2020
Harris Directory of
Delaware
Businesses

Published April 2020 next update April 2021

WARNING: Purchasers and users of this directory may not use this directory to compile mailing lists, other marketing aids and other types of data, which are sold or otherwise provided to third parties. Such use is wrongful, illegal and a violation of the federal copyright laws.

CAUTION: Because of the many thousands of establishment listings contained in this directory and the possibilities of both human and mechanical error in processing this information, Mergent Inc. cannot assume liability for the correctness of the listings or information on which they are based. Hence, no information contained in this work should be relied upon in any instance where there is a possibility of any loss or damage as a consequence of any error or omission in this volume.

Publisher
Mergent Inc.
444 Madison Ave
New York, NY 10022

©Mergent Inc All Rights Reserved
2020 Mergent Business Press
ISSN 1080-2614
ISBN 978-1-64141-603-0

TABLE OF CONTENTS

Summary of Contents & Explanatory Notes 4
User's Guide to Listings 6

Geographic Section
County/City Cross-Reference Index 9
Establishments Listed by City 11

Standard Industrial Classification (SIC) Section
SIC Alphabetical Index 443
SIC Numerical Index 447
Establishments Listed by SIC 451

Alphabetic Section
Establishments Listed by Establishment Name 581

Products & Services Section
Products & Services Index 751
Establishments Listed by Product or Service Category 767

SUMMARY OF CONTENTS

Number of Companies	13,368
Number of Decision Makers	20,688
Minimum Number of Employees (Services)	4
Minimum Number of Employees (Manufacturers)	1

EXPLANATORY NOTES

How to Cross-Reference in This Directory

Sequential Entry Numbers. Each establishment in the Geographic Section is numbered sequentially (G-0000). The number assigned to each establishment is referred to as its "entry number." To make cross-referencing easier, each listing in the Geographic, SIC, Alphabetic and Product Sections includes the establishment's entry number. To facilitate locating an entry in the Geographic Section, the entry numbers for the first listing on the left page and the last listing on the right page are printed at the top of the page next to the city name.

Source Suggestions Welcome

Although all known sources were used to compile this directory, it is possible that companies were inadvertently omitted. Your assistance in calling attention to such omissions would be greatly appreciated. A special form on the facing page will help you in the reporting process.

Analysis

Every effort has been made to contact all firms to verify their information. The one exception to this rule is the annual sales figure, which is considered by many companies to be confidential information. Therefore, estimated sales have been calculated by multiplying the nationwide average sales per employee for the firm's major SIC/NAICS code by the firm's number of employees. Nationwide averages for sales per employee by SIC/NAICS codes are provided by the U.S. Department of Commerce and are updated annually. All sales—sales (est)—have been estimated by this method. The exceptions are parent companies (PA), division headquarters (DH) and headquarter locations (HQ) which may include an actual corporate sales figure—sales (corporate-wide) if available.

Types of Companies

Descriptive and statistical data are included for companies in the entire state. These comprise manufacturers, machine shops, fabricators, assemblers and printers. Also identified are corporate offices in the state.

Employment Data

The employment figure shown in the Products & Services Section includes male and female employees and embraces all levels of the company. This directory includes manufacturing companies with 1 or more employees and service companies with 4 or more employees. This figure is for the facility listed and does not include other plants or offices. It should be recognized that these figures represent an approximate year-round average. These employment figures are broken into codes A through F and used in the Alphabetic and Geographic Sections to further help you in qualifying a company. Be sure to check the footnotes at the bottom of the page for the code breakdowns.

Standard Industrial Classification (SIC)

The Standard Industrial Classification (SIC) system used in this directory was developed by the federal government for use in classifying establishments by the type of activity they are engaged in. The SIC classifications used in this directory are from the 1987 edition published by the U.S. Government's Office of Management and Budget. The SIC system separates all activities into broad industrial divisions (e.g., manufacturing, mining, retail trade). It further subdivides each division. The range of manufacturing industry classes extends from two-digit codes (major industry group) to four-digit codes (product).

For example:

Industry Breakdown	Code	Industry, Product, etc.
*Major industry group	20	Food and kindred products
Industry group	203	Canned and frozen foods
*Industry	2033	Fruits and vegetables, etc.

*Classifications used in this directory

Only two-digit and four-digit codes are used in this directory.

Arrangement

1. The **Geographic Section** contains complete in-depth corporate data. This section is sorted by cities listed in alphabetical order and companies listed alphabetically within each city. A County/City Index for referencing cities within counties precedes this section.

> IMPORTANT NOTICE: It is a violation of both federal and state law to transmit an unsolicited advertisement to a facsimile machine. Any user of this product that violates such laws may be subject to civil and criminal penalties, which may exceed $500 for each transmission of an unsolicited facsimile. Mergent Inc. provides fax numbers for lawful purposes only and expressly forbids the use of these numbers in any unlawful manner.

2. The **Standard Industrial Classification (SIC) Section** lists companies under approximately 500 four-digit SIC codes. An alphabetical and a numerical index precedes this section. A company can be listed under several codes. The codes are in numerical order with companies listed alphabetically under each code.

3. The **Alphabetic Section** lists all companies with their full physical or mailing addresses and telephone number.

4. The **Product & Services Section** lists companies under unique Harris categories. An index precedes this section. Companies can be listed under several categories.

USER'S GUIDE TO LISTINGS

GEOGRAPHIC SECTION

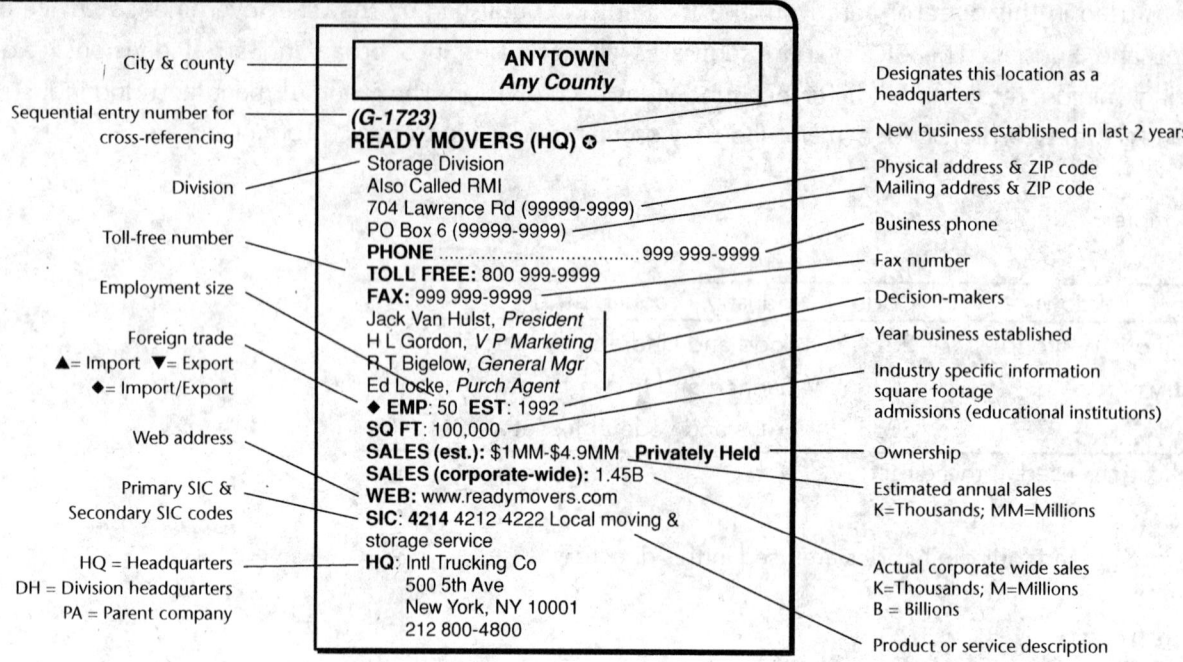

SIC SECTION

ALPHABETIC SECTION

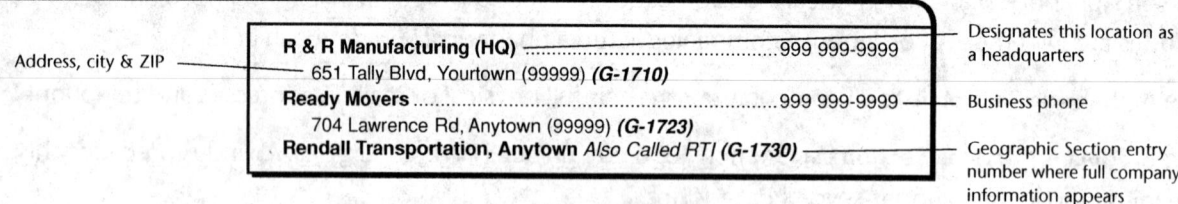

PRODUCTS & SERVICES SECTION

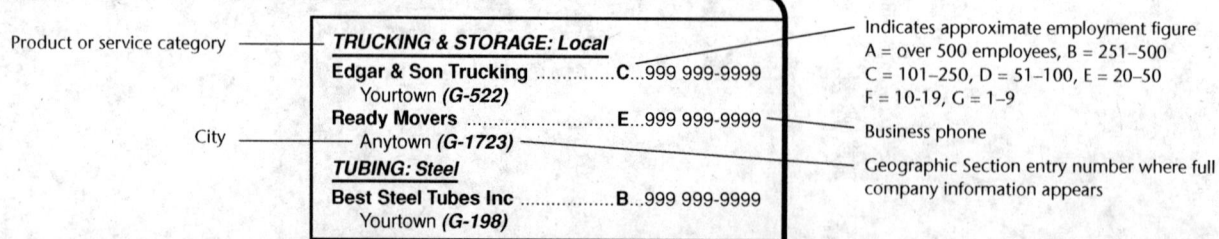

GEOGRAPHIC SECTION
Companies sorted by city in alphabetical order
In-depth company data listed

STANDARD INDUSTRIAL CLASSIFICATIONS
Alphabetical index of classifcation descriptions
Numerical index of classifcation descriptions
Companies sorted by SIC product groupings

ALPHABETIC SECTION
Company listings in alphabetical order

PRODUCTS & SERVICES INDEX
Products & Services categories listed in alphabetical order

PRODUCTS & SERVICES SECTION
Companies sorted by product & service classifications

Delaware
County Map

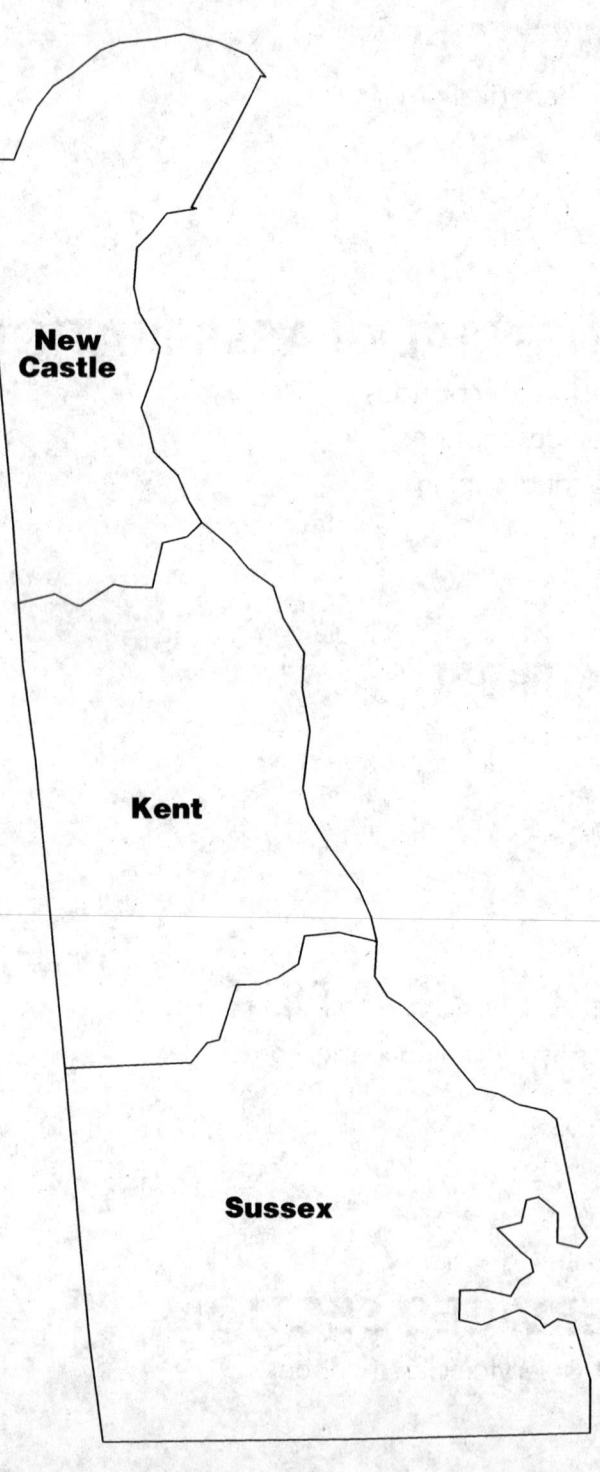

COUNTY/CITY CROSS-REFERENCE INDEX

	ENTRY #		ENTRY #		ENTRY #		ENTRY #		ENTRY #
Kent		Magnolia	(G-3876)	Montchanin	(G-4984)	**Sussex**		Harbeson	(G-2771)
Camden	(G-535)	Marydel	(G-3915)	New Castle	(G-4988)	Bethany Beach	(G-382)	Laurel	(G-3188)
Camden Wyoming	(G-609)	Smyrna	(G-8558)	Newark	(G-5850)	Bethel	(G-440)	Lewes	(G-3315)
Cheswold	(G-663)	Viola	(G-8834)	Newport	(G-7744)	Bridgeville	(G-441)	Lincoln	(G-3838)
Clayton	(G-830)	Wyoming	(G-13358)	Odessa	(G-7825)	Dagsboro	(G-876)	Milford	(G-4296)
Dover	(G-1062)	**New Castle**		Port Penn	(G-7834)	Delmar	(G-969)	Millsboro	(G-4617)
Felton	(G-2269)	Bear	(G-1)	Rockland	(G-8122)	Dewey Beach	(G-1051)	Millville	(G-4832)
Frederica	(G-2400)	Christiana	(G-664)	Saint Georges	(G-8125)	Ellendale	(G-2257)	Milton	(G-4859)
Harrington	(G-2803)	Claymont	(G-683)	Talleyville	(G-8749)	Farmington	(G-2265)	Ocean View	(G-7753)
Hartly	(G-2912)	Delaware City	(G-945)	Townsend	(G-8753)	Fenwick Island	(G-2328)	Rehoboth Beach	(G-7835)
Houston	(G-3176)	Hockessin	(G-2945)	Wilmington	(G-8840)	Frankford	(G-2342)	Seaford	(G-8132)
Kenton	(G-3184)	Marshallton	(G-3914)	Winterthur	(G-13356)	Georgetown	(G-2416)	Selbyville	(G-8446)
Leipsic	(G-3313)	Middletown	(G-3924)	Yorklyn	(G-13364)	Greenwood	(G-2710)		

GEOGRAPHIC SECTION

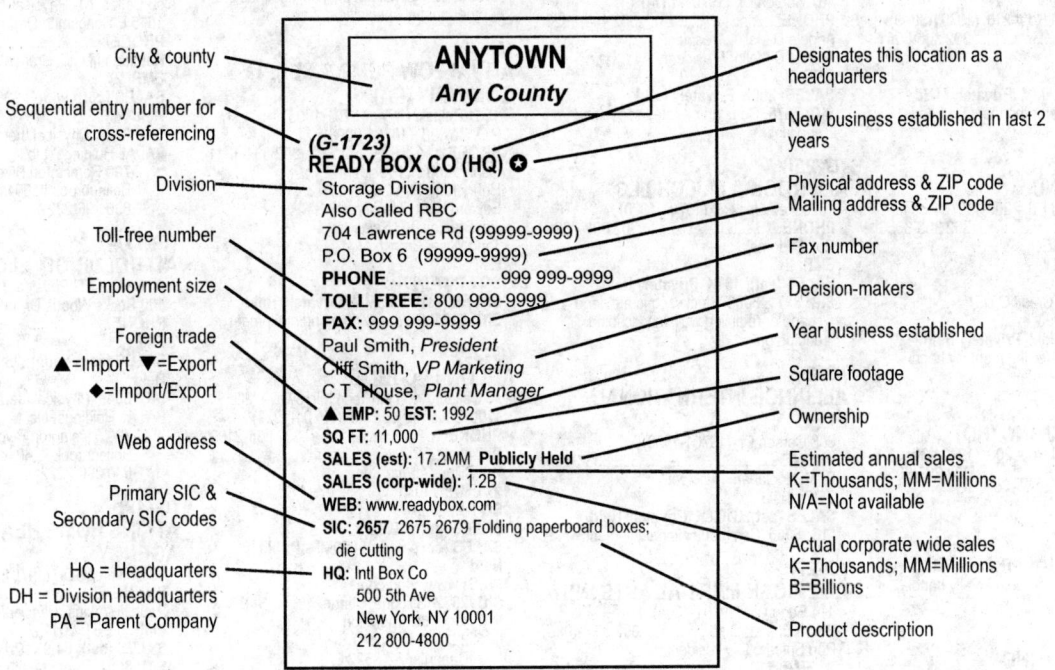

See footnotes for symbols and codes identification.
- This section is in alphabetical order by city.
- Companies are sorted alphabetically under their respective cities.
- To locate cities within a county refer to the County/City Cross Reference Index.

IMPORTANT NOTICE: It is a violation of both federal and state law to transmit an unsolicited advertisement to a facsimile machine. Any user of this product that violates such laws may be subject to civil and criminal penalties which may exceed $500 for each transmission of an unsolicited facsimile. Harris InfoSource provides fax numbers for lawful purposes only and expressly forbids the use of these numbers in any unlawful manner.

Bear
New Castle County

(G-1)
431 CORPORATION
4185 Krkwood St Georges (19701-2272)
PHONE.................................352 385-1427
Greg Harrison, *Director*
EMP: 7
SALES (corp-wide): 1.8MM **Privately Held**
SIC: 8732 Commercial nonphysical research
PA: 431 Corporation
   28334 Churchill Smith Ln
   Mount Dora FL 32757
   352 383-0988

(G-2)
A & G LAWN CARE LLC
13 Hackney Dr (19701-2210)
PHONE.................................302 584-8719
Gregory Haynes, *Owner*
EMP: 4
SALES (est): 118.3K **Privately Held**
SIC: 0782 Lawn care services

(G-3)
A AND H NURSING ADMINISTRA
94 Dasher Ave (19701-1174)
PHONE.................................302 544-4474
Holly A McConomy, *Principal*
EMP: 6
SALES (est): 156.7K **Privately Held**
SIC: 8059 Nursing & personal care

(G-4)
A CHILDS WORLD LLC
300 Bear Christiana Rd (19701-1040)
PHONE.................................302 322-9386
Stephanie Fagles, *Director*
EMP: 11
SALES (est): 261.1K **Privately Held**
SIC: 8351 Preschool center

(G-5)
A COLLINS TRUCKING INC
314 Turnberry Ct (19701-4720)
PHONE.................................302 438-8334
Aubrey Collins Sr, *CEO*
Bryan J Collins, *Vice Pres*
EMP: 5
SALES: 750K **Privately Held**
SIC: 4212 Local trucking, without storage

(G-6)
A-STOVER MANAGEMENT GROUP LLC
238 Turnberry Ct Ste A (19701-4723)
PHONE.................................866 299-0709
Aubrey Stover,
EMP: 15
SALES (est): 4MM **Privately Held**
SIC: 6512 6531 Nonresidential building operators; real estate agents & managers

(G-7)
AAMCO TRANSMISSIONS
819 Pulaski Hwy (19701-1239)
PHONE.................................302 322-3454
Lane Carey, *Owner*
EMP: 5
SALES (est): 510.7K **Privately Held**
SIC: 7537 Automotive transmission repair shops

(G-8)
AARDVARK PARTY RENTALS LLC
37 Deer Cir (19701-2718)
PHONE.................................302 331-1929
Ronald Jester, *Principal*
EMP: 4 EST: 2013
SALES (est): 174.8K **Privately Held**
SIC: 7359 Party supplies rental services

(G-9)
AC ENGINEERING
135 Emerald Ridge Dr (19701-2280)
PHONE.................................215 873-6482
Victor Changlee, *Principal*
EMP: 2 EST: 2012
SALES (est): 122.5K **Privately Held**
SIC: 3621 Armatures, industrial

(G-10)
ACADEMY MASSAGE & BDY WORK LTD
1218 Pulaski Hwy Ste 324 (19701-1344)
PHONE.................................302 392-6768
Gheorghe Nastase, *Partner*
Elsa Nastase, *Partner*
EMP: 7
SQ FT: 3,550
SALES (est): 518.7K **Privately Held**
WEB: www.massage-academy.com
SIC: 8331 Job training & vocational rehabilitation services

(G-11)
ACTIVE SUPPLY LLC
465 Carson Dr (19701-1314)
PHONE.................................888 843-0243
EMP: 4
SALES (est): 142.4K **Privately Held**
SIC: 5099 Durable goods

(G-12)
ADDALLI LANDSCAPING
2546 Red Lion Rd (19701-2429)
PHONE.................................302 836-2002
Sebastian Addalli, *Owner*
EMP: 5
SALES (est): 254.8K **Privately Held**
SIC: 0781 Landscape services

(G-13)
ADKESS TRANSPORT SERVICES LLC
14 Winchester Ct (19701-2232)
PHONE.................................978 235-3924
Godwin Adansi, *Principal*
EMP: 4
SALES (est): 88.1K **Privately Held**
SIC: 4789 Transportation services

(G-14)
ADVANTAGE DELAWARE
134 Antlers Ln (19701-3710)
PHONE.................................302 365-5398
Nancy J Wolf, *Principal*
EMP: 8 **Privately Held**
SIC: 6712 Bank holding companies

(G-15)
ADVANTAGE TRAVEL INC
1218 Pulaski Hwy Ste 336 (19701-1344)
PHONE.................................302 674-8747
EMP: 6
SALES (est): 491.4K **Privately Held**
SIC: 4729 4724 Passenger Transportation Arrangement Travel Agency

Bear - New Castle County (G-16)

(G-16)
ADVO OPCO LLC (PA)
Also Called: Advoserv
2520 Wrangle Hill Rd # 210 (19701-3849)
PHONE 302 365-8051
Judith Favell,
EMP: 600
SALES (est): 26.5MM Privately Held
SIC: 8361 Home for the mentally handicapped

(G-17)
ADVOSERV INC
2520 Wrangle Hill Rd # 200 (19701-3849)
PHONE 302 365-8050
Kelly McCrann, CEO
Robert Bacon, COO
Kathy Shea, CFO
Judith Favell, Ch Credit Ofcr
EMP: 25 EST: 1996
SALES (est): 2.2MM Privately Held
SIC: 8361 Home for the mentally handicapped

(G-18)
ADVOSERV NJ INC (HQ)
2520 Wrangle Hill Rd # 200 (19701-3849)
PHONE 302 365-8050
Kelly McCrann, CEO
Robert Bacon, COO
Kathleen Shea, CFO
EMP: 15
SALES (est): 1.1MM Privately Held
SIC: 8361 Home for the mentally handicapped

(G-19)
ADVOSERV NJ INC
2520 Wrangle Hill Rd # 200 (19701-3856)
PHONE 302 365-8050
EMP: 99
SALES (est): 1.8MM Privately Held
SIC: 8361 Residential Care Services
PA: Gi Advo Opco, Llc
    2520 Wrangle Hill Rd # 210
    Bear DE 19701

(G-20)
AFFINITY WOMENS HEALTH LLC
121 Becks Woods Dr # 100 (19701-3851)
PHONE 302 468-4320
Stanley Wiercinski, Principal
EMP: 4
SALES (est): 100.8K Privately Held
SIC: 8011 Gynecologist

(G-21)
AFFORDABLE INSUR NETWRK DEL
1218 Pulaski Hwy Ste 490 (19701-4300)
PHONE 302 392-4500
Sam Peppelman, Principal
Mary Peppelman, Agent
EMP: 5
SALES (est): 590.5K Privately Held
WEB: www.ainofde.com
SIC: 6411 Insurance agents, brokers & service

(G-22)
AFFORDABLE INSURANCE
Also Called: Amato & Associates Insurance
1218 Pulaski Hwy Ste 490 (19701-4300)
PHONE 302 834-9641
Samuel Peptelman, President
David Welch, Vice Pres
Susan Amato, Treasurer
EMP: 4
SQ FT: 1,200
SALES: 150K Privately Held
SIC: 6411 Insurance agents, brokers & service

(G-23)
AFFORDABLE TAX SERVICES LLC
241 Shai Cir (19701-3607)
PHONE 302 399-3867
Cheryl Apparicio, Principal
EMP: 4
SALES (est): 36.1K Privately Held
SIC: 7291 Tax return preparation services

(G-24)
AIT ADVANCED INFOTECH INC
467 Carson Dr (19701-1314)
PHONE 302 454-8620
Angelo D Mello, President
Angelo D'Mello, President
EMP: 9
SALES: 200K Privately Held
SIC: 7379 Computer related consulting services

(G-25)
ALL ROCK & MULCH LLC
1570 Red Lion Rd (19701-1870)
PHONE 302 838-7625
Roy Stidoms,
EMP: 2
SALES (est): 161K Privately Held
SIC: 3271 5083 Blocks, concrete: landscape or retaining wall; landscaping equipment

(G-26)
ALLIANCE INTERNATIONAL ELEC
608 Carson Dr (19701-1450)
PHONE 302 838-3880
Brian Hoolahan, Principal
EMP: 4
SALES (est): 310.6K Privately Held
SIC: 5065 Communication equipment

(G-27)
AMERICAN MARTIAL ARTS INST
414 Eden Cir (19701-4304)
PHONE 302 834-4060
Ron Sutcarotte, President
▼ EMP: 11
SALES: 600K Privately Held
SIC: 7999 7991 Martial arts school; physical fitness clubs with training equipment

(G-28)
AMSPEC CHEMICAL CORPORATION
703 Carson Dr (19701-1454)
PHONE 302 392-1702
Maria Bernal, CEO
Kay Pali, President
▲ EMP: 3
SALES (est): 631.3K Privately Held
WEB: www.amspecorp.com
SIC: 2819 Industrial inorganic chemicals

(G-29)
ANDREW NOWAKOWSKI MD PA
22 Riva Ridge Ln (19701-3357)
PHONE 410 838-8900
Andrew Nowakowski, Owner
EMP: 4
SALES (est): 308.8K Privately Held
SIC: 8011 Internal medicine practitioners; nephrologist

(G-30)
ANGELS MESSIAHS FOUNDATION
360 Fox Hunt Dr (19701-2537)
P.O. Box 1151 (19701-7151)
PHONE 302 465-1647
Michael Higgin, Director
EMP: 10
SALES (est): 272.5K Privately Held
SIC: 8322 Adult day care center

(G-31)
ANIMAL HAVEN VETERINARY CENTER
757 Pulaski Hwy Ste 6 (19701-5215)
PHONE 302 326-1400
Charlotte Fagraeus, Principal
EMP: 6
SALES (est): 309.2K Privately Held
WEB: www.animalhavenvetcenter.com
SIC: 0742 Animal hospital services, pets & other animal specialties

(G-32)
ANIMAL VETERINARY CENTER LLC
160 Bear Christiana Rd (19701-1042)
PHONE 302 322-6488
Jim Berg Dvm Dvm, Principal
EMP: 12
SALES (est): 434.4K Privately Held
WEB: www.animalvetcenter.com
SIC: 0742 Animal hospital services, pets & other animal specialties

(G-33)
AQUAFLOW PUMP & SUPPLY COMPANY (PA)
1561 Pulaski Hwy (19701-1303)
P.O. Box 98 (19701-0098)
PHONE 302 834-1311
Henry King Jr, President
Henry King III, Vice Pres
Edward King, Treasurer
Jim Bradley, VP Sales
Todd Wise, Branch Mgr
EMP: 15
SQ FT: 14,000
SALES (est): 19.5MM Privately Held
SIC: 5084 Pumps & pumping equipment

(G-34)
ARLON LLC (HQ)
Also Called: Arlon Mtl Tech Microwave Mtls
1100 Governor Lea Rd (19701-1927)
PHONE 302 834-2100
Bob Carini, President
Pat Dillon, Admin Sec
▲ EMP: 140
SQ FT: 7,500
SALES (est): 60MM
SALES (corp-wide): 879MM Publicly Held
WEB: www.arlon.com
SIC: 2822 Silicone rubbers
PA: Rogers Corporation
    2225 W Chandler Blvd
    Chandler AZ 85224
    480 917-6000

(G-35)
ARLON PARTNERS INC
1100 Governor Lea Rd (19701-1927)
PHONE 302 595-1234
Anthony Welo, Technical Staff
EMP: 5
SALES (est): 342K Privately Held
SIC: 5085 Abrasives

(G-36)
ARROW LEASING CORP
Also Called: Arrow Sanitary Service
1772 Pulaski Hwy (19701-1712)
PHONE 302 834-4546
Albert T Sammons Jr, President
EMP: 17
SQ FT: 5,200
SALES (est): 2MM Privately Held
WEB: www.arrowsanitary.com
SIC: 7359 7699 Equipment rental & leasing; septic tank cleaning service

(G-37)
ARROW SHUTTLE SERVICE
105 Ascot Ct (19701-2365)
PHONE 302 836-5658
EMP: 4
SALES (est): 122.6K Privately Held
SIC: 4111 Airport transportation

(G-38)
ARTISANS BANK INC
1124 Pulaski Hwy (19701-1306)
PHONE 302 834-8800
Alice Candeloro, Manager
EMP: 8
SALES (corp-wide): 22.8MM Privately Held
WEB: www.artisansbank.com
SIC: 6036 6029 State savings banks, not federally chartered; commercial banks
PA: Artisans Bank Inc
    2961 Centerville Rd # 101
    Wilmington DE 19808
    302 658-6881

(G-39)
ASAP AUTOMOTIVE
807 Pulaski Hwy (19701-1239)
PHONE 302 444-8659
Dan Salter, Owner
EMP: 4 EST: 2015
SALES (est): 57.9K Privately Held
SIC: 7538 General automotive repair shops

(G-40)
ATI HOLDINGS LLC
Also Called: ATI Physical Therapy
1015 E Songsmith Dr (19701-1194)
PHONE 302 836-5670
Kathleen Iffland, Branch Mgr
EMP: 21
SALES (corp-wide): 338.3MM Privately Held
SIC: 8049 Physical therapist
PA: Ati Holdings, Llc
    790 Remington Blvd
    Bolingbrook IL 60440
    630 296-2222

(G-41)
ATI HOLDINGS LLC
Also Called: ATI Physical Therapy
100 Becks Woods Dr (19701-3835)
PHONE 302 392-3400
EMP: 21
SALES (corp-wide): 338.3MM Privately Held
SIC: 8049 Physical therapist
PA: Ati Holdings, Llc
    790 Remington Blvd
    Bolingbrook IL 60440
    630 296-2222

(G-42)
ATKINS HOME HEALTH AID AGENCY
18 Calvarese Dr (19701-6006)
PHONE 302 832-0315
Paulette Atkins, Principal
EMP: 5 EST: 2011
SALES (est): 64.9K Privately Held
SIC: 8082 Home health care services

(G-43)
AUTO EQUITY LOANS
1146 Pulaski Hwy (19701-1306)
PHONE 302 834-2500
Glen Douglas, Owner
EMP: 4
SALES (corp-wide): 3.1MM Privately Held
SIC: 6141 Automobile loans, including insurance
PA: Auto Equity Loans
    15231 N 87th St Ste 115b
    Scottsdale AZ 85260
    480 307-6388

(G-44)
BAKER SAFETY EQUIPMENT INC
107 Delilah Dr (19701-4833)
PHONE 302 376-9302
Ralph T Baker, CEO
Dawn Nutter, President
Mark D Baker, Vice Pres
EMP: 6
SQ FT: 600,000
SALES (est): 600K Privately Held
WEB: www.lifechute.com
SIC: 5047 2221 Industrial safety devices: first aid kits & masks; nylon broadwoven fabrics

(G-45)
BE BLESSED DESIGN GROUP LLC
Also Called: Bbdg
808 Lowell Dr (19701-4948)
PHONE 302 561-3793
Kiara Irby,
EMP: 3
SALES (est): 121.3K Privately Held
SIC: 2396 5699 7389 2299 Apparel & other linings, except millinery; customized clothing & apparel; apparel designers, commercial; apparel filling: cotton waste, kapok & related material; department stores

(G-46)
BEAR CHIROPRACTIC CENTER DC
811 Governors Pl (19701-3046)
PHONE 302 836-8361
Alexander Bohatiuk, Owner
Alexander N Bohativk DC, Owner
EMP: 5

GEOGRAPHIC SECTION   Bear - New Castle County (G-78)

SALES (est): 249.3K **Privately Held**
SIC: 8041 Offices & clinics of chiropractors

(G-47)
BEAR FORGE AND MACHINE CO INC
Also Called: Stafford Precision
147 School Bell Rd (19701-1191)
PHONE.........................302 322-5199
William Stafford, *President*
EMP: 2
SQ FT: 7,000
SALES (est): 297.3K **Privately Held**
WEB: www.staffordprecision.com
SIC: 3469 7692 Machine parts, stamped or pressed metal; welding repair

(G-48)
BEAR HOSPITALITY INC
Also Called: Best Western Plus
875 Pulaski Hwy (19701-1252)
PHONE.........................302 326-2500
Ann Watkins, *Principal*
EMP: 7
SALES (est): 696.6K **Privately Held**
SIC: 7011 Hotels & motels

(G-49)
BEAR-GLASGOW DENTAL LLC
1106 Pulaski Hwy (19701-1332)
PHONE.........................302 836-9330
Neil Woloshin, *Principal*
EMP: 4
SALES (est): 73.6K **Privately Held**
SIC: 8021 Offices & clinics of dentists

(G-50)
BELLWETHER BEHAVIORAL HEALTH
2520 Wrangle Hill Rd # 200 (19701-3849)
PHONE.........................856 769-2042
Katina Saunders, *Principal*
EMP: 10
SALES (est): 570.5K **Privately Held**
SIC: 8322 General counseling services

(G-51)
BERNIEFACE PRODUCTIONS LLC ✪
11 Wildfields Ct (19701-1410)
PHONE.........................302 561-0273
EMP: 8 **EST:** 2019
SALES (est): 63K **Privately Held**
SIC: 7822 Motion picture & tape distribution

(G-52)
BLESSED BEGINNINGS LRNG CTR
117 Portside Ct (19701-2287)
PHONE.........................302 838-9112
Randee Briggs, *Principal*
EMP: 5
SALES (est): 110.9K **Privately Held**
SIC: 8351 Child day care services

(G-53)
BLUE HEN PHOTOGRAPHY
111 Clear Creek Dr (19701-3339)
PHONE.........................302 690-3259
Geoffrey Heath, *Principal*
EMP: 4
SALES (est): 46K **Privately Held**
SIC: 7221 Photographer, still or video

(G-54)
BLUE HERON ENT INC
Also Called: Blue Heron Discount Cards
600 Garron Point Pass (19701-1992)
PHONE.........................302 834-1521
Samantha Young, *Principal*
EMP: 2
SALES (est): 154.7K **Privately Held**
SIC: 2754 Business form & card printing, gravure

(G-55)
BRADLEY & SONS DESIGNER CON
1 Tammie Dr (19701-1758)
PHONE.........................302 836-8031
Bob Bradley, *Owner*
Robin Bradley, *Office Mgr*
EMP: 5

SALES: 260K **Privately Held**
SIC: 1771 Concrete work

(G-56)
BRANDYWINE ELECTRONICS CORP
Also Called: Brandywine Elec Ltd Belcom
611 Carson Dr (19701-1450)
PHONE.........................302 324-9992
Joseph Dombroski, *President*
Ronald Casalvera, *Vice Pres*
Sharon Dombroski, *Vice Pres*
Trena Cook, *Office Mgr*
Kaitlin Mayhorn, *Producer*
EMP: 18
SQ FT: 10,084
SALES (est): 2.4MM **Privately Held**
WEB: www.bel.com
SIC: 7812 1731 5064 3651 Music video production; sound equipment specialization; video camera-audio recorders (camcorders); household audio & video equipment; audio-visual equipment & supply rental; video cameras, recorders & accessories

(G-57)
BURTON ENTERPRISES INC
241 Rice Dr (19701-1896)
PHONE.........................302 838-0115
James Burton, *Principal*
EMP: 4
SALES (est): 282.7K **Privately Held**
SIC: 8748 Business consulting

(G-58)
BYERS INDUSTRIAL SERVICES LLC
1501 Porter Rd (19701-2111)
PHONE.........................302 836-4790
Tom Moore, *Manager*
EMP: 30
SALES (est): 1.8MM **Privately Held**
SIC: 1731 General electrical contractor
PA: Byers Industrial Services, Llc.
    1100 Grant Ave
    Franklinville NJ 08322

(G-59)
C & K BUILDERS LLC
Also Called: Kokoszka Ent
334 Bear Christiana Rd (19701-1040)
PHONE.........................302 324-9811
Jospeh Kokoszka, *Mng Member*
EMP: 6
SALES (est): 657.6K **Privately Held**
SIC: 1521 General remodeling, single-family houses; new construction, single-family houses

(G-60)
C&G DENTAL STUDIO LLC
3 Lotus Cir N (19701-6327)
PHONE.........................302 345-4995
Steven Stokes,
EMP: 1 **EST:** 2015
SALES (est): 88.4K **Privately Held**
SIC: 3843 7389 Dental equipment & supplies;

(G-61)
CADTECH INC
2500 Wrangle Hill Rd # 105 (19701-3840)
PHONE.........................302 832-2255
Arturo Lemus, *President*
Haridel Gonzalez, *Vice Pres*
EMP: 10
SALES: 1.2MM **Privately Held**
SIC: 7389 Design, commercial & industrial;

(G-62)
CALATLANTIC GROUP INC
8 Meridian Blvd (19701-6803)
PHONE.........................302 834-5472
EMP: 5
SALES (corp-wide): 20.5B **Publicly Held**
SIC: 6531 Real estate agent, residential
HQ: Calatlantic Group, Inc.
    1100 Wilson Blvd Ste 2100
    Arlington VA 22209
    240 532-3806

(G-63)
CALVIN SHEETS
Also Called: Nationwide
254 Foxhunt Dr (19701-2536)
PHONE.........................302 832-0600
Calvin Sheets, *Owner*
EMP: 4
SALES (est): 274.3K **Privately Held**
SIC: 6411 Insurance agents, brokers & service

(G-64)
CARDENTI ELECTRIC
109 E Scotland Dr (19701-1756)
PHONE.........................302 834-1278
Lori Cardenti, *Manager*
Michael D Cardenti,
Maria Cardenti, *Admin Sec*
EMP: 15
SQ FT: 2,500
SALES (est): 1MM **Privately Held**
SIC: 1731 Electrical work

(G-65)
CARRIER RENTAL SYSTEMS INC
500 Carson Dr (19701-1318)
PHONE.........................302 836-3000
George Doring, *Manager*
EMP: 20
SALES (corp-wide): 66.5B **Publicly Held**
SIC: 7359 Equipment rental & leasing
HQ: Carrier Rental Systems, Inc.
    1 Carrier Pl
    Farmington CT 06032

(G-66)
CARTER KAREN DMD
1991 Pulaski Hwy (19701-1708)
PHONE.........................302 832-2200
Karen Carter, *Principal*
EMP: 4 **EST:** 2007
SALES (est): 127.2K **Privately Held**
SIC: 8021 Dental surgeon

(G-67)
CATCH-A-WEB CLEANING INC
2099 Red Lion Rd (19701-1853)
PHONE.........................302 836-1970
Wendell Raulston, *President*
EMP: 20
SALES (est): 250K **Privately Held**
SIC: 7349 Janitorial service, contract basis

(G-68)
CEDAR HARDSCAPING L L C
1782 Red Lion Rd (19701-1834)
PHONE.........................877 569-9859
Alfonso Lopez, *President*
EMP: 4
SALES (est): 227K **Privately Held**
WEB: www.cedarhardscaping.com
SIC: 0782 0781 Lawn services; landscape services

(G-69)
CELEBREE HOLDING INC
Also Called: Celebree Learning Centers
1205 Quintilio Dr (19701-6005)
PHONE.........................302 834-0436
Lisa Henkel, *Branch Mgr*
EMP: 5 **Privately Held**
SIC: 8351 Group day care center
PA: Celebree Holding, Inc.
    1306 Bellona Ave Ste A
    Lutherville Timonium MD 21093

(G-70)
CFT AMBULANCE SERVICE INC
33 Pear Dr (19701-4135)
PHONE.........................302 984-2255
Denette Lawson, *President*
EMP: 45
SQ FT: 2,000
SALES (est): 1.2MM **Privately Held**
SIC: 4119 Ambulance service

(G-71)
CHRISTIANA FIRE COMPANY
1714 Porter Rd (19701-2110)
PHONE.........................302 834-2433
Jeff Tillinghast, *Chief*
EMP: 8

SALES (corp-wide): 4MM **Privately Held**
WEB: www.christianafc.org
SIC: 9224 4119 ; ambulance service
PA: Christiana Fire Company
    2 E Main St
    Christiana DE 19702
    302 737-2433

(G-72)
CHRISTINA NEWTON
925 Bear Corbitt Rd (19701-1323)
PHONE.........................302 454-2400
Christina Newton, *Principal*
EMP: 8
SALES (est): 65.7K **Privately Held**
SIC: 8049 Offices of health practitioner

(G-73)
CITIFINANCIAL INC
619 Governors Pl (19701-3034)
PHONE.........................302 834-6677
John Barkley, *Branch Mgr*
EMP: 4
SALES (corp-wide): 72.8B **Publicly Held**
SIC: 7389 6141 Financial services; personal credit institutions
HQ: Citifinancial, Inc.
    300 Saint Paul St Fl 3
    Baltimore MD 21202
    410 332-3000

(G-74)
CITIFINANCIAL CREDIT COMPANY
619 Governors Pl (19701-3034)
P.O. Box 598 (19701-0598)
PHONE.........................302 834-6677
John Barkley, *Manager*
EMP: 6
SALES (corp-wide): 72.8B **Publicly Held**
WEB: www.citifinancial.com
SIC: 6153 6141 Short-term business credit; personal credit institutions
HQ: Citifinancial Credit Company
    300 Saint Paul St Fl 3
    Baltimore MD 21202
    410 332-3000

(G-75)
CITIZENS BANK NATIONAL ASSN
146 Foxhunt Dr (19701-2535)
PHONE.........................302 834-2611
Eric Quinones, *Branch Mgr*
EMP: 10
SALES (corp-wide): 7.3B **Publicly Held**
WEB: www.ccoinvest.com
SIC: 6022 State commercial banks
HQ: Citizens Bank, National Association
    1 Citizens Plz Ste 1 # 1
    Providence RI 02903
    401 282-7000

(G-76)
CLARK SERVICES INC DELAWARE
900 Julian Ln (19701-2277)
PHONE.........................302 834-0556
Mark Clark, *President*
Kathleen Clark, *Vice Pres*
EMP: 5 **EST:** 1997
SQ FT: 5,000
SALES (est): 647.1K **Privately Held**
SIC: 1711 5983 Heating & air conditioning contractors; fuel oil dealers

(G-77)
CLEANPRO DETAIL CENTER
200 Connor Blvd (19701-1741)
PHONE.........................302 834-6878
Chris Anacay, *Owner*
EMP: 4
SALES (est): 138K **Privately Held**
SIC: 7542 Washing & polishing, automotive

(G-78)
CLICK FOR SAVINGS LLC
5104 Christiana Mdws (19701-1156)
PHONE.........................302 300-0202
Adam Cotter, *Principal*
EMP: 5 **EST:** 2016
SALES (est): 176.4K **Privately Held**
SIC: 8399 Advocacy group

(PA)=Parent Co (HQ)=Headquarters (DH)=Div Headquarters
✪ = New Business established in last 2 years

2020 Harris Directory of Delaware Businesses

Bear - New Castle County (G-79)

(G-79)
CLUB BRENNAN
1 Primrose Dr (19701-6393)
PHONE................................302 838-9530
Jack Hilman, *President*
EMP: 9
SALES: 74.7K **Privately Held**
SIC: 7997 Swimming club, membership

(G-80)
COMMUNITY PWERED FEDERAL CR UN (PA)
1758 Pulaski Hwy (19701-1712)
PHONE................................302 392-2930
Anthony Hinds, *CEO*
Michelle Cross, *Loan Officer*
EMP: 11
SALES: 3.8MM **Privately Held**
SIC: 6061 Federal credit unions

(G-81)
COMPUTER JOCKS
726 Pulaski Hwy (19701-5210)
PHONE................................302 544-6448
Richard Veid, *Principal*
EMP: 5 **EST:** 2008
SALES (est): 410.4K **Privately Held**
SIC: 7378 Computer maintenance & repair

(G-82)
CONCRETE WALLS INC
3415 Wrangle Hill Rd # 2 (19701-4812)
P.O. Box 4434, Wilmington (19807-0434)
PHONE................................302 293-7061
EMP: 5
SALES (est): 442.5K **Privately Held**
SIC: 1611 Concrete construction: roads, highways, sidewalks, etc.

(G-83)
CONSTRUCTION UNLIMITED INC
705 Elizabeth Ln (19701-2603)
PHONE................................302 836-3140
Jim Cammock, *President*
Cathie Filipkowski, *Corp Secy*
Debbie Cammock, *Vice Pres*
EMP: 7
SALES: 1MM **Privately Held**
SIC: 1542 1751 Commercial & office building contractors; carpentry work

(G-84)
COOPER LEVENSON PA
30 Foxhunt Dr U30 (19701-2534)
PHONE................................302 838-2600
Gregory A Kraemer, *Associate*
EMP: 5
SALES (corp-wide): 20.7MM **Privately Held**
SIC: 8111 General practice attorney, lawyer
PA: Cooper Levenson, P.A.
  1125 Atlantic Ave Fl 3
  Atlantic City NJ
  609 344-3161

(G-85)
CORNERSTONE SENIOR CENTER
3135 Summit Bridge Rd (19701-2001)
PHONE................................302 836-6463
Victoria Lyons, *Director*
EMP: 4
SALES (est): 106.5K **Privately Held**
SIC: 8322 Geriatric social service

(G-86)
CORRIN TREE & LANDSCAPE CO
Also Called: Corrin Expert Tree Care
1276 Porter Rd (19701-1311)
PHONE................................302 753-8733
Kenneth M Corrin, *President*
EMP: 5 **EST:** 2011
SALES: 85K **Privately Held**
SIC: 0781 Landscape services

(G-87)
CREATIVE LEARNING ACADEMY INC
Also Called: Creative Learning Preschool
1458 Bear Corbitt Rd (19701-1535)
PHONE................................302 834-5259
Fine Washington, *President*
EMP: 9
SQ FT: 3,000
SALES (est): 320K **Privately Held**
SIC: 8351 Child day care services

(G-88)
CRESCENT DENTAL ASSOCIATES
100 Becks Woods Dr (19701-3835)
PHONE................................302 836-6968
EMP: 4
SALES (est): 67.6K **Privately Held**
SIC: 8021 Dentists' office

(G-89)
CROSSFIT BEAR
2611 Del Laws Rd (19701-1706)
PHONE................................302 540-4394
EMP: 4
SALES (est): 93.3K **Privately Held**
SIC: 7991 Health club

(G-90)
CRUISE SHOPPE INC
26 Valerie Dr (19701-1749)
PHONE................................302 737-7220
Carl Shanofk, *President*
Donna Shanofk, *Vice Pres*
EMP: 7
SQ FT: 750
SALES (est): 1.1MM **Privately Held**
SIC: 4724 Travel agencies

(G-91)
CYBERWOLF SOFTWARE INC
8 Willhelen Ct (19701-4818)
PHONE................................302 324-8442
Dennis Debeve, *President*
Dennis Debevec, *Info Tech Dir*
EMP: 1
SALES (est): 96.7K **Privately Held**
WEB: www.cyberwolf-software.com
SIC: 7372 Prepackaged software

(G-92)
D M PEOPLES INVESTMENT CORP
2750 Wrangle Hill Rd (19701-1732)
PHONE................................302 836-1500
Dorothy M Peoples, *President*
Harrison B Peoples, *Vice Pres*
Robert C Peoples Jr, *Vice Pres*
W Thomas Peoples, *Vice Pres*
EMP: 4
SQ FT: 4,000
SALES (est): 313.7K **Privately Held**
SIC: 6799 Real estate investors, except property operators

(G-93)
DANA E HERBERT
Also Called: Desserts By Dana
22 Peterson Pl (19701-3082)
PHONE................................302 721-5798
Dana E Herbert, *Principal*
EMP: 5
SALES (est): 446.3K **Privately Held**
SIC: 2024 Ice cream & frozen desserts

(G-94)
DANS PALLETS & SERVICES
8 Andrew Ln (19701-1542)
PHONE................................302 836-4848
Daniel K Carnley, *Principal*
EMP: 1 **EST:** 2010
SALES (est): 91.2K **Privately Held**
SIC: 2448 Pallets, wood & wood with metal

(G-95)
DAVID BRIDGE
245 Benjamin Blvd (19701-1693)
PHONE................................302 429-3317
David Bridge, *Owner*
EMP: 4
SALES (est): 209.9K **Privately Held**
SIC: 1623 Water, sewer & utility lines

(G-96)
DAVID JENKINS
Also Called: Diamond Glo Cleaning Solutions
522 Liam Pl (19701-2442)
PHONE................................302 304-5568
David Jenkins, *Owner*
EMP: 6 **EST:** 2014

SALES (est): 137.7K **Privately Held**
SIC: 7349 Janitorial service, contract basis

(G-97)
DAVID M SARTIN SR
1984 Porter Rd (19701-2189)
PHONE................................302 838-1074
David Sartin, *Principal*
EMP: 4
SALES (est): 387.4K **Privately Held**
SIC: 1611 Highway & street paving contractor

(G-98)
DAVID M WAGNER
Also Called: Daves Lawn Care & Landscaping
812 Archer Pl (19701-2712)
PHONE................................302 832-8336
David M Wagner, *Owner*
EMP: 4
SALES (est): 261K **Privately Held**
SIC: 0782 Lawn care services; landscape contractors

(G-99)
DAVIN MANAGEMENT GROUP LLC
808 Jeffrey Pine Dr (19701-2162)
PHONE................................302 367-6563
Craig Holmes, *President*
EMP: 15
SALES: 1.5MM **Privately Held**
SIC: 8741 7389 Management services;

(G-100)
DBW TAX SERVICES
222 Guilford St (19701-4702)
PHONE................................302 276-0428
Dorothy Williams, *Principal*
EMP: 4 **EST:** 2017
SALES (est): 39.7K **Privately Held**
SIC: 7291 Tax return preparation services

(G-101)
DE NEST STUDIO
216 Lake Arrowhead Cir (19701-1796)
PHONE................................302 836-1316
Nick Denest, *President*
EMP: 4
SALES (est): 207.9K **Privately Held**
SIC: 7336 Commercial art & graphic design

(G-102)
DEAFINITIONS & INTERPRETING
1148 Pulaski Hwy Ste 236 (19701-1306)
PHONE................................302 563-7714
Andrea Mattie, *Coordinator*
EMP: 15
SALES (est): 699.7K **Privately Held**
SIC: 7389 Translation services

(G-103)
DELAWARE ARTS CONSERVATORY
723 Rue Madora Ste 4 (19701-2597)
PHONE................................302 595-4160
Tracy Friswell Jacobs, *Partner*
Scott Jacobs, *Partner*
Bryan Russo, *Partner*
Laura Russo, *Partner*
EMP: 16
SALES (est): 173K **Privately Held**
SIC: 8999 7911 Artist's studio; dance studio & school

(G-104)
DELAWARE BEER WORKS INC
Also Called: Stewart's Brewing Company
219 Governors Pl (19701-3026)
PHONE................................302 836-2739
Forrest Stewart, *President*
EMP: 35
SQ FT: 5,600
SALES (est): 1.4MM **Privately Held**
WEB: www.stewartsbrewingcompany.com
SIC: 5812 2082 American restaurant; beer (alcoholic beverage)

(G-105)
DELAWARE CLEAN SERVICE
4 Winchester Ct (19701-2232)
PHONE................................302 838-1650
EMP: 4

SALES (est): 219.5K **Privately Held**
SIC: 8721 Billing & bookkeeping service

(G-106)
DELAWARE COBRAS INC
122 Honora Dr (19701-2042)
PHONE................................302 983-3500
Richard Edwards, *Principal*
EMP: 4
SALES: 181.4K **Privately Held**
SIC: 7997 Baseball club, except professional & semi-professional

(G-107)
DELAWARE CURATIVE
609 Governors Pl (19701-3034)
PHONE................................302 836-5670
Beth Gilliland, *Director*
EMP: 5
SALES (est): 72.1K **Privately Held**
SIC: 8049 Physical therapist

(G-108)
DELAWARE HEATING & AC
Also Called: Honeywell Authorized Dealer
713 Millcreek Ln (19701-3011)
PHONE................................302 738-4669
Frank J Bartuski, *President*
EMP: 14
SALES (est): 2.2MM **Privately Held**
SIC: 1711 Warm air heating & air conditioning contractor

(G-109)
DELAWARE LAWN & TREE SERVICE
1756 Bear Corbitt Rd (19701-1538)
PHONE................................302 834-7406
Edward R Vickers, *President*
Edward R Vicker Jr, *Vice Pres*
EMP: 10
SQ FT: 3,500
SALES (est): 627.3K **Privately Held**
SIC: 0781 5261 Landscape architects; nursery stock, seeds & bulbs

(G-110)
DELAWARE MOVING & STORAGE INC
214 Bear Christiana Rd (19701-1041)
PHONE................................302 322-0311
James D Hopkins, *President*
David Hopkins, *Vice Pres*
Andrew Hopkins, *Treasurer*
Drew Hopkins, *Sales Executive*
EMP: 51
SQ FT: 8,700
SALES (est): 5.6MM **Privately Held**
SIC: 4214 4225 4213 Household goods moving & storage, local; general warehousing & storage; trucking, except local

(G-111)
DELAWARE ROCK GYM INC
520 Carson Dr (19701-1318)
PHONE................................302 838-5850
Matt McCorquodal, *Principal*
EMP: 6
SALES (est): 137K **Privately Held**
SIC: 7991 Athletic club & gymnasiums, membership

(G-112)
DELAWARE SECRETARY OF STATE
Also Called: State Del Veterans Mem Cmtry
2465 Chesapeake City Rd (19701-2344)
PHONE................................302 834-8046
Estelle Tecker, *Director*
EMP: 7 **Privately Held**
SIC: 0782 9199 9451 Cemetery upkeep services; general government administration; ; administration of veterans' affairs;
HQ: Delaware Secretary of State
  401 Federal St Ste 3
  Dover DE 19901
  302 739-4111

(G-113)
DELAWARE SIDING COMPANY INC
723 Rue Madora Ste 8 (19701-2597)
PHONE................................302 836-6971
Jason Whitaker, *President*
EMP: 6

GEOGRAPHIC SECTION

Bear - New Castle County (G-146)

SALES (est): 754.4K **Privately Held**
SIC: 1761 Siding contractor

(G-114)
DELAWARE WOMENS BOWLING ASSN
9 Winchester Ct (19701-2232)
PHONE.................302 834-7002
Barbara Bardsley, *President*
Ruth-Ann Sydnor, *Corp Secy*
Carolyn Powell, *Vice Pres*
EMP: 11
SALES (est): 198.6K **Privately Held**
SIC: 7933 Ten pin center

(G-115)
DEWITT HEATING AND AC INC
1 Joanne Ct (19701-1884)
PHONE.................267 228-7355
Stanley Wiley, *President*
EMP: 8 **EST:** 2012
SALES: 20K **Privately Held**
SIC: 1711 7389 Warm air heating & air conditioning contractor;

(G-116)
DIAMOND STATE COMMERCIAL CLG
9 S Sherman Dr (19701-3088)
PHONE.................215 888-2575
Walter Sellers, *Principal*
EMP: 4
SALES (est): 57.7K **Privately Held**
SIC: 7349 7342 Building & office cleaning services; building cleaning service; rest room cleaning service

(G-117)
DIAMOND STATE PROPS
463 Granger Dr (19701-2175)
PHONE.................302 528-7146
Joe Winnington, *Principal*
EMP: 4
SALES (est): 192K **Privately Held**
SIC: 3369 Nonferrous foundries

(G-118)
DIAMOND STATE TIRE INC
3482 Wrangle Hill Rd (19701-1845)
PHONE.................302 836-1919
Ed Long, *President*
Steve Bailey, *Vice Pres*
EMP: 10
SQ FT: 12,000
SALES (est): 2.1MM **Privately Held**
SIC: 5531 7534 Automotive tires; tire retreading & repair shops

(G-119)
DIMPLE CONSTRUCTION INC
3310 Wrangle Hill Rd # 112 (19701-1874)
P.O. Box 1250 (19701-7250)
PHONE.................302 559-7535
Amrinder Singh, *CEO*
EMP: 5
SALES: 600K **Privately Held**
SIC: 1521 Single-family housing construction

(G-120)
DISCOUNT OIL LLC
2126 Old Kirkwood Rd (19701-2249)
P.O. Box 9100, Newark (19714-9100)
PHONE.................302 737-6560
Kathleen M Warne, *Mng Member*
EMP: 5
SALES: 1.3MM **Privately Held**
SIC: 2911 Petroleum refining

(G-121)
DIVISION-DEVELOPMENTAL DSBLTS
2540 Wrangle Hill Rd (19701-3848)
PHONE.................302 836-2110
Warren Ellis, *Principal*
EMP: 2
SALES (est): 74.4K **Privately Held**
SIC: 2821 Plastics materials & resins

(G-122)
DOCS MEDICAL LLC
25 Dynasty Dr (19701-4011)
PHONE.................301 401-1489
Marvin Nune, *Principal*
Sandra Anderson, *Principal*

Jesse Longoria, *Principal*
EMP: 3
SALES (est): 117.4K **Privately Held**
SIC: 3841 2676 3827 5021 Surgical & medical instruments; sanitary paper products; optical instruments & lenses; furniture

(G-123)
DOLPHIN SHIP SERVICES LTD (PA)
235 Hope Ct W (19701-3373)
PHONE.................302 832-0410
Will Schmidt, *President*
EMP: 6
SALES (est): 305.3K **Privately Held**
SIC: 4789 Cargo loading & unloading services

(G-124)
DOROSHOW PASQUALE KARWITZ SIEG
1701 Pulaski Hwy (19701-1711)
PHONE.................302 832-3200
Kristine Wallace, *Branch Mgr*
Shakuntla L Bhaya,
Erin K Brignola,
EMP: 7
SALES (corp-wide): 10.6MM **Privately Held**
SIC: 8111 Bankruptcy law
PA: Doroshow Pasquale Krawitz Siegel Bhaya
 1202 Kirkwood Hwy
 Wilmington DE 19805
 302 998-2397

(G-125)
DOT FOODS INC
301 American Blvd (19701)
PHONE.................302 300-4239
Joe Little, *General Mgr*
EMP: 100
SALES (corp-wide): 1.1B **Privately Held**
SIC: 4225 5142 General warehousing & storage; packaged frozen goods
PA: Dot Foods, Inc.
 1 Dot Way
 Mount Sterling IL 62353
 217 773-4411

(G-126)
DOUBLE S DEVELOPERS INC
Also Called: Double S Co
1919 Red Lion Rd (19701-1855)
PHONE.................302 838-8880
Alvin T Schwartz, *President*
Jeffrey Schwartz, *Vice Pres*
Agnes Tinucci, *Office Mgr*
EMP: 15
SQ FT: 2,100
SALES (est): 1.3MM **Privately Held**
WEB: www.doublescompanies.com
SIC: 1521 Single-family housing construction

(G-127)
DR WEIDONG YANG DENTAL OFFICE
131 Becks Woods Dr (19701-3833)
PHONE.................302 409-3050
EMP: 4
SALES (est): 61.5K **Privately Held**
SIC: 8021 Offices & clinics of dentists

(G-128)
DS PAVING
426 Woods Rd (19701-2102)
PHONE.................302 832-3748
Stanley Daniel, *President*
EMP: 5 **EST:** 2010
SALES (est): 423.6K **Privately Held**
SIC: 1611 Surfacing & paving

(G-129)
DUNCAN S CONCRETE
324 N Red Lion Ter (19701-1029)
PHONE.................302 395-1552
EMP: 5
SALES (est): 242.4K **Privately Held**
SIC: 1771 Concrete work

(G-130)
DUQUE NIEVA MD PA
121 Becks Woods Dr (19701-3851)
PHONE.................302 838-9712
Nieva T Duque MD, *Principal*
EMP: 5
SALES (corp-wide): 944.5K **Privately Held**
SIC: 8011 Gynecologist
PA: Duque Nieva Md Pa
 1010 N Bancroft Pkwy L3
 Wilmington DE 19805
 302 655-2048

(G-131)
DYNAMIC THERAPY SERVICES LLC
Also Called: Aquatic Rehabilitation
1651-53 Pulaski Hwy (19701)
PHONE.................302 834-1550
Heather Browne, *Manager*
EMP: 23
SALES (corp-wide): 12.9MM **Privately Held**
WEB: www.dynamicpt.com
SIC: 8049 Physical therapist
PA: Dynamic Therapy Services Llc
 1501 Blueball Ave
 Linwood PA 19061
 610 859-8850

(G-132)
E I DU PONT DE NEMOURS & CO
407 Cheer Ct (19701-3366)
PHONE.................302 695-7141
Ellen Kullman, *Branch Mgr*
EMP: 339
SALES (corp-wide): 30.6B **Publicly Held**
SIC: 2879 Agricultural chemicals
HQ: E. I. Du Pont De Nemours And Company
 974 Centre Rd Bldg 735
 Wilmington DE 19805
 302 485-3000

(G-133)
EAGLE ERECTORS INC
3500 Wrangle Hill Rd (19701-1843)
PHONE.................302 832-9586
Al.Klerlein, *President*
John Klerlein, *Vice Pres*
Melissa Klerlein, *Manager*
EMP: 42
SQ FT: 30,000
SALES (est): 9.5MM **Privately Held**
SIC: 3441 3312 Fabricated structural metal; blast furnaces & steel mills

(G-134)
EAGLE EYE AMERICA INC
405 Bergenia Loop (19701-4881)
PHONE.................302 392-3600
Srini Lokula, *President*
EMP: 1 **EST:** 2011
SALES (est): 506.2K **Privately Held**
SIC: 7379 7375 7371 7372 Computer related maintenance services; information retrieval services; custom computer programming services; prepackaged software; computer maintenance & repair

(G-135)
EAR ENTERPRISE LLC
123 Pinion Pl (19701-2161)
PHONE.................302 836-8334
Evelyn Russell,
EMP: 4
SALES (est): 254.6K **Privately Held**
WEB: www.rcpeoples.com
SIC: 6531 Real estate agents & managers

(G-136)
EAST COAST GAMES INC
24 Eaton Pl (19701-2370)
PHONE.................302 838-0669
James Servia, *President*
EMP: 10
SALES (est): 735.1K **Privately Held**
SIC: 3577 Computer peripheral equipment

(G-137)
EAST WEST ENGINEERING INC
130 Wynnefield Rd (19701-4854)
P.O. Box 32 (19701-0032)
PHONE.................302 528-0652

William W LI, *President*
EMP: 7
SALES (est): 799.6K **Privately Held**
SIC: 8711 Engineering services

(G-138)
EASTERN AUTO BODY INC
700 Elizabeth Ln (19701-2603)
PHONE.................302 731-1200
Mike Filipkowski, *Principal*
EMP: 4
SALES (est): 490K **Privately Held**
SIC: 7532 Body shop, automotive

(G-139)
EASTERN MAIL TRANSPORT INC
900 Julian Ln (19701-2277)
PHONE.................302 838-0500
Byron D Williams, *President*
Marjorie Williams, *Vice Pres*
EMP: 18
SALES (est): 1.6MM **Privately Held**
SIC: 4213 4212 Trucking, except local; contract haulers; mail carriers, contract

(G-140)
EDWARD LAND CONSULTING INC
27 Rose Hill Dr (19701-2398)
PHONE.................302 838-7003
Edward Land, *Owner*
EMP: 4
SALES (est): 178.1K **Privately Held**
SIC: 7379 Computer related consulting services

(G-141)
EDYTHE L PRIDGEN
450 S Hyde Pl (19701-1070)
PHONE.................302 652-8887
EMP: 2
SALES (est): 92.3K **Privately Held**
SIC: 2752 Commercial printing, lithographic

(G-142)
ELANCO INC
723 Rue Madora Ste 6 (19701-2597)
PHONE.................302 731-8500
Anthony Gonzon, *Principal*
EMP: 5
SALES (est): 785.3K **Privately Held**
SIC: 3443 Fabricated plate work (boiler shop)

(G-143)
ELS
13 Dunleary Dr (19701-6357)
PHONE.................302 312-3645
EMP: 2 **EST:** 2015
SALES (est): 116.3K **Privately Held**
SIC: 2879 Agricultural chemicals

(G-144)
ENVISION IT PUBLICATIONS LLC
Also Called: Stylish Stylus, The
1148 Pulaski Hwy (19701-1306)
PHONE.................800 329-9411
Candice Huddy, *President*
Thomas Kenny, *Vice Pres*
EMP: 2 **EST:** 2009
SALES (est): 99.5K **Privately Held**
SIC: 2721 8999 7389 8732 Periodicals: publishing & printing; commercial & literary writings; apparel designers, commercial; survey service: marketing, location, etc.; graphic arts & related design

(G-145)
EROSION CONTROL SERVICES DE
1432 Elk Way (19701-3707)
PHONE.................302 218-8913
Robert McGowan, *President*
EMP: 25
SALES (est): 2.5MM **Privately Held**
SIC: 1731 Environmental system control installation

(G-146)
EWS FUNERAL HOME
219 Niobrara Ln (19701-4805)
PHONE.................302 494-1847

Bear - New Castle County (G-147)

Evan Smith, *Principal*
EMP: 4
SALES (est): 64.4K **Privately Held**
SIC: 7261 Funeral home

(G-147)
F & S BOAT WORKS
353 Summit Pointe Cir (19701-2604)
PHONE...................302 838-5500
James Floyd, *Owner*
EMP: 21
SALES (est): 3.1MM **Privately Held**
WEB: www.fsboatworks.com
SIC: 3732 Boats, fiberglass: building & repairing

(G-148)
FACTORS ETC INC
1218 Pulaski Hwy Ste 484 (19701-4300)
PHONE...................302 834-1625
Harry Lee Geissler Jr, *President*
EMP: 55
SALES (est): 3.6MM **Privately Held**
SIC: 2752 2759 Transfers, decalcomania or dry; lithographed; screen printing

(G-149)
FAIRWINDS BAPTIST CHURCH INC
Also Called: Fairwinds Christian School
801 Seymour Rd (19701-1121)
PHONE...................302 322-1029
Carlo Destefano, *Pastor*
EMP: 7
SALES (est): 355.5K **Privately Held**
SIC: 8661 8699 Baptist Church; charitable organization

(G-150)
FEENEY CHROPRACTIC CARE CTR PA
Also Called: Feeney Chrprctic Care Cntre PA
835 Pulaski Hwy (19701-1240)
PHONE...................302 328-0200
John Feeney, *Owner*
EMP: 11
SQ FT: 5,000
SALES (est): 744K **Privately Held**
WEB: www.unitedspinecentre.com
SIC: 8041 Offices & clinics of chiropractors

(G-151)
FIRST CHOICE HEALTH CARE INC
12 Fox Hunt Dr (19701-2534)
PHONE...................302 836-6150
Ronald Saggese, *President*
EMP: 7
SQ FT: 1,400
SALES (est): 361.1K **Privately Held**
SIC: 8041 Offices & clinics of chiropractors

(G-152)
FIRST MONTGOMERY PROPERTIES
Also Called: Fox Run Apartments
900 Woodchuck Pl (19701-2775)
PHONE...................302 834-8272
Kelly Crowley, *Manager*
EMP: 20
SALES (corp-wide): 3.7MM **Privately Held**
WEB: www.morgan-properties.com
SIC: 6531 6513 Real estate leasing & rentals; apartment building operators
PA: First Montgomery Properties, Ltd.
160 Clubhouse Rd
King Of Prussia PA 19406
610 265-2800

(G-153)
FIRST STATE LANDSCAPING
214 Springwood Dr (19701-3602)
P.O. Box 1369 (19701-7369)
PHONE...................302 420-8604
Brad Wortman,
EMP: 10
SALES (est): 827K **Privately Held**
SIC: 4971 Irrigation systems

(G-154)
FIRST STATE PHYSICIA NS (PA)
12 Fox Hunt Dr (19701-2534)
PHONE...................302 836-6150
Kevin McDermott, *Owner*
EMP: 5
SALES (est): 564.2K **Privately Held**
SIC: 8041 Offices & clinics of chiropractors

(G-155)
FLADGER & ASSOCIATES INC
204 Stewards Ct (19701-2296)
PHONE...................302 836-3100
Michael Fladger, *CEO*
EMP: 30 **EST:** 1992
SQ FT: 2,500
SALES (est): 5MM **Privately Held**
WEB: www.fladgerassociates.com
SIC: 7363 Employee leasing service

(G-156)
FLOWRITE INC
Also Called: Flowrite Plumbing
102 Country Woods Dr (19701-1436)
PHONE...................302 547-5657
Bill Ebert, *Principal*
EMP: 5
SALES (est): 542.7K **Privately Held**
SIC: 1711 Plumbing contractors

(G-157)
FOLEY INCORPORATED
Also Called: Caterpillar Authorized Dealer
720 Pulaski Hwy (19701-5210)
PHONE...................302 328-4131
Charles Racine, *Manager*
EMP: 30
SALES (corp-wide): 253.8MM **Privately Held**
WEB: www.ransome.com
SIC: 5082 Contractors' materials
PA: Foley Incorporated
855 Centennial Ave
Piscataway NJ 08854
732 885-5555

(G-158)
FOX & ROACH LP
Also Called: Prudential Fox Roach Realtors
1126 Pulaski Hwy (19701-1306)
PHONE...................302 836-2888
Brenda Murray, *Partner*
Connie Wilson, *Sales Staff*
EMP: 45
SALES (corp-wide): 16.3MM **Privately Held**
WEB: www.prufoxroach.com
SIC: 6531 Real estate agent, residential
PA: Fox & Roach Lp
431 W Lancaster Ave
Devon PA 19333
610 722-7851

(G-159)
FOX RUN AUTOMOTIVE INC
610 Connor Blvd (19701-1745)
PHONE...................302 834-1200
Michael Defino, *President*
Michael Accursi, *General Mgr*
Rick Taraumina, *Vice Pres*
EMP: 18
SQ FT: 7,000
SALES (est): 2MM **Privately Held**
WEB: www.foxrunautomotive.com
SIC: 7538 General automotive repair shops

(G-160)
FRANK FALCO MD
Also Called: Comprhnsive Spine Spt Medicine
100 Becks Woods Dr # 102 (19701-3835)
PHONE...................302 392-6501
Frank Falco MD, *Owner*
EMP: 10
SALES (est): 321.5K **Privately Held**
SIC: 8011 Physical medicine, physician/surgeon

(G-161)
FRESENIUS MEDICAL CARE NEPHR
Also Called: Fresenius Medical Care Fox Run
2520 Wrangle Hill Rd (19701-3849)
PHONE...................302 836-6093
Mary Garber, *Manager*
EMP: 8
SALES (corp-wide): 18.3B **Privately Held**
SIC: 8092 Kidney dialysis centers
HQ: Fresenius Medical Care Nephrology And Internal Medicine Dialysis Centers, Llc
920 Winter St
Waltham MA 02451

(G-162)
FURNITURE WHL CONNECTION INC
Also Called: Furniture Solution
1890 Pulaski Hwy (19701-1710)
PHONE...................302 836-6000
Robert Cohen, *President*
Janice Cohen, *Vice Pres*
EMP: 12
SQ FT: 8,000
SALES (est): 2.5MM **Privately Held**
SIC: 5712 5021 Furniture stores; furniture

(G-163)
G2 GROUP INC
Also Called: G2 Lab Group
88 Loblolly Ln (19701-2167)
PHONE...................302 836-4202
Gerald V Holmes, *President*
John K Holmes, *Vice Pres*
Susan D Holmes, *Admin Sec*
EMP: 7
SALES (est): 1.6MM **Privately Held**
SIC: 5712 1751 Customized furniture & cabinets; cabinet building & installation

(G-164)
GAMMA THETA LAMBDA ED
2 N Sherman Dr (19701-3087)
P.O. Box 25209, Wilmington (19899-5209)
PHONE...................302 983-9429
Michael Yancey, *President*
Charles Baylor Jr, *Principal*
Reginald Hughes, *Principal*
El Cid Jones, *Principal*
Kevin McAllister, *Principal*
EMP: 6
SALES (est): 83.3K **Privately Held**
SIC: 4832 Educational

(G-165)
GLASGOW SHOPPING CENTER CORP
2750 Wrangle Hill Rd (19701-1732)
PHONE...................302 836-1503
W Thomas Peoples, *Vice Pres*
Harrison B Peoples, *Vice Pres*
Robert C Peoples Jr, *Vice Pres*
Ms Jesse Moxley, *Manager*
EMP: 5
SQ FT: 2,000
SALES (est): 520K **Privately Held**
SIC: 6512 Commercial & industrial building operation

(G-166)
GOLDENOPP RE SOLUTIONS
936 King James Ct (19701-4737)
PHONE...................908 565-0510
Timothy Oppelt, *Principal*
EMP: 7
SALES (est): 170.5K **Privately Held**
SIC: 6531 Real estate agent, residential

(G-167)
GOLDMINE ENTERPRISES INC
930 Woods Rd (19701-2106)
PHONE...................302 834-4314
Joseph Dugan, *President*
▲ **EMP:** 2
SALES (est): 107.6K **Privately Held**
SIC: 3961 Jewelry apparel, non-precious metals

(G-168)
GOTSHADEONLINE INC
Also Called: Formula One Tinting Graphics
1700 Firedancer Ln (19701-5216)
PHONE...................302 832-8468
Sylvia Gourley, *President*
EMP: 6
SALES: 400K **Privately Held**
SIC: 1799 3993 7319 Glass tinting, architectural or automotive; signs & advertising specialties; transit advertising services; car card advertising

(G-169)
GPE CONSTRUCTION LLC
129 Mendel Ct (19701-3062)
PHONE...................267 595-8942
Paul Wilson,
EMP: 5
SALES (est): 195.7K **Privately Held**
SIC: 1521 New construction, single-family houses

(G-170)
GREAT NEW BEGINNINGS
14 Saint Andrews Dr (19701-4762)
PHONE...................302 218-8332
Linda Clark, *President*
EMP: 5
SALES (est): 227.9K **Privately Held**
SIC: 8351 Child day care services

(G-171)
GREEN DOT CAPITAL LLC
203 Cornwell Dr (19701-3103)
PHONE...................302 395-0500
Ernest Green, *Principal*
EMP: 5 **EST:** 2017
SALES (est): 302.9K **Privately Held**
SIC: 6799 Investors

(G-172)
GREENBROOK TMS NEUROHEALTH CTR
121 Becks Woods Dr # 204 (19701-3851)
PHONE...................302 994-4010
EMP: 1
SALES (corp-wide): 1.8MM **Privately Held**
SIC: 3312 Blast furnaces & steel mills
PA: Greenbrook Tms Neurohealth Center
8405 Greensboro Dr # 120
Mc Lean VA 22102
703 356-1568

(G-173)
GREGGO & FERRARA INC
Also Called: Bear Concrete
595 Walther Rd (19701)
PHONE...................302 834-3333
Mike Mayhugh, *Branch Mgr*
EMP: 25
SALES (corp-wide): 74.7MM **Privately Held**
SIC: 3273 Ready-mixed concrete
PA: Greggo & Ferrara, Inc.
4048 New Castle Ave
New Castle DE 19720
302 658-5241

(G-174)
H&R BLOCK INC
Also Called: H & R Block
54 Foxhunt Dr (19701-2534)
PHONE...................302 836-2700
George Manz, *General Mgr*
EMP: 12
SALES (corp-wide): 3B **Publicly Held**
WEB: www.hrblock.com
SIC: 7291 Tax return preparation services
PA: H&R Block, Inc.
1 H&R Block Way
Kansas City MO 64105
816 854-3000

(G-175)
HAGE TOOL AND MACHINE INC
3415 Wrangle Hill Rd # 7 (19701-4812)
PHONE...................302 836-4850
George Kennedy Jr, *Owner*
EMP: 5
SALES (est): 640.3K **Privately Held**
SIC: 3599 Machine shop, jobbing & repair

(G-176)
HALPERN EYE ASSOCIATES INC
1237 Quintilio Dr (19701-6005)
PHONE...................302 838-0800
Dana Hobbs, *Branch Mgr*
EMP: 8
SALES (corp-wide): 4.3MM **Privately Held**
SIC: 8042 Offices & clinics of optometrists
PA: Halpern Eye Associates, Inc.
885 S Governors Ave
Dover DE 19904
302 734-5861

GEOGRAPHIC SECTION
Bear - New Castle County (G-211)

(G-177)
HARMAN HAY PUBLICATIONS INC
221 Cornwell Dr (19701-3103)
PHONE..................................302 669-9144
EMP: 1 EST: 2016
SALES (est): 37.5K Privately Held
SIC: 2741 Miscellaneous publishing

(G-178)
HARVARD ENVIRONMENTAL INC
760 Pulaski Hwy (19701-5200)
PHONE..................................302 326-2333
Wesley Morrison, President
Ashley Mote, Manager
EMP: 17
SQ FT: 2,500
SALES (est): 1.7MM Privately Held
WEB: www.harvardenvironmental.com
SIC: 8748 Environmental consultant

(G-179)
HAUNTED INDUSTRIES
457 Buck Jersey Rd (19701-2339)
PHONE..................................302 836-5823
James T Jones, Principal
EMP: 1
SALES (est): 56K Privately Held
SIC: 3999 Manufacturing industries

(G-180)
HEALING ADULTS & ADOLESCENTS
Also Called: Haart Program
3560 Wrangle Hill Rd (19701-1843)
PHONE..................................302 836-4000
EMP: 5 EST: 2015
SALES (est): 198.4K Privately Held
SIC: 8049 Offices of health practitioner

(G-181)
HEIDIS ACADEMY OF PRFRMG ARTS
1218 Pulaski Hwy (19701-4318)
PHONE..................................302 293-7868
Heidi Yancey, Exec Dir
Joanne Irby, Administration
EMP: 10
SALES: 90K Privately Held
SIC: 7922 Performing arts center production

(G-182)
HERTIAGE BUILDERS & IMPROVEMEN
9 Linn Ct (19701-1351)
PHONE..................................302 275-8675
Tom Miller, Owner
EMP: 5
SALES (est): 213.3K Privately Held
SIC: 1799 Special trade contractors

(G-183)
HIDDEN HITCH & TRAILER PARTS
304 Connor Blvd (19701-1742)
PHONE..................................410 398-5949
William Harrington, President
EMP: 6
SQ FT: 4,000
SALES: 500K Privately Held
SIC: 7539 Trailer repair

(G-184)
HIGHDEF TRANSPORTATION LLC
8 Dover Ct (19701-1618)
PHONE..................................610 212-8596
Macy Robinson,
Samual Sanders,
EMP: 7
SALES (est): 144.1K Privately Held
SIC: 8748 Business consulting

(G-185)
HIGHLAND CONSTRUCTION LLC
3415 Wrangle Hill Rd # 10 (19701-4812)
PHONE..................................302 286-6990
Edward Neal, Owner
EMP: 17
SQ FT: 4,800

SALES: 500K Privately Held
SIC: 1611 1771 4212 Concrete construction: roads, highways, sidewalks, etc.; blacktop (asphalt) work; local trucking, without storage

(G-186)
HOME CARE ASSISTANCE DE
11 Mcmahon Dr (19701-2049)
PHONE..................................856 625-9934
Susan Imam, Manager
EMP: 8
SALES (est): 61.1K Privately Held
SIC: 8082 Home health care services

(G-187)
I AM CONSULTING GROUP INC
12 Dunleary Dr (19701-6355)
P.O. Box 884 (19701-0884)
PHONE..................................302 521-4999
Valerie Brown Baul, President
EMP: 10
SALES (est): 544.2K Privately Held
SIC: 8748 Business consulting

(G-188)
INNPROS INC
Also Called: AmericInn Lodge & Suites
875 Pulaski Hwy (19701-1252)
PHONE..................................302 326-2500
Ann Watkins, CEO
Ginny Wilkins, General Mgr
EMP: 10
SALES (est): 224.4K Privately Held
WEB: www.derooms.com
SIC: 7041 Membership-basis organization hotels

(G-189)
INTERNTIONAL MKT SUPPLIERS INC
Also Called: IMS
400 Carson Dr (19701-1314)
PHONE..................................302 392-1840
Bruce Hugelmeyer, CEO
Francis Nuzzi, President
EMP: 12
SQ FT: 21,000
SALES (est): 5.2MM Privately Held
SIC: 5169 Chemicals & allied products

(G-190)
INTERSTATE AERIALS LLC
900 Julian Ln (19701-2277)
PHONE..................................302 838-1117
Ray Wenger, CFO
Michael Love, Sales Mgr
Matt Lang,
EMP: 4
SALES (est): 355.8K Privately Held
SIC: 7353 Heavy construction equipment rental

(G-191)
INUMSOFT INC
2500 Wrangle Hill Rd # 222 (19701-3836)
PHONE..................................302 533-5403
Pbvs Lakshmi Meka, President
EMP: 6
SALES (est): 460K Privately Held
SIC: 7371 7379 Computer software development; computer related consulting services

(G-192)
IRENE C SZETO MD
121 Becks Woods Dr # 100 (19701-3851)
PHONE..................................302 832-1560
Irene C Szeto MD, Owner
EMP: 5
SALES (est): 261.9K Privately Held
SIC: 8011 Internal medicine, physician/surgeon

(G-193)
ITEA INC
Also Called: Springhaus Landscape Company
370 School Bell Rd (19701-1129)
PHONE..................................302 328-3716
Steve Price, President
George Price, Principal
Debbie Mulholland, Vice Pres
EMP: 9

SALES: 1.1MM Privately Held
WEB: www.itea.com
SIC: 0782 5261 Landscape contractors; nursery stock, seeds & bulbs

(G-194)
J & K AUTO REPAIR INC
Also Called: J&K Fleet Service
3310 Wrangle Hill Rd # 103 (19701-1874)
PHONE..................................302 834-8025
Jim Brinkley, President
EMP: 7
SALES (est): 639.7K Privately Held
SIC: 7538 7539 General automotive repair shops; brake services

(G-195)
J N HOOKER INC
Also Called: All About Kidz
1799 Pulaski Hwy (19701-1711)
PHONE..................................302 838-5650
Jahara Hooker, President
EMP: 24
SQ FT: 9,000
SALES (est): 143.7K Privately Held
SIC: 8351 Child day care services

(G-196)
JAED CORPORATION (PA)
Also Called: Studio Jaed
2500 Wrangle Hill Rd # 110 (19701-3840)
PHONE..................................302 832-1652
James A Hutchison III, CEO
Philip Conte, Principal
Joseph Skinner, Principal
David Spangler, Principal
Edward Lupineck, Senior VP
EMP: 19
SQ FT: 5,500
SALES (est): 3MM Privately Held
WEB: www.studiojaed.com
SIC: 8712 8711 Architectural engineering; engineering services

(G-197)
JAIRUS ENTERPRISES INC
1218 Pulaski Hwy Ste 484 (19701-4300)
PHONE..................................302 834-1625
Richard Thomas, President
EMP: 5
SQ FT: 6,000
SALES: 220K Privately Held
SIC: 2396 Screen printing on fabric articles

(G-198)
JBA ENTERPRISES
109 Peace Ct W (19701-3372)
PHONE..................................302 834-6685
Charles Jones, Owner
EMP: 14
SALES: 150K Privately Held
SIC: 7349 7389 Janitorial service, contract basis;

(G-199)
JCHOLLEY LLC
Also Called: Connie's Market
3661 Wrangle Hill Rd (19701-1906)
PHONE..................................302 653-6659
EMP: 7
SALES (est): 1.1MM Privately Held
SIC: 5141 Whol General Groceries

(G-200)
JERRY O THOMPSON PRNTNG
4 Ogden Ct (19701-2056)
PHONE..................................302 832-1309
Jerry Thompson, Principal
EMP: 2
SALES (est): 160.6K Privately Held
SIC: 2752 Commercial printing, lithographic

(G-201)
JJID INC
100 Julian Ln (19701-2274)
PHONE..................................302 836-0414
Joseph R Julian, President
James J Julian, President
Doc Conn, Safety Mgr
Cheryl Ayares, Accounting Mgr
Dylan Norris, Manager
EMP: 50

SALES (est): 21.6MM Privately Held
SIC: 1611 1629 General contractor, highway & street construction; waste water & sewage treatment plant construction

(G-202)
JMT INTER LLC
415 Aldwych Dr (19701-2586)
PHONE..................................302 312-5177
Jean Marie Tuete,
▲ EMP: 4
SALES: 172K Privately Held
SIC: 3411 Food & beverage containers

(G-203)
JOHN WASNIEWSKI III DMD
262 Foxhunt Dr (19701-2536)
PHONE..................................302 832-1371
EMP: 4
SALES (est): 61.5K Privately Held
SIC: 8021 Offices & clinics of dentists

(G-204)
JOHNS AUTO PARTS INC
10 Nick Ct (19701-1120)
PHONE..................................302 322-3273
John Elasic, President
Deborah Elasic, Vice Pres
EMP: 12
SALES (est): 1MM Privately Held
SIC: 5013 Automotive supplies & parts

(G-205)
JT HOOVER CONCRETE INC
3415 Wrangle Hill Rd # 1 (19701-4812)
PHONE..................................302 832-7699
John T Hoover, President
EMP: 45
SALES (est): 6.3MM Privately Held
SIC: 1771 Concrete work

(G-206)
JUST ONE EMBROIDERER
17 Decidedly Ln (19701-3347)
PHONE..................................302 832-9655
Joe Loughlin, Principal
EMP: 2
SALES (est): 100.2K Privately Held
SIC: 2395 Embroidery & art needlework

(G-207)
JUST RIGHT TIRES INC
1148 Pulaski Hwy Ste 331 (19701-1306)
PHONE..................................302 268-2825
EMP: 13 EST: 2017
SALES: 100K Privately Held
SIC: 7539 5531 Automotive Repair Ret Auto/Home Supplies

(G-208)
JV S CLEANING SERVICES
1148 Pulaski Hwy Ste 151 (19701-1306)
PHONE..................................302 345-7679
Joan Virgil, Principal
EMP: 5
SALES (est): 70.8K Privately Held
SIC: 7349 Cleaning service, industrial or commercial

(G-209)
JWR 1 LLC
11 Biltmore Ct (19701-4005),
PHONE..................................302 379-9951
Erin Rautio, Owner
EMP: 6
SALES (est): 71.1K Privately Held
SIC: 7218 Industrial launderers

(G-210)
K & R SEAL COATING LLC
135 Willamette Dr (19701-4803)
PHONE..................................302 530-3649
Kenneth Spicer,
EMP: 4
SALES: 60K Privately Held
WEB: www.krsealcoatingandpressure.com
SIC: 1799 Coating, caulking & weather, water & fireproofing

(G-211)
K K AMERICAN CORPORATION
231 Shai Cir (19701-3606)
PHONE..................................302 738-8982
Ching Tsai, President
▲ EMP: 4
SQ FT: 1,600

(PA)=Parent Co (HQ)=Headquarters (DH)=Div Headquarters
✪ = New Business established in last 2 years

2020 Harris Directory of Delaware Businesses

Bear - New Castle County (G-212)   GEOGRAPHIC SECTION

SALES: 1MM **Privately Held**
SIC: 5199 Packaging materials
PA: Taiwan K.K. Corporation
  5f, 14, Lane 235, Paoqiao Rd.,
  New Taipei City TAP 23145

(G-212)
KATLYN CO CERAMICS
9 Moores Dr (19701-1402)
PHONE..................302 528-1322
EMP: 2
SALES (est): 105.9K **Privately Held**
SIC: 3269 Pottery products

(G-213)
KAUFFMAN WOODWORKS
1967 Pulaski Hwy (19701-1708)
PHONE..................302 836-1976
EMP: 1
SALES (est): 54.1K **Privately Held**
SIC: 2431 Millwork

(G-214)
KELLY WALKER DDS
1991 Pulaski Hwy (19701-1708)
PHONE..................302 832-2200
Kelly Walker, *Owner*
EMP: 5
SALES (est): 242.8K **Privately Held**
SIC: 8021 Dentists' office

(G-215)
KENNETH DEITCH
Also Called: Office Furnish & Sup Bus Ctr
95 Loblolly Ln (19701-2167)
PHONE..................302 838-2808
Kenneth Deitch, *Owner*
EMP: 4 EST: 1993
SQ FT: 750
SALES: 500K **Privately Held**
SIC: 5021 Office & public building furniture

(G-216)
KEVIN GARBER
Also Called: Carpentry Unlimited
148 Carlotta Dr (19701-2104)
PHONE..................302 834-0639
Kevin Garber, *Owner*
EMP: 8
SALES (est): 496.2K **Privately Held**
SIC: 1751 Carpentry work

(G-217)
KFS STRATEGIC MGT SVCS LLC
125 Rickey Blvd Unit 1650 (19701-8669)
PHONE..................302 545-7640
Frederick Smith Jr, *CEO*
EMP: 12
SALES (est): 332.8K **Privately Held**
SIC: 8748 8742 Business consulting; business consultant

(G-218)
KIDZ INK (PA)
1703 Porter Rd (19701-2119)
PHONE..................302 838-1500
Linda Clark, *President*
EMP: 40 EST: 1998
SQ FT: 7,800
SALES (est): 2.4MM **Privately Held**
WEB: www.gnbkids.com
SIC: 8351 Preschool center

(G-219)
KITE
446 School Bell Rd (19701-1147)
PHONE..................302 324-9569
Elaine Kite, *Principal*
EMP: 2 EST: 2010
SALES (est): 116.3K **Privately Held**
SIC: 3944 Kites

(G-220)
KORTECH CONSULTING INC
13 Primrose Dr (19701-6317)
PHONE..................302 559-4612
Alioune Tounkara, *CEO*
EMP: 10 EST: 2015
SALES (est): 414.3K **Privately Held**
SIC: 7379 7371 8742 8243 Computer related consulting services; computer software development; management consulting services; software training, computer; systems software development services;

(G-221)
KPV ENTERPRISES LLC ✪
125 Mendel Ct (19701-3077)
PHONE..................302 500-9669
Patricia Harris,
EMP: 4 EST: 2019
SALES: 100K **Privately Held**
SIC: 6799 Investors

(G-222)
KRAEMER & SONS LLC
4077 Wrangle Hill Rd (19701-1921)
PHONE..................302 832-1534
Jeffrey Kraemer, *Principal*
EMP: 4 EST: 2008
SALES (est): 202.8K **Privately Held**
SIC: 7549 Towing services

(G-223)
KRESKE KARES LLC
4 Cottage Ct (19701-1420)
PHONE..................302 893-5600
Renee Kreske,
EMP: 4
SALES (est): 117.2K **Privately Held**
SIC: 8059 Personal care home, with health care

(G-224)
KRISALLIS
2419 Porter Rd (19701-2019)
PHONE..................610 522-7273
Carmen Anderson, *CEO*
EMP: 2
SALES (est): 73.4K **Privately Held**
SIC: 2231 Apparel & outerwear broadwoven fabrics

(G-225)
KW SOLAR SOLUTIONS INC
2444 Denny Rd (19701-2314)
PHONE..................302 838-8400
Dale Wolf, *President*
Jackie Johnson, *Manager*
Ann Wolf, *Administration*
EMP: 8
SALES (est): 1MM **Privately Held**
SIC: 1711 Solar energy contractor

(G-226)
KW SOLAR SOLUTIONS INC
2444 Denny Rd (19701-2314)
PHONE..................302 838-8400
Dale Wolf, *President*
EMP: 8 EST: 2012
SALES (est): 403.9K **Privately Held**
SIC: 1711 Solar energy contractor

(G-227)
LABORATORY CORPORATION AMERICA
101 Becks Woods Dr (19701-3855)
PHONE..................302 834-6845
EMP: 8
SALES (est): 87K **Publicly Held**
SIC: 8071 Testing laboratories
HQ: Laboratory Corporation Of America
  358 S Main St Ste 458
  Burlington NC 27215
  336 229-1127

(G-228)
LADY PS HAIR DESIGNS INC
117 Emerald Ridge Dr (19701-2280)
PHONE..................302 832-2668
Paula Wright, *President*
EMP: 4
SALES (est): 108.8K **Privately Held**
SIC: 7231 Beauty shops

(G-229)
LASER IMAGES OF DELAWARE INC
100 E Scotland Dr (19701-1756)
PHONE..................302 836-8610
Ed Bell, *President*
Nancy Bell, *Vice Pres*
EMP: 7
SQ FT: 5,000
SALES (est): 520K **Privately Held**
SIC: 7378 5734 Computer & data processing equipment repair/maintenance; computer software & accessories

(G-230)
LAUREN FARMS GROUP HOME
Also Called: Martin Luther Homes
116 Walls Way (19701-1803)
PHONE..................302 836-1379
Terry Olson, *Owner*
EMP: 8
SALES (est): 127.3K **Privately Held**
SIC: 8059 Home for the mentally retarded, exc. skilled or intermediate

(G-231)
LAWN QUENCHERS INC
2633 Denny Rd (19701-2307)
PHONE..................302 218-1909
Richard L Hindt, *President*
EMP: 4
SALES (est): 238.3K **Privately Held**
SIC: 0782 Lawn care services

(G-232)
LEADERSHIP CADDIE
15 Waterton Dr (19701-4915)
PHONE..................302 743-6456
EMP: 10
SALES (est): 540K **Privately Held**
SIC: 8331 8748 Leading Edge Coaching And Consulting

(G-233)
LEARNING CIRCLE CHILD CARE
765 Old Porter Rd (19701-1841)
PHONE..................302 834-1473
Diane Callaway, *Owner*
EMP: 5 EST: 1998
SALES (est): 99.3K **Privately Held**
SIC: 8351 Child day care services

(G-234)
LIBERTY ELECTRIC LLC
1102 Varsity Ln (19701-3913)
P.O. Box 8 (19701-0008)
PHONE..................410 275-9200
Aimee Smith, *Principal*
EMP: 6
SALES (est): 322.9K **Privately Held**
SIC: 1731 Electrical work

(G-235)
LIMESTONE OPEN MRI LLC
101 Becks Woods Dr # 103 (19701-3854)
PHONE..................302 834-4500
Chris Coyne, *Branch Mgr*
EMP: 6
SALES (est): 322.8K
SALES (corp-wide): 1.3MM **Privately Held**
SIC: 8011 Radiologist
PA: Limestone Open Mri, Llc
  2060 Limestone Rd
  Wilmington DE 19808
  302 246-2001

(G-236)
LINDA PUTNAM DAY CARE
525 Deer Run (19701-2716)
PHONE..................302 836-1033
Linda Putnam, *Principal*
EMP: 5
SALES (est): 121.2K **Privately Held**
SIC: 8351 Child day care services

(G-237)
LITTLE POPLE CHILD DEV CTR INC
3843 Wrangle Hill Rd (19701-1919)
PHONE..................302 836-5900
Janice Palmer, *President*
Nathaniel L Marks, *Vice Pres*
EMP: 13
SALES (est): 750.9K **Privately Held**
SIC: 8351 Preschool center

(G-238)
LOWES HOME CENTERS LLC
800 Eden Cir (19701-4308)
PHONE..................302 834-8508
Tony Starkper, *Store Mgr*
Ken Taylor, *Manager*
EMP: 150
SALES (corp-wide): 71.3B **Publicly Held**
SIC: 5211 5031 5722 5064 Home centers; building materials, exterior; building materials, interior; household appliance stores; electrical appliances, television & radio
HQ: Lowe's Home Centers, Llc
  1605 Curtis Bridge Rd
  Wilkesboro NC 28697
  336 658-4000

(G-239)
LST INSVESTMENT LLC
Also Called: AAMCO Transmissions
819 Pulaski Hwy (19701-1239)
PHONE..................302 322-3454
Lane Carey, *Principal*
EMP: 7
SQ FT: 5,000
SALES (est): 480K **Privately Held**
SIC: 7537 Automotive transmission repair shops

(G-240)
LUMS POND ANIMAL HOSPITAL INC
3052 Wrangle Hill Rd (19701-1714)
PHONE..................302 836-5585
Robert Thompson, *President*
Betsy Helm, *Technician*
EMP: 50
SALES (est): 3.1MM **Privately Held**
SIC: 0742 Animal hospital services, pets & other animal specialties

(G-241)
LUX SPA & NAILS
122 Foxhunt Dr (19701-2535)
PHONE..................302 834-4899
EMP: 4
SALES (est): 28.8K **Privately Held**
SIC: 7231 Manicurist, pedicurist

(G-242)
M D ELECTRIC LLC
Also Called: Action Security
325 Meadow Glen Dr (19701-3377)
PHONE..................302 838-2852
Michael Doto, *President*
EMP: 4
SALES: 750K **Privately Held**
SIC: 1731 Fire detection & burglar alarm systems specialization

(G-243)
MANOR EXXON INC
131 W Savannah Dr (19701-1638)
PHONE..................302 834-6691
Cliff Galvin, *President*
EMP: 8
SQ FT: 20,000
SALES (est): 911K **Privately Held**
SIC: 5541 7538 Filling stations, gasoline; general automotive repair shops

(G-244)
MANUFACTURERS & TRADERS TR CO
Also Called: M&T
10 Foxhunt Dr (19701-2534)
PHONE..................302 651-8828
Nancy Choma, *Manager*
EMP: 15
SALES (corp-wide): 6.4B **Publicly Held**
WEB: www.binghamlegg.com
SIC: 6022 State commercial banks
HQ: Manufacturers And Traders Trust Company
  1 M&T Plz Fl 3
  Buffalo NY 14203
  716 842-4200

(G-245)
MARJANO LLC
Also Called: Sign-A-Rama
14 Orchid Dr (19701-6330)
PHONE..................302 454-7446
Mark Janocha,
EMP: 3
SALES: 250K **Privately Held**
SIC: 3993 Signs & advertising specialties

GEOGRAPHIC SECTION
Bear - New Castle County (G-280)

(G-246)
MARK WIECZOREK DMD PC
Also Called: Newtown Family Dentistry
494 Bear Christiana Rd (19701-1039)
PHONE..................302 838-3384
Mark Wieczorek, *Principal*
Wanda Ayala, *Principal*
EMP: 10
SALES (est): 300K **Privately Held**
SIC: 8021 Dentists' office

(G-247)
MASTER TECH INC
Also Called: Master Tech Pnt Collision Ctr
743 Rue Madora (19701-2543)
PHONE..................302 832-1660
Jim Hill, *President*
Enoch Anderson, *Vice Pres*
EMP: 30
SQ FT: 9,000
SALES (est): 2.4MM **Privately Held**
WEB: www.mastertechcollision.com
SIC: 7532 Body shop, automotive

(G-248)
MAVEN SECURITY CONSULTING INC
512 Portrush Pass (19701-1986)
P.O. Box 243, Ashburn VA (20146-0243)
PHONE..................302 365-6862
David Rhoades, *President*
EMP: 6
SALES (est): 450K **Privately Held**
WEB: www.mavensecurity.com
SIC: 7379

(G-249)
MAX ONE PRINTING
310 Chattahoochee Dr (19701-4808)
PHONE..................302 897-9050
David Dale, *Owner*
EMP: 2
SALES (est): 89.1K **Privately Held**
SIC: 2759 Commercial printing

(G-250)
MEDICAL ASSOCIATES BEAR INC
121 Becks Woods Dr # 100 (19701-3853)
PHONE..................302 832-6768
Rene Padillo MD, *President*
EMP: 7
SALES (est): 764.5K **Privately Held**
SIC: 8011 Surgeon

(G-251)
MICAHS GENERAL CONTRACTING
37 Primrose Dr (19701-6307)
PHONE..................302 437-4068
Michael Degraphenreed, *Owner*
EMP: 1
SALES: 250K **Privately Held**
SIC: 3253 Ceramic wall & floor tile

(G-252)
MICAN TECHNOLOGIES INC (PA)
2500 Wrangle Hill Rd (19701-3836)
PHONE..................302 703-0708
Satya S Kusampudi, *President*
Siva Kanumuri, *Vice Pres*
EMP: 14 EST: 2007
SQ FT: 1,100
SALES: 11.5MM **Privately Held**
SIC: 7371 Computer software development & applications

(G-253)
MICHAEL A SINCLAIR INC
705 Connell Dr (19701-2241)
PHONE..................302 834-8144
Michael Sinclair, *President*
EMP: 5
SALES: 695K **Privately Held**
SIC: 4212 0781 Truck rental with drivers; landscape services

(G-254)
MICHAEL GALLAGHER JEWELERS
102 Fox Hunt Dr (19701-2535)
PHONE..................302 836-2925
Michael E Gallagher, *President*
Kathleen M Gallagher, *Vice Pres*
EMP: 5
SQ FT: 1,400
SALES (est): 782.8K **Privately Held**
WEB: www.mgallagherjewelers.com
SIC: 5944 7631 Jewelry, precious stones & precious metals; jewelry repair services

(G-255)
MICHAEL WOODY PRODUCTIONS
210 Skeet Cir W (19701-2728)
PHONE..................302 584-2082
Michael Woody, *Owner*
EMP: 10
SALES (est): 123.1K **Privately Held**
SIC: 7822 Motion picture & tape distribution

(G-256)
MILLENNIUM PRCESS CONTRLS SVCS
105 Carson Dr (19701-1319)
P.O. Box 7138, Newark (19714-7138)
PHONE..................302 455-1717
EMP: 12 EST: 1997
SQ FT: 10,000
SALES: 1.6MM **Privately Held**
SIC: 3829 Mfg Measuring/Controlling Devices

(G-257)
MOLECULAR IMAGING SERVICES INC
10 Whitaker Ct (19701-2383)
PHONE..................302 450-4505
Frank Digregorio, *President*
EMP: 5
SALES (est): 897.8K **Privately Held**
SIC: 8071 X-ray laboratory, including dental

(G-258)
MS GOVERNORS SQUARE SHOPPING C
1229 Quintilio Dr (19701-6005)
PHONE..................302 838-3384
Tim Marrisey, *Principal*
EMP: 4 EST: 2009
SALES (est): 104K **Privately Held**
SIC: 8021 Dentists' office

(G-259)
N AND J DELIVERY SERVICE LLC
125 Rickey Blvd Unit 246 (19701-8610)
PHONE..................302 562-3220
Neil A Rayman, *Principal*
EMP: 4
SALES (est): 285.2K **Privately Held**
SIC: 4212 Delivery service, vehicular

(G-260)
N U FRIENDSHIP OUTREACH INC
20 Waterton Dr (19701-4914)
P.O. Box 2172, Wilmington (19899-2172)
PHONE..................302 836-0404
Kevin Evans, *CEO*
Howard Sharps, *Executive*
EMP: 5
SALES: 1K **Privately Held**
SIC: 8322 Outreach program

(G-261)
N&D NAIL SALON
14 Foxhunt Dr (19701-2534)
PHONE..................302 834-4899
Dung Nguyen, *Owner*
EMP: 5
SALES (est): 95.1K **Privately Held**
SIC: 7231 Manicurist, pedicurist

(G-262)
NEW CASTLE COUNTY HEAD START
931 Bear Corbitt Rd (19701-1323)
PHONE..................302 832-2212
Nannette Ziemba, *Branch Mgr*
EMP: 15
SALES (corp-wide): 6.1MM **Privately Held**
SIC: 8351 Head start center, except in conjunction with school
PA: New Castle County Head Start Inc
256 Chapman Rd Ste 103
Newark DE 19702
302 452-1500

(G-263)
NEW CASTLE DANCE ACADEMY
Also Called: New Castle Dance & Mus Academy
460 Eden Cir (19701-4304)
PHONE..................302 836-2060
Valerie Gooding, *Owner*
EMP: 10
SALES (est): 253.9K **Privately Held**
SIC: 7911 Dance studios, schools & halls

(G-264)
NEWARK GLASS & MIRROR INC
151 Rickey Blvd (19701-2540)
P.O. Box 1462 (19701-7462)
PHONE..................302 834-1158
Martha Joseph, *President*
Walter E Joseph, *Vice Pres*
EMP: 12
SALES (est): 1MM **Privately Held**
SIC: 5231 1793 Glass; glass & glazing work

(G-265)
NEWCOSMOS LLC
52 Blue Spruce Dr (19701-4128)
PHONE..................302 838-1935
Xiang Yu, *Partner*
EMP: 2
SALES (est): 120.8K **Privately Held**
SIC: 3663 Satellites, communications

(G-266)
NO PLACE LIKE HOME LLC
1017 Bear Corbitt Rd (19701-1325)
PHONE..................302 528-8682
Bill Miller, *Principal*
EMP: 4
SALES (est): 125.1K **Privately Held**
SIC: 8082 Home health care services

(G-267)
NOVA INDUSTRIES LLC
47 Courtland Cir (19701-1205)
PHONE..................302 218-4837
Anthony W Stewart,
Anthony Stewart,
EMP: 2
SALES (est): 106.6K **Privately Held**
SIC: 3999 Atomizers, toiletry

(G-268)
NOVACARE REHABILITATION
256 Foxhunt Dr (19701-2536)
PHONE..................302 597-9256
EMP: 8
SALES (est): 73.3K **Privately Held**
SIC: 8093 Rehabilitation center, outpatient treatment

(G-269)
O MORALES STUCCO PLASTER INC
7 Hawkins Ct (19701-1622)
PHONE..................302 834-8891
Orlando Morales, *President*
EMP: 6
SALES (est): 342.1K **Privately Held**
SIC: 1771 1742 Exterior concrete stucco contractor; plastering, plain or ornamental

(G-270)
OCEANSTAR TECHNOLOGIES INC
203 Mariners Way (19701-2291)
PHONE..................302 542-1900
Fred Eisele, *President*
Mary Eisele, *Vice Pres*
EMP: 5
SALES (est): 295.3K **Privately Held**
SIC: 8742 Management consulting services

(G-271)
OLD SCHOOL PLATING
757 Rue Madora (19701-2555)
PHONE..................302 345-0350
EMP: 2
SALES (est): 76.8K **Privately Held**
SIC: 3471 Plating of metals or formed products

(G-272)
ON THE SPOT MASSAGE
2871 Red Lion Rd (19701-2425)
PHONE..................302 545-5200
Patricia Ann Reilly, *Principal*
EMP: 8
SALES (est): 73.3K **Privately Held**
SIC: 8093 Rehabilitation center, outpatient treatment

(G-273)
ONEMAIN FINANCIAL GROUP LLC
619 Governors Pl (19701-3034)
PHONE..................302 834-6677
EMP: 5
SALES (corp-wide): 4.2B **Publicly Held**
SIC: 6282 Investment advice
HQ: Onemain Financial Group, Llc
100 International Dr # 150
Baltimore MD 21202
855 663-6246

(G-274)
OUR CHILDRENS LEARNING CTR
313 Sun Blvd (19701-6807)
PHONE..................302 565-1272
EMP: 4 EST: 2010
SALES (est): 58.8K **Privately Held**
SIC: 8351 Child day care services

(G-275)
PALMER & ASSOCIATES INC
14 Lauren Dr (19701-1805)
PHONE..................302 834-9329
Thomas Palmer, *President*
Barbara Palmer, *Corp Secy*
EMP: 9
SQ FT: 3,200
SALES (est): 735.3K **Privately Held**
SIC: 1611 1794 Highway & street paving contractor; excavation & grading, building construction

(G-276)
PANDA EARLY EDUCATION CTR INC (PA)
105 Emerald Ridge Dr (19701-2280)
PHONE..................302 832-1891
Daniel Frost, *President*
Leslie Frost, *Vice Pres*
EMP: 12
SALES: 950K **Privately Held**
SIC: 8351 Preschool center

(G-277)
PARADIGM HEALTH LLC
709 Observatory Dr (19701-6835)
P.O. Box 1190 (19701-7190)
PHONE..................301 233-7221
Chisa Harris,
EMP: 4
SALES (est): 98.6K **Privately Held**
SIC: 8099 Health & allied services

(G-278)
PASSION CARE SERVICES INC
3727 Wrangle Hill Rd (19701-1918)
P.O. Box 1307 (19701-7307)
PHONE..................302 832-2622
Lola Mayo, *President*
EMP: 12
SALES (est): 453.2K **Privately Held**
SIC: 8351 Preschool center

(G-279)
PAT PRESS
8 Eaton Pl (19701-2370)
PHONE..................302 836-2955
EMP: 1
SALES (est): 37.5K **Privately Held**
SIC: 2741 Miscellaneous publishing

(G-280)
PATRICIA MCKAY
Also Called: Patty Cakes Childcare
337 Starboard Dr (19701-2299)
PHONE..................302 563-5334
Patricia McKay, *Principal*
EMP: 5 EST: 2011

Bear - New Castle County (G-281)

SALES (est): 65.1K **Privately Held**
SIC: **8351** Preschool center

(G-281)
PENN DEL ADJUSTMENT SERVICE
7 Lake Dr (19701-1061)
P.O. Box 5244, Wilmington (19808-0244)
PHONE..................302 999-0196
EMP: 7
SQ FT: 3,000
SALES (est): 1MM **Privately Held**
SIC: **6411** Insurance Claim Administrator's

(G-282)
PHONECANDIESCOM
507 Grinnell Ct (19701-4938)
PHONE..................215 385-1818
Cherelle Thomas, *Principal*
EMP: 4
SALES (est): 101.5K **Privately Held**
SIC: **4899** Communication services

(G-283)
PHYLLIS M GREEN
Also Called: Hannahs Christian HM Day Care
329 N Red Lion Ter (19701-1028)
PHONE..................302 354-6986
Phyllis M Green, *Principal*
EMP: 7 EST: 2011
SALES (est): 136.9K **Privately Held**
SIC: **8082** Home health care services

(G-284)
PNC BANK NATIONAL ASSOCIATION
100 Eden Cir (19701-4301)
PHONE..................302 832-8750
Laura Mestro, *Manager*
EMP: 12
SALES (corp-wide): 19.9B **Publicly Held**
WEB: www.pncfunds.com
SIC: **6021** National trust companies with deposits, commercial
HQ: Pnc Bank, National Association
   222 Delaware Ave
   Wilmington DE 19801
   877 762-2000

(G-285)
PNC BANK NATIONAL ASSOCIATION
100 Eden Cir (19701-4301)
PHONE..................302 838-6782
Crystal Dixon, *Branch Mgr*
EMP: 12
SALES (corp-wide): 19.9B **Publicly Held**
WEB: www.pncfunds.com
SIC: **6021** National trust companies with deposits, commercial
HQ: Pnc Bank, National Association
   222 Delaware Ave
   Wilmington DE 19801
   877 762-2000

(G-286)
PNC BANK NATIONAL ASSOCIATION
250 Foxhunt Dr (19701-2536)
PHONE..................302 832-6180
Joan Galli, *Branch Mgr*
EMP: 12
SALES (corp-wide): 19.9B **Publicly Held**
SIC: **6021** National commercial banks
HQ: Pnc Bank, National Association
   222 Delaware Ave
   Wilmington DE 19801
   877 762-2000

(G-287)
POST SHIPPER LLC
601 Carson Dr (19701-1450)
PHONE..................302 444-8144
Mahmuoud Alshoushan, *President*
EMP: 10
SALES (est): 557.9K **Privately Held**
SIC: **4731** Agents, shipping

(G-288)
PREFERRED SECURITY INC
1570 Red Lion Rd (19701-1870)
P.O. Box 127 (19701-0127)
PHONE..................302 834-7800
Paul Pennachi, *President*
Cynthia Pennachi, *Vice Pres*
EMP: 6
SQ FT: 4,500
SALES (est): 543.6K **Privately Held**
WEB: www.preferredsecurity.com
SIC: **1731** **1799** Safety & security specialization; sound equipment specialization; closed circuit television installation; central vacuum cleaning system installation

(G-289)
PREFERRED TRAVEL
11 Mystic Dr (19701-4006)
PHONE..................302 838-8966
Luisa Georgov, *Principal*
EMP: 4
SALES (est): 454.8K **Privately Held**
SIC: **4724** Travel agencies

(G-290)
PREFERRED TRNSP SYSTEMS LLC
101 E Beaver Ct (19701-1082)
P.O. Box 867 (19701-0867)
PHONE..................302 323-0828
Gary Arters, *Mng Member*
EMP: 6
SALES (est): 600K **Privately Held**
SIC: **4119** **4111** Vanpool operation; airport limousine, scheduled service

(G-291)
PREPAID LEGAL SERVICE INC
Also Called: Prepaid Legal Svc USA & Canada
214 Palermo Dr (19701-2524)
PHONE..................302 836-1985
Sultan Whitney, *President*
EMP: 15
SALES (est): 1.1MM **Privately Held**
SIC: **5099** Novelties, durable

(G-292)
PRO TRANS INC
807 Pulaski Hwy (19701-1239)
PHONE..................302 328-1550
Dan Salter, *President*
EMP: 5
SALES: 500K **Privately Held**
WEB: www.protrans.net
SIC: **7538** General automotive repair shops

(G-293)
PROFESSIONSALE INC
1148 Pulaski Hwy Ste 134 (19701-1306)
PHONE..................646 262-9101
Xiangdong Zhou, *President*
EMP: 4
SALES (est): 221K **Privately Held**
SIC: **7374** Computer graphics service

(G-294)
PRUDENTIAL FOX AND ROACH REALT
1126 Pulaski Hwy (19701-1306)
PHONE..................302 378-9500
EMP: 6
SALES (est): 322.1K **Privately Held**
SIC: **6531** Real Estate Agent/Manager

(G-295)
PURUSHAS PICKS INC
Also Called: My Baby's Heartbeat Bear
3310 Wrangle Hill Rd # 107 (19701-1874)
PHONE..................302 918-7663
Purusha Rivera, *President*
Sheldon Thomas, *Vice Pres*
EMP: 6
SALES: 1.1MM **Privately Held**
SIC: **5047** **5999** Medical equipment & supplies; medical apparatus & supplies

(G-296)
R D COLLINS & SONS
19 Shellbark Dr (19701-2141)
PHONE..................302 834-3409
Doug Collins, *Owner*
EMP: 10
SQ FT: 1,500
SALES (est): 303.8K **Privately Held**
SIC: **0782** **0781** Lawn services; landscape services

(G-297)
RATNER COMPANIES LC
Also Called: Creative Hairdressers
1009 Governors Pl (19701-3048)
PHONE..................302 836-3749
Ann Magargal, *Manager*
EMP: 18 **Privately Held**
WEB: www.haircuttery.com
SIC: **7231** Unisex hair salons
HQ: Ratner Companies, L.C.
   1577 Spring Hill Rd # 500
   Vienna VA 22182
   703 269-5400

(G-298)
RED BIRD EGG FARM INC (PA)
1701 Red Lion Rd (19701-1813)
PHONE..................302 834-2571
Kenneth Steele, *President*
Shirley Steele, *Corp Secy*
EMP: 38
SQ FT: 2,000
SALES (est): 5.6MM **Privately Held**
WEB: www.redbirdeggs.com
SIC: **0252** Chicken eggs

(G-299)
REGIS CORPORATION
1233 Quintilio Dr (19701-6005)
PHONE..................302 834-1272
Stacey Noble, *Branch Mgr*
EMP: 8
SALES (corp-wide): 1B **Publicly Held**
SIC: **7231** Unisex hair salons
PA: Regis Corporation
   7201 Metro Blvd
   Edina MN 55439
   952 947-7777

(G-300)
REGIS CORPORATION
Also Called: Holiday Hair 238
420 Eden Cir (19701-4304)
PHONE..................302 834-9916
Loriann Carey, *Manager*
EMP: 10
SALES (corp-wide): 1B **Publicly Held**
WEB: www.regiscorp.com
SIC: **7231** Unisex hair salons
PA: Regis Corporation
   7201 Metro Blvd
   Edina MN 55439
   952 947-7777

(G-301)
REIS ENTERPRISES LLC
504 Connor Blvd (19701-1744)
PHONE..................302 740-8382
Soner Kece, *President*
EMP: 5 EST: 2016
SALES (est): 140.9K **Privately Held**
SIC: **1721** Residential painting

(G-302)
RENT-A-CENTER INC
38 Foxhunt Dr 40 (19701-2534)
PHONE..................302 838-7333
J R Mallon, *Manager*
EMP: 5
SALES (corp-wide): 2.6B **Publicly Held**
WEB: www.rentacenter.com
SIC: **7359** Appliance rental; furniture rental; home entertainment equipment rental; television rental
PA: Rent-A-Center, Inc.
   5501 Headquarters Dr
   Plano TX 75024
   972 801-1100

(G-303)
RETRO FITNESS
835 Pulaski Hwy (19701-1240)
PHONE..................302 276-0828
Ryan Sykes, *General Mgr*
EMP: 24
SALES (est): 439.8K **Privately Held**
SIC: **7991** Physical fitness facilities

(G-304)
REYBOLD CONSTRUCTION CORP
116 E Scotland Dr (19701-1766)
PHONE..................302 832-7100
Jerome Heisler Sr, *President*
Jerome S Heisler Jr, *President*
Zach Brown, *Superintendent*
Mike Clineff, *Project Mgr*
Bill Davis, *Project Mgr*
EMP: 45
SQ FT: 12,000
SALES (est): 8.9MM **Privately Held**
SIC: **6552** **1542** **1541** Land subdividers & developers, residential; commercial & office building, new construction; warehouse construction

(G-305)
REYBOLD GROUP OF COMPANIES INC (PA)
116 E Scotland Dr (19701-1766)
PHONE..................302 832-7100
Anthony Bielicki, *General Mgr*
Kevin McDonough, *Superintendent*
Angela Irato, *Controller*
James R Grygiel, *VP Finance*
Phyllis Dubose, *Finance Mgr*
EMP: 40
SQ FT: 6,450
SALES (est): 23.6MM **Privately Held**
SIC: **6531** Real estate managers

(G-306)
REYBOLD GROUP OF COMPANIES INC
Also Called: Hunters Run Associates
114 E Scotland Dr (19701-1756)
PHONE..................302 832-2544
Kevin Rieneke, *Branch Mgr*
EMP: 8
SALES (corp-wide): 23.6MM **Privately Held**
SIC: **6515** Mobile home site operators
PA: The Reybold Group Of Companies Inc
   116 E Scotland Dr
   Bear DE 19701
   302 832-7100

(G-307)
RIVERSIDE SPECIALTY CHEM INC
400 Carson Dr (19701-1314)
PHONE..................212 769-3440
George Murray, *Branch Mgr*
EMP: 8 **Privately Held**
SIC: **2869** **5169** Industrial organic chemicals; chemicals & allied products
PA: Riverside Specialty Chemicals, Inc.
   316 W 79th St Apt 7w
   New York NY 10024

(G-308)
ROBERT C PEOPLES INC
Also Called: Peoples, R C
2750 Wrangle Hill Rd (19701-1732)
PHONE..................302 834-5268
Dorothy M Peoples, *President*
Carol Manubay, *Corp Secy*
Harrison B Peoples, *Vice Pres*
Robert C Peoples Jr, *Vice Pres*
W Thomas Peoples, *Vice Pres*
EMP: 55
SQ FT: 4,000
SALES (est): 7.8MM **Privately Held**
SIC: **1521** **1542** New construction, single-family houses; commercial & office building, new construction

(G-309)
ROBERT F MULLEN INSURANCE AGCY
Also Called: State Farm Insurance
887 Pulaski Hwy (19701-1252)
PHONE..................302 322-5331
Robert F Mullen, *Owner*
Brian Dawson, *Manager*
EMP: 6
SALES (est): 875.6K **Privately Held**
SIC: **6411** Insurance agents & brokers

(G-310)
ROCKY LAC LLC
1012 San Remo Ct Ste A (19701-2519)
PHONE..................302 440-5561
EMP: 10
SALES: 2.5MM **Privately Held**
SIC: **6531** Real estate agents & managers

GEOGRAPHIC SECTION
Bear - New Castle County (G-342)

(G-311)
ROCLA CONCRETE TIE INC
268 E Scotland Dr (19701-1738)
PHONE.................................302 836-5304
Mark Gaworowski, *Purchasing*
Robert Andrews, *Sales Staff*
EMP: 50
SALES (corp-wide): 959.3MM **Privately Held**
WEB: www.roclatie.com
SIC: 3272 2421 Ties, railroad: concrete; sawmills & planing mills, general
HQ: Rocla Concrete Tie, Inc
    1819 Denver West Dr # 450
    Lakewood CO 80401
    303 296-3500

(G-312)
ROGERS CORPORATION
1100 Governor Lea Rd (19701-1927)
PHONE.................................302 834-2100
Tom Magnani, *Branch Mgr*
EMP: 150
SALES (corp-wide): 879MM **Publicly Held**
WEB: www.arlon.com
SIC: 2822 3672 Synthetic rubber; printed circuit boards
PA: Rogers Corporation
    2225 W Chandler Blvd
    Chandler AZ 85224
    480 917-6000

(G-313)
S T PROGRESSIVE STRIDES
718 Thyme Dr (19701-6018)
PHONE.................................410 775-8103
Jackie Smith, *CEO*
EMP: 4
SALES (est): 77.2K **Privately Held**
SIC: 8093 Rehabilitation center, outpatient treatment

(G-314)
SCHOOL BELL APARTMENTS LP
2000 Varsity Ln (19701-3900)
PHONE.................................302 328-9500
Yvonne Ryder, *Manager*
EMP: 6
SALES (est): 893.2K **Privately Held**
SIC: 6513 Apartment building operators

(G-315)
SCHOOLHOUSE TRUST INC
Also Called: Christiana Meadows Apartments
265 Bear Christiana Rd (19701-1047)
PHONE.................................302 322-6161
Brock Vinton, *President*
Carmen Facciolo, *Vice Pres*
EMP: 12
SALES (est): 1.4MM **Privately Held**
WEB: www.christiana-meadows.com
SIC: 6513 Apartment hotel operation

(G-316)
SCHWERMAN TRUCKING CO
3340 Wrangle Hill Rd (19701-1846)
PHONE.................................302 832-3103
Paul Womax, *Branch Mgr*
EMP: 29
SALES (corp-wide): 374.5MM **Privately Held**
SIC: 4213 Contract haulers
HQ: Schwerman Trucking Co.
    611 S 28th St
    Milwaukee WI 53215
    414 671-1600

(G-317)
SERPRO OF BEAR NEW CASTLE
301 Carson Dr (19701-1374)
PHONE.................................302 392-6000
Richard Massey, *Principal*
EMP: 5
SALES (est): 289.4K **Privately Held**
SIC: 7349 Building maintenance services

(G-318)
SHEAR MAGIC HAIR DESIGN
106 Foxhunt Dr (19701-2535)
PHONE.................................302 836-4001
Donna Mozer, *Owner*
EMP: 11
SALES (est): 227.8K **Privately Held**
SIC: 7231 Hairdressers

(G-319)
SHEET METAL CONTRACTING CO
3445 Wrangle Hill Rd (19701-1831)
P.O. Box 307 (19701-0307)
PHONE.................................302 834-3727
Jeffrey Bupp, *President*
Thomas R Douglas, *Treasurer*
EMP: 20
SQ FT: 24,000
SALES (est): 3.7MM **Privately Held**
WEB: www.sheetmetalcontracting.com
SIC: 3444 3599 Sheet metal specialties, not stamped; machine shop, jobbing & repair

(G-320)
SHEETS INSURANCE INC
Also Called: Sheets Insurance Agency
254 Foxhunt Dr (19701-2536)
PHONE.................................302 832-0441
Calvin Sheets, *President*
EMP: 4
SALES (est): 429.6K **Privately Held**
SIC: 6411 Insurance agents, brokers & service

(G-321)
SIEMENS AG
217 Benjamin Blvd (19701-1692)
PHONE.................................302 836-2933
Wayne Tiedeman, *Manager*
EMP: 2
SALES (est): 88.3K **Privately Held**
SIC: 3661 Telephones & telephone apparatus

(G-322)
SIMON EYE ASSOCIATES PA
116 Foxhunt Dr Ste 116 # 116 (19701-2535)
PHONE.................................302 834-4305
Simon Charles, *Branch Mgr*
EMP: 20
SALES (corp-wide): 4.7MM **Privately Held**
SIC: 8042 Offices & clinics of optometrists
PA: Simon Eye Associates, P.A.
    5301 Limestone Rd Ste 128
    Wilmington DE 19808
    302 239-1389

(G-323)
SITE SOURCE CONTRACTOR SUPPLY
613 Pulaski Hwy (19701-1235)
PHONE.................................302 322-0444
Richard Sweeny, *President*
Mike Stears, *Principal*
Nicholas Stellini, *Vice Pres*
EMP: 4
SQ FT: 2,000
SALES (est): 1.4MM **Privately Held**
SIC: 5199 General merchandise, nondurable

(G-324)
SITEONE LANDSCAPE SUPPLY LLC
711 Carson Dr (19701-1454)
PHONE.................................302 836-3903
Brian Clements, *Branch Mgr*
EMP: 4
SALES (corp-wide): 2.1B **Publicly Held**
SIC: 0781 Landscape services
HQ: Siteone Landscape Supply, Llc
    300 Colonial Center Pkwy # 600
    Roswell GA 30076
    770 255-2100

(G-325)
SMARTY PANTS EARLY EDUCATION
146 Willamette Dr (19701-4802)
PHONE.................................302 985-3770
EMP: 5
SALES (est): 48.6K **Privately Held**
SIC: 8351 Child day care services

(G-326)
SMID AEROSPACE CORPORATION
104 Dorothy Dr (19701-1773)
PHONE.................................443 205-0881
Lou Harrigan, *CEO*
Markisha Greene, *COO*
Howard Greene, *Vice Pres*
EMP: 4 **EST:** 2015
SALES (est): 109.5K **Privately Held**
SIC: 8733 Noncommercial research organizations

(G-327)
SOLAR HEATING INC
Also Called: Sussex Electric
21 E Savannah Dr (19701-1663)
PHONE.................................302 836-3943
William C Anderson, *President*
Julie Anderson, *Vice Pres*
Jack Pfleger, *Manager*
EMP: 25
SQ FT: 3,000
SALES (est): 1.3MM **Privately Held**
SIC: 1731 1711 General electrical contractor; warm air heating & air conditioning contractor

(G-328)
SOPHISTICUTS INC
3 Rice Dr (19701-1890)
PHONE.................................302 834-7427
Theresa Williams, *President*
EMP: 6
SALES (est): 159.7K **Privately Held**
SIC: 7231 Unisex hair salons

(G-329)
SOUTH JERSEY PAVING
518 Turnberry Ct (19701-4729)
PHONE.................................856 498-8647
Rochelle Reilly, *Principal*
EMP: 5
SALES (est): 334K **Privately Held**
SIC: 1611 Highway & street paving contractor

(G-330)
SPACE MAKERS INC
Also Called: S P A C E-Makers
600 Pulaski Hwy (19701-1228)
P.O. Box 808 (19701-0808)
PHONE.................................302 322-4325
Samuel Glick, *President*
EMP: 4
SQ FT: 1,000
SALES (est): 409.7K **Privately Held**
SIC: 1521 1542 Single-family home remodeling, additions & repairs; garage construction

(G-331)
SPEARHEAD INC
2306 Porter Rd (19701-2021)
PHONE.................................347 670-2699
Harjeet Singh, *CEO*
Kit Cheng, *Principal*
EMP: 4
SALES: 10K **Privately Held**
SIC: 7371 Computer software development & applications

(G-332)
SPEC PROCESSING GROUP INC
Also Called: Spg
2266 Porter Rd (19701-2022)
PHONE.................................302 295-2197
James Mentz, *President*
EMP: 6
SALES (est): 426.1K **Privately Held**
SIC: 0711 Soil preparation services

(G-333)
SPIRIT-TRANS INC
832 N Gwynn Ct (19701-3012)
PHONE.................................302 290-9830
John McDevitt, *CEO*
EMP: 4 **EST:** 2011
SALES (est): 271.6K **Privately Held**
SIC: 4789 Transportation services

(G-334)
ST ANDREWS APARTMENTS
50 Turnberry Ct (19701-4700)
PHONE.................................302 834-8600
Jerry Heisler, *Owner*
EMP: 15
SALES (est): 700.8K **Privately Held**
SIC: 6531 Rental agent, real estate

(G-335)
ST ANDREWS MAINTENANCE
104 E Scotland Dr (19701-1756)
PHONE.................................302 832-2675
Rechel Riley, *Principal*
EMP: 5
SALES (est): 155.7K **Privately Held**
SIC: 7349 Building maintenance services

(G-336)
STAFFMARK INVESTMENT LLC
1867 Pulaski Hwy (19701-1731)
PHONE.................................302 834-2303
Kalli Medina, *Branch Mgr*
EMP: 42 **Privately Held**
SIC: 7363 Temporary help service
HQ: Staffmark Investment Llc
    201 E 4th St Ste 800
    Cincinnati OH 45202

(G-337)
STAR ART INC
1272 Porter Rd (19701-1311)
P.O. Box 828 (19701-0828)
PHONE.................................302 261-6732
EMP: 2
SALES (est): 92.3K **Privately Held**
SIC: 2752 Commercial printing, lithographic

(G-338)
STAY TRUE PLUMBING
693 Old Porter Rd (19701-1864)
PHONE.................................302 464-1198
EMP: 6
SALES (est): 396.6K **Privately Held**
SIC: 1711 Plumbing contractors

(G-339)
STEVEN AUGUSIEWICZ INC
25 Monticello Dr (19701-2078)
P.O. Box 1246 (19701-7246)
PHONE.................................302 738-1919
Steven Augusiewicz, *President*
EMP: 4 **EST:** 1990
SALES: 600K **Privately Held**
SIC: 1795 Wrecking & demolition work

(G-340)
SUMMIT MECHANICAL INC
304 Carson Dr (19701-1374)
P.O. Box 1398 (19701-7398)
PHONE.................................302 836-8814
Edward M Mendez, *President*
EMP: 35
SQ FT: 13,000
SALES: 4MM **Privately Held**
SIC: 1711 Mechanical contractor

(G-341)
SUMMIT NORTH MARINA
3000 Summit Harbour Pl (19701-2609)
PHONE.................................302 836-1800
Henry Heiman, *President*
Darrell Baker, *Vice Pres*
Ed Falkowski, *Shareholder*
Albert Forwood, *Shareholder*
William Freas, *Admin Sec*
EMP: 15
SQ FT: 1,800
SALES (est): 1.4MM **Privately Held**
WEB: www.summitnorthmarina.net
SIC: 5941 4493 Sporting goods & bicycle shops; marinas

(G-342)
SUPERIOR FOUNDATIONS INC
445 County Rd (19701-1811)
PHONE.................................302 293-7061
Matthew Kirbi, *President*
EMP: 21
SALES (est): 649.4K **Privately Held**
SIC: 1771 Concrete work

Bear - New Castle County (G-343)

(G-343)
SUPERIOR SEALING SERVICES D
613 Pulaski Hwy (19701-1235)
P.O. Box 3539, Wilmington (19807-0539)
PHONE.................................610 717-6237
Mark Mitchell, *President*
EMP: 4
SALES (est): 314K **Privately Held**
SIC: 1771 Concrete work

(G-344)
T&T CUSTOM EMBROIDERY INC
51 Rawlings Dr (19701-1519)
PHONE.................................302 420-9454
Terrance Wiggins, *President*
Monique Springer, *Admin Sec*
EMP: 2 **EST:** 2007
SALES (est): 127K **Privately Held**
SIC: 2395 Embroidery products, except schiffli machine

(G-345)
T-MOBILE USA INC
1102 Quintilio Dr (19701-6004)
PHONE.................................302 838-4500
Diane Strong, *Principal*
EMP: 12
SALES (corp-wide): 83.9B **Publicly Held**
WEB: www.voicestream.com
SIC: 4812 Cellular telephone services
HQ: T-Mobile Usa, Inc.
    12920 Se 38th St
    Bellevue WA 98006
    425 378-4000

(G-346)
TAEKWONDO FITNESS CTR OF DEL
Also Called: Doctor Laubers Karate Plus
1230 Pulaski Hwy (19701-1321)
PHONE.................................302 836-8264
Harold Lauber PHD, *President*
EMP: 6
SALES (est): 180.6K
SALES (corp-wide): 287.4K **Privately Held**
SIC: 7991 Physical fitness facilities
PA: Taekwondo Fitness Center Of Delaware, Inc
    515 E Basin Rd
    New Castle DE
    302 328-5755

(G-347)
TAT TRUCKING INC
3482 Wrangle Hill Rd (19701-1845)
PHONE.................................302 261-5444
Mike Atack, *President*
EMP: 15
SALES: 2MM **Privately Held**
SIC: 7513 Truck rental & leasing, no drivers

(G-348)
TAX MASTERS OF DELAWARE
37 Carrick Ln (19701-6344)
PHONE.................................302 832-1313
Keith Dorman, *Principal*
EMP: 4 **EST:** 2016
SALES (est): 36.1K **Privately Held**
SIC: 7291 Tax return preparation services

(G-349)
TC LOGISTICS INCORPORATED
934 Roger Chaffee Sq C (19701-6854)
PHONE.................................302 470-8357
Sean King, *President*
EMP: 14
SALES (est): 389.4K **Privately Held**
SIC: 4213 Trucking, except local

(G-350)
TECHNOSECURE CORPORATION
705 Thyme Dr (19701-6017)
PHONE.................................732 302-9005
Bindu Batra, *Principal*
EMP: 24
SALES (est): 871.9K **Privately Held**
WEB: www.technosecure.com
SIC: 7371 Custom computer programming services

(G-351)
THERAPY CONCIERGE
516 Daniels Ct (19701-1178)
PHONE.................................302 319-3040
Nicole Sult, *Principal*
EMP: 8
SALES (est): 73.3K **Privately Held**
SIC: 8093 Rehabilitation center, outpatient treatment

(G-352)
THIRST 2 LEARN
891 Pulaski Hwy (19701-1252)
PHONE.................................302 293-2304
Pierre Smythe, *Director*
EMP: 8 **EST:** 2011
SALES (est): 217.6K **Privately Held**
SIC: 8351 Child day care services

(G-353)
TIMOTHY W MCHUGH
121 Becks Woods Dr # 100 (19701-3851)
PHONE.................................302 633-1280
Timothy McHugh, *Principal*
EMP: 8
SALES (est): 65.7K **Privately Held**
SIC: 8049 Offices of health practitioner

(G-354)
TLALOC BUILDING SERVICES INC
738 Pulaski Hwy Trlr 29b (19701-1248)
PHONE.................................302 559-6459
Ecequier Kyon, *President*
EMP: 14
SALES: 53K **Privately Held**
SIC: 7349 Building cleaning service

(G-355)
TOSS THAT JUNK LLC
300 S Dragon Dr (19701-2214)
PHONE.................................302 326-3867
EMP: 5
SALES (est): 231.5K **Privately Held**
SIC: 4953 Refuse collection & disposal services

(G-356)
TOWN AND COUNTRY TRUST
Also Called: Brandywine Wods Aprtmnts Sites
270 Brandywine Dr (19701-3201)
PHONE.................................302 328-8700
Jennifer Tyre, *Manager*
EMP: 12
SALES (corp-wide): 52.4MM **Privately Held**
WEB: www.tctrust.com
SIC: 6513 Apartment building operators
PA: The Town And Country Trust
    75 2nd Ave Ste 200
    Needham MA 02494
    781 449-6650

(G-357)
TRANSPORTATION DELAWARE DEPT
Also Called: North District Engrg Cnstr
250 Bear Christiana Rd (19701-1041)
PHONE.................................302 326-8950
Mark Alexander, *Branch Mgr*
EMP: 300 **Privately Held**
WEB: www.dartfirststate.com
SIC: 1611 9621 Highway & street construction; regulation, administration of transportation;
HQ: Delaware Department Of Transportation
    800 S Bay Rd
    Dover DE 19901

(G-358)
TRI-STATE UNDERGROUND INC
2141 Old Kirkwood Rd (19701-2248)
PHONE.................................302 293-9352
Richard Hess, *President*
EMP: 6
SQ FT: 1,100
SALES: 480K **Privately Held**
SIC: 1623 Underground utilities contractor

(G-359)
TRINITY 3 ENTERPRISES INC
38 Ayrshire St (19701-4710)
PHONE.................................267 973-2666
Sandy Brown, *President*
Harry Brown, *Vice Pres*
EMP: 5
SALES: 200K **Privately Held**
SIC: 4213 Trucking, except local

(G-360)
TROY FARMER
16 Catherine Ct (19701-2298)
PHONE.................................888 711-0094
Troy Farmer, *Principal*
EMP: 4
SALES (est): 42.4K **Privately Held**
SIC: 8322 Individual & family services

(G-361)
TRUE LIFE CHURCH NEWARK INC (PA)
33 Lotus Cir N (19701-6321)
PHONE.................................302 283-9003
Mykal Smith, *CEO*
EMP: 4
SALES: 1K **Privately Held**
SIC: 8661 7371 Miscellaneous denomination church; computer software development & applications

(G-362)
U HAUL NEIGHBORHOOD DEALER
214 Bear Christiana Rd (19701-1041)
PHONE.................................302 613-0207
J D Hopkins, *Owner*
EMP: 6
SALES (est): 122.3K **Privately Held**
SIC: 7513 Truck rental & leasing, no drivers

(G-363)
UDAAN INC
5 Brittany Ln (19701-6384)
PHONE.................................267 408-3001
Sandhitsu Das, *Treasurer*
Kalol Ray, *Director*
EMP: 11
SALES (est): 452.4K **Privately Held**
SIC: 6732 Trusts: educational, religious, etc.

(G-364)
UET INTERNATIONAL INC
9 Riva Ridge Ln (19701-3355)
PHONE.................................302 834-0234
Charles Chen, *President*
▲ **EMP:** 4
SALES (est): 635.5K **Privately Held**
SIC: 5084 Industrial machinery & equipment

(G-365)
UNITED MEDICAL CLINICS OF DE
121 Becks Woods Dr # 100 (19701-3853)
PHONE.................................302 451-5607
EMP: 12
SALES (est): 594.9K **Privately Held**
SIC: 8099 Health & allied services

(G-366)
VADER LLC
Also Called: Vader.ro
108 E Scotland Dr (19701-1756)
PHONE.................................302 565-9684
Vili Vatafu, *Mng Member*
Sorin Isac,
EMP: 10 **EST:** 2013
SQ FT: 1,000
SALES (est): 700K **Privately Held**
SIC: 4424 Intercoastal transportation, freight

(G-367)
VSG BUSINESS SOLUTIONS LLC
221 Cornwell Dr (19701-3103)
PHONE.................................302 261-3209
Vivek Kapoor,
EMP: 50
SALES (est): 766.2K **Privately Held**
SIC: 7379

(G-368)
W LEE MACKEWIZ OD PA
Also Called: Bear Eye Assoc
725 Pulaski Hwy (19701-1236)
PHONE.................................302 834-2020
W Lee Mackewiz, *President*
Tara Marty, *Manager*
EMP: 4
SALES (est): 520.9K **Privately Held**
WEB: www.beareye.com
SIC: 5995 8011 Contact lenses, prescription; offices & clinics of medical doctors

(G-369)
WALLEYS TRUCKING INC
29 Emerald Ridge Dr (19701-2233)
P.O. Box 11624, Wilmington (19850-1624)
PHONE.................................302 893-8652
Lyn Walters, *President*
Marcia Walters, *Vice Pres*
EMP: 9
SALES (est): 854.7K **Privately Held**
SIC: 4212 Dump truck haulage

(G-370)
WANAMAKERS ASSOCIATES LLC
203 Cornwell Dr (19701-3103)
P.O. Box 83, Bala Cynwyd PA (19004-0083)
PHONE.................................302 834-3491
Ernest Green,
EMP: 4
SQ FT: 3,500
SALES: 100K **Privately Held**
SIC: 6531 Real estate agent, residential; real estate agent, commercial

(G-371)
WATERFORD MHC INC
205 Joan Dr (19701-1300)
PHONE.................................302 834-9514
Howard Walker, *CEO*
Donna Caroll, *Manager*
EMP: 4
SALES (est): 240K **Privately Held**
SIC: 6515 Mobile home site operators

(G-372)
WAYNE I TUCKER
100 Becks Woods Dr # 202 (19701-3835)
PHONE.................................302 838-1100
Cheryl Tucker, *Principal*
EMP: 6
SALES (est): 507.7K **Privately Held**
SIC: 8011 General & family practice, physician/surgeon

(G-373)
WB PAVING LLC
1387 Red Lion Rd (19701-1818)
PHONE.................................302 838-1886
Charlott Baker, *Principal*
EMP: 5
SALES (est): 597.2K **Privately Held**
SIC: 1611 Highway & street paving contractor; surfacing & paving

(G-374)
WELLS FARGO BANK NATIONAL ASSN
1601 Governors Pl (19701-3054)
PHONE.................................302 832-6104
Meg Thomas, *Branch Mgr*
EMP: 5
SALES (corp-wide): 101B **Publicly Held**
SIC: 6021 National commercial banks
HQ: Wells Fargo Bank, National Association
    101 N Phillips Ave
    Sioux Falls SD 57104
    605 575-6900

(G-375)
WENDY CPA LLC
Also Called: Cornerstone CPA
39 Maureen Way (19701-6341)
PHONE.................................302 377-7165
Wendy Hassiepen, *Principal*
EMP: 4
SALES (est): 242.4K **Privately Held**
SIC: 8721 Certified public accountant

(G-376)
WESTSIDE FAMILY HEALTHCARE INC
404 Foxhunt Dr (19701-2538)
PHONE.................................302 836-2864
EMP: 17

GEOGRAPHIC SECTION

Bethany Beach - Sussex County (G-406)

SALES (corp-wide): 22.8MM **Privately Held**
SIC: **8011** 8021 General & family practice, physician/surgeon; offices & clinics of dentists
PA: Westside Family Healthcare, Inc.
 300 Water St Ste 200
 Wilmington DE 19801
 302 656-8292

(G-377)
WILMINGTON SAVINGS FUND SOC
210 Foxhunt Dr (19701-2536)
PHONE................................302 838-6300
Carol Edge, *President*
Cindy Crompton-Barone, *Vice Pres*
Nancy Pflum, *Branch Mgr*
EMP: 5
SALES (corp-wide): 455.5MM **Publicly Held**
SIC: **6029** Commercial banks
HQ: Wilmington Savings Fund Society
 500 Delaware Ave Ste 500 # 500
 Wilmington DE 19801
 302 792-6000

(G-378)
WILSON PUBLICATIONS LLC
331 N Red Lion Ter (19701-1028)
PHONE................................215 237-2344
EMP: 1 EST: 2016
SALES (est): 44.8K **Privately Held**
SIC: **2741** Miscellaneous publishing

(G-379)
WNA INFOTECH LLC
2306 Porter Rd (19701-2021)
PHONE................................302 668-5977
Amit Dudani,
EMP: 25
SALES (est): 560.4K **Privately Held**
SIC: **2741** 5961 7371 ; ; software programming applications

(G-380)
WORLD HOSPITAL INC
102 Sweethollow Dr (19701-3376)
PHONE................................609 254-3391
Marinus Ndikum, *Principal*
EMP: 9
SALES: 81.2K **Privately Held**
SIC: **8062** General medical & surgical hospitals

(G-381)
WRECK MASTERS DEMO DERBY
221 Kline St (19701-2218)
PHONE................................302 368-5544
Joe Fields, *Owner*
EMP: 10
SALES (est): 458.4K **Privately Held**
SIC: **5531** 7514 Automotive & home supply stores; rent-a-car service

---
Bethany Beach
Sussex County

(G-382)
ADDY SEA
Also Called: Addy Sea, The
99 Ocean View Pkwy (19930-9262)
P.O. Box 275 (19930-0275)
PHONE................................302 539-3707
Leroy Gravatte, *President*
EMP: 5
SALES (est): 230K **Privately Held**
SIC: **7011** Bed & breakfast inn

(G-383)
BEACH BREAK & BAKRIE
123 Garfield Pkwy (19930-7747)
PHONE................................302 537-3800
Beth Webb, *Owner*
EMP: 5
SALES (est): 176K **Privately Held**
SIC: **5149** Bakery products

(G-384)
BEACH HOUSE RESOURCES
29l Atlantic Ave 199 (19930)
PHONE................................703 980-3336
Paul Denault, *Principal*
EMP: 5
SALES (est): 249.8K **Privately Held**
SIC: **7011** Bed & breakfast inn

(G-385)
BETHANY BEACH BED & BREAKFAST
33391 Ocean Pines Ln (19930-3735)
PHONE................................301 651-2278
EMP: 6
SALES (est): 90.5K **Privately Held**
SIC: **7011** Motel, franchised

(G-386)
BETHANY BEACH BOOKS
99 Garfield Pkwy (19930-7703)
P.O. Box 904 (19930-0904)
PHONE................................302 539-2522
Jacklyn Inman, *Owner*
Amanda Zirn, *Manager*
EMP: 9
SQ FT: 800
SALES (est): 1.5MM **Privately Held**
WEB: www.bethanybeachbooks.com
SIC: **5192** Books

(G-387)
BETHANY BEACH OCEAN
99 Hollywood St (19930-7749)
PHONE................................302 539-3201
Patrick Staib, *General Mgr*
EMP: 40
SALES (est): 288.1K **Privately Held**
SIC: **7011** Resort hotel

(G-388)
BETHANY BEACH VLNTR FIRE CO (PA)
215 Hollywood St (19930)
P.O. Box 950 (19930-0950)
PHONE................................302 539-7700
Michael Suit, *President*
Steve Lett, *President*
Rick Parrett, *Vice Pres*
Heather Murphy, *Admin Asst*
EMP: 50
SALES: 315.3K **Privately Held**
SIC: **7389** 8699 Fire protection service other than forestry or public; charitable organization

(G-389)
BETHANY DENTAL ASSOCIATION
32895 Coastal Hwy # 102 (19930-3783)
PHONE................................302 537-1200
Alfred Brown, *Principal*
EMP: 4
SALES (est): 326.6K **Privately Held**
SIC: **8621** Professional membership organizations

(G-390)
BETHANY PRIMARY CARE
33188 Coastal Hwy Unit 4 (19930-3779)
PHONE................................302 537-1100
K T Mohan MD, *Owner*
Vidya Mave, *Co-Owner*
EMP: 4
SALES (est): 452.4K **Privately Held**
SIC: **8011** Internal medicine, physician/surgeon

(G-391)
CARL M FREEMAN ASSOCIATES INC
Also Called: Sea Colony
Pennsylvania Ave Rr 1 (19930)
P.O. Box 480 (19930-0480)
PHONE................................302 539-6961
Patrick Davis, *General Mgr*
EMP: 200
SALES (corp-wide): 57.3MM **Privately Held**
SIC: **1531** 6531 6519 6513 Condominium developers; real estate agents & managers; real property lessors; apartment building operators
PA: Carl M. Freeman Associates, Inc.
 111 Rckvlle Pike Ste 1100
 Rockville MD 20850
 240 453-3000

(G-392)
COLDWELL BANKER
39682 Sunrise Ct (19930-3469)
P.O. Box 640 (19930-0640)
PHONE................................302 539-4086
Cindi Wolfe, *Manager*
EMP: 15
SALES (est): 1.1MM **Privately Held**
WEB: www.bethany-rehoboth.com
SIC: **6531** Real estate agent, residential

(G-393)
CUSTOM MECHANICAL INC
Custom Sheet Metal
State Routes 370 (19930)
PHONE................................302 537-5611
Patti Roberts, *Treasurer*
Chris McGee, *Office Mgr*
Mike Blades, *Manager*
EMP: 1
SALES (corp-wide): 5.7MM **Privately Held**
SIC: **3444** 3446 3441 Sheet metalwork; architectural metalwork; fabricated structural metal
PA: Custom Mechanical, Inc.
 34799 Daisey Rd
 Frankford DE 19945
 302 537-1150

(G-394)
CUT ABOVE HAIR GALLERY
1 N Pennsylvania Ave (19930)
P.O. Box 356 (19930-0356)
PHONE................................302 539-0622
Eddie Gabor, *Owner*
EMP: 4
SALES (est): 72.6K **Privately Held**
SIC: **7231** Beauty shops

(G-395)
D M F ASSOCIATES INC
Also Called: Bennett Realty
Evergreen St Rr 1 (19930)
PHONE................................302 539-0606
Edgar C Bennett, *President*
Durwood Bennett, *Vice Pres*
Judy Bennett, *Treasurer*
EMP: 5
SALES (est): 472.6K **Privately Held**
WEB: www.bennett-realty.com
SIC: **6531** Real estate brokers & agents

(G-396)
DAVID MARSHALL & ASSOCIATES
Kent Avenue Westley Dr (19930)
P.O. Box 1472 (19930-1472)
PHONE................................302 539-4488
David Marshall, *Owner*
EMP: 40
SALES: 400K **Privately Held**
WEB: www.tennisadvantage.com
SIC: **7999** Tennis services & professionals

(G-397)
DELAWARE BOTANIC GARDENS INC
201 Ashwood St (19930)
P.O. Box 360 (19930-0360)
PHONE................................202 262-9501
Raymond Sander, *Principal*
Sheryl Swed, *Principal*
EMP: 6
SALES (est): 132.9K **Privately Held**
SIC: **7389**

(G-398)
DIESTE MARK DESIGN BUILD LLC
32895 Coastal Hwy # 201 (19930-3784)
PHONE................................301 921-9050
Walter H Magruder,
Mark Dieste,
EMP: 10
SALES (est): 787.3K **Privately Held**
SIC: **1522** Remodeling, multi-family dwellings

(G-399)
FRESH ACCENTS LLC
Also Called: Green Outfitters
134 New Castle Dr (19930-9742)
PHONE................................301 717-3757
Margo Lee Fitzpatrick,
Donna Poindexter,
EMP: 2
SALES (est): 153.4K **Privately Held**
SIC: **2311** 2337 2326 Men's & boys' uniforms; uniforms, except athletic: women's, misses' & juniors'; work uniforms

(G-400)
FRONTGATE LLC
Also Called: Julesk
33258 Kent Ave (19930-3787)
PHONE................................302 245-6654
Nick Kypreos, *Mng Member*
Julie Kypreos, *Mng Member*
EMP: 2 EST: 2011
SALES: 50K **Privately Held**
SIC: **3171** Women's handbags & purses

(G-401)
GALLO REALTY INC
33292 Coastal Hwy (19930-3703)
PHONE................................888 624-6794
Elizabeth D Gallo, *Branch Mgr*
Cindy Baker, *Asst Broker*
EMP: 6
SALES (corp-wide): 1.9MM **Privately Held**
SIC: **6531** Real estate agent, residential
PA: Gallo Realty Inc
 37230 Rehoboth Avenue Ext
 Rehoboth Beach DE 19971
 302 945-7368

(G-402)
GW SOLUTIONS LLC
237 Oyster Shell Cv (19930-9001)
PHONE................................240 578-5981
Wilson Mann,
EMP: 5
SQ FT: 3,570
SALES (est): 204.1K **Privately Held**
WEB: www.gwsolutions.net
SIC: **7371** Computer software development

(G-403)
HUGH H HICKMAN & SONS INC
300 Ocean View Pkwy (19930-9211)
P.O. Box 1000 (19930-1000)
PHONE................................302 539-9741
Tim Tribbitt, *President*
EMP: 11 EST: 1957
SQ FT: 703
SALES (est): 1.4MM **Privately Held**
WEB: www.hughhhickman.com
SIC: **1521** New construction, single-family houses

(G-404)
INTOUCH BODY THERAPY LLC
33012 Coastal Hwy Unit 4 (19930-3777)
PHONE................................302 537-0510
Dianna Moesce, *Principal*
EMP: 4
SALES (est): 108.3K **Privately Held**
SIC: **8093** Rehabilitation center, outpatient treatment

(G-405)
ISLAND BOY ENTERPRISE LLC
35 Inlet View Ct (19930-9251)
PHONE................................904 347-4563
Joe Cole, *Mng Member*
EMP: 2
SALES: 100K **Privately Held**
SIC: **7372** Application computer software

(G-406)
JACK HICKMAN REAL ESTATE
Also Called: White's Creek Manor
33188 Coastal Hwy Unit 2 (19930-3779)
P.O. Box 1 (19930-0001)
PHONE................................302 539-8000
Jack Hickman, *President*
Chad Hickman, *Vice Pres*
Jaclyn Hills, *Broker*
EMP: 10
SALES (est): 1.8MM **Privately Held**
WEB: www.jackhickmanrealestate.com
SIC: **6552** 1521 4493 Land subdividers & developers, residential; new construction, single-family houses; marinas

Bethany Beach - Sussex County (G-407)

(G-407)
JOE MAGGIO REALTY
8 N Pennsylvania Ave (19930-9746)
PHONE................................302 539-9300
EMP: 6
SALES (corp-wide): 500K Privately Held
SIC: 6531 Real estate brokers & agents
PA: Joe Maggio Realty
  37169 Rehoboth Avenue Ext # 11
  Rehoboth Beach DE 19971
  302 251-8792

(G-408)
LEGUM & NORMAN MID-WEST LLC
4 4 Edgewater House Rd (19930)
PHONE................................302 537-9499
Craig Clarke, Branch Mgr
Kristine Warner, Manager
Ann McGinley, Admin Asst
EMP: 7
SALES (corp-wide): 8.8MM Privately Held
SIC: 6531 Real estate managers
PA: Legum & Norman Mid-West, Llc
  3130 Frview Pk Dr Ste 200
  Falls Church VA 22042
  703 600-6000

(G-409)
LESLIE KOPP INC
33298 Coastal Hwy (19930-3781)
P.O. Box 1301 (19930-1301)
PHONE................................302 541-5207
Leslie Kopp, Owner
EMP: 10
SALES (est): 537.7K Privately Held
SIC: 6531 Real estate agent, residential

(G-410)
LONG & FOSTER COMPANIES INC
1150 S Coastal Hwy (19930)
PHONE................................302 539-9040
Marie Cahill, Principal
EMP: 40
SALES (corp-wide): 225.3B Publicly Held
WEB: www.longandfoster.com
SIC: 6531 Real estate brokers & agents
HQ: The Long & Foster Companies Inc
  14501 George Carter Way # 1
  Chantilly VA 20151
  703 653-8500

(G-411)
LONG & FOSTER COMPANIES INC
33298 Coastal Hwy Unit 1 (19930-3781)
PHONE................................302 539-9767
James R Hubal, Principal
Linda Regan, Real Est Agnt
EMP: 7
SALES (corp-wide): 225.3B Publicly Held
SIC: 6531 Real estate brokers & agents
HQ: The Long & Foster Companies Inc
  14501 George Carter Way # 1
  Chantilly VA 20151
  703 653-8500

(G-412)
MANUFACTURERS & TRADERS TR CO
Also Called: M&T
33364 S Pennsylvania Ave (19930-3446)
PHONE................................302 539-3471
Debbie Crago, Manager
EMP: 4
SALES (corp-wide): 6.4B Publicly Held
WEB: www.binghamlegg.com
SIC: 6022 State commercial banks
HQ: Manufacturers And Traders Trust Company
  1 M&T Plz Fl 3
  Buffalo NY 14203
  716 842-4200

(G-413)
MARK B BROWN DDS
32895 Coastal Hwy # 102 (19930-3782)
PHONE................................302 537-1200
Mark Brown, Office Mgr
EMP: 4
SALES (est): 61.5K Privately Held
SIC: 8021 Offices & clinics of dentists

(G-414)
MERIS GARDENS BED & BREAKFAST
33309 Kent Ave (19930-3730)
PHONE................................302 752-4962
EMP: 4
SALES (est): 94.4K Privately Held
SIC: 7011 Bed & breakfast inn

(G-415)
MIND BODY & SOLE
32892 Coastal Hwy Unit 3 (19930-3788)
PHONE................................302 537-3668
EMP: 4 EST: 2010
SALES (est): 431.2K Privately Held
SIC: 1542 Nonresidential Construction

(G-416)
NAGORKA
303 Wellington Pkwy (19930-9543)
PHONE................................302 537-2392
Diane S Nagorka, Principal
EMP: 2
SALES (est): 114.9K Privately Held
SIC: 2389 Clergymen's vestments

(G-417)
NATIONAL FITNESS LLC
726 Fox Tail Dr (19930-9012)
PHONE................................301 841-8066
Richard Bumford,
EMP: 4
SALES: 270K Privately Held
SIC: 7991 Physical fitness facilities

(G-418)
NINETY ONE HOLDING INC
56140 Pine Cone Ln (19930)
PHONE................................212 203-7900
Bleron Baraliu, CEO
Eleonora Gashi, President
EMP: 21
SALES (est): 390.1K Privately Held
SIC: 7371 Custom computer programming services

(G-419)
PATRICIA HOFFMANN
Also Called: Stitch-Stash
98 Garfield Pkwy (19930-7753)
PHONE................................203 247-2635
EMP: 1
SALES (est): 26.4K Privately Held
SIC: 2395 Embroidery & art needlework

(G-420)
PAUL AMOS
Also Called: Holiday Inn
39642 Jefferson Bridge Rd (19930-3723)
PHONE................................302 541-9200
Brad Clark, Manager
EMP: 15 EST: 2001
SALES (est): 1.2MM Privately Held
SIC: 7011 Hotels & motels

(G-421)
PETER PATELLIS
32895 Coastal Hwy # 102 (19930-3782)
P.O. Box 862 (19930-0862)
PHONE................................302 537-1200
Peter Patellis, Principal
EMP: 4 EST: 2013
SALES (est): 95.5K Privately Held
SIC: 8021 Offices & clinics of dentists

(G-422)
PIVOTAL MEDICAL
413 Salt Pond Rd (19930-9595)
PHONE................................302 299-5795
Charles Davis, Principal
EMP: 8
SALES (est): 76K Privately Held
SIC: 8099 Health & allied services

(G-423)
PNC BANK NATIONAL ASSOCIATION
2 S Pennsylvania Ave (19930-9772)
PHONE................................302 537-2600
Barbara Howard, Site Mgr
Jane McCabe, Manager
EMP: 14
SALES (corp-wide): 19.9B Publicly Held
WEB: www.pncfunds.com
SIC: 6021 National trust companies with deposits, commercial
HQ: Pnc Bank, National Association
  222 Delaware Ave
  Wilmington DE 19801
  877 762-2000

(G-424)
PROPERTY IMPROVEMENTS LLC
144 Elizabeth Way (19930-9167)
PHONE................................610 692-5343
Stephan Walker, Principal
EMP: 5
SALES (est): 308.6K Privately Held
SIC: 6512 Nonresidential building operators

(G-425)
RASKAUKAS JOSEPH C ATY LAW
33176 Coastal Hwy (19930-3758)
P.O. Box 1509 (19930-1509)
PHONE................................302 537-2000
J C Raskaukas, Owner
Joseph C Raskaukas, Owner
EMP: 6
SALES (est): 619K Privately Held
SIC: 8111 General practice attorney, lawyer

(G-426)
RAYMOND JAMES FINCL SVCS INC
701 Bethany Loop (19930-9257)
PHONE................................302 539-3323
Raymond Jsander, Branch Mgr
EMP: 4
SALES (corp-wide): 8B Publicly Held
SIC: 6211 Brokers, security
HQ: Raymond James Financial Services, Inc.
  880 Carillon Pkwy
  Saint Petersburg FL 33716
  727 567-1000

(G-427)
REMAX BY SEA
R 1 5th D St (19930)
P.O. Box 1499 (19930-1499)
PHONE................................302 541-5000
Frank Serio, Partner
Clover Simpler, Real Est Agnt
EMP: 22
SALES (est): 1.2MM Privately Held
SIC: 6531 Real estate agent, residential; real estate brokers & agents

(G-428)
RESORTQUEST DELAWARE RE LLC (DH)
Also Called: Resort Quest Delaware Beaches
33546 Market Pl (19930-4269)
P.O. Box 480 (19930-0480)
PHONE................................302 541-8999
Patrick Davis, General Mgr
Ann Baker, Real Est Agnt
EMP: 17
SALES (est): 4.7MM Publicly Held
SIC: 6531 6519 Real estate leasing & rentals; real property lessors

(G-429)
ROBERTS PROPERTY MGT LLC
107 Canal Rd (19930-9507)
PHONE................................302 537-5371
Dennis Roberts, Principal
EMP: 5 EST: 2010
SALES (est): 399.8K Privately Held
SIC: 8741 Management services

(G-430)
SALT POND ASSOCIATES
Also Called: Salt Pond Golf Club
400 Bethany Loop (19930-9020)
PHONE................................302 539-2750
Ken Simpler, Managing Prtnr
Rupert Smith, Partner
Bill Janke, Partner
Robert Kent, Partner
Shirley Kent, Partner
EMP: 12
SALES (est): 2.8MM Privately Held
SIC: 6552 7997 Land subdividers & developers, residential; golf club, membership

(G-431)
SEA COLONY TENNIS CENTER
Also Called: Resort Quest
Westway & Kent Ave (19930)
PHONE................................302 539-4488
Thomas Johnson, Director
EMP: 4
SALES (est): 352.8K Privately Held
SIC: 7999 Tennis courts, outdoor/indoor: non-membership

(G-432)
SUNSHINE CREPES
100 Garfield Pkwy (19930-7705)
PHONE................................302 537-1765
Pavla Glovcikova, Owner
EMP: 5
SALES (est): 289.9K Privately Held
SIC: 2024 Ice cream & frozen desserts

(G-433)
SUSSEX SHORES WATER CO CORP
Rr 1 (19930)
P.O. Box 170 (19930-0170)
PHONE................................302 539-7611
Richard Russo, Ch of Bd
Pamela Short, Ch of Bd
Christine Mason, President
Glenn Kelly, Admin Asst
EMP: 7
SALES (est): 955.7K Privately Held
WEB: www.sussexshoreswater.com
SIC: 4941 Water supply

(G-434)
T K O DESIGNS INC
100 Garfield Pkwy (19930-7705)
P.O. Box 146 (19930-0146)
PHONE................................302 539-6992
Alice Klein, President
Bryant Poark, Vice Pres
EMP: 3
SALES (est): 242K Privately Held
SIC: 3961 5944 Costume jewelry; jewelry stores

(G-435)
TECH MANAGEMENT SERVICES INC
134 Henlopen Dr (19930-9740)
P.O. Box 636 (19930-0636)
PHONE................................302 539-4837
Elaine Wilkinson, CEO
George Wilkinson, Vice Pres
EMP: 7
SALES: 350K Privately Held
SIC: 8748 Business consulting

(G-436)
WARNER TANSEY INC
Pennsylvania Ave (19930)
P.O. Box 337 (19930-0337)
PHONE................................302 539-3001
Deborha Conneen, President
EMP: 7
SALES (est): 440K Privately Held
WEB: www.tanseywarner.com
SIC: 6531 Real estate brokers & agents

(G-437)
WAVE NEWSPAPER
Coastal Hwy (19930)
P.O. Box 1420 (19930-1420)
PHONE................................302 537-1881
Rick Jensen, Principal
Glenn Ankenbrand, Engineer
David Tancredi, Engineer
Ron Pousson, Adv Dir
Lori Fields, Business Anlyst
EMP: 17
SALES (est): 443.6K Privately Held
WEB: www.thewavenewspaper.com
SIC: 2711 Newspapers, publishing & printing

(G-438)
WILGUS ASSOCIATES INC (PA)
32904 Coastal Hwy (19930)
PHONE................................302 539-7511
Michael W Wilgus, President

GEOGRAPHIC SECTION

Bridgeville - Sussex County (G-469)

David Wilgus, *Corp Secy*
Cody Ayers, *Manager*
Cindy Hall, *Agent*
EMP: 23
SQ FT: 8,000
SALES (est): 8.3MM **Privately Held**
WEB: www.wilgusassociates.com
SIC: 6411 6531 Insurance brokers; real estate brokers & agents; appraiser, real estate

(G-439)
WOMENS CIVIC CLUB BETHANY BCH
332 Sandpiper Dr (19930-9086)
P.O. Box 935 (19930-0935)
PHONE....................302 539-7515
Cheryl Dorfman, *Principal*
William Makowski, *Agent*
EMP: 6
SALES (est): 180.6K **Privately Held**
SIC: 7997 Membership sports & recreation clubs

Bethel
Sussex County

(G-440)
APPLIED CONSTRUCTAL INC
7730 Main St (19931)
P.O. Box 300 (19931-0300)
PHONE....................203 606-1656
Adam P Dixon, *President*
EMP: 4
SALES (est): 388.1K **Privately Held**
SIC: 5085 Bearings

Bridgeville
Sussex County

(G-441)
36 BUILDERS INC
16255 Sussex Hwy (19933-2968)
PHONE....................302 349-9480
Heather Holt, *President*
EMP: 13
SALES (est): 2MM **Privately Held**
SIC: 1521 New construction, single-family houses

(G-442)
A C SCHULTES OF DELAWARE INC (HQ)
16289 Sussex Hwy (19933-2968)
P.O. Box 188 (19933-0188)
PHONE....................302 337-0700
R Michael Collison, *President*
EMP: 15 **EST:** 1921
SQ FT: 1,500
SALES (est): 2.2MM **Privately Held**
SIC: 1781 Water well servicing

(G-443)
ACORN SITE FURNISHINGS
5218 Federalsburg Rd (19933-3552)
PHONE....................302 249-4979
Anthony Corum, *Sales Mgr*
EMP: 2
SALES (est): 121.3K **Privately Held**
SIC: 2531 7389 Picnic tables or benches, park;

(G-444)
ALL-SPAN INC (PA)
9347 Allspan Dr (19933-2982)
PHONE....................302 349-9460
David Miller, *President*
Craig Beard, *COO*
Jj Carter, *Vice Pres*
Herb Troyer, *Vice Pres*
Ed Kielbasa, *Plant Mgr*
▼ **EMP:** 38
SQ FT: 34,000
SALES (est): 7.1MM **Privately Held**
WEB: www.allspaninc.com
SIC: 3448 Trusses & framing: prefabricated metal

(G-445)
AMH ENTERPRISES LLC
8805 Newton Rd (19933-2946)
PHONE....................302 337-0300
Austin Hubbard, *Mng Member*
Traci Creighton,
EMP: 28
SALES (est): 4.7MM **Privately Held**
SIC: 4731 Freight forwarding

(G-446)
AMP ELECTRIC LLC
302 Earlee Ave (19933-1304)
PHONE....................302 337-8050
Steve McCarron, *Principal*
Phillip Andrew, *Principal*
EMP: 9
SALES (est): 582K **Privately Held**
SIC: 1731 Electrical work

(G-447)
ARCTEC AIR HEATING & COOLING
21965 Palomino Way (19933-4575)
PHONE....................302 629-7129
Jeremy Booros, *Owner*
EMP: 6
SALES (est): 512.6K **Privately Held**
SIC: 1711 Warm air heating & air conditioning contractor

(G-448)
ASI TRANSPORT LLC
9347 Allspan Dr (19933-2982)
PHONE....................302 349-9460
David Miller, *President*
James Carter, *Vice Pres*
EMP: 6
SQ FT: 5,000
SALES (est): 468.9K **Privately Held**
WEB: www.allspaninc.com
SIC: 4212 4213 Local trucking, without storage; trucking, except local
PA: All-Span, Inc.
9347 Allspan Dr
Bridgeville DE 19933

(G-449)
ATLANTIC BUSINESS CONTRACTING
18089 Sussex Hwy (19933-4082)
PHONE....................302 337-7490
EMP: 6
SALES (est): 283.6K **Privately Held**
SIC: 1799 Special trade contractors

(G-450)
AUTOMATION AIR INC
16782 Oak Rd (19933-3910)
PHONE....................973 875-6676
William Schnabel, *President*
EMP: 7
SALES (est): 890K **Privately Held**
WEB: www.automationair.com
SIC: 5084 Drilling equipment, excluding bits

(G-451)
BALDWIN SAYRE INC
17882 Potato Ln (19933-3154)
PHONE....................302 337-0309
Daniel Baldwin, *President*
Diane Baldwin, *Vice Pres*
EMP: 5
SQ FT: 20,000
SALES (est): 460K **Privately Held**
SIC: 0161 5153 Corn farm, sweet; corn; soybeans; wheat

(G-452)
BASE ENTERPRISE INC
Also Called: Information Retrieval Services
14021 Quiddity Way (19933-4200)
P.O. Box 268, Georgetown (19947-0268)
PHONE....................302 337-0548
Kelly R Jansen, *President*
EMP: 4
SALES (est): 250K **Privately Held**
WEB: www.basede.com
SIC: 7381 Detective agency

(G-453)
BG WELDING LLC
14047 Redden Rd (19933-4175)
PHONE....................302 228-7260
Jose Angel Campos Jr, *Principal*
EMP: 8
SALES (est): 88.7K **Privately Held**
SIC: 7692 Welding repair

(G-454)
BRIDGEVILLE AUTO CENTER INC
Rr 13 Box S (19933)
P.O. Box 185 (19933-0185)
PHONE....................302 337-3100
Joseph Johnson, *President*
Toni Johnson, *Vice Pres*
EMP: 13
SQ FT: 20,000
SALES (est): 1.6MM **Privately Held**
SIC: 5015 Motor vehicle parts, used

(G-455)
BRIDGEVILLE LIONS CLUB INC
P.O. Box 414 (19933-0414)
PHONE....................302 629-9543
Willis Dewey, *President*
Richard Tull, *Treasurer*
EMP: 25
SQ FT: 4,000
SALES (est): 25K **Privately Held**
SIC: 7997 Membership sports & recreation clubs

(G-456)
BRIDGEVILLE SENIOR CENTER
414 Market St (19933-1133)
PHONE....................302 337-8771
Fran Smith, *Director*
Paula Williams, *Director*
EMP: 5
SALES (est): 184.3K **Privately Held**
SIC: 8322 Senior citizens' center or association

(G-457)
CANNON COLD STORAGE LLC
500 Market St (19933-1155)
P.O. Box 550 (19933-0550)
PHONE....................302 337-5500
Bob Huntsberger, *Mng Member*
EMP: 30
SALES (est): 2.6MM **Privately Held**
WEB: www.cannoncold.com
SIC: 4225 8748 General warehousing & storage; business consulting

(G-458)
CHICK/BROOK LLC
20015 Wilson Farm Rd (19933-3740)
PHONE....................302 337-7141
Kenneth Wilson, *Principal*
EMP: 4 **EST:** 2008
SALES (est): 583.5K **Privately Held**
SIC: 5159 Chicks

(G-459)
CIRCLE C OUTFIT LLC
9801 Orchards End (19933-4054)
PHONE....................302 337-8828
Wayne Conner, *Mng Member*
EMP: 1
SALES (est): 110K **Privately Held**
SIC: 3799 Carriages, horse drawn

(G-460)
CLEAR BROOK FARMS INC
18800 Wesley Church Rd (19933-3710)
PHONE....................302 337-7678
Howard W Allen, *President*
Jeff Allen, *Vice Pres*
EMP: 4
SQ FT: 2,400
SALES (est): 343.5K **Privately Held**
SIC: 0119 0111 Barley farm; wheat

(G-461)
COVERDALE COMMUNITY COUNCIL
11575 Fisher Cir (19933-4389)
P.O. Box 646 (19933-0646)
PHONE....................302 337-7179
Evelyn Wilson, *President*
EMP: 6
SALES (est): 279.9K **Privately Held**
SIC: 8399 Community development groups

(G-462)
CREATIVE ASSEMBLIES INC
17053 Tatman Farm Rd (19933-4193)
PHONE....................302 956-6194
Raymond Hance, *President*
EMP: 10 **EST:** 1982
SQ FT: 9,000
SALES (est): 1.1MM **Privately Held**
WEB: www.creativeassemblies.com
SIC: 3443 3585 Cooling towers, metal plate; dehumidifiers electric, except portable

(G-463)
DATA GUARD RECYCLING INC
9174 Redden Rd (19933-4723)
PHONE....................302 337-8870
Clint Phillips, *Mng Member*
EMP: 5
SALES (est): 320.8K **Privately Held**
SIC: 4953 Recycling, waste materials

(G-464)
DEANGELIS & SON INC (PA)
19489 Handy Rd (19933-3217)
PHONE....................302 337-8699
James M Deangelis, *President*
Jamie L Deangelis, *Admin Sec*
EMP: 1
SALES (est): 250K **Privately Held**
SIC: 5084 7699 3599 7389 Printing trades machinery, equipment & supplies; printing trades machinery & equipment repair; machine & other job shop work;

(G-465)
DELMARVA BUILDERS INC
20846 Camp Rd (19933-4626)
PHONE....................302 629-9123
John A Mc Farland, *President*
EMP: 8
SALES (est): 671.1K **Privately Held**
SIC: 1521 1542 1781 New construction, single-family houses; commercial & office building, new construction; specialized public building contractors; water well drilling

(G-466)
DELMARVA RUBBER & GASKET CO
16356 Sussex Hwy (19933-3056)
P.O. Box 249 (19933-0249)
PHONE....................302 424-8300
Richard Phillips, *President*
EMP: 8
SALES (est): 1.9MM **Privately Held**
SIC: 5085 Rubber goods, mechanical; hose, belting & packing

(G-467)
DOWN UNDER BOXING CLUB
19124 Wesley Church Rd (19933-3764)
P.O. Box 605 (19933-0605)
PHONE....................302 745-4392
Bruce Hibbs Sr, *Owner*
EMP: 5
SALES (est): 64K **Privately Held**
SIC: 7997 Membership sports & recreation clubs

(G-468)
DRIVEWAY MINT PVNG/SLCTING LLC
7031 Cannon Rd (19933-3722)
PHONE....................302 228-2644
John R Hawkins,
EMP: 2
SALES: 150K **Privately Held**
SIC: 2951 Asphalt paving mixtures & blocks

(G-469)
EVANS FARMS LLC
9843 Seashore Hwy (19933-4620)
PHONE....................302 337-8130
Kevin Evans, *Mng Member*
EMP: 6
SALES (est): 1.2MM **Privately Held**
SIC: 0161 7389 Vegetables & melons;

Bridgeville - Sussex County (G-470)

(G-470)
FIRESIDE HEART & HOME
18109 Sussex Hwy (19933-4010)
P.O. Box 395 (19933-0395)
PHONE 302 337-3025
Mark Johnson, *Manager*
EMP: 1
SALES (est): 54.8K **Privately Held**
SIC: 5719 5023 3429 Fireplace equipment & accessories; fireplace equipment & accessories; hardware: andirons, grates, screens

(G-471)
FIRING DISTANCE
6515 Ray Rd (19933-3130)
PHONE 302 337-9094
EMP: 5
SALES (est): 178.6K **Privately Held**
SIC: 4813 Long distance telephone communications

(G-472)
FOUR PAWS ANIMAL HOSPITAL PA
21804 Eskridge Rd (19933-4509)
PHONE 302 629-7297
Michael Metzler Dvm, *President*
EMP: 13
SALES (est): 825.8K **Privately Held**
SIC: 0742 Animal hospital services, pets & other animal specialties

(G-473)
FRESENIUS MEDICAL CARE
Also Called: Fresenius Kdney Care Brdgville
9115 Antique Aly Unit 1 (19933-4681)
PHONE 302 337-8789
Mary Garber, *Principal*
Bradford Schultz, *Principal*
EMP: 25
SALES (est): 266.2K **Privately Held**
SIC: 8092 Kidney dialysis centers

(G-474)
GENES LIMOUSINE SERVICE INC
501 Market St (19933-1156)
PHONE 410 479-8470
Howard Mullins, *President*
EMP: 30
SALES (est): 1.4MM **Privately Held**
SIC: 4119 Limousine rental, with driver

(G-475)
GOODWILL INDUSTRIES DELAWARE
18178 Sussex Hwy (19933-4009)
PHONE 302 337-8561
EMP: 1
SALES (est): 11.2K **Privately Held**
SIC: 3999 Manufacturing industries

(G-476)
GREENWOOD PALLET CO
16849 Road Runner Dr (19933-2996)
PHONE 302 337-8181
T Tennefos, *Principal*
EMP: 4
SALES (est): 415.6K **Privately Held**
SIC: 2448 5031 Pallets, wood & wood with metal; pallets, wood

(G-477)
H C DAVIS INC
Also Called: Shore Pride Foods
Pine Aly (19933)
P.O. Box 346 (19933-0346)
PHONE 302 337-7001
Harry C Davis III, *President*
Matt Davis, *Vice Pres*
Jenny Davis, *Treasurer*
Wanda S Davis, *Admin Sec*
EMP: 8 **EST:** 1919
SQ FT: 5,000
SALES (est): 1.8MM **Privately Held**
SIC: 5143 5142 5147 Dairy products, except dried or canned; packaged frozen goods; meats, fresh

(G-478)
HAB NAB TRUCKING INC
8805 Newton Rd (19933-2946)
PHONE 302 245-6900
Michael J Hubbard, *President*
Janet Hubbard, *Corp Secy*
EMP: 40
SQ FT: 10,700
SALES (est): 4.4MM **Privately Held**
SIC: 4213 4212 Contract haulers; local trucking, without storage

(G-479)
HARRY A LEHMAN III MD PA
38 Snowy Egret Ct (19933-2404)
PHONE 302 629-5050
Harry A Lehman III, *Principal*
Harry Lehman, *Med Doctor*
Michelle L Mitchell, *Practice Mgr*
EMP: 12
SALES (est): 1MM **Privately Held**
SIC: 8011 Offices & clinics of medical doctors

(G-480)
HEALTH & SOCIAL SVCS DEL DEPT
Also Called: Bridgeville State Services
400 Mill St (19933-1114)
PHONE 302 337-8261
Ruthie Adams Hunter, *Director*
EMP: 15 **Privately Held**
SIC: 8322 9441 Individual & family services; administration of social & manpower programs;
HQ: Delaware Dept Of Health And Social Services
1901 N Dupont Hwy
New Castle DE 19720

(G-481)
HELENA AGRI-ENTERPRISES LLC
16635 Adams Rd (19933-2906)
PHONE 302 337-3881
Trace Hall, *Office Mgr*
Rick Adams, *Branch Mgr*
EMP: 6 **Privately Held**
WEB: www.helenachemical.com
SIC: 5191 Chemicals, agricultural
HQ: Helena Agri-Enterprises, Llc
255 Schilling Blvd # 300
Collierville TN 38017
901 761-0050

(G-482)
HOPKINS CONSTRUCTION INC
18904 Maranatha Way # 1 (19933-4057)
PHONE 302 337-3366
R Keller Hopkins, *President*
Joanne Hopkins, *Corp Secy*
Susan Collins, *Controller*
Joann Hopkins, *Marketing Staff*
Cynthia Lopez, *Officer*
EMP: 13
SQ FT: 12,000
SALES (est): 6.3MM **Privately Held**
WEB: www.hopkins-inc.com
SIC: 1623 Sewer line construction; water main construction

(G-483)
HORNEY INDUSTRIAL ELECTRONICS (PA)
Also Called: Hie
114 N Main St (19933-1146)
P.O. Box 700 (19933-0700)
PHONE 302 337-3600
Ray Horney, *President*
EMP: 4
SALES (est): 720K **Privately Held**
WEB: www.horneyonline.com
SIC: 3829 Measuring & controlling devices

(G-484)
INTERNAL MEDICINE BRIDGEVILLE
Also Called: Smith, Kenneth MD
8991 Redden Rd (19933-4746)
PHONE 302 337-3300
Kenneth Smith, *Owner*
EMP: 6
SALES (est): 560.5K **Privately Held**
SIC: 8011 Internal medicine, physician/surgeon; general & family practice, physician/surgeon

(G-485)
J CULVER CONSTRUCTION INC
18731 Progress School Rd (19933-3502)
PHONE 302 337-8136
Fax: 302 337-9662
EMP: 5
SALES (est): 400K **Privately Held**
SIC: 1521 Single-Family House Construction

(G-486)
JERSEY CLIPPERS LLC
Also Called: Great Clips
134 Widgeon Way (19933-2421)
PHONE 302 956-0138
Robert Yasher,
Cindy Yasher,
EMP: 25
SALES (est): 750K **Privately Held**
SIC: 7231 Unisex hair salons

(G-487)
JL MECHANICAL INC
Also Called: Honeywell Authorized Dealer
5460 Hartzell Rd (19933-3458)
PHONE 302 337-7855
Jerome Layton, *Principal*
EMP: 4
SALES (est): 419.4K **Privately Held**
SIC: 7389 Design services

(G-488)
KENNY BROTHERS PRODUCE LLC
16440 Adams Rd (19933-2910)
P.O. Box 728 (19933-0728)
PHONE 302 337-3007
Michael Kenny, *Mng Member*
EMP: 5
SQ FT: 1,500
SALES (est): 528.3K **Privately Held**
SIC: 2035 Cucumbers, pickles & pickle salting

(G-489)
KROEGERS SALVAGE INC
15896 White Pine Ln (19933-4184)
PHONE 302 381-7082
Joel H Kroeger, *President*
Joel Kroeger, *President*
EMP: 17
SALES: 5MM **Privately Held**
SIC: 4953 Recycling, waste materials

(G-490)
LYNNS HOME DAYCARE
412 S Laws St (19933-1326)
PHONE 302 337-0186
EMP: 5
SALES (est): 150K **Privately Held**
SIC: 8351 Child Day Care Services

(G-491)
MACK CONSTRUCTION & HANDY
3100 Craft Rd (19933-3241)
PHONE 302 337-3448
Mack McIntire, *Owner*
EMP: 4
SALES (est): 164.8K **Privately Held**
SIC: 1521 Single-family housing construction

(G-492)
MARBLE SOURCE UNLIMITED INC
18089 Sussex Hwy (19933-4082)
PHONE 302 337-7665
Ritchie Woodland, *President*
EMP: 20
SALES (est): 874.4K **Privately Held**
SIC: 5032 Marble building stone

(G-493)
MARK IV TRANSPORTATION CO INC
617 Market St (19933)
P.O. Box 248 (19933-0248)
PHONE 302 337-9898
Mark Hunsberger, *President*
EMP: 25
SALES (est): 4.2MM
SALES (corp-wide): 1.7B **Privately Held**
SIC: 4213 Trucking, except local
HQ: Simmons Feed Ingredients, Inc.
601 N Hico St
Siloam Springs AR 72761

(G-494)
MARLETTE R LOFLAND
Also Called: Colorful World Daycare
20255 Wilson Farm Rd (19933-3742)
PHONE 302 628-1521
Arthur Lofland, *Principal*
EMP: 5
SALES (est): 63.3K **Privately Held**
SIC: 8351 Group day care center

(G-495)
MCCLUNG-LOGAN EQUIPMENT CO INC
17941 Sussex Hwy (19933-4083)
PHONE 302 337-3400
Logan McClung, *Branch Mgr*
EMP: 11
SALES (corp-wide): 125.3MM **Privately Held**
SIC: 5082 Excavating machinery & equipment
HQ: Mcclung-Logan Equipment Company, Inc.
4601 Washington Blvd A
Baltimore MD 21227
410 242-6500

(G-496)
MEHERRIN AG & CHEM CO
18441 Wesley Church Rd (19933-3702)
PHONE 302 337-0330
Chris Griffith, *Manager*
EMP: 6
SALES (corp-wide): 1.1B **Privately Held**
WEB: www.hamptonfarms.com
SIC: 2879 4226 Agricultural chemicals; special warehousing & storage
PA: Meherrin Agricultural & Chemical Co
413 Main St
Severn NC 27877
252 585-1744

(G-497)
MESSICK & GRAY CNSTR INC (PA)
Also Called: Bridgeville Machining
9003 Fawn Rd (19933-2941)
PHONE 302 337-8777
Alan Messick, *President*
Shirley Messick, *Corp Secy*
Thomas Messick, *Vice Pres*
Gary Leonard, *Foreman/Supr*
Jason Smith, *Engineer*
EMP: 50 **EST:** 1963
SQ FT: 7,000
SALES (est): 32.1MM **Privately Held**
WEB: www.messickandgray.com
SIC: 5084 5083 7699 3441 Industrial machinery & equipment; agricultural machinery; industrial machinery & equipment repair; agricultural equipment repair services; fabricated structural metal

(G-498)
MESSICK & GRAY CNSTR INC
17016 N Main St (19933-2920)
PHONE 302 337-8445
James Sigmon, *Branch Mgr*
EMP: 12
SALES (corp-wide): 32.1MM **Privately Held**
WEB: www.messickandgray.com
SIC: 3599 5083 7699 3441 Air intake filters, internal combustion engine, except auto; agricultural machinery; industrial machinery & equipment repair; agricultural equipment repair services; fabricated structural metal
PA: Messick & Gray Construction, Inc.
9003 Fawn Rd
Bridgeville DE 19933
302 337-8777

(G-499)
METRIE INC
617 Market St Unit 4 (19933)
PHONE 302 337-0269
EMP: 7
SALES (corp-wide): 89.6MM **Privately Held**
SIC: 5031 Whol Millwork

GEOGRAPHIC SECTION — Bridgeville - Sussex County (G-527)

HQ: Metrie Inc.
2200 140th Ave E Ste 600
Sumner WA 98390
253 470-5050

(G-500)
MID-SHORE ENVMTL SVCS INC
7481 Federalsburg Rd (19933-3656)
PHONE....................302 736-5504
Michael Stang, *President*
Paul M Pearson, *Exec VP*
Paul Pearson, *Vice Pres*
EMP: 16
SALES (est): 867.5K **Privately Held**
SIC: 4953 Refuse systems

(G-501)
MILLER METAL FABRICATION INC
16356 Sussex Hwy Unit 4 (19933-3056)
P.O. Box 249 (19933-0249)
PHONE....................302 337-2291
Martin W Miller Jr, *President*
Dave Morris, *VP Opers*
Jeff Passwaters, *Foreman/Supr*
Jeffrey Passwaters, *Foreman/Supr*
Chris Esterson, *Project Engr*
▲ **EMP:** 100
SQ FT: 50,000
SALES: 17.1MM **Privately Held**
WEB: www.millermetal.com
SIC: 3441 3053 5051 3542 Fabricated structural metal; gaskets, all materials; sheets, metal; mechanical (pneumatic or hydraulic) metal forming machines

(G-502)
NEWS PRINT SHOP
16694 Emma Jane Ln (19933-2904)
P.O. Box 127 (19933-0127)
PHONE....................302 337-8283
Sandy Rementer, *President*
EMP: 7 **EST:** 1951
SQ FT: 1,000
SALES (est): 973.2K **Privately Held**
SIC: 2752 Commercial printing, offset

(G-503)
O A NEWTON & SON CO
16356 Sussex Hwy (19933-3056)
P.O. Box 397 (19933-0397)
PHONE....................302 337-8211
John Korschgen, *Partner*
Dean Hetrick, *Project Mgr*
Mike Descoteaux, *Engineer*
Alan Moore, *Controller*
Susan Rider, *Human Res Dir*
EMP: 35
SALES (est): 199.6K **Privately Held**
SIC: 0191 General farms, primarily crop

(G-504)
O A NEWTON & SON COMPANY
16356 Sussex Hwy Unit 1 (19933-3056)
P.O. Box 397 (19933-0397)
PHONE....................302 337-3782
Robert F Rider Jr, *President*
Bill Warner, *Vice Pres*
▲ **EMP:** 32 **EST:** 1916
SQ FT: 100,000
SALES (est): 22MM **Privately Held**
WEB: www.oanewton.com
SIC: 5083 3599 5084 Irrigation equipment; machine shop, jobbing & repair; materials handling machinery

(G-505)
OLD DOMINION FREIGHT LINE INC
1664 Emma Jane Ln (19933)
PHONE....................302 337-8793
Rich Molnar, *Manager*
EMP: 48
SALES (corp-wide): 4B **Publicly Held**
WEB: www.odfl.com
SIC: 4213 Contract haulers
PA: Old Dominion Freight Line Inc
500 Old Dominion Way
Thomasville NC 27360
336 889-5000

(G-506)
PASSWATERS LANDSCAPING
18956 Sussex Hwy (19933-4604)
PHONE....................302 542-8077
EMP: 4 **EST:** 2015
SALES (est): 109.9K **Privately Held**
SIC: 0781 Landscape services

(G-507)
PERDUE FARMS INC
16447 Adams Rd (19933-2911)
PHONE....................302 337-2210
Charles Broderick, *Manager*
Gail Wallace, *Analyst*
EMP: 44
SALES (corp-wide): 5.9B **Privately Held**
WEB: www.perdue.com
SIC: 2015 Poultry slaughtering & processing
PA: Perdue Farms Inc.
31149 Old Ocean City Rd
Salisbury MD 21804
410 543-3000

(G-508)
PET POULTRY PRODUCTS LLC
7494 Federalsburg Rd (19933-3662)
P.O. Box 128 (19933-0128)
PHONE....................302 337-8223
Robert Hunsberger, *President*
Wanda Stewart, *Corp Secy*
Mark Hunsberger, *Vice Pres*
▼ **EMP:** 38
SQ FT: 145,000
SALES (est): 14.8MM
SALES (corp-wide): 1.7B **Privately Held**
WEB: www.petpoultry.com
SIC: 5144 5113 Poultry products; boxes & containers
HQ: Simmons Feed Ingredients, Inc.
601 N Hico St
Siloam Springs AR 72761

(G-509)
PICTSWEET COMPANY
18215 Wesley Church Rd (19933)
P.O. Box 398 (19933-0398)
PHONE....................302 337-8206
Edward Carey, *Manager*
EMP: 55
SALES (corp-wide): 421.8MM **Privately Held**
SIC: 2038 Ethnic foods, frozen
PA: The Pictsweet Company
10 Pictsweet Dr
Bells TN 38006
731 663-7600

(G-510)
PINE BREEZE FARMS INC
3583 Buck Fever Rd (19933-2517)
PHONE....................302 337-7717
Richard Carlisrle, *President*
Katheerine Carlisrle, *Vice Pres*
EMP: 7
SALES (est): 948.9K **Privately Held**
SIC: 0161 Vegetables & melons

(G-511)
PNC BANK NATIONAL ASSOCIATION
100 S Laws St (19933-1108)
PHONE....................302 337-3500
Denise Taylor, *Manager*
EMP: 9
SALES (corp-wide): 19.9B **Publicly Held**
WEB: www.pncfunds.com
SIC: 6021 National trust companies with deposits, commercial
HQ: Pnc Bank, National Association
222 Delaware Ave
Wilmington DE 19801
877 762-2000

(G-512)
POWER TRANS INC
9029 Fawn Rd (19933-2941)
PHONE....................302 337-3016
Alan Messick, *President*
Justin Bailey, *Manager*
Steven Small, *Admin Sec*
EMP: 17
SQ FT: 12,000
SALES (est): 8.4MM **Privately Held**
WEB: www.powertrans.com
SIC: 5084 5999 Industrial machine parts; materials handling machinery; electronic parts & equipment

(G-513)
PROVIDENCE AT HERITAGE SH
21 White Pelican Ct (19933-2403)
PHONE....................302 337-1040
Dorothy Harper, *Principal*
EMP: 6
SALES (est): 251.2K **Privately Held**
SIC: 8741 Construction management

(G-514)
PYRAMID TRANSPORT INC
18119 Sussex Hwy Unit 2 (19933-4095)
PHONE....................302 337-9340
Jim Hitchens, *President*
Sam Ennis, *Opers Mgr*
Mera Hitchens, *Human Res Mgr*
Billy Griffith, *Area Spvr*
Dawn Ellsworth,
EMP: 50
SQ FT: 10,000
SALES (est): 17.7MM **Privately Held**
WEB: www.pyramidtransport.com
SIC: 4731 Truck transportation brokers

(G-515)
QUALITY CONSTRUCTION CLEANING
8902 Cannon Rd (19933-4639)
PHONE....................302 956-0752
Roxana Flores, *Owner*
EMP: 30 **EST:** 2013
SALES (est): 710.2K **Privately Held**
SIC: 1521 Single-family housing construction

(G-516)
R & S FABRICATION INC
7159 Seashore Hwy (19933-3111)
P.O. Box 903, Seaford (19973-0903)
PHONE....................302 629-0377
Larry Rust, *President*
Richard Ray, *Vice Pres*
EMP: 15
SQ FT: 80,000
SALES (est): 1.1MM **Privately Held**
SIC: 1796 Machinery installation

(G-517)
RALPH AND PAUL ADAMS INC
Also Called: Rapa Scrapple
103 Railroad Ave (19933-1153)
PHONE....................800 338-4727
Phillip Jones, *CEO*
Donna Seefried, *General Mgr*
EMP: 350
SALES (est): 51MM
SALES (corp-wide): 57.6MM **Privately Held**
SIC: 2013 5147 Scrapple from purchased meat; meats, fresh; meats, cured or smoked
PA: Jones Dairy Farm
800 Jones Ave
Fort Atkinson WI 53538
920 563-2432

(G-518)
RAWLINS FERGUSON JONES & LEWIS
119 Market St (19933-1139)
PHONE....................302 337-8231
Allen Jones, *President*
W Allen Jones, *President*
EMP: 5 **EST:** 1906
SQ FT: 1,620
SALES (est): 530K **Privately Held**
SIC: 6411 Insurance agents

(G-519)
RENTOKIL NORTH AMERICA INC
Also Called: Ehlrlich, J C Pest Control
18904 Maranatha Way (19933-4057)
PHONE....................302 337-8100
Mark Masten, *Finance*
EMP: 16
SALES (corp-wide): 3.2B **Privately Held**
WEB: www.ehrlichdistribution.com
SIC: 7342 Pest control in structures; termite control
HQ: Rentokil North America, Inc.
1125 Berkshire Blvd # 15
Wyomissing PA 19610
610 372-9700

(G-520)
SHARK SERVICE CENTER LLC
616a Market St (19933)
PHONE....................302 337-8233
Donald Breeding,
EMP: 9
SQ FT: 7,000
SALES (est): 1.5MM **Privately Held**
WEB: www.sharksservicecenter.com
SIC: 7699 7538 Industrial machinery & equipment repair; general truck repair

(G-521)
SP AUTO PARTS INC
7514 Federalsburg Rd (19933-3660)
PHONE....................302 337-8897
Paul Samuel Machenry, *Branch Mgr*
EMP: 4
SALES (corp-wide): 18.3MM **Privately Held**
SIC: 5013 Automotive supplies & parts
PA: Sp Auto Parts, Inc.
201 Executive Dr
Moorestown NJ 08057
856 273-9252

(G-522)
SUSSEX PROTECTION SERVICE LLC (PA)
100 Market St (19933-1127)
P.O. Box 568 (19933-0568)
PHONE....................302 337-0209
Gregory Rafail,
Kevin Evans,
EMP: 15 **EST:** 1998
SQ FT: 4,000
SALES (est): 2.9MM **Privately Held**
WEB: www.sussexprotection.com
SIC: 7359 5084 Work zone traffic equipment (flags, cones, barrels, etc.); safety equipment

(G-523)
SUSSEX TREE INC
20350 Nelson Dr (19933-4557)
PHONE....................302 629-9899
Jeff Meredith, *President*
Jeffrey Meredith, *Vice Pres*
EMP: 8
SALES (est): 1.3MM **Privately Held**
SIC: 0783 Planting, pruning & trimming services

(G-524)
T S SMITH & SONS INC
8899 Redden Rd (19933-4749)
P.O. Box 275 (19933-0275)
PHONE....................302 337-8271
Matthew W Smith, *President*
Thomass S Smith, *Corp Secy*
EMP: 20
SALES (est): 1.5MM **Privately Held**
SIC: 0175 0251 0116 0111 Apple orchard; peach orchard; broiler, fryer & roaster chickens; soybeans; wheat; corn; barley farm

(G-525)
THAT GRANITE PLACE LLC
18089 Sussex Hwy (19933-4082)
PHONE....................302 337-7490
Robert M Lisle,
EMP: 6 **EST:** 2008
SALES (est): 549.3K **Privately Held**
SIC: 1799 Counter top installation

(G-526)
UTILICON SOLUTIONS LTD
18109 Sussex Hwy (19933-4010)
PHONE....................302 337-9980
EMP: 5
SALES (corp-wide): 4.5B **Privately Held**
SIC: 1623 1521 Underground utilities contractor; single-family housing construction
HQ: Utilicon Solutions, Ltd.
708 Blair Mill Rd
Willow Grove PA 19090

(G-527)
UTILITY LINES CNSTR SVCS LLC
18109 Sussex Hwy (19933-4010)
PHONE....................302 337-9980
Tim Jahnigen, *Branch Mgr*
EMP: 19

Bridgeville - Sussex County (G-528)

SALES (corp-wide): 63MM **Privately Held**
SIC: 1623 Underground utilities contractor
HQ: Utility Lines Construction Services, Llc
   708 Blair Mill Rd
   Willow Grove PA 19090
   215 784-4463

(G-528)
UTILITY/EASTERN
9126 Redden Rd (19933-4723)
P.O. Box 159 (19933-0159)
PHONE...............................302 337-7400
Kenneth Abbott, *President*
EMP: 20
SALES (est): 1.4MM **Privately Held**
SIC: 5599 3715 5012 5013 Utility trailers; truck trailers; trailers for trucks, new & used; trailer parts & accessories

(G-529)
VINTAGE CANDLE COMPANY
16734 Oak Rd (19933-3910)
PHONE...............................302 643-9343
Michelle Clouser, *Principal*
EMP: 2 **EST:** 2013
SALES (est): 85.8K **Privately Held**
SIC: 3999 Candles

(G-530)
WARREN TRUSS CO
16632 Nates Way (19933-2994)
PHONE...............................302 337-9470
Doug Warren, *Branch Mgr*
EMP: 5
SALES (est): 455.1K
SALES (corp-wide): 2.1MM **Privately Held**
SIC: 2439 Trusses, wooden roof
PA: Warren Truss Co.
   10 Aleph Dr
   Newark DE 19702
   302 368-8566

(G-531)
WELLERS TIRE SERVICE INC
Also Called: Weller's Utility Trailers
16889 N Main St (19933-2976)
PHONE...............................302 337-8228
James J Weller Jr, *President*
Tom Patton, *Manager*
Terry Spencer, *Manager*
Jason Troyer, *Manager*
Sherry Pearson, *Assistant*
EMP: 10
SQ FT: 3,600
SALES (est): 1.6MM **Privately Held**
WEB: www.pacetrailers.com
SIC: 5531 5014 5511 Automotive tires; automotive accessories; automobile tires & tubes; truck tires & tubes; trucks, tractors & trailers: new & used

(G-532)
WESTERN SUSSEX ANIMAL HOSP INC
16487 Sussex Hwy (19933-2991)
PHONE...............................302 337-7387
Craig Metzner, *Principal*
EMP: 6
SALES (est): 350.2K **Privately Held**
SIC: 0742 Animal hospital services, pets & other animal specialties

(G-533)
WESTMOR INDUSTRIES
16941 Sussex Hwy (19933-4011)
P.O. Box 219 (19933-0219)
PHONE...............................302 956-0243
EMP: 3
SALES (est): 194.3K **Privately Held**
SIC: 3999 Manufacturing industries

(G-534)
WHEATLEY FARMS INC
19115 Freeland Ln (19933-4072)
PHONE...............................302 337-7286
E Dale Wheatley, *President*
Gail Wheatley, *Corp Secy*
Jeffrey Wheatley, *Vice Pres*
Lynda Hoover, *Office Mgr*
EMP: 9
SALES (est): 1.1MM **Privately Held**
SIC: 0191 General farms, primarily crop

Camden
Kent County

(G-535)
ALL UNITED PRPTS SOLUTIONS LLC
4034 Willow Grove Rd (19934-3148)
PHONE...............................310 853-2223
Michael McPherson Jr, *Mng Member*
EMP: 13
SALES (est): 348.7K **Privately Held**
SIC: 6798 Real estate investment trusts

(G-536)
ALPHA PHI DELTA FRATERNITY
257 E Camden Wyoming Ave A (19934-1298)
PHONE...............................302 531-7854
Joseph Piras, *Principal*
Joseph Rahtelli, *Vice Pres*
EMP: 25
SALES: 243.6K **Privately Held**
SIC: 8641 University club

(G-537)
ALVIS D BURRIS
199 South St (19934-1300)
PHONE...............................302 697-3125
Alvis Burris, *Principal*
EMP: 4 **EST:** 2014
SALES (est): 325.3K **Privately Held**
SIC: 8021 Dental surgeon

(G-538)
ANDREWS & WELLS LLC
195 Captain Davis Dr (19934-1751)
PHONE...............................302 359-5417
Rod Harrison, *Mng Member*
EMP: 4
SALES (est): 132.7K **Privately Held**
SIC: 7322 Adjustment & collection services

(G-539)
BARCLAY FARMS
1 Paynters Way (19934-4556)
PHONE...............................302 697-6939
Sam Sobel, *President*
EMP: 7
SALES (est): 794.6K **Privately Held**
WEB: www.barclay-farms.com
SIC: 6552 Land subdividers & developers, residential

(G-540)
BARUTOPIA INC
2140 S Dupont Hwy (19934-1249)
PHONE...............................858 284-8830
EMP: 5
SALES (est): 104.7K **Privately Held**
SIC: 7389 Business Services, Nec, Nsk

(G-541)
BONNIE M BENSON PA (PA)
306 E Camden Wyoming Ave (19934-1304)
PHONE...............................302 697-4900
Bonnie Benson, *President*
EMP: 7
SQ FT: 2,875
SALES (est): 835.6K **Privately Held**
WEB: www.bonniebenson.com
SIC: 8111 General practice attorney, lawyer

(G-542)
BUZLIN INC
2140 S Dupont Hwy (19934-1249)
PHONE...............................800 829-0115
Mohamad Alrashidi, *Engineer*
EMP: 4
SALES (est): 105.9K **Privately Held**
SIC: 7371 Computer software development

(G-543)
C L BURCHENAL OIL CO INC
109 S Main St (19934-1320)
PHONE...............................302 697-1517
Terry Burchenal, *President*
Paullinia Burchenal, *Corp Secy*
EMP: 6 **EST:** 1945
SQ FT: 2,000
SALES: 1MM **Privately Held**
SIC: 5983 5172 Fuel oil dealers; fuel oil; kerosene

(G-544)
CAMDENWYOMING SEWER & WTR AUTH
16 S West St (19934-1324)
P.O. Box 405, Camden Wyoming (19934-0405)
PHONE...............................302 697-6372
Harold Scott, *Superintendent*
EMP: 18
SALES (est): 761.5K **Privately Held**
SIC: 4952 4941 Sewerage systems; water supply

(G-545)
CARING MATTERS HOME CARE
283 Orchard Grove Dr (19934-4908)
PHONE...............................302 993-1121
Stacy Mullin, *President*
EMP: 9
SALES (est): 214.7K **Privately Held**
SIC: 8082 Home health care services

(G-546)
CARL KING TIRE CO INC (PA)
109 S Main St (19934-1320)
P.O. Box 1004, Camden Wyoming (19934-0504)
PHONE...............................302 697-9506
Bruce King, *President*
Carl King, *President*
Richard Hawes, *Vice Pres*
EMP: 32
SQ FT: 20,000
SALES (est): 12.8MM **Privately Held**
SIC: 5014 5013 5531 Automotive tires & tubes; truck tires & tubes; automotive batteries; automotive tires; batteries, automotive & truck

(G-547)
CELLCO PARTNERSHIP
Also Called: Verizon Wireless
386 Walmart Dr (19934-1374)
PHONE...............................302 697-8340
EMP: 71
SALES (corp-wide): 130.8B **Publicly Held**
SIC: 4812 Cellular telephone services
HQ: Cellco Partnership
   1 Verizon Way
   Basking Ridge NJ 07920

(G-548)
CHILDRENS PLACE
3377 S Dupont Hwy (19934-1378)
PHONE...............................302 698-0969
Teresa Perez, *Director*
EMP: 5
SALES (est): 102.4K **Privately Held**
SIC: 8351 Child day care services

(G-549)
CHRISTIANA CARE HOME HEALTH
Also Called: Christiana Care Dover
2116 S Dupont Hwy Ste 2 (19934-1259)
PHONE...............................302 698-4300
Melinda Stevens, *Branch Mgr*
EMP: 13
SALES (corp-wide): 1.5B **Privately Held**
WEB: www.christianacare.com
SIC: 8082 7361 Visiting nurse service; nurses' registry
HQ: Christiana Care Home Health And Community Services Inc
   1 Reads Way Ste 100
   New Castle DE 19720
   302 327-5583

(G-550)
CK CONSTRUCTION INC
4181 Berrytown Rd (19934-2576)
P.O. Box 129, Viola (19979-0129)
PHONE...............................302 698-3207
Charles Kazlauskas, *President*
Wanda Kazlauskas, *Admin Sec*
EMP: 4
SALES (est): 502.6K **Privately Held**
SIC: 1521 General remodeling, single-family houses

(G-551)
CONDOR TECHNOLOGIES INC
110 N Main St Ste H (19934-1232)
PHONE...............................302 698-4444
Andrew Nowak, *CEO*
Jennifer Nowak, *Vice Pres*
EMP: 7
SQ FT: 1,000
SALES: 1.8MM **Privately Held**
WEB: www.condortechnologies.com
SIC: 5074 Water softeners

(G-552)
CONTINUUM MEDIA LLC
2140 S Dupont Hwy (19934-1249)
PHONE...............................310 295-9997
Sonia Mudbhatkal, *President*
EMP: 10
SALES (est): 217.5K **Privately Held**
SIC: 7371 7812 7929 Computer software development; motion picture & video production; entertainment service

(G-553)
CREATIVE PROMOTIONS
38 South St (19934-1337)
PHONE...............................302 697-7896
Betsy Gustafson, *Owner*
EMP: 3
SALES (est): 194.5K **Privately Held**
WEB: www.creativepromos.com
SIC: 2759 5199 5943 Commercial printing; advertising specialties; office forms & supplies

(G-554)
CURVES INTERNATIONAL INC
103 South St 2 (19934-1338)
PHONE...............................302 698-1481
Christina Grellch, *President*
EMP: 6
SALES (est): 74.4K **Privately Held**
SIC: 7991 Physical fitness facilities

(G-555)
DAL CONSTRUCTION
8331 Willow Grove Rd (19934-2538)
PHONE...............................302 538-5310
Dan Irwin, *Partner*
EMP: 20
SALES (est): 225.6K **Privately Held**
SIC: 1542 Commercial & office building, new construction

(G-556)
DAWSON BUS SERVICE INC (PA)
405 E Camden Wyoming Ave (19934-1211)
PHONE...............................302 697-9501
Willaim A Dawson, *President*
John Thomas Dawson, *Vice Pres*
William R Dawson, *Vice Pres*
Lisa Dawson, *Admin Sec*
EMP: 100 **EST:** 1941
SQ FT: 5,000
SALES: 2.3MM **Privately Held**
SIC: 4142 4151 Bus charter service, except local; school buses

(G-557)
DELAWARE ADLESCENT PROGRAM INC
Also Called: Tot's Turf Child Care Center
185 South St (19934-1300)
PHONE...............................302 531-0257
Gene Miner, *Director*
EMP: 20
SALES (corp-wide): 820.4K **Privately Held**
SIC: 8322 Individual & family services
PA: Delaware Adolescent Program Incorporated
   1901 S College Ave
   Newark DE

(G-558)
DELAWARE INSTITUE PAIN MGT
6 E Camden Wyoming Ave (19934-1301)
PHONE...............................302 698-3994
Nazim Ameer, *CEO*
EMP: 4
SQ FT: 2,640

GEOGRAPHIC SECTION

Camden - Kent County (G-589)

SALES (est): 427.9K **Privately Held**
WEB: www.delawareantiaging.com
SIC: **8011** Internal medicine, physician/surgeon

(G-559)
DELAWARE SPCA
32 Shelter Cir (19934-2293)
PHONE..................302 698-3006
Murray Goldwaite, *Director*
EMP: 4
SALES (est): 152.7K **Privately Held**
SIC: **8699** Animal humane society

(G-560)
DELAWARE STATE FARM BUREAU
Also Called: DELAWARE FARM BUREAU
233 S Dupont Hwy (19934)
PHONE..................302 697-3183
Gary Warren, *President*
Laura Faircloth, *Principal*
Pamela Bakerain, *Exec Dir*
EMP: 5
SQ FT: 6,000
SALES: 1MM **Privately Held**
SIC: **8611** Business associations

(G-561)
DIGITAL WHALE LLC
110 N Main St Ste F (19934-1232)
PHONE..................302 526-0115
Jonathan Hazelwood,
EMP: 5
SALES (est): 109.1K **Privately Held**
SIC: **7375** Information retrieval services

(G-562)
DINING SOFTWARE GROUP INC
2140 S Dupont Hwy (19934-1249)
P.O. Box 271148, Louisville CO (80027-5021)
PHONE..................720 236-9572
Jaspal Singh, *President*
EMP: 9
SALES: 150K **Privately Held**
SIC: **7371** Computer software development & applications

(G-563)
DISABLED AMERICAN VETERANS
183 South St (19934-1300)
P.O. Box 407, Camden Wyoming (19934-0407)
PHONE..................302 697-9061
Paul Lardizzone, *Principal*
EMP: 32
SALES (corp-wide): 137MM **Privately Held**
SIC: **8641** Veterans' organization
PA: Disabled American Veterans
    3725 Alexandria Pike
    Cold Spring KY 41076
    859 441-7300

(G-564)
DISH NETWORK LLC
2 S Main St (19934-1319)
PHONE..................302 387-0341
EMP: 44 **Publicly Held**
SIC: **4841** Direct broadcast satellite services (DBS)
HQ: Dish Network L.L.C.
    9601 S Meridian Blvd
    Englewood CO 80112
    303 723-1000

(G-565)
DOVER FAMILY CHIROPRACTIC
120 Old Camden Rd Ste C (19934-5501)
PHONE..................302 531-1900
Brian Errico, *Owner*
EMP: 5
SALES (est): 180K **Privately Held**
WEB: www.doverfamilychiro.com
SIC: **8041** Offices & clinics of chiropractors

(G-566)
EASTERN SHORE ENERGY INC
11550 Willow Grove Rd (19934-2297)
P.O. Box 158, Camden Wyoming (19934-0158)
PHONE..................302 697-9230
Fred Ellingsworth, *President*

Leslie Betts, *Corp Secy*
EMP: 26
SQ FT: 5,000
SALES (est): 2.5MM **Privately Held**
SIC: **1711** Warm air heating & air conditioning contractor

(G-567)
EKSAB CORPORATION
2140 S Dupont Hwy (19934-1249)
PHONE..................319 371-1669
Aly Mahmoud, *President*
EMP: 3
SALES (est): 71.1K **Privately Held**
SIC: **7372** Application computer software

(G-568)
ELEGANT IMAGES LLP
10 S West St (19934-1324)
PHONE..................302 698-5250
Carol Smith, *Partner*
Brian Smith, *Partner*
EMP: 9
SALES (est): 189.1K **Privately Held**
SIC: **7231** Beauty shops

(G-569)
EVEREST HOTEL GROUP LLC (PA)
2140 S Dupont Hwy (19934-1249)
PHONE..................213 272-0088
Marshall Young, *CEO*
Li Hui Lo, *COO*
EMP: 15
SQ FT: 5,000
SALES: 1.2MM **Privately Held**
SIC: **7011** 8741 Hotels; hotel or motel management

(G-570)
EVEREST SONOMA MANAGEMENT LLC
2140 S Dupont Hwy (19934-1249)
PHONE..................213 272-0088
Marshall Young, *Mng Member*
Li Hui Lo,
EMP: 60
SALES: 14MM
SALES (corp-wide): 1.2MM **Privately Held**
SIC: **7011** Hotels
PA: Everest Hotel Group, Llc
    2140 S Dupont Hwy
    Camden DE 19934
    213 272-0088

(G-571)
FEVER LABS INC (PA)
2140 S Dupont Hwy (19934-1249)
PHONE..................646 781-7359
Ignacio Strohlein, *Ch of Bd*
EMP: 1 EST: 2011
SALES (est): 143.3K **Privately Held**
SIC: **7371** 7372 Software programming applications; application computer software

(G-572)
FIRST NATIONAL BNK OF WYOMING
4566 S Dupont Hwy (19934-1363)
PHONE..................302 697-2666
Joseph E Chippie, *President*
Mary E Benham, *Vice Pres*
EMP: 74 EST: 1909
SALES: 13.2MM **Privately Held**
WEB: www.fnbwyomingde.com
SIC: **6021** National commercial banks

(G-573)
FUTURE BRIGHT PEDIATRICS LLC (PA)
Also Called: Bright Future Pediatrics
120 Old Camden Rd Ste B (19934-5501)
PHONE..................302 538-6258
Elsayed Abdelsalam, *Med Doctor*
EMP: 11 EST: 2011
SALES (est): 2.1MM **Privately Held**
SIC: **8011** Pediatrician

(G-574)
HANDY & HARMAN
12244 Willow Grove Rd (19934-2281)
PHONE..................302 697-9521
John Coates, *Branch Mgr*

EMP: 8
SALES (corp-wide): 1.5B **Publicly Held**
SIC: **3317** Steel pipe & tubes
HQ: Handy & Harman
    C/O Steel Partners
    New York NY 10022
    212 520-2300

(G-575)
HANDYTUBE CORPORATION
Also Called: Camdel Metals
12244 Willow Grove Rd (19934-2281)
PHONE..................302 697-9521
Dan Carley, *Branch Mgr*
EMP: 100
SALES (corp-wide): 1.5B **Publicly Held**
SIC: **3317** Tubing, mechanical or hypodermic sizes; cold drawn stainless
HQ: Handytube Corporation
    12244 Willow Grove Rd
    Camden DE 19934

(G-576)
HANDYTUBE CORPORATION
Also Called: Camden Metals
124 Vepco Blvd (19934-2286)
PHONE..................302 697-9521
Tim Karly, *Manager*
EMP: 70
SALES (corp-wide): 1.5B **Publicly Held**
SIC: **3317** Steel pipe & tubes
HQ: Handytube Corporation
    12244 Willow Grove Rd
    Camden DE 19934

(G-577)
HANDYTUBE CORPORATION (DH)
Also Called: Handy & Harman
12244 Willow Grove Rd (19934-2281)
PHONE..................302 697-9521
John Coates, *President*
▲ EMP: 92
SALES (est): 41.1MM
SALES (corp-wide): 1.5B **Publicly Held**
SIC: **3317** Steel pipe & tubes
HQ: Handy & Harman
    C/O Steel Partners
    New York NY 10022
    212 520-2300

(G-578)
HENRY EASHUM & SON INC
20 S Dupont Hwy (19934-1309)
PHONE..................302 697-6164
Mildred Eashum, *President*
EMP: 10
SALES: 800K **Privately Held**
SIC: **1711** Warm air heating & air conditioning contractor; plumbing contractors

(G-579)
HIGH VUE LOGGING INC
12090 Willow Grove Rd (19934-2269)
PHONE..................302 697-3606
Charles Harvey, *Partner*
Herbert Harvey, *Partner*
EMP: 2
SALES (est): 153.2K **Privately Held**
SIC: **2411** Logging camps & contractors

(G-580)
HILTON BUS SERVICE
168 Vepco Blvd (19934)
P.O. Box 394, Camden Wyoming (19934-0394)
PHONE..................302 697-7676
James D Hilton, *Owner*
EMP: 50
SALES (est): 644.2K **Privately Held**
SIC: **4131** Intercity & rural bus transportation

(G-581)
IDRCH3 MINISTRIES
49 Brenda Ln (19934-2282)
PHONE..................302 344-6957
Ira D Roach III, *Pastor*
EMP: 7
SALES: 43K **Privately Held**
SIC: **8322** Individual & family services

(G-582)
INTEGRATED DYNMC SOLUTIONS LLC
2140 S Dupont Hwy (19934-1249)
PHONE..................818 406-8500
Allan Burgess, *Partner*
EMP: 4
SALES (est): 151.2K **Privately Held**
SIC: **4785** 4522 Inspection services connected with transportation; air transportation, nonscheduled

(G-583)
J I BEILER HOMES LLC
Also Called: John I Beiler Developers
106 Orchard Grove Way (19934-9610)
PHONE..................302 697-1553
John Beiler,
Clayton Beiler,
EMP: 5
SALES (est): 351.8K **Privately Held**
SIC: **1521** New construction, single-family houses

(G-584)
JAMES L WEBB PAVING CO INC
11804 Willow Grove Rd (19934-2266)
PHONE..................302 697-2000
James L Webb, *President*
Henrietta Webb, *Corp Secy*
EMP: 6
SQ FT: 300
SALES (est): 577.5K **Privately Held**
SIC: **1771** 1611 Concrete work; surfacing & paving

(G-585)
JAREL INDUSTRIES LLC
3411 S Dupont Hwy (19934-1371)
PHONE..................336 782-0697
Jonathan Howlett,
Amy Diem,
Ronnie Diem,
Elyse Howlett,
Lucy Howlett,
EMP: 5
SALES (est): 373.6K **Privately Held**
SIC: **3842** 3199 7389 Personal safety equipment; harness or harness parts;

(G-586)
KATIE BENNETT
Also Called: State Farm Insurance
2150 S Dupont Hwy (19934-1249)
PHONE..................302 697-2650
Katie Bennett, *Owner*
Paula Bowmen, *Manager*
EMP: 9
SALES (est): 849.8K **Privately Held**
SIC: **6411** Insurance agents & brokers

(G-587)
KENT COUNTY SCTY FOR THE PRVNT
Also Called: KENT COUNTY SPCA
32 Shelter Cir (19934-2293)
PHONE..................302 698-3006
Alex Moore, *President*
Frank Newon, *Treasurer*
EMP: 50
SQ FT: 10,000
SALES: 2.6MM **Privately Held**
WEB: www.kentcountyspca.com
SIC: **8699** Animal humane society

(G-588)
KENT LANDSCAPING CO LLC
109 S Main St (19934-1320)
PHONE..................302 535-4296
Justin King, *Principal*
Justin T King, *Principal*
EMP: 10
SALES (est): 781.3K **Privately Held**
SIC: **0781** Landscape services

(G-589)
LOWES HOME CENTERS LLC
516 Walmart Dr (19934-1360)
PHONE..................302 697-0700
Mike Snowden, *Manager*
EMP: 150

Camden - Kent County (G-590)

SALES (corp-wide): 71.3B **Publicly Held**
SIC: 5211 5031 5722 5064 Lumber & other building materials; building materials, exterior; building materials, interior; household appliance stores; electrical appliances, television & radio
HQ: Lowe's Home Centers, Llc
1605 Curtis Bridge Rd
Wilkesboro NC 28697
336 658-4000

(G-590)
MID ATLANTIC INDUSTRIAL SALES
26 Kathleen Ct (19934-4740)
PHONE 302 698-6356
Ron Cook, *Owner*
EMP: 2
SALES (est): 232.1K **Privately Held**
SIC: 3592 Valves

(G-591)
MILLER JOHN H PLUMBING & HTG
Also Called: John H Miller Sons Plbg Htg AC
220 Old North Rd (19934-1242)
PHONE 302 697-1012
John H Miller III, *President*
John H Miller IV, *Vice Pres*
David Miller, *Treasurer*
Joanie L Miller, *Admin Sec*
EMP: 10
SALES: 625K **Privately Held**
SIC: 1711 Plumbing contractors; warm air heating & air conditioning contractor

(G-592)
MINOR FIGURES INC
2140 S Dupont Hwy (19934-1249)
PHONE 714 875-3449
Stuart Forsyth, *CEO*
EMP: 1
SALES (est): 39.5K **Privately Held**
SIC: 2086 Soft drinks: packaged in cans, bottles, etc.

(G-593)
NORTHEASTERN SUPPLY INC
100 S Dupont Hwy (19934-1311)
PHONE 302 698-1414
Dave Deason, *Manager*
EMP: 5
SALES (corp-wide): 202MM **Privately Held**
WEB: www.gagedoctr.com
SIC: 5074 Plumbing fittings & supplies
PA: Northeastern Supply, Inc.
8323 Pulaski Hwy
Baltimore MD 21237
410 574-0010

(G-594)
NURSE NEXT DOOR HOME CARE SVCS
110 N Main St Ste A (19934-1232)
PHONE 302 264-1021
EMP: 9 **EST:** 2015
SALES (est): 70.4K **Privately Held**
SIC: 8082 8049 Home health care services; nurses, registered & practical

(G-595)
PARAGON CONTRACTING INC
220 Weeks Dr (19934-1246)
P.O. Box 78, Viola (19979-0078)
PHONE 302 697-6565
George Voshell Jr, *President*
Goerge Voshell Sr, *Treasurer*
Micheal Voshell, *Treasurer*
EMP: 4
SALES: 500K **Privately Held**
SIC: 1521 General remodeling, single-family houses

(G-596)
PENCO CORPORATION
2000 S Dupont Hwy (19934-1375)
PHONE 302 698-3108
David Blades, *Branch Mgr*
EMP: 6
SALES (corp-wide): 18.4MM **Privately Held**
WEB: www.pencocorp.com
SIC: 5074 Plumbing & hydronic heating supplies
PA: Penco Corporation
1503 W Stein Hwy
Seaford DE 19973
302 629-7911

(G-597)
QUALITY BUILDERS INC
213 Willow Ave (19934-1356)
PHONE 302 697-0664
Mary Ressler, *President*
EMP: 5
SALES (est): 510K **Privately Held**
SIC: 1521 General remodeling, single-family houses

(G-598)
REGIS CORPORATION
263 Walmart Dr (19934-1308)
PHONE 302 697-6220
Alicia Lopez, *Branch Mgr*
EMP: 8
SALES (corp-wide): 1B **Publicly Held**
SIC: 7231 Unisex hair salons
PA: Regis Corporation
7201 Metro Blvd
Edina MN 55439
952 947-7777

(G-599)
SHORE UNITED BANK
4580 S Dupont Hwy (19934-1363)
PHONE 302 698-1432
Robin Deputy, *President*
EMP: 11
SALES (corp-wide): 64.9MM **Publicly Held**
SIC: 6022 State commercial banks
HQ: Shore United Bank
18 E Dover St
Easton MD 21601
410 758-1600

(G-600)
SILICON VALLEY HT PARTNERS LP
2140 S Dupont Hwy (19934-1249)
PHONE 213 272-0088
Marshall Young, *CEO*
EMP: 5
SALES (est): 146.1K **Privately Held**
SIC: 7361 Labor contractors (employment agency)

(G-601)
SUMURI LLC
49 Brenda Ln Ste A (19934-2282)
P.O. Box 252, Camden Wyoming (19934-0252)
PHONE 302 570-0015
Steve Whalen, *CEO*
Ailyn Whalen, *President*
Jason Roslewicz, *Opers Staff*
EMP: 5
SALES: 5.4MM **Privately Held**
SIC: 5072 7371 7372 8243 Builders' hardware; custom computer programming services; operating systems computer software; operator training, computer; electronic computers

(G-602)
TURNING PT COUNSELING CTR LLC
1 N Main St (19934-1227)
PHONE 214 883-5148
Laura Pruitt,
EMP: 8 **EST:** 2017
SALES (est): 64K **Privately Held**
SIC: 8059 Personal care home, with health care

(G-603)
TWYNE INC
2140 S Dupont Hwy (19934-1249)
PHONE 213 675-9518
Robert Tam, *President*
Lee Silor, *CFO*
George Grama, *CTO*
EMP: 4
SALES: 100K **Privately Held**
SIC: 4729 7371 Passenger transportation arrangement; computer software development & applications

(G-604)
US BORTEK LLC
2140 S Dupont Hwy (19934-1249)
PHONE 888 203-7686
Kevin Cook, *President*
EMP: 15
SALES (est): 528.9K **Privately Held**
SIC: 1623 Oil & gas pipeline construction

(G-605)
WILMINGTON SAVINGS FUND SOC
4566 S Dupont Hwy (19934-1363)
PHONE 302 697-8891
EMP: 21
SALES (corp-wide): 455.5MM **Publicly Held**
SIC: 6022 State commercial banks
HQ: Wilmington Savings Fund Society
500 Delaware Ave Ste 500 # 500
Wilmington DE 19801
302 792-6000

(G-606)
WITORS AMERICA LLC
2140 S Dupont Hwy (19934-1249)
PHONE 646 247-4836
Rossano Bonetti, *Mng Member*
EMP: 1
SQ FT: 1,000
SALES: 6MM
SALES (corp-wide): 89.3MM **Privately Held**
SIC: 2066 Chocolate & cocoa products
PA: Witor's Spa
Via Levata 2
Corte De' Frati CR 26010
037 293-0311

(G-607)
WYOMING MILLWORK CO (PA)
140 Vepco Blvd (19934-2286)
P.O. Box 387, Camden Wyoming (19934-0387)
PHONE 302 697-8650
David Failing, *President*
Craig Failing, *Vice Pres*
EMP: 45
SALES: 61.5MM **Privately Held**
WEB: www.wyomingmillwork.com
SIC: 2431 Millwork

(G-608)
X/L MECHANICAL INC
282 Apple Blossom Dr (19934-1943)
PHONE 203 233-3329
Paul F Lande, *President*
EMP: 4
SALES: 250K **Privately Held**
SIC: 1711 Mechanical contractor

Camden Wyoming
Kent County

(G-609)
A + FLOOR STORE INC
Also Called: A Plus Floor Store
166 Roundabout Trl (19934-9672)
PHONE 302 698-2166
Robert S Dashiell, *President*
EMP: 11
SQ FT: 5,000
SALES: 713.3K **Privately Held**
SIC: 5713 5023 Floor covering stores; floor coverings

(G-610)
AAA PORTABLE RESTROOM CO INC
108 Gardengate Rd (19934-9648)
PHONE 909 981-0090
Samuel B Roth, *President*
Leslie Roth, *Vice Pres*
EMP: 9
SALES: 1.4MM **Privately Held**
SIC: 7359 Portable toilet rental

(G-611)
ADVANCE CONSTRUCTION CO DEL
280 Banning Rd (19934-1758)
PHONE 302 697-9444
Robert C Sylvester, *President*
Judith Ann Sylvester, *Corp Secy*
Robert T Sylvester, *Vice Pres*
EMP: 10
SQ FT: 4,500
SALES: 2.1MM **Privately Held**
SIC: 1521 1542 1541 General remodeling, single-family houses; new construction, single-family houses; commercial & office building, new construction; commercial & office buildings, renovation & repair; prefabricated building erection, industrial

(G-612)
ALFRED B LAUDER DDS
508 Eagle Nest Dr (19934-2024)
PHONE 302 697-7188
Alfred Lauder, *Principal*
EMP: 4
SALES (est): 105.1K **Privately Held**
SIC: 8021 Offices & clinics of dentists

(G-613)
ALL RESTORED INC
1638 Thicket Rd (19934-2350)
PHONE 302 222-3537
Dallas Glass, *Principal*
EMP: 6
SALES (est): 692.6K **Privately Held**
SIC: 1799 Special trade contractors

(G-614)
APPLIED TECHNOLOGIES INC
169 Roundabout Trl (19934-9673)
PHONE 302 670-4601
Brian T Valeski, *President*
EMP: 6
SALES: 950K **Privately Held**
SIC: 7379

(G-615)
AUSTIN SIGNS
351 Captain Davis Dr (19934-1749)
PHONE 302 697-7321
William Austin, *Owner*
EMP: 1
SALES (est): 71.9K **Privately Held**
SIC: 3993 Signs & advertising specialties

(G-616)
B & T CONTRACTING
4158 Westville Rd (19934-1427)
PHONE 302 492-8415
Allen Troyer, *Partner*
EMP: 16
SQ FT: 3,262
SALES: 992K **Privately Held**
SIC: 1799 Special trade contractors

(G-617)
B DIAMOND FEED COMPANY
2140 Jebb Rd (19934-3630)
PHONE 302 697-7576
Sam Berry, *Owner*
EMP: 2
SALES (est): 103.6K **Privately Held**
SIC: 2048 5191 Livestock feeds; animal feeds

(G-618)
BAYSIDE SEALCOATING SUPPLY
6453 Mud Mill Rd (19934-3415)
PHONE 302 697-6441
Charles D Wallace, *Branch Mgr*
EMP: 5 **Privately Held**
SIC: 1611 Surfacing & paving
PA: Bayside Sealcoating Supply
540 S Bedford St
Georgetown DE

(G-619)
BOYDS TRAILOR HITCHES
Also Called: Boyds Crane
3178 S State St (19934-1830)
PHONE 302 697-9000
Ken Boyd, *President*
EMP: 6
SALES: 460K **Privately Held**
SIC: 5051 7692 1799 5531 Steel; welding repair; special trade contractors; trailer hitches, automotive

GEOGRAPHIC SECTION
Camden Wyoming - Kent County (G-652)

(G-620)
BOYDS WELDING INC
3178 S State St (19934-1830)
PHONE.................302 697-9000
M Kenneth Boyd, *President*
Janet Boyd, *Corp Secy*
EMP: 7
SQ FT: 5,000
SALES (est): 1MM **Privately Held**
SIC: 7692 Welding repair

(G-621)
BRAUN ENGINEERING & SURVEYING
863 Allabands Mill Rd (19934-2132)
PHONE.................302 698-0701
David Braun, *President*
Patricia Braun, *Vice Pres*
Janette Lafashia, *Officer*
EMP: 15
SQ FT: 4,000
SALES: 900K **Privately Held**
WEB: www.braunengineering.net
SIC: 8713 7334 Surveying services; photocopying & duplicating services

(G-622)
CAMDEN-WYOMING ROTARY CLUB
6 Bob White Pl (19934-9522)
P.O. Box 223 (19934-0223)
PHONE.................302 697-2724
David Walczak, *Principal*
EMP: 5
SALES (est): 99.3K **Privately Held**
SIC: 7997 Membership sports & recreation clubs

(G-623)
CHARLES E CARLSON
Also Called: Blue Hen Courier
3670 Willow Grove Rd (19934-3144)
PHONE.................302 284-3184
Charles E Carlson, *Principal*
EMP: 5
SALES (est): 282.8K **Privately Held**
SIC: 4215 Courier services, except by air

(G-624)
COMPLETE PROPERTIES SERVICES
116 Sarah Cir Ste D (19934-2203)
PHONE.................302 242-8666
John Fuchs, *President*
Buddy Snyder, *Manager*
EMP: 8
SALES (est): 238.7K **Privately Held**
SIC: 0781 Landscape services

(G-625)
CONTRUCTION JONES AND LDSCPG
5169 Mud Mill Rd (19934-2913)
PHONE.................302 423-6456
Chris Jones, *Principal*
EMP: 4
SALES (est): 148K **Privately Held**
SIC: 0781 Landscape services

(G-626)
COUNTRY COMFORTS
6309 Mud Mill Rd (19934-3416)
PHONE.................302 242-8527
Charlie R Jarman, *Owner*
EMP: 5
SALES (est): 100K **Privately Held**
SIC: 0272 Horses & other equines

(G-627)
CROTHERS DOORS AND MORE I
11361 Willow Grove Rd (19934-2251)
PHONE.................302 678-3667
Bryan Crothers, *Owner*
EMP: 4
SALES (est): 340.8K **Privately Held**
SIC: 5031 Door frames, all materials

(G-628)
CRUISE ONE
159 Orchard Grove Ct (19934-4901)
PHONE.................302 698-6468
Elaine Nolan, *Manager*
Donna Smeal, *Manager*
EMP: 5 EST: 2008
SALES (est): 618.9K **Privately Held**
SIC: 4724 4481 Travel agencies; deep sea passenger transportation, except ferry

(G-629)
CURRENT SOLUTIONS INC
1100 Apple Grove Schl Rd (19934-4112)
PHONE.................302 736-5210
Christina Wolf, *President*
Gary Wolf, *Admin Sec*
Juliet Cavallaro, *Graphic Designe*
EMP: 7 EST: 1996
SALES (est): 615.1K **Privately Held**
SIC: 1731 General electrical contractor

(G-630)
DOMINOS BODY SHOP
467 Moose Lodge Rd (19934-2234)
PHONE.................302 697-3801
Frank Domino, *Owner*
EMP: 5
SQ FT: 4,600
SALES (est): 601K **Privately Held**
SIC: 7532 Body shop, automotive

(G-631)
DUNAMIS-HOMES OF DIVINE
1328 Rising Sun Rd Ste 1 (19934-1914)
P.O. Box 37, Lincoln (19960-0037)
PHONE.................302 393-5778
Vanessa Johnson Brinkley, *President*
Vanessa Brinkley, *Principal*
EMP: 5
SALES (est): 58.4K **Privately Held**
SIC: 8361 8322 Residential care; emergency shelters

(G-632)
E A SLACK BUS SERVICE INC
751 Oak Point School Rd (19934-3860)
PHONE.................302 697-2012
EMP: 9 EST: 1998
SALES (est): 321.7K **Privately Held**
SIC: 4151 School Bus Service

(G-633)
EASTERN SHORE EQUIPMENT CO
Also Called: Eseco
Vepco Indus Park Bldg 7 (19934)
P.O. Box 1001 (19934-0501)
PHONE.................302 697-3300
Robert Bole, *President*
Theodore Bole, *President*
Thomas Bole, *Vice Pres*
Alma Bole, *Treasurer*
Elizabeth Boaman, *Admin Sec*
EMP: 5 EST: 1961
SQ FT: 3,500
SALES (est): 946.2K **Privately Held**
WEB: www.eseco.com
SIC: 5087 5085 Cleaning & maintenance equipment & supplies; industrial supplies; hose, belting & packing; valves, pistons & fittings

(G-634)
ELECTRIC MOTOR WHOLESALE INC
2629 Morgans Choice Rd (19934-3654)
PHONE.................302 222-2090
Edward Frye Jr, *Principal*
Wendy Frye, *Principal*
EMP: 14
SALES (est): 235.4K **Privately Held**
SIC: 7389

(G-635)
ELECTRIC MOTOR WHOLESALE INC
2575 Morgans Choice Rd (19934-3655)
PHONE.................302 653-1844
Wendy L Frye, *President*
Ed Frye, *Vice Pres*
Edward Frye, *Vice Pres*
EMP: 17
SQ FT: 4,000
SALES (est): 330.8K **Privately Held**
WEB: www.electricmotorwholesale.com
SIC: 5063 5085 Motor controls, starters & relays; electric; power transmission equipment & apparatus

(G-636)
FALASCO MASONRY INC
3152 S State St (19934-1809)
PHONE.................302 697-8971
Joseph Falasco, *President*
Trish Alexander, *Admin Sec*
EMP: 6
SQ FT: 3,500
SALES (est): 342.7K **Privately Held**
SIC: 1741 Masonry & other stonework

(G-637)
FIFER ORCHARDS INC
1919 Allabands Mill Rd (19934-2121)
PHONE.................302 697-2141
Carlton C Fifer, *President*
Curt Fifer, *Vice Pres*
Mary Fennemore, *Treasurer*
Robert S Fifer, *Manager*
▼ EMP: 125
SQ FT: 150,000
SALES (est): 17.4MM **Privately Held**
WEB: www.fiferorchards.com
SIC: 0161 0175 Asparagus farm; apple orchard

(G-638)
FIRST COMMAND FINCL PLG INC
1378 Rising Sun Rd (19934-1922)
PHONE.................302 535-8132
Cliff Weddington, *Branch Mgr*
EMP: 12
SALES (corp-wide): 467.4MM **Privately Held**
SIC: 6282 Investment advice
HQ: First Command Financial Planning, Inc.
1 Firstcomm Plz
Fort Worth TX 76109
817 731-8621

(G-639)
FIRST STATE SEALCOATING
787 Darling Farm Rd (19934-1455)
PHONE.................302 632-1234
Larry A Prince, *Principal*
EMP: 4
SALES (est): 226.1K **Privately Held**
SIC: 8748 Business consulting

(G-640)
FIRST STATE STRINGS INC
140 Metz Dr (19934-1702)
PHONE.................302 331-7362
Steve Gaston, *Principal*
EMP: 5
SALES: 10.2K **Privately Held**
SIC: 7929 Orchestras or bands

(G-641)
FORWARD DISCOVERY INC
27 Milbourn Manor Dr (19934-3638)
PHONE.................703 647-6364
Art Ehuan, *President*
EMP: 6 EST: 2007
SALES (est): 800K **Privately Held**
SIC: 7379 Computer related consulting services

(G-642)
GELFAND GROUP INC
341 Raven Cir (19934-4033)
PHONE.................310 666-2362
Dimitiy Gelfand, *CEO*
EMP: 1
SALES: 1.6MM **Privately Held**
SIC: 3355 3942 Aluminum wire & cable; dolls & stuffed toys

(G-643)
GOLDSBORO SAND AND GRAVEL
2904 Willow Grove Rd (19934-3211)
PHONE.................410 310-0402
Arlene Seaman, *Principal*
EMP: 2
SALES (est): 66K **Privately Held**
SIC: 1442 Construction sand & gravel

(G-644)
HARTS TWO
Also Called: Curves Franchise
204 Grouse Trl (19934-9542)
PHONE.................302 741-2119
Pauline Blehart, *President*
Jack Blehart, *Corp Secy*
EMP: 4
SALES (est): 62.4K **Privately Held**
SIC: 7991 Physical fitness facilities

(G-645)
HIGHWAY TRAFFIC CONTROLLERS
6236 Mud Mill Rd (19934-3406)
PHONE.................302 697-7117
Karen Pollard, *President*
Sue Snyder, *Admin Sec*
EMP: 50
SALES (est): 1.6MM **Privately Held**
SIC: 7389 Flagging service (traffic control)

(G-646)
INOV8 INC
45 Milbourn Manor Dr (19934-3638)
PHONE.................302 465-5124
Penelope L H Farley, *CEO*
Mark Farley, *Consultant*
EMP: 4 EST: 2011
SALES (est): 242.4K **Privately Held**
SIC: 8741 8243 7379 9441 Personnel management; software training, computer; data processing consultant; administration of social & human resources;

(G-647)
JMSP USA LLC
341 Rven Cir Cnty Of Kent County Of Kent (19934)
PHONE.................337 254-1451
Michael Hook, *Partner*
EMP: 1
SALES (est): 64K **Privately Held**
SIC: 2833 Medicinals & botanicals

(G-648)
JOHN HIOTT REFRIGERATION & AC
9166 Willow Grove Rd (19934-2437)
PHONE.................302 697-3050
John Hiott, *President*
Brenda Hiott, *Treasurer*
Debbie Hiott, *Admin Sec*
EMP: 10
SALES: 900K **Privately Held**
SIC: 1711 Refrigeration contractor; warm air heating & air conditioning contractor

(G-649)
MILFORD EARLY LEARNING CENTER
592 Ashland Ave (19934-2481)
PHONE.................302 331-6612
Esther Graham, *Principal*
EMP: 5
SALES (est): 78K **Privately Held**
SIC: 8351 Preschool center

(G-650)
MITCHELL S WELDING LLC
1106 Steeles Ridge Rd (19934-2422)
PHONE.................302 632-1089
Christina Mitchell, *Principal*
EMP: 1
SALES (est): 39.1K **Privately Held**
SIC: 7692 Welding repair

(G-651)
QUAIL ASSOCIATES INC
Also Called: Wild Quail Golf & Country Club
1 Clubhouse Dr (19934-9501)
PHONE.................302 697-4660
Ric McCall, *General Mgr*
EMP: 45
SQ FT: 20,000
SALES (est): 2.6MM **Privately Held**
SIC: 7997 7299 Golf club, membership; country club, membership; banquet hall facilities

(G-652)
QUALITY LAWN CARE HOME RE
4 Turtle Dr (19934-1801)
PHONE.................302 331-5892
EMP: 4 EST: 2009
SALES (est): 73.3K **Privately Held**
SIC: 8059 Nursing & personal care

Camden Wyoming - Kent County (G-653)

(G-653)
RIGHT WAY FLAGGING AND SIGN CO
173 Brenda Ln Ste C (19934-2292)
P.O. Box 1013 (19934-0513)
PHONE...................................302 698-5229
Roger E Satterfield, *President*
Ann M Satterfield, *Vice Pres*
Melissa B Button, *Admin Sec*
EMP: 35
SQ FT: 32,000
SALES (est): 900K **Privately Held**
SIC: 7389 7359 Flagging service (traffic control); equipment rental & leasing

(G-654)
ROBERT LARIMORE
328 Moose Lodge Rd (19934-2216)
PHONE...................................302 730-8682
Robert Larimore, *Owner*
EMP: 6
SQ FT: 5,000
SALES (est): 280K **Privately Held**
SIC: 8713 Surveying services

(G-655)
ROCKY MTN ELK FOUNDATION INC
34 Milbourn Manor Dr (19934-3600)
PHONE...................................302 697-3621
Ken Starke, *Chairman*
EMP: 20
SALES (corp-wide): 53.2MM **Privately Held**
WEB: www.rmef.com
SIC: 0971 Wildlife management
PA: Rocky Mountain Elk Foundation, Inc.
5705 Grant Creek Rd
Missoula MT 59808
406 523-4500

(G-656)
RTCP FARM PARTNERSHIP
1095 Hollering Hill Rd (19934-3043)
PHONE...................................302 584-3584
Richard Lester Jr, *Partner*
EMP: 4 EST: 2000
SALES (est): 119.9K **Privately Held**
SIC: 0191 0212 General farms, primarily crop; beef cattle except feedlots

(G-657)
SJM SALES INC
500 Eagle Nest Dr (19934-2024)
PHONE...................................302 697-6748
Tony Marano, *President*
Deborah Marano, *Vice Pres*
EMP: 2
SALES (est): 153.2K **Privately Held**
WEB: www.sjmsales.net
SIC: 3949 Sporting & athletic goods

(G-658)
TA FARMS LLC
4664 Mud Mill Rd (19934-3010)
PHONE...................................302 492-3030
Daniel C Palmer,
EMP: 4
SALES (est): 529.3K **Privately Held**
WEB: www.danielcpalmer.com
SIC: 0191 General farms, primarily crop

(G-659)
TIMOTHY BLAWN
Also Called: Tim's Upholstry
11178 Willow Grove Rd (19934-2246)
PHONE...................................302 697-3843
EMP: 8 EST: 2011
SALES (est): 71.7K **Privately Held**
SIC: 7641 Upholstery work

(G-660)
TOTAL PEST SOLUTIONS
309 Quail Run (19934-9518)
PHONE...................................302 275-7159
Joel Mick, *Principal*
EMP: 6
SALES (est): 151.2K **Privately Held**
SIC: 7342 Pest control in structures

(G-661)
WADE KIMBALL CONSTRUCTION INC
1736 Henry Cowgill Rd (19934-2615)
PHONE...................................302 284-4732
EMP: 10
SALES (est): 918.5K **Privately Held**
SIC: 1521 Single-Family House Construction

(G-662)
ZIMMER US INC
82 Brookwood Dr (19934-3677)
PHONE...................................617 272-0062
EMP: 3 EST: 2018
SALES (est): 140.2K
SALES (corp-wide): 7.9B **Publicly Held**
SIC: 3842 Orthopedic appliances
PA: Zimmer Biomet Holdings, Inc.
345 E Main St
Warsaw IN 46580
574 267-6131

Cheswold
Kent County

(G-663)
ROYS ELECTRICAL SERVICE INC
543 Main St (19936)
P.O. Box 178 (19936-0178)
PHONE...................................302 674-3199
James Roy Jr, *President*
Nancy P Roy, *Admin Sec*
EMP: 7
SQ FT: 1,840
SALES (est): 1.2MM **Privately Held**
SIC: 7629 7694 5999 Generator repair; motor repair services; alcoholic beverage making equipment & supplies

Christiana
New Castle County

(G-664)
ACRE MORTGAGE & FINANCIAL
56 W Main St Ste 107 (19702-1539)
PHONE...................................302 737-5853
Sandy Cline, *Manager*
EMP: 5
SALES (est): 484.1K **Privately Held**
SIC: 6162 Mortgage bankers & correspondents

(G-665)
ADIRONDACK BHVRAL HLTHCARE LLC
Also Called: Allied Behavioral Health
1400 Peoples Plz Ste 204 (19702-5708)
PHONE...................................302 832-1282
Neil Kaye, *Principal*
EMP: 5
SALES (est): 318.8K **Privately Held**
SIC: 8322 General counseling services

(G-666)
CHRISTIANA COMMUNITY CTR INC
50 N Old Baltimore Pike (19702)
PHONE...................................302 353-6796
EMP: 6 EST: 2014
SALES (est): 117.1K **Privately Held**
SIC: 8322 Individual/Family Services

(G-667)
EMPLOYERS BENCH INC
40 W Main St Ste 855 (19702)
PHONE...................................973 757-1912
Sushil Kumar, *Director*
EMP: 10
SALES (est): 222.7K **Privately Held**
SIC: 7363 Labor resource services

(G-668)
EPIC HEALTH SERVICES INC
56 W Main St Ste 211 (19702-1500)
PHONE...................................302 504-4092
Keith G Frey, *CFO*
EMP: 5
SALES (corp-wide): 402.6MM **Privately Held**
SIC: 8082 Home health care services
HQ: Epic Health Services, Inc.
5220 Spring Valley Rd
Dallas TX 75254
214 466-1340

(G-669)
GT WORLD MACHINERIES USA INC
40 W Main St (19702-1501)
PHONE...................................800 242-4935
Majid Tahmassbi, *CEO*
EMP: 12
SQ FT: 4,500
SALES (est): 411.7K **Privately Held**
SIC: 5064 Air conditioning appliances

(G-670)
JR WALTER J KAMINSKI DDS
100 Chrstana Vlg Prof Ctr (19702-1510)
PHONE...................................302 738-3666
Walter J Kaminski Jr, *Owner*
Julianne Lin, *Bd of Directors*
EMP: 11
SALES (est): 216K **Privately Held**
SIC: 8021 Specialized dental practitioners

(G-671)
KIMMEL CARTER ROMAN & PELTZ (PA)
56 W Main St Ste 400 (19702-1575)
P.O. Box 8149, Newark (19714-8149)
PHONE...................................302 565-6100
Morton Richard Kimmel, *President*
Lawrance Kimmel, *Managing Prtnr*
Kimmel Carter, *Principal*
Carter Edw Jr,
Emily Laursen, *Associate*
EMP: 17
SQ FT: 2,500
SALES (est): 3.8MM **Privately Held**
WEB: www.kcrlaw.com
SIC: 8111 General practice law office

(G-672)
KIRK & ASSOCIATES LLC
56 W Main St Ste 305 (19702-1503)
PHONE...................................302 444-4733
Maryann Kirk, *Exec Dir*
EMP: 10 EST: 2013
SALES (est): 2.2MM **Privately Held**
SIC: 8742 Management consulting services

(G-673)
LITTLE PEOPLE CHILD DEV
122 E Main St (19702-3100)
PHONE...................................302 328-1481
EMP: 5 EST: 2016
SALES (est): 54.4K **Privately Held**
SIC: 8351 Child day care services

(G-674)
PANDA EARLY EDUCATION CTR INC
122 E Main St (19702-3100)
PHONE...................................302 832-1891
Collen Corkey, *Director*
EMP: 20 **Privately Held**
SIC: 8351 Preschool center
PA: Early Panda Education Center Inc
105 Emerald Ridge Dr
Bear DE 19701

(G-675)
PHILADELPHIA CONTROL SYSTEMS
56 W Main St Ste 103 (19702-1539)
P.O. Box 11682, Wilmington (19850-1682)
PHONE...................................302 368-4333
Kevin L Wade, *President*
Gary K Wade, *Vice Pres*
EMP: 4 EST: 1981
SQ FT: 2,000
SALES (est): 385.4K **Privately Held**
WEB: www.pcs4automation.com
SIC: 8711 Professional engineer

(G-676)
PLASTI PALLETS CORP
6 Albe Dr (19702-1322)
PHONE...................................302 737-1977
Melvin Messinger, *President*
Carmen Micucio, *Vice Pres*
EMP: 6
SALES (est): 300K **Privately Held**
SIC: 3089 Pallets, plastic

(G-677)
POINT OF HOPE INC
19 Peddlers Row (19702-1525)
PHONE...................................302 731-7676
EMP: 6
SALES (est): 118.7K **Privately Held**
SIC: 8322 Social service center

(G-678)
PRESSLEY RIDGE FOUNDATION
Also Called: Treatment Foster Care - Newark
56 W Main St Ste 203 (19702-1503)
PHONE...................................302 366-0490
Chatanya Lankford, *Manager*
EMP: 6 **Privately Held**
SIC: 8211 8361 School for physically handicapped; group foster home
PA: Pressley Ridge Foundation
5500 Corporate Dr Ste 400
Pittsburgh PA 15237

(G-679)
REGAL CINEMAS INC
Also Called: Peoples Plaza Cinema 17
1100 Peoples Plz (19702-5606)
PHONE...................................302 834-8515
Ken Owens, *Manager*
EMP: 70 **Privately Held**
WEB: www.regalcinemas.com
SIC: 7832 Motion picture theaters, except drive-in
HQ: Regal Cinemas, Inc.
101 E Blount Ave Ste 100
Knoxville TN 37920
865 922-1123

(G-680)
STEINEBACH ROBERT AND ASSOC
Also Called: Nationwide
20 Peddlers Row (19702-1525)
P.O. Box 1713, Bear (19701-7713)
PHONE...................................302 328-1212
EMP: 6
SALES (est): 1MM **Privately Held**
SIC: 6411 Insurance agents, brokers & service

(G-681)
SYNERGY DIRECT MORTGAGE
9 Peddlers Village Ctr (19702-1525)
PHONE...................................302 283-0833
Don Scioli, *President*
Randy Reddick, *Loan Officer*
EMP: 15
SALES (est): 5MM **Privately Held**
SIC: 6163 Mortgage brokers arranging for loans, using money of others

(G-682)
TAYLOR MCCORMICK INC
56 W Main St Ste 300 (19702-1503)
PHONE...................................302 738-0203
Ted Foglietta, *Vice Pres*
EMP: 42
SALES (corp-wide): 81.5MM **Privately Held**
SIC: 8711 Consulting engineer
PA: Taylor Mccormick Inc
1818 Market St Fl 16
Philadelphia PA 19103
215 592-4200

Claymont
New Castle County

(G-683)
1 A LIFESAFER INC
333 Naamans Rd Ste 41 (19703-2808)
PHONE...................................800 634-3077
EMP: 1
SALES (corp-wide): 4.3MM **Privately Held**
SIC: 3829 Measuring & controlling devices
PA: 1 A Lifesafer, Inc.
4290 Glendale Milford Rd
Blue Ash OH 45242
513 651-9560

GEOGRAPHIC SECTION
Claymont - New Castle County (G-718)

(G-684)
A PLACE TO GROW FMLY CHLD CARE
3067 W Court Ave (19703-2020)
PHONE..................302 897-8944
EMP: 5
SALES (est): 46.9K **Privately Held**
SIC: 8351 Child day care services

(G-685)
ADV FUEL POLISHING SERVICE
950 Ridge Rd Ste A6 (19703-3526)
PHONE..................302 477-1040
EMP: 2
SALES (est): 72K **Privately Held**
SIC: 1389 Bailing, cleaning, swabbing & treating of wells

(G-686)
ADVANCED POWER GENERATION
950 Ridge Rd Ste A6 (19703-3526)
PHONE..................302 375-6145
Donald Depew, *Principal*
EMP: 8
SALES (est): 890K **Privately Held**
SIC: 1731 Electrical work

(G-687)
ADVANCED TREATMENT SYSTEMS
2999 Philadelphia Pike (19703-2507)
PHONE..................302 792-0700
Nicole Moore, *Director*
EMP: 15
SALES (est): 463.5K **Privately Held**
SIC: 8069 Drug addiction rehabilitation hospital

(G-688)
ALLPOWER GENERATOR SALES & SVC
100 Naamans Rd Ste 1h (19703-2735)
PHONE..................302 793-1690
Don Depew, *Owner*
EMP: 5
SALES (est): 992.9K **Privately Held**
SIC: 5063 Generators

(G-689)
AMC - COMMERCIAL INC
316 Governor Printz Blvd (19703-2911)
PHONE..................302 229-0051
Charles Lee, *President*
EMP: 7
SALES (est): 100K **Privately Held**
SIC: 8741 Management services

(G-690)
AMEARS CONTRACTORS INC
905 Cedartree Ln Apt 6 (19703-1619)
PHONE..................302 791-7767
Angela Miller, *President*
EMP: 4
SALES (est): 330K **Privately Held**
SIC: 1611 Highway & street construction

(G-691)
AMEKEN NETWORK GROUP INC
405 Maple Ln (19703-1824)
PHONE..................302 545-3472
Samuel Mwangi, *President*
EMP: 10
SALES (est): 325.8K **Privately Held**
SIC: 8741 Management services

(G-692)
APARTMENT COMMUNITIES INC
Also Called: Harbor House Apts
31 Harbor Dr Apt 2 (19703-2946)
PHONE..................302 798-9100
Beth Mc Hugh, *Manager*
EMP: 10
SALES (est): 872.7K **Privately Held**
WEB: www.harborhouseapts.com
SIC: 6513 Apartment building operators

(G-693)
AR SOLUTIONS INC
650 Naamans Rd Ste 207 (19703-2318)
PHONE..................609 751-9611
Srinivas Chitturi, *President*
EMP: 18
SALES: 1.6MM **Privately Held**
SIC: 5045 Computer software

(G-694)
ARENARTS INC
619 New York Ave (19703-1957)
PHONE..................302 408-0887
Grigori Sigalov, *Principal*
Serhii Surhanov, *Principal*
Oleksii Zrazhevskyi, *Principal*
EMP: 10
SALES (est): 198.7K **Privately Held**
SIC: 8711 Engineering services

(G-695)
ASK CONNOISSEUR LLC
2093 Philadelphia Pike # 3353 (19703-2424)
PHONE..................302 482-8026
EMP: 7
SALES (est): 135.2K **Privately Held**
SIC: 5812 7371 Eating places; computer software development & applications

(G-696)
AURISTA TECHNOLOGIES INC
100 Naamans Rd Ste 3c (19703-2737)
PHONE..................302 792-4900
Ronald D Graf, *President*
Ronald Graf, *President*
Ron Graf, *Accounts Mgr*
EMP: 15
SQ FT: 3,500
SALES: 1MM **Privately Held**
WEB: www.aurista.com
SIC: 5094 3471 3873 Clocks, watches & parts; plating & polishing; watches & parts, except crystals & jewels

(G-697)
AXIAL MEDICAL PRINTING INC
2803 Philadelphia Pike B (19703-2506)
PHONE..................518 620-4479
EMP: 2
SALES (est): 83.9K **Privately Held**
SIC: 2752 Commercial printing, lithographic

(G-698)
AZZOTA CORPORATION
Also Called: Labshops
100 Naamans Rd Ste 5i (19703-2700)
PHONE..................877 649-2746
Xiaoli He, *CEO*
EMP: 2
SALES (est): 389.7K **Privately Held**
SIC: 3821 Laboratory equipment: fume hoods, distillation racks, etc.

(G-699)
BANE CLENE WAY
Also Called: Quality Clene
950 Ridge Rd Ste B25 (19703-3533)
PHONE..................610 485-1234
Jeff Poehlmann, *Owner*
EMP: 4
SALES (est): 161.1K **Privately Held**
SIC: 7217 Carpet & upholstery cleaning on customer premises

(G-700)
BC HOME HEALTH CARE SERVICES
Also Called: Home Helpers
3301 Green St (19703-2052)
PHONE..................302 746-7844
Joseph Munis, *President*
EMP: 7
SALES (est): 108.1K **Privately Held**
SIC: 8082 Home health care services

(G-701)
BENCHMARK TRANSMISSION INC
2610 Philadelphia Pike 1a (19703-2574)
PHONE..................302 792-2300
Michael Neubauer, *CEO*
EMP: 5
SALES (est): 403.5K **Privately Held**
SIC: 7539 7537 Automotive repair shops; automotive transmission repair shops

(G-702)
BILLS PRINTERS SERVICE
718 Elmtree Ln (19703-1608)
PHONE..................302 798-0482
William Warren, *Owner*
EMP: 1
SALES (est): 58K **Privately Held**
SIC: 2752 Commercial printing, lithographic

(G-703)
BNAI BRITH SNIOR CTZENS HSING
Also Called: B'Nai B'Rith House
8000 Society Dr (19703-1702)
PHONE..................302 798-6846
David Schlaker, *President*
Jack Levine, *Vice Pres*
EMP: 8
SQ FT: 150,000
SALES: 869.4K **Privately Held**
SIC: 6513 Retirement hotel operation

(G-704)
BRANDY WINE SENIOR CENTER
3301 Green St (19703-2052)
PHONE..................302 798-5562
Phyllis Hicks, *Director*
Beverly Henry, *Admin Sec*
EMP: 9
SALES: 220K **Privately Held**
SIC: 8322 Senior citizens' center or association

(G-705)
BRANDYWINE CLUB INC
135 Princeton Ave (19703-2608)
PHONE..................302 798-9891
John Raughley, *President*
Lloyd Godshalk, *Vice Pres*
EMP: 6
SQ FT: 6,500
SALES (est): 164.6K **Privately Held**
SIC: 8641 Fraternal associations

(G-706)
CANDLE PARLOUR
12 Commonwealth Ave (19703-2012)
PHONE..................302 408-0890
EMP: 1
SALES (est): 39.6K **Privately Held**
SIC: 3999 Candles

(G-707)
CARMEN R BENITEZ
3047 Greenshire Ave (19703-2000)
PHONE..................302 793-2061
Carmen R Benitez, *Principal*
EMP: 5
SALES (est): 88.6K **Privately Held**
SIC: 8351 Preschool center

(G-708)
CATALYST HANDLING RESOURCES
950 Ridge Rd Ste E3 (19703-3520)
PHONE..................302 798-2200
John Wooten, *Owner*
EMP: 20
SALES (est): 1.6MM **Privately Held**
SIC: 5084 Materials handling machinery

(G-709)
CD DIAGNOSTICS INC (HQ)
650 Naamans Rd Ste 100 (19703-2301)
PHONE..................302 367-7770
Richard Birkmyer, *President*
Carl Deirmengian, *Chief Mktg Ofcr*
EMP: 11
SALES (est): 9.5MM
SALES (corp-wide): 7.9B **Publicly Held**
SIC: 8071 Medical laboratories
PA: Zimmer Biomet Holdings, Inc.
345 E Main St
Warsaw IN 46580
574 267-6131

(G-710)
CDA GROUP INC
15 Delaware Ave (19703-1901)
PHONE..................302 793-0693
Curtis Anderson, *Owner*
EMP: 4
SALES (est): 148.9K **Privately Held**
WEB: www.cda-europe.com
SIC: 8748 Business consulting

(G-711)
CELEBRATIONS DESIGN GROUP LTD
950 Ridge Rd Ste D8 (19703-3529)
PHONE..................302 793-3893
Tom Covello, *President*
EMP: 6
SQ FT: 1,400
SALES: 100K **Privately Held**
SIC: 7299 Party planning service

(G-712)
CENTURY 21 FANTINI REALTY
3724 Philadelphia Pike (19703-3412)
PHONE..................302 798-6688
George Fantini, *Owner*
EMP: 10
SALES (est): 490K **Privately Held**
SIC: 6531 Real estate agent, residential

(G-713)
CHARLES MOON PLUMBING & HTG (PA)
2505 Philadelphia Pike C (19703-2522)
PHONE..................302 798-6666
Carl Moon, *President*
EMP: 8
SQ FT: 3,800
SALES: 600K **Privately Held**
SIC: 1711 Plumbing contractors

(G-714)
CHART EXCHANGE
3001 Philadelphia Pike (19703-2580)
PHONE..................850 376-6435
EMP: 2
SALES: 43.5K **Privately Held**
SIC: 7372 Prepackaged software

(G-715)
CHOCOLATE EDITIONS INC
2614 Philadelphia Pike (19703-2504)
PHONE..................302 479-8400
Edward Przelomski, *CEO*
Cher L Przelomski, *President*
EMP: 3
SQ FT: 1,200
SALES (est): 729K **Privately Held**
SIC: 2066 Chocolate

(G-716)
CHRISS AUTO REPAIR
950 Ridge Rd Ste A3 (19703-3526)
PHONE..................302 791-0699
Chris Borris, *Owner*
EMP: 4
SALES (est): 152.5K **Privately Held**
SIC: 7538 General automotive repair shops

(G-717)
CHRISTIANA CARE HEALTH SYS INC
2401 Philadelphia Pike (19703-2430)
PHONE..................302 428-4110
EMP: 8
SALES (corp-wide): 1.5B **Privately Held**
SIC: 8011 Primary care medical clinic; general & family practice, physician/surgeon
HQ: Christiana Care Health System, Inc.
200 Hygeia Dr
Newark DE 19713
302 733-1000

(G-718)
CIGNA GLOBAL HOLDINGS INC (DH)
590 Naamans Rd (19703-2308)
PHONE..................302 797-3469
Paul B Lukens, *Ch of Bd*
Joanne Dorak, *President*
EMP: 11
SALES (est): 59.8MM
SALES (corp-wide): 141.6B **Publicly Held**
SIC: 6311 6512 6411 Life insurance; non-residential building operators; property & casualty insurance agent

Claymont - New Castle County (G-719) GEOGRAPHIC SECTION

HQ: Cigna Holdings, Inc.
590 Naamans Rd
Claymont DE 19703
215 761-1000

(G-719)
CIGNA HOLDINGS INC (DH)
590 Naamans Rd (19703-2308)
PHONE.................................215 761-1000
Paul B Lukens, *Ch of Bd*
William C Hartman, *President*
Samuel E Larosa, *Vice Pres*
Maureen H Ryan, *Treasurer*
Jim Blesto, *Director*
EMP: 11
SALES (est): 8.5B
SALES (corp-wide): 141.6B **Publicly Held**
SIC: 6311 6321 6331 6512 Life insurance; health insurance carriers; fire, marine & casualty insurance; commercial & industrial building operation; residential building, four or fewer units: operation; investment advice
HQ: Cigna Holding Company
900 Cottage Grove Rd
Bloomfield CT 06002
860 226-6000

(G-720)
CITY WIDE TRANSPORTATION INC
6705 Governor Printz Blvd (19703)
PHONE.................................302 792-1225
Vitor Thomas, *President*
Victor Thomas, *Owner*
EMP: 15
SALES: 700K **Privately Held**
SIC: 4111 Airport transportation

(G-721)
CLAYMONT COMMUNITY CENTER INC
Also Called: Brandywine Com Rsrc Cncl
3301 Green St (19703-2062)
PHONE.................................302 792-2757
James Thornton, *Exec Dir*
EMP: 20
SALES (est): 1.9MM **Privately Held**
WEB: www.claymontcenter.org
SIC: 8322 Community center

(G-722)
CLAYMONT METHADONE CLINIC
2999 Philadelphia Pike (19703-2507)
PHONE.................................855 244-7803
Nicole Moore, *Manager*
EMP: 6
SALES (est): 91.9K **Privately Held**
SIC: 8099 Health & allied services

(G-723)
CONTINENTAL WARRANTY CORP
99 Wiltshire Rd (19703-3307)
P.O. Box 207 (19703-0207)
PHONE.................................302 375-0401
Mario Volpe, *President*
Dorothy A Volpe, *Vice Pres*
EMP: 38
SQ FT: 6,550
SALES (est): 3.1MM **Privately Held**
WEB: www.continentalwarranty.com
SIC: 7549 Automotive customizing services, non-factory basis

(G-724)
CRESSONA ASSOCIATES LLC
1308 Society Dr (19703-1743)
PHONE.................................302 792-2737
Donald Jaffey,
EMP: 15
SALES (est): 756.8K **Privately Held**
SIC: 6531 Real estate managers

(G-725)
CROSS OVER CAMO LLC
7205 Governor Printz Blvd (19703-2470)
PHONE.................................302 798-1898
Todd Stroh, *Principal*
EMP: 2
SALES (est): 119.1K **Privately Held**
SIC: 2311 Military uniforms, men's & youths': purchased materials

(G-726)
DACK REALTY CORP (PA)
Also Called: Donald Jaffey Enterprises
1308 Society Dr (19703-1743)
PHONE.................................302 792-2737
Donald Jaffey, *President*
EMP: 8
SQ FT: 2,000
SALES (est): 1.4MM **Privately Held**
SIC: 6531 6512 6513 Real estate managers; shopping center, property operation only; apartment building operators

(G-727)
DANE WATERS
1 Hillside Rd (19703-2602)
PHONE.................................302 377-9999
Dane Waters, *Partner*
EMP: 7 **EST:** 2000
SALES (est): 414.5K **Privately Held**
WEB: www.danewaters.com
SIC: 3629 Static elimination equipment, industrial

(G-728)
DANS TAXI & SHUTTLE
152 Bayard Dr (19703)
PHONE.................................302 383-8826
Daniel Thurpe, *Owner*
EMP: 4
SALES (est): 130.6K **Privately Held**
SIC: 4111 Local & suburban transit

(G-729)
DAVE SMAGALA
Also Called: Independent Electrical Svcs
26 Rolling Rd (19703-2464)
PHONE.................................302 383-2761
Dave Smagala, *Principal*
EMP: 3 **EST:** 2013
SALES (est): 293.9K **Privately Held**
SIC: 1731 7539 3699 General electrical contractor; electrical services; electrical equipment & supplies

(G-730)
DD INC DE LLC
907 Providence Ave (19703-1862)
PHONE.................................302 669-9269
Renee Kreske, *Principal*
EMP: 5
SALES (est): 377.8K **Privately Held**
SIC: 5012 Automobiles & other motor vehicles

(G-731)
DELAMED SUPPLIES INC
950 Ridge Rd Ste C29 (19703-3538)
PHONE.................................917 517-4492
Issam Barajat, *President*
EMP: 1
SALES (est): 55K **Privately Held**
SIC: 3841 Surgical & medical instruments

(G-732)
DELAWARE HOTEL ASSOCIATES LP
Also Called: Crowne Plaza Wilmington North
630 Naamans Rd (19703-2310)
PHONE.................................302 792-2700
Tim Zezulka, *General Mgr*
Keisha Jacobs, *Sales Mgr*
Kevin Cushing, *Marketing Staff*
Heather Harrison, *Manager*
EMP: 80
SALES: 2MM **Privately Held**
SIC: 7011 Hotels & motels

(G-733)
DELDEO BUILDERS INC
100 Naamans Rd Ste 3f (19703-2737)
PHONE.................................302 791-0243
Louis M Deldeo, *President*
Marc T Wolfe, *Corp Secy*
Marion E Deldeo, *Vice Pres*
EMP: 10
SQ FT: 1,200
SALES: 1.5MM **Privately Held**
SIC: 1542 1522 Commercial & office building, new construction; residential construction

(G-734)
DOOR & GATE CO LLC
130 Hickman Rd Ste 26 (19703-3552)
PHONE.................................888 505-6962
Frank Burger, *Principal*
EMP: 8
SALES (est): 1.5MM **Privately Held**
SIC: 5039 Prefabricated structures; glass construction materials

(G-735)
DRAGONS LAIR PRINTING LLC
Also Called: D L Printing
130 Hickman Rd Ste 24 (19703-3552)
PHONE.................................302 798-4465
Bob Chavis, *Principal*
EMP: 4
SALES (est): 252.8K **Privately Held**
WEB: www.dragonslairprint.com
SIC: 2759 Screen printing

(G-736)
DREAMSCAPE LANDSCAPING
60 Colby Ave (19703-2708)
P.O. Box 730 (19703-0730)
PHONE.................................302 354-5247
Steve Reese, *Principal*
EMP: 4
SALES (est): 186K **Privately Held**
SIC: 0781 Landscape services

(G-737)
DURKEE AUTOMOTIVE INC
8400 Governor Printz Blvd (19703-3219)
PHONE.................................302 798-5656
Doug Durkee, *President*
EMP: 4
SQ FT: 3,500
SALES (est): 374.1K **Privately Held**
SIC: 7538 General truck repair

(G-738)
EAGLE ONE FEDERAL CREDIT UNION
3301 Philadelphia Pike (19703-3102)
P.O. Box 543 (19703-0543)
PHONE.................................302 798-7749
Jerry Piper, *Principal*
Terri Kelly, *Vice Pres*
Sandy Shenk,
EMP: 6
SALES (corp-wide): 3.8MM **Privately Held**
SIC: 6062 State credit unions
PA: Eagle One Federal Credit Union
7500 Lindbergh Blvd
Philadelphia PA 19176
267 298-1480

(G-739)
EPIC KINGS LLC
2093 Philadelphia Pike (19703-2424)
PHONE.................................302 669-9018
Alexander Nasonov,
EMP: 6
SALES (est): 123.5K **Privately Held**
SIC: 7371 Computer software development & applications

(G-740)
ESTABLISHING BLACK MEN LLC
P.O. Box 182 (19703-0182)
PHONE.................................215 432-7469
Mark Nelson,
EMP: 8
SALES (est): 81.5K **Privately Held**
SIC: 8611 Community affairs & services

(G-741)
ESTIA HOSPITALITY GROUP INC (PA)
Also Called: Claymont Foods
3526 Philadelphia Pike (19703-3109)
PHONE.................................302 798-5319
Spiro Demetratos, *Partner*
Bob Hionis, *Partner*
EMP: 15 **EST:** 1969
SQ FT: 1,600
SALES: 1.2MM **Privately Held**
SIC: 5812 5147 5148 Sandwiches & submarines shop; pizza restaurants; meats & meat products; fresh fruits & vegetables

(G-742)
EVAN HURST PROPERTY MANAGEMENT
Also Called: Evan Hurst Lawn & Landscaping
100 Naamans Rd (19703-2737)
PHONE.................................302 375-0398
Chris Evans, *President*
EMP: 8
SALES: 350K **Privately Held**
SIC: 0782 Lawn services

(G-743)
EVRAZ CLYMONT STL HOLDINGS INC
4001 Philadelphia Pike (19703-2727)
PHONE.................................302 792-5400
Allen Egner, *CFO*
David Miltenberger, *Manager*
Kevin Oltmann, *Software Engr*
Michael Reed, *Technical Staff*
Randall Coan, *Maintence Staff*
◆ **EMP:** 400
SALES (est): 6.1MM
SALES (corp-wide): 177.9K **Privately Held**
SIC: 3312 Plate, steel
PA: Evraz Group Sa
Avenue Monterey 13
Luxembourg

(G-744)
FAITH VICTORY CHRISTN ACADEMY
301 Commonwealth Ave (19703-2063)
PHONE.................................302 333-0855
Alvin Walker, *Principal*
Vernee Davis, *Principal*
EMP: 10
SALES (est): 157.2K **Privately Held**
SIC: 8351 Child day care services

(G-745)
FIRST STATE MOTOR SPORTS
950 Ridge Rd Ste B18 (19703-3535)
PHONE.................................302 798-7000
Erik Iswod, *Principal*
EMP: 4
SALES (est): 617.5K **Privately Held**
SIC: 6022 State commercial banks

(G-746)
FMJ ELECTRICAL CONTRACTING
912 Parkside Blvd (19703-1022)
P.O. Box 23555, Philadelphia PA (19143-8555)
PHONE.................................215 669-2085
Frank Montgomery Jr, *President*
EMP: 4
SALES: 200K **Privately Held**
SIC: 5082 General construction machinery & equipment

(G-747)
FOX POINT PROGRAMS INC
3001 Philadelphia Pike # 1 (19703-2580)
PHONE.................................800 499-7242
Glenn W Clark, *President*
Karl Stukis, *Vice Pres*
EMP: 11
SALES (est): 1.3MM **Privately Held**
SIC: 6411 Insurance agents

(G-748)
FRASCELLA ENTERPRISES INC
Also Called: Cashtoday Financial Centers
650 Naamans Rd Ste 300 (19703-2300)
PHONE.................................267 467-4496
David Frascella, *President*
EMP: 29
SQ FT: 4,500
SALES (est): 3.7MM **Privately Held**
SIC: 6159 Small business investment companies

(G-749)
GB SHADES LLC (PA)
Also Called: Goodwin Brothers Shading & Spc
100 Naamans Rd Ste 5f (19703-2700)
PHONE.................................302 798-3028
John Goodwin, *President*
Charles Goodwin, *Vice Pres*
Steve Fouts, *Project Mgr*
Tom Scanlan, *Project Mgr*

GEOGRAPHIC SECTION
Claymont - New Castle County (G-779)

Gene Kurtz, *Master*
EMP: 9
SQ FT: 4,800
SALES (est): 14.8MM **Privately Held**
SIC: **5023** Window furnishings

(G-750)
GEBHART FUNERAL HOME INC
3401 Philadelphia Pike (19703-3105)
PHONE.................302 798-7726
Chandler Gebhart III, *President*
Chandler Gebhart IV, *Vice Pres*
EMP: 50
SALES (est): 1.5MM **Privately Held**
WEB: www.gebhartfuneralhomes.com
SIC: **7261** Funeral home

(G-751)
GENESEC INC
62 Lake Forest Blvd (19703)
PHONE.................917 656-5742
John Entwistle, *President*
Andrew Entwistle, *General Counsel*
EMP: 5 EST: 2015
SALES (est): 260K **Privately Held**
SIC: **7379** Computer hardware requirements analysis; ; computer related consulting services

(G-752)
GENUINE PARTS COMPANY
Also Called: NAPA Auto Parts
319 Ridge Rd (19703-3508)
PHONE.................610 494-6355
Stanley Wielosik, *General Mgr*
EMP: 5
SALES (corp-wide): 18.7B **Publicly Held**
WEB: www.qcmponline.com
SIC: **5531** 5013 Automobile & truck equipment & parts; automotive supplies & parts
PA: Genuine Parts Company
2999 Wildwood Pkwy
Atlanta GA 30339
678 934-5000

(G-753)
GIAN-CO
Also Called: Brandywine Vending
2 Stockdale Ave (19703-2917)
PHONE.................302 798-7100
Charles Gianakis, *President*
Cynthia Contis, *Corp Secy*
EMP: 20
SQ FT: 5,400
SALES (est): 856.5K **Privately Held**
SIC: **7359** Vending machine rental

(G-754)
GLOBAL SHIPPING CENTER LLC
2803 Philadelphia Pike B (19703-2506)
PHONE.................302 798-4321
Rona Mendosia, *Owner*
EMP: 4
SALES (est): 344.4K **Privately Held**
SIC: **7389** Mailbox rental & related service

(G-755)
GLOBAL VISION XTREME CORP
Also Called: Gvx
21 Benning Rd (19703-1205)
PHONE.................302 287-4822
Sean Bryant, *CEO*
Dante Broxton, *Opers Staff*
EMP: 12
SQ FT: 3,000
SALES: 8.3MM **Privately Held**
SIC: **8742** New products & services consultants

(G-756)
GO MOZAIC LLC
3042 Greenshire Ave (19703-2058)
P.O. Box 11 (19703-0011)
PHONE.................302 438-4141
Daniel Boddie,
EMP: 3
SALES: 100K **Privately Held**
SIC: **2761** Manifold business forms

(G-757)
GRANDMA ZS MAPLE HAUS
171 Harbor Dr Apt 1 (19703-2960)
PHONE.................412 297-3324
Brittany Zehr, *Owner*
EMP: 1 EST: 2012

SALES (est): 87.7K **Privately Held**
SIC: **2099** Maple syrup

(G-758)
GRASSY CREEK QUILTING
4 W Rivers End Dr (19703-2611)
PHONE.................302 528-1653
EMP: 1
SALES (est): 39.7K **Privately Held**
SIC: **2395** Pleating/Stitching Services

(G-759)
GTECH CLEANING SERVICES LLC
950 Ridge Rd Ste B5 (19703-3527)
P.O. Box 33 (19703-0033)
PHONE.................302 494-2102
Tyreese Green, *Mng Member*
EMP: 50
SALES: 625K **Privately Held**
SIC: **7699** Cleaning services

(G-760)
HALOALI TEETH WHITENING LLC
409 Fillmore Ct (19703-2254)
PHONE.................302 300-4042
Aliha Walker, *Mng Member*
EMP: 5
SALES (est): 117.4K **Privately Held**
SIC: **5999** 7389 Toiletries, cosmetics & perfumes

(G-761)
HISTORICAL & CULTURAL AFAIRS
Also Called: Robinson House, The
1 Naamans Rd (19703-2701)
PHONE.................302 792-0285
Gerry Chillas, *Principal*
EMP: 10 **Privately Held**
SIC: **8412** 9111 Museum; executive offices;
HQ: Delaware Division Of Historical & Cultural Afairs
21 The Grn
Dover DE

(G-762)
HOLIDAY INN SELECT
630 Naamans Rd (19703-2310)
PHONE.................302 792-2700
Joe Podolinsky, *Owner*
EMP: 55 EST: 2001
SALES (est): 1.6MM **Privately Held**
SIC: **7011** Hotels & motels

(G-763)
HONEYWELL INTERNATIONAL INC
6100 Philadelphia Pike (19703-2716)
PHONE.................302 791-6700
Connie Bevito, *Principal*
Harry Faulkner, *Principal*
Troy Vincent, *Principal*
Amado Vidin, *Branch Mgr*
EMP: 95
SALES (corp-wide): 41.8B **Publicly Held**
WEB: www.honeywell.com
SIC: **2819** 2911 2899 2869 Boron compounds, not from mines; petroleum refining; chemical preparations; industrial organic chemicals; cyclic crudes & intermediates
PA: Honeywell International Inc.
300 S Tryon St
Charlotte NC 28202
973 455-2000

(G-764)
HORIZON HOUSE INC
134 Unit A Princeton Ave (19703)
PHONE.................302 798-1960
Rosanne Saust, *Principal*
EMP: 4
SALES (est): 95.4K **Privately Held**
SIC: **8069** Alcoholism rehabilitation hospital

(G-765)
INTEGRA SERVICES TECH INC
100 Naamans Rd Ste 1f (19703-2735)
PHONE.................302 792-0346
Scott Ball, *Branch Mgr*
EMP: 12

SALES (corp-wide): 7.6MM **Privately Held**
SIC: **5085** Fasteners, industrial: nuts, bolts, screws, etc.
HQ: Integra Services Technologies, Inc.
5812 Genoa Red Bluff Rd
Pasadena TX 77507

(G-766)
INTERSTATE HOTELS RESORTS INC
Also Called: Holiday Inn
630 Naamans Rd (19703-2310)
PHONE.................302 792-2700
Walter Conner, *Branch Mgr*
EMP: 20 **Privately Held**
WEB: www.sheratonokc.com
SIC: **7011** Hotels & motels
HQ: Interstate Hotels & Resorts, Inc.
2011 Crystal Dr Ste 1100
Arlington VA 22202
703 387-3100

(G-767)
JAMES MACHINE SHOP INC
3102 W Brandywine Ave (19703-2010)
PHONE.................302 798-5679
Frank James, *President*
Harry James, *Treasurer*
Thomas James, *Shareholder*
EMP: 3
SQ FT: 5,341
SALES (est): 203K **Privately Held**
SIC: **3599** Machine shop, jobbing & repair

(G-768)
JEWISH FAMILY SERVICE OF DEL
8000 Society Dr (19703-1702)
PHONE.................302 798-0600
Dori Zatecuchni, *Director*
EMP: 4
SALES (est): 85.9K **Privately Held**
SIC: **8322** General counseling services

(G-769)
JOHNS WASHER REPAIR
Also Called: Johns Maytag
3309 Philadelphia Pike (19703-3102)
PHONE.................302 792-2333
John Passero, *Owner*
EMP: 9
SALES (est): 416.2K **Privately Held**
WEB: www.johnsmaytag.com
SIC: **7629** 5722 Electrical household appliance repair; household appliance stores

(G-770)
JORDAN CABINETRY & WD TURNING
84 S Avon Dr (19703-1405)
PHONE.................302 792-1009
Timothy R Jordan, *Owner*
EMP: 2
SALES: 50K **Privately Held**
SIC: **2517** Home entertainment unit cabinets, wood

(G-771)
K & J AUTOMOTIVE INC (PA)
Also Called: AAMCO Transmissions
3111 Philadelphia Pike (19703-2509)
PHONE.................302 798-3635
Ken Rickoski, *President*
EMP: 5
SALES: 300K **Privately Held**
SIC: **7537** Automotive transmission repair shops

(G-772)
KRISTIN KONSTRUCTION COMPANY
Also Called: Kristin Construction
950 Ridge Rd Ste C14 (19703-3536)
PHONE.................302 791-9670
Albert Stavola, *President*
Joseph Stavola, *Vice Pres*
EMP: 5 EST: 1980
SQ FT: 1,600

SALES (est): 1.1MM **Privately Held**
SIC: **1521** 1522 1542 1541 Single-family home remodeling, additions & repairs; hotel/motel & multi-family home renovation & remodeling; commercial & office buildings, renovation & repair; renovation, remodeling & repairs: industrial buildings

(G-773)
LEON N WEINER & ASSOCIATES INC
Also Called: Stoneybrook Apts
1114 Andrea Ct (19703-2242)
PHONE.................302 798-3446
Robin Cheemes, *Branch Mgr*
EMP: 6
SALES (corp-wide): 54MM **Privately Held**
SIC: **6513** Apartment building operators
PA: Leon N. Weiner & Associates, Inc.
1 Fox Pt Ctr 4 Denny Rd
Wilmington DE 19809
302 656-1354

(G-774)
LITTLE LEARNER INC
41 N Avon Dr (19703-1503)
PHONE.................302 798-5570
Sandra V Desmond, *President*
EMP: 18
SALES (est): 325.4K **Privately Held**
SIC: **8351** Preschool center

(G-775)
LIVEWARE INC
1506 Society Dr (19703-1740)
PHONE.................302 791-9446
Daniel Levin, *CEO*
Christian Strasser, *Exec VP*
Chris Strasser, *Manager*
EMP: 10
SQ FT: 3,000
SALES (est): 710.4K **Privately Held**
WEB: www.workbigger.com
SIC: **7379** 2731 Computer related consulting services; books: publishing only

(G-776)
LOAN TILL PAYDAY LLC
2604 Philadelphia Pike (19703-2504)
PHONE.................302 792-5001
EMP: 22
SALES (corp-wide): 1.3MM **Privately Held**
SIC: **6163** Loan agents
PA: Loan Till Payday Llc
1901 W 4th St &Lincln
Wilmington DE
302 428-3925

(G-777)
M L PARKER CONSTRUCTION INC
950 Ridge Rd Ste C6 (19703-3528)
PHONE.................302 798-8530
Michael L Parker, *President*
EMP: 15
SQ FT: 10,000
SALES (est): 1.4MM **Privately Held**
SIC: **1521** 1542 New construction, single-family houses; single-family home remodeling, additions & repairs; commercial & office building, new construction; commercial & office buildings, renovation & repair

(G-778)
MADISON ADOPTION ASSOCIATES (PA)
1102 Society Dr (19703-1780)
PHONE.................302 475-8977
Aleda Madison, *President*
Laura Taylor, *Supervisor*
Diana Bramble, *Exec Dir*
Diana Madison, *Director*
EMP: 10
SALES: 1.6MM **Privately Held**
WEB: www.madisonadoption.com
SIC: **8322** Adoption services

(G-779)
MAGEN TACTICAL DEFENSE
2083 Philadelphia Pike (19703-2424)
PHONE.................484 589-0670
EMP: 3 EST: 2017

Claymont - New Castle County (G-780)

SALES (est): 170.5K **Privately Held**
SIC: 3812 Defense systems & equipment

(G-780)
MANUFACTURERS & TRADERS TR CO
Also Called: M&T
3503 Philadelphia Pike (19703-3106)
PHONE....................302 472-3262
Anthony Watts, *Branch Mgr*
EMP: 5
SALES (corp-wide): 6.4B **Publicly Held**
WEB: www.binghamlegg.com
SIC: 6022 State commercial banks
HQ: Manufacturers And Traders Trust Company
1 M&T Plz Fl 3
Buffalo NY 14203
716 842-4200

(G-781)
MESSER LLC
6000 Philadelphia Pike (19703-2717)
P.O. Box 590 (19703-0590)
PHONE....................302 798-9342
Todd Quintard, *Branch Mgr*
EMP: 45
SALES (corp-wide): 1.4B **Privately Held**
SIC: 2813 Nitrogen; oxygen, compressed or liquefied
HQ: Messer Llc
200 Somerset Corp Blvd # 7000
Bridgewater NJ 08807
908 464-8100

(G-782)
MILL CREEK METALS INC
3 1/2 Yale Ave (19703-2975)
P.O. Box 7493, Wilmington (19803-0493)
PHONE....................302 529-7020
Mark Gillan, *President*
Tina Gillan, *Admin Sec*
EMP: 12
SQ FT: 4,500
SALES (est): 2.4MM **Privately Held**
SIC: 5033 1761 Roofing & siding materials; roofing, siding & sheet metal work

(G-783)
MITHRIL CABLE NETWORK INC
2093 Philadelphia Pike (19703-2424)
PHONE....................213 373-4381
Jun LI, *Principal*
EMP: 11
SALES (est): 234.5K **Privately Held**
SIC: 7371 Computer software development & applications

(G-784)
MITTELMAN DENTAL LAB
108 Delaware Ave (19703-1904)
PHONE....................302 798-7440
Larry Mittelman, *Owner*
EMP: 11
SQ FT: 800
SALES (est): 436.6K **Privately Held**
SIC: 8072 Crown & bridge production

(G-785)
MORAN FOODS LLC
401 Naamans Dr Ste 3 (19703)
PHONE....................302 798-5042
EMP: 18
SALES (corp-wide): 4.5B **Privately Held**
SIC: 5141 Groceries, general line
HQ: Moran Foods, Llc
400 Northwest Plaza Dr
Saint Ann MO 63074
314 592-9100

(G-786)
MR WINDOW WASHER
126 Glenrock Dr (19703-1321)
PHONE....................302 588-3624
Blase Maitland, *Principal*
EMP: 2
SALES (est): 235.2K **Privately Held**
SIC: 3452 Washers

(G-787)
MUNTERS CORPORATION
100 Naamans Rd Ste 5l (19703-2731)
PHONE....................302 798-2455
Larry Waltmenire, *Manager*
EMP: 10
SALES (corp-wide): 749.8MM **Privately Held**
WEB: www.muntersamerica.com
SIC: 3585 Refrigeration & heating equipment
HQ: Munters Corporation
79 Monroe St
Amesbury MA 01913

(G-788)
NESMITH & COMPANY INC
Academy Electrical Contractors
100 Naamans Rd Ste 2d (19703-2736)
PHONE....................215 755-4570
William J Galbraith Jr, *Branch Mgr*
EMP: 30
SALES (corp-wide): 3.6MM **Privately Held**
SIC: 1731 General electrical contractor
PA: Nesmith & Company, Inc.
2440 Tasker St
Philadelphia PA 19145
215 755-4570

(G-789)
NEURO OPHTHALMOLOGIC ASSO
1201 Society Dr (19703-1777)
PHONE....................302 792-1616
EMP: 5
SALES (est): 364.8K **Privately Held**
SIC: 8011 Neurologist

(G-790)
NEW R V ASSOCIATES L P
2610 Philadelphia Pike B6 (19703-2526)
PHONE....................302 798-6878
Michael Cohen, *Partner*
EMP: 8
SALES (est): 386.6K **Privately Held**
SIC: 6513 6512 Apartment building operators; shopping center, property operation only

(G-791)
OCEANPORT LLC
6200 Philadelphia Pike (19703-2715)
PHONE....................302 792-2212
William Creighton, *Mng Member*
Lisa Stapleford,
▲ EMP: 15
SALES (est): 3.3MM **Privately Held**
SIC: 1479 Rock salt mining

(G-792)
PARAGON GROUP
1304 Society Dr (19703-1743)
PHONE....................302 798-5777
Fax: 302 798-4277
EMP: 15
SALES (est): 1.2MM **Privately Held**
SIC: 8748 Business Consulting, Nec, Nsk

(G-793)
PARKER CONSTRUCTION INC
950 Ridge Rd Ste C6 (19703-3528)
PHONE....................302 798-8530
Michael Parker, *President*
Allison Pini, *Admin Asst*
EMP: 5
SQ FT: 1,914
SALES (est): 522.2K **Privately Held**
SIC: 1521 General remodeling, single-family houses

(G-794)
PGW AUTO GLASS LLC
Also Called: Pgw Autoglass
130 Hickman Rd Ste 19 (19703-3552)
PHONE....................302 793-1486
EMP: 6
SALES (corp-wide): 11.8B **Publicly Held**
SIC: 5013 Automobile glass
HQ: Pgw Auto Glass, Llc
51 Dutilh Rd Ste 310
Cranberry Township PA 16066
878 208-4001

(G-795)
PIXXY SOLUTIONS LLC
2093 Philadelphia Pike # 4 (19703-2424)
PHONE....................631 609-6686
David Miller, *CEO*
EMP: 40
SALES (est): 595.4K **Privately Held**
SIC: 7336 Graphic arts & related design

(G-796)
PRISCILLA LANCASTER
302 Harvey Rd (19703-1942)
PHONE....................302 792-8305
Priscilla Lancaster, *Principal*
EMP: 2
SALES (est): 98K **Privately Held**
SIC: 3315 Wire & fabricated wire products

(G-797)
PROSPECT CROZER LLC
Also Called: Grobman, Marc Do
2999 Philadelphia Pike (19703-2507)
PHONE....................302 798-8785
Marc Grobman, *Branch Mgr*
EMP: 4
SALES (corp-wide): 1.2B **Privately Held**
SIC: 8011 Internal medicine, physician/surgeon
HQ: Ckhs, Inc.
100 W Sproul Rd
Springfield PA 19064
610 338-8200

(G-798)
QREPUBLIK INC
2093 Philadelphia Pike # 2012 (19703-2424)
PHONE....................559 475-8262
Sergey Vishchipnov, *CEO*
EMP: 2
SALES (est): 56.5K **Privately Held**
SIC: 7372 Prepackaged software

(G-799)
RC HELLINGS INC
Also Called: Hellings Builders
950 Ridge Rd Ste D3 (19703-3529)
PHONE....................302 798-6850
Ross Hellings, *CEO*
Jay Thuer, *Vice Pres*
EMP: 12
SQ FT: 2,100
SALES (est): 2.4MM **Privately Held**
WEB: www.rchellings.com
SIC: 1521 General remodeling, single-family houses; new construction, single-family houses

(G-800)
RICHARD S JACOBS DDS
3716 Philadelphia Pike (19703-3412)
PHONE....................302 792-2648
Richard S Jacobs DDS, *Owner*
EMP: 4
SALES (est): 249.1K **Privately Held**
SIC: 8021 Dentists' office

(G-801)
RP MANAGEMENT INC
Also Called: East Pointe Apartments
2610 Philadelphia Pike B6 (19703-2567)
PHONE....................302 798-6878
Candy McVey, *Manager*
EMP: 4 **Privately Held**
WEB: www.rpmgt.com
SIC: 6513 Apartment hotel operation
PA: Rp Management, Inc.
308 E Lancaster Ave # 235
Wynnewood PA 19096

(G-802)
SECURITY INC
Also Called: Ace Monitoring
8000 Society Dr (19703-1702)
P.O. Box 7357, Wilmington (19803-0357)
PHONE....................302 652-5276
John A Melson, *President*
Nancy Melson, *Vice Pres*
John Orr, *Manager*
EMP: 10 EST: 1977
SQ FT: 6,000
SALES (est): 1MM **Privately Held**
SIC: 7382 1731 Burglar alarm maintenance & monitoring; fire detection & burglar alarm systems specialization

(G-803)
SELLING DREAMS LLC
2901 Philadelphia Pike (19703-2507)
PHONE....................302 746-7999
Clif D'Mello, *Owner*
EMP: 9
SALES (est): 689K **Privately Held**
SIC: 5023 Decorative home furnishings & supplies

(G-804)
SERVICE KING HOLDINGS LLC
Also Called: Service King Cllision Repr Ctr
130 Hickman Rd (19703-3552)
PHONE....................302 797-8783
EMP: 36
SALES (corp-wide): 366.8MM **Privately Held**
SIC: 7538 General automotive repair shops
PA: Service King Holdings, Llc
2375 N Glenville Dr
Richardson TX 75082
972 960-7595

(G-805)
SID HARVEY INDUSTRIES INC
130 Hickman Rd Ste 32 (19703-3552)
PHONE....................302 746-7760
John Dobies, *Branch Mgr*
EMP: 6
SALES (corp-wide): 2.3MM **Privately Held**
SIC: 5074 Heating equipment (hydronic)
PA: Sid Harvey Industries, Inc.
605 Locust St Ste A
Garden City NY 11530
516 745-9200

(G-806)
SOUTH GATE REALTY ASSOC LLP
Also Called: South Gate Apartments
1308 Society Dr (19703-1743)
PHONE....................302 368-4535
Craig Jossey, *Managing Prtnr*
EMP: 4
SALES (est): 410K **Privately Held**
SIC: 6513 Apartment building operators

(G-807)
STOLTZ REALTY CO
Also Called: Society Hill Apts
7120 Society Dr (19703-1773)
PHONE....................302 798-8500
Sue Carson, *Manager*
EMP: 10
SALES (corp-wide): 7.4MM **Privately Held**
WEB: www.stoltzusa.com
SIC: 6531 6513 Real estate brokers & agents; apartment building operators
PA: Stoltz Realty Co
3704 Kennett Pike Ste 200
Wilmington DE
302 656-2852

(G-808)
STORYWORTH INC
2093 Philadelphia Pike (19703-2424)
PHONE....................415 967-1531
Nicholas Baum, *CEO*
Krista Baum,
EMP: 4
SALES (est): 40K **Privately Held**
SIC: 7299 Information services, consumer

(G-809)
TASTEABLES (PA)
333 Naamans Rd Ste 17b (19703-2805)
PHONE....................267 777-9143
La Vette Beasley, *CEO*
EMP: 4 EST: 2015
SALES (est): 298.6K **Privately Held**
SIC: 5149 Health foods

(G-810)
TERRA SYSTEMS INC
130 Hickman Rd Ste 1 (19703-3519)
PHONE....................302 798-9553
Richard L Raymond Jr, *President*
Michael Lee, *Vice Pres*
Free Michael, *VP Sales*
EMP: 15
SQ FT: 1,500
SALES (est): 2.2MM **Privately Held**
WEB: www.terrasystems.net
SIC: 8748 4959 Environmental consultant; environmental cleanup services

(G-811)
THI (US) INC (DH)
650 Naamans Rd Ste 307 (19703-2300)
PHONE....................302 792-1444
EMP: 1

GEOGRAPHIC SECTION

Clayton - Kent County (G-841)

SALES (est): 30MM
SALES (corp-wide): 4.1B **Publicly Held**
SIC: **2731** Holding Company
HQ: Thomson Reuters Corporation
3 Times Sq Lbby Mailroom
New York NY 10036
646 223-4000

(G-812)
TRI-STATE DRYWALL LLC
2803b Philadelphia Pike (19703-2506)
PHONE................................302 798-2709
Dean Ganoudis, *President*
EMP: 42
SALES: 2.7MM **Privately Held**
SIC: **1742** Drywall

(G-813)
UNITED CHECK CASHING
95 Naamans Rd Ste 37a (19703)
PHONE................................302 792-2545
Glen Fritzgerald, *President*
EMP: 5
SQ FT: 1,600
SALES (est): 609.9K **Privately Held**
SIC: **6099** Check cashing agencies

(G-814)
VET HOUSECALL SERVICE
2602 Jefferson Ave (19703-1851)
PHONE................................302 656-7291
Alfred Olsen, *Principal*
EMP: 4
SALES (est): 129.5K **Privately Held**
SIC: **0742** Animal hospital services, pets & other animal specialties

(G-815)
VICTOR KORNBLUTH
Also Called: Printz Picks
106 Governor Printz Blvd (19703-2909)
PHONE................................302 791-9777
Vic Kornbluth, *Principal*
EMP: 2
SALES (est): 90.7K **Privately Held**
SIC: **3931** 5571 Musical instruments; bicycles, motorized

(G-816)
VISUAL COMMUNICATIONS INC
Also Called: Vci
3724 Philadelphia Pike (19703-3412)
PHONE................................302 792-9500
Robert S Burt, *President*
EMP: 7
SQ FT: 1,800
SALES (est): 684.5K **Privately Held**
WEB: www.1stchoiceleddisplays.com
SIC: **7629** 5999 Business machine repair, electric; communication equipment

(G-817)
WAYDEN INC (PA)
Also Called: Wayden Paper
205 Ridge Rd (19703-3506)
PHONE................................302 798-1642
Wayne Todd, *President*
Denise Todd, *Vice Pres*
EMP: 4
SALES (est): 799.2K **Privately Held**
SIC: **5113** Bags, paper & disposable plastic

(G-818)
WEELWORK INC
619 New York Ave (19703-1957)
PHONE................................800 546-8607
Serhii Surhanov, *CEO*
EMP: 5
SALES (est): 124.8K **Privately Held**
SIC: **8742** Human resource consulting services

(G-819)
WHEREBYUS ENTERPRISES INC
2093 Philadelphia Pike (19703-2424)
PHONE................................305 988-0808
Christopher Sopher, *President*
EMP: 1
SALES (est): 45.4K **Privately Held**
SIC: **2741** 8732 ; survey service: marketing, location, etc.

(G-820)
WILCON NORTH INC
Also Called: Meineke Discount Mufflers
3005 Philadelphia Pike (19703-2524)
PHONE................................302 798-1699
Barry Conrad, *President*
Jake Williams, *Treasurer*
EMP: 4
SALES (est): 448.3K **Privately Held**
SIC: **7533** Muffler shop, sale or repair & installation

(G-821)
WILMINGTON SAVINGS FUND SOC
Also Called: Claymont Branch
3512 Philadelphia Pike (19703-3109)
PHONE................................302 792-6043
M Pindell, *Manager*
EMP: 4
SALES (corp-wide): 455.5MM **Publicly Held**
WEB: www.wsfsbank.com
SIC: **6035** Federal savings banks
HQ: Wilmington Savings Fund Society
500 Delaware Ave Ste 500 # 500
Wilmington DE 19801
302 792-6000

(G-822)
WILMINGTON SAVINGS FUND SOC
Also Called: Wsfs Bank
2105 Philadelphia Pike (19703-2426)
PHONE................................302 792-6435
Albert Roop, *Vice Pres*
Malisa Pindell, *Branch Mgr*
Kathleen Gathagan, *Sr Project Mgr*
Ken Kafel, *Manager*
Matthew Walsh, *Manager*
EMP: 5
SALES (corp-wide): 455.5MM **Publicly Held**
SIC: **6022** State commercial banks
HQ: Wilmington Savings Fund Society
500 Delaware Ave Ste 500 # 500
Wilmington DE 19801
302 792-6000

(G-823)
WINDY WEATHER WORLD INC
2093 Philadelphia Pike # 7 (19703-2424)
PHONE................................650 204-7941
EMP: 5
SALES (est): 450K **Privately Held**
SIC: **7371** Computer software development & applications

(G-824)
WIRE WORKS
Also Called: Creative Spaces
302 Harvey Rd (19703-1942)
PHONE................................302 792-8305
Percella Lancaster, *Owner*
EMP: 1
SALES (est): 56.7K **Privately Held**
SIC: **3496** 3315 Miscellaneous fabricated wire products; wire & fabricated wire products

(G-825)
WOLFE RESOURCES LTD (PA)
Also Called: Country Maid Launderette
2087 Philadelphia Pike (19703-2424)
PHONE................................302 798-6397
Alan Wolfe, *Owner*
Paul Wolfe, *Admin Sec*
EMP: 10
SALES (est): 220K **Privately Held**
SIC: **7215** Laundry, coin-operated

(G-826)
WOODACRES ASSOCIATES LP
Also Called: Woodacres Apts
915 Cedartree Ln (19703-1687)
PHONE................................302 792-0243
Cheri Prather, *Partner*
EMP: 10
SQ FT: 30,000
SALES (est): 750.8K **Privately Held**
SIC: **6513** Apartment building operators

(G-827)
WRIGHT CHOICE CHILD CARE
3031 W Court Ave (19703-2020)
PHONE................................302 798-0758
Carmen Wright, *Principal*
EMP: 5
SALES (est): 121.1K **Privately Held**
SIC: **8351** Child day care services

(G-828)
YES HARDSOFT SOLUTIONS INC
351 Lenape Way (19703-3323)
PHONE................................609 632-0397
Raj Kumar, *Senior Mgr*
EMP: 5
SALES (corp-wide): 1.7MM **Privately Held**
SIC: **7379** Computer related consulting services
PA: Yes Hardsoft Solutions, Inc
3626 Silverside Rd
Wilmington DE 19810
609 632-0397

(G-829)
ZENBANX HOLDING LTD
650 Naamans Rd Ste 300 (19703-2300)
PHONE................................310 749-3101
Arkadi Kuhlmann, *CEO*
Arkadi Kuhlman, *CEO*
EMP: 6
SALES (est): 575.3K
SALES (corp-wide): 262.9MM **Privately Held**
SIC: **7371** Computer software development
PA: Social Finance, Inc.
234 1st St
San Francisco CA 94105
415 930-4467

Clayton
Kent County

(G-830)
A & H PLUMBING & HEATING INC
811 Clayton Delaney Rd (19938-9789)
PHONE................................302 223-8027
EMP: 9
SALES (est): 766.9K **Privately Held**
SIC: **1711** Plumbing & Heating Contractor

(G-831)
ABRAHAMS SEED LLC
246 Coldwater Dr (19938-3902)
P.O. Box 374 (19938-0374)
PHONE................................302 588-1913
Khalilah Ling,
EMP: 6
SALES: 15K **Privately Held**
SIC: **7349** Building maintenance services

(G-832)
ALLIANCE BUS DEV CONCEPTS LLC
1480 Alley Corner Rd (19938-2630)
PHONE................................803 814-4004
Bryan Danboise,
EMP: 10
SALES (est): 215.3K **Privately Held**
SIC: **8742** 8748 7389 Construction project management consultant; new business start-up consultant; training & development consultant; telecommunications consultant; ;

(G-833)
ANGLIN ASSOCIATES LLC
Also Called: Anglin Aircraft Recovery Svc
4901 Holletts Corner Rd (19938-3156)
PHONE................................302 653-3500
D Scott Anglin,
EMP: 10 **Privately Held**
SIC: **6719** Personal holding companies, except banks

(G-834)
ANTA IMPORT/EXPORT LLC
428 Christiana River Dr (19938-3926)
PHONE................................302 653-4542
Fanta Bamba,
EMP: 2 EST: 2016
SALES (est): 62.6K **Privately Held**
SIC: **3281** Household articles, except furniture: cut stone

(G-835)
ATLANTIC TRACTOR LLC
Also Called: John Deere Authorized Dealer
315 Main St (19938-7702)
P.O. Box 1125 (19938-1125)
PHONE................................302 653-8536
Mike Asche, *General Mgr*
Bill Cooper, *Vice Pres*
Jim Torbert, *Parts Mgr*
Josh Martin, *Sales Staff*
Mike Kern, *Manager*
EMP: 30
SALES (corp-wide): 86.5MM **Privately Held**
WEB: www.atlantictractor.com
SIC: **5083** Farm & garden machinery
PA: Atlantic Tractor Llc
720 Wheeler School Rd
Whiteford MD 21160
410 457-3696

(G-836)
BALLARD BUILDERS LLC
101 S Bassett St (19938-7714)
PHONE................................302 363-1677
Michael J Bandurski,
Dennis Ballard,
EMP: 11
SQ FT: 1,500
SALES (est): 1.4MM **Privately Held**
SIC: **1542** Commercial & office buildings, prefabricated erection

(G-837)
BARRYS CLEANING SERVICE
2472 Chance Rd (19938-3012)
PHONE................................302 653-0110
Barry Larkin, *Owner*
EMP: 7
SALES (est): 300K **Privately Held**
SIC: **5084** Cleaning equipment, high pressure, sand or steam

(G-838)
BARTLETT & BARTLETT LLC
Also Called: B B Construction
392 Hopewell Dr (19938-2226)
PHONE................................302 653-7200
Wilson Bartlett, *Mng Member*
EMP: 5
SALES (est): 442.8K **Privately Held**
SIC: **1521** Single-family housing construction

(G-839)
CLARK SEED COMPANY INC
1467 Seven Hickories Rd (19938-3277)
PHONE................................302 653-9249
Donald M Clark, *President*
D James Clark, *Vice Pres*
Ruth Clark, *Treasurer*
Jeff Clark, *Admin Sec*
EMP: 4
SALES (est): 1.2MM **Privately Held**
WEB: www.clatsopcounty.us
SIC: **5191** 5261 5990 Seeds: field, garden & flower; nursery stock, seeds & bulbs; feed & farm supply

(G-840)
COUNTRY ROADS VETERINARY SVC
2681 Shaws Corner Rd (19938-3222)
PHONE................................302 514-9087
EMP: 5 EST: 2012
SALES (est): 169.4K **Privately Held**
SIC: **0742** Animal hospital services, pets & other animal specialties

(G-841)
D E ENTERPRISES LLC
1826 Clayton Delaney Rd (19938-9778)
PHONE................................302 653-5493
Edwin Poore, *Principal*
EMP: 4
SALES (est): 227.7K **Privately Held**
SIC: **8748** Business consulting

Clayton - Kent County

(G-842)
DULIN BROTHERS
938 Blackiston Church Rd (19938-2301)
PHONE..................302 653-5365
Lee Dulin Jr, *Partner*
Donald Dulin, *Partner*
Norman Dulin, *Partner*
William Dulin, *Partner*
EMP: 6
SALES (est): 898.9K **Privately Held**
SIC: 0241 0119 Dairy farms; feeder grains

(G-843)
DUNNINGS BODY SHOP
2399 Sudlersville Rd (19938-3097)
PHONE..................302 653-9615
Robert Dunning, *President*
EMP: 4
SALES (est): 434.4K **Privately Held**
SIC: 7532 Body shop, automotive

(G-844)
E D CUSTOM CONTRACTING INC
94 Green Heather Ln (19938-2102)
PHONE..................302 653-2646
Earl Dawlery, *President*
EMP: 4
SALES: 500K **Privately Held**
SIC: 1761 1521 Roofing, siding & sheet metal work; general remodeling, single-family houses

(G-845)
EAGLE BLDG & GROUNDS MAINT LLC
3507 Sudlersville Rd (19938-3085)
PHONE..................302 264-7058
EMP: 4
SALES (est): 46.6K **Privately Held**
SIC: 0782 Lawn & garden services

(G-846)
EAGLE BUILDING AND GROUNDS
2817 Shaws Corner Rd (19938-3220)
PHONE..................302 508-5403
Ken Duphily, *Principal*
EMP: 4 EST: 2017
SALES (est): 148.2K **Privately Held**
SIC: 0782 Lawn & garden services

(G-847)
EAGLE MHC COMPANY
Also Called: Eagle Group
100 Industrial Blvd (19938-8900)
PHONE..................302 653-3000
Larry McAllister, *President*
▲ EMP: 380
SALES (est): 127.5MM **Privately Held**
SIC: 3589 8099 Commercial cooking & foodwarming equipment; blood related health services
PA: Metal Masters Foodservice Equipment Co., Inc.
100 Industrial Blvd
Clayton DE 19938
302 653-3000

(G-848)
EASTERN SHORE LITE INDUSTRIES
5908 Judith Rd (19938-2827)
PHONE..................302 653-8687
Michael A Briggs, *Principal*
EMP: 2
SALES (est): 92.8K **Privately Held**
SIC: 3999 Manufacturing industries

(G-849)
EZ MANUFACTURING COMPANY LLC
500 N Bassett St (19938)
P.O. Box 63, Smyrna (19977-0063)
PHONE..................302 653-6567
Eugene Fox, *Mng Member*
EMP: 5
SALES (est): 718.8K **Privately Held**
SIC: 5014 Tire & tube repair materials

(G-850)
FIRST CLASS CARDS LLC
131 Stirrup Rd (19938-4671)
PHONE..................302 653-0111
EMP: 2
SALES (est): 108.5K **Privately Held**
SIC: 2759 Commercial printing

(G-851)
FOREST VIEW NURSERY
1313 Blackbird Forest Rd (19938-9747)
PHONE..................302 653-7757
John Ellingsworth III, *President*
Irene Ellingsworth, *Corp Secy*
EMP: 22 EST: 1951
SQ FT: 5,800
SALES: 900K **Privately Held**
SIC: 0181 Shrubberies grown in field nurseries

(G-852)
GATEWAY CONSTRUCTION INC
498 Sudlersville Rd (19938-2772)
P.O. Box 308, Hartly (19953-0308)
PHONE..................302 653-4400
Mark Kohout, *President*
Cynthia Swyka, *Vice Pres*
EMP: 7
SQ FT: 1,500
SALES (est): 776.9K **Privately Held**
SIC: 1799 Building site preparation

(G-853)
GEORGE SWIRE SR
790 Daisey Rd (19938-2971)
PHONE..................302 690-6995
EMP: 1 EST: 2016
SALES (est): 25K **Privately Held**
SIC: 7692 Welding repair

(G-854)
GIBSON INDUSTRIES
2712 Shaws Corner Rd (19938-3218)
PHONE..................302 653-7874
EMP: 2
SALES (est): 74K **Privately Held**
SIC: 3999 Mfg Misc Products

(G-855)
HANOVER FOODS CORPORATION
Duck Creek Rd Rr 6 (19938)
P.O. Box 1150 (19938-1150)
PHONE..................302 653-9281
Arnold Bowman, *Manager*
EMP: 220
SALES (corp-wide): 353.3MM **Publicly Held**
WEB: www.hanoverfoods.com
SIC: 2033 2037 2038 2034 Vegetables: packaged in cans, jars, etc.; tomato sauce: packaged in cans, jars, etc.; vegetables, quick frozen & cold pack, excl. potato products; dinners, frozen & packaged; vegetables, freeze-dried; manufactured ice; canned specialties; soups & broths: canned, jarred, etc.
PA: Hanover Foods Corporation
1486 York St
Hanover PA 17331
717 632-6000

(G-856)
INTEGRITY CLEANING SVCS LLC
331 Coldwater Dr (19938-3916)
P.O. Box 1431, Bear (19701-7431)
PHONE..................302 353-9315
Kerry Cerdan,
EMP: 6
SALES (est): 82K **Privately Held**
SIC: 7699 Cleaning services

(G-857)
INTEGRITY MGT SOLUTION INC
312 Seeneytown Rd (19938-3248)
PHONE..................302 270-8976
Henry Mast, *Principal*
EMP: 5 EST: 2014
SALES (est): 263.6K **Privately Held**
SIC: 1521 Single-family housing construction

(G-858)
JEFFS MOBILE POWER WASHING
62 Old Creek Dr (19938-3866)
PHONE..................302 753-4726
Jeff Lively,
EMP: 1
SALES (est): 89.6K **Privately Held**
SIC: 2842 Specialty cleaning preparations

(G-859)
KENTON CHAIR SHOP
291 Blackiston Rd (19938-2266)
PHONE..................302 653-2411
Fred Zimmerman, *Partner*
EMP: 10
SALES (est): 1.1MM **Privately Held**
SIC: 2511 5712 Chairs, household, except upholstered: wood; furniture stores

(G-860)
KRM STABLES
1225 Clyton Grenspring Rd (19938-9731)
PHONE..................302 653-3838
John Melnick,
EMP: 5 EST: 2008
SALES: 20K **Privately Held**
SIC: 0752 Training services, horses (except racing horses)

(G-861)
LARKINS BUS SERVICE LLC
512 S Bassett St (19938-7736)
PHONE..................302 653-5855
Sandra Larkin,
EMP: 17
SALES (est): 524.6K **Privately Held**
SIC: 4151 School buses

(G-862)
LIBERTY PARKS AND PLAYGROUNDS
319 Wheatleys Pond Rd (19938)
PHONE..................302 659-5083
Charles Walker, *President*
EMP: 3
SALES: 3MM **Privately Held**
SIC: 3949 Playground equipment

(G-863)
METAL MSTERS FDSERVICE EQP INC (PA)
Also Called: Eagle Foodservice
100 Industrial Blvd (19938-8900)
PHONE..................302 653-3000
Larry N McAllister, *President*
Glenn Dorris, *Vice Pres*
Betty McAllister, *Vice Pres*
David Ezeani, *Research*
Randolph Fox, *Admin Sec*
▲ EMP: 132 EST: 1978
SQ FT: 475,000
SALES (est): 127.5MM **Privately Held**
WEB: www.eaglegrp.com
SIC: 3589 3556 Commercial cooking & foodwarming equipment; food products machinery

(G-864)
MGL SCREEN PRINTING
47 S Longwood Ln (19938-1934)
PHONE..................302 450-6250
EMP: 2
SALES (est): 118.1K **Privately Held**
SIC: 2752 Commercial printing, lithographic

(G-865)
MONROE MECHANICAL CONTRACTING
370 Christiana River Dr (19938-3925)
PHONE..................302 223-6020
Jay R Beers, *President*
Wanda Beers, *Bookkeeper*
EMP: 5
SALES (est): 391.4K **Privately Held**
SIC: 1711 Warm air heating & air conditioning contractor

(G-866)
NEXSIGNS LLC
711 Coldwater Dr (19938-3911)
PHONE..................302 508-2615
EMP: 2
SALES (est): 83.9K **Privately Held**
SIC: 2752 Commercial printing, lithographic

(G-867)
POINT OF SALE TECHNOLOGIES
Also Called: Pos Technologies
412 Bryn Zion Rd (19938-2602)
PHONE..................302 659-5119
EMP: 7 EST: 2000
SALES (est): 360K **Privately Held**
SIC: 7372 Ret Software

(G-868)
POWER ELECTRONICS INC
310 S Bassett St (19938-7711)
P.O. Box 537 (19938-0537)
PHONE..................302 653-4822
Karen Taylor, *Corp Secy*
John Hubbard, *Vice Pres*
Dennis Szabo, *Project Mgr*
Charlie Racine, *Mfg Spvr*
EMP: 35
SQ FT: 20,000
SALES (est): 8.6MM **Privately Held**
WEB: www.powerelec.com
SIC: 3444 3613 Sheet metalwork; control panels, electric

(G-869)
PREFERRED ENVIROMENTAL
2300 W Fourth St Ste E104 (19938)
PHONE..................610 364-1106
Edward Darrah, *Mng Member*
EMP: 8
SALES: 400K **Privately Held**
SIC: 4959 Environmental cleanup services

(G-870)
RUSSELL D EARNEST & ASSOC
P.O. Box 1132 (19938-1132)
PHONE..................302 659-0730
Russell Earnest, *Principal*
EMP: 2
SALES (est): 107.3K **Privately Held**
SIC: 2741 Miscellaneous publishing

(G-871)
SELECT STAINLESS PRODUCTS LLC
100 Industrial Blvd (19938-8900)
P.O. Box 1129 (19938-1129)
PHONE..................302 653-3062
Jason Keller, *Manager*
EMP: 7
SALES (est): 1.4MM **Privately Held**
SIC: 3914 Silverware & plated ware

(G-872)
VALET CLEANING SERVICE
3234 Downs Chapel Rd (19938-2020)
PHONE..................302 653-0233
Linda Reed, *Owner*
EMP: 4
SALES (est): 84.5K **Privately Held**
SIC: 7349 Building cleaning service

(G-873)
VITALUS TECHNOLOGIES INC
5644 Millington Rd (19938-2515)
PHONE..................302 383-9100
Hong Vu-Leanza, *Principal*
EMP: 4
SALES (est): 50.1K **Privately Held**
SIC: 7379 Computer related consulting services

(G-874)
WILLIAM BYLER JR ARCHITECT INC
2652 Chance Rd (19938-3014)
PHONE..................302 653-3550
William Byler Jr, *President*
EMP: 4
SALES: 217.1K **Privately Held**
SIC: 8712 Architectural services

(G-875)
YERKIE CORP
Also Called: Yerkie Enterprises
567 Seeneytown Rd (19938-3255)
PHONE..................302 653-1321
James B Yerkie Sr, *President*
Jim Yerkie, *President*
Cheryl Yerkie, *Vice Pres*
EMP: 4
SQ FT: 1,200

GEOGRAPHIC SECTION — Dagsboro - Sussex County (G-906)

SALES (est): 392.7K **Privately Held**
SIC: **1711** 5999 Mechanical contractor; telephone & communication equipment; communication equipment; telephone equipment & systems

Dagsboro
Sussex County

(G-876)
A G CONCRETE WORKS LLC
Also Called: AG Concrete Works
31883 New St (19939-3832)
PHONE.................................302 841-2227
EMP: 5
SALES (est): 226.3K **Privately Held**
SIC: **1771** Concrete work

(G-877)
ALLEN HARIM FOODS LLC
26867 Nine Foot Rd (19939-4429)
PHONE.................................302 732-9511
Frank Wills, *Engnr/R&D Mgr*
EMP: 26 **Privately Held**
SIC: **0254** Poultry hatcheries
HQ: Allen Harim Foods, Llc
126 N Shipley St
Seaford DE 19973
302 629-9136

(G-878)
ATLANTIC ELEVATORS
Also Called: De Atlantic Elevator
31023 Country Gdns Sf3 (19939-5436)
PHONE.................................302 537-8304
Bruce E Brosnahan, *Owner*
EMP: 7
SALES (est): 610K **Privately Held**
SIC: **5084** 3534 Elevators; elevators & moving stairways

(G-879)
AUTO WORKS COLLISION CTR LLC
27420 Auto Works Ave (19939-5426)
PHONE.................................302 732-3902
David Jones,
Christine Jones,
EMP: 15
SQ FT: 15,000
SALES (est): 2.1MM **Privately Held**
SIC: **7532** Body shop, automotive

(G-880)
BANK OF DELMAR
601 Main St (19939)
P.O. Box 98 (19939-0098)
PHONE.................................302 732-3610
Crystal Hudson, *Branch Mgr*
EMP: 4
SALES (corp-wide): 24.7MM **Publicly Held**
WEB: www.bankofdelmarvahb.com
SIC: **6022** State commercial banks
HQ: The Bank Of Delmarva
2245 Northwood Dr
Salisbury MD 21801
410 548-1100

(G-881)
BANKS FARM LLC
30190 Whites Neck Rd (19939-3468)
PHONE.................................302 542-4100
David Banks, *Mng Member*
EMP: 5
SALES: 500K **Privately Held**
SIC: **0191** 4213 General farms, primarily crop; heavy hauling

(G-882)
BETTERLVING PTIO SNROMS DLMRVA
32442 Royal Blvd Unit 1 (19939-5427)
PHONE.................................302 251-0000
Michael J Cummings, *Owner*
EMP: 5
SALES: 580K **Privately Held**
SIC: **3448** Sunrooms, prefabricated metal

(G-883)
BLACKWATER VILLAGE ASSOCIATION
31275 Mohican Dr (19939-4157)
PHONE.................................302 541-4700
Gary Lee, *President*
Caroline Miller, *Corp Secy*
EMP: 7
SALES: 35K **Privately Held**
SIC: **8699** Membership organizations

(G-884)
BLADES H V A C SERVICES
Also Called: Honeywell Authorized Dealer
32798 Swamp Rd (19939-4425)
PHONE.................................302 539-4436
Brandon Blades, *Owner*
EMP: 5
SALES (est): 1.1MM **Privately Held**
SIC: **7699** Boiler & heating repair services

(G-885)
BRAFMAN FAMILY DENTISTRY PC
31381 Dogwood Acres Dr # 2 (19939-4076)
PHONE.................................302 732-3852
Wendy Brafman DMD, *President*
Kevin Brafman DMD, *Vice Pres*
Wendy Brafman, *Fmly & Gen Dent*
EMP: 12
SALES (est): 810K **Privately Held**
SIC: **8021** Dentists' office

(G-886)
BUNTINGS GARAGE INC
28506 Carebear Ln (19939-3943)
PHONE.................................302 732-9021
Ellison Bunting, *President*
Keith Bunting, *Vice Pres*
Sara Bunting, *Treasurer*
EMP: 13
SALES (est): 885.5K **Privately Held**
SIC: **4492** 7539 4214 Towing & tugboat service; automotive repair shops; local trucking with storage

(G-887)
BURTON HG & COMPANY INC
32973 Main St (19939-3842)
PHONE.................................302 245-3384
Dallas Burton Hudson, *President*
Miguel R Garcia, *Senior VP*
Bradon M Hudson, *Vice Pres*
Bradon Hudson, *Vice Pres*
Evelyn Hudson, *Manager*
EMP: 11
SALES: 2.2MM **Privately Held**
SIC: **0781** 1389 Landscape counseling & planning; construction, repair & dismantling services

(G-888)
CAREY INS & FIN SERVICES INC
30618 Dupont Blvd Unit 1 (19939-5402)
PHONE.................................302 934-8383
Scott Carey, *Principal*
EMP: 4
SALES (est): 854.8K **Privately Held**
SIC: **6282** Investment advice

(G-889)
CAREY JR JAMES E INC (PA)
30618 Dupont Blvd Unit 1 (19939-5402)
P.O. Box 1500, Millsboro (19966-5500)
PHONE.................................302 934-8383
James E Carey Jr, *President*
EMP: 9
SQ FT: 1,200
SALES (est): 2MM **Privately Held**
SIC: **6411** Insurance agents

(G-890)
CECO INC
27515 Hodges Ln Unit N1 (19939-5404)
PHONE.................................302 732-3919
Dell Morsberger, *Manager*
EMP: 40
SALES (corp-wide): 14MM **Privately Held**
SIC: **4225** General warehousing & storage
PA: Ceco, Inc.
6770 Oak Hall Ln Ste 117
Columbia MD 21045
410 995-6270

(G-891)
CEDAR NECK DECOR LLC
30980 Country Gdns Q1 (19939-5441)
PHONE.................................918 497-7179
Josh Lobecker,
EMP: 2
SALES (est): 50.2K **Privately Held**
SIC: **2499** Decorative wood & woodwork

(G-892)
CHRISTINE E FOX DDS
31059 Dupont Blvd (19939-4439)
PHONE.................................302 732-9850
Christine Fox, *Principal*
EMP: 4
SALES (est): 89.7K **Privately Held**
SIC: **8021** Dentists' office

(G-893)
COMMUNICATIONS & WIRING CO
Also Called: 1 Smart Home
34423 Sylvan Vue Dr (19939-4106)
PHONE.................................302 539-0809
Lew Reeves, *Owner*
Bonnie Reeves, *Co-Owner*
EMP: 6
SQ FT: 2,500
SALES (est): 332.5K **Privately Held**
WEB: www.communicationswiring.com
SIC: **1731** Telephone & telephone equipment installation

(G-894)
CRIPPLE CREEK GOLF & CNTRY CLB
29494 Cripple Creek Dr (19939-3423)
PHONE.................................302 539-1446
Don Pharr, *President*
William Clarke, *Vice Pres*
Brenda Bove, *Manager*
Marry Alice Senneman, *Admin Sec*
EMP: 45
SQ FT: 8,800
SALES (est): 3.6MM **Privately Held**
WEB: www.cripplecreekgolf.com
SIC: **7997** Country club, membership

(G-895)
DELAWARE LEARNING INSTITUE OF
32448 Royal Blvd Unit 1 (19939-3899)
PHONE.................................302 732-6704
Melody Morgan, *Principal*
Danielle Kunkel, *Asst Mgr*
Cindy Dunham, *Director*
John Cook, *Director*
EMP: 12
SALES (est): 541.3K **Privately Held**
SIC: **7231** 7999 Cosmetology school; massage instruction

(G-896)
DELMARVA AUTO GLASS INC
30667 Dupont Blvd (19939-4451)
PHONE.................................302 934-8600
David Drane, *Manager*
EMP: 4
SALES (corp-wide): 2.1MM **Privately Held**
WEB: www.delmarvaautoglass.com
SIC: **7536** Automotive glass replacement shops
PA: Delmarva Auto Glass Inc
2121 W Zion Rd
Salisbury MD 21801
410 546-3600

(G-897)
DELMARVALOUS
30748 Long Leaf Rd (19939-4025)
PHONE.................................302 200-2001
EMP: 2 EST: 2018
SALES (est): 88.9K **Privately Held**
SIC: **3442** Metal doors, sash & trim

(G-898)
DISCOVERY ISLAND PRESCHOOL
32532 Smith Dr (19939)
PHONE.................................302 732-7529
Kerry Clark, *Owner*
EMP: 10
SALES (est): 136.1K **Privately Held**
SIC: **8351** Preschool center

(G-899)
ELITE MECHANICAL
29810 Beach A Landing Rd (19939)
PHONE.................................302 321-9215
EMP: 4
SALES (est): 314.7K **Privately Held**
SIC: **1711** Plumbing/Heating/Air Cond Contractor

(G-900)
ENTERPRISE LSG PHLADELPHIA LLC
Also Called: Enterprise Rent-A-Car
27424 Auto Works Ave (19939-5426)
PHONE.................................302 732-3534
Nicole Delmastro, *Branch Mgr*
EMP: 6
SALES (corp-wide): 4.5B **Privately Held**
SIC: **7514** Rent-a-car service
HQ: Enterprise Leasing Company Of Philadelphia, Llc
2434 W Main St 2436
Norristown PA 19403

(G-901)
FIRST CHOICE SERVICES INC
33334 Main St (19939-3812)
PHONE.................................302 648-7877
Joe Ernest, *Owner*
EMP: 20 EST: 2017
SALES (est): 1MM **Privately Held**
SIC: **1521** Repairing fire damage, single-family houses

(G-902)
FLW WOOD PRODUCTS INC
33290 Bayberry Ct (19939-4923)
PHONE.................................410 259-4674
EMP: 4
SALES (corp-wide): 4.7MM **Privately Held**
SIC: **5099** Wood & wood by-products
PA: F.L.W. Wood Products, Inc.
100 Prnctn S Corpt Ctr # 270
Ewing NJ 08628
609 520-8333

(G-903)
GEORGES CUSTOM WOODWORKING
34885 Wingate Ct (19939-3458)
PHONE.................................302 541-4599
EMP: 1
SALES (est): 105.8K **Privately Held**
SIC: **2431** Millwork

(G-904)
GULLS WAY CAMPGROUND
Rr 26 (19939)
PHONE.................................302 732-6383
Lina Cropper, *President*
Wayne Cropper, *President*
Dawn Cropper, *Vice Pres*
EMP: 6
SALES (est): 332.9K **Privately Held**
SIC: **7033** Campgrounds

(G-905)
GULLS WAY INC
Also Called: Gull's Way Campground
Rural Route 2 Box 45
PHONE.................................302 732-9629
Lina Cropper, *President*
Dawn Farmer, *Corp Secy*
Wayne Cropper, *Vice Pres*
EMP: 6
SALES (est): 166.9K **Privately Held**
SIC: **7033** Campgrounds

(G-906)
H&K GROUP INC
Dagsboro Material
30548 Thoroughgood Rd (19939)
PHONE.................................302 934-7635
Steve Nelson, *Office Mgr*
EMP: 6
SALES (corp-wide): 71.6MM **Privately Held**
WEB: www.hkgroup.com
SIC: **3281** Stone, quarrying & processing of own stone products
PA: H&K Group, Inc.
2052 Lucon Rd
Skippack PA 19474
610 584-8500

Dagsboro - Sussex County (G-907) — GEOGRAPHIC SECTION

(G-907)
HARVEST CONSUMER PRODUCTS LLC
350 Clayton St (19939)
PHONE.....................302 732-6624
Joe Kollock III, *President*
Edward Humes, *Vice Pres*
EMP: 38 Privately Held
WEB: www.coastalsupplyinc.com
SIC: 2499 5191 5193 2875 Mulch, wood & bark; hay; straw; soil, potting & planting; flowers & florists' supplies; fertilizers, mixing only
HQ: Harvest Consumer Products, Llc
215 Overhill Dr 200
Mooresville NC 28117
980 444-2000

(G-908)
HEATHER KRAFT
33094 Main St (19939-3807)
PHONE.....................302 927-0072
EMP: 3
SALES (est): 146.5K Privately Held
SIC: 2022 Mfg Cheese

(G-909)
HICKORY HILL BUILDERS INC
25714 Timmons Ln (19939-4472)
PHONE.....................302 934-6109
Todd Timmons, *President*
Ralph Timmons Jr, *Vice Pres*
Pauline Timmons, *Admin Sec*
EMP: 5
SALES (est): 705.3K Privately Held
SIC: 1521 New construction, single-family houses

(G-910)
HIGGINS HOUSE VICTORIAN B & B
140 River Bend Dr (19939-9715)
PHONE.....................407 324-9238
Lou Jobin, *Owner*
EMP: 7
SALES (est): 76.9K Privately Held
SIC: 7011 Bed & breakfast inn

(G-911)
INDIAN RIVER POWER LLC
29416 Power Plant Rd (19939-4906)
PHONE.....................302 934-3527
EMP: 19
SALES (est): 22.6MM Publicly Held
SIC: 4931 Electric & other services combined
PA: Nrg Energy, Inc.
804 Carnegie Ctr
Princeton NJ 08540

(G-912)
ISLAND OF MISFITS LLC
32448 Royal Blvd Ste A (19939-3899)
PHONE.....................302 732-6704
John Cook, *Principal*
EMP: 9
SALES (est): 55.4K Privately Held
SIC: 7231 Cosmetology school

(G-913)
KIDZ AKADEMY CORP
32442 Royal Blvd (19939-5427)
PHONE.....................302 732-6077
Alison Taylor, *Director*
Allison Taylor, *Director*
EMP: 6
SALES (est): 104.4K Privately Held
SIC: 8351 Group day care center

(G-914)
KIMBERLY SUE KESTER
Also Called: Chicken Little Child Care
32315 Spring Ct (19939-4001)
PHONE.....................302 732-1093
EMP: 5 EST: 2011
SALES (est): 140K Privately Held
SIC: 8351 Child Day Care Services

(G-915)
LYCON INVESTMENT COMPANY
Also Called: Lyon 784
30983 Country Gdns Unit 1 (19939-5405)
PHONE.....................302 732-0940
Dion Wright, *Branch Mgr*
EMP: 8
SALES (corp-wide): 20.7B Privately Held
SIC: 5075 Warm air heating & air conditioning
HQ: Lycon Investment Company
4501 Hollins Ferry Rd # 140
Baltimore MD 21227
410 540-4880

(G-916)
MAIN OFFICE INC
32096 Sussex St (19939-3861)
PHONE.....................302 732-3460
Lisa Blanchette, *President*
EMP: 2
SALES (est): 253.6K Privately Held
SIC: 3694 Distributors, motor vehicle engine

(G-917)
MARVEL PORTABLE WELDING INC
32887 Dupont Blvd (19939-4466)
P.O. Box 27 (19939-0027)
PHONE.....................302 732-9480
Kendall R Marvel, *President*
Linda M Marvel, *Vice Pres*
EMP: 9
SQ FT: 3,300
SALES (est): 2.8MM Privately Held
SIC: 7692 Welding repair

(G-918)
MAXWELL WORLD (PA)
Also Called: Maxwell Historic Preservation
29092a Piney Neck Rd (19939-3819)
PHONE.....................937 463-3579
Dwight L Dowson, *President*
EMP: 4
SQ FT: 3,200
SALES: 500K Privately Held
SIC: 8412 7812 1751 Historical society; motion picture & video production; carpentry work

(G-919)
MCCOMRICK INSURANCE SERVICES
3394 N Main St (19939)
P.O. Box 8 (19939-0008)
PHONE.....................302 732-6655
Calvin McComrick, *President*
Jane McComrick, *Vice Pres*
Kelly Collins, *Manager*
Harriet Hannah,
EMP: 8
SALES (est): 1.1MM Privately Held
WEB: www.mccomrickinsurance.com
SIC: 6411 Insurance agents

(G-920)
MCGINNIS FARMS LLC
32738 Dupont Blvd (19939-4463)
P.O. Box 14 (19939-0014)
PHONE.....................302 841-8175
John Sertich, *President*
McGinnis Richard, *Co-Owner*
EMP: 1
SALES (est): 67.8K Privately Held
SIC: 3634 0251 Roasters, electric; broiling chickens, raising of

(G-921)
MEDIACOM LLC
32441 Royal Blvd (19939-3860)
PHONE.....................302 732-9332
David Kane, *Manager*
EMP: 65
SALES (corp-wide): 2.7B Privately Held
WEB: www.ridgenet.net
SIC: 4841 Cable television services
HQ: Mediacom Llc
1 Mediacom Way
Mediacom Park NY 10918

(G-922)
MICHAEL BUTTERWORTH DR
31059 Dupont Blvd (19939-4439)
PHONE.....................302 732-9850
Amy R Hall, *Principal*
Michael Butterworth, *Fmly & Gen Dent*
EMP: 7
SALES (est): 530K Privately Held
SIC: 8011 8021 Physicians' office, including specialists; offices & clinics of dentists

(G-923)
MORNING STAR CONSTRUCTION LLC
103 Wood Duck Ct (19939-2005)
PHONE.....................302 539-0791
Robert T Stephens,
Sherry Stephens,
EMP: 14
SALES (est): 1.2MM Privately Held
SIC: 1521 New construction, single-family houses

(G-924)
MORRIS E JUSTICE INC
33897 Em Calhoun Ln (19939-4171)
PHONE.....................302 539-7731
Morris Justice, *President*
Sara Justice, *Principal*
EMP: 5
SALES (est): 390K Privately Held
SIC: 4212 Dump truck haulage

(G-925)
NORTH STAR HEATING & AIR INC
Also Called: Honeywell Authorized Dealer
30968 Vines Creek Rd (19939-4357)
PHONE.....................302 732-3967
Harry Jarvis, *President*
Tina Jarvis, *Vice Pres*
EMP: 25
SQ FT: 10,000
SALES: 3MM Privately Held
WEB: www.northstar-hvac.com
SIC: 1711 Warm air heating & air conditioning contractor; heating & air conditioning contractors

(G-926)
NVR INC
32448 Royal Blvd Ste B (19939-3899)
PHONE.....................302 732-9900
Todd Hickman, *Manager*
EMP: 35 Publicly Held
WEB: www.nvrinc.com
SIC: 1521 New construction, single-family houses
PA: Nvr, Inc.
11704 Plaza America Dr # 500
Reston VA 20190

(G-927)
OCEAN VIEW PLUMBING INC
Also Called: Ocean View Plumbing & Heating
Rr 4 Box 21a (19939)
PHONE.....................302 732-9117
Richard Shaubach, *President*
Eric Ankrom, *Vice Pres*
Mariann Shaubach, *Treasurer*
EMP: 19
SQ FT: 9,999
SALES: 1MM Privately Held
WEB: www.oceanviewplumbing.com
SIC: 1711 Plumbing contractors

(G-928)
OX POND INDUSTRIES
29489 Colony Dr (19939-3319)
PHONE.....................703 608-7769
Bill McGrail, *Principal*
EMP: 2 EST: 2016
SALES (est): 83.2K Privately Held
SIC: 3544 Special dies, tools, jigs & fixtures

(G-929)
PENINSULA REGIONAL MEDICAL CTR
Also Called: Dagsboro Family Practice
Rts 113 & 26th (19939)
PHONE.....................302 732-8400
Ron Fisher, *Director*
EMP: 10
SALES (corp-wide): 411.6MM Privately Held
WEB: www.abilityrehab.com
SIC: 8062 8011 General medical & surgical hospitals; general & family practice, physician/surgeon
PA: Peninsula Regional Medical Center
100 E Carroll St
Salisbury MD 21801
410 546-6400

(G-930)
PIERSON CULVER LLC
27517 Hodges Ln (19939-5401)
PHONE.....................302 732-1145
Dean Pierson, *Principal*
EMP: 5
SALES (est): 390K Privately Held
SIC: 1521 4213 Mobile home repair, on site; mobile homes transport

(G-931)
PREFERRED AUTO AND CYCLE LLC
100 Deer Run (19939-9754)
PHONE.....................302 855-0169
Louis A Perticari,
EMP: 5 EST: 2011
SALES (est): 394K Privately Held
SIC: 7538 5521 General automotive repair shops; used car dealers

(G-932)
RIVER ASPHALT LLC
30548 Thorogoods Rd (19939-4528)
PHONE.....................302 934-0881
Steve Green, *Principal*
EMP: 5
SALES (est): 369.9K Privately Held
SIC: 1771 Blacktop (asphalt) work

(G-933)
SHUBERT ENTERPRISES INC
28091 Nine Foot Rd (19939-4432)
PHONE.....................714 595-5762
EMP: 4
SALES (est): 182.4K Privately Held
SIC: 0782 Landscape contractors

(G-934)
SOUTHERN STATES COOP INC
Also Called: Dagsboro Serv-Dagsboro BR
302 Clayton St (19939)
P.O. Box 278 (19939-0278)
PHONE.....................302 732-6651
Brian Schilling, *Branch Mgr*
EMP: 12
SALES (corp-wide): 1.9B Privately Held
SIC: 2048 2875 Prepared feeds; fertilizers, mixing only
PA: Southern States Cooperative, Incorporated
6606 W Broad St Ste B
Richmond VA 23230
804 281-1000

(G-935)
SUPERIOR DRYWALL INC
30996 Country Gdns Ste R1 (19939-5429)
P.O. Box 730, Millsboro (19966-0730)
PHONE.....................302 732-9800
Michael Myers, *President*
EMP: 10
SQ FT: 1,600
SALES (est): 1.1MM Privately Held
SIC: 1742 1721 Drywall; exterior residential painting contractor; interior residential painting contractor

(G-936)
SUSSEX VETERINARY HOSPITAL
30053 Vine St Rd (19939)
PHONE.....................302 732-9433
Gary Farmer Dvm, *Owner*
EMP: 5
SALES (est): 277.8K Privately Held
SIC: 0742 Animal hospital services, pets & other animal specialties

(G-937)
SYSTEMS TECH & SCIENCE LLC
34394 Indian River Dr (19939-3304)
PHONE.....................703 757-2010
William Evers, *President*
EMP: 6
SALES: 1MM Privately Held
SIC: 8748 Business consulting

(G-938)
THORO-GOODS CONCRETE CO INC (PA)
30548 Thorogoods Rd (19939-4528)
P.O. Box 407, Millsboro (19966-0407)
PHONE.....................302 934-8102
Frank W Thoroughgood, *President*

GEOGRAPHIC SECTION

Delaware City - New Castle County (G-966)

Glenn B Thoroughgood, *Vice Pres*
Shirley Wilson, *Treasurer*
EMP: 25
SALES (est): 2.8MM **Privately Held**
WEB: www.thorogoodsconcrete.com
SIC: 3273 Ready-mixed concrete

(G-939)
TRACY PEOPLES LLC
31039 Country Gdns (19939-5407)
PHONE...............................302 927-0280
Tracy Peoples, *Principal*
EMP: 4
SALES (est): 455.6K **Privately Held**
SIC: 6021 National commercial banks

(G-940)
TUCKAHOE ACRES CAMPING RESORT
36031 Tuckahoe Trl (19939-2003)
P.O. Box 7 (19939-0007)
PHONE...............................302 539-1841
Mark Browne, *President*
Van Browne, *Vice Pres*
EMP: 9 **EST:** 1966
SALES (est): 738.3K **Privately Held**
SIC: 7033 Trailer park

(G-941)
UNITED ELECTRIC SUPPLY CO INC
27519 Hodges Ln Bldg P (19939-5401)
PHONE...............................302 732-1291
Nick O'Lone, *Manager*
EMP: 7
SALES (corp-wide): 221.3MM **Privately Held**
WEB: www.unitedelectric.com
SIC: 5063 Electrical supplies
PA: United Electric Supply Company, Inc.
10 Bellecor Dr
New Castle DE 19720
800 322-3374

(G-942)
VIACARD CONCEPTS
322 Baywinds Ct (19939-9665)
PHONE...............................302 537-4602
Joseph Harris, *Principal*
EMP: 7
SALES (est): 882.4K **Privately Held**
SIC: 3089 Identification cards, plastic

(G-943)
WEST THIRD ENTERPRISES LLC
Also Called: Natural Lawn Care of America
30996 Country Gdns (19939-5429)
PHONE...............................302 732-3133
Thomas Deemido,
EMP: 4
SALES (est): 258.9K **Privately Held**
SIC: 0782 Lawn care services

(G-944)
WILKINS ENTERPRISES
Also Called: Clayton Theatre
E S Main St (19939)
PHONE...............................302 732-3744
Ronald Wilkins Jr, *Partner*
Ronald Wilkins Sr, *Partner*
Susan Wilkins, *Partner*
EMP: 4
SQ FT: 2,000
SALES (est): 194.8K **Privately Held**
SIC: 7832 Motion picture theaters, except drive-in

Delaware City
New Castle County

(G-945)
ABSOLUTE EQUITY
501 Clinton St (19706-7713)
PHONE...............................302 983-2591
Paul Zugehoer, *Partner*
Linda Zugehoer, *Partner*
EMP: 15
SQ FT: 1,000
SALES (est): 983K **Privately Held**
SIC: 1542 Commercial & office building contractors

(G-946)
AIRGAS USA LLC
4442 Wrangle Rd (19706)
P.O. Box 272 (19706-0272)
PHONE...............................302 834-7404
Ted Salazar, *Manager*
EMP: 30
SALES (corp-wide): 121.9MM **Privately Held**
WEB: www.airliquide.com
SIC: 5169 2813 Carbon dioxide; industrial gases
HQ: Airgas Usa, Llc
259 N Radnor Chester Rd
Radnor PA 19087
610 687-5253

(G-947)
AMAKOR INC
72 Clinton St (19706-7702)
P.O. Box 636 (19706-0636)
PHONE...............................302 834-8664
Ryan Jackson, *President*
Barbara Serbu, *Corp Secy*
Steve Serbu, *Vice Pres*
EMP: 10
SQ FT: 3,500
SALES (est): 4.5MM **Privately Held**
WEB: www.amakor.com
SIC: 1542 Commercial & office building, new construction; commercial & office buildings, renovation & repair

(G-948)
AMERICAN BIRDING ASSN INC (PA)
93 Clinton St Ste Aba (19706-7701)
P.O. Box 744 (19706-0744)
PHONE...............................302 838-3660
Lou Morrell, *Chairman*
EMP: 5
SALES (est): 1.3MM **Privately Held**
SIC: 8621 Scientific membership association

(G-949)
BILCARE RESEARCH INC
1389 School House Rd (19706)
P.O. Box 537 (19706-0537)
PHONE...............................302 838-3200
Kevin Stevens, *President*
William Timm, *Engineer*
Vineet Mehrota, *Exec Dir*
◆ **EMP:** 100
SALES (est): 45.3MM
SALES (corp-wide): 111.6MM **Privately Held**
WEB: www.ineosfilms.com
SIC: 2821 Vinyl resins
HQ: Bilcare Research Gmbh
Radebeulstr. 1
Staufen Im Breisgau 79219
763 381-10

(G-950)
CD CREAM
Also Called: Crabby Dick's Creamery
32 Clinton St (19706-7700)
PHONE...............................302 832-5425
EMP: 6 **EST:** 2015
SALES (est): 309.8K **Privately Held**
SIC: 2021 Creamery butter

(G-951)
CUTTING EDGE
511 5th St (19706)
P.O. Box 104 (19706-0104)
PHONE...............................302 834-8723
Sean Johnson, *Partner*
Steve Divirgilio, *Partner*
EMP: 12
SALES (est): 865.1K **Privately Held**
SIC: 0782 Lawn services

(G-952)
DELAWARE CITY FIRE CO NO 1
815 5th St (19706-7723)
P.O. Box 251 (19706-0251)
PHONE...............................302 834-9336
Paul H Johnson Sr, *President*
Donna Hensley, *Comp Spec*
Sharon Hart, *Director*
Robert Costango, *Assistant*
EMP: 4
SALES: 1.7MM **Privately Held**
SIC: 5099 Fire extinguishers

(G-953)
DELAWARE CITY RECREATION CLUB
5th And Wahington (19706)
P.O. Box 538 (19706-0538)
PHONE...............................302 834-9900
Shawn Wagner, *President*
Charles Hall, *President*
Lillard Brown, *Vice Pres*
Sandra Rynolds, *Admin Sec*
EMP: 7
SALES: 198.7K **Privately Held**
SIC: 8641 Bars & restaurants, members only; social club, membership; recreation association

(G-954)
DELAWARE CITY REFINING CO LLC
4550 Wrangle Hill Rd (19706)
P.O. Box 7000 (19706-7000)
PHONE...............................302 834-6000
Thomas Nimbley, *Branch Mgr*
EMP: 130
SALES (corp-wide): 27.1B **Publicly Held**
SIC: 1629 Oil refinery construction
HQ: Delaware City Refining Company Llc
1 Sylvan Way Ste 2
Parsippany NJ 07054

(G-955)
DELAWARE CY VLNTR FIRE CO NO 1
815 5th St (19706-7723)
P.O. Box 251 (19706-0251)
PHONE...............................302 834-9336
Wally Poppe, *President*
James D Rosseel, *Chief*
Edward A Kalinowski Sr, *Vice Pres*
EMP: 125
SQ FT: 27,000
SALES: 1.5MM **Privately Held**
SIC: 4119 0851 Ambulance service; fire prevention services, forest

(G-956)
DESIGN CRAFT
104 Clark Cir (19706-8720)
P.O. Box 4072 (19706-4072)
PHONE...............................302 834-3720
April Debendictis, *Owner*
Ozzie Debendictis, *Owner*
EMP: 3
SALES (est): 109.8K **Privately Held**
SIC: 2759 Commercial printing

(G-957)
FORAKER OIL INC
5th & Clinton St (19706)
P.O. Box 298 (19706-0298)
PHONE...............................302 834-7595
Warner T Foraker Jr, *President*
Lynn Foraker, *Treasurer*
EMP: 8
SQ FT: 2,000
SALES (est): 1.8MM **Privately Held**
SIC: 5983 4212 Fuel oil dealers; local trucking, without storage

(G-958)
FORMOSA PLASTICS CORP DELAWARE
Schoolhouse Rd (19706)
P.O. Box 320 (19706-0320)
PHONE...............................302 836-2200
Jason Lin, *President*
Ken Mounger, *Exec VP*
David Lin, *Treasurer*
Jung Rock Toss, *Manager*
EMP: 117
SQ FT: 225,000
SALES (est): 33.6MM **Privately Held**
WEB: www.fpcusa.com
SIC: 2821 Polyvinyl chloride resins (PVC)
HQ: Formosa Plastics Corporation, U.S.A.
9 Peach Tree Hill Rd
Livingston NJ 07039
973 992-2090

(G-959)
FORT DELAWARE SOCIETY
33 Staff Ln (19706)
P.O. Box 553 (19706-0553)
PHONE...............................302 834-1630
William Robelen, *President*

Edith Mahoney, *Vice Pres*
Kay Keenan, *Treasurer*
Thomas Smith, *Admin Sec*
EMP: 5
SALES: 42.4K **Privately Held**
SIC: 8999 Natural resource preservation service

(G-960)
MALGIERO HELEN A DAY CARE
311 Monroe St (19706-7743)
P.O. Box 4118 (19706-4118)
PHONE...............................302 834-9060
H Malgiero, *Principal*
EMP: 5
SALES (est): 62.4K **Privately Held**
SIC: 8351 Child day care services

(G-961)
NICKLE INSURANCE AGENCY INC
Also Called: Nationwide
119 Washington St (19706-7783)
P.O. Box 4080 (19706-4080)
PHONE...............................302 834-9700
Henry Nickle, *President*
EMP: 7
SQ FT: 1,500
SALES (est): 1.1MM **Privately Held**
SIC: 6411 6531 Insurance brokers; real estate brokers & agents

(G-962)
P S C CONTRACTING INC
704 5th St (19706-7810)
P.O. Box 319 (19706-0319)
PHONE...............................302 838-2998
Preston Carden, *President*
P Carden, *Owner*
EMP: 10
SALES: 3MM **Privately Held**
WEB: www.psccontracting.com
SIC: 1731 Electrical work

(G-963)
P S C ELECTRIC CONTRACTOR INC
704 5th St (19706-7810)
P.O. Box 319 (19706-0319)
PHONE...............................302 838-2998
Preston Carden, *CEO*
Bart Quick, *Sales Executive*
EMP: 15
SALES (est): 1MM **Privately Held**
SIC: 1731 General electrical contractor

(G-964)
PRO CLEAN WILMINGTON INC
Also Called: Pro Clean Company
210 Clinton St (19706-7708)
P.O. Box 638 (19706-0638)
PHONE...............................302 836-8080
William Baker, *President*
EMP: 5
SALES (est): 316.6K **Privately Held**
SIC: 1522 Residential construction

(G-965)
PROCLEAN INC
P.O. Box 638 (19706-0638)
PHONE...............................302 656-8080
William G Baker Sr, *President*
EMP: 20
SQ FT: 8,000
SALES (est): 670.8K **Privately Held**
SIC: 1799 7217 7216 5713 Cleaning building exteriors; carpet & furniture cleaning on location; curtain cleaning & repair; carpets

(G-966)
RALPH BURDICK DO
900 5th St (19706-7736)
P.O. Box 300 (19706-0300)
PHONE...............................302 834-3600
Ralph Burdick, *Owner*
Debbie S Romanoski, *Office Mgr*
EMP: 5 **EST:** 1987
SALES (est): 208.8K **Privately Held**
SIC: 8031 Offices & clinics of osteopathic physicians

(G-967)
SLICE OF WOOD LLC
70 Clinton St (19706-7702)
PHONE..................315 335-0917
Steve Redmond, *Owner*
EMP: 2
SALES (est): 95.5K **Privately Held**
SIC: 2511 Wood household furniture

(G-968)
VALLEN DISTRIBUTION INC
Also Called: Hagemeyer - Site X4
4550 Wrangle Hill Rd (19706)
PHONE..................856 542-1453
Nancy Kalinowsky, *Opers Mgr*
EMP: 4
SALES (corp-wide): 11.3MM **Privately Held**
SIC: 5084 Industrial machinery & equipment
HQ: Vallen Distribution, Inc.
    2100 The Oaks Pkwy
    Belmont NC 28012

Delmar
Sussex County

(G-969)
ALPHA TO OMEGA SIGNS
14413 Pepperbox Rd (19940-4155)
PHONE..................302 846-3865
EMP: 1
SALES (est): 46K **Privately Held**
SIC: 3993 Mfg Signs/Advertising Specialties

(G-970)
AMICK FARMS LLC
10392 Allens Mill Rd (19940-3517)
P.O. Box 269 (19940-0269)
PHONE..................302 846-9511
Scott Lee, *Manager*
Ricky Martinson, *Manager*
EMP: 60
SALES (est): 3.2MM **Privately Held**
SIC: 0191 General farms, primarily crop

(G-971)
APPLIANCES ZONE
34936 Sussex Hwy (19940-3351)
PHONE..................302 280-6073
Jose Correa, *Owner*
EMP: 4
SALES (est): 353.1K **Privately Held**
SIC: 5064 Electrical appliances, major

(G-972)
ATLANTIC IRRIGATION SPC INC
14413 Pepperbox Rd (19940-4155)
PHONE..................302 846-3527
Dale Carey, *Branch Mgr*
EMP: 4
SALES (corp-wide): 2.1B **Publicly Held**
SIC: 4971 Irrigation systems
HQ: Atlantic Irrigation Specialties, Inc.
    111 Lafayette Ave
    White Plains NY 10603
    914 686-0008

(G-973)
BAUSUM & DUCKETT ELC CO INC
38190 Old Stage Rd (19940-3550)
PHONE..................302 846-0536
John Dorsey, *Vice Pres*
EMP: 4
SALES (est): 245K
SALES (corp-wide): 15.5MM **Privately Held**
SIC: 1731 General electrical contractor
PA: Bausum & Duckett Electric Company, Inc.
    3481 Pike Ridge Rd
    Edgewater MD 21037
    410 269-6761

(G-974)
BRYAN & BRITTINGHAM INC
38148 Bi State Blvd (19940-3435)
P.O. Box 156 (19940-0156)
PHONE..................302 846-9500
Robert Messick, *President*
Margaret Messick, *Vice Pres*
EMP: 10
SQ FT: 22,500
SALES (est): 4MM **Privately Held**
WEB: www.bryanandbrittingham.com
SIC: 5191 5999 5251 Feed; feed & farm supply; hardware

(G-975)
BURKE EQUIPMENT COMPANY
Also Called: Kubota Authorized Dealer
11196 E Snake Rd (19940-3452)
PHONE..................302 248-7070
Chris Wagner, *Sales Staff*
Mark Timmons, *Branch Mgr*
EMP: 22
SALES (corp-wide): 9.7MM **Privately Held**
SIC: 5046 5083 Commercial equipment; farm & garden machinery
PA: Burke Equipment Company
    54 Andrews Lake Rd
    Felton DE 19943
    302 697-3200

(G-976)
BURKE EQUIPMENT COMPANY
11196 E Snake Rd (19940-3452)
PHONE..................302 248-7070
Chris Babbitt, *General Mgr*
Keith Pettit, *Branch Mgr*
EMP: 7
SALES (est): 584.6K
SALES (corp-wide): 9.7MM **Privately Held**
WEB: www.burkeequipment.com
SIC: 5046 Commercial equipment
PA: Burke Equipment Company
    54 Andrews Lake Rd
    Felton DE 19943
    302 697-3200

(G-977)
BURKE EQUIPMENT COMPANY
11196 E Snake Rd (19940-3452)
PHONE..................302 629-7500
Tim McUllem, *Branch Mgr*
EMP: 19
SALES (corp-wide): 9.7MM **Privately Held**
WEB: www.burkeequipment.com
SIC: 7514 Passenger car rental
PA: Burke Equipment Company
    54 Andrews Lake Rd
    Felton DE 19943
    302 697-3200

(G-978)
CAP MANAGMENT SERVICES LLC
10977 State St Unit 6 (19940-2442)
PHONE..................302 846-0120
EMP: 5
SALES (est): 240K **Privately Held**
SIC: 8741 Management Services

(G-979)
CARR COURIER SERVICE INC
12294 Coachmen Ln (19940-2432)
PHONE..................302 846-9826
Norman Carr, *Principal*
EMP: 5 EST: 2009
SALES (est): 150K **Privately Held**
SIC: 4215 Courier services, except by air

(G-980)
CASH ADVANCE PLUS
38650 Sussex Hwy Unit 8 (19940-3527)
PHONE..................302 846-3900
Ed Wilgus, *Owner*
EMP: 5
SALES (corp-wide): 3.4MM **Privately Held**
SIC: 6141 Personal credit institutions
PA: Cash Advance Plus
    N607 N 607 N Dual Hwy Rr
    Seaford DE 19973
    302 629-6266

(G-981)
CAT WELDING LLC
37544 Horsey Church Rd (19940-3279)
PHONE..................302 846-3509
Chad Avery Timmons, *Principal*
EMP: 1
SALES (est): 34.5K **Privately Held**
SIC: 7692 Welding repair

(G-982)
CHANCELLOR CARE CTR OF DELMAR
Also Called: Chancellor Care Center Delmar
101 Delaware Ave (19940-1110)
PHONE..................302 846-3077
Michel Augsburger, *President*
EMP: 101
SQ FT: 30,000
SALES (est): 3.7MM **Privately Held**
SIC: 8051 8052 Skilled nursing care facilities; intermediate care facilities

(G-983)
CHESLANTIC OVERHEAD DOOR
23 Shannon St (19940-1176)
PHONE..................443 880-0378
Philip L Donoway Jr, *Principal*
EMP: 3
SALES (est): 146.1K **Privately Held**
SIC: 3442 Garage doors, overhead: metal

(G-984)
CLASSIC CANVAS LLC
3505 May Twilley Rd (19940-3077)
PHONE..................443 359-0150
Joshua Littleton, *Principal*
EMP: 1
SALES (est): 51.2K **Privately Held**
SIC: 2211 Canvas

(G-985)
COLUMBIA VENDING SERVICE INC
10000 Old Racetrack Rd (19940-3495)
P.O. Box 449 (19940-0449)
PHONE..................302 856-7000
Mike Tyler, *Manager*
EMP: 10
SQ FT: 1,000
SALES (corp-wide): 6.7MM **Privately Held**
SIC: 5962 7699 Sandwich & hot food vending machines; vending machine repair
PA: Columbia Vending Service, Inc.
    6424 Frankford Ave 26
    Baltimore MD 21206
    410 485-3700

(G-986)
CONCRETE BLDG SYSTEMS DEL INC
Also Called: CBS
9283 Old Racetrack Rd (19940-3398)
P.O. Box 48 (19940-0048)
PHONE..................302 846-3645
Todd Stephens, *President*
Renae Stephens, *Admin Sec*
EMP: 25
SQ FT: 2,000
SALES (est): 4.1MM **Privately Held**
WEB: www.cbs-incorp.com
SIC: 3272 Prestressed concrete products

(G-987)
CRYSTAL PENN AVENUE LP
9317 Old Racetrack Rd (19940-3365)
PHONE..................302 846-0613
William Lo, *Partner*
Crystal Penn Avenue LLC, *Partner*
Shaun Smith, *QC Mgr*
Richard Gast, *Manager*
EMP: 80 **Privately Held**
SIC: 6719 Investment holding companies, except banks

(G-988)
CRYSTAL STEEL FABRICATORS INC
N 2nd (19940)
PHONE..................302 846-0277
Micheal Smith, *Manager*
Lisa Brenner, *Executive Asst*
EMP: 1 **Privately Held**
SIC: 3441 Fabricated structural metal
PA: Crystal Steel Fabricators Inc
    9317 Old Racetrack Rd
    Delmar DE 19940

(G-989)
CRYSTAL STEEL FABRICATORS INC (PA)
9317 Old Racetrack Rd (19940-3365)
PHONE..................302 846-0613
William Lo, *President*
Jeff Lo, *Director*
EMP: 128
SQ FT: 50,000
SALES (est): 54MM **Privately Held**
WEB: www.crystalsteel.com
SIC: 3441 Building components, structural steel

(G-990)
D&C LOGGING
16075 Russell Rd (19940-4137)
PHONE..................302 846-3982
David Carptner, *Owner*
EMP: 4
SALES (est): 273.2K **Privately Held**
SIC: 2411 Logging camps & contractors

(G-991)
DELMAR VAPOR LOUNGE
38660 Sussex Hwy Unit 2 (19940-3529)
PHONE..................302 907-0125
Sharon Donovan, *President*
EMP: 4 EST: 2014
SALES (est): 394.3K **Privately Held**
SIC: 5194 Smokeless tobacco

(G-992)
DELMARVA REFRIGERATION INC
504 N Pennsylvania Ave (19940-1137)
P.O. Box 38 (19940-0038)
PHONE..................302 846-2727
Lou Alberti, *President*
Cathy Alberti, *Vice Pres*
EMP: 9 EST: 1983
SQ FT: 3,000
SALES (est): 976.3K **Privately Held**
SIC: 7623 1711 5078 5074 Refrigeration repair service; warm air heating & air conditioning contractor; commercial refrigeration equipment; heating equipment (hydronic); air conditioning & ventilation equipment & supplies; electric household appliances

(G-993)
DICKERSON FENCE CO INC
36947 Saint George Rd (19940-3324)
PHONE..................302 846-2227
Scott Dickerson, *President*
Ronald Dickerson, *Vice Pres*
EMP: 7
SALES (est): 342.7K **Privately Held**
SIC: 1799 Fence construction

(G-994)
DUANE EDWARD RUARK
6988 Beagle Dr (19940-3171)
PHONE..................302 846-2332
Ketteh Ruark, *President*
EMP: 3
SALES: 400K **Privately Held**
SIC: 3531 Bulldozers (construction machinery)

(G-995)
E Z CASH OF DELAWARE INC (PA)
300 N Bi State Blvd Ste 1 (19940-1235)
PHONE..................302 846-2920
Marion Adkins, *President*
EMP: 6
SALES (est): 4MM **Privately Held**
SIC: 6099 Check cashing agencies

(G-996)
EGOLF FOREST HARVESTING INC
36642 Horsey Church Rd (19940-3269)
PHONE..................302 846-0634
Arthur Egolf, *President*
EMP: 1
SALES: 63K **Privately Held**
SIC: 3523 Planting, haying, harvesting & processing machinery

GEOGRAPHIC SECTION

Delmar - Sussex County (G-1028)

(G-997)
ELLIOTT JOHN
36411 August Rd (19940-2343)
PHONE 302 846-2487
John Elliott, *Owner*
EMP: 5 EST: 1945
SALES (est): 132.1K **Privately Held**
SIC: 0111 0115 0116 Wheat; corn; soybeans

(G-998)
EZ CASH OF NEW HAMPSHIRE INC
300 N Bi State Blvd Ste 2 (19940-1235)
PHONE 302 846-0464
Barbara Waters, *CEO*
EMP: 4
SALES (est): 368.8K **Privately Held**
SIC: 6099 6141 Check cashing agencies; personal credit institutions

(G-999)
GENERAL REFRIGERATION COMPANY (PA)
36615 Old Stage Rd (19940-2420)
P.O. Box 140 (19940-0140)
PHONE 302 846-3073
Rudolph Nechay, *President*
Frank Nechay, *President*
Eva M Nechay, *Corp Secy*
David Hartig, *Vice Pres*
EMP: 49
SQ FT: 18,000
SALES: 15.7MM **Privately Held**
WEB: www.generalrefrig.com
SIC: 1711 Refrigeration contractor

(G-1000)
H & J WRIGHT FAMILY FARMS LLC
4814 Blackwater Branch Rd (19940-3058)
PHONE 302 841-9002
Jeffrey Wright,
EMP: 4
SALES (est): 229.4K **Privately Held**
SIC: 0191 General farms, primarily crop

(G-1001)
HARRY H MC ROBIE
Also Called: Harry McRobie Farm
6872 Delmar Rd (19940-3161)
PHONE 302 846-9784
Harry Mc Robie, *Owner*
Barbara McRobie, *Owner*
EMP: 4
SALES (est): 166.5K **Privately Held**
SIC: 0291 7389 General farms, primarily animals;

(G-1002)
HARVEST MINISTRIES INC
305 N Bi State Blvd (19940-1212)
P.O. Box 506 (19940-0506)
PHONE 302 846-3001
Mark Frazier, *President*
EMP: 25
SALES: 55.7K **Privately Held**
SIC: 8699 Food co-operative

(G-1003)
HIGH TIDE TRUCKING INC
10256 Beauchamp Ln (19940-3453)
PHONE 302 846-3537
Robert Davis, *President*
EMP: 4
SALES: 497K **Privately Held**
SIC: 4212 Light haulage & cartage, local

(G-1004)
ILLUMINATION TECHNOLOGY INC
38024 N Spring Hill Rd (19940-3113)
PHONE 410 430-5349
EMP: 2
SALES (est): 88.3K **Privately Held**
SIC: 3646 Commercial indusl & institutional electric lighting fixtures

(G-1005)
J & A OVERHEAD DOOR INC
16937 Whitesville Rd (19940-4032)
PHONE 302 846-9915
Jason A Yoder Jr, *Owner*
Amy J Yoder, *Admin Sec*
EMP: 5
SQ FT: 2,400
SALES (est): 950K **Privately Held**
SIC: 1751 Garage door, installation or erection

(G-1006)
J WILLIAM GORDY FUEL CO (PA)
Also Called: Tiger Mart
106 N Pennsylvania Ave (19940-1133)
P.O. Box 268 (19940-0268)
PHONE 302 846-3425
J William Gordy, *President*
William E Gordy, *President*
Karen Gordy, *Treasurer*
EE Gordy, *Admin Sec*
EMP: 16
SQ FT: 3,000
SALES (est): 2.8MM **Privately Held**
SIC: 5411 5172 5541 Convenience stores; gasoline; gasoline service stations

(G-1007)
JERRY A FLETCHER
Also Called: Jerry A Fletcher Catering
34301 Rider Rd (19940-3001)
PHONE 302 875-9057
Jerry A Fletcher, *Principal*
EMP: 8
SALES (est): 362.3K **Privately Held**
SIC: 4899 Communication services

(G-1008)
JOB PRINTING
36729 Bi State Blvd (19940-3427)
PHONE 302 907-0416
Jeffrey F Walbert, *Principal*
EMP: 2
SALES (est): 141.8K **Privately Held**
SIC: 2752 Commercial printing, lithographic

(G-1009)
JOHNSON CONTROLS INC
34898 Sussex Hwy (19940-3395)
PHONE 302 715-5208
EMP: 3 **Privately Held**
SIC: 2531 Seats, automobile
HQ: Johnson Controls Inc
    5757 N Green Bay Ave
    Milwaukee WI 53209
    414 524-1200

(G-1010)
JONES FRANCINA
Also Called: Illuminations Training, Coachi
36114 Horsey Church Rd (19940-3222)
PHONE 302 245-4139
Francina Jones, *Owner*
EMP: 5 EST: 2011
SALES (est): 111.1K **Privately Held**
SIC: 8621 Education & teacher association

(G-1011)
JUDD BROOK 5 LLC
Also Called: Bobcat of Sussex County
36322 Sussex Hwy (19940-3573)
PHONE 302 846-3355
Daryl F Scott,
David R Scott,
EMP: 4
SALES (est): 884.8K **Privately Held**
SIC: 5083 5082 7353 Tractors, agricultural; construction & mining machinery; heavy construction equipment rental

(G-1012)
K AND B HVAC SVCS LLC
Also Called: Honeywell Authorized Dealer
18228 Whitesville Rd (19940-4024)
PHONE 302 846-3111
Brett Elkington, *Mng Member*
Keith Hornsby,
EMP: 7
SALES: 140K **Privately Held**
SIC: 1711 Heating & air conditioning contractors

(G-1013)
KENCO TROPHY SALES
301 Lincoln Ave (19940-1237)
PHONE 302 846-3339
Kenneth W Birch Sr, *Owner*
EMP: 2
SALES: 100K **Privately Held**
SIC: 2499 Trophy bases, wood

(G-1014)
LADYBUG PEST MANAGEMENT INC
15307 Britt Ln (19940-4167)
PHONE 302 846-2295
Sandra Honess, *Principal*
EMP: 7
SALES (est): 602.2K **Privately Held**
SIC: 7342 Pest control services

(G-1015)
LARRY HILL FARMS INC
Rr 1 Box 518 (19940)
PHONE 302 875-0886
Larry Hill, *President*
Alex Hill, *Vice Pres*
Bonnie Hill, *Treasurer*
Wade Hill, *Admin Sec*
EMP: 15
SALES (est): 1.4MM **Privately Held**
SIC: 1542 Farm building construction

(G-1016)
LARRY HILL FARMS LLC
36292 Old Stage Rd (19940-2411)
PHONE 302 245-6657
Larry Hill,
EMP: 10
SALES (est): 136.6K **Privately Held**
SIC: 0251 Broiling chickens, raising of

(G-1017)
LIL RED HEN NURSERY SCHL INC
400 N Bi State Blvd (19940-1205)
PHONE 302 846-2777
Ann Atkinson, *President*
Tom Atkinson, *Principal*
EMP: 24
SALES (est): 872.7K **Privately Held**
SIC: 8351 Group day care center

(G-1018)
MANUFACTURERS & TRADERS TR CO
Also Called: M&T
38716 Sussex Hwy (19940-3516)
PHONE 302 855-2297
Keith Atkins, *Branch Mgr*
EMP: 15
SALES (corp-wide): 6.4B **Publicly Held**
WEB: www.binghamlegg.com
SIC: 6022 State commercial banks
HQ: Manufacturers And Traders Trust Company
    1 M&T Plz Fl 3
    Buffalo NY 14203
    716 842-4200

(G-1019)
MCCALL HANDLING CO
38431 Sussex Hwy (19940-3511)
PHONE 302 846-2334
Kevin Harris, *Manager*
EMP: 14
SALES (corp-wide): 45.1MM **Privately Held**
WEB: www.mccallhandling.com
SIC: 5084 Materials handling machinery
PA: Mccall Handling Co.
    8801 Wise Ave Ste 200
    Baltimore MD 21222
    410 388-2600

(G-1020)
METAL SHOP
10690 Allens Mill Rd (19940-3532)
PHONE 302 846-2988
Sherry Disharoon, *Owner*
John Disharoon, *Co-Owner*
EMP: 12
SALES: 1MM **Privately Held**
SIC: 7699 7389 Welding equipment repair; metal cutting services

(G-1021)
MIRWORTH ENTERPRISE INC
Also Called: Children's Theater of Delmarva
404 Lincoln Ave (19940-1240)
P.O. Box 531 (19940-0531)
PHONE 302 846-0218
Carlos Mir, *Owner*
Ruth Colbourne, *E-Business*
EMP: 25
SALES (est): 407.4K **Privately Held**
SIC: 7922 Amateur theatrical company

(G-1022)
MONRO INC
Also Called: Mr Tire 1210
5 Gerald Ct (19940-3566)
PHONE 302 846-2732
William Hamm, *Branch Mgr*
EMP: 6
SALES (corp-wide): 1.2B **Publicly Held**
SIC: 5531 7549 7538 Automotive tires; automotive maintenance services; general automotive repair shops
PA: Monro, Inc.
    200 Holleder Pkwy
    Rochester NY 14615
    585 647-6400

(G-1023)
MOTION INDUSTRIES INC
38541 Sussex Hwy (19940-3512)
PHONE 302 462-3130
Berk Ruark, *General Mgr*
Kelly Larger, *Manager*
Andrew Manders, *Manager*
EMP: 12
SQ FT: 24,750
SALES (corp-wide): 18.7B **Publicly Held**
WEB: www.motion-ind.com
SIC: 5085 Industrial supplies
HQ: Motion Industries, Inc.
    1605 Alton Rd
    Birmingham AL 35210
    205 956-1122

(G-1024)
PENINSULA ANMAL HOSP ORTHPDICS
38375 Old Stage Rd (19940-3569)
PHONE 302 846-9011
Frances Haberstroh Ms, *Principal*
EMP: 9
SALES (est): 637.6K **Privately Held**
SIC: 0742 Animal hospital services, pets & other animal specialties

(G-1025)
PENINSULA TECHNICAL SERVICES I
38224 Old Stage Rd (19940-3547)
P.O. Box 149 (19940-0149)
PHONE 302 907-0554
Mark A Frazier, *Principal*
EMP: 3
SALES (est): 165.8K **Privately Held**
SIC: 7692 Welding repair

(G-1026)
PET MEDICAL CENTER
Rr 13 (19940)
PHONE 302 846-2869
Richard Long, *Owner*
EMP: 7
SALES (est): 291.2K **Privately Held**
SIC: 0742 Veterinarian, animal specialties

(G-1027)
REDHEAD FARMS LLC
34841 Columbia Rd (19940-3015)
PHONE 443 235-3990
Jerry Rider, *Principal*
EMP: 2
SALES (est): 500K **Privately Held**
SIC: 3523 Driers (farm): grain, hay & seed

(G-1028)
SHORT FUNERAL HOME INC (PA)
13 E Grove St (19940-1114)
P.O. Box 204 (19940-0204)
PHONE 302 846-9814
Amy Short, *President*
Tom Jewel, *Vice Pres*
EMP: 6
SQ FT: 5,800
SALES (est): 522K **Privately Held**
WEB: www.shortfh.com
SIC: 7261 5999 Funeral home; vaults & safes

Delmar - Sussex County (G-1029) — GEOGRAPHIC SECTION

(G-1029)
SHUBERT ENTERPRISES INC
Also Called: Scott & Sons Landscaping
11077 Iron Hill Rd (19940-3523)
PHONE 302 846-3122
Scott Shubert, *President*
Janie Shubert, *Corp Secy*
Monica Shubert, *Vice Pres*
EMP: 40 **EST:** 1997
SALES: 45K **Privately Held**
SIC: 0782 Landscape contractors

(G-1030)
SIMMONS ELECTRICAL SERVICE LLC
4663 White Deer Rd B (19940-3050)
PHONE 410 543-1480
Kermit Simmons, *President*
Gina Simmons, *General Mgr*
EMP: 4
SALES: 310K **Privately Held**
SIC: 1731 General electrical contractor

(G-1031)
STANLEY STEEMER INTL INC
1 Gerald Ct (19940-3566)
PHONE 302 907-0062
Lisa Farrell, *President*
EMP: 35
SALES (corp-wide): 227.2MM **Privately Held**
SIC: 7217 Carpet & furniture cleaning on location
PA: Stanley Steemer International, Inc.
  5800 Innovation Dr
  Dublin OH 43016
  614 764-2007

(G-1032)
SUNBELT RENTALS INC
36412 Sussex Hwy (19940-3501)
PHONE 302 907-1921
Joseph Bussard, *Branch Mgr*
EMP: 19
SALES (corp-wide): 5.9B **Privately Held**
SIC: 7353 Heavy construction equipment rental
HQ: Sunbelt Rentals, Inc.
  2341 Deerfield Dr
  Fort Mill SC 29715
  803 578-5811

(G-1033)
SUSSEX HYDRAULICS SALES & SVCS
12619 Line Rd (19940-2438)
PHONE 302 846-9702
Edward Thompson, *President*
Henry Mc Cann, *Corp Secy*
EMP: 4
SQ FT: 3,000
SALES (est): 590.1K **Privately Held**
SIC: 7699 5084 Hydraulic equipment repair; hydraulic systems equipment & supplies

(G-1034)
SVN COMMERCIAL REAL ESTATE
286 E Main St (19940)
PHONE 410 543-2440
Tom Knopp, *Principal*
EMP: 15
SALES (est): 327.4K **Privately Held**
SIC: 6531 Real estate agent, commercial

(G-1035)
TAX FREE LIQUORS
38627 Benro Dr Unit 7 (19940-3572)
PHONE 302 846-0410
Kirtin Patel, *Owner*
Melissa Anderson, *Broker*
EMP: 5
SALES (est): 384.9K **Privately Held**
SIC: 5182 Liquor

(G-1036)
TELCO ENVIROTROLS INC
105 E State St (19940-1155)
P.O. Box 467 (19940-0467)
PHONE 302 846-9103
Jeffrey Vernon, *Vice Pres*
Amber Ball, *Marketing Staff*
EMP: 10

SALES (est): 736.5K **Privately Held**
SIC: 4813 Local & long distance telephone communications

(G-1037)
TERRA FIRMA OF DELMARVA INC
36393 Sussex Hwy (19940-3500)
P.O. Box 478 (19940-0478)
PHONE 302 846-3350
Phillip W Pusey, *Principal*
Vicki Pusey, *Principal*
Chris Pusey, *Vice Pres*
Joyce Kayser, *Accounting Mgr*
Barbara Pusey, *Office Admin*
EMP: 12
SALES: 950K **Privately Held**
WEB: www.terrafirmacorp.com
SIC: 1794 1771 Excavation & grading, building construction; parking lot construction

(G-1038)
THERMO KING CORPORATION
Also Called: Thermo King Chesapeake
36550 Sussex Hwy (19940-3503)
PHONE 302 907-0345
Donald Hall, *Branch Mgr*
EMP: 20 **Privately Held**
WEB: www.thermoking.com
SIC: 5078 Refrigeration equipment & supplies
HQ: Thermo King Corporation
  314 W 90th St
  Minneapolis MN 55420
  952 887-2200

(G-1039)
THERMO KING CORPORATION
Also Called: Thermo King of Delaware
36550 Sussex Hwy (19940-3503)
P.O. Box 1642, Seaford (19973-8942)
PHONE 302 907-0345
Donald Hall, *Manager*
EMP: 24 **Privately Held**
WEB: www.thermoking.com
SIC: 5078 Refrigeration equipment & supplies
HQ: Thermo King Corporation
  314 W 90th St
  Minneapolis MN 55420
  952 887-2200

(G-1040)
TRIGLIA EXPRESS INC
38001 Bi State Blvd (19940-3433)
PHONE 302 846-2248
Joseph S Triglia III, *President*
Bernie Motkowski, *Treasurer*
Tracy Triglia, *Admin Sec*
EMP: 20
SQ FT: 100,000
SALES (est): 3.1MM **Privately Held**
SIC: 4731 Freight forwarding

(G-1041)
TRIGLIA TRANS CO
Bystate Blvd (19940)
P.O. Box 218 (19940-0218)
PHONE 302 846-3795
Rosemary Lynch, *President*
Toney Triglia, *Vice Pres*
Carrie Williams, *Manager*
EMP: 25
SALES (est): 505.3K **Privately Held**
SIC: 7363 Truck driver services

(G-1042)
TRIGLIAS TRANSPORTATION CO
Rr 13 Box A (19940)
P.O. Box 187 (19940-0187)
PHONE 302 846-2141
Rosemary Lynch, *President*
Anthony Triglia, *Vice Pres*
Justin Lych, *Treasurer*
George Lynch, *Admin Sec*
EMP: 20 **EST:** 1940
SQ FT: 7,200
SALES: 1.5MM **Privately Held**
SIC: 4212 4213 Delivery service, vehicular; contract haulers

(G-1043)
TRINITY MEDICAL CENTER PA
8 E Grove St (19940-1115)
PHONE 302 846-0618
Khalil Gorgui, *Principal*
EMP: 5 **EST:** 2008
SALES (est): 316.3K **Privately Held**
SIC: 8031 8011 Offices & clinics of osteopathic physicians; medical centers

(G-1044)
U S 13 DRAGWAY INC (PA)
Also Called: Delaware Intl Speedway
36952 Sussex Hwy (19940-3507)
PHONE 302 875-1911
Charles Cathell, *President*
Hal Cathell, *Vice Pres*
Juanita Cathell, *Treasurer*
Joyce Cathell, *Admin Sec*
EMP: 66
SQ FT: 8,000
SALES (est): 3.3MM **Privately Held**
WEB: www.us13dragway.com
SIC: 7948 Automotive race track operation

(G-1045)
UNITED RENTALS NORTH AMER INC
38352 Sussex Hwy (19940-3508)
PHONE 302 846-0955
Bruce Austin, *Manager*
EMP: 10
SALES (corp-wide): 8B **Publicly Held**
WEB: www.unitedrentals.com
SIC: 7359 Rental store, general
HQ: United Rentals (North America), Inc.
  100 Frederick St 700
  Stamford CT 06902
  203 622-3131

(G-1046)
UNITED RENTALS NORTH AMER INC
38190 Old Stage Rd A (19940-3550)
PHONE 302 907-0292
Kenny Midgett, *Manager*
EMP: 5
SALES (corp-wide): 8B **Publicly Held**
WEB: www.thompsonpump.com
SIC: 5084 Pumps & pumping equipment
HQ: United Rentals (North America), Inc.
  100 Frederick St 700
  Stamford CT 06902
  203 622-3131

(G-1047)
WELDING BY JACKSON
10178 Jackson St (19940-3301)
P.O. Box 39 (19940-0039)
PHONE 302 846-3090
Helen Jackson, *Principal*
EMP: 2
SALES (est): 132.4K **Privately Held**
SIC: 7692 Welding repair

(G-1048)
WHITETAIL COUNTRY LOG & HLG
Also Called: Whitetail Country Log & Hlg
16075 Russell Rd (19940-4137)
PHONE 302 846-3982
David Carpenter, *President*
EMP: 4
SALES (est): 416.6K **Privately Held**
WEB: www.whitetaillogging.com
SIC: 2411 0811 4212 Logging; timber tracts; local trucking, without storage

(G-1049)
WIDGEON ENTERPRISES INC
38204 Old Stage Rd (19940-3547)
P.O. Box 468 (19940-0468)
PHONE 302 846-9763
David P Widgeon, *President*
Faye Widgeon, *Corp Secy*
Larry Widgeon, *Vice Pres*
EMP: 6
SALES (est): 582.1K **Privately Held**
SIC: 7699 5046 Scale repair service; scales, except laboratory

(G-1050)
YODER OVERHEAD DOOR COMPANY
Also Called: Yoder Overhead Door Co.
36318 Sussex Hwy (19940-3573)
PHONE 302 875-0663
Nolan Brunk, *General Mgr*
Joe Centineo, *Sales Staff*
Dave Bear, *Traffic Dir*
EMP: 6
SQ FT: 3,300
SALES (est): 736.6K **Privately Held**
SIC: 1751 7699 Garage door, installation or erection; door & window repair

---

Dewey Beach
Sussex County

(G-1051)
ADAMS OCEANFRONT RESORT
Also Called: Adams Oceanfront Villas
4 Read Ave (19971-2311)
PHONE 302 227-3030
Harold E Dukes Jr, *Owner*
EMP: 12 **EST:** 1976
SQ FT: 14,000
SALES (est): 444.1K **Privately Held**
WEB: www.adamsoceanfront.com
SIC: 7011 Motels

(G-1052)
ATLANTIC VIEW MOTEL
2 Clayton St (19971-2307)
PHONE 302 227-3878
Kenneth Simpler, *Owner*
EMP: 12
SALES: 800K **Privately Held**
SIC: 7011 Motels

(G-1053)
BAKED LLC
2000 Coastal Hwy (19971-2355)
PHONE 302 212-5202
Pam Minhas, *Owner*
EMP: 5 **EST:** 2014
SALES (est): 375.5K **Privately Held**
SIC: 5149 Bakery products

(G-1054)
BELL BUOY MOTEL
Also Called: Bellbuoy Inn
21 Vandyke St (19971-2510)
PHONE 302 227-6000
Tim Mahoney, *Partner*
EMP: 5
SALES (est): 214.2K **Privately Held**
WEB: www.bellbuoyinn.com
SIC: 7011 Motels

(G-1055)
DEWEY BEACH HOUSE
Also Called: Beach House Dewey Hotel
1710 Coastal Hwy (19971-2333)
PHONE 302 227-4000
Stuart Beinstbin, *President*
Michael Fitzmaurice, *General Mgr*
Doug Compher, *Agent*
EMP: 20
SALES (est): 1.1MM **Privately Held**
SIC: 7011 Motels

(G-1056)
DEWEY BEER & FOOD COMPANY LLC
Also Called: Dewey Beer Company
2100 Coastal Hwy (19971-2317)
PHONE 302 227-1182
Brandon Smith, *Principal*
Scot Kaufman, *Principal*
Mike Reilly, *Principal*
EMP: 3 **EST:** 2016
SALES (est): 136.2K **Privately Held**
SIC: 2082 5813 Beer (alcoholic beverage); beer garden (drinking places)

(G-1057)
FELLS POINT SURF CO LLC
23 Bellevue St (19971-2301)
PHONE 302 212-2005
EMP: 2
SALES (est): 115.1K **Privately Held**
SIC: 3949 Surfboards

GEOGRAPHIC SECTION
Dover - Kent County (G-1090)

(G-1058)
GRACELAND GROUP INC
113 Dickinson St (19971-2403)
PHONE.....................302 226-1373
EMP: 4
SALES (est): 215K **Privately Held**
SIC: 8748 Business consulting

(G-1059)
MOORE PARTNERSHIP
Also Called: Bay Resort Motel
126 Bellevue St (19971-3202)
P.O. Box 461, Rehoboth Beach (19971-0461)
PHONE.....................302 227-5253
Robert H Moore, *Partner*
Ronald T Moore, *Partner*
EMP: 15
SQ FT: 20,700
SALES (est): 913.8K **Privately Held**
WEB: www.bayresort.com
SIC: 7011 Motels

(G-1060)
SURF CLUB
1 Read Ave (19971-2311)
PHONE.....................302 227-7059
Carol Smith, *Manager*
Charlie Hammer, *Manager*
EMP: 6
SALES (est): 406.8K **Privately Held**
SIC: 7011 Resort hotel; motels

(G-1061)
VENUS ON HALFSHELL
136 Dagsworthy Ave (19971)
PHONE.....................302 227-9292
Bill Galbraith, *Principal*
EMP: 7
SALES (est): 229.7K **Privately Held**
SIC: 5812 5146 Eating places; fish & seafoods

Dover
Kent County

(G-1062)
1 A LIFESAFER INC
280 N Dupont Hwy (19901-7510)
PHONE.....................800 634-3077
EMP: 1
SALES (corp-wide): 4.3MM **Privately Held**
SIC: 3829 Measuring & controlling devices
PA: 1 A Lifesafer, Inc.
4290 Glendale Milford Rd
Blue Ash OH 45242
513 651-9560

(G-1063)
1080 SLVER LK BLVD OPRTONS LLC
Also Called: Silver Lake Center
1080 Silver Lake Blvd (19904-2410)
PHONE.....................610 444-6350
Dave Almquist,
Mike Reitz,
EMP: 205
SALES (est): 6.1MM **Privately Held**
SIC: 8051 Convalescent home with continuous nursing care

(G-1064)
1203 WALKER RD OPERATIONS LLC
Also Called: Heritage At Dover
1203 Walker Rd (19904-6541)
PHONE.....................302 735-8800
Michele Weeks, *Human Res Dir*
EMP: 112
SALES (est): 849.6K **Publicly Held**
WEB: www.genesishcc.com
SIC: 8051 Skilled nursing care facilities
HQ: Genesis Healthcare Llc
101 E State St
Kennett Square PA 19348

(G-1065)
1203 WALKER RD OPERATIONS LLC
Also Called: Heritage At Dover
1203 Walker Rd (19904-6541)
PHONE.....................610 444-6350
EMP: 811
SALES (est): 4.7MM **Publicly Held**
SIC: 8051 Skilled nursing care facilities
HQ: Genesis Healthcare Llc
101 E State St
Kennett Square PA 19348

(G-1066)
1ST CAPITOL MORTGAGE INC
9 E Loockerman St Ste 207 (19901-7347)
PHONE.....................302 674-5540
Larry Knopf, *General Mgr*
EMP: 4
SQ FT: 3,606
SALES (est): 536.7K **Privately Held**
SIC: 6162 Mortgage bankers & correspondents

(G-1067)
1ST STATE POWER CLEAN LLC
1609 Forrest Ave (19904-9725)
PHONE.....................302 735-7974
Dennis W Rogers Jr,
EMP: 5
SALES (est): 264.2K **Privately Held**
SIC: 7699 Cleaning services

(G-1068)
302 AQUATICS LLC
79 Aintree Ln (19904-1062)
PHONE.....................302 222-4807
Joe Olive,
EMP: 5
SALES (est): 221K **Privately Held**
SIC: 3644 Scrubbers for CATV systems

(G-1069)
3RDGP LLC
8 The Grn Ste A (19901-3618)
PHONE.....................905 330-3335
Brian Semkiw, *CEO*
Rui Mendes,
EMP: 10
SALES (est): 217.5K **Privately Held**
SIC: 7371 Computer software development & applications

(G-1070)
44 AASHA HOSPITALITY ASSOC LLC
Also Called: Hilton
1706 N Dupont Hwy (19901-2219)
PHONE.....................302 674-3784
Nuveen Karkura,
EMP: 31
SALES (est): 985K **Privately Held**
SIC: 7011 Hotels & motels

(G-1071)
764 DOVER LEIPSIC LLC
Also Called: Comfort Suites
1654 N Dupont Hwy (19901-2217)
PHONE.....................302 736-1204
Mahesh Patel,
EMP: 10
SALES (est): 761.9K **Privately Held**
SIC: 7011 Hotel, franchised

(G-1072)
A & G KRAMEDAS ASSOCIATES LLC
Also Called: Comfort Inn
222 S Dupont Hwy (19901-3797)
PHONE.....................302 674-3300
Tom Kimmetas,
EMP: 14
SALES (est): 965.2K **Privately Held**
SIC: 7011 Hotels & motels

(G-1073)
A & G REALTY LLC
Also Called: Comfort Inn
222 S Dupont Hwy (19901-3797)
PHONE.....................302 674-3300
Tom Kimmetas,
Abelina Kramedas,
EMP: 50
SALES (est): 1.4MM **Privately Held**
SIC: 7011 Hotels & motels

(G-1074)
A CENTER FOR MNTAL WLLNESS INC
121 W Loockerman St (19904-7325)
PHONE.....................302 674-1397
Lauren E Tinsley, *President*
EMP: 15
SALES (est): 1.8MM **Privately Held**
SIC: 8011 Offices & clinics of medical doctors

(G-1075)
AAA CLUB ALLIANCE INC
Also Called: AAA Dover
124 Greentree Dr (19904-7648)
PHONE.....................302 674-8020
Donna Jackson, *General Mgr*
EMP: 12
SALES (corp-wide): 528.9MM **Privately Held**
WEB: www.aaamidatlantic.net
SIC: 8699 4724 6331 Automobile owners' association; travel agencies; fire, marine & casualty insurance
PA: Aaa Club Alliance Inc.
1 River Pl
Wilmington DE 19801
302 299-4700

(G-1076)
AAFTON RESEARCH & MEDIA INC
73 Greentree Dr 47 (19904-7646)
PHONE.....................617 407-6619
James A Scott, *President*
EMP: 1
SALES (est): 74.8K **Privately Held**
SIC: 2732 Book printing

(G-1077)
AAG LA LLC
160 Greentree Dr Ste 101 (19904-7620)
PHONE.....................305 801-7900
Mohammad Ali, *Principal*
EMP: 1
SALES (est): 40.5K **Privately Held**
SIC: 2741

(G-1078)
ABSOLUTE CYBER DEFENSE
8 The Grn Ste A (19901-3618)
PHONE.....................850 532-0233
EMP: 2
SALES (est): 87.4K **Privately Held**
SIC: 3812 Defense systems & equipment

(G-1079)
ACCELERTRAIN COMPANY LIMITED
8 The Grn Ste A (19901-3618)
PHONE.....................413 599-0450
Matthew Spriegel, *CEO*
EMP: 4
SALES: 40K **Privately Held**
SIC: 7371 Computer software development & applications

(G-1080)
ACCESS DENTAL LLC
446a S New St (19904-6725)
PHONE.....................302 674-3303
Karen Rose,
Russell Rose,
EMP: 8
SALES (est): 200K **Privately Held**
SIC: 8021 Dentists' office

(G-1081)
ACCESS LABOR SERVICE INC
1102 S State St Ste 1 (19901-4124)
PHONE.....................302 741-2575
Butch Brooks, *Branch Mgr*
EMP: 45
SALES (corp-wide): 3.5MM **Privately Held**
SIC: 7363 Temporary help service
PA: Access Labor Service Inc
2203 N Dupont Hwy
New Castle DE 19720
302 326-2575

(G-1082)
ACCUTAX
408 Martin St (19901-4530)
PHONE.....................302 735-9747
Debbie Clough, *Owner*
EMP: 5
SALES (est): 306.2K **Privately Held**
SIC: 8721 Accounting, auditing & bookkeeping

(G-1083)
ACM CORP
Also Called: American Consumer Marketing
218 Canal St (19904-5729)
PHONE.....................302 736-3864
EMP: 15
SQ FT: 4,000
SALES: 2.2MM **Privately Held**
SIC: 5141 Whol General Groceries

(G-1084)
ACTORS ATTIC
Also Called: Bewitched
540 Otis Dr (19901-4630)
PHONE.....................302 734-8214
Susan Betts, *Owner*
EMP: 2
SQ FT: 8,000
SALES (est): 300K **Privately Held**
WEB: www.actorsattic.com
SIC: 5999 7359 2395 Theatrical equipment & supplies; equipment rental & leasing; embroidery & art needlework

(G-1085)
ACUPOINT THERAPEUTICS
165 Chucker Xing (19904-5574)
PHONE.....................302 734-7716
EMP: 8
SALES (est): 73.3K **Privately Held**
SIC: 8093 Rehabilitation center, outpatient treatment

(G-1086)
ADFERNS MEDIA LLC
8 The Grn (19901-3618)
PHONE.....................315 444-7720
Ankitt Kumar Pathak, *Mng Member*
EMP: 6
SALES: 80K **Privately Held**
SIC: 7371 7389 Computer software development & applications;

(G-1087)
ADMIRAL TIRE
Also Called: Edge Water Tire
280 Cowgill St (19901-4500)
P.O. Box 699, Edgewater MD (21037-0699)
PHONE.....................302 734-5911
Bob Wilson, *President*
EMP: 9 **EST:** 1979
SQ FT: 6,400
SALES (est): 1.1MM **Privately Held**
SIC: 7538 5531 5014 General automotive repair shops; automotive tires; automobile tires & tubes

(G-1088)
ADVANCED BIO-ENERGY TECH INC
3500 S Dupont Hwy (19901-6041)
PHONE.....................347 363-9927
EMP: 1
SALES (est): 72K **Privately Held**
SIC: 2869 Fuels

(G-1089)
ADVANCED ENDOSCOPY CENTER LLC
742 S Governors Ave Ste 2 (19904-4111)
PHONE.....................302 678-0725
Natwarlal V Ramani MD, *Mng Member*
V Ramani, *Manager*
EMP: 6
SALES (est): 384.2K **Privately Held**
WEB: www.aec-gi.com
SIC: 8011 Endocrinologist

(G-1090)
ADVANTECH INCORPORATED
151 Garrison Oak Dr (19901-3364)
PHONE.....................302 674-8405
Eric Schaeffer, *President*
Melville Warren, *Treasurer*
John Gampp, *Director*
EMP: 40
SQ FT: 4,500

Dover - Kent County (G-1091) — GEOGRAPHIC SECTION

SALES (est): 7.6MM **Privately Held**
WEB: www.advantechsecurity.net
SIC: **7382** Security systems services

(G-1091)
AFFINITY HOMECARE SERVICES
1040 S State St (19901-6925)
PHONE.................................302 264-9363
EMP: 7
SALES (est): 67.2K **Privately Held**
SIC: **8082** Home health care services

(G-1092)
AFRICAN MARKETS FUND LLC
8 The Grn Ste A (19901-3618)
PHONE.................................703 944-1514
EMP: 1
SALES (est): 37K **Privately Held**
SIC: **7389** 6726 1099 1061 Fund raising organizations; management investment funds, closed-end; tin ore mining; tantalite mining

(G-1093)
AFTERMATH SERVICES LLC
160 Greentree Dr Ste 101 (19904-7620)
PHONE.................................302 357-3780
Amanda Ellison, *Owner*
EMP: 35
SALES (corp-wide): 16.1MM **Privately Held**
SIC: **6512** Commercial & industrial building operation
HQ: Aftermath Services Llc
  75 Executive Dr Ste 200
  Aurora IL 60504
  630 551-0735

(G-1094)
AGFIRST FARM CREDIT BANK
1410 S State St (19901-4948)
P.O. Box 418 (19903-0418)
PHONE.................................302 734-7534
Steven O'Shea, *Vice Pres*
Martin Desmond, *Manager*
EMP: 8
SALES (corp-wide): 883.9MM **Privately Held**
WEB: www.countrymortgages.com
SIC: **6111** Federal & federally sponsored credit agencies
PA: Agfirst Farm Credit Bank
  1901 Main St
  Columbia SC 29201
  803 799-5000

(G-1095)
AGRICULTURE UNITED STATES DEPT
800 S Bay Rd Ste 2 (19901-4685)
PHONE.................................302 741-2600
Edwin Alexander, *Branch Mgr*
EMP: 8 **Publicly Held**
SIC: **8999** Artists & artists' studios
HQ: United States Department Of Agriculture
  1400 Independence Ave Sw
  Washington DC 20250
  202 720-3631

(G-1096)
AHL ORTHODONTICS
1004 S State St (19901-6901)
PHONE.................................302 678-3000
Jamie Ahl, *Owner*
EMP: 8
SALES (est): 531.5K **Privately Held**
SIC: **8021** Orthodontist

(G-1097)
AIRESPA WORLDWIDE WHL LLC
8 The Grn (19901-3618)
PHONE.................................908 227-4441
J Henry Scott,
EMP: 2
SALES: 1MM **Privately Held**
SIC: **3599** Air intake filters, internal combustion engine, except auto

(G-1098)
AIRWAVE TECHNOLOGY
1238 Forrest Ave (19904-3311)
PHONE.................................302 734-7838
David Moses, *Owner*
Cecilia V Moses, *Partner*
EMP: 4
SALES: 200K **Privately Held**
SIC: **5731** 1731 Antennas, satellite dish; high fidelity stereo equipment; television sets; communications specialization

(G-1099)
AIVO AMERICA CORP
160 Greentree Dr (19904-7620)
PHONE.................................415 849-2288
Martin Sebastian Frascaroli, *CEO*
Augusto Oliva, *Administration*
EMP: 2
SALES (est): 32.7K **Privately Held**
SIC: **7372** Prepackaged software

(G-1100)
AJS CROCHETS
1679 S State St Trlr A32 (19901-5111)
PHONE.................................302 257-0381
Amanda Givens, *Principal*
EMP: 1
SALES (est): 48.8K **Privately Held**
SIC: **2399** Hand woven & crocheted products

(G-1101)
ALBERT S LAMBERTSON INC
2433 Central Church Rd (19904-1221)
P.O. Box 491 (19903-0491)
PHONE.................................302 734-9649
EMP: 8 EST: 1950
SQ FT: 600
SALES (est): 880K **Privately Held**
SIC: **1542** 1521 Nonresidential Construction Single-Family House Construction

(G-1102)
ALEX VAUGHAN MOBILE ENTRTNMNT
509 Dyke Branch Rd (19901-1548)
P.O. Box 1921 (19903-1921)
PHONE.................................302 674-2464
Alex Vaughan, *Owner*
EMP: 6
SALES (est): 113.2K **Privately Held**
SIC: **7929** Entertainers & entertainment groups

(G-1103)
ALFRED LAUDER DDS
33 Gooden Ave (19904-4143)
PHONE.................................302 678-9742
Alfred Lauder DDS, *Owner*
EMP: 5
SALES (est): 199.5K **Privately Held**
SIC: **8021** Dentists' office

(G-1104)
ALICE M MEHAFFEY
Also Called: Kitten's Quilting & Embroidery
1896 Upper King Rd (19904-6400)
PHONE.................................302 697-1893
Alice Mehaffey, *Principal*
EMP: 1
SALES (est): 71.4K **Privately Held**
SIC: **2395** Embroidery & art needlework

(G-1105)
ALL IN ONE BRANDS LLC
8 The Grn Ste 6817 (19901-3618)
PHONE.................................301 323-8144
Luis Correa, *Principal*
Daniel Guadalupe,
Angela Guadalupe,
Gloria Guadalupe,
Miguel Guadalupe,
EMP: 5
SALES (est): 124.8K **Privately Held**
SIC: **8742** Management consulting services

(G-1106)
ALL LIVES MATTER LLC
8 The Grn Ste A (19901-3618)
PHONE.................................252 767-9291
Nilin Patel, *Principal*
EMP: 3
SALES (est): 71.1K **Privately Held**
SIC: **7372** 7389 Application computer software;

(G-1107)
ALL SMILES FAMILY & COSME
95 Wolf Creek Blvd Ste 3 (19901-4965)
PHONE.................................302 734-5303
Neena Mukkamala, *Principal*
EMP: 5
SALES (est): 431.1K **Privately Held**
SIC: **8021** Dentists' office

(G-1108)
ALLAN MYERS MATERIALS INC
3700 S Bay Rd (19901-5905)
PHONE.................................302 734-8632
James Miller, *Branch Mgr*
EMP: 4
SALES (corp-wide): 881MM **Privately Held**
SIC: **5211** 5032 Masonry materials & supplies; paving materials
HQ: Allan Myers Materials, Inc.
  1805 Berks Rd
  Worcester PA 19490
  610 560-7900

(G-1109)
ALLAN MYERS MD INC
440 Twin Oak Dr (19904-1908)
PHONE.................................302 883-3501
Bobby Shade, *Manager*
EMP: 154
SALES (corp-wide): 881MM **Privately Held**
SIC: **1611** General contractor, highway & street construction
HQ: Allan Myers Md, Inc.
  2011 Bel Air Rd
  Fallston MD 21047
  410 776-2000

(G-1110)
ALLIED ANESTHESIA ASSOC LLC
75 Old Mill Rd (19901-6290)
PHONE.................................302 547-3620
Steven Shields, *Principal*
EMP: 5
SALES (est): 178.8K **Privately Held**
SIC: **8011** Anesthesiologist

(G-1111)
ALOE & CARR PA
Also Called: Cammarato & Aloe PA
850 S State St Ste 2 (19901-4113)
PHONE.................................302 736-6631
Vincent Cammarato, *Owner*
EMP: 6
SALES (est): 545.9K **Privately Held**
SIC: **8021** Endodontist

(G-1112)
ALS POWER WASHING SERVICE
Also Called: Al's Vinyl Cleaning Service
213 Rose Bowl Rd (19904-1106)
PHONE.................................302 399-3406
Alfred S Tunnell, *President*
EMP: 4
SALES (est): 124.3K **Privately Held**
WEB: www.alspowerwashingservice.com
SIC: **7349** Exhaust hood or fan cleaning

(G-1113)
ALTEA RESOURCES LLC
3500 S Dupont Hwy (19901-6041)
PHONE.................................713 242-1460
Armand Pasteur,
EMP: 77
SQ FT: 764
SALES (est): 3.7MM **Privately Held**
SIC: **8711** 7361 Petroleum, mining & chemical engineers; employment agencies

(G-1114)
ALTR SOLUTIONS LLC
8 The Grn Ste A (19901-3618)
PHONE.................................888 757-2587
Pete Martin,
EMP: 10
SALES (est): 221.8K **Privately Held**
SIC: **7372** 5734 Business oriented computer software; software, business & non-game

(G-1115)
AMAA MANAGEMENT CORPORATION
Also Called: Comfort Inn
764 Dover Leipsic Rd (19901-2055)
PHONE.................................302 677-0505
Shalin Patel, *President*
Nilesh Patel, *Vice Pres*
EMP: 15
SALES (est): 781.8K **Privately Held**
SIC: **7011** Hotels & motels

(G-1116)
AMC MUSEUM FOUNDATION
1301 Heritage Rd (19902)
P.O. Box 2050 (19902-2050)
PHONE.................................302 677-5938
Michael Quarnaccio, *Chairman*
Mike Leister, *Director*
EMP: 8
SALES (est): 204.7K **Privately Held**
SIC: **5399** 7997 8412 Army-Navy goods; aviation club, membership; museum

(G-1117)
AMEDISYS INC
Also Called: Home Hlth Care Amer An Amdisys
1221 College Park Dr # 203 (19904-8726)
PHONE.................................302 678-4764
Patti Contino, *Branch Mgr*
EMP: 28 **Publicly Held**
SIC: **8082** Home health care services
PA: Amedisys, Inc.
  3854 American Way Ste A
  Baton Rouge LA 70816

(G-1118)
AMERICAN CHIROPRACTIC CENTER
230 Beiser Blvd Ste 101 (19904-7791)
PHONE.................................302 450-3153
Michael Sharkey, *Principal*
EMP: 8
SALES (est): 77.4K **Privately Held**
SIC: **8041** Offices & clinics of chiropractors

(G-1119)
AMERICAN GEN TRDG CONTG US INC
Also Called: Agtus
73 Greentree Dr 519 (19904-7646)
PHONE.................................804 739-1480
Courtney Sledge, *President*
EMP: 4
SALES (est): 206.1K **Privately Held**
WEB: www.agtus.com
SIC: **8748** Business consulting

(G-1120)
AMERICAN LUNG ASSOCIATION
Also Called: American Lung Assn In Del
422 S Governors Ave (19904-6735)
PHONE.................................302 674-9701
Deb Brown, *CEO*
EMP: 7
SALES (corp-wide): 42.8MM **Privately Held**
WEB: www.alase.org
SIC: **8621** Health association
PA: American Lung Association
  55 W Wacker Dr Ste 1150
  Chicago IL 60601
  312 801-7600

(G-1121)
AMPX2 INC
615 S Dupont Hwy (19901-4517)
P.O. Box 7188, Tempe AZ (85281-0007)
PHONE.................................650 521-5750
Thomas Clements, *President*
EMP: 9
SALES: 1.6MM **Privately Held**
SIC: **7371** 7389 Computer software development;

(G-1122)
ANAMO INC
28 Old Rudnick Ln (19901-4912)
PHONE.................................702 852-2992
Harry McNab, *Director*
Alex Podobas, *Director*
Jonathan Goetsch, *Admin Sec*
EMP: 3

SALES (est): 71.1K **Privately Held**
SIC: 7372 Prepackaged software

(G-1123)
ANATROPE INC
3500 S Dupont Hwy (19901-6041)
PHONE..............................202 507-9441
Tiffany RAD, *CEO*
Teague Newman, *Co-Owner*
EMP: 2
SALES (est): 85.9K **Privately Held**
SIC: 3571 Electronic computers

(G-1124)
ANDREAS RAUER MD PA
16 Old Rudnick Ln (19901-4912)
PHONE..............................302 734-1760
Andreas Rauer, *Owner*
EMP: 9
SALES (est): 572.3K **Privately Held**
SIC: 8011 General & family practice, physician/surgeon

(G-1125)
ANDY MAST
Also Called: Mast Harness Shop
1269 Seeneytown Rd (19904-4442)
PHONE..............................302 653-5014
Andy Mast, *Owner*
EMP: 1
SALES (est): 82.4K **Privately Held**
SIC: 3199 5159 Feed bags for horses; horses

(G-1126)
ANGLE PLANNING CONCEPTS
31 Saulsbury Rd B (19904-3444)
PHONE..............................302 735-7526
John Rowley, *President*
EMP: 15
SALES (est): 1.8MM **Privately Held**
SIC: 7389 Design services

(G-1127)
ANIMAL INN INC
2308 Seeneytown Rd (19904-1650)
PHONE..............................302 653-5560
Gail Warren, *President*
Debbie Eckels, *Vice Pres*
EMP: 6
SALES (est): 210K **Privately Held**
SIC: 0752 Boarding services, kennels; grooming services, pet & animal specialties

(G-1128)
ANTHONY STREETT
Also Called: Executive Touch
24 Verona Ct (19904-0985)
PHONE..............................302 528-2861
Anthony Streett, *Owner*
EMP: 1
SALES (est): 53.2K **Privately Held**
SIC: 3721 Aircraft

(G-1129)
ANTITOXIN TECHNOLOGIES INC
8 The Grn Ste A (19901-3618)
PHONE..............................650 304-0608
Zohar Levkovitz, *Principal*
EMP: 24
SALES (est): 433.3K **Privately Held**
SIC: 7371 Computer software development

(G-1130)
APPA INC
8 The Grn Ste 7868 (19901-3618)
PHONE..............................302 440-1448
Luisa Manyoma, *COO*
EMP: 8
SALES (est): 113.1K **Privately Held**
SIC: 4812 Cellular telephone services

(G-1131)
APPIC STARS LLC
8 The Grn Ste 4524 (19901-3618)
PHONE..............................903 224-6469
Aliaksandr Istamianok, *CEO*
EMP: 5
SALES: 500K **Privately Held**
SIC: 7371 Computer software development & applications

(G-1132)
APPLIED BIOFEEDBACK SOLUTIONS
1485 S Governors Ave (19904-7017)
PHONE..............................302 674-3225
Robert A Gorkin, *Principal*
EMP: 5 EST: 2010
SALES (est): 109.4K **Privately Held**
SIC: 8093 Mental health clinic, outpatient

(G-1133)
APPLIED RESEARCH ASSOC INC
Also Called: Mantech
909 Arnold Drive Ext (19902-5009)
P.O. Box 2063 (19902-2063)
PHONE..............................302 677-4147
Timothy McHale, *Manager*
EMP: 62
SALES (corp-wide): 251.9MM **Privately Held**
WEB: www.ara.com
SIC: 8731 8748 Engineering laboratory, except testing; environmental consultant
PA: Applied Research Associates, Inc.
4300 San Mateo Blvd Ne
Albuquerque NM 87110
505 883-3636

(G-1134)
ARDEXO INC
Also Called: Ardexo Housing Solutions
8 The Grn Ste 4810 (19901-3618)
PHONE..............................855 617-7500
Robert Caskey, *CEO*
EMP: 6
SQ FT: 500
SALES (est): 135.8K **Privately Held**
SIC: 7371 7373 8741 7372 Computer software systems analysis & design, custom; office computer automation systems integration; business management; prepackaged software; document & office records storage

(G-1135)
AREAS USA DD LLC
1131 N Dupont Hwy (19901-2008)
PHONE..............................302 674-1946
EMP: 5
SALES (est): 260K **Privately Held**
SIC: 8021 Dentist's Office

(G-1136)
ARIIO INC
8 The Grn Ste 8074 (19901-3618)
PHONE..............................562 481-8717
Armand Atinkpahoun, *Principal*
EMP: 5
SALES (est): 178.9K **Privately Held**
SIC: 4226 Special warehousing & storage

(G-1137)
ARMED FORCES MED EXAMINER SYS
115 Purple Heart Ave (19902-5051)
PHONE..............................302 346-8653
Lauryne Morris, *Comptroller*
Lanelle Chisolm, *Administration*
EMP: 99
SQ FT: 117,000
SALES (est): 3.1MM **Privately Held**
SIC: 8071 9711 Pathological laboratory; Army

(G-1138)
ARMY & AIR FORCE EXCHANGE SVC
Also Called: Dover Afb Child Care Center
260 Chad St (19902-5260)
PHONE..............................302 677-3716
Patty Porter, *Director*
EMP: 65 **Publicly Held**
WEB: www.aafes.com
SIC: 8351 9711 Group day care center; Air Force;
HQ: Army & Air Force Exchange Service
3911 S Walton Walker Blvd
Dallas TX 75236
214 312-2011

(G-1139)
ARMY & AIR FORCE EXCHANGE SVC
Also Called: Dover Afb Aero Club
447 Tuskegee Blvd (19902-5447)
PHONE..............................302 677-6365
EMP: 4 **Publicly Held**
WEB: www.aafes.com
SIC: 7997 9711 Aviation club, membership; Air Force;
HQ: Army & Air Force Exchange Service
3911 S Walton Walker Blvd
Dallas TX 75236
214 312-2011

(G-1140)
ARMY & AIR FORCE EXCHANGE SVC
Also Called: Dover Afb Beauty Salon
266 Galaxy St (19902-5266)
PHONE..............................302 734-8262
EMP: 6 **Publicly Held**
SIC: 7231 9711 Beauty Shop
HQ: Army & Air Force Exchange Service
3911 S Walton Walker Blvd
Dallas TX 75236
214 312-2011

(G-1141)
ARTHUR W HENRY DDS INC
748 S New St (19904-3573)
PHONE..............................302 734-8101
Arthur W Henry DDS, *President*
EMP: 6
SALES (est): 295K **Privately Held**
SIC: 8021 Dentists' office

(G-1142)
ARTISANS BANK INC
1555 S Governors Ave (19904-7019)
PHONE..............................302 674-3214
Kathleen Cooper, *Manager*
EMP: 8
SALES (corp-wide): 22.8MM **Privately Held**
WEB: www.artisansbank.com
SIC: 6036 6035 State savings banks, not federally chartered; savings institutions, federally chartered
PA: Artisans Bank Inc
2961 Centerville Rd # 101
Wilmington DE 19808
302 658-6881

(G-1143)
ARYVVE TECHNOLOGIES LLC
1675 S State St Ste B (19901-5140)
PHONE..............................678 977-1252
Ray Lee, *Mng Member*
EMP: 5 EST: 2018
SALES (est): 86.8K **Privately Held**
SIC: 4121 Taxicabs

(G-1144)
ASHER B CAREY III (PA)
Also Called: Center For Plastic/Rconstructv
200 Banning St Ste 370 (19904-3490)
PHONE..............................302 678-3443
Asher B Carey III, *Owner*
EMP: 6
SALES (est): 622.7K **Privately Held**
SIC: 8011 Plastic surgeon

(G-1145)
ASLIN INC
Also Called: Simpson Log Homes
2143 Lockwood Chapel Rd (19904-5021)
PHONE..............................302 674-1900
EMP: 3
SQ FT: 10,000
SALES (est): 309.1K **Privately Held**
SIC: 1521 2411 Log Home Mfg & Construction

(G-1146)
ASPIRE ENERGY LLC
909 Silver Lake Blvd (19904-2409)
PHONE..............................330 682-7726
Sydney H Davis, *General Mgr*
EMP: 6
SALES (est): 262.1K **Privately Held**
SIC: 4911 Distribution, electric power

(G-1147)
ASPLUNDH TREE EXPERT CO
100 Carlsons Way Ste 14 (19901-2365)
PHONE..............................302 678-4702
Steve Miller, *Vice Pres*
EMP: 300
SALES (corp-wide): 4.5B **Privately Held**
WEB: www.asplundh.com
SIC: 1629 1623 Railroad & subway construction; land clearing contractor; water, sewer & utility lines
PA: Asplundh Tree Expert, Llc
708 Blair Mill Rd
Willow Grove PA 19090
215 784-4200

(G-1148)
ASSISTED LIVING CONCEPTS LLC
Also Called: Dover Place
1203 Walker Rd (19904-6541)
PHONE..............................302 735-8800
Beth Kelly, *Branch Mgr*
EMP: 8
SALES (corp-wide): 298.2MM **Privately Held**
SIC: 8361 Residential care
HQ: Assisted Living Concepts, Llc
330 N Wabash Ave Ste 3700
Chicago IL 60611

(G-1149)
ASSOCIATED SVC SPECIALIST INC
Also Called: Psycho Therapeutic Services
630 W Division St Ste E (19904-2760)
PHONE..............................302 672-7159
Sharon Stevens, *Branch Mgr*
EMP: 10
SALES (corp-wide): 86.2MM **Privately Held**
SIC: 8361 Children's home
PA: Associated Service Specialist, Inc.
870 High St Ste 2
Chestertown MD 21620
410 778-9114

(G-1150)
ASSOCIATES CONTRACTING INC
Also Called: Honeywell Authorized Dealer
1661 S Dupont Hwy (19901-5129)
P.O. Box 796 (19903-0796)
PHONE..............................302 734-4311
James Morris, *President*
Wayne Reed, *Treasurer*
George Brown, *Admin Sec*
EMP: 14
SQ FT: 6,000
SALES (est): 1.8MM **Privately Held**
SIC: 1711 1731 Plumbing contractors; warm air heating & air conditioning contractor; general electrical contractor

(G-1151)
AT HOME CARE AGENCY
57 Saulsbury Rd (19904-3479)
PHONE..............................302 883-2059
EMP: 8
SALES (est): 61.1K **Privately Held**
SIC: 8082 Home health care services

(G-1152)
AT HOME INFUCARE LLC
373 W North St Ste A (19904-6748)
PHONE..............................302 883-2059
George Aboagye, *Principal*
EMP: 5
SALES (est): 127.9K **Privately Held**
SIC: 8082 Home health care services

(G-1153)
AT&T MOBILITY LLC
Also Called: Cingular Wireless
275 N Dupont Hwy (19901-7509)
PHONE..............................302 674-4888
Felicia Baker, *Manager*
EMP: 10
SALES (corp-wide): 170.7B **Publicly Held**
WEB: www.cingular.com
SIC: 4812 Cellular telephone services

Dover - Kent County (G-1154)   GEOGRAPHIC SECTION

HQ: At&T Mobility Llc
 1025 Lenox Park Blvd Ne
 Brookhaven GA 30319
 800 331-0500

(G-1154)
ATHARI INC
278 Jordan Dr (19904-2005)
PHONE..................312 358-4933
Oluwapelumi Adeleke, *Principal*
EMP: 10
SALES (est): 57.1K **Privately Held**
SIC: **8699** Charitable organization

(G-1155)
ATI HOLDINGS LLC
Also Called: ATI Physical Therapy
1288 S Governors Ave (19904-4802)
PHONE..................302 677-0100
Jamie Smoot, *Branch Mgr*
EMP: 21
SALES (corp-wide): 338.3MM **Privately Held**
SIC: **8049** Physical therapist
PA: Ati Holdings, Llc
 790 Remington Blvd
 Bolingbrook IL 60440
 630 296-2222

(G-1156)
ATI HOLDINGS LLC
Also Called: ATI Physical Therapy
260 Beiser Blvd Ste 102 (19904-5773)
PHONE..................302 741-0200
Chris Bethard, *Branch Mgr*
EMP: 21
SALES (corp-wide): 338.3MM **Privately Held**
SIC: **8049** Physical therapist
PA: Ati Holdings, Llc
 790 Remington Blvd
 Bolingbrook IL 60440
 630 296-2222

(G-1157)
ATLANTIC MARKETING INC
5 Maggies Way Ste 6 (19901-4893)
P.O. Box 518 (19903-0518)
PHONE..................302 674-7036
Phillip A Adams, *President*
EMP: 5
SQ FT: 3,000
SALES (est): 600K **Privately Held**
WEB: www.atlantic-marketing.com
SIC: **5045** Computers, peripherals & software

(G-1158)
ATRIA MEDICAL INC (PA)
160 Greentree Dr Ste 101 (19904-7620)
PHONE..................407 334-5190
Ori Ben-Amotz, *CEO*
Nissim Darvish, *Chairman*
EMP: 4
SQ FT: 1,400
SALES (est): 811K **Privately Held**
SIC: **8733** Medical research

(G-1159)
AUDTRA BENEFIT CORP
8 The Grn Ste A (19901-3618)
PHONE..................800 991-5156
B Van Dam, *CEO*
EMP: 1
SALES (est): 33.1K **Privately Held**
SIC: **7372** Application computer software

(G-1160)
AURUM CAPITAL VENTURES INC
3500 S Dupont Hwy (19901-6041)
PHONE..................877 467-7780
John Paul Baric, *Principal*
EMP: 5 EST: 2018
SALES (est): 164.3K **Privately Held**
SIC: **6799** Venture capital companies

(G-1161)
AVIAN PRODUCTIONS INC
8 The Grn Ste 4876 (19901-3618)
PHONE..................302 526-0542
Darran Ingretolli, *CEO*
EMP: 4
SALES (est): 58.6K **Privately Held**
SIC: **7812** Motion picture & video production

(G-1162)
AXIA MANAGEMENT
222 S Dupont Hwy Frnt (19901-3778)
PHONE..................302 674-2200
Tom Kramedas, *Partner*
Greg Kramedas, *Partner*
Tina Kramedas, *Partner*
EMP: 300
SALES (est): 18.8MM **Privately Held**
SIC: **8741** Hotel or motel management

(G-1163)
AXIOM RESOURCES LLC
160 Greentree Dr Ste 101 (19904-7620)
PHONE..................410 756-0440
Brandon Kaissi, *General Mgr*
EMP: 10 EST: 2016
SALES (est): 215.9K **Privately Held**
SIC: **7379**

(G-1164)
B JAMES ROGGE DDS
838 Walker Rd Ste 21-1 (19904-2751)
PHONE..................302 736-1423
B James Rogge DDS, *Owner*
EMP: 6
SALES (est): 273.1K **Privately Held**
SIC: **8021** Oral pathologist; dentists' office

(G-1165)
B M A CENTRAL DELAWARE
655 S Bay Rd Ste 4m (19901-4656)
PHONE..................302 678-5718
EMP: 4
SALES (est): 73.7K **Privately Held**
SIC: **8069** Specialty Hospital

(G-1166)
B P SERVICES
Also Called: BP
547 N Bradford St (19904-7205)
PHONE..................302 399-4132
Joseph Mesick, *Executive Asst*
EMP: 6
SALES (est): 149.2K **Privately Held**
SIC: **8999** Personal services

(G-1167)
B SAFE INC
Also Called: Delaware Electric Signal
1490 E Lebanon Rd (19901-5833)
PHONE..................302 422-3916
EMP: 25
SALES (corp-wide): 6.9MM **Privately Held**
SIC: **1731** **7382** Fire detection & burglar alarm systems specialization; telephone & telephone equipment installation; burglar alarm maintenance & monitoring; fire alarm maintenance & monitoring
PA: B Safe, Inc.
 109 Baltimore Ave
 Wilmington DE 19805
 302 633-1533

(G-1168)
BAIRD MANDALAS BROCKSTEDT LLC (PA)
6 S State St (19901-7363)
PHONE..................302 677-0061
Kevin Baird, *Principal*
Karen Baird, *Controller*
Ed Tarlov, *Admin Sec*
EMP: 17
SALES (est): 2.8MM **Privately Held**
SIC: **8111** General practice attorney, lawyer

(G-1169)
BANFIELD & TEMPERLEY INC
8 The Grn Ste A (19901-3618)
PHONE..................347 878-6057
James Marlow, *Director*
EMP: 3
SALES (est): 105.2K **Privately Held**
SIC: **5052** 1011 Coal & other minerals & ores; iron ores

(G-1170)
BANK AMERICA NATIONAL ASSN
1404 Forrest Ave Ste 5 (19904-3478)
PHONE..................302 674-5379
EMP: 7
SALES (corp-wide): 101.7B **Publicly Held**
SIC: **6162** Mortgage Banker/Correspondent
HQ: Bank Of America, National Association
 101 S Tryon St Ste 1000
 Charlotte NC 28202
 704 386-5000

(G-1171)
BAQ LOGISTICS LLC
8 The Grn Ste 8118 (19901-3618)
PHONE..................302 401-6466
Tonya Bailey,
EMP: 4
SALES (est): 141K **Privately Held**
SIC: **4213** Trucking, except local

(G-1172)
BARBARAS DANCE ACADEMY
1151 E Lebanon Rd Ste F (19901-5829)
PHONE..................302 883-4355
Barbara McDonald, *Owner*
EMP: 4
SALES (est): 65.8K **Privately Held**
SIC: **7911** Dance studio & school

(G-1173)
BARRETT BUSINESS SERVICES INC
Also Called: Bbsi
116 E Water St (19901-3614)
PHONE..................302 674-2206
Larry Lewis, *Manager*
EMP: 5
SQ FT: 1,375
SALES (corp-wide): 940.7MM **Publicly Held**
SIC: **7361** 7363 Employment agencies; temporary help service
PA: Barrett Business Services Inc
 8100 Ne Parkway Dr # 200
 Vancouver WA 98662
 360 828-0700

(G-1174)
BARROS MC NAMARA MALKWCZ & TAY
2 W Loockerman St (19904-7324)
P.O. Box 1298 (19903-1298)
PHONE..................302 734-8400
Edward McNamara, *President*
Michael Malkiewicz, *Vice Pres*
Patk Scanlon,
EMP: 25
SALES (est): 2.7MM **Privately Held**
SIC: **8111** General practice attorney, lawyer

(G-1175)
BARRY USA INC
874 Walker Rd Ste C (19904-2778)
PHONE..................800 305-2673
Peter Barry, *President*
EMP: 1
SALES (corp-wide): 1MM **Privately Held**
SIC: **2298** Wire rope centers
PA: Barry Usa Inc.
 104 Alan Dr
 Newark DE 19711
 800 305-2673

(G-1176)
BASCO PHYSICAL THERAPY
1410 Joshua Clayton Rd (19904-7006)
PHONE..................302 730-1294
Willie Basco, *Principal*
EMP: 5
SALES (est): 87.5K **Privately Held**
SIC: **8049** Physical therapist

(G-1177)
BASEMARK INC (PA)
3500 S Dupont Hwy (19901-6041)
PHONE..................832 483-7093
Tero Sarkkinen, *CEO*
Eric Zapalac, *Vice Pres*
EMP: 2
SALES: 3MM **Privately Held**
SIC: **7372** Application computer software

(G-1178)
BATTLE PROVEN FOUNDATION
368 Artis Dr (19904-5643)
P.O. Box 710672, Herndon VA (20171-0672)
PHONE..................703 216-1986
Terrence Hill, *Chairman*
Stephen Fails, *Exec Dir*
EMP: 7 EST: 2012
SALES (est): 75.9K **Privately Held**
SIC: **8641** Veterans' organization

(G-1179)
BAY DEVELOPERS INC
200 Weston Dr (19904-2786)
PHONE..................302 736-0924
Henry S Mast, *President*
Donna Seibert, *Admin Asst*
Tammy Mast, *Real Est Agnt*
EMP: 12
SALES (est): 8MM **Privately Held**
SIC: **1542** 1521 Commercial & office building, new construction; new construction, single-family houses

(G-1180)
BAYHEALTH MED CTR INC-OCC HLTH
Also Called: Healthworks
1275 S State St (19901-6927)
PHONE..................302 678-1303
Dennis E Klima, *Chairman*
John T Fifer, *Vice Chairman*
Gerald L White, *CFO*
EMP: 25
SALES (est): 2.2MM **Privately Held**
SIC: **8062** General medical & surgical hospitals

(G-1181)
BAYHEALTH MEDICAL CENTER INC
Purchasing Department
35 Commerce Way Ste 100 (19904-5747)
PHONE..................302 744-7033
Debbie Betts, *Manager*
EMP: 60 **Privately Held**
SIC: **8099** Health screening service
PA: Bayhealth Medical Center, Inc.
 640 S State St
 Dover DE 19901

(G-1182)
BAYHEALTH MEDICAL CENTER INC (PA)
640 S State St (19901-3530)
PHONE..................302 422-3311
Kathy Kucek, *CEO*
Terry Murphy, *President*
Diane Andrews, *Counsel*
Eric Gloss, *Vice Pres*
John Vangorp, *Vice Pres*
EMP: 32
SALES (est): 677.8MM **Privately Held**
SIC: **8062** General medical & surgical hospitals

(G-1183)
BEACH ASSOCIATES INC
Also Called: R.R. Beach Associates
9 E Loockerman St Ste 2a (19901-7343)
PHONE..................866 744-9911
Jay Schukoske, *President*
Shelby Truesdale, *Vice Pres*
Mike Scher, *Engineer*
Jennifer Truesdale, *Treasurer*
Kaci Townsend, *Assistant*
EMP: 19
SQ FT: 2,000
SALES (est): 1.6MM **Privately Held**
WEB: www.beachassoc.com
SIC: **7322** Collection agency, except real estate

(G-1184)
BEAR ASSOCIATES LLC
209 Massey Dr (19904-5882)
PHONE..................302 735-5558
Mark Mougel,
Laurie Mougel,
EMP: 5
SQ FT: 2,201
SALES (est): 362K **Privately Held**
SIC: **7336** Art design services

GEOGRAPHIC SECTION — Dover - Kent County (G-1218)

(G-1185)
BEATDAPP INC
9 E Loockerman St Ste 311 (19901-8305)
PHONE 310 903-0244
Morgan Hayduk, *Mng Member*
EMP: 6
SALES (est): 133.8K **Privately Held**
SIC: 8731 7372 Commercial physical research; prepackaged software

(G-1186)
BEAUTY MAX INC
1634 S Governors Ave (19904-7004)
PHONE 302 735-1705
Sung Kim, *President*
EMP: 2 EST: 1997
SALES (est): 224.4K **Privately Held**
SIC: 2842 7231 Specialty cleaning, polishes & sanitation goods; beauty shops

(G-1187)
BEAUTY PURSE INC
3500 S Dupont Hwy (19901-6041)
P.O. Box 1276, Madison AL (35758-5276)
PHONE 424 210-7474
Josiah Harry, *CEO*
EMP: 4
SALES (est): 92.1K **Privately Held**
SIC: 7389 Business services

(G-1188)
BECAUSE LOVE ALLOWS COMPASSION
270 Beechwood Ave (19901-5233)
PHONE 302 674-2496
Anne Coleman, *Owner*
Shakira Hameen, *Admin Sec*
EMP: 25
SALES (est): 225.4K **Privately Held**
SIC: 8699 Charitable organization

(G-1189)
BECKER MORGAN GROUP INC
309 S Governors Ave (19904-6705)
PHONE 302 734-7950
Christopher Weeks, *Business Mgr*
Gregory Z Moore, *Branch Mgr*
EMP: 11
SALES (corp-wide): 17.1MM **Privately Held**
WEB: www.beckermorgan.com
SIC: 8711 8712 Civil engineering; architectural services
PA: Becker Morgan Group Inc
    312 W Main St Ste 3fl
    Salisbury MD 21801
    410 546-9100

(G-1190)
BEGINNINGS AND BEYOND INC
402 Cowgill St (19901-4512)
PHONE 302 734-2464
Danielle Harrison, *President*
EMP: 11
SALES (est): 338.7K **Privately Held**
SIC: 8351 Preschool center

(G-1191)
BENEVLENT PRTECTIVE ORDER ELKS
Also Called: ELKS LODGE 1903
200 Saulsbury Rd (19904-2721)
PHONE 302 736-1903
Richard Woodhall, *President*
EMP: 25
SQ FT: 4,000
SALES: 322.9K **Privately Held**
SIC: 8699 Charitable organization

(G-1192)
BENNETT DET PRTECTIVE AGCY INC (PA)
Also Called: Bennett Security Service
335 Martin St (19901-4527)
P.O. Box 344 (19903-0344)
PHONE 302 734-2480
Edward J Bennett, *CEO*
Judy L Bennett, *Corp Secy*
EMP: 6
SQ FT: 2,200
SALES (est): 4MM **Privately Held**
SIC: 7381 Protective services, guard; detective agency

(G-1193)
BENNIE SMITH FUNERAL HOME INC (PA)
717 W Division St (19904-2731)
P.O. Box 691 (19903-0691)
PHONE 302 678-8747
Bennie Smith, *President*
EMP: 9
SALES (est): 1.6MM **Privately Held**
WEB: www.benniesmithfuneralhome.com
SIC: 7261 Funeral home; funeral director

(G-1194)
BERNARD A LEWIS DDS
149 Great Geneva Dr (19901-5870)
PHONE 302 943-0456
Bernard Lewis, *Principal*
EMP: 4
SALES (est): 255K **Privately Held**
SIC: 8021 Offices & clinics of dentists

(G-1195)
BERNARD LIMPERT
Also Called: Stage One
1465 S Governors Ave (19904-7017)
PHONE 302 674-8280
Billy J Smith, *President*
Bernard Limpert, *Owner*
EMP: 5
SALES (est): 324.8K **Privately Held**
SIC: 7538 7539 7533 General automotive repair shops; brake services; muffler shop, sale or repair & installation

(G-1196)
BERRY INTERNATIONAL INC
606 Pear St Unit 1 (19904)
PHONE 302 674-1300
W Brock Berry, *President*
EMP: 9
SQ FT: 105,000
SALES: 1MM **Privately Held**
SIC: 4212 Moving services
PA: Diamond State Corporation
    602 Pear St
    Dover DE 19904

(G-1197)
BEST ROOFING AND SIDING CO
5091 N Dupont Hwy (19901-2346)
PHONE 302 678-5700
John Gearhart, *Owner*
EMP: 8
SALES (est): 393.9K **Privately Held**
SIC: 1761 Roofing contractor

(G-1198)
BESTEMPS
Also Called: Bestemps of Dover
385 W North St (19904-6748)
PHONE 302 674-4357
Patsy Ware, *President*
Kari Jenkins, *Treasurer*
EMP: 5 EST: 2007
SALES (est): 397.4K **Privately Held**
SIC: 7363 Help supply services

(G-1199)
BETH SHOLOM CONGREGATION
Also Called: Sisterhood of Congregation
340 N Queen St (19904-3026)
PHONE 302 734-5578
Frank Ceback, *President*
EMP: 60 EST: 1945
SALES (est): 2.6MM **Privately Held**
SIC: 5947 8399 Gift shop; fund raising organization, non-fee basis

(G-1200)
BFPE INTERNATIONAL INC
155 Commerce Way (19904-8306)
PHONE 302 346-4800
Michelle Herdman, *Manager*
EMP: 18
SALES (corp-wide): 109.1MM **Privately Held**
SIC: 8322 Community center
PA: Bfpe International, Inc.
    7512 Connelley Dr
    Hanover MD 21076
    410 768-2200

(G-1201)
BIGGS SWELL C MSEUM AMERCN ART
Also Called: Biggs Museum of American Art
406 Federal St (19901-3615)
P.O. Box 711 (19903-0711)
PHONE 302 674-2111
Terry Jackson, *President*
Jennifer Sauselein, *Marketing Staff*
Linda Danko, *Director*
EMP: 4
SALES (est): 1MM **Privately Held**
WEB: www.biggsmuseum.org
SIC: 8412 Museum

(G-1202)
BILL TORBERT
335 Grey Fox Ln (19904-1099)
PHONE 302 734-9804
Bill Torbert, *Principal*
William C Torbert, *Principal*
EMP: 10
SALES (est): 301.7K **Privately Held**
SIC: 7389

(G-1203)
BILLS HOME CARE SERVICE LLC
160 Beech Dr (19904-9439)
PHONE 302 526-2071
Mark Wojtkiewicz, *Principal*
EMP: 8 EST: 2018
SALES (est): 61.1K **Privately Held**
SIC: 8082 Home health care services

(G-1204)
BIOMECHSYS INCORPORATED
160 Greentree Dr Ste 101 (19904-7620)
PHONE 818 305-4436
Brian Gyss, *CEO*
EMP: 1
SALES (est): 61K **Privately Held**
SIC: 7372 Prepackaged software

(G-1205)
BIRDIE SSOT LLC
3500 S Dupont Hwy (19901-6041)
PHONE 857 361-6883
Alexandre Abdo Hadade,
EMP: 8
SALES (est): 182.5K **Privately Held**
SIC: 7371 Computer software development & applications

(G-1206)
BIRITEK LLC
8 The Grn Ste A (19901-3618)
PHONE 949 556-3943
Hatice Ozcan, *Branch Mgr*
EMP: 1
SALES (corp-wide): 25K **Privately Held**
SIC: 7372 7379 Application computer software; computer related consulting services
PA: Biritek Llc
    300 Spectrum Center Dr # 414
    Irvine CA 92618
    224 813-4331

(G-1207)
BITS & BYTES INC
3895 N Dupont Hwy (19901-1568)
P.O. Box 751 (19903-0751)
PHONE 302 674-2999
Henry Forester, *President*
Michelle Rae Condon, *Treasurer*
Debbie Caffo, *Admin Sec*
EMP: 7
SQ FT: 1,000
SALES (est): 1.5MM **Privately Held**
SIC: 5045 5734 8243 7371 Computers, peripherals & software; computer & software stores; software training, computer; computer software systems analysis & design, custom

(G-1208)
BLACK MATH LABS INC
8 The Grn Ste A (19901-3618)
PHONE 858 349-9446
Mohammad Kurabi, *Director*
EMP: 5
SALES (est): 107K **Privately Held**
SIC: 7371 Software programming applications

(G-1209)
BLAZE COIN LLC
Also Called: Information Technology
8 The Grn Ste B (19901-3618)
PHONE 509 768-2249
Ankush Sood, *Principal*
Shamik Kundu, *Principal*
EMP: 7
SALES (est): 136.4K **Privately Held**
SIC: 7389

(G-1210)
BLJ&D FLAGGING LLC
820 Carvel Dr (19901-6671)
P.O. Box 1383 (19903-1383)
PHONE 302 272-0574
Corlet Demby, *Owner*
EMP: 15 EST: 17
SALES (est): 273.4K **Privately Held**
SIC: 7389 Metal cutting services

(G-1211)
BLOCKWEATHER HOLDINGS LLC
8 The Grn Ste 6338 (19901-3618)
PHONE 844 644-6837
Shane Shields, *Managing Prtnr*
David Henry, *Managing Prtnr*
EMP: 5 **Privately Held**
SIC: 6719 Investment holding companies, except banks

(G-1212)
BLOG - CARE FIRST DENTAL TEAM
1250 S Governors Ave (19904-4802)
PHONE 302 741-2044
EMP: 8 EST: 2017
SALES (est): 84.5K **Privately Held**
SIC: 8021 Offices & clinics of dentists

(G-1213)
BLUE HEN AUCTION CO LLC
1528 E Lebanon Rd (19901-5834)
PHONE 302 697-6096
EMP: 5
SALES (est): 320K **Privately Held**
SIC: 7389 Business Services, Nec, Nsk

(G-1214)
BLUE MARLIN ICE LLC
273 Walnut Shade Rd (19904-6474)
PHONE 302 697-7800
Jon Nichols Jr, *CEO*
EMP: 4
SQ FT: 4,800
SALES: 50K **Privately Held**
SIC: 4222 2097 Warehousing, cold storage or refrigerated; block ice

(G-1215)
BLUE RIDGE HOME CARE INC
9 E Loockerman St Ste 210 (19901-7347)
PHONE 302 397-8211
EMP: 7
SALES (est): 67.2K **Privately Held**
SIC: 8082 Home health care services

(G-1216)
BOB SIMMONS AGENCY
Also Called: State Farm Insurance
1460 E Lebanon Rd (19901-5833)
PHONE 302 698-1970
Bob Simmons, *Owner*
EMP: 5
SALES (est): 620.2K **Privately Held**
WEB: www.bobsimmonsinsurance.com
SIC: 6411 Insurance agents & brokers

(G-1217)
BOBBY WILSON ENTERTAINMENT LLC
1561 Nthaniel Mitchell Rd (19904-7011)
PHONE 302 233-6463
Bobby Wilson,
EMP: 4
SALES: 50K **Privately Held**
SIC: 7929 Entertainment service

(G-1218)
BOBOLA FARM & FLORIST
Also Called: Bobola Farms
5268 Forrest Ave (19904-5108)
PHONE 302 492-3367
Ted P Bobola Jr, *Owner*

Dover - Kent County (G-1219)   **GEOGRAPHIC SECTION**

EMP: 4
SALES (est): 356.1K **Privately Held**
SIC: **0171** 0161 0251 Strawberry farm; corn farm, sweet; cantaloupe farm; broiler, fryer & roaster chickens

(G-1219)
BOEING COMPANY
639 Evreux St (19902-5139)
P.O. Box 2047 (19902-2047)
PHONE..................................302 735-2922
EMP: 996
SALES (corp-wide): 101.1B **Publicly Held**
SIC: **3721** Airplanes, fixed or rotary wing
PA: The Boeing Company
100 N Riverside Plz
Chicago IL 60606
312 544-2000

(G-1220)
BOLT INNOVATION LLC
Also Called: Buddycable
8 The Grn 4594 (19901-3618)
P.O. Box 30, Hartly (19953-0030)
PHONE..................................800 293-5249
Daniel Poliseno, *Principal*
Chelsea Carr, *Principal*
Alexander Loffreda, *Principal*
Cody Poliseno, *Principal*
Marylou Poliseno, *Principal*
EMP: 5
SQ FT: 600
SALES (est): 458.8K **Privately Held**
SIC: **5961** 7371 7389 Computer equipment & electronics, mail order; computer software development & applications;

(G-1221)
BOOTHE INVESTMENT GROUP
450 Kings Hwy (19901-7507)
PHONE..................................302 734-7526
EMP: 4
SALES (est): 515.5K **Privately Held**
SIC: **6211** 6733 8742 Security Broker/Dealer Trust Management Management Consulting Services

(G-1222)
BOSCO INSURANCE AGENCY
625 S Dupont Hwy Ste 101 (19901-4504)
PHONE..................................302 678-0647
James A Watkins, *Partner*
Jim Watkins, *Vice Pres*
EMP: 6
SALES (est): 442.6K **Privately Held**
SIC: **6411** Insurance agents, brokers & service

(G-1223)
BOTTLE OF SMOKE PRESS
902 Wilson Dr (19904-2437)
P.O. Box 66, Wallkill NY (12589-0066)
PHONE..................................302 399-1856
Bill Roberts, *Principal*
EMP: 2
SALES (est): 187K **Privately Held**
SIC: **2741** Miscellaneous publishing

(G-1224)
BOYS & GIRLS CLUB OF DE
864 Center Rd (19901-5908)
PHONE..................................302 677-6376
Roxanne Lee, *Manager*
EMP: 6
SALES (est): 91.5K **Privately Held**
SIC: **8641** Youth organizations

(G-1225)
BOYS & GIRLS CLUBS DEL INC
Also Called: Boys & Girls Club of Dover
375 Simon Cir (19904-3437)
PHONE..................................302 678-3180
Renata Stewart, *Director*
EMP: 5
SALES (corp-wide): 20.8MM **Privately Held**
SIC: **8641** Youth organizations
PA: Boys & Girls Clubs Of Delaware, Inc.
669 S Union St
Wilmington DE 19805
302 658-1870

(G-1226)
BOYS & GIRLS CLUBS DEL INC
Also Called: Wesley College
9 E Loockerman St Ste 2c (19901-7343)
PHONE..................................302 678-5182
EMP: 7
SALES (corp-wide): 18.3MM **Privately Held**
SIC: **8641** Civic And Social Associations
PA: Boys & Girls Clubs Of Delaware, Inc.
669 S Union St
Wilmington DE 19805
302 658-1870

(G-1227)
BRADFORD FAMILY PHYSICIANS LLC
1055 S Bradford St (19904-4141)
PHONE..................................302 730-3750
EMP: 5 EST: 2016
SALES (est): 256.3K **Privately Held**
SIC: **8011** Offices & clinics of medical doctors

(G-1228)
BRAIN INJURY ASSOCIATION DEL
Also Called: BIAD
840 Walker Rd Ste A (19904-2727)
P.O. Box 1897 (19903-1897)
PHONE..................................302 346-2083
Jim Mills, *President*
Sharon Lyons, *Vice Pres*
EMP: 13
SALES (est): 38.6K **Privately Held**
SIC: **8699** Charitable organization

(G-1229)
BRENFORD ANIMAL HOSPITAL P A (PA)
Also Called: Hammer, Greg S
4118 N Dupont Hwy (19901-1523)
PHONE..................................302 678-9418
Craig Stonesifer, *Partner*
Greg Hammer, *Partner*
Paul Hanebutt, *Manager*
EMP: 25 EST: 1974
SQ FT: 3,875
SALES (est): 2.8MM **Privately Held**
SIC: **0742** 0752 Animal hospital services, pets & other animal specialties; animal boarding services

(G-1230)
BRIAN GARNSEY
Also Called: Husband 4 Hire
34 Debs Way (19901-2892)
PHONE..................................302 463-1985
Brian Garnsey, *Principal*
EMP: 4 EST: 2010
SALES (est): 261.5K **Privately Held**
SIC: **4581** Airports, flying fields & services

(G-1231)
BRICK DOCTOR INC (PA)
130 Kruser Blvd (19901-3265)
PHONE..................................302 678-3380
Jason Goodnight, *President*
Ellen Capitan, *Vice Pres*
EMP: 9
SQ FT: 1,600
SALES (est): 1MM **Privately Held**
SIC: **1741** 1611 1771 Unit paver installation; sidewalk construction; sidewalk contractor

(G-1232)
BRIDGESTONE RET OPERATIONS LLC
Also Called: Firestone
625 S Bay Rd (19901-4601)
PHONE..................................302 734-4522
Joseph Litz, *Manager*
EMP: 11 **Privately Held**
WEB: www.bfis.com
SIC: **5531** 7534 Automotive tires; rebuilding & retreading tires
HQ: Bridgestone Retail Operations, Llc
333 E Lake St Ste 300
Bloomingdale IL 60108
630 259-9000

(G-1233)
BROAD ACRES INC
8853 Bayside Dr (19901-1316)
PHONE..................................302 734-2910
Dan M Zimmerman, *President*
Fred D Zimmerman, *Vice Pres*
Elizabeth A Zimmerman, *Admin Sec*
EMP: 4
SALES (est): 430K **Privately Held**
SIC: **0191** General farms, primarily crop

(G-1234)
BROCKS SOY CANDLES
105 Hobbyhorse Ct (19904-7117)
PHONE..................................609 841-5121
EMP: 2
SALES (est): 62.5K **Privately Held**
SIC: **3999** Candles

(G-1235)
BROOKS MACHINE INC (PA)
Also Called: BROOKS METAL SAWS REPAIR
716 S West St (19904-3513)
PHONE..................................302 674-5900
Linda Brooks, *President*
Paul A Brooks II, *Vice Pres*
John W Brooks, *Shareholder*
EMP: 7
SQ FT: 4,800
SALES: 3.1MM **Privately Held**
WEB: www.brooks-saws.com
SIC: **7699** 5084 Industrial machinery & equipment repair; metalworking machinery

(G-1236)
BROWN SHIELS & OBRIEN
108 E Water St (19901-3614)
P.O. Box F (19903-1556)
PHONE..................................302 734-4766
Roy Shiels, *Partner*
Herman Cubbiage Brown, *Partner*
John E O'Brien, *Partner*
Mary A Sherlock,
EMP: 19
SALES (est): 1.5MM **Privately Held**
WEB: www.del-law.com
SIC: **8111** General practice attorney, lawyer

(G-1237)
BROWN SHELS BAUREGARD LLC
148 S Bradford St (19904-7318)
PHONE..................................302 226-2270
Andre M Beauregard, *President*
EMP: 8
SALES (est): 136.7K **Privately Held**
SIC: **8111** Legal services

(G-1238)
BRUNSWICK DOVERAMA
1600 S Governors Ave (19904-7004)
PHONE..................................302 734-7501
Carmine Alessandro, *Manager*
EMP: 6
SALES (est): 180.6K **Privately Held**
SIC: **7933** Bowling centers

(G-1239)
BRYAN K STERLING LLC
773 S Queen St Ste A (19904-3574)
PHONE..................................302 734-3511
Bryan K Sterling, *Owner*
EMP: 4
SALES (est): 253.2K **Privately Held**
SIC: **8042** Specialized optometrists

(G-1240)
BSR TRADE LLC
8 The Grn Ste 6258 (19901-3618)
PHONE..................................646 250-4409
Apdullah Adiloglu,
EMP: 5
SALES (est): 164.3K **Privately Held**
SIC: **6799** Commodity contract trading companies

(G-1241)
BUILDING BLOCKS FOR LEARNI
88 Beech Dr (19904-9428)
PHONE..................................302 677-0248
Patricia C Slentz, *Principal*
EMP: 5

SALES (est): 76.4K **Privately Held**
SIC: **8351** Child day care services

(G-1242)
BURKE DERMATOLOGY (PA)
95 Wolf Creek Blvd Ste 1 (19901-4965)
PHONE..................................302 734-3376
Thomas Burke, *Principal*
EMP: 9 EST: 2010
SALES (est): 1.3MM **Privately Held**
SIC: **8011** Dermatologist

(G-1243)
BURNS & ELLIS REALTY CO
490 N Dupont Hwy (19901-3906)
P.O. Box 105 (19903-0105)
PHONE..................................302 674-4220
Tom Burns, *Partner*
Terry Burns, *Partner*
Angela Ringgold, *Admin Asst*
Ellen Pfeiffer, *Real Est Agnt*
Peter Shade, *Real Est Agnt*
EMP: 20
SQ FT: 1,000
SALES (est): 1.5MM **Privately Held**
WEB: www.burnsandellis.com
SIC: **6531** Real estate agent, residential

(G-1244)
BYLER SAWMILL
2846 Yoder Dr (19904-5845)
PHONE..................................302 730-4208
Crist Byler, *Owner*
EMP: 3
SALES (est): 20K **Privately Held**
SIC: **2421** Sawmills & planing mills, general

(G-1245)
C EDGAR WOOD INC (PA)
Also Called: L&W Insurance Agency
1154 S Governors Ave (19904-6904)
P.O. Box 918 (19903-0918)
PHONE..................................302 674-3500
Davis H Wood, *President*
Andy Cousins, *Vice Pres*
Chelsea Clark, *Personnel*
Terry Myers, *Sales Associate*
Jeff Eanes, *Agent*
EMP: 40
SALES (est): 7.3MM **Privately Held**
WEB: www.lwinsurance.com
SIC: **6411** Insurance agents

(G-1246)
C4-NVIS USA LLC
8 The Grn Ste 6794 (19901-3618)
PHONE..................................213 465-5089
Paul Morabito,
EMP: 2
SALES (est): 33.1K **Privately Held**
SIC: **4813** 3663 8748 7389 Long distance telephone communications; voice telephone communications; radio broadcasting & communications equipment; receivers, radio communications; telecommunications consultant;

(G-1247)
CABE ASSOCIATES INC
144 S Governors Ave (19904-3223)
P.O. Box 877 (19903-0877)
PHONE..................................302 674-9280
Lee J Beetschen, *President*
Shaun Condron, *Engineer*
Scott Hoffman, *Senior Engr*
Brian Lyncha, *Senior Engr*
Robert W Kerr, *Treasurer*
EMP: 16 EST: 1976
SQ FT: 12,000
SALES (est): 1.4MM **Privately Held**
WEB: www.cabe.com
SIC: **8711** Consulting engineer

(G-1248)
CAESAR RODNEY SCHOOL DISTRICT
Also Called: W B Simpson Elementary School
950 Center Rd (19901)
PHONE..................................302 697-3207
Michael Kijowski, *Principal*
EMP: 63
SALES (corp-wide): 53.4MM **Privately Held**
SIC: **8211** 8351 Public elementary school; child day care services

GEOGRAPHIC SECTION   Dover - Kent County (G-1275)

PA: Caesar Rodney School District
7 Front St
Wyoming DE 19934
302 698-4800

(G-1249)
CANCER CARE CTRS AT BAY HLTH
Also Called: Costleigh, Brian J MD
793 S Queen St (19904-3568)
PHONE.................................302 674-4401
Luther Brady MD, *President*
William Holden, *Principal*
Dennis Klima, *Treasurer*
Mark Menendez, *Med Doctor*
Sean Mace, *Manager*
EMP: 12
SQ FT: 7,000
SALES: 500K
SALES (corp-wide): 3.1MM **Privately Held**
SIC: 8062 General medical & surgical hospitals
PA: Bay Health Development Inc
640 S State St
Dover DE 19901
302 744-7994

(G-1250)
CAPITAL SCHOOL DISTRICT
Also Called: Dover Mntessori Cntry Day Schl
88 Carpenter St (19901-9266)
PHONE.................................302 678-8394
Margaret Kling, *Director*
EMP: 5
SALES (corp-wide): 64.8MM **Privately Held**
WEB: www.k12.de.us
SIC: 8211 8351 Public elementary school; Montessori child development center
PA: Capital School District
198 Commerce Way
Dover DE 19904
302 672-1500

(G-1251)
CAPITOL CLEANERS & LAUNDERERS (PA)
Also Called: Capitol Uniform & Linen Svc
195 Commerce Way (19904-8224)
PHONE.................................302 674-1511
E Stuart Outten Jr, *President*
EMP: 68 EST: 1933
SQ FT: 28,000
SALES: 5.5MM **Privately Held**
WEB: www.capitolcleaners.com
SIC: 7212 7213 Laundry & drycleaner agents; pickup station, laundry & drycleaning; linen supply; uniform supply

(G-1252)
CAPITOL CLEANERS & LAUNDERERS
217 S New St (19904-6708)
PHONE.................................302 674-0500
Stuart Otten, *Manager*
EMP: 4
SALES (corp-wide): 5.5MM **Privately Held**
SIC: 7212 7216 Laundry & drycleaner agents; curtain cleaning & repair
PA: Capitol Cleaners & Launderers Inc
195 Commerce Way
Dover DE 19904
302 674-1511

(G-1253)
CAPITOL CREDIT SERVICES INC (PA)
872 Walker Rd Ste B (19904-2700)
P.O. Box 102, Lewes (19958-0102)
PHONE.................................302 678-1735
Matthew J Spinella, *President*
Tracy Hynes, *Vice Pres*
Shirley Spinella, *Treasurer*
Judith R Snarsky, *Admin Sec*
EMP: 17
SQ FT: 2,000
SALES (est): 2.7MM **Privately Held**
SIC: 7322 8111 Collection agency, except real estate; legal services

(G-1254)
CAPITOL NURSG & RHB CNTR LLC
Also Called: CAPITAL HEALTHCARE SERVICES, N
1225 Walker Rd (19904-6541)
PHONE.................................302 734-1199
Steven Silver, *Partner*
Ronald Schafer, *Partner*
Yoko Imai, *Education*
EMP: 150
SALES: 14.2MM **Privately Held**
SIC: 8059 8093 8051 Nursing home, except skilled & intermediate care facility; rehabilitation center, outpatient treatment; skilled nursing care facilities

(G-1255)
CAREER ASSOCIATES INC
Also Called: Bestemps Career Asso Resume Sv
385 W North St Ste A (19904-6748)
PHONE.................................302 674-4357
Patsy Ware, *Manager*
EMP: 5
SALES (corp-wide): 2.5MM **Privately Held**
WEB: www.careerassociatesinc.com
SIC: 7363 Temporary help service
PA: Career Associates Inc
100 Clemwood St
Salisbury MD
410 546-0250

(G-1256)
CARMIKE CINEMAS INC
1365 N Dupont Hwy # 3020 (19901-8710)
PHONE.................................302 734-5249
Neill A McLean, *Manager*
EMP: 20
SALES (corp-wide): 7.3MM **Publicly Held**
WEB: www.carmike.com
SIC: 7832 Exhibitors, itinerant: motion picture
HQ: Carmike Cinemas, Llc
11500 Ash St
Leawood KS 66211
913 213-2000

(G-1257)
CARPEDIEM HEALTH LLC
8 The Grn Ste 240 (19901-3618)
PHONE.................................347 467-4444
Jess Yliniemi,
EMP: 2
SALES (est): 67K **Privately Held**
SIC: 2339 2329 Women's & misses' athletic clothing & sportswear; men's & boys' sportswear & athletic clothing

(G-1258)
CARZATY INC
874 Walker Rd Ste C (19904-2778)
PHONE.................................650 396-0144
Hassan Jaffar, *CEO*
EMP: 14
SALES (est): 367.9K **Privately Held**
SIC: 5961 7371 ; computer software development & applications

(G-1259)
CATHERINE KOTALIS
540 S Governors Ave (19904-3530)
PHONE.................................302 526-1470
Catherine Kotalis, *Principal*
EMP: 5
SALES (est): 65.7K **Privately Held**
SIC: 8049 Offices of health practitioner

(G-1260)
CATHOLIC CHARITIES INC
Also Called: Energy Assistance Program
2099 S Dupont Hwy (19901-5568)
PHONE.................................302 674-1600
Katrina A Furlong, *Branch Mgr*
EMP: 5
SALES (corp-wide): 6.8MM **Privately Held**
WEB: www.ccwilm.org
SIC: 8322 Social service center
PA: Catholic Charities Inc
2601 W 4th St
Wilmington DE 19805
302 655-9624

(G-1261)
CATHOLIC CHARITIES INC
Also Called: Delaware Day Treatment
1155 Walker Rd (19904-6539)
PHONE.................................302 674-1600
Vallerie Roach, *Partner*
EMP: 6
SALES (corp-wide): 6.8MM **Privately Held**
WEB: www.ccwilm.org
SIC: 8322 8351 General counseling services; group day care center
PA: Catholic Charities Inc
2601 W 4th St
Wilmington DE 19805
302 655-9624

(G-1262)
CELLCO PARTNERSHIP
Also Called: Verizon
1045 N Dupont Hwy (19901-2006)
PHONE.................................302 730-5200
Peris Street, *Branch Mgr*
EMP: 14
SALES (corp-wide): 130.8B **Publicly Held**
SIC: 4812 Cellular telephone services
HQ: Cellco Partnership
1 Verizon Way
Basking Ridge NJ 07920

(G-1263)
CENTRAL DEL CHMBER OF COMMERCE
Also Called: CHAMBER OF COMMERCE OF CENTRAL
435 N Dupont Hwy (19901-3907)
PHONE.................................302 734-7513
Judy Diogo, *President*
Jennette Wessel, *Exec VP*
EMP: 5
SALES: 537.4K **Privately Held**
WEB: www.cdcc.net
SIC: 8611 Chamber of Commerce

(G-1264)
CENTRAL DEL ENDOSCOPY UNIT (PA)
644 S Queen St Ste 105 (19904-3543)
PHONE.................................302 677-1617
William Kaplan MD, *President*
EMP: 5
SQ FT: 4,066
SALES (est): 832.8K **Privately Held**
SIC: 8062 General medical & surgical hospitals

(G-1265)
CENTRAL DELAWARE COMMITTEE (PA)
Also Called: Kent County Counseling Svcs
1241 College Park Dr (19904-8713)
PHONE.................................302 735-7790
James Lark, *Exec Dir*
James Larks, *Exec Dir*
EMP: 30
SQ FT: 12,000
SALES: 3.8MM **Privately Held**
SIC: 8093 Substance abuse clinics (outpatient)

(G-1266)
CENTRAL DELAWARE FMLY MEDICINE
95 Wolf Creek Blvd Ste 2 (19901-4965)
PHONE.................................302 735-1616
Theresa Little, *Owner*
Tim A Breyer, *Office Mgr*
Elaine Balcraek, *Asst Office Mgr*
EMP: 15
SALES (est): 1.2MM **Privately Held**
SIC: 8011 General & family practice, physician/surgeon

(G-1267)
CENTRAL DELAWARE HABITAT FOR
2311 S Dupont Hwy (19901-5514)
PHONE.................................302 526-2366
Tammy Ordway, *President*
Angel Stark, *Bookkeeper*
Katie Gillis, *Marketing Staff*
Harvey Carrow, *Manager*
Jocelyn Tice, *Administration*
EMP: 9
SALES: 1.4MM **Privately Held**
SIC: 8399 Community development groups

(G-1268)
CENTRAL DELAWARE SURGERY CTR
Also Called: Central Delaware Surgery Ctr
640 S State St (19901-3530)
PHONE.................................302 744-6801
EMP: 12
SALES (est): 375.3K **Privately Held**
SIC: 8062 General Hospital

(G-1269)
CENTRAL STORAGE
650 W Division St (19904-2702)
PHONE.................................302 678-1919
Bill Clark, *Owner*
EMP: 4
SALES (est): 206.1K **Privately Held**
WEB: www.centralstorage.net
SIC: 4225 Warehousing, self-storage

(G-1270)
CENTURY ENGINEERING INC
550 S Bay Rd (19901-4603)
PHONE.................................302 734-9188
Scott L Rathfon, *Branch Mgr*
EMP: 85
SALES (corp-wide): 44.2MM **Privately Held**
WEB: www.centuryeng.com
SIC: 8711 Consulting engineer
PA: Century Engineering, Inc.
10710 Gilroy Rd
Hunt Valley MD 21031
443 589-2400

(G-1271)
CETARIS INC (PA)
73 Greentree Dr 540 (19904-7646)
PHONE.................................416 679-9555
Ric Bedard, *President*
David Crawford, *Treasurer*
Adam Becker, *Sales Staff*
EMP: 6
SALES (est): 309.6K **Privately Held**
SIC: 8741 Administrative management

(G-1272)
CHABBOTT PTROSKY COML REALTORS
2 N State St (19901-3833)
PHONE.................................302 678-3276
George Chabbott, *Partner*
Joseph Petrosky, *Partner*
EMP: 5
SALES (est): 300K **Privately Held**
SIC: 6512 Commercial & industrial building operation

(G-1273)
CHARLES DEMPSEY FARMS
1708 Fast Landing Rd (19901-2718)
PHONE.................................302 734-4937
Alice May Dempsey, *Partner*
Bruce Dempsey, *Partner*
Greg Dempsey, *Partner*
EMP: 9
SALES: 250K **Privately Held**
SIC: 0119 0241 Feeder grains; milk production

(G-1274)
CHESAPEAKE UTILITIES CORP (PA)
909 Silver Lake Blvd (19904-2472)
P.O. Box 615 (19903-0615)
PHONE.................................302 734-6799
John R Schimkaitis, *Ch of Bd*
Michael P McMasters, *President*
Stacie L Roberts, *President*
Kevin J Webber, *President*
Sharon Sturgis, *General Mgr*
EMP: 170 EST: 1859
SALES: 717.4MM **Publicly Held**
WEB: www.chpk.com
SIC: 4924 4911 Natural gas distribution; distribution, electric power

(G-1275)
CHILDREN FIRST LRNG CTR INC
760 Townsend Blvd (19901-2515)
PHONE.................................302 674-5227

Dover - Kent County (G-1276)   GEOGRAPHIC SECTION

Quiana Nieves, *President*
EMP: 9
SALES (est): 346.1K Privately Held
SIC: 8351 Group day care center

(G-1276)
CHILDREN FMILIES FIRST DEL INC
91 Wolf Creek Blvd (19901-4914)
PHONE...................302 674-8384
Alais Erickson, *Manager*
EMP: 5
SALES (corp-wide): 16.8MM Privately Held
SIC: 8322 8399 Social service center; council for social agency
PA: Children & Families First Delaware Inc.
  809 N Washington St
  Wilmington DE 19801
  302 658-5177

(G-1277)
CHILDREN S SECRET GARDEN
717 Hatchery Rd (19901-1509)
PHONE...................302 730-1717
Pamela Harper, *Owner*
EMP: 12 EST: 2000
SALES (est): 284.9K Privately Held
SIC: 8351 Group day care center

(G-1278)
CHILDRENS ADVOCACY CTR OF DEL (PA)
611 S Dupont Hwy Ste 201 (19901-4507)
PHONE...................302 741-2123
Randall Williams, *CEO*
EMP: 14
SALES: 1.3MM Privately Held
SIC: 8399 Council for social agency

(G-1279)
CHIMES INC
3499 Cypress St (19901)
PHONE...................302 678-3270
Calvin Mackey, *Principal*
EMP: 6
SALES (corp-wide): 10.6MM Privately Held
SIC: 8361 Residential care for the handicapped
HQ: The Chimes Inc
  4815 Seton Dr
  Baltimore MD 21215
  410 358-6400

(G-1280)
CHOICE FOR COMMUNITY
210 Hiawatha Ln (19904-2461)
PHONE...................302 734-9020
EMP: 4 EST: 2007
SALES (est): 180K Privately Held
SIC: 8361 Self-help group home

(G-1281)
CHUCK B BARKER PT DPT OCS ATC
1015 S Governors Ave (19904-6901)
PHONE...................302 730-4800
Chuck Barker, *President*
EMP: 4
SALES (est): 128.7K Privately Held
SIC: 8049 8093 Physical therapist; rehabilitation center, outpatient treatment

(G-1282)
CHURCH OF GOD IN CHRIST
Also Called: Drop A Tot Pre-School Day Care
120a S Governors Ave (19904-3223)
P.O. Box 174 (19903-0174)
PHONE...................302 678-1949
Kemuel Butler, *Director*
EMP: 15
SALES (est): 155.5K Privately Held
SIC: 8351 8661 Child day care services; churches, temples & shrines

(G-1283)
CITIFINANCIAL CREDIT COMPANY
Also Called: Commercial Credit
1057 N Dupont Hwy (19901-2006)
P.O. Box 1214 (19903-1214)
PHONE...................302 678-8226
EMP: 4

SALES (corp-wide): 92.5B Publicly Held
SIC: 6153 6141 Short-Term Business Credit Institution Personal Credit Institution
HQ: Citifinancial Credit Company
  300 Saint Paul St Fl 3
  Baltimore MD 21202
  410 332-3000

(G-1284)
CITIZENS BANK NATIONAL ASSN
8 W Loockerman St (19904-7385)
PHONE...................302 734-0200
Vicky Antoniou, *Manager*
EMP: 15
SALES (corp-wide): 7.3B Publicly Held
SIC: 6022 State commercial banks
HQ: Citizens Bank, National Association
  1 Citizens Plz Ste 1 # 1
  Providence RI 02903
  401 282-7000

(G-1285)
CITIZENS BANK NATIONAL ASSN
1399 Forrest Ave (19904-3312)
PHONE...................302 734-0231
Vicky Shockley, *Manager*
EMP: 6
SALES (corp-wide): 7.3B Publicly Held
SIC: 6022 State trust companies accepting deposits, commercial
HQ: Citizens Bank, National Association
  1 Citizens Plz Ste 1 # 1
  Providence RI 02903
  401 282-7000

(G-1286)
CITY CAB OF DELWARE INC
716 S Governors Ave (19904-4106)
PHONE...................302 734-5968
Joyce Vickers, *Branch Mgr*
EMP: 4 Privately Held
SIC: 4121 Taxicabs
PA: City Cab Of Delware Inc
  1203 State College Rd
  Dover DE 19904

(G-1287)
CITY CAB OF DELWARE INC (PA)
1203 State College Rd (19904)
PHONE...................302 734-5968
Tom Antionio, *President*
Vicki Antiono, *Vice Pres*
EMP: 4
SALES (est): 990.9K Privately Held
SIC: 4121 Taxicabs

(G-1288)
CITY OF DOVER
Also Called: Finance Department
5 E Reed St (19901-7334)
PHONE...................302 736-7018
Donna Mitchell, *Controller*
EMP: 8 Privately Held
SIC: 8721 Payroll accounting service
PA: Dover, City Of (Inc)
  15 Loockerman Plz
  Dover DE 19901
  302 736-7004

(G-1289)
CITY OF DOVER
Also Called: Customer Services Department
5 E Reed St Ste 100 (19901-7334)
PHONE...................302 736-7035
Kirby Hudson, *Manager*
EMP: 21 Privately Held
SIC: 7389 9199 Financial services;
PA: Dover, City Of (Inc)
  15 Loockerman Plz
  Dover DE 19901
  302 736-7004

(G-1290)
CITY OF DOVER
Also Called: Electric Department
860 Buttner Pl (19904-2405)
P.O. Box 475 (19903-0475)
PHONE...................302 736-7070
Harry Maloney III, *Director*
EMP: 48 Privately Held
SIC: 4911 9611 Distribution, electric power; energy development & conservation agency, government

PA: Dover, City Of (Inc)
  15 Loockerman Plz
  Dover DE 19901
  302 736-7004

(G-1291)
CITY OF DOVER - MCKEE RUN
880 Buttner Pl (19904-2405)
PHONE...................302 672-6306
EMP: 6
SALES (est): 49.5K Privately Held
SIC: 7389

(G-1292)
CLASSERIUM CORPORATION
Also Called: Photodemy.com
8 The Grn Ste 4534 (19901-3618)
PHONE...................773 306-3297
Kennard Wottowa, *Principal*
Dmitry Fedotov, *Principal*
Brian Jensen, *Principal*
Yuriy Seleznev, *Principal*
EMP: 4
SALES (est): 101.3K Privately Held
SIC: 7389

(G-1293)
CLIFTON LEASING CO INC (PA)
Also Called: Delmarva Kenworth Trucks
613 Clara St (19904-3011)
P.O. Box 603 (19903-0603)
PHONE...................302 674-2300
Richard Weyandt, *President*
Matt Weyandt, *Vice Pres*
Lynne Bergold, *Treasurer*
Pam Weyandt, *Admin Sec*
EMP: 21 EST: 1964
SQ FT: 5,000
SALES (est): 9.5MM Privately Held
SIC: 5511 7513 7699 Trucks, tractors & trailers: new & used; truck leasing, without drivers; marine engine repair

(G-1294)
CLIQUE DIGITAL MEDIA MKTG LLC ◆
8 The Grn Ste A (19901-3618)
PHONE...................305 704-2128
EMP: 4 EST: 2019
SALES (est): 22.8K Privately Held
SIC: 4899 Communication services

(G-1295)
CLOUDXPERTS LLC
8 The Grn Ste 5210 (19901-3618)
PHONE...................302 257-5686
Salman Khan, *CEO*
Muzzamil Mubeen, *Principal*
EMP: 5
SALES (est): 240.3K Privately Held
SIC: 7373 Computer systems analysis & design

(G-1296)
CNC INSURANCE ASSOCIATES INC
20 E Division St Ste A (19901-7366)
P.O. Box 831 (19903-0831)
PHONE...................302 678-3860
Kevin Nemith, *President*
Jeffery Lord, *Corp Secy*
EMP: 12 EST: 1978
SQ FT: 3,506
SALES: 2MM
SALES (corp-wide): 165.5MM Privately Held
WEB: www.cncinsurance.com
SIC: 6411 Insurance agents
PA: The Hilb Group Llc
  8720 Stony Point Pkwy # 125
  Richmond VA 23235
  804 414-6501

(G-1297)
CNTRL DE GSTROENTEROLGYASSOC I
644 S Queen St Ste 106 (19904-3543)
PHONE...................302 678-9002
Wendy Silicato, *Office Mgr*
EMP: 5
SALES (est): 240.2K Privately Held
SIC: 8011 Pediatrician

(G-1298)
CNU FIT LLC
1404 Forrest Ave Ste 9 (19904-3478)
PHONE...................302 744-9037
Evans Armantrading, *Mng Member*
EMP: 8
SQ FT: 1,500
SALES: 130K Privately Held
SIC: 7991 7299 Exercise salon; massage parlor

(G-1299)
CNWYNN PUBLICATIONS
1102 Dwight Ct (19904-2690)
P.O. Box 328, Cheswold (19936-0328)
PHONE...................484 753-1568
Chistian Wynn, *Principal*
EMP: 1
SALES (est): 37.5K Privately Held
SIC: 2741 Miscellaneous publishing

(G-1300)
COASTAL CREDIT LLC
1406 Forrest Ave Ste 2 (19904-3398)
PHONE...................302 734-1312
Teresa Metheny, *Branch Mgr*
EMP: 4
SALES (corp-wide): 25.8MM Privately Held
SIC: 6141 Financing: automobiles, furniture, etc., not a deposit bank
HQ: Coastal Credit, L.L.C.
  10333 N Meridian St # 400
  Indianapolis IN 46290
  757 340-6000

(G-1301)
COGENCY GLOBAL INC
850 New Burton Rd (19904-5785)
PHONE...................800 483-1140
Bruce Jacobi, *Ch of Bd*
EMP: 4
SALES (corp-wide): 40.6MM Privately Held
SIC: 8111 Legal services
PA: Cogency Global Inc.
  10 E 40th St Fl 10 # 10
  New York NY 10016
  212 947-7200

(G-1302)
COGNITIVE GROUP LLC
160 Greentree Dr Ste 101 (19904-7620)
PHONE...................301 585-1444
EMP: 15
SALES (est): 680K Privately Held
SIC: 8744 8748 Facilities Support Services Business Consulting Services

(G-1303)
COLONIAL INV MANAGMENT CO
Also Called: Dover Garden Court Apartments
9 E Loockerman St Ste C (19901-8306)
PHONE...................302 736-0674
Mary Anne Fannin, *Partner*
Adelle Welzel, *Manager*
EMP: 6
SALES (est): 608.1K Privately Held
SIC: 6513 Apartment building operators

(G-1304)
COMCAST OF DELMARVA LLC
5729 W Denneys Rd (19904-1365)
PHONE...................215 286-3345
Marc Sirota, *Vice Pres*
Terrence Connell, *Vice Pres*
EMP: 99
SALES: 950K
SALES (corp-wide): 94.5B Publicly Held
SIC: 4841 Cable television services
PA: Comcast Corporation
  1701 Jfk Blvd
  Philadelphia PA 19103
  215 286-1700

(G-1305)
COMMERCIAL RECOVERY GROUP INC
1012 College Rd Ste 203 (19904-6506)
PHONE...................302 730-4040
John Yursha, *President*
David Simmons, *Vice Pres*
EMP: 14
SQ FT: 2,500

GEOGRAPHIC SECTION
Dover - Kent County (G-1340)

SALES (est): 1.1MM **Privately Held**
WEB: www.crgcollect.com
SIC: 7322 Collection agency, except real estate

(G-1306)
COMMUNITY LEGAL AID SOCIETY
Also Called: Disabilities Law Program
840 Walker Rd (19904-2727)
PHONE.................................302 674-8500
Gottschalk E Deborah I, *Project Dir*
James G McGiffin Jr, *Exec Dir*
Christopher White, *Director*
William H Sudell Jr,
Peter K Mitchell Jr, *Representative*
EMP: 8
SALES (est): 610.4K
SALES (corp-wide): 5.2MM **Privately Held**
SIC: 8111 General practice law office
PA: Community Legal Aid Society Inc
100 W 10th St Ste 801
Wilmington DE 19801
302 757-7001

(G-1307)
COMPLETE RSRVTION SLUTIONS LLC
8 The Grn Ste 5863 (19901-3618)
PHONE.................................800 672-8522
Sean Engler, *Mng Member*
Leornardis Ramirez,
EMP: 14
SALES: 250K **Privately Held**
SIC: 7519 Travel, camping or recreational trailer rental

(G-1308)
COMPLIANCE ENVIRONMENTAL INC
150 S Bradford St (19904-7318)
PHONE.................................302 674-4427
Valentino Derocili, *President*
Debra J Derocili, *Vice Pres*
EMP: 5
SALES (est): 500K **Privately Held**
SIC: 8748 Environmental consultant

(G-1309)
COMPUTER SERVICES OF DELAWARE
Also Called: Payroll Services of Delaware
1991 S State St Ste B (19901-5811)
PHONE.................................302 697-8644
Bill Orth, *President*
Ray Kowalick, *Vice Pres*
EMP: 6
SALES (est): 50K **Privately Held**
SIC: 7374 Data processing service

(G-1310)
CONCRETE SERVICES INC
794 Rose Valley School Rd (19904-5508)
PHONE.................................302 883-2883
Brian Lilly, *President*
Barbara Lily, *Corp Secy*
Mark Lily, *Vice Pres*
EMP: 16
SALES: 3MM **Privately Held**
SIC: 1771 Concrete work

(G-1311)
CONNECTIONS CSP INC DOVER
698 S Bay Rd (19901)
PHONE.................................302 672-9276
EMP: 8
SALES (est): 73.3K **Privately Held**
SIC: 8093 Substance abuse clinics (outpatient)

(G-1312)
CONTACT INFO INC
8 The Grn Ste A (19901-3618)
PHONE.................................917 817-7939
Thomas Fast, *President*
EMP: 4
SALES (est): 89.7K **Privately Held**
SIC: 7371 Computer software development & applications

(G-1313)
CORP1 INC
614 N Dupont Hwy Ste 210 (19901-3900)
PHONE.................................720 644-6144
Kelly A McKown, *President*
Glenda K Hallett, *Vice Pres*
EMP: 10
SALES (est): 276.7K **Privately Held**
SIC: 8111 Legal services

(G-1314)
CORPORATE KIDS LRNG CTR INC
605 S Bay Rd (19901-4601)
PHONE.................................302 678-0688
Tracey L Preskenis, *President*
EMP: 25
SQ FT: 1,800
SALES (est): 824.2K **Privately Held**
SIC: 8351 Preschool center

(G-1315)
COUNTRY MEADOW PROPCO LLC
850 New Burton Rd (19904-5785)
PHONE.................................330 633-0555
EMP: 8
SALES (est): 75.4K **Privately Held**
SIC: 8051 Skilled nursing care facilities

(G-1316)
COUNTRY VILLAGE APARTMENTS
480 Country Dr (19901-5612)
PHONE.................................302 674-0991
Joanne Kelly, *Manager*
Jim Hall, *Manager*
EMP: 8
SALES (est): 540K **Privately Held**
SIC: 6513 Apartment building operators

(G-1317)
COUNTY OF KENT
Also Called: 911 Emergency
911 Public Safety Blvd (19901-4524)
PHONE.................................302 735-2180
Colin Faulkner, *Director*
EMP: 56 **Privately Held**
WEB: www.kentnet.org
SIC: 7363 Help supply services
PA: County Of Kent
555 S Bay Rd
Dover DE 19901
302 744-2305

(G-1318)
COURTLAND MANOR INC
889 S Little Creek Rd (19904-4721)
PHONE.................................302 674-0566
Irma C Schurman, *President*
Sandy Schurman, *Vice Pres*
Richard Schurman, *Admin Sec*
EMP: 100
SQ FT: 4,200
SALES (est): 5.3MM **Privately Held**
WEB: www.courtlandmanor.com
SIC: 8059 8051 Convalescent home; nursing home, except skilled & intermediate care facility; skilled nursing care facilities

(G-1319)
CR NEWLIN TRUCKING INC
2199 Fast Landing Rd (19901-2725)
PHONE.................................302 678-9124
Christopher Newlin, *President*
Renee Newlin, *Vice Pres*
EMP: 5 EST: 1998
SALES (est): 191.3K **Privately Held**
SIC: 4212 Local trucking, without storage

(G-1320)
CRATIS SOLUTIONS INC
8 The Grn Ste 5910 (19901-3618)
PHONE.................................515 423-7259
Stanley Wilson, *President*
EMP: 5
SALES (est): 107K **Privately Held**
SIC: 7371 Custom computer programming services

(G-1321)
CREDIT SHARE CLUB LLC
8 The Grn Ste 8360 (19901-3618)
PHONE.................................302 401-6450
EMP: 4 EST: 2018
SALES (est): 38.1K **Privately Held**
SIC: 7997 Membership sports & recreation clubs

(G-1322)
CREST CENTRAL
300 W Water St (19904-6743)
PHONE.................................302 736-0576
Theresa Evans Carter, *Director*
Samantha Hurd, *Director*
EMP: 12
SALES (est): 284.7K **Privately Held**
SIC: 8069 Drug addiction rehabilitation hospital

(G-1323)
CRIMSON STRATEGY GROUP LLP
8 The Grn Ste 10235 (19901-3618)
PHONE.................................302 503-5698
Greg Brown, *Partner*
EMP: 5
SALES (est): 124.8K **Privately Held**
SIC: 8742 Management consulting services

(G-1324)
CROSSKNOWLEDGE
874 Walker Rd Ste C (19904-2778)
PHONE.................................646 699-5983
Mickael Ohana, *CEO*
EMP: 98
SALES (est): 1.5MM **Privately Held**
SIC: 7372 Educational computer software

(G-1325)
CROSSROADS OF DELAWARE
2 Forest St (19904-3211)
PHONE.................................302 744-9999
Mike Barbier, *Owner*
EMP: 5 EST: 2012
SALES (est): 76.5K **Privately Held**
SIC: 8322 Family (marriage) counseling

(G-1326)
CROWN SHIPPING
15 Brittingham Dr (19904-5765)
PHONE.................................617 909-3357
EMP: 4
SALES (est): 148.3K **Privately Held**
SIC: 4789 Transportation services

(G-1327)
CRUDE GOLD RESEARCH LLC
8 The Grn Ste A (19901-3618)
PHONE.................................646 681-7317
Ramnarayan Sharma, *Mng Member*
EMP: 14
SQ FT: 850
SALES: 100K **Privately Held**
SIC: 6282 Investment advice

(G-1328)
CRUZ PUBLISHING GROUP
64 Representative Ln (19904-2491)
PHONE.................................302 287-2938
Laura Cruz, *Principal*
EMP: 1
SALES (est): 37.5K **Privately Held**
SIC: 2741 Miscellaneous publishing

(G-1329)
CURLEY & BENTON LLC
Also Called: Curley and Funk
250 Beiser Blvd Ste 202 (19904-7795)
PHONE.................................302 674-3333
Edward Curley, *Owner*
EMP: 6
SALES (est): 649.6K **Privately Held**
SIC: 8111 General practice attorney, lawyer

(G-1330)
CURRENT SOLUTIONS
1160 Rose Valley Schl Rd (19904-5513)
PHONE.................................302 724-5243
EMP: 4 EST: 2016
SALES (est): 281.2K **Privately Held**
SIC: 1623 Pipeline construction

(G-1331)
CURRY INDUSTRIES LLC
380 David Hall Rd (19904-5416)
PHONE.................................732 858-1794
Jamaal Curry, *Principal*
EMP: 2
SALES (est): 62.5K **Privately Held**
SIC: 3999 Manufacturing industries

(G-1332)
CUSTOM DECOR INC
1585 Mckee Rd 1 (19904-1380)
P.O. Box 336, Cheswold (19936-0336)
PHONE.................................302 735-7600
William Scotton, *President*
Lesterlee Scotton, *Treasurer*
◆ EMP: 20 EST: 1973
SALES (est): 4.6MM **Privately Held**
WEB: www.customdecornet.com
SIC: 5199 Gifts & novelties

(G-1333)
CUTS R US INC
51 Roosevelt Ave (19901-4459)
PHONE.................................302 674-2223
Carla Russum, *President*
EMP: 4
SALES (est): 90.1K **Privately Held**
SIC: 7231 Beauty shops

(G-1334)
CYNTHIA P MANGUBAT MD
22 Old Rudnick Ln (19901-4912)
PHONE.................................302 674-1356
Cynthia Mangubat, *Principal*
EMP: 4
SALES (est): 86.6K **Privately Held**
SIC: 8031 8011 Offices & clinics of osteopathic physicians; physicians' office, including specialists

(G-1335)
D BY D PRINTING LLC
5083 N Dupont Hwy (19901-2346)
PHONE.................................302 659-3373
Dennis Connell, *Mng Member*
EMP: 3
SQ FT: 2,500
SALES (est): 434.5K **Privately Held**
SIC: 2261 3993 Screen printing of cotton broadwoven fabrics; signs & advertising specialties

(G-1336)
D-STAFFING CONSULTING SVCS LLC
8 The Grn Ste 6060 (19901-3618)
PHONE.................................302 402-5678
Shaik Sher Ali,
EMP: 75
SALES (est): 730.8K **Privately Held**
SIC: 7361 Employment agencies

(G-1337)
DALE MAPLE COUNTRY CLUB INC
180 Mapledale Cir (19904-7118)
PHONE.................................302 674-2505
Larry Mc Allister, *President*
EMP: 40 EST: 1925
SQ FT: 8,750
SALES (est): 2.1MM **Privately Held**
SIC: 7997 Country club, membership; golf club, membership

(G-1338)
DAMON BACA
Also Called: Cross Border It
8 The Grn Ste 8 # 8 (19901-3618)
PHONE.................................858 837-0800
Damon Baca, *Owner*
EMP: 6
SQ FT: 15,000
SALES (est): 135.3K **Privately Held**
SIC: 7372 7389 Prepackaged software; drawback service, customs

(G-1339)
DANCE CONSERVATORY
Also Called: Ballet Theatre of Dover
522 Otis Dr (19901-4630)
P.O. Box 493 (19903-0493)
PHONE.................................302 734-9717
Teresa Emmons, *Owner*
EMP: 9
SALES (est): 203.1K **Privately Held**
SIC: 7911 Dance studio & school; dance instructor & school services

(G-1340)
DANIEL A YODER
2956 Yoder Dr (19904-5846)
PHONE.................................302 730-4076
Daniel Yoder, *Principal*

Dover - Kent County (G-1341)

EMP: 2
SALES (est): 145.8K **Privately Held**
SIC: 2431 Millwork

(G-1341)
DAS FINANCIAL HEALTH LLC
53 Chatham Ct (19901-3933)
PHONE.................570 947-7931
Nandita Das, *Principal*
EMP: 8
SALES (est): 76K **Privately Held**
SIC: 8099 Health & allied services

(G-1342)
DAVES DISC MFFLERS OF DVER DE
Also Called: Meineke Discount Mufflers
1312 S Dupont Hwy (19901-4404)
PHONE.................302 678-8803
David Kaplan, *President*
EMP: 6
SQ FT: 3,200
SALES: 1MM **Privately Held**
SIC: 7533 Muffler shop, sale or repair & installation

(G-1343)
DAVES TOWING INC
1927 Peachtree Run Rd (19901-7734)
P.O. Box 361 (19903-0361)
PHONE.................302 697-9073
David Pallam, *Principal*
EMP: 4
SALES (est): 147.5K **Privately Held**
SIC: 7549 Towing services

(G-1344)
DAVID G REYES MD
Also Called: Integrated Care of Dover
29 Gooden Ave (19904-4143)
P.O. Box 813 (19903-0813)
PHONE.................302 735-7780
EMP: 4 EST: 2001
SALES (est): 180K **Privately Held**
SIC: 8011 Medical Doctor's Office

(G-1345)
DAWSON BUS SERVICE INC
1 Weston Dr Ste A (19904-2769)
PHONE.................302 678-2594
Betty Bell, *General Mgr*
EMP: 13
SALES (corp-wide): 2.3MM **Privately Held**
SIC: 4142 4151 Bus charter service, except local; school buses
PA: Dawson Bus Service, Inc
   405 E Camden Wyoming Ave
   Camden DE 19934
   302 697-9501

(G-1346)
DAYS INN DOVER DOWNTOWN
272 N Dupont Hwy (19901-7510)
PHONE.................302 674-8002
Hatal Christian, *Owner*
EMP: 20
SALES: 999K **Privately Held**
SIC: 7011 Hotels & motels

(G-1347)
DE COLORES FAMILY CHILD CARE
917 Monroe Ter (19904-4119)
PHONE.................302 883-3298
Sarita Medero, *Principal*
EMP: 5
SALES (est): 57.5K **Privately Held**
SIC: 8351 Child day care services

(G-1348)
DEDICATED TO WOMEN OB GYN
200 Banning St Ste 320 (19904-3488)
PHONE.................302 674-0223
Robert Q Scacheri, *Partner*
Pat Randell, *Partner*
EMP: 50
SALES (est): 4.1MM **Privately Held**
SIC: 8011 Gynecologist

(G-1349)
DEE & DOREENS TEAM
1671 S State St (19901-5148)
PHONE.................302 677-0030
Dee Demolen, *Owner*
EMP: 12
SALES (est): 473.7K **Privately Held**
WEB: www.deeanddoreen.com
SIC: 6531 Real estate brokers & agents

(G-1350)
DEL BAY RETRIEVER CLUB
68 Mcbry Dr (19901-4408)
PHONE.................302 678-8583
Theodore Finley, *Treasurer*
EMP: 4
SALES: 26.3K **Privately Held**
SIC: 7997 Membership sports & recreation clubs

(G-1351)
DEL HOMES INC
1567 Mckee Rd (19904-1380)
PHONE.................302 730-1479
EMP: 29
SALES (corp-wide): 3.4MM **Privately Held**
SIC: 1521 Single-family housing construction
PA: Del Homes Inc
   1309 Ponderosa Dr
   Magnolia DE 19962
   302 697-8204

(G-1352)
DEL-MAR APPLIANCE OF DELAWARE (PA)
230 S Governors Ave (19904-6704)
PHONE.................302 674-2414
Jo Ann Mandarano, *President*
Bruce Nygard, *Vice Pres*
EMP: 9 EST: 1968
SQ FT: 12,000
SALES (est): 1.4MM **Privately Held**
SIC: 7629 5722 Electrical household appliance repair; electric household appliances

(G-1353)
DEL-ONE FEDERAL CREDIT UNION
150 E Water St Ste 1 (19901-3619)
PHONE.................302 739-2390
Sharee Coleman, *Vice Pres*
John Ricca, *Officer*
EMP: 19 **Privately Held**
SIC: 6061 Federal credit unions
PA: Del-One Federal Credit Union
   270 Beiser Blvd
   Dover DE 19904

(G-1354)
DEL-ONE FEDERAL CREDIT UNION
270 Beiser Blvd (19904-7790)
PHONE.................302 739-4496
EMP: 5 EST: 2015
SALES (est): 272.1K **Privately Held**
SIC: 6061 Federal Credit Unions

(G-1355)
DEL-ONE FEDERAL CREDIT UNION (PA)
270 Beiser Blvd (19904-7790)
PHONE.................302 739-4496
Ron Baron, *President*
Jennifer Ellis, *Opers Staff*
Kellie Rychwalski, *CFO*
Beth Pritchett, *Loan Officer*
Amy Durham, *Business Anlyst*
EMP: 45
SALES: 19MM **Privately Held**
WEB: www.del-one.org
SIC: 6061 6163 Federal credit unions; loan brokers

(G-1356)
DEL-ONE FEDERAL CREDIT UNION
635 S Bay Rd (19901-4601)
PHONE.................302 739-6389
Lisa Brewer, *Branch Mgr*
EMP: 4 **Privately Held**
WEB: www.del-one.org
SIC: 6061 Federal credit unions
PA: Del-One Federal Credit Union
   270 Beiser Blvd
   Dover DE 19904

(G-1357)
DELAWARE AG MUSEUM & VLG
866 N Dupont Hwy (19901-2003)
PHONE.................302 734-1618
Joyce Farmer, *Business Mgr*
Carolyn Claypoole, *Exec Dir*
EMP: 9
SQ FT: 300,000
SALES: 350K **Privately Held**
WEB: www.agriculturalmuseum.org
SIC: 8412 7299 Museum; facility rental & party planning services

(G-1358)
DELAWARE BAIL BONDS
414 Denison St (19901)
PHONE.................302 734-9881
Berry Udoff, *Manager*
EMP: 8
SALES (est): 330.4K **Privately Held**
WEB: www.delawarebailbonds.com
SIC: 7389 Bail bonding

(G-1359)
DELAWARE BOAT REGISTRATION
89 Kings Hwy (19901-7305)
PHONE.................302 739-9916
Vicki Rhodes, *Manager*
EMP: 5 EST: 2015
SALES (est): 79.2K **Privately Held**
SIC: 7997 Boating club, membership

(G-1360)
DELAWARE BREAST CANCER COALIT
Also Called: Delaware Brast Cncer Coalition
165 Commerce Way Ste 2 (19904-8224)
PHONE.................302 672-6435
Lois Wilkinson, *Branch Mgr*
EMP: 4
SALES (est): 127.4K
SALES (corp-wide): 1.2MM **Privately Held**
SIC: 8322 Individual & family services
PA: Delaware Breast Cancer Coalition, Inc.
   100 W 10th St Ste 209
   Wilmington DE 19801
   302 778-1102

(G-1361)
DELAWARE BRICK COMPANY
492 Webbs Ln (19904-5440)
PHONE.................302 883-2807
Jim Pelaclathan, *Manager*
EMP: 6
SALES (corp-wide): 10.3MM **Privately Held**
SIC: 5032 5082 Brick, stone & related material; masonry equipment & supplies
PA: Delaware Brick Company
   1114 Centerville Rd
   Wilmington DE 19804
   302 994-0948

(G-1362)
DELAWARE CRDOVASCULAR ASSOC PA
1113 S State St Ste 100 (19901-4112)
PHONE.................302 734-7676
Teri Flores, *Manager*
Stephen Blumberg, *Cardiovascular*
Kahlad Eljazzar, *Cardiovascular*
Michael Shea, *Cardiovascular*
Gurmeet Singh, *Cardiovascular*
EMP: 19 **Privately Held**
WEB: www.delawarecardiovascular.com
SIC: 8011 Cardiologist & cardio-vascular specialist
PA: Delaware Cardiovascular Associates, P.A.
   1403 Foulk Rd Ste 101a
   Wilmington DE 19803

(G-1363)
DELAWARE DENTAL CARE CENTERS
73 Greentree Dr 407 (19904-7646)
PHONE.................410 474-5520
Jeffrey M Wilson DDS, *Principal*
EMP: 5
SALES: 500K **Privately Held**
SIC: 8021 Offices & clinics of dentists

(G-1364)
DELAWARE DEPARTMENT FINANCE
Also Called: Delaware State Lottery
1575 Mckee Rd Ste 102 (19904-1382)
PHONE.................302 739-5291
Vernon Kirk, *Director*
Judy Everett, *Administration*
EMP: 24 **Privately Held**
WEB: www.delottery.com
SIC: 8111 9311 Legal services; lottery control board, government;
HQ: Delaware Department Of Finance
   820 N French St Ste 8
   Wilmington DE 19801

(G-1365)
DELAWARE DEPT TRANSPORTATION
Also Called: Dart First State
655 S Bay Rd Ste 4g (19901-4656)
PHONE.................302 577-3278
Steve Williams, *Buyer*
Jennifer Wilson, *Controller*
EMP: 124 **Privately Held**
WEB: www.dartfirststate.com
SIC: 8611 9621 Business associations; regulation, administration of transportation;
HQ: Delaware Department Of Transportation
   800 S Bay Rd
   Dover DE 19901

(G-1366)
DELAWARE DERMATOLGY PA
Also Called: Andrews, Joseph F MD
737 S Queen St Ste 1 (19904-3529)
PHONE.................302 736-1800
Joseph Andrews MD, *Owner*
EMP: 5
SALES (est): 447.6K **Privately Held**
SIC: 8011 Dermatologist

(G-1367)
DELAWARE DRNKING DRVER PROGRAM (PA)
1661 S Dupont Hwy (19901-5129)
PHONE.................302 736-4326
Walter Mc Cann, *President*
Bruce Lorenz, *Vice Pres*
EMP: 8
SQ FT: 1,500
SALES (est): 559.7K **Privately Held**
SIC: 8322 Alcoholism counseling, nontreatment

(G-1368)
DELAWARE EYE CARE CENTER (PA)
833 S Governors Ave (19904-4158)
PHONE.................302 674-1121
Gary Markowitz MD, *President*
Dr Gary I Markowitz, *Founder*
EMP: 25
SALES (est): 3.4MM **Privately Held**
SIC: 8042 Offices & clinics of optometrists

(G-1369)
DELAWARE FFA FOUNDATION INC
35 Commerce Way Ste 1 (19904-5747)
PHONE.................302 857-6493
Lisa Falconetti, *President*
Robert Lawson, *Vice Pres*
James Testerman, *Treasurer*
Amber Bullock, *Admin Sec*
EMP: 9
SALES: 44.2K **Privately Held**
SIC: 8641 Civic social & fraternal associations

(G-1370)
DELAWARE FIRST MEDIA CORP
1200 N Dupont Hwy (19901-2202)
PHONE.................302 857-7096
Nancy L Karibjanian, *Principal*
Jane Vincent, *Manager*
EMP: 7
SALES: 630.9K **Privately Held**
SIC: 4899 Communication services

Dover - Kent County (G-1400)

(G-1371)
DELAWARE FNCL EDCATN ALNCE INC
8 W Loockerman St Ste 200 (19904-7324)
P.O. Box 494 (19903-0494)
PHONE.................................302 674-0288
Sarah Long, *President*
EMP: 7
SALES: 746.9K **Privately Held**
SIC: 8299 7389 Educational services;

(G-1372)
DELAWARE FRIENDS OF FOLK
275 Simms Woods Rd (19901-2330)
PHONE.................................302 678-1423
Jonathan Kidd, *Chairman*
EMP: 7
SALES (est): 111.4K **Privately Held**
SIC: 8699 Personal interest organization

(G-1373)
DELAWARE GUIDANCE SER
Also Called: Act Program
103 Mont Blanc Blvd (19904-7615)
PHONE.................................302 678-3020
Rhonda Quin, *Director*
EMP: 35
SALES (corp-wide): 10.1MM **Privately Held**
WEB: www.delawareguidance.org
SIC: 8322 Individual & family services
PA: Delaware Guidance Services For Children And Youth, Inc.
1213 Delaware Ave
Wilmington DE 19806
302 652-3948

(G-1374)
DELAWARE HEALTH CARE COMM
Oneill Bldg 410 Federal (19901)
PHONE.................................302 739-2730
Paula Roy, *Exec Dir*
EMP: 10
SALES (est): 623.9K **Privately Held**
SIC: 8621 Health association

(G-1375)
DELAWARE HEALTH INFO NETWRK
107 Wolf Creek Blvd Ste 2 (19901-4970)
PHONE.................................302 678-0220
Amanda Gamble, *Principal*
Michael Macdonald, *Manager*
Garrett Murawski, *Manager*
Jamie Rocke, *Manager*
Ed Seaton, *Manager*
EMP: 11
SALES (est): 1.5MM **Privately Held**
SIC: 8621 Health association

(G-1376)
DELAWARE HEALTHCARE ASSN
1280 S Governors Ave (19904-4802)
PHONE.................................302 674-2853
Wayne Smith, *President*
Suzanne Raab-Long, *Vice Pres*
Christina C Bryan, *Director*
EMP: 4
SALES: 1.2MM **Privately Held**
WEB: www.deha.org
SIC: 8611 8742 Trade associations; hospital & health services consultant

(G-1377)
DELAWARE HEART & VASCULAR PA
200 Banning St Ste 340 (19904-3490)
PHONE.................................302 734-1414
Terry Flores, *President*
Terri Rosetta, *Office Mgr*
EMP: 8
SALES (est): 1.1MM **Privately Held**
SIC: 8011 Cardiologist & cardio-vascular specialist

(G-1378)
DELAWARE HOSPICE INC
911 S Dupont Hwy (19901-4468)
PHONE.................................302 678-4444
Judi Tulak, *Manager*
EMP: 25
SALES (corp-wide): 27.4MM **Privately Held**
SIC: 8082 Home health care services
PA: Delaware Hospice Inc.
16 Polly Drmmd Shpg Ctr 2
Newark DE 19711
302 478-5707

(G-1379)
DELAWARE INTERVENTIONAL SPINE
Also Called: Delaware Spine Institute
1673 S State St Ste B (19901-5148)
PHONE.................................302 674-8444
Ron Lieberman, *Mng Member*
EMP: 7
SQ FT: 2,000
SALES (est): 1.1MM **Privately Held**
SIC: 8011 Physicians' office, including specialists

(G-1380)
DELAWARE LANDSCAPING INC
106 Semans Dr (19904-6460)
P.O. Box 501, Camden Wyoming (19934-5001)
PHONE.................................302 698-3001
Steve Gedney, *President*
EMP: 6
SQ FT: 6,000
SALES (est): 270K **Privately Held**
SIC: 0782 Landscape contractors

(G-1381)
DELAWARE MOBILE DENTISTRY
189 S Fairfield Dr (19901-5756)
PHONE.................................302 698-9901
Terry Bryan, *Principal*
EMP: 4
SALES (est): 127.7K **Privately Held**
SIC: 8021 Offices & clinics of dentists

(G-1382)
DELAWARE NATIVE PLANTS SOCIETY
163 Mitscher Rd (19901-7424)
PHONE.................................302 735-8918
Eric Zuelke, *President*
EMP: 4
SALES (est): 202.5K **Privately Held**
SIC: 8733 Noncommercial biological research organization

(G-1383)
DELAWARE OBGYN & WOMENS HEALTH
1057 S Bradford St (19904-4141)
PHONE.................................302 730-0633
Mark Anthony, *Principal*
EMP: 5 **EST:** 2009
SALES (est): 255.2K **Privately Held**
SIC: 8011 Gynecologist

(G-1384)
DELAWARE OPEN M R I & C T
1030 Forrest Ave Ste 105 (19904-3382)
PHONE.................................302 734-5800
Victoria Sanchez, *Principal*
EMP: 4
SALES (est): 215.6K **Privately Held**
SIC: 8011 Radiologist

(G-1385)
DELAWARE ORTHOPEDIC
230 Beiser Blvd Ste 100 (19904-7791)
PHONE.................................302 730-0840
Eric Todd Schwartz, *Principal*
EMP: 4
SALES (est): 358.8K **Privately Held**
SIC: 8011 Orthopedic physician

(G-1386)
DELAWARE PARENTS ASSOCIATION
101 W Loockerman St 3a (19904-7328)
PHONE.................................302 678-9288
Harold E Stafford, *Exec Dir*
Earlene Jackson, *Exec Dir*
EMP: 12
SALES (est): 390K **Privately Held**
WEB: www.delparents.org
SIC: 8641 Parent-teachers' association

(G-1387)
DELAWARE PODIATRIST MEDICINE (PA)
22 Old Rudnick Ln (19901-4912)
PHONE.................................302 674-9255
Ronald Kahn, *Owner*
Kathlene Khan, *Manager*
EMP: 8
SALES (est): 667.3K **Privately Held**
SIC: 8043 Offices & clinics of podiatrists

(G-1388)
DELAWARE PRIMARY CARE LLC
810 New Burton Rd Ste 3 (19904-5488)
PHONE.................................302 730-0554
Osun Koya,
EMP: 8
SALES (est): 565.8K **Privately Held**
SIC: 8011 Internal medicine, physician/surgeon

(G-1389)
DELAWARE SECRETARY OF STATE
Also Called: Delaware St Historic Pres
21 The Grn A (19901-3611)
PHONE.................................302 736-7400
Cherie Biron, *Sales Mgr*
Kimberly Judy, *Manager*
Timothy Slavin, *Director*
Laurie Corsa, *Officer*
EMP: 10 **Privately Held**
SIC: 8999 9199 Natural resource preservation service; general government administration;
HQ: Delaware Secretary Of State
401 Federal St Ste 3
Dover DE 19901
302 739-4111

(G-1390)
DELAWARE SENIOR OLYMPICS INC
1121 Forrest Ave (19904-3308)
PHONE.................................302 736-5698
Gene J Mirolli, *President*
Conny Wertz, *Exec Dir*
EMP: 6
SALES: 100.3K **Privately Held**
SIC: 8322 Senior citizens' center or association

(G-1391)
DELAWARE SKATING CENTER LTD
Also Called: Dover Skating Center
2201 S Dupont Hwy (19901-5512)
PHONE.................................302 697-3218
Virgil Dooley, *Manager*
EMP: 25
SALES (corp-wide): 3.6MM **Privately Held**
WEB: www.delaware.entertainment.com
SIC: 7999 Roller skating rink operation
PA: Delaware Skating Center Ltd Inc
801 Christiana Rd
Newark DE 19713
302 366-0473

(G-1392)
DELAWARE SOLID WASTE AUTHORITY (PA)
1128 S Bradford St (19904-6919)
P.O. Box 455 (19903-0455)
PHONE.................................302 739-5361
Pasquale S Canzano Pe Dee, *CEO*
Richard V Pryor, *Ch of Bd*
Joseph Koskey, *General Mgr*
Toby Ryan, *Principal*
Tim Sheldon, *Principal*
EMP: 50
SQ FT: 14,000
SALES (est): 85.8MM **Privately Held**
WEB: www.dswa.com
SIC: 4953 Recycling, waste materials

(G-1393)
DELAWARE SOLID WASTE AUTHORITY
Also Called: Cherry Island Landfill
1128 S Bradford St (19904-6919)
PHONE.................................302 764-2732
Robin Roddie, *Manager*
EMP: 31

SALES (corp-wide): 85.8MM **Privately Held**
WEB: www.dswa.com
SIC: 4953 Sanitary landfill operation
PA: Delaware Solid Waste Authority
1128 S Bradford St
Dover DE 19904
302 739-5361

(G-1394)
DELAWARE SPINE REHABILITATION
642 S Queen St (19904-3506)
PHONE.................................302 883-2292
EMP: 8
SALES (est): 73.3K **Privately Held**
SIC: 8093 Rehabilitation center, outpatient treatment

(G-1395)
DELAWARE SSTNBLE ENRGY UTILITY
500 W Loockerman St # 400 (19904-7309)
PHONE.................................302 883-3038
Tony Deprima, *Principal*
EMP: 4
SALES: 15.5MM **Privately Held**
SIC: 8731 Energy research

(G-1396)
DELAWARE STATE EDUCATION ASSN (PA)
136 E Water St (19901-3614)
PHONE.................................302 734-5834
Judy Anderson, *Business Mgr*
EMP: 25
SALES: 6MM **Privately Held**
SIC: 8631 8742 Labor unions & similar labor organizations; management consulting services

(G-1397)
DELAWARE STATE PRINTING
110 Galaxy Dr (19901-9262)
PHONE.................................302 228-9431
EMP: 2
SALES (est): 92.3K **Privately Held**
SIC: 2752 Commercial printing, lithographic

(G-1398)
DELAWARE STNDRDBRE OWNRS ASSC
830 Walker Rd (19904-2748)
PHONE.................................302 678-3058
Charles Lockart, *Principal*
Francis Pitts, *Principal*
Ralph Holloway, *Vice Pres*
Presley Moore, *Treasurer*
Sal Dimario, *Exec Dir*
EMP: 5 **EST:** 1997
SQ FT: 1,350
SALES: 4MM **Privately Held**
WEB: www.deharnessracing.com
SIC: 8611 Business associations

(G-1399)
DELAWARE STORAGE & PIPELINE CO
987 Port Mahon Rd (19901-4833)
P.O. Box 313 (19903-0313)
PHONE.................................302 736-1774
Charles Denault, *CEO*
George Steady, *Terminal Mgr*
EMP: 8 **Privately Held**
WEB: www.delawarespc.com
SIC: 1389 Pumping of oil & gas wells
HQ: Delaware Storage & Pipeline Co Inc
400 Amherst St Ste 202
Nashua NH
603 886-7300

(G-1400)
DELAWARE STOREFRONTS LLC
720 S Governors Ave (19904-4106)
PHONE.................................302 697-1850
John E Layton Jr, *Mng Member*
EMP: 9
SQ FT: 40,000
SALES (est): 842.6K **Privately Held**
SIC: 1793 Glass & glazing work

Dover - Kent County (G-1401)   GEOGRAPHIC SECTION

(G-1401)
DELAWARE SURGERY CENTER LLC
200 Banning St Ste 110 (19904-3486)
PHONE...................................302 730-0217
Kathy Freshwater, *Materials Mgr*
Jeffrey Barton, *Med Doctor*
Thomas Barnett, *Anesthesiology*
Jennifer Anderson, *Director*
Asher Carey,
▲ **EMP:** 48
SALES: 7.9MM **Privately Held**
WEB: www.desurgery.com
SIC: 8011 Surgeon

(G-1402)
DELAWARE TIRE CENTER INC
207 S Governors Ave (19904-6703)
PHONE...................................302 674-0234
Tom Lindale, *Manager*
EMP: 10
SALES (corp-wide): 10.2MM **Privately Held**
SIC: 5531 5014 5013 Automotive tires; batteries, automotive & truck; automobile tires & tubes; automotive batteries
PA: Delaware Tire Center, Inc.
  616 S College Ave
  Newark DE 19713
  302 368-2531

(G-1403)
DELAWARE TRANSPORTATION AUTH
800 S Bay Rd (19901-4685)
PHONE...................................302 760-2000
Shailene Bhatt, *Regional Mgr*
EMP: 13
SALES (est): 459K **Privately Held**
SIC: 4111 Local & suburban transit

(G-1404)
DELAWARE TRNSP SVCS INC
130 Falmouth Way (19904-5391)
PHONE...................................302 981-6562
Nicole Jenkins, *Owner*
EMP: 4 **EST:** 2007
SALES (est): 136.4K **Privately Held**
SIC: 4111 4731 Airport transportation; transportation agents & brokers

(G-1405)
DELAWARE WIC PROGRAM (PA)
Also Called: Administrative Office
635 S Bay Rd 1c (19901-4601)
PHONE...................................302 741-2900
Joanne Whire, *Director*
Joanne White, *Director*
EMP: 8
SALES (est): 711.3K **Privately Held**
SIC: 8322 Individual & family services

(G-1406)
DELAWARE WIC PROGRAM
Also Called: Wic State Office of Delaware
805 River Rd (19901-3753)
PHONE...................................302 857-5000
Steve Dettweyler, *Principal*
EMP: 7
SALES (corp-wide): 711.3K **Privately Held**
SIC: 8322 Individual & family services
PA: Delaware Wic Program
  635 S Bay Rd 1c
  Dover DE 19901
  302 741-2900

(G-1407)
DELMARV ORTHTCS & PROSTHTCS
30 E Division St (19901-7302)
PHONE...................................302 678-8311
Robert E McElligott, *Mng Member*
EMP: 2
SALES: 370.3K **Privately Held**
SIC: 3842 Orthopedic appliances; prosthetic appliances

(G-1408)
DELMARVA ANMAL EMRGNCY CTR LLC
1482 E Lebanon Rd (19901-5833)
PHONE...................................302 697-0850
Bernie Brown, *Principal*
EMP: 4
SALES (est): 241.5K **Privately Held**
SIC: 0742 Animal hospital services, pets & other animal specialties; veterinarian, animal specialties

(G-1409)
DELMARVA CLEANING & MAINT INC
1131 N Dupont Hwy Fl 2 (19901-2008)
P.O. Box 936 (19903-0936)
PHONE...................................302 734-1856
Charlotte E Mathes, *President*
EMP: 150
SQ FT: 2,000
SALES (est): 2.7MM **Privately Held**
SIC: 7349 Janitorial service, contract basis; cleaning service, industrial or commercial

(G-1410)
DELMARVA EQUINE CLINIC
Also Called: Egli, Michelle D Dvm
1008 S Governors Ave (19904-6902)
PHONE...................................302 735-4735
Janice Sosnowski, *Owner*
Julianna Scarangelli, *Office Admin*
EMP: 6
SALES (est): 370K **Privately Held**
SIC: 0742 Veterinarian, animal specialties

(G-1411)
DELMARVA PROSTHODONTICS
871 S Governors Ave Ste 1 (19904-4115)
PHONE...................................302 674-8331
Christopher David Burns, *Principal*
EMP: 5 **EST:** 2008
SALES (est): 421.3K **Privately Held**
SIC: 8021 Prosthodontist

(G-1412)
DELMARVA WATER SOLUTIONS
1039 Fowler Ct (19901-4638)
PHONE...................................302 674-0509
John Sensi, *President*
Steven Cropper, *Vice Pres*
EMP: 5
SALES (est): 432.1K **Privately Held**
SIC: 7389 Water softener service

(G-1413)
DEMPSEY FARMS LLC
1708 Fast Landing Rd (19901-2718)
PHONE...................................302 734-4937
Alice Mae Jacobs, *Principal*
Charles Dempsey Jr, *Principal*
EMP: 17
SALES (est): 997K **Privately Held**
SIC: 0241 7389 Dairy farms;

(G-1414)
DEO TRUCKING
2505 White Oak Rd (19901-3345)
PHONE...................................302 744-9832
Surinder Singh, *Principal*
EMP: 4
SALES (est): 215K **Privately Held**
SIC: 4212 Local trucking, without storage

(G-1415)
DERBY SOFTWARE LLC (PA)
8 The Grn Ste A (19901-3618)
PHONE...................................502 435-1371
Jordan Cox,
EMP: 1
SALES (est): 71.5K **Privately Held**
SIC: 7372 7389 Prepackaged software;

(G-1416)
DESS MACHINE & MANUFACTURING
5049 N Dupont Hwy (19901-2346)
PHONE...................................302 736-7457
Martin Graham, *President*
Susan Graham, *Vice Pres*
Evan Graham, *Treasurer*
Stacey Graham, *Admin Sec*
EMP: 2
SQ FT: 7,200
SALES (est): 288.8K **Privately Held**
SIC: 3599 Machine shop, jobbing & repair; custom machinery

(G-1417)
DEVARY ELECTRIC INC
3 Forrest Hills Ct (19904-9443)
PHONE...................................302 674-4560
EMP: 8
SALES: 2MM **Privately Held**
SIC: 1731 Electrical Contractor

(G-1418)
DEVON SADLOWSKI DMD
882 Walker Rd Ste A (19904-2792)
PHONE...................................302 735-8940
Devon Sadlowski DMD, *Owner*
EMP: 12
SALES (est): 584.8K **Privately Held**
SIC: 8021 Dental surgeon

(G-1419)
DFS CORPORATE SERVICES LLC
34 Starlifter Ave (19901-9245)
PHONE...................................302 735-3902
Bianca Albarran, *Sales Staff*
Richard Palmer, *Manager*
Betty Garrett, *Manager*
EMP: 275
SALES (corp-wide): 12.8B **Publicly Held**
WEB: www.discovercard.com
SIC: 7389 6153 Credit card service; short-term business credit
HQ: Dfs Corporate Services Llc
  2500 Lake Cook Rd 2
  Riverwoods IL 60015
  224 405-0900

(G-1420)
DIAMOND COMPUTER INC
4608 S Dupont Hwy Ste 4 (19901-6408)
PHONE...................................302 674-4064
Philip Malmstrom, *President*
Karl Wojcik, *Partner*
EMP: 4
SQ FT: 3,400
SALES (est): 315K **Privately Held**
WEB: www.diamondcomputer.com
SIC: 7378 5734 Computer maintenance & repair; computer peripheral equipment

(G-1421)
DIAMOND ELECTRIC INC
3566 Peachtree Run Rd # 1 (19901-7661)
P.O. Box 996 (19903-0996)
PHONE...................................302 697-3296
Tom J Hartley, *President*
Chuck Arnott, *Project Mgr*
Dawn Godfrey, *Controller*
Jerry Craig, *Technology*
EMP: 36 **EST:** 1969
SQ FT: 7,500
SALES: 11.8MM **Privately Held**
SIC: 1731 General electrical contractor

(G-1422)
DIAMOND MECHANICAL INC
3588 Peachtree Run Rd (19901-7647)
PHONE...................................302 697-7694
EMP: 20
SALES (est): 37.2K **Privately Held**
SIC: 8711 Mechanical engineering

(G-1423)
DIAMOND MOTOR SPORTS INC
Also Called: Price Honda
4595 S Dupont Hwy (19901-6034)
PHONE...................................302 697-3222
Warren A Price, *President*
Alvin Atkinson, *Sales Mgr*
Stewart Crouch, *IT/INT Sup*
Linda Topping, *Admin Sec*
EMP: 100 **EST:** 1966
SQ FT: 16,000
SALES (est): 34.9MM **Privately Held**
WEB: www.ridedms.com
SIC: 5511 5012 Automobiles, new & used; automobiles & other motor vehicles

(G-1424)
DIAMOND STATE CLT INC
Also Called: DIAMOND STATE COMMUNITY LAND T
9 E Loockerman St Ste 205 (19901-7347)
P.O. Box 1484 (19903-1484)
PHONE...................................800 282-0477
Amy Walls, *President*
Jeannine Knight, *Principal*
Van Temple, *Exec Dir*
EMP: 10
SALES: 271K **Privately Held**
SIC: 8748 Urban planning & consulting services

(G-1425)
DIAMOND STATE CORPORATION (PA)
Also Called: Berry Van Lines
602 Pear St (19904-2832)
PHONE...................................302 674-1300
W Leland Berry, *President*
EMP: 54
SQ FT: 100,000
SALES (est): 12.3MM **Privately Held**
SIC: 4213 4214 Trucking, except local; local trucking with storage

(G-1426)
DILLS ELECTRIC
4508 N Dupont Hwy (19901-1563)
PHONE...................................302 674-3444
Charles Dill, *Owner*
EMP: 2
SALES: 70.1K **Privately Held**
SIC: 7694 Electric motor repair

(G-1427)
DIPPOLD MARBLE GRANITE
101 Hatchery Rd (19901-1502)
PHONE...................................302 734-8505
EMP: 5
SALES (corp-wide): 1MM **Privately Held**
SIC: 1743 Terrazzo, tile, marble, mosaic work
PA: Dippold Marble Granite
  110 W Main St
  Middletown DE 19709
  302 324-9101

(G-1428)
DIRECTRESTORE LLC
3500 S Dupont Hwy (19901-6041)
PHONE...................................650 276-0384
Emil Sildos,
EMP: 19
SALES (est): 78K
SALES (corp-wide): 6.6MM **Privately Held**
SIC: 7372 Business oriented computer software
HQ: Axcient, Inc.
  1161 San Antonio Rd
  Mountain View CA 94043
  650 314-7300

(G-1429)
DISRUPT INDUSTRIES DELEWARE
8 The Grn (19901-3618)
PHONE...................................424 229-9300
Gary Elphick, *CEO*
EMP: 3
SALES (est): 85.6K **Privately Held**
SIC: 3949 Sporting & athletic goods

(G-1430)
DISRUPT PHARMA TECH AFRICA INC
8 The Grn Ste A (19901-3618)
PHONE...................................312 945-8002
Vivian Nwakah, *Principal*
EMP: 7
SALES (est): 198.8K **Privately Held**
SIC: 5122 Drugs & drug proprietaries

(G-1431)
DISTILLATE MEDIA LLC
141 Shinnecock Rd (19904-9446)
PHONE...................................302 270-7945
Michael Pillsbury,
EMP: 1 **EST:** 2017 **Privately Held**
SIC: 8299 2741 Educational services;

(G-1432)
DITROCCHIO MARIA ANTONETTA
Also Called: Busy Bees Home Learning Center
814 S Governors Ave (19904-4107)
PHONE...................................302 450-6790
Ree Ditrocchio, *Principal*
EMP: 5

2020 Harris Directory of Delaware Businesses

▲ = Import ▼ = Export
◆ = Import/Export

GEOGRAPHIC SECTION
Dover - Kent County (G-1461)

SALES (est): 60.1K **Privately Held**
SIC: 8351 Child day care services

(G-1433)
DIVINE ELEMENT HBB
405 W Lebanon Rd (19901-6155)
PHONE....................302 538-5209
Tamara Vicere, *Principal*
EMP: 3
SALES (est): 174K **Privately Held**
SIC: 2819 Elements

(G-1434)
DIXON CONTRACTING INC
1614 Seeneytown Rd (19904-4437)
PHONE....................302 653-4623
Lee Dixon, *President*
EMP: 8
SQ FT: 5,662
SALES (est): 1.1MM **Privately Held**
SIC: 1794 Excavation & grading, building construction

(G-1435)
DNREC AIR WASTE MANAGEMENT
30 S American Ave (19901-7346)
PHONE....................302 739-9406
Wanda Hurley, *Manager*
Sergio Huerta, *Administration*
EMP: 9
SALES: 5MM **Privately Held**
SIC: 8741 Management services

(G-1436)
DOCTORS PATHOLOGY SERVICES PA
1253 College Park Dr (19904-8713)
PHONE....................302 677-0000
Raman Fukumar, *President*
Theresa Smith, *COO*
Jenna Murfree, *Info Tech Dir*
EMP: 32
SQ FT: 10,000
SALES (est): 3.4MM **Privately Held**
WEB: www.dpspa.com
SIC: 8011 Pathologist

(G-1437)
DONALD C SAVOY INC
Also Called: Health Insurance Associates
5158 S Dupont Hwy (19901-6411)
PHONE....................302 697-4100
Jay Moriello, *Branch Mgr*
EMP: 8
SALES (corp-wide): 12.8MM **Privately Held**
SIC: 6411 Insurance brokers
PA: Donald C. Savoy, Inc.
25b Hanover Rd Ste 220
Florham Park NJ
973 377-2220

(G-1438)
DOROSHOW PASQUALE KARWITZ SIEG
Also Called: Law Offices Doroshow Pasquele
500 W Loockerman St # 120 (19904-7309)
PHONE....................302 674-7100
Donald Grogery, *Manager*
EMP: 12
SALES (corp-wide): 10.6MM **Privately Held**
SIC: 8111 General practice attorney, lawyer
PA: Doroshow Pasquale Krawitz Siegel Bhaya
1202 Kirkwood Hwy
Wilmington DE 19805
302 998-2397

(G-1439)
DOT MATRIX INC (PA)
3500 S Dupont Hwy (19901-6041)
PHONE....................917 657-4918
Huayang Guo, *Vice Pres*
EMP: 5
SALES (est): 461.2K **Privately Held**
SIC: 5961 7389 General merchandise, mail order; business services

(G-1440)
DOUGLAS BENNETTI INSUR AGCY (PA)
43 Voshell Mill Rd (19904-6025)
PHONE....................302 724-4490
Douglas F Bennetti, *Owner*
EMP: 6
SALES (est): 489.8K **Privately Held**
SIC: 6411 Insurance agents

(G-1441)
DOVER ANIMAL HOSPITAL
Also Called: Coon, Chris E Dvm
1151 S Governors Ave (19904-6998)
PHONE....................302 746-2688
Bernard L Brown Dvm, *Owner*
Kathy Study, *Corp Secy*
A G Howie Dvm, *Vice Pres*
EMP: 12
SALES (est): 402K **Privately Held**
SIC: 0742 Animal hospital services, pets & other animal specialties

(G-1442)
DOVER BEHAVORL HLTH 249
725 Horsepond Rd (19901-7232)
PHONE....................302 741-0140
William Weaver, *Manager*
EMP: 9
SALES (est): 458K **Privately Held**
SIC: 8099 Health & allied services

(G-1443)
DOVER CONSULTING SERVICES INC
555 E Loockerman St # 102 (19901-3779)
PHONE....................302 736-1365
Phillip McGinnis, *President*
EMP: 4
SALES (est): 358.8K **Privately Held**
SIC: 6531 Real estate brokers & agents

(G-1444)
DOVER DENTAL ASSOCIATES
65 N Dupont Hwy (19901-4265)
PHONE....................302 734-7634
John Russo, *Owner*
EMP: 17
SALES (est): 449.8K **Privately Held**
SIC: 8021 Dentists' office

(G-1445)
DOVER DOWNS INC
Also Called: Dover Downs Hotel & Casino
1131 N Dupont Hwy (19901-2008)
P.O. Box 843 (19903-0843)
PHONE....................302 674-4600
Denis McGlynn, *Ch of Bd*
Edward Sutor, *President*
Klaus M Belohoubek, *Vice Pres*
Janie Libby, *Vice Pres*
EMP: 803
SQ FT: 90,000
SALES (est): 55MM **Publicly Held**
WEB: www.nashvillesuperspeedway.com
SIC: 7948 7999 Harness horse racing; gambling machines, operation
HQ: Premier Entertainment Iii, Llc
1131 N Dupont Hwy
Dover DE 19901
302 674-4600

(G-1446)
DOVER EDUCATIONAL & CMNTY CTR
744 River Rd (19901-3752)
PHONE....................302 883-3092
Juliette Jones, *Director*
EMP: 18
SALES: 215.3K **Privately Held**
SIC: 8351 8322 Group day care center; individual & family services

(G-1447)
DOVER ELECTRIC SUPPLY CO INC (PA)
1631 S Dupont Hwy (19901-5199)
PHONE....................302 674-0115
Bernard Tudor, *President*
Scott Noll, *Vice Pres*
Bruce Emerson, *Software Dev*
Mary Alice Noll, *Admin Sec*
EMP: 31 EST: 1948
SQ FT: 30,000
SALES (est): 10.9MM **Privately Held**
WEB: www.doverelectric.com
SIC: 5063 Electrical supplies

(G-1448)
DOVER FAMILY PHYSICIANS PA
1342 S Governors Ave (19904-4804)
PHONE....................302 734-2500
Jerome L Abrams MD, *President*
Michael J Bradley Do, *Treasurer*
Jerome Abrams, *Med Doctor*
Joseph F Rubacky III Do, *Admin Sec*
Shalini Shah, *Family Practiti*
EMP: 32
SQ FT: 10,000
SALES (est): 4.6MM **Privately Held**
WEB: www.doverfamilyphysicians.com
SIC: 8011 General & family practice, physician/surgeon

(G-1449)
DOVER FEDERAL CREDIT UNION (PA)
1075 Silver Lake Blvd (19904-2411)
P.O. Box 2009 (19902-2009)
PHONE....................302 678-8000
Chaz Rzewnicki, *CEO*
EMP: 80 EST: 1958
SQ FT: 12,000
SALES: 18.2MM **Privately Held**
WEB: www.doverfcu.com
SIC: 6061 6062 Federal credit unions; state credit unions

(G-1450)
DOVER FMLY CSMTC DENTISTRY LLC
1113 S State St Ste 201 (19901-4112)
PHONE....................302 672-7766
Vanessa Dover, *Manager*
Junior A Dover,
EMP: 5
SQ FT: 2,700
SALES (est): 552.4K **Privately Held**
SIC: 8021 Offices & clinics of dentists

(G-1451)
DOVER GOLF CENTER
924 Artis Dr (19904-5639)
PHONE....................302 674-8275
Rick Jones, *President*
EMP: 6
SALES (est): 220.5K **Privately Held**
SIC: 7992 Public golf courses

(G-1452)
DOVER HEALTH CARE CENTER LLC
212 S Queen St (19904-3550)
PHONE....................302 270-5238
Cheryl Epps,
EMP: 4
SALES (est): 220.1K **Privately Held**
SIC: 8082 Home health care services

(G-1453)
DOVER HOSPITALITY GROUP LLC
Also Called: Fairfield Inn
655 N Dupont Hwy (19901-3936)
PHONE....................302 677-0900
Dan Orledge, *Mng Member*
EMP: 30
SALES (est): 1.4MM **Privately Held**
SIC: 7011 Hotels & motels

(G-1454)
DOVER INTERFAITH MISSION FR HO
684 Forest St (19904-3204)
P.O. Box 1148 (19903-1148)
PHONE....................302 736-3600
Jeanine Kleimo, *Ch of Bd*
Herbert Konowitz, *Vice Chairman*
Katherine Lessard, *Treasurer*
Dorothy Kashner, *Admin Sec*
EMP: 10
SALES (est): 579.8K **Privately Held**
SIC: 8322 Emergency shelters

(G-1455)
DOVER INTL SPEEDWAY INC
1131 N Dupont Hwy (19901-2008)
P.O. Box 843 (19903-0843)
PHONE....................302 857-2114
Denis McGlynn, *President*
EMP: 4
SALES (est): 1.2MM
SALES (corp-wide): 47MM **Publicly Held**
SIC: 7948 Automotive race track operation
PA: Dover Motorsports, Inc.
1131 N Dupont Hwy
Dover DE 19901
302 883-6500

(G-1456)
DOVER LEASING CO INC
613 Clara St (19904-3011)
P.O. Box 603 (19903-0603)
PHONE....................302 674-2300
Richard Weyandt, *President*
Lynne Bergold, *Treasurer*
Pam Weyandt, *Admin Sec*
Robert Zimmerman, *Administration*
EMP: 15 EST: 1955
SQ FT: 5,000
SALES (est): 1.1MM **Privately Held**
SIC: 7513 4111 Truck leasing, without drivers; bus line operations

(G-1457)
DOVER LITHO PRINTING CO
21 Chadwick Dr (19901-5828)
PHONE....................302 698-5292
Michael Frebert, *President*
EMP: 18
SQ FT: 13,500
SALES (est): 1.7MM **Privately Held**
WEB: www.doverlitho.com
SIC: 2752 Commercial printing, offset

(G-1458)
DOVER LUBRICANTS INC
Also Called: Jiffy Lube
236 S Dupont Hwy (19901-4733)
PHONE....................302 674-8282
Edward Arnold, *President*
John Gosnell, *Treasurer*
Roland Bounds, *Admin Sec*
EMP: 11
SALES: 700K **Privately Held**
SIC: 7549 Lubrication service, automotive

(G-1459)
DOVER MALL LLC
Also Called: Dover Security
1365 N Dupont Hwy # 5061 (19901-8710)
PHONE....................302 678-4000
Michele Dousette, *Office Mgr*
EMP: 12 **Publicly Held**
SIC: 6512 Shopping center, property operation only
HQ: Dover Mall, Llc
225 W Washington St
Indianapolis IN 46204

(G-1460)
DOVER MOTORSPORTS INC (PA)
1131 N Dupont Hwy (19901-2008)
P.O. Box 843 (19903-0843)
PHONE....................302 883-6500
Henry B Tippie, *Ch of Bd*
Denis McGlynn, *President*
Michael A Tatoian, *COO*
Klaus M Belohoubek, *Senior VP*
Jerry Dunning, *Vice Pres*
EMP: 57
SALES: 47MM **Publicly Held**
WEB: www.doverdowns.com
SIC: 7948 Automotive race track operation

(G-1461)
DOVER NUNAN LLC
Also Called: SERVPRO of Dover/Middletown
607 Otis Dr (19901-4644)
P.O. Box 485 (19903-0485)
PHONE....................302 697-9776
Charles Nunan III,
EMP: 9
SQ FT: 2,500
SALES (est): 468.6K **Privately Held**
SIC: 7349 Building maintenance se

Dover - Kent County (G-1462) GEOGRAPHIC SECTION

(G-1462)
DOVER OPHTHALMOLOGY ASC LLC
Also Called: Blue Hen Surgery Center The
655 S Bay Rd Ste 5b (19901-4660)
PHONE.................302 724-4720
Christopher A Holden, *President*
EMP: 18 **EST:** 2000
SALES (est): 2MM
SALES (corp-wide): 643.1MM **Privately Held**
WEB: www.amsurg.com
SIC: 8011 Ambulatory surgical center
HQ: Envision Healthcare Corporation
1a Burton Hills Blvd
Nashville TN 37215
615 665-1283

(G-1463)
DOVER ORAL AND MAXILLOFACIAL S
1004 S State St Ste 1 (19901-6901)
PHONE.................302 674-1140
Franklin X Pancko, *Principal*
Jennifer O' Connell,
EMP: 4
SALES (est): 232.2K **Privately Held**
SIC: 8011 Surgeon

(G-1464)
DOVER PLUMBING SUPPLY CO
3626 N Dupont Hwy (19901-1500)
P.O. Box 342 (19903-0342)
PHONE.................302 674-0333
Orlan T Kelley Jr, *President*
Herbert E Kelley, *President*
Orlan T Kelly III, *Treasurer*
Megan Kelley, *Admin Sec*
EMP: 15 **EST:** 1946
SQ FT: 21,000
SALES (est): 6.5MM **Privately Held**
SIC: 5074 Plumbing fittings & supplies

(G-1465)
DOVER POOL & PATIO CENTER INC (PA)
1255 S State St Ste 1 (19901-6932)
PHONE.................302 346-7665
Randy D Anderson, *President*
Vonda Calhoun, *Vice Pres*
EMP: 27
SQ FT: 12,000
SALES (est): 3.8MM **Privately Held**
WEB: www.doverpools.com
SIC: 1799 5999 Swimming pool construction; swimming pool chemicals, equipment & supplies

(G-1466)
DOVER POST CO INC (PA)
Also Called: Smyrna-Clayton Sun Times
609 E Division St (19901-4201)
P.O. Box 664 (19903-0664)
PHONE.................302 653-2083
James A Flood Jr, *President*
James A Flood Sr, *Chairman*
Fred Kaltreider, *Vice Pres*
Mary Kaltreider, *Vice Pres*
Donald G Flood, *Treasurer*
EMP: 100
SQ FT: 18,000
SALES (est): 9.8MM **Privately Held**
WEB: www.doverpost.com
SIC: 2711 2752 Newspapers, publishing & printing; commercial printing, offset

(G-1467)
DOVER POST CO INC
Also Called: Dover Post Web Printing
1196 S Little Creek Rd (19901-4727)
PHONE.................302 678-3616
Mark Whidden, *Principal*
Brian Dawson, *Creative Dir*
EMP: 80
SALES (corp-wide): 9.8MM **Privately Held**
WEB: www.doverpost.com
SIC: 7383 2791 2789 2752 Press service; typesetting; bookbinding & related work; commercial printing, lithographic
PA: The Dover Post Co Inc
609 E Division St
Dover DE 19901
302 653-2083

(G-1468)
DOVER PULMONARY PA
31 Gooden Ave (19904-4143)
PHONE.................302 734-0400
Brian J Walsh, *Partner*
David Jawahar, *Partner*
EMP: 7
SALES (est): 666.4K **Privately Held**
SIC: 8011 Specialized medical practitioners, except internal

(G-1469)
DOVER RENT-ALL INC
Also Called: Dover Rental
35 Commerce Way Ste 180 (19904-5747)
PHONE.................302 739-0860
George C Clapp Jr, *President*
David Clapp, *Corp Secy*
EMP: 18 **EST:** 1973
SALES (est): 3.3MM **Privately Held**
SIC: 6512 7359 Commercial & industrial building operation; equipment rental & leasing

(G-1470)
DOVER SOFT TOUCH CAR WASH
226 N Dupont Hwy (19901-7510)
PHONE.................302 736-6011
Fax: 302 736-8011
EMP: 20
SALES (est): 465.6K **Privately Held**
SIC: 7542 Carwash

(G-1471)
DOVER SYMPHONY ORCHESTRA INC
P.O. Box 163 (19903-0163)
PHONE.................302 734-1701
Robert Moyer, *President*
EMP: 9
SALES: 30K **Privately Held**
SIC: 7929 Symphony orchestras

(G-1472)
DOVER VOLKSWAGEN INC
1387 N Dupont Hwy (19901-8702)
PHONE.................302 734-4761
Arthur R Carlson Jr, *President*
EMP: 45
SQ FT: 10,000
SALES (est): 16.2MM **Privately Held**
WEB: www.dovervw.com
SIC: 5511 7538 Automobiles, new & used; general automotive repair shops

(G-1473)
DOVERS CHILDRENS VILLAG
726 Woodcrest Dr (19904-2439)
PHONE.................302 672-6476
Daisy Callaway, *Director*
EMP: 11
SALES (est): 271.4K **Privately Held**
SIC: 8351 Group day care center

(G-1474)
DR ANDREW BERMAN
446 S New St (19904-6725)
PHONE.................302 678-1000
Andrew Berman, *Owner*
EMP: 7
SALES (est): 380.2K **Privately Held**
SIC: 8042 Offices & clinics of optometrists

(G-1475)
DR CHRISTOPHER BURNS
871 S Governors Ave Ste 1 (19904-4115)
PHONE.................302 674-8331
Dr Christopher Burns, *Owner*
EMP: 7
SALES (est): 226.9K **Privately Held**
SIC: 8021 Dentists' office

(G-1476)
DR DAWN GRANDISON DDS
429 S Governors Ave (19904-6707)
PHONE.................302 678-3384
EMP: 4
SALES (est): 66.1K **Privately Held**
SIC: 8021 Dentists' office

(G-1477)
DR JOHN FONTANA III
910 Walker Rd Ste A (19904-2759)
PHONE.................302 734-1950
John Fontana, *Principal*
EMP: 5
SALES (est): 216.9K **Privately Held**
SIC: 8021 Offices & clinics of dentists

(G-1478)
DR MARISA E CONTI DO
725 S Queen St (19904-3568)
PHONE.................302 678-4488
Marisa E Conti, *Principal*
EMP: 5 **EST:** 2011
SALES (est): 161.5K **Privately Held**
SIC: 8031 Offices & clinics of osteopathic physicians

(G-1479)
DR ROBERT WEBSTER
1522 S State St (19901-4950)
PHONE.................302 674-1080
Peter Schaeffer, *Principal*
Robert W Webster, *Fmly & Gen Dent*
EMP: 7
SALES (est): 432.5K **Privately Held**
SIC: 8021 Dentists' office

(G-1480)
DRESSLIKEME LLC
8 The Grn Ste 1 (19901-3618)
PHONE.................302 450-1046
Dylan Stamer,
EMP: 4
SALES (est): 98.3K **Privately Held**
SIC: 7372 Application computer software

(G-1481)
DRW FUNDING LLC
8 The Grn Ste B (19901-3618)
PHONE.................404 631-7127
Darryl Wright,
EMP: 5
SQ FT: 1,200
SALES (est): 124.8K **Privately Held**
SIC: 8742 Management consulting services

(G-1482)
DSS - INTEGRITY LLC
1679 S Dupont Hwy Ste 5 (19901-5101)
PHONE.................302 677-0111
Dwayne Holmes,
Antonius Hines,
EMP: 25 **EST:** 2012
SQ FT: 1,200
SALES (est): 250K **Privately Held**
SIC: 7349 Janitorial service, contract basis

(G-1483)
DSS SERVICES INC
373 W North St Ste B (19904-6748)
PHONE.................302 677-0111
Dwayne Holmes, *President*
Stanford Belfield, *Vice Pres*
EMP: 18 **EST:** 2008
SALES (est): 350K **Privately Held**
SIC: 7349 Janitorial service, contract basis

(G-1484)
DSS URBAN JOINT VENTURE LLC
373 W North St Ste B (19904-6748)
PHONE.................302 677-0111
Dwayne Holmes, *President*
Stephen Bryant, *President*
EMP: 26
SALES (est): 456.1K **Privately Held**
SIC: 7349 Janitorial service, contract basis

(G-1485)
DSU STUDENT HOUSING LLC
430 College Rd (19904-2210)
PHONE.................302 857-7966
Shekeetah Allan, *Manager*
EMP: 5
SALES (est): 250K **Privately Held**
SIC: 7021 Lodging house, except organization

(G-1486)
DUNCAN ELISABETH D MD
300 Tuskegee Blvd (19902-5003)
PHONE.................302 677-2730
Elisabeth Duncan, *Manager*
EMP: 6
SALES (est): 80.5K **Privately Held**
SIC: 8011 Offices & clinics of medical doctors

(G-1487)
DUPONT DE NEMOURS EI & CO
1238 Lynnbury Woods Rd (19904-1744)
PHONE.................302 659-1079
EMP: 2
SALES (est): 82K **Privately Held**
SIC: 2879 Mfg Agricultural Chemicals

(G-1488)
DUSHUTTLE RICHARD P MD PA
240 Beiser Blvd Ste 101 (19904-8208)
PHONE.................302 678-8447
Richard P Dushuttle MD, *Owner*
Richard Dushuttle, *Med Doctor*
EMP: 12
SALES (est): 1.2MM **Privately Held**
SIC: 8011 Orthopedic physician

(G-1489)
DYNAMIC THERAPY SERVICES LLC
487 S Queen St (19904-3572)
PHONE.................302 526-2148
EMP: 16
SALES (corp-wide): 12.9MM **Privately Held**
SIC: 8049 8011 Physical therapist; offices & clinics of medical doctors
PA: Dynamic Therapy Services Llc
1501 Blueball Ave
Linwood PA 19061
610 859-8850

(G-1490)
E & M ENTERPRISES INC
Also Called: Dover Auto Repair
5102 N Dupont Hwy (19901-2338)
PHONE.................302 736-6391
Edward Piecuski, *President*
EMP: 5
SALES: 350K **Privately Held**
SIC: 7538 General automotive repair shops

(G-1491)
E N T ASSOCIATES
Also Called: Cooper, Stephen MD
826 S Governors Ave (19904-4107)
PHONE.................302 674-3752
Stephen Cooper, *Partner*
EMP: 16
SALES (est): 784.5K **Privately Held**
SIC: 8011 Eyes, ears, nose & throat specialist: physician/surgeon; physicians' office, including specialists

(G-1492)
E-LYTE TRANSPORTATION
8 The Grn (19901-3618)
PHONE.................808 269-0283
Joel Deners, *Principal*
EMP: 5
SALES (est): 242.1K **Privately Held**
SIC: 4789 Transportation services

(G-1493)
EAGLE HOSPITALITY GROUP LLC
201 Stover Blvd (19901-4675)
P.O. Box 996 (19903-0996)
PHONE.................302 678-8388
Sandra Caloway, *Info Tech Mgr*
Robert Hartley,
EMP: 18 **EST:** 2008
SALES (est): 1.1MM **Privately Held**
SIC: 8741 Hotel or motel management

(G-1494)
EAN HOLDINGS LLC
580 S Bay Rd (19901-4603)
PHONE.................302 674-5553
EMP: 8
SALES (corp-wide): 4.5B **Privately Held**
SIC: 7514 Passenger car rental
HQ: Ean Holdings, Llc
600 Corporate Park Dr
Saint Louis MO 63105

GEOGRAPHIC SECTION
Dover - Kent County (G-1525)

(G-1495)
EARLE TEATE MUSIC (PA)
3098 N Dupont Hwy (19901-8793)
PHONE.................................302 736-1937
Dale Teat, *CEO*
Nancy Teat, *Corp Secy*
Dean Teat, *Vice Pres*
EMP: 6
SQ FT: 10,000
SALES (est): 1MM **Privately Held**
WEB: www.earleteatmusic.com
SIC: 5736 7922 Organs; pianos; sheet music; theatrical producers & services

(G-1496)
EARLY CHILDHOOD LAB
1200 N Dupont Hwy (19901-2202)
PHONE.................................302 857-6731
Constance Williams, *Director*
EMP: 8
SALES (est): 71.5K **Privately Held**
SIC: 8351 Head start center, except in conjunction with school

(G-1497)
EARTHSCAPES LLC
6336 Pearsons Corner Rd (19904-0919)
PHONE.................................302 678-0478
William Daniels,
Brian Daniels,
EMP: 5
SALES (est): 409.9K **Privately Held**
SIC: 0782 Landscape contractors

(G-1498)
EAST COAST AUTO BODY INC
216 South St (19904)
P.O. Box 432, Camden Wyoming (19934-0432)
PHONE.................................302 265-6830
Mark Sammak, *President*
Norman Mullen, *Vice Pres*
EMP: 6
SQ FT: 2,871
SALES (est): 425.6K **Privately Held**
SIC: 7532 Body shop, automotive

(G-1499)
EASTER SEAL DELAWARE
100 Enterprise Pl Ste 1 (19904-8202)
PHONE.................................302 678-3353
Diane Schilling, *Manager*
Gary Cassidy, *Director*
Gary Cassedy, *Director*
EMP: 50
SALES (corp-wide): 34.3MM **Privately Held**
SIC: 8331 8093 Job training & vocational rehabilitation services; rehabilitation center, outpatient treatment
PA: Easter Seals Delaware & Marylands Eastern Shore, Inc.
61 Corporate Cir
New Castle DE 19720
302 324-4444

(G-1500)
EASTERN SHORE NATURAL GAS CO
Also Called: CHESAPEAKE
909 Silver Lake Blvd (19904-2409)
P.O. Box 615 (19903-0615)
PHONE.................................302 734-6716
John R Schimkaitis, *CEO*
Stephen C Thompson, *President*
Paul M Barbas, *Exec VP*
Michael P McMasters, *Senior VP*
Beth W Cooper, *Vice Pres*
EMP: 10 EST: 1955
SQ FT: 4,000
SALES: 64.8MM
SALES (corp-wide): 717.4MM **Publicly Held**
WEB: www.chpk.com
SIC: 4922 Pipelines, natural gas
PA: Chesapeake Utilities Corporation
909 Silver Lake Blvd
Dover DE 19904
302 734-6799

(G-1501)
EASY DIAGNOSTICS
160 Greentree Dr Ste 101 (19904-7620)
PHONE.................................302 674-4089
EMP: 3 EST: 2016
SALES (est): 132.1K **Privately Held**
SIC: 2835 Diagnostic Substances, Nsk

(G-1502)
ECOMO INC
160 Greentree Dr Ste 101 (19904-7620)
PHONE.................................412 567-3867
Zhiqiang LI, *CEO*
EMP: 6
SALES (est): 245.6K **Privately Held**
SIC: 3571 3823 7389 Electronic computers; water quality monitoring & control systems,

(G-1503)
ED HUNT INC (PA)
8 The Grn Ste 9487 (19901-3618)
PHONE.................................302 339-8443
Edward E Hunt, *President*
EMP: 5
SALES (est): 50K **Privately Held**
SIC: 7032 4789 Sporting camps; transportation services

(G-1504)
EDEN HILL EXPRESS CARE LLC
200 Banning St Ste 170 (19904-3491)
PHONE.................................302 674-1999
Carolyn M Apple, *Director*
EMP: 20
SALES (est): 1.2MM **Privately Held**
SIC: 7363 Medical help service

(G-1505)
EDEN HILL MEDICAL CENTER LLC
200 Banning St Ste 330 (19904-3490)
P.O. Box 577 (19903-0577)
PHONE.................................302 883-0097
Thomas P Barnett, *President*
Sean Mace, *Mng Member*
Thomas Barnett,
EMP: 4
SQ FT: 140,000
SALES (est): 1MM **Privately Held**
SIC: 8011 Clinic, operated by physicians; medical centers

(G-1506)
EDGEWELL PERSONAL CARE LLC
50 N Dupont Hwy (19901-4261)
PHONE.................................302 678-6000
Chris Kroll, *Branch Mgr*
Thomas Tarburton, *Planning*
EMP: 500
SALES (corp-wide): 2.1B **Publicly Held**
SIC: 2676 Tampons, sanitary: made from purchased paper
HQ: Edgewell Personal Care, Llc
1350 Timberlake Mano
Chesterfield MO 63017
314 594-1900

(G-1507)
EDGEWELL PERSONAL CARE COMPANY
185 Saulsbury Rd (19904-2719)
P.O. Box 7016 (19903-1516)
PHONE.................................302 678-6191
James Walker, *Superintendent*
Thomas Zaremba, *Superintendent*
Bryan Harrison, *Area Mgr*
Nick Powell, *Vice Pres*
Stephen Young, *Project Mgr*
EMP: 600
SALES (corp-wide): 2.1B **Publicly Held**
SIC: 2676 Panty liners: made from purchased paper
PA: Edgewell Personal Care Company
1350 Tmberlake Manor Pkwy
Chesterfield MO 63017
314 594-1900

(G-1508)
EDUQC LLC
3500 S Dupont Hwy (19901-6041)
PHONE.................................800 346-4646
Victor Maia,
EMP: 19
SALES (est): 299.4K **Privately Held**
SIC: 7389 Business services

(G-1509)
EDWARDS PAUL CRPT INSTALLATION
Also Called: Paul Edwards Carpet Cleaning
547 Otis Dr (19901-4645)
PHONE.................................302 672-7847
Paul Edwards, *Owner*
EMP: 5
SQ FT: 1,500
SALES: 750K **Privately Held**
SIC: 5713 1752 7217 Carpets; carpet laying; carpet & upholstery cleaning on customer premises

(G-1510)
ELDAS KITCHEN LLC (PA)
Also Called: ELDAS KITCHEN COOKING & GRILLI
8 The Grn 6947 (19901-3618)
PHONE.................................925 260-6156
Aldo Abronzino, *Mng Member*
EMP: 3
SALES (est): 683.1K **Privately Held**
SIC: 2099 Sauces: gravy, dressing & dip mixes

(G-1511)
ELDERWOOD VILLAGE DOVER LLC
21 N State St (19901-3802)
PHONE.................................516 496-1505
Lisa Havelow, *Director*
EMP: 74 EST: 1999
SALES (est): 3.9MM **Privately Held**
WEB: www.statestreetal.com
SIC: 8361 Residential care

(G-1512)
ELEC INTEGRITY
6253 N Dupont Hwy (19901-2610)
PHONE.................................302 388-3430
EMP: 11
SALES (est): 1MM **Privately Held**
SIC: 4911 Electric services

(G-1513)
ELECTRIC BEACH TANNING COMPANY
650 S Bay Rd (19901-4616)
PHONE.................................302 730-8266
EMP: 1 **Privately Held**
SIC: 7299 3699 Tanning salon; electrical equipment & supplies
PA: Electric Beach Tanning Company
5350 Smmt Brdge Rd 111
Middletown DE 19709

(G-1514)
ELITE OFFICE STAFF INC
8 The Grn Ste 5421 (19901-3618)
PHONE.................................302 387-4158
Ibtihaj Khan, *President*
EMP: 60
SALES (est): 613.1K **Privately Held**
SIC: 7361 Labor contractors (employment agency)

(G-1515)
ELIZABETH W MURPHEY SCHOOL INC
42 Kings Hwy (19901-3817)
PHONE.................................302 734-7478
Michael Kopp, *Exec Dir*
EMP: 52
SALES: 2.7MM **Privately Held**
SIC: 8361 Group foster home

(G-1516)
EMERALD CITY WASH WORLD
730 W Division St (19904-2732)
PHONE.................................302 734-1230
Robin Holt, *President*
EMP: 8
SALES (est): 294.1K **Privately Held**
SIC: 7215 Laundry, coin-operated

(G-1517)
EMERITUS CORPORATION
Also Called: Green Meadows At Latrobe
150 Saulsbury Ave (19904-2776)
PHONE.................................302 674-4407
Terry Reardon, *Director*
EMP: 38
SALES (corp-wide): 4.5B **Publicly Held**
WEB: www.emeraldestatesllc.org
SIC: 8051 Skilled nursing care facilities
HQ: Emeritus Corporation
3131 Elliott Ave Ste 500
Milwaukee WI 53214

(G-1518)
EMIL W TETZNER D M D
804 S State St Ste 1 (19901-4123)
PHONE.................................302 744-9900
Emil Tetzner, *Owner*
EMP: 7
SALES (est): 354K **Privately Held**
SIC: 8021 Periodontist

(G-1519)
EMLYN CONSTRUCTION CO
1341 Walnut Shade Rd (19901-7761)
PHONE.................................302 697-8247
Bob Joyner, *President*
EMP: 5 EST: 1977
SQ FT: 7,000
SALES: 3MM **Privately Held**
SIC: 1791 Structural steel erection

(G-1520)
EMORY MASSAGE THERAPY
155 Willis Rd Apt G (19901-4030)
P.O. Box 422 (19903-0422)
PHONE.................................302 290-0003
Teresa Wilson, *Principal*
EMP: 5
SALES (est): 92.3K **Privately Held**
SIC: 8093 Rehabilitation center, outpatient treatment

(G-1521)
ENDOCRINOLOGY CONSULTANT
111 Wolf Creek Blvd (19901-4969)
PHONE.................................302 734-2782
Judy L Reynolds, *Principal*
EMP: 7
SALES (est): 670.7K **Privately Held**
SIC: 8748 Business consulting

(G-1522)
ENERGIZER HOLDINGS INC
50 N Dupont Hwy (19901-4261)
PHONE.................................302 678-6767
Larry Babst, *Principal*
EMP: 2
SALES (est): 111.6K **Privately Held**
SIC: 3692 Primary batteries, dry & wet

(G-1523)
ENERGY CENTER DOVER LLC
1280 W North St (19904-7756)
PHONE.................................302 678-4666
William Grow, *Chief Mktg Ofcr*
Amy Emeigh, *Manager*
Donald Spencer, *Supervisor*
Brian Haskell, *Admin Asst*
EMP: 18
SALES (est): 8.2MM
SALES (corp-wide): 1B **Publicly Held**
SIC: 4911 Generation, electric power
PA: Clearway Energy, Inc.
300 Carnegie Ctr Ste 300 # 300
Princeton NJ 08540
609 608-1525

(G-1524)
ENGLISH TECH LLC
3500 S Dupont Hwy (19901-6041)
PHONE.................................844 707-9904
EMP: 8
SALES (est): 182.5K **Privately Held**
SIC: 7371 Custom Computer Programing

(G-1525)
ENVIRONMENTAL PROTECTION AGCY
Also Called: EPA
89 Kings Hwy (19901-7305)
PHONE.................................302 739-9917
John Hues, *Director*
EMP: 700 **Publicly Held**
WEB: www.epa.gov
SIC: 8731 Environmental research
HQ: Environmental Protection Agency
1200 Pennsylvania Ave Nw
Washington DC 20460
202 564-4700

Dover - Kent County (G-1526)

(G-1526)
EQUIDENTAL
21 Wilder Rd (19904-6064)
PHONE 302 423-0851
EMP: 4
SALES (est): 77.6K **Privately Held**
SIC: 8021 Offices & clinics of dentists

(G-1527)
ERA HARRINGTON REALTY (PA)
Also Called: Prudential Emerson and Company
1404 Forrest Ave Ste A (19904-3478)
PHONE 302 674-4663
Ralph Pennell Emerson, *President*
EMP: 28 EST: 1974
SQ FT: 2,000
SALES (est): 1.7MM **Privately Held**
SIC: 6531 Real estate brokers & agents

(G-1528)
ERA HARRINGTON REALTY
516 Jefferic Blvd Ste C (19901-2023)
PHONE 302 363-1796
Linda Brannock, *Branch Mgr*
EMP: 30
SALES (corp-wide): 1.7MM **Privately Held**
SIC: 6531 Real estate agent, residential
PA: Era Harrington Realty
1404 Forrest Ave Ste A
Dover DE 19904
302 674-4663

(G-1529)
ERANGA CARDIOLOGY
200 Banning St Ste 310 (19904-3488)
PHONE 302 747-7486
Eranga Haththotuwa, *Principal*
Danielle Taylor, *Administration*
EMP: 9 EST: 2013
SALES (est): 681.7K **Privately Held**
SIC: 8011 Cardiologist & cardio-vascular specialist

(G-1530)
ERGOSIX CORPORATION
615 S Dupont Hwy (19901-4517)
PHONE 844 603-1181
EMP: 6
SALES (est): 350K **Privately Held**
SIC: 5045 Computers, Peripherals, And Software, Nsk

(G-1531)
ESSIES KITCHEN LLC
218 Samuel Paynter Dr (19904-5431)
PHONE 302 465-2856
Shadrack Minor,
EMP: 4
SALES (est): 188.4K **Privately Held**
SIC: 1541 Food products manufacturing or packing plant construction

(G-1532)
EUGENE E GODFREY DO
22 Old Rudnick Ln 2 (19901-4912)
PHONE 302 674-1356
Eugene Godfrey, *Owner*
EMP: 5
SALES (est): 185K **Privately Held**
SIC: 8011 Anesthesiologist

(G-1533)
EVOCATI GROUP CORPORATION
9 E Loockerman St Ste 3a (19901-7316)
PHONE 206 551-9087
Alejandro Thornton, *CEO*
EMP: 10
SALES: 500K **Privately Held**
SIC: 8711 7379 Engineering services;

(G-1534)
EXO WORKS INC
3500 S Dupont Hwy Yy101 (19901-6041)
PHONE 302 531-1139
Lily Safrani, *Mng Member*
Salim Ismail,
EMP: 4 EST: 2015
SALES (est): 124.8K **Privately Held**
SIC: 8742 7389 General management consultant;

(G-1535)
EYE35DESIGN LLC
28 Old Rudnick Ln (19901-4912)
P.O. Box 2036, Mableton GA (30126-1017)
PHONE 470 236-3933
Jalila Bobb-Semple,
EMP: 5
SALES (est): 115.9K **Privately Held**
SIC: 7336 7389 Graphic arts & related design;

(G-1536)
F H EVERETT & ASSOCIATES INC
Also Called: Life Reach / Eap Systems
1151 Walker Rd Ste 100 (19904-6600)
PHONE 302 674-2380
Frank H Everett, *President*
EMP: 8
SALES (est): 321.8K **Privately Held**
SIC: 8322 8011 Individual & family services; psychiatrist

(G-1537)
FAMILY DENTAL ASSOCIATES INC
385 Saulsbury Rd (19904-2722)
PHONE 302 674-8810
Chris A Nacrelli, *President*
EMP: 13
SALES (est): 798.7K **Privately Held**
SIC: 8021 Dentists' office

(G-1538)
FAMILY HEALTH DELAWARE INC
640 S Queen St (19904-3565)
PHONE 302 734-2444
Tutse Thonwe, *President*
Tutse Tonwe, *Med Doctor*
EMP: 7
SALES (est): 410K **Privately Held**
WEB: www.familyhealthofdelaware.com
SIC: 8011 General & family practice, physician/surgeon

(G-1539)
FAMILY MEDICAL CENTRE PA
111 Wolf Creek Blvd Ste 2 (19901-4969)
PHONE 302 678-0510
Jose Austria MD, *Principal*
Kenny K Vu, *Med Doctor*
EMP: 14
SALES (est): 1.1MM **Privately Held**
SIC: 8011 Medical centers

(G-1540)
FANTAST COSTUMES INC
8 The Grn Ste A (19901-3618)
PHONE 302 455-2006
Lijun Jin, *President*
EMP: 10
SALES (est): 339.8K **Privately Held**
SIC: 2389 Costumes

(G-1541)
FARMERS HARVEST INC
Also Called: Sweet Potato Equipments
2826 Seven Hickories Rd (19904-1687)
PHONE 302 734-7708
Kevin Pinelli, *President*
Diane Pinelli, *Vice Pres*
▲ EMP: 2
SALES (est): 297.1K **Privately Held**
SIC: 3523 5999 Farm machinery & equipment; farm equipment & supplies

(G-1542)
FAST INTRCNNECT TCHOLOGIES INC
73 Greentree Dr Ste 30 (19904-7646)
PHONE 302 465-5344
R Balasubramanian, *Principal*
EMP: 5
SALES (est): 165.5K **Privately Held**
SIC: 8732 Business research service

(G-1543)
FAVORED CHILDCARE ACADEMY INC
2319 S Dupont Hwy (19901-5514)
PHONE 302 698-1266
Vincent Ikwuagwu, *President*
EMP: 5 EST: 2013
SALES (est): 31.1K **Privately Held**
SIC: 8299 8351 Airline training; group day care center

(G-1544)
FAW CASSON & CO LLP
Also Called: Faw Casson & Co
160 Greentree Dr Ste 203 (19904-7620)
PHONE 302 674-4305
Lisa Hastings, *Managing Prtnr*
James Arthur, *Partner*
Kimberly Fonda, *Partner*
Lauren Harper, *Partner*
Alison Houck, *Partner*
EMP: 36 EST: 1944
SALES: 5.4MM **Privately Held**
WEB: www.fawcasson.com
SIC: 8721 Accounting services, except auditing; certified public accountant; auditing services

(G-1545)
FEAST KITCHEN INC
1679 S Dupont Hwy Ste 100 (19901-5164)
PHONE 415 758-8779
EMP: 4 EST: 2014
SALES (est): 103.1K **Privately Held**
SIC: 7379 Computer Related Services

(G-1546)
FEASTFOX INC
8 The Grn (19901-3618)
PHONE 650 250-6887
Daniel Petz, *President*
EMP: 4
SALES (est): 108.2K **Privately Held**
SIC: 7372 Application computer software

(G-1547)
FEDERAL TECHNICAL ASSOCIATES
50 Westview Ave (19901-6229)
PHONE 302 697-7951
Frank Minnick, *Owner*
EMP: 5
SALES (est): 224.3K **Privately Held**
SIC: 7389 Pipeline & power line inspection service

(G-1548)
FERGUSON ENTERPRISES LLC
10 Maggies Way (19901-4887)
PHONE 302 747-2032
EMP: 5
SALES (corp-wide): 20.7B **Privately Held**
SIC: 5074 3432 Plumbing fittings & supplies; plumbing fixture fittings & trim
HQ: Ferguson Enterprises, Llc
12500 Jefferson Ave
Newport News VA 23602
757 874-7795

(G-1549)
FESSENDEN HALL INCORPORATED
Also Called: Fessenden Hall of Deleware
1037 Fowler Ct (19904-4638)
PHONE 302 674-4505
Patrick Shearon, *Branch Mgr*
Chris Kilbride, *Manager*
EMP: 13
SALES (corp-wide): 47MM **Privately Held**
SIC: 5031 Plywood
PA: Hall Fessenden Incorporated
1050 Sherman Ave
Pennsauken NJ 08110
856 665-2210

(G-1550)
FIDELITY MNTAL HLTH SLTONS LLC
365 United Way (19901-3769)
PHONE 302 304-2974
Angela Robinson, *Principal*
EMP: 7 EST: 2016
SALES (est): 70.3K **Privately Held**
SIC: 8099 Health & allied services

(G-1551)
FIRESIDE PARTNERS INC
60 Starlifter Ave (19901-9254)
P.O. Box 213 (19903-0213)
PHONE 302 613-2165
Don Chupp, *CEO*
Donald Chupp, *President*
EMP: 9 EST: 2016
SALES (est): 257.2K **Privately Held**
SIC: 8748 Safety training service

(G-1552)
FIRST CLASS PROPERTIES DEL LLC (PA)
1641 E Lebanon Rd (19901-5841)
PHONE 302 677-0770
Audrey Brodie,
EMP: 5
SQ FT: 3,200
SALES (est): 1.4MM **Privately Held**
SIC: 6531 6519 Buying agent, real estate; selling agent, real estate; real property lessors

(G-1553)
FIRST STATE CMNTY ACTION AGCY
655 S Bay Rd Ste 4j (19901-4656)
PHONE 302 674-1355
Bernice Edwards, *Branch Mgr*
EMP: 75
SALES (corp-wide): 8MM **Privately Held**
SIC: 8322 Settlement house
PA: First State Community Action Agency Inc
308 N Railroad Ave
Georgetown DE 19947
302 856-7761

(G-1554)
FIRST STATE COIN CO
53 Greentree Dr (19904-2685)
PHONE 302 734-7776
Ray Gesualdo, *President*
Kathleen Gesualdo, *Corp Secy*
EMP: 5
SALES (est): 780.3K **Privately Held**
SIC: 5094 5999 5944 Precious metals; coins; stamps (philatelist); jewelry, precious stones & precious metals

(G-1555)
FIRST STATE CPAS LLC
970 N State St (19901-3903)
PHONE 302 736-6657
Kathy Sarchett, *President*
EMP: 6
SALES (est): 184.8K **Privately Held**
SIC: 8721 Certified public accountant

(G-1556)
FIRST STATE FEDERAL CREDIT UN
58 Carver Rd (19904-2716)
PHONE 302 674-5281
Bea Conrad, *President*
EMP: 10
SQ FT: 1,500
SALES (est): 1MM **Privately Held**
WEB: www.firststatefcu.com
SIC: 6061 Federal credit unions

(G-1557)
FIRST STATE GASTROENTEROLOGY A
644 S Queen St Ste 106 (19904-3543)
PHONE 302 677-1617
EMP: 4 EST: 2015
SALES (est): 146K **Privately Held**
SIC: 8011 Gastronomist

(G-1558)
FIRST STATE ORAL & M
1004 S State St Ste 1 (19901-6901)
PHONE 302 674-4450
Kim Deo, *Office Mgr*
Wanda Connors, *Manager*
Douglas Ditty, *Fmly & Gen Dent*
EMP: 5
SALES: 500K **Privately Held**
SIC: 8021 Dental surgeon

(G-1559)
FIRST STATE SIGNS INC
122 Rosemary Rd (19901-7243)
PHONE 302 744-9990
Dale McCalister, *President*
EMP: 12
SQ FT: 8,000
SALES: 1.6MM **Privately Held**
SIC: 3993 Electric signs

GEOGRAPHIC SECTION
Dover - Kent County (G-1590)

(G-1560)
FLUTTERBY STITCHES & EMB
203 Doveview Dr Unit 403 (19904-3699)
PHONE....................302 531-7784
Paulette Leggs, *Principal*
EMP: 1
SALES (est): 51.4K **Privately Held**
SIC: 2395 Embroidery & art needlework

(G-1561)
FOREVER FIT FOUNDATION
1510 E Lebanon Rd (19901-5834)
P.O. Box 44, Camden Wyoming (19934-0044)
PHONE....................302 698-5201
Nancy Hawkins-Rigg, *President*
EMP: 5 **EST:** 1994
SALES (est): 175.5K **Privately Held**
SIC: 7991 Health club

(G-1562)
FORREST AVENUE ANIMAL HOSPITAL
3156 Forrest Ave (19904-5317)
PHONE....................302 736-3000
Vance Sciver, *President*
Kim Geines, *Vice Pres*
John G Vansciver,
EMP: 12 **EST:** 2000
SQ FT: 2,561
SALES (est): 948.4K **Privately Held**
SIC: 0742 Animal hospital services, pets & other animal specialties

(G-1563)
FOUNDTION FOR A BTTER TOMORROW
121 W Loockerman St (19904-7325)
PHONE....................302 674-1397
Lauren Tinsley, *President*
Christine Gordon, *Principal*
Jenna Mahoney, *Principal*
Cyndi McLaughlin, *Principal*
EMP: 7
SQ FT: 6,000
SALES (est): 3.3K **Privately Held**
SIC: 8011 8093 Primary care medical clinic; psychiatric clinic; substance abuse clinics (outpatient)

(G-1564)
FOX POINTE
352 Fox Pointe Dr (19904-1415)
PHONE....................302 744-9442
EMP: 2
SALES (est): 86.7K **Privately Held**
SIC: 2452 Prefabricated wood buildings

(G-1565)
FRANKLIN PANCKO DDS
712 S Governors Ave (19904-4106)
PHONE....................302 674-1140
EMP: 4
SALES (est): 61.5K **Privately Held**
SIC: 8021 Offices & clinics of dentists

(G-1566)
FREE PSYCHIC READING LLC
8 The Grn Ste 7048 (19901-3618)
PHONE....................305 439-1455
Jordan Siberry,
EMP: 2
SALES: 100K **Privately Held**
SIC: 7372 Application computer software

(G-1567)
FRESENIUS MEDICAL CARE
Also Called: Dover Home Dialysis Center
1198 S Governors Ave (19904-6930)
PHONE....................302 736-1340
Mary Garber, *Principal*
William Valle, *Principal*
EMP: 20
SALES (est): 194K **Privately Held**
SIC: 8092 Kidney dialysis centers

(G-1568)
FRESENIUS MEDICAL CARE SOUTHER
Also Called: Fresenius Kidney Care N Dover
80 Salt Creek Dr (19901-2436)
PHONE....................302 678-2181
Mary Garber, *Principal*
EMP: 20 **EST:** 2018
SALES (est): 302.1K **Privately Held**
SIC: 8011 Offices & clinics of medical doctors

(G-1569)
FRESH START MARKETPLACE LLC
8 The Grn (19901-3618)
PHONE....................302 240-3002
Eric Moore, *Mng Member*
EMP: 15
SALES (est): 87.3K **Privately Held**
SIC: 7299 Debt counseling or adjustment service, individuals

(G-1570)
FRIENDS OF CAPITOL THEATER INC
Also Called: Schwartz Center For The Arts
226 S State St (19901-6728)
PHONE....................302 678-3583
William Jonhnston, *President*
EMP: 5
SQ FT: 36,000
SALES (est): 437.1K **Privately Held**
SIC: 7922 Community theater production

(G-1571)
FSHERY MID-ATLNTIC MGT COUNCIL
800 N State St Ste 201 (19901-3925)
PHONE....................302 674-2331
Kiley Dancy, *Manager*
Dr Jos L Montaez, *Manager*
Mary Sabo, *Manager*
Dr C M Moore, *Exec Dir*
Christopher Moore, *Exec Dir*
EMP: 11
SALES (est): 804.2K **Privately Held**
SIC: 8748 Environmental consultant

(G-1572)
FUN BAKERY LLC
3500 S Dupont Hwy (19901-6041)
PHONE....................858 220-0946
Rhonda Woerner, *Manager*
EMP: 2
SALES (est): 110K **Privately Held**
SIC: 7372 Home entertainment computer software

(G-1573)
FURRS TIRE SERVICE INC
1251 S Bay Rd (19901-4613)
P.O. Box 943 (19903-0943)
PHONE....................302 678-0800
Frank F Furr, *President*
Frank Furr III, *President*
EMP: 5
SQ FT: 3,500
SALES (est): 480K **Privately Held**
SIC: 5531 7538 Automotive tires; general automotive repair shops

(G-1574)
FUTURE BRIGHT PEDIATRICS
Also Called: BRIGHT FUTURE PEDIATRICS
938 S Bradford St (19904-4140)
P.O. Box 1082 (19903-1082)
PHONE....................302 883-3266
Mamoon Mahmoud, *Branch Mgr*
EMP: 15
SALES (corp-wide): 2.1MM **Privately Held**
SIC: 8011 Pediatrician
PA: Future Bright Pediatrics Llc
120 Old Camden Rd Ste B
Camden DE 19934
302 538-6258

(G-1575)
G & G FLIGHT SERVICE INC
144 Cherry St (19904-3412)
PHONE....................302 674-3264
EMP: 4
SQ FT: 6,000
SALES (est): 437.6K **Privately Held**
SIC: 4522 Air Transportation, Nonscheduled, Nsk

(G-1576)
G L K INC (PA)
Also Called: Milford Stitching Co
55 Beloit Ave (19901-5704)
PHONE....................302 697-3838
Herbert Konowitz, *President*
EMP: 6 **EST:** 1952
SQ FT: 75,000
SALES (est): 1.3MM **Privately Held**
SIC: 2392 2391 Bedspreads & bed sets: made from purchased materials; comforters & quilts: made from purchased materials; draperies, plastic & textile: from purchased materials

(G-1577)
G T PAINTING INC
1206 White Oak Rd (19901-4052)
PHONE....................302 734-7771
Gene Tipsword, *President*
EMP: 12
SQ FT: 700
SALES: 400K **Privately Held**
SIC: 1721 Commercial painting

(G-1578)
GALE AND ASSOCIATES LLC
113 Jillian Dr (19901-5415)
PHONE....................302 698-4253
Wendy E Gale, *Principal*
EMP: 4
SALES (est): 364.6K **Privately Held**
SIC: 8742 Management consulting services

(G-1579)
GARRISON CALPINE
450 Garrison Oak Dr (19901-3369)
PHONE....................302 562-5661
EMP: 9 **EST:** 2015
SALES (est): 873.4K **Privately Held**
SIC: 4911 Generation, electric power

(G-1580)
GARY QUIROGA
34 S Fairfield Dr (19901-5723)
PHONE....................302 697-3352
Gary T Quiroga MD, *Owner*
EMP: 5
SALES (est): 299.5K **Privately Held**
SIC: 8011 Internal medicine, physician/surgeon; cardiologist & cardio-vascular specialist

(G-1581)
GARY SJ CPA
809 Monroe Ter (19904-4117)
PHONE....................302 730-3737
Shari Gary, *Owner*
EMP: 4
SALES (est): 235.6K **Privately Held**
SIC: 8721 Certified public accountant

(G-1582)
GAS & GO INC
Also Called: Westside Car Wash
805 Forest St (19904-3417)
PHONE....................302 734-8234
Vic Giangrant, *President*
Lynn Giangrant, *Admin Sec*
EMP: 7
SQ FT: 800
SALES (est): 364.8K **Privately Held**
SIC: 7542 7532 Carwash, automatic; top & body repair & paint shops

(G-1583)
GATEHOUSE MEDIA INC
Also Called: Dover Post News Paper
1196 S Little Creek Rd (19901-4727)
P.O. Box 664 (19903-0664)
PHONE....................302 678-3616
Mike Reed, *President*
Nanette Kreiser, *Accounting Mgr*
Linda Miller, *Director*
EMP: 75
SALES (est): 20MM **Privately Held**
SIC: 2711 Newspapers

(G-1584)
GATEHUSE MDIA DEL HOLDINGS INC
1196 S Little Creek Rd (19901-4727)
PHONE....................302 678-3616
Garrett J Cummings,
EMP: 1
SALES (est): 62.4K
SALES (corp-wide): 1.5B **Publicly Held**
SIC: 2711 Commercial printing & newspaper publishing combined
PA: Gannett Co., Inc.
7950 Jones Branch Dr
Mc Lean VA 22102
703 854-6000

(G-1585)
GAUDLITZ INC
Also Called: Gaudlitz Plastic Technologies
160 Greentree Dr Ste 101 (19904-7620)
PHONE....................202 468-3876
Peter Wallace, *Officer*
Reiner Leifhelm, *Officer*
Thomas Pick, *Officer*
Niels Roelofsen, *Officer*
EMP: 4
SALES (est): 122.6K **Privately Held**
SIC: 7389 5047 3089 5013 ; medical laboratory equipment; injection molded finished plastic products; motor vehicle supplies & new parts

(G-1586)
GEARHALO US INC
8 The Grn (19901-3618)
PHONE....................780 239-2120
Demetrius Bazos, *President*
EMP: 2 **EST:** 2018
SALES: 100K **Privately Held**
SIC: 2842 Sanitation preparations, disinfectants & deodorants

(G-1587)
GEARHART CONSTRUCTION INC
Also Called: J & L Construction Co
5075 N Dupont Hwy (19901-2463)
PHONE....................302 674-5466
Jerry Gearhart, *President*
Linda Gearhart, *Treasurer*
EMP: 6
SALES (est): 676K **Privately Held**
SIC: 1761 1531 Roofing contractor; siding contractor; speculative builder, single-family houses

(G-1588)
GENESIS ELDERCARE NAT CTRS INC
1080 Silver Lake Blvd (19904-2410)
PHONE....................302 734-5990
Donna Brown, *Human Res Dir*
Jim Adams, *Manager*
James Adams, *Manager*
EMP: 125 **Publicly Held**
WEB: www.pleasantviewretirement.com
SIC: 8051 Convalescent home with continuous nursing care
HQ: Genesis Eldercare National Centers, Inc.
101 E State St
Kennett Square PA 19348
610 444-6350

(G-1589)
GEO-FENCE INC
8 The Grn Ste A (19901-3618)
PHONE....................763 516-8934
Evan Lundeen, *CEO*
EMP: 2
SALES (est): 88.3K **Privately Held**
SIC: 3663 5531 7371 ; automotive accessories; computer software development & applications

(G-1590)
GEORGE & LYNCH INC (PA)
150 Lafferty Ln (19901-7205)
PHONE....................302 736-3031
William B Robinson, *CEO*
Dennis J Dinger, *President*
Leonard Brooks, *Vice Pres*
Jeffrey I Norman, *Vice Pres*
David W McGuigan, *Vice Pres*
EMP: 122 **EST:** 1923
SQ FT: 12,000
SALES (est): 111.8MM **Privately Held**
WEB: www.geolyn.com
SIC: 1623 1611 1629 1731 Water, sewer & utility lines; highway & street construction; marine construction; environmental system control installation

Dover - Kent County (G-1591)   GEOGRAPHIC SECTION

(G-1591)
GEORVE V SAWYER
Also Called: Buck's Barber Shop
2296 Forrest Ave (19904-5308)
PHONE.................................302 736-1474
George V Sawyer, *Owner*
EMP: 7
SALES (est): 55.1K **Privately Held**
SIC: 7241 Barber shops

(G-1592)
GI ASSOCIATES OF DELAWARE
Also Called: G I Associates of Delaware
742 S Governors Ave Ste 3 (19904-4111)
PHONE.................................302 678-5008
Natwarlal V Ramani MD, *CEO*
EMP: 7
SQ FT: 5,000
SALES (est): 902.8K **Privately Held**
SIC: 8011 Gastronomist

(G-1593)
GLIMPSE GLOBAL INC
8 The Grn Ste A (19901-3618)
PHONE.................................305 216-7667
Reinaldo Ramos, *Principal*
EMP: 1
SALES (est): 37.5K **Privately Held**
SIC: 2741

(G-1594)
GLOBAL CHILDRENS ADVOCACY LLC
Also Called: Limitless Project, The
8 The Grn Ste B (19901-3618)
PHONE.................................484 383-3900
Miriam Roth,
EMP: 4
SALES (est): 59.7K **Privately Held**
SIC: 8399 Advocacy group

(G-1595)
GLYCOMIRA LLC
160 Greentree Dr Ste 101 (19904-7620)
PHONE.................................704 651-9789
Thomas Kennedy,
EMP: 2
SALES (est): 97.7K **Privately Held**
SIC: 2834 Pharmaceutical preparations

(G-1596)
GO-GLASS CORPORATION
Also Called: Mr Go-Glass
3895 N Dupont Hwy (19901-1568)
PHONE.................................302 674-3390
Thomas Huff, *President*
EMP: 14
SALES (corp-wide): 12.3MM **Privately Held**
SIC: 1793 7536 5231 Glass & glazing work; automotive glass replacement shops; glass
PA: Go-Glass Joy, Llc
  805 Snow Hill Rd
  Salisbury MD 21804
  410 742-1151

(G-1597)
GOLAGE INC
8 The Grn Ste 5568 (19901-3618)
PHONE.................................302 526-1181
Furkan Contar, *CEO*
EMP: 1
SALES (est): 56K **Privately Held**
SIC: 3699 Security control equipment & systems

(G-1598)
GOLDEN CHARIOT TRANSPORTAION
622 W Division St (19904-2702)
PHONE.................................302 730-3882
Adamolekun Olukayode, *President*
EMP: 8
SALES: 130K **Privately Held**
SIC: 7514 Hearse or limousine rental, without drivers

(G-1599)
GOLDEN SHELL CORP
8 The Grn (19901-3618)
PHONE.................................917 951-6118
Jingyu Meng,
EMP: 5

SALES (est): 107K **Privately Held**
SIC: 7371 Computer software development & applications

(G-1600)
GOLDFINCH GROUP INC
9 E Loockerman St Ste 3a (19901-7316)
PHONE.................................646 300-0716
Dion Clark, *Ch of Bd*
EMP: 5
SALES (est): 250K **Privately Held**
SIC: 8111 7389 Corporate, partnership & business law;

(G-1601)
GOOD MANUFACTURING PRACTICES
80 Coventry Ct (19901-6552)
PHONE.................................302 222-6808
EMP: 2
SALES (est): 82.7K **Privately Held**
SIC: 3999 Manufacturing industries

(G-1602)
GOTIT INC
3500 S Dupont Hwy (19901-6041)
PHONE.................................408 382-1300
Tal Agassi, *CEO*
EMP: 12
SALES (est): 285.2K **Privately Held**
SIC: 7371 Computer software development & applications

(G-1603)
GOVBIZCONNECT INC
850 New Burton Rd (19904-5451)
PHONE.................................860 341-1925
Tom Skypek, *CEO*
EMP: 3
SALES (est): 86.5K **Privately Held**
SIC: 2741

(G-1604)
GOVERNMENT INFORMATION CENTER
121 Martin Luther King (19901-3638)
PHONE.................................302 857-3020
Mike Mahafee, *Branch Mgr*
EMP: 8
SALES (est): 111.2K **Privately Held**
SIC: 8999 Information bureau

(G-1605)
GOVERNORS AVE ANIMAL HOSPITAL
Also Called: The Dog House
1008 S Governors Ave (19904-6902)
PHONE.................................302 734-5588
Janice Sosnowski, *President*
Annette Von Stetten, *Practice Mgr*
EMP: 20
SALES (est): 1.2MM **Privately Held**
SIC: 0742 Animal hospital services, pets & other animal specialties

(G-1606)
GRADY & HAMPTON LLC
6 N Bradford St (19904-3102)
PHONE.................................302 678-1265
John S Grady, *Mng Member*
Steven A Hampton,
Anthony Panicola, *Associate*
EMP: 6
SQ FT: 700
SALES (est): 671.7K **Privately Held**
WEB: www.gradyhampton.com
SIC: 8111 General practice attorney, lawyer; general practice law office

(G-1607)
GRAYS PEAK LLC (PA)
8 The Grn Ste A (19901-3618)
PHONE.................................302 288-0670
Scott Stevens, *Mng Member*
EMP: 2
SALES (est): 257.6K **Publicly Held**
SIC: 3999

(G-1608)
GREAT GRAPHIC ORIGINALS LTD
5374 Pearsons Corner Rd (19904-4971)
PHONE.................................302 734-7600
Marsha Holler, *President*
Bill Holler, *Exec Dir*

EMP: 6
SALES (est): 450K **Privately Held**
WEB: www.ggoltd.com
SIC: 2253 2393 5136 5137 T-shirts & tops, knit; bags & containers, except sleeping bags: textile; shirts, men's & boys'; women's & children's clothing

(G-1609)
GREATER DOVER FOUNDATION
101 W Loockerman St 1b (19904-7328)
PHONE.................................302 734-2513
EMP: 5
SALES (est): 141.4K **Privately Held**
SIC: 8641 Civic/Social Association

(G-1610)
GREEN CLINICS LABORATORY LLC
740 S New St Ste B (19904-3571)
PHONE.................................302 734-5050
Fady Gerges, *Principal*
Fady J Gerges,
EMP: 8
SALES (est): 67.7K **Privately Held**
SIC: 8099 Health & allied services

(G-1611)
GREEN CRESCENT LLC
Also Called: Green Crescent Translations
8 The Grn Ste 4710 (19901-3618)
P.O. Box 19912, Kalamazoo MI (49019-0912)
PHONE.................................800 735-9620
Jonathan W Fabian, *Mng Member*
EMP: 5
SALES: 100K **Privately Held**
SIC: 7389 7336 Translation services; graphic arts & related design

(G-1612)
GREEN INTEREST ENTERPRISES LLC
81 Rye Oak Ct (19904)
PHONE.................................228 355-0708
Clarissa O Anderson, *Principal*
Derrick Kimbrough, *Admin Asst*
EMP: 6
SALES (est): 343.3K **Privately Held**
SIC: 8742 Management consulting services

(G-1613)
GREENE BUSINESS SUPPORT S
3 Heritage Dr (19904-6518)
PHONE.................................302 480-3725
EMP: 4
SALES (est): 44.6K **Privately Held**
SIC: 8399 Advocacy group

(G-1614)
GUIDANCE GAMING
1033 High St (19901-7912)
PHONE.................................724 708-2321
Cameron Swink, *Principal*
EMP: 10
SALES (est): 1MM **Privately Held**
SIC: 5092 Video games

(G-1615)
GULAB MANAGEMENT INC (PA)
Also Called: Dover Budget Inn
1426 N Dupont Hwy (19901-2213)
PHONE.................................302 734-4433
Ernest Gulab, *President*
Asim Gulab, *Treasurer*
EMP: 20
SALES (est): 3.6MM **Privately Held**
SIC: 7011 Hotels & motels

(G-1616)
GUSHEN AMERICA INC
1679 S Dupont Hwy Ste 100 (19901-5164)
PHONE.................................630 853-3135
Shiwei LI, *President*
Zulin Shi, *Admin Sec*
EMP: 2
SALES (est): 90K **Privately Held**
SIC: 2869 Perfumes, flavorings & food additives

(G-1617)
GUTTER CONNECTION LLC
2559 Mckee Rd (19904-1217)
PHONE.................................302 736-0105

Debra Carney, *President*
EMP: 5
SALES (est): 51.5K **Privately Held**
SIC: 7349 Building maintenance services

(G-1618)
GUY & LADY BARREL LLC
Also Called: Guy & Lady Barrel Cigars
198 Hatteras Dr (19904-3883)
PHONE.................................302 399-3069
Maurice J Williams, *President*
Grace K Williams, *Vice Pres*
EMP: 5
SALES (est): 110K **Privately Held**
SIC: 5993 5194 7389 Cigar store; cigars;

(G-1619)
GUY BUG
1017 Westview Ter (19904-4344)
PHONE.................................302 242-5254
Jean Taylor, *Owner*
EMP: 7
SALES (est): 217.3K **Privately Held**
SIC: 7342 Pest control services

(G-1620)
GYST INC
8 The Grn Ste A (19901-3618)
P.O. Box 871, Larchmont NY (10538-0871)
PHONE.................................631 680-4307
Daniel O'Sullivan, *CEO*
EMP: 7
SALES (est): 164.3K **Privately Held**
SIC: 7371 7373 Computer software development & applications; computer integrated systems design

(G-1621)
H & A ELECTRIC CO
59 Roosevelt Ave (19901-4459)
PHONE.................................302 678-8252
Richard W Arndt, *President*
Patricia Arndt, *Treasurer*
EMP: 9 EST: 1973
SQ FT: 700
SALES (est): 1.1MM **Privately Held**
WEB: www.cmielectric.com
SIC: 1731 Electrical work

(G-1622)
H H BUILDERS INC
3947 Forrest Ave (19904-5216)
PHONE.................................302 735-9900
H Lbaker, *Principal*
EMP: 5
SALES (est): 500.4K **Privately Held**
SIC: 1521 New construction, single-family houses

(G-1623)
HALPERN EYE ASSOCIATES INC (PA)
Also Called: Halpern Eye Care
885 S Governors Ave (19904-4158)
P.O. Box 762 (19903-0762)
PHONE.................................302 734-5861
Ryan Halpern, *President*
Troy Raber, *Vice Pres*
EMP: 25
SQ FT: 1,000
SALES (est): 4.3MM **Privately Held**
WEB: www.halperneye.com
SIC: 8042 Specialized optometrists

(G-1624)
HALPERN OPTHALMOLOGY ASSOC
200 Banning St (19904-3485)
PHONE.................................302 678-2210
Dawn Wolford, *Principal*
EMP: 5
SALES (est): 398K **Privately Held**
SIC: 8011 Ophthalmologist

(G-1625)
HAMPTON INN-DOVER
Also Called: Hampton Inn Dover
1568 N Dupont Hwy (19901-2215)
PHONE.................................302 736-3500
Avelina Kramedas,
EMP: 7
SALES (est): 527.5K **Privately Held**
SIC: 7011 Hotels & motels

GEOGRAPHIC SECTION
Dover - Kent County (G-1654)

(G-1626)
HANCO INC
3975 Leipsic Rd (19901-2924)
PHONE..................................302 734-9782
James Hanna, *President*
Mike Akers, *Vice Pres*
Albert Biddle, *Vice Pres*
EMP: 9
SALES (est): 484.6K **Privately Held**
WEB: www.hanco.info
SIC: 1521 General remodeling, single-family houses

(G-1627)
HARDWOOD MILLS INC
5237 S Dupont Hwy (19901-6434)
PHONE..................................302 697-7195
Catherine Michalski, *Principal*
EMP: 1
SALES (est): 68.9K **Privately Held**
SIC: 2273 Carpets & rugs

(G-1628)
HARREL STEFONI
1040 Harvest Grove Trl (19901-2783)
PHONE..................................302 344-3269
Stefoni Harrell, *Owner*
EMP: 4
SALES (est): 92.1K **Privately Held**
SIC: 7389

(G-1629)
HARRINGTON INSURANCE
736 N Dupont Hwy (19901-3939)
PHONE..................................302 883-5000
Mike Harrington Sr, *President*
EMP: 4
SQ FT: 10,000
SALES (est): 460K **Privately Held**
WEB: www.harringtoninsurance.net
SIC: 6321 6361 Accident & health insurance; real estate title insurance

(G-1630)
HARRINGTON REALTY INC (PA)
Also Called: ERA
516 Jefferic Blvd Ste C (19901-2023)
PHONE..................................302 736-0800
Michael Harrington Sr, *President*
Donna Harrington, *Corp Secy*
Christy Wilkins, *Sales Staff*
Larry Harrison, *Branch Mgr*
Bill Ulmer, *Manager*
EMP: 50
SALES (est): 12.6MM **Privately Held**
SIC: 6411 6531 Insurance agents, brokers & service; real estate agents & managers

(G-1631)
HARRINGTON REALTY INC
Also Called: ERA
736 N Dupont Hwy B (19901-3939)
PHONE..................................302 422-2424
Michael Harrington Jr, *Manager*
Jim Wirick, *Real Estate*
EMP: 20
SALES (corp-wide): 12.6MM **Privately Held**
SIC: 6531 Real estate agent, residential
PA: Harrington Realty Inc
516 Jefferic Blvd Ste C
Dover DE 19901
302 736-0800

(G-1632)
HARRIS TOWING AND AUTO SERVICE
5360 N Dupont Hwy (19901-2340)
P.O. Box 347, Cheswold (19936-0347)
PHONE..................................302 736-9901
Luke Harris, *President*
Miriam Harris, *Admin Sec*
EMP: 7
SALES (est): 720.9K **Privately Held**
SIC: 7549 7538 Towing service, automotive; general automotive repair shops

(G-1633)
HARRISONS ASPHALT PAVING
51 Union St (19904-1114)
PHONE..................................302 674-1255
William Harrison, *President*
Henry Harrison, *Partner*
Rowdy Harrison, *Partner*
Allysan Harrison, *Admin Sec*
EMP: 4
SALES: 50K **Privately Held**
SIC: 1611 Highway & street paving contractor

(G-1634)
HARRY LOUIES LAUNDRY & DRY CLG
Also Called: Louie Harry Laundry & Dry Clg
129 S Governors Ave (19904-3222)
PHONE..................................302 734-8195
David Mercer Louie, *Owner*
EMP: 13 **EST:** 1949
SQ FT: 3,204
SALES (est): 322.9K **Privately Held**
SIC: 7216 7211 7219 Drycleaning plants, except rugs; power laundries, family & commercial; laundry, except power & coin-operated

(G-1635)
HARSHA TANKALA MD
Also Called: Patel, Ashok MD
1055 S Bradford St (19904-4141)
PHONE..................................302 674-1818
Ashok Patel, *Partner*
Harsha Tankala, *Partner*
EMP: 8
SALES (est): 749.6K **Privately Held**
SIC: 8011 Internal medicine, physician/surgeon

(G-1636)
HART GROUP LLC
8 The Grn Ste A (19901-3618)
PHONE..................................302 782-9742
Timothy Reynolds II,
EMP: 8
SALES (est): 151.6K **Privately Held**
SIC: 7389 Financial services

(G-1637)
HARVEY MILLER CONSTRUCTION
371 Blue Heron Rd (19904-4731)
PHONE..................................302 674-4128
Harvey Miller, *Owner*
EMP: 4
SALES (est): 250K **Privately Held**
SIC: 1521 Single-family housing construction

(G-1638)
HAZARDOUS WASTE
89 Kings Hwy (19901-7305)
PHONE..................................302 739-9403
Nancy Marker, *Manager*
EMP: 4
SALES (est): 164.6K **Privately Held**
SIC: 4959 Environmental cleanup services

(G-1639)
HEALTH & SOCIAL SVCS DEL DEPT
Also Called: James Williams State Svc Ctr
805 River Rd (19901-3753)
PHONE..................................302 857-5000
Linda Melvin, *Director*
EMP: 100 **Privately Held**
SIC: 8322 8093 9431 Individual & family services; specialty outpatient clinics;
HQ: Delaware Dept Of Health And Social Services
1901 N Dupont Hwy
New Castle DE 19720

(G-1640)
HEALTH & SOCIAL SVCS DEL DEPT
Division Health Care Comm
410 Federal St Ste 7 (19901-3640)
PHONE..................................302 255-9500
Rosanne Mahaney, *Branch Mgr*
EMP: 10 **Privately Held**
SIC: 8322 9441 Child related social services;
HQ: Delaware Dept Of Health And Social Services
1901 N Dupont Hwy
New Castle DE 19720

(G-1641)
HEALTHPARTNERS DELMARVA LLC
640 S State St (19901-3530)
PHONE..................................302 744-6008
Terence Murphy, *Vice Pres*
Peggy Naleppa, *Vice Pres*
Michael Tretina, *Treasurer*
Susan Doughty, *Controller*
EMP: 4
SALES (est): 66.8K **Privately Held**
SIC: 8062 General medical & surgical hospitals

(G-1642)
HERTZ LOCAL EDITION CORP
1679 S Dupont Hwy Ste 17 (19901-5114)
PHONE..................................302 678-0700
Luke Parson, *Manager*
EMP: 6
SALES (corp-wide): 9.5B **Publicly Held**
SIC: 7514 Rent-a-car service
HQ: Hertz Local Edition Corp.
8501 Williams Rd
Estero FL 33928
239 301-7000

(G-1643)
HICKORY HILL METAL FABRICATION
2134 Seven Hickories Rd (19904-1645)
PHONE..................................302 382-6727
EMP: 1 **EST:** 2008
SALES (est): 111K **Privately Held**
SIC: 3499 Fabricated metal products

(G-1644)
HIGHER POWER YOGA AND FITNESS
96 Salt Creek Dr Unit 3 (19901-2437)
PHONE..................................302 526-2077
Jessica Coyne, *President*
EMP: 5
SALES (est): 111.3K **Privately Held**
SIC: 7991 Health club

(G-1645)
HIGHMARKS INC
Also Called: Health Care Center of Dover
870 S Governors Ave (19904-4108)
PHONE..................................302 674-8492
Fax: 302 674-8213
EMP: 6
SALES (corp-wide): 468.7MM **Privately Held**
SIC: 6321 Accident/Health Insurance Carrier
PA: Highmarks, Inc.
800 Delaware Ave Ste 900
Wilmington DE 19801
302 421-3000

(G-1646)
HILLIS-CARNES ENGRG ASSOC INC
1277 Mcd Dr (19904-4639)
PHONE..................................302 744-9855
Tom Schick, *Branch Mgr*
EMP: 26
SQ FT: 2,312
SALES (corp-wide): 72.2MM **Privately Held**
SIC: 8711 Consulting engineer
PA: Hillis-Carnes Engineering Associates, Inc.
10975 Guilford Rd Ste A
Annapolis Junction MD 20701
410 880-4788

(G-1647)
HIMALAYA TRADING INC
8 The Grn (19901-3618)
PHONE..................................702 833-0485
Dawei Wang, *President*
EMP: 4
SALES: 10.6MM **Privately Held**
SIC: 7371 5961 Computer software development & applications; general merchandise, mail order

(G-1648)
HIRSH INDUSTRIES INC
631 Ridgely St (19904-2772)
PHONE..................................302 678-4990
▼ **EMP:** 2

SALES (corp-wide): 174.5MM **Privately Held**
SIC: 3999 Barber & beauty shop equipment
PA: Hirsh Industries, Inc.
3636 Westown Pkwy Ste 100
West Des Moines IA 50266
515 299-3200

(G-1649)
HIRSH INDUSTRIES INC
1525 Mckee Rd (19904-1380)
PHONE..................................302 678-3456
Diane Nagyiski, *President*
Joe Antonelli, *Vice Pres*
Ken Murr, *Vice Pres*
Mark Woodward, *Transportation*
Sandy Weishaupt, *Purch Mgr*
EMP: 220
SALES (corp-wide): 174.5MM **Privately Held**
WEB: www.hirshindustries.com
SIC: 2522 Filing boxes, cabinets & cases: except wood; desks, office: except wood
PA: Hirsh Industries, Inc.
3636 Westown Pkwy Ste 100
West Des Moines IA 50266
515 299-3200

(G-1650)
HISTORICAL & CULTURAL AFFAIRS
Also Called: John Dickinson Plantation
340 Kitts Hummock Rd (19901-7016)
PHONE..................................302 739-3277
James Stewart, *Branch Mgr*
EMP: 10 **Privately Held**
SIC: 8412 9111 Museum; executive offices;
HQ: Delaware Division Of Historical & Cultural Afairs
21 The Grn
Dover DE

(G-1651)
HODGES INTERNATIONAL INC
8 The Grn (19901-3618)
PHONE..................................310 874-8516
Deanna Hodges, *President*
EMP: 4
SALES (est): 147.6K **Privately Held**
SIC: 2299 Textile goods

(G-1652)
HOME DEPOT USA INC
Also Called: Home Depot, The
801 N Dupont Hwy (19901-2002)
PHONE..................................302 735-8864
Herb Speech, *Manager*
EMP: 200
SALES (corp-wide): 108.2B **Publicly Held**
WEB: www.homerentalsdepot.com
SIC: 5211 7359 Home centers; tool rental
HQ: Home Depot U.S.A., Inc.
2455 Paces Ferry Ave
Atlanta GA 30339

(G-1653)
HOME HEALTH CORP AMERICA INC
Also Called: Professional Home Health Care
1221 College Park Dr # 203 (19904-8727)
PHONE..................................302 678-4764
Terri Twilley, *Manager*
EMP: 15
SALES (corp-wide): 12.6MM **Privately Held**
SIC: 8082 Home health care services
PA: Home Health Corporation Of America, Inc.
425 Se 26th Ave
Fort Lauderdale FL

(G-1654)
HOME INSTEAD SENIOR CARE
755 Walker Rd Ste A (19904-2801)
P.O. Box 39, Camden Wyoming (19934-0039)
PHONE..................................302 697-6435
Robert Ware, *Principal*
EMP: 5
SALES (est): 45.1K **Privately Held**
SIC: 8082 Home health care services

Dover – Kent County (G-1655)

(G-1655)
HOMEIMPROVEMENT E B&S
19 Carpenter St (19901-9249)
PHONE.................................302 465-1828
Abu Mansaray, *President*
EMP: 5
SQ FT: 350
SALES (est): 14.6K **Privately Held**
SIC: 7699 General household repair services

(G-1656)
HORTY & HORTY PA
3702 N Dupont Hwy (19901-1555)
PHONE.................................302 730-4560
Doug Phillips, *Branch Mgr*
EMP: 20
SALES (corp-wide): 3.4MM **Privately Held**
SIC: 8721 7291 Certified public accountant; tax return preparation services
PA: Horty & Horty Pa
   503 Carr Rd Ste 120
   Wilmington DE 19809
   302 652-4194

(G-1657)
HOUSE OF HAIR
1462 E Lebanon Rd (19901-5833)
PHONE.................................302 697-6088
Richard Shulpitie, *President*
EMP: 4
SALES (est): 83.4K **Privately Held**
SIC: 7241 Hair stylist, men

(G-1658)
HRNX LLC
874 Walker Rd Ste C (19904-2778)
PHONE.................................844 700-0090
Paul Mladineo, *CEO*
Richard Barbut, *CTO*
EMP: 10 EST: 2014
SQ FT: 200
SALES (est): 292.7K **Privately Held**
SIC: 8322 Individual & family services

(G-1659)
HUAWEI TECHNOLOGIES SVC LLC
8 The Grn Ste A (19901-3618)
PHONE.................................888 548-2934
Joel Martinez,
EMP: 1
SALES (est): 54.5K **Privately Held**
SIC: 3578 Point-of-sale devices

(G-1660)
HUB ASSOCIATES
222 S Dupont Hwy (19901-3797)
PHONE.................................302 674-2200
Greg Kramedas, *Owner*
EMP: 9
SALES (est): 18MM **Privately Held**
SIC: 6513 Residential hotel operation

(G-1661)
HUDSON JNES JAYWORK FISHER LLC (PA)
225 S State St (19901-6756)
PHONE.................................302 734-7401
Harry M Fisher III, *Partner*
John Terence Jaywork, *Partner*
R Brandon Jones, *Partner*
Ron B Philips, *Partner*
Ronald D Smith, *Partner*
EMP: 24 EST: 1964
SALES (est): 3.8MM **Privately Held**
WEB: www.delawarelaw.com
SIC: 8111 General practice attorney, lawyer

(G-1662)
HULLO INC
3500 S Dupont Hwy (19901-6041)
PHONE.................................415 939-6534
Taher Khorakiwala, *CEO*
Angad Nadkarni, *COO*
EMP: 4 EST: 2015
SALES (est): 98.3K **Privately Held**
SIC: 7372 Application computer software

(G-1663)
HYPEBEAST INC
Also Called: Hbnyc
3500 S Dupont Hwy (19901-6041)
PHONE.................................714 791-0755
Huan Nguyen, *President*
EMP: 30
SQ FT: 1,600
SALES: 500K **Privately Held**
SIC: 2721 Magazines: publishing & printing

(G-1664)
HYPERTEC USA INC
73 Greentree Dr (19904-7646)
PHONE.................................480 626-9000
Robert Ahdoot, *President*
EMP: 5 EST: 2014
SALES (est): 752.5K **Privately Held**
SIC: 5045 Computer peripheral equipment

(G-1665)
I N I HOLDINGS INC (PA)
110 Galaxy Dr (19901-9262)
PHONE.................................302 674-3600
Joe Smith, *Director*
Chris Engel, *Bd of Directors*
EMP: 4
SALES (est): 81.8MM **Privately Held**
SIC: 2711 2752 Newspapers: publishing only, not printed on site; newspapers, publishing & printing; commercial printing, offset

(G-1666)
IHEARTCOMMUNICATIONS INC
Also Called: Wdov AM
1575 Mckee Rd Ste 206 (19904-1382)
PHONE.................................302 674-1410
Martha Burns, *Sales Mgr*
EMP: 21 **Publicly Held**
SIC: 4832 Country
HQ: Iheartcommunications, Inc.
   20880 Stone Oak Pkwy
   San Antonio TX 78258
   210 822-2828

(G-1667)
III JOHN F GLENN MD
737 S Queen St Ste 2 (19904-3529)
P.O. Box 576 (19903-0576)
PHONE.................................302 735-8850
John F Glenn III, *Owner*
Michelle Dominique, *Co-Owner*
EMP: 7
SALES (est): 206.2K **Privately Held**
SIC: 8011 General & family practice, physician/surgeon

(G-1668)
IN A STITCH
526 Rose Dale Ln (19904-1606)
PHONE.................................302 678-2260
Lisa Mummert, *Owner*
EMP: 1
SALES (est): 45.7K **Privately Held**
SIC: 2395 Embroidery & art needlework

(G-1669)
INBIT INC
8 The Grn Ste 10159 (19901-3618)
PHONE.................................302 603-7437
Evgeny Sporyshev, *Director*
EMP: 9
SALES (est): 200K **Privately Held**
SIC: 7371 Computer software development & applications

(G-1670)
IND SWIFT LABORATORIES INC
3500 S Dupont Hwy (19901-6041)
PHONE.................................302 233-1564
Nirmal Aggarwal, *Principal*
EMP: 5
SALES (est): 119.7K **Privately Held**
SIC: 8082 Home health care services

(G-1671)
INDEPENDENT METAL STRAP CO INC
883 Horsepond Rd (19901-7214)
PHONE.................................516 621-0030
Paul Maslar, *President*
Michael Maslar, *Senior VP*
Michael Bertram, *Opers Mgr*
Anthony Mariano, *Marketing Mgr*
Kerry C Cleary, *Manager*
▲ EMP: 20
SQ FT: 40,000
SALES (est): 6.5MM **Privately Held**
WEB: www.indmetalstrap.com
SIC: 5085 Tools

(G-1672)
INDEPENDENT NEWSMEDIA USA INC (HQ)
110 Galaxy Dr (19901-9262)
PHONE.................................302 674-3600
Edward Dulin, *CEO*
Joe Smyth, *Ch of Bd*
Wanda Ford-Waring, *Vice Pres*
Darryl Laprade, *Vice Pres*
Toni Jackson, *Treasurer*
▲ EMP: 90 EST: 1953
SALES (est): 81.8MM **Privately Held**
WEB: www.inweekly.net
SIC: 2711 2752 Newspapers: publishing only, not printed on site; newspapers, publishing & printing; commercial printing, offset

(G-1673)
INDEPENDENT NEWSMEDIA USA INC
Also Called: Delaware State News
110 Galaxy Dr (19901-9262)
P.O. Box 737 (19903-0737)
PHONE.................................302 674-3600
Richard Dyer, *Editor*
Mike Pelrine, *Manager*
EMP: 200 **Privately Held**
WEB: www.inweekly.net
SIC: 2711 Newspapers, publishing & printing; newspapers publishing only, not printed on site
HQ: Independent Newsmedia Usa, Inc.
   110 Galaxy Dr
   Dover DE 19901
   302 674-3600

(G-1674)
INDEPENDENT RESOURCES INC
154 S Governors Ave (19904-3223)
PHONE.................................302 735-4599
Deborah Justice, *Director*
EMP: 15
SALES (est): 320K
SALES (corp-wide): 653.7K **Privately Held**
SIC: 8322 Social service center
PA: Independent Resources, Inc.
   6 Denny Rd Ste 101
   Wilmington DE 19809
   302 765-0191

(G-1675)
INFARM - INDOOR URBAN FARMING
8 The Grn Ste 7929 (19901-3618)
PHONE.................................561 809-5183
Matthias Lebherz, *Owner*
EMP: 200
SALES (est): 1.2MM **Privately Held**
SIC: 0762 Farm management services

(G-1676)
INFO TITAN LLC
32 Loockerman Plz Ste 109 (19901)
PHONE.................................510 495-4117
WEI Lin,
EMP: 3
SALES (est): 92K **Privately Held**
SIC: 2711 Newspapers

(G-1677)
INFUSION SOLUTIONS OF DE
1100 Forrest Ave (19904-3309)
PHONE.................................302 674-4627
Robert Anthony Moyer, *Principal*
Ramesh Vemulapalli, *Infectious Dis*
EMP: 14
SALES (est): 1.8MM **Privately Held**
SIC: 8011 Internal medicine, physician/surgeon

(G-1678)
INSPECTION LANES
415 Transportation Cir (19901-4672)
P.O. Box 698 (19903-0698)
PHONE.................................302 744-2514
Fax: 302 744-2641
EMP: 7
SALES (est): 95.6K **Privately Held**
SIC: 7933 Bowling Center

(G-1679)
INSTANT GLOBAL SERVICES CORP
8 The Grn Ste 8301 (19901-3618)
PHONE.................................302 514-1047
Christopher A Palmer Jr, *President*
EMP: 9 **Privately Held**
SIC: 6719 Holding companies

(G-1680)
INSTANTUPTIME INC
Also Called: Pointstrekker
8 The Grn Ste A (19901-3618)
PHONE.................................302 608-0890
Robert Tilley Jr, *President*
EMP: 15
SALES (est): 317.3K **Privately Held**
SIC: 7389

(G-1681)
INTERNAL MEDICINE DOVER PA
725 S Queen St (19904-3568)
PHONE.................................302 678-4488
Pam Poore, *Office Mgr*
EMP: 7
SALES (est): 106.2K **Privately Held**
SIC: 8011 Internal medicine, physician/surgeon

(G-1682)
INTERNATIONAL GAME TECHNOLOGY
1281 Mcd Dr (19901-4639)
PHONE.................................302 674-3177
Chuck Mathewson, *Principal*
EMP: 14
SALES (corp-wide): 4.8B **Privately Held**
WEB: www.igt.com
SIC: 5099 Game machines, coin-operated
HQ: Igt Inc.
   9295 Prototype Dr
   Reno NV 89521

(G-1683)
INTOUCH INC (PA)
160 Greentree Dr Ste 101 (19904-7620)
PHONE.................................302 313-2594
Aliaksei Adamovitch,
EMP: 2
SALES (est): 280.3K **Privately Held**
SIC: 2741 7371 ; computer software development & applications

(G-1684)
IRONHOUSE SECURITY GROUP INC
8 The Grn Ste A (19901-3618)
PHONE.................................443 312-9932
Brett Mabrie, *CEO*
Thomas Hernandez, *President*
EMP: 6 EST: 2017
SALES (est): 108.8K **Privately Held**
SIC: 7381 Guard services

(G-1685)
ITCONNECTUS INC
3500 S Dupont Hwy (19901-6041)
PHONE.................................302 531-1139
Ankit Kashyap, *Technology*
Yash Pal, *Director*
Puneet Khehra, *Tech Recruiter*
EMP: 5
SALES (corp-wide): 2.9MM **Privately Held**
SIC: 7389 Mailing & messenger services
PA: Itconnectus Inc.
   1375 Ste W Remington Rd
   Schaumburg IL 60173
   847 258-9595

(G-1686)
J & J BUS SERVICE
315 Billy Mitchell Ln E209 (19901-5390)
PHONE.................................302 744-9002
Terry Grim Jr, *Owner*
EMP: 10
SALES (est): 321.4K **Privately Held**
SIC: 4789 Transportation services

GEOGRAPHIC SECTION — Dover - Kent County

(G-1687)
J KENNETH MOORE & SON INC
1876 E Denneys Rd (19901-2755)
PHONE....................302 736-0563
J Kenneth Moore, *President*
Josephine Moore, *Admin Sec*
EMP: 4
SALES: 1.7MM **Privately Held**
SIC: 1521 Single-family housing construction

(G-1688)
J R WILLIAMSON DDS
Also Called: Richard Williamson
900 Forest St (19904-3402)
PHONE....................302 734-8887
Jesse R Williamson DDS, *Owner*
Richard S Williamson, *Fmly & Gen Dent*
EMP: 5
SALES (est): 345.7K **Privately Held**
SIC: 8021 Dentists' office

(G-1689)
JACKSON CONTRACTING INC
7242 Pearsons Corner Rd (19904-0928)
PHONE....................302 678-2011
Gary Jackson, *President*
Joe Corrado, *Vice Pres*
EMP: 14
SALES (est): 1.1MM **Privately Held**
SIC: 8748 Business consulting

(G-1690)
JACKSON THMAS C ATTRNEY AT LAW
438 S State St (19901-6724)
PHONE....................302 736-1723
Thomas C Jackson, *Owner*
EMP: 5
SQ FT: 2,500
SALES (est): 223K **Privately Held**
SIC: 8111 General practice attorney, lawyer

(G-1691)
JAMES FRIESA ACUPUNCTURE
1326 S Governors Ave (19904-4800)
PHONE....................302 674-4204
EMP: 8
SALES (est): 65.7K **Privately Held**
SIC: 8049 Acupuncturist

(G-1692)
JAMES S PILLSBURY DDS
125 Greentree Dr B (19904-7656)
PHONE....................302 734-0330
James S Pillsbury DDS, *Owner*
EMP: 7
SALES (est): 410.6K **Privately Held**
SIC: 8021 Dentists' office

(G-1693)
JAMMIN PRODUCTIONS
2178 S State St (19901-6315)
PHONE....................302 670-7302
Jeff Neitzelt, *Owner*
EMP: 5
SALES (est): 73.6K **Privately Held**
SIC: 7929 Entertainment service

(G-1694)
JARRELL BENSON GILES & SWEENEY
Also Called: Giles, Christopher MD
725 S Queen St (19904-3568)
PHONE....................302 678-4488
T Noble Jarrell, *Partner*
EMP: 15
SALES (est): 1.2MM **Privately Held**
SIC: 8011 Internal medicine practitioners

(G-1695)
JEFFERSON URIAN DANE STRNER PA
107 Wolf Creek Blvd Ste 1 (19901-4970)
P.O. Box 830, Georgetown (19947-0830)
PHONE....................302 678-1425
David Doan, *President*
EMP: 10
SALES (corp-wide): 5.8MM **Privately Held**
WEB: www.juds.com
SIC: 8721 Certified public accountant

PA: Jefferson, Urian, Doane & Sterner, P.A.
651 N Bedford St
Georgetown DE 19947
302 856-3900

(G-1696)
JETSET TRAVEL INC
222 S Dupont Hwy Ste 102 (19901-3778)
PHONE....................302 678-5050
Angela Armutcu, *President*
EMP: 5
SALES (est): 828.7K **Privately Held**
SIC: 4724 Tourist agency arranging transport, lodging & car rental

(G-1697)
JK TANGLES HAIR SALON
Also Called: Ciseaux Hair Design Studio
1151 E Lebanon Rd Ste E (19901-5829)
PHONE....................302 698-1006
Denise Moore, *President*
EMP: 11
SALES (est): 238K **Privately Held**
SIC: 7231 Unisex hair salons

(G-1698)
JKB CORP
Also Called: Two Men and A Truck
1169 S Dupont Hwy (19901-4423)
PHONE....................302 734-5017
Jeremy Brown, *President*
EMP: 35
SQ FT: 2,400
SALES: 1.6MM **Privately Held**
SIC: 4212 Local trucking, without storage

(G-1699)
JOBS FOR DELAWARE GRADUATES
381 W North St (19904-6748)
PHONE....................302 734-9341
Suzzanna Lee, *President*
EMP: 20
SALES (corp-wide): 3.9MM **Privately Held**
WEB: www.jobsfordelawaregraduates.org
SIC: 7361 Employment agencies
PA: Jobs For Delaware Graduates Inc
5157 W Woodmill Dr Ste 16
Wilmington DE 19808
302 995-7175

(G-1700)
JOEL R TEMPLE MD
9 E Loockerman St Ste 303 (19901-8305)
PHONE....................302 678-1343
Joel Temple, *Owner*
▲ EMP: 5
SALES (est): 571.5K **Privately Held**
SIC: 8011 Allergist

(G-1701)
JOHN A CAPODANNO DDS PA
75 W Fairfield Dr (19901-5757)
PHONE....................302 697-7859
EMP: 4 EST: 2010
SALES (est): 180K **Privately Held**
SIC: 8021 Dentist's Office

(G-1702)
JOHN B COLL DO
1074 S State St (19901-6925)
PHONE....................302 678-8100
John B Coll Do, *Principal*
EMP: 4 EST: 2001
SALES (est): 121.8K **Privately Held**
SIC: 8031 Offices & clinics of osteopathic physicians

(G-1703)
JOHN BORDEN
Also Called: State Farm Insurance
450 S Dupont Hwy Ofc B (19901-4502)
PHONE....................302 674-2992
John Borden, *Owner*
EMP: 5
SALES (est): 438.4K **Privately Held**
SIC: 6411 Insurance agents & brokers

(G-1704)
JOHN D MANNION M D
540 S Governors Ave 101a (19904-3530)
PHONE....................302 744-7980
John Mannion, *Owner*
EMP: 5

SALES (est): 82.1K **Privately Held**
SIC: 8011 Offices & clinics of medical doctors

(G-1705)
JOHN H HATFIELD DDS
1390 Lochmeath Way (19901-6514)
PHONE....................302 698-0567
John Hatfield, *Principal*
EMP: 4
SALES (est): 91.2K **Privately Held**
SIC: 8021 Offices & clinics of dentists

(G-1706)
JOINCUBE INC
3500 S Dupont Hwy (19901-6041)
PHONE....................214 532-9997
Mariano Rodriguez, *CEO*
EMP: 10
SALES (est): 453.9K **Privately Held**
SIC: 7371 Computer software development & applications

(G-1707)
JONATHAN L KATES M D
540 S Governors Ave # 201 (19904-3530)
PHONE....................302 730-4366
Cristobal Alvarado, *Owner*
EMP: 6
SALES (est): 80.5K **Privately Held**
SIC: 8011 Offices & clinics of medical doctors

(G-1708)
JONNY NICHOLS LDSCP MAINT INC
273 Walnut Shade Rd (19904-6474)
P.O. Box 419, Woodside (19980-0419)
PHONE....................302 697-2200
Jon Nichols Jr, *President*
Jon Nichols Sr, *Vice Pres*
EMP: 9
SALES (est): 1.5MM **Privately Held**
WEB: www.jonnynichols.com
SIC: 0782 Landscape contractors

(G-1709)
JOSEPH PARISE DO
793 S Queen St (19904-3568)
PHONE....................302 735-8855
Joseph Parise Do, *Owner*
EMP: 5
SALES (est): 388.1K **Privately Held**
SIC: 8031 Offices & clinics of osteopathic physicians

(G-1710)
JR BOARD OF KENT GEN HOSPITAL
640 S State St (19901-3530)
PHONE....................302 744-7128
EMP: 6
SALES (est): 157K **Privately Held**
SIC: 8062 General medical & surgical hospitals

(G-1711)
JS AUTOMOTIVE AAMCO
Also Called: AAMCO Transmissions
3729 N Dupont Hwy (19901-1574)
PHONE....................302 678-5660
John Snyder, *Owner*
EMP: 6
SALES: 750K **Privately Held**
SIC: 7537 Automotive transmission repair shops

(G-1712)
JSC VENTURES LLC
9 E Loockerman St Ste 202 (19901-7347)
PHONE....................302 336-8151
Fj Johnson,
EMP: 65
SALES (est): 1.3MM **Privately Held**
SIC: 6799 Venture capital companies

(G-1713)
JSD MANAGEMENT INC
Also Called: JAMES, STEVENS & DANIELS
1283 College Park Dr (19904-8713)
PHONE....................302 735-4628
Kelly Hedrick, *President*
Joe Vanzego, *Business Mgr*
Cindy Lee, *Vice Pres*
Aron Johnson, *QC Dir*

Lyn Boyd, *Engineer*
EMP: 48
SQ FT: 8,000
SALES: 2.3MM **Privately Held**
WEB: www.jsdinc.net
SIC: 7322 Collection agency, except real estate

(G-1714)
JUAN SAUCEDO
Also Called: Saucedos Landscaping
1133 S Little Creek Rd (19901-4772)
PHONE....................302 233-4539
Juan Saucedo, *Principal*
EMP: 4
SALES (est): 185.7K **Privately Held**
SIC: 0781 Landscape services

(G-1715)
JULIE Q NIES DDS
1380 S State St (19901-4946)
PHONE....................302 242-9085
Julie Nies, *Principal*
EMP: 4
SALES (est): 61.5K **Privately Held**
SIC: 8021 Offices & clinics of dentists

(G-1716)
JUNGLE GYM LLC
1418 S State St (19901-4948)
PHONE....................302 734-1515
Deborah Simmons,
Tracy Goff,
EMP: 12
SALES (est): 281.6K **Privately Held**
SIC: 8322 Rehabilitation services

(G-1717)
K BS PLUMBING INCORPORATED
518 Lochmeath Way (19904-6452)
PHONE....................302 678-2757
Kenneth R Boots, *President*
EMP: 5
SQ FT: 1,850
SALES (est): 440K **Privately Held**
SIC: 1711 Plumbing contractors

(G-1718)
K W LANDS LLC
Also Called: Hampton Inn
222 S Dupont Hwy (19901-3797)
PHONE....................302 674-2200
Thomas Kramedas, *Manager*
Avelina Kramedas,
Tom Kramedas,
Davis H Wood,
EMP: 37
SALES (est): 1MM **Privately Held**
WEB: www.axiamgt.com
SIC: 7011 8741 Hotels & motels; management services

(G-1719)
K W LANDS NORTH LLC
Also Called: Holiday Inn
1780 N Dupont Hwy (19901-2219)
PHONE....................302 678-0600
Gregory Kramedas, *Owner*
Tanya Forero, *Sales Staff*
Joyce Mak, *Sales Staff*
Cynthia Marcial, *Sales Staff*
EMP: 40
SALES (est): 2.4MM **Privately Held**
SIC: 7011 Hotels & motels

(G-1720)
KA ANALYTICS & TECH LLC
1024 Avocado Ave (19901-7908)
PHONE....................800 520-8178
Dr Kankoe Assiongbon, *CEO*
EMP: 6
SALES (est): 146.2K **Privately Held**
SIC: 8732 Business analysis

(G-1721)
KAIROS HOME PROS LLC
8 The Grn Ste 8086 (19901-3618)
PHONE....................302 233-7044
Warren Falden, *CEO*
EMP: 5 EST: 2016
SALES (est): 285.5K **Privately Held**
SIC: 1521 General remodeling, single-family houses

Dover - Kent County (G-1722)

(G-1722)
KAREN Y VCKS LAW OFFCES OF LLC
500 W Loockerman St # 102 (19904-7309)
PHONE..................302 674-1100
Karen Vicks,
EMP: 6
SQ FT: 1,000
SALES (est): 609.7K **Privately Held**
SIC: 8111 General practice law office

(G-1723)
KATHRYN L FORD FMLY PRACTICE
870 S Governors Ave (19904-4108)
PHONE..................302 674-8088
Paul W Ford, *Partner*
EMP: 8
SALES (est): 936K **Privately Held**
SIC: 8011 General & family practice, physician/surgeon

(G-1724)
KATHY SAFFORD
Also Called: State Farm Insurance
1 S Independence Blvd (19904-3381)
PHONE..................302 734-8268
Kathy Safford, *Owner*
EMP: 4
SALES (est): 500.8K **Privately Held**
SIC: 6411 Insurance agents & brokers

(G-1725)
KAZA MEDICAL GROUP INC
Also Called: Kaza, Janaki B MD
18 Old Rudnick Ln (19901-4912)
PHONE..................302 674-2616
Janaki B Kaza, *President*
EMP: 15
SQ FT: 3,053
SALES (est): 1.5MM **Privately Held**
SIC: 8011 Pediatrician

(G-1726)
KCS SENSATIONAL VACATIONS
1206 S Farmview Dr (19904-3370)
PHONE..................267 886-0991
EMP: 4
SALES (est): 532.7K **Privately Held**
SIC: 4724 Travel agencies

(G-1727)
KEARNS BRINEN & MONAGHAN INC
20 E Division St Ste B (19901-7366)
P.O. Box 314, Camden Wyoming (19934-0314)
PHONE..................302 736-6481
Mark Lefevre, *President*
Joshua David, *Senior Mgr*
EMP: 16
SQ FT: 3,800
SALES (est): 1.8MM **Privately Held**
SIC: 7322 Collection agency, except real estate

(G-1728)
KEEN COMPRESSED GAS CO
Also Called: K C G
226 S New St (19904-6709)
PHONE..................302 736-6814
Paul Kenney, *Branch Mgr*
EMP: 4
SALES (corp-wide): 28.8MM **Privately Held**
WEB: www.keengas.com
SIC: 5085 Welding supplies
PA: Keen Compressed Gas Co.
   101 Rogers Rd Ste 200
   Wilmington DE 19801
   302 594-4545

(G-1729)
KEGLERS KORNER PRO SHOP
1600 S Governors Ave (19904-7004)
PHONE..................302 526-2249
Brian Knauer, *Owner*
EMP: 5
SALES (est): 120.9K **Privately Held**
SIC: 7933 Bowling centers

(G-1730)
KELLER WILLIAMS REALTY CE
1671 S State St (19901-5148)
PHONE..................302 653-3624
Doreen Lucas, *Principal*
Betty J Corey, *Sales Staff*
Doreen I Lucas, *Sales Staff*
Kimberly R Jones, *Sales Staff*
Mason McGill, *Real Est Agnt*
EMP: 5
SALES (est): 420.2K **Privately Held**
SIC: 6531 Real estate agent, residential

(G-1731)
KELLY SERVICES INC
160 Greentree Dr Ste 103 (19904-7620)
PHONE..................302 674-8087
Bonnie Share, *Branch Mgr*
EMP: 4
SALES (corp-wide): 5.5B **Publicly Held**
WEB: www.kellyservices.com
SIC: 7363 Temporary help service
PA: Kelly Services, Inc.
   999 W Big Beaver Rd
   Troy MI 48084
   248 362-4444

(G-1732)
KENT CNTY CMNTY ACTN AGNCY INC
120a S Governors Ave (19904-3223)
PHONE..................302 678-1949
Rev Larry Blinon, *Treasurer*
Sara Butler, *Exec Dir*
EMP: 12
SALES (est): 482.2K **Privately Held**
SIC: 8322 Children's aid society

(G-1733)
KENT COUNTY TOURISM CORP
435 N Dupont Hwy (19901-3907)
P.O. Box 576 (19903-0576)
PHONE..................302 734-1736
Cindy Small, *Manager*
EMP: 4
SALES (est): 598.7K **Privately Held**
WEB: www.visitdover.com
SIC: 7389 Tourist information bureau

(G-1734)
KENT GENERAL HOSPITAL
Also Called: Saint Jnes Ctr For Bhvral Hlth
725 Horsepond Rd (19901-7232)
PHONE..................302 744-7688
Janis Chester, *Director*
EMP: 9 **Privately Held**
SIC: 8062 General medical & surgical hospitals
HQ: Kent General Hospital
   640 S State St
   Dover DE 19901
   302 674-4700

(G-1735)
KENT GENERAL HOSPITAL (HQ)
Also Called: Milford Memorial Hospital
640 S State St (19901-3599)
PHONE..................302 674-4700
Terry M Murphy, *Principal*
Richard Dushuttle, *Med Doctor*
Courtney Breasure, *Hlthcr Dir*
Heather Pellrin, *Analyst*
Adrianne Fisher, *Nurse*
EMP: 63
SQ FT: 335,000
SALES: 537.3MM **Privately Held**
SIC: 8062 Hospital, affiliated with AMA residency

(G-1736)
KENT LEASING COMPANY INC
2181 S Dupont Hwy (19901-5556)
P.O. Box 456 (19903-0456)
PHONE..................302 697-3000
John W Whitby Jr, *President*
Audrey Whitby, *Vice Pres*
EMP: 50
SQ FT: 3,000
SALES (est): 1.2MM **Privately Held**
SIC: 7514 Rent-a-car service

(G-1737)
KENT PEDIATRICS LLC
1102 S Dupont Hwy Ste 1 (19901-4493)
PHONE..................302 264-9691
Osama Hussein, *Principal*
EMP: 4
SALES (est): 267.6K **Privately Held**
SIC: 8011 Pediatrician

(G-1738)
KENT PULMONARY ASSOCIATES LLC
807 S Bradford St (19904-4137)
PHONE..................302 674-7155
David A Jawahar, *Principal*
Charlotte Bird, *Office Mgr*
EMP: 5
SALES (est): 637.2K **Privately Held**
SIC: 8011 Pulmonary specialist, physician/surgeon; internal medicine practitioners

(G-1739)
KENT SIGN COMPANY INC
2 E Bradys Ln (19901-6310)
PHONE..................302 697-2181
William S Craven, *President*
Leona Cravens, *Corp Secy*
Riley McCalister, *Vice Pres*
Kim Diehl, *Admin Sec*
EMP: 17 **EST:** 1958
SALES (est): 1.5MM **Privately Held**
WEB: www.kentsigns.net
SIC: 5046 1799 7539 3993 Signs, electrical; sign installation & maintenance; electrical services; electric signs

(G-1740)
KENT SUSSEX COMMUNITY SERVICES
1241 College Park Dr (19904-8713)
PHONE..................302 384-6926
Alan Hash, *Controller*
Natalie Andrews, *Info Tech Mgr*
Irene Curry, *Admin Asst*
EMP: 14
SALES (est): 1.1MM **Privately Held**
SIC: 8093 Mental health clinic, outpatient

(G-1741)
KENT SWIMMING CLUB INC
295 Cardinal Hills Pkwy (19904-5666)
PHONE..................302 674-3283
Lisa Cutrnona, *President*
EMP: 15
SALES (est): 234.5K **Privately Held**
SIC: 7997 Swimming club, membership

(G-1742)
KENTON CHILD CARE
1298 Mckee Rd (19904-1381)
P.O. Box 340, Kenton (19955-0340)
PHONE..................302 674-8142
Donna Revel, *Owner*
EMP: 7
SALES (est): 195.3K **Privately Held**
SIC: 8351 Child day care services

(G-1743)
KERA CABLE PRODUCTS LLC
8 The Grn Ste A (19901-3618)
PHONE..................917 383-4013
Kera Thompson,
EMP: 2
SALES (est): 56.5K **Privately Held**
SIC: 7372 Application computer software

(G-1744)
KEY ADVISORS GROUP LLC (PA)
31 Saulsbury Rd (19904-3444)
PHONE..................302 735-9909
Ferros Doher,
Eddie Gubhor,
EMP: 4
SALES (est): 1MM **Privately Held**
SIC: 8742 Financial consultant

(G-1745)
KHAN OB GYN ASSOCIATES
1113 S State St (19901-4112)
PHONE..................302 735-8720
Nasreen Khan, *Owner*
EMP: 10
SQ FT: 6,586
SALES (est): 550K **Privately Held**
SIC: 8011 Gynecologist

(G-1746)
KID AGAINS INC
33 Lindley Dr (19904-3807)
PHONE..................631 830-5228
Frank Ko, *CEO*
Michael Prendergast, *President*
▲ **EMP:** 2 **EST:** 2013
SALES (est): 204K **Privately Held**
SIC: 3944 7389 Board games, puzzles & models, except electronic;

(G-1747)
KIDD ROBERT W III DDS
850 S State St (19901-4113)
P.O. Box 657 (19903-0657)
PHONE..................302 678-1440
Robert W Kidd III DDS, *Owner*
EMP: 12
SQ FT: 1,800
SALES (est): 450.9K **Privately Held**
SIC: 8021 Orthodontist

(G-1748)
KIDS R US LEARNING CENTER INC
Also Called: Kids-R-Us Learning Center
425 Webbs Ln (19904-5439)
PHONE..................302 678-1234
Sylvia Davis, *Principal*
EMP: 6
SALES (est): 197.7K **Privately Held**
SIC: 8351 Child day care services

(G-1749)
KIDS TEENS PEDIATRICS OF DOVER
125 Greentree Dr Ste 1 (19904-7656)
PHONE..................302 538-5624
Amal Ouad, *Principal*
EMP: 6
SALES (est): 104.3K **Privately Held**
SIC: 8011 Pediatrician

(G-1750)
KING OF SWEETS INC
47 S West St (19904-3265)
PHONE..................302 730-8200
Janine Altenkirch, *President*
EMP: 17 **EST:** 2013
SALES (est): 412.7K **Privately Held**
SIC: 5812 5441 5145 Eating places; candy, nut & confectionery stores; confectionery

(G-1751)
KINGS CONTRACTING INC
Also Called: General Contractor
378 Kentland Ave (19901-5288)
PHONE..................302 677-0363
Harold King, *President*
Dawn King, *Corp Secy*
Valerie King, *Office Mgr*
EMP: 5
SALES (est): 450K **Privately Held**
SIC: 1521 General remodeling, single-family houses

(G-1752)
KINGS SEALCOATING
416 Dogwood Ave (19904-4879)
PHONE..................302 674-1568
Ryan Cushman, *Principal*
EMP: 2
SALES (est): 90.7K **Privately Held**
SIC: 2952 Asphalt felts & coatings

(G-1753)
KNA SOLUTIONS LLC
8 The Grn Ste 4372 (19901-3618)
PHONE..................302 709-1215
Kimberly Smitz,
Amelia Christy,
Samar Hatoum,
Nickalaus Killip,
EMP: 4
SALES (est): 143.3K **Privately Held**
SIC: 7361 Labor contractors (employment agency)

(G-1754)
KNEPPER & STRATTON
309 S State St Ste C (19901-6753)
PHONE..................302 658-1717
E Knepper, *Manager*
EMP: 6 **Privately Held**
WEB: www.knepperstratton.com
SIC: 8111 General practice attorney, lawyer
PA: Knepper & Stratton
   1228 N King St
   Wilmington DE 19801

GEOGRAPHIC SECTION
Dover - Kent County (G-1786)

(G-1755)
KNIGHT CAPITAL FUNDING LLC
9 E Lockmerman St Ste (19901)
PHONE.................................888 523-4363
EMP: 25
SALES (est): 2.1MM **Privately Held**
SIC: 6159 Miscellaneous Business Credit Institutions, Nsk

(G-1756)
KNS09 INC
Also Called: Maaco Collision Repr Auto Pntg
1062 Lafferty Ln (19901-4642)
PHONE.................................302 697-3499
Scott Koenig, *Treasurer*
EMP: 11
SALES: 350K **Privately Held**
SIC: 7532 Paint shop, automotive

(G-1757)
KPKM INC
Also Called: Maaco Collision Repr Auto Pntg
1062 Lafferty Ln (19901-4642)
PHONE.................................302 678-0271
Mark Lopisz, *President*
EMP: 8
SALES (est): 640.3K **Privately Held**
SIC: 7532 Paint shop, automotive

(G-1758)
KRAFT HEINZ COMPANY
Kraft Foods
1250 W North St (19904-7756)
PHONE.................................302 734-6100
M Shah, *Principal*
Randy Klongland, *Manager*
Jason Hoelscher, *Info Tech Mgr*
Patterson Scott, *Associate Dir*
EMP: 800
SALES (corp-wide): 26.2B **Publicly Held**
WEB: www.kraftfoods.com
SIC: 2099 2066 2051 2041 Gelatin dessert preparations; chocolate & cocoa products; bread, cake & related products; flour & other grain mill products; canned fruits & specialties; fluid milk
PA: The Kraft Heinz Company
   1 Ppg Pl Fl 34
   Pittsburgh PA 15222
   412 456-5700

(G-1759)
KW GARDEN
Also Called: Sleep Inn
1784 N Dupont Hwy (19901-2219)
PHONE.................................302 735-7770
Tad Fox, *General Mgr*
EMP: 24
SALES: 750K **Privately Held**
SIC: 7011 Hotels & motels

(G-1760)
L & W INSURANCE INC
1154 S Governors Ave (19904-6904)
P.O. Box 918 (19903-0918)
PHONE.................................302 674-3500
Gary Wyatt, *Accountant*
Tim Conley, *Accounts Exec*
Sharon Daube, *Accounts Exec*
Ed Brown, *Sales Staff*
Cheri Fuchs, *Marketing Staff*
EMP: 4
SALES (est): 703.3K **Privately Held**
SIC: 6411 Insurance agents

(G-1761)
L3D LLC
1671 S State St (19901-5148)
PHONE.................................302 677-0031
Doreen Lucas,
EMP: 6
SALES (est): 420K **Privately Held**
WEB: www.l3d.com
SIC: 6531 Multiple listing service, real estate

(G-1762)
LA BELLA VITA SALON & DAY SPA
525 S Red Haven Ln (19901-6483)
PHONE.................................302 883-2597
Dawn Dicecco, *Owner*
EMP: 6 EST: 2010
SALES (est): 164.9K **Privately Held**
SIC: 7991 Spas

(G-1763)
LABORATORY CORPORATION AMERICA
200 Banning St Ste 160 (19904-3491)
PHONE.................................302 735-4694
Connie Seth, *Branch Mgr*
EMP: 4 **Publicly Held**
SIC: 8071 Medical laboratories
HQ: Laboratory Corporation Of America
   358 S Main St Ste 458
   Burlington NC 27215
   336 229-1127

(G-1764)
LAN RACK INC (PA)
8 The Grn Ste 8284 (19901-3618)
PHONE.................................949 587-5168
John Fagan, *President*
EMP: 5 EST: 1996
SALES (est): 1.1MM **Privately Held**
SIC: 5045 5021 Computer peripheral equipment; racks

(G-1765)
LANDMARK HOMES
68 Representative Ln (19904-2491)
P.O. Box 1037, Middletown (19709-7037)
PHONE.................................302 388-8557
Landmark Homes, *Principal*
EMP: 4
SALES (est): 255.7K **Privately Held**
SIC: 6799 Investors

(G-1766)
LASER & PLASTIC SURGERY CENTER
200 Banning St Ste 230 (19904-3487)
PHONE.................................302 674-4865
David Smith, *President*
EMP: 5
SQ FT: 5,750
SALES (est): 328.8K **Privately Held**
SIC: 8011 Plastic surgeon

(G-1767)
LAW OFFICE LAURA A YIENGST LLC
314 S State St (19901-6730)
PHONE.................................302 264-9780
Donna Juhrden, *President*
Laura Yiengst, *Counsel*
EMP: 6 EST: 2010
SALES (est): 430K **Privately Held**
SIC: 8111 Legal services

(G-1768)
LAW OFFICES GARY R DODGE PA
250 Beiser Blvd Ste 202 (19904-7795)
PHONE.................................302 674-5400
Gary R Dodge, *President*
Tara Hayhurst, *Office Mgr*
EMP: 5
SALES (est): 432.5K **Privately Held**
SIC: 8111 General practice law office

(G-1769)
LAWALL PROSTHETICS - ORTHOTICS
514 N Dupont Hwy (19901-3961)
PHONE.................................302 677-0693
Doug Davis, *Manager*
EMP: 5 **Privately Held**
SIC: 8011 8069 Specialized medical practitioners, except internal; children's hospital
PA: Lawall Prosthetics - Orthotics Inc.
   1822 Augustine Cut Off
   Wilmington DE 19803

(G-1770)
LAWRENCE A LOUIE DMD
250 Beiser Blvd Ste 101 (19904-7795)
PHONE.................................302 674-5437
Lawrence A Louie DMD, *Owner*
EMP: 6
SALES (est): 304.4K **Privately Held**
SIC: 8021 Pedodontist

(G-1771)
LAWRENCE M LEWANDOSKI MD
4601 S Dupont Hwy Ste 2 (19901-6405)
PHONE.................................302 698-1100
Lawrence M Lewandoski MD, *Principal*
EMP: 5
SALES (est): 206K **Privately Held**
SIC: 8011 General & family practice, physician/surgeon

(G-1772)
LAWTER PLANNING GROUP INC
1305 S Governors Ave (19904-4803)
P.O. Box 1457 (19903-1457)
PHONE.................................302 736-6065
Dallas A Lawter, *President*
Sandra Lawter O'Toole, *Vice Pres*
EMP: 8
SALES: 600K **Privately Held**
SIC: 8742 Financial consultant

(G-1773)
LEADERSHIP FORUM LLC
850 New Burton Rd Ste 201 (19904-5786)
PHONE.................................919 309-4025
Wanda Wallace, *Principal*
Liam Fahey, *Principal*
Peter Wright, *Principal*
EMP: 4
SALES (est): 92.1K **Privately Held**
SIC: 7389

(G-1774)
LEARNING YEARS PRESCHOOL
2 Riverside Rd (19904-5723)
PHONE.................................302 241-4781
Kattie R Gibson, *Owner*
EMP: 5
SALES (est): 70K **Privately Held**
SIC: 8351 Preschool center

(G-1775)
LEE LYNN INC
Also Called: Melvin's Sunoco
1020 S State St (19901-6925)
PHONE.................................302 678-9978
James C Davis, *President*
Lisa Davis, *Vice Pres*
EMP: 10
SQ FT: 3,000
SALES (est): 950K **Privately Held**
SIC: 7699 7538 Engine repair & replacement, non-automotive; general automotive repair shops

(G-1776)
LEE M DENNIS MD
960 Forest St (19904-3470)
PHONE.................................302 735-1888
Lee M Dennis, *Owner*
Janette L Dennis, *Office Mgr*
Bob C Hoffner, *Administration*
Pat A Hoffner,
Trish Worthy, *Assistant*
▲ EMP: 5
SALES (est): 413.9K **Privately Held**
SIC: 8011 General & family practice, physician/surgeon

(G-1777)
LEE NAILS
63 Greentree Dr (19904-2685)
PHONE.................................302 674-5001
Phana Vuong, *Owner*
EMP: 5
SALES (est): 87.5K **Privately Held**
SIC: 7231 Manicurist, pedicurist

(G-1778)
LEE TOWNSEND ELECTRICAL CONTR
2577 Upper King Rd (19904-6438)
PHONE.................................302 697-3432
Lee Townsend, *President*
Sharon Townsend, *Admin Sec*
EMP: 4
SALES (est): 364K **Privately Held**
SIC: 1731 General electrical contractor

(G-1779)
LEGALNATURE LLC (PA)
8 The Grn Ste 1 (19901-3618)
PHONE.................................888 881-1139
Corey Bray, *CEO*
Bernard Bray, *Principal*
Michael Curtis, *CTO*
EMP: 4
SALES (est): 1.5MM **Privately Held**
SIC: 8111 Legal services

(G-1780)
LEHVOSS NORTH AMER HOLDG INC (HQ)
615 S Dupont Hwy (19901-4517)
PHONE.................................302 734-1450
EMP: 4 EST: 2012
SALES (est): 2.1MM
SALES (corp-wide): 366MM **Privately Held**
SIC: 2899 Mfg Chemical Preparations
PA: Lehmann & Voss & Co. Kg
   Alsterufer 19
   Hamburg 20354
   404 419-70

(G-1781)
LEO RITTER & CO
Also Called: Woodcrest Apartments
892 Woodcrest Dr (19904-2444)
PHONE.................................302 674-1375
Marge Cirillo, *Manager*
EMP: 4
SALES (corp-wide): 1MM **Privately Held**
SIC: 6513 Apartment building operators
PA: Leo Ritter & Co
   1776 Broadway Fl 17
   New York NY 10019
   212 757-4646

(G-1782)
LIBERTO DEVELOPMENT LTD
Also Called: Chruch Creek
1500 E Lebanon Rd (19901-5834)
PHONE.................................302 698-1104
Anthony J Liberto, *President*
EMP: 7
SALES (est): 700K **Privately Held**
SIC: 1521 Prefabricated single-family house erection

(G-1783)
LIDS CORPORATION
Also Called: Hat World
1365 N Dupont Hwy # 4018 (19901-8723)
PHONE.................................302 736-8465
Daniel Andrews, *Manager*
EMP: 4
SALES (corp-wide): 2.1B **Publicly Held**
WEB: www.hatworld.com
SIC: 5699 2395 Caps & gowns (academic vestments); embroidery products, except schiffli machine
HQ: Lids Corporation
   7555 Woodland Dr
   Indianapolis IN 46278

(G-1784)
LIFESOURCE CONSULTING SVCS LLC
8 The Grn Ste 8155 (19901-3618)
PHONE.................................302 257-6247
Blake Silliman,
EMP: 15
SALES: 500K **Privately Held**
SIC: 8742 Management consulting services

(G-1785)
LIFESQUARED INC
1679 S Dupont Hwy (19901-5101)
PHONE.................................415 475-9090
Zhou Yu, *CEO*
Tingting Hu, *Principal*
EMP: 2 EST: 2013
SALES (est): 110K **Privately Held**
SIC: 7379 7372 7389 ; application computer software;

(G-1786)
LIFETOUCH PORTRAIT STUDIOS INC
5000 Dover Mall (19901-8726)
PHONE.................................302 734-9870
Betsy Harrington, *Manager*
EMP: 10
SALES (corp-wide): 1.9B **Privately Held**
WEB: www.jcpportraits.com
SIC: 7221 Photographic studios, portrait
HQ: Lifetouch Portrait Studios Inc.
   11000 Viking Dr
   Eden Prairie MN 55344
   952 826-4335

Dover - Kent County (G-1787) — GEOGRAPHIC SECTION

(G-1787)
LIGHT MY FIRE INC
48 Old Rudnick Ln (19901)
PHONE 239 777-0878
Calill Odbist Jagush, *CEO*
Michael Holtz, *General Mgr*
EMP: 4
SALES (est): 106.1K
SALES (corp-wide): 4MM **Privately Held**
SIC: 5091 Camping equipment & supplies
PA: Light My Fire Sweden Ab
Vastkustvagen 7
Malmo 211 2
406 601-660

(G-1788)
LIGUORI MORRIS & REDDIN
46 The Grn (19901-3612)
PHONE 302 678-9900
Jim Liguori, *Partner*
Gregg Morris, *Partner*
Lori Reddin, *Partner*
EMP: 8
SALES (est): 1MM **Privately Held**
SIC: 8111 General practice attorney, lawyer

(G-1789)
LILLYS PERSONAL TRAINING
106 Mast Cir (19901-6845)
PHONE 302 538-6723
EMP: 4
SALES (est): 54.2K **Privately Held**
SIC: 7991 Physical fitness facilities

(G-1790)
LINDA & RICHARD PARTNERSHIP
107 Lake Front Dr (19904-6421)
PHONE 302 697-9758
EMP: 2
SALES (est): 66.3K **Privately Held**
SIC: 7699 3942 Repair Services Mfg Dolls/Stuffed Toys

(G-1791)
LINE-X DELAWARE INC
1053 Barl Ct (19901-4629)
PHONE 302 672-7005
Donald Tallman, *President*
EMP: 10
SALES (est): 491K **Privately Held**
SIC: 1799 Corrosion control installation

(G-1792)
LITTLE SCHOOL INC
Also Called: Afternoon Little
105 Mont Blanc Blvd (19904-7615)
PHONE 302 734-3040
Shannon K Mercer, *Manager*
M Jane Richter, *Director*
EMP: 13
SALES (est): 462.1K **Privately Held**
SIC: 8351 Preschool center

(G-1793)
LKQ NORTHEAST INC
1575 Mckee Rd Ste 5 (19904-1382)
PHONE 800 223-0171
EMP: 4
SALES: 317.9K
SALES (corp-wide): 11.8B **Publicly Held**
SIC: 5093 5015 3714 Automotive wrecking for scrap; motor vehicle parts, used; motor vehicle parts & accessories
PA: Lkq Corporation
500 W Madison St Ste 2800
Chicago IL 60661
312 621-1950

(G-1794)
LOCAL VERTICAL
69 Oakcrest Dr (19901-5730)
PHONE 302 242-2552
EMP: 2 EST: 2014
SALES (est): 126.8K **Privately Held**
SIC: 2591 Blinds vertical

(G-1795)
LONE STAR GLOBAL SERVICES INC
9 E Loockerman St Ste 3a (19901-7316)
PHONE 302 744-9800
Markus Vogt, *President*
EMP: 2 EST: 2012

SALES (est): 86.3K **Privately Held**
SIC: 1389 Oil & gas field services

(G-1796)
LOOKINN INC
8 The Grn Ste 5154 (19901-3618)
PHONE 302 839-2088
Temel Sari, *CEO*
EMP: 8
SALES (est): 151.6K **Privately Held**
SIC: 7389 7372 Hotel & motel reservation service; application computer software

(G-1797)
LOVE N LEARN NURSERY TOO
1598 Forrest Ave (19904-3329)
PHONE 302 678-0445
Yvonne Biddle, *Manager*
EMP: 9
SALES (est): 310K **Privately Held**
SIC: 8351 Child day care services

(G-1798)
LOWES HOME CENTERS LLC
1450 N Dupont Hwy (19901-2213)
PHONE 302 735-7500
Craig Hurd, *Principal*
Rodney Simons, *Store Mgr*
EMP: 150
SQ FT: 2,014
SALES (corp-wide): 71.3B **Publicly Held**
SIC: 5211 5031 5722 5064 Lumber & other building materials; building materials, exterior; building materials, interior; household appliance stores; electrical appliances, television & radio
HQ: Lowe's Home Centers, Llc
1605 Curtis Bridge Rd
Wilkesboro NC 28697
336 658-4000

(G-1799)
LURIWARE CONSULTING AGRICULTUR
155 S Bradford St 200a (19904-7367)
PHONE 302 244-1947
Tendai J Mutenje,
EMP: 5 EST: 2017
SALES (est): 144.5K **Privately Held**
SIC: 8711 Consulting engineer

(G-1800)
LUTHER MARTIN FOUNDATION DOVER
430 Kings Hwy Ofc 727 (19901-7521)
PHONE 302 674-1408
Arthur Kringel, *President*
EMP: 5
SALES: 63.1K **Privately Held**
SIC: 6531 Rental agent, real estate

(G-1801)
LUTHER TOWERS III DOVER INC
430 Kings Hwy (19901-7512)
PHONE 302 674-1408
Gary Coy, *Exec Dir*
EMP: 27
SALES: 310.9K **Privately Held**
SIC: 6513 Retirement hotel operation

(G-1802)
LUTHER TOWERS IV DOVER INC
430 Kings Hwy Ofc 1021 (19901-7512)
PHONE 302 674-1408
Gary Coy, *Exec Dir*
EMP: 10
SALES: 281.3K **Privately Held**
SIC: 6513 Apartment building operators

(G-1803)
LUTHER TOWERS OF DOVER INC
430 Kings Hwy Ofc 727 (19901-7521)
PHONE 302 674-1408
Gary Coy, *Exec Dir*
EMP: 27
SALES: 417.8K **Privately Held**
SIC: 6513 Retirement hotel operation

(G-1804)
LUTHER VILLAGE I DOVER INC
430 Kings Hwy Ofc 727 (19901-7521)
PHONE 302 674-1408
Sharon Poisson, *Info Tech Mgr*
Gary Coy, *Exec Dir*
EMP: 10
SALES: 412.7K **Privately Held**
SIC: 6513 Apartment building operators

(G-1805)
LUTHER VILLAGE II DOVER INC
430 Kings Hwy (19901-7512)
PHONE 302 674-1408
Gary Coy, *Exec Dir*
EMP: 10
SALES: 432.6K **Privately Held**
SIC: 6513 Retirement hotel operation

(G-1806)
LUTHER VILLAGE OF DOVER
101 Babb Dr Unit 1000 (19901-8865)
PHONE 302 674-3780
EMP: 4
SALES (est): 175.9K **Privately Held**
SIC: 6513 Retirement hotel operation

(G-1807)
LUTHERAN SENIOR SVCS OF DOVER
Also Called: LUTHER TOWERS OF DOVER
430 Kings Hwy Ofc 727 (19901-7521)
PHONE 302 674-1408
Arthur Kringel, *President*
Elizabeth Barrett, *Vice Pres*
Robert E Bunnell, *Director*
Gary Coy, *Director*
EMP: 15
SQ FT: 135,000
SALES: 1.8MM **Privately Held**
SIC: 6531 Housing authority operator

(G-1808)
LYNN HOLIDAY SHYNEA
540 S Governors Ave 101b (19904-3530)
PHONE 302 674-4700
Shynea Holiday, *Principal*
EMP: 8
SALES (est): 65.7K **Privately Held**
SIC: 8049 Offices of health practitioner

(G-1809)
LYNX GOLF LTD
160 Greentree Dr Ste 101 (19904-7620)
PHONE 778 755-4107
EMP: 4
SALES (est): 54.7K **Privately Held**
SIC: 7992 Public golf courses

(G-1810)
M K CUSTOMER ELEVATOR PADS
1644 Sorghum Mill Rd (19901-6813)
PHONE 302 698-3110
Minet Bhagwandin, *Owner*
EMP: 2
SALES (est): 169.8K **Privately Held**
SIC: 3534 Elevators & moving stairways

(G-1811)
MAINSTAY SUITES
201 Stover Blvd (19901-4675)
PHONE 302 678-8383
Francine Dobson, *Executive*
EMP: 12 EST: 2008
SALES (est): 501K **Privately Held**
SIC: 7011 Hotels & motels

(G-1812)
MAKAVE INTERNATIONAL TRDG LLC
8 The Grn Ste A (19901-3618)
PHONE 302 288-0670
AMR Bassiouny,
EMP: 26
SALES: 30K **Privately Held**
SIC: 7371 Computer software development & applications

(G-1813)
MANPOWERGROUP INC
1012 College Rd (19904-6506)
PHONE 302 674-8600
Dawn Ford, *Branch Mgr*
EMP: 4 **Publicly Held**

WEB: www.manpower.com
SIC: 7363 Manpower pools
PA: Manpowergroup Inc.
100 W Manpower Pl
Milwaukee WI 53212

(G-1814)
MANUFACTURERS & TRADERS TR CO
Also Called: M&T
139 S State St (19901-7313)
PHONE 302 735-2010
Paul Frick, *Vice Pres*
Gail Fink, *Manager*
EMP: 18
SALES (corp-wide): 6.4B **Publicly Held**
WEB: www.binghamlegg.com
SIC: 6022 State trust companies accepting deposits, commercial
HQ: Manufacturers And Traders Trust Company
1 M&T Plz Fl 3
Buffalo NY 14203
716 842-4200

(G-1815)
MANUFACTURERS & TRADERS TR CO
Also Called: M&T
1001 Walker Rd (19904-6572)
PHONE 302 735-2075
Helen Armstrong, *Branch Mgr*
EMP: 11
SALES (corp-wide): 6.4B **Publicly Held**
WEB: www.binghamlegg.com
SIC: 6022 State commercial banks
HQ: Manufacturers And Traders Trust Company
1 M&T Plz Fl 3
Buffalo NY 14203
716 842-4200

(G-1816)
MANUFACTURERS & TRADERS TR CO
Also Called: M&T
1001 E Lebanon Rd (19901-5855)
PHONE 302 735-2020
John Breda, *Vice Pres*
Ellen Pride, *Manager*
EMP: 10
SALES (corp-wide): 6.4B **Publicly Held**
WEB: www.binghamlegg.com
SIC: 6022 State commercial banks
HQ: Manufacturers And Traders Trust Company
1 M&T Plz Fl 3
Buffalo NY 14203
716 842-4200

(G-1817)
MANVEEN DUGGAL MD
Also Called: TP Indira and Mdpa
874 Walker Rd Ste B (19904-2778)
PHONE 302 734-5438
Senbhab Kumar MD, *President*
EMP: 6
SALES (est): 285.4K **Privately Held**
SIC: 8011 Endocrinologist

(G-1818)
MARK D GARRETT
Also Called: Magic Office Supply
4 Michael Ct (19904-2263)
PHONE 302 674-2825
Mark D Garrett, *Owner*
Ann Garrett, *Manager*
EMP: 4
SALES (est): 234.8K **Privately Held**
SIC: 5999 7629 Business machines & equipment; business machine repair, electric

(G-1819)
MARK ONE LLC
Also Called: Best Western
1700 E Lebanon Rd (19901-5845)
PHONE 302 735-4700
Manu Patel,
EMP: 14
SQ FT: 18,000
SALES (est): 869.5K **Privately Held**
SIC: 7011 Hotels & motels

GEOGRAPHIC SECTION — Dover - Kent County (G-1852)

(G-1820)
MARTEL & SON FOREIGN CAR CTR
1161 Horsepond Rd (19901-7218)
PHONE..................302 674-5556
Karl Martel, *President*
EMP: 5
SALES (est): 425.6K **Privately Held**
SIC: 7538 7549 General automotive repair shops; towing service, automotive

(G-1821)
MARTEL INC
4608 S Dupont Hwy Ste 1 (19901-6408)
PHONE..................302 744-9566
Mark Carlson, *President*
EMP: 11
SQ FT: 1,000
SALES (est): 1MM **Privately Held**
WEB: www.martelinc.com
SIC: 7629 1731 Telephone set repair; communications specialization

(G-1822)
MARTHANN PRINT CENTER LLC
1130 Charles Dr (19904-4328)
PHONE..................267 884-8130
Yaya G Bruce, *Principal*
EMP: 2
SALES (est): 88.4K **Privately Held**
SIC: 2752 Commercial printing, lithographic

(G-1823)
MARTIN J BURKE INC
Also Called: Burke Roofing
22 N Sandpiper Dr (19901-7106)
PHONE..................302 741-2638
Martin Burke, *President*
EMP: 4
SALES (est): 263.8K **Privately Held**
SIC: 1761 Roofing contractor

(G-1824)
MASTERCRAFT WELDING
4010 S Dupont Hwy (19901-6007)
P.O. Box 101, Woodside (19980-0101)
PHONE..................302 697-3932
Chuck Moller, *Owner*
EMP: 5
SQ FT: 5,000
SALES: 420K **Privately Held**
SIC: 3444 1761 7692 Sheet metalwork; sheet metalwork; welding repair

(G-1825)
MASTERCRAFTERS INC
1234 S Governors Ave A (19904-4895)
PHONE..................302 678-1470
Brian Larson, *President*
Marilyn Larson, *Admin Sec*
EMP: 25
SQ FT: 5,000
SALES: 3MM **Privately Held**
SIC: 1751 1799 Carpentry work; counter top installation

(G-1826)
MASTERCUTS
Dupont Hwy Dover Mall 8 (19901)
PHONE..................302 674-0300
Molly Dobos, *Manager*
EMP: 9
SALES (corp-wide): 1B **Publicly Held**
WEB: www.mastercuts.com
SIC: 7231 Unisex hair salons
HQ: Mastercuts
7850 Mentor Ave Ste 376
Mentor OH

(G-1827)
MATTERN & PICCIONI MD PA
260 Beiser Blvd Ste 1 (19904-5773)
PHONE..................302 730-8060
Michael L Mattern, *President*
Michael Mattern, *Med Doctor*
Lawrence Piccioni, *Med Doctor*
EMP: 12
SALES (est): 915.4K **Privately Held**
SIC: 8021 Orthodontist

(G-1828)
MATTHEW SMITH BUS SERVICE
206 N Queen St (19904-3152)
PHONE..................302 734-9311
Matthew Smith, *President*
EMP: 5
SALES (est): 805.1K **Privately Held**
SIC: 4131 4142 Intercity & rural bus transportation; bus charter service, except local

(G-1829)
MATTHEWS PIERCE & LLOYD INC (PA)
830 Walker Rd Ste 12 (19904-2748)
PHONE..................302 678-5500
Alan Nadler, *President*
Charles Hill, *Technology*
Basil Marcial, *Technology*
EMP: 20
SQ FT: 3,200
SALES (est): 3.4MM **Privately Held**
WEB: www.mpli.net
SIC: 7322 Collection agency, except real estate

(G-1830)
MAUDE BURTON
Also Called: Dust Your Stuff Cleaning Svc
657 Vista Ave (19901-4307)
PHONE..................302 674-4210
Maudie Burton,
EMP: 4
SQ FT: 1,980
SALES (est): 123.7K **Privately Held**
WEB: www.dustsquad.com
SIC: 7349 Building cleaning service

(G-1831)
MC GINNIS COMMERCIAL RE
Also Called: McGinnis Commercial RE Co
555 E Loockerman St # 102 (19901-3793)
P.O. Box 556 (19903-0556)
PHONE..................302 736-2700
James Mc Ginnis, *President*
Phillip Mc Ginnis, *Partner*
EMP: 5
SQ FT: 28,000
SALES (est): 572.5K **Privately Held**
SIC: 4225 Miniwarehouse, warehousing

(G-1832)
MCDONALDS
1424 Forrest Ave (19904-3315)
PHONE..................302 674-2095
Ilana Sanders, *President*
EMP: 5
SALES (est): 233.5K
SALES (corp-wide): 1.5MM **Privately Held**
SIC: 5812 8741 Fast-food restaurant, chain; restaurant management
PA: Sanders Management Corp
755 Walker Rd Ste A
Dover DE

(G-1833)
MD FREIGHT & LOGISTICS LLC
8 The Grn Ste A (19901-3618)
PHONE..................804 347-1196
Morrell M Davidson,
Morrell Davidson,
EMP: 5
SQ FT: 2,300
SALES (est): 327.5K **Privately Held**
SIC: 4731 Freight transportation arrangement

(G-1834)
MDNEWSLINE INC
28 Old Rudnick Ln (19901-4912)
PHONE..................773 759-4363
Jeffrey O Osuji, *Principal*
EMP: 6
SALES (est): 120.8K **Privately Held**
SIC: 7389 Courier or messenger service

(G-1835)
MEDEVICE SERVICES LLC
3500 S Dupont Hwy (19901-6041)
PHONE..................877 202-1588
Jing LI,
EMP: 8
SALES: 100K **Privately Held**
SIC: 8748 Business consulting

(G-1836)
MEDICAL TECHNOLOGIES INTL
8 The Grn Ste 1 (19901-3618)
PHONE..................760 837-4778
Gary Thompson, *President*
EMP: 50
SALES (est): 5.7MM **Privately Held**
SIC: 5047 Medical equipment & supplies

(G-1837)
MELISSA A MACKEL DO
655 S Bay Rd Ste 1f (19901-4694)
PHONE..................302 674-4070
Melissa Mackel, *Principal*
EMP: 6
SALES (est): 80.5K **Privately Held**
SIC: 8011 Offices & clinics of medical doctors

(G-1838)
MERGE INDUSTRIAL SOLUTIONS LLC
3500 S Dupont Hwy (19901-6041)
PHONE..................302 400-2157
Candela Iribarren,
EMP: 20 EST: 2017
SALES (est): 394.3K **Privately Held**
SIC: 8711 Engineering services

(G-1839)
MERIDIAN LIMO LLC
8 The Grn (19901-3618)
PHONE..................800 462-1550
Cesar Tedesco,
EMP: 6 EST: 2010
SALES: 500K **Privately Held**
SIC: 4789 Transportation services

(G-1840)
MERRILL LYNCH PIERCE FENNER
55 Kings Hwy (19901-3816)
P.O. Box 1367 (19903-1367)
PHONE..................302 736-7700
Lisa Primeck, *Manager*
Patricia H Thatcher, *Assistant*
Kristopher Todd, *Advisor*
EMP: 30
SALES (corp-wide): 110.5B **Publicly Held**
WEB: www.merlyn.com
SIC: 6211 Stock brokers & dealers
HQ: Merrill Lynch, Pierce, Fenner & Smith Incorporated
111 8th Ave
New York NY 10011
800 637-7455

(G-1841)
MERRY MAIDS INC
753 Walker Rd Ste A (19904-2724)
PHONE..................302 698-9038
Robert Ware, *President*
Christen Maroulis, *Director*
EMP: 15
SQ FT: 1,500
SALES (est): 349K **Privately Held**
WEB: www.mmhisc.com
SIC: 7349 Maid services, contract or fee basis

(G-1842)
MESSINA CHARLES PLBG & ELC CO
3681 S Little Creek Rd (19901-4864)
PHONE..................302 674-5696
Charles Messina, *President*
Carolyn Messina, *Vice Pres*
EMP: 65
SALES (est): 8.1MM **Privately Held**
SIC: 1731 General electrical contractor

(G-1843)
METATRON INC (PA)
160 Greentree Dr Ste 101 (19904-7620)
PHONE..................619 550-4668
Diane Troyer, *President*
Denis Sluka, *COO*
Mike Sunyich, *CTO*
EMP: 5
SALES (est): 527.4K **Publicly Held**
SIC: 3699 Photographic control systems, electronic

(G-1844)
METROPOLITAN LIFE INSUR CO
Also Called: MetLife
160 Greentree Dr Ste 105 (19904-7620)
PHONE..................302 734-5803
Rick Walker, *Manager*
EMP: 10
SALES (corp-wide): 67.9B **Publicly Held**
SIC: 6411 Insurance agents & brokers
HQ: Metropolitan Life Insurance Company (Inc)
1095 Ave Of The Americas
New York NY 10036
908 253-1000

(G-1845)
MICHAEL L MATTERN MD PA
724 S New St (19904-3540)
PHONE..................302 734-3416
Michael L Mattern MD, *President*
EMP: 12
SQ FT: 4,646
SALES (est): 669.8K **Privately Held**
SIC: 8011 Orthopedic physician; general & family practice, physician/surgeon

(G-1846)
MICHAELANGELOS HAIR DESIGNS
696 N Dupont Hwy (19901-3937)
PHONE..................302 734-8343
Michael Williams, *President*
EMP: 7
SALES (est): 147.1K **Privately Held**
SIC: 7231 Hairdressers

(G-1847)
MID ATLANTIC FARM CREDIT ACA
1410 S State St (19901-4948)
PHONE..................302 734-7534
Robert Frazee, *CEO*
EMP: 100
SALES (est): 12.8MM **Privately Held**
SIC: 6159 6111 Production credit association, agricultural; Federal Land Banks

(G-1848)
MID ATLANTIC RENEWABLE ENERGY
29 N State St Ste 300 (19901-3873)
PHONE..................302 672-0741
EMP: 6
SALES (est): 163K **Privately Held**
SIC: 4911 Electric Services

(G-1849)
MID DELAWARE IMAGING INC
710 S Queen St (19904-3567)
PHONE..................302 734-9888
Mahendra Parikh, *President*
Bharati Parikh, *Treasurer*
EMP: 15
SQ FT: 7,000
SALES (est): 2.8MM **Privately Held**
SIC: 8011 Radiologist

(G-1850)
MID-ATLANTIC PACKAGING COMPANY
14 Starlifter Ave (19901-9200)
PHONE..................800 284-1332
Herbert Glanden, *President*
Kimberly Glanden, *Corp Secy*
Donald T Glanden, *Vice Pres*
Andrew Pierson, *Vice Pres*
Tracy Mascelli, *Accounting Mgr*
◆ EMP: 30
SQ FT: 32,000
SALES (est): 13.1MM **Privately Held**
SIC: 5199 Packaging materials

(G-1851)
MID-ATLNTIC DISMANTLEMENT CORP
913 Horsepond Rd (19901-7221)
P.O. Box 1192 (19903-1192)
PHONE..................302 678-9300
Mathew Mitten, *President*
Matthew Mitten, *President*
EMP: 10
SALES (est): 1.5MM **Privately Held**
SIC: 1795 Demolition, buildings & other structures

(G-1852)
MIDATLANTIC FARM CREDIT
Also Called: Dover
1410 S State St (19901-4948)
PHONE..................302 734-7534

Dover - Kent County (G-1853)

Lloyd Webb, *Branch Mgr*
EMP: 11
SALES (corp-wide): 179.7MM **Privately Held**
WEB: www.mfc.com
SIC: 6159 Agricultural credit institutions; machinery & equipment finance leasing
PA: Midatlantic Farm Credit
45 Aileron Ct
Westminster MD 21157
410 848-1033

(G-1853)
MIDDELAWARE FAMILY MEDICINE
1813 Windswept Cir (19901-5850)
PHONE 302 724-5125
EMP: 6 **EST:** 2016
SALES (est): 91.9K **Privately Held**
SIC: 8099 Health & allied services

(G-1854)
MIGHTYINVOICE LLC
Also Called: Invoicegenius
8 The Grn Ste B (19901-3618)
PHONE 302 415-3000
David Reynier, *Mng Member*
EMP: 5
SALES: 450K **Privately Held**
SIC: 7371 Computer software development & applications

(G-1855)
MIKE WALSH PHYSICAL THERAPY
810 New Burton Rd Ste 2 (19904-5488)
PHONE 302 724-5593
Michael Walsh, *Principal*
EMP: 4
SALES (est): 287.9K **Privately Held**
SIC: 8049 8011 Physical therapist; offices & clinics of medical doctors

(G-1856)
MILFORD HOUSING DEVELOPMENT
200 Harmony Ln (19904-6601)
PHONE 302 678-0300
EMP: 30
SALES (corp-wide): 9.8MM **Privately Held**
SIC: 6513 Apartment building operators
PA: Milford Housing Development Corp
977 E Masten Cir
Milford DE 19963
302 422-8255

(G-1857)
MILFORD RENTAL CENTER INC
1679 S Dupont Hwy (19901-5101)
PHONE 302 422-0315
Joseph Wiley, *President*
EMP: 6
SQ FT: 6,000
SALES (est): 418.3K **Privately Held**
SIC: 7359 Party supplies rental services; lawn & garden equipment rental

(G-1858)
MIMESIS SIGNS
1035 Fowler Ct (19901-4638)
PHONE 302 674-5566
EMP: 1
SALES (est): 46K **Privately Held**
SIC: 3993 Signs & advertising specialties

(G-1859)
MIMIX COMPANY
8 The Grn Ste 6236 (19901-3618)
PHONE 305 916-8602
David Bethune, *President*
Xavier Bethune, *Vice Pres*
EMP: 3
SALES (est): 71.1K **Privately Held**
SIC: 7372 Prepackaged software

(G-1860)
MIND AND BODY CONSORTIUM LLC
156 S State St (19901-7314)
PHONE 302 674-2380
Lisa A Gantt, *Principal*
EMP: 20 **EST:** 2010
SALES (est): 1.8MM **Privately Held**
SIC: 8322 General counseling services

(G-1861)
MITTEN & WINTERS CPA
119 W Loockerman St (19904-7325)
P.O. Box 492 (19903-0492)
PHONE 302 736-6100
William Winters, *Partner*
David Mitten, *Partner*
Kevin Mitten, *Accountant*
Sandra L Mitten, *Accountant*
Jodi Arthur, *CPA*
EMP: 10
SALES (est): 748.9K **Privately Held**
SIC: 8721 Accounting services, except auditing

(G-1862)
MITTEN CONSTRUCTION CO
1420 E Lebanon Rd (19901)
P.O. Box 904 (19903-0904)
PHONE 302 697-2124
William B Mitten III, *Principal*
Wendy Mitten, *Vice Pres*
Eben P Roberts, *Treasurer*
Jacqueline M Robert, *Admin Sec*
EMP: 25 **EST:** 1968
SQ FT: 2,000
SALES (est): 3.3MM **Privately Held**
SIC: 1611 1542 1541 Highway & street paving contractor; commercial & office building, new construction; industrial buildings, new construction

(G-1863)
MITUSHA INTERNATIONAL CORP
626 Roberta Ave (19901-4612)
PHONE 302 674-2977
Amit Kalyani, *President*
▲ **EMP:** 5
SALES (est): 704.6K **Privately Held**
SIC: 5084 5085 Industrial machine parts; pulp (wood) manufacturing machinery; petroleum industry machinery; industrial fittings; valves & fittings, fasteners & fastening equipment

(G-1864)
MM MOBILE LLC
874 Walker Rd Ste C (19904-2778)
PHONE 917 297-9534
Masa Pezdirc,
EMP: 1 **EST:** 2015
SALES (est): 39.6K **Privately Held**
SIC: 7372 Application computer software

(G-1865)
MMR ASSOCIATES INC
Also Called: Pennisula Glass
679 Horsepond Rd (19901-7238)
PHONE 302 883-2984
Michael D Rooney, *President*
EMP: 6
SALES (est): 524.4K **Privately Held**
SIC: 1793 Glass & glazing work

(G-1866)
MNR INDUSTRIES LLC
200 Banning St Ste 170 (19904-3491)
PHONE 443 485-6213
EMP: 1
SALES (est): 39.6K **Privately Held**
SIC: 3999 Manufacturing industries

(G-1867)
MOBILE ALERTS LLC
160 Greentree Dr Ste 101 (19904-7620)
PHONE 202 596-8709
EMP: 4 **EST:** 2013
SALES (est): 180K **Privately Held**
SIC: 7371 Mobile Application Development

(G-1868)
MODERN MASTERS INC
8 The Grn Ste A (19901-3618)
P.O. Box 331, Sagle ID (83860-0331)
PHONE 240 800-6622
John Lund, *President*
EMP: 4
SALES (est): 89.7K **Privately Held**
SIC: 7371 7389 Computer software development & applications;

(G-1869)
MODERN MATURITY CENTER INC
1121 Forrest Ave (19904-3308)
PHONE 302 734-1200
Carolyn Fredricks, *Exec Dir*
EMP: 120 **EST:** 1969
SQ FT: 73,000
SALES: 8.1MM **Privately Held**
SIC: 8322 Senior citizens' center or association

(G-1870)
MOMS HOUSE INC
864 S State St (19901-4148)
P.O. Box 1138 (19903-1138)
PHONE 302 678-8688
D Renee Bullock, *President*
Terri Brown, *Vice Pres*
Leslie Cote, *Vice Pres*
EMP: 7
SALES: 130K **Privately Held**
SIC: 8351 Group day care center

(G-1871)
MORALES SCREEN PRINTING
201 Cassidy Dr Ste C (19901-4899)
PHONE 302 465-8179
EMP: 2
SALES (est): 83.9K **Privately Held**
SIC: 2752 Commercial printing, lithographic

(G-1872)
MORNING REPORT RESEARCH INC
Also Called: Gaming Morning Report
32 W Loockerman St 101a (19904-7352)
P.O. Box 1676 (19903-1676)
PHONE 302 730-3793
Frank Fantini, *President*
Hannah Wilmarth, *Assistant*
EMP: 7
SQ FT: 400
SALES (est): 537.3K **Privately Held**
WEB: www.gaminginvestments.com
SIC: 2711 8742 Commercial printing & newspaper publishing combined; management consulting services

(G-1873)
MORRIS JAMES LLP
Also Called: Morris, James
850 New Burton Rd Ste 101 (19904-5786)
PHONE 302 678-8815
Glenn E Hitchens, *Manager*
EMP: 7
SALES (corp-wide): 21.2MM **Privately Held**
SIC: 8111 General practice attorney, lawyer; general practice law office
PA: Morris James Llp
500 Delaware Ave Ste 1500
Wilmington DE 19801
302 888-6863

(G-1874)
MOSCASE INC
3500 S Dupont Hwy (19901-6041)
PHONE 786 520-8062
Akos Balogh, *President*
Laszlo Viragos, *President*
Mary Hogan, *CFO*
EMP: 4
SALES: 100K **Privately Held**
SIC: 7371 8731 7389 Computer software development & applications; computer (hardware) development; business services

(G-1875)
MOTOPODS LLC
8 The Grn Ste 8095 (19901-3618)
PHONE 818 641-4299
Sozum Dogan,
EMP: 1
SALES (est): 49.1K **Privately Held**
SIC: 3861 Photographic equipment & supplies

(G-1876)
MOUNTAIN CONSULTING INC
103 S Bradford St (19904-7317)
P.O. Box 558 (19903-0558)
PHONE 302 744-9875
Kim Adams, *CEO*
Troy Adams, *Vice Pres*
EMP: 6
SALES (est): 1.2MM **Privately Held**
WEB: www.mountainconsultinginc.com
SIC: 8711 8742 Civil engineering; construction project management consultant

(G-1877)
MSSGME INC
3500 S Dupont Hwy (19901-6041)
PHONE 786 233-7592
Dmitriy Prosvirnov, *President*
EMP: 8
SALES (est): 182.5K **Privately Held**
SIC: 7371 Custom computer programming services

(G-1878)
MULTICULTURAL A DELAWARE
365 United Way (19901-3769)
PHONE 302 399-6118
Michael H Casson Jr, *President*
Enwan Casson, *Principal*
EMP: 10
SALES: 314.3K **Privately Held**
SIC: 8748 Testing service, educational or personnel

(G-1879)
MUNCIE INSURANCE SERVICES
Also Called: Nationwide
1889 S Dupont Hwy (19901-5128)
PHONE 302 678-2800
Marvin Muncie, *Branch Mgr*
EMP: 4
SALES (est): 202.6K **Privately Held**
SIC: 6411 Insurance agents
PA: Muncie Insurance Services
1011 Norman Eskridge Hwy
Seaford DE 19973

(G-1880)
N DAISY JAX INC
1585 Mckee Rd Ste 3 (19904-1380)
PHONE 302 387-3543
Tina Dennis, *CEO*
George Dennis, *President*
EMP: 20
SQ FT: 9,000
SALES: 3.5MM **Privately Held**
SIC: 2844 Shampoos, rinses, conditioners: hair; lotions, shaving

(G-1881)
NAIL IT DOWN GENERAL CONTRS
Also Called: Nail It Down General Contrs
1474 E Lebanon Rd (19901-5833)
PHONE 302 698-3073
Brian Dawson, *CEO*
Jess Manning, *President*
Kim Dawson, *Manager*
EMP: 7 **EST:** 2000
SALES: 60K **Privately Held**
SIC: 1522 Residential construction

(G-1882)
NAIL PROS
1365 N Dupont Hwy # 5008 (19901-8726)
PHONE 302 674-2988
Pat Tang, *Owner*
EMP: 5 **EST:** 1998
SALES (est): 104.3K **Privately Held**
SIC: 7231 Manicurist, pedicurist

(G-1883)
NAKUURUQ SOLUTIONS
206 Atlantic St (19902-5206)
PHONE 302 526-2223
EMP: 3
SALES (est): 185K **Privately Held**
SIC: 3728 Aircraft training equipment

(G-1884)
NATIONWIDE INSURANCE CO
1252 Forrest Ave (19904-3311)
PHONE 302 678-2223
Doug Bennetti, *Owner*
Angela Muncie, *Prdtn Mgr*
Glenn Deaton, *Manager*
EMP: 6
SALES (est): 781.3K **Privately Held**
SIC: 6411 Insurance agents, brokers & service

GEOGRAPHIC SECTION
Dover - Kent County (G-1918)

(G-1885)
NATURES GOURMET CANDLES
2189 S State St (19901-6301)
PHONE.................................302 697-2785
Frances Avery, *Principal*
EMP: 1
SALES (est): 39.6K Privately Held
SIC: 3999 Candles

(G-1886)
NAZAR DOVER LLC
Also Called: Holiday Inn
561 N Dupont Hwy (19901-3960)
PHONE.................................302 747-5050
Muhammad Zulfiqar, *CEO*
EMP: 25 EST: 2015
SALES (est): 535K Privately Held
SIC: 7011 Hotels & motels

(G-1887)
NAZHAT ENTERPRISES HOLDINGS
8 The Grn Ste 7361 (19901-3618)
PHONE.................................415 670-9262
Enayat Nazhat, *Principal*
EMP: 5 Privately Held
SIC: 6719 Holding companies

(G-1888)
NCALL RESEARCH INC (PA)
363 Saulsbury Rd (19904-2722)
PHONE.................................302 678-9400
Joe L Myer, *Exec Dir*
Will Grimes, *Director*
Randall Kunkle, *Bd of Directors*
Karen Speakman, *Deputy Dir*
Marie Dube, *Admin Asst*
EMP: 28
SQ FT: 6,000
SALES (est): 4.6MM Privately Held
SIC: 8748 Urban planning & consulting services

(G-1889)
NCS PEARSON INC
1012 College Rd (19904-6506)
PHONE.................................302 736-8006
EMP: 99
SALES (corp-wide): 5.4B Privately Held
SIC: 3577 Optical scanning devices
HQ: Ncs Pearson Inc
5601 Green Valley Dr # 220
Bloomington MN 55437
952 681-3000

(G-1890)
NEENA MUKKAMALA DDS
95 Wolf Creek Blvd Ste 3 (19901-4965)
PHONE.................................302 734-5305
Neena Mukkamala, *Principal*
EMP: 4
SALES (est): 67.6K Privately Held
SIC: 8021 Dentists' office

(G-1891)
NEENEE WEES DAYCARE
208 Mifflin Rd (19904-3321)
PHONE.................................302 730-3630
Patricia Williams, *Principal*
EMP: 5
SALES (est): 64.4K Privately Held
SIC: 8351 Group day care center

(G-1892)
NEON DOJO LLC
3500 S Dupont Hwy (19901-6041)
PHONE.................................650 275-2395
EMP: 1 EST: 2012
SALES (est): 67K Privately Held
SIC: 7372 Prepackaged Software Services

(G-1893)
NEON FUN LLC
3500 S Dupont Hwy (19901-6041)
PHONE.................................858 220-0946
Rhonda Woerner, *Manager*
EMP: 2 EST: 2012
SALES (est): 110K Privately Held
SIC: 7372 Home entertainment computer software

(G-1894)
NERD BOY LLC
800 N State St Ste 402 (19901-3925)
P.O. Box 383, Pine Brook NJ (07058-0383)
PHONE.................................302 857-0243
Deniz Turgut, *Mng Member*
Michael Aviles,
Andrew Hansen,
Oscar Lakra,
EMP: 5 EST: 2017
SALES: 100K Privately Held
SIC: 7372 Prepackaged software

(G-1895)
NETWORK SECURITY SERVICES INC
32 W Loockerman St # 108 (19904-7311)
PHONE.................................703 319-0411
EMP: 18
SALES: 700K Privately Held
SIC: 7379 Computer Related Services

(G-1896)
NEUTEC CORP
29 Emerson Dr (19901-5819)
PHONE.................................302 697-6752
Lachhman Gupta, *President*
Surender Gupta, *Vice Pres*
EMP: 5
SALES: 100K Privately Held
SIC: 7371 Computer software development & applications

(G-1897)
NEWPHOENIX SCREEN PRINTING
305 Lotus St (19901-4461)
PHONE.................................302 747-8991
Wayne L Newsome Sr, *Owner*
EMP: 2
SALES (est): 136.9K Privately Held
SIC: 2752 Commercial printing, lithographic

(G-1898)
NOBLE EAGLE SALES LLC
Also Called: Shooter's Choice
5105 N Dupont Hwy (19901-2345)
PHONE.................................302 736-5166
Beth Parsons, *Manager*
EMP: 18 EST: 2012
SALES (est): 1.1MM Privately Held
SIC: 5941 7999 Firearms; shooting range operation

(G-1899)
NOBLE FINANCE CORP
1708 E Lebanon Rd Ste 4 (19901-5813)
PHONE.................................302 995-2760
EMP: 4
SALES (corp-wide): 36.2MM Privately Held
SIC: 6141 Personal Credit Institution
PA: Noble Finance Corp.
25331 W Interstate 10 # 101
San Antonio TX 78257
210 698-0448

(G-1900)
NORMAN M LIPPMAN DDS
712 S Governors Ave (19904-4106)
PHONE.................................302 674-1140
Norman Lippman, *Owner*
Candice Sheppard, *Office Mgr*
Franklyn X Pancko, *Med Doctor*
Cindy Jones,
Jenny Oconnell, *Receptionist Se*
EMP: 8
SALES (est): 310K Privately Held
SIC: 8021 Dentists' office

(G-1901)
NORTH EASTERN WAFFLES LLC
4003 S Dupont Hwy # 1753 (19901-6005)
PHONE.................................302 697-2226
Lance Clark, *Officer*
EMP: 4
SALES (est): 77.2K Privately Held
SIC: 8059 Nursing & personal care

(G-1902)
NORTHEASTERN TITLE LOANS
105 N Dupont Hwy (19901-4263)
PHONE.................................302 672-7895
Jose Torres, *Manager*
EMP: 4
SALES (est): 525.4K Privately Held
SIC: 6141 Automobile loans, including insurance

(G-1903)
NOVA PANGAEA TECHNOLOGIES INC
160 Greentree Dr Ste 101 (19904-7620)
PHONE.................................612 743-6266
John Nicholas, *President*
EMP: 3
SALES (est): 159K Privately Held
SIC: 2869 Industrial organic chemicals

(G-1904)
NOVACARE REHABILITATION
128 Greentree Dr (19904-7648)
PHONE.................................302 674-4192
EMP: 6
SALES (est): 80.5K Privately Held
SIC: 8011 Offices & clinics of medical doctors

(G-1905)
NOVACARE REHABILITATION DOVER
230 Beiser Blvd Ste 103 (19904-7791)
PHONE.................................302 760-9966
EMP: 8
SALES (est): 73.3K Privately Held
SIC: 8093 Rehabilitation center, outpatient treatment

(G-1906)
NOVO FINANCIAL CORP
850 New Burton Rd Ste 201 (19904-5786)
PHONE.................................844 260-6800
Tyler McIntyre, *President*
EMP: 10 EST: 2016
SALES (est): 239.3K Privately Held
SIC: 7371 7389 Computer software development & applications; financial services

(G-1907)
NRAI SERVICES LLC
160 Greentree Dr Ste 101 (19904-7620)
PHONE.................................302 674-4089
Dominic Gatto, *Marketing Staff*
Tina Bonovich,
EMP: 12 EST: 2000
SQ FT: 3,000
SALES (est): 1MM Privately Held
WEB: www.nraiservices.com
SIC: 7389 Document storage service

(G-1908)
NU ATTITUDE STYLING SALON LTD
49 S Dupont Hwy (19901-7430)
PHONE.................................302 734-8638
Willie White, *Managing Prtnr*
Tanya Dullsworth, *Partner*
Valerie Laughlin, *Partner*
EMP: 9
SALES (est): 141.5K Privately Held
SIC: 7231 Unisex hair salons

(G-1909)
NU WORLD BUILDING SERVICE
148 Willis Rd Apt F (19901-4023)
P.O. Box 368 (19903-0368)
PHONE.................................302 678-2578
Leroy Sage, *Owner*
EMP: 11
SALES: 200K Privately Held
SIC: 7349 Building cleaning service

(G-1910)
NU-LOOK PAINTING CONTRACTORS
149 Beech Dr (19904-9439)
PHONE.................................302 734-9203
Jeff Dickey, *Owner*
EMP: 4
SALES: 105K Privately Held
SIC: 1721 Exterior residential painting contractor; interior residential painting contractor; exterior commercial painting contractor; interior commercial painting contractor

(G-1911)
NURSING BOARD
861 Silver Lake Blvd (19904-2467)
PHONE.................................302 744-4500
Iva Boardman, *Exec Dir*
EMP: 7
SALES (est): 153.6K Privately Held
SIC: 8051 Skilled nursing care facilities

(G-1912)
OB-GYN ASSOCIATES OF DOVER P A
200 Banning St Ste 320 (19904-3488)
PHONE.................................302 674-0223
Robert Scacheri MD, *President*
Robert H Radnick MD, *Vice Pres*
EMP: 29
SALES (est): 2.3MM Privately Held
SIC: 8011 Obstetrician; gynecologist

(G-1913)
OCONNOR ORTHODONTICS
1004 S State St (19901-6901)
PHONE.................................302 678-1441
Oconnor Orthodontics, *Principal*
EMP: 5
SALES (est): 298.2K Privately Held
SIC: 8021 Orthodontist

(G-1914)
OINK OINK LLC
8 The Grn Ste A (19901-3618)
PHONE.................................302 924-5034
Cesar Espitia,
Camilo Millon,
EMP: 8
SALES (est): 81.4K Privately Held
SIC: 7299 6099 6153 7389 Personal financial services; money order issuance; factoring services; financial services

(G-1915)
OLD REPUBLIC NAT TITLE INSUR
32 The Grn (19901-3612)
PHONE.................................302 734-3570
Kathy B-Endicott, *Manager*
EMP: 6
SALES (corp-wide): 6B Publicly Held
WEB: www.orbitinfo.net
SIC: 6361 Real estate title insurance
HQ: Old Republic National Title Insurance Company
400 2nd Ave S
Minneapolis MN 55401
612 371-1111

(G-1916)
OMEGA INDUSTRIES INC
7 Messina Hill Rd (19904-1831)
P.O. Box 407, Cheswold (19936-0407)
PHONE.................................302 734-3835
George Diakos, *President*
Peter Diakos, *Admin Sec*
EMP: 9
SALES (est): 1.7MM Privately Held
SIC: 3585 Air conditioning equipment, complete; refrigeration equipment, complete

(G-1917)
OMEGA PSI PHI FRATERNITY
1300 S Farmview Dr (19904-3374)
P.O. Box 392 (19903-0392)
PHONE.................................908 463-2197
EMP: 4
SALES (est): 59.5K Privately Held
SIC: 8641 Civic social & fraternal associations

(G-1918)
ONEMAIN FINANCIAL GROUP LLC
1057 N Dupont Hwy (19901-2006)
PHONE.................................302 674-3900
EMP: 4
SALES (corp-wide): 4.2B Publicly Held
SIC: 6282 Investment advice
HQ: Onemain Financial Group, Llc
100 International Dr # 150
Baltimore MD 21202
855 663-6246

Dover - Kent County (G-1919)

(G-1919)
OPENEXO INC
3500 S Dupont Hwy (19901-6041)
PHONE...................617 965-5057
Salim Ismail, *President*
Lawrence Pensack, *CFO*
EMP: 10
SALES: 1MM **Privately Held**
SIC: 8742 Management consulting services

(G-1920)
ORTH & KOWALICK PA
1991 S State St (19901-5811)
PHONE...................302 697-2159
P William Orth, *President*
Raymond J Kowalick, *Principal*
EMP: 5
SALES (est): 295.4K **Privately Held**
SIC: 8721 Certified public accountant

(G-1921)
ORTHODONTICS ON SILVER LAKE
42 Hiawatha Ln (19904-2401)
PHONE...................302 672-7776
EMP: 4 EST: 2010
SALES (est): 180K **Privately Held**
SIC: 8021 Dentist's Office

(G-1922)
ORTHODONTICS ON SILVER LAKE PA
Also Called: Stephanie E Steckel DDS, Ms
42 Hiawatha Ln (19904-2401)
PHONE...................302 672-7776
Stephanie E Steckl DDS, *Owner*
Steve Artz, *Manager*
EMP: 7
SALES (est): 481K **Privately Held**
SIC: 8021 Orthodontist

(G-1923)
ORTHOPEDIC SPINE CENTER P A
260 Beiser Blvd (19904-5773)
PHONE...................302 734-9700
Stephen L Malone, *Principal*
EMP: 5
SALES (est): 370.1K **Privately Held**
SIC: 8011 Orthopedic physician

(G-1924)
ORVILLE SAMMONS ARDENS
4272 Judith Rd (19904-5069)
PHONE...................302 492-8620
Orville Sammons, *Owner*
EMP: 5
SALES (est): 296.8K **Privately Held**
SIC: 3479 Painting, coating & hot dipping

(G-1925)
OTIS KAMARA
Also Called: Veteran Owned Cleaning Svcs
P.O. Box 960 (19903-0960)
PHONE...................443 207-2643
Otis Kamara, *Owner*
Spencer Biah, *Co-Owner*
EMP: 5
SALES (est): 56.8K **Privately Held**
SIC: 7349 Janitorial service, contract basis

(G-1926)
OTW TECHNOLOGIES INC
8 The Grn Ste A (19901-3618)
PHONE...................813 230-4212
Victor Obi, *Exec Dir*
EMP: 4
SALES (est): 89.7K **Privately Held**
SIC: 7371 Computer software development & applications

(G-1927)
OUTREACH TEAM LLC
8 The Grn Ste R (19901-3618)
PHONE...................302 744-9550
EMP: 4
SALES (est): 42.4K **Privately Held**
SIC: 8322 Outreach program

(G-1928)
P A CNMRI
1074 S State St (19901-6925)
PHONE...................302 678-8100
Robert Varipapa, *President*
John Coll, *Corp Secy*
Jeannie Virdin, *Research*
Audry Lenox, *Office Mgr*
Stephen F Penny, *Med Doctor*
EMP: 90
SQ FT: 4,000
SALES (est): 8MM **Privately Held**
SIC: 8011 7389 Neurologist;

(G-1929)
PAIN MGT & REHABILITATION CTR
240 Beiser Blvd Ste 201a (19904-8208)
PHONE...................302 734-7246
Ganesh Balu, *Owner*
EMP: 14
SALES (est): 458.7K **Privately Held**
WEB: www.painrehab.net
SIC: 8011 Specialized medical practitioners, except internal

(G-1930)
PAMELA M D LECLAIRE
300 Tuskegee Blvd (19902-5003)
PHONE...................302 677-2600
Pamela Leclaire, *Principal*
EMP: 6
SALES (est): 80.5K **Privately Held**
SIC: 8011 Offices & clinics of medical doctors

(G-1931)
PANDA SLEEP INC
8 The Grn Ste A (19901-3618)
PHONE...................302 760-9754
Qingwei Wang, *CEO*
EMP: 1
SALES: 5MM **Privately Held**
SIC: 2515 Sleep furniture

(G-1932)
PAPEN FARMS INC
847 Papen Ln (19904-5733)
PHONE...................302 697-3291
Jeffrey Papen, *President*
Janet Meyer, *Corp Secy*
Richard G Papen, *Vice Pres*
EMP: 16
SALES (est): 4.4MM **Privately Held**
WEB: www.papenfarms.com
SIC: 0161 Cabbage farm; corn farm, sweet; cucumber farm; snap bean farm (bush & pole)

(G-1933)
PAPERBASKET LLC
8 The Grn Ste A (19901-3618)
PHONE...................516 360-3500
Dulcina Belcher, *CEO*
Tammy Farrell, *Principal*
EMP: 2
SALES (est): 56.5K **Privately Held**
SIC: 7372 Educational computer software

(G-1934)
PAR 3 INC
924 Artis Dr (19904-5639)
PHONE...................302 674-8275
Rick Jones, *President*
EMP: 4
SALES (est): 235.2K **Privately Held**
SIC: 7992 Public golf courses

(G-1935)
PARCELS INC
Also Called: Delaware Document Retrieval
1111 B S Govenanvce Ave (19904)
PHONE...................302 736-1777
Shelly Miles, *Branch Mgr*
EMP: 7
SALES (corp-wide): 15MM **Privately Held**
SIC: 4215 Package delivery, vehicular
PA: Parcels, Inc.
    230 N Market St
    Wilmington DE 19801
    302 888-1718

(G-1936)
PARKOWSKI GUERKE & SWAYZE PA (PA)
Also Called: Dunkle, Mark F
116 W Water St (19904-6739)
P.O. Box 598 (19903-0598)
PHONE...................302 678-3262
F Michael Parkowski, *President*
EMP: 22
SALES (est): 2.5MM **Privately Held**
SIC: 8111 General practice law office

(G-1937)
PARTS PLUS MORE LLC
8 The Grn Ste 4469 (19901-3618)
PHONE...................302 300-4913
Esteban Anderson,
EMP: 30
SALES (est): 621.4K **Privately Held**
SIC: 5015 Automotive supplies, used

(G-1938)
PARTY GAS
5200 N Dupont Hwy (19901-2339)
P.O. Box 716 (19903-0716)
PHONE...................302 730-3880
Jane Jensen, *Principal*
EMP: 1
SALES (est): 55.7K **Privately Held**
SIC: 1321 Propane (natural) production

(G-1939)
PATHAO INC (PA)
8 The Grn Ste A (19901-3618)
PHONE...................845 242-3834
Fahim Saleh, *President*
EMP: 7
SALES: 250K **Privately Held**
SIC: 7371 Computer software development & applications

(G-1940)
PATRIOT AUTO & TRUCK CARE LLC
Also Called: General Automotive Repair
497 S Dupont Hwy (19901-4513)
PHONE...................302 257-5715
Kathy De Angleis,
EMP: 5
SALES: 500K **Privately Held**
SIC: 7538 General automotive repair shops

(G-1941)
PATTERSON & KELLY PA
18 S State St (19901-7312)
PHONE...................302 736-6657
John P Kelly, *Owner*
EMP: 4
SALES (est): 236.3K **Privately Held**
SIC: 8721 Certified public accountant

(G-1942)
PATTERSON-SCHWARTZ & ASSOC INC
Also Called: Patterson Schwartz Real Estate
140 Greentree Dr (19904-7648)
PHONE...................302 672-9400
Mark Levering, *Manager*
EMP: 40
SQ FT: 3,543
SALES (est): 1.3MM
SALES (corp-wide): 32.2MM **Privately Held**
WEB: www.pacinihomes.com
SIC: 6531 Real estate brokers & agents
PA: Patterson-Schwartz And Associates, Inc.
    7234 Lancaster Pike
    Hockessin DE 19707
    302 234-5250

(G-1943)
PEEPER VEHICLE TECHNOLOGY CORP
8 The Grn Ste A (19901-3618)
PHONE...................800 971-4134
Thomas A Jackson, *CEO*
EMP: 1
SALES (est): 29.2K **Privately Held**
SIC: 7371 7372 3829 7389 Computer software development & applications; application computer software; instrument board gauges, automotive: computerized;

(G-1944)
PENINSULA ALLERGY AND ASTHMA
200 Banning St Ste 280 (19904-3489)
PHONE...................302 734-4434
Shankar L Lakhani, *Principal*
EMP: 5 EST: 2008
SALES (est): 403.7K **Privately Held**
SIC: 8011 Allergist

(G-1945)
PENINSULA ENERGY SVCS CO INC (HQ)
909 Silver Lake Blvd (19904-2409)
P.O. Box 615 (19903-0615)
PHONE...................302 734-6799
Stephen C Thompson, *President*
William D Hancock, *Assistant VP*
Paul Barbas, *Vice Pres*
Beth W Cooper, *Treasurer*
Ralph J Askins, *Director*
EMP: 10
SALES (est): 518.7K
SALES (corp-wide): 717.4MM **Publicly Held**
WEB: www.chpk.com
SIC: 4932 Gas & other services combined
PA: Chesapeake Utilities Corporation
    909 Silver Lake Blvd
    Dover DE 19904
    302 734-6799

(G-1946)
PENNSYLVANIA BRAND CO
550 S New St (19904-3536)
PHONE...................302 674-5774
EMP: 4
SALES (est): 211.5K **Privately Held**
SIC: 2051 Bread, cake & related products

(G-1947)
PEOPLE OVER PROFIT LLC
8 The Grn Ste A (19901-3618)
PHONE...................718 612-0328
Ahmed Attoh,
EMP: 4
SALES (est): 89.7K **Privately Held**
SIC: 7371 Computer software development & applications

(G-1948)
PEOPLES PLACE II INC
165 Commerce Way (19904-2824)
PHONE...................302 730-1321
Linda Burris, *Manager*
EMP: 60
SALES (corp-wide): 7.1MM **Privately Held**
SIC: 8351 Child day care services
PA: People's Place Ii, Inc.
    1129 Airport Rd
    Milford DE 19963
    302 422-8033

(G-1949)
PERCEBE MUSIC INC
8 The Grn Ste A (19901-3618)
PHONE...................850 341-9594
Pitagoras Goncalves, *President*
Joel Becker, *Principal*
EMP: 1 EST: 2016
SALES (est): 37.5K **Privately Held**
SIC: 2741 7372 7389 Music book & sheet music publishing; educational computer software;

(G-1950)
PERCERI LLC
160 Greentree Dr Ste 101 (19904-7620)
PHONE...................217 721-8731
David Tarvin, *Manager*
Sean McCrimmon, *Manager*
Aaron Wiener, *Manager*
Andrew Gordon,
Jeremy Leval,
EMP: 2
SALES (est): 120K **Privately Held**
SIC: 7372 7389 Business oriented computer software;

(G-1951)
PETROLEUM EQUIPMENT INC (PA)
Also Called: Poores Propane Gas Service
3799 N Dupont Hwy (19901-1574)
P.O. Box 1000, Cheswold (19936-1000)
PHONE...................302 734-7433
Donald Steiner, *President*
Micheal Steiner, *Vice Pres*
▲ EMP: 40
SQ FT: 4,000

GEOGRAPHIC SECTION
Dover - Kent County (G-1981)

SALES (est): 42.3MM **Privately Held**
SIC: **5172** 5984 Petroleum products; liquefied petroleum gas dealers

(G-1952)
PETROLEUM EQUIPMENT INC
Also Called: Poore's Propane Gas Service
3799 N Dupont Hwy (19901-1574)
P.O. Box 658 (19903-0658)
PHONE..................302 422-4281
Michael Steiner, *Vice Pres*
EMP: 6 **Privately Held**
SIC: **5172** Petroleum products
PA: Petroleum Equipment, Inc.
3799 N Dupont Hwy
Dover DE 19901

(G-1953)
PFISTER INSURANCE INC
625 S Dupont Hwy Ste 101 (19901-4504)
P.O. Box 756 (19903-0756)
PHONE..................302 674-3100
Mel Warren, *President*
Scott Soltz, *Vice Pres*
James Watkins, *Vice Pres*
Kim Ritter, *Administration*
EMP: 8
SALES (est): 1MM
SALES (corp-wide): 165.5MM **Privately Held**
WEB: www.pfisterins.com
SIC: **6411** Insurance agents
PA: The Hilb Group Llc
8720 Stony Point Pkwy # 125
Richmond VA 23235
804 414-6501

(G-1954)
PHIL HILL
Also Called: State Farm Insurance
3728 N Dupont Hwy (19901-1555)
PHONE..................302 678-0499
Phil Hill, *Owner*
EMP: 5
SALES (est): 732.1K **Privately Held**
SIC: **6411** Insurance agents & brokers

(G-1955)
PHYSICAL THERAPY SERVICES INC (PA)
725 Walker Rd (19904-2724)
PHONE..................302 678-3100
Vincent Deleo, *President*
Gary T Nowell, *Owner*
Phillip N Barkins, *Vice Pres*
Jean T Deleo, *Treasurer*
Gary Nowle, *Admin Sec*
EMP: 26
SQ FT: 4,800
SALES: 1MM **Privately Held**
SIC: **8049** Physiotherapist

(G-1956)
PHYSICIANS BEAUTY GROUP LLC
9 E Loockerman St Ste 202 (19901-7347)
PHONE..................866 270-9290
Gregory Socherman, *President*
EMP: 30
SALES (est): 729.6K **Privately Held**
SIC: **5122** Cosmetics, perfumes & hair products

(G-1957)
PHYSIOTHERAPY ASSOCIATES INC
Also Called: Barker-Mtrix Thrapy Rhbltation
642 Suth Queen St Ste 101 (19904)
PHONE..................302 674-1269
David Wylderman, *Manager*
EMP: 10 **Privately Held**
WEB: www.myphysio.com
SIC: **8049** Physical therapist
HQ: Physiotherapy Associates, Inc.
680 American Ave Ste 200
King Of Prussia PA 19406
610 644-7824

(G-1958)
PIERCE DESIGN & TOOL
20 Bailey Cir (19901-6063)
PHONE..................302 222-3339
Franklin Frementer, *Mng Member*
EMP: 2

SALES (est): 170.3K **Privately Held**
SIC: **7389** 3679 3568 Design services; electronic components; power transmission equipment

(G-1959)
PIERCE FENCE COMPANY INC
5751 N Dupont Hwy (19901-2603)
PHONE..................302 674-1996
Robert Pierce, *President*
Karen Pierce, *Office Mgr*
EMP: 13
SQ FT: 5,000
SALES (est): 641.8K **Privately Held**
SIC: **1799** Fence construction

(G-1960)
PINEWOOD ACRES MBL HM PK LLC
Also Called: Pinewood Acres Mobile Home Pk
1 Pinewood Acres Ave (19901-1916)
PHONE..................302 678-1004
Todd Nelson,
Walter A Nelson,
EMP: 4
SQ FT: 800
SALES (est): 495.7K **Privately Held**
SIC: **6515** Mobile home site operators

(G-1961)
PIXSTORM LLC
160 Greentree Dr Ste 101 (19904-7620)
PHONE..................617 365-4949
Erik Bunce, *Chief Engr*
Quinn Lipin, *Manager*
EMP: 4
SALES (est): 47.2K **Privately Held**
SIC: **2741** 7389 ;

(G-1962)
PLAI APPS INC
850 New Burton Rd Ste 201 (19904-5786)
PHONE..................661 678-3740
Eldrin Cruz, *CEO*
EMP: 8 EST: 2016
SALES (est): 168.1K **Privately Held**
SIC: **7375** 7389 Information retrieval services;

(G-1963)
PLANNED PARENTHOOD OF DELAWARE
805 S Governors Ave (19904-4158)
PHONE..................302 678-5200
Karla McFarland, *Director*
EMP: 4
SALES (corp-wide): 4.9MM **Privately Held**
WEB: www.ppde.org
SIC: **8093** Family planning clinic
PA: Planned Parenthood Of Delaware Inc
625 N Shipley St
Wilmington DE 19801
302 655-7293

(G-1964)
PLAY GAME SPORTS
222 Kentwood Dr (19901-8737)
PHONE..................302 736-0606
EMP: 6
SALES (est): 159.2K **Privately Held**
SIC: **4832** Radio Broadcast Station

(G-1965)
PLAY US MEDIA LLC
Also Called: Wild Bets
8 The Gree Ste 8136 Dover (19901)
PHONE..................302 924-5034
Cesar Espitia, *Mng Member*
EMP: 8
SALES (est): 200.8K **Privately Held**
SIC: **7371** 7372 7373 7379 Computer software development & applications; application computer software; systems software development services;

(G-1966)
PLAYHOUSE NURSERY SCHOOL
1925 S Dupont Hwy (19901-5152)
PHONE..................302 747-7007
Colleen Endicott, *Director*
EMP: 9
SALES (est): 141.1K **Privately Held**
SIC: **8351** Nursery school

(G-1967)
PLAYPHONE INC
3500 S Dupont Hwy (19901-6041)
PHONE..................415 307-0246
Ron Czerny, *CEO*
EMP: 5 EST: 2006
SALES (est): 486.9K **Privately Held**
SIC: **7371** Computer software development & applications
PA: Gungho Online Entertainment,Inc.
1-11-1, Marunouchi
Chiyoda-Ku TKY 100-0

(G-1968)
PLAYTEX INVESTMENT CORPORATION
50 N Dupont Hwy (19901-4261)
PHONE..................302 678-6000
Chris Crowell, *Principal*
EMP: 6
SALES (est): 2.1MM
SALES (corp-wide): 2.1B **Publicly Held**
SIC: **6282** Investment advice
PA: Edgewell Personal Care Company
1350 Tmberlake Manor Pkwy
Chesterfield MO 63017
314 594-1900

(G-1969)
PLAYTEX MANUFACTURING INC (DH)
50 N Dupont Hwy (19901-4261)
PHONE..................302 678-6000
Michael R Gallagher, *CEO*
EMP: 90
SALES (est): 100.9MM
SALES (corp-wide): 2.1B **Publicly Held**
WEB: www.playtexproductsinc.com
SIC: **2676** 2844 2842 Sanitary paper products; toilet preparations; specialty cleaning, polishes & sanitation goods
HQ: Playtex Products, Llc
6 Research Dr Ste 400
Shelton CT 06484
203 944-5500

(G-1970)
PLAYTEX MARKETING CORP
800 Silver Lake Blvd # 103 (19904-2402)
P.O. Box 7016 (19903-1516)
PHONE..................302 678-6000
Michael Gallagher, *Chairman*
Donald J Franceschini, *Vice Pres*
Calvin J Gauss, *Vice Pres*
Hercules P Sotos, *Vice Pres*
Glenn A Forbes, *Treasurer*
EMP: 7 **Privately Held**
SIC: **6719** Personal holding companies, except banks

(G-1971)
PLAYTEX PRODUCTS LLC
50 N Dupont Hwy (19901-4261)
PHONE..................302 678-6000
Glenn Forbes, *Principal*
EMP: 15
SALES (corp-wide): 2.1B **Publicly Held**
WEB: www.playtexproductsinc.com
SIC: **2676** Sanitary paper products
HQ: Playtex Products, Llc
6 Research Dr Ste 400
Shelton CT 06484
203 944-5500

(G-1972)
PLUGDIN INC
8 The Grn Ste A (19901-3618)
PHONE..................347 726-1831
David J Montini, *CEO*
EMP: 5
SALES: 50K **Privately Held**
SIC: **7336** Creative services to advertisers, except writers

(G-1973)
PNC BANK NATIONAL ASSOCIATION
3 Loockerman Plz Frnt (19901-7335)
PHONE..................302 735-3117
June Allin, *Branch Mgr*
EMP: 25
SALES (corp-wide): 19.9B **Publicly Held**
SIC: **6021** National commercial banks

HQ: Pnc Bank, National Association
222 Delaware Ave
Wilmington DE 19801
877 762-2000

(G-1974)
PNC BANK NATIONAL ASSOCIATION
87 Greentree Dr (19904-7647)
PHONE..................302 735-2160
Aaron Bowers, *Manager*
EMP: 10
SALES (corp-wide): 19.9B **Publicly Held**
WEB: www.pncfunds.com
SIC: **6021** National trust companies with deposits, commercial
HQ: Pnc Bank, National Association
222 Delaware Ave
Wilmington DE 19801
877 762-2000

(G-1975)
POINTLESS TECHNOLOGY LLC
9 E Loockerman St Ste 215 (19901-7347)
PHONE..................917 403-2264
Jeremy Schoenherr,
EMP: 1
SALES (est): 40.7K **Privately Held**
SIC: **7372** Application computer software

(G-1976)
POOF POWER WASH & LDSCPG LLC
182 Hatteras Dr (19904-3883)
PHONE..................302 595-1576
Rodney Holloman, *CEO*
EMP: 4
SALES (est): 68.7K **Privately Held**
SIC: **0781** 7699 Landscape services; cleaning services

(G-1977)
PORTER BROADCASTING
1991 S State St (19901-5811)
PHONE..................302 535-8809
EMP: 5
SALES (est): 92.4K **Privately Held**
SIC: **4832** Radio broadcasting stations

(G-1978)
POWER PLUS ELECTRICAL CONTG
10 Janis Dr (19901-5752)
PHONE..................302 736-5070
William M Kriss, *President*
EMP: 11
SALES (est): 1.5MM **Privately Held**
SIC: **1731** General electrical contractor

(G-1979)
PRECIOUS MOMENTS EDU
4607 S Dupont Hwy (19901-6413)
PHONE..................302 697-9374
Angela C Wilson, *President*
EMP: 17
SQ FT: 3,171
SALES (est): 874.7K **Privately Held**
SIC: **8322** Community center

(G-1980)
PREGNANCY HEALTH CENTER
Also Called: PREGNANCY HELP CENTER OF KENT
811 S Governors Ave (19904-4158)
PHONE..................302 698-9311
Pat Dundas, *Director*
EMP: 4
SALES: 103.9K **Privately Held**
SIC: **8011** Obstetrician

(G-1981)
PREMIER CAPITAL HOLDING (PA)
1675 S State St (19901-5140)
PHONE..................302 730-1010
Hanh Nguyen, *Principal*
EMP: 6
SALES (est): 450.8K **Privately Held**
SIC: **6162** Mortgage bankers

Dover - Kent County (G-1982) — GEOGRAPHIC SECTION

(G-1982)
PREMIER ENTERTAINMENT III LLC (HQ)
Also Called: Dover Downs Gaming & Entrmt
1131 N Dupont Hwy (19901-2008)
PHONE...................302 674-4600
George Papanier, *President*
John E Taylor Jr, *Chairman*
Craig Eaton, *Exec VP*
Stephen Capp, *CFO*
EMP: 47
SALES: 179.9MM **Publicly Held**
WEB: www.doverdownsslots.com
SIC: 7929 7999 7011 7948 Entertainment service; card & game services; hotels; racing, including track operation; harness horse racing

(G-1983)
PREMIER SPINE & REHAB
111 S West St Ste 5 (19904-3219)
PHONE...................302 730-4878
Roberto Thelusma, *President*
EMP: 5
SALES (est): 97.6K **Privately Held**
SIC: 8093 Rehabilitation center, outpatient treatment

(G-1984)
PRESBYTERIAN SENIOR LIVING
Also Called: Westminster Village Health Ctr
1175 Mckee Rd (19904-2268)
PHONE...................302 744-3600
Janette Ring, *Human Res Dir*
Sue Post, *Sales Mgr*
Laura Garvine, *Office Mgr*
Rob Kratz, *Systems Dir*
Joan Beebe, *Director*
EMP: 145 **Privately Held**
WEB: www.phi.org
SIC: 8059 8069 8051 Nursing home, except skilled & intermediate care facility; specialty hospitals, except psychiatric; skilled nursing care facilities
HQ: Presbyterian Homes, Inc.
1 Trinity Dr E Ste 201
Dillsburg PA 17019
717 502-8840

(G-1985)
PRESSLEY RIDGE FOUNDATION
Also Called: Pressley Ridge of Delaware
942 Walker Rd Ste A (19904-2757)
PHONE...................302 677-1590
Cha-Tanya Lankford, *Director*
EMP: 6 **Privately Held**
SIC: 8322 Child related social services
PA: Pressley Ridge Foundation
5500 Corporate Dr Ste 400
Pittsburgh PA 15237

(G-1986)
PRIMARY CARE DELAWARE L L C
200 Banning St Ste 210 (19904-3487)
PHONE...................302 744-9645
Vineet Puri, *Med Doctor*
Vinet Puri,
EMP: 6
SALES (est): 325.2K **Privately Held**
SIC: 8049 Offices of health practitioner

(G-1987)
PRINTIT SOLUTIONS
1155 E Lebanon Rd (19901-5830)
PHONE...................302 380-3838
EMP: 2 EST: 2017
SALES (est): 88.5K **Privately Held**
SIC: 2752 Commercial printing, lithographic

(G-1988)
PRIVATE FAMILY NETWORK LLC
8 The Grn Ste A (19901-3618)
PHONE...................302 760-9684
Patrick Mc Cann, *Managing Dir*
Brian Donohoe, *Finance*
EMP: 10
SALES: 1MM **Privately Held**
SIC: 7379 7389 ;

(G-1989)
PROCTER & GAMBLE PAPER PDTS CO
1340 W North St (19904-7796)
P.O. Box 7010 (19903-1510)
PHONE...................302 678-2600
Ken Marsh, *Engineer*
Francisco Pribyl, *Department Mgr*
Laytrice Henson, *Manager*
EMP: 275
SALES (corp-wide): 67.6B **Publicly Held**
SIC: 2676 Towels, paper: made from purchased paper
HQ: The Procter & Gamble Paper Products Company
1 Procter And Gamble Plz
Cincinnati OH 45202
513 983-1100

(G-1990)
PROGRESSIVE CASUALTY INSUR CO
Also Called: Progressive Insurance
1241 N Dupont Hwy (19901-8703)
PHONE...................302 734-7360
Mark Bushy, *Branch Mgr*
EMP: 7
SALES (corp-wide): 31.9B **Publicly Held**
WEB: www.progressinsurance.com
SIC: 6331 6411 Fire, marine & casualty insurance; insurance agents & brokers
HQ: Progressive Casualty Insurance Company
6300 Wilson Mills Rd
Mayfield Village OH 44143
440 461-5000

(G-1991)
PROSIFT LLC
1239 N Farmview Dr (19904-3367)
PHONE...................302 678-2386
Uma Pinaghapani, *Mng Member*
Vali Umapathy,
EMP: 4
SALES: 280K **Privately Held**
WEB: www.prosift.com
SIC: 7372 Business oriented computer software

(G-1992)
PROVIDENT FEDERAL CREDIT UNION
401 S New St (19904-6715)
PHONE...................302 734-1133
Ellen Garnett, *Loan Officer*
Francine Wilson, *Manager*
EMP: 10
SALES: 497.7K **Privately Held**
WEB: www.providentfcu.com
SIC: 6061 6163 Federal credit unions; loan brokers

(G-1993)
PRUDENTIAL INSUR CO OF AMER
9 E Looockerman St (19901-8306)
PHONE...................302 734-7877
EMP: 26
SQ FT: 2,198
SALES (corp-wide): 57.1B **Publicly Held**
SIC: 6411 Insurance Agent/Broker
HQ: The Prudential Insurance Company Of America
751 Broad St
Newark NJ 07102
973 802-6000

(G-1994)
PSYCHOTHERAPEUTIC SERVICES
630 W Division St Ste D (19904-2760)
PHONE...................302 672-7159
Randall L Cooper, *CFO*
Charles Gibbs, *Case Mgr*
John C Sigler, *Manager*
Sherry Johnson,
EMP: 40
SALES (corp-wide): 86.2MM **Privately Held**
SIC: 8063 Hospital for the mentally ill
HQ: Psychotherapeutic Services Inc
870 High St Ste 2
Chestertown MD 21620
410 778-1933

(G-1995)
PSYCHOTHERAPEUTIC SERVICES
942 Walker Rd Ste B (19904-2757)
PHONE...................302 678-9962
Sherry Debra Jones, *Owner*
Friendoll Tucker, *Technology*
EMP: 6
SALES (corp-wide): 86.2MM **Privately Held**
SIC: 8049 Acupuncturist
HQ: Psychotherapeutic Services Inc
870 High St Ste 2
Chestertown MD 21620
410 778-1933

(G-1996)
PSYCHOTHERAPEUTIC SVC ASSN INC
Also Called: Felton Residential Trtmnt Ctr
2015 Peachtree Run Rd (19901-7733)
PHONE...................302 284-8370
Nakita Sy, *Branch Mgr*
EMP: 5
SALES (corp-wide): 86.2MM **Privately Held**
SIC: 8093 Mental health clinic, outpatient
HQ: Psychotherapeutic Service Association, Inc.
870 High St Ste 2
Chestertown MD 21620
410 778-9114

(G-1997)
PSYCHOTHERAPEUTIC SVCS ASSOC
630 W Division St Ste D (19904-2760)
PHONE...................302 672-7159
Sharon Stevenson, *Branch Mgr*
EMP: 30
SALES (corp-wide): 86.2MM **Privately Held**
SIC: 8999 Psychological consultant
HQ: Psychotherapeutic Service Association, Inc.
870 High St Ste 2
Chestertown MD 21620
410 778-9114

(G-1998)
PTERIS GLOBAL (USA) INC
615 S Dupont Hwy (19901-4517)
PHONE...................516 593-5633
David Haddaway, *General Mgr*
Daniel Goh, *Vice Pres*
Angel Amadeo, *Project Mgr*
Tony Mathis, *Project Mgr*
Dana Bark, *Opers Staff*
EMP: 7
SALES (est): 618.6K
SALES (corp-wide): 240.4MM **Privately Held**
SIC: 4731 Freight forwarding
PA: Pteris Global Limited
28 Quality Road
Singapore 61882
686 128-28

(G-1999)
PUGHS SERVICE INC
728 Dover Leipsic Rd (19901-2055)
PHONE...................302 678-2408
Horrace Pugh Jr, *President*
EMP: 14
SQ FT: 500
SALES: 1.5MM **Privately Held**
SIC: 7538 7549 7699 5261 Engine repair; towing services; lawn mower repair shop; lawn & garden equipment

(G-2000)
PXE GROUP LLC
8 The Grn Ste A (19901-3618)
PHONE...................561 295-1451
Robert Scaduto, *Managing Prtnr*
EMP: 8
SQ FT: 500
SALES (est): 182.5K **Privately Held**
SIC: 7371 Computer software development

(G-2001)
QUANTUMFLY LLC
9 E Looockerman St Ste 215 (19901-7347)
PHONE...................312 618-5739
Suri Surinder, *CEO*
Narasimhan Surinder, *Co-Owner*
Sunil Dixit, *Co-Owner*
Anoop Mohan, *Co-Owner*
EMP: 10
SALES (est): 450K **Privately Held**
SIC: 7375 On-line data base information retrieval

(G-2002)
QUEEN B TBL CHAIR RENTALS LLC
8 The Grn 8105 (19901-3618)
PHONE...................215 960-6303
Balil Brown,
Kiyanna Thompson,
EMP: 5
SALES (est): 124.1K **Privately Held**
SIC: 7359 Equipment rental & leasing

(G-2003)
QUEST DIAGNOSTICS INCORPORATED
190 John Hunn Brown Rd (19901-4708)
PHONE...................302 735-4555
EMP: 6
SALES (corp-wide): 7.5B **Publicly Held**
SIC: 8071 Medical laboratories
PA: Quest Diagnostics Incorporated
500 Plaza Dr Ste G
Secaucus NJ 07094
973 520-2700

(G-2004)
QUINN PEDIATRIC DENTISTRY
1380 S State St (19901-4946)
PHONE...................302 674-8000
Richard M Quinn, *Principal*
EMP: 4
SALES (est): 188.3K **Privately Held**
SIC: 8011 Pediatrician

(G-2005)
QUINTASIAN LLC
Also Called: Hilton
1706 N Dupont Hwy (19901-2219)
PHONE...................302 674-3784
Clifford Weber, *General Mgr*
Dorothy Cheung, *Treasurer*
Andrew Cheung, *Mng Member*
EMP: 35
SALES: 3.2MM **Privately Held**
SIC: 7011 Hotels & motels

(G-2006)
R E MICHEL COMPANY LLC
550 S Queen St (19904-3563)
PHONE...................302 678-0250
Kenneth Childers, *Sales Staff*
Eric Smith, *Manager*
EMP: 5
SALES (corp-wide): 898.2MM **Privately Held**
WEB: www.remichel.com
SIC: 5075 5078 Warm air heating equipment & supplies; refrigeration equipment & supplies
PA: R. E. Michel Company, Llc
1 Re Michel Dr
Glen Burnie MD 21060
410 760-4000

(G-2007)
R M QUINN DDS
1380 S State St Ste 2 (19901-4911)
PHONE...................302 674-8000
Richard M Quinn, *Owner*
EMP: 11
SALES (est): 439.8K **Privately Held**
SIC: 8021 Dentists' office

(G-2008)
R T ACCOUNTANTS CO
39 S Turnberry Dr (19904-2348)
PHONE...................302 670-5117
William R Tyson, *Principal*
EMP: 6
SALES (est): 443.2K **Privately Held**
SIC: 8721 Accounting, auditing & bookkeeping

(G-2009)
RANGELAND NM LLC
1675 S State St Ste B (19901-5140)
PHONE...................800 316-6660

GEOGRAPHIC SECTION
Dover - Kent County (G-2042)

Christopher W Keene, *CEO*
Paul Broker, *COO*
EMP: 4
SALES (est): 179.4K **Publicly Held**
SIC: 1382 Oil & gas exploration services
HQ: Rio Andeavor Holdings Llc
2150 Town Square Pl # 700
Sugar Land TX 77479

(G-2010)
RATNER COMPANIES LC
Also Called: Hair Cuttery
1005 N Dupont Hwy (19901-2006)
PHONE.................................302 678-8081
Mary Conners, *Branch Mgr*
EMP: 11 **Privately Held**
WEB: www.haircuttery.com
SIC: 7231 Unisex hair salons
HQ: Ratner Companies, L.C.
1577 Spring Hill Rd # 500
Vienna VA 22182
703 269-5400

(G-2011)
RAYMOND F BOOK III (PA)
Also Called: Ray Book & Co
220 Beiser Blvd (19904-7790)
PHONE.................................302 734-5826
Raymond F Book III, *Owner*
Angela Balcerak, *Site Mgr*
Donna Austin, *CPA*
EMP: 20
SALES (est): 1.7MM **Privately Held**
WEB: www.rfbookcpas.com
SIC: 8721 Certified public accountant

(G-2012)
RBS AUTO REPAIR INC
Also Called: Meineke Car Care Center
1312 S Dupont Hwy (19901-4404)
PHONE.................................302 678-8803
James R Kramer Jr, *President*
EMP: 6
SALES: 1MM **Privately Held**
SIC: 7538 General automotive repair shops

(G-2013)
RE/MAX HORIZONS INC
1198 S Governors Ave (19904-6930)
PHONE.................................302 678-4300
Edward Hammond Jr, *President*
George Becker, *Broker*
Erin Fortney, *Broker*
Shawna Kirlin, *Broker*
Steven Smiertka, *Sales Staff*
EMP: 29
SALES (est): 3.2MM **Privately Held**
SIC: 6531 Real estate agent, residential

(G-2014)
READHOWYOUWANT LLC
3702 N Dupont Hwy (19901-1555)
PHONE.................................302 730-4560
EMP: 2 **EST:** 2004
SALES (est): 52.8K **Privately Held**
SIC: 8211 8732 2731 Specialty education; commercial sociological & educational research; book publishing

(G-2015)
READYB INC
8 The Grn Ste A (19901-3618)
PHONE.................................323 813-8710
Edna Mimran, *Principal*
EMP: 3
SALES (est): 71.1K **Privately Held**
SIC: 7372 Prepackaged software

(G-2016)
RECORD STORAGE CENTER INC
602 Pear St (19904-2832)
PHONE.................................302 674-8571
Leland Berry, *President*
Armando Herrera, *Comptroller*
EMP: 4
SALES (est): 199.9K **Privately Held**
SIC: 4225 Miniwarehouse, warehousing

(G-2017)
RED BARN INC
Also Called: Maaco Auto Painting
1062 Lafferty Ln (19901-4642)
PHONE.................................302 678-0271
Elmore Smith, *President*
EMP: 13
SQ FT: 6,200
SALES (est): 758.3K **Privately Held**
SIC: 7532 Paint shop, automotive

(G-2018)
REESE AGENCY INC
575 N Dupont Hwy (19901-3960)
PHONE.................................302 678-5656
Billy Reese, *President*
EMP: 4 **EST:** 2010
SALES (est): 235K **Privately Held**
SIC: 6331 6411 Automobile insurance; property & casualty insurance agent

(G-2019)
REGAL CONTRACTORS LLC
13 Nobles Pond Xing (19904-1296)
PHONE.................................302 736-5000
Mary Field,
EMP: 6
SALES (est): 337.3K **Privately Held**
SIC: 1542 Custom builders, non-residential

(G-2020)
REGEN SOLUTIONS LLC
32 W Loockerman St # 201 (19904-7352)
PHONE.................................323 362-4336
Houston Evans,
EMP: 2
SALES (est): 400K **Privately Held**
SIC: 3449 Miscellaneous metalwork

(G-2021)
REGULATORY INSURANCE SERVICES
841 Silver Lake Blvd # 201 (19904-2465)
P.O. Box 835 (19903-0835)
PHONE.................................302 678-2444
John T Tinsley III, *President*
Tony Meisenheimer, *Corp Secy*
George Donhauser, *Vice Pres*
Donna Parry, *Administration*
EMP: 5
SALES (est): 1.2MM **Privately Held**
SIC: 6411 Insurance information & consulting services

(G-2022)
RELIG STAFFING INC
8 The Grn Ste 7460 (19901-3618)
PHONE.................................312 219-6786
Juzar Motorwala, *Director*
Jwalant Patel, *Director*
Ankit Rathod, *Director*
EMP: 20
SALES (est): 236.7K **Privately Held**
SIC: 7361 Employment agencies

(G-2023)
RELYTV LLC
8 The Grn Ste 8422 (19901-3618)
PHONE.................................213 373-5988
Eric Vasquez, *Mng Member*
EMP: 2
SALES (est): 275K **Privately Held**
SIC: 7372 Home entertainment computer software

(G-2024)
RENAISSANCE SQUARE LLC
1534 S Governors Ave B (19904-7054)
PHONE.................................302 943-5118
Andre Boggerty,
EMP: 7
SALES (est): 144.1K **Privately Held**
SIC: 8748 Business consulting

(G-2025)
RENAL CARE CENTER DOVER
Also Called: Fresenius Medical Care
655 S Bay Rd Ste 4m (19901-4656)
PHONE.................................302 678-5718
Fax: 302 678-5732
EMP: 20
SALES (est): 149.8M **Privately Held**
SIC: 8092 Kidney Dialysis Centers

(G-2026)
RENAL CARE GROUP INC
748 S New St (19904-3573)
PHONE.................................302 678-8744
Sharon Simmons, *Branch Mgr*
EMP: 26
SALES (corp-wide): 18.3B **Privately Held**
WEB: www.bamap.com
SIC: 8092 Kidney dialysis centers
HQ: Renal Care Group Alaska, Inc.
2525 West End Ave Ste 600
Nashville TN

(G-2027)
RENDERAPPS LLC
8 The Grn Ste A (19901-3618)
PHONE.................................919 274-0582
Bobby Ren, *Mng Member*
EMP: 5 **EST:** 2016
SALES: 10K **Privately Held**
SIC: 7372 7389 Prepackaged software;

(G-2028)
RENE DELYN DESIGNS INC
Also Called: Rene Delyn Hair Design Studio
1744 N Dupont Hwy (19901-2219)
PHONE.................................302 736-6070
Rene Brickman, *President*
Gladys T Brickman, *Partner*
Jacob R Brickman, *Vice Pres*
EMP: 10
SALES (est): 276.8K **Privately Held**
WEB: www.renedelyn.com
SIC: 7231 Hairdressers

(G-2029)
RENT CO INC
35 Commerce Way Ste 180 (19904-5747)
PHONE.................................302 674-1177
George C Clapp Jr, *President*
David W Clapp, *Admin Sec*
EMP: 16
SQ FT: 8,500
SALES (est): 1.7MM **Privately Held**
WEB: www.doverrentall.com
SIC: 7359 Party supplies rental services

(G-2030)
RENT-A-CENTER INC
1013 N Dupont Hwy (19901-2006)
PHONE.................................302 678-4676
Wandfa Hill, *Manager*
EMP: 5
SALES (corp-wide): 2.6B **Publicly Held**
WEB: www.rentacenter.com
SIC: 7359 Appliance rental; furniture rental; home entertainment equipment rental; television rental
PA: Rent-A-Center, Inc.
5501 Headquarters Dr
Plano TX 75024
972 801-1100

(G-2031)
RENT-A-CENTER INC
288 S Dupont Hwy (19901-4733)
PHONE.................................302 674-5060
Elbert Hicks, *Manager*
EMP: 5
SALES (corp-wide): 2.6B **Publicly Held**
WEB: www.rentacenter.com
SIC: 7359 Appliance rental; furniture rental; home entertainment equipment rental; television rental
PA: Rent-A-Center, Inc.
5501 Headquarters Dr
Plano TX 75024
972 801-1100

(G-2032)
RENT-A-CENTER INC
1688 S Governors Ave (19904-7004)
PHONE.................................302 734-3505
Billy Strickland, *Owner*
EMP: 5
SALES (corp-wide): 2.6B **Publicly Held**
SIC: 7359 Appliance rental
PA: Rent-A-Center, Inc.
5501 Headquarters Dr
Plano TX 75024
972 801-1100

(G-2033)
RESIDENCE INN DOVER
600 Jefferic Blvd (19901-2019)
PHONE.................................302 677-0777
Diana Carter, *Principal*
EMP: 14
SALES (est): 727.3K **Privately Held**
SIC: 7011 Hotels

(G-2034)
RFX ANALYST INC
8 The Grn 5875 (19901-3618)
PHONE.................................302 244-5650
Ryan Champion, *President*
EMP: 5
SALES (est): 171.6K **Privately Held**
SIC: 7372 Business oriented computer software

(G-2035)
RICHARD A PARSONS AGENCY INC
57 Saulsbury Rd Ste C (19904-3472)
PHONE.................................302 674-2810
Richard Parsons, *President*
Kristin Parsons, *Vice Pres*
EMP: 6
SALES (est): 758.7K **Privately Held**
SIC: 6411 Insurance agents

(G-2036)
RIGBYS KARATE ACADEMY
560 Otis Dr (19901-4630)
PHONE.................................302 735-9637
Reese Rigby, *Owner*
Judy Rigby, *Co-Owner*
EMP: 5
SALES (est): 260K **Privately Held**
SIC: 5941 7999 Martial arts equipment & supplies; martial arts school

(G-2037)
ROBERT J VARIPAPA MD
1074 S State St (19901-6925)
PHONE.................................302 678-8100
Robert J Varipapa MD, *Principal*
EMP: 4 **EST:** 2001
SALES (est): 145.4K **Privately Held**
SIC: 8011 Neurologist

(G-2038)
ROBINO MANAGEMENT GROUP INC
Also Called: Mifflin Run Apts
1300 S Farmview Dr Bldg O (19904-3374)
PHONE.................................302 734-2944
EMP: 8
SALES (corp-wide): 7.3MM **Privately Held**
SIC: 6513 Apartment Building Operator
HQ: Robino Management Group Inc
5189 W Woodmill Dr 30a
Wilmington DE 19808

(G-2039)
ROBOTICK NEW MEDIA NETWORK LLC
Also Called: Robotick Media
8 The Grn Ste A (19901-3618)
PHONE.................................213 219-3083
Dennis Grant Jr,
EMP: 1
SALES (est): 37.5K **Privately Held**
SIC: 2741

(G-2040)
ROGER C ALLEN DC
Also Called: Allen Chiropractic
884 Walker Rd Ste A (19904-2758)
PHONE.................................302 734-9824
Roger C Allen, *Owner*
EMP: 4
SALES (est): 217.6K **Privately Held**
SIC: 8041 Offices & clinics of chiropractors

(G-2041)
RONALD MIDAUGH
Also Called: Jackson Hewitt Tax Service
1030 Forrest Ave Ste 104 (19904-3382)
PHONE.................................410 860-1040
Jennifer Lynch, *Manager*
EMP: 10
SALES (est): 143.2K **Privately Held**
SIC: 7291 Tax return preparation services
PA: Ronald Midaugh
13600 Annapolis Rd
Bowie MD 20720

(G-2042)
ROOAH LLC
768 Townsend Blvd Ste 3 (19901-2515)
PHONE.................................305 233-7557
Robert Njoku, *Principal*
EMP: 5

Dover - Kent County (G-2043)   GEOGRAPHIC SECTION

SALES (est): 115.2K **Privately Held**
SIC: 7389

(G-2043)
ROSAS GREEK BTQ
338 Blue Heron Rd (19904-4724)
PHONE.................302 678-2147
Rosa Smith, *Owner*
EMP: 2
SALES (est): 149.8K **Privately Held**
SIC: 3999 Models, general, except toy

(G-2044)
ROUSE INSURANCE AND FINCL LL
1252 Forrest Ave (19904-3311)
PHONE.................302 678-2223
Doug Bennetti, *Owner*
EMP: 4
SALES (est): 675K **Privately Held**
SIC: 6282 Investment advice

(G-2045)
RUBY INDUSTRIAL TECH LLC
Also Called: Kaman Industrial Technology
521 Otis Dr (19901-4645)
PHONE.................302 674-2943
Brenda Deveau, *Manager*
EMP: 4
SALES (corp-wide): 770.7MM **Privately Held**
SIC: 5085 Bearings
PA: Ruby Industrial Technologies, Llc
1 Vision Way
Bloomfield CT 06002
860 687-5000

(G-2046)
RYAN C GOUGH MD
300 Tuskegee Blvd (19902-5003)
PHONE.................302 677-6527
Ryan Gough, *Executive*
EMP: 6 EST: 2017
SALES (est): 80.5K **Privately Held**
SIC: 8011 Offices & clinics of medical doctors

(G-2047)
S & B PRO SECURITY LLC
Also Called: Electronic Security
1300 E Lebanon Rd (19901-5832)
PHONE.................800 841-9907
David V Snook Sr,
Vincent Barranco,
EMP: 8
SALES: 800K **Privately Held**
SIC: 7382 5065 Protective devices, security; security control equipment & systems

(G-2048)
S & S WINES AND SPIRITS
1007 Walker Rd (19904-6572)
PHONE.................302 678-9987
Ralph Mills, *President*
EMP: 5
SALES (est): 299.7K **Privately Held**
SIC: 5182 Wine

(G-2049)
S D NEMCIC DDS
910 Walker Rd Ste A (19904-2759)
PHONE.................302 734-1950
Steven D Nemcic DDS, *Fmly & Gen Dent*
EMP: 6
SALES (est): 300.7K **Privately Held**
SIC: 8021 Specialized dental practitioners

(G-2050)
S G WILLIAMS OF DOVER INC
580 Lafferty Ln (19901-7201)
PHONE.................302 678-1080
John D Griffith, *President*
William M Kinnamon, *Corp Secy*
Helen Griffith, *Vice Pres*
EMP: 12
SQ FT: 20,000
SALES (est): 4.3MM
SALES (corp-wide): 15MM **Privately Held**
SIC: 5033 Roofing, asphalt & sheet metal; siding, except wood
PA: S. G. Williams & Bros. Co.
301 N Tatnall St
Wilmington DE 19801
302 656-8167

(G-2051)
S&H LOGISTICS LLC
8 The Grn 6451 (19901-3618)
PHONE.................708 548-8982
Halimah Clay, *Mng Member*
EMP: 1
SALES (est): 54.6K **Privately Held**
SIC: 3724 Aircraft engines & engine parts

(G-2052)
SAFELITE FULFILLMENT INC
Also Called: Safelite Autoglass
746 N Du Pont Hwy (19901)
PHONE.................302 678-9600
James Peel Jr, *Branch Mgr*
EMP: 6
SALES (corp-wide): 177.9K **Privately Held**
WEB: www.belronus.com
SIC: 7536 Automotive glass replacement shops
HQ: Safelite Fulfillment, Inc.
7400 Safelite Way
Columbus OH 43235
614 210-9000

(G-2053)
SAFELITE GLASS CORP
Also Called: Safelite Autoglass
4200 N Dupont Hwy Ste 6 (19901-2400)
PHONE.................877 800-2727
Kim Cordrey, *Manager*
EMP: 5
SALES (corp-wide): 177.9K **Privately Held**
SIC: 7536 5013 Automotive glass replacement shops; automobile glass
HQ: Safelite Glass Corp.
7400 Safelite Way
Columbus OH 43235
614 210-9000

(G-2054)
SAILNOVO LIMITED
108 S Governors Ave (19904-3246)
PHONE.................213 550-3897
Chunsan Xiang, *CEO*
EMP: 95
SALES: 330K **Privately Held**
SIC: 7371 Computer software development & applications

(G-2055)
SAINT JOHNS LUTHERAN CHURCH
Also Called: St Johns Early Learning Center
113 Lotus St (19901-4435)
PHONE.................302 734-7078
Rick Murphy, *President*
Arthur Kringel, *Pastor*
Dorothy Kringil, *Director*
EMP: 35
SALES (est): 1.1MM **Privately Held**
SIC: 8351 Child day care services

(G-2056)
SALLY BEAUTY SUPPLY LLC
Also Called; Sally Beauty Supply 712
283 N Dupont Hwy Ste D (19901-7532)
PHONE.................302 674-2201
Erin Dudley, *Manager*
EMP: 7 **Publicly Held**
WEB: www.sallybeauty.com
SIC: 5087 Beauty parlor equipment & supplies
HQ: Sally Beauty Supply Llc
3001 Colorado Blvd
Denton TX 76210
940 898-7500

(G-2057)
SANDPIPER ENERGY INC
909 Silver Lake Blvd (19904-2409)
PHONE.................302 736-7656
Thomas Mahn, *Treasurer*
EMP: 20
SQ FT: 8,000
SALES (est): 624.9K
SALES (corp-wide): 717.4MM **Publicly Held**
SIC: 4923 Gas transmission & distribution
PA: Chesapeake Utilities Corporation
909 Silver Lake Blvd
Dover DE 19904

(G-2058)
SANDRA S GULLEDGE CPA
Also Called: National Income Tax Service
1037 S Dupont Hwy (19901-4421)
PHONE.................302 674-1585
Sandra Gulledge, *Owner*
EMP: 5 EST: 1998
SALES (est): 232.7K **Privately Held**
SIC: 7291 Tax return preparation services

(G-2059)
SCHMITTINGER & RODRIGUEZ PA (PA)
414 S State St (19901-6702)
PHONE.................302 674-0140
Nicholas H Rodriguez, *President*
John J Schmittinger, *Treasurer*
Bruce C Ennis, *Asst Treas*
Paul H Boswell, *Admin Sec*
Puddie Torgerson, *Legal Staff*
EMP: 79 EST: 1962
SQ FT: 9,000
SALES: 6.1MM **Privately Held**
WEB: www.schmittrod.com
SIC: 8111 General practice attorney, lawyer

(G-2060)
SCHWARTZ & SCHWARTZ ATTY AT LA
1140 S State St (19901-6926)
P.O. Box 541 (19903-0541)
PHONE.................302 678-8700
Steven Schwartz, *President*
EMP: 6
SALES (est): 686.4K **Privately Held**
WEB: www.benschwartz.com
SIC: 8111 General practice attorney, lawyer

(G-2061)
SCOPE ONE INC
8 The Grn Ste D (19901-3618)
PHONE.................415 429-9347
Sergey Stelmakh, *Principal*
EMP: 4
SALES (est): 89.7K **Privately Held**
SIC: 7371 Computer software development

(G-2062)
SCOTT ENGINEERING INC
22 Old Rudnick Ln Ste 2 (19901-4912)
PHONE.................302 736-3058
Greg Scott, *President*
Carol Scott, *Administration*
EMP: 5
SQ FT: 5,000
SALES (est): 569.9K **Privately Held**
WEB: www.scottengineering.com
SIC: 8711 8713 Consulting engineer; surveying services

(G-2063)
SCOTT MUFFLER LLC (PA)
1465 S Governors Ave (19904-7017)
PHONE.................302 674-8280
Bernard Limpert,
Lynn Limpert,
EMP: 8
SALES (est): 758.6K **Privately Held**
SIC: 7533 Muffler shop, sale or repair & installation

(G-2064)
SCUBA WORLD INC
Also Called: Commercial Residential Contrs
4004 S Dupont Hwy Ste B (19901-2577)
PHONE.................302 698-1117
Darrell Louder, *President*
Tracy Louder, *Corp Secy*
EMP: 12
SQ FT: 1,200
SALES: 400K **Privately Held**
SIC: 5941 1522 Skin diving, scuba equipment & supplies; residential construction

(G-2065)
SECURE DATA CMPT SOLUTIONS INC
910 Walker Rd Ste B (19904-2759)
P.O. Box 458 (19903-0458)
PHONE.................302 346-7327
David Green, *President*
EMP: 4

SALES (est): 328.4K **Privately Held**
SIC: 7378 5734 Computer & data processing equipment repair/maintenance; computer & software stores

(G-2066)
SEDATION CENTER PA
429 S Governors Ave (19904-6707)
PHONE.................302 678-3384
Dawn M Grandison, *Principal*
EMP: 5
SALES (est): 381.1K **Privately Held**
SIC: 8021 Dental clinic

(G-2067)
SELECT PHYSICAL THERAPY
230 Beiser Blvd Ste 100 (19904-7791)
PHONE.................302 760-9966
EMP: 4
SALES (corp-wide): 15.3MM **Privately Held**
SIC: 8049 Nutritionist
PA: Select Physical Therapy Holdings, Inc.
680 American Ave Ste 200
King Of Prussia PA 19406
800 331-8840

(G-2068)
SELECT SUPPLIERS LTD
30 Old Rudnick Ln (19901-4912)
PHONE.................303 523-1813
EMP: 5
SALES: 100K **Privately Held**
SIC: 5063 Mfr's Representatives For Overseas Sales

(G-2069)
SEPARE INC
529 Weaver Dr (19901-1377)
PHONE.................302 736-5000
Harry Miller, *President*
EMP: 30
SALES: 15MM **Privately Held**
SIC: 1522 Residential construction

(G-2070)
SEPER 8 MOTEL
Also Called: Red Carpet Inn
348 N Dupont Hwy (19901-3935)
PHONE.................302 734-5701
Pradip Parikh, *President*
EMP: 20
SALES (est): 282K **Privately Held**
SIC: 7011 Hotels & motels

(G-2071)
SERVICE ENERGY LLC (PA)
3799 N Dupont Hwy (19901-1574)
P.O. Box 1000, Cheswold (19936-1000)
PHONE.................302 734-7433
Jack Grant, *General Mgr*
Park McDaniel, *Opers Mgr*
Donald Steiner,
Edward Steiner,
EMP: 66
SQ FT: 5,000
SALES: 55MM **Privately Held**
WEB: www.serviceenergy.com
SIC: 5172 5983 5411 Petroleum products; fuel oil dealers; convenience stores

(G-2072)
SERVICE OIL COMPANY
Also Called: Poores Propane
3799 N Dupont Hwy (19901-1574)
P.O. Box 279, Milford (19963-0279)
PHONE.................302 734-7433
Don Steiner, *Owner*
EMP: 20
SALES (corp-wide): 3.8MM **Privately Held**
SIC: 5171 Petroleum bulk stations & terminals
HQ: Service Oil Company
Cedar Beach Rd
Milford DE 19963
302 422-6631

(G-2073)
SEWELL C BIGGS TRUST
406 Federal St (19901-3615)
P.O. Box 711 (19903-0711)
PHONE.................302 674-2111
C Terry Jackson, *President*
Kathryn Marro, *Manager*
Angela S Moore, *Manager*

GEOGRAPHIC SECTION
Dover - Kent County (G-2106)

Linda Danko, *Exec Dir*
Charles Guerin, *Exec Dir*
EMP: 10
SALES: 2.1MM **Privately Held**
SIC: 8412 Museum

(G-2074)
SHADYBROOK FARMS LLC
6401 Bayside Dr (19901-3429)
PHONE.................................302 734-9966
Sandra Cartanza, *Owner*
Chris Cartanza,
Mark Cartanza,
Paul Cartanza,
EMP: 17
SQ FT: 3,000
SALES (est): 1.6MM **Privately Held**
SIC: 0115 0134 0111 0116 Corn; Irish potatoes; wheat; soybeans; barley farm

(G-2075)
SHELATIA J DENNIS
9 E Loockerman St Ste 302 (19901-8305)
PHONE.................................302 465-0630
Shelatia J Dennis Lcsw, *Owner*
EMP: 4
SALES (est): 42.4K **Privately Held**
SIC: 8322 Individual & family services

(G-2076)
SHEPHERD PLACE INC
1362 S Governors Ave (19904-4804)
PHONE.................................302 678-1909
Lakena Hammond, *Exec Dir*
EMP: 13
SALES: 423.2K **Privately Held**
WEB: www.shepherdplace.org
SIC: 8322 Individual & family services

(G-2077)
SHIV BABA LLC
Also Called: Wireless Traders
100 Carlsons Way Ste 15 (19901-2365)
PHONE.................................703 314-1203
Mayam Patel, *Mng Member*
Pandre Prabhu, *Mng Member*
EMP: 10 **EST:** 2018
SALES (est): 542.3K **Privately Held**
SIC: 3661 Telephone dialing devices, automatic

(G-2078)
SHIV SAGAR INC
Also Called: Microtel
1703 E Lebanon Rd (19901-5844)
PHONE.................................302 674-3800
Nita Patel, *Principal*
EMP: 10 **EST:** 2013
SALES (est): 550.6K **Privately Held**
SIC: 7011 Hotels & motels

(G-2079)
SHOOTERS CHOICE INC
5105 N Dupont Hwy (19901-2345)
PHONE.................................302 736-5166
David Lawson, *President*
David G Lawson, *COO*
Charles Spiegelman, *Vice Pres*
Adrienne Spiegelman, *Treasurer*
EMP: 9
SQ FT: 7,000
SALES (est): 954.8K **Privately Held**
WEB: www.shootersline.com
SIC: 5941 7999 Firearms; shooting range operation

(G-2080)
SHORECARE OF DELAWARE ✪
874 Walker Rd Ste D (19904-2778)
PHONE.................................302 724-5235
EMP: 8 **EST:** 2019
SALES (est): 61.1K **Privately Held**
SIC: 8082 Home health care services

(G-2081)
SHORECARE OF DELAWARE
874 Walker Rd (19904-2778)
PHONE.................................302 724-5235
EMP: 4
SALES (est): 94.2K **Privately Held**
SIC: 8082 Home Health Care Services

(G-2082)
SHREE LALJI LLC
Also Called: Red Roof Inn
652 N Dupont Hwy (19901-3937)
PHONE.................................302 730-8009
Vinaykumar Patel, *Principal*
Vijay Shroff, *Principal*
EMP: 9 **EST:** 2013
SQ FT: 45,000
SALES (est): 557.5K **Privately Held**
SIC: 7011 Hotels & motels

(G-2083)
SHRI SAI DOVER LLC
Also Called: Holiday Inn
561 N Dupont Hwy (19901-3960)
PHONE.................................302 747-5050
Mehul Khatiwala,
EMP: 30
SALES (est): 1.4MM **Privately Held**
SIC: 7011 Hotels & motels

(G-2084)
SIMPLY CLEAN JANTR SVCS INC
100 Carlsons Way Ste 6 (19901-2365)
PHONE.................................302 744-9100
Michael Devault, *Vice Pres*
EMP: 25
SALES: 350K **Privately Held**
SIC: 7349 Janitorial service, contract basis

(G-2085)
SITE WORK SAFETY SUPPLIES INC
4020 Hickories Rd (19904)
PHONE.................................302 672-7011
Peter D Coker, *President*
EMP: 5 **EST:** 2008
SALES: 1.8MM **Privately Held**
SIC: 3561 Cylinders, pump

(G-2086)
SITENGLE TECHNOLOGY LLC
8 The Grn Ste A (19901-3618)
PHONE.................................719 822-0710
Yumei Huang,
EMP: 10
SALES (est): 309.2K **Privately Held**
SIC: 5961 7371 7389 Catalog sales; computer software development & applications;

(G-2087)
SKAB INTERNATIONAL CORPORATION
15 Loockerman Plz (19901-7327)
PHONE.................................412 475-2221
EMP: 4
SALES (est): 450K **Privately Held**
SIC: 5084 Whol Industrial Equipment

(G-2088)
SLACUM & DOYLE TAX SERVICE LLC
Also Called: Liberty Tax Service
838 Walker Rd Ste 22-2 (19904-2751)
PHONE.................................302 734-1850
Doug Doyle,
Scott Slacum,
EMP: 32
SALES (est): 723.3K **Privately Held**
SIC: 7291 Tax return preparation services

(G-2089)
SMARTIS
Also Called: Home Theater
73 Greentree Dr (19904-7646)
PHONE.................................302 653-8355
Christopher Hargett, *President*
EMP: 5
SALES (est): 641.8K **Privately Held**
WEB: www.smartisinc.com
SIC: 7373 1731 Systems integration services; sound equipment specialization; voice, data & video wiring contractor; access control systems specialization

(G-2090)
SNAP FITNESS
1030 Forrest Ave Ste 100 (19904-3382)
PHONE.................................302 741-2444
Roger Bradley, *Manager*
EMP: 4
SALES (est): 94.6K **Privately Held**
SIC: 7991 7299 Physical fitness facilities; personal appearance services

(G-2091)
SOCIAL HEALTH INNOVATIONS INC
8 The Grn Ste 5175 (19901-3618)
PHONE.................................917 476-9355
Amanda Johnstone, *CEO*
EMP: 8
SALES (est): 82.2K **Privately Held**
SIC: 8063 Psychiatric hospitals

(G-2092)
SOCIAL SECURITY ADMINISTRATION
655 S Bay Rd Ste 3j (19901-4992)
PHONE.................................302 736-3688
EMP: 5 **Publicly Held**
SIC: 7381 Guard services
HQ: Social Security Administration
6401 Security Blvd
Baltimore MD 21235

(G-2093)
SOCIAL WORK HELPER PBC
8 The Grn Ste 8043 (19901-3618)
PHONE.................................302 233-7422
Deona Cooper, *President*
EMP: 9
SALES (est): 264.3K **Privately Held**
SIC: 7313 Electronic media advertising representatives

(G-2094)
SOMETHING UNIQUE INC
1014 Lafferty Ln (19901-4642)
PHONE.................................302 678-0555
Susan Whitney, *President*
EMP: 4
SALES (est): 104.9K **Privately Held**
SIC: 7231 Manicurist, pedicurist

(G-2095)
SOUTHERN DELAWARE MED GROUP
200 Banning St Ste 380 (19904-3493)
P.O. Box 337, Milford (19963-0337)
PHONE.................................302 424-3900
EMP: 4
SALES (est): 169K **Privately Held**
SIC: 8031 8011 Offices & clinics of osteopathic physicians; offices & clinics of medical doctors

(G-2096)
SOUTHSIDE FAMILY PRACTICE
230 Beiser Blvd Ste 200 (19904-7792)
PHONE.................................302 735-1880
Andrew Willet MD, *Owner*
Charlene Mailey, *Office Mgr*
EMP: 17
SQ FT: 1,500
SALES: 450K **Privately Held**
SIC: 8011 General & family practice, physician/surgeon

(G-2097)
SPEEDRID LTD
625 S Dupont Hwy (19901-4504)
PHONE.................................213 550-5462
Guiyun Wang, *Mng Member*
EMP: 98
SALES (est): 1.3MM **Privately Held**
SIC: 7371 Computer software development & applications

(G-2098)
SPENCES BAZAAR & AUCTION LLC
550 S New St (19904-3536)
PHONE.................................302 734-3441
Richard Spence,
EMP: 17
SALES (est): 1.1MM **Privately Held**
SIC: 7389 Auctioneers, fee basis; speakers' bureau

(G-2099)
SQUARE ONE ELECTRIC SERVICE CO
347 Fork Branch Rd (19904-1230)
PHONE.................................302 678-0400
Ed Crumbock, *President*
Amber Reed, *IT/INT Sup*
EMP: 18
SQ FT: 12,000
SALES (est): 9.9MM **Privately Held**
WEB: www.sqone.com
SIC: 5084 7699 3462 Water pumps (industrial); industrial machinery & equipment repair; iron & steel forgings

(G-2100)
ST DELWARE ELECTRICAL
245 Mckee Rd (19904-2232)
PHONE.................................302 857-5316
EMP: 5
SALES (est): 152.6K **Privately Held**
SIC: 4911 Electric services

(G-2101)
ST MATTHEW GRAND CHAPTER
450 Topaz Cir (19904-3711)
PHONE.................................302 834-9552
EMP: 4
SALES (est): 74.2K **Privately Held**
SIC: 8399 Advocacy group

(G-2102)
STANDARD DISTRIBUTING CO INC
Horse Pond Rd Lafferty Ln (19901)
PHONE.................................302 674-4591
Chris Tigani, *General Mgr*
Steven Tigani, *Manager*
Jim Dawson, *Manager*
Ryan Freebery, *Manager*
Wayne Brzoska, *Officer*
EMP: 34
SALES (corp-wide): 46.5MM **Privately Held**
WEB: www.standardde.com
SIC: 4225 General warehousing
PA: Standard Distributing Co Inc
100 Mews Dr
New Castle DE 19720
302 655-5511

(G-2103)
STATE EDUCATION AGENCY DI
401 Federal St Ste 2 (19901-3639)
PHONE.................................302 739-4111
Ana Luisa Cardona, *President*
Lynn Tuttle, *Treasurer*
Debora Hanses, *Admin Sec*
EMP: 14
SALES: 200.2K **Privately Held**
SIC: 8621 Professional membership organizations

(G-2104)
STATE JANITORIAL SUPPLY CO
525 Otis Dr (19901-4645)
PHONE.................................302 734-4814
Chris Lebendig, *President*
EMP: 8 **EST:** 1960
SQ FT: 18,500
SALES (est): 5.8MM **Privately Held**
WEB: www.statejanitorial.com
SIC: 5087 Janitors' supplies

(G-2105)
STATE STREET INN
228 N State St (19901-3837)
PHONE.................................302 734-2294
Yvonne Hall, *Principal*
EMP: 7 **EST:** 2005
SALES (est): 308.2K **Privately Held**
SIC: 7011 Bed & breakfast inn

(G-2106)
STEADFAST INSURANCE COMPANY (DH)
2 Loockerman Plz Ste 202 (19901)
PHONE.................................847 605-6000
Martin Senn, *CEO*
Michael Foley, *Chairman*
Tom De Swaan, *Chairman*
David A Bowers, *Vice Pres*
Wayne Fisher, *Vice Pres*
EMP: 7
SALES: 8.4MM
SALES (corp-wide): 48.2B **Privately Held**
SIC: 6331 Automobile insurance
HQ: Zurich American Insurance Company
1299 Zurich Way
Schaumburg IL 60196
800 987-3373

Dover - Kent County (G-2107)   GEOGRAPHIC SECTION

(G-2107)
STEALTHORG LLC
8 The Grn Ste 8295 (19901-3618)
PHONE.................................302 724-6461
James Stroud, *Mng Member*
EMP: 2
SALES: 200K **Privately Held**
SIC: 7372 7389 Application computer software;

(G-2108)
STEPHEN F PENNY MD
1074 S State St (19901-6925)
PHONE.................................302 678-8100
Robert Varipapa, *President*
Judy Ridgeway, *Principal*
Stephen F Penny, *Med Doctor*
▼ **EMP:** 4
SALES (est): 98.5K **Privately Held**
SIC: 8011 Neurologist

(G-2109)
STORMBLADE INC
73 Greentree Dr 311 (19904-7646)
PHONE.................................302 206-1631
EMP: 6
SQ FT: 700
SALES (est): 346K **Privately Held**
SIC: 6531 Consulting Goverment Contracting

(G-2110)
STREET & ELLIS P A
426 S State St (19901-6724)
PHONE.................................302 735-8408
Gerald I Street, *President*
John I Ellis,
EMP: 9
SQ FT: 2,500
SALES (est): 947.8K **Privately Held**
WEB: www.streetellis.com
SIC: 8111 General practice law office; general practice attorney, lawyer

(G-2111)
SUDS BAR SOAP & ESSENTIALS LLC
Also Called: Suds and Company
31 W Loockerman St (19904-7350)
PHONE.................................302 674-1303
Kimberly Aigle,
Agnes Aigle,
EMP: 2 **EST:** 2013
SALES: 75K **Privately Held**
SIC: 2841 Soap & other detergents

(G-2112)
SUK-YOUNG CARR DDS
850 S State St Ste 2 (19901-4113)
PHONE.................................302 736-6631
Suk-Young Carr, *Owner*
EMP: 4
SALES (est): 61.5K **Privately Held**
SIC: 8021 Endodontist

(G-2113)
SUN PHARMACEUTICALS CORP
Also Called: Banana Boat Products
50 S Dupont Hwy (19901)
PHONE.................................302 678-6000
Max Recone, *President*
Glenn Forbes, *CFO*
John Mc Colgan, *Finance Dir*
William B Stammer, *Asst Sec*
◆ **EMP:** 15
SQ FT: 10,000
SALES (est): 2.7MM
SALES (corp-wide): 2.1B **Publicly Held**
WEB: www.playtex.com
SIC: 2844 Cosmetic preparations; suntan lotions & oils
HQ: Playtex Products, Llc
    6 Research Dr Ste 400
    Shelton CT 06484
    203 944-5500

(G-2114)
SUNNYFIELD CONTRACTORS INC
Also Called: Bartsch John C
150 Sunnyfield Ln (19904-1657)
PHONE.................................302 674-8610
John Bartsch, *President*
Jeffery Bartsch, *Vice Pres*
EMP: 11
SALES (est): 865.5K **Privately Held**
SIC: 1799 Building site preparation

(G-2115)
SUNSHINE GRAPHICS AND PRINTING
511 N West St (19904-2930)
PHONE.................................302 724-5127
EMP: 1
SALES (est): 52.8K **Privately Held**
SIC: 7336 2759 Graphic arts & related design; commercial printing

(G-2116)
SUNSHINE HOME DAYCARE
370 Mimosa Ave (19904-4839)
PHONE.................................302 674-2009
EMP: 5
SALES (est): 73.2K **Privately Held**
SIC: 8351 Group day care center

(G-2117)
SUPER EIGHT DOVER
348 N Dupont Hwy (19901-3935)
PHONE.................................302 734-5701
Chirayush Parikh, *Manager*
EMP: 7
SALES (est): 312.8K **Privately Held**
SIC: 7011 Hotels & motels

(G-2118)
SUPREME HAIR DESIGN
309 Northdown Dr (19904-9793)
PHONE.................................302 672-7255
EMP: 4 **EST:** 2015
SALES (est): 28.8K **Privately Held**
SIC: 7231 Beauty shops

(G-2119)
SURGICAL ASSOCIATES PA
Also Called: Eden Hill Medical Center
200 Banning St Ste 200 # 200 (19904-3487)
PHONE.................................302 346-4502
Tina Mitelmal, *Principal*
EMP: 19
SALES (est): 1.8MM **Privately Held**
SIC: 8011 Surgeon

(G-2120)
SUSSEX COUNTIAN
1196 S Little Creek Rd (19901-4727)
PHONE.................................302 856-0026
Adam Huber, *Principal*
EMP: 2
SALES (est): 62.9K **Privately Held**
SIC: 2711 Newspapers

(G-2121)
SUSSEX ORTHODONTICS
1004 S State St Ste 3 (19901-6910)
PHONE.................................302 644-4100
Jonathan Hall, *Principal*
EMP: 4
SALES (est): 123.6K **Privately Held**
SIC: 8021 Orthodontist

(G-2122)
SVEA REAL ESTATE GROUP LLC (PA)
1675 S State St Ste B (19901-5140)
PHONE.................................855 262-9665
Harry J Kuper,
EMP: 15
SALES (est): 970.6K **Privately Held**
SIC: 6799 Real estate investors, except property operators

(G-2123)
SWEAT SOCIAL LLC
8 The Grn Ste 7379 (19901-3618)
PHONE.................................504 510-1973
Rupa Mohan, *Mng Member*
EMP: 5
SALES (est): 124.8K **Privately Held**
SIC: 8742 7372 Hospital & health services consultant; application computer software

(G-2124)
SYSTMADE TECHNOLOGIES LLC
8 The Grn Ste 6233 (19901-3618)
PHONE.................................888 944-3546
Vibhu Kaushik,
EMP: 10

(G-2125)
T & J MURRAY WORLDWIDE SVCS
283 Persimmon Tree Ln (19901-1308)
P.O. Box 214 (19903-0214)
PHONE.................................302 736-1790
Nancy L Murray, *President*
Thomas Murray, *President*
John Murray, *Vice Pres*
▼ **EMP:** 10
SALES: 700K **Privately Held**
SIC: 5531 5013 3713 Automobile & truck equipment & parts; truck parts & accessories; truck bodies & parts

(G-2126)
T J LANE CONSTRUCTION INC
267 Fork Branch Rd (19904-1231)
PHONE.................................302 734-1099
Thomas Hammund, *Manager*
EMP: 5 **Privately Held**
SIC: 1521 New construction, single-family houses
PA: T J Lane Construction Inc
    711 Sharon Hill Rd
    Dover DE 19904

(G-2127)
T&T CLEANING LLC
2888 Fast Landing Rd (19901-3106)
PHONE.................................609 575-0458
Travis Williams,
EMP: 12
SALES (est): 208K **Privately Held**
SIC: 7699 Cleaning services

(G-2128)
T-MOBILE USA INC
Also Called: T-Mobile Store 9730
1141 N Dupont Hwy Ste 3 (19901-2024)
PHONE.................................302 736-1980
EMP: 6
SALES (corp-wide): 83.9B **Publicly Held**
SIC: 4812 Cellular telephone services
HQ: T-Mobile Usa, Inc.
    12920 Se 38th St
    Bellevue WA 98006
    425 378-4000

(G-2129)
TAPLY LLC
3500 S Dupont Hwy (19901-6041)
PHONE.................................650 275-2395
EMP: 2 **EST:** 2012
SALES (est): 100K **Privately Held**
SIC: 7372 Prepackaged Software Services

(G-2130)
TAQ INCORPORATED
874 Walker Rd Ste C (19904-2778)
PHONE.................................302 734-8300
Michael Barr, *President*
EMP: 5
SALES (est): 400.2K **Privately Held**
SIC: 8732 Business economic service

(G-2131)
TAYLOR WOODWORKS
34 Clearview Dr (19901-5713)
PHONE.................................302 745-2049
Jeff Taylor, *Principal*
EMP: 2
SALES (est): 252.9K **Privately Held**
SIC: 2434 Wood kitchen cabinets

(G-2132)
TAZELAAR ROOFING SERVICE INC
4869 S Dupont Hwy (19901-6430)
PHONE.................................302 697-2643
John J Tazelaar, *Owner*
Sharon Tazelaar, *Admin Sec*
EMP: 7
SALES: 450K **Privately Held**
SIC: 1761 Roofing contractor

(G-2133)
TDP WIRELESS INC
34 Salt Creek Dr (19901-2436)
PHONE.................................302 424-1900
Tajesh Patel, *Owner*
EMP: 12 **EST:** 2007
SALES (est): 1.2MM **Privately Held**
SIC: 4812 Cellular telephone services

(G-2134)
TEAL CONSTRUCTION INC
612 Mary St (19904-3024)
P.O. Box 779 (19903-0779)
PHONE.................................302 276-6034
Robert Edgell, *President*
Dale Kohout, *Superintendent*
Charles Reed III, *Project Mgr*
David Redick, *Materials Mgr*
EMP: 70
SQ FT: 1,200
SALES (est): 14.4MM **Privately Held**
WEB: www.tealconstruction.com
SIC: 1611 1623 Highway & street paving contractor; sewer line construction

(G-2135)
TECOT ELECTRIC SUPPLY CO
1251 College Park Dr (19904-8713)
PHONE.................................302 735-3300
Joe Eooth, *Manager*
EMP: 4
SALES (corp-wide): 220.5MM **Privately Held**
SIC: 5063 Electrical apparatus & equipment
HQ: Tecot Electric Supply Co (Inc)
    55 Lukens Dr
    New Castle DE
    302 429-9100

(G-2136)
TELAMON CORPORATION
195 Willis Rd (19901-4085)
PHONE.................................302 736-5933
Yolanda Evans, *Manager*
EMP: 40
SALES (corp-wide): 70.5MM **Privately Held**
SIC: 8351 Head start center, except in conjunction with school
PA: Telamon Corporation
    5560 Munford Rd Ste 201
    Raleigh NC 27612
    919 851-7611

(G-2137)
TELEMED HEALTH GROUP
8 The Grn Ste D (19901-3618)
PHONE.................................561 922-3953
Lester K Stockett, *Mng Member*
EMP: 8
SALES (est): 76K **Privately Held**
SIC: 8099 Health & allied services

(G-2138)
TENDER HEARTS
1339 S Governors Ave (19904-4803)
PHONE.................................302 674-2565
Linda Ohlig, *President*
EMP: 10
SALES (est): 161.2K **Privately Held**
SIC: 8351 Child day care services

(G-2139)
TERRY BRYAN
189 S Fairfield Dr (19901-5756)
PHONE.................................302 698-9901
Terry Bryan, *Principal*
EMP: 4
SALES (est): 122.9K **Privately Held**
SIC: 8021 Offices & clinics of dentists

(G-2140)
TESLA NOOTROPICS INC
8 The Grn Ste 5757 (19901-3618)
PHONE.................................514 718-2270
Angela Kahn, *CEO*
EMP: 2
SALES: 300K **Privately Held**
SIC: 2023 Dietary supplements, dairy & non-dairy based

(G-2141)
THERESA LITTLE MD
Also Called: Little Thresa P MD Fmly Mdcine
1001 S Bradford St Ste 5 (19904-4153)
PHONE.................................302 735-1616
Theresa Little, *Owner*
EMP: 9

▲ = Import ▼=Export
◆ =Import/Export

GEOGRAPHIC SECTION
Dover - Kent County (G-2172)

SALES (est): 159.2K **Privately Held**
SIC: 8011 General & family practice, physician/surgeon

(G-2142)
THINKRUPTIVE MEDIA INC
Also Called: Thinkrupter Magazine
8 The Grn Ste R (19901-3618)
PHONE..................310 779-4748
Munif Ali, *President*
EMP: 10
SALES: 100K **Privately Held**
SIC: 7371 7389 Computer software development & applications; subscription fulfillment services: magazine, newspaper, etc.

(G-2143)
THOMAS POSTLETHWAIT DDS
1592 Lochmeath Way (19901-6516)
PHONE..................302 674-8283
Thomas Postlethwait, *Owner*
EMP: 7
SALES (est): 263.8K **Privately Held**
SIC: 8021 Dentists' office

(G-2144)
THOMAS W MERCER DMD
Also Called: Mercer Dental Associates
77 Saulsbury Rd (19904-3444)
PHONE..................302 678-2942
Thomas W Mercer DMD, *Principal*
Tom Mercer, *Fmly & Gen Dent*
Adam Sydell, *Fmly & Gen Dent*
EMP: 6
SALES (est): 791.9K **Privately Held**
SIC: 8021 Dental surgeon

(G-2145)
THREADS N DENIMS
8 Senator Ave (19901-5243)
PHONE..................302 678-0642
Herbert Watkins, *Principal*
EMP: 1
SALES (est): 56.1K **Privately Held**
SIC: 2211 Denims

(G-2146)
THREATSTOP INC (PA)
615 S Dupont Hwy (19901-4517)
PHONE..................760 542-1550
Tom Byrnes, *CEO*
Tomas Byrnes, *CEO*
Boris Veksler, *COO*
Karen Byrnes, *Controller*
Dave Carlyon, *Administration*
EMP: 11
SALES (est): 100K **Privately Held**
SIC: 7379 Computer related maintenance services

(G-2147)
TIDEWATER UTILITIES INC
1100 S Little Creek Rd (19901-4727)
PHONE..................302 674-8056
Bruce O'Connor, *President*
Jeremy Kalmbacher, *Pastor*
Bruce Patrick, *Vice Pres*
Dennis Grimm, *Foreman/Supr*
Neil Gerardi, *Maint Spvr*
EMP: 100
SQ FT: 7,000
SALES (est): 20.3MM
SALES (corp-wide): 138MM **Publicly Held**
WEB: www.tuiwater.com
SIC: 4941 Water supply
PA: Middlesex Water Company
   485c Route 1 S Ste 400
   Iselin NJ 08830
   732 634-1500

(G-2148)
TIMBER HEART LEARNING CENTER
1339 S Governors Ave (19904-4803)
PHONE..................302 674-2565
Lindy Ohaig, *Owner*
EMP: 15
SALES (est): 459K **Privately Held**
SIC: 8351 Head start center, except in conjunction with school

(G-2149)
TITANIUM BLACK EXEC SLTONS LLC
850 New Burton Rd (19904-5785)
PHONE..................813 785-7842
EMP: 2
SALES (est): 90.8K **Privately Held**
SIC: 3356 Titanium

(G-2150)
TOM MILLER REMODELING
416 N State St (19901-3841)
PHONE..................302 674-1637
Tom Miller, *Owner*
EMP: 1
SALES (est): 51.7K **Privately Held**
SIC: 7372 Prepackaged software

(G-2151)
TONY ASHBURN INC
872 Walker Rd Ste A (19904-2700)
PHONE..................302 677-1940
Tony Ashburn, *President*
Theresa Ashburn, *Vice Pres*
Jackie McCann, *Accountant*
EMP: 7
SALES (est): 1.9MM **Privately Held**
WEB: www.ashburnhomes.net
SIC: 6552 Land subdividers & developers, residential

(G-2152)
TOOZE & EASTER MD PA
Also Called: Moyer, Robert A MD
720 S Queen St (19904-3500)
P.O. Box 1416 (19903-1416)
PHONE..................302 735-8700
J H Easter MD, *Principal*
EMP: 30
SALES (est): 2.6MM **Privately Held**
WEB: www.tooze.net
SIC: 8011 General & family practice, physician/surgeon; orthopedic physician

(G-2153)
TORBERT FUNERAL CHAPEL INC
Also Called: Capital Crematorium
61 S Bradford St (19904-7315)
PHONE..................302 734-3341
William Covell Torbert, *President*
EMP: 13
SQ FT: 1,200
SALES (est): 1MM **Privately Held**
SIC: 7261 Funeral home

(G-2154)
TOWLES ELECTRIC INC
621 W Div St Dover Dover (19904)
P.O. Box 1012 (19903-1012)
PHONE..................302 674-4985
Nick Sebastian, *President*
EMP: 5 EST: 1978
SALES (est): 890.1K **Privately Held**
WEB: www.towleselectric.com
SIC: 1731 General electrical contractor

(G-2155)
TOWNSEND BROS INC
21 Emerson Dr (19901-5819)
PHONE..................302 674-0100
Jeffrey S Townsend Sr, *President*
S T Ebe, *Vice Pres*
Ebe S Townsend Jr, *Vice Pres*
Amy Mosley, *Manager*
Wanda Townsend, *Admin Sec*
EMP: 57
SQ FT: 32,000
SALES (est): 19.3MM **Privately Held**
WEB: www.townsendchevy.com
SIC: 5511 5013 Automobiles, new & used; pickups, new & used; automotive supplies & parts

(G-2156)
TOXTRAP INC
12 S Springview Dr (19901-5550)
P.O. Box 241, Magnolia (19962-0241)
PHONE..................302 698-1400
Donald R Wilkinson, *President*
Carol Wilkinson, *Corp Secy*
J Robert Zettle, *Vice Pres*
EMP: 5
SQ FT: 1,300
SALES (est): 225K **Privately Held**
WEB: www.toxtrap.com
SIC: 3829 5049 Breathalyzers; law enforcement equipment & supplies

(G-2157)
TPP ACQUISITION INC
1365 N Dupont Hwy # 4012 (19901-8710)
PHONE..................302 674-4805
Renee McPoyle, *Manager*
EMP: 11
SALES (corp-wide): 168.6MM **Privately Held**
WEB: www.picturepeople.com
SIC: 7221 Photographer, still or video
PA: Tpp Acquisition Inc
   1155 Kas Dr Ste 180
   Richardson TX 75081

(G-2158)
TRADER FUNERAL HOME INC
12 Lotus St (19901-4426)
PHONE..................302 734-4620
Thomas R Trader, *President*
Ross Trader, *Corp Secy*
EMP: 4
SQ FT: 2,000
SALES (est): 342.8K **Privately Held**
WEB: www.traderfh.com
SIC: 7261 Funeral home

(G-2159)
TRANSCORE LP
26 Old Rudnick Ln (19901-4912)
PHONE..................302 677-7262
EMP: 20
SALES (corp-wide): 5.1B **Publicly Held**
WEB: www.transcore.com
SIC: 1731 Electrical work
HQ: Transcore, Lp
   150 4th Ave N Ste 1200
   Nashville TN 37219
   615 988-8962

(G-2160)
TRANSSTATE JET SERVICE INC
139 Davis Cir (19904-3466)
PHONE..................302 346-3102
Gerald Franklin, *Principal*
EMP: 2
SALES (est): 250K **Privately Held**
SIC: 2911 Jet fuels

(G-2161)
TRAPS PLUMBING HEATING A/C
Also Called: Honeywell Authorized Dealer
1851 S Dupont Hwy (19901-5128)
PHONE..................302 677-1775
Trap Tracksem, *Owner*
EMP: 5
SALES (est): 528.4K **Privately Held**
SIC: 1711 Heating & air conditioning contractors

(G-2162)
TRAUMA FILM PRODUCTION PR LLC
8 The Grn Ste A (19901-3618)
PHONE..................623 582-2287
EMP: 8
SALES (est): 63K **Privately Held**
SIC: 7822 Motion picture & tape distribution

(G-2163)
TREVOR ENNIS DC
200 Banning St (19904-3485)
PHONE..................302 730-8848
Trevor Ennis, *Med Doctor*
EMP: 8
SALES (est): 77.4K **Privately Held**
SIC: 8041 Offices & clinics of chiropractors

(G-2164)
TROUTMAN MACHINE COMPANY INC
Also Called: A M T General Contracting
1175 S Governors Ave (19904-6903)
PHONE..................302 674-3540
Todd Troutman, *President*
EMP: 4
SALES (est): 547.6K **Privately Held**
SIC: 3599 Machine shop, jobbing & repair

(G-2165)
TUDOR ELECTRIC INC
801 Otis Dr (19901-4647)
PHONE..................302 736-1444
Robert H Tudor, *President*
Susan P Tudor, *Treasurer*
Patty Brough, *Admin Sec*
EMP: 27 EST: 1952
SQ FT: 8,400
SALES (est): 4.1MM **Privately Held**
SIC: 1731 General electrical contractor

(G-2166)
TUDOR ENTERPRISES L L C
1031 Fowler Ct (19901-4638)
PHONE..................302 736-8255
Robert H Tudor,
EMP: 5
SALES (est): 614.1K **Privately Held**
SIC: 6512 Commercial & industrial building operation

(G-2167)
TWIN HEARTS MANAGEMENT LLC
200 Banning St Ste 340 (19904-3490)
PHONE..................302 777-5700
Anthony Alfieri, *Principal*
EMP: 5
SALES (est): 368.2K **Privately Held**
SIC: 8741 Management services

(G-2168)
TY LIN INTERNATIONAL GROUP
222 S Dupont Hwy (19901-3797)
PHONE..................302 883-3662
William Detwiler, *President*
EMP: 5
SALES (corp-wide): 160MM **Privately Held**
SIC: 8711 Consulting engineer
PA: T.Y.Lin International Group, Ltd.
   345 California St Fl 23
   San Francisco CA 94104
   415 291-3700

(G-2169)
U AND I BUILDERS INC
1633 Sorghum Mill Rd (19901-6810)
PHONE..................302 697-1645
Usman Sandhu, *President*
EMP: 6 EST: 2008
SALES (est): 891.2K **Privately Held**
SIC: 1521 New construction, single-family houses

(G-2170)
U TAN INC
650 S Bay Rd Ste 11 (19901-4636)
PHONE..................302 674-8040
Lillian Kingsford, *President*
Aaron Kingsford, *Vice Pres*
EMP: 6
SQ FT: 1,400
SALES (est): 198.6K **Privately Held**
SIC: 7299 Tanning salon

(G-2171)
UBLERB
9 E Loockerman St Ste 215 (19901-7347)
PHONE..................773 569-9686
Gerard Hartman, *CEO*
Keith Harris, *CFO*
EMP: 6
SQ FT: 500
SALES (est): 185.6K **Privately Held**
SIC: 7379

(G-2172)
UDR INC
Also Called: Cedar Chase Apartments
1700 N Dupont Hwy Ste 1 (19901-7812)
PHONE..................302 674-8887
Tracey Lund, *Branch Mgr*
EMP: 7
SALES (corp-wide): 1B **Publicly Held**
WEB: www.udrt.com
SIC: 6513 Apartment building operators
PA: Udr, Inc.
   1745 Shea Center Dr # 200
   Highlands Ranch CO 80129
   720 283-6120

Dover - Kent County (G-2173)

(G-2173)
UMIYA INC
Also Called: Dover Inn
428 N Dupont Hwy (19901-3906)
PHONE.................302 674-4011
Ram Patel, *President*
EMP: 6
SALES (est): 361.3K **Privately Held**
SIC: 7011 Motels

(G-2174)
UNADORI LLC
8 The Grn Ste A (19901-3618)
PHONE.................917 539-2128
Lyn Dee,
EMP: 1
SALES (est): 32.7K **Privately Held**
SIC: 7372 Application computer software

(G-2175)
UNCORKED CANVAS PARTIES
125 W Loockerman St (19904-7325)
PHONE.................302 724-7625
EMP: 1
SALES (est): 51.2K **Privately Held**
SIC: 2211 Canvas

(G-2176)
UNFOLD CREATIVE LLC (PA)
9 E Loockerman St Ste 311 (19901-8305)
PHONE.................509 850-1337
Alfonso Cobo, *CEO*
EMP: 2 EST: 2018
SALES: 500K **Privately Held**
SIC: 7372 Application computer software

(G-2177)
UNIKIE INC
615 S Dupont Hwy (19901-4517)
PHONE.................408 839-1920
Seppo Kolari, *Ch of Bd*
EMP: 10 EST: 2015
SALES (est): 470K **Privately Held**
SIC: 7371 7389 Software programming applications;

(G-2178)
UNIQUE MASSAGE THERAPY
124 Lynnbroom Ln (19904-1463)
PHONE.................302 359-5982
Nnenna Amadi, *Principal*
EMP: 5 EST: 2015
SALES (est): 97.6K **Privately Held**
SIC: 8093 Rehabilitation center, outpatient treatment

(G-2179)
UNISEX PALACE
1365 N Dupont Hwy # 2046 (19901-8720)
PHONE.................302 674-0950
Michael Maddalena, *Manager*
EMP: 20
SALES (corp-wide): 638.1K **Privately Held**
SIC: 7231 Beauty shops
PA: Unisex Palace
75 W Route 59 Ste 2024
Nanuet NY 10954
845 623-4327

(G-2180)
UNITED ELECTRIC SUPPLY CO INC
551 S Dupont Hwy (19901-4515)
PHONE.................302 674-8351
Mike Caloway, *Branch Mgr*
EMP: 15
SALES (corp-wide): 221.3MM **Privately Held**
WEB: www.unitedelectric.com
SIC: 5063 Electrical supplies
PA: United Electric Supply Company, Inc.
10 Bellecor Dr
New Castle DE 19720
800 322-3174

(G-2181)
UPPERCUT INC
Also Called: Upper Cut The
119 S Dupont Hwy (19901-7432)
PHONE.................302 736-1661
Carol Brennan, *President*
EMP: 17

SALES (est): 529.8K **Privately Held**
WEB: www.uppercut.com
SIC: 7231 Unisex hair salons

(G-2182)
UROLOGY ASSOCIATES DOVER PA
200 Banning St Ste 250 (19904-3492)
PHONE.................302 674-1728
J Henry Kim, *President*
Dr Jason Walther, *Treasurer*
EMP: 30 EST: 1963
SQ FT: 3,000
SALES: 5MM **Privately Held**
WEB: www.urologyassociatesofdover.com
SIC: 8011 Urologist

(G-2183)
US DEPT OF THE AIR FORCE
Also Called: 436th Medical Group
300 Tuskegee Blvd 1b22 (19902-5003)
PHONE.................302 677-2525
Timothy Tendergrass, *Manager*
EMP: 300 **Publicly Held**
WEB: www.af.mil
SIC: 8093 9711 Specialty outpatient clinics; Air Force
HQ: United States Department Of The Air Force
1000 Air Force Pentagon
Washington DC 20330

(G-2184)
UZIN UTZ MANUFACTURING N AMER
200 Garrison Oak Dr (19901-3365)
PHONE.................336 456-4624
Phillip Utz, *Manager*
EMP: 4 EST: 2015
SALES (est): 330.7K **Privately Held**
SIC: 3999 Manufacturing industries

(G-2185)
UZUAKOLI DEV & CULTURAL ASSN
2319 S Dupont Hwy (19901-5514)
PHONE.................302 465-3266
Ihuoma Chuks, *Vice Pres*
EMP: 6 **Privately Held**
SIC: 8399 Community development groups
PA: Uzuakoli Development And Cultural Association
10311 Adams St
Omaha NE 68127

(G-2186)
VALLEY LANDSCAPING AND CON INC
8 The Grn (19901-3618)
PHONE.................302 922-5020
Paul Kantner, *President*
EMP: 5 EST: 2016
SALES (est): 207.9K **Privately Held**
SIC: 3271 Blocks, concrete: landscape or retaining wall

(G-2187)
VANGUARD CONSTRUCTION INC
2089 S Dupont Hwy (19901-5566)
PHONE.................302 697-9187
William L Stayton Jr, *President*
EMP: 7
SQ FT: 1,000
SALES (est): 787.7K **Privately Held**
SIC: 1542 1521 Commercial & office building, new construction; new construction, single-family houses

(G-2188)
VCG LLC
9 E Loockerman St 3a-522 (19901-8306)
PHONE.................302 336-8151
Frank Johnson, *Mng Member*
EMP: 5 EST: 2013
SQ FT: 600
SALES (est): 212.9K **Privately Held**
SIC: 8742 Construction project management consultant; financial consultant; management information systems consultant

(G-2189)
VENDING SOLUTIONS LLC
1624 N Little Creek Rd (19901-4706)
PHONE.................302 674-2222
Schuyler Sills,
EMP: 3
SALES (est): 94.4K **Privately Held**
SIC: 5999 5046 5087 5962 Alarm & safety equipment stores; vending machines, coin-operated; vending machines & supplies; candy & snack food vending machines; cold drinks vending machines; automatic vending machines

(G-2190)
VERISOFT INC
48 Kings Hwy (19901-3817)
PHONE.................602 908-7151
Robert Almoney, *President*
Jeanette Almoney, *Admin Sec*
EMP: 2
SALES: 150K **Privately Held**
SIC: 3589 Water treatment equipment, industrial

(G-2191)
VICKS COMMERCIAL CLG & MAINT
378 Mannering Dr (19901-5407)
P.O. Box 1433 (19903-1433)
PHONE.................302 697-9591
Leah Dickerson, *Principal*
EMP: 7
SALES (est): 157K **Privately Held**
SIC: 7349 Building maintenance services

(G-2192)
VICTORIAN APARTMENTS LLC
123 W Loockerman St (19904-7325)
PHONE.................302 678-0968
EMP: 4
SALES (est): 258.7K **Privately Held**
SIC: 6513 Apartment Operators

(G-2193)
VILLAGE GRAPHICS LLC
69 Peyton St # 3 (19901-5296)
PHONE.................302 697-9288
Ken Sweeney, *Owner*
EMP: 4
SQ FT: 1,500
SALES (est): 385.1K **Privately Held**
SIC: 2759 Commercial printing

(G-2194)
VINSYS CORPORATION
160 Greentree Dr Ste 101 (19904-7620)
PHONE.................732 983-4150
Vikrant Patil, *CEO*
EMP: 80
SALES (est): 928K **Privately Held**
SIC: 7389

(G-2195)
VISIONARY ENERGY SYSTEMS INC
325 Alder Rd (19904-4819)
PHONE.................410 739-4342
Steven R Rock, *President*
EMP: 3
SALES (est): 158.8K **Privately Held**
SIC: 3499 Fabricated metal products

(G-2196)
VISIONQUEST EYE CARE CENTER
820 Walker Rd (19904-2727)
PHONE.................302 678-3545
Philip Gross, *Principal*
Robin Willey, *Payroll Mgr*
EMP: 45
SALES (est): 1.7MM **Privately Held**
WEB: www.vqeyecare.com
SIC: 8011 General & family practice, physician/surgeon

(G-2197)
VISIONQUEST NONPROFIT CORP
1001 S Bradford St Ste 1 (19904-4153)
PHONE.................302 735-1666
Marlene Devonshire, *Manager*
EMP: 30 **Privately Held**
WEB: www.vq.com

SIC: 8361 Residential care
PA: Visionquest Nonprofit Corporation
600 N Swan St
Tucson AZ 85711

(G-2198)
VOITLEX CORP
8 The Grn Ste A (19901-3618)
PHONE.................302 288-0670
Aliaksandr Vaitovich, *Principal*
EMP: 10 EST: 2017
SALES (est): 180.6K **Privately Held**
SIC: 7389 Business services

(G-2199)
VOSHELL BROS WELDING INC
Also Called: Voshell Brothers
1769 Kenton Rd (19904-1350)
PHONE.................302 674-1414
Gale Voshell, *President*
Diana Voshell, *Corp Secy*
EMP: 49 EST: 1957
SQ FT: 10,000
SALES (est): 6.5MM **Privately Held**
SIC: 1623 1611 Oil & gas pipeline construction; underground utilities contractor; highway & street paving contractor

(G-2200)
VSHIELD SOFTWARE CORP
3500 S Dupont Hwy (19901-6041)
PHONE.................302 531-0855
Marino Kriheli, *Principal*
EMP: 2
SALES (est): 110K **Privately Held**
SIC: 7372 Prepackaged software

(G-2201)
VTMS LLC
Also Called: Mymortgageready.com
3 Mineral Ct (19904-3704)
PHONE.................302 264-9094
Kevin Phillipson,
EMP: 6
SALES (est): 360K **Privately Held**
WEB: www.mymortgageready.com
SIC: 8748 8742 7389 Business consulting; marketing consulting services;

(G-2202)
W H THOMAS DDS
1981 S State St (19901-5811)
PHONE.................302 697-1152
W H Thomas, *Owner*
EMP: 6
SALES (est): 242.5K **Privately Held**
SIC: 8021 Dentists' office

(G-2203)
WALNUT GROVE CABINETS LLC
308 Rose Valley School Rd (19904-5504)
PHONE.................302 678-2694
EMP: 2
SALES (est): 215.5K **Privately Held**
SIC: 2434 Wood kitchen cabinets

(G-2204)
WALO US HOLDINGS INC
1675 S State St Ste B (19901-5140)
PHONE.................212 691-4537
Walo Bertschinger, *President*
Jerry Reece, *COO*
Davide Di Falco, *Vice Pres*
David Wilson, *Vice Pres*
Michel Bsiger, *Director*
EMP: 8
SALES (est): 289.2K **Privately Held**
SIC: 1611 Highway & street construction

(G-2205)
WALTER L FOX POST 2 INC
835 S Bay Rd (19901-4632)
PHONE.................302 674-1741
Danny Seeman, *President*
Michael Cohill, *Vice Pres*
EMP: 35
SALES (est): 130.8K **Privately Held**
SIC: 8641 Veterans' organization

(G-2206)
WARREN W SEAVER
Also Called: S & S Trucking
3619 Bayside Dr (19901-7175)
PHONE.................302 674-8969
Warren W Seaver, *Owner*
EMP: 1

GEOGRAPHIC SECTION

Dover - Kent County (G-2238)

SALES: 120K **Privately Held**
SIC: 4213 3999 Contract haulers; honeycomb foundations (beekeepers' supplies)

(G-2207)
WBOC INC
Also Called: Wboc-TV
1839 S Dupont Hwy (19901-5128)
PHONE.....................302 734-9262
William Kenton, *General Mgr*
EMP: 12
SALES (corp-wide): 30MM **Privately Held**
WEB: www.wboc.com
SIC: 4833 8732 Television broadcasting stations; commercial nonphysical research
HQ: Wboc, Inc.
  1729 N Salisbury Blvd
  Salisbury MD 21801
  410 749-1111

(G-2208)
WE DESERVE IT SHS FOR KIDS INC
363 Frear Dr (19901-6612)
PHONE.....................302 521-7255
Jackie Yates, *CEO*
EMP: 5
SALES (est): 53.1K **Privately Held**
SIC: 8322 Children's aid society

(G-2209)
WEBER GALLAGHER SIMPSON (PA)
19 S State St Ste 102 (19901-7318)
PHONE.....................302 346-6377
Mary Sherlock, *Manager*
EMP: 4
SALES (est): 273.5K **Privately Held**
SIC: 8111 General practice attorney, lawyer

(G-2210)
WELCOME ABOARD TRAVEL LTD
57 Saulsbury Rd Ste C (19904-3472)
PHONE.....................302 678-9480
Shelley Brocklehurst, *President*
EMP: 5
SALES (est): 976.6K **Privately Held**
WEB: www.welcomeaboard.net
SIC: 4724 Tourist agency arranging transport, lodging & car rental

(G-2211)
WELLS FARGO BANK NATIONAL ASSN
101 W Loockerman St (19904-7328)
PHONE.....................302 736-2910
EMP: 13
SALES (corp-wide): 94.1B **Publicly Held**
SIC: 6021 National Commercial Bank
HQ: Wells Fargo Bank, National Association
  420 Montgomery St
  San Francisco CA 57104
  415 396-7392

(G-2212)
WELLS FARGO BANK NATIONAL ASSN
Also Called: Delaware Trust 208
100 N Du Pont Hwy (19901)
PHONE.....................302 736-2920
Mary Schreiber, *Branch Mgr*
EMP: 8
SALES (corp-wide): 101B **Publicly Held**
SIC: 6021 National commercial banks
HQ: Wells Fargo Bank, National Association
  101 N Phillips Ave
  Sioux Falls SD 57104
  605 575-6900

(G-2213)
WESLEY PLAY CARE CENTER
Also Called: Wesley Preschool
209 S State St (19901-6727)
PHONE.....................302 678-8987
Brian Belcher, *Superintendent*
Wanda Anderson, *Dean*
Joseph Bottiglieri, *COO*
Barbara Bayers, *Vice Pres*
Kenny Scharnick, *Opers Staff*
EMP: 12
SALES (est): 243K **Privately Held**
SIC: 8351 Child day care services

(G-2214)
WEST DOVER BUTCHER SHOP INC
3997 Hazlettville Rd (19904-5615)
PHONE.....................302 734-5447
Jeffrey Dean Haass, *Owner*
▲ EMP: 6
SALES (est): 2.7MM **Privately Held**
SIC: 5147 5421 Meats, fresh; meat markets, including freezer provisioners

(G-2215)
WEST MINSTER MANAGEMENT
Also Called: Mapleton Square Apartments
177 Willis Rd (19901-4082)
PHONE.....................302 678-4515
Lynn Beulah, *Branch Mgr*
EMP: 4
SALES (corp-wide): 1.2MM **Privately Held**
SIC: 6513 Apartment building operators
PA: West Minster Management
  4345 Us Highway 9
  Freehold NJ

(G-2216)
WESTMINSTER VILLAGE DOVER
181 Westminster Dr (19904-8730)
PHONE.....................302 744-3527
Karen Kerstetter, *Mktg Dir*
Mary A Poling, *Exec Dir*
EMP: 9
SALES (est): 329.8K **Privately Held**
SIC: 8361 Home for the aged

(G-2217)
WESTSIDE FAMILY HEALTHCARE INC
1020 Forrest Ave (19904-2799)
PHONE.....................302 678-4622
Christopher Fraser, *Principal*
Shannon Bartow, *Manager*
EMP: 20
SALES (corp-wide): 22.8MM **Privately Held**
SIC: 8021 Offices & clinics of dentists
PA: Westside Family Healthcare, Inc.
  300 Water St Ste 200
  Wilmington DE 19801
  302 656-8292

(G-2218)
WHAT IF Y NOT EVERYTHING INC
8 The Grn Ste A (19901-3618)
PHONE.....................732 898-0241
Shakeem Durden, *Principal*
EMP: 1
SALES: 100K **Privately Held**
SIC: 3999 Manufacturing industries

(G-2219)
WHATCOAT CHRISTIAN PRESCHOOL
16 Main St (19901)
PHONE.....................302 698-2108
Leanne Jackson, *Director*
Lee Anne Jackson, *Director*
EMP: 7 EST: 2007
SALES (est): 105.3K **Privately Held**
SIC: 8351 Preschool center

(G-2220)
WHATCOAT SOCIAL SERVICE AGENCY
Also Called: Ruth N Dorsey Relief Shelter
381 College Rd (19904-2236)
PHONE.....................302 734-0319
Ruth Pugh, *Director*
EMP: 16
SALES (est): 355.8K **Privately Held**
SIC: 8322 Social service center; emergency shelters

(G-2221)
WHATCOAT VILLAGE ASSOC LLC
992 Whatcoat Dr Apt 12 (19904-2755)
P.O. Box 994, Marlton NJ (08053-0994)
PHONE.....................856 596-0500
John J O'Donnell, *President*
Michael J Levitt, *Vice Pres*
EMP: 10
SQ FT: 69,000
SALES (est): 168.6K **Privately Held**
SIC: 6513 Apartment building operators

(G-2222)
WHEN POETS DREAM INC
1679 S Dupont Hwy Ste 100 (19901-5164)
PHONE.....................818 738-6954
Sarah Evans, *Treasurer*
EMP: 1
SALES (est): 38.3K **Privately Held**
SIC: 2731 7389 Book publishing;

(G-2223)
WHISPERING MEADOWS LLC
4110b Connecticut Ln (19901-6337)
PHONE.....................302 698-1073
Michael Hunt,
EMP: 8
SQ FT: 950
SALES (est): 499.3K
SALES (corp-wide): 581.2MM **Privately Held**
SIC: 8741 Management services
HQ: Hunt Elp, Ltd
  4401 N Mesa St
  El Paso TX 79902
  915 298-0474

(G-2224)
WHITE OAK HEAD START
195 Willis Rd (19901-4085)
PHONE.....................302 736-5933
EMP: 5 EST: 2010
SALES (est): 78.5K **Privately Held**
SIC: 8351 Head start center, except in conjunction with school

(G-2225)
WILD MEADOWS HOMES
529 Weaver Dr (19901-1377)
PHONE.....................302 730-4700
Harry Miller, *Owner*
EMP: 100
SALES (est): 2.4MM **Privately Held**
WEB: www.wildmeadowshomes.com
SIC: 6514 Residential building, four or fewer units: operation

(G-2226)
WILKISONS MARKING SERVICE INC
22 Stevens St (19901-5533)
PHONE.....................302 697-3669
Robert Wilkison, *President*
Patricia Faye Adcox, *Vice Pres*
EMP: 5
SQ FT: 3,500
SALES: 500K **Privately Held**
SIC: 1721 Residential painting; exterior commercial painting contractor; pavement marking contractor

(G-2227)
WILLIAM R KNOTTS & SON INC
4786 Forrest Ave (19904-5225)
PHONE.....................302 674-3496
William R Knotts, *President*
Edward Knotts, *Admin Sec*
EMP: 10
SALES (est): 1.1MM **Privately Held**
SIC: 4213 Refrigerated products transport

(G-2228)
WILLIES AUTO DETAIL SERVICE
17 Weston Dr (19904-2713)
PHONE.....................302 734-1010
Willie Mills, *Owner*
EMP: 5
SALES (est): 120.6K **Privately Held**
SIC: 7542 Carwashes

(G-2229)
WILLIS GROUP LLC
4 The Grn (19901-3617)
PHONE.....................302 632-9898
Lincoln Willis, *CEO*
EMP: 5 EST: 2016
SALES (est): 166.6K **Privately Held**
SIC: 8743 Lobbyist

(G-2230)
WILMINGTON SAVINGS FUND SOC
1486 Forrest Ave (19904-3380)
PHONE.....................302 677-1891
Diane Simone, *Manager*
EMP: 6
SALES (corp-wide): 455.5MM **Publicly Held**
SIC: 6029 Commercial banks
HQ: Wilmington Savings Fund Society
  500 Delaware Ave Ste 500 # 500
  Wilmington DE 19801
  302 792-6000

(G-2231)
WINDHAM ENTERPRISES INC
Also Called: Windham Travel
435 S Dupont Hwy (19901-4513)
PHONE.....................302 678-5777
Troy Windham, *President*
EMP: 4
SALES (est): 550.2K **Privately Held**
SIC: 4724 Travel agencies

(G-2232)
WINDHAM TRAVEL INC
435 S Dupont Hwy (19901-4513)
PHONE.....................302 678-5777
Troy Windham, *CEO*
EMP: 4
SALES (est): 713.6K **Privately Held**
WEB: www.windhamtravel.com
SIC: 4724 Tourist agency arranging transport, lodging & car rental

(G-2233)
WINDSWEPT ENTERPRISES
Also Called: Windswept Enterprising
251 N Dupont Hwy (19901-7539)
PHONE.....................302 678-0805
William McPoyle, *Owner*
EMP: 7
SALES: 1MM **Privately Held**
SIC: 7334 Blueprinting service

(G-2234)
WINDY INC
8 The Grn Ste A (19901-3618)
PHONE.....................224 707-0442
EMP: 10
SALES (est): 180.6K **Privately Held**
SIC: 7389 Financial services

(G-2235)
WOLF CREEK SURGEONS PA
103 Wolf Creek Blvd Ste 1 (19901-4967)
PHONE.....................302 678-3627
Wendy Newell, *Principal*
Rahul Singh, *Med Doctor*
EMP: 10
SALES (est): 720.1K **Privately Held**
SIC: 8011 Surgeon

(G-2236)
WOODS HOLE GROUP INC
301 Cassidy Dr Ste D (19901-4973)
PHONE.....................302 222-6720
Stephen O'Malley, *Manager*
EMP: 5
SALES (corp-wide): 4.2MM **Privately Held**
SIC: 8748 Environmental consultant
HQ: The Woods Hole Group Inc
  107 Waterhouse Rd
  Bourne MA 02532
  301 925-4411

(G-2237)
WORKPLACE REBELS LLC
310 Alder Rd (19904-4820)
PHONE.....................917 771-8286
Nicholas Terzi, *Co-Owner*
EMP: 4
SALES (est): 216.7K **Privately Held**
SIC: 5092 7371 Video games; computer software development & applications

(G-2238)
WORKWEEK INC
160 Greentree Dr Ste 101 (19904-7620)
PHONE.....................423 708-4565
Travis Dunn, *CEO*
EMP: 5

Dover - Kent County (G-2239)

SALES: 50K **Privately Held**
SIC: 7371 Computer software development & applications

(G-2239)
WORLD TRANSMISSIONS INC
2860 N Dupont Hwy (19901-8783)
PHONE..........................302 735-5535
Tom Monforte, *President*
Larry Novellino, *Treasurer*
EMP: 5
SALES (est): 340K **Privately Held**
SIC: 7537 Automotive transmission repair shops

(G-2240)
WUJI INC
8 The Grn Ste A (19901-3618)
PHONE..........................815 274-6777
Stephen M Cutter, *CEO*
Brenden Dougherty, *COO*
EMP: 5
SALES (est): 104.7K **Privately Held**
SIC: 7389

(G-2241)
WUTOPIA GROUP US LTD
Also Called: Wutopia Comics
8 The Grn Ste 501 (19901-3618)
PHONE..........................302 488-0248
Jingping Lai, *CEO*
EMP: 11
SALES: 400K **Privately Held**
SIC: 2721 7371 Comic books: publishing & printing; computer software development & applications

(G-2242)
XCUTIVESCOM INC
3500 S Dupont Hwy (19901-6041)
PHONE..........................888 245-9996
EMP: 9
SALES (corp-wide): 746K **Privately Held**
SIC: 8742 General management consultant
PA: Xcutives.Com Inc.
 1510 Oakridge Ct
 Decatur GA 30033
 888 245-9996

(G-2243)
XYNOMIC PHARMACEUTICALS INC
3500 S Dupont Hwy (19901-6041)
PHONE..........................650 430-7510
Mark Xu, *President*
Yong Cui, *Vice Pres*
Wentao Wu, *CFO*
EMP: 12
SALES (est): 898.3K **Privately Held**
SIC: 5122 Pharmaceuticals

(G-2244)
YESLLAMA LLC
8 The Grn Ste A (19901-3618)
PHONE..........................714 270-8731
Minh Reigen, *CEO*
EMP: 3 EST: 2016
SALES (est): 106.7K **Privately Held**
SIC: 2741

(G-2245)
YIELD NEXUS LLC
1679 S Dupont Hwy Ste 100 (19901-5164)
PHONE..........................308 380-3788
Omer Latif, *CEO*
Loren Wilson, *President*
EMP: 10
SALES (est): 237.3K **Privately Held**
SIC: 7313 Electronic media advertising representatives

(G-2246)
YOUNG & MCNELIS
300 S State St (19901-6730)
PHONE..........................302 674-8822
Jeff Young, *Partner*
Brian McNelis, *Partner*
EMP: 7
SALES (est): 699.4K **Privately Held**
SIC: 8111 General practice law office

(G-2247)
YOUNG AND MALMBERG PA
Also Called: Malmberg Firm, The
30 The Grn (19901-3612)
PHONE..........................302 672-5600
Kenneth Young, *Partner*
Constantine F Malmberg III, *Partner*
Alice W Stark,
EMP: 10 EST: 1996
SALES (est): 1.2MM **Privately Held**
WEB: www.youngmalmberg.com
SIC: 8111 General practice attorney, lawyer

(G-2248)
YOUNGS STUDIO OF PHOTOGRAPHY
4 Carolee Dr (19901-5118)
PHONE..........................302 736-2661
Ross E Young, *Owner*
EMP: 4 EST: 1953
SALES (est): 160.8K **Privately Held**
SIC: 7221 Photographer, still or video

(G-2249)
YOUSHOP INC
3500 S Dupont Hwy (19901-6041)
PHONE..........................302 526-0521
Ke Wang, *CEO*
EMP: 20 EST: 2014
SALES (est): 473.3K **Privately Held**
SIC: 7371 Computer software development & applications

(G-2250)
YPH CONSULTANTS LLC
Also Called: Your Personal Health Center
700 Otis Dr (19901-4649)
PHONE..........................302 674-4766
EMP: 7
SQ FT: 9,999
SALES (est): 600K **Privately Held**
SIC: 8748 Business Consulting Services

(G-2251)
YVONNE HALL INC
Also Called: Yvonne Hall Realty
1671 S State St (19901-5148)
PHONE..........................302 677-1300
Yvonne Hall, *CEO*
EMP: 5
SALES (est): 260K **Privately Held**
SIC: 6531 Real estate brokers & agents

(G-2252)
ZIMPLE INC
1679 S Dupont Hwy Ste 10 (19901-5101)
P.O. Box 11500, Bainbridge Island WA (98110-5500)
PHONE..........................877 494-6753
Steven Rabago, *CEO*
Scott McGarrigle, *CTO*
EMP: 3
SQ FT: 1,500
SALES (est): 164.5K **Privately Held**
SIC: 7372 Business oriented computer software

(G-2253)
ZOBER CONTRACTING SERVICES INC
155 Old Mill Rd (19901-6255)
PHONE..........................302 270-3078
Rosalie A Zober, *President*
EMP: 5
SALES: 1.1MM **Privately Held**
SIC: 1623 Water, sewer & utility lines

(G-2254)
ZONE LASER TAG INC
419 Webbs Ln (19904-5439)
PHONE..........................302 730-8888
Adnrew L Jiranek, *Administration*
EMP: 13
SALES (est): 560.2K **Privately Held**
SIC: 7929 Entertainment service

(G-2255)
ZONE SYSTEMS INC
419 Webbs Ln (19904-5439)
PHONE..........................302 730-8888
Kate Holmes, *President*
Erik Guthrie, *Vice Pres*
Pat Holmes, *Vice Pres*
Simon Willetts, *Vice Pres*

Jeremy Gaddy, *Opers Staff*
▲ EMP: 11
SQ FT: 5,000
SALES (est): 2MM
SALES (corp-wide): 220.8K **Privately Held**
SIC: 3944 Electronic game machines, except coin-operated
HQ: P & C Micros Pty. Ltd.
 12-14 Ricketts Rd
 Mount Waverley VIC 3149

(G-2256)
ZUHATREND LLC
207 W Loockerman St (19904-3247)
PHONE..........................302 883-2656
Hassan Azhar,
EMP: 2 EST: 2009
SALES (est): 293.8K **Privately Held**
SIC: 2311 Tuxedos: made from purchased materials

Ellendale
Sussex County

(G-2257)
ARTISTS AT WORK INC
20879 Hummingbird Rd (19941-2545)
PHONE..........................302 424-4427
Kimberly Donald, *Principal*
EMP: 1
SALES (est): 83.3K **Privately Held**
SIC: 3952 Artists' equipment

(G-2258)
BRIGGS SERVICES LLC
14546 S Old State Rd (19941-3340)
PHONE..........................302 569-5230
EMP: 5 EST: 2014
SALES (est): 186.8K **Privately Held**
SIC: 7349 Janitorial service, contract basis

(G-2259)
DELMARVA CLERGY UNITED INC
13726 S Old State Rd (19941-3330)
PHONE..........................302 422-2350
Bhisop M Foster, *CEO*
EMP: 15
SALES (est): 700.7K **Privately Held**
SIC: 8331 Community service employment training program

(G-2260)
HAND -N- HAND EARLY LRNG CTR
13724 S Old State Rd (19941-3330)
PHONE..........................302 422-0702
Cassie Malinger, *Director*
Elizabeth Williams, *Director*
Tony Austin,
Cheryl Clendaniel,
Terrance Neal,
EMP: 12
SALES: 68K **Privately Held**
SIC: 8351 Child day care services

(G-2261)
KEENE ENTERPRISES INC
14247 Oakley Rd (19941-3012)
PHONE..........................302 422-2856
Homer Keene, *President*
Rebecca Keene, *Corp Secy*
EMP: 4
SALES (est): 396K **Privately Held**
SIC: 7699 1799 Compressor repair; service station equipment installation & maintenance

(G-2262)
PHILADLPHIA ARMS TOWN HMES INC
18527 Pentecostal St (19941-3359)
PHONE..........................302 503-7216
Leah Brown, *Exec Dir*
EMP: 10 EST: 2016
SALES (est): 219.7K **Privately Held**
SIC: 1521 Single-family housing construction

(G-2263)
ROBBINS NEST FARM INC
16900 Robbins Nest Rd (19941-3202)
PHONE..........................302 422-4722
Raymond Robbins, *President*
EMP: 4
SQ FT: 10,000
SALES: 285K **Privately Held**
SIC: 0251 Broiling chickens, raising of

(G-2264)
WHITES FAMILY TRUCKING LLC
714 Main St (19941-2066)
PHONE..........................302 393-1401
Ronald C White, *Principal*
EMP: 4
SALES (est): 328.9K **Privately Held**
SIC: 4212 Local trucking, without storage

Farmington
Sussex County

(G-2265)
AUTO PARTS OF GREENWOOD
8316 Greenwood Rd (19950-4845)
P.O. Box 630, Greenwood (19950-0630)
PHONE..........................302 349-9601
Devin Johnson, *Owner*
Mark Case, *Family Practiti*
EMP: 5
SALES (est): 260.5K **Privately Held**
SIC: 5015 Automotive parts & supplies, used

(G-2266)
BAY TO BEACH BUILDERS INC
11582 Sussex Hwy (19950)
PHONE..........................302 349-5099
Derrick Parker, *President*
Monty Sarig, *Director*
EMP: 6
SALES (est): 937.8K **Privately Held**
SIC: 1521 New construction, single-family houses

(G-2267)
DIAMOND STATE MACHINING INC (PA)
207 Main St (19950-2183)
PHONE..........................302 398-8437
Donald Huey, *President*
Joann Huey, *Corp Secy*
Jennifer Huey, *VP Opers*
EMP: 13
SQ FT: 32,000
SALES: 1.5MM **Privately Held**
SIC: 3599 Machine shop, jobbing & repair

(G-2268)
WILLARD AGRI SERVICE GREENW
22272 S Dupont Hwy (19950-2311)
PHONE..........................302 349-4100
Ken Fry, *Principal*
EMP: 6
SALES (est): 456.9K **Privately Held**
SIC: 5083 Agricultural machinery & equipment

Felton
Kent County

(G-2269)
ADAM HOBBS & SON INC
344 Fitzbrian Dr (19943-3377)
PHONE..........................302 697-2090
Adam Hobbs, *President*
Shelly Hobbs, *Vice Pres*
EMP: 16
SALES: 1MM **Privately Held**
SIC: 4213 Trucking, except local

(G-2270)
ALBAN TRACTOR CO INC
Also Called: Caterpillar Authorized Dealer
13074 S Dupont Hwy (19943-4027)
PHONE..........................302 284-4100
Ed Mosley, *Manager*
EMP: 25

SALES (corp-wide): 266.4MM **Privately Held**
WEB: www.albancat.com
SIC: 5082 Construction & mining machinery
PA: Alban Tractor Co., Inc.
8531 Pulaski Hwy
Baltimore MD 21237
410 686-7777

(G-2271)
AMERESCO INC
1119 Willow Grove Rd (19943-2926)
PHONE..................302 284-1480
Christopher Clay, *Branch Mgr*
EMP: 5
SALES (corp-wide): 787.1MM **Publicly Held**
SIC: 8748 Energy conservation consultant
PA: Ameresco, Inc.
111 Speen St Ste 410
Framingham MA 01701
508 661-2200

(G-2272)
ATLANTIC CONTROL SYSTEMS INC
7873 S Dupont Hwy Ste 2 (19943-5700)
PHONE..................302 284-9700
Gary Reddish, *President*
Eric Linz, *Engineer*
EMP: 8
SALES (est): 840K **Privately Held**
WEB: www.acsd.net
SIC: 3613 Control panels, electric

(G-2273)
AZTECH CONTRACTING INC
68 Elijah Ln (19943-7362)
P.O. Box 701 (19943-0701)
PHONE..................302 526-2145
Henry Mast, *President*
EMP: 15 **EST:** 2009
SQ FT: 100
SALES: 1.2MM **Privately Held**
SIC: 1799 Service station equipment installation & maintenance

(G-2274)
BFI WASTE SERVICES LLC
Also Called: Site 426
907 Willow Grove Rd (19943-2924)
PHONE..................302 284-4440
Don Lucas, *Manager*
EMP: 60
SALES (corp-wide): 10B **Publicly Held**
SIC: 4953 Refuse systems
HQ: Bfi Waste Services, Llc
18500 N Allied Way # 100
Phoenix AZ 85054
480 627-2700

(G-2275)
BK LORD TRUCKING
1428 Turkey Point Rd (19943-1720)
PHONE..................302 284-7890
EMP: 4
SALES (est): 200K **Privately Held**
SIC: 4212 Local Trucking Operator

(G-2276)
BRYANT TECHNOLOGIES INC
2368 Paradise Alley Rd (19943-4133)
PHONE..................302 289-2044
Jeannette Bryant, *President*
EMP: 5
SALES (est): 277K **Privately Held**
WEB: www.bryant-technologies.com
SIC: 7371 Computer software development

(G-2277)
BUILDING BLOCKS ACADEMY LTD
333 Ludlow Ln (19943-1794)
PHONE..................302 284-8797
Maryjean Bladas, *Owner*
EMP: 11
SALES (est): 312.3K **Privately Held**
SIC: 8351 Preschool center

(G-2278)
BURKE EQUIPMENT COMPANY (PA)
Also Called: Kubota Authorized Dealer
54 Andrews Lake Rd (19943-4633)
PHONE..................302 697-3200
Mark Babbitt, *President*
Stephen Bridges, *General Mgr*
Mac Wiggam, *Purchasing*
Lucienne Babbitt, *Treasurer*
Andy McCullen, *Sales Dir*
EMP: 60 **EST:** 1949
SQ FT: 8,000
SALES (est): 9.7MM **Privately Held**
WEB: www.burkeequipment.com
SIC: 5261 7359 5083 Lawnmowers & tractors; equipment rental & leasing; farm & garden machinery

(G-2279)
CANTERBURY HOMES INC (PA)
120 Crestwood Dr Ste A (19943-9546)
PHONE..................302 284-0351
Joyce A Voshell, *President*
EMP: 4
SALES (est): 1MM **Privately Held**
SIC: 6515 Mobile home site operators

(G-2280)
CARL DEPUTY & SON BUILDERS LLC
5564 Lttle Mstens Crnr Rd (19943-4565)
PHONE..................302 284-3041
Carl A Deputy,
Patricia M Deputy,
EMP: 7
SALES: 2.2MM **Privately Held**
SIC: 1521 1542 New construction, single-family houses; commercial & office building, new construction

(G-2281)
CENTER FOR A PSTIVE HMNITY LLC
Also Called: Williams-Garcia & Associates
86 Ludlow Ln (19943-1764)
PHONE..................302 703-1036
Ronald Williams-Garcia, *Principal*
EMP: 5
SALES (est): 106K **Privately Held**
SIC: 8322 7389 General counseling services;

(G-2282)
CHARLES R REED
93 Paradise Cove Way (19943-4000)
PHONE..................302 284-3353
Charles R Reed, *Principal*
EMP: 5
SALES (est): 366.8K **Privately Held**
SIC: 1521 New construction, single-family houses

(G-2283)
CHESAPEAKE SUPPLY & EQP CO
12915 S Dupont Hwy (19943-4854)
PHONE..................302 284-1000
Dave Goulet, *Branch Mgr*
EMP: 9
SALES (corp-wide): 4.8MM **Privately Held**
SIC: 5082 7359 7353 General construction machinery & equipment; equipment rental & leasing; heavy construction equipment rental
PA: Chesapeake Supply & Equipment Company
8366 Washington Blvd
Savage MD 20763
410 792-4750

(G-2284)
COSEY GABRE
23 Lake Cove Ln (19943-5352)
PHONE..................302 233-0658
Gabre Cosey, *Owner*
EMP: 4
SALES (est): 42.4K **Privately Held**
SIC: 8322 Individual & family services

(G-2285)
DELAWARE SIGN CO
411 E Railroad Ave (19943-7354)
PHONE..................302 469-5656
EMP: 1
SALES (est): 46K **Privately Held**
SIC: 3993 Signs & advertising specialties

(G-2286)
DIAMOND STATE POLE BLDINGS LLC (PA)
7288 S Dupont Hwy (19943-5704)
P.O. Box 163, Magnolia (19962-0163)
PHONE..................302 387-1710
Michelle Sartin, *Sales Staff*
Nick Alessandro,
Dave Mason,
EMP: 9 **EST:** 2008
SALES: 5MM **Privately Held**
SIC: 1522 1542 Residential construction; commercial & office building contractors

(G-2287)
DOVINGTON TRAINING CENTER LLC
595 Black Swamp Rd (19943-3647)
PHONE..................302 284-2114
Alan Lovely, *President*
Jeffery Franklin, *Vice Pres*
Carolyn Franklin, *Treasurer*
Lorraine Lovely, *Admin Sec*
EMP: 5
SALES (est): 500K **Privately Held**
WEB: www.dovington.com
SIC: 0752 Training services, horses (except racing horses)

(G-2288)
DUCTS R US LLC
6084 Hopkins Cemetery Rd (19943-2366)
PHONE..................302 284-4006
John Caynor, *Principal*
EMP: 5
SALES (est): 81K **Privately Held**
SIC: 7349 Air duct cleaning

(G-2289)
EARLS PLACE LLC
9989 S Dupont Hwy Ste 4 (19943-5677)
PHONE..................302 538-8909
James Knox, *Mng Member*
EMP: 7 **EST:** 2017
SALES (est): 411.2K **Privately Held**
SIC: 7699 Repair services

(G-2290)
ECKELS FAMILY LLC
Also Called: Office Pride
141 Hunters Run Blvd (19943-5772)
PHONE..................302 465-5224
Mark Eckels,
Kelly Eckels,
EMP: 31 **EST:** 2014
SALES: 200K **Privately Held**
SIC: 7349 Janitorial service, contract basis

(G-2291)
FELTON COMMUNITY FIRE CO INC
9 E Main St (19943-7323)
P.O. Box 946 (19943-9046)
PHONE..................302 284-9552
William A Chandler, *President*
Lawrence R Sipple, *Chief*
David Wood, *Vice Pres*
Ken Ryder, *Treasurer*
Rodney Simons, *Director*
EMP: 136
SALES: 1.1MM **Privately Held**
SIC: 4119 Ambulance service

(G-2292)
FIRST STATE CRANE SERVICE
13326 S Dupont Hwy (19943-4030)
PHONE..................302 398-8885
John P Hayden, *President*
Jim Hauer, *Office Mgr*
EMP: 17 **EST:** 1974
SQ FT: 10,000
SALES (est): 2MM **Privately Held**
WEB: www.firststatecrane.com
SIC: 7353 1622 1629 Cranes & aerial lift equipment, rental or leasing; bridge construction; pile driving contractor

(G-2293)
FRANCIS BERGOLD
Also Called: By Feel Farms
918 Midstate Rd (19943-4701)
PHONE..................302 284-8101
Francis Bergold, *Owner*
EMP: 6
SALES (est): 216.7K **Privately Held**
SIC: 0134 0119 0115 Irish potatoes; barley farm; bean (dry field & seed) farm; corn

(G-2294)
HUGHES DELAWARE MAID SCRAPPLE
8873 Burnite Mill Rd (19943-4552)
PHONE..................302 284-4370
David Quillen, *President*
Dolly Womack, *Corp Secy*
EMP: 8
SALES (est): 200K **Privately Held**
SIC: 5141 Food brokers

(G-2295)
J & M FENCING INC
Also Called: Forrest Fencing
9867 S Dupont Hwy (19943-5620)
P.O. Box 21 (19943-0021)
PHONE..................302 284-9674
John Forrest, *President*
John P Forrest, *President*
Amber Lighthall, *Office Admin*
Karen Forrest, *Officer*
EMP: 10
SQ FT: 2,100
SALES (est): 645.7K **Privately Held**
SIC: 1799 5039 Fence construction; wire fence, gates & accessories

(G-2296)
J R BROOKS CUSTOM FRAMING LLC
1791 Peach Basket Rd (19943-5650)
PHONE..................302 538-3637
John Brooks, *Mng Member*
EMP: 4
SALES (est): 140K **Privately Held**
SIC: 1751 Framing contractor

(G-2297)
J W HUMPHRIES MASONARY
1185 Berrytown Rd (19943-6252)
PHONE..................302 284-0510
EMP: 6
SALES (est): 263.5K **Privately Held**
SIC: 1741 Masonry/Stone Contractor

(G-2298)
JD RELLEK COMPANY INC
Also Called: Inspection of Gas/Chemical
693 Irish Hill Rd (19943-5445)
P.O. Box 309, Viola (19979-0309)
PHONE..................302 284-7042
Ruth Noseworthy, *President*
Jeff Noseworthy, *Vice Pres*
Scott Smith, *Admin Sec*
EMP: 4
SALES (est): 408.8K **Privately Held**
SIC: 8748 Agricultural consultant

(G-2299)
JS KNOTTS INC
918 Midstate Rd (19943-4701)
PHONE..................302 284-4888
Jeff Knotts, *President*
EMP: 7
SQ FT: 2,400
SALES (est): 2.4MM **Privately Held**
SIC: 0721 7692 Irrigation system operation, not providing water; welding repair

(G-2300)
KENCO DRYWALL
Also Called: Kenco Cnstr Drywall Special
7093 S Dupont Hwy (19943-5718)
P.O. Box 957 (19943-0957)
PHONE..................302 697-6489
Kenneth Collins, *Owner*
Alyce Collins, *Office Mgr*
EMP: 20
SALES (est): 806.8K **Privately Held**
WEB: www.kencoconstruction.com
SIC: 1742 Drywall

Felton - Kent County (G-2301)

(G-2301)
KEVINS MASONRY CONCRETE CO
526 Reeves Crossing Rd (19943-4064)
P.O. Box 827 (19943-0827)
PHONE...................302 382-7259
Kevin Gay, *Principal*
EMP: 5
SALES (est): 335.5K Privately Held
SIC: 1771 Concrete work

(G-2302)
LELAND OAKLEY WELDING
93 Paradise Cove Way (19943-4000)
PHONE...................302 469-5746
Leland Oakley, *Principal*
EMP: 1
SALES (est): 25K Privately Held
SIC: 7692 Welding repair

(G-2303)
LEROY BETTS CONSTRUCTION INC
4020 Hopkins Cemetery Rd (19943-3729)
PHONE...................302 284-9193
Leroy Betts, *President*
Mary Lou Betts, *Corp Secy*
EMP: 9
SALES (est): 1.1MM Privately Held
SIC: 1794 Excavation work

(G-2304)
LIMOUSINE UNLIMITED LLC
12600 S Dupont Hwy (19943-4847)
PHONE...................302 284-1100
Lloyd Wheatley,
EMP: 12
SQ FT: 1,600
SALES: 240K Privately Held
SIC: 4119 Limousine rental, with driver

(G-2305)
LINCARE INC
7012 S Dupont Hwy (19943-5714)
PHONE...................302 424-8302
Barry Krenbrink, *Manager*
EMP: 8 Privately Held
SIC: 7352 Medical equipment rental
HQ: Lincare Inc.
    19387 Us Highway 19 N
    Clearwater FL 33764
    727 530-7700

(G-2306)
MARY ANNES LANDSCAPING INC
96 Windward Dr (19943-5356)
PHONE...................302 335-5433
Mary Anne Whidby, *President*
Dominick Whidby, *Vice Pres*
EMP: 6
SALES (est): 410K Privately Held
SIC: 0782 1711 Landscape contractors; irrigation sprinkler system installation

(G-2307)
MJM PUBLISHING
719 Tomahawk Ln (19943-6230)
PHONE...................302 943-3590
EMP: 1
SALES (est): 41.3K Privately Held
SIC: 2741 Miscellaneous publishing

(G-2308)
PENWOOD PROPERTY PRESERVATION
125 Dickens Ln (19943-9287)
PHONE...................302 469-5318
Keith Penawell, *President*
EMP: 4
SALES (est): 84.2K Privately Held
SIC: 0782 7349 Lawn care services; building maintenance services

(G-2309)
PERSPECTIVE COUNSELING CENTER
393 Fork Landing Rd (19943-4467)
PHONE...................302 677-1758
Janet Asay, *President*
EMP: 6
SALES (est): 307.7K Privately Held
SIC: 8011 Psychiatrist

(G-2310)
PINNACLE GARAGE DOOR COMPANY
764 Midstate Rd (19943-4808)
PHONE...................302 505-4531
Shawn Hollar, *Principal*
EMP: 1
SALES (est): 63.3K Privately Held
SIC: 1751 7699 2431 5015 Garage door, installation or erection; garage door repair; garage doors, overhead: wood; garage service equipment, used; garage doors, overhead: metal

(G-2311)
PIONEER MATERIALS
401 Lombard St (19943-4576)
PHONE...................302 284-3580
Richard Baker, *Manager*
EMP: 2
SALES (est): 66K Privately Held
SIC: 1429 Crushed & broken stone

(G-2312)
PIZZADILI PARTNERS LLC
1683 Peach Basket Rd (19943-5649)
PHONE...................302 284-9463
Pete Pizzadili,
Jean Pizzadili,
Kathy Pizzadili,
EMP: 5 EST: 2007
SALES (est): 386.8K Privately Held
SIC: 5921 2084 Wine; wines

(G-2313)
POND PUBLISHING & PRODUCTIONS
5012 Killens Pond Rd (19943-1904)
PHONE...................302 284-0200
Robert Crimmins, *Owner*
EMP: 1
SALES (est): 34K Privately Held
SIC: 2731 7336 7812 Book publishing; creative services to advertisers, except writers; video tape production

(G-2314)
RAD PETS INC
685 Roesville Rd (19943-4450)
PHONE...................302 335-5718
Robert Draper II, *President*
EMP: 5
SALES (est): 142.7K Privately Held
SIC: 0752 Animal specialty services

(G-2315)
RAYS PLUMBING & HEATING SVCS
Also Called: Ray's & Sons
7244 S Dupont Hwy (19943-5704)
P.O. Box 288 (19943)
PHONE...................302 697-3936
Craig Jones, *President*
EMP: 10
SALES (est): 1.2MM Privately Held
SIC: 1711 1731 1521 Plumbing contractors; warm air heating & air conditioning contractor; general electrical contractor; new construction, single-family houses; general remodeling, single-family houses

(G-2316)
RELIABLE TRAILER INC
1603 Andrews Lake Rd (19943-5260)
PHONE...................856 962-7900
Cory Nelson, *President*
Melissa Nelson, *Vice Pres*
Marlene Garbowski, *Admin Sec*
EMP: 11
SALES (est): 1.1MM Privately Held
WEB: www.reliabletrailerinc.com
SIC: 7699 7539 Nautical repair services; industrial machinery & equipment repair; tractor repair; trailer repair

(G-2317)
RITE WAY DISTRIBUTORS (PA)
Also Called: Value Furniture
7385 S Dupont Hwy (19943-5721)
PHONE...................302 535-8507
Lucian Szczepanski, *Owner*
EMP: 8
SALES: 780K Privately Held
WEB: www.ritewaydistributors.com
SIC: 6799 5712 5023 Commodity investors; furniture stores; home furnishings

(G-2318)
ROCK BOTTOM PAVING INC
8191 S Dupont Hwy (19943-5729)
PHONE...................800 728-3160
Selena Broadway, *President*
EMP: 5
SALES (est): 539.9K Privately Held
WEB: www.rockbottompaving.com
SIC: 1611 Surfacing & paving

(G-2319)
SEAFOOD CITY INC
9996 S Dupont Hwy (19943-5615)
P.O. Box 710 (19943-0710)
PHONE...................302 284-8486
Michael Harris, *President*
EMP: 28
SALES (est): 1.2MM Privately Held
SIC: 5421 5146 5812 Fish & seafood markets; fish & seafoods; eating places

(G-2320)
SENIOR HOME HELP LLC
266 Lake Cove Ln (19943-5351)
PHONE...................302 335-4243
Graeme Doughty, *Mng Member*
EMP: 4
SALES (est): 60K Privately Held
SIC: 8082 Home health care services

(G-2321)
SHINING TIME DAY CARE CENTER
220 Fox Chase Rd (19943-5504)
PHONE...................302 335-2770
Michelle Toothman, *Owner*
EMP: 9 EST: 1992
SALES: 297K Privately Held
SIC: 8351 Child day care services

(G-2322)
SHORE UNITED BANK
120 W Main St (19943-7328)
PHONE...................302 284-4600
EMP: 5
SALES (corp-wide): 64.9MM Publicly Held
SIC: 6022 State commercial banks
HQ: Shore United Bank
    18 E Dover St
    Easton MD 21601
    410 758-1600

(G-2323)
SUPERIOR MAIDS
1391 Chandlers Rd (19943-2457)
PHONE...................302 284-2012
Sharon Creed, *Owner*
EMP: 10
SALES (est): 342.6K Privately Held
SIC: 7699 Cleaning services

(G-2324)
UNITED CEREBRAL PALSY OF DE
3249 Midstate Rd (19943-4910)
PHONE...................302 335-3739
Carma Carpenter, *Director*
EMP: 4
SALES (corp-wide): 1.6MM Privately Held
SIC: 8322 Association for the handicapped
PA: United Cerebral Palsy Of De, Inc
    700 River Rd Apt A
    Wilmington DE 19809
    302 764-2400

(G-2325)
WAGNER N J & SONS TRUCKING
5972 Hopkins Cemetery Rd (19943-2365)
PHONE...................302 242-7731
N J Wagner, *Partner*
Christopher Wagner, *Partner*
Emily Wagner, *Partner*
Kenneth Wagner, *Partner*
Matthew Wagner, *Partner*
EMP: 10
SALES (est): 931.2K Privately Held
SIC: 4212 Dump truck haulage

(G-2326)
WEAVERS CONSTRUCTION INC
6806 Canterbury Rd (19943-4388)
PHONE...................302 270-8876
Vernon Weaver, *Principal*
EMP: 4
SQ FT: 1,474
SALES: 120K Privately Held
SIC: 1799 Athletic & recreation facilities construction

(G-2327)
YENCER BUILDERS INC
925 Marshyhope Rd (19943-3837)
PHONE...................302 284-9989
David R Yencer, *President*
Kevin J Yencer, *Vice Pres*
EMP: 8
SALES (est): 1.3MM Privately Held
SIC: 1521 New construction, single-family houses

Fenwick Island
Sussex County

(G-2328)
ACTION ENTERPRISE INC
Also Called: Delmarva Sports Action Mag
27 W Bayard St (19944-4503)
P.O. Box 914, Bethany Beach (19930-0914)
PHONE...................302 537-7223
Susan Taylor-Walls, *President*
EMP: 20
SALES (est): 1.4MM Privately Held
SIC: 2721 Magazines: publishing only, not printed on site

(G-2329)
BANK OF OCEAN CITY
904 Coastal Hwy (19944-4410)
P.O. Box 150, Ocean City MD (21843-0150)
PHONE...................410 723-4944
Patty Gray, *Manager*
EMP: 4
SALES (corp-wide): 13.7MM Privately Held
WEB: www.bankofoceancity.com
SIC: 6022 6162 State commercial banks; mortgage bankers & correspondents
PA: Bank Of Ocean City
    10005 Golf Course Rd
    Ocean City MD 21842
    410 213-0173

(G-2330)
BEAM CONSTRUCTION INC
1 E Atlantic St (19944-4446)
PHONE...................302 537-2787
Mark Beam, *President*
EMP: 5
SALES (est): 529.4K Privately Held
SIC: 1521 General remodeling, single-family houses; new construction, single-family houses

(G-2331)
BETHANY-FENWICK CHAMBER
36913 Coastal Hwy (19944-4079)
PHONE...................302 539-2100
Emilie Bonano, *Comms Mgr*
Lauren Weaber, *Exec Dir*
Kori Gassaway, *Director*
EMP: 5
SALES (est): 423.3K Privately Held
SIC: 8611 Chamber of Commerce

(G-2332)
CAROLINA STREET GARDEN & HOME
40118 E Sc St (19944)
PHONE...................302 539-2405
Betty Phillips, *Managing Prtnr*
Paul Phillips, *Managing Prtnr*
EMP: 6
SQ FT: 2,000
SALES: 750K Privately Held
WEB: www.carolinastreet.com
SIC: 7389 5712 Interior decorating; furniture stores

GEOGRAPHIC SECTION

(G-2333)
COASTAL IMAGES INC
Also Called: Beach-Net.com
711 Coastal Hwy (19944-4416)
PHONE.....................302 539-6001
Peter Roenke, *President*
Gloria Webster, *Vice Pres*
Michelle Roenke, *Treasurer*
EMP: 7
SQ FT: 2,000
SALES (est): 873.2K **Privately Held**
WEB: www.cafelocale.com
SIC: 4813 2741 ; directories, telephone: publishing only, not printed on site; shopping news: publishing only, not printed on site

(G-2334)
DR RONALD R BLANCK DO
1613 Bay St (19944-4506)
PHONE.....................302 541-4137
Ronald Ray Blanck, *Principal*
EMP: 4
SALES (est): 125.4K **Privately Held**
SIC: 8031 Offices & clinics of osteopathic physicians

(G-2335)
FENWICK MEDICAL CENTER
1209 Coastal Hwy (19944-4401)
PHONE.....................302 539-2399
Fax: 302 539-5988
EMP: 9
SALES (est): 564.4K **Privately Held**
SIC: 8011 Offices And Clinics Of Medical Doctors, Nsk

(G-2336)
FISHERS POPCORN FENWICK LLC
37081 Coastal Hwy (19944-4057)
PHONE.....................302 539-8833
Martha F Hall, *Owner*
EMP: 35
SALES (est): 2.1MM **Privately Held**
SIC: 5441 2096 Popcorn, including caramel corn; potato chips & similar snacks

(G-2337)
ICY PUP
35432 Coastal Hwy (19944-4030)
PHONE.....................302 777-1776
EMP: 1
SALES (est): 45.5K **Privately Held**
SIC: 3999 Pet supplies

(G-2338)
OCEAN WAVES LLC
Rr 3 Box 286d (19944)
PHONE.....................302 344-1282
Adam Ask, *Sales Mgr*
Eric Hemming,
EMP: 4
SALES (est): 267.4K **Privately Held**
SIC: 7542 Carwashes

(G-2339)
RAYMOND E TOMASSETTI ESQ (PA)
1209 Coastal Hwy Fl 2 (19944-4401)
PHONE.....................302 539-3041
Raymond Tomassetti Jr, *Owner*
EMP: 5
SALES (est): 944.7K **Privately Held**
SIC: 8111 General practice attorney, lawyer

(G-2340)
SEASIDE INN
1401 Coastal Hwy (19944-4421)
PHONE.....................302 251-5000
Jayson Vit, *Principal*
EMP: 15
SALES (est): 426.6K **Privately Held**
SIC: 7011 Inns; motels

(G-2341)
SUSSEX SANDS INC
Also Called: Sands Motel
1501 Coastal Hwy (19944-4422)
P.O. Box 228, Selbyville (19975-0228)
PHONE.....................302 539-8200
Susan B Caldwell, *Principal*
EMP: 7
SALES (est): 329.7K **Privately Held**
SIC: 7011 Motels

Frankford
Sussex County

(G-2342)
A & A AIR SERVICES INC (PA)
Also Called: Honeywell Authorized Dealer
35130 Bennett Rd (19945-4061)
P.O. Box 610, Selbyville (19975-0610)
PHONE.....................302 436-4800
Gregory Allen, *President*
EMP: 45
SQ FT: 2,000
SALES (est): 5.4MM **Privately Held**
SIC: 1711 Warm air heating & air conditioning contractor

(G-2343)
A & A ELECTRICAL INC
35130 Bennett Rd (19945-4061)
PHONE.....................302 436-4800
Greg Allen, *President*
Christopher Allen, *Vice Pres*
EMP: 10
SALES (est): 672.7K **Privately Held**
SIC: 1731 General electrical contractor

(G-2344)
A DOUGLAS MELSON
Also Called: Melson Funeral Services
40 Thatcher St (19945-9401)
P.O. Box 100 (19945-0100)
PHONE.....................302 732-6606
A Douglas Melson, *Owner*
Sharon H Melson, *Principal*
EMP: 4
SQ FT: 10,000
SALES (est): 244.2K **Privately Held**
SIC: 7261 Funeral home

(G-2345)
B & E TIRE ALIGNMENT INC
Rr 113 (19945)
P.O. Box 325 (19945-0325)
PHONE.....................302 732-6091
Kenneth Evans, *President*
EMP: 5
SQ FT: 3,600
SALES: 500K **Privately Held**
SIC: 7539 Wheel alignment, automotive

(G-2346)
BAR CODE SOFTWARE INC
34295 Wilgus Cemetery Rd (19945-4514)
PHONE.....................410 360-7455
Frederick Cody, *President*
EMP: 4
SQ FT: 1,000
SALES: 375K **Privately Held**
WEB: www.barcodesoftwareinc.com
SIC: 7371 Computer software development

(G-2347)
BLUEBERRY LNE BRRY FRM & ORCHD
24133 Blueberry Ln (19945-3831)
PHONE.....................302 238-7067
EMP: 4
SALES: 125K **Privately Held**
SIC: 0171 Berry Crop Farm

(G-2348)
BOLD INDUSTRIES LLC
37424 Dale Earnhardt Blvd (19945-3676)
PHONE.....................302 858-7237
Ashlee Justice, *Principal*
EMP: 1
SALES (est): 39.6K **Privately Held**
SIC: 3999 Manufacturing industries

(G-2349)
BRASURES BODY SHOP INC
Rr 113 (19945)
P.O. Box 118 (19945-0118)
PHONE.....................302 732-6157
James Brasure, *President*
Paulette Brasure, *Corp Secy*
EMP: 6
SQ FT: 4,000
SALES (est): 682.8K **Privately Held**
SIC: 7532 5521 Body shop, automotive; automobiles, used cars only

(G-2350)
BRENNAN TITLE COMPANY
31634 Hickory Manor Rd (19945-3142)
PHONE.....................302 541-0400
EMP: 5 **Privately Held**
SIC: 6541 Title & trust companies
PA: Brennan Title Company
    5865 Allentown Rd
    Suitland MD 20746

(G-2351)
BUNTING & BERTRAND INC
15 Hickory St (19945-2032)
P.O. Box 639 (19945-0639)
PHONE.....................302 732-6836
Walter H Bunting, *President*
EMP: 12 EST: 1963
SALES (est): 7.7MM **Privately Held**
WEB: www.buntingandbertrand.com
SIC: 5083 Poultry equipment; livestock equipment; grain elevators equipment & supplies

(G-2352)
C&B COMPLETE CLEANING & CNSTR
36007 Zion Church Rd (19945-4544)
PHONE.....................302 436-9622
William Craig Conover, *Principal*
EMP: 4
SALES (est): 51.3K **Privately Held**
SIC: 7699 Cleaning services

(G-2353)
CHESAPEAKE CLIMATE CONTROL LLC
Also Called: Honeywell Authorized Dealer
34913 Delaware Ave (19945-3890)
PHONE.....................302 732-6006
Travis Martin, *Owner*
EMP: 28 EST: 2017
SALES (est): 723.4K **Privately Held**
SIC: 1711 Heating & air conditioning contractors

(G-2354)
CHESAPEAKE PLUMBING & HTG INC
34913 Delaware Ave (19945-3890)
PHONE.....................302 732-6006
Travis Martin, *President*
Jessie Martin, *Vice Pres*
EMP: 27
SALES (est): 7.6MM **Privately Held**
WEB: www.cpnhinc.com
SIC: 1711 Plumbing contractors

(G-2355)
COASTAL SUN ROMS PRCH ENCLSRES
36017 Pine Bark Ln (19945-3571)
PHONE.....................302 537-3679
David Goodman, *Principal*
EMP: 2
SALES (est): 287.6K **Privately Held**
SIC: 1521 3448 5999 Patio & deck construction & repair; sunrooms, prefabricated metal; awnings

(G-2356)
CONNECTIONS DEVELOPMENT CORP
35906 Zion Church Rd (19945-4540)
PHONE.....................302 436-3292
Catherine D McKay, *CEO*
EMP: 4
SALES (est): 56.3K **Privately Held**
SIC: 8351 Group day care center
PA: Connections Development Corp
    3821 Lancaster Pike
    Wilmington DE 19805

(G-2357)
COZY CRITTERS CHILD CARE CORP
35371 Beaver Dam Rd (19945-3227)
PHONE.....................302 541-8210
Lora Collins, *Owner*
Dale Collins, *Co-Owner*
Laura Collins, *Director*
EMP: 27
SALES (est): 773K **Privately Held**
SIC: 8351 Group day care center

(G-2358)
CUSTOM MECHANICAL INC (PA)
Also Called: Honeywell Authorized Dealer
34799 Daisey Rd (19945-3530)
P.O. Box 1479, Bethany Beach (19930-1479)
PHONE.....................302 537-1150
Glen S Roberts, *President*
Patti Roberts, *Corp Secy*
Belinda Dyson, *Purchasing*
Chris Megee, *CFO*
Heather Kaufman, *Sales Staff*
EMP: 42
SQ FT: 3,200
SALES (est): 5.7MM **Privately Held**
WEB: www.custommechanical.com
SIC: 1711 3444 Mechanical contractor; sheet metalwork

(G-2359)
DELMARVA CONCRETE PUMPING INC
34090 Central Ave (19945-3555)
Rural Route 2 Box 174b (19945)
PHONE.....................302 537-4118
Joseph Schroeder, *President*
EMP: 5
SALES (est): 466.1K **Privately Held**
SIC: 1771 Concrete pumping

(G-2360)
DPS CUSTOM PAINTING LLC
33099 Thunder Rd (19945-2917)
PHONE.....................302 732-3232
Dennis Pierce,
EMP: 5
SALES: 200K **Privately Held**
SIC: 1721 Painting & paper hanging

(G-2361)
EAST SUSSEX MOOSE LODGE
35993 Zion Church Rd (19945-4500)
PHONE.....................302 436-2088
Glen Densmore, *Administration*
EMP: 5
SALES: 236.1K **Privately Held**
SIC: 8641 8699 Civic associations; charitable organization

(G-2362)
EUROPEAN COACH WERKES INC
Rr 20 (19945)
PHONE.....................302 436-2277
Jack Barranger, *President*
EMP: 6
SQ FT: 6,500
SALES (est): 1.3MM **Privately Held**
SIC: 5521 7389 Automobiles, used cars only; automobile recovery service

(G-2363)
FRANKFORD CUSTOM WOODWORKS INC
34139 Dupont Blvd (19945-3807)
PHONE.....................302 732-9570
Maynard Esender, *President*
EMP: 11
SALES (est): 1.2MM **Privately Held**
SIC: 2431 Millwork

(G-2364)
GARTH TROESCHER JR LLC
34105 Shockley Town Rd (19945-2600)
PHONE.....................302 927-0106
Garth Troescher, *Principal*
EMP: 4
SALES (est): 121.9K **Privately Held**
SIC: 7389

(G-2365)
GERONE C HUDSON ELEC CONTR
35944 Bayard Rd (19945-4573)
PHONE.....................302 539-3332
Guy Hudson, *President*
Pat Hudson, *Corp Secy*
EMP: 11 EST: 1969
SQ FT: 2,500
SALES (est): 1.2MM **Privately Held**
SIC: 1731 General electrical contractor

Frankford - Sussex County (G-2366) GEOGRAPHIC SECTION

(G-2366)
GUMBORO SERVICE CENTER INC
22181 Charles West Rd (19945-2431)
PHONE...................................302 238-7040
Margarite Davis, *President*
EMP: 6
SALES (est): 515.8K **Privately Held**
SIC: 7538 General automotive repair shops

(G-2367)
H2O PRO LLC
31765 Hickory Manor Rd (19945-3134)
PHONE...................................302 321-7077
Elizabeth Keefer, *COO*
EMP: 4
SALES (est): 346.4K **Privately Held**
SIC: 1799 8744 Waterproofing;

(G-2368)
HOWARD WIMBROW CPA
35288 Honeysuckle Rd (19945-4518)
PHONE...................................302 539-0829
Cindy Wimbrow, *Owner*
EMP: 4
SALES (est): 256.5K **Privately Held**
SIC: 8721 Certified public accountant

(G-2369)
JAMES POWELL
Also Called: Robinsons Sewage Disposial
34309 Burton Farm Rd (19945-2957)
PHONE...................................302 539-2351
James R Powell, *Principal*
EMP: 5 **EST:** 2011
SALES (est): 247.2K **Privately Held**
SIC: 4953

(G-2370)
KOALA ENTERPRISES INC
Also Called: Honeywell Authorized Dealer
36382 Bayard Rd (19945-4572)
PHONE...................................302 436-9950
Peter Bernsten, *Principal*
EMP: 4 **EST:** 2008
SALES (est): 420.7K **Privately Held**
SIC: 8748 Business consulting

(G-2371)
MAG TOWING
35001 Roxana Rd (19945-3281)
PHONE...................................302 462-5686
Mark Eiblin, *Owner*
EMP: 4
SALES (est): 343.6K **Privately Held**
SIC: 7549 Towing service, automotive

(G-2372)
MATTS MANAGEMENT FAMILY LLC
Also Called: Matt's Line Painting
32397 Omar Rd (19945-2807)
PHONE...................................302 732-3715
Angela Matthews, *Mng Member*
Gary Matthews, *Mng Member*
Gary W Matthews Sr,
EMP: 14
SALES (est): 1.6MM **Privately Held**
SIC: 1611 Highway & street construction

(G-2373)
MELSON FUNERAL SERVICES LTD
Also Called: Melsons Henlipen Creammatury
43 Thatcher St (19945)
P.O. Box 100 (19945-0100)
PHONE...................................302 732-9000
A Douglas Melson, *Owner*
Sharon Nelson, *Partner*
EMP: 5
SALES (est): 618.5K **Privately Held**
SIC: 7261 Funeral director; funeral home

(G-2374)
MELSONS CAPE HNLOPEN CREMATORY
41 Thatcher St (19945-9400)
P.O. Box 100 (19945-0100)
PHONE...................................302 537-2441
Sharon Melson, *General Mgr*
Alvin D Melson, *Director*
Lisa A Banks, *Admin Sec*
EMP: 9 **EST:** 1980
SALES (est): 162K **Privately Held**
SIC: 7261 Crematory

(G-2375)
MOUNTAIRE FARMS INC
Also Called: Mountaire Farms of Delmarva
11 Daisey St (19945-2030)
P.O. Box 88 (19945-0088)
PHONE...................................302 732-6611
Charletta McCray, *Purchasing*
Justin Tomlinson, *Branch Mgr*
EMP: 45
SALES (corp-wide): 1.4B **Privately Held**
SIC: 2048 Chicken feeds, prepared
HQ: Mountaire Farms Inc.
1901 Napa Valley Dr
Little Rock AR 72212
501 372-6524

(G-2376)
MR NATURAL BOTTLED WATER
32482 Mccary Rd (19945-4032)
PHONE...................................302 436-7700
Eileen C Short, *President*
EMP: 1
SALES (est): 78.1K **Privately Held**
SIC: 2086 Pasteurized & mineral waters, bottled & canned

(G-2377)
MULTI KOASTAL SERVICES
34756 Roxana Rd (19945-3242)
P.O. Box 276, Ocean View (19970-0276)
PHONE...................................302 436-8822
Kenneth Walsh, *Owner*
EMP: 8
SALES (est): 1MM **Privately Held**
SIC: 7699 Septic tank cleaning service

(G-2378)
NATIONAL RIG RENTAL LLC
35322 Bayard Rd (19945-4557)
PHONE...................................302 539-1963
Michael Jahnigan, *Mng Member*
Shra Carlson, *Mng Member*
EMP: 4
SALES (est): 330.4K **Privately Held**
SIC: 7359 Equipment rental & leasing

(G-2379)
PAULS PAVING INC
37425 Dale Earnhardt Blvd (19945-3662)
P.O. Box 232, Bethany Beach (19930-0232)
PHONE...................................302 539-9123
Anita Justice, *President*
Michael Justice, *Vice Pres*
Maureen Justice, *Admin Sec*
EMP: 15
SALES (est): 732K **Privately Held**
SIC: 1771 1629 Driveway contractor; parking lot construction; land clearing contractor

(G-2380)
PREMIER GLASS & SCREEN INC
Also Called: Premier Porch & Patio
33937 Premire Dr (19945-3830)
PHONE...................................302 732-3101
Joe Kauffman, *President*
Frank Tharby, *Vice Pres*
EMP: 19
SQ FT: 6,000
SALES (est): 2.6MM **Privately Held**
SIC: 1793 Glass & glazing work

(G-2381)
PROGRESSIVE SYSTEMS INC
Also Called: PSI
25 Hickory St (19945-2032)
P.O. Box 35 (19945-0035)
PHONE...................................302 732-3321
Joseph P Carney, *President*
EMP: 6
SQ FT: 8,000
SALES (est): 2.7MM **Privately Held**
WEB: www.progressivesystemsinc.com
SIC: 5084 5169 7699 Cleaning equipment, high pressure, sand or steam; chemicals & allied products; industrial equipment services

(G-2382)
PYLE CHILD DEVELOPMENT CENTER
34314 Pyle Center Rd (19945-3277)
PHONE...................................302 732-1443
April Kelly, *Director*
EMP: 12
SALES (est): 346.2K **Privately Held**
SIC: 8351 Child day care services

(G-2383)
ROBERT GEARS
Also Called: Gears Mechanical Company
34696 Daisey Rd (19945-3531)
PHONE...................................302 834-7487
Robert Gears, *Owner*
EMP: 5
SQ FT: 1,500
SALES: 500K **Privately Held**
SIC: 1711 Plumbing contractors; warm air heating & air conditioning contractor

(G-2384)
RONALD P WILSON
Also Called: Wilson's Welding
Rr 2 Box 182 (19945-9802)
PHONE...................................302 539-4139
Ronald P Wilson, *Owner*
EMP: 1
SALES (est): 102K **Privately Held**
SIC: 7692 3444 3441 Welding repair; sheet metalwork; fabricated structural metal

(G-2385)
SALTED VINES VINEYARD WINERY
32512 Blackwater Rd (19945-2940)
PHONE...................................302 829-8990
EMP: 12
SALES (est): 1.3MM **Privately Held**
SIC: 5182 Wine

(G-2386)
SCOTTS REFRIGERATION & AC
32327 Wingate Rd (19945-2825)
PHONE...................................302 732-3736
Scott Barnfield, *President*
Nancy Barnfield, *Treasurer*
EMP: 4
SALES (est): 603.4K **Privately Held**
SIC: 1711 Warm air heating & air conditioning contractor

(G-2387)
SIMPLER SURVEYING & ASSOCIATES
32486 Powell Farm Rd (19945-3344)
PHONE...................................302 539-7873
Greg Hook, *Owner*
Michael Loveland, *Project Mgr*
EMP: 9 **EST:** 2000
SALES (est): 704.7K **Privately Held**
WEB: www.kimhook.com
SIC: 8713 Surveying services

(G-2388)
SNOW PHARMACEUTICALS LLC
35998 Zion Church Rd (19945-4501)
PHONE...................................302 436-8855
Ron Howard,
Eric Howard,
Paul E Howard MD,
▲ **EMP:** 6
SALES (est): 638K **Privately Held**
SIC: 2834 Pharmaceutical preparations

(G-2389)
SOUTH COASTAL
33711 S Coastal Ln (19945-4221)
PHONE...................................302 542-5668
Kevin Vanauken, *Principal*
EMP: 6
SALES (est): 157.3K **Privately Held**
SIC: 8322 Community center

(G-2390)
STEPHEN CROPPER
35029 Dupont Blvd (19945-3867)
PHONE...................................302 732-3730
Stephen Cropper, *Owner*
EMP: 2 **EST:** 1988
SALES (est): 72.7K **Privately Held**
SIC: 7389 2752 2396 2754 Embroidering of advertising on shirts, etc.; promotional printing, lithographic; screen printing on fabric articles; business form & card printing, gravure

(G-2391)
SUN MARINE MAINTENANCE INC
35322 Bayard Rd (19945-4557)
PHONE...................................302 539-6756
Michael R Jahnigen, *President*
▼ **EMP:** 15
SQ FT: 3,000
SALES (est): 1.8MM **Privately Held**
WEB: www.sunmarinemaint.com
SIC: 1629 Marine construction; dredging contractor; pile driving contractor

(G-2392)
SUN PILEDRIVING EQUIPMENT LLC
35322 Bayard Rd (19945-4557)
PHONE...................................302 539-6756
Sondra Connor, *Comptroller*
Michael Jahnigen,
Harry Montgomery, *Technician*
▲ **EMP:** 6
SQ FT: 1,500
SALES (est): 4MM **Privately Held**
WEB: www.sunpiledrivingequipment.com
SIC: 5082 Road construction equipment

(G-2393)
TJ S PLUMBING HEATING L
26577 Blueberry Ln (19945-3934)
PHONE...................................302 228-7129
Travis Lee Justice Sr, *President*
EMP: 6
SALES (est): 340.8K **Privately Held**
SIC: 1711 Plumbing contractors

(G-2394)
TROTTYS CONCRETE PUMPING INC
34107 Dupont Blvd (19945-3807)
PHONE...................................302 732-3100
Richard Trott, *President*
EMP: 15
SALES (est): 1.1MM **Privately Held**
SIC: 1771 Concrete pumping

(G-2395)
TUNE-UP III OF MD INC (PA)
Also Called: Precision Tune Auto Care
112 Setting Sun Way (19945-4703)
PHONE...................................410 655-9500
Gary L Marsiglia, *President*
Bradley K Marsiglia, *Vice Pres*
EMP: 4 **EST:** 1984
SQ FT: 2,500
SALES (est): 370.9K **Privately Held**
SIC: 7538 General automotive repair shops

(G-2396)
V B TOWING INC
22167 Cypress Rd (19945-2319)
PHONE...................................302 238-7705
Victor Baker, *Principal*
EMP: 4 **EST:** 2008
SALES (est): 181.6K **Privately Held**
SIC: 7549 Towing services

(G-2397)
WAYNE BENNETT
Also Called: Bennett Electric
35484 Honeysuckle Rd (19945-4520)
PHONE...................................302 436-2379
Wayne Bennett, *Owner*
EMP: 5
SALES (est): 260K **Privately Held**
SIC: 1731 General electrical contractor

(G-2398)
WEBER SIGN CO
Also Called: Weber Sign & Art Studio
16 Hickory St (19945)
P.O. Box 131, Dagsboro (19939-0131)
PHONE...................................302 732-1429
Rick Weber, *Owner*
EMP: 10
SALES (est): 878K **Privately Held**
SIC: 3993 Signs & advertising specialties

Frederica
Kent County

(G-2399)
WINIFRED ELLEN ERBE
Also Called: Blue Sky Management
38397 Hemlock Dr (19945-4617)
PHONE..................302 541-0889
John Buono, *Principal*
EMP: 5 EST: 2009
SALES (est): 382.7K **Privately Held**
SIC: 8741 Management services

(G-2400)
COMMISSION ON ARCHVS IN HSTORY (PA)
Also Called: Annual Conf of United Meth Ch
6362 Bay Rd (19946-1505)
P.O. Box 668 (19946-0668)
PHONE..................302 335-5544
Barbara Duffin, *Administration*
EMP: 5
SQ FT: 2,370
SALES (est): 320.8K **Privately Held**
WEB: www.barrattschapel.org
SIC: 8412 Museum

(G-2401)
DIANE SPENCE DAY CARE
19 Ruyter Dr (19946-1916)
PHONE..................302 335-4460
Diane Spence, *Director*
EMP: 4
SALES (est): 81.4K **Privately Held**
SIC: 8351 Child day care services

(G-2402)
FREDERICA SENIOR CENTER INC
216 Market St (19946-4606)
P.O. Box 165 (19946-0165)
PHONE..................302 335-4555
Wilbur Jones, *President*
Renee Hoffman, *Director*
EMP: 8
SALES: 592.5K **Privately Held**
SIC: 8322 Senior citizens' center or association

(G-2403)
GRAYLING INDUSTRIES INC
1 Moonwalker Rd (19946-2080)
PHONE..................770 751-9095
Kurt David Ross, *President*
Carlos Rubio, *CFO*
Dorothy Pahner, *Admin Mgr*
Dorothy R Pahner, *Admin Sec*
▲ EMP: 25
SQ FT: 20,000
SALES: 16.9MM **Privately Held**
WEB: www.graylingindustries.com
SIC: 5169 2673 3081 2869 Polyurethane products; plastic bags: made from purchased materials; unsupported plastics film & sheet; industrial organic chemicals
HQ: Ilc Dover Lp
 1 Moonwalker Rd
 Frederica DE 19946
 302 335-3911

(G-2404)
GRAYLING INDUSTRIES INC
2 Moonwalker Rd (19946-2080)
PHONE..................302 629-6860
EMP: 2
SALES (est): 188.6K **Privately Held**
SIC: 3999 Manufacturing industries

(G-2405)
HABITAT DESIGN GROUP
192 Bowers Beach Rd (19946-1714)
PHONE..................302 335-4452
Coleman Morris Jr, *Owner*
EMP: 5
SQ FT: 1,352
SALES: 150K **Privately Held**
SIC: 0781 Landscape planning services

(G-2406)
HUGHES NETWORK SYSTEMS LLC
1 E David St (19946-4617)
PHONE..................302 335-4138
EMP: 4 **Publicly Held**
SIC: 7375 On-line data base information retrieval
HQ: Hughes Network Systems, Llc
 11717 Exploration Ln
 Germantown MD 20876
 301 428-5500

(G-2407)
ILC DOVER LP (HQ)
1 Moonwalker Rd (19946-2080)
PHONE..................302 335-3911
Fran Dinuzzo, *Managing Prtnr*
William Wallach, *General Ptnr*
Daniel Herring, *Vice Pres*
John Griffin, *Mfg Staff*
David Graziosi, *Chief Engr*
▲ EMP: 420
SQ FT: 270,000
SALES (est): 133MM **Privately Held**
WEB: www.ilcdover.com
SIC: 3842 3721 Personal safety equipment; space suits; balloons, hot air (aircraft)

(G-2408)
JVL AUTOMOTIVE
Also Called: J V L Automotive & Custom Wldg
411 Buffalo Rd (19946-1561)
PHONE..................302 335-3942
John Vaina, *Owner*
EMP: 1
SALES (est): 41.6K **Privately Held**
SIC: 7692 Automotive welding

(G-2409)
KENT COUNTY
Also Called: De Turf Sports Complex
4000 Bay Rd (19946-2129)
PHONE..................302 330-8873
Christopher Giacomucci, *CEO*
William Strickland, *President*
EMP: 6 EST: 2012
SALES: 635.8K **Privately Held**
SIC: 7999 Outfitters, recreation

(G-2410)
NEW ILC DOVER INC (PA)
1 Moonwalker Rd (19946-2080)
PHONE..................302 335-3911
William Wallach, *President*
Adrienne Kenyon, *Opers Staff*
Mark Puzzo, *Buyer*
Olga Rodarte, *Buyer*
Michelle Scott, *Engineer*
EMP: 17
SALES (est): 133MM **Privately Held**
SIC: 3842 Personal safety equipment

(G-2411)
ROBERTS CONST CO
Frnt Main Sts (19946)
PHONE..................302 335-4141
EMP: 20 EST: 1974
SQ FT: 20,000
SALES: 2.1MM **Privately Held**
SIC: 1542 Nonresidential Construction

(G-2412)
ROLL-A-BOUT CORPORATION
3240 Barratts Chapel Rd (19946-1808)
PHONE..................302 736-6151
Lola Accetta, *President*
Susan Accetta, *Vice Pres*
EMP: 2
SALES (est): 295.6K **Privately Held**
WEB: www.roll-a-bout.com
SIC: 3842 Crutches & walkers

(G-2413)
SUN COMMUNITIES INC
Also Called: High Point Mobil Park
2 Willow Dr (19946-2668)
PHONE..................302 335-5444
Jarvis Moore, *Manager*
EMP: 4
SALES (corp-wide): 1.1B **Publicly Held**
WEB: www.suncommunities.com
SIC: 6515 Mobile home site operators
PA: Sun Communities, Inc.
 27777 Franklin Rd Ste 200
 Southfield MI 48034
 248 208-2500

(G-2414)
SWAN FINANCIAL GROUP
251 Saundra St (19946-2937)
PHONE..................302 689-6095
Jose Echeverri, *Principal*
EMP: 4
SALES (est): 307.8K **Privately Held**
SIC: 6282 Investment advice

(G-2415)
VIVID COLORS CARPET LLC
43 Bayview Ave (19946-1304)
PHONE..................302 335-3933
Albert C Ebert,
EMP: 2
SALES: 69K **Privately Held**
SIC: 1741 2273 7217 Tuckpointing or restoration; dyeing & finishing of tufted rugs & carpets; carpet & upholstery cleaning

Georgetown
Sussex County

(G-2416)
1 A LIFESAFER INC
23095 Lwes Georgetown Hwy (19947-5302)
PHONE..................800 634-3077
EMP: 1
SALES (corp-wide): 4.3MM **Privately Held**
SIC: 3829 Measuring & controlling devices
PA: 1 A Lifesafer, Inc.
 4290 Glendale Milford Rd
 Blue Ash OH 45242
 513 651-9560

(G-2417)
4N CAR INC
Also Called: 4-N Car
20185 Dupont Blvd (19947-3138)
PHONE..................302 856-7434
Randy Gooner, *President*
Jennifer Buckley, *Vice Pres*
Edward Buckley, *Admin Sec*
EMP: 4
SQ FT: 2,400
SALES: 300K **Privately Held**
SIC: 7538 5521 General automotive repair shops; automobiles, used cars only

(G-2418)
5 JS SANITATION
21754 Simpler Branch Rd (19947-6624)
PHONE..................302 945-7086
Jacob Kabino, *Owner*
EMP: 4
SALES: 200K **Privately Held**
SIC: 7699 Septic tank cleaning service

(G-2419)
A P CROLL & SON INC
22997 Lwes Georgetown Hwy (19947-5301)
P.O. Box 748 (19947-0748)
PHONE..................302 856-6177
A P Croll III, *CEO*
A P Croll Jr, *Vice Pres*
Thomas C Hudson, *CFO*
EMP: 55 EST: 1921
SQ FT: 2,000
SALES (est): 12MM **Privately Held**
WEB: www.apcroll.com
SIC: 1611 General contractor, highway & street construction

(G-2420)
A R NAILS
401 College Park Ln (19947-2114)
PHONE..................302 858-4592
EMP: 4
SALES (est): 28.8K **Privately Held**
SIC: 7231 Manicurist, pedicurist

(G-2421)
ABBY L ALLEN FNP
20797 Professional Prk Bl (19947-3198)
PHONE..................302 856-1773
Abby Allen, *Owner*
Curt Watkins, *Co-Owner*
EMP: 5
SALES (est): 131.2K **Privately Held**
SIC: 8011 Allergist

(G-2422)
AD-ART SIGNS GEORGETOWN INC
24383 Mariner Cir (19947-2677)
PHONE..................302 856-7446
Gordon Mariner, *Principal*
EMP: 7
SALES (est): 14.9K **Privately Held**
SIC: 3993 Signs & advertising specialties

(G-2423)
ADAMS KEMP ASSOCIATES INC
217 S Race St (19947-1911)
PHONE..................302 856-6699
Charles E Adams Jr, *President*
Roy B Kemp, *Corp Secy*
Roy Kemp, *Admin Sec*
EMP: 5
SALES (est): 380.1K **Privately Held**
WEB: www.adamskemp.com
SIC: 8713 Photogrammetric engineering

(G-2424)
ADRIANE HOHMANN
501 College Park Ln (19947-2113)
PHONE..................302 253-2020
Adriane Hohmann, *Principal*
EMP: 5
SALES (est): 82.1K **Privately Held**
SIC: 8011 Offices & clinics of medical doctors

(G-2425)
AGFIRST FARM CREDIT BANK
20816 Dupont Blvd (19947-3179)
PHONE..................302 856-9081
Chamayne Busker, *Manager*
EMP: 8
SALES (corp-wide): 883.9MM **Privately Held**
WEB: www.countrymortgages.com
SIC: 6111 Federal & federally sponsored credit agencies
PA: Agfirst Farm Credit Bank
 1901 Main St
 Columbia SC 29201
 803 799-5000

(G-2426)
AIR METHODS CORPORATION
21479 Rudder Ln (19947-2024)
PHONE..................302 363-3168
Aaron Todd, *CEO*
EMP: 6
SALES (corp-wide): 1.6B **Privately Held**
SIC: 4522 Ambulance services, air
HQ: Air Methods Corporation
 5500 S Quebec St Ste 300
 Greenwood Village CO 80111
 303 792-7400

(G-2427)
AKU TRANSPORT INC (PA)
24559 Dupont Blvd (19947-2627)
PHONE..................302 500-8127
Halil Camci, *President*
EMP: 6
SALES (est): 2.5MM **Privately Held**
SIC: 4731 Truck transportation brokers

(G-2428)
ALIAS TECHNOLOGY LLC
25100 Trinity Dr (19947-6585)
PHONE..................302 856-9488
David Middleton, *Technology*
Thomas Sombar, *Technology*
Carole E Chaski PHD,
EMP: 5
SALES: 100K **Privately Held**
SIC: 7371 8734 Software programming applications; forensic laboratory

Georgetown - Sussex County (G-2429)   GEOGRAPHIC SECTION

(G-2429)
ALTERNATIVE SOLUTIONS
532 S Bedford St (19947-1852)
PHONE....................................302 542-9081
Wade Jones, *Principal*
EMP: 8
SALES (est): 82.2K **Privately Held**
SIC: 8063 Psychiatric hospitals

(G-2430)
AMERESCO INC
29086 Landfill Ln (19947-6068)
PHONE....................................302 875-0696
Mike Gruben, *Manager*
EMP: 6
SALES (corp-wide): 787.1MM **Publicly Held**
SIC: 8748 Energy conservation consultant
PA: Ameresco, Inc.
111 Speen St Ste 410
Framingham MA 01701
508 661-2200

(G-2431)
AMERICAN HARDSCAPES LLC
20099 Gravel Hill Rd (19947-5359)
PHONE....................................302 253-8237
John D Glenn,
EMP: 10
SALES (est): 1.5MM **Privately Held**
SIC: 8711 Building construction consultant

(G-2432)
AQUILA OF DELAWARE INC
6 N Railroad Ave (19947-1242)
PHONE....................................302 856-9746
April Lasthbury, *Manager*
Tyler Hohman, *Director*
EMP: 5 **Privately Held**
SIC: 8069 Drug addiction rehabilitation hospital
PA: Aquila Of Delaware Inc.
1812 Newport Gap Pike
Wilmington DE 19808

(G-2433)
ARCHER & GREINER PC
Also Called: Harold W.T. Purnell II
406 S Bedford St Ste 1 (19947-1854)
P.O. Box 977 (19947-0977)
PHONE....................................302 858-5151
Harold Purnell II, *Owner*
EMP: 4
SALES (est): 277.6K
SALES (corp-wide): 57.5MM **Privately Held**
SIC: 8111 General practice attorney, lawyer
PA: Archer & Greiner, P.C.
33 E Euclid Ave
Haddonfield NJ 08033
856 795-2121

(G-2434)
ARCHER EXTERIORS INC
22295 Lwes Georgetown Hwy (19947-5526)
PHONE....................................302 877-0650
Michael Sykes, *Opers Staff*
Mike Sykes, *Manager*
EMP: 11
SALES (corp-wide): 58.2MM **Privately Held**
SIC: 1761 Skylight installation; siding contractor
PA: Archer Exteriors Inc.
341 Harding Hwy
Elmer NJ 08318
856 363-7000

(G-2435)
AROUND CLOCK HTG AC INC
22343 Bunting Rd (19947)
PHONE....................................302 856-9306
Phil Daisey, *President*
EMP: 4
SALES (est): 232.3K **Privately Held**
SIC: 1711 Warm air heating & air conditioning contractor

(G-2436)
ATLANTIC CHIROPRACTIC ASSOCIAT
2 Lee Ave Unit 103 (19947-2149)
PHONE....................................302 854-9300
Andrew Riddle, *Branch Mgr*
EMP: 5 **Privately Held**
SIC: 8041 Offices & clinics of chiropractors
PA: Atlantic Chiropractic Associat
375 Mullet Run
Milford DE 19963

(G-2437)
ATLANTIC FAMILY PHYSICIAN LLC
2 Lee Ave Unit 103 (19947-2149)
PHONE....................................302 856-4092
Fabricio Alarcon, *Owner*
EMP: 5
SALES (est): 134.8K **Privately Held**
SIC: 8011 General & family practice, physician/surgeon

(G-2438)
ATLANTIC INDUSTRIAL OPTICS
Also Called: A I O
21348 Cedar Creek Ave (19947-6305)
PHONE....................................302 856-7905
Richard Vanderhook, *President*
EMP: 8
SALES (est): 1.1MM **Privately Held**
SIC: 3679 3299 3827 Quartz crystals, for electronic application; tubing for electrical purposes, quartz; optical instruments & lenses

(G-2439)
ATLANTIC LAW GROUP LLC
512 E Market St (19947-2255)
PHONE....................................302 854-0380
Craig Trumbull, *Branch Mgr*
EMP: 20 **Privately Held**
SIC: 8111 General practice law office
PA: Atlantic Law Group, Llc
1602 Vllge Mrkt Se 310
Leesburg VA 20175

(G-2440)
ATLANTIS INDUSTRIES CORP
21490 Baltimore Ave (19947-6415)
PHONE....................................302 684-8542
Thad Schippereit, *President*
Dave Bunting, *General Mgr*
Thorne Gould, *Vice Pres*
Doug McGarvey, *Vice Pres*
Chuck McClure, *Opers Mgr*
▲ **EMP:** 45
SALES (est): 12.3MM **Privately Held**
SIC: 3089 Injection molding of plastics

(G-2441)
AUSTIN COX HOME SERVICES
22945 E Piney Grove Rd (19947-5962)
PHONE....................................410 334-6406
Marty Batze, *Principal*
EMP: 4
SALES (est): 329.6K **Privately Held**
SIC: 7261 Funeral home

(G-2442)
B & M ELECTRIC INC
19460 Savannah Rd (19947-3094)
PHONE....................................302 745-3807
George Bailey, *President*
Lori Bradley, *Vice Pres*
EMP: 6 **EST:** 1994
SALES (est): 466.2K **Privately Held**
SIC: 1731 General electrical contractor

(G-2443)
B WALLS SON HTG & A CONDITIONS
22424 Peterkins Rd (19947-2717)
PHONE....................................302 856-4045
Virginia Walls, *President*
Sharon Lewis, *Principal*
Robert J Lewis, *Vice Pres*
Barry Walls, *Vice Pres*
Charles Steiner, *Admin Sec*
EMP: 18
SALES: 350K **Privately Held**
SIC: 1711 Warm air heating & air conditioning contractor; plumbing contractors

(G-2444)
BAHARS COMPANY
Also Called: Service General
110 N Race St Ste 101 (19947-1495)
PHONE....................................302 856-2966
Banda Bahar, *Owner*
EMP: 10
SALES (est): 1.3MM **Privately Held**
SIC: 6099 Check cashing agencies

(G-2445)
BARBOSA MANUFACTURING
24965 Kruger Rd (19947-2640)
PHONE....................................302 856-6343
Mario A Barbosa, *Principal*
EMP: 2
SALES (est): 95.7K **Privately Held**
SIC: 3999 Candles

(G-2446)
BARNETT TOM D LAW FIRM
512 E Market St (19947-2255)
PHONE....................................302 855-9252
Tom Barnett, *Owner*
EMP: 5
SALES (est): 290K **Privately Held**
SIC: 8111 Legal services

(G-2447)
BAXTER FARMS INC
23073 Zoar Rd (19947-6801)
PHONE....................................302 856-1818
James H Baxter Jr, *President*
Ruth D Baxter, *Vice Pres*
James Baxter IV, *Treasurer*
EMP: 5
SQ FT: 5,000
SALES (est): 820K **Privately Held**
SIC: 5159 5083 Farm animals; agricultural machinery & equipment

(G-2448)
BAYHEALTH MEDICAL GROUP ENT
20930 Dupont Blvd # 202 (19947-1725)
PHONE....................................302 339-8040
Debbie B Betts, *Purch Mgr*
Michelle Gosnell, *Office Mgr*
EMP: 5
SALES (est): 87.2K **Privately Held**
SIC: 8011 Offices & clinics of medical doctors

(G-2449)
BB CUSTOM INSTRUMENTS
300a Nancy St (19947-2324)
PHONE....................................302 339-3826
EMP: 2
SALES (est): 137.1K **Privately Held**
SIC: 3931 Musical instruments

(G-2450)
BEACHVIEW MGMT INC
Also Called: Sign-A-Rama
24049 Lews Georgtwn Hwy # 22 (19947-5433)
PHONE....................................302 227-3280
Pamela K Handy, *President*
Gwen K Osborne, *Owner*
Gwendolyn Osborne, *Vice Pres*
EMP: 4
SQ FT: 2,400
SALES (est): 339.4K **Privately Held**
SIC: 8741 3993 Management services; advertising artwork

(G-2451)
BEACON ENGINEERING LLC
23318 Cedar Ln (19947-2755)
PHONE....................................302 864-8825
Robert Palmer, *Principal*
EMP: 5
SALES (est): 324.6K **Privately Held**
SIC: 8711 Engineering services

(G-2452)
BEACON HOSPITALITY
Also Called: Microtel
22297 Dupont Blvd (19947-3182)
PHONE....................................302 249-0502
Chad Moore, *Owner*
EMP: 7
SALES (est): 280K **Privately Held**
SIC: 7011 7021 Hotels & motels; dormitory, commercially operated

(G-2453)
BEEBE MEDICAL CENTER INC
Also Called: Beebe Imaging
21635 Biden Ave (19947-4574)
PHONE....................................302 856-9729
Jan Hickman, *Director*
EMP: 7
SALES (corp-wide): 447.8MM **Privately Held**
SIC: 8062 8011 General medical & surgical hospitals; offices & clinics of medical doctors
PA: Beebe Medical Center, Inc.
424 Savannah Rd
Lewes DE 19958
302 645-3300

(G-2454)
BETTS & ABRAM PA LLC
15 S Race St (19947-1907)
P.O. Box 770 (19947-0770)
PHONE....................................302 856-7755
Irene Hudson, *Officer*
A D Betts Jr,
EMP: 6
SQ FT: 2,500
SALES (est): 465.1K **Privately Held**
SIC: 8111 General practice law office

(G-2455)
BLAIR CARMEAN MASONRY
24373 Gravel Hill Rd (19947-6567)
PHONE....................................302 934-6103
Carmean Blair, *Owner*
EMP: 5
SALES (est): 186.3K **Privately Held**
SIC: 1741 Masonry & other stonework

(G-2456)
BLESSED GIVING
40 Ingramtown Rd (19947-1610)
PHONE....................................302 856-4551
Rhonda Reynolds, *Principal*
EMP: 5
SALES (est): 54.7K **Privately Held**
SIC: 8699 Charitable organization

(G-2457)
BOYS & GIRLS CLUBS DEL INC
Also Called: Georgetown
115 N Race St (19947-1406)
PHONE....................................302 856-4903
Christopher Couch, *Manager*
Amber Cooper, *Director*
Renee Hickman, *Director*
EMP: 10
SALES (corp-wide): 20.8MM **Privately Held**
SIC: 8641 Youth organizations
PA: Boys & Girls Clubs Of Delaware, Inc.
669 S Union St
Wilmington DE 19805
302 658-1870

(G-2458)
BRAMBLE CONSTRUCTION CO INC
812 E Market St (19947-2224)
PHONE....................................302 856-6723
Sammuel Bramble III, *President*
Dawn Bramble, *Corp Secy*
EMP: 10
SALES: 1.5MM **Privately Held**
WEB: www.brambleconstruction.com
SIC: 1623 1611 1794 Underground utilities contractor; grading; excavation work

(G-2459)
BRIDGE COUNSELING CENTER LLC
21635 Biden Ave (19947-4574)
PHONE....................................302 856-9190
Joel Van Ini, *Mng Member*
Joel Vanini, *Mng Member*
EMP: 4
SALES (est): 175.5K **Privately Held**
WEB: www.bridgecounseling.com
SIC: 8322 General counseling services

(G-2460)
BRUCE A ROGERS PA
12 S Front St (19947-1869)
PHONE....................................302 856-7161
Bruce A Rogers, *Owner*
EMP: 4
SALES (est): 280K **Privately Held**
SIC: 8111 General practice attorney, lawyer

GEOGRAPHIC SECTION
Georgetown - Sussex County (G-2488)

(G-2461)
C H P T MANUFACTURING INC
Also Called: Chpt Manufacturing
21388 Cedar Creek Ave (19947-6305)
PHONE..................................302 856-7660
Matthew A Koch, *President*
Douglas C Hicks, *President*
John E Protack, *Vice Pres*
EMP: 7
SQ FT: 4,500
SALES (est): 1.4MM **Privately Held**
SIC: 3561 7699 Pumps & pumping equipment; industrial machinery & equipment repair

(G-2462)
CAREYS FOREIGN & DOMESTIC REPR
7 Bridgeville Rd (19947-2105)
PHONE..................................302 856-2779
Archie Carey, *President*
EMP: 4
SALES (est): 370K **Privately Held**
SIC: 7538 General automotive repair shops

(G-2463)
CATHOLIC CHARITIES INC
406 S Bedford St (19947-1853)
PHONE..................................302 856-9578
Maureen Murphy, *Controller*
Teddi Millerline, *Admin Sec*
EMP: 6
SALES (corp-wide): 6.8MM **Privately Held**
WEB: www.ccwilm.org
SIC: 8322 Social service center
PA: Catholic Charities Inc
2601 W 4th St
Wilmington DE 19805
302 655-9624

(G-2464)
CATO CORPORATION
509 N Dupont Hwy (19947)
PHONE..................................302 854-9548
Britney Holmes, *Manager*
EMP: 7
SALES (corp-wide): 829.6MM **Publicly Held**
SIC: 5621 5632 5137 5699 Ready-to-wear apparel, women's; women's accessory & specialty stores; women's & children's clothing; sports apparel; department stores; children's & infants' wear stores; children's wear
PA: The Cato Corporation
8100 Denmark Rd
Charlotte NC 28273
704 554-8510

(G-2465)
CENTRAL AMERICA DISTRS LLC
Also Called: Central Amer Hlth Buty Distrs
11 E Market St Ste 2 (19947-1511)
PHONE..................................302 628-4178
Evelio Velasquez,
EMP: 10
SALES (est): 1.8MM **Privately Held**
SIC: 5087 Beauty parlor equipment & supplies

(G-2466)
CENTRAL DELAWARE COMMITTEE
Also Called: Sussex County Counseling Svcs
20728 Dupont Blvd # 315 (19947-3199)
PHONE..................................302 854-0172
Valerie Chastain, *Manager*
EMP: 6
SALES (corp-wide): 3.8MM **Privately Held**
SIC: 8069 Alcoholism rehabilitation hospital
PA: Central Delaware Committee
1241 College Park Dr
Dover DE 19904
302 735-7790

(G-2467)
CHEER INC (PA)
546 S Bedford St (19947-1852)
PHONE..................................302 856-5641
Don Wood, *Manager*
Beckett Harman, *Info Tech Mgr*
Kevin Mutch, *Technology*
Arlene Littleton, *Director*
Carolyn Oneal, *Director*
EMP: 13
SQ FT: 2,500
SALES: 8.6MM **Privately Held**
SIC: 8322 Senior citizens' center or association

(G-2468)
CHILDREN FMILIES FIRST DEL INC
410 S Bedford St (19947-1850)
PHONE..................................302 856-2388
Al Sneider, *Exec Dir*
EMP: 30
SALES (corp-wide): 16.8MM **Privately Held**
SIC: 8069 8322 Alcoholism rehabilitation hospital; individual & family services
PA: Children & Families First Delaware Inc.
809 N Washington St
Wilmington DE 19801
302 658-5177

(G-2469)
CHILDRENS ADVOCACY CTR OF DEL
410 S Bedford St (19947-1850)
PHONE..................................302 854-0323
Randall Williams, *Branch Mgr*
EMP: 15
SALES (corp-wide): 1.3MM **Privately Held**
SIC: 8322 Child related social services
PA: Children's Advocacy Center Of Delaware Inc
611 S Dupont Hwy Ste 201
Dover DE 19901
302 741-2123

(G-2470)
CHOICE BUILDERS LLC
23105 Parker Rd (19947-4716)
PHONE..................................302 856-7234
Greg Fritzpatrick,
Melinfa Fritzpatrick,
EMP: 4
SALES (est): 469.4K **Privately Held**
WEB: www.choicebuilders.net
SIC: 1542 Commercial & office building, new construction

(G-2471)
CHUDASAMA ENTERPRISES LLC
Also Called: Knights Inn
313 N Dupont Hwy (19947)
PHONE..................................302 856-7532
Hitesh Chudasama, *Owner*
EMP: 8
SALES (corp-wide): 709.4K **Privately Held**
SIC: 7011 Hotels & motels
PA: Chudasama Enterprises Llc
521 W Dupont Hwy
Millsboro DE 19966
302 934-7968

(G-2472)
CINDY L SZABO
9 N Front St (19947-1413)
P.O. Box 574 (19947-0574)
PHONE..................................302 855-9505
Cindy Szabo, *Manager*
Steve Ellis,
Susie Davis, *Legal Staff*
EMP: 8 **EST:** 2015
SALES (est): 189.9K **Privately Held**
SIC: 8111 General practice attorney, lawyer

(G-2473)
CITIZENS BANK NATIONAL ASSN
13 The Cir (19947-1501)
PHONE..................................302 856-4231
Lee Walls, *Branch Mgr*
EMP: 7
SALES (corp-wide): 7.3B **Publicly Held**
SIC: 6022 State commercial banks
HQ: Citizens Bank, National Association
1 Citizens Plz Ste 1 # 1
Providence RI 02903
401 282-7000

(G-2474)
CLARK & SONS INC
500 W Market St (19947-2322)
PHONE..................................302 856-3372
David J Clark, *Manager*
EMP: 9
SALES (corp-wide): 9.5MM **Privately Held**
WEB: www.clarkandsonsdoors.com
SIC: 1751 Garage door, installation or erection
PA: Clark & Sons, Inc.
314 E Ayre St
Wilmington DE 19804
302 998-7552

(G-2475)
COASTAL WOODCRAFT
404 Robinson St (19947-1148)
PHONE..................................302 856-7947
James Debastiani, *Owner*
EMP: 1
SALES (est): 79.4K **Privately Held**
SIC: 2499 Woodenware, kitchen & household

(G-2476)
COATINGS WITH A PURPOSE INC
21166 Greenway Pl (19947-4373)
PHONE..................................302 462-1465
Mark Lyon, *President*
EMP: 3
SALES (est): 386.6K **Privately Held**
SIC: 2851 Removers & cleaners

(G-2477)
COMCAST CABLEVISION OF DEL (HQ)
426a N Dupont Hwy (19947)
PHONE..................................302 856-4591
Henry Pearl, *General Mgr*
EMP: 12
SALES (est): 8.3MM
SALES (corp-wide): 94.5B **Publicly Held**
SIC: 4841 Cable television services
PA: Comcast Corporation
1701 Jfk Blvd
Philadelphia PA 19103
215 286-1700

(G-2478)
COMMUNITY AUTO REPAIR
514 W Market St (19947-2322)
PHONE..................................302 856-3333
EMP: 6
SALES (est): 103.2K **Privately Held**
SIC: 7699 Repair services

(G-2479)
COMMUNITY LEGAL AID SOCIETY
Also Called: Disabilities Law Program
20151 Office Cir (19947-3197)
PHONE..................................302 856-0038
Elanoe Kiesel, *Branch Mgr*
EMP: 12
SALES (est): 745K
SALES (corp-wide): 5.2MM **Privately Held**
SIC: 8111 General practice attorney, lawyer
PA: Community Legal Aid Society Inc
100 W 10th St Ste 801
Wilmington DE 19801
302 757-7001

(G-2480)
COMPASSIONATE CARE HOSPICE
20165 Office Cir (19947-3197)
PHONE..................................302 856-1486
Judith I Grey, *COO*
EMP: 5
SALES (est): 122.4K **Privately Held**
SIC: 8069 Specialty hospitals, except psychiatric

(G-2481)
CONFLUENT CORPORATION
19640 Buck Run (19947-5336)
PHONE..................................301 440-4100
Douglas A Spooner, *President*
EMP: 7
SQ FT: 5,500
SALES (est): 523.1K **Privately Held**
WEB: www.confluent-it.com
SIC: 7378 Computer & data processing equipment repair/maintenance

(G-2482)
CONNOR CHARLES & SONS PAINTING
14219 Road 526 (19947)
P.O. Box 235, Nassau (19969-0235)
PHONE..................................302 945-1746
Charles Connor, *Owner*
EMP: 5
SALES: 220K **Privately Held**
SIC: 1721 Exterior commercial painting contractor

(G-2483)
CONVENTIONEER PUBG CO INC
Also Called: P & R Printing
24948 Green Fern Dr (19947-2776)
PHONE..................................301 487-3907
David Stein, *President*
EMP: 4
SQ FT: 3,000
SALES (est): 426.4K **Privately Held**
SIC: 2752 Commercial printing, lithographic

(G-2484)
COOPER BEARINGS INC
21629 Baltimore Ave (19947-6312)
PHONE..................................302 858-5056
Paul Foster, *President*
▲ **EMP:** 12
SQ FT: 35,000
SALES (est): 1.4MM
SALES (corp-wide): 56.1MM **Privately Held**
WEB: www.epowerrail.com
SIC: 7699 Industrial machinery & equipment repair
PA: Powerrail Holdings, Inc.
205 Clark Rd
Duryea PA 18642
570 883-7005

(G-2485)
CORINTHIAN HOUSE
219 S Race St (19947-1911)
PHONE..................................302 858-1493
EMP: 6 **EST:** 2017
SALES (est): 86.2K **Privately Held**
SIC: 8093 Substance abuse clinics (outpatient)

(G-2486)
CORNERSTONE MEDIA PRODUCTION
41 Bramhall St (19947-2145)
P.O. Box 487 (19947-0487)
PHONE..................................302 855-9380
Rick Greenberg, *President*
Diane Greenberg, *Vice Pres*
EMP: 4
SQ FT: 3,500
SALES: 400K **Privately Held**
WEB: www.cornerstonemedia.com
SIC: 7812 Video production

(G-2487)
CORRECTION DELAWARE DEPARTMENT
Also Called: Sussex Correctional Instn
23203 Dupont Blvd (19947)
P.O. Box 500 (19947-0599)
PHONE..................................302 856-5280
G R Johnson, *Warden*
EMP: 350 **Privately Held**
SIC: 8361 9223 Residential care; correctional institutions;
HQ: Delaware Department Of Correction
245 Mckee Rd
Dover DE 19904

(G-2488)
COUNTY BANK
13 N Bedford St (19947-1497)
PHONE..................................302 855-2000
Robin Parker, *Manager*
EMP: 7 **Privately Held**
WEB: www.countybankdel.com
SIC: 6021 National commercial banks

Georgetown - Sussex County (G-2489)

PA: County Bank
19927 Shuttle Rd
Rehoboth Beach DE 19971

(G-2489)
COUNTY OF SUSSEX
Also Called: Suffex County Ems
22215 Dupont Blvd (19947-3165)
P.O. Box 589 (19947-0589)
PHONE..................302 854-5050
Bill Lecates, *Branch Mgr*
Jay Shine,
EMP: 80 **Privately Held**
SIC: 7363 Medical help service
PA: County Of Sussex
2 The Cir
Georgetown DE 19947
302 855-7700

(G-2490)
COUNTY OF SUSSEX ▲
Also Called: Sussex County Planning & Zng
2 The Cir (19947-1502)
P.O. Box 417 (19947-0417)
PHONE..................302 855-7878
Lawrence Lank, *Director*
EMP: 25 **Privately Held**
SIC: 8742 Administrative services consultant
PA: County Of Sussex
2 The Cir
Georgetown DE 19947
302 855-7700

(G-2491)
CROWN EQUINE LLC
14274 Cokesbury Rd (19947-4622)
PHONE..................302 629-2782
Krystal Lyn Harrell Dvm, *Principal*
EMP: 4 **EST:** 2012
SALES (est): 189K **Privately Held**
SIC: 0272 Horses & other equines

(G-2492)
D C MEDICAL SERVICES LLC
Also Called: Jona D Gorra MD
10 W Laurel St (19947-1424)
PHONE..................302 855-0915
Jona D Gorra,
EMP: 4
SALES (est): 373.3K **Privately Held**
SIC: 8011 Internal medicine practitioners

(G-2493)
DAVID WENTWORTH
Also Called: H & R Block
418 N Dupont Hwy (19287)
PHONE..................302 856-3272
David Wentworth, *Partner*
Elizabeth Wentworth, *Partner*
EMP: 4
SALES (est): 173.5K **Privately Held**
SIC: 7291 Tax return preparation services

(G-2494)
DAVIS CHIROPRACTIC INC
20461 Dupont Blvd Ste 1 (19947-3174)
PHONE..................302 856-2225
John C Davis, *President*
EMP: 4
SALES (est): 329.4K **Privately Held**
SIC: 8041 Offices & clinics of chiropractors

(G-2495)
DCAT TRANSIT LLC
18800 Whaleys Corner Rd (19947-4929)
PHONE..................302 855-1231
EMP: 4
SALES (est): 170.5K **Privately Held**
SIC: 4111 Local/Suburban Transportation

(G-2496)
DECRANE AIRCRAFT SYSTEMS
21583 Baltimore Ave (19947-6313)
PHONE..................302 253-0390
Harvey O Patrick, *President*
Larry Ohler, *CFO*
EMP: 600 **EST:** 1974
SQ FT: 2,000
SALES (est): 41.4MM **Privately Held**
SIC: 3728 Aircraft body assemblies & parts
HQ: Pats Aircraft, Llc
21652 Nanticoke Ave
Georgetown DE 19947
855 236-1638

(G-2497)
DEITER INC
27840 Woodcrest Dr. (19947-6041)
PHONE..................302 875-9167
EMP: 4 **EST:** 1998
SALES (est): 500K **Privately Held**
SIC: 1542 Nonresidential Construction

(G-2498)
DEL-ONE FEDERAL CREDIT UNION
30 Georgetown Plz (19947-2300)
P.O. Box 490 (19947-0490)
PHONE..................302 856-5100
Debbie Harriger, *Branch Mgr*
EMP: 4 **Privately Held**
WEB: www.del-one.org
SIC: 6061 Federal credit unions
PA: Del-One Federal Credit Union
270 Beiser Blvd
Dover DE 19904

(G-2499)
DELAWARE DRNKING DRVER PROGRAM
Also Called: Thresholds
20505 Dupont Blvd Unit 1 (19947-3173)
PHONE..................302 856-1835
Andy Burlingame, *Manager*
EMP: 10
SALES (corp-wide): 559.7K **Privately Held**
SIC: 8322 Alcoholism counseling, nontreatment
PA: Delaware Drinking Driver Program Inc
1661 S Dupont Hwy
Dover DE 19901
302 736-4326

(G-2500)
DELAWARE HOME HEALTH CARE
22251 Lews Georgtwn Hwy (19947-5526)
PHONE..................302 856-3600
Janet Chorman, *Branch Mgr*
EMP: 10
SALES (est): 176.3K **Privately Held**
SIC: 8082 Home health care services
PA: Delaware Home Health Care Inc
22251 Lews Georgtwn Hwy
Georgetown DE 19947

(G-2501)
DELAWARE INTEGRATIVE MEDICAL C
20930 Dupont Blvd # 203 (19947-1724)
PHONE..................302 559-5959
Henry Childers, *Principal*
EMP: 5
SALES (est): 267K **Privately Held**
SIC: 8099 Blood related health services

(G-2502)
DELAWARE S P C A
Also Called: Sussex Chapter
22918 Dupont Blvd (19947-8803)
PHONE..................302 856-6361
EMP: 8
SALES (corp-wide): 1.9MM **Privately Held**
SIC: 8699 Membership Organization
PA: Delaware S P C A
455 Stanton Christiana Rd
Newark DE 19713
302 998-2281

(G-2503)
DELAWARE STATE POLICE FEDERAL (PA)
700 N Bedford St (19947-2151)
P.O. Box 717 (19947-0717)
PHONE..................302 856-3501
Jeffery Weaver, *Ch of Bd*
Stephen Cimo, *President*
Blanche Jackson, *Vice Pres*
Diane Short, *Vice Pres*
Tracey Jackson, *CFO*
EMP: 19
SQ FT: 6,000
SALES: 3.8MM **Privately Held**
WEB: www.dspfcu.com
SIC: 6061 Federal credit unions

(G-2504)
DELAWARE TCHNCAL CMNTY COLLEGE
Also Called: Jack F Owens Campus
21179 College Dr (19947-4193)
PHONE..................302 259-6160
Ileana Smith, *Admin Director*
EMP: 230 **Privately Held**
WEB: www.dtcc.edu
SIC: 8222 8111 Junior college; legal services
PA: Delaware Technical & Community College
100 Campus Dr
Dover DE 19904

(G-2505)
DELAWARE VEIN CENTER
20930 Dupont Blvd # 202 (19947-1725)
PHONE..................302 258-8853
Henry Childers, *Owner*
EMP: 5
SALES (est): 87.5K **Privately Held**
SIC: 8049 Offices of health practitioner

(G-2506)
DELMACO MANUFACTURING INC
21424 Cedar Creek Ave (19947-6305)
PHONE..................302 856-6345
G Bennett, *President*
S Allan Davey, *Chairman*
▼ **EMP:** 14
SQ FT: 11,200
SALES (est): 2.5MM **Privately Held**
WEB: www.delmacomfg.com
SIC: 3499 3495 Reels, cable: metal; wire springs

(G-2507)
DELMARVA POULTRY INDUSTRY INC
Also Called: DPI
16686 County Seat Hwy (19947-4881)
PHONE..................302 856-9037
Roger Marino, *President*
Lori Morrow, *Corp Secy*
Wayne Evans, *Vice Pres*
J William Satterfield, *Exec Dir*
Bill Satterfield, *Exec Dir*
EMP: 4
SQ FT: 1,800
SALES: 744.1K **Privately Held**
WEB: www.dpichicken.com
SIC: 8611 Trade associations

(G-2508)
DELMARVA SIGN CO
24835 Lawson Rd (19947-6659)
PHONE..................302 934-6188
Anna McDonough, *Owner*
EMP: 2
SALES (est): 174.7K **Privately Held**
SIC: 3993 Signs & advertising specialties

(G-2509)
DELMARVA SPRAY FOAM LLC
22976 Sussex Ave (19947-6310)
PHONE..................302 752-1080
Robert Devere,
Gerald Palmer,
EMP: 13
SALES (est): 188.1K
SALES (corp-wide): 15.1MM **Privately Held**
SIC: 1799 1742 Spraying contractor, non-agricultural; insulation, buildings
PA: Southland Insulators, Inc.
8521 Quarry Rd
Manassas VA 20110
703 368-1965

(G-2510)
DELORES WELCH
Also Called: Dee's Cleaning Service
22812 Cedar Ln (19947-6320)
PHONE..................302 856-7989
Delores Welch, *Owner*
EMP: 8
SALES (est): 150K **Privately Held**
SIC: 7349 Janitorial service, contract basis; maid services, contract or fee basis; office cleaning or charring

(G-2511)
DIXIE CONSTRUCTION COMPANY INC
22237 Lwes Georgetown Hwy (19947-5526)
PHONE..................302 858-5007
Keith Jacobi, *Branch Mgr*
EMP: 25
SALES (corp-wide): 150MM **Privately Held**
SIC: 1611 1623 General contractor, highway & street construction; resurfacing contractor; water, sewer & utility lines
PA: Dixie Construction Company, Inc.
260 Hpwell Rd Churchville
Churchville MD 21028
410 879-8055

(G-2512)
DIY TOOL SUPPLY LLC
23135 Lewes Georgetown (19947-5395)
PHONE..................302 253-8461
EMP: 1
SALES (est): 75.7K **Privately Held**
SIC: 3541 Machine tools, metal cutting type

(G-2513)
DOREY FINANCIAL SERVICES INC
13 Bridgeville Rd (19947-2105)
PHONE..................302 856-0970
Terry Dorey, *President*
EMP: 6
SALES (est): 346.4K **Privately Held**
SIC: 8742 Financial consultant

(G-2514)
DRAPER & GOLDBERG PLLC
512 E Market St (19947-2255)
PHONE..................302 448-4040
Thomas Barnet, *Manager*
EMP: 6
SALES (est): 383.4K
SALES (corp-wide): 6.8MM **Privately Held**
SIC: 8111 General practice law office
PA: Draper & Goldberg, Pllc
44050 Ashbrn Shpg Plz
Ashburn VA 20147
703 777-7101

(G-2515)
DREAM VIEW EXTERIORS GROUP LLC
201 Primary Ave (19947-2805)
PHONE..................302 358-9530
Christopher W Vidro,
Chris Vidro,
EMP: 5 **EST:** 2013
SALES (est): 360K **Privately Held**
SIC: 1761 Roofing, siding & sheet metal work

(G-2516)
DUNBARTON OAKS ASSOCIATES
301 Dunbarton (19947-1173)
PHONE..................302 856-7719
EMP: 5
SALES (est): 225.3K **Privately Held**
SIC: 6513 Legal Entity

(G-2517)
EAST COAST CSTM CABINETRY LLC
23636 Saulsbury Ln (19947-6389)
PHONE..................302 245-3040
Kevin Minor, *Principal*
EMP: 4
SALES (est): 286K **Privately Held**
SIC: 2434 Wood kitchen cabinets

(G-2518)
EAST COAST SEED LLC
17741 Davis Rd (19947-4430)
PHONE..................302 856-7018
Mark Davis,
EMP: 4
SALES (est): 387.4K **Privately Held**
SIC: 8748 Agricultural consultant

Georgetown - Sussex County (G-2547)

(G-2519)
EASTER SEAL DELAWARE
22317 Dupont Blvd (19947-2153)
PHONE...................302 856-7364
Pam Reuther, *Manager*
EMP: 35
SALES (corp-wide): 34.3MM **Privately Held**
SIC: 8331 8399 Job training & vocational rehabilitation services; health & welfare council
PA: Easter Seals Delaware & Marylands Eastern Shore, Inc.
61 Corporate Cir
New Castle DE 19720
302 324-4444

(G-2520)
EASTERN SHORE POULTRY COMPANY
21724 Broad Creek Ave (19947-6307)
PHONE...................302 855-1350
Harry Dukes, *President*
Edward Pion, *Vice Pres*
EMP: 356
SQ FT: 22,000
SALES (est): 101.8MM **Privately Held**
SIC: 5144 Poultry & poultry products

(G-2521)
ELOHIM COMMUNITY DEV CORP
40 Ingramtown Rd (19947-1610)
P.O. Box 756 (19947-0756)
PHONE...................302 856-4551
Patricia Kasinath, *Ch of Bd*
EMP: 4
SALES (est): 137.3K **Privately Held**
SIC: 8322 Individual & family services

(G-2522)
EMORY AGENCY INC
20650 Dupont Blvd (19947-3177)
PHONE...................302 855-2100
Emory Pusey, *Principal*
EMP: 4
SALES (est): 193.5K **Privately Held**
SIC: 6411 Insurance agents & brokers

(G-2523)
EPIC HEALTH SERVICES INC
20093 Office Cir 205 (19947-3196)
PHONE...................302 422-3176
EMP: 4
SALES (corp-wide): 402.6MM **Privately Held**
SIC: 8099 Blood related health services
HQ: Epic Health Services, Inc.
5220 Spring Valley Rd
Dallas TX 75254
214 466-1340

(G-2524)
ERIC S BALLIET
Also Called: Lord & Wheeler
212 W Market St (19947-1441)
PHONE...................302 856-7423
Eric S Balliet, *Principal*
EMP: 15
SQ FT: 2,650
SALES (est): 692.8K **Privately Held**
SIC: 8021 Dentists' office

(G-2525)
FAMILY PLANNING
544 S Bedford St (19947-1852)
PHONE...................302 856-5225
Nieca Lietzan, *Principal*
EMP: 4
SALES (est): 85K **Privately Held**
SIC: 8093 Specialty outpatient clinics

(G-2526)
FARM FINANCIAL SERVICES INC
Also Called: Stracar Insurance Group
P.O. Box 769 (19947-0769)
PHONE...................302 854-9760
Edward A Stracar, *President*
Lisa Stracar, *President*
EMP: 4
SQ FT: 700
SALES: 1MM **Privately Held**
SIC: 6411 Insurance agents

(G-2527)
FBK MEDICAL TUBING INC
21649 Cedar Creek Ave (19947-6396)
PHONE...................302 855-0585
Bartlett Bretz, *CEO*
Edwin Finch III, *Ch of Bd*
Jim Kieth, *President*
Betty Edkins, *Vice Pres*
Alan Drenneb III, *Admin Sec*
EMP: 21
SQ FT: 21,750
SALES (est): 2.4MM **Privately Held**
SIC: 8731 3082 3841 3083 Medical research, commercial; tubes, unsupported plastic; surgical & medical instruments; laminated plastics plate & sheet

(G-2528)
FELLOWSHIP HLTH RESOURCES INC
Also Called: New England Fellowship
505 W Market St Ste 110 (19947-2344)
PHONE...................302 854-0626
Joseph Dziobek, *Exec Dir*
EMP: 12
SALES (corp-wide): 38.7MM **Privately Held**
WEB: www.fellowshiphr.org
SIC: 8361 8322 Halfway group home, persons with social or personal problems; general counseling services
PA: Fellowship Health Resources, Inc.
24 Albion Rd Ste 420
Lincoln RI 02865
401 333-3980

(G-2529)
FELLOWSHIP HLTH RESOURCES INC
23769 Shortly Rd (19947-4754)
PHONE...................302 856-7642
Lois Cortese, *Manager*
EMP: 10
SALES (corp-wide): 38.7MM **Privately Held**
WEB: www.fellowshiphr.org
SIC: 8361 8661 Halfway group home, persons with social or personal problems; religious organizations
PA: Fellowship Health Resources, Inc.
24 Albion Rd Ste 420
Lincoln RI 02865
401 333-3980

(G-2530)
FERRY JOSEPH & PEARCE PA
6 W Market St (19947-1484)
PHONE...................302 856-3706
David J Ferry Jr, *Branch Mgr*
Brian Ferry, *Associate*
EMP: 5
SALES (est): 307.3K
SALES (corp-wide): 2.9MM **Privately Held**
SIC: 8111 General practice attorney, lawyer
PA: Ferry, Joseph & Pearce Pa
824 N Market St Ste 1000
Wilmington DE 19801
302 575-1555

(G-2531)
FIRST AMERICAN TITLE INSUR CO
106 N Bedford St (19947-1466)
PHONE...................302 855-2120
David Toomey, *Branch Mgr*
EMP: 10 **Publicly Held**
WEB: www.fatc.com
SIC: 6361 Real estate title insurance
HQ: First American Title Insurance Company
1 First American Way
Santa Ana CA 92707
800 854-3643

(G-2532)
FIRST STATE CMNTY ACTION AGCY (PA)
308 N Railroad Ave (19947-1252)
P.O. Box 877 (19947-0877)
PHONE...................302 856-7761
Bernice Edwards, *Exec Dir*
Helen McAdory, *Associate Dir*
EMP: 75
SALES: 8MM **Privately Held**
SIC: 8399 8322 Antipoverty board; individual & family services

(G-2533)
FISHER AUTO PARTS INC
Also Called: Manlove Auto Parts
117 E Market St (19947-1405)
PHONE...................302 856-2507
Bill Fisher, *Manager*
EMP: 5
SALES (corp-wide): 891.9MM **Privately Held**
WEB: www.fisherautoparts.com
SIC: 5013 Automotive supplies & parts
PA: Fisher Auto Parts, Inc.
512 Greenville Ave
Staunton VA 24401
540 885-8901

(G-2534)
FRETS4VETSORG
300a Nancy St (19947-2324)
PHONE...................302 382-1426
Isaiah Baker, *Principal*
EMP: 4
SALES (est): 97.2K **Privately Held**
SIC: 8699 Charitable organization

(G-2535)
FRUITBEARER PUBLISHING LLC
107 Elizabeth St (19947-1427)
PHONE...................302 856-6649
Candy Abbott, *Managing Prtnr*
Pam Halter, *Editor*
Kim Sponaugle, *Art Dir*
EMP: 4
SALES (est): 296.6K **Privately Held**
SIC: 2741 Miscellaneous publishing

(G-2536)
FUQUA & YORI P A
Also Called: Fuqua, James A Jr
26 The Cir (19947-1500)
P.O. Box 250 (19947-0250)
PHONE...................302 856-7777
James Fuqua, *President*
EMP: 12
SALES (est): 1.3MM **Privately Held**
WEB: www.fuquaandyori.com
SIC: 8111 General practice law office

(G-2537)
GALVIN INDUSTRIES LLC
202 W Laurel St (19947-2308)
PHONE...................703 505-7860
Tom Sherman,
EMP: 8
SALES (est): 186K **Privately Held**
SIC: 8733 Research institute

(G-2538)
GEO-TECHNOLOGY ASSOCIATES INC
Also Called: Gga
21133 Sterling Ave Unit 7 (19947-5572)
PHONE...................302 855-5775
Amin Rahman, *Vice Pres*
Greg Sauter, *Branch Mgr*
EMP: 5 **Privately Held**
SIC: 8748 Environmental consultant
HQ: Geo-Technology Associates Inc
3445 Box Hll Corp Ctr Dr A
Abingdon MD 21009
410 515-9446

(G-2539)
GEORGETOWN AIR SERVICES
21553 Rudder Ln Unit 1 (19947-2029)
P.O. Box 760 (19947-0760)
PHONE...................302 855-2355
Gerrett Dernoga, *Owner*
EMP: 5
SALES (est): 320.1K **Privately Held**
WEB: www.georgetownairservices.com
SIC: 4581 Aircraft maintenance & repair services

(G-2540)
GEORGETOWN AIR SERVICES LLC
Also Called: Sussex Aero Maintenance
21553 Rudder Ln Unit 1 (19947-2029)
PHONE...................302 855-2355
John F Kenney, *Principal*
Lisa Brown, *CFO*
Garrett Dernoga, *Manager*
EMP: 10
SQ FT: 6,400
SALES (est): 691.7K **Privately Held**
SIC: 4581 Aircraft maintenance & repair services

(G-2541)
GEORGETOWN ANIMAL HOSPITAL PA
20784 Dupont Blvd (19947-3178)
PHONE...................302 856-2623
John Gooss, *Partner*
EMP: 7
SALES (est): 361.7K **Privately Held**
SIC: 0742 Animal hospital services, pets & other animal specialties

(G-2542)
GEORGETOWN BOYS AND GIRLS CLUB
115 N Race St (19947-1406)
PHONE...................302 856-4903
Renee Hickman, *Director*
Geanne Guckes, *Director*
EMP: 15
SALES (est): 130.1K **Privately Held**
SIC: 8641 Youth organizations

(G-2543)
GEORGETOWN CHAMBER COMMERCE
87 E Market St (19947-1401)
P.O. Box 1 (19947-0001)
PHONE...................302 856-1544
EMP: 18
SALES: 124.9K **Privately Held**
SIC: 8611 Business Association

(G-2544)
GEORGETOWN CONSTRUCTION CO
25136 Dupont Blvd (19947-2610)
PHONE...................302 856-7601
Kenneth Adams, *President*
Joe Ann Adams, *Principal*
EMP: 60
SALES (est): 2.3MM **Privately Held**
WEB: www.melvinjoseph.com
SIC: 8748 Business consulting

(G-2545)
GEORGETOWN FAMILY MEDICINE
201 W Market St (19947-1440)
PHONE...................302 856-4092
Ryan Scot Davis, *Principal*
Fabricio J Alarcon, *Med Doctor*
EMP: 12 **EST:** 2001
SALES (est): 1.1MM **Privately Held**
SIC: 8011 General & family practice, physician/surgeon

(G-2546)
GEORGETOWN MEDICAL ASSOC LLC
20930 Dupont Blvd # 101 (19947-1723)
PHONE...................302 856-3737
Beshara Helou, *Principal*
Stacey Dixon, *Office Mgr*
Sharon Moyer, *Office Mgr*
EMP: 10
SALES (est): 717.6K **Privately Held**
SIC: 8011 Internal medicine, physician/surgeon

(G-2547)
GEORGETOWN PLAYGROUND & PK INC
212 Wilson St (19947-2328)
PHONE...................302 856-7111
Christine Lecates, *President*
EMP: 6
SALES: 51.6K **Privately Held**
SIC: 8399 Fund raising organization, non-fee basis

Georgetown - Sussex County (G-2548)

(G-2548)
GILL EDWARD LAW OFFICES OF
16 N Bedford St (19947-1463)
P.O. Box 824 (19947-0824)
PHONE..................302 854-5400
Edward Gill, *President*
EMP: 11
SALES (est): 1.6MM **Privately Held**
SIC: 8111 General practice law office

(G-2549)
GODS WAY TO RECOVERY INC
20785 Dupont Blvd (19947-3170)
PHONE..................302 856-7375
Roger Wood, *Branch Mgr*
EMP: 8
SALES (corp-wide): 1.1MM **Privately Held**
SIC: 8699 Charitable organization
PA: God's Way To Recovery Inc
  1 N Maple Ave
  Milford DE 19963
  302 422-3033

(G-2550)
GOLDEN CAR CARE
19395 Substation Rd (19947-4760)
PHONE..................302 856-2219
EMP: 4
SALES (est): 133.8K **Privately Held**
SIC: 7538 General automotive repair shops

(G-2551)
GS RACING PHOTOS
18063 Deer Forest Rd (19947-3414)
PHONE..................302 855-1165
EMP: 5 EST: 1999
SALES: 100K **Privately Held**
SIC: 7221 Photo Portrait Studio

(G-2552)
GUARDIAN ANGEL DAY CARE
25193 Zoar Rd (19947-6523)
PHONE..................302 934-0130
Shirley Davis, *President*
Sharon Moore, *Vice Pres*
EMP: 5
SALES (est): 170K **Privately Held**
SIC: 8351 Child day care services

(G-2553)
HABITAT FOR HUMANITY INTL INC
107 Depot St (19947-1471)
P.O. Box 759 (19947-0759)
PHONE..................302 855-1156
Kevin Gilmore, *Exec Dir*
EMP: 6
SALES (corp-wide): 349.9MM **Privately Held**
SIC: 8322 Individual & family services
PA: Habitat For Humanity International, Inc.
  270 Peachtree St Nw # 1300
  Atlanta GA 30303
  800 422-4828

(G-2554)
HALLER & HUDSON
101 S Bedford St (19947-1843)
PHONE..................302 856-4525
Karl Haller, *Partner*
Howard Hudson, *Partner*
EMP: 5
SALES (est): 330K **Privately Held**
SIC: 8111 General practice attorney, lawyer

(G-2555)
HARRISON SNIOR LVING GORGETOWN
110 W North St (19947-2137)
PHONE..................302 856-4574
Carol Daniels, *Administration*
EMP: 5
SALES: 14.8MM
SALES (corp-wide): 33.1MM **Privately Held**
SIC: 8051 Skilled nursing care facilities
PA: Harrison Holdings Corporation
  300 Strode Ave
  Coatesville PA 19320
  610 383-4225

(G-2556)
HEALTH & SOCIAL SVCS DEL DEPT
Also Called: Division of Child Spprt &
20105 Office Cir (19947-3197)
PHONE..................302 856-5586
Gary Bellkot, *Director*
EMP: 15 **Privately Held**
SIC: 8322 9111 Child related social services; executive offices;
HQ: Delaware Dept Of Health And Social Services
  1901 N Dupont Hwy
  New Castle DE 19720

(G-2557)
HEALTHY OUTCOMES LLC
2 Lee Ave Unit 103 (19947-2149)
PHONE..................302 856-4022
Jennifer Morelli, *Office Mgr*
EMP: 9 EST: 2011
SALES (est): 246.7K **Privately Held**
SIC: 8011 Offices & clinics of medical doctors

(G-2558)
HIPPO TRAILER
14 Evergreen Dr (19947-9483)
PHONE..................302 854-6661
Walter Hyler, *President*
Elaine Hyler, *Admin Sec*
EMP: 2
SALES (est): 129.7K **Privately Held**
SIC: 2451 Mobile homes

(G-2559)
HOLLINGSEAD INTERNATIONAL LLC
21583 Baltimore Ave (19947-6313)
PHONE..................302 855-5888
John Martin, *President*
Sandra Taras, *CFO*
Christopher Mikola, *Finance*
Matthew Hill, *Sales Staff*
Brian Neal, *Sales Staff*
EMP: 300 EST: 2011
SQ FT: 100,000
SALES (est): 11.2MM **Privately Held**
SIC: 3679 Electronic switches; harness assemblies for electronic use: wire or cable
HQ: Pats Aircraft, Llc
  21652 Nanticoke Ave
  Georgetown DE 19947
  855 236-1638

(G-2560)
HOME MEDIA ONE LLC
22344 Lwes Georgetown Hwy (19947-5535)
PHONE..................302 644-0307
Marc J Green,
EMP: 7
SALES (est): 650.5K **Privately Held**
SIC: 4813 Telephone communication, except radio

(G-2561)
HOMESTEAD CAMPING INC
25165 Prettyman Rd (19947-5207)
PHONE..................302 684-4278
William Prettyman, *President*
Irma Prettyman, *President*
EMP: 5
SALES (est): 346.7K **Privately Held**
SIC: 7033 Campsite

(G-2562)
HOY EN DELAWARE LLC
105 Depot St (19947-1471)
P.O. Box 593 (19947-0593)
PHONE..................302 854-0240
Jose Somalo,
EMP: 6
SALES (est): 256.1K **Privately Held**
SIC: 2711 Commercial printing & newspaper publishing combined

(G-2563)
HUDSON HOUSE SERVICES
11 W Pine St (19947-1825)
PHONE..................302 856-4363
Cindy Witt, *Principal*
EMP: 7
SALES (est): 80.6K **Privately Held**
SIC: 8093 Substance abuse clinics (outpatient)

(G-2564)
INDIAN RIVER TRUST (PA)
22855 Dupont Blvd (19947-8801)
PHONE..................302 661-2320
P C Townsend, *Owner*
Jay Moorehead, *Exec VP*
Patrick Johnston, *Vice Pres*
Greg Kapsch, *Vice Pres*
George White, *Vice Pres*
EMP: 7
SALES (est): 2.3MM **Privately Held**
SIC: 6733 Trusts

(G-2565)
INFINITY CHOPPERS
24655 Dupont Blvd (19947-2626)
PHONE..................302 249-7282
Michael Pizzola, *Principal*
EMP: 1
SALES (est): 61K **Privately Held**
SIC: 3751 Motorcycles & related parts

(G-2566)
INSPECTION LANES
23737 Dupont Blvd (19947-8805)
PHONE..................302 853-1003
Pam Smith, *Manager*
EMP: 5
SALES (est): 79.3K **Privately Held**
SIC: 7933 Ten pin center

(G-2567)
INTEGRATED SOLUTIONS PLANNING
Also Called: Solutions, I.P.E.M.
303 N Bedford St (19947-1151)
P.O. Box 416 (19947-0416)
PHONE..................302 297-9215
Frank M Kea, *Mng Member*
Peirce Kea, *Graphic Designe*
Jason Palkewicz,
EMP: 4
SQ FT: 1,450
SALES: 450K **Privately Held**
SIC: 8711 0781 8741 7336 Civil engineering; landscape architects; management services; graphic arts & related design

(G-2568)
IRON SOURCE LLC
25113 Dupont Blvd (19947-2621)
PHONE..................302 856-7545
Joby Lewis, *General Mgr*
James Wilczynski, *General Mgr*
Gary Hutton, *Cust Mgr*
Chess Hedrick, *Mng Member*
Kenneth P Adams,
▼ EMP: 8
SQ FT: 5,500
SALES: 8.6MM **Privately Held**
SIC: 5082 7353 Construction & mining machinery; heavy construction equipment rental

(G-2569)
J & P MANAGEMENT INC
Also Called: Comfort Inn
20530 Dupont Blvd (19947-3176)
PHONE..................302 854-9400
Raj Patel, *CEO*
Sashi Patel, *President*
EMP: 15
SALES: 1.2MM **Privately Held**
SIC: 7011 Hotels & motels

(G-2570)
J ROCCO CONSTRUCTION LLC
22476 Deep Branch Rd (19947-6351)
PHONE..................302 856-4100
Joe Rocco, *Mng Member*
Joseph Rocco, *Mng Member*
Mary Ann Rocco,
EMP: 4
SALES (est): 179K **Privately Held**
SIC: 1721 1522 1521 Residential painting; residential construction; single-family housing construction

(G-2571)
JANE L STAYTON CPA
117 S Bedford St (19947-1843)
PHONE..................302 856-4141
Jane L Stayton, *Owner*
EMP: 10
SALES (est): 474.6K **Privately Held**
SIC: 8721 Certified public accountant

(G-2572)
JED T JAMES
Also Called: Current Services
18066 Asketum Branch Rd (19947-6047)
PHONE..................302 875-0101
Jed T James, *Owner*
EMP: 5
SALES (est): 429.1K **Privately Held**
SIC: 0191 7389 General farms, primarily crop;

(G-2573)
JEFFERSON URIAN DANE STRNER PA (PA)
651 N Bedford St (19947-2159)
P.O. Box 830 (19947-0830)
PHONE..................302 856-3900
David C Doan, *President*
David Urian, *Vice Pres*
Charles Sterner, *Treasurer*
Stephanie Barry, *Accountant*
Nikita Massey, *Accountant*
EMP: 30
SALES (est): 5.8MM **Privately Held**
WEB: www.juds.com
SIC: 8721 Certified public accountant

(G-2574)
JG TOWNSEND JR & CO INC (PA)
316 N Race St (19947-1166)
P.O. Box 430 (19947-0430)
PHONE..................302 856-2525
Paul G Townsend, *President*
EMP: 40 EST: 1937
SQ FT: 52,554
SALES: 79MM **Privately Held**
SIC: 6531 6519 5099 5142 Selling agent, real estate; farm land leasing; timber products, rough; packaged frozen goods; frozen fruits & vegetables

(G-2575)
JG TOWNSEND JR FRZ FOODS INC
316 N Race St (19947-1166)
P.O. Box 430 (19947-0430)
PHONE..................302 856-2525
J G Townsend IV, *President*
Steven C Nett, *Treasurer*
Lisa Workman, *Admin Sec*
EMP: 40
SALES (est): 8.7MM
SALES (corp-wide): 79MM **Privately Held**
SIC: 5142 Packaged frozen goods
PA: J.G. Townsend Jr & Co Inc
  316 N Race St
  Georgetown DE 19947
  302 856-2525

(G-2576)
JOES PAINT & BODY SHOP INC
Also Called: Capes & Open Glass
501 N Bedford St (19947-2123)
PHONE..................302 855-0281
Joe Weemstein, *President*
EMP: 8
SALES (est): 238.7K **Privately Held**
SIC: 7532 Body shop, automotive

(G-2577)
JOHN L BRIGGS & CO
Also Called: Briggs Company
106 E Laurel St (19947-1430)
P.O. Box 90 (19947-0090)
PHONE..................302 856-7033
Charles D Dolson, *President*
W F Carlsten, *Corp Secy*
EMP: 12 EST: 1947
SQ FT: 2,500

GEOGRAPHIC SECTION

Georgetown - Sussex County (G-2605)

SALES (est): 3.5MM **Privately Held**
SIC: **1542** 1541 Commercial & office building, new construction; commercial & office buildings, renovation & repair; industrial buildings, new construction; renovation, remodeling & repairs: industrial buildings

(G-2578)
JOSEPH M L SAND & GRAVEL CO
25136 Dupont Blvd (19947-2610)
PHONE 302 856-7396
Melvin L Joseph, *President*
Joanne Adams, *Corp Secy*
Rick Webster, *Technology*
Bob Stickels, *Director*
EMP: 11
SQ FT: 700
SALES (est): 1.1MM **Privately Held**
SIC: **1442** 5191 Sand mining; gravel mining; farm supplies

(G-2579)
JUSTIN TANKS LLC
21413 Cedar Creek Ave (19947-6306)
PHONE 302 856-3521
Edward Short,
Emil Cattle,
Richard Terfinger,
EMP: 30
SQ FT: 35,000
SALES (est): 7.7MM **Privately Held**
WEB: www.justintanks.com
SIC: **3089** Plastic & fiberglass tanks

(G-2580)
KEEN CONSULTING INC
26229 Prettyman Rd (19947-5251)
PHONE 302 684-5270
G Anthony Keen, *President*
Todd Keen, *Vice Pres*
EMP: 4
SALES: 450K **Privately Held**
WEB: www.keenconsulting.net
SIC: **8742** Management consulting services

(G-2581)
KEITHS BOAT CANVAS
16408 Seashore Hwy (19947-4205)
PHONE 302 841-8081
EMP: 1
SALES (est): 46.5K **Privately Held**
SIC: **2211** Canvas

(G-2582)
KIMBLES AVI LGISTICAL SVCS INC
Also Called: Kimbles DLS
21785 Aviation Ave (19947-5574)
PHONE 334 663-4954
Mark Langley, *President*
Sean Carroll, *Vice Pres*
EMP: 9
SALES (est): 958.7K **Privately Held**
SIC: **4231** Trucking terminal facilities

(G-2583)
KRUGER FARMS INC
24306 Dupont Blvd (19947-2602)
PHONE 302 856-2577
Alvin Kruger, *President*
Paul Kruger, *Corp Secy*
Frank Kruger, *Vice Pres*
EMP: 5
SALES (est): 693.1K **Privately Held**
SIC: **0119** Barley farm

(G-2584)
KRUGER TRAILERS INC
24306 Dupont Blvd (19947-2602)
PHONE 302 856-2577
Alvin Kruger, *President*
Paul Kruger, *Corp Secy*
Frank Kruger, *Vice Pres*
EMP: 8 EST: 1958
SQ FT: 15,000
SALES (est): 770K **Privately Held**
SIC: **3715** 3713 Trailer bodies; farm truck bodies

(G-2585)
LA ESPERANZA INC
Also Called: LA ESPERANZA COMMUNITY CENTER
216 N Race St (19947-1409)
PHONE 302 854-9262
Charles Burton, *President*
Claudia Pena Porretti, *Exec Dir*
EMP: 13
SALES: 708.7K **Privately Held**
SIC: **8322** 8111 Social service center; immigration & naturalization law

(G-2586)
LA RED HEALTH CARE
23659 Saulsbury Ln (19947-6388)
PHONE 757 709-5072
Magali Tellez Blancas, *Manager*
EMP: 8
SALES (est): 61.1K **Privately Held**
SIC: **8082** Home health care services

(G-2587)
LA RED HEALTH CENTER INC
21444 Carmean Way (19947-4572)
PHONE 302 855-1233
Brian Olson, *CEO*
Angel Rivera, *Project Engr*
Beatrice Chiemelu, *CFO*
Judy Johnson, *Treasurer*
Sue Bardsley, *Med Doctor*
EMP: 100
SQ FT: 25,000
SALES: 10.9MM **Privately Held**
WEB: www.laredhealthcenter.com
SIC: **8099** Medical services organization

(G-2588)
LABORERS INTL UN N AMER
Also Called: Liuna
26351 Patriots Way (19947-2575)
PHONE 302 934-7376
Shiela Littleton, *Manager*
EMP: 12
SALES (corp-wide): 98.7MM **Privately Held**
SIC: **8631** Labor union
PA: Laborers International Union Of North America
 905 16th St Nw
 Washington DC 20006
 202 737-8320

(G-2589)
LEGACY VULCAN LLC
28272 Landfill Ln (19947-6071)
PHONE 302 875-0748
EMP: 2 **Publicly Held**
SIC: **1442** Construction sand & gravel
HQ: Legacy Vulcan, Llc
 1200 Urban Center Dr
 Vestavia AL 35242
 205 298-3000

(G-2590)
LEON N WEINER & ASSOCIATES INC
Also Called: Georgetown Apts
200 Ingramtown Rd (19947-1626)
PHONE 302 856-2251
Kathy Toomey, *Manager*
EMP: 4
SALES (corp-wide): 54MM **Privately Held**
SIC: **6513** Apartment building operators
PA: Leon N. Weiner & Associates, Inc.
 1 Fox Pt Ctr 4 Denny Rd
 Wilmington DE 19809
 302 656-1354

(G-2591)
LIFESTYLE DOCUMENT MGT INC
22277 Lwes Georgetown Hwy (19947-5526)
P.O. Box 822 (19947-0822)
PHONE 302 856-6387
David Parker, *President*
EMP: 5 EST: 2000
SQ FT: 5,000
SALES: 300K **Privately Held**
SIC: **4226** Document & office records storage

(G-2592)
LITTLE GYM
21500 Carmean Way Unit 4 (19947-4581)
PHONE 302 856-2310
EMP: 4
SALES (est): 38.1K **Privately Held**
SIC: **7997** Membership sports & recreation clubs

(G-2593)
M DAVIS FARMS LLC
17741 Davis Rd (19947-4430)
PHONE 302 856-7018
Mark Davis,
EMP: 5
SALES (est): 469.6K **Privately Held**
SIC: **0191** General farms, primarily crop

(G-2594)
MACKLYN HOME CARE
6 W Market St (19947-1484)
PHONE 302 253-8208
EMP: 8
SALES (est): 61.1K **Privately Held**
SIC: **8082** 8059 Home health care services; personal care home, with health care

(G-2595)
MANUFACTURERS & TRADERS TR CO
Also Called: M&T
22205 Dupont Blvd (19947-3165)
PHONE 302 856-4410
Linda Johnson, *Branch Mgr*
EMP: 52
SALES (corp-wide): 6.4B **Publicly Held**
WEB: www.binghamlegg.com
SIC: **6022** State commercial banks
HQ: Manufacturers And Traders Trust Company
 1 M&T Plz Fl 3
 Buffalo NY 14203
 716 842-4200

(G-2596)
MANUFACTURERS & TRADERS TR CO
Also Called: M&T
7 W Market St (19947-1492)
PHONE 302 856-4405
Linda Jones, *Branch Mgr*
EMP: 8
SALES (corp-wide): 6.4B **Publicly Held**
WEB: www.binghamlegg.com
SIC: **6022** State trust companies accepting deposits, commercial
HQ: Manufacturers And Traders Trust Company
 1 M&T Plz Fl 3
 Buffalo NY 14203
 716 842-4200

(G-2597)
MARK PENUEL
Also Called: State Farm Insurance
522 E Market St (19947-2255)
PHONE 302 856-7724
Bruce Penuel, *Owner*
Lindsey Steele, *Representative*
EMP: 7
SALES (est): 921.3K **Privately Held**
SIC: **6411** Insurance agents & brokers

(G-2598)
MARKET STREET CENTER INC
Also Called: Barnett, Norman C
9 Chestnut St (19947-1901)
P.O. Box 755 (19947-0755)
PHONE 302 856-9024
William Schab, *President*
Norman C Barnett, *Vice Pres*
EMP: 8
SALES (est): 579.2K **Privately Held**
SIC: **6512** Nonresidential building operators

(G-2599)
MCCABES MECHANICAL SERVICE INC
16689 Seashore Hwy (19947-4221)
P.O. Box 488 (19947-0488)
PHONE 302 854-9001
Allen Mc Cabe, *President*
Debra McCabe, *Vice Pres*
EMP: 10
SQ FT: 60,000
SALES: 2MM **Privately Held**
SIC: **5084** 3444 3823 Industrial machinery & equipment; sheet metalwork; industrial instrmnts msrmnt display/control process variable

(G-2600)
MEGEE PLUMBING & HEATING CO
Also Called: Honeywell Authorized Dealer
22965 Lwes Georgetown Hwy (19947-5301)
P.O. Box 745 (19947-0745)
PHONE 302 856-6311
B Darrow McLaughlin, *President*
Ernest E Megee Jr, *Corp Secy*
Larry Faist, *Sales Engr*
EMP: 65
SQ FT: 18,000
SALES (est): 9.9MM **Privately Held**
WEB: www.megeeco.com
SIC: **1711** 1731 Warm air heating & air conditioning contractor; general electrical contractor

(G-2601)
MEGHAN HOUSE INC
210 Rosa St (19947-1248)
PHONE 302 253-8261
Douglas Hall, *Principal*
EMP: 6
SALES (est): 83.5K **Privately Held**
SIC: **8399** Social services

(G-2602)
MELVIN L JOSEPH CNSTR CO
25136 Dupont Blvd (19947-2610)
PHONE 302 856-7396
Ken Adams, *President*
Melvin L Joseph Sr, *President*
Joe Ann Adams, *Vice Pres*
Traci Toomey, *Vice Pres*
EMP: 50 EST: 1940
SQ FT: 42,000
SALES (est): 9.1MM **Privately Held**
SIC: **1629** 1611 Land clearing contractor; highway & street paving contractor

(G-2603)
MID SOUTH AUDIO LLC
Also Called: MSA Recording
52 Bramhall St (19947-2104)
PHONE 302 856-6993
Kevin H Short,
EMP: 4
SQ FT: 3,100
SALES (est): 522.9K **Privately Held**
WEB: www.midsouthaudio.com
SIC: **7389** 7359 Recording studio, non-commercial records; audio-visual equipment & supply rental

(G-2604)
MIDATLANTIC FARM CREDIT ACA
20816 Dupont Blvd (19947-3179)
PHONE 302 856-9081
Charmayne Busker, *Branch Mgr*
EMP: 8
SALES (corp-wide): 179.7MM **Privately Held**
WEB: www.mfc.com
SIC: **6159** Agricultural credit institutions; machinery & equipment finance leasing
PA: Midatlantic Farm Credit
 45 Aileron Ct
 Westminster MD 21157
 410 848-1033

(G-2605)
MOONEY & ANDREW PA
11 S Race St (19947-1907)
PHONE 302 856-3070
Eric Mooney, *Owner*
Eric G Mooney, *Owner*
Michael W Andrew, *Principal*
Linda Dulis, *Admin Sec*
EMP: 6
SALES (est): 227.5K **Privately Held**
SIC: **8111** General practice attorney, lawyer

Georgetown - Sussex County (G-2606) — GEOGRAPHIC SECTION

(G-2606)
MOORE FARMS
14619 Cokesbury Rd (19947-4364)
PHONE.................................302 629-4999
Donald Moore Jr, *Partner*
Laura Lindo, *Admin Sec*
EMP: 12
SALES (est): 2.5MM **Privately Held**
SIC: 1542 Commercial & office building, new construction

(G-2607)
MORRIS & RITCHIE ASSOC INC
8 W Market St (19947-1437)
PHONE.................................302 855-5734
Kenneth Usab, *Branch Mgr*
EMP: 20 **Privately Held**
SIC: 8711 8713 Designing: ship, boat, machine & product; surveying services
HQ: Morris & Ritchie Associates, Inc.
3445 Box Hll Corp Ctr Dr B
Abingdon MD
410 515-9000

(G-2608)
NANTICOKE HEALTH SERVICES INC
Also Called: Anthony, Harry C MD
503 W Market St Ste 110b (19947-2321)
PHONE.................................302 856-7099
Joseph Karnish, *Family Practiti*
EMP: 42 **Privately Held**
SIC: 8011 General & family practice, physician/surgeon
PA: Nanticoke Health Services, Inc.
801 Middleford Rd
Seaford DE 19973

(G-2609)
NICKLE ELEC COMPANIES INC
540 S Bedford St (19947-1852)
PHONE.................................302 856-1006
Steve Dignan, *Branch Mgr*
EMP: 30
SALES (corp-wide): 32.4MM **Privately Held**
WEB: www.panickle.com
SIC: 1731 General electrical contractor
PA: Nickle Electrical Companies, Inc.
14 Mill Park Ct Ste E
Newark DE 19713
302 453-4000

(G-2610)
NO NONSENSE OFFICE MCHS LLC
22416 Lwes Georgetown Hwy (19947-5534)
P.O. Box 931 (19947-0931)
PHONE.................................302 856-7381
Richard Fowler,
EMP: 5
SALES (est): 440K **Privately Held**
SIC: 5044 Office equipment

(G-2611)
OM SHIV GROCERIES INC (PA)
Also Called: Bodies Dar Mkts Coin Laundries
208 N Bedford St (19947-1468)
P.O. Box 1111 (19947-5111)
PHONE.................................302 856-7014
Ashok Patel, *President*
EMP: 4
SQ FT: 1,400
SALES (est): 6.3MM **Privately Held**
SIC: 5411 5541 7215 Convenience stores, chain; filling stations, gasoline; laundry, coin-operated

(G-2612)
PATRICK AIRCRAFT GROUP LLC
21583 Baltimore Ave (19947-6313)
PHONE.................................302 854-9300
Harvey Patrick, *Principal*
EMP: 25 **EST:** 1999
SALES: 8K **Privately Held**
SIC: 3728 Refueling equipment for use in flight, airplane

(G-2613)
PATS AIRCRAFT LLC (HQ)
Also Called: Aloft Aeroarchitects
21652 Nanticoke Ave (19947-6308)
PHONE.................................855 236-1638
Robert Sundin, *President*
Wilhelm Wieland, *President*
Cameron Burr, *Exec VP*
Duncan Clark, *Vice Pres*
Matthew Hill, *Vice Pres*
EMP: 108
SQ FT: 90,000
SALES (est): 81.8MM **Privately Held**
SIC: 4581 3728 3721 Aircraft upholstery repair; fuselage assembly, aircraft; aircraft

(G-2614)
PENINSULA HEALTH ALLIANCE INC
Also Called: Masten Insurance & Fincl Svcs
13 Bridgeville Rd (19947-2105)
PHONE.................................302 856-9778
Michael Johnson, *President*
EMP: 4
SQ FT: 1,800
SALES (est): 430.2K **Privately Held**
SIC: 6411 Insurance agents, brokers & service

(G-2615)
PENINSULA PAVE & SEAL LLC
Also Called: Peninsula Paving
20288 Asphalt Aly (19947-5392)
PHONE.................................302 226-7283
David Fletcher Kenton, *Principal*
EMP: 4 **EST:** 2014
SALES (est): 208.8K **Privately Held**
SIC: 1611 Highway & street paving contractor; surfacing & paving

(G-2616)
PENUEL SIGN CO
22832 E Trap Pond Rd (19947-4727)
PHONE.................................302 856-7265
John Penuel, *Owner*
EMP: 1
SALES (est): 95.9K **Privately Held**
SIC: 3993 7532 Signs & advertising specialties; truck painting & lettering

(G-2617)
PEP-UP INC (PA)
24987 Dupont Blvd (19947-2623)
P.O. Box 556 (19947-0556)
PHONE.................................302 856-2555
William C Pepper, *President*
Bryan Pepper, *President*
Nancy West, *General Mgr*
Martin Pepper, *Vice Pres*
April Harris, *Safety Dir*
EMP: 12
SQ FT: 3,000
SALES (est): 38.2MM **Privately Held**
WEB: www.pep-up.com
SIC: 5984 5172 Liquefied petroleum gas, delivered to customers' premises; service station supplies, petroleum

(G-2618)
PERDUE FARMS INCORPORATED
20621 Savannah Rd (19947-2252)
PHONE.................................302 855-5635
David Jones, *Principal*
Jim Perdue, *Chairman*
Brenda Wilson, *Buyer*
Sharon Cook, *Technician*
EMP: 2
SALES (est): 353.1K **Privately Held**
SIC: 2015 Poultry slaughtering & processing

(G-2619)
PINEAPPLE STITCHERY
26005 Gvernor Stockley Rd (19947-2568)
PHONE.................................302 500-8050
Stacy L Henningan, *Owner*
EMP: 1
SALES (est): 55.3K **Privately Held**
SIC: 2395 Embroidery & art needlework

(G-2620)
PLANT RETRIEVERS WHL NURS
13418 Seashore Hwy (19947-4395)
PHONE.................................302 337-9833
John Briggs, *Partner*
EMP: 8
SALES (est): 947.5K **Privately Held**
WEB: www.pr-wn.com
SIC: 0782 Landscape contractors

(G-2621)
PNC BANK NATIONAL ASSOCIATION
Alfred St Rr 113 (19947)
PHONE.................................302 855-0400
Sheryl Lynch, *Manager*
EMP: 9
SALES (corp-wide): 19.9B **Publicly Held**
WEB: www.pncfunds.com
SIC: 6021 National trust companies with deposits, commercial
HQ: Pnc Bank, National Association
222 Delaware Ave
Wilmington DE 19801
877 762-2000

(G-2622)
POWELL CONSTRUCTION L L C
100 Murrays Ln (19947-2232)
PHONE.................................302 745-1146
Bruce Powell, *Principal*
EMP: 5
SALES (est): 389.7K **Privately Held**
SIC: 1521 Single-family housing construction

(G-2623)
PRECIOUS MOMENTS DAY CARE
18943 Shingle Point Rd (19947-5233)
PHONE.................................302 856-2346
Lester Maloney, *Principal*
EMP: 5
SALES (est): 107.3K **Privately Held**
SIC: 8351 Group day care center

(G-2624)
PRELA S LYNCH
409 N Front St (19947-1133)
PHONE.................................302 856-2130
Prela S Lynch, *Principal*
EMP: 2 **EST:** 2010
SALES (est): 125.4K **Privately Held**
SIC: 3531 Automobile wrecker hoists

(G-2625)
PREMIER STAFFING SOLUTIONS INC (PA)
123 W Market St (19947-1415)
PHONE.................................302 344-5996
Christopher Washington, *CEO*
Cameron Scotton, *President*
EMP: 7 **EST:** 2015
SALES (est): 3.6MM **Privately Held**
SIC: 7361 Labor contractors (employment agency)

(G-2626)
PRESSLEY RIDGE FOUNDATION
Also Called: Treatment Fster Care - Grgtown
20461 Dupont Blvd Ste 2 (19947-3174)
PHONE.................................302 854-9782
Cha-Tanya Lankford, *Director*
EMP: 6 **Privately Held**
SIC: 8699 8299 Charitable organization; educational service, nondegree granting: continuing educ.
PA: Pressley Ridge Foundation
5500 Corporate Dr Ste 400
Pittsburgh PA 15237

(G-2627)
PRIMEROS PASOS INC
Also Called: FIRST STEPS PRIMEROS PASOS
20648 Savannah Rd (19947-2261)
PHONE.................................302 856-7406
Ann Camasso, *President*
EMP: 5
SALES (est): 494.5K **Privately Held**
SIC: 8351 Preschool center

(G-2628)
PRO-GRADE ELECTRIC LLC
20151 Sand Hill Rd (19947-5509)
PHONE.................................302 258-7745
Ramiro Ramirez,
EMP: 4
SALES (est): 162.7K **Privately Held**
SIC: 1731 General electrical contractor

(G-2629)
PROFESSNAL ARFICATION SVCS INC
4 Hollyberry Dr (19947-9427)
PHONE.................................302 752-7003
Benito A Peta, *President*
Benito Peta, *President*
EMP: 7
SALES (est): 248.1K **Privately Held**
SIC: 0782 Lawn services

(G-2630)
PUBLIC HEALTH NURSING
544 S Bedford St (19947-1852)
PHONE.................................302 856-5136
John Kennedy, *Principal*
EMP: 13
SALES (est): 441.7K **Privately Held**
SIC: 8051 Skilled nursing care facilities

(G-2631)
QUESTAR CAPITAL CORPORATION
13 Bridgeville Rd (19947-2105)
PHONE.................................302 856-9778
Michael Johnson, *President*
Terry Dorey, *Principal*
EMP: 7
SALES (est): 467.1K **Privately Held**
SIC: 6799 Investors

(G-2632)
R AND H FILTER CO INC
21646 Baltimore Ave (19947-6311)
PHONE.................................302 856-2129
David F Davidson, *President*
Renee Davidson, *Vice Pres*
Mamie E Reese, *Shareholder*
EMP: 3
SQ FT: 4,100
SALES: 253K **Privately Held**
WEB: www.glassfilter.com
SIC: 3229 Scientific glassware

(G-2633)
REDI CALL CORP
Also Called: Redi-Call Communications
543 S Bedford St (19947-1851)
P.O. Box 571 (19947-0571)
PHONE.................................302 856-9000
Randy K Murray, *President*
Aubrey P Murray, *Vice Pres*
Sharyn A Murray, *Admin Sec*
EMP: 20
SQ FT: 1,500
SALES (est): 2.3MM **Privately Held**
WEB: www.redicall.com
SIC: 5731 4812 Radio, television & electronic stores; cellular telephone services

(G-2634)
REGIS CORPORATION
6 College Park Ln Ste 1 (19947-2179)
PHONE.................................302 856-2575
Tracy Lear, *Branch Mgr*
EMP: 4
SALES (corp-wide): 1B **Publicly Held**
SIC: 7231 Hairdressers
PA: Regis Corporation
7201 Metro Blvd
Minneapolis MN 55439
952 947-7777

(G-2635)
RENEWABLE ENERGY RESOURCES INC
105 S Race St Ste A (19947-1909)
PHONE.................................302 544-0054
EMP: 3
SALES: 100K **Privately Held**
SIC: 3621 Mfg Electrical Motors/Generators

(G-2636)
RENT-A-CENTER INC
12 Georgetown Plz (19947-2300)
PHONE.................................302 856-9200
Jennifer Aguirre, *Manager*
EMP: 6
SALES (corp-wide): 2.6B **Publicly Held**
WEB: www.rentacenter.com
SIC: 7359 Appliance rental; furniture rental; home entertainment equipment rental; television rental

GEOGRAPHIC SECTION

Georgetown - Sussex County (G-2669)

PA: Rent-A-Center, Inc.
5501 Headquarters Dr
Plano TX 75024
972 801-1100

(G-2637)
REPOTMECOM INC
21657 Paradise Rd (19947-5899)
PHONE.................................301 315-2344
EMP: 8
SALES (est): 330.3K **Privately Held**
SIC: 8099 Health/Allied Services

(G-2638)
RICHARD ALLEN COALITION
16950 Deer Forest Rd (19947-3404)
P.O. Box 624 (19947-0624)
PHONE.................................302 258-7182
Jane Hovington, *Principal*
EMP: 4
SALES (est): 81.2K **Privately Held**
SIC: 8399 Advocacy group

(G-2639)
RICHARD BELOTTI
Also Called: Belotti R Landscaping & Nurs
22988 Lawson Rd (19947-6663)
PHONE.................................302 934-7585
Richard Belotti,
EMP: 14
SALES (est): 340.9K **Privately Held**
SIC: 0181 5261 0782 Nursery stock, growing of; nursery stock, seeds & bulbs; landscape contractors

(G-2640)
RIGID BUILDERS LLC
24491 Blackberry Dr (19947-2780)
PHONE.................................732 425-3443
Craig Pfeifer,
EMP: 12
SALES (est): 387.3K **Privately Held**
SIC: 1711 Solar energy contractor

(G-2641)
ROGERS GRAPHICS INC (PA)
Also Called: Copy Print
32 Bridgeville Rd (19947-2106)
P.O. Box 189 (19947-0189)
PHONE.................................302 856-0028
Charles J Rogers, *President*
Frank E Rogers, *Vice Pres*
EMP: 18
SQ FT: 12,000
SALES (est): 2.3MM **Privately Held**
SIC: 2752 Commercial printing, offset

(G-2642)
RONALD D JR ATTORNEY AT LAW
Also Called: Murrayphillipspa
215 E Market St (19947-1233)
PHONE.................................302 856-9860
Ronald D Phillips Jr, *Principal*
EMP: 6
SALES (est): 137.9K **Privately Held**
SIC: 8111 Criminal law

(G-2643)
ROUTE 9 AUTO CENTER
23422 Park Ave (19947-6370)
PHONE.................................302 856-3941
Robert Lawson, *President*
Diana Lawson, *Vice Pres*
EMP: 6
SALES: 310K **Privately Held**
SIC: 7538 General automotive repair shops

(G-2644)
ROWE INDUSTRIES INC
21649 Cedar Creek Ave (19947-6396)
P.O. Box 189, Annapolis MD (21404-0189)
PHONE.................................443 458-5569
Gerald L Rowe, *Principal*
EMP: 6
SALES (est): 178.9K **Privately Held**
SIC: 3999 Manufacturing industries

(G-2645)
S DORMAN LAWN CARE INC
24676 Mallard Pond Ln (19947-6767)
PHONE.................................302 947-2858
EMP: 4

SALES (est): 85K **Privately Held**
SIC: 0782 Lawn care services

(G-2646)
SAFELITE FULFILLMENT INC
Also Called: Safelite Autoglass
22834 Dupont Blvd (19947-8804)
PHONE.................................302 856-7175
Raymond Plymire, *Branch Mgr*
EMP: 7
SALES (corp-wide): 177.9K **Privately Held**
WEB: www.belronus.com
SIC: 7536 Automotive glass replacement shops
HQ: Safelite Fulfillment, Inc.
7400 Safelite Way
Columbus OH 43235
614 210-9000

(G-2647)
SANDY HILL GREENHOUSES INC
18303 Sand Hill Rd (19947-3726)
PHONE.................................302 856-2412
Mark Folke, *President*
Maria Folke, *Vice Pres*
EMP: 10
SALES (est): 200K **Privately Held**
SIC: 0181 Bulbs & seeds

(G-2648)
SCHAB & BARNETT PA
9 Chestnut St (19947-1901)
PHONE.................................302 856-9024
Norman Barnett, *Partner*
William Schab, *Partner*
EMP: 15
SALES (est): 1.1MM **Privately Held**
SIC: 8111 General practice law office

(G-2649)
SERGOVIC & CARMEAN P A
231 S Race St (19947-1911)
PHONE.................................302 855-1260
John A Sergovic Jr, *Principal*
EMP: 4
SALES (est): 384.6K **Privately Held**
SIC: 8111 Real estate law

(G-2650)
SERGOVIC CARMEAN WEIDMAN (PA)
406 S Bedford St Ste 1 (19947-1854)
PHONE.................................302 855-0551
Deirdre McCartney, *Principal*
Shannon Carmean Burton, *Principal*
Shannon R Owens, *Principal*
John Sergovic Jr, *Principal*
Elizabeth L Soucek, *Principal*
EMP: 15
SALES (est): 1.4MM **Privately Held**
SIC: 8111 Real estate law

(G-2651)
SERVICE GENERAL CORP
Also Called: Crestwood Garden Apts
120 N Race St (19947-1483)
PHONE.................................302 856-3500
Bamdad Bahar, *President*
EMP: 200
SQ FT: 50,000
SALES: 2MM **Privately Held**
SIC: 6513 8741 7361 3582 Apartment building operators; management services; employment agencies; washing machines, laundry: commercial, incl. coin-operated; check cashing agencies

(G-2652)
SERVICEXPRESS CORPORATION (PA)
120 N Ray St (19947)
PHONE.................................302 856-3500
Bamdad Bahar, *President*
EMP: 9
SALES: 10MM **Privately Held**
SIC: 7361 Labor contractors (employment agency)

(G-2653)
SHECHINAH EMPOWER CENTER INC
231 S Race St (19947-1911)
PHONE.................................302 858-4467

Ronnie Hovington, *President*
Haronda Sheppard, *Treasurer*
EMP: 4
SQ FT: 2,500
SALES: 59.5K **Privately Held**
SIC: 8299 7299 8322 Educational services; debt counseling or adjustment services, individuals; general counseling services

(G-2654)
SHORE ANSWER LLC
Also Called: Telephone Answering Service
543 S Bedford St (19947-1851)
PHONE.................................302 253-8381
Randy Murrey,
Carol L Heck,
EMP: 19
SALES (est): 1.1MM **Privately Held**
WEB: www.shoreanswer.com
SIC: 7389 Telephone answering service

(G-2655)
SHURE LINE ELECTRICAL INC
24207 Dupont Blvd (19947-2630)
P.O. Box 249, Kenton (19955-0249)
PHONE.................................302 856-3110
EMP: 8 EST: 2011
SALES (est): 875.4K **Privately Held**
SIC: 1731 General electrical contractor

(G-2656)
SLEEPER CREEPER INC
17015 Sand Hill Rd (19947-3729)
PHONE.................................302 519-4553
EMP: 5
SALES (est): 222.3K **Privately Held**
SIC: 7389 Business Services At Non-Commercial Site

(G-2657)
SMITH FNBERG MCCRTNEY BERL LLP (PA)
406 S Bedford St (19947-1853)
P.O. Box 588 (19947-0588)
PHONE.................................302 856-7082
Richard E Berl, *Managing Prtnr*
George Smith, *Partner*
Buck Smith, *Counsel*
Tanya Cassup, *Bookkeeper*
Amber Nelson, *Admin Asst*
EMP: 21
SALES (est): 2.4MM **Privately Held**
WEB: www.shopllp.com
SIC: 8111 General practice law office

(G-2658)
SOFTBALL WORLD LLC
Also Called: Sports At The Beach
22518 Lwes Georgetown Hwy (19947-5533)
PHONE.................................302 856-7922
Ronald Barrows, *Owner*
Darren Kraljev, *Info Tech Dir*
Bobbi Brooks, *Executive*
EMP: 6
SALES (est): 769.3K **Privately Held**
WEB: www.sportsatthebeach.com
SIC: 7997 Indoor/outdoor court clubs

(G-2659)
SOMBAR & CO CPA PA (PA)
109 S Bedford St (19947-1843)
P.O. Box 127 (19947-0127)
PHONE.................................302 856-6712
Seth Thomas Sombar, *Owner*
EMP: 6
SALES (est): 479.1K **Privately Held**
SIC: 8721 Certified public accountant

(G-2660)
SOUTHERN DEL PHYSCL THERAPY
2 Lee Ave Unit 101 (19947-2149)
PHONE.................................302 854-9600
Southern Therpy, *Branch Mgr*
EMP: 4 **Privately Held**
SIC: 8049 Physical therapist
PA: Southern Delaware Physical Therapy Inc
701 Savannah Rd Ste A
Lewes DE 19958

(G-2661)
SOUTHERN DELAWARE DENTAL SPEC
20785 Prof Pk Blvd (19947)
PHONE.................................302 855-9499
EMP: 4
SALES (est): 80.1K **Privately Held**
SIC: 8021 Offices & clinics of dentists

(G-2662)
SOUTHLAND INSULATORS DEL LLC
Also Called: Delmarva Insulation
22976 Sussex Ave (19947-6310)
PHONE.................................302 854-0344
Robert Devere,
Gerald Palmer,
EMP: 89
SALES (est): 8.3MM **Privately Held**
WEB: www.delmarvainsulation.com
SIC: 1742 Insulation, buildings

(G-2663)
SPLASH LNDRMAT LLC - GORGETOWN
201 E Laurel St (19947-1202)
PHONE.................................302 249-8231
Enrique Nunez, *Principal*
EMP: 6
SALES (est): 73.9K **Privately Held**
SIC: 7215 Coin-operated laundries & cleaning

(G-2664)
SPRINT COMMUNICATIONS INC
Also Called: Sprint Sprint
6 College Park Ln (19947-2179)
PHONE.................................302 604-6125
EMP: 36 **Publicly Held**
SIC: 4813 Local & long distance telephone communications
HQ: Sprint Communications, Inc.
6200 Sprint Pkwy
Overland Park KS 66251
855 848-3280

(G-2665)
STAFFMARK INVESTMENT LLC
132 E Market St (19947-1508)
PHONE.................................302 854-0650
EMP: 4 **Privately Held**
SIC: 7361 Labor contractors (employment agency)
HQ: Staffmark Investment Llc
201 E 4th St Ste 800
Cincinnati OH 45202

(G-2666)
STOCKLEY MATERIALS LLC
25154 Dupont Blvd (19947-2610)
PHONE.................................302 856-7601
Joe Adams, *Owner*
EMP: 3 EST: 2012
SALES (est): 238.4K **Privately Held**
SIC: 2499 3531 1446 Mulch or sawdust products, wood; pavers; industrial sand

(G-2667)
STONEGATE GRANITE
25029 Dupont Blvd (19947-2622)
PHONE.................................302 500-8081
Naim Celik, *Owner*
EMP: 4 EST: 2015
SALES (est): 111.5K **Privately Held**
SIC: 1741 Masonry & other stonework

(G-2668)
STRAIGHT LINE STRIPING LLC
17865 Hudson Ln (19947-4417)
PHONE.................................302 228-3335
William Robert Hall III, *President*
EMP: 5
SALES (est): 389.7K **Privately Held**
SIC: 1611 Surfacing & paving

(G-2669)
STUMPF VICKERS AND SANDY
8 W Market St (19947-1437)
PHONE.................................302 856-3561
Vincent Vickers, *Partner*
Brian Dolan, *Partner*
Tom Gay, *Partner*
John Sandy, *Partner*
Thomas J Stumpf, *Partner*
EMP: 12

Georgetown - Sussex County (G-2670)

SALES (est): 1.3MM **Privately Held**
WEB: www.svslaw.com
SIC: 8111 General practice law office

(G-2670)
SUFFEX CONSERVATION
23818 Shortly Rd (19947-4755)
PHONE.................................302 856-2105
Debbie Absher, *Manager*
EMP: 8
SALES (est): 284.4K **Privately Held**
SIC: 8748 Energy conservation consultant

(G-2671)
SUNRISE MEDICAL CENTER
Also Called: Office of Ruben Tejeira MD The
22549 Little St (19947-4759)
PHONE.................................302 854-9006
Ruben Tejeira MD, *Principal*
Lilian Vassallo, *Office Mgr*
EMP: 6
SALES (est): 616.9K **Privately Held**
SIC: 8099 Childbirth preparation clinic

(G-2672)
SURE LINE ELECTRICAL INC
281 W Commerce St (19947)
PHONE.................................302 856-3110
Ed Hitch, *President*
EMP: 20
SALES (est): 1.2MM **Privately Held**
SIC: 1731 General electrical contractor

(G-2673)
SUSAN STRAUGHEN
Also Called: Teddy Bear Enterprises
205 N Front St (19947-1129)
PHONE.................................302 856-7703
EMP: 2 EST: 1989
SALES: 120K **Privately Held**
SIC: 3942 7389 Mfg Dolls/Stuffed Toys Business Services

(G-2674)
SUSSEX CNTY HABITAT FOR HUMANI
206 Academy St (19947-1947)
P.O. Box 759 (19947-0759)
PHONE.................................302 855-1153
Susan Webb, *Finance Mgr*
Kevin Gilmore, *Exec Dir*
Jay Gundy, *Director*
EMP: 8
SALES: 5.1MM **Privately Held**
SIC: 1521 Single-family housing construction

(G-2675)
SUSSEX COMMUNITY CRISIS
204 E North St (19947-1243)
PHONE.................................302 856-2246
Marie Morole, *CEO*
EMP: 12
SALES (est): 398.6K **Privately Held**
SIC: 8322 Emergency social services

(G-2676)
SUSSEX CONSERVATION DISTRICT
23818 Shortly Rd (19947-4755)
PHONE.................................302 856-2105
Debra Absher, *President*
Matt Messina, *Project Mgr*
Gina Wolken, *Records Dir*
EMP: 23
SALES (est): 1.5MM **Privately Held**
WEB: www.de.nacdnet.net
SIC: 8999 Natural resource preservation service

(G-2677)
SUSSEX COUNTY ASSN REALTORS
23407 Park Ave (19947-6373)
PHONE.................................302 855-2300
Patricia Anderson, *CEO*
Andrew Mason, *Mktg Dir*
Benjamin Kunde, *IT/INT Sup*
EMP: 4
SALES: 1.2MM **Privately Held**
WEB: www.scaor.com
SIC: 8611 Real Estate Board

(G-2678)
SUSSEX COUNTY SENIOR SVCS INC
Also Called: Sand Hill Adult Program
20520 Sand Hill Rd (19947-5504)
PHONE.................................302 854-2882
A S Littleton, *Exec Dir*
Arlene S Littleton, *Exec Dir*
EMP: 5
SALES (est): 103.1K **Privately Held**
SIC: 8322 Adult day care center

(G-2679)
SUSSEX EYE CENTER PA (PA)
502 W Market St (19947-2322)
P.O. Box 400 (19947-0400)
PHONE.................................302 856-2020
Carl Maschauer, *Owner*
Karen Duffield, *Exec Dir*
EMP: 6 EST: 1997
SALES (est): 1.5MM **Privately Held**
SIC: 8042 Specialized optometrists

(G-2680)
SUSSEX FAMILY COUNSELING LLC
26114 Kits Burrow Ct (19947-5390)
PHONE.................................302 864-7970
Matthew W Turley, *Owner*
EMP: 4
SALES (est): 42.4K **Privately Held**
SIC: 8322 Family counseling services

(G-2681)
SUSSEX PAIN RELIEF CENTER LLC
18229 Dupont Blvd (19947-3127)
PHONE.................................302 519-0100
Antony Manonmani, *Mng Member*
EMP: 24
SALES: 2MM **Privately Held**
SIC: 8041 8011 Offices & clinics of chiropractors; physicians' office, including specialists

(G-2682)
SUSSEX PINES COUNTRY CLUB
22426 Sussex Pines Rd (19947-6445)
PHONE.................................302 856-6283
Jim King, *President*
Tom Love, *Vice Pres*
Dennis Fitzgerald, *Treasurer*
EMP: 48
SALES: 1MM **Privately Held**
SIC: 7997 Country club, membership; golf club, membership; swimming club, membership

(G-2683)
SUSSEX PREGNANCY CARE CENTER
5 Burger King Dr (19947-2176)
PHONE.................................302 856-4344
Rita Denney, *Director*
EMP: 5
SALES (est): 221.2K **Privately Held**
WEB: www.sussexpregnancy.com
SIC: 8322 8093 Individual & family services; family planning clinic

(G-2684)
SUSSEX SUITES LLC
22339 Sussex Pines Rd (19947-6452)
P.O. Box 252 (19947-0252)
PHONE.................................302 856-3351
Ira Brittingham, *President*
Matthew Birttingham, *Vice Pres*
Shawn Birttingham, *Treasurer*
Monica Birttingham, *Admin Sec*
EMP: 4
SALES: 400K **Privately Held**
SIC: 7519

(G-2685)
SWIFT CONSTRUCTION CO INC
24892 Pebblestone Ln (19947-2553)
PHONE.................................302 855-1011
EMP: 9 EST: 1998
SALES: 1.5MM **Privately Held**
SIC: 1794 Excavation Contractor

(G-2686)
TAYLOR & SONS INC
26511 E Trap Pond Rd (19947-5721)
PHONE.................................302 856-6962
Thomas Taylor, *President*
EMP: 6
SALES (est): 386.1K **Privately Held**
SIC: 1721 Painting & paper hanging

(G-2687)
TC TRANS INC
24557 Dupont Blvd (19947)
PHONE.................................302 339-7952
Ismail Sen, *President*
EMP: 8
SQ FT: 1,000
SALES: 800K **Privately Held**
SIC: 4731 Freight forwarding

(G-2688)
TECHGAS INC
22251 Lwes Georgetown Hwy (19947-5526)
PHONE.................................302 856-4111
Avic Rickards, *President*
Ray Medan, *Vice Pres*
EMP: 4
SALES (est): 407.8K **Privately Held**
SIC: 7389 Personal service agents, brokers & bureaus

(G-2689)
TEFF INC
Also Called: SERVPRO
109 E Laurel St (19947-1429)
P.O. Box 70 (19947-0070)
PHONE.................................302 856-9768
Raymond T Hopkins, *President*
Joanne Hopkins, *Vice Pres*
Kathleen Hargrove, *Officer*
EMP: 10 EST: 1979
SALES (est): 437.1K **Privately Held**
SIC: 7349 Building maintenance services

(G-2690)
TELAMON CORP/EARLY CHLDHD PGRM
26351 Patriots Way (19947-2575)
PHONE.................................302 934-1642
Nancy Shaffer, *Principal*
EMP: 5
SALES (est): 174.1K **Privately Held**
SIC: 8331 Job training services

(G-2691)
THOMAS JFFRSON LRNG FOUNDATION
Also Called: JEFFERSON SCHOOL, THE
22051 Wilson Rd (19947-3770)
PHONE.................................302 856-3300
Constance Hendricks, *Principal*
Donna Melton, *Pub Rel Dir*
Beverly Wenner, *Admin Sec*
Jennifer Chowdhry, *Teacher*
Bill Nelson, *Education*
EMP: 19
SALES: 1.1MM **Privately Held**
SIC: 8351 Head start center, except in conjunction with school

(G-2692)
THOROUGHBRED SOFTWARE INTL
22536 Lakeshore Dr (19947-2563)
PHONE.................................302 339-8383
Charles Gilman, *Principal*
EMP: 2
SALES (est): 97K **Privately Held**
SIC: 7372 Prepackaged software

(G-2693)
TIDEWATER PHYSCL THRPY AND REB
10 Georgetown Plz (19947-2300)
PHONE.................................302 856-2446
Michelle Lowe, *Branch Mgr*
EMP: 5
SALES (corp-wide): 2.6MM **Privately Held**
SIC: 8049 Physical therapist
PA: Tidewater Physical Therapy And Rehabilitation Associates Pa
406 Marvel Ct
Easton MD 21601
410 822-3116

(G-2694)
TPI PARTNERS INC (PA)
Also Called: Thermoplastic Processes
21649 Cedar Creek Ave (19947-6396)
PHONE.................................302 855-0139
D Brooke Kinney, *Principal*
Betty Adkins, *Vice Pres*
EMP: 75
SALES (est): 22.6MM **Privately Held**
SIC: 3082 Tubes, unsupported plastic; rods, unsupported plastic

(G-2695)
TRU BY HILTON GEORGETOWN LLC
301 College Park Ln (19947-2111)
PHONE.................................302 515-2100
Steven Silver, *CEO*
EMP: 20
SALES (est): 109.1K **Privately Held**
SIC: 7011 Hotels & motels

(G-2696)
TUNNELL & RAYSOR PA (PA)
30 E Pine St (19947-1904)
P.O. Box 151 (19947-0151)
PHONE.................................302 856-7313
Harold E Dukes Jr, *President*
Craig De Mariana Alem, *Dean*
Heidi Balliet, *Vice Pres*
Kelly Dunn Gelof, *Vice Pres*
Tina Timmons, *Receptionist*
EMP: 48
SALES (est): 6.4MM **Privately Held**
WEB: www.tunnellraysor.com
SIC: 8111 General practice attorney, lawyer

(G-2697)
UNDERGROUND LOCATING SERVICES
24497 Dupont Blvd (19947-2628)
PHONE.................................302 856-9626
Alton Stack, *Owner*
EMP: 9
SALES (est): 734.2K **Privately Held**
SIC: 1623 Underground utilities contractor

(G-2698)
UNITED CEREBRAL PALSY OF DE
Also Called: P A C T T Child Care Center
17099 County Seat Hwy (19947-4865)
P.O. Box 351 (19947-0351)
PHONE.................................302 856-3490
Kathy Moore, *Director*
EMP: 14
SALES (corp-wide): 1.6MM **Privately Held**
SIC: 8351 Preschool center
PA: United Cerebral Palsy Of De, Inc
700 River Rd Apt A
Wilmington DE 19809
302 764-2400

(G-2699)
UNIVERSAL FOREST PRODUCTS ◆
22976 Sussex Ave (19947-6310)
PHONE.................................302 855-1250
EMP: 2 EST: 2019
SALES (est): 86.7K **Privately Held**
SIC: 2439 Structural wood members

(G-2700)
VEST MANAGEMENT INC
18591 Sand Hill Rd (19947-3723)
PHONE.................................302 856-3100
EMP: 4
SALES (est): 366.7K **Privately Held**
SIC: 8741 Management services

(G-2701)
VOICE RADIO LLC
20254 Dupont Blvd (19947-3105)
PHONE.................................302 858-5118
Tracy Baker, *Office Mgr*
Kevin Andrade, *Director*
EMP: 6
SALES (est): 50.6K **Privately Held**
SIC: 4832 Radio broadcasting stations

GEOGRAPHIC SECTION

Greenwood - Sussex County (G-2731)

(G-2702)
WAY HOME INC
413 E Market St (19947-2215)
P.O. Box 1103 (19947-5103)
PHONE..................................302 856-9870
Ronald Kerchner, *Finance Dir*
Barbara Carter, *Director*
Barbara Del Mastro, *Director*
EMP: 4
SALES: 303K **Privately Held**
SIC: 8322 Social service center

(G-2703)
WEST PHOTOGRAPHY
16848 Old Furnace Rd (19947-4839)
PHONE..................................302 858-6003
Ryan West, *Principal*
EMP: 4
SALES (est): 46K **Privately Held**
SIC: 7221 Photographer, still or video

(G-2704)
WILSON CONSTRUCTION CO INC
23054 Park Ave (19947-6364)
PHONE..................................302 856-3115
Richard Wilson, *President*
Joan Wilson, *Corp Secy*
EMP: 5
SALES (est): 460K **Privately Held**
SIC: 1521 New construction, single-family houses; general remodeling, single-family houses

(G-2705)
WILSON HALBROOK & BAYARD PA
Also Called: Bayard, Eugene H
107 W Market St (19947-1438)
P.O. Box 690 (19947-0690)
PHONE..................................302 856-0015
Eugene H Bayard, *President*
Clayton E Bunting, *Vice Pres*
Eric C Howard, *Director*
Mark D Olson, *Director*
Robert G Gibbs, *Admin Sec*
EMP: 19
SALES (est): 1.7MM **Privately Held**
WEB: www.whblaw.com
SIC: 8111 General practice law office

(G-2706)
WJWK
20200 Dupont Blvd (19947-3105)
PHONE..................................302 856-2567
EMP: 7
SALES (est): 153.2K **Privately Held**
SIC: 4832 Radio Broadcast Station

(G-2707)
WOODLAND FERRY BEAGLE CLUB
26858 Johnson Rd (19947-6610)
PHONE..................................302 856-2186
Paul Eckrich, *Principal*
EMP: 6
SALES (est): 126.3K **Privately Held**
SIC: 7997 Membership sports & recreation clubs

(G-2708)
WOODS GENERAL CONTRACTING
22403 Peterkins Rd (19947-2733)
P.O. Box 240, Millsboro (19966-0240)
PHONE..................................302 856-4047
William B Wood, *President*
Karen Wood, *Vice Pres*
EMP: 5
SQ FT: 3,200
SALES (est): 2.5MM **Privately Held**
SIC: 1542 1521 Commercial & office building, new construction; new construction, single-family houses

(G-2709)
WORKMANS INC
20135 Hardscrabble Rd (19947-6124)
PHONE..................................302 934-9228
Mark Workman, *President*
Charles Workman, *Vice Pres*
EMP: 5
SQ FT: 5,500
SALES (est): 535.3K **Privately Held**
SIC: 0111 0115 0116 0119 Wheat; corn; soybeans; barley farm

Greenwood
Sussex County

(G-2710)
A & B ELECTRIC
25 Adamsville Rd (19950-8400)
PHONE..................................302 349-4050
Alan Warren, *President*
Andrew Warren, *Vice Pres*
Brenda Warren, *Admin Sec*
EMP: 9
SALES: 600K **Privately Held**
SIC: 1731 Electrical work

(G-2711)
ADANDY FARM
13450 Adandy Farm Ln (19950-5766)
P.O. Box 2016 (19950-0606)
PHONE..................................302 349-5116
Cathrine Vincent, *Owner*
Edith Vincent, *Co-Owner*
EMP: 5
SALES: 500K **Privately Held**
WEB: www.adandyfarm.com
SIC: 0752 Training services, horses (except racing horses)

(G-2712)
ALL AMERICAN ELECTRIC SVCS LLC
680 Hickman Rd (19950-1749)
PHONE..................................410 479-0277
Bonnie Ellwanger,
EMP: 1
SALES (est): 180.9K **Privately Held**
SIC: 3621 Motors & generators; electric motor & generator parts; generators & sets, electric

(G-2713)
ATLANTIC ALUMINUM PRODUCTS INC
12136 Sussex Hwy (19950-5414)
PHONE..................................302 349-9091
Daniel Schlabach, *President*
Brenda M Feathers, *Financial Exec*
Patricia Gillespie, *Credit Staff*
Richard Fischer, *Sales Mgr*
Todd Anderson, *Sales Staff*
EMP: 57 EST: 1996
SQ FT: 165,000
SALES: 14MM **Privately Held**
WEB: www.atlanticproducts.com
SIC: 3089 3446 2431 Fences, gates & accessories: plastic; railings, bannisters, guards, etc.: made from metal pipe; railings, prefabricated metal; fences or posts, ornamental iron or steel; staircases, stairs & railings

(G-2714)
BEAVERDAM PET FOOD
12933 Sussex Hwy (19950-6070)
PHONE..................................302 349-5299
E Truman Schrock, *Owner*
EMP: 8
SALES (est): 875.9K **Privately Held**
SIC: 5149 Pet foods

(G-2715)
BENDER FARMS LLC
13060 Bender Farm Rd (19950-5050)
PHONE..................................302 349-5574
Loyal Bender,
EMP: 6 EST: 2008
SALES (est): 317.6K **Privately Held**
SIC: 0191 General farms, primarily crop

(G-2716)
BERACAH HOMES INC
9590 Nantcke Bus Pk Dr (19950-5453)
PHONE..................................302 349-4561
Wayne Collison, *CEO*
Jeffrey Bowers, *President*
Johnathan Fair, *Plant Mgr*
Jamie Hammond, *Opers Staff*
Emory Rick, *Purch Mgr*
EMP: 50
SALES (est): 9.5MM **Privately Held**
WEB: www.beracahhomes.com
SIC: 1521 2452 New construction, single-family houses; prefabricated buildings, wood

(G-2717)
BILLY WARREN SON
286 Burrsville Rd (19950-1725)
PHONE..................................302 349-5767
Billy Warren Sr, *Owner*
EMP: 8
SALES (est): 1.8MM **Privately Held**
SIC: 5093 5084 Ferrous metal scrap & waste; industrial machinery & equipment

(G-2718)
BLUE HEN MASONRY INC
3296 Andrewville Rd (19950-2206)
PHONE..................................302 398-8737
Norman Woodall, *President*
Jason W Woodall, *Vice Pres*
EMP: 6 EST: 1993
SALES (est): 359K **Privately Held**
SIC: 1741 Masonry & other stonework

(G-2719)
CARLISLE FARMS INC
12733 Shawnee Rd (19950-5327)
PHONE..................................302 349-5692
Keith Carlisle, *President*
Carol Carlisle, *Corp Secy*
Richard Carlisle, *Vice Pres*
EMP: 8
SALES (est): 678.9K **Privately Held**
SIC: 0191 General farms, primarily crop

(G-2720)
CLIMATE CONTROL HEATING INC
9703 Woodyard Rd (19950-5429)
PHONE..................................302 349-5778
Frank Umstetter, *President*
Lynn Umstetter, *Co-Owner*
EMP: 4
SALES (est): 332.4K **Privately Held**
SIC: 1711 Heating & air conditioning contractors

(G-2721)
COLONIAL MASONRY LTD
219 Wheatfield Rd (19950-1841)
PHONE..................................302 349-4945
Sylvia Propes, *President*
Bill Propes, *Vice Pres*
EMP: 4
SALES (est): 190.2K **Privately Held**
SIC: 1741 Stone masonry

(G-2722)
COMCAST CORPORATION
2 Schulze Rd (19950-5357)
PHONE..................................302 495-5612
EMP: 55
SALES (corp-wide): 94.5B **Publicly Held**
SIC: 4841 Cable television services
PA: Comcast Corporation
1701 Jfk Blvd
Philadelphia PA 19103
215 286-1700

(G-2723)
COUNTERPARTS LLC
12952 Sussex Hwy (19950-6006)
P.O. Box 580 (19950-0580)
PHONE..................................302 349-0400
Mark Mihalik, *Executive Asst*
EMP: 4
SALES (est): 556.3K **Privately Held**
SIC: 2541 Counter & sink tops

(G-2724)
COUNTRY KIDS CHILD
12400 Sussex Hwy (19950-5447)
P.O. Box 46 (19950-0046)
PHONE..................................302 349-5888
Catherine Porter,
EMP: 5
SALES (est): 170K **Privately Held**
SIC: 8351 Child day care services

(G-2725)
CUSTOM CABINET SHOP INC
Also Called: Campbell's Custom Cabinet Shop
Rr 13 (19950)
P.O. Box 2 (19950-0002)
PHONE..................................302 337-8241
Gerald Campbell, *President*
Valerie Campbell, *Admin Sec*
EMP: 11
SQ FT: 3,000
SALES (est): 1.2MM **Privately Held**
SIC: 2434 5211 Wood kitchen cabinets; lumber & other building materials

(G-2726)
D & C MECHANICAL LLC
13500 Wolf Rd (19950-5522)
PHONE..................................302 604-9025
EMP: 4 EST: 2011
SALES (est): 269.2K **Privately Held**
SIC: 1711 Mechanical contractor

(G-2727)
D & D SCREEN PRINTING
12794 Shawnee Rd (19950-5331)
PHONE..................................302 349-4231
David Friedel, *Principal*
EMP: 2
SALES (est): 141.5K **Privately Held**
SIC: 2759 Commercial printing

(G-2728)
DELMARVA ROOFING & COATING INC
12982 Mennonite School Rd (19950-5310)
P.O. Box 489 (19950-0489)
PHONE..................................302 349-5174
Sheldon L Swartzentruber, *President*
Verle D Schlabach, *Vice Pres*
Sylvia Swartzentruber, *Manager*
EMP: 22
SQ FT: 12,000
SALES (est): 2.9MM **Privately Held**
SIC: 1761 1799 Roofing contractor; waterproofing

(G-2729)
DELMARVA TRANSPORTATION INC
101 Maryland Ave (19950-7728)
PHONE..................................302 349-0840
Debbie Freeman, *President*
EMP: 8
SALES (est): 621.1K **Privately Held**
SIC: 4121 Taxicabs

(G-2730)
DFS CORPORATE SERVICES LLC
502 E Market St (19950-9700)
PHONE..................................302 349-4512
Rodney Caldwell, *Project Mgr*
Benjamin Harrsch, *Project Mgr*
Laura Bretz, *Corp Comm Staff*
Milind Bengeri, *Manager*
Dawn Gunn, *Manager*
EMP: 4
SALES (est): 174.9K
SALES (corp-wide): 12.8B **Publicly Held**
SIC: 6061 Federal credit unions
PA: Discover Financial Services
2500 Lake Cook Rd
Riverwoods IL 60015
224 405-0900

(G-2731)
DISCOVER BANK (HQ)
502 E Market St (19950-9700)
PHONE..................................302 349-4512
Christina Favilla, *President*
James J Roszkowski, *President*
David Digiacoma, *Director*
Josh Kessler, *Director*
EMP: 23
SALES: 12.1B
SALES (corp-wide): 12.8B **Publicly Held**
SIC: 6022 State trust companies accepting deposits, commercial
PA: Discover Financial Services
2500 Lake Cook Rd
Riverwoods IL 60015
224 405-0900

Greenwood - Sussex County (G-2732)

(G-2732)
DRAW INCORPORATED
Also Called: 1-800 Got Junk
12528 Utica Rd (19950-5245)
PHONE.................410 208-9513
Ward Halverson, *President*
EMP: 4
SALES (est): 401.1K **Privately Held**
SIC: 4953 Rubbish collection & disposal

(G-2733)
E & J TRUCKING INC
14907 Nichols Run Rd (19950-5571)
P.O. Box 313, Seaford (19973-0313)
PHONE.................302 349-4284
Janet Nichols, *Principal*
Melinda Nichols, *Admin Sec*
EMP: 4
SALES (est): 430K **Privately Held**
SIC: 4213 Trucking, except local

(G-2734)
EAST COAST MACHINE WORKS
12773 Tuckers Rd (19950-5609)
PHONE.................302 349-5180
George Mihalik, *Owner*
EMP: 5
SALES (est): 240K **Privately Held**
SIC: 3599 3444 7692 Machine shop, jobbing & repair; sheet metalwork; welding repair

(G-2735)
EASTERN BISON ASSOCIATION
10685 Buffalo Rd (19950-5700)
PHONE.................434 660-6036
Mike Morris, *CEO*
Bobbi Lester, *Corp Secy*
EMP: 10 EST: 1996
SALES: 8.8K **Privately Held**
SIC: 8641 7389 Social associations;

(G-2736)
EASY LAWN INC
9599 Nantcke Bus Pk Dr # 1 (19950-5448)
P.O. Box 316, Bridgeville (19933-0316)
PHONE.................302 815-6500
Robert N Lisle, *President*
Marcia Lisle, *Treasurer*
Mark Williamson, *Sales Staff*
▼ EMP: 28
SQ FT: 80,000
SALES (est): 5.3MM **Privately Held**
WEB: www.easylawn.com
SIC: 3524 3423 3561 3523 Lawn & garden equipment; hand & edge tools; pumps & pumping equipment; farm machinery & equipment; air & gas compressors

(G-2737)
ELVIN SCHROCK AND SONS INC
10725 Beach Hwy (19950-5710)
PHONE.................302 349-4384
Merlin Schrock, *President*
Linda Schrock, *Corp Secy*
Marlin J Schrock, *Vice Pres*
EMP: 8
SALES (est): 906.6K **Privately Held**
SIC: 1711 Plumbing contractors; septic system construction

(G-2738)
ENSINGER PENN FIBRE INC
220 S Church & Snider St (19950)
P.O. Box 160 (19950-0160)
PHONE.................302 349-4505
Jimmy Walls, *Opers Staff*
Mark Kreisher, *Sales Mgr*
EMP: 45
SALES (corp-wide): 533.1MM **Privately Held**
WEB: www.pennfibre.com
SIC: 3089 Plastic processing
HQ: Ensinger Penn Fibre, Inc.
2434 Bristol Rd
Bensalem PA 19020
215 702-9551

(G-2739)
EROSION CONTROL PRODUCTS CORP
9599 Nantcke Bus Pk Dr (19950-5448)
PHONE.................302 815-6500
Kirc Horne, *General Mgr*
EMP: 12
SQ FT: 85,000
SALES (est): 535.5K **Privately Held**
SALES (corp-wide): 26.4MM **Privately Held**
SIC: 3524 5999 Lawn & garden equipment; farm equipment & supplies; farm machinery
PA: Dhg Inc.
9281 Le Saint Dr
West Chester OH
513 874-2818

(G-2740)
EXECUTIVE TRANSPORTATION INC
12643 Rock Rd (19950-5364)
P.O. Box 203, Bridgeville (19933-0203)
PHONE.................302 337-3455
Robin Lynn Mullins, *President*
EMP: 5 EST: 1997
SALES (est): 143.3K **Privately Held**
SIC: 4119 Local passenger transportation; local rental transportation

(G-2741)
GREENWOOD LIQUOR INC
12599 Sussex Hwy (19950)
P.O. Box 452 (19950-0452)
PHONE.................302 349-4767
Andy Patel, *Principal*
EMP: 5
SALES (est): 322.6K **Privately Held**
SIC: 5182 Liquor

(G-2742)
GROFF TRACTOR & EQUIPMENT LLC
12420 Sussex Hwy (19950-5447)
P.O. Box 338 (19950-0338)
PHONE.................302 349-5760
Mike Youse, *Principal*
EMP: 10
SALES (corp-wide): 100.5MM **Privately Held**
WEB: www.folcomer.com
SIC: 5084 7699 7359 Industrial machinery & equipment; industrial machinery & equipment repair; equipment rental & leasing
PA: Groff Tractor & Equipment, Llc
6779 Carlisle Pike
Mechanicsburg PA 17050
717 766-7671

(G-2743)
H & C INSULATION LLC
14329 Saint Johnstown Rd (19950-6055)
PHONE.................302 448-0777
Joseph Caudell, *Owner*
EMP: 6
SALES: 750K **Privately Held**
SIC: 1742 Insulation, buildings

(G-2744)
HUMPHRIES CONSTRUCTION COMPANY
11533 Holly Tree Ln (19950-5458)
PHONE.................302 349-9277
Danny Humphries, *President*
EMP: 5
SALES (est): 488.4K **Privately Held**
SIC: 1542 1521 Farm building construction; single-family housing construction

(G-2745)
HYDROSEEDING COMPANY LLC
Also Called: Epic Manufacturing
9599 Nantcke Bus Pk Dr # 3 (19950-5448)
PHONE.................302 815-6500
Jeff Clouser, *President*
Robert M Lisle, *Mng Member*
EMP: 30
SQ FT: 2,000
SALES (est): 3.4MM **Privately Held**
SIC: 3524 5999 Lawn & garden equipment; farm equipment & supplies; farm machinery

(G-2746)
J B S CONSTRUCTION LLC
8801 Greenwood Rd (19950-4878)
PHONE.................302 349-5705
Bruce Wardwell, *Mng Member*
EMP: 7
SQ FT: 3,500
SALES (est): 3MM **Privately Held**
WEB: www.jbsconstructionllc.com
SIC: 1521 New construction, single-family houses

(G-2747)
J E BAILEY & SONS INC
2135 Seashore Hwy (19950-4146)
PHONE.................302 349-4376
Jeffery Bailey, *President*
Alan Bailey, *Treasurer*
EMP: 5
SALES (est): 796.1K **Privately Held**
SIC: 0241 0254 Milk production; chicken hatchery

(G-2748)
JAMES THOMPSON & COMPANY INC
301 S Church St (19950-7726)
P.O. Box 2013 (19950-0603)
PHONE.................302 349-4501
Steve Luchansky, *Manager*
EMP: 37
SQ FT: 135,000
SALES (corp-wide): 13MM **Privately Held**
WEB: www.jamesthompson.com
SIC: 2843 2269 2261 Textile finishing agents; finishing plants; finishing plants, cotton
PA: James Thompson & Company, Inc.
463 7th Ave Rm 1603
New York NY 10018
212 686-4242

(G-2749)
JUDY TIM FUEL INC
12386 Beach Hwy (19950-5728)
PHONE.................302 349-5895
Timothy F Judy, *Owner*
EMP: 7
SALES (est): 942.6K **Privately Held**
SIC: 2869 Fuels

(G-2750)
M/S HOLLOW METAL WHOLESALE LLC
9644 Nantcke Bus Pk Dr (19950-5454)
PHONE.................302 349-9471
Jim Schroeder, *General Mgr*
Alan Miller,
Rics Schmitt,
EMP: 20
SALES (est): 2.4MM **Privately Held**
SIC: 5031 Metal doors, sash & trim; door frames, all materials; window frames, all materials

(G-2751)
MENNOS WOODWORKS
10147 Shawnee Rd (19950-4954)
PHONE.................302 381-5525
EMP: 1
SALES (est): 101.9K **Privately Held**
SIC: 2431 Millwork

(G-2752)
MEREDITH SALVAGE
12206 Woodbridge Rd (19950-4553)
PHONE.................302 349-4776
Meredith Salvage, *Principal*
EMP: 1
SALES (est): 50K **Privately Held**
SIC: 3531 Scrapers (construction machinery)

(G-2753)
MJ WEBB FARMS INC
12608 Webb Farm Rd (19950-5111)
PHONE.................302 349-4453
M J Webb III, *President*
Michael B Webb, *Treasurer*
Louise Webb, *Admin Sec*
EMP: 7
SQ FT: 2,400
SALES (est): 662.4K **Privately Held**
SIC: 0191 General farms, primarily crop

(G-2754)
MYRLE MANUFACTURING LLC
14866 Adamsville Rd (19950-4163)
PHONE.................302 249-9408
Betsy Ellingsworth, *Mng Member*
EMP: 1
SALES (est): 39.6K **Privately Held**
SIC: 3999 Manufacturing industries

(G-2755)
NANTICOKE CONSULTING INC
Also Called: Nanticoke Consulting and McHy
7707 Lindale Rd (19950-4914)
PHONE.................302 424-0750
Kevin Huey, *CEO*
Brent Huey, *Vice Pres*
EMP: 9
SALES (est): 1.4MM **Privately Held**
SIC: 3599 7389 Machine & other job shop work;

(G-2756)
NATIONAL CONCRETE PRODUCTS LLC
9466 Beach Hwy (19950-5302)
P.O. Box 2001 (19950-0501)
PHONE.................302 349-5528
Albert Croll III,
EMP: 30
SALES (est): 4.1MM **Privately Held**
SIC: 3272 Steps, prefabricated concrete

(G-2757)
NEW PROCESS FIBRE COMPANY INC
12655 N 1st St (19950-4864)
P.O. Box 2009 (19950-0510)
PHONE.................302 349-4535
Carl Peters, *President*
William Rust, *Vice Pres*
Scott Jerman, *QC Mgr*
Denise Jefferson, *Cust Mgr*
EMP: 70 EST: 1927
SQ FT: 65,000
SALES (est): 17.6MM **Privately Held**
WEB: www.newprocess.com
SIC: 3089 3083 Plastic processing; extruded finished plastic products; laminated plastics plate & sheet

(G-2758)
PB TRUCKING INC
8940 Greenwood Rd (19950-4861)
PHONE.................302 841-3209
Perry Butler, *President*
Nicole Callahan, *Manager*
EMP: 10 EST: 1983
SALES (est): 800K **Privately Held**
SIC: 4212 Local trucking, without storage

(G-2759)
RELAXING TOURS LLC
11546 Adamsville Rd (19950-4202)
PHONE.................610 905-3852
Hildegard Rieger, *President*
EMP: 8
SALES (est): 83.2K **Privately Held**
SIC: 8093 Rehabilitation center, outpatient treatment

(G-2760)
ROBERT T MINNER JR
Also Called: Rt Minner & Sons
2181 Deep Grass Ln (19950-2450)
P.O. Box 63, Houston (19954-0063)
PHONE.................302 422-9206
Robert T Minner Jr, *Owner*
Mary Minner, *Co-Owner*
EMP: 5
SALES: 320K **Privately Held**
SIC: 5148 Fruits

(G-2761)
SAKURA INC
600 Cattail Branch Rd (19950-1703)
PHONE.................302 349-4628
Kaz Hosaka, *President*
EMP: 5
SQ FT: 3,366
SALES (est): 82K **Privately Held**
SIC: 0752 Boarding services, kennels

(G-2762)
SAM YODER AND SON LLC
9387 Memory Rd (19950-4924)
PHONE.................302 398-4711
Maylon Mast,
Sam Yoder, *Chairman*
Ronald Yoder, *Vice Pres*

▲ = Import ▼ = Export
◆ = Import/Export

Ramona Carter, *Treasurer*
Curtis Yoder, *Sales Associate*
EMP: 114
SQ FT: 57,200
SALES (est): 17.1MM **Privately Held**
WEB: www.samyoder.com
SIC: 2439 Trusses, wooden roof; trusses, except roof: laminated lumber; arches, laminated lumber

(G-2763)
SHIRKEY TRUCKING CORP
734 Cattail Branch Rd (19950-1704)
PHONE..................302 349-2791
Rosanne G Ford, *Principal*
EMP: 4
SALES (est): 328.9K **Privately Held**
SIC: 4212 Local trucking, without storage

(G-2764)
STATE LINE CONSTRUCTION INC
650 Hickman Rd (19950-1749)
PHONE..................302 349-4244
EMP: 12
SALES (est): 1.2MM **Privately Held**
SIC: 1521 Steel Building Construction

(G-2765)
TED JOHNSON ENTERPRISES
14403 Adamsville Rd (19950-4110)
PHONE..................302 349-5925
Ted Johnson, *Owner*
EMP: 2
SALES (est): 160K **Privately Held**
SIC: 3663 Space satellite communications equipment

(G-2766)
TERRYS WELDING LLC
1477 Hickman Rd (19950-1766)
PHONE..................302 349-5260
Terry Algier, *Principal*
EMP: 1 EST: 2010
SALES (est): 54.6K **Privately Held**
SIC: 7692 Welding repair

(G-2767)
TRANSITIONAL YOUTH
8748 Greenwood Rd (19950-4858)
PHONE..................302 423-7543
Shannies Felipa, *Principal*
Rhona Mahl, *Director*
EMP: 10
SALES (est): 107.8K **Privately Held**
SIC: 8322 Individual & family services

(G-2768)
WILLEY KNIVES INC
14210 Sugar Hill Rd (19950-6065)
PHONE..................302 349-4070
W Gerald Willey, *Owner*
Geri Elliott, *Store Mgr*
EMP: 4
SALES (est): 376.8K **Privately Held**
SIC: 5719 7699 Cutlery; knife, saw & tool sharpening & repair

(G-2769)
WORTHYS TOWING LLC
9763 Blacksmith Shop Rd (19950-5040)
P.O. Box 1004, Seaford (19973-1004)
PHONE..................302 259-5265
EMP: 5
SALES (est): 101.1K **Privately Held**
SIC: 7549 Automotive Services

(G-2770)
YELLOW LIGHT PUBLISHING LLC
25 Governors Ave (19950-6090)
PHONE..................302 242-0990
EMP: 1 EST: 2017
SALES (est): 37.5K **Privately Held**
SIC: 2741 Miscellaneous publishing

Harbeson
Sussex County

(G-2771)
1 A LIFESAFER INC
26905 Lwes Georgetown Hwy (19951-2865)
PHONE..................800 634-3077
EMP: 1
SALES (corp-wide): 4.3MM **Privately Held**
SIC: 3829 Measuring & controlling devices
PA: 1 A Lifesafer, Inc.
   4290 Glendale Milford Rd
   Blue Ash OH 45242
   513 651-9560

(G-2772)
ARTISAN WOODWORKS LLC
28205 Johnson Ln (19951-2827)
PHONE..................302 841-5182
EMP: 3
SALES (est): 157.8K **Privately Held**
SIC: 2499 Decorative wood & woodwork

(G-2773)
ASPHALT PAVING EQP & SUPS
26822 Lwes Georgetown Hwy (19951-2856)
PHONE..................302 683-0105
Andy Pennington, *Owner*
EMP: 7
SALES (est): 1.8MM **Privately Held**
SIC: 5032 Paving materials; asphalt mixture

(G-2774)
B RITTER LLC
20478 Beaver Dam Rd (19951-3016)
PHONE..................302 945-7294
Howard Ritter, *Principal*
EMP: 4
SALES (est): 163.7K **Privately Held**
SIC: 0722 Field crops, except cash grains, machine harvesting services

(G-2775)
CLASSIC AUTO SALES & SERVICE
26905 Lwes Georgetown Hwy (19951-2865)
PHONE..................302 684-8126
Troy Hazzard, *Owner*
EMP: 4
SALES (est): 337.7K **Privately Held**
SIC: 7538 General automotive repair shops

(G-2776)
COASTAL CONCRETE WORKS LLC
27220 Buckskin Trl (19951-2717)
PHONE..................302 381-5261
EMP: 4
SALES (est): 116.8K **Privately Held**
SIC: 1771 Concrete work

(G-2777)
COMPASS POINT ASSOCIATES LLC
26373 Lwes Georgetown Hwy (19951-2869)
P.O. Box 246 (19951-0246)
PHONE..................302 684-2980
Mary Walch, *Mng Member*
EMP: 5
SQ FT: 2,800
SALES (est): 340K **Privately Held**
WEB: www.compasspointassociates.org
SIC: 8713 Surveying services

(G-2778)
COSTLINE CLEANING SERVICE
22791 Dozer Ln Unit 5 (19951-3023)
PHONE..................302 420-3000
Jonah Walls, *Opers Mgr*
EMP: 4
SALES (est): 112.7K **Privately Held**
SIC: 7699 Cleaning services

(G-2779)
COUNTRY LAWN CARE & MAINT
30435 Hollymount Rd (19951-2938)
PHONE..................302 593-3393
Jerry Dougherty, *Principal*
EMP: 4
SALES (est): 214.5K **Privately Held**
SIC: 0782 Lawn care services

(G-2780)
CREATIVE BUILDERS INC
20593 Rust Rd (19951-2828)
PHONE..................302 228-8153
Brian Ware, *President*
EMP: 5 EST: 1992
SQ FT: 4,000
SALES (est): 2MM **Privately Held**
SIC: 1531 Speculative builder, single-family houses

(G-2781)
CUSTOM FRAMERS INC
Also Called: At The Bch Repr & Maintainance
26526 Lwes Georgetown Hwy (19951-2858)
P.O. Box 261 (19951-0261)
PHONE..................302 684-5377
William Payden, *Partner*
Karen Payden, *Partner*
Tom Shinn, *Partner*
EMP: 20
SALES (est): 1.7MM **Privately Held**
SIC: 1751 1799 Framing contractor; athletic & recreation facilities construction

(G-2782)
E F AG PRODUCTS & SERVICE
26805 Anderson Corner Rd (19951-2922)
PHONE..................302 945-2415
Eric W Fogg, *Owner*
EMP: 4
SALES (est): 330K **Privately Held**
SIC: 5191 Animal feeds

(G-2783)
FLEXERA INC
22791 Dozer Ln Unit 8 (19951-3023)
P.O. Box 884, Selbyville (19975-0884)
PHONE..................302 945-6870
Robert Light, *CEO*
Brian Lisiewski, *President*
Alice Lisiewski, *COO*
Benjamin Farr, *Vice Pres*
EMP: 20 EST: 2006
SQ FT: 1,000
SALES (est): 2.4MM **Privately Held**
SIC: 8748 Energy conservation consultant

(G-2784)
HELLENS HEATING & AIR I
20949 Harbeson Rd (19951-2914)
PHONE..................302 945-1875
Mike Hellen, *Principal*
EMP: 6
SALES (est): 590K **Privately Held**
SIC: 1711 Warm air heating & air conditioning contractor

(G-2785)
HOT SHOT CONCEPTS
4 Sassafras Ln (19951-9469)
PHONE..................302 947-1808
Karin Snoots, *Owner*
EMP: 2 EST: 2008
SALES (est): 30K **Privately Held**
SIC: 3953 Stencils, painting & marking

(G-2786)
HYETT REFRIGERATION INC
Also Called: Honeywell Authorized Dealer
26451 Lwes Georgetown Hwy (19951-2860)
PHONE..................302 684-4600
Ernest Hyett, *President*
EMP: 13
SQ FT: 4,000
SALES (est): 1.7MM **Privately Held**
SIC: 1711 Warm air heating & air conditioning contractor

(G-2787)
J D MASONRY INC
Rr 5 (19951)
P.O. Box 111 (19951-0111)
PHONE..................302 684-1009
John Davison, *President*
EMP: 12
SALES (est): 759.4K **Privately Held**
SIC: 1741 Masonry & other stonework

(G-2788)
JAYKAL LED SOLUTIONS INC
26832 Lewes Georgetown Hw (19951)
PHONE..................302 295-0015
Sanjay Kapuria, *President*
Frank Gayzur, *Principal*
Brian Asher, *Director*
▲ **EMP:** 3
SALES (est): 310K **Privately Held**
SIC: 3648 3674 Lighting fixtures, except electric: residential; light emitting diodes

(G-2789)
LULLABY LEARNING CENTER INC
26324 Lwes Georgetown Hwy (19951-2867)
PHONE..................302 703-2871
Joseph Gebbia, *President*
Sheri Gebbia, *Exec Dir*
EMP: 14
SQ FT: 4,500
SALES (est): 129K **Privately Held**
SIC: 8351 Child day care services

(G-2790)
MAKO SWIM CLUB LLC
P.O. Box 231 (19951-0231)
PHONE..................631 682-2131
Matthew Morgan,
EMP: 5
SALES (est): 93.3K **Privately Held**
SIC: 7997 Membership sports & recreation clubs

(G-2791)
MCCREA EQUIPMENT COMPANY INC
22787 Dozer Ln Unit 2 (19951-3032)
PHONE..................302 945-0821
EMP: 60
SALES (corp-wide): 40.6MM **Privately Held**
SIC: 1711 Plumbing/Heating/Air Cond Contractor
PA: Mccrea Equipment Company, Inc.
   4463 Beech Rd
   Temple Hills MD 20748
   301 423-6623

(G-2792)
MIDSHORE ELECTRICAL SERVICES
22787 Dozer Ln Unit A1 (19951-3032)
PHONE..................302 945-2555
James Bailey, *President*
EMP: 4
SALES (est): 381.6K **Privately Held**
SIC: 1731 General electrical contractor

(G-2793)
MOLD BUSTERS LLC
27221 Buckskin Trl (19951-2719)
PHONE..................302 339-2204
Larry Hobman, *Mng Member*
EMP: 1
SALES: 86K **Privately Held**
SIC: 3544 Industrial molds

(G-2794)
OLD WOOD & CO LLC
26804 Lwes Georgetown Hwy (19951-2856)
PHONE..................302 684-3600
Martin Bueneman, *Mng Member*
Mary Bueneman,
EMP: 18
SALES (est): 2MM **Privately Held**
SIC: 2426 Flooring, hardwood

(G-2795)
PENINSULA MASONRY INC
26822 Lwes Georgetown Hwy (19951-2856)
P.O. Box 9174, Newark (19714-9174)
PHONE..................302 684-3410
John Eisenbrey, *President*
Susan Eisenbrey, *Corp Secy*
Larry Terettyman, *Vice Pres*
EMP: 50
SQ FT: 2,500

Harbeson - Sussex County (G-2796)

SALES: 4MM **Privately Held**
WEB: www.pmasonry.com
SIC: **1741** 1771 Masonry & other stonework; concrete work

(G-2796)
R F GENTNER & SON
22797 Dozer Ln Unit 15 (19951-3024)
PHONE.................................302 947-2733
Richard F Gentner, *Owner*
EMP: 5
SALES (est): 294.8K **Privately Held**
SIC: **1741** Masonry & other stonework

(G-2797)
ROGERS GRAPHICS INC
26836 Lwes Georgetown Hwy (19951)
P.O. Box 231, Milford (19963-0231)
PHONE.................................302 422-6694
Elba Wise, *Manager*
EMP: 2
SALES (corp-wide): 2.3MM **Privately Held**
SIC: **2752** Commercial printing, offset
PA: Rogers Graphics Inc
  32 Bridgeville Rd
  Georgetown DE 19947
  302 856-0028

(G-2798)
RW HEATING & AIR INC
20801 Doddtown Rd (19951-2845)
P.O. Box 385, Georgetown (19947-0385)
PHONE.................................302 856-4330
Ronald Witke, *Principal*
EMP: 7
SALES (est): 547K **Privately Held**
SIC: **1711** Warm air heating & air conditioning contractor

(G-2799)
SHORE PROPERTY MAINTENANCE
28828 Four Of Us Rd (19951-2890)
PHONE.................................302 947-4440
Ted Nowakowski, *Owner*
EMP: 15
SALES (est): 356.9K **Privately Held**
SIC: **0781** Landscape services

(G-2800)
SHORE TINT & MORE INC
22797 Dozer Ln Unit 13 (19951-3024)
PHONE.................................302 947-4624
Jared Becker, *President*
EMP: 5
SALES (est): 300K **Privately Held**
SIC: **7549** 1799 Glass tinting, automotive; glass tinting, architectural or automotive

(G-2801)
SUNDEW PAINTING INC
26836 L Georgetown Hwyb1e (19951)
PHONE.................................302 684-5858
Dino Mardo, *President*
Nardo Nick, *President*
Jenny Wottes, *Admin Sec*
EMP: 25
SALES (est): 783.8K **Privately Held**
SIC: **1721** Residential painting

(G-2802)
WEBSTUDY INC (PA)
30649 Hollymount Rd (19951-3010)
PHONE.................................888 326-4058
Joseph Curt Corbi, *CEO*
Michael Adams, *President*
EMP: 5
SALES (est): 831.7K **Privately Held**
SIC: **7371** 7372 7373 7374 Computer software development; prepackaged software; computer integrated systems design; data processing & preparation; information retrieval services;

Harrington
Kent County

(G-2803)
1 A LIFESAFER INC
101 Clark St (19952-1246)
PHONE.................................800 634-3077
EMP: 1
SALES (corp-wide): 4.3MM **Privately Held**
SIC: **3829** Measuring & controlling devices
PA: 1 A Lifesafer, Inc.
  4290 Glendale Milford Rd
  Blue Ash OH 45242
  513 651-9560

(G-2804)
A LITTLE VETERINARY CLINIC PA
6902 Mlford Hrrington Hwy (19952)
PHONE.................................302 398-3367
Sharon Little Dvm, *President*
Larry Little, *Software Dev*
EMP: 10
SALES (est): 653.6K **Privately Held**
SIC: **0742** Animal hospital services, pets & other animal specialties

(G-2805)
AGRO LAB
101 Clukey Dr (19952-2372)
PHONE.................................302 265-2734
Jennifer Shaner, *Principal*
EMP: 4 EST: 2010
SALES (est): 159.9K **Privately Held**
SIC: **8071** Testing laboratories

(G-2806)
AGROLAB INC
101 Clukey Dr (19952-2372)
PHONE.................................302 535-6591
Bill Rohrer, *Owner*
EMP: 7 EST: 2010
SALES (est): 450K **Privately Held**
SIC: **0711** Soil preparation services

(G-2807)
ALPHA CARE MEDICAL LLC (PA)
1000 Midway Dr Ste 3 (19952-2448)
PHONE.................................302 398-0888
Nihar Gala,
EMP: 7
SALES (est): 1.1MM **Privately Held**
SIC: **8011** Primary care medical clinic

(G-2808)
AMERICAN FINANCE LLC
17507 S Dupont Hwy (19952-2370)
PHONE.................................302 674-0365
Frank Moore, *President*
EMP: 60
SQ FT: 22,000
SALES: 27MM **Privately Held**
SIC: **6159** Agricultural credit institutions

(G-2809)
AMERICAN LEGION
Also Called: American Legion Ckrt Post 7
17448 S Dupont Hwy (19952-2481)
PHONE.................................302 398-3566
Chris Werner, *Principal*
EMP: 5 EST: 1972
SALES (est): 310.3K **Privately Held**
SIC: **8641** Veterans' organization

(G-2810)
AMERICINN INTERNATIONAL LLC
1259 Corn Crib Rd (19952-2266)
PHONE.................................302 398-3900
Nancy Roberts, *Manager*
EMP: 10 **Publicly Held**
SIC: **7011** Hotels & motels
HQ: Americinn By Wyndham
  250 Lake Dr E
  Chanhassen MN 55317

(G-2811)
ANGELS IN HEAVEN
Also Called: Angel's In Heaven Daycare
333 Weiner Ave (19952-1140)
PHONE.................................302 398-7820
EMP: 5 EST: 2009
SALES (est): 150K **Privately Held**
SIC: **8351** Child Day Care Services

(G-2812)
ARCADIA FENCING INC
166 Hopkins Cemetery Rd (19952-3235)
P.O. Box 97 (19952-0097)
PHONE.................................302 398-7700
Steve Scott, *President*
EMP: 5
SALES (est): 557.5K **Privately Held**
SIC: **1799** Fence construction

(G-2813)
ARUNDEL TRAILER SALES
344 Jefferson Woods Dr (19952-6032)
PHONE.................................302 398-6288
Bill Hoovler, *CEO*
EMP: 5
SALES (est): 650.4K **Privately Held**
SIC: **5013** 5015 Trailer parts & accessories; trailer parts & accessories, used

(G-2814)
ATI HOLDINGS LLC
Also Called: ATI Physical Therapy
16819 S Dupont Hwy # 500 (19952-3192)
PHONE.................................302 786-3008
EMP: 21
SALES (corp-wide): 338.3MM **Privately Held**
SIC: **8049** Physical therapist
PA: Ati Holdings, Llc
  790 Remington Blvd
  Bolingbrook IL 60440
  630 296-2222

(G-2815)
ATLANTIC CONCRETE COMPANY INC
Newworf Rd (19952)
P.O. Box 321, Milford (19963-0321)
PHONE.................................302 398-8920
David Jones, *President*
EMP: 1
SALES (corp-wide): 10.8MM **Privately Held**
SIC: **3273** Ready-mixed concrete
PA: Atlantic Concrete Company Inc
  New Wharf Rd
  Milford DE 19963
  302 422-8017

(G-2816)
BAUER FARMS
396 Hayfield Rd (19952-5733)
PHONE.................................302 284-9722
Joseph Bauer, *Principal*
EMP: 5
SQ FT: 1,540
SALES (est): 419.3K **Privately Held**
SIC: **0191** General farms, primarily crop

(G-2817)
BI-STATE FEEDERS LLC
16054 S Dupont Hwy (19952-3121)
PHONE.................................302 398-3408
EMP: 2
SALES (est): 131K **Privately Held**
SIC: **0213** 2048 Hog feedlot; feed supplements

(G-2818)
BILL RUST PLUMBING
64 Deer Valley Rd (19952-1706)
PHONE.................................302 422-6061
EMP: 6
SALES (est): 474.5K **Privately Held**
SIC: **1711** Plumbing/Heating/Air Cond Contractor

(G-2819)
BRS CONSULTING INC
293 Jackson Ditch Rd (19952-2432)
P.O. Box 237 (19952-0237)
PHONE.................................302 786-2326
Robin Schurman, *President*
Brian Schurman, *Vice Pres*
EMP: 8
SALES (est): 1.2MM **Privately Held**
SIC: **8742** 1542 Construction project management consultant; nonresidential construction; commercial & office buildings, renovation & repair

(G-2820)
BURRIS LOGISTICS
Burris Retail Food System
111 Reese Ave (19952-1316)
PHONE.................................302 398-5050
Larry Passwater, *Vice Pres*
EMP: 80
SQ FT: 200,000
SALES (corp-wide): 1.4B **Privately Held**
SIC: **4225** 5143 5142 General warehousing & storage; dairy products, except dried or canned; packaged frozen goods
PA: Burris Logistics
  501 Se 5th St
  Milford DE 19963
  302 839-4531

(G-2821)
BW ELECTRIC INC
Also Called: Bwe Electric
15342 S Dupont Hwy (19952-3114)
PHONE.................................302 566-6248
Bryon S Warren, *President*
Kelly Warren, *Vice Pres*
EMP: 28
SQ FT: 2,500
SALES: 3.8MM **Privately Held**
SIC: **1731** General electrical contractor

(G-2822)
CABELL CORP
Also Called: Heritage Manor
131 W Center St Apt 33 (19952-1073)
PHONE.................................302 398-8125
Emily Wothers, *Manager*
EMP: 4
SALES (corp-wide): 750K **Privately Held**
WEB: www.cabellcorp.com
SIC: **6531** 6513 Housing authority operator; apartment building operators
PA: Cabell Corp
  410 Market St
  Denton MD 21629
  410 479-3655

(G-2823)
CALLAWAY FURNITURE INC
15152 S Dupont Hwy (19952-3112)
PHONE.................................302 398-8858
Paul S Callaway, *President*
Paul R Callaway, *President*
EMP: 8 EST: 1947
SQ FT: 15,000
SALES (est): 1.5MM **Privately Held**
WEB: www.callawayfurniture.net
SIC: **5712** 2394 5713 Office furniture; awnings, fabric: made from purchased materials; carpets

(G-2824)
CHICK HARNESS & SUPPLY INC (PA)
Also Called: Equine Wholesalers
18011 S Dupont Hwy (19952-2135)
PHONE.................................302 398-4630
Robert L Fleming, *President*
Tom Dunlop, *Accountant*
Robert Fieming, *Sales Executive*
Sam Chick, *Manager*
Linda Chick, *Admin Sec*
◆ EMP: 30
SQ FT: 20,000
SALES (est): 7.2MM **Privately Held**
WEB: www.chicksaddlery.com
SIC: **5941** 5699 5661 5191 Saddlery & equestrian equipment; western apparel; men's boots; equestrian equipment; commercial printing, lithographic

(G-2825)
CHOICES FOR COMMUNITY LIVING (PA)
100 Kings Ct (19952-2553)
PHONE.................................302 398-0446
Belinda Smith, *Manager*
EMP: 8
SALES (est): 206.6K **Privately Held**
SIC: **8361** Residential care for the handicapped

(G-2826)
COASTAL PUMP & TANK INC
17401 S Dupont Hwy (19952-2312)
PHONE.................................302 398-3061
William E Towers Jr, *President*
William Thompson, *Treasurer*
EMP: 14
SQ FT: 1,500
SALES (est): 1.3MM **Privately Held**
SIC: **1799** Gasoline pump installation

Harrington - Kent County

(G-2827)
COASTAL WOOD INDUSTRIES
6621 Mlford Hrrington Hwy (19952)
P.O. Box 296 (19952-0296)
PHONE..................302 398-9601
Pat Garey, *Principal*
EMP: 3
SALES (est): 201.2K **Privately Held**
SIC: 3999 Manufacturing industries

(G-2828)
COLLINS MECHANICAL INC
15294 S Dupont Hwy (19952-3113)
PHONE..................302 398-8877
Bruce Collins, *President*
Gregory Collins, *Vice Pres*
Barbara Collins, *Treasurer*
Sara Collins, *Admin Sec*
EMP: 40
SQ FT: 2,200
SALES (est): 6MM **Privately Held**
SIC: 5999 1711 Plumbing & heating supplies; plumbing contractors

(G-2829)
D A B PRODUCTIONS
Also Called: Axe Bail Bonds
604 Fernwood Dr (19952-6012)
PHONE..................302 670-9407
Dwayne Breeding, *Principal*
EMP: 5 EST: 2011
SALES (est): 312.3K **Privately Held**
SIC: 7389 Bail bonding

(G-2830)
DELAWARE RURAL WATER ASSN
27 Commerce St Ste 27c (19952-1500)
PHONE..................302 398-9633
Finley Jones, *President*
Allen Atkins, *Vice Pres*
EMP: 8
SQ FT: 500
SALES: 804K **Privately Held**
SIC: 7699 Waste cleaning services

(G-2831)
DELAWARE STATE FAIR INC (PA)
18500 S Dupont Hwy (19952)
P.O. Box 28 (19952-0028)
PHONE..................302 398-3269
Brent M Adams Jr, *Ch of Bd*
W Leroy Betts, *President*
R Ronald Draper, *President*
Danny R Aguilar, *General Mgr*
William Dimondi, *General Mgr*
EMP: 26
SQ FT: 15,000
SALES: 7.4MM **Privately Held**
WEB: www.delawarestatefair.com
SIC: 7999 Agricultural fair

(G-2832)
DELMARVA PLASTICS CO
800 Pine Pitch Rd (19952-3432)
PHONE..................302 398-1000
Dirk Gleysteen, *President*
EMP: 5
SQ FT: 1,000
SALES (est): 912.4K **Privately Held**
WEB: www.delmarvaplastics.com
SIC: 2821 Plastics materials & resins

(G-2833)
DISCOUNT CIGARETTE DEPOT
1 Liberty Plz (19952-1248)
PHONE..................302 398-4447
Askol Patel, *Owner*
EMP: 2
SALES (est): 97K **Privately Held**
SIC: 3999 Cigar & cigarette holders

(G-2834)
DONALD WALKER
Also Called: Innovative Music Group
142 W Milby St (19952-1023)
PHONE..................240 507-9805
Donald Walker, *Principal*
Lonyai Downing, *Principal*
EMP: 4
SALES (est): 101.3K **Privately Held**
SIC: 7389 Music & broadcasting services

(G-2835)
DOVER MILLWORK INC
Also Called: Dover Windows and Doors
10862 Shawnee Rd (19952-6836)
PHONE..................302 349-5070
Larry Yoder, *President*
Jeanette Yoder, *Vice Pres*
Rita Zehr, *Office Mgr*
▲ EMP: 18
SALES (est): 2.8MM **Privately Held**
SIC: 2431 Doors & door parts & trim, wood; doors, wood; windows, wood

(G-2836)
DYNAMIC THERAPY SERVICES LLC
2000 Midway Dr (19952-2449)
PHONE..................302 566-6624
EMP: 6 EST: 2016
SALES (est): 88.2K **Privately Held**
SIC: 8093 Rehabilitation center, outpatient treatment

(G-2837)
ENVIROCORP INC
51 Clark St (19952-1242)
PHONE..................302 398-3869
H Joseph Gannon Jr, *President*
H Jpseph Gannon 3rd, *Vice Pres*
Howard J Gannon III, *Vice Pres*
Erin Bichy, *Admin Sec*
EMP: 10
SQ FT: 5,000
SALES (est): 1.3MM **Privately Held**
SIC: 8734 Water testing laboratory

(G-2838)
ERCO CEILINGS & INTERIORS INC
Also Called: Erco Ceilings & Blinds
512 Shaw Ave (19952-1233)
PHONE..................302 398-3200
Frank Castiglione, *Branch Mgr*
EMP: 11
SALES (corp-wide): 32.5MM **Privately Held**
SIC: 5039 5211 Ceiling systems & products; lumber & other building materials
HQ: Erco Ceilings & Interiors Inc
2 S Dupont Rd
Wilmington DE 19805
302 994-6200

(G-2839)
FAIRWAY MANUFACTURING COMPANY (HQ)
51 Clark St (19952-1242)
PHONE..................302 398-4630
Linda Chick, *President*
James Fleming, *Vice Pres*
Rebecca Fleming, *Treasurer*
Frank Chick, *Shareholder*
Scott Fleming, *Admin Sec*
EMP: 6
SALES (est): 1.3MM
SALES (corp-wide): 7.2MM **Privately Held**
SIC: 3199 2399 3111 Equestrian related leather articles; horse blankets; saddlery leather
PA: Chick Harness & Supply, Inc.
18011 S Dupont Hwy
Harrington DE 19952
302 398-4630

(G-2840)
FAMILY COMB & SCISSORS
100 W Milby St (19952)
PHONE..................302 398-8570
Mary Layton, *Owner*
EMP: 4
SALES (est): 102.2K **Privately Held**
SIC: 7231 Hairdressers

(G-2841)
FIRST STATE PETROLEUM SERVICES
714 Gallo Rd (19952-4454)
PHONE..................302 398-9704
Stacey Gallo, *President*
Helen Gallo, *Owner*
Frank Gallo, *Vice Pres*
Fred Gallo, *Vice Pres*
Carmine Gallo, *Shareholder*
EMP: 7
SALES (est): 93.7K **Privately Held**
SIC: 1799 Gasoline pump installation

(G-2842)
GRAPHICS UNLIMITED INC
Also Called: Chicks Graphics Unlimited
51 Clark St (19952-1242)
P.O. Box 59 (19952-0059)
PHONE..................302 398-3898
Linda Chick, *President*
EMP: 4
SALES (est): 178.2K **Privately Held**
SIC: 7336 Commercial art & graphic design

(G-2843)
GRIFF SON HOMETOWN AUTO REP
201 Delaware Ave (19952-1236)
PHONE..................302 786-2143
James Griffith, *Owner*
EMP: 5 EST: 2013
SALES (est): 557.7K **Privately Held**
SIC: 7538 General automotive repair shops

(G-2844)
GULAB MANAGEMENT INC
Also Called: Super 8 Motel
17101 Dupont Hwy (19952)
PHONE..................302 398-4206
Asim Gulab, *Manager*
EMP: 5
SALES (corp-wide): 3.6MM **Privately Held**
SIC: 7011 Hotels & motels
PA: Gulab Management Inc
1426 N Dupont Hwy
Dover DE 19901
302 734-4433

(G-2845)
HARRINGTON RACEWAY INC
15 W Rider Rd (19952-3322)
P.O. Box 28 (19952-0028)
PHONE..................302 398-4920
William Chasanov, *President*
Leroy Detts, *Vice Pres*
Larry Mannering, *Manager*
Adam Straka, *Manager*
Brian Gillis, *Exec Dir*
▲ EMP: 15 EST: 1946
SQ FT: 12,000
SALES (est): 2.3MM
SALES (corp-wide): 7.4MM **Privately Held**
WEB: www.harringtonraceway.com
SIC: 7948 0752 Harness horse racing; animal specialty services
PA: The Delaware State Fair Inc
18500 S Dupont Hwy
Harrington DE 19952
302 398-3269

(G-2846)
HARRINGTON RACEWAY INC
Also Called: Harrington Raceway and Casino
Rr 13 (19952)
P.O. Box 310 (19952-0310)
PHONE..................302 398-5346
Patricia Key, *CEO*
Bruce McKee, *General Mgr*
EMP: 450
SQ FT: 72,000
SALES (est): 12.5MM **Privately Held**
WEB: www.midwayslots.com
SIC: 7999 7993 5813 5812 Gambling & lottery services; gambling establishments operating coin-operated machines; drinking places; eating places

(G-2847)
HARRINGTON SENIOR CENTER INC
102 Fleming St (19952-1145)
PHONE..................302 398-4224
Karen Crouse, *Exec Dir*
EMP: 5
SALES: 248.4K **Privately Held**
SIC: 8322 Senior citizens' center or association

(G-2848)
HEAD START HARRINGTON
112 East St (19952-3375)
PHONE..................302 398-9196
Cheryl Pritchett, *Principal*
Jose Garcia, *Director*
EMP: 5
SALES (est): 80.3K **Privately Held**
SIC: 8351 Head start center, except in conjunction with school

(G-2849)
HENSCO LLC
Also Called: Hensco Glass Company
155 Argos Choice (19952-2641)
PHONE..................302 423-1638
Kenneth Bailey, *President*
Joseph Scott, *Vice Pres*
EMP: 5
SALES: 100K **Privately Held**
SIC: 3231 6519 1742 Insulating glass; made from purchased glass; real property lessors; plastering, drywall & insulation

(G-2850)
HOLIDAY INN EXPRESS
17271 S Dupont Hwy (19952-2484)
PHONE..................302 398-8800
Alina Keller, *General Mgr*
EMP: 20
SALES (est): 1.3MM **Privately Held**
SIC: 7011 Hotels & motels

(G-2851)
HOT ROD WELDING
258 Sika Dr (19952-1705)
PHONE..................302 725-5485
EMP: 1 EST: 2017
SALES (est): 28.1K **Privately Held**
SIC: 7692 Welding repair

(G-2852)
HRUPSA FARMS LTD PARTNERSHIP
3418 Hopkins Cemetery Rd (19952-3522)
PHONE..................302 270-1817
Frank G Hrupsa, *Principal*
EMP: 4
SALES (est): 509.5K **Privately Held**
SIC: 0191 General farms, primarily crop

(G-2853)
HUDSON FARM SUPPLY CO INC
Also Called: Souther States Co-Op
213 Harrington Ave (19952-1117)
PHONE..................302 398-3654
E Ruth Hudson, *President*
EMP: 7
SQ FT: 7,000
SALES: 100K **Privately Held**
SIC: 5261 5191 Nursery stock, seeds & bulbs; fertilizer; farm supplies

(G-2854)
JAMES ATKINSON
1911 Prospect Church Rd (19952-4361)
PHONE..................302 236-7499
James Atkinson, *Principal*
EMP: 1
SALES (est): 91.2K **Privately Held**
SIC: 3523 Farm machinery & equipment

(G-2855)
JD SIGN COMPANY LLC
515 Smith Ave (19952-1227)
P.O. Box 937, Felton (19943-0937)
PHONE..................302 786-2761
Jason Dean, *President*
EMP: 2
SALES (est): 228K **Privately Held**
SIC: 3993 Electric signs

(G-2856)
JJS LEARNING EXPERIENCE LLC
17001 S Dupont Hwy (19952-2486)
PHONE..................302 398-9000
Keith Shawanda, *Mng Member*
EMP: 15
SALES (est): 73.9K **Privately Held**
SIC: 8351 Child day care services

(G-2857)
JLJ ENTERPRISES INC
6465 Mlford Hrrington Hwy (19952)
PHONE..................302 398-0229
Jerry L Jerman, *President*
Tom Callahan, *Human Res Mgr*
Mellisa Esquivel, *Info Tech Mgr*

Harrington - Kent County (G-2858)

Elizabeth Jerman, *Admin Sec*
▼ **EMP:** 14
SALES (est): 4.4MM **Privately Held**
SIC: 5084 Food industry machinery

(G-2858)
JOHN T BROWN INC
4795 Mlford Hrrington Hwy (19952)
PHONE 302 398-8518
John T Brown, *President*
Linda Brown, *Admin Sec*
EMP: 4
SALES (est): 286.7K **Privately Held**
SIC: 4212 Local trucking, without storage

(G-2859)
JOSEPH T RICHARDSON INC
105 E Center St (19952-1105)
P.O. Box 269 (19952-0269)
PHONE 302 398-8101
John Dunbar, *President*
Virginia Richardson, *Corp Secy*
EMP: 18 **EST:** 1952
SALES (est): 1MM **Privately Held**
SIC: 1711 Plumbing contractors; warm air heating & air conditioning contractor

(G-2860)
K L VINCENT WELDING SVC INC
19456 S Dupont Hwy (19952-2116)
PHONE 302 398-9357
Kenneth L Vincent, *President*
EMP: 15
SALES (est): 1.2MM **Privately Held**
SIC: 7692 Welding repair

(G-2861)
KEY TO BEAUTY
7184 Mlford Hrrington Hwy (19952)
PHONE 302 398-9460
Barbara Pitts, *Owner*
EMP: 4
SALES (est): 210.5K **Privately Held**
SIC: 5699 7231 Wigs, toupees & wiglets; beauty shops

(G-2862)
KIDZ KOTTAGE CLUB INC
17001 S Dupont Hwy (19952-2486)
PHONE 302 398-4067
EMP: 15
SALES (est): 480K **Privately Held**
SIC: 8351 Child Day Care Services

(G-2863)
KIRBY & HOLLOWAY PROVISIONS CO
Also Called: K & H Provision Co
966 Jackson Ditch Rd (19952-2417)
P.O. Box 222 (19952-0222)
PHONE 302 398-3705
Russell Kirby II, *President*
Blanche Kirby, *Corp Secy*
Ruth Ann Argo, *Admin Sec*
EMP: 50 **EST:** 1946
SQ FT: 5,000
SALES (est): 8.9MM **Privately Held**
SIC: 2013 Sausages from purchased meat

(G-2864)
LAKE FOREST SCHOOL DISTRICT
Also Called: Delaware Early Childhood Ctr
100 W Mispillion St (19952-1027)
PHONE 302 398-8945
Janet Cornwell, *Director*
EMP: 15
SALES (corp-wide): 26.1MM **Privately Held**
WEB: www.lf.k12.de.us
SIC: 8211 8351 Public special education school; child day care services
PA: Lake Forest School District
5423 Killens Pond Rd
Felton DE 19943
302 284-3020

(G-2865)
LILY WREATHS
133 W Lucky Estates Dr (19952-2471)
PHONE 202 251-6004
EMP: 2
SALES (est): 62.5K **Privately Held**
SIC: 3999 Wreaths, artificial

(G-2866)
MEDICAL CENTER OF HARRINGTON
Also Called: Harrington Medical & Optical
203 Shaw Ave 205 (19952-1220)
P.O. Box 179 (19952-0179)
PHONE 302 398-8704
Vincent Lobo Do, *Owner*
EMP: 6
SALES (est): 352.6K **Privately Held**
SIC: 8011 General & family practice, physician/surgeon

(G-2867)
MESSICKS MOBILE HOMES INC
17959 S Dupont Hwy (19952-2136)
PHONE 302 398-9166
Ronald Messick, *President*
EMP: 10
SALES (est): 1.1MM **Privately Held**
SIC: 4213 1799 Mobile homes transport; mobile home site setup & tie down

(G-2868)
MICHAEL MATTHEW SPONAUGLE
Also Called: Happy Hoofer
2427 Flatiron Rd (19952-3926)
PHONE 302 566-1010
Michael Sponaugle, *Owner*
EMP: 7
SALES (est): 452.7K **Privately Held**
SIC: 7699 0752 Horseshoeing; training services, horses (except racing horses)

(G-2869)
MOUNTAIRE FARMS DELAWARE INC
615 Fairground Rd (19952-3318)
P.O. Box 218 (19952-0218)
PHONE 302 398-3296
Scott Brittingham, *Manager*
EMP: 5
SALES (corp-wide): 1.4B **Privately Held**
SIC: 5153 Grain elevators
HQ: Mountaire Farms Of Delaware, Inc.
29005 John J Williams Hwy
Millsboro DE 19966
302 934-1100

(G-2870)
OBRYAN WOODWORKS
5400 Vernon Rd (19952-4166)
PHONE 302 398-8202
Robert Obryan, *Principal*
EMP: 1 **EST:** 2016
SALES (est): 54.1K **Privately Held**
SIC: 2431 Millwork

(G-2871)
PEPSI BOTTLING VENTURES LLC
Also Called: Pepsico
58 Clukey Dr (19952-2330)
PHONE 302 398-3415
Wayne Farrare, *Branch Mgr*
EMP: 75 **Privately Held**
WEB: www.pbpllc.com
SIC: 2086 Carbonated soft drinks, bottled & canned
HQ: Pepsi Bottling Ventures Llc
4141 Parklake Ave Ste 600
Raleigh NC 27612
919 865-2300

(G-2872)
PERFECT FINISH POWDER COATING
3845 Whiteleysburg Rd (19952-5334)
PHONE 302 566-6189
Steve Curtiss, *President*
William Brown, *General Mgr*
EMP: 5 **EST:** 2013
SALES (est): 674.8K **Privately Held**
SIC: 3479 Coating of metals & formed products

(G-2873)
PETROSERV INC
17436 S Dupont Hwy (19952)
PHONE 302 398-3260
William Thompson, *President*
EMP: 5
SALES (est): 996.4K **Privately Held**
SIC: 5051 5072 5085 Pipe & tubing, steel; nozzles; drums, new or reconditioned

(G-2874)
PHILLIP L HRRS FD/CNSLTNT
40 Meadowood Ln (19952-1329)
PHONE 302 270-2905
Phillip L Harris, *Owner*
EMP: 1
SALES (est): 70K **Privately Held**
SIC: 2099 Food preparations

(G-2875)
PORTER SAND & GRAVEL INC
640 Sandbox Rd (19952-2707)
PHONE 302 335-5132
Frank Porter, *President*
EMP: 8
SALES (est): 1.4MM **Privately Held**
SIC: 5032 Gravel; sand, construction

(G-2876)
QUALITY EXTERIORS INC
60 Hopkins Cemetery Rd (19952-3149)
P.O. Box 9303, Warwick RI (02889-0303)
PHONE 302 398-9283
Micheal Makdad, *President*
Jason Stallings, *Manager*
EMP: 18
SALES (est): 2.8MM **Privately Held**
SIC: 1761 Roofing & gutter work

(G-2877)
R S BAUER LLC
17584 S Dupont Hwy (19952-2300)
PHONE 302 398-4668
Randy S Bauer, *President*
Belinda Bauer, *Vice Pres*
EMP: 16
SALES (est): 2.3MM **Privately Held**
SIC: 1711 Hydronics heating contractor; warm air heating & air conditioning contractor

(G-2878)
R STANLEY COLLIER & SON INC
1832 Brownsville Rd (19952-5017)
PHONE 302 398-7855
R Stanley Collier Jr, *President*
Faye Collier, *Corp Secy*
R Thomas Collier, *Vice Pres*
EMP: 5
SALES (est): 525.2K **Privately Held**
SIC: 0241 Dairy farms

(G-2879)
RAPID RENOVATION AND REPR LLC
79 Pleasant Pine Ct (19952-6403)
PHONE 302 475-5400
Brent Applebaum, *President*
EMP: 16 **EST:** 2011
SALES (est): 1.1MM **Privately Held**
SIC: 1522 Residential construction

(G-2880)
RONS MOBILE HOME SALES INC
17959 S Dupont Hwy (19952-2136)
PHONE 302 398-9166
Jason Browning, *General Mgr*
Michael Smith, *Controller*
EMP: 5
SQ FT: 3,000
SALES (est): 970K **Privately Held**
WEB: www.ronsmobilehomes.com
SIC: 5271 1521 Mobile homes; single-family housing construction

(G-2881)
ROUTZHAN JESSMAN
Also Called: Super 8 Motel
17010 S Dupont Hwy (19952-2477)
PHONE 302 398-4206
Jessman Routzhan, *General Mgr*
EMP: 15
SALES (est): 383.3K **Privately Held**
SIC: 7011 5812 Hotels & motels; eating places

(G-2882)
S BROWN APPRAISALS LLC
16819 S Dupont Hwy # 300 (19952-3192)
PHONE 302 672-0694
Scott Brown, *Mng Member*
EMP: 9
SALES (est): 273.1K **Privately Held**
SIC: 7389 Appraisers, except real estate

(G-2883)
SCHATZ MESSICK ENTERPRISES LLC
705 Andrewville Rd (19952-4443)
PHONE 302 398-8646
John Schatzschneider, *Principal*
EMP: 6 **EST:** 2008
SALES (est): 657.3K **Privately Held**
SIC: 8748 Business consulting

(G-2884)
SCHIFF FARMS INC (PA)
16054 S Dupont Hwy (19952-3121)
PHONE 302 398-8014
James Schiff, *President*
Carol Schiff, *Admin Sec*
EMP: 20
SALES (est): 9.3MM **Privately Held**
WEB: www.schifffarms.com
SIC: 0212 0115 0116 0111 Beef cattle except feedlots; corn; soybeans; wheat

(G-2885)
SCHIFF TRANSPORT LLC
16054 S Dupont Hwy (19952-3121)
PHONE 302 398-8014
Terrence Schiff, *Principal*
EMP: 7
SALES (est): 632.7K **Privately Held**
SIC: 4789 Transportation services

(G-2886)
SHARON ALGER-LITTLE DR
6902 Mlford Hrrington Hwy (19952)
PHONE 302 398-3367
Sharon Alger-Little, *Owner*
EMP: 13
SALES (est): 203.7K **Privately Held**
SIC: 0742 Veterinarian, animal specialties

(G-2887)
SHARP RAINGUTTERS
Rr 36 (19952)
PHONE 302 398-4873
Glen Sharp, *Owner*
EMP: 10
SALES (est): 398.2K **Privately Held**
SIC: 1761 Gutter & downspout contractor

(G-2888)
SHELLS CHILD CARE CENTER III
5332 Mlford Hrrington Hwy (19952)
PHONE 302 398-9778
Michelle Malavet, *Owner*
EMP: 11
SALES (est): 135.9K **Privately Held**
SIC: 8351 Group day care center

(G-2889)
SIMPSON GARY CONTRACTING LLC
1994 Fox Hunters Rd (19952-4063)
PHONE 302 398-7733
Gary Simpson, *Owner*
EMP: 6
SALES (est): 794.6K **Privately Held**
SIC: 1542 Commercial & office building contractors

(G-2890)
SMITTYS AUTO REPAIR INC
17378 S Dupont Hwy (19952-2464)
PHONE 302 398-8419
Anthony W Smith, *President*
EMP: 5
SALES (est): 580.4K **Privately Held**
SIC: 7538 General automotive repair shops

(G-2891)
SMOOTH SOUND DANCE BAND
201 Dorman St (19952-1002)
PHONE 302 398-8467
Tony Perrone, *Director*
EMP: 20 **EST:** 2010

GEOGRAPHIC SECTION
Hartly - Kent County (G-2924)

SALES: 38K **Privately Held**
SIC: 7929 Dance bands

(G-2892)
SNOWDEN CANDLES
7184 Mlford Hrrington Hwy (19952)
PHONE.................302 398-4373
James Snowden, *Owner*
EMP: 1 EST: 2018
SALES (est): 39.6K **Privately Held**
SIC: 3999 Candles

(G-2893)
STARS TRANSPORTATION LLC
311 Cams Fortune Way (19952-2574)
PHONE.................770 530-1843
Arlande M Mesidor, *Principal*
EMP: 4
SALES (est): 214.4K **Privately Held**
SIC: 4119 Limousine rental, with driver

(G-2894)
STEVE O QUILLIN OD
203 Shaw Ave 205 (19952-1220)
PHONE.................302 398-8404
Vincent Lobo, *Owner*
EMP: 6
SALES (est): 156K **Privately Held**
SIC: 8042 Specialized optometrists

(G-2895)
SUNNY HOSPITALITY LLC
Also Called: AmericInn Ldge Stes Harrington
1259 Corn Crib Rd (19952-2266)
PHONE.................302 398-3900
Nancy Roberts, *General Mgr*
Ted Watkins,
Anne Watkins,
EMP: 16
SALES: 700K **Privately Held**
SIC: 7011 Hotels & motels

(G-2896)
SYLVESTER CUSTOM CABINETRY
16869 S Dupont Hwy (19952-2488)
PHONE.................302 398-6050
Greg Sylvester, *Owner*
EMP: 4
SALES (est): 222.3K **Privately Held**
SIC: 2434 3261 Wood kitchen cabinets; closet bowls, vitreous china

(G-2897)
TAYLOR AND MESSICK INC
Also Called: John Deere Authorized Dealer
325 Walt Messick Rd (19952-3300)
PHONE.................302 398-3729
James W Messick, *President*
Rhonda Lee Shalzschnider, *Treasurer*
Maryann Wilson, *Admin Sec*
EMP: 17 EST: 1951
SQ FT: 7,000
SALES (est): 15.1MM **Privately Held**
WEB: www.taylormessick.com
SIC: 5083 Agricultural machinery & equipment

(G-2898)
TELAMON CORPORATION
112 East St (19952-3375)
PHONE.................302 398-9196
Lurys Fuhrman, *Manager*
EMP: 19
SALES (corp-wide): 70.5MM **Privately Held**
SIC: 8331 Job training services
PA: Telamon Corporation
    5560 Munford Rd Ste 201
    Raleigh NC 27612
    919 851-7611

(G-2899)
THOMAS E MELVIN SON INC
Also Called: Melvin Funeral Home
15522 S Dupont Hwy (19952-3116)
PHONE.................302 398-3884
Thomas E Melvin, *President*
Gene Melvin, *Director*
EMP: 4
SALES (est): 538.6K **Privately Held**
WEB: www.melvinfuneralhome.com
SIC: 7261 Funeral home

(G-2900)
TIDEWATER PHYSCL THRPY AND REB
610 Gordon St (19952-1217)
PHONE.................302 398-7982
Patrick McKenzie, *Branch Mgr*
EMP: 6
SALES (corp-wide): 2.6MM **Privately Held**
SIC: 8049 Physical therapist
PA: Tidewater Physical Therapy And Rehabilitation Associates Pa
    406 Marvel Ct
    Easton MD 21601
    410 822-3116

(G-2901)
TUSCAN/LEHIGH DAIRIES INC
Also Called: HI Grade Dairy
17267 S Dupont Hwy (19952-2484)
PHONE.................302 398-8321
Steve Moore, *Branch Mgr*
EMP: 16 **Publicly Held**
SIC: 2026 5143 5149 Milk processing (pasteurizing, homogenizing, bottling); milk; juices
HQ: Tuscan/Lehigh Dairies, Inc.
    117 Cumberland Blvd
    Burlington NJ 08016
    570 385-1884

(G-2902)
UNITED ADULT CARE LTD
3 Commerce St (19952-1075)
PHONE.................302 725-0708
A J Patel, *Mng Member*
EMP: 8 EST: 2017
SALES (est): 64K **Privately Held**
SIC: 8059 Nursing & personal care

(G-2903)
UTILITY AUDIT GROUP INC
93 Clark St (19952-1246)
PHONE.................302 398-8505
James Elliott Jr, *President*
Jacqueline D Elliott, *CFO*
EMP: 4
SQ FT: 1,800
SALES: 400K **Privately Held**
SIC: 4813 Telephone communication, except radio

(G-2904)
VEER HOTELS INC
Also Called: Quality Inn
1259 Corn Crib Rd (19952-2266)
PHONE.................302 398-3900
Jigar Patel, *President*
EMP: 8 EST: 2013
SALES (est): 645.1K **Privately Held**
SIC: 7011 Hotels & motels

(G-2905)
VINCENT LOBO DR PA
203 Shaw Ave 205 (19952-1220)
P.O. Box 179 (19952-0179)
PHONE.................302 398-8163
Vincent Lobo Jr, *President*
EMP: 5
SQ FT: 2,400
SALES (est): 151K **Privately Held**
SIC: 8031 Offices & clinics of osteopathic physicians

(G-2906)
WESTMOR INDUSTRIES
17409 S Dupont Hwy (19952-2312)
P.O. Box 219, Bridgeville (19933-0219)
PHONE.................302 398-3253
EMP: 2 EST: 2016
SALES (est): 125.4K **Privately Held**
SIC: 3999 Manufacturing industries

(G-2907)
WILMINGTON SAVINGS FUND SOC
Also Called: First National Bank
7 Commerce St (19952-1075)
PHONE.................302 398-3232
Benjamin Outten, *Branch Mgr*
EMP: 16
SALES (corp-wide): 455.5MM **Publicly Held**
WEB: www.firstnationalbankoftexas.com
SIC: 6021 National commercial banks
HQ: Wilmington Savings Fund Society
    500 Delaware Ave Ste 500 # 500
    Wilmington DE 19801
    302 792-6000

(G-2908)
WILSON MASONRY CORP
78 Pond View Ln (19952-2001)
PHONE.................302 398-8240
Linda Wilson, *Owner*
EMP: 14
SQ FT: 3,518
SALES (est): 914.8K **Privately Held**
SIC: 1741 Masonry & other stonework

(G-2909)
WONDER YEARS KIDS CLUB
17629 S Dupont Hwy (19952-2369)
PHONE.................302 398-0563
Kathleen Kagle, *Owner*
Judy Williams, *Owner*
Denise Halcomb, *Director*
EMP: 10
SALES (est): 294K **Privately Held**
SIC: 8351 Child day care services

(G-2910)
WYATT & BROWN INC
15602 S Dupont Hwy (19952-3117)
PHONE.................302 786-2793
EMP: 8
SALES (est): 462.8K **Privately Held**
SIC: 7322 Collection agency, except real estate

(G-2911)
XERGY INC
299 Cluckey Dr Ste A (19952-2376)
PHONE.................302 629-5768
Bamdad Bahar, *President*
Richard L Williams, *CFO*
EMP: 3
SALES (est): 419.5K **Privately Held**
SIC: 3677 Filtration devices, electronic

Hartly
Kent County

(G-2912)
AIR DOCTORX INC
Also Called: Honeywell Authorized Dealer
4639 Halltown Rd Ste B (19953-2614)
P.O. Box 267 (19953-0267)
PHONE.................302 492-1333
Mark Sabean, *President*
Lauren Leto, *Admin Sec*
EMP: 10
SALES (est): 1.4MM **Privately Held**
WEB: www.airdoctorx.com
SIC: 1711 Warm air heating & air conditioning contractor; heating & air conditioning contractors

(G-2913)
BYLERS WOODWORKING SHOP
2021 Pearsons Corner Rd (19953-2528)
PHONE.................302 492-1375
William Byler, *Principal*
EMP: 1
SALES (est): 89.4K **Privately Held**
SIC: 2434 Wood kitchen cabinets

(G-2914)
CARING HEARTS HOME CARE LLC
971 Burris Rd (19953-3515)
PHONE.................302 734-9000
EMP: 9
SALES (est): 73.9K **Privately Held**
SIC: 8082 Home health care services

(G-2915)
CHETS WELDING SERVICE
1308 Taraila Rd (19953-1802)
PHONE.................302 492-1003
Chester Tleasanton, *Owner*
EMP: 1
SALES (est): 55.8K **Privately Held**
SIC: 7692 Welding repair

(G-2916)
CISCO SYSTEMS INC
850 Arthursville Rd (19953-3301)
PHONE.................302 492-1735
Dan Radke, *Chairman*
EMP: 3
SALES (corp-wide): 51.9B **Publicly Held**
SIC: 3577 Data conversion equipment, media-to-media: computer
PA: Cisco Systems, Inc.
    170 W Tasman Dr
    San Jose CA 95134
    408 526-4000

(G-2917)
D GINGERICH CONCRETE & MASNRY
952 Myers Dr (19953-3034)
P.O. Box 242 (19953-0242)
PHONE.................302 492-8662
Connie Gingerich, *President*
David Ginerich, *Vice Pres*
EMP: 20
SQ FT: 500
SALES (est): 1.9MM **Privately Held**
SIC: 1771 Concrete work

(G-2918)
DAN H BEACHY & SONS INC
1298 Lockwood Chapel Rd (19953-3050)
PHONE.................302 492-1493
Alva Beachy, *President*
EMP: 9
SALES (est): 1.1MM **Privately Held**
WEB: www.danhbeachy.com
SIC: 1542 1541 Farm building construction; garage construction; warehouse construction

(G-2919)
DETWEILERS LIGHTING
285 Pearsons Corner Rd R (19953-2364)
PHONE.................302 678-5804
EMP: 2
SALES (est): 233.6K **Privately Held**
SIC: 3648 Lighting equipment

(G-2920)
DOTTY SWEICICKI DVM
748 Hazlettville Rd (19953-2346)
PHONE.................302 674-1380
Dotty Sweiciciki Dvm, *Owner*
EMP: 4
SALES (est): 157.3K **Privately Held**
SIC: 0742 Veterinarian, animal specialties

(G-2921)
ELECTRICAL ASSOCIATES INC
959 Hazlettville Rd (19953-2417)
P.O. Box 381, Camden Wyoming (19934-0381)
PHONE.................302 678-1068
William Webb, *President*
Glenn Cillen, *Vice Pres*
EMP: 5
SALES: 890K **Privately Held**
SIC: 1731 General electrical contractor

(G-2922)
FENCEMAXCOM INC
2210 Bryants Corner Rd (19953-2236)
PHONE.................302 343-9063
Jeff Lighthall, *President*
Jennifer Weiss, *Vice Pres*
EMP: 3
SQ FT: 2,000
SALES: 506K **Privately Held**
SIC: 3452 Gate hooks

(G-2923)
HARTLY FAMILY LEARNING CTR LLC
21 North St (19953-2936)
P.O. Box 138 (19953-0138)
PHONE.................302 492-1152
Connie Richards, *Owner*
EMP: 11
SALES (est): 291.1K **Privately Held**
SIC: 8351 Preschool center

(G-2924)
HARTLY RURITAN CLUB
683 Hartly Rd (19953-2922)
P.O. Box 105 (19953-0105)
PHONE.................302 492-8337

Hartly - Kent County (G-2925)

Suzanne Morris, *Principal*
EMP: 4
SALES (est): 43.8K **Privately Held**
SIC: 7997 Membership sports & recreation clubs

(G-2925)
HERITAGE SPORTS RDO NETWRK LLC
1841 Bryants Corner Rd (19953-2247)
PHONE..................302 492-1132
David Jones, *Principal*
EMP: 9 EST: 2007
SALES (est): 342.8K **Privately Held**
SIC: 4832 Radio broadcasting stations

(G-2926)
HILLANDALE FARMS DELAWARE INC
Also Called: Sydell-Hillandale Farms
149 Sydell Dr (19953-3584)
P.O. Box 269 (19953-0269)
PHONE..................302 492-3644
Ian Sydell, *General Mgr*
Daniel Kelly, *Opers Mgr*
Chuck Vincent, *CFO*
Rita Fabi, *Manager*
EMP: 30
SALES (est): 4.4MM **Privately Held**
SIC: 2499 Food handling & processing products, wood

(G-2927)
HILLANDALE FARMS OF PA INC
Also Called: Hillandale Farms of Delaware
149 Sydell Dr (19953-3584)
P.O. Box 269 (19953-0269)
PHONE..................302 492-1537
Ian Sydell, *General Mgr*
EMP: 25
SALES (corp-wide): 88.2MM **Privately Held**
SIC: 5144 5143 Eggs; dairy products, except dried or canned
PA: Hillandale Farms Of Pa., Inc.
    4001 Crooked Run Rd Ste 2
    North Versailles PA 15137
    412 672-9685

(G-2928)
JOHN MOBILE SNDBLST & PAIN
683 Hartly Rd (19953-2922)
PHONE..................302 270-5627
John Kohout, *Principal*
EMP: 8
SALES (est): 352.1K **Privately Held**
SIC: 1721 Painting & paper hanging

(G-2929)
JOHNS WOODWORKING LLC
84 Tack Shop Ln (19953-1860)
PHONE..................302 492-3527
EMP: 1
SALES (est): 54.1K **Privately Held**
SIC: 2431 Millwork

(G-2930)
JOSEPH SMITH & SONS INC
3221 Hartly Rd (19953-2744)
PHONE..................302 492-8091
Ronald Demoss, *Branch Mgr*
EMP: 7 **Privately Held**
SIC: 5093 Metal scrap & waste materials
HQ: Joseph Smith & Sons, Inc.
    2001 Kenilworth Ave
    Capitol Heights MD 20743
    301 773-1266

(G-2931)
KINGDOM KIDS DAY CARE
Also Called: Kingdom of God Fellowship
2899 Arthursville Rd (19953-3141)
P.O. Box 196 (19953-0196)
PHONE..................302 492-0207
Judy P Nazelrod, *Director*
EMP: 10
SALES (est): 419.1K **Privately Held**
SIC: 8351 Group day care center

(G-2932)
KRISS CONTRACTING INC
1523 Gunter Rd (19953)
P.O. Box 246 (19953-0246)
PHONE..................302 492-3502
Veronica Kriss, *President*

Kathleen Kriss, *Vice Pres*
EMP: 20
SALES (est): 6.7MM **Privately Held**
SIC: 1731 7389 Electrical work;

(G-2933)
LAMAR BAGS
2090 Hartly Rd (19953-2729)
PHONE..................302 492-8566
EMP: 2 EST: 2010
SALES (est): 60K **Privately Held**
SIC: 3171 7389 Mfg Women's Handbags/Purses Business Services At Non-Commercial Site

(G-2934)
LEROY A COBLENTZ
Also Called: Coblentz Woodworking
5024 Halltown Rd (19953-2532)
PHONE..................302 343-7434
EMP: 2
SALES (est): 109.3K **Privately Held**
SIC: 2431 Mfg Millwork

(G-2935)
MIA BELLAS CANDLES
697 Judith Rd (19953-2663)
PHONE..................302 331-7038
Dawn Walker, *Principal*
EMP: 1
SALES (est): 39.6K **Privately Held**
SIC: 3999 Candles

(G-2936)
MORNING AFTER INC
5006 Halltown Rd (19953-2532)
PHONE..................302 562-5190
Harriet W Glover, *Exec Dir*
EMP: 5
SALES (est): 123.3K **Privately Held**
SIC: 8699 7389 Charitable organization;

(G-2937)
PONY RUN KITCHENS LLC
5066 Westville Rd (19953-2106)
PHONE..................302 492-3006
Ivan Miller, *Mng Member*
EMP: 5
SALES (est): 350K **Privately Held**
SIC: 2514 3089 3263 Kitchen cabinets: metal; kitchenware, plastic; kitchen articles, semivitreous earthenware

(G-2938)
PRECISION LDSCPG & LAWN CARE
286 Judith Rd (19953-2648)
PHONE..................302 492-1583
Mike Nagyiski, *Partner*
EMP: 9
SALES (est): 516K **Privately Held**
SIC: 0781 Landscape services

(G-2939)
REXMEX DRYWALL LLC
449 Gibbs Chapel Rd (19953-3427)
PHONE..................302 343-9140
EMP: 5 EST: 2010
SALES (est): 217.1K **Privately Held**
SIC: 1742 Drywall

(G-2940)
ROBERT C THOMPSON
Also Called: Thompson's Farm
671 Bryants Corner Rd (19953-1974)
PHONE..................302 492-1053
Robert C Thompson, *Owner*
EMP: 5
SQ FT: 3,288
SALES (est): 647.6K **Privately Held**
SIC: 0241 Dairy farms

(G-2941)
RUSSELL D EARNEST ASSOC
1278 Fords Corner Rd (19953-3527)
PHONE..................302 659-0730
Russell Earnest, *Principal*
EMP: 1
SALES (est): 46.3K **Privately Held**
SIC: 2741 Miscellaneous publishing

(G-2942)
SWARTZENTRUBER SAWMILL CO
1191 Pearsons Corner Rd (19953-2355)
PHONE..................302 492-1665
Norman Wilkerson, *President*
Henry Swartzentruber, *President*
Gertrude Swartzentruber, *Corp Secy*
EMP: 8
SALES (est): 930K **Privately Held**
SIC: 2421 Sawmills & planing mills, general

(G-2943)
T & T SMALL ENGINES INC
6503 Halltown Rd (19953)
PHONE..................302 492-8677
William Thompson, *President*
Barbara Thompson, *Corp Secy*
EMP: 4
SQ FT: 5,000
SALES (est): 541.7K **Privately Held**
SIC: 7699 5251 5261 Engine repair & replacement, non-automotive; chainsaws; lawnmowers & tractors

(G-2944)
WSD CONTRACTING INC
952 Myers Dr (19953-3034)
P.O. Box 242 (19953-0242)
PHONE..................302 492-8606
EMP: 6
SALES (est): 326.5K **Privately Held**
SIC: 1771 Concrete Contractor

Hockessin
New Castle County

(G-2945)
100 ST CLIRE DRV OPRATIONS LLC
Also Called: Brackenville Center
100 Saint Claire Dr (19707-8906)
PHONE..................610 444-6350
Michael Sherman, *Exec VP*
J Richard Edwards, *Treasurer*
EMP: 123
SALES (est): 2.1MM **Privately Held**
SIC: 8051 Skilled nursing care facilities

(G-2946)
100 ST CLIRE DRV OPRATIONS LLC
100 Saint Claire Dr (19707-8906)
PHONE..................302 234-5420
George V Hager Jr, *CEO*
EMP: 107 EST: 2014
SALES (est): 715.2K **Publicly Held**
SIC: 8051 Skilled nursing care facilities
HQ: Genesis Healthcare Llc
    101 E State St
    Kennett Square PA 19348

(G-2947)
3D TECH LLC
7454 Lancaster Pike 308 (19707-9399)
PHONE..................610 268-2350
Thomas E Boyle,
Laura Boyle,
EMP: 5
SALES (est): 202.4K **Privately Held**
SIC: 7379 Data processing consultant

(G-2948)
3TI COATINGS LLC
780 Brookwood Ln (19707-9536)
PHONE..................302 379-1265
Mercedes Overcash,
Glenn Evers,
Kathleen Evers,
Derric Overcash,
EMP: 4
SALES (est): 92.1K **Privately Held**
SIC: 7389

(G-2949)
A & A MECHANICAL SERVICE INC
517 Erickson Ave (19707-1128)
P.O. Box 1197 (19707-5197)
PHONE..................302 234-9949
John W Adcock, *President*

Tracey Hayes, *Buyer*
Gerry Lewis, *Manager*
EMP: 4
SALES (est): 517.8K **Privately Held**
SIC: 1711 5075 Mechanical contractor; ventilation & duct work contractor; refrigeration contractor; warm air heating & air conditioning

(G-2950)
ACHIEVE SOLUTIONS
1 Foxview Cir (19707-2503)
PHONE..................302 598-1457
Justin Dinorscia, *Principal*
EMP: 6
SALES (est): 92.9K **Privately Held**
SIC: 8322 Community center

(G-2951)
ACUMEN STRATEGIES INC
7454 Lancaster Pike # 334 (19707-9399)
PHONE..................302 218-3949
Albert Chang, *President*
EMP: 4 EST: 1999
SALES (est): 138.1K **Privately Held**
SIC: 8748 Business consulting

(G-2952)
AECOM ENERGY & CNSTR INC
Also Called: Washington Group
2 York Way (19707-1345)
PHONE..................302 234-1445
EMP: 10
SALES (corp-wide): 20.1B **Publicly Held**
WEB: www.wgint.com
SIC: 1542 Commercial & office building, new construction
HQ: Aecom Energy & Construction, Inc.
    1999 Avenue Of The Stars
    Los Angeles CA 90067
    213 593-8100

(G-2953)
AIM RESEARCH CO
5936 Limestone Rd Ste 302 (19707-8932)
PHONE..................302 235-5940
Dian Y Lee, *President*
Diana Z Lee, *COO*
EMP: 8
SQ FT: 600
SALES (est): 1.2MM **Privately Held**
SIC: 3825 Lab standards, electric: resistance, inductance, capacitance

(G-2954)
ALARM SYSTEMS CO OF DELAWARE
735 Montgomery Woods Dr (19707-9324)
PHONE..................302 239-7754
Thomas S Hounsell, *President*
EMP: 5
SALES (est): 346.8K **Privately Held**
SIC: 1731 Fire detection & burglar alarm systems specialization; general electrical contractor

(G-2955)
ALDAS REFINISHING COMPANY
606 Chanin Ct (19707-9541)
PHONE..................302 528-5028
German Aldas Jr, *President*
Juan Aldas, *Vice Pres*
EMP: 3
SALES (est): 500K **Privately Held**
SIC: 2431 7389 Millwork;

(G-2956)
ALEXIS A SENHOLZI DMD
720 Yorklyn Rd Ste 120 (19707-8730)
PHONE..................302 234-2728
Raymond L Para DDS, *Owner*
EMP: 4 EST: 2012
SALES (est): 115.2K **Privately Held**
SIC: 8021 Dentists' office

(G-2957)
AMSTEL BARBERSHOP LLC
7313 Lancaster Pike Ste 4 (19707-9278)
PHONE..................302 635-7686
EMP: 4
SALES (est): 26.6K **Privately Held**
SIC: 7241 Barber shops

GEOGRAPHIC SECTION
Hockessin - New Castle County (G-2990)

(G-2958)
ANGITA PHARMARD LLC
24 Tall Oaks Dr (19707-2041)
PHONE..................................302 234-6794
Yanhe Huang,
EMP: 2
SQ FT: 1,000
SALES (est): 14.9K **Privately Held**
SIC: 2834 Pharmaceutical preparations

(G-2959)
AQUILA TRADING LLC
17 Amberfield Ln (19707-2079)
PHONE..................................302 290-5566
Cuong Pham, *Owner*
EMP: 1
SALES (est): 136.4K **Privately Held**
SIC: 3412 Metal barrels, drums & pails

(G-2960)
ATLANTIC REMEDIATION
Also Called: Arrc
1074 Yorklyn Rd E (19707-9769)
PHONE..................................610 444-5513
Harry Weatherby, *Mng Member*
EMP: 10
SALES (est): 1.1MM **Privately Held**
SIC: 3826 Moisture analyzers

(G-2961)
BAS HOME AND LANDSCAPE SVCS
416 Hockessin Hills Rd (19707-9677)
PHONE..................................302 354-0178
EMP: 4
SALES (est): 170.4K **Privately Held**
SIC: 0781 Landscape services

(G-2962)
BASHER & SON ENTERPRISES INC
Also Called: Basher & Son Welding
1072 Yorklyn Rd (19707-9769)
P.O. Box 1615 (19707-5615)
PHONE..................................302 239-6584
Warren Basher, *President*
Kim Mavil, *Treasurer*
EMP: 4
SALES (est): 280K **Privately Held**
SIC: 7549 7692 Trailer maintenance; welding repair

(G-2963)
BERKSHIRE HATAWAY HOME SVCS
88 Lantana Dr (19707-8814)
PHONE..................................302 235-6431
EMP: 14 EST: 2014
SALES (est): 604.1K **Privately Held**
SIC: 6531 Real estate agent, residential

(G-2964)
BGP PUBLICITY INC
1214 Old Lancaster Pike # 1 (19707-9401)
PHONE..................................302 234-9500
Bridget Gillespie Paverd, *President*
EMP: 7
SALES (est): 492.7K **Privately Held**
SIC: 8743 Public relations & publicity

(G-2965)
BOB REYNOLDS BACKHOE SERVICES
1124 Old Wilmington Rd (19707-9367)
PHONE..................................302 239-4711
Bob Reynolds, *Manager*
EMP: 1
SALES (est): 62.5K **Privately Held**
SIC: 3531 Backhoes

(G-2966)
BONNA-AGELA TECHNOLOGIES INC
217 Cherry Blossom Pl (19707-2047)
PHONE..................................302 438-8798
Zhixin Yang, *Manager*
EMP: 85 **Privately Held**
SIC: 3826 Analytical instruments
PA: Bonna-Agela Technologies Inc
    2038a Telegraph Rd
    Wilmington DE

(G-2967)
BORSELLO INC
720 Yorklyn Rd Ste 5 (19707-8729)
P.O. Box 1598 (19707-5598)
PHONE..................................302 472-2600
Thomas M Borsello Jr, *President*
Tammy Booth-Rice, *Manager*
EMP: 20 EST: 2009
SALES (est): 1.1MM **Privately Held**
SIC: 0781 0782 Landscape services; landscape counseling services; landscape contractors

(G-2968)
BRANDYWINE TRUST CO
7234 Lancaster Pike 300a (19707-9295)
PHONE..................................302 234-5750
Richard E Carlson, *President*
Scott Campbell, *Senior VP*
Jonathan Criswell, *Assistant VP*
Veronica Fischer, *Assistant VP*
Steven Petlev, *Assistant VP*
EMP: 33
SALES (est): 4.4MM **Privately Held**
WEB: www.brandytrust.com
SIC: 6733 Trusts, except educational, religious, charity: management

(G-2969)
BRENDEN BAILEY & CHANDLER VFW
Also Called: VFW Post 5892
7620 Lancaster Pike (19707-9755)
P.O. Box 231 (19707-0231)
PHONE..................................302 239-0797
Gayle Bledens, *President*
Mike Farley, *President*
EMP: 6
SALES (est): 147.7K **Privately Held**
SIC: 8641 Veterans' organization

(G-2970)
BROOKDALE SENIOR LIVING INC
6677 Lancaster Pike (19707-9503)
PHONE..................................302 239-3200
Susan Varnes, *Manager*
EMP: 30
SALES (corp-wide): 4.5B **Publicly Held**
SIC: 8059 8052 Nursing home, except skilled & intermediate care facility; intermediate care facilities
PA: Brookdale Senior Living
    111 Westwood Pl Ste 400
    Brentwood TN 37027
    615 221-2250

(G-2971)
BRUCE E MATTHEWS DDS PA
451 Hockessin Cors (19707-9586)
PHONE..................................302 234-2440
Daniel E Matthews, *Principal*
EMP: 5
SALES (est): 586.5K
SALES (corp-wide): 962.5K **Privately Held**
SIC: 8021 Dentists' office
PA: Bruce E Matthews Dds Pa
    1403 Silverside Rd Ste A
    Wilmington DE 19810
    302 475-9220

(G-2972)
BUFORD MANLOVE GRDNS ASSOC LP
722 Yorklyn Rd Ste 350 (19707-8740)
PHONE..................................302 652-3991
EMP: 20
SALES (est): 1MM **Privately Held**
SIC: 6513 Apartment Building Operator

(G-2973)
C WALLACE & ASSOCIATES
Also Called: Wallce & Associates
805 Grande Ln (19707-9350)
PHONE..................................302 528-2182
Brady Harris, *Managing Prtnr*
Charles N Wallace, *Partner*
EMP: 6
SALES (est): 597.4K **Privately Held**
SIC: 1521 General remodeling, single-family houses

(G-2974)
CACC MONTESSORI SCHOOL
1313 Little Baltimore Rd (19707-9701)
P.O. Box 892 (19707-0892)
PHONE..................................302 239-2917
Elizabeth Simmon, *Director*
EMP: 22
SALES (est): 810.3K **Privately Held**
SIC: 8211 8351 Private elementary & secondary schools; kindergarten; child day care services

(G-2975)
CAMBRIDGE CLUB ASSOC PARTN
726 Yorklyn Rd Ste 200 (19707-8701)
PHONE..................................302 674-3500
EMP: 5
SALES (est): 109.3K **Privately Held**
SIC: 7997 Membership sports & recreation clubs

(G-2976)
CAROLYN PALMATARY
Also Called: Hockessin Sanitation
519 Pershing Rd (19707-1106)
P.O. Box 222 (19707-0222)
PHONE..................................302 239-5744
Carolyn Palmatary, *Owner*
EMP: 4
SALES (est): 330K **Privately Held**
SIC: 4953 Garbage: collecting, destroying & processing

(G-2977)
CARRIE CONSTRUCTION INC
403 Hockessin Hills Rd (19707-9699)
PHONE..................................302 239-5386
Robert Wilkinson, *President*
Frederick Charles Wilkinson, *Vice Pres*
EMP: 5
SALES (est): 557.6K **Privately Held**
SIC: 1521 General remodeling, single-family houses

(G-2978)
CARTESSA AESTHETICS
210 Peoples Way (19707-1904)
PHONE..................................302 332-1991
Joe Amon, *Principal*
EMP: 4 EST: 2017
SALES (est): 28.8K **Privately Held**
SIC: 7231 Cosmetology & personal hygiene salons

(G-2979)
CASE HNDYMAN SVCS W CHSTER LLC
510 Thorndale Dr (19707-2332)
PHONE..................................302 234-6558
George Gardner,
EMP: 6
SALES (est): 275.9K **Privately Held**
SIC: 1521 General remodeling, single-family houses

(G-2980)
CAVEMAN DESIGN INC
359 Lower Snuff Mill Rd (19707-9389)
P.O. Box 235, Yorklyn (19736-0235)
PHONE..................................302 234-9969
Tom Long, *President*
EMP: 3
SALES (est): 306.5K **Privately Held**
WEB: www.caveman.com
SIC: 3841 Medical instruments & equipment, blood & bone work

(G-2981)
CDB VENTURES INC
Also Called: The Goddard School
157 Lantana Dr (19707-8808)
PHONE..................................302 235-0414
Genelle Craig, *President*
Christian Craig, *Vice Pres*
EMP: 26
SALES (est): 990.6K **Privately Held**
SIC: 8351 Preschool center

(G-2982)
CEO-HQCOM LLC
Also Called: Consulting Experts Online
7209 Lancaster Pike # 41023 (19707-9292)
PHONE..................................302 883-8555
Jayson Peppar,
John Bogle,
Richelle Feniak,
Brenda Howard,
Donavin Howard,
EMP: 6
SALES (est): 155.8K **Privately Held**
SIC: 8741 Business management

(G-2983)
CHARLES SLANINA
724 Yorklyn Rd Ste 210 (19707-8704)
PHONE..................................302 234-1605
Charles Slanina, *Owner*
EMP: 5
SALES (est): 338.4K **Privately Held**
SIC: 8111 General practice attorney, lawyer

(G-2984)
CHEAP-SCAPE INC
Also Called: Borsello Landscaping
720 Yorklyn Rd Ste 5 (19707-8729)
P.O. Box 9281, Wilmington (19809-0281)
PHONE..................................302 472-2600
Thomas M Borsello Jr, *President*
EMP: 22
SQ FT: 3,000
SALES (est): 1.5MM **Privately Held**
SIC: 0782 Landscape contractors

(G-2985)
CHILDREN FIRST PRESCHOOL
728 Yorklyn Rd (19707-9770)
PHONE..................................302 239-3544
Rick McKenny, *CFO*
Anna Traudt, *Director*
EMP: 9
SALES (est): 299.3K **Privately Held**
WEB: www.childrenfirstpreschool.org
SIC: 8351 Preschool center

(G-2986)
CHILIMIDOS LLC
7209 Lancaster Pike Ste 4 (19707-9292)
PHONE..................................302 388-1880
Jerry Chilimidos,
EMP: 6
SALES (est): 312.9K **Privately Held**
SIC: 1542 Nonresidential construction

(G-2987)
CHOICE RMDLG & RESTORATION INC
110 Ramunno Cir (19707-9743)
PHONE..................................717 917-0601
John Paoletti, *President*
EMP: 5 EST: 2009
SALES (est): 102K **Privately Held**
SIC: 1521 General remodeling, single-family houses

(G-2988)
CHRISTOPHER H WENDEL MD PA
P.O. Box 250 (19707-0250)
PHONE..................................302 540-2979
Christopher Wendel, *Principal*
EMP: 5
SALES (est): 199.3K **Privately Held**
SIC: 8011 General & family practice, physician/surgeon

(G-2989)
CITIZENS BANK NATIONAL ASSN
128 Lantana Dr (19707-8800)
PHONE..................................302 235-4321
Jennifer Lyons, *Branch Mgr*
EMP: 10
SALES (corp-wide): 7.3B **Publicly Held**
SIC: 6022 State commercial banks
HQ: Citizens Bank, National Association
    1 Citizens Plz Ste 1 # 1
    Providence RI 02903
    401 282-7000

(G-2990)
CMC CORPORATION OF HOCKESSIN
Also Called: U S Male Mens Hair Care Ctrs
721 Yorklyn Rd (19707-9279)
P.O. Box 1269 (19707-5269)
PHONE..................................302 239-1960
Clinton Vick Sr, *President*

Hockessin - New Castle County (G-2991)

EMP: 7
SQ FT: 1,200
SALES: 250K **Privately Held**
SIC: **7231** 7241 Beauty shops; barber shops

(G-2991)
COFFEE RUN CONDO COUNCIL INC
614 Loveville Rd Ofc (19707-1623)
PHONE.................302 239-4134
John Bryans, *President*
EMP: 5
SQ FT: 800
SALES (est): 303.1K **Privately Held**
SIC: **8641** Condominium association

(G-2992)
COLTON CLEANERS
146 Lantana Dr (19707-8800)
PHONE.................302 234-9422
Sherry Thorngate, *Manager*
EMP: 10
SALES (est): 109.5K **Privately Held**
SIC: **7216** Drycleaning plants, except rugs

(G-2993)
COMFORT SUITES MOTEL
181 Thompson Dr (19707-1913)
PHONE.................302 266-6600
Paresh Patel, *Owner*
EMP: 7 EST: 1998
SALES (est): 196.3K **Privately Held**
SIC: **7011** Hotel, franchised

(G-2994)
COMMONSPIRIT HEALTH
100 Saint Claire Dr (19707-8906)
PHONE.................302 234-5420
Earl Kimball, *Branch Mgr*
EMP: 100 **Privately Held**
WEB: www.chi-national.org
SIC: **8051** Skilled nursing care facilities
PA: Commonspirit Health
444 W Lake St Ste 2500
Chicago IL 60606

(G-2995)
COMPREHENSIVE BUS CONS INC
3 Larchmont Ct (19707-9682)
PHONE.................302 635-7711
Ann Emely, *CEO*
Charles H Emely, *President*
EMP: 4
SALES (est): 350K **Privately Held**
WEB: www.cbc.org
SIC: **8742** Management consulting services

(G-2996)
CROSSLAND AND ASSOCIATES
724 Yorklyn Rd Ste 100 (19707-8734)
PHONE.................302 658-2100
Daniel Crossland, *Owner*
EMP: 5
SALES (est): 494.4K **Privately Held**
WEB: www.conaty.com
SIC: **8111** General practice attorney, lawyer

(G-2997)
CRUISE HOLIDAYS BRANDYWINE VLY
7460 Lancaster Pike Ste 6 (19707-9276)
PHONE.................302 239-6400
Shirley McCreary, *Owner*
James McCreary, *Principal*
EMP: 10
SALES: 700K **Privately Held**
WEB: www.cruisedel.com
SIC: **4724** Travel agencies

(G-2998)
CS WEBB DAUGHTERS & SON INC
1028 Yorklyn Rd (19707-9769)
P.O. Box 84, Yorklyn (19736-0084)
PHONE.................302 239-2801
Charles Webb, *President*
EMP: 6
SALES: 750K **Privately Held**
SIC: **1711** Septic system construction

(G-2999)
D C PAINTING CORP
410 Uxbridge Way (19707-1937)
PHONE.................302 218-1211
Derek Cuthrell, *President*
Stacey Cuthrell, *Owner*
EMP: 4
SALES (est): 270K **Privately Held**
WEB: www.dcpainting.com
SIC: **1721** Residential painting

(G-3000)
DAVID P ROSER INC (PA)
19 Roser Ln (19707-9551)
P.O. Box 104 (19707-0104)
PHONE.................302 239-7605
David P Roser, *President*
EMP: 20
SALES (est): 3.1MM **Privately Held**
SIC: **1794** Excavation & grading, building construction

(G-3001)
DAVID WATERS & SON
1862 Graves Rd (19707-9131)
PHONE.................302 235-8653
David Waters, *Owner*
EMP: 4
SALES (est): 476K **Privately Held**
SIC: **1521** Single-family housing construction

(G-3002)
DE WORKERS CMPNSTION LEGAL CTR (PA)
Also Called: Law Firm Michael P Freebery PA
32 Barley Glen Ct (19707-3403)
P.O. Box 8888, Wilmington (19899-8888)
PHONE.................302 888-1111
Mark Houghton, *Partner*
Michael Freebery, *Partner*
EMP: 5
SALES (est): 551.8K **Privately Held**
SIC: **8111** General practice attorney, lawyer

(G-3003)
DEBORAH A WINGEL DO
724 Yorklyn Rd Ste 125 (19707-8731)
PHONE.................302 239-6200
Deborah A Wingel, *Owner*
EMP: 7
SALES (est): 307.9K **Privately Held**
SIC: **8011** Offices & clinics of medical doctors

(G-3004)
DELAWARE HEALTH AND FITNES LLC ◆
204 Lantana Dr (19707-8805)
PHONE.................302 584-7531
EMP: 8 EST: 2019
SALES (est): 76K **Privately Held**
SIC: **8099** Health & allied services

(G-3005)
DELAWARE MONUMENT AND VAULT
203 Wyndtree Ct S (19707-2316)
PHONE.................302 540-2387
EMP: 3
SALES (est): 145.4K **Privately Held**
SIC: **3272** Burial vaults, concrete or pre-cast terrazzo

(G-3006)
DELAWARE NATURE SOCIETY (PA)
3511 Barley Mill Rd (19707-9393)
P.O. Box 700 (19707-0700)
PHONE.................302 239-1283
Bernard Dempsey, *President*
Jim White, *Associate Dir*
Helen Fischel, *Education*
Annalie Mallon, *Education*
George Fisher,
EMP: 69 EST: 1962
SALES (est): 3.1MM **Privately Held**
SIC: **8631** 8641 8733 Labor unions & similar labor organizations; civic social & fraternal associations; noncommercial research organizations

(G-3007)
DELAWARE VALLEY DEV LLC
726 Yorklyn Rd Ste 150 (19707-8701)
PHONE.................302 235-2500
George Beer,
EMP: 10
SALES (est): 1.2MM **Privately Held**
SIC: **6531** Real estate managers

(G-3008)
DESIGNER CONSIGNER INC (PA)
7185 Lancaster Pike (19707-9270)
PHONE.................302 239-4034
Scott Michele, *Principal*
EMP: 6
SALES (est): 886.8K **Privately Held**
SIC: **7389** Design services

(G-3009)
DIAMOND STATE CURLING CLUB
8 E Aldine Dr (19707-1814)
PHONE.................856 577-3747
Frank Sharp, *President*
EMP: 4
SALES (est): 51.8K **Privately Held**
SIC: **7997** Membership sports & recreation clubs

(G-3010)
DMG CLEARANCES INC
13 Robin Dr (19707-1144)
PHONE.................302 239-6337
Deborah Mannisgardner, *President*
EMP: 6
SALES (est): 498.3K **Privately Held**
WEB: www.dmgclearances.com
SIC: **7389** Music distribution systems

(G-3011)
DR AMIT DUA
500 Lantana Dr (19707-8813)
PHONE.................302 239-5917
Amit Dua, *Executive*
EMP: 4
SALES (est): 113.5K **Privately Held**
SIC: **8021** Dentists' office

(G-3012)
DR BRUCE MATTHEWS DDS
451 Hockessin Cors (19707-9586)
PHONE.................302 234-2440
Bruce Matthews, *Principal*
EMP: 4
SALES (est): 81.6K **Privately Held**
SIC: **8021** Dentists' office

(G-3013)
DSOUZA AND ASSOCIATES INC
530 Schoolhouse Rd Ste A (19707-9526)
PHONE.................302 239-2300
Mabel Dsouza, *President*
Rudy D'Souza, *Vice Pres*
Rohan Dsouza, *Vice Pres*
Connie Rice,
Cynthia Urbanik,
EMP: 19
SQ FT: 1,400
SALES (est): 1.6MM **Privately Held**
WEB: www.dsouzainc.com
SIC: **8721** Billing & bookkeeping service

(G-3014)
E2E LLC
177 Thompson Dr Ste 888 (19707-1913)
PHONE.................703 906-5353
Mow Chung,
EMP: 5
SALES: 200K **Privately Held**
SIC: **7379** 7371 Computer related consulting services; computer software development & applications

(G-3015)
EARLY LEARNING CENTER
7250 Lancaster Pike (19707-9263)
PHONE.................302 239-3033
Kelly Mervine, *Director*
Kim Simmons, *Director*
EMP: 26
SALES (est): 540K **Privately Held**
WEB: www.earlylearningcenter.com
SIC: **8351** Preschool center

(G-3016)
EASTERN ATHLETIC CLUBS LLC
Also Called: Hockessin Athletic Club
100 Fitness Way (19707-2423)
PHONE.................302 239-6688
Gina Luck, *HR Admin*
Donna Healy, *Asst Mgr*
Maria Crennan, *Director*
Rachael Ling, *Director*
Bob Carpenter,
EMP: 52
SALES (est): 4.7MM **Privately Held**
SIC: **7997** Tennis club, membership

(G-3017)
ECONOMIC LAUNDRY SOLUTIONS
Also Called: Alpha Chemicals
14 Cinnamon Dr (19707-1349)
PHONE.................302 234-7627
Michael Schulte, *Owner*
EMP: 20
SALES (est): 1.1MM **Privately Held**
SIC: **2899** Household tints or dyes

(G-3018)
EKWW INC
720 Yorklyn Rd Ste 100 (19707-8730)
PHONE.................302 234-2877
Bernard E Erwin, *President*
EMP: 4
SQ FT: 700
SALES (est): 289.1K **Privately Held**
SIC: **8721** 7291 8741 Certified public accountant; tax return preparation services; financial management for business

(G-3019)
EMERALD BIOAGRICULTURE CORP (PA)
726 Yorklyn Rd Ste 420 (19707-8700)
PHONE.................517 882-7370
John McIntyre, *President*
John L McIntyre, *President*
▲ EMP: 10
SQ FT: 6,500
SALES (est): 2.5MM **Privately Held**
WEB: www.emeraldbio.com
SIC: **2875** 5191 8748 Fertilizers, mixing only; chemicals, agricultural; agricultural consultant

(G-3020)
EMERSON & KLAIR
853 Old Wilmington Rd (19707-9510)
PHONE.................302 239-6362
Barbara Klair, *Partner*
EMP: 2
SALES (est): 129.9K **Privately Held**
SIC: **2391** Curtains & draperies

(G-3021)
EMPOWERED THERAPY SERVICES
118 Dandelion Dr (19707-9778)
PHONE.................302 234-4820
Brittany N Dallas, *Principal*
EMP: 8
SALES (est): 73.3K **Privately Held**
SIC: **8093** Rehabilitation center, outpatient treatment

(G-3022)
EMW PUBLICATIONS
351 Mockingbird Hill Rd (19707-9723)
P.O. Box 400 (19707-0400)
PHONE.................302 438-9879
Edith M Warren, *Owner*
EMP: 1
SALES (est): 37.5K **Privately Held**
SIC: **2741** Miscellaneous publishing

(G-3023)
ESSENCIA SALON AND DAY SPA
1240 Old Lancaster Pike (19707-8727)
PHONE.................302 234-9144
Janet Conigaril, *Owner*
EMP: 8
SALES (est): 258.2K **Privately Held**
WEB: www.essenciasalon.com
SIC: **7299** Massage parlor & steam bath services

GEOGRAPHIC SECTION
Hockessin - New Castle County (G-3056)

(G-3024)
EVERGREEN WASTE SERVICES LLC
839 Valley Rd (19707-9151)
PHONE...................302 635-7055
Raphael Morado,
EMP: 30
SALES: 3.5MM **Privately Held**
SIC: 4953 Garbage: collecting, destroying & processing

(G-3025)
EXCLUSIVELY LEGAL INC
7301 Lancaster Pike Ste 2 (19707-9589)
P.O. Box 1436 (19707-5436)
PHONE...................302 239-5990
Sueann M Hall, *President*
EMP: 10
SALES (est): 652K **Privately Held**
WEB: www.exclusivelylegal.com
SIC: 7361 Placement agencies

(G-3026)
FAIRVILLE MANAGEMENT CO LLC (PA)
726 Yorklyn Rd Ste 200 (19707-8701)
PHONE...................302 489-2000
John Marinangeli, *General Mgr*
Maria Kempski,
EMP: 12
SALES (est): 2.3MM **Privately Held**
SIC: 6531 Rental agent, real estate

(G-3027)
FAMILY PRACTICE HOCKESSIN PA
5936 Limestone Rd Ste 202 (19707-8931)
PHONE...................302 239-4500
Alessandro Bianchi, *Principal*
EMP: 5
SALES (est): 520.4K **Privately Held**
SIC: 8031 8011 Offices & clinics of osteopathic physicians; general & family practice, physician/surgeon

(G-3028)
FIELDS & COMPANY INC
7460 Lancaster Pike Ste 3 (19707-9276)
PHONE...................302 234-2775
William F Fields Jr, *President*
Chris Fields, *Manager*
EMP: 4
SALES (est): 303.2K **Privately Held**
SIC: 8721 Accounting, auditing & bookkeeping

(G-3029)
FIRST STATE HEALTH & WELLNESS
Also Called: Midway Chiropractic
310 Lantana Dr (19707-8807)
PHONE...................302 239-1600
Bradley Meier, *Principal*
EMP: 4
SALES (corp-wide): 757.1K **Privately Held**
SIC: 8041 Offices & clinics of chiropractors
PA: First State Health And Wellness
  18585 Coastal Hwy Unit 26
  Rehoboth Beach DE 19971
  302 645-6681

(G-3030)
FLO MECHANICAL LLC
507 Baxter Ct (19707-1916)
PHONE...................302 239-7299
EMP: 13
SALES (est): 1.6MM **Privately Held**
SIC: 1711 Mechanical contractor

(G-3031)
FOX & ROACH LLC
Also Called: Prudential Fox Roach Realtors
88 Lantana Dr (19707-8814)
PHONE...................302 239-2343
Jerry Strusowski, *Sales Executive*
Susan Taylor, *Manager*
EMP: 40
SALES (corp-wide): 16.3MM **Privately Held**
WEB: www.prufoxroach.com
SIC: 6531 Real estate brokers & agents
PA: Fox & Roach Lp
  431 W Lancaster Ave
  Devon PA 19333
  610 722-7851

(G-3032)
FRESENIUS MED CRE N DELAWARE
Also Called: Fresenius Kidney Care Lantana
704 Lantana Dr (19707-8811)
PHONE...................302 239-4704
William Valle, *Branch Mgr*
EMP: 25
SALES (corp-wide): 675.7K **Privately Held**
SIC: 8092 Kidney dialysis centers
PA: Fresenius Medical Care Northern Delaware, Llc
  920 Winter St
  Waltham MA 02451
  781 699-4404

(G-3033)
G FEDALE GENERAL CONTRS LLC
Also Called: G Fedale Roofing & Siding
160 Thompson Dr (19707-1911)
PHONE...................302 225-7663
Jake Domanski, *Project Mgr*
Benjamin Lyons, *Project Mgr*
Judy Lorenzoni, *Accounting Mgr*
Joe Santucci, *Consultant*
Michael Small, *Consultant*
EMP: 17
SALES (est): 2.1MM **Privately Held**
SIC: 1761 Roofing contractor

(G-3034)
GARDEN DESIGN GROUP INC
787 Valley Rd (19707-9150)
P.O. Box 1143 (19707-5143)
PHONE...................302 234-3000
Richard Hollender, *President*
EMP: 8
SALES (est): 777.2K **Privately Held**
SIC: 0781 Landscape architects; landscape services

(G-3035)
GARY A BRYDE PA
724 Yorklyn Rd Ste 100 (19707-8734)
PHONE...................302 239-3700
Gary Bryde, *President*
EMP: 6
SALES (est): 420K **Privately Held**
SIC: 8111 General practice law office

(G-3036)
GENOVESIUS SOLUTIA LLC
521 Cabot Dr (19707-1138)
PHONE...................302 252-7506
Kevin Genovesius,
EMP: 5
SALES: 280K **Privately Held**
SIC: 8742 7379 Quality assurance consultant; computer related consulting services

(G-3037)
GEORGE AND SON SEAFOOD MARKET
1216 Old Lancaster Pike (19707-9401)
PHONE...................302 239-7204
EMP: 4
SALES (est): 417.3K **Privately Held**
SIC: 5146 Fish & seafoods

(G-3038)
GET REAL ON LINE CLASSIFIEDS
30 Robin Dr (19707-1143)
PHONE...................302 234-6522
Al Sammarco, *President*
EMP: 1
SALES (est): 62.2K **Privately Held**
SIC: 2711 Newspapers

(G-3039)
GONCE WILLIAM E DR DDS PA
1127 Valley Rd Ste 4 (19707-8515)
PHONE...................302 235-2400
William E Gonce DDS, *Owner*
William Gonce, *Fmly & Gen Dent*
EMP: 5
SALES (est): 508.8K **Privately Held**
SIC: 8021 Dentists' office

(G-3040)
GREG ELECT
547 Ashland Ridge Rd (19707-9662)
PHONE...................215 651-1477
George Eichelberger, *Principal*
EMP: 5
SALES (est): 395.7K **Privately Held**
SIC: 1796 Installing building equipment

(G-3041)
GTV LIVE SHOPPING LLC
724 Yorklyn Rd Ste 248 (19707-8732)
PHONE...................844 694-8688
EMP: 7
SALES (est): 198.6K **Privately Held**
SIC: 4833 Television broadcasting stations

(G-3042)
H DEAN MCSPADDEN DDS
500 Lantana Dr (19707-8813)
PHONE...................302 239-5917
H Dean McSpadden, *Principal*
EMP: 4
SALES (est): 74.4K **Privately Held**
SIC: 8021 Dentists' office

(G-3043)
HARTNETT & HARTNETT
7301 Lancaster Pike Ste 2 (19707-9589)
P.O. Box 220 (19707-0220)
PHONE...................302 239-4220
Lawrence Hartnett, *Partner*
Jennifer Hartnett, *Partner*
EMP: 7
SALES (est): 332.8K **Privately Held**
SIC: 8111 General practice attorney, lawyer

(G-3044)
HCSG REGAL HGHTS REGAL41
6525 Lancaster Pike (19707-9582)
PHONE...................302 998-0181
Ben Friedman, *Principal*
EMP: 4
SALES (est): 167K **Privately Held**
SIC: 8011 Clinic, operated by physicians

(G-3045)
HECKESSIN HEALTH PARTNERS
5850 Limestone Rd (19707-9819)
PHONE...................302 234-2597
EMP: 4
SALES (est): 102.8K **Privately Held**
SIC: 8099 Physical examination & testing services

(G-3046)
HERBERT R MARTIN ASSOCIATES
489 Valley Brook Dr (19707-9113)
PHONE...................302 239-1700
Herbert Martin, *Owner*
EMP: 5
SALES: 210K **Privately Held**
WEB: www.childassist.com
SIC: 7376 Computer facilities management

(G-3047)
HOCKESSIN ANIMAL HOSPITAL
Also Called: Windcrest Animal Hospital
643 Yorklyn Rd (19707-9248)
PHONE...................302 239-9464
Bruce Damme Dvm, *Owner*
Janet Mitchell, *Associate*
EMP: 6
SALES (est): 232K **Privately Held**
SIC: 0742 Animal hospital services, pets & other animal specialties; veterinarian, animal specialties

(G-3048)
HOCKESSIN CHRPRACTIC CENTRE PA
Also Called: Blossic, Tamara DC
724 Yorklyn Rd Ste 150 (19707-8735)
PHONE...................302 239-8550
Tamara Blossic, *President*
EMP: 9
SALES (est): 704.1K **Privately Held**
WEB: www.hockessinchiro.com
SIC: 8041 5499 8049 Offices & clinics of chiropractors; health & dietetic food stores;

(G-3049)
HOCKESSIN CLEANERS
7313 Lancaster Pike Ste 1 (19707-9278)
PHONE...................302 239-6071
Young Gong Son, *Owner*
Jodi Wagner, *Manager*
EMP: 4
SALES (est): 180.2K **Privately Held**
SIC: 7216 Cleaning & dyeing, except rugs

(G-3050)
HOCKESSIN DAY SPA
1304 Old Lancaster Pike C (19707-8806)
PHONE...................302 234-7573
Jean Boland, *Principal*
EMP: 6
SALES (est): 187.6K **Privately Held**
SIC: 7991 7231 Spas; beauty shops

(G-3051)
HOCKESSIN DENTAL
6300 Limestone Rd (19707-9178)
PHONE...................302 239-7277
Trevor Scheff, *Principal*
EMP: 4
SALES (est): 303.2K **Privately Held**
SIC: 8021 Dental surgeon

(G-3052)
HOCKESSIN ELECTRIC INC
6 Fritze Ct (19707-1042)
P.O. Box 72 (19707-0072)
PHONE...................302 239-9332
Mark Denney, *President*
Paul Dieleuterio, *Vice Pres*
EMP: 8
SALES (est): 750K **Privately Held**
SIC: 1731 Electrical work

(G-3053)
HOCKESSIN MONTESSORI SCHOOL
1000 Old Lancaster Pike (19707-9522)
PHONE...................302 234-1240
Marcia Kinnamen, *President*
EMP: 24
SQ FT: 24,000
SALES: 1.8MM **Privately Held**
WEB: www.hockmont.org
SIC: 8351 Montessori child development center

(G-3054)
HOCKESSIN SOCCER CLUB
740 Evanson Rd (19707-9114)
PHONE...................302 234-1444
Pete Hayes, *President*
Tom Braatz, *Vice Pres*
Mike Lupichuk, *Director*
Justin Romano, *Administration*
EMP: 12
SALES: 1.2MM **Privately Held**
WEB: www.hockessinsoccerclub.com
SIC: 7997 Membership sports & recreation clubs

(G-3055)
HOCKESSIN TRACTOR INC
Also Called: Gravely Hockessin
654 Yorklyn Rd (19707-9688)
P.O. Box 203 (19707-0203)
PHONE...................302 239-4201
John Langille, *President*
Louise Langille, *Treasurer*
Betty Rector, *Admin Sec*
EMP: 8
SQ FT: 10,000
SALES (est): 1.2MM **Privately Held**
WEB: www.gravelyhockessin.com
SIC: 5261 7699 Lawnmowers & tractors; garden tractors & tillers; tractor repair; lawn mower repair shop

(G-3056)
HOTEL ENVIRONMENTS INC
Also Called: Select Amenities,
359 Mockingbird Hill Rd (19707-9723)
PHONE...................302 234-9294
Vince McIntosh, *President*
Adele McIntosh CPA, *Vice Pres*

EMP: 4
SALES: 2MM **Privately Held**
WEB: www.selectamenities.com
SIC: 5122 Toiletries; toilet soap

(G-3057)
IN VISION EYE CARE INC
Also Called: Fairfax Vision Center
210 Lantana Dr (19707-8805)
PHONE..................302 235-7031
Roger D Ammon, *President*
EMP: 6
SALES (est): 477.3K **Privately Held**
SIC: 8042 Specialized optometrists

(G-3058)
INDEPENDENCE WEALTH ADVISORS
726 Yorklyn Rd Ste 300 (19707-8701)
PHONE..................302 763-1180
Louanne Hammer, *Principal*
Thomas J Grabowski, *CPA*
Jacquelynn M Simon, *Manager*
Raymond S Babiarz, *Advisor*
David V Duncan, *Advisor*
EMP: 4 EST: 2008
SALES (est): 356.4K **Privately Held**
SIC: 6282 Investment advisory service

(G-3059)
INDEPENDENT TRANSFER OPERATORS
P.O. Box 1443 (19707-5443)
PHONE..................302 420-4289
EMP: 5
SALES (est): 286.1K **Privately Held**
SIC: 4953 Refuse collection & disposal services

(G-3060)
IRWIN LANDSCAPING INC
1080 Old Lancaster Pike (19707-9514)
P.O. Box 186 (19707-0186)
PHONE..................302 239-9229
Peter D Irwin, *President*
EMP: 15
SQ FT: 3,000
SALES: 800K **Privately Held**
SIC: 0781 0782 Landscape counseling & planning; landscape contractors

(G-3061)
J M INDUSTRIES
845 Old Public Rd (19707-9631)
PHONE..................302 893-0363
EMP: 2
SALES (est): 87.7K **Privately Held**
SIC: 3999 Manufacturing industries

(G-3062)
J&D MANAGEMENT
1174 Old Wilmington Rd (19707-9368)
PHONE..................302 239-2489
Donna Malloy, *Principal*
EMP: 5
SALES (est): 296.1K **Privately Held**
SIC: 8741 Management services

(G-3063)
J&J SYSTEMS
10 Ridgewood Dr (19707-1413)
PHONE..................302 239-2969
Frank Jaksky, *Owner*
EMP: 6
SALES (est): 460.3K **Privately Held**
WEB: www.jjsystems.com
SIC: 1521 Patio & deck construction & repair

(G-3064)
JACK KELLYS LDSCPG & TREE SVC
Also Called: Jack Kelly's Landscaping
6 Crest Dr (19707-9772)
PHONE..................302 239-7185
Jack Kelly, *President*
EMP: 5
SALES (est): 250K **Privately Held**
WEB: www.jackkellylandscaping.com
SIC: 0782 Landscape contractors

(G-3065)
JAMES HUGHES COMPANY INC
508 Pershing Ct (19707-1102)
PHONE..................302 239-4529
James Hughes Jr, *President*
Marie Hughes, *Admin Sec*
EMP: 4 EST: 1971
SALES (est): 187.3K **Privately Held**
SIC: 1721 Residential painting

(G-3066)
JILLANN I HOUNSELL DDS
7197 Lancaster Pike (19707-9270)
PHONE..................302 239-5917
Jillann Hounsell, *Principal*
EMP: 4
SALES (est): 70.1K **Privately Held**
SIC: 8021 Offices & clinics of dentists

(G-3067)
JOHN CAMPANELLI & SONS INC
7460 Lancaster Pike (19707-9294)
PHONE..................302 239-8573
John E Campanelli, *President*
Mary Jane Campanelli, *Admin Sec*
EMP: 6
SALES (est): 660K **Privately Held**
SIC: 1521 1522 1542 New construction, single-family houses; apartment building construction; commercial & office building contractors

(G-3068)
JOHN KOZIOL INC
Also Called: Nationwide
724 Yorklyn Rd Ste 370 (19707-8704)
PHONE..................302 234-5430
John Koziol, *President*
EMP: 7
SQ FT: 1,500
SALES: 5MM **Privately Held**
SIC: 6282 6411 Investment advice; insurance agents, brokers & service

(G-3069)
JOSEPH CORNATZER DDS
500 Lantana Dr (19707-8813)
PHONE..................302 239-5917
Joseph Cornatzer, *Principal*
EMP: 4 EST: 2007
SALES (est): 120.8K **Privately Held**
SIC: 8021 Dentists' office

(G-3070)
JSI GROUP LLC
7217 Lancaster Pike Ste F (19707-9587)
PHONE..................267 582-5850
Joel Iagovino,
EMP: 5
SALES (est): 186.7K **Privately Held**
SIC: 7371 4813 Custom computer programming services; telephone communication, except radio

(G-3071)
KINDERCARE LEARNING CTRS LLC
Also Called: Hockessin Kinder Care 1633
6696 Lancaster Pike (19707-9596)
PHONE..................302 234-8680
Heather Schorah, *Director*
EMP: 35
SALES (corp-wide): 963.9MM **Privately Held**
WEB: www.kindercare.com
SIC: 8351 Group day care center
HQ: Kindercare Learning Centers, Llc
650 Ne Holladay St # 1400
Portland OR 97232
503 872-1300

(G-3072)
KUBOTA RESEARCH ASSOCIATES
100 Hobson Dr (19707-2106)
PHONE..................302 683-0199
Masanori Kubota, *President*
Ayako Kubota, *CFO*
EMP: 5
SQ FT: 1,500
SALES: 180.7K **Privately Held**
WEB: www.kubotaresearch.com
SIC: 8711 Consulting engineer

(G-3073)
L & D INSURANCE SERVICES LLC
Also Called: Nationwide
1 Isabella Ct (19707-9298)
PHONE..................302 235-2288
EMP: 4
SALES (est): 67.5K **Privately Held**
SIC: 6411 Insurance agents

(G-3074)
L&J TRANSPORTATION LLC
4 Fox Run Dr (19707-1409)
PHONE..................302 234-3366
Leyla Didehvar, *Principal*
EMP: 4
SALES (est): 269.5K **Privately Held**
SIC: 4789 Transportation services

(G-3075)
LA PETITE ACADEMY INC
5986 Limestone Rd (19707-9157)
PHONE..................302 234-2574
Valerie Miller, *Director*
EMP: 35
SALES (corp-wide): 164MM **Privately Held**
WEB: www.lapetite.com
SIC: 8351 Preschool center
HQ: La Petite Academy, Inc.
21333 Haggerty Rd Ste 300
Novi MI 48375
877 861-5078

(G-3076)
LABORATORY CORPORATION AMERICA
722 Yorklyn Rd Ste 154 (19707-8703)
PHONE..................302 234-0493
Dana McFadden, *Branch Mgr*
EMP: 25 **Publicly Held**
WEB: www.labcorp.com
SIC: 8071 Blood analysis laboratory
HQ: Laboratory Corporation Of America
358 S Main St Ste 458
Burlington NC 27215
336 229-1127

(G-3077)
LANTANA VETERINARY CENTER INC
306 Lantana Dr (19707-8807)
PHONE..................302 234-3275
Lon Schlussel, *President*
EMP: 12
SALES (est): 903.1K **Privately Held**
SIC: 0742 Animal hospital services, pets & other animal specialties

(G-3078)
LAURIE JACOBS
730 Brookwood Ln (19707-9536)
PHONE..................302 239-6257
EMP: 4
SALES (est): 100K **Privately Held**
SIC: 8021 Dentist's Office

(G-3079)
LC ASSOCIATES LLC
726 Yorklyn Rd Ste 150 (19707-8701)
PHONE..................302 235-2500
George Beer,
George P Beer,
EMP: 10
SALES (est): 714.9K **Privately Held**
SIC: 6799 Real estate investors, except property operators

(G-3080)
LCD WEALTH MANAGEMENT LLC
42 Piersons Rdg (19707-9275)
PHONE..................302 294-0013
Liang Huang,
EMP: 4
SALES (est): 470.7K **Privately Held**
SIC: 6799 Investors

(G-3081)
LENS TOLIC LLC
7209 Lancaster Pike (19707-9292)
PHONE..................800 343-5697
Edwin Zivuku,
EMP: 5

SALES (est): 195.9K **Privately Held**
SIC: 8748 Business consulting

(G-3082)
LIMESTONE VETERINARY HOSPITAL
6102 Limestone Rd (19707-9158)
PHONE..................302 239-5415
John Williams, *Owner*
EMP: 10
SALES (est): 450.1K **Privately Held**
WEB: www.limestonevet.com
SIC: 0742 Animal hospital services, pets & other animal specialties

(G-3083)
M W FOGARTY INC
22 Bernard Blvd (19707-9756)
PHONE..................302 658-5547
Michael W Fogarty, *President*
EMP: 5
SALES (est): 647.8K **Privately Held**
SIC: 1521 1542 General remodeling, single-family houses; commercial & office buildings, renovation & repair

(G-3084)
MACKNYFE SPECIALTIES
Also Called: Macknife Specialties
862 Auburn Mill Rd (19707-8502)
PHONE..................302 239-4904
C J McLaughlin III, *Owner*
EMP: 2
SALES (est): 139.2K **Privately Held**
SIC: 3421 3523 3999 Scissors, shears, clippers, snips & similar tools; clippers, for animal use: hand or electric; manufacturing industries

(G-3085)
MALINS JIM E PLUMBING & HTG
538 Basher Ln (19707)
P.O. Box 1135 (19707-5135)
PHONE..................302 239-2755
James E Malin, *CEO*
Eileen M Malin, *Corp Secy*
EMP: 6
SALES: 700K **Privately Held**
SIC: 1711 Plumbing contractors

(G-3086)
MALLARD ADVISORS LLC
7234 Lancaster Pike 220a (19707-8751)
PHONE..................302 239-1654
Paul S Baumbach, *Branch Mgr*
EMP: 15
SALES (corp-wide): 2.7MM **Privately Held**
SIC: 8742 6282 Financial consultant; investment advisory service
PA: Mallard Advisors Llc
750 Barksdale Rd Ste 3
Newark DE 19711
302 737-4546

(G-3087)
MANUFACTURERS & TRADERS TR CO
Also Called: M&T
151 Lantana Dr (19707-8808)
PHONE..................302 472-3177
Gale Dibble, *Manager*
EMP: 10
SALES (corp-wide): 6.4B **Publicly Held**
WEB: www.binghamlegg.com
SIC: 6022 State commercial banks
HQ: Manufacturers And Traders Trust Company
1 M&T Plz Fl 3
Buffalo NY 14203
716 842-4200

(G-3088)
MARIACHI HOUSE
7313 Lancaster Pike Ste 3 (19707-9278)
PHONE..................302 635-7361
Carlos Rivera, *Owner*
EMP: 3
SALES (est): 128.5K **Privately Held**
SIC: 2032 Mexican foods: packaged in cans, jars, etc.

Hockessin - New Castle County (G-3120)

(G-3089)
MARK VENTRESCA ASSOCIATES INC
19 Bernard Blvd (19707-9758)
PHONE..................302 239-3925
Mark Ventresca, *Owner*
EMP: 5
SALES (est): 471K **Privately Held**
SIC: 1521 1751 5211 Single-family home remodeling, additions & repairs; carpentry work; door & window products

(G-3090)
MARK W WINGEL
Also Called: Hockessin Family Medicine
724 Yorklyn Rd Ste 125 (19707-8731)
PHONE..................302 239-6200
Mark Wingel, *Owner*
Debra Wingel, *Co-Owner*
EMP: 6
SALES (est): 450.8K **Privately Held**
SIC: 8011 General & family practice, physician/surgeon

(G-3091)
MARTYS CONTRACTING
1072 Yorklyn Rd (19707-9769)
P.O. Box 289, Yorklyn (19736-0289)
PHONE..................302 234-8690
Martin Mellinger, *Owner*
Dawn Mellinger, *Office Mgr*
EMP: 4
SALES: 1.1MM **Privately Held**
WEB: www.martyscontracting.com
SIC: 1611 6513 7389 General contractor, highway & street construction; apartment building operators;

(G-3092)
MAX RE CENTRAL
1302 Old Lancaster Pike (19707-9557)
PHONE..................302 234-3800
John W Ford, *Sales Staff*
John Ford, *Manager*
Daniel Thomforde, *Associate*
EMP: 11
SALES (corp-wide): 3.9MM **Privately Held**
SIC: 6531 Real estate agent, residential
PA: Max Re Central
   228 Suburban Dr
   Newark DE

(G-3093)
MEDI-WEIGHTLOSS CLINICS
502 Lantana Dr (19707-8813)
PHONE..................302 763-3455
EMP: 8
SALES (est): 73.3K **Privately Held**
SIC: 8093 Weight loss clinic, with medical staff

(G-3094)
MICHAEL W FOGARTY GEN CONTR
22 Bernard Blvd (19707-9756)
PHONE..................302 658-5547
Michael W Fogarty, *President*
EMP: 4
SALES (est): 550K **Privately Held**
SIC: 1521 Single-family housing construction

(G-3095)
MIKE MOLITOR CONTRACTOR LLC
754 Morris Rd (19707-9697)
PHONE..................302 528-6300
Mike Molitor, *Principal*
Natali Molitor, *Principal*
EMP: 5
SALES: 500K **Privately Held**
SIC: 1542 Nonresidential construction

(G-3096)
MILLCREEK FOUNDATION
3713 Mill Creek Rd (19707-9725)
PHONE..................302 239-3811
Michael B Leach, *President*
EMP: 4
SALES: 1.5K **Privately Held**
SIC: 8641 Environmental protection organization

(G-3097)
MJL INDUSTRIAL INC
405 Uxbridge Way (19707-1938)
PHONE..................302 234-0898
Maijane Lin, *President*
Jia-Shyong Lin, *Principal*
◆ **EMP:** 4
SALES (est): 841.1K **Privately Held**
WEB: www.mjlindustrial.com
SIC: 5169 Industrial chemicals

(G-3098)
MONSECO LEATHER LLC
724 Yorklyn Rd Ste 260 (19707-8738)
PHONE..................302 235-1777
Robert Rothman,
Ulf Demberger,
▲ **EMP:** 12
SQ FT: 20,000
SALES (est): 1.1MM **Privately Held**
SIC: 5199 Leather & cut stock

(G-3099)
MORNINGSTAR MAIDS LLC
987 Old Lancaster Pike (19707-9561)
PHONE..................302 829-3030
Nana Tandoh,
EMP: 7
SALES (est): 136.4K **Privately Held**
SIC: 7389

(G-3100)
MYMEDCHOICES INC
407 Valley Brook Dr (19707-9113)
PHONE..................302 932-1920
Mary Schreiber Swenson, *President*
EMP: 7
SALES: 7MM **Privately Held**
SIC: 8011 7371 Offices & clinics of medical doctors; computer software development

(G-3101)
NATIONWIDE MUTUAL INSURANCE CO
724 Yorklyn Rd Ste 200 (19707-8732)
PHONE..................302 234-5430
John Koziol, *Manager*
EMP: 10
SALES (corp-wide): 13.2B **Privately Held**
WEB: www.nirassn.com
SIC: 6411 Insurance agents, brokers & service
PA: Nationwide Mutual Insurance Company
   1 Nationwide Plz
   Columbus OH 43215
   614 249-7111

(G-3102)
NAUDAIN ENTERPRISES LLC
5840 Limestone Rd (19707-9731)
PHONE..................302 239-6840
Lynn B Naudain,
EMP: 40 **EST:** 1977
SALES: 3MM **Privately Held**
SIC: 1611 Highway & street paving contractor; grading

(G-3103)
NEWARK CHROPRACTIC HLTH CTR PA
Also Called: Lantana Chiropratic
310 Lantana Dr (19707-8807)
PHONE..................302 239-1600
Lydia Cohen, *Principal*
Cindy Ferguson, *Manager*
EMP: 7 **Privately Held**
SIC: 8041 Offices & clinics of chiropractors
PA: Newark Chiropractic Health Center Pa
   1536 Capitol Trl
   Newark DE 19711

(G-3104)
NICOLE L SCOTT NP-C ADULT
45 Forest Creek Dr (19707-2017)
PHONE..................302 690-1692
Nicole L Scott, *Agent*
EMP: 8
SALES (est): 64K **Privately Held**
SIC: 8059 Nursing & personal care

(G-3105)
NOOR FOUNDATION INTERNATIONAL
249 Peoples Way (19707-1908)
PHONE..................302 234-8860
Samuel Mingo, *Principal*
EMP: 5
SALES (est): 175.5K **Privately Held**
SIC: 8641 Civic social & fraternal associations

(G-3106)
NORTH STAR PTA
1340 Little Baltimore Rd (19707-9733)
PHONE..................302 234-7200
Jen Woottnen, *President*
Debra Davenport, *HR Admin*
EMP: 9
SALES: 34.1K **Privately Held**
SIC: 8641 Parent-teachers' association

(G-3107)
OCCUPATIONAL THERAPY SOUR
14 Winding Hill Dr (19707-2014)
PHONE..................302 234-2273
EMP: 8 **EST:** 2018
SALES (est): 73.3K **Privately Held**
SIC: 8093 Specialty Outpatient Clinic

(G-3108)
OTOLARYNGOLOGY CONSULTANTS (PA)
Also Called: New Castle Hearing Speech Ctr
10 Foxview Cir (19707-2504)
PHONE..................302 328-1331
Emilio Valdes Jr, *President*
EMP: 15
SQ FT: 5,000
SALES (est): 1.4MM **Privately Held**
SIC: 8011 Ears, nose & throat specialist: physician/surgeon

(G-3109)
P A CHADLEY
Also Called: Corrective Chiropractic
7503 Lancaster Pike Ste A (19707-9593)
PHONE..................302 234-1115
Chad Evan Laurence, *CEO*
Chad Laurence, *Chiropractor*
EMP: 4
SQ FT: 1,700
SALES (est): 419.6K **Privately Held**
SIC: 8041 Offices & clinics of chiropractors

(G-3110)
PAINTBALL ACTION OF DELWARE
102 Lucia Ln (19707-1032)
PHONE..................302 234-1735
Barry Vansant, *President*
EMP: 16
SALES (est): 259.5K **Privately Held**
WEB: www.paintballactiongames.com
SIC: 7999 Amusement & recreation

(G-3111)
PAT T CLEAN INC
519 Cabot Dr (19707-1138)
PHONE..................302 239-5354
Pat Turtoro, *President*
Josepg Turtoro, *Vice Pres*
Pat Tuney, *Manager*
EMP: 5 **EST:** 1980
SALES (est): 258.5K **Privately Held**
SIC: 7699 Cleaning services

(G-3112)
PATTERSON-SCHWARTZ & ASSOC INC (PA)
Also Called: Patterson-Schwartz Real Estate
7234 Lancaster Pike (19707-9295)
PHONE..................302 234-5250
Richard Christopher, *President*
Christopher Patterson, *Vice Pres*
Susan Cleal, *Treasurer*
Charles Schwartz II, *Admin Sec*
EMP: 450
SALES (est): 32.2MM **Privately Held**
WEB: www.pacinihomes.com
SIC: 6531 Real estate brokers & agents

(G-3113)
PENINSULA UNTD MTHDST HMES INC
Also Called: Cokesbury Village
726 Loveville Rd Ste 3000 (19707-1536)
PHONE..................302 235-6810
Alan Johnson, *CEO*
Debra Croker, *Marketing Staff*
Katie Nemeth, *Social Dir*
EMP: 322
SALES (corp-wide): 24.6MM **Privately Held**
SIC: 8051 Skilled nursing care facilities
PA: Peninsula United Methodist Homes, Inc.
   726 Loveville Rd Ste 3000
   Hockessin DE 19707
   302 235-6800

(G-3114)
PENINSULA UNTD MTHDST HMES INC (PA)
Also Called: Pumh
726 Loveville Rd Ste 3000 (19707-1536)
PHONE..................302 235-6800
Charles W Coxson III, *President*
Robert Supper, *Vice Pres*
EMP: 8
SQ FT: 11,000
SALES (est): 24.6MM **Privately Held**
SIC: 8361 Home for the aged; rest home, with health care incidental

(G-3115)
PERFORMANCE PHYSCL THERAPY INC (PA)
720 Yorklyn Rd Ste 150 (19707-8729)
PHONE..................302 234-2288
Steve Rapposelli, *President*
Dino Carpentieri, *Opers Staff*
Rosann Bryant, *CFO*
Cheryl Botwick, *Human Resources*
Krista Eckrote, *Manager*
EMP: 13
SALES (est): 1MM **Privately Held**
WEB: www.pptandfitness.com
SIC: 8049 Physical therapist

(G-3116)
PERKWIZ INC
7209 Lancaster Pike (19707-9292)
PHONE..................702 866-9122
Leon Lapel, *CEO*
EMP: 7
SALES (est): 100K **Privately Held**
SIC: 7389 7371 Credit card service; computer software development & applications

(G-3117)
PERRY AND ASSOCIATES INC
540 Waterford Rd (19707-9545)
P.O. Box 1521 (19707-5521)
PHONE..................302 898-2327
Yvonne Dollar-Perry, *President*
EMP: 10
SALES (est): 858.5K **Privately Held**
SIC: 8742 Management consulting services

(G-3118)
PETER DOMANSKI & SONS
1562 Brackenville Rd (19707-9525)
PHONE..................302 475-3214
EMP: 6 **EST:** 1947
SALES: 300K **Privately Held**
SIC: 1611 1761 Paving Contractors

(G-3119)
PHARMA E MARKET LLC
Also Called: Monitor for Hire. Com
726 Loveville Rd Apt 99 (19707-1524)
PHONE..................302 737-3711
Louis Freedman, *Mng Member*
Scott Freedman, *Mng Member*
EMP: 11
SALES: 9MM **Privately Held**
SIC: 2834 Pharmaceutical preparations

(G-3120)
PIEDMONT BASEBALL LEAGUE INC
102 Wyeth Way (19707-1200)
P.O. Box 425 (19707-0425)
PHONE..................302 234-9437

Hockessin - New Castle County (G-3121)

Ron Pena, *President*
Roger Leach, *Admin Sec*
EMP: 5
SALES: 312.2K **Privately Held**
SIC: 8699 Athletic organizations

(G-3121)
PNC BANK NATIONAL ASSOCIATION
7421 Lancaster Pike (19707-9272)
PHONE 302 235-4000
Janet Desmond, *Manager*
EMP: 12
SALES (corp-wide): 19.9B **Publicly Held**
SIC: 6022 State commercial banks
HQ: Pnc Bank, National Association
  222 Delaware Ave
  Wilmington DE 19801
  877 762-2000

(G-3122)
POLYMART INC
710 Yorklyn Rd Ste 200 (19707-8749)
PHONE 302 656-1470
Don Priester, *Manager*
EMP: 6
SALES (corp-wide): 726.6K **Privately Held**
SIC: 5162 5085 Plastics materials; rubber goods, mechanical
PA: Polymart Inc
  129 Ridgway Dr
  Bordentown NJ 08505
  610 444-4274

(G-3123)
POSH CUPCAKE
50 Westwoods Blvd (19707-2062)
PHONE 302 234-4451
Tricia Matthews, *Principal*
EMP: 4
SALES (est): 160.7K **Privately Held**
SIC: 2051 Bread, cake & related products

(G-3124)
PRADHAN ENERGY PROJECTS
104 Hawthorne Ct W (19707-1800)
PHONE 305 428-2123
Ravi Pradhan, *CEO*
Maya Pradhan, *President*
Vinay Pradhan, *Vice Pres*
EMP: 8
SALES: 1MM **Privately Held**
SIC: 1796 7389 Pollution control equipment installation;

(G-3125)
PREMIER IMMEDIATE MED CARE LLC
316 Lantana Dr (19707-8807)
PHONE 610 226-6200
Edward M Silverman, *Branch Mgr*
EMP: 4
SALES (corp-wide): 10.8MM **Privately Held**
SIC: 8082 Home health care services
PA: Premier Immediate Medical Care, Llc
  278 Eagleview Blvd
  Exton PA 19341
  610 561-6400

(G-3126)
PRODUCE FOR BTTER HLTH FNDTION (PA)
7465 Lancaster Pike (19707-9583)
PHONE 302 235-2329
Patricia Zecca, *Ch of Bd*
Elizabeth Pivonka, *President*
Kristen Stevens, *COO*
Connie Fisher, *Senior VP*
Barbara T Berry, *Vice Pres*
EMP: 22
SQ FT: 11,000
SALES: 1.8MM **Privately Held**
WEB: www.5aday.org
SIC: 8099 Nutrition services

(G-3127)
QUALITY FAMILY PHYSICIANS PA
722 Yorklyn Rd Ste 400 (19707-8740)
PHONE 302 235-2351
Kathleen H Willey MD, *Partner*
Bonnie L Kelly, *Partner*
EMP: 4
SALES (est): 924.8K **Privately Held**
SIC: 8011 General & family practice, physician/surgeon

(G-3128)
RAMA CORPORATION
181 Thompson Dr (19707-1913)
PHONE 302 266-6600
Paresh Patel, *President*
Ranjan Patel, *Vice Pres*
EMP: 25
SALES: 1.4MM **Privately Held**
SIC: 7011 Hotel, franchised

(G-3129)
RAYCO AUTO & MARINE UPHL INC
113 Carriage Dr (19707-1329)
PHONE 302 323-8844
Rudolph Tiberi,
Megan Tiberi,
EMP: 5
SALES (est): 306.2K **Privately Held**
SIC: 4581 7532 Aircraft upholstery repair; upholstery & trim shop, automotive

(G-3130)
RAYMOND L PARA DDS
720 Yorklyn Rd Ste 120 (19707-8730)
PHONE 302 234-2728
Raymond L Para, *Owner*
Linda Dicampli, *Manager*
EMP: 10
SALES (est): 546.5K **Privately Held**
SIC: 8021 Dentists' office

(G-3131)
RCW RENOVATIONS INC
828 Westridge Dr (19707-2306)
P.O. Box 1242 (19707-5242)
PHONE 302 239-3714
Richard Curry, *President*
Richard S Williams, *Senior VP*
EMP: 4
SALES (est): 334.2K **Privately Held**
SIC: 1521 Single-family home remodeling, additions & repairs; general remodeling, single-family houses

(G-3132)
RED CLAY INC
2388 Brackenville Rd (19707-9306)
PHONE 302 239-2018
David Ford, *President*
Susan Ford, *Admin Sec*
EMP: 2
SALES (est): 294.5K **Privately Held**
SIC: 3599 8731 8742 Machine shop, jobbing & repair; commercial physical research; industrial & labor consulting services

(G-3133)
REGAL HGTS HLTHCRE CTR LLC
6525 Lancaster Pike (19707-9582)
PHONE 302 998-0181
Meir Gelley, *Mng Member*
Ben Friedman,
EMP: 99
SALES: 19MM **Privately Held**
SIC: 8051 Convalescent home with continuous nursing care

(G-3134)
RESONATE FORWARD LLC
503 Ridgeview Dr (19707-2313)
PHONE 302 893-9504
Ingrid Pretzer-Aboff, *Partner*
EMP: 5
SALES (est): 237.6K **Privately Held**
SIC: 3699 Sound signaling devices, electrical

(G-3135)
RH GALLERY AND STUDIOS
1304 Old Lancaster Pike D (19707-8806)
PHONE 302 218-5182
EMP: 4
SALES (est): 38.5K **Privately Held**
SIC: 8412 Art gallery

(G-3136)
RIGGIN GROUP
530 Schoolhouse Rd Ste E (19707-9526)
PHONE 302 235-2903
Eddie Riggin, *Owner*
EMP: 6 **EST:** 2001
SALES (est): 349.6K **Privately Held**
WEB: www.riggingrouprealestate.com
SIC: 6531 Real estate agent, residential

(G-3137)
RK ADVISORS LLC
104 Country Center Ln (19707-9335)
PHONE 302 561-5258
Richard Klumpp, *Principal*
EMP: 4
SALES (est): 561.3K **Privately Held**
SIC: 6282 Investment advice

(G-3138)
ROBERT A CHAGNON
726 Loveville Rd Apt 126 (19707-1506)
PHONE 302 489-1932
Robert A Chagnon, *Principal*
Robert Chagnon, *Principal*
EMP: 5
SALES (est): 334.6K **Privately Held**
SIC: 8711 Consulting engineer

(G-3139)
ROBERT KEATING EXCAVATING
1610 Old Wilmington Rd (19707-9231)
PHONE 302 239-4670
Robert Keating, *Owner*
Charlene Keating, *Vice Pres*
EMP: 4
SALES (est): 637.7K **Privately Held**
SIC: 1794 Excavation work

(G-3140)
ROSAURI BUILDERS & REMODELERS
1797 Yeatmans Mill Rd (19707)
P.O. Box 1088 (19707-5088)
PHONE 302 234-8464
Sam Rosauri, *President*
EMP: 4
SALES (est): 2MM **Privately Held**
SIC: 1521 1542 New construction, single-family houses; general remodeling, single-family houses; commercial & office buildings, renovation & repair

(G-3141)
SALON BY DOMINIC
130 Lantana Dr (19707-8800)
PHONE 302 239-8282
Dominic Rappuci, *Owner*
EMP: 18
SALES (est): 481.2K **Privately Held**
WEB: www.salonbydominic.com
SIC: 7231 Unisex hair salons

(G-3142)
SCHWARTZ ERIC WM MD
726 Yorklyn Rd Ste 100 (19707-8745)
PHONE 302 234-5770
Eric Schwartz MD, *Principal*
EMP: 20
SALES (est): 375.3K **Privately Held**
SIC: 8011 General & family practice, physician/surgeon

(G-3143)
SENIORTECH INC
Also Called: Senior Helpers
726 Yorklyn Rd Ste 410 (19707-8700)
PHONE 302 234-1274
Barbara A Hartz, *Principal*
EMP: 9
SALES (est): 280.5K **Privately Held**
SIC: 8082 Home health care services

(G-3144)
SERVICE QUEST
217 Louis Ln (19707-9767)
P.O. Box 1637 (19707-5637)
PHONE 302 235-0173
P Fitzharris, *Principal*
Brian Bair, *Vice Pres*
EMP: 6
SALES (est): 165.9K **Privately Held**
SIC: 8331 Job training & vocational rehabilitation services

(G-3145)
SHARDA USA LLC
7217 Lancaster Pike Ste A (19707-9587)
P.O. Box 640 (19707-0640)
PHONE 610 350-6930
◆ **EMP:** 5
SALES (est): 668.4K **Privately Held**
SIC: 2879 Insecticides, agricultural or household

(G-3146)
SHORTY USA INC
Also Called: Airsoft Shortyusa.com
141 Ramunno Cir (19707-9727)
PHONE 302 234-7750
David W Smyth, *President*
EMP: 6
SQ FT: 1,000
SALES (est): 1.2MM **Privately Held**
WEB: www.shortyusa.com
SIC: 5091 5941 Sporting & recreation goods; sporting goods & bicycle shops

(G-3147)
SPEECH THERAPEUTICS INC
15 Elderberry Ct (19707-2131)
PHONE 302 234-9226
Judy Roberson, *Owner*
EMP: 7
SALES (est): 277.1K **Privately Held**
SIC: 8049 Speech specialist

(G-3148)
STATE DRYWALL CO INC
12 Ridon Dr (19707-1002)
P.O. Box 717 (19707-0717)
PHONE 302 239-2843
Eugene R Radka, *Vice Pres*
EMP: 35 **EST:** 1965
SALES (est): 1.8MM **Privately Held**
SIC: 1742 Drywall

(G-3149)
STEPHEN G PUZIO DC
7460 Lancaster Pike Ste 8 (19707-9276)
PHONE 302 234-4045
Stephen G Puzio, *Owner*
Carmen Garcia, *Co-Owner*
EMP: 4
SALES (est): 118K **Privately Held**
SIC: 8041 Offices & clinics of chiropractors

(G-3150)
STREET CORE UTILITY SERVICE
501 Erickson Ave (19707-1129)
PHONE 302 239-4110
Scott Bell, *President*
Michael McMahon, *Vice Pres*
EMP: 10
SALES: 680K **Privately Held**
SIC: 3448 Farm & utility buildings

(G-3151)
SUI TRADING CO
Also Called: Reima Sportswear
406 Hawthorne Ct E (19707-1805)
P.O. Box 1720 (19707-5720)
PHONE 302 239-2012
Frank Jornlin, *President*
Diane Hyman, *Sales Staff*
EMP: 6
SALES (est): 853.1K **Privately Held**
SIC: 5136 Gloves, men's & boys'

(G-3152)
SUMMERS LOGGING LLC
364 Skyline Orchard Dr (19707-9354)
PHONE 302 234-8725
EMP: 2
SALES (est): 81.7K **Privately Held**
SIC: 2411 Logging

(G-3153)
SUMMIT AT HOCKESSIN
5850 Limestone Rd (19707-9819)
PHONE 302 235-8388
Melissa Hurlock, *Human Res Dir*
Scott Thomas, *Director*
EMP: 7
SALES (est): 449K **Privately Held**
SIC: 8052 Intermediate care facilities

(G-3154)
SUMMIT RETIREMENT COMMUNITY
5850 Limestone Rd Ofc 1 (19707-9828)
PHONE..................................888 933-2300
EMP: 13 EST: 2015
SALES (est): 316.6K Privately Held
SIC: 8051 Skilled nursing care facilities

(G-3155)
SUPERIOR YARDWORKS INC
211 Cherry Blossom Pl (19707-2047)
PHONE..................................610 274-2255
Christopher Kane, *President*
EMP: 6
SALES (est): 302.8K Privately Held
SIC: 0781 Landscape architects

(G-3156)
TAKE LEAD DANCE STUDIO
320 Lantana Dr (19707-8807)
PHONE..................................302 234-0909
Luann D'Agostino, *Owner*
EMP: 4
SALES (est): 110K Privately Held
SIC: 7911 Dance studio & school

(G-3157)
TD BANK NA
7330 Lancaster Pike (19707-9264)
PHONE..................................302 234-8570
Michael Tryon, *Branch Mgr*
EMP: 13
SALES (corp-wide): 22.8B Privately Held
SIC: 6022 State commercial banks
HQ: Td Bank, N.A.
    1701 Route 70 E Ste 200
    Cherry Hill NJ 08003
    856 751-2739

(G-3158)
THERAPY SERVICES OF DELAW
24 Gates Cir (19707-9686)
PHONE..................................302 239-2285
EMP: 8
SALES (est): 73.3K Privately Held
SIC: 8093 Rehabilitation center, outpatient treatment

(G-3159)
THERMAL TRANSF COMPOSITES LLC (PA)
724 Yorklyn Rd Ste 200 (19707-8732)
PHONE..................................302 635-7156
Dan White,
Mark Schillinger,
EMP: 8
SALES: 1.2MM Privately Held
WEB: www.thermaltransfercomposites.com
SIC: 3699 Electrical equipment & supplies

(G-3160)
THERMO STACK LLC
7460 Lancaster Pike (19707-9294)
PHONE..................................401 885-7781
Hans Wenghoefer, *Vice Pres*
EMP: 1
SALES: 160K Privately Held
SIC: 3567

(G-3161)
TIMBER RIDGE INC
710 Yorklyn Rd (19707-8747)
PHONE..................................302 239-9239
Matt Minker, *President*
Robert Blanck, *Vice Pres*
Mark Price, *Vice Pres*
Kevin Lucas, *Treasurer*
Carol Minker, *Admin Sec*
EMP: 50
SQ FT: 6,000
SALES (est): 1.3MM Privately Held
WEB: www.timberridge.com
SIC: 7363 Help supply services

(G-3162)
TOLTON BUILDERS INC
7301 Lancaster Pike (19707-9588)
P.O. Box 811 (19707-0811)
PHONE..................................302 239-5357
Randy R Tolton, *President*
EMP: 5
SQ FT: 200
SALES: 1MM Privately Held
SIC: 1542 Commercial & office buildings, renovation & repair

(G-3163)
TOM WRIGHT REAL ESTATE
7234 Lancaster Pike # 101 (19707-9295)
PHONE..................................302 234-6026
Tom Wright, *Owner*
EMP: 70
SALES (est): 1.2MM Privately Held
SIC: 6531 Real estate agent, residential

(G-3164)
TRITEK CORPORATION
Also Called: Tritek Technologies
103 E Bridle Path (19707-9409)
PHONE..................................302 239-1638
James Malatesta, *President*
EMP: 10
SALES: 2MM Privately Held
SIC: 3579 Mailing, letter handling & addressing machines

(G-3165)
TRITEK TECHNOLOGIES INC (PA)
103 E Bridle Path (19707-9409)
PHONE..................................302 239-1638
James Malatesta, *President*
EMP: 12
SALES (est): 1.2MM Privately Held
WEB: www.tritektech.com
SIC: 3579 Mailing, letter handling & addressing machines

(G-3166)
VEL MICRO WORKS INCORPORATED
726 Yorklyn Rd Ste 400 (19707-8700)
PHONE..................................302 239-4661
Sakthi Vel, *President*
Kamatchi Vel, *Vice Pres*
Murugesan Nagappan, *Software Engr*
EMP: 7
SQ FT: 150
SALES (est): 703.8K Privately Held
SIC: 7373 Computer systems analysis & design

(G-3167)
VETERAN IT PRO LLC
37 Staten Dr (19707-1338)
PHONE..................................302 824-3111
Luke Bernhardt, *CEO*
Amrinder Romana, *COO*
EMP: 10
SALES (est): 260.5K Privately Held
SIC: 8742 7389 7375 7371 Management consulting services; ; information retrieval services; custom computer programming services; computer facilities management

(G-3168)
VICTORIA MEWS LP DELNWARE VALL
722 Yorklyn Rd Ste 350 (19707-8740)
PHONE..................................302 489-2000
EMP: 4 EST: 2013
SALES (est): 188.2K Privately Held
SIC: 6513 Apartment building operators

(G-3169)
WELLS FARGO BANK NATIONAL ASSN
Also Called: Delaware Trust 221
7270 Lancaster Pike (19707-9263)
PHONE..................................302 235-4300
Cathy McVaugh, *Branch Mgr*
EMP: 15
SALES (corp-wide): 101B Publicly Held
SIC: 6021 National commercial banks
HQ: Wells Fargo Bank, National Association
    101 N Phillips Ave
    Sioux Falls SD 57104
    605 575-6900

(G-3170)
WELLS FARGO BANK NATIONAL ASSN
5801 Limestone Rd (19707-9732)
PHONE..................................302 235-4304
Pat Ponzo, *Principal*
EMP: 8
SALES (corp-wide): 101B Publicly Held
SIC: 6021 National commercial banks
HQ: Wells Fargo Bank, National Association
    101 N Phillips Ave
    Sioux Falls SD 57104
    605 575-6900

(G-3171)
WELLS FARGO HOME MORTGAGE INC
7465 Lancaster Pike Ste C (19707-9578)
PHONE..................................302 239-6300
Chritopher Tally, *Branch Mgr*
EMP: 6
SALES (corp-wide): 101B Publicly Held
WEB: www.wfhm.com
SIC: 6021 6162 National commercial banks; mortgage bankers
HQ: Wells Fargo Home Mortgage Inc
    1 Home Campus
    Des Moines IA 50328
    515 324-3707

(G-3172)
WELSH FAMILY DENTISTRY
Also Called: Sharon A Welsh DDS
34 Withers Way (19707-2514)
PHONE..................................302 836-3711
Sharon Welsh, *Owner*
EMP: 8
SALES (est): 480.9K Privately Held
SIC: 8072 Dental laboratories

(G-3173)
WILMINGTON SAVINGS FUND SOC
7450 Lancaster Pike (19707-9265)
PHONE..................................302 235-7600
Tracey Stegemeier, *Manager*
EMP: 5
SALES (corp-wide): 455.5MM Publicly Held
SIC: 6022 State commercial banks
HQ: Wilmington Savings Fund Society
    500 Delaware Ave Ste 500 # 500
    Wilmington DE 19801
    302 792-6000

(G-3174)
WINDSOR PLACE
6677 Lancaster Pike (19707-9503)
PHONE..................................302 239-3200
John Place, *Principal*
EMP: 4
SALES (est): 123.2K Privately Held
SIC: 8361 Residential care

(G-3175)
WOODCHUCK ENTERPRISES INC
1070 Sharpless Rd (19707-9664)
PHONE..................................302 239-8336
John Fauerbach, *Principal*
EMP: 3 EST: 2011
SALES (est): 185.2K Privately Held
SIC: 2421 Sawmills & planing mills, general

Houston
Kent County

(G-3176)
APEX ARABIANS INC
Also Called: Apex Stable
671 Williamsville Rd (19954-2618)
PHONE..................................302 242-6272
P O Robichaud, *President*
Pamela Onusko, *President*
Nancy Onusko, *Admin Sec*
EMP: 6
SQ FT: 40,000
SALES: 120K Privately Held
SIC: 0752 Breeding services, horses: racing & non-racing

(G-3177)
CONVENTIONAL BUILDERS INC
846 School St (19954-2018)
P.O. Box 47 (19954-0047)
PHONE..................................302 422-2429
Gregory Thompson, *President*
W Pierce Thompson Sr, *President*
W Pierce Thompson Jr, *Vice Pres*
Dawn Layton, *Admin Sec*
EMP: 14 EST: 1975
SQ FT: 10,000
SALES: 8MM Privately Held
SIC: 1542 1541 Commercial & office building, new construction; commercial & office buildings, renovation & repair; industrial buildings, new construction; renovation, remodeling & repairs: industrial buildings

(G-3178)
GEORGE W OPPEL
3202 Gun And Rod Club Rd (19954-2601)
PHONE..................................302 398-4433
George W Oppel, *Owner*
EMP: 5
SALES (est): 343.5K Privately Held
SIC: 4213 Trucking, except local

(G-3179)
HILL FARMS INC
2007 School St (19954-2325)
PHONE..................................302 422-0219
Marvin Hill, *President*
EMP: 4
SALES (est): 326K Privately Held
SIC: 0115 Corn

(G-3180)
PTS PROFESSIONAL WELDING
609 Broad St (19954-2009)
PHONE..................................302 632-2079
Philip Taubler, *Principal*
EMP: 2 EST: 2013
SALES (est): 151.4K Privately Held
SIC: 7692 Welding repair

(G-3181)
R J K TRANSPORTATION INC
1118 School St (19954-2303)
PHONE..................................302 422-3188
Robert J Koppenhaver, *President*
Mary Koppenhaver, *Vice Pres*
EMP: 14
SALES: 170K Privately Held
SIC: 4141 Local bus charter service

(G-3182)
RE CALLOWAY TRNSP INC
897 School St (19954-2019)
PHONE..................................302 422-2471
Barbara J Calloway, *President*
EMP: 46
SALES: 3MM Privately Held
SIC: 4131 Intercity highway transport, special service

(G-3183)
TANTROUGH FARM
234 Blairs Pond Rd (19954-2326)
PHONE..................................302 422-5547
EMP: 5
SALES (est): 451.5K Privately Held
SIC: 0116 0161 0211 Soybean Farm Vegetable/Melon Farm Beef Cattle Feedlot

---

Kenton
Kent County

(G-3184)
COUNTRY STORE
11 S Main St (19955)
P.O. Box 328 (19955-0328)
PHONE..................................302 653-5111
Nona Porter, *Owner*
Patricia Clark, *Partner*
EMP: 12 EST: 1971
SQ FT: 2,500
SALES (est): 973.6K Privately Held
SIC: 5399 0251 Country general stores; broiling chickens, raising of

(G-3185)
SHURE-LINE CONSTRUCTION INC
Also Called: Electric
281 W Commerce St (19955)
PHONE..................................302 653-4610
J A Stoneberger, *President*
Vernon Wright, *Vice Pres*
Ron Pryor, *Treasurer*

Kenton - Kent County (G-3186)

Gary Everett, *Admin Sec*
EMP: 45
SQ FT: 4,600
SALES (est): 27.7MM **Privately Held**
WEB: www.shure-line.com
SIC: 1542 Commercial & office buildings, renovation & repair

(G-3186)
THOMAS E MOORE INC
6 Marlyn Ln (19955)
P.O. Box 794, Dover (19903-0794)
PHONE..................................302 653-2000
Thomas Cullen, *Vice Pres*
EMP: 1
SALES (corp-wide): 10.9MM **Privately Held**
SIC: 3842 Welders' hoods
PA: Thomas E. Moore, Inc.
  696 S Bay Rd
  Dover DE 19901

(G-3187)
THOMAS E MOORE INC
6 Maryland Ave (19955)
PHONE..................................302 674-1500
Thomas D Cullen, *Vice Pres*
EMP: 10
SALES (corp-wide): 10.9MM **Privately Held**
SIC: 5148 5141 Vegetables; food brokers
PA: Thomas E. Moore, Inc.
  696 S Bay Rd
  Dover DE 19901

Laurel
Sussex County

(G-3188)
3D MICROWAVE LLC
7795 Bethel Rd (19956-3921)
PHONE..................................302 497-0223
Donald Dubinski,
EMP: 2
SALES: 25K **Privately Held**
SIC: 3663 Radio & TV communications equipment

(G-3189)
ACCURATE PEST CONTROL COMPANY
Also Called: Accurate Termite & Pest Ctrl
30139 Sussex Hwy (19956-3826)
P.O. Box 1686, Salisbury MD (21802-1686)
PHONE..................................302 875-2725
Gordon R Benson, *President*
David Register, *Vice Pres*
Ruth Ann Taylor, *Treasurer*
Mary Register, *Admin Sec*
EMP: 30
SQ FT: 1,500
SALES: 2MM **Privately Held**
WEB: www.accuratepestcontrol.com
SIC: 7342 Pest control in structures; pest control services

(G-3190)
AEG INTERNATIONAL LLC
30931 Sussex Hwy (19956-4426)
P.O. Box 461, Dagsboro (19939-0461)
PHONE..................................302 750-6411
Asher Gulab, *Mng Member*
EMP: 3
SALES: 1MM **Privately Held**
WEB: www.aeginternational.com
SIC: 4789 7372 Transportation services; application computer software

(G-3191)
AGRICLTRAL ASSSSMNTS INTL CORP
101 Lake Dr (19956-1707)
PHONE..................................240 463-6677
William H Wigton, *President*
Dr Sohail J Malik, *Vice Pres*
EMP: 5
SALES: 100K **Privately Held**
SIC: 8748 7389 Agricultural consultant;

(G-3192)
ALLEN BODY WORKS INC
421 N Central Ave (19956-1127)
PHONE..................................302 875-3208
Steve Allen, *President*
Bonnie Allen, *Vice Pres*
EMP: 4
SALES: 450K **Privately Held**
SIC: 7532 Body shop, automotive

(G-3193)
ARMIGERS AUTO CENTER INC (PA)
28866 Sussex Hwy (19956-3825)
PHONE..................................302 875-7642
Jay E Armiger, *President*
Jed E Armiger, *Vice Pres*
Junior E Armiger, *Shareholder*
Judith Armiger, *Admin Sec*
EMP: 6
SQ FT: 2,400
SALES: 2.3MM **Privately Held**
WEB: www.armigers.com
SIC: 5521 7532 Automobiles, used cars only; body shop, automotive

(G-3194)
B & R BOYER PRESSURE WASHING
16835 Arvey Rd (19956-3051)
PHONE..................................302 875-3603
Robert Boyer, *Owner*
EMP: 1
SALES (est): 56.4K **Privately Held**
SIC: 0751 3589 Poultry services; car washing machinery

(G-3195)
BANK OF DELMAR
200 E Market St (19956-1535)
PHONE..................................302 875-5901
Don Dykes, *Manager*
EMP: 5
SALES (corp-wide): 24.7MM **Publicly Held**
WEB: www.bankofdelmarvahb.com
SIC: 6022 6029 State commercial banks; commercial banks
HQ: The Bank Of Delmarva
  2245 Northwood Dr
  Salisbury MD 21801
  410 548-1100

(G-3196)
BAYNUM ENTERPRISES INC
Also Called: Pizza King
307 N Central Ave Unit A (19956-1751)
PHONE..................................302 875-4477
Becky Hastings, *Branch Mgr*
EMP: 35
SALES (corp-wide): 5MM **Privately Held**
SIC: 5812 6514 Pizza restaurants; dwelling operators, except apartments
PA: Baynum Enterprises, Inc.
  300 W Stein Hwy
  Seaford DE 19973
  302 629-6104

(G-3197)
BEGINNING BRIDGES CHILD CARE
6721 Sharptown Rd (19956-4148)
PHONE..................................302 875-7428
EMP: 5
SALES (est): 94.8K **Privately Held**
SIC: 8351 Child Day Care Services

(G-3198)
BETTER HOMES LAUREL II INC
Also Called: Carvel Gardens Annex
2600 Daniel St 3000 (19956-1775)
P.O. Box 635 (19956-0635)
PHONE..................................302 875-4282
Andrew Harstein, *President*
EMP: 5
SALES: 287.5K **Privately Held**
SIC: 6531 Real estate agents & managers

(G-3199)
BETTER HOMES OF LAUREL INC
Also Called: CARVEL GARDEN
3000 Daniel St (19956)
P.O. Box 635 (19956-0635)
PHONE..................................302 875-4281
David T Boyce, *President*
June Woodward, *Manager*
EMP: 5
SALES: 290K **Privately Held**
SIC: 6513 Apartment building operators

(G-3200)
BG FARMS INC
Watson Rd (19956)
PHONE..................................302 875-2167
EMP: 4
SALES (est): 260K **Privately Held**
SIC: 0251 Chicken Farm

(G-3201)
BLU H2O LTD
120 Horsey Ave (19956-1212)
PHONE..................................302 875-4810
Anthony M Ruggio, *President*
John Kohlman, *Vice Pres*
EMP: 4
SALES (est): 330K **Privately Held**
SIC: 5099 Luggage

(G-3202)
BOS CONSTRUCTION COMPANY
7045 Sharptown Rd (19956-4153)
PHONE..................................302 875-9120
Paul Collins, *Owner*
EMP: 2
SALES (est): 197.3K **Privately Held**
SIC: 3531 Buckets, excavating: clamshell, concrete, dragline, etc.

(G-3203)
BOYCES ELECTRICAL SERVICE
229 E Market St (19956-1534)
P.O. Box 373 (19956-0373)
PHONE..................................302 875-5877
Brent J Boyce Sr, *Owner*
EMP: 4
SALES (est): 185.4K **Privately Held**
SIC: 1731 General electrical contractor

(G-3204)
BOYS & GIRLS CLUBS OF AMERICA
454 N Central Ave (19956)
PHONE..................................302 875-1200
Brian Daisey, *Director*
EMP: 9
SALES (corp-wide): 141.3MM **Privately Held**
WEB: www.careerlaunch.net
SIC: 8641 Youth organizations
PA: Boys & Girls Clubs Of America
  1275 Peachtree St Ne # 500
  Atlanta GA 30309
  404 487-5700

(G-3205)
BULLFEATHERS AUTO SOUND INC
28368 Beaver Dam Br Rd (19956-2548)
PHONE..................................302 846-0434
Heather Byrd, *President*
EMP: 6
SQ FT: 2,700
SALES (est): 612K **Privately Held**
SIC: 5511 7538 New & used car dealers; general automotive repair shops

(G-3206)
C&S FARMS INC
8947 Woodland Ferry Rd (19956-3887)
PHONE..................................302 249-0458
Scot Bennett Givens, *President*
EMP: 5
SALES (est): 430K **Privately Held**
SIC: 0191 General farms, primarily crop

(G-3207)
CAREYS INC
Also Called: Careys Towing
30986 Sussex Hwy (19956-4429)
PHONE..................................302 875-5674
Robert Carey, *President*
Grace Carey, *Treasurer*
EMP: 20
SQ FT: 5,080
SALES: 2MM **Privately Held**
SIC: 7538 5541 7549 Diesel engine repair: automotive; filling stations, gasoline; towing service, automotive

(G-3208)
CARVEL GARDENS ASSOCIATES LP
801 Daniel St (19956-1633)
PHONE..................................302 875-4281
EMP: 4 **EST:** 2011
SALES (est): 250K **Privately Held**
SIC: 6513 Apartment Building Operator

(G-3209)
CB PRODUCTIONS
33434 Ellis Grove Rd (19956-4175)
PHONE..................................302 715-1015
Cody Belote, *Principal*
EMP: 4 **EST:** 2011
SALES (est): 93.6K **Privately Held**
SIC: 7822 Motion picture & tape distribution

(G-3210)
CBD PRO LLC
6625 Millcreek Rd (19956-3221)
PHONE..................................443 736-9002
Barrett Morrison, *Principal*
EMP: 2
SALES (est): 107.7K **Privately Held**
SIC: 3999

(G-3211)
CHARLES OFFROAD
33418 Horsey Church Rd (19956-4167)
PHONE..................................443 365-0630
Charles Toler, *Mng Member*
EMP: 4
SALES (est): 195K **Privately Held**
SIC: 7699 5571 Motorcycle repair service; motorcycle parts & accessories

(G-3212)
CHESAPEAKE DESIGN CENTER LLC
32852 Sussex Hwy (19956-4564)
PHONE..................................302 875-8570
Warren Reid, *Mng Member*
EMP: 9
SALES (est): 540K **Privately Held**
SIC: 7389 Design services

(G-3213)
CHETS AUTO BODY INC
425 N Central Ave (19956-1127)
PHONE..................................302 875-3376
Chester H Parches Jr, *President*
Sharon Parches, *Treasurer*
EMP: 4
SQ FT: 4,000
SALES (est): 292K **Privately Held**
SIC: 7532 Body shop, automotive

(G-3214)
CITIFINANCIAL SERVICES INC
11212 Trussum Pond Rd (19956-4592)
PHONE..................................302 875-2813
EMP: 5
SALES (corp-wide): 69.8B **Publicly Held**
SIC: 6141 Personal Credit Institution
HQ: Citifinancial Services, Inc.
  300 Saint Paul St Fl 3
  Baltimore MD 21202
  813 604-0402

(G-3215)
CLARAVALL ODILON
1124 S Central Ave (19956-1418)
PHONE..................................302 875-7753
Odilon Claravall MD, *Partner*
Antonio Pedro MD, *Partner*
Odilon Y Claravall, *Med Doctor*
EMP: 6
SALES (est): 383K **Privately Held**
SIC: 8011 Offices & clinics of medical doctors

(G-3216)
CLARKE SERVICE GROUPDOTCOM LLC
109 E Front St (19956-1721)
PHONE..................................302 875-0300
Fax: 302 875-2575
EMP: 13
SALES (est): 960K **Privately Held**
SIC: 1711 Plumbing/Heating/Air Cond Contractor

GEOGRAPHIC SECTION
Laurel - Sussex County (G-3249)

(G-3217)
COMMON SENSE SOLUTIONS LLC
14127 Rottwaller Rd (19956-2746)
PHONE.................................302 875-4510
EMP: 9
SALES (est): 844K **Privately Held**
SIC: 0782 Landscape contractors

(G-3218)
CURTIS A SMITH
314 S Central Ave (19956-1525)
PHONE.................................302 875-6800
Curtis Smith, *Owner*
EMP: 8
SALES (est): 444.1K **Privately Held**
WEB: www.curtisasmith.com
SIC: 8011 General & family practice, physician/surgeon

(G-3219)
DADS WORKWEAR INC (PA)
Also Called: Dad's Workwear
11480 Commercial Ln (19956-4585)
PHONE.................................302 663-0068
Mitchell Brittingham, *President*
Anissa Brittingham, *Vice Pres*
EMP: 2
SALES: 2MM **Privately Held**
SIC: 3842 5611 Personal safety equipment; men's & boys' clothing stores

(G-3220)
DANIEL GEORGE BEBEE INC
Also Called: Tri County Electrical Services
32353 Cobbs Creek Rd (19956-4087)
PHONE.................................443 359-1542
Dan Bebee, *President*
EMP: 9
SALES (est): 991.5K **Privately Held**
SIC: 1731 General electrical contractor

(G-3221)
DAVID G HORSEY & SONS INC
Also Called: Horsey Family, The
28107 Beaver Dam Br Rd (19956-2543)
PHONE.................................302 875-3033
David G Horsey, *President*
Patricia L Horsey, *Corp Secy*
Michael A Horsey, *Vice Pres*
EMP: 75
SALES (est): 20.9MM **Privately Held**
SIC: 1611 1794 7389 Surfacing & paving; excavation work; business services

(G-3222)
DELMARVA HARDWOOD PRODUCTS
28950 Seaford Rd (19956-3868)
PHONE.................................302 349-4101
Ben Gordy, *President*
EMP: 10
SALES: 420K **Privately Held**
SIC: 2426 Lumber, hardwood dimension

(G-3223)
DEVASTATOR GAME CALLS LLC
12009 Lahoba Ln (19956-2776)
PHONE.................................302 875-5328
Roger L Baker,
Roger Baker,
EMP: 2
SALES: 150K **Privately Held**
SIC: 3949 Game calls

(G-3224)
DSI LAUREL LLC
Also Called: US Renal Care Laurel Dialysis
30214 Sussex Hwy (19956-3880)
P.O. Box 638754, Cincinnati OH (45263-8754)
PHONE.................................302 715-3060
Stephen Pirri, *President*
EMP: 87
SALES (est): 873.8K **Privately Held**
SIC: 8092 Kidney dialysis centers
HQ: Dialysis Newco, Inc.
424 Church St Ste 1900
Nashville TN 37219

(G-3225)
DYNAMIC THERAPY SERVICES LLC
400 S Central Ave (19956-1571)
PHONE.................................302 280-6953
Patricia Petrecca, *Principal*
EMP: 5
SALES (est): 188.2K **Privately Held**
SIC: 8093 Rehabilitation center, outpatient treatment

(G-3226)
EASTERN LIFT TRUCK CO INC
11512 Commercial Ln (19956-4585)
PHONE.................................302 875-4031
Lori Zakrzewski, *Office Mgr*
Peggy Berest, *Branch Mgr*
EMP: 12
SALES (corp-wide): 175.6MM **Privately Held**
SIC: 5084 Materials handling machinery
PA: Eastern Lift Truck Co., Inc.
549 E Linwood Ave
Maple Shade NJ 08052
856 779-8880

(G-3227)
EASTERN SHORE VETERINARY HOSP
32384 Sussex Hwy (19956-4642)
P.O. Box 586 (19956-0586)
PHONE.................................302 875-5941
Sarah Dykstra, *President*
EMP: 13 EST: 1998
SQ FT: 8,700
SALES (est): 903.9K **Privately Held**
SIC: 0742 Animal hospital services, pets & other animal specialties

(G-3228)
EMECA/SPE USA LLC
200 W 10th St (19956-1966)
PHONE.................................302 875-0760
Michael R Jahnigen,
▲ **EMP:** 5
SALES (est): 995.9K **Privately Held**
SIC: 3317 Steel pipe & tubes

(G-3229)
F AND M EQUIPMENT LTD
Also Called: Mardlantic Machinery
28587 Sussex Hwy (19956-3729)
PHONE.................................302 715-5382
Paul Berkey, *Branch Mgr*
EMP: 4 **Privately Held**
SIC: 7699 5039 Industrial machinery & equipment repair; prefabricated structures
HQ: F And M Equipment, Ltd.
2240 Bethlehem Pike
Hatfield PA 19440
215 822-0145

(G-3230)
FLEMINGS ELECTRICAL SERVICE
15199 Trap Pond Rd (19956-3133)
PHONE.................................302 258-9386
Brandon Fleming, *Principal*
EMP: 8 EST: 2016
SALES (est): 620.9K **Privately Held**
SIC: 4911 Electric services

(G-3231)
FUN 2 LEARN DAY CARE
7119 Airport Rd (19956-4239)
PHONE.................................302 875-3393
EMP: 5 EST: 2015
SALES (est): 56.1K **Privately Held**
SIC: 8351 Child day care services

(G-3232)
GOOD BEGINNINGS PRESCHOOL
10024 Woodland Ferry Rd (19956-3860)
PHONE.................................302 875-5507
Hazel P Glover, *Principal*
EMP: 5
SALES (est): 79.1K **Privately Held**
SIC: 8351 Preschool center

(G-3233)
GOOD SAMARITAN AID
Also Called: GOOD SAMARITAN THRIFT SHOP, TH
115 W Market St (19956-1001)
P.O. Box 643 (19956-0643)
PHONE.................................302 875-2425
Dale Doice, *President*
Henretta Koch, *Manager*
EMP: 9

SALES: 119.9K **Privately Held**
SIC: 8322 5947 Individual & family services; gift shop

(G-3234)
GORDYS LUMBER INC
28950 Seaford Rd (19956-3868)
PHONE.................................302 875-3502
John B Gordy, *President*
EMP: 11
SALES (est): 830K **Privately Held**
SIC: 2421 2426 Sawmills & planing mills, general; hardwood dimension & flooring mills

(G-3235)
GROWMARK FS LLC
31052 N Poplar St (19956-3911)
PHONE.................................302 875-7511
Mike Pochop, *Sales Mgr*
Robbie Givens, *Manager*
EMP: 11
SALES (corp-wide): 8.7B **Privately Held**
WEB: www.growmarkfs.com
SIC: 5191 Seeds: field, garden & flower
HQ: Growmark Fs, Llc
308 Ne Front St
Milford DE 19963
302 422-3002

(G-3236)
HABITAT AMERICA LLC
101 Laurel Commons Ln (19956-1408)
PHONE.................................302 875-3525
EMP: 45 **Privately Held**
SIC: 6512 Nonresidential building operators
PA: Habitat America Llc
180 Admiral Cochrane Dr # 200
Annapolis MD 21401

(G-3237)
HANNIGAN SHORT DISHAROONK
700 West St (19956-1928)
PHONE.................................302 875-3637
Holly Hannigan, *Owner*
EMP: 5
SALES (est): 447.8K **Privately Held**
SIC: 7261 Funeral home

(G-3238)
HORSEY TURF FARM LLC
28107 Beaver Dam Br Rd (19956-2543)
PHONE.................................302 875-7299
Robert Horsey,
David Wayne Horsey,
Michael Horsey,
EMP: 14
SALES: 3.5MM **Privately Held**
SIC: 0782 Sodding contractor

(G-3239)
INSURANCE MARKET INC (PA)
310 N Central Ave (19956-1750)
P.O. Box 637 (19956-0637)
PHONE.................................302 875-7591
Stephen Hartstein, *President*
James J Hartstein, *Vice Pres*
John L Downes, *Treasurer*
Shirley Lane, *Personnel*
Sharon Melone, *Personnel*
EMP: 24
SQ FT: 2,000
SALES (est): 6.2MM **Privately Held**
WEB: www.insurancemarket.net
SIC: 6411 Insurance agents

(G-3240)
INTELEXMICRO INC
Also Called: Lexatys,
10253 Stone Creek Dr 1 (19956-4700)
PHONE.................................302 907-9545
Walter Gordon, *President*
EMP: 3
SALES (est): 193.8K **Privately Held**
SIC: 3679 Microwave components

(G-3241)
INTERNET BUSINESS PUBG CORP
Also Called: Delmarva Digital Media Group
220 Laureltowne (19956)
PHONE.................................302 875-7700
Tim Smith, *President*

Alan Cole, *Vice Pres*
Andrew Gladish, *Prgrmr*
EMP: 12 EST: 1997
SALES (est): 1.3MM **Privately Held**
SIC: 7373 Computer integrated systems design

(G-3242)
JAMES F GIVENS INC
11213 County Seat Hwy (19956-3652)
PHONE.................................302 875-5436
Iris T Given, *President*
EMP: 6
SALES (est): 416K **Privately Held**
SIC: 1731 General electrical contractor

(G-3243)
JOHNNY JANOSIK INC (PA)
Also Called: Johnny Janosik World Furniture
11151 Trussum Pond Rd (19956-4522)
PHONE.................................302 875-5955
David Koehler, *CEO*
Kim Manzoni, *Purch Mgr*
Steve Price, *Buyer*
Dan Ringer, *CFO*
Debi Quillen, *Sales Dir*
▲ **EMP:** 200
SQ FT: 80,000
SALES (est): 58MM **Privately Held**
WEB: www.johnnyjanosik.com
SIC: 5712 7389 Beds & accessories; mattresses; office furniture; design services

(G-3244)
JOSEPH & CUMMINGS BUILDER
34629 Hudson Rd (19956-3061)
PHONE.................................302 875-4279
Al Joseph, *Partner*
EMP: 4
SALES (est): 255.1K **Privately Held**
SIC: 1521 New construction, single-family houses

(G-3245)
JOSEPH L HINKS
Also Called: Quality Masonry
32053 Gordy Rd (19956-4504)
PHONE.................................302 875-2260
Joseph Hinks, *Principal*
EMP: 5 EST: 2010
SALES (est): 221.1K **Privately Held**
SIC: 1741 Masonry & other stonework

(G-3246)
JUNTTAN USA INC
10253 Stone Creek Dr (19956-4700)
PHONE.................................302 500-1274
Pasi Poranen, *President*
James Massey, *Opers Mgr*
Tim Boyd, *Admin Sec*
EMP: 1
SALES (est): 240.7K **Privately Held**
SIC: 3511 3549 3621 7359 Hydraulic turbine generator set units, complete; rotary slitters (metalworking machines); rotary converters (electrical equipment); electronic equipment rental, except computers

(G-3247)
K E SMART & SONS INC
29110 Discount Land Rd (19956-3662)
PHONE.................................302 875-7002
Kenneth Smart, *President*
Joyce Smart, *Treasurer*
EMP: 5 EST: 1970
SALES: 300K **Privately Held**
SIC: 1521 General remodeling, single-family houses

(G-3248)
KAREN SCHREIBER
Also Called: Discovery Cove Learning Center
12034 County Seat Hwy (19956-2634)
PHONE.................................302 875-7733
Karen Schreiber, *Owner*
EMP: 9
SALES (est): 156.3K **Privately Held**
SIC: 8351 Preschool center

(G-3249)
L & J SHEET METAL
8095 Airport Rd (19956-4218)
PHONE.................................302 875-2822
Leroy Smith, *Owner*
Larry Smith,
EMP: 10

Laurel - Sussex County (G-3250)

SALES (est): 740.1K **Privately Held**
SIC: **1761** 7692 3444 Sheet metalwork; welding repair; sheet metalwork

(G-3250)
LAKESIDE GREENHOUSES INC (PA)
Also Called: Windsors Flowers Plants Shrubs
31494 Greenhouse Ln (19956-3583)
PHONE..................................302 875-2457
James C Windsor, *President*
Janet Windsor, *Vice Pres*
EMP: 5
SALES (est): 1.5MM **Privately Held**
SIC: **5992** 5193 0181 Flowers, fresh; plants, potted; flowers, fresh; nursery stock; flowers: grown under cover (e.g. greenhouse production)

(G-3251)
LAKESIDE PHYSICAL THERAPY LLC
200 Laurel Ct Unit 202 (19956-1969)
PHONE..................................302 280-6920
Metodio A Pamplona, *CEO*
Rowena Pamplona, *Principal*
EMP: 10
SALES (est): 276.1K **Privately Held**
SIC: **8049** 8011 Physical therapist; offices & clinics of medical doctors

(G-3252)
LAUREL DENTAL
10250 Stone Creek Dr # 1 (19956-4703)
PHONE..................................302 875-4271
Richard Tananis, *Owner*
EMP: 5
SALES (est): 195.5K **Privately Held**
SIC: **8021** Dentists' office

(G-3253)
LAUREL GRAIN COMPANY
10717 Georgetown Rd (19956-3823)
P.O. Box 422 (19956-0422)
PHONE..................................302 875-4231
Burton Massick, *President*
Dawn Brittingham, *Manager*
Mike Spangler, *Manager*
Craig Truitt,
EMP: 5
SQ FT: 20,000
SALES (est): 1.2MM **Privately Held**
SIC: **5153** Grains

(G-3254)
LAUREL HIGHSCHOOL WELLNESS CTR
1133 S Central Ave (19956-1417)
PHONE..................................302 875-6164
Karen L Hearn, *Director*
EMP: 7
SALES: 155K **Privately Held**
SIC: **8099** Medical services organization

(G-3255)
LAUREL MEDICAL GROUP
1124 S Central Ave (19956-1418)
PHONE..................................302 875-7753
Odilon Y Claravall, *Med Doctor*
Kathy Tyler, *Manager*
EMP: 5
SALES (est): 509.2K **Privately Held**
SIC: **8011** Internal medicine, physician/surgeon

(G-3256)
LAUREL SENIOR CENTER INC
Also Called: Laurel Adult Day Care
113 N Central Ave (19956-1723)
P.O. Box 64 (19956-0064)
PHONE..................................302 875-2536
Dee Renshaw, *President*
Harriet Tulliet, *Principal*
Robbin Lecates, *Director*
EMP: 5
SALES: 376.5K **Privately Held**
SIC: **8322** Senior citizens' center or association

(G-3257)
LAYTONS UMBRELLAS
35527 Jamie Ave (19956-4602)
PHONE..................................302 249-1958
Jonathan Layton, *Owner*
EMP: 4

SALES (est): 166.6K **Privately Held**
SIC: **3999** 5021 Manufacturing industries; furniture

(G-3258)
LEROY H SMITH
8095 Airport Rd (19956-4218)
PHONE..................................302 875-5976
Leroy H Smith, *Owner*
EMP: 1
SALES (est): 50.9K **Privately Held**
SIC: **7692** Welding repair

(G-3259)
LEXATYS LLC
10253 Stone Creek Dr 1 (19956-4700)
PHONE..................................302 715-5029
Walter E Gordon, *Principal*
EMP: 18
SALES: 5.1MM **Privately Held**
SIC: **3679** Electronic circuits; electronic switches

(G-3260)
MAMIE STURGIS HANDY DAY CARE
31732 Old Stage Rd (19956-3445)
PHONE..................................302 875-4703
EMP: 5 **EST:** 2005
SALES (est): 160K **Privately Held**
SIC: **8351** Child Day Care Services

(G-3261)
MANUFACTURERS & TRADERS TR CO
Also Called: M&T
101 W Market St (19956-1001)
PHONE..................................302 855-2873
David Engelhardt, *Branch Mgr*
Nancy Hearn, *Manager*
EMP: 8
SALES (corp-wide): 6.4B **Publicly Held**
WEB: www.binghamlegg.com
SIC: **6022** State commercial banks
HQ: Manufacturers And Traders Trust Company
 1 M&T Plz Fl 3
 Buffalo NY 14203
 716 842-4200

(G-3262)
MARY BRYAN INC
4679 Old Sharptown Rd (19956-4013)
PHONE..................................302 875-5099
Mary Bryan, *Principal*
Wede Bryan, *Vice Pres*
EMP: 12
SALES (est): 2.2MM **Privately Held**
SIC: **6411** Insurance agents

(G-3263)
MAXINES HAIR HAPPENINGS INC
206 Laureltowne (19956)
PHONE..................................302 875-4055
Maxine Lynch, *President*
EMP: 5
SALES (est): 130.1K **Privately Held**
SIC: **7231** Unisex hair salons

(G-3264)
MICHAEL C RAPA
Also Called: Mk Krawlers
10596 Georgetown Rd (19956-3820)
PHONE..................................302 236-4423
Michael C Rapa, *Owner*
EMP: 2 **EST:** 2010
SALES (est): 98.9K **Privately Held**
SIC: **3799** Off-road automobiles, except recreational vehicles

(G-3265)
MIDDLE DEPT INSPTN AGCY INC
11508 Commercial Ln (19956-4582)
PHONE..................................302 875-4514
Sam Trice, *Manager*
EMP: 4
SALES (corp-wide): 9MM **Privately Held**
SIC: **7389** Building inspection service
PA: Middle Department Inspection Agency, Inc.
 1337 W Chester Pike
 West Chester PA 19382
 610 696-3900

(G-3266)
NORTHEAST AGRI SYSTEMS INC
28527 Boyce Rd (19956-3877)
PHONE..................................302 875-1886
Frank Pusey, *Branch Mgr*
EMP: 7
SALES (corp-wide): 29.1MM **Privately Held**
WEB: www.neagri.com
SIC: **5083** Agricultural machinery & equipment
PA: Northeast Agri Systems, Inc.
 139a W Airport Rd
 Lititz PA 17543
 717 569-2702

(G-3267)
NR HUDSON CONSULTING INC
14617 Arvey Rd (19956-3069)
PHONE..................................302 875-5276
Nathan R Hudson, *Principal*
EMP: 7
SALES (est): 554.6K **Privately Held**
SIC: **8748** Business consulting

(G-3268)
ONEAL J C & SONS AUCTIONEERS
1112 Laurel Rd (19956)
PHONE..................................302 875-5261
EMP: 9 **EST:** 1971
SALES (est): 526.3K **Privately Held**
SIC: **7389** Business Services

(G-3269)
PEGASUS AIR INC
32524 Aero Dr (19956-4394)
PHONE..................................302 875-3540
EMP: 2
SALES (est): 152.2K **Privately Held**
SIC: **3721** Mfg Aircraft

(G-3270)
PENINSULA POULTRY EQP CO INC
30709 Sussex Hwy (19956-4425)
PHONE..................................302 875-0889
Larry Hill, *Owner*
EMP: 18 **Privately Held**
SIC: **5083** Poultry equipment
PA: Peninsula Poultry Equipment Company, Inc.
 201 N Dual Hwy
 Laurel DE

(G-3271)
PERDUE FARMS INC
Also Called: Laurel DMV North Growout Off
10262 Stone Creek Dr (19956-4701)
PHONE..................................302 855-5681
Marilyn O'Neal, *Branch Mgr*
EMP: 422
SALES (corp-wide): 5.9B **Privately Held**
SIC: **0251** Broiler, fryer & roaster chickens
PA: Perdue Farms Inc.
 31149 Old Ocean City Rd
 Salisbury MD 21804
 410 543-3000

(G-3272)
PHILLIPS FABRICATION
32846 Shockley Rd (19956-4047)
PHONE..................................302 875-4424
Bruce Philps, *Owner*
Bruce Phillips, *Owner*
EMP: 3
SQ FT: 1,700
SALES (est): 301.9K **Privately Held**
SIC: **3444** 3441 Sheet metal specialties, not stamped; fabricated structural metal

(G-3273)
PLANNED POULTRY RENOVATION
16244 Sycamore Rd (19956-2558)
PHONE..................................302 875-4196
Jay James, *Partner*
Brian Ramey, *Partner*
EMP: 32 **EST:** 1995
SQ FT: 21,000
SALES (est): 4.4MM **Privately Held**
WEB: www.plannedpoultryrenovations.com
SIC: **1796** Machinery installation

(G-3274)
PROVIDENCE MEDIA LLC
119 Lake Dr (19956-1707)
PHONE..................................302 715-1757
Steven Howard, *President*
Stephen Howard, *IT/INT Sup*
EMP: 5 **EST:** 2011
SALES: 200K **Privately Held**
SIC: **4899** Data communication services

(G-3275)
PROXIMITY MALT LLC
33222 Bi State Blvd (19956-4644)
PHONE..................................414 755-8388
Matt Musial, *Branch Mgr*
EMP: 16
SALES (corp-wide): 13.6MM **Privately Held**
SIC: **2083** Barley malt; rye malt; wheat malt
PA: Proximity Malt, Llc
 644 S 5th St
 Milwaukee WI 53204
 414 755-8388

(G-3276)
R & J WELDING & FABRICATION
32812 Bi State Blvd (19956-4533)
PHONE..................................302 236-5618
EMP: 1
SALES (est): 48.2K **Privately Held**
SIC: **7692** Welding repair

(G-3277)
R J BAKER DISTILLERY
34171 Rider Rd (19956-4067)
PHONE..................................302 745-0967
EMP: 3
SALES (est): 112.7K **Privately Held**
SIC: **2085** Distilled & blended liquors

(G-3278)
RAM ELECTRIC INC
34779 Whaleys Rd (19956-3015)
P.O. Box 1680, Seaford (19973-8980)
PHONE..................................302 875-2356
Rodney A Morton, *President*
EMP: 9
SALES (est): 834K **Privately Held**
SIC: **1731** Electrical work

(G-3279)
RELAX INN
30702 Sussex Hwy (19956-4424)
PHONE..................................302 875-1554
Rk Gadani, *Principal*
EMP: 7
SALES (est): 234.5K **Privately Held**
SIC: **7011** Inns

(G-3280)
RICHARD E SMALL INC
1130 S Central Ave (19956-1418)
P.O. Box 697 (19956-0697)
PHONE..................................302 875-7199
EMP: 4
SALES (est): 370K **Privately Held**
SIC: **6411** Insurance Agent/Broker

(G-3281)
RICHARD J TANANIS DDS LLC
10250 Stone Creek Dr # 1 (19956-4703)
PHONE..................................302 875-4271
Richard J Tananis, *Executive Asst*
EMP: 5
SALES (est): 237.6K **Privately Held**
SIC: **8021** Dentists' office

(G-3282)
RIVERA TRANSPORTATION INC
205 W 7th St (19956-1939)
PHONE..................................302 258-9023
Erlin I Rivera, *Principal*
EMP: 8 **EST:** 2010
SALES (est): 492.2K **Privately Held**
SIC: **4789** Transportation services

(G-3283)
ROBERT BAYLY
Also Called: Bayly's Garage
Dual Hwy Rr 13 (19956)
PHONE..................................302 846-9752
Robert Bayly, *Owner*
◆ **EMP:** 4

GEOGRAPHIC SECTION
Lewes - Sussex County (G-3315)

SALES (est): 163.5K **Privately Held**
SIC: 7549 7539 Towing services; automotive repair shops

(G-3284)
ROBERT BRYAN
4679 Old Sharptown Rd (19956-4013)
PHONE.................302 875-5099
Robert Bryan, *Principal*
EMP: 4
SALES (est): 357.6K **Privately Held**
SIC: 4789 Transportation services

(G-3285)
ROUTE 13 OUTLET MARKET
11290 Trussum Pond Rd (19956-4592)
P.O. Box 32 (19956-0032)
PHONE.................302 875-4800
David Roeberg, *Owner*
Mark Handler, *Partner*
EMP: 4
SALES (est): 575.2K **Privately Held**
SIC: 6512 Shopping center, property operation only

(G-3286)
ROYAL MISSION & MINISTRIES
9751 Randall St (19956-4315)
PHONE.................302 249-8863
Gerry Royal, *Principal*
EMP: 5
SALES (est): 78.6K **Privately Held**
SIC: 8399 Social services

(G-3287)
SANDY KNOLL ENTERPRISES LLC
12254 Laurel Rd (19956-3432)
PHONE.................302 875-3916
Charles C Hudson, *Principal*
EMP: 4
SALES (est): 248.6K **Privately Held**
SIC: 8748 Business consulting

(G-3288)
SHORT FUNERAL HOME INC
700 West St (19956-1928)
PHONE.................302 875-3637
EMP: 4
SALES (corp-wide): 522K **Privately Held**
WEB: www.shortfh.com
SIC: 7261 5999 Funeral home; vaults & safes
PA: Short Funeral Home Inc
  13 E Grove St
  Delmar DE 19940
  302 846-9814

(G-3289)
SMOOTHIES SOUP AND SANDWICHES
11290 Trussum Pond Rd (19956-4592)
PHONE.................302 280-6183
EMP: 3
SALES (est): 71.4K **Privately Held**
SIC: 2037 Frozen fruits & vegetables

(G-3290)
SMW SALES LLC
11432 Trussum Pond Rd (19956-3412)
PHONE.................302 875-7958
Richard Carmine, *Principal*
EMP: 17
SALES (est): 3.1MM **Privately Held**
SIC: 3272 3531 3594 Irrigation pipe, concrete; rakes, land clearing: mechanical; fluid power pumps & motors

(G-3291)
SOLID IMAGE INC
11244 Whitesville Rd (19956-3318)
PHONE.................302 877-0901
Warren Reid, *President*
EMP: 7
SALES (est): 446.4K **Privately Held**
SIC: 2541 Counter & sink tops

(G-3292)
SOUTHERN DEL TRCK GROWERS ASSN
Dual Hwy & Georgestwn Rd (19956)
PHONE.................302 875-3147
George Collins, *President*
Robert L Whaley, *Vice Pres*
Joseph C O'Neal, *Treasurer*
Thomas Wright, *Admin Sec*
EMP: 25 EST: 1940
SALES (est): 1.2MM **Privately Held**
SIC: 7389 Auctioneers, fee basis

(G-3293)
SOUTHERN STATES COOP INC
Also Called: S S C 7714-1
102 Deshields St (19956-1951)
PHONE.................302 875-3635
Brian Shelly, *Sales/Mktg Mgr*
EMP: 5
SALES (corp-wide): 1.9B **Privately Held**
SIC: 8748 2875 Agricultural consultant; fertilizers, mixing only
PA: Southern States Cooperative, Incorporated
  6606 W Broad St Ste B
  Richmond VA 23230
  804 281-1000

(G-3294)
SPORTZ TEES
16536 Adams Rd (19956-2922)
PHONE.................302 280-6076
Chris Otwell, *Owner*
EMP: 1 EST: 2012
SALES (est): 83.2K **Privately Held**
SIC: 2759 Screen printing

(G-3295)
STATE LINE MACHINE INC
1154 S Central Ave (19956-1418)
PHONE.................302 875-2248
EMP: 2
SALES (est): 81.4K **Privately Held**
SIC: 3599 Industrial machinery

(G-3296)
STUDIO J ENTRMT & AP & COF BAR
11290 Trussum Pond Rd F32 (19956-4592)
Rural Route 706 Wadena, Salisbury MD (21801)
PHONE.................410 422-3155
Jenelle Flythe-Brownlow, *CEO*
Thomas Brownlow, *Principal*
EMP: 5
SALES (est): 57.5K **Privately Held**
SIC: 7929 5651 5735 Entertainers & entertainment groups; family clothing stores; record & prerecorded tape stores

(G-3297)
SUSSEX MACHINE WORKS INC
11432 Trussum Pond Rd (19956-3412)
PHONE.................302 875-7958
Richard Charmina, *President*
EMP: 8
SALES (est): 903.3K **Privately Held**
SIC: 1799 Welding on site

(G-3298)
TAMMY S BENNETT
30668 Sussex Hwy (19956-4421)
PHONE.................302 875-6550
Tammy Bennett, *Executive*
EMP: 7
SALES (est): 60.9K **Privately Held**
SIC: 8049 Offices of health practitioner

(G-3299)
TELAMON CORPORATION HEADSTART
Also Called: Telamon - Laurel Head Start
30125 Discount Land Rd (19956-3679)
PHONE.................302 875-7718
Selina Houston, *Principal*
EMP: 10
SALES (est): 123.5K **Privately Held**
SIC: 8351 Preschool center

(G-3300)
V P PRODUCE INC
32228 Old Hickory Rd (19956-4227)
PHONE.................302 249-0718
Vance Phillips, *President*
EMP: 4
SALES: 150K **Privately Held**
SIC: 0161 Vegetables & melons

(G-3301)
VANCE PHILLIPS INC
7472 Portsville Rd (19956-3958)
PHONE.................302 542-1501
Vance Phillips, *President*
EMP: 4
SALES: 200K **Privately Held**
SIC: 0161 6519 6513 0971 Watermelon farm; farm land leasing; apartment building operators; hunting services

(G-3302)
VINCENT FARMS INC
12487 Salt Barn Rd (19956-3337)
P.O. Box 219, Delmar (19940-0219)
PHONE.................302 875-5707
Raymond Thomas Vincent, *President*
EMP: 125
SQ FT: 25,000
SALES (est): 13.6MM **Privately Held**
SIC: 0191 4971 General farms, primarily crop; irrigation systems

(G-3303)
W ENTERPRISES LLC
12793 Laurel Rd (19956-3439)
PHONE.................302 875-0430
George Whaley Jr,
Kathy Whaley,
Kirk Whaley,
EMP: 4
SQ FT: 2,400
SALES (est): 470.6K **Privately Held**
SIC: 1542 5999 5191 5083 Agricultural building contractors; farm equipment & supplies; farm supplies; lawn & garden machinery & equipment

(G-3304)
WARREN REID
Also Called: Warren A Reid Custon Builders
14234 Sycamore Rd (19956-2738)
PHONE.................302 877-0901
Warren A Reid, *President*
EMP: 25 EST: 1999
SALES: 750K **Privately Held**
SIC: 1522 Residential construction

(G-3305)
WASTE MANAGEMENT INC
11323 Trussum Pond Rd (19956-4520)
PHONE.................302 854-5304
Shannon Argo, *Principal*
EMP: 10
SALES (corp-wide): 14.9B **Publicly Held**
SIC: 8741 Management services
PA: Waste Management, Inc.
  1001 Fannin St Ste 4000
  Houston TX 77002
  713 512-6200

(G-3306)
WASTE MANAGEMENT DELAWARE INC
11323 Trussum Pond Rd (19956-4520)
PHONE.................302 854-5301
Shannon Argo, *Branch Mgr*
EMP: 7
SALES (corp-wide): 14.9B **Publicly Held**
SIC: 4953 Refuse systems
HQ: Waste Management Of Delaware Inc.
  1001 Fannin St Ste 4000
  Houston TX 77002
  713 512-6200

(G-3307)
WASTEFLO LLC
207 N Poplar St (19956-1009)
PHONE.................410 202-0802
Wilson Handy, *Owner*
EMP: 5
SALES (est): 254.1K **Privately Held**
SIC: 4212 4953 Garbage collection & transport, no disposal; rubbish collection & disposal

(G-3308)
WHALEYS SEED STORE INC
106 W 8th St (19956-1900)
PHONE.................302 875-7833
W Douglas Whaley, *President*
Lisa Jester, *Vice Pres*
Patricia Whaley, *Treasurer*
EMP: 6
SALES: 770K **Privately Held**
SIC: 5191 5083 7349 Farm supplies; garden machinery & equipment; lawn machinery & equipment; building maintenance services

(G-3309)
WHAYLAND COMPANY INC
30613 Sussex Hwy (19956-4420)
PHONE.................302 875-5445
Robert Wheatley, *President*
John Wilson, *Superintendent*
Shirley Prettyman, *VP Finance*
Sonya Hicks, *Admin Asst*
EMP: 12
SQ FT: 1,200
SALES (est): 3.6MM **Privately Held**
WEB: www.whayland.com
SIC: 1542 1541 Commercial & office building, new construction; industrial buildings, new construction

(G-3310)
WHAYLAND COMPANY LLC
100 W 10th St (19956-1904)
PHONE.................302 875-5445
Steven Hentschel, *Principal*
EMP: 12
SALES (est): 1.7MM **Privately Held**
SIC: 1542 Commercial & office building, new construction

(G-3311)
WILLEY AND CO
11588 Commercial Ln (19956-4640)
P.O. Box 60, Seaford (19973-0060)
PHONE.................302 629-3327
Micheal Willey, *Owner*
EMP: 9 EST: 1974
SALES (est): 133.1K **Privately Held**
SIC: 1711 1389 Heating systems repair & maintenance; plumbing contractors; septic system construction; cleaning wells

(G-3312)
ZINGER ENTERPRIZES INC
9224 Sharptown Rd (19956-4310)
PHONE.................302 381-6761
Carl Schirtzinger, *CEO*
EMP: 5
SALES: 150K **Privately Held**
SIC: 8733 Research institute

Leipsic
Kent County

(G-3313)
CAREYS DIESEL INC
168 Denny St (19901-1763)
PHONE.................302 678-3797
John J Carey, *President*
Louise Carey, *Corp Secy*
◆ EMP: 18
SALES (est): 2MM **Privately Held**
WEB: www.careysdiesel.com
SIC: 7538 5084 Diesel engine repair: automotive; engines & parts, diesel

(G-3314)
SAWYERS SANITATION SERVICE
184 Front St (19901-1715)
P.O. Box 538, Smyrna (19977-0538)
PHONE.................302 678-8240
Daniel Fox, *Owner*
EMP: 5
SALES (est): 325.2K **Privately Held**
SIC: 7699 Cesspool cleaning

Lewes
Sussex County

(G-3315)
1 A LIFESAFER INC
32393 Lwes Georgetown Hwy (19958-1676)
PHONE.................800 634-3077
EMP: 1

Lewes - Sussex County (G-3316)

SALES (corp-wide): 4.3MM **Privately Held**
SIC: 3829 Measuring & controlling devices
PA: 1 A Lifesafer, Inc.
4290 Glendale Milford Rd
Blue Ash OH 45242
513 651-9560

(G-3316)
313DESIGN LAB INC
16192 Coastal Hwy (19958-3608)
PHONE............................929 399-6426
Yohan Ku, *CEO*
EMP: 4
SALES (est): 92.1K **Privately Held**
SIC: 7389 Design services

(G-3317)
7P NETWORKS LLC
16192 Coastal Hwy (19958-3608)
PHONE............................938 777-7662
Andrew Rosen, *Mng Member*
EMP: 13
SALES (est): 134.9K **Privately Held**
SIC: 4813

(G-3318)
A CHANCE TO WRITE IT LLC
16192 Coastal Hwy (19958-3608)
PHONE............................202 256-4524
Terraine Manley, *Manager*
Lawrence Manley, *Manager*
EMP: 7
SALES: 35K **Privately Held**
SIC: 2731 Book publishing

(G-3319)
A CHILDS POTENTIAL
12 Gosling Dr (19958-9570)
PHONE............................302 249-6929
Candace Shetzler, *Principal*
EMP: 5 EST: 2010
SALES (est): 68K **Privately Held**
SIC: 8351 Montessori child development center

(G-3320)
A2A INTGRTED PHRMCEUTICALS LLC
16192 Coastal Hwy (19958-3608)
PHONE............................270 202-2461
Jack Downing,
Addie Towery,
EMP: 5
SALES: 4.5MM **Privately Held**
SIC: 2834 5122 7389 Druggists' preparations (pharmaceuticals); pharmaceuticals;

(G-3321)
ABA TRAVL & ENT INC
16192 Coastal Hwy (19958-3608)
PHONE............................305 374-0838
Wenceslao Lora, *CEO*
EMP: 5
SQ FT: 1,100
SALES (est): 824.9K **Privately Held**
SIC: 4724 Travel agencies; tourist agency arranging transport, lodging & car rental

(G-3322)
ACCESS4U INC
510 Railroad Ave (19958-1432)
P.O. Box 2535, Lower Burrell PA (15068-0747)
PHONE............................800 355-7025
Robert B Heffernan, *President*
Kirit Patel, *Vice Pres*
EMP: 1
SALES (est): 224.7K **Privately Held**
WEB: www.access4uinc.com
SIC: 3446 Stairs, staircases, stair treads: prefabricated metal

(G-3323)
ACCURATE-ENERGY LLC
35180 South Dr (19958-3244)
P.O. Box 293 (19958-0293)
PHONE............................302 947-9560
Paul McDaniel,
EMP: 4
SALES (est): 316.3K **Privately Held**
SIC: 1389 Oil field services

(G-3324)
ACTIV PEST & LAWN INC
16861 New Rd (19958-3706)
PHONE............................302 645-1502
Bailey McMahon, *Owner*
Chrissy Powell, *Office Mgr*
Chris Kiker, *Director*
EMP: 14
SALES (est): 1.5MM **Privately Held**
SIC: 7342 Pest control services

(G-3325)
ADVANCE AUTO PARTS INC
17884 Coastal Hwy Unit 1 (19958-6323)
PHONE............................302 644-0141
Tommy Rubino, *Principal*
EMP: 9
SALES (corp-wide): 9.5B **Publicly Held**
SIC: 5531 5013 Batteries, automotive & truck; automotive supplies & parts
PA: Advance Auto Parts, Inc.
2635 E Millbrook Rd Ste A
Raleigh NC 27604
540 362-4911

(G-3326)
ADVANCED BEHAVIORAL CARE INC
19 Cedarwood Dr (19958-9583)
PHONE............................410 599-7400
Leonard Francis Stielper, *Principal*
EMP: 5
SALES (est): 146.8K **Privately Held**
SIC: 8093 Mental health clinic, outpatient

(G-3327)
AFFORDABLE RECREATION LLC
16192 Coastal Hwy (19958-3608)
PHONE............................603 635-2101
EMP: 2 EST: 2006
SALES (est): 160K **Privately Held**
SIC: 3799 Mfg Transportation Equipment

(G-3328)
AGRIMA POSTAL SOLUTIONS LLC
16192 Coastal Hwy (19958-3608)
PHONE............................302 394-6939
Anmol Gupta, *Mng Member*
EMP: 51 EST: 2011
SALES (est): 278K **Privately Held**
SIC: 4731 4215 Shipping documents preparation; parcel delivery, vehicular

(G-3329)
AGVISORY LLC
125 Lakeside Dr (19958-8937)
PHONE............................302 270-5165
Jodi Pries, *CEO*
EMP: 8
SALES (est): 585.8K **Privately Held**
SIC: 6531 Appraiser, real estate

(G-3330)
AIDBITS INC
16192 Coastal Hwy (19958-3608)
PHONE............................647 692-3494
Feras Nasr, *CEO*
EMP: 7
SALES (est): 320K **Privately Held**
SIC: 7375 On-line data base information retrieval

(G-3331)
AIGC GAMES INC
16192 Coastal Hwy (19958-3608)
PHONE............................214 499-8654
Mohammed Ammous, *CEO*
Maram Amous, *Vice Pres*
EMP: 7
SQ FT: 2,000
SALES (est): 350K **Privately Held**
SIC: 7373 Computer integrated systems design

(G-3332)
ALAMAD INVESTMENTS LLC
16192 Coastal Hwy (19958-3608)
PHONE............................833 311-8799
Malik Mukhametkaliyev,
EMP: 5
SALES (est): 162.9K **Privately Held**
SIC: 5094 Precious stones & metals

(G-3333)
ALBATROSS INDUSTRIES LLC
16192 Coastal Hwy (19958-3608)
PHONE............................850 447-2150
EMP: 1
SALES (est): 39.6K **Privately Held**
SIC: 3999 Manufacturing industries

(G-3334)
ALL PRO MAIDS INC
1546 Savannah Rd (19958-1624)
PHONE............................302 645-9247
James Sprinkle, *President*
Michele Sprinkle, *Corp Secy*
EMP: 30
SALES (est): 800K **Privately Held**
WEB: www.allpromaids.com
SIC: 7349 Janitorial service, contract basis

(G-3335)
AMERICAN CEDAR & MILLWORK INC (PA)
17993 American Way (19958-4799)
PHONE............................302 645-9580
Michael Neal, *President*
Paul Sessum, *General Mgr*
Julie A Neal, *Corp Secy*
John Ritson, *CFO*
Wanda Kilgore, *Credit Mgr*
EMP: 62
SQ FT: 24,000
SALES (est): 39.2MM **Privately Held**
SIC: 5031 5211 Building materials, interior; lumber & other building materials

(G-3336)
AMERICAN CLASSIC GOLF CLUB LLC
18485 Bethpage Dr Ste 1 (19958-4853)
PHONE............................302 703-6662
Bonnie Morrison, *Principal*
Harry Morrison Jr, *Principal*
EMP: 8
SALES (est): 278.7K **Privately Held**
SIC: 7992 Public golf courses

(G-3337)
AMY DONOVAN
32855 Ocean Reach Dr (19958-4666)
PHONE............................302 245-8957
Amy Donovan, *President*
EMP: 8
SALES (est): 65.7K **Privately Held**
SIC: 8049 Offices of health practitioner

(G-3338)
AN INN BY BAY
205 E Savannah Rd (19958-1128)
PHONE............................302 644-8878
EMP: 19 EST: 2001
SALES (est): 760K **Privately Held**
SIC: 7011 Hotel/Motel Operation

(G-3339)
ANGELIC THERAPY
17436 Slipper Shell Way # 11 (19958-6319)
PHONE............................717 870-4618
Angel Ic Therapy, *Principal*
EMP: 7 EST: 2017
SALES (est): 75.3K **Privately Held**
SIC: 8093 Rehabilitation center, outpatient treatment

(G-3340)
ANGLERS MARINA
Also Called: Anglers Fishing Center
213 Anglers Rd (19958-1151)
PHONE............................302 644-4533
Ted Moulinier, *Branch Mgr*
EMP: 9
SALES (est): 289.4K **Privately Held**
WEB: www.anglersfishingcenter.com
SIC: 7999 Fishing boats, party: operation
PA: Marina Anglers
400 Anglers Rd
Lewes DE 19958

(G-3341)
ANGOLA BY BAY PRPRTY OWNR ASSN
33457 Woodland Cir (19958-5179)
PHONE............................302 945-2700
Kim Rogers, *General Mgr*
EMP: 10 EST: 1968
SQ FT: 1,200
SALES: 300K **Privately Held**
SIC: 8641 Homeowners' association

(G-3342)
ANIMATRA INC (PA)
16192 Coastal Hwy (19958-3608)
PHONE............................303 350-9264
James Esch Duran, *President*
EMP: 8
SALES (est): 309.2K **Privately Held**
SIC: 8099 7371 Health & allied services; computer software development & applications

(G-3343)
ANOTHERAI INC (PA)
16192 Coastal Hwy (19958-3608)
PHONE............................408 987-1927
Andrew Doherty, *CEO*
EMP: 8
SALES (est): 182.5K **Privately Held**
SIC: 7371 Computer software development & applications

(G-3344)
APPS COMPLEX LLC
16192 Coastal Hwy (19958-3608)
PHONE............................705 600-0729
Faizan Siddiqui,
EMP: 12
SALES (est): 249.2K **Privately Held**
SIC: 7379 Computer related consulting services

(G-3345)
ARENA SIGNS
34696 Jiffy Way (19958-4931)
PHONE............................302 644-8300
Ed Martin, *Owner*
EMP: 2
SALES (est): 203.8K **Privately Held**
SIC: 3993 Signs, not made in custom sign painting shops

(G-3346)
ARNOLD POWERWASH LLC
18197 Robinsonville Rd (19958-4403)
PHONE............................302 542-9783
Charles R Arnold Jr, *Mng Member*
EMP: 5
SALES: 150K **Privately Held**
WEB: www.arnoldpowerwash.com
SIC: 1799 Cleaning building exteriors

(G-3347)
ARPAGO CORP
Also Called: Midway Par 3 Golf Course & Dri
34578 Pinnacle Rd (19958-9697)
PHONE............................302 645-7955
H Walton Jones, *President*
Barbara Moore, *Manager*
EMP: 4
SQ FT: 2,400
SALES (est): 330K **Privately Held**
SIC: 7992 Public golf courses

(G-3348)
ARTISAN ELECTRICAL INC
119 S Washington Ave (19958-1443)
PHONE............................302 645-5844
Charles T Malewski, *President*
Thomas Malewski, *Vice Pres*
Mary Ann Malewski, *Treasurer*
EMP: 5
SALES: 400K **Privately Held**
SIC: 5064 1731 Fans, household: electric; electrical work

(G-3349)
ARTISTIC DESIGNS SALON
20361 John J Williams Hwy (19958-4305)
PHONE............................302 644-2009
Arlin Berlinger, *President*
EMP: 8
SALES (est): 288.9K **Privately Held**
SIC: 7231 Hairdressers

(G-3350)
ASSOCIATES IN MEDICINE PA
1302 Savannah Rd (19958-1526)
PHONE............................302 645-6644
Mark Schatz, *Manager*
EMP: 8

SALES (est): 166K **Privately Held**
SIC: 8011 Internal medicine, physician/surgeon

(G-3351)
ATAPY SOFTWARE LLC
16192 Coastal Hwy (19958-3608)
PHONE 657 221-9370
EMP: 2
SALES (est): 56.5K **Privately Held**
SIC: 7372 Prepackaged software

(G-3352)
ATLANTIC ADULT & PEDIATRIC
34453 King Street Row # 1 (19958-4787)
PHONE 302 644-1300
Charles Stanislav, *Owner*
EMP: 10
SALES (est): 516K **Privately Held**
SIC: 8011 Pediatrician

(G-3353)
ATLANTIC CHIROPRACTIC ASSOCIAT
12001 Old Vine Blvd (19958-1688)
PHONE 302 703-6108
EMP: 12 **Privately Held**
SIC: 8041 Offices & clinics of chiropractors
PA: Atlantic Chiropractic Associat
 375 Mullet Run
 Milford DE 19963

(G-3354)
ATLANTIC CONCRETE COMPANY INC
1 Country Ln (19958-9650)
P.O. Box 321, Milford (19963-0321)
PHONE 302 856-7847
David A Jones, *President*
EMP: 20
SALES (corp-wide): 10.8MM **Privately Held**
SIC: 3273 Ready-mixed concrete
PA: Atlantic Concrete Company Inc
 New Wharf Rd
 Milford DE 19963
 302 422-8017

(G-3355)
ATLANTIC ENTERPRISES LLC
20684 John J Williams Hwy # 1 (19958-4393)
PHONE 302 542-5427
Mark Grahne,
EMP: 8
SALES: 950K **Privately Held**
SIC: 1521 General remodeling, single-family houses

(G-3356)
ATLANTIC HOMES LLC
20684 John J Williams Hwy # 1 (19958-4393)
PHONE 302 947-0223
Mark Grahne, *Mng Member*
Linda Grahne, *Administration*
EMP: 5
SQ FT: 256
SALES (est): 644.5K **Privately Held**
WEB: www.atlanticcustomhomes.com
SIC: 1522 Residential construction

(G-3357)
ATLANTIC KITCHEN & BATH LLC
18355 Coastal Hwy (19958-4778)
PHONE 302 947-9001
Mark Grahne, *Mng Member*
EMP: 7 EST: 2009
SALES (est): 623.2K **Privately Held**
SIC: 1799 Kitchen & bathroom remodeling

(G-3358)
ATLANTIC REFRIGERATION INC
Also Called: Atlantic Refrigeration & AC
17553 Nassau Commons Blvd (19958-6284)
PHONE 302 645-9321
David Jones, *President*
Jamie Nickerson, *Vice Pres*
EMP: 32
SALES (est): 7MM **Privately Held**
WEB: www.atlanticrefrigeration.net
SIC: 1711 Warm air heating & air conditioning contractor; heating & air conditioning contractors

(G-3359)
ATLANTIC SOURCE CONTG INC
35 Bridge Ridge Cir (19958)
PHONE 302 645-5207
Michael Mattia, *President*
Linda Mattia, *Vice Pres*
EMP: 2
SALES: 285K **Privately Held**
SIC: 3088 1799 Shower stalls, fiberglass & plastic; closet organizers, installation & design

(G-3360)
AVATAR INSTRUMENTS INC
16587 Coastal Hwy (19958-3605)
P.O. Box 496 (19958-0496)
PHONE 302 703-6865
Paul Evalds, *President*
EMP: 5
SQ FT: 8,000
SALES: 1.1MM **Privately Held**
WEB: www.avatarinstruments.com
SIC: 3829 Measuring & controlling devices

(G-3361)
AXXESS MARINE LLC
16192 Coastal Hwy (19958-3608)
PHONE 954 225-1744
Kym Petrie, *Chief Mktg Ofcr*
Dennis Sokke, *Mng Member*
EMP: 5
SALES: 1.5MM **Privately Held**
SIC: 4899 Data communication services

(G-3362)
BARSGR LLC (PA)
Also Called: Holly Lake Campsites
32193 Winery Way (19958-6208)
PHONE 302 645-6665
John P Hall, *Trustee*
Robert A Raley,
Susan G Raley,
EMP: 4 EST: 1962
SQ FT: 2,000
SALES: 2MM **Privately Held**
SIC: 7033 0139 0254 0251 Campsite; hay farm; chicken hatchery; broiler, fryer & roaster chickens; marinas

(G-3363)
BAYSIDE EXTERIORS LLC
32295 Nassau Rd (19958-3712)
PHONE 302 727-5288
Andrzej Lfwandowski, *Mng Member*
EMP: 4
SALES (est): 451.2K **Privately Held**
SIC: 1761 Roofing contractor

(G-3364)
BAYSIDE HEALTH ASSN CHARTERED (PA)
Also Called: Bahtiarian, Gregory Do
1535 Savannah Rd (19958-1611)
P.O. Box 538, Millsboro (19966-0538)
PHONE 302 645-4700
Vincent B Killeen MD, *President*
Newell R Washburn MD, *Treasurer*
Susan L Rogers MD, *Admin Sec*
EMP: 43
SQ FT: 5,000
SALES (est): 6.2MM **Privately Held**
WEB: www.baysidehealth.com
SIC: 8011 Obstetrician; gynecologist; general & family practice, physician/surgeon

(G-3365)
BAYVIEW ENDOSCOPY CENTER
Also Called: Eastern Shore Gastroenterology
33663 Bayview Med Dr 3 (19958)
PHONE 302 644-0455
Harry Anagnostakos, *President*
Robert Decmann, *Officer*
Palow Piginnie, *Officer*
EMP: 14
SALES (est): 610.4K **Privately Held**
SIC: 8062 General medical & surgical hospitals

(G-3366)
BEACH BABIES CHILD CARE (PA)
31169 Learning Ln (19958-3686)
PHONE 302 644-1585
Deborah Toner, *Owner*
Thomas Toner, *Owner*
EMP: 40 EST: 1997
SALES (est): 2.5MM **Privately Held**
WEB: www.beachbabieschildcare.com
SIC: 8351 Preschool center

(G-3367)
BEACH TIME
32191 Nassau Rd (19958-3762)
PHONE 302 644-2850
Greg Christmas, *Owner*
Mary Ann Christmas, *Owner*
EMP: 8
SALES: 50K **Privately Held**
SIC: 2085 Distilled & blended liquors

(G-3368)
BEACON MOTEL
514 E Savannah Rd (19958-1161)
PHONE 302 645-4888
Janice Lingo, *Owner*
EMP: 30 EST: 1997
SALES (est): 843K **Privately Held**
WEB: www.beaconmotel.com
SIC: 7011 Motels

(G-3369)
BEEBE HOSPITAL HS
424 E Savannah Rd (19958)
PHONE 302 645-3565
Andrew Fitzee, *Owner*
EMP: 8
SALES (est): 174.2K **Privately Held**
SIC: 8062 General medical & surgical hospitals

(G-3370)
BEEBE MEDICAL CENTER INC (PA)
Also Called: BEEBE MEDICAL CENTER HOME HEAL
424 Savannah Rd (19958-1462)
P.O. Box 226 (19958-0226)
PHONE 302 645-3300
Rick Schaffner, *CEO*
Paul T Cowan, *Principal*
David A Herbert, *Principal*
Christopher J Weeks, *Principal*
Kathy Ellis, *Regional Mgr*
EMP: 800
SQ FT: 196,556
SALES: 447.8MM **Privately Held**
SIC: 8062 General medical & surgical hospitals

(G-3371)
BEEBE MEDICAL CENTER INC
440 Market St (19958-1308)
PHONE 302 645-3300
Jeffrey M Fried, *President*
EMP: 124
SALES (corp-wide): 447.8MM **Privately Held**
SIC: 8062 General medical & surgical hospitals
PA: Beebe Medical Center, Inc.
 424 Savannah Rd
 Lewes DE 19958
 302 645-3300

(G-3372)
BEEBE MEDICAL CENTER INC
Also Called: Beebe Healthcare
431 Savannah Rd Bldg C (19958-1460)
PHONE 302 645-3629
James Bartle, *Branch Mgr*
Beebe Stories, *Med Doctor*
EMP: 21
SALES (corp-wide): 447.8MM **Privately Held**
SIC: 8062 General medical & surgical hospitals
PA: Beebe Medical Center, Inc.
 424 Savannah Rd
 Lewes DE 19958
 302 645-3300

(G-3373)
BEEBE MEDICAL FOUNDATION (HQ)
Also Called: BEEBE MEDICAL CENTER HOME HEAL
902 Savannah Rd (19958-1511)
P.O. Box 226 (19958-0226)
PHONE 302 644-2900
Paul Townsend, *Principal*
Alex Sydnor, *Exec Dir*
EMP: 6
SALES: 4.1MM
SALES (corp-wide): 447.8MM **Privately Held**
SIC: 7389 Fund raising organizations
PA: Beebe Medical Center, Inc.
 424 Savannah Rd
 Lewes DE 19958
 302 645-3300

(G-3374)
BEEBE PHYSICIAN NETWORK INC
Also Called: BEEBE MEDICAL CENTER HOME HEAL
1515 Savannah Rd Ste 103 (19958-1675)
P.O. Box 226 (19958-0226)
PHONE 302 645-1805
EMP: 50
SALES: 37.3MM
SALES (corp-wide): 447.8MM **Privately Held**
SIC: 8011 Medical centers
PA: Beebe Medical Center, Inc.
 424 Savannah Rd
 Lewes DE 19958
 302 645-3300

(G-3375)
BEEBE SCHOOL OF NURSING
424 Savannah Rd (19958-1462)
PHONE 302 645-3251
Connie Bushey, *Principal*
EMP: 11
SALES (est): 354.7K **Privately Held**
SIC: 8051 Skilled nursing care facilities

(G-3376)
BELL MANUFACTURING COMPANY INC
31971 Carneros Ave (19958-2501)
PHONE 302 703-2684
Thomas Bell, *Owner*
EMP: 2
SALES (est): 116.1K **Privately Held**
SIC: 3999 Manufacturing industries

(G-3377)
BESECURE LLC
16192 Coastal Hwy (19958-3608)
PHONE 855 897-0650
Andreas Lalos, *CEO*
EMP: 25
SALES: 5MM **Privately Held**
SIC: 7382 Security systems services

(G-3378)
BEST GRANITE LLC
95 Tulip Dr (19958-1612)
PHONE 302 644-8302
Christine A Becker,
▲ EMP: 6 EST: 2008
SALES (est): 1.3MM **Privately Held**
SIC: 5032 Granite building stone

(G-3379)
BETHEL UNITED METHODIST CHURCH
129 W 4th St (19958-1333)
PHONE 302 645-9426
Rev Fred W Duncan, *Pastor*
Earle Baker, *Pastor*
Donna Dickey, *Assistant*
EMP: 25
SALES (est): 990K **Privately Held**
WEB: www.bethellewes.org
SIC: 8661 8351 Methodist Church; nursery school

(G-3380)
BETTAN TRUCKING LLC
19347 Beaver Dam Rd (19958-5539)
PHONE 302 841-3834
Jonathan Hall,
EMP: 20
SALES: 500K **Privately Held**
SIC: 4731 Freight transportation arrangement

(G-3381)
BHASKAR PALEKAR MD PA
1526 Savannah Rd Ste 1 (19958-1683)
P.O. Box 519, Georgetown (19947-0519)
PHONE 302 645-1805
Bhaskar Palekar MD, *Owner*

Lewes - Sussex County (G-3382)

EMP: 8
SALES (est): 95K **Privately Held**
SIC: 8011 General & family practice, physician/surgeon

(G-3382)
BHASKAR S PALEKAR MD PA
1526 Savannah Rd Ste 2 (19958-1683)
PHONE..................................302 645-1806
Bhaskar Palekar, *Principal*
EMP: 4
SALES (est): 130.1K **Privately Held**
SIC: 8011 Offices & clinics of medical doctors

(G-3383)
BIBLION
205 2nd St (19958-1354)
PHONE..................................302 644-2210
Jen Mason, *Owner*
EMP: 5
SALES: 150K **Privately Held**
SIC: 5942 8999 Comic books; editorial service

(G-3384)
BIHBRAND INC
16192 Coastal Hwy (19958-3608)
PHONE..................................302 223-4330
Grace Enow Maximuangu, *Director*
EMP: 10
SALES (est): 46.5K **Privately Held**
SIC: 7929 Entertainers & entertainment groups

(G-3385)
BILL M DOUTHAT JR
Also Called: Unicare Transport Service
17468 Slipper Shell Way # 16 (19958-6316)
P.O. Box 677802, Orlando FL (32867-7802)
PHONE..................................407 977-2273
Bill Douthat Jr, *Owner*
EMP: 12
SALES: 350K **Privately Held**
SIC: 4119 Ambulance service

(G-3386)
BLAIR A JONES DDS
34359 Carpenters Way (19958-4910)
PHONE..................................302 226-1115
Blair Jones, *Executive*
EMP: 8
SALES (est): 84.5K **Privately Held**
SIC: 8021 Offices & clinics of dentists

(G-3387)
BLOCKFREIGHT INC
16192 Coastal Hwy (19958-3608)
PHONE..................................614 350-2252
EMP: 14
SALES (est): 532.3K **Privately Held**
SIC: 4731 Freight Transportation Arrangement

(G-3388)
BLUENT LLC
16192 Coastal Hwy (19958-3608)
PHONE..................................832 476-8459
Sajeel Khanna, *Mng Member*
Mandy Goldman,
Tanya Kumar,
Norman Moore,
◆ EMP: 75
SQ FT: 6,000
SALES: 3MM **Privately Held**
WEB: www.bluent.com
SIC: 7379 7373 Computer related consulting services; computer-aided system services

(G-3389)
BLUEWATER WIND LLC
700 Pilottown Rd (19958-1242)
PHONE..................................302 731-7020
Peter Mandelstam, *President*
EMP: 5
SALES (est): 5.9MM **Publicly Held**
SIC: 5083 Wind machines (frost protection equipment)
PA: Nrg Energy, Inc.
804 Carnegie Ctr
Princeton NJ 08540

(G-3390)
BOARD OF PUBLIC WORKS INC
Also Called: Lewes Waste Water Trtmnt Plant
116 American Legion Rd (19958-1194)
PHONE..................................302 645-6450
Walter Baumer, *Manager*
EMP: 4 **Privately Held**
WEB: www.ci.lewes.de.us
SIC: 7699 Waste cleaning services
PA: Lewes Board Of Public Works
107 Franklin Ave
Lewes DE 19958
302 645-6228

(G-3391)
BREAKTHRUGH CPITL PARTNERS LLC
16192 Coastal Hwy (19958-3608)
PHONE..................................212 381-4420
Will Bermender,
EMP: 4 EST: 2017
SALES (est): 183.8K **Privately Held**
SIC: 6726 Investment offices

(G-3392)
BSBV INC
16192 Coastal Hwy (19958-3608)
PHONE..................................631 201-2044
Juergen Schmitt,
EMP: 8
SALES (est): 182.5K **Privately Held**
SIC: 7371 Computer software development & applications

(G-3393)
BUCHSPOT LLC
16192 Coastal Hwy (19958-3608)
PHONE..................................302 715-1253
Elena Buettner,
EMP: 1 EST: 2017
SALES (est): 37.5K **Privately Held**
SIC: 2741 Miscellaneous publishing

(G-3394)
BUSINESS AT INTERNATIONAL LLC
16192 Coastal Hwy (19958-3608)
PHONE..................................605 610-4885
Hoang Dinh Chinh,
EMP: 20
SALES (est): 311.7K **Privately Held**
SIC: 7389 Financial services

(G-3395)
BUSINESS SERVICES CORP
11 New Hampshire Ave (19958-1020)
PHONE..................................302 645-0400
Donald Bland, *President*
EMP: 1
SQ FT: 500
SALES (est): 105.1K **Privately Held**
SIC: 7372 Business oriented computer software

(G-3396)
BYTE TECHNOLOGY SYSTEMS INC
16192 Coastal Hwy (19958-3608)
PHONE..................................347 687-7240
Syed Safeeullah Shah, *CEO*
EMP: 5
SALES: 100K **Privately Held**
SIC: 7389 Business services

(G-3397)
C AND C ALPACA FACTORY
17219 Sweetbriar Rd (19958-4028)
PHONE..................................609 752-7894
Christian Addor, *Principal*
EMP: 2
SALES (est): 163.7K **Privately Held**
SIC: 2211 Alpacas, cotton

(G-3398)
C KS HAIRPORT LTD SALON & SPA
Also Called: C K'S Hair Port
34410 Tenley Ct Unit 5 (19958-4202)
PHONE..................................302 645-2246
Kay Barnett, *Owner*
EMP: 7
SALES (est): 155.1K **Privately Held**
SIC: 7231 Hairdressers

(G-3399)
CADBURY AT LEWES INC
17028 Cadbury Cir (19958-7022)
PHONE..................................302 644-6382
Victor D Amey, *CEO*
Kathleen Horton, *CFO*
EMP: 100
SALES: 14.7MM **Privately Held**
SIC: 8051 Convalescent home with continuous nursing care

(G-3400)
CAPE FINANCIAL SERVICES INC
Also Called: CFS Construction
16117 Willow Creek Rd (19958-3620)
P.O. Box 758 (19958-0758)
PHONE..................................302 645-6274
L Thomas Miller, *President*
Kevin Miller, *Vice Pres*
Linda F Miller, *Vice Pres*
EMP: 14
SQ FT: 3,200
SALES (est): 1.9MM **Privately Held**
SIC: 1521 1531 1542 New construction, single-family houses; general remodeling, single-family houses; speculative builder, single-family houses; commercial & office building, new construction

(G-3401)
CAPE GAZETTE LTD
17585 Nassau Commons Blvd # 6 (19958-6286)
P.O. Box 213 (19958-0213)
PHONE..................................302 645-7700
Dennis Forney, *President*
Trish Vernon, *Advt Staff*
EMP: 25
SALES (est): 1.8MM **Privately Held**
WEB: www.capegazette.com
SIC: 2711 Newspapers, publishing & printing

(G-3402)
CAPE MEDICAL ASSOCIATES PA
Also Called: James Marvel Jr MD
701 Savannah Rd Ste B (19958-1557)
PHONE..................................302 645-2805
James Marvel Jr, *President*
Mark J Boytim, *Principal*
Paul J Harriot MD, *Principal*
EMP: 15
SQ FT: 2,500
SALES (est): 1.6MM **Privately Held**
SIC: 8011 Orthopedic physician

(G-3403)
CAPE SURGICAL ASSOCIATES PA
750 Kings Hwy Ste 103 (19958-1772)
PHONE..................................302 645-7050
Alae Zarif MD, *Principal*
Erik D Stancofski, *Med Doctor*
EMP: 4
SALES (est): 440.6K **Privately Held**
SIC: 8011 Surgeon

(G-3404)
CAPSTONE HOMES LLC
33712 Wescoats Rd Unit 5 (19958-4926)
P.O. Box 212 (19958-0212)
PHONE..................................302 644-0300
Scott Dailey,
EMP: 7
SALES (est): 573.7K **Privately Held**
SIC: 8748 Business consulting

(G-3405)
CARDIOLOGY CONSULTANTS
16704 Kings Hwy (19958-4929)
PHONE..................................302 645-1233
Judy Callaghan, *Branch Mgr*
Barry S Denenberg, *Med Doctor*
Rob Myers, *Cardiology*
Kenneth Sunnergren, *Cardiology*
Ajith Kumar, *Cardiovascular*
EMP: 15
SQ FT: 9,000
SALES (est): 1.7MM **Privately Held**
SIC: 8011 Cardiologist & cardio-vascular specialist
PA: Cardiology Consultants
35141 Atlantic Ave Unit 3
Millville DE 19967

(G-3406)
CARL KING TIRE CO INC
96 Tulip Dr (19958-1689)
PHONE..................................302 644-4070
Carl King, *CEO*
EMP: 10
SALES (corp-wide): 12.8MM **Privately Held**
SIC: 5014 5531 Automobile tires & tubes; automotive tires
PA: Carl King Tire Co., Inc.
109 S Main St
Camden DE 19934
302 697-9506

(G-3407)
CAROL BOYD HERON
Also Called: Peninsula Gallery
520 E Savannah Rd (19958-1161)
PHONE..................................302 645-0551
Carol Boyd-Heron, *Owner*
EMP: 2
SALES (est): 120K **Privately Held**
WEB: www.peninsula-gallery.com
SIC: 2499 5999 Picture frame molding, finished; alcoholic beverage making equipment & supplies

(G-3408)
CAROLYN A DRKOWSKI HT ASCP LLC
20845 Crest Ct (19958-5597)
PHONE..................................443 831-4854
Carolyn Durkowski, *Principal*
EMP: 1 EST: 2009
SALES: 20K **Privately Held**
SIC: 2835 In vitro & in vivo diagnostic substances

(G-3409)
CARTER POOL MANAGEMENT LLC
35740 Cutter Ct (19958-5020)
P.O. Box 288 (19958-0288)
PHONE..................................302 236-6952
Laura Draper Carter,
EMP: 16
SALES (est): 783.1K **Privately Held**
SIC: 7389 Swimming pool & hot tub service & maintenance

(G-3410)
CARUSO RICHARD F MD PA
Also Called: Seaside Gstrointerology Conslt
130 Savannah Rd Ste B (19958-1463)
P.O. Box 472 (19958-0472)
PHONE..................................302 645-6698
Richard F Caruso MD, *Owner*
David V Reindl, *Gastroenterlgy*
EMP: 8
SALES (est): 830K **Privately Held**
SIC: 8011 Gastronomist

(G-3411)
CENTRAL PACIFIC HELICOPTERS
16192 Coastal Hwy (19958-3608)
PHONE..................................760 786-4163
Kenneth Norman, *CEO*
EMP: 1
SALES: 960K **Privately Held**
SIC: 3721 Helicopters

(G-3412)
CHEER INC
Also Called: Lewes Cheer Center
34211 Woods Edge Dr (19958-4917)
PHONE..................................302 645-9239
Fax: 302 644-8327
EMP: 4
SALES (est): 135.8K
SALES (corp-wide): 7.7MM **Privately Held**
SIC: 8322 Individual/Family Services
PA: Cheer, Inc.
546 S Bedford St
Georgetown DE 19947
302 856-5641

(G-3413)
CHILDRENS BEACH HOUSE INC
1800 Bay Ave (19958-1859)
PHONE..................................302 645-9184
Richard Garret, *Exec Dir*
EMP: 10

GEOGRAPHIC SECTION   Lewes - Sussex County (G-3445)

SALES (est): 410.8K
SALES (corp-wide): 2.4MM **Privately Held**
SIC: 7999 8351 Instruction schools, camps & services; preschool center
PA: Children's Beach House Inc
100 W 10th St Ste 411
Wilmington DE 19801
302 655-4288

(G-3414)
CHILDS PLAY AT HOME LLC
11 Hartford Way (19958-9419)
PHONE.................................302 644-3445
Alisha Melesky, *Principal*
EMP: 5
SALES (est): 88.8K **Privately Held**
SIC: 8351 Child day care services

(G-3415)
CHILDS PLAY BY BAY
1510 Savannah Rd (19958-1624)
PHONE.................................302 703-6234
Alisia Melesky, *Owner*
Alesia Griffith, *Co-Owner*
Sarah Dickey, *Director*
EMP: 8
SALES (est): 240.8K **Privately Held**
SIC: 8351 Child day care services

(G-3416)
CHOCOLETTE DISTRIBUTION LLC
16192 Coastal Hwy (19958-3608)
PHONE.................................917 547-8905
Janet Candullo, *Sales Staff*
Arnold W E A Vahrenwald, *Mng Member*
Sergey Stepanov, *Director*
EMP: 5
SALES (est): 119.2K **Privately Held**
SIC: 5149 Chocolate

(G-3417)
CHPT MFG INC
100 Dock Dr (19958-1190)
PHONE.................................302 645-4314
Hicks Douglas, *Owner*
EMP: 2
SALES (est): 176K **Privately Held**
SIC: 3599 Machine shop, jobbing & repair

(G-3418)
CHRIST CARE CARDIAC SURGERY
400 Savannah Rd Ste C (19958-1499)
PHONE.................................302 644-4282
Fernando M Garzia, *Med Doctor*
EMP: 5 EST: 2007
SALES (est): 168.3K **Privately Held**
SIC: 8351 Child day care services

(G-3419)
CHRISTINE FOX DDS
32792 Ocean Reach Dr (19958-4662)
PHONE.................................302 703-2838
Christine Fox, *Principal*
EMP: 4
SALES (est): 180K **Privately Held**
SIC: 8021 Offices & clinics of dentists

(G-3420)
CHRISTMAS CORPORATION
16192 Coastal Hwy (19958-3608)
PHONE.................................424 645-5001
Eduardus Christmas, *CEO*
EMP: 4
SALES (est): 92.1K **Privately Held**
SIC: 7389 Business services

(G-3421)
CHT HOLDINGS LLC
16192 Coastal Hwy (19958-3608)
PHONE.................................954 864-2008
Harrison Vargas, *Mng Member*
Miriam Jimenez, *Executive Asst*
EMP: 15
SQ FT: 1,500
SALES (est): 624.2K **Privately Held**
SIC: 8741 Business management

(G-3422)
CIRCUS ASSOCIATES INTELLIGENCE
Also Called: Circus Associates, The
16192 Coastal Hwy (19958-3608)
PHONE.................................757 663-7864
Paul Flowers,
Amanda Valcik, *Master*
EMP: 41
SALES (est): 663.6K **Privately Held**
SIC: 8742 8732 Business consultant; research services, except laboratory

(G-3423)
CITIZENS BANK NATIONAL ASSN
34161 Citizen Dr (19958-4722)
PHONE.................................302 360-6101
Erin Baker, *Branch Mgr*
EMP: 10
SALES (corp-wide): 7.3B **Publicly Held**
SIC: 6022 State commercial banks
HQ: Citizens Bank, National Association
1 Citizens Plz Ste 1 # 1
Providence RI 02903
401 282-7000

(G-3424)
CITIZENS BANK NATIONAL ASSN
131 2nd St (19958-1323)
PHONE.................................302 645-2024
Dennise Durton, *Branch Mgr*
EMP: 7
SALES (corp-wide): 7.3B **Publicly Held**
SIC: 6022 State commercial banks
HQ: Citizens Bank, National Association
1 Citizens Plz Ste 1 # 1
Providence RI 02903
401 282-7000

(G-3425)
CLARIUS MOBILE HEALTH CORP
16192 Coastal Hwy (19958-3608)
PHONE.................................778 800-9975
Don Wright, *CFO*
EMP: 2
SALES (est): 86.6K **Privately Held**
SIC: 3841 Surgical & medical instruments

(G-3426)
CLASSROOMAPP INC
16192 Coastal Hwy (19958-3608)
PHONE.................................833 257-7761
Ramez Rafla, *President*
EMP: 10
SALES (est): 2MM **Privately Held**
SIC: 7371 Computer software development & applications

(G-3427)
CLEAN DELAWARE LLC
33852 Clay Rd (19958-6321)
P.O. Box 123, Milton (19968-0123)
PHONE.................................302 684-4221
Gerry Desmonz, *Mng Member*
EMP: 30 EST: 2011
SALES (est): 100.3K **Privately Held**
SIC: 7699 1711 Cleaning services; septic system construction

(G-3428)
CLEANERS SUNNY
17601 Coastal Hwy (19958-6217)
PHONE.................................302 827-2095
Sunhui Seo, *Owner*
EMP: 5
SALES (est): 105.4K **Privately Held**
SIC: 7349 Building & office cleaning services

(G-3429)
CLINIC BY SEA
16295 Willow Creek Rd (19958-3614)
PHONE.................................302 644-0999
Zeina Jeha, *Principal*
EMP: 6
SALES (est): 601.1K **Privately Held**
SIC: 8011 Cardiologist & cardio-vascular specialist

(G-3430)
CLOUDBEES INC
16192 Coastal Hwy (19958-3608)
PHONE.................................804 767-5481
Austin Morris, *Opers Staff*
Zackery Mahon, *Manager*
Martha Samper, *Manager*
Derek Dougherty, *Executive*
EMP: 12 **Privately Held**
SIC: 7371 Software programming applications
PA: Cloudbees, Inc.
16192 Coastal Hwy
Lewes DE 19958

(G-3431)
CLOUDBEES INC (PA)
16192 Coastal Hwy (19958-3608)
PHONE.................................323 842-7783
Sacha Labourey, *CEO*
Susan Lally, *Vice Pres*
Andre Pino, *Vice Pres*
Matt Parson, *CFO*
Laurence Poussot, *VP Finance*
EMP: 15
SALES (est): 700K **Privately Held**
SIC: 7371 Computer software development

(G-3432)
CLYDE BERGEMANN PWR GROUP LLC
16192 Coastal Hwy (19958-3608)
PHONE.................................770 557-3600
Franz Bartels, *Mng Member*
EMP: 60 **Privately Held**
SIC: 6719 Investment holding companies, except banks
PA: Clyde Bergemann Power Group Americas Inc.
4015 Presidential Pkwy
Atlanta GA 30340

(G-3433)
CLYMENE LLC
16192 Coastal Hwy (19958-3608)
PHONE.................................888 679-3310
Kambiz Behi, *Director*
EMP: 5 EST: 2015
SALES (est): 189.5K **Privately Held**
SIC: 7371 Custom computer programming services

(G-3434)
COAST SURVEY
32261 Nassau Rd (19958-4071)
P.O. Box 117, Nassau (19969-0117)
PHONE.................................302 645-7184
Robert Rykel, *President*
Yvonne Moore, *Manager*
EMP: 6
SALES (est): 280K **Privately Held**
SIC: 8713 Surveying services

(G-3435)
COASTAL CLUB SCHELL BROTHERS
31605 Exeter Way (19958-5827)
PHONE.................................302 966-0063
EMP: 4
SALES (est): 56.3K **Privately Held**
SIC: 7997 Membership sports & recreation clubs

(G-3436)
COASTAL COATINGS INC
17993 American Way (19958-4799)
PHONE.................................302 645-1399
EMP: 2
SALES (est): 144K **Privately Held**
SIC: 3479 Metal coating & allied service

(G-3437)
COASTAL CONCERTS INC
Bethel United Methodist (19958)
P.O. Box 685 (19958-0685)
PHONE.................................302 645-1539
Denise Emery, *President*
Edna V Ellett, *Exec Dir*
EMP: 9
SALES: 128K **Privately Held**
SIC: 7929 Entertainers & entertainment groups

(G-3438)
COASTAL PAIN CARE PHYSCIANS PA
1606 Savannah Rd Ste 8 (19958-1656)
PHONE.................................302 644-8330
Gabriel Somori, *Principal*
EMP: 12
SALES (est): 910K **Privately Held**
SIC: 8011 Medical centers

(G-3439)
COASTAL TOWING INC
33012 Cedar Grove Rd (19958-4644)
PHONE.................................302 645-6300
Charles Moore, *President*
EMP: 9
SALES (est): 848.8K **Privately Held**
SIC: 7549 7539 7538 Towing service, automotive; automotive repair shops; general truck repair

(G-3440)
CODESHIP INC
16192 Coastal Hwy (19958-3608)
PHONE.................................617 515-3664
Moritz Plassnig, *President*
Chris Wolfgang, *Editor*
Dmitry Belakhov, *Vice Pres*
Manuel Weiss, *Vice Pres*
Daniel Curtis, *CFO*
EMP: 15
SQ FT: 2,000
SALES (est): 84K **Privately Held**
SIC: 7371 Computer software development
PA: Cloudbees, Inc.
16192 Coastal Hwy
Lewes DE 19958

(G-3441)
CODITAS INC
16192 Coastal Hwy (19958-3608)
PHONE.................................888 220-6200
EMP: 2
SALES (est): 56.5K **Privately Held**
SIC: 7372 Application computer software

(G-3442)
COLONIAL EAST LP
16 Manor House Ln (19958-4165)
PHONE.................................302 644-4758
Stevan Class, *Partner*
Deborah Coverdale, *Controller*
EMP: 12
SALES (est): 2.2MM **Privately Held**
SIC: 6515 Mobile home site operators

(G-3443)
COMMTRAK CORPORATION
17493 Nassau Commons Blvd (19958-6283)
P.O. Box 1100, Rehoboth Beach (19971-5100)
PHONE.................................302 644-1600
Gene Wilson, *President*
Roger Miersch, *Vice Pres*
EMP: 8
SQ FT: 1,800
SALES (est): 721.8K **Privately Held**
WEB: www.commtrak.com
SIC: 7322 7371 Collection agency, except real estate; custom computer programming services

(G-3444)
COMMUNITY BANK DELAWARE (PA)
16982 Kings Hwy (19958-4785)
P.O. Box 742 (19958-0742)
PHONE.................................302 348-8600
Jack Riddle, *President*
Angie Warrell, *CFO*
EMP: 30
SALES: 8.9MM **Privately Held**
WEB: www.communitybankdelaware.com
SIC: 6022 State trust companies accepting deposits, commercial

(G-3445)
COUNTY BANK
Also Called: Five Points
1609 Savannah Rd (19958-1625)
PHONE.................................302 645-8880
Gavin Radka, *Manager*
EMP: 9 **Privately Held**

Lewes - Sussex County (G-3446)   GEOGRAPHIC SECTION

WEB: www.countybankdel.com
SIC: 6021 National commercial banks
PA: County Bank
   19927 Shuttle Rd
   Rehoboth Beach DE 19971

(G-3446)
COUNTY WOMEN S JOURNAL
17252 N Village Main Blvd # 9 (19958-6292)
P.O. Box 57 (19958-0057)
PHONE..................302 236-1435
EMP: 4 **EST:** 2008
SALES (est): 206.9K **Privately Held**
SIC: 2711 Newspapers, publishing & printing

(G-3447)
CYCOLOGY 202 LLC (PA)
23924 Sunny Cove Ct (19958-5695)
PHONE..................610 202-0518
Ellen Spell,
EMP: 12
SALES: 500K **Privately Held**
SIC: 7991 7389 Exercise facilities;

(G-3448)
DAVID I WALSH ESQUIRE PA
20640 Hopkins Rd (19958-5521)
P.O. Box 1217, Bear (19701-7217)
PHONE..................302 498-0760
EMP: 4
SALES (est): 259K
SALES (corp-wide): 283.1K **Privately Held**
SIC: 8111 Specialized law offices, attorneys
PA: David I. Walsh, Esquire, P.A.
   1 Langley Ct
   Newark DE 19702
   302 498-0760

(G-3449)
DEBAY SURGICAL SERVICE
Also Called: Delaware Surgical Service
33664 Bayview Medical Dr (19958-1687)
PHONE..................302 644-4954
Mayer Catz, *President*
EMP: 12
SALES (est): 666.8K **Privately Held**
SIC: 8011 Orthopedic physician

(G-3450)
DECOY MAGAZINE
102 2nd St (19958-1324)
P.O. Box 787 (19958-0787)
PHONE..................302 644-9001
Joe Engers, *Owner*
EMP: 1 **EST:** 2007
SALES (est): 114.4K **Privately Held**
SIC: 2721 8748 Magazines: publishing & printing; publishing consultant

(G-3451)
DEIRDE A MCCARTNEY
Also Called: MCCARTNEY DEIRDE A
34382 Carpenters Way # 1 (19958-4919)
PHONE..................302 644-8330
Ellen Feinberg, *Principal*
EMP: 4
SALES (corp-wide): 1.4MM **Privately Held**
SIC: 8111 General practice attorney, lawyer
PA: Sergovic Carmean Weidman Mccartney & Owens, P.A
   406 S Bedford St Ste 1
   Georgetown DE 19947
   302 855-0551

(G-3452)
DEL MARVA HAND SPECIALISTS LLC
701 Savannah Rd Ste B (19958-1550)
PHONE..................302 644-0940
Scott M Schulze, *Owner*
EMP: 6
SALES (est): 372.3K **Privately Held**
SIC: 8011 Surgeon

(G-3453)
DELAWARE BAY & RIVER
700 Pilottown Rd (19958-1242)
PHONE..................302 645-7861
Gene Johnson, *President*
EMP: 17

SALES (est): 842.6K **Privately Held**
SIC: 4959 Oil spill cleanup

(G-3454)
DELAWARE BAY SURGICAL SVC PA
33664 Bayvw Med Dr Ste 2 (19958-1687)
PHONE..................302 645-5650
Mayer M Katz, *President*
EMP: 16
SALES (est): 1.3MM **Privately Held**
SIC: 8062 General medical & surgical hospitals

(G-3455)
DELAWARE BREAST CANCER COALIT
16529 Coastal Hwy (19958-3696)
PHONE..................302 644-6844
Cheryl Doucette, *Principal*
EMP: 6
SALES (est): 152.5K
SALES (corp-wide): 1.2MM **Privately Held**
SIC: 8322 Social service center
PA: Delaware Breast Cancer Coalition, Inc.
   100 W 10th St Ste 209
   Wilmington DE 19801
   302 778-1102

(G-3456)
DELAWARE CRDOVASCULAR ASSOC PA
34453 King Street Row (19958-4787)
PHONE..................302 644-7676
Tina Ruggeri, *Office Mgr*
Dimitrios Barmpouletos, *Med Doctor*
Grace Walls Do, *Manager*
Ehtasham Qureshi, *Cardiovascular*
EMP: 15 **Privately Held**
WEB: www.delawarecardiovascular.com
SIC: 8011 Cardiologist & cardio-vascular specialist
PA: Delaware Cardiovascular Associates, P.A.
   1403 Foulk Rd Ste 101a
   Wilmington DE 19803

(G-3457)
DELAWARE RIVER & BAY AUTHORITY
Also Called: Cape May-Lewes Ferry
43 Cape Henlopen Dr (19958-3142)
P.O. Box 517 (19958-0517)
PHONE..................800 643-3779
Richard Castrati, *Manager*
EMP: 25
SALES (corp-wide): 139.5MM **Privately Held**
WEB: www.drba.net
SIC: 4482 9621 Ferries operating across rivers or within harbors; water vessels & port regulating agencies;
PA: Delaware River & Bay Authority
   Interstate 295 New Castle
   New Castle DE 19720
   302 571-6303

(G-3458)
DELAWARE TITLE LOANS INC
17672 Coastal Hwy (19958-6214)
PHONE..................302 644-3640
Christine Stclair, *Manager*
EMP: 8
SALES (corp-wide): 7.7MM **Privately Held**
SIC: 6163 Loan agents
PA: Delaware Title Loans, Inc.
   8601 Dunwoody Pl Ste 406
   Atlanta GA 30350
   770 552-9840

(G-3459)
DELMARVA BARIATRIC FITNES CTR
17487 Taramino Pl (19958-6243)
PHONE..................410 341-6180
EMP: 6
SALES (est): 695.6K **Privately Held**
SIC: 8011 Medical Doctor's Office

(G-3460)
DELMARVAVOIP LLC
16557 Coastal Hwy (19958-3605)
PHONE..................855 645-8647

Larry Poli, *Vice Pres*
EMP: 4
SALES (est): 264.1K **Privately Held**
SIC: 7379

(G-3461)
DENTAL GROUP
Also Called: Barnhart, Ryan DDS
34359 Carpenters Way (19958-4910)
PHONE..................302 645-8993
Blair A Jones DMD, *Principal*
Melissa Jones, *Financial Exec*
Charles J Labin, *Med Doctor*
EMP: 8
SALES (est): 750K **Privately Held**
SIC: 8021 Dental clinic

(G-3462)
DESIGN DELMARVA
1304 Savannah Rd (19958-1526)
PHONE..................302 644-8884
Stephen E Wagner, *Owner*
Travis Durant, *Internal Med*
EMP: 5
SALES (est): 250K **Privately Held**
SIC: 8712 House designer

(G-3463)
DESTINY RESCUE INTL INC
16192 Coastal Hwy (19958-3608)
P.O. Box 25684, Fort Wayne IN (46825-0684)
PHONE..................574 529-2238
Tony Kirwan, *President*
EMP: 7 **EST:** 2015
SALES (est): 437.1K **Privately Held**
SIC: 8999 Search & rescue service

(G-3464)
DICK ENNIS INC
22357 John J Williams Hwy (19958-4370)
PHONE..................302 945-2627
Harold R Ennis Jr, *President*
Richard Ennis, *President*
EMP: 6
SALES (est): 1.2MM **Privately Held**
SIC: 5211 1389 0782 4492 Modular homes; construction, repair & dismantling services; lawn care services; marine towing services; landscape services

(G-3465)
DIEHL & CO CPA
18306 Coastal Hwy (19958-4772)
PHONE..................302 644-4441
Mark Diehl, *Owner*
Don Foraker, *Mng Member*
EMP: 4
SALES (est): 277.1K **Privately Held**
SIC: 8721 Certified public accountant

(G-3466)
DIRT WORKS INC
22547 Waterview Rd (19958-5749)
P.O. Box 511 (19958-0511)
PHONE..................302 947-2429
Clint Fluharty, *President*
EMP: 16
SALES: 1.5MM **Privately Held**
SIC: 1794 Excavation work

(G-3467)
DISCOVERY SOLUTIONS INC
16192 Coastal Hwy (19958-3608)
PHONE..................410 929-0025
Don McLaughlin, *President*
EMP: 6
SALES (est): 483K **Privately Held**
SIC: 0782 Lawn services

(G-3468)
DOGFISH INN
105 Savannah Rd (19958-1437)
PHONE..................302 644-8292
EMP: 5 **EST:** 2014
SALES (est): 116K **Privately Held**
SIC: 7011 Inns

(G-3469)
DONE AGAIN SOFTWARE LLC
31736 Marsh Island Ave (19958-3351)
P.O. Box 366, Nassau (19969-0366)
PHONE..................301 466-7858
Gerald Donegan,
EMP: 1

SALES (est): 35.4K **Privately Held**
SIC: 7371 7372 Computer software systems analysis & design, custom; computer software development & applications; computer software development; application computer software

(G-3470)
DOUBLE R HOLDINGS INC
1009 Kings Hwy (19958-1731)
PHONE..................302 645-5555
Robert Burton, *President*
Jeffrey Burton, *Vice Pres*
EMP: 5
SALES (est): 242.6K **Privately Held**
SIC: 6519 Real property lessors

(G-3471)
DOUGLAS DITTY DMD MD
37718 Wescoats Rd (19958)
PHONE..................302 644-2977
Douglas Ditty, *Principal*
EMP: 4
SALES (est): 92.4K **Privately Held**
SIC: 8021 Dental surgeon

(G-3472)
DREAMVILLE LLC
16192 Coastal Hwy (19958-3608)
PHONE..................662 524-0917
Justin Bobo,
EMP: 6
SALES (est): 144K **Privately Held**
SIC: 8742 6531 Management consulting services; real estate leasing & rentals

(G-3473)
DRFISH LLC
16192 Coastal Hwy (19958-3608)
PHONE..................978 393-1212
Yang Wenjun,
EMP: 4
SALES (est): 92.1K **Privately Held**
SIC: 7389 Personal service agents, brokers & bureaus

(G-3474)
DRIFTWOOD CABINETRY LLC
1009 Kings Hwy (19958-1731)
PHONE..................302 645-4876
EMP: 2 **EST:** 2010
SALES (est): 132.4K **Privately Held**
SIC: 2434 Wood kitchen cabinets

(G-3475)
DRONE DELIVERY SYSTEMS CORP
33572 Westgate Cir Unit 1 (19958-6508)
PHONE..................757 903-5006
Brandon T Pargoe, *CEO*
Will Stavanja, *CTO*
Dr Jeremy Tucker, *Director*
Lukas Wrede, *Director*
EMP: 6
SALES (est): 72.7K **Privately Held**
SIC: 4212 Delivery service, vehicular

(G-3476)
DYNAMIC THERAPY SERVICES LLC
1415 Savannah Rd Unit 1 (19958-1794)
PHONE..................302 703-2355
Holly Firuta, *Branch Mgr*
EMP: 16
SALES (corp-wide): 12.9MM **Privately Held**
SIC: 8049 Physical therapist
PA: Dynamic Therapy Services Llc
   1501 Blueball Ave
   Linwood PA 19061
   610 859-8850

(G-3477)
EAGER GEAR
19413 Jingle Shell Way # 6 (19958-6307)
PHONE..................302 727-5831
EMP: 1 **EST:** 2015
SALES (est): 71K **Privately Held**
SIC: 3462 Gear & chain forgings

(G-3478)
EDC LLC
Also Called: Element Design Group
115 W Market St Fl 2 (19958-1309)
PHONE..................302 645-0777

GEOGRAPHIC SECTION

Lewes - Sussex County (G-3510)

Katie Harp, *Office Mgr*
Douglas M Warner, *Mng Member*
Douglas Warner, *Mng Member*
EMP: 11
SALES: 1.7MM **Privately Held**
WEB: www.elementdg.com
SIC: 8712 8711 0781 Architectural services; structural engineering; landscape architects

(G-3479)
EDOKK LLC ✪
16192 Coastal Hwy (19958-3608)
PHONE..................................305 434-7227
Mariano Cariola, *Principal*
EMP: 8 EST: 2019
SALES (est): 151.6K **Privately Held**
SIC: 7389 Business services

(G-3480)
ELEMENT
115 W Market St (19958-1309)
PHONE..................................302 645-0777
Douglas M Warner, *Principal*
EMP: 3
SALES (est): 176.5K **Privately Held**
SIC: 2819 Industrial inorganic chemicals

(G-3481)
ELZUFON AUSTIN REARDON TARLOV
1413 Savannah Rd Unit 1 (19958-1792)
PHONE..................................302 644-0144
Edward A Tarlov, *President*
EMP: 5
SALES (corp-wide): 4.9MM **Privately Held**
SIC: 8111 General practice attorney, lawyer
PA: Elzufon Austin Reardon Tarlov & Mondell, P.A.
300 Delaware Ave Ste 1700
Wilmington DE 19801
302 428-3181

(G-3482)
ENCLAVE DIGITAL DEVELOPMENT CO (PA)
16192 Coastal Hwy (19958-3608)
PHONE..................................203 807-0400
Rory John Diverall Semple, *President*
EMP: 1
SALES: 50K **Privately Held**
SIC: 7372 7389 Application computer software;

(G-3483)
ENVIROTECH ENVMTL CONSULTING
17605 Nassau Commons Blvd (19958-6284)
PHONE..................................302 684-5201
Todd Fritchman, *President*
Patty Benson, *Business Mgr*
EMP: 6
SQ FT: 1,500
SALES (est): 722.8K **Privately Held**
SIC: 8748 Environmental consultant

(G-3484)
ENVIRTECH ENVIROMENTAL CONSLTG
34634 Bay Crossing Blvd (19958-2737)
PHONE..................................302 645-6491
Todd Fritchman, *President*
Glenn Mandalas, *Mng Member*
Kelly Fritchman, *Admin Sec*
EMP: 9
SALES (est): 482.8K **Privately Held**
WEB: www.envirotechecinc.com
SIC: 7389 Aquatic weed maintenance

(G-3485)
ENVISION HEALTHCARE CORP
Also Called: Seaside Endoscopy Pavillion
1451 Kings Hwy Ste 4a (19958)
PHONE..................................302 644-3852
Sandy Kennedy, *Manager*
EMP: 10
SALES (corp-wide): 643.1MM **Privately Held**
SIC: 8062 General medical & surgical hospitals

HQ: Envision Healthcare Corporation
1a Burton Hills Blvd
Nashville TN 37215
615 665-1283

(G-3486)
EQUITY LIFESTYLE PRPTS INC
Also Called: Whispering Pines Community Ctr
32045 Janice Rd (19958-2004)
PHONE..................................302 645-5770
Steven Affer, *Principal*
EMP: 4 **Publicly Held**
SIC: 6515 Mobile home site operators
PA: Equity Lifestyle Properties, Inc.
2 N Riverside Plz Ste 800
Chicago IL 60606

(G-3487)
ERIK M D STANCOFSKI
431 Savannah Rd (19958-1460)
PHONE..................................302 645-7050
E Stancofski, *Executive Asst*
EMP: 6
SALES (est): 80.5K **Privately Held**
SIC: 8011 Offices & clinics of medical doctors

(G-3488)
EVERLIFT WIND TECHNOLOGY
31798 Carneros Ave (19958-2523)
PHONE..................................240 683-9787
George Syrovy, *Owner*
EMP: 4
SALES (est): 165.9K **Privately Held**
SIC: 3511 Turbines & turbine generator sets

(G-3489)
FACTORY SPORTS
17543 Nassau Commons Blvd (19958-6284)
PHONE..................................302 313-4186
EMP: 7 EST: 2016
SALES (est): 178.8K **Privately Held**
SIC: 7997 Membership sports & recreation clubs

(G-3490)
FAITH FMLY FRIENDS HOLDG LLC
16192 Coastal Hwy (19958-3608)
PHONE..................................202 256-4524
Lawrence Manley, *Principal*
EMP: 10
SALES: 120K **Privately Held**
SIC: 6719 Holding companies

(G-3491)
FAMILY PRACTICE CENTER
7 Dunes Ter (19958-3128)
PHONE..................................302 645-2833
Connie Groll, *Executive Asst*
Amy Robinson, *Gnrl Med Prac*
EMP: 10
SALES (est): 963.8K **Privately Held**
SIC: 8011 General & family practice, physician/surgeon

(G-3492)
FARPATH FOUNDATION
800 Bay Ave (19958-1005)
PHONE..................................302 645-8328
Clifford Diver, *Director*
EMP: 6
SALES: 0 **Privately Held**
SIC: 8641 Civic social & fraternal associations

(G-3493)
FAUST SHEET METAL WORKS INC
1636 Savannah Rd Ste A (19958-1657)
P.O. Box 181 (19958-0181)
PHONE..................................302 645-9509
Mike Faust, *President*
EMP: 2
SQ FT: 2,400
SALES: 385K **Privately Held**
SIC: 3444 Metal ventilating equipment; ducts, sheet metal

(G-3494)
FEMMEPAL CORPORATION
Also Called: Underground
16192 Coastal Hwy (19958-3608)
PHONE..................................888 406-0804
Andrew Linney, *CEO*
Rebecca Knuth, *Opers Staff*
EMP: 27
SALES (est): 2.5MM **Privately Held**
SIC: 8742 Management consulting services

(G-3495)
FINDING A VOICE INC
16193 Coastal Hwy (19958)
PHONE..................................315 333-7567
Bjarke Mrythu, *CEO*
Nancy Wolf, *Administration*
EMP: 3
SALES: 100K **Privately Held**
SIC: 2741

(G-3496)
FINE LINE IT CONSULTING LLP
16678 Kings Hwy Ste 1 (19958-4927)
PHONE..................................302 645-4549
Thomas Brown, *Managing Prtnr*
Carney Kinnamon, *Partner*
Zee Sage, *Web Dvlpr*
Thomas B Brown Jr, *Software Dev*
EMP: 6
SALES: 459K **Privately Held**
SIC: 7374 Computer graphics service

(G-3497)
FIRST ATLANTIC MRTG SVCS LLC
Also Called: First Atlantic Mortgage Svcs
16678 Kings Hwy Ste 2 (19958-4927)
PHONE..................................302 841-8435
Brian Grammer,
EMP: 6
SALES (est): 444.7K **Privately Held**
SIC: 6163 Mortgage brokers arranging for loans, using money of others

(G-3498)
FIRST STATE DISPOSAL
15 Bridle Reach Ct (19958-8912)
PHONE..................................302 644-3885
Tom Grogas, *Owner*
EMP: 10
SALES (est): 615.7K **Privately Held**
SIC: 4953 Refuse collection & disposal services

(G-3499)
FIRSTCHOICE GROUP AMERICA LLC
16192 Coastal Hwy (19958-3608)
PHONE..................................425 242-8626
Suresh Jagtiani, *Mng Member*
EMP: 5 **Privately Held**
SIC: 5084 Industrial machinery & equipment
PA: Firstchoice Group America Llc
169 Lewfield Cir Ste 169 # 169
Winter Park FL 32792

(G-3500)
FIRSTCOLLECT INC
12000 Old Vine Blvd (19958-1700)
P.O. Box 102 (19958-0102)
PHONE..................................302 644-6804
Tracy M Hynes, *Principal*
EMP: 8 EST: 2009
SALES (est): 721.1K **Privately Held**
SIC: 7322 Collection agency, except real estate

(G-3501)
FLUENT FOREVER INC
16192 Coastal Hwy (19958-3608)
PHONE..................................262 725-1707
Gabriel Wyner, *CEO*
John Rush, *CTO*
EMP: 10
SALES: 850K **Privately Held**
SIC: 7372 Educational computer software

(G-3502)
FOOT LIGHT PRODUCTION INC
516 Kings Hwy (19958-1456)
PHONE..................................302 645-7220
John Warrener, *President*

EMP: 10
SALES: 200K **Privately Held**
SIC: 7832 Motion picture theaters, except drive-in

(G-3503)
FORT MILES HISTORICAL ASSN INC
120 E Wild Rabbit Run (19958-1632)
PHONE..................................302 645-0753
Gary Wray, *President*
EMP: 4
SALES: 38.5K **Privately Held**
SIC: 8399 Neighborhood development group

(G-3504)
FRONTLINE LLC
16192 Coastal Hwy (19958-3608)
PHONE..................................302 526-0877
Kenneth Rhule, *Principal*
EMP: 5
SQ FT: 1,000
SALES (est): 130.1K **Privately Held**
SIC: 6531 Fiduciary, real estate

(G-3505)
FTL TECHNOLOGIES CORPORATION
Also Called: Silis Security Group
16192 Coastal Hwy (19958-3608)
PHONE..................................703 873-7801
Robert Bass, *Exec Dir*
Alexandra Maria Gomez-Gamboa, *Administration*
EMP: 15
SALES (est): 299.3K **Privately Held**
SIC: 7371 Custom computer programming services

(G-3506)
FULTON BANK NATIONAL ASSN
Also Called: Fulton Financial Advisors
34346 Carpenters Way (19958-4910)
PHONE..................................302 644-4900
Adrianne Morre, *Branch Mgr*
EMP: 5
SALES (corp-wide): 954MM **Publicly Held**
WEB: www.delawarenational.com
SIC: 6021 National commercial banks
HQ: Fulton Bank, National Association
1 Penn Sq Ste 1 # 1
Lancaster PA 17602
717 581-3166

(G-3507)
FX-EDGE LLC
16192 Coastal Hwy (19958-3608)
PHONE..................................718 404-9362
Imran Firoz, *Managing Dir*
EMP: 20
SALES (est): 424.1K **Privately Held**
SIC: 7371 Computer software development & applications

(G-3508)
GARRISON CUSTOM HOMES
19413 Jingle Shell Way # 5 (19958-6307)
PHONE..................................302 644-4008
Jeffrey M Garrison, *Owner*
Trudean Morris, *Finance Mgr*
EMP: 8
SALES (est): 981.7K **Privately Held**
SIC: 1521 New construction, single-family houses

(G-3509)
GCG CAPITAL LLC
16192 Coastal Hwy (19958-3608)
PHONE..................................302 703-7610
Rashad Naqawah,
EMP: 371
SALES: 269.8MM **Privately Held**
SIC: 6719 Investment holding companies, except banks

(G-3510)
GEM MERCHANT LLC
16192 Coastal Hwy (19958-3608)
PHONE..................................734 274-1280
Aaron Savit, *Principal*
EMP: 1

Lewes - Sussex County (G-3511)

SALES (est): 46.7K **Privately Held**
SIC: **5094** 3915 Precious stones (gems); jewelers' materials & lapidary work

(G-3511)
GEORGE W PLUMMER & SON INC
18370 Coastal Hwy (19958-4772)
PHONE..................................302 645-9531
George Plummer III, *President*
Greg E Plummer, *Treasurer*
▲ **EMP:** 7
SQ FT: 8,000
SALES (est): 930.5K **Privately Held**
SIC: 7692 Welding repair

(G-3512)
GET CENTS LLC
16192 Coastal Hwy (19958-3608)
PHONE..................................203 856-0841
Matt Kalmans, *Mng Member*
EMP: 30
SALES (est): 512.1K **Privately Held**
SIC: 7319 Distribution of advertising material or sample services

(G-3513)
GET TAKEOUT LLC
Also Called: Gettakeout.com
16192 Coastal Hwy (19958-3608)
P.O. Box 25653, Portland OR (97298-0653)
PHONE..................................800 785-6218
Frank Halpin, *Managing Prtnr*
EMP: 3
SALES (est): 131.4K **Privately Held**
SIC: 7372 7389 Business oriented computer software;

(G-3514)
GIGKLOUD INC
16192 Coastal Hwy (19958-3608)
PHONE..................................301 375-5008
D William Zero, *CEO*
Jaime Wong Luna, *Vice Pres*
Brett Nelson, *Vice Pres*
Brandon Robinson, *Vice Pres*
Bradley Sackmann, *Vice Pres*
EMP: 10
SALES: 100MM **Privately Held**
SIC: 7371 Computer software development & applications

(G-3515)
GLEN PLAYA INC
16192 Coastal Hwy (19958-3608)
PHONE..................................302 703-7512
Heather Hargett, *CEO*
EMP: 8
SALES (est): 1MM **Privately Held**
SIC: 8741 Financial management for business

(G-3516)
GLOBAL DATA MINING LLC
16192 Coastal Hwy (19958-3608)
PHONE..................................551 208-1316
Boris Tolkachev, *CEO*
EMP: 4
SALES (est): 290K **Privately Held**
SIC: 8742 Marketing consulting services

(G-3517)
GO GO GO INC
Also Called: Estacionamiento Inteligente
16192 Coastal Hwy (19958-3608)
PHONE..................................302 645-7400
Fernando Poch, *Director*
EMP: 6
SALES (est): 55.9K **Privately Held**
SIC: 7521 7372 Automobile parking; application computer software

(G-3518)
GOLDEN COASTAL REALTY
33815 Clay Rd Ste 5 (19958-6297)
PHONE..................................302 360-0226
Carol Golden, *Owner*
EMP: 10
SALES (est): 437.4K **Privately Held**
SIC: 6531 Real estate brokers & agents

(G-3519)
GOLDEN THORNS INC
16192 Coastal Hwy (19958-3608)
PHONE..................................861 598-6748
Xiaohong Bin, *President*
EMP: 8
SALES (est): 180.6K **Privately Held**
SIC: 8742 Retail trade consultant

(G-3520)
GOSSAMER GAMES LLC
16192 Coastal Hwy (19958-3608)
PHONE..................................302 645-7400
Thomas Sharpe,
Jameela Wahlgren,
EMP: 4
SALES (est): 89.7K **Privately Held**
SIC: 7371 Computer software development & applications

(G-3521)
GREEN ACRES FARM INC
18186 Dairy Farm Rd (19958-4505)
PHONE..................................302 645-8652
Walter C Hopkins Sr, *President*
William Hopkins, *Vice Pres*
EMP: 12
SALES (est): 1.4MM **Privately Held**
WEB: www.greenacresfarm.com
SIC: 0191 General farms, primarily crop

(G-3522)
GREEN ROOTS LLC
16192 Coastal Hwy (19958-3608)
PHONE..................................516 643-2621
Manan Patel,
EMP: 5
SALES: 100K **Privately Held**
SIC: 5149 Organic & diet foods

(G-3523)
GREENLEAF SERVICES INC
20393 John J Williams Hwy (19958-4305)
PHONE..................................302 836-9050
Joseph B Winemiller, *President*
Cynthia Winemiller, *Office Mgr*
EMP: 7
SALES: 1.5MM **Privately Held**
SIC: 0782 Landscape contractors

(G-3524)
GRIZZLYS LANDSCAPE SUP & SVCS
20144 John J Williams Hwy (19958-4339)
PHONE..................................302 644-0654
Richard Pack, *Principal*
EMP: 4
SALES (est): 225.2K **Privately Held**
SIC: 0782 Landscape contractors

(G-3525)
GUARDIAN PROPERTY MGT LLC
17298 Coastal Hwy Unit 1 (19958-6226)
PHONE..................................302 227-7878
Susan Jimenez,
Christie Bond, *Associate*
EMP: 20
SALES (est): 1.9MM **Privately Held**
SIC: 6531 Real estate managers

(G-3526)
GULL HOUSE ADULT ACTIVITY
34382 Carpenters Way # 1 (19958-4919)
PHONE..................................302 226-2160
Kay Edman, *Exec Dir*
Kathy Schlitter, *Director*
EMP: 7
SALES (est): 113.1K **Privately Held**
SIC: 8322 Adult day care center

(G-3527)
H & M CONSTRUCTION
4 Bradford Ln (19958-9500)
PHONE..................................302 645-6639
Bernard Meyers, *Partner*
Michael Heck, *Partner*
EMP: 4
SALES (est): 340K **Privately Held**
SIC: 1751 1522 Framing contractor; residential construction

(G-3528)
HAGUE SURFBOARDS
102 Gosling Creek Rd (19958-9592)
PHONE..................................302 745-9336
EMP: 2
SALES (est): 188.3K **Privately Held**
SIC: 3949 Surfboards

(G-3529)
HAIR ARTISTRY
33995 Clay Rd (19958-6310)
PHONE..................................302 645-7167
Dorothy Darley, *Owner*
EMP: 4
SQ FT: 900
SALES (est): 122.7K **Privately Held**
SIC: 7231 Hairdressers

(G-3530)
HALLIGAN INC
16192 Coastal Hwy (19958-3608)
PHONE..................................314 488-9400
Alexander Montgomery, *President*
Alexander Krill, *Treasurer*
EMP: 2
SALES (est): 56.5K **Privately Held**
SIC: 7372 Application computer software

(G-3531)
HAP LLC
16192 Coastal Hwy (19958-3608)
PHONE..................................302 645-7400
Eyal Ramakrishnan, *Mng Member*
EMP: 5
SALES (est): 141.7K **Privately Held**
SIC: 7374 Computer processing services

(G-3532)
HARBIN LLC
16192 Coastal Hwy (19958-3608)
PHONE..................................302 219-3320
Abdelmalek Bellaoune, *Mng Member*
Billel Amiour,
Amine Smida,
EMP: 3
SALES (est): 71.1K **Privately Held**
SIC: 7372 7389 Application computer software;

(G-3533)
HARBOUR TOWNE ASSOCIATES LP
34232 Woods Edge Dr # 313 (19958-4912)
PHONE..................................302 645-1003
Linda Chantler, *Principal*
EMP: 4
SALES (est): 350K **Privately Held**
SIC: 6513 Apartment building operators

(G-3534)
HARVARD BUSINESS SERVICES INC
Also Called: Hbs
16192 Coastal Hwy (19958-3608)
PHONE..................................302 645-7400
Richard H Bell II, *CEO*
Michael J Bell, *Vice Pres*
Justin Damiani, *Sales Executive*
Rakesh Khurana, *Professor*
EMP: 30
SQ FT: 8,500
SALES (est): 10MM **Privately Held**
WEB: www.delawareinc.com
SIC: 8111 Specialized legal services; corporate, partnership & business law

(G-3535)
HAT BLUE GROUP LLC
16192 Coastal Hwy (19958-3608)
PHONE..................................225 288-2962
EMP: 18
SALES (est): 341.9K **Privately Held**
SIC: 8742 3061 Business consultant; automotive rubber goods (mechanical)

(G-3536)
HATFIELD GAS CONNECTIONS INC
59 Aintree Dr (19958-9473)
PHONE..................................302 945-2354
Michael Hatfield, *President*
EMP: 4
SALES (est): 427K **Privately Held**
SIC: 5722 7389 Gas household appliances;

(G-3537)
HAYMY RESOURCES LLC
Also Called: HM Defense Resources
16192 Coastal Hwy (19958-3608)
PHONE..................................402 218-6787
Philip Gunn, *Branch Mgr*
EMP: 5
SALES (corp-wide): 288.3K **Privately Held**
SIC: 8299 7389 7363 Airline training; photogrammatic mapping; pilot service, aviation
PA: Haymy Resources Llc
20218 Kings Camp Dr
Katy TX 77450
402 218-6787

(G-3538)
HAZZARD ELECTRICAL CONTRACTORS
1 American Legion Rd (19958)
P.O. Box 252 (19958-0252)
PHONE..................................302 645-8457
David Hazzard, *President*
EMP: 7 **EST:** 1946
SQ FT: 3,000
SALES (est): 1MM **Privately Held**
SIC: 1731 General electrical contractor

(G-3539)
HEART TO HAND DAYCARE LLC
16192 Coastal Hwy (19958-3608)
PHONE..................................202 256-4524
Loretha Daniel, *Manager*
Lawrence Manley, *Manager*
EMP: 6
SALES: 65K **Privately Held**
SIC: 8351 Child day care services

(G-3540)
HENLOPEN DESIGN LLC
16192 Coastal Hwy (19958-3608)
PHONE..................................302 265-4330
David E Dougherty,
EMP: 2
SALES: 15K **Privately Held**
SIC: 2721 Periodicals

(G-3541)
HENLOPEN HOMES INC
17644 Coastal Hwy (19958-6257)
P.O. Box 476, Georgetown (19947-0476)
PHONE..................................302 684-0860
Tim Parker, *President*
EMP: 5
SALES (est): 338.7K **Privately Held**
SIC: 1521 2452 New construction, single-family houses; modular homes, prefabricated, wood

(G-3542)
HENLOPEN MUSIC THERAPY SE
31618 Holly Ct (19958-2051)
PHONE..................................302 593-7784
EMP: 8
SALES (est): 73.3K **Privately Held**
SIC: 8093 Rehabilitation center, outpatient treatment

(G-3543)
HOENEN & MITCHELL INC
18548 Arabian Acres Rd (19958-3920)
PHONE..................................302 645-6193
Richard Hoenen, *President*
Wayne Mitchell, *Treasurer*
EMP: 6
SALES (est): 800K **Privately Held**
SIC: 1521 New construction, single-family houses

(G-3544)
HOMETOWN AMERICA LLC
22971 Suburban Blvd (19958-5273)
PHONE..................................302 945-5186
Tara Edmonds, *Branch Mgr*
EMP: 4
SALES (corp-wide): 36.7MM **Privately Held**
SIC: 6515 Mobile home site operators
PA: Hometown America, L.L.C.
150 N Wacker Dr Ste 2800
Chicago IL 60606
312 604-7500

Lewes - Sussex County (G-3578)

(G-3545)
HOMEWATCH CAREGIVERS
17527 Nassau Commons Blvd (19958-6283)
PHONE.....................302 644-1888
EMP: 5
SALES (est): 70.7K Privately Held
SIC: 8082 Home health care services

(G-3546)
HONEY ALTERATION
17370 Coastal Hwy (19958-6209)
PHONE.....................302 519-2031
Honey Kang, Principal
EMP: 4
SALES (est): 41.8K Privately Held
SIC: 7219 Laundry & garment services

(G-3547)
HOST INTEGRADO INC
16192 Coastal Hwy (19958-3608)
PHONE.....................277 326-6719
Andries Come, President
EMP: 5
SALES: 100K Privately Held
SIC: 4813

(G-3548)
HPLUSMEDIA LLC
16192 Coastal Hwy (19958-3608)
PHONE.....................347 480-8996
EMP: 5
SALES (est): 115.9K Privately Held
SIC: 7336 Commercial Art And Graphic Design

(G-3549)
IBOPE MEDIA LLC
16192 Coastal Hwy (19958-3608)
PHONE.....................305 529-0062
Fernando Oliveira,
EMP: 7
SALES (est): 470K Privately Held
SIC: 8732 Market analysis or research

(G-3550)
ICASE LLC
16192 Coastal Hwy (19958-3608)
PHONE.....................302 703-7854
EMP: 15
SALES (est): 248.6K Privately Held
SIC: 7389

(G-3551)
IDENTISOURCE LLC
16192 Coastal Hwy (19958-3608)
PHONE.....................888 716-7498
Roberto Ruiz,
EMP: 3
SALES: 600K Privately Held
WEB: www.identisource.net
SIC: 3955 Carbon paper & inked ribbons

(G-3552)
IGNIS GROUP LLC
16192 Coastal Hwy (19958-3608)
PHONE.....................302 645-7400
Senton Kacaniku,
EMP: 21
SALES (est): 386K Privately Held
SIC: 8742 Management consulting services

(G-3553)
IMCG GLOBAL INC (PA)
Also Called: Imcg Global Asia
16192 Coastal Hwy (19958-3608)
PHONE.....................800 559-6140
Ying Shi-Bryant, President
William Thomas Bryant, Exec Dir
▲ EMP: 1
SALES: 15MM Privately Held
SIC: 3089 7922 7812 Injection molded finished plastic products; concert management service; motion picture & video production

(G-3554)
IMPRESS
616 Kings Hwy (19958-1446)
P.O. Box 328 (19958-0328)
PHONE.....................302 645-8411
Edward L Zygmonski, Owner
EMP: 1
SALES: 90K Privately Held
WEB: www.impressrubberstamps.com
SIC: 2741 Miscellaneous publishing

(G-3555)
IMPULSE CONSTRUCTION
31622 Madison Dr (19958)
PHONE.....................302 644-0464
Golbs Brough, Owner
EMP: 5
SALES (est): 223.1K Privately Held
SIC: 1521 Single-family housing construction

(G-3556)
INCLIND INC
119 W 3rd St Ste 6 (19958-1315)
P.O. Box 265, Milton (19968-0265)
PHONE.....................302 856-2802
Shaun Tyndall, President
Jessica Tyndall, Marketing Staff
Phil Everton, Web Dvlpr
Veronica Severyn, Web Dvlpr
Dalton Tyndall, Web Dvlpr
EMP: 8
SQ FT: 2,250
SALES: 750K Privately Held
WEB: www.inclind.com
SIC: 7371 7373 Computer software systems analysis & design, custom; computer software development & applications; computer software development; software programming applications; systems software development services

(G-3557)
INDELIBLE BLUE INC
16192 Coastal Hwy (19958-3608)
PHONE.....................302 231-5200
Valerie Kestenbaum, Vice Pres
EMP: 10
SQ FT: 3,000
SALES (est): 343.2K Privately Held
SIC: 7373 Computer systems analysis & design; local area network (LAN) systems integrator

(G-3558)
INETWORKZ LLC
16192 Coastal Hwy (19958-3608)
PHONE.....................407 401-9384
Nareen Biswass,
EMP: 10
SALES (est): 570K Privately Held
SIC: 7379 7389 Computer related consulting services;

(G-3559)
INRG OF DELAWARE INC
16949 Hudsons Turn (19958-4840)
PHONE.....................302 369-1412
Bill McCarten, President
EMP: 5
SALES: 350K Privately Held
SIC: 8748 Business consulting

(G-3560)
INSTADAPP LABS LLC
16192 Coastal Hwy (19958-3608)
PHONE.....................469 605-1661
Sowmay Jain,
EMP: 4
SALES (est): 87.5K Privately Held
SIC: 7379

(G-3561)
INT INVESTIGATION SECURITY INC
16192 Coastal Hwy (19958-3608)
PHONE.....................609 727-8317
Collin Innis, CFO
Onori Ajong, Exec Dir
EMP: 5
SALES (est): 63.1K
SALES (corp-wide): 454.8K Privately Held
SIC: 7381 7382 Protective services, guard; security guard service; security systems services
PA: Ihsan Ibadah Infrastructure Construction, Llc
327 E Union St 2
Burlington NJ 08016
609 727-8317

(G-3562)
IROI MANAGEMENT LLC
16192 Coastal Hwy (19958-3608)
PHONE.....................516 373-5269
Liu Zihao, Principal
EMP: 10
SALES (est): 217.5K Privately Held
SIC: 7371 Computer software development & applications

(G-3563)
ISIS NORTH AMERICA INC
16192 Coastal Hwy (19958-3608)
PHONE.....................508 653-7318
Laura Alwir, General Counsel
EMP: 4
SALES (est): 240K Privately Held
SIC: 8742 Management consulting services

(G-3564)
IT S APPLES ORANGES IN
121 Jefferson Ave (19958-1415)
PHONE.....................301 333-3696
EMP: 2
SALES (est): 150K Privately Held
SIC: 3571 Mfg Electronic Computers

(G-3565)
IT TIGERS LLC
16192 Coastal Hwy (19958-3608)
PHONE.....................732 898-2793
Niraj Kumar,
EMP: 5 EST: 2018
SALES (est): 124.8K Privately Held
SIC: 8742 7379 Management information systems consultant;

(G-3566)
J B LANDSCAPING
Also Called: JB Landscaping
15468 New Rd (19958-3700)
P.O. Box 72 (19958-0072)
PHONE.....................302 645-7202
Chris Valenti,
EMP: 22
SQ FT: 1,400
SALES (est): 970K Privately Held
WEB: www.jblandscaping.com
SIC: 0781 Landscape services

(G-3567)
J G M ASSOCIATES
Also Called: John Mancuso and Associates
17569 Nassau Commons Blvd (19958-6284)
PHONE.....................302 645-2159
John Mancuso, Owner
EMP: 6
SALES (est): 311.4K Privately Held
SIC: 1721 Residential painting

(G-3568)
JACK LINGO INC REALTOR
1240 Kings Hwy (19958-1735)
P.O. Box 789 (19958-0789)
PHONE.....................302 947-9030
John Lingo, Opers-Prdtn-Mfg
Carol Lynch, Human Res Mgr
Claudia McCloskey, Sales Associate
Lou Cristaldi, Asst Broker
Derrick Lingo, Asst Broker
EMP: 13
SALES (corp-wide): 4.6MM Privately Held
WEB: www.jacklingo.com
SIC: 6531 Real estate brokers & agents
PA: Jack Lingo Inc Realtor
246 Rehoboth Ave
Rehoboth Beach DE 19971
302 227-3883

(G-3569)
JACK LINGO REALTOR
1240 Kings Hwy (19958-1735)
PHONE.....................302 645-2207
Paul Townsend, Principal
David Lambert, Real Est Agnt
EMP: 35
SALES (est): 1.5MM Privately Held
WEB: www.wolfepointe.com
SIC: 6531 Real estate brokers & agents

(G-3570)
JAMES F PALMER
Also Called: Nanticoke Podiatry
33664 Bayview Medical Dr (19958-1687)
PHONE.....................302 644-3980
James F Palmer, Podiatrist
Roman C Orsini, Podiatrist
EMP: 5 Privately Held
SIC: 8043 Offices & clinics of podiatrists
PA: James F Palmer
8857 Riverside Dr
Seaford DE 19973

(G-3571)
JOANNE REUTHER
Also Called: Hair Dimensions
20750 John J Williams Hwy # 17 (19958-4399)
PHONE.....................302 945-8707
Joanne Reuther, Owner
EMP: 5
SALES (est): 122.4K Privately Held
SIC: 7231 Manicurist, pedicurist

(G-3572)
JOBES LANDSCAPE INC
20934 Robinsonville Rd (19958-6045)
PHONE.....................302 945-0195
Joy Tomer, President
Jobe Tomer, Admin Sec
EMP: 9
SALES (est): 365.9K Privately Held
WEB: www.jobeslandscape.com
SIC: 0781 4971 Landscape services; irrigation systems

(G-3573)
JOHN M COOPER REVERAND
Tall Pnes (19958)
PHONE.....................302 684-8639
John Cooper, Principal
EMP: 2
SALES (est): 105K Privately Held
SIC: 2389 Clergymen's vestments

(G-3574)
JOHN SNOW LABS INC
16192 Coastal Hwy (19958-3608)
PHONE.....................302 786-5227
John Snow, President
EMP: 30
SQ FT: 5,000
SALES: 1MM Privately Held
SIC: 7374 Data processing service

(G-3575)
JOHNNY WALKER ENTERPRISES LLC
16192 Coastal Hwy Ste 346 (19958-3608)
PHONE.....................408 500-6439
Jonathan Walker,
EMP: 1
SQ FT: 80
SALES: 50K Privately Held
SIC: 4212 8099 7372 Local trucking, without storage; health screening service; application computer software

(G-3576)
JOSE A PANDO MD
Also Called: Rheumatology Consultant Del
20268 Plantations Rd (19958-4622)
PHONE.....................302 644-2302
Jose Pando, Owner
EMP: 10
SALES (est): 540K Privately Held
SIC: 8011 Rheumatology specialist, physician/surgeon

(G-3577)
JOSE H AUSTRIA MD (PA)
10 Pilot Pt (19958-1154)
PHONE.....................302 645-8954
Jose Austria MD, Owner
EMP: 5
SALES (est): 384.1K Privately Held
SIC: 8011 Offices & clinics of medical doctors

(G-3578)
JOSELOW BETH LPCMH
1307 Savannah Rd (19958-1514)
PHONE.....................302 644-0130
Loretta Higgins, Principal
Marianne Walch, Research

Lewes - Sussex County (G-3579) — GEOGRAPHIC SECTION

EMP: 4 EST: 2007
SALES (est): 122.9K **Privately Held**
SIC: 8093 Mental health clinic, outpatient

(G-3579)
JOSEPH SCHWARTZ PSYD
17021 Old Orchard Rd # 1 (19958-4832)
PHONE................302 213-3287
EMP: 6
SALES (est): 80.5K **Privately Held**
SIC: 8011 Offices & clinics of medical doctors

(G-3580)
K BANK
17021 Old Orchard Rd A (19958-4832)
PHONE................302 645-9700
Julie Brown, *Branch Mgr*
EMP: 5
SALES (corp-wide): 31.2MM **Privately Held**
SIC: 6029 6022 Commercial banks; state commercial banks
PA: K Bank
11407 Cronhill Dr Ste N
Owings Mills MD 21117
443 271-6491

(G-3581)
KATHRYN M GEHRET
Also Called: Kate Gehret Ms
17124 Poplar Dr (19958-3873)
PHONE................610 420-7233
Kathryn M Gehret, *Principal*
EMP: 4 EST: 2012
SALES (est): 143.6K **Privately Held**
SIC: 8049 Clinical psychologist

(G-3582)
KITSCHY STITCH
18419 Berkeley Rd (19958-4692)
PHONE................302 200-9889
EMP: 1
SALES (est): 31.2K **Privately Held**
SIC: 2395 Embroidery & art needlework

(G-3583)
KLH INDUSTRIES LLC
16192 Coastal Hwy (19958-3608)
PHONE................800 348-0758
Eric Hemphill,
EMP: 2
SALES (est): 86.8K **Privately Held**
SIC: 3999 Barber & beauty shop equipment

(G-3584)
KNOWLAND GROUP LLC
115 W Market St (19958-1309)
P.O. Box 476 (19958-0476)
PHONE................302 645-9777
Jeff Haslow, *Branch Mgr*
EMP: 15
SALES (est): 743.5K **Privately Held**
SIC: 7299 Party planning service
PA: Knowland Group, Llc
1735 N Lynn St Ste 600
Arlington VA 22209

(G-3585)
KNOWT INC
16192 Coastal Hwy (19958-3608)
PHONE................848 391-0575
Abheek Pandoh, *CEO*
Daniel Like, *President*
EMP: 11
SALES (est): 234.5K **Privately Held**
SIC: 7371 7372 7389 Computer software development & applications; application computer software; business services

(G-3586)
KRATOM FOUNDATION LLC
16192 Coastal Hwy (19958-3608)
PHONE................302 645-7400
Mark Baits,
EMP: 5
SALES (est): 111.2K **Privately Held**
SIC: 5099 Durable goods

(G-3587)
LACHALL LEE LLP
17563 Nassau Commons Blvd (19958-1793)
PHONE................302 644-9952
James Lachall, *Owner*

EMP: 4
SALES (est): 283.9K **Privately Held**
SIC: 8721 Accounting services, except auditing

(G-3588)
LAIMA V ANTHANEY DMD
1200 Savannah Rd (19958-1525)
PHONE................302 645-4726
Anthaney Laima, *Owner*
EMP: 5
SALES (est): 229.7K **Privately Held**
SIC: 8021 Dentists' office

(G-3589)
LAMBERTSON SIGNS
30444 Lwes Georgetown Hwy (19958-4172)
PHONE................302 645-6700
Barry Lamberton, *Owner*
EMP: 1 EST: 1976
SALES (est): 54.2K **Privately Held**
SIC: 3993 Signs & advertising specialties

(G-3590)
LANDMARK ASSOCIATES OF DEL
Also Called: Piper, Glenn T
9 Bradford Ln (19958-9511)
PHONE................302 645-7070
Glenn Piper, *President*
Barbara Piper, *Vice Pres*
EMP: 5
SALES: 500K **Privately Held**
SIC: 6531 Appraiser, real estate

(G-3591)
LANE BUILDERS LLC
1009 Kings Hwy (19958-1731)
PHONE................302 645-5555
Mark Beam, *Superintendent*
Greg Goodwin, *Superintendent*
Mary E Rozell, *Accounting Mgr*
Kara Joseph, *Marketing Mgr*
Jeff Burtun, *Mng Member*
EMP: 17
SALES (est): 2MM **Privately Held**
WEB: www.lanebuilders.com
SIC: 1521 New construction, single-family houses

(G-3592)
LANTRANSIT ENTERPRISES LLC
Also Called: U S Mail Transport
16192 Coastal Hwy (19958-3608)
PHONE................302 722-4800
Deborah Holcomb, *President*
Ramaj St James, *Senior VP*
Linda Portrum, *Vice Pres*
Madison Walsh,
Campbell Stepp,
EMP: 11
SQ FT: 1,500
SALES (est): 550K **Privately Held**
SIC: 4789 Freight car loading & unloading

(G-3593)
LEFTYS ALLEY & EATS
36450 Plaza Blvd (19958-4211)
PHONE................302 864-6000
EMP: 11 EST: 2017
SALES (est): 466K **Privately Held**
SIC: 7933 Bowling centers

(G-3594)
LEGUM & NORMAN MID-WEST LLC
Also Called: Legum & Norman Realty
12000 Old Vine Blvd # 114 (19958-1717)
PHONE................302 227-8448
Pam Counti, *Principal*
EMP: 6
SALES (corp-wide): 8.8MM **Privately Held**
SIC: 6531 Real estate brokers & agents
PA: Legum & Norman Mid-West, Llc
3130 Frview Pk Dr Ste 200
Falls Church VA 22042
703 600-6000

(G-3595)
LESTER & CO PC
17021 Old Orchard Rd # 4 (19958-4832)
PHONE................302 684-5980

Norman Lester, *Owner*
EMP: 4
SALES (est): 187.6K **Privately Held**
SIC: 8721 Certified public accountant

(G-3596)
LEWES BODY WORKS INC
16205 New Rd (19958-3707)
PHONE................302 645-5595
Richard Perez, *President*
EMP: 6
SALES (est): 1.2MM **Privately Held**
SIC: 7532 Collision shops, automotive

(G-3597)
LEWES CHIROPRACTIC CENTER
Also Called: Elrod, Michael E DC
1527 Savannah Rd (19958-1611)
PHONE................302 645-9171
Michael Elrod, *Owner*
EMP: 5
SALES (est): 206.1K **Privately Held**
WEB: www.leweschiro.com
SIC: 8041 Offices & clinics of chiropractors

(G-3598)
LEWES DAIRY INC
660 Pilottown Rd (19958-1299)
P.O. Box 207 (19958-0207)
PHONE................302 645-6281
Archie Brittingham Jr, *President*
Robert E Brittingham, *Vice Pres*
Judy B Bye, *Treasurer*
Tracy Mascelli, *Office Mgr*
Henry L Brittingham, *Admin Sec*
EMP: 22 EST: 1946
SQ FT: 20,000
SALES (est): 1.1MM **Privately Held**
SIC: 0241 Dairy farms

(G-3599)
LEWES EXPRESSIVE THERAPY
105 Dove Dr (19958-1622)
PHONE................302 727-3275
Sarah Smith, *Principal*
EMP: 8
SALES (est): 73.3K **Privately Held**
SIC: 8093 Rehabilitation center, outpatient treatment

(G-3600)
LEWES FISHHOUSE & PRODUCE INC
17696 Coastal Hwy (19958-6214)
PHONE................302 827-4074
Charles Donohue, *President*
Diane Donohue, *Corp Secy*
EMP: 25
SQ FT: 1,500
SALES (est): 7.3MM **Privately Held**
SIC: 5147 5421 5146 Meats & meat products; meat & fish markets; fish & seafoods

(G-3601)
LEWES HISTORICAL SOCIETY
110 Shipcarpenter St (19958-1210)
PHONE................302 645-7670
S Rogers Jones, *President*
Jennifer Manning, *Mktg Coord*
EMP: 4
SALES: 1.1MM **Privately Held**
SIC: 8412 Museum

(G-3602)
LEWES MONTESSORI SCHOOL
32234 Conleys Chapel Rd (19958-6023)
PHONE................302 644-7482
Lisa Desombre, *Principal*
EMP: 5
SALES (est): 114.1K **Privately Held**
SIC: 8351 Montessori child development center

(G-3603)
LEWES ORTHOPEDIC CTR
16704 Kings Hwy 2 (19958-4929)
PHONE................302 645-4939
David Sopa, *Owner*
EMP: 5
SALES (est): 202.9K **Privately Held**
SIC: 8011 Orthopedic physician

(G-3604)
LEWES SENIOR CITIZENS CENTER
Also Called: LEWES SENIOR CENTER
32083 Janice Rd (19958-2004)
PHONE................302 645-9293
Dennis Nealen, *Director*
EMP: 5
SALES: 633.1K **Privately Held**
WEB: www.verizo.net
SIC: 8322 8699 Senior citizens' center or association; charitable organization

(G-3605)
LEWES SURGERY CENTER
17015 Old Orchard Rd # 4 (19958-4849)
P.O. Box 495 (19958-0495)
PHONE................302 644-3466
John E Spieker, *Managing Prtnr*
Wilson Choy, *Partner*
Gina McClanahan, *Partner*
EMP: 8
SQ FT: 5,000
SALES (est): 1.5MM **Privately Held**
SIC: 8011 Surgeon; orthopedic physician

(G-3606)
LEWIS RESEARCH INC
33712 Wescoats Rd Unit 1 (19958-4926)
PHONE................302 644-0881
Robert B Lewis, *President*
Andy Lewis, *Manager*
EMP: 4
SALES (est): 370K **Privately Held**
SIC: 8734 Testing laboratories

(G-3607)
LICENSING ASSURANCE LLC
16192 Coastal Hwy (19958-3608)
PHONE................305 851-3545
Walter Lora, *CEO*
EMP: 10
SALES (est): 367.9K **Privately Held**
SIC: 7379 Computer related services

(G-3608)
LIELLES INVESTMENTS LLC
16192 Coastal Hwy (19958-3608)
PHONE................215 874-0770
Inbal Altit, *Owner*
EMP: 25
SQ FT: 4,000
SALES (est): 1MM **Privately Held**
SIC: 6531 Real estate agents & managers

(G-3609)
LIGHTHOUSE MASONRY INC
20090 Beaver Dam Rd (19958-5517)
PHONE................302 945-1392
James McIlreavy Jr, *President*
EMP: 7
SALES (est): 366.9K **Privately Held**
SIC: 1741 Masonry & other stonework

(G-3610)
LOCKSIGN LLC
16192 Coastal Hwy (19958-3608)
PHONE................917 573-6582
Nikitas Alexiades, *Mng Member*
EMP: 1
SALES (est): 32.7K **Privately Held**
SIC: 7372 Application computer software

(G-3611)
LOVE CREEK MARINA MBL HM SITE (PA)
Also Called: Laurel Storage Center
31136 Conleys Chapel Rd (19958-5511)
PHONE................302 448-6492
Milton Chaski Jr, *President*
Mary Lee Chaski, *Corp Secy*
Diana Chaski, *Vice Pres*
Carol Chaski, *Shareholder*
Hilda Chaski, *Shareholder*
EMP: 10
SQ FT: 10,000
SALES: 390K **Privately Held**
SIC: 5271 6515 4493 4225 Mobile homes; mobile home site operators; marinas; miniwarehouse, warehousing

(G-3612)
LOWES HOME CENTERS LLC
20364 Plantations Rd (19958-5814)
PHONE................302 645-0900

Kerilyn Urvan, *Branch Mgr*
EMP: 150
SALES (corp-wide): 71.3B **Publicly Held**
SIC: **5211** 5031 5722 5064 Home centers; building materials, exterior; building materials, interior; household appliance stores; electrical appliances, television & radio
HQ: Lowe's Home Centers, Llc
1605 Curtis Bridge Rd
Wilkesboro NC 28697
336 658-4000

(G-3613)
LOYAL ORDER MOSE LWES REHOBOTH
28971 Lwes Georgetown Hwy (19958-3910)
PHONE..................302 684-4004
Randy Betts, *Manager*
EMP: 4
SALES (est): 468.8K **Privately Held**
SIC: **8641** Civic associations

(G-3614)
M & P ADVENTURES INC
Also Called: Lighthse Rstrnt Fshrmans Wharf
Corner Of Savannah Angler (19958)
PHONE..................302 645-6271
Paul Buchness, *President*
Mary Buchness, *Vice Pres*
EMP: 50
SALES (est): 2.5MM **Privately Held**
SIC: **7299** 5812 Banquet hall facilities; eating places

(G-3615)
MAAN SOFTWARES INC
16192 Coastal Hwy (19958-3608)
P.O. Box 41214, Arlington VA (22204-8214)
PHONE..................531 203-9141
Aditya Dwivedi, *President*
EMP: 22
SALES: 11.4K **Privately Held**
SIC: **7379** 7371 7389 Computer related consulting services; computer software development & applications;

(G-3616)
MAD DELAWARE CHAPTER
34013 Woodland Cir (19958-5212)
PHONE..................910 284-6386
Hector Reyes, *Principal*
EMP: 4 EST: 2016
SALES (est): 58K **Privately Held**
SIC: **8399** Advocacy group

(G-3617)
MAID FOR SHORE
22 Chesterfield Dr (19958-9407)
PHONE..................302 344-1857
Juliana Vantol, *Principal*
EMP: 5
SALES (est): 166.3K **Privately Held**
SIC: **7349** Cleaning service, industrial or commercial

(G-3618)
MANUFACTURERS & TRADERS TR CO
Also Called: M&T
1515 Savannah Rd Ste 103 (19958-1675)
PHONE..................302 644-9930
EMP: 4
SALES (corp-wide): 6.4B **Publicly Held**
SIC: **6022** 6021 6029 State commercial banks; national commercial banks; commercial banks
HQ: Manufacturers And Traders Trust Company
1 M&T Plz Fl 3
Buffalo NY 14203
716 842-4200

(G-3619)
MARK MENENDEZ
33759 Clay Rd Unit 2 (19958-6294)
PHONE..................302 644-8500
Mark Menendez, *Owner*
EMP: 5
SALES (est): 116.3K **Privately Held**
SIC: **8011** Offices & clinics of medical doctors

(G-3620)
MARLENKA AMERICA LLC (PA)
16192 Coastal Hwy (19958-3608)
PHONE..................502 530-0720
Cezary Wlodarczyk, *CEO*
Galina Blinetsky, *Principal*
Alec Blinetsky, *Director*
Jenya Cherny, *Director*
EMP: 1
SALES (est): 343.2K **Privately Held**
SIC: **2051** Cakes, pies & pastries

(G-3621)
MARTIN GREY LLC
16192 Coastal Hwy (19958-3608)
PHONE..................302 990-0675
Aleksandr Popov, *Principal*
EMP: 3
SALES (est): 91.3K **Privately Held**
SIC: **2099** Tea blending

(G-3622)
MARUKO HOLDINGS USA LLC
16192 Coastal Hwy (19958-3608)
PHONE..................917 515-2776
Christian Bustamante, *Principal*
EMP: 4 **Privately Held**
SIC: **6719** Holding companies

(G-3623)
MARYANN METRINKO LLC
Also Called: Metrinko Office Interiors
401 Samantha Dr (19958-4145)
PHONE..................410 643-1472
EMP: 4
SALES (est): 380K **Privately Held**
SIC: **7389** 5712 8748 Business Services Ret Furniture Business Consulting Services

(G-3624)
MATTS FISH CAMP LEWES DE LLC
34401 Tenley Ct (19958-4200)
PHONE..................302 539-4415
Jack Temple, *General Mgr*
EMP: 4
SALES (est): 60.5K **Privately Held**
SIC: **7032** Sporting & recreational camps

(G-3625)
MAX SEAL INC
Also Called: Teleborg Pipe Seals US
16192 Coastal Hwy (19958-3608)
PHONE..................619 946-2650
Alan Guzowski, *President*
Alejandro Castro, *Principal*
▼ EMP: 10
SQ FT: 10,000
SALES (est): 175.3K **Privately Held**
SIC: **2891** Sealing compounds, synthetic rubber or plastic

(G-3626)
MAXBRIGHT INC
16192 Coastal Hwy (19958-3608)
P.O. Box 841688, Pearland TX (77584-0021)
PHONE..................281 616-7999
Jeff Shen, *Manager*
EMP: 40
SALES: 1MM **Privately Held**
SIC: **5065** 3651 Electronic parts & equipment; home entertainment equipment, electronic

(G-3627)
MAXILLOFACIAL SOUTHERN DE ORAL
17605 Nassau Commons Blvd (19958-6284)
P.O. Box 400, Nassau (19969-0400)
PHONE..................302 644-2977
Bruce D Fisher, *Principal*
EMP: 4
SALES (est): 264.7K **Privately Held**
SIC: **8021** Oral pathologist

(G-3628)
MAYJUUN LLC (PA)
16192 Coastal Hwy (19958-3608)
PHONE..................865 300-7738
John Manning,
EMP: 6

SALES (est): 256.9K **Privately Held**
SIC: **8082** 7371 7389 Home health care services; computer software development & applications;

(G-3629)
MCCLAIN CUSTODIAL SERVICE
418 Burton Ave (19958-1238)
PHONE..................302 645-6597
Tacolla Mc Clain, *Owner*
EMP: 5
SALES (est): 138.4K **Privately Held**
SIC: **7349** Building maintenance services

(G-3630)
MCMAHON HEATING & AC
20378 John J Williams Hwy (19958-4303)
PHONE..................302 945-4300
Rick McMahon, *Owner*
EMP: 10
SALES (est): 431.9K **Privately Held**
SIC: **1711** Heating & air conditioning contractors

(G-3631)
MEALS ON WHELS OF LWES RHOBOTH
32409 Lwes Georgetown Hwy (19958-1646)
PHONE..................302 645-7449
Robert Derrickson, *President*
Kathleen Keuski, *Exec Dir*
EMP: 5
SALES: 862.6K **Privately Held**
WEB: www.beachmeals.com
SIC: **8322** Meal delivery program

(G-3632)
MEDTIX LLC
16337 Coastal Hwy (19958-3607)
P.O. Box 428, Elkton MD (21922-0428)
PHONE..................302 265-4550
Jack Berberian, *Principal*
EMP: 16
SALES (corp-wide): 20.5MM **Privately Held**
SIC: **5047** Medical equipment & supplies
PA: Medtix Llc
221 S Rehoboth Blvd
Milford DE 19963
302 645-8070

(G-3633)
MELCAR UNDERGROUND LTD
16192 Coastal Hwy (19958-3608)
PHONE..................484 653-8259
James McIntyre, *CEO*
EMP: 23
SALES (est): 628.5K **Privately Held**
SIC: **1623** Underground utilities contractor

(G-3634)
MELCHIORRE AND MELCHIORRE
Also Called: J Melchiore & Sons
17352 Coastal Hwy (19958-6209)
PHONE..................302 645-6311
J G Melchiorre Sr, *President*
EMP: 10
SQ FT: 6,000
SALES (est): 875.3K **Privately Held**
SIC: **6512** 6514 Commercial & industrial building operation; residential building, four or fewer units: operation

(G-3635)
MELISSA A WOLF
18512 Belle Grove Rd # 6 (19958-4699)
PHONE..................716 465-7093
Melissa Wolf, *Owner*
EMP: 8
SALES (est): 65.7K **Privately Held**
SIC: **8049** Offices of health practitioner

(G-3636)
MELROYS FURNITURE REFINISHING
20597 Mulberry Knoll Rd (19958-2645)
PHONE..................302 645-1856
Melody Ruark, *Principal*
EMP: 5
SALES (est): 245.3K **Privately Held**
SIC: **7641** Furniture refinishing

(G-3637)
MERESTONE CONSULTANTS INC
33516 Crossing Ave Unit 1 (19958-1697)
PHONE..................302 226-5880
Mike Early, *Branch Mgr*
EMP: 10
SALES (corp-wide): 1.4MM **Privately Held**
WEB: www.merestoneconsultants.com
SIC: **8713** 8711 Surveying services; construction & civil engineering
PA: Merestone Consultants, Inc.
5215 W Woodmill Dr Ste 38
Wilmington DE 19808
302 992-7900

(G-3638)
MERIX LLC (PA)
16192 Coastal Hwy (19958-3608)
PHONE..................425 659-1425
Nithin Yadav, *Director*
EMP: 1
SALES: 10K **Privately Held**
SIC: **7372** 7375 7389 Application computer software; on-line data base information retrieval;

(G-3639)
MICHAEL A POLECK DDS
1632 Savannah Rd (19958-1659)
PHONE..................302 644-4100
Micheal Poleck, *Principal*
EMP: 4
SALES (est): 190K **Privately Held**
SIC: **8021** Dentists' office

(G-3640)
MICHAEL L CAHOON DR
750 Kings Hwy Ste 107 (19958-1772)
PHONE..................302 644-4171
Michael Cahoon, *Principal*
EMP: 4
SALES (est): 321.8K **Privately Held**
SIC: **8021** Dental surgeon

(G-3641)
MID-ATLANTIC FMLY PRACTICE LLC (PA)
20251 John J Williams Hwy (19958-4314)
P.O. Box 465 (19958-0465)
PHONE..................302 644-6860
Jeffrey Heckert,
Mark Sordi, *Family Practiti*
EMP: 14
SALES (est): 3.9MM **Privately Held**
SIC: **8011** General & family practice, physician/surgeon

(G-3642)
MILTON FAMILY PRACTICE
16529 Coastal Hwy (19958-3696)
PHONE..................302 684-2000
Charles G Wagner, *Principal*
EMP: 10
SALES (est): 701.9K **Privately Held**
SIC: **8011** General & family practice, physician/surgeon

(G-3643)
MINDER FOUNDATION
16192 Coastal Hwy (19958-3608)
PHONE..................917 477-7661
Natalie Moore, *Director*
EMP: 5
SALES (est): 107.6K **Privately Held**
SIC: **8733** Research institute

(G-3644)
MINOTI INC
16192 Coastal Hwy (19958-3608)
PHONE..................720 725-0720
Robin Paul, *President*
EMP: 13 EST: 2017
SALES: 5K **Privately Held**
SIC: **7371** Computer software development & applications

(G-3645)
MITCHELL C STICKLER MD INC (PA)
Also Called: Cape Hnlpen Nntcoke Drmatology
750 Kings Hwy Ste 110 (19958-1772)
PHONE..................302 644-6400

Lewes - Sussex County (G-3646)   GEOGRAPHIC SECTION

Mitchell C Stickler MD, *President*
EMP: 16
SALES (est): 1.3MM **Privately Held**
WEB: www.skinsite.com
SIC: 8011 Dermatologist

(G-3646)
MONEY BAX LLC
33692 Reservoir Dr (19958-6862)
PHONE...................302 360-8577
Rose Jacques,
Greg Reaves,
EMP: 4
SQ FT: 4,000
SALES: 210K **Privately Held**
WEB: www.moneybax.com
SIC: 8742 Marketing consulting services

(G-3647)
MOON SHOT ENERGY LLC
16192 Coastal Hwy (19958-3608)
PHONE...................512 297-2626
John Lee, *President*
EMP: 3
SALES (est): 140K **Privately Held**
SIC: 2086 Bottled & canned soft drinks

(G-3648)
MOONLIGHT ARCHITECHTURE INC
29003 Lwes Georgetown Hwy (19958-3909)
PHONE...................302 645-9361
Robert Rollins, *President*
Fredrick T Bada, *Vice Pres*
EMP: 4
SALES (est): 658.6K **Privately Held**
WEB: www.moonlightarch.com
SIC: 8712 Architectural engineering

(G-3649)
MOOSE INTERNATIONAL INC
Also Called: Moose Family Center 646
28971 Lwes Georgetown Hwy (19958-3910)
PHONE...................302 684-4004
Richard Stec, *Administration*
EMP: 4
SALES (corp-wide): 48.4MM **Privately Held**
WEB: www.thalist.com
SIC: 8641 Civic associations
PA: Moose International, Incorporated
    155 S International Dr
    Mooseheart IL 60539
    630 859-2000

(G-3650)
MORTON ELECTRIC CO
Also Called: U-Haul
16867 Kings Hwy (19958-4783)
PHONE...................302 645-9414
Todd Fritchman, *President*
EMP: 5 **EST:** 2011
SALES (est): 266.7K **Privately Held**
SIC: 7519 7513 7359 7629 Utility trailer rental; truck rental & leasing, no drivers; equipment rental & leasing; electrical repair shops

(G-3651)
MOVEMENT MORTGAGE LLC
19413 Jingle Shell Way (19958-6307)
PHONE...................302 344-6758
Trish Raber, *Branch Mgr*
EMP: 6 **Privately Held**
SIC: 6162 Mortgage bankers & correspondents
PA: Movement Mortgage, Llc
    8024 Calvin Hall Rd
    Indian Land SC 29707

(G-3652)
MURPHY ELECTRIC INC
30731 Sassafras Dr (19958-3875)
P.O. Box 392 (19958-0292)
PHONE...................302 644-0404
June Murphy, *President*
James Murphy, *Vice Pres*
EMP: 16
SALES: 1MM **Privately Held**
SIC: 1731 General electrical contractor

(G-3653)
MY LIP STUFF
21002 Robinsonville Rd (19958-6069)
PHONE...................302 945-5922
My Lip Stuff, *Principal*
EMP: 2 **EST:** 2008
SALES (est): 174.6K **Privately Held**
SIC: 2844 Toilet preparations

(G-3654)
NANCY A UNION MD
Also Called: Aponte, Lourdes MD
1302 Savannah Rd (19958-1526)
PHONE...................302 645-6644
Nancy Union MD, *President*
Janette R Boyer, *Nurse Practr*
EMP: 9
SALES (est): 350.8K **Privately Held**
SIC: 8011 Offices & clinics of medical doctors

(G-3655)
NASSAU VLY VINEYARDS & WINERY
32165 Winery Way (19958-6326)
PHONE...................302 645-9463
Margaret Raley, *Owner*
Robert Raley, *Co-Owner*
EMP: 4
SALES (est): 292.3K **Privately Held**
SIC: 2084 Wines

(G-3656)
NATURAL STACKS INC
16192 Coastal Hwy (19958-3608)
PHONE...................855 678-2257
Ryan Munsey, *Chief*
Abelard Lindsay, *Director*
EMP: 6
SALES (est): 368.8K **Privately Held**
SIC: 2834 Vitamin, nutrient & hematinic preparations for human use

(G-3657)
NETPROTEUS
Also Called: Netproteus.com
33107 Perrydale Grn (19958-5402)
PHONE...................206 203-2525
EMP: 9
SALES (est): 150K **Privately Held**
SIC: 5199 Retail Nondurable Goods

(G-3658)
NEVER NEVER LND KENNEL CATTERY
34377 Neverland Rd (19958-4651)
PHONE...................302 645-6140
Allen Quillen, *President*
Dorothy Guillen, *President*
EMP: 5
SALES (est): 150.1K **Privately Held**
WEB: www.neverlandkennel.com
SIC: 0752 Boarding services, kennels

(G-3659)
NIKKO CAPITAL INVESTMENTS LTD
16192 Coastal Hwy (19958-3608)
PHONE...................832 324-5335
Phong Lai, *CEO*
EMP: 20
SALES (est): 722.5K **Privately Held**
SIC: 6799 Venture capital companies

(G-3660)
NOBLE MASTER
Also Called: Noble Master Games
16192 Coastal Hwy (19958-3608)
PHONE...................302 261-2018
Christoph Aschwanden,
EMP: 2
SALES (est): 110.2K **Privately Held**
SIC: 7372 7371 Application computer software; custom computer programming services

(G-3661)
NOVA RE & BUS CONSULTING LLC
16192 Coastal Hwy (19958-3608)
PHONE...................302 258-2193
John Nickerson,
EMP: 12 **EST:** 2006
SQ FT: 1,200

SALES (est): 899.1K **Privately Held**
SIC: 8742 Management consulting services

(G-3662)
NUVIM INC
18327 Port Cir (19958-2525)
PHONE...................302 827-4052
Richard P Kundrat, *Ch of Bd*
Michael H Maizes, *Partner*
EMP: 1
SALES (est): 134.1K **Privately Held**
WEB: www.nuvim.com
SIC: 2023 Dietary supplements, dairy & non-dairy based

(G-3663)
OAK CONSTRUCTION
788 Kings Hwy (19958-1704)
PHONE...................302 703-2013
Michael Purnell, *Principal*
Sharon Purnell, *Treasurer*
EMP: 5 **EST:** 2008
SALES (est): 421.3K **Privately Held**
SIC: 1521 New construction, single-family houses

(G-3664)
OCEANIC VENTURES INC
32292 Nassau Rd Unit 1 (19958-3721)
PHONE...................302 645-5872
John Nelson, *President*
Lisa Nelson, *Vice Pres*
EMP: 8
SQ FT: 5,000
SALES (est): 1.2MM **Privately Held**
SIC: 1751 Cabinet & finish carpentry

(G-3665)
OCEANSIDE ELITE CLG BLDG SVCS
33033 Nassau Loop (19958-3730)
PHONE...................302 339-7777
Noreen Kushner, *Principal*
EMP: 25 **EST:** 2017
SQ FT: 250
SALES (est): 175.4K **Privately Held**
SIC: 7349 7217 Building & office cleaning services; office cleaning or charring; carpet & upholstery cleaning on customer premises

(G-3666)
OCEANSIDE SEAFOOD MKT DELI LLC
109 Savannah Rd (19958-1475)
PHONE...................302 313-5158
Christine Becker, *Principal*
EMP: 5
SALES (est): 94.6K **Privately Held**
SIC: 5812 5146 Delicatessen (eating places); fish & seafoods

(G-3667)
OLIVAR & GREB CAPITAL MGT LLC
16192 Coastal Hwy (19958-3608)
PHONE...................508 598-7590
Thomas Greb, *Principal*
EMP: 10
SALES (est): 180.6K **Privately Held**
SIC: 7389

(G-3668)
ONE HOUR TRANSLATION INC
16192 Coastal Hwy (19958-3608)
PHONE...................800 720-3722
Lior Libman, *President*
EMP: 5
SALES (est): 299.4K
SALES (corp-wide): 23.1MM **Privately Held**
SIC: 7389 Translation services
PA: One Hour Translation Ltd
    3 Golda Meir
    Ness Ziona 74036
    779 555-316

(G-3669)
ONEILL WOODWORKING LLC
23292 Bridgeway Dr W (19958-5115)
PHONE...................443 669-3458
EMP: 1 **EST:** 2018
SALES (est): 54.1K **Privately Held**
SIC: 2431 Millwork

(G-3670)
OPEN BARN INC
16192 Coastal Hwy (19958-3608)
PHONE...................669 254-7747
Hema Sakthivel, *Director*
EMP: 1
SALES (est): 32.7K **Privately Held**
SIC: 7372 Application computer software

(G-3671)
OPPA INC
16192 Coastal Hwy (19958-3608)
PHONE...................732 540-0308
Hung C Ho, *CEO*
EMP: 6
SQ FT: 700
SALES (est): 135.3K **Privately Held**
SIC: 7372 Application computer software

(G-3672)
OPPAMEET LLC
16192 Coastal Hwy (19958-3608)
PHONE...................732 540-0308
Hung C Ho, *CEO*
EMP: 6
SQ FT: 6,486
SALES (est): 290K **Privately Held**
SIC: 7372 Application computer software

(G-3673)
ORTHOPDIC ASSOC SUTHERN DEL PA
17005 Old Orchard Rd (19958-4828)
PHONE...................302 644-3311
EMP: 21 **EST:** 1990
SALES (est): 3.7MM **Privately Held**
SIC: 8011 Orthopedic physician
PA: First State Orthopaedics, P.A.
    4745 Ogletown Stanton Rd # 225
    Newark DE 19713
    302 731-2888

(G-3674)
OVERFALLS MARITIME MUSEUM
219 Pilottown Rd (19958)
P.O. Box 413 (19958-0413)
PHONE...................302 644-8050
Tracy Muveny, *Exec Dir*
EMP: 60
SALES (est): 1MM
SALES (corp-wide): 143K **Privately Held**
SIC: 8412 Museum
PA: Overfalls Maritime Museum
    13 Harborview Rd
    Lewes DE 19958
    302 645-0761

(G-3675)
P A ABA INTL INC
Also Called: Aba PA
16192 Coastal Hwy (19958-3608)
PHONE...................800 979-5106
Manuel P Lora, *CEO*
Aycher Carbonell, *Admin Sec*
EMP: 13
SQ FT: 1,500
SALES (est): 1.2MM **Privately Held**
SIC: 8742 Banking & finance consultant

(G-3676)
PAGETECH
20418 Oakney St (19958-5820)
PHONE...................845 624-4911
EMP: 1
SALES (est): 37.5K **Privately Held**
SIC: 2741 Miscellaneous publishing

(G-3677)
PANGEAMART INC
16192 Coastal Hwy (19958-3608)
PHONE...................914 374-0913
EMP: 4 **EST:** 2016
SALES (est): 98.3K **Privately Held**
SIC: 7372 Prepackaged Software Services

(G-3678)
PAPALEO ROSEN CHELF & PINDER
135 2nd St (19958-1347)
PHONE...................302 644-8600
Harry Papaleo, *President*
EMP: 15

GEOGRAPHIC SECTION
Lewes - Sussex County (G-3709)

SALES (est): 207.4K **Privately Held**
SIC: 7291 8721 Tax return preparation services; accounting, auditing & bookkeeping

(G-3679)
PARSELL FUNERAL ENTPS INC
Also Called: Parsell Fnrl Homes Crematorium
16961 Kings Hwy (19958-4782)
PHONE..................................302 645-9520
Keith Parsell, *President*
Andrew Parsell, *Principal*
Johnathan Parsell, *Principal*
Andrea Parsell, *Vice Pres*
EMP: 7
SALES (est): 620K **Privately Held**
WEB: www.parsellfuneralhomes.com
SIC: 7261 Funeral home; funeral director

(G-3680)
PATIO SYSTEMS INC
16083 New Rd (19958-3710)
PHONE..................................302 644-6540
Ronald Simmons, *President*
Jim Holdridge, *Consultant*
Karen Truitt, *Admin Sec*
EMP: 5
SQ FT: 1,300
SALES: 913.2K **Privately Held**
SIC: 1799 Awning installation

(G-3681)
PATRICK SWIER MDPA KAR
1400 Savannah Rd (19958-1623)
PHONE..................................302 645-7737
Patrick Swier, *Principal*
EMP: 5
SALES (est): 474.3K **Privately Held**
SIC: 8011 Offices & clinics of medical doctors

(G-3682)
PAYBYSKY INC
16192 Coastal Hwy (19958-3608)
PHONE..................................519 641-1771
Roger D'Hollander, *President*
EMP: 8 **EST:** 2014
SQ FT: 1,000
SALES (est): 320K **Privately Held**
SIC: 4785 Toll operations

(G-3683)
PEPPERS INC (PA)
17601 Coastal Hwy Unit 1 (19958-6217)
PHONE..................................302 645-0812
Chip Hearn, *President*
Luther Hearn, *Vice Pres*
EMP: 15
SALES (est): 4.7MM **Privately Held**
WEB: www.peppers.com
SIC: 5149 Sauces

(G-3684)
PEPPERS INC
15608 Coastal Hwy (19958)
PHONE..................................302 644-6900
Nicole Cooper, *Office Mgr*
EMP: 10
SALES (corp-wide): 4.7MM **Privately Held**
SIC: 2033 Chili sauce, tomato: packaged in cans, jars, etc.
PA: Peppers Inc
17601 Coastal Hwy Unit 1
Lewes DE 19958
302 645-0812

(G-3685)
PETAL PUSHERS LLC
31341 Kendale Rd (19958-4480)
PHONE..................................302 945-0350
Harriet Allen, *Principal*
EMP: 2 **EST:** 2008
SALES (est): 100K **Privately Held**
SIC: 3545 Pushers

(G-3686)
PHARMACY TECHNOLOGIES INC
16192 Coastal Hwy (19958-3608)
PHONE..................................877 655-3846
Jonathan Haski, *Director*
Ray Cheng, *Director*
EMP: 4
SQ FT: 100

SALES (est): 180K **Privately Held**
SIC: 7372 Prepackaged software

(G-3687)
PHILLIP T BRADLEY INC
33057 Angola Rd (19958-5699)
PHONE..................................302 947-2741
Phillip Bradley, *Principal*
EMP: 5
SALES (est): 409.7K **Privately Held**
SIC: 7389

(G-3688)
PHOCAL THERAPY INC
16192 Coastal Hwy (19958-3608)
PHONE..................................917 803-7168
Jonathan Shapiro, *CEO*
Shia Halpern, *Agent*
EMP: 5
SALES (est): 198.4K **Privately Held**
SIC: 3843 Dental equipment & supplies

(G-3689)
PHOENIX INTL RESOURCES LLC
Also Called: Infant Acid Reflux Solutions
16192 Coastal Hwy (19958-3608)
PHONE..................................954 309-0120
Kira Volpi, *Manager*
EMP: 2
SALES (est): 81.8K **Privately Held**
SIC: 2833 Vitamins, natural or synthetic: bulk, uncompounded

(G-3690)
PILOTS ASSN FOR BAY RIVER DEL
41 Cape Henlopen Dr (19958-3142)
PHONE..................................302 645-2229
John Vaughn, *Director*
EMP: 28
SALES (corp-wide): 5.5MM **Privately Held**
SIC: 3812 Search & navigation equipment
PA: Pilots Association For The Bay And River Delaware
800 S Columbus Blvd
Philadelphia PA
215 465-2851

(G-3691)
PILOTTOWN ENGINEERING LLC
17585 Nssau Cmmons Blvd S (19958)
PHONE..................................302 703-1770
Jim Baker,
Mark Nauman,
EMP: 4
SALES (est): 129.5K **Privately Held**
SIC: 8711 Engineering services

(G-3692)
PINE ACRES INC
Also Called: Leisure Pt MBL HM Pk Cmpground
34385 Carpenters Way B (19958-4910)
PHONE..................................302 945-2000
George H Harrison Jr, *President*
Thelma Corso, *Corp Secy*
Judith Harrison, *Vice Pres*
EMP: 15
SALES (est): 943.6K **Privately Held**
SIC: 7033 6515 Campsite; mobile home site operators

(G-3693)
PKS & COMPANY PA
1143 Savannah Rd (19958-1516)
PHONE..................................302 645-5757
Ronald E Derr, *Branch Mgr*
Michelle Grager, *Supervisor*
EMP: 6
SALES (corp-wide): 7.2MM **Privately Held**
SIC: 7371 Computer software development
PA: Pks & Company, P.A.
1801 Sweetbay Dr
Salisbury MD 21804
410 219-3345

(G-3694)
PNC BANK NATIONAL ASSOCIATION
17725 Coastal Hwy (19958-6215)
PHONE..................................302 645-4500
David Crouse, *Vice Pres*

Vanita Vanegas, *Administration*
EMP: 12
SALES (corp-wide): 19.9B **Publicly Held**
WEB: www.pncfunds.com
SIC: 6021 National trust companies with deposits, commercial
HQ: Pnc Bank, National Association
222 Delaware Ave
Wilmington DE 19801
877 762-2000

(G-3695)
POLAR STRATEGY INC
16192 Coastal Hwy (19958-3608)
PHONE..................................703 628-0001
Omar Mahmood, *Principal*
EMP: 5
SQ FT: 150
SALES (est): 107K **Privately Held**
SIC: 7371 7373 Computer software systems analysis & design, custom; value-added resellers, computer systems

(G-3696)
PREMIER RESTORATION INC
145 Heather Dr (19958-6042)
PHONE..................................302 645-1611
William Baughman, *President*
Bill Baughman, *President*
EMP: 10
SALES (est): 1.2MM **Privately Held**
SIC: 8711 Construction & civil engineering

(G-3697)
PRINT COAST 2 COAST
33073 E Light Dr (19958-4661)
PHONE..................................302 381-4610
Melody Diaz, *Principal*
EMP: 2
SALES (est): 168.4K **Privately Held**
SIC: 2752 Commercial printing, lithographic

(G-3698)
PRO REHAB CHIROPRACTIC
105 W 4th St (19958-1311)
PHONE..................................302 200-9102
EMP: 1
SALES (est): 73.3K **Privately Held**
SIC: 8093 8041 Rehabilitation center, outpatient treatment; offices & clinics of chiropractors

(G-3699)
PROGAR & CO
Also Called: Progar & Company PA
33815 Clay Rd Ste 1 (19958-6297)
PHONE..................................302 645-6216
Gary A Progar, *Owner*
Marc Samuels, *Office Mgr*
EMP: 8
SALES (est): 280K **Privately Held**
WEB: www.1040pro.com
SIC: 8721 Certified public accountant

(G-3700)
PRUDENTIAL GALLO REALTY
16712 Kings Hwy (19958-4929)
PHONE..................................302 645-6661
Salvatore Gallo, *Owner*
Adriane Gallagher, *Purch Mgr*
Gayle Doughten, *Broker*
Maureen Kyritsis, *Broker*
Adrienne Klase, *Sales Associate*
EMP: 15
SALES (est): 1MM **Privately Held**
SIC: 6531 6512 6513 6514 Real estate agent, residential; commercial & industrial building operation; apartment building operators; dwelling operators, except apartments

(G-3701)
PSC TECHNOLOGY INCORPORATED (PA)
16192 Coastal Hwy (19958-3608)
PHONE..................................866 866-1466
Paul Brooks, *President*
EMP: 8 **EST:** 2008
SALES: 5MM **Privately Held**
SIC: 8059 Personal care home, with health care

(G-3702)
QUALITY CARE HOMES LLC
20366 Hopkins Rd (19958-5533)
PHONE..................................302 858-3999
Dominic Drummond, *Principal*
EMP: 9 **EST:** 2015
SALES (est): 103.1K **Privately Held**
SIC: 8059 Nursing & personal care

(G-3703)
QUALITY ROFG SUP LANCASTER INC
1312 Hwy 1 (19958)
PHONE..................................302 644-4115
William Boylen, *Manager*
Kevin Mitchell, *Manager*
EMP: 12
SALES (corp-wide): 7.1B **Publicly Held**
SIC: 5033 Roofing & siding materials
HQ: Quality Roofing Supply Company Of Lancaster, Inc.
737 Flory Mill Rd
Lancaster PA 17601
717 569-2661

(G-3704)
R E MICHEL COMPANY LLC
32437 Lwes Georgetown Hwy (19958-1646)
PHONE..................................302 645-0585
Carl Mears, *Manager*
EMP: 7
SALES (corp-wide): 898.2MM **Privately Held**
WEB: www.remichel.com
SIC: 5075 5078 Warm air heating equipment & supplies; air conditioning & ventilation equipment & supplies; refrigeration equipment & supplies
PA: R. E. Michel Company, Llc
1 Re Michel Dr
Glen Burnie MD 21060
410 760-4000

(G-3705)
R M BELL INDUSTRIES INC
1504 Savannah Rd (19958-1624)
PHONE..................................302 542-3747
EMP: 2
SALES (est): 94.5K **Privately Held**
SIC: 3999 Manufacturing industries

(G-3706)
RADIANCE VR INC
16192 Coastal Hwy (19958-3608)
PHONE..................................937 818-3988
Nini Hinsche, *Principal*
EMP: 2
SALES (est): 104.7K **Privately Held**
SIC: 3571 Personal computers (microcomputers)

(G-3707)
RAMACHANDRA U HOSMANE MD
1408 Savannah Rd (19958-1623)
P.O. Box 648 (19958-0648)
PHONE..................................302 645-2274
Ramachandr U Hosmane MD, *Owner*
EMP: 6
SQ FT: 1,000
SALES (est): 370K **Privately Held**
SIC: 8011 Surgeon; urologist

(G-3708)
RAVE BUSINESS SYSTEMS LLC
16192 Coastal Hwy (19958-3608)
PHONE..................................302 407-2270
Mohsin Khan,
EMP: 15
SALES (est): 297K **Privately Held**
SIC: 7379 7373 ; systems software development services

(G-3709)
RAYMOND JAMES FINCL SVCS INC
34346 Carpenters Way (19958-4910)
PHONE..................................302 645-8592
Adrianne Moore, *Vice Pres*
EMP: 11
SALES (corp-wide): 8B **Publicly Held**
SIC: 6211 Brokers, security

Lewes - Sussex County (G-3710) GEOGRAPHIC SECTION

HQ: Raymond James Financial Services, Inc.
880 Carillon Pkwy
Saint Petersburg FL 33716
727 567-1000

(G-3710)
RDS ENGINEERING LLC
16192 Coastal Hwy (19958-3608)
PHONE..................417 763-3727
EMP: 2
SQ FT: 700
SALES (est): 102.9K **Privately Held**
SIC: 3861 8711 Mfg Photographic Equipment/Supplies Engineering Services

(G-3711)
RED MILL INN
16218 Coastal Hwy (19958-3609)
PHONE..................302 645-9736
Roger Mall, *Mng Member*
Percilla Mall,
EMP: 4
SALES (est): 170K **Privately Held**
SIC: 7011 Motels

(G-3712)
REDDIX TRANSPORTATION INC
31014 Oak Leaf Dr (19958-5596)
PHONE..................302 249-9331
George I Reddix, *Principal*
George Reddix, *Principal*
EMP: 10
SALES (est): 714.4K **Privately Held**
SIC: 4789 Pipeline terminal facilities, independently operated

(G-3713)
REDDIX TRUCKING INC
31342 Kendale Rd (19958-4486)
PHONE..................302 745-1277
George Reddix, *President*
EMP: 4 EST: 2012
SALES (est): 537K **Privately Held**
SIC: 4212 Dump truck haulage

(G-3714)
REMAX COAST & COUNTRY
Also Called: Re/Max
16392 Coastal Hwy (19958-3611)
PHONE..................302 645-0800
Kathy Engel, *Owner*
Susan Malone, *Broker*
Brooke Davis, *Real Est Agnt*
EMP: 4
SALES (est): 264K **Privately Held**
WEB: www.rccde.com
SIC: 6531 Real estate agent, residential

(G-3715)
RENDEZVOUS INC
16192 Coastal Hwy (19958-3608)
PHONE..................302 645-7400
Adonis Peralta, *CEO*
EMP: 1
SALES (est): 50K **Privately Held**
SIC: 7299 7372 7389 Dating service; prepackaged software;

(G-3716)
RESORT BROADCASTING CO LP
Also Called: Wgmd
31549 Dutton Ln (19958-4512)
P.O. Box 530, Rehoboth Beach (19971-0530)
PHONE..................302 945-2050
David Schoumacher, *Partner*
Joseph Giuliani, *General Ptnr*
Walt Palmer, *Engineer*
Laura Duvall, *Marketing Staff*
Sandy Christensen, *Manager*
EMP: 30 EST: 1975
SALES (est): 1.4MM **Privately Held**
WEB: www.wgmd.com
SIC: 4832 Radio broadcasting stations, music format

(G-3717)
RESORT CUSTOM HOMES
18355 Coastal Hwy (19958-4778)
PHONE..................302 645-8222
EMP: 8 EST: 2017
SALES (est): 74.8K **Privately Held**
SIC: 7011 Hotels

(G-3718)
RICHARD BRYAN
Also Called: Long & Foster Realtors
117 Savannah Rd (19958-1447)
P.O. Box 34 (19958-0034)
PHONE..................302 645-6100
Richard Bryan, *Owner*
EMP: 12
SALES (est): 530.7K **Privately Held**
SIC: 6531 Real estate agent, residential

(G-3719)
RICHARD WOINSKI TRUCKING
17157 Minos Conaway Rd (19958-3807)
PHONE..................302 644-1579
Richard Woinski, *Owner*
EMP: 4
SALES (est): 197.5K **Privately Held**
SIC: 4212 Local trucking, without storage

(G-3720)
ROAD SITE CONSTRUCTION INC
Also Called: Clean Cut Interlocking Pavers
16192 Coastal Hwy (19958-3608)
PHONE..................302 645-1922
Rich Bell, *President*
EMP: 14
SQ FT: 24,001
SALES (est): 2MM **Privately Held**
SIC: 1611 Surfacing & paving

(G-3721)
ROBIN S WRIGHT
Also Called: Lotus Blossom Learning Center
19305 Beaver Dam Rd (19958-5539)
PHONE..................302 249-2105
Robin Wright, *Director*
EMP: 5
SALES (est): 165.7K **Privately Held**
SIC: 8351 Child day care services

(G-3722)
ROCKET SIGNS
18388 Coastal Hwy Unit 4 (19958-4204)
P.O. Box 332, Nassau (19969-0332)
PHONE..................302 645-1425
Rocket Arena, *Principal*
EMP: 2
SALES (est): 139.3K **Privately Held**
SIC: 3993 Signs & advertising specialties

(G-3723)
ROCKEY & ASSOCIATES INC
Also Called: Rockteam
18306 Coastal Hwy (19958-4772)
PHONE..................610 640-4880
Patience Rockey, *President*
EMP: 5
SQ FT: 6,000
SALES (est): 578.3K **Privately Held**
SIC: 7371 Computer software systems analysis & design, custom

(G-3724)
ROGUE ELEPHANTS LLC
16192 Coastal Hwy (19958-3608)
PHONE..................979 264-2845
Affan Farooq,
Rajiv Tyal,
Najam Wasty,
EMP: 3
SALES (est): 73.4K **Privately Held**
SIC: 7389 7372 Business services; educational computer software

(G-3725)
ROSE HEALTH CENTER INC
31347 Point Cir (19958-3869)
PHONE..................302 441-5987
Romina Thomas, *Admin Sec*
EMP: 5
SALES: 209.6K **Privately Held**
SIC: 8099 Health & allied services

(G-3726)
ROSS BICYCLES LLC (PA)
16192 Coastal Hwy (19958-3608)
PHONE..................888 392-5628
Shaun Ross, *CEO*
EMP: 3
SALES (est): 1.4MM **Privately Held**
SIC: 3751 Bicycles & related parts

(G-3727)
RYAN MEDIA LAB INC
31794 Carneros Ave (19958-2523)
PHONE..................302 360-8847
Mark Ryan, *CEO*
EMP: 2 EST: 2014
SALES (est): 110.2K **Privately Held**
SIC: 2741

(G-3728)
SAFERWATCH LLC
16192 Coastal Hwy (19958-3608)
PHONE..................844 449-2824
EMP: 20
SALES (est): 375.4K **Privately Held**
SIC: 7371 Computer software development & applications

(G-3729)
SANDWICH INC
16192 Coastal Hwy (19958-3608)
PHONE..................647 360-8300
Tanuj Sethi, *CEO*
EMP: 1 EST: 2014
SALES (est): 39.6K **Privately Held**
SIC: 3999 Manufacturing industries

(G-3730)
SAVANNAH INN
55 N Atlantic Dr (19958)
PHONE..................302 645-0330
Gina Kaye, *Principal*
EMP: 5 EST: 2008
SALES (est): 203.9K **Privately Held**
SIC: 7011 Bed & breakfast inn

(G-3731)
SAXTON MARITIME SERVICES LLC
16192 Coastal Hwy (19958-3608)
PHONE..................415 870-3881
Matt Saxton,
EMP: 1
SALES (est): 54.6K **Privately Held**
SIC: 3732 Boat building & repairing

(G-3732)
SCANTA INC
16192 Coastal Hwy (19958-3608)
PHONE..................302 645-7400
Chaitanya Hiremath, *CEO*
EMP: 22 **Privately Held**
SIC: 7371 Computer software development & applications

(G-3733)
SCHOLARJET PBC
16192 Coastal Hwy (19958-3608)
PHONE..................617 407-9851
Tuan Ho, *CEO*
Joseph Alim, *CEO*
EMP: 2
SALES (est): 56.5K **Privately Held**
SIC: 7372 Educational computer software

(G-3734)
SEARCH LLC
16192 Coastal Hwy (19958-3608)
PHONE..................858 348-4584
Abhishek Singh, *Principal*
EMP: 31
SALES (est): 541.1K **Privately Held**
SIC: 4813

(G-3735)
SEASIDE SERVICE LLC
36360 Tarpon Dr (19958-5055)
PHONE..................302 827-3775
EMP: 2
SALES (est): 94.5K **Privately Held**
SIC: 3444 3312 Casings, sheet metal; structural shapes & pilings, steel

(G-3736)
SECURENETMD LLC
16557 Coastal Hwy (19958-3605)
PHONE..................302 645-7770
Casey Bradham, *Vice Pres*
Tammie Draine, *Accounting Mgr*
Jeff Gennusa, *IT/INT Sup*
Alexander Cruz, *Network Enginr*
Rob Nicholson, *Business Dir*
EMP: 40

SALES (est): 4.7MM **Privately Held**
SIC: 7379 Computer related maintenance services

(G-3737)
SERVICE ENERGY LLC
47 Clay Rd (19958-1741)
P.O. Box 24, Milford (19963-0024)
PHONE..................302 645-9050
Charles Sackritter, *Manager*
EMP: 10 **Privately Held**
WEB: www.serviceenergy.com
SIC: 5172 5983 Petroleum products; fuel oil dealers
PA: Service Energy, L.L.C.
3799 N Dupont Hwy
Dover DE 19901

(G-3738)
SHAMROCK SERVICES LLC
Also Called: Shamrock Taxi
22576 Waterview Rd (19958-5703)
PHONE..................302 519-7609
Jason Wells, *Manager*
EMP: 4
SALES (est): 164.5K **Privately Held**
SIC: 4111 Local & suburban transit

(G-3739)
SHOOLEX LLC (PA)
16192 Coastal Hwy (19958-3608)
PHONE..................866 697-3330
Joseph Ghahari,
EMP: 1 EST: 2017
SALES (est): 145K **Privately Held**
SIC: 3131 5139 Boot & shoe accessories; shoe accessories

(G-3740)
SHORE ELECTRIC INC
34697 Jiffy Way Unit 4 (19958-4932)
PHONE..................302 645-4503
Joseph Johnson, *President*
EMP: 6
SALES: 1MM **Privately Held**
SIC: 1731 General electrical contractor

(G-3741)
SHOULDR LLC
16192 Coastal Hwy (19958-3608)
PHONE..................917 331-1384
Mohashin Azad, *CEO*
Adam Thiessen, *COO*
EMP: 5
SALES (est): 107K **Privately Held**
SIC: 7371 Computer software development & applications

(G-3742)
SIGN LNGUAGE BLITZ PBLC BENFT ◯
16192 Coastal Hwy (19958-3608)
PHONE..................928 925-3842
EMP: 1 EST: 2019
SALES (est): 46K **Privately Held**
SIC: 3993 Signs & advertising specialties

(G-3743)
SIGNAL GARDEN RESEARCH CORP
16192 Coastal Hwy (19958-3608)
PHONE..................708 715-3646
Danny Bernal, *Administration*
EMP: 4
SALES (est): 90.2K **Privately Held**
SIC: 8733 Research institute

(G-3744)
SIGNATURE FITNESS EQP LLC
16192 Coastal Hwy (19958-3608)
PHONE..................888 657-5357
EMP: 4
SALES (est): 250K **Privately Held**
SIC: 5091 Sporting And Recreation Goods

(G-3745)
SIGNATURE PROPERTY MANAGEMENT
20375 John J Williams Hwy (19958-4305)
PHONE..................302 212-2381
Harry Burroughs, *Owner*
Stuart Galkin, *Vice Pres*
EMP: 5 EST: 2014
SALES (est): 261.5K **Privately Held**
SIC: 8741 Business management

Lewes - Sussex County (G-3780)

(G-3746)
SITEAGE LLC
16192 Coastal Hwy (19958-3608)
PHONE..................302 380-3709
Adil Hussain,
EMP: 10
SALES (est): 111.9K Privately Held
SIC: 4813

(G-3747)
SLEEP DISORDERS CENTER
424 Savannah Rd (19958-1462)
PHONE..................302 645-3186
Jeffrey Freed, CEO
EMP: 5 EST: 1993
SALES (est): 240K Privately Held
SIC: 8099 Health screening service

(G-3748)
SLEEP INN & SUITES
18451 Coastal Hwy (19958-4930)
PHONE..................302 645-6464
Tom Kramedas, Owner
EMP: 20 EST: 2001
SALES (est): 823.1K Privately Held
WEB: www.rehobothsleepinn.com
SIC: 7011 Hotels & motels

(G-3749)
SMF DELIVERIES LLC
17 Amberwood Way (19958-9467)
PHONE..................302 945-6693
Stacey Furman, Principal
EMP: 4
SALES (est): 243.1K Privately Held
SIC: 4212 Delivery service, vehicular

(G-3750)
SMITH FNBERG MCCRTNEY BERL LLP
34382 Carpenters Way # 1 (19958-4919)
PHONE..................302 644-8330
George Smith, Managing Prtnr
EMP: 21 Privately Held
SIC: 8111 General practice attorney, lawyer
PA: Smith Feinberg Mccartney & Berl Llp
406 S Bedford St
Georgetown DE 19947

(G-3751)
SOCAL AUTO SUPPLY INC (PA)
16192 Postal Hwy (19958)
PHONE..................818 717-9982
Jonathan Robert Noori, CEO
Kos Noori, Exec VP
Khoforw Noori, Vice Pres
EMP: 65
SQ FT: 5,000
SALES (est): 510.3K Privately Held
SIC: 7213 2676 Towel supply; towels, napkins & tissue paper products

(G-3752)
SOCIETY FOR ACPUNCTURE RES INC
108 Dewey Ave (19958-1713)
PHONE..................302 222-1832
Rosa Schnyer, President
Richard Harris, Vice Pres
Roni D Posner, Exec Dir
EMP: 15
SALES: 58.1K Privately Held
SIC: 8733 7389 Noncommercial research organizations;

(G-3753)
SOCIOMATRY PRESS
103 Hornbill Ct (19958-2318)
PHONE..................302 313-5341
EMP: 1
SALES (est): 43.6K Privately Held
SIC: 2741 Miscellaneous publishing

(G-3754)
SOLAR UNLIMITED NORTH AMER LLC
11 Kentucky Ave (19958-1838)
PHONE..................302 542-4580
George Chambers, Mng Member
Herbert Edwards,
Beverly Yankwitt,
EMP: 3

SALES: 500K Privately Held
SIC: 3494 3674 7389 Valves & pipe fittings; solar cells;

(G-3755)
SOLID IDEA SOLUTIONS LLC
16192 Coastal Hwy (19958-3608)
PHONE..................646 982-2890
Travis Vance, CEO
EMP: 5
SALES (est): 104.3K Privately Held
SIC: 7379 Computer related consulting services

(G-3756)
SOUCIALIZE INC
16192 Coastal Hwy (19958-3608)
PHONE..................916 803-1057
Monique Rice, CEO
EMP: 7
SALES (est): 37.9K Privately Held
SIC: 7929 Entertainment service

(G-3757)
SOUTHERN DEL PHYSCL THERAPY (PA)
Also Called: Lewes Physical Therapy
701 Savannah Rd Ste A (19958-1550)
PHONE..................302 644-2530
Julie Moyer Knowles, President
EMP: 10
SALES (est): 765.5K Privately Held
SIC: 8049 Physical therapist

(G-3758)
SOUTHERN DELAWARE IMAGING LLP
Also Called: Southern Del Imaging Assoc
17503 Nassau Commons Blvd (19958-6283)
P.O. Box 263 (19958-0263)
PHONE..................302 645-7919
Norman Boyer MD, Partner
Ellen Bahtiarian, Partner
Binzhi Zhang, Internal Med
Dennis Flamini, Radiology
EMP: 17
SALES (est): 1MM Privately Held
WEB: www.sdiassociates.com
SIC: 8011 Radiologist

(G-3759)
SOUTHERN DELAWARE SIGNS
18388 Coastal Hwy Unit 4 (19958-4204)
PHONE..................302 645-1425
D J Baker, Owner
EMP: 1
SALES (est): 50.6K Privately Held
SIC: 3993 Signs & advertising specialties

(G-3760)
SPECIAL CARE INC
16698 Kings Hwy Ste D (19958-4936)
PHONE..................302 644-6990
Cheryl Jankowski, Branch Mgr
Beth Copeland, Director
EMP: 11
SALES (corp-wide): 7.4MM Privately Held
SIC: 8082 Home health care services
PA: Special Care, Inc.
800 Bethlehem Pike
Glenside PA 19038
215 402-0200

(G-3761)
SQRIN TECHNOLOGIES LLC
16192 Coastal Hwy (19958-3608)
PHONE..................540 330-1379
Olajide Makinde,
EMP: 4 EST: 2018
SALES: 15K Privately Held
SIC: 7371 Computer software development & applications

(G-3762)
STAMPS BY IMPRESSION
102 Dove Dr (19958-1602)
P.O. Box 641 (19958-0641)
PHONE..................302 645-7191
Paul Tyrrell, Partner
Paul Terryle, Partner
Bob Tyrrell, Partner
EMP: 2

SALES: 220K Privately Held
WEB: www.stampsbyimpression.com
SIC: 3953 Marking devices

(G-3763)
STEAMBOAT LANDING
Coastal Hwy 1 (19958)
P.O. Box 300 (19958-0300)
PHONE..................302 645-6500
Linda Pride, Owner
EMP: 5 EST: 1970
SALES: 270K Privately Held
SIC: 7033 Campgrounds

(G-3764)
STEEL BUILDINGS INC
Also Called: Northern Steel International
17515 Nassau Commons Blvd (19958-6283)
PHONE..................302 644-0444
Joss Hudson, President
EMP: 2
SQ FT: 4,500
SALES (est): 192.7K Privately Held
WEB: www.nsteel.com
SIC: 3448 Buildings, portable: prefabricated metal

(G-3765)
STEVEN P COPP
Also Called: Copp Seafood
Rr 3 Box 254a (19958)
PHONE..................302 645-9112
Clifford Copp, Owner
EMP: 4
SALES (est): 187.4K Privately Held
SIC: 2092 Seafoods, frozen: prepared

(G-3766)
STRIKE EXCHANGE INC
Also Called: Strike Social
16192 Coastal Hwy (19958-3608)
PHONE..................310 995-5653
Patrick McKenna, CEO
Tim Helfrey, Principal
EMP: 12
SALES (est): 480K Privately Held
SIC: 7389 ;

(G-3767)
STUDIO ON 24 INC
20231 John J Williams Hwy (19958-4314)
PHONE..................302 644-4424
Debra Applebey, President
EMP: 3
SALES: 125K Privately Held
SIC: 3229 Pressed & blown glass

(G-3768)
SUMMIT ORTHOPAEDIC HM CARE LLC
1632 Savannah Rd Ste 8 (19958-1659)
PHONE..................302 703-0800
Eric Reinhold, Mng Member
EMP: 7 EST: 2014
SALES (est): 81.3K Privately Held
SIC: 8011 Orthopedic physician

(G-3769)
SUN EXCHANGE INC (PA)
16192 Coastal Hwy 1 (19958-3608)
PHONE..................917 747-9527
Abraham Campbridge, CEO
Lawrence Temlock, CFO
EMP: 6 EST: 2016
SALES: 1MM Privately Held
SIC: 7389 Financial services

(G-3770)
SUNSHINE NUT COMPANY LLC
16192 Coastal Hwy (19958-3608)
PHONE..................781 352-7766
Don Larson,
▲ EMP: 20
SALES (est): 1.1MM Privately Held
SIC: 2068 Salted & roasted nuts & seeds

(G-3771)
SUSSEX COUNTY FEDERAL CR UN
34686 Oldm Postal Ln (19958)
PHONE..................302 644-7111
Karen Jefferson, Branch Mgr
EMP: 9

SALES (corp-wide): 9.7MM Privately Held
SIC: 6061 Federal credit unions
PA: Sussex County Federal Credit Union
1941 Bridgeville Hwy
Seaford DE 19973
302 629-0100

(G-3772)
SUSSEX EYE CARE & MEDICAL ASSO
1306 Savannah Rd (19958-1526)
PHONE..................302 644-8007
Roldolfo J Rios, Principal
Rodolfo Rios, Principal
▲ EMP: 9
SALES (est): 226.2K Privately Held
SIC: 8099 Health & allied services

(G-3773)
SUSSEX PODIATRY GROUP
Also Called: Kulina, Patrick F MD
1532 Savannah Rd (19958-1624)
PHONE..................302 645-8555
Patrick F Kulina, President
EMP: 8
SALES (est): 440K Privately Held
SIC: 8043 Offices & clinics of podiatrists

(G-3774)
SUTHAR HOLDING CORPORATION
16192 Coastal Hwy (19958-3608)
PHONE..................302 291-2490
Jay Suthar, President
Parkash Suthar, Corp Secy
EMP: 35 Privately Held
SIC: 6719 Investment holding companies, except banks

(G-3775)
SWITCHEDON INC
16192 Coastal Hwy (19958-3608)
PHONE..................415 271-1172
Jason Collins, CEO
EMP: 22 EST: 2015
SALES (est): 1.1MM Privately Held
SIC: 7372 Business oriented computer software

(G-3776)
TALK AWARE LLC
16192 Coastal Hwy (19958-3608)
PHONE..................302 645-7400
James Morrissette,
EMP: 2
SQ FT: 1,500
SALES (est): 56.5K Privately Held
SIC: 7372 Operating systems computer software

(G-3777)
TALL PINES ASSOCIATES LLC
Also Called: Tall Pines Campground
29551 Persimmon Rd (19958-3954)
PHONE..................302 684-0300
Richard Berman, President
Malcolm Berman,
EMP: 12
SALES (est): 599.5K Privately Held
SIC: 7033 Campgrounds

(G-3778)
TARGUS U S A
32884 Ocean Reach Dr (19958-4658)
PHONE..................302 644-2311
Wesley Kirschner, Principal
EMP: 1
SALES (est): 74.6K Privately Held
SIC: 3661 Telephone & telegraph apparatus

(G-3779)
TDC PARTNERS LTD
31781 Marsh Island Ave (19958-3350)
PHONE..................302 827-2137
Theodore R Ferragut, President
EMP: 5 EST: 2008
SALES: 310K Privately Held
SIC: 8741 Business management

(G-3780)
TECHNO GOOBER
17527 Nssau Cmmons Blvd S (19958)
PHONE..................302 645-7177

Lewes - Sussex County (G-3781) — GEOGRAPHIC SECTION

Frank Payton, *Owner*
Michele Glanden, *Office Mgr*
EMP: 10
SALES (est): 327.6K **Privately Held**
SIC: 7374 Computer graphics service

(G-3781)
THERAPY AT BEACH
34444 King Street Row (19958-4787)
PHONE.................................302 313-5555
EMP: 7
SALES (est): 97.6K **Privately Held**
SIC: 7299 Massage parlor

(G-3782)
THOMAS R WYSHOCK
Also Called: American Heritage
32832 Pear Tree Ct (19958-3724)
PHONE.................................302 645-5070
EMP: 6 **EST:** 1975
SQ FT: 1,800
SALES (est): 440K **Privately Held**
SIC: 6411 Insurance Agent/Broker

(G-3783)
THRESHOLDS INC
17577 Nassau Commons Blvd # 202 (19958-6288)
PHONE.................................302 827-4478
EMP: 4
SALES (est): 111.9K **Privately Held**
SIC: 8069 Drug addiction rehabilitation hospital

(G-3784)
TIDEWATER PHYSCL THRPY AND REB
20750 John J Williams Hwy # 1 (19958-4399)
PHONE.................................302 945-5111
Susan Goldstein, *Manager*
EMP: 8
SALES (corp-wide): 2.6MM **Privately Held**
WEB: www.tidewaterpt.com
SIC: 8049 8093 Physical therapist; rehabilitation center, outpatient treatment
PA: Tidewater Physical Therapy And Rehabilitation Associates Pa
406 Marvel Ct
Easton MD 21601
410 822-3116

(G-3785)
TIKI INTERACTIVE INC
16192 Coastal Hwy (19958-3608)
PHONE.................................408 306-4393
Anil Neela, *Principal*
EMP: 5
SALES (est): 107K **Privately Held**
SIC: 7371 Computer software development & applications

(G-3786)
TILE MARKET OF DELAWARE INC
17701 Dartmouth Dr Unit 1 (19958-4205)
PHONE.................................302 644-7100
Paul Anderson, *General Mgr*
Kim Watson, *Vice Pres*
EMP: 4
SALES (est): 283.6K **Privately Held**
SIC: 1743 Tile installation, ceramic
PA: Tile Market Of Delaware, Inc.
405 Marsh Ln Ste 3
Wilmington DE 19804

(G-3787)
TLBC LLC
Also Called: Lewes Building Co, The
105 2nd St (19958-1356)
PHONE.................................302 797-8700
Jeff Dawson, *Owner*
EMP: 5 **EST:** 2011
SALES (est): 430.3K **Privately Held**
SIC: 1521 New construction, single-family houses

(G-3788)
TOP NAILS
17601 Coastal Hwy Unit 2 (19958-6217)
PHONE.................................302 644-2261
Luong Nguyen, *Managing Prtnr*
Minh Tram, *Partner*
EMP: 4
SALES: 170K **Privately Held**
SIC: 7231 Manicurist, pedicurist

(G-3789)
TOP NOTCH HTG & A C & RFRGN
33806 Dreamweaver Ln (19958-1653)
PHONE.................................302 645-7171
Robert Willin, *Principal*
EMP: 6
SALES (est): 441K **Privately Held**
SIC: 1711 Heating systems repair & maintenance; heating & air conditioning contractors

(G-3790)
TOP OF THE LINE JANTR SVCS
19602 Mulberry Knoll Rd (19958-4358)
P.O. Box 668 (19958-0668)
PHONE.................................302 645-2668
Robert W Shipe, *President*
Sandra Shipe, *Treasurer*
EMP: 12
SALES (est): 267.5K **Privately Held**
SIC: 7349 Janitorial service, contract basis

(G-3791)
TOUCH OF ITALY BAKERY LLC
33323 E Chesapeake St # 31 (19958-7242)
PHONE.................................302 827-2132
Carrie Greenleaf, *Manager*
EMP: 8
SALES (est): 640.4K **Privately Held**
SIC: 5149 Bakery products

(G-3792)
TOUGH LUCK LLC
1030 Hwy One (19958)
PHONE.................................302 644-8001
Alex Dunn, *Principal*
EMP: 3
SALES (est): 237.6K **Privately Held**
SIC: 3199 Leather garments

(G-3793)
TPW MANAGEMENT LLC
17577 Nassau Commons Blvd # 103 (19958-6288)
PHONE.................................302 227-7878
EMP: 5
SALES (est): 319.3K **Privately Held**
SIC: 8741 Management services
PA: Tpw Management Llc
4903 Main St
Manchester Center VT 05255

(G-3794)
TRAVEL AGENCY
101 Breakwater Reach (19958-3125)
P.O. Box 366, Nassau (19969-0366)
PHONE.................................302 381-0205
Mudit NASA, *Principal*
EMP: 4
SALES (est): 120.2K **Privately Held**
SIC: 4512 7389 Air passenger carrier, scheduled;

(G-3795)
TRUCK LAGBE INC
16192 Coastal Hwy (19958-3608)
PHONE.................................860 810-8677
Anayet Rashid, *CEO*
EMP: 42
SALES: 10MM **Privately Held**
SIC: 7371 Computer software development & applications

(G-3796)
TRUITT INSURANCE AGENCY INC
Also Called: Nationwide
365 Savannah Rd (19958-1438)
P.O. Box 248 (19958-0248)
PHONE.................................302 645-9344
Thad Truitt, *President*
Nick Hibbs, *Agent*
EMP: 5
SQ FT: 2,200
SALES (est): 920.2K **Privately Held**
WEB: www.truittins.com
SIC: 6411 Insurance agents, brokers & service

(G-3797)
TRUMOVE INC
16192 Coastal Hwy (19958-3608)
PHONE.................................917 379-7427
Chiao-WEI Lee, *Director*
EMP: 3
SALES (est): 71.1K **Privately Held**
SIC: 7372 Application computer software

(G-3798)
TUNNELL & RAYSOR PA
770 Kings Hwy (19958-1704)
PHONE.................................302 644-4442
Heidi Balliet, *Branch Mgr*
EMP: 5
SALES (corp-wide): 6.4MM **Privately Held**
WEB: www.tunnellraysor.com
SIC: 8111 General practice attorney, lawyer
PA: Tunnell & Raysor, P.A.
30 E Pine St
Georgetown DE 19947
302 856-7313

(G-3799)
TURNKEY LENDER INC
16192 Coastal Hwy (19958-3608)
PHONE.................................888 299-4892
Elena Ionenko, *CFO*
EMP: 5
SALES (est): 112.7K **Privately Held**
SIC: 7371 Computer software development

(G-3800)
U-HAUL NEIGHBORHOOD DEALER
33012 Cedar Grove Rd (19958-4644)
PHONE.................................302 644-4316
EMP: 8
SALES (est): 101.1K **Privately Held**
SIC: 7513 Truck rental & leasing, no drivers

(G-3801)
U-HAUL NEIGHBORHOOD DEALER
17649 Coastal Hwy (19958-6213)
PHONE.................................302 703-0376
EMP: 8
SALES (est): 101.1K **Privately Held**
SIC: 7513 Truck rental & leasing, no drivers

(G-3802)
UFO DEVELOPMENT GROUP INC
16192 Coastal Hwy (19958-3608)
PHONE.................................408 995-3217
Mike Ross, *Principal*
EMP: 2
SQ FT: 1,000
SALES (est): 61.7K **Privately Held**
SIC: 7372 Application computer software

(G-3803)
URBN STEAMLAB LLC
16192 Coastal Hwy (19958-3608)
PHONE.................................267 738-3096
Shivanthi Anandan, *Mng Member*
EMP: 2
SALES (est): 74.4K **Privately Held**
SIC: 2869 Laboratory chemicals, organic

(G-3804)
US ENGINEERING CORPORATION
16192 Coastal Hwy (19958-3608)
PHONE.................................302 645-7400
Prometheus George, *President*
EMP: 10
SALES (est): 880K **Privately Held**
SIC: 3533 Oil & gas field machinery

(G-3805)
US LAWNS DOVER
16856 Ketch Ct (19958-5012)
PHONE.................................302 703-2818
Bruce Maloomian, *Principal*
EMP: 4
SALES (est): 133.7K **Privately Held**
SIC: 0782 Lawn care services

(G-3806)
UTILISITE INC
20721 Robinsonville Rd (19958-6044)
PHONE.................................302 945-5022
Sharon Hart, *President*
EMP: 12
SALES: 2MM **Privately Held**
SIC: 1623 Water, sewer & utility lines

(G-3807)
VALIU INC
16192 Coastal Hwy (19958-3608)
PHONE.................................317 853-5081
Simon Chamorro, *CEO*
EMP: 6
SALES: 100K **Privately Held**
SIC: 7374 Data processing service

(G-3808)
VERTRIUS CORP
16192 Coastal Hwy (19958-3608)
PHONE.................................800 770-1913
Joe Ruiz, *CEO*
EMP: 10
SQ FT: 7,500
SALES (est): 373.3K **Privately Held**
SIC: 7371 Computer software development & applications

(G-3809)
VIVIANS STYLE
33516 Crossing Ave Unit 2 (19958-1697)
PHONE.................................302 645-9444
Vivan Mills, *CEO*
EMP: 5
SALES (est): 100.8K **Privately Held**
WEB: www.viviansstyle.com
SIC: 7231 Hairdressers

(G-3810)
VPN VPN VPN PROXY
16192 Coastal Hwy (19958-3608)
PHONE.................................415 758-8354
Robin Kumar Paul, *President*
EMP: 5
SALES (est): 107K **Privately Held**
SIC: 7371 Computer software development & applications

(G-3811)
VPS INTERNATIONAL LLC
16192 Coastal Hwy (19958-3608)
PHONE.................................800 493-9356
Carlos Sanchez, *Mng Member*
Alice Weiner,
EMP: 12
SALES (est): 726.1K **Privately Held**
SIC: 4813 Telephone communication, except radio

(G-3812)
VVS INC
115 Rodney Ave (19958-1207)
PHONE.................................302 827-2525
EMP: 4
SALES: 50K **Privately Held**
SIC: 1522 Residential Construction

(G-3813)
WAHED INC (PA)
16192 Coastal Hwy (19958-3608)
PHONE.................................646 961-7063
Junaid Wahedna, *CEO*
EMP: 39
SALES: 4.2K **Privately Held**
SIC: 7379

(G-3814)
WALLOR WEARABLES LLC
16192 Coastal Hwy (19958-3608)
PHONE.................................505 310-6099
Viorel Nicolae Cretu,
EMP: 4
SALES: 17K **Privately Held**
SIC: 7371 Computer software development & applications

(G-3815)
WALLTAG INC
16192 Coastal Hwy (19958-3608)
PHONE.................................917 725-1715
Chris Hanson, *CEO*
EMP: 1
SALES (est): 32.7K **Privately Held**
SIC: 7372 Prepackaged software

GEOGRAPHIC SECTION
Lincoln - Sussex County (G-3849)

(G-3816)
WASH-N-WAG
34680 Jiffy Way (19958-4931)
PHONE.................................302 644-2466
Joyce Stillwel, *President*
EMP: 5
SALES (est): 116.9K **Privately Held**
SIC: 0752 Grooming services, pet & animal specialties

(G-3817)
WEBCASTING MEDIA LLC
16192 Coastal Hwy (19958-3608)
PHONE.................................302 261-5178
EMP: 4
SALES (est): 108.3K **Privately Held**
SIC: 2741 Internet Publishing And Broadcasting

(G-3818)
WELLNESS FROM WITHIN
33253 Waterview Ct (19958-5317)
PHONE.................................717 884-3908
Emma Newman, *Principal*
EMP: 8 **EST:** 2016
SALES (est): 76K **Privately Held**
SIC: 8099 Health & allied services

(G-3819)
WHARTONS LANDSCAPING LLC
20503 Wil King Rd (19958-6024)
PHONE.................................302 947-0913
Joshua Wharton, *Principal*
EMP: 4
SALES (est): 545K **Privately Held**
WEB: www.whartonlandscapes.com
SIC: 0781 Landscape services

(G-3820)
WHAT IS YOUR VOICE INC
30428 E Barrier Reef Blvd (19958-6820)
P.O. Box 657, Georgetown (19947-0657)
PHONE.................................443 653-2067
Jacqueline Sterbach, *CEO*
Walter Sterbach, *Vice Pres*
Steve Folsom, *Treasurer*
Maria Grace Folsom, *Director*
Michelle Gallagher, *Advisor*
EMP: 15
SALES: 58.8K **Privately Held**
SIC: 8699 Charitable organization

(G-3821)
WHOLE CHILD APP INC
16192 Coastal Hwy (19958-3608)
PHONE.................................302 570-2002
Claudia Sasndor, *Principal*
EMP: 12
SALES (est): 192.9K
SALES (corp-wide): 200K **Privately Held**
SIC: 5942 8999 Book stores; personal services
PA: Whole Child Parenting, Inc.
    16192 Coastal Hwy
    Lewes DE 19958
    305 454-8285

(G-3822)
WIEDMANN ENTERPRISES INC
18013 Robinsonville Rd (19958-4401)
PHONE.................................302 645-2028
Karen Wiedmann, *Principal*
EMP: 4
SALES (est): 248.3K **Privately Held**
SIC: 8748 Business consulting

(G-3823)
WILGUS ASSOCIATES INC
1520 Savannah Rd (19958-1624)
PHONE.................................302 644-2960
Michele Ewing, *Personnel*
Joe Polichetti, *Manager*
EMP: 15
SALES (est): 1MM
SALES (corp-wide): 8.3MM **Privately Held**
SIC: 6411 6519 6531 Insurance brokers; real property lessors; real estate agents & managers
PA: Wilgus Associates Inc
    32904 Coastal Hwy
    Bethany Beach DE 19930
    302 539-7511

(G-3824)
WILKINS ENTERPRISES INC
34994 Holly Dr (19958-3231)
P.O. Box 250, Harbeson (19951-0250)
PHONE.................................302 945-4142
Scott Wilkins, *President*
EMP: 4
SALES (est): 306.9K **Privately Held**
SIC: 1799 7349 Cleaning building exteriors; cleaning service, industrial or commercial

(G-3825)
WILLIAMSON BUILDING CORP
130 New Rd (19958-9573)
PHONE.................................302 644-0605
Jeff Williamson, *President*
Mayumi Williamson, *Vice Pres*
EMP: 5
SALES (est): 378.8K **Privately Held**
SIC: 1521 7389 Single-family home remodeling, additions & repairs;

(G-3826)
WILLOW TREE EQUITY HOLDING LLC
16192 Coastal Hwy (19958-3608)
PHONE.................................213 479-4077
Oleksandr Martynov,
EMP: 10 **Privately Held**
SIC: 6719 Holding companies

(G-3827)
WILLOWFLARE LLC
16192 Coastal Hwy (19958-3608)
PHONE.................................312 428-0159
Rui Liu,
Richard Zhang,
Wanqi Zhu,
EMP: 4
SALES (est): 100.6K **Privately Held**
SIC: 8732 Market analysis, business & economic research

(G-3828)
WING2WIND TECHNOLOGY INC
31798 Carneros Ave (19958-2523)
PHONE.................................240 683-9787
EMP: 4
SALES (est): 199K **Privately Held**
SIC: 3511 Mfg Turbines/Generator Sets

(G-3829)
WIRELISITY INC
16192 Coastal Hwy (19958-3608)
PHONE.................................213 816-1957
EMP: 2
SALES (est): 88.3K **Privately Held**
SIC: 3629 Battery chargers, rectifying or nonrotating

(G-3830)
WRITINGWIZARDS INC
16192 Coastal Hwy (19958-3608)
PHONE.................................650 382-1357
Atay Kula, *Principal*
EMP: 5
SALES (est): 107K **Privately Held**
SIC: 7371 Computer software writers, freelance

(G-3831)
X LEADER LLC
16192 Coastal Hwy (19958-3608)
PHONE.................................800 345-2677
Sayd Farook,
EMP: 2
SALES (est): 59.2K **Privately Held**
SIC: 2741

(G-3832)
XENOPIA LLC
16192 Coastal Hwy (19958-3608)
PHONE.................................302 703-7050
Avram Cheaney,
◆ **EMP:** 5
SALES (est): 390K **Privately Held**
SIC: 5999 7389 Electronic parts & equipment;

(G-3833)
YELLO TECHNOLOGIES INC (PA)
16192 Coastal Hwy (19958-3608)
PHONE.................................954 802-6089
Adrian Corrente, *CEO*
EMP: 4
SALES (est): 92.1K **Privately Held**
SIC: 7389 7371 Courier or messenger service; computer software development & applications

(G-3834)
ZEINA JEHA MD MPH
16295 Willow Creek Rd (19958-3614)
PHONE.................................302 503-4200
EMP: 6 **EST:** 2018
SALES (est): 80.5K **Privately Held**
SIC: 8011 Offices & clinics of medical doctors

(G-3835)
ZIR LLC
16192 Coastal Hwy (19958-3608)
PHONE.................................203 524-1215
Anthony Pollak, *Principal*
EMP: 5
SALES: 100K **Privately Held**
SIC: 7371 8742 Computer software development & applications; marketing consulting services

(G-3836)
ZUMRA SOLUTIONS LLC
16192 Coastal Hwy (19958-3608)
PHONE.................................302 504-4423
Nouf Alfares, *CEO*
EMP: 8
SALES (est): 100K **Privately Held**
SIC: 8742 7371 Marketing consulting services; computer software development & applications

(G-3837)
ZWAANENDAEL LLC
142 2nd St (19958-1396)
PHONE.................................302 645-6466
Michael J Cryne,
EMP: 9 **EST:** 1952
SQ FT: 20,000
SALES (est): 472.3K **Privately Held**
SIC: 7261 7011 6513 6514 Funeral home; hotels; apartment building operators; residential building, four or fewer units: operation

Lincoln
Sussex County

(G-3838)
BELLA TERRA LANDSCAPES LLC
21429 Bella Terra Dr (19960-3725)
PHONE.................................302 422-9000
Mike Schimmel, *Mng Member*
Katharine Schimmel, *Mng Member*
EMP: 30
SALES: 3MM **Privately Held**
SIC: 0782 Landscape contractors

(G-3839)
BYRON H JEFFERSON ENGINEERING
10045 Clendaniel Pond Rd (19960-3015)
P.O. Box 161 (19960-0161)
PHONE.................................302 422-9568
Byron H Jefferson, *Owner*
EMP: 4
SALES (est): 300K **Privately Held**
WEB: www.byronlee.com
SIC: 4952 Sewerage systems

(G-3840)
CALVIN R CLENDANIEL ASSOCIATES
1 Buttler Ave (19960)
P.O. Box 125 (19960-0125)
PHONE.................................302 422-5347
Robert Calvin, *President*
EMP: 4
SALES (est): 339.7K **Privately Held**
SIC: 8711 Engineering services

(G-3841)
CHANGING FACES INC
19500 Pine Rd (19960-3016)
PHONE.................................302 397-4164
Deneen Smith-Roe, *Principal*
EMP: 12
SALES: 100K **Privately Held**
SIC: 8361 Residential care

(G-3842)
CLUB MANTIS BOXING LLC
16424 Fitzgeralds Rd (19960-3220)
PHONE.................................302 943-2580
Christopher Johnson, *Principal*
EMP: 4
SALES (est): 38.1K **Privately Held**
SIC: 7997 Membership sports & recreation clubs

(G-3843)
COMMUNITY HEATING & AC
10511 N Union Church Rd (19960-3519)
PHONE.................................302 422-6839
John Garbrick, *President*
Mary Garbrick, *Vice Pres*
EMP: 4 **EST:** 1998
SALES (est): 444.6K **Privately Held**
SIC: 1711 Warm air heating & air conditioning contractor

(G-3844)
DEAN DSIGN/MARKETING GROUP INC
13 Water St (19960-9728)
P.O. Box 605, Lewes (19958-0605)
PHONE.................................717 898-9800
EMP: 9
SQ FT: 3,000
SALES (est): 742K **Privately Held**
SIC: 7336 Commercial Art/Graphic Design

(G-3845)
ELIZABETH MALBERT
Also Called: Jireh Trucking
242 Cedar Dr (19960-2822)
PHONE.................................302 422-9015
Elizabeth Malbert, *Principal*
EMP: 4
SALES (est): 241.1K **Privately Held**
SIC: 4212 Local trucking, without storage

(G-3846)
F & N VAZQUEZ CONCRETE LLC
18577 Sherman Ave (19960-3143)
PHONE.................................302 725-5305
Fernando Vazquez, *Principal*
EMP: 9
SALES (est): 688.2K **Privately Held**
SIC: 1771 Concrete work

(G-3847)
FAMILY OUTRCH MULTI-PURPSE COM
19227 Young Ln (19960-2941)
PHONE.................................302 422-2158
Stephanie Dukes, *Exec Dir*
EMP: 8
SALES (est): 102.3K **Privately Held**
SIC: 8399 Community development groups

(G-3848)
FIRST STATE MANAGEMENT LLC
37 Major St (19960-2836)
PHONE.................................302 268-8176
Cody Ayers,
Vivian Vasilikos,
EMP: 4
SALES (est): 227.1K **Privately Held**
SIC: 8741 Management services

(G-3849)
FITZGERALD AUTO SALVAGE INC
17115 Fitzgeralds Rd (19960-3265)
P.O. Box 26 (19960-0026)
PHONE.................................302 422-7584
John Fitzgerald III, *President*
Kim Attix, *Managing Prtnr*
Karen Fitzgerald, *Corp Secy*
Scott Fitzgerald, *Vice Pres*
EMP: 70
SQ FT: 2,000
SALES (est): 5.4MM **Privately Held**
SIC: 7389 5013 5531 Salvaging of damaged merchandise, service only; automotive supplies & parts; automotive parts

Lincoln - Sussex County (G-3850)

(G-3850)
GGC INC
Also Called: Delight Housing Complex
19544 Pine Rd (19960-3016)
P.O. Box 113 (19960-0113)
PHONE.....................267 893-8052
Krystal Blackwell, *President*
EMP: 5 **EST:** 2016
SALES (est): 53.8K **Privately Held**
SIC: 8399 Neighborhood development group

(G-3851)
GIBBONS INNOVATIONS INC
P.O. Box 99 (19960-0099)
PHONE.....................302 265-4220
Christopher Gibbons, *President*
EMP: 3
SALES (est): 314.6K **Privately Held**
SIC: 3429 Manufactured hardware (general)

(G-3852)
GREENVIEW GARDENS INC
Sherman Ave (19960)
P.O. Box 21 (19960-0021)
PHONE.....................302 422-8109
Bruce Morgan, *President*
Woodrow W Morgan, *Owner*
EMP: 8
SQ FT: 13,400
SALES: 650K **Privately Held**
WEB: www.greenviewgardens.com
SIC: 5191 Greenhouse equipment & supplies

(G-3853)
HACCP NAVIGATOR LLC
10256 Webb Farm Rd (19960-3434)
PHONE.....................302 531-7922
Larry David Bowe,
EMP: 7
SALES (est): 331.4K **Privately Held**
SIC: 8742 Food & beverage consultant

(G-3854)
HAPPYLAND CHILDCARE
18073 Johnson Rd (19960-3209)
PHONE.....................302 424-3868
Sharon McPhatter, *Principal*
EMP: 5 **EST:** 2010
SALES (est): 60.8K **Privately Held**
SIC: 8351 Child day care services

(G-3855)
HOOD MAN LLC
10421 Jasmine Dr (19960-3634)
PHONE.....................302 422-4564
Rob Hill, *Principal*
EMP: 4
SALES (est): 135.9K **Privately Held**
SIC: 7349 Exhaust hood or fan cleaning

(G-3856)
HOWARD WILKINS & SONS INC
7630 Wilkins Rd (19960-2616)
PHONE.....................302 270-4183
Ken Wilkins, *President*
David Wilkins, *Corp Secy*
George Wilkins, *Vice Pres*
EMP: 4
SALES (est): 397.3K **Privately Held**
SIC: 0191 0241 0251 General farms, primarily crop; dairy farms; broiling chickens, raising of

(G-3857)
JBM PETROLEUM SERVICE LLC
8913 Clendaniel Pond Rd (19960-2979)
PHONE.....................302 752-6105
Dean Vincent, *Principal*
EMP: 3
SALES (est): 353.6K **Privately Held**
SIC: 1799 7389 7699 1389 Petroleum storage tanks, pumping & draining; petroleum refinery inspection service; service station equipment repair; testing, measuring, surveying & analysis services

(G-3858)
KAMPRODUCTIONS
7768 Dobbin Ct (19960-2654)
P.O. Box 122, Lewes (19958-0122)
PHONE.....................302 228-1852
Keith Mosher, *Principal*
EMP: 4
SALES (est): 148.7K **Privately Held**
SIC: 7822 Motion picture & tape distribution

(G-3859)
LINCOLN COMMUNITY HALL INC
18881 Washington St (19960-3131)
P.O. Box 77 (19960-0077)
PHONE.....................302 242-1747
EMP: 9
SALES: 11K **Privately Held**
SIC: 8641 Civic social & fraternal associations

(G-3860)
LISA M HORSEY
Also Called: Lisa M Horsey Bus Service
8868 Cedar Creek Rd (19960-2764)
P.O. Box 160, Harbeson (19951-0160)
PHONE.....................302 725-5767
EMP: 6
SALES: 100K **Privately Held**
SIC: 4119 Local Passenger Transportation

(G-3861)
MIDWAY SERVICES INC
9446 Willow Pond Ln (19960-2778)
PHONE.....................302 422-8603
Robert Bower, *President*
EMP: 5
SALES (est): 600K **Privately Held**
SIC: 1711 1794 Septic system construction; excavation work

(G-3862)
MILFORD GUTTER GUYS LLC
7074 Marshall St (19960-3155)
PHONE.....................302 424-1931
Randolph Adams, *Mng Member*
EMP: 5
SALES (est): 448.2K **Privately Held**
SIC: 1761 Gutter & downspout contractor

(G-3863)
MISSION MOVEMENT TRANSPORT LLC
8604 First Born Church Rd (19960-3235)
PHONE.....................302 480-9401
Tonya Snead, *Principal*
EMP: 5 **EST:** 2016
SALES (est): 115.2K **Privately Held**
SIC: 7389

(G-3864)
R W MORGAN FARMS INC
18126 Haflinger Rd (19960-3318)
PHONE.....................302 542-7740
Ron W Morgan, *President*
Ron Morgan, *President*
EMP: 5
SALES (est): 450K **Privately Held**
SIC: 4213 Trucking, except local

(G-3865)
RICHARD Y JOHNSON & SON INC
18404 Johnson Rd (19960-3112)
P.O. Box 105 (19960-0105)
PHONE.....................302 422-3732
Dean Johnson, *CEO*
EMP: 25
SQ FT: 2,000
SALES (est): 6.3MM **Privately Held**
SIC: 1542 1521 Commercial & office building, new construction; commercial & office buildings, renovation & repair; new construction, single-family houses; general remodeling, single-family houses

(G-3866)
RPR ENVIRONMENTAL SOLUTIONS
20758 Jefferson Rd (19960-3024)
PHONE.....................302 362-0687
Ryan Rae, *Principal*
EMP: 4
SALES (est): 176.9K **Privately Held**
SIC: 1799 7389 Exterior cleaning, including sandblasting

(G-3867)
SAMSON COMMUNICATIONS INC
Also Called: Wxpz FM 101.3
9078 Attles Rd (19960)
PHONE.....................302 424-1013
Fax: 302 424-2358
EMP: 15
SQ FT: 2,200
SALES (est): 790K **Privately Held**
SIC: 4832 8661 Radio Broadcasting Stations

(G-3868)
SAPPS WELDING SERVICE
8547 Sophies Way (19960-2679)
PHONE.....................302 491-6319
EMP: 1
SALES (est): 25K **Privately Held**
SIC: 7692 Welding repair

(G-3869)
SHOCKLEY BROTHERS CONSTRUCTION
8772 Herring Branch Rd (19960-3933)
PHONE.....................302 424-3255
Vernon Shockley, *President*
Ivan Shockley, *Corp Secy*
Marvel Shockley, *Vice Pres*
EMP: 5
SQ FT: 388
SALES: 250K **Privately Held**
SIC: 1521 Single-family housing construction

(G-3870)
SLAUGHTER NECK EDUCATIONAL AND
22942 Slaughter Neck Rd (19960-3911)
PHONE.....................302 684-1834
Grace A Young, *President*
Ellen Parker, *Vice Pres*
Roslyn Harris, *Director*
EMP: 6
SALES (est): 178.6K **Privately Held**
SIC: 8351 Group day care center

(G-3871)
STEVES PAINTING PLUS
22235 Jefferson Rd (19960-4015)
PHONE.....................302 684-8938
Steve Fletcher, *Owner*
EMP: 1
SALES (est): 58K **Privately Held**
WEB: www.artcycles.com
SIC: 2851 Paints & allied products

(G-3872)
SWAIN EXCAVATION INC
18678 Sherman Ave Unit 1 (19960-3132)
P.O. Box 46 (19960-0046)
PHONE.....................302 422-4349
Lee Chaney, *President*
Robert Bower, *Vice Pres*
EMP: 7
SQ FT: 7,500
SALES (est): 1MM **Privately Held**
SIC: 1794 Excavation work

(G-3873)
WHITE DRILLING CORP
Us 113 (19960)
PHONE.....................302 422-4057
Roy White, *President*
Francis White, *Treasurer*
R Allen White, *Admin Sec*
EMP: 7
SALES (est): 761.2K **Privately Held**
SIC: 1781 1799 Water well drilling; hydraulic equipment, installation & service

(G-3874)
WILSONS AUCTION SALES INC
10120 Dupont Blvd (19960-3604)
P.O. Box 84 (19960-0084)
PHONE.....................302 422-3454
David Wilson, *President*
EMP: 7
SQ FT: 22,000
SALES (est): 639.7K **Privately Held**
SIC: 7389 6531 Auctioneers, fee basis; inventory computing service; real estate agents & managers

(G-3875)
WORTHYS PROPERTY MGT LLC
8989 Herring Branch Rd (19960-3930)
PHONE.....................302 265-8301
Tykesha Garland, *Principal*
EMP: 15
SALES (est): 101.2K **Privately Held**
SIC: 7217 Carpet & furniture cleaning on location

Magnolia
Kent County

(G-3876)
1ST STATE PC TRAINING
500 E Cherry Dr (19962-1926)
PHONE.....................302 697-0347
Karen M Michaels, *Owner*
EMP: 4
SALES (est): 640.7K **Privately Held**
SIC: 6022 State commercial banks

(G-3877)
A AND D PLUMBING LLC
128 Glenn Forest Rd (19962-1702)
PHONE.....................302 387-9232
Dyshone Jack, *Mng Member*
EMP: 1
SALES (est): 96K **Privately Held**
SIC: 1711 3432 7389 Plumbing contractors; hydronics heating contractor; faucets & spigots, metal & plastic; plastic plumbing fixture fittings, assembly; water softener service;

(G-3878)
AIR ENTERPRISES INC
4403 Irish Hill Rd (19962-1415)
PHONE.....................302 335-5141
Alfred F Johnson Jr, *President*
EMP: 4 **EST:** 1959
SQ FT: 220,000
SALES (est): 567.6K **Privately Held**
SIC: 0721 Crop dusting services

(G-3879)
AKHTAR JAVED
658 W Birdie Ln (19962-3108)
PHONE.....................606 515-3698
Javed Akhtar, *CEO*
EMP: 8
SALES (est): 65.7K **Privately Held**
SIC: 8049 Offices of health practitioner

(G-3880)
ANTHONY J NAPPA
Also Called: Nappa Trading Company
56 Cedarfield Rd (19962-9300)
PHONE.....................716 888-0553
Anthony Nappa, *Owner*
Anthony J Nappa, *Principal*
EMP: 1
SALES (est): 55.2K **Privately Held**
SIC: 3443 3452 Metal parts; bolts, metal

(G-3881)
BEIMAC LLC
859 Golf Links Ln (19962-1188)
PHONE.....................302 677-1965
Robert C Macleish, *Mng Member*
Robert Macleish,
Megan Glick,
Mike Grek,
Angela J Macleish,
EMP: 4
SALES (est): 220K **Privately Held**
SIC: 6531 Real estate leasing & rentals

(G-3882)
BJK PLUMBING & HEATING LLC
49 Macintosh Cir. (19962-3647)
PHONE.....................215 828-2556
Jamal Patterson, *Owner*
EMP: 4
SALES: 400K **Privately Held**
SIC: 1711 Heating systems repair & maintenance; plumbing contractors

(G-3883)
C & W AUTO PARTS CO INC
851 Sorghum Mill Rd (19962-1228)
PHONE.....................302 697-2684
Craig Conner, *President*

EMP: 9 EST: 1958
SQ FT: 5,600
SALES: 1MM **Privately Held**
SIC: 5013 5531 Automotive supplies & parts; automotive parts

(G-3884)
CHAMPIONS CLUB
488 Augusta National Dr (19962-3199)
PHONE.................................215 380-1273
EMP: 5
SALES (est): 41.9K **Privately Held**
SIC: 7997 Membership sports & recreation clubs

(G-3885)
CHEMLIME NJ INC
Also Called: Despatch Section
198 Records Dr (19962-4630)
PHONE.................................302 697-2115
Al Rogall, *Manager*
EMP: 4
SALES (corp-wide): 1.4MM **Privately Held**
SIC: 5032 Lime, except agricultural
PA: Chemlime Nj Inc
32 Commerce Dr
Cranford NJ
908 272-0330

(G-3886)
CHILD INC
Also Called: Children's Place, The
776 Tullamore Ct (19962-2602)
PHONE.................................302 335-8652
Carol Mitchell, *President*
EMP: 10
SALES (est): 330K **Privately Held**
SIC: 8351 Child day care services

(G-3887)
CONVENTION COACH
554 Lexington Mill Rd (19962-1545)
PHONE.................................302 335-5459
Cynthia Baker, *Owner*
EMP: 7
SALES (est): 395.6K **Privately Held**
WEB: www.conventioncoach.com
SIC: 5199 7311 Advertising specialties; advertising consultant

(G-3888)
CROSSFIT DOVER LLC
177 Windrow Way (19962-3617)
PHONE.................................302 242-5400
EMP: 4 EST: 2012
SALES (est): 72.8K **Privately Held**
SIC: 7991 Health club

(G-3889)
DEL HOMES INC (PA)
1309 Ponderosa Dr (19962-1165)
P.O. Box 8 (19962-0008)
PHONE.................................302 697-8204
Jacquelyn I West, *President*
John T Beiser, *Shareholder*
EMP: 6 EST: 1964
SALES (est): 3.4MM **Privately Held**
SIC: 1521 1542 1531 6552 New construction, single-family houses; commercial & office building, new construction; condominium developers; subdividers & developers

(G-3890)
EAST COAST KITE SPORTS
10 N Main St (19962-4002)
P.O. Box 139 (19962-0139)
PHONE.................................302 359-0749
Rian Davis, *Owner*
EMP: 1
SALES (est): 44.9K **Privately Held**
SIC: 3944 Kites

(G-3891)
GL GRAY CONSULTING SERVICES LL
1563 Autumn Moon Ln (19962-1824)
PHONE.................................302 698-3339
Gerald Gray, *Principal*
EMP: 4
SALES (est): 205.8K **Privately Held**
SIC: 8748 Business consulting

(G-3892)
GRACELAND DAYCARE
342 Ponderosa Dr (19962-1204)
PHONE.................................302 698-0414
Alfred Wieczorek, *Principal*
EMP: 5
SALES (est): 65.5K **Privately Held**
SIC: 8351 Group day care center

(G-3893)
GREEN BLADE IRRIGATION & TURF
2203 Ponderosa Dr (19962-1256)
PHONE.................................302 736-8873
Todd Burger, *Principal*
EMP: 6 EST: 2007
SALES (est): 426.8K **Privately Held**
SIC: 0782 Turf installation services, except artificial

(G-3894)
H G INVESTMENTS LLC
Also Called: Two Men and A Truck
27 E Walnut St (19962-9304)
PHONE.................................302 734-5017
Jennifer Gondolfo,
EMP: 25
SQ FT: 1,500
SALES (est): 1.9MM **Privately Held**
SIC: 4212 Local trucking, without storage

(G-3895)
HODGES L WOOTEN
Also Called: Bbg2x Transportation
120 Limerick Ln (19962-2623)
P.O. Box 33 (19962-0033)
PHONE.................................302 335-5162
Hodges L Wooten, *Principal*
EMP: 4
SALES (est): 333.1K **Privately Held**
SIC: 4789 Car loading

(G-3896)
JONATHANS LANDING
Also Called: Jonathans Landing Pub Golf CLB
1309 Ponderosa Dr (19962-1165)
PHONE.................................302 697-8204
Jack Beiser, *Owner*
EMP: 35
SALES (est): 852.4K **Privately Held**
WEB: www.jonathanslanding.com
SIC: 7992 Public golf courses

(G-3897)
KMH CONTRACTING
133 Moores Dr (19962-2073)
PHONE.................................302 331-4894
Kathleen Hutson, *Owner*
EMP: 4
SALES (est): 140K **Privately Held**
SIC: 8742 Merchandising consultant

(G-3898)
LIGHTHOUSE CONSTRUCTION INC
859 Golf Ln Ste 1 (19962)
PHONE.................................302 677-1965
Robert C Macleish, *President*
Michael Glick, *Vice Pres*
Angela Macleish, *Vice Pres*
EMP: 10
SALES (est): 2MM **Privately Held**
SIC: 1521 1542 8741 New construction, single-family houses; commercial & office building contractors; construction management

(G-3899)
MICHAEL J MUNROE
811 Augusta National Dr (19962-3257)
PHONE.................................804 240-7188
J Munroe, *Principal*
EMP: 1
SALES (est): 39.6K **Privately Held**
SIC: 3999 Manufacturing industries

(G-3900)
MILLIES SCENTED ROCKS LLC
83 Pitch Kettle Ct (19962-1590)
PHONE.................................302 331-9232
Millie Hughes,
EMP: 1
SALES: 70K **Privately Held**
SIC: 3999 Potpourri

(G-3901)
NKOGNITO PRODUCTIONS LLC
80 Braeburn Ter (19962-1670)
PHONE.................................302 943-0399
Chris Larson, *Mng Member*
EMP: 4
SALES (est): 60K **Privately Held**
SIC: 7822 Motion picture & tape distribution

(G-3902)
PERSONA GROUP LLC
Also Called: Persona Ink
74 Wildflower Cir W (19962-9350)
PHONE.................................302 335-5221
Justin Spivey,
EMP: 1
SALES (est): 89.6K **Privately Held**
SIC: 3993 6719 Signs & advertising specialties; investment holding companies, except banks

(G-3903)
PIERCE PROFESSIONAL SERVICES
501 Cypress Dr (19962-1234)
PHONE.................................302 331-1154
Gerald Pierce, *Owner*
EMP: 4
SALES (est): 203.5K **Privately Held**
SIC: 8742 Management consulting services

(G-3904)
PLUME SERUM LLC
1059 Ponderosa Dr (19962-1168)
PHONE.................................302 697-9044
Daniel Dunkleberger, *Principal*
EMP: 2
SALES (est): 74.4K **Privately Held**
SIC: 2836 Serums

(G-3905)
PROPERTY DOCTORS LLC
309 Millchop Ln (19962-2008)
PHONE.................................302 249-7731
James Shuford, *Principal*
EMP: 2
SALES (est): 150.3K **Privately Held**
SIC: 1389 Construction, repair & dismantling services

(G-3906)
REVNATION LTD LIABILITY CO
64 Olde Field Dr (19962-3806)
PHONE.................................202 672-4120
Dominique Nelson, *Mng Member*
EMP: 2
SALES: 52K **Privately Held**
SIC: 3711 3743 Motor vehicles & car bodies; streetcars & car equipment

(G-3907)
ROBERTS ELECTRIC INC
165 Barkers Landing Rd (19962-1117)
PHONE.................................302 233-3017
Mike Roberts, *President*
EMP: 5
SALES: 200K **Privately Held**
SIC: 1731 Electric power systems contractors

(G-3908)
ROCK SOLID SERVICING LLC
89 Mandrake Dr (19962-3670)
PHONE.................................302 233-2569
EMP: 2
SALES (est): 84.5K **Privately Held**
SIC: 1389 Roustabout service

(G-3909)
STOCKMARKET
2573 Woodlytown Rd (19962-1452)
PHONE.................................302 697-8878
Bruce Ney, *Principal*
EMP: 2
SALES (est): 93.5K **Privately Held**
SIC: 3484 Shotguns or shotgun parts, 30 mm. & below

(G-3910)
TAYLOR WOODWORKS
5140 S State St (19962-1466)
PHONE.................................302 697-0155
EMP: 1 EST: 2015

SALES (est): 63K **Privately Held**
SIC: 2431 Mfg Millwork

(G-3911)
VERSION 40 SOFTWARE LLC
662 Tullamore Ct (19962-2603)
PHONE.................................302 270-0245
EMP: 2
SALES (est): 112.4K **Privately Held**
SIC: 7372 Application computer software

(G-3912)
WAYMAN TRANSPORTATION SVC
160 Carnation Dr (19962-1579)
PHONE.................................302 363-5139
Clarence Wayman, *Principal*
EMP: 4
SALES (est): 156K **Privately Held**
SIC: 4789 Transportation services

(G-3913)
ZACS INC
31 Par Ct (19962-1153)
PHONE.................................302 242-4653
Billy Zaccardelli, *Principal*
EMP: 5
SQ FT: 37,000
SALES: 100K **Privately Held**
SIC: 1542 Commercial & office buildings, renovation & repair

Marshallton
New Castle County

(G-3914)
SHACRAFT
1904 Lincoln Ave (19808-6110)
PHONE.................................302 995-6385
Sue Howell, *Owner*
EMP: 1
SALES (est): 47K **Privately Held**
SIC: 2395 Embroidery & art needlework

Marydel
Kent County

(G-3915)
DELMARVA PUMP CENTER INC (PA)
Also Called: Dpc Emergency Equipment
335 Strauss Ave (19964-2218)
P.O. Box 340 (19964-0340)
PHONE.................................302 492-1245
Richard Strauss Sr, *President*
Mary Pardee, *Treasurer*
EMP: 30
SQ FT: 25,000
SALES: 12MM **Privately Held**
WEB: www.dpcemergency.com
SIC: 7538 5511 5012 General truck repair; new & used car dealers; fire trucks; ambulances

(G-3916)
FM ELECTRIC INC
436 Strauss Ave (19964-2202)
P.O. Box 65 (19964-0065)
PHONE.................................302 492-3900
John A Fabhees, *President*
EMP: 4 EST: 1992
SALES: 353.2K **Privately Held**
WEB: www.fmelectric.com
SIC: 1731 General electrical contractor

(G-3917)
HARVEST RIDGE WINERY LLC
447 Westville Rd (19964-1820)
PHONE.................................302 250-6583
Kristi May Wyatt, *Sales Mgr*
Chuck Nunan, *Mng Member*
Chris Nunan, *Mng Member*
Jason Hopwood, *Manager*
EMP: 7
SALES (est): 743K **Privately Held**
SIC: 2084 Wines

Marydel - Kent County (G-3918)

(G-3918)
HIDDEN ACRES REST HOME INC
265 Mowely Ln (19964-1839)
PHONE.................................302 492-1962
Denise Madden, *Director*
EMP: 14
SALES: 535K **Privately Held**
SIC: 8399 Social services

(G-3919)
JEFFREY HATCH
Also Called: Hatch's Home Improvement
233 Westville Rd (19964-1800)
PHONE.................................443 496-0449
Jeffrey Hatch Sr, *Owner*
EMP: 4
SALES (est): 315.8K **Privately Held**
SIC: 1541 1521 1799 7389 Renovation, remodeling & repairs: industrial buildings; single-family home remodeling, additions & repairs; general remodeling, single-family houses; kitchen & bathroom remodeling; post-disaster renovations;

(G-3920)
M D PLUMBING DRAIN CLEANING
1500 Gunter Rd (19964-2251)
PHONE.................................302 492-8880
Mike Megill, *President*
Tammy Megill, *Vice Pres*
EMP: 9
SALES (est): 440K **Privately Held**
SIC: 1711 Plumbing contractors

(G-3921)
NATIONAL DCUMENT MGT SOLUTIONS
301 Westville Rd (19964-1821)
PHONE.................................302 535-9263
Jose Dancel, *Partner*
EMP: 5
SALES: 100K **Privately Held**
SIC: 7374 Data processing service

(G-3922)
SPG INTERNATIONAL LLC
841 Mud Mill Rd (19964-1921)
PHONE.................................404 823-3934
EMP: 2
SALES (est): 87.4K **Privately Held**
SIC: 3441 Fabricated structural metal

(G-3923)
THOMAS FAMILY FARMS LLC
896 Sandy Bend Rd (19964-1948)
PHONE.................................302 492-3688
John W Thomas, *Partner*
Carolyn Thomas, *Partner*
EMP: 7
SALES (est): 580.1K **Privately Held**
SIC: 0191 General farms, primarily crop

Middletown
New Castle County

(G-3924)
321 DOWN STREET PRESS INC
62 Chancellorsville Cir (19709-3826)
PHONE.................................302 376-3965
Christopher Popp, *Principal*
EMP: 1
SALES: 9.8K **Privately Held**
SIC: 2741 Miscellaneous publishing

(G-3925)
3D INTERNET GROUP INC
609 Colchester Ct (19709-2139)
PHONE.................................302 376-7900
Ian Frisbie, *President*
EMP: 5
SALES (est): 263.1K **Privately Held**
WEB: www.3dig.com
SIC: 4813

(G-3926)
AA SMITH & ASSOCIATES LLC
364 E Main St Ste 403 (19709-1482)
PHONE.................................973 477-3052
Alvin Smith, *Mng Member*
Betty Smith,
EMP: 12
SALES (est): 493.3K **Privately Held**
SIC: 8742 Management consulting services

(G-3927)
ABRA AUTO BODY & GLASS LP
5077 Summit Bridge Rd (19709-9591)
PHONE.................................302 279-1007
Michael Levasseur, *Branch Mgr*
EMP: 13 **Privately Held**
WEB: www.keenanautobody.com
SIC: 7532 Body shop, automotive
HQ: Abra Auto Body & Glass Lp
7225 Northland Dr N # 110
Brooklyn Park MN 55428
888 872-2272

(G-3928)
ABRIDGE PARTNERS LLC (PA)
6 Crawford St (19709-1117)
PHONE.................................302 378-1882
Michael Flanagan,
EMP: 4
SALES (est): 464.6K **Privately Held**
SIC: 8742 Financial consultant

(G-3929)
ACCOUNTING & BOOKKEEPING SVC
18 Manassas Dr (19709-3802)
PHONE.................................302 376-7857
Christopher Acevedo, *Principal*
EMP: 4
SALES (est): 180.7K **Privately Held**
SIC: 8721 Billing & bookkeeping service

(G-3930)
ACUHEALTH & WELLNESS
134 Tywyn Dr (19709-8701)
PHONE.................................302 438-4493
Patricia Yancey, *Principal*
EMP: 7
SALES (est): 83.6K **Privately Held**
SIC: 8099 Health & allied services

(G-3931)
ADVANCED METAL CONCEPTS INC
1823 Choptank Rd (19709-9047)
PHONE.................................302 421-9905
Greg Sachetta, *President*
Beth Sachetta, *Vice Pres*
EMP: 12 EST: 2001
SQ FT: 2,000
SALES (est): 302.4K **Privately Held**
SIC: 3545 Precision tools, machinists'

(G-3932)
AEZI ELECTRICAL SERVICES LLC
131 Azbury Loop (19709)
PHONE.................................302 547-5734
Danyelle Purdie,
Karim Purdie,
EMP: 5 EST: 2014
SALES (est): 244.3K **Privately Held**
SIC: 1731 Electrical work

(G-3933)
AI CONSTRUCTION SERVICES LLC
651 N Broad St Ste 206 (19709-6402)
PHONE.................................619 732-0250
Ayodeji Babaniyi,
Frederick Bowman,
EMP: 4
SALES: 200K **Privately Held**
SIC: 8711 Engineering services

(G-3934)
ALERIC INTERNATIONAL INC
116 Saint Andrews Ct (19709-8851)
PHONE.................................302 547-4846
Alain Ratsimbazafy, *President*
Eric Ratsimbazafy, *Director*
EMP: 10
SALES: 500K **Privately Held**
SIC: 7379 Computer related consulting services

(G-3935)
ALL THERAPY LLC
212 Carter Dr Ste C (19709-5837)
P.O. Box 856 (19709-0856)
PHONE.................................302 376-5578

Aisha Ryan, *Branch Mgr*
EMP: 4 **Privately Held**
SIC: 8049 Physical therapist
PA: All Therapy Llc
1201 Franklin St Ne # 105
Washington DC 20017

(G-3936)
ALLIED PRECISION INC
106 Sleepy Hollow Dr C (19709-9191)
PHONE.................................302 376-6844
John R Lees, *President*
Sandra Hartzel, *Mfg Staff*
Sandee Hartzel, *CFO*
EMP: 6
SQ FT: 5,000
SALES (est): 1.4MM **Privately Held**
SIC: 7692 3444 3599 Welding repair; sheet metalwork; machine shop, jobbing & repair

(G-3937)
AMERICAN K9 DOGGIE DAYCARE & T
128 Patriot Dr Unit 12 (19709-8770)
PHONE.................................302 376-9663
Laurie Brown, *Mng Member*
Michael Brown,
EMP: 10
SALES (est): 288K **Privately Held**
SIC: 0752 Training services, pet & animal specialties (not horses)

(G-3938)
ANDERSON LAWN & HOME CARE
813 W Creek Ln (19709-8835)
PHONE.................................302 376-7115
Daniel Anderson, *Principal*
EMP: 8
SALES (est): 61.1K **Privately Held**
SIC: 8082 Home health care services

(G-3939)
ANGEL NAILS
480 Middletown Warwick Rd (19709-9192)
PHONE.................................302 449-5067
Tony Nguyen, *Owner*
EMP: 16
SALES (est): 94.3K **Privately Held**
SIC: 7231 Manicurist, pedicurist

(G-3940)
ANNETTE RICKOLT
350 Noxontown Rd (19709-1621)
PHONE.................................302 285-4200
Annette Rickolt Aprn, *Owner*
EMP: 8
SALES (est): 65.7K **Privately Held**
SIC: 8049 Offices of health practitioner

(G-3941)
APERTURE PHOTOGRAPHY
106 Redden Ln (19709-1707)
PHONE.................................302 377-6590
Marcus Williams, *Principal*
EMP: 4
SALES (est): 46K **Privately Held**
SIC: 7221 Photographer, still or video

(G-3942)
APPOQUINIMINK DEVELOPMENT INC
Also Called: Norris Village
103 E Park Pl (19709-1429)
PHONE.................................302 378-0878
Geraldine Hellams, *President*
Maggie Cook-Pleasant, *Principal*
EMP: 7
SALES: 5K **Privately Held**
SIC: 6513 Apartment building operators

(G-3943)
ARUANNO ENTERPRISES INC
524 E Creek Ln (19709-8836)
PHONE.................................302 530-1217
Michael Aruanno, *President*
EMP: 8
SALES: 1MM **Privately Held**
SIC: 1522 1521 Remodeling, multi-family dwellings; single-family home remodeling, additions & repairs

(G-3944)
ASSOC COMMUNITY TALENTS INC
41 W Main St (19709-1017)
PHONE.................................302 378-7038
EMP: 4
SALES (est): 82.2K **Privately Held**
SIC: 7832 Motion Picture Theater

(G-3945)
ASSOCIATED CMNTY TALENTS INC
Also Called: EVERETT THEATRE
45 W Main St (19709-1017)
PHONE.................................302 378-1200
Hedley C Davis, *Ch of Bd*
Joe Hortiz, *Chairman*
Noreen Tully, *Admin Sec*
Jay Greene,
Larry Hirsch,
EMP: 7
SALES: 241K **Privately Held**
SIC: 7832 Motion picture theaters, except drive-in

(G-3946)
ASTEC INC
1554 Lorewood Grove Rd (19709-9480)
PHONE.................................302 378-2717
Io J Betley, *President*
Thomas P Betley, *Vice Pres*
EMP: 17
SQ FT: 2,200
SALES (est): 1.5MM **Privately Held**
SIC: 1799 Asbestos removal & encapsulation

(G-3947)
ATI HOLDINGS LLC
Also Called: ATI Physical Therapy
114 Sandhill Dr Ste 103 (19709-5805)
PHONE.................................302 285-0700
Kevin Calvey, *Director*
EMP: 21
SALES (corp-wide): 338.3MM **Privately Held**
SIC: 8049 Physical therapist
PA: Ati Holdings, Llc
790 Remington Blvd
Bolingbrook IL 60440
630 296-2222

(G-3948)
ATLANTIC BROADBAND
5350 Summit Bridge Rd # 101 (19709-4802)
PHONE.................................302 378-0780
Gina Agron, *Manager*
Thomas Chaplin, *Technical Staff*
EMP: 5
SALES (est): 247.3K **Privately Held**
SIC: 4841 Cable television services

(G-3949)
ATLANTIC BULK CARRIERS
364 E Main St (19709-1482)
PHONE.................................302 378-6300
George Smith, *Vice Pres*
EMP: 14
SALES (est): 2.7MM **Privately Held**
SIC: 4213 Trucking, except local

(G-3950)
ATLANTIC BULK LTD
421 Boyds Corner Rd (19709-9547)
PHONE.................................302 378-6300
Jennifer Rice, *President*
EMP: 12
SALES (est): 738.5K **Privately Held**
SIC: 4789 Cargo loading & unloading services

(G-3951)
ATLANTIC TRAINING LLC
101 N Broad St (19709-1034)
P.O. Box 44 (19709-0044)
PHONE.................................302 464-0341
Anthony Lafazia, *General Mgr*
Cassandra Abel, *Accounts Mgr*
Michele Carey, *Accounts Mgr*
Lauren Cook, *Accounts Mgr*
Susana Correia, *Accounts Mgr*
EMP: 10
SQ FT: 3,500

GEOGRAPHIC SECTION
Middletown - New Castle County (G-3984)

SALES (est): 710K **Privately Held**
SIC: 8748 Safety training service

(G-3952)
ATLANTIC VETERINARY SVCS INC
Also Called: Atlantic Veterinary Center
741 N Broad St (19709-1166)
PHONE..................................302 376-7506
John Weiher, *President*
EMP: 6
SALES (est): 386.4K **Privately Held**
WEB: www.atlanticvetcenter.com
SIC: 0742 Animal hospital services, pets & other animal specialties

(G-3953)
ATLAS WORLD EXPRESS LLC
119 Plymouth Pl (19709-8314)
PHONE..................................202 536-5238
Fred M Scott,
EMP: 5
SALES (est): 340.4K **Privately Held**
SIC: 4212 Delivery service, vehicular

(G-3954)
ATR ELECTRICAL SERVICES INC
14 Manassas Dr (19709-3802)
PHONE..................................302 373-7769
Sean McCarron, *Principal*
EMP: 4
SQ FT: 2,500
SALES (est): 257.5K **Privately Held**
SIC: 1731 7389 Electrical work;

(G-3955)
AUTOMOTIVE ACCOUNTING SERVICE
680 N Broad St (19709-1030)
P.O. Box 5000 (19709-5000)
PHONE..................................302 378-9551
James Duckworth, *President*
William Stackhouse, *Vice Pres*
EMP: 15 EST: 1958
SQ FT: 2,000
SALES (est): 578.4K
SALES (corp-wide): 18.7B **Publicly Held**
WEB: www.qcmponline.com
SIC: 8721 Accounting services, except auditing; billing & bookkeeping service
PA: Genuine Parts Company
2999 Wildwood Pkwy
Atlanta GA 30339
678 934-5000

(G-3956)
AUTOTYPE HOLDINGS (USA) INC
701 Industrial Rd (19709-1085)
PHONE..................................302 378-3100
Frank J Monteiro, *President*
John L Cordanis, *Admin Sec*
▲ EMP: 125 EST: 1975
SALES (est): 9.4MM
SALES (corp-wide): 1.9B **Publicly Held**
WEB: www.autotype.com
SIC: 5043 5084 Printing apparatus, photographic; developing apparatus, photographic; industrial machinery & equipment
PA: Element Solutions Inc
500 E Broward Blvd # 1860
Fort Lauderdale FL 33394
561 207-9600

(G-3957)
B RICH ENTERPRISES
808 Sweet Hollow Ct (19709-8645)
PHONE..................................302 530-6865
David Rich, *CEO*
Veronica Rich, *Administration*
EMP: 5
SALES (est): 310K **Privately Held**
SIC: 8748 Business consulting

(G-3958)
BACK CREEK GOLF SHOP
Also Called: Back Creek Golf Course
101 Back Creek Dr (19709-8843)
PHONE..................................302 378-6499
Frank Horton, *Managing Prtnr*
Allen Liddicoat, *General Ptnr*
Dan Flood, *Director*
EMP: 25

SALES (est): 1MM **Privately Held**
SIC: 7992 Public golf courses

(G-3959)
BAILEYS LAWN AND LANDSCAPE LLC
5101 Summit Bridge Rd (19709-8821)
PHONE..................................302 376-9113
Brian Bailey,
EMP: 4
SALES (est): 313.3K **Privately Held**
SIC: 0781 Landscape services

(G-3960)
BAKER & SONS PAVING
116 Bakerfield Dr (19709-9451)
PHONE..................................302 945-6333
William Baker, *Principal*
EMP: 5
SALES (est): 446.4K **Privately Held**
SIC: 1611 Surfacing & paving

(G-3961)
BAKER FARMS INC
665 Shallcross Lake Rd (19709-9440)
P.O. Box 312, Odessa (19730-0312)
PHONE..................................302 378-3750
EMP: 5
SALES: 1MM **Privately Held**
SIC: 0115 Corn Farm

(G-3962)
BALANCED MIND CNSELING CTR LLC
115 N Broad St Ste 4a (19709-1045)
PHONE..................................302 377-6911
Jennifer Ewald, *Principal*
Nicole Geiser, *Office Mgr*
EMP: 6
SALES (est): 203.3K **Privately Held**
SIC: 8322 General counseling services

(G-3963)
BASE LINE TRANSPORTS L
452 Goodwick Dr (19709-0180)
PHONE..................................302 438-3092
Trina McKinney, *Principal*
EMP: 4
SALES (est): 220.5K **Privately Held**
SIC: 4789 Transportation services

(G-3964)
BEAZER HOMES CORP
202 Ann Dr (19709-2621)
PHONE..................................302 378-4161
EMP: 17
SALES (corp-wide): 1.4B **Publicly Held**
SIC: 1521 Single-Family House Construction
HQ: Beazer Homes Corp.
1000 Abernathy Rd
Atlanta GA 30328
770 829-3700

(G-3965)
BEELINE SERVICES LLC
865 Vance Neck Rd (19709-9135)
PHONE..................................302 376-7399
Steve Jacono, *Mng Member*
Carolyn Stanley, *Manager*
EMP: 5 EST: 2007
SALES (est): 2MM **Privately Held**
SIC: 1751 7389 Carpentry work; automobile recovery service

(G-3966)
BETH A RENZULLI M D
102 Sleepy Hollow Dr # 200 (19709-5841)
PHONE..................................302 449-0420
Beth Renzulli, *Principal*
EMP: 6
SALES (est): 80.5K **Privately Held**
SIC: 8011 Offices & clinics of medical doctors

(G-3967)
BG TRUCK & TRAILOR REPAIR
4917 Summit Bridge Rd (19709-8819)
PHONE..................................302 455-9171
Floyd Bettts, *Owner*
EMP: 4
SALES (est): 301.7K **Privately Held**
SIC: 7699 Repair services

(G-3968)
BIRDSONG BOOKS
1322 Bayview Rd (19709-2152)
PHONE..................................302 378-7274
Nancy Carol Willis, *Owner*
EMP: 1
SALES (est): 49K **Privately Held**
WEB: www.nancycarolwillis.com
SIC: 2731 Books: publishing only

(G-3969)
BIZZY BEES HOME DAYCARE LLC
815 S Cass St (19709-1334)
PHONE..................................302 376-9245
EMP: 5
SALES (est): 76K **Privately Held**
SIC: 8351 Child day care services

(G-3970)
BLOOMFIELD TRUCKING INC
P.O. Box 1284 (19709-7284)
PHONE..................................302 834-6922
EMP: 4
SALES (est): 296.3K **Privately Held**
SIC: 4212 Local trucking, without storage

(G-3971)
BOXHERO INC
651 N Broad St Ste 205 (19709-6402)
PHONE..................................827 867-4320
Heehong Moon, *CEO*
Jeongbong Seo, *CTO*
Sangchul Lim,
EMP: 4
SALES (est): 89.7K **Privately Held**
SIC: 7371 Custom computer programming services

(G-3972)
BRIAN MCALLISTER DDS
200 Cleaver Farms Rd # 101 (19709-1630)
PHONE..................................302 376-0617
Brian McAllister DDS, *Owner*
EMP: 5
SALES (est): 303K **Privately Held**
SIC: 8021 Dentists' office

(G-3973)
BRIGHT DENTAL
600 N Broad St Ste 7 (19709-1032)
PHONE..................................302 376-7882
Jeffrey Bright, *Owner*
EMP: 23
SALES (est): 578K **Privately Held**
WEB: www.brightdental.net
SIC: 8021 Offices & clinics of dentists

(G-3974)
BRIGHT FUTURES INC
125 Sleepy Hollow Dr (19709-8895)
PHONE..................................610 905-0506
Jessica Deshong, *CEO*
EMP: 20
SALES (est): 232.6K **Privately Held**
SIC: 8351 Child day care services

(G-3975)
BRIGHT STARS HOME DAYCARE
302 Northhampton Way (19709-8338)
PHONE..................................302 378-8142
Reshina Wells, *Principal*
EMP: 5
SALES (est): 72.5K **Privately Held**
SIC: 8351 Group day care center

(G-3976)
BRILLIANT LITTLE MINDS
102 Sandhill Dr (19709-5806)
PHONE..................................302 376-9889
Jennifer Phipps, *Director*
EMP: 5
SALES (est): 236.5K **Privately Held**
SIC: 8351 Group day care center

(G-3977)
BROADMEADOW INVESTMENT LLC
Also Called: BROADMEADOW HEALTHCARE
500 S Broad St (19709-1443)
PHONE..................................302 449-3400
Frank Reimbold, *Mng Member*
Maryann Connor, *Director*
Teresa Manko, *Records Dir*

EMP: 180
SALES (est): 16.5MM **Privately Held**
SIC: 8059 Nursing home, except skilled & intermediate care facility

(G-3978)
C&H ENVIRONMENTAL SERVICES
112 Gillespie Ave (19709-8303)
PHONE..................................302 376-0178
Charles Hairston, *Principal*
EMP: 4
SALES (est): 129.9K **Privately Held**
SIC: 4959 Environmental cleanup services

(G-3979)
CAHILL CONTRACTING
Also Called: Cahill Electrical Contractors
104 Sleepy Hollow Dr # 201 (19709-5842)
PHONE..................................302 378-9650
Kevin Cahill, *President*
EMP: 10
SQ FT: 6,700
SALES (est): 1.6MM **Privately Held**
WEB: www.cahillelectricalcontractors.com
SIC: 1731 General electrical contractor

(G-3980)
CAMP CHIROPRACTIC INC
272 Carter Dr Ste 120 (19709-5850)
PHONE..................................302 378-2899
Trent Camp, *President*
EMP: 7
SALES (est): 470.6K **Privately Held**
WEB: www.campchiropractic.com
SIC: 8041 8011 Offices & clinics of chiropractors; physicians' office, including specialists

(G-3981)
CAPITOL CLEANERS & LAUNDERERS
Also Called: Middletown Shopping Center
600 N Broad St Ste 14 (19709-1032)
PHONE..................................302 378-4744
Christina Smith, *Manager*
EMP: 4
SQ FT: 1,200
SALES (corp-wide): 5.5MM **Privately Held**
WEB: www.capitolcleaners.com
SIC: 7212 Retail agent, laundry & drycleaning; laundry & drycleaner agents
PA: Capitol Cleaners & Launderers Inc
195 Commerce Way
Dover DE 19904
302 674-1511

(G-3982)
CELERA SERVICES INC
364 E Main St (19709-1482)
PHONE..................................302 378-7778
Linda Lushbaugh, *President*
Ed Lushbaugh, *Vice Pres*
EMP: 6
SALES (est): 540K **Privately Held**
SIC: 7359 Home appliance, furniture & entertainment rental services

(G-3983)
CELLCO PARTNERSHIP
Also Called: Verizon Wireless
580 W Main St (19709-1057)
PHONE..................................302 376-6049
EMP: 14
SALES (corp-wide): 130.8B **Publicly Held**
SIC: 5999 4813 4812 Telephone equipment & systems; telephone communication, except radio; cellular telephone services
HQ: Cellco Partnership
1 Verizon Way
Basking Ridge NJ 07920

(G-3984)
CEMEX MATERIALS LLC
Rinker Materials
800 Industrial Rd (19709-1065)
P.O. Box 167 (19709-0167)
PHONE..................................302 378-8920
Tim Meyer, *Manager*
EMP: 50 **Privately Held**
WEB: www.rinkermaterials.com
SIC: 3273 Ready-mixed concrete

Middletown - New Castle County (G-3985)

HQ: Cemex Materials Llc
1501 Belvedere Rd
West Palm Beach FL 33406
561 833-5555

(G-3985)
CHAS POOLS INC
600 N Broad St Ste 11 (19709-1032)
PHONE.................................302 737-9224
Joseph Chas II, *Owner*
EMP: 15
SALES: 450K **Privately Held**
SIC: 1799 Swimming pool construction

(G-3986)
CHIEFFO ELECTRIC INC
108 W Cedarwood Dr (19709-4022)
PHONE.................................302 292-6813
Joseph F Chieffo, *President*
EMP: 20
SALES (est): 1.8MM **Privately Held**
SIC: 1731 Electrical work

(G-3987)
CHOPTANK EXCAVATION
410 Joshua Ln (19709-8006)
PHONE.................................302 378-8114
Keith Biddle, *Principal*
EMP: 7
SALES (est): 914.7K **Privately Held**
SIC: 1794 Excavation work

(G-3988)
CHRISTIANA CARE HEALTH SYS INC
124 Sleepy Hollow Dr # 203 (19709-5838)
PHONE.................................302 449-3000
Todd S Cumming, *Partner*
Charlotte Williams, *Exec Dir*
Theresa Romanowski, *Executive Asst*
Lisa Timmons, *Admin Asst*
Alison Segal, *Physician Asst*
EMP: 8
SALES (corp-wide): 1.5B **Privately Held**
SIC: 8062 General medical & surgical hospitals
HQ: Christiana Care Health System, Inc.
200 Hygeia Dr
Newark DE 19713
302 733-1000

(G-3989)
CHRISTIANA MECHANICAL INC
Also Called: CMI
109 Sleepy Hollow Dr A (19709-8895)
PHONE.................................302 378-7308
Theresa A Sill, *President*
Gary Marshall, *Manager*
Kelsey Sill, *Office Admin*
EMP: 13
SQ FT: 1,200
SALES (est): 2.5MM **Privately Held**
SIC: 1711 Mechanical contractor

(G-3990)
CHRISTOPHERS HAIR DESIGN
Also Called: Christopher's Salon & Spa
423 N Broad St Ste 5 (19709-1092)
PHONE.................................302 378-1988
Ann Caminiti, *Partner*
Christopher Caminiti, *Partner*
EMP: 8
SALES (est): 259.7K **Privately Held**
SIC: 7231 7991 Hairdressers; spas

(G-3991)
CINDYS HOME AWAY FROM HME FAM
22 Canary Ct (19709-2184)
PHONE.................................302 378-0487
Cindy Shaw, *Principal*
EMP: 5
SALES (est): 88.4K **Privately Held**
SIC: 8082 Home health care services

(G-3992)
CITIZENS BANK NATIONAL ASSN
460 E Main St (19709-1462)
PHONE.................................302 376-3641
Danielle Cummins, *Manager*
EMP: 7
SALES (corp-wide): 7.3B **Publicly Held**
WEB: www.ccoinvest.com
SIC: 6022 State commercial banks

HQ: Citizens Bank, National Association
1 Citizens Plz Ste 1 # 1
Providence RI 02903
401 282-7000

(G-3993)
CIVIL ENGINEERING ASSOC LLC
55 W Main St (19709-1017)
PHONE.................................302 376-8833
Ronald Sutton, *Mng Member*
EMP: 5
SQ FT: 2,880
SALES: 700K **Privately Held**
SIC: 8711 Civil engineering

(G-3994)
CLARIOS LLC
Also Called: Johnson Controls
700 N Broad St (19709-1050)
PHONE.................................302 378-9885
Mario Alvarez, *CFO*
EMP: 300
SALES (corp-wide): 42.9B **Publicly Held**
SIC: 3691 Storage batteries
HQ: Clarios, Llc
5757 N Green Bay Ave
Milwaukee WI 53209

(G-3995)
CLARIOS LLC
Also Called: Johnson Controls
50 Patriot Dr (19709-8769)
PHONE.................................302 696-3221
EMP: 10
SALES (corp-wide): 42.9B **Publicly Held**
SIC: 3691 Storage batteries
HQ: Clarios, Llc
5757 N Green Bay Ave
Milwaukee WI 53209

(G-3996)
CLEAN AS A WHISTLE INC
107 Lynn Cir (19709-9253)
PHONE.................................302 376-1388
Carla Briccotto, *Principal*
EMP: 2 **EST:** 2008
SALES (est): 150.6K **Privately Held**
SIC: 3999 Whistles

(G-3997)
CLIFFORD L ANZILOTTI DDS PC
112 Saint Annes Church Rd (19709-1495)
PHONE.................................302 378-2778
Dr Clifford Anzilotti, *Branch Mgr*
EMP: 15
SALES (est): 477K
SALES (corp-wide): 976.7K **Privately Held**
SIC: 8021 Orthodontist
PA: Clifford L Anzilotti Dds Pc
2101 Foulk Rd
Wilmington DE 19810
302 475-2050

(G-3998)
CLIFTON L BAKHSH JR INC
Also Called: Bakhsh Surveyors
4450 Summit Bridge Rd (19709-9344)
PHONE.................................302 378-8009
Clifton L Bakhsh Jr, *President*
Sue Bakhsh, *Vice Pres*
Roger Brickley, *Project Mgr*
EMP: 16
SQ FT: 2,000
SALES (est): 1.4MM **Privately Held**
WEB: www.cbakhsh.com
SIC: 8713 Surveying services

(G-3999)
CLINTON CRADDOCK
Also Called: Delaware Protection Agency
511 Cilantro Ct (19709-8783)
PHONE.................................267 505-2671
Clinton Craddock, *Owner*
EMP: 10
SALES (est): 180.6K **Privately Held**
SIC: 7389

(G-4000)
COINTIGO LLC
651 N Broad St Ste 205 (19709-6402)
PHONE.................................817 681-7131
Guillermo Graa,
Raspal Bhatia,
Jonathan Kohn,
Jamie Owens,

EMP: 10
SALES (est): 180.6K **Privately Held**
SIC: 7389

(G-4001)
COMMUNICATE U MEDIA LLC
1010 Camelot Dr (19709-7526)
PHONE.................................610 453-6501
Steffan Roots,
EMP: 1
SALES (est): 39.9K **Privately Held**
SIC: 2711 7372 Job printing & newspaper publishing combined; application computer software

(G-4002)
COMMUNITY PUBLICATIONS INC
Also Called: Greenville Community Newspaper
24 W Main St (19709-1039)
P.O. Box 536, Hockessin (19707-0536)
PHONE.................................302 239-4644
Joseph Amom, *President*
EMP: 15
SALES (est): 560.2K **Privately Held**
SIC: 2711 Newspapers: publishing only, not printed on site

(G-4003)
COMPASS GRAPHICS
137 Back Creek Dr (19709-8843)
PHONE.................................302 378-1977
D Clendening, *Principal*
EMP: 2
SALES (est): 146.8K **Privately Held**
SIC: 2759 Commercial printing

(G-4004)
COMPASSONATE CERTIFICATION CTR
364 E Main St Ste 2001 (19709-1482)
PHONE.................................888 316-9085
Bryan Doner, *Owner*
EMP: 4
SALES (est): 82.7K **Privately Held**
SIC: 8099 Health & allied services

(G-4005)
COMPD HOLDINGS INC
651 N Broad St Ste 205 (19709-6402)
PHONE.................................929 436-5252
Jan T Strzelecki, *President*
EMP: 4
SALES (est): 87.5K **Privately Held**
SIC: 7379

(G-4006)
CONNOR MARKETING INC
434 Boxwood Ln (19709-9658)
PHONE.................................302 376-6037
Dan Conner, *President*
EMP: 1
SALES (est): 81.9K **Privately Held**
SIC: 3423 Hand & edge tools

(G-4007)
CONREP INC
292 Carter Dr Ste C (19709-5846)
PHONE.................................302 528-8383
SAI Kumar, *Associate*
EMP: 4
SALES (est): 371K **Privately Held**
SIC: 7371 Computer software development

(G-4008)
CONVENTRA LLC
25 S Cummings Dr (19709-1663)
PHONE.................................302 378-4461
Priya Dubey, *Vice Pres*
EMP: 6
SALES (est): 283.8K **Privately Held**
SIC: 7379 7371 8243 7372 Computer related consulting services; software programming applications; software training, computer; application computer software

(G-4009)
COOK G LEGIH DDS& COOK JEFRY
12 Pennington St Ste 300 (19709-1026)
PHONE.................................302 378-4416
Gordon Leigh Cook DDS, *Partner*
Dr G Leigh Cook DDS, *Partner*
Dr Jeffrey L Cook, *Partner*

▲ **EMP:** 6
SQ FT: 650
SALES (est): 807.9K **Privately Held**
SIC: 8021 Dentists' office

(G-4010)
COOK HAULING LLC
350 Misty Vale Dr (19709-2124)
PHONE.................................302 378-6451
Melvin Cook,
EMP: 5
SALES (est): 419.8K **Privately Held**
SIC: 1442 Construction sand & gravel

(G-4011)
COOPER-WILBERT VAULT CO INC
4971 Summit Bridge Rd (19709-8819)
PHONE.................................302 376-1331
Paul Cooper, *General Mgr*
EMP: 4
SALES (corp-wide): 4.5MM **Privately Held**
SIC: 3272 Burial vaults, concrete or precast terrazzo
PA: Cooper-Wilbert Vault Co Inc
621 Atlantic Ave
Barrington NJ 08007
856 547-8405

(G-4012)
COUNTY BUILDING SERVICES INC
8 Knightsbridge Rd (19709-9706)
PHONE.................................302 377-4213
Jack Reede, *President*
EMP: 52
SALES: 450K **Privately Held**
SIC: 7349 Building cleaning service

(G-4013)
CRAZY COATINGS
4783 Summit Bridge Rd (19709-8815)
PHONE.................................302 378-0888
Dave Seemans, *Manager*
EMP: 2
SALES (est): 159.7K **Privately Held**
SIC: 3479 Coating of metals & formed products

(G-4014)
CREATIVE DEVICES INC
361 Misty Vale Dr (19709-2125)
PHONE.................................302 378-5433
Robert Urstadt, *President*
Sandra Urstadt, *Corp Secy*
▲ **EMP:** 2
SALES (est): 500K **Privately Held**
WEB: www.creativedevices.com
SIC: 3826 Analytical optical instruments

(G-4015)
CRISTY ANNA CARE PHYSCL THRAPY
Also Called: Schwezers Thrapy Rhabilitation
200 Cleaver Farms Rd (19709-1630)
PHONE.................................302 378-6111
Traci Butler, *Manager*
EMP: 6
SALES (est): 93.7K **Privately Held**
SIC: 8049 Physical therapist

(G-4016)
CRYSTAL GRAHAM
Also Called: Commercial & Trauma Clg Entp
415 E Main St (19709-1463)
P.O. Box 415 (19709-0415)
PHONE.................................302 669-9318
Crystal Graham, *Owner*
Clarissa Crawford, *Principal*
EMP: 15
SALES (est): 198.8K **Privately Held**
SIC: 7217 7342 7349 7389 Carpet & upholstery cleaning; rest room cleaning service; building & office cleaning services; building cleaning service; office cleaning or charring;

(G-4017)
CYBERSECURITY TRUST LLC
45 Millwood Dr (19709-8879)
PHONE.................................844 240-2287
Matthew Taylor, *CEO*
Delon J Taylor, *COO*
EMP: 4

SALES (est): 92.1K **Privately Held**
SIC: 7389 Business services

(G-4018)
D&S CONSTRUCTION COMPANY
58 Millwood Dr (19709-9746)
PHONE..................302 650-3209
Kathy Yetter, *Principal*
EMP: 4
SALES: 336K **Privately Held**
SIC: 1521 Single-family housing construction

(G-4019)
DATWYLER PHARMA PACKG USA INC
571 Merrimac Ave (19709-4647)
PHONE..................302 603-8020
EMP: 2
SALES (corp-wide): 1.3B **Privately Held**
SIC: 3841 Surgical instruments & apparatus
HQ: Datwyler Pharma Packaging Usa Inc.
9012 Pennsauken Hwy
Pennsauken NJ 08110
856 663-2202

(G-4020)
DAWN L CONLY
266 Bucktail Dr (19709-6131)
PHONE..................302 378-1890
Dawn L Conly, *Principal*
EMP: 5
SALES (est): 77.3K **Privately Held**
SIC: 8351 Child day care services

(G-4021)
DE TECHNOLOGIES INC
118 Sleepy Hollow Dr # 1 (19709-5836)
PHONE..................302 285-0353
Mark Majerus, *Principal*
EMP: 4
SALES (est): 267.2K **Privately Held**
WEB: www.detechnologies.com
SIC: 8711 Consulting engineer
PA: De Technologies, Inc.
100 Queens Dr
King Of Prussia PA 19406

(G-4022)
DEANNE NAPLES FAMILY DAYCARE
225 Manchester Way (19709-2131)
PHONE..................302 376-1408
David Naples, *Principal*
EMP: 5
SALES (est): 71.4K **Privately Held**
SIC: 8351 Group day care center

(G-4023)
DEBBIE GILL
Also Called: Made Just For You
108 Fox Hunt Ln (19709-8995)
PHONE..................302 547-5182
Debbie Gill, *Owner*
EMP: 1
SALES (est): 80K **Privately Held**
SIC: 2819 Chemicals, reagent grade: refined from technical grade

(G-4024)
DEDICATED TO WOMEN OBGYN
209 E Main St (19709-1449)
PHONE..................302 285-5545
Michelle H Cooper, *Partner*
EMP: 10
SALES (est): 439.6K **Privately Held**
SIC: 8011 Gynecologist

(G-4025)
DEL-MAR DOOR SERVICES INC
515 Janvier Dr (19709-1745)
P.O. Box 170 (19709-0170)
PHONE..................800 492-2392
James Murphy, *President*
Dave Rowan, *Division Mgr*
Dave W Rowan, *Vice Pres*
EMP: 4
SALES (est): 950K **Privately Held**
WEB: www.delmardoor.com
SIC: 1751 Garage door, installation or erection

(G-4026)
DELA BELLE INV GROUP CORP
651 N Broad St Ste 205 (19709-6402)
PHONE..................901 279-2742
Juanita Wilson, *COO*
Tehren Wilson, *Vice Pres*
EMP: 6
SALES (est): 114.7K **Privately Held**
SIC: 7514 Rent-a-car service

(G-4027)
DELAWARE DETECTIVE GROUP LLC
364 E Main St (19709-1482)
PHONE..................302 373-3678
Stephen Kemtski, *Principal*
EMP: 4 EST: 2009
SALES (est): 170.3K **Privately Held**
SIC: 7381 Detective agency; private investigator

(G-4028)
DELAWARE IMAGING NETWORK
Also Called: Papastavros Assoc Med Imaging
114 Sandhill Dr Ste 201 (19709-5805)
PHONE..................302 449-5400
Dick Palmer, *Manager*
EMP: 5 **Publicly Held**
SIC: 8011 8071 Radiologist; X-ray laboratory, including dental
HQ: Delaware Imaging Network
40 Polly Drmmnd Hl Rd 4
Newark DE 19711
302 652-3016

(G-4029)
DELAWARE MILLWORK
110 W Green St (19709-1317)
PHONE..................302 376-8324
EMP: 1
SALES (est): 54.1K **Privately Held**
SIC: 2431 Millwork

(G-4030)
DELAWARE OPEN M R I LLC
Also Called: Tri State Imaging Consultants
374 E Main St (19709-1482)
PHONE..................302 449-2300
Steven Edell MD,
EMP: 4
SALES (est): 179.4K **Privately Held**
SIC: 8011 Radiologist

(G-4031)
DELAWARE SCREEN PRINTING INC
350 Strawberry Ln (19709-9641)
PHONE..................302 378-4231
Dennis Cowan, *President*
EMP: 3
SALES: 300K **Privately Held**
WEB: www.delawarescreenprinting.com
SIC: 2759 2752 2396 Commercial printing; commercial printing, lithographic; automotive & apparel trimmings

(G-4032)
DELAWARE SMILE CENTER
201 Carter Dr Ste A (19709-5833)
PHONE..................302 285-7645
Saqib Usmani, *Principal*
EMP: 8
SALES (est): 68.5K **Privately Held**
SIC: 3843 Enamels, dentists'

(G-4033)
DELAWRES FNEST HARDWOOD FLOORS
1461 Cedar Lane Rd (19709-9317)
PHONE..................302 376-0742
Jack Lashonb, *Owner*
EMP: 6 EST: 1999
SALES (est): 333.4K **Privately Held**
SIC: 1752 Floor laying & floor work

(G-4034)
DELSTAR TECHNOLOGIES INC (DH)
Also Called: Delnet
601 Industrial Rd (19709-1083)
PHONE..................302 378-8888
Mark Abrahams, *President*
James Dickson, *Vice Pres*
Dennis Eckels, *Vice Pres*
William Geissler, *Vice Pres*
Andrew Platt, *Vice Pres*
◆ EMP: 130
SQ FT: 145,000
SALES (est): 149.4MM **Publicly Held**
SIC: 3081 Polypropylene film & sheet
HQ: Delstar Holding Corp.
100 N Point Ctr E Ste 600
Alpharetta GA 30022
800 514-0186

(G-4035)
DENTAL ASSOCIATES DELAWARE PA
Also Called: Dental Assoc Del Mddletown Off
106 Saint Annes Church Rd (19709-1495)
PHONE..................302 378-8600
Dr Greg Hansen, *Manager*
EMP: 20
SALES (corp-wide): 5.9MM **Privately Held**
SIC: 8021 Dentists' office
PA: Dental Associates Of Delaware Pa
1415 Foulk Rd Ste 200
Wilmington DE 19803
302 477-4900

(G-4036)
DEPENDABLE LAWN CARE INC
1421 Pole Bridge Rd (19709-2167)
PHONE..................302 834-0159
Herbert Strohl Jr, *President*
Elizabeth Strohl, *Admin Sec*
EMP: 4
SQ FT: 1,000
SALES (est): 135.7K **Privately Held**
SIC: 0782 Lawn care services

(G-4037)
DESIGNER BRAIDS AND TRADE
148 Vincent Cir (19709-3059)
PHONE..................718 783-9078
Marion Council-George, *President*
Anita Hill, *Vice Pres*
EMP: 6
SQ FT: 1,700
SALES: 150K **Privately Held**
SIC: 7231 5999 5611 5621 Beauty shops; hair care products; clothing, men's & boys': everyday, except suits & sportswear; women's clothing stores

(G-4038)
DIAMOND CAR WASH INC
104 Sandhill Dr (19709-5806)
PHONE..................302 449-5896
Christophe McQuaide, *Principal*
EMP: 4
SALES (est): 278.5K **Privately Held**
SIC: 7542 Washing & polishing, automotive

(G-4039)
DIENAY DISTRIBUTION CORP
101 Trupenny Turn Ste 1b (19709-8965)
PHONE..................732 766-0814
Dan Dagadu, *President*
EMP: 5
SALES (est): 466.2K **Privately Held**
SIC: 5047 Medical & hospital equipment

(G-4040)
DOLAN MANUFACTURING SOLUTIONS
424 Spring Hollow Dr (19709-7893)
PHONE..................302 378-4981
Robert Dolan, *Principal*
EMP: 4
SALES (est): 206K **Privately Held**
SIC: 8748 Business consulting

(G-4041)
DOMAIN HR SOLUTIONS
364 E Main St Ste 1012 (19709-1482)
PHONE..................302 357-9401
Irshad Beg, *Accounts Mgr*
EMP: 10 EST: 2016
SALES (est): 74K **Privately Held**
SIC: 7218 Industrial equipment launderers

(G-4042)
DONALD BRIGGS
Also Called: Don Noel Professional Services
400 W Harvest Ln (19709-3046)
PHONE..................267 476-2712
Donald Briggs, *Owner*
EMP: 5
SALES (est): 177.8K **Privately Held**
SIC: 7538 7549 General automotive repair shops; high performance auto repair & service

(G-4043)
DORIS V OBENSHAIN
Also Called: Doris Obenshain Counseling
100 W Green St (19709-1398)
PHONE..................302 448-1450
Doris Venetta Obenshain, *Principal*
EMP: 5 EST: 2011
SALES (est): 106.9K **Privately Held**
SIC: 8093 Mental health clinic, outpatient

(G-4044)
DOVER POST CO INC
Also Called: Middletown Transcript
24 W Main St (19709-1039)
PHONE..................302 378-9531
Josh Trust, *Manager*
EMP: 6
SALES (corp-wide): 9.8MM **Privately Held**
WEB: www.doverpost.com
SIC: 2711 Newspapers: publishing only, not printed on site
PA: The Dover Post Co Inc
609 E Division St
Dover DE 19901
302 653-2083

(G-4045)
DOVER SURGICENTER LLC
108 Patriot Dr Ste A (19709-8803)
PHONE..................302 346-3171
Larry Piccioni, *Principal*
EMP: 28
SALES (est): 4.9MM **Privately Held**
SIC: 8011 Ambulatory surgical center

(G-4046)
DYNAMIC THERAPY SERVICES LLC
432 E Main St (19709-1462)
PHONE..................302 376-4315
Marta Gospodarek, *Exec Dir*
EMP: 16
SALES (corp-wide): 12.9MM **Privately Held**
SIC: 8049 Physical therapist
PA: Dynamic Therapy Services Llc
1501 Blueball Ave
Linwood PA 19061
610 859-8850

(G-4047)
EAN HOLDINGS LLC
5207 Summit Bridge Rd (19709-8823)
PHONE..................302 376-5606
Anthony Jacobs, *Branch Mgr*
EMP: 8
SALES (corp-wide): 4.5B **Privately Held**
SIC: 7514 Passenger car rental
HQ: Ean Holdings, Llc
600 Corporate Park Dr
Saint Louis MO 63105

(G-4048)
ECONAT INC
651 N Broad St Ste 206 (19709-6402)
PHONE..................201 925-5239
Selcuk Yesil, *President*
EMP: 1
SALES (est): 61.6K **Privately Held**
SIC: 3634 Heating units, for electric appliances

(G-4049)
ECONERD
117 Zachary Ln (19709-9896)
PHONE..................302 669-9279
EMP: 6
SALES (est): 517.2K **Privately Held**
SIC: 7699 Repair services

(G-4050)
EDLYNCARE LLC
261 Ann Dr (19709-2605)
PHONE..................267 474-0486
Linda K Agyapong, *Principal*
EMP: 8

Middletown - New Castle County (G-4051)

SALES (est): 206.3K **Privately Held**
SIC: **8059** Personal care home, with health care

(G-4051)
EJ USA INC
401 Industrial Rd (19709-1079)
P.O. Box 510 (19709-0510)
PHONE..................................302 378-1100
Charles White, *General Mgr*
EMP: 12 **Privately Held**
WEB: www.ejiw.com
SIC: **3321** Manhole covers, metal
HQ: Ej Usa, Inc.
   301 Spring St
   East Jordan MI 49727
   800 874-4100

(G-4052)
ELAINE LEONARD
Also Called: Early Essentials
111 Patriot Dr Ste A&B (19709-8771)
PHONE..................................302 376-5553
Elaine Leonard, *Owner*
EMP: 12
SALES (est): 74.7K **Privately Held**
SIC: **8351** Preschool center

(G-4053)
ELAYNE JAMES SALON & SPA LLC
462 W Main St (19709-1063)
PHONE..................................302 376-5290
James Galoff, *Principal*
EMP: 6
SALES (est): 236.6K **Privately Held**
SIC: **7231** Beauty shops

(G-4054)
ELITE AUTO LLC
364 E Main St Ste 204 (19709-1482)
PHONE..................................302 690-2948
Maurice Curtis, *CEO*
Dawn A Roberts, *Managing Prtnr*
EMP: 5
SALES (est): 223.3K **Privately Held**
SIC: **7538** General automotive repair shops

(G-4055)
ELITE FEET LLC
5238 Summit Bridge Rd (19709-8822)
PHONE..................................302 464-1028
Jason Hunt, *Mng Member*
Joy Hunt,
EMP: 8
SALES: 500K **Privately Held**
SIC: **5139** 5661 Footwear; footwear, athletic

(G-4056)
ELLIOTT HOLDINGS CORPORATION
651 N Broad St Ste 20512 (19709-6400)
PHONE..................................650 241-8646
Omar Benchemsi, *CEO*
EMP: 10
SALES (est): 440.5K **Privately Held**
SIC: **6722** Management investment, open-end

(G-4057)
EMERALD GREEN
992 Port Penn Rd (19709-8932)
PHONE..................................302 836-6909
Laura Moyer, *Manager*
EMP: 4
SALES (est): 230.3K **Privately Held**
SIC: **0782** Lawn care services

(G-4058)
ENCOMPASS HEALTH CORPORATION
Also Called: HealthSouth
250 E Hampden Rd (19709-5303)
PHONE..................................302 464-3400
Melissa Boney, *Marketing Staff*
EMP: 129
SALES (corp-wide): 4.2B **Publicly Held**
SIC: **8069** Specialty hospitals, except psychiatric
PA: Encompass Health Corporation
   9001 Liberty Pkwy
   Birmingham AL 35242
   205 967-7116

(G-4059)
ENVIRONMENTAL CONSULTING SVCS (PA)
100 S Cass St (19709-1354)
P.O. Box 138 (19709-0138)
PHONE..................................302 378-9881
Alvin Maiden, *President*
Gary A Hayes, *Vice Pres*
EMP: 12
SQ FT: 3,800
SALES (est): 2.5MM **Privately Held**
SIC: **8731** 8748 Environmental research; environmental consultant

(G-4060)
ENVIRONMENTAL TESTING INC
100 S Cass St (19709-1354)
P.O. Box 138 (19709-0138)
PHONE..................................302 378-5341
Gary Hayes, *President*
C C Miller, *Vice Pres*
Alvin Maiden, *Treasurer*
Cathy Grimm, *Info Tech Mgr*
A L Maiden, *Admin Sec*
EMP: 6
SQ FT: 3,800
SALES (est): 710.6K
SALES (corp-wide): 2.5MM **Privately Held**
WEB: www.ecsi-del.com
SIC: **8748** 8731 Environmental consultant; natural resource research
PA: Environmental Consulting Services, Inc
   100 S Cass St
   Middletown DE 19709
   302 378-9881

(G-4061)
EPIC MARKETING CONS CORP
10 Jackie Cir (19709-9369)
PHONE..................................302 285-9790
Nancy Dibert, *CEO*
Donald Dibert, *President*
Michael Dibert, *Vice Pres*
EMP: 20
SALES (est): 678.7K **Privately Held**
SIC: **7311** 8742 Advertising agencies; marketing consulting services

(G-4062)
ESQUIRE PLUMBING & HEATING CO
7 Wood St (19709-1048)
P.O. Box 441 (19709-0441)
PHONE..................................302 378-7001
Virginia Briccotto, *President*
Virginia Bricotto, *President*
Robert Briccotto Jr, *Vice Pres*
EMP: 7
SQ FT: 3,500
SALES (est): 440K **Privately Held**
SIC: **1711** Warm air heating & air conditioning contractor; plumbing contractors

(G-4063)
EUGENE M DAMICO III DDS PA
114 Saint Annes Church Rd (19709-1495)
PHONE..................................302 376-3700
Eugene M D'Amico III DDS, *Branch Mgr*
EMP: 4
SALES (est): 94.1K **Privately Held**
SIC: **8021** Dentists' office
PA: Eugene M D'amico Iii Dds Pa
   4735 Ogletown Stanton Rd # 1115
   Newark DE 19713

(G-4064)
EVANIX ENTERPRISES LLC
49 W Sarazen Dr (19709-9358)
PHONE..................................302 384-1806
Istvan Gabor, *President*
EMP: 5
SALES (est): 290.5K **Privately Held**
SIC: **4731** Freight forwarding

(G-4065)
EVENTS A LA CARTE
3 N Cummings Dr (19709-1666)
PHONE..................................302 753-7462
Kimberly Olson, *Owner*
EMP: 4
SALES (est): 107.8K **Privately Held**
SIC: **7299** Facility rental & party planning services

(G-4066)
EXPERT HOME CARE
504 Silverhill Xing (19709-6842)
PHONE..................................856 870-6691
Agememnon M Davis, *Manager*
EMP: 8
SALES (est): 61.1K **Privately Held**
SIC: **8082** Home health care services

(G-4067)
EZANGACOM INC
222 Carter Dr Ste 201 (19709-5857)
PHONE..................................888 439-2642
Richard K Kahn, *President*
Beth Kahn, *CFO*
Brian Samson, *Web Dvlpr*
Mary Holland, *Administration*
EMP: 42
SQ FT: 7,500
SALES (est): 8MM **Privately Held**
WEB: www.ezanga.com
SIC: **7311** Advertising agencies

(G-4068)
F AND D EQUIPMENT & REPAIR LLC
213 W Lake St Unit F (19709-1757)
PHONE..................................302 378-1999
David Neugebauer,
Frank Sinkko,
EMP: 4
SALES (est): 57.6K **Privately Held**
SIC: **7694** Motor repair services

(G-4069)
FARRELL ROOFING INC
201 W Lake St (19709-1755)
PHONE..................................302 378-7663
T Paul Farrell, *President*
Paula J Farrel, *Vice Pres*
Paula Farrel, *Vice Pres*
Frank E Clark, *Director*
EMP: 22
SQ FT: 5,000
SALES (est): 3.8MM **Privately Held**
SIC: **1761** 1799 Roofing contractor; waterproofing

(G-4070)
FILE RIGHT LLC
364 E Main St (19709-1482)
PHONE..................................302 757-7107
Justin Workman, *Principal*
EMP: 4 EST: 2011
SALES (est): 233.8K **Privately Held**
SIC: **7371** Computer software development & applications

(G-4071)
FIRST CHICE AUTO TRCK MDDLTOWN
128 Patriot Dr (19709-8770)
PHONE..................................302 376-6333
Kenneth Williams, *President*
EMP: 4
SALES (est): 268K **Privately Held**
SIC: **4212** Local trucking, without storage

(G-4072)
FIRST STATE INSPECTION AGENCY
811 N Broad St Ste 201 (19709-1173)
PHONE..................................302 449-5383
Robert Smith, *Branch Mgr*
EMP: 5
SALES (corp-wide): 2.5MM **Privately Held**
SIC: **7389** Building inspection service
PA: First State Inspection Agency Inc
   1001 Mattlind Way
   Milford DE 19963
   302 422-3859

(G-4073)
FITWISE INC
651 N Broad St (19709-6400)
PHONE..................................812 929-2696
Jeffry Smith, *Vice Pres*
EMP: 4
SALES: 100K **Privately Held**
SIC: **7371** Computer software development & applications

(G-4074)
FIVE STARS EMBROIDERY
224 Milford Dr (19709-9417)
PHONE..................................443 466-9692
Tamara Lewis, *Owner*
Marion Hughes, *Owner*
EMP: 2
SALES (est): 80.9K **Privately Held**
SIC: **2395** Embroidery products, except schiffli machine; embroidery & art needlework

(G-4075)
FOOT CARE GROUP INC
272 Carter Dr Ste 220 (19709-5851)
PHONE..................................302 285-0292
Chris Bailey, *Manager*
EMP: 13 **Privately Held**
WEB: www.footcaregroup.org
SIC: **8043** Offices & clinics of podiatrists
PA: Foot Care Group Inc
   1601 Milltown Rd Ste 24
   Wilmington DE 19808

(G-4076)
FOREVER INC
Also Called: Fulton Paper
328 E Main St (19709-1482)
PHONE..................................302 449-2100
Lisa Stoddard, *President*
EMP: 7
SALES (est): 474.8K
SALES (corp-wide): 2.8MM **Privately Held**
SIC: **5113** Paper & products, wrapping or coarse
PA: Forever, Inc.
   1006 W 27th St
   Wilmington DE 19802
   302 594-0400

(G-4077)
FREEDOM CTR FOR IND LIVING INC
400 N Broad St Ste A (19709-1004)
PHONE..................................302 376-4399
Lauren Reynolds, *Director*
EMP: 5
SALES: 219.5K **Privately Held**
WEB: www.fcilde.org
SIC: **8322** Individual & family services

(G-4078)
FRIGHTLAND LLC
309 Port Penn Rd (19709-9732)
PHONE..................................302 838-0256
EMP: 4 EST: 2011
SALES (est): 130.3K **Privately Held**
SIC: **7999** Amusement & recreation

(G-4079)
FROG HOLLOW GOLF COURSE
1 Wittington Way (19709-7906)
PHONE..................................302 376-6500
Alan Liddicoat, *Partner*
Ken Kershaw, *Partner*
EMP: 20
SALES (est): 1MM **Privately Held**
SIC: **7992** Public golf courses

(G-4080)
FULTON BANK NATIONAL ASSN
Also Called: Fulton Financial Advisors
468 W Main St (19709-1063)
PHONE..................................302 378-4575
Vicky Buckley, *Site Mgr*
EMP: 9
SALES (corp-wide): 954MM **Publicly Held**
SIC: **6021** National commercial banks
HQ: Fulton Bank, National Association
   1 Penn Sq Ste 1 # 1
   Lancaster PA 17602
   717 581-3166

(G-4081)
G B TECH INC
651 N Broad St Ste 301 (19709-6403)
PHONE..................................302 378-5600
Sudheer Bathula, *President*
EMP: 50
SALES (est): 204K **Privately Held**
SIC: **7379**

GEOGRAPHIC SECTION
Middletown - New Castle County (G-4113)

(G-4082)
G G + A LLC
1050 Industrial Rd # 110 (19709-2802)
PHONE.................................302 376-6122
Lori Grayson,
David Grayson,
EMP: 16 **EST:** 2005
SALES (est): 3.4MM **Privately Held**
WEB: www.vtechconstruction.com
SIC: 1521 Single-family housing construction

(G-4083)
GANNETT FLEMING INC
651 N Broad St (19709-6400)
PHONE.................................302 378-2256
Brian J Smith, *Office Mgr*
EMP: 37
SALES (corp-wide): 462MM **Privately Held**
SIC: 8711 Consulting engineer
HQ: Fleming Gannett Inc
    207 Senate Ave
    Camp Hill PA 17011
    717 763-7211

(G-4084)
GB JACOBS LLC
Also Called: Grow & Learn Childcare Center
2486 N Dupont Pkwy (19709-9653)
PHONE.................................302 378-9100
Kari Kroll,
EMP: 27
SQ FT: 5,500
SALES (est): 125.5K **Privately Held**
SIC: 8351 Preschool center

(G-4085)
GENALYZE LLC
410 N Ramunno Dr Ut1806 (19709-3003)
PHONE.................................732 917-4893
Hui-Ju Tsai, *Principal*
EMP: 1
SALES (est): 70K **Privately Held**
SIC: 2836 Biological products, except diagnostic

(G-4086)
GEORGE PRODUCTS COMPANY INC
110 Sleepy Hollow Dr (19709-8894)
PHONE.................................302 449-0199
Fred Land, *President*
Dawn Land, *Vice Pres*
Dawn L Land, *Purch Mgr*
George Kreshock, *Treasurer*
Kenya Smith, *Sales Staff*
EMP: 18 **EST:** 1951
SQ FT: 20,000
SALES (est): 3.9MM **Privately Held**
WEB: www.gprod.com
SIC: 3469 Ornamental metal stampings

(G-4087)
GLASS TECHNOLOGISTS INC
32 S Main St (19709-9736)
PHONE.................................240 682-0966
John Michael Trembly, *President*
EMP: 1
SALES (est): 80K **Privately Held**
SIC: 3231 3221 3641 3272 Products of purchased glass; glass containers; electric lamps; concrete products

(G-4088)
GLOBAL COMPUTERS NETWORKS LLC
718 Pinewood Dr Ste 2 (19709-8643)
PHONE.................................484 686-8374
Dominique Pereira, *Principal*
Harlen King, *Principal*
EMP: 7
SALES (est): 310K **Privately Held**
SIC: 8243 7372 Repair training, computer; application computer software

(G-4089)
GLOBAL EXTERIOR LLC
1057 Boyds Corner Rd (19709-9227)
PHONE.................................302 722-1969
Peppe Longato, *Mng Member*
EMP: 7
SALES (est): 1MM **Privately Held**
SIC: 7371 Computer software development & applications

(G-4090)
GO TEES LLC
101 Arcadia Pkwy (19709-1329)
PHONE.................................708 703-1788
Christine Degliobizzi, *Principal*
EMP: 2
SALES (est): 125.4K **Privately Held**
SIC: 2759 Screen printing

(G-4091)
GORDON C HONIG DMD PA
104 Sleepy Hollow Dr (19709-5842)
PHONE.................................302 696-4020
Gordon Hornig, *Branch Mgr*
EMP: 5
SALES (corp-wide): 904.8K **Privately Held**
SIC: 8021 Orthodontist
PA: Gordon C Honig Dmd Pa
    2707 Kirkwood Hwy
    Newark DE 19711
    302 737-6333

(G-4092)
GREENHILL EXPRESS CAR WASH
299 E Main St (19709-1449)
PHONE.................................302 464-1031
EMP: 7
SALES (est): 65.6K **Privately Held**
SIC: 7542 Carwash, automatic

(G-4093)
GREENWICH AEROGROUP INC
4200 Summit Bridge Rd (19709-9340)
P.O. Box 258 (19709-0258)
PHONE.................................302 834-5400
EMP: 3
SALES (est): 207.4K
SALES (corp-wide): 7.6B **Publicly Held**
SIC: 3724 Research & development on aircraft engines & parts
PA: W. R. Berkley Corporation
    475 Steamboat Rd Fl 1
    Greenwich CT 06830
    203 629-3000

(G-4094)
GROWING PALACE
111 Patriot Dr Ste A (19709-8771)
PHONE.................................302 376-5553
Drexann Fields, *Principal*
EMP: 10
SALES (est): 85.6K **Privately Held**
SIC: 8351 Child day care services

(G-4095)
GROWING PALACE III
Also Called: Growing Palace 3, The
111 Patriot Dr Ste A (19709-8771)
PHONE.................................302 376-5553
Ranika Holmes, *Owner*
EMP: 13
SALES (est): 186K **Privately Held**
SIC: 8351 Child day care services

(G-4096)
GT DESIGNS INC
109 Wellington Way (19709-9406)
PHONE.................................302 275-8100
Greg Tweddell, *President*
EMP: 5
SALES (est): 299.8K **Privately Held**
SIC: 7389 Design services

(G-4097)
GUARDIAN FENCE CO
4783 Summit Bridge Rd (19709-8815)
PHONE.................................302 834-3044
Ruth Ann Seemans, *President*
David Seemans, *Vice Pres*
Terri Seemans, *Admin Sec*
EMP: 12 **EST:** 1957
SALES (est): 2MM **Privately Held**
WEB: www.guardianpoolfence.com
SIC: 1799 Fence construction

(G-4098)
H B P INC (PA)
110 W Green St (19709-1317)
PHONE.................................302 378-9693
Danny Burris, *President*
EMP: 32

SALES (est): 5.3MM **Privately Held**
SIC: 1522 Remodeling, multi-family dwellings

(G-4099)
H&H CUSTOMS INC
708 Lorewood Grove Rd (19709-9428)
PHONE.................................302 378-0810
Allan Hutton, *President*
EMP: 2
SALES (est): 138.8K **Privately Held**
SIC: 2449 Rectangular boxes & crates, wood

(G-4100)
H&R BLOCK INC
Also Called: H & R Block
Middletown Shopping Ctr (19709)
PHONE.................................302 378-8931
George Manz, *Manager*
EMP: 12
SALES (corp-wide): 3B **Publicly Held**
WEB: www.hrblock.com
SIC: 7291 Tax return preparation services
PA: H&R Block, Inc.
    1 H&R Block Way
    Kansas City MO 64105
    816 854-3000

(G-4101)
HAIR 2 PLEASE
2484 Rte 13 (19709)
PHONE.................................302 378-3349
Joe Balien, *Owner*
EMP: 5
SALES (est): 111.4K **Privately Held**
SIC: 7231 Hairdressers

(G-4102)
HALPERN EYE ASSOCIATES INC
223 E Main St (19709-1449)
PHONE.................................302 734-5861
Joel Halpern, *Owner*
EMP: 5
SALES (corp-wide): 4.3MM **Privately Held**
WEB: www.halperneye.com
SIC: 8042 Contact lense specialist optometrist
PA: Halpern Eye Associates, Inc.
    885 S Governors Ave
    Dover DE 19904
    302 734-5861

(G-4103)
HAMPTON INN MIDDLETOWN
117 Sandhill Dr (19709-5813)
PHONE.................................302 378-5656
Linda Dunn, *Executive*
EMP: 19
SALES (est): 761.9K **Privately Held**
SIC: 7011 Hotels & motels

(G-4104)
HARDING LIMO BUS CNNECTION LLC
21 W Green St (19709-1315)
PHONE.................................302 376-1818
EMP: 5
SALES (est): 115K **Privately Held**
SIC: 4142 4119 Bus charter service, except local; limousine rental, with driver

(G-4105)
HARDWOOD DIRECT LLC
4390 Smmit Brdge Rd Ste 5 (19709)
PHONE.................................302 378-3692
Lorraine Demers, *CFO*
John Demers, *Mng Member*
EMP: 4
SQ FT: 1,200
SALES: 1.3MM **Privately Held**
SIC: 5999 2426 Alarm signal systems; blanks, wood: bowling pins, handles, etc.

(G-4106)
HEAD QUARTERS BARBERSHOP
217 E Main St (19709-1449)
PHONE.................................646 423-6767
Pheob Milford, *Owner*
EMP: 4
SQ FT: 1,100

SALES (est): 97K **Privately Held**
SIC: 7231 Hairdressers

(G-4107)
HELIX INC TA AUDIOWORKS
478 Middletown Warwick Rd (19709-9192)
PHONE.................................302 285-0555
Ben Holland, *Principal*
EMP: 1
SALES (est): 79.1K **Privately Held**
SIC: 3651 Audio electronic systems

(G-4108)
HOMSELF LIMITED
200 Cleaver Farms Rd (19709-1630)
PHONE.................................213 269-5469
Zurong Huang, *Sales Staff*
EMP: 70
SALES: 255K **Privately Held**
SIC: 7371 Computer software development & applications

(G-4109)
HOOBER INC
Also Called: Hoober Equipment
1130 Middletown Warwick Rd (19709-9096)
P.O. Box 107 (19709-0107)
PHONE.................................717 768-8231
Charles Hoober, *Branch Mgr*
Howie Andrew, *Manager*
Bubba Nicely, *Manager*
Ralph Saner, *Manager*
Nicole Manley, *Administration*
EMP: 69
SALES (corp-wide): 72MM **Privately Held**
WEB: www.hoober.com
SIC: 5083 Farm implements; tractors, agricultural; harvesting machinery & equipment; cultivating machinery & equipment
PA: Hoober, Inc.
    3452 Old Phladelphia Pike
    Intercourse PA 17534
    717 768-8231

(G-4110)
HX INNOVATIONS INC
372 Northhampton Way (19709-8341)
PHONE.................................302 983-9705
Von Homer, *CEO*
Kehlin Swain, *President*
Isis Ashford, *COO*
David Cannady, *Director*
EMP: 4
SALES (est): 92.1K **Privately Held**
SIC: 7389

(G-4111)
INTERNAL MEDICINE DELAWARE LLC
411 Hawks Nest Ct (19709-4107)
PHONE.................................302 261-2269
Rodrigo C Tanchanco,
EMP: 5 **EST:** 2010
SALES (est): 479.8K **Privately Held**
SIC: 8011 General & family practice, physician/surgeon

(G-4112)
J & G ACOUSTICAL CO
Also Called: J&G Building Group
118 Sleepy Hollow Dr (19709-5836)
PHONE.................................302 285-3630
Gladys D King, *CEO*
Paul A King, *President*
G Keith Hopkins, *Vice Pres*
Keith Hopkins, *Vice Pres*
Alexis King, *Admin Asst*
EMP: 25
SQ FT: 4,500
SALES (est): 3.2MM **Privately Held**
SIC: 1742 1799 Acoustical & ceiling work; demountable partition installation

(G-4113)
JEFFREY A BRIGHT DMD
600 N Broad St Ste 7 (19709-1032)
PHONE.................................302 832-1371
Jeffrey A Bright DMD, *President*
EMP: 20
SALES (est): 689.9K **Privately Held**
SIC: 8021 Dentists' office

Middletown - New Castle County (G-4114)
GEOGRAPHIC SECTION

(G-4114)
JESCO INC
Also Called: John Deere Authorized Dealer
1001 Industrial Rd (19709-1097)
PHONE..................302 376-6946
EMP: 6
SALES (corp-wide): 1.5B **Privately Held**
SIC: 5046 5082 Commercial equipment; construction & mining machinery
HQ: Jesco, Inc.
  2020 Mccullough Blvd
  Tupelo MS 38801
  662 842-3240

(G-4115)
JOEL GONZALEZ
Also Called: Custom Ceramics
21 Silver Lake Dr (19709-1360)
PHONE..................302 562-6878
Gina Gonzalez, Principal
EMP: 2
SALES (est): 111.3K **Privately Held**
SIC: 3269 Pottery products

(G-4116)
JOSEPH A DUDECK
739 Idlewyld Dr (19709-7844)
PHONE..................302 559-5552
Debra Dudeck, Principal
EMP: 4
SALES (est): 46K **Privately Held**
SIC: 7221 Photographer, still or video

(G-4117)
JOSEPH M PRESS MR
Also Called: Press, Christine M. Mrs.
375 Misty Vale Dr (19709-2125)
PHONE..................302 378-2053
Joseph Press, Principal
EMP: 1
SALES (est): 59.1K **Privately Held**
SIC: 2741 Miscellaneous publishing

(G-4118)
JUMPERS WELDING INC
808 Lorewood Grove Rd (19709-9346)
PHONE..................302 519-7941
Robert Jumper, Principal
EMP: 1 EST: 2012
SALES (est): 67.6K **Privately Held**
SIC: 7692 Welding repair

(G-4119)
K & S IRONWORKS
406 Draper Ln (19709-8018)
PHONE..................302 658-0040
Scott Swarter, President
Keith Swarter, Vice Pres
EMP: 12
SQ FT: 4,000
SALES: 1.5MM **Privately Held**
SIC: 3441 Fabricated structural metal

(G-4120)
KENT GENERAL HOSPITAL
Also Called: Bayhealth Medical Center
209 E Main St (19709-1449)
PHONE..................302 378-1199
Deana Rigby, Director
Gregory Burton, Assistant
EMP: 8 **Privately Held**
SIC: 8062 General medical & surgical hospitals
HQ: Kent General Hospital
  640 S State St
  Dover DE 19901
  302 674-4700

(G-4121)
KERSHAW INDUSTRIES
110 W Main St (19709-1040)
PHONE..................302 464-1051
EMP: 1
SALES (est): 43.3K **Privately Held**
SIC: 3999 Manufacturing industries

(G-4122)
KIDDIE ACADEMY OF MIDDLETOWN
915 Boyds Corner Rd (19709-9713)
PHONE..................302 376-5112
Susan Tudor, Mng Member
Christine Wisler, Director
EMP: 26
SALES (est): 500.9K **Privately Held**
SIC: 8351 Child day care services

(G-4123)
KIDZ INK
125 Sleepy Hollow Dr (19709-8895)
PHONE..................302 376-1700
Phil Kitson, Owner
EMP: 5
SALES (est): 135K
SALES (corp-wide): 2.3MM **Privately Held**
SIC: 8351 Preschool center
PA: Kidz Ink
  1703 Porter Rd
  Bear DE 19701
  302 838-1500

(G-4124)
KINDHEART HOMECARE
207 Parker Dr (19709-2623)
PHONE..................484 479-6582
Oluyemi Taiwo, Principal
EMP: 8
SALES (est): 61.1K **Privately Held**
SIC: 8082 Home health care services

(G-4125)
KRISTINA BRANDIS
208 Wickerberry Dr (19709-7806)
PHONE..................516 457-2717
Kristina Brandis, Principal
EMP: 4
SALES (est): 46.7K **Privately Held**
SIC: 8322 Individual & family services

(G-4126)
LABORATORY CORPORATION AMERICA
Also Called: Labcorp of America
120 Sandhill Dr Ste 1 (19709-5864)
PHONE..................302 376-6146
EMP: 5 **Publicly Held**
SIC: 8071 Testing laboratories
HQ: Laboratory Corporation Of America
  358 S Main St Ste 458
  Burlington NC 27215
  336 229-1127

(G-4127)
LABORATORY CORPORATION AMERICA
Also Called: Labcorp of America
366 E Main St (19709-1482)
PHONE..................302 449-0246
EMP: 5 **Publicly Held**
SIC: 8071 Testing laboratories
HQ: Laboratory Corporation Of America
  358 S Main St Ste 458
  Burlington NC 27215
  336 229-1127

(G-4128)
LENAPE BUILDERS INC
700 Ash Blvd (19709-8871)
PHONE..................302 376-3971
EMP: 11
SQ FT: 13,000
SALES (est): 1.5MM **Privately Held**
SIC: 1521 New construction, single-family houses

(G-4129)
LES NAILS
372 E Main St (19709-1482)
PHONE..................302 449-5290
Le Le, Principal
EMP: 6
SALES (est): 84.5K **Privately Held**
SIC: 7231 Manicurist, pedicurist

(G-4130)
LETICA CORPORATION
801 Industrial Rd (19709-1066)
P.O. Box 443 (19709-0443)
PHONE..................302 378-9853
Ed Foraker, Plant Mgr
Edward Foraker, Manager
EMP: 150 **Publicly Held**
WEB: www.letica.com
SIC: 3089 Plastic containers, except foam
HQ: Letica Corporation
  52585 Dequindre Rd
  Rochester Hills MI 48307
  248 652-0557

(G-4131)
LIESKE E2E HOME HLTH CARE INC
Also Called: Shorecare of Delaware
53 Meadow Dr (19709-4103)
PHONE..................302 898-1563
Jacqueline Lieske, President
EMP: 25
SALES: 200K **Privately Held**
SIC: 8082 Home health care services

(G-4132)
LIFETIME SKILLS SERVICES LLC
Also Called: Digen Auto Group
300 Brady Ln (19709-9010)
PHONE..................302 378-2911
Digen Ballayan, Mng Member
EMP: 35
SALES (est): 94.4K **Privately Held**
SIC: 8082 5521 Home health care services; automobiles, used cars only

(G-4133)
LILA KESHAV HOSPITALITY LLC
Also Called: Holiday Inn Express & Suites
315 Auto Park Dr (19709-9983)
PHONE..................302 696-2272
Bakulesh Patel,
EMP: 15
SALES (est): 118.2K **Privately Held**
SIC: 7011 Hotels & motels

(G-4134)
LITTLE PEOPLE DAY CARE
17 Cole Blvd (19709-1617)
PHONE..................302 528-4336
EMP: 5
SALES (est): 54.5K **Privately Held**
SIC: 8351 Child day care services

(G-4135)
LITTLE TROOPER DAY CARE
329 Senator Dr (19709-8023)
PHONE..................302 378-7355
Bonnie Aube, Director
EMP: 5
SALES (est): 71.8K **Privately Held**
SIC: 8351 Child day care services

(G-4136)
LLC SCHELL BROTHERS
758 Idlewyld Dr (19709-7836)
PHONE..................302 376-0355
EMP: 35
SALES (corp-wide): 13.3MM **Privately Held**
SIC: 1521 Single-Family House Construction
PA: Schell Brothers Llc
  20184 Phillips St
  Rehoboth Beach DE 19971
  302 226-1994

(G-4137)
LOWES HOME CENTERS LLC
500 W Main St (19709-9651)
PHONE..................302 376-3006
Paul Bateman, Branch Mgr
EMP: 150
SALES (corp-wide): 71.3B **Publicly Held**
SIC: 5211 5031 5722 5064 Home centers; building materials, exterior; building materials, interior; household appliance stores; electrical appliances, television & radio
HQ: Lowe's Home Centers, Llc
  1605 Curtis Bridge Rd
  Wilkesboro NC 28697
  336 658-4000

(G-4138)
M O T SENIOR CITIZEN CENTER
300 S Scott St (19709-1355)
PHONE..................302 378-3041
Jack Tellman, President
Maxine Barton, Exec Dir
EMP: 13
SQ FT: 2,500
SALES: 502.7K **Privately Held**
SIC: 8322 Senior citizens' center or association

(G-4139)
MABEL R COLE
139 Wellington Way (19709-9406)
PHONE..................302 378-2792
Mabel Cole, Principal
EMP: 2
SALES (est): 209.4K **Privately Held**
SIC: 1389 Oil field services

(G-4140)
MAGIC CANVAS
900 S Cass St (19709-1337)
PHONE..................302 312-4122
Jeannie White, Principal
EMP: 1
SALES (est): 46.5K **Privately Held**
SIC: 2211 Canvas

(G-4141)
MAHAFFY & ASSOCIATES INC
4 Brightham Ln (19709-2112)
PHONE..................302 656-8381
Hugh Mahaffy, President
Edward Fayda, Vice Pres
Scott D Parlow, Vice Pres
EMP: 20
SALES (est): 1.9MM **Privately Held**
WEB: www.mahaffyengineers.com
SIC: 8711 Consulting engineer; heating & ventilation engineering; electrical or electronic engineering

(G-4142)
MAINLINE MASONRY INC
415 Boxwood Ln (19709-9659)
PHONE..................302 998-2499
EMP: 35
SALES (est): 2.2MM **Privately Held**
SIC: 7389 1741 Business Services Masonry/Stone Contractor

(G-4143)
MANUFACTURERS & TRADERS TR CO
Also Called: M&T
399 E Main St (19709-1450)
PHONE..................302 285-3277
Dona Jester, Manager
EMP: 9
SALES (corp-wide): 6.4B **Publicly Held**
WEB: www.binghamlegg.com
SIC: 6022 State trust companies accepting deposits, commercial
HQ: Manufacturers And Traders Trust Company
  1 M&T Plz Fl 3
  Buffalo NY 14203
  716 842-4200

(G-4144)
MANUFACTURERS & TRADERS TR CO
Also Called: M&T
405 W Main St (19709-1064)
PHONE..................302 449-2780
Deborah Wisniewski, Branch Mgr
Betty Whitlock, Manager
Kari Kroll, Consultant
EMP: 8
SALES (corp-wide): 6.4B **Publicly Held**
WEB: www.binghamlegg.com
SIC: 6022 State commercial banks
HQ: Manufacturers And Traders Trust Company
  1 M&T Plz Fl 3
  Buffalo NY 14203
  716 842-4200

(G-4145)
MARINE CORPS UNITED STATES
705 N Broad St (19709-1166)
PHONE..................302 376-3590
EMP: 4 **Publicly Held**
SIC: 7361 Labor contractors (employment agency)
HQ: United States Marine Corps
  Pentagon Rm 4b544
  Washington DC 20380

(G-4146)
MARLYN MEADOW ARABIANS
Also Called: Maryland Meadow Arabians
1210 Sharp Ln (19709-8806)
PHONE..................302 378-8642

GEOGRAPHIC SECTION

Middletown - New Castle County (G-4181)

Mark Ashley, *Owner*
EMP: 5
SALES (est): 164.1K **Privately Held**
SIC: 0752 Animal training services

(G-4147)
MARTIAL INDUSTRIES LLC
526 Barrymore Pkwy (19709-6614)
PHONE...................302 983-5742
EMP: 2 EST: 2016
SALES (est): 87.8K **Privately Held**
SIC: 3999 Manufacturing industries

(G-4148)
MAYSE PAINTING & CONTG LLC
2250 Audubon Trl (19709-9844)
PHONE...................443 553-6503
Justin Mayse,
EMP: 5
SALES: 150K **Privately Held**
SIC: 1721 Residential painting; commercial painting

(G-4149)
MCCORMICK ASSOC MIDDLETOWN LLC
5350 Summit Bridge Rd # 107 (19709-4802)
PHONE...................302 449-0710
Caren Coffy-Mccormick, *Principal*
EMP: 8
SALES (est): 286.8K **Privately Held**
SIC: 8093 Mental health clinic, outpatient

(G-4150)
MCKENZIE PAVING INC
114 Bakerfield Dr (19709-9451)
PHONE...................302 376-8560
Margaret McKenzie, *President*
EMP: 14
SALES (est): 1.9MM **Privately Held**
SIC: 1611 Surfacing & paving

(G-4151)
MDM HAIR STUDIO
187 Gloucester Blvd (19709-8332)
PHONE...................302 312-6052
Patricia Howell, *Principal*
EMP: 4
SALES (est): 28.8K **Privately Held**
SIC: 7231 Hairdressers

(G-4152)
MERCY LAND ACADEMY INC
211 E Main St (19709-1449)
PHONE...................302 378-2013
Adeola Salako, *Principal*
EMP: 5
SALES (est): 37.3K **Privately Held**
SIC: 8351 Child day care services

(G-4153)
MICHAEL J RYAN DDS
106 Saint Annes Church Rd (19709-1495)
PHONE...................302 378-8600
Michael J Ryan, *Executive*
EMP: 4 EST: 1998
SALES (est): 95.8K **Privately Held**
SIC: 8021 Dentists' office

(G-4154)
MIDDLETOWN CAR CARE
50 E Main St (19709-1427)
PHONE...................302 449-1550
Sean J McDade, *Owner*
Sean McDade, *Owner*
EMP: 5 EST: 2010
SALES (est): 820.3K **Privately Held**
SIC: 7538 General automotive repair shops

(G-4155)
MIDDLETOWN COUNSELING
401 N Broad St (19709-1037)
PHONE...................302 376-0621
Sandra Lee Lnauer, *Principal*
EMP: 9
SALES (est): 292.8K **Privately Held**
SIC: 8322 General counseling services

(G-4156)
MIDDLETOWN FAMILY DENTIST
122 Sandhill Dr Ste 101 (19709-5861)
PHONE...................302 376-1959
Scott Anthony Arrighi, *Principal*
Scott Arrighi, *Principal*
EMP: 8 EST: 2007
SALES (est): 575.3K **Privately Held**
WEB: www.middletownfamilydentistry.com
SIC: 8021 Dentists' office

(G-4157)
MIDDLETOWN INK LLC
126 Patriot Dr (19709-8762)
PHONE...................302 725-0705
Megan Haines, *Owner*
Brian Haines, *Owner*
▲ EMP: 2
SALES (est): 17.5K **Privately Held**
SIC: 2759 Screen printing

(G-4158)
MIDDLETOWN KITCHEN AND BATH
987 Marl Pit Rd (19709-9604)
PHONE...................302 376-5766
EMP: 5
SALES (est): 699.6K **Privately Held**
SIC: 5023 Kitchenware

(G-4159)
MIDDLETOWN MAIN STREET INC
216 N Broad St (19709-1002)
PHONE...................302 378-2977
N Manerthia, *Exec Dir*
Nick Manerthia, *Exec Dir*
EMP: 4
SALES: 60.4K **Privately Held**
SIC: 8743 Promotion service

(G-4160)
MIDDLETOWN SPORTS COMPLEX LLC
407 Draper Ln (19709-8017)
PHONE...................302 299-8630
EMP: 6
SALES (est): 242.2K **Privately Held**
SIC: 7997 Membership sports & recreation clubs

(G-4161)
MIDDLETOWN VETERINARY HOSPITAL
366 Warwick Rd (19709-9537)
PHONE...................302 378-2342
David Beste Dvm, *Owner*
Julia Chant,
EMP: 6
SALES (est): 269.8K **Privately Held**
WEB: www.middletownveterinaryhospital.com
SIC: 0742 Animal hospital services, pets & other animal specialties

(G-4162)
MIDDLTOWN FAMILYCARE ASSOC LLC
114 Sandhill Dr Ste 101 (19709-5805)
PHONE...................302 378-4779
Guni Dedhia, *Office Mgr*
Lax Dedhia MD, *Mng Member*
EMP: 12
SALES (est): 1.2MM **Privately Held**
SIC: 8011 General & family practice, physician/surgeon

(G-4163)
MIDDLTOWN ODSSA TWNSEND SNIOR
Also Called: MOT SENIOR CENTER
300 S Scott St (19709-1355)
PHONE...................302 378-4758
Cecillai Rocunalski, *Director*
EMP: 13
SALES: 703.5K **Privately Held**
SIC: 8322 Senior citizens' center or association

(G-4164)
MIDWAY LLC
102 Dungarvan Dr (19709-9455)
PHONE...................302 378-9156
George D Baker,
Patricia E S Baker,
Scott S Baker,
EMP: 7 **Privately Held**
SIC: 6719 Investment holding companies, except banks

(G-4165)
MIKES CERAMIC TILE INC
624 Nesting Ln (19709-6124)
PHONE...................302 376-5743
EMP: 4
SALES (est): 410K **Privately Held**
SIC: 1752 Ceramic Tile Installation

(G-4166)
MILLER JW WLDG BOILER REPR CO
Also Called: J W Miller Wldg Boiler Repr Co
4917 Summit Bridge Rd (19709-8819)
P.O. Box 862 (19709-0862)
PHONE...................302 449-1575
James W Miller, *President*
Grace Miller, *Treasurer*
EMP: 6
SALES: 500K **Privately Held**
SIC: 7692 Welding repair

(G-4167)
MISSY MULLER
Also Called: Done Done Fitness
5350 Summit Bridge Rd (19709-4801)
PHONE...................302 376-0760
Missy Muller, *Owner*
EMP: 5 EST: 2014
SALES (est): 85.2K **Privately Held**
SIC: 7991 Health club

(G-4168)
MONRO INC
Also Called: Mr. Tire
430 Haveg Rd (19709-1723)
PHONE...................302 378-3801
Cindy Hawes, *Manager*
EMP: 11
SALES (corp-wide): 1.2B **Publicly Held**
SIC: 7538 General automotive repair shops
PA: Monro, Inc.
   200 Holleder Pkwy
   Rochester NY 14615
   585 647-6400

(G-4169)
MOORE QUALITY WELDING FAB
328 W Dickerson Ln (19709-8832)
PHONE...................302 250-7136
Dan Moore, *Principal*
EMP: 8
SALES (est): 88.7K **Privately Held**
SIC: 7692 Welding repair

(G-4170)
MOORES CABINET REFINISHING INC
939 Bethel Church Rd (19709-9757)
PHONE...................302 378-3055
John D Moore, *President*
Joanne Moore, *Corp Secy*
EMP: 6
SALES (est): 468.4K **Privately Held**
WEB: www.moorescabinets.com
SIC: 2434 Wood kitchen cabinets

(G-4171)
MUMFORD AND MILLER CON INC
1005 Industrial Rd (19709-1097)
PHONE...................302 378-7736
Richard L Mumford, *President*
Bernadette Mumford, *Admin Sec*
EMP: 140
SQ FT: 11,500
SALES (est): 32.2MM **Privately Held**
SIC: 1629 1611 1771 Land preparation construction; highway & street construction; concrete work

(G-4172)
NEW COVENANT ELEC SVCS INC
Also Called: Nces
806 Old School House Rd (19709-9066)
PHONE...................302 454-1165
Kimberly Creek, *President*
Kimberly Irene Creek, *President*
Kevin Elwood Creek, *Vice Pres*
EMP: 9
SALES (est): 902.3K **Privately Held**
SIC: 8748 Business consulting

(G-4173)
NEWARC WELDING INC
222 Chestnut Way (19709-9348)
PHONE...................302 376-1801
Bruce D Blair, *Principal*
EMP: 1
SALES (est): 44.3K **Privately Held**
SIC: 7692 Welding repair

(G-4174)
NEWREZ LLC
651 N Broad St (19709-6400)
PHONE...................302 455-6600
EMP: 4
SALES (corp-wide): 1.6B **Publicly Held**
SIC: 8742 7389 Financial consultant; financial services
HQ: Newrez Llc
   1100 Virginia Dr Ste 125
   Fort Washington PA 19034

(G-4175)
NORBERTINE FATHERS
1269 Bayview Rd (19709-2147)
PHONE...................302 449-1840
John Logan, *Plant Mgr*
EMP: 8
SALES (est): 226.6K **Privately Held**
SIC: 8699 Charitable organization

(G-4176)
NORTHEASTERN SUPPLY INC
104 Patriot Dr (19709-8762)
PHONE...................302 378-7880
Greg Cook, *Accounts Exec*
Jarrod Moore, *Branch Mgr*
EMP: 5
SALES (corp-wide): 202MM **Privately Held**
WEB: www.gagedoctr.com
SIC: 5074 Plumbing fittings & supplies
PA: Northeastern Supply, Inc.
   8323 Pulaski Hwy
   Baltimore MD 21237
   410 574-0010

(G-4177)
OBSIDIAN INVESTORS LLC
2336 E Palladio Pl (19709-9891)
PHONE...................954 560-1499
Sobers Brooks,
EMP: 4
SALES (est): 146.1K **Privately Held**
SIC: 6799 6531 Investors; real estate leasing & rentals

(G-4178)
OMNIMAVEN INC
103 Cazier Dr (19709-8852)
PHONE...................302 378-8918
Manuel Duarte, *Principal*
EMP: 5
SALES (est): 510.7K **Privately Held**
WEB: www.compsolonline.com
SIC: 8731 7373 Computer (hardware) development; systems software development services

(G-4179)
ONE OFF ROD & CUSTOM INC
118 Sleepy Hollow Dr (19709-5836)
PHONE...................302 449-1489
Ray Bartlett, *President*
Garyson Corkell, *President*
Theresa Faust, *Vice Pres*
EMP: 14 EST: 2009
SALES (est): 627.3K **Privately Held**
SIC: 5012 Automobiles

(G-4180)
PATEL SANJAY
Also Called: Middletown Liquors
745 N Broad St (19709-1166)
PHONE...................302 376-0136
Sanjay Patel, *Principal*
EMP: 5 EST: 2009
SALES (est): 336.2K **Privately Held**
SIC: 5182 Liquor

(G-4181)
PATTERSON PRICE RE LLC (PA)
5 E Green St (19709-1420)
PHONE...................302 378-9550
A John Price,
David W Baker,
Andrew John Price,

Middletown - New Castle County (G-4182)

EMP: 16
SALES (est): 1.3MM **Privately Held**
WEB: www.pattersonprice.com
SIC: 6531 6552 Real estate agent, residential; subdividers & developers

(G-4182)
PATTERSON-SCHWARTZ & ASSOC INC
Also Called: Patterson Schwartz Real Estate
4485 Summit Bridge Rd (19709-9549)
PHONE..................302 285-5100
Michael C Dunning, *Manager*
EMP: 16
SALES (est): 700K
SALES (corp-wide): 32.2MM **Privately Held**
WEB: www.pacinihomes.com
SIC: 6531 Real estate brokers & agents
PA: Patterson-Schwartz And Associates, Inc.
 7234 Lancaster Pike
 Hockessin DE 19707
 302 234-5250

(G-4183)
PAUL A LANGE
7 Claddagh Ct (19709-9003)
PHONE..................302 378-1706
Paul A Lange, *Owner*
EMP: 4 EST: 1956
SALES (est): 159.2K **Privately Held**
SIC: 3541 Machine tools, metal cutting type

(G-4184)
PAUL R CHRISTIAN DMD
423 E Main St (19709-1463)
PHONE..................302 376-9600
Paul R Christian DMD, *Owner*
EMP: 4
SALES (est): 340.7K **Privately Held**
SIC: 8021 Dentists' office

(G-4185)
PAWS & PEOPLE TOO
4390 Summit Bridge Rd # 4 (19709-9828)
PHONE..................302 376-8234
Theresa Overbey, *Owner*
EMP: 5
SALES (est): 167.2K **Privately Held**
SIC: 0752 Animal specialty services

(G-4186)
PCK ASSOCIATES INC
Also Called: Candyland Farm
1343 Bohemia Mill Rd (19709-9021)
PHONE..................302 378-7192
Herbert Moelis, *President*
Ellen Moelis, *Treasurer*
EMP: 5
SALES (est): 500K **Privately Held**
SIC: 0272 Horses & other equines

(G-4187)
PEIRCE JAMES TOWNSEND III
Also Called: A & J Custom Woodworking
19 Canary Ct (19709-2183)
PHONE..................302 449-2279
James Peirce, *Principal*
EMP: 2
SALES (est): 115K **Privately Held**
SIC: 2431 Millwork

(G-4188)
PENSKE TRUCK LEASING CORP
921 Middletown Warwick Rd (19709-9099)
PHONE..................302 449-9294
EMP: 4
SALES (corp-wide): 9.6B **Privately Held**
SIC: 7513 4214 Truck rental & leasing, no drivers; local trucking with storage
HQ: Penske Truck Leasing Corporation
 2675 Morgantown Rd
 Reading PA 19607
 610 775-6000

(G-4189)
PERFECTION LAWNCARE LTD
129 Gazebo Ln (19709-4601)
PHONE..................215 624-7410
Walt Beuttenmuller, *Owner*
EMP: 9
SALES (est): 411.3K **Privately Held**
SIC: 0782 Lawn care services

(G-4190)
PHYSICAL THERAPIST
503 Pierce Ct (19709-9697)
PHONE..................302 983-4151
Amy Delaney, *Principal*
EMP: 8 EST: 2016
SALES (est): 65.7K **Privately Held**
SIC: 8049 Physical therapist

(G-4191)
PIERCE TOTAL COMFORT LLC
Also Called: Honeywell Authorized Dealer
24 Chancellorsville Cir (19709-3825)
PHONE..................302 378-7714
Gary Lee Pierce Jr,
EMP: 12
SALES (est): 657.2K **Privately Held**
SIC: 1711 Heating & air conditioning contractors

(G-4192)
PIKE CREEK PSYCHLOGICAL CTR PA
252 Carter Dr Ste 100 (19709-5858)
PHONE..................302 449-2223
Stacey Staunton, *Branch Mgr*
EMP: 4
SALES (est): 131.7K **Privately Held**
SIC: 8049 Clinical psychologist
PA: Pike Creek Psychological Center Pa
 8 Polly Drummond Hill Rd
 Newark DE 19711

(G-4193)
PINE VALLEY CORVETTES
108 Pine Valley Dr (19709-9793)
PHONE..................302 834-1268
EMP: 4 EST: 2011
SALES (est): 183.4K **Privately Held**
SIC: 7532 Top & body repair & paint shops

(G-4194)
PNC BANK NATIONAL ASSOCIATION
460 W Main St (19709-1063)
PHONE..................302 378-4441
William Neal, *Manager*
EMP: 5
SALES (corp-wide): 19.9B **Publicly Held**
WEB: www.pncfunds.com
SIC: 6021 National trust companies with deposits, commercial
HQ: Pnc Bank, National Association
 222 Delaware Ave
 Wilmington DE 19801
 877 762-2000

(G-4195)
POSITIVE SIGNS
14 Spring Arbor Dr (19709-4608)
PHONE..................302 378-9559
Dominic Albi, *Owner*
EMP: 2 EST: 1998
SALES (est): 87K **Privately Held**
SIC: 3993 Signs & advertising specialties

(G-4196)
PRAYON INC
231 Casper Way (19709-7964)
PHONE..................302 449-0875
Michael Hamlin, *Principal*
Noel Daniel, *Human Res Mgr*
EMP: 1
SALES (est): 77.4K **Privately Held**
SIC: 2844 Toilet preparations

(G-4197)
PREMIER COMPREHENSIVE DENTAL
212 Celebration Ct (19709-8777)
PHONE..................302 378-3131
Kate Oshea, *Principal*
Hans Liu, *Fmly & Gen Dent*
EMP: 5 EST: 2010
SALES (est): 292.4K **Privately Held**
SIC: 8021 Dentists' office

(G-4198)
PREMIER RESTORATION CNSTR INC (PA)
Also Called: Premier Restorations
703 Industrial Rd (19709-1085)
PHONE..................302 832-1288
Kenneth M Mazik, *President*

Richard R Clark, *Vice Pres*
Thomas L Deemedio, *Treasurer*
EMP: 13
SALES (est): 2.8MM **Privately Held**
SIC: 1741 Tuckpointing or restoration

(G-4199)
PRODUCTIONS FOR PURPOSE INC
10 Little Cir (19709-7956)
PHONE..................302 388-9883
Dawn Mosley, *Exec Dir*
EMP: 6
SALES (est): 149.8K **Privately Held**
SIC: 7812 Motion picture & video production

(G-4200)
PROSPERITY UNLIMITED ENTE
32 E Sarazen Dr (19709-7960)
PHONE..................302 379-2494
EMP: 4
SALES (est): 205.1K **Privately Held**
SIC: 8741 Management services

(G-4201)
PRUDENTIAL INSUR CO OF AMER
208 N Broad St (19709-1002)
PHONE..................302 378-8811
Craig Socie, *Manager*
EMP: 4
SALES (corp-wide): 62.9B **Publicly Held**
SIC: 6411 Insurance agents, brokers & service
HQ: The Prudential Insurance Company Of America
 751 Broad St
 Newark NJ 07102
 973 802-6000

(G-4202)
PUGLISI EGG FARMS DELAWARE LLC
1881 Middle Neck Rd (19709-9646)
PHONE..................302 376-1200
Daniel Velasquez,
EMP: 27
SALES (est): 2MM **Privately Held**
SIC: 0252 Chicken eggs

(G-4203)
PULTE HOME CORPORATION
3 Garcia Dr (19709-2423)
PHONE..................302 378-9091
John Inman, *Manager*
EMP: 26
SALES (corp-wide): 10.1B **Publicly Held**
SIC: 1531 Speculative builder, single-family houses
HQ: Pulte Home Company, Llc
 3350 Peachtree Rd Ne # 150
 Atlanta GA 30326
 248 647-2750

(G-4204)
PURE WELLNESS LLC
708 Ash Blvd (19709-8871)
PHONE..................302 449-0149
EMP: 8
SALES (corp-wide): 1.9MM **Privately Held**
SIC: 8041 Offices & clinics of chiropractors
PA: Pure Wellness, Llc
 550 Christiana Rd # 302
 Newark DE 19713
 302 365-5470

(G-4205)
QUEST DIAGNOSTICS INCORPORATED
114 Sandhill Dr Ste 202 (19709-5807)
PHONE..................302 376-8675
Bijoy Ghosh, *Branch Mgr*
EMP: 5
SALES (corp-wide): 7.5B **Publicly Held**
WEB: www.questdiagnostics.com
SIC: 8071 Testing laboratories
PA: Quest Diagnostics Incorporated
 500 Plaza Dr Ste G
 Secaucus NJ 07094
 973 520-2700

(G-4206)
QUILTED HEIRLOOMS
123 Back Creek Dr (19709-8843)
PHONE..................302 354-6061
Michelle Smith, *Principal*
EMP: 1
SALES (est): 102.7K **Privately Held**
SIC: 2511 Wood household furniture

(G-4207)
R D ARNOLD CONSTRUCTION INC
33 E Stonewall Dr (19709-3810)
P.O. Box 26, Kemblesville PA (19347-0026)
PHONE..................610 255-4739
Rudy Arnold, *President*
Greg Fletcher, *Vice Pres*
Chris Gordon, *Admin Sec*
Christy Kane, *Admin Sec*
EMP: 12
SALES (est): 1.2MM **Privately Held**
SIC: 1521 New construction, single-family houses

(G-4208)
R G ARCHITECTS LLC
200 W Main St (19709-1041)
PHONE..................302 376-8100
Robert A Grove,
Christopher M Bowen, *Associate*
EMP: 4
SALES (est): 429.9K **Privately Held**
WEB: www.rgarchitects.net
SIC: 8712 Architectural engineering

(G-4209)
RACQUETEER
125 Crystal Run Dr (19709-6009)
PHONE..................302 378-1596
Thomas W Bennett, *Owner*
EMP: 1
SALES (est): 65.1K **Privately Held**
SIC: 3949 5941 Strings, tennis racket; team sports equipment

(G-4210)
RAM TECH SYSTEMS INC (PA)
1050 Industrial Rd # 110 (19709-2802)
PHONE..................302 832-6600
Srinivas Lokula, *CEO*
EMP: 41
SQ FT: 1,300
SALES (est): 4.9MM **Privately Held**
WEB: www.rtsiusa.com
SIC: 7371 7373 7372 7629 Computer software systems analysis & design, custom; value-added resellers, computer systems; prepackaged software; business machine repair, electric; computer related maintenance services; computers, peripherals & software

(G-4211)
RATNER COMPANIES LC
659 Middletown Warwick Rd (19709-9639)
PHONE..................302 378-8565
EMP: 4 **Privately Held**
SIC: 7241 Barber shops
HQ: Ratner Companies, L.C.
 1577 Spring Hill Rd # 500
 Vienna VA 22182
 703 269-5400

(G-4212)
RATNER COMPANIES LC
Also Called: Hair Cuttery
282 Dove Run Dr (19709-7971)
PHONE..................302 376-3568
Peaches Lacona, *Branch Mgr*
EMP: 12 **Privately Held**
WEB: www.haircuttery.com
SIC: 7231 Unisex hair salons
HQ: Ratner Companies, L.C.
 1577 Spring Hill Rd # 500
 Vienna VA 22182
 703 269-5400

(G-4213)
RED GHOST INTERACTIVE LLC
651 N Broad St Ste 205 (19709-6402)
PHONE..................385 485-9100
Simon M James,
EMP: 2
SALES (est): 59.2K **Privately Held**
SIC: 2741

Middletown - New Castle County (G-4246)

(G-4214)
REGIS CORPORATION
705 Middletown Warwick Rd (19709-9095)
PHONE 302 376-6165
Lucy Martinez, *Branch Mgr*
EMP: 8
SALES (corp-wide): 1B **Publicly Held**
SIC: 7231 Unisex hair salons
PA: Regis Corporation
7201 Metro Blvd
Edina MN 55439
952 947-7777

(G-4215)
RELIANCE MORTGAGE COMPANY INC
101 S Broad St (19709-1405)
PHONE 302 376-7234
EMP: 5
SALES: 5MM **Privately Held**
SIC: 6163 Mortgage Broker

(G-4216)
REMARLE
427 Smee Rd (19709-9939)
PHONE 215 245-6448
Renee Lemasney, *Principal*
EMP: 4 EST: 2011
SALES (est): 315.1K **Privately Held**
SIC: 2844 Lotions, shaving

(G-4217)
REMAX 1ST CHOICE LLC
Also Called: Re/Max
100 S Broad St (19709-1467)
PHONE 302 378-8700
Michael Blaisdell, *Broker*
Ronald Haberstroh, *Broker*
Karla Saffos, *Broker*
Helena Davidson, *Sales Staff*
John Ticknor,
EMP: 5
SALES (est): 701.8K **Privately Held**
SIC: 6531 Real estate agent, residential

(G-4218)
RENOVATE LLC
786 Old School House Rd (19709-9692)
PHONE 302 378-1768
Michael Biliunas, *Principal*
EMP: 4 EST: 2011
SALES (est): 401.9K **Privately Held**
SIC: 1542 Commercial & office buildings, renovation & repair

(G-4219)
RETAINED LOGIC GROUP INC
1070a Shallcross Lake Rd (19709-9705)
PHONE 302 530-3692
Lila Grkovic, *Co-Owner*
Kenneth Monroe, *Project Mgr*
Aleksandar Grkovic, *Development*
EMP: 4
SALES (est): 173.3K **Privately Held**
SIC: 8713 8711 Surveying services; photogrammetric engineering; ; construction & civil engineering

(G-4220)
RICHARD J WADSLEY
108 Sleepy Hollow Dr (19709-5847)
PHONE 302 545-7162
Richard Wadsley, *Owner*
EMP: 2
SALES (est): 85.7K **Privately Held**
SIC: 2759 Commercial printing

(G-4221)
ROBERTS WILBERT
Also Called: R&R Contractors
303 E Harvest Ln (19709-3039)
PHONE 215 867-5655
Wilbert Roberts, *Owner*
EMP: 4
SALES (est): 219.9K **Privately Held**
SIC: 1542 1522 Nonresidential construction; residential construction

(G-4222)
RODNEY BALTAZAR
Also Called: Baltazar Women's Care
120 Sandhill Dr (19709-5864)
PHONE 302 283-3300
Rodney Baltazar, *Owner*
EMP: 5
SALES (est): 161.9K **Privately Held**
SIC: 8011 Endocrinologist

(G-4223)
ROGER RULLO BRICK POINTING
915 Waterlilly Ln (19709-9308)
PHONE 302 378-8100
EMP: 5 EST: 1999
SALES (est): 290.3K **Privately Held**
SIC: 1741 Masonry/Stone Contractor

(G-4224)
ROTARY INTERNATIONAL
109 Stephen Ct (19709-9466)
PHONE 302 378-2488
EMP: 12
SALES (corp-wide): 503.3MM **Privately Held**
WEB: www.rotary5340.org
SIC: 8641 Civic associations
PA: Rotary International
1 Rotary Ctr
Evanston IL 60201
847 866-3000

(G-4225)
RUAN T119
819 Middletown Warwick Rd (19709-9097)
PHONE 302 376-9300
EMP: 8
SALES (est): 471.8K **Privately Held**
SIC: 4789 Transportation services

(G-4226)
RUAN TRANSPORT CORPORATION
50 Patriot Dr (19709-8769)
PHONE 302 696-3270
EMP: 4
SALES (corp-wide): 1.7B **Privately Held**
SIC: 4213 Trucking, except local
HQ: Ruan Transport Corporation
666 Grand Ave Ste 3100
Des Moines IA 50309
515 245-2500

(G-4227)
RUTKOSKE BROS INC
819 Middletown Warwick Rd (19709-9097)
P.O. Box 227 (19709-0227)
PHONE 302 378-8181
Felix Rutkoske, *President*
Mark A Rutkoske, *Vice Pres*
EMP: 7
SALES (est): 1MM **Privately Held**
SIC: 0134 0115 Irish potatoes; corn

(G-4228)
RUTLEDGE DENTAL ASSOC INC
410 N Cass St (19709-1038)
PHONE 302 378-8705
Jane C Rutledge, *Admin Sec*
EMP: 4
SALES (est): 255.6K **Privately Held**
SIC: 8021 Offices & clinics of dentists

(G-4229)
SACHETTA MACHINE & DEVELOPMENT
1823 Choptank Rd (19709-9047)
PHONE 302 378-5468
Gregory L Sachetta, *President*
Pamela Sue Sachetta, *Corp Secy*
EMP: 10
SQ FT: 6,200
SALES (est): 580K **Privately Held**
SIC: 3599 Machine shop, jobbing & repair

(G-4230)
SAVANNAH LOGISTICS LLC
278 Liborio Dr (19709-3109)
PHONE 302 893-7251
Njenga Benson, *Principal*
EMP: 4
SALES (est): 215.6K **Privately Held**
SIC: 4789 Transportation services

(G-4231)
SCASSOCIATES INC
651 N Broad St Ste 103 (19709-6401)
PHONE 302 454-1100
Sharron Cirillo, *President*
EMP: 10
SQ FT: 3,000
SALES: 682K **Privately Held**
SIC: 8721 Certified public accountant

(G-4232)
SCHAGRIN GAS CO (PA)
Also Called: Schagringas Company
1000 N Broad St (19709-1062)
P.O. Box 427 (19709-0427)
PHONE 302 378-2000
Eric Levinson, *President*
Andrew Levinson, *Vice Pres*
Andy Lambert, *VP Opers*
Mark Wood, *Opers Mgr*
Susan Wood, *Finance Mgr*
EMP: 35 EST: 1932
SQ FT: 4,000
SALES (est): 14.7MM **Privately Held**
WEB: www.schagringas.com
SIC: 5984 5722 5074 Propane gas, bottled; gas household appliances; water purification equipment

(G-4233)
SCOTT MUFFLER LLC
308 W Main St (19709-1701)
PHONE 302 378-9247
Chuck Linpert, *Owner*
EMP: 7
SALES (est): 594.4K
SALES (corp-wide): 758.6K **Privately Held**
SIC: 7538 7537 5013 General automotive repair shops; automotive transmission repair shops; automotive supplies & parts
PA: Scott Muffler Llc
1465 S Governors Ave
Dover DE 19904
302 674-8280

(G-4234)
SECURE MANAGEMENT
1050 Industrial Rd # 100 (19709-2802)
PHONE 302 999-8342
Shane Malek, *Manager*
EMP: 5
SALES (est): 509K **Privately Held**
SIC: 8741 Business management

(G-4235)
SECURITY SATELLITE
Also Called: Security Satellite Systems
5101 Summit Bridge Rd (19709-8821)
P.O. Box 12 (19709-0012)
PHONE 302 376-0241
Steve Kacprzyk, *President*
Steve Kacpryzyk, *President*
EMP: 2
SALES (est): 121.8K **Privately Held**
SIC: 3643 Current-carrying wiring devices

(G-4236)
SEMPER PROGRAM LLC
304 Bohemia Mill Pond Dr (19709-6058)
PHONE 302 535-6769
Steven Rommel,
EMP: 4
SALES (est): 230.1K **Privately Held**
SIC: 7539 Fuel system repair, motor vehicle

(G-4237)
SERENITY GARDENS ASSISTED LIVI
Also Called: Serenity Grdns Assisted Living
207 Ruth Dr (19709-9470)
P.O. Box 9541, Wilmington (19809-0541)
PHONE 302 442-5330
Heather Bressi, *Exec Dir*
EMP: 11
SQ FT: 4,000
SALES (est): 193.3K **Privately Held**
SIC: 8059 Personal care home, with health care

(G-4238)
SEVEN TECH LLC
600 N Broad St (19709-1032)
PHONE 302 464-6488
Hari Prasath,
EMP: 5
SALES: 100K **Privately Held**
SIC: 7371 Software programming applications

(G-4239)
SHARP FARM
1214 Sharp Ln (19709-8806)
PHONE 302 378-9606
Michael Zwiesler, *Manager*
EMP: 10
SALES (corp-wide): 532.9K **Privately Held**
SIC: 0752 7948 Breeding services, horses: racing & non-racing; horses, racing
PA: Sharp Farm
5727 Kennett Pike
Wilmington DE 19807
302 652-7729

(G-4240)
SHIPSHAP LLC
651 N Road St Ste 205478 (19709)
PHONE 425 298-5215
EMP: 4
SALES (est): 213.7K **Privately Held**
SIC: 4731 7371 Agents, shipping; computer software development & applications

(G-4241)
SILVER LAKE ELEM SCH PTA
200 E Cochran St (19709-1496)
PHONE 302 378-5023
Traci Smith, *Principal*
Cari Papellas, *Bookkeeper*
EMP: 70
SALES (est): 614.9K **Privately Held**
SIC: 8641 Parent-teachers' association

(G-4242)
SKINARY APP INC
651 N Broad St Ste 205 (19709-6402)
PHONE 773 744-5407
EMP: 7
SALES (est): 94.4K **Privately Held**
SIC: 7371 Computer software development & applications

(G-4243)
SMACKERALS BY MICHELLE LLC
109 Fox Hunt Ln (19709-8996)
PHONE 302 376-8272
Michelle L Fox,
EMP: 3 EST: 2009
SALES (est): 211K **Privately Held**
SIC: 2051 Bread, cake & related products

(G-4244)
SMILES JOLLY PA
102 Sleepy Hollow Dr # 100 (19709-5841)
PHONE 302 378-3384
Jeena M Jolly, *Owner*
Sharon Jolly, *Med Doctor*
EMP: 5
SALES (est): 280K **Privately Held**
SIC: 8021 Dentists' office

(G-4245)
SMOKEYS GULF SERVICE INC
48 E Main St (19709-1427)
P.O. Box 16 (19709-0016)
PHONE 302 378-2451
William K Smith, *President*
Dorothy H Smith, *Treasurer*
EMP: 4
SQ FT: 3,600
SALES (est): 740.7K **Privately Held**
SIC: 5983 5541 5172 Fuel oil dealers; filling stations, gasoline; fuel oil

(G-4246)
SOUTHERN STATES COOP INC
Also Called: S S C 7777-1
900 N Broad St (19709-1068)
P.O. Box 155 (19709-0155)
PHONE 302 378-9841
Samuel Mitchell, *Manager*
EMP: 15
SALES (corp-wide): 1.9B **Privately Held**
SIC: 2048 2873 0181 2874 Prepared feeds; nitrogenous fertilizers; bulbs & seeds; phosphatic fertilizers; fertilizers, mixing only

Middletown - New Castle County (G-4247) — GEOGRAPHIC SECTION

PA: Southern States Cooperative, Incorporated
6606 W Broad St Ste B
Richmond VA 23230
804 281-1000

(G-4247)
SOUTHGATE CONCRETE COMPANY
600 Industrial Rd (19709-1082)
PHONE..................302 376-5280
Dennis Partrillo, *Manager*
EMP: 15 Privately Held
SIC: 3273 Ready-mixed concrete
PA: Southgate Concrete Company
204 Marsh Ln
New Castle DE

(G-4248)
STEVEN SCHMITH
Also Called: Sas Contracting
408 Maplewood Dr (19709-4002)
PHONE..................302 584-8394
Steven Schmith, *Owner*
EMP: 12
SALES: 118K Privately Held
SIC: 1521 Single-family housing construction

(G-4249)
STONE EXPRESS
5093 Summit Bridge Rd (19709-9591)
PHONE..................302 376-8876
EMP: 3
SALES (est): 117K Privately Held
SIC: 3281 Marble, building: cut & shaped

(G-4250)
SUMMIT AVIATION INC (HQ)
4200 Summit Bridge Rd (19709-9340)
P.O. Box 258 (19709-0258)
PHONE..................302 834-5400
Caroline Dupont Prickett, *Ch of Bd*
Finn K Neilsen, *President*
Ralph Kunz, *General Mgr*
Edward J Scully, *Vice Pres*
Joyce Morales, *CFO*
EMP: 73
SQ FT: 68,000
SALES (est): 35MM Privately Held
WEB: www.summit-aviation.com
SIC: 4581 7699 7622 5088 Airport terminal services; aircraft flight instrument repair; aircraft radio equipment repair; transportation equipment & supplies; industrial supplies

(G-4251)
SUNWISE DRMATOLOGY SURGERY LLC
102 Sleepy Hollow Dr (19709-5841)
PHONE..................302 378-7981
Jennifer Larusso, *Owner*
EMP: 4
SALES (est): 59.5K Privately Held
SIC: 8011 Surgeon

(G-4252)
T & B INVSTGTIONS SEC AGCY LLC
68 Haggis Rd (19709-8751)
PHONE..................302 476-4087
Thomas Haile,
EMP: 7
SALES (est): 74.8K Privately Held
SIC: 7381 7389 Security guard service; personal investigation service

(G-4253)
TAJAN HOLDINGS & INVESTMENTS
600 N Broad St Ste 5 (19709-1032)
PHONE..................302 300-1183
Latoya Roberts, *CEO*
EMP: 2
SALES (est): 90.8K Privately Held
SIC: 3324 Steel investment foundries

(G-4254)
TEK ELECTRONICS LLC
865 Bullen Dr (19709-8973)
P.O. Box 853 (19709-0853)
PHONE..................302 449-6947
Tom Voytek, *Principal*
EMP: 7

SALES (est): 813.1K Privately Held
SIC: 8748 Systems engineering consultant, ex. computer or professional

(G-4255)
TEN TALENTS ENTERPRISES INC (PA)
Also Called: ABG Designs
316 Braemar St (19709-8733)
PHONE..................302 409-0718
Jason Clifton, *President*
Jessica Clifton, *Vice Pres*
◆ EMP: 4
SALES (est): 485.7K Privately Held
SIC: 2759 7359 Screen printing; home cleaning & maintenance equipment rental services

(G-4256)
TENDER LOVING KARE
400 N Ramunno Dr (19709-3001)
PHONE..................302 464-1014
Samuel Q Johnson, *President*
Julie Johnson, *Financial Exec*
Megan Coats, *Director*
EMP: 35
SALES (est): 817.5K Privately Held
WEB: www.tenderlovingkare.com
SIC: 8351 Group day care center

(G-4257)
THOMAS E OGRADY MASONRY
305 N Scott St (19709-1044)
PHONE..................302 378-8245
Thomas E O'Grady, *Owner*
EMP: 5
SALES (est): 182K Privately Held
SIC: 1741 Masonry & other stonework

(G-4258)
THRIVE PHYSICAL THERAPY
834 Kohl Ave (19709-4703)
PHONE..................302 834-8400
Kevin Calvey, *Principal*
EMP: 5
SALES (est): 126.5K Privately Held
SIC: 8049 Physical therapist

(G-4259)
TMK TRUCKING LLC
53 Cantwell Dr (19709-6835)
PHONE..................302 449-5131
Thomas M Kennedy, *Principal*
EMP: 4 EST: 2009
SALES (est): 271.8K Privately Held
SIC: 4212 Local trucking, without storage

(G-4260)
TODAYS LATINO MAGAZINE
217 N Broad St (19709-1035)
PHONE..................302 981-5131
Celton Delgado, *Owner*
EMP: 1
SALES (est): 62K Privately Held
SIC: 2721 Periodicals

(G-4261)
TODD A RICHARDSON DCPA
708 Ash Blvd (19709-8871)
PHONE..................302 449-0149
Todd Richardson, *Principal*
EMP: 4
SALES (est): 179.1K Privately Held
SIC: 8041 Offices & clinics of chiropractors

(G-4262)
TODDS JANITORIAL SERVICE INC
407 E Lake St (19709-1137)
PHONE..................302 378-8212
Unitas Todd, *President*
Charmaine Todd Butcher, *Owner*
Devin M Todd Second, *Vice Pres*
Norman H Todd Jr, *Vice Pres*
EMP: 9
SALES (est): 152.4K Privately Held
SIC: 7349 Janitorial service, contract basis

(G-4263)
TOTALLY CLEAN
13 Kingfisher Ct (19709-9171)
P.O. Box 798 (19709-0798)
PHONE..................302 376-3626
Jennifer Howard, *Owner*
EMP: 18

SALES: 20K Privately Held
SIC: 7349 Cleaning service, industrial or commercial

(G-4264)
TOWN OF MIDDLETOWN
Also Called: Middletown Police Department
130 Hampden Rd (19709-5302)
PHONE..................302 376-9950
Daniel Yeager, *Chief*
David Potter, *Network Tech*
EMP: 30 Privately Held
SIC: 9221 7371 ; custom computer programming services
PA: Town Of Middletown
19 W Green St
Middletown DE 19709
302 378-1171

(G-4265)
TOWN OF MIDDLETOWN
Also Called: It Dept
19 W Green St (19709-1315)
PHONE..................302 378-2711
Craig Zorn, *IT/INT Sup*
EMP: 4
SALES (est): 186.5K Privately Held
SIC: 7371 Custom computer programming services
PA: Town Of Middletown
19 W Green St
Middletown DE 19709
302 378-1171

(G-4266)
TRANSCORE LP
2111 Dupont Pkwy (19709-9332)
PHONE..................302 838-7429
Joseph Morris, *Branch Mgr*
EMP: 35
SALES (corp-wide): 5.1B Publicly Held
WEB: www.transcore.com
SIC: 4731 Domestic freight forwarding
HQ: Transcore, Lp
150 4th Ave N Ste 1200
Nashville TN 37219
615 988-8962

(G-4267)
TRANSPORTATION DELAWARE DEPT
Also Called: Highway Operations
5369 Summit Bridge Rd (19709-1493)
PHONE..................302 653-4128
Maria Titeri, *Branch Mgr*
EMP: 25 Privately Held
WEB: www.dartfirststate.com
SIC: 1611 9621 Highway & street maintenance; regulation, administration of transportation.
HQ: Delaware Department Of Transportation
800 S Bay Rd
Dover DE 19901

(G-4268)
TRIFECTA HEALTH SOLUTIONS INC
651 N Broad St Ste 20515 (19709-6400)
PHONE..................614 582-4184
Derek Rine, *CEO*
EMP: 4
SALES: 400K Privately Held
SIC: 7371 Computer software systems analysis & design, custom

(G-4269)
TRU BEAUTI LLC
Also Called: Bodied By Tru
307 Bald Eagle Way (19709-4112)
PHONE..................302 353-9249
Sharmayne Weatherbee,
EMP: 30
SQ FT: 2,000
SALES (est): 206K Privately Held
SIC: 8011 Offices & clinics of medical doctors

(G-4270)
TRUE PEST CONTROL SERVICES (PA)
48 Loblolly Ln (19709-9781)
PHONE..................302 834-0867
Bruce York, *President*
EMP: 6

SALES (est): 548.9K Privately Held
SIC: 7342 Pest control in structures

(G-4271)
TWO DDS LLC
153 Jane Ct (19709-9408)
PHONE..................302 300-1259
EMP: 4 EST: 2010
SALES (est): 210K Privately Held
SIC: 8021 Dentist's Office

(G-4272)
U-HAUL NEIGHBORHOOD DEALER
5101 Summit Bridge Rd (19709-8821)
PHONE..................302 449-7379
EMP: 8
SALES (est): 101.1K Privately Held
SIC: 7513 Truck rental & leasing, no drivers

(G-4273)
UNIVERSAL BEV IMPORTERS LLC
505 E Glen Mare Dr (19709-8773)
PHONE..................302 276-0619
Alexander A Rivera, *Managing Prtnr*
Alexander Rivera, *Mng Member*
EMP: 7
SALES (est): 1.6MM Privately Held
SIC: 2084 Wine coolers (beverages)

(G-4274)
V QUINTON INC
400 N Ramunno Dr (19709-3001)
PHONE..................302 449-1711
Samuel Q Johnson, *Principal*
EMP: 13
SALES (est): 466.7K Privately Held
SIC: 8351 Group day care center

(G-4275)
VALUEWRITE
204 Tralee Dr (19709-9006)
PHONE..................302 593-0694
Valerie Stewart, *Principal*
EMP: 1 EST: 2009
SALES (est): 75.6K Privately Held
SIC: 3269 Pottery florists' articles

(G-4276)
VILLAGE WINES & SPIRITS
718 Ash Blvd (19709-8871)
PHONE..................302 376-5583
John Weaver, *Manager*
EMP: 5
SALES (est): 383.9K Privately Held
SIC: 5182 Wine

(G-4277)
VOLUNTEER BREWING COMPANY LLC
120 W Main St (19709-1040)
PHONE..................610 721-2836
EMP: 3 EST: 2015
SALES (est): 68.6K Privately Held
SIC: 2082 Malt beverages

(G-4278)
VPS SERVICES LLC
651 N Broad St Ste 308 (19709-6403)
PHONE..................302 376-6710
Reyner Meikle,
EMP: 9
SALES (est): 198.1K Privately Held
SIC: 8111 Legal services

(G-4279)
WALLIS REPAIR INC
106 Patriot Dr (19709-8762)
PHONE..................302 378-4301
Norman Wallis, *President*
Phyllis Wallis, *Treasurer*
EMP: 8
SQ FT: 20,000
SALES: 1.2MM Privately Held
SIC: 7538 General automotive repair shops

(G-4280)
WALTER W SNYDER
Also Called: W W Snyder Excavating & Masnry
1844 Choptank Rd (19709-9648)
PHONE..................302 378-1817

Walter W Snyder, *Owner*
EMP: 5
SALES (est): 330K **Privately Held**
SIC: 1741 1794 Masonry & other stonework; excavation work

(G-4281)
WELLS FARGO BANK NATIONAL ASSN
310 Dove Run Centre Dr (19709-7912)
PHONE..................302 449-5485
Joan B Hitchens, *Branch Mgr*
EMP: 8
SALES (corp-wide): 101B **Publicly Held**
SIC: 6021 National commercial banks
HQ: Wells Fargo Bank, National Association
101 N Phillips Ave
Sioux Falls SD 57104
605 575-6900

(G-4282)
WESTOVER CARDIOLOGY
222 Carter Dr (19709-5854)
PHONE..................302 482-2035
EMP: 5
SALES (est): 223.8K **Privately Held**
SIC: 8011 Cardiologist & cardio-vascular specialist

(G-4283)
WESTOWN MOVIES LLC
150 Commerce Dr (19709-9039)
PHONE..................330 244-1633
Art Helmick,
EMP: 5
SALES: 5MM **Privately Held**
SIC: 7832 Motion picture theaters, except drive-in

(G-4284)
WHITE EAGLE ELECTRICAL CONTG
709 Guido Dr (19709-1480)
PHONE..................302 378-3366
Al Rutkowski, *President*
EMP: 10
SALES (est): 833K **Privately Held**
SIC: 1731 Electrical work

(G-4285)
WHITE EAGLE INTEGRATIONS
635 Lorewood Grove Rd (19709-9235)
PHONE..................302 464-0550
Walter White, *Principal*
EMP: 4
SALES (est): 692.3K **Privately Held**
SIC: 1542 7299 Commercial & office building contractors; home improvement & renovation contractor agency

(G-4286)
WHITTINGTON & AULGUR
651 N Broad St Ste 206 (19709-6402)
P.O. Box 1040 (19709-7040)
PHONE..................302 378-1661
Robert T Aulgur Jr, *Manager*
EMP: 10
SALES (corp-wide): 2.5MM **Privately Held**
SIC: 8111 General practice law office
PA: Whittington & Aulgur
2979 Barley Mill Rd
Yorklyn DE 19736
302 235-5800

(G-4287)
WILLOW WINTERS PUBLISHING LLC
164 N Bayberry Pkwy (19709-9855)
PHONE..................570 885-2513
EMP: 2
SALES (est): 82.4K **Privately Held**
SIC: 2741 Miscellaneous publishing

(G-4288)
WINDVIEW INC (PA)
1482 Levels Rd (19709-9084)
PHONE..................610 345-9001
Christopher McCardell, *President*
Timothy McCardell, *Principal*
EMP: 7
SALES (est): 968.8K **Privately Held**
SIC: 8699 Athletic organizations

(G-4289)
WOLOSHIN AND LYNCH ASSOCIATES
22 W Main St (19709-1039)
PHONE..................302 449-2606
Stacy Murphy, *Branch Mgr*
EMP: 12
SALES (corp-wide): 2.8MM **Privately Held**
SIC: 8111 General practice attorney, lawyer
PA: Woloshin And Lynch Associates
3200 Concord Pike
Wilmington DE 19803
302 477-3200

(G-4290)
WOODIN + ASSOCIATES LLC
111 Patriot Dr Ste D (19709-8771)
PHONE..................302 378-7300
Richard C Woodin,
EMP: 13
SQ FT: 3,000
SALES (est): 770K **Privately Held**
SIC: 8711 8713 Civil engineering; surveying services

(G-4291)
WOODWARD ENTERPRISES INC
Also Called: Woodward Outdoor Equipment
226 W Main St (19709-1041)
PHONE..................302 378-2849
Christopher Woodward, *CEO*
Susan Woodward, *Corp Secy*
Ray Woodward, *Vice Pres*
EMP: 13
SQ FT: 6,000
SALES: 3MM **Privately Held**
SIC: 5261 7699 5083 Lawn & garden equipment; general household repair services; lawn & garden machinery & equipment

(G-4292)
XANADU CONCEPTS LLC
104 W Main St Ste 4a (19709-4400)
PHONE..................302 449-2677
Andrea Patterson, *Mng Member*
EMP: 5 **EST:** 2010
SQ FT: 1,200
SALES: 50K **Privately Held**
SIC: 7231 Unisex hair salons

(G-4293)
YARDSCAPE INC
303 Bald Eagle Way (19709-4112)
PHONE..................302 540-0311
Adam Sierocinski, *President*
EMP: 5
SALES (est): 284.9K **Privately Held**
SIC: 1771 Driveway contractor

(G-4294)
YESAMERICA CORPORATION
651 N Broad St 205-908 (19709-6400)
PHONE..................800 872-1548
Kirill Zhukov, *CEO*
EMP: 10
SALES: 500K **Privately Held**
SIC: 7379

(G-4295)
ZEST-INDEX INVESTMENTS LLC
651 N Broad St Ste 205 (19709-6402)
PHONE..................503 908-2110
Ukpeba Godspower,
EMP: 4
SALES: 410K **Privately Held**
SIC: 7389 Business services

Milford
Sussex County

(G-4296)
1 A LIFESAFER INC
317 S Rehoboth Blvd (19963-1531)
PHONE..................800 634-3077
EMP: 1
SALES (corp-wide): 4.3MM **Privately Held**
SIC: 3829 Measuring & controlling devices
PA: 1 A Lifesafer, Inc.
4290 Glendale Milford Rd
Blue Ash OH 45242
513 651-9560

(G-4297)
500 SOUTH DUPONT BOULE
Also Called: Milford Place
500 S Dupont Blvd (19963-1758)
PHONE..................302 422-8700
EMP: 25
SALES (est): 545.6K **Publicly Held**
WEB: www.genesishcc.com
SIC: 8051 Convalescent home with continuous nursing care
HQ: Genesis Healthcare Llc
101 E State St
Kennett Square PA 19348

(G-4298)
700 MARVEL ROAD OPERATIONS LLC
Also Called: Milford Center
700 Marvel Rd (19963-1740)
PHONE..................302 422-3303
Shirlyn Shafer, *Mng Member*
EMP: 5135
SALES (est): 2.1MM **Publicly Held**
WEB: www.pleasantviewretirement.com
SIC: 8051 Skilled nursing care facilities
HQ: Genesis Healthcare Llc
101 E State St
Kennett Square PA 19348

(G-4299)
887 THE BRIDGE
1977 Bay Rd (19963-6134)
P.O. Box 680 (19963-0680)
PHONE..................302 422-6909
William T Sammons, *General Mgr*
EMP: 16
SALES (est): 608K **Privately Held**
SIC: 4832 Radio broadcasting stations

(G-4300)
A BETTER CHNCE FOR OUR CHLDREN
805 S Dupont Blvd (19963-2232)
PHONE..................302 725-5008
EMP: 5
SALES (est): 97.4K **Privately Held**
SIC: 8351 Child day care services

(G-4301)
A DANCE CLASS
Also Called: Diamond Dance Co
107 S Maple Ave (19963-1951)
PHONE..................302 422-2633
Louie Voshell, *Owner*
EMP: 4
SALES: 31.6K **Privately Held**
SIC: 7911 Dance studio & school

(G-4302)
ADDUS HEALTHCARE INC
1675 S State St (19963)
PHONE..................302 424-4842
Sheila Zook, *Manager*
EMP: 20 **Publicly Held**
WEB: www.addus.com
SIC: 8082 Home health care services
HQ: Addus Healthcare, Inc.
2300 Warrenville Rd # 100
Downers Grove IL 60515
630 296-3400

(G-4303)
ADKINS MANAGEMENT COMPANY
421 Kings Hwy (19963-1763)
P.O. Box 316 (19963-0316)
PHONE..................302 684-3000
Chris Adkins, *Principal*
EMP: 13
SALES (est): 534.6K **Privately Held**
SIC: 7997 Golf club, membership

(G-4304)
ALL ABOUT ME DAY CARE
104 Mccoy St (19963-2310)
PHONE..................302 424-8322
Cherie Kersey, *Owner*
EMP: 10
SALES (est): 141.8K **Privately Held**
SIC: 8351 Child day care services

(G-4305)
AMAZON STEEL CONSTRUCTION INC
2537 Bay Rd (19963-6020)
PHONE..................302 751-1146
Martin Heesh, *President*
Kristin Couden, *Info Tech Mgr*
▼ **EMP:** 9
SQ FT: 13,000
SALES: 850K **Privately Held**
SIC: 1799 1796 3441 1791 Welding on site; millwright; fabricated structural metal; structural steel erection; conveyors & conveying equipment

(G-4306)
AMERICAN NEON PRODUCTS COMPANY
Also Called: Tetrus Led Co
715c S Washington St (19963-2305)
PHONE..................302 856-3400
Lance Mueller, *President*
EMP: 10
SQ FT: 8,000
SALES: 700K **Privately Held**
WEB: www.americansignandlighting.com
SIC: 5063 Lighting fixtures, commercial & industrial

(G-4307)
ANDREW PIPON
Also Called: Embroidery Enterprises
8231 Woods Edge Cir (19963-4803)
PHONE..................949 337-2249
Andrew Pipon, *Owner*
EMP: 4 **EST:** 2017
SALES (est): 113.1K **Privately Held**
SIC: 2395 Embroidery & art needlework

(G-4308)
AP LINENS INC
Also Called: A P Linen Service
713 S Washington St (19963-2305)
PHONE..................302 430-0851
Michael G Attix, *President*
EMP: 26
SALES: 3MM **Privately Held**
SIC: 7211 Power laundries, family & commercial

(G-4309)
ARTISANS BANK INC
100 Aerenson Dr (19963-1236)
PHONE..................302 430-7681
Kathleen Cooper, *Manager*
EMP: 7
SALES (corp-wide): 22.8MM **Privately Held**
WEB: www.artisansbank.com
SIC: 6036 6029 State savings banks, not federally chartered; commercial banks
PA: Artisans Bank Inc
2961 Centerville Rd # 101
Wilmington DE 19808
302 658-6881

(G-4310)
ATI HOLDINGS LLC
Also Called: ATI Physical Therapy
941 N Dupont Blvd Ste C (19963-1069)
PHONE..................302 422-6670
Jennifer Hilliard, *Branch Mgr*
EMP: 21
SALES (corp-wide): 338.3MM **Privately Held**
SIC: 8049 Physical therapist
PA: Ati Holdings, Llc
790 Remington Blvd
Bolingbrook IL 60440
630 296-2222

(G-4311)
ATLANTIC CHIROPRACTIC ASSOCIAT (PA)
375 Mullet Run (19963-5373)
PHONE..................302 422-3100
Andrew W Riddle, *Owner*
Kelly Keener, *Education*
EMP: 12
SALES (est): 1.9MM **Privately Held**
SIC: 8041 Offices & clinics of chiropractors

(G-4312)
ATLANTIC CONCRETE COMPANY INC (PA)
New Wharf Rd (19963)
P.O. Box 321 (19963-0321)
PHONE.....................302 422-8017
David A Jones, *President*
Cynthia Jones, *Corp Secy*
EMP: 60 **EST:** 1946
SQ FT: 10,000
SALES (est): 10.8MM **Privately Held**
SIC: 3273 Ready-mixed concrete

(G-4313)
ATTITUDE LLC NONE
808 Seabury Ave (19963-2223)
PHONE.....................302 422-3356
Cheryl O'Connor, *Manager*
EMP: 5 **EST:** 2007
SALES (est): 195.8K **Privately Held**
SIC: 8011 Dermatologist

(G-4314)
AV LOGISTICS LLC
14 Patriots Pass (19963-4002)
PHONE.....................302 725-5407
Alexis Viana Saez, *Principal*
EMP: 4
SALES (est): 198.9K **Privately Held**
SIC: 4789 Transportation services

(G-4315)
AVE PRESCHOOL
20 N Church Ave (19963-1021)
PHONE.....................302 422-8775
Andrea Prettyman, *Exec Dir*
Cheryl Waldon, *Director*
EMP: 10
SALES (est): 228.1K **Privately Held**
SIC: 8351 Preschool center

(G-4316)
AVIADO DOMINGO G MD
18 S Dupont Blvd (19963-1027)
PHONE.....................302 430-7600
Domingo Aviado, *Principal*
EMP: 5
SALES (est): 294.1K **Privately Held**
SIC: 8011 General & family practice, physician/surgeon

(G-4317)
BALTIMORE AIRCOIL COMPANY INC
Also Called: B A C
1162 Holly Hill Rd (19963-6339)
P.O. Box 402 (19963-0402)
PHONE.....................302 424-2583
Paul Marsiglia, *Human Res Mgr*
Richard Green, *Branch Mgr*
Jason Langley, *Manager*
Leah Vilkanskas, *Manager*
EMP: 140
SQ FT: 60,000
SALES (corp-wide): 2.4B **Privately Held**
WEB: www.baltimoreaircoil.com
SIC: 3585 3443 3498 Evaporative condensers, heat transfer equipment; lockers, refrigerated; heat exchangers: coolers (after, inter), condensers, etc.; fabricated pipe & fittings
HQ: Baltimore Aircoil Company, Inc.
7600 Dorsey Run Rd
Jessup MD 20794
410 799-6200

(G-4318)
BAY AREA WOMENS CARE
306 Polk Ave (19963-1818)
PHONE.....................302 424-2200
Albert French, *Principal*
EMP: 4 **EST:** 2001
SALES (est): 372.7K **Privately Held**
SIC: 8011 Gynecologist

(G-4319)
BAYADA HOME HEALTH CARE INC
1016 N Walnut St (19963-1244)
PHONE.....................302 424-8200
Steve P Flannery, *Branch Mgr*
EMP: 84
SALES (corp-wide): 672.5MM **Privately Held**
SIC: 8082 8049 8011 Visiting nurse service; nurses & other medical assistants; pediatrician
PA: Bayada Home Health Care, Inc.
1 W Main St
Moorestown NJ 08057
856 231-1000

(G-4320)
BAYHEALTH MEDICAL CENTER INC
21 W Clarke Ave (19963-1840)
PHONE.....................302 422-3311
Terry Murphy, *CEO*
Greg Springer, *Opers Staff*
Garrett Reece, *Engineer*
Chaitanya Mandadi, *Business Anlyst*
Jennifer Dailey, *Marketing Staff*
EMP: 1500 **Privately Held**
SIC: 8062 General medical & surgical hospitals
PA: Bayhealth Medical Center, Inc.
640 S State St
Dover DE 19901

(G-4321)
BEEBE MEDICAL CENTER INC
810 Seabury Ave (19963-2223)
PHONE.....................302 393-2056
EMP: 62
SALES (corp-wide): 447.8MM **Privately Held**
SIC: 8011 Medical centers
PA: Beebe Medical Center, Inc.
424 Savannah Rd
Lewes DE 19958
302 645-3300

(G-4322)
BENEVOLENT & PROTECTIVE ORDER
Also Called: Milford Lodge 2401
18951 Elks Lodge Rd (19963)
P.O. Box 63 (19963-0063)
PHONE.....................302 424-2401
Jeffrey Spatz, *Owner*
EMP: 4
SALES: 154.4K
SALES (corp-wide): 28.1MM **Privately Held**
SIC: 8641 Fraternal associations
PA: Benevolent And Protective Order Of Elks
2750 N Lakeview Ave
Chicago IL 60614
773 755-4700

(G-4323)
BENNETT FARMS INC
24139 Sugar Hill Rd (19963-4713)
PHONE.....................302 684-1627
Fred Bennett, *Principal*
EMP: 5
SALES (est): 535.4K **Privately Held**
SIC: 0191 General farms, primarily crop

(G-4324)
BERRY SHORT FUNERAL HOME INC
Also Called: Short Funeral Services
119 Nw Front St (19963-1022)
PHONE.....................302 422-8091
George Short, *President*
Janet Short, *Vice Pres*
EMP: 4
SQ FT: 5,000
SALES (est): 310K **Privately Held**
SIC: 7261 Funeral director; funeral home

(G-4325)
BETTYS
140 N Landing Dr (19963-5382)
PHONE.....................302 233-2675
EMP: 5
SALES (est): 289.9K **Privately Held**
SIC: 2087 Beverage bases

(G-4326)
BIG STONE HUNTING CLUB
687 New Wharf Rd (19963-1389)
PHONE.....................302 424-7592
Peter Renzi, *Principal*
EMP: 4 **EST:** 2009

SALES (est): 69.7K **Privately Held**
SIC: 7997 Membership sports & recreation clubs

(G-4327)
BLUE HEN INSULATION INC
2844 Deer Valley Rd (19963-6234)
PHONE.....................302 424-4482
Joann Carter, *President*
Constance Warren, *Vice Pres*
John P Carter, *Shareholder*
EMP: 8
SALES (est): 576K **Privately Held**
SIC: 1742 Insulation, buildings

(G-4328)
BLUE HEN SPRING WORKS INC
112 N Rehoboth Blvd (19963-1339)
PHONE.....................302 422-6600
Billie Lynn Thompson, *President*
Mathew Thompson, *Corp Secy*
EMP: 11
SALES: 1.2MM **Privately Held**
WEB: www.bluehensprings.com
SIC: 7539 7538 Brake repair, automotive; automotive springs, rebuilding & repair; general truck repair

(G-4329)
BOUTIQUE THE BRIDAL LTD
2454 Bay Rd (19963-6003)
PHONE.....................302 335-5948
Patricia S Davis, *Owner*
EMP: 8
SALES (est): 75K **Privately Held**
SIC: 5621 7299 Bridal shops; tuxedo rental

(G-4330)
BOYS & GIRLS CLUB OF MILFORD
105 Ne Front St (19963-1429)
PHONE.....................302 422-4453
Maria Edgerton, *Principal*
EMP: 5
SALES (est): 119.4K **Privately Held**
SIC: 8641 Youth organizations

(G-4331)
BOYS & GIRLS CLUBS DEL INC
Also Called: Milford Boys & Girls Club
101 Dlaware Veterans Blvd (19963-5398)
PHONE.....................302 422-3757
Dorian Menz-Vaz, *Director*
EMP: 15
SALES (corp-wide): 20.8MM **Privately Held**
SIC: 8641 Youth organizations
PA: Boys & Girls Clubs Of Delaware, Inc.
669 S Union St
Wilmington DE 19805
302 658-1870

(G-4332)
BRADLEY ARTHUR & SON CNSTR
Also Called: Arthur Bradley & Son
720 Meadow Brook Ln (19963-3008)
PHONE.....................302 422-9391
EMP: 5
SALES: 1MM **Privately Held**
SIC: 1521 Single-Family House Construction

(G-4333)
BRDLY M WINSTON PDRTCS PRCTC
375 Mullet Run (19963-5373)
PHONE.....................302 424-1650
Bradley M Winston, *Owner*
EMP: 4
SALES (est): 376.5K **Privately Held**
SIC: 8049 8011 Nutrition specialist; pediatrician

(G-4334)
BRENDON T WARFEL CONSTRUCTION
940 Ne Front Street Ext (19963-1371)
PHONE.....................302 422-7814
Brendon T Warfel, *President*
EMP: 4

SALES (est): 695.9K **Privately Held**
WEB: www.brendonwarfel.com
SIC: 1521 1542 New construction, single-family houses; commercial & office building contractors

(G-4335)
BRIDGESTONE RET OPERATIONS LLC
Also Called: Firestone
103 Causey Ave Bldg 103 # 103 (19963-1933)
PHONE.....................302 422-4508
Brandy Ward, *Manager*
EMP: 7 **Privately Held**
WEB: www.bfis.com
SIC: 5531 5014 5013 Automotive tires; automobile tires & tubes; automotive supplies & parts
HQ: Bridgestone Retail Operations, Llc
333 E Lake St Ste 300
Bloomingdale IL 60108
630 259-9000

(G-4336)
BURRIS FREIGHT MANAGEMENT LLC
501 Se 5th St (19963-2022)
PHONE.....................800 805-8135
Nick Falk, *President*
Anthony Megale, *Vice Pres*
EMP: 59
SALES (est): 2.9MM
SALES (corp-wide): 1.4B **Privately Held**
SIC: 4731 Transportation agents & brokers
PA: Burris Logistics
501 Se 5th St
Milford DE 19963
302 839-4531

(G-4337)
BURRIS LOGISTICS (PA)
Also Called: Burris Retail Logistics
501 Se 5th St (19963-2022)
P.O. Box 219 (19963-0219)
PHONE.....................302 839-4531
Jeff Swain, *Ch of Bd*
Donnan R Burris, *President*
Greg Cyganiewicz, *General Mgr*
Nick Falk, *General Mgr*
Tim Peifley, *General Mgr*
◆ **EMP:** 60
SQ FT: 10,000
SALES (est): 1.4B **Privately Held**
WEB: www.burrislogistics.com
SIC: 4789 Freight car loading & unloading

(G-4338)
C & B CONSTRUCT
150 Vickers Rd (19963-5393)
PHONE.....................302 378-9862
John Burton, *Co-Owner*
EMP: 5
SALES (est): 576.6K **Privately Held**
SIC: 1521 New construction, single-family houses

(G-4339)
C & S CONSULTANTS INC
6 E Clarke Ave (19963-1803)
PHONE.....................302 236-5211
Chuck Culotta, *President*
EMP: 5
SALES (est): 393.2K **Privately Held**
SIC: 8741 Construction management

(G-4340)
CAPRIOTTIS OF MILFORD
684 N Dupont Blvd (19963-1002)
PHONE.....................302 424-3309
Ray Rodriguez, *Owner*
EMP: 6
SALES (est): 724.8K **Privately Held**
SIC: 2841 Soap & other detergents

(G-4341)
CEDAR CREEK CUSTOM CABINETS
7816 Cedar Creek Ct (19963-4784)
PHONE.....................302 542-7794
Brandon Ritter, *Principal*
EMP: 1 **EST:** 2018
SALES (est): 53.7K **Privately Held**
SIC: 2434 Wood kitchen cabinets

GEOGRAPHIC SECTION

Milford - Sussex County (G-4374)

(G-4342)
CEDAR CREEK MARINA
100 Marina Ln (19963-4922)
PHONE.................302 422-2040
Marvin Kahl, *Owner*
EMP: 4
SALES (est): 441.3K **Privately Held**
WEB: www.cedarcreekmarina.com
SIC: 4493 5551 Boat yards, storage & incidental repair; boat dealers

(G-4343)
CENTER FOR COMMUNITY JUSTICE
1129 Airport Rd (19963-6418)
PHONE.................302 424-0890
Natalie Way, *Director*
EMP: 5 **EST:** 1996
SALES (est): 232.1K **Privately Held**
SIC: 7389 Arbitration & conciliation service

(G-4344)
CENTER FOR NEUROLOGY
Also Called: Physical Medical Rehab Assoc
111 Neurology Way (19963-5368)
PHONE.................302 422-0800
Jay I Freid, *Med Doctor*
Peter Koveleski, *Manager*
EMP: 65
SALES (est): 1.8MM **Privately Held**
WEB: www.cnmri.com
SIC: 8011 Neurologist

(G-4345)
CENTRAL AND SOUTHERN DELAWARE
221 S Rehoboth Blvd (19963-1568)
PHONE.................302 545-8067
Paul Lakeman, *Exec Dir*
EMP: 9
SALES (est): 287K **Privately Held**
SIC: 8621 Health association

(G-4346)
CENTRAL DEL ENDOSCOPY UNIT
302 Polk Ave (19963-1818)
P.O. Box 406 (19963-0406)
PHONE.................302 422-3393
William M Kaplan, *Branch Mgr*
EMP: 13
SALES (est): 1.2MM **Privately Held**
SIC: 8011 Gastronomist
PA: Central Delaware Endoscopy Unit, Inc
  644 S Queen St Ste 105
  Dover DE 19904

(G-4347)
CENTRAL DEL GSTRNTROLOGY ASSOC
302 Polk Ave (19963-1818)
PHONE.................302 422-3393
EMP: 5
SALES (est): 291.6K **Privately Held**
SIC: 8011 Medical Doctor's Office

(G-4348)
CHARLES D MURPHY ASSOCIATES
14 S Maple Ave (19963-1950)
PHONE.................302 422-7327
Robert W Nash, *President*
EMP: 13
SQ FT: 2,200
SALES (est): 1MM **Privately Held**
SIC: 8713 Surveying services

(G-4349)
CHARLES H WEST FARMS INC
2953 Tub Mill Pond Rd (19963-5910)
PHONE.................302 335-3936
Stanley West, *President*
Charles West, *Exec VP*
Sandra L Mitchell, *Treasurer*
Lorraine B West, *Admin Sec*
Steven H West, *Asst Sec*
EMP: 26
SQ FT: 1,500
SALES (est): 2.5MM **Privately Held**
SIC: 0161 0119 Rooted vegetable farms; feeder grains

(G-4350)
CHEMSTAR CORP
686 N Dupont Blvd (19963-1002)
PHONE.................302 465-3175
EMP: 3 **EST:** 2018
SALES (est): 160.8K **Privately Held**
SIC: 2951 Asphalt & asphaltic paving mixtures (not from refineries)

(G-4351)
CHOY WILSON CDGN
Also Called: Waverly Orthopaedic
329 Mullet Run (19963-5373)
PHONE.................302 424-4141
Wilson Choy, *Principal*
EMP: 3
SALES (est): 230K **Privately Held**
SIC: 3842 Prosthetic appliances

(G-4352)
CHRISTOPHER FORTIN DDS
214 S Walnut St (19963-1958)
PHONE.................302 422-9791
Christopher Fortin, *Principal*
EMP: 4
SALES (est): 61.5K **Privately Held**
SIC: 8021 Offices & clinics of dentists

(G-4353)
CITIZENS BANK NATIONAL ASSN
610 N Dupont Blvd (19963-1002)
PHONE.................302 422-5010
Michelle Cavello, *Manager*
EMP: 6
SALES (corp-wide): 7.3B **Publicly Held**
SIC: 6022 State commercial banks
HQ: Citizens Bank, National Association
  1 Citizens Plz Ste 1 # 1
  Providence RI 02903
  401 282-7000

(G-4354)
CITY OF MILFORD
Also Called: Electric Department
180 Vickers Rd (19963-5393)
PHONE.................302 422-1110
Rick Carmean, *Superintendent*
EMP: 40 **Privately Held**
SIC: 4911 Electric services
PA: Milford, City Of (Inc)
  201 S Walnut St
  Milford DE 19963
  302 424-3712

(G-4355)
CLEAN SWEEP
5862 Old Shawnee Rd (19963-3352)
PHONE.................302 422-6085
Ernest Hostedler, *Owner*
EMP: 5
SALES (est): 269.8K **Privately Held**
SIC: 1741 7349 Chimney construction & maintenance; chimney cleaning

(G-4356)
CLEARVIEW WINDOWS LLC
Also Called: Fish Window Cleaning Services
600 Ne Front Street Ext H (19963-1391)
PHONE.................302 491-6768
Paul Garnett,
EMP: 5
SALES: 110K **Privately Held**
SIC: 7349 5031 Window cleaning; doors & windows

(G-4357)
CLIFTON FARMS INC
306 Warner Rd (19963-5834)
PHONE.................302 424-8340
William Clifton, *President*
EMP: 4
SALES (est): 376.9K **Privately Held**
SIC: 0182 Vegetable crops grown under cover

(G-4358)
CLOSE CUTS LAWN SVC & LDSCPG
24 Ne 10th St (19963-1363)
PHONE.................302 422-2248
Cyle Hostedler, *Owner*
EMP: 2
SALES (est): 136.4K **Privately Held**
SIC: 3999 Grasses, artificial & preserved

(G-4359)
CLOVER YARNS INC (PA)
Also Called: Steiner Company
715 S Washington St (19963-2305)
P.O. Box 354 (19963-0354)
PHONE.................302 422-4518
Edward Steiner, *President*
Donald Steiner, *Vice Pres*
▲ **EMP:** 2
SQ FT: 40,000
SALES (est): 64.8MM **Privately Held**
SIC: 2282 Rewinding of yarn

(G-4360)
CNMRI
111 Neurology Way (19963-5368)
PHONE.................302 422-0800
EMP: 6
SALES (est): 80.5K **Privately Held**
SIC: 8011 Offices & clinics of medical doctors

(G-4361)
COHAWK
611 Abbott Dr (19963-2401)
PHONE.................302 422-5176
Ben Cohee, *CEO*
Benjiman Cohee, *CEO*
Cathy Cohee, *CFO*
EMP: 4
SALES (est): 121.2K **Privately Held**
SIC: 8711 Engineering services

(G-4362)
COMMUNITY INTEGRATED SERVICES
24 Nw Front St Ste 300 (19963-1463)
PHONE.................215 238-7411
Susan Schonfeld, *Exec Dir*
EMP: 50
SALES (corp-wide): 8.9MM **Privately Held**
SIC: 7361 Employment agencies
PA: Community Integrated Services
  441 N 5th St Ste 210
  Philadelphia PA 19123
  215 238-7411

(G-4363)
COMPLEXIONS TANNING SALON
280 N Rehoboth Blvd (19963-1304)
PHONE.................302 430-0150
Jody Roberts, *Owner*
EMP: 4
SQ FT: 2,032
SALES (est): 45K **Privately Held**
SIC: 7231 Beauty shops

(G-4364)
COMSTOCK CUSTOM CABINETS INC
6706 Shawnee Rd (19963-3427)
PHONE.................302 422-2928
Janice Comstock, *President*
Butch Comstock, *Treasurer*
EMP: 4
SQ FT: 4,800
SALES: 500K **Privately Held**
SIC: 1521 1751 Single-family housing construction; carpentry work

(G-4365)
COUNTRY LIFE HOMES MILFORD DE
610 Marshall St (19963-2308)
PHONE.................302 265-2257
Elmer Fannin, *Principal*
EMP: 5
SALES (est): 687.9K **Privately Held**
SIC: 1521 New construction, single-family houses

(G-4366)
COUNTRY VILLA MOTEL
1036 N Walnut St (19963-1222)
PHONE.................814 938-8330
Monica Haag, *Owner*
EMP: 13
SALES (est): 435.4K **Privately Held**
WEB: www.countryvillamotel.com
SIC: 7011 5812 5813 Motels; restaurant, family: independent; bar (drinking places)

(G-4367)
COUNTY BANK
100 E Masten Cir (19963-1062)
PHONE.................302 424-2500
Priscilla Rogers, *President*
EMP: 6 **Privately Held**
WEB: www.countybankdel.com
SIC: 6021 National commercial banks
PA: County Bank
  19927 Shuttle Rd
  Rehoboth Beach DE 19971

(G-4368)
D & J RECYCLING INC
5688 Betty St (19963-3304)
P.O. Box 411 (19963-0411)
PHONE.................302 422-0163
Duane A Kenton, *President*
Joyce A Kenton, *Vice Pres*
EMP: 6
SALES (est): 556.7K **Privately Held**
SIC: 4953 Recycling, waste materials

(G-4369)
D&N BUS SERVICE INC
140 Vickers Rd (19963)
PHONE.................302 422-3869
Neil Moore, *President*
EMP: 10
SQ FT: 1,500
SALES (est): 476.1K **Privately Held**
SIC: 4151 School buses

(G-4370)
DANNY G PEREZ EA MST
233 Ne Front St (19963-1431)
PHONE.................302 422-2600
Danny Perez, *Owner*
EMP: 4
SALES (est): 203.5K **Privately Held**
SIC: 8721 Certified public accountant

(G-4371)
DAVIS BOWEN & FRIEDEL INC
1 Park Ave (19963-1441)
PHONE.................302 424-1441
Brenda Horstic, *Manager*
Ring Lardner, *Associate*
EMP: 45
SALES (corp-wide): 10.4MM **Privately Held**
WEB: www.dbfinc.com
SIC: 8713 8712 Surveying services; architectural engineering
PA: Davis, Bowen & Friedel, Inc.
  601 E Main St Ste 100
  Salisbury MD 21804
  410 543-9091

(G-4372)
DEL RAY FOUNDATINS LLC
48 Goosebriar Ln (19963-6348)
PHONE.................302 272-6153
Raynold Garcia, *Principal*
EMP: 5
SALES (est): 165.4K **Privately Held**
SIC: 8641 Civic social & fraternal associations

(G-4373)
DEL-ONE FEDERAL CREDIT UNION
100 Credit Union Way (19963-1071)
PHONE.................302 424-2969
Amy Vest, *Manager*
EMP: 6 **Privately Held**
WEB: www.del-one.org
SIC: 6061 Federal credit unions
PA: Del-One Federal Credit Union
  270 Beiser Blvd
  Dover DE 19904

(G-4374)
DELAWARE ANIMAL PRODUCTS LLC
Also Called: Dap
662 Log Cabin Rd (19963-6952)
PHONE.................302 423-7754
Scott Peterman, *Mng Member*
Brian Shanklin, *Mng Member*
EMP: 2
SALES: 400K **Privately Held**
SIC: 2499 Mulch or sawdust products, wood

(PA)=Parent Co (HQ)=Headquarters (DH)=Div Headquarters
○ = New Business established in last 2 years

Milford - Sussex County (G-4375) — GEOGRAPHIC SECTION

(G-4375)
DELAWARE ARCHITECTS LLC
16558 Retreat Cir (19963-3028)
PHONE..............................302 491-6047
Martin D Dusbiber,
EMP: 5 EST: 2010
SALES (est): 458.1K Privately Held
SIC: 8712 Architectural services

(G-4376)
DELAWARE BAY LAUNCH SERVICE
100 Passwaters Dr (19963-4921)
PHONE..............................302 422-7604
H Hickman Rowland Jr, *President*
Christopher Rowland, *Treasurer*
EMP: 10 EST: 1973
SALES (est): 1.4MM
SALES (corp-wide): 7.1MM Privately Held
WEB: www.delawarebaylaunch.com
SIC: 4493 4489 4449 Marinas; water taxis; river transportation, except on the St. Lawrence Seaway
PA: Tug Wilmington Inc
 11 Gist Rd Ste 200
 Wilmington DE 19801
 302 652-1666

(G-4377)
DELAWARE BUILDING SUPPLY CORP
141 Mullet Run (19963-5376)
PHONE..............................302 424-3505
Darin Hobbs, *President*
Kelly Hobbs, *Vice Pres*
EMP: 20
SQ FT: 30,000
SALES (est): 11.1MM Privately Held
SIC: 5031 Building materials, exterior

(G-4378)
DELAWARE COAST LINE RR CO (PA)
8266 N Union Church Rd (19963-3633)
PHONE..............................302 422-9200
Elaine Herholdt, *President*
Michael Herholdt, *President*
Dan Herholdt, *Treasurer*
EMP: 9
SQ FT: 500
SALES (est): 1.4MM Privately Held
SIC: 4011 Railroads, line-haul operating

(G-4379)
DELAWARE HOSPICE INC
100 Patriots Way (19963-5800)
PHONE..............................302 856-7717
Susan Lloyd, *President*
EMP: 30
SALES (corp-wide): 27.4MM Privately Held
SIC: 8082 Home health care services
PA: Delaware Hospice Inc.
 16 Polly Drmmd Shpg Ctr 2
 Newark DE 19711
 302 478-5707

(G-4380)
DELAWARE RURAL WATER ASSN
210 Vickers Rd (19963-5374)
PHONE..............................302 424-3792
Allen Atkins, *President*
David Baird, *Vice Pres*
Richard A Duncan, *Exec Dir*
EMP: 9
SALES: 904.1K Privately Held
SIC: 8621 Professional membership organizations

(G-4381)
DELAWARE THRMPLASTIC SPECIALTY
720 Mccolley St Ste D (19963-2393)
PHONE..............................302 424-4722
John Dorofee Jr, *President*
EMP: 2
SALES (est): 203.9K Privately Held
SIC: 3053 Gaskets & sealing devices

(G-4382)
DELAWARE VETERANS HOME INC
100 Dlaware Veterans Blvd (19963-5395)
PHONE..............................302 424-6000
Bill Peterson, *Director*
EMP: 100
SQ FT: 110,000
SALES: 617K Privately Held
SIC: 8641 Veterans' organization

(G-4383)
DELMARVA BROADCASTING CO INC
Wafl
1666 Blairs Pond Rd (19963-5263)
PHONE..............................302 422-7575
Steve Jordan, *Vice Pres*
Florence Joyce, *Sales Mgr*
Melody Booker, *Branch Mgr*
Rafael Dosman, *Program Dir*
EMP: 25
SALES (corp-wide): 30.4MM Privately Held
WEB: www.delmarvabroadcasting.com
SIC: 4832 Radio broadcasting stations
PA: Delmarva Broadcasting Co Inc
 2727 Shipley Rd
 Wilmington DE 19810
 302 478-2700

(G-4384)
DELMARVA PRECISION GRINDING
906 Se 2nd St (19963-1514)
PHONE..............................302 393-3008
Mary Jo Hill, *Owner*
William Hill, *Co-Owner*
EMP: 2
SALES: 50K Privately Held
SIC: 3599 Grinding castings for the trade

(G-4385)
DELMARVA RV CENTER INC
702 Milford Harrington Hw (19963-5308)
PHONE..............................302 424-4505
Ryan Clough, *CEO*
Louis Clough, *CEO*
George Kover, *CFO*
EMP: 23
SQ FT: 15,000
SALES: 18.8MM Privately Held
SIC: 7538 5561 Recreational vehicle repairs; camper & travel trailer dealers

(G-4386)
DENIM DUO-VERS
113 Lovers Ln (19963-1529)
PHONE..............................302 632-6943
EMP: 1
SALES (est): 46.5K Privately Held
SIC: 2211 Denims

(G-4387)
DENTSPLY SIRONA INC
38 W Clarke Ave (19963-1805)
PHONE..............................302 422-4511
Grace Champagne, *Buyer*
George Ellis, *Buyer*
Sonja Frey, *Design Engr*
Robert Size, *Branch Mgr*
Curtis Merriman, *Manager*
EMP: 5
SALES (corp-wide): 3.9B Publicly Held
SIC: 5047 5999 Dental equipment & supplies; medical apparatus & supplies
PA: Dentsply Sirona Inc.
 13320 Bllntyne Crprtate P
 Charlotte NC 28277
 844 848-0137

(G-4388)
DENTSPLY SIRONA INC
Dentsply Caulk
38 W Clarke Ave (19963-1805)
P.O. Box 359 (19963-0359)
PHONE..............................302 422-4511
Dan Berner, *District Mgr*
Mark Pheasant, *Area Mgr*
Jim Daniels, *Facilities Mgr*
Walter Dias, *Research*
Eugene Dorff, *Branch Mgr*
EMP: 100

SALES (corp-wide): 3.9B Publicly Held
WEB: www.dentsply.com
SIC: 3843 Dental equipment & supplies
PA: Dentsply Sirona Inc.
 13320 Bllntyne Crprtate P
 Charlotte NC 28277
 844 848-0137

(G-4389)
DENTSPLY SIRONA INC
779 E Masten Cir (19963-1030)
P.O. Box 359 (19963-0359)
PHONE..............................302 422-1043
Wayne Starkey, *Planning Mgr*
Judy Cole, *Administration*
EMP: 80
SALES (corp-wide): 3.9B Publicly Held
WEB: www.dentsply.com
SIC: 3843 Dental equipment & supplies
PA: Dentsply Sirona Inc.
 13320 Bllntyne Crprtate P
 Charlotte NC 28277
 844 848-0137

(G-4390)
DENTSPLY SIRONA INC
Dentsply Caulk
412 Mccolley St (19963-2068)
PHONE..............................302 430-7474
Alice Caulk, *Branch Mgr*
EMP: 111
SALES (corp-wide): 3.9B Publicly Held
SIC: 3843 Dental equipment & supplies
PA: Dentsply Sirona Inc.
 13320 Bllntyne Crprtate P
 Charlotte NC 28277
 844 848-0137

(G-4391)
DOROSHOW PASQUALE KARWITZ SIEG
903 Lakeview Ave (19963-1731)
PHONE..............................302 424-7744
Eric Doroshow, *Branch Mgr*
EMP: 19
SALES (corp-wide): 10.6MM Privately Held
SIC: 8111 Bankruptcy law
PA: Doroshow Pasquale Krawitz Siegel Bhaya
 1202 Kirkwood Hwy
 Wilmington DE 19805
 302 998-2397

(G-4392)
DOVER POOL & PATIO CENTER INC
1055 N Walnut St (19963-1201)
PHONE..............................302 839-3300
Joann Roberts, *Manager*
EMP: 5
SALES (est): 270.9K
SALES (corp-wide): 3.8MM Privately Held
WEB: www.doverpools.com
SIC: 1799 Swimming pool construction
PA: Dover Pool & Patio Center, Inc.
 1255 S State St Ste 1
 Dover DE 19901
 302 346-7665

(G-4393)
DOVER POST INC
12 S Walnut St (19963-1954)
PHONE..............................304 222-6025
John Trumpower, *Principal*
EMP: 3
SALES (est): 117.7K Privately Held
WEB: www.milfordbeacon.com
SIC: 2711 Newspapers, publishing & printing

(G-4394)
DOWNS INSURANCE ASSOCIATES
1047 N Walnut St (19963-1201)
PHONE..............................302 422-8863
Gary Downs, *President*
EMP: 4
SALES (est): 794.4K Privately Held
SIC: 6411 Insurance agents

(G-4395)
DRAPERIES ETC INC
723 Mccolley St (19963-2313)
P.O. Box 91 (19963-0091)
PHONE..............................302 422-7323
Kevin P Lonergan, *President*
Karen Warren, *Corp Secy*
Joanne L Warren, *Vice Pres*
EMP: 19 EST: 1970
SQ FT: 7,200
SALES (est): 1.8MM Privately Held
SIC: 2391 Draperies, plastic & textile; from purchased materials

(G-4396)
DRNATURALHEALING INC
Also Called: Drhealing
111 Mccoy St (19963-2309)
PHONE..............................302 265-2213
James Liu, *CEO*
Scott McCaig, *Vice Pres*
Dr Jiatyu Zhou, *Manager*
▲ EMP: 8
SQ FT: 38,000
SALES (est): 1.2MM Privately Held
WEB: www.techworldcorp.com
SIC: 2834 Pills, pharmaceutical

(G-4397)
E Z CASH OF DELAWARE INC
658 N Dupont Blvd (19963-1002)
PHONE..............................302 424-4013
Loraine Kemp, *Manager*
EMP: 4
SALES (corp-wide): 4MM Privately Held
SIC: 6141 Personal credit institutions
PA: E Z Cash Of Delaware Inc.
 300 N Bi State Blvd Ste 1
 Delmar DE 19940
 302 846-2920

(G-4398)
EAN HOLDINGS LLC
411 N Rehoboth Blvd (19963-1307)
PHONE..............................302 422-1167
Michael Bryant, *Branch Mgr*
EMP: 8
SALES (corp-wide): 4.5B Privately Held
SIC: 7514 Passenger car rental
HQ: Ean Holdings, Llc
 600 Corporate Park Dr
 Saint Louis MO 63105

(G-4399)
EAST COAST POURED WALLS INC
331 S Rehoboth Blvd (19963-1531)
PHONE..............................302 430-0630
Fred Fowler, *President*
EMP: 20
SALES (est): 1.7MM Privately Held
SIC: 1771 Concrete work

(G-4400)
EAST COAST PROPERTY MGT INC (HQ)
977 E Masten Cir (19963-1085)
P.O. Box 1510, Seaford (19973-5510)
PHONE..............................302 629-8612
Patricia Batchelor, *CEO*
Sharon Kensinger, *President*
Christina Stanley, *Director*
Linda Marvel, *Admin Sec*
EMP: 14
SQ FT: 2,800
SALES (est): 2.1MM
SALES (corp-wide): 9.8MM Privately Held
SIC: 6531 6513 Real estate managers; apartment building operators
PA: Milford Housing Development Corp
 977 E Masten Cir
 Milford DE 19963
 302 422-8255

(G-4401)
EAST COAST SIGNS & GRAPH
853 S Bowers Rd (19963-6822)
PHONE..............................302 335-5824
David Mosley, *Owner*
EMP: 1
SALES: 250K Privately Held
SIC: 3993 Signs & advertising specialties

GEOGRAPHIC SECTION

Milford - Sussex County (G-4430)

(G-4402)
EASTERN ORNAMENTALS LLC
24675 Bakerfield Rd (19963-4723)
PHONE...................302 684-8733
Thomas Russell,
EMP: 8
SALES (est): 480K Privately Held
SIC: 0783 Planting services, ornamental bush

(G-4403)
EDWIN M MOW DPM FACFAS
Also Called: Mow Foot & Ankle Center
505 Lakeview Ave (19963-2917)
P.O. Box 165 (19963-0165)
PHONE...................302 424-1760
Edwin M Mow, Owner
Edwin Mow, Podiatrist
EMP: 4
SALES (est): 230K Privately Held
SIC: 8043 Offices & clinics of podiatrists

(G-4404)
EMERALD LAWN AND LDSCPG LLC
701 Lindsay Ln (19963-2130)
PHONE...................302 228-1468
John Davis, President
EMP: 4
SALES (est): 118.2K Privately Held
SIC: 0781 Landscape services

(G-4405)
EMORY & MARIER PA
Also Called: Marier, Robert P DDS
771 E Masten Cir Ste 107 (19963-1088)
PHONE...................302 422-2020
Fax: 302 424-0850
EMP: 12
SALES (est): 500K Privately Held
SIC: 8021 Dentist's Office

(G-4406)
ESTHER V GRAHAM
Also Called: Milford Early Learning Center
901 N Dupont Blvd (19963-1092)
PHONE...................302 422-6667
Oleta Fullmun, Director
EMP: 5
SALES (est): 138.8K Privately Held
SIC: 8351 Child day care services

(G-4407)
F D HAMMOND ENTERPRISES INC
Also Called: Trans Products
1111 N Dupont Blvd (19963-1075)
P.O. Box 898 (19963-0898)
PHONE...................302 424-8455
Wyatt F Hammond, President
Elizabeth A Hammond, Vice Pres
Elizabeth Hammond, Vice Pres
EMP: 10
SQ FT: 7,200
SALES (est): 987.8K Privately Held
WEB: www.transproducts.com
SIC: 8742 5961 Business consultant; mail order house

(G-4408)
FA WEBB & SONS
3277 Milford Neck Rd (19963-6751)
PHONE...................302 335-4548
Thomas E Webb, Partner
Barry Maloney, Partner
Richard L Webb, Partner
Thomas P Webb, Partner
EMP: 4 EST: 1950
SALES (est): 360K Privately Held
SIC: 0115 0251 0111 0116 Corn; broiler, fryer & roaster chickens; wheat; soybeans; barley farm

(G-4409)
FAMILY DENTISTRY MILFORD PA
100 Sussex Ave (19963-1823)
PHONE...................302 422-6924
John Bausch DDS, President
EMP: 8
SQ FT: 2,200
SALES (est): 555.5K Privately Held
SIC: 8021 Dentists' office

(G-4410)
FARMERS FIRST SERVICES INC (PA)
306 Warner Rd (19963-5834)
PHONE...................302 424-8340
William Cliston II, CEO
EMP: 4
SALES (est): 1MM Privately Held
WEB: www.farmersfirstservices.com
SIC: 5083 Farm & garden machinery

(G-4411)
FASTENAL COMPANY
205 Mullet Run (19963-5394)
PHONE...................302 424-4149
Philip Anderson, Manager
EMP: 4
SALES (corp-wide): 4.9B Publicly Held
WEB: www.fastenal.com
SIC: 5085 Fasteners, industrial: nuts, bolts, screws, etc.
PA: Fastenal Company
    2001 Theurer Blvd
    Winona MN 55987
    507 454-5374

(G-4412)
FELLOWSHIP HLTH RESOURCES INC
7549 Wilkins Rd (19963-4106)
PHONE...................302 422-6699
Antonio Ojongtambia, Director
EMP: 9
SALES (corp-wide): 38.7MM Privately Held
WEB: www.fellowshiphr.org
SIC: 8093 Mental health clinic, outpatient
PA: Fellowship Health Resources, Inc.
    24 Albion Rd Ste 420
    Lincoln RI 02865
    401 333-3980

(G-4413)
FIRST STATE INSPECTION AGENCY (PA)
1001 Mattlind Way (19963-5369)
PHONE...................302 422-3859
Theodore Morrison, President
Frances Morrison, Vice Pres
EMP: 9
SQ FT: 720
SALES (est): 2.5MM Privately Held
SIC: 7389 Industrial & commercial equipment inspection service; inspection & testing services

(G-4414)
FIRST STATE MANUFACTURING INC
301 Se 4th St (19963-2011)
PHONE...................302 424-4520
Eliseo Valenzuela, President
Cheryl Valenzuela, Vice Pres
Paul Fazzini, Prdtn Mgr
Joseph A Wolfe, Exec Dir
Andrea Cisneros, Administration
EMP: 63
SQ FT: 5,000
SALES (est): 12.9MM Privately Held
WEB: www.firststatemfg.com
SIC: 2531 Seats, aircraft

(G-4415)
FIRST STEPS PRESCHOOL-MILFORD
104 Mccoy St (19963-2310)
PHONE...................302 424-4470
Carrie Singer, Director
EMP: 5
SALES (est): 85.6K Privately Held
SIC: 8351 Preschool center

(G-4416)
FOOD BANK OF DELAWARE INC
1040 Mattlind Way (19963-5366)
PHONE...................302 424-3301
Patricia Bebe, President
Melissa Holochwost, Warehouse Mgr
Caitlin Custer, Manager
Tiarra Thomas, Instructor
Iskeisha Stuckey, Education
EMP: 50
SALES (corp-wide): 21.9MM Privately Held
SIC: 8399 Community development groups
PA: Food Bank Of Delaware, Inc.
    222 Lake Dr
    Newark DE 19702
    302 292-1305

(G-4417)
FRESENIUS USA INC
656 N Dupont Blvd (19963-1094)
PHONE...................302 422-9739
Kenneth Lanza, Manager
EMP: 15
SALES (corp-wide): 18.3B Privately Held
SIC: 8092 Kidney dialysis centers
HQ: Fresenius Usa, Inc.
    4040 Nelson Ave
    Concord CA 94520
    925 288-4218

(G-4418)
FRY FARMS INC
5846 Williamsville Rd (19963-5250)
PHONE...................302 422-9112
Michael Fry, President
Jeff Fry, Vice Pres
EMP: 4
SALES (est): 392.7K Privately Held
SIC: 0191 General farms, primarily crop

(G-4419)
G & S TV & ANTENNA
20450 Sapp Rd (19963-4243)
PHONE...................302 422-5733
Eugene D Smith Jr, Partner
Sue Smith, Partner
EMP: 5 EST: 1981
SALES (est): 317.7K Privately Held
SIC: 7622 5731 Television repair shop; television sets

(G-4420)
GARY I MARKOWITZ MD
110 Ne Front St (19963-1430)
PHONE...................302 422-5155
Gary Markowitz, Principal
EMP: 4
SALES (est): 100.4K Privately Held
SIC: 8011 Ophthalmologist

(G-4421)
GCORA CORP
30 Rosebush Ct (19963-2128)
PHONE...................302 310-1000
EMP: 7
SQ FT: 5,000
SALES: 1.2MM Privately Held
SIC: 8711 Engineering And Consulting

(G-4422)
GENESIS HEALTHCARE CORPORATION
700 Marvel Rd (19963-1740)
PHONE...................302 422-3754
Jean Franks, Office Mgr
Barbara Stumpf, Executive
EMP: 8 Publicly Held
SIC: 8051 Skilled nursing care facilities
HQ: Genesis Healthcare Corporation
    101 E State St
    Kennett Square PA 19348
    610 444-6350

(G-4423)
GERALD BROWN
3232 Thompsonville Rd (19963-6919)
PHONE...................302 335-5211
Gerald Brown, Partner
EMP: 4
SALES (est): 330K Privately Held
SIC: 0251 Roasting chickens, raising of

(G-4424)
GROW USA PRESS
503 Gilcrest St (19963-2306)
PHONE...................302 725-5195
EMP: 2
SALES (est): 78K Privately Held
SIC: 2741 Misc Publishing

(G-4425)
GROWMARK FS LLC (HQ)
Also Called: Milford Fertilizer
308 Ne Front St (19963-1434)
PHONE...................302 422-3002
Michael Macoy, Plant Mgr
Daniel Peachey, Opers Staff
Bonnie Difebo, Human Res Mgr
Denise Goedel, Sales Staff
Sam Grove, Sales Associate
◆ EMP: 75
SQ FT: 351,500
SALES (est): 66.7MM
SALES (corp-wide): 8.7B Privately Held
WEB: www.growmarkfs.com
SIC: 2875 2873 2874 5191 Fertilizers, mixing only; nitrogenous fertilizers; nitrogen solutions (fertilizer); phosphatic fertilizers; pesticides; seeds: field, garden & flower
PA: Growmark, Inc.
    1701 Towanda Ave
    Bloomington IL 61701
    309 557-6000

(G-4426)
GROWMARK FS LLC
Also Called: Shopworks
339 Mlford Harrington Hwy (19963)
PHONE...................302 422-3001
Paul Masula, General Mgr
Norman Hamstead, Prdtn Mgr
Larry Dumbleton, Opers Staff
Joann Carter, Cust Mgr
Keith Keily, Manager
EMP: 5
SALES (corp-wide): 8.7B Privately Held
WEB: www.growmarkfs.com
SIC: 2874 5191 Phosphatic fertilizers; pesticides
HQ: Growmark Fs, Llc
    308 Ne Front St
    Milford DE 19963
    302 422-3002

(G-4427)
GULAB MANAGEMENT INC
Also Called: Travelers Inn
1036 N Walnut St (19963-1222)
PHONE...................302 422-8089
Asim Gulab, Treasurer
EMP: 10
SALES (corp-wide): 3.6MM Privately Held
SIC: 7011 Resort hotel
PA: Gulab Management Inc
    1426 N Dupont Hwy
    Dover DE 19901
    302 734-4433

(G-4428)
GULAB MANAGEMENT INC
Also Called: Super 8 Motel
729 Bay Rd (19963-6122)
PHONE...................302 934-6126
Asim Gulab, Manager
EMP: 60
SALES (corp-wide): 3.6MM Privately Held
SIC: 7011 Hotels & motels
PA: Gulab Management Inc
    1426 N Dupont Hwy
    Dover DE 19901
    302 734-4433

(G-4429)
H & T BUILDERS INC
6650 Shawnee Rd (19963-3426)
PHONE...................302 422-0745
Kevin Troyer, Owner
EMP: 4
SALES: 150K Privately Held
SIC: 1791 1522 Structural steel erection; residential construction

(G-4430)
H R PHILLIPS INC (PA)
715 S Washington St (19963-2305)
P.O. Box 354 (19963-0354)
PHONE...................302 422-4518
Edward J Steiner, President
EMP: 21

Milford - Sussex County (G-4431) — GEOGRAPHIC SECTION

SALES (est): 3.8MM **Privately Held**
WEB: www.hrphillips.com
SIC: 5172 5983 6512 Gasoline; fuel oil dealers; commercial & industrial building operation

(G-4431)
HALLS WE CLEAN SERVICE LLC
16332 Sarah St (19963-3670)
PHONE..................................302 422-7787
Gary Hall, *Mng Member*
EMP: 5
SALES: 200K **Privately Held**
SIC: 7699 Cleaning services

(G-4432)
HALPERN EYE ASSOCIATES INC
Also Called: Helpern Eye Associates
771 E Masten Cir Ste 109 (19963-1088)
PHONE..................................302 422-2020
Juan Rodriguez, *Manager*
EMP: 7
SALES (corp-wide): 4.3MM **Privately Held**
WEB: www.halperneye.com
SIC: 8042 Specialized optometrists
PA: Halpern Eye Associates, Inc.
   885 S Governors Ave
   Dover DE 19904
   302 734-5861

(G-4433)
HAMMOND ENTERPRISES INC
1111 N Dupont Blvd (19963-1075)
P.O. Box 820, Millsboro (19966-0820)
PHONE..................................302 934-1700
Ricky Hammond, *Owner*
EMP: 5
SALES (est): 247.8K **Privately Held**
SIC: 5015 Tires, used

(G-4434)
HAMPTON INN
800 Karken Pit Rd (19963)
PHONE..................................302 422-4320
Jenifer Barto, *General Mgr*
EMP: 15 **EST:** 2010
SALES (est): 842.6K **Privately Held**
SIC: 7011 Hotels & motels

(G-4435)
HAPPY HOURS
2908 Milford Hrrington Hwy (19963)
PHONE..................................302 422-9766
Fax: 302 422-5635
EMP: 5
SALES (est): 241.7K **Privately Held**
SIC: 1711 Plumbing/Heating/Air Cond Contractor

(G-4436)
HAVEN LAKE ANIMAL HOSPITAL
300 Milford Harrington Hw (19963-5304)
PHONE..................................302 422-8100
Chris Coon, *Owner*
EMP: 15 **EST:** 1999
SALES (est): 597.7K **Privately Held**
SIC: 0742 Animal hospital services, pets & other animal specialties

(G-4437)
HEARSAY SERVICES OF DELAWARE
104 Ne Front St (19963-1430)
PHONE..................................302 422-3312
Pamela J P Robinson, *President*
Ronniere Robinson, *Vice Pres*
EMP: 5 **EST:** 2007
SALES (est): 383.9K **Privately Held**
SIC: 8011 5999 Ears, nose & throat specialist: physician/surgeon; eyes, ears, nose & throat specialist: physician/surgeon; hearing aids

(G-4438)
HENDERSON SERVICES INC
Also Called: Pools & Spas Unlimited Milford
219 N Rehoboth Blvd (19963-1303)
PHONE..................................302 424-1999
Mark Henderson, *President*
Susan Henderson, *Vice Pres*
EMP: 10
SALES (est): 1.1MM **Privately Held**
SIC: 7389 1799 Swimming pool & hot tub service & maintenance; athletic & recreation facilities construction

(G-4439)
HERITAGE AT MILFORD
500 S Dupont Blvd (19963-1758)
PHONE..................................302 422-8700
Eileen Hanhauser, *Principal*
EMP: 16
SALES (est): 682.5K **Privately Held**
SIC: 8361 Residential care

(G-4440)
HERTRICH COLLISION CTR OF
1449 Bay Rd (19963-6129)
PHONE..................................302 839-0550
Ben Filer,
EMP: 4
SALES (est): 191.1K **Privately Held**
SIC: 7532 Collision shops, automotive

(G-4441)
HICKMAN OVERHEAD DOOR COMPANY
Also Called: Springhill Seamless Gutter
1625 Bay Rd (19963-6131)
PHONE..................................302 422-4249
Phyllis Walker, *President*
Paul E Walker Jr, *Vice Pres*
Phillip E Hickman, *Treasurer*
EMP: 17
SALES (est): 3.7MM **Privately Held**
WEB: www.hickmandoor.com
SIC: 5211 7699 5031 1761 Garage doors, sale & installation; garage door repair; doors, garage; gutter & downspout contractor

(G-4442)
HITHER CREEK PRESS
197 Meadow Brook Ln (19963-3020)
PHONE..................................603 387-3444
EMP: 1
SALES (est): 37.5K **Privately Held**
SIC: 2741 Miscellaneous publishing

(G-4443)
HOLLINGSWORTH HEATING & AC
719 S Dupont Blvd (19963-2230)
P.O. Box 493, Denton MD (21629-0493)
PHONE..................................302 422-7525
Robert Hollingsworth, *President*
EMP: 8
SALES: 1MM **Privately Held**
SIC: 1711 Warm air heating & air conditioning contractor

(G-4444)
HOOK EM & COOK EM LLC
24603 Bay Ave (19963-4900)
PHONE..................................302 226-8220
Albert Adams III,
EMP: 5
SALES (est): 406K **Privately Held**
SIC: 7999 Fishing boats, party: operation

(G-4445)
HOUSERS AUTO TRIM INC
112 Park Ave (19963-1444)
PHONE..................................302 422-1290
Lawrence Houser Sr, *President*
EMP: 4
SQ FT: 5,000
SALES (est): 585.6K **Privately Held**
SIC: 5013 7532 Automotive supplies & parts; top & body repair & paint shops

(G-4446)
HOWARD M JOSEPH INC (PA)
3235 Bay Rd (19963-6027)
PHONE..................................302 335-1300
Howard M Joseph, *President*
Nadina Joseph, *Corp Secy*
EMP: 8
SQ FT: 8,000
SALES (est): 1.2MM **Privately Held**
SIC: 6531 2452 Broker of manufactured homes, on site; prefabricated buildings, wood

(G-4447)
IG BURTON & COMPANY INC (PA)
Also Called: I G Burton Imports
793 Bay Rd (19963-6122)
PHONE..................................302 422-3041
Charles Burton, *President*
Daniel Hall, *General Mgr*
Irwin G Burton III, *Vice Pres*
Jim Pagden, *Maintenance Dir*
Caleb Ashley, *Parts Mgr*
EMP: 70
SQ FT: 25,000
SALES: 225MM **Privately Held**
WEB: www.igburton.com
SIC: 5511 7538 Automobiles, new & used; pickups, new & used; trucks, tractors & trailers: new & used; general automotive repair shops

(G-4448)
IG BURTON & COMPANY INC
Also Called: I G Burton Chrysler
605 Bay Rd (19963-6121)
PHONE..................................302 424-3041
Charlie Burton, *President*
Dylan Housman, *Sales Staff*
Allan Moran, *Sales Staff*
Roger Whitney, *Sales Associate*
Kimberly Ekas, *Receptionist*
EMP: 45
SALES (corp-wide): 225MM **Privately Held**
WEB: www.igburton.com
SIC: 5511 7538 5531 Automobiles, new & used; pickups, new & used; trucks, tractors & trailers: new & used; general automotive repair shops; automotive parts
PA: I.G. Burton & Company, Inc.
   793 Bay Rd
   Milford DE 19963
   302 422-3041

(G-4449)
INDEPENDENT NEWSMEDIA INC USA
Chronicle The
37a Walnut St (19963)
PHONE..................................302 422-1200
Cat Porterfield, *Manager*
Gwen Guerke, *Systems Mgr*
EMP: 8
SQ FT: 4,000 **Privately Held**
WEB: www.inweekly.net
SIC: 2711 Newspapers, publishing & printing
HQ: Independent Newsmedia Usa, Inc.
   110 Galaxy Dr
   Dover DE 19901
   302 674-3600

(G-4450)
INTERNET WORKING TECHNOLOGIES
12 S Walnut St A (19963-1954)
P.O. Box 852 (19963-0852)
PHONE..................................302 424-1855
David Dolan, *President*
James Allen Wagaman, *Vice Pres*
EMP: 8
SQ FT: 2,500
SALES (est): 743.2K **Privately Held**
WEB: www.itnt.com
SIC: 7379 Computer related consulting services

(G-4451)
INTOYOU INC
203 Ne Front St Ste 101 (19963-1431)
PHONE..................................818 309-5115
Hayden Commans, *Branch Mgr*
EMP: 4
SALES (corp-wide): 368.8K **Privately Held**
SIC: 7371 Computer software development & applications
PA: Intoyou, Inc.
   5208 Carmento Dr
   Oak Park CA 91377
   818 309-5115

(G-4452)
J & J SERVICES
2908 Mlford Hrrington Hwy (19963)
PHONE..................................302 422-2684
Jonathan J Plump, *Owner*
EMP: 6
SALES (est): 320.5K **Privately Held**
SIC: 8999 Services

(G-4453)
J & V SHOOTERS SUPPLY
7369 Shawnee Rd (19963-3436)
PHONE..................................302 422-5417
Joseph Heeger, *Owner*
Victoria Heeger, *Owner*
EMP: 2
SALES (est): 121K **Privately Held**
SIC: 3949 Shooting equipment & supplies, general

(G-4454)
J AND J HAIR FASHIONS
971 N Dupont Blvd (19963-1072)
PHONE..................................302 422-5117
Judith Breeding, *Partner*
EMP: 4
SALES (est): 50K **Privately Held**
SIC: 7231 Cosmetologist

(G-4455)
J C WELLS & SONS LP
7481 Wells Rd (19963-4728)
PHONE..................................302 422-4732
Mark Wells, *Partner*
Dawn Wells, *Partner*
EMP: 5
SALES (est): 173.8K **Privately Held**
SIC: 8748 Agricultural consultant

(G-4456)
J H WILKERSON & SON INC
Also Called: Wilkerson Water Co
Ne Front St (19963)
P.O. Box 78 (19963-0078)
PHONE..................................302 422-4306
Charles H Wilkerson, *President*
David Wilerson, *Corp Secy*
Arlene D Wilkerson, *Corp Secy*
Elizabeth Wilkerson, *Vice Pres*
EMP: 5 **EST:** 1919
SQ FT: 3,840
SALES (est): 1MM **Privately Held**
SIC: 5983 4941 Fuel oil dealers; water supply

(G-4457)
JERRYS INC
17776 Oak Hill Dr (19963-3400)
PHONE..................................302 422-7676
Jerry Kovach, *CEO*
Jan Kovach, *Vice Pres*
Beth Workman, *Admin Asst*
EMP: 18
SALES (est): 2.4MM **Privately Held**
SIC: 1794 1611 Excavation work; surfacing & paving

(G-4458)
JITEN PATEL DDS
100 Sussex Ave (19963-1823)
PHONE..................................302 690-8629
EMP: 8
SALES (est): 84.5K **Privately Held**
SIC: 8021 Offices & clinics of dentists

(G-4459)
JOHN R STUMP MD
200 Kona Cir (19963-5396)
PHONE..................................302 422-3937
John R Stump MD, *Owner*
EMP: 6
SALES (est): 260K **Privately Held**
SIC: 8011 Ophthalmologist

(G-4460)
JOHN T MALCYNSKI MD
Also Called: Atlantic Surgical
100 Wellness Way (19963-4364)
P.O. Box 412 (19963-0412)
PHONE..................................302 424-7522
David Clooney MD, *Owner*
EMP: 7
SALES (est): 439K **Privately Held**
SIC: 8011 Surgeon

(G-4461)
JOR-LIN INC
Also Called: Jor-Lin Charter Bus Service
309 S Rehoboth Blvd (19963-1531)
PHONE..................................302 424-4445

GEOGRAPHIC SECTION
Milford - Sussex County (G-4491)

Alan Mitchell, *President*
EMP: 20
SALES (est): 1.5MM **Privately Held**
WEB: www.jor-lin.com
SIC: 4142 Bus charter service, except local

(G-4462)
JOSEPHINE KEIR LIMITED
27 S Walnut St (19963-1953)
PHONE..................302 422-0270
EMP: 2
SALES (est): 117.2K **Privately Held**
SIC: 2273 Carpets & rugs

(G-4463)
KENT GENERAL HOSPITAL
Also Called: Milford Memorial Hospital
100 Wellness Way (19963-4364)
PHONE..................302 430-5731
Joe Whiting, *COO*
Nicole Jackson, *Director*
EMP: 49 **Privately Held**
SIC: 8062 General medical & surgical hospitals
HQ: Kent General Hospital
  640 S State St
  Dover DE 19901
  302 674-4700

(G-4464)
KENT GENERAL HOSPITAL INC
301 Jefferson Ave (19963-1800)
PHONE..................302 430-5705
Craig Crouch, *Owner*
EMP: 7 **Privately Held**
SIC: 8099 8011 Blood related health services; clinic, operated by physicians
HQ: Kent General Hospital
  640 S State St
  Dover DE 19901
  302 674-4700

(G-4465)
KENT SUSSEX AUTO CARE INC
914 N Walnut St (19963-1220)
PHONE..................302 422-3337
Sam Shah, *President*
EMP: 4
SALES (est): 369.2K **Privately Held**
SIC: 7538 General automotive repair shops

(G-4466)
KENT-SUSSEX INDUSTRIES INC
Also Called: KSI CARTRIDGE SERVICE
301 N Rehoboth Blvd (19963-1305)
PHONE..................302 422-4014
B Craig Crouch, *CEO*
EMP: 313
SQ FT: 75,000
SALES: 7.2MM **Privately Held**
WEB: www.ksiinc.org
SIC: 3955 Print cartridges for laser & other computer printers

(G-4467)
KIDS INC
613 Lakeview Ave (19963-2919)
PHONE..................302 422-9099
Mary Wilson, *Principal*
Paige Evers, *Pastor*
EMP: 5
SALES (est): 80.3K **Privately Held**
SIC: 8351 Group day care center

(G-4468)
KUSTOM KUTZ
1007 N Walnut St (19963-1201)
PHONE..................302 424-7556
Joetta Hopkins, *Owner*
Joetta Lowbray, *Owner*
EMP: 6
SALES (est): 86.7K **Privately Held**
SIC: 7231 Beauty shops

(G-4469)
LA VERE ELECTRIC INC
840 Church Hill Rd (19963-5537)
P.O. Box 208 (19963-0208)
PHONE..................302 422-9185
Ronald La Vere, *President*
Debbie La Vere, *Corp Secy*
EMP: 4
SALES (est): 419.9K **Privately Held**
SIC: 1731 General electrical contractor

(G-4470)
LANK JOHNSON AND TULL (PA)
268 Milford Harrington Hw (19963-5303)
P.O. Box 253 (19963-0253)
PHONE..................302 422-3308
Robert B Lank, *Partner*
Terrance Johnson, *Partner*
Richard Tull, *Partner*
Robyn Hutzulak, *Accountant*
Mark Johnson, *CPA*
EMP: 8
SALES (est): 2.3MM **Privately Held**
SIC: 8721 Accounting services, except auditing; certified public accountant

(G-4471)
LASER TONE BUS SYSTEMS LLC
1973 Bay Rd (19963-6134)
PHONE..................302 335-2510
Steven Martin, *President*
EMP: 6
SQ FT: 4,000
SALES (est): 1.3MM **Privately Held**
WEB: www.ltone.com
SIC: 7699 5044 Office equipment & accessory customizing; office equipment

(G-4472)
LAWRENCE LEGATES MASNRY CO INC
2891 Mlford Hrrington Hwy (19963)
P.O. Box 199, Houston (19954-0199)
PHONE..................302 422-8043
Lawrence D Legates, *President*
Margaret Legates, *Vice Pres*
EMP: 6
SALES: 250K **Privately Held**
SIC: 1741 Masonry & other stonework

(G-4473)
LEON N WEINER & ASSOCIATES INC
Also Called: Milford Crossing Apartments
806a Moyer Cir E (19963-9602)
PHONE..................302 422-3343
Karen Lambden, *Branch Mgr*
EMP: 4
SALES (corp-wide): 54MM **Privately Held**
SIC: 6513 Apartment building operators
PA: Leon N. Weiner & Associates, Inc.
  1 Fox Pt Ctr 4 Denny Rd
  Wilmington DE 19809
  302 656-1354

(G-4474)
LILY INTRNL MEDICINE ASSCS LLC
1019 Mattlind Way (19963-5369)
PHONE..................302 424-1000
Ifeanyi A Udezulu, *Principal*
EMP: 5
SALES (est): 239.3K **Privately Held**
SIC: 8099 Health & allied services

(G-4475)
LNP MEDIA GROUP INC
Also Called: Delmarva Broadcasting
1666 Blairs Pond Rd (19963-5263)
P.O. Box 808 (19963-0808)
PHONE..................302 422-7575
Melody Booker, *Manager*
EMP: 30
SALES (corp-wide): 110.9MM **Privately Held**
WEB: www.lanccounty.com
SIC: 4832 Radio broadcasting stations
PA: Lnp Media Group, Inc.
  8 W King St
  Lancaster PA 17603
  717 291-8811

(G-4476)
LOFLAND FUNERAL HOME INC
102 Lakeview Ave (19963-1719)
PHONE..................302 422-5416
J Sudler Lofland III, *President*
EMP: 4 **EST:** 1917
SQ FT: 4,500
SALES (est): 312.7K **Privately Held**
SIC: 7261 Funeral home

(G-4477)
LONG TERM CARE RESIDENTS DIV
24 Nw Front St (19963-1463)
PHONE..................302 424-8600
Kim Reed, *Principal*
EMP: 15 **EST:** 2010
SALES (est): 200.5K **Privately Held**
SIC: 8399 Health systems agency

(G-4478)
LOWELL SCOTT MD PA
Also Called: Scott Pediatrics
807 Hickory Ln (19963-1317)
PHONE..................302 684-1119
Lowell Scott MD, *President*
EMP: 6
SALES (est): 531.3K **Privately Held**
SIC: 8011 General & family practice, physician/surgeon

(G-4479)
LUFF & ASSOCIATES CPA PA
Also Called: Luff & Associates PA
223 S Rehoboth Blvd (19963-1568)
PHONE..................302 422-9699
George Luff, *President*
Donna R Keily, *Office Admin*
EMP: 7
SALES (est): 609K **Privately Held**
SIC: 8721 Certified public accountant

(G-4480)
LUIS L DAVID MD PA
204 S Walnut St (19963-1958)
P.O. Box 482 (19963-0482)
PHONE..................302 422-9768
Luis L David, *President*
EMP: 6
SALES (est): 380K **Privately Held**
SIC: 8011 Pediatrician

(G-4481)
LYNCH HEIGHTS FUEL CORP
840 Bay Rd (19963-6107)
PHONE..................302 422-9195
Liz Garcia, *Manager*
EMP: 6
SALES (est): 646.2K **Privately Held**
SIC: 2869 Fuels

(G-4482)
LYNN AND RACHEL WALSH
6028 Old Shawnee Rd (19963-3355)
PHONE..................302 422-2893
Rachel Walsh, *Principal*
EMP: 4
SALES (est): 151.4K **Privately Held**
SIC: 7389 Interior design services

(G-4483)
MAIL CENTER
686 N Dupont Blvd (19963-1002)
PHONE..................302 422-2200
Debbie Tappan, *CEO*
EMP: 4
SALES (est): 366.4K **Privately Held**
SIC: 7331 Mailing service

(G-4484)
MAKE WAVE
628 Mlford Harrington Hwy (19963)
PHONE..................302 422-1247
Michael Thompson, *President*
EMP: 6
SALES (est): 170K **Privately Held**
SIC: 7231 Beauty shops

(G-4485)
MANUFACTURERS & TRADERS TR CO
Also Called: M&T
673 N Dupont Blvd (19963-1001)
PHONE..................302 855-2160
Gail Dickerson, *Manager*
EMP: 11
SALES (corp-wide): 6.4B **Publicly Held**
WEB: www.binghamlegg.com
SIC: 6022 State trust companies accepting deposits, commercial
HQ: Manufacturers And Traders Trust Company
  1 M&T Plz Fl 3
  Buffalo NY 14203
  716 842-4200

(G-4486)
MARKET STREET PRESERVATION INC
977 E Masten Cir (19963-1085)
PHONE..................302 422-8255
David Moore, *President*
Russell Huxtable, *Vice Pres*
Christina Stanley, *Vice Pres*
Jennifer Kintz, *Treasurer*
EMP: 4
SALES (est): 111K
SALES (corp-wide): 9.8MM **Privately Held**
SIC: 6513 Apartment building operators
PA: Milford Housing Development Corp
  977 E Masten Cir
  Milford DE 19963
  302 422-8255

(G-4487)
MARKET STREET PRESERVATION LP
977 E Masten Cir (19963-1085)
PHONE..................302 422-8255
David Moore, *President*
Russell Huxtable, *Vice Pres*
Christina Stanley, *Vice Pres*
Jennifer Kintz, *Treasurer*
EMP: 4
SALES (est): 111K
SALES (corp-wide): 9.8MM **Privately Held**
SIC: 6513 Apartment building operators
PA: Milford Housing Development Corp
  977 E Masten Cir
  Milford DE 19963
  302 422-8255

(G-4488)
MARVEL AGENCY INC
Also Called: Allstate
15 N Walnut St (19963-1445)
P.O. Box 358 (19963-0358)
PHONE..................302 422-7844
Harvey G Marvel Jr, *President*
Randy Marvel, *Treasurer*
Annette Cerasaro, *Admin Sec*
EMP: 25
SQ FT: 5,000
SALES (est): 4.4MM **Privately Held**
WEB: www.marvelagency.com
SIC: 6411 6531 Insurance agents, brokers & service; real estate brokers & agents

(G-4489)
MASTER INTERIORS INC
160 Mullet Run (19963-5367)
PHONE..................302 368-9361
Mary C Humpton, *President*
Lyle Humpton, *Manager*
EMP: 9
SALES (corp-wide): 3.5MM **Privately Held**
SIC: 1742 Acoustical & ceiling work
PA: Master Interiors, Inc.
  113 Sandy Dr
  Newark DE 19713
  302 368-9361

(G-4490)
MATRIX REHABILITATION DELAWARE
Also Called: Barker Therapy Rehabilitation
800 Airport Rd Ste 102 (19963-6469)
PHONE..................302 424-1714
Courtney Twilley, *Owner*
EMP: 6
SALES (est): 130.9K
SALES (corp-wide): 5B **Publicly Held**
SIC: 8093 Rehabilitation center, outpatient treatment
PA: Select Medical Holdings Corporation
  4714 Gettysburg Rd
  Mechanicsburg PA 17055
  717 972-1100

(G-4491)
MEDING & SON SEAFOOD
3697 Bay Rd (19963-6031)
PHONE..................302 335-3944
Henry D Meding, *Owner*
EMP: 15
SALES (est): 2MM **Privately Held**
SIC: 5146 5812 5421 Seafoods; seafood restaurants; seafood markets

Milford - Sussex County (G-4492)   GEOGRAPHIC SECTION

(G-4492)
MEDTIX LLC (PA)
Also Called: Medtix Medical Supply
221 S Rehoboth Blvd (19963-1568)
P.O. Box 188, Bear (19701-0188)
PHONE...................302 645-8070
Jack Berberian,
EMP: 30 EST: 2009
SALES (est): 20.5MM Privately Held
SIC: 5047 Medical equipment & supplies

(G-4493)
MH CUSTOM CABINETS
624 Marshall St (19963-2308)
PHONE...................302 422-7082
Michael Hitchens, *Owner*
EMP: 1
SALES (est): 129.4K Privately Held
SIC: 2434 Wood kitchen cabinets

(G-4494)
MID ATLANTIC PAIN INSTITUTE
550 S Dupont Blvd Ste C (19963-1704)
PHONE...................302 369-1700
Rhonda Biddle, *Principal*
EMP: 5
SALES (est): 206.2K Privately Held
SIC: 8733 Noncommercial research organizations

(G-4495)
MIDATLNTIC AUTO RSTRATION SUPS
6930 Shawnee Rd (19963-3430)
PHONE...................302 422-3812
Fred Golden, *Owner*
EMP: 7
SALES (est): 430K Privately Held
WEB: www.midatlanticstangs.org
SIC: 5099 Durable goods

(G-4496)
MILFORD BOWLING LANES INC
809 N Dupont Blvd (19963-1066)
PHONE...................302 422-9456
Ernest Fry, *President*
Doris Fry, *Corp Secy*
EMP: 22
SQ FT: 30,000
SALES (est): 788.5K Privately Held
SIC: 7933 Ten pin center

(G-4497)
MILFORD COMMUNITY BAND INC
616 Cedarwood Ave (19963-2357)
PHONE...................302 422-6304
Joe Lear, *Manager*
EMP: 75
SALES (est): 643.8K Privately Held
SIC: 7929 Musical entertainers

(G-4498)
MILFORD GRAIN CO INC
6789 Shawnee Rd (19963-3444)
PHONE...................302 422-6752
David Wilkins, *President*
Donald Calhoun, *President*
Hugh Rowan, *General Mgr*
EMP: 4
SALES (est): 387.3K Privately Held
SIC: 4221 Grain elevator, storage only

(G-4499)
MILFORD HOUSING DEVELOPMENT (PA)
977 E Masten Cir (19963-1085)
PHONE...................302 422-8255
David Moore, *CEO*
Russel Huxtable, *Vice Pres*
Russell Huxtable, *Vice Pres*
Rob Ament, *Manager*
Dan Vanvorst, *Manager*
EMP: 18
SALES (est): 9.8MM Privately Held
WEB: www.milfordhousing.com
SIC: 6531 Real estate managers

(G-4500)
MILFORD LODGING LLC
Also Called: AmericInn Lodging & Suites
699 N Dupont Blvd (19963-1001)
PHONE...................302 839-5000
Wilma Besnoska, *Manager*
Ted Watkins,
EMP: 20
SALES: 700K Privately Held
SIC: 7011 Hotels

(G-4501)
MILFORD MEDICAL ASSOCIATES PA (PA)
310 Mullet Run (19963-5371)
PHONE...................302 424-0600
G M Edmondson MD, *Partner*
Mary L Hawkins MD, *Partner*
Loretta I Edmondson, *Partner*
Susan Sufit MD, *Partner*
EMP: 13
SALES (est): 1.9MM Privately Held
SIC: 8011 General & family practice, physician/surgeon

(G-4502)
MILFORD PULMONARY ASSOC LLC
39 W Clarke Ave (19963-1839)
PHONE...................302 424-3100
Angela Messick, *President*
EMP: 5
SALES (est): 253.3K Privately Held
SIC: 8011 Pulmonary specialist, physician/surgeon

(G-4503)
MILFORD RENT ALL INC
601 Marshall St (19963-2307)
PHONE...................302 422-0100
Joseph Wiley, *Principal*
EMP: 4
SALES (est): 458.5K Privately Held
SIC: 7359 Rental store, general

(G-4504)
MILFORD SENIOR CENTER INC
111 Park Ave (19963-1443)
PHONE...................302 422-3385
Daphne Bumbrey, *Exec Dir*
EMP: 17 EST: 1973
SALES: 646K Privately Held
SIC: 8322 Senior citizens' center or association

(G-4505)
MIND MECHANIX
556 S Dupont Blvd Ste I (19963-1706)
PHONE...................302 503-5142
EMP: 7
SALES (est): 70.3K Privately Held
SIC: 8099 Health & allied services

(G-4506)
MISPILLION ART LEAGUE INC
5 N Walnut St (19963-1456)
PHONE...................302 430-7646
Judy Struck, *President*
Sharon Hepford, *Director*
EMP: 9
SALES (est): 79.4K Privately Held
SIC: 8412 Art gallery, noncommercial; art gallery

(G-4507)
MISPILLION III
504 Mispillion Apts (19963-2348)
PHONE...................302 422-4429
Arthur W Edwards, *CEO*
Arthur Edwards, *Owner*
EMP: 5
SALES (est): 222.4K Privately Held
SIC: 6513 Apartment building operators

(G-4508)
MISPILLION RIVER BREWING LLC
233 Mullet Run (19963)
PHONE...................302 491-6623
Eric Williams,
EMP: 5 EST: 2012
SALES (est): 429.6K Privately Held
SIC: 2082 Ale (alcoholic beverage)

(G-4509)
MOHAWK ELECTRICAL SYSTEMS INC
251 S Rehoboth Blvd (19963-1568)
P.O. Box 630 (19963-0630)
PHONE...................302 422-2500
Scott M Welch, *President*
Linda Welch,
EMP: 25
SQ FT: 24,000
SALES (est): 7.3MM Privately Held
WEB: www.mohawkelectrical.com
SIC: 3699 Electrical equipment & supplies

(G-4510)
MOHAWK PLASTIC PRODUCTS INC
251 S Rehoboth Blvd (19963-1568)
PHONE...................302 424-4324
Scott Welch, *President*
Stephen Welch, *Vice Pres*
EMP: 1
SQ FT: 24,000
SALES (est): 131.1K Privately Held
SIC: 3089 Injection molding of plastics

(G-4511)
MOM HOME DAYCARE
8351 Collett Ln (19963-3666)
PHONE...................302 265-2668
M Maldonado-Hernandez, *Principal*
EMP: 5
SALES (est): 72.1K Privately Held
SIC: 8351 Child day care services

(G-4512)
NEMOURS FOUNDATION
Also Called: Nemours Dpont Pdatrics Milford
703 N Dupont Blvd (19963-1003)
PHONE...................302 422-4559
Kelly Thomas, *Office Mgr*
Susan Wagenhoffer, *Manager*
EMP: 7
SALES (corp-wide): 1.3B Privately Held
SIC: 8011 Pediatrician
PA: Nemours Foundation
   10140 Centurion Pkwy N
   Jacksonville FL 32256
   904 697-4100

(G-4513)
NKS DISTRIBUTORS INC
759 E Masten Cir (19963-1030)
PHONE...................302 422-1220
Joanne Lee, *Vice Pres*
Edward Walsen, *Opers Mgr*
Rich Godwin, *Sales Staff*
Jeff Morris, *Sales Executive*
EMP: 27
SALES (est): 1.8MM
SALES (corp-wide): 38.1MM Privately Held
WEB: www.nksdistributors.com
SIC: 5181 Beer & other fermented malt liquors
PA: N.K.S. Distributors, Inc.
   399 Churchmans Rd
   New Castle DE 19720
   302 322-1811

(G-4514)
NORMAN S STEWARD DDS PA
214 S Walnut St (19963-1958)
PHONE...................302 422-9791
Norman S Steward DDS, *Owner*
EMP: 8
SALES (est): 435.6K Privately Held
SIC: 8021 Dentists' office

(G-4515)
NURSES N KIDS INC
Also Called: Nurses N Kids Southern Del
705 North St (19963-2707)
PHONE...................302 424-1770
Tanya Pennington, *Director*
EMP: 25
SALES (corp-wide): 4.3MM Privately Held
WEB: www.nursesnkids.com
SIC: 8082 Home health care services
PA: Nurses N Kids, Inc
   904 Churchmans Road Ext
   New Castle DE 19720
   302 323-1118

(G-4516)
NUTRIEN AG SOLUTIONS INC
200 N Rehoboth Blvd (19963-1304)
PHONE...................302 422-3570
Jimmy Warren, *Branch Mgr*
EMP: 10 Privately Held
WEB: www.cropproductionservices.com
SIC: 5191 Fertilizer & fertilizer materials
HQ: Nutrien Ag Solutions, Inc.
   3005 Rocky Mountain Ave
   Loveland CO 80538
   970 685-3300

(G-4517)
ODD FELLOWS CMTRY OF MILFORD
300 S Rehoboth Blvd (19963-1532)
PHONE...................302 422-4619
James Greenly, *President*
Bill Sipple, *President*
EMP: 6
SALES: 111.5K Privately Held
SIC: 6553 Cemetery subdividers & developers

(G-4518)
ONE STOP MEDICAL INC
515 S Dupont Blvd Bldg C (19963-1757)
PHONE...................302 450-4479
Dorothy Harmon, *President*
Alisa Miller, *Vice Pres*
EMP: 8
SALES (est): 85.3K Privately Held
SIC: 8099 Health & allied services

(G-4519)
ONEMAIN FINANCIAL GROUP LLC
660 N Dupont Blvd (19963-1002)
PHONE...................302 422-9657
Deborah Hoopengardner, *Manager*
EMP: 4
SALES (corp-wide): 4.2B Publicly Held
SIC: 6282 Investment advice
HQ: Onemain Financial Group, Llc
   100 International Dr # 150
   Baltimore MD 21202
   855 663-6246

(G-4520)
OVERHEAD DOOR CO DELMAR INC
603 Marshall St (19963-2307)
PHONE...................302 424-4400
Robert S Gross, *President*
Paul Cummings III, *Vice Pres*
EMP: 20
SQ FT: 8,000
SALES (est): 2.2MM Privately Held
SIC: 1751 Garage door, installation or erection

(G-4521)
OWNERS MANAGEMENT COMPANY
Also Called: Silver Lakes Estates
5 Linstone Ln Ofc 100 (19963-1174)
PHONE...................302 422-0740
Martin Auckland, *Manager*
EMP: 4
SALES (corp-wide): 38.4MM Privately Held
WEB: www.hawthornevalleycc.com
SIC: 6513 Apartment building operators
HQ: Owner's Management Company Inc
   25250 Rockside Rd Ste 1
   Cleveland OH 44146
   440 439-3800

(G-4522)
PARSON THORNE REALTY ASSOC LP
Also Called: Parson Thorne Apartments
505 Nw Front St Apt A24 (19963)
PHONE...................302 422-9367
Donald Jaffey, *Partner*
Spring Kapper, *Manager*
EMP: 20
SALES (est): 750K Privately Held
SIC: 6513 Apartment building operators

(G-4523)
PATRICK SCANLON PA
203 Ne Front St Ste 101 (19963-1431)
PHONE...................302 424-1996
Patrick Scanlon, *President*
EMP: 7
SALES (est): 561K Privately Held
WEB: www.delcollections.com
SIC: 8111 Debt collection law

GEOGRAPHIC SECTION
Milford - Sussex County (G-4556)

(G-4524)
PEOPLES PLACE II INC (PA)
1129 Airport Rd (19963-6418)
PHONE.................................302 422-8033
Denise Jackson, *Program Mgr*
Leon Kelly, *Program Mgr*
Mike Rowe, *Program Mgr*
Michael Kersteter, *Exec Dir*
Del Failing, *Associate Dir*
EMP: 7 EST: 1972
SALES: 7.1MM Privately Held
WEB: www.peoplesplace2.com
SIC: 8322 Social service center

(G-4525)
PERDUE FARMS INC
225 S Rehoboth Blvd (19963-1568)
PHONE.................................302 424-2600
Ron Darnell, *Production*
Isaac Ferreira, *Engineer*
Maria Rivera, *Manager*
EMP: 100
SALES (corp-wide): 5.9B Privately Held
WEB: www.perdue.com
SIC: 2015 Poultry, processed
PA: Perdue Farms Inc.
    31149 Old Ocean City Rd
    Salisbury MD 21804
    410 543-3000

(G-4526)
PHOENIX REHABILITATION AND HEA
401 S Dupont Blvd (19963-1787)
PHONE.................................302 725-5720
Jason Mohacey, *Branch Mgr*
EMP: 4
SALES (corp-wide): 14.8MM Privately Held
SIC: 8049 Physical therapist
PA: Phoenix Rehabilitation And Health
    Services, Inc.
    430 Innovation Dr
    Blairsville PA 15717
    724 463-7478

(G-4527)
PNC BANK NATIONAL ASSOCIATION
655 N Dupont Blvd (19963-1001)
PHONE.................................302 422-1015
Wayne Davis, *General Mgr*
EMP: 12
SALES (corp-wide): 19.9B Publicly Held
SIC: 6021 National commercial banks
HQ: Pnc Bank, National Association
    222 Delaware Ave
    Wilmington DE 19801
    877 762-2000

(G-4528)
PRECISION JEWELRY INC
Also Called: EKA Jewelers
607 N Dupont Blvd (19963-1099)
PHONE.................................302 422-7138
Robert Addonizio, *President*
Amanda N Phipps, *Advt Staff*
EMP: 5
SQ FT: 1,100
SALES (est): 556.5K Privately Held
WEB: www.ekajewelers.com
SIC: 5944 7631 Jewelry, precious stones & precious metals; watch, clock & jewelry repair

(G-4529)
PREMIER OTHPDIC BONE JINT CARE
329 Mullet Run (19963-5373)
PHONE.................................302 422-6506
EMP: 5 EST: 2010
SALES (est): 350K Privately Held
SIC: 8011 Medical Doctor's Office

(G-4530)
PRIMECARE MEDICAL TRNSPT LLC
568 Milford Harrington Hw (19963-5306)
P.O. Box 839 (19963-0839)
PHONE.................................302 422-0900
Charles Bradley, *President*
Efmarie Bradley, *Vice Pres*
EMP: 25
SALES (est): 814.7K Privately Held
SIC: 4119 Ambulance service

(G-4531)
PROUSE ENTERPRISES LLC
Also Called: Old Mill Crab House
120 Mullet Run (19963-5367)
PHONE.................................302 846-9000
EMP: 1
SALES (est): 47K Privately Held
SIC: 3949 Scoops, crab & fish

(G-4532)
QUEST DIAGNOSTICS INCORPORATED
975 N Dupont Blvd (19963-1026)
PHONE.................................302 424-4504
Kim Tiller, *Branch Mgr*
EMP: 21
SALES (corp-wide): 7.5B Publicly Held
SIC: 8071 Testing laboratories
PA: Quest Diagnostics Incorporated
    500 Plaza Dr Ste G
    Secaucus NJ 07094
    973 520-2700

(G-4533)
RCD PRINTING
623 Abbott Dr (19963-2401)
PHONE.................................302 424-8467
EMP: 2
SALES (est): 83.9K Privately Held
SIC: 2752 Lithographic Commercial Printing

(G-4534)
REAGAN-WATSON AUCTIONS LLC
115 N Washington St (19963-1457)
PHONE.................................302 422-2392
Scott Reagan, *Marketing Staff*
Glenn Watson Jr,
EMP: 5
SALES: 950K Privately Held
SIC: 7389 Auctioneers, fee basis

(G-4535)
REGIS CORPORATION
939 N Dupont Blvd (19963-1072)
PHONE.................................302 430-0881
Peggy Tice, *Branch Mgr*
EMP: 8
SALES (corp-wide): 1B Publicly Held
SIC: 7231 Unisex hair salons
PA: Regis Corporation
    7201 Metro Blvd
    Edina MN 55439
    952 947-7777

(G-4536)
REMCO ELECTRIC
125 Causey Ave (19963-1909)
PHONE.................................302 422-6833
EMP: 4 EST: 1976
SQ FT: 200
SALES: 30K Privately Held
SIC: 1731 Electrical Contractor

(G-4537)
RENT-A-CENTER INC
678 N Dupont Blvd (19963-1002)
PHONE.................................302 422-1230
Robert Bliss, *Manager*
EMP: 5
SALES (corp-wide): 2.6B Publicly Held
WEB: www.rentacenter.com
SIC: 7359 Appliance rental; furniture rental; home entertainment equipment rental; television rental
PA: Rent-A-Center, Inc.
    5501 Headquarters Dr
    Plano TX 75024
    972 801-1100

(G-4538)
RENZI RUST INC
Also Called: Almost Home Child Care Center
6722 Griffith Lake Dr (19963-3510)
PHONE.................................302 424-4470
Christine Rust, *President*
EMP: 14
SALES (est): 243.5K Privately Held
SIC: 8351 Group day care center

(G-4539)
RESERVES AT SAWMILL
100a Valley Dr (19963-1184)
PHONE.................................302 424-1910

EMP: 3 EST: 2016
SALES (est): 220.7K Privately Held
SIC: 2421 Sawmills & planing mills, general

(G-4540)
RESPONSE COMPUTER GROUP INC
213 W Liberty Way (19963-5399)
PHONE.................................302 335-3400
Robert Stone, *President*
Randy Ennis, *Corp Secy*
Faith Ennis, *Office Mgr*
Pat Coulter, *Manager*
Curt Ennis, *Prgrmr*
EMP: 10
SQ FT: 2,500
SALES (est): 1MM Privately Held
WEB: www.rcgweb.com
SIC: 7378 5734 Computer & data processing equipment repair/maintenance; computer & software stores

(G-4541)
REW MATERIAL
150 Vickers Rd (19963-5393)
PHONE.................................302 424-2125
Jhonny Emm, *Principal*
EMP: 8
SALES (est): 686K Privately Held
SIC: 5039 Prefabricated structures

(G-4542)
RHUE & ASSOCIATES INC
Also Called: Rhue Insurance
628 Mlford Harrington Hwy (19963)
P.O. Box 569 (19963-0569)
PHONE.................................302 422-3058
Edward B Rhue, *President*
Nancy C Rhue, *Corp Secy*
EMP: 5
SALES: 300K Privately Held
SIC: 6411 Insurance agents

(G-4543)
RICHARD ADDINGTON CO
316 N Rehoboth Blvd (19963-1306)
PHONE.................................302 422-2668
Richard Addington, *Owner*
Donna Addington, *Co-Owner*
EMP: 6
SALES (est): 1MM Privately Held
SIC: 5511 7542 New & used car dealers; washing & polishing, automotive

(G-4544)
RITA LYNN INC
501 Point Dr (19963-1673)
PHONE.................................302 422-3904
Joe Wells, *President*
Rita Wells, *Treasurer*
EMP: 4
SALES (est): 185.2K Privately Held
SIC: 6531 Real estate agent, residential

(G-4545)
ROBERT G STARKEY CPA
1043 N Walnut St (19963-1201)
PHONE.................................302 422-0108
Robert G Starkey, *Owner*
Lois Palmer, *Accountant*
Lori Webb, *Accountant*
Judith Parsons, *Officer*
Mary Naylor, *Administration*
EMP: 5
SALES (est): 402.8K Privately Held
SIC: 8721 Certified public accountant

(G-4546)
ROBERT GRANT INC
Also Called: Grant & Sons Roofing & Siding
606 Mlford Harrington Hwy (19963)
PHONE.................................302 422-6090
Robert Grant, *President*
EMP: 16
SALES (est): 959.4K Privately Held
SIC: 1761 Roofing contractor; siding contractor

(G-4547)
ROGER ALEXANDER MD
306 Lakeview Ave (19963-2914)
PHONE.................................302 422-5223
Rodger Alexander MD, *Owner*
EMP: 4

SALES (est): 288.1K Privately Held
SIC: 8011 Physicians' office, including specialists

(G-4548)
ROOKERY GOLF COURSES SOUTH
6152 S Rehoboth Blvd (19963-4140)
PHONE.................................302 422-7010
Glenda Adkins, *Manager*
EMP: 5
SALES (est): 194.5K Privately Held
SIC: 7992 Public golf courses

(G-4549)
RUMPSTICH MACHINE WORKS INC
305 S Rehoboth Blvd (19963-1531)
PHONE.................................302 422-4816
John L Allen, *President*
Joan A Maloney, *Corp Secy*
Ronald R Allen, *Vice Pres*
EMP: 5
SQ FT: 3,600
SALES: 250K Privately Held
SIC: 3599 Machine shop, jobbing & repair

(G-4550)
S J PASSWATER GENERAL CNSTR
715a S Washington St (19963-2305)
PHONE.................................302 422-1061
Samuel Passwater, *Owner*
EMP: 5
SALES (est): 351.6K Privately Held
SIC: 1521 General remodeling, single-family houses

(G-4551)
SAINT HOME HEALTH CARE
1017 Mattlind Way (19963-5369)
PHONE.................................302 514-9597
Tina Chambers, *CEO*
EMP: 7
SALES (est): 217.3K Privately Held
SIC: 8082 Home health care services

(G-4552)
SAMAHA MICHEL R MD
39 W Clarke Ave (19963-1839)
PHONE.................................302 422-3100
Michel Samaha, *Principal*
EMP: 5
SALES (est): 165.4K Privately Held
SIC: 8011 Offices & clinics of medical doctors

(G-4553)
SATTERFIELD & RYAN INC
8266 N Union Church Rd (19963-3633)
PHONE.................................302 422-4919
Michael Herholdt, *President*
Michael D Herholdt Jr, *Treasurer*
EMP: 15 EST: 1931
SQ FT: 30,000
SALES (est): 2.2MM Privately Held
SIC: 1731 General electrical contractor

(G-4554)
SCHANNE MARK STATE FARM INSUR
915 S Dupont Blvd (19963-2234)
PHONE.................................302 422-7231
Mark Schanne, *Owner*
EMP: 8
SALES (est): 773.4K Privately Held
SIC: 6411 Insurance agents & brokers

(G-4555)
SELECT FINANCIAL GROUP
556 S Dupont Blvd Ste G (19963-1706)
PHONE.................................302 424-7777
Drew Sammons, *Principal*
EMP: 4
SALES (est): 76.9K Privately Held
SIC: 6411 Insurance agents

(G-4556)
SERVICEXPRESS CORPORATION
340 Ne Front St (19963-1434)
PHONE.................................302 424-3500
Bamdad Bahar, *Branch Mgr*
EMP: 221 Privately Held

Milford - Sussex County (G-4557) — **GEOGRAPHIC SECTION**

SIC: 7361 Labor contractors (employment agency)
PA: Servicexpress Corporation
120 N Ray St
Georgetown DE 19947

(G-4557)
SHAWNEE WOOD FARMS INC
7237 Calhoun Rd (19963-3614)
PHONE 302 422-3534
Donald Calhoun Jr, *President*
EMP: 4
SALES (est): 410K **Privately Held**
SIC: 0111 0115 0116 Wheat; corn; soybeans

(G-4558)
SHEA CONCRETE LTD
4th & Montgomery St (19963)
PHONE 302 422-7221
Mike Shea, *President*
EMP: 25
SQ FT: 5,400
SALES (est): 1.9MM **Privately Held**
SIC: 1771 Concrete work

(G-4559)
SHORE UNITED BANK
698a N Dupont Blvd (19963-1002)
PHONE 302 424-4600
Dee Andrews, *President*
EMP: 11
SALES (corp-wide): 64.9MM **Publicly Held**
SIC: 6022 State commercial banks
HQ: Shore United Bank
18 E Dover St
Easton MD 21601
410 758-1600

(G-4560)
SHREE KISHNA INC
699 N Dupont Blvd (19963-1001)
PHONE 302 839-5000
Arvid Patel, *President*
EMP: 10 **EST:** 2013
SALES (est): 345.5K **Privately Held**
SIC: 7011 Motel, franchised

(G-4561)
SLING WITH ME
809 Ne 10th St (19963-1346)
PHONE 302 424-0111
EMP: 2
SALES (est): 140.1K **Privately Held**
SIC: 3949 Mfg Sporting/Athletic Goods

(G-4562)
SMITH CONCRETE INC
8473 N Union Church Rd (19963-3638)
PHONE 302 270-9251
Robbi Smith, *President*
EMP: 5
SALES (est): 285K **Privately Held**
SIC: 1771 Concrete work

(G-4563)
SOUND-N-SECURE INC
20444 Pingue Dr (19963-4276)
PHONE 302 424-3670
Melissa E Pingue, *CEO*
Robert Pingue, *Vice Pres*
EMP: 7
SQ FT: 20,000
SALES: 600K **Privately Held**
SIC: 7382 3651 Burglar alarm maintenance & monitoring; audio electronic systems

(G-4564)
SOUTH BOWERS LADIES AUXILIARY
57 Scotts Corner Rd (19963-7129)
P.O. Box 314 (19963-0314)
PHONE 302 335-4135
Jo Ann Webb, *President*
Michele Melvin, *President*
EMP: 20
SALES (est): 260.4K **Privately Held**
SIC: 8641 Civic social & fraternal associations

(G-4565)
SOUTH BOWERS VOLUNTEER FIRE CO
57 Scotts Corner Rd (19963)
P.O. Box 314 (19963-0314)
PHONE 302 335-4666
Dennis Dean, *Fire Chief*
EMP: 35
SALES: 520.7K **Privately Held**
SIC: 8711 Fire protection engineering

(G-4566)
SOUTHERN DELAWARE MED GROUP PA
119 Neurology Way (19963-5368)
P.O. Box 337 (19963-0337)
PHONE 302 424-3900
Cedric Barnes, *President*
Cedric T Barnes, *Principal*
Sott A Hammer, *Principal*
EMP: 20
SALES (est): 1.4MM **Privately Held**
SIC: 8011 Offices & clinics of medical doctors

(G-4567)
SPECIALIZED CARIER SYSTEMS INC
256 N Rehoboth Blvd (19963-1304)
P.O. Box 198 (19963-0198)
PHONE 302 424-4548
Tom Noll, *President*
EMP: 5
SQ FT: 12,000
SALES (est): 560K **Privately Held**
SIC: 4212 7389 Local trucking, without storage; crane & aerial lift service

(G-4568)
SPRINT SPECTRUM LP
120 Aerenson Dr (19963-1236)
PHONE 302 393-2060
EMP: 20 **Publicly Held**
SIC: 4813 Local & long distance telephone communications
HQ: Sprint Spectrum L.P.
6800 Sprint Pkwy
Overland Park KS 66251

(G-4569)
STAFFMARK INVESTMENT LLC
242 S Rehoboth Blvd (19963-1569)
PHONE 302 422-0606
Brenda Bill, *Principal*
EMP: 9 **Privately Held**
SIC: 7361 Labor contractors (employment agency)
HQ: Staffmark Investment Llc
201 E 4th St Ste 800
Cincinnati OH 45202

(G-4570)
STEVEN ALBAN DDS PA
3 Sussex Ave (19963-1853)
PHONE 302 422-9637
Steven M Alban, *Principal*
EMP: 5 **EST:** 2008
SALES (est): 451.2K **Privately Held**
SIC: 8021 Dentists' office

(G-4571)
STEVENSON VENTURES LLC
Also Called: Scj
26 N Walnut St (19963)
PHONE 302 752-4449
Baron Stevenson,
EMP: 8 **EST:** 2015
SQ FT: 2,450
SALES (est): 289.5K **Privately Held**
SIC: 7322 Collection agency, except real estate

(G-4572)
SURVEY SUPPLY INC
726 Mccolley St (19963-2314)
P.O. Box 403 (19963-0403)
PHONE 302 422-3338
Jerry H McPherson, *President*
Kevin S McPherson, *Vice Pres*
EMP: 6
SQ FT: 10,000
SALES (est): 940.8K **Privately Held**
WEB: www.surveysupplyinc.com
SIC: 5049 Surveyors' instruments

(G-4573)
SUSSEX COUNTY FEDERAL CR UN
140 Aerenson Dr (19963-1236)
PHONE 302 422-9110
Richard Stoops, *Branch Mgr*
EMP: 7
SALES (corp-wide): 9.7MM **Privately Held**
SIC: 6061 Federal credit unions
PA: Sussex County Federal Credit Union
1941 Bridgeville Hwy
Seaford DE 19973
302 629-0100

(G-4574)
SUSSEX POST
37 N Walnut St (19963-1445)
PHONE 302 629-5505
Kitt Parker, *Manager*
EMP: 3
SALES (est): 112.7K **Privately Held**
SIC: 2711 Newspapers

(G-4575)
TAX MANAGEMENT SERVICE INC
233 Ne Front St (19963-1431)
PHONE 703 845-5900
Danny G Perez, *President*
Maria Perez, *Corp Secy*
EMP: 6
SALES (est): 388K **Privately Held**
SIC: 8721 7291 Accounting, auditing & bookkeeping; tax return preparation services

(G-4576)
TAYLOR ELECTRIC SERVICE INC
8 Columbia St (19963-1536)
PHONE 302 422-3966
William C Taylor Jr, *President*
Michael Taylor, *Vice Pres*
EMP: 5
SALES: 600K **Privately Held**
SIC: 1731 General electrical contractor

(G-4577)
TELAMON CORPORATION
Also Called: Telamon Corp Lincoln Hs
518 N Church Ave (19963-1129)
PHONE 302 424-2335
Sedonia Worthy, *Branch Mgr*
EMP: 6
SALES (corp-wide): 70.5MM **Privately Held**
SIC: 8331 Job training services
PA: Telamon Corporation
5560 Munford Rd Ste 201
Raleigh NC 27612
919 851-7611

(G-4578)
TERESA H KELLER MD
16 S Dupont Blvd (19963-1027)
PHONE 302 422-2022
Teresa H Keller MD, *Owner*
EMP: 6
SALES (est): 462.8K **Privately Held**
SIC: 8011 General & family practice, physician/surgeon

(G-4579)
TOMALL INC
Also Called: Muffler Mart
1109 N Dupont Blvd (19963-1075)
PHONE 302 424-4004
Thomas Munz, *President*
EMP: 4
SALES (est): 450.9K **Privately Held**
WEB: www.tomall.sk
SIC: 7539 7533 Brake services; muffler shop, sale or repair & installation

(G-4580)
TURNING POINT AT PEOPLES PLACE
1131 Airport Rd (19963-6418)
PHONE 302 424-2420
Linda Haussine, *Manager*
Cherelyn Homlish, *Director*
EMP: 8
SALES (est): 455.3K **Privately Held**
SIC: 8322 Social service center

(G-4581)
TWIN CREEK FARMS LLC
638 Canterbury Rd (19963-5328)
PHONE 302 249-2294
Bentley Blessing,
EMP: 5
SALES (est): 231.9K **Privately Held**
SIC: 0119 7389 Cash grains;

(G-4582)
U HAUL CO INDEPENDENT DEALERS
Also Called: U-Haul
601 Marshall St (19963-2307)
PHONE 302 424-3189
Joe Wiley, *Owner*
Gerald Wiley, *Owner*
EMP: 5
SALES (est): 170.4K **Privately Held**
SIC: 7513 Truck rental & leasing, no drivers

(G-4583)
UNDER/COMM INC
198 Mullet Run (19963-5367)
PHONE 302 424-1554
David L Hermansader, *President*
Scott Hermansader, *Vice Pres*
EMP: 15
SQ FT: 480
SALES (est): 3.1MM **Privately Held**
WEB: www.undercomm.com
SIC: 4813 Telephone communication, except radio

(G-4584)
UNITED STATES COLD STORAGE INC
Also Called: American Ice
419 Milford Harrington Hwy (19963)
P.O. Box 242 (19963-0242)
PHONE 302 422-7536
Ronald Longhany, *Warehouse Mgr*
Ron Longhany, *Manager*
EMP: 22
SALES (corp-wide): 13.9B **Privately Held**
WEB: www.uscold.com
SIC: 4222 Warehousing, cold storage or refrigerated
HQ: United States Cold Storage, Inc.
2 Aquarium Dr Ste 400
Camden NJ 08103
856 354-8181

(G-4585)
UNITED STATES COLD STORAGE INC
P.O. Box 242 (19963-0242)
PHONE 302 422-7536
Ron LInghany, *Branch Mgr*
EMP: 45
SALES (corp-wide): 13.9B **Privately Held**
SIC: 4222 Warehousing, cold storage or refrigerated
HQ: United States Cold Storage, Inc.
2 Aquarium Dr Ste 400
Camden NJ 08103
856 354-8181

(G-4586)
UNITRACK INDUSTRIES INC
967 E Masten Cir (19963-1085)
PHONE 302 424-5050
Clayton Marchetti, *President*
EMP: 30
SQ FT: 34,000
SALES (est): 2.7MM **Privately Held**
WEB: www.unitrackind.com
SIC: 8711 Engineering services

(G-4587)
UNITY PERSPECTIVES INC
702 North St (19963-2708)
P.O. Box 555 (19963-0555)
PHONE 302 265-2854
Merlyn Brown, *Exec Dir*
EMP: 9
SALES: 17K **Privately Held**
SIC: 8322 Individual & family services

(G-4588)
UROLOGY ASSOC SOUTHERN DEL PA
810 Seabury Ave (19963-2223)
PHONE 302 422-5569

GEOGRAPHIC SECTION
Millsboro - Sussex County (G-4618)

Richard Paul, *Branch Mgr*
EMP: 9
SALES (est): 681.7K
SALES (corp-wide): 365.5K **Privately Held**
SIC: 8011 8031 Urologist; offices & clinics of osteopathic physicians
PA: Urology Associates Of Southern Delaware Pa
34431 King Street Row
Lewes DE 19958
302 645-2666

(G-4589)
VECTOR SECURITY INC
409 S Dupont Blvd (19963-1787)
PHONE..................302 422-7031
Chris Adamcik, *Branch Mgr*
EMP: 32
SALES (corp-wide): 444.1MM **Privately Held**
SIC: 7382 1731 Burglar alarm maintenance & monitoring; fire detection & burglar alarm systems specialization
HQ: Vector Security Inc.
2000 Ericsson Dr Ste 250
Warrendale PA 15086
724 741-2200

(G-4590)
VERIZON DELAWARE LLC
2 S Industrial Ln (19963-1080)
PHONE..................302 422-1430
Janice Porter, *General Mgr*
EMP: 50
SALES (corp-wide): 130.8B **Publicly Held**
SIC: 4813 Telephone communication, except radio
HQ: Verizon Delaware Llc
901 N Tatnall St Fl 2
Wilmington DE 19801
302 571-1571

(G-4591)
VFW POST 6483
77 Veterans Cir (19963)
PHONE..................302 422-4412
Henry Waudby, *Principal*
EMP: 7
SALES (est): 230K **Privately Held**
SIC: 8641 Veterans' organization

(G-4592)
WAFL WYUS BROADCASTING INC
Also Called: Eagle 97.7 FM
1666 Blairs Pond Rd (19963-5263)
PHONE..................302 422-7575
Melody Booker, *President*
EMP: 23
SQ FT: 2,500
SALES (est): 789.9K **Privately Held**
WEB: www.eagle977.com
SIC: 4832 Radio broadcasting stations

(G-4593)
WAGAMON TECHNOLOGY GROUP LLC
12 S Walnut St A (19963-1954)
P.O. Box 852 (19963-0852)
PHONE..................302 424-1855
Allan Wagamon,
EMP: 4
SALES (est): 276.8K **Privately Held**
SIC: 8748 Business consulting

(G-4594)
WALLS FARM AND GARDEN CTR INC
833 S Dupont Blvd (19963-2232)
PHONE..................302 422-4565
Robert E Walls, *President*
Robert B Walls, *Vice Pres*
Bonnie Walls, *Treasurer*
Lisa Walls, *Admin Sec*
EMP: 5
SQ FT: 5,000
SALES (est): 931.9K **Privately Held**
SIC: 5571 5012 5261 5719 All-terrain vehicles; recreation vehicles, all-terrain; lawnmowers & tractors; fireplaces & wood burning stoves

(G-4595)
WALLS IRRIGATION INC (PA)
833 S Dupont Blvd (19963-2232)
PHONE..................302 422-2262
Robert E Walls, *President*
Rob Chambers, *Vice Pres*
Garry Chops, *Parts Mgr*
Jay Reibsome, *Sales Staff*
Bonnie Walls, *Admin Sec*
EMP: 12
SQ FT: 10,000
SALES (est): 3.3MM **Privately Held**
WEB: www.wallsirrigation.com
SIC: 5083 Irrigation equipment

(G-4596)
WALLS SERVICE CENTER INC
220 Ne Front St (19963-1432)
PHONE..................302 422-8110
Colin Walls, *President*
John W Walls Jr, *President*
EMP: 6 **EST:** 1956
SQ FT: 3,000
SALES (est): 882.2K **Privately Held**
WEB: www.wallsrx.com
SIC: 7537 7533 5541 Automotive transmission repair shops; muffler shop, sale or repair & installation; gasoline service stations

(G-4597)
WALSH CHIROPRACTIC CENTER
800 Airport Rd Ste 103 (19963-6469)
PHONE..................302 422-0622
Lynn Walsh, *Owner*
EMP: 5
SALES (est): 168K **Privately Held**
SIC: 8041 Offices & clinics of chiropractors

(G-4598)
WARFEL CONSTRUCTION CO INC
246 S Rehoboth Blvd (19963-1569)
PHONE..................302 422-8927
Rob Warfel, *President*
Jay Schlabach, *Vice Pres*
Weston Yutzy, *Vice Pres*
Missy Kenton, *Admin Sec*
EMP: 35 **EST:** 1972
SQ FT: 14,000
SALES (est): 5.4MM **Privately Held**
WEB: www.warfelconstruction.com
SIC: 1521 1542 New construction, single-family houses; general remodeling, single-family houses; farm building construction; commercial & office building, new construction

(G-4599)
WATSONS AUCTION & REALTY SVC
Also Called: Re/Max Twin Counties
115 N Washington St (19963-1457)
PHONE..................302 422-2392
Glen Watson, *President*
EMP: 5
SALES (est): 574.7K **Privately Held**
WEB: www.watsonsauction.com
SIC: 6531 Real estate agent, residential

(G-4600)
WEBBIT
6200 Kirby Rd (19963-4146)
PHONE..................302 725-6024
Kit Creighton, *Owner*
EMP: 5
SALES: 150K **Privately Held**
SIC: 7379 Computer related consulting services

(G-4601)
WELLNESS HEALTH INC
Also Called: Wellness Health Center
106 Nw Front St (19963-1023)
PHONE..................302 424-4100
Pierre Moise, *Owner*
EMP: 5
SALES (est): 139K **Privately Held**
SIC: 8041 8049 Offices & clinics of chiropractors; physical therapist

(G-4602)
WELLS AGENCY INC
995 N Dupont Blvd (19963-1072)
P.O. Box 599 (19963-0599)
PHONE..................302 422-2121
Fax: 302 422-2898
EMP: 6 **EST:** 1954
SALES (est): 360K **Privately Held**
SIC: 6531 Appraisal Real Estate

(G-4603)
WELLS FARMS INC
7481 Wells Rd (19963-4728)
PHONE..................302 422-4732
James C Wells Jr, *President*
Dawn H Wells, *Admin Sec*
EMP: 6
SALES: 500K **Privately Held**
SIC: 0191 General farms, primarily crop

(G-4604)
WHIPPER SNAPPER TRANSPORT LLC
278 Canterbury Rd (19963-5323)
PHONE..................302 265-2437
George S Godwin, *Mng Member*
Evetta Godwin, *Admin Sec*
EMP: 4
SALES: 590K **Privately Held**
SIC: 4214 7389 Local trucking with storage;

(G-4605)
WILKINS FUEL CO
701 S Washington St (19963-2305)
P.O. Box 167 (19963-0167)
PHONE..................302 422-5597
Howard C Wilkins II, *President*
Aileen Wilkins, *Corp Secy*
Sandy Wilkins, *Admin Sec*
EMP: 6
SQ FT: 1,500
SALES (est): 1.2MM **Privately Held**
SIC: 5983 1711 Fuel oil dealers; heating systems repair & maintenance

(G-4606)
WILLIAM M KAPLAN MD
302 Polk Ave (19963-1818)
P.O. Box 406 (19963-0406)
PHONE..................302 422-3393
William Kaplan, *Manager*
EMP: 4 **Privately Held**
SIC: 8011 Gastronomist
PA: William M Kaplan Md
644 S Queen St
Dover DE 19904

(G-4607)
WILLIAM STELE WLDG FABRICATION
200 Mullet Run (19963-5372)
PHONE..................302 422-7444
Steele William, *Owner*
EMP: 4
SALES (est): 217.4K **Privately Held**
SIC: 7692 Welding repair

(G-4608)
WILLIAM T WADKINS GARAGE INC
Also Called: U-Save Auto
402 Ne Front St (19963-1436)
PHONE..................302 422-0265
William T Wadkins, *President*
EMP: 7
SALES (est): 746.3K **Privately Held**
SIC: 7538 General automotive repair shops

(G-4609)
WILSON FAMILY PRACTICE
901 Lakeview Ave (19963-1731)
PHONE..................302 422-6677
Robert Wilson, *Owner*
Harvey Mast MD, *Owner*
EMP: 4
SALES (est): 439K **Privately Held**
SIC: 8011 General & family practice, physician/surgeon

(G-4610)
WILSON FLEET & EQUIPMENT
961 E Masten Cir (19963-1085)
PHONE..................302 422-7159

Rick Wilson, *Partner*
EMP: 7
SALES (est): 483.5K **Privately Held**
SIC: 7549 Automotive services

(G-4611)
WM V SIPPLE & SON INC
300 S Rehoboth Blvd (19963-1532)
PHONE..................302 422-4214
Scott G Sipple, *President*
EMP: 3
SALES (est): 377.5K **Privately Held**
SIC: 3272 Monuments, concrete

(G-4612)
WRENCHES
1958 Bloomfield Dr (19963-6231)
PHONE..................302 422-2690
EMP: 4
SALES (est): 287.4K **Privately Held**
SIC: 5013 Whol Auto Parts/Supplies

(G-4613)
WSFS FINANCIAL CORPORATION
688 N Dupont Blvd (19963-1002)
PHONE..................302 346-2930
Brian Warnock, *Branch Mgr*
EMP: 5
SALES (corp-wide): 455.5MM **Publicly Held**
SIC: 6022 State commercial banks
PA: Wsfs Financial Corporation
500 Delaware Ave
Wilmington DE 19801
302 792-6000

(G-4614)
X SCREEN GRAPHIX
1514 Bay Rd (19963-6114)
P.O. Box 6 (19963-0006)
PHONE..................302 422-4550
Richard Dix, *Owner*
EMP: 2
SALES (est): 120K **Privately Held**
SIC: 3993 Signs & advertising specialties

(G-4615)
YANKEE CLIPPERS HAIR DESIGNER
30 Nw 10th St Ste A (19963-1267)
PHONE..................302 422-2748
Paul Holmes, *Owner*
EMP: 5
SALES (est): 86.6K **Privately Held**
SIC: 7231 Hairdressers

(G-4616)
ZARRAGA & ZARRAGA INTERNL MEDC
219 S Walnut St (19963-1957)
P.O. Box 258 (19963-0258)
PHONE..................302 422-9140
Antonio Zarraga, *President*
Cindy Zarraga, *Vice Pres*
EMP: 8
SALES (est): 638.8K **Privately Held**
SIC: 8011 Infectious disease specialist, physician/surgeon; internal medicine, physician/surgeon

---

Millsboro
Sussex County

(G-4617)
1 A LIFESAFER INC
27380 William Street Rd (19966-3924)
PHONE..................800 634-3077
EMP: 1
SALES (corp-wide): 4.3MM **Privately Held**
SIC: 3829 Measuring & controlling devices
PA: 1 A Lifesafer, Inc.
4290 Glendale Milford Rd
Blue Ash OH 45242
513 651-9560

(G-4618)
1ST STATE HOME SERVICES
25935 Starboard Dr (19966-6606)
PHONE..................302 339-5573
EMP: 4

Millsboro - Sussex County (G-4619)   GEOGRAPHIC SECTION

SALES (est): 710.8K **Privately Held**
SIC: 6022 State commercial banks

(G-4619)
4 SEASONS NAILS & SPA
28662 Dupont Blvd (19966-4794)
PHONE..................302 663-9474
EMP: 4
SALES (est): 28.8K **Privately Held**
SIC: 7231 Manicurist, pedicurist

(G-4620)
A E MOORE INCORPORATED
25872 W State St (19966-1551)
P.O. Box 638 (19966-0638)
PHONE..................302 934-7055
Steve Kern, *President*
Tom White, *Vice Pres*
David Wharton, *Treasurer*
EMP: 12 EST: 1988
SQ FT: 10,000
SALES (est): 4.5MM **Privately Held**
SIC: 5169 5113 5145 Specialty cleaning & sanitation preparations; paper & products, wrapping or coarse; confectionery

(G-4621)
ACCESS QUALITY HEALTHCARE
32026 Long Neck Rd (19966-6228)
PHONE..................302 947-4437
Aaron Green, *Principal*
EMP: 5 EST: 2007
SALES (est): 423.2K **Privately Held**
SIC: 8099 Health & allied services

(G-4622)
ACCESSIBLE HOME BUILDERS INC
28412 Dupont Blvd Ste 103 (19966-1227)
PHONE..................302 628-9571
Scott Lanham, *President*
EMP: 6
SQ FT: 1,000
SALES (est): 740K **Privately Held**
WEB: www.accessiblehomebuilders.com
SIC: 1521 New construction, single-family houses; general remodeling, single-family houses

(G-4623)
AECOM GLOBAL II LLC
28485 Dupont Blvd (19966-4749)
PHONE..................302 933-0200
Kyle Gulbronson, *Branch Mgr*
Brandt Butler, *Sr Consultant*
EMP: 84
SALES (corp-wide): 20.1B **Publicly Held**
SIC: 8711 Consulting engineer
HQ: Aecom Global Ii, Llc
1999 Avenue Of The Stars
Los Angeles CA 90067
213 593-8100

(G-4624)
AFTER HOURS HEATING & AIR
Also Called: Honeywell Authorized Dealer
24436 Hollyville Rd (19966-2608)
PHONE..................302 945-3310
Clarence A Edgens, *Owner*
EMP: 4
SALES (est): 466.4K **Privately Held**
SIC: 1711 Warm air heating & air conditioning contractor

(G-4625)
AKZO NOBEL INC
Also Called: Intervet USA
29160 Intervet Ln (19966-4217)
P.O. Box 318 (19966-0318)
PHONE..................312 544-7000
David Kukula, *Accounts Mgr*
Chris Raglind, *Manager*
EMP: 5
SALES (corp-wide): 11.3B **Privately Held**
WEB: www.akzonobelusa.com
SIC: 8059 Personal care home, with health care
HQ: Akzo Nobel Inc.
525 W Van Buren St Fl 16
Chicago IL 60607

(G-4626)
ALLEN BIOTECH LLC
Also Called: Allen Harim
29984 Pinnacle Way (19966)
P.O. Box 1380 (19966-5380)
PHONE..................302 629-9136
Joseph Moran, *CEO*
Brian G Hildreth, *CFO*
Pam Good Trice, *Credit Mgr*
EMP: 1000
SALES (est): 160.1MM **Privately Held**
SIC: 2015 Poultry, processed
HQ: Allen Harim Foods, Llc
126 N Shipley St
Seaford DE 19973
302 629-9136

(G-4627)
ALLEN HARIM FARMS LLC
29984 Pinnacle Way (19966)
PHONE..................302 629-9136
Key Lee, *Exec Dir*
Steven Evans,
Brian Hildreth,
EMP: 24
SALES (est): 3.6MM **Privately Held**
SIC: 0751 Poultry services

(G-4628)
ALPHA CARE MEDICAL LLC
29787 John J Williams Hwy # 8 (19966-4097)
PHONE..................800 818-8680
EMP: 9
SALES (corp-wide): 1.1MM **Privately Held**
SIC: 8011 Primary care medical clinic
PA: Alpha Care Medical, L.L.C.
1000 Midway Dr Ste 3
Harrington DE 19952
302 398-0888

(G-4629)
AM CUSTOM TACKLE INC
25889 Kings Ln (19966-6632)
PHONE..................302 945-7921
EMP: 1
SALES (est): 99.9K **Privately Held**
SIC: 3861 Fishing Reel Repair Mfg Fishing Rigs

(G-4630)
AMERICAN PRTABLE MINI STOR INC
24139 Fishers Pt (19966-4723)
P.O. Box 779 (19966-0779)
PHONE..................302 934-9898
Jeffrey Scott Burton, *President*
EMP: 4
SALES (est): 448.1K **Privately Held**
SIC: 4225 General warehousing & storage

(G-4631)
ATI HOLDINGS LLC
Also Called: ATI Physical Therapy
28535 Dupont Blvd Unit 1 (19966-4799)
PHONE..................302 297-0700
Dave Pinkerton, *Director*
EMP: 21
SALES (corp-wide): 338.3MM **Privately Held**
SIC: 8049 Physical therapist
PA: Ati Holdings, Llc
790 Remington Blvd
Bolingbrook IL 60440
630 296-2222

(G-4632)
ATLANTIC BUDGET INN MILLSBORO
28534 Dupont Blvd (19966-4777)
PHONE..................302 934-6711
EMP: 30
SALES (est): 1.2MM **Privately Held**
SIC: 7011 Hotel Franchised

(G-4633)
BACK BAY PLUMBING
34140 Meadow Ln (19966-6360)
PHONE..................302 945-1210
Craig Rahn, *Owner*
Tracy Rahn, *Co-Owner*
EMP: 7
SALES (est): 250K **Privately Held**
SIC: 1711 Plumbing contractors

(G-4634)
BARSGR LLC
Also Called: Holly Lake Campsite
32087 Holly Lake Rd (19966-4472)
P.O. Box 141 (19966-0141)
PHONE..................302 945-3410
Kenny Hopkins, *Manager*
EMP: 20
SALES (corp-wide): 2MM **Privately Held**
SIC: 7033 Campsite; campgrounds
PA: Barsgr Llc
32193 Winery Way
Lewes DE 19958
302 645-6665

(G-4635)
BAYNUM ENTERPRISES INC
Also Called: T/A Pizza King
28632 Dupont Blvd Unit 20 (19966-4793)
PHONE..................302 934-8699
Todd Ruark, *Branch Mgr*
EMP: 30
SALES (corp-wide): 5MM **Privately Held**
SIC: 5812 6514 Pizza restaurants; dwelling operators, except apartments
PA: Baynum Enterprises, Inc.
300 W Stein Hwy
Seaford DE 19973
302 629-6104

(G-4636)
BAYSIDE LIMOUSINE
34026 Annas Way Unit 1 (19966-3213)
PHONE..................302 644-6999
Tyrone Gale, *President*
EMP: 10
SALES (est): 500K **Privately Held**
SIC: 4119 Limousine rental, with driver

(G-4637)
BAYWOOD GREENS
34026 Annas Way Unit 5 (19966-3213)
PHONE..................302 947-9800
Mark Coty, *Principal*
Daniel Kerley, *VP Bus Dvlpt*
EMP: 4 EST: 2010
SALES (est): 220.2K **Privately Held**
SIC: 8641 Homeowners' association

(G-4638)
BAYWOOD GREENS GOLF CLUB
24 Ofc Rte (19966)
PHONE..................302 947-9225
Robert Tunnell Jr, *Branch Mgr*
EMP: 20
SALES (corp-wide): 4.9MM **Privately Held**
SIC: 7992 5941 5812 Public golf courses; golf goods & equipment; eating places
PA: Baywood Greens Golf Club
32267 Clubhouse Way
Millsboro DE 19966
302 947-9800

(G-4639)
BAYWOOD GREENS GOLF CLUB (PA)
32267 Clubhouse Way (19966-6259)
PHONE..................302 947-9800
Robert Tunnell Jr, *President*
EMP: 44 EST: 1998
SALES (est): 4.9MM **Privately Held**
WEB: www.baywoodgreens.com
SIC: 7992 Public golf courses

(G-4640)
BEACH MOBILE HOME SUPPLY
32695 Long Neck Rd Unit 1 (19966-6693)
PHONE..................302 945-5611
EMP: 2
SALES (est): 79.9K **Privately Held**
SIC: 3585 Refrigeration & heating equipment

(G-4641)
BEEBE HEALTHCARE
28538 Dupont Blvd Unit 2 (19966-4791)
PHONE..................302 934-5052
EMP: 8
SALES (est): 82.2K **Privately Held**
SIC: 8062 General medical & surgical hospitals

(G-4642)
BEEBE MEDICAL CENTER INC
Long Neck Rd (19966)
PHONE..................302 947-9767
EMP: 20
SALES (corp-wide): 447.8MM **Privately Held**
SIC: 8062 General medical & surgical hospitals
PA: Beebe Medical Center, Inc.
424 Savannah Rd
Lewes DE 19958
302 645-3300

(G-4643)
BENNIE SMITH FUNERAL HOME INC
216 S Washington St (19966)
PHONE..................302 934-9019
Bennie Smith, *Manager*
EMP: 6 **Privately Held**
WEB: www.benniesmithfuneralhome.com
SIC: 7261 Funeral director
PA: Bennie Smith Funeral Home, Inc.
717 W Division St
Dover DE 19904

(G-4644)
BETHANY TRAVEL INC
Also Called: Dream Vacations
28412 Dupont Blvd Ste 103 (19966-1227)
PHONE..................302 933-0955
Cynthia McCabe, *President*
Lonny Groton, *Agent*
Linda Sprows, *Agent*
EMP: 5
SQ FT: 800
SALES (est): 1MM **Privately Held**
WEB: www.bethanytravel.com
SIC: 4724 Travel agencies

(G-4645)
BLM INDUSTRIES INC
Also Called: Vickers Heating & Air
19930 Lowes Crossing Rd (19966-2962)
PHONE..................302 238-7745
William Vickers, *President*
Charles L Graves, *Vice Pres*
Janice Vickers, *Treasurer*
EMP: 3
SALES (est): 308.8K **Privately Held**
SIC: 1711 7692 Heating & air conditioning contractors; automotive welding

(G-4646)
BLUE HEN BZZRDS DSPOSE-ALL LLC
34026 Annas Way Unit 3 (19966-3213)
PHONE..................302 856-0913
Rob Tunnel, *Partner*
John Atkins, *Partner*
Gary Conaway, *Partner*
EMP: 14 EST: 2000
SALES (est): 2.1MM **Privately Held**
SIC: 4953 Refuse systems

(G-4647)
BOTTS INDUSTRIES
29535 Whitstone Ln (19966-4752)
PHONE..................302 934-1628
John Botts, *Principal*
EMP: 1
SALES (est): 64.8K **Privately Held**
SIC: 3999 Manufacturing industries

(G-4648)
BREAKWATER CONSTRUCTION ENVMTL
4 Chief Joseph Trl (19966-2018)
PHONE..................302 945-5800
John Fink, *President*
Shaun Fink, *Vice Pres*
EMP: 20
SALES (est): 133.2K **Privately Held**
SIC: 1629 Athletic & recreation facilities construction

(G-4649)
BRIGHT BEGINNINGS CHILD CARE C
29753 John J Williams Hwy (19966-3921)
PHONE..................302 934-1249
EMP: 5
SALES (est): 110.7K **Privately Held**
SIC: 8351 Child day care services

GEOGRAPHIC SECTION
Millsboro - Sussex County (G-4682)

(G-4650)
BURTON REALTY INC
24808 John J Williams Hwy (19966-4983)
PHONE.................302 945-5100
Kathrine Louheed, *President*
EMP: 5
SALES (est): 306.5K **Privately Held**
SIC: 6531 Real estate brokers & agents

(G-4651)
BUZZARDS INC
Longneck Rd (19966)
PHONE.................302 945-3500
Robert Tunnell, *President*
EMP: 4
SALES (est): 270K **Privately Held**
SIC: 4212 4953 Garbage collection & transport, no disposal; rubbish collection & disposal

(G-4652)
C&M CONSTRUCTION COMPANY LLC
Also Called: C & M Roofing & Siding
27324 Johan Williams Hwy (19966)
PHONE.................302 663-0936
Cindy Cruz, *Mng Member*
EMP: 24 **EST:** 2016
SALES (est): 159.1K **Privately Held**
SIC: 1521 General remodeling, single-family houses

(G-4653)
CAKES BY DEE
30790 Hickory Hill Rd (19966-3504)
P.O. Box 1344 (19966-5344)
PHONE.................302 934-7483
Debbie Daisey, *Owner*
EMP: 1
SALES (est): 61.1K **Privately Held**
SIC: 2051 Cakes, bakery; except frozen

(G-4654)
CANDLELIGHT BRIDAL FORMAL TLRG
314 Main St (19966-8414)
P.O. Box 777 (19966-0777)
PHONE.................302 934-8009
Hope T Mitchell, *Partner*
Julia R Cornell, *Partner*
Hope Mitchell, *Partner*
EMP: 6
SQ FT: 1,800
SALES (est): 492.6K **Privately Held**
WEB: www.candlelightbridalshop.com
SIC: 5699 7219 7299 Formal wear; tailor shop, except custom or merchant tailor; clothing rental services

(G-4655)
CAPTAINS GRANT SOLAR 1 INC
Also Called: Captains Grant Hoa
32499 Captains Way (19966-4840)
PHONE.................410 375-2092
Joey Johnson, *President*
EMP: 4
SALES (est): 279.2K **Privately Held**
SIC: 4911 7389 Generation, electric power;

(G-4656)
CARROLL BROTHERS ELECTRIC LLC
24853 Rivers Edge Rd (19966-7217)
PHONE.................302 947-4754
John Ehartshorn, *Principal*
EMP: 5
SALES (est): 142.8K **Privately Held**
SIC: 4911 Electric services

(G-4657)
CASTROL INDUSTRIAL N AMER INC
Also Called: Castrol Premium Lube Express
28569 Dupont Blvd (19966-4798)
PHONE.................302 934-9100
EMP: 57
SALES (corp-wide): 298.7B **Privately Held**
SIC: 2992 Lubricating oils & greases
HQ: Castrol Industrial North America Inc.
150 W Warrenville Rd
Naperville IL 60563
877 641-1600

(G-4658)
CEDAR TREE SURGICAL CENTER
32711 Long Neck Rd (19966-6678)
PHONE.................302 945-9766
Barbara Campilano, *Director*
EMP: 11
SALES (est): 712.9K **Privately Held**
SIC: 8062 General medical & surgical hospitals

(G-4659)
CHILDRENS PLACE CHILD DEV CE
32362 Long Neck Rd Unit 1 (19966-9062)
PHONE.................302 947-4808
EMP: 5
SALES (est): 23.3K **Privately Held**
SIC: 8351 Child day care services

(G-4660)
CHIP VICKIO
30845 Phillips Branch Rd (19966-6405)
PHONE.................302 448-0211
EMP: 1
SALES (est): 37.5K **Privately Held**
SIC: 2741 Miscellaneous publishing

(G-4661)
CHRISTOPHER HANDY
Also Called: Handy Man Maintenance
24872 Doe Bridge Ln (19966-1670)
PHONE.................302 934-1018
Christopher Handy, *Principal*
EMP: 4
SALES (est): 86.8K **Privately Held**
SIC: 7349 Building maintenance services

(G-4662)
CHRISTOPHER T PARSONS
Also Called: Sussex Landscaping & Lawn Care
162 White Pine Dr (19966-8749)
PHONE.................302 947-2380
Christopher T Parsons, *Principal*
EMP: 4
SALES (est): 98.2K **Privately Held**
SIC: 0782 Lawn care services

(G-4663)
COASTAL CHIROPRACTIC LLC
28467 Dupont Blvd Unit 1 (19966-3749)
PHONE.................302 933-0700
Robert Laduca, *Principal*
EMP: 4
SALES (est): 69.2K **Privately Held**
SIC: 8041 Offices & clinics of chiropractors

(G-4664)
COFFEE ARTISAN LLC
718 Phillips Hill Dr (19966-1764)
PHONE.................302 297-8800
Geoffrey Elliott,
Jill Elliott,
◆ **EMP:** 2
SALES (est): 180.3K **Privately Held**
SIC: 3589 Coffee brewing equipment

(G-4665)
COFFIN HARDWOOD FLOORING INC
28539 Dupont Blvd (19966-4798)
P.O. Box 1677 (19966-5677)
PHONE.................302 934-6414
Rolf Albright, *President*
Ronald Coffin, *Vice Pres*
Donna Coffin, *Admin Sec*
EMP: 6
SALES (est): 510.4K **Privately Held**
SIC: 1752 Wood floor installation & refinishing

(G-4666)
COLLINS BROTHERS FARMS
37161 Millsboro Hwy (19966-4169)
PHONE.................302 238-7822
Allan Collins, *Principal*
EMP: 4
SALES: 1MM **Privately Held**
SIC: 0251 0116 Broiling chickens, raising of; soybeans

(G-4667)
COMPLETE TREE CARE INC
Also Called: Complete Lawn Care
30598 Cordrey Rd (19966-4041)
PHONE.................302 945-8289
Dan Atkinson, *President*
EMP: 6
SALES (est): 404.7K **Privately Held**
SIC: 0783 Ornamental shrub & tree services

(G-4668)
COSMIC CUSTOM SCREEN PRINTING
28116 John J Williams Hwy (19966-4002)
PHONE.................302 933-0920
Debbie Bochaud, *Branch Mgr*
EMP: 1 **Privately Held**
SIC: 2759 Screen printing
PA: Cosmic Custom Screen Printing Llc
935 S Black Horse Pike
Williamstown NJ 08094

(G-4669)
COUNTY BANK
25933 School Ln (19966-6265)
PHONE.................302 947-7300
Kathy Coffin, *Branch Mgr*
EMP: 7 **Privately Held**
SIC: 6021 National commercial banks
PA: County Bank
19927 Shuttle Rd
Rehoboth Beach DE 19971

(G-4670)
COUNTY OF SUSSEX
Inland Bays Rgnal Wstwtr Fclty
29445 Inland Bay Rd (19966-2632)
PHONE.................302 947-0864
Justin Mitchell, *District Mgr*
EMP: 13 **Privately Held**
SIC: 4971 Water distribution or supply systems for irrigation
PA: County Of Sussex
2 The Cir
Georgetown DE 19947
302 855-7700

(G-4671)
CROSSINGS AT OAK ORCHARD
Also Called: Suffix Cutlers Sales
27825 Sandy Dr (19966-4605)
PHONE.................302 231-8243
Kathy Foglio, *Vice Pres*
EMP: 4
SALES (est): 166.3K **Privately Held**
SIC: 0175 Apple orchard

(G-4672)
CRUISEONE
32317 Mulligan Way (19966-6267)
PHONE.................302 945-4620
Robert Cardaneo, *Owner*
EMP: 4
SALES (est): 531.7K **Privately Held**
SIC: 4724 Travel agencies

(G-4673)
DAVID G MAJOR ASSOCIATES INC
Also Called: Ci Centre
30165 Ethan Allen Ct (19966-8300)
PHONE.................703 642-7450
David G Major, *President*
Mary Major, *Exec VP*
EMP: 20
SALES (est): 740.5K **Privately Held**
WEB: www.spytrek.com
SIC: 8742 Training & development consultant

(G-4674)
DAVIS TRUCKING & FAMILY LLC
38254 Millsboro Hwy (19966-4164)
PHONE.................302 381-6358
Shannen Davis, *Principal*
Raymond Davis, *Principal*
EMP: 12
SALES (est): 1.2MM **Privately Held**
SIC: 4214 Local trucking with storage

(G-4675)
DELAWARE HOSPICE
315 Old Landing Rd Unit 1 (19966-1210)
PHONE.................302 934-9018
Bill Law, *Technology*
Sandy Farrell, *Administration*
Rose Benn, *Executive Asst*
EMP: 5 **EST:** 2007
SALES (est): 135.3K **Privately Held**
SIC: 8052 Personal care facility

(G-4676)
DELMARVA SPACE SCNCES FNDATION
Also Called: Dssf
10046 Iron Pointe Drv Ext (19966-4264)
PHONE.................302 236-2761
Bob Lingo, *President*
Michael Potter, *Principal*
Jeff Geidel, *Principal*
Ryan Goodwin, *Principal*
Jeremy Kirkendall, *Principal*
EMP: 5
SALES (est): 104.7K **Privately Held**
SIC: 7389

(G-4677)
DENNEY ELECTRIC SUPPLY DEL INC
28635 Dupont Blvd (19966-4784)
PHONE.................302 934-8885
John McCormick, *Principal*
Mark McCormick, *Treasurer*
Rod Gowen, *Director*
John Bruce, *Administration*
EMP: 9
SQ FT: 12,000
SALES (est): 5.8MM **Privately Held**
WEB: www.denneyelectric.com
SIC: 5063 5999 5719 Electrical supplies; electronic parts & equipment; lighting fixtures

(G-4678)
DIAMOND STATE CABINETRY
32627 Millsboro Hwy (19966-3010)
PHONE.................302 250-3531
EMP: 2 **EST:** 2012
SALES (est): 152.1K **Privately Held**
SIC: 2434 Wood kitchen cabinets

(G-4679)
DM HOME MAINTENANCE
34079 Taylor Dr S (19966-6017)
PHONE.................302 945-5050
Donna Messick, *Principal*
EMP: 5
SALES (est): 122.8K **Privately Held**
SIC: 7349 Building maintenance services

(G-4680)
DONAWAY CORPORATION (PA)
Also Called: Donaway Service Station
Rr 24 (19966)
PHONE.................302 934-6226
Bart Donaway, *President*
EMP: 1
SALES (est): 50K **Privately Held**
SIC: 7692 7538 Automotive welding; general automotive repair shops

(G-4681)
DOROSHOW PASQUALE KARWITZ SIEG
Also Called: Doroshow Pasquale Law Offices
28535 Dupont Blvd Unit 2 (19966-4799)
PHONE.................302 934-9400
Debra Aldrich, *Manager*
EMP: 11
SQ FT: 2,194
SALES (corp-wide): 10.6MM **Privately Held**
SIC: 8111 Bankruptcy law
PA: Doroshow Pasquale Krawitz Siegel Bhaya
1202 Kirkwood Hwy
Wilmington DE 19805
302 998-2397

(G-4682)
DOUBLE DIAMONE BUILDERS INC
25187 Banks Rd (19966-4482)
PHONE.................302 945-2512
Brandee East, *President*
EMP: 10
SALES: 110K **Privately Held**
SIC: 1521 New construction, single-family houses

Millsboro - Sussex County (G-4683) GEOGRAPHIC SECTION

(G-4683)
EAST COAST PERENNIALS INC
30366 Cordrey Rd (19966-4042)
PHONE.................................302 945-5853
Andres Burgos, *Principal*
EMP: 1 **EST:** 1989
SALES (est): 110K **Privately Held**
SIC: 3524 Lawn & garden equipment

(G-4684)
EAST MILLSBORO ELEM SCHOOL PTO
29343 Iron Branch Rd (19966)
PHONE.................................302 238-0176
Mary Bixler, *Principal*
EMP: 4
SALES: 54.5K **Privately Held**
SIC: 8641 Parent-teachers' association

(G-4685)
ENTERPRISE RENT-A-CAR
28656 Dupont Blvd (19966-4794)
PHONE.................................302 934-1216
EMP: 8
SALES (est): 101.1K **Privately Held**
SIC: 7514 Passenger car rental

(G-4686)
EQUITY LIFESTYLE PRPTS INC
Also Called: Mariner's Cove
126 Pine St (19966)
PHONE.................................302 945-1544
Tiffany Hernandez,
EMP: 4 **Publicly Held**
SIC: 6515 Mobile home site operators
PA: Equity Lifestyle Properties, Inc.
    2 N Riverside Plz Ste 800
    Chicago IL 60606

(G-4687)
ERIC M DOROSHOW
213 E Dupont Hwy (19966)
PHONE.................................302 934-9400
Eric Doroshow, *Owner*
EMP: 7
SALES (est): 241.7K **Privately Held**
SIC: 8111 General practice attorney, lawyer

(G-4688)
EZ LOANS INC (PA)
28273 Dupont Blvd (19966-4747)
PHONE.................................302 934-5563
John Adkins, *President*
EMP: 17
SALES (est): 4.8MM **Privately Held**
WEB: www.ezloans.com
SIC: 6141 Personal credit institutions

(G-4689)
FERGUSON ENTERPRISES LLC
118 E Dupont Hwy (19966)
PHONE.................................302 934-6040
Steve Boyette, *Manager*
EMP: 8
SALES (corp-wide): 20.7B **Privately Held**
WEB: www.ferguson.com
SIC: 5074 Plumbing fittings & supplies
HQ: Ferguson Enterprises, Llc
    12500 Jefferson Ave
    Newport News VA 23602
    757 874-7795

(G-4690)
FIRST CLASS HEATING & AC INC
28418 Dupont Blvd (19966-1226)
P.O. Box 1264 (19966-5264)
PHONE.................................302 934-8900
Tim Tulice, *Owner*
Mike Kardos, *Division Mgr*
Paula Weir, *Office Mgr*
Rj Hitch, *Manager*
Connor McDonald, *Manager*
EMP: 13
SALES (est): 2.7MM **Privately Held**
WEB: www.firstclass-heating-cooling.net
SIC: 1711 Warm air heating & air conditioning contractor; heating & air conditioning contractors

(G-4691)
FISHERS AUTO PARTS INC
Also Called: NAPA
422 Union St (19966-1203)
PHONE.................................302 934-8088
Wayne Nagee, *Manager*
EMP: 5
SALES (corp-wide): 5.3MM **Privately Held**
WEB: www.fishersautoparts.com
SIC: 5531 5013 Automobile & truck equipment & parts; automotive accessories; automotive supplies & parts
PA: Fisher's Auto Parts Inc
    211 W Market St
    Georgetown DE 19947
    302 856-9591

(G-4692)
FOOT & ANKLE CTR OF DELAWARE
26744 John J Williams Hwy (19966-4667)
PHONE.................................302 945-1221
James Palmer DPM, *Principal*
EMP: 5
SALES (est): 176K **Privately Held**
SIC: 8043 Offices & clinics of podiatrists

(G-4693)
FOX LANDSCAPING CORP
24659 Banks Rd (19966-4487)
PHONE.................................302 945-5656
Chandler Fox, *Principal*
EMP: 4
SALES (est): 169.7K **Privately Held**
SIC: 0782 Landscape contractors

(G-4694)
FRESENIUS MED CARE S DELAWARE
Also Called: Fresenius Med Care Millsboro
30164 Commerce Dr (19966-3585)
PHONE.................................302 934-6342
Pam Cooper, *Manager*
EMP: 15
SALES (corp-wide): 18.3B **Privately Held**
SIC: 8092 Kidney dialysis centers
HQ: Fresenius Medical Care Southern Delaware, Llc
    920 Winter St
    Waltham MA 02451

(G-4695)
FULTON BANK NATIONAL ASSN
Also Called: Property Management Dept., of
28412 Dupont Blvd Ste 106 (19966-1227)
P.O. Box 520, Georgetown (19947-0520)
PHONE.................................302 934-5911
Sandy Craig, *Branch Mgr*
Sandy Chandler, *Manager*
Linda Price, *Admin Sec*
EMP: 8
SALES (corp-wide): 954MM **Publicly Held**
SIC: 6022 State commercial banks
HQ: Fulton Bank, National Association
    1 Penn Sq Ste 1 # 1
    Lancaster PA 17602
    717 581-3166

(G-4696)
GENERAL COATINGS LLC
26492 Shasta Way (19966-4305)
PHONE.................................302 841-7958
EMP: 2 **EST:** 2010
SALES (est): 86.8K **Privately Held**
SIC: 3479 Metal coating & allied service

(G-4697)
GEORGE & LYNCH INC
20631 Betts Rd (19966-4115)
PHONE.................................302 238-7289
Will Robbinson, *Branch Mgr*
EMP: 30
SALES (corp-wide): 111.8MM **Privately Held**
SIC: 1521 Single-family housing construction
PA: George & Lynch, Inc.
    150 Lafferty Ln
    Dover DE 19901
    302 736-3031

(G-4698)
GRAHAMS WIRELESS SOLUTIONS INC
24817 Rivers Edge Rd (19966-7216)
PHONE.................................717 943-0717
Joseph Graham, *President*
EMP: 12
SALES (est): 275K **Privately Held**
SIC: 4812 7389 Cellular telephone services;

(G-4699)
GREEN ACRES HEALTH SYSTEMS
Also Called: Green Valley Terrance
231 S Washington St (19966-1236)
PHONE.................................302 934-7300
Allen Segal, *President*
EMP: 150
SALES (est): 1.2MM
SALES (corp-wide): 29.5MM **Privately Held**
WEB: www.gahsi.com
SIC: 8051 Extended care facility
PA: Green Acres Health Systems Inc
    4 Ivybrook Blvd
    Warminster PA

(G-4700)
GREEN VALLEY TERRACE SNF LLC
Also Called: ATLANTIC SHORES REHABILITATION
231 S Washington St (19966-1236)
PHONE.................................302 934-7300
Allen Segal, *President*
Gary Segal, *Exec VP*
Juliet Fountain, *Office Mgr*
EMP: 185 **EST:** 1960
SQ FT: 37,020
SALES (est): 21.2MM **Privately Held**
SIC: 8051 Convalescent home with continuous nursing care

(G-4701)
H & V FARMS INC
341 Grace St (19966-1906)
PHONE.................................302 934-1320
Vernon Baker Sr, *President*
Harriet Baker, *Principal*
Vernon Baker Jr, *Corp Secy*
EMP: 4
SALES: 900K **Privately Held**
SIC: 0116 0115 0251 Soybeans; corn; broiler, fryer & roaster chickens

(G-4702)
H&R BLOCK INC
Also Called: H & R Block
28417 Dupont Blvd Unit 4 (19966-1209)
PHONE.................................302 934-6178
Elizabeth Whetler, *Owner*
EMP: 6
SALES (corp-wide): 3B **Publicly Held**
SIC: 7291 Tax return preparation services
PA: H&R Block, Inc.
    1 H&R Block Way
    Kansas City MO 64105
    816 854-3000

(G-4703)
HAIR STUDIO II
Long Neck Rd (19966)
P.O. Box 12 (19966-0012)
PHONE.................................302 945-5110
Pam Johnston, *Owner*
EMP: 5
SALES (est): 120K **Privately Held**
SIC: 7241 7231 Barber shops; beauty shops

(G-4704)
HARRY CASWELL INC
32645 Long Neck Rd (19966-6677)
PHONE.................................302 945-5322
Lynne Caswell, *President*
Harry Caswell, *Treasurer*
EMP: 49
SQ FT: 15,000
SALES (est): 8.2MM **Privately Held**
WEB: www.harrycaswellplumbing.com
SIC: 1711 Plumbing contractors

(G-4705)
HENNINGER PRINTING CO INC
208 Main St (19966-8411)
P.O. Box 550 (19966-0550)
PHONE.................................302 934-8119
Judith M Henninger, *President*
Paul Henninger Jr, *Vice Pres*
EMP: 6
SQ FT: 4,000
SALES (est): 1MM **Privately Held**
SIC: 2621 5943 5999 5947 Stationery, envelope & tablet papers; stationery stores; flags; party favors; signs, not made in custom sign painting shops; bridal supplies

(G-4706)
HOOPIN IT UP EMBROIDERY
34491 Sunset Dr (19966-6061)
PHONE.................................302 945-5511
Deborah A Hooper, *Principal*
EMP: 1
SALES (est): 64.4K **Privately Held**
SIC: 2395 Embroidery products, except schiffli machine

(G-4707)
HUNT WANDENDALE CLUB
34068 Village Way (19966-6728)
PHONE.................................302 945-3369
Hank Gonelli, *President*
EMP: 4 **EST:** 2011
SALES (est): 56.5K **Privately Held**
SIC: 7997 Membership sports & recreation clubs

(G-4708)
INDIAN RIVER GOLF CARS DR WLDG
26246 Kathys Way (19966-3218)
PHONE.................................302 947-2044
Mike M Curdy, *Principal*
EMP: 3
SALES (est): 224.5K **Privately Held**
SIC: 8011 7692 5511 Offices & clinics of medical doctors; welding repair; new & used car dealers

(G-4709)
INSURANCE MARKET INC
17 Main St (19966-8408)
P.O. Box 312, Georgetown (19947-0312)
PHONE.................................302 934-9006
Terri L Moor, *Manager*
EMP: 5
SALES (corp-wide): 6.2MM **Privately Held**
SIC: 6411 Insurance agents
PA: The Insurance Market Inc
    310 N Central Ave
    Laurel DE 19956
    302 875-7591

(G-4710)
INTERVET INC (HQ)
29160 Intervet Ln (19966-4217)
PHONE.................................302 934-4341
Christopher Ragland, *President*
Mark Thompson, *Research*
Terri Debord, *Sales Staff*
Terry Stajcar, *Supervisor*
Lynn Miller, *Administration*
◆ **EMP:** 500
SQ FT: 100,000
SALES (est): 138.5MM
SALES (corp-wide): 42.2B **Publicly Held**
WEB: www.intervetusa.com
SIC: 2836 Veterinary biological products
PA: Merck & Co., Inc.
    2000 Galloping Hill Rd
    Kenilworth NJ 07033
    908 740-4000

(G-4711)
JACK DONOVAN
Also Called: Donovan, Jack, Seminars
23868 Samuel Adams Cir (19966-8206)
PHONE.................................410 715-0504
Jack Donovan, *Owner*
EMP: 5
SALES (est): 250K **Privately Held**
WEB: www.jdseminars.com
SIC: 8742 Programmed instruction service

GEOGRAPHIC SECTION
Millsboro - Sussex County (G-4745)

(G-4712)
JACKSON HEWITT INC
Also Called: Jackson Hewitt Tax Service
28412 Dupont Blvd Ste 102 (19966-1227)
PHONE.................................302 934-7430
Joyce Rosas, *Manager*
EMP: 6 **Privately Held**
WEB: www.fremontcomp.com
SIC: 7291 Tax return preparation services
HQ: Jackson Hewitt Inc.
  10 Exchange Pl Fl 27
  Jersey City NJ 07302
  973 630-0617

(G-4713)
JASON M BRADFORD
Also Called: Ever Green Lawns
24681 Wesley Dr (19966-7401)
PHONE.................................302 236-8236
Jason Bradford, *Principal*
EMP: 4 EST: 2009
SALES (est): 155.5K **Privately Held**
SIC: 0782 Lawn care services

(G-4714)
JBR CONTRACTORS INC
30853 Short Cove Ct (19966-7234)
PHONE.................................856 296-9594
Airton Pinto Maria Jr, *President*
Carlos Vicente Ferreira, *Vice Pres*
EMP: 27
SQ FT: 2,000
SALES: 2.1MM **Privately Held**
SIC: 1751 7389 Framing contractor;

(G-4715)
JOHN T ROGERS JR
Rr 6 Box 87a (19966-9806)
PHONE.................................302 945-3016
John T Rogers Jr, *Owner*
EMP: 4
SALES (est): 245.9K **Privately Held**
WEB: www.johntrogers.com
SIC: 1629 Harbor construction

(G-4716)
KENYA GATHER FOUNDATION
23246 Country Living Rd (19966-2848)
PHONE.................................302 382-8227
Alayna Aiken, *Principal*
Tom Angote, *Principal*
Karen Johnson, *Principal*
EMP: 15
SALES (est): 248.6K **Privately Held**
SIC: 7389

(G-4717)
KERSEY HOMES INC
23090 Lakewood Cir (19966-2842)
PHONE.................................302 934-8434
EMP: 8
SALES (est): 665.9K **Privately Held**
SIC: 1521 Single-Family House Construction

(G-4718)
LAURIE ANN FISHINGER
29441 Glenwood Dr (19966-7504)
PHONE.................................570 460-4370
Laurie Fishinger, *Owner*
EMP: 8
SALES (est): 65.7K **Privately Held**
SIC: 8049 Offices of health practitioner

(G-4719)
LEWES SURGICAL AND MED ASSOC
Also Called: Cedar Tree Medical Center
32711 Long Neck Rd (19966-6678)
PHONE.................................302 945-9730
Semaan M Abboud, *Principal*
EMP: 17
SALES (est): 2.2MM **Privately Held**
SIC: 8011 Internal medicine, physician/surgeon

(G-4720)
LEWIS SAND AND GRAVEL LLC
38227 Firemans Rd (19966-3122)
PHONE.................................302 238-0169
Ray Lewis, *Owner*
EMP: 6
SALES (est): 473.2K **Privately Held**
SIC: 1442 Construction sand & gravel

(G-4721)
LITTLE EINSTEINS PRESCHOOL
28253 Dupont Blvd (19966-1223)
PHONE.................................302 933-0600
Lindsey Cannon, *Director*
EMP: 5
SALES (est): 135.1K **Privately Held**
SIC: 8351 Preschool center

(G-4722)
LNS DELIVERY INC
25905 Pear St (19966-6520)
PHONE.................................302 448-6848
EMP: 4 EST: 2010
SALES (est): 376.7K **Privately Held**
SIC: 4212 Delivery service, vehicular

(G-4723)
LONG NECK MED ENTREPRISES LLC
32711 Long Neck Rd (19966-6678)
PHONE.................................302 945-9730
Semaan Abboud MD,
Semaan M Abboud,
EMP: 4
SALES (est): 338.8K **Privately Held**
SIC: 8011 Offices & clinics of medical doctors

(G-4724)
LONG NECK WATER CO
32783 Long Neck Rd Unit 6 (19966-6692)
PHONE.................................302 947-9600
Jim Mooney, *Director*
EMP: 8
SALES (est): 581K **Privately Held**
SIC: 4941 Water supply

(G-4725)
LONGNECK BACKHOE
25509 Guinea Hollow Rd (19966-4921)
PHONE.................................302 945-3429
David Shepherd, *Owner*
EMP: 2
SALES (est): 158.6K **Privately Held**
SIC: 3531 Backhoes

(G-4726)
LONGNECK FAMILY PRACTICE
26744 J J Wllms Hwy 3 (19966)
PHONE.................................302 947-9767
Jeffrey Hawtof MD, *Principal*
EMP: 8
SALES (est): 362.3K **Privately Held**
SIC: 8011 General & family practice, physician/surgeon

(G-4727)
LOWES HOME CENTERS LLC
26688 Centerview Dr (19966-3750)
PHONE.................................302 934-3740
Frank Guidry, *Manager*
EMP: 158
SALES (corp-wide): 71.3B **Publicly Held**
SIC: 5211 5031 5722 5064 Lumber & other building materials; building materials, exterior; building materials, interior; household appliance stores; electrical appliances, television & radio
HQ: Lowe's Home Centers, Llc
  1605 Curtis Bridge Rd
  Wilkesboro NC 28697
  336 658-4000

(G-4728)
LWECO GROUP LLC
Also Called: Master Industrical Catalog
28428 Cedar Ridge Dr (19966-2710)
P.O. Box 368 (19966-0368)
PHONE.................................302 296-8035
Walter J Gurczenski, *Mng Member*
Louise M Gurczenski,
EMP: 6
SQ FT: 1,500
SALES: 1.7MM **Privately Held**
SIC: 5084 Industrial machinery & equipment

(G-4729)
M & D POULTRY SERVICE
26518 Gravel Hill Rd (19966-3417)
PHONE.................................302 934-7050
EMP: 4

SALES (est): 216.8K **Privately Held**
SIC: 0751 8999 Livestock Services Services-Misc

(G-4730)
MA TRANSPORTATION LLC
34016 Sea Otter Way (19966-6465)
PHONE.................................302 588-5435
Murtada Alatta, *Mng Member*
EMP: 8
SALES (est): 385.2K **Privately Held**
SIC: 4731 Freight transportation arrangement

(G-4731)
MAIL STOP
24832 John J Williams Hwy # 1 (19966-4997)
PHONE.................................302 947-4704
Laura Gregory, *Manager*
EMP: 5 EST: 2011
SALES (est): 519.8K **Privately Held**
SIC: 7389 Mailbox rental & related service

(G-4732)
MANUFACTURERS & TRADERS TR CO
Also Called: M&T
499 Mitchell St (19966-9408)
PHONE.................................302 934-2400
John Borges, *Vice Pres*
Jason Joseph, *Manager*
Michelle Rossi, *Manager*
Jay Wiley, *Director*
EMP: 6
SALES (corp-wide): 6.4B **Publicly Held**
WEB: www.mandtbank.com
SIC: 6022 State commercial banks
HQ: Manufacturers And Traders Trust Company
  1 M&T Plz Fl 3
  Buffalo NY 14203
  716 842-4200

(G-4733)
MANUFACTURERS & TRADERS TR CO
Also Called: M&T
28529 Dupont Blvd (19966-4798)
PHONE.................................302 855-2891
Lenny Brittingham, *Manager*
Kelly Sellers, *Manager*
EMP: 8
SALES (corp-wide): 6.4B **Publicly Held**
WEB: www.binghamlegg.com
SIC: 6022 State commercial banks
HQ: Manufacturers And Traders Trust Company
  1 M&T Plz Fl 3
  Buffalo NY 14203
  716 842-4200

(G-4734)
MANUFCTURED HSING CONCEPTS LLC
Also Called: Longneck Housing Specialist
28862 Dupont Blvd (19966-4781)
P.O. Box 1048 (19966-1048)
PHONE.................................302 934-8848
EMP: 64
SALES (est): 2.3MM **Privately Held**
SIC: 6531 Broker of manufactured homes, on site; selling agent, real estate

(G-4735)
MARK WILSON DIGUARDI
Also Called: Champion Exterminators
27046 Merchantman Dr (19966-4512)
PHONE.................................302 897-6625
Mark Wilson Diguardi, *Owner*
EMP: 1
SALES (est): 81K **Privately Held**
SIC: 2879 Exterminating products, for household or industrial use

(G-4736)
MASSEYS LANDING PARK INC
Also Called: Resort At Massey's Landing
20628 Long Beach Dr (19966-4331)
PHONE.................................302 947-2600
Patricia Lavanceau, *President*
EMP: 5 EST: 2001
SALES (est): 124.5K **Privately Held**
SIC: 7033 Campgrounds

(G-4737)
MASTERMARK WOODWORKING INC
25205 Mastermark Ln (19966-2615)
PHONE.................................302 945-9131
Mark K Miller, *Principal*
EMP: 2 EST: 2011
SALES (est): 176.6K **Privately Held**
SIC: 2431 Millwork

(G-4738)
MCNEIL PAVING
32758 Spring Water Dr (19966-7126)
PHONE.................................302 945-7131
Jimmy Neal, *Principal*
EMP: 5 EST: 2008
SALES (est): 356.8K **Privately Held**
SIC: 1611 Surfacing & paving

(G-4739)
MEARS BASEBALL INSTRUCTION
24975 Radish Rd (19966-3335)
PHONE.................................302 448-9713
EMP: 4
SALES (est): 38.1K **Privately Held**
SIC: 7997 Baseball club, except professional & semi-professional

(G-4740)
MEDICAL REIMBURSEMENT SOL
29517 Glenwood Dr (19966-7503)
PHONE.................................516 809-6812
Paul Newman, *Principal*
EMP: 5
SALES (est): 229.2K **Privately Held**
SIC: 8099 Health & allied services

(G-4741)
MELSON FUNERAL SERVICES
Longneck Rd (19966)
P.O. Box 100, Frankford (19945-0100)
PHONE.................................302 945-9000
A Douglas Melson, *Owner*
EMP: 6
SALES (est): 299.9K **Privately Held**
SIC: 7261 Funeral home

(G-4742)
MERCK & CO INC
28387 Dupont Blvd (19966-4789)
P.O. Box 537 (19966-0537)
PHONE.................................410 860-2227
Larry Manogue, *Branch Mgr*
EMP: 45
SALES (corp-wide): 42.2B **Publicly Held**
SIC: 2834 Pharmaceutical preparations
PA: Merck & Co., Inc.
  2000 Galloping Hill Rd
  Kenilworth NJ 07033
  908 740-4000

(G-4743)
MERCK AND COMPANY INC
Also Called: Merck Animal Health
29160 Intervet Ln (19966-4217)
PHONE.................................302 934-8051
Rose Collins, *Principal*
Theodore Larason, *COO*
Staci Kleven, *Opers Staff*
Mike Hammond, *Production*
Brandon Hudson, *Production*
▲ EMP: 34
SALES (est): 9.6MM **Privately Held**
SIC: 2834 Pharmaceutical preparations

(G-4744)
MID SUSSEX RESCUE SQUAD INC
31738 Indian Mission Rd (19966-4911)
PHONE.................................302 945-2680
Raymond Johnson, *President*
Henry Colon, *Bd of Directors*
EMP: 23
SALES: 1.3MM **Privately Held**
WEB: www.midsussexrescuesquad.com
SIC: 8999 Search & rescue service

(G-4745)
MID-ATLANTIC ELEC SVCS INC
24556 Betts Pond Rd (19966-1560)
PHONE.................................302 945-2555
Joseph Noble, *President*

Millsboro - Sussex County (G-4746) — GEOGRAPHIC SECTION

EMP: 48 EST: 2010
SQ FT: 3,200
SALES (est): 7.8MM Privately Held
SIC: 1731 General electrical contractor

(G-4746)
MID-ATLANTIC FMLY PRACTICE LLC
28538 Dupont Blvd Unit 1 (19966-4791)
PHONE.................302 934-0944
Daryl G Sharman, *Representative*
EMP: 24
SALES (corp-wide): 3.9MM Privately Held
SIC: 8011 General & family practice, physician/surgeon
PA: Mid-Atlantic Family Practice, Llc
20251 John J Williams Hwy
Lewes DE 19958
302 644-6860

(G-4747)
MID-COUNTY ELECTRIC INC
24556 Betts Pond Rd (19966-1560)
P.O. Box 951 (19966-0951)
PHONE.................302 934-8304
Judith K Doughty, *President*
EMP: 12
SQ FT: 1,600
SALES: 740K Privately Held
SIC: 1731 General electrical contractor

(G-4748)
MILLSBORO ART LEAGUE INC
103 Main St (19966-8410)
P.O. Box 1043 (19966-1043)
PHONE.................302 934-6440
Deborah Duseth, *President*
Ron Lightcap, *Vice Pres*
EMP: 4
SALES (est): 145.6K Privately Held
SIC: 8699 Charitable organization

(G-4749)
MILLSBORO FAMILY PRACTICE PA
201 Laurel Rd (19966-1732)
PHONE.................302 934-5626
Lisa A Martin MD, *President*
EMP: 7
SALES (est): 498.9K Privately Held
SIC: 8011 General & family practice, physician/surgeon

(G-4750)
MILLSBORO LANES INC
Also Called: Millsboro Bowling Center
213 Mitchell St (19966-9402)
PHONE.................302 934-0400
Craig Smith, *Partner*
EMP: 12
SQ FT: 20,000
SALES (est): 566.3K Privately Held
SIC: 7933 5813 Ten pin center; bar (drinking places)

(G-4751)
MILLSBORO LITTLE LEAGUE
262 W State St (19966-1507)
PHONE.................302 934-1806
Mark Cordrey, *Principal*
EMP: 10
SALES (est): 69.9K Privately Held
SIC: 7997 Membership sports & recreation clubs

(G-4752)
MILLSBORO VILLAGE I LLC
701 Stanford Bratton Dr (19966-1268)
PHONE.................302 678-9400
William B Duffy Jr,
Maggie Cook Pleasant,
EMP: 9
SALES (est): 454.5K Privately Held
SIC: 6513 Apartment building operators

(G-4753)
MOORE & LIND INC
Also Called: Indian River Land Company
28448 Dupont Blvd (19966-4707)
PHONE.................302 934-8818
Lynn W Moore, *President*
Cathi Lind, *Vice Pres*
Carlton Moore, *Vice Pres*
Terry L Lind, *Treasurer*
Judy A Moore, *Admin Sec*
EMP: 5
SQ FT: 2,000
SALES: 315K Privately Held
WEB: www.indianriverland.com
SIC: 6531 Real estate agent, commercial; real estate agent, residential; rental agent, real estate; real estate managers

(G-4754)
MOTHER GOOSE CHILDRENS CENTER
27275 Dagsboro Rd (19966-3721)
P.O. Box 233 (19966-0233)
PHONE.................302 934-8454
Sarah Thoroughgood, *President*
EMP: 5
SALES (est): 198.4K Privately Held
SIC: 8351 Preschool center

(G-4755)
MOUNT AIRE FARMS OF DELAWA
29005 John J Williams Hwy (19966-4095)
P.O. Box 1320 (19966-5320)
PHONE.................302 934-4048
EMP: 5 EST: 2007
SALES (est): 210K Privately Held
SIC: 0191 General Crop Farm

(G-4756)
MOUNTAIRE FARMS DELAWARE INC (HQ)
29005 John J Williams Hwy (19966-4095)
P.O. Box 1320 (19966-5320)
PHONE.................302 934-1100
Paul Downs, *CEO*
Ronald Cameron, *Ch of Bd*
Dee Ann English, *Exec VP*
Phil Plylar, *Vice Pres*
Quinton Hull, *Export Mgr*
◆ EMP: 15
SQ FT: 20,000
SALES (est): 427.9MM
SALES (corp-wide): 1.4B Privately Held
SIC: 2015 Poultry slaughtering & processing
PA: Mountaire Corporation
1901 Napa Valley Dr
Little Rock AR 72212
501 372-6524

(G-4757)
MSB ENTERPRISE PARTNERS LLC
24912 Pot Bunker Way (19966-6279)
PHONE.................302 947-0736
Martha McKinley,
EMP: 5
SALES (est): 161.1K Privately Held
SIC: 7389 Purchasing service;

(G-4758)
NANTICOKE INDIAN MUSEUM
27073 John J Williams Hwy (19966-4642)
PHONE.................302 945-7022
Herman Robbins, *Chief*
Leoya Wright, *Director*
EMP: 5
SALES: 101.1K Privately Held
SIC: 8412 Museum

(G-4759)
NANTICOKE SHORES ASSOC LLC
Also Called: Rehoboth Shores
26335 Goosepond Rd (19966-6945)
PHONE.................302 945-1500
Richard Berman,
Malcolm Bermen,
EMP: 11
SALES (est): 890.6K Privately Held
WEB: www.rehobothshores.com
SIC: 6515 6531 Mobile home site operators; real estate agents & managers

(G-4760)
NATIONAL MENTOR HOLDINGS INC
Also Called: Delaware Mentor
28417 Dupont Blvd (19966-1209)
PHONE.................732 627-9890
EMP: 21
SALES (corp-wide): 1.4B Publicly Held
SIC: 8082 8361 Home Health Care Services Residential Care Services
HQ: National Mentor Holdings, Inc.
313 Congress St Fl 5
Boston MA 02210
617 790-4800

(G-4761)
NATIONAL MENTOR HOLDINGS INC
Also Called: Delaware Mentor
230 Mitchell St (19966-9402)
PHONE.................302 934-0512
EMP: 10
SALES (corp-wide): 310.7MM Privately Held
SIC: 8082 8361 Home health care services; home for the mentally handicapped
HQ: National Mentor Holdings, Inc.
313 Congress St Fl 5
Boston MA 02210
617 790-4800

(G-4762)
NORTHEAST RALLY CLUB
213 Dodd St (19966-1138)
P.O. Box 547 (19966-0547)
PHONE.................302 934-1246
EMP: 4 EST: 2010
SALES (est): 82.3K Privately Held
SIC: 7997 Membership sports & recreation clubs

(G-4763)
NRG ENERGY INC
Burton Island Rd (19966)
PHONE.................302 934-3537
Jim Spencer, *Branch Mgr*
EMP: 180 Publicly Held
WEB: www.nrgenergy.com
SIC: 4911 Electric services
PA: Nrg Energy, Inc.
804 Carnegie Ctr
Princeton NJ 08540

(G-4764)
NU-TECH MASONRY INC
Rr 2 Box 332f (19966-9802)
P.O. Box 806 (19966-0806)
PHONE.................302 934-5660
Steven Short, *President*
EMP: 12 EST: 1992
SALES: 900K Privately Held
WEB: www.nutechstone.com
SIC: 1741 Masonry & other stonework

(G-4765)
O B PNTG & POWERWASHING INC
23031 Dennis Ln (19966-3144)
PHONE.................302 238-7384
EMP: 5 EST: 2008
SALES: 397K Privately Held
SIC: 1721 Painting/Paper Hanging Contractor

(G-4766)
OAK ORCHARD-RIVERDALE AMERICAN
Also Called: Oak Orchard AM Legion 28
31768 Legion Rd (19966-7114)
PHONE.................302 945-1673
Casmere Stasack, *President*
EMP: 15
SQ FT: 1,600
SALES: 1.4MM Privately Held
SIC: 8641 Veterans' organization

(G-4767)
OLD LANDING II LP
29320 White St Unit 400 (19966-1124)
PHONE.................302 934-1871
William Duffy, *Principal*
EMP: 8
SALES (est): 315.3K Privately Held
SIC: 6513 Apartment building operators

(G-4768)
PARADISE GRILL
27344 Bay Walk (19966-6392)
PHONE.................302 945-4500
EMP: 6
SALES (est): 769.3K Privately Held
SIC: 5099 Durable goods

(G-4769)
PARKER BLOCK CO INC (HQ)
30234 Millsboro Hwy (19966)
PHONE.................302 934-9237
Marvin McCray, *Principal*
Brad Black, *Principal*
Doug Clarke, *Principal*
Jimmy Conley, *Principal*
Mike Tang, *Principal*
EMP: 25
SQ FT: 1,000
SALES (est): 8.1MM
SALES (corp-wide): 65.8MM Privately Held
SIC: 5032 Brick, stone & related material
PA: Ernest Maier, Inc.
4700 Annapolis Rd
Bladensburg MD 20710
301 927-8300

(G-4770)
PATRICIA DEGIROLANO DAY CARE
32909 Long Neck Rd (19966-6690)
P.O. Box 344 (19966-0344)
PHONE.................302 947-2874
Patricia Degirolano, *Principal*
EMP: 5
SALES (est): 76.9K Privately Held
SIC: 8351 Group day care center

(G-4771)
PAUL G COLLINS DDS
560 W Dupont Hwy (19966)
PHONE.................302 934-8005
Paul Collins, *Principal*
EMP: 4
SALES (est): 233.8K Privately Held
SIC: 8021 Dentists' office

(G-4772)
PEARL CLINIC LLC
230 Mitchell St Ste B (19966-9402)
P.O. Box 489, Dagsboro (19939-0489)
PHONE.................302 648-2099
Sherin Ibrahim, *Principal*
EMP: 5
SALES (est): 347.5K Privately Held
SIC: 8099 Health & allied services

(G-4773)
PELICAN BAY GROUP INC
Also Called: Sea Esta Motel 2
100 Rudder Rd (19966-6636)
P.O. Box 4 (19966-0004)
PHONE.................302 945-5900
George A Metz III, *President*
EMP: 8
SQ FT: 325
SALES: 620K Privately Held
SIC: 7011 Motels

(G-4774)
PENINSULA
32981 Peninsula Esplanade (19966-7300)
PHONE.................302 945-4768
Sarah Shoemaker, *Principal*
EMP: 4
SALES (est): 284.1K Privately Held
SIC: 7997 Country club, membership

(G-4775)
PENINSULA AT LONG NECK LLC
468 Bay Farm Rd (19966)
PHONE.................302 947-4717
EMP: 6
SALES (est): 270.8K Privately Held
SIC: 7992 Public golf courses

(G-4776)
PENINSULA DENTAL LLC
26670 Centerview Dr # 19 (19966-3584)
PHONE.................302 297-3750
John T Moore, *Principal*
EMP: 5
SALES (est): 430.1K Privately Held
SIC: 8021 Dental clinic

(G-4777)
PENINSULA HEALTH LLC
26744 J J Williams 7 (19966)
PHONE.................302 945-0440
Joseph Baran, *Principal*
EMP: 5

GEOGRAPHIC SECTION
Millsboro - Sussex County (G-4809)

SALES (est): 297K **Privately Held**
SIC: 8099 Health & allied services

(G-4778)
PENINSULA PLASTIC SURGERY PC
30265 Commerce Dr # 208 (19966-3728)
PHONE................302 663-0119
Vincent Perrotta MD, *President*
EMP: 9
SALES (est): 431.2K **Privately Held**
SIC: 8011 Plastic surgeon

(G-4779)
PENINSULA VETERINARY SVCS LLC
32038 Long Neck Rd (19966-6228)
PHONE................302 947-0719
April Reid,
EMP: 5
SALES (est): 204.1K **Privately Held**
SIC: 0742 Animal hospital services, pets & other animal specialties

(G-4780)
PEOPLES PLACE II INC
30265 Commerce Dr # 201 (19966-3593)
PHONE................302 934-0300
Del Failing Jr, *Branch Mgr*
EMP: 96
SALES (corp-wide): 7.1MM **Privately Held**
SIC: 8351 Child day care services
PA: People's Place Ii, Inc.
1129 Airport Rd
Milford DE 19963
302 422-8033

(G-4781)
PETITE HAIR DESIGNS
Long Neck Rd Palmer Shpng (19966)
PHONE................302 945-2595
Terry Roberts Beiner, *Owner*
Terry Roberts-Beiner, *Owner*
EMP: 8 EST: 1992
SALES (est): 134K **Privately Held**
SIC: 7231 Hairdressers

(G-4782)
PLANTATION LAKES HOMEOWNERS
29787 Plntn Lakes Blvd (19966)
PHONE................302 934-5200
Keith Hines, *Principal*
EMP: 4
SALES (est): 56K **Privately Held**
SIC: 8699 Membership organizations

(G-4783)
PNC BANK NATIONAL ASSOCIATION
104 Main St (19966-8409)
P.O. Box 507 (19966-0507)
PHONE................302 934-3106
Scott E Bagshaw, *Branch Mgr*
Sheree Silva, *Branch Mgr*
EMP: 25
SALES (corp-wide): 19.9B **Publicly Held**
WEB: www.pncfunds.com
SIC: 6021 National trust companies with deposits, commercial
HQ: Pnc Bank, National Association
222 Delaware Ave
Wilmington DE 19801
877 762-2000

(G-4784)
POULTRY LITTER SOLUTIONS LLC
28194 Fox Run Rd (19966-1524)
PHONE................302 245-5377
David Size,
Bryan Hospic,
Janit London,
EMP: 1
SALES (est): 35.4K **Privately Held**
SIC: 2873 Fertilizers: natural (organic), except compost

(G-4785)
POWERBACK SERVICE LLC
30148 Mitchell St (19966)
PHONE................302 934-1901
Matt Williams, *Owner*
EMP: 6 EST: 2008

SALES (est): 576.6K **Privately Held**
SIC: 5063 Generators

(G-4786)
POWERS PUBLISHING GROUP
29549 Whitstone Ln (19966-4752)
PHONE................302 519-8575
Bryan Powers, *Principal*
EMP: 1
SALES (est): 72.2K **Privately Held**
SIC: 2741 Miscellaneous publishing

(G-4787)
POWERSCAPE LLC
34438 Dog Wood Rd (19966-6386)
PHONE................302 945-4626
Michael Humphrey,
Russel Snyder Jr,
EMP: 6
SALES: 500K **Privately Held**
WEB: www.powerscape.com
SIC: 3589 Sewer cleaning equipment, power

(G-4788)
RENT-A-CENTER INC
28544 Dupont Blvd Unit 9 (19966-4792)
PHONE................302 934-6700
Cathy Rogers, *Manager*
EMP: 5
SALES (corp-wide): 2.6B **Publicly Held**
WEB: www.rentacenter.com
SIC: 7359 Appliance rental
PA: Rent-A-Center, Inc.
5501 Headquarters Dr
Plano TX 75024
972 801-1100

(G-4789)
RICHARD D WHALEY CNSTR LLC
29952 Lewis Rd (19966-4740)
PHONE................302 934-9525
Richard D Whaley,
EMP: 5
SQ FT: 2,400
SALES (est): 456.6K **Privately Held**
SIC: 1521 1771 Single-family housing construction; concrete work

(G-4790)
RICKARDS AUTO BODY
28656 Dupont Blvd (19966-4794)
PHONE................302 934-9600
EMP: 5
SALES (est): 94.4K **Privately Held**
SIC: 7532 Paint shop, automotive

(G-4791)
RIDDLES MASONRY
22689 Riddle Rd (19966-3090)
PHONE................302 238-7225
Russell Allen, *Owner*
EMP: 6
SALES (est): 304.3K **Privately Held**
SIC: 1741 Bricklaying

(G-4792)
RIVERDALE PARK LLC
28301 Chief Rd (19966-4582)
PHONE................302 945-2475
Kenneth S Clark Sr, *Owner*
Charles C Clark, *Co-Owner*
Kenneth Clark Jr, *Co-Owner*
EMP: 5
SQ FT: 600
SALES: 800K **Privately Held**
SIC: 7011 0191 Resort hotel; general farms, primarily crop

(G-4793)
ROBERT HOYT & CO
Also Called: Hoyt, Robert M & Co LLC CPA
218 N Dupont (19966)
P.O. Box 818 (19966-0818)
PHONE................302 934-6688
W H Pusey, *Owner*
EMP: 8
SALES (est): 707.5K **Privately Held**
SIC: 8721 Certified public accountant

(G-4794)
ROBINSON EXPORT & IMPORT CORP
Also Called: Reico Kitchen & Bath
28412 Dupont Blvd Ste 106 (19966-1227)
PHONE................410 219-7200
Tessa Hammer, *Branch Mgr*
EMP: 5
SALES (corp-wide): 105.2MM **Privately Held**
WEB: www.reico.com
SIC: 5031 Kitchen cabinets
PA: Robinson Export And Import Corporation
6790 Commercial Dr
Springfield VA 22151
703 245-8322

(G-4795)
ROSA M CUSTIS
Also Called: Kidz Korner Home Daycare
436 Old Landing Rd (19966-1809)
PHONE................302 934-0541
Rosa M Custis, *Principal*
EMP: 5
SALES (est): 49.5K **Privately Held**
SIC: 8351 Group day care center

(G-4796)
ROUTE 24 ANIMAL HOSPITAL
26984 John J Williams Hwy (19966-4640)
PHONE................302 945-2330
EMP: 7
SALES (est): 268K **Privately Held**
SIC: 8062 0742 General medical & surgical hospitals; animal hospital services, pets & other animal specialties

(G-4797)
SALVATION ARMY
559 E Dupont Hwy (19966-1914)
PHONE................302 934-3730
Christy Cugno, *Branch Mgr*
EMP: 150
SALES (corp-wide): 2.2B **Privately Held**
WEB: www.salvationarmy-usaeast.org
SIC: 8322 8661 Individual & family services; religious organizations
HQ: The Salvation Army
440 W Nyack Rd Ofc
West Nyack NY 10994
845 620-7200

(G-4798)
SAMS SIGN
25768 Salt Grass Rd (19966-7242)
PHONE................302 947-8152
Sam Debella, *Principal*
EMP: 1 EST: 2011
SALES (est): 76.5K **Privately Held**
SIC: 3993 Signs & advertising specialties

(G-4799)
SCHRIDER ENTERPRISES INC
398 W State St (19966)
PHONE................302 934-1900
William Schrider, *President*
Rita Schrider, *Admin Sec*
EMP: 15
SALES (est): 970K **Privately Held**
SIC: 7539 7549 Automotive repair shops; lubrication service, automotive

(G-4800)
SHORE MASONRY INC
32405 Mermaid Run (19966-4462)
PHONE................302 945-5933
Donald Ireland, *President*
April Ireland, *Vice Pres*
EMP: 7
SALES: 1MM **Privately Held**
SIC: 1741 1771 Masonry & other stonework; concrete work

(G-4801)
SHORE SHUTTERS AND SHADE
26760 Meadowlark Loop (19966-6829)
PHONE................302 569-1738
Todd Ellis, *Principal*
EMP: 3
SALES (est): 179.2K **Privately Held**
SIC: 3442 Shutters, door or window: metal

(G-4802)
SOUTHERN DEL PHYSCL THERAPY
26089 Shpps At Long Nck (19966-5981)
PHONE................302 947-4460
Deanna Call, *Exec Dir*
EMP: 4 **Privately Held**
SIC: 8049 Physical therapist
PA: Southern Delaware Physical Therapy Inc
701 Savannah Rd Ste A
Lewes DE 19958

(G-4803)
SPRING COMMUNICATIONS INC
Also Called: AT&T Authorized Retailer
26670 Centerview Dr # 14 (19966-3584)
PHONE................302 297-2000
EMP: 5
SALES (corp-wide): 280MM **Privately Held**
SIC: 4812 Radio telephone communication
HQ: Spring Communications, Inc.
12550 Reed Rd Ste 100
Sugar Land TX 77478
801 277-7777

(G-4804)
STOP TRAFFIC
408 Circle Rd (19966-8730)
PHONE................302 604-1176
EMP: 2
SALES (est): 98.3K **Privately Held**
SIC: 3993 Signs & advertising specialties

(G-4805)
STRANDS PRPRTY PRSERVATION LLC
26035 Oak St Ste 101 (19966-3430)
PHONE................302 381-9792
Tashyne Strand,
EMP: 8
SALES (est): 294.4K **Privately Held**
SIC: 8741 7389 Business management;

(G-4806)
SUSSEX CNTY MANUFACTRD HOUSING
35124 Seahawk Ln (19966-6960)
PHONE................302 945-2122
EMP: 6
SALES (est): 94.7K **Privately Held**
SIC: 8641 Civic/Social Association

(G-4807)
SUSSEX FENCING
John J Williams Hwy (19966)
PHONE................302 945-7008
Rob Haas, *Owner*
EMP: 5
SALES: 2MM **Privately Held**
SIC: 1799 Fence construction

(G-4808)
SUSSEX LUMBER COMPANY INC
655 Mitchell St (19966-9432)
P.O. Box 509 (19966-0509)
PHONE................302 934-8128
Jeffrey Revell, *President*
Donna Revell, *Vice Pres*
Barbara Betts, *Sales Staff*
Allen Hudson, *Sales Associate*
Debbie Ash, *Sales Executive*
EMP: 29 EST: 2001
SQ FT: 32,500
SALES (est): 9.3MM **Privately Held**
SIC: 5031 Lumber, plywood & millwork

(G-4809)
T & C ENTERPRISE INCORPORATED
Also Called: Tri-State Mobile Home Supply
26007 Pugs Xing (19966-3995)
PHONE................302 934-8080
Greson Duox, *President*
Patricia L Taylor, *President*
Willie Taylor, *Vice Pres*
EMP: 5
SQ FT: 6,400
SALES (est): 794.2K **Privately Held**
SIC: 5039 5271 5072 Mobile homes; mobile home equipment; mobile home parts & accessories; builders' hardware

Millsboro - Sussex County (G-4810)

(G-4810)
TAIL BANGERS INC
24546 Betts Pond Rd (19966-1560)
PHONE..................302 947-4900
Lisa Sinclair, *President*
EMP: 28
SQ FT: 5,000
SALES (est): 3.7MM **Privately Held**
SIC: 5149 Dog food

(G-4811)
TAILBANGERS
24546 Betts Pond Rd (19966-1560)
PHONE..................302 934-1125
Lisa St Clair, *Owner*
EMP: 60
SALES (est): 4.2MM **Privately Held**
SIC: 5149 Dog food

(G-4812)
TH WHITE GENERAL CONTRACT
32783 Long Neck Rd Unit 2 (19966-6692)
PHONE..................302 945-1829
Thomas H White, *Principal*
EMP: 5
SALES (est): 681.4K **Privately Held**
SIC: 5082 General construction machinery & equipment

(G-4813)
TO DO YARD GUYS
28244 Chippewa Ave (19966-2536)
PHONE..................302 947-9475
Don Hocker, *Principal*
EMP: 4
SALES (est): 104.9K **Privately Held**
SIC: 8031 Offices & clinics of osteopathic physicians

(G-4814)
TRIPLE D CHARTERS LLC
24386 Godwin School Rd (19966-3682)
PHONE..................302 934-6837
EMP: 4
SALES (est): 154.2K **Privately Held**
SIC: 4141 Local Bus Charter Service

(G-4815)
TSC ENTERPRISES LLC
27380 William Street Rd (19966-3924)
P.O. Box 1267 (19966-5267)
PHONE..................302 934-6158
Tony Hudson, *Pres*
EMP: 4
SALES (est): 550.4K **Privately Held**
SIC: 7538 General automotive repair shops

(G-4816)
TUNNELL COMPANIES LP (PA)
Also Called: Tunnel Industries
34026 Annas Way Unit 1 (19966-3213)
PHONE..................302 945-9300
Robert W Tunnell III, *Partner*
Robert Tunnell Jr, *General Ptnr*
Dawn Haeffner, *Comms Dir*
EMP: 40
SQ FT: 10,000
SALES (est): 15.2MM **Privately Held**
WEB: www.potnets.com
SIC: 6515 6531 6519 Mobile home site operators; real estate agents & managers; real property lessors

(G-4817)
UNITED3 SERVICES INC
24789 Rivers Edge Rd (19966-7215)
PHONE..................302 233-5985
Christopher Birney, *President*
Edwin Nanavati, *Vice Pres*
EMP: 4
SALES (est): 179.9K **Privately Held**
SIC: 7373 Computer integrated systems design

(G-4818)
URIS LLC (PA)
Also Called: Uris Salvage Auto Inspections
32783 Long Neck Rd Unit 3 (19966-6692)
PHONE..................302 469-7000
Leo Sticinski, *President*
EMP: 5
SALES (est): 623.9K **Privately Held**
SIC: 7549 Inspection & diagnostic service, automotive

(G-4819)
V F W SUSSEX MEM POST 7422
28659 Dupont Blvd (19966-4784)
P.O. Box 606 (19966-0606)
PHONE..................302 934-9967
EMP: 6
SALES: 24.7K **Privately Held**
SIC: 8641 Civic/Social Association

(G-4820)
VIRGIL P ELLWANGER
Mllsboro Vlg Grn Rr 24 (19966)
P.O. Box 216 (19966-0216)
PHONE..................302 934-8083
Virgil Ellwanger, *Owner*
EMP: 6
SALES (est): 628.9K **Privately Held**
SIC: 6411 Insurance agents, brokers & service

(G-4821)
VISION SALON & BARBERSHOP
401 W Dupont Hwy Ste 103 (19966)
PHONE..................302 934-9301
Keith Harmon, *Owner*
EMP: 4
SALES (est): 82.1K **Privately Held**
SIC: 7241 7231 Barber shops; beauty shops

(G-4822)
W T SCHRIDER & SONS INC
24572 Betts Pond Rd (19966-1560)
PHONE..................302 934-1900
William Schrider, *President*
EMP: 10
SQ FT: 6,000
SALES (est): 2.3MM **Privately Held**
SIC: 5085 Industrial supplies

(G-4823)
WASTE INDUSTRIES LLC
28471 John J Williams Hwy (19966-4098)
PHONE..................302 934-1364
EMP: 5
SALES (corp-wide): 1.1B **Privately Held**
SIC: 4953 Garbage: collecting, destroying & processing
HQ: Waste Industries, Llc
3301 Benson Dr Ste 601
Raleigh NC 27609
919 325-3000

(G-4824)
WATSON FUNERAL HOME INC
Also Called: Rkb Funeral Inc Trading
211 S Washington St (19966-8425)
P.O. Box 125 (19966-0125)
PHONE..................302 934-7842
Robert Herrington, *President*
Tia Watson, *Treasurer*
EMP: 12
SALES (est): 1.1MM **Privately Held**
SIC: 7261 Funeral home

(G-4825)
WELLNESS AND REJUVENATION
30996 Puseys Rd (19966-2913)
PHONE..................732 977-6958
Tiffany Siegler, *Principal*
EMP: 6 **EST:** 2017
SALES (est): 78.3K **Privately Held**
SIC: 8099 Health & allied services

(G-4826)
WESTWOOD FARMS INCORPORATED
21906 Esham Ln (19966-3032)
PHONE..................302 238-7141
Bruce Esham, *President*
EMP: 10
SALES: 2MM **Privately Held**
SIC: 1542 0111 0251 Farm building construction; wheat; broiler, fryer & roaster chickens

(G-4827)
WHITE HOUSE BEACH INC
35266 Fishermans Rd # 2 (19966-6755)
PHONE..................302 945-3032
William H Showell, *President*
John Showell, *Corp Secy*
Sam Showell, *Vice Pres*
EMP: 10
SALES (est): 600K **Privately Held**
SIC: 6515 Mobile home site operators

(G-4828)
WILMINGTON SAVINGS FUND SOC
25926 Plaza Dr (19966-4998)
PHONE..................302 360-0020
Cliff Wiggins, *Opers Staff*
Sarah Slaysman, *Branch Mgr*
EMP: 4
SALES (corp-wide): 455.5MM **Publicly Held**
SIC: 6022 State commercial banks
HQ: Wilmington Savings Fund Society
500 Delaware Ave Ste 500 # 500
Wilmington DE 19801
302 792-6000

(G-4829)
WOOLEY BULLY INC
Also Called: Labrador, The
25605 Rogers Rd (19966-4943)
PHONE..................302 542-3613
Roger B Wooleyhan Jr, *President*
Elizebeth M Wooleyhan, *Admin Sec*
EMP: 6 **EST:** 2004
SALES (est): 324K **Privately Held**
SIC: 5146 Fish & seafoods

(G-4830)
WWC III
34564 Pear Tree Rd (19966-3040)
PHONE..................302 238-7778
William W Clifton III, *Principal*
EMP: 10 **EST:** 2009
SALES (est): 630K **Privately Held**
SIC: 4212 Local trucking, without storage

(G-4831)
WWC III TRUCKING LLC
34564 Pear Tree Rd (19966-3040)
PHONE..................302 238-7778
Mary Clifton, *Principal*
EMP: 4
SALES (est): 589.1K **Privately Held**
SIC: 3537 Industrial trucks & tractors

Millville
Sussex County

(G-4832)
AFTERGLO BEAUTY SPA
22 Cedar Dr (19967)
PHONE..................302 537-7546
Sheila Rebbingham, *Owner*
EMP: 6 **EST:** 2011
SALES (est): 138.9K **Privately Held**
SIC: 7991 7231 Spas; beauty shops

(G-4833)
ALL ABOUT U EVADA CONCEPT (PA)
35825 Atlantic Ave (19967-6908)
PHONE..................302 539-1925
Cathy Lynch, *Owner*
EMP: 7
SALES (est): 304.8K **Privately Held**
SIC: 7231 Unisex hair salons

(G-4834)
BEACHVIEW CHIROPRACTIC CENTER
35202 Atlantic Ave (19967-6901)
PHONE..................302 539-7063
Donald Hattier, *Owner*
EMP: 4
SALES (est): 230K **Privately Held**
SIC: 8041 Offices & clinics of chiropractors

(G-4835)
BEACHVIEW FAMILY HEALTH
35202 Atlantic Ave (19967-6901)
PHONE..................302 537-8318
Julie Hattier, *Principal*
EMP: 5
SALES (est): 199.2K **Privately Held**
SIC: 8099 Health & allied services

(G-4836)
BEEBE MEDICAL CENTER INC
32550 Docs Pl (19967-6975)
PHONE..................302 541-4175
EMP: 99
SALES (corp-wide): 447.8MM **Privately Held**
SIC: 8011 Medical centers
PA: Beebe Medical Center, Inc.
424 Savannah Rd
Lewes DE 19958
302 645-3300

(G-4837)
BETHANY BCH HAIR SNIPPERY INC
32566 Docs Pl Unit 6 (19967-6959)
P.O. Box 923, Bethany Beach (19930-0923)
PHONE..................302 539-8344
John Scordo, *President*
EMP: 5
SALES (est): 128.5K **Privately Held**
SIC: 7241 7231 Barber shops; beauty shops

(G-4838)
CARDIOLOGY CONSULTANTS (PA)
35141 Atlantic Ave Unit 3 (19967-6954)
PHONE..................302 541-8138
Judy Callaghan, *Manager*
EMP: 7
SALES (est): 1.1MM **Privately Held**
SIC: 8011 Cardiologist & cardio-vascular specialist

(G-4839)
COASTAL KID WATCH
32566 Docs Pl (19967-6959)
PHONE..................302 537-0793
Paula R Nadig, *Owner*
EMP: 10
SALES (est): 673.2K **Privately Held**
SIC: 8011 Pediatrician

(G-4840)
COASTAL RENTALS HYDRAULICS LLC
35283 Atlantic Ave (19967-6912)
PHONE..................302 251-3103
Michael G McCarthy, *Pres*
EMP: 6
SALES (est): 530K **Privately Held**
SIC: 7359 Equipment rental & leasing

(G-4841)
COUNTY BANK
36754 Old Mill Rd (19967-6951)
PHONE..................302 537-0900
Dick Reed, *Manager*
EMP: 6 **Privately Held**
WEB: www.countybankdel.com
SIC: 6021 6029 National commercial banks; commercial banks
PA: County Bank
19927 Shuttle Rd
Rehoboth Beach DE 19971

(G-4842)
DICKENS PARLOUR THEATRE
35715 Atlantic Ave (19967-6944)
PHONE..................302 829-1071
Rich Bloch, *Owner*
EMP: 4
SALES (est): 230K **Privately Held**
SIC: 7922 Legitimate live theater producers

(G-4843)
DRIFTWOOD CANDLES LLC
23 Thornberry Rd (19967-6764)
PHONE..................302 858-1600
Stephanie Wright,
EMP: 1
SALES (est): 65K **Privately Held**
SIC: 3999 Candles

(G-4844)
EXCEL PROPERTY MANAGEMENT LLC
35370 Atlantic Ave (19967-6903)
PHONE..................302 541-5312
David Baldo, *Mng Member*

EMP: 9 EST: 2001
SQ FT: 1,500
SALES (est): 955.6K **Privately Held**
WEB: www.excelpropertymanagement.com
SIC: 6531 Real estate managers

(G-4845)
FRIENDS & FAMILY PRACTICE
35141 Atlantic Ave Unit 1 (19967-6954)
PHONE..................................302 537-3740
Kimberly Gallagher, *Director*
EMP: 6
SALES (est): 475.8K **Privately Held**
SIC: 8322 Individual & family services

(G-4846)
HALPERN EYE ASSOCIATES INC
35786 Atlantic Ave Unit 1 (19967-6955)
PHONE..................................302 537-0234
P Zakrochimski, *Branch Mgr*
EMP: 8
SALES (corp-wide): 4.3MM **Privately Held**
WEB: www.halperneye.com
SIC: 8042 Specialized optometrists
PA: Halpern Eye Associates, Inc.
   885 S Governors Ave
   Dover DE 19904
   302 734-5861

(G-4847)
LORDS LANDSCAPING INC
35577 Atlantic Ave (19967-6961)
PHONE..................................302 539-6119
William Lord, *President*
Donna Lord, *Vice Pres*
EMP: 20
SQ FT: 7,000
SALES (est): 1.5MM **Privately Held**
SIC: 0782 5261 Landscape contractors; garden supplies & tools

(G-4848)
MANUFACTURERS & TRADERS TR CO
Also Called: M&T
204 Atlantic Ave (19967-6728)
PHONE..................................302 541-8700
Marsha Phillips, *Manager*
EMP: 7
SALES (corp-wide): 6.4B **Publicly Held**
WEB: www.binghamlegg.com
SIC: 6022 State commercial banks
HQ: Manufacturers And Traders Trust Company
   1 M&T Plz Fl 3
   Buffalo NY 14203
   716 842-4200

(G-4849)
MERCANTILE PROCESSING INC
32695 Roxana Rd (19967)
PHONE..................................302 524-8000
Kyle Morgan, *President*
EMP: 8
SALES (est): 273.4K **Privately Held**
SIC: 7389 Credit card service

(G-4850)
MICHAEL MCCARTHY STONES
35283 Atlantic Ave (19967-6912)
PHONE..................................302 539-8056
EMP: 7 EST: 2016
SALES (est): 460.8K **Privately Held**
SIC: 5032 Brick, stone & related material

(G-4851)
MIKEN BUILDERS INC
32782 Cedar Dr Unit 1 (19967-6919)
PHONE..................................302 537-4444
T Michael Nally, *CEO*
Gary Pitman, *Superintendent*
Mike Cummings, *COO*
Michael McKone, *COO*
Sean Cummings, *Project Mgr*
EMP: 28
SALES (est): 7.6MM **Privately Held**
WEB: www.mikenbuilders.com
SIC: 1542 1541 1521 Commercial & office building, new construction; industrial buildings, new construction; new construction, single-family houses

(G-4852)
PENINSULA REGIONAL MEDICAL CTR
35786 Atlantic Ave Unit 3 (19967-6955)
PHONE..................................302 537-1457
EMP: 129
SALES (corp-wide): 411.6MM **Privately Held**
SIC: 8099 Childbirth preparation clinic
PA: Peninsula Regional Medical Center
   100 E Carroll St
   Salisbury MD 21801
   410 546-6400

(G-4853)
QUEST DIAGNOSTICS INCORPORATED
38025 Town Center Dr (19967-6904)
PHONE..................................302 537-3862
Michelle Krissinger, *Branch Mgr*
EMP: 18
SALES (corp-wide): 7.5B **Publicly Held**
SIC: 8071 Testing laboratories
PA: Quest Diagnostics Incorporated
   500 Plaza Dr Ste G
   Secaucus NJ 07094
   973 520-2700

(G-4854)
RATNER COMPANIES LC
Also Called: Hair Cuttery
38069 Town Center Dr # 4 (19967-6968)
PHONE..................................302 537-4624
Jessica Johnson, *Manager*
EMP: 12 **Privately Held**
WEB: www.haircuttery.com
SIC: 7231 Unisex hair salons
HQ: Ratner Companies, L.C.
   1577 Spring Hill Rd # 500
   Vienna VA 22182
   703 269-5400

(G-4855)
RESORT INVESTIGATION & PATROL
19 Pine St (19970)
PHONE..................................302 539-5808
Joseph J Kansak Sr, *President*
Janet Rae Kansak, *Vice Pres*
EMP: 30
SALES (est): 497.8K **Privately Held**
SIC: 7381 Detective agency; protective services, guard

(G-4856)
TRANSFORMING WELLNESS LLC
35802 Atlantic Ave (19967-6907)
PHONE..................................302 249-2526
Marcia Moon, *Principal*
EMP: 7
SALES (est): 78K **Privately Held**
SIC: 8099 Health & allied services

(G-4857)
VICKIE YORK AT BEACH REALTY (PA)
518 Atlantic Ave (19967)
PHONE..................................302 539-2145
Vickie York, *Owner*
EMP: 5
SALES (est): 766.9K **Privately Held**
SIC: 6531 Real estate agent, residential; real estate brokers & agents

(G-4858)
WELLS FARGO BANK NATIONAL ASSN
38011 Town Center Dr (19967-6969)
PHONE..................................302 541-8660
Michelle Gallagher, *Branch Mgr*
EMP: 16
SALES (corp-wide): 101B **Publicly Held**
SIC: 6021 National commercial banks
HQ: Wells Fargo Bank, National Association
   101 N Phillips Ave
   Sioux Falls SD 57104
   605 575-6900

Milton
Sussex County

(G-4859)
A&V LANDSCAPING
704 Chestnut St (19968-1324)
PHONE..................................302 684-8609
Victor Gomez, *Principal*
EMP: 4
SALES (est): 50.7K **Privately Held**
SIC: 0781 Landscape services

(G-4860)
ADAM C SYDELL DDS
524 Union St (19968-1016)
PHONE..................................302 684-1100
EMP: 4
SALES (est): 77.3K **Privately Held**
SIC: 8021 Dentist's Office

(G-4861)
ALLEN CHORMAN INC
Also Called: Allen Chorman & Son
30475 E Mill Run (19968-3457)
PHONE..................................302 684-2770
Allen Chorman, *President*
Jeffrey A Chorman, *Vice Pres*
EMP: 4
SALES (est): 663.2K **Privately Held**
SIC: 0721 Crop dusting services; crop related entomological services (insect control); crop spraying services

(G-4862)
ALWAYS BEST CARE
624 Mulberry St (19968-1516)
PHONE..................................302 409-3710
EMP: 8
SALES (est): 61.1K **Privately Held**
SIC: 8082 Home health care services

(G-4863)
AMERICAN INDUSTRIES LLC
124 Broadkill Rd Ste 436 (19968-1008)
PHONE..................................302 585-0129
Angelo Casino,
EMP: 5
SALES (est): 150.7K **Privately Held**
SIC: 3999 Manufacturing industries

(G-4864)
ATLANTIC FAMILY PHYSICIANS
100 Eaton Ln (19968-1336)
PHONE..................................302 856-4092
Fabricio Alarcon, *Principal*
EMP: 5
SALES (est): 297.7K **Privately Held**
SIC: 8011 General & family practice, physician/surgeon

(G-4865)
ATLANTIC SCREEN & MFG INC
Also Called: A S I
142 Broadkill Rd (19968-1008)
PHONE..................................302 684-3197
Patricia Lawson, *President*
Jeffrey Lawson, *Corp Secy*
Bill Lawson, *Vice Pres*
EMP: 4
SQ FT: 28,000
SALES (est): 722.4K **Privately Held**
WEB: www.atlantic-screen.com
SIC: 3444 3569 3498 Irrigation pipe, sheet metal; mail chutes, sheet metal; filters & strainers, pipeline; pipe sections fabricated from purchased pipe

(G-4866)
AUTOMATION & CONTROLS TECH LLC
16610 Bluestone Ter (19968-3916)
PHONE..................................913 908-4344
Bill Breitmayer,
EMP: 2
SALES (est): 114K **Privately Held**
SIC: 3491 Automatic regulating & control valves

(G-4867)
BEACH HOUSE SERVICES
26 Cripple Creek Run (19968-9731)
PHONE..................................302 645-2554
Rick Trasati, *Owner*
EMP: 7
SALES (est): 249.3K **Privately Held**
SIC: 7011 Resort hotel

(G-4868)
BEEBE MEDICAL FOUNDATION
611 Federal St Ste 2 (19968-1157)
PHONE..................................302 684-8579
EMP: 5
SALES (corp-wide): 447.8MM **Privately Held**
SIC: 8071 Medical laboratories
HQ: Beebe Medical Foundation
   902 Savannah Rd
   Lewes DE 19958

(G-4869)
BLAKE COMPUTERS
438 S Lake Dr (19968-9647)
PHONE..................................540 843-0656
Kenneth W Lawson, *Owner*
EMP: 3
SALES (est): 17.7K **Privately Held**
WEB: www.blakecomputers.com
SIC: 3571 Personal computers (microcomputers)

(G-4870)
BOOZER EXCAVATION CO INC
18208 Beech Tree Path (19968-2618)
PHONE..................................302 542-0290
Douglas L Boozer, *Principal*
EMP: 5 EST: 2015
SALES (est): 128.5K **Privately Held**
SIC: 1771 Concrete work

(G-4871)
BY THE SHORE
5005 Beverly Ln (19968-9373)
PHONE..................................302 462-0496
EMP: 4
SALES (est): 61.1K **Privately Held**
SIC: 8082 Home health care services

(G-4872)
BYZANTIUM SKY PRESS
27567 Bristol Ct (19968-3742)
PHONE..................................302 258-6116
EMP: 1 EST: 2018
SALES (est): 37.5K **Privately Held**
SIC: 2741 Miscellaneous publishing

(G-4873)
C&J PAVING INC
Also Called: C & J Paving
12518 Union Street Ext (19968-2655)
PHONE..................................302 684-0211
Clarence J Reed, *Principal*
EMP: 10
SALES (est): 680.8K **Privately Held**
SIC: 4212 1771 1611 Local trucking, without storage; driveway, parking lot & blacktop contractors; surfacing & paving

(G-4874)
CAPE CANVAS
12 Meadowridge Ln (19968-9694)
PHONE..................................302 684-8201
Dave Vitella, *President*
EMP: 1
SALES (est): 50.4K **Privately Held**
SIC: 2394 Canvas covers & drop cloths

(G-4875)
CAPSTONE HOMES
27423 Walking Run (19968-3087)
PHONE..................................302 684-4480
Scott Dailey, *Director*
EMP: 4 EST: 2010
SALES (est): 328.7K **Privately Held**
SIC: 1521 Single-family housing construction

(G-4876)
CATHOLIC CHARITIES INC
Also Called: Casa San Francisco
127 Broad St (19968-1601)
P.O. Box 38 (19968-0038)
PHONE..................................302 684-8694
Melinda Wolf, *Manager*
EMP: 7
SALES (corp-wide): 6.8MM **Privately Held**
WEB: www.ccwilm.org
SIC: 8322 Social service center

Milton - Sussex County (G-4877) — GEOGRAPHIC SECTION

PA: Catholic Charities Inc
2601 W 4th St
Wilmington DE 19805
302 655-9624

(G-4877)
CENTRAL BACKHOE SERVICE
28247 Rund Pole Bridge Rd (19968-3093)
PHONE..................302 398-6420
Debbie Craft, *Principal*
Randall Craft,
EMP: 3
SALES (est): 328.6K **Privately Held**
SIC: 3531 1794 Backhoes; excavation work

(G-4878)
CHELSEA MCHUGH MUSIC THERAPY
28784 Fisher Rd (19968-3283)
PHONE..................302 827-2335
Chelsea M McHugh, *Owner*
EMP: 8
SALES (est): 73.3K **Privately Held**
SIC: 8093 Rehabilitation center, outpatient treatment

(G-4879)
CLEAN DELAWARE INC
Rr 404 (19968)
P.O. Box 123 (19968-0123)
PHONE..................302 684-4221
Gerry Desmonz, *Manager*
EMP: 12
SQ FT: 3,000
SALES (est): 1.4MM **Privately Held**
SIC: 4953 7699 1794 Liquid waste, collection & disposal; septic tank cleaning service; excavation & grading, building construction

(G-4880)
CLENDANIEL PLBG HTG & COOLG
Also Called: Clendaniel Plbg Htg & Coolg
18052 Gravel Hill Rd (19968-2510)
PHONE..................302 684-3152
Arthur Clendaniel, *Owner*
EMP: 8
SALES (est): 591.2K **Privately Held**
SIC: 1711 Plumbing contractors

(G-4881)
CLIPPERS & CURLS HAIR DESIGN
620 Clipper Sq 620 Mulbry (19968)
PHONE..................302 684-1522
Patricia Moore, *Owner*
EMP: 4
SALES (est): 62.2K **Privately Held**
SIC: 7231 Beauty shops

(G-4882)
COMFORT ZONE JAZZ LLC
14620 Oyster Rocks Rd (19968-3750)
PHONE..................302 745-2019
Emmett Nixon, *Manager*
Michael Dominquez,
EMP: 7
SALES (est): 111.8K **Privately Held**
SIC: 7929 Entertainers & entertainment groups

(G-4883)
CORE & MAIN LP
25414 Primehook Rd # 100 (19968-2706)
PHONE..................302 684-3452
EMP: 5
SALES (corp-wide): 2.6B **Privately Held**
SIC: 5074 4941 4952 Plumbing fittings & supplies; water supply; sewerage systems
PA: Core & Main Lp
1830 Craig Park Ct
Saint Louis MO 63146
314 432-4700

(G-4884)
COUNTY BANK
140 Broadkill Rd (19968-1008)
PHONE..................302 684-2300
Sonja Davis, *Vice Pres*
EMP: 7 **Privately Held**
SIC: 6022 State commercial banks

PA: County Bank
19927 Shuttle Rd
Rehoboth Beach DE 19971

(G-4885)
D E I FARMS INC
114 S White Cedar Dr (19968-9700)
PHONE..................302 684-3415
David E Isaacs, *President*
EMP: 5
SALES (est): 422.1K **Privately Held**
SIC: 0751 Poultry services

(G-4886)
DEL BAY CHARTER FISHING LLC
23602 Harvest Run Reach (19968-2470)
PHONE..................302 542-1930
Richard M Cornell, *Principal*
EMP: 4 EST: 2008
SALES (est): 249.9K **Privately Held**
SIC: 7999 Fishing boats, party: operation

(G-4887)
DELAWARE EYE CLINICS
16924 Lilly Pad Dr (19968-3422)
PHONE..................302 645-2338
EMP: 5 EST: 2009
SALES (est): 244.9K **Privately Held**
SIC: 8099 Health/Allied Services

(G-4888)
DELAWARE MEDICAL COURIER
17048 W Holly Dr (19968-3435)
PHONE..................302 670-1247
EMP: 5
SALES (est): 254.4K **Privately Held**
SIC: 4215 Courier services, except by air

(G-4889)
DELMARVA 2000 LTD
21 Shay Ln (19968-3048)
PHONE..................302 645-2226
Chuck Betyeman, *President*
John Marsillo, *Vice Pres*
Katrina Bethard, *Treasurer*
EMP: 8
SALES (est): 487.7K **Privately Held**
SIC: 3843 Dental equipment & supplies

(G-4890)
DELMARVA ENERGY SOLUTIONS LLC
115 Atlantic Ave (19968-1205)
P.O. Box 228 (19968-0228)
PHONE..................302 684-3418
EMP: 7 EST: 2010
SALES: 500K **Privately Held**
SIC: 8711 Energy conservation engineering

(G-4891)
DELMARVA LABORATORIES INC
21 Shay Ln (19968-3048)
PHONE..................302 645-2226
Chuck Bettieman, *President*
EMP: 2
SALES (corp-wide): 295.5MM **Privately Held**
SIC: 3843 3842 Dental equipment; surgical appliances & supplies
HQ: Delmarva Laboratories, Inc.
3200 Meacham Blvd
Fort Worth TX

(G-4892)
DESIGN CONSULTANTS GROUP LLC
10872d Davidson Dr (19968)
PHONE..................302 684-8030
Mark Davidson,
EMP: 20
SALES (est): 1.1MM **Privately Held**
WEB: www.dcgengineering.com
SIC: 8713 Photogrammetric engineering

(G-4893)
DEVILS PARTY PRESS
204 Sundance Ln (19968-1360)
PHONE..................310 904-3660
Dianne Pearce, *Principal*
EMP: 1
SALES (est): 37.5K **Privately Held**
SIC: 2741 Miscellaneous publishing

(G-4894)
DIAMOND STATE WELDING LLC
13307 Jefferson Rd (19968-2988)
PHONE..................302 644-8489
Christopher O'Callaghan, *Principal*
EMP: 1
SALES (est): 43.4K **Privately Held**
SIC: 7692 Welding repair

(G-4895)
DIGITAL WISH INC
15187 Hudson Rd (19968-3616)
P.O. Box 255 (19968-0255)
PHONE..................802 375-6721
Heather Chirtea, *Ch of Bd*
Gordon Woodrow, *Exec Dir*
EMP: 8
SQ FT: 600
SALES: 300K **Privately Held**
SIC: 8732 Commercial nonphysical research

(G-4896)
DOGFISH HEAD COMPANIES LLC
6 Cannery Vlg (19968-1308)
PHONE..................302 684-1000
Nick Benz, *CEO*
Mariah Calagione, *President*
Ken Woodward, *Division Mgr*
Neal Stewart, *Vice Pres*
Amy Heers, *Opers Staff*
EMP: 5 EST: 2017
SALES (est): 134.1K **Privately Held**
SIC: 2085 Distilled & blended liquors

(G-4897)
DOGFISH HEAD CRAFT BREWERY LLC
Cannery Vlg Ctr Ste 6 (19968)
PHONE..................302 684-1000
Sam Calagione, *CEO*
George Pastrana, *President*
Mariah Calagione, *Exec VP*
Harriet Warwick-Smith, *CFO*
Katie Crudele, *Regl Sales Mgr*
▲ EMP: 100
SQ FT: 102,000
SALES (est): 35.2MM **Privately Held**
WEB: www.dogfish.com
SIC: 2082 Ale (alcoholic beverage)

(G-4898)
DRAPER COMMUNICATIONS INC
1 Square (19968)
PHONE..................302 684-8962
Thomas H Draper, *Branch Mgr*
EMP: 15
SALES (corp-wide): 30MM **Privately Held**
SIC: 4833 Television broadcasting stations
PA: Draper Communications Inc
1729 N Salisbury Blvd
Salisbury MD 21801
410 749-1111

(G-4899)
DRYZONE LLC
115 Atlantic Ave (19968-1205)
P.O. Box 135 (19968-0135)
PHONE..................302 684-5034
Brian Barczak, *Sales Mgr*
Lydia Lawson, *Office Mgr*
Gary Lawson,
William Anderson,
EMP: 8
SALES (est): 487.1K **Privately Held**
SIC: 7349 Building maintenance, except repairs

(G-4900)
E A ZANDO CUSTOM DESIGNS INC
210 Chandler St (19968-1236)
PHONE..................302 684-4601
Elizabeth A Zando, *President*
EMP: 10
SALES (est): 401K **Privately Held**
SIC: 0781 1522 Landscape planning services; residential construction

(G-4901)
EDWARD S JAOUDE
28322 Lwes Georgetown Hwy (19968-3117)
PHONE..................302 684-2020
Edward Jaoude, *Owner*
EMP: 20
SALES (est): 299.8K **Privately Held**
SIC: 8011 Internal medicine, physician/surgeon

(G-4902)
EISELE CELINE
Also Called: Shell Recreation Center
225 Bayport Business Park (19968)
P.O. Box 277 (19968-0277)
PHONE..................302 684-3201
Celine Eisele Dir, *Principal*
EMP: 8
SALES (est): 190.1K **Privately Held**
SIC: 8351 Group day care center

(G-4903)
EMENTUM INC (PA)
2841 S Bay Shore Dr Mlton Milton (19968)
PHONE..................866 984-1999
Carolyn Merek, *President*
Robert C Randa, *Surgery Dir*
EMP: 22
SQ FT: 3,000
SALES (est): 5.9MM **Privately Held**
WEB: www.ementum.com
SIC: 8748 Business consulting

(G-4904)
ESPOSITOS WOODWORKING & CNSTR
99 Falls Rd (19968-9374)
PHONE..................302 245-5474
EMP: 1
SALES (est): 54.1K **Privately Held**
SIC: 2431 Millwork

(G-4905)
FIFTY PLUS MONTHLY
16587 John Rowland Trl (19968-3539)
PHONE..................302 645-2938
Jose Cintron, *Principal*
EMP: 2
SALES (est): 62.9K **Privately Held**
SIC: 2711 Newspapers

(G-4906)
FIRST STATE HEALTH & WELLNESS
113 Union St Unit A (19968-1600)
PHONE..................302 684-1995
EMP: 8
SALES (est): 76K **Privately Held**
SIC: 8099 Health & allied services

(G-4907)
FOOTCARE TECHNOLOGIES INC
124 Broadkill Rd Ste 472 (19968-1008)
PHONE..................704 301-6966
Tyler McCracken, *President*
EMP: 1
SALES (est): 39.6K **Privately Held**
SIC: 3999 Manufacturing industries

(G-4908)
GG SHUTTLE SERVICE
28379 Martins Farm Rd (19968-3206)
PHONE..................302 684-8818
George Lofland, *CEO*
EMP: 4
SALES (est): 122.2K **Privately Held**
SIC: 4111 Local & suburban transit

(G-4909)
GRACE VISITATION SERVICES
Also Called: Visiting Angel of Sussex, De
28350 Lwes Georgetown Hwy (19968-3115)
PHONE..................302 329-9475
David Forman, *President*
Karen Reed, *Director*
EMP: 60 EST: 2011
SALES (est): 117.4K **Privately Held**
SIC: 8082 Home health care services

▲ = Import ▼=Export
◆ =Import/Export

GEOGRAPHIC SECTION

Milton - Sussex County (G-4944)

(G-4910)
GREENS AT BROADVIEW LLC
Also Called: Rookery, The
27052 Broadkill Rd (19968-3736)
PHONE...................................302 684-3000
Chris Akins, *Managing Prtnr*
Chris Adkins, *Manager*
EMP: 40
SALES (est): 1.7MM Privately Held
SIC: 7992 Public golf courses

(G-4911)
HARRY JOSEPH
18749 Josephs Rd (19968-3268)
PHONE...................................302 684-3243
Harry Joseph, *Owner*
EMP: 4
SALES (est): 237.5K Privately Held
SIC: 0115 Corn

(G-4912)
HEALTH CARE ASSOC PA
616 Mulberry St (19968-1516)
PHONE...................................302 684-2033
Paul E Gorrin, *Principal*
EMP: 7
SALES (est): 201.1K Privately Held
SIC: 8011 Internal medicine, physician/surgeon

(G-4913)
HENLOPEN HOMES LLC
18427 Josephs Rd (19968-3269)
P.O. Box 476, Georgetown (19947-0476)
PHONE...................................302 684-0860
Timothy Parker, *Managing Prtnr*
EMP: 5
SALES (est): 339K Privately Held
SIC: 1522 Residential construction

(G-4914)
HERRING CREEK BUILDERS INC
26085 Williams Farm Rd (19968-2928)
PHONE...................................302 684-3015
Alan Steele, *President*
Allen Steel, *President*
EMP: 8
SQ FT: 1,800
SALES (est): 989K Privately Held
SIC: 1521 New construction, single-family houses

(G-4915)
HOPKINS GRANARY INC
611 Federal St (19968-1157)
PHONE...................................302 684-8525
John A Hopkins Jr, *President*
Donna Hopkins Gooner, *Corp Secy*
John A Hopkins III, *Vice Pres*
EMP: 4
SQ FT: 3,000
SALES (est): 582.4K Privately Held
SIC: 5153 Grains

(G-4916)
HTS 20 LLP
16394 Samuel Paynter Blvd # 103
(19968-3560)
PHONE...................................800 690-2029
Steve Parsons, *Owner*
Gavin Furlong, *Owner*
EMP: 6
SQ FT: 900
SALES (est): 61.3K Privately Held
SIC: 1731 7389 Sound equipment specialization;

(G-4917)
HUDSON MANAGEMENT & ENTPS LLC
30045 Eagles Crest Rd (19968-3624)
PHONE...................................302 645-9464
Joseph R Hudson,
EMP: 9
SALES (est): 810K Privately Held
SIC: 1531 Condominium developers

(G-4918)
IRON WORKS INC
14726 Gravel Hill Rd 1 (19968-2449)
PHONE...................................302 684-1887
Robert Klerlein, *President*
EMP: 15
SQ FT: 1,500

SALES: 900K Privately Held
SIC: 3441 Fabricated structural metal

(G-4919)
J L CARPENTER FARMS LLC
27113 Carpenter Rd (19968-3129)
PHONE...................................302 684-8601
James L Carpenter Jr, *President*
Tammy Carpenter,
EMP: 8
SALES (est): 312.8K Privately Held
SIC: 0115 0161 7389 Corn; vegetables & melons;

(G-4920)
JACO LLC
Also Called: Macan Manufacturing
21 Shay Ln (19968-3048)
PHONE...................................302 645-8068
John Marsillo, *Mng Member*
EMP: 8
SALES: 500K Privately Held
SIC: 5047 Medical equipment & supplies

(G-4921)
JAMES L CARPENTER & SON INC
27113 Carpenter Rd (19968-3129)
PHONE...................................302 684-8601
James L Carpenter Jr, *President*
Kay C Dukes, *Admin Sec*
EMP: 7
SALES (est): 701.7K Privately Held
SIC: 0241 0161 0119 Dairy farms; vegetables & melons; feeder grains

(G-4922)
KEYSTONE SWINE SERVICES
14356 Clydes Dr (19968-2987)
PHONE...................................302 329-9731
Mike Mullady, *Owner*
EMP: 6
SALES (est): 223.9K Privately Held
SIC: 0213 Hogs

(G-4923)
LEARNING TREE NETWORK
16581 John Rowland Trl (19968-3539)
PHONE...................................302 645-7199
EMP: 5 EST: 2017
SALES (est): 44.6K Privately Held
SIC: 8351 Child day care services

(G-4924)
LINDSAY AND ASSOCIATES LIMITED
1610 Beach Plum Dr (19968-9480)
PHONE...................................703 631-5840
EMP: 4
SALES: 1.2MM Privately Held
SIC: 8711 Engineering Services

(G-4925)
LOCKWOOD DESIGN CONSTRUCTION
26412 Broadkill Rd Fl 1 (19968-2955)
PHONE...................................302 684-4844
Donald H Lockwood, *CEO*
Don A Lockwood, *President*
EMP: 7
SQ FT: 9,000
SALES (est): 1.1MM Privately Held
WEB: www.lockwoodesign.com
SIC: 1542 1521 Commercial & office building, new construction; commercial & office buildings, renovation & repair; new construction, single-family houses; general remodeling, single-family houses

(G-4926)
LOWELL SCOTT MD PA
611 Federal St Ste 3 (19968-1157)
PHONE...................................302 684-1119
Scott Lowell, *Principal*
EMP: 5
SALES (est): 307.1K Privately Held
SIC: 8011 Pediatrician

(G-4927)
LUTHERAN SNR SRVCS SSX CNTY
Also Called: LUTHER TOWERS OF MILTON, THE
500 Palmer St (19968-1006)
PHONE...................................302 684-1668

John Ranney, *President*
John Barton, *Vice Pres*
Sandra Wachter-Myers, *Admin Sec*
EMP: 6
SALES: 523.8K Privately Held
SIC: 6513 Retirement hotel operation

(G-4928)
M R DESIGNS INC
26342 Broadkill Rd (19968-2956)
PHONE...................................302 684-8082
Matthew Dotterer, *President*
Stephanie Parker, *Vice Pres*
EMP: 4
SALES (est): 205.1K Privately Held
SIC: 7389 Design services

(G-4929)
M T O CLEAN OF SUSSEX COUNTY
2 N Aquarius Way (19968-9483)
PHONE...................................302 854-0204
Sandra Connelly, *President*
Rodney Connelly, *Senior VP*
April Connelly, *Vice Pres*
EMP: 6
SALES: 213K Privately Held
SIC: 7349 Building & office cleaning services

(G-4930)
MANUFACTURERS & TRADERS TR CO
Also Called: M&T
107 Front St (19968-1427)
P.O. Box 217 (19968-0217)
PHONE...................................302 855-2184
Beverly White, *Manager*
EMP: 6
SALES (corp-wide): 6.4B Publicly Held
WEB: www.binghamlegg.com
SIC: 6022 State commercial banks
HQ: Manufacturers And Traders Trust Company
1 M&T Plz Fl 3
Buffalo NY 14203
716 842-4200

(G-4931)
MARY ZIOMEK DDS
317 Mariners Cir (19968-2236)
PHONE...................................301 984-9646
Mary Ziomek, *Principal*
EMP: 7
SALES (est): 566K Privately Held
SIC: 8021 Dentists' office

(G-4932)
MAWS TAILS MFG
29621 Riverstone Dr (19968-3927)
PHONE...................................302 740-7664
EMP: 2
SALES (est): 94.6K Privately Held
SIC: 3999 Manufacturing industries

(G-4933)
MEDICINE WOMAN
503 Canning House Row (19968-1314)
PHONE...................................302 684-8048
EMP: 8
SALES (est): 76K Privately Held
SIC: 8099 Health & allied services

(G-4934)
MERCER DENTAL ASSOCIATES
Also Called: Mercer and Sydell Dental
524 Union St (19968-1016)
PHONE...................................302 664-1385
Sean M Mercer, *Principal*
EMP: 5
SALES (est): 405K Privately Held
SIC: 8021 Dentists' office

(G-4935)
MERIDIAN ARCHITECTS ENGINEERS
26412 Broadkill Rd (19968-2955)
PHONE...................................302 643-9928
EMP: 25
SALES (est): 1.6MM Privately Held
SIC: 8711 Engineering Architectural And Surveying Services

(G-4936)
MF STONEWORKS LLC
23844 Dakotas Reach (19968-2480)
PHONE...................................302 265-7732
EMP: 4 EST: 2013
SALES (est): 194.2K Privately Held
SIC: 0781 Landscape services

(G-4937)
MILFORD MEDICAL ASSOCIATES PA
611 Federal St (19968-1157)
PHONE...................................302 329-9517
Adam Brownstein, *Branch Mgr*
EMP: 5
SALES (est): 276.2K
SALES (corp-wide): 1.9MM Privately Held
SIC: 8031 8011 Offices & clinics of osteopathic physicians; offices & clinics of medical doctors
PA: Milford Medical Associates, P.A.
310 Mullet Run
Milford DE 19963
302 424-0600

(G-4938)
MILLSBORO EYE CARE LLC
Also Called: Delaware Eye Clinic
28322 L Georgetown Hwy (19968)
PHONE...................................302 684-2020
Mireille Jaoude, *Office Mgr*
Edward S Jaoude,
EMP: 23
SALES (est): 236.8K Privately Held
SIC: 8011 Ophthalmologist

(G-4939)
MILTON ENTERPRISES INC
Also Called: Milton Family Practice
424 Mulberry St Ste 2 (19968-1628)
PHONE...................................302 684-2000
Charles G Wagner MD, *President*
EMP: 6 EST: 1981
SALES (est): 550K Privately Held
SIC: 8011 General & family practice, physician/surgeon

(G-4940)
MILTON GARDEN CLUB
14354 Sand Hill Rd (19968-2562)
P.O. Box 203 (19968-0203)
PHONE...................................302 684-8315
Sandy Winterbottom, *Principal*
EMP: 4
SALES (est): 38.1K Privately Held
SIC: 7997 Membership sports & recreation clubs

(G-4941)
MILTON HISTORICAL SOCIETY
210 Union St (19968-1620)
P.O. Box 112 (19968-0112)
PHONE...................................302 684-1010
Melinda Huff, *Director*
EMP: 12 EST: 1970
SALES: 235K Privately Held
SIC: 8412 Historical society

(G-4942)
NATIONAL WATERWORKS INC
25414 Primehook Rd # 100 (19968-2706)
PHONE...................................302 653-9096
EMP: 8 EST: 2008
SALES (est): 680K Privately Held
SIC: 4941 Water Supply Service

(G-4943)
OCEAN MEDICAL IMAGING DEL LLC
611 Federal St Ste 4 (19968-1157)
PHONE...................................302 684-5151
Jonathan L Patterson,
Jonathan Patterson,
EMP: 8
SALES (est): 912.3K Privately Held
SIC: 8011 Medical centers; radiologist

(G-4944)
OCKELS ACRES LLC
17120 Ockles Ln (19968-2458)
PHONE...................................302 684-0456
Dale Ockels,
EMP: 7

Milton - Sussex County (G-4945)

SALES (est): 139.3K **Privately Held**
SIC: 0191 General farms, primarily crop

(G-4945)
OCKELS FARMS INC
17120 E Redden Rd (19968)
PHONE..................................302 684-0456
Dale Ockels, *President*
Dennis Ockels, *Vice Pres*
Gary Ockels, *Vice Pres*
Cynthia Ockels, *Treasurer*
EMP: 7
SALES (est): 707.5K **Privately Held**
SIC: 0191 0213 0252 General farms, primarily crop; hogs; chicken eggs

(G-4946)
PEDIATRIC & ADOLESCENT CENTER
424 Mulberry St (19968-1628)
PHONE..................................302 684-0561
John Ludwicki, *President*
Brandy Little,
EMP: 7
SALES (est): 798.1K **Privately Held**
SIC: 8011 Pediatrician

(G-4947)
PENNONI ASSOCIATES INC
18072 Davidson Dr (19968-2598)
PHONE..................................302 684-8030
Mark Davidson, *President*
Stephen McCabe, *Senior Engr*
EMP: 39
SALES (corp-wide): 191.8MM **Privately Held**
SIC: 8711 Consulting engineer
PA: Pennoni Associates Inc.
    1900 Market St Fl 3
    Philadelphia PA 19103
    215 222-3000

(G-4948)
PEPPER GREENHOUSES
13034 Mulberry Street Ext (19968)
PHONE..................................302 684-8092
Fred Pepper, *Partner*
EMP: 4
SALES (est): 762.1K **Privately Held**
SIC: 5191 5211 Greenhouse equipment & supplies; greenhouse kits, prefabricated

(G-4949)
PETTYJOHN FARMS INC
16771 Gravel Hill Rd (19968-2515)
PHONE..................................302 684-4383
Arthur Pettyjohn, *President*
EMP: 5
SALES (est): 352.6K **Privately Held**
SIC: 0111 Wheat

(G-4950)
PETTYJOHNS CUSTOM ENGINE
Also Called: Pettyjohn's Parts & Repair
601 Federal St (19968-1115)
PHONE..................................302 684-8888
William Pettyjohn, *Owner*
EMP: 4
SALES (est): 263.9K **Privately Held**
SIC: 7538 5531 General automotive repair shops; automotive parts

(G-4951)
PHOTOGRAPHY BY DENNIS MCD
5 W Greenwing Dr (19968-9558)
PHONE..................................610 678-0318
EMP: 4
SALES (est): 46K **Privately Held**
SIC: 7221 Photographer, still or video

(G-4952)
PIONEER DISTRIBUTORS INC
16612 Howard Millman Ln (19968-3528)
P.O. Box 90, Seaford (19973-0090)
PHONE..................................302 644-0791
William Furman, *President*
Edward Ross, *Vice Pres*
EMP: 7
SQ FT: 5,000
SALES (est): 680K **Privately Held**
SIC: 5149 Bakery products

(G-4953)
PREMIER HEATING & AC
25111 Williams Farm Rd (19968-2929)
PHONE..................................302 684-1888
Patrick C Brown, *Owner*
EMP: 4
SALES (est): 257.5K **Privately Held**
SIC: 1711 Warm air heating & air conditioning contractor

(G-4954)
QUILLEN SIGNS LLC
523 Federal St (19968-1113)
PHONE..................................302 684-3661
Patrick Quillen, *Partner*
Margaret Quillen, *Partner*
Theresa Townsend, *Partner*
EMP: 4
SALES (est): 300K **Privately Held**
WEB: www.quillensigns.com
SIC: 3993 7532 Signs, not made in custom sign painting shops; lettering & painting services; truck painting & lettering

(G-4955)
REED TRUCKING COMPANY
522 Chestnut St (19968-1320)
P.O. Box 216 (19968-0216)
PHONE..................................302 684-8585
Blake Reed, *President*
George Reed, *Vice Pres*
Beulah Reed, *Treasurer*
Nancy Reed, *Admin Sec*
EMP: 60 EST: 1933
SQ FT: 1,800
SALES (est): 10.7MM **Privately Held**
SIC: 4213 Trucking, except local

(G-4956)
REMENTER BROTHERS INC
Also Called: Budget Blinds
28348 Lwes Georgetown Hwy (19968-3115)
PHONE..................................302 249-4250
Christopher Rementer, *President*
Anthony Rementer, *Vice Pres*
EMP: 6
SALES: 700K **Privately Held**
SIC: 5719 1751 Window furnishings; cabinet & finish carpentry

(G-4957)
RICHARD L SAPP FARMS LLC
12698 Union Street Ext (19968-2656)
PHONE..................................302 684-4727
Barbara Sapp,
Richard Sapp,
EMP: 11
SALES (est): 346.7K **Privately Held**
SIC: 0191 7389 General farms, primarily crop;

(G-4958)
RICHARD L TODD PHD
28312 Lwes Georgetown Hwy (19968-3115)
PHONE..................................302 853-0559
Richard L Todd, *Principal*
EMP: 5 EST: 2011
SALES (est): 135.5K **Privately Held**
SIC: 8093 Mental health clinic, outpatient

(G-4959)
RICHARD M WHITE WELDING
14443 Collins St (19968-2640)
PHONE..................................302 684-4461
Richard White, *Owner*
EMP: 1
SALES (est): 65.1K **Privately Held**
SIC: 7692 Welding repair

(G-4960)
RICHARD SAPP FARMS
12698 Union Street Ext (19968-2656)
PHONE..................................302 684-4727
Richard Sapp, *Owner*
Barbara Sapp, *Co-Owner*
EMP: 4
SALES (est): 230K **Privately Held**
SIC: 0161 5083 Green lima bean farm; green pea farm (except dry peas); agricultural machinery & equipment; farm equipment parts & supplies

(G-4961)
RICHERT INC (PA)
2836 S Bay Shore Dr (19968-9451)
PHONE..................................302 684-0696
Allyn I Richert, *President*
EMP: 22
SQ FT: 2,500
SALES (est): 3.2MM **Privately Held**
SIC: 5021 Office furniture

(G-4962)
RICKS FITNESS & HEALTH INC
22893 Neptune Rd (19968-2536)
PHONE..................................302 684-0316
Richard G Moore, *President*
EMP: 6
SALES (est): 122K **Privately Held**
SIC: 7991 8011 Health club; offices & clinics of medical doctors

(G-4963)
RMV WORKFORCE CORP
124 Broadkill Rd Ste 380 (19968-1008)
PHONE..................................302 408-1061
Rohit Sood, *Principal*
EMP: 10
SALES (est): 180.6K **Privately Held**
SIC: 7389

(G-4964)
ROBERT MCMANN
Also Called: Frst State Ceramics & Marble
13259 Sunland Dr (19968-2992)
PHONE..................................302 329-9413
Robert McMann, *Principal*
EMP: 2
SALES (est): 145.4K **Privately Held**
SIC: 3269 Pottery products

(G-4965)
ROGERS SIGN COMPANY INC
110 Lavinia St (19968-1126)
PHONE..................................302 684-8338
Lynn Rogers, *President*
Keith Revelle, *Vice Pres*
Linda Rogers, *Treasurer*
Deb Breneman, *Admin Sec*
Jarred Knorr, *Graphic Designe*
EMP: 18
SQ FT: 14,000
SALES (est): 1.4MM **Privately Held**
WEB: www.rogerssign.com
SIC: 7389 Sign painting & lettering shop

(G-4966)
SECURITY INSTRUMENT CORP DEL
28226 Lwes Georgetown Hwy (19968)
PHONE..................................302 674-2891
Mike Cork, *Manager*
EMP: 10
SALES (corp-wide): 17MM **Privately Held**
WEB: www.securityinstrument.com
SIC: 7382 Protective devices, security
PA: Security Instrument Corp Of Delaware
    309 W Newport Pike
    Wilmington DE 19804
    302 998-2261

(G-4967)
SENSOFUSION INC
30061 Clam Shell Ln (19968-3793)
PHONE..................................570 239-4912
Kaveh Haroun Mahdavi, *Vice Pres*
EMP: 15 EST: 2016
SALES (est): 390.2K **Privately Held**
SIC: 7373 7371 7389 Systems software development services; systems integration services; computer software development & applications;
HQ: Sensofusion Oy
    Hakamaenkuja 1
    Vantaa 01510
    985 619-420

(G-4968)
SHERMAN HEATING OILS INC
223 Bay Front Rd G (19968-9563)
P.O. Box 206 (19968-0206)
PHONE..................................302 684-4008
Harold Sheets Jr, *Director*
EMP: 9

SALES (corp-wide): 8.3MM **Privately Held**
SIC: 5172 Gases, liquefied petroleum (propane); fuel oil; kerosene
PA: Sherman Heating Oils Inc
    223g Bay Ave
    Milton DE 19968
    302 684-4008

(G-4969)
SHERMAN HEATING OILS INC (PA)
223g Bay Ave (19968-1217)
P.O. Box 326 (19968-0326)
PHONE..................................302 684-4008
Dean W Sherman, *President*
Orville Mills, *Vice Pres*
Harold A Sheets Jr, *Admin Sec*
EMP: 10
SQ FT: 3,000
SALES (est): 8.3MM **Privately Held**
SIC: 5172 Gases, liquefied petroleum (propane); fuel oil; kerosene

(G-4970)
SLEIGH FINANCIAL INC
28266 Lwes Georgetown Hwy (19968-3107)
PHONE..................................302 684-2929
Randy Reed, *President*
EMP: 7 EST: 2004
SQ FT: 5,000
SALES (est): 1.4MM **Privately Held**
SIC: 5182 Wine & distilled beverages

(G-4971)
SPOSATO IRRIGATION COMPANY
16181 Hudson Rd (19968-3612)
PHONE..................................302 645-4773
David Anthony Sposato, *Principal*
John Frederick Sposato, *Principal*
Mark Payne, *Plant Mgr*
Katy Hopkins, *Marketing Staff*
Terry Bomar, *Manager*
EMP: 26
SALES (est): 3.3MM **Privately Held**
SIC: 0781 Landscape services

(G-4972)
SPOSATO LANDSCAPE COMPANY INC
16181 Hudson Rd (19968-3612)
PHONE..................................302 645-4773
Tony Sposato, *Owner*
Tim McMahon, *Accounts Mgr*
Brad Bos, *Manager*
EMP: 7
SALES (est): 702.4K **Privately Held**
SIC: 0781 Landscape services

(G-4973)
SPOSATO LAWN CARE
Rr 4 Box 265-B (19968-9804)
PHONE..................................302 645-4773
David Sposato, *Owner*
EMP: 20
SALES (est): 648K **Privately Held**
SIC: 0782 Lawn services

(G-4974)
SUBURBAN FARMHOUSE
108 Federal St (19968-1603)
PHONE..................................302 250-6254
Kristen Latham, *Principal*
EMP: 5
SALES (est): 380.1K **Privately Held**
SIC: 0191 General farms, primarily crop

(G-4975)
TELAMON CORPORATION
28607 W Meadowview Dr (19968-3118)
PHONE..................................302 684-3234
EMP: 4
SALES (corp-wide): 70.5MM **Privately Held**
SIC: 8331 Job training services
PA: Telamon Corporation
    5560 Munford Rd Ste 201
    Raleigh NC 27612
    919 851-7611

GEOGRAPHIC SECTION

New Castle - New Castle County (G-5005)

(G-4976)
TIDEWATER PHYSCL THRPY AND REB
611 Federal St Ste 1 (19968-1157)
PHONE...................................302 684-2829
Richard Recicar, *Branch Mgr*
Shawn Carter, *Director*
EMP: 6
SALES (corp-wide): 2.6MM **Privately Held**
SIC: 8049 8322 Physical therapist; rehabilitation services
PA: Tidewater Physical Therapy And Rehabilitation Associates Pa
406 Marvel Ct
Easton MD 21601
410 822-3116

(G-4977)
TRENTON BLOCK DELAWARE INC
701 Federal St (19968-1117)
PHONE...................................302 684-0112
Richard Kilian, *President*
EMP: 5
SALES (est): 342.2K **Privately Held**
SIC: 1741 Masonry & other stonework

(G-4978)
TRI STATE TREE SERVICE
30534 E Mill Run (19968-3424)
PHONE...................................302 645-7412
Ronald Baker, *Owner*
EMP: 4
SALES (est): 150K **Privately Held**
SIC: 0783 Pruning services, ornamental tree; removal services, bush & tree

(G-4979)
W SHARP PAYNTER & SONS INC
28443 Paynter Rd (19968-3702)
PHONE...................................302 684-8508
William P Sharp Jr, *President*
Henry Sharp, *Vice Pres*
EMP: 4
SALES (est): 350K **Privately Held**
SIC: 1629 1794 Dock construction; excavation work

(G-4980)
WILKINS ENTERPRISES INC
Pettyjohn Rd (19968)
PHONE...................................302 945-4142
Scott Wilkins, *President*
EMP: 5
SALES (est): 300K **Privately Held**
SIC: 7542 Carwashes

(G-4981)
WORCESTER GOLF CLUB INC
121 W Shore Dr (19968-1145)
PHONE...................................610 222-0200
Michael Malone, *President*
EMP: 10
SQ FT: 2,500
SALES (est): 357K **Privately Held**
SIC: 7992 7299 Public golf courses; banquet hall facilities

(G-4982)
WRIGHTS LAWN CARE INC
14174 Union Street Ext (19968-2662)
PHONE...................................302 684-3058
Jill Wright, *President*
Bill Wright, *Vice Pres*
EMP: 10
SALES: 200K **Privately Held**
SIC: 0782 Landscape contractors

(G-4983)
WYOMING MILLWORK CO
23000 Tracks End Ln (19968-2620)
PHONE...................................302 684-3150
EMP: 1
SALES (est): 54.1K **Privately Held**
SIC: 2431 Millwork

Montchanin
New Castle County

(G-4984)
DAN LICALE
Also Called: Inn At Montchanin Village, The Corner Kirk Rd And 100 (19710)
P.O. Box 130 (19710-0130)
PHONE...................................302 888-2133
Ann Licale, *Owner*
Dan Licale, *Owner*
EMP: 85
SALES (est): 1.8MM **Privately Held**
WEB: www.montchanin.com
SIC: 7011 Bed & breakfast inn

(G-4985)
DAVIS INSURANCE GROUP INC
And Rockland Rd Rr 100 (19710)
PHONE...................................302 652-4700
William H Davis Jr, *CEO*
Robert H Davis Jr, *President*
Robert Davis, *President*
Janet Matarese, *Accounts Mgr*
Janet McNulty, *Agent*
EMP: 9
SQ FT: 3,500
SALES (est): 1.4MM **Privately Held**
WEB: www.davisinsurancegroup.com
SIC: 6411 Insurance agents; life insurance agents; property & casualty insurance agent

(G-4986)
MALVERN FEDERAL SAVINGS BANK
10 W Rockland Rd (19710-2008)
PHONE...................................302 477-7305
George H Trapnell, *Manager*
EMP: 9
SALES (corp-wide): 43.9MM **Privately Held**
SIC: 6035 Federal savings banks
PA: Malvern Federal Savings Bank
42 E Lancaster Ave Unit A
Paoli PA 19301
610 644-9400

(G-4987)
MORROW LIMITED
4 W Rockland Rd (19710-2008)
PHONE...................................213 631-3534
Lan Fu, *Sales Mgr*
EMP: 61
SALES: 275K **Privately Held**
SIC: 7371 Computer software development & applications

New Castle
New Castle County

(G-4988)
1122 CONDOMINIUM (PA)
Also Called: Eleven Twenty Two Condominium
610 W 11th St (19720-6075)
PHONE...................................302 234-4860
EMP: 4
SALES (est): 620.8K **Privately Held**
SIC: 8641 Condominium association

(G-4989)
166TH MEDICAL SQUADRON
2600 Spruance Dr (19720-1615)
PHONE...................................302 323-3385
Rick Collier, *Manager*
EMP: 60 EST: 2010
SALES (est): 749.3K **Privately Held**
SIC: 8099 Health & allied services

(G-4990)
326 ASSOCIATES LP
Also Called: New Castle Farmers Market
110 N Dupont Hwy (19720-3102)
PHONE...................................302 328-4101
Richard Stat, *Partner*
EMP: 6
SQ FT: 2,000
SALES (est): 608.1K **Privately Held**
SIC: 5149 Groceries & related products

(G-4991)
A B FAB & MACHINING LLC
170 Earland Dr (19720)
PHONE...................................302 293-4945
Allen Beiler,
EMP: 2
SQ FT: 23,000
SALES: 500K **Privately Held**
SIC: 3499 Machine bases, metal

(G-4992)
A BAIL BOND BY RESTO & CO INC
Also Called: Bond Network, The
7 Corkwood Ln (19720-7670)
PHONE...................................302 312-7714
William Resto, *President*
EMP: 4
SALES (est): 283.5K **Privately Held**
SIC: 8322 Individual & family services

(G-4993)
A DUIE PYLE INC
204 Quigley Blvd (19720-4106)
PHONE...................................302 326-9440
Duie Latta, *President*
EMP: 71
SALES (corp-wide): 398MM **Privately Held**
SIC: 4213 Trucking, except local
PA: A. Duie Pyle Inc.
650 Westtown Rd
West Chester PA 19382
610 696-5800

(G-4994)
A STITCH IN TIME
101 Harrison Ave (19720-2526)
PHONE...................................302 395-1306
Connie Mc Grory, *Owner*
EMP: 4
SALES: 50K **Privately Held**
SIC: 2395 Embroidery products, except schiffli machine; embroidery & art needlework

(G-4995)
A-1 SANITATION SERVICE INC
1009 River Rd (19720-5103)
P.O. Box 336 (19720-0336)
PHONE...................................302 322-1074
Anthony Smiertka Jr, *President*
Anthony A Smiertka Jr, *Vice Pres*
Steven Smiertka, *Vice Pres*
Joanne Smiertka, *Admin Sec*
EMP: 15
SQ FT: 3,800
SALES (est): 2.4MM **Privately Held**
WEB: www.a1sanitation.com
SIC: 7359 7699 Portable toilet rental; sewer cleaning & rodding

(G-4996)
AARONS INC
511 E Basin Rd (19720-4230)
PHONE...................................302 221-1200
Sirena Rich, *Manager*
Jeff Mc Cant, *Manager*
EMP: 4
SALES (corp-wide): 3.8B **Publicly Held**
WEB: www.aaronrents.com
SIC: 7359 Home appliance, furniture & entertainment rental services
PA: Aaron's, Inc.
400 Galleria Pkwy Se # 30
Atlanta GA 30339
678 402-3000

(G-4997)
ABC PAYDAY & TITLE LENDING
624 E Basin Rd (19720-2189)
PHONE...................................302 322-0233
Aneesah Michaels, *Manager*
EMP: 4
SALES (est): 368.4K **Privately Held**
SIC: 6163 Loan brokers

(G-4998)
ABOVE BEYOND UNISEX HAIR SALON
1111 Wilmington Rd (19720-3641)
PHONE...................................302 276-0187
Natasha Boney, *Owner*
EMP: 4 EST: 2009
SALES (est): 57.7K **Privately Held**
SIC: 7231 Unisex hair salons

(G-4999)
ACANTHUS & REED LTD
Also Called: Acanthus and Reed
106 E 3rd St (19720-4537)
PHONE...................................212 628-9290
Adrian Alganaraz, *President*
EMP: 4
SQ FT: 1,500
SALES (est): 675.4K **Privately Held**
WEB: www.acanthus-reed.com
SIC: 7699 Picture framing, custom

(G-5000)
ACCESS LABOR SERVICE INC (PA)
2203 N Dupont Hwy (19720-6302)
PHONE...................................302 326-2575
Butch Brooks, *President*
EMP: 15
SALES (est): 3.5MM **Privately Held**
SIC: 7361 Placement agencies

(G-5001)
ACTION UNLIMITED RESOURCES INC
230 Quigley Blvd (19720-4106)
PHONE...................................302 323-1455
Aaron Glazar, *President*
Chuck Epperson, *COO*
Wayne Dippold, *Store Mgr*
Michael Pinto, *Safety Mgr*
EMP: 21
SQ FT: 35,000
SALES (est): 4.3MM **Privately Held**
WEB: www.action-industries.com
SIC: 7359 2621 5169 Stores & yards equipment rental; paper mills; chemicals & allied products

(G-5002)
ACUITY BRANDS LIGHTING INC
Also Called: Whiteoptics
19 Blevins Dr (19720-4153)
PHONE...................................302 476-2055
Eric Teather, *Branch Mgr*
EMP: 20
SALES (corp-wide): 3.6B **Publicly Held**
SIC: 3646 3645 3641 Commercial indusl & institutional electric lighting fixtures; residential lighting fixtures; electric lamps
HQ: Acuity Brands Lighting, Inc.
1 Acuity Way
Conyers GA 30012

(G-5003)
ADECCO USA INC
40 Reads Way (19720-1649)
PHONE...................................302 669-4005
Sandie Milligan, *Branch Mgr*
EMP: 7
SALES (corp-wide): 26.4B **Privately Held**
SIC: 7361 Employment agencies
HQ: Adecco Usa, Inc.
10151 Deerwood Park Blvd
Jacksonville FL 32256
940 360-2000

(G-5004)
ADERYN WOODWORKS
11 Villas Dr Apt 9 (19720-2846)
PHONE...................................219 229-5070
Sean Billups, *Principal*
EMP: 1
SALES (est): 54.1K **Privately Held**
SIC: 2431 Millwork

(G-5005)
ADESIS INC
27 Mccullough Dr (19720-2080)
PHONE...................................302 323-4880
Charles Chuck Beard, *CEO*
Bill Wiley, *General Mgr*
Jianfei Zheng, *Business Mgr*
Andrew Cottone, *Vice Pres*
Jack Church, *Facilities Mgr*
▲ EMP: 40
SALES (est): 10.4MM **Publicly Held**
SIC: 2834 Medicines, capsuled or ampuled
PA: Universal Display Corporation
375 Phillips Blvd Ste 1
Ewing NJ 08618

New Castle - New Castle County (G-5006) GEOGRAPHIC SECTION

(G-5006)
ADT LLC
140 Quigley Blvd (19720-4104)
PHONE 302 325-3125
Eric Orosco, *Manager*
EMP: 12
SALES (corp-wide): 4.5B **Publicly Held**
WEB: www.brinks-home-security-system.com
SIC: **7382** Burglar alarm maintenance & monitoring
HQ: Adt Llc
1501 W Yamato Rd
Boca Raton FL 33431
561 988-3600

(G-5007)
ADVANCE AMERICA CASH ADVANCE
527 E Basin Rd (19720-4230)
PHONE 302 999-0145
EMP: 10
SALES (corp-wide): 5.3B **Privately Held**
SIC: **6141** Personal Credit Institution
HQ: Advance America, Cash Advance Centers, Inc.
135 N Church St
Spartanburg SC 29306
864 342-5600

(G-5008)
ADVANCE OFFICE INSTLLTIONS INC
37 Lukens Dr Ste B (19720-7710)
PHONE 302 777-5599
Joseph Culter, *Vice Pres*
Armin Kostic, *Vice Pres*
Felix Marrero, *Opers Mgr*
EMP: 40
SALES: 2MM **Privately Held**
WEB: www.advanceofficeinstallations.com
SIC: **1799** 4214 7641 4225 Office furniture installation; furniture moving & storage, local; office furniture repair & maintenance; general warehousing & storage; office & public building furniture; office furniture

(G-5009)
ADVANCED MACHINERY SALES INC
2 Mccullough Dr Ste 2 # 2 (19720-2092)
P.O. Box 312 (19720-0312)
PHONE 302 322-2226
Wolfgang Derke, *President*
Hanns J Derke, *Vice Pres*
Hanns Derke, *Vice Pres*
▲ EMP: 11
SQ FT: 11,000
SALES (est): 2.7MM **Privately Held**
SIC: **5084** Sawmill machinery & equipment; woodworking machinery

(G-5010)
ADVANCED THERMAL PACKAGING
420 Churchmans Rd (19720-3157)
PHONE 302 326-2222
Marshall Suplee, *Manager*
EMP: 2
SALES (est): 157.5K **Privately Held**
SIC: **2621** Paper mills

(G-5011)
AEGISNET INC (PA)
42 Reads Way (19720-1649)
P.O. Box 3897, Merrifield VA (22116-3897)
PHONE 302 325-2122
Michael Callihan, *President*
Mario Hyland, *Senior VP*
Tom Lourenco, *Vice Pres*
Monica Hozle, *CFO*
EMP: 25
SALES (est): 6.1MM **Privately Held**
WEB: www.aegis.net
SIC: **7379**

(G-5012)
AEGLE HEALTH
27 Chelwynne Rd (19720-3535)
PHONE 302 468-0235
Alton Williams, *President*
EMP: 8
SALES (est): 81.8K **Privately Held**
SIC: **8082** Home health care services

(G-5013)
AERES CORPORATION
2035 Sunset Lk Rd Ste B-2 (19720)
PHONE 858 926-8626
Safa Mahzari, *CEO*
EMP: 1 EST: 2015
SALES (est): 71K **Privately Held**
SIC: **7372** 7389 Prepackaged software;

(G-5014)
AERO WAYS INC
131 N Dupont Hwy (19720-3135)
PHONE 302 324-9970
Duane Brown, *President*
Charles Belmont, *President*
Ron Beckson, *COO*
Edward T Bohn, *COO*
Ronald M Beckson, *CFO*
EMP: 10 EST: 1999
SQ FT: 24,000
SALES (est): 2.3MM **Privately Held**
WEB: www.aeroways.com
SIC: **7363** Pilot service, aviation

(G-5015)
AEROTEK INC
100 W Cmmons Blvd Ste 425 (19720)
PHONE 302 561-6300
Matt Bramblett, *President*
EMP: 22
SALES (corp-wide): 13.4B **Privately Held**
SIC: **7363** Temporary help service
HQ: Aerotek, Inc.
7301 Parkway Dr
Hanover MD 21076
410 694-5100

(G-5016)
AFFORDABLE DELIVERY SVCS LLC
Also Called: ADS
217 Lisa Dr Ste D (19720-8404)
PHONE 302 276-0246
Miguel Marrero,
EMP: 20
SALES: 1.3MM **Privately Held**
SIC: **4212** 1799 Delivery service, vehicular; office furniture installation

(G-5017)
AFFORDABLE HEATING & AC
1700 Wilmington Rd (19720-2749)
PHONE 302 328-9220
William J Burns, *President*
EMP: 5
SALES (est): 730.4K **Privately Held**
SIC: **1711** Warm air heating & air conditioning contractor; heating & air conditioning contractors

(G-5018)
AIA
4058 New Castle Ave (19720-1434)
PHONE 302 407-2252
Brian Darby, *Owner*
EMP: 2
SALES (est): 73.2K **Privately Held**
SIC: **2759** Commercial printing

(G-5019)
AIRBASE CARPET MART ABCT DIST
76 Southgate Blvd (19720-2068)
PHONE 302 323-8800
Michael Longwood, *Owner*
EMP: 4
SALES (est): 210K **Privately Held**
SIC: **5099** 1752 Firearms & ammunition, except sporting; carpet laying

(G-5020)
AJACKS TIRE SERVICE INC
819 S Dupont Hwy (19720-4610)
PHONE 302 834-5200
Anthony Micucio Jr, *President*
EMP: 4 EST: 1976
SQ FT: 2,400
SALES (est): 315K **Privately Held**
SIC: **7534** 5531 Tire repair shop; automotive tires

(G-5021)
ALDERMAN AUTOMOTIVE ENTERPRISE
Also Called: Alderman Automotive Machine Sp
2317 N Dupont Hwy (19720-6304)
PHONE 302 652-3733
George Alderman, *President*
Paul Alderman, *Vice Pres*
EMP: 6
SALES: 350K **Privately Held**
SIC: **7538** General automotive repair shops

(G-5022)
ALFREDA HICKS LLC
701 E Hazeldell Ave Ste 2 (19720-6121)
PHONE 302 312-8721
Phillip Dillard Jr, *Principal*
EMP: 4
SALES (est): 217.4K **Privately Held**
SIC: **4789** Passenger train services

(G-5023)
ALMARS OUTBOARD SERVICE & SLS
701 Washington St (19720-6046)
PHONE 302 328-8541
Albert Marinelli Jr, *President*
Jack Aukamp, *Sales Staff*
EMP: 9
SQ FT: 16,000
SALES (est): 1.4MM **Privately Held**
SIC: **7699** 5551 Marine engine repair; outboard motors

(G-5024)
ALOFT CANVAS LLC
511 Delaware St (19720-5045)
PHONE 302 893-0144
Dionne G Rhoades, *Principal*
EMP: 1 EST: 2014
SALES (est): 65K **Privately Held**
SIC: **2211** Canvas

(G-5025)
ALPHA OMEGA INVSTGTONS WRKMANS
42 Reads Way (19720-1649)
PHONE 302 323-8111
Dorothy Wesley, *Owner*
EMP: 5
SALES: 200K **Privately Held**
SIC: **7381** Private investigator

(G-5026)
ALPHA OMEGA SCIENTIFIC LLC
129 Freedom Trl (19720-3849)
PHONE 302 415-4499
Saki Koudis, *Vice Pres*
EMP: 5
SALES (est): 103.9K **Privately Held**
SIC: **8731** Commercial physical research

(G-5027)
ALSCO INC
30 Mccullough Dr (19720-2066)
PHONE 302 322-2136
Jared Wantoch, *General Mgr*
EMP: 40
SALES (corp-wide): 922.9MM **Privately Held**
WEB: www.palacelaundry.com
SIC: **7213** Uniform supply
PA: Alsco Inc,
505 E 200 S Ste 101
Salt Lake City UT 84102
801 328-8331

(G-5028)
ALVINS PROFESSIONAL SERVICES
Also Called: APS Cleaning Services
241 Old Churchmans Rd (19720-1529)
PHONE 302 544-6634
Alvin R Emory Jr, *President*
Brandt Emory, *Vice Pres*
EMP: 10
SALES (est): 279.8K **Privately Held**
WEB: www.apscleaning.org
SIC: **7349** 7699 Janitorial service, contract basis; cleaning services

(G-5029)
AMEMG INC
Also Called: Adventures Lrning Erly Chood
32 Phoebe Farms Ln (19720-8769)
PHONE 302 220-7132
Joanne Steicher, *President*
EMP: 13 EST: 2006
SALES (est): 618.8K **Privately Held**
SIC: **8351** Child day care services

(G-5030)
AMER MASONRY T A MARINO
Also Called: Marino & Sons
811 Reybold Dr (19720-4616)
PHONE 302 834-1511
Thomas Marino Jr, *President*
EMP: 5
SALES (est): 331.2K **Privately Held**
SIC: **1741** Masonry & other stonework

(G-5031)
AMERICAN FEDERATION OF STATE
Also Called: Afscme-Council 81
91 Christiana Rd (19720-3104)
PHONE 302 323-2121
Michael Beagetto, *Exec Dir*
EMP: 10
SALES (corp-wide): 177.7MM **Privately Held**
WEB: www.afscme512.org
SIC: **8631** Labor unions & similar labor organizations
PA: American Federation Of State County & Municipal Employees
1625 L St Nw
Washington DC 20036
202 429-1000

(G-5032)
AMERICAN FURNITURE RENTALS INC
Also Called: A F R
490 W Basin Rd (19720-6408)
PHONE 302 323-1682
Frank McCall, *Branch Mgr*
EMP: 50
SALES (corp-wide): 98.6MM **Privately Held**
WEB: www.rentfurniture.com
SIC: **7359** Furniture rental
PA: American Furniture Rentals, Inc.
720 Hylton Rd
Pennsauken NJ 08110
856 406-1200

(G-5033)
AMERICAN MINERALS INC
301 Pigeon Point Rd (19720-1400)
PHONE 302 652-3301
Jim Murphy, *Manager*
EMP: 8
SALES (corp-wide): 1.5MM **Privately Held**
WEB: www.princeminerals.com
SIC: **1446** 3313 Silica sand mining; electrometallurgical products
HQ: American Minerals Inc
21 W 46th St Fl 14
New York NY 10036
646 747-4222

(G-5034)
AMERICAN MINERALS PARTNERSHIP
301 Pigeon Point Rd (19720-1400)
PHONE 302 652-3301
Frank Nefoske, *Principal*
▲ EMP: 200
SALES (est): 9.5MM **Privately Held**
SIC: **1061** 1011 1099 Manganese ores mining; manganite mining; iron ores; bauxite mining; zirconium ore mining

(G-5035)
AMERICAN POSTAL WORKERS UNION
271 Christiana Rd (19720-2907)
P.O. Box 311 (19720-0311)
PHONE 302 322-8994
Steve Collins, *President*
EMP: 20

GEOGRAPHIC SECTION

New Castle - New Castle County (G-5064)

SALES (corp-wide): 56.8MM **Privately Held**
WEB: www.denverapwu.com
SIC: 8631 Labor union
PA: American Postal Workers Union
1300 L St Nw Ste 200
Washington DC 20005
202 842-4200

(G-5036)
AMSTEL MECHANICAL CONTRACTORS
Also Called: Honeywell Authorized Dealer
1183 S Dupont Hwy (19720-5203)
PHONE..................................302 836-6469
John Nobel, *President*
EMP: 8
SQ FT: 5,000
SALES (est): 1.3MM **Privately Held**
SIC: 1711 Warm air heating & air conditioning contractor; plumbing contractors

(G-5037)
ANCHOR ELECTRIC INC
185 Old Churchmans Rd (19720-3115)
P.O. Box 12591, Wilmington (19850-2591)
PHONE..................................302 221-6111
Charles Saxton, *President*
EMP: 8
SALES (est): 783.2K **Privately Held**
SIC: 1731 General electrical contractor

(G-5038)
ANDRE NOEL THALIA
Also Called: Mistress of Spice
550 S Dupont Hwy Apt 11b (19720-5115)
PHONE..................................302 747-0813
Andre Noel Thalia, *Owner*
EMP: 1
SALES (est): 68.6K **Privately Held**
SIC: 2099 5499 Seasonings & spices; spices & herbs

(G-5039)
ANGELS LINDAS
6 Parkway Ct (19720-4020)
PHONE..................................302 328-3700
Linda Bright, *Owner*
EMP: 30
SALES (est): 71.8K **Privately Held**
SIC: 8351 Group day care center

(G-5040)
ANTONIOS LAWN SERVICE LLC
8 W 9th St (19720-6003)
PHONE..................................302 293-1200
Paul Antonio, *Principal*
EMP: 4
SALES (est): 207.7K **Privately Held**
SIC: 0782 Lawn care services

(G-5041)
APPLEBY APARTMENTS ASSOC LP
401 Bedford Ln (19720-3936)
PHONE..................................302 219-5014
Trudy Carter, *Manager*
EMP: 5
SALES (est): 479.7K **Privately Held**
SIC: 6513 Apartment hotel operation

(G-5042)
ARGO FINANCIAL SERVICES INC
Also Called: United Check Cashing
104 Penn Mart Shopg Ctr (19720-4209)
PHONE..................................302 322-7788
David Argo, *Manager*
EMP: 6
SQ FT: 1,000
SALES (est): 658.3K **Privately Held**
SIC: 6099 Check clearing services

(G-5043)
ARISE AFRICA FOUNDATION INC
10 Elks Trl (19720-3855)
PHONE..................................877 829-5500
Damilola Junaid, *President*
Archit Joshi, *Director*
EMP: 6 **EST:** 2016
SALES (est): 95.6K **Privately Held**
SIC: 8641 Civic social & fraternal associations

(G-5044)
ARKION LIFE SCIENCES LLC (PA)
551 Mews Dr Ste J (19720-2798)
PHONE..................................302 504-7400
Earnest W Porta, *President*
Thomas A Jerrell, *Vice Pres*
Harvey L Weaver, *Vice Pres*
Rick L Stejskal, *CFO*
Tony Simei, *Controller*
▲ **EMP:** 28
SQ FT: 7,998
SALES (est): 5.6MM **Privately Held**
WEB: www.airepel.com
SIC: 5999 8731 Feed & farm supply; biological research; biotechnical research, commercial; environmental research

(G-5045)
ARMSTRONG RELOCATION CO LLC
20 E Commons Blvd (19720-1734)
PHONE..................................302 323-9000
EMP: 5
SALES (est): 544.3K **Privately Held**
SIC: 4213 Trucking, except local

(G-5046)
ARS NEW CASTLE LLC
263 Quigley Blvd Ste 1b (19720-8126)
PHONE..................................302 323-9400
Daniel Ennis, *Mng Member*
EMP: 5
SALES (est): 199.6K **Privately Held**
SIC: 8093 Drug clinic, outpatient

(G-5047)
ART GUILD INC
Also Called: Artguild
200 Anchor Mill Rd (19720-2264)
PHONE..................................302 420-8056
Nick Giordano, *Branch Mgr*
EMP: 1
SALES (corp-wide): 18.2MM **Privately Held**
SIC: 3993 Signs & advertising specialties
PA: Art Guild Inc.
300 Wolf Dr
West Deptford NJ 08086
856 853-7500

(G-5048)
ASSOCTED BLDRS CNTRS DEL CHPTE (PA)
Also Called: ASSOCIATED BUILDERS & CONTRACT
31 Blevins Dr Ste B (19720-4170)
PHONE..................................302 328-1111
Edward J Capodanno, *President*
EMP: 5
SALES: 1MM **Privately Held**
SIC: 8611 Contractors' association

(G-5049)
ASW MACHINERY INC (DH)
Also Called: Felder USA
2 Lukens Dr Ste 300 (19720-2796)
PHONE..................................899 792-5288
Ruan Du Toit, *CEO*
Geoffrey Doubet, *Sales Staff*
Mark Mullenhour, *Manager*
◆ **EMP:** 16
SQ FT: 7,800
SALES (est): 10.1MM
SALES (corp-wide): 12.5MM **Privately Held**
WEB: www.format-4-usa.com
SIC: 5084 Woodworking machinery
HQ: Felder Kg
Kr-Felder-StraBe 1
Hall In Tirol 6060
522 358-500

(G-5050)
ATI HOLDINGS LLC
Also Called: ATI Physical Therapy
2032 New Castle Ave (19720-7703)
PHONE..................................302 654-1700
EMP: 21
SALES (corp-wide): 338.3MM **Privately Held**
SIC: 8049 Physical therapist
PA: Ati Holdings, Llc
790 Remington Blvd
Bolingbrook IL 60440
630 296-2222

(G-5051)
ATLANTIC AVIATION CORPORATION
120 Old Churchmans Rd (19720-3116)
PHONE..................................302 613-4747
Dave Hill, *Branch Mgr*
Mark Anderson, *Manager*
EMP: 25
SALES (corp-wide): 1.7B **Publicly Held**
SIC: 4581 Aircraft servicing & repairing
HQ: Atlantic Aviation Corporation
5201 Tennyson Pkwy # 150
Plano TX 75024
972 905-2500

(G-5052)
ATLANTIC WATER PRODUCTS
74 Southgate Blvd (19720-2068)
PHONE..................................302 326-1166
Curtis Wunder, *Owner*
Timothy Way, *General Mgr*
EMP: 24
SALES (est): 1.5MM **Privately Held**
WEB: www.atlanticwaterproducts.com
SIC: 7389 4971 Water softener service; water distribution or supply systems for irrigation

(G-5053)
ATLAS WLDG & FABRICATION INC
728 Grantham Ln (19720-4802)
PHONE..................................302 326-1900
Christopher Ramsey, *President*
Kurt Schmid, *Vice Pres*
Tracey Schmid, *Admin Sec*
EMP: 21
SQ FT: 3,000
SALES: 6.2MM **Privately Held**
SIC: 3444 1791 Sheet metalwork; structural steel erection

(G-5054)
AUDIOSCIENCE INC (PA)
42 Reads Way (19720-1649)
PHONE..................................302 324-5333
Richard Gross, *President*
Stephen Turner, *Vice Pres*
Nicole Santiago, *Sales Mgr*
Andrew Elder, *Shareholder*
▲ **EMP:** 11 **EST:** 1996
SQ FT: 3,697
SALES (est): 2.3MM **Privately Held**
WEB: www.audioscience.com
SIC: 3577 Data conversion equipment, media-to-media: computer

(G-5055)
AUTO COLLISION SERVICE (PA)
501 Churchmans Rd (19720-3154)
PHONE..................................302 328-5611
Tom Henry, *Principal*
EMP: 4
SALES (est): 459.2K **Privately Held**
SIC: 7532 Collision shops, automotive

(G-5056)
AUTO SUN ROOF INC
26 Parkway Cir Ste 5 (19720-4070)
PHONE..................................302 325-3001
Dave Hoffman, *Manager*
EMP: 10
SALES (corp-wide): 5.2MM **Privately Held**
WEB: www.autosunroof.com
SIC: 7549 Automotive customizing services, non-factory basis; sun roof installation, automotive
PA: Auto Sun Roof, Inc.
1305 Industrial Hwy
Cinnaminson NJ 08077
856 786-0600

(G-5057)
AUTOPORT INC
203 Pigeon Point Rd (19720-2177)
PHONE..................................302 658-5100
Roy Kirchner, *President*
Grace McGrath, *Business Mgr*
John Lovett, *Vice Pres*
Melissa Arocha, *Terminal Mgr*
Susan Schofield, *Marketing Mgr*
▼ **EMP:** 40
SQ FT: 29,000
SALES (est): 6.8MM **Privately Held**
WEB: www.autoportinc.com
SIC: 7532 7549 5012 3714 Top & body repair & paint shops; automotive customizing services, non-factory basis; truck bodies; acceleration equipment, motor vehicle

(G-5058)
AVIS RENT A CAR SYSTEM INC
Also Called: Avis Rent A Car Systems
151 N Dupont Hwy (19720-3136)
PHONE..................................302 322-2092
Pat Boyer, *Principal*
EMP: 17
SALES (corp-wide): 9.1B **Publicly Held**
SIC: 7514 Rent-a-car service
HQ: Avis Rent A Car System, Inc.
6 Sylvan Way Ste 1
Parsippany NJ 07054
973 496-3500

(G-5059)
AVKIN INC
113 J And M Dr Fl 2 (19720-3142)
PHONE..................................302 562-7468
Amy Cowperthwait, *CEO*
Mike Patterson, *COO*
Amy Bucha, *Security Dir*
EMP: 12 **EST:** 2015
SALES (est): 1.4MM **Privately Held**
SIC: 5999 8299 3999 Education aids, devices & supplies; educational services; education aids, devices & supplies

(G-5060)
AVS INDUSTRIES LLC
21 Bellecor Dr Ste C (19720-1743)
PHONE..................................302 221-1705
David Sydow, *CEO*
Robert Colwell, *Natl Sales Mgr*
▲ **EMP:** 7
SALES (est): 1.9MM **Privately Held**
WEB: www.avsind.com
SIC: 5023 Sheets, textile

(G-5061)
AXESS CORPORATION (PA)
91 Lukens Dr Ste E (19720-2799)
PHONE..................................302 292-8500
Richard Giacco, *President*
Robert E Davis, *Managing Dir*
Alexander F Giacco, *Managing Dir*
EMP: 3
SALES (est): 2.2MM **Privately Held**
WEB: www.empowermaterials.com
SIC: 3826 3089 3081 Analytical instruments; plastic containers, except foam; unsupported plastics film & sheet

(G-5062)
B & F TOWING & SALVAGE CO INC
449 Old Airport Rd (19720-1001)
PHONE..................................302 328-4146
Robert Fenimore, *President*
Henry Fenimore, *Corp Secy*
EMP: 20 **EST:** 1966
SQ FT: 3,000
SALES (est): 2.6MM **Privately Held**
WEB: www.bftowing.com
SIC: 7549 7538 Towing service, automotive; general truck repair

(G-5063)
B G HALKO & SONS INC
204 Old Churchmans Rd (19720-1530)
PHONE..................................302 322-2020
Thomas G Halko, *President*
EMP: 6
SQ FT: 4,000
SALES (est): 675.9K **Privately Held**
SIC: 1799 Fence construction

(G-5064)
BAINES SHAPIRO & ASSOCIATES
30 Queen Ave (19720-2031)
PHONE..................................302 384-2322
Maverick Robinson, *Owner*
EMP: 4
SALES (est): 160K **Privately Held**
SIC: 7322 Adjustment & collection services

New Castle - New Castle County (G-5065)

(G-5065)
BALL ROOM BY BILL
166 S Du Pont Pkwy (19720-4168)
PHONE.....................302 328-4014
EMP: 1
SALES (est): 61K **Privately Held**
SIC: 3993 Mfg Signs/Advertising Specialties

(G-5066)
BANK OF NEW CASTLE
Also Called: DISCOVER
12 Reads Way (19720-1649)
PHONE.....................800 347-3301
Beverly Ballard, *Principal*
EMP: 5
SALES: 316K
SALES (corp-wide): 12.8B **Publicly Held**
WEB: www.discoverdriverspremier.com
SIC: 6141 Personal credit institutions
PA: Discover Financial Services
2500 Lake Cook Rd
Riverwoods IL 60015
224 405-0900

(G-5067)
BARITC LAWN CARE LLC
621 Delaware St (19720-5073)
PHONE.....................302 420-6072
EMP: 4
SALES (est): 120.7K **Privately Held**
SIC: 0782 Lawn care services

(G-5068)
BATHWA LIMITED
702 Delaware St (19720-5060)
PHONE.....................213 550-3812
Zhisha Yang,
EMP: 83
SALES: 280K **Privately Held**
SIC: 7371 Computer software development & applications

(G-5069)
BATTAGLIA ASSOCIATES INC
11 Industrial Blvd (19720-2087)
PHONE.....................302 325-6100
Christine Meyer, *President*
Jennifer Sidwell, *Vice Pres*
Bill Broomall, *Project Mgr*
EMP: 4 EST: 2016
SALES (est): 174K **Privately Held**
SIC: 1711 1731 Plumbing contractors; heating & air conditioning contractors; mechanical contractor; electric power systems contractors; general electrical contractor

(G-5070)
BATTAGLIA ELECTRIC INC
11 Industrial Blvd (19720-2087)
P.O. Box 630 (19720-0630)
PHONE.....................302 325-6100
Gene Battaglia, *President*
Louis J Orsini, *Vice Pres*
Jennifer Sidwell, *Vice Pres*
Scott Hibbard, *Project Mgr*
Jim McNeal, *Project Mgr*
EMP: 175
SQ FT: 20,000
SALES (est): 34.8MM **Privately Held**
WEB: www.battagliaelectric.com
SIC: 1731 1711 General electrical contractor; mechanical contractor

(G-5071)
BATTAGLIA MECHANICAL INC
11 Industrial Blvd (19720-2087)
P.O. Box 630 (19720-0630)
PHONE.....................302 325-6100
Eugene Battaglia, *President*
Jean Battaglia, *Corp Secy*
Anthony Iorii, *Vice Pres*
EMP: 28
SQ FT: 20,000
SALES (est): 2.1MM **Privately Held**
WEB: www.battagliamechanical.com
SIC: 1521 Single-family housing construction

(G-5072)
BAY SHIPPERS LLC
1535 Matassino Rd (19720-3353)
P.O. Box 650 (19720-0650)
PHONE.....................302 652-5005
Robert Higgins, *Principal*
EMP: 8
SALES (est): 639.3K **Privately Held**
SIC: 4789 Cargo loading & unloading services

(G-5073)
BAYADA HOME HEALTH CARE INC
32 Reads Way (19720-1649)
PHONE.....................856 231-1000
Patricia Watson, *Director*
EMP: 16
SALES (corp-wide): 672.5MM **Privately Held**
WEB: www.bayada.com
SIC: 8082 Visiting nurse service
PA: Bayada Home Health Care, Inc.
1 W Main St
Moorestown NJ 08057
856 231-1000

(G-5074)
BAYADA HOME HEALTH CARE INC
15 Reads Way Ste 205 (19720-1600)
PHONE.....................302 322-2300
Mary Agnes, *Branch Mgr*
EMP: 5
SALES (corp-wide): 672.5MM **Privately Held**
SIC: 8082 Home health care services
PA: Bayada Home Health Care, Inc.
1 W Main St
Moorestown NJ 08057
856 231-1000

(G-5075)
BAYSHORE FORD TRUCK SALES INC (PA)
4003 N Dupont Hwy (19720-6323)
P.O. Box 627 (19720-0627)
PHONE.....................302 656-3160
Dale Brewer, *President*
Mike Branca, *General Mgr*
Nikki Mohr, *Finance Dir*
John Christof, *Sales Mgr*
Todd Willard, *Sales Mgr*
▼ EMP: 69
SQ FT: 26,000
SALES (est): 16.4MM **Privately Held**
WEB: www.bayshoreford.com
SIC: 7513 5511 7538 Truck rental & leasing, no drivers; automobiles, new & used; trucks, tractors & trailers: new & used; general automotive repair shops

(G-5076)
BCD SYSTEMS
34 Blevins Dr Ste 1 (19720-4177)
PHONE.....................302 328-2070
George Finnan, *President*
Linda Finnan, *Corp Secy*
EMP: 7
SQ FT: 6,000
SALES: 500K **Privately Held**
WEB: www.bcdsys.com
SIC: 7331 Mailing list compilers

(G-5077)
BEACON AIR INC
23 Parkway Cir Ste 9 (19720-4019)
P.O. Box 10806, Wilmington (19850-0806)
PHONE.....................302 323-1688
Dennis Mellott, *President*
Jennifer Rydlewski, *Manager*
EMP: 8
SALES (est): 1MM **Privately Held**
WEB: www.beaconair.com
SIC: 1731 Computer installation

(G-5078)
BEAR MATERIALS LLC (PA)
4048 New Castle Ave (19720-1455)
PHONE.....................302 658-5241
Nicholas Ferrera Sr,
Nicholas Ferrera Jr,
Vincent Greggo,
EMP: 9 EST: 1998
SQ FT: 8,000
SALES (est): 3MM **Privately Held**
SIC: 1442 Construction sand & gravel

(G-5079)
BEAST OF EAST BASEBALL LLC
916 Gray St (19720-6036)
PHONE.....................302 545-9094
EMP: 4
SALES (est): 101.3K **Privately Held**
SIC: 7997 Baseball club, except professional & semi-professional

(G-5080)
BEGINNING BLSSNGS CHLDCARE LLC
Also Called: Beginning Blessings Daycare
23 Karen Ct (19720-5171)
PHONE.....................302 893-1726
Deborah Omowunmi, *President*
Rotimi Omowunmi, *Principal*
EMP: 5
SALES: 150K **Privately Held**
SIC: 8351 Child day care services

(G-5081)
BENNETT & BENNETT INC
122 Delaware St (19720-4814)
PHONE.....................302 990-8939
EMP: 15
SQ FT: 1,500
SALES: 1.7MM **Privately Held**
SIC: 8742 4214 7299 Mgmt Consulting Svcs Local Truck-With Storage Misc Personal Service

(G-5082)
BENZ HYDRAULICS INC (PA)
Also Called: Benz Hydraulic Service
153 S Dupont Hwy (19720-4127)
PHONE.....................302 328-6648
Timothy J Dougherty, *President*
John E Dougherty, *Vice Pres*
Shelley Dougherty, *Vice Pres*
Ken Parramore, *Foreman/Supr*
Joann Christian, *Accounts Mgr*
EMP: 14
SQ FT: 3,800
SALES: 2.8MM **Privately Held**
SIC: 5084 Hydraulic systems equipment & supplies

(G-5083)
BERMAN DEVELOPMENT CORP
Also Called: Scotch Hills Apartments
30 Highland Blvd (19720-6980)
PHONE.....................302 323-1197
Sara Farmer, *Manager*
EMP: 5
SALES (corp-wide): 7.9MM **Privately Held**
SIC: 6513 Apartment building operators
PA: Berman Development Corp
901 S Trooper Rd
Valley Forge PA

(G-5084)
BERMAN DEVELOPMENT CORP
Also Called: Stonebridge Apartments
2801 Stonebridge Blvd (19720-6738)
PHONE.....................302 323-9522
Page Leland, *Branch Mgr*
EMP: 4
SALES (corp-wide): 7.9MM **Privately Held**
SIC: 1531 Cooperative apartment developers
PA: Berman Development Corp
901 S Trooper Rd
Valley Forge PA

(G-5085)
BERRODIN SOUTH INC
20 Mccullough Dr (19720-2066)
PHONE.....................302 575-0500
John Berrodin, *President*
James Berrodin, *Corp Secy*
Lou Berrodin, *Vice Pres*
EMP: 20
SQ FT: 25,000
SALES (est): 5.6MM
SALES (corp-wide): 11.6MM **Privately Held**
WEB: www.berrodin.com
SIC: 5013 Automotive supplies & parts; automotive supplies
PA: Berrodin Co.
790 Burmont Rd
Drexel Hill PA 19026
610 259-8700

(G-5086)
BEST STUCCO LLC
304 Jefferson Ave (19720-2506)
PHONE.....................302 650-3620
Edgar Morales, *Principal*
EMP: 1
SALES (est): 80.4K **Privately Held**
SIC: 3299 Stucco

(G-5087)
BESTRANS INC
19 Davidson Ln Fmt Frnt (19720-2207)
PHONE.....................302 824-0909
Brian E Simmons, *President*
Tracey Simmons, *Vice Pres*
EMP: 68
SQ FT: 4,000
SALES: 9MM **Privately Held**
SIC: 4953 Hazardous waste collection & disposal

(G-5088)
BETHRANT INDUSTRIES LLC
7 Midfield Rd (19720-3439)
PHONE.....................484 343-5435
Ashly Bethrant, *Mng Member*
EMP: 2
SQ FT: 1,500
SALES: 50K **Privately Held**
SIC: 2392 Household furnishings

(G-5089)
BETTER BUSINESS BUREAU OF DE
60 Reads Way (19720-1649)
PHONE.....................302 221-5255
Frances West, *President*
Jon Bell, *Director*
Shari Heartsong, *Representative*
EMP: 7
SALES: 622.4K **Privately Held**
WEB: www.wilmington.bbb.org
SIC: 8611 Better Business Bureau

(G-5090)
BIMBO BAKERIES USA INC
78 Southgate Blvd (19720-2078)
PHONE.....................302 328-7970
Walter Johnson, *Manager*
EMP: 25 **Privately Held**
SIC: 2051 Bakery: wholesale or wholesale/retail combined
HQ: Bimbo Bakeries Usa, Inc
255 Business Center Dr # 200
Horsham PA 19044
215 347-5500

(G-5091)
BIMBO BAKERIES USA INC
Also Called: Stroehmann Bakeries 62
32 Parkway Cir (19720-4077)
PHONE.....................302 328-0837
Rob Towers, *Manager*
EMP: 40 **Privately Held**
SIC: 5461 5149 Bread; bakery products
HQ: Bimbo Bakeries Usa, Inc
255 Business Center Dr # 200
Horsham PA 19044
215 347-5500

(G-5092)
BIOTEK REMEDYS INC (PA)
2 Penns Way Ste 404 (19720-2407)
PHONE.....................877 246-9104
Chai Gadde, *CEO*
Carla Sparkler, *Chief Mktg Ofcr*
Andrew Babb, *Pharmacist*
EMP: 40 EST: 2011
SQ FT: 5,000
SALES: 7MM **Privately Held**
SIC: 8082 Home health care services

(G-5093)
BLUCHILL INC
19 Davidson Ln Bldg 7 (19720-2207)
PHONE.....................302 658-2638
Bob Onorato, *President*
Carl Warren, *Vice Pres*
EMP: 5
SQ FT: 5,000

GEOGRAPHIC SECTION
New Castle - New Castle County (G-5121)

SALES: 700K **Privately Held**
SIC: 3585 Refrigeration equipment, complete

(G-5094)
BLUE HEN UTILITY SERVICES INC
473 Old Airport Rd Bldg 4 (19720-1017)
PHONE.................................302 273-3167
Michele Reynolds, *President*
Ted Kelly, *Vice Pres*
Mike Reynolds, *Vice Pres*
EMP: 6
SQ FT: 7,000
SALES: 1MM **Privately Held**
SIC: 4911 Distribution, electric power; transmission, electric power

(G-5095)
BLUE RIBBON OIL COMPANY INC
Also Called: Blue Ribbon Petroleum
819 S Dupont Hwy (19720-4610)
PHONE.................................302 832-7601
Cheryl Kehnast, *Principal*
EMP: 10
SALES (est): 1.1MM **Privately Held**
SIC: 5169 Chemicals & allied products

(G-5096)
BLUE RIDGE AIR INC
137 N Dupont Hwy (19720-3135)
PHONE.................................302 323-4800
Steve Williams, *President*
EMP: 4
SQ FT: 2,500
SALES (est): 372.8K **Privately Held**
WEB: www.blueridgeair.com
SIC: 8742 Business consultant

(G-5097)
BLUE SKIES SOLAR & WIND POWER
261 Airport Rd (19720-1540)
PHONE.................................302 326-0856
Bruce Wanex, *Owner*
Linda Wanex, *Co-Owner*
EMP: 20
SALES (est): 828.7K **Privately Held**
WEB: www.wanex.com
SIC: 1711 7629 Solar energy contractor; electrical repair shops

(G-5098)
BOBCAT OF NEW CASTLE LLC (PA)
325 Quigley Blvd (19720-4107)
PHONE.................................732 780-6880
Robert Woods, *President*
EMP: 10
SALES (est): 3.9MM **Privately Held**
SIC: 1794 Excavation work

(G-5099)
BOMBONAIS CABLE TECH LLC
218 Mccalmont Rd (19720-3332)
PHONE.................................302 444-1199
Salvador Gonzalez, *President*
EMP: 8
SALES (est): 440.6K **Privately Held**
SIC: 4841 Cable television services

(G-5100)
BOWLERAMA INC
3031 New Castle Ave Ste 2 (19720-2297)
PHONE.................................302 654-0704
Barbara Cocharn, *General Mgr*
Jeff Benson, *General Mgr*
Karyn Wilson, *Director*
EMP: 25
SALES (corp-wide): 1.3MM **Privately Held**
SIC: 7933 Ten pin center
PA: Bowlerama Inc
   15 Mccullough Dr
   New Castle DE

(G-5101)
BOXWOOD ELECTRIC INC
10 King Ave (19720-1512)
PHONE.................................302 368-3257
David Fink, *Principal*
EMP: 8
SALES (est): 422.9K **Privately Held**
SIC: 1731 Electrical work

(G-5102)
BOYS & GIRLS CLUBS DEL INC
Also Called: New Castle Boys & Girls Clubs
19 Lambson Ln (19720-2118)
PHONE.................................302 655-8569
Leandra Brown, *Manager*
EMP: 10
SALES (corp-wide): 20.8MM **Privately Held**
SIC: 8641 Youth organizations
PA: Boys & Girls Clubs Of Delaware, Inc.
   669 S Union St
   Wilmington DE 19805
   302 658-1870

(G-5103)
BRAINCORE INC
35 Industrial Blvd (19720-2091)
PHONE.................................302 999-9221
EMP: 18
SALES (est): 1MM **Privately Held**
SIC: 7375 Information Retrieval Services

(G-5104)
BRANDYWINE CHEMICAL COMPANY
600 Terminal Ave Ste 1 (19720-1457)
PHONE.................................302 656-5428
Valerie C Hahn, *President*
Ken Shockley, *Vice Pres*
Betty Schockley, *Admin Sec*
EMP: 2
SQ FT: 23,000
SALES (est): 150K **Privately Held**
SIC: 4225 2819 Warehousing, self-storage; industrial inorganic chemicals

(G-5105)
BRANDYWINE CONSTRUCTION CO
101 Pigeon Point Rd (19720-2197)
PHONE.................................302 571-9773
Kathleen Thomas, *President*
Kelly Humphrey, *Vice Pres*
John Olson, *Vice Pres*
EMP: 80 EST: 1957
SQ FT: 8,000
SALES (est): 11MM **Privately Held**
WEB: www.bccico.com
SIC: 1794 1623 1611 Excavation & grading, building construction; water, sewer & utility lines; surfacing & paving

(G-5106)
BRANDYWINE CONTRACTORS INC
Also Called: BCI
34 Industrial Blvd (19720-2091)
PHONE.................................302 325-2700
Michael J Peters, *President*
John Bradley, *Superintendent*
Ken Coldiron, *Vice Pres*
Michael Pergeorelis, *Vice Pres*
Greg Pappas, *Project Mgr*
EMP: 30
SQ FT: 1,000
SALES (est): 3.2MM **Privately Held**
WEB: www.bci-online.com
SIC: 1542 Commercial & office building, new construction; commercial & office buildings, renovation & repair

(G-5107)
BRANDYWINE CONTRACTORS INC
34 Industrial Blvd (19720-2091)
PHONE.................................302 325-2700
Michael Peters, *President*
EMP: 8
SALES (est): 1MM **Privately Held**
SIC: 1521 1542 1711 8741 New construction, single-family houses; nonresidential construction; plumbing, heating, air-conditioning contractors; construction management

(G-5108)
BRAVO BUILDING SERVICES INC
34 Blevins Dr Ste 7 (19720-4177)
PHONE.................................302 322-5959
Sally Denton, *Vice Pres*
Rubens Dufau, *Vice Pres*
Jamie Blevins, *Opers Staff*
EMP: 1484
SALES (corp-wide): 45.4MM **Privately Held**
SIC: 7349 Janitorial service, contract basis
PA: Bravo Building Services, Inc.
   1140 Rte 22 Ste 202
   Bridgewater NJ 08807
   732 465-0707

(G-5109)
BREAKTHRU BEVERAGE GROUP LLC
Also Called: Breakthru Beverage Delaware
411 Churchmans Rd (19720-3156)
P.O. Box 10370, Wilmington (19850-0370)
PHONE.................................302 356-3500
Jennifer Youngman, *Sales Staff*
Paul Tigani, *Manager*
EMP: 150
SALES (corp-wide): 1B **Privately Held**
SIC: 2085 2869 Rum (alcoholic beverage); alcohols, non-beverage
PA: Breakthru Beverage Group, Llc
   60 E 42nd St Ste 1915
   New York NY 10165
   212 699-7000

(G-5110)
BRESLIN CONTRACTING INC
18 King Ct (19720-1519)
PHONE.................................302 322-0320
Patrick Breslin, *President*
Anita Breslin, *Vice Pres*
Mike Parodi, *Vice Pres*
Patrick Beaston, *Project Mgr*
Carol Breslin, *Treasurer*
EMP: 43
SQ FT: 6,000
SALES: 4.6MM **Privately Held**
WEB: www.breslincorp.com
SIC: 1541 1542 Renovation, remodeling & repairs: industrial buildings; commercial & office buildings, renovation & repair

(G-5111)
BREWSTER PRODUCTS INC
3020 Bowlarama Dr (19720-1317)
PHONE.................................302 798-1988
EMP: 4
SALES (est): 254.3K **Privately Held**
SIC: 7822 Motion picture & tape distribution

(G-5112)
BRIDGESTONE RET OPERATIONS LLC
Also Called: Firestone
2098 New Castle Ave (19720-7704)
PHONE.................................302 656-2529
Brian Williams, *Manager*
EMP: 7 **Privately Held**
WEB: www.bfrs.com
SIC: 5531 7534 Automotive tires; rebuilding & retreading tires
HQ: Bridgestone Retail Operations, Llc
   333 E Lake St Ste 300
   Bloomingdale IL 60108
   630 259-9000

(G-5113)
BRIDGEWATER JEWELERS
318 Delaware St (19720-5038)
P.O. Box 44 (19720-0044)
PHONE.................................302 328-2101
Mary F Lenhoff, *Owner*
Lesli Neel, *Sales Associate*
EMP: 5
SQ FT: 2,000
SALES (est): 514.7K **Privately Held**
WEB: www.bridgewaterjewelers.com
SIC: 7631 5944 Watch repair; jewelry repair services; watches

(G-5114)
BRIGGS COMPANY (PA)
3 Bellecor Dr (19720-1763)
PHONE.................................302 328-9471
Constance Newman, *Ch of Bd*
Robert J Newman, *President*
Debbie McMahon, *Vice Pres*
Lillian Reynolds, *Sales Staff*
Gibson Yoder, *Manager*
EMP: 21 EST: 1937
SQ FT: 25,000
SALES (est): 11.1MM **Privately Held**
WEB: www.briggsco.net
SIC: 5074 5085 Pipes & fittings, plastic; hose, belting & packing

(G-5115)
BRISTOL INDUSTRIAL CORPORATION
1010 River Rd (19720-5104)
P.O. Box 12304, Wilmington (19850-2304)
PHONE.................................302 322-1100
Felicia Enuha, *President*
EMP: 10
SALES (est): 1.7MM **Privately Held**
SIC: 1541 5074 5085 5082 Industrial buildings, new construction; plumbing & heating valves; pistons & valves; bailey bridges; electrical fittings & construction materials; piling, iron & steel

(G-5116)
BROWNE USA INC
802 Centerpoint Blvd (19720-8123)
PHONE.................................302 326-4802
▼ EMP: 32
SALES (est): 4.3MM **Privately Held**
SIC: 5021 Whol Furniture

(G-5117)
BROWNSTONE LLC
200 Centerpoint Blvd A (19720-4175)
PHONE.................................302 300-4370
EMP: 5 EST: 2016
SALES (est): 368.2K **Privately Held**
SIC: 8741 Business management

(G-5118)
BRUCE INDUSTRIAL CO INC
4049 New Castle Ave (19720-1496)
P.O. Box 10485, Wilmington (19850-0485)
PHONE.................................302 655-9616
Christian Johnston, *President*
Mark Davis, *Project Mgr*
Keith Cordrey, *Sales Mgr*
▲ EMP: 75
SQ FT: 50,000
SALES: 15MM **Privately Held**
WEB: www.bruceindustrial.com
SIC: 5084 7699 1796 Materials handling machinery; industrial machinery & equipment repair; machinery installation

(G-5119)
BUCHI CORPORATION (HQ)
19 Lukens Dr Ste 400 (19720-2787)
PHONE.................................302 652-3000
Thomas Liner, *CEO*
Herve Lacombe, *President*
John Donahue, *Warehouse Mgr*
Jacquelyn Johnson, *Accountant*
Brad Miller, *Sales Mgr*
▲ EMP: 74
SALES (est): 30.3MM
SALES (corp-wide): 41.9MM **Privately Held**
WEB: www.buchi.com
SIC: 5049 Laboratory equipment, except medical or dental
PA: Buchi Labortechnik Ag
   Meierseggstrasse 40
   Flawil SG 9230
   713 946-363

(G-5120)
BUDGET ROOTER INC
1015 River Rd (19720-5103)
P.O. Box 1708, Bear (19701-7708)
PHONE.................................302 322-3011
Suzanne Palady, *President*
Jen Conway, *Business Mgr*
Jeffrey Palady, *Vice Pres*
Andrea Myers, *Admin Sec*
EMP: 10
SQ FT: 4,000
SALES (est): 2MM **Privately Held**
SIC: 1711 7699 Plumbing contractors; sewer cleaning & rodding

(G-5121)
BURNS & MCBRIDE INC (PA)
18 Boulden Cir Ste 30 (19720-3494)
P.O. Box 11287, Wilmington (19850-1287)
PHONE.................................302 656-5110
Thomas G Mc Bride, *President*
James R Mc Bride, *Vice Pres*
Terrace Mc Bride, *Vice Pres*

New Castle - New Castle County (G-5122)

Terrence McBride, *Human Resources*
EMP: 60
SQ FT: 8,000
SALES (est): 9.9MM **Privately Held**
WEB: www.burnsandmcbride.com
SIC: 1711 5983 7623 7699 Boiler & furnace contractors; heating & air conditioning contractors; fuel oil dealers; air conditioning repair; oil burner repair service

(G-5122)
BURRIS LOGISTICS
Also Called: Burris Refrigerated Logistics
1000 Centerpoint Blvd (19720-8124)
PHONE..................302 221-4100
Megan Caruso, *Accounts Exec*
Eric Fears, *Branch Mgr*
Christine Collins, *Manager*
EMP: 20
SALES (corp-wide): 1.4B **Privately Held**
SIC: 4225 4222 4213 General warehousing & storage; storage, frozen or refrigerated goods; refrigerated products transport
PA: Burris Logistics
  501 Se 5th St
  Milford DE 19963
  302 839-4531

(G-5123)
BUSHWICK METALS LLC
100 Steel Dr (19720-7708)
PHONE..................302 328-0590
EMP: 4
SALES (est): 723.2K
SALES (corp-wide): 225.3B **Publicly Held**
SIC: 5051 Steel
PA: Berkshire Hathaway Inc.
  3555 Farnam St Ste 1140
  Omaha NE 68131
  402 346-1400

(G-5124)
BUSINESS MOVE SOLUTIONS INC
Also Called: Office Movers
11 Boulden Cir (19720-3400)
PHONE..................302 324-0080
David Greenblatt, *President*
Carol Cathell, *Vice Pres*
Betty Greenblatt, *Vice Pres*
Lashunda Smith, *Sales Staff*
EMP: 30
SQ FT: 53,000
SALES (est): 5.6MM **Privately Held**
SIC: 7389 Relocation service

(G-5125)
C B JOE TV & APPLIANCES INC
348 Churchmans Rd (19720-3112)
PHONE..................302 322-7600
Joseph M Williams, *President*
Alice Williams, *Vice Pres*
EMP: 18
SQ FT: 6,000
SALES (est): 2.5MM **Privately Held**
SIC: 5722 5731 7622 Electric household appliances, major; electric household appliances, small; radios, two-way, citizens' band, weather, short-wave, etc.; television sets; radio repair shop; television repair shop

(G-5126)
C&C WELDING
50 N Purdue Ave (19720-4315)
PHONE..................402 414-2485
Cesar J Torres Jr, *Principal*
EMP: 1
SALES (est): 33.8K **Privately Held**
SIC: 7692 Welding repair

(G-5127)
C-MET INC
Also Called: Midas Muffler
1604 N Dupont Hwy (19720-1904)
PHONE..................302 652-1884
Ernest Natal, *President*
EMP: 8
SALES: 1MM **Privately Held**
SIC: 7533 Muffler shop, sale or repair & installation

(G-5128)
CAD IMPORT INC
650 Centerpoint Blvd (19720-8108)
PHONE..................302 628-4178
Vicky Deleon, *Principal*
Hugo Torres, *Sales Mgr*
Tanya Roblero, *Manager*
Evelio Velasquez, *Master*
▲ **EMP:** 30
SALES (est): 8.5MM **Privately Held**
SIC: 5087 7389 Beauty parlor equipment & supplies; labeling bottles, cans, cartons, etc.

(G-5129)
CAMMOCKS AUTO WORKS LLC
Also Called: Cammock Boy Auto
314 Bay West Blvd Ste 5a (19720-5195)
PHONE..................302 597-0204
Garfield Cammock,
EMP: 4 **EST:** 2012
SQ FT: 4,200
SALES: 80K **Privately Held**
SIC: 7538 5531 General automotive repair shops; automobile air conditioning equipment, sale, installation

(G-5130)
CANADA DRY DSTRG WILMINGTON DE (PA)
Also Called: Canada Dry Distrg Wilmington
650 Ships Landing Way (19720-4577)
PHONE..................302 322-1856
Lou Morsa, *Sales Mgr*
Greg Check, *Sales Staff*
Julius Wiggins, *Manager*
Harold Honickman, *Admin Sec*
Diane Baskin, *Executive Asst*
EMP: 30
SQ FT: 22,000
SALES (est): 5.9MM **Privately Held**
WEB: www.cddelval.com
SIC: 2086 Bottled & canned soft drinks

(G-5131)
CANNON SLINE LLC
103 Carroll Dr (19720-4873)
PHONE..................302 658-1420
Ted Mansfield, *CEO*
Mark Chuplis, *President*
Glenn Baughman, *Vice Pres*
Rich Bartell, *CFO*
Marcy Miller, *CFO*
EMP: 65
SQ FT: 5,000
SALES (est): 3.5MM
SALES (corp-wide): 2.8B **Privately Held**
SIC: 1721 Industrial painting
HQ: K2 Industrial Services, Inc.
  3838 N Sam Houston Pkwy E
  Houston TX 77032
  850 477-6437

(G-5132)
CAREERS USA INC
2 Reads Way Ste 224 (19720-1630)
PHONE..................302 737-3600
Rosa Catalano, *Manager*
EMP: 4
SALES (corp-wide): 433.2MM **Privately Held**
WEB: www.careersusa.com
SIC: 7361 Employment agencies
PA: Careers Usa, Inc.
  6501 Congress Ave Ste 200
  Boca Raton FL 33487
  561 995-7000

(G-5133)
CARING FOR LIFE INC
Also Called: Comfort Keepers
92 Reads Way Ste 207 (19720-1631)
PHONE..................302 892-2214
Sharon Powell, *President*
Jim Powell, *Vice Pres*
EMP: 35
SALES (est): 878.8K **Privately Held**
SIC: 8082 Home health care services

(G-5134)
CARLYLE COCOA CO LLC
23 Harbor View Dr (19720-2179)
PHONE..................302 428-3800
Micheal Kostic,
◆ **EMP:** 13
SQ FT: 20,000
SALES (est): 2.2MM **Privately Held**
SIC: 2099 Food preparations

(G-5135)
CARTER PRINTING AND DESIGN
427 Martin Dr (19720-2759)
PHONE..................302 655-2343
Robert Carter, *President*
EMP: 3
SALES (est): 166.2K **Privately Held**
SIC: 2261 Screen printing of cotton broadwoven fabrics

(G-5136)
CASTLE CONSTRUCTION DEL INC
185 Old Churchmans Rd (19720-3115)
PHONE..................302 326-3600
Dennis W Yanick, *President*
EMP: 33
SQ FT: 4,000
SALES (est): 4.6MM **Privately Held**
SIC: 1794 Excavation work

(G-5137)
CATHOLIC HEALTH EAST
612 Ferry Cut Off St (19720-4549)
PHONE..................302 325-4900
EMP: 7
SALES (corp-wide): 6.4B **Privately Held**
SIC: 8062 Hospital
HQ: Catholic Health East
  3805 West Chester Pike # 100
  Newtown Square PA 19073
  610 355-2000

(G-5138)
CBI SERVICES LLC
24 Reads Way (19720-1649)
PHONE..................302 325-8400
James Rhudy, *Vice Pres*
Alan Black, *Manager*
EMP: 10
SALES (corp-wide): 6.7B **Privately Held**
WEB: www.cbi.com
SIC: 1629 Dams, waterways, docks & other marine construction
HQ: Cbi Services, Llc
  14107 S Route 59
  Plainfield IL 60544
  815 439-6668

(G-5139)
CEDAR LANE INC
Also Called: Oak Knoll Books
310 Delaware St (19720-5038)
PHONE..................302 328-7232
Robert D Fleck Jr, *President*
Mildred Fleck, *Vice Pres*
▲ **EMP:** 10
SQ FT: 15,000
SALES (est): 1.5MM **Privately Held**
WEB: www.oakknoll.com
SIC: 5961 2731 Book club, mail order; book publishing

(G-5140)
CENTER STAGE AUTO AUCTION
741 Hamburg Rd (19720-5101)
PHONE..................302 325-2277
Albert Rossi, *Principal*
EMP: 4
SALES: 600K **Privately Held**
SIC: 5012 Automobile auction

(G-5141)
CHAMBERS LDSCPG & LAWNCARE INC
41 Don Ave (19720-1507)
PHONE..................302 328-1312
Woodrow Chambers, *President*
EMP: 8
SALES (est): 704.3K **Privately Held**
SIC: 0782 Lawn care services; landscape contractors

(G-5142)
CHELTEN PRESERVATION ASSOC LLC
Also Called: Chelten Apartments
431 Old Forge Rd (19720-3764)
PHONE..................302 322-6323
William Demarco, *Managing Prtnr*
EMP: 13

SALES (est): 280K **Privately Held**
SIC: 6514 Dwelling operators, except apartments

(G-5143)
CHEMAX MANUFACTURING CORP
1025 River Rd (19720-5103)
PHONE..................302 328-2440
Susan H Rappa, *President*
Charles J Rappa, *Vice Pres*
EMP: 4 **EST:** 1953
SQ FT: 2,000
SALES (est): 694K **Privately Held**
WEB: www.chemaxcorp.com
SIC: 3999 Barber & beauty shop equipment

(G-5144)
CHERRY ISLAND LLC
4048 New Castle Ave (19720-1455)
PHONE..................302 658-5241
Maryann Kowalski, *Office Mgr*
Vincent N Greggo,
Vincent Greggo,
EMP: 18
SALES: 950K **Privately Held**
SIC: 4953 Sanitary landfill operation

(G-5145)
CHESAPEAKE INSURANCE ADVISORS
10 Corporate Cir Ste 215 (19720-2418)
PHONE..................302 544-6900
Michael V Buchler, *President*
Robert Houser, *President*
Linda Dean, *CFO*
EMP: 12
SQ FT: 5,000
SALES (est): 1MM **Privately Held**
SIC: 6411 Insurance agents, brokers & service

(G-5146)
CHESAPEAKE SEC INVESTIGATIONS
122 Delaware St 5 (19720-4814)
PHONE..................302 429-7505
Marla Sturgill, *President*
Holly Jankiewicz, *Vice Pres*
EMP: 30
SALES (est): 1.4MM **Privately Held**
WEB: www.chesapeakesecurityinvestigation.com
SIC: 7382 Protective devices, security

(G-5147)
CHILDREN YOUTH & THEIR FAM
Also Called: Terry Chld Psychiatric Ctr
10 Central Ave (19720-1152)
PHONE..................302 577-4270
Sterling Seemans, *Principal*
EMP: 100 **Privately Held**
SIC: 8063 9431 Psychiatric hospitals; administration of public health programs;
HQ: Children, Youth & Their Families, Delaware Dept Of Services For
  1825 Faulkland Rd
  Wilmington DE 19805

(G-5148)
CHIMES INC
Also Called: New Beginnings
130 Quigley Blvd (19720-4104)
PHONE..................302 382-4500
EMP: 4
SALES (corp-wide): 10.6MM **Privately Held**
SIC: 8331 Vocational training agency; vocational rehabilitation agency
HQ: The Chimes Inc
  4815 Seton Dr
  Baltimore MD 21215
  410 358-6400

(G-5149)
CHIMES METRO INC
323 E 14th St (19720-4509)
PHONE..................302 452-3400
EMP: 5
SALES (corp-wide): 10.6MM **Privately Held**
SIC: 3699 Chimes, electric

GEOGRAPHIC SECTION   New Castle - New Castle County (G-5175)

HQ: Chimes Metro, Inc.
4815 Seton Dr
Baltimore MD 21215

(G-5150)
CHIMPARK LLC
257 Old Churchmans Rd (19720-1529)
PHONE.............................226 219-7771
Juan Gonzalez,
EMP: 1
SALES: 30K **Privately Held**
SIC: **3999** Manufacturing industries

(G-5151)
CHOICE FOR CMNTY LVNG-BYVIEW 1
713 Dora Moors Ln (19720-8766)
PHONE.............................302 328-4176
Carrie Ann Brown, *Director*
EMP: 4
SALES (est): 71.2K **Privately Held**
SIC: **8361** Residential care for the handicapped

(G-5152)
CHRISTANA CARE HM HLTH CMNTY S (HQ)
Also Called: Christana Care Vsting Nrse Ass
1 Reads Way Ste 100 (19720-1605)
PHONE.............................302 327-5583
Lynn Jones, *President*
Gerald Manley, *Finance Dir*
Brenda K Pierce, *Admin Sec*
EMP: 300 EST: 1922
SQ FT: 22,000
SALES: 47.5MM
SALES (corp-wide): 1.5B **Privately Held**
WEB: www.christianacare.com
SIC: **8082** Visiting nurse service
PA: Christiana Care Health Services, Inc.
4755 Ogletown Stanton Rd
Newark DE 19718
302 733-1000

(G-5153)
CHRISTIANA CARE HEALTH SYS INC
Also Called: Cchs Logistics Center
11 Boulden Cir (19720-3400)
PHONE.............................302 623-3970
Janice E Nevin, *CEO*
Salena Giddings, *Analyst*
EMP: 13
SALES (corp-wide): 1.5B **Privately Held**
SIC: **4119** Ambulance service
HQ: Christiana Care Health System, Inc.
200 Hygeia Dr
Newark DE 19713
302 733-1000

(G-5154)
CHRISTIANA CARE HLTH SVCS INC
11 Reads Way (19720-1648)
PHONE.............................302 327-5820
Ken Bates, *Principal*
William Schmitt, *Manager*
Laura Pizonka, *Info Tech Dir*
EMP: 17
SALES (corp-wide): 1.5B **Privately Held**
SIC: **8062** General medical & surgical hospitals
PA: Christiana Care Health Services, Inc.
4755 Ogletown Stanton Rd
Newark DE 19718
302 733-1000

(G-5155)
CHRISTIANA CARE HLTH SVCS INC
Also Called: Information Services
1 Reads Way Ste 200 (19720-1605)
PHONE.............................302 327-3959
Corbin Ellsaesser, *Senior Engr*
Andy Tracey, *Senior Engr*
Lynn Jones, *Branch Mgr*
William Reid, *Manager*
James Banger, *Analyst*
EMP: 200
SALES (corp-wide): 1.5B **Privately Held**
SIC: **8062** General medical & surgical hospitals

PA: Christiana Care Health Services, Inc.
4755 Ogletown Stanton Rd
Newark DE 19718
302 733-1000

(G-5156)
CHRISTIANA CARE HLTH SVCS INC
Also Called: Schwezers Thrapy Rhabilitation
100 W Cmmons Blvd Ste 100 (19720)
PHONE.............................302 327-5555
Paul Schweizer, *Branch Mgr*
EMP: 24
SALES (corp-wide): 1.5B **Privately Held**
SIC: **8049** Physical therapist
PA: Christiana Care Health Services, Inc.
4755 Ogletown Stanton Rd
Newark DE 19718
302 733-1000

(G-5157)
CHRISTIANA MOTOR FREIGHT INC (PA)
520 Terminal Ave Ste C (19720-1459)
P.O. Box 668 (19720-0668)
PHONE.............................302 655-6271
Imari Bollman, *President*
Herbert Bollman, *President*
Evelyn Bollman, *Admin Sec*
EMP: 10 EST: 1981
SQ FT: 15,000
SALES (est): 1.1MM **Privately Held**
SIC: **4213** 4214 Trucking, except local; local trucking with storage

(G-5158)
CHRISTIANA WOOD LLC
Also Called: Villas Apartments
218 Villas Dr (19720)
PHONE.............................302 322-1172
Michael Acierno,
EMP: 6
SALES: 1.9MM **Privately Held**
SIC: **6513** Apartment building operators

(G-5159)
CHRISTINA CARE VNA
1 Reads Way Ste 100 (19720-1605)
PHONE.............................302 327-5212
Steven Rombach, *Owner*
EMP: 20 EST: 2001
SALES (est): 720K **Privately Held**
SIC: **8093** Respiratory therapy clinic

(G-5160)
CHRISTINA CTR FOR ORAL SURGERY
112 2nd Ave (19720-4118)
PHONE.............................302 328-3053
EMP: 8 EST: 2004
SALES (est): 410K **Privately Held**
SIC: **8021** Oral Surgeon

(G-5161)
CIM CONCEPTS INCORPORATED
100 W Cmmons Blvd Ste 101 (19720)
PHONE.............................302 613-5400
Randall C Herbein, *President*
Joachim Hirche, *Vice Pres*
Kyle Herbein, *Prgrmr*
EMP: 12
SQ FT: 2,500
SALES (est): 1.6MM **Privately Held**
WEB: www.cimconcepts.com
SIC: **7373** 7371 Systems integration services; systems software development services; computer systems analysis & design; custom computer programming services

(G-5162)
CIRILLO BROS INC
761 Grantham Ln (19720-4801)
PHONE.............................302 326-1540
Michael Cirillo, *President*
Mark Cirillo, *Treasurer*
EMP: 50
SQ FT: 1,000
SALES (est): 12.9MM **Privately Held**
WEB: www.cirillobros.com
SIC: **1794** 1542 1522 Excavation & grading, building construction; commercial & office building contractors; residential construction

(G-5163)
CITIBANK NATIONAL ASSOCIATION
1 Penns Way (19721-2300)
PHONE.............................302 477-5418
Vickram Pandit, *President*
EMP: 13
SALES (corp-wide): 72.8B **Publicly Held**
WEB: www.citibank.com
SIC: **6021** National commercial banks
HQ: Citibank, National Association
701 E 60th St N
Sioux Falls SD 57104
605 331-2626

(G-5164)
CITIBANK OVERSEAS INV CORP (DH)
1 Penns Way (19720-2408)
PHONE.............................302 323-3600
Michael Humes, *Assistant VP*
EMP: 11
SALES (est): 3.7MM
SALES (corp-wide): 72.8B **Publicly Held**
SIC: **6211** Investment bankers
HQ: Citibank, National Association
701 E 60th St N
Sioux Falls SD 57104
605 331-2626

(G-5165)
CITICORP BANKING CORPORATION (HQ)
Also Called: Citigroup
1 Penns Way (19721-2300)
PHONE.............................302 323-3140
Richard Collins, *President*
Martin Blake, *President*
Sameer Patil, *President*
Charles Mogilevsky, *Managing Dir*
James Bourget, *Assistant VP*
EMP: 200
SALES (est): 1.9B
SALES (corp-wide): 72.8B **Publicly Held**
SIC: **6021** National commercial banks
PA: Citigroup Inc.
388 Greenwich St
New York NY 10013
212 559-1000

(G-5166)
CITICORP DEL-LEASE INC (HQ)
1 Penns Way (19721-2300)
PHONE.............................302 323-3801
William Silver, *President*
Timothy Cormany, *Vice Pres*
Abhishek Kumar, *Vice Pres*
Luis Meneses, *Vice Pres*
James Chan, *Project Mgr*
EMP: 100
SALES (est): 91.3MM
SALES (corp-wide): 72.8B **Publicly Held**
SIC: **6022** 6311 6321 State commercial banks; life insurance; disability health insurance
PA: Citigroup Inc.
388 Greenwich St
New York NY 10013
212 559-1000

(G-5167)
CITICORP DELAWARE SERVICES INC
1 Penns Way (19721-2300)
PHONE.............................302 323-3124
William Wolf, *President*
EMP: 10
SALES (est): 3MM
SALES (corp-wide): 72.8B **Publicly Held**
SIC: **6021** National commercial banks
HQ: Citicorp Banking Corporation
1 Penns Way
New Castle DE 19721
302 323-3140

(G-5168)
CITICORP TRUST BANK (HQ)
1 Penns Way (19721-2300)
PHONE.............................302 737-7803
Virginia M Russell, *Manager*
EMP: 4
SALES (est): 1.7MM
SALES (corp-wide): 72.8B **Publicly Held**
SIC: **6021** National commercial banks

PA: Citigroup Inc.
388 Greenwich St
New York NY 10013
212 559-1000

(G-5169)
CITIGROUP ASIA PCF HOLDG CORP (DH)
Also Called: Citibank
1 Penns Way Fl 1 # 1 (19721-2300)
PHONE.............................302 323-3100
Edward C Salvitti, *President*
Micahel F Brisgone, *Vice Pres*
Robert Hangacsi, *Vice Pres*
Scott A Lyons, *Vice Pres*
William H Wolf, *Vice Pres*
▲ EMP: 5 EST: 1964
SQ FT: 1,000
SALES (est): 6.7MM
SALES (corp-wide): 72.8B **Publicly Held**
WEB: www.citcorp.com
SIC: **6021** National commercial banks
HQ: Citibank, National Association
701 E 60th St N
Sioux Falls SD 57104
605 331-2626

(G-5170)
CITIZENS BANK NATIONAL ASSN
130 N Dupont Hwy (19720-3102)
PHONE.............................302 322-0525
Jennifer McKenna, *Branch Mgr*
EMP: 10
SALES (corp-wide): 7.3B **Publicly Held**
SIC: **6022** State commercial banks
HQ: Citizens Bank, National Association
1 Citizens Plz Ste 1 # 1
Providence RI 02903
401 282-7000

(G-5171)
CITY MIST LLC
Also Called: City Mist Logistics
1005 Willings Way (19720-3955)
PHONE.............................302 342-1377
Bruce Omwoyo,
EMP: 8
SQ FT: 5,000
SALES (est): 663.1K **Privately Held**
SIC: **4213** 4731 Trucking, except local; freight transportation arrangement

(G-5172)
CLARK ASSOCIATES INC
Also Called: Clarke Association
3065 New Castle Ave (19720-2245)
PHONE.............................302 421-9950
Barry Martin, *Principal*
EMP: 22
SALES (corp-wide): 182.4MM **Privately Held**
WEB: www.noblechemical.com
SIC: **8611** Merchants' association
PA: Clark Associates, Inc.
2205 Old Phladelphia Pike
Lancaster PA 17602
717 392-7550

(G-5173)
CLARK BFFONE MTTHEWS INSUR AGC
Also Called: Nationwide
100 W Cmmons Blvd Ste 302 (19720)
PHONE.............................302 322-2261
Brandon Baffone, *Partner*
EMP: 20
SALES (est): 325.1K **Privately Held**
SIC: **6411** Insurance agents

(G-5174)
CLARK SERVICES INC OF DEL
107 J And M Dr (19720-3147)
PHONE.............................302 322-1118
EMP: 10
SALES (est): 660K **Privately Held**
SIC: **1711** Plumbing/Heating/Air Cond Contractor

(G-5175)
CLARKS GLASGOW POOLS INC (PA)
Also Called: Clarks Pool and Spa
109 J And M Dr (19720-3147)
PHONE.............................302 834-0200

New Castle - New Castle County (G-5176) GEOGRAPHIC SECTION

Cary Pitman, *President*
Nathan Myers, *Project Mgr*
EMP: 19
SQ FT: 10,000
SALES (est): 2.8MM **Privately Held**
WEB: www.clarkspools.com
SIC: 1799 1771 Swimming pool construction; blacktop (asphalt) work

(G-5176)
CLASSIC IMAGE INC
Also Called: Classic Image Clrs Laundromat
21 Stamm Blvd (19720-6604)
PHONE.................................302 658-7281
Richard Willis, *Manager*
EMP: 4
SALES (corp-wide): 584.6K **Privately Held**
SIC: 5699 7215 Custom tailor; drycleaning, coin-operated
PA: Classic Image, Inc
  Wilmington DE

(G-5177)
CLEAN EARTH NEW CASTLE INC
94 Pyles Ln (19720-1420)
PHONE.................................302 427-6633
Willaim R Massa, *CEO*
Michael Goebner, *President*
Paul Lane, *Vice Pres*
Tricia Papile, *Treasurer*
EMP: 20
SALES (est): 3.6MM
SALES (corp-wide): 1.7B **Publicly Held**
SIC: 4953 5722 Hazardous waste collection & disposal; non-hazardous waste disposal sites; garbage disposals
HQ: Clean Earth, Inc.
  334 S Warminster Rd
  Hatboro PA 19040

(G-5178)
CLYDE SPINELLI
Also Called: Pinevalley Apartments
500 S Dupont Hwy Apt 225 (19720-4631)
PHONE.................................302 328-7679
Clyde Spinelli, *Owner*
EMP: 6 **EST:** 1969
SALES: 1MM **Privately Held**
SIC: 6513 Apartment building operators

(G-5179)
COCHRAN-TRIVITS INC
Also Called: Firestone
401 S Dupont Hwy (19720-4605)
PHONE.................................302 328-2945
C M Cochran III, *President*
Jeff M Hall, *Technician*
EMP: 5 **EST:** 1952
SQ FT: 5,000
SALES (est): 570K **Privately Held**
SIC: 5531 5014 5013 Automotive tires; automotive parts; automotive accessories; tires & tubes; automotive supplies & parts; automotive supplies

(G-5180)
COLE AND LATZ INC
38 Phoebe Farms Ln (19720-8769)
P.O. Box 9828, Wilmington (19809-0828)
PHONE.................................702 234-2784
Augustus Coleman, *President*
EMP: 4 **EST:** 2016
SALES (est): 143.9K **Privately Held**
SIC: 2086 2051 Iced tea & fruit drinks, bottled & canned; cakes, pies & pastries

(G-5181)
COLONIAL ELECTRIC SUPPLY CO
Also Called: Brite Lite Supply
88 Quigley Blvd (19720-4150)
PHONE.................................302 998-9993
John Przychodzien, *Manager*
EMP: 10
SALES (corp-wide): 270MM **Privately Held**
SIC: 5063 5719 Lighting fixtures; lighting fixtures
PA: The Colonial Electric Supply Company
  201 W Church Rd Ste 100
  King Of Prussia PA 19406
  610 312-8100

(G-5182)
COLONIAL SCHOOL DISTRICT
Also Called: Transportation Department
1617 Matassino Rd (19720-2086)
PHONE.................................302 323-2700
Donald R Hartwig, *Director*
EMP: 115
SALES (corp-wide): 62.7MM **Privately Held**
WEB: www.e2t2c2.net
SIC: 4151 School buses
PA: Colonial School District
  318 E Basin Rd
  New Castle DE 19720
  302 323-2700

(G-5183)
COLOR WORKS PAINTING INC
251 Edwards Ave (19720-4857)
PHONE.................................302 324-8411
Sean O Histed, *President*
EMP: 10
SQ FT: 5,500
SALES (est): 1.1MM **Privately Held**
WEB: www.colorworkspainting.com
SIC: 1721 Painting & paper hanging

(G-5184)
COLORIMETRIX INC
122 Delaware St Ste M (19720-4814)
PHONE.................................347 560-0037
Juan Leonardo Martinez, *CEO*
Dominik Westner, *CTO*
EMP: 2
SALES: 1MM **Privately Held**
SIC: 7372 Application computer software

(G-5185)
COMCAST CABLEVISION OF DEL
5 Bellecor Dr (19720-1763)
PHONE.................................302 661-4465
Jim Maguire, *Manager*
Pat Kain, *Representative*
EMP: 27
SALES (corp-wide): 94.5B **Publicly Held**
SIC: 4841 Cable television services
HQ: Comcast Cablevision Of Delaware Inc
  426a N Dupont Hwy
  Georgetown DE 19947
  302 856-4591

(G-5186)
COMCAST CBLE CMMUNICATIONS LLC
22 Reads Way (19720-1649)
PHONE.................................302 323-9200
Karen Barksdale, *Advt Staff*
Patrick Dellecave, *Manager*
EMP: 11
SALES (corp-wide): 94.5B **Publicly Held**
WEB: www.comcastmediacenter.com
SIC: 4841 Cable television services
HQ: Comcast Cable Communications, Llc
  1701 John F Kennedy Blvd
  Philadelphia PA 19103

(G-5187)
COMMUNITY ALTERNATIVES IND INC
Also Called: Rp New Churchmans
908 Churchmans Road Ext B (19720-3109)
PHONE.................................302 323-1436
Deena Ombres, *Manager*
EMP: 11
SALES (corp-wide): 2B **Privately Held**
SIC: 8052 Home for the mentally retarded, with health care
HQ: Community Alternatives Indiana, Inc.
  1400 E Pugh Dr Ste 10
  Terre Haute IN
  812 235-6202

(G-5188)
COMMUNITY PWERED FEDERAL CR UN
4 Quigley Blvd (19720-4150)
PHONE.................................302 324-1441
John Watterson, *Branch Mgr*
Marie Wileman, *Assistant*
EMP: 9
SALES (corp-wide): 3.8MM **Privately Held**
SIC: 6061 Federal credit unions

PA: Community Powered Federal Credit Union
  1758 Pulaski Hwy
  Bear DE 19701
  302 392-2930

(G-5189)
COMMUNITY SYSTEMS AND SVCS INC
2 Penns Way Ste 301 (19720-2407)
PHONE.................................302 325-1500
David Paige, *Branch Mgr*
EMP: 180
SQ FT: 400
SALES (corp-wide): 22.6MM **Privately Held**
SIC: 8052 Home for the mentally retarded, with health care
PA: Community Systems And Services, Inc.
  7926 Jones Branch Dr # 105
  Mc Lean VA 22102
  703 448-0606

(G-5190)
CONNECTIONS
204 Gordy Pl (19720-4704)
PHONE.................................302 221-6605
Catheryn Murry, *Manager*
EMP: 5 **EST:** 2008
SALES (corp-wide): 102.4K **Privately Held**
SIC: 8093 Mental health clinic, outpatient

(G-5191)
CONNOLLY OPTIONS LLC
Also Called: Two Men and A Truck
83 Christiana Rd (19720-3104)
PHONE.................................302 998-2016
Thomas P Connolly,
Don Connolly,
EMP: 25
SALES: 1.2MM **Privately Held**
SIC: 4212 Local trucking, without storage

(G-5192)
CONTEMPRARY STFFING SLTONS INC
10 Corporate Cir Ste 210 (19720-2418)
PHONE.................................302 328-1300
Kieth Pierson, *Branch Mgr*
EMP: 5 **Privately Held**
SIC: 7361 8631 Employment agencies; employees' association
PA: Contemporary Staffing Solutions, Inc.
  161 Gaither Dr Ste 210
  Mount Laurel NJ 08054

(G-5193)
CONTRACTOR MATERIALS LLC
Also Called: Contractors Materials
4048 New Castle Ave (19720-1455)
PHONE.................................302 658-5241
Vincent N Greggo,
Nicholas Ferrara,
Vincent Greggo,
EMP: 27
SALES (est): 5.6MM **Privately Held**
WEB: www.contractormaterials.com
SIC: 3443 Mixers, for hot metal

(G-5194)
COOPER BROS INC
62 Southgate Blvd Frnt (19720-2077)
PHONE.................................302 323-0717
Walter D Cooper, *President*
George Cooper, *Vice Pres*
Sandra L Cooper, *Treasurer*
Debra Scully, *Admin Sec*
EMP: 16 **EST:** 1963
SQ FT: 5,200
SALES (est): 1.9MM **Privately Held**
SIC: 1711 Plumbing contractors; heating & air conditioning contractors

(G-5195)
CORPORATE INTERIORS INC (PA)
Also Called: Corporate Interiors Delaware
223 Lisa Dr (19720-4193)
PHONE.................................302 322-1008
Janice K Leone, *President*
Jake Leone, *General Mgr*
Neil Marshall, *Vice Pres*
Patricia Tobin, *Vice Pres*
Nick Zammer, *Vice Pres*
▲ **EMP:** 81

SALES (est): 88.8MM **Privately Held**
WEB: www.corporate-interiors.com
SIC: 5021 2521 Office furniture; wood office furniture

(G-5196)
CORRADO AMERICAN LLC
200 Marsh Ln (19720-1175)
PHONE.................................302 655-6501
Martin R Bienkowski, *President*
EMP: 50 **EST:** 1945
SQ FT: 16,366
SALES (est): 7.7MM **Privately Held**
WEB: www.corrado.com
SIC: 1794 1741 Excavation & grading, building construction; foundation building

(G-5197)
CORRADO CONSTRUCTION CO LLC
210 Marsh Ln (19720-1175)
PHONE.................................302 652-3339
Joseph J Corrado Jr, *President*
James Brown, *Vice Pres*
Jerry Denney, *Vice Pres*
Kelly Jones, *Human Res Dir*
Kelly D Jones, *Admin Sec*
EMP: 66
SQ FT: 9,180
SALES (est): 7MM **Privately Held**
SIC: 1794 Excavation & grading, building construction

(G-5198)
CORRADO MANAGEMENT SVCS LLC
204 Marsh Ln (19720-1175)
PHONE.................................302 225-0700
Joseph Corrado Sr, *President*
Walter G Meisinger III, *Vice Pres*
William Price, *Project Mgr*
Rick Civita, *Safety Mgr*
Terri L Bertrando, *Admin Sec*
EMP: 30
SQ FT: 21,309
SALES (est): 3.3MM **Privately Held**
WEB: www.heliconis.com
SIC: 8741 Financial management for business; administrative management

(G-5199)
COTTMAN TRANSMISSION
1600 N Dupont Hwy (19720-1904)
PHONE.................................302 322-4600
Greg Dittbrenner, *Owner*
Carolyn Dittbrenner, *General Mgr*
EMP: 6
SALES (est): 449K **Privately Held**
SIC: 7537 Automotive transmission repair shops

(G-5200)
COUNTERMEASURES ASSESSMENT
Also Called: Case
110 Quigley Blvd (19720-4104)
PHONE.................................302 322-9600
Ernest Frazier Sr, *Mng Member*
EMP: 7
SQ FT: 3,080
SALES (est): 553.9K **Privately Held**
SIC: 8748 8742 8111 Business consulting; business planning & organizing services; legal services

(G-5201)
COUNTY ENVIRONMENTAL INC
Also Called: County Group Companies
461 Churchmans Rd (19720-3156)
PHONE.................................302 322-8946
James W Bently, *President*
Nelson Constanza, *Division Mgr*
Joseph Waninger, *General Mgr*
Larry Johnson, *Vice Pres*
Virgel Cassel, *Project Mgr*
EMP: 40
SQ FT: 10,000
SALES (est): 4.6MM **Privately Held**
SIC: 1799 4959 Asbestos removal & encapsulation; environmental cleanup services

GEOGRAPHIC SECTION

New Castle - New Castle County (G-5232)

(G-5202)
COUNTY INSULATION CO
461 Churchmans Rd (19720-3186)
PHONE...................................302 322-8946
James W Betley, *President*
Warren Flowers, *General Mgr*
Larry C Johnson, *Vice Pres*
Charles Abbott, *Project Mgr*
Ryan Foster, *Project Mgr*
EMP: 80 EST: 1971
SQ FT: 12,000
SALES (est): 8.6MM **Privately Held**
SIC: 1799 Insulation of pipes & boilers

(G-5203)
COURTESY TRNSP SVCS INC
Also Called: Global Logistics and Trnsp
4 Parkway Cir (19720-4077)
PHONE...................................302 322-9722
Henry Kamau, *President*
EMP: 52
SQ FT: 10,000
SALES (est): 3.8MM **Privately Held**
WEB: www.globallogisticstrans.com
SIC: 4212 Local trucking, without storage

(G-5204)
COUTURE DENIM LLC
Also Called: MSA
3 Silsbee Rd (19720-3227)
PHONE...................................302 220-8339
Lisa D Moore, *Mng Member*
EMP: 5
SALES: 200K **Privately Held**
SIC: 5712 7389 Furniture stores;

(G-5205)
COVENANT ASSET MGMT & FINANCL
42 Reads Way (19720-1649)
PHONE...................................302 324-5655
EMP: 6 EST: 1999
SALES (est): 110.2K **Privately Held**
SIC: 8661 7299 Religious Organization Misc Personal Services

(G-5206)
COWIE TECHNOLOGY CORP
18 Boulden Cir Ste 28 (19720-3494)
P.O. Box 6036, Wilmington (19804-0636)
PHONE...................................856 692-2828
George Cowie, *Owner*
EMP: 2
SALES (est): 197.8K **Privately Held**
SIC: 2822 Ethylene-propylene rubbers, EPDM polymers

(G-5207)
CPR CONSTRUCTION INC
106 E 14th St (19720-4506)
P.O. Box 10845, Wilmington (19850-0845)
PHONE...................................302 322-5770
Fransis Deascnais, *President*
EMP: 7
SALES (est): 635.6K **Privately Held**
SIC: 1521 New construction, single-family houses

(G-5208)
CRODA INC
321 Cherry Ln (19720-2780)
PHONE...................................302 429-5249
EMP: 12
SALES (corp-wide): 1.8B **Privately Held**
SIC: 2899 Chemical preparations
HQ: Croda, Inc.
300 Columbus Cir Ste A
Edison NJ 08837
732 417-0800

(G-5209)
CRODA INC
315 Cherry Ln (19720-2780)
PHONE...................................302 429-5200
Cindy Brungard, *Regional*
EMP: 15
SALES (corp-wide): 1.8B **Privately Held**
SIC: 5169 2899 Industrial chemicals; chemical preparations
HQ: Croda, Inc.
300 Columbus Cir Ste A
Edison NJ 08837
732 417-0800

(G-5210)
CRODA UNIQEMA INC
Also Called: Croda Atlas Point
315 Cherry Ln (19720-2780)
PHONE...................................302 429-5599
Kevin Gallagher, *President*
▲ EMP: 37
SALES (est): 7.9MM
SALES (corp-wide): 1.8B **Privately Held**
SIC: 1629 Chemical plant & refinery construction
PA: Croda International Public Limited Company
Cowick Hall
Goole N HUMBS DN14
140 586-0551

(G-5211)
D C J L PARTNERSHIP (PA)
A-1 Paisely Ln (19720)
PHONE...................................302 328-8040
Donald T Capparo, *Partner*
John J Lapone, *Partner*
Ron Rose, *General Mgr*
Maryann Rose, *Systems Mgr*
EMP: 9
SALES (est): 335.2K **Privately Held**
SIC: 6513 Apartment building operators

(G-5212)
D C S COMPANY
233 Gordy Pl (19720-4733)
PHONE...................................302 328-5138
Debra Wolfe, *Partner*
Robert Wolfe, *Partner*
EMP: 8
SALES (est): 200K **Privately Held**
SIC: 7349 Cleaning service, industrial or commercial

(G-5213)
DALE INSULATION CO OF DELAWARE
13 King Ct Ste 5 (19720-1523)
PHONE...................................302 324-9332
Thomas J Dale Jr, *President*
EMP: 9
SQ FT: 2,100
SALES: 1.2MM **Privately Held**
SIC: 1742 Insulation, buildings

(G-5214)
DASSAULT AIRCRAFT SVCS CORP
191 N Dupont Hwy (19720-3121)
PHONE...................................302 322-7000
Tony Lowarty, *Office Mgr*
EMP: 7
SALES (corp-wide): 47.6MM **Privately Held**
SIC: 4581 Aircraft maintenance & repair services
HQ: Dassault Aircraft Services Corp.
200 Riser Rd
Little Ferry NJ 07643

(G-5215)
DATA MGT INTERNATIONALE INC (PA)
Also Called: D M I
55 Lukens Dr Ste A (19720-2788)
PHONE...................................302 656-1151
Carol Swezey, *CEO*
William Swezey Sr, *Corp Secy*
Susan Hendley, *Technician*
▲ EMP: 50
SQ FT: 50,000
SALES (est): 9MM **Privately Held**
WEB: www.dmi-inc.com
SIC: 7389 Microfilm recording & developing service

(G-5216)
DAVID E DRIBAN
239 Christiana Rd (19720-2907)
PHONE...................................302 322-0860
EMP: 8
SALES (est): 82.2K **Privately Held**
SIC: 8062 General medical & surgical hospitals

(G-5217)
DAWN ARROW INC
602 Brant Ave (19720)
PHONE...................................302 328-9695
Donald Dalton, *President*
EMP: 25
SALES (est): 1MM **Privately Held**
SIC: 4212 Local trucking, without storage

(G-5218)
DAY SCHOOL FOR CHILDREN
3071 New Castle Ave (19720-2245)
PHONE...................................302 652-4651
R Dorsey, *Exec Dir*
EMP: 5
SALES (est): 122.9K **Privately Held**
SIC: 8351 Child day care services

(G-5219)
DE CHEAPER TRASH LLC
29 Prosperity Rd (19720-1568)
PHONE...................................302 325-0670
Bruce Stabley,
EMP: 5
SALES (est): 375.1K **Privately Held**
SIC: 7389

(G-5220)
DEDICATED TO HOME CARE LLC
2 Yorktown Rd (19720-4222)
PHONE...................................484 470-5013
Haywood Lewis, *Principal*
EMP: 8 EST: 2017
SALES (est): 61.1K **Privately Held**
SIC: 8082 Home health care services

(G-5221)
DEL-ONE FEDERAL CREDIT UNION
80 Christiana Rd (19720-3118)
PHONE...................................302 323-4578
Amy Draper, *Branch Mgr*
Todd Smith, *Officer*
EMP: 5 **Privately Held**
WEB: www.del-one.org
SIC: 6061 Federal credit unions
PA: Del-One Federal Credit Union
270 Beiser Blvd
Dover DE 19904

(G-5222)
DELASOFT INC
92 Reads Way Ste 204 (19720-1631)
PHONE...................................302 533-7912
Sateesh Dola, *President*
Jyothsna Dola, *Director*
Tom Stoffel, *Business Dir*
EMP: 175
SQ FT: 2,400
SALES (est): 17MM **Privately Held**
SIC: 7379 Computer related consulting services

(G-5223)
DELAWARE ACDEMY PUB SAFETY SEC
179 Stanton Christiana Rd (19720)
PHONE...................................302 377-1465
Charles Hughes, *Principal*
EMP: 19
SALES: 3.9MM **Privately Held**
SIC: 7381 Guard services

(G-5224)
DELAWARE ALIANCE FEDERAL CR UN
2320 N Dupont Hwy (19720-6327)
PHONE...................................302 429-0404
Dawn Sutcliffe, *CEO*
Betsy Cole, *Ch of Bd*
Sherry Ford, *Technology*
EMP: 7
SALES: 706.8K **Privately Held**
WEB: www.delall.com
SIC: 6061 Federal credit unions

(G-5225)
DELAWARE AUTO SALVAGE INC
445 Old Airport Rd (19720-1001)
PHONE...................................302 322-2328
Johnnie Sue Russell, *President*
EMP: 5 EST: 1974
SQ FT: 2,400
SALES (est): 862.2K **Privately Held**
SIC: 5015 5093 Automotive parts & supplies, used; automotive wrecking for scrap

(G-5226)
DELAWARE BUSINESS SYSTEMS INC
Also Called: D B S
191 Airport Rd (19720-2379)
PHONE...................................302 395-0900
Mike Hynson, *Vice Pres*
Dan Stubblebine, *Project Mgr*
Tim Farrow, *Purch Agent*
Mike Fischer, *Sales Mgr*
Christina Butler, *Sales Staff*
EMP: 31
SQ FT: 10,000
SALES (est): 8.1MM **Privately Held**
WEB: www.dbs4pos.com
SIC: 7373 Value-added resellers, computer systems

(G-5227)
DELAWARE DETAILING SERVICES
800 Washington St (19720-6049)
PHONE...................................302 414-0755
EMP: 7
SALES (est): 65.6K **Privately Held**
SIC: 7542 Washing & polishing, automotive

(G-5228)
DELAWARE ENTERPRISES INC
Also Called: Buffalo Consulting Group
42 Reads Way (19720-1649)
P.O. Box 539, Kemblesville PA (19347-0539)
PHONE...................................302 324-5660
Kurt Sarac, *CEO*
EMP: 25
SQ FT: 800
SALES (est): 1.3MM **Privately Held**
WEB: www.de-enter.com
SIC: 8742 New products & services consultants

(G-5229)
DELAWARE FLEET SERVICE INC
550 Pigeon Point Rd (19720-1444)
P.O. Box 9866, Wilmington (19809-0866)
PHONE...................................302 778-5000
Andrew Newcastle, *President*
EMP: 5
SALES (est): 788.7K **Privately Held**
SIC: 7538 General truck repair

(G-5230)
DELAWARE FLOORING SUPPLY INC
Also Called: Eztread
520 South St (19720-5024)
PHONE...................................302 276-0031
Max T Maurer, *President*
Sharon Maurer, *CFO*
Sharon Moorer, *Marketing Staff*
EMP: 7
SQ FT: 13,000
SALES (est): 643.5K **Privately Held**
SIC: 3446 5031 Stairs, staircases, stair treads: prefabricated metal; building materials, interior

(G-5231)
DELAWARE IMPORTERS INC
615 Lambson Ln (19720-2100)
P.O. Box 10887, Wilmington (19850-0887)
PHONE...................................302 656-4487
Edward J Stegemeier, *President*
Terry Arnold, *Vice Pres*
Kenneth Beach, *Treasurer*
▲ EMP: 100
SQ FT: 100,000
SALES (est): 18.2MM **Privately Held**
WEB: www.delimporters.com
SIC: 5182 5181 Liquor; wine; beer & other fermented malt liquors

(G-5232)
DELAWARE MOTEL AND RV PARK
235 S Dupont Hwy (19720-4141)
PHONE...................................302 328-3114
David Shah, *Owner*
EMP: 5
SALES (est): 166.5K **Privately Held**
SIC: 7033 7011 Trailer park; motels

New Castle - New Castle County (G-5233) — **GEOGRAPHIC SECTION**

(G-5233)
DELAWARE PLUMBING SUPPLY CO
2309 N Dupont Hwy (19720-6300)
PHONE..................302 656-5437
Henry King Jr, *President*
EMP: 11
SQ FT: 15,000
SALES (est): 3.1MM
SALES (corp-wide): 19.5MM **Privately Held**
WEB: www.deplumbingsupply.com
SIC: 5074 5999 Plumbing & hydronic heating supplies; plumbing & heating supplies
PA: Aquaflow Pump & Supply Company
    1561 Pulaski Hwy
    Bear DE 19701
    302 834-1311

(G-5234)
DELAWARE PUBLIC AUTO AUCTION
2323 N Dupont Hwy (19720-6304)
PHONE..................302 656-0500
Doug Powell, *Owner*
Brandon Price, *Manager*
EMP: 20
SALES (est): 2.7MM **Privately Held**
SIC: 5012 5521 Automobile auction; used car dealers

(G-5235)
DELAWARE RECYCLABLE PRODUCTS
246 Marsh Ln (19720-1175)
PHONE..................302 655-1360
Matt Williams, *Ch of Bd*
Jonathan Barber, *Principal*
Chris Isakov, *District Mgr*
EMP: 15
SALES (est): 5.1MM
SALES (corp-wide): 14.9B **Publicly Held**
WEB: www.wm.com
SIC: 4953 Recycling, waste materials
PA: Waste Management, Inc.
    1001 Fannin St Ste 4000
    Houston TX 77002
    713 512-6200

(G-5236)
DELAWARE RIVER & BAY AUTHORITY
Also Called: New Castle Airport
I 295 N Rte 9 (19720)
PHONE..................302 571-6474
Jim Johnson, *Exec Dir*
EMP: 25
SALES (corp-wide): 139.5MM **Privately Held**
WEB: www.drba.net
SIC: 4785 4581 Toll bridge operation; airports, flying fields & services
PA: Delaware River & Bay Authority
    Interstate 295 New Castle
    New Castle DE 19720
    302 571-6303

(G-5237)
DELAWARE RIVER & BAY AUTHORITY (PA)
Interstate 295 New Castle (19720)
P.O. Box 71 (19720-0071)
PHONE..................302 571-6303
William Lowe, *Chairman*
Vincent P Meconi, *COO*
Joseph Larotonda, *Finance Dir*
Lewis B Finch Jr, *Manager*
Scott A Green, *Exec Dir*
EMP: 200 EST: 1962
SALES: 139.5MM **Privately Held**
WEB: www.drba.net
SIC: 4785 Toll bridge operation

(G-5238)
DELAWARE RVER BAY AUTH EMPLYEE
P.O. Box 71 (19720-0071)
PHONE..................302 571-6320
Scott W Reese Jr, *President*
Jack Cawman, *President*
Rich Standarowsky, *Vice Pres*
Greg Pawlowski, *Engineer*
Frances Sweeney, *Treasurer*
EMP: 7
SALES: 132.7K **Privately Held**
SIC: 6061 Federal credit unions

(G-5239)
DELAWARE SAFETY COUNCIL INC
2 Penns Way Ste 201 (19720-2407)
PHONE..................302 276-0660
Frances M West, *President*
Bruce Swayze, *Vice Pres*
R B Swayze, *Vice Pres*
Anthony Nardone, *Treasurer*
E A Nardone, *Treasurer*
EMP: 8
SALES: 488.2K **Privately Held**
WEB: www.delawaresafetycouncil.org
SIC: 8748 Safety training service

(G-5240)
DELAWARE STATE POLICE FEDERAL
235 Christiana Rd (19720-2907)
P.O. Box 800, Georgetown (19947-0800)
PHONE..................302 324-8141
Lexine Starling, *Manager*
EMP: 5
SALES (est): 638.2K **Privately Held**
SIC: 6061 Federal credit unions
PA: Delaware State Police Federal Credit Union
    700 N Bedford St
    Georgetown DE 19947

(G-5241)
DELAWARE TITLE LOANS INC
505 N Dupont Hwy (19720-6442)
PHONE..................302 328-7482
EMP: 7
SALES (corp-wide): 7.7MM **Privately Held**
SIC: 6159 Loan institutions, general & industrial
PA: Delaware Title Loans, Inc.
    8601 Dunwoody Pl Ste 406
    Atlanta GA 30350
    770 552-9840

(G-5242)
DELAWARE VALLEY FENCE & IRON
47 University Ave (19720-4319)
PHONE..................302 322-8193
Tom F Odonnell, *President*
EMP: 3 EST: 2008
SALES (est): 172.2K **Privately Held**
SIC: 1799 2411 3089 3312 Fence construction; rails, fence: round or split; fences, gates & accessories: plastic; fence posts, iron & steel; fence gates posts & fittings: steel; fencing

(G-5243)
DELCON BUILDERS INC (PA)
124 Delaware St Fl 3 (19720-4859)
PHONE..................609 499-7747
Antonio Santos, *President*
EMP: 10 EST: 2012
SALES (est): 2.7MM **Privately Held**
SIC: 1542 Commercial & office building contractors

(G-5244)
DELMARVA COMMUNICATIONS INC
113 J And M Dr (19720-3142)
P.O. Box 11725, Wilmington (19850-1725)
PHONE..................302 324-1230
Jeff D Tillinghast, *President*
Mike Cavazzini, *Director*
Mike Napier, *Director*
EMP: 10
SQ FT: 9,500
SALES (est): 2.3MM **Privately Held**
WEB: www.delmarvacom.com
SIC: 5065 5731 8999 1731 Radio & television equipment & parts; radios, two-way, citizens' band, weather, short-wave, etc.; communication services; electrical work

(G-5245)
DELPA BUILDERS LLC
10 King Ave (19720-1512)
PHONE..................302 731-7304
Larry Zeccola, *Mng Member*
EMP: 14 EST: 2013
SALES (est): 738.3K **Privately Held**
SIC: 1521 New construction, single-family houses

(G-5246)
DELPORT HOLDING COMPANY
529 Terminal Ave (19720-1426)
PHONE..................302 655-7300
Mary Thomas, *President*
James B Thomas Sr, *Chairman*
Madeleine Tucker, *Treasurer*
Margaret Knotts, *Admin Sec*
EMP: 6
SALES (est): 520K **Privately Held**
SIC: 6512 Nonresidential building operators

(G-5247)
DELTA ENGINEERING CORPORATION
13 Drba Way (19720-3129)
PHONE..................302 325-9320
John Moritz, *President*
Jonathan Moritz, *Vice Pres*
Janine Nagle, *Treasurer*
Bob Conover, *Program Mgr*
Virginia A Moritz, *Admin Sec*
EMP: 15
SALES (est): 2.4MM **Privately Held**
WEB: www.delta-engineering.com
SIC: 8711 5088 Aviation &/or aeronautical engineering; aircraft equipment & supplies

(G-5248)
DEPENDABLE TRUCKING INC
520 Terminal Ave (19720-1459)
P.O. Box 668 (19720-0668)
PHONE..................302 655-6271
Herbert Bollman, *President*
E Marie Bollman, *Admin Sec*
EMP: 15
SQ FT: 15,000
SALES (est): 829.1K
SALES (corp-wide): 1.1MM **Privately Held**
WEB: www.dependabletrucking.com
SIC: 7513 4212 Truck leasing, without drivers; local trucking, without storage
PA: Christiana Motor Freight, Inc
    520 Terminal Ave Ste C
    New Castle DE 19720
    302 655-6271

(G-5249)
DFC INDUSTRIES INC
4 Bellecor Dr Unit B (19720-2218)
PHONE..................215 292-1572
Jeffrey D Wright, *President*
EMP: 6
SQ FT: 14,000
SALES (est): 960K **Privately Held**
WEB: www.dfcind.us
SIC: 5085 Filters, industrial

(G-5250)
DFS CORPORATE SERVICES LLC
Also Called: Discover Financial Services
12 Reads Way (19720-1649)
PHONE..................302 323-7191
Richard Howard, *Manager*
EMP: 1200
SALES (corp-wide): 12.8B **Publicly Held**
WEB: www.discovercard.com
SIC: 8742 Human resource consulting services
HQ: Dfs Corporate Services Llc
    2500 Lake Cook Rd 2
    Riverwoods IL 60015
    224 405-0900

(G-5251)
DIAMOND HILL INC
34 Industrial Blvd 104 (19720-2091)
PHONE..................302 999-0302
Michael E Sheehan, *President*
EMP: 8
SALES (est): 2.2MM **Privately Held**
SIC: 1542 Commercial & office building, new construction

(G-5252)
DIAMOND STATE GRAPHICS INC
200 Century Park (19720-3122)
PHONE..................302 325-1100
David Hood, *President*
Douglas Hood, *Vice Pres*
Carlos Vasquez, *Technology*
EMP: 15
SQ FT: 5,500
SALES (est): 2.1MM **Privately Held**
SIC: 2759 Screen printing

(G-5253)
DIMARQUEZ INTL MINISTRIES INC
Also Called: Bells of Hope
417 Moores Ln (19720-4476)
PHONE..................302 256-4847
Hope Bell, *President*
EMP: 18
SALES (est): 207K **Privately Held**
SIC: 8322 Individual & family services

(G-5254)
DIMO CORP
46 Industrial Blvd (19720-2091)
PHONE..................302 324-8100
Sohrab Naghshineh, *President*
Nasim Sadr-Fala, *General Mgr*
Omid Naghshineh, *COO*
Andre Baarsma, *Senior VP*
Lisa Rana Arasteh, *VP Finance*
EMP: 28
SQ FT: 18,500
SALES: 17.3MM **Privately Held**
WEB: www.dimo.com
SIC: 5088 5599 Aircraft & parts; aircraft instruments, equipment or parts

(G-5255)
DIVISION SVCS FOR AGNG ADLTS
1901 N Dupont Hwy Fl 1 (19720-1100)
PHONE..................302 255-9390
Guy Peroppi, *Director*
EMP: 45
SALES (est): 948.8K **Privately Held**
SIC: 8322 Senior citizens' center or association

(G-5256)
DJ FIRST CLASS
20 Robins Nest Ln (19720-1860)
P.O. Box 961 (19720-0961)
PHONE..................302 345-0602
Valerie C Chaney, *CEO*
EMP: 10
SALES (est): 87.7K **Privately Held**
SIC: 7929 8999 Entertainment service; music arranging & composing

(G-5257)
DMC POWER INC
98 Quigley Blvd (19720-4150)
PHONE..................302 276-0303
Francisco Vega, *Human Res Mgr*
EMP: 10 **Privately Held**
SIC: 3643 Current-carrying wiring devices
PA: Dmc Power, Inc.
    623 E Artesia Blvd
    Carson CA 90746

(G-5258)
DOVER FEDERAL CREDIT UNION
499 Pulaski Hwy (19720-3901)
PHONE..................302 322-4230
Gladie Brogan, *Branch Mgr*
EMP: 8
SALES (corp-wide): 18.2MM **Privately Held**
SIC: 6061 Federal credit unions
PA: Dover Federal Credit Union
    1075 Silver Lake Blvd
    Dover DE 19904
    302 678-8000

(G-5259)
DOVER MOTORSPORTS INC
162 Old Churchmans Rd (19720-3116)
PHONE..................302 328-6820
Joseph Ruggiero, *Manager*
EMP: 5

GEOGRAPHIC SECTION
New Castle - New Castle County (G-5287)

SALES (corp-wide): 47MM **Publicly Held**
WEB: www.doverdowns.com
SIC: 7948 7929 Automotive race track operation; entertainment service
PA: Dover Motorsports, Inc.
1131 N Dupont Hwy
Dover DE 19901
302 883-6500

(G-5260)
DRBA POLICE FUND
And I 295 Rr 9 (19720)
PHONE.................................302 571-6326
Paul Hyland, *Buyer*
James T Johnson, *Director*
Joe Martini, *Lab Dir*
EMP: 99
SALES (est): 3.5MM **Privately Held**
SIC: 4785 Inspection & fixed facilities

(G-5261)
DREAM GRAPHICS
9 King Ave (19720-1511)
PHONE.................................302 328-6264
Kathy Stabley, *Partner*
Susan Rawheiser, *Partner*
EMP: 2
SALES: 125K **Privately Held**
SIC: 2396 Screen printing on fabric articles

(G-5262)
DRY WALL INC
13 King Ct Ste 3 (19720-1523)
PHONE.................................302 838-6500
Bryan Hannum, *Owner*
EMP: 28
SALES (est): 3.7MM **Privately Held**
SIC: 1742 Drywall

(G-5263)
DSM DESOTECH INC
Also Called: DSM Somos Technology Center
52 Reads Way (19720-1649)
PHONE.................................302 328-5435
Connie Mitchell, *Branch Mgr*
EMP: 100
SALES (corp-wide): 10.2B **Privately Held**
WEB: www.dsmdesotech.com
SIC: 5169 Chemicals & allied products
HQ: Dsm Desotech Inc.
1122 Saint Charles St
Elgin IL 60120
847 697-0400

(G-5264)
DUMONT AVIATION LLC (PA)
2000 Brett Rd (19720-2428)
PHONE.................................302 777-1003
Dan Piraino, *CEO*
Daniel Piraino, *CEO*
Robert Flansburg, *COO*
Jim McGroarty, *Sales Staff*
Ashley Pfender, *Supervisor*
EMP: 4
SALES (est): 1.7MM **Privately Held**
SIC: 4581 Aircraft maintenance & repair services

(G-5265)
DUMONT GROUP LLC
Also Called: Dumont Aviation
2000 Brett Rd (19720-2428)
PHONE.................................302 777-1003
Katrina Brown, *Accountant*
Amber Martin, *Manager*
Darrin Price, *Maintence Staff*
EMP: 7 EST: 2014
SALES (est): 395.7K **Privately Held**
SIC: 8742 Management consulting services

(G-5266)
DUPONT AVIATION CORP
199 N Dupont Hwy (19720-3121)
PHONE.................................302 996-8000
Keith Shelburn, *Director*
EMP: 30
SALES (est): 2.3MM
SALES (corp-wide): 30.6B **Publicly Held**
WEB: www.dupont.com
SIC: 8711 Aviation &/or aeronautical engineering

HQ: E. I. Du Pont De Nemours And Company
974 Centre Rd Bldg 735
Wilmington DE 19805
302 485-3000

(G-5267)
DURALEX USA INC
802 Centerpoint Blvd (19720-8123)
PHONE.................................302 326-4804
Alan Senior, *President*
Jacques Henry, *Shareholder*
▲ EMP: 60
SQ FT: 44,000
SALES: 2MM **Privately Held**
SIC: 5023 Glassware

(G-5268)
DUTCH VILLAGE MOTEL INC
Also Called: Rodeway Inn
111 S Dupont Hwy (19720-4127)
PHONE.................................302 328-6246
Harshad Amin, *President*
Pierre L Olivero, *President*
Margaret L Olivero, *Vice Pres*
EMP: 11
SQ FT: 21,000
SALES (est): 499.2K **Privately Held**
SIC: 7011 Hotels & motels

(G-5269)
DYCOM INDUSTRIES INC
34 Blevins Dr Ste 5 (19720-4177)
PHONE.................................302 613-0958
Jeff Drzymala, *Principal*
EMP: 4 EST: 2016
SALES (est): 224.7K **Privately Held**
SIC: 1623 Water, sewer & utility lines

(G-5270)
DYNAMIC THERAPY SERVICES LLC
1218 Beaver Brook Plz A (19720-8632)
PHONE.................................302 544-4388
EMP: 16
SALES (corp-wide): 12.9MM **Privately Held**
SIC: 8049 Physical therapist
PA: Dynamic Therapy Services Llc
1501 Blueball Ave
Linwood PA 19061
610 859-8850

(G-5271)
E I DU PONT DE NEMOURS & CO
Also Called: Dupont
1001 Lambson Ln (19720-2107)
PHONE.................................302 772-0016
Harry Abock, *Manager*
EMP: 4
SALES (corp-wide): 30.6B **Publicly Held**
WEB: www.dupont.com
SIC: 2911 5171 5541 Petroleum refining; petroleum bulk stations & terminals; gasoline service stations
HQ: E. I. Du Pont De Nemours And Company
974 Centre Rd Bldg 735
Wilmington DE 19805
302 485-3000

(G-5272)
E-CARAUCTIONS LLC (PA)
1602 N Dupont Hwy (19720-1904)
P.O. Box 272, Wilmington (19899-0272)
PHONE.................................302 677-1552
Kathleen Stevenson, *Principal*
EMP: 8
SALES (est): 1.5MM **Privately Held**
SIC: 7389 Auction, appraisal & exchange services

(G-5273)
EAGLE LIMOUSINE INC (PA)
Also Called: Eagle Transportation
77 Mccullough Dr Ste 5 (19720-2089)
PHONE.................................302 325-4200
Kristin Aulendach, *President*
EMP: 150
SQ FT: 15,000
SALES (est): 8.1MM **Privately Held**
WEB: www.eaglelimo.com
SIC: 4119 Limousine rental, with driver

(G-5274)
EAGLE POWER AND EQUIPMENT CORP
2211 N Du Pont Pkwy (19720-6302)
P.O. Box 889 (19720-0889)
PHONE.................................302 652-3028
Bob McCullough, *Manager*
Frank Beck, *Manager*
Pat Dicicco, *Manager*
EMP: 10 **Privately Held**
WEB: www.eaglepowerandequipment.com
SIC: 5082 7353 General construction machinery & equipment; heavy construction equipment rental
PA: Eagle Power And Equipment Corp.
953 Bethlehem Pike
Montgomeryville PA 18936

(G-5275)
EAST COAST ERECTORS INC
1144 River Rd (19720-5106)
P.O. Box 448 (19720-0448)
PHONE.................................302 323-1800
Michael A Williams, *President*
Thomas Williams, *Vice Pres*
William Zern, *Treasurer*
David Brooks, *Manager*
EMP: 25
SALES (est): 3.9MM **Privately Held**
SIC: 1791 3441 Structural steel erection; fabricated structural metal

(G-5276)
EASTER SEAL DELAWARE (PA)
61 Corporate Cir (19720-2405)
PHONE.................................302 324-4444
Kenan J Sklenar, *CEO*
Laura McKeown, *Facilities Mgr*
Shannon Pencek, *HR Admin*
EMP: 250
SQ FT: 20,000
SALES: 34.3MM **Privately Held**
SIC: 8322 8331 Social services for the handicapped; general counseling services; vocational training agency

(G-5277)
EASTERN HOSPITALITY MANAGEMENT
Also Called: Super 8 Motel
215 S Dupont Hwy (19720-4141)
PHONE.................................302 322-9480
Chuck Pitts, *Principal*
Charles Le Ferguson, *Manager*
EMP: 15 **Privately Held**
SIC: 7011 Hotels & motels
PA: Eastern Hospitality Management, Inc
1910 8th Ave Ne
Aberdeen SD 57401

(G-5278)
EASTERN INDUSTRIAL SVCS INC
Also Called: Eisi
196 Quigley Blvd Ste A (19720-4176)
PHONE.................................302 455-1400
Louis Faverio, *CEO*
Tim Shelton, *Corp Secy*
Ronald Galloway, *COO*
Trevor Eshelman, *Project Mgr*
Kevin Evans, *Project Mgr*
EMP: 80
SALES (est): 10.6MM **Privately Held**
SIC: 1742 1799 Insulation, buildings; coating, caulking & weather, water & fireproofing; rigging & scaffolding

(G-5279)
EBANKS CONSTRUCTION LLC
507 Florence Fields Ln (19720-8752)
PHONE.................................302 420-7584
Stacy Ebanks,
EMP: 15
SALES (est): 1.8MM **Privately Held**
SIC: 1542 1522 Commercial & office building, new construction; residential construction

(G-5280)
ELCRITON INC
15 Reads Way (19720-1600)
PHONE.................................864 921-5146
Bryan Tracy, *CEO*
Eleftherios Papoutsakis, *President*
Shawn Jones, *Development*

Carrissa Kesler, *Development*
Daniel Mitchell, *Development*
EMP: 4
SALES (est): 380K **Privately Held**
SIC: 2869 Industrial organic chemicals

(G-5281)
ELECTRIC MOTOR REPAIR SVC
263 Quigley Blvd Ste 12 (19720-8112)
PHONE.................................302 322-1179
Caroline Kauffman, *Principal*
EMP: 2 EST: 2016
SALES (est): 40.5K **Privately Held**
SIC: 7694 Electric motor repair

(G-5282)
ELECTRICAL INTEGRITY LLC
117 J And M Dr (19720-3147)
PHONE.................................302 388-3430
EMP: 4
SALES (est): 117.2K **Privately Held**
SIC: 4911 Electric services

(G-5283)
ELECTRICAL POWER SYSTEMS INC (PA)
240a Churchmans Rd (19720-3110)
PHONE.................................302 325-3502
Stephen Yovanov, *President*
EMP: 7
SQ FT: 2,700
SALES: 700K **Privately Held**
SIC: 1731 Electric power systems contractors; switchgear & related devices installation

(G-5284)
ELECTRO-ART SIGN COMPANY
107 J And M Dr (19720-3147)
P.O. Box 281 (19720-0281)
PHONE.................................302 322-1108
Thomas Rash Jr, *President*
Tony Tettoruto, *Vice Pres*
Nick Tettoruto, *Treasurer*
Dave Tettoruto, *Admin Sec*
EMP: 6
SQ FT: 3,000
SALES (est): 712.3K **Privately Held**
SIC: 3993 Electric signs

(G-5285)
ELECTRONICS EXCHANGE INC
282 Quigley Blvd (19720-4163)
P.O. Box 7550, Wilmington (19803-0550)
PHONE.................................302 322-5401
Roberta Mostovoy, *President*
Stanley Mostovoy, *Admin Sec*
EMP: 7 EST: 1978
SQ FT: 2,500
SALES (est): 2.1MM **Privately Held**
WEB: www.eedelaware.com
SIC: 5065 Electronic parts

(G-5286)
ELIZABETH BEVERAGE COMPANY LLC
Also Called: Elizabeth Bottling Company
650 Ships Landing Way (19720-4577)
PHONE.................................302 322-9895
Robert Dalvano, *Vice Pres*
Jack Keller, *Vice Pres*
EMP: 9
SALES (est): 2.7MM **Privately Held**
SIC: 5149 Soft drinks
PA: Elizco Inc
650 Ships Landing Way
New Castle DE 19720

(G-5287)
EMORY HILL & COMPANY (PA)
10 Corporate Cir Ste 100 (19720-2418)
PHONE.................................302 322-4400
Robert H Hill, *President*
Carmen Facciolo Jr, *Vice Pres*
Joe Fox, *Project Mgr*
Ed Kotsay, *Project Mgr*
Fred Wise, *Project Mgr*
EMP: 60
SQ FT: 4,000
SALES: 16.7MM **Privately Held**
SIC: 8742 Construction project management consultant

New Castle - New Castle County (G-5288) GEOGRAPHIC SECTION

(G-5288)
EMORY HILL RE SVCS INC (PA)
10 Corporate Cir (19720-2418)
PHONE....................302 322-9500
Carmen J Facciolo Jr, *President*
Robert H Hill, *Vice Pres*
Fred Wise, *Project Mgr*
Dave Morrison, *Sales Staff*
Stephen Dobraniecki, *Property Mgr*
EMP: 55
SQ FT: 3,500
SALES: 6.3MM **Privately Held**
SIC: 6512 Commercial & industrial building operation

(G-5289)
EMPIRE INVESTMENTS INC
201 Jestan Blvd (19720-5214)
PHONE....................302 838-0631
Pasquale Muzzi, *President*
Bernadette Hanson, *Manager*
Sylvester Aiello, *Admin Sec*
EMP: 7
SQ FT: 3,000
SALES (est): 1MM **Privately Held**
SIC: 1521 1542 New construction, single-family houses; nonresidential construction

(G-5290)
EMPOWER MATERIALS INC
91 Lukens Dr Ste E (19720-2799)
PHONE....................302 225-0100
Richard J Giacco, *President*
Peter Ferraro, *Director*
EMP: 12
SALES (est): 1.2MM
SALES (corp-wide): 2.2MM **Privately Held**
SIC: 2822 Ethylene-propylene rubbers, EPDM polymers
PA: Axess Corporation
     91 Lukens Dr Ste E
     New Castle DE 19720
     302 292-8500

(G-5291)
ENTERPRISE RENT-A-CAR
190 S Dupont Hwy (19720-4149)
PHONE....................302 323-0850
EMP: 6
SALES (corp-wide): 4.5B **Privately Held**
SIC: 7514 Passenger car rental
HQ: Enterprise Rent-A-Car Company Of Los Angeles, Llc
     333 City Blvd W Ste 1000
     Orange CA 92868
     657 221-4400

(G-5292)
ENVIRONMENTAL SERVICES INC
461 Churchmans Rd (19720-3156)
PHONE....................302 669-6812
Jennifer Bailey, *Owner*
Howard Morrison, *Info Tech Mgr*
EMP: 6
SALES (est): 468K **Privately Held**
SIC: 8748 Environmental consultant

(G-5293)
EPSTEIN KPLAN OPTHLMLOGIST LLP
169 Christiana Rd (19720-3040)
PHONE....................302 322-4444
Matt Epstein, *Partner*
EMP: 8
SALES (est): 424.5K **Privately Held**
SIC: 8011 Ophthalmologist

(G-5294)
ESTELLES CHILD DEV CTR INC
132 Colesbery Dr (19720-3204)
PHONE....................302 792-9065
Estelle Turner, *CEO*
EMP: 15
SALES (est): 236.2K **Privately Held**
WEB: www.ncchs.net
SIC: 8351 Head start center, except in conjunction with school

(G-5295)
ESTEP DOUGLAS E PUB ACCOUNTANT
193 Christiana Rd (19720-3038)
PHONE....................302 322-4621
Douglas E Estep, *Owner*
EMP: 4
SQ FT: 1,200
SALES (est): 286K **Privately Held**
SIC: 8721 Certified public accountant

(G-5296)
ET COMMUNICATIONS LLC
270 Quigley Blvd (19720-4106)
PHONE....................302 322-2222
Eddie Traynham, *Principal*
Amy Harper, *Technology*
EMP: 15
SALES (est): 930K **Privately Held**
SIC: 7622 Communication equipment repair

(G-5297)
EUROFINS QC INC
Also Called: Qc Laboratories
272 Quigley Blvd (19720-4106)
PHONE....................302 276-0432
Ruth Pyle, *Manager*
EMP: 48
SALES (corp-wide): 34.3MM **Privately Held**
SIC: 8734 Water testing laboratory
PA: Eurofins Qc, Inc.
     702 Electronic Dr
     Horsham PA 19044
     215 355-3900

(G-5298)
EVOQUA WATER TECHNOLOGIES LLC
259 Quigley Blvd (19720-4186)
PHONE....................302 322-6247
EMP: 6
SALES (corp-wide): 1.4B **Publicly Held**
SIC: 3589 Sewage & water treatment equipment
HQ: Evoqua Water Technologies Llc
     210 6th Ave Ste 3300
     Pittsburgh PA 15222
     724 772-0044

(G-5299)
EXCELLENT HOME CARE
122 Delaware St (19720-4814)
PHONE....................302 327-0147
EMP: 8 EST: 2017
SALES (est): 61.1K **Privately Held**
SIC: 8082 Home health care services

(G-5300)
EXECUTIVE OFFICES INC
42 Reads Way (19720-1649)
P.O. Box 9085, Newark (19714-9085)
PHONE....................302 323-8100
Allan Strawhacker, *CEO*
Wendy Strawhacker, *President*
EMP: 4
SALES (est): 488.2K **Privately Held**
WEB: www.eoinc.com
SIC: 6512 Commercial & industrial building operation

(G-5301)
EXPERIENCED AUTO PARTS INC
461 Old Airport Rd (19720-1001)
PHONE....................302 322-3344
John Dudziec, *President*
Debra Dudziec, *Vice Pres*
EMP: 4
SALES (est): 1MM **Privately Held**
SIC: 5084 Industrial machinery & equipment

(G-5302)
FACEPAINTING
260 Christiana Rd Apt F10 (19720-2970)
PHONE....................302 344-3145
Daria Lewis, *Principal*
EMP: 7 EST: 2016
SALES (est): 94.4K **Privately Held**
SIC: 1721 Painting & paper hanging

(G-5303)
FAMOID TECHNOLOGY LLC
607 Deemer Pl (19720-5043)
PHONE....................530 601-7284
Canberk Demirci,
EMP: 2
SALES (est): 50.7K **Privately Held**
SIC: 7371 7372 5734 Computer software development & applications; application computer software; software, business & non-game

(G-5304)
FEDERAL EXPRESS CORPORATION
Also Called: Fedex
2 W Commons Blvd (19720-2497)
PHONE....................800 463-3339
EMP: 34
SALES (corp-wide): 69.6B **Publicly Held**
SIC: 4513 Package delivery, private air
HQ: Federal Express Corporation
     3610 Hacks Cross Rd
     Memphis TN 38125
     901 369-3600

(G-5305)
FEDERAL MECHANICAL CONTRACTORS
Also Called: Cochran Oil
229 Hillview Ave (19720-2204)
PHONE....................302 656-2998
Thomas H Cochran Jr, *President*
EMP: 10
SQ FT: 6,000
SALES (est): 1.7MM **Privately Held**
SIC: 1711 Plumbing contractors; warm air heating & air conditioning contractor

(G-5306)
FEDEX FREIGHT CORPORATION
617 Lambson Ln (19720-2103)
PHONE....................800 218-6570
EMP: 20
SALES (corp-wide): 69.6B **Publicly Held**
SIC: 4213 Less-than-truckload (LTL) transport
HQ: Fedex Freight Corporation
     1715 Aaron Brenner Dr
     Memphis TN 38120

(G-5307)
FEDEX GROUND PACKAGE SYS INC
6 Dock View Dr (19720-2206)
PHONE....................800 463-3339
EMP: 4
SALES (corp-wide): 69.6B **Publicly Held**
SIC: 4513 Air courier services
HQ: Fedex Ground Package System, Inc.
     1000 Fed Ex Dr
     Coraopolis PA 15108
     800 463-3339

(G-5308)
FELIXCEM CORPORATION INC
314 Bay West Blvd (19720-5195)
PHONE....................302 324-9101
Earl Pearce, *Principal*
EMP: 3
SALES (est): 170K **Privately Held**
SIC: 3471 Cleaning, polishing & finishing

(G-5309)
FERGUSON ENTERPRISES LLC
Also Called: Ferguson 1991
77 Mccullough Dr Ste 12 (19720-2089)
PHONE....................302 322-2836
Rick Massaro, *Branch Mgr*
EMP: 9
SALES (corp-wide): 20.7B **Privately Held**
WEB: www.ferguson.com
SIC: 5074 Plumbing fittings & supplies
HQ: Ferguson Enterprises, Llc
     12500 Jefferson Ave
     Newport News VA 23602
     757 874-7795

(G-5310)
FIRSD TEA NORTH AMERICA LLC (HQ)
34 Blevins Dr Ste 1&2 (19720-4177)
PHONE....................302 322-1255
Kurt Kumagai, *Sales Mgr*
Shengyuan Chen, *Exec Dir*
▲ EMP: 6
SQ FT: 7,578
SALES: 3.3MM
SALES (corp-wide): 75.3MM **Privately Held**
SIC: 5149 2099 2393 Tea; beverage concentrates; tea bagging; tea blending; tea bags, fabric: made from purchased materials
PA: Zhejiang Tea Group Co., Ltd.
     No.218, Tiyuchang Road, Xiacheng District
     Hangzhou 31001
     571 850-5355

(G-5311)
FIRST CHOICE AUTO & TRUCK REPR
533 Rogers Rd (19720-1323)
PHONE....................302 656-1433
Kenneth Williams, *President*
EMP: 5
SALES (est): 1.3MM **Privately Held**
SIC: 7538 General automotive repair shops

(G-5312)
FIRST CHOICE HOME MED EQUIPT (PA)
259 Quigley Blvd Ste 1 (19720-4186)
PHONE....................302 323-8700
Craig Rotenberry, *Partner*
Mark Havrilla, *Opers Mgr*
Michael Eddy,
Richard Kreider,
EMP: 30
SALES (est): 11.9MM **Privately Held**
SIC: 5047 Medical equipment & supplies

(G-5313)
FIRST CLASS LIMOUSINE (PA)
734 Staghorn Dr (19720-7652)
PHONE....................302 836-9500
Kevin Jones, *Partner*
Cleopatra Jones, *Partner*
EMP: 4
SALES: 170K **Privately Held**
WEB: www.firstclassonline.com
SIC: 4119 Limousine rental, with driver

(G-5314)
FIRST STATE AUTOMATION LLC
34 Blevins Dr Ste 3 (19720-4177)
PHONE....................302 743-4798
Daniel T McVey,
EMP: 5
SALES: 100K **Privately Held**
SIC: 5084 Industrial machinery & equipment

(G-5315)
FIRST STATE ELECTRIC COMPANY
25 King Ct (19720-1519)
PHONE....................302 322-0140
Nicola J Aievoli, *President*
Edward P Twitchell, *Treasurer*
EMP: 25 EST: 1979
SQ FT: 6,000
SALES (est): 3.3MM **Privately Held**
WEB: www.firststateelectric.com
SIC: 1731 General electrical contractor

(G-5316)
FIRST STATE FIREARMS & ACC LLC
178 S Dupont Hwy (19720-4149)
PHONE....................302 322-1126
Diana Carry, *Mng Member*
Larry Hudson, *Manager*
EMP: 7
SQ FT: 2,000
SALES: 1.5MM **Privately Held**
SIC: 5091 Firearms, sporting

(G-5317)
FIRST STATE REFINERY
118 Jestan Blvd (19720-5299)
PHONE....................302 838-8303
Dora Conlen, *President*
EMP: 4
SALES: 139.3K **Privately Held**
SIC: 6061 Federal credit unions

GEOGRAPHIC SECTION

New Castle - New Castle County (G-5348)

(G-5318)
FIRST STATE STEEL DRUM CO
4030 New Castle Ave (19720-1455)
PHONE..................302 655-2422
John D Ryan III, *Partner*
Jane Ryan, *Partner*
Robert S Ryan, *Partner*
William R Ryan, *Partner*
EMP: 6
SQ FT: 2,000
SALES (est): 952.7K **Privately Held**
WEB: www.firststatesteeldrum.com
SIC: 5085 Drums, new or reconditioned

(G-5319)
FIRST STATE WAREHOUSING
Also Called: Diamond State Whsng & Dist
300 Pigeon Blvd (19720)
PHONE..................302 426-0802
Patrick Bastian, *Owner*
Richard Bastian, *Co-Owner*
EMP: 65
SALES (est): 4.1MM **Privately Held**
SIC: 4225 General warehousing

(G-5320)
FLOOR COATINGS ETC INC
110 J And M Dr (19720-3147)
PHONE..................302 322-4177
Bill Deveney, *CEO*
John Pennington, *President*
Anthony Watkins, *Vice Pres*
Patty Weicker, *Manager*
EMP: 25
SQ FT: 3,000
SALES (est): 5.1MM **Privately Held**
WEB: www.floorcoatingsetc.com
SIC: 1771 Flooring contractor

(G-5321)
FLYADVANCED LLC
131 N Dupont Hwy (19720-3135)
PHONE..................302 324-9970
Regis De Ramel, *Principal*
Sean Loolian, *Opers Mgr*
Benjamin Koontz, *Controller*
Caroline Ramos, *Manager*
EMP: 4
SALES (est): 424.8K **Privately Held**
SIC: 4581 Airports, flying fields & services

(G-5322)
FOCUS HEALTH CARE DELAWARE LLC
Also Called: Meadowwood Behavioral Health
575 S Dupont Hwy (19720-4606)
PHONE..................302 395-1111
Patty Wright, *Administration*
EMP: 55
SALES (est): 20.3MM **Privately Held**
SIC: 8093 Mental health clinic, outpatient

(G-5323)
FORESITE ASSOC INC
208 Delaware St (19720-4850)
PHONE..................302 351-3421
Andrew Hayes, *President*
EMP: 4
SALES (est): 350K **Privately Held**
SIC: 8711 Civil engineering

(G-5324)
FOREVER GREEN LANDSCAPING INC
340 Churchmans Rd (19720-3112)
PHONE..................302 322-9535
Elly Nadot, *President*
Susan King, *Software Engr*
EMP: 11
SALES (est): 1.2MM **Privately Held**
SIC: 0782 Landscape contractors

(G-5325)
FOUR STATES LLC
520 Terminal Ave Ste D (19720-1447)
P.O. Box 891 (19720-0891)
PHONE..................302 655-3400
Jim Byrne, *Owner*
EMP: 10
SQ FT: 25,000
SALES (est): 1.1MM **Privately Held**
WEB: www.fourstatesllc.com
SIC: 7538 5084 Truck engine repair, except industrial; trucks, industrial

(G-5326)
FOX SPECIALTIES INC
Also Called: Encompass Elements
1500 Johnson Way (19720-8110)
PHONE..................302 322-5200
Phillip Murray, *Branch Mgr*
EMP: 14
SALES (est): 1.9MM
SALES (corp-wide): 20.1MM **Privately Held**
SIC: 2789 Binding only: books, pamphlets, magazines, etc.
PA: Fox Specialties, Inc.
2750 Morris Rd Ste C
Lansdale PA 19446
215 822-5775

(G-5327)
FRANCIS ENTERPRISES LLC
Also Called: Sheep Skin Gifts
261 Quigley Blvd Ste 10 (19720-4187)
PHONE..................302 276-1316
Joseph Francis,
▲ EMP: 12
SALES (est): 1MM **Privately Held**
SIC: 5699 5199 Leather garments; leather, leather goods & furs

(G-5328)
FRANK DERAMO & SON INC
10 King Ct (19720-1519)
PHONE..................302 328-0102
S Elizabeth Deramo, *President*
Frank Deramo Jr, *Shareholder*
EMP: 10
SQ FT: 3,480
SALES (est): 500K **Privately Held**
SIC: 1771 Concrete work

(G-5329)
FREEHOLD CARTAGE INC
350 Pigeon Point Rd (19720-1464)
PHONE..................302 658-2005
Norm Gaitens, *General Mgr*
EMP: 6
SALES (corp-wide): 60.4MM **Privately Held**
WEB: www.freeholdcartage.com
SIC: 4213 Trucking, except local
PA: Freehold Cartage Inc.
825 State Route 33
Freehold NJ 07728
732 462-1001

(G-5330)
FRESENIUS MEDICAL CARE N AMER
Also Called: First State
608 Ferry Cut Off St (19720-4549)
PHONE..................302 328-9044
John Grandson, *Branch Mgr*
Debbie Baker, *Director*
EMP: 15
SALES (corp-wide): 18.3B **Privately Held**
SIC: 8092 Kidney dialysis centers
HQ: Fresenius Usa Manufacturing, Inc.
920 Winter St
Waltham MA 02451

(G-5331)
FRIENDS OF BELLACA AIRFIELD
Ctr Pt Blvd Rr 273 (19720)
P.O. Box 267 (19720-0267)
PHONE..................302 322-3816
Sally Monigle, *Vice Pres*
EMP: 5
SALES (est): 20.2K **Privately Held**
SIC: 8412 Historical society

(G-5332)
FRONTLINE CROSSFIT
4060 N Dupont Hwy 1 (19720-6325)
PHONE..................302 229-6467
EMP: 7
SALES (est): 81.9K **Privately Held**
SIC: 7991 Health club

(G-5333)
FUJI FILM
233 Cherry Ln (19720-2779)
PHONE..................302 477-8000
Brian Meldrum, *Principal*
John Ackerman, *Executive*
Kathleen Ryan, *Executive*
EMP: 13
SALES (est): 2.6MM **Privately Held**
SIC: 3081 Photographic & X-ray film & sheet

(G-5334)
FUJIFILM IMAGING COLORANTS INC (DH)
233 Cherry Ln (19720-2779)
PHONE..................302 477-8022
Ian Wilkinson, *President*
Clayton Gaskill, *Engineer*
Ashley Yu, *Finance*
Jennifer Handlin, *Cust Mgr*
Maureen Concordia, *Director*
◆ EMP: 30
SQ FT: 5,000
SALES (est): 56.5MM **Privately Held**
WEB: www.fujifilmimagingcolorants.com
SIC: 5043 Photographic equipment & supplies

(G-5335)
FUJIFILM IMAGING COLORANTS INC
233 Cherry Ln (19720-2779)
PHONE..................302 472-1245
Peter Ciocys, *Branch Mgr*
EMP: 80 **Privately Held**
WEB: www.fujifilmimagingcolorants.com
SIC: 7384 Photofinish laboratories
HQ: Fujifilm Imaging Colorants, Inc.
233 Cherry Ln
New Castle DE 19720
302 477-8022

(G-5336)
FURSAN CONSULTING SERVICES
42 Reads Way (19720-1649)
PHONE..................240 654-5784
Aysha Kayani, *Managing Dir*
EMP: 10
SALES (est): 480K **Privately Held**
SIC: 8249 8331 8742 Business training services; job training services; manpower training; human resource consulting services

(G-5337)
FUSCO ENTERPRISES (PA)
200 Airport Rd (19720-1520)
PHONE..................302 328-6251
Anthony Fusco, *Owner*
EMP: 8 EST: 2008
SALES (est): 922.8K **Privately Held**
SIC: 6512 Shopping center, property operation only

(G-5338)
FUSCO MANAGEMENT INC
Also Called: Fusco Enterprises
200 Airport Rd (19720-1520)
P.O. Box 665 (19720-0665)
PHONE..................302 328-6251
Anthony Fusco, *President*
Catherine Fusco, *Vice Pres*
EMP: 29
SQ FT: 26,000
SALES (est): 3.1MM **Privately Held**
SIC: 6512 Nonresidential building operators

(G-5339)
G & E WELDING SUPPLY CO
281 Airport Rd (19720-1540)
PHONE..................302 322-9353
Wayne E Rapine, *President*
Hansen James, *COO*
Pam S Rapine, *Vice Pres*
EMP: 15
SQ FT: 4,000
SALES (est): 5.2MM **Privately Held**
WEB: www.geweldingsupply.com
SIC: 5084 5085 Welding machinery & equipment; welding supplies

(G-5340)
G4S SECURE SOLUTIONS (USA)
38 Reads Way (19720-1649)
PHONE..................302 395-9920
Dave Zabala, *Branch Mgr*
EMP: 4 **Privately Held**
SIC: 7381 Security guard service
HQ: G4s Secure Solutions (Usa) Inc.
1395 University Blvd
Jupiter FL 33458
561 622-5656

(G-5341)
GALLOWAY COURT APTS
400 S Dupont Hwy Ofc 125 (19720-7624)
PHONE..................302 328-0488
Barbara Petree, *President*
EMP: 4
SALES (est): 288.2K **Privately Held**
SIC: 6513 Apartment hotel operation

(G-5342)
GALLUCIOS LAWN CARE
24 Farragut Ln (19720-2919)
PHONE..................302 324-8182
Donna Gallucio, *Principal*
EMP: 4 EST: 2011
SALES (est): 134.7K **Privately Held**
SIC: 0782 Lawn care services

(G-5343)
GANNETT CO INC
Also Called: News Journal
950 W Basin Rd (19720-1008)
P.O. Box 15505, Wilmington (19850-5505)
PHONE..................302 325-6600
Curtis Riddle, *Manager*
Verna Thompson, *Producer*
Anthony Calvarese, *Maintence Staff*
EMP: 77
SALES (corp-wide): 1.5B **Publicly Held**
WEB: www.gannett.com
SIC: 2711 2752 Newspapers: publishing only, not printed on site; commercial printing, lithographic
HQ: Gannett Media Corp.
7950 Jones Branch Dr
Mc Lean VA 22102
703 854-6000

(G-5344)
GARCIA LANDSCAPING SERVICES
14 Mark Dr (19720-1749)
PHONE..................302 324-8789
Paolo Garcia, *Principal*
EMP: 4
SALES (est): 176.7K **Privately Held**
SIC: 0782 Landscape contractors

(G-5345)
GATEWAY INTERNATIONAL 360 LLC
260 Quigley Blvd Ste 135 (19720-9012)
PHONE..................302 250-4990
Daniel Mozey, *Marketing Staff*
EMP: 4
SALES: 540.5K **Privately Held**
SIC: 8742 Management consulting services

(G-5346)
GBA ENTERPRISES INC
Also Called: Everest Grocery
208 Churchmans Rd (19720-3110)
PHONE..................302 323-1080
Jackie Greene, *Partner*
David Kabasa, *Partner*
Prasad Ammatta, *Vice Pres*
EMP: 4
SALES (est): 272.8K **Privately Held**
SIC: 7379 5411 Computer related consulting services; grocery stores

(G-5347)
GC NEW CASTLE INC
Also Called: Great Clips Hair Cut Salon
1508 Beaver Creek Xing (19720)
PHONE..................302 544-6128
John A Llughren, *President*
EMP: 8
SQ FT: 1,600
SALES: 150K **Privately Held**
SIC: 7231 Unisex hair salons

(G-5348)
GENERAL CRPT-MECH SPLY
4 Nonesuch Pl (19720-2209)
PHONE..................302 322-1847
Stanley Cometz, *President*
David Cometz, *Shareholder*
Michael Cometz, *Shareholder*

New Castle - New Castle County (G-5349)

Steven Cometz, *Shareholder*
Sonia Cometz, *Admin Sec*
EMP: 5
SALES (est): 675K **Privately Held**
WEB: www.generalfloor.com
SIC: 5023 Floor coverings; carpets; resilient floor coverings: tile or sheet; wood flooring
PA: General Floor Industries, Inc.
190 Benigno Blvd
Bellmawr NJ 08031

(G-5349)
GENERAL TEAMSTERS LOCAL UN 326
451 Churchmans Rd (19720-3156)
PHONE.............................302 328-2387
John Ryan, *President*
EMP: 4
SALES: 999.6K **Privately Held**
SIC: 8631 Labor union

(G-5350)
GENS TRUCKING INC
512 Golding Ave (19720-1461)
PHONE.............................302 421-3522
Genevieve English, *Principal*
EMP: 4
SALES (est): 166.7K **Privately Held**
SIC: 4212 Local trucking, without storage

(G-5351)
GEO-TECHNOLOGY ASSOCIATES INC
18 Boulden Cir Ste 36 (19720-3494)
PHONE.............................302 326-2100
Chris Reith, *Branch Mgr*
EMP: 25 **Privately Held**
SIC: 8748 8734 Environmental consultant; soil analysis
HQ: Geo-Technology Associates Inc
3445 Box Hll Corp Ctr Dr A
Abingdon MD 21009
410 515-9446

(G-5352)
GEORGETOWN MANOR APARTMENTS
260 Christiana Rd Ofc B4 (19720-2964)
PHONE.............................302 328-6231
Pam Abel, *Manager*
Jodi E Walters, *Manager*
EMP: 8
SALES (est): 580K **Privately Held**
SIC: 6513 Apartment building operators

(G-5353)
GILES & RANSOME INC
Also Called: Caterpillar
2225 N Dupont Hwy (19720-6302)
PHONE.............................302 777-5800
Fax: 302 777-2433
EMP: 8 **Privately Held**
SIC: 5082 Whol Construction/Mining Equipment
PA: Giles & Ransome, Inc.
2975 Galloway Rd
Bensalem PA 19020
215 639-4300

(G-5354)
GIRLS AUTO CLINIC LLC
35 Antioch Ct (19720-3704)
P.O. Box 686, Montchanin (19710-0686)
PHONE.............................484 679-6394
Patrice Banks, *President*
Crystal Lewis, *Mng Member*
EMP: 7
SALES (est): 148K **Privately Held**
SIC: 7538 7231 General automotive repair shops; cosmetology & personal hygiene salons

(G-5355)
GOBOS TOGO INC
136 Quigley Blvd (19720-4104)
PHONE.............................302 426-1898
EMP: 9 **EST:** 2003
SALES (est): 420K **Privately Held**
SIC: 7922 Theatrical Producers/Services

(G-5356)
GORDY MANAGEMENT INC
Also Called: Gordy Enterprises
265 N Dupont Hwy Fl 2 (19720-6400)
P.O. Box 687 (19720-0687)
PHONE.............................302 322-3723
Ralph E Gordy Jr, *President*
Peter Gordy, *Vice Pres*
EMP: 5
SALES (est): 713K **Privately Held**
SIC: 6512 Commercial & industrial building operation

(G-5357)
GORE FUNERAL SERVICES
812 Arthur Springs Ln (19720-8771)
PHONE.............................610 364-9900
Derick Gore, *Owner*
EMP: 4
SALES (corp-wide): 232.2K **Privately Held**
SIC: 7261 Funeral director
PA: Gore Funeral Services
406 Marsh Rd
Wilmington DE 19809
610 364-9900

(G-5358)
GRACELAWN MEMORIAL PARK INC (PA)
2220 N Dupont Hwy (19720-6319)
P.O. Box 714 (19720-0714)
PHONE.............................302 654-6158
Earl J Reed, *Ch of Bd*
Lee W Hagenbach, *President*
EMP: 25
SQ FT: 5,000
SALES: 2MM **Privately Held**
WEB: www.gracelawn.com
SIC: 7011 Hotels & motels

(G-5359)
GRAY AUDOGRAPH AGENCY INC
2340 N Dupont Hwy (19720-6327)
P.O. Box 726 (19720-0726)
PHONE.............................302 658-1700
John P Collins, *President*
Paul J Collins, *Treasurer*
Pea Marshall, *Admin Sec*
EMP: 20
SQ FT: 8,000
SALES (est): 1.9MM **Privately Held**
SIC: 1731 1799 5999 Telephone & telephone equipment installation; office furniture installation; business machines & equipment; telephone equipment & systems

(G-5360)
GRAYBAR ELECTRIC COMPANY INC
43 Boulden Blvd (19720-2082)
PHONE.............................302 322-2200
Robert Gibson, *Manager*
EMP: 30
SALES (corp-wide): 7.2B **Privately Held**
WEB: www.graybar.com
SIC: 5063 Electrical supplies
PA: Graybar Electric Company, Inc.
34 N Meramec Ave
Saint Louis MO 63105
314 573-9200

(G-5361)
GREAT I AM PROD STUDIOS INC
25 Rose Ln (19720-2140)
P.O. Box 30412, Wilmington (19805-7412)
PHONE.............................302 463-2483
Candy Watkins, *CEO*
EMP: 5
SALES (est): 313.2K **Privately Held**
SIC: 7389 Recording studio, noncommercial records

(G-5362)
GREEN RECOVERY TECH LLC
42 Lukens Dr Ste 100 (19720-2700)
PHONE.............................302 317-0062
Kenneth Laubsch, *President*
Josh Dube, *Engineer*
Matt Grivnovics, *Engineer*
EMP: 6
SALES (est): 843.8K **Privately Held**
SIC: 2048 Prepared feeds

(G-5363)
GRINDSTONE AVIATION LLC
13 1/2 Penns Way (19720-2437)
PHONE.............................302 324-1993
EMP: 2
SALES (est): 86K **Privately Held**
SIC: 3721 Aircraft

(G-5364)
GROSSMAN ELECTRIC SUPPLY INC
Also Called: Gross Lighting Center
30 W 5th St (19720-5022)
PHONE.............................302 655-5561
Phil Gross, *President*
Sidney Gross, *Vice Pres*
EMP: 4
SQ FT: 5,000
SALES: 480K **Privately Held**
WEB: www.grosslightingcenter.com
SIC: 5719 5063 Lighting fixtures; lighting, lamps & accessories; lighting fixtures; electrical supplies

(G-5365)
GUARDIAN CONSTRUCTION CO INC (HQ)
1617 Matassino Rd (19720-2086)
P.O. Box 11607, Wilmington (19850-1607)
PHONE.............................302 834-1000
Nona J Cunane, *Ch of Bd*
Teresa Miller, *Principal*
Joseph Cunane Jr, *Exec VP*
Craig Allen, *Project Mgr*
Paul Dimino, *Controller*
EMP: 90
SQ FT: 50,000
SALES (est): 39.4MM
SALES (corp-wide): 41.9MM **Privately Held**
WEB: www.guardiancompanies.com
SIC: 1542 Commercial & office building, new construction
PA: Guardian Companies, Inc.
101 Rogers Rd Ste 101 # 101
Wilmington DE 19801
302 834-1000

(G-5366)
GURUKRUPA INC
Also Called: Knights Inn
133 S Dupont Hwy (19720-4127)
PHONE.............................302 328-6691
Raman Patel, *President*
Amball Patel, *Shareholder*
EMP: 6
SQ FT: 5,400
SALES (est): 510.1K **Privately Held**
SIC: 7011 Hotels & motels

(G-5367)
H & R HEATING & AC
7 King Ct (19720-1519)
PHONE.............................302 323-9919
Rodney Husfelt, *President*
Charles Reeve, *Vice Pres*
EMP: 40
SALES (est): 5.6MM **Privately Held**
SIC: 1711 Warm air heating & air conditioning contractor; heating & air conditioning contractors

(G-5368)
H T G CONSULTING LLC
2 Penns Way Ste 300 (19720-2407)
PHONE.............................302 322-4100
Rod Turner, *Principal*
Robert J Mercer, *Principal*
David Passero, *Principal*
Christopher J Urban, *Principal*
Robert Mercer,
EMP: 20
SALES (est): 1.7MM **Privately Held**
WEB: www.hermanturner.com
SIC: 6531 Real estate agents & managers

(G-5369)
H&H SERVICES ELECTRICAL CONTRS
507 Sterling Ave (19720-4780)
PHONE.............................302 373-4950
James J Howard, *Principal*
EMP: 5
SALES (est): 74.3K **Privately Held**
SIC: 7539 Electrical services

(G-5370)
H&R BLOCK INC
Also Called: H & R Block
196 Penn Mart Ctr Unit 11 (19720-4209)
PHONE.............................302 328-7320
Bernie Brittingham, *Branch Mgr*
EMP: 12
SALES (corp-wide): 3B **Publicly Held**
WEB: www.hrblock.com
SIC: 7291 Tax return preparation services
PA: H&R Block, Inc.
1 H&R Block Way
Kansas City MO 64105
816 854-3000

(G-5371)
H&R BLOCK INC
Also Called: H & R Block
232 New Castle Ave (19720-2701)
PHONE.............................302 652-3286
Bernie Brittingham, *Manager*
EMP: 12
SALES (corp-wide): 3B **Publicly Held**
WEB: www.hrblock.com
SIC: 7291 8244 Tax return preparation services; business & secretarial schools
PA: H&R Block, Inc.
1 H&R Block Way
Kansas City MO 64105
816 854-3000

(G-5372)
HAIR SENSATIONS INC
55 Herbert Dr (19720-3231)
PHONE.............................302 731-0920
Renee Greenlee, *President*
EMP: 7 **EST:** 1976
SQ FT: 1,600
SALES (est): 270K **Privately Held**
SIC: 7231 Unisex hair salons

(G-5373)
HALOSIL INTERNATIONAL INC
91 Lukens Dr Ste A (19720-2799)
PHONE.............................302 543-8095
Chris Ungermann, *CEO*
David Stclair, *Chairman*
Mary Alice St Clair, *Vice Pres*
Maryalice Stclair, *VP Business*
▼**EMP:** 7
SQ FT: 5,000
SALES (est): 1.1MM **Privately Held**
SIC: 2842 Disinfectants, household or industrial plant

(G-5374)
HARDCORE CMPSTES OPRATIONS LLC
618 Lambson Ln (19720-2187)
PHONE.............................302 442-5900
Scott Hemphill, *Partner*
EMP: 75
SQ FT: 108,000
SALES (est): 299.2K **Privately Held**
SIC: 3441 8711 Fabricated structural metal for bridges; engineering services

(G-5375)
HARRISON HSE CMNTY PRGRAMS INC
6 Halcyon Dr (19720-1239)
PHONE.............................302 427-8438
Lateasa L Scott, *President*
EMP: 5
SQ FT: 18,500
SALES: 1.9MM **Privately Held**
SIC: 8322 Community center

(G-5376)
HARRY KENYON INCORPORATED
259 Quigley Blvd Ste 1 (19720-4186)
PHONE.............................302 762-7776
E Kenyon Still, *President*
John H Still, *Treasurer*
Betty Lee Bradley, *Admin Sec*
Harry K Still, *Asst Sec*
EMP: 50
SQ FT: 30,000
SALES (est): 6.9MM **Privately Held**
SIC: 5194 5145 Cigars; cigarettes; smoking tobacco; confectionery

▲ = Import ▼=Export
◆ =Import/Export

GEOGRAPHIC SECTION
New Castle - New Castle County (G-5403)

(G-5377)
HARRY L ADAMS INC
23 Parkway Cir Ste 14 (19720-4019)
PHONE..................................302 328-5268
Lee Adams, *President*
EMP: 6
SALES (est): 615.7K **Privately Held**
SIC: 1711 Heating & air conditioning contractors

(G-5378)
HARRYMIRIMAX LOGISITICS
26 Bellecor Dr Ste B (19720-2188)
P.O. Box 10364, Wilmington (19850-0364)
PHONE..................................302 784-5578
Harrison Sintim,
EMP: 14
SALES (est): 692.7K **Privately Held**
WEB: www.harrymirimax.com
SIC: 4789 4215 Cargo loading & unloading services; courier services, except by air

(G-5379)
HARTLE BRIAN STATE FARM AGENCY
Also Called: State Farm Insurance
239 Christiana Rd Ste C (19720-2907)
PHONE..................................302 322-1741
Brian Hartle, *Owner*
EMP: 5 EST: 2007
SALES (est): 554.3K **Privately Held**
SIC: 6411 Insurance agents & brokers

(G-5380)
HARTZELL INDUSTRIES INC
Also Called: Kad Industrial Rubber Products
115 Quigley Blvd (19720-4103)
PHONE..................................302 322-4900
Jay Williams, *President*
Marion Williams, *Treasurer*
EMP: 7
SALES (est): 2.3MM **Privately Held**
SIC: 5085 Hose, belting & packing; pistons & valves; industrial fittings; rubber goods, mechanical

(G-5381)
HARVEY DEVELOPMENT CO
29 E Commons Blvd Ste 100 (19720-1736)
PHONE..................................302 323-9300
Edgar Thomas Harvey III, *President*
Debra Harvey, *Corp Secy*
E Harvey, *Opers Staff*
EMP: 175
SALES (est): 9MM **Privately Held**
SIC: 8741 6531 Management services; real estate agents & managers

(G-5382)
HARVEY MACK SALES & SVC INC (PA)
Also Called: Harvey Truck Center
29 E Commons Blvd Ste 300 (19720-1739)
PHONE..................................302 324-8340
Debrah Layton-Harvey, *President*
Joe Jacoby, *Business Mgr*
Jeffrey Layton, *Vice Pres*
Dennis Haley, *Parts Mgr*
Alex Bialek, *Sales Associate*
EMP: 50
SQ FT: 34,000
SALES (est): 15.7MM **Privately Held**
WEB: www.harveytruckcenter.com
SIC: 5012 5013 5511 Trailers for trucks, new & used; truck parts & accessories; pickups, new & used

(G-5383)
HEALTH & SOCIAL SVCS DEL DEPT
Also Called: Division For Visually Impaired
1901 N Dupont Hwy (19720-1100)
PHONE..................................302 255-9800
Alan Wingrove, *Principal*
EMP: 35 **Privately Held**
SIC: 8331 3993 2752 2396 Job training & vocational rehabilitation services; signs & advertising specialties; commercial printing, lithographic; automotive & apparel trimmings;
HQ: Delaware Dept Of Health And Social Services
1901 N Dupont Hwy
New Castle DE 19720

(G-5384)
HEALTH & SOCIAL SVCS DEL DEPT
Also Called: Delaware Psychiatric Center
1901 N Dupont Hwy (19720-1100)
PHONE..................................302 255-2700
Elizabeth Hurley, *Manager*
EMP: 13 **Privately Held**
SIC: 8063 Psychiatric hospitals
HQ: Delaware Dept Of Health And Social Services
1901 N Dupont Hwy
New Castle DE 19720

(G-5385)
HEALTH & SOCIAL SVCS DEL DEPT
Also Called: Delaware Industries For Blind
1901 N Dupont Hwy (19720-1100)
PHONE..................................302 255-9855
Edna Newsome, *Branch Mgr*
EMP: 35 **Privately Held**
SIC: 9431 8331 3993 2752 ; job training & vocational rehabilitation services; signs & advertising specialties; commercial printing, lithographic; automotive & apparel trimmings
HQ: Delaware Dept Of Health And Social Services
1901 N Dupont Hwy
New Castle DE 19720

(G-5386)
HEALTH & SOCIAL SVCS DEL DEPT
Also Called: Delaware State Hospital
1901 N Dupont Hwy Fl 1 (19720-1100)
PHONE..................................302 255-2700
EMP: 3500 **Privately Held**
SIC: 8063 9431 Psychiatric hospitals; administration of public health programs;
HQ: Delaware Dept Of Health And Social Services
1901 N Dupont Hwy
New Castle DE 19720

(G-5387)
HEALTH & SOCIAL SVCS DEL DEPT
Division of Services For Aging
1901 N Dupont Hwy (19720-1100)
PHONE..................................302 391-3505
Herman Holloway, *Director*
EMP: 62 **Privately Held**
SIC: 8322 9441 9431 Geriatric social service; administration of social & manpower programs; ; administration of public health programs;
HQ: Delaware Dept Of Health And Social Services
1901 N Dupont Hwy
New Castle DE 19720

(G-5388)
HEAVY EQUIPMENT RENTAL INC
Also Called: Corrado Fleet Services
218 Marsh Ln (19720-1175)
PHONE..................................302 654-5716
Frank L Corrado, *President*
Joseph J Corrado Sr, *Vice Pres*
EMP: 17
SALES (est): 5.2MM **Privately Held**
SIC: 7353 7699 Heavy construction equipment rental; construction equipment repair

(G-5389)
HEAVY KEY STUDIOS LLC
320 N Dupont Hwy (19720-6434)
PHONE..................................302 356-6732
Jesse Lavigne,
EMP: 3
SALES (est): 113.9K **Privately Held**
SIC: 7372 Prepackaged software

(G-5390)
HERTZ CORPORATION
100 Mrtin Lther King Blvd (19720)
PHONE..................................302 428-0637
J Bonney, *Branch Mgr*
EMP: 23
SALES (corp-wide): 9.5B **Publicly Held**
SIC: 7514 Rent-a-car service
HQ: The Hertz Corporation
8501 Williams Rd
Estero FL 33928
239 301-7000

(G-5391)
HERTZ CORPORATION
191 N Dupont Hwy (19720-3121)
PHONE..................................302 428-0637
EMP: 23
SALES (corp-wide): 9.5B **Publicly Held**
SIC: 7514 Rent-a-car service
HQ: The Hertz Corporation
8501 Williams Rd
Estero FL 33928
239 301-7000

(G-5392)
HERTZ CORPORATION
162 Old Churchmans Rd (19720-3116)
PHONE..................................302 428-0637
EMP: 23
SALES (corp-wide): 9.5B **Publicly Held**
SIC: 7514 Rent-a-car service
HQ: The Hertz Corporation
8501 Williams Rd
Estero FL 33928
239 301-7000

(G-5393)
HES SIGN SERVICES LLC
Also Called: Yesco Sign Ltg Southeastern PA
459 Old Airport Rd (19720-1001)
PHONE..................................302 232-2100
William Eyler, *President*
Michael Hewitt, *Vice Pres*
John Reith, *Sales Mgr*
EMP: 4
SALES (est): 294.6K **Privately Held**
SIC: 3993 Electric signs

(G-5394)
HIBBERT COMPANY
Also Called: Hibbert Group, The
890 Ships Landing Way (19720-4575)
PHONE..................................609 394-7500
Paul Zukowski, *Branch Mgr*
EMP: 48
SALES (corp-wide): 80.3MM **Privately Held**
SIC: 7331 Direct mail advertising services
PA: The Hibbert Company
400 Pennington Ave
Trenton NJ 08618
609 392-0478

(G-5395)
HILL & SMITH INC
18 Blevins Dr (19720-4152)
PHONE..................................302 328-3220
Todd Hartnett, *Director*
EMP: 22
SALES (corp-wide): 840.5MM **Privately Held**
SIC: 3669 Transportation signaling devices
HQ: Hill & Smith Inc.
987 Buckeye Park Rd
Columbus OH 43207

(G-5396)
HISTORICAL & CULTURAL AFAIRS
Also Called: New Castle Court House Museum
211 Delaware St (19720-4815)
PHONE..................................302 323-4453
Cynthia Schneider, *Director*
EMP: 10 **Privately Held**
SIC: 8412 9111 Museum; executive offices;
HQ: Delaware Division Of Historical & Cultural Affairs
21 The Grn
Dover DE

(G-5397)
HISTORICAL SOCIETY OF DEL INC
Also Called: George Read II House
42 The Strand (19720-4826)
PHONE..................................302 322-8411
Michelle Ainstine, *Manager*
David Young, *Exec Dir*
EMP: 25

SALES (corp-wide): 1.3MM **Privately Held**
WEB: www.hsd.org
SIC: 8412 Historical society; museum
PA: The Historical Society Of Delaware
505 N Market St
Wilmington DE 19801
302 655-7161

(G-5398)
HOLMAN MOVING SYSTEMS LLC (PA)
20 E Commons Blvd (19720-1734)
P.O. Box 3043, Wilmington (19804-0043)
PHONE..................................302 323-9000
Darla Chaffin, *General Mgr*
Paul Melanson, *Vice Pres*
Robert Webster, *Vice Pres*
Rose Huhn, *Sales Associate*
Greg Lefkowitz, *Director*
◆ EMP: 275 EST: 1885
SQ FT: 60,000
SALES (est): 17.8MM **Privately Held**
WEB: www.xonex.com
SIC: 4213 4214 Trucking, except local; local trucking with storage

(G-5399)
HOLMAN MOVING SYSTEMS LLC
20 E Commons Blvd (19720-1734)
PHONE..................................302 323-9000
Robert Webster, *Vice Pres*
EMP: 60
SALES (corp-wide): 17.8MM **Privately Held**
WEB: www.xonex.com
SIC: 4213 4214 Household goods transport; local trucking with storage
PA: Holman Moving Systems Llc
20 E Commons Blvd
New Castle DE 19720
302 323-9000

(G-5400)
HOME DEPOT USA INC
Also Called: Home Depot, The
138 Sunset Blvd (19720-4100)
PHONE..................................302 395-1260
Rob Garbacz, *Manager*
EMP: 175
SALES (corp-wide): 108.2B **Publicly Held**
WEB: www.homerentalsdepot.com
SIC: 5211 7359 Home centers; tool rental
HQ: Home Depot U.S.A., Inc.
2455 Paces Ferry Ave
Atlanta GA 30339

(G-5401)
HOME PARAMOUNT PEST CONTROL
769 S Dupont Hwy (19720-4609)
PHONE..................................302 894-9201
Jeff Fuge, *Manager*
EMP: 6
SALES (corp-wide): 73.9MM **Privately Held**
SIC: 7342 Exterminating & fumigating; pest control in structures
PA: Home Paramount Pest Control Companies, Inc.
2011 Rock Spring Rd
Forest Hill MD 21050
410 638-0800

(G-5402)
HONEYWELL INTERNATIONAL INC
3 Boulden Cir (19720-3400)
PHONE..................................302 322-4071
EMP: 673
SALES (corp-wide): 41.8B **Publicly Held**
SIC: 3724 Aircraft engines & engine parts
PA: Honeywell International Inc.
300 S Tryon St
Charlotte NC 28202
973 455-2000

(G-5403)
HOOPTY DO
5 Palmer Pl (19720-3852)
PHONE..................................302 324-1742
EMP: 1

New Castle - New Castle County (G-5404)   GEOGRAPHIC SECTION

SALES (est): 46K **Privately Held**
SIC: **3993** Signs & advertising specialties

(G-5404)
HORIZON SYSTEMS INC
42 Reads Way (19720-1649)
PHONE..................................302 983-3203
EMP: 8 EST: 2005
SALES (est): 580K **Privately Held**
SIC: **7371** 5045 7373 7379 Computer Programming Svc Whol Computer/Peripheral Computer Systems Design Computer Related Svcs

(G-5405)
HOSPITAL BLLING CLLCTN SVC LTD (PA)
Also Called: Hbcs
118 Lukens Dr (19720-2727)
PHONE..................................302 552-8000
Brain J Wasilewski, *President*
Maureen Dieleuterio, *Vice Pres*
Joe Dudek, *Vice Pres*
Joseph Dudek, *Vice Pres*
Stacey Lumb, *Vice Pres*
EMP: 370
SQ FT: 43,000
SALES: 29.6MM **Privately Held**
WEB: www.hbcs.org
SIC: **8721** Billing & bookkeeping service

(G-5406)
HOWARD WESTON SENIOR CENTER
1 Bassett Ave Ste 1 # 1 (19720-2088)
PHONE..................................302 328-6425
Sandy Krett, *Exec Dir*
EMP: 5
SALES: 722.9K **Privately Held**
SIC: **8322** Senior citizens' center or association

(G-5407)
IAA INC
417 Old Airport Rd (19720-1001)
PHONE..................................302 322-1808
Paul Weeks, *Branch Mgr*
EMP: 4 Publicly Held
SIC: **5012** Automobile auction
HQ: Insurance Auto Auctions, Inc.
   2 Westbrook Corporate Ctr # 1000
   Westchester IL 60154
   708 492-7000

(G-5408)
IBG ENTERPRISE INC
9 Nieole Ave (19720-1206)
PHONE..................................302 494-5017
Shirley Woodlin, *President*
EMP: 6
SALES (est): 180.9K **Privately Held**
SIC: **8999** Music arranging & composing

(G-5409)
IEXPERIENCEILEARN LLC
66 Buttonwood Ave (19720-3604)
PHONE..................................718 704-4870
Dennis Scott,
EMP: 2
SALES (est): 62.1K **Privately Held**
SIC: **7372** Educational computer software

(G-5410)
IGNACIO S GISPERT DDS
189 Christiana Rd (19720-3039)
PHONE..................................302 322-2303
Ignacio S Gispert DDS, *Owner*
EMP: 4
SALES (est): 228.7K **Privately Held**
SIC: **8021** Dentists' office

(G-5411)
IHEARTMEDIA INC
Also Called: News Radio 1450 Wilm
920 W Basin Rd Ste 400 (19720-1013)
PHONE..................................302 395-9800
Mark Fowser, *Director*
EMP: 100 Publicly Held
SIC: **4832** Radio broadcasting stations
PA: Iheartmedia, Inc.
   20880 Stone Oak Pkwy
   San Antonio TX 78258

(G-5412)
II EXTREME ENTERTAINMENT
100 Schafer Blvd (19720-4722)
P.O. Box 293, Clayton (19938-0293)
PHONE..................................302 389-8525
Warner Knowland, *Owner*
EMP: 7
SALES (est): 1.3K **Privately Held**
SIC: **7911** Dance studios, schools & halls

(G-5413)
INDEPENDENCE SUPPORT SVCS LLC
637 Dane Ct (19720-5639)
PHONE..................................484 450-6662
Harold Brady,
EMP: 6 EST: 2018
SALES (est): 104.3K **Privately Held**
SIC: **8399** Advocacy group

(G-5414)
INDUSTRIAL PHYSICS INC (PA)
40 Mccullough Dr (19720-2227)
PHONE..................................302 613-5600
James Neville, *CEO*
Andrew Lawrisuk, *Vice Pres*
EMP: 6
SALES (est): 1.4MM **Privately Held**
SALES (corp-wide): 2.8MM **Privately Held**
WEB: www.benzhydraulics.com
SIC: **5085** 5082 3441 Industrial supplies; general construction machinery & equipment; fabricated structural metal
PA: Benz Hydraulics, Inc.
   153 S Dupont Hwy
   New Castle DE 19720
   302 328-6648

(G-5415)
INDUSTRIAL PRODUCTS OF DEL
153 S Dupont Hwy (19720-4127)
PHONE..................................302 328-6648
John E Dougherty, *President*
Timothy J Dougherty, *Vice Pres*
EMP: 12
SALES (est): 1.9MM
SALES (corp-wide): 2.8MM **Privately Held**
WEB: www.benzhydraulics.com
SIC: **5085** 5082 3441 Industrial supplies; general construction machinery & equipment; fabricated structural metal
PA: Benz Hydraulics, Inc.
   153 S Dupont Hwy
   New Castle DE 19720
   302 328-6648

(G-5416)
INDUSTRIAL STL STRUCTURES INC
4049 New Castle Ave (19720-1414)
PHONE..................................302 275-8892
EMP: 30 EST: 2012
SALES (est): 292.8K **Privately Held**
SIC: **5051** Steel

(G-5417)
INDUSTRIAL VALVES & FITTINGS
Also Called: I V F
55 Mccullough Dr (19720-2080)
PHONE..................................302 326-2494
Julio C Daponte Sr, *President*
Justin Suchanec, *General Mgr*
Maureen L Daponte, *Vice Pres*
Paul Powell, *Engineer*
Chris Yandell, *Associate*
EMP: 14
SQ FT: 10,000
SALES (est): 3.7MM **Privately Held**
WEB: www.ivfinc.com
SIC: **3052** 5085 Rubber & plastics hose & beltings; hose, belting & packing

(G-5418)
INFO SOLUTIONS NORTH AMER LLC
12 Penns Way (19720-2414)
P.O. Box 1025, Bear (19701-7025)
PHONE..................................302 793-9200
Mark R Olazagasti,
EMP: 11
SALES (est): 1.4MM **Privately Held**
SIC: **8999** Information bureau

(G-5419)
INSTA SIGNS PLUS INC
107 J And M Dr (19720-3147)
PHONE..................................302 324-8800
Anthony Pettoruto, *President*
David Pettoruto, *Vice Pres*
Josh Krautwald, *Sales Staff*
David Mitchell, *Manager*
EMP: 11
SQ FT: 4,500
SALES (est): 1.2MM **Privately Held**
WEB: www.instasignsplus.com
SIC: **3993** Signs, not made in custom sign painting shops

(G-5420)
INTEGRATED TECH SYSTEMS LLC
42 Reads Way (19720-1649)
PHONE..................................302 613-2111
Daniela Santos, *Director*
EMP: 5
SALES (est): 143.8K **Privately Held**
SIC: **7382** Security systems services

(G-5421)
INTEGRITY TESTLABS LLC (PA)
258 Quigley Blvd (19720-4106)
PHONE..................................302 325-2365
Stacey Spike,
EMP: 55
SQ FT: 5,000
SALES: 6MM **Privately Held**
WEB: www.integritytestlab.com
SIC: **8734** Testing laboratories

(G-5422)
INTERIM HEALTH CARE
Also Called: Interim Services
2 Reads Way Ste 209 (19720-1630)
PHONE..................................302 322-2743
Lynda Kupishke, *President*
EMP: 6 EST: 1966
SALES (est): 1.3MM **Privately Held**
SIC: **7363** Temporary help service

(G-5423)
ION POWER INC
720 Governor Lea Rd (19720-5501)
PHONE..................................302 832-9550
Steven Grot, *President*
Andi Debold, *Opers Mgr*
Wendy Grot, *Controller*
EMP: 7
SALES (est): 2.8MM **Privately Held**
WEB: www.ion-power.com
SIC: **5162** Resins

(G-5424)
IPM INC
247 Old Churchmans Rd (19720-1529)
PHONE..................................302 328-4030
EMP: 3
SALES (est): 106.2K **Publicly Held**
SIC: **3296** 2952 Fiberglass insulation; insulation: rock wool, slag & silica minerals; acoustical board & tile, mineral wool; roofing mats, mineral wool; asphalt felts & coatings
PA: Owens Corning
   1 Owens Corning Pkwy
   Toledo OH 43659

(G-5425)
IRON MOUNTAIN INCORPORATED
6 Dock View Dr Ste 200 (19720-2208)
PHONE..................................610 636-1424
Charlie Crompton, *Principal*
EMP: 7
SALES (corp-wide): 4.2B **Publicly Held**
SIC: **4226** Document & office records storage
PA: Iron Mountain Incorporated
   1 Federal St Fl 7
   Boston MA 02110
   617 535-4766

(G-5426)
ISAAC FAIR CORPORATION
100 W Cmmons Blvd Ste 400 (19720)
PHONE..................................302 324-8015
Mark Greene, *Branch Mgr*
Joan Mangan, *Director*
EMP: 24
SALES (corp-wide): 1B **Publicly Held**
WEB: www.fairisaac.com
SIC: **7372** 3575 Operating systems computer software; computer terminals
PA: Fair Isaac Corporation
   181 Metro Dr Ste 700
   San Jose CA 95110
   408 535-1500

(G-5427)
J & L BUILDING MATERIALS INC
59 Lukens Dr (19720-2718)
PHONE..................................302 504-0350
John Rash, *Principal*
Jonathan Fritts, *Sales Associate*
EMP: 16
SALES (corp-wide): 72.6MM **Privately Held**
SIC: **5033** Roofing, asphalt & sheet metal
PA: J & L Building Materials, Inc.
   600 Lancaster Ave
   Malvern PA 19355
   610 644-6311

(G-5428)
J CHANCE PRODUCTIONS
5 Stevens Ave (19720-4046)
PHONE..................................302 322-2251
Jabari Chancey, *Principal*
EMP: 9
SALES (est): 116.1K **Privately Held**
SIC: **7822** Motion picture & tape distribution

(G-5429)
J J WHITE INC
101 Cirillo Cir (19720-4865)
PHONE..................................215 722-1000
James J White IV, *President*
EMP: 725
SALES (corp-wide): 238.5MM **Privately Held**
SIC: **1711** Plumbing, heating, air-conditioning contractors
PA: J. J. White, Inc.
   5500 Bingham St
   Philadelphia PA 19120
   215 722-1000

(G-5430)
J R FORSHEY DMD PA
702 E Basin Rd Ste 1 (19720-4263)
PHONE..................................302 322-0245
James R Forshey DMD, *President*
Jennifer Greenley DDS, *Vice Pres*
Jennifer R Greenley, *Fmly & Gen Dent*
EMP: 10
SALES (est): 411.9K **Privately Held**
SIC: **8021** Dentists' office

(G-5431)
J T MICAN & ASSOCIATES INC
42 Reads Way (19720-1649)
PHONE..................................302 323-8152
James Mirtinovich, *President*
Shery Myers, *President*
Richard Holmes, *Director*
EMP: 5 EST: 1989
SQ FT: 2,000
SALES (est): 417.1K **Privately Held**
SIC: **8741** Construction management

(G-5432)
J&S LEASING CO INC
729 Grantham Ln Ste 12 (19720-4898)
PHONE..................................302 328-1066
Sharon Ash, *Principal*
EMP: 4
SALES (est): 287.9K **Privately Held**
SIC: **7359** Equipment rental & leasing

(G-5433)
JAA INDUSTRIES LLC
Also Called: Jaa's Crane Service and Eqp
16 W Point Ave (19720-4326)
PHONE..................................302 332-0388
Jaime Ahumada, *Mng Member*
Eunice Ahumada, *Mng Member*
EMP: 3
SALES: 600K **Privately Held**
SIC: **3589** 5084 Commercial cooking & foodwarming equipment; cranes, industrial

(G-5434)
JACKS BSTRO AT DVID FNNEY INN
222 Delaware St (19720-4855)
PHONE..................................302 544-5172
EMP: 7

SALES (est): 131.7K **Privately Held**
SIC: 7011 5812 Hotel/Motel Operation Eating Place

(G-5435)
JAMES SUTTON
Also Called: Training Center, The
807 Churchmans Road Ext (19720-3152)
PHONE............................302 328-5438
James Sutton, *Owner*
EMP: 10
SALES (est): 752.1K **Privately Held**
SIC: 5091 Fitness equipment & supplies

(G-5436)
JAY AMBE INC
Also Called: Days Inn
3 Memorial Dr (19720-1310)
PHONE............................302 654-5400
Pramod Patel, *President*
EMP: 10
SQ FT: 50,000
SALES: 1MM **Privately Held**
SIC: 7011 Hotels & motels

(G-5437)
JAY DEVI INC
Also Called: Fairfield Inn
2117 N Dupont Hwy (19720-6308)
PHONE............................302 777-4700
Mehul Patel, *President*
EMP: 12
SALES (est): 831.7K **Privately Held**
SIC: 7011 Hotels & motels

(G-5438)
JAY GANESH LLC
140 S Dupont Hwy (19720-4149)
PHONE............................302 322-1800
Premal Patel, *Mng Member*
EMP: 4
SALES (est): 254.2K **Privately Held**
SIC: 7011 Hotels & motels

(G-5439)
JCR SYSTEMS LLC
621 Delaware St (19720-5073)
PHONE............................302 420-6072
Mark Lumer, *Business Mgr*
Doug Salter, *Mng Member*
EMP: 2
SALES (est): 185.2K **Privately Held**
SIC: 2493 2899 Insulation & roofing material, reconstituted wood; waterproofing compounds

(G-5440)
JM VIRGIN HAIR COMPANY
12 Briarcliff Dr (19720-1304)
PHONE............................856 383-8588
Monique Smith, *Principal*
EMP: 4
SALES (est): 28.8K **Privately Held**
SIC: 7231 Hairdressers

(G-5441)
JOHN R SEIBERLICH INC
Also Called: Seiberlich Trane
66 Southgate Blvd (19720-2068)
PHONE............................302 356-2400
John Seiberlich, *President*
Frank Kempski, *Project Mgr*
Ronald Hess, *Treasurer*
John Walker, *Accounts Mgr*
Samantha Walton, *Accounts Mgr*
EMP: 72
SQ FT: 24,000
SALES (est): 33.2MM **Privately Held**
SIC: 5063 5065 5075 5078 Electronic wire & cable; capacitors, electronic; air filters; commercial refrigeration equipment; cleaning equipment, high pressure, sand or steam; valves & fittings

(G-5442)
JOHNSON CNTRLS SEC SLTIONS LLC
18 Boulden Cir Ste 24 (19720-3494)
PHONE............................302 328-2800
Pat Feeley, *Manager*
EMP: 60 **Privately Held**
WEB: www.adt.com
SIC: 7382 Burglar alarm maintenance & monitoring; fire alarm maintenance & monitoring

HQ: Johnson Controls Security Solutions Llc
6600 Congress Ave
Boca Raton FL 33487
561 264-2071

(G-5443)
JORC INDUSTRIAL LLC
1146 River Rd Ste 100 (19720-5106)
PHONE............................302 395-0310
Eugene White,
▲ **EMP:** 7
SQ FT: 4,500
SALES (est): 1.3MM **Privately Held**
WEB: www.jorc.com
SIC: 5084 Compressors, except air conditioning

(G-5444)
JOSEPH DEVANE ENTERPRISES INC
Also Called: Allstate
240 S Dupont Hwy Ste 200 (19720-8403)
PHONE............................302 703-0493
Joseph Devane, *President*
EMP: 10
SALES (est): 1MM **Privately Held**
SIC: 1521 Single-family home remodeling, additions & repairs

(G-5445)
JOSEPH RIZZO & SONS CNSTR CO
13 Rizzo Ave (19720-2139)
PHONE............................302 656-8116
Anthony A Rizzo, *President*
Anthony Rizzo, *President*
Mark Rizzo, *Corp Secy*
John Rizzo, *Vice Pres*
EMP: 30 **EST:** 1942
SQ FT: 3,000
SALES (est): 2.7MM **Privately Held**
SIC: 1741 Stone masonry

(G-5446)
JOSEPH T HARDY & SON INC (PA)
Also Called: Hardy Environmental Services
425 Old Airport Rd (19720-1001)
PHONE............................302 328-9457
Jack J Hardy, *President*
John J Hardy, *President*
Robert P Hopkins, *Vice Pres*
EMP: 40 **EST:** 1921
SQ FT: 2,000
SALES (est): 7.2MM **Privately Held**
WEB: www.hardyservices.com
SIC: 1623 8748 Underground utilities contractor; environmental consultant

(G-5447)
JUICEPLUS+
15 W 3rd St (19720-5009)
PHONE............................302 322-2616
Marilyn Del Duca, *Principal*
EMP: 3
SALES (est): 166.3K **Privately Held**
SIC: 2037 Fruit juices

(G-5448)
K V ASSOCIATES INC
Also Called: Family Care Associates
191 Christiana Rd Ste 3 (19720-3024)
PHONE............................302 322-1353
Khaja G Yezdani, *President*
Dr Vijaya Yezdani, *Vice Pres*
EMP: 7
SALES (est): 1MM **Privately Held**
SIC: 8011 General & family practice, physician/surgeon; pediatrician

(G-5449)
KAESER COMPRESSORS INC
77 Mccullough Dr Ste 3 (19720-2079)
PHONE............................410 242-8793
Dan Leviness, *Branch Mgr*
EMP: 8
SALES (corp-wide): 1.6MM **Privately Held**
WEB: www.kaeser.com
SIC: 5084 Compressors, except air conditioning

HQ: Kaeser Compressors, Inc.
511 Sigma Dr
Fredericksburg VA 22408
540 898-5500

(G-5450)
KAMARA LLC
260 Christiana Rd (19720-2921)
PHONE............................302 220-9570
Emmanuel Kamara,
EMP: 5
SALES (est): 192.3K **Privately Held**
SIC: 7389

(G-5451)
KARRIES DAYCARE
44 Lesley Ln (19720-3341)
PHONE............................302 328-7369
EMP: 5 **EST:** 2011
SALES (est): 160K **Privately Held**
SIC: 8351 Child Day Care Services

(G-5452)
KATHERINE KLYC INTL LLC
108 W 3rd St (19720-4832)
PHONE............................917 312-0789
EMP: 1 **EST:** 2001
SALES: 5K **Privately Held**
SIC: 2392 Mfg Household Furnishings

(G-5453)
KATHY STABLEY
9 King Ave (19720-1511)
PHONE............................302 322-7884
Kathy Stabley, *Principal*
EMP: 1
SALES (est): 53.8K **Privately Held**
SIC: 2396 Screen printing on fabric articles

(G-5454)
KAUL GLOVE AND MFG CO
Also Called: Choctaw- Kaul Distribution Co
599 Ships Landing Way (19720-4578)
PHONE............................302 292-2660
Janice Watson, *Sales Staff*
Judy McDilda, *Manager*
EMP: 89
SALES (corp-wide): 50.1MM **Privately Held**
WEB: www.choctawkaul.com
SIC: 2381 3151 5136 Fabric dress & work gloves; gloves, leather: work; work clothing, men's & boys'
PA: Kaul Glove And Mfg. Co.
3540 Vinewood St
Detroit MI 48208
313 894-9494

(G-5455)
KBF ASSOCIATES LP
Also Called: William Penn Vlg Appartment
595 Tulip Ln (19720-5800)
PHONE............................302 328-5400
Diane Gay, *Branch Mgr*
EMP: 4
SALES (corp-wide): 27.9MM **Privately Held**
SIC: 6513 Apartment building operators
PA: Kbf Associates, L.P.
160 Clubhouse Rd
King Of Prussia PA 19406
610 265-2800

(G-5456)
KEEN COMPRESSED GAS CO
4063 New Castle Ave (19720-1497)
PHONE............................302 594-4545
David Haas, *CFO*
Justin Johnson, *Sales Mgr*
Bryan Keen, *Branch Mgr*
Mike Keen, *Manager*
EMP: 50
SALES (corp-wide): 28.8MM **Privately Held**
WEB: www.keengas.com
SIC: 5085 5169 5984 2813 Welding supplies; gases, compressed & liquefied; propane gas, bottled; industrial gases
PA: Keen Compressed Gas Co.
101 Rogers Rd Ste 200
Wilmington DE 19801
302 594-4545

(G-5457)
KEEN COMPRESSED GAS CO INC (PA)
4063 New Castle Ave (19720-1497)
PHONE............................610 583-8770
Peter Giorgi, *President*
Rich Fleming, *General Mgr*
Dave Haas, *Exec VP*
Carol Giorgi, *Treasurer*
Justin Johnson, *Sales Mgr*
EMP: 4 **EST:** 1982
SQ FT: 3,500
SALES (est): 1MM **Privately Held**
SIC: 5085 Welding supplies

(G-5458)
KEEP SELLING PROPERTY LLC
2 Penns Way Ste 301 (19720-2407)
PHONE............................302 235-3066
Shayvette Hunter,
Kimberly Broomer,
EMP: 4
SALES (est): 337.4K **Privately Held**
SIC: 8741 Construction management

(G-5459)
KELLY SERVICES INC
34 Reads Way (19720-1649)
PHONE............................302 323-4748
George Freas, *Manager*
EMP: 15
SALES (corp-wide): 5.5B **Publicly Held**
WEB: www.kellyservices.com
SIC: 7363 Temporary help service
PA: Kelly Services, Inc.
999 W Big Beaver Rd
Troy MI 48084
248 362-4444

(G-5460)
KEOGHS CONTRACTING COMPANY
Also Called: Keogh & Son Contracting Co
9 Bellecor Dr (19720-1763)
P.O. Box 690 (19720-0690)
PHONE............................302 656-0058
Peter Keogh, *President*
Michael Keogh, *Vice Pres*
EMP: 7 **EST:** 1971
SALES (est): 400K **Privately Held**
SIC: 1611 Surfacing & paving

(G-5461)
KEYSTONE AUTOMOTIVE INDS INC
62 Southgate Blvd Ste D (19720-2090)
PHONE............................302 764-8010
Darren Lane, *Manager*
EMP: 16
SALES (corp-wide): 11.8B **Publicly Held**
WEB: www.kool-vue.com
SIC: 5013 Automotive supplies & parts
HQ: Keystone Automotive Industries, Inc.
5846 Crossings Blvd
Antioch TN 37013
615 781-5200

(G-5462)
KEYSTONE GRANITE AND TILE INC
217 Lisa Dr Ste C (19720-8404)
PHONE............................302 323-0200
▲ **EMP:** 3
SALES (est): 138.6K **Privately Held**
SIC: 1743 3281 Tile installation, ceramic; granite, cut & shaped

(G-5463)
KHAJA YEZDANI MD
191 Christiana Rd Ste 3 (19720-3024)
PHONE............................302 322-1794
Khaja Yezdani MD, *Owner*
EMP: 10
SALES (est): 484K **Privately Held**
SIC: 8011 Offices & clinics of medical doctors

(G-5464)
KIDSCOM DAYCARE
25 Wardor Ave (19720-3532)
PHONE............................302 544-5655
EMP: 5
SALES (est): 60.6K **Privately Held**
SIC: 8351 Child Day Care Services

New Castle - New Castle County (G-5465)

GEOGRAPHIC SECTION

(G-5465)
KINDERCARE LEARNING CTRS LLC
327 Old State Rd (19720-4618)
PHONE..................302 322-3102
Megan Williams, *Branch Mgr*
EMP: 19
SALES (corp-wide): 963.9MM **Privately Held**
SIC: 8351 Group day care center
HQ: Kindercare Learning Centers, Llc
   650 Ne Holladay St # 1400
   Portland OR 97232
   503 872-1300

(G-5466)
KIRKIN ROOFING LLC
1053 Lower Twin Lane Rd (19720-5502)
PHONE..................302 483-7135
EMP: 4
SALES (est): 413.3K **Privately Held**
SIC: 1761 Roofing contractor

(G-5467)
KNOTTS INCORPORATED
700 Wilmington Rd (19720-3698)
PHONE..................302 322-0554
Edna J Knotts, *President*
Paul H Knotts, *Vice Pres*
Philip L Knotts, *Treasurer*
EMP: 65
SQ FT: 14,500
SALES (est): 1.9MM **Privately Held**
SIC: 4151 School buses

(G-5468)
KOKOSZKA & SONS INC
68 Skyline Dr (19720-2943)
PHONE..................302 328-4807
Edward Kokoszka Sr, *President*
EMP: 5 **EST:** 1970
SALES (est): 554K **Privately Held**
SIC: 1521 1731 1721 New construction, single-family houses; general remodeling, single-family houses; general electrical contractor; wallcovering contractors

(G-5469)
KOMPRESSED AIR DELAWARE INC
144 Quigley Blvd Ste 100 (19720-4199)
PHONE..................302 275-1985
Jay Williams, *President*
Marian Williams, *Vice Pres*
Kristi Spence, *Manager*
EMP: 8
SQ FT: 14,000
SALES (est): 2.4MM **Privately Held**
SIC: 5075 7699 Compressors, air conditioning; compressor repair

(G-5470)
KUEHNE CHEMICAL COMPANY INC
Chloramone Co
1645 River Rd (19720-5194)
P.O. Box 294, Delaware City (19706-0294)
PHONE..................302 834-4557
Charles McCun, *Branch Mgr*
EMP: 45
SQ FT: 30,000
SALES (corp-wide): 107.9MM **Privately Held**
SIC: 2812 2819 Chlorine, compressed or liquefied; industrial inorganic chemicals
PA: Kuehne Chemical Company, Inc.
   86 N Hackensack Ave
   Kearny NJ 07032
   973 589-0700

(G-5471)
L F SYSTEMS CORP
249 Old Churchmans Rd (19720-1529)
PHONE..................302 322-0460
Gerald Holmes, *President*
EMP: 14
SQ FT: 9,800
SALES: 784.9K **Privately Held**
WEB: www.lfsystems.com
SIC: 5021 3821 Furniture; laboratory furniture

(G-5472)
LABORATORY CORPORATION AMERICA
212 Cherry Ln (19720-2776)
PHONE..................302 655-5673
Danielle Mitchell, *President*
EMP: 7 **Publicly Held**
SIC: 8071 Medical laboratories
HQ: Laboratory Corporation Of America
   358 S Main St Ste 458
   Burlington NC 27215
   336 229-1127

(G-5473)
LANDMARK HOMES INC
2 Reads Way Ste 224 (19720-1630)
P.O. Box 1037, Middletown (19709-7037)
PHONE..................302 242-1394
EMP: 4
SALES (est): 318.3K **Privately Held**
SIC: 1521 Single-family housing construction

(G-5474)
LAVISH STRANDS 1
1408 Stonebridge Blvd (19720-6724)
PHONE..................302 333-5742
Candace Duckett, *Principal*
EMP: 4
SALES (est): 28.8K **Privately Held**
SIC: 7231 Beauty shops

(G-5475)
LEHANES BUS SERVICE INC
1705 Wilmington Rd (19720-2750)
P.O. Box 349 (19720-0349)
PHONE..................302 328-7100
Joan Russell, *President*
Jerry Lehanes, *Vice Pres*
EMP: 31
SQ FT: 10,000
SALES (est): 2MM **Privately Held**
SIC: 4151 School buses

(G-5476)
LEHIGH TESTING LABORATORIES
308 W Basin Rd (19720-6406)
PHONE..................302 328-0500
J Barry McCrudden, *President*
Jeffrey L Donaldson, *Admin Sec*
EMP: 23
SQ FT: 13,625
SALES: 2.5MM
SALES (corp-wide): 11.4MM **Privately Held**
WEB: www.mmr-group.com
SIC: 8734 Testing laboratories
PA: The Mmr Group Inc
   308 W Basin Rd
   New Castle DE 19720
   302 328-0500

(G-5477)
LEHIGH VLY SAFETY SUP CO INC
Also Called: Shoemobile Services
1f King Ave (19720-1511)
PHONE..................302 323-9166
Nancy Hinkel, *Cust Mgr*
Brad Shapiro, *Med Doctor*
Don Tyndall, *Manager*
EMP: 7
SALES (corp-wide): 16.4MM **Privately Held**
WEB: www.safetyshoes.com
SIC: 5139 5661 Shoes; shoe stores
PA: Lehigh Valley Safety Supply Co., Inc.
   1105 E Susquehanna St
   Allentown PA 18103
   610 791-1577

(G-5478)
LEKUE USA INC
802 Centerpoint Blvd (19720-8123)
PHONE..................302 326-4805
Alan Senior, *President*
Charles Quinn, *CFO*
Patrick Lobo, *Sales Mgr*
▲ **EMP:** 64
SQ FT: 60,000
SALES (est): 2.9MM **Privately Held**
SIC: 5023 Kitchen tools & utensils

(G-5479)
LEON N WEINER & ASSOCIATES INC
Also Called: Chelten Apartments
431 Old Forge Rd Ofc Ofc (19720-3765)
PHONE..................302 322-6323
William Demarco, *Vice Pres*
EMP: 13
SALES (corp-wide): 54MM **Privately Held**
SIC: 6513 Apartment building operators
PA: Leon N. Weiner & Associates, Inc.
   1 Fox Pt Ctr 4 Denny Rd
   Wilmington DE 19809
   302 656-1354

(G-5480)
LEONS GARDEN WORLD EJ INC
137 S Dupont Hwy (19720-4127)
PHONE..................410 392-8630
Evan Macguinness, *Principal*
EMP: 12
SALES (est): 284.8K **Privately Held**
SIC: 5261 5191 0781 Nurseries & garden centers; garden supplies; landscape services

(G-5481)
LIGHT ACTION INC
31 Blevins Dr Ste C (19720-4170)
PHONE..................302 328-7800
Scott Humphrey, *President*
Andy Rougvie, *Project Mgr*
Charlie Lyon, *Sales Mgr*
Vickielynne Newcomer, *Office Mgr*
Paula A De Luca, *Manager*
EMP: 13
SALES: 3MM **Privately Held**
WEB: www.lightactioninc.com
SIC: 7922 1731 5719 Lighting, theatrical; lighting contractor; lighting fixtures

(G-5482)
LIMO EXCHANGE
800 Washington St (19720-6049)
PHONE..................302 322-1200
Greg Zelano, *President*
EMP: 10
SALES (est): 583.1K **Privately Held**
WEB: www.limo-exchange.com
SIC: 4119 Limousine rental, with driver

(G-5483)
LINARDUCCI & BUTLER PA
910 W Basin Rd Ste 100 (19720-1015)
PHONE..................302 325-2400
Gary Linarducci, *Partner*
Steven Butler, *Partner*
EMP: 8
SALES (est): 940.7K **Privately Held**
WEB: www.linarducci.com
SIC: 8111 General practice attorney, lawyer; specialized law offices, attorneys

(G-5484)
LINDAS ANGELS CHLDCARE DEV CTR
6 Parkway Ct (19720-4020)
PHONE..................302 328-3700
Linda Bright, *Owner*
EMP: 14 **EST:** 2010
SALES (est): 487K **Privately Held**
SIC: 8351 Child day care services

(G-5485)
LITECURE LLC
Also Called: Companion Therapy Lasers
101 Lukens Dr Ste G (19720-2791)
PHONE..................302 709-0408
Brian Pryor, *CEO*
John Hoffer, *VP Opers*
Charles Spyres, *Mfg Mgr*
Andy Wood, *Export Mgr*
Kamie Mech, *Accounting Mgr*
▲ **EMP:** 22
SALES (est): 5.3MM **Privately Held**
SIC: 3845 Laser systems & equipment, medical

(G-5486)
LITTLE LEAGUE BASEBALL INC
23 Blount Rd (19720-3221)
PHONE..................302 276-0375
James Raab, *Branch Mgr*
EMP: 9
SALES (corp-wide): 27.6MM **Privately Held**
WEB: www.littleleaguebaseball.net
SIC: 8699 7997 Athletic organizations; membership sports & recreation clubs
PA: Little League Baseball Inc
   539 Us Route 15 Hwy
   Williamsport PA 17702
   570 326-1921

(G-5487)
LOST AND FOUND DOG RESCUE ADOP
70 Ivy Ln (19720-2339)
PHONE..................302 613-0394
Marleen Oetzel, *Principal*
EMP: 6
SALES (est): 137.2K **Privately Held**
SIC: 8322 Adoption services

(G-5488)
LOWES HOME CENTERS LLC
2225 Hessler Blvd (19720-6305)
PHONE..................302 252-3228
EMP: 150
SALES (corp-wide): 71.3B **Publicly Held**
SIC: 5211 5031 5722 5064 Home centers; building materials, exterior; building materials, interior; household appliance stores; electrical appliances, television & radio
HQ: Lowe's Home Centers, Llc
   1605 Curtis Bridge Rd
   Wilkesboro NC 28697
   336 658-4000

(G-5489)
LUCILA CARMICHAEL RN
1101 Delaware St (19720-6033)
PHONE..................302 324-8901
Lucila Carmichael, *Principal*
EMP: 8
SALES (est): 65.7K **Privately Held**
SIC: 8049 Offices of health practitioner

(G-5490)
LUMBER JACKS AXE CLUB LLC
44 E 4th St (19720-5014)
PHONE..................215 900-0318
Mark Chaump,
EMP: 10
SALES (est): 59.4K **Privately Held**
SIC: 7997 Outdoor field clubs

(G-5491)
LUXOTTICA OF AMERICA INC
124 Sunset Blvd (19720-4100)
PHONE..................302 322-4131
EMP: 101
SALES (corp-wide): 1.4MM **Privately Held**
SIC: 3851 Eyeglasses, lenses & frames
HQ: Luxottica Of America Inc.
   4000 Luxottica Pl
   Mason OH 45040

(G-5492)
M & W TRUCKING INC
44 Glen Ave (19720-2008)
PHONE..................302 655-6994
Willie L Mc Reynolds, *President*
Marjorie Mc Reynolds, *Vice Pres*
EMP: 6
SALES: 500K **Privately Held**
SIC: 4212 Local trucking, without storage

(G-5493)
M G HAMEX CORPORATION
1063 Twin Lane Rd (19720-5502)
PHONE..................302 832-9072
Michael Hamm, *Principal*
Georgia Hamm, *Vice Pres*
EMP: 12 **EST:** 1997
SQ FT: 2,250
SALES: 3MM **Privately Held**
SIC: 1794 Excavation work

(G-5494)
M3R & ASSOC INC
Also Called: Allstate Accounting Services
287 Christiana Rd Ste 24 (19720-2978)
P.O. Box 11131, Wilmington (19850-1131)
PHONE..................302 324-1040
EMP: 4

GEOGRAPHIC SECTION
New Castle - New Castle County (G-5523)

SALES (est): 293.8K **Privately Held**
SIC: 8721 Accounting, auditing & book-keeping

(G-5495)
MAGIC TOUCH
1707 New Castle Ave (19720-7711)
PHONE.................302 655-6430
Richard M Collins, *Partner*
Richard F Hickman, *Partner*
EMP: 12 EST: 1979
SALES (est): 692.8K **Privately Held**
SIC: 7542 Carwash, automatic

(G-5496)
MAGIC YRS CHILD CARE LRNG CNTR
327 Old State Rd (19720-4618)
PHONE.................302 322-3102
Madeline Robinson, *Director*
EMP: 10
SALES (corp-wide): 963.9MM **Privately Held**
WEB: www.klccorp.com
SIC: 8351 Child day care services
HQ: Magic Yrs Child Care & Lrng Cntr Inc
560 B St
King Of Prussia PA

(G-5497)
MAGNUS ENVIRONMENTAL CORP
220 Marsh Ln (19720-1175)
PHONE.................302 655-4443
Joseph R Matteo, *President*
EMP: 20
SQ FT: 70,000
SALES (est): 2.9MM **Privately Held**
SIC: 4953 Recycling, waste materials

(G-5498)
MAGRON INC
31 Palmetto Dr (19720-4657)
PHONE.................302 324-8094
Ronald L Salter, *President*
EMP: 4
SALES (est): 280K **Privately Held**
SIC: 6531 Real estate agents & managers

(G-5499)
MAICHLE S HEATING AIR
105 J And M Dr (19720-3147)
PHONE.................302 328-4822
Donna Maichle, *Owner*
EMP: 16
SALES (est): 771.3K **Privately Held**
SIC: 1711 Warm air heating & air conditioning contractor

(G-5500)
MAIDS FOR YOU INC
3 Scottie Ln (19720-3922)
PHONE.................302 328-9050
Joe Mc Donald, *Vice Pres*
EMP: 15
SQ FT: 750
SALES (est): 288K **Privately Held**
SIC: 7349 Maid services, contract or fee basis

(G-5501)
MAILLIE LLP
15 Reads Way Ste 200 (19720-1600)
PHONE.................302 324-0780
EMP: 14
SALES (corp-wide): 11.8MM **Privately Held**
SIC: 8721 Certified public accountant
PA: Maillie Llp
140 Whitaker Ave Ste A
Mont Clare PA
610 935-1420

(G-5502)
MAINTENANCE TECH
10 Strawbridge Ave (19720-1536)
PHONE.................302 322-6410
Rita Skinner, *Manager*
EMP: 5
SALES (est): 187.8K **Privately Held**
SIC: 7349 Building maintenance services

(G-5503)
MAKESHOPNCOMPANY INC
312 Cherry Ln Ste 300 (19720-2784)
PHONE.................302 999-9961
Seungkook Ko, *Branch Mgr*
EMP: 10
SALES (corp-wide): 33.5MM **Privately Held**
SIC: 4731 5122 Transportation agents & brokers; vitamins & minerals
PA: Makeshopncompany, Inc.
15627 S Broadway
Gardena CA 90248
213 748-5118

(G-5504)
MALIKS AUTO REPAIR
95 Christiana Rd (19720-3104)
PHONE.................302 325-2555
Anadil Aslam, *Owner*
EMP: 7
SALES (est): 359K **Privately Held**
SIC: 7538 General automotive repair shops

(G-5505)
MANUFACTURERS & TRADERS TR CO
Also Called: M&T
287 Christiana Rd Ste 16 (19720-2978)
PHONE.................302 472-3249
Katrine Hutchison, *Branch Mgr*
EMP: 35
SALES (corp-wide): 6.4B **Publicly Held**
WEB: www.binghamlegg.com
SIC: 6022 State commercial banks
HQ: Manufacturers And Traders Trust Company
1 M&T Plz Fl 3
Buffalo NY 14203
716 842-4200

(G-5506)
MARINIS BROS INC
755 Grantham Ln (19720-4801)
PHONE.................302 322-9663
Nick Marinis, *President*
Sothiere Marinis, *Vice Pres*
Sophia Marinis, *Admin Sec*
EMP: 10 EST: 1966
SALES (est): 1.1MM **Privately Held**
WEB: www.marinisbros.com
SIC: 1721 Bridge painting; commercial painting

(G-5507)
MARITA F FALLORINA MD
1 Catherine St Ste 1 # 1 (19720-3001)
PHONE.................302 322-0660
Marita F Fallorina MD, *Owner*
EMP: 5
SALES (est): 538.7K **Privately Held**
SIC: 8011 General & family practice, physician/surgeon

(G-5508)
MARLEX PHARMACEUTICALS INC
65 Lukens Dr New Castle (19720)
PHONE.................302 328-3355
Amrish Patel, *President*
Payal Patel, *Technology*
Samir Patel, *Admin Sec*
Maria Martinez, *Admin Asst*
EMP: 40
SQ FT: 80,000
SALES (est): 8MM **Privately Held**
WEB: www.marlexpharm.com
SIC: 4783 2834 Packing goods for shipping; pharmaceutical preparations

(G-5509)
MARLINGS INC
Also Called: Marling's Emergency Water
710 Wilmington Rd (19720-3634)
PHONE.................302 325-1759
John Marling, *President*
Khristian Toolan, *Business Mgr*
EMP: 14
SALES (est): 1.6MM **Privately Held**
SIC: 7349 1799 7217 Building maintenance services; post-disaster renovations; carpet & upholstery cleaning

(G-5510)
MAROSA SURGICAL INDUSTRIES
Also Called: Avenue Medical
243 Quigley Blvd Ste J (19720-4191)
PHONE.................302 674-0907
Adam Samuel, *President*
Sara Samuel, *Vice Pres*
EMP: 11
SQ FT: 12,000
SALES (est): 4.1MM **Privately Held**
WEB: www.avemed.com
SIC: 5047 5999 Medical equipment & supplies; surgical equipment & supplies; medical apparatus & supplies

(G-5511)
MATERIAL HANDLING SUPPLY INC
Also Called: MHS Lift of Delaware
243 Quigley Blvd Ste I (19720-4191)
PHONE.................302 571-0176
Dave Brown, *Manager*
Chris Humes, *Manager*
Ben Miller, *Manager*
EMP: 12
SALES (corp-wide): 70.5MM **Privately Held**
WEB: www.mhslift.com
SIC: 5084 7359 Materials handling machinery; equipment rental & leasing
PA: Material Handling Supply, Inc.
6965 Airport Highway Ln
Pennsauken NJ 08109
877 647-9320

(G-5512)
MATERIAL TRANSIT INC
Also Called: Material Supply
255 Airport Rd (19720-1539)
PHONE.................302 395-0556
Blaise Saienni, *President*
William Saienni Jr, *Corp Secy*
Quinton Saienni, *Vice Pres*
Elmer Saienne, *Shareholder*
William Saienni Sr, *Shareholder*
EMP: 12
SQ FT: 5,000
SALES (est): 588.9K **Privately Held**
SIC: 1442 3273 4213 Construction sand & gravel; ready-mixed concrete; heavy hauling

(G-5513)
MECHANICS PARADISE INC
Also Called: Tools & More
2335 N Dupont Hwy (19720-6304)
PHONE.................302 652-8863
William Baron, *CEO*
Suzanne Baron, *Treasurer*
EMP: 10
SQ FT: 15,400
SALES (est): 7MM **Privately Held**
WEB: www.toolsandmorestore.com
SIC: 5084 5211 5251 Industrial machinery & equipment; lumber & other building materials; hardware; builders' hardware

(G-5514)
MEDLAB ENVIRONMENTAL TESTING
212 Cherry Ln (19720-2776)
PHONE.................302 655-5227
Jame Diguglielmo, *President*
EMP: 4
SALES (est): 103.9K **Privately Held**
SIC: 8071 Testing laboratories

(G-5515)
MEMORIAL SUPER FUEL
3006 New Castle Ave (19720-2244)
PHONE.................215 512-1012
Jassveer Singh, *Manager*
EMP: 6 EST: 2011
SALES (est): 505.8K **Privately Held**
SIC: 2869 Fuels

(G-5516)
MERAKEY USA
2 Penns Way (19720-2407)
PHONE.................302 325-3540
Rose Stewart, *Branch Mgr*
EMP: 54
SALES (corp-wide): 381.9MM **Privately Held**
SIC: 8322 Individual & family services
PA: Merakey Usa
620 Germantown Pike
Lafayette Hill PA 19444
610 260-4600

(G-5517)
METAL PARTNERS REBAR LLC
Also Called: Metal Partners International
20 Davidson Ln (19720-2214)
PHONE.................215 791-3491
Mike Poff, *Manager*
EMP: 12 **Privately Held**
SIC: 5051 Metals service centers & offices
PA: Metal Partners Rebar, Llc
3933 75th St Ste 101
Aurora IL 60504

(G-5518)
METAL-TECH INC
265 Airport Rd (19720-1540)
PHONE.................302 322-7770
Hugh Hood, *President*
Tony Morris, *General Mgr*
Erika Hood, *Vice Pres*
Tammy Hood, *Manager*
EMP: 22
SQ FT: 50,000
SALES (est): 3.6MM **Privately Held**
WEB: www.metaltech-de.com
SIC: 3599 3444 7692 3479 Machine shop, jobbing & repair; sheet metalwork; welding repair; painting of metal products

(G-5519)
METRO STEEL INCORPORATED
4049 New Castle Ave (19720-1414)
P.O. Box 12808, Wilmington (19850-2808)
PHONE.................302 778-2288
Robert Cordrey, *President*
EMP: 20 EST: 1998
SQ FT: 5,000
SALES (est): 6MM **Privately Held**
SIC: 1541 Industrial buildings & warehouses

(G-5520)
METROPOLITAN REVENUE ASSOC LLC
29 E Commons Blvd Ste 100 (19720-1736)
P.O. Box 47, Middletown (19709-0047)
PHONE.................302 449-7490
John P Eldridge, *Principal*
EMP: 8 EST: 2011
SALES (est): 659K **Privately Held**
SIC: 8742 Hospital & health services consultant

(G-5521)
MICHAELS HOME REPAIR SERVICES
550 S Dupont Hwy Apt 22k (19720-5135)
PHONE.................302 333-2235
Michael Dobey, *Vice Pres*
EMP: 6
SALES (est): 154.3K **Privately Held**
SIC: 7389 Business services

(G-5522)
MID ATLANTIC GRAND PRIX LLC
4060 N Dupont Hwy Ste 11 (19720-6325)
PHONE.................302 656-5278
Jeff Schwarz,
Robert Schwarz,
EMP: 20
SALES (est): 626.3K **Privately Held**
WEB: www.midatlanticgrandprix.com
SIC: 7929 8741 7999 Entertainers & entertainment groups; management services; indoor court clubs

(G-5523)
MID ATLANTIC WASTE SYSTEM
314 Bay West Blvd Ste 3 (19720-5195)
PHONE.................610 497-2405
Richard Weinstein, *Owner*
EMP: 15
SALES (est): 869.4K **Privately Held**
SIC: 4953 Refuse systems

New Castle - New Castle County (G-5524)

(G-5524)
MID ATLNTIC SCIENTIFIC SVC INC
62 Southgate Blvd Ste Ab (19720-2075)
P.O. Box 880 (19720-0880)
PHONE..................302 328-4440
James Twenge, *CEO*
Robert Reissman, *President*
Lorie Twenge, *COO*
EMP: 5 **EST:** 1995
SQ FT: 6,000
SALES (est): 900K **Privately Held**
SIC: 7699 5999 Scientific equipment repair service; medical apparatus & supplies

(G-5525)
MID-ATLANTIC ENVMTL LABS INC
30 Lukens Dr Ste A (19720-2700)
PHONE..................302 654-1340
Akhter Mehmood, *President*
Nuzhat Mehmood, *Admin Sec*
EMP: 15
SQ FT: 3,200
SALES: 1.5MM **Privately Held**
WEB: www.midatlanticenvlabs.com
SIC: 8734 Testing laboratories

(G-5526)
MID-ATLANTIC REALTY CO INC
Also Called: Emory Hill
10 Corporate Cir Ste 100 (19720-2418)
PHONE..................302 322-9500
Donna Carroll, *Manager*
EMP: 4
SALES (corp-wide): 4.6MM **Privately Held**
SIC: 6513 Apartment building operators
PA: Mid-Atlantic Realty Co Inc
39 Abbey Ln
Newark DE 19711
302 658-7642

(G-5527)
MID-ATLANTIC STEEL LLC
1144 River Rd (19720-5106)
PHONE..................302 323-1800
Mike Williams,
Tom Williams,
EMP: 31
SALES (est): 5.2MM **Privately Held**
SIC: 1791 Structural steel erection

(G-5528)
MIDWAY TOWING INC
443 Old Airport Rd (19720-1001)
PHONE..................302 323-4850
Steven Mullins, *Manager*
Roger Crannell, *Manager*
EMP: 7
SALES: 300K **Privately Held**
SIC: 7549 Towing services

(G-5529)
MILLENNIA CONTRACTING INC
3075 New Castle Ave (19720-2245)
PHONE..................302 654-6200
Kevin Dougherty, *President*
EMP: 16
SQ FT: 2,000
SALES (est): 1.8MM **Privately Held**
WEB: www.millenniacontracting.com
SIC: 1799 Antenna installation

(G-5530)
MILLERS GUN CENTER INC
97 Jackson Ave (19720-6431)
PHONE..................302 328-9747
John Miller Jr, *President*
Robert Miller, *Treasurer*
EMP: 9
SQ FT: 2,500
SALES (est): 2.4MM **Privately Held**
WEB: www.millersguns.com
SIC: 5941 5091 Firearms; firearms, sporting

(G-5531)
MMR GROUP INC (PA)
Also Called: Connecticut Metallurgical
308 W Basin Rd (19720-6406)
PHONE..................302 328-0500
Francis S Shoreys, *President*
Jerry Creswell, *Project Mgr*
Jennifer Wegner, *Treasurer*
Kevin Pelletier, *Sales Staff*
Deborah Keiser, *Manager*
EMP: 28
SQ FT: 25,000
SALES (est): 11.4MM **Privately Held**
WEB: www.mmr-group.com
SIC: 8731 8734 Commercial physical research; metallurgical testing laboratory

(G-5532)
MODERN CONTROLS INC
7 Bellecor Dr (19720-1763)
PHONE..................302 325-6800
Michael Peet, *President*
William Schatzman, *Vice Pres*
Lisa Hicken, *Purch Mgr*
Chase Lockard, *Sales Engr*
Jim Dryden, *Sales Staff*
EMP: 45
SQ FT: 8,000
SALES: 10.5MM **Privately Held**
WEB: www.moderncontrols.com
SIC: 1711 7699 7629 Mechanical contractor; pumps & pumping equipment repair; electrical repair shops

(G-5533)
MODERN WATER INC
15 Reads Way Ste 100 (19720-1600)
PHONE..................302 669-6900
Sejal Patel, *Opers Mgr*
Clayton Albright, *Sales Staff*
Kathy Miklas, *Manager*
EMP: 21
SALES (est): 3.1MM **Privately Held**
SIC: 8731 Commercial physical research

(G-5534)
MODULAR CARPET RECYCLING INC
239 Lisa Dr (19720-4193)
P.O. Box 370, Unionville PA (19375-0370)
PHONE..................484 885-5890
Ron Simonetti, *CEO*
EMP: 16 **EST:** 2008
SALES (est): 2.2MM **Privately Held**
SIC: 4953 1752 Recycling, waste materials; carpet laying

(G-5535)
MONRO INC
Also Called: Monro Muffler Brake
401 S Dupont Hwy (19720-4605)
PHONE..................302 328-2945
Bryan Boone, *Branch Mgr*
EMP: 5
SALES (corp-wide): 1.2B **Publicly Held**
WEB: www.monro.com
SIC: 7539 7533 Wheel alignment, automotive; muffler shop, sale or repair & installation
PA: Monro, Inc.
200 Holleder Pkwy
Rochester NY 14615
585 647-6400

(G-5536)
MORRIS & RITCHIE ASSOC INC
18 Boulden Cir Ste 36 (19720-3494)
PHONE..................302 326-2200
Phillip Tolliver, *Manager*
EMP: 15 **Privately Held**
SIC: 8711 8713 Designing: ship, boat, machine & product; surveying services
HQ: Morris & Ritchie Associates, Inc.
3445 Box Hll Corp Ctr Dr B
Abingdon MD
410 515-9000

(G-5537)
MOVE CREW
14 Fresconi Ct (19720-3011)
PHONE..................302 290-4684
George Williams, *President*
EMP: 4
SALES (est): 323.1K **Privately Held**
SIC: 4212 Moving services

(G-5538)
MTC DELAWARE LLC
2 Dock View Dr (19720-2180)
PHONE..................302 654-3400
Harry Halpert, *President*
EMP: 7
SALES (est): 755.6K **Privately Held**
SIC: 4225 General warehousing & storage

(G-5539)
MUNICIPAL SERVICES COMMISSION (PA)
216 Chestnut St (19720-4834)
P.O. Box 208 (19720-0208)
PHONE..................302 323-2330
Robert S Appleby, *President*
Maryjane Stubbs, *Business Mgr*
George Freebery, *Commissioner*
Hickman Rolling, *Commissioner*
Chip Patterson, *Admin Sec*
EMP: 17
SALES (est): 5.8MM **Privately Held**
WEB: www.newcastlecity.com
SIC: 4911 4941 Electric services; water supply

(G-5540)
MURRYS OF MARYLAND INC
Also Called: Murry's Steaks 8262
1400 S Dupont Hwy (19720-5514)
PHONE..................302 328-3361
EMP: 5
SALES (corp-wide): 88.5MM **Privately Held**
SIC: 5421 5142 Frozen Meats Poultry Seafood And Other Related Food Products
HQ: Murry's Of Maryland, Inc.
7852 Walker Dr Ste 420
Greenbelt MD 20770
301 420-6400

(G-5541)
NABERTHERM INC
64 Reads Way (19720-1649)
PHONE..................302 322-3665
Martin Naber, *Principal*
Samuel Forsythe, *Sales Engr*
John Crowther, *Technical Staff*
Melanie Clements, *Administration*
▲ **EMP:** 5
SALES (est): 1.1MM
SALES (corp-wide): 71.2MM **Privately Held**
WEB: www.nabertherm.com
SIC: 3567 Industrial furnaces & ovens
HQ: Nabertherm Gmbh
Bahnhofstr. 20
Lilienthal 28865
429 892-20

(G-5542)
NAES CORPORATION
13 Reads Way Ste 100 (19720-1609)
PHONE..................856 299-0020
Steve Goers, *Manager*
EMP: 12 **Privately Held**
SIC: 7629 Electrical equipment repair services
HQ: Naes Corporation
1180 Nw Maple St Ste 200
Issaquah WA 98027
425 961-4700

(G-5543)
NALCO COMPANY LLC
204 Quigley Blvd (19720-4106)
PHONE..................856 423-6417
Brian Devlin, *Branch Mgr*
EMP: 35
SALES (corp-wide): 14.6B **Publicly Held**
WEB: www.nalco.com
SIC: 2899 Corrosion preventive lubricant
HQ: Nalco Company Llc
1601 W Diehl Rd
Naperville IL 60563
630 305-1000

(G-5544)
NATIONAL DENTEX LLC
Also Called: Dodd Dental Laboratory
24 Lukens Dr (19720-2700)
P.O. Box 1005 (19720-7005)
PHONE..................302 661-6000
Donna Jarman, *Branch Mgr*
Mark Dodd, *Technical Staff*
EMP: 90
SALES (corp-wide): 151.4MM **Privately Held**
WEB: www.nationaldentex.com
SIC: 8072 Crown & bridge production
HQ: National Dentex, Llc
11601 Kew Gardens Ave # 200
Palm Beach Gardens FL 33410
561 537-8300

(G-5545)
NATIONAL GUARD ASSOCIATION DEL
1 Vavala Way (19720-2417)
PHONE..................302 326-7125
Leonard Gratteri, *CEO*
David Rice, *Principal*
Susan Lewis, *Med Doctor*
EMP: 15
SALES (est): 161.5K **Privately Held**
SIC: 8699 Membership organizations

(G-5546)
NATIONAL HVAC SERVICE
Also Called: Honeywell Authorized Dealer
42a Southgate Blvd (19720-2068)
PHONE..................302 323-1776
Pat Cunningham, *General Mgr*
John Chido, *Mktg Dir*
EMP: 30
SALES (est): 3.7MM **Privately Held**
WEB: www.nationalhvacservice.com
SIC: 1711 Warm air heating & air conditioning contractor; ventilation & duct work contractor
PA: National H.V.A.C. Service, Ltd
100 Bradford Rd Ste 120
Wexford PA 15090

(G-5547)
NATIONAL OPPRTNITIES UNLIMITED
42 Reads Way Ste 5 (19720-1649)
PHONE..................913 905-2261
Joshua Landy, *President*
EMP: 17
SALES (est): 691.6K **Privately Held**
SIC: 7389 Financial services

(G-5548)
NATIONWIDE CORPORATION
100 Penn Mart Shopg Ctr (19720-4209)
PHONE..................302 761-9611
Thomas McKenney, *Branch Mgr*
EMP: 4
SALES (corp-wide): 13.2B **Privately Held**
SIC: 6411 Insurance agents, brokers & service
HQ: Nationwide Corporation
1 Nationwide Plz
Columbus OH 43215
614 249-7111

(G-5549)
NEGRI BOSSI NORTH AMERICA INC
311 Carroll Dr (19720-4858)
PHONE..................302 328-8020
Sandra Ryan, *Accounts Mgr*
▲ **EMP:** 2
SALES (est): 1.1MM **Privately Held**
SIC: 3089 Injection molded finished plastic products

(G-5550)
NEGRI BOSSI USA INC
311 Carroll Dr 100 (19720-4858)
PHONE..................302 328-8020
Luca Berrone, *President*
Colin Drewek, *Regl Sales Mgr*
Mark Brackett, *Manager*
▲ **EMP:** 11
SALES (est): 3.8MM
SALES (corp-wide): 177.9K **Privately Held**
WEB: www.negribossiusa.com
SIC: 3559 Plastics working machinery
HQ: Negri Bossi Spa
Viale Europa 64
Cologno Monzese MI 20093
022 538-264

(G-5551)
NESSUS INVESTMENT CORPORATION
1 Penns Way (19721-2300)
PHONE..................302 323-3104
EMP: 4

GEOGRAPHIC SECTION

New Castle - New Castle County (G-5582)

SALES (est): 476.6K
SALES (corp-wide): 90.5B **Publicly Held**
SIC: 6021 National Commercial Bank
HQ: Citigroup Asia Pacific Holding Corporation
1 Penns Way Fl 1
New Castle DE 19721
302 323-3100

(G-5552)
NESTLE USA INC
200 Lisa Dr (19720-4167)
PHONE..................302 325-0300
EMP: 135
SALES (corp-wide): 92.8B **Privately Held**
SIC: 2023 Evaporated milk
HQ: Nestle Usa, Inc.
1812 N Moore St Ste 118
Rosslyn VA 22209
818 549-6000

(G-5553)
NEW CAR CONNECTION
174 N Dupont Hwy (19720-3103)
PHONE..................302 328-7000
Chris Dagesse, *Owner*
Ron Miller, *Owner*
Bill Russo, *Vice Pres*
EMP: 12
SALES (est): 1.1MM **Privately Held**
WEB: www.nucar.com
SIC: 5511 7538 7532 7515 Automobiles, new & used; general automotive repair shops; top & body repair & paint shops; passenger car leasing; automotive dealers; used car dealers

(G-5554)
NEW CASTLE CNTY SHOPPERS GUIDE
950 W Basin Rd (19720-1008)
PHONE..................302 325-6600
Curtis Riddle, *President*
EMP: 20
SALES (est): 847.6K **Privately Held**
SIC: 8748 2741 Business consulting; miscellaneous publishing

(G-5555)
NEW CASTLE COUNTY SCHOOL EMPLO
Also Called: NCCSEFCU
113 W 6th St (19720-5070)
P.O. Box 232 (19720-0232)
PHONE..................302 613-5350
Terri L Keene, *General Mgr*
Colin Feeney, *Teacher*
Stephanie Mitchell, *Teacher*
EMP: 11
SALES: 1.9MM **Privately Held**
SIC: 6061 Federal credit unions

(G-5556)
NEW CASTLE DENTAL ASSOC PA
Also Called: Chamish, Steven E
92 Reads Way Ste 200 (19720-1631)
PHONE..................302 328-1513
Steven Chamish, *President*
EMP: 17
SALES (est): 1.1MM **Privately Held**
SIC: 8021 Dentists' office

(G-5557)
NEW CASTLE ENGRAVING CO
133 Festone Ave (19720-2049)
PHONE..................302 652-7551
Jim Cain, *Owner*
EMP: 2
SALES: 85K **Privately Held**
SIC: 3089 Engraving of plastic

(G-5558)
NEW CASTLE GLASS INC
38 Lesley Ln (19720-3340)
P.O. Box 10984, Wilmington (19850-0984)
PHONE..................302 322-6164
George R Glanden, *President*
Joanne Glanden, *Treasurer*
EMP: 8
SQ FT: 1,400
SALES (est): 700K **Privately Held**
SIC: 1793 Glass & glazing work

(G-5559)
NEW CASTLE HEALTH&REHAB CNTR
Also Called: New Castle Health&Rehab Cntr
32 Buena Vista Dr (19720-4660)
PHONE..................302 328-2580
Richard Powell, *Manager*
Sarah Depompei, *Assistant*
EMP: 126
SALES (est): 338.6K **Privately Held**
SIC: 8051 Skilled nursing care facilities

(G-5560)
NEW CASTLE HISTORICAL SOCIETY
30 Market St (19720-4830)
PHONE..................302 322-2794
Michael Connolly, *Exec Dir*
EMP: 12
SALES: 394.1K **Privately Held**
WEB: www.newcastlehistoricalsociety.com
SIC: 8412 Historical society

(G-5561)
NEW CASTLE INSURANCE LTD
621 Delaware St Ste 100 (19720-5073)
PHONE..................302 328-6111
Dennis Salter, *President*
Michelle Fidance, *Manager*
Patricia Flynn, *Admin Sec*
EMP: 16
SQ FT: 5,600
SALES (est): 1.9MM **Privately Held**
WEB: www.newcastleinsure.com
SIC: 6411 Insurance brokers

(G-5562)
NEW CASTLE LODGING CORPORATION
Also Called: New Castle Travelodge
1213 West Ave (19720-6250)
PHONE..................302 654-5544
Peter Bhai, *President*
Pinky Bhai, *Admin Sec*
EMP: 18
SALES (est): 584.3K **Privately Held**
SIC: 7011 Motels

(G-5563)
NEW CASTLE PRECISION MCH LLC
729 Grantham Ln Ste 2 (19720-4898)
PHONE..................302 650-7849
Guy Anderson, *Mng Member*
EMP: 3
SALES: 96K **Privately Held**
SIC: 3599 Machine shop, jobbing & repair

(G-5564)
NEW CASTLE SAILING CLUB
614 South St (19720-5026)
P.O. Box 46 (19720-0046)
PHONE..................302 307-3060
John G Ingram, *Principal*
EMP: 4
SALES: 45.7K **Privately Held**
SIC: 5813 7997 Drinking places; membership sports & recreation clubs

(G-5565)
NEW CASTLE SENIOR CENTER
400 South St (19720-5057)
P.O. Box 30 (19720-0030)
PHONE..................302 326-4209
Natalie Kaplan, *Asst Director*
EMP: 4
SALES: 314.4K **Privately Held**
SIC: 8322 Senior citizens' center or association

(G-5566)
NEW CASTLE SHUTTLE AND TAXI SE
38 Stevens Ave (19720-4047)
PHONE..................302 326-1855
Carolyn Propson, *Owner*
EMP: 7
SALES (est): 202.3K **Privately Held**
SIC: 4119 Limousine rental, with driver

(G-5567)
NEW CASTLE WEEKLY INC
203 Delaware St (19720-4815)
PHONE..................302 328-6005
Mimi Carpenter, *President*
EMP: 2
SALES (est): 110K **Privately Held**
SIC: 2711 Newspapers: publishing only, not printed on site

(G-5568)
NEW CSTLE CNTY DEL EM FDRAL CR
100 Churchmans Rd (19720-3108)
PHONE..................302 395-5350
Merideth Jefferies, *CEO*
EMP: 4
SALES: 635.6K **Privately Held**
SIC: 6061 Federal credit unions

(G-5569)
NEWS-JOURNAL COMPANY
950 W Basin Rd (19720-1006)
PHONE..................302 324-2500
Jane Amari, *Principal*
Craig Monti, *Plant Engr Mgr*
Lynette Scott, *Manager*
Eileen Cox, *Director*
Alexis Ziobro, *Director*
EMP: 20
SALES (est): 4MM **Privately Held**
SIC: 2711 Commercial printing & newspaper publishing combined; newspapers, publishing & printing

(G-5570)
NIXON UNF RNTL SVC OF LNCASTER (PA)
42 Lukens Dr Ste 100 (19720-2700)
PHONE..................302 656-2774
Brian Bear, *President*
EMP: 5
SQ FT: 23,000
SALES (est): 4.6MM **Privately Held**
WEB: www.patient-gowns.com
SIC: 7299 Clothing rental services

(G-5571)
NIXON UNIFORM SERVICE INC (PA)
Also Called: Nixon Uniform Service & Med Wr
500 Centerpoint Blvd (19720-8106)
PHONE..................302 325-2875
Jason Berstein, *President*
Robert L Schecter, *Vice Pres*
Dan Berstein, *Site Mgr*
Stephanie Thomas, *Opers Staff*
Michael Small, *Regl Sales Mgr*
EMP: 170
SQ FT: 75,000
SALES (est): 32.7MM **Privately Held**
WEB: www.nixonuniform.com
SIC: 7218 2326 Industrial equipment launderers; medical & hospital uniforms, men's

(G-5572)
NKS DISTRIBUTORS INC (PA)
399 Churchmans Rd (19720-3111)
P.O. Box 758 (19720-0758)
PHONE..................302 322-1811
James V Tigani Sr, *Ch of Bd*
Robert Tigani, *President*
John Leyh, *Human Res Dir*
Mike Lashomb, *Sales Mgr*
Alyse Alvini, *Sales Staff*
▲ EMP: 105 EST: 1946
SQ FT: 50,000
SALES (est): 38.1MM **Privately Held**
WEB: www.nksdistributors.com
SIC: 5181 5182 Beer & other fermented malt liquors; wine

(G-5573)
NO JOKE I LLC
Also Called: Champion Builders
16 Stockton Dr (19720-4318)
PHONE..................302 395-0882
Micheal Stewart, *Mng Member*
Lisa Stewart,
EMP: 7
SALES: 98K **Privately Held**
SIC: 1531 7389 Operative builders;

(G-5574)
NORA LEES FRNCH QUARTER BISTRO
124 Delaware St (19720-4859)
PHONE..................302 322-7675

EMP: 3
SALES (est): 244K **Privately Held**
SIC: 3131 Quarters

(G-5575)
NORTH AMERICAN TRNSPT CO INC
92 Reads Way Ste 202 (19720-1631)
PHONE..................856 696-5483
Stephanie Wood, *Branch Mgr*
EMP: 5
SALES (est): 506.1K
SALES (corp-wide): 5.9MM **Privately Held**
SIC: 4731 Truck transportation brokers
PA: North American Transport Company Inc.
1830 Gallagher Dr Ste 101
Vineland NJ 08360
856 696-5483

(G-5576)
NORTH ATL INTL OCEAN CARIER
35 Davidson Ln (19720-2213)
PHONE..................786 275-5352
Olga Fred, *General Mgr*
EMP: 3
SALES (est): 340.4K **Privately Held**
SIC: 3711 Motor vehicles & car bodies

(G-5577)
NORTH ATLANTIC OCEAN SHIP
19 Davidson Ln (19720-2246)
PHONE..................302 652-3782
Efren Jimenez, *Principal*
Christian Rabateau, *Sales Executive*
Susan Gurry, *VP Mktg*
EMP: 8
SALES (est): 420K **Privately Held**
SIC: 4789 Cargo loading & unloading services

(G-5578)
NORTH DUPONT SHELL
102 N Dupont Hwy (19720-3102)
PHONE..................301 375-6000
EMP: 2
SALES (est): 74.4K **Privately Held**
SIC: 2879 Agricultural chemicals

(G-5579)
NORTHEASTERN TITLE LOANS
Also Called: Select Management Resources
1560 N Dupont Hwy (19720-1902)
PHONE..................302 326-2210
Rod Aycox, *President*
John Henry, *General Mgr*
EMP: 9
SALES (est): 886.1K **Privately Held**
SIC: 6141 Personal finance licensed loan companies, small

(G-5580)
NOTHING BUT NET INC
83 Charles Dr (19720-4679)
PHONE..................302 476-0453
Lonnie Wright, *Principal*
EMP: 5
SALES (est): 58K **Privately Held**
SIC: 7999 Basketball instruction school

(G-5581)
NOVA CONSULTANTS LTD
245 Quigley Blvd Ste B (19720-4192)
P.O. Box 10125, Wilmington (19850-0125)
PHONE..................302 328-1686
Ray Lyons, *President*
Janet Brandt, *Purchasing*
EMP: 10
SALES (est): 910K **Privately Held**
WEB: www.novaconsultants.com
SIC: 8748 2899 Business consulting; chemical preparations

(G-5582)
NUMAKE-1 LLC
239 Lisa Dr (19720-4193)
PHONE..................302 220-4760
Bryan Tracy, *CEO*
EMP: 1
SALES: 39.5K
SALES (corp-wide): 2.4MM **Privately Held**
SIC: 2048 Feed concentrates

New Castle - New Castle County (G-5583)   **GEOGRAPHIC SECTION**

PA: White Dog Labs, Inc.
239 Lisa Dr
New Castle DE 19720
302 220-4760

(G-5583)
NURSES N KIDS INC (PA)
904 Churchmans Road Ext (19720-3151)
PHONE..................302 323-1118
Janet Carroll, *CEO*
Missy Mahoney-Roche, *Principal*
Melissa Cappelli, *Vice Pres*
Missy Cappelli, *Vice Pres*
David Carroll, *Treasurer*
EMP: 50
SQ FT: 25,000
SALES (est): 4.3MM **Privately Held**
WEB: www.nursesnkids.com
SIC: 8351 Child day care services

(G-5584)
OAK HRC NEW CASTLE LLC
Also Called: New Cstle Hlth Rhblitation Ctr
32 Buena Vista Dr (19720-4660)
PHONE..................302 328-2580
Howard Jaffe, *President*
Wayne Barrett, *Treasurer*
Karen Thomas, *Administration*
EMP: 99
SQ FT: 40,000
SALES (est): 2.4MM **Privately Held**
SIC: 8051 Mental retardation hospital

(G-5585)
OCCIDENTAL CHEMICAL CORP
1657 River Rd (19720-5194)
PHONE..................302 834-3800
Charles J Zullo, *President*
EMP: 3
SALES (est): 327K **Privately Held**
SIC: 2813 Hydrogen

(G-5586)
OHMYZIP
599 Ships Landing Way (19720-4578)
PHONE..................302 322-8792
Hyelim Song, *Branch Mgr*
EMP: 20
SALES (corp-wide): 2.8MM **Privately Held**
SIC: 4731 Freight transportation arrangement
PA: Ohmyzip
14400 Industry Cir
La Mirada CA 90638
714 676-7274

(G-5587)
ON BOARD ENGINEERING CORP
2 Penns Way Ste 400 (19720-2407)
PHONE..................302 613-5030
Richard Jervis, *Manager*
EMP: 60
SALES (corp-wide): 26MM **Privately Held**
SIC: 8711 Consulting engineer
PA: On Board Engineering Corporation
50 Millstone Rd # 300110
East Windsor NJ 08520
609 945-8000

(G-5588)
ON-DEMAND SERVICES LLC
412 Park Ave (19720-4794)
PHONE..................302 388-1215
Olanrewaju Akinola,
EMP: 4
SALES (est): 240.4K **Privately Held**
SIC: 4214 4212 4783 4213 Household goods moving & storage, local; local trucking, without storage; packing & crating; trucking, except local; general warehousing & storage

(G-5589)
OPPORTUNITY CENTER INC (PA)
Also Called: Oci
13 Reads Way Ste 101 (19720-1609)
P.O. Box 254, Wilmington (19899-0254)
PHONE..................302 762-0300
Janet Samuelson, *President*
Michelle Lee, *Vice Chairman*
Robin Portman, *Vice Chairman*
Bruce Patterson, *COO*
Mark Hall, *Exec VP*

EMP: 100
SALES: 9.1MM **Privately Held**
SIC: 8331 7361 Job counseling; placement agencies

(G-5590)
ORCHARD PARK GROUP INC
42 Reads Way (19720-1649)
PHONE..................302 356-1139
Ray Garcia, *President*
EMP: 50
SALES: 1,000K **Privately Held**
SIC: 8748 Business consulting

(G-5591)
ORKIN LLC
Also Called: Orkin Pest Control 314
101 Johnson Way (19720-8115)
PHONE..................302 322-9569
Walter Fitzpatrick, *Manager*
EMP: 18
SALES (corp-wide): 1.8B **Publicly Held**
WEB: www.orkin.com
SIC: 7342 Pest control services
HQ: Orkin, Llc
2170 Piedmont Rd Ne
Atlanta GA 30324
404 888-2000

(G-5592)
ORPHEUS COMPANIES LTD
255 Old Churchmans Rd (19720-1529)
P.O. Box 10863, Wilmington (19850-0863)
PHONE..................302 328-3451
Neeshard Ahamad, *President*
EMP: 4
SALES (est): 610.9K **Privately Held**
WEB: www.oclmedia.com
SIC: 7379 Data processing consultant

(G-5593)
OTOLARYNGOLOGY CONSULTANTS
Also Called: New Castle Hearing/Spch/Vstblr
100 Christiana Rd (19720-3003)
P.O. Box 993, Wilmington (19899-0993)
PHONE..................302 328-1331
Dr Emilio Valdes, *Owner*
EMP: 8
SALES (corp-wide): 1.4MM **Privately Held**
SIC: 8069 Eye, ear, nose & throat hospital
PA: Otolaryngology Consultants, Inc
10 Foxview Cir
Hockessin DE 19707
302 328-1331

(G-5594)
OVER RAINBOW DAYCARE
713 W 12th St (19720-4947)
PHONE..................302 328-6574
Robert Gibbons, *Principal*
EMP: 5
SALES (est): 89.4K **Privately Held**
SIC: 8351 Group day care center

(G-5595)
P & C ROOFING INC
35 Southgate Blvd (19720-2069)
PHONE..................302 322-6767
Angela Papa Mariano, *President*
Randy Mariano, *Vice Pres*
Peter A Papa Jr, *Vice Pres*
Vincent Papa, *Vice Pres*
Mathew Papa, *Admin Sec*
EMP: 45
SQ FT: 30,000
SALES (est): 6.5MM **Privately Held**
WEB: www.pcroofinginc.com
SIC: 1761 Roofing contractor

(G-5596)
P A ANESTHESIA SERVICES
2 Reads Way Ste 201 (19720-1630)
PHONE..................302 709-4709
Richard Stern, *Principal*
EMP: 6
SALES (est): 1.2MM **Privately Held**
SIC: 8011 Anesthesiologist

(G-5597)
PAGODA HOTEL INC
Also Called: Pagoda Hotel & Floating Rest
599 Ships Landing Way (19720-4578)
PHONE..................808 922-1233
Herbert T Hayashi, *Ch of Bd*

Harry Hayashi, *Vice Pres*
Kery Kamita, *Treasurer*
John Hayashi, *Admin Sec*
EMP: 600 EST: 1963
SALES (est): 14.6MM
SALES (corp-wide): 23.6MM **Privately Held**
WEB: www.pagodahotel.com
SIC: 5812 7011 Restaurant, family: independent; hotels
PA: Hth Asset Management, Llc
1668 S King St Fl 2
Honolulu HI 96826
808 469-4111

(G-5598)
PALACE LAUNDRY INC
Also Called: Linens of The Week
30 Mccullough Dr (19720-2066)
PHONE..................302 322-2136
Ken Bubes, *Branch Mgr*
EMP: 45
SALES (corp-wide): 20.1MM **Privately Held**
WEB: www.palacelaundry.com
SIC: 7213 Uniform supply
PA: Palace Laundry, Inc.
713 Lamont St Nw
Washington DC 20010
202 291-9200

(G-5599)
PANDACITI LLC
257 Old Churchmans Rd (19720-1529)
PHONE..................226 219-7771
Juan Gonzalez,
EMP: 1
SALES: 40K **Privately Held**
SIC: 3999 Manufacturing industries

(G-5600)
PANELMATIC INC
11 Southgate Blvd (19720-2069)
PHONE..................302 324-9193
Edward F Reschka, *Vice Pres*
EMP: 7
SALES (corp-wide): 38MM **Privately Held**
WEB: www.panelmatic.com
SIC: 3613 8711 Control panels, electric; cubicles (electric switchboard equipment); designing: ship, boat, machine & product
PA: Panelmatic, Inc.
258 Donald Dr
Fairfield OH 45014
513 829-3666

(G-5601)
PANELMATIC EAST INC
11 Southgate Blvd (19720-2069)
PHONE..................302 324-9193
Richard Leach, *President*
David D Adamson, *CFO*
▼ EMP: 10
SALES (est): 2MM
SALES (corp-wide): 38MM **Privately Held**
WEB: www.panelmatic.com
SIC: 3613 8711 Control panels, electric; designing: ship, boat, machine & product
PA: Panelmatic, Inc.
258 Donald Dr
Fairfield OH 45014
513 829-3666

(G-5602)
PARKER EXPRESS INC
152 S Dupont Hwy (19720-4149)
P.O. Box 12585, Wilmington (19850-2585)
PHONE..................302 221-5777
Linda Parker, *President*
EMP: 25
SALES (est): 189.5K **Privately Held**
SIC: 4213 Trucking, except local

(G-5603)
PARKWAY GRAVEL INC
4048 New Castle Ave (19720-1455)
PHONE..................302 658-5241
Nicholas Ferrara Jr, *President*
Henry S Alisa, *Comptroller*
EMP: 99

SALES: 1,000K **Privately Held**
WEB: www.sigmadatainc.com
SIC: 6519 6552 6512 Real property lessors; subdividers & developers; non-residential building operators

(G-5604)
PARKWAY GRAVEL INC
13 Parkway Cir (19720-4077)
PHONE..................302 326-0554
EMP: 2
SALES (est): 66K **Privately Held**
SIC: 1442 Construction sand & gravel

(G-5605)
PARTNERS PLUS INC
2 Tenns Way Ste 403 (19720)
PHONE..................302 529-3700
William Hogan, *President*
EMP: 5
SALES (est): 745.6K **Privately Held**
SIC: 7379 Computer related consulting services

(G-5606)
PASCALE INDUSTRIES INC
National Roll Kote
55 Harbor View Dr (19720-2179)
PHONE..................302 421-9400
Joe Ferma, *Branch Mgr*
EMP: 10 **Privately Held**
WEB: www.nationalrollkote.com
SIC: 3069 5084 Rubber rolls & roll coverings; industrial machinery & equipment
PA: Pascale Industries, Inc.
1301 Ridgway Rd
Pine Bluff AR 71603

(G-5607)
PAT CIRELLI
Also Called: New Castel, West Coast Video
622 E Basin Rd (19720-4202)
PHONE..................302 322-6751
EMP: 6 EST: 1988
SQ FT: 1,680
SALES: 240K **Privately Held**
SIC: 7841 Video Rental Store

(G-5608)
PATIO PRINTING CO INC
197 Airport Rd (19720-2379)
PHONE..................302 328-6881
George T Fox II, *President*
George Fox, *Contractor*
EMP: 3 EST: 1981
SQ FT: 2,600
SALES (est): 376.4K **Privately Held**
SIC: 2759 Commercial printing

(G-5609)
PAULS PLASTERING INC
19 Davidson Ln Bldg 1 (19720-2210)
PHONE..................302 654-5583
Donald L Jester, *President*
Helen Marie Jester, *Corp Secy*
Ken P Jester, *Vice Pres*
EMP: 20
SQ FT: 2,500
SALES (est): 1.9MM **Privately Held**
WEB: www.paulsplastering.com
SIC: 1742 Plastering, plain or ornamental

(G-5610)
PCI OF VIRGINIA LLC (HQ)
529 Terminal Ave (19720-1426)
PHONE..................302 655-7300
Mary Anna Thomas, *Mng Member*
EMP: 12
SALES (est): 2.7MM
SALES (corp-wide): 20.2MM **Privately Held**
SIC: 4789 Freight car loading & unloading
PA: Port Contractors, Inc.
529 Terminal Ave
New Castle DE 19720
302 655-7300

(G-5611)
PEARCE & MORETTO INC
314 Bay West Blvd Ste 4 (19720-5195)
PHONE..................302 326-0707
Earl Pearce, *President*
Joseph Moretto, *Vice Pres*
EMP: 31 EST: 2000

GEOGRAPHIC SECTION

SALES (est): 7.5MM **Privately Held**
WEB: www.pearce-moretto.com
SIC: **1794** Excavation work

(G-5612)
PENINSULA COMPOST COMPANY LLC
529 Terminal Ave (19720-1426)
PHONE..............................215 595-4218
Nathan Widell,
EMP: 1
SALES (est): 127.9K **Privately Held**
SIC: **2875** Compost

(G-5613)
PENN ACRES SWIM CLUB
30 Fithian Dr (19720)
P.O. Box 694 (19720-0694)
PHONE..............................302 322-6501
Mike Shaw, *President*
EMP: 21
SALES: 55.5K **Privately Held**
SIC: **7997** Swimming club, membership

(G-5614)
PENN DEL CARRIERS LLC
110 W Edinburgh Dr (19720-2317)
PHONE..............................484 424-3768
Raymond Lamont Butts, *Mng Member*
EMP: 6
SALES (est): 1.5MM **Privately Held**
SIC: **4731** Freight transportation arrangement

(G-5615)
PENNY COOPER SPORTSWEAR & EMB
204 Christiana Rd (19720-3010)
PHONE..............................302 325-3710
Penny Weingardner, *Owner*
EMP: 6
SALES (est): 285K **Privately Held**
SIC: **2395** Embroidery products, except schiffli machine

(G-5616)
PENOBSCOT PROPERTIES LLC (PA)
135 N Dupont Hwy Hngr B (19720-3135)
PHONE..............................302 322-4477
Leonard Abrahmson, *President*
Madelyn Abrahmson,
EMP: 9
SALES (est): 1.4MM **Privately Held**
SIC: **4512** 4522 4513 Air transportation, scheduled; air transportation, nonscheduled; air courier services

(G-5617)
PENSKE TRUCK LEASING CO LP
51 Boulden Blvd (19720-2065)
PHONE..............................302 325-9290
Bill Mc Anally, *Branch Mgr*
EMP: 36
SALES (corp-wide): 9.6B **Privately Held**
WEB: www.penusketruckleasing.com
SIC: **7513** 7519 7359 Truck rental & leasing, no drivers; utility trailer rental; equipment rental & leasing
HQ: Penske Truck Leasing Co., L.P.
2675 Morgantown Rd
Reading PA 19607
610 775-6000

(G-5618)
PEOPLE IN TRANSITION INC
39 Smyrn Ln (19720-2151)
PHONE..............................302 784-5214
Doreen S Watson, *Director*
EMP: 8
SALES (est): 136K **Privately Held**
SIC: **8361** Residential care

(G-5619)
PETES BIG TVS INC (PA)
22 Lukens Dr (19720-2700)
P.O. Box 1156, Columbia MD (21044-0156)
PHONE..............................302 328-3551
Peter Daniel, *President*
Guy Benjamin, *Vice Pres*
Juan Rapegna, *Opers Mgr*
Jack Miller, *Warehouse Mgr*
Anne Johnston, *Representative*
▲ EMP: 6

SQ FT: 44,000
SALES (est): 7.5MM **Privately Held**
WEB: www.petesbigtvs.com
SIC: **7812** Audio-visual program production

(G-5620)
PHARMADEL LLC
600 Ships Landing Way (19720-4577)
PHONE..............................302 322-1329
Evilio Velasquez, *CEO*
▲ EMP: 15
SQ FT: 28,000
SALES: 4MM **Privately Held**
SIC: **5122** Cosmetics

(G-5621)
PHC INC (HQ)
Also Called: Pioneer Behavioral Health
575 S Dupont Hwy (19720-4606)
PHONE..............................313 831-3500
Bruce A Shear, *President*
EMP: 14
SALES (est): 11.1MM **Publicly Held**
WEB: www.highlandridgehospital.com
SIC: **8063** 8322 Psychiatric hospitals; rehabilitation services

(G-5622)
PHOTON PROGRAMMING
58 Stockton Dr (19720-4318)
PHONE..............................302 328-2925
Thomas Shustack, *Principal*
EMP: 2
SALES (est): 120.6K **Privately Held**
SIC: **3661** Fiber optics communications equipment

(G-5623)
PJ FITZPATRICK INC (PA)
Also Called: Rt Stover
21 Industrial Blvd (19720-2087)
PHONE..............................302 325-2360
Rick Stover, *President*
Scott Schmoyer, *CFO*
Kevin Krapf, *Accountant*
Almena Faux, *Director*
EMP: 70
SQ FT: 26,500
SALES (est): 24MM **Privately Held**
WEB: www.pjfitz.com
SIC: **1761** 1521 Siding contractor; single-family home remodeling, additions & repairs

(G-5624)
PKWY GRAVEL
820 Federal School Ln (19720-5185)
PHONE..............................302 328-5182
Richard Withington, *Owner*
EMP: 2 EST: 2018
SALES (est): 66K **Privately Held**
SIC: **1442** Construction sand & gravel

(G-5625)
PLANET PAYMENT SOLUTIONS INC (HQ)
Also Called: Ipay
100 W Cmmons Blvd Ste 200 (19720)
PHONE..............................516 670-3200
Carl J Williams, *President*
Philip D Beck, *Chairman*
Graham N Arad, *Senior VP*
Andrew Lieberman, *Info Tech Mgr*
EMP: 22
SALES (est): 5.3MM
SALES (corp-wide): 54.3MM **Privately Held**
SIC: **7374** 6411 Data processing service; insurance agents, brokers & service
PA: Planet Payment, Inc.
670 Long Beach Blvd
Long Beach NY 11561
516 670-3200

(G-5626)
PNC BANK NATIONAL ASSOCIATION
1 Penn Mart Ctr (19720-4206)
PHONE..............................302 326-4710
Rick Modell, *Principal*
EMP: 6
SALES (corp-wide): 19.9B **Publicly Held**
SIC: **6799** Investors

HQ: Pnc Bank, National Association
222 Delaware Ave
Wilmington DE 19801
877 762-2000

(G-5627)
PNC BANK NATIONAL ASSOCIATION
1 E Basin Rd (19720-4264)
PHONE..............................302 326-4701
Pedro Viero Jr, *Branch Mgr*
EMP: 24
SALES (corp-wide): 19.9B **Publicly Held**
SIC: **6021** National commercial banks
HQ: Pnc Bank, National Association
222 Delaware Ave
Wilmington DE 19801
877 762-2000

(G-5628)
PNC BANK NATIONAL ASSOCIATION
4643 Stanton Ogletwown Rd (19720)
PHONE..............................302 733-7192
Tony Saimre, *Manager*
EMP: 11
SALES (corp-wide): 19.9B **Publicly Held**
SIC: **6022** State trust companies accepting deposits, commercial
HQ: Pnc Bank, National Association
222 Delaware Ave
Wilmington DE 19801
877 762-2000

(G-5629)
POINT HOPE BRAIN INJURY SPPORT
34 Blevins Dr Ste 5 (19720-4177)
PHONE..............................302 731-7676
Damian Robinson, *Principal*
EMP: 7
SALES (est): 233.6K **Privately Held**
SIC: **8093** Mental health clinic, outpatient

(G-5630)
POLICE & FIRE ROD & GUN CLUB
1 Glen Ave (19720-3528)
PHONE..............................302 655-0304
Fred Durham, *President*
EMP: 5
SALES: 69.3K **Privately Held**
SIC: **7997** 5941 Gun club, membership; firearms

(G-5631)
POLICE ATHLETIC LEAGUE DEL (PA)
Also Called: Police Athletic Leag Del Inc-P
26 Karlyn Dr (19720-1253)
PHONE..............................302 656-9501
Capt Steward Snyder, *President*
Jimmy Riggs, *Exec Dir*
EMP: 8
SALES (est): 244.2K **Privately Held**
WEB: www.palde.org
SIC: **8641** Youth organizations

(G-5632)
PORT CONTRACTORS INC (PA)
529 Terminal Ave (19720-1426)
PHONE..............................302 655-7300
Jean Luc Decaux, *Principal*
Bernard Parisot, *Principal*
Nicolas Clochard Bossuet, *COO*
Mary Anna Thomas, *Vice Pres*
Tom Mason, *Vice Pres*
EMP: 64
SQ FT: 5,000
SALES (est): 20.2MM **Privately Held**
WEB: www.portcontractors.com
SIC: **4789** Freight car loading & unloading

(G-5633)
PORT TO PORT INTL CORP
32 Pyles Ln (19720-1420)
PHONE..............................302 654-2444
Anabel Panayotti, *President*
Gwen North, *Vice Pres*
Dunia Flores, *Sales Executive*
Tania Alfaro, *Marketing Staff*
Karen Ramos, *Office Mgr*
EMP: 40 EST: 1998

SALES (est): 9.5MM **Privately Held**
WEB: www.porttoportintl.com
SIC: **4731** Foreign freight forwarding; freight forwarding

(G-5634)
POWER TRANS INC
12 Mccullough Dr Ste 2 (19720-2076)
PHONE..............................302 322-7110
Hank Warner, *Principal*
EMP: 4
SALES (est): 309K **Privately Held**
SIC: **5085** Bearings

(G-5635)
PRECIOUS YEARS CHILD CARE LLC
200 Robinson Dr (19720-1826)
PHONE..............................302 322-1701
EMP: 5
SALES (est): 72.8K **Privately Held**
SIC: **8351** Child day care services

(G-5636)
PRECISION FLOW LLC
62 Southgate Blvd Ste L (19720-2090)
P.O. Box 875, Clementon NJ (08021-0875)
PHONE..............................302 544-4417
Charles Lafferty III,
EMP: 10
SALES (est): 8MM **Privately Held**
WEB: www.precisionflow.com
SIC: **5085** Valves & fittings

(G-5637)
PREFERRED CONSTRUCTION INC
505 Churchmans Rd (19720-3154)
PHONE..............................302 322-9568
Joseph A Sparco, *President*
John Paul, *Vice Pres*
EMP: 8
SQ FT: 1,500
SALES (est): 865.6K **Privately Held**
WEB: www.preferredconstruction.net
SIC: **1542** 1522 Commercial & office building contractors; residential construction

(G-5638)
PREFERRED ELECTRIC INC
505 Churchmans Rd (19720-3154)
PHONE..............................302 322-1217
Catherine L Sparco, *President*
Joseph Sparco, *Corp Secy*
John Paul Sparco, *Vice Pres*
Larry Buyarski, *Project Mgr*
Terry Short, *Project Mgr*
EMP: 70
SQ FT: 15,000
SALES (est): 10.1MM **Privately Held**
SIC: **1731** General electrical contractor; voice, data & video wiring contractor

(G-5639)
PREVENT ALARM COMPANY LLC
Also Called: Prevent Security and Tech
91 Lukens Dr Ste B (19720-2799)
PHONE..............................302 478-6647
B Painter, *Regl Sales Mgr*
Eric Taylor,
EMP: 6
SALES (est): 967.1K
SALES (corp-wide): 170MM **Privately Held**
SIC: **7382** Burglar alarm maintenance & monitoring
PA: Unified Door And Hardware Group, Llc
1650 Suckle Hwy
Pennsauken NJ 08110
856 320-4868

(G-5640)
PREZOOM LLC
262 Quigley Blvd (19720-9004)
PHONE..............................302 414-8204
Claire Davids, *Mng Member*
EMP: 7
SQ FT: 12,000
SALES (est): 470K **Privately Held**
SIC: **3086** Packaging & shipping materials, foamed plastic

New Castle - New Castle County (G-5641)

(G-5641)
PRINCE MANUFACTURING CO
301 Pigeon Point Rd (19720-1448)
PHONE..................646 747-4208
Elizabeth Reinhart, *Principal*
◆ **EMP:** 10
SALES (est): 1.5MM **Privately Held**
SIC: 2752 Commercial printing, lithographic

(G-5642)
PRINCE MINERALS LLC
301 Pigeon Point Rd (19720-1448)
P.O. Box 251, Quincy IL (62306-0251)
PHONE..................646 747-4200
Mike Fix, *Branch Mgr*
Fred Feazel, *Manager*
EMP: 13
SALES (corp-wide): 1.5MM **Privately Held**
SIC: 3295 Blast furnace slag
HQ: Prince Minerals Llc
  15311 Vantage Pkwy W
  Houston TX 77032
  646 747-4222

(G-5643)
PRINCE TELECOM LLC (HQ)
Also Called: Leading Communication Contrs
551 Mews Dr Ste A (19720-2798)
PHONE..................302 324-1800
Hector Cabrera, *Area Mgr*
Joe Sanchez, *Area Mgr*
Barry L Fischer, *Vice Pres*
Tom Tideman, *Vice Pres*
Jay Linden, *Project Mgr*
EMP: 60
SQ FT: 6,000
SALES (est): 174.3MM
SALES (corp-wide): 3.1B **Publicly Held**
SIC: 1731 Cable television installation
PA: Dycom Industries, Inc.
  11780 Us Highway 1 # 600
  Palm Beach Gardens FL 33408
  561 627-7171

(G-5644)
PRINTCUREMENT
122 Delaware St Ste 300 (19720-4814)
PHONE..................302 249-6100
EMP: 2
SALES (est): 83.9K **Privately Held**
SIC: 2752 Commercial printing, lithographic

(G-5645)
PRINTPACK INC
Also Called: Flexible Packaging Group
600 Grantham Ln (19720-4852)
P.O. Box 110 (19720-0110)
PHONE..................302 323-4000
Steve Aguillard, *Branch Mgr*
EMP: 200
SALES (corp-wide): 1.3B **Privately Held**
WEB: www.printpack.com
SIC: 2673 3081 2671 Bags: plastic, laminated & coated; plastic film & sheet; packaging paper & plastics film, coated & laminated
HQ: Printpack, Inc.
  2800 Overlook Pkwy Ne
  Atlanta GA 30339
  404 460-7000

(G-5646)
PRINTPACK ENTERPRISES INC (HQ)
River Rd & Grantham Ln (19720)
PHONE..................302 323-0900
Gay M Love, *Ch of Bd*
John Casula, *President*
Dennis M Love, *President*
James E Love III, *Vice Pres*
▲ **EMP:** 1 EST: 1998
SALES: 1.3B **Privately Held**
SIC: 2673 Bags: plastic, laminated & coated
PA: Printpack Holdings, Inc.
  2800 Overlook Pkwy Ne
  Atlanta GA 30339
  404 460-7000

(G-5647)
PRO PHYSICAL THERAPY PA
Also Called: ATI
2032 New Castle Ave (19720-7703)
PHONE..................302 654-1700
Matthew Haney, *President*
EMP: 10
SALES (est): 327.4K **Privately Held**
SIC: 8049 Physical therapist

(G-5648)
PRO-BOND AUTO GLASS
23 Parkway Cir Ste 7 (19720-4019)
PHONE..................302 324-8500
Tony Milam, *Owner*
EMP: 4
SALES (est): 213.3K **Privately Held**
SIC: 7536 Automotive glass replacement shops

(G-5649)
PROCLEAN
28 Mifflin Ave (19720-1157)
PHONE..................302 654-1074
EMP: 6
SALES: 52K **Privately Held**
SIC: 7349 7389 Repair Services

(G-5650)
PROTECH DELIVERY & ASSEMBLY
106 Somers Ave (19720-2011)
PHONE..................302 449-5003
Lisa Gaorfal, *President*
George Gaorfal, *Vice Pres*
EMP: 18
SALES (est): 998.7K **Privately Held**
WEB: www.protechassembly.net
SIC: 7389 Bicycle assembly service

(G-5651)
PTM MANUFACTURING LLC
196 Quigley Blvd Ste A (19720-4176)
PHONE..................302 455-9733
Pete Faverio IV, *Manager*
Timothy Shelton,
Michale Zimmy,
▲ **EMP:** 8
SALES (est): 1.9MM **Privately Held**
SIC: 3564 Air cleaning systems

(G-5652)
PUBLIC SYSTEMS INC
Also Called: P S I Maximus
2 Penns Way Ste 406 (19720-2407)
PHONE..................302 326-4500
Reese Robinson, *CEO*
Clark Brown Sr, *President*
Michael Moore, *Treasurer*
EMP: 30
SALES (est): 1.9MM **Privately Held**
WEB: www.publicsystems.com
SIC: 7373 Systems software development services

(G-5653)
PULSAR PRINT LLC
243 Quigley Blvd Ste K (19720-4191)
PHONE..................302 394-9202
EMP: 2 EST: 2016
SALES (est): 111.6K **Privately Held**
SIC: 2752 Commercial printing, lithographic

(G-5654)
PULTE HOME CORPORATION
206 Jestan Blvd (19720-5214)
PHONE..................302 999-9525
Steve Anderson, *Branch Mgr*
EMP: 45
SALES (corp-wide): 10.1B **Publicly Held**
SIC: 1521 Single-family housing construction
HQ: Pulte Home Company, Llc
  3350 Peachtree Rd Ne # 150
  Atlanta GA 30326
  248 647-2750

(G-5655)
PYRAMID EDUCATIONAL CONS
350 Churchmans Rd Ste B (19720-3146)
PHONE..................302 368-2515
Andrew Bondy, *President*
EMP: 30

SALES (est): 3MM **Privately Held**
WEB: www.pecs.com
SIC: 8748 Educational consultant

(G-5656)
QORO LLC
166 S Dupont Hwy Ste B (19720-4159)
PHONE..................302 322-5900
Col Frank D Davis, *CEO*
E William Jensen, *President*
Katherine Griffith, *Corp Secy*
EMP: 7
SALES: 100K **Privately Held**
WEB: www.kitchensforcooks.com
SIC: 2741 Art copy & poster publishing

(G-5657)
QUALITY FINISHERS INC
1 Merit Dr (19720-3683)
P.O. Box 288 (19720-0288)
PHONE..................302 325-1963
John Stachowski, *President*
Korang Stachowski, *Treasurer*
EMP: 8
SQ FT: 5,000
SALES (est): 543K **Privately Held**
WEB: www.qualityfinishers.com
SIC: 1721 1521 Exterior residential painting contractor; general remodeling, single-family houses

(G-5658)
QUALITY ROFG SUP LANCASTER INC
9 Parkway Cir (19720-4077)
PHONE..................302 322-8322
Todd Doussard, *Opers-Prdtn-Mfg*
Todd Bussard, *Branch Mgr*
EMP: 9
SALES (corp-wide): 7.1B **Publicly Held**
SIC: 5033 Roofing, asphalt & sheet metal
HQ: Quality Roofing Supply Company Of Lancaster, Inc.
  737 Flory Mill Rd
  Lancaster PA 17601
  717 569-2661

(G-5659)
QUEST DIAGNOSTICS INCORPORATED
525 E Basin Rd (19720-4230)
PHONE..................302 322-4651
C Clements, *Manager*
EMP: 12
SALES (corp-wide): 7.5B **Publicly Held**
WEB: www.questdiagnostics.com
SIC: 8071 Medical laboratories
PA: Quest Diagnostics Incorporated
  500 Plaza Dr Ste G
  Secaucus NJ 07094
  973 520-2700

(G-5660)
R & E EXCAVATION LLC
226 Harlequin Dr (19720-8900)
PHONE..................302 750-5226
Eric Knabe, *Principal*
EMP: 5
SALES (est): 310.1K **Privately Held**
SIC: 1794 Excavation work

(G-5661)
R A CHANCE PLUMBING INC
23 Parkway Cir Ste 5 (19720-4019)
PHONE..................302 324-8200
Richard A Chance, *President*
EMP: 8
SALES (est): 677.2K **Privately Held**
SIC: 1711 Plumbing contractors

(G-5662)
R E MICHEL COMPANY LLC
184 Quigley Blvd (19720-4104)
PHONE..................302 322-7480
Robert Rapposelli, *Manager*
EMP: 4
SALES (corp-wide): 898.2MM **Privately Held**
WEB: www.remichel.com
SIC: 5075 Air conditioning equipment, except room units
PA: R. E. Michel Company, Llc
  1 Re Michel Dr
  Glen Burnie MD 21060
  410 760-4000

(G-5663)
R L LABORATORIES INC
245 Quigley Blvd Ste B (19720-4192)
P.O. Box 326, Claymont (19703-0326)
PHONE..................302 328-1686
Ray Lyons, *President*
EMP: 10
SQ FT: 1,700
SALES (est): 1.1MM **Privately Held**
SIC: 8734 Water testing laboratory

(G-5664)
RABSPAN INC
13 King Ct Ste 1 (19720-1523)
PHONE..................302 324-8104
Fax: 302 324-8105
EMP: 7
SALES (est): 560K **Privately Held**
SIC: 1711 Plumbing/Heating/Air Cond Contractor

(G-5665)
RANDOLPHS REFUSE SERVICE INC
28 Dover Ave (19720)
P.O. Box 2718, Wilmington (19805-0718)
PHONE..................302 658-5674
Fred Randolph, *President*
EMP: 6
SQ FT: 5,000
SALES (est): 137.5K **Privately Held**
SIC: 4953 Rubbish collection & disposal

(G-5666)
RAPID RECYCLING INC
42 Reads Way (19720-1649)
PHONE..................302 324-5360
Kathi Guy, *Manager*
EMP: 4
SALES (corp-wide): 123.3MM **Privately Held**
SIC: 4953 Recycling, waste materials
HQ: Rapid Recycling, Inc.
  5 Brower Ave
  Oaks PA 19456

(G-5667)
RAVEN CRANE & EQUIPMENT CO LLC
196 Quigley Blvd Ste B (19720-4176)
PHONE..................302 998-1000
Charles Adams, *Mng Member*
EMP: 6
SALES (est): 906.5K **Privately Held**
SIC: 7353 Cranes & aerial lift equipment, rental or leasing

(G-5668)
RCD TIMBER PRODUCTS INC (PA)
1699 Matassino Rd (19720-2086)
PHONE..................302 778-5700
Robert C Donehower, *President*
Greg Longchamp, *General Mgr*
Joanne Donehower, *Corp Secy*
EMP: 9
SALES (est): 2MM **Privately Held**
WEB: www.rcdtimber.com
SIC: 2448 5031 Pallets, wood; pallets, wood

(G-5669)
RE COMMUNITY HOLDINGS II INC
Also Called: Recommunity
1101 Lambson Ln (19720-2186)
PHONE..................302 778-9793
Steven Bodman, *Manager*
EMP: 9
SALES (corp-wide): 10B **Publicly Held**
SIC: 4953 Recycling, waste materials
HQ: Re Community Holdings Ii, Inc.
  2440 Whitehall Park Dr # 800
  Charlotte NC 28273

(G-5670)
REFRATING LLC
92 Reads Way Ste 104 (19720-1631)
PHONE..................617 358-2789
Mark Williams,
EMP: 5
SALES (est): 117.2K **Privately Held**
SIC: 7372 Application computer software

GEOGRAPHIC SECTION
New Castle - New Castle County (G-5703)

(G-5671)
RENT-A-CENTER INC
185 Penn Mart Shopping Ct (19720-4208)
PHONE 302 322-4335
Juan Perez, *Branch Mgr*
EMP: 20
SALES (corp-wide): 2.6B **Publicly Held**
WEB: www.rentcenter.com
SIC: 7359 Appliance rental; furniture rental; home entertainment equipment rental; television rental
PA: Rent-A-Center, Inc.
5501 Headquarters Dr
Plano TX 75024
972 801-1100

(G-5672)
REPROGRAPHICS CENTER INC
Also Called: Rci
298 Churchmans Rd (19720-3110)
PHONE 302 328-5019
Joan A Janis, *President*
Michael J Janis, *Vice Pres*
EMP: 8 **EST:** 1959
SQ FT: 6,000
SALES (est): 900K **Privately Held**
WEB: www.rciplot.com
SIC: 7334 5049 Blueprinting service; drafting supplies

(G-5673)
RES-CARE INC
908 Churchmans Road Ext (19720-3109)
PHONE 302 323-1436
Meloni Palmer, *Branch Mgr*
EMP: 48
SALES (corp-wide): 2B **Privately Held**
SIC: 8052 Home for the mentally retarded, with health care
HQ: Res-Care, Inc.
805 N Whittington Pkwy
Louisville KY 40222
502 394-2100

(G-5674)
RESH LLC
206 Jestan Blvd (19720-5214)
PHONE 302 543-5469
Sherell Flagg, *Mng Member*
Michael Flagg,
EMP: 13 **EST:** 2009
SALES (est): 481.3K **Privately Held**
SIC: 7231 5122 Cosmetologist; cosmetics, perfumes & hair products

(G-5675)
RESOURCE INTL INC
18 Boulden Cir Ste 10 (19720-3494)
PHONE 302 762-4501
Michael Sullivan, *President*
▲ **EMP:** 10
SQ FT: 3,000
SALES: 3MM **Privately Held**
SIC: 3089 Automotive parts, plastic

(G-5676)
REVOLUTION RECOVERY DEL LLC
1101 Lambson Ln (19720-2186)
PHONE 302 356-3000
Fern Gookin, *Director*
EMP: 11 **EST:** 2012
SALES (est): 432.1K **Privately Held**
SIC: 2611 Pulp manufactured from waste or recycled paper

(G-5677)
REYES REBECA
Also Called: Kidd Mc
1303 Goldeneye Dr (19720-8923)
PHONE 302 276-9132
Rebeca Reyes, *Owner*
Ivalisse King, *Principal*
EMP: 5
SALES (est): 104.7K **Privately Held**
SIC: 7389

(G-5678)
RICORE INC
13 Rizzo Ave (19720-2139)
PHONE 302 656-8158
Joseph Rizzo, *President*
EMP: 4
SALES (est): 446.9K **Privately Held**
SIC: 8748 Business consulting

(G-5679)
RIDGAWAY PHILIPS OF DELAWARE
908 Churchmans Road Ext B (19720-3109)
PHONE 302 323-1436
Jacqueline Moore, *President*
EMP: 6
SALES (est): 132.5K **Privately Held**
SIC: 8082 Home health care services

(G-5680)
ROBERT J PEOPLES INC
3020 Bowlarama Dr (19720-1317)
P.O. Box 65 (19720-0065)
PHONE 302 984-2017
Steven M Pedrick, *Owner*
EMP: 17
SALES (est): 960.5K **Privately Held**
SIC: 1721 Painting & paper hanging

(G-5681)
ROBERT P HART DDS
92 Reads Way Ste 101 (19720-1631)
PHONE 302 328-1513
Robert P Hart DMD, *Owner*
EMP: 4
SALES (est): 61.5K **Privately Held**
SIC: 8021 Offices & clinics of dentists

(G-5682)
RON ELL HARDWARE INC
16 Darlington Rd (19720-2313)
PHONE 302 328-8997
Ronald Fields, *President*
Mary Ellen Fields, *Treasurer*
EMP: 12
SALES (est): 1.2MM **Privately Held**
SIC: 5072 Hardware

(G-5683)
RONDO SPECIALTY FOODS LTD
118 Quigley Blvd (19720-4104)
PHONE 800 724-6636
P J Leary, *Principal*
◆ **EMP:** 4
SALES (est): 626.3K **Privately Held**
WEB: www.rondofoods.com
SIC: 5149 Specialty food items

(G-5684)
ROSE HILL COMMUNITY CENTER
19 Lambson Ln (19720-2118)
PHONE 302 656-8513
Dara Dupont, *Deputy Dir*
Deborah Deubert, *Administration*
EMP: 12
SQ FT: 47,000
SALES: 1MM **Privately Held**
SIC: 8322 8299 8351 Senior citizens' center or association; educational services; head start center, except in conjunction with school

(G-5685)
ROSLE U S A CORP
802 Centerpoint Blvd (19720-8123)
PHONE 302 326-4801
Eric Jones, *General Mgr*
▲ **EMP:** 33
SALES (est): 3.2MM **Privately Held**
WEB: www.rosleusa.com
SIC: 5023 Kitchen tools & utensils; stainless steel flatware

(G-5686)
ROYAL INSTRUMENTS INC
266 Quigley Blvd (19720-4106)
PHONE 302 328-5900
Dominick Paladinetti, *Manager*
EMP: 6
SALES (corp-wide): 4.4MM **Privately Held**
WEB: www.royalinstruments.com
SIC: 5085 Valves & fittings
PA: Royal Instruments Inc
835 Industrial Hwy Ste 2
Cinnaminson NJ 08077
856 829-9888

(G-5687)
ROYAL PEST MANAGEMENT
53 Mccullough Dr (19720-2080)
PHONE 302 322-3600
George Milyo, *General Mgr*
Phil Mullen, *Principal*
EMP: 7
SALES (est): 490K **Privately Held**
SIC: 7342 Pest control in structures

(G-5688)
ROYAL PEST SOLUTIONS INC
53 Mccullough Dr (19720-2080)
PHONE 302 322-6665
Roy Richardson, *President*
Roger Richardson, *Exec VP*
James Conroy, *CFO*
EMP: 35
SALES (est): 5MM
SALES (corp-wide): 14.6B **Publicly Held**
WEB: www.royalfume.com
SIC: 7342 Exterminating & fumigating; pest control services
PA: Ecolab Inc.
1 Ecolab Pl
Saint Paul MN 55102
800 232-6522

(G-5689)
ROYAL TERMITE & PEST CTRL INC
Also Called: Royal Termite and Pest Control
53 Mccullough Dr (19720-2080)
PHONE 302 322-3600
Roy Richardson, *President*
Donna Richardson, *Corp Secy*
EMP: 38
SQ FT: 1,800
SALES (est): 3.4MM **Privately Held**
SIC: 7342 Pest control in structures; termite control

(G-5690)
RP VENTURES AND HOLDINGS INC (PA)
9 Bellecor Dr (19720-1763)
PHONE 410 398-3000
Richard Piendak, *President*
EMP: 35
SQ FT: 8,000
SALES (est): 5.5MM **Privately Held**
WEB: www.richardspaving.com
SIC: 1771 1611 Blacktop (asphalt) work; driveway contractor; parking lot construction; highway & street construction

(G-5691)
RUSSELL PLYWOOD INC
3 Mccullough Dr (19720-2007)
PHONE 302 689-0137
Paul Koronoski, *Branch Mgr*
EMP: 12
SALES (corp-wide): 20.6MM **Privately Held**
SIC: 5031 Plywood
PA: Russell Plywood, Inc.
401 Old Wyomissing Rd
Reading PA 19611
610 374-3206

(G-5692)
SABRE AMB LLC
Also Called: Clarion Hotel - The Belle
1612 N Dupont Hwy (19720-1904)
PHONE 302 299-1400
EMP: 37
SALES (est): 2.6MM
SALES (corp-wide): 1B **Publicly Held**
SIC: 7011 Hotels
PA: Choice Hotels International, Inc.
1 Choice Hotels Cir
Rockville MD 20850
301 592-5000

(G-5693)
SAINT ANTHONYS CLUB
1017 Gray St (19720-6747)
PHONE 302 328-9440
Butch Deangelo, *President*
EMP: 4
SALES (est): 214.4K **Privately Held**
SIC: 7997 Country club, membership

(G-5694)
SANOSIL INTERNATIONAL LLC
91 Lukens Dr Ste A (19720-2799)
PHONE 302 454-8102
Christopher Ungermann, *CEO*
EMP: 19

SALES (est): 2.4MM **Privately Held**
SIC: 8732 2842 3589 Market analysis or research; ammonia, household; water treatment equipment, industrial

(G-5695)
SCOTTISH VENTURES LLC
5 Wildfire Ln (19720-3859)
PHONE 302 382-6057
Andrew P McDannels,
EMP: 8 **EST:** 2009
SALES (est): 741.3K **Privately Held**
WEB: www.scottishventuresllc.com
SIC: 8742 7389 6799 Marketing consulting services; ; real estate investors, except property operators

(G-5696)
SDG DEFENSE INDUSTRY LLC
42 N Independence Blvd (19720-4457)
PHONE 302 526-4800
EMP: 2
SALES (est): 62.5K **Privately Held**
SIC: 3999 Mfg Misc Products

(G-5697)
SEAN E CHIPMAN
200 Centerpoint Blvd A (19720-4175)
PHONE 302 300-4307
Sean E Chipman, *Owner*
EMP: 18
SALES (est): 286.9K **Privately Held**
SIC: 7389 8721 Financial services; payroll accounting service

(G-5698)
SECURE SELF STORAGE (PA)
1020 Bear Rd (19720-4602)
PHONE 302 832-0400
Ken Newberry, *Principal*
EMP: 7 **EST:** 2007
SALES (est): 2.2MM **Privately Held**
SIC: 4225 4226 Warehousing, self-storage; household goods & furniture storage

(G-5699)
SERVICE ENERGY LLC
29 Harbor View Dr (19720-2179)
PHONE 302 734-7433
Michael Steiner, *Branch Mgr*
EMP: 4 **Privately Held**
SIC: 5172 Petroleum products
PA: Service Energy, L.L.C.
3799 N Dupont Hwy
Dover DE 19901

(G-5700)
SERVICE UNLIMITED INC
Also Called: S U I
19 Southgate Blvd Unit A (19720-2231)
PHONE 302 326-2665
Carl R Wolf, *President*
Brian Martinenza Jr, *Vice Pres*
Ralph R Rose, *Vice Pres*
Ralph Rose, *Vice Pres*
EMP: 36 **EST:** 1962
SQ FT: 15,000
SALES (est): 6.4MM **Privately Held**
WEB: www.serviceunlimitedinc.com
SIC: 1711 1731 Warm air heating & air conditioning contractor; electronic controls installation

(G-5701)
SEVYS AUTO SERVICE INC
245 Christiana Rd (19720-2907)
PHONE 302 328-0839
Allan Hammond, *Owner*
EMP: 6
SALES (est): 501.9K **Privately Held**
SIC: 7538 7539 General automotive repair shops; brake services

(G-5702)
SF EXPRESS CORPORATION
1140 River Rd (19720)
PHONE 302 407-6155
EMP: 15
SALES (est): 1MM **Privately Held**
SIC: 4212 Delivery service, vehicular

(G-5703)
SF LOGISTICS LIMITED
1140 River Rd (19720)
PHONE 302 317-3954
Boris Tikhonov, *Director*

New Castle - New Castle County (G-5704)

EMP: 50
SALES (est): 127.9K **Privately Held**
SIC: 4731 Freight transportation arrangement

(G-5704)
SHAVONE LOVES KIDS DAY CARE
Also Called: Little Sunshines
6 Darien Ct (19720-3804)
PHONE.................302 544-6170
Kevin Thomas, *Principal*
EMP: 5
SALES (est): 64K **Privately Held**
SIC: 8351 Child day care services

(G-5705)
SHOP TALK INC
101 E Franklin Ave (19720-3309)
PHONE.................302 322-5860
EMP: 4
SALES (est): 130K **Privately Held**
SIC: 7231 Beauty Shop

(G-5706)
SHRIJI HOSPITALITY (NOT LLC)
Also Called: New Castle Travelodge
1213 West Ave (19720-6250)
PHONE.................302 654-5544
Peter Bhai,
EMP: 12 EST: 2001
SQ FT: 600
SALES (est): 294.6K **Privately Held**
SIC: 7011 Motels

(G-5707)
SID TOOL CO INC
Also Called: Holloway Bros Tools
19 E Commons Blvd (19720-1734)
PHONE.................302 322-5441
Donald Macmaon, *Branch Mgr*
EMP: 18 **Publicly Held**
WEB: www.screwshop.com
SIC: 5085 Industrial supplies
HQ: Sid Tool Co., Inc.
  75 Maxess Rd
  Melville NY 11747
  516 812-2000

(G-5708)
SIECK WHOLESALE FLORIST INC
11 Southgate Blvd (19720-2069)
P.O. Box 1166, Hockessin (19707-5166)
PHONE.................302 356-2000
Don Freeburn, *President*
Ed Michel, *Vice Pres*
EMP: 12
SALES (est): 672.2K **Privately Held**
SIC: 5193 Flowers & florists' supplies

(G-5709)
SIEMENS CORPORATION
800 Centerpoint Blvd A (19720-8123)
PHONE.................302 220-1544
EMP: 4
SALES (corp-wide): 96.9B **Privately Held**
SIC: 3661 Telephones & telephone apparatus
HQ: Siemens Corporation
  300 New Jersey Ave Nw # 10
  Washington DC 20001
  202 434-4800

(G-5710)
SIEMENS HEALTHCARE DIAGNOSTICS
200 Centerpoint Blvd (19720-4175)
PHONE.................302 631-8006
Tony Oleck, *Branch Mgr*
EMP: 90
SALES (corp-wide): 96.9B **Privately Held**
WEB: www.dpcweb.com
SIC: 2835 In vitro & in vivo diagnostic substances
HQ: Siemens Healthcare Diagnostics Inc.
  511 Benedict Ave
  Tarrytown NY 10591
  914 631-8000

(G-5711)
SIGNATURE CNSTR SVCS LLC
Also Called: Signature Cnstr & Design
3029 Bowlarama Dr (19720-1316)
P.O. Box 10285, Wilmington (19850-0285)
PHONE.................302 691-1010
Eric Holloway, *Principal*
EMP: 10
SALES (est): 337.6K **Privately Held**
SIC: 1521 Single-family home remodeling, additions & repairs

(G-5712)
SIGNATURE FURNITURE SVCS LLC
Also Called: Signature Construction Svcs
3029 Bowlarama Dr (19720-1316)
P.O. Box 10285, Wilmington (19850-0285)
PHONE.................302 691-1010
Eric Holloway,
EMP: 40
SQ FT: 54,000
SALES (est): 8.1MM **Privately Held**
WEB: www.salessolutionsgroupllc.com
SIC: 1542 Commercial & office building contractors

(G-5713)
SIGNATURE GROUP MANAGEMENT CO
3029 Bowlarama Dr (19720-1316)
P.O. Box 10285, Wilmington (19850-0285)
PHONE.................302 691-1010
Eric Holloway, *Principal*
EMP: 4
SALES (est): 113.2K **Privately Held**
SIC: 8741 Office management

(G-5714)
SIMPLEX TIME RECORDER LLC
Also Called: Simplex Time Recorder 557
18 Boulden Cir Ste 36 (19720-3494)
PHONE.................302 325-6300
Joe Cerasino, *Manager*
EMP: 16 **Privately Held**
WEB: www.comtec-alaska.com
SIC: 5063 1731 Fire alarm systems; electrical work
HQ: Simplex Time Recorder Llc
  50 Technology Dr
  Westminster MA 01441

(G-5715)
SKY NAILS
287 Christiana Rd Ste 15 (19720-2978)
PHONE.................302 322-5949
Kuoc Len, *Owner*
EMP: 4
SALES (est): 79.4K **Privately Held**
SIC: 7231 Manicurist, pedicurist

(G-5716)
SKYWAYS MOTOR LODGE CORP
Also Called: Quality Inn
147 N Dupont Hwy (19720-3135)
PHONE.................302 328-6666
Alan Spiro, *President*
Mark Mattei, *Admin Sec*
EMP: 25 EST: 1961
SQ FT: 8,000
SALES (est): 1.1MM **Privately Held**
SIC: 7011 Hotels & motels

(G-5717)
SMART
12 Varmar Dr (19720-2036)
PHONE.................302 655-6084
Nelson Seeney, *Branch Mgr*
EMP: 10
SALES (corp-wide): 27.7MM **Privately Held**
SIC: 8631 Labor unions & similar labor organizations
PA: Smart
  24950 Country Club Blvd # 340
  North Olmsted OH 44070
  216 228-9400

(G-5718)
SMARTER HOME & OFFICE LLC
18 Monticello Blvd (19720-3404)
PHONE.................302 723-9313
Brian T Owens,
EMP: 5

SALES: 500K **Privately Held**
SIC: 1542 Nonresidential construction

(G-5719)
SNICKERS DITCH TRUNK COMPANY
182 E 4th St (19720-4539)
PHONE.................302 325-1762
Kenneth Sturgis, *Owner*
EMP: 3
SALES (est): 212.1K **Privately Held**
SIC: 3161 Trunks

(G-5720)
SOCIAL ENTERPRISE LLC
Also Called: Interrupcion Fair Trade
250 Centerpoint Blvd (19720-4197)
PHONE.................718 417-4076
Rafael Goldberg, *CEO*
Diego Gonzales, *President*
Michela Calabrese, *Vice Pres*
▲ EMP: 8
SALES (est): 3.4MM **Privately Held**
WEB: www.interruption.com
SIC: 6799 Commodity contract trading companies

(G-5721)
SOLAR FOUNDATIONS USA INC
1142 River Rd (19720-5106)
PHONE.................855 738-7200
EMP: 12
SALES (est): 511.8K **Privately Held**
SIC: 8641 Civic social & fraternal associations

(G-5722)
SOLUTION ON-CALL SERVICES LLC
19 Lambson Ln Ste 108-B (19720-2118)
PHONE.................302 353-4328
Dorothy Jones-Britton,
EMP: 27
SQ FT: 160
SALES (est): 357K **Privately Held**
SIC: 8059 Personal care home, with health care

(G-5723)
SOURCE SUPPLY INC
6 Bellecor Dr Ste 104 (19720-1744)
P.O. Box 3318, Wilmington (19804-4318)
PHONE.................302 328-5110
Dave Brown, *President*
Bianca Gaidos, *Sales Mgr*
Donna Shamblin, *Director*
EMP: 17 EST: 2000
SALES (est): 3.2MM **Privately Held**
SIC: 5087 Janitors' supplies

(G-5724)
SOUTHERN GLAZERS WINE
615 Lambson Ln (19720-2103)
PHONE.................302 656-4487
Jim Miller, *General Mgr*
EMP: 30
SALES (corp-wide): 12.3B **Privately Held**
SIC: 5181 5182 Beer & ale; bottling wines & liquors
PA: Southern Glazer's Wine And Spirits, Llc
  1600 Nw 163rd St
  Miami FL 33169
  305 625-4171

(G-5725)
SOUTHERN PRINTING
1053 Lower Twin Lane Rd (19720)
PHONE.................302 832-3475
EMP: 2 EST: 2008
SALES (est): 159.9K **Privately Held**
SIC: 2752 Lithographic Commercial Printing

(G-5726)
SOUTHERN WINE SPIRITS DEL LLC
Also Called: Southern Glazers Wine Spirits
615 Lambson Ln (19720-2103)
PHONE.................800 292-7890
Ashley Nichols, *Division Mgr*
Tam Jessica, *Accounts Mgr*
Evan Grabowski, *Sales Staff*
Hernandez Linda, *Administration*
▲ EMP: 14

SALES (est): 2MM **Privately Held**
SIC: 2084 Wines, brandy & brandy spirits

(G-5727)
SPACECON LLC (HQ)
292 Churchmans Rd (19720-3110)
PHONE.................302 322-9285
Leonard Woerner, *President*
B G Dicarlo, *Corp Secy*
EMP: 9
SALES (est): 15.9MM **Privately Held**
SIC: 1742 1752 Drywall; floor laying & floor work
PA: Smucker Company
  15 Newport Rd
  Leola PA 17540
  717 396-8900

(G-5728)
SPARK
950 W Basin Rd (19720-1008)
PHONE.................302 324-2203
Kelly Housen, *Principal*
Desiray Raposa, *Accounts Mgr*
Kelly McDonald, *Manager*
EMP: 3 EST: 2007
SALES (est): 114.8K **Privately Held**
SIC: 2711 Newspapers, publishing & printing

(G-5729)
SPICER MULLIKIN FUNERAL HOMES (PA)
1000 N Dupont Hwy (19720-2537)
PHONE.................302 368-9500
Harvey C Smith Jr, *President*
Frank C Mayer Jr, *Vice Pres*
Katherine Angell, *Consultant*
William King, *Director*
John Meyer, *Director*
EMP: 20
SQ FT: 8,000
SALES (est): 2.5MM **Privately Held**
SIC: 7261 Funeral home

(G-5730)
SPRING FLOOR TECH LLC
1m King Ave (19720-1511)
PHONE.................302 528-3474
Jeffrey Martino,
EMP: 4
SQ FT: 1,800
SALES (est): 340.9K **Privately Held**
SIC: 5091 Gymnasium equipment

(G-5731)
SPRINT COMMUNICATIONS INC
Also Called: Sprint Sprint
1505 N Dupont Hwy (19720-1901)
PHONE.................302 613-4004
EMP: 36 **Publicly Held**
SIC: 4813 Local & long distance telephone communications
HQ: Sprint Communications, Inc.
  6200 Sprint Pkwy
  Overland Park KS 66251
  855 848-3280

(G-5732)
SPRINT SPECTRUM LP
118 N Dupont Hwy (19720-3102)
PHONE.................302 322-1712
Jonathon Yi, *Branch Mgr*
EMP: 22 **Publicly Held**
SIC: 4813 Local & long distance telephone communications
HQ: Sprint Spectrum L.P.
  6800 Sprint Pkwy
  Overland Park KS 66251

(G-5733)
SSS CLUTCH COMPANY INC
610 W Basin Rd (19720-6448)
PHONE.................302 322-8080
Morgan Hendry, *President*
Randall Attix, *Manager*
▲ EMP: 7 EST: 1984
SQ FT: 10,000
SALES (est): 1.6MM **Privately Held**
SIC: 3568 Clutches, except vehicular

(G-5734)
ST FRANCIS FAMILY CARE
612 Ferry Cut Off St (19720-4549)
PHONE.................302 554-5127
EMP: 8

SALES (est): 82.2K **Privately Held**
SIC: 8062 General Hospital

(G-5735)
STAGING DIMENSIONS INC
31 Blevins Dr Ste A (19720-4170)
PHONE....................302 328-4100
Scott Humphrey, *President*
Chris Bates, *Sales Staff*
Chris Bogia, *Sales Staff*
Ashley McDonough, *Graphic Designe*
EMP: 10
SQ FT: 10,000
SALES (est): 1.7MM **Privately Held**
SIC: 3999 Stage hardware & equipment, except lighting

(G-5736)
STAGING DIMESIONS INC
Also Called: Mathias
31 Blevins Dr Ste A (19720-4170)
PHONE....................302 328-4100
Scott Humphrey, *President*
Kim Moore, *Manager*
EMP: 16 **EST:** 2001
SQ FT: 8,000
SALES: 1.2MM **Privately Held**
SIC: 3999 Stage hardware & equipment, except lighting

(G-5737)
STANDARD DISTRIBUTING CO INC (PA)
100 Mews Dr (19720-2792)
PHONE....................302 655-5511
Eugene M Tigani, *President*
F Gregory Tigani, *Vice Pres*
J Vincent Tigani Jr, *Vice Pres*
▲ **EMP:** 100 **EST:** 1933
SQ FT: 115,000
SALES (est): 46.5MM **Privately Held**
WEB: www.standardde.com
SIC: 5181 5182 Beer & other fermented malt liquors; wine

(G-5738)
STANDARD INSURANCE COMPANY
10 Corporate Cir (19720-2418)
PHONE....................302 322-9922
J Greg Ness, *Branch Mgr*
EMP: 4 **Privately Held**
SIC: 6411 Insurance agents, brokers & service
HQ: Standard Insurance Company
920 Sw 6th Ave Ste 1100
Portland OR 97204
971 321-7000

(G-5739)
STEEL AND METAL SERVICE (PA)
407 Old Airport Rd (19720-1001)
PHONE....................302 322-9960
Sam Caputo, *President*
Maureen Allen, *CFO*
EMP: 4
SALES (est): 2.5MM **Privately Held**
WEB: www.steelliq.com
SIC: 5051 5093 Steel; metal scrap & waste materials

(G-5740)
SUM INC
Also Called: Stanley Steamer Carpet
31 Southgate Blvd (19720-2069)
P.O. Box 195, Hockessin (19707-0195)
PHONE....................302 322-0831
Jane Moore, *President*
Janice Underwood, *Corp Secy*
EMP: 20
SQ FT: 5,000
SALES (est): 2MM **Privately Held**
SIC: 7217 Carpet & furniture cleaning on location; upholstery cleaning on customer premises

(G-5741)
SUMMIT STEEL INC
201 Edwards Ave (19720-4857)
P.O. Box 730 (19720-0730)
PHONE....................302 325-3220
Jerry Tompkins, *President*
Joseph L Irwin, *Vice Pres*
EMP: 55

SQ FT: 13,000
SALES (est): 15MM **Privately Held**
SIC: 3441 1791 Building components, structural steel; structural steel erection

(G-5742)
SUN HOTEL INC
Also Called: Econo Lodge
232 S Dupont Hwy (19720-4130)
PHONE....................302 322-0711
Debbie Patel, *General Mgr*
EMP: 8
SQ FT: 34,000
SALES (est): 836.7K **Privately Held**
SIC: 7011 Hotels & motels

(G-5743)
SUNBELT RENTALS INC
453 Pulaski Hwy (19720-3901)
PHONE....................302 669-0595
Cindy Blevins, *Branch Mgr*
EMP: 5
SALES (corp-wide): 5.9B **Privately Held**
SIC: 7353 Heavy construction equipment rental
HQ: Sunbelt Rentals, Inc.
2341 Deerfield Dr
Fort Mill SC 29715
803 578-5811

(G-5744)
SUSAN R AUSTIN
Also Called: Guiding Hearts Family Daycare
103 Lesley Ln (19720-3329)
PHONE....................302 322-4685
Sue Austin, *Principal*
EMP: 5
SALES (est): 54.6K **Privately Held**
SIC: 8351 Child day care services

(G-5745)
SUSSEX COUNTY FEDERAL CR UN
121 Centerpoint Blvd (19720-4180)
PHONE....................302 322-7777
Paula Campbell, *Branch Mgr*
EMP: 18
SALES (corp-wide): 9.7MM **Privately Held**
SIC: 6061 Federal credit unions
PA: Sussex County Federal Credit Union
1941 Bridgeville Hwy
Seaford DE 19973
302 629-0100

(G-5746)
SWARTHMORE FINANCIAL SERVICES
15 Reads Way Ste 210 (19720-1600)
PHONE....................302 325-0700
Charles Pass, *Principal*
EMP: 25
SALES (est): 3MM **Privately Held**
SIC: 6282 Investment advisory service

(G-5747)
SWIFT SERVICES INC
2 3rd Ave (19720-4120)
PHONE....................302 328-1145
Michael Salemi, *President*
EMP: 7
SALES (est): 278.4K **Privately Held**
SIC: 7349 Chimney cleaning

(G-5748)
SWIFT TOWING & RECOVERY
469 Old Airport Rd (19720-1001)
PHONE....................302 650-4579
Ron Bennett, *Owner*
EMP: 6
SALES (est): 416.1K **Privately Held**
SIC: 7549 Towing services

(G-5749)
T P COMPOSITES INC
1600 Johnson Way (19720-8199)
PHONE....................610 358-9001
Anna Romanowski, *Principal*
EMP: 2
SALES (est): 97.5K **Privately Held**
SIC: 2821 Plastics materials & resins

(G-5750)
T SHANE PALMER DC
Also Called: Palmer Chiropractic
191 Christiana Rd Ste 1 (19720-3024)
PHONE....................302 328-2656
T Shane Palmer DC, *Owner*
EMP: 5
SALES (est): 274K **Privately Held**
SIC: 8041 Offices & clinics of chiropractors

(G-5751)
TA INSTRUMENTS - WATERS LLC (DH)
159 Lukens Dr (19720-2795)
PHONE....................302 427-4000
Jonathan M Pratt, *President*
Jim Schilthuis, *Vice Pres*
Ernie Smith, *Facilities Mgr*
Armando Lujan, *Mfg Spvr*
John Rokicki, *Mfg Staff*
▲ **EMP:** 200
SQ FT: 200,000
SALES (est): 85.2MM **Publicly Held**
WEB: www.tainstruments.com
SIC: 3826 Instruments measuring thermal properties
HQ: Waters Technologies Corporation,
34 Maple St
Milford MA 01757
508 478-2000

(G-5752)
TALOSTECH LLC
274 Quigley Blvd (19720-4106)
PHONE....................302 332-9236
Hansan Liu, *President*
EMP: 4
SALES (est): 273.1K **Privately Held**
SIC: 3691 3692 Storage batteries; primary batteries, dry & wet

(G-5753)
TARABICOS GROSSO
100 W Commons Blvd # 415 (19720-2419)
PHONE....................302 757-7800
Larry J Tarabicos, *Principal*
Megan Good, *Administration*
EMP: 6 **EST:** 2013
SALES (est): 648.8K **Privately Held**
SIC: 8111 General practice attorney, lawyer

(G-5754)
TAYLOR KLINE INC
298b Churchmans Rd (19720-3110)
PHONE....................302 328-8306
Jeffrey Kline, *President*
Gary Place, *Vice Pres*
EMP: 15
SQ FT: 6,400
SALES: 3.5MM **Privately Held**
SIC: 1542 Commercial & office building, new construction

(G-5755)
TDW DELAWARE INC (HQ)
43 Harbor View Dr (19720-2179)
PHONE....................302 594-9880
Richard B Williamson, *President*
EMP: 3
SALES (est): 405.4K
SALES (corp-wide): 378.6MM **Privately Held**
SIC: 3533 Gas field machinery & equipment
PA: T. D. Williamson, Inc.
6120 S Yale Ave Ste 1700
Tulsa OK 74136
918 493-9494

(G-5756)
TDW SERVICES INC
Also Called: Northeast Coast Service Center
261 Quigley Blvd Ste 18 (19720-4187)
PHONE....................302 594-9880
EMP: 12
SALES (corp-wide): 586.6MM **Privately Held**
SIC: 1389 Pipeline Service Company
HQ: Tdw Services, Inc.
6801 S 65th West Ave
Tulsa OK 74131
918 447-5000

(G-5757)
TEC-CON INC
Also Called: Keen Compressed Gas
4063 New Castle Ave (19720-1414)
PHONE....................610 583-8770
Rich Fleming, *Branch Mgr*
EMP: 3
SALES (est): 123.3K **Privately Held**
SIC: 1389 Gas compressing (natural gas) at the fields

(G-5758)
TECHMER ENGINEERED SOLUTIONS
1600 Johnson Way (19720-8199)
PHONE....................800 401-8181
Henry Piacitelli, *Maintence Staff*
EMP: 6
SALES (est): 74.3K **Privately Held**
SIC: 8711 Engineering services

(G-5759)
TECHMER ENGNERED SOLUTIONS LLC
Also Called: T E S
1600 Johnson Way (19720-8199)
PHONE....................610 548-5032
EMP: 75
SALES (corp-wide): 228.1MM **Privately Held**
SIC: 2821 Mfg Plastic Materials/Resins
HQ: Techmer Engineered Solutions, Llc
1 Quality Cir
Clinton TN 37716
865 457-6700

(G-5760)
TELEPLAN VDEOCOM SOLUTIONS INC
100 W Cmmons Blvd Ste 415 (19720)
PHONE....................302 323-8503
Joe Neff, *CEO*
Aivar Elbrecht, *General Mgr*
EMP: 150
SALES (est): 7.5MM
SALES (corp-wide): 2.6MM **Privately Held**
WEB: www.teleplan.com
SIC: 7378 Computer maintenance & repair
HQ: Teleplan International N.V.
Schiphol Boulevard 201
Luchthaven Schiphol 1118
852 733-674

(G-5761)
TERMINIX INTL CO LTD PARTNR
284 Quigley Blvd (19720-4106)
PHONE....................302 653-4866
Brian Searle, *Manager*
EMP: 35
SALES (corp-wide): 1.9B **Publicly Held**
SIC: 7342 Pest control services
HQ: The Terminix International Company Limited Partnership
150 Peabody Pl
Memphis TN 38103
901 766-1400

(G-5762)
TERRACE ATHLETIC CLUB INC
208 New Castle Ave (19720-2701)
P.O. Box 421 (19720-0421)
PHONE....................302 652-9059
Walter Kendall, *President*
EMP: 4
SALES: 143.3K **Privately Held**
SIC: 7997 Membership sports & recreation clubs

(G-5763)
TESLA INDUSTRIES INC (PA)
101 109 Centerpoint Blvd (19720)
PHONE....................302 324-8910
David Masilotti, *President*
Frank Mooney, *General Mgr*
Keith Edwards, *Manager*
▲ **EMP:** 35
SQ FT: 20,000
SALES (est): 7.5MM **Privately Held**
SIC: 3724 3812 Starting vibrators, aircraft engine; aircraft control instruments

New Castle - New Castle County (G-5764)

(G-5764)
TESTING MACHINES INC (PA)
Also Called: T M I Div
40 Mccullough Dr Unit A (19720-2228)
PHONE..................302 613-5600
John L Sullivan, *President*
Jim Graham, *President*
Heather Crawford, *General Mgr*
Dave Muchorski, *Vice Pres*
Kevin Marrin, *Electrical Engi*
▲ **EMP:** 30 **EST:** 1931
SQ FT: 15,000
SALES (est): 13.4MM **Privately Held**
WEB: www.testingmachines.com
SIC: 3829 5084 Physical property testing equipment; measuring & testing equipment, electrical

(G-5765)
THALES INC
100 W Cmmons Blvd (19720)
PHONE..................302 326-0830
Rod Manning, *President*
EMP: 6
SALES (corp-wide): 253.9MM **Privately Held**
SIC: 6726 Investment offices
HQ: Thales, Inc.
2733 Crystal Dr Ste 1200
Arlington VA 22202
703 838-9685

(G-5766)
THALES HOLDING CORPORATION
100 W Cmmons Blvd Ste 302 (19720)
PHONE..................302 326-0830
Rod Mannig, *CEO*
Daniel H O'Brien, *President*
EMP: 593
SQ FT: 4,800
SALES (corp-wide): 253.9MM **Privately Held**
SIC: 6719 4833 Public utility holding companies; television broadcasting stations
HQ: Thales Usa, Inc.
2733 Crystal Dr
Arlington VA 22202
703 413-6029

(G-5767)
THINK CLEAN & GROUNDS UP LLC
11 W 9th St (19720-6002)
PHONE..................904 250-1614
Marc Foraker,
EMP: 10
SALES (est): 147.7K **Privately Held**
SIC: 7342 Disinfecting services

(G-5768)
THOMAS A COCHRAN & SONS INC (PA) ◆
807 Washington St (19720-6079)
PHONE..................302 656-6054
John Cochren, *Principal*
EMP: 11 **EST:** 2019
SALES (est): 1.9MM **Privately Held**
SIC: 1711 Plumbing, heating, air-conditioning contractors

(G-5769)
THRUPORE TECHNOLOGIES INC (PA)
15 Reads Way Ste 107 (19720-1600)
PHONE..................205 657-0714
Franchessa Sayler, *CEO*
Martin G Bakker, *COO*
EMP: 1
SALES (est): 167.8K **Privately Held**
SIC: 2899 Chemical preparations

(G-5770)
TIMKEN GEARS & SERVICES INC
Also Called: Philadelphia Gear
100 Anchor Mill Rd (19720-4572)
PHONE..................302 633-4600
Rich Chrivnowski, *Manager*
EMP: 17
SALES (corp-wide): 3.5B **Publicly Held**
WEB: www.philagear.com
SIC: 3462 Gear & chain forgings; gears, forged steel; anchors, forged

HQ: Timken Gears & Services Inc.
901 E 8th Ave Ste 100
King Of Prussia PA 19406

(G-5771)
TIRE RACK INC
300 Anchor Mill Rd (19720-4574)
PHONE..................302 325-8260
Chris Lagkowski, *Manager*
EMP: 60
SALES (corp-wide): 1.3B **Privately Held**
SIC: 5014 Tires & tubes
PA: The Tire Rack Inc
7101 Vorden Pkwy
South Bend IN 46628
888 541-1777

(G-5772)
TIRE SALES LLC
70 Mccullough Dr (19720-9010)
PHONE..................302 994-2900
John Morrone, *Mng Member*
EMP: 26
SALES (est): 4.8MM **Privately Held**
SIC: 5014 Tire & tube repair materials

(G-5773)
TOLL BROTHERS INC
1100 Casey Dr (19720-5683)
PHONE..................302 832-1700
Mike Kline, *Manager*
EMP: 39
SALES (corp-wide): 7.2B **Publicly Held**
SIC: 1521 New construction, single-family houses
PA: Toll Brothers, Inc.
250 Gibraltar Rd
Horsham PA 19044
215 938-8000

(G-5774)
TORNADO II JANITORIAL SERVICE
336 Hackberry Dr (19720-7696)
P.O. Box 12936, Wilmington (19850-2936)
PHONE..................302 898-1370
Danita Mosley, *Partner*
EMP: 10
SALES (est): 75K **Privately Held**
SIC: 7349 Building maintenance services

(G-5775)
TOTAL CONSTRUCTION RENTALS INC
Also Called: T C R
19 Davidson Ln Bldg 4 (19720-2207)
P.O. Box 7454, Wilmington (19803-0454)
PHONE..................302 575-1132
Timothy Cairo, *President*
Stephanie Cairo, *Info Tech Mgr*
EMP: 10
SALES (est): 1.6MM **Privately Held**
SIC: 7359 Propane equipment rental

(G-5776)
TOTAL SERVICES INC
19 Davidson Ln Bldg 4 (19720-2207)
PHONE..................302 575-1132
Timothy M Cairo, *Principal*
EMP: 5
SALES (est): 493.7K **Privately Held**
SIC: 5112 Office supplies

(G-5777)
TOTALTRANSLOGISTICS LLC
8 Mccullough Dr (19720-2066)
PHONE..................302 325-4245
Zurab Zubitashbili, *CEO*
Paul Cullen,
EMP: 6
SQ FT: 6,500
SALES (est): 512.6K **Privately Held**
SIC: 8741 Business management

(G-5778)
TOTALTRAX INC
920 W Basin Rd Ste 400 (19720-1013)
PHONE..................302 514-0600
Frank Cavallaro, *CEO*
Larry G Mahan, *President*
Neil O'Connell, *COO*
Philip B Van Wormer, *Exec VP*
Monty Taylor, *Research*
▲ **EMP:** 60

SALES (est): 12.1MM **Privately Held**
SIC: 3825 3621 5084 Building services monitoring controls, automatic; control equipment for buses or trucks, electric; safety equipment

(G-5779)
TOUCHSTONE SYSTEMS INC
42c Reads Way (19720-1649)
PHONE..................302 324-5322
Sanford S Stone, *President*
EMP: 10
SALES (est): 354.4K **Privately Held**
SIC: 7371 Computer software development

(G-5780)
TOWER BUSINESS MACHINES INC
Also Called: Tower Business Systems
278 Quigley Blvd (19720-4106)
PHONE..................302 395-1445
Kevin Laird, *President*
EMP: 5
SQ FT: 2,500
SALES (est): 817.3K **Privately Held**
WEB: www.towerbiz.com
SIC: 5734 5999 7378 7629 Computer peripheral equipment; business machines & equipment; computer maintenance & repair; business machine repair, electric

(G-5781)
TOY BOX CHILD CARE CENTER
Also Called: Toy Box Child Care Ctr
6 Halcyon Dr (19720-1239)
PHONE..................302 427-8438
Elisha Gresham, *Owner*
Arie Harrison, *Owner*
EMP: 4
SALES (est): 110K **Privately Held**
SIC: 8351 Child day care services

(G-5782)
TRADEWAY CORPORATION
549 Mason Dr (19720-7683)
PHONE..................302 834-1957
Rosmarie Odomwadalam, *Owner*
EMP: 1
SALES (est): 70K **Privately Held**
SIC: 3171 Women's handbags & purses

(G-5783)
TRANE US INC
66 Southgate Blvd (19720-2068)
PHONE..................302 395-0200
John Seiberlich, *District Mgr*
Mark Cresitello, *Admin Sec*
EMP: 20 **Privately Held**
SIC: 3585 Refrigeration & heating equipment
HQ: Trane U.S. Inc.
3600 Pammel Creek Rd
La Crosse WI 54601
608 787-2000

(G-5784)
TRANS PLUS INC
423 W 7th St (19720-4904)
PHONE..................302 323-3051
Charles Cox, *President*
EMP: 4 **EST:** 2015
SALES (est): 374.8K **Privately Held**
SIC: 7537 Automotive transmission repair shops

(G-5785)
TRANSAXLE LLC
4060 N Dupont Hwy Ste 6 (19720-6325)
PHONE..................302 322-8300
Sam Palmucci, *Branch Mgr*
EMP: 5
SALES (corp-wide): 80.9MM **Privately Held**
SIC: 5013 5531 Truck parts & accessories; truck equipment & parts
PA: Transaxle Llc
2501 Route 73
Cinnaminson NJ 08077
856 665-4445

(G-5786)
TRASH TECH LLC
755 Governor Lea Rd (19720-5512)
P.O. Box 987 (19720-0987)
PHONE..................302 832-8000

Lou Matos, *Accounts Exec*
Kevin Shegog,
EMP: 4 **EST:** 2015
SALES (est): 295.1K **Privately Held**
SIC: 4953 Garbage: collecting, destroying & processing

(G-5787)
TRI-STATE CHEERNASTICS INC
1 King Ave (19720-1511)
PHONE..................302 322-4020
Jeffrey Martino, *Principal*
EMP: 4 **EST:** 2007
SALES (est): 111.6K **Privately Held**
SIC: 7911 7991 7999 8322 Dance studio & school; physical fitness clubs with training equipment; gymnastic instruction, non-membership; geriatric social service

(G-5788)
TRI-STATE FBRCTION MCHNING LLC
251 Airport Rd (19720-1539)
PHONE..................302 232-3133
Andrew Studzinski, *Mng Member*
EMP: 24 **EST:** 2014
SALES: 550K **Privately Held**
SIC: 3599 1761 1791 1799 Machine shop, jobbing & repair; architectural sheet metal work; building front installation metal; ornamental metal work; metal household furniture; fabricated structural metal

(G-5789)
TRI-STATE TRUCK & EQP SLS LLC
201 E 6th St (19720-4556)
PHONE..................302 276-1253
Patrick Walsh,
Lori Walsh,
EMP: 5
SALES (est): 805.3K **Privately Held**
WEB: www.tristatetrucksales.com
SIC: 5012 Trucks, commercial

(G-5790)
TRI-STATE WASTE SOLUTIONS INC
1600 Matassino Rd (19720-2085)
PHONE..................302 622-8600
Kevin Shegog, *CEO*
EMP: 21
SALES (est): 1.9MM **Privately Held**
WEB: www.tristatewaste.com
SIC: 4953 Refuse systems

(G-5791)
TRIAD CONSTRUCTION COMPANY LLC
210 Marsh Ln (19720-1175)
PHONE..................302 652-3339
Christopher Modesto, *President*
Marty Bienkowski, *Treasurer*
Jerry Denney, *Admin Sec*
EMP: 50
SALES (est): 1.9MM **Privately Held**
SIC: 1771 Blacktop (asphalt) work

(G-5792)
TRIANGLE FASTENER CORPORATION
243 Quigley Blvd Ste C (19720-4191)
PHONE..................302 322-0600
Larry Ratliff, *Purch Agent*
Tony Gutowski, *Manager*
EMP: 10
SQ FT: 12,500
SALES (corp-wide): 66.6MM **Privately Held**
SIC: 5072 Miscellaneous fasteners
PA: Triangle Fastener Corporation
1925 Preble Ave
Pittsburgh PA 15233
412 321-5000

(G-5793)
TRICON CONSTRUCTION MGT INC
13 King Ct Ste 3 (19720-1523)
PHONE..................302 838-6500
James Marcus, *CFO*
EMP: 50

GEOGRAPHIC SECTION

New Castle - New Castle County (G-5823)

SALES (est): 1.2MM **Privately Held**
SIC: 1521 Single-family housing construction

(G-5794)
TRINITY LOGISTICS INC
23 Fantail Ct (19720-4674)
PHONE..................302 595-2116
Dismas Makori, *Branch Mgr*
EMP: 4
SALES (corp-wide): 1.4B **Privately Held**
SIC: 4731 Freight transportation arrangement
HQ: Trinity Logistics, Inc.
  50 Fallon Ave
  Seaford DE 19973
  302 253-3900

(G-5795)
TRITON CONSTRUCTION CO INC
101 Pigeon Point Rd (19720-2108)
PHONE..................516 780-8100
Joe Dimenna, *President*
EMP: 22
SQ FT: 1,800
SALES (est): 2.3MM **Privately Held**
WEB: www.tccico.com
SIC: 1623 Water, sewer & utility lines

(G-5796)
TRUCK TECH INC
1600 Matassino Rd (19720-2085)
P.O. Box 987 (19720-0987)
PHONE..................302 832-8000
Kevin Shegop, *President*
Jeannie Forgie, *Office Mgr*
EMP: 16
SALES (est): 2.5MM **Privately Held**
SIC: 7538 7692 General truck repair; welding repair

(G-5797)
TRUE MOBILITY INC
773 S Dupont Hwy (19720-4609)
PHONE..................302 836-4110
Patricia Castoria, *President*
Michael Castoria, *Vice Pres*
Gary Demaine, *CFO*
EMP: 6
SALES (est): 737.2K **Privately Held**
SIC: 5999 7699 5531 Medical apparatus & supplies; recreational vehicle repair services; automobile & truck equipment & parts

(G-5798)
TRUE-PACK LTD (PA)
Also Called: Mail Box Outlet
420 Churchmans Rd (19720-3157)
PHONE..................302 326-2222
William W Bane III, *President*
Theresa Groves, *Vice Pres*
EMP: 30
SQ FT: 35,000
SALES (est): 5.8MM **Privately Held**
WEB: www.truepack.com
SIC: 2653 5999 Boxes, corrugated: made from purchased materials; packaging materials: boxes, padding, etc.

(G-5799)
U S EXPRESS TAXI COMPANY LLC
260 Christiana Rd Apt N18 (19720-2963)
PHONE..................302 357-1908
Abdoulaye Kamagate, *Principal*
EMP: 4 EST: 2015
SALES (est): 110.8K **Privately Held**
SIC: 4121 Taxicabs

(G-5800)
U-HAUL NEIGHBORHOOD DEALER
1713 Wilmington Rd (19720-2750)
PHONE..................302 326-1875
EMP: 8
SALES (est): 101.1K **Privately Held**
SIC: 7513 Truck rental & leasing, no drivers

(G-5801)
ULTRACHEM INC
900 Centerpoint Blvd (19720-8121)
PHONE..................302 325-9880
Robert Whiting, *President*
Cindy Lingerfelt, *Regional Mgr*
David Mitchell, *Regional Mgr*
Bruce Jewett, *Vice Pres*
John Pelle, *Plant Mgr*
▼ EMP: 17
SQ FT: 58,000
SALES (est): 7.8MM **Privately Held**
WEB: www.ultracheminc.com
SIC: 2992 Lubricating oils

(G-5802)
UNI PRINTING SOLUTIONS LLC
42 Reads Way (19720-1649)
PHONE..................631 438-6045
EMP: 2 EST: 2018
SALES (est): 83.9K **Privately Held**
SIC: 2752 Commercial printing, lithographic

(G-5803)
UNITED AUTO SALES INC
300 Churchmans Rd (19720-3112)
PHONE..................302 325-3000
Brian Wolf, *President*
EMP: 5
SQ FT: 7,500
SALES (est): 1.1MM **Privately Held**
WEB: www.unitedautosales.com
SIC: 5521 7538 Automobiles, used cars only; general automotive repair shops

(G-5804)
UNITED ELECTRIC SUPPLY CO INC (PA)
10 Bellecor Dr (19720-1763)
P.O. Box 10287, Wilmington (19850-0287)
PHONE..................800 322-3374
George Vorwick, *CEO*
Gayle Davis, *Vice Pres*
Angela Holowka, *Engineer*
Rich Stagliano, *CFO*
Brian Dunnigan, *Branch Mgr*
EMP: 112 EST: 1965
SQ FT: 80,000
SALES (est): 221.3MM **Privately Held**
WEB: www.unitedelectric.com
SIC: 5063 Electrical supplies

(G-5805)
UNITED GROUP REAL ESTATE LLC
607 Deemer Pl (19720-5043)
PHONE..................929 999-1277
Thamer Alamry, *Mng Member*
EMP: 25
SALES: 100K **Privately Held**
SIC: 6531 Real estate leasing & rentals

(G-5806)
UNITED REFRIGERATION INC
Also Called: Johnson Contrls Authorized Dlr
818 W Basin Rd (19720-1708)
PHONE..................302 322-1836
William Stapleton, *Manager*
EMP: 9
SALES (corp-wide): 50MM **Privately Held**
WEB: www.uri.com
SIC: 5078 5075 Refrigeration equipment & supplies; warm air heating & air conditioning
PA: United Refrigeration, Inc.
  11401 Roosevelt Blvd
  Philadelphia PA 19154
  215 698-9100

(G-5807)
UNITED RENTALS NORTH AMER INC
248 S Dupont Hwy (19720-4130)
PHONE..................302 328-2900
Tom Ghigliotty, *Branch Mgr*
Mike Roberts, *Manager*
EMP: 25
SALES (corp-wide): 8B **Publicly Held**
WEB: www.unitedrentals.com
SIC: 7359 Equipment rental & leasing
HQ: United Rentals (North America), Inc.
  100 Frederick St 700
  Stamford CT 06902
  203 622-3131

(G-5808)
UNITED TECHNOLOGIES CORP
276 Quigley Blvd (19720-4106)
PHONE..................800 227-7437
Doug Ergod, *Branch Mgr*
Tony Dinger, *Manager*
EMP: 10
SALES (corp-wide): 66.5B **Publicly Held**
SIC: 7623 Refrigeration service & repair
PA: United Technologies Corporation
  10 Farm Springs Rd
  Farmington CT 06032
  860 728-7000

(G-5809)
UNIVERSAL DESIGN COMPANY
18 Baldt Ave (19720-4512)
PHONE..................302 328-8391
James Dugan, *Principal*
EMP: 5
SALES (est): 77.4K **Privately Held**
SIC: 8351 Group day care center

(G-5810)
UNIVERSALFLEET
2019 Walmsley Dr (19720)
PHONE..................302 428-0661
Gary Merritt, *Owner*
EMP: 5
SALES (est): 264K **Privately Held**
SIC: 7538 General truck repair

(G-5811)
URBAN ENGINEERS INC
2 Penns Way Ste 400 (19720-2407)
PHONE..................302 689-0260
John Pietrobono, *Branch Mgr*
EMP: 5
SALES (corp-wide): 97.1MM **Privately Held**
SIC: 8711 Consulting engineer
PA: Urban Engineers, Inc.
  530 Walnut St Fl 7
  Philadelphia PA 19106
  215 922-8080

(G-5812)
US GREEN BATTERY INC
157 S Dupont Hwy Fl 2 (19720-4138)
PHONE..................347 723-5963
Falguni R Trivedi, *Vice Pres*
EMP: 2
SALES (est): 62.5K **Privately Held**
SIC: 3999 Manufacturing industries

(G-5813)
VANNIES HATS
4 Andover Ct (19720-3905)
PHONE..................302 765-7094
EMP: 2 EST: 2015
SALES (est): 76.5K **Privately Held**
SIC: 2353 Hats, caps & millinery

(G-5814)
VEHATTIRE LLC
174 N Dupont Hwy (19720-3103)
PHONE..................302 221-2000
Michael Gedz,
Mike Ricchiuti,
EMP: 16
SQ FT: 12,000
SALES (est): 1.3MM **Privately Held**
WEB: www.vehattire.com
SIC: 5015 Automotive accessories, used

(G-5815)
VERIZON COMMUNICATIONS INC
Also Called: Verizon Wireless
124 Sunset Blvd (19720-4100)
PHONE..................302 324-1385
EMP: 17
SALES (corp-wide): 115.8B **Publicly Held**
SIC: 4812 Radiotelephone Communication
PA: Verizon Communications Inc.
  140 West St
  New York NY 10036
  212 395-1000

(G-5816)
VETERINARY SPECIALTY CTR DEL PA
Also Called: Veterinary Emergency Ctr Del
290 Churchmans Rd (19720-3110)
PHONE..................302 322-6933
Mark Cofone, *President*
Robin Pullen, *Corp Secy*
Mike Miller, *Vice Pres*
Shirley A Lockhart, *Director*
R Jankowski, *Shareholder*
EMP: 24 EST: 2000
SALES (est): 3.2MM **Privately Held**
WEB: www.vscdel.com
SIC: 0742 Animal hospital services, pets & other animal specialties

(G-5817)
VIDEO WALLTRONICS INC
Also Called: Rent Big Screens
22 Lukens Dr (19720-2700)
PHONE..................302 328-4511
Mitchell Kaplan, *President*
Mike Quinn, *Sales Staff*
▲ EMP: 4
SALES (est): 1.3MM **Privately Held**
WEB: www.videowalltronics.com
SIC: 5065 Video equipment, electronic

(G-5818)
VINCES PRODUCE INC
380 Pulaski Hwy (19720-4668)
PHONE..................302 322-0386
EMP: 4
SALES: 500K **Privately Held**
SIC: 5431 5148 Ret & Whol Produce

(G-5819)
VISAMTION LLC
607 Deemer Pl (19720-5043)
PHONE..................302 268-2177
Siraj Mahmood,
EMP: 4
SALES (est): 239.4K **Privately Held**
SIC: 4724 Travel agencies

(G-5820)
VOIGT & SCHWEITZER LLC
Also Called: V and S Phldelphia Galvanizing
511 Carroll Dr (19720-4871)
PHONE..................302 322-1420
Tammy Kinsey, *Manager*
EMP: 15
SALES (corp-wide): 840.5MM **Privately Held**
WEB: www.hotdipgalvanizing.com
SIC: 3479 Galvanizing of iron, steel or end-formed products; hot dip coating of metals or formed products
HQ: Voigt & Schweitzer Llc
  987 Buckeye Park Rd
  Columbus OH 43207
  614 449-8281

(G-5821)
WAHID CONSULTANTS LLC
51 Villas Dr Apt 8 (19720-2842)
P.O. Box 12006, Wilmington (19850-2006)
PHONE..................315 400-0955
Asma Rashid, *Mng Member*
Farham Dafar,
EMP: 26
SALES: 60K **Privately Held**
SIC: 8721 7379 7389 7291 Accounting, auditing & bookkeeping; computer related consulting services; ; tax return preparation services

(G-5822)
WANEX ELECTRICAL SERVICE LLC
261 Airport Rd (19720-1540)
PHONE..................302 326-1700
William Wanex,
Bruce Wanex,
Linda Wanex,
EMP: 15
SALES (est): 1.8MM **Privately Held**
SIC: 1731 General electrical contractor

(G-5823)
WAREHOUSE TECHNOLOGY INC
2 Lukens Dr Ste 600 (19720-2796)
PHONE..................302 516-7791

New Castle - New Castle County (G-5824)

Mike Struempfler, *President*
EMP: 4
SALES (est): 55.2K **Privately Held**
SIC: 8731 Commercial physical research

(G-5824)
WASTE MANAGEMENT MICHIGAN INC
246 Marsh Ln (19720-1175)
PHONE 302 655-1360
Anne Krolicki, *Branch Mgr*
EMP: 4
SALES (corp-wide): 14.9B **Publicly Held**
SIC: 4953 Refuse systems
HQ: Waste Management Of Michigan, Inc.
48797 Alpha Dr Ste 100
Wixom MI 48393
586 574-2760

(G-5825)
WASTE MASTERS SOLUTIONS LLC
19 Davidson Ln (19720-2246)
PHONE 302 824-0909
Brian Simmons, *President*
Carly Devirgilio, *Business Mgr*
Rich Lober, *Vice Pres*
Ronald Tuder, *Opers Staff*
EMP: 6
SALES (est): 1.6MM **Privately Held**
SIC: 4953 Refuse collection & disposal services

(G-5826)
WATERLOGIC USA INC
77 Mccullough Dr Ste 9 (19720-2089)
PHONE 302 323-2100
Brian Brady, *CFO*
Andrea Baker, *Sales Staff*
Matt Deiter, *Manager*
Aaron Giersch, *Manager*
Veronica Johnson, *Manager*
EMP: 145
SALES (corp-wide): 38.2MM **Privately Held**
SIC: 5074 Water purification equipment
PA: Waterlogic Usa, Inc.
11710 Stonegate Cir
Omaha NE 68164
800 288-1891

(G-5827)
WATKINS SYSTEM INC
Also Called: Watkins Dealership
4031 New Castle Ave (19720-1414)
PHONE 302 658-8561
Stan Lenanski, *Manager*
EMP: 25
SALES (est): 338.5K
SALES (corp-wide): 18.9MM **Privately Held**
SIC: 7513 Truck rental & leasing, no drivers
PA: Watkins System Inc
1516 Rt 202
Concordville PA

(G-5828)
WELLS FARGO BANK NATIONAL ASSN
1424 N Dupont Hwy (19720-1844)
PHONE 302 326-4304
Susan Robinson, *Manager*
EMP: 18
SALES (corp-wide): 101B **Publicly Held**
SIC: 6021 National commercial banks
HQ: Wells Fargo Bank, National Association
101 N Phillips Ave
Sioux Falls SD 57104
605 575-6900

(G-5829)
WENOVA INC (PA)
42 Reads Way (19720-1649)
PHONE 847 477-0489
Suparna Namburi, *President*
EMP: 6
SALES (est): 2.1MM **Privately Held**
SIC: 7379 Computer related consulting services

(G-5830)
WEST VENTURES INC
Also Called: Glass Doctor of Delaware
13 King Ct Ste 1 (19720-1523)
PHONE 307 737-9900
Bill Schlatterback, *President*
EMP: 4 **EST:** 2010
SALES (est): 538.8K **Privately Held**
SIC: 1793 Glass & glazing work

(G-5831)
WESTSIDE FAMILY HEALTHCARE INC
2 Penns Way Ste 412 (19720-2407)
PHONE 302 652-2455
EMP: 123
SALES (corp-wide): 22.8MM **Privately Held**
SIC: 8011 Offices & clinics of medical doctors
PA: Westside Family Healthcare, Inc.
300 Water St Ste 200
Wilmington DE 19801
302 656-8292

(G-5832)
WHITE DOG LABS INC (PA)
239 Lisa Dr (19720-4193)
PHONE 302 220-4760
Bryan Tracy, *CEO*
Aharon Eyal, *Security Dir*
EMP: 13 **EST:** 2011
SALES (est): 2.4MM **Privately Held**
SIC: 8731 Biotechnical research, commercial

(G-5833)
WHOLESALE AUTO INC
53 Collingsdale Ave (19720-1571)
PHONE 302 322-6190
John Killeen, *President*
EMP: 4 **EST:** 2009
SALES (est): 420.4K **Privately Held**
SIC: 5013 Automotive supplies & parts

(G-5834)
WILCOX LANDSCAPING
230 S Dupont Hwy (19720-4130)
P.O. Box 629 (19720-0629)
PHONE 302 322-3002
Tom Wilcox, *Owner*
Janice Hopkins, *Office Mgr*
EMP: 50
SALES (est): 2.8MM **Privately Held**
SIC: 0782 Landscape contractors

(G-5835)
WILMINGTON AQUATIC CLUB INC
Also Called: Wac
212 W Grant Ave (19720-2525)
PHONE 302 322-2487
EMP: 5
SALES (est): 113.7K **Privately Held**
SIC: 7997 Membership sports & recreation clubs

(G-5836)
WILMINGTON FIBRE SPECIALTY CO
700 Washington St (19720-6065)
P.O. Box 192 (19720-0192)
PHONE 302 328-7525
John W Morris III, *Ch of Bd*
B Scott Morris, *President*
David Celli, *Opers Mgr*
Chris Mathe, *Engineer*
▲ **EMP:** 30 **EST:** 1904
SQ FT: 40,000
SALES (est): 5.9MM **Privately Held**
WEB: www.wilmfibre.com
SIC: 3089 3081 3714 Thermoformed finished plastic products; polyethylene film; motor vehicle parts & accessories

(G-5837)
WILMINGTON SAVINGS FUND SOC
Also Called: Airport Plaza Branch
144 N Dupont Hwy (19720-3102)
PHONE 302 324-5800
Becky Lockwood, *Manager*
EMP: 15
SALES (corp-wide): 455.5MM **Publicly Held**
WEB: www.wsfsbank.com
SIC: 6022 State commercial banks
HQ: Wilmington Savings Fund Society
500 Delaware Ave Ste 500 # 500
Wilmington DE 19801
302 792-6000

(G-5838)
WINDSOR FOREST TOWN HOMES
101 Paisley Ln (19720-3841)
P.O. Box 897, Lakewood NJ (08701-0897)
PHONE 302 328-1260
David Hasenfeld, *Owner*
EMP: 4
SALES (est): 283.8K **Privately Held**
SIC: 6513 Apartment building operators

(G-5839)
WJC OF DELAWARE LLC (PA)
Also Called: Johnstone Supply
19 E Commons Blvd Ste 3 (19720-2262)
PHONE 302 323-9600
Richard Comunale, *CEO*
Dean Mader, *Manager*
EMP: 10
SALES (est): 4.2MM **Privately Held**
SIC: 5075 Warm air heating & air conditioning

(G-5840)
WRDX
920 W Basin Rd Ste 400 (19720-1013)
PHONE 302 395-9739
Valerie Alston, *Principal*
EMP: 6
SALES (est): 165.9K **Privately Held**
SIC: 4832 Radio broadcasting stations

(G-5841)
WS ONE INVESTMENT USA LLC
298 Cherry Ln (19720-2776)
PHONE 302 317-2610
Donald Godwin, *Branch Mgr*
EMP: 15
SALES (corp-wide): 27.8MM **Privately Held**
SIC: 6799 Investors
PA: Ws One Investment Usa, Llc
1263 S Chillicothe Rd
Aurora OH 44202
855 895-3728

(G-5842)
WW GRAINGER INC
Also Called: Grainger 595
117 Quigley Blvd (19720-4188)
PHONE 302 322-1840
Rick Bliss, *Manager*
EMP: 18
SALES (corp-wide): 11.2B **Publicly Held**
WEB: www.grainger.com
SIC: 5063 5084 5075 5078 Motors, electric; motor controls, starters & relays: electric; power transmission equipment, electric; generators; fans, industrial; pumps & pumping equipment; compressors, except air conditioning; pneumatic tools & equipment; warm air heating equipment & supplies; air conditioning equipment, except room units; refrigeration equipment & supplies; electric tools; power tools & accessories; hand tools
PA: W.W. Grainger, Inc.
100 Grainger Pkwy
Lake Forest IL 60045
847 535-1000

(G-5843)
XONEX RELOCATION LLC
20 E Commons Blvd (19720-1734)
P.O. Box 3496, Wilmington (19804-0496)
PHONE 302 323-9000
Katherine Holman, *President*
Robin Wagner, *General Mgr*
Robert B Holman, *Vice Pres*
Robert Webster, *CFO*
Robert Downey-Webster, *VP Finance*
EMP: 65
SALES (est): 9.5MM **Privately Held**
SIC: 8742 Management consulting services

(G-5844)
YRC INC
Also Called: Yellow Transportation
316 Churchmans Rd (19720-3112)
PHONE 302 322-5111
Thomas Giordano, *Manager*
EMP: 7
SALES (corp-wide): 5B **Publicly Held**
WEB: www.roadway.com
SIC: 4213 Automobiles, transport & delivery; contract haulers
HQ: Yrc Inc.
10990 Roe Ave
Overland Park KS 66211
913 696-6100

(G-5845)
ZENITH HOME CORP
Also Called: Zhc
400 Lukens Dr (19720-2772)
PHONE 302 326-8200
Mary Beth Martino, *CEO*
David Ronge, *CFO*
Kevin Orcutt, *Director*
EMP: 400
SQ FT: 20,000
SALES (est): 121MM
SALES (corp-wide): 419.3K **Privately Held**
SIC: 3431 5211 Bathroom fixtures, including sinks; bathroom fixtures, equipment & supplies
HQ: Decolin Inc
9150 Av Du Parc
Montreal QC H2N 1
514 384-2910

(G-5846)
ZENITH PRODUCTS
499 Ships Landing Way (19720-4579)
PHONE 302 322-2190
EMP: 2
SALES (corp-wide): 419.3K **Privately Held**
SIC: 2434 Vanities, bathroom: wood
HQ: Maytex Mills
9150 Av Du Parc
Montreal QC H2N 1
514 384-2910

(G-5847)
ZIMNY & ASSOCIATES PA
92 Reads Way Ste 104 (19720-1631)
PHONE 302 325-6900
Richard Zimny, *President*
EMP: 7
SQ FT: 3,800
SALES (est): 640.3K **Privately Held**
SIC: 8721 Certified public accountant

(G-5848)
ZWD PRODUCTS CORPORATION (DH)
Also Called: India Ink
400 Lukens Dr (19720-2728)
PHONE 302 326-8200
Richard Benaron, *President*
◆ **EMP:** 470 **EST:** 1939
SQ FT: 480,000
SALES (est): 147.8MM
SALES (corp-wide): 419.3K **Privately Held**
WEB: www.zenith-products.com
SIC: 2434 2514 Vanities, bathroom: wood; medicine cabinets & vanities: metal
HQ: Maytex Mills
9150 Av Du Parc
Montreal QC H2N 1
514 384-2910

(G-5849)
ZZHOUSE INC
34 Blevins Dr Ste 1 (19720-4177)
PHONE 302 354-3474
Rick Pulling, *Accounts Exec*
EMP: 2
SALES (est): 215.9K **Privately Held**
SIC: 2759 Commercial printing

GEOGRAPHIC SECTION   Newark - New Castle County (G-5881)

Newark
New Castle County

(G-5850)
1 A LIFESAFER INC
280 E Main St (19711-7333)
PHONE..................800 634-3077
EMP: 1
SALES (corp-wide): 4.3MM **Privately Held**
SIC: 3829 Measuring & controlling devices
PA: 1 A Lifesafer, Inc.
   4290 Glendale Milford Rd
   Blue Ash OH 45242
   513 651-9560

(G-5851)
1 SOFTWARE PLACE
18 Ethan Allen Ct (19711-3227)
PHONE..................302 533-0344
Mamatou Wann, *Partner*
EMP: 4
SALES (est): 4MM **Privately Held**
SIC: 7371 Computer software development & applications

(G-5852)
1ST IMPRESSION INC
933 Branch Rd (19711-2320)
P.O. Box 910, Hockessin (19707-0910)
PHONE..................302 738-4918
Berry Frank, *President*
EMP: 32
SALES: 1.2MM **Privately Held**
SIC: 0782 Landscape contractors

(G-5853)
24 HR TRUCK SERVICES LLC
1 Innovation Way Ste 400 (19711-5463)
PHONE..................609 516-7307
Aaron Swan,
EMP: 3
SALES: 50K **Privately Held**
SIC: 3715 Truck trailers

(G-5854)
2NU PHOTONICS LLC
113 E Main St Unit 404 (19711-7380)
PHONE..................302 388-2261
David Chase,
Matthew Doty,
Joshua Zide,
EMP: 3
SALES (est): 121.3K **Privately Held**
SIC: 3661 Fiber optics communications equipment

(G-5855)
3-D FABRICATIONS INC
100 Gabor Dr (19711-6629)
PHONE..................302 292-3501
Greg Brant, *President*
Steve Friedman, *Vice Pres*
EMP: 32
SQ FT: 17,500
SALES (est): 5.1MM **Privately Held**
WEB: www.3dfabrication.com
SIC: 2541 Cabinets, except refrigerated: show, display, etc.: wood

(G-5856)
302 PROPERTIES LLC
250 Corporate Blvd Ste L (19702-3329)
PHONE..................302 753-8383
Lou Honick, *CEO*
EMP: 5
SALES (est): 499K **Privately Held**
SIC: 6512 Nonresidential building operators

(G-5857)
34M LLC
40 E Main St 1196 (19711-4639)
PHONE..................302 444-8290
Rory Opanasets, *Business Mgr*
EMP: 20
SALES (est): 1MM **Privately Held**
SIC: 7379 5045 7377 Computer hardware requirements analysis; computer software; computer hardware rental or leasing, except finance leasing

(G-5858)
360TOVISIT INC
2035 Sunset Lake Rd (19702-2600)
PHONE..................302 526-0575
Morgan Riche, *Director*
EMP: 11
SALES: 1.5MM **Privately Held**
SIC: 7371 Computer software development & applications

(G-5859)
3M COMPANY
650 Dawson Dr (19713-3412)
PHONE..................302 286-2480
Tom Flaherty, *Principal*
Joyce McGuire, *QC Mgr*
Thomas Stroz, *Executive*
EMP: 150
SALES (corp-wide): 32.7B **Publicly Held**
SIC: 3537 Industrial trucks & tractors
PA: 3m Company
   3m Center
   Saint Paul MN 55144
   651 733-1110

(G-5860)
51 AND PROSPECT
227 S Dillwyn Rd (19711-5549)
PHONE..................443 944-1934
Meaghan Daugherty, *Principal*
EMP: 4
SALES (est): 264.9K **Privately Held**
SIC: 5194 Smokeless tobacco

(G-5861)
6 STAR FUNDRAISING LLC
16 Revelstone Ct (19711-2981)
P.O. Box 1435, Hockessin (19707-5435)
PHONE..................302 250-5085
Doug Mostrom, *Sales Staff*
EMP: 25
SALES: 12MM **Privately Held**
SIC: 7389 Fund raising organizations;

(G-5862)
9193 4323 QUEBEC INC
Also Called: Dml Creation
2915 Ogletown Rd # 2385 (19713-1927)
PHONE..................855 824-0795
Ron De Moor, *President*
EMP: 3
SALES (corp-wide): 177.5K **Privately Held**
SIC: 3993 7336 Signs & advertising specialties; graphic arts & related design
PA: 9193-4323 Quebec Inc
   800 Rue Price
   Saint-Jerome QC J7Y 4
   514 750-0795

(G-5863)
A & H METALS INC
249 E Chestnut Hill Rd (19713-3734)
PHONE..................302 366-7540
Brian Perry, *President*
Anne Farnan, *Treasurer*
Antoinette Armento, *Admin Sec*
EMP: 35 EST: 1971
SQ FT: 26,000
SALES (est): 8.5MM **Privately Held**
WEB: www.ahmetals.com
SIC: 3444 Sheet metal specialties, not stamped; machine guards, sheet metal; hoods, range: sheet metal; flues & pipes, stove or furnace: sheet metal

(G-5864)
A & R FENCE CO INC
1126 Ralph Rd (19713-3249)
PHONE..................302 366-8550
Richard Read, *President*
Ronald Read Sr, *Corp Secy*
Ronald Read Jr, *Vice Pres*
EMP: 7
SALES: 700K **Privately Held**
SIC: 1799 7699 Fence construction; general household repair services

(G-5865)
A CARING DOCTOR MINNESOTA PA
1291 Churchmans Rd (19713-2149)
PHONE..................302 266-0122
Jessica Berkeridge, *Branch Mgr*
EMP: 20
SALES (corp-wide): 37.6B **Privately Held**
WEB: www.banfield.net
SIC: 0742 Animal hospital services, pets & other animal specialties
HQ: A Caring Doctor Minnesota Pa
   8000 Ne Tillamook St
   Portland OR 97213
   503 922-5000

(G-5866)
A FIELDS UNLIMITED LLC
200 Continental Dr (19713-4334)
PHONE..................800 484-2331
Regina Fields,
EMP: 4
SALES (est): 40.8K **Privately Held**
SIC: 7299 1521 Home improvement & renovation contractor agency; single-family housing construction

(G-5867)
A FRESH START CLG SVCS CORP
3 Linette Ct (19702-6815)
PHONE..................302 257-1099
EMP: 5 EST: 2017
SALES (est): 44.1K **Privately Held**
SIC: 8699 Membership Organization

(G-5868)
A L N CONSTRUCTION INC
104 Sandy Dr (19713-1147)
P.O. Box 7959 (19714-7959)
PHONE..................302 292-1580
Greg Peterson, *President*
EMP: 85
SQ FT: 3,500
SALES (est): 7.7MM **Privately Held**
SIC: 1742 Drywall

(G-5869)
A PLUS ELECTRIC & SECURITY
94 Stardust Dr (19702-4771)
PHONE..................302 455-1725
David Johnson, *Owner*
EMP: 6
SALES (est): 302.5K **Privately Held**
SIC: 1731 5065 5999 7382 General electrical contractor; security control equipment & systems; alarm & safety equipment stores; security systems services

(G-5870)
A S A P INSULATION INC
3019 Mcdaniel Ln (19702-4506)
PHONE..................302 836-9040
Helen W Kline, *President*
Thomas W Kline, *Vice Pres*
EMP: 11
SALES: 2MM **Privately Held**
SIC: 1742 Insulation, buildings

(G-5871)
A-DEL CONSTRUCTION COMPANY INC
10 Adel Dr (19702-1331)
PHONE..................302 453-8286
Barry J Baker, *President*
Sonny Johnson, *Vice Pres*
Harry G Johnson, *Admin Sec*
EMP: 100
SQ FT: 5,000
SALES (est): 35.6MM **Privately Held**
WEB: www.a-del.com
SIC: 1611 Highway & street paving contractor

(G-5872)
A1 STRIPING INC
902 Irish Bank Rd (19702-2135)
P.O. Box 3, Bear (19701-0003)
PHONE..................302 738-5016
Joseph Shortlidge, *Principal*
EMP: 8
SALES (est): 473.9K **Privately Held**
SIC: 1721 4959 7349 Pavement marking contractor; sweeping service: road, airport, parking lot, etc.; building maintenance services

(G-5873)
AAA CLUB ALLIANCE INC
200 Commerce Dr (19713-6804)
PHONE..................302 368-8175
Janyce Smalley, *Branch Mgr*
Mark Goodman, *Director*
EMP: 423
SALES (corp-wide): 528.9MM **Privately Held**
SIC: 8699 Automobile owners' association
PA: Aaa Club Alliance Inc.
   1 River Pl
   Wilmington DE 19801
   302 299-4700

(G-5874)
AAA CLUB ALLIANCE INC
200 Continental Dr # 402 (19713-4334)
PHONE..................302 283-4300
Margret Mary Burke, *Branch Mgr*
EMP: 12
SALES (corp-wide): 528.9MM **Privately Held**
WEB: www.aaamidatlantic.net
SIC: 6411 Insurance agents, brokers & service
PA: Aaa Club Alliance Inc.
   1 River Pl
   Wilmington DE 19801
   302 299-4700

(G-5875)
AAL DRTC
200 Gbc Dr (19702-2462)
PHONE..................302 229-5891
Christian Dussarrat, *Principal*
Vasuhi Rasanayagam, *Manager*
EMP: 6
SALES (est): 995.4K **Privately Held**
SIC: 2813 Oxygen, compressed or liquefied

(G-5876)
AARK NETWORK INC
1142 Elkton Rd (19711-3509)
PHONE..................302 399-3945
Pradip Saha, *President*
Bhupen Mandal, *Manager*
EMP: 70
SALES (est): 3.5MM **Privately Held**
SIC: 8741 Restaurant management

(G-5877)
AARON B POLECK D M D LLC
4735 Ogletown Stanton Rd # 1101 (19713-2089)
PHONE..................302 623-4190
EMP: 4
SALES (est): 208.3K **Privately Held**
SIC: 8021 Dentist's Office

(G-5878)
AARON B POLECK DDS
50 Omega Dr (19713-2060)
PHONE..................302 533-7649
Aaron B Poleck, *Principal*
EMP: 4
SALES (est): 67.6K **Privately Held**
SIC: 8021 Offices & clinics of dentists

(G-5879)
AB GROUP PACKAGING INC
1800 Ogletown Rd (19711-5472)
PHONE..................302 607-3281
◆ EMP: 4 EST: 2015
SALES (est): 148.1K **Privately Held**
SIC: 2674 Paper bags: made from purchased materials
PA: Premier Liveaboard Diving Limited
   19 Allington Garden
   Boston LINCS

(G-5880)
ABBA MONUMENT CO INC
94 Albe Dr Ste 1 (19702-1364)
PHONE..................302 738-0272
Theodore Kusters, *President*
EMP: 1
SALES: 180K **Privately Held**
SIC: 5999 2759 7389 3281 Monuments, finished to custom order; engraving; tombstone engraving; monuments, cut stone (not finishing or lettering only); tombstones, cut stone (not finishing or lettering only)

(G-5881)
ABBEY LEIN INC
28 Meteor Ct (19711-3026)
PHONE..................302 239-2712

Jeff Robinson, *President*
EMP: 5
SALES (est): 271.7K **Privately Held**
SIC: 3949 Golf equipment

(G-5882)
ABBY MEDICAL CENTER
Also Called: Gold Care Center
1 Centurian Dr Ste 301 (19713-2127)
PHONE..................302 999-0003
Arlen D Stone, *Partner*
Laurie Cox, *Office Mgr*
EMP: 5
SALES (est): 443.5K **Privately Held**
SIC: 8011 8031 Medical centers; offices & clinics of osteopathic physicians

(G-5883)
ABC SYSTEMS INC
92 White Clay Cres (19711-4847)
PHONE..................302 528-8875
Steve French, *President*
EMP: 8
SALES: 490K **Privately Held**
WEB: www.abc-systems-inc.com
SIC: 8748 Telecommunications consultant

(G-5884)
ABIGAIL FAMILY MEDICINE LLC
Also Called: Abbycare
412 Suburban Dr (19711-3564)
P.O. Box 147 (19715-0147)
PHONE..................302 738-3770
Christine Horah, *Owner*
EMP: 6
SALES: 750K **Privately Held**
SIC: 8011 General & family practice, physician/surgeon

(G-5885)
ABOVE ALL GTTER GARDENING SVCS
44 Fairway Rd Apt 2a (19711-5663)
PHONE..................302 478-0762
Paul Eirmann, *Owner*
EMP: 4 EST: 2014
SALES: 90K **Privately Held**
SIC: 0782 Garden services

(G-5886)
ABS ENGINEERING LLC
417 Jaymar Blvd (19702-2853)
PHONE..................302 595-9081
Taiseer Habib,
EMP: 4 EST: 2012
SQ FT: 1,600
SALES: 213K **Privately Held**
SIC: 7389 8742 Design, commercial & industrial; automation & robotics consultant

(G-5887)
ABSOLUTE COMPUTER SUPPORT LLC
249 E Main St Ste 1 (19711-7323)
PHONE..................717 917-8900
Kimberly M Crew,
Chris Acevedo,
Kimberly Erle,
Paul Kreamer,
EMP: 25
SQ FT: 1,000
SALES: 250K **Privately Held**
WEB: www.absolutecomputersupport.com
SIC: 7376 Computer facilities management

(G-5888)
ABSOLUTELY GREEN INC
Also Called: Lawn Doctor of Newark
995 S Chapel St Ste 3 (19713-3441)
P.O. Box 8130 (19714-8130)
PHONE..................302 731-1616
Brian Singleton, *President*
EMP: 15
SQ FT: 4,200
SALES (est): 1MM **Privately Held**
WEB: www.dnrec.state.de.us
SIC: 0782 Lawn care services

(G-5889)
ACCUDYNE SYSTEMS INC (PA)
210 Executive Dr Ste 5 (19702-3335)
PHONE..................302 369-5390
Ralph D Cope, *President*
Ralph Cope, *Senior Partner*
Mark Gruber, *Partner*
Curtis Ebersold, *Engineer*
Nan Gopez, *Engineer*
EMP: 30
SQ FT: 15,000
SALES (est): 10.4MM **Privately Held**
WEB: www.accudyne.com
SIC: 5084 Industrial machinery & equipment

(G-5890)
ACCUGENIX INC
223 Lake Dr (19702-3320)
PHONE..................302 292-8888
Douglas Smith, *President*
Ulrich Herber, *Managing Dir*
Patricia Wray, *COO*
Michael Waddington, *Vice Pres*
Joseph Martini, *CFO*
EMP: 41
SQ FT: 12,000
SALES (est): 4.1MM
SALES (corp-wide): 2.2B **Publicly Held**
WEB: www.accugenix.com
SIC: 8734 Testing laboratories
HQ: Charles River Laboratories, Inc.
251 Ballardvale St
Wilmington MA 01887
781 222-6000

(G-5891)
ACE CASH EXPRESS INC
14 Marrows Rd Ste B (19713-3702)
PHONE..................302 737-3785
Jason Raysor, *District Mgr*
EMP: 4
SALES (corp-wide): 2.5B **Privately Held**
SIC: 6099 Check cashing agencies
HQ: Populus Financial Group, Inc
1231 Greenway Dr Ste 600
Irving TX 75038
972 550-5000

(G-5892)
ACE RENT-A-CAR INC
915 S Chapel St (19713-3419)
PHONE..................302 368-5950
EMP: 22
SALES (corp-wide): 18.1MM **Privately Held**
SIC: 7514 Passenger car rental
PA: Ace Rent-A-Car, Inc.
4529 W 96th St
Indianapolis IN 46268
317 243-6536

(G-5893)
ACOPIA LLC
220 Continental Dr # 203 (19713-4312)
PHONE..................302 286-5172
EMP: 78
SALES (corp-wide): 46MM **Privately Held**
SIC: 6799 Investors
PA: Acopia, Llc
306 Northcreek Blvd # 100
Goodlettsville TN 37072
615 859-5537

(G-5894)
ACTION RENTAL INC
8 Mill Park Ct (19713-1986)
PHONE..................302 366-0749
Gregory Kerstey, *President*
EMP: 5 EST: 1969
SALES (est): 460K **Privately Held**
SIC: 7359 7513 Party supplies rental services; tool rental; furniture rental; home entertainment equipment rental; truck rental, without drivers

(G-5895)
ACTION SECURITY
100 Peoples Dr (19702-1306)
PHONE..................302 838-2852
Michael Doto, *Chief*
EMP: 6
SALES (est): 176.6K **Privately Held**
SIC: 7382 Security systems services

(G-5896)
ACTIVE DAY INC
Also Called: University De Active Day Ctr
200 Whitechapel Dr (19713-3811)
PHONE..................302 831-6774
Sharon Beard, *Manager*
EMP: 15 **Privately Held**
WEB: www.acsr.com
SIC: 8322 8361 Adult day care center; residential care
PA: Active Day, Inc.
6 Neshaminy Interplex Dr # 401
Trevose PA 19053

(G-5897)
ACUREN INSPECTION INC
6 Verdun Ct (19702-5525)
PHONE..................302 836-0165
Duane Edwards, *Manager*
EMP: 4
SALES (corp-wide): 1.7B **Privately Held**
SIC: 1389 Testing, measuring, surveying & analysis services
HQ: Acuren Inspection, Inc.
30 Main St Ste 402
Danbury CT 06810
203 702-8740

(G-5898)
ADAM BASEMENT (PA)
563 Walther Rd (19702-2903)
PHONE..................302 983-8446
EMP: 7
SALES (est): 970.1K **Privately Held**
SIC: 1799 Waterproofing

(G-5899)
ADECCO USA INC
Also Called: Adecco Staffing
1000 Samoset Dr (19713-6000)
PHONE..................302 457-4059
EMP: 7
SALES (corp-wide): 26.4B **Privately Held**
WEB: www.usadecco.com
SIC: 7363 Temporary help service
HQ: Adecco Usa, Inc.
10151 Deerwood Park Blvd
Jacksonville FL 32256
940 360-2000

(G-5900)
ADJUVANT RESEARCH SERVICES INC
1 Innovation Way Ste 400 (19711-5463)
PHONE..................302 737-5513
James Cinquina, *President*
EMP: 15
SQ FT: 1,000
SALES (est): 1MM **Privately Held**
WEB: www.adjres.com
SIC: 8742 Industry specialist consultants

(G-5901)
ADMIRALS CLUB APTS2C
Also Called: Admirals Club Apartments
41 Fairway Rd Ofc 2c (19711-5660)
PHONE..................302 737-8496
Fair Joyce, *Manager*
EMP: 20
SALES (est): 835.5K **Privately Held**
SIC: 6513 Apartment building operators

(G-5902)
ADT LLC
Also Called: Protection One
130 Executive Dr Ste 2 (19702-3349)
PHONE..................302 918-1016
Mark Costa, *Manager*
Christopher Siburt, *Manager*
Jamie R Haenggi, *Officer*
EMP: 13
SALES (corp-wide): 4.5B **Publicly Held**
SIC: 7381 Guard services
HQ: Adt Llc
1501 W Yamato Rd
Boca Raton FL 33431
561 988-3600

(G-5903)
ADVANCE WNDW/SPRIOR SIDING INC
11 Mcmillan Way Ste A (19713-3456)
PHONE..................302 324-8890
Gary Derrick, *President*
Doug Derrick, *Vice Pres*
Audery Derrick, *Admin Sec*
EMP: 13
SQ FT: 5,500
SALES (est): 1.7MM **Privately Held**
WEB: www.advancewindowsiding.com
SIC: 1521 Single-family home remodeling, additions & repairs

(G-5904)
ADVANCED COATINGS ENGRG LLC
2915 Ogletown Rd (19713-1927)
PHONE..................888 607-0000
Michael Draven,
EMP: 33
SALES (est): 812.5K **Privately Held**
SIC: 1731 Safety & security specialization

(G-5905)
ADVANCED FOOT & ANKLE CENTER
774 Christiana Rd Ste 105 (19713-4248)
PHONE..................302 355-0056
Raymond Dipretoro, *Owner*
EMP: 6
SALES (est): 536K **Privately Held**
SIC: 8043 Offices & clinics of podiatrists

(G-5906)
ADVANCED PLASTIC SURGERY CENTE
4735 Ogletown Stanton Rd (19713-2072)
PHONE..................302 623-4004
Theresa A Adams, *Principal*
Lawrence Chang, *Med Doctor*
Joseph Thornton, *Practice Mgr*
EMP: 11
SALES (est): 1.2MM **Privately Held**
SIC: 8011 Plastic surgeon

(G-5907)
ADVANCED POWER CONTROL INC (HQ)
Also Called: Albireo Energy
126 Sandy Dr (19713-1147)
PHONE..................302 368-0443
Paul E Czerwin, *President*
Paul Fuller, *Project Mgr*
Ken Gildea, *Purch Agent*
Toni Hartman, *Project Engr*
Timothy Krohn, *Senior Engr*
EMP: 64 EST: 1980
SQ FT: 10,000
SALES (est): 11.5MM
SALES (corp-wide): 55MM **Privately Held**
WEB: www.adv-power.com
SIC: 1731 Energy management controls
PA: Albireo Energy, Llc
3 Ethel Rd Ste 300
Edison NJ 08817
732 512-9100

(G-5908)
ADVANCED SYSTEMS INC
202 Cheltenham Rd (19711-3681)
P.O. Box 8032 (19714-8032)
PHONE..................302 368-1211
Marlene O Moore, *President*
EMP: 5
SALES (est): 200K **Privately Held**
SIC: 8742 Quality assurance consultant

(G-5909)
ADVANCED TRAINING ACADMEY
9 Prospect Ave (19711-2261)
PHONE..................302 369-8800
Bowen Wang, *Principal*
EMP: 12 EST: 1999
SALES: 150K **Privately Held**
SIC: 8331 Skill training center

(G-5910)
ADVANCEXING PAIN & REHABLTATN
620 Stanton Christiana Rd # 202 (19713-2130)
PHONE..................302 384-7439
Selina Xing, *Owner*
EMP: 12 EST: 2010
SALES (est): 400K **Privately Held**
SIC: 8093 Rehabilitation center, outpatient treatment

(G-5911)
ADVANTDGE HLTHCARE SLTIONS INC
307 Ruthar Dr (19711-8016)
P.O. Box 41263, Staten Island NY (10304-7263)
PHONE..................302 224-5678

GEOGRAPHIC SECTION

Newark - New Castle County (G-5941)

EMP: 7
SALES (corp-wide): 69.6MM **Privately Held**
SIC: 8721 Billing & bookkeeping service
PA: Advantedge Healthcare Solutions, Inc.
30 Technology Dr Ste 1n
Warren NJ 07059
908 279-8111

(G-5912)
ADVERTISING HEALTHY INC
210 Sweetgrass Run (19702-1154)
P.O. Box 1415, Bear (19701-7415)
PHONE 302 366-7502
Lori Copes, *President*
EMP: 4
SALES: 25K **Privately Held**
SIC: 7311 Advertising agencies

(G-5913)
AEARO TECHNOLOGIES LLC
E-A-R Specialty Composites Div
650 Dawson Dr (19713-3412)
PHONE 302 283-5497
George Klett, *Manager*
EMP: 75
SALES (corp-wide): 32.7B **Publicly Held**
WEB: www.aearo.com
SIC: 3081 3086 2821 Unsupported plastics film & sheet; plastics foam products; plastics materials & resins
HQ: Aearo Technologies Llc
5457 W 79th St
Indianapolis IN 46268
317 692-6666

(G-5914)
AES FOODS
83 Albe Dr Ste F (19702-1374)
PHONE 302 420-8377
Patrick Kinyanga, *President*
EMP: 2 **EST:** 2014
SALES (est): 127K **Privately Held**
SIC: 2013 Sausages & other prepared meats

(G-5915)
AESOPS GABLES INC
9 Whitfield Rd (19711-4817)
PHONE 302 737-2683
EMP: 4
SALES (est): 320K **Privately Held**
SIC: 5039 Whol Construction Materials

(G-5916)
AETNA HOSE HOOK & LADDER CO 9
Also Called: Aetna Banquet Hall
400 Ogletown Rd (19711-5402)
PHONE 302 454-3305
EMP: 50 **Privately Held**
SIC: 6324 Health maintenance organization (HMO), insurance only
PA: Aetna Hose Hook & Ladder Co.
31 Academy St
Newark DE 19711
302 454-3300

(G-5917)
AETNA HOSE HOOK AND LADDER CO
31 Academy St (19711-4608)
P.O. Box 148 (19715-0148)
PHONE 302 454-3300
Jim Wood, *President*
EMP: 3
SALES: 4.4MM **Privately Held**
SIC: 3711 Fire department vehicles (motor vehicles), assembly of

(G-5918)
AETNA INC
750 Prides Xing Ste 200 (19713-6105)
PHONE 860 808-3458
Jamie McCarrick, *Manager*
EMP: 6
SALES (corp-wide): 194.5B **Publicly Held**
SIC: 6324 Health maintenance organization (HMO), insurance only
HQ: Aetna Inc.
151 Farmington Ave
Hartford CT 06156

(G-5919)
AFFORDABLE SOD INC
1 S Wynwyd Dr (19711-7426)
PHONE 302 545-0275
Stan Spoor, *Owner*
EMP: 5
SALES (est): 195.4K **Privately Held**
SIC: 0181 Sod farms

(G-5920)
AGORA NET INC
314 E Main St Ste 1 (19711-7195)
PHONE 302 224-2475
John Gray, *President*
Lorie Miller, *Vice Pres*
Tom Way, *Vice Pres*
Loris Miller, *Treasurer*
Betsy Warren, *Office Mgr*
EMP: 12
SALES: 500K **Privately Held**
WEB: www.agora-net.com
SIC: 7371 Computer software development

(G-5921)
AIKIKAI FOUNDATION OF DELAWARE
103 Jupiter Rd Ste A (19711-3426)
PHONE 302 369-2454
Zenko Okimura, *Branch Mgr*
EMP: 6
SALES (est): 180.4K **Privately Held**
WEB: www.aikidoda.org
SIC: 7999 Martial arts school
PA: Aikikai Foundation Of Delaware Inc
667 Dawson Dr Ste A
Newark DE

(G-5922)
AILA PTY INC
2035 Sunset Lake Rd B2 (19702-2600)
PHONE 626 693-0598
Rongde Lu, *CEO*
EMP: 20
SALES (est): 375.4K **Privately Held**
SIC: 7371 Computer software development & applications

(G-5923)
AION PRIDES COURT LLC
Also Called: Liberty Square
6 Sussex Rd Ofc F (19713-3119)
PHONE 302 737-2085
Robin Flagler,
EMP: 4
SALES (est): 111K
SALES (corp-wide): 3.6MM **Privately Held**
SIC: 6513 Apartment building operators
PA: Aion Management Llc
1 S Broad St Ste 1860
Philadelphia PA 19107
215 999-2849

(G-5924)
AION UNIVERSITY VILLAGE LLC
Also Called: Liberty Pointe
2017 Mederia Cir (19702)
PHONE 302 366-8000
Robin Flagler,
EMP: 5
SALES (est): 167.7K
SALES (corp-wide): 3.6MM **Privately Held**
SIC: 6513 Apartment building operators
PA: Aion Management Llc
1 S Broad St Ste 1860
Philadelphia PA 19107
215 999-2849

(G-5925)
AIR LQIDE ADVANCED TECH US LLC
200 Gbc Dr (19702-2462)
PHONE 302 225-1100
EMP: 2
SALES (corp-wide): 121.9MM **Privately Held**
SIC: 2813 Industrial gases
HQ: Air Liquide Advanced Technologies Us Llc
9807 Katy Fwy
Houston TX 77024

(G-5926)
AIR NATURES WAY INC
5 Myers Rd (19713-2316)
PHONE 302 738-3063
Patricia Sutton, *Principal*
EMP: 2
SALES (est): 144.7K **Privately Held**
SIC: 3564 Purification & dust collection equipment

(G-5927)
AIRGAS USA LLC
200 Gbc Dr (19702-2462)
PHONE 302 286-5400
Trapti Chaubey, *Research*
Robert Baird, *Financial Analy*
Patricia McQueeney, *Branch Mgr*
EMP: 17
SALES (corp-wide): 121.9MM **Privately Held**
SIC: 5084 Welding machinery & equipment
HQ: Airgas Usa, Llc
259 N Radnor Chester Rd
Radnor PA 19087
610 687-5253

(G-5928)
AIRSLED INC
70 Aleph Dr Ste A (19702-1359)
PHONE 302 292-8911
Steve Wolfgang, *CEO*
Bruce F Harvey, *Ch of Bd*
Karen Edwards, *Vice Pres*
EMP: 5
SALES (est): 1.1MM **Privately Held**
WEB: www.airsled.com
SIC: 3535 5084 3537 Conveyors & conveying equipment; materials handling machinery; industrial trucks & tractors

(G-5929)
AJEDIUM FILM GROUP LLC
100 Interchange Blvd (19711-3549)
PHONE 302 452-6609
Peter Woldson, *CEO*
Richard Giacco, *President*
▲ **EMP:** 6
SALES (est): 1.5MM **Privately Held**
WEB: www.ajedium.com
SIC: 3081 Plastic film & sheet

(G-5930)
ALEX AND ANI LLC
132 Christiana Mall (19702-3202)
PHONE 302 731-1420
EMP: 6 **Privately Held**
SIC: 5944 3911 Jewelry, precious stones & precious metals; jewelry, precious metal
PA: Alex And Ani, Llc
2000 Chapel View Blvd # 360
Cranston RI 02920

(G-5931)
ALI S HUSAIN ORTHODONTIST (PA)
Also Called: Husain, Ali S DMD Msd
1400 Peoples Plz Ste 312 (19702-5708)
PHONE 302 838-1400
Ali S Husain, *Owner*
EMP: 14
SQ FT: 2,800
SALES (est): 797.9K **Privately Held**
WEB: www.delawareorthodontics.com
SIC: 8021 Orthodontist

(G-5932)
ALL ABOUT WOMEN LLC
4735 Ogletown Stanton Rd # 2300 (19713-8005)
PHONE 302 224-8400
Diane McCracken, *Principal*
Tara Hood, *Obstetrician*
Veronica Mahon, *Obstetrician*
Regina Smith, *Obstetrician*
EMP: 21
SALES (est): 3.5MM **Privately Held**
SIC: 8011 General & family practice, physician/surgeon

(G-5933)
ALL CLASSICS LTD
66 Albe Dr (19702-1322)
P.O. Box 5 (19715-0005)
PHONE 302 738-2190
Darren Hussey, *Owner*
▲ **EMP:** 4
SALES (est): 499.8K **Privately Held**
WEB: www.allclassics.com
SIC: 5199 Statuary

(G-5934)
ALL HKED UP TWING RECOVERY LLC
102 Pattie Dr (19702-2803)
PHONE 302 545-1205
William Conner, *Principal*
EMP: 4 **EST:** 2010
SALES (est): 176.7K **Privately Held**
SIC: 7549 Towing service, automotive

(G-5935)
ALL PEOPLES FOOD LLC
62 Albe Dr Ste B (19702-1370)
PHONE 302 690-4881
Frederick Ebede, *Principal*
▲ **EMP:** 1
SALES (est): 640.3K **Privately Held**
SIC: 2099 Food preparations

(G-5936)
ALL THE DIFFERENCE INC
119 Saint Regis Dr (19711-3822)
PHONE 302 738-6353
Kristina Stroh, *Exec Dir*
EMP: 12
SALES: 304K **Privately Held**
WEB: www.allthedifference.org
SIC: 8093 Rehabilitation center, outpatient treatment

(G-5937)
ALL TRANS TRANSMISSION INC
18 Albe Dr Ste F (19702-1353)
PHONE 302 366-0104
Mark Bulovas, *President*
EMP: 5
SQ FT: 4,000
SALES (est): 502.2K **Privately Held**
WEB: www.alltranstransmission.com
SIC: 7537 Automotive transmission repair shops

(G-5938)
ALLEGIANT FIRE PROTECTION LLC
118 Sandy Dr Ste 6 (19713-1177)
PHONE 302 276-1300
Frank Rivera, *Superintendent*
Frederick Hill, *Vice Pres*
Fred Hill, *Vice Pres*
Robert Hill, *Vice Pres*
EMP: 5
SALES (est): 726.5K **Privately Held**
SIC: 7389 Fire protection service other than forestry or public

(G-5939)
ALLERGY ASSOCIATES PA
2600 Glasgow Ave Ste 201 (19702-5704)
PHONE 302 834-3401
Micheal Wydila, *CEO*
EMP: 7
SALES (est): 445.9K **Privately Held**
SIC: 8011 Medical centers; allergist

(G-5940)
ALLIANCE ELECTRIC INC
1003 S Chapel St Ste D (19702-1357)
PHONE 302 366-0295
Kevin Morgan, *President*
EMP: 12
SQ FT: 2,068
SALES: 3MM **Privately Held**
WEB: www.alliance-electric.net
SIC: 1731 General electrical contractor

(G-5941)
ALLOSENTRY LLC
2035 Sunset Lake Rd B2 (19702-2600)
PHONE 617 838-7608
Laird Choi, *CEO*
Lulu Fan, *President*
EMP: 2
SQ FT: 1,000
SALES (est): 56.5K **Privately Held**
SIC: 7372 Application computer software

Newark - New Castle County (G-5942)

(G-5942)
ALLOW ME ERRAND SERVICE LLC
5 Peddlers Row (19702-1525)
PHONE....................302 480-0954
Lebonne Jerome Mathis, *Owner*
EMP: 13
SALES (est): 656.3K **Privately Held**
SIC: 8322 Individual & family services

(G-5943)
ALLSTATE VAN & STORAGE CORP
910 Interchange Blvd (19711-3563)
PHONE....................302 369-0230
Thomas Bennett III, *President*
EMP: 20
SALES (est): 1.2MM **Privately Held**
SIC: 4225 General warehousing & storage

(G-5944)
ALLURA BATH & KITCHEN INC
704 Interchange Blvd (19711-3595)
PHONE....................302 731-2851
Alan J Pannaccione, *President*
EMP: 6
SQ FT: 5,144
SALES (est): 1.2MM **Privately Held**
SIC: 1799 5031 Kitchen & bathroom remodeling; kitchen cabinets

(G-5945)
ALMA COMPANY
625 Barksdale Rd (19711-4535)
PHONE....................302 731-4427
Jeffrey Morton, *President*
EMP: 5
SALES (est): 300K **Privately Held**
SIC: 8721 Accounting services, except auditing

(G-5946)
ALMOST HOME DAY CARE
1129 Capitol Trl (19711-3921)
PHONE....................302 220-6731
EMP: 5
SALES (est): 89.8K **Privately Held**
SIC: 8082 Home health care services

(G-5947)
ALTERED IMAGES HAIR STUDIO
45 Abelia Ln (19711-3415)
PHONE....................302 234-2151
Nancy Marenco, *Partner*
Kimberly Willis, *Partner*
EMP: 4
SALES (est): 103.4K **Privately Held**
SIC: 7231 7241 Hairdressers; barber shops

(G-5948)
ALTERNATIVE ECO ENERGY LLC
6 S Dillwyn Rd (19711-5544)
PHONE....................404 434-0660
M Steven Gronka,
EMP: 1
SALES: 950K **Privately Held**
SIC: 3714 Motor vehicle parts & accessories

(G-5949)
ALTERNATIVE THERAPY LLC
4629 Ogletown Stanton Rd (19713-2006)
PHONE....................302 368-0800
Rachele Louis, *Mng Member*
EMP: 7
SALES (est): 143.1K **Privately Held**
SIC: 7299 7991 Massage parlor; spas

(G-5950)
AMERICAN EXPRESS SHUTTLE INC
Also Called: AES Foods
83 Albe Dr Ste F (19702-1374)
PHONE....................302 420-8377
Patrick Kinyanga, *President*
EMP: 1
SALES (est): 65.2K **Privately Held**
SIC: 2015 Poultry sausage, luncheon meats & other poultry products

(G-5951)
AMERICAN FEDERATION
698 Old Baltimore Pike (19702-1312)
PHONE....................302 283-1330
Sam Lathem, *President*
EMP: 4
SALES (corp-wide): 154.8MM **Privately Held**
WEB: www.aflcio.org
SIC: 8631 Collective bargaining unit
PA: American Federation Of Labor & Congress Of Industrial Organzation
815 16th St Nw
Washington DC 20006
202 637-5000

(G-5952)
AMERICAN HEART ASSOCIATION INC
200 Continental Dr # 101 (19713-4303)
PHONE....................302 454-0613
Jim Rezac, *Branch Mgr*
Mary Merritt, *Exec Dir*
EMP: 12
SALES (corp-wide): 460.7MM **Privately Held**
WEB: www.americanheart.org
SIC: 8621 Professional membership organizations
PA: American Heart Association, Inc.
7272 Greenville Ave
Dallas TX 75231
214 373-6500

(G-5953)
AMERICAN HOMEPATIENT INC
701 Interchange Blvd (19711-3594)
PHONE....................302 454-4941
Joseph Cozza, *Manager*
EMP: 68 **Privately Held**
WEB: www.ahom.com
SIC: 7352 5999 Medical equipment rental; medical apparatus & supplies
HQ: American Homepatient, Inc.
5213 Linbar Dr Ste 408
Nashville TN 37211
615 221-8884

(G-5954)
AMERICAN KARATE STUDIOS
Also Called: Academy Bind Body Arts
1150 Capitol Trl (19711-3933)
P.O. Box 9102 (19714-9102)
PHONE....................302 737-9500
Jim Clapp, *Owner*
EMP: 20
SALES (est): 580K **Privately Held**
SIC: 7999 7991 Martial arts school; aerobic dance & exercise classes

(G-5955)
AMERICAN LUNG ASSN OF DEL
630 Churchmans Rd Ste 202 (19702-1944)
PHONE....................302 737-6414
Debra P Brown, *Director*
Debra Brown, *Director*
EMP: 8
SQ FT: 3,000
SALES (est): 551.2K
SALES (corp-wide): 42.8MM **Privately Held**
WEB: www.alase.org
SIC: 8621 Professional membership organizations
PA: American Lung Association
55 W Wacker Dr Ste 1150
Chicago IL 60601
312 801-7600

(G-5956)
AMERICAN PHILOSOPHICAL ASSN
Also Called: UNIVERSITY OF DELAWARE
31 Amstel Ave (19716-4200)
PHONE....................302 831-1112
Kevin Rose, *COO*
William Mann, *Exec Dir*
Amy Ferrer, *Director*
Joseph I Daniel, *Director*
Theresa Derose, *Executive*
EMP: 10
SALES: 1.6MM **Privately Held**
SIC: 8621 Education & teacher association

(G-5957)
AMERICAN SLEEP MEDICINE LLC
200 Continental Dr # 112 (19713-4369)
PHONE....................302 366-0111
Raj Mangat, *Manager*
EMP: 31
SALES (corp-wide): 29.6MM **Privately Held**
SIC: 8099 Blood related health services
PA: American Sleep Medicine, Llc
7900 Blfort Pkwy Ste 301b
Jacksonville FL 32256
904 517-5500

(G-5958)
AMERICAN SPIRIT FEDERAL CR UN
1110 Elkton Rd (19711-3509)
PHONE....................302 738-4515
Maurice Dawkins, *President*
Jack Cable, *Info Tech Dir*
Susanne Spaulding,
EMP: 14
SALES: 2.2MM **Privately Held**
SIC: 6061 6163 Federal credit unions; loan brokers

(G-5959)
AMERICAN SPIRIT FEDERAL CR UN
1110 Elkton Rd (19711-3509)
PHONE....................302 738-4515
Robert L Watson Jr, *President*
Lewis O Reisinger, *Vice Pres*
George Bush Jr, *Treasurer*
Elijah Wright Jr, *Admin Sec*
EMP: 14
SALES: 2.3MM **Privately Held**
WEB: www.americanspirit.org
SIC: 6061 Federal credit unions

(G-5960)
AMERICAN UNIVERSAL LLC
Also Called: American Kidney Care
1415 Pulaski Hwy Ste 2 (19702-5104)
PHONE....................302 836-9790
John J McDonough, *COO*
EMP: 5
SALES (est): 161.8K **Publicly Held**
SIC: 8351 Child day care services
PA: American Renal Associates Holdings, Inc.
500 Cummings Ctr Ste 6550
Beverly MA 01915

(G-5961)
AMERICAN VAN STORAGE CORP
Also Called: American Records Management
900 Interchange Blvd (19711-3563)
PHONE....................302 369-0900
Thomas Bennett III, *President*
Marc Quirk, *Opers Staff*
EMP: 20
SQ FT: 40,000
SALES (est): 2.4MM **Privately Held**
WEB: www.americande.com
SIC: 4213 4225 Household goods transport; general warehousing

(G-5962)
AMETEK INC
Ametek Prcess Anlytical Instrs
455 Corporate Blvd (19702-3332)
PHONE....................302 456-4400
Kenneth Spencer, *Warehouse Mgr*
Diana DEA, *Buyer*
Paul Baatz, *Engineer*
Jim Burns, *Branch Mgr*
Joe Orzechowski, *Sr Software Eng*
EMP: 65
SALES (corp-wide): 4.8B **Publicly Held**
SIC: 3399 3621 3826 3823 Powder, metal; motors & generators; moisture analyzers; industrial instrmnts msrmnt display/control process variable; plotters, computer
PA: Ametek, Inc.
1100 Cassatt Rd
Berwyn PA 19312
610 647-2121

(G-5963)
AMPLIFIED GCHMICAL IMAGING LLC
210 Executive Dr Ste 1 (19702-3335)
PHONE....................302 266-2428
Harry S Anderson, *COO*
Grant J Tonkin, *CFO*
Paul Harrington, *Sales Staff*
EMP: 6 EST: 2007
SALES (est): 494.4K **Privately Held**
SIC: 8713

(G-5964)
AMY M FARRALL OD LLC
317 E Main St (19711-7152)
PHONE....................302 737-5777
Dr Amy Farrall, *Owner*
EMP: 6
SALES (est): 235.3K **Privately Held**
SIC: 8042 Offices & clinics of optometrists

(G-5965)
ANACONDA PRTCTIVE CONCEPTS INC
210 Executive Dr Ste 6 (19702-3335)
PHONE....................302 834-1125
Nancy L Dunfee, *President*
EMP: 10
SALES (est): 2.2MM **Privately Held**
SIC: 7382 1731 Burglar alarm maintenance & monitoring; general electrical contractor

(G-5966)
ANCAR ENTERPRISES LLC
Also Called: AlphaGraphics
703 Interchange Blvd (19711-3594)
PHONE....................302 453-2600
Atul Chugh, *President*
EMP: 11
SALES (corp-wide): 1.2MM **Privately Held**
WEB: www.thompsonsearchconsultants.com
SIC: 2752 Commercial printing, lithographic
PA: Ancar Enterprises Llc
3411 Silverside Rd 103
Wilmington DE 19810
302 477-1884

(G-5967)
ANDRE M D HOFFMAN
1090 Old Churchmans Rd (19713-2102)
PHONE....................302 892-2710
Andre Hoffman, *Med Doctor*
EMP: 6
SALES (est): 80.5K **Privately Held**
SIC: 8011 Offices & clinics of medical doctors

(G-5968)
ANDREY GEORGIEFF MD
83 E Main St 3 (19716-0600)
PHONE....................302 998-1866
David Wien MD, *Owner*
EMP: 4
SALES (est): 230K **Privately Held**
SIC: 8011 Offices & clinics of medical doctors

(G-5969)
ANGLE WIRELESS WHOLESALE LLC
11 Avignon Dr (19702-5511)
PHONE....................302 883-7788
EMP: 4
SALES (est): 157.8K **Privately Held**
SIC: 4812 Cellular telephone services

(G-5970)
ANGLER PLUMBING LLC
37 Dempsey Dr (19713-1930)
PHONE....................302 293-5691
Robert Grabowski,
EMP: 7
SALES (est): 470K **Privately Held**
SIC: 1711 Plumbing contractors

(G-5971)
ANGRY 8 LLC (PA)
200 Continental Dr # 401 (19713-4334)
PHONE....................203 304-9256
Frank H Brady,
EMP: 10

SALES: 2MM Privately Held
SIC: 5149 Beverages, except coffee & tea

(G-5972)
ANNS FAMILY DAYCARE
30 Reubens Cir (19702-3034)
PHONE...................................302 836-8910
Shawn Ennis, *Principal*
EMP: 5
SALES (est): 74.5K Privately Held
SIC: 8351 Child day care services

(G-5973)
ANTENNA HOUSE INC
500 Creek View Rd Ste 107 (19711-8549)
PHONE...................................302 427-2456
Tokushige Kobayashi, *President*
Michael Miller, *Exec VP*
EMP: 6
SALES (est): 1MM Privately Held
WEB: www.xslformatter.com
SIC: 7379 5734 Computer related maintenance services; computer & software stores

(G-5974)
ANTHONY LEE CUCUZZELLA MD
Also Called: Physiatrist Assoc
4735 Ogletown Stanton Rd # 3302 (19713-2094)
PHONE...................................302 623-4370
Anthony L Cucuzzella, *Owner*
Anthony Cucuzzella, *Principal*
EMP: 16
SALES (est): 1.8MM Privately Held
SIC: 8011 Physical medicine, physician/surgeon

(G-5975)
ANTONIO C NARVAEZ MD
2602 Eastburn Ctr (19711-7285)
PHONE...................................302 453-1002
Antonio C Narvaez MD, *Owner*
EMP: 5
SALES (est): 114.3K Privately Held
SIC: 8011 Offices & clinics of medical doctors

(G-5976)
ANYA INTERNATIONAL LLC
113 Barksdale Pro Ctr (19711-3258)
PHONE...................................847 850-0920
Tamara Khazin, *Mng Member*
EMP: 25
SQ FT: 1,500
SALES (est): 961.6K Privately Held
SIC: 3961 Costume jewelry

(G-5977)
ANYTHING UNDER SUN LLC
3027 Rosetree Ln (19702-2131)
PHONE...................................302 292-1023
John Day Jr,
EMP: 1
SALES (est): 39.6K Privately Held
SIC: 3999 Pet supplies

(G-5978)
ANYTIME FITNESS
201 Louviers Dr (19711-4164)
PHONE...................................302 738-3040
Troy Rinker, *Principal*
EMP: 6
SALES (est): 188K Privately Held
SIC: 7991 Physical fitness clubs with training equipment

(G-5979)
AOZ FOOD AND GAS LLC
9 Wenark Dr Apt 8 (19713-1418)
PHONE...................................302 981-2966
Syed Jaffery, *Principal*
EMP: 4
SALES (est): 201.3K Privately Held
SIC: 4212 Local trucking, without storage

(G-5980)
APEX DENTAL CENTER LLC
537 Stanton Christn Rd # 211 (19713-2148)
PHONE...................................302 633-7550
Veena Reddy, *Executive*
EMP: 4

SALES (est): 307.8K Privately Held
SIC: 8021 Dental clinic

(G-5981)
APEX MANUFACTURING GROUP INC
825 Dawson Dr Ste 1&2 (19712-0824)
PHONE...................................484 888-6252
Mary Kuklinski, *Admin Sec*
EMP: 1
SALES (corp-wide): 392K Privately Held
SIC: 3599 Machine shop, jobbing & repair
PA: Apex Manufacturing Group Inc.
    825 Dawson Dr Ste 1
    Newark DE 19713
    484 888-6252

(G-5982)
APEX MANUFACTURING GROUP INC (PA)
825 Dawson Dr Ste 1 (19713-3438)
PHONE...................................484 888-6252
John Kuklinski, *Principal*
Mary Kuklinski, *Admin Sec*
EMP: 3 EST: 2016
SQ FT: 10,000
SALES (est): 392K Privately Held
SIC: 3599 Machine shop, jobbing & repair

(G-5983)
APOLLO SCITECH LLC
18 Shea Way Ste 108 (19713-3448)
PHONE...................................302 861-6557
Yanping Amy Chen, *President*
EMP: 3 EST: 2014
SQ FT: 2,250
SALES (est): 321K Privately Held
SIC: 3826 Gas analyzing equipment

(G-5984)
APPHIVE INC
2035 Sunset Lake Rd (19702-2600)
PHONE...................................240 898-4661
Jonatan Vazquez Pia, *CEO*
EMP: 8 Privately Held
SIC: 7371 7389 Computer software development & applications; business services

(G-5985)
APPLIED ANALYTICS INC
113 Barksdale Pro Ctr (19711-3258)
PHONE...................................781 791-5005
Giselle Ridderplaat, *President*
Grogory Elias, *Director*
EMP: 30
SQ FT: 12,000
SALES: 5.5MM Privately Held
SIC: 3823 Industrial process measurement equipment

(G-5986)
APPLIED BANK
660 Plaza De Rte 89 (19713)
PHONE...................................302 326-4200
Loreen Newman, *Branch Mgr*
EMP: 15 Privately Held
SIC: 6021 National commercial banks
PA: Applied Bank
    2200 Concord Pike Ste 102
    Wilmington DE 19803

(G-5987)
APPLIED CONTROL ENGRG INC (PA)
700 Creek View Rd (19711-8544)
P.O. Box 520, Hockessin (19707-0520)
PHONE...................................302 738-8800
Ian P Burns, *President*
Shawn T Coughlan, *Vice Pres*
David N Erby, *Vice Pres*
Gary A Hida, *Vice Pres*
Michael A Lennon, *Vice Pres*
EMP: 60
SQ FT: 20,800
SALES: 26MM Privately Held
WEB: www.ace-net.com
SIC: 7371 7373 7379 Custom computer programming services; computer systems analysis & design; computer related consulting services

(G-5988)
APPLIED VIRTUAL SOLUTIONS LLC
16 N Bellwoode Dr (19702-3415)
P.O. Box 1625, Bear (19701-7625)
PHONE...................................302 312-8548
Willa Lee,
EMP: 6 EST: 2015
SALES: 20K Privately Held
SIC: 7389 Telephone answering service

(G-5989)
APPLOYE INC
2035 Sunset Lake Rd B2 (19702-2600)
PHONE...................................925 452-6102
Mohammad Sheikh, *Principal*
Mohammad Nazrul Islam Sheikh, *Principal*
EMP: 4
SALES: 10K Privately Held
SIC: 7372 7371 Business oriented computer software; computer software development & applications

(G-5990)
APRIA HEALTHCARE LLC
225 Lake Dr (19702-3320)
PHONE...................................302 737-7979
David Sikorsky, *Branch Mgr*
EMP: 22 Privately Held
WEB: www.apria.com
SIC: 7352 Medical equipment rental
HQ: Apria Healthcare Llc
    26220 Enterprise Ct
    Lake Forest CA 92630
    949 639-2000

(G-5991)
AQUA FLOW SPRINKLERS
52 W Stephen Dr (19713-1867)
PHONE...................................302 369-3629
Jamie Waltz, *Owner*
EMP: 1
SALES: 30K Privately Held
SIC: 3432 7929 Lawn hose nozzles & sprinklers; disc jockey service

(G-5992)
AQUA WASH INC
4142 Ogletown Stanton Rd (19713-4169)
PHONE...................................302 994-1720
Amy Grubb, *President*
Mark Grubb, *Vice Pres*
EMP: 5
SALES (est): 107.5K Privately Held
SIC: 7349 Building & office cleaning services; cleaning service, industrial or commercial

(G-5993)
AQUACAST LINER LLC
100 Lake Dr Ste 200 (19702-3361)
PHONE...................................302 535-3728
Mark Monahan,
EMP: 75
SQ FT: 2,000
SALES: 10MM Privately Held
SIC: 2899 Waterproofing compounds

(G-5994)
ARGILLA BREWING COMPANY
2667 Kirkwood Hwy (19711-7242)
PHONE...................................302 731-8200
EMP: 5
SALES (est): 432.6K Privately Held
SIC: 5181 Beer & ale

(G-5995)
ARMED FORCES DRIVING SCHOOL
14 Waltham St (19713-1627)
PHONE...................................302 981-6903
EMP: 4
SALES (est): 270K Privately Held
SIC: 4213 Trucking Operator-Nonlocal

(G-5996)
ARMOR GRAPHICS INC
1102 Ogletown Rd (19711-5416)
P.O. Box 386, Cheswold (19936-0386)
PHONE...................................302 737-8790
Margaret Allen, *President*
David Allen, *Vice Pres*
EMP: 5 EST: 2001
SQ FT: 1,500

SALES (est): 605.9K Privately Held
WEB: www.armorgraphics.com
SIC: 2752 Commercial printing, offset; photo-offset printing

(G-5997)
ARNAB MOBILITY INC
2035 Sunset Lake Rd B2 (19702-2600)
PHONE...................................774 316-6767
Hamad Obaid Rashid Obaid, *CEO*
Hamad Obaid Rashid Obaid Alsha, *CEO*
EMP: 15
SALES (est): 299.3K Privately Held
SIC: 7371 Software programming applications

(G-5998)
ARNOLD INTERNATIONAL INC
573 Bellevue Rd Ste B (19713-5801)
PHONE...................................302 266-4441
John Michael Arnold, *President*
Margaret Arnold, *Vice Pres*
▲ EMP: 5
SQ FT: 4,500
SALES: 560K Privately Held
SIC: 5084 Machine tools & accessories

(G-5999)
ART BEAT
2431 Sunset Lake Rd (19702-4038)
PHONE...................................302 834-5700
Donna L Del Grosso, *Owner*
EMP: 2
SALES (est): 114.2K Privately Held
SIC: 3993 Signs & advertising specialties

(G-6000)
ARTESIAN RESOURCES CORPORATION (PA)
664 Churchmans Rd (19702-1934)
P.O. Box 15004, Wilmington (19850-5004)
PHONE...................................302 453-6900
Dian C Taylor, *Ch of Bd*
Nicholle R Taylor, *COO*
Joseph A Dinunzio, *Exec VP*
John M Thaeder, *Senior VP*
Pierre A Anderson, *Vice Pres*
EMP: 8 EST: 1905
SALES: 80.4MM Publicly Held
WEB: www.artesianwater.com
SIC: 4941 Water supply

(G-6001)
ARTESIAN UTILITY DEV INC
664 Churchmans Rd (19702-1934)
P.O. Box 15004, Wilmington (19850-5004)
PHONE...................................800 332-5114
Dian C Taylor, *CEO*
EMP: 40 EST: 2015
SALES (est): 76.8K
SALES (corp-wide): 80.4MM Publicly Held
SIC: 4941 Water supply
PA: Artesian Resources Corporation
    664 Churchmans Rd
    Newark DE 19702
    302 453-6900

(G-6002)
ARTESIAN WASTEWATER MD INC
664 Churchmans Rd (19702-1934)
P.O. Box 15004, Wilmington (19850-5004)
PHONE...................................302 453-6900
Dian C Taylor, *President*
EMP: 20
SALES (est): 121.7K
SALES (corp-wide): 80.4MM Publicly Held
SIC: 1629 Waste water & sewage treatment plant construction
PA: Artesian Resources Corporation
    664 Churchmans Rd
    Newark DE 19702
    302 453-6900

(G-6003)
ARTESIAN WASTEWATER MGT INC
664 Churchmans Rd (19702-1934)
PHONE...................................302 453-6900
Dian C Taylor, *CEO*
David B Spacht, *President*
EMP: 20 EST: 2015

Newark - New Castle County (G-6004)

GEOGRAPHIC SECTION

SALES (est): 173K
SALES (corp-wide): 80.4MM **Publicly Held**
SIC: **1629** Waste water & sewage treatment plant construction
PA: Artesian Resources Corporation
664 Churchmans Rd
Newark DE 19702
302 453-6900

(G-6004)
ARTESIAN WATER COMPANY INC
664 Churchmans Rd (19702-1938)
P.O. Box 15004, Wilmington (19850-5004)
PHONE..................302 453-6900
Dian C Taylor, *President*
Joseph A Dinunzio, *Exec VP*
Nicki Taylor, *Vice Pres*
Stanley Siegfried, *Project Mgr*
Rob Penman, *Opers Staff*
EMP: 30
SQ FT: 35,000
SALES (est): 49.7MM
SALES (corp-wide): 80.4MM **Publicly Held**
WEB: www.artesianwater.com
SIC: **4941** Water supply
PA: Artesian Resources Corporation
664 Churchmans Rd
Newark DE 19702
302 453-6900

(G-6005)
ARTESIAN WATER MARYLAND INC
664 Churchmans Rd (19702-1934)
P.O. Box 15004, Wilmington (19850-5004)
PHONE..................302 453-6900
EMP: 50 EST: 2015
SALES (est): 76.8K
SALES (corp-wide): 80.4MM **Publicly Held**
SIC: **4941** Water supply
PA: Artesian Resources Corporation
664 Churchmans Rd
Newark DE 19702
302 453-6900

(G-6006)
ARTHUR L YOUNG DENTIST JR
6 Millbourne Dr (19711-3900)
PHONE..................302 737-9065
Arthur Young, *Principal*
EMP: 4
SALES (est): 109.7K **Privately Held**
SIC: **8021** Offices & clinics of dentists

(G-6007)
ARTISANS BANK INC
Also Called: Artisans Bank Clefco Branch
2424 Pulaski Hwy (19702-3906)
PHONE..................302 838-6700
Alice Candeloro, *Manager*
EMP: 7
SALES (corp-wide): 22.8MM **Privately Held**
SIC: **6036** State savings banks, not federally chartered
PA: Artisans Bank Inc
2961 Centerville Rd # 101
Wilmington DE 19808
302 658-6881

(G-6008)
ARTTISTA ACCESSORIES
105 Woodring Ln (19702-1411)
PHONE..................302 455-0195
Dennis Arttista, *Owner*
EMP: 1
SALES (est): 74.3K **Privately Held**
WEB: www.arttista.com
SIC: **3269** Figures: pottery, china, earthenware & stoneware

(G-6009)
ASHBY MANAGEMENT CORPORATION
108 W Main St (19711-3229)
PHONE..................302 894-1200
Robert E Ashby, *President*
EMP: 5
SALES (est): 307.7K **Privately Held**
SIC: **8741** Restaurant management

(G-6010)
ASHISH B PARIKH
Also Called: Heart and Vascular Clinic
620 Stanton Christiana Rd # 203 (19713-2130)
PHONE..................302 338-9444
Ashish B Parikh, *Owner*
EMP: 12
SQ FT: 1,600
SALES (est): 1.5MM **Privately Held**
SIC: **8011** Cardiologist & cardio-vascular specialist

(G-6011)
ASPIRA OF DELAWARE INC
326 Ruthar Dr (19711-8017)
PHONE..................302 292-1463
Margaret Rivera, *Ch of Bd*
Jari Santana-Wynn, *Principal*
EMP: 5
SQ FT: 103,000
SALES (est): 133.8K **Privately Held**
SIC: **8748** Testing service, educational or personnel

(G-6012)
ASSOCIATED PRESS
100 Addison Dr (19702-1939)
PHONE..................302 737-1628
EMP: 9
SALES (corp-wide): 595.7MM **Privately Held**
SIC: **7383** News Syndicate
PA: The Associated Press
450 W 33rd St Fl 16
New York NY 10281
212 621-1500

(G-6013)
ASTRAZENECA PHARMACEUTICALS LP
587 Old Baltimore Pike (19702-1307)
P.O. Box 4520 (19714-4520)
PHONE..................302 286-3500
Eric Voigt, *Mfg Spvr*
John Devine, *Maint Spvr*
Elizabeth Keener, *Production*
Matt Milks, *Production*
Omar Poventud, *Engineer*
EMP: 701
SALES (corp-wide): 22B **Privately Held**
WEB: www.astrazeneca-us.com
SIC: **2834** Pharmaceutical preparations
HQ: Astrazeneca Pharmaceuticals Lp
1 Medimmune Way
Gaithersburg MD 20878

(G-6014)
ATHENA T JOLLY M D
24 Brookhill Dr (19702-1301)
PHONE..................302 454-3020
Athena Jolly, *Owner*
EMP: 5 EST: 2017
SALES (est): 85.3K **Privately Held**
SIC: **8011** Offices & clinics of medical doctors

(G-6015)
ATI FLAT RLLED PDTS HLDNGS LLC
48 Prestbury Sq 18 (19713-2690)
PHONE..................302 368-7350
Mark Thomason, *Branch Mgr*
EMP: 1 **Publicly Held**
WEB: www.alleghenyludlum.com
SIC: **3312** Stainless steel
HQ: Ati Flat Rolled Products Holdings, Llc
1000 Six Ppg Pl
Pittsburgh PA 15222
412 394-3047

(G-6016)
ATI HOLDINGS LLC
Also Called: ATI Physical Therapy
4051 Ogletown Rd Ste 104 (19713-3101)
PHONE..................302 894-1600
Katie Newcomb, *Partner*
EMP: 21
SALES (corp-wide): 338.3MM **Privately Held**
SIC: **8049** Physical therapist
PA: Ati Holdings, Llc
790 Remington Blvd
Bolingbrook IL 60440
630 296-2222

(G-6017)
ATI HOLDINGS LLC
Also Called: ATI Physical Therapy
2600 Glasgow Ave Ste 105 (19702-5703)
PHONE..................302 838-2165
John Records, *Branch Mgr*
EMP: 21
SALES (corp-wide): 338.3MM **Privately Held**
SIC: **8049** Physical therapist
PA: Ati Holdings, Llc
790 Remington Blvd
Bolingbrook IL 60440
630 296-2222

(G-6018)
ATLANTIC CITY ELECTRIC COMPANY (DH)
500 N Wakefield Dr Fl 2 (19702-5440)
P.O. Box 231, Wilmington (19899-0231)
PHONE..................202 872-2000
David M Velazquez, *President*
Sean Buckle, *Engineer*
Jeffrey Mercanti, *Engineer*
Alexis Louie, *Senior Engr*
Frederick J Boyle, *CFO*
EMP: 50
SALES: 1.2B
SALES (corp-wide): 35.9B **Publicly Held**
SIC: **4911** Distribution, electric power
HQ: Conectiv, Llc
800 N King St Ste 400
Wilmington DE 19801
202 872-2680

(G-6019)
ATLANTIC DAWN LTD
Also Called: Little Caboose The
430 Old Baltimore Pike (19702-8410)
PHONE..................302 737-8854
Ms Kim B, *Owner*
Michelle Spencer, *Director*
EMP: 14
SALES (est): 601.6K **Privately Held**
SIC: **8351** Group day care center

(G-6020)
ATLANTIC DUNCAN INC
5 Magil Ct (19702-8636)
PHONE..................302 383-0740
Janinder Kalsi, *CEO*
EMP: 10
SALES (est): 294.3K **Privately Held**
SIC: **8748** Business consulting

(G-6021)
ATLANTIC SUN SCREEN PRTG INC
700 Peoples Plz (19702-5601)
PHONE..................302 731-5100
John Whitehead, *President*
EMP: 10
SALES (est): 110K **Privately Held**
SIC: **2396** **7389** Screen printing on fabric articles; embroidering of advertising on shirts, etc.

(G-6022)
ATLANTIC TRACTOR LLC
Also Called: John Deere Authorized Dealer
2688 Pulaski Hwy (19702-3915)
PHONE..................302 834-0114
Thomas Patrick, *General Mgr*
Tom Patrick, *Branch Mgr*
EMP: 12
SALES (corp-wide): 86.5MM **Privately Held**
WEB: www.atlantictractor.com
SIC: **5261** **5082** Lawn & garden equipment; construction & mining machinery
PA: Atlantic Tractor Llc
720 Wheeler School Rd
Whiteford MD 21160
410 457-3696

(G-6023)
ATLAS GLASS & METAL LLC
110 Coopers Dr (19702-2119)
PHONE..................302 456-5958
Anthony Jones,
EMP: 4
SALES: 400K **Privately Held**
SIC: **1793** Glass & glazing work

(G-6024)
ATLAS VAN LINES AGENTS
900 Interchange Blvd (19711-3563)
PHONE..................302 369-0900
Thomas Bennett III, *President*
EMP: 20 EST: 1955
SALES (est): 1MM **Privately Held**
SIC: **4783** Packing & crating

(G-6025)
ATOZE INC
2035 Sunset Lake Rd B2 (19702-2600)
PHONE..................415 992-7936
EMP: 4
SALES (est): 89.7K **Privately Held**
SIC: **7371** Custom Computer Programming

(G-6026)
AUSTIN & BEDNASH CONSTRUCTION
32 Brookhill Dr (19702-1301)
PHONE..................302 376-5590
Mike Austin, *Principal*
Sam Bednash, *Vice Pres*
EMP: 45
SQ FT: 43,560
SALES (est): 7.5MM **Privately Held**
SIC: **1611** General contractor, highway & street construction

(G-6027)
AUTISM DELAWARE INC
924 Old Harmony Rd # 201 (19713-4186)
PHONE..................302 224-6020
Theda Ellis, *Exec Dir*
Brian Hall, *Associate Dir*
Ann Athas, *Admin Asst*
EMP: 13
SALES: 3.6MM **Privately Held**
SIC: **8322** Social services for the handicapped

(G-6028)
AUTO EQUITY LOANS
1241 Churchmans Rd (19713-2149)
PHONE..................302 731-0073
EMP: 4
SALES (corp-wide): 3.1MM **Privately Held**
SIC: **6141** Automobile loans, including insurance
PA: Auto Equity Loans
15231 N 87th St Ste 115b
Scottsdale AZ 85260
480 307-6388

(G-6029)
AUTOTOTE CANADA INC
100 Bellevue Rd (19713-3426)
PHONE..................302 737-4300
Keith Dodwell, *Exec VP*
William J Huntley, *Vice Pres*
EMP: 160
SALES (est): 411.4K
SALES (corp-wide): 3.3B **Publicly Held**
SIC: **5044** Office equipment
HQ: Autotote Systems, Inc.
1500 Bluegrass Lakes Pkwy
Alpharetta GA 30004
770 664-3700

(G-6030)
AVALON DENTAL LLC BLDG G4
420 Christiana Med Ctr (19702-1654)
PHONE..................302 292-8899
Adeline Farhi, *Principal*
EMP: 4
SALES (est): 95.4K **Privately Held**
SIC: **8021** Offices & clinics of dentists

(G-6031)
AVANTIX LABRATORIES INC
100 Biddle Ave Ste 202 (19702-3983)
PHONE..................302 832-1008
Dr Linyee Shum, *CEO*
Chad T Westhoven, *QC Mgr*
Krysta Wriston, *Manager*
EMP: 10
SQ FT: 10,000
SALES (est): 920K **Privately Held**
WEB: www.avantixlabs.com
SIC: **8733** Scientific research agency

GEOGRAPHIC SECTION
Newark - New Castle County (G-6063)

(G-6032)
B & W TEK INC
18 Shea Way Ste 103 (19713-3448)
PHONE..................302 368-7788
Sean Wang, *President*
Thomas Zawislak, *General Mgr*
Jack Zhou, *COO*
Jessy Fu, *Engineer*
Dick Jollay, *Engineer*
▲ **EMP:** 60
SQ FT: 20,000
SALES (est): 16.2MM **Privately Held**
WEB: www.bwtek.com
SIC: 3826 Analytical instruments

(G-6033)
B E & K INC
Ashford Bldg 242 Chpmn Rd 242 Chapman (19702)
PHONE..................302 452-9000
Robert Pinson, *General Mgr*
EMP: 378 **Publicly Held**
WEB: www.bek.com
SIC: 8711 Construction & civil engineering
HQ: B E & K, Inc.
2000 International Pk Dr
Birmingham AL 35243
205 972-6000

(G-6034)
B E & K ENGINEERING COMPANY
Also Called: BE&k
242 Chapman Rd (19702-5405)
PHONE..................302 452-9000
Keith Reece, *Branch Mgr*
EMP: 4 **Publicly Held**
SIC: 8711 Construction & civil engineering
HQ: B E & K Engineering Company (Inc)
2000 International Pk Dr
Birmingham AL 35243
205 972-6000

(G-6035)
B FIT ENTERPRISES (PA)
35 Salem Church Rd Ste 23 (19713-4927)
PHONE..................302 292-1785
Marcellus Beasley, *Owner*
EMP: 10
SALES (est): 282.8K **Privately Held**
SIC: 7991 Health club

(G-6036)
B&H INSURANCE LLC
Also Called: Nationwide Insurance
111 Ruthar Dr (19711-8025)
PHONE..................302 995-2247
John Boykin, *Mng Member*
Mark Doughty, *Director*
Jennifer Wilson, *Director*
Alicia Luff, *Executive Asst*
Megan Gallagher, *Commercial*
EMP: 28
SALES (est): 74.3K **Privately Held**
SIC: 6411 7371 Insurance agents; computer software development & applications

(G-6037)
B&W TEK LLC
19 Shea Way Ste 301 (19713-3452)
PHONE..................302 368-7824
EMP: 4
SALES (est): 92.1K **Privately Held**
SIC: 7389 Business Services, Nec, Nsk

(G-6038)
B&W TEK LLC
19 Shea Way Ste 301 (19713-3452)
PHONE..................302 368-7824
Jack Zhou, *CEO*
Kristen Frano, *Engineer*
Julie Tang, *Accountant*
Nick Maclean, *Sales Engr*
Brenden Lui, *Administration*
EMP: 60
SALES (est): 2MM **Privately Held**
SIC: 3826 Analytical instruments

(G-6039)
BABILONIA INC
2035 Sunset Lake Rd B2 (19702-2600)
PHONE..................415 237-3339
Freddy Linares, *CEO*
Andrs Osterling, *Principal*

EMP: 8
SALES (est): 163.3K **Privately Held**
SIC: 6531 7371 Real estate agents & managers; computer software development & applications

(G-6040)
BABY TEL COMMUNICATIONS INC
727 Art Ln (19713-1208)
PHONE..................302 368-3969
Benjamin Raphael, *President*
Catherine P Raphael, *Admin Sec*
EMP: 5 **EST:** 1981
SALES (est): 389.6K **Privately Held**
WEB: www.babytel.com
SIC: 1731 Sound equipment specialization; telephone & telephone equipment installation

(G-6041)
BAMBOOZLE WEB SERVICES INC
2035 Sunset Lake Rd (19702-2600)
PHONE..................833 380-4600
Patrick Swoboda, *CEO*
EMP: 7
SALES (est): 163K **Privately Held**
SIC: 7379

(G-6042)
BAMBU CANDLES LLC
210 Cullen Way (19711-6112)
PHONE..................917 903-2563
Altagracia Mena,
EMP: 1
SALES (est): 39.6K **Privately Held**
SIC: 3999 Manufacturing industries

(G-6043)
BANCROFT BEHAVIORAL HEALTH INC
1107 Drummond Plz (19711-5705)
PHONE..................302 502-3255
EMP: 7
SALES (est): 70.3K **Privately Held**
SIC: 8099 Health & allied services

(G-6044)
BANGUS BUSINESS SERVICES
18 Marvin Dr Apt B4 (19713-1362)
P.O. Box 7751 (19714-7751)
PHONE..................302 266-7285
Shu Chow, *Owner*
EMP: 6
SALES (est): 355.8K **Privately Held**
WEB: www.bangus-express.com
SIC: 7389 Business services

(G-6045)
BANK AMERICA NATIONAL ASSN
655 Paper Mill Rd (19711-7500)
PHONE..................302 464-1745
Teresa Chopko, *Assistant VP*
Cynthia Klemencic, *Vice Pres*
Cristina Brounce, *Vice Pres*
EMP: 19
SALES (corp-wide): 110.5B **Publicly Held**
WEB: www.bofa.com
SIC: 6021 National commercial banks
HQ: Bank Of America, National Association
100 S Tryon St
Charlotte NC 28202
704 386-5681

(G-6046)
BARBARA L MCKINNEY
Also Called: Kiddie Express
5 Knickerbocker Dr (19713-3708)
PHONE..................302 266-9594
Barbara L McKinney, *Principal*
EMP: 5 **EST:** 2009
SALES (est): 77.6K **Privately Held**
SIC: 8351 Child day care services

(G-6047)
BARRETTES RUN APARTMENTS
Also Called: Village of Barrett's Run The
100 N Barrett Ln (19702-2927)
PHONE..................302 368-3400
Lewis Capano, *Owner*
EMP: 8

SALES (est): 433.9K **Privately Held**
SIC: 6513 Apartment hotel operation

(G-6048)
BARRY KAYNE DDS
58 Omega Dr Ste F58 (19713-2062)
PHONE..................302 456-0400
Barry Kayne, *Owner*
EMP: 7
SALES (est): 344.3K **Privately Held**
SIC: 8021 Periodontist

(G-6049)
BARRY USA INC (PA)
104 Alan Dr (19711-8027)
PHONE..................800 305-2673
Peter Barry, *President*
Claire Murphy,
EMP: 2 **EST:** 2014
SQ FT: 2,000
SALES (est): 1MM **Privately Held**
SIC: 2298 Wire rope centers

(G-6050)
BASTIANELLI GROUP INC
231 Executive Dr Ste 15 (19702-3324)
PHONE..................302 658-1500
Paul Bastianelli, *President*
EMP: 5 **EST:** 1995
SALES (est): 460K **Privately Held**
WEB: www.bastianelligroup.com
SIC: 8748 8721 Business consulting; accounting, auditing & bookkeeping

(G-6051)
BATTA INC
6 Garfield Way (19713-3450)
PHONE..................302 737-3376
Neeraj K Batta, *President*
Naresh Batta, *Treasurer*
EMP: 35
SALES (est): 1.4MM **Privately Held**
SIC: 8748 Environmental consultant

(G-6052)
BATTA ENVIRONMENTAL ASSOC INC (PA)
Also Called: Batta Laboratory
6 Garfield Way (19713-3450)
PHONE..................302 737-3376
Naresh C Batta, *President*
Neelam Batta, *Vice Pres*
EMP: 24
SQ FT: 6,000
SALES (est): 8.8MM **Privately Held**
WEB: www.battaenv.com
SIC: 8748 Environmental consultant

(G-6053)
BAUGUESS ELECTRICAL SVCS INC
1400 Interchange Blvd (19711-1818)
PHONE..................302 737-5614
Mark Bauguess, *Principal*
EMP: 6
SALES (est): 937.7K **Privately Held**
SIC: 1731 General electrical contractor

(G-6054)
BAULS TOWING & SERVICES LLC
543 Old Baltimore Pike (19702-1307)
PHONE..................302 999-9919
Rashan Baul, *Principal*
EMP: 4
SALES (est): 425.4K **Privately Held**
SIC: 7549 Towing services

(G-6055)
BAYADA HOME HEALTH CARE INC
Also Called: Bayada Nurses
200 Biddle Ave Ste 101 (19702-3967)
PHONE..................302 836-1000
Carla Young, *Manager*
EMP: 11
SALES (corp-wide): 672.5MM **Privately Held**
WEB: www.bayada.com
SIC: 8082 Visiting nurse service
PA: Bayada Home Health Care, Inc.
1 W Main St
Moorestown NJ 08057
856 231-1000

(G-6056)
BAYMONT INN & SUITES NEWARK
630 S College Ave (19713-1315)
PHONE..................302 453-1700
Stephen Holmes, *CEO*
Thomas Conforti, *CFO*
EMP: 8
SALES (est): 167.1K
SALES (corp-wide): 1.8B **Publicly Held**
SIC: 7011 Inns
HQ: Wyndham Hotel Group, Llc
22 Sylvan Way
Parsippany NJ 07054

(G-6057)
BAYSHORE COMMUNICATIONS INC
Also Called: Telsec Answering Service
2839 Ogletown Rd (19713-1837)
PHONE..................302 737-2164
Mary Lou Bayshore, *President*
EMP: 12
SALES (est): 868.8K **Privately Held**
SIC: 7389 7311 Telephone answering service; advertising agencies

(G-6058)
BAYSHORE RECORDS MGT LLC
300 Pencader Dr (19702-3342)
PHONE..................302 731-4477
Brad Mundy,
EMP: 6
SALES (est): 310.6K **Privately Held**
WEB: www.bayshoreallied.com
SIC: 8741 Management services

(G-6059)
BAYSHORE TRNSP SYS INC (PA)
901 Dawson Dr (19713-5802)
PHONE..................302 366-0220
Linda L Piazza, *President*
Andy Larmore, *Vice Pres*
Matt Larmore, *Vice Pres*
Mark Muddiman, *CFO*
Ralph E Piazza, *Treasurer*
▲ **EMP:** 60
SQ FT: 193,500
SALES: 33.8MM **Privately Held**
WEB: www.bayshoreteam.com
SIC: 4213 4214 Household goods transport; local trucking with storage

(G-6060)
BAYSHORE TRNSP SYS INC
300 Pencader Dr (19702-3342)
PHONE..................302 366-0220
Matthew Larrmore, *Branch Mgr*
EMP: 15
SALES (corp-wide): 33.8MM **Privately Held**
SIC: 4214 Household goods moving & storage, local
PA: Bayshore Transportation System, Inc.
901 Dawson Dr
Newark DE 19713
302 366-0220

(G-6061)
BAYTOWN PACKHOUSE INC
Also Called: Day Town Pack House
112 Capitol Trl (19711-3716)
PHONE..................936 340-2122
Laryssa Ferreira, *Manager*
EMP: 9
SALES (est): 3MM **Privately Held**
SIC: 3086 Packaging & shipping materials, foamed plastic

(G-6062)
BEAR CONCRETE CONSTRUCTION
595 Walther Rd (19702-2903)
PHONE..................302 834-3333
Vincent N Greggo, *Mng Member*
EMP: 20
SALES (est): 1.1MM **Privately Held**
SIC: 4213 Heavy hauling

(G-6063)
BEAR EARLY EDUCATION CENTER
2884 Glasgow Ave (19702)
PHONE..................302 836-5000
Jacqui Mullen, *Principal*

Newark - New Castle County (G-6064) GEOGRAPHIC SECTION

EMP: 5
SALES (est): 109.9K **Privately Held**
SIC: 8351 Preschool center

(G-6064)
BEAR GLASGOW DENTAL
1290 Peoples Plz (19702-5701)
PHONE..................302 836-3750
Glen Goleburn, *Partner*
EMP: 12
SALES (est): 1.7MM **Privately Held**
WEB: www.bearglasgowdental.com
SIC: 8021 Dental clinic

(G-6065)
BEAR INDUSTRIES INC
15 Albe Dr (19702-1321)
P.O. Box 9174 (19714-9174)
PHONE..................302 368-1311
John R Eisenbrey Jr, *President*
Sue Eisenbrey, *Corp Secy*
Lou Annas IV, *Vice Pres*
Charles Johnston, *Vice Pres*
EMP: 80
SQ FT: 10,000
SALES (est): 15.3MM **Privately Held**
SIC: 1711 Sprinkler contractors

(G-6066)
BEAR-GLASGOW YMCA
351 George Williams Way (19702-3518)
PHONE..................302 836-9622
Terry Mullen, *Owner*
Angie Riley, *Director*
EMP: 5
SALES (est): 194.4K **Privately Held**
SIC: 8641 7991 8351 7032 Youth organizations; physical fitness facilities; child day care services; youth camps; individual & family services

(G-6067)
BEECH HILL PRESS
85 Beech Hill Dr (19711-2945)
PHONE..................302 588-0315
Steven Leech, *Principal*
EMP: 1 **EST:** 2010
SALES (est): 60.7K **Privately Held**
SIC: 2741 Miscellaneous publishing

(G-6068)
BEETLES PLAYHOUSE DAY CARE
1 Coronet Ct (19713-1975)
PHONE..................302 593-7321
EMP: 5
SALES (est): 74.3K **Privately Held**
SIC: 8351 Child day care services

(G-6069)
BELL PAINTING & WALL COVERING
667 Dawson Dr Ste F (19713-3437)
PHONE..................302 738-8854
Harry W Bell Jr, *President*
Donna Bell, *Corp Secy*
Robert Mark Geary, *Vice Pres*
EMP: 14
SALES (est): 1MM **Privately Held**
SIC: 1721 Residential painting; commercial painting

(G-6070)
BELLES AND BEAUS PHOTOGRAPHY
238 E Seneca Dr (19702-1933)
PHONE..................302 368-2468
EMP: 4 **EST:** 2014
SALES (est): 46K **Privately Held**
SIC: 7221 Photographer, still or video

(G-6071)
BELMONT VILLA CONDOMINIUMS
Also Called: Villa Belmont
60 Welsh Tract Rd Ste 2b (19713-2265)
PHONE..................302 368-1633
Lisa Thornton, *Manager*
EMP: 8
SALES (est): 653.1K
SALES (corp-wide): 7.4MM **Privately Held**
WEB: www.villabelmont.com
SIC: 6513 Apartment building operators

PA: Stoltz Realty Co
3704 Kennett Pike Ste 200
Wilmington DE
302 656-2852

(G-6072)
BEN-DOM PRINTING COMPANY
Also Called: Bendom Printing
35 Salem Church Rd 43e (19713-4928)
P.O. Box 7649 (19714-7649)
PHONE..................302 737-9144
Carla Mancari, *President*
Nick Mancari, *Vice Pres*
EMP: 10
SQ FT: 5,500
SALES (est): 732K **Privately Held**
WEB: www.ben-dom.com
SIC: 2752 2791 2789 Commercial printing, offset; typesetting; bookbinding & related work

(G-6073)
BERRY REFRIGERATION CO
Also Called: Honeywell Authorized Dealer
2 Garfield Way (19713-5807)
PHONE..................302 733-0933
Louis G Perna, *President*
William Hentkowski, *General Mgr*
Paul Perna, *Treasurer*
Lou Perna Jr, *Shareholder*
EMP: 38 **EST:** 1960
SQ FT: 9,000
SALES (est): 8.8MM **Privately Held**
WEB: www.berryrefrigeration.com
SIC: 7623 5075 5078 Air conditioning repair; refrigeration repair service; warm air heating equipment & supplies; air conditioning & ventilation equipment & supplies; refrigeration equipment & supplies; refrigerators, commercial (reach-in & walk-in)

(G-6074)
BEST WESTERN NEWARK
260 Chapman Rd (19702-5490)
PHONE..................302 738-3400
EMP: 4
SALES (est): 215.5K **Privately Held**
SIC: 7011 Hotel/Motel Operation

(G-6075)
BETH TRUCKING INC
129 Crikmoe Blvd (19702)
PHONE..................918 814-2970
Beth Kamau, *Co-Owner*
Elijah Kamau, *Vice Pres*
EMP: 7
SALES (est): 178.2K **Privately Held**
SIC: 4212 Local trucking, without storage

(G-6076)
BETTS TEXACO AND B & G GL INC
Also Called: Betts Garage
2806 Pulaski Hwy (19702-3913)
PHONE..................302 834-2284
William W Betts Sr, *Principal*
David Betts Jr, *Principal*
EMP: 8
SALES (est): 799.7K **Privately Held**
SIC: 7532 Collision shops, automotive

(G-6077)
BGI PRINT SOLUTIONS
4142 Ogletown Stanton Rd (19713-4169)
PHONE..................302 234-2825
Ernie Lehnan, *Owner*
EMP: 4
SALES (est): 192.9K **Privately Held**
SIC: 2752 Commercial printing, lithographic

(G-6078)
BGI PRINT SOLUTIONS
1109 Oakland Ct (19711-3450)
PHONE..................302 234-2825
Ernie Lehan, *Principal*
EMP: 4
SALES (est): 280.1K **Privately Held**
WEB: www.bgisolutions.com
SIC: 2752 Commercial printing, lithographic

(G-6079)
BIDDLE CAPITAL MANAGEMENT INC
220 Continental Dr # 202 (19713-4311)
PHONE..................302 369-6789
Dave Biddle, *President*
Bill Knopka, *Director*
EMP: 4 **EST:** 1996
SALES (est): 350K **Privately Held**
SIC: 6282 Investment advisory service

(G-6080)
BIJAN K SOROURI MD PA
10 Darwin Dr Ste C (19711-6658)
PHONE..................302 453-9171
Bijan Sorouri, *President*
EMP: 4
SALES (est): 300K **Privately Held**
SIC: 8011 Offices & clinics of medical doctors

(G-6081)
BIO-MDCAL APPLICATIONS DEL INC
Also Called: Fresenius Kidney Care Main St
230 E Main St Ste 325 (19711)
PHONE..................302 366-0129
Alex Safavi, *Branch Mgr*
EMP: 7
SALES (corp-wide): 18.3B **Privately Held**
SIC: 8092 Kidney dialysis centers
HQ: Bio-Medical Applications Of Delaware, Inc.
920 Winter St
Waltham MA 02451

(G-6082)
BIO-MDICAL APPLICATIONS OF DEL
Also Called: Fresenius Medcl Care Brndywine
4923 Ogletown Stanton Rd (19713-2081)
PHONE..................302 998-7568
Mary Garber, *Manager*
EMP: 28
SALES (est): 628.5K **Privately Held**
SIC: 8092 Kidney dialysis centers

(G-6083)
BIRTH CENTER HOLISTIC WOMEN
620 Churchmans Rd Ste 101 (19702-1945)
PHONE..................302 658-2229
Kathleen McCarthy,
Sarah Webster, *Nurse*
EMP: 15
SALES (est): 1.3MM **Privately Held**
SIC: 8011 8051 Gynecologist; skilled nursing care facilities

(G-6084)
BISHOP ASSOCIATES
1235 Peoples Plz (19702-5701)
PHONE..................302 838-1270
Walter Bishop, *Owner*
EMP: 6
SALES (est): 810.8K **Privately Held**
SIC: 6411 Insurance agents

(G-6085)
BITTA MONK ENTERTAINMENT INC
25 Winchester Rd Apt G (19713-3124)
PHONE..................916 969-4430
Marcellus Brady, *President*
EMP: 5
SALES (est): 330K **Privately Held**
SIC: 7389 Music recording producer;

(G-6086)
BLACK & DECKER CORPORATION
1207 Drummond Plz (19711-5790)
PHONE..................302 738-0250
Les Chadwick, *Manager*
EMP: 8
SQ FT: 1,000
SALES (corp-wide): 13.9B **Publicly Held**
WEB: www.blackanddecker.com
SIC: 3546 Power-driven handtools
HQ: The Black & Decker Corporation
701 E Joppa Rd
Towson MD 21286
410 716-3900

(G-6087)
BLACK & DECKER INC (DH)
1207 Drummond Plz (19711-5790)
PHONE..................860 827-3861
Don Graber, *President*
Charles Fenton, *Treasurer*
EMP: 8
SQ FT: 220,000
SALES (est): 210.4MM
SALES (corp-wide): 13.9B **Publicly Held**
SIC: 3452 3579 3423 3949 Bolts, nuts, rivets & washers; rivets, metal; nuts, metal; screws, metal; stapling machines (hand or power); garden & farm tools, including shovels; shafts, golf club; locks or lock sets
HQ: The Black & Decker Corporation
701 E Joppa Rd
Towson MD 21286
410 716-3900

(G-6088)
BLACK DOG CONSTRUCTION LLC
1104 Oakland Ct (19711-3450)
PHONE..................302 530-4967
Tim Supplee,
EMP: 5 **EST:** 2013
SALES (est): 800K **Privately Held**
SIC: 1521 Single-family housing construction

(G-6089)
BLACK DRAGON CORPORATION
40 E Main St 1010 (19711-4639)
PHONE..................617 470-9230
Helder Gavaia, *CEO*
EMP: 99
SALES (est): 950K **Privately Held**
SIC: 7381 Detective & armored car services

(G-6090)
BLACKTOP SEALCOATING INC
511 Paisley Pl (19711-3453)
PHONE..................302 234-2243
Thomas P Harkins, *Principal*
EMP: 5 **EST:** 2009
SALES (est): 240K **Privately Held**
SIC: 1771 Blacktop (asphalt) work

(G-6091)
BLAIR COMPUTING SYSTEMS INC
500 Creek View Rd Ste 200 (19711-8549)
PHONE..................302 453-8947
Mark Blair, *President*
Bronson Hokuf, *Manager*
Fred Beam, *Software Engr*
Chris Hoffman, *Software Engr*
Harold Jordan, *Software Engr*
EMP: 18
SALES (est): 1.8MM **Privately Held**
WEB: www.bcs-inc.com
SIC: 7371 Computer software development

(G-6092)
BLAZE SYSTEMS CORPORATION
300 Creek View Rd Ste 204 (19711-8548)
PHONE..................302 733-7235
Lawrence E Deheer, *President*
Kevin M Winter, *Shareholder*
EMP: 9
SALES (est): 960K **Privately Held**
WEB: www.blazesystems.com
SIC: 7372 7371 Prepackaged software; computer software development

(G-6093)
BLENHEIM MANAGEMENT COMPANY
Also Called: Blenheim Homes
220 Continental Dr # 410 (19713-4315)
PHONE..................302 254-0100
Jay Sonecha, *President*
EMP: 38
SQ FT: 2,800
SALES (est): 7.3MM **Privately Held**
WEB: www.blenheimhomes.com
SIC: 1521 New construction, single-family houses

GEOGRAPHIC SECTION — Newark - New Castle County (G-6125)

(G-6094)
BLIX INC
40 E Main St Ste 556 (19711-4639)
PHONE................347 753-8035
Dotan Volach, *President*
EMP: 40
SALES (est): 117.7K **Privately Held**
SIC: 7371 Computer software development & applications

(G-6095)
BLOOD BANK OF DELMARVA INC (PA)
100 Hygeia Dr (19713-2085)
PHONE................302 737-1151
Elizabeth McQuail, *CEO*
Elizabeth J McQuail, *Exec VP*
David Graham, *Vice Pres*
Anne Ho, *Accountant*
Nancy Descano, *Train & Dev Mgr*
EMP: 19
SALES: 22.7MM **Privately Held**
SIC: 8099 Blood bank

(G-6096)
BLOOM ENERGY CORPORATION
611 Interchange Blvd (19711-3561)
PHONE................302 733-7524
▲ EMP: 20
SALES (est): 3.1MM **Privately Held**
SIC: 3674 Mfg Semiconductors/Related Devices

(G-6097)
BLU DRAGON STUDIO INC
2035 Sunset Lake Rd B2 (19702-2600)
PHONE................302 722-6227
Isaac Ortega, *CEO*
EMP: 4
SALES: 1K **Privately Held**
SIC: 7371 7373 Computer software development & applications; computer integrated systems design

(G-6098)
BLUE ARROW CONTRACT MANUFACTUR
115 Pencader Dr (19702-3322)
PHONE................302 738-2583
Gonc Tez, *Owner*
EMP: 4
SALES (est): 519.4K **Privately Held**
SIC: 3641 Electric lamps

(G-6099)
BLUE HEN HOTEL LLC
400 David Hollowell Dr (19716-7448)
PHONE................302 266-0354
Tracy Holmes, *Manager*
EMP: 6
SALES (est): 278.8K **Privately Held**
SIC: 7011 Hotel, franchised

(G-6100)
BLUE HEN PHYSICAL THERAPY INC
Also Called: Novacare Rehabilitation
1501 Casho Mill Rd Ste 6 (19711-3567)
PHONE................302 453-1588
Jim Taylor, *Director*
EMP: 20
SALES: 820K
SALES (corp-wide): 5B **Publicly Held**
SIC: 8049 Physiotherapist
HQ: Select Medical Corporation
4714 Gettysburg Rd
Mechanicsburg PA 17055
717 972-1100

(G-6101)
BLUE MOUNTAIN APPAREL LA LLC
40 E Main St Ste 899 (19711-4639)
PHONE................646 787-5679
Dennis Slapo, *President*
EMP: 9
SQ FT: 2,000
SALES: 5MM **Privately Held**
SIC: 2325 Jeans: men's, youths' & boys'

(G-6102)
BLUEDOT TECHNOLOGIES INC
2035 Sunset Lake Rd B2 (19702-2600)
PHONE................415 800-1890
Ferhat Babacan, *CEO*
EMP: 8
SALES (est): 155.7K **Privately Held**
SIC: 4789 Transportation services

(G-6103)
BODY EASE THERAPY
105 Louviers Dr (19711-4163)
PHONE................610 314-0780
EMP: 8 EST: 2017
SALES (est): 73.3K **Privately Held**
SIC: 8093 Rehabilitation center, outpatient treatment

(G-6104)
BODY/MIND & SPIRIT MASSAGE THR
1215 Janice Dr (19713-2354)
PHONE................302 453-8151
Shirl Lord, *Owner*
EMP: 4
SALES (est): 137.1K **Privately Held**
SIC: 8093 Rehabilitation center, outpatient treatment

(G-6105)
BOOKAWAY
2035 Sunset Lake Rd (19702-2600)
PHONE................888 250-3414
Omer Chehmer, *Principal*
EMP: 50 EST: 2017
SALES (est): 641.1K **Privately Held**
SIC: 7389 Reservation services

(G-6106)
BOOKING BULLET INC (PA)
2035 Sunset Lake Rd B2 (19702-2600)
PHONE................416 988-2354
Eli Azoulay, *CEO*
EMP: 4
SALES: 10K **Privately Held**
SIC: 7371 Computer software systems analysis & design, custom

(G-6107)
BOOTHS SERVICES PLBG HTG & AC
1088 1/2 S Chapel St (19702)
PHONE................302 454-7385
Brian Booth, *President*
Pam Edwards, *Vice Pres*
EMP: 9
SQ FT: 3,900
SALES: 400K **Privately Held**
SIC: 1711 Plumbing, heating, air-conditioning contractors

(G-6108)
BOTHUB AI LIMITED
113 Darksdale Prof Ctr (19711)
PHONE................669 278-7485
Wenhao Xu, *CEO*
EMP: 10 EST: 2017
SALES: 500K **Privately Held**
SIC: 7373 Systems software development services

(G-6109)
BOWLAMISHA LLC
105 Holiday Pl (19702-2314)
PHONE................302 727-4969
EMP: 7 EST: 2014
SALES (est): 210K **Privately Held**
SIC: 7997 Membership Sport/Recreation Club

(G-6110)
BOWMAN LINDA GROUP DAY CARE
Also Called: Ms Linda's
21 Oklahoma State Dr (19713-1143)
PHONE................302 737-5479
Linda Bowman, *Owner*
EMP: 4
SALES (est): 85.4K **Privately Held**
SIC: 8351 Child day care services

(G-6111)
BOYD JEFFREY MD
4102 Ogletown Stanton Rd (19713-4183)
PHONE................302 454-8800
Jeffrey Boyd, *Manager*
EMP: 5
SALES (est): 88.5K **Privately Held**
SIC: 8011 Ophthalmologist

(G-6112)
BOYS & GIRLS CLUBS DEL INC
Also Called: Boys Girls CLB Greater Newark
109 Glasgow Dr (19702-4155)
PHONE................302 836-6464
Stuart Sherman, *Director*
EMP: 30
SALES (corp-wide): 20.8MM **Privately Held**
SIC: 8641 Youth organizations
PA: Boys & Girls Clubs Of Delaware, Inc.
669 S Union St
Wilmington DE 19805
302 658-1870

(G-6113)
BPG HOTEL PARTNERS X LLC
Also Called: Homewood Suites
640 S College Ave (19713-1315)
PHONE................302 453-9700
Greg Miller, *Partner*
EMP: 99
SALES (est): 3.2MM **Privately Held**
SIC: 7011 Hotels & motels

(G-6114)
BRANDYWINE BALUSTRADES
1225 Old Coochs Bridge Rd (19713-2333)
PHONE................302 893-1837
Keith Fleming, *Principal*
EMP: 7 EST: 2007
SALES (est): 1MM **Privately Held**
SIC: 3534 Elevators & moving stairways

(G-6115)
BRANDYWINE COSMETIC SURGERY
Medical Arts Pvilion 13 (19713)
PHONE................302 652-3331
Christopher Saunders, *Med Doctor*
EMP: 5
SALES (corp-wide): 763.3K **Privately Held**
SIC: 8011 Plastic surgeon
PA: Brandywine Cosmetic Surgery
410 Foulk Rd Ste 201
Wilmington DE 19803
302 652-3331

(G-6116)
BRANDYWINE COUNSELING
24 Brookhill Dr (19702-1301)
PHONE................302 454-3020
Matthew Shalk, *QA Dir*
Lynn M Fahey, *Manager*
Dionne Cornish, *Director*
Kattie Kotowski,
Nicole Manelski,
EMP: 15
SALES (est): 504.4K
SALES (corp-wide): 12.4MM **Privately Held**
SIC: 8069 Alcoholism rehabilitation hospital
PA: Brandywine Counseling & Community Services, Inc.
2713 Lancaster Ave
Wilmington DE 19805
302 655-9880

(G-6117)
BREAST IMAGING CENTER
4735 Ogletown Stanton Rd # 2112 (19713-8000)
P.O. Box 16015 (19718-0001)
PHONE................302 623-9729
Bob Garrett, *Vice Pres*
EMP: 20
SALES (est): 276.3K **Privately Held**
SIC: 8071 X-ray laboratory, including dental

(G-6118)
BRIDAL & TUXEDO OUTLET INC (PA)
Also Called: Bridal & Tuxedo Shoppe
124 Astro Shopping Ctr (19711-7254)
PHONE................302 731-8802
Vaughn Sawdon, *President*
Cathy Sawdon, *Vice Pres*
EMP: 5
SQ FT: 3,300
SALES: 350K **Privately Held**
SIC: 5621 7299 Bridal shops; tuxedo rental

(G-6119)
BRIGHT HORIZONS CHLD CTRS LLC
Also Called: Bank of America Child Dev Ctr
950 Samoset Dr (19713-6003)
P.O. Box 442, Bel Air MD (21014-0442)
PHONE................302 456-8913
Tracey Kuhn, *Director*
EMP: 60
SALES (corp-wide): 1.9B **Publicly Held**
WEB: www.atlantaga.ncr.com
SIC: 8351 Group day care center
HQ: Bright Horizons Children's Centers Llc
200 Talcott Ave
Watertown MA 02472
617 673-8000

(G-6120)
BRIGHT HORIZONS CHLD CTRS LLC
Also Called: MBNA Bank Great Expectations
1089 Prides Xing (19713-6106)
PHONE................302 453-2050
Linda Whitehead, *Director*
EMP: 27
SALES (corp-wide): 1.9B **Publicly Held**
WEB: www.atlantaga.ncr.com
SIC: 8351 Group day care center
HQ: Bright Horizons Children's Centers Llc
200 Talcott Ave
Watertown MA 02472
617 673-8000

(G-6121)
BRIGHT KIDZ INC
273 Old Baltimore Pike (19702-1420)
PHONE................302 369-6929
Medhat Banoub, *President*
EMP: 13
SALES: 500K **Privately Held**
SIC: 8351 Child day care services

(G-6122)
BRIGHTVIEW LANDSCAPES LLC
22 Brookhill Dr (19702-1301)
PHONE................302 731-4162
Jamie Sharp, *Vice Pres*
Mark Smolko, *Human Res Dir*
Jake Campion, *Manager*
EMP: 56
SALES (corp-wide): 2.4B **Publicly Held**
SIC: 0781 Landscape services
HQ: Brightview Landscapes, Llc
980 Jolly Rd Ste 300
Blue Bell PA 19422
484 567-7204

(G-6123)
BRISCOE TRUCKING INC
28 Chambord Dr (19702-5547)
PHONE................302 836-1327
Brenda Briscoe, *CEO*
Bernard Briscoe, *President*
Brian Briscoe, *Vice Pres*
EMP: 10
SALES (est): 814K **Privately Held**
SIC: 4731 Freight transportation arrangement

(G-6124)
BROOKSIDE LAUNDROMAT
69 Marrows Rd (19713-3701)
PHONE................302 369-3366
Young Choe, *Owner*
EMP: 5
SALES (est): 156.2K **Privately Held**
SIC: 7215 Laundry, coin-operated

(G-6125)
BROOKSIDE PLAZA APARTMENTS LLC
885 Marrows Rd Apt D6 (19713-1571)
P.O. Box 627 (19715-0627)
PHONE................302 737-2008
Lauren Demichael,
EMP: 5
SALES (est): 609.4K **Privately Held**
SIC: 6513 Apartment hotel operation

Newark - New Castle County (G-6126) — GEOGRAPHIC SECTION

(G-6126)
BROWN LISHA
Also Called: Sprinkles Christian Daycare
33 Wellington Dr (19702-4225)
PHONE.................302 832-9529
Lisha Brown, *Principal*
EMP: 5
SALES (est): 57.7K **Privately Held**
SIC: 8351 Group day care center

(G-6127)
BROWNSTARR THERAPY
6 Bristol Ct (19702-4234)
PHONE.................302 838-2645
Monique Brown, *Principal*
EMP: 4
SALES (est): 85K **Privately Held**
SIC: 8093 Rehabilitation center, outpatient treatment

(G-6128)
BRUCE C TURNER MD
8 Sunrise Cir (19713-1176)
PHONE.................302 366-0938
Bruce C Turner MD, *Owner*
Bruce Turner, *Director*
EMP: 4
SALES (est): 195.2K **Privately Held**
SIC: 8011 General & family practice, physician/surgeon

(G-6129)
BUILDERS FIRSTSOURCE INC
54 Albe Dr (19702-1322)
PHONE.................302 731-0678
Silvio Serrari, *Branch Mgr*
EMP: 27
SALES (corp-wide): 7.7B **Publicly Held**
WEB: www.hopelumber.com
SIC: 5031 Wallboard; metal doors, sash & trim; door frames, all materials
PA: Builders Firstsource, Inc.
2001 Bryan St Ste 1600
Dallas TX 75201
214 880-3500

(G-6130)
BUILDERS LLC GENERAL
99 Albe Dr Ste A (19702-1363)
PHONE.................302 533-6528
Jeff Scarangelli, *Owner*
EMP: 6
SALES (est): 591.2K **Privately Held**
SIC: 1799 Special trade contractors

(G-6131)
BUILDING CONCEPTS AMERICA INC
101 Peoples Dr (19702-1306)
PHONE.................302 292-0200
Anthony Ferrara, *President*
EMP: 25
SQ FT: 2,000
SALES (est): 15MM **Privately Held**
SIC: 5039 1541 Metal buildings; prefabricated buildings; structural assemblies, prefabricated: non-wood; prefabricated building erection, industrial

(G-6132)
BUILDING FASTENERS INC
955 Dawson Dr Ste 1 (19713-5803)
PHONE.................302 738-0671
Jeffrey Dalton, *President*
Joseph F Dalton, *President*
Susan Fritsch, *Corp Secy*
EMP: 8
SQ FT: 8,000
SALES (est): 3.8MM **Privately Held**
WEB: www.buildingfasteners.net
SIC: 5085 5072 Fasteners, industrial: nuts, bolts, screws, etc.; bolts; nuts (hardware); power handtools

(G-6133)
BUILDING INSPECTION UNDRWRTR
Also Called: Building Insptn Underwriters
1 Liberty Plz Ste C (19711-5589)
PHONE.................302 266-9057
Mark Mc Laucklin, *President*
Mark McLaucklin, *President*
EMP: 4
SALES (est): 286.8K **Privately Held**
SIC: 7389 Building inspection service

(G-6134)
BUILT-RITE FENCE CO INC
34 Hidden Valley Dr (19711-7466)
PHONE.................302 366-8329
John T Milotte, *President*
EMP: 4
SALES: 190K **Privately Held**
SIC: 1799 Fence construction

(G-6135)
BUKER LIMOUSINE & TRNSP SVC
517 Paisley Pl (19711-3457)
PHONE.................302 234-7600
Robert Buker, *President*
EMP: 10 EST: 1996
SALES: 620K **Privately Held**
SIC: 4119 Limousine rental, with driver

(G-6136)
BURKE DERMATOLOGY (PA)
774 Christiana Rd Ste 107 (19713-4248)
PHONE.................302 230-3376
Thomas John Burke Do, *President*
EMP: 7 EST: 2015
SALES (est): 1.7MM **Privately Held**
SIC: 8011 Dermatologist

(G-6137)
BURNS & FIORINA DEMOLITION
46 Vansant Rd (19711-4839)
PHONE.................732 888-1076
Ronald Fiorina, *President*
Maureen Fiorina, *Vice Pres*
EMP: 4
SQ FT: 4,000
SALES: 600K **Privately Held**
SIC: 1795 Demolition, buildings & other structures

(G-6138)
BURRIS & BAXTER COMMUNICATIONS
Also Called: Computer User
256 Chapman Rd Ste 201 (19702-5415)
PHONE.................302 454-8511
Craig Burris, *President*
EMP: 2
SALES (est): 180K **Privately Held**
SIC: 2721 7313 Periodicals; radio, television, publisher representatives

(G-6139)
BUSINESS INTEGRATION SOLUTION
220 Continental Dr # 213 (19713-4312)
PHONE.................302 355-3512
Raju Enduri, *CEO*
EMP: 8
SALES: 950K **Privately Held**
SIC: 8741 Business management

(G-6140)
C & A INK
42 Stallion Dr (19713-3571)
PHONE.................302 565-9866
EMP: 2 EST: 2016
SALES (est): 108.4K **Privately Held**
SIC: 2893 Printing ink

(G-6141)
C M-TEC INC
1 Innovation Way Ste 100 (19711-5462)
PHONE.................302 369-6166
Xiaoqun Daniel Wu, *President*
Huifang Chen, *Principal*
Xiaoqun Wu, *Marketing Staff*
EMP: 6
SQ FT: 1,000
SALES (est): 220K **Privately Held**
WEB: www.cmtec-inc.com
SIC: 8731 Commercial physical research

(G-6142)
C21 GOLD KEY REALTY
260 E Main St Frnt (19711-7357)
PHONE.................302 250-6801
Ed Adams, *Principal*
Gia Ford, *Vice Pres*
Jan Ward, *Sales Staff*
Tami Xue, *Sales Staff*
Robert Lee, *Executive Asst*
EMP: 4
SALES (est): 333.5K **Privately Held**
SIC: 6531 Real estate agent, residential

(G-6143)
CADAPULT LTD
2644 Kirkwood Hwy Ste 140 (19711-7231)
PHONE.................302 733-0477
Richard Woltemate, *CEO*
Karen Greisman, *President*
EMP: 11
SALES (est): 2.7MM **Privately Held**
WEB: www.cadapult.net
SIC: 5045 5734 Computer software; computer & software stores

(G-6144)
CAHILL PLUMBING & HEATING INC
325 Markus Ct (19713-1157)
P.O. Box 250, Lewisville PA (19351-0250)
PHONE.................302 894-1802
EMP: 8
SQ FT: 4,500
SALES (est): 625K **Privately Held**
SIC: 1711 Plumbing contractors

(G-6145)
CALMEET INC
113 Barksdale Pro Ctr (19711-3258)
PHONE.................469 223-0863
Sahil Naik, *Director*
Aditya Rahalkar, *Director*
EMP: 2
SALES (est): 56.5K **Privately Held**
SIC: 7372 Application computer software

(G-6146)
CAMERAS ETC INC
Also Called: Cameras Etc TV & Video
165 E Main St (19711-7350)
PHONE.................302 453-9400
EMP: 6
SALES (est): 235.4K
SALES (corp-wide): 1.3MM **Privately Held**
WEB: www.camerasetcinc.com
SIC: 5946 7384 Cameras; film developing & printing
PA: Cameras, Etc Inc
2303 Baynard Blvd
Wilmington DE 19802
302 764-9400

(G-6147)
CAMPBELLS LANDSCAPE SVC INC
22 Deer Run (19711-2424)
P.O. Box 1631, Hockessin (19707-5631)
PHONE.................302 266-0117
Jeff Campbell, *CEO*
EMP: 7
SALES (est): 466.2K **Privately Held**
SIC: 0781 Landscape architects

(G-6148)
CANNONS CAKE AND CANDY SUPS
2638 Kirkwood Hwy (19711-7252)
PHONE.................302 738-3321
Leah J Cannon, *Managing Prtnr*
Stephen J Cannon, *Partner*
EMP: 5
SQ FT: 6,000
SALES (est): 2.2MM **Privately Held**
SIC: 5999 5199 Cake decorating supplies; candy making goods & supplies

(G-6149)
CAPANO MANAGEMENT COMPANY
33 Marrows Rd (19713)
PHONE.................302 737-8056
Michelle Malizia, *CFO*
Candy McVey, *Admin Sec*
EMP: 4
SALES (est): 358.6K **Privately Held**
SIC: 6513 6531 1522 Apartment building operators; real estate managers; residential construction

(G-6150)
CAPITOL ENVIRONMENTAL SVCS INC
Also Called: Capitaql Environmental
200 Biddle Ave Ste 205 (19702-3966)
PHONE.................302 652-8999
Mike Schubert, *Principal*
EMP: 6
SALES (corp-wide): 8.1MM **Privately Held**
SIC: 8748 Environmental consultant
PA: Capitol Environmental Services, Inc.
200 Biddle Ave Ste 205
Newark DE 19702
302 380-3737

(G-6151)
CAR TECH AUTO CENTER
102 Albe Dr Ste A (19702-1347)
PHONE.................302 368-4104
Curt Geesaman, *Owner*
EMP: 7
SALES (est): 423.5K **Privately Held**
SIC: 7532 Top & body repair & paint shops

(G-6152)
CARDIO-KINETICS INC
52 N Chapel St Ste 101 (19711-2363)
PHONE.................302 738-6635
Tom Hall, *CEO*
Richard Shaw, *President*
Josh Hall, *Exec VP*
Matt Katie, *Opers Staff*
Phillis Mc Gee, *Assistant*
EMP: 20 EST: 1979
SQ FT: 6,500
SALES (est): 1.6MM **Privately Held**
WEB: www.cardiokinetics.com
SIC: 8093 8011 Rehabilitation center, outpatient treatment; offices & clinics of medical doctors

(G-6153)
CARDIOLOGY PHYSICANS PA INC
Also Called: Leidig, Gilbert A MD
1 Centurian Dr Ste 200 (19713-2150)
PHONE.................302 366-8600
John J Kelly III, *President*
EMP: 30
SQ FT: 10,000
SALES (est): 6MM **Privately Held**
SIC: 8011 Cardiologist & cardio-vascular specialist

(G-6154)
CARDNO INC
121 Continental Dr # 308 (19713-4342)
PHONE.................302 395-1919
Susan Lee, *VP Human Res*
Rich Hubner, *Branch Mgr*
EMP: 17 **Privately Held**
SIC: 8748 Environmental consultant
HQ: Cardno, Inc.
10004 Park Meadows Dr # 300
Lone Tree CO 80124
720 257-5800

(G-6155)
CARING N ACTION NURSING
15 Prestbury Sq (19713-2608)
PHONE.................302 368-2273
Yvette Hall, *Mng Member*
EMP: 5
SALES (est): 190.8K **Privately Held**
SIC: 7361 Employment agencies

(G-6156)
CARLO PORTER MICHAEL
Also Called: Porter Trucking
2015 Cervantes Ct (19702-4401)
PHONE.................267 709-6370
EMP: 4
SALES (est): 201.8K **Privately Held**
SIC: 5181 Whol Beer/Ale

(G-6157)
CARME LLC
Also Called: School - Del Paul Mitchell
1420 Pulaski Hwy (19702-5108)
PHONE.................302 832-8418
Trina Carter, *Principal*
Vera Genwright, *Manager*
Eric Brown, *Info Tech Mgr*
EMP: 10
SQ FT: 9,000
SALES (est): 913.5K **Privately Held**
SIC: 7231 Beauty schools

GEOGRAPHIC SECTION
Newark - New Castle County (G-6190)

(G-6158)
CARMINE POTTER & ASSOCIATES
1400 Peoples Plz Ste 104 (19702-5706)
PHONE...................302 832-6000
Stephen Potter, *Branch Mgr*
EMP: 8
SALES (est): 594.6K
SALES (corp-wide): 1.5MM Privately Held
SIC: 8111 General practice attorney, lawyer
PA: Carmine Potter & Associates
840 N Union St
Wilmington DE 19805
302 658-8940

(G-6159)
CAROL INC
106 Peoples Plz (19702-4794)
PHONE...................302 386-4362
Carol Holladay, *President*
EMP: 41
SALES (est): 2MM Privately Held
SIC: 7231 Unisex hair salons

(G-6160)
CAROL A TAVANI MD
Also Called: Christiana Psychiatric Svcs
4745 Ogltn Stntn Rd # 124 (19713-1390)
PHONE...................302 454-9900
Carol A Tavani MD, *Owner*
Mehdi Balakhani, *Plastic Surgeon*
EMP: 5
SALES (est): 465.9K Privately Held
SIC: 8011 Psychiatrist

(G-6161)
CARPE DIA ORGANIZATION
241 Goldfinch Turn (19711-4119)
PHONE...................302 333-7546
Martha Essick, *Exec Dir*
EMP: 6
SALES (est): 175.3K Privately Held
SIC: 8322 Rehabilitation services; emergency shelters; temporary relief service

(G-6162)
CARTERS INC
3132 Fashion Center Blvd (19702-3246)
PHONE...................302 731-1432
EMP: 2
SALES (corp-wide): 3.4B Publicly Held
SIC: 2361 5641 Girls' & children's dresses, blouses & shirts; children's wear
PA: Carter's, Inc.
3438 Peachtree Rd Ne # 18
Atlanta GA 30326
678 791-1000

(G-6163)
CARTHAGE GROUP INC
407 Stanley Plaza Blvd (19713-2983)
PHONE...................610 931-8493
Victor Nathan Morlee, *Managing Prtnr*
EMP: 4 EST: 2016
SALES (est): 120.8K Privately Held
SIC: 6531 Real estate brokers & agents

(G-6164)
CASE CONSTRUCTION INC
Also Called: A Toll Building Systems
17 Mcmillan Way (19713-3420)
PHONE...................302 737-3800
Arnold Toller, *President*
EMP: 20
SQ FT: 17,000
SALES (est): 1.8MM Privately Held
SIC: 5211 5251 5085 Lumber & other building materials; tools; tools

(G-6165)
CASH CONNECT INC
Also Called: W S M S Bank
500 Creek View Rd Ste 100 (19711-8549)
PHONE...................302 283-4100
Thomas E Stevenson, *President*
Allan Matyger, *Vice Pres*
EMP: 30 EST: 1985
SALES (est): 4.5MM Privately Held
WEB: www.cash-connect.com
SIC: 6099 Automated teller machine (ATM) network

(G-6166)
CASSCELLS ORTHOPAEDICS SP
2600 Glasgow Ave Ste 104 (19702-5703)
PHONE...................302 832-6220
Christopher Casscells, *Surgeon*
EMP: 8
SALES (est): 615K Privately Held
SIC: 8011 Orthopedic physician

(G-6167)
CASTLE MORTAGE SERVICES INC
4 Vantage Ct (19711-4814)
PHONE...................302 366-0912
Jeff McGowan, *President*
EMP: 10
SALES: 10MM Privately Held
WEB: www.castlemortgageco.com
SIC: 6162 Mortgage bankers

(G-6168)
CATARACT AND LASER CENTER LLC
4102 Ogltn Stntn Rd # 1 (19713-4183)
PHONE...................302 454-8802
Frank R Owczarek, *Owner*
EMP: 10 EST: 2007
SALES (est): 674K Privately Held
SIC: 8011 Ophthalmologist

(G-6169)
CATHOLIC DOCESE WILMINGTON INC
Also Called: Holy Angels School
82 Possum Park Rd (19711-3858)
PHONE...................302 731-2210
Barbara Snively, *Principal*
Kathy Brown, *Teacher*
EMP: 40
SALES (corp-wide): 26.1MM Privately Held
SIC: 8211 8351 Elementary school; pre-school center
PA: Catholic Diocese Of Wilmington, Inc.
1925 Delaware Ave
Wilmington DE 19806
302 573-3100

(G-6170)
CATHOLIC MNSTRY TO ELDERLY INC
Also Called: MARYDALE RETIREMENT VILLAGE
135 Jeandell Dr (19713-2962)
PHONE...................302 368-2784
W Francis Malooly, *President*
Ray Lloyd, *Administration*
EMP: 10
SALES: 611K Privately Held
WEB: www.catholicdeaf.org
SIC: 8361 Geriatric residential care; home for the mentally handicapped

(G-6171)
CATHY L HARRIS DDS
220 Christiana Med Ctr (19702-1652)
PHONE...................302 453-1400
Cathy Harris, *Manager*
EMP: 4
SALES (est): 61.5K Privately Held
SIC: 8021 Offices & clinics of dentists

(G-6172)
CAVALIER GROUP
Also Called: Cavalier Apts
25 Golf View Dr Ofc A4 (19702-1721)
PHONE...................302 368-7437
Ann McDonald, *Branch Mgr*
EMP: 20
SALES (corp-wide): 7MM Privately Held
WEB: www.thecavaliergroup.com
SIC: 6513 Apartment building operators
PA: The Cavalier Group
105 Foulk Rd
Wilmington DE 19803
302 429-8700

(G-6173)
CAVALIERS OF DELAWARE INC
Also Called: Cavaliers Country Club
100 Addison Dr (19702-1939)
PHONE...................302 731-5600
Stan Minka, *President*
Randy Park, *General Mgr*
EMP: 80 EST: 1958
SQ FT: 18,000
SALES (est): 2.6MM Privately Held
SIC: 7997 Country club, membership

(G-6174)
CBI GROUP LLC (PA)
Also Called: Outside In
1501 Casho Mill Rd Ste 9 (19711-3500)
PHONE...................302 266-0860
Kim Burkhard, *Vice Pres*
Kelly Hocutt, *Marketing Staff*
Don Klumbach, *Marketing Staff*
Greg Moore, *Manager*
Rena Conklin, *Consultant*
EMP: 32
SALES (est): 7.6MM Privately Held
WEB: www.thecbigroup.com
SIC: 7361 Executive placement

(G-6175)
CC ENTERPRISES LLC
105 Anita Dr (19713-2341)
PHONE...................302 265-3677
EMP: 5
SALES (est): 246.3K Privately Held
SIC: 1021 Copper ores

(G-6176)
CENTER FOR BLACK CULTURE
192 S College Ave (19716-6115)
PHONE...................302 831-2991
Kasandra Moye, *Exec Dir*
EMP: 4 EST: 2003
SALES (est): 32.8K Privately Held
SIC: 7231 Beauty culture school

(G-6177)
CENTER FOR CHILD DEVELOPEMENT
256 Chapman Rd Ste 201 (19702-5415)
PHONE...................302 292-1334
Lisa R Savage, *Principal*
EMP: 5 EST: 2010
SALES (est): 178.8K Privately Held
SIC: 8351 Child day care services

(G-6178)
CENTER FOR HUMAN REPRODUCTION (PA)
Also Called: Delaware Inst For Rep
4745 Ogletown Stanton Rd (19713-2067)
PHONE...................302 738-4600
Jeffrey Russell, *President*
Jeffrey B Russell, *Director*
EMP: 17
SALES (est): 2.3MM Privately Held
SIC: 8011 Endocrinologist; fertility specialist, physician

(G-6179)
CENTURY 21 TOM LIVIZOS INC
701 Capitol Trl (19711-3913)
PHONE...................302 737-9000
Tom Livizos, *President*
EMP: 9
SQ FT: 3,000
SALES (est): 630K Privately Held
SIC: 6531 Real estate agent, residential

(G-6180)
CERAMIC TILE SUPPLY CO
375 Bellevue Rd (19713-3429)
PHONE...................302 737-4968
Pauline Campbell, *Branch Mgr*
EMP: 70
SALES (corp-wide): 39.7MM Privately Held
SIC: 1743 Tile installation, ceramic
PA: Ceramic Tile Supply Co.
103 Greenbank Rd
Wilmington DE 19808
302 992-9200

(G-6181)
CGE LANDSCAPE DESIGN
15 Fox Den Rd (19711-4204)
PHONE...................302 983-4847
Gordon Everts, *Principal*
EMP: 4 EST: 2010
SALES (est): 158K Privately Held
SIC: 0781 Landscape services

(G-6182)
CHA MOON DDS
1290 Peoples Plz (19702-5701)
PHONE...................302 297-3750
Cha Moon, *Fmly & Gen Dent*
EMP: 4 EST: 2017
SALES (est): 61.5K Privately Held
SIC: 8021 Offices & clinics of dentists

(G-6183)
CHAFFIN CLEANING SERVICE INC
3 Whitfield Rd (19711-4817)
PHONE...................302 369-2704
Jamie Chaffin, *President*
Robert Chaffin, *General Mgr*
EMP: 25
SALES (est): 250.4K Privately Held
SIC: 7349 Janitorial service, contract basis

(G-6184)
CHAMELEON CITY INC (PA)
2035 Sunset Lake Rd (19702-2600)
PHONE...................415 964-0054
Peter Naujoks, *Principal*
EMP: 1
SALES (est): 71.5K Privately Held
SIC: 7372 Application computer software

(G-6185)
CHAMPIONS FOR CHILDRENS MH
119 Timberline Dr (19711-7443)
PHONE...................302 249-6788
Barbara Messick, *Principal*
EMP: 5
SALES (est): 75.4K Privately Held
SIC: 8399 Advocacy group

(G-6186)
CHAMPIONSHIP APPAREL CORP
60 N College Ave (19711-2246)
PHONE...................302 731-5917
William O Dell, *President*
EMP: 5
SQ FT: 2,800
SALES (est): 310K Privately Held
SIC: 2395 Embroidery & art needlework

(G-6187)
CHANGE SHOP LLC
2035 Sunset Lake Rd B2 (19702-2600)
PHONE...................301 363-7188
EMP: 6
SALES: 20K Privately Held
SIC: 7371 Computer software development & applications

(G-6188)
CHANNELPRO MOBILE LLC
19 Kris Ct (19702-6843)
PHONE...................757 620-4635
Jonathan Cooper,
Charles R Lewis,
EMP: 10
SALES (est): 217.5K Privately Held
SIC: 7371 Custom computer programming services

(G-6189)
CHAPMAN HOSPITALITY INC
Also Called: Ramada Inn
260 Chapman Rd (19702-5490)
PHONE...................302 738-3400
David Shah, *President*
Pragna Shah, *Vice Pres*
EMP: 25
SALES (est): 1.9MM Privately Held
WEB: www.bestwerndelaware.com
SIC: 7011 Hotels & motels

(G-6190)
CHARLES RIVER LABS INTL INC
Also Called: Accugenix
614 Interchange Blvd (19711-3560)
PHONE...................302 292-8888
Gary Merkel, *President*
EMP: 7
SALES (corp-wide): 2.2B Publicly Held
SIC: 8731 Biological research

Newark - New Castle County (G-6191) — GEOGRAPHIC SECTION

PA: Charles River Laboratories International, Inc.
251 Ballardvale St
Wilmington MA 01887
781 222-6000

(G-6191)
CHASEMONT APARTMENTS
54 Cheswold Blvd (19713-4178)
PHONE..................302 731-0784
Robin Reich, *Principal*
EMP: 4
SALES (est): 262.4K **Privately Held**
SIC: 6513 Apartment building operators

(G-6192)
CHERRYRICH PUBLISHING
4 Four Seasons Pkwy (19702-2300)
PHONE..................302 533-6354
EMP: 2 **EST:** 2010
SALES (est): 85K **Privately Held**
SIC: 2741 Misc Publishing

(G-6193)
CHESAPEAKE PERL INC (PA)
Also Called: C-Perl
7 Mcmillan Way Ste 7 # 7 (19713-3459)
PHONE..................302 533-3540
John Lee Compton, *Ch of Bd*
David Davis, *Manager*
▲ **EMP:** 13
SQ FT: 4,200
SALES (est): 1.8MM **Privately Held**
SIC: 2824 Protein fibers

(G-6194)
CHESAPEAKE REHAB EQUIPMENT INC
810 Interchange Blvd (19711-3570)
PHONE..................302 266-6234
Kari Queen, *Branch Mgr*
EMP: 7
SALES (corp-wide): 3B **Privately Held**
WEB: www.chesrehab.com
SIC: 5999 6321 Medical apparatus & supplies; health insurance carriers
HQ: Chesapeake Rehab Equipment, Inc.
2700 Lord Baltimore Dr
Baltimore MD 21244
410 298-4555

(G-6195)
CHEVEUX INC
1115 Churchmans Rd (19713-2112)
PHONE..................302 731-9202
Mario Rispoli, *President*
Dorothy Rosica, *Corp Secy*
Lisa Rispoli, *Vice Pres*
EMP: 28
SALES: 750K **Privately Held**
SIC: 7231 Hairdressers

(G-6196)
CHILAY INC
Also Called: Consumer Injury Alert
40 E Main St 111 (19711-4639)
PHONE..................302 559-6014
Michelle Rizza, *President*
EMP: 6
SQ FT: 1,000
SALES (est): 331.3K **Privately Held**
SIC: 7311 Advertising agencies

(G-6197)
CHILD INC
148 Flamingo Dr (19702-4147)
PHONE..................302 832-5451
Earline Vann, *Manager*
EMP: 118
SALES (corp-wide): 5.2MM **Privately Held**
SIC: 8322 Social service center
PA: Child, Inc.
507 Philadelphia Pike
Wilmington DE 19809
302 762-8989

(G-6198)
CHILDRENS CHOICE INC
25 S Old Baltmre Pike # 101 (19702-1540)
PHONE..................302 731-9512
Erin Bates, *Manager*
EMP: 8
SALES (corp-wide): 3.1MM **Privately Held**
SIC: 8322 Individual & family services

PA: Children's Choice, Inc.
211 Benigno Blvd 100
Bellmawr NJ 08031
856 754-0914

(G-6199)
CHIMES INC
514 Interchange Blvd (19711-3557)
PHONE..................302 452-3400
Pete Dakchunak, *Director*
EMP: 60
SALES (corp-wide): 10.6MM **Privately Held**
SIC: 8361 Residential care for the handicapped
HQ: The Chimes Inc
4815 Seton Dr
Baltimore MD 21215
410 358-6400

(G-6200)
CHIORINO INC (PA)
125 Ruthar Dr Harm K Y Business Par (19711)
PHONE..................302 292-1906
Gregory Chiorino, *President*
David Pickrell, *Vice Pres*
Ken Balogh, *Regl Sales Mgr*
▲ **EMP:** 20
SQ FT: 33,000
SALES (est): 3MM **Privately Held**
WEB: www.chiorino.com
SIC: 3568 Drives: belt, cable or rope

(G-6201)
CHISTINE E WOODS
111 Continental Dr # 412 (19713-4306)
PHONE..................302 709-4497
Chistine E Woods, *Principal*
EMP: 7 **EST:** 2013
SALES (est): 191K **Privately Held**
SIC: 8011 Offices & clinics of medical doctors

(G-6202)
CHOICE MEDWASTE LLC
16 Tyre Ave (19711-7142)
PHONE..................302 366-1187
EMP: 5
SALES (est): 286.8K **Privately Held**
SIC: 4953 Recycling, waste materials

(G-6203)
CHRISTANA CARE VSCLAR SPCALIST
4765 Ogletown Stanton Rd 1e20 (19713-8003)
PHONE..................302 733-5700
Todd F Harad, *President*
Sonya Tuerff MD, *Principal*
EMP: 10
SALES (est): 819.4K **Privately Held**
SIC: 8062 General medical & surgical hospitals

(G-6204)
CHRISTANA CTR FOR WNS WELLNESS
4745 Ogletown Stanton Rd (19713-2067)
PHONE..................302 454-9800
EMP: 3
SALES (est): 115.4K **Privately Held**
SIC: 8011 3842 Gynecologist; supports: abdominal, ankle, arch, kneecap, etc.

(G-6205)
CHRISTIAN RAYMOND F & ASSOC
226 W Park Pl (19711-4565)
PHONE..................302 738-3016
Fax: 302 738-3016
EMP: 5 **EST:** 1986
SALES (est): 280K **Privately Held**
SIC: 8713 Surveying Services

(G-6206)
CHRISTIAN SCIENCE READING ROOM
92 E Main St Ste 7 (19711-4623)
PHONE..................302 456-1428
Peggy Schultz, *Relg Ldr*
EMP: 7
SALES (est): 320K **Privately Held**
SIC: 8699 Reading room, religious materials

(G-6207)
CHRISTIANA CARE HEALTH SYS INC
Also Called: Christianity Care Pathology
4755 Stanton Ogletown (19718-0001)
P.O. Box 6001 (19714-6001)
PHONE..................302 733-1601
Cheryle Katz, *Vice Pres*
Adam Raben, *Med Doctor*
Kelly J Whitmarsh, *Recruiter*
EMP: 400
SALES (corp-wide): 1.5B **Privately Held**
SIC: 8741 8071 Hospital management; pathological laboratory
HQ: Christiana Care Health System, Inc.
200 Hygeia Dr
Newark DE 19713
302 733-1000

(G-6208)
CHRISTIANA CARE HEALTH SYS INC
200 Hygeia Dr (19713-2049)
PHONE..................302 623-0390
Bill Padmonsky, *Manager*
EMP: 11
SALES (corp-wide): 1.5B **Privately Held**
SIC: 8741 8093 Hospital management; respiratory therapy clinic
HQ: Christiana Care Health System, Inc.
200 Hygeia Dr
Newark DE 19713
302 733-1000

(G-6209)
CHRISTIANA CARE HEALTH SYS INC
300 Biddle Ave Ste 200 (19702-3972)
PHONE..................302 838-4750
Nancy Howard, *Manager*
EMP: 12
SALES (corp-wide): 1.5B **Privately Held**
SIC: 8099 Childbirth preparation clinic
HQ: Christiana Care Health System, Inc.
200 Hygeia Dr
Newark DE 19713
302 733-1000

(G-6210)
CHRISTIANA CARE HEALTH SYS INC
Also Called: Christany Care Healthcare
4745 Ogltwn Stn Mp 1 217 (19718-0001)
PHONE..................302 733-2410
Michael Antunes, *Principal*
Michael Pushkarewicz, *Med Doctor*
EMP: 10
SALES (corp-wide): 1.5B **Privately Held**
SIC: 8011 Offices & clinics of medical doctors
HQ: Christiana Care Health System, Inc.
200 Hygeia Dr
Newark DE 19713
302 733-1000

(G-6211)
CHRISTIANA CARE HEALTH SYS INC
Also Called: Christana Care Crdiolgy Conslt
252 Chapman Rd Ste 150 (19702-5438)
PHONE..................302 366-1929
Edward Goldenberg, *Branch Mgr*
Raymond Miller, *Cardiovascular*
EMP: 9
SALES (corp-wide): 1.5B **Privately Held**
SIC: 8741 Hospital management
HQ: Christiana Care Health System, Inc.
200 Hygeia Dr
Newark DE 19713
302 733-1000

(G-6212)
CHRISTIANA CARE HEALTH SYS INC (HQ)
Also Called: Christiana Hospital
200 Hygeia Dr (19713-2049)
PHONE..................302 733-1000
Robert Laskowski MD, *President*
Matthew Hoffman, *Vice Chairman*
Buddy Elmore, *Senior VP*
Barry Dahllof, *Accounting Mgr*
Janice E Nevin, *Chief Mktg Ofcr*
EMP: 6
SQ FT: 600,000

SALES (est): 538.5MM
SALES (corp-wide): 1.5B **Privately Held**
SIC: 8062 General medical & surgical hospitals
PA: Christiana Care Health Services, Inc.
4755 Ogletown Stanton Rd
Newark DE 19718
302 733-1000

(G-6213)
CHRISTIANA CARE HEALTH SYS INC
4755 Ogletown Stanton Rd (19718-2200)
P.O. Box 6001 (19714-6001)
PHONE..................302 733-5700
Joyce Breinlinger, *Business Mgr*
Joanne McAuliffe, *Vice Pres*
Shawn Smith, *Vice Pres*
Scott Pentecost, *Opers Staff*
Bernice Bumpers, *Train & Dev Mgr*
EMP: 6
SALES (corp-wide): 1.5B **Privately Held**
SIC: 8062 General medical & surgical hospitals
HQ: Christiana Care Health System, Inc.
200 Hygeia Dr
Newark DE 19713
302 733-1000

(G-6214)
CHRISTIANA CARE HLTH SVCS INC
200 Hygeia Dr Unit B (19713-2049)
PHONE..................302 623-0100
EMP: 11
SALES (corp-wide): 1.5B **Privately Held**
SIC: 8011 Internal medicine, physician/surgeon
PA: Christiana Care Health Services, Inc.
4755 Ogletown Stanton Rd
Newark DE 19718
302 733-1000

(G-6215)
CHRISTIANA CARE HLTH SVCS INC
4755 Ogle Town (19718-0001)
PHONE..................302 733-1900
Eric Kmiec, *Research*
Robert Laskowski, *Branch Mgr*
David Driban, *Med Doctor*
Shauna Vogl, *Supervisor*
Mark Cadungog, *Surgeon*
EMP: 327
SALES (corp-wide): 1.5B **Privately Held**
SIC: 8062 General medical & surgical hospitals
PA: Christiana Care Health Services, Inc.
4755 Ogletown Stanton Rd
Newark DE 19718
302 733-1000

(G-6216)
CHRISTIANA CARE HLTH SVCS INC
Also Called: Imaginations
4755 Ogletown Stanton Rd (19718-2200)
PHONE..................302 733-5437
Margo Hobson, *Manager*
EMP: 28
SALES (corp-wide): 1.5B **Privately Held**
SIC: 8062 General medical & surgical hospitals
PA: Christiana Care Health Services, Inc.
4755 Ogletown Stanton Rd
Newark DE 19718
302 733-1000

(G-6217)
CHRISTIANA CARE HLTH SVCS INC
200 Hygeia Dr (19713-2049)
P.O. Box 2653, Wilmington (19805-0653)
PHONE..................302 623-7201
Charles Smith, *President*
EMP: 200
SALES (corp-wide): 1.5B **Privately Held**
SIC: 8062 8721 Hospital, AMA approved residency; accounting, auditing & bookkeeping
PA: Christiana Care Health Services, Inc.
4755 Ogletown Stanton Rd
Newark DE 19718
302 733-1000

▲ = Import ▼=Export
◆ =Import/Export

GEOGRAPHIC SECTION
Newark - New Castle County (G-6247)

(G-6218)
CHRISTIANA CARE HLTH SVCS INC
Also Called: Nursing Resources
4755 Ogletown Stanton Rd # 1249 (19718-2200)
P.O. Box 6001 (19714-6001)
PHONE..................302 733-6510
Shirley Morane, *Director*
EMP: 13
SALES (corp-wide): 1.5B **Privately Held**
SIC: **8051** Skilled nursing care facilities
PA: Christiana Care Health Services, Inc.
   4755 Ogletown Stanton Rd
   Newark DE 19718
   302 733-1000

(G-6219)
CHRISTIANA CARE INFUSION
600 White Clay Center Dr (19715-5455)
PHONE..................302 623-0345
Barbara Knightly, *Manager*
EMP: 6 EST: 2010
SALES (est): 163.6K **Privately Held**
SIC: **8082** Home health care services

(G-6220)
CHRISTIANA CHIROPRACTIC LLC
Also Called: First State Health & Wellness
1 Centurian Dr Ste 303 (19713-2127)
PHONE..................302 633-6335
Stacy S Cohen,
Tiffany Garcia,
EMP: 4
SALES (est): 160.9K **Privately Held**
SIC: **8041** 8049 Offices & clinics of chiropractors; acupuncturist

(G-6221)
CHRISTIANA CONSULTING INC
2608 Eastburn Ctr (19711-7285)
PHONE..................302 454-7000
G Jerry Litalien, *President*
Richard O Collins, *Vice Pres*
Barbara Litalien, *Treasurer*
EMP: 4
SQ FT: 500
SALES (est): 407.3K **Privately Held**
WEB: www.searchconsult.com
SIC: **7361** Executive placement

(G-6222)
CHRISTIANA CSMTC SRGRY CNSLTNT
Also Called: Christiana Cosmetics Surgery
62e Omega Dr (19713-2061)
PHONE..................302 368-9611
Julia W Macrae, *Plastic Surgeon*
Jonathan Saunders MD,
EMP: 10
SALES (est): 920K **Privately Held**
SIC: **8011** Plastic surgeon

(G-6223)
CHRISTIANA EXCAVATING COMPANY
2016 Sunset Lake Rd (19702-2630)
PHONE..................302 738-8660
Mike Conner, *President*
Paul Connor, *Senior VP*
Nancy McKinley, *Bookkeeper*
EMP: 35
SQ FT: 5,000
SALES (est): 5.6MM **Privately Held**
WEB: www.cecde.com
SIC: **1794** Excavation & grading, building construction

(G-6224)
CHRISTIANA FAMILY DENTAL CARE
50 Omega Dr (19713-2060)
PHONE..................302 623-4190
EMP: 4
SALES (est): 61.5K **Privately Held**
SIC: **8021** Offices & clinics of dentists

(G-6225)
CHRISTIANA MEDICAL GROUP PA
131 Continental Dr # 410 (19713-4308)
P.O. Box 8288, Wilmington (19803-8288)
PHONE..................302 366-1800
EMP: 5
SALES (est): 521.7K
SALES (corp-wide): 287.4MM **Privately Held**
SIC: **8011** Health/Allied Services
HQ: Ipc Healthcare, Inc.
   4605 Lankershim Blvd
   North Hollywood CA 91602
   888 447-2362

(G-6226)
CHRISTIANA NEONATAL PRACTICE
4745 Ogltn Stntn Rd # 217 (19713-2074)
PHONE..................302 733-2410
Deborah Tuttle, *Partner*
EMP: 15
SALES (est): 587.7K **Privately Held**
SIC: **8011** General & family practice, physician/surgeon

(G-6227)
CHRISTIANNA DENTAL CENTER
330 Christiana Med Ctr (19702-1653)
PHONE..................302 369-3200
Dr William Rectinov, *Owner*
EMP: 7
SALES (est): 722.4K **Privately Held**
SIC: **8021** Dental surgeon; dental clinic

(G-6228)
CHRISTINA EDUCATION ASSN
4135 Ogletown Stanton Rd (19713-4179)
PHONE..................302 454-7700
Arthur Wolf, *President*
EMP: 13
SALES: 104.4K **Privately Held**
SIC: **8631** Employees' association

(G-6229)
CHRISTINA SCHOOL DISTRICT
Also Called: School Transportation Dept
400 Wyoming Rd (19713-7189)
PHONE..................302 454-2281
Ron G Albence, *Principal*
Heather Bordas, *Director*
Bernadine Lopez, *Admin Asst*
Sara Deflaviis, *Teacher*
EMP: 400
SALES (corp-wide): 130.1MM **Privately Held**
WEB: www.christina.k12.de.us
SIC: **4151** School buses
PA: Christina School District
   600 N Lombard St
   Wilmington DE 19801
   302 552-2600

(G-6230)
CHRISTINE W MAYNARD M D
4735 Ogletown Stanton Rd (19713-2072)
PHONE..................302 225-6110
Christine Maynard, *Manager*
EMP: 6 EST: 2017
SALES (est): 80.5K **Privately Held**
SIC: **8011** Offices & clinics of medical doctors

(G-6231)
CHRISTOPHER A BOWENS MD
Also Called: Deleware Heart Group
2600 Glasgow Ave Ste 108 (19702-5703)
PHONE..................302 834-3700
Christophe A Bowens MD, *Partner*
Dr Joseph West, *Partner*
EMP: 8
SALES (est): 298.1K **Privately Held**
SIC: **8011** 8049 Cardiologist & cardio-vascular specialist; offices of health practitioner

(G-6232)
CHRISTOPHER CASSCELLS MD
Glasgow Med Ctr Ste 104 (19702)
PHONE..................302 832-6220
Christopher Casscells, *Principal*
EMP: 8
SALES (est): 258.7K **Privately Held**
SIC: **8011** Orthopedic physician

(G-6233)
CHROMIUM DENTAL LLC
300 Creek View Rd Ste 105 (19711-8547)
PHONE..................302 731-5582
David Anderson,
EMP: 13
SALES: 1.5MM **Privately Held**
SIC: **8072** Dental laboratories

(G-6234)
CHURCHMAN VILLAGE CENTER LLC
Also Called: Churman Village Center
4949 Ogletown Stanton Rd (19713-2068)
PHONE..................302 998-6900
Terence Walls, *Maintenance Dir*
Richard Powell, *Exec Dir*
EMP: 9
SQ FT: 90,820
SALES (est): 152.5K **Privately Held**
SIC: **8051** 8361 Convalescent home with continuous nursing care; geriatric residential care

(G-6235)
CIGARETTE CITY INC (PA)
460 Peoples Plz (19702-4797)
PHONE..................302 836-4889
Frank Speciale, *President*
EMP: 24
SALES (est): 3MM **Privately Held**
WEB: www.cigar-ettecity.com
SIC: **5194** 5993 Cigars; tobacco stores & stands

(G-6236)
CIMENTUM
17 Springbrook Ln (19711-2497)
PHONE..................302 635-7262
Ghulam Haider, *Owner*
EMP: 1
SALES (est): 49.8K **Privately Held**
SIC: **3241** Cement, hydraulic

(G-6237)
CITIGROUP INC
500 White Clay Center Dr (19711-5469)
PHONE..................302 631-3530
Edward Handelman, *Managing Dir*
Kay Ambrose, *Vice Pres*
Dominic Anepete, *Vice Pres*
Allison Barone, *Vice Pres*
Lalit Derashri, *Vice Pres*
EMP: 21
SALES (est): 4.9MM
SALES (corp-wide): 72.8B **Publicly Held**
SIC: **6099** 7389 Check clearing services; financial services
PA: Citigroup Inc.
   388 Greenwich St
   New York NY 10013
   212 559-1000

(G-6238)
CITIZENS BANK NATIONAL ASSN
100 Suburban Dr (19711-3597)
PHONE..................302 292-6401
Michael Vaught, *Branch Mgr*
EMP: 10
SALES (corp-wide): 7.3B **Publicly Held**
WEB: www.ccoinvest.com
SIC: **6022** State commercial banks
HQ: Citizens Bank, National Association
   1 Citizens Plz Ste 1 # 1
   Providence RI 02903
   401 282-7000

(G-6239)
CITIZENS BANK NATIONAL ASSN
117 E Main St (19711-7312)
PHONE..................302 456-7100
Jonica Clay, *Branch Mgr*
EMP: 10
SALES (corp-wide): 7.3B **Publicly Held**
WEB: www.ccoinvest.com
SIC: **6022** State commercial banks
HQ: Citizens Bank, National Association
   1 Citizens Plz Ste 1 # 1
   Providence RI 02903
   401 282-7000

(G-6240)
CITIZENS BANK NATIONAL ASSN
1 University Plz (19702-1549)
PHONE..................302 283-5600
Belinda Hawes, *Branch Mgr*
EMP: 7
SALES (corp-wide): 7.3B **Publicly Held**
WEB: www.ccoinvest.com
SIC: **6022** State commercial banks
HQ: Citizens Bank, National Association
   1 Citizens Plz Ste 1 # 1
   Providence RI 02903
   401 282-7000

(G-6241)
CITIZENS BANK NATIONAL ASSN
40 Chestnut Hill Plz (19713-2701)
PHONE..................302 456-7111
Edie Moore, *Principal*
EMP: 10
SALES (corp-wide): 7.3B **Publicly Held**
SIC: **6022** State commercial banks
HQ: Citizens Bank, National Association
   1 Citizens Plz Ste 1 # 1
   Providence RI 02903
   401 282-7000

(G-6242)
CITY OF NEWARK
Also Called: Downtown Parking
45 E Main St Ste 205 (19711-4600)
PHONE..................302 366-0457
Marvin Howard, *Manager*
EMP: 15 **Privately Held**
WEB: www.newark.de.us
SIC: **7521** 9111 Parking lots; mayors' offices
PA: City Of Newark
   220 S Main St
   Newark DE 19711
   302 366-7000

(G-6243)
CITY OF NEWARK
Also Called: Parks Rcreation Dept Cy Newark
220 S Main St (19711-4594)
PHONE..................302 366-7060
Charles Emerson, *CTO*
Charlie Emerson, *Director*
EMP: 22 **Privately Held**
WEB: www.newark.de.us
SIC: **9512** 7999 Recreational program administration, government; recreation center
PA: City Of Newark
   220 S Main St
   Newark DE 19711
   302 366-7000

(G-6244)
CITY THEATER CO INC
110 Tanglewood Ln (19711-3120)
PHONE..................302 831-2206
John Suchanec, *Principal*
EMP: 2
SALES (est): 67K **Privately Held**
SIC: **2339** Women's & misses' outerwear

(G-6245)
CLAY WHITE DENTAL ASSOCIATES
Also Called: Bond, Donald T DDS
12 Polly Drummond Hill Rd (19711-5703)
PHONE..................302 731-4225
Donald Bond, *President*
EMP: 10
SALES (est): 970.1K **Privately Held**
SIC: **8021** Dentists' office

(G-6246)
CLEAN AS A WHISTLE
46 Cheswold Blvd (19713-4153)
PHONE..................302 757-5024
EMP: 2 EST: 2012
SALES (est): 104K **Privately Held**
SIC: **3999** Mfg Misc Products

(G-6247)
CLEAN FORCE BUILDING SERVICES
36 Ashkirk Pl (19702-4099)
PHONE..................302 494-9330
Ronnie James, *Owner*
EMP: 11
SALES (est): 130.1K **Privately Held**
SIC: **7349** Janitorial service, contract basis

Newark - New Castle County (G-6248) — GEOGRAPHIC SECTION

(G-6248)
CLEANING FRENZY LLC
2860 Ogletown Rd Bldg 6-1 (19713-1820)
PHONE.............................302 453-8800
Ashley Dematt, *Mng Member*
EMP: 8
SALES (est): 149.6K **Privately Held**
SIC: 7699 Cleaning services

(G-6249)
CLEMENTES CLUBHOUSE
321 Shisler Ct (19702-1341)
PHONE.............................302 455-0936
EMP: 4 EST: 2011
SALES (est): 66.7K **Privately Held**
SIC: 7997 Membership sports & recreation clubs

(G-6250)
CLIENT MONSTER LLC
1300 Helen Dr Unit 112 (19702-1672)
PHONE.............................866 799-5433
Francis Frisby III,
EMP: 5
SALES (est): 172.4K **Privately Held**
SIC: 7371 Computer software development & applications

(G-6251)
CLINICAL CRDLGY SPCIALISTS LLC
1400 Peoples Plz Ste 111 (19702-5706)
PHONE.............................302 834-3700
Christopher A Bowens, *Principal*
EMP: 5
SALES (est): 452.7K **Privately Held**
SIC: 8011 Cardiologist & cardio-vascular specialist

(G-6252)
CLOUTO INC
40 E Main St 1202 (19711-4639)
PHONE.............................302 966-9282
EMP: 4 EST: 2013
SALES (est): 190K **Privately Held**
SIC: 4813 Telephone Communications

(G-6253)
CMI ELECTRIC INC
83 Albe Dr Ste E (19702-1374)
PHONE.............................302 731-5556
Linda Davis, *Vice Pres*
EMP: 24
SALES (corp-wide): 3.5MM **Privately Held**
SIC: 7629 1711 Electrical repair shops; solar energy contractor
PA: Cmi Electric, Inc.
    83 Albe Dr Ste A
    Newark DE 19702
    302 731-5556

(G-6254)
CMI ELECTRIC INC (PA)
Also Called: CMI Solar Electric
83 Albe Dr Ste A (19702-1373)
PHONE.............................302 731-5556
Dale W Davis, *President*
Linda A Davis, *Vice Pres*
EMP: 24
SQ FT: 6,000
SALES: 3.5MM **Privately Held**
SIC: 4911 1711 ; solar energy contractor

(G-6255)
CMP FIRE LLC
1820 Otts Chapel Rd (19702-2016)
PHONE.............................410 620-2062
Samantha Pearce, *President*
EMP: 9
SALES (est): 587.8K **Privately Held**
SIC: 1711 7389 Fire sprinkler system installation; fire extinguisher servicing

(G-6256)
CMY SOLUTIONS LLC
2035 Sunset Lake Rd B2 (19702-2600)
PHONE.............................321 732-1866
Joseph Buran, *Partner*
Bryan Cianchetti, *Partner*
Paul Malkewicz, *Partner*
Baldwin Yeung, *Partner*
EMP: 4
SALES (est): 121.2K **Privately Held**
SIC: 8711 8742 1731 Public utilities consultant; electric power systems contractors; electrical or electronic engineering

(G-6257)
CNS CONSTRUCTION CORP
116 Sandy Dr Ste B (19713-1187)
PHONE.............................302 224-0450
Charles Showell, *President*
EMP: 20
SQ FT: 500
SALES (est): 1.8MM **Privately Held**
SIC: 1521 Single-family housing construction

(G-6258)
CO FS HOLDING COMPANY LLC
502 S College Ave (19713-1338)
PHONE.............................302 894-1244
Bob Pfeifer, *Branch Mgr*
EMP: 7
SALES (corp-wide): 577MM **Privately Held**
WEB: www.farrell-lines.com
SIC: 4213 Automobiles, transport & delivery
HQ: Co Fs Holding Company, Llc
    624 Steele St
    Denver CO 80206
    800 624-3256

(G-6259)
COGTEST INC
Topkis Bldg Ste 100254c (19702-5413)
PHONE.............................302 454-1265
Rishi Barkataki, *Director*
EMP: 10 EST: 2015
SALES (est): 71.7K **Privately Held**
SIC: 8071 Testing laboratories

(G-6260)
COLDWELL BNKR COML AMATO ASSOC
100 Christiana Med Ctr (19702-1697)
PHONE.............................302 224-7700
Susan Amato, *Principal*
Susan M Amato, *Director*
EMP: 5
SALES (est): 441.5K **Privately Held**
SIC: 6531 6519 Real estate agent, residential; real property lessors

(G-6261)
COLLINS ASSOCIATES
38 Peoples Plz (19702-4727)
PHONE.............................302 834-4000
Ronald E Collins, *Partner*
Lynn Collins DDS, *Partner*
EMP: 18
SQ FT: 6,636
SALES (est): 1.2MM **Privately Held**
SIC: 8021 Dentists' office

(G-6262)
COLON RECTAL SURGERY ASSOC DEL
4745 Ogletown Stanton Rd # 216 (19713-2074)
PHONE.............................302 737-5444
Joseph Damico MD, *Partner*
Frederick Denstman MD, *Partner*
Carey Mason, *Partner*
Shanthi Shakamori, *Partner*
Carey Ann Nathan, *Med Doctor*
EMP: 12
SALES (est): 1.2MM **Privately Held**
SIC: 8011 Surgeon

(G-6263)
COLONIAL CHAPTER OF
700 Barksdale Rd Ste 6 (19711-3260)
PHONE.............................302 861-6671
Allyson Swartzentruber, *Administration*
EMP: 4
SALES: 360.5K **Privately Held**
SIC: 8399 Advocacy group

(G-6264)
COLONIAL RLTY ASSOC LTD PARTNR
Also Called: Colonial Garden Apartments
334 E Main St Bldg B (19711-7151)
PHONE.............................302 737-1254
Jonathan De Young, *Partner*
Mitchell Horenstein Do, *Partner*
Robert Levin DDS, *Partner*
Philip Pearlstein Do, *Partner*
EMP: 10
SALES (est): 680.3K **Privately Held**
SIC: 6513 Apartment building operators

(G-6265)
COLOR DYE SYSTEMS AND CO
Also Called: Trim Shop
663 Dawson Dr Ste B (19713-3461)
PHONE.............................302 454-1754
Greg Culbertson, *Owner*
Debera S Culbertson, *Co-Owner*
EMP: 7
SALES (est): 353.4K **Privately Held**
SIC: 7641 Upholstery work

(G-6266)
COMFORT CARE AT HOME INC
260 Chapman Rd Ste 201 (19702-5491)
PHONE.............................302 737-8078
Adwoa Tina Brew, *Exec Dir*
EMP: 28
SALES: 950K **Privately Held**
SIC: 8082 Home health care services

(G-6267)
COMFORT INN & SUITES
3 Concord Ln (19713-3577)
PHONE.............................302 737-3900
Rodney Perkins, *General Mgr*
EMP: 15
SALES (est): 884.4K **Privately Held**
SIC: 7011 Hotels & motels

(G-6268)
COMMERCIAL INSURANCE ASSOC
256 Chapman Rd Ste 203 (19702-5415)
PHONE.............................610 436-4608
Victoria Tester, *President*
EMP: 5
SQ FT: 10,000
SALES: 2MM **Privately Held**
SIC: 6411 Insurance agents

(G-6269)
COMMODITIES PLUS INC
Also Called: Buy and Sell Rags
132 Sandy Dr (19713-1147)
P.O. Box 517, Middletown (19709-0517)
PHONE.............................302 376-5219
Lallind Nalwattie, *President*
Brian Harris, *Opers Staff*
Vavita Jagnanan, *Manager*
EMP: 5
SQ FT: 10,000
SALES (est): 4.8K **Privately Held**
SIC: 4953 Recycling, waste materials

(G-6270)
COMMUNICATIONS PRINTING INC
2850 Ogletown Rd (19713-1838)
P.O. Box 7790 (19714-7790)
PHONE.............................302 229-9369
Vincent Mercante, *President*
Alice Mercante, *Corp Secy*
EMP: 4
SQ FT: 1,000
SALES (est): 450.8K **Privately Held**
SIC: 2752 Commercial printing, offset; lithographing on metal

(G-6271)
COMMUNITY BUSINESS DEV CORP
25 Hempstead Dr (19702-7713)
PHONE.............................302 544-1709
Roger Turner, *President*
Carlton Gray, *Vice Pres*
EMP: 5
SALES (est): 77.7K **Privately Held**
SIC: 8641 Civic social & fraternal associations

(G-6272)
COMMUNITY SERVICES CORPORATION
116 Haines St (19711-5367)
PHONE.............................302 368-4400
Mark Smith Jr, *President*
EMP: 17
SQ FT: 1,400
SALES (est): 1.1MM **Privately Held**
WEB: www.dewindows.com
SIC: 7299 7349 Home improvement & renovation contractor agency; building cleaning service

(G-6273)
COMMUNITY TWERED FEDERAL CR UN (PA)
401 Eagle Run Rd (19702-1602)
P.O. Box 7739 (19714-7739)
PHONE.............................302 368-2396
Anthony Hinds, *CEO*
Robert Oaks, *President*
Bill Thompson, *Controller*
Beverly Minsberg, *Finance Mgr*
Doris Davidson, *Branch Mgr*
EMP: 11
SALES: 3.4MM **Privately Held**
WEB: www.dplfcu.org
SIC: 6061 6062 Federal credit unions; state credit unions

(G-6274)
COMPREHENSIVE BUS SVCS LLC (PA)
112 Capitol Trl (19711-3716)
PHONE.............................302 994-2000
Dean Brand, *CEO*
Robert Dotey, *Principal*
Mark Marinzoli, *CFO*
EMP: 11 EST: 1993
SQ FT: 3,500
SALES (est): 2MM **Privately Held**
SIC: 7389 Financial services

(G-6275)
COMPRHENSIVE NEUROLOGY CTR LLC
537 Stanton Christiana Rd # 106 (19713-2145)
PHONE.............................302 996-9010
Carl Yacoub, *Owner*
EMP: 12
SALES (est): 1.4MM **Privately Held**
SIC: 8011 Neurologist

(G-6276)
COMPUTER AID INC
500 Creek View Rd Ste 300 (19711-8549)
PHONE.............................302 831-5500
Tom Salvaggio, *Manager*
EMP: 204
SALES (corp-wide): 603.3MM **Privately Held**
SIC: 7371 7374 Computer software systems analysis & design, custom; data processing & preparation
PA: Computer Aid, Inc.
    1390 Ridgeview Dr Ste 300
    Allentown PA 18104
    610 530-5000

(G-6277)
COMPUTER SCIENCES CORPORATION
500 Creek View Rd (19711-8549)
PHONE.............................302 391-8347
Anthony Kowal, *Manager*
EMP: 400
SALES (corp-wide): 20.7B **Publicly Held**
WEB: www.csc.com
SIC: 7379 Computer related consulting services
HQ: Computer Sciences Corporation
    1775 Tysons Blvd Ste 1000
    Tysons VA 22102
    703 245-9675

(G-6278)
COMPUTER STAFFING SERVICES LLC (PA)
Also Called: CSS Technical Staffing
263 E Main St Ste A (19711-7314)
PHONE.............................302 737-4920
Tom Clarke, *Vice Pres*
Robert Fishman, *Vice Pres*
Kimberly Crew,
EMP: 30
SQ FT: 1,000
SALES (est): 1.7MM **Privately Held**
WEB: www.cssnow.com
SIC: 7361 Employment agencies

GEOGRAPHIC SECTION

Newark - New Castle County (G-6308)

(G-6279)
CONCENTRA INC
4110 Stanton Ogletown Rd (19713-4169)
PHONE.................................302 738-0103
Gail Phaton, *Manager*
Michael Kennedy, *Director*
EMP: 15
SALES (corp-wide): 5B **Publicly Held**
WEB: www.concentra.com
SIC: 8011 Medical centers
HQ: Concentra Inc.
5080 Spectrum Dr Ste 400w
Addison TX 75001
972 364-8000

(G-6280)
CONCORD TOWERS INC
Also Called: Holiday Inn
1201 Christiana Rd (19713-3503)
PHONE.................................302 737-2700
Paul Isken, *President*
Donald Isken, *Corp Secy*
Laura Isken Doyle, *Director*
EMP: 70
SQ FT: 80,000
SALES (est): 5.5MM **Privately Held**
SIC: 7011 Hotels & motels

(G-6281)
CONECTIV LLC
375 N Wakefield Dr (19702-5416)
P.O. Box 6066 (19714-6066)
PHONE.................................302 429-3018
Bruce Pawling, *Director*
EMP: 20
SALES (corp-wide): 35.9B **Publicly Held**
WEB: www.conectiv.com
SIC: 4911 Distribution, electric power
HQ: Conectiv, Llc
800 N King St Ste 400
Wilmington DE 19801
202 872-2680

(G-6282)
CONECTIV COMMUNICATIONS INC (HQ)
252 Chapman Rd (19702-5436)
P.O. Box 6066 (19714-6066)
PHONE.................................302 224-1177
EMP: 25
SALES (est): 4.7MM
SALES (corp-wide): 588MM **Privately Held**
SIC: 1731 7379 4813 Electrical Contractor Computer Related Services Telephone Communications
PA: Cavalier Telephone, L.L.C.
2134 W Laburnum Ave
Richmond VA 23227
804 422-4100

(G-6283)
CONECTIV ENERGY SUPPLY INC (DH)
500 N Wakefield Dr (19702-5440)
P.O. Box 6066 (19714-6066)
PHONE.................................302 454-0300
Howard Cosgrove, *CEO*
Jerrold Jacobs, *Vice Ch Bd*
David Hughes, *Vice Pres*
Bernie Fowler, *Engineer*
EMP: 96 EST: 1998
SQ FT: 2,500
SALES (est): 40.8MM
SALES (corp-wide): 9.5B **Privately Held**
SIC: 5063 1731 4924 4925 Antennas, receiving, satellite dishes; cable television installation; natural gas distribution; gas production and/or distribution; gas transmission & distribution
HQ: Calpine Mid-Atlantic Energy, Llc
717 Texas St Ste 1000
Houston TX 77002
713 830-2000

(G-6284)
CONFERENCE GROUP LLC
254 Chapman Rd Ste 200 (19702-5422)
PHONE.................................302 224-8255
Karen Smythe, *Human Res Mgr*
John Riggins, *Mng Member*
Kim Lyons, *Supervisor*
Ian Williams, *Prgrmr*
Andrew Schelling, *Executive*
EMP: 40
SQ FT: 6,500
SALES (est): 4.8MM **Privately Held**
WEB: www.conferencegroup.com
SIC: 7389 Teleconferencing services

(G-6285)
CONFORMIT
2915 Ogletown Rd Ste 2636 (19713-1927)
PHONE.................................302 451-9167
EMP: 2
SALES (est): 118.6K **Privately Held**
SIC: 7372 Prepackaged software

(G-6286)
CONGRUENCE CONSULTING GROUP
87 Madison Dr Ste A (19711-4403)
PHONE.................................320 290-6155
Kelli Collins, *Principal*
EMP: 7 EST: 2013
SALES (est): 258K **Privately Held**
SIC: 7361 8742 8748 7379 Labor contractors (employment agency); human resource consulting services; business consulting; computer related consulting services; custom computer programming services; computer systems analysis & design

(G-6287)
CONNELL CONSTRUCTION CO
808 N Country Club Dr (19711-2751)
PHONE.................................302 738-9428
David Connell, *Owner*
EMP: 6
SALES (est): 318.2K **Privately Held**
WEB: www.connellconstruction.com
SIC: 1521 Single-family home remodeling, additions & repairs

(G-6288)
CONNOR SWEEPING INC
2016 Sunset Lake Rd (19702-2630)
PHONE.................................302 368-2210
Patrick Connor, *President*
EMP: 4
SALES (est): 200.2K **Privately Held**
WEB: www.connorsweeping.com
SIC: 4959 Sweeping service: road, airport, parking lot, etc.

(G-6289)
CONSTRUCTION LAYOUT SERVICES
304 Mason Dr (19711-2568)
PHONE.................................302 998-1800
Anthony Di Campli Jr, *Owner*
EMP: 4
SALES (est): 400K **Privately Held**
SIC: 1531 Condominium developers

(G-6290)
CONSULTTIVE RVIEW RHBILITATION
630 Churchmans Rd Ste 105 (19702-1943)
PHONE.................................302 366-0356
Robert Pare, *Branch Mgr*
EMP: 7
SQ FT: 1,300 **Privately Held**
SIC: 8748 Business consulting
PA: Consultative Review And Rehabilitation Inc
20 Lee Ann Dr
Blackwood NJ

(G-6291)
CONTINENTAL CASE
64 Shields Ln (19702-3111)
PHONE.................................302 322-1765
James Broomall, *Owner*
Bonnie Broomall, *Corp Secy*
EMP: 3
SALES (est): 217.8K **Privately Held**
SIC: 3161 Cases, carrying; trunks

(G-6292)
CONTRACTUAL CARRIERS INC
104 Alan Dr (19711-8027)
PHONE.................................302 453-1420
Karl E Schneider, *President*
Stephen Dawson, *Vice Pres*
Joachim Schneider, *Treasurer*
Karen Thompson, *Admin Sec*
EMP: 35
SQ FT: 2,000
SALES (est): 4.2MM **Privately Held**
SIC: 4214 4213 Local trucking with storage; contract haulers

(G-6293)
CONWAY CONSTRUCTION LLC
521 Dougfield Rd (19713-2731)
PHONE.................................302 453-9260
EMP: 4
SALES (est): 320.7K **Privately Held**
SIC: 1521 Single-Family House Construction

(G-6294)
CONZURGE INC
2035 Sunset Lake Rd B2 (19702-2600)
PHONE.................................267 507-6039
Jees Raj, *CEO*
EMP: 10
SALES (est): 180.6K **Privately Held**
SIC: 7389 Business services

(G-6295)
COOK PLASTERING INC
1026 Summit View Dr (19713-1124)
PHONE.................................302 737-0778
Steve Cook, *President*
EMP: 12
SALES (est): 500K **Privately Held**
SIC: 1742 Plaster & drywall work

(G-6296)
CORDJIA LLC (PA)
131 Continental Dr # 409 (19713-4308)
PHONE.................................302 743-1297
David Anderson, *Vice Pres*
Samantha Wallace, *Vice Pres*
Michael Cahill, *Production*
Tim Lambert, *CFO*
Kristy Adkins, *Accountant*
EMP: 21
SALES (est): 4.1MM **Privately Held**
SIC: 7389 Financial services

(G-6297)
CORE & MAIN LP
22 Garfield Way (19713-3450)
PHONE.................................302 737-1500
EMP: 7
SALES (corp-wide): 2.6B **Privately Held**
SIC: 1623 4941 4952 Water, sewer & utility lines; water supply; sewerage systems
PA: Core & Main Lp
1830 Craig Park Ct
Saint Louis MO 63146
314 432-4700

(G-6298)
CORIZON HEALTH INC
111 Continental Dr # 211 (19713-4306)
PHONE.................................302 266-8230
Barbara Bailey, *Admin Sec*
EMP: 55
SALES (corp-wide): 1.2B **Privately Held**
SIC: 8011 Dispensary, operated by physicians
HQ: Corizon Health, Inc.
103 Powell Ct
Brentwood TN 37027
800 729-0069

(G-6299)
CORLO SERVICES INC ✪
100 Peoples Dr (19702-1306)
PHONE.................................302 737-3207
EMP: 2 EST: 2019
SALES (est): 73.2K **Privately Held**
SIC: 2759 Commercial printing

(G-6300)
CORPORATE RELOCATION ASSN
663 Arbour Dr (19713-1205)
P.O. Box 1679, Hockessin (19707-5679)
PHONE.................................302 239-9314
EMP: 5 EST: 1999
SALES (est): 300K **Privately Held**
SIC: 8611 Business Association

(G-6301)
CORROSION TESTING LABORATORIES
60 Blue Hen Dr (19713-3406)
PHONE.................................302 454-8200
Richard A Corbett, *President*
Robert Nixon, *General Mgr*
Douglas Sherman, *Engineer*
Barbara Corbett, *Admin Sec*
Brad Krantz, *Administration*
EMP: 10
SQ FT: 6,500
SALES (est): 1.6MM **Privately Held**
WEB: www.corrosionlab.com
SIC: 8711 8734 Engineering services; testing laboratories

(G-6302)
CORVANT LLC
131 Continental Dr # 409 (19713-4308)
PHONE.................................302 299-1570
Navroze Eduljee, *CEO*
Sukumar Narayanan, *COO*
Greg Miller, *Vice Pres*
Carol Lambert, *Controller*
Adam Orescan, *Software Dev*
EMP: 12
SALES (est): 785.4K **Privately Held**
SIC: 7371 Computer software development

(G-6303)
COUNTRY INNS SUITES
Also Called: Country Suites By Carlson
1024 Old Churchmans Rd (19713-2102)
PHONE.................................302 266-6400
Perry Patel, *Owner*
EMP: 7
SALES (est): 1MM **Privately Held**
SIC: 7011 Hotels & motels

(G-6304)
COUNTRYSIDE LAWN & LANDSCAPE
Also Called: Countryside Nursery & Grdn Ctr
1604 Pulaski Hwy (19702-4105)
PHONE.................................302 832-1320
Keith Harris, *President*
EMP: 25
SQ FT: 4,000
SALES (est): 1.5MM **Privately Held**
WEB: www.countrysidegardencenter.com
SIC: 0181 5261 0782 Nursery stock, growing of; nurseries & garden centers; lawn care services; landscape contractors

(G-6305)
COURTYARD MANAGEMENT CORP
Also Called: Courtyard By Marriott
48 Geoffrey Dr (19713-3603)
PHONE.................................302 456-3800
Jason Abbey, *General Mgr*
EMP: 23
SALES (corp-wide): 20.7B **Publicly Held**
SIC: 7011 Hotels & motels
HQ: Courtyard Management Corporation
10400 Fernwood Rd
Bethesda MD 20817

(G-6306)
COURTYARD NEWARK AT UD
400 David Hollowell Dr (19716-7448)
PHONE.................................302 737-0900
Bill Sullivan, *Director*
EMP: 11
SALES (est): 661K **Privately Held**
SIC: 7011 Motels

(G-6307)
COVANT SOLUTIONS INC
220 Continental Dr # 314 (19713-4314)
PHONE.................................302 607-2678
Haris Koya, *President*
EMP: 35
SQ FT: 1,500
SALES (est): 2.6MM **Privately Held**
SIC: 7371 Custom computer programming services

(G-6308)
COVENTRY HEALTH CARE INC
750 Prides Xing Ste 200 (19716-6105)
PHONE.................................302 995-6100
EMP: 5 **Publicly Held**
SIC: 6324 Hospital/Medical Service Plan
HQ: Coventry Health Care, Inc.
6720 Rockledge Dr 700b
Bethesda MD 20817
301 581-0600

Newark - New Castle County (G-6309)

(G-6309)
COVENTRY HEALTH CARE INC
Also Called: Ceventry Health Care Delaware
750 Prdes Crssing Ste 200 (19713)
PHONE..................800 833-7423
Kalpana Mody, *Accountant*
Delores Plank, *Director*
EMP: 6
SALES (corp-wide): 194.5B **Publicly Held**
SIC: 8741 6324 Management services; hospital & medical service plans
HQ: Coventry Health Care, Inc.
6720 Rockledge Dr 700b
Bethesda MD 20817
301 581-0600

(G-6310)
COX INDUSTRIES INC
111 Lake Dr Ste C (19702-3334)
PHONE..................302 332-8470
Alan Cox, *President*
EMP: 5
SALES: 3.5MM **Privately Held**
SIC: 3449 Miscellaneous metalwork

(G-6311)
CRAMARO TARPAULIN SYSTEMS INC
131 Sandy Dr (19713-1149)
PHONE..................302 292-2170
Ernie Dempsey, *Manager*
EMP: 19
SALES (corp-wide): 28.4MM **Privately Held**
WEB: www.cramarotarps.com
SIC: 5199 3089 Tarpaulins; floor coverings, plastic
PA: Cramaro Tarpaulin Systems Inc
600 North Dr
Melbourne FL 32934
321 757-7611

(G-6312)
CREAFORM USA INC
220 E Delaware Ave (19711)
PHONE..................407 732-4103
Charled Mony, *President*
Jackie Cheng, *Sales Staff*
Yoyo Han, *Sales Staff*
Jennifer Duquette, *Manager*
EMP: 6
SALES (est): 555.8K
SALES (corp-wide): 4.8B **Publicly Held**
SIC: 7374 Optical scanning data service
PA: Ametek, Inc.
1100 Cassatt Rd
Berwyn PA 19312
610 647-2121

(G-6313)
CREATIVE FLOORS INC
105 Sandy Dr (19713-1148)
PHONE..................302 455-9045
Ronald Wollaston, *President*
Roger Wollaston, *Vice Pres*
EMP: 10
SQ FT: 9,500
SALES (est): 1.9MM **Privately Held**
SIC: 1752 Floor laying & floor work

(G-6314)
CREATIVE MICRO DESIGNS INC
645 Dawson Dr Ste B (19713-3443)
PHONE..................302 456-5800
Ralph Page, *President*
Phillip Emms, *Exec VP*
EMP: 8
SQ FT: 3,900
SALES (est): 907.1K **Privately Held**
WEB: www.cmdfab.com
SIC: 8748 5734 3577 Systems engineering consultant, ex. computer or professional; computer peripheral equipment; computer peripheral equipment

(G-6315)
CREATIVE TRAVEL INC
Also Called: Rainbow Charter Service
908 Old Harmony Rd (19713-4107)
P.O. Box 30798, Wilmington (19805-7798)
PHONE..................302 658-2900
Bob Older, *President*
EMP: 17
SALES (est): 2.3MM **Privately Held**
WEB: www.creativetravelinc.com
SIC: 4724 Tourist agency arranging transport, lodging & car rental

(G-6316)
CRIMSON GROUP LLC
17 Dubb Dr (19702-6825)
PHONE..................301 252-3779
John McCleod,
Lynda Steward,
EMP: 7
SALES (est): 294.3K **Privately Held**
SIC: 1629 Waste water & sewage treatment plant construction

(G-6317)
CROWN MOLDING MAN
187 Scottfield Dr (19713-2453)
PHONE..................302 455-1204
John Feeney, *Owner*
EMP: 1
SALES (est): 68.9K **Privately Held**
SIC: 3089 Molding primary plastic

(G-6318)
CRUISE SHIP CENTERS
760 Peoples Plz (19702-5601)
PHONE..................302 999-0202
James Devoe, *Owner*
Dave Devoe, *Owner*
EMP: 5
SALES (est): 419.9K **Privately Held**
SIC: 4724 Tourist agency arranging transport, lodging & car rental

(G-6319)
CRYSTAL DIAMOND PUBLISHING
1 Mabry Ct (19702-2156)
PHONE..................302 737-2130
Delilah Jackson-Britt, *Principal*
EMP: 2 EST: 2009
SALES (est): 90.2K **Privately Held**
SIC: 2741 Miscellaneous publishing

(G-6320)
CSI SOLUTIONS LLC
200 Continental Dr # 401 (19713-4334)
PHONE..................202 506-7573
Roger Chaufournier, *CEO*
EMP: 10
SALES (est): 826.7K **Privately Held**
SIC: 8742 Management consulting services

(G-6321)
CSL PLASMA INC
Also Called: Center 213
77 Marrows Rd (19713-3701)
PHONE..................302 565-0003
EMP: 7 **Privately Held**
SIC: 8099 Blood bank
HQ: Csl Plasma Inc.
900 Broken Sound Pkwy Nw # 400
Boca Raton FL 33487
561 981-3700

(G-6322)
CSOLS INC
750 Prdes Crssing Ste 305 (19713)
PHONE..................302 731-5290
Kyle McDuffie, *President*
Don Jennings, *General Mgr*
Joe Roamer, *Business Mgr*
Sandy Ahmed, *Vice Pres*
Marian Button, *Controller*
EMP: 30
SQ FT: 1,575
SALES: 5MM **Privately Held**
WEB: www.csolsinc.com
SIC: 7379 Computer related consulting services

(G-6323)
CTA ROOFING & WATERPROOFING
91 Blue Hen Dr (19713-3405)
P.O. Box 7109 (19714-7109)
PHONE..................302 454-8551
Mark Cribb, *President*
Candace Tomlinson, *Finance Dir*
Michael Keywan, *Director*
EMP: 13
SALES (est): 1.9MM **Privately Held**
SIC: 1799 1761 Waterproofing; roofing & gutter work

(G-6324)
CUBICS INC
Also Called: Online
2035 Sunset Lake Rd B2 (19702-2600)
PHONE..................302 261-5751
Rustam Gasimov, *President*
EMP: 7
SALES (est): 164.3K **Privately Held**
SIC: 7371 Computer software development & applications

(G-6325)
CUHIANA CARE HEALTH SYSTEM
4755 Ogletown Stanton Rd (19718-2200)
PHONE..................302 733-1780
Anzilotti Kert, *Director*
EMP: 9 EST: 2012
SALES (est): 384.3K **Privately Held**
SIC: 8062 General medical & surgical hospitals

(G-6326)
CUNNINGHAM HOMES LLC
5 Rudloff Ct (19702-2863)
PHONE..................267 473-0895
EMP: 1
SALES (est): 41K **Privately Held**
SIC: 1389 Construction, repair & dismantling services

(G-6327)
CURRAN JAMES P LAW OFFICES
Also Called: James P Curran
256 Chapman Rd Ste 107 (19702-5417)
PHONE..................302 894-1111
James Curran, *Owner*
EMP: 7
SALES (est): 836.9K **Privately Held**
SIC: 8111 General practice law office

(G-6328)
CURVATURE INC
Also Called: SMS Systems Maintenance
645 Paper Mill Rd (19711-7515)
PHONE..................302 525-9525
EMP: 8
SALES (corp-wide): 359.7MM **Privately Held**
SIC: 7378 Computer maintenance & repair
PA: Curvature, Inc.
2810 Coliseum Centre Dr # 600
Charlotte NC 28217
704 921-1620

(G-6329)
CURVES
7 Chestnut Hill Plz (19713-2701)
PHONE..................302 731-2617
EMP: 4
SALES (est): 55.2K **Privately Held**
SIC: 7991 Physical Fitness Facility

(G-6330)
CUSTOM DRYWALL INC
Also Called: Larry's Custom Drywall
573 Bellevue Rd Ste C (19713-5801)
PHONE..................302 369-3266
Larry Stevens, *President*
EMP: 7
SALES (est): 1MM **Privately Held**
SIC: 1742 Drywall

(G-6331)
CUSTOM HOUSE ULC
132 Christiana Mall (19702-3202)
PHONE..................302 737-4085
EMP: 18
SALES (corp-wide): 5.6B **Publicly Held**
SIC: 6099 Depository Banking Services
HQ: Western Union Business Solutions (Usa), Llc
1152 15th St Nw Ste 700
Washington DC 20005
202 408-1200

(G-6332)
CUSTOM IMPROVERS INC
89 Albe Dr (19702-1321)
PHONE..................302 731-9246
Richard Altemus, *President*
Ann Altemus, *Corp Secy*
EMP: 5
SQ FT: 3,800
SALES (est): 699.5K **Privately Held**
SIC: 1522 1521 Residential construction; general remodeling, single-family houses

(G-6333)
CUT OUT IMAGE INC
2035 Sunset Lake Rd B2 (19702-2600)
PHONE..................844 866-5577
Atik Rahman, *CEO*
EMP: 9
SALES (est): 29.3K **Privately Held**
SIC: 7335 Photographic studio, commercial

(G-6334)
CYBER 20/20 INC
1 Innovation Way Unit 2 (19711-5442)
PHONE..................203 802-8742
N Macdonnell Ulsch, *CEO*
John Modi, *COO*
Victoria Kumaran, *Exec Dir*
EMP: 10
SALES (est): 82.4K **Privately Held**
SIC: 7372 7389 Prepackaged software;

(G-6335)
CYBER SEVEN TECHNOLOGIES LLC
465 Upper Pike Creek Rd (19711-4336)
PHONE..................302 635-7122
Jamees Fraley, *Principal*
EMP: 1
SALES (est): 58K **Privately Held**
SIC: 7373 7371 7372 7389 Systems engineering, computer related; computer software development & applications; operating systems computer software;

(G-6336)
CYBERDAPTIVE INC
P.O. Box 7989 (19714-7989)
PHONE..................302 388-3506
Jason Graham, *President*
Greg Silver, *Principal*
Tristan Graham, *Vice Pres*
EMP: 4 EST: 2011
SALES: 120K **Privately Held**
SIC: 5734 7374 Computer & software stores; data processing & preparation

(G-6337)
CYCLESOLV LLC
301 Ruthar Dr Ste C (19711-8031)
PHONE..................302 894-9400
Marat Niazoff,
EMP: 4
SALES (est): 329K **Privately Held**
WEB: www.cyclesolv.com
SIC: 8748 Environmental consultant

(G-6338)
CYNTHIA L CARROLL
262 Chapman Rd Ste 108 (19702-5412)
PHONE..................302 733-0411
Cynthia L Carroll, *Owner*
EMP: 5
SALES (est): 430K **Privately Held**
SIC: 8111 General practice attorney, lawyer

(G-6339)
D & B PRINTING AND MAILING INC
3 Brookmont Dr (19702-4141)
PHONE..................302 838-7111
Craig McClintock, *President*
Ken Kerns, *Vice Pres*
EMP: 5
SQ FT: 3,600
SALES (est): 259.1K **Privately Held**
SIC: 2752 7331 Commercial printing, lithographic; mailing service

(G-6340)
D & H CREDIT SERVICES INC
171 Haut Brion Ave (19702-4537)
PHONE..................302 832-6980
Harold Schaeffer Jr, *President*
EMP: 10

SALES (est): 567.4K **Privately Held**
WEB: www.dandhcredit.com
SIC: 8748 7323 Business consulting; credit investigation service

(G-6341)
D & S WAREHOUSING INC
104 Alan Dr (19711-8027)
PHONE.................................302 731-7440
Stephen Dawson, *President*
Monika Fulton, *Vice Pres*
EMP: 40
SQ FT: 550,000
SALES (est): 6.8MM **Privately Held**
WEB: www.wedistribute.com
SIC: 4225 General warehousing

(G-6342)
D M S STUCCO CONSTRUCTION CO
47 Wedgewood Rd (19711-2055)
P.O. Box 7738 (19714-7738)
PHONE.................................302 368-2618
Darren Cavanaugh, *Owner*
EMP: 10
SALES (est): 623.1K **Privately Held**
SIC: 1742 Stucco work, interior

(G-6343)
DA VINCI PAINTING
5 Wenark Dr Apt 11 (19713-1410)
PHONE.................................302 229-0644
EMP: 4
SALES (est): 256.5K **Privately Held**
SIC: 3993 Signs, not made in custom sign painting shops

(G-6344)
DAIMLERCHRYSLER N AMRCA FINANC
131 Continental Dr (19713-4305)
PHONE.................................302 292-6840
Anthony Turner, *General Mgr*
Mark Werner, *Engineer*
Antonio Briceno, *Accounting Mgr*
EMP: 13
SALES (est): 908.9K **Privately Held**
SIC: 8742 Financial consultant

(G-6345)
DANA S WRIGHT
Also Called: B D Welding
94 Albe Dr (19702-1364)
PHONE.................................610 563-6070
EMP: 1
SALES (est): 43.4K **Privately Held**
SIC: 7692 Welding repair

(G-6346)
DARLINGTON POSTAL COMPANY LLC
1217 Cooches Bridge Rd (19713-2333)
PHONE.................................410 917-4147
Louis F Haber II,
EMP: 5
SALES (corp-wide): 1.1MM **Privately Held**
SIC: 4215 Courier services, except by air
PA: Darlington Postal Company, Llc
   2434 Shuresville Rd
   Darlington MD 21034
   410 917-4147

(G-6347)
DATA DRUM INC
2035 Sunset Lake Rd (19702-2600)
PHONE.................................347 502-8485
Girish Gupta, *CEO*
EMP: 5
SALES (est): 82.9K **Privately Held**
SIC: 7374 Data processing service

(G-6348)
DAVID B ETTINGER DMD MD
131 E Chestnut Hill Rd (19713-4043)
PHONE.................................302 369-1000
David B Ettinger MD, *Owner*
EMP: 5
SALES (est): 157.9K **Privately Held**
SIC: 8011 Eyes, ears, nose & throat specialist: physician/surgeon

(G-6349)
DAVID OPPENHEIMER AND CO I LLC
Also Called: Oppenheimer Group, The
200 Continental Dr # 301 (19713-4334)
PHONE.................................302 533-0779
Brett Libke, *Branch Mgr*
EMP: 35 **Privately Held**
SIC: 5148 Fruits
HQ: David Oppenheimer And Company I, L.L.C.
   180 Nickerson St Ste 211
   Seattle WA 98109
   206 284-1705

(G-6350)
DAY AND ZIMMERMANN INC
504 Interchange Blvd (19711-3557)
PHONE.................................302 368-1609
EMP: 151
SALES (corp-wide): 2.2B **Privately Held**
SIC: 8744 Facilities support services
HQ: Day And Zimmermann, Incorporated
   1500 Spring Garden St
   Philadelphia PA 19130
   215 299-8000

(G-6351)
DAYS OF KNIGHTS
173 E Main St Lowr (19711-7330)
PHONE.................................302 366-0963
Daniel W Farrow IV, *President*
John M Corradin, *Vice Pres*
Frank Givonnazzi, *Treasurer*
EMP: 8
SQ FT: 3,000
SALES (est): 560K **Privately Held**
SIC: 5945 7999 Games (chess, backgammon & other durable games); arts & crafts supplies; game parlor

(G-6352)
DCMFM AT CHRISTIANA CARE
1 Centurian Dr Ste 312 (19713-2127)
PHONE.................................302 543-7543
A C Sciscione, *Partner*
Anthony C Sciscione, *Partner*
Philip Shlossman, *Med Doctor*
Jennifer Merriman, *Assistant*
EMP: 5
SALES (est): 416.7K **Privately Held**
SIC: 8011 Gynecologist

(G-6353)
DDH ADVANCED MTLS SYSTEMS INC
625 Dawson Dr Ste B (19713-3433)
PHONE.................................515 441-1313
Yulin Huang, *CEO*
Fei Deng, *Vice Pres*
EMP: 2 EST: 2013
SALES (est): 570K **Privately Held**
SIC: 2819 Catalysts, chemical

(G-6354)
DE SALES AND SERVICE
1210 Janice Dr (19713-2355)
PHONE.................................302 456-1660
EMP: 3
SALES (est): 250.5K **Privately Held**
SIC: 3563 Air & gas compressors

(G-6355)
DEADCOW COMPUTERS
14 Deer Track Ln (19711-2968)
PHONE.................................302 239-5974
Brian Henriquez, *Principal*
EMP: 1
SALES (est): 57.5K **Privately Held**
SIC: 2621 Paper mills

(G-6356)
DEBORAH J HALLIGAN DDS
414 Capitol Trl (19711-3865)
PHONE.................................302 738-5766
Deborah Halligan, *Owner*
EMP: 4
SALES (est): 311.2K **Privately Held**
SIC: 8021 Dentists' office

(G-6357)
DECISIVEDGE LLC (PA)
131 Continental Dr # 409 (19713-4308)
PHONE.................................302 299-1570
Anthony Handa, *General Mgr*
Sandip Sharma, *Managing Dir*
Andrew Macdowell, *Vice Pres*
Navroze Eduljee,
Sukumar Narayanan,
EMP: 5 EST: 2007
SALES (est): 7.5MM **Privately Held**
SIC: 7371 8742 Computer software systems analysis & design, custom; computer software writing services; computer software development & applications; computer software development; management consulting services

(G-6358)
DEDC LLC
315 S Chapel St (19711-5307)
PHONE.................................302 738-7172
Michael Acevedo, *Engineer*
David Barton, *Engineer*
John Leslie, *Engineer*
Steven Krinsky, *Mng Member*
EMP: 60 EST: 2010
SALES (est): 5.8MM **Privately Held**
SIC: 8711 Consulting engineer

(G-6359)
DEES LEARNING CARE
128 Auckland Dr (19702-6206)
PHONE.................................908 623-7685
Diedrean Patton, *Principal*
EMP: 5
SALES (est): 56.4K **Privately Held**
SIC: 8351 Child day care services

(G-6360)
DEGUSSA INTERNATIONAL INC
220 Continental Dr # 204 (19713-4362)
PHONE.................................302 731-9250
Eric Dawson, *Corp Secy*
EMP: 8
SALES (est): 902.9K
SALES (corp-wide): 2.5B **Privately Held**
SIC: 5169 Chemicals & allied products
HQ: Evonik Corporation
   299 Jefferson Rd
   Parsippany NJ 07054
   973 929-8000

(G-6361)
DEL HAVEN OF WILMINGTON INC (PA)
Also Called: Jewelers of Wilmington
152 Kane Dr (19702-2801)
PHONE.................................302 999-9040
Leonard Lewkowitz, *President*
EMP: 9
SQ FT: 2,000
SALES (est): 1.6MM **Privately Held**
SIC: 5944 7631 Jewelry, precious stones & precious metals; jewelry repair services

(G-6362)
DEL LAWN SERVICE
5 Matthews Rd (19713-2554)
PHONE.................................302 525-4148
EMP: 4 EST: 2009
SALES (est): 136.6K **Privately Held**
SIC: 0782 Lawn services

(G-6363)
DELAWARE ACDEMY OF MDICINE INC
4765 Ogletown Stanton Rd (19713-8003)
PHONE.................................302 733-3900
Liz Lenz, *Opers Mgr*
Tim Gibbs, *Exec Dir*
EMP: 12
SQ FT: 3,000
SALES (est): 501.3K **Privately Held**
SIC: 8733 Educational research agency

(G-6364)
DELAWARE BACK PAIN&SPRTS REHAB
2006 Foulk Rd Ste B (19702)
PHONE.................................302 529-8783
EMP: 60
SALES (est): 2.8MM **Privately Held**
SIC: 8093 Specialty Outpatient Clinic

(G-6365)
DELAWARE BARTER CORP
Also Called: Atlantic Barter
4 Mill Park Ct F (19713-1901)
PHONE.................................800 343-1322
Mattew Hepworth, *President*
Renee Skibicki, *Admin Sec*
EMP: 9
SQ FT: 1,200
SALES: 100K **Privately Held**
SIC: 7389 Barter exchange

(G-6366)
DELAWARE CENTER FOR DIGESTIVE
71 Omega Dr Bldg D (19713-2063)
PHONE.................................302 565-6596
EMP: 15
SALES (est): 1MM **Privately Held**
SIC: 8399 Advocacy group

(G-6367)
DELAWARE CENTER FOR ORAL SRGRY
131 E Chestnut Hill Rd (19713-4043)
PHONE.................................302 369-1000
David Ettinger, *President*
EMP: 10
SALES (est): 900K **Privately Held**
WEB: www.deoms.com
SIC: 8062 General medical & surgical hospitals

(G-6368)
DELAWARE CHIROPRACTIC AT LOUVI
105 Louviers Dr (19711-4163)
PHONE.................................302 738-7300
John Glenn, *Owner*
EMP: 4
SALES (est): 375.1K **Privately Held**
SIC: 8041 Offices & clinics of chiropractors

(G-6369)
DELAWARE CHPR AMER ACDMY PEDTC
4765 Ogletown Stanton Rd (19713-8003)
PHONE.................................302 218-1075
Katie Hamilton, *Exec Dir*
EMP: 6
SALES: 72.7K **Privately Held**
WEB: www.cpam.pcc.com
SIC: 8699 Charitable organization

(G-6370)
DELAWARE CLNCAL LAB PHYSCANS P (PA)
4701 Ogletown Stanton Rd (19713-2055)
PHONE.................................302 737-7700
Gary Witkin, *President*
Frank Beardell, *Vice Pres*
Cynthia Flynn, *Vice Pres*
R Bradley Slease, *Treasurer*
Janet Shetzler, *Office Mgr*
EMP: 39
SQ FT: 1,000
SALES (est): 1.3MM **Privately Held**
WEB: www.delawarephysicianscare.com
SIC: 8011 Hematologist; pathologist; internal medicine, physician/surgeon

(G-6371)
DELAWARE CRDOVASCULAR ASSOC PA
537 Stanton Christiana Rd (19713-2146)
PHONE.................................302 993-7676
Missy Henderson, *Branch Mgr*
Mark Zweben, *Cardiovascular*
EMP: 5 **Privately Held**
SIC: 8011 Cardiologist & cardio-vascular specialist
PA: Delaware Cardiovascular Associates, P.A.
   1403 Foulk Rd Ste 101a
   Wilmington DE 19803

(G-6372)
DELAWARE CREDIT UNION LEAG INC
262 Chapman Rd Ste 101 (19702-5412)
PHONE.................................302 322-9341
Patrick Mahaney, *President*
EMP: 5
SALES: 91.2K **Privately Held**
WEB: www.dcul.org
SIC: 8611 Trade associations

Newark - New Castle County (G-6373) — GEOGRAPHIC SECTION

(G-6373)
DELAWARE D G CO LLC
Also Called: Delaware Dry Goods
1007 S Chapel St (19702-1305)
P.O. Box 10424, Wilmington (19850-0424)
PHONE..................................302 731-0500
Jason Strassner,
◆ EMP: 16
SQ FT: 30,000
SALES: 8MM Privately Held
WEB: www.delawaredg.com
SIC: 5131 Sewing supplies & notions

(G-6374)
DELAWARE DANCE COMPANY INC
168 S Main St Ste 101 (19711-7966)
PHONE..................................302 738-2023
Martin Hopkins, President
Mary Roth, Manager
Sunshine Latshaw, Director
EMP: 27
SALES: 467.4K Privately Held
SIC: 7911 Dance studio & school

(G-6375)
DELAWARE DESIGN COMPANY
Also Called: Dolphin Design & Communic
29 S Old Baltimore Pike (19702-1533)
P.O. Box 412, Odessa (19730-0412)
PHONE..................................302 737-9700
Janice Garbini, President
EMP: 5
SALES (est): 692.1K Privately Held
SIC: 7311 Advertising consultant

(G-6376)
DELAWARE DIAGNOSTIC LABS LLC
1 Centurian Dr Ste 103 (19713-2154)
PHONE..................................302 996-9585
Qing Liu, Principal
EMP: 5 EST: 2017
SALES (est): 353.7K Privately Held
SIC: 8071 Medical laboratories

(G-6377)
DELAWARE EAR NOSE & THROAT HEA
4745 Ogletown Stanton Rd # 112 (19713-2070)
PHONE..................................302 738-6014
Robert L Witt, Principal
EMP: 5 EST: 2007
SALES (est): 370.9K Privately Held
SIC: 8011 Ears, nose & throat specialist; physician/surgeon

(G-6378)
DELAWARE ENGINEERING & DESIGN
315 S Chapel St (19711-5320)
PHONE..................................302 738-7172
Robert Krinsky, President
EMP: 60 EST: 1965
SQ FT: 2,200
SALES (est): 6.3MM Privately Held
WEB: www.dedc-eng.com
SIC: 8711 Heating & ventilation engineering

(G-6379)
DELAWARE FINANCIAL CAPITAL (PA)
22 Polly Drummond Hill Rd (19711-5703)
PHONE..................................302 266-9500
Sam Collins, President
Samuel A Collins III, President
EMP: 10
SALES (est): 1.3MM Privately Held
WEB: www.delawarefinancial.com
SIC: 6163 Mortgage brokers arranging for loans, using money of others

(G-6380)
DELAWARE FOOT & ANKLE ASSOC
Also Called: Troisi, Ernest DPM PA
2600 Glasgow Ave Ste 101 (19702-5703)
PHONE..................................302 834-3575
Ernest Troisi, Owner
EMP: 6
SALES (est): 694K Privately Held
SIC: 8043 Offices & clinics of podiatrists

(G-6381)
DELAWARE GRAPEVINE LLC
16 Martine Ct (19711-5909)
PHONE..................................302 731-8400
John Daniello, Principal
EMP: 1
SALES (est): 67.5K Privately Held
SIC: 2711 Newspapers, publishing & printing

(G-6382)
DELAWARE GUIDANCE SERVICES FOR
Also Called: Dgs
Polly Drummond Ofc (19711)
PHONE..................................302 455-9333
C Molina, Branch Mgr
EMP: 19
SALES (corp-wide): 10.1MM Privately Held
SIC: 8322 Family counseling services
PA: Delaware Guidance Services For Children And Youth, Inc.
1213 Delaware Ave
Wilmington DE 19806
302 652-3948

(G-6383)
DELAWARE HEATING & AC SVCS INC
11 Mcmillan Way (19713-3456)
PHONE..................................302 738-4669
Frank Bartuski, President
Karen Bartuski, Manager
EMP: 30
SQ FT: 1,500
SALES (est): 4.9MM Privately Held
SIC: 1711 Warm air heating & air conditioning contractor; heating & air conditioning contractors

(G-6384)
DELAWARE HOSPICE INC (PA)
16 Polly Drmmd Shpg Ctr 2 (19711-4861)
PHONE..................................302 478-5707
Susan Lloyd, CEO
John Ward, President
Sharon Leyhow, Vice Pres
Luanne Holland, Accounts Exec
Barbie Sheldon, Accounts Exec
EMP: 55
SQ FT: 10,200
SALES: 27.4MM Privately Held
SIC: 8052 Personal care facility

(G-6385)
DELAWARE IMAGING NETWORK
Also Called: Papastavros Assoc Med Imaging
40 Polly Drummond Hill Rd (19711-5703)
PHONE..................................302 737-5990
Thomas Fiss, President
Anthony Scola, Diag Radio
EMP: 6 Publicly Held
SIC: 8099 Blood related health services
HQ: Delaware Imaging Network
40 Polly Drmmnd Hl Rd 4
Newark DE 19711
302 652-3016

(G-6386)
DELAWARE IMAGING NETWORK
2600 Glasgow Ave Ste 122 (19702-4777)
PHONE..................................302 836-4200
Anna Allen, Manager
EMP: 5 Publicly Held
SIC: 8011 Radiologist
HQ: Delaware Imaging Network
40 Polly Drmmnd Hl Rd 4
Newark DE 19711
302 652-3016

(G-6387)
DELAWARE IMAGING NETWORK (HQ)
40 Polly Drmmnd Hl Rd 4 (19711-5703)
PHONE..................................302 652-3016
Michael Leviton, Diag Radio
Garth A Koniver MD,
EMP: 50
SALES (est): 19.7MM Publicly Held
SIC: 8011 Radiologist

(G-6388)
DELAWARE IMAGING NETWORK
Also Called: Radiology Associates
40 Polly Drmmnd Hl Rd 4 (19711-5703)
PHONE..................................302 644-2590
Lisa Daniello, Principal
EMP: 16 Publicly Held
SIC: 8011 8071 Radiologist; X-ray laboratory, including dental
HQ: Delaware Imaging Network
40 Polly Drmmnd Hl Rd 4
Newark DE 19711
302 652-3016

(G-6389)
DELAWARE INSTRUMENT LAB LLC
2106 Chelmsford Cir (19713-2912)
PHONE..................................302 737-6250
Xiaochun Kennedy, Principal
EMP: 1 EST: 2015
SALES (est): 52.9K Privately Held
SIC: 3841 Instruments, microsurgical: except electromedical

(G-6390)
DELAWARE INSUR GUARANTEE ASSN
220 Continental Dr # 309 (19713-4311)
PHONE..................................302 456-3656
John Falkenbach, Director
EMP: 4 EST: 1972
SALES: 3MM Privately Held
SIC: 6411 Insurance claim adjusters, not employed by insurance company

(G-6391)
DELAWARE JUNIORS VOLLEYBALL
4142 Ogletown Stanton Rd # 229 (19713-4169)
PHONE..................................302 463-4218
Steve Lenderman, Director
EMP: 6 EST: 2013
SALES (est): 121.3K Privately Held
SIC: 8322 Individual & family services

(G-6392)
DELAWARE LAW OFFICE OF LARRY
111 Barksdale Pro Ctr (19711-3258)
PHONE..................................302 286-6336
Larry D Sullivan, Principal
EMP: 4
SQ FT: 1,250
SALES (est): 315.5K Privately Held
WEB: www.delawoffice.com
SIC: 8111 General practice attorney, lawyer

(G-6393)
DELAWARE MED CARE ASSOC LLC
550 Stanton Christiana Rd # 103 (19713-2131)
PHONE..................................302 633-9033
Hummayun Ismail, Principal
EMP: 5 EST: 2008
SALES (est): 398.1K Privately Held
SIC: 8099 Health & allied services

(G-6394)
DELAWARE MEDICAL MGT SVCS LLC
Also Called: Dmms
71 Omega Dr (19713-2063)
PHONE..................................302 283-3300
Justine Cahill, Sales Mgr
Ira Lobis,
Jean Marie Taylor,
EMP: 33
SQ FT: 2,500
SALES (est): 3.3MM Privately Held
SIC: 8721 Billing & bookkeeping service

(G-6395)
DELAWARE MFG EXT PARTNR INC
Also Called: DEMEP
400 Stanton Christiana Rd (19713-2111)
PHONE..................................302 283-3131
Rustyn Stoops, Exec Dir
EMP: 8
SQ FT: 1,000
SALES: 1.3MM Privately Held
WEB: www.demep.org
SIC: 8742 Manufacturing management consultant

(G-6396)
DELAWARE MODERN DENTAL LLC
850 Library Ave Ste 102 (19711-7170)
PHONE..................................302 366-8668
Donald Puglisi, Principal
EMP: 4
SALES (est): 420.8K Privately Held
SIC: 8021 Dentists' office

(G-6397)
DELAWARE MODERN PEDIATRICS
300 Biddle Ave Ste 206 (19702-3972)
PHONE..................................302 392-2077
Janet Storch, Office Mgr
David M Epstein, Pediatrics
Joan Leary, Receptionist
EMP: 10
SALES (est): 752.3K Privately Held
SIC: 8011 Pediatrician

(G-6398)
DELAWARE MOSQUITO CONTROL LLC
Also Called: Mosquito Joe of Delaware
4 Cobblestone Xing (19702-1150)
PHONE..................................302 504-6757
Ken Alkire, Mng Member
EMP: 6
SALES (est): 109.8K Privately Held
SIC: 7342 7389 Pest control services;

(G-6399)
DELAWARE NUROSURGICAL GROUP PA
774 Christiana Rd Ste 202 (19713-4221)
PHONE..................................302 731-3017
Yakov U Koysman MD, President
Matthew J Eppley MD, Principal
Michael G Sugarman MD, Corp Secy
Pawan Rastogi, Med Doctor
EMP: 10
SALES (est): 2.1MM Privately Held
SIC: 8011 Neurosurgeon

(G-6400)
DELAWARE OCCUPATIONAL HEALTH S
Also Called: Omega Medical Center
15 Omega Dr Bldg K15 (19713-2057)
PHONE..................................302 368-5100
Siobhan Hawkins, Sales Mgr
Mary Roeshler, Office Mgr
Deirdre Oconnell,
Barbara Jaffee, Administration
Linda Conley,
EMP: 28
SQ FT: 14,500
SALES (est): 2.4MM Privately Held
WEB: www.omegamedicalcenter.com
SIC: 8099 8721 6512 Medical services organization; billing & bookkeeping service; nonresidential building operators

(G-6401)
DELAWARE OUTPATIENT CENTER
774 Christiana Rd Ste 2 (19713-4219)
PHONE..................................302 738-0300
Cherrie Records, Manager
Kaleigh Macpherson, Manager
Nicole Carrington, Business Dir
EMP: 69
SALES (est): 99.5K
SALES (corp-wide): 1.7B Publicly Held
SIC: 8062 General medical & surgical hospitals
HQ: Surgery Partners, Inc.
310 Sven Sprng Way Ste 50
Brentwood TN 37027
615 234-5900

(G-6402)
DELAWARE PLASTIC & RECON
Also Called: Delaware Plastic & Recon
1 Centurian Dr Ste 301 (19713-2127)
PHONE..................................302 994-8492
Abdollah Malek MD, President

GEOGRAPHIC SECTION

Newark - New Castle County (G-6432)

EMP: 10
SALES (est): 803K **Privately Held**
SIC: 8011 Plastic surgeon

(G-6403)
DELAWARE PLSTIC/RECONS SRGY PA
1 Centurian Dr Ste 301 (19713-2127)
PHONE.................................302 994-8492
EMP: 5
SALES (est): 390K **Privately Held**
SIC: 8011 Medical Doctor's Office

(G-6404)
DELAWARE PROF FNRL SVCS INC
Also Called: Strano-Feely Funeral Home
635 Churchmans Rd (19702-1917)
PHONE.................................302 731-5459
Vincent Strano, *President*
Joseph Feeley, *Vice Pres*
EMP: 20
SALES (est): 1.7MM **Privately Held**
SIC: 7261 Funeral home

(G-6405)
DELAWARE RACING ASSOCIATION
2701 Kirkwood Hwy (19711-6810)
PHONE.................................302 355-1000
Bill Fasy, *Branch Mgr*
EMP: 445
SALES (corp-wide): 79.8MM **Privately Held**
SIC: 7948 7993 Horse race track operation; slot machines
PA: Delaware Racing Association
   777 Delaware Park Blvd
   Wilmington DE 19804
   302 994-2521

(G-6406)
DELAWARE REGISTERED AGENTS
19 Kris Ct (19702-6843)
PHONE.................................302 733-0600
David Walsh, *Partner*
Kathleen Moore, *Partner*
EMP: 4
SALES (est): 353.5K **Privately Held**
SIC: 8742 Business planning & organizing services

(G-6407)
DELAWARE REHABILITATION INST
540 S College Ave Rm 201k (19713-1302)
PHONE.................................302 831-0315
EMP: 8 EST: 2015
SALES (est): 73.3K **Privately Held**
SIC: 8093 Rehabilitation center, outpatient treatment

(G-6408)
DELAWARE RESTAURANT ASSN
500 Creek View Rd Ste 103 (19711-8549)
P.O. Box 7838 (19714-7838)
PHONE.................................302 738-2545
Carrie Leishman, *CEO*
Xavier Teixido, *President*
EMP: 8
SALES: 208.1K **Privately Held**
SIC: 8611 Trade associations

(G-6409)
DELAWARE S P C A (PA)
455 Stanton Christiana Rd (19713-2119)
P.O. Box 398, Georgetown (19947-0398)
PHONE.................................302 998-2281
Andrea Terlack, *Director*
John Caldwell, *Director*
EMP: 50
SQ FT: 3,000
SALES (est): 1.9MM **Privately Held**
WEB: www.delspca.com
SIC: 8699 8322 0742 0752 Animal humane society; adoption services; veterinary services, specialties; vaccinating services, pet & animal specialties

(G-6410)
DELAWARE SAENGERBUND LIB ASSN
49 Salem Church Rd (19713-2933)
PHONE.................................302 366-9454
Richard Grieb, *President*
George Schweiger, *Vice Pres*
Crystal Coffee, *Treasurer*
EMP: 7 EST: 1903
SQ FT: 3,000
SALES (est): 405K **Privately Held**
WEB: www.delawaresaengerbund.org
SIC: 8641 Social club, membership

(G-6411)
DELAWARE SETTLEMENT SERVICES
930 Old Harmony Rd Ste F1 (19713-4161)
PHONE.................................302 731-2500
Patricia Green,
EMP: 7
SALES (est): 601.1K **Privately Held**
SIC: 6541 Title abstract offices

(G-6412)
DELAWARE SKATING CENTER LTD (PA)
Also Called: Christiana Skating Center
801 Christiana Rd (19713-3262)
PHONE.................................302 366-0473
Charles Wahlig, *President*
Constance Wahlig, *Vice Pres*
EMP: 40
SALES (est): 3.6MM **Privately Held**
WEB: www.delaware.entertainment.com
SIC: 7999 Roller skating rink operation

(G-6413)
DELAWARE SOC ORTHPD SURGEONS
900 Prides Xing (19713-6100)
PHONE.................................302 366-1400
EMP: 4
SALES: 51.4K **Privately Held**
SIC: 8011 Medical Doctor's Office

(G-6414)
DELAWARE STATE DENTAL SOCIETY
200 Continental Dr # 111 (19713-4380)
PHONE.................................302 368-7634
Beetty Dencler, *Exec Dir*
EMP: 12
SALES: 484K **Privately Held**
WEB: www.delawarestatedentalsociety.org
SIC: 8621 Dental association

(G-6415)
DELAWARE STATE EDUCATION ASSN
4135 Ogltn Stntn Rd # 101 (19713-4180)
PHONE.................................302 366-8440
Laura Rowe, *Administration*
EMP: 6
SALES (corp-wide): 6MM **Privately Held**
SIC: 8631 Labor unions & similar labor organizations
PA: Delaware State Education Association Inc
   136 E Water St
   Dover DE 19901
   302 734-5834

(G-6416)
DELAWARE SURGICAL ARTS
537 Stanton Christn Rd # 109 (19713-2145)
PHONE.................................302 225-0177
Peter Panzer, *Principal*
EMP: 5
SALES (est): 319.7K **Privately Held**
SIC: 8011 Internal medicine, physician/surgeon

(G-6417)
DELAWARE TECHNOLOGY PARK INC
1 Innovation Way Ste 300 (19711-5490)
PHONE.................................302 452-1700
J Michael Bowman, *Ch of Bd*
Angela Giliberti, *Admin Asst*
EMP: 3

SALES: 3.8MM **Privately Held**
WEB: www.deltechpark.org
SIC: 3821 Incubators, laboratory

(G-6418)
DELAWARE TIRE CENTER INC (PA)
616 S College Ave (19713-1314)
PHONE.................................302 368-2531
James Baxter Jr, *CEO*
James P Walling, *Vice Pres*
EMP: 12
SQ FT: 15,000
SALES (est): 10.2MM **Privately Held**
SIC: 5531 5014 Automotive tires; automobile tires & tubes

(G-6419)
DELAWARE TITLE LOANS INC
2431 Pulaski Hwy Ste 1 (19702-3905)
PHONE.................................302 368-2131
EMP: 11
SALES (corp-wide): 7.7MM **Privately Held**
SIC: 6159 Loan institutions, general & industrial
PA: Delaware Title Loans, Inc.
   8601 Dunwoody Pl Ste 406
   Atlanta GA 30350
   770 552-9840

(G-6420)
DELAWARE TRAIL SPINNERS
1013 Tulip Tree Ln (19713-1128)
PHONE.................................302 738-0177
Rick Henry, *President*
EMP: 5
SALES: 19.5K **Privately Held**
SIC: 7997 Membership sports & recreation clubs

(G-6421)
DELAWARE VLY OUTCOMES RES LLC
17 Henderson Hill Rd (19711-5958)
PHONE.................................302 444-9363
James M Gill, *CEO*
Wendy C Gill, *Business Mgr*
EMP: 4
SALES: 525K **Privately Held**
SIC: 8733 Research institute

(G-6422)
DELAWARE WOMENS IMAGING LLC
Also Called: Womens Imaging Center Delaware
J24 26 Omega Dr (19713)
PHONE.................................302 738-9100
Joseph R Peacock,
Philip Seluchins,
EMP: 30
SALES: 950K
SALES (corp-wide): 4.2MM **Privately Held**
SIC: 8071 Medical laboratories
PA: Omega Imaging Associates, L.L.C.
   6 Omega Dr
   Newark DE 19713
   302 738-9300

(G-6423)
DELAWAREBLACK COM LLC
560 Peoples Plz Ste 288 (19702-4798)
PHONE.................................302 388-1444
Leonard Young,
EMP: 1
SALES (est): 68.4K **Privately Held**
SIC: 2711 Newspapers, publishing & printing

(G-6424)
DELAWRE CTR FOR MTRNAL & FETAL
1 Centurian Dr Ste 312 (19713-2127)
PHONE.................................302 319-5680
Anthony Sciscione, *President*
Elizabeth A Williams, *Principal*
EMP: 25 EST: 2007
SALES (est): 3.8MM **Privately Held**
SIC: 8011 Gynecologist; physicians' office, including specialists

(G-6425)
DELL OEM INC
705 Dawson Dr (19713-3413)
PHONE.................................302 294-0060
Guru Singh, *President*
EMP: 5
SALES: 110K **Privately Held**
SIC: 5961 7389

(G-6426)
DELMARVA POWER & LIGHT COMPANY (DH)
500 N Wakefield Dr Fl 2 (19702-5440)
P.O. Box 231, Wilmington (19899-0231)
PHONE.................................302 454-0300
David M Velazquez, *President*
Tae Koh, *Opers Mgr*
Carlton Bradshaw, *Engineer*
Michael Kraft, *Engineer*
Kevin Lane, *Engineer*
EMP: 132
SALES (corp-wide): 35.9B **Publicly Held**
SIC: 4911 Distribution, electric power
HQ: Conectiv, Llc
   800 N King St Ste 400
   Wilmington DE 19801
   202 872-2680

(G-6427)
DELMARVA POWER & LIGHT COMPANY
401 Eagle Run Rd (19702-1598)
PHONE.................................302 454-4040
David M Velazquez, *President*
Monica Lake, *Accounts Mgr*
EMP: 8
SALES (corp-wide): 35.9B **Publicly Held**
SIC: 8711 Engineering services
HQ: Delmarva Power & Light Company
   500 N Wakefield Dr Fl 2
   Newark DE 19702
   302 454-0300

(G-6428)
DELMARVA POWER & LIGHT COMPANY
I 95 Rr 273 (19714)
P.O. Box 9239 (19714-9239)
PHONE.................................302 454-4450
Wayne Yerkes, *Vice Pres*
EMP: 200
SALES (corp-wide): 35.9B **Publicly Held**
SIC: 4911 Generation, electric power; distribution, electric power
HQ: Delmarva Power & Light Company
   500 N Wakefield Dr Fl 2
   Newark DE 19702
   302 454-0300

(G-6429)
DELMARVA SURGERY CENTER
139 E Chestnut Hill Rd (19713-4043)
PHONE.................................302 369-1700
Frank Falco, *Principal*
Frank J Falco, *Principal*
EMP: 5
SALES (est): 390K **Privately Held**
SIC: 8011 Surgeon

(G-6430)
DELMARVA SURGERY CTR
100 Biddle Ave Ste 101 (19702-3982)
PHONE.................................443 245-3470
Ray Krett, *Office Mgr*
EMP: 7 EST: 2017
SALES (est): 80.6K **Privately Held**
SIC: 8093 Specialty outpatient clinics

(G-6431)
DELT LLC
201 Ruthar Dr Ste 4 (19711-8029)
PHONE.................................215 869-7409
EMP: 4
SALES (est): 381.6K **Privately Held**
SIC: 7379

(G-6432)
DELTA MACHINE & TOOL COMPANY
201 Ruthar Dr Ste 3 (19711-8029)
PHONE.................................302 738-1788
Andrew R Alessi, *President*
Michele Alessi, *Admin Sec*
EMP: 6 EST: 1975

SQ FT: 5,000
SALES (est): 960.2K **Privately Held**
WEB: www.deltamachineandtool.com
SIC: 3599 Machine shop, jobbing & repair

(G-6433)
DELTRANS INC
759 Old Baltimore Pike (19702-1316)
PHONE..................................302 453-8213
Edward Lee, *President*
Susanna Lee, *Corp Secy*
Bill Harris, *Manager*
EMP: 16
SQ FT: 10,000
SALES (est): 2.6MM **Privately Held**
WEB: www.deltransinc.com
SIC: 5015 5531 Automotive parts & supplies, used; automotive parts

(G-6434)
DELUX ENGINEERING LLC
550 S College Ave (19716-1307)
PHONE..................................610 304-0606
Brendan Delacy, *CEO*
Mark Mirotznik, *COO*
Zachary Larimore,
Paul Parsons,
EMP: 4
SALES (est): 98K **Privately Held**
SIC: 8711 Chemical engineering; electrical or electronic engineering

(G-6435)
DEMPSEYS SERVICE CENTER INC
604 Corner Ketch Rd (19711-2901)
P.O. Box 15114 (19711-0114)
PHONE..................................302 239-4996
William Dempsey, *President*
Warren Dempsey, *Admin Sec*
EMP: 8
SQ FT: 3,000
SALES (est): 1.4MM **Privately Held**
SIC: 7538 Engine repair

(G-6436)
DEMPSEYS SPECIALIZED SERVICES
304b Markus Ct (19713-1151)
PHONE..................................302 530-7856
EMP: 2
SALES (est): 142K **Privately Held**
SIC: 7692 Welding repair

(G-6437)
DENICES RAGGED WREATH
691 Churchmans Rd (19702-1918)
PHONE..................................302 220-7377
Denice Montero, *Principal*
EMP: 3 EST: 2017
SALES (est): 138.1K **Privately Held**
SIC: 3999 Wreaths, artificial

(G-6438)
DENNIS WOLTEMATE LAWN CORP
117 N Dillwyn Rd (19711-5555)
PHONE..................................302 738-5266
Denis C Woltemate, *Principal*
EMP: 4
SALES (est): 219K **Privately Held**
SIC: 0782 Lawn care services

(G-6439)
DERIDE IGO
28 Findail Dr (19711-2972)
PHONE..................................302 234-4121
Kevin Igo, *Principal*
EMP: 2
SALES (est): 167.7K **Privately Held**
SIC: 3613 Distribution cutouts

(G-6440)
DESHONG & SONS CONTRACTORS
2606 Ogletown Rd (19713-1824)
P.O. Box 7498 (19714-7498)
PHONE..................................302 453-8500
Marc Deshong, *President*
Ryan R Deshong, *Corp Secy*
EMP: 7
SQ FT: 4,500
SALES (est): 4.5MM **Privately Held**
SIC: 1542 1541 1521 Commercial & office building, new construction; commercial & office buildings, renovation & repair; industrial buildings, new construction; new construction, single-family houses; general remodeling, single-family houses

(G-6441)
DEW SOFTECH INC
200 Biddle Ave Ste 212 (19702-3966)
PHONE..................................302 834-2555
David Merigala, *President*
Sam Merigala, *Director*
Nirmala Grace, *Tech Recruiter*
EMP: 35
SQ FT: 1,000
SALES (est): 2MM **Privately Held**
SIC: 7379 Computer related consulting services

(G-6442)
DIAGNOSTIC MEDICAL SERVICES
25 S Old Baltimore Pike # 104 (19702-1540)
PHONE..................................302 292-2700
Fax: 302 239-5349
EMP: 5
SALES (est): 500K **Privately Held**
SIC: 8099 Mobile Diagnostic Testing Service

(G-6443)
DIAMOND CHIROPRACTIC INC
Also Called: Diamond State Chiropractic
1101 Twin Ceiling Ln 20 (19713)
PHONE..................................302 892-9355
Cristina Holstein, *President*
EMP: 10
SALES (est): 809.4K **Privately Held**
WEB: www.diamondchiropractic.com
SIC: 8041 Offices & clinics of chiropractors

(G-6444)
DIAMOND STATE FINCL GROUP INC
121 Continental Dr # 110 (19713-4326)
PHONE..................................302 366-0366
Raymond F Bree, *President*
Raymond Bree, *Managing Prtnr*
Shaun Jones, *Partner*
Todd Hudson, *COO*
Leanne Eilola, *Marketing Staff*
EMP: 20
SALES (est): 2.2MM **Privately Held**
WEB: www.dsfg.com
SIC: 8742 Financial consultant

(G-6445)
DIGITAL GENERATION INC
450 Corporate Blvd (19702-3330)
PHONE..................................302 368-0002
Delwin Bothof, *Manager*
EMP: 15 **Privately Held**
SIC: 7311 Advertising consultant
HQ: Digital Generation, Inc.
    75 2nd Ave Ste 720
    Needham Heights MA 02494

(G-6446)
DIGITAL HEART PRODUCTIONS
112 Entre Ln (19702-2077)
PHONE..................................302 737-6158
Joshua J Delorimier, *Owner*
EMP: 4
SALES (est): 83.2K **Privately Held**
SIC: 7822 Motion picture & tape distribution

(G-6447)
DIGITAL OFFICE SOLUTIONS INC
Also Called: Copy Systems
101 Sandy Dr (19713-1148)
PHONE..................................302 286-6706
Annette Simms, *President*
Connie Cooper, *CFO*
EMP: 12
SALES (est): 2.5MM **Privately Held**
SIC: 5044 Office equipment

(G-6448)
DIGITAL PENGUIN INC
625 Dawson Dr Ste A (19713-3433)
PHONE..................................484 387-7803
Jing LI, *Principal*
EMP: 1
SALES (est): 35.4K **Privately Held**
SALES (corp-wide): 6.7K **Privately Held**
SIC: 7371 7372 Computer software development & applications; application computer software
PA: Shanghai Digital Penguin Information Technology Co., Ltd.
    Building C, Floor 9, No.588, Yingkou Road, Yangpu District
    Shanghai 20043
    215 230-5336

(G-6449)
DILIGENT BUS SOLUTIONS LLC
1 Marra Pl (19702-5200)
PHONE..................................302 897-5993
Vidyashankar Narayanan, *Partner*
EMP: 6
SALES (est): 226.6K **Privately Held**
SIC: 7379 Computer related consulting services

(G-6450)
DINGLE & KANE PA
356 E Main St Ste A (19711-7194)
PHONE..................................302 731-5200
Fred Dingle, *President*
William Kane, *Shareholder*
Keith Thompson, *Shareholder*
EMP: 6
SALES (est): 582.7K **Privately Held**
WEB: www.dingle-peninsula.ie
SIC: 8721 Certified public accountant

(G-6451)
DIRECT IMPORTER LLC
843 Salem Church Rd (19702-4015)
PHONE..................................302 838-2183
Feng Guo,
EMP: 5
SALES (est): 390K **Privately Held**
SIC: 5099 Durable goods

(G-6452)
DIRECT RADIOGRAPHY CORP
600 Technology Dr (19702-2463)
PHONE..................................302 631-2700
Peter Soltani, *Senior VP*
▲ EMP: 155
SQ FT: 164,000
SALES (est): 18.6MM
SALES (corp-wide): 3.3B **Publicly Held**
WEB: www.hologic.com
SIC: 3845 3844 Electromedical equipment; X-ray apparatus & tubes
PA: Hologic, Inc.
    250 Campus Dr
    Marlborough MA 01752
    508 263-2900

(G-6453)
DIS INC (PA)
Also Called: G.C.E.
268 Cornell Dr (19702-4163)
PHONE..................................302 834-1633
Sam Diferdinando, *President*
Kelli L Disabatino, *Managing Prtnr*
Paul Disabatino, *Vice Pres*
EMP: 10
SALES (est): 2.2MM **Privately Held**
SIC: 6515 Mobile home site operators

(G-6454)
DISASTER RESEARCH CENTER
111 Academy St Rm 166 (19716-7399)
PHONE..................................302 831-6618
James Kendra, *Director*
EMP: 45
SALES (est): 1.6MM **Privately Held**
SIC: 8733 Noncommercial research organizations

(G-6455)
DISCIDIUM TECHNOLOGY INC
Also Called: Discidium Technologies
100 Cullen Way (19711-6108)
PHONE..................................347 220-5979
Renee Casanova, *Principal*
Joshua Schuller, *Principal*
EMP: 2

SALES (est): 56.5K **Privately Held**
SIC: 7379 8243 7372 7371 Computer related consulting services; software training, computer; application computer software; custom computer programming services; value-added resellers, computer systems

(G-6456)
DIXON BROTHERS LLC
3 Francis Cir (19711-2625)
PHONE..................................302 377-8289
Vincent Dixon,
EMP: 10
SALES (est): 212.3K **Privately Held**
SIC: 4789 Transportation services

(G-6457)
DMI COMMODITIES INC
2915 Ogletown Rd (19713-1927)
PHONE..................................877 364-3644
Martin Choquette, *President*
EMP: 10
SALES (est): 553.2K **Privately Held**
SIC: 6221 Commodity brokers, contracts

(G-6458)
DOG ANYA
918 Kenilworth Ave (19711-2638)
PHONE..................................302 456-0108
Dog Anya, *Principal*
EMP: 2
SALES (est): 93.6K **Privately Held**
SIC: 3999 Pet supplies

(G-6459)
DOG WORKS SOUTH
2201 Ogletown Rd (19711-5401)
PHONE..................................302 366-8161
Sarah Hawks, *Owner*
EMP: 5
SALES (est): 107.7K **Privately Held**
SIC: 0752 Boarding services, kennels

(G-6460)
DONALD C SAVOY INC
200 Continental Dr # 209 (19713-4334)
PHONE..................................888 992-6755
Chris Handley, *Branch Mgr*
EMP: 8
SALES (corp-wide): 12.8MM **Privately Held**
SIC: 6411 6311 Insurance brokers; life insurance
PA: Donald C. Savoy, Inc.
    25b Hanover Rd Ste 220
    Florham Park NJ
    973 377-2220

(G-6461)
DONALD G VARNES & SONS INC
27 Albe Dr Ste A (19702-1325)
PHONE..................................302 737-5953
Steven D Varnes, *President*
Allen Varnes, *Vice Pres*
Lisa Varnes, *Admin Sec*
EMP: 9 EST: 1960
SALES (est): 901.3K **Privately Held**
SIC: 1752 Wood floor installation & refinishing

(G-6462)
DONNE DELLE & ASSOCIATES INC (PA)
200 Continental Dr # 200 (19713-4334)
PHONE..................................302 325-1111
Ernest Delle Donne, *President*
James P Collins, *Exec VP*
Nan Schulte, *Vice Pres*
Anthony Barba, *Property Mgr*
EMP: 23
SQ FT: 9,000
SALES (est): 7.7MM **Privately Held**
WEB: www.dda1.com
SIC: 6552 Land subdividers & developers, commercial

(G-6463)
DOUG RICHMONDS BODY SHOP
Also Called: Richmonds Automotive
854 Dawson Dr (19713-3416)
PHONE..................................302 453-1173
Douglas Richmond, *Owner*
EMP: 11 EST: 1976
SQ FT: 5,275

GEOGRAPHIC SECTION

Newark - New Castle County (G-6491)

SALES (est): 755.9K **Privately Held**
WEB: www.richmondsautomotive.com
SIC: 7532 Body shop, automotive; paint shop, automotive

(G-6464)
DOUGLAS C LOEW & ASSOCIATES
248 E Chestnut Hill Rd # 4 (19713-3700)
PHONE..................302 453-0550
Douglas C Loew, *Owner*
EMP: 6
SQ FT: 800
SALES (est): 413.8K **Privately Held**
SIC: 8742 6411 Financial consultant; insurance agents

(G-6465)
DOUGLAS J LAVENBURG MD PA (PA)
1 Centurian Dr Ste 114 (19713-2154)
PHONE..................302 993-0722
Douglas J Lavenburg MD, *President*
EMP: 10
SALES (est): 1.4MM **Privately Held**
SIC: 8011 Ophthalmologist

(G-6466)
DOVER JUNIOR A DDS
1290 Peoples Plz (19702-5701)
PHONE..................302 836-3750
Junior A Dover, *Principal*
EMP: 4 EST: 2011
SALES (est): 84.9K **Privately Held**
SIC: 8021 Dentists' office

(G-6467)
DOW CHEMICAL COMPANY
451 Bellevue Rd Bldg 9 (19713-3431)
PHONE..................302 368-4169
Tony Khouri, *President*
EMP: 350
SALES (corp-wide): 61B **Publicly Held**
SIC: 2842 2297 3291 Specialty cleaning, polishes & sanitation goods; nonwoven fabrics; abrasive products
HQ: The Dow Chemical Company
2211 H H Dow Way
Midland MI 48642
989 636-1000

(G-6468)
DOW CHEMICAL COMPANY
231 Lake Dr (19702-3320)
PHONE..................302 366-0500
EMP: 120
SALES (corp-wide): 61B **Publicly Held**
SIC: 2819 2821 Industrial inorganic chemicals; plastics materials & resins
HQ: The Dow Chemical Company
2211 H H Dow Way
Midland MI 48642
989 636-1000

(G-6469)
DPNL LLC
Also Called: Staybrdge Stes - Nwrk/Wlmngton
270 Chapman Rd (19702-5406)
PHONE..................302 366-8097
Michelle Fones, *General Mgr*
Stephanie Walker, *Sales Staff*
EMP: 17
SALES (est): 1.2MM **Privately Held**
SIC: 7011 Hotels & motels

(G-6470)
DR DEBRA WOLF ENCORE HEALTH
19 Green Meadow Ct (19711-2583)
PHONE..................302 737-1918
EMP: 8
SALES (est): 76K **Privately Held**
SIC: 8099 Health & allied services

(G-6471)
DR MONIKA GUPTA PA
314 E Main St Ste 404 (19711-7182)
PHONE..................302 737-5074
Monika Gupta, *Principal*
EMP: 5
SALES (est): 256.5K **Privately Held**
SIC: 8011 Internal medicine, physician/surgeon

(G-6472)
DRAFTING BY DESIGN INC (PA)
170 E Main St Ste 1 (19711-7318)
P.O. Box 8062 (19714-8062)
PHONE..................302 292-8304
Neil Brenner, *President*
EMP: 8
SQ FT: 1,000
SALES (est): 682.1K **Privately Held**
WEB: www.draftingbydesign.com
SIC: 8711 7389 Industrial engineers; building construction consultant; design, commercial & industrial

(G-6473)
DREAM CLEAN TEAM LP
Also Called: Dct
217 Sleepy Hollow Ct (19711-3436)
PHONE..................302 981-5154
Davonne Roye,
Leanora Bassett,
Alethia Jones,
Jonathan Mayfield,
Donna Roye- Morton,
EMP: 17 EST: 2012
SALES (est): 203.5K **Privately Held**
SIC: 7299 7349 Home improvement & renovation contractor agency; janitorial service, contract basis

(G-6474)
DRUMMOND HILL SWIM CLUB
Alton Dr (19711)
PHONE..................302 366-9882
Ed Broadbelt, *President*
EMP: 6 EST: 1971
SALES (est): 250K **Privately Held**
SIC: 7997 Swimming club, membership

(G-6475)
DRY WALL ASSOCIATES LTD
58 Albe Dr (19702-1375)
PHONE..................302 737-3220
David Bull, *President*
Helena Ellingsworth, *Admin Sec*
EMP: 60
SQ FT: 5,000
SALES (est): 11.6MM **Privately Held**
SIC: 1542 Commercial & office buildings, renovation & repair; commercial & office building contractors

(G-6476)
DSS INTERNATIONAL LLC
203 Peoples Plz (19702)
PHONE..................302 836-0270
Patricia A King, *Partner*
EMP: 4 EST: 2001
SALES (est): 487.7K **Privately Held**
SIC: 8742 8721 Business planning & organizing services; accounting, auditing & bookkeeping

(G-6477)
DUHADAWAY TOOL AND DIE SP INC
801 Dawson Dr (19713-3415)
PHONE..................302 366-0113
Robert W Duhadaway, *President*
Cathy Duhadaway, *Corp Secy*
▲ EMP: 80 EST: 1957
SQ FT: 49,000
SALES (est): 18.6MM **Privately Held**
WEB: www.duhadawaytool.com
SIC: 3599 Machine shop, jobbing & repair

(G-6478)
DUPONT NUTRITION AND HEALTH
1301 Ogletown Rd (19711-5419)
PHONE..................302 451-0112
EMP: 6
SALES (corp-wide): 1.6MM **Privately Held**
SIC: 2834 Pharmaceutical preparations
PA: Dupont Nutrition And Health
2 Boulden Cir Ste 6
New Castle DE 19720
302 695-5300

(G-6479)
DUPONT SPECIALTY PDTS USA LLC
350 Bellevue Rd (19713-3430)
P.O. Box 6100 (19714-6100)
PHONE..................302 774-1000
Kay Willien, *General Mgr*
Robert J Phillip, *Plant Mgr*
Stephen Constable, *Engineer*
John Cunningham, *Engineer*
Mark Dwhitmarsh II, *Engineer*
EMP: 50
SALES (corp-wide): 85.9B **Publicly Held**
WEB: www.dupont.com
SIC: 2821 Plastics materials & resins
HQ: Dupont Specialty Products Usa, Llc
974 Centre Rd
Wilmington DE 19805
302 774-1000

(G-6480)
DUPONT SPECIALTY PDTS USA LLC
5 Tralee Industrial Park (19711-5444)
P.O. Box 6098 (19714-6098)
PHONE..................302 451-0717
Ellen Balh, *Branch Mgr*
EMP: 170
SALES (corp-wide): 85.9B **Publicly Held**
SIC: 2822 Synthetic rubber
HQ: Dupont Specialty Products Usa, Llc
974 Centre Rd
Wilmington DE 19805
302 774-1000

(G-6481)
DURRELL SANDBLASTING & PNTG CO
Also Called: Friendly Oil Co
829 Salem Church Rd (19702-4015)
PHONE..................302 836-1113
Mark Durrell, *President*
EMP: 4
SALES (est): 316.4K **Privately Held**
SIC: 1799 1721 5983 8351 Sandblasting of building exteriors; steam cleaning of building exteriors; pavement marking contractor; fuel oil dealers; child day care services

(G-6482)
DXC TECHNOLOGY COMPANY
645 Paper Mill Rd (19711-7515)
PHONE..................302 391-2762
EMP: 3
SALES (corp-wide): 20.7B **Publicly Held**
SIC: 7372 Prepackaged software
PA: Dxc Technology Company
1775 Tysons Blvd Fl 8
Tysons VA 22102
703 245-9675

(G-6483)
DYNAMIC CONVERTERS LLC
122 Sandy Dr Ste F (19713-1188)
PHONE..................302 454-9203
Frank Lupo,
EMP: 6 EST: 1998
SALES (est): 653.9K **Privately Held**
SIC: 7537 Automotive transmission repair shops

(G-6484)
DYNAMIC PACKET CORP
40 E Main St Ste 4000 (19711-4639)
PHONE..................302 448-2222
Robert Pedraza, *President*
EMP: 18
SQ FT: 2,000
SALES (est): 761.6K **Privately Held**
SIC: 8999 Communication services

(G-6485)
DYNAMIC THERAPY SERVICES LLC
550 Stanton Christn Rd # 203 (19712-2125)
PHONE..................302 691-5603
Andrew G Laws, *President*
EMP: 16
SALES (corp-wide): 12.9MM **Privately Held**
SIC: 8049 Physical therapist
PA: Dynamic Therapy Services Llc
1501 Blueball Ave
Linwood PA 19061
610 859-8850

(G-6486)
DYNAMIC THERAPY SERVICES LLC
Also Called: Dynamic Physical Therapy
2717 Pulaski Hwy (19702-3960)
PHONE..................302 292-3454
Jody Riddle, *Branch Mgr*
EMP: 6
SALES (corp-wide): 12.9MM **Privately Held**
SIC: 8049 Physical therapist
PA: Dynamic Therapy Services Llc
1501 Blueball Ave
Linwood PA 19061
610 859-8850

(G-6487)
E C I MOTORSPORTS INC
9 Polaris Dr (19711-3056)
PHONE..................302 239-6376
EMP: 2 EST: 2012
SALES (est): 74.4K **Privately Held**
SIC: 2879 Agricultural chemicals

(G-6488)
E I DU PONT DE NEMOURS & CO
Also Called: Dupont
6 Meteor Ln (19711-3042)
PHONE..................302 239-9424
Ram Kahanna, *Branch Mgr*
EMP: 3
SALES (corp-wide): 30.6B **Publicly Held**
SIC: 2879 Agricultural chemicals
HQ: E. I. Du Pont De Nemours And Company
974 Centre Rd Bldg 735
Wilmington DE 19805
302 485-3000

(G-6489)
E I DU PONT DE NEMOURS & CO
Also Called: Dupont Stine Haskell RES Ctr
1090 Elkton Rd (19711-3507)
PHONE..................302 774-1000
Chuck Corrigan, *Principal*
EMP: 33
SALES (corp-wide): 30.6B **Publicly Held**
SIC: 8059 Personal care home, with health care
HQ: E. I. Du Pont De Nemours And Company
974 Centre Rd Bldg 735
Wilmington DE 19805
302 485-3000

(G-6490)
E I DU PONT DE NEMOURS & CO
Also Called: Dupont
1007 Mkt St De Nmurs Bldg (19702)
PHONE..................302 774-1000
David Timmons, *Consultant*
William Conlin, *Director*
EMP: 52
SALES (corp-wide): 30.6B **Publicly Held**
WEB: www.dupont.com
SIC: 8748 Systems analysis & engineering consulting services
HQ: E. I. Du Pont De Nemours And Company
974 Centre Rd Bldg 735
Wilmington DE 19805
302 485-3000

(G-6491)
E I DU PONT DE NEMOURS & CO
Also Called: Haskell Laboratory
1090 Elkton Rd (19711-3507)
PHONE..................302 366-5763
Kathleen Reed, *General Mgr*
Carol Ashman, *Manager*
EMP: 4
SALES (corp-wide): 30.6B **Publicly Held**
WEB: www.dupont.com
SIC: 2813 Industrial gases
HQ: E. I. Du Pont De Nemours And Company
974 Centre Rd Bldg 735
Wilmington DE 19805
302 485-3000

Newark - New Castle County (G-6492)

(G-6492)
E I DU PONT DE NEMOURS & CO
Also Called: Dupont
242 Chapman Rd (19702-5405)
P.O. Box 8255 (19714-8255)
PHONE....................302 452-9000
Robert Pinson, *General Mgr*
Michelle Robinson, *Engineer*
EMP: 31
SALES (corp-wide): 30.6B **Publicly Held**
WEB: www.dupont.com
SIC: 2911 Petroleum refining
HQ: E. I. Du Pont De Nemours And Company
974 Centre Rd Bldg 735
Wilmington DE 19805
302 485-3000

(G-6493)
E-MERGE SYSTEMS INC
254 Cadmin Rd (19702)
PHONE....................302 894-3860
Mike Kalajin, *General Mgr*
EMP: 4
SALES (corp-wide): 4.2MM **Privately Held**
SIC: 8711 Consulting engineer
PA: E-Merge Systems, Inc.
8715 Bollman Pl
Savage MD 20763
240 456-0930

(G-6494)
EAST COAST LAWN SERVICES INC
2860 Ogletown Rd Apt 2 (19713-1856)
PHONE....................302 453-8400
Keith Allen Lefebvre, *Principal*
EMP: 4
SALES (est): 125K **Privately Held**
SIC: 0782 Lawn services

(G-6495)
EAST COAST STAINLESS INC
30 Albe Dr Ste E (19702-1352)
PHONE....................302 366-0675
James Adie, *President*
Debra Adie, *Chairman*
Art Adie, *Exec VP*
Frank Shilkitus, *Sales Mgr*
EMP: 7
SQ FT: 6,000
SALES (est): 4MM **Privately Held**
SIC: 5051 Steel

(G-6496)
EAST COAST STAINLESS & ALLOYS
30 Albe Dr Ste E (19702-1352)
PHONE....................302 366-0675
Art Adie, *Vice Pres*
EMP: 10
SALES (est): 82.3K **Privately Held**
SIC: 5051 Steel

(G-6497)
EASTERN GROUP INC
Also Called: Eastern Marine
931 S Chapel St (19713-3419)
PHONE....................302 737-6603
Glenn Hojnowski, *General Mgr*
Tom Bidgood, *Vice Pres*
George Long, *Store Mgr*
Mike Bourne, *Buyer*
John H Hollingsworth, *Shareholder*
▼ **EMP:** 40 **EST:** 1912
SQ FT: 10,000
SALES (est): 9.9MM **Privately Held**
WEB: www.polytarps.net
SIC: 5551 5088 5091 Marine supplies; outboard motors; marine supplies; outboard motors

(G-6498)
EASTERN LIFT TRUCK CO INC
137 Sandy Dr (19713-1149)
PHONE....................302 286-6660
Jim Testerman, *Sales Staff*
Max Bielat, *Manager*
Adam Garrett, *Manager*
Scott Thatcher, *Manager*
Bob Zak, *Manager*
EMP: 25

SALES (corp-wide): 175.6MM **Privately Held**
SIC: 5084 Materials handling machinery
PA: Eastern Lift Truck Co., Inc.
549 E Linwood Ave
Maple Shade NJ 08052
856 779-8880

(G-6499)
EASTERN METALS INC
679 Dawson Dr (19713-3411)
P.O. Box 674, Bear (19701-0674)
PHONE....................302 454-7886
Walter J Moulder Jr, *President*
Michael J Moulder, *Vice Pres*
Walter J Moulder Sr, *Treasurer*
EMP: 11
SALES (est): 1.3MM **Privately Held**
SIC: 1761 1541 Roofing contractor; siding contractor; prefabricated building erection, industrial

(G-6500)
EBENEZER UNITED METHDST CHRUCH
Also Called: Ebenezer Preschool
525 Polly Drummond Hl Rd (19711-4342)
PHONE....................302 731-9495
Kathleen M Bieri, *Director*
EMP: 10
SALES (est): 470K **Privately Held**
SIC: 8661 8351 Methodist Church; preschool center

(G-6501)
EBUBE GROUP & CO LLC
40 E Main St (19711-4639)
PHONE....................215 821-7490
Uchenna Emeche, *Mng Member*
EMP: 4
SALES (est): 92.1K **Privately Held**
SIC: 7389 Business services

(G-6502)
ECG INDUSTRIES INC (PA)
254 Chapman Rd Ste 203 (19702-5422)
PHONE....................302 453-0535
Enemute Oduaran, *President*
EMP: 3
SALES: 1MM **Privately Held**
SIC: 8744 4953 1799 1389 Facilities support services; sanitary landfill operation; petroleum storage tanks, pumping & draining; testing, measuring, surveying & analysis services; soil analysis; pollution testing

(G-6503)
EDWARD VARNES HARDWOOD FLOORS
634 Old Baltimore Pike (19702-1311)
PHONE....................302 292-0919
Edward Varnes, *President*
EMP: 10
SALES (est): 900K **Privately Held**
WEB: www.edvarnes.com
SIC: 1752 Wood floor installation & refinishing

(G-6504)
EDWIN C KATZMAN MD
Also Called: Kids First Newark
210 Christiana Med Ctr (19702-1652)
PHONE....................302 368-2501
Edwin C Katzman MD, *Principal*
EMP: 5
SALES (est): 280.9K **Privately Held**
SIC: 8011 Pediatrician

(G-6505)
EDWIN S KUIPERS DDS
210 W Park Pl (19711-4519)
PHONE....................302 455-0333
Edwin S Kuipers, *Principal*
EMP: 4
SALES (est): 66.1K **Privately Held**
SIC: 8021 Offices & clinics of dentists

(G-6506)
EECO INC (HQ)
850 Library Ave Ste 204c (19711-7170)
PHONE....................302 456-1448
Michael Lefkowitz, *CFO*
EMP: 1

SALES (est): 5.1B
SALES (est): 18.3B **Publicly Held**
SIC: 3491 3621 3585 3546 Industrial valves; automatic regulating & control valves; process control regulator valves; valves, automatic control; motors & generators; motors, electric; refrigeration & heating equipment; heating equipment, complete; refrigeration equipment, complete; parts for heating, cooling & refrigerating equipment; power-driven handtools; saws & sawing equipment; drills & drilling tools; grinders, portable: electric or pneumatic; electronic circuits; industrial flow & liquid measuring instruments
PA: Emerson Electric Co.
8000 West Florissant Ave
Saint Louis MO 63136
314 553-2000

(G-6507)
EECOO LLC
19 Kris Ct (19702-6843)
PHONE....................315 503-1477
Chun Luo,
EMP: 50
SALES: 1.8MM **Privately Held**
SIC: 5199 General merchandise, nondurable

(G-6508)
EF TECHNOLOGIES INC
119b Sandy Dr (19713-1148)
PHONE....................302 451-1088
William Groft, *President*
Beverly Groft, *Corp Secy*
David Groft, *Vice Pres*
Michael Groft, *Vice Pres*
EMP: 7
SQ FT: 5,000
SALES (est): 1.3MM **Privately Held**
WEB: www.eft-inc.com
SIC: 3548 Electric welding equipment

(G-6509)
EGGPLANT INC
1918 Kirkwood Hwy (19711-5724)
PHONE....................302 737-1073
Dave Richardson, *President*
EMP: 4
SQ FT: 6,000
SALES (est): 270K **Privately Held**
SIC: 0181 5992 Shrubberies grown under cover (e.g. greenhouse production); flowers: grown under cover (e.g. greenhouse production); florists; flowers, fresh

(G-6510)
ELECTRONIC SYSTEMS SPECIALIST
Polly Drummond Shr Bldg 1 (19711)
PHONE....................302 738-4165
Matthew Kearns, *President*
EMP: 6
SALES (est): 331.2K **Privately Held**
SIC: 1731 Electrical work

(G-6511)
ELEGANT STONE VENEER LLC
4 Carriage Ln (19711-2044)
PHONE....................302 547-4780
Shane Cavanaugh,
EMP: 1 **EST:** 2017
SALES (est): 83.6K **Privately Held**
SIC: 3271 Concrete block & brick

(G-6512)
ELEMENTS BEAUTY SUPPLY NORTH
1309 Churchmans Rd (19713-2100)
PHONE....................302 738-7732
Steven Roberts, *Owner*
EMP: 4
SALES (est): 240K **Privately Held**
SIC: 5122 Cosmetics, perfumes & hair products

(G-6513)
ELITE CHEMICAL AND SUPPLY INC
630 Churchmans Rd Ste 106 (19702-1943)
PHONE....................302 366-8900
Sheryl Ecton, *Principal*
EMP: 5

SALES (est): 290K **Privately Held**
SIC: 7699 Cleaning services

(G-6514)
ELITE COMMERCIAL CLEANING INC
Also Called: Elite Cleaning Company
630 Churchmans Rd Ste 106 (19702-1943)
PHONE....................302 366-8900
Henry Winchester, *President*
Cheryl Ecton, *Owner*
EMP: 60
SALES (est): 1.3MM **Privately Held**
SIC: 7349 Janitorial service, contract basis

(G-6515)
ELIZABETH JACKOVIC MD
200 Hygeia Dr (19713-2049)
PHONE....................302 623-0240
Elizabeth Jackovic MD, *Principal*
EMP: 4
SALES (est): 94.5K **Privately Held**
SIC: 8011 Offices & clinics of medical doctors

(G-6516)
ELKTON EXTERMINATING CO INC
1040 S Chapel St (19702-1303)
PHONE....................302 368-9116
Philip Kreer, *Principal*
EMP: 11
SALES (est): 717.2K
SALES (corp-wide): 2.9MM **Privately Held**
SIC: 7342 Pest control services
PA: Elkton Exterminating Company, Inc.
913 N Bridge St
Elkton MD 21921
410 398-4378

(G-6517)
ELLINGSEN & ASSOCIATES
113 Barksdale Pro Ctr (19711-3258)
PHONE....................302 650-6437
Mary Ellingsen, *Owner*
Myra McCourt, *Mktg Dir*
EMP: 15
SALES: 46K **Privately Held**
SIC: 8049 Speech therapist

(G-6518)
ELS TIRE SERVICE INC
2724 Pulaski Hwy (19702-3911)
PHONE....................302 834-1997
El Van Blarcom, *President*
Joyce Van Blarcom, *Vice Pres*
EMP: 15
SQ FT: 5,200
SALES (est): 2.1MM **Privately Held**
SIC: 5531 5014 7539 Automotive tires; truck tires & tubes; automotive repair shops; brake services; wheel alignment, automotive; shock absorber replacement

(G-6519)
ELSICON INC
5 Innovation Way Ste 100 (19711-5459)
PHONE....................302 266-7030
Shao-Tang Sun, *President*
Wayne Gibbons, *Dir Ops-Prd-Mfg*
Eric Fahnoe, *Finance Dir*
Paul Shannon, *Technology*
EMP: 15 **EST:** 1997
SQ FT: 14,000
SALES (est): 1.5MM **Privately Held**
WEB: www.elsicon.com
SIC: 5049 Optical goods

(G-6520)
ELUKTRONICS INC
9 Albe Dr Ste E (19702-1380)
PHONE....................302 380-3242
William Kiryluk, *CEO*
John Kindred, *COO*
Brian Rappaport, *Engineer*
▲ **EMP:** 10
SQ FT: 7,920
SALES: 13.5MM **Privately Held**
SIC: 3571 Personal computers (microcomputers)

GEOGRAPHIC SECTION

Newark - New Castle County (G-6550)

(G-6521)
ELVA G PEARSON MD
4735 Ogletown Stanton Rd (19713-2072)
PHONE...........................302 623-4144
Anthony L Cucuzzella, *Principal*
EMP: 4
SALES (est): 121.8K **Privately Held**
SIC: 8011 General & family practice, physician/surgeon

(G-6522)
EM PHOTONICS INC
51 E Main St Ste 203 (19711-4685)
PHONE...........................302 456-9003
Eric Kelmelis, *CEO*
Dennis Prather, *President*
Amol Apte, *Business Mgr*
Evenie Chao, *Engineer*
Aaron Paolini, *Engineer*
EMP: 15 **EST:** 2001
SQ FT: 1,500
SALES: 2MM **Privately Held**
WEB: www.emphotonics.com
SIC: 8711 Electrical or electronic engineering

(G-6523)
EMBLEM AT CHRISTIANA CLUBHOUSE
1150 Helen Dr (19702-1650)
PHONE...........................302 525-6692
EMP: 4 **EST:** 2017
SALES (est): 87.8K **Privately Held**
SIC: 7997 Membership sports & recreation clubs

(G-6524)
EMPIRE CONSTRUCTION COMPANY
Also Called: Empire Building and Dev
1 Tenby Chase Dr (19711-2440)
PHONE...........................302 235-2093
Pat Mussey, *President*
Sylvester Aiello, *Corp Secy*
Bonnie Dimichele, *Vice Pres*
▼ **EMP:** 4
SALES: 2MM **Privately Held**
SIC: 1522 Residential construction

(G-6525)
ENCIMA GROUP INC
1 Innovation Way Ste 400 (19711-5463)
PHONE...........................302 352-1714
David Clunes, *President*
Shouvanik Chatterjee, *COO*
Junaid Khan, *Vice Pres*
Michael Aherne, *Opers Staff*
Carl Wall, *Engineer*
EMP: 60
SALES: 950K **Privately Held**
SIC: 8742 Marketing consulting services
HQ: Indegene Pharmaceutical Solutions, Inc.
  4727 Wilshire Blvd
  Los Angeles CA 90010
  323 900-4900

(G-6526)
ENDLESS SUMMER TANNING SALON (PA)
60 N College Ave Ste A (19711-2246)
PHONE...........................302 369-0455
John Thornton, *Owner*
EMP: 6
SALES (est): 219.7K **Privately Held**
SIC: 7299 5699 Tanning salon; bathing suits

(G-6527)
ENDOSCOPY CENTER OF DELEWARE
Also Called: Endoscopy Center of Delaware
1090 Old Churchmans Rd (19713-2102)
PHONE...........................302 892-2710
Joseph S Hacker III, *President*
Donald Girard MD, *Vice Pres*
George Benes MD, *Treasurer*
Warren G Butt MD, *Admin Sec*
Gloria Congleton, *Administration*
EMP: 17
SALES (est): 2.3MM **Privately Held**
SIC: 8062 General medical & surgical hospitals

(G-6528)
ENERGY SYSTEMS TECH INC
126a Sandy Dr (19713-1147)
PHONE...........................302 368-0443
Paul E Czerwin, *President*
Joan Czerwin, *Admin Sec*
EMP: 5
SALES (est): 578.5K
SALES (corp-wide): 55MM **Privately Held**
SIC: 3822 Auto controls regulating residntl & coml environmt & applncs
PA: Albireo Energy, Llc
  3 Ethel Rd Ste 300
  Edison NJ 08817
  732 512-9100

(G-6529)
ENHANCED CORPORATE PRFMCE LLC
Also Called: McCoy Enterprises
1 Morning Glen Ln (19711-4396)
P.O. Box 5338, Deptford NJ (08096-0338)
PHONE...........................302 545-8541
Joseph McCoy,
Robert Madonna,
Joseph Murray,
EMP: 35
SALES (est): 780.7K **Privately Held**
SIC: 8299 8742 Educational services; training & development consultant

(G-6530)
ENT AND ALLERGY DELAWARE LLC
2600 Glasgow Ave Ste 221 (19702-5704)
PHONE...........................302 832-8700
Michelle O'Neil, *Office Mgr*
EMP: 5
SALES (corp-wide): 5.7MM **Privately Held**
SIC: 8011 Allergist
PA: Ent And Allergy Of Delaware, Llc
  1401 Foulk Rd Ste 205
  Wilmington DE 19803
  302 478-8467

(G-6531)
ENTERPRISE LSG PHILADELPHIA LLC
Also Called: Enterprise Rent-A-Car
409 E Cleveland Ave (19711-3714)
PHONE...........................302 266-7777
EMP: 6
SALES (corp-wide): 4.5B **Privately Held**
SIC: 7514 Passenger car rental
HQ: Enterprise Leasing Company Of Philadelphia, Llc
  2434 W Main St 2436
  Norristown PA 19403

(G-6532)
ENTERPRISE LSG PHLADELPHIA LLC
Also Called: Enterprise Rent-A-Car
430 Newark Shopping Ctr (19711-7304)
PHONE...........................302 292-0524
Kathyn Volpe, *Manager*
Kevin Reinsel, *Manager*
EMP: 7
SALES (corp-wide): 4.5B **Privately Held**
SIC: 7514 Passenger car rental
HQ: Enterprise Leasing Company Of Philadelphia, Llc
  2434 W Main St 2436
  Norristown PA 19403

(G-6533)
ENTERPRISE SERVICES LLC
248 Chapman Rd Ste 100 (19702-5425)
P.O. Box 907 (19715-0907)
PHONE...........................302 454-7622
Lance Rogers, *Branch Mgr*
EMP: 125
SALES (corp-wide): 11.1B **Publicly Held**
WEB: www.eds.com
SIC: 7373 Computer integrated systems design
HQ: Perspecta Enterprise Solutions Llc
  13600 Eds Dr A3s
  Herndon VA 20171
  703 245-9675

(G-6534)
ENVOY FLIGHT SYSTEMS INC
201 Ruthar Dr Ste 3 (19711-8029)
PHONE...........................302 738-1788
Jason Amato, *Principal*
EMP: 2 **EST:** 2013
SQ FT: 2,000
SALES (est): 85.9K **Privately Held**
SIC: 3728 Research & dev by manuf., aircraft parts & auxiliary equip

(G-6535)
EPILEPSY FOUNDATION OF DEL (PA)
527 Stanton Christiana Rd (19713-2106)
PHONE...........................302 999-9313
Barbara Blair, *Director*
EMP: 4
SALES (est): 153.6K **Privately Held**
WEB: www.efde.org
SIC: 8322 Social service center

(G-6536)
ERIC BARSKY
19 Autumnwood Dr (19711-6218)
PHONE...........................856 495-6988
Eric Barsky, *Manager*
EMP: 7
SALES (est): 72.3K **Privately Held**
SIC: 8049 Offices of health practitioner

(G-6537)
ERICKSON MANAGEMENT
447 Coldspring Run (19711-2466)
PHONE...........................302 235-0855
Thomas Erickson, *Principal*
Eileen Anderson, *Accounts Exec*
Kathleen O'Donnell, *Accounts Exec*
Pat Walega, *Administration*
EMP: 4
SALES (est): 275.7K **Privately Held**
SIC: 8741 Management services

(G-6538)
ERIN N MACKO DDS LLC
625 Barksdale Rd Ste 101 (19711-4535)
PHONE...........................302 368-7463
Erin N Macko DDS, *Principal*
EMP: 4
SALES (est): 93.1K **Privately Held**
SIC: 8021 Offices & clinics of dentists

(G-6539)
ESA P PORTFOLIO LLC
Also Called: Extended Stay America, Inc.
333 Continental Dr (19713-4329)
PHONE...........................302 283-0800
EMP: 15
SALES (corp-wide): 1.2B **Publicly Held**
WEB: www.homesteadgs.com
SIC: 7011 Hotels & motels
HQ: Esa P Portfolio Llc
  11525 N Commnty House 1
  Charlotte NC 28277
  980 345-1600

(G-6540)
ESTATE SERVICING LLC
901 Barksdale Rd (19711-3205)
PHONE...........................302 731-1119
George Zielinski, *Principal*
EMP: 2 **EST:** 2008
SALES (est): 82.9K **Privately Held**
SIC: 1389 Roustabout service

(G-6541)
ET INTERNATIONAL INC
10 Fountainview Dr (19713-3859)
PHONE...........................302 266-6426
Guang R Gao, *Chairman*
Ashwin Alankar, *Director*
Nicholas Gao, *Director*
EMP: 16
SALES (est): 1.6MM **Privately Held**
WEB: www.etinternational.com
SIC: 7371 Computer software development

(G-6542)
ETECHPUBLISH INC
35 Stature Dr (19713-3565)
PHONE...........................302 294-1678
EMP: 7 **EST:** 2012
SALES (est): 346.7K **Privately Held**
SIC: 8748 Business Consulting Services

(G-6543)
ETS & YCP LLC
113 Barksdale Pro Ctr (19711-3258)
PHONE...........................302 525-4111
Tommie Price, *Mng Member*
EMP: 5
SALES: 250K **Privately Held**
SIC: 7379 Computer related consulting services

(G-6544)
EUGENE M DAMICO III DDS PA (PA)
4735 Ogletown Stanton Rd # 1115 (19713-2089)
PHONE...........................302 292-1600
Eugene M D'Amico III DDS, *President*
EMP: 7
SALES (est): 542.2K **Privately Held**
WEB: www.christianaoms.com
SIC: 8021 8011 Dental surgeon; offices & clinics of medical doctors

(G-6545)
EVENTC2 LLC
23 Oklahoma State Dr (19713-1143)
PHONE...........................301 467-5780
Ronald Siarnicki, *Partner*
B Tilman Jolly, *Partner*
Ed Klima, *Partner*
David Statter, *Partner*
EMP: 4 **EST:** 2012
SALES (est): 108.7K **Privately Held**
SIC: 7299 Facility rental & party planning services

(G-6546)
EVEREST AUTOWORKS AUTO SPA LLC
690 Kirkwood Hwy (19711)
PHONE...........................302 737-8424
Christian Porter,
EMP: 5
SALES (est): 449.1K **Privately Held**
SIC: 7538 General automotive repair shops

(G-6547)
EWINGS TOWING SERVICE INC
1111 Elkton Rd (19711-3508)
PHONE...........................302 366-8806
Kevin Cox, *President*
Joe Reilly, *Vice Pres*
Dale Duncan, *Director*
EMP: 8
SQ FT: 1,000
SALES: 1MM **Privately Held**
SIC: 7549 7539 Towing services; automotive repair shops

(G-6548)
EXA SOLUTIONS INC
2035 Sunset Lake Rd B2 (19702-2600)
PHONE...........................302 273-9320
Manuel Cabrera, *CEO*
Sulna Held, *Principal*
EMP: 5
SALES (est): 107K **Privately Held**
SIC: 7371 Computer software development & applications

(G-6549)
EXAM MASTER CORPORATION
100 Lake Dr Ste 6 (19702-3346)
PHONE...........................302 378-3842
Matthew Bader, *President*
A Stuart Markham, *Chairman*
Gene Bergey, *Vice Pres*
Ann Marie Mylar, *Treasurer*
Chip Noonan, *Sales Mgr*
EMP: 21
SALES: 1.2MM **Privately Held**
WEB: www.exammaster.com
SIC: 8099 Physical examination & testing services

(G-6550)
EXCEL BUSINESS SYSTEMS INC (PA)
201 Ruthar Dr Ste 10 (19711-8029)
PHONE...........................302 453-1500
Frank Montisano, *President*
Joseph Di Marco, *Vice Pres*
Joseph Dimarco, *Vice Pres*
Connie Merchant, *Transportation*

Newark - New Castle County (G-6551)

Don Peterson, *Sales Executive*
EMP: 23
SQ FT: 5,500
SALES (est): 4.8MM **Privately Held**
WEB: www.exceldigital.com
SIC: 5999 7629 Business machines & equipment; photocopy machines; facsimile equipment; business machine repair, electric

(G-6551)
EXCEPTIONAL CARE FOR CHILDREN
11 Independence Way (19713-1159)
PHONE 302 894-1001
Stephen J Falchek, *Principal*
Bill Ludlam, *Facilities Mgr*
Donna Hartzell, *Supervisor*
Tracie Martin, *Nursing Dir*
Annette V Moore, *Administration*
EMP: 80
SALES: 12MM **Privately Held**
SIC: 8051 Convalescent home with continuous nursing care

(G-6552)
EXECUTIVE BROADBAND
Also Called: Executive Brdband Cmmnications
6 Jaymar Blvd (19702-2877)
PHONE 302 463-4335
Peter F Daly Jr, *Mng Member*
Craig Viar,
EMP: 5
SALES: 1.5MM **Privately Held**
SIC: 3663 4841 Cable television equipment; cable television services; satellite master antenna systems services (SMATV)

(G-6553)
EXPRESS ELECTRIC INC
P.O. Box 9560 (19714-9560)
PHONE 302 456-1919
EMP: 2
SALES (est): 135.7K **Privately Held**
SIC: 2353 Hats, caps & millinery

(G-6554)
EXPRESS VPN LLC
113 Barksdale Pro Ctr (19711-3258)
PHONE 310 601-8492
EMP: 5
SALES (est): 370.6K **Privately Held**
SIC: 5045 Computer software

(G-6555)
EXTREME AUDIO & VIDEO
19a Albe Dr (19702-1321)
PHONE 302 533-7404
Alfred Barone, *Principal*
EMP: 5
SALES (est): 203.3K **Privately Held**
SIC: 7841 Video tape rental

(G-6556)
EXTREME MACHINING LLC
111 Lake Dr Ste A (19702-3334)
PHONE 302 368-7595
Mark Kreshock, *President*
Donald Urie, *Vice Pres*
EMP: 10
SQ FT: 80,000
SALES (est): 2.5MM **Privately Held**
SIC: 3599 Machine shop, jobbing & repair

(G-6557)
EXTREME REACH INC
450 Corporate Blvd (19702-3330)
PHONE 302 366-7538
EMP: 19 **Privately Held**
SIC: 7311 Advertising agencies
PA: Extreme Reach, Inc.
75 2nd Ave Ste 720
Needham Heights MA 02494

(G-6558)
EXTREME SCALE SOLUTIONS LLC
256 Chapman Rd Ste 107 (19702-5417)
PHONE 302 540-7149
Rishi Khan,
EMP: 16
SQ FT: 1,500
SALES: 3.8MM **Privately Held**
SIC: 7371 Computer software systems analysis & design, custom

(G-6559)
EYE CARE OF DELAWARE
4102 Ogletown Rd Ste 1 (19713)
PHONE 302 454-8800
Jane Baker, *Manager*
EMP: 20
SALES (est): 1.5MM **Privately Held**
WEB: www.eyetopics.com
SIC: 8011 Ophthalmologist

(G-6560)
EZPROHUB LLC
100 Biddle Ave Ste 112 (19702-3982)
PHONE 302 327-4222
Shirisha Kathoju, *Mng Member*
Nag Raj, *Executive*
EMP: 4 **EST:** 2012
SALES (est): 176.9K **Privately Held**
SIC: 8742 General management consultant

(G-6561)
F SCHUMACHER & CO
Also Called: F S C Wallcoverings
131 Continental Dr # 300 (19713-4305)
P.O. Box 7960, New York NY (10116-7960)
PHONE 302 454-3200
Richard Malin, *Manager*
EMP: 180
SALES (corp-wide): 102.8MM **Privately Held**
WEB: www.fsco.com
SIC: 5023 5131 5198 Draperies; carpets; yard goods, woven; paints, varnishes & supplies
PA: F. Schumacher & Co.
875 Ave Of The Amrcs 14
New York NY 10001
212 213-7900

(G-6562)
FABREEKA INTL HOLDINGS INC
Fabreeka-Fablene Division
315 Ruthar Dr (19711-8016)
PHONE 302 452-2500
Paul Oconnor, *Manager*
EMP: 15
SALES (corp-wide): 428.8K **Privately Held**
WEB: www.fabreeka.com
SIC: 3069 Molded rubber products
HQ: Fabreeka International Holdings, Inc.
1023 Turnpike St
Stoughton MA 02072
781 341-3655

(G-6563)
FACTORY TECHNOLOGIES INC
2035 Sunset Lake Rd B2 (19702-2600)
PHONE 302 266-1290
Valentine Oleka, *CEO*
EMP: 9 **EST:** 2017
SALES (est): 166.3K **Privately Held**
SIC: 7389 Business services

(G-6564)
FAITH FAMILY MANAGEMENT CO
63 Marrows Rd (19713-3701)
PHONE 302 832-5936
Lan Nguyen, *Partner*
EMP: 5 **EST:** 2013
SALES (est): 370.1K **Privately Held**
SIC: 8741 Management services

(G-6565)
FAMEALY INC (PA)
2035 Sunset Lake Rd B2 (19702-2600)
PHONE 650 492-5009
Manish Malik, *Principal*
EMP: 1 **EST:** 2017
SALES: 25K **Privately Held**
SIC: 7372 Prepackaged software

(G-6566)
FAMILY CARE ASSOCIATES
510 Christiana Med Ctr (19702-1655)
PHONE 302 454-8880
Crystal Mason, *Office Mgr*
EMP: 7
SALES (est): 72.3K **Privately Held**
SIC: 8049 Offices of health practitioner

(G-6567)
FAMILY DENISTRY
179 W Chestnut Hill Rd # 4 (19713-2210)
PHONE 302 368-0054
EMP: 4
SALES (est): 61.5K **Privately Held**
SIC: 8021 Offices & clinics of dentists

(G-6568)
FAMILY DOCTORS
Also Called: Bilski, William F Do
4 Polly Drummond Hill Rd (19711)
PHONE 302 368-3600
William F Bilski, *Partner*
EMP: 6
SALES (est): 321.6K **Privately Held**
SIC: 8031 Offices & clinics of osteopathic physicians

(G-6569)
FAMILY PRACTICE CNTR OF NEW CA
Also Called: Abby Family Practice
1 Centurian Dr Ste 105 (19713-2154)
PHONE 302 999-0933
Arlen D Stone, *Principal*
EMP: 5 **EST:** 2010
SALES (est): 389.8K **Privately Held**
SIC: 8011 General & family practice, physician/surgeon

(G-6570)
FAR REZOLUTIONS INC
218 Margaux Cir (19702-4548)
PHONE 302 547-6850
Steve Resnick, *President*
EMP: 5
SALES (est): 110.8K **Privately Held**
SIC: 7622 Television repair shop

(G-6571)
FAR TRUCKING LLC
23 O Rourke Ct (19702-6837)
PHONE 302 266-8034
Cora Robinson, *Principal*
EMP: 4
SALES (est): 164.2K **Privately Held**
SIC: 4212 Local trucking, without storage

(G-6572)
FARMERS RADIATOR & AC
Also Called: Farmers Radiator & AC Sho
15 Deer Track Ln (19711-2966)
PHONE 302 235-5922
Mike J Sprinkle, *Owner*
EMP: 4
SALES (est): 148.2K **Privately Held**
SIC: 7539 Radiator repair shop, automotive

(G-6573)
FAS MART / SHORE STOP 286 LLC
Also Called: Shore Stop Store 286
1400 Capitol Trl (19711-5782)
PHONE 302 366-9694
Gene Daunno, *Principal*
EMP: 5
SALES (est): 452K **Privately Held**
SIC: 6799 Investors

(G-6574)
FAST PIPE LINING EAST INC
563 Walther Rd (19702-2903)
P.O. Box 99, Bear (19701-0099)
PHONE 302 368-7414
Robin Quinn, *CEO*
EMP: 10
SALES (est): 517.9K **Privately Held**
SIC: 1623 Water, sewer & utility lines

(G-6575)
FATANEH M ZIARI MD
2600 Glasgow Ave Ste 212 (19702-5704)
PHONE 302 836-8533
Fataneh Ziari MD, *Owner*
EMP: 8
SALES (est): 437.3K **Privately Held**
SIC: 8011 Pediatrician

(G-6576)
FEDEX OFFICE & PRINT SVCS INC
132 S Main St (19711-7935)
PHONE 302 368-5080
EMP: 16
SALES (corp-wide): 69.6B **Publicly Held**
WEB: www.kinkos.com
SIC: 7334 Photocopying & duplicating services
HQ: Fedex Office And Print Services, Inc.
7900 Legacy Dr
Plano TX 75024
800 463-3339

(G-6577)
FIBER ONE INC
2812 Old County Rd (19702-4602)
PHONE 302 834-0890
Ruth Filippone, *President*
Joseph Filippone, *Vice Pres*
EMP: 13
SALES: 496.2K **Privately Held**
WEB: www.fiber-one.com
SIC: 1731 Communications specialization

(G-6578)
FIGGO INC
2035 Sunset Lake Rd B2 (19702-2600)
PHONE 734 560-1300
Danny Joseph Daniels, *Director*
EMP: 10
SALES (est): 217.5K **Privately Held**
SIC: 7371 Computer software development & applications

(G-6579)
FILIPINO HERITG & ARTS MUSEUM
58 S Skyward Dr (19713-2843)
PHONE 302 731-5899
Manuelita Camomot, *Exec Dir*
EMP: 5
SALES: 15.4K **Privately Held**
SIC: 8412 Museum

(G-6580)
FIRST CLASS HEATING AC
6 Shea Way (19713-3422)
PHONE 302 834-1036
Tom Minio, *President*
EMP: 30
SALES (est): 2.9MM **Privately Held**
SIC: 1711 Warm air heating & air conditioning contractor

(G-6581)
FIRST STATE ANESTHESIA SVCS
537 Stanton Christiana Rd # 201 (19713-2148)
PHONE 302 225-2990
Prasad Kanchana, *Principal*
Kellie McFadden, *Buyer*
Denise Drolet, *Manager*
Susan Suglia, *Assistant*
EMP: 4 **EST:** 2007
SALES (est): 174.3K **Privately Held**
SIC: 8011 Anesthesiologist

(G-6582)
FIRST STATE CARPENTRY LLC
14 Thomas Ln N (19711-4865)
PHONE 302 738-8849
EMP: 6 **EST:** 1999
SALES (est): 410K **Privately Held**
SIC: 1751 Carpentry Contractor

(G-6583)
FIRST STATE CONTAINER LLC
100 Lake Dr Ste 106 (19702-3351)
PHONE 603 888-1315
EMP: 26
SALES (est): 3.3MM **Privately Held**
SIC: 3085 Plastics bottles
PA: Carr Management, Inc.
1 Tara Blvd Ste 303
Nashua NH 03062

(G-6584)
FIRST STATE PEDIATRICS LLC (PA)
210 Christiana Med Ctr (19702-1652)
PHONE 302 292-1559
John W Murphy, *Principal*
EMP: 13 **EST:** 2009
SALES (est): 1.8MM **Privately Held**
SIC: 8011 Pediatrician

GEOGRAPHIC SECTION

Newark - New Castle County (G-6616)

(G-6585)
FIRST STATE PRESS LLC
14 Eileen Dr (19711-3814)
PHONE...................302 731-9058
John Micklos, *Principal*
EMP: 4
SALES (est): 114.9K **Privately Held**
SIC: 2711 Newspapers: publishing only, not printed on site

(G-6586)
FIRST STATE SURGERY CENTER LLC
Also Called: First State Orthopaedics
1000 Twin C Ln Ste 200 (19713-2142)
PHONE...................302 683-0700
William A Newcomb, *Partner*
Lucy Knappenberger,
Michael J Axe,
Alex P Bodenstab,
Evan H Crain,
EMP: 13 **EST:** 2000
SQ FT: 12,000
SALES (est): 3.3MM **Privately Held**
SIC: 8011 Surgeon

(G-6587)
FIRST STUDENT INC
750 Stanton Christiana Rd (19713-2028)
PHONE...................302 995-9607
Joy Miller, *Branch Mgr*
EMP: 150
SALES (corp-wide): 9.1B **Privately Held**
WEB: www.firststudentinc.com
SIC: 4142 4151 Bus charter service, except local; school buses
HQ: First Student, Inc.
600 Vine St Ste 1400
Cincinnati OH 45202

(G-6588)
FISCAL ASSOCIATES
16 Fairfield Dr (19711-2767)
PHONE...................302 894-0500
G William Bailey, *Principal*
EMP: 10
SALES (est): 399.6K **Privately Held**
WEB: www.fiscal-associates.com
SIC: 8742 Business consultant

(G-6589)
FIT ME BY CRYSTAL
1600 Helen Dr Unit 205 (19702-1685)
PHONE...................302 573-1235
Crystal Mitchell, *CEO*
EMP: 1
SALES: 80K **Privately Held**
SIC: 2339 Athletic clothing: women's, misses' & juniors'

(G-6590)
FIVE 1 FIVE ICE SPORTS GROUP L
101 John F Campbell Rd (19711-5457)
PHONE...................302 266-0777
EMP: 4
SALES (est): 38.1K **Privately Held**
SIC: 7997 Ice sports

(G-6591)
FIVE IN ONE OVEN INC
200 Continental Dr # 401 (19713-4334)
PHONE...................888 401-3911
John McDavitt, *President*
EMP: 5
SALES (est): 216K **Privately Held**
SIC: 3631 Microwave ovens, including portable: household

(G-6592)
FIVE STAR QUALITY CARE INC
Also Called: Somerford House Newark
501 S Harmony Rd (19713-3338)
PHONE...................302 266-9255
Brenda Cuart, *Branch Mgr*
EMP: 6 **Publicly Held**
WEB: www.fivestarqualitycare.com
SIC: 8051 Skilled nursing care facilities
PA: Five Star Senior Living Inc.
400 Centre St
Newton MA 02458

(G-6593)
FIVE STAR QUALITY CARE INC
Also Called: Millcroft
255 Possum Park Rd (19711-3877)
PHONE...................302 366-0160
Goeff Henry, *Manager*
EMP: 8 **Publicly Held**
WEB: www.fivestarqualitycare.com
SIC: 8051 Skilled nursing care facilities
PA: Five Star Senior Living Inc.
400 Centre St
Newton MA 02458

(G-6594)
FIVE STAR SENIOR LIVING INC
Also Called: Somerford Place Newark
4175 Ogletown Rd (19713)
PHONE...................302 283-0540
Sue Russ, *Branch Mgr*
EMP: 63 **Publicly Held**
WEB: www.fivestarqualitycare.com
SIC: 8051 Skilled nursing care facilities
PA: Five Star Senior Living Inc.
400 Centre St
Newton MA 02458

(G-6595)
FLAPDOODLES INC (PA)
725 Dawson Dr (19713-3413)
P.O. Box 4675, Wilmington (19807-4675)
PHONE...................302 731-9793
Marc A Ham, *President*
Carole A Bieber, *Vice Pres*
EMP: 92
SQ FT: 60,000
SALES (est): 6.3MM **Privately Held**
SIC: 2253 5137 Knit outerwear mills; children's goods

(G-6596)
FMC CORPORATION
Also Called: F M C Biopolymore
1301 Ogletown Rd (19711-5496)
PHONE...................302 451-0100
James Cronin, *Opers-Prdtn-Mfg*
Signe Kleinot, *Administration*
EMP: 100
SALES (corp-wide): 4.7B **Publicly Held**
WEB: www.fmc.com
SIC: 2823 2834 Cellulosic manmade fibers; pharmaceutical preparations
PA: Fmc Corporation
2929 Walnut St
Philadelphia PA 19104
215 299-6000

(G-6597)
FOCUS SOLUTIONS SERVICES INC
262 Chapman Rd Ste 200 (19702-5442)
PHONE...................302 318-1345
Troy Husser, *CEO*
Darrell Hervey, *President*
EMP: 10
SALES (est): 93.8K **Privately Held**
SIC: 7349 8744 Cleaning service, industrial or commercial; facilities support services

(G-6598)
FOOD BANK OF DELAWARE INC (PA)
222 Lake Dr (19702-3319)
PHONE...................302 292-1305
Patricia Bebe, *President*
Naty Moreta, *Partner*
Erik Klair, *Opers Staff*
Sanjay Malik, *Finance Dir*
Kim Turner, *Comms Dir*
EMP: 50
SQ FT: 16,000
SALES: 21.9MM **Privately Held**
WEB: www.fbd.org
SIC: 8399 Community development groups

(G-6599)
FOOD FOR PETS USA INC
2915 Ogletown Rd Ste 2846 (19713-1927)
PHONE...................514 831-4876
Dominique Martin, *Principal*
EMP: 5 **EST:** 2018
SALES: 650K **Privately Held**
SIC: 5149 Pet foods

(G-6600)
FOODLINER INC
206 Hansen Ct (19713-1150)
PHONE...................302 368-4204
Bob Houston, *Branch Mgr*
EMP: 94
SALES (corp-wide): 95.7MM **Privately Held**
SIC: 4213 Trucking, except local
PA: Foodliner, Inc.
2099 Southpark Ct Ste 1
Dubuque IA 52003
563 584-2670

(G-6601)
FOOT STEPS TWO HEAVEN DAYCARE
606 Lisbeth Rd (19713-1742)
PHONE...................302 738-5519
EMP: 5
SALES (est): 170K **Privately Held**
SIC: 8351 Child day care services

(G-6602)
FORESEE PHARMACEUTICALS INC
3 Innovation Way Ste 240 (19711-5456)
PHONE...................302 396-5243
Jennifer Yen, *Administration*
EMP: 4 **EST:** 2014
SALES (est): 235.6K **Privately Held**
SIC: 5122 Pharmaceuticals

(G-6603)
FOREST OAK ELEMENTARY PTA
55 S Meadowood Dr (19711-6755)
PHONE...................302 540-2873
Diane Dambach, *Principal*
EMP: 6
SALES: 66.7K **Privately Held**
SIC: 8641 Parent-teachers' association

(G-6604)
FOREVER INC
Also Called: Fulton Paper Co
334 Suburban Dr (19711-3599)
PHONE...................302 368-1440
Jay Pirolo, *Manager*
EMP: 4
SALES (corp-wide): 2.8MM **Privately Held**
SIC: 5943 5947 5113 Stationery stores; party favors; industrial & personal service paper; bags, paper & disposable plastic; paper & products, wrapping or coarse
PA: Forever, Inc.
1006 W 27th St
Wilmington DE 19802
302 594-0400

(G-6605)
FOREWINDS HOSPITALITY LLC (HQ)
507 Thompson Station Rd (19711-7504)
PHONE...................302 368-6640
Ron Winarck,
EMP: 9
SALES (est): 4.4MM
SALES (corp-wide): 35.8MM **Privately Held**
SIC: 7997 Golf club, membership
PA: Sawyer Property Management Of Maryland, Inc.
9658 Baltimore Ave # 300
College Park MD 20740
781 449-6650

(G-6606)
FORMAL AFFAIRS INC
257 E Main St 100 (19711-7382)
PHONE...................302 737-1519
Christopher Locke, *President*
EMP: 12
SALES (est): 591.5K **Privately Held**
SIC: 7299 5699 Tuxedo rental; formal wear

(G-6607)
FORTE SPORTS INCORPORATED
314 E Main St Ste 1 (19711-7195)
P.O. Box 422 (19715-0422)
PHONE...................302 731-0776
James L Manniso, *CEO*
Mark Manniso, *President*
EMP: 5
SQ FT: 3,600
SALES (est): 681.3K **Privately Held**
WEB: www.fortesports.com
SIC: 3069 Toys, rubber

(G-6608)
FOUR POINTS BY SHERATON
56 S Old Baltimore Pike (19702-1596)
PHONE...................302 266-6600
Bryan Chiaramante, *General Mgr*
EMP: 6
SALES (est): 329.7K **Privately Held**
SIC: 7011 Hotels & motels

(G-6609)
FOXFIRE INDUSTRIES LLC
2035 Sunset Lake Rd B2 (19702-2600)
PHONE...................817 602-4900
Jared McCluskey,
EMP: 1 **EST:** 2016
SALES (est): 32.2K **Privately Held**
SIC: 7372 7371 Application computer software; business oriented computer software; computer software writing services

(G-6610)
FOXWOOD APTS REHAB
15 Fox Hall Ofc (19711-5941)
PHONE...................302 366-8790
Sandy Esposito, *Manager*
EMP: 4
SALES (est): 368.1K **Privately Held**
SIC: 6513 Apartment hotel operation

(G-6611)
FRANCHISE COMMAND INC
40 E Main St Ste 70 (19711-4639)
PHONE...................714 832-7767
John Simons, *CEO*
Brent Slezak, *CTO*
EMP: 35
SALES: 500K **Privately Held**
SIC: 7371 Computer software development & applications

(G-6612)
FRANKLIN JESTER PA
603 Lisbeth Rd (19713-1741)
PHONE...................302 368-3080
Franklin Jester, *Owner*
EMP: 5
SALES (est): 362.5K **Privately Held**
SIC: 2899 Patching plaster, household

(G-6613)
FRAUNHOFER USA INC
Also Called: Fraunhofer Center For Molecula
9 Innovation Way (19711-5449)
PHONE...................302 369-1708
Vidadi Yusibov, *Exec Dir*
Stephen Streatfield, *Director*
EMP: 52
SALES (corp-wide): 2.7B **Privately Held**
SIC: 8731 Biotechnical research, commercial
HQ: Fraunhofer Usa, Inc.
44792 Helm St
Plymouth MI 48170

(G-6614)
FREDERICK K FUNK
24 Polly Drummond Hill Rd (19711-5703)
PHONE...................302 368-6233
Frederick K Funk, *Owner*
EMP: 4
SALES (est): 485.5K **Privately Held**
WEB: www.fredfunkesq.com
SIC: 8111 General practice attorney, lawyer

(G-6615)
FREEDOM CYCLE LLC
1110 Ogletown Rd (19711-5416)
PHONE...................302 286-6900
Frank Lamaina,
EMP: 5
SALES (est): 377.5K **Privately Held**
SIC: 7699 Motorcycle repair service

(G-6616)
FREEDOM DENTAL MANAGEMENT INC
1290 Peoples Plz (19702-5701)
PHONE...................302 836-3750

Newark - New Castle County (G-6617) GEOGRAPHIC SECTION

EMP: 5 EST: 2015
SALES (est): 145.9K **Privately Held**
SIC: 8021 Offices & clinics of dentists

(G-6617)
FREEDOM MATERIALS
721 Dawson Dr (19713-3413)
PHONE..................................302 281-0085
Silvio Ferrari, *Principal*
EMP: 6
SALES (est): 2.7MM **Privately Held**
SIC: 5099 Firearms & ammunition, except sporting

(G-6618)
FREEDOM MORTGAGE CORPORATION
220 Continental Dr # 315 (19713-4314)
PHONE..................................302 368-7100
John Turner, *General Mgr*
EMP: 17 **Privately Held**
WEB: www.fhmc.com
SIC: 6162 Mortgage bankers
PA: Freedom Mortgage Corporation
   907 Pleasant Valley Ave # 3
   Mount Laurel NJ 08054

(G-6619)
FREELEE FOUNDATION
1400 Helen Dr Unit 104 (19702-1678)
PHONE..................................302 607-8053
Keonna Freeman, *President*
Varleisha Gibbs, *President*
Lachema Manigault, *President*
Renae Pritchett, *President*
Vacinqua Rogers, *President*
EMP: 5
SALES (est): 89.6K **Privately Held**
SIC: 8641 Civic social & fraternal associations

(G-6620)
FREMONT HALL
82 Possum Park Rd (19711-3858)
PHONE..................................302 731-2431
Richard Reissmann, *Pastor*
Elaine Montoro, *Manager*
R Elaine Montoro, *Manager*
EMP: 7
SALES (est): 128K **Privately Held**
SIC: 7299 Banquet hall facilities

(G-6621)
FRESENIUS MEDICAL CARE VERO BE
Also Called: Rcc Christiana
63 University Plz (19702-1549)
PHONE..................................302 453-8834
Allison Jenks, *Manager*
EMP: 50
SALES (corp-wide): 18.3B **Privately Held**
WEB: www.bamap.com
SIC: 8092 Kidney dialysis centers
HQ: National Medical Care, Inc.
   920 Winter St Ste A
   Waltham MA 02451

(G-6622)
FRESENIUS USA INC
61 University Plz (19702-1549)
PHONE..................................302 455-0454
EMP: 20
SALES (corp-wide): 20.9B **Privately Held**
SIC: 8092 Kidney Dialysis Centers
HQ: Fresenius Usa, Inc.
   4040 Nelson Ave
   Concord CA 94520
   925 288-4218

(G-6623)
FRESH START TRANSFORMATIONS
4604 Tracy Dr (19702-8104)
PHONE..................................302 219-0221
Joyce Nichols, *CEO*
EMP: 5
SALES (est): 150.2K **Privately Held**
SIC: 7299 7389 Personal appearance services;

(G-6624)
FRIENDS AND SIGN
61 Matthews Rd (19713-2555)
PHONE..................................302 368-4794
Erin Barthel, *Principal*

EMP: 1
SALES (est): 46K **Privately Held**
SIC: 3993 Signs & advertising specialties

(G-6625)
FROM GROUND UP CONSTRUCTION
26 Evergreen Dr (19702-3712)
PHONE..................................302 747-0996
James E Furlow Jr, *Principal*
EMP: 7
SALES (est): 462.9K **Privately Held**
SIC: 1542 Nonresidential construction

(G-6626)
FRONTIER SCIENTIFIC INC
Also Called: Frontier Agricultural Sciences
601 Interchange Blvd (19711-3561)
PHONE..................................302 266-6891
Kelly Sauder, *Principal*
EMP: 1
SALES (corp-wide): 10.2MM **Privately Held**
SIC: 8731 2899 Biological research; chemical preparations
PA: Frontier Scientific, Inc.
   195 S 700 W
   Logan UT
   435 753-1901

(G-6627)
FRONTIER SCIENTIFIC SVCS INC
Also Called: Asdi
601 Interchange Blvd (19711-3561)
PHONE..................................302 266-6891
W Tim Miller, *President*
Kabana Perkins, *Senior VP*
Megan Black, *Project Mgr*
Will Ortiz, *Opers Mgr*
Anthony Guida, *Site Mgr*
EMP: 2
SALES (est): 55.4K **Privately Held**
SIC: 8731 2899 Commercial research laboratory; chemical preparations

(G-6628)
FULTON BANK NATIONAL ASSN
Also Called: Fulton Financial Advisors
281 E Main St (19711-7315)
PHONE..................................302 737-7766
Deborah Blyskal, *Branch Mgr*
Aaron Wright, *Manager*
EMP: 5
SALES (corp-wide): 954MM **Publicly Held**
SIC: 6022 State commercial banks
HQ: Fulton Bank, National Association
   1 Penn Sq Ste 1 # 1
   Lancaster PA 17602
   717 581-3166

(G-6629)
FUNSTEP INC
1805 Capitol Trl (19711-5721)
PHONE..................................302 731-9618
Kim Libus, *Director*
EMP: 15
SALES (est): 505.5K **Privately Held**
WEB: www.funstep.org
SIC: 8351 Preschool center

(G-6630)
FUTURETECH INV GROUP INC
Also Called: Future Option Trading Company
12 Timber Creek Ln (19711-2606)
PHONE..................................302 476-9529
Wayne L Branch, *Ch of Bd*
EMP: 10
SQ FT: 1,500
SALES: 2MM **Privately Held**
SIC: 6211 Traders, security

(G-6631)
G LEIGH COOK DMD
16 Peddlers Row (19702-1525)
PHONE..................................302 453-8700
EMP: 12
SALES (est): 256.6K **Privately Held**
SIC: 8021 Dentist's Office

(G-6632)
GAI COMMUNICATIONS INC
560 Peoples Plz 136 (19702-4798)
PHONE..................................609 254-1470

Miguel Graham, *President*
EMP: 2
SALES (est): 99.7K **Privately Held**
SIC: 4899 Communication services

(G-6633)
GALLOWAY ELECTRIC CO INC
19 Albe Dr (19702-1321)
PHONE..................................302 453-8385
J Paul Galloway Jr, *President*
Janice Galloway, *Corp Secy*
Ronald Galloway, *Vice Pres*
EMP: 15 EST: 1948
SALES (est): 50K **Privately Held**
SIC: 1731 Electrical work

(G-6634)
GALLOWAY LEASING INC
19 Albe Dr (19702-1321)
PHONE..................................302 453-8385
J Paul Galloway Jr, *President*
Ronald Galloway, *Vice Pres*
EMP: 16
SALES (est): 950K **Privately Held**
SIC: 6531 Real estate leasing & rentals

(G-6635)
GALMAN GROUP INC
Also Called: Buckingham Pl Twnhuse Aprtmnts
25b Windsor Cir (19702-9430)
PHONE..................................302 737-5550
John Chelsey, *Property Mgr*
Gina Plunto, *Manager*
EMP: 8
SALES (est): 647.3K **Privately Held**
SIC: 6513 Apartment building operators

(G-6636)
GAMERS4GAMERS LLC
40 E Main St Ste 649 (19711-4639)
PHONE..................................302 722-6289
Zenijanin Vikovic,
EMP: 6
SALES (est): 123.5K **Privately Held**
SIC: 7371 7389 Computer software development & applications;

(G-6637)
GAMESTOP INC
326 Suburban Dr (19711-3599)
PHONE..................................302 266-7362
Bryan McMilina, *Manager*
EMP: 10
SALES (corp-wide): 8.2B **Publicly Held**
WEB: www.babbages.com
SIC: 5092 5734 5945 Video games; computer & software stores; hobby, toy & game shops
HQ: Gamestop, Inc.
   625 Westport Pkwy
   Grapevine TX 76051

(G-6638)
GARAGE
132 Christiana Mall (19702-3202)
PHONE..................................302 453-1930
EMP: 2
SALES (est): 50.8K **Privately Held**
SIC: 5651 5632 5621 2299 Family clothing stores; women's dancewear, hosiery & lingerie; women's clothing stores; jute & flax textile products

(G-6639)
GARILE INC
Also Called: Sir Speedy
311 Ruthar Dr (19711-8016)
PHONE..................................302 366-0848
Alan Gardner, *President*
Harvey Banning, *Principal*
John Riley, *Corp Secy*
Aileen Huester, *Vice Pres*
Brynn Hudson, *Sales Executive*
EMP: 20
SQ FT: 3,200
SALES (est): 3.8MM **Privately Held**
WEB: www.sirspeedyofnewark.com
SIC: 2752 7334 2791 2789 Commercial printing, lithographic; photocopying & duplicating services; typesetting; bookbinding & related work; secretarial & court reporting

(G-6640)
GARY M MUNCH INC
Also Called: Sign-A-Rama
995 S Chapel St Ste 1 (19713-3441)
PHONE..................................302 525-8301
Gary M Munch, *President*
Barbara Munch, *Corp Secy*
EMP: 3
SQ FT: 4,000
SALES (est): 44.1K **Privately Held**
WEB: www.signaramaofnewark.com
SIC: 3993 Signs & advertising specialties

(G-6641)
GASTROENTEROLOGY ASSOCIATES PA (PA)
4745 Ogletown Stanton Rd # 134 (19713-1342)
PHONE..................................302 738-5300
Ira Lobiz MD, *President*
Ira Lobis MD, *Partner*
Warren G Butt, *Vice Pres*
Bernard Hamrowitz, *Vice Pres*
Oscar J Martinez, *Vice Pres*
EMP: 20 EST: 1970
SALES (est): 3.2MM **Privately Held**
SIC: 8011 Gastronomist

(G-6642)
GAURI INC
306 Suburban Dr (19711-3599)
PHONE..................................302 731-5300
Piyush Upadhyay, *President*
EMP: 4
SALES (est): 258K **Privately Held**
SIC: 0132 Tobacco

(G-6643)
GEM-GRADUALLY EXPANDING MINDS
523 Concord Bridge Pl (19702-5205)
PHONE..................................302 322-3701
Kenyesta Haughton, *President*
EMP: 6
SALES: 400K **Privately Held**
SIC: 8322 Individual & family services

(G-6644)
GENERAL ELECTRIC COMPANY
400 Bellevue Rd (19713-3432)
PHONE..................................302 631-1300
Katrina Dean, *Branch Mgr*
EMP: 240
SALES (corp-wide): 121.6B **Publicly Held**
SIC: 3724 Aircraft engines & engine parts
PA: General Electric Company
   5 Necco St
   Boston MA 02210
   617 443-3000

(G-6645)
GENERAL SEPARATION TECH INC
Also Called: Gs - Tek
625 Dawson Dr Ste A (19713-3433)
PHONE..................................302 533-5646
Zhenghua Ji, *President*
Sean Wang, *Sales Staff*
Lu Wang, *Office Mgr*
EMP: 4
SALES (est): 133.1K **Privately Held**
WEB: www.abel-industries.com
SIC: 7699 Laboratory instrument repair

(G-6646)
GENERATION CONSULTANTS LLC
Also Called: Codemessaging
362 Wedgewood Rd Ste 2a (19711-2053)
PHONE..................................302 722-4884
Christopher Gorzynski, *General Mgr*
EMP: 4
SALES: 50K **Privately Held**
SIC: 4822 Telegraph & other communications

(G-6647)
GENEX TECHNOLOGIES INC
100 Lake Dr Ste 6 (19702-3346)
PHONE..................................302 266-6161
Pushpavathi Kanumri, *President*
Sushanta Basu, *COO*
Venkat Kanumuri, *Vice Pres*
EMP: 76

SQ FT: 1,200
SALES: 4.4MM **Privately Held**
SIC: **7373** 7372 7371 Computer integrated systems design; publishers' computer software; software programming applications

(G-6648)
GEORGE P STEWART
488 Walther Rd (19702-2902)
PHONE.................................302 737-4927
George Stewart, *Principal*
EMP: 5
SALES (est): 360.1K **Privately Held**
SIC: **1611** Surfacing & paving

(G-6649)
GEOTECH LLC
13 Shull Dr (19711-7715)
PHONE.................................302 353-9769
Victoria Esposito, *Mng Member*
EMP: 9
SALES: 750K **Privately Held**
SIC: **1795** 1799 4212 Wrecking & demolition work; building site preparation; dump truck haulage

(G-6650)
GERIS AUTO FINANCIAL SERVICES
23 Geneva Ct Apt B4 (19702-2619)
PHONE.................................302 660-9719
Geraldine Rilley, *Partner*
EMP: 6
SALES (est): 271.5K **Privately Held**
SIC: **6163** Loan agents

(G-6651)
GI SPECIALISTS OF DE
2600 Glasgow Ave Ste 106 (19702-5703)
PHONE.................................302 832-1545
EMP: 5
SALES (est): 399.3K **Privately Held**
SIC: **8011** Gastronomist

(G-6652)
GIBELLINO CONSTRUCTION CO
1213 Old Coochs Bridge Rd (19713-2333)
PHONE.................................302 455-0500
Aldo Gibellino, *President*
Diane C Gibellino, *Analyst*
EMP: 5
SALES (est): 979.2K **Privately Held**
SIC: **1521** Repairing fire damage, single-family houses

(G-6653)
GIESELA INC
2035 Sunset Lake Rd B2 (19702-2600)
PHONE.................................855 556-4338
Shikhir Arora, *President*
Simon Berger, *Vice Pres*
EMP: 2
SALES (est): 56.5K **Privately Held**
SIC: **7372** 7371 7389 Application computer software; computer software development;

(G-6654)
GIFT SOLUTIONS LLC
16 Townsend Rd (19711-7904)
PHONE.................................585 317-4465
James Corbett, *President*
EMP: 4
SALES (est): 198.5K
SALES (corp-wide): 5.8B **Publicly Held**
SIC: **8748** Business consulting
HQ: First Data Corporation
225 Liberty St Fl 29
New York NY 10281
800 735-3362

(G-6655)
GINCH GONCH CORP
2915 Ogletown Rd (19713-1927)
PHONE.................................713 240-9900
Robert Chouecke, *President*
Neil Rohr, *Treasurer*
EMP: 2
SALES: 2.5MM **Privately Held**
SIC: **2254** Knit underwear mills

(G-6656)
GIRL SCOUTS OF THE CHEASAPEA (PA)
225 Old Baltimore Pike (19702-8409)
PHONE.................................302 456-7150
Anne T Hogan, *CEO*
EMP: 40
SQ FT: 20,000
SALES: 6.6MM **Privately Held**
SIC: **8322** 8641 Youth center; Girl Scout organization

(G-6657)
GIVFOLIO LLC (PA)
2035 Sunset Lake Rd B2 (19702-2600)
PHONE.................................213 949-1964
Amanda Yiu, *CEO*
EMP: 2
SALES (est): 231.5K **Privately Held**
SIC: **7372** Application computer software

(G-6658)
GJ CHALFANT WELDING
1123 Mayflower Dr (19711-6822)
PHONE.................................302 545-6404
Greg Chalfant, *Owner*
EMP: 1
SALES (est): 56.4K **Privately Held**
SIC: **7692** Welding repair

(G-6659)
GJV INC (PA)
Also Called: UPS
4142 Ogletown Stanton Rd (19713-4169)
PHONE.................................302 455-1600
Greg Vaghini, *President*
Jason Warden, *Manager*
EMP: 5
SALES (est): 598.4K **Privately Held**
SIC: **7389** 4731 Mailbox rental & related service; freight transportation arrangement

(G-6660)
GLASGOW CHIROPRACTIC
650 Plaza Dr (19702-6369)
PHONE.................................302 453-4043
Stacy Cohen DC, *President*
EMP: 4 **EST:** 2001
SALES (est): 497.1K **Privately Held**
WEB: www.glasgowchiropractic.com
SIC: **8041** Offices & clinics of chiropractors

(G-6661)
GLASGOW MEDICAL ASSOCIATES PA
2600 Glasgow Ave Ste 106 (19702-5703)
PHONE.................................302 836-3539
EMP: 9 **Privately Held**
SIC: **8011** Surgeon
PA: Glasgow Medical Associates Pa
2600 Glasgow Ave Ste 126
Newark DE 19702

(G-6662)
GLASGOW MEDICAL ASSOCIATES PA
2600 Glasgow Ave Ste 100 (19702-5703)
PHONE.................................302 836-8350
Arthur Kretz, *Branch Mgr*
EMP: 5 **Privately Held**
SIC: **6552** Subdividers & developers
PA: Glasgow Medical Associates Pa
2600 Glasgow Ave Ste 126
Newark DE 19702

(G-6663)
GLASGOW MEDICAL ASSOCIATES PA (PA)
Also Called: Glasgow Medical Center
2600 Glasgow Ave Ste 126 (19702-4778)
PHONE.................................302 836-8350
Curt Blacklock Do, *President*
John O'Neil Do, *Vice Pres*
Jean Lockwood, *Manager*
Janine Orth, *Nursing Dir*
Arthur Kretz, *Officer*
EMP: 18
SALES (est): 3.8MM **Privately Held**
SIC: **8011** Physicians' office, including specialists

(G-6664)
GLASGOW MEDICAL CENTER LLC
Also Called: Medical Aid Unit At Christiana
2600 Glasgow Ave Ste 226 (19702-5709)
PHONE.................................302 836-8350
Arthur Kretz, *COO*
EMP: 114
SALES (est): 3.8MM **Privately Held**
WEB: www.glasgowmedicalcenter.com
SIC: **8011** Clinic, operated by physicians
PA: Glasgow Medical Associates Pa
2600 Glasgow Ave Ste 126
Newark DE 19702

(G-6665)
GLOBAL AIR STRATEGY INC
40 E Main St Ste 275 (19711-4639)
PHONE.................................302 229-5889
Luiz Sette, *President*
S Hughes, *Principal*
EMP: 5
SALES (est): 298.7K **Privately Held**
SIC: **3728** Aircraft parts & equipment

(G-6666)
GLOBAL INSTITUTE
10 Eileen Dr (19711-3814)
P.O. Box 7137 (19714-7137)
PHONE.................................732 776-7360
Susanne Richert, *Principal*
E S Richert, *Real Est Agnt*
EMP: 5
SALES (est): 318.4K **Privately Held**
SIC: **8733** Noncommercial research organizations

(G-6667)
GLOBAL RECRUITERS NETWORK INC
Also Called: Grn Wilmington
3202 Drummond Plz (19711-5746)
PHONE.................................302 455-9500
Jamie Mosberg, *Principal*
EMP: 4
SALES (est): 406.4K **Privately Held**
SIC: **7361** Executive placement

(G-6668)
GO AHEAD MAKE MY RING
1 Great Circle Rd (19711-2336)
PHONE.................................302 235-8172
Friday Nelson, *Owner*
EMP: 1
SALES (est): 57.3K **Privately Held**
SIC: **3961** Costume jewelry, ex. precious metal & semiprecious stones

(G-6669)
GOBLIN TECHNOLOGIES LLC
63 Bay Blvd (19702-4838)
PHONE.................................844 733-5724
Stephen Hoops, *CEO*
EMP: 5
SALES (est): 82.9K **Privately Held**
SIC: **7374** Data processing & preparation

(G-6670)
GOLD LABEL TRANSPORTATION LLC
36 Cardenti Ct (19702-6841)
PHONE.................................302 668-2383
Corey Brisco-Bey, *Principal*
EMP: 5
SALES (est): 155.9K **Privately Held**
SIC: **4111** Airport transportation

(G-6671)
GOLD STAR SERVICES
Also Called: Honeywell Authorized Dealer
665 Dawson Dr Ste A (19713-3434)
PHONE.................................302 376-7677
Shane Donahue, *President*
EMP: 13
SQ FT: 3,000
SALES: 2MM **Privately Held**
SIC: **1711** Heating & air conditioning contractors

(G-6672)
GOLDEN MERGER CORP
Also Called: VCA Hockessin Animal Hospital
245 E Cleveland Ave (19711-3710)
PHONE.................................302 737-8100
Shirley Lockhart, *Manager*
Scott Amtsberg, *Director*
EMP: 10
SALES (corp-wide): 37.6B **Privately Held**
WEB: www.goldenlegend.com
SIC: **0742** Animal hospital services, pets & other animal specialties
HQ: Golden Merger Corp
12401 W Olympic Blvd
Los Angeles CA 90064

(G-6673)
GOLO LLC
630 Churchmans Rd Ste 200 (19702-1944)
P.O. Box 247, Bear (19701-0247)
PHONE.................................302 635-7245
Chris Lundin, *Mng Member*
EMP: 4 **EST:** 2010
SALES (est): 512.8K **Privately Held**
SIC: **8093** Weight loss clinic, with medical staff

(G-6674)
GOODALES NATURALS
84 Warren Dr (19702-6822)
PHONE.................................302 743-6455
EMP: 2
SALES (est): 128K **Privately Held**
SIC: **2844** Toilet preparations

(G-6675)
GOODCHILD INC
6 Brookhill Dr (19702-1395)
PHONE.................................302 368-1681
Paul R Goodchild Sr, *President*
Paula Henderson Newton, *Admin Sec*
EMP: 6
SQ FT: 11,500
SALES (est): 480K **Privately Held**
WEB: www.goodchild.com
SIC: **7539** 5015 7549 Automotive repair shops; automotive supplies, used; towing services

(G-6676)
GOODMAN MANUFACTURING CO LP
230 Executive Dr Ste 5 (19702-3338)
PHONE.................................302 894-1010
Matt Brubraker, *Manager*
EMP: 6 **Privately Held**
SIC: **5199** Advertising specialties
HQ: Goodman Manufacturing Company, Lp
5151 San Felipe St # 500
Houston TX 77056
713 861-2500

(G-6677)
GOODYEAR TIRE & RUBBER COMPANY
1929 Kirkwood Hwy (19711-5725)
PHONE.................................302 737-2461
Chris Lee, *Branch Mgr*
EMP: 5
SALES (corp-wide): 15.4B **Publicly Held**
SIC: **5531** 7538 Automotive tires; general automotive repair shops
PA: The Goodyear Tire & Rubber Company
200 E Innovation Way
Akron OH 44316
330 796-2121

(G-6678)
GORDON C HONIG DMD PA (PA)
Also Called: Honig, Gordon C DMD
2707 Kirkwood Hwy (19711-6828)
PHONE.................................302 737-6333
Gordon C Honig, *Owner*
Chantel Imran, *Obstetrician*
EMP: 5
SALES (est): 897.1K **Privately Held**
WEB: www.honigortho.com
SIC: **8021** Orthodontist

(G-6679)
GOVERNMENT MRKTPLACE LTD LBLTY
200 Continental Dr 401o (19713-4334)
PHONE.................................302 297-9694
Steven Stone, *Opers Staff*
Tanya Warren, —
EMP: 44
SALES (est): 3.8MM **Privately Held**
SIC: **8742** Business consultant; marketing consulting services

Newark - New Castle County (G-6680) — GEOGRAPHIC SECTION

(G-6680)
GRAHAM PACKAGING CO EUROPE LLC
1601 Ogletown Rd (19711-5425)
PHONE....................302 453-9464
Bob Doyle, *Manager*
EMP: 40
SALES (corp-wide): 14.1MM **Privately Held**
WEB: www.liquidcontainer.com
SIC: 3089 Plastic containers, except foam
HQ: Graham Packaging Company Europe Llc
   2401 Pleasant Valley Rd # 2
   York PA 17402

(G-6681)
GRANT PHARMACEUTICALS INC
200 Continental Dr # 401 (19713-4334)
PHONE....................855 364-7268
Michael Banks, *Principal*
EMP: 2
SALES (est): 74.4K **Privately Held**
SIC: 2834 Pharmaceutical preparations

(G-6682)
GRASS BUSTERS LANDSCAPING CO
935 Rahway Dr (19711-2687)
PHONE....................302 292-1166
Richard Crouse, *President*
EMP: 50
SALES (est): 5.7MM **Privately Held**
SIC: 0782 Landscape contractors

(G-6683)
GRAVER SEPARATIONS INC
200 Lake Dr (19702-3327)
PHONE....................302 731-1700
Angelo Pantelao, *President*
Robert Gluth, *Treasurer*
Patrick Allen, *Admin Sec*
EMP: 4
SQ FT: 6,000
SALES (est): 1.2MM
SALES (corp-wide): 225.3B **Publicly Held**
SIC: 3569 Filters
HQ: Graver Technologies Llc
   200 Lake Dr
   Newark DE 19702

(G-6684)
GRAVER TECHNOLOGIES LLC (DH)
Also Called: Liquid Filter Division
200 Lake Dr (19702-3327)
PHONE....................302 731-1700
John Schroeder, *President*
John J Goody, *Director*
Robert Webb, *Admin Sec*
◆ EMP: 200
SQ FT: 43,000
SALES (est): 59MM
SALES (corp-wide): 225.3B **Publicly Held**
WEB: www.gravertech.com
SIC: 5999 5074 3589 Water purification equipment; water purification equipment; water treatment equipment, industrial
HQ: Marmon Industrial Llc
   181 W Madison St Fl 26
   Chicago IL 60602
   312 372-9500

(G-6685)
GREATER NEWARK BASEBALL L
P.O. Box 7212 (19714-7212)
PHONE....................302 635-0562
EMP: 4
SALES (est): 61.6K **Privately Held**
SIC: 7997 Baseball club, except professional & semi-professional

(G-6686)
GREEN PAGES TECHNOLOGIES INC
2035 Sunset Lake Rd B2 (19702-2600)
PHONE....................626 497-6363
Andy Tai, *Principal*
EMP: 1

SALES (est): 42.6K **Privately Held**
SIC: 2741

(G-6687)
GREENLEAF TURF SOLUTIONS INC
9 Albe Dr Ste C (19702-1380)
PHONE....................302 731-1075
David Greenleaf, *Principal*
EMP: 4
SALES (est): 472.5K **Privately Held**
SIC: 0782 Turf installation services, except artificial

(G-6688)
GREG SMITH EQUIPMENT SALES
250 Executive Dr Ste 1 (19702-3336)
PHONE....................302 894-9333
Gavin Smith, *Owner*
EMP: 6
SALES (corp-wide): 5.5MM **Privately Held**
SIC: 5013 Tools & equipment, automotive
PA: Greg Smith Equipment Sales Inc
   5800 Massachusetts Ave
   Indianapolis IN 46218
   317 333-8444

(G-6689)
GREGORY D THACKER
Also Called: Glass Works Company, The
20 Lamatan Rd (19711-2316)
PHONE....................302 239-0879
Gregory D Thacker, *Owner*
EMP: 1
SALES (est): 68K **Privately Held**
SIC: 3231 1793 3229 Leaded glass; stained glass: made from purchased glass; glass & glazing work; pressed & blown glass

(G-6690)
GRIER SIGNS
4 Bridgeview Ct (19711-7454)
PHONE....................302 737-4823
Robert Grier, *Owner*
EMP: 3
SALES (est): 140.5K **Privately Held**
SIC: 3993 Signs & advertising specialties

(G-6691)
GRIFFITH INDUSTRIAL SUPPLY
153 Scottfield Dr (19713-2452)
PHONE....................302 731-0574
Bruce W Griffith, *President*
Cynthia Griffith, *Vice Pres*
EMP: 4
SALES: 300K **Privately Held**
WEB: www.griffithindustrial.com
SIC: 5063 5085 Electrical supplies; industrial supplies

(G-6692)
GRIME BUSTERS USA INC
3 Misty Ct (19702-4726)
PHONE....................302 834-7006
Edward Wilberg Jr, *President*
EMP: 6
SALES (est): 0 **Privately Held**
SIC: 7217 5087 Carpet & upholstery cleaning on customer premises; carpet & rug cleaning equipment & supplies, commercial

(G-6693)
GROFOS INTERNATIONAL LLC (PA)
Also Called: 5 Roads
1 Innovation Way Ste 426 (19711-5463)
PHONE....................302 635-4805
Ram Bala,
EMP: 6
SALES (est): 5K **Privately Held**
SIC: 7299 8742 Information services, consumer; management consulting services

(G-6694)
GROWTH INC
311 Ruthar Dr (19711-8016)
PHONE....................302 366-8586
John Riley, *CEO*
EMP: 13

SALES (est): 2MM **Privately Held**
SIC: 7336 Commercial art & graphic design

(G-6695)
GUARDIAN ENVMTL SVCS CO INC
70 Albe Dr (19702-1322)
PHONE....................302 918-3070
Joseph A Cunane, *President*
Nona M Vandeusen, *Corp Secy*
Herbert G Vandeusen, *Vice Pres*
Sherry Maule, *CFO*
EMP: 65
SQ FT: 6,000
SALES: 29.3MM **Privately Held**
WEB: www.gesoncall.com
SIC: 1541 4959 Industrial buildings, new construction; environmental cleanup services

(G-6696)
GWANTEL INTL CORP ENGRG & TECH
Also Called: Gwantel-Usa
21 Hidden Valley Dr Fl B (19711-7463)
PHONE....................302 377-6235
Frank Gao, *President*
Gilbert Tellez, *Vice Pres*
Harry Wang, *CFO*
EMP: 8
SALES (est): 324.4K **Privately Held**
SIC: 8748 Environmental consultant

(G-6697)
H I E CONTRACTORS INC
324 Markus Ct (19713-1151)
PHONE....................302 224-3032
James Houston, *CEO*
Judy Houston, *Admin Sec*
EMP: 16
SALES (est): 1.7MM **Privately Held**
SIC: 1623 Sewer line construction; water main construction

(G-6698)
H K GRIFFITH INC
115 Happy Ln (19711-8020)
PHONE....................302 368-4635
John McLaughlin, *President*
Ronald Jackson, *Treasurer*
EMP: 40
SQ FT: 20,000
SALES (est): 8.3MM **Privately Held**
WEB: www.hkgriffith.com
SIC: 1761 Roofing contractor; sheet metal-work

(G-6699)
H&R BLOCK INC
Also Called: H & R Block
860 Peoples Plz (19702-5602)
PHONE....................302 479-5717
EMP: 12
SALES (corp-wide): 3B **Publicly Held**
SIC: 7291 Tax Return Preparation Services
PA: H&R Block, Inc.
   1 H&R Block Way
   Kansas City MO 64105
   816 854-3000

(G-6700)
HACKNEY BUSINESS SOLUTIONS LLC
930 Alexandria Dr (19711-7701)
PHONE....................843 496-7236
Matthew Hackney,
EMP: 9
SALES (est): 401.4K **Privately Held**
SIC: 6311 Life insurance

(G-6701)
HAIR ACADEMY LLC
Also Called: Hair Acdemy Schl Brbering Buty
160 Pencader Plz (19713-3408)
PHONE....................302 738-6251
Raymond Noel, *Mng Member*
Christopher Arnold,
Kelsey Holveck,
Jonathan Otano,
EMP: 5
SALES (est): 42.3K **Privately Held**
SIC: 7231 Beauty schools; cosmetology school

(G-6702)
HAIRCUT & COMPANY INC
47 Tenby Chase Dr (19711-2440)
PHONE....................302 239-3236
William Gioffre, *President*
EMP: 14 EST: 1979
SQ FT: 800
SALES (est): 131.2K **Privately Held**
SIC: 7241 Hair stylist, men

(G-6703)
HALE BYRNES HOUSE
606 Stanton Christiana Rd (19713-2109)
PHONE....................302 998-3792
Barbara White, *Chairman*
EMP: 12 EST: 1750
SALES (est): 11K **Privately Held**
WEB: www.halebyrnes.org
SIC: 8412 Museum

(G-6704)
HAMMOND M KNOX DDS
13 Thomas Ln N (19711-4865)
PHONE....................302 383-6696
Hammond Knox, *President*
EMP: 4
SALES (est): 63.3K **Privately Held**
SIC: 8021 Offices & clinics of dentists

(G-6705)
HANBANG GROUP
201 Ruthar Dr (19711-8029)
PHONE....................626 506-7585
EMP: 2 EST: 2015
SALES (est): 198.6K **Privately Held**
SIC: 3829 Measuring & controlling devices

(G-6706)
HAPPY KIDS ACADEMY INC
273 Old Baltimore Pike (19702-1420)
PHONE....................302 369-6929
Mariam Banoub, *President*
EMP: 40
SALES (est): 670.3K **Privately Held**
SIC: 8351 Preschool center

(G-6707)
HAPPY PLACE DAY CARE LLC
4638 Ogletown Stanton Rd (19713-2007)
PHONE....................302 737-7603
Sameh Tawfik, *Principal*
EMP: 6 EST: 2012
SALES (est): 132.6K **Privately Held**
SIC: 8351 Child day care services

(G-6708)
HARBOR CLUB APARTMENTS
26 Cheswold Blvd Apt 2a (19713-4135)
PHONE....................302 738-3561
Paul Lawrence, *Managing Prtnr*
EMP: 25
SALES (est): 817.1K **Privately Held**
WEB: www.harborclubapartments.com
SIC: 6513 Apartment building operators

(G-6709)
HARMONY CONSTRUCTION INC
350 Salem Church Rd (19702-1415)
PHONE....................302 737-8700
William Saienni Jr, *President*
Joe Cannon, *Vice Pres*
Gerald Denney, *Vice Pres*
Carolyn Hamby, *Treasurer*
EMP: 10
SALES (est): 2.3MM **Privately Held**
WEB: www.harmonyconstruction.net
SIC: 1611 1799 Highway & street paving contractor; building site preparation

(G-6710)
HARRISON HOUSE CMNTY PROGRAM
1415 Pulaski Hwy (19702-5104)
PHONE....................302 595-5370
Leticia Scott, *President*
EMP: 30
SALES (est): 95.8K **Privately Held**
SIC: 8699 8351 Charitable organization; child day care services

(G-6711)
HARRY HE DDS
1400 Peoples Plz Ste 207 (19702-5708)
PHONE....................302 836-3711
EMP: 4 EST: 2016

▲ = Import ▼=Export
◆ =Import/Export

SALES (est): 61.5K Privately Held
SIC: 8021 Offices & clinics of dentists

(G-6712)
HART CONSTRUCTION CO INC
Also Called: Hart Management Group
109 Dallas Ave (19711-5125)
P.O. Box 721 (19715-0721)
PHONE..................302 737-7886
William B Hart, *President*
Lawrence J Hart, *Exec VP*
EMP: 12
SQ FT: 900
SALES (est): 1.3MM Privately Held
SIC: 1542 1541 Commercial & office building, new construction; commercial & office buildings, renovation & repair; industrial buildings, new construction; renovation, remodeling & repairs: industrial buildings

(G-6713)
HASHR8 SOFTWARE LLC
2035 Sunset Lake Rd B2 (19702-2600)
PHONE..................702 473-0426
EMP: 5
SALES (est): 107K Privately Held
SIC: 7371 Computer software development & applications

(G-6714)
HCAC
301 Ruthar Dr Ste C (19711-8031)
PHONE..................302 266-8100
Kimberly Hamill, *Manager*
EMP: 4
SALES (est): 448.5K Privately Held
SIC: 6282 7389 Investment advice; financial services

(G-6715)
HEADQUARTERS 2 INC
6 Polly Drummond Shpg Ctr (19711-4859)
PHONE..................302 731-9600
Margaret Woodock, *President*
Mary Bacchetta, *Vice Pres*
EMP: 16
SALES (est): 412.5K Privately Held
SIC: 7231 Hairdressers

(G-6716)
HEALTH & SOCIAL SVCS DEL DEPT
Also Called: Hudson State Service Center
501 Ogletown Rd (19711-5403)
PHONE..................302 368-6700
Darleissa Robertson, *Director*
EMP: 17 Privately Held
SIC: 8093 9431 Mental health clinic, outpatient; administration of public health programs;
HQ: Delaware Dept Of Health And Social Services
1901 N Dupont Hwy
New Castle DE 19720

(G-6717)
HEALTH & SOCIAL SVCS DEL DEPT
Also Called: New Cstle Cmnty Mntal Hlth Ctr
501 Ogletown Rd Fl 3 (19711-5403)
PHONE..................302 283-7500
Neil McLaughlin, *Branch Mgr*
EMP: 5 Privately Held
SIC: 8093 9431 Mental health clinic, outpatient; administration of public health programs
HQ: Delaware Dept Of Health And Social Services
1901 N Dupont Hwy
New Castle DE 19720

(G-6718)
HEARTLAND HOSPICE SERVICES LLC
Also Called: Heartland Hospice Svcs 4668
256 Chapman Rd Ste 102 (19702-5417)
PHONE..................302 737-7080
Karen Netta, *Manager*
EMP: 56
SALES (corp-wide): 8.2B Privately Held
SIC: 8082 Home health care services
HQ: Heartland Hospice Services, Llc
333 N Summit St
Toledo OH 43604

(G-6719)
HEARTLAND HOSPICE SERVICES LLC
750 Prides Xing Ste 110 (19713-6107)
PHONE..................419 252-5743
Linda Lewis, *Director*
EMP: 56
SALES (corp-wide): 8.2B Privately Held
SIC: 8082 Home health care services
HQ: Heartland Hospice Services, Llc
333 N Summit St
Toledo OH 43604

(G-6720)
HEDGEFORCE LLC
9 Majestic Dr (19713-3070)
PHONE..................305 600-0085
Rj Bonifacino, *Principal*
EMP: 8
SALES (est): 226.1K Privately Held
SIC: 8748 Business consulting

(G-6721)
HELIUM3 TECH AND SERVICES LLC
197 Harriet Ct (19711-8521)
PHONE..................302 766-2856
EMP: 3
SALES (est): 135.6K Privately Held
SIC: 2813 Helium

(G-6722)
HELLS KITCHEN SOFTWARE LTD
12 Furman Ct (19713-1611)
PHONE..................302 983-5644
Rob Epler, *Software Dev*
EMP: 2
SALES (est): 109.9K Privately Held
SIC: 7372 Prepackaged software

(G-6723)
HERA SPORTS SURFACES LLC
2915 Ogletown Rd (19713-1927)
PHONE..................781 392-4094
EMP: 20
SALES (est): 311.7K Privately Held
SIC: 7389 Business Serv Non-Commercial Site

(G-6724)
HERBERT STUDIOS
131 Canal Way (19702-4841)
PHONE..................302 836-3122
Jeff Herbert, *President*
EMP: 5
SQ FT: 3,160
SALES (est): 233.2K Privately Held
WEB: www.herbertstudios.com
SIC: 7335 Photographic studio, commercial

(G-6725)
HERITAGE INTERIORS INC
113 Sandy Dr (19713-1148)
PHONE..................302 369-3199
Roger Humpton, *President*
Jeffrey Faull, *Vice Pres*
EMP: 50 EST: 1998
SALES (est): 4.4MM Privately Held
WEB: www.heritageinteriors.com
SIC: 1742 Drywall

(G-6726)
HEXACT INC
2035 Sunset Lake Rd B2 (19702-2600)
PHONE..................850 716-1616
Stepan Aslanyan, *CEO*
Tigran Bayburtsyan, *CTO*
EMP: 4
SALES: 500K Privately Held
SIC: 7371 Computer software development & applications

(G-6727)
HFM INVESTMENT ADVISORS INC
5 Hunting Ct (19711-2962)
PHONE..................302 234-9777
Steve L Hyde, *CEO*
EMP: 4
SALES (est): 350K Privately Held
SIC: 8741 Financial management for business

(G-6728)
HILL PUBLISHING INC
2035 Sunset Lake Rd (19702-2600)
PHONE..................917 826-3722
EMP: 1
SALES (est): 37.5K Privately Held
SIC: 2741 Miscellaneous publishing

(G-6729)
HILLSIDE OIL COMPANY INC
Also Called: Meter Service
40 Brookhill Dr (19702-1328)
PHONE..................302 738-4144
James L Sellers, *President*
James Mackenzie, *Vice Pres*
EMP: 28
SQ FT: 3,700
SALES (est): 8.2MM Privately Held
SIC: 5983 1711 Fuel oil dealers; warm air heating & air conditioning contractor

(G-6730)
HISPANIC AMERICAN ASSN OF DEL (PA)
92 S Gerald Dr Ste A (19713-3216)
PHONE..................302 562-2705
Ronald Tello-Marzol, *Ch of Bd*
Aurora Colin, *Principal*
Noe Trujillo Medina, *Principal*
Elder Ayala, *Treasurer*
Ana Fields, *Admin Sec*
EMP: 4
SALES: 4.4K Privately Held
SIC: 8699 Membership organizations

(G-6731)
HISPANIC PERSONAL DEV LLC
2 Rolling Dr (19713-2020)
PHONE..................302 738-4782
Ronald Tello-Marzol, *Principal*
EMP: 4 EST: 2017
SALES (est): 77K Privately Held
SIC: 8399 Advocacy group

(G-6732)
HOBO NEWS PRESS INC
8 Willow Creek Ln (19711-3422)
PHONE..................302 235-1066
EMP: 1 EST: 2008
SALES (est): 58K Privately Held
SIC: 2741 Misc Publishing

(G-6733)
HOCKESSIN DANCE CENTER INC
Also Called: Dance Hdc
216 Louviers Dr (19711-4167)
PHONE..................302 738-3838
Michelle Buglio, *President*
EMP: 4
SALES (est): 71.2K Privately Held
SIC: 7911 Dance studio & school

(G-6734)
HOESCHEL INV & INSUR GROUP
106 Haines St Ste A (19711-5365)
PHONE..................302 738-3535
Andre Hoeschel, *Owner*
EMP: 10
SALES (est): 332.6K Privately Held
SIC: 6411 Insurance agents

(G-6735)
HOLA DELAWARE LLC
Also Called: El Tiempo Hispano
100 Hickory Pl (19702-5800)
PHONE..................302 832-3620
Marianelly Vera,
EMP: 2
SALES: 100K Privately Held
SIC: 2711 Newspapers

(G-6736)
HOLLYWOOD GRILL RESTAURANT
Also Called: Hampton Inn
3 Concord Ln (19713-3577)
PHONE..................302 737-3900
Rodney Perkins, *Manager*
EMP: 35
SALES (corp-wide): 15.5MM Privately Held
SIC: 7011 Hotels & motels
PA: Hollywood Grill Restaurant Inc
1811 Concord Pike
Wilmington DE 19803
302 655-1348

(G-6737)
HOLOGIC INC
18 Bay Blvd (19702-4800)
PHONE..................302 631-2846
Shusheng He, *Manager*
EMP: 195
SALES (corp-wide): 3.3B Publicly Held
WEB: www.hologic.com
SIC: 3844 X-ray apparatus & tubes
PA: Hologic, Inc.
250 Campus Dr
Marlborough MA 01752
508 263-2900

(G-6738)
HOLOGIC INC
600 Technology Dr (19702-2463)
PHONE..................302 631-2700
Peter Soltani, *Vice Pres*
EMP: 21
SALES (corp-wide): 3.3B Publicly Held
SIC: 3841 Surgical & medical instruments
PA: Hologic, Inc.
250 Campus Dr
Marlborough MA 01752
508 263-2900

(G-6739)
HOME DEPOT USA INC
Also Called: Home Depot, The
2000 Peoples Plz (19702-5702)
PHONE..................302 838-6818
Rob Garbacc, *Manager*
EMP: 150
SALES (corp-wide): 108.2B Publicly Held
WEB: www.homerentalsdepot.com
SIC: 5211 7359 Home centers; tool rental
HQ: Home Depot U.S.A., Inc.
2455 Paces Ferry Ave
Atlanta GA 30339

(G-6740)
HOME SERVICES UNLIMITED
22 Sailboat Cir (19702-2319)
PHONE..................302 293-8726
Rick Smith, *Owner*
EMP: 8 EST: 2008
SALES (est): 399.6K Privately Held
SIC: 1761 Siding contractor

(G-6741)
HOMEWARD BOUND INC
34 Continental Ave (19711-5310)
P.O. Box 9740 (19714-9740)
PHONE..................302 737-2241
Mariellen Green, *President*
EMP: 10
SALES (est): 68K Privately Held
SIC: 8399 Social services

(G-6742)
HOMEWOOD SUITES NEWARK
640 S College Ave (19713-1315)
PHONE..................302 453-9700
Aaron Smith, *Principal*
EMP: 9
SALES (est): 513.2K Privately Held
SIC: 7011 Hotels & motels

(G-6743)
HOOPES FIRE PREVENTION INC
124 Sandy Dr (19713-1147)
P.O. Box 7839 (19714-7839)
PHONE..................302 323-0220
Jaclyn Eastburn, *President*
Anthony Long, *General Mgr*
Jeff Eastburn, *Vice Pres*
Jessica Eastburn, *Office Mgr*
EMP: 18 EST: 1962
SQ FT: 8,000
SALES: 1.5MM Privately Held
WEB: www.hoopesfp.com
SIC: 5087 Firefighting equipment

(G-6744)
HOPE RISING THERAPY
262 Chapman Rd (19702-5448)
PHONE..................302 273-3194
EMP: 8

Newark - New Castle County (G-6745)

SALES (est): 73.3K **Privately Held**
SIC: 8093 Rehabilitation center, outpatient treatment

(G-6745)
HORIZON HELICOPTERS INC
2035 Sunset Lake Rd Ste A (19702-2665)
PHONE..................302 368-5135
Harry Griffith, *President*
Judy Trella, *Vice Pres*
EMP: 8
SQ FT: 2,000
SALES (est): 1.2MM **Privately Held**
SIC: 4522 8299 7335 Helicopter carriers, nonscheduled; flying instruction; aerial photography, except mapmaking

(G-6746)
HORIZONS FAMILY PRACTICE PA
2600 Glasgow Ave Ste 102 (19702-5703)
PHONE..................302 918-6300
Rosanna Moran, *Manager*
EMP: 14 EST: 2008
SALES (est): 1.4MM **Privately Held**
SIC: 8011 General & family practice, physician/surgeon

(G-6747)
HORTON AND BROS INC
Also Called: Horton Brothers Towing
80 Aleph Dr (19702-1319)
PHONE..................302 738-7221
EMP: 6
SQ FT: 2,500
SALES (est): 1MM **Privately Held**
SIC: 5541 7538 Gasoline Service Station General Auto Repair

(G-6748)
HORTON BROTHERS RECOVERY INC
1001 S Chapel St Ste A (19702-1356)
PHONE..................302 266-7339
EMP: 10
SQ FT: 2,000
SALES (est): 1.2MM **Privately Held**
SIC: 7549 Automotive Services

(G-6749)
HOTELRUNNER INC
2035 Sunset Lake Rd (19702-2600)
PHONE..................302 956-9616
Arden Agopyan, *President*
EMP: 25
SALES (est): 670.6K **Privately Held**
SIC: 2741

(G-6750)
HOUGH ASSOCIATES INC
2605 Eastburn Ctr (19711-7285)
PHONE..................302 322-7800
Tom Bombico, *President*
Dennis Dever, *Vice Pres*
David Fraczkowski, *Vice Pres*
Mitchell Hill, *Vice Pres*
James J Cuff, *Treasurer*
EMP: 19
SQ FT: 10,000
SALES (est): 333.9K **Privately Held**
WEB: www.houghassociates.com
SIC: 8711 Consulting engineer

(G-6751)
HOWARD B STROMWASSER
Also Called: Vision Optik
210 Suburban Dr (19711-3596)
PHONE..................302 368-4424
Howard B Stromwasser, *Owner*
Howard Stromwasser,
EMP: 6
SQ FT: 1,500
SALES (est): 310.4K **Privately Held**
SIC: 8042 Specialized optometrists

(G-6752)
HOWROYD-WRIGHT EMPLYMNT AGCY
Also Called: Apple One
131 Continental Dr # 207 (19713-4305)
PHONE..................302 738-4022
EMP: 8
SALES (corp-wide): 200.6MM **Privately Held**
WEB: www.appleone.com
SIC: 7361 Executive placement
HQ: Howroyd-Wright Employment Agency, Inc.
327 W Broadway
Glendale CA 91204
818 240-8688

(G-6753)
HP MOTORS INC
Also Called: H P Electric Motors
38 Albe Dr Ste 14 (19702-1351)
PHONE..................302 368-4543
Richard Hamory, *President*
Charles Perkins, *Vice Pres*
EMP: 5
SQ FT: 3,000
SALES (est): 1.1MM **Privately Held**
SIC: 7694 5999 3599 Electric motor repair; motors, electric; machine shop, jobbing & repair

(G-6754)
HRD PRODUCTS INC
68d Omega Dr (19713-2063)
PHONE..................302 757-3587
Saurabh Sheth, *Principal*
EMP: 2 EST: 2016
SALES (est): 83.9K **Privately Held**
SIC: 2899 Chemical preparations

(G-6755)
HSI SERVICE CORP
220 Continental Dr # 115 (19713-4311)
PHONE..................302 369-3709
David Dwire, *President*
EMP: 10 **Privately Held**
SIC: 6719 Personal holding companies, except banks

(G-6756)
HUZALA INC (PA)
Also Called: WEANAS
4c Aleph Dr New Castle Co (19702)
PHONE..................313 404-6941
WEI Zhang, *President*
EMP: 4 EST: 2013
SQ FT: 5,000
SALES (est): 75.6K **Privately Held**
SIC: 5699 2329 5137 Sports apparel; men's & boys' sportswear & athletic clothing; women's & children's sportswear & swimsuits

(G-6757)
HYPER JOBS LLC
40 E Main St Ste 1212 (19711-4639)
PHONE..................786 667-0905
Denis Madureira,
EMP: 20
SALES: 180K **Privately Held**
SIC: 7372 7361 Application computer software; employment agencies

(G-6758)
IAAD
Also Called: Indoor American Assn Del
113 Jupiter Rd (19711-3426)
PHONE..................302 234-0214
Jitu Asthana, *President*
Pidren Tandon, *Vice Pres*
Vishal Tandon, *Admin Sec*
EMP: 15
SALES (est): 25K **Privately Held**
WEB: www.iaadso.org
SIC: 8699 Charitable organization

(G-6759)
IAN MYERS MD LLC
2600 Glasgow Ave Ste 218 (19702-5704)
PHONE..................302 832-7600
Ian Myers, *Principal*
EMP: 6
SALES (est): 495.7K **Privately Held**
SIC: 8011 General & family practice, physician/surgeon

(G-6760)
IBR GROUP INC
1098 Elkton Rd (19711-3507)
PHONE..................610 986-8545
Ibrahim Sanni, *President*
EMP: 12

SALES (est): 248.5K **Privately Held**
SIC: 8742 Management consulting services

(G-6761)
ICUELAB LLC
51 W Kyla Marie Dr (19702-5431)
PHONE..................302 983-8924
Rouslan Zenetl,
EMP: 4
SALES: 200K **Privately Held**
WEB: www.icuelab.com
SIC: 7379

(G-6762)
IEC
451 Wyoming Rd (19716-5901)
PHONE..................302 831-6231
Robert Brikmire, *Director*
EMP: 20
SALES (est): 277.4K **Privately Held**
SIC: 8731 Energy research

(G-6763)
IERARDI VASCULAR CLINIC LLC
Also Called: Ivc
1 Centurian Dr Ste 307 (19713-2127)
PHONE..................302 655-8272
Ralph P Ierardi, *Mng Member*
EMP: 4
SALES (est): 242.7K **Privately Held**
SIC: 8011 8099 Cardiologist & cardio-vascular specialist; childbirth preparation clinic

(G-6764)
IFI INC
2035 Sunset Lake Rd B2 (19702-2600)
PHONE..................718 791-7669
Russell Khaimov, *CEO*
EMP: 1 EST: 2015
SALES (est): 37.9K **Privately Held**
SIC: 7372 Utility computer software

(G-6765)
IGAL BIOCHEMICAL LLC
4142 Ogletown Stanton Rd (19713-4169)
PHONE..................302 525-2090
Igor Shkodin, *Business Mgr*
EMP: 5
SALES (est): 147.7K **Privately Held**
SIC: 7699 5049 Scientific equipment repair service; scientific instruments

(G-6766)
IK SOLUTIONS INC (PA)
100 Commerce Dr Ste 201 (19713-2850)
PHONE..................302 861-6775
Subba Indukuri, *CEO*
Devi Indukuri, *President*
Sudhakar Datla, *Vice Pres*
EMP: 7
SQ FT: 3,000
SALES (est): 16.8MM **Privately Held**
WEB: www.iksolutionsinc.com
SIC: 7379 Data processing consultant

(G-6767)
IMAGINE TECHNOLOGIES
110 Coopers Dr (19702-2119)
PHONE..................240 428-8406
Wayne Roberts, *Principal*
EMP: 10
SALES: 10K **Privately Held**
SIC: 7371 Computer software development

(G-6768)
IMAGING NEUROSCIENCE REAL EST
774 Christiana Rd (19713-4236)
PHONE..................302 731-9656
John R Townsend, *Principal*
EMP: 5
SALES (est): 293.8K **Privately Held**
SIC: 6531 Real estate brokers & agents

(G-6769)
IMPLIFY INC
260 Chapman Rd Ste 201c (19702-5491)
PHONE..................302 533-2345
Ravi Kondapalli, *CEO*
EMP: 50

SALES (est): 3.4MM **Privately Held**
SIC: 7371 7379 Computer software development; data processing consultant

(G-6770)
INDEPENDENCE PROSTHTCS-ORTHO (PA)
31 Meadowood Dr (19711-7202)
PHONE..................302 369-9476
John Horne, *CEO*
Cassandra Gorman,
EMP: 2
SQ FT: 2,000
SALES (est): 527.2K **Privately Held**
SIC: 5999 3842 Orthopedic & prosthesis applications; abdominal supporters, braces & trusses

(G-6771)
INDEPENDENCE SCHOOL INC
1300 Paper Mill Rd (19711-3408)
PHONE..................302 239-0330
Catherine Pomeroy, *Director*
EMP: 90
SQ FT: 60,000
SALES (est): 8.3MM **Privately Held**
WEB: www.theindependenceschool.org
SIC: 8211 8351 Private combined elementary & secondary school; child day care services

(G-6772)
INDO-AMERICAN ASSOCIATION DEL
113 Jupiter Rd (19711-3426)
PHONE..................302 234-0214
Jitender Asthana, *Principal*
EMP: 16
SALES: 85.6K **Privately Held**
SIC: 8641 Educator's association

(G-6773)
INDONESIAN CULTURAL INSTITUTE
15 Anthony Dr (19702-8431)
PHONE..................302 981-7780
Lidia Darmawan, *Principal*
Rissa Asnan, *Principal*
EMP: 4
SALES (est): 90.2K **Privately Held**
SIC: 8733 Noncommercial research organizations

(G-6774)
INDUSTRIAL TRAINING CONS INC
Also Called: Itc Specialty
13 Garfield Way (19713-3450)
PHONE..................302 266-6100
Louis M Mene, *President*
EMP: 19
SALES (est): 3.2MM **Privately Held**
WEB: www.itcawards.com
SIC: 7311 8331 7389 Advertising agencies; skill training center; product endorsement service

(G-6775)
INFECTIOUS DISEASE ASSOCIATION
Also Called: Bacon, Alfred
78 Omega Dr C (19713-2064)
PHONE..................302 368-2883
Alfred Bacon MD, *Owner*
Julian Serio, *Manager*
EMP: 9
SALES (est): 1.2MM **Privately Held**
SIC: 8011 Internal medicine, physician/surgeon

(G-6776)
INFECTIOUS DISEASES CONS PA
537 Stanton Christiana Rd # 201 (19713-2146)
PHONE..................302 994-9692
Marshall T Williams, *President*
Wesley W Emmons, *Med Doctor*
Marshall Williams, *Med Doctor*
EMP: 10
SALES (est): 985.2K **Privately Held**
SIC: 4959 Disease control

GEOGRAPHIC SECTION   Newark - New Castle County (G-6806)

(G-6777)
INFEVO TECHNOLOGIES CO LTD
200 Continental Dr # 401 (19713-4334)
PHONE..................................626 703-8197
Yuting Sun, *Principal*
EMP: 6
SALES (est): 123.5K **Privately Held**
SIC: 7371 Computer software development & applications

(G-6778)
INFINITY INTELLECTUALS INC
113 Barksdale Pro Ctr (19711-3258)
PHONE..................................302 565-4830
S Shiva Kumar, *President*
M Soma Shekar, *Chairman*
Sapna Savant, *CFO*
Bruce Wayne, *Manager*
Scott Williams, *Business Dir*
EMP: 185
SQ FT: 4,000
SALES (est): 18MM **Privately Held**
SIC: 7374 Computer graphics service

(G-6779)
INFLECTION POINT VENTURES LP
1 Innovation Way Ste 500 (19711-5464)
PHONE..................................302 452-1120
Jeff Davidson, *Partner*
Michael Omalley, *Partner*
Tim Webb, *Partner*
EMP: 4
SALES (est): 316.6K **Privately Held**
SIC: 8742 Financial consultant

(G-6780)
INFORMAL INC
2035 Sunset Lake Rd B2 (19702-2600)
PHONE..................................415 504-2106
Mathais Holzmann, *CEO*
Simon Hamancher, *COO*
EMP: 5
SALES (est): 107K **Privately Held**
SIC: 7371 Computer software development & applications

(G-6781)
INN LLC A-1 DASH
380 E Chestnut Hill Rd (19713-2759)
PHONE..................................302 368-7964
EMP: 4 **EST:** 2011
SALES (est): 182.6K **Privately Held**
SIC: 7011 Inns

(G-6782)
INNOSPEC INC
200 Executive Dr (19702-3315)
PHONE..................................302 454-8100
Patrick William, *President*
Andrew Hartley, *President*
David Daniels, *Research*
Graeme Kay, *Finance*
Kevin Barrett, *Manager*
EMP: 12
SQ FT: 13,000
SALES (est): 2MM
SALES (corp-wide): 34.9MM **Privately Held**
WEB: www.octelcorp.com
SIC: 2911 Petroleum refining
PA: Innospec Fuel Specialties Llc
  8310 S Valley Hwy Ste 350
  Englewood CO 80112
  303 792-5554

(G-6783)
INNOSPEC INC
220 Continental Dr # 115 (19713-4311)
PHONE..................................302 454-8100
Dave Biddle, *President*
Alexander A Dobbie, *Exec VP*
Thomas Entwistle, *Vice Pres*
EMP: 2 **EST:** 2006
SALES (est): 163.2K **Privately Held**
SIC: 2911 7319 Fuel additives; display advertising service

(G-6784)
INSLEY INSURANCE & FINCL SVC
Also Called: Nationwide
110 Christiana Med Ctr (19702-1697)
PHONE..................................302 286-0777
Harry Insley, *Manager*
EMP: 9 **EST:** 2009
SALES (est): 667.8K **Privately Held**
SIC: 6411 Insurance agents, brokers & service

(G-6785)
INSTITUTE OF CHRISTIANA
Also Called: Chrias
537 Stanton Christiana Rd # 102 (19713-2145)
PHONE..................................302 892-9900
Isaias Irgau, *President*
Gail M Wynn, *Co-Founder*
Sydney Manbeck, *Physician Asst*
EMP: 12
SALES (est): 380.5K **Privately Held**
WEB: www.chrias.com
SIC: 8011 Surgeon

(G-6786)
INSURANCE ASSOCIATES INC
720 New London Rd (19711-2100)
PHONE..................................302 368-0888
Dennis Barba, *President*
Anne Dilks, *Office Mgr*
Rachel Ferrell, *Manager*
EMP: 15
SQ FT: 4,500
SALES (est): 2.9MM **Privately Held**
WEB: www.iai-de.com
SIC: 6411 Insurance agents

(G-6787)
INTECH SERVICES
136 Pawnee Ct (19702-1920)
PHONE..................................302 366-1442
Tom McNulty, *Owner*
EMP: 4
SALES (est): 149.8K **Privately Held**
SIC: 3795 Tanks & tank components

(G-6788)
INTECH SERVICES INC
211 Lake Dr Ste J (19702-3320)
PHONE..................................302 366-8530
Michael Paterson, *President*
Chris Dohl, *Vice Pres*
Monica Trout, *Accounting Mgr*
Ken Barnes, *Accounts Mgr*
Dave Jones, *Accounts Mgr*
▲ **EMP:** 5
SQ FT: 6,000
SALES (est): 2.6MM **Privately Held**
WEB: www.intechservices.com
SIC: 2821 Polytetrafluoroethylene resins (teflon)

(G-6789)
INTEGRATED TURF MANAGEMENT SYS
Also Called: I T M S
200 Ruthar Dr Ste 7 (19711-8000)
PHONE..................................302 266-8000
Stephen Lange, *President*
EMP: 10 **EST:** 1998
SALES (est): 937.4K **Privately Held**
WEB: www.itms-turf.com
SIC: 0782 Lawn care services

(G-6790)
INTEGRITY CORPORATION INC (PA)
Also Called: Integrity Supply & Service
1 Innovation Way (19711-5442)
PHONE..................................410 392-8665
Brandon McGowan, *CEO*
James Evenson, *President*
EMP: 10
SQ FT: 45,000
SALES (est): 3.6MM **Privately Held**
SIC: 5072 Hardware

(G-6791)
INTEGRITY STAFFING SOLUTIONS
700 Prides Xing Ste 300 (19713-6109)
PHONE..................................520 276-7775
EMP: 1115
SALES (corp-wide): 427.9MM **Privately Held**
SIC: 7363 Help supply services
PA: Integrity Staffing Solutions Inc
  700 Prides Xing Ste 300
  Newark DE 19713
  302 661-8770

(G-6792)
INTEGRITY STAFFING SOLUTIONS (PA)
700 Prides Xing Ste 300 (19713-6109)
PHONE..................................302 661-8770
Todd B Bavol, *President*
Ken Bode, *Area Mgr*
Adam Hebenstreich, *Business Mgr*
Neil McGeehan, *Business Mgr*
Sean Montgomery, *COO*
EMP: 1472
SQ FT: 15,150
SALES (est): 427.9MM **Privately Held**
SIC: 7361 Employment agencies

(G-6793)
INTEGRITY TECH SOLUTIONS INC
200 Continental Dr # 401 (19713-4334)
PHONE..................................302 369-9093
James R Draper, *President*
Pam Draper, *Vice Pres*
EMP: 5
SALES (est): 475.1K **Privately Held**
WEB: www.itscableinc.com
SIC: 1731 Electrical work

(G-6794)
INTELLIGENT BUILDING MTLS LLC
40 E Main St Ste 611 (19711-4639)
PHONE..................................302 261-9922
Bernhard Kinpel, *CEO*
EMP: 2 **EST:** 2010
SALES: 500K **Privately Held**
SIC: 3253 3269 Ceramic wall & floor tile; chemical porcelain; china decorating

(G-6795)
INTELLIGENT SYSTEMS INC
601 Interchange Blvd (19711-3561)
PHONE..................................302 388-0566
Herbert Gregory Silber, *President*
Jason T Graham, *Vice Pres*
EMP: 4
SQ FT: 7,000
SALES (est): 234.1K **Privately Held**
WEB: www.isyoursolution.com
SIC: 7371 Computer software development

(G-6796)
INTERACTIVE MARKETING SERVICES
200 University Plz (19702-1550)
PHONE..................................302 456-9810
Herb Spatola, *Manager*
EMP: 30
SALES (corp-wide): 14.9MM **Privately Held**
SIC: 7389 Telemarketing services
PA: Interactive Marketing Services, Inc
  2 N Maple Ave
  Ridgely MD 21660
  410 634-2060

(G-6797)
INTERNATIONAL LITERACY ASSN (PA)
Also Called: Ila
800 Barksdale Rd (19711-3204)
P.O. Box 8139 (19714-8139)
PHONE..................................302 731-1600
Mark Mullen, *Principal*
Nicola Wedderburn, *Marketing Staff*
Linda Marston, *Info Tech Mgr*
Lakshay Puniani, *Web Dvlpr*
Marcie Craig Post, *Exec Dir*
EMP: 55
SQ FT: 30,000
SALES (est): 12.5MM **Privately Held**
SIC: 8621 Education & teacher association

(G-6798)
INTERSTATE CONSTRUCTION INC
1000 Dawson Dr Ste A (19713-5805)
P.O. Box 9949 (19714-5049)
PHONE..................................302 369-3590
Gordon B Lester, *President*
James P Insley, *Principal*
EMP: 20
SQ FT: 2,000
SALES: 2MM **Privately Held**
SIC: 1629 Dams, waterways, docks & other marine construction

(G-6799)
INTERSTATE MORTGAGE CORP INC
Also Called: Lowe, Robert W Agency
1933 Kirkwood Hwy (19711-5708)
PHONE..................................302 733-7620
Robert W Lowe, *President*
EMP: 7
SQ FT: 5,000
SALES (est): 543K **Privately Held**
SIC: 6163 Mortgage brokers arranging for loans, using money of others

(G-6800)
INTERSTATE STEEL CO INC
11 Taylors Farm Dr (19711-2964)
PHONE..................................302 598-5159
William F Drupieski Jr, *President*
Laura J Drupieski, *Corp Secy*
EMP: 20
SALES (est): 1.5MM **Privately Held**
SIC: 1761 Siding contractor

(G-6801)
INVISTA CAPITAL MANAGEMENT LLC
150 Red Mill Rd (19711-6632)
PHONE..................................302 731-6882
EMP: 517
SALES (corp-wide): 40.6B **Privately Held**
WEB: www.kosa.com
SIC: 2821 Plastics materials & resins
HQ: Invista Capital Management, Llc
  2801 Centerville Rd
  Wilmington DE 19808
  302 683-3000

(G-6802)
INVISTAS APPLIED RES CENTRE
150 Red Mill Rd (19711-6632)
PHONE..................................302 731-6800
Greg Weeks, *Principal*
EMP: 11
SALES (est): 580K **Privately Held**
SIC: 8733 Research institute

(G-6803)
IPC HEALTHCARE
111 Continental Dr # 406 (19713-4306)
PHONE..................................302 984-2577
EMP: 4
SALES (est): 74.6K **Privately Held**
SIC: 8011 Offices & clinics of medical doctors

(G-6804)
IPC HEALTHCARE INC
111 Continental Dr (19713-4306)
PHONE..................................302 368-2630
Adam Singer, *Branch Mgr*
EMP: 27
SALES (corp-wide): 287.4MM **Privately Held**
SIC: 8011 Primary care medical clinic
HQ: Ipc Healthcare, Inc.
  4605 Lankershim Blvd
  North Hollywood CA 91602
  888 447-2362

(G-6805)
IPD TECHNOLOGIES LLC
240 Goldfinch Turn (19711-4112)
PHONE..................................302 533-8850
Dan Molligan,
EMP: 2
SALES (est): 104.6K **Privately Held**
SIC: 3083 Laminated plastics plate & sheet

(G-6806)
IRON HILL APARTMENTS ASSOC
2 Burleigh Ct Ofc A4 (19702-2605)
PHONE..................................302 366-8228
Anne Andreas, *General Mgr*
Robin Reich, *General Mgr*
Aaron Pomares, *General Ptnr*
Arnon Perry, *Admin Sec*

Newark - New Castle County (G-6807) — GEOGRAPHIC SECTION

EMP: 6
SALES: 720K **Privately Held**
WEB: www.ironhillapartments.com
SIC: 6513 Apartment hotel operation

(G-6807)
IRON HILL FENCE
1565 Old Baltimore Pike (19702-2008)
PHONE.....................302 453-9060
David E Waugh, *Owner*
EMP: 5
SALES: 150K **Privately Held**
SIC: 1799 Fence construction

(G-6808)
IRON HL APRSAL PRPERTY MGT LLC
1 Penn State Dr (19713-1166)
PHONE.....................302 454-1404
John McMahan,
EMP: 4
SALES (est): 240.8K **Privately Held**
SIC: 7389 Auction, appraisal & exchange services

(G-6809)
IT RESOURCES INC
220 Continental Dr # 104 (19713-4304)
PHONE.....................203 521-6945
Hari Koya, *Director*
EMP: 40
SALES: 1.9MM **Privately Held**
SIC: 7379 Computer related consulting services

(G-6810)
ITENNISYOU LLC
2035 Sunset Lake Rd B2 (19702-2600)
PHONE.....................305 890-3234
Xavier Vaguer,
EMP: 4
SALES (est): 38.1K **Privately Held**
SIC: 7997 7371 Membership sports & recreation clubs; computer software development & applications

(G-6811)
IVYCHAT INC
2035 Sunset Lake Rd B2 (19702-2600)
PHONE.....................201 567-5694
EMP: 10
SALES: 25K **Privately Held**
SIC: 8732 7371 Commercial Nonphysical Research Custom Computer Programing

(G-6812)
J & A GRINDING INC
307 Markus Ct (19713-1151)
PHONE.....................302 368-8760
Jeff T Coffin, *President*
EMP: 15 EST: 1978
SQ FT: 5,000
SALES (est): 2.2MM **Privately Held**
WEB: www.jagrinding.com
SIC: 7699 Industrial tool grinding; knife, saw & tool sharpening & repair

(G-6813)
J & S MOVING & DLVRY SVC LLC
603 Franklin Bldg (19702-5231)
PHONE.....................302 357-5675
James Brown,
EMP: 6
SQ FT: 450
SALES: 30K **Privately Held**
SIC: 4212 Delivery service, vehicular

(G-6814)
J & T CONCRETE INC
84 Salem Church Rd (19713-2935)
PHONE.....................302 368-4949
Julio Vasquez Sr, *President*
EMP: 13
SALES (est): 1MM **Privately Held**
SIC: 1771 Flooring contractor; foundation & footing contractor

(G-6815)
J D CONSTRUCTION
5 Radnor Rd (19713-1817)
PHONE.....................302 292-8789
Jeff Denyes, *Owner*
EMP: 4

SALES (est): 515.6K **Privately Held**
SIC: 1531 Operative builders

(G-6816)
J FREDERICKS & SON ELEC C
16 Flint Hill Dr (19702-2835)
PHONE.....................302 733-0307
V S Marioni, *Principal*
EMP: 5
SALES (est): 189.6K **Privately Held**
SIC: 4911 Electric services

(G-6817)
J MICHAELS PAINTING INC
108 Unami Trl (19711-7507)
P.O. Box 7767 (19714-7767)
PHONE.....................302 738-8465
James Purvis, *President*
EMP: 17
SALES (est): 910.2K **Privately Held**
SIC: 1721 1742 Painting & paper hanging; drywall

(G-6818)
J P MORGAN SERVICES INC
500 Stanton Christiana Rd (19713-2105)
P.O. Box 6070 (19714)
PHONE.....................302 634-1000
Rich J Johnson, *President*
EMP: 1000
SQ FT: 635,000
SALES (est): 52.3MM
SALES (corp-wide): 131.4B **Publicly Held**
WEB: www.jpmorganchase.com
SIC: 7374 8741 Data processing service; management services
PA: Jpmorgan Chase & Co.
   383 Madison Ave
   New York NY 10179
   212 270-6000

(G-6819)
J R PINI ELECTRICAL CONTRS
104 Sandy Dr (19713-1147)
PHONE.....................302 368-2311
Joseph R Pini, *President*
Susan J Pini, *Vice Pres*
EMP: 10
SQ FT: 2,000
SALES (est): 690K **Privately Held**
SIC: 1731 General electrical contractor

(G-6820)
J R RENTS INC (PA)
Also Called: Aaron's Rental Purchase
59 Marrows Rd (19713-3701)
PHONE.....................302 266-8090
Jay Richards, *President*
EMP: 10
SALES (est): 5.1MM **Privately Held**
SIC: 7359 Home appliance, furniture & entertainment rental services

(G-6821)
J&J STAFFING RESOURCES INC
200 Continental Dr # 107 (19713-4303)
PHONE.....................302 738-7800
Virginia Schrann, *Manager*
EMP: 5
SALES (corp-wide): 72.8MM **Privately Held**
WEB: www.jjstaff.com
SIC: 7363 Temporary help service
PA: J&J Staffing Resources, Inc.
   1814 Marlton Pike E # 210
   Cherry Hill NJ 08003
   856 751-5050

(G-6822)
JACKSON MASSAGE AND CFT
124 Wren Way (19711-8330)
PHONE.....................302 525-6808
Christopher A Jackson, *Principal*
EMP: 8 EST: 2017
SALES (est): 65.7K **Privately Held**
SIC: 8049

(G-6823)
JACQUELINE ALLENS DAYCARE
17 Timberline Dr (19711-7413)
PHONE.....................302 368-3633
Jacqualine Allen, *Owner*
EMP: 9

SALES (est): 88.6K **Privately Held**
SIC: 8351 Child day care services

(G-6824)
JAM PRODUCTIONS
8 Hillcroft Rd (19711-5513)
P.O. Box 9585 (19714-9585)
PHONE.....................302 369-3629
Jamie Waltz, *Principal*
EMP: 9
SALES (est): 138.7K **Privately Held**
SIC: 7822 Motion picture & tape distribution

(G-6825)
JAMES A PEEL & SONS INC
118 Sandy Dr Ste 1 (19713-1177)
PHONE.....................302 738-1468
Glen D Peel, *President*
EMP: 5
SQ FT: 4,000
SALES: 800K **Privately Held**
SIC: 1521 General remodeling, single-family houses

(G-6826)
JAMES RICE JR CONSTRUCTION CO
122 Upper Pike Creek Rd (19711-5802)
P.O. Box 7276 (19714-7276)
PHONE.....................302 731-9323
James Rice Jr, *President*
EMP: 6
SALES: 700K **Privately Held**
SIC: 1521 1542 General remodeling, single-family houses; commercial & office buildings, renovation & repair

(G-6827)
JAMESTOWN PAINTING & DCTG INC
830 Dawson Dr (19713-3416)
PHONE.....................302 454-7344
Christopher S Blackwell, *President*
Frank Kovach, *Project Mgr*
Chris Beatson, *Opers Mgr*
EMP: 50
SALES (est): 5.7MM **Privately Held**
SIC: 1721 Interior residential painting contractor; exterior residential painting contractor; interior commercial painting contractor; exterior commercial painting contractor

(G-6828)
JANICE TILDON-BURTON MD (PA)
2600 Glasgow Ave Ste 207 (19702-5704)
PHONE.....................302 832-1124
Janice Tildon-Burton, *Owner*
EMP: 5
SALES (est): 786.4K **Privately Held**
SIC: 8011 Pediatrician

(G-6829)
JAY J HARRIS PC
Also Called: Wild Smiles
220 Christiana Med Ctr (19702-1652)
PHONE.....................302 453-1400
Jay J Harris, *Owner*
Jay Harris, *Principal*
EMP: 8
SALES: 350K **Privately Held**
SIC: 8021 Dentists' office

(G-6830)
JEANES RADIOLOGY ASSOCIATES PC
Also Called: Delaware Open M R I
42 Omega Dr Ste H (19713-2078)
PHONE.....................302 738-1700
Linda Collin, *Manager*
EMP: 8
SALES (corp-wide): 2.5MM **Privately Held**
SIC: 8011 Radiologist
PA: Jeanes Radiology Associates, Llc
   888 Fox Chase Rd
   Jenkintown PA 19046
   215 728-3767

(G-6831)
JEFFREY L COOK D M D
16 Peddlers Row Ste 16 # 16 (19702-1525)
PHONE.....................302 453-8700
Jeffrey Cook, *Principal*
EMP: 5
SALES (est): 347.2K **Privately Held**
SIC: 8021 Offices & clinics of dentists

(G-6832)
JENNIFER LOPEZ MOYA RPT
8 Three Rivers Ct (19702-4262)
PHONE.....................302 836-1495
Jennifer Lopez Moya, *Principal*
EMP: 4
SALES (est): 83.7K **Privately Held**
SIC: 8093 Respiratory therapy clinic

(G-6833)
JENNIFERS SPA
4 S Merriment Dr (19702-5300)
PHONE.....................302 740-6363
Jennifer Allegretti, *Principal*
EMP: 5
SALES (est): 178.1K **Privately Held**
SIC: 7991 Spas

(G-6834)
JENNY CRAIG WGHT LOSS CTRS INC
108 Astro Shopping Ctr (19711-7254)
PHONE.....................302 454-0991
Joyce Michers, *Manager*
EMP: 4
SALES (corp-wide): 127MM **Privately Held**
SIC: 7299 Diet center, without medical staff
HQ: Jenny Craig Weight Loss Centers, Inc.
   5770 Fleet St
   Carlsbad CA 92008

(G-6835)
JEROME C KAYATTA DDS
192 Kenneth Ct (19711-8504)
PHONE.....................302 737-6761
Jerome Kayatta, *Owner*
EMP: 7
SALES (est): 370.9K **Privately Held**
SIC: 8021 Dentists' office

(G-6836)
JES-MADE BAKERY (PA)
314 N Dillwyn Rd (19711-5505)
PHONE.....................610 558-2131
Delaware County, *Principal*
EMP: 9
SALES (est): 748.6K **Privately Held**
SIC: 5149 Bakery products

(G-6837)
JEWELL ENTERPRISES INC
Also Called: Maaco Auto Painting
729 Dawson Dr (19713-3413)
PHONE.....................302 737-8460
William Jewell, *President*
William H Jewell Sr, *Treasurer*
EMP: 11
SQ FT: 12,000
SALES: 1.1MM **Privately Held**
SIC: 7532 Paint shop, automotive

(G-6838)
JHONSTON AND ASSOCIATES
16 Farmhouse Rd (19711-7460)
PHONE.....................302 368-9790
Thomas Johnston, *Owner*
EMP: 5
SALES (est): 273.5K **Privately Held**
WEB: www.johnstonassoc.com
SIC: 7379 Computer related consulting services

(G-6839)
JIFFY LUBE INTERNATIONAL INC
29 Liberty Plz (19711-5591)
PHONE.....................302 738-5494
Dennis Schmidt, *Manager*
EMP: 10
SALES (corp-wide): 388.3B **Privately Held**
WEB: www.jiffylube.com
SIC: 7549 Lubrication service, automotive

GEOGRAPHIC SECTION

Newark - New Castle County (G-6870)

HQ: Jiffy Lube International, Inc.
700 Milam St
Houston TX 77002
713 546-1400

(G-6840)
JIM SELLERS
Also Called: Hill-Billy Towing Services
40 Brookhill Dr (19702-1301)
PHONE.................302 738-4149
Bill Betts, *Partner*
EMP: 4
SALES (est): 240K **Privately Held**
SIC: 7549 Towing service, automotive

(G-6841)
JOHN A DONOVAN
Also Called: Donovan Transport
131 E Rutherford Dr (19713-2024)
PHONE.................302 540-7512
Jeffrey M Donovan, *Principal*
EMP: 4 EST: 2012
SALES (est): 184.3K **Privately Held**
SIC: 4789 Transportation services

(G-6842)
JOHN F REINHARDT MD PA
4745 Ogletown Stanton Rd # 138 (19713-2074)
PHONE.................302 731-0800
John F Reinhardt MD, *President*
EMP: 4
SALES (est): 698.4K **Privately Held**
SIC: 8011 Infectious disease specialist, physician/surgeon

(G-6843)
JOHN LOVETT INC
Also Called: Prime America
520 Christiana Med Ctr (19702-1655)
PHONE.................302 455-9460
Steele Lovett, *President*
EMP: 60
SALES (est): 2.6MM **Privately Held**
WEB: www.johnlovett.com
SIC: 6163 6153 6141 6211 Mortgage brokers arranging for loans, using money of others; working capital financing; consumer finance companies; mortgages, buying & selling

(G-6844)
JOHN M OTTO OD
Also Called: Christiana Hosp Satellite Off
200 Hygeia Dr Ste 1420 (19713-2049)
PHONE.................302 623-0170
John M Otto, *Principal*
EMP: 5
SALES (est): 100.1K **Privately Held**
SIC: 8042 Offices & clinics of optometrists

(G-6845)
JOHN NISTA DDS
74 Omega Dr (19713-2063)
PHONE.................302 292-1552
John Nista, *Principal*
EMP: 4
SALES (est): 174.4K **Privately Held**
SIC: 8021 Dentists' office

(G-6846)
JOHN WASNIEWSKI DMD
103 Louviers Dr (19711-4163)
PHONE.................302 266-0200
John Wasniewski III DMD, *Principal*
EMP: 5
SALES (est): 108.9K **Privately Held**
SIC: 8021 Dentists' office

(G-6847)
JOHNSON MIRMIRAN THOMPSON INC
Also Called: Jmt
121 Continental Dr # 300 (19713-4342)
PHONE.................302 266-9600
Dave Duplessis, *Vice Pres*
EMP: 28
SALES (corp-wide): 259.1MM **Privately Held**
SIC: 8711 Civil engineering
PA: Johnson, Mirmiran & Thompson, Inc.
40 Wight Ave
Hunt Valley MD 21030
410 329-3100

(G-6848)
JOHNSTON ASSOCIATES
5 Winsome Way (19702-6311)
PHONE.................302 521-2984
Dean Johnston, *Principal*
EMP: 4
SALES (est): 382.6K **Privately Held**
SIC: 8742 Management consulting services

(G-6849)
JOINT ANLYTCL SYSTMS (AMRCS)
134a Sandy Dr (19713-1147)
PHONE.................302 607-0088
Joachim Gerstel, *Owner*
Ken Ellis, *Service Mgr*
EMP: 4
SALES (est): 504.9K
SALES (corp-wide): 619.5K **Privately Held**
SIC: 3826 5049 Chromatographic equipment, laboratory type; analytical instruments
HQ: Joint Analytical Systems Gmbh
Carl-Zeiss-Str. 49
Moers 47445
284 198-7110

(G-6850)
JOSE PICAZO M D P A
600 Christiana Med Ctr (19702-1656)
PHONE.................302 738-6535
Jose Picazo, *Principal*
EMP: 5
SALES (est): 469.3K **Privately Held**
SIC: 8011 Obstetrician

(G-6851)
JOSEPH T RYERSON & SON INC
700 Pencader Dr (19702-3310)
PHONE.................302 366-0555
Mike Burke, *Branch Mgr*
EMP: 33 **Publicly Held**
SIC: 1081 3499 Metal mining services; friction material, made from powdered metal
HQ: Joseph T. Ryerson & Son, Inc.
227 W Monroe St Fl 27
Chicago IL 60606
312 292-5000

(G-6852)
JOSHUA KALIN MD
314 E Main St Ste 302 (19711-7181)
PHONE.................302 737-6900
Joshua Kalin, *President*
Harriet Kalin, *Vice Pres*
EMP: 5
SALES (est): 281.2K **Privately Held**
SIC: 8011 Offices & clinics of medical doctors

(G-6853)
JP MORGAN TRUST COMPANY DEL
500 Stanton Christiana Rd (19713-2105)
PHONE.................302 634-3800
Hung Ngo, *Associate*
Jorge Reyes, *Associate*
EMP: 17 EST: 1911
SALES (est): 5.6MM **Privately Held**
SIC: 6021 National commercial banks

(G-6854)
JP SIGNDESIGN CO
205 Tamara Cir (19711-6946)
PHONE.................302 733-7547
Paul Piscaria, *President*
EMP: 1
SALES (est): 22K **Privately Held**
SIC: 3993 Signs & advertising specialties

(G-6855)
JPMORGAN CHASE & CO
500 Stanton Christiana Rd (19713-2105)
PHONE.................312 732-2801
Ted Dewoody, *Vice Pres*
Steven Hope, *Vice Pres*
Kyle Knestaut, *Vice Pres*
John Podesta, *Vice Pres*
Gayatri Satpathy, *Vice Pres*
EMP: 36
SALES (corp-wide): 131.4B **Publicly Held**
SIC: 6021 National commercial banks
PA: Jpmorgan Chase & Co.
383 Madison Ave
New York NY 10179
212 270-6000

(G-6856)
JPMORGAN CHASE BANK NAT ASSN
Also Called: Chase Manhattan
200 White Clay Center Dr (19711-5466)
PHONE.................302 634-1000
Michael Bearett, *Branch Mgr*
Yesny Winkels, *Analyst*
EMP: 1400
SALES (corp-wide): 131.4B **Publicly Held**
WEB: www.chase.com
SIC: 6021 National commercial banks
HQ: Jpmorgan Chase Bank, National Association
1111 Polaris Pkwy
Columbus OH 43240
614 436-3055

(G-6857)
JUDITH E MCCANN DMD
101 Barksdale Pro Ctr (19711-3258)
PHONE.................302 368-7463
Judith E McCann DMD, *Owner*
EMP: 7
SALES (est): 294.4K **Privately Held**
SIC: 8021 Offices & clinics of dentists

(G-6858)
JUNIOR BD OF CHRISTIANA CARE
Glass Box, The
4755 Stanton Ogletown Rd (19718-0001)
PHONE.................302 733-1100
Noreen West, *Opers-Prdtn-Mfg*
EMP: 5
SALES (corp-wide): 648.8K **Privately Held**
SIC: 5047 5947 Hospital equipment & furniture; gift shop
PA: Junior Board Of Christiana Care Inc
501 W 14th St
Wilmington DE 19801
302 428-2246

(G-6859)
JUST BE HOLDINGS LLC
200 Continental Dr # 401 (19713-4334)
PHONE.................833 454-5273
Christopher Kastigar, *Mng Member*
EMP: 5 **Privately Held**
SIC: 6719 Investment holding companies, except banks

(G-6860)
JUST FOR WOMEN OB/GYN PA
875 Aaa Blvd (19713-3624)
PHONE.................302 224-9400
Alexander Kirifides, *Principal*
EMP: 14
SALES (est): 1.2MM **Privately Held**
SIC: 8011 Gynecologist

(G-6861)
JZ ROAD & AIR CARGO LINES INC
40 E Main St Ste 1437 (19711-4639)
PHONE.................302 468-5988
Janos Karszky, *President*
Istvan Pal, *Vice Pres*
EMP: 4
SALES (est): 460.2K **Privately Held**
SIC: 4513 4522 4213 Air courier services; air cargo carriers, nonscheduled; less-than-truckload (LTL) transport

(G-6862)
K & L RENOVATIONS LLC
5 Garfield Way Ste A (19713-3457)
PHONE.................302 456-0373
EMP: 13
SQ FT: 2,000
SALES (est): 1.2MM **Privately Held**
SIC: 1795 Wrecking/Demolition Contractor

(G-6863)
K & S GARAGE INC
1060 S Chapel St (19702-1304)
PHONE.................302 731-7997
John D Smith, *President*
EMP: 4
SALES (est): 100K **Privately Held**
SIC: 7538 General automotive repair shops

(G-6864)
K & S TECHNICAL SERVICES INC
941 New London Rd (19711-2113)
P.O. Box 9827 (19714-4927)
PHONE.................302 737-9133
Ted Schreiber, *President*
EMP: 4
SALES (est): 580K **Privately Held**
WEB: www.kstechservices.com
SIC: 5049 8734 Scientific instruments; testing laboratories

(G-6865)
K F W MEDICAL INST DE LLC
1423 Capitol Trl Ste 3105 (19711)
PHONE.................302 533-6406
EMP: 5 EST: 2010
SALES (est): 400K **Privately Held**
SIC: 8011 Medical Doctor's Office

(G-6866)
KALIN EYE ASSOC
Also Called: Kalin, Neil S MD
314 E Main St Ste 302 (19711-7181)
PHONE.................302 292-2020
Neil Kalin, *Owner*
EMP: 5
SALES (est): 518.9K **Privately Held**
SIC: 8011 8049 Ophthalmologist; nutrition specialist

(G-6867)
KARINS ENGINEERING INC
Also Called: Karins & Associates
17 Polly Drummond Shpg Ct (19711-4820)
PHONE.................302 369-2900
Dev Sitaram, *President*
Bruce Buker, *Vice Pres*
John Johnson, *Vice Pres*
Ubaidur Quabili, *Project Engr*
John Barwick, *Design Engr*
EMP: 27 EST: 1973
SALES (est): 4.8MM **Privately Held**
WEB: www.karinsengineering.com
SIC: 8711 Consulting engineer; civil engineering

(G-6868)
KARLI FLANAGAN DVM
Also Called: In Home Veterinary Care
18 Silverwood Blvd (19711-8306)
PHONE.................302 893-7872
Karli Flanagan, *Owner*
EMP: 6
SALES (est): 231.8K **Privately Held**
SIC: 0742 Veterinarian, animal specialties

(G-6869)
KCH VENTURES LLC
12 Timber Creek Ln (19711-2606)
PHONE.................302 737-6260
Kathy Hundley, *Owner*
EMP: 4
SALES (est): 341K **Privately Held**
SIC: 8742 Business consultant

(G-6870)
KCI PROTECTION TECH LLC
1352 Marrows Rd Ste 100 (19711-5476)
PHONE.................302 543-8340
John C Fannin III, *CEO*
EMP: 4
SALES (est): 273.8K
SALES (corp-wide): 185.6MM **Privately Held**
SIC: 8711 Consulting engineer
HQ: Kci Technologies, Inc.
936 Ridgebrook Rd
Sparks MD 21152
410 316-7800

Newark - New Castle County (G-6871) — GEOGRAPHIC SECTION

(G-6871)
KCI TECHNOLOGIES INC
1352 Marrows Rd (19711-5475)
PHONE.................302 731-9176
Michael Ebner, *Office Mgr*
Dwight Walters, *Branch Mgr*
EMP: 30
SALES (corp-wide): 185.6MM **Privately Held**
SIC: 8711 8712 Civil engineering; architectural services; architectural engineering
HQ: Kci Technologies, Inc.
   936 Ridgebrook Rd
   Sparks MD 21152
   410 316-7800

(G-6872)
KEENER-SENSENIG CO
491 Gender Rd (19713-2828)
PHONE.................302 453-8584
Dana Ressler, *Partner*
Allen Ressler, *Partner*
James Ressler, *Partner*
EMP: 14
SQ FT: 4,000
SALES (est): 675K **Privately Held**
SIC: 0782 Lawn care services; spraying services, lawn; landscape contractors

(G-6873)
KELLY ROBERT & ASSOC LLC
Also Called: Liberty Tax Service
418 Suburban Dr (19711-3564)
PHONE.................302 737-7785
Robert Kelly,
EMP: 10
SALES (est): 349.1K **Privately Held**
SIC: 7291 Tax return preparation services

(G-6874)
KENNETH BUTLER
Also Called: Vet Spa, The
34 Cheswold Blvd Apt 1b (19713-4141)
PHONE.................302 561-8114
EMP: 4
SALES (est): 140K **Privately Held**
SIC: 8093 Specialty Outpatient Clinics, Nec

(G-6875)
KERCHER GROUP INC (PA)
254 Chapman Rd Ste 202 (19702-5422)
PHONE.................302 894-1098
Alan Kercher, *President*
Steve Lander, *Opers Staff*
Qazi Aurangzeb, *Engineer*
Jim Lober, *Engineer*
Aaron Gerber, *Project Engr*
EMP: 10
SALES (est): 1.6MM **Privately Held**
SIC: 8711 Civil engineering

(G-6876)
KERRY S KIRIFIDES MD PA
Also Called: Just Kids Pediatrics
875 Aaa Blvd Ste C (19713-3624)
PHONE.................302 918-6400
Kerry Kirifides MD, *President*
Pam Bevenour, *Practice Mgr*
EMP: 9
SALES (est): 821.7K **Privately Held**
SIC: 8011 Pediatrician

(G-6877)
KEVAL CORP
Also Called: Comfort Inn
100 Mcintosh Plz (19713-3232)
PHONE.................302 453-9100
Jack Patel, *Owner*
EMP: 10
SALES (est): 346.5K **Privately Held**
SIC: 7011 Hotels & motels

(G-6878)
KEVIN LAMMERS INS
18 Carriage Ln (19711-2045)
PHONE.................302 283-1210
Kevin Lammers, *Owner*
EMP: 4
SALES (est): 177.1K **Privately Held**
SIC: 6411 Insurance agents, brokers & service

(G-6879)
KEYSTACK INC
2035 Sunset Lake Rd (19702-2600)
PHONE.................510 629-5099
Khoa Do, *Principal*
EMP: 1
SALES: 20K **Privately Held**
SIC: 7372 Application computer software

(G-6880)
KEYSTONE AUTISM SERVICES
7 Firethorn Ct (19711-4900)
PHONE.................302 731-3115
John Pengsir, *Director*
EMP: 1
SALES (est): 188.1K **Privately Held**
SIC: 8361 Halfway group home, persons with social or personal problems

(G-6881)
KEYSTONE SERVICE SYSTEMS INC
300 Creek View Rd (19711-8546)
PHONE.................302 286-7234
Denise Cragg, *Manager*
EMP: 104
SALES (corp-wide): 12.1MM **Privately Held**
SIC: 8361 Home for the mentally handicapped
HQ: Keystone Service Systems, Inc.
   4391 Sturbridge Dr
   Harrisburg PA 17110
   717 232-7509

(G-6882)
KEYSTONE SERVICE SYSTEMS INC
824 N Barrett Ln (19702-6906)
PHONE.................302 273-3952
EMP: 4
SALES (corp-wide): 12.1MM **Privately Held**
SIC: 8361 8322 Home for the mentally handicapped; individual & family services
HQ: Keystone Service Systems, Inc.
   4391 Sturbridge Dr
   Harrisburg PA 17110
   717 232-7509

(G-6883)
KHA-NEKE INC
Also Called: RC Turner Collection
25 Hempstead Dr (19702-7713)
PHONE.................302 440-4728
Roger Turner, *President*
EMP: 3
SQ FT: 1,000
SALES (est): 344.8K **Privately Held**
SIC: 2329 Shirt & slack suits: men's, youths' & boys'

(G-6884)
KHAN PEDIATRICS INC (PA)
266 S College Ave (19711-5235)
PHONE.................302 449-5791
Mohammad A Khan, *Principal*
EMP: 8
SALES (est): 801.8K **Privately Held**
SIC: 8011 Pediatrician

(G-6885)
KHANNA ENTPS LTD A LTD PARTNR
Also Called: Country Suites By Carlson
1024 Old Churchmans Rd (19713-2102)
PHONE.................302 266-6400
Richard Carter, *Manager*
EMP: 30
SALES (corp-wide): 7.1MM **Privately Held**
WEB: www.kehotels.com
SIC: 7011 Hotels & motels
PA: Khanna Enterprises, Ltd., A Limited Partnership
   2601 Main St Ste 320
   Irvine CA 92614
   949 502-7892

(G-6886)
KIDS NEST DAY CARE
24 Donaldson Dr (19713-1783)
PHONE.................302 731-7017
EMP: 5
SALES (est): 57.6K **Privately Held**
SIC: 8351 Preschool center

(G-6887)
KIMBERTON APARTMENTS ASSOC LP
Also Called: Carrington Way Apartments
100 Kimberton Dr (19713-1676)
PHONE.................302 368-0116
William Demarco, *Partner*
Jackie Edmanson, *Principal*
Michael Stahler, *Controller*
EMP: 13 EST: 2009
SALES: 950K **Privately Held**
SIC: 6513 Apartment building operators

(G-6888)
KINDERCARE LEARNING CTRS LLC
100 Paxson Dr (19702-4738)
PHONE.................302 834-6931
Irene Kerrigan, *Director*
EMP: 19
SALES (corp-wide): 963.9MM **Privately Held**
SIC: 8351 8211 Group day care center; kindergarten
HQ: Kindercare Learning Centers, Llc
   650 Ne Holladay St # 1400
   Portland OR 97232
   503 872-1300

(G-6889)
KINOLAND LOGISTICS LLC
256 Chapman Rd Ste 105 (19702-5417)
PHONE.................302 565-4505
Mariam N Kamwani, *President*
EMP: 4
SALES (est): 89K **Privately Held**
SIC: 4789 Transportation services

(G-6890)
KIRKS FLOWERS INC
Also Called: Kirk Flowers
7 Ash Ave (19711-5500)
PHONE.................302 737-3931
John Mayer, *President*
Elizabeth Mayer, *Vice Pres*
EMP: 23
SQ FT: 6,000
SALES (est): 1.5MM **Privately Held**
WEB: www.kirksflowers.com
SIC: 5992 7389 Flowers, fresh; interior decorating

(G-6891)
KIRKWOOD ANMAL BRDING GROOMING
Also Called: V C A Kirkwood Animal Hospital
1501 Capitol Trl (19711-5715)
PHONE.................302 737-1098
Linda Simione, *Manager*
EMP: 21
SALES: 544.3K
SALES (corp-wide): 37.6B **Privately Held**
SIC: 0742 Animal hospital services, pets & other animal specialties
HQ: Vca Inc.
   12401 W Olympic Blvd
   Los Angeles CA 90064
   310 571-6500

(G-6892)
KIRKWOOD DENTAL ASSOCIATES PA
1200 Peoples Plz Ste 1260 (19702-5701)
PHONE.................302 834-7700
Peggy Cusatis, *Manager*
EMP: 6
SALES (corp-wide): 2.9MM **Privately Held**
WEB: www.kdental.com
SIC: 8021 Dentists' office
PA: Kirkwood Dental Associates Pa
   710 Greenbank Rd Ste A
   Wilmington DE 19808
   302 994-2582

(G-6893)
KIRKWOOD SMOKE SHOP
151 E Main St (19711-7313)
PHONE.................302 525-6718
EMP: 4 EST: 2010
SALES (est): 364.5K **Privately Held**
SIC: 5159 Tobacco distributors & products

(G-6894)
KIRKWOOD TIRES INC
1929 Kirkwood Hwy (19711-5773)
PHONE.................302 737-2460
Clarence E Ward Jr, *President*
EMP: 5 EST: 1963
SQ FT: 4,000
SALES (est): 572.8K **Privately Held**
WEB: www.kirkwoodtireinc.com
SIC: 5531 7538 Automotive tires; general automotive repair shops

(G-6895)
KISSANGEN INC
Also Called: Ksn
113 Barksdale Pro Ctr (19711-3258)
PHONE.................414 446-4182
Mark Hufham, *CEO*
Jeff Hunter, *COO*
EMP: 25 EST: 2013
SQ FT: 20,000
SALES (est): 1.3MM **Privately Held**
SIC: 3569 3511 3621 Gas producers, generators & other gas related equipment; turbines & turbine generator sets; storage battery chargers, motor & engine generator type

(G-6896)
KITTY JAZZY PUBLISHING
702 Cobble Creek Curv (19702-2421)
PHONE.................302 897-8842
Kevin Attaway, *Owner*
EMP: 2
SALES (est): 45.4K **Privately Held**
SIC: 2741 Miscellaneous publishing

(G-6897)
KLEEN-COMP LLC
32 Edgebrooke Way (19702-1642)
PHONE.................302 981-0791
Adeniran Emiola, *Director*
EMP: 4
SALES (est): 43.3K **Privately Held**
SIC: 7349 7389 Building & office cleaning services; janitorial service, contract basis; office cleaning or charring; cleaning service, industrial or commercial;

(G-6898)
KMP MECHANICAL LLC
406 Suburban Dr 155 (19711-3566)
PHONE.................410 392-6126
Mark Miller,
EMP: 6 **Privately Held**
SIC: 1711 Mechanical contractor
PA: Kmp Mechanical Llc
   45 Appleton Rd
   Elkton MD 21921

(G-6899)
KNEISLEY EYE CARE PA
45 E Main St Ste 201 (19711-4600)
PHONE.................302 224-3000
Yvonne Kneisley, *President*
EMP: 5
SALES (est): 673.1K **Privately Held**
SIC: 8042 Specialized optometrists

(G-6900)
KNIGHTS YORK CROSS OF HONOUR
208 Sypherd Dr (19711-3627)
PHONE.................302 731-4817
Don Thomas, *President*
EMP: 5 EST: 1983
SALES (est): 123K **Privately Held**
SIC: 8399 8699 Fund raising organization, non-fee basis; charitable organization

(G-6901)
KOGUT TECH CONSULTING INC
Also Called: Ktc
24 Ohio State Dr (19713-1164)
PHONE.................302 455-0388
Spence Kogut, *President*
EMP: 5
SALES (est): 205.4K **Privately Held**
SIC: 7379 Computer related consulting services

GEOGRAPHIC SECTION
Newark - New Castle County (G-6933)

(G-6902)
KRAL ELECTRONICS INC
Also Called: Clark Video Productions
2403 Ogletown Rd (19711-5487)
PHONE..................302 737-1300
EMP: 10
SQ FT: 5,000
SALES: 3MM Privately Held
SIC: 7629 Electrical Repair

(G-6903)
KRISTOL CTR FOR JEWISH LF INC
47 W Delaware Ave (19711-4635)
PHONE..................302 453-0479
Donna Schewartz, *Exec Dir*
EMP: 5
SALES: 784.6K Privately Held
SIC: 8641 Youth organizations

(G-6904)
KS KITCHEN LLC
6 Smalleys Ct (19702-5263)
PHONE..................302 743-4349
Kristopher Moore,
EMP: 4
SALES (est): 124.8K Privately Held
SIC: 8742 Marketing consulting services

(G-6905)
L & B PUBLISHING
44 Lakewood Cir (19711-2343)
PHONE..................302 743-4061
Kelly Penoyer, *Principal*
EMP: 2
SALES (est): 45.4K Privately Held
SIC: 2741 Miscellaneous publishing

(G-6906)
L & L CARPET DISCOUNT CTRS INC
Also Called: Lane Carpet Company
900 Interchange Blvd # 901 (19711-3563)
PHONE..................302 292-3712
Mike Geisler, *Branch Mgr*
EMP: 6
SALES (corp-wide): 43.9MM Privately Held
SIC: 5023 5713 Floor coverings; carpets
PA: L & L Carpet Discount Centers, Inc.
7459 Mason King Ct
Manassas VA 20109
703 368-5025

(G-6907)
L A MASONARY INC
125 Sun Ct (19711-3413)
P.O. Box 6272, Wilmington (19804-0872)
PHONE..................302 239-6833
Leon T Ashcraft, *President*
Faith A Smith, *Corp Secy*
EMP: 15
SALES: 2.3MM Privately Held
SIC: 1741 Masonry & other stonework

(G-6908)
LABORATORY CORPORATION AMERICA
2600 Glasgow Ave (19702-4773)
PHONE..................302 834-1359
EMP: 8
SALES (est): 87K Publicly Held
SIC: 8071 Testing laboratories
HQ: Laboratory Corporation Of America
358 S Main St Ste 458
Burlington NC 27215
336 229-1127

(G-6909)
LABORATORY CORPORATION AMERICA
4623 Ogletown Stanton Rd (19713-2006)
PHONE..................302 737-3525
Leanne Greg, *Branch Mgr*
EMP: 25 Publicly Held
WEB: www.labcorp.com
SIC: 8071 Testing laboratories
HQ: Laboratory Corporation Of America
358 S Main St Ste 458
Burlington NC 27215
336 229-1127

(G-6910)
LABORATORY CORPORATION AMERICA
314 E Main St Ste 105 (19711-7180)
PHONE..................302 731-0244
Dana Mc Fadden, *Principal*
EMP: 7 Publicly Held
WEB: www.labcorp.com
SIC: 8071 Pathological laboratory
HQ: Laboratory Corporation Of America
358 S Main St Ste 458
Burlington NC 27215
336 229-1127

(G-6911)
LABORERS INTL UN N AMER
Also Called: LOCAL 199
308 Markus Ct (19713-1151)
PHONE..................302 654-2880
James Marvelias, *Business Mgr*
EMP: 5
SQ FT: 2,000
SALES: 1.1MM Privately Held
WEB: www.local199.com
SIC: 8631 Labor union

(G-6912)
LACIEAH INC
14 Creek Ln (19702-5937)
PHONE..................302 365-5585
Lorraine Green, *CEO*
EMP: 5
SALES (est): 235.7K Privately Held
SIC: 1799 Special trade contractors

(G-6913)
LAKE THERAPY CREATIONS
2271 Sunset Lake Rd (19702-2633)
PHONE..................410 920-7130
EMP: 8
SALES (est): 73.3K Privately Held
SIC: 8093 Rehabilitation center, outpatient treatment

(G-6914)
LAMED LLC
2915 Ogletown Rd (19713-1927)
PHONE..................302 597-9018
Stephane Megioni, *CEO*
EMP: 7
SALES (est): 164.3K Privately Held
SIC: 7371 Computer software systems analysis & design, custom

(G-6915)
LANDMARK ENGINEERING INC (PA)
Also Called: Landmark Science & Engineering
200 Continental Dr # 400 (19713-4337)
PHONE..................302 323-9377
Bruce J Tease, *Ch of Bd*
Ted Williams, *President*
Joseph Charma, *COO*
Keith Kooker, *Exec VP*
John Gonzalez, *Project Engr*
EMP: 55
SQ FT: 10,000
SALES: 6.2MM Privately Held
SIC: 8711 8713 8748 8999 Civil engineering; surveying services; environmental consultant; natural resource preservation service

(G-6916)
LANDMARK ENGINEERING INC
Also Called: L E I
200 Continental Dr # 400 (19713-4337)
PHONE..................302 734-9597
Keith Cooker, *Manager*
EMP: 8
SALES (corp-wide): 6.2MM Privately Held
SIC: 8711 8713 Civil engineering; surveying services
PA: Landmark Engineering, Inc.
200 Continental Dr # 400
Newark DE 19713
302 323-9377

(G-6917)
LAP STUDIOS INC
2035 Sunset Lake Rd (19702-2600)
PHONE..................213 357-0825
Anping LI, *CEO*
EMP: 10
SALES: 100K Privately Held
SIC: 7371 Computer software development & applications

(G-6918)
LARSON ENGINEERING INC
910 S Chapel St Ste 200 (19713-3469)
PHONE..................302 731-7434
George Larson Jr, *President*
Doug Liberman, *Vice Pres*
Douglas J Liberman, *Vice Pres*
EMP: 9
SALES (est): 1MM Privately Held
SIC: 8711 Civil engineering

(G-6919)
LAUREL BRIDGE SOFTWARE INC
500 Creek View Rd Ste 200 (19711-8549)
PHONE..................302 453-0222
Mark M Blair, *President*
John Stonkus, *Sales Staff*
Bronson Hokuf, *Manager*
Gregory Muller, *Manager*
Suzan Ragean, *Manager*
EMP: 3
SALES: 500K Privately Held
WEB: www.laurelbridge.com
SIC: 7372 Business oriented computer software

(G-6920)
LAW OFFICE OF JAMES CURRA
256 Chapman Rd Ste 107 (19202-5417)
PHONE..................302 894-1111
James Curran, *Owner*
EMP: 4
SALES (est): 222.7K Privately Held
SIC: 8111 General practice law office

(G-6921)
LAW OFFICE OF R I MASTEN JR
500 Creek View Rd Ste 304 (19711-8549)
PHONE..................302 358-2044
Robert I Masten, *Principal*
EMP: 5
SALES (est): 303.4K Privately Held
SIC: 8111 General practice attorney, lawyer

(G-6922)
LAWNWORKS INC
667 Dawson Dr Ste D (19713-3437)
P.O. Box 5538 (19714-5538)
PHONE..................302 368-5699
William F Hobbs III, *President*
Bonnie M Hobbs, *Vice Pres*
EMP: 10 EST: 1992
SQ FT: 1,250
SALES: 400K Privately Held
SIC: 0782 Lawn care services

(G-6923)
LAWRENCE KENNEDY
Also Called: Ikeno Tech Business Solutions
262 Chapman Rd Ste 107 (19702-5412)
PHONE..................302 533-5880
Lawrence Kennedy, *Owner*
EMP: 10
SALES (est): 281.2K Privately Held
SIC: 8741 Business management

(G-6924)
LAYERCAKE LLC
42 Hawthorne Ave (19711-5566)
PHONE..................571 449-7538
Emmanuel T'Chawi, *CEO*
EMP: 6
SALES (est): 144.4K Privately Held
SIC: 7379

(G-6925)
LEADERSHIP INSTITUTE INC
76 Omega Dr (19713-2064)
PHONE..................302 368-7292
James Bettle, *President*
Deborah A Bettle, *Corp Secy*
EMP: 16
SQ FT: 1,300
SALES (est): 226.6K Privately Held
WEB: www.leadershipinstitute.org
SIC: 8331 Job training & vocational rehabilitation services

(G-6926)
LEARNING EXPRESS ACADEMY
302 Darling St (19702-3775)
PHONE..................302 737-8260
Jennifer Valentine, *Owner*
Becky Pullin, *Admin Asst*
EMP: 22 EST: 2007
SALES: 609.3K Privately Held
SIC: 8351 Preschool center

(G-6927)
LEARNING EXPRESS PRESCHOOL
300 Darling St (19702-3775)
PHONE..................302 737-8990
Beth Smith, *Director*
EMP: 10
SALES (est): 303.2K Privately Held
SIC: 8351 Preschool center

(G-6928)
LEARNING PATCH KIDS
25 Red Mill Rd (19711-6665)
PHONE..................302 368-7208
EMP: 5
SALES (est): 68.4K Privately Held
SIC: 8351 Child Day Care Services

(G-6929)
LEARNING TRAIN LLC
309 Possum Park Rd (19711-3853)
PHONE..................302 731-0944
Jasmine Prince,
EMP: 15 EST: 2018
SALES: 100K Privately Held
SIC: 8351 Child day care services

(G-6930)
LEEBER LIMITED USA
Also Called: Elegance
115 Pencader Dr (19702-3322)
PHONE..................302 733-0991
Alice Ho, *President*
Floyd Ho, *Vice Pres*
Willy Ho, *Vice Pres*
◆ EMP: 14
SQ FT: 33,000
SALES (est): 2.6MM Privately Held
WEB: www.leeber.com
SIC: 3914 Silverware

(G-6931)
LENDING MANAGER HOLDINGS LLC
152 E Main St (19711-7308)
PHONE..................888 501-0335
EMP: 9
SALES (est): 366.8K
SALES (corp-wide): 7.1MM Privately Held
SIC: 6163 Loan brokers
PA: Volly
53 Commerce Way
Woburn MA 01801
781 938-1175

(G-6932)
LEON N WEINER & ASSOCIATES INC
Also Called: Main Towers
330 E Main St Apt 214 (19711-8406)
PHONE..................302 737-9574
Lynn Makowski, *Branch Mgr*
EMP: 4
SALES (corp-wide): 54MM Privately Held
SIC: 6513 Apartment building operators
PA: Leon N. Weiner & Associates, Inc.
1 Fox Pt Ctr 4 Denny Rd
Wilmington DE 19809
302 656-1354

(G-6933)
LEXINGTON GREEN APARTMENTS
1201 Kingston Bldg (19702-5261)
PHONE..................302 322-8959
Diane Grant, *General Mgr*
Sue Rimel, *General Mgr*
EMP: 7
SALES (est): 520.5K Privately Held
WEB: www.lexingtongreenapartments.com
SIC: 6513 Apartment building operators

(G-6934)
LIBERTY ELEVATOR EXPERTS LLC
625 Barksdale Rd Ste 113 (19711-4535)
PHONE.................................302 650-4688
Christopher Dodds, *Principal*
EMP: 4
SALES (est): 263.4K **Privately Held**
SIC: 5084 Elevators

(G-6935)
LIFETOUCH PORTRAIT STUDIOS INC
Christina Mall Ste 606 (19702)
PHONE.................................302 453-8080
Tracy Telletier, *Branch Mgr*
EMP: 6
SALES (corp-wide): 1.9B **Privately Held**
WEB: www.jcpportraits.com
SIC: 7221 Photographic studios, portrait
HQ: Lifetouch Portrait Studios Inc.
   11000 Viking Dr
   Eden Prairie MN 55344
   952 826-4335

(G-6936)
LINGUATEXT LTD
103 Walker Way (19711-6119)
PHONE.................................302 453-8695
Tom Lathrop, *President*
EMP: 2
SALES (est): 200K **Privately Held**
WEB: www.juandelacuesta.com
SIC: 5192 2731 Books; textbooks: publishing & printing

(G-6937)
LINKS OUTBOARD LLC
20 Brookhill Dr (19702-1301)
PHONE.................................302 368-2860
Ted Link,
EMP: 4
SALES (est): 505.5K **Privately Held**
WEB: www.linksmarine.com
SIC: 7699 Boat repair

(G-6938)
LINNE INDUSTRIES LLC
11 Bridlebrook Ln (19711-2003)
P.O. Box 9856 (19714-4956)
PHONE.................................302 454-1439
Sandra Burton, *Principal*
Craig Burton, *Principal*
EMP: 2 **EST:** 2013
SALES (est): 288.3K **Privately Held**
SIC: 3563 Air & gas compressors

(G-6939)
LISA BROADBENT INSURANCE INC
Also Called: Nationwide
20 Polly Drummond Hill Rd (19711-5703)
PHONE.................................302 731-0044
Lisa Broadbent, *President*
Caron Blackwell, *Manager*
Jo Dougherty, *Agent*
Julia Wang, *Agent*
Scott Wilson, *Agent*
EMP: 11
SALES (est): 1.8MM **Privately Held**
SIC: 6411 Insurance agents

(G-6940)
LISA R SAVAGE
260 Chapman Rd Ste 100b (19702-5410)
PHONE.................................302 353-7052
Lisa R Savage, *Executive*
EMP: 4
SALES (est): 42.4K **Privately Held**
SIC: 8322 Individual & family services

(G-6941)
LITTLE SISTERS OF THE POOR
Also Called: Jeanne Jugan Residence
185 Salem Church Rd (19713-2997)
PHONE.................................302 368-5886
Margaret Halloran, *President*
Cecile Zeringue, *Vice Pres*
EMP: 80
SALES: 6.2MM **Privately Held**
WEB: www.littlesistersofthepoor.net
SIC: 8059 8361 8052 Rest home, with health care; residential care; intermediate care facilities

(G-6942)
LITTLE STARS INC
947 Old Harmony Rd (19713-4106)
PHONE.................................302 737-9759
Elizabeth Cahill, *President*
EMP: 10
SALES (est): 451.8K **Privately Held**
SIC: 8351 Preschool center

(G-6943)
LIVING WELL MAGAZINE
1519 Old Coach Rd (19711-5803)
PHONE.................................302 355-0929
Brian Strauss, *Owner*
Diane Strauss, *Treasurer*
EMP: 1
SALES (est): 89.6K **Privately Held**
SIC: 2721 7389 Magazines: publishing only, not printed on site;

(G-6944)
LIVINGSTON HEALTHCARE SVCS INC
220 Lake Dr (19702-3353)
PHONE.................................302 631-5000
EMP: 272
SALES (est): 14.4MM
SALES (corp-wide): 71.8B **Publicly Held**
SIC: 4215 4513 7513 4522 Package delivery, vehicular; parcel delivery, vehicular; letter delivery, private air; package delivery, private air; parcel delivery, private air; truck rental & leasing, no drivers; flying charter service
HQ: Ups Logistics Group Inc
   55 Glenlake Pkwy
   Atlanta GA 30328
   678 746-4100

(G-6945)
LNH INC
Also Called: Hosting.com
650 Pencader Dr (19702-3348)
PHONE.................................302 731-4948
Art Zeile, *Principal*
EMP: 13
SALES (est): 1MM **Privately Held**
SIC: 4813

(G-6946)
LOCKER CONSTRUCTION INC
314 Cox Rd (19713-3025)
PHONE.................................302 239-2859
Roy Locker, *President*
EMP: 5
SQ FT: 1,000
SALES (est): 430K **Privately Held**
SIC: 8741 1521 1542 Construction management; general remodeling, single-family houses; new construction, single-family houses; commercial & office building, new construction; commercial & office buildings, renovation & repair

(G-6947)
LON SPA INC
330 Suburban Dr (19711-3599)
PHONE.................................302 368-4595
Carol Cook, *President*
EMP: 7
SALES (est): 221.8K **Privately Held**
SIC: 7999 7231 Tennis courts, outdoor/indoor: non-membership; manicurist, pedicurist

(G-6948)
LOOMCRAFT TEXTILE & SUPPLY CO
Also Called: Interior Alternative, The
211 Executive Dr Ste 13 (19702-3358)
PHONE.................................302 454-3232
Victoria Moulen, *Manager*
EMP: 10
SALES (corp-wide): 28.4MM **Privately Held**
WEB: www.fsco.com
SIC: 5131 5949 Piece goods & other fabrics; fabric stores piece goods
PA: Loomcraft Textile & Supply Company
   2801 Lawndale Dr
   Greensboro NC 27408
   336 282-1100

(G-6949)
LORI EMORY
35 Winsome Way (19702-6313)
PHONE.................................302 737-7352
Lori Emory, *Owner*
EMP: 1
SALES (est): 71.4K **Privately Held**
SIC: 2393 Textile bags

(G-6950)
LORIS HANDS INC
100 Discovery Blvd Fl 4 (19713-1313)
PHONE.................................302 440-5454
Sarah Lafave, *CEO*
Maggie Ratnayake, *Director*
EMP: 6 **EST:** 2009
SALES (est): 133.8K **Privately Held**
SIC: 8399 Community development groups

(G-6951)
LOUIS CAPANO AND ASSOCIATES
6502 Winterhaven Dr (19702-8325)
PHONE.................................302 738-8000
Louis Capano, *Owner*
EMP: 4
SALES (est): 252.3K **Privately Held**
SIC: 6513 Apartment building operators

(G-6952)
LOUVIERS FEDERAL CREDIT UNION (PA)
185 S Main St (19711-7941)
PHONE.................................302 733-0426
Christopher J Davis, *CEO*
EMP: 10
SQ FT: 3,600
SALES: 5.5MM **Privately Held**
WEB: www.louviers.com
SIC: 6061 Federal credit unions

(G-6953)
LOWES HOME CENTERS LLC
2000 Ogletown Rd (19711-5439)
PHONE.................................302 781-1154
Kevin Andrews, *Office Mgr*
EMP: 157
SALES (corp-wide): 71.3B **Publicly Held**
SIC: 5211 5031 5722 5064 Lumber & other building materials; building materials, exterior; building materials, interior; household appliance stores; electrical appliances, television & radio
HQ: Lowe's Home Centers, Llc
   1605 Curtis Bridge Rd
   Wilkesboro NC 28697
   336 658-4000

(G-6954)
LSREF4 LIGHTHOUSE CORP ACQSTN
146 Chestnut Crossing Dr (19713-2600)
PHONE.................................302 737-8500
Annmarie Hobson, *Branch Mgr*
EMP: 7 **Privately Held**
WEB: www.homeproperties.com
SIC: 6513 Apartment building operators
PA: Lsref4 Lighthouse Corporate Acquisitions, Llc
   11459 Cronhill Dr
   Owings Mills MD 21117

(G-6955)
LUKE DESTEFANO INC
Also Called: First State Printing
107b Albe Dr Ste B (19702-1336)
PHONE.................................302 455-0710
Luke Destefano, *President*
EMP: 2
SQ FT: 1,000
SALES (est): 120K **Privately Held**
WEB: www.firststateprinting.com
SIC: 2752 Commercial printing, offset

(G-6956)
LUMI CASES LLC
501 Capitol Trl Apt 201 (19711-5507)
PHONE.................................302 525-6971
EMP: 2
SALES (est): 104.7K **Privately Held**
SIC: 3523 Farm machinery & equipment

(G-6957)
LUMULABS INC
2035 Sunset Lake Rd B2 (19702-2600)
PHONE.................................302 261-5284
Stas Stankovic, *CEO*
EMP: 5
SALES: 50K **Privately Held**
SIC: 7371 Computer software development & applications

(G-6958)
LUNDBERG TECH INC - AMERICA
667 Dawson Dr Ste C (19713-3437)
P.O. Box 1234, Bear (19701-7234)
PHONE.................................302 738-2500
Charlotte Lercke, *Finance Asst*
Kai Hornetz, *Sales Staff*
EMP: 4
SALES (est): 404.1K **Privately Held**
SIC: 5084 Industrial machinery & equipment

(G-6959)
LUZ D REYNOSO
179 W Chestnut Hill Rd # 6 (19713-2210)
PHONE.................................302 358-6237
Luz Del Alba Reynoso Lcsw, *Principal*
EMP: 4
SALES (est): 42.4K **Privately Held**
SIC: 8322 Individual & family services

(G-6960)
LYCRA COMPANY LLC
150 Red Mill Rd (19711-6632)
PHONE.................................302 731-6800
EMP: 2
SALES (corp-wide): 40.6B **Privately Held**
SIC: 2221 Textile mills, broadwoven: silk & manmade, also glass
HQ: The Lycra Company Llc
   2711 Centerville Rd # 300
   Wilmington DE 19808
   316 226-9361

(G-6961)
LYNX GENERAL CONTRACTING
1267 Old Cooches Brdg Rd (19713-2336)
PHONE.................................302 368-9401
Mark Willhoite,
Jeff Stapen,
EMP: 4
SALES: 350K **Privately Held**
SIC: 1541 1799 Factory construction; athletic & recreation facilities construction

(G-6962)
LYRA SOFTWARE INC
2035 Sunset Lake Rd B2 (19702-2600)
PHONE.................................347 506-5287
March Rogers, *Principal*
EMP: 5
SALES (est): 117.2K **Privately Held**
SIC: 7372 Educational computer software

(G-6963)
M A K ROOFING INC
10 Deerborne Trl (19702-2041)
PHONE.................................302 737-5380
Kenneth M Horkey, *President*
EMP: 4
SALES (est): 228.3K **Privately Held**
SIC: 1761 Gutter & downspout contractor

(G-6964)
M CUBED TECHNOLOGIES INC
1300 Marrows Rd (19711-5445)
PHONE.................................302 454-8600
Elmer Miller, *Branch Mgr*
EMP: 100
SALES (corp-wide): 1.3B **Publicly Held**
WEB: www.mmmt.com
SIC: 3444 Sheet metalwork
HQ: M Cubed Technologies, Inc.
   31 Pecks Ln Ste 8
   Newtown CT 06470
   203 304-2940

(G-6965)
M DIANA METZGER MD
665 Churchmans Rd (19702-1918)
PHONE.................................302 731-0942
M D Metzger MD, *Owner*
EMP: 10

GEOGRAPHIC SECTION

Newark - New Castle County (G-6996)

SALES (est): 199.5K **Privately Held**
SIC: 8011 General & family practice, physician/surgeon

(G-6966)
M IMRAN MD
2707 Kirkwood Hwy Ste 1 (19711-6828)
PHONE 302 453-7399
Mohammad Imran MD, *Owner*
EMP: 6
SALES (est): 210.9K **Privately Held**
SIC: 8011 Gynecologist; obstetrician; physicians' office, including specialists

(G-6967)
M&M MASS SPEC CONSULTING LLC
Also Called: ASAP Mass Spectrometry
28 Tenby Chase Dr (19711-2441)
P.O. Box 191, Hockessin (19707-0191)
PHONE 302 250-4488
Richard McKay,
EMP: 2
SALES: 50K **Privately Held**
SIC: 3826 Analytical instruments

(G-6968)
M3 CONTRACTING LLC
13 Garfield Way (19713-3450)
PHONE 302 781-3143
Louis Mene,
EMP: 30
SALES (est): 5.4MM **Privately Held**
SIC: 1742 Drywall; acoustical & ceiling work; insulation, buildings

(G-6969)
MAALIKA K LLC
35 Stature Dr (19713-3565)
PHONE 844 622-5452
Krystina Muhammad, *Mng Member*
EMP: 1
SALES: 24K **Privately Held**
SIC: 2337 Women's & misses' suits & skirts

(G-6970)
MADE BY TILDE INC
2035 Sunset Lake Rd B2 (19702-2600)
PHONE 302 766-7215
EMP: 4
SALES (est): 89.7K **Privately Held**
SIC: 7371 Computer software development & applications

(G-6971)
MAESTRIK INC
2035 Sunset Lake Rd D2 (19702-2600)
PHONE 312 925-3116
Mario Tobon, *President*
EMP: 32
SALES (est): 543.4K **Privately Held**
SIC: 7371 Custom computer programming services

(G-6972)
MAGOWI CONSULTING GROUP LLC
262 Chapman Rd Ste 107 (19702-5412)
PHONE 832 301-9230
Alovett King, *Mng Member*
Lawrence Kennedy,
Joe Mulbah,
Jones Williams,
EMP: 10
SALES (est): 251.4K **Privately Held**
SIC: 8711 1771 1794 8243 Building construction consultant; parking lot construction; excavation & grading, building construction; operator training, computer; software training, computer

(G-6973)
MAIN EVENT INC
2601 Eastburn Ctr (19711-7285)
PHONE 302 737-2225
Gene Chudzik, *President*
EMP: 5
SALES: 48K **Privately Held**
SIC: 7231 Beauty shops

(G-6974)
MAIN STREET FMLY CHIROPRACTIC
Also Called: New Castle Chiropractic Ctr PA
280 E Main St Ste 111 (19711-7324)
PHONE 302 737-8667
Patrick Roberts, *President*
EMP: 4
SALES (est): 240K **Privately Held**
SIC: 8041 Offices & clinics of chiropractors

(G-6975)
MAIN TWERS PRSRVTION ASSOC LLC
330 E Main St (19711-8416)
PHONE 302 737-9574
David Curtis, *Exec VP*
William Demarco, *Vice Pres*
EMP: 13
SALES (est): 620.4K **Privately Held**
SIC: 6513 Apartment building operators

(G-6976)
MAINTENANCE TROUBLESHOOTING
2860 Ogletown Rd (19713-1857)
PHONE 302 692-0871
Thomas B Davis, *Owner*
EMP: 9
SQ FT: 4,000
SALES: 250K **Privately Held**
WEB: www.mtroubleshooting.com
SIC: 8742 5192 5099 3829 Management consulting services; books; video cassettes, accessories & supplies; measuring & controlling devices

(G-6977)
MAJDELL GROUP USA INC
40 E Main St 790 (19711-4639)
PHONE 302 722-8223
Gary Majdell, *President*
▲ EMP: 4 EST: 2012
SALES (est): 331.6K **Privately Held**
SIC: 2329 5136 Men's & boys' sportswear & athletic clothing; bathing suits & swimwear; men's & boys'; underwear, men's & boys'

(G-6978)
MALEK ABDOLLAH DR
1 Centurian Dr Ste 301 (19713-2127)
PHONE 302 994-8492
EMP: 5
SALES (est): 280K **Privately Held**
SIC: 8011 Medical Doctor's Office

(G-6979)
MALLARD ADVISORS LLC (PA)
750 Barksdale Rd Ste 3 (19711-3245)
PHONE 302 737-4546
Paul Baumbach,
William Starnes,
EMP: 20 EST: 1996
SQ FT: 1,315
SALES (est): 2.7MM **Privately Held**
WEB: www.mallardadvisors.com
SIC: 6282 Investment advisory service

(G-6980)
MANAGEMENT OPTIONS INC
Also Called: Toroville
4142 Ogletown Stanton Rd (19713-4169)
PHONE 302 234-0836
Kenrick Fraser, *President*
EMP: 15 EST: 1994
SQ FT: 1,000
SALES: 500K **Privately Held**
WEB: www.managementoptions.biz
SIC: 8742 5961 Management consulting services; catalog & mail-order houses

(G-6981)
MANUFACTURERS & TRADERS TR CO
Also Called: M&T
82 E Main St (19711-4640)
PHONE 302 651-1618
Amy Plant, *Branch Mgr*
EMP: 21
SALES (corp-wide): 6.4B **Publicly Held**
WEB: www.binghamlegg.com
SIC: 6022 State commercial banks
HQ: Manufacturers And Traders Trust Company
1 M&T Plz Fl 3
Buffalo NY 14203
716 842-4200

(G-6982)
MANUFACTURERS & TRADERS TR CO
Also Called: M&T
550 Suburban Dr (19711-1808)
PHONE 302 472-3335
Barbara French, *Branch Mgr*
EMP: 8
SALES (corp-wide): 6.4B **Publicly Held**
WEB: www.binghamlegg.com
SIC: 6022 State commercial banks
HQ: Manufacturers And Traders Trust Company
1 M&T Plz Fl 3
Buffalo NY 14203
716 842-4200

(G-6983)
MANUFACTURERS & TRADERS TR CO
Also Called: M&T
102 Astro Shopping Ctr (19711-7254)
PHONE 302 292-6060
Fax: 302 455-0580
EMP: 15
SALES (corp-wide): 5.7B **Publicly Held**
SIC: 6022 State Commercial Bank
HQ: Manufacturers And Traders Trust Company
1 M And T Plz
Buffalo NY 14203
716 842-4200

(G-6984)
MARCUS MATERIALS CO
9 Renee Ct (19711-2759)
PHONE 302 731-7519
David McElwee, *General Mgr*
EMP: 5
SALES: 2MM **Privately Held**
WEB: www.mcelwee.net
SIC: 5032 Ceramic construction materials, excluding refractory

(G-6985)
MARGHERITA VINCENT & ANTHONY
5 Misty Ct (19702-4726)
PHONE 302 834-9023
Vincent Margherita, *Principal*
EMP: 4
SALES (est): 291.8K **Privately Held**
SIC: 1752 Floor laying & floor work

(G-6986)
MARIA LAZAR MD
1400 Peoples Plz Ste 305 (19702-5708)
PHONE 302 838-2210
Maria Lazar, *Owner*
Quan Nguyen, *Vice Pres*
EMP: 5 EST: 1998
SALES (est): 269.5K **Privately Held**
SIC: 8071 Medical laboratories

(G-6987)
MARINHRDWREMFG/FORCEBEYOND INC
201 Ruthar Dr Ste 2 (19711-8029)
PHONE 302 691-4787
EMP: 2
SALES (est): 73.4K **Privately Held**
SIC: 3429 Mfg Hardware

(G-6988)
MARJAM SUPPLY CO INC
200 Bellevue Rd (19713-3428)
PHONE 302 283-1020
Jeff Benson, *Branch Mgr*
EMP: 10
SALES (corp-wide): 484.1MM **Privately Held**
WEB: www.marjam.com
SIC: 5031 5211 Building materials, exterior; building materials, interior; lumber & other building materials
PA: Marjam Supply Co., Inc.
885 Conklin St
Farmingdale NY 11735
631 249-4900

(G-6989)
MARK GLASSNER MD
324 E Main St Ste 202 (19711-7150)
PHONE 302 369-9002
Mark Glassner, *Owner*
EMP: 10
SALES (est): 820.5K **Privately Held**
SIC: 8011 General & family practice, physician/surgeon

(G-6990)
MARK IV BEAUTY SALON INC
Also Called: Mark IV Hair Design
240 College Sq (19711-5451)
PHONE 302 737-4994
Debra Demaio, *President*
EMP: 8
SQ FT: 1,500
SALES (est): 306.4K **Privately Held**
SIC: 7231 Hairdressers

(G-6991)
MARRIOTT INTERNATIONAL INC
400 David Hollowell Dr (19716-7448)
PHONE 800 441-7048
Bruce Admier, *Principal*
EMP: 5
SALES (est): 146.4K
SALES (corp-wide): 20.7B **Publicly Held**
SIC: 7011 Hotels & motels
PA: Marriott International, Inc.
10400 Fernwood Rd
Bethesda MD 20817
301 380-3000

(G-6992)
MARSHALL T WILLIAMS MD PHD
537 Stanton Christiana Rd (19713-2146)
PHONE 302 994-9692
Marshall Williams MD, *Owner*
EMP: 11
SALES (est): 177.9K **Privately Held**
SIC: 8011 Infectious disease specialist, physician/surgeon

(G-6993)
MARTA GROUP
885 Marrows Rd Apt D6 (19713-1571)
P.O. Box 1066 (19715-1066)
PHONE 302 737-2008
Lauren Demichiel, *President*
EMP: 5
SALES (est): 648.8K **Privately Held**
WEB: www.martagroup.com
SIC: 8741 Management services

(G-6994)
MARTIN CONSTRUCTION SVCS LLC
340 W Chestnut Hill Rd (19713-1101)
PHONE 302 200-0885
Richard Martin, *Mng Member*
Carole Martin,
EMP: 18
SQ FT: 1,000
SALES: 2MM **Privately Held**
SIC: 1542 1522 Commercial & office building contractors; residential construction

(G-6995)
MARTIN DEALERSHIP
298 E Cleveland Ave (19711-3711)
PHONE 302 738-5200
Homi Poursaied, *Principal*
Gino Marra, *Sales Staff*
Al Rasin, *Manager*
Tom Baker, *Director*
EMP: 7
SALES (est): 470K **Privately Held**
SIC: 7532 5511 Body shop, automotive; new & used car dealers

(G-6996)
MARTIN NEWARK DEALERSHIP INC
Also Called: Martin Honda
298 E Cleveland Ave (19711-3711)
PHONE 302 454-9300
Scott Lustgarten, *President*
Laura Hanby, *General Mgr*
Ron Roark, *Business Mgr*
Linda Lustgarten, *Vice Pres*
Joe St John, *Parts Mgr*

Newark - New Castle County (G-6997) — **GEOGRAPHIC SECTION**

EMP: 225
SALES (est): 68.1MM **Privately Held**
WEB: www.martinhonda.com
SIC: 5511 7538 7515 7513 Automobiles, new & used; general automotive repair shops; passenger car leasing; truck rental & leasing, no drivers; automotive & home supply stores

(G-6997)
MARY KOBAK MD
200 Hygeia Dr (19713-2049)
PHONE 302 623-0260
Paul King, *President*
Mary Kobak, *Principal*
EMP: 4
SALES (est): 144.1K **Privately Held**
SIC: 8011 General & family practice, physician/surgeon

(G-6998)
MARYRUTH L NICH
86 Omega Dr (19713-2065)
PHONE 302 623-1929
Maryruth Nich, *Principal*
EMP: 8
SALES (est): 65.7K **Privately Held**
SIC: 8049 Offices of health practitioner

(G-6999)
MASON BUILDING GROUP INC
35 Albe Dr (19702-1321)
PHONE 302 292-0600
Christopher Mason, *President*
Rita Thomas, *Corp Secy*
EMP: 150
SQ FT: 11,000
SALES (est): 24.7MM **Privately Held**
WEB: www.masonbuilding.com
SIC: 1542 1751 Commercial & office building, new construction; framing contractor

(G-7000)
MASTER INTERIORS INC (PA)
113 Sandy Dr (19713-1148)
PHONE 302 368-9361
Mary Humpton, *President*
EMP: 25
SQ FT: 10,000
SALES (est): 3.5MM **Privately Held**
WEB: www.masteracoustical.com
SIC: 1742 Acoustical & ceiling work; drywall

(G-7001)
MASTER SIDLOW & ASSOCIATES PA
750 Prides Xing Ste 100 (19713-6108)
P.O. Box 4080, Wilmington (19807-0080)
PHONE 302 384-9780
William H Master, *President*
Michael T McCudden, *Vice Pres*
John Still, *Accountant*
Jennifer Watson, *CPA*
Greg Moser, *Manager*
EMP: 50
SALES (est): 6.2MM **Privately Held**
WEB: www.smspa.com
SIC: 8721 Certified public accountant

(G-7002)
MATERNITY GYNECOLOGY ASSOC PA
4745 Ogletown Stanton Rd # 207
(19713-2074)
PHONE 302 368-9000
George Liarkos MD, *President*
Cathi Ratasiewicc, *Manager*
Sarah Wagner, *Physician Asst*
EMP: 20
SALES (est): 1.7MM **Privately Held**
SIC: 8011 Obstetrician; gynecologist

(G-7003)
MATTLEMAN WEINROTH & MILLER PC
200 Continental Dr # 215 (19713-4335)
PHONE 302 731-8349
Adam Elgart, *Manager*
John Denney, *Associate*
James Edwards, *Associate*
John Stephenson, *Associate*
EMP: 8

SALES (est): 554.2K
SALES (corp-wide): 7MM **Privately Held**
SIC: 8111 General practice attorney, lawyer
PA: Mattleman, Weinroth & Miller, P.C.
   401 Rte 70 Marlton
   Cherry Hill NJ 08034
   856 429-5507

(G-7004)
MAWULI LOGISTICS LLC
262 Chapman Rd 205-222 (19702-5448)
PHONE 302 544-5129
Anthony K Sorkpah, *President*
EMP: 4
SALES (est): 170.6K **Privately Held**
SIC: 4213 Trucking, except local

(G-7005)
MAX RE ASSOCIATES INC
Also Called: Re/Max
228 Suburban Dr (19711-3596)
PHONE 302 453-3200
Paul Saulk, *General Mgr*
EMP: 37
SALES (est): 1.2MM **Privately Held**
WEB: www.donash.com
SIC: 6531 Real estate agent, residential
PA: Max Re Associates Inc
   3302 Concord Pike
   Wilmington DE 19803

(G-7006)
MAX VIRTUAL LLC
40 E Main St 766 (19711-4639)
PHONE 302 525-8112
EMP: 3
SALES (est): 187.1K **Privately Held**
SIC: 3699 Mfg Electrical Equipment/Supplies

(G-7007)
MAZINDUSTRIES
103 Greenfield Rd (19713-2004)
PHONE 302 292-3636
Nicole Moretti, *Principal*
EMP: 1 EST: 2007
SALES (est): 45.8K **Privately Held**
SIC: 3999 Manufacturing industries

(G-7008)
MAZZOLA SYSTEMS INC
Also Called: Mazzola Construction
560 Peoples Plz Ste 112 (19702-4798)
PHONE 302 738-6808
Donato Mazzola, *President*
EMP: 12
SALES (est): 2MM **Privately Held**
SIC: 1521 1522 Single-family housing construction; residential construction

(G-7009)
MAZZPAC LLC
94 Salem Church Rd (19713-2935)
PHONE 973 641-9159
Wolfgang Maslo, *Owner*
EMP: 4
SALES (est): 374.5K **Privately Held**
SIC: 3541 7389 Machine tool replacement & repair parts, metal cutting types;

(G-7010)
MBANZA COFFEE INC
2035 Sunset Lake Rd (19702-2600)
PHONE 813 403-8724
Nikesh Patel, *Vice Pres*
EMP: 1
SALES (est): 39.5K **Privately Held**
SIC: 2095 Roasted coffee

(G-7011)
MCBRIDE AND ZIEGLER INC
2607 Eastburn Ctr (19711-7267)
PHONE 302 737-9138
Mark Ziegler, *President*
Trevor Furr, *Project Mgr*
EMP: 25
SALES (est): 1.7MM **Privately Held**
SIC: 8713 Surveying services

(G-7012)
MCCRAY INVESTMENTS
76 Three Rivers Dr (19702-4209)
PHONE 302 836-8569
Jacqueline McCray, *Owner*
EMP: 4

SALES (est): 175.5K **Privately Held**
SIC: 6799 Real estate investors, except property operators

(G-7013)
MEADOWOOD MOBIL STATION
2650 Kirkwood Hwy (19711-7241)
PHONE 302 731-5602
Jeff Ozdmer, *Owner*
EMP: 5 EST: 1958
SQ FT: 2,800
SALES (est): 540.1K **Privately Held**
SIC: 5541 7539 Filling stations, gasoline; brake repair, automotive

(G-7014)
MECHANICAL SYSTEMS INTL CORP
9 Lewis St (19711)
PHONE 302 453-8315
Charles Rudd, *President*
Barbara Rudd, *Vice Pres*
EMP: 12
SALES: 1MM **Privately Held**
SIC: 3545 Tools & accessories for machine tools

(G-7015)
MEDICAL BILLING & MGT SVCS INC (PA)
111 Continental Dr # 101 (19713-4302)
PHONE 610 564-5314
Tom Schovee, *CEO*
Cathy Sells, *President*
Tischa Roberts, *COO*
Larry Buller Jr, *Exec VP*
Matt Ostrum, *Exec VP*
EMP: 6
SQ FT: 4,000
SALES (est): 2.8MM **Privately Held**
SIC: 8721 Billing & bookkeeping service

(G-7016)
MEDICAL MASSAGE DELAWARE LLC (PA)
254 Chapman Rd Ste 112 (19702-5413)
PHONE 888 757-1951
Jackie Staker, *Partner*
Zac Meiyu, *Partner*
Linda Ogilvie, *Partner*
Patricia Peterson, *Partner*
EMP: 7
SALES (est): 389.6K **Privately Held**
SIC: 8049

(G-7017)
MEDICAL ONCOLOGY HEMATOLOGY
Also Called: Delduca, Vincent Jr MD
4701 Ogltn Stntn Rd # 2200 (19713-7000)
PHONE 302 999-8095
Dr Stephen Grubbs, *Partner*
Michael Griliano, *Partner*
Sujung Park, *Internal Med*
Gregory A Masters, *Oncology*
EMP: 35
SALES (est): 1.2MM **Privately Held**
SIC: 8011 Oncologist

(G-7018)
MEDICAL SOCIETY OF DELAWARE (PA)
900 Prides Xing (19713-6100)
PHONE 302 366-1400
Michelle Seymour, *Manager*
Mark Thompson, *Exec Dir*
Antje Arnold, *Education*
EMP: 20
SQ FT: 1,500
SALES: 1.6MM **Privately Held**
SIC: 8621 2731 Medical field-related associations; book publishing

(G-7019)
MERIT MECHANICAL CO INC
39 Albe Dr (19702-1321)
PHONE 302 366-8601
John Rettig, *Vice Pres*
EMP: 70
SALES (est): 8.9MM **Privately Held**
SIC: 1711 Mechanical contractor

(G-7020)
MERIT SERVICES INC
39 Albe Dr (19702-1321)
PHONE 302 366-8601
Richard M Rettig, *President*
John Travis Rettig, *Vice Pres*
Virginia Rettig, *Treasurer*
EMP: 80 EST: 1958
SQ FT: 14,000
SALES (est): 6.7MM **Privately Held**
SIC: 1711 Mechanical contractor

(G-7021)
METROPOLITAN LIFE INSUR CO
Also Called: MetLife
111 Continental Dr # 305 (19713-4317)
PHONE 302 738-0888
Rickey Walker, *Manager*
Mike Sava, *Director*
EMP: 30
SALES (corp-wide): 67.9B **Publicly Held**
SIC: 6411 Insurance agents & brokers
HQ: Metropolitan Life Insurance Company (Inc)
   1095 Ave Of The Americas
   New York NY 10036
   908 253-1000

(G-7022)
MI-DEE INC
Also Called: Edu-Care Preschool & Daycare
345 Polly Drummond Hl (19711-4809)
PHONE 302 453-7326
Helen Shih, *President*
Lynne Magrogan, *Principal*
Neda Horne, *Director*
EMP: 40
SALES (est): 1MM **Privately Held**
SIC: 8351 Group day care center; preschool center

(G-7023)
MICHAEL W LANKIEWICZ MD
Also Called: Delaware Clinical & Lab Physcn
4701 Ogletown Stanton Rd # 4200 (19713-2055)
PHONE 302 737-7700
Michael W Lankiewicz MD, *Principal*
Robert Slease, *Internal Med*
EMP: 5
SALES (est): 410K **Privately Held**
SIC: 8011 Hematologist

(G-7024)
MICHELIN CORPORATION
2724 Pulaski Hwy (19702-3911)
PHONE 864 458-4698
EMP: 2
SALES (corp-wide): 992.7MM **Privately Held**
SIC: 3011 Tires & inner tubes
HQ: Michelin Corporation
   1 Parkway S
   Greenville SC 29615
   864 458-5000

(G-7025)
MICROSOFT CORPORATION
137 Christiana Mall (19702-3201)
PHONE 302 669-0200
Eric Bentley, *President*
Shawni Jernigan, *Technical Staff*
EMP: 35
SALES (corp-wide): 125.8B **Publicly Held**
SIC: 7371 Computer software development
PA: Microsoft Corporation
   1 Microsoft Way
   Redmond WA 98052
   425 882-8080

(G-7026)
MID ATLANTIC INDUS BELTING
15 Garfield Way (19713-3450)
P.O. Box 1518, Hockessin (19707-5518)
PHONE 302 453-7353
Rick Miller, *President*
EMP: 4
SQ FT: 10,000
SALES (est): 598.2K **Privately Held**
SIC: 3496 Conveyor belts

GEOGRAPHIC SECTION

Newark - New Castle County (G-7056)

(G-7027)
MID ATLANTIC SPINE
100 Biddle Ave Ste 101 (19702-3982)
PHONE..................302 369-1700
Frank Falco, *Owner*
EMP: 15
SALES (est): 1MM **Privately Held**
SIC: 8011 Orthopedic physician

(G-7028)
MID-ATLANTIC BALLET INC
506 Interchange Blvd (19713-3557)
P.O. Box 161 (19715-0161)
PHONE..................302 266-6362
Dawn Calzada, *Director*
EMP: 5
SALES: 209K **Privately Held**
WEB: www.midatlanticballet.org
SIC: 7911 Dance instructor & school services

(G-7029)
MID-ATLANTIC REALTY CO INC (PA)
39 Abbey Ln (19711-6869)
PHONE..................302 658-7642
Edward L Davidson, *President*
Verino Pettinaro, *Vice Pres*
Susanne Jarome, *VP Finance*
EMP: 20
SQ FT: 1,662
SALES (est): 4.6MM **Privately Held**
SIC: 6531 Condominium manager

(G-7030)
MID-ATLANTIC REALTY CO INC
Also Called: Salem Village
911 Village Cir Ofc D (19713-4917)
PHONE..................302 738-5325
Debbie Lawhorn, *Branch Mgr*
EMP: 4
SALES (corp-wide): 4.6MM **Privately Held**
SIC: 6531 6513 Real estate managers; apartment building operators
PA: Mid-Atlantic Realty Co Inc
39 Abbey Ln
Newark DE 19711
302 658-7642

(G-7031)
MID-ATLANTIC REALTY CO INC
Also Called: Abbey Walk Apts
39 Abbey Ln (19711-6869)
PHONE..................302 737-3110
Kim Dreyer, *Manager*
EMP: 6
SALES (corp-wide): 4.6MM **Privately Held**
SIC: 6531 6513 Real estate managers; apartment building operators
PA: Mid-Atlantic Realty Co Inc
39 Abbey Ln
Newark DE 19711
302 658-7642

(G-7032)
MID-ATLANTIC SYSTEMS DPN INC (PA)
802 Interchange Blvd (19711-3570)
PHONE..................301 206-9510
Charles Levine, *President*
Eric Tullio, *COO*
Edwin Fennell, *Admin Sec*
EMP: 7
SQ FT: 5,500
SALES: 5.9MM **Privately Held**
SIC: 1799 Waterproofing

(G-7033)
MID-ATLNTIC WTRPROOFING MD INC
Also Called: Mid-Atlantic Systems of D P N
802 Interchange Blvd (19711-3570)
PHONE..................855 692-4668
Robert Cunliffe, *Principal*
EMP: 5
SALES (corp-wide): 9.6MM **Privately Held**
SIC: 1799 Waterproofing
PA: Mid-Atlantic Waterproofing Md, Inc.
9145 Guilford Rd Ste 180
Columbia MD 21046
301 206-9500

(G-7034)
MIDATLANTIC PAIN INSTITUTE
Also Called: Midatlantic Spine
100 Biddle Ave Ste 101 (19702-3982)
PHONE..................302 369-1700
Frank Falco, *President*
EMP: 54
SALES: 5.5MM **Privately Held**
SIC: 8093 Specialty outpatient clinics

(G-7035)
MIDI LABS INC
125 Sandy Dr (19713-1148)
PHONE..................302 737-4297
Myron Sasser, *President*
Craig Kunitsky, *Mktg Dir*
EMP: 25
SALES (est): 1.6MM **Privately Held**
WEB: www.midilabs.com
SIC: 8734 Testing laboratories
PA: Midi, Inc
125 Sandy Dr
Newark DE

(G-7036)
MIDNITE AIR CORP
35 Salem Church Rd (19713-4928)
PHONE..................614 296-1678
Paul J Martins, *Branch Mgr*
EMP: 21
SALES (corp-wide): 1B **Privately Held**
SIC: 4513 Air courier services
HQ: Midnite Air Corp.
5001 Arprt Plz Dr Ste 250
Long Beach CA 90815
310 910-9199

(G-7037)
MIDWAY LITTLE LEAGUE
55 S Meadowood Dr (19711-6755)
PHONE..................302 737-3104
Joseph Phillip, *President*
EMP: 15
SALES (est): 171.4K **Privately Held**
SIC: 7997 Baseball club, except professional & semi-professional; outdoor field clubs

(G-7038)
MIH INTERNATIONAL LLC
112 Capitol Trl (19711-3716)
PHONE..................301 908-4233
EMP: 3
SALES (est): 364.8K **Privately Held**
SIC: 3842 Surgical appliances & supplies

(G-7039)
MILES SCIENTIFIC CORPORATION
Also Called: Analtech
75 Blue Hen Dr (19713-3405)
P.O. Box 7558 (19714-7558)
PHONE..................302 737-6960
Steven Miles, *President*
Terry Mc Vey, *Prdtn Mgr*
Steven C Miles, *Director*
◆ **EMP:** 13 **EST:** 1961
SQ FT: 10,000
SALES (est): 1.9MM **Privately Held**
WEB: www.analtech.com
SIC: 3231 5049 3826 Laboratory glassware; laboratory equipment, except medical or dental; chromatographic equipment, laboratory type

(G-7040)
MILESTONE CONSTRUCTION CO INC
4 Mill Park Ct Ste A (19713-1901)
PHONE..................302 442-4252
Steven Sieja, *President*
EMP: 19 **EST:** 2009
SALES (est): 2.7MM **Privately Held**
SIC: 1542 Commercial & office building contractors

(G-7041)
MILFORD ANESTHESIA ASSOC LLC
111 Continental Dr # 412 (19713-4332)
PHONE..................203 783-1831
Jeffrey A Wagner MD, *Mng Member*
Thomas Verdone MD,
EMP: 2943
SQ FT: 2,667
SALES (est): 31.1MM
SALES (corp-wide): 643.1MM **Privately Held**
SIC: 8011 Anesthesiologist
HQ: Emcare, Inc.
13737 Noel Rd Ste 1600
Dallas TX 75240
214 712-2000

(G-7042)
MINDCENTRAL INC
2035 Sunset Lake Rd B2 (19702-2600)
PHONE..................302 273-1011
Petar Vojvodic, *CEO*
EMP: 1
SALES (est): 32.7K **Privately Held**
SIC: 7372 Business oriented computer software

(G-7043)
MINIMALLY INVASIVE SURGCL & NE
774 Christiana Rd Ste 2 (19713-4219)
PHONE..................302 738-0300
Suzanne Rodenheiser, *CEO*
Fred Hyde, *Principal*
Nicole Carrington, *CFO*
EMP: 50
SALES (est): 7.4MM
SALES (corp-wide): 1.7B **Publicly Held**
WEB: www.delmarvablood.org
SIC: 8011 Surgeon; neurosurgeon
HQ: Surgery Partners, Inc.
310 Sven Sprng Way Ste 50
Brentwood TN 37027
615 234-5900

(G-7044)
MINKERS CONSTRUCTION INC
830 Dawson Dr (19713-3416)
PHONE..................302 239-9239
Matt Minker, *President*
Robert Blanck, *Vice Pres*
Mark Price, *Vice Pres*
Kevin Lucas, *Treasurer*
Carol Minker, *Admin Sec*
EMP: 50
SQ FT: 6,000
SALES (est): 5.5MM **Privately Held**
SIC: 1521 Single-family housing construction

(G-7045)
MITSDRFER BROS LAWN LDSCPG INC
Also Called: Mitsdarfer Bros Lawn Ldscpg I
715 Stanton Christiana Rd (19713-2141)
PHONE..................302 633-1150
Fredrick H Mitsdarfer Jr, *President*
EMP: 4
SALES (est): 458.4K **Privately Held**
SIC: 0782 0781 Lawn services; fertilizing services, lawn; lawn care services; mowing services, lawn; landscape services

(G-7046)
MJ WILMINGTON HOTEL ASSOC LP
Also Called: Hilton Christiana
100 Continental Dr (19713-4327)
PHONE..................302 454-1500
Vince Difonzo, *Branch Mgr*
EMP: 20
SALES (corp-wide): 3.7MM **Privately Held**
SIC: 7011 Hotels & motels
PA: Mj Wilmington Hotel Associates Lp
7 W Kenosia Ave
Danbury CT 06810
203 798-1099

(G-7047)
MJ WILMINGTON HOTEL ASSOC LP
Also Called: Hilton Christiana
100 Continental Dr (19713-4327)
PHONE..................302 454-1500
Brad Wenger, *General Mgr*
Richard Jabara, *General Ptnr*
William Meyer, *General Ptnr*
Corey Williamson, *Facilities Dir*
Michelle Goad, *Sales Staff*
EMP: 159
SALES (est): 9MM **Privately Held**
SIC: 7011 Hotels & motels
PA: Meyer Jabara Hotels
7 Kenosia Ave Ste 2a
Danbury CT 06810

(G-7048)
ML NEWARK LLC
Also Called: Christina Mill Apartments
100 Christina Mill Dr (19711-3572)
PHONE..................302 737-2868
Grace Grey, *Mng Member*
EMP: 15
SALES (est): 1.2MM
SALES (corp-wide): 865.7MM **Privately Held**
SIC: 6513 Apartment building operators
HQ: Lowe Enterprises Investment Management, Inc
11777 San Vicente Blvd # 900
Los Angeles CA 90049

(G-7049)
MMI HOLDINGS INC
1360 Marrows Rd (19711-5458)
PHONE..................302 455-2021
Lisa Garrett, *Asst Mgr*
EMP: 4
SALES (corp-wide): 37.6B **Privately Held**
SIC: 0742 Veterinarian, animal specialties
HQ: Mmi Holdings, Inc.
18101 Se 6th Way
Vancouver WA 98683
360 784-5422

(G-7050)
MONGE WOODWORKING
4 Barnard St (19711-4345)
PHONE..................302 455-0175
EMP: 1
SALES (est): 54.1K **Privately Held**
SIC: 2431 Millwork

(G-7051)
MONICA MEHRING DDS
179 W Chestnut Hill Rd # 4 (19713-2210)
PHONE..................302 368-0054
Monica Mehring, *Owner*
EMP: 12
SALES (est): 444.4K **Privately Held**
SIC: 8021 Dentists' office

(G-7052)
MONOGRAM SPECIALTIES
701 Valley Rd (19711-2580)
PHONE..................302 292-2424
Nancy Franklin, *Owner*
Chuck Franklin, *Principal*
EMP: 2
SALES (est): 148.2K **Privately Held**
SIC: 3999 Embroidery kits

(G-7053)
MONTEREY ENTERPRISES LLC
111 Continental Dr # 114 (19713-4302)
PHONE..................302 504-4901
Barbara Bailey, *Principal*
EMP: 4 **EST:** 2011
SALES (est): 184.8K **Privately Held**
SIC: 8748 Business consulting

(G-7054)
MONTEREY SW LLC
111 Continental Dr # 114 (19713-4306)
PHONE..................302 504-4901
Peter Jones,
EMP: 10 **EST:** 2012
SALES (est): 630K **Privately Held**
SIC: 6221 Commodity contracts brokers, dealers

(G-7055)
MONTEREY SWF LLC
111 Continental Dr # 114 (19713-4306)
PHONE..................302 504-4901
Peter Jones, *Managing Dir*
EMP: 10 **EST:** 2012
SALES (est): 630K **Privately Held**
SIC: 6221 Commodity contracts brokers, dealers

(G-7056)
MOORE QLTY WLDG FBRICATION LLC
522 Stafford Ave (19711-5577)
PHONE..................302 731-4818
Daniel Moore, *Principal*

Newark - New Castle County (G-7057)   GEOGRAPHIC SECTION

EMP: 1 **EST:** 2013
SALES (est): 99.2K **Privately Held**
SIC: 7692 Welding repair

(G-7057)
MORAN ENVMTL RECOVERY LLC
9 Garfield Way (19713-3450)
PHONE.................302 322-6008
Justin Woodard, *Manager*
EMP: 12
SALES (corp-wide): 64.9MM **Privately Held**
SIC: 8999 Earth science services
PA: Moran Environmental Recovery Llc
75 York Ave Ste D
Randolph MA 02368
781 815-1100

(G-7058)
MORGAN GARANTY INTL FINCL CORP
500 Stanton Christiana Rd (19713-2105)
PHONE.................302 634-1000
Richard McLoughlin, *President*
EMP: 50
SALES (est): 7.3MM
SALES (corp-wide): 131.4B **Publicly Held**
SIC: 6211 Investment firm, general brokerage
PA: Jpmorgan Chase & Co.
383 Madison Ave
New York NY 10179
212 270-6000

(G-7059)
MORRIS JMES HTCHENS WLLAMS LLP
16 Polly Drummond Hill Rd (19711-5703)
PHONE.................302 368-4200
Eleanor Vigliotta, *Technology*
Catherine Bukowski, *Admin Asst*
EMP: 4
SALES (est): 122.1K **Privately Held**
SIC: 8111 General practice attorney, lawyer

(G-7060)
MOSAIC
Also Called: Charlan Neighborhood Home
8 Stoddard Dr (19702-2205)
PHONE.................302 456-5995
Terry Oflin, *Director*
EMP: 112
SALES (corp-wide): 257.7MM **Privately Held**
WEB: www.lsa-dn.org
SIC: 8052 Home for the mentally retarded, with health care
PA: Mosaic
4980 S 118th St
Omaha NE 68137
402 896-3884

(G-7061)
MOSAIC
Also Called: Woods Neighborhood Home
223 E Seneca Dr (19702-1929)
PHONE.................302 366-0257
Terry Olsen, *Director*
EMP: 8
SALES (corp-wide): 257.7MM **Privately Held**
WEB: www.lsa-dn.org
SIC: 8361 Self-help group home
PA: Mosaic
4980 S 118th St
Omaha NE 68137
402 896-3884

(G-7062)
MOSAIC
Also Called: Marthin Luther Homes of Del
261 Chapman Rd Ste 201 (19702-5428)
PHONE.................302 456-5995
Terry Olsen, *Director*
EMP: 115
SALES (corp-wide): 257.7MM **Privately Held**
WEB: www.lsa-dn.org
SIC: 8322 8741 8052 Association for the handicapped; management services; intermediate care facilities

PA: Mosaic
4980 S 118th St
Omaha NE 68137
402 896-3884

(G-7063)
MOTHER HUBBARD CHILD CARE CTR
2050 S College Ave (19702-3302)
PHONE.................302 368-7584
April Hubbard, *President*
EMP: 14
SALES (est): 181K **Privately Held**
SIC: 8351 Group day care center

(G-7064)
MOVETEC FITNESS EQUIPMENT LLC (PA)
790 Salem Church Rd (19702-3623)
PHONE.................302 563-4487
Robert Piane Jr, *Mng Member*
EMP: 5
SALES (est): 1.2MM **Privately Held**
SIC: 3949 7389 Exercise equipment;

(G-7065)
MOZEWEB LLC
40 E Main St (19711-4639)
PHONE.................302 355-0692
EMP: 4 **EST:** 2010
SALES (est): 87.5K **Privately Held**
SIC: 7379 8742 Computer Related Services Management Consulting Services

(G-7066)
MR GREGORY MICHAEL HAUSMANN
39 Tremont Ct (19711-1903)
PHONE.................302 635-7675
EMP: 5
SALES (est): 220K **Privately Held**
SIC: 7389 Business Services At Non-Commercial Site

(G-7067)
MRI CONSULTANTS LLC
1 Centurian Dr Ste 107 (19713-2154)
PHONE.................302 295-3367
Philip W Chao,
EMP: 7
SALES (est): 583.9K **Privately Held**
SIC: 8011 Radiologist

(G-7068)
MSTM LLC
28 Tenby Chase Dr (19711-2441)
PHONE.................302 239-4447
Sarah Trimpin, *Partner*
Charles McEwen,
EMP: 2 **EST:** 2013
SALES (est): 243K **Privately Held**
SIC: 3826 Mass spectrometers

(G-7069)
MTC USA LLC
Also Called: M T C
411 Woodlawn Ave (19711-5535)
PHONE.................980 999-8888
Wenyi Tiang, *Mng Member*
EMP: 10
SQ FT: 2,000
SALES (est): 1.5MM **Privately Held**
SIC: 5734 8742 Software, business & non-game; marketing consulting services

(G-7070)
MTK ENTERPRISES LLC
210 Nathan Ct (19711-3932)
PHONE.................302 266-9611
Matthew R Longo Esq, *Principal*
EMP: 4 **EST:** 2013
SALES (est): 312K **Privately Held**
SIC: 8748 Business consulting

(G-7071)
MTO HOSE SOLUTIONS INC (PA)
214 Interchange Blvd (19711)
PHONE.................302 266-6555
Don Malizia, *President*
Shane Carter, *Vice Pres*
Jennifer Karahalis, *Office Mgr*
▲ **EMP:** 8
SQ FT: 10,000

PA: Mosaic
4980 S 118th St
Omaha NE 68137
402 896-3884

SALES: 3MM **Privately Held**
SIC: 5013 3492 Motor vehicle supplies & new parts; hose & tube fittings & assemblies, hydraulic/pneumatic

(G-7072)
MULTI-PRO BUSINESS SVCS LLC
200 Continental Dr (19713-4334)
PHONE.................800 571-7017
Camille Lewis,
EMP: 4
SALES (est): 75.1K **Privately Held**
SIC: 8721 Accounting, auditing & bookkeeping; payroll accounting service

(G-7073)
MURPHY STEEL INC
727 Dawson Dr (19713-3495)
P.O. Box 9071 (19714-9071)
PHONE.................302 366-8676
Nancy Baffone, *President*
Aleseo Baffone, *Corp Secy*
EMP: 20
SALES (est): 3.9MM **Privately Held**
SIC: 1521 3446 3444 Single-family housing construction; architectural metalwork; sheet metalwork

(G-7074)
MUSHROOM SUPPLY & SERVICES INC
227 Cullen Way (19711-6115)
P.O. Box 1360, Hockessin (19707-5360)
PHONE.................302 998-2008
David Iaconi, *President*
◆ **EMP:** 11
SALES (est): 1.6MM **Privately Held**
SIC: 2033 Mushrooms: packaged in cans, jars, etc.

(G-7075)
MY EASY TEAM LLC
200 Continental Dr (19713-4334)
PHONE.................302 722-6821
Donna Dutta,
EMP: 2
SALES (est): 50K **Privately Held**
SIC: 7372 Application computer software

(G-7076)
MY SISTERS PLACE INC
50 Currant Dr (19702-2852)
PHONE.................302 737-5303
Robert E Young, *President*
EMP: 5
SALES (est): 1.1K **Privately Held**
SIC: 8322 Individual & family services

(G-7077)
MYMOROCCANBAZAR INC
2035 Sunset Lake Rd (19702-2600)
PHONE.................323 238-5747
Oualid Ben Naid,
EMP: 2
SALES (est): 50.5K **Privately Held**
SIC: 2389 5961 4724 Apparel & accessories; ; travel agencies

(G-7078)
N MALLARI GC CORP
44 Bastille Loop (19702-5528)
PHONE.................302 516-7738
EMP: 4
SALES (est): 103.5K **Privately Held**
SIC: 1799 Special trade contractors

(G-7079)
N O BIASOTTO DO
620 Stanton Christn Rd # 2 (19713-2133)
PHONE.................302 998-1211
N O Biasotto Do, *Owner*
EMP: 4
SALES (est): 159.7K **Privately Held**
SIC: 8031 Offices & clinics of osteopathic physicians

(G-7080)
NABSTAR HOSPITALITY
630 S College Ave (19713-1315)
PHONE.................302 453-1700
Bharet Patel, *Owner*
EMP: 5
SALES (est): 293.9K **Privately Held**
SIC: 8748 Business consulting

(G-7081)
NACSTAR
Also Called: Sleep Inn
630 S College Ave (19713-1315)
PHONE.................302 453-1700
Alice Yang, *President*
Hsu-Yuh Chen, *Shareholder*
Kuo-Jui Chen, *Shareholder*
Tinny Chiu, *Shareholder*
Gour-Tyh Yeh, *Shareholder*
EMP: 22
SALES (est): 713.1K **Privately Held**
SIC: 7011 Hotels & motels

(G-7082)
NAIVA SOLUTIONS INC
100 Biddle Ave Ste 124 (19702-3982)
PHONE.................612 987-6350
Naresh Kumar Chitipolu, *President*
Nareh K Chitipolu, *President*
EMP: 4
SALES (est): 58.9K **Privately Held**
SIC: 7379 7371 Computer related services; custom computer programming services

(G-7083)
NARINDER SINGH MD
295 E Main St Ste 100 (19711-7338)
PHONE.................302 737-2600
Narinder Singh, *Owner*
EMP: 6
SALES (est): 723.3K **Privately Held**
SIC: 8011 General & family practice, physician/surgeon

(G-7084)
NATHANIEL JON BENT DDS PA
625 Barksdale Rd Ste 117 (19711-4535)
PHONE.................302 731-4907
Nathaniel Jon Bent, *Principal*
EMP: 5 **EST:** 2015
SALES (est): 125.1K **Privately Held**
SIC: 8021 Dentists' office

(G-7085)
NATIONAL CRICKET ASSOCIATES
12 Rocky Rd (19702-8634)
PHONE.................302 454-7294
Shuja Khan, *President*
EMP: 1
SALES (est): 79.7K **Privately Held**
SIC: 3949 Cricket equipment, general

(G-7086)
NATURAL DAIRY PRODUCTS CORP
Also Called: Natural By Nature
316 Markus Ct (19713-1151)
PHONE.................302 455-1261
Edward R Macarthur, *President*
Ned Macarthur, *Vice Pres*
Susan Macarthur, *Admin Sec*
EMP: 7
SQ FT: 8,000
SALES (est): 5.5MM **Privately Held**
SIC: 5143 Dairy products, except dried or canned

(G-7087)
NATURAL HOUSE INC
2515 Kirkwood Hwy (19711-7249)
PHONE.................302 218-0338
Yoo Won Jang, *President*
EMP: 5
SALES (est): 536.5K **Privately Held**
SIC: 8741 Business management

(G-7088)
NEAR AND DEAR HOME CARE
1002 Birchwood Dr (19713-3010)
PHONE.................302 530-6498
Samantha Pfeifer, *Principal*
EMP: 6 **EST:** 2016
SALES (est): 67.1K **Privately Held**
SIC: 8082 Home health care services

(G-7089)
NEIL G MCANENY DDS
400 New London Rd (19711-7010)
PHONE.................302 368-0329
Neil McAneny, *Executive*
EMP: 4

▲ = Import ▼=Export
◆ =Import/Export

GEOGRAPHIC SECTION
Newark - New Castle County (G-7120)

SALES (est): 61.5K Privately Held
SIC: 8021 Offices & clinics of dentists

(G-7090)
NEIL G MCANENY DDS PC
117 Barksdale Pro Ctr (19711-3258)
PHONE..................................302 731-4907
Neil McAneny, *President*
EMP: 11
SALES (est): 370K Privately Held
WEB: www.barksdaledental.com
SIC: 8021 Dentists' office

(G-7091)
NEMOURS FUNDATION PENSION PLAN
1400 Peoples Plz Ste 300 (19702-5708)
PHONE..................................302 836-7820
William Higginbotham, *Systems Dir*
Steven Sparks, *Systems Dir*
Jackie Donnelly, *Executive*
EMP: 101
SALES (corp-wide): 77.3MM Privately Held
SIC: 8011 Pediatrician
PA: The Nemours Foundation Pension Plan
  10140 Centurion Pkwy N
  Jacksonville FL 32256
  904 697-4100

(G-7092)
NEMOURS HLTH & PREVENTION SVCS (PA)
252 Chapman Rd Ste 200 (19702-5437)
P.O. Box 269, Wilmington (19899-0269)
PHONE..................................302 366-1929
David Bailey, *CEO*
EMP: 7
SALES (est): 625.8K Privately Held
SIC: 8742 8611 Hospital & health services consultant; community affairs & services

(G-7093)
NEPHROLOGY ASSOCIATES PA
4923 Ogletown Stanton Rd # 200 (19713-6005)
PHONE..................................302 225-0451
William E Miller MD, *President*
Rena Titus, *Office Mgr*
William Lyndon, *Med Doctor*
Gina Johnston, *Info Tech Mgr*
Mary Polk, *Administration*
EMP: 25
SALES (est): 9.4MM Privately Held
SIC: 8011 Nephrologist

(G-7094)
NETRAGY LLC
10 Cheswold Blvd Apt 1d (19713-4121)
PHONE..................................973 846-7018
David Callender,
Edward Callender,
EMP: 6 EST: 2012
SALES (est): 150.4K Privately Held
SIC: 8748 Business consulting

(G-7095)
NEUROLOGY ASSOCIATES PA
Also Called: Edelsohn, Lanny MD
774 Christiana Rd Ste 201 (19713-4221)
PHONE..................................302 731-3017
Sung H Bae MD, *CEO*
Lanny Edelsohn, *President*
Ted E Chronister MD, *Vice Pres*
Thomas Vates Jr, *Admin Sec*
Malisa Yarrusso, *Admin Sec*
EMP: 50 EST: 1970
SQ FT: 2,500
SALES (est): 2.7MM Privately Held
SIC: 8011 Neurologist

(G-7096)
NEUROSURGERY CONSULTANTS PA
79 Omega Dr Bldg C (19713-2080)
PHONE..................................302 738-9145
Bikash Bose MD, *President*
EMP: 5
SQ FT: 3,000
SALES (est): 770.4K Privately Held
SIC: 8011 Neurosurgeon; neurologist

(G-7097)
NEUROSURGICAL ASSOCIATES PA
249 E Main St Apt K (19711-7320)
PHONE..................................302 738-9543
EMP: 5 EST: 1990
SALES (est): 310K Privately Held
SIC: 8011 Ofcsclns Of Mdl Dr

(G-7098)
NEW ARK PEDIATRICS INC
314 E Main St Ste 101 (19711-7180)
PHONE..................................302 738-4800
Barbara Cimino, *Office Mgr*
EMP: 12
SALES (est): 1MM Privately Held
SIC: 8011 Pediatrician

(G-7099)
NEW CASTLE CONSERVATION DST
2430 Old County Rd (19702-4702)
PHONE..................................302 832-3100
Larry Irelan, *Coordinator*
EMP: 30
SALES (est): 889.5K Privately Held
SIC: 8999 Natural resource preservation service

(G-7100)
NEW CASTLE COUNTY FLOORING
2923 Ogletown Rd (19713-1927)
PHONE..................................302 218-0507
Eric Parsons, *President*
EMP: 6
SQ FT: 3,000
SALES (est): 765K Privately Held
SIC: 1752 1611 Carpet laying; general contractor, highway & street construction

(G-7101)
NEW CASTLE COUNTY HEAD START (PA)
256 Chapman Rd Ste 103 (19702-5417)
PHONE..................................302 452-1500
Jeff Benatti, *Exec Dir*
Jeffrey Benatti, *Exec Dir*
Janelle Dorsey, *Assistant*
Mabel Roberts-Cole, *Assistant*
Lisa Schneider, *Assistant*
EMP: 13
SALES (est): 6.1MM Privately Held
SIC: 8351 Head start center, except in conjunction with school

(G-7102)
NEW CASTLE FAMILY CARE PA
14 Magil Ct (19702-8636)
PHONE..................................302 275-3428
Mike James, *President*
EMP: 7
SALES (est): 695K Privately Held
SIC: 8011 Offices & clinics of medical doctors

(G-7103)
NEW CREATION LOGISTICS INC
6 Sussex Rd Apt J (19713-3119)
PHONE..................................302 438-3154
Makori Danvas, *President*
Helen Maina, *Vice Pres*
EMP: 10
SQ FT: 1,200
SALES: 300K Privately Held
SIC: 4214 4731 5531 4225 Local trucking with storage; freight transportation arrangement; automotive & home supply stores; general warehousing & storage

(G-7104)
NEW DIRECTION EARLY HEADSTART
321 S College Ave (19716-3366)
PHONE..................................302 831-0584
Heidi Beck, *Director*
EMP: 41
SALES (est): 360.3K Privately Held
SIC: 8351 Head start center, except in conjunction with school

(G-7105)
NEW ERA MEDIA LLC
31 Cordele Rd (19711-5613)
PHONE..................................302 731-2003
Brandon Clark, *Managing Prtnr*
EMP: 4
SALES (est): 600K Privately Held
SIC: 7311 7389 Advertising agencies;

(G-7106)
NEW IMAGE INC
2401 Ogletown Rd Ste A (19711-6403)
P.O. Box 369, Cheswold (19936-0369)
PHONE..................................302 738-6824
Nancy Quade, *CEO*
Ronald M Cox, *President*
Carolyn F Selway, *Admin Asst*
EMP: 6
SQ FT: 4,000
SALES (est): 625.4K Privately Held
WEB: www.nuimage.com
SIC: 2759 5199 2752 Screen printing; advertising specialties; commercial printing, lithographic

(G-7107)
NEW LONDON VETERINARY CENTER
437 New London Rd (19711-7009)
PHONE..................................302 738-5000
Mickey King, *Owner*
EMP: 11
SALES: 350K Privately Held
SIC: 0742 Animal hospital services, pets & other animal specialties

(G-7108)
NEW VISION SERVICES INC
Also Called: McKie Foundation, The
812 Village Cir Apt B (19713-4907)
PHONE..................................484 350-6495
Khari McKie, *CEO*
EMP: 13
SALES (est): 167.4K Privately Held
SIC: 8361 7389 Residential care for children; group foster home;

(G-7109)
NEW VISIONS INV GROUP LLC
31 Phoenix Ave (19702-2406)
PHONE..................................302 299-6234
Steven Coleman, *Mng Member*
EMP: 5 EST: 2016
SALES (est): 199.3K Privately Held
SIC: 6282 Investment advice

(G-7110)
NEW YORK LIFE INSURANCE CO
200 Continental Dr # 306 (19713-4371)
PHONE..................................302 369-8500
Marlene Waters, *Manager*
EMP: 20
SALES (corp-wide): 10.8B Privately Held
WEB: www.newyorklife.com
SIC: 6411 Insurance agents & brokers
PA: New York Life Insurance Company
  51 Madison Ave Bsmt 1b
  New York NY 10010
  212 576-7000

(G-7111)
NEWARK BUILDING SERVICES LLC
9 Cartier Ct (19711-5951)
PHONE..................................302 377-7687
Stephen Davis, *Mng Member*
EMP: 5
SALES (est): 187.5K Privately Held
SIC: 1522 Residential construction

(G-7112)
NEWARK CHINESE LDRY & DRY CLRS
810 Hilltop Rd (19711-2712)
PHONE..................................302 368-3305
EMP: 4
SQ FT: 1,200
SALES (est): 290K Privately Held
SIC: 7211 7216 Laundry & Dry Cleaning

(G-7113)
NEWARK CHRISTIAN CHILDCARE
680 S Chapel St (19713-1541)
PHONE..................................302 369-3000
James Fulghum, *Owner*
Clara Orlando, *Director*
EMP: 5
SALES (est): 191.4K Privately Held
SIC: 8351 Preschool center

(G-7114)
NEWARK COUNTRY CLUB
300 W Main St (19711-3287)
PHONE..................................302 368-7008
Ron Gardner, *President*
Todd Ladutko, *Vice Pres*
Tom Demedio, *Treasurer*
Guy Johnson, *Admin Sec*
EMP: 25
SQ FT: 18,000
SALES: 1.3MM Privately Held
WEB: www.newarkcc.com
SIC: 7997 5812 Country club, membership; eating places

(G-7115)
NEWARK CTR FOR CREATIVE LRNG
401 Phillips Ave (19711-5166)
PHONE..................................302 368-7772
Betty Balder, *Administration*
Carolyn Bartoo, *Education*
EMP: 12 EST: 1971
SALES (est): 937.2K Privately Held
WEB: www.ncclschool.com
SIC: 8211 8351 Private elementary school; child day care services

(G-7116)
NEWARK DAY-NURSERY ASSOCIATION
Also Called: NEWARK DAY NURSERY AND CHILDRE
921 Barksdale Rd (19711-3205)
PHONE..................................302 731-4925
William Carl, *Exec Dir*
Bobbi Budin, *Program Dir*
EMP: 50
SALES (est): 1.8MM Privately Held
SIC: 8351 Preschool center

(G-7117)
NEWARK DENTAL ASSOC INC
344 E Main St (19711-7187)
PHONE..................................302 737-5170
Joseph Stout DDS, *President*
Katy Brown, *General Mgr*
Edward Stout DDS, *Corp Secy*
William H Ralston DDS, *Treasurer*
EMP: 25
SALES (est): 2MM Privately Held
WEB: www.dentaldots.com
SIC: 8021 Dentists' office

(G-7118)
NEWARK EMERGENCY CENTER INC
324 E Main St Ste 100 (19711-7169)
PHONE..................................302 738-4300
Amir Mansoori, *President*
Robert Lynn, *Administration*
EMP: 50
SQ FT: 2,300
SALES (est): 2.1MM Privately Held
SIC: 8011 Freestanding emergency medical center; medical centers

(G-7119)
NEWARK FAMILY COUNCELING CTR
Also Called: Heyden, Edward B
501 Ogletown Rd (19711-5403)
PHONE..................................302 368-6895
Gregory K Brown, *Partner*
EMP: 5
SALES (est): 110.1K Privately Held
SIC: 8322 Family counseling services

(G-7120)
NEWARK FENCE CO
24 Briarcliffe Ct (19702-2214)
PHONE..................................302 368-5329
Robert Rash, *Principal*

Newark - New Castle County (G-7121) — GEOGRAPHIC SECTION

EMP: 6
SALES (est): 421.2K **Privately Held**
WEB: www.newarkfence.com
SIC: 1799 Fence construction

(G-7121)
NEWARK HERITAGE PARTNERS I LLC
501 S Harmony Rd (19713-3338)
PHONE..................302 283-0540
EMP: 16
SALES (est): 107.7K **Publicly Held**
SIC: 8748 Business consulting
PA: Five Star Senior Living Inc.
400 Centre St
Newton MA 02458

(G-7122)
NEWARK INSULATION CO INC
68 Albe Dr A (19702-1322)
P.O. Box 1095 (19715-1095)
PHONE..................302 731-8970
Dominic J Maida Jr, *President*
Gail Maida, *Vice Pres*
EMP: 15
SQ FT: 5,000
SALES: 2MM **Privately Held**
SIC: 1742 Insulation, buildings

(G-7123)
NEWARK KUBOTA INC
Also Called: Kubota Authorized Dealer
2063 Pulaski Hwy (19702-3503)
PHONE..................302 365-6000
Mark Babbit, *President*
Chris Wagner, *General Mgr*
Jeff Pontak, *Parts Mgr*
Josh Lord, *Sales Staff*
EMP: 10
SALES (est): 1.3MM **Privately Held**
WEB: www.burke-equip.com
SIC: 5999 5083 Farm tractors; farm & garden machinery

(G-7124)
NEWARK MONTESSORI PRESCHOOL
1031 S Chapel St (19702-1305)
PHONE..................302 366-1481
Penny Escobar, *Director*
EMP: 6
SALES (est): 189.2K **Privately Held**
SIC: 8351 Montessori child development center

(G-7125)
NEWARK NATIONAL LITTLE LEAGUE
P.O. Box 15031 (19711-0031)
PHONE..................302 738-0881
Danny Balint, *Principal*
EMP: 26
SALES (est): 119.9K **Privately Held**
SIC: 7997 Outdoor field clubs

(G-7126)
NEWARK PEDIATRICIAN INC
314 E Main St Ste 101 (19711-7180)
PHONE..................302 738-4800
Jay B Stewart MD, *Principal*
Joann Villanarin MD, *Principal*
Sangita P Modi, *Med Doctor*
EMP: 13
SALES (est): 870K **Privately Held**
SIC: 8011 Pediatrician

(G-7127)
NEWARK RECYCLING CENTER INC
6 Albe Dr (19702-1322)
PHONE..................302 737-7300
Carmen Micucio Jr, *President*
EMP: 6
SQ FT: 10,000
SALES (est): 1MM **Privately Held**
SIC: 5093 Scrap & waste materials

(G-7128)
NEWARK SENIOR CENTER INC
200 Whitechapel Dr (19713-3811)
PHONE..................302 737-2336
Katiana Foizen, *COO*
Laura Greene, *COO*
Wendell Davis, *Facilities Dir*
Carla Grygiel, *Exec Dir*
EMP: 20 EST: 1966
SQ FT: 29,000
SALES: 3.7MM **Privately Held**
WEB: www.newarkseniorcenter.com
SIC: 8322 Senior citizens' center or association

(G-7129)
NEWARK UNITED METHODIST
69 E Main St (19711-4645)
PHONE..................302 368-8774
Randy Weins, *Principal*
Bernard Keels, *Pastor*
Tammy Sharp, *Manager*
Ned Perwo, *Director*
EMP: 28
SALES (est): 1MM **Privately Held**
WEB: www.newark-umc.org
SIC: 8661 8351 Methodist Church; preschool center

(G-7130)
NEWTON ONE ADVISORS
131 Continental Dr # 206 (19713-4333)
PHONE..................302 731-1326
H Thomas Hollinger, *President*
EMP: 10
SALES (est): 1.2MM **Privately Held**
WEB: www.newtononeadvisors.com
SIC: 8742 Financial consultant

(G-7131)
NICHOLAS J PUNTURIERI
1200 Peoples Plz (19702-5701)
PHONE..................302 834-7700
Nicholas Punturieri, *Officer*
EMP: 4
SALES (est): 105.4K **Privately Held**
SIC: 8021 Dentists' office

(G-7132)
NICHOLAS O BIASOTTO CO
620 Stanton Christiana Rd # 205 (19713-2130)
PHONE..................302 998-1235
N Biasotto, *Principal*
EMP: 5
SALES (est): 295.2K **Privately Held**
SIC: 8031 Offices & clinics of osteopathic physicians

(G-7133)
NICHOLS NURSERY INC
Also Called: Nichols Excavation and Ldscp
324 Markus Ct (19713-1151)
PHONE..................302 834-2426
Stephen Nichols, *President*
Charlene Nichols, *Vice Pres*
EMP: 49
SALES (est): 6.7MM **Privately Held**
SIC: 0781 Landscape planning services

(G-7134)
NICKLE ELEC COMPANIES INC (PA)
14 Mill Park Ct Ste E (19713-1986)
PHONE..................302 453-4000
Steven Dignan, *President*
John Dematteis, *Vice Pres*
Jeromy Newton, *Vice Pres*
Brandon Cale, *Project Mgr*
Dave Schreffler, *Project Mgr*
EMP: 120
SQ FT: 4,000
SALES: 32.4MM **Privately Held**
WEB: www.panickle.com
SIC: 1731 General electrical contractor

(G-7135)
NOLAN WILLIAMS & PLUMHOFF
Also Called: Glushakow, Robert S
4132 Ogletown Stanton Rd (19713-4169)
PHONE..................410 823-7800
Steve Nolan, *Owner*
EMP: 20
SALES (est): 760.7K **Privately Held**
SIC: 8111 General practice attorney, lawyer

(G-7136)
NORKOL CONVERTING CORPORATION
1800 Ogletown Rd (19711-5472)
PHONE..................302 283-1080
Eric Holzer, *Principal*
EMP: 20
SALES (corp-wide): 164.5MM **Privately Held**
SIC: 2621 Paper mills
PA: Norkol Converting Corporation
11650 W Grand Ave
Melrose Park IL 60164
708 531-1000

(G-7137)
NORTH BAY MEDICAL ASSOCIATES
313 W Main St Ste A (19711-3217)
PHONE..................302 731-4620
Gary A Beste MD, *President*
Gary Beste, *Med Doctor*
EMP: 11
SALES (est): 807.4K **Privately Held**
SIC: 8011 Physicians' office, including specialists

(G-7138)
NORTH EAST CONTRACTORS INC
87 Blue Hen Dr (19713-3405)
PHONE..................302 286-6324
Kevin Garber, *President*
Donald Smith, *Vice Pres*
EMP: 20
SALES (est): 5.8MM **Privately Held**
SIC: 1542 Commercial & office building, new construction

(G-7139)
NOTIFY TECHNOLOGY INC
2035 Sunset Lake Rd (19702-2600)
PHONE..................505 818-5888
James Pine, *CEO*
EMP: 4
SALES (est): 53.5K **Privately Held**
SIC: 4813

(G-7140)
NVR INC
Also Called: Ryan Homes
1302 Drummond Plz 1032 (19711-5741)
PHONE..................302 731-5770
Jon Moats, *Manager*
EMP: 30 **Publicly Held**
WEB: www.nvrinc.com
SIC: 1531 1522 1521 Operative builders; residential construction; single-family housing construction
PA: Nvr, Inc.
11700 Plaza America Dr # 500
Reston VA 20190

(G-7141)
OCEAN CLB RSORT RSERVATION CTR
153 E Chestnut Hill Rd # 200 (19713-4046)
PHONE..................302 369-1420
Laurie Uriani, *General Mgr*
EMP: 6
SALES (est): 510.5K **Privately Held**
SIC: 7997 Swimming club, membership

(G-7142)
OCONNOR BELTING INTL INC
Also Called: Derco USA
728 Dawson Dr (19713-3414)
PHONE..................302 452-2500
Paul O'Connors Jr, *President*
Eric O'Connors Sr, *Vice Pres*
▲ EMP: 27
SQ FT: 53,000
SALES: 6MM **Privately Held**
SIC: 3496 Conveyor belts

(G-7143)
ODYSSEY TECHNOLOGIES LLC
2915 Ogletown Rd 1072 (19713-1927)
PHONE..................302 525-8184
EMP: 75
SALES (est): 1.4MM **Privately Held**
SIC: 7372 Educational computer software

(G-7144)
OGLETOWN BAPTIST CHURCH
316 Red Mill Rd (19713-1990)
PHONE..................302 737-2511
Drew Landry, *Pastor*
Sharon Spruill, *Admin Sec*
Evan Collier, *Assoc Pastor*
EMP: 20
SALES (est): 961.9K **Privately Held**
WEB: www.ogletown.org
SIC: 8661 8351 Baptist Church; child day care services

(G-7145)
OILMINERS CBD LLC
22 Gershwin Cir (19702-3039)
PHONE..................484 885-9417
George Lee Crampton Jr, *Mng Member*
EMP: 2
SALES (est): 73.4K **Privately Held**
SIC: 2299 Hemp yarn, thread, roving & textiles

(G-7146)
OMEGA IMAGING ASSOCIATES LLC (PA)
Also Called: Diagnostic Imaging Associates
6 Omega Dr (19713-2056)
PHONE..................302 738-9300
Magdy Boulos MD, *Ltd Ptnr*
Bruce A Fellows MD, *Ltd Ptnr*
Camillo A Gopez MD, *Ltd Ptnr*
Stephen L Hershey MD, *Ltd Ptnr*
Leonard Katz MD, *Ltd Ptnr*
EMP: 25
SQ FT: 5,554
SALES (est): 4.2MM **Privately Held**
SIC: 8011 Radiologist

(G-7147)
OMNIWAY CORPORATION (PA)
Also Called: Water's Edge
2300 Waters Edge Dr (19702-6355)
PHONE..................302 738-5076
Hugh Martin, *President*
Margaret Martin, *Vice Pres*
EMP: 17
SQ FT: 4,460
SALES (est): 965.9K **Privately Held**
WEB: www.omni-way.com
SIC: 8741 8742 7532 Construction management; management consulting services; distribution channels consultant; antique & classic automobile restoration

(G-7148)
ON DEMAND SERVICES LLC
Also Called: On Demand Moving Services
46 Chambord Dr (19702-5548)
PHONE..................302 388-1215
EMP: 4
SALES (est): 386.5K **Privately Held**
SIC: 3577 Printers & plotters

(G-7149)
ONCOLOGY CARE HOME
267 E Main St (19711-7314)
PHONE..................610 274-2437
EMP: 8 EST: 2018
SALES (est): 64K **Privately Held**
SIC: 8059 Nursing & personal care

(G-7150)
ONE HOUR PRINTING
122 Balmoral Way (19702-5253)
PHONE..................302 220-1684
EMP: 2
SALES (est): 83.9K **Privately Held**
SIC: 2752 Commercial printing, lithographic

(G-7151)
ONE MAIN FINANCIAL
Also Called: Citifinancial
420 Suburban Dr (19711-3564)
PHONE..................302 737-9456
Douglas Trauber, *Managing Dir*
Casey Baritz, *Assistant VP*
Zhan Sun, *Vice Pres*
EMP: 4
SALES (corp-wide): 4.2B **Publicly Held**
WEB: www.citifinancial.com
SIC: 6153 6141 Short-term business credit; personal credit institutions
HQ: One Main Financial
601 Nw 2nd St
Evansville IN 47708
812 424-8031

(G-7152)
ONE STEP AHEAD CHILDCARE
432 Salem Church Rd (19702-2707)
PHONE..................302 292-1162
Dawn Sheehan-Reilly, *Director*

EMP: 5
SALES (est): 155.4K **Privately Held**
SIC: 7231 Beauty shops

(G-7153)
ONENESS MASSAGE THERAPY
10 Blue Jay Dr (19713-1210)
PHONE..................302 893-0348
Wendy Forrest, *Principal*
EMP: 4
SALES (est): 128.2K **Privately Held**
SIC: 8093 Rehabilitation center, outpatient treatment

(G-7154)
ONPOINT ONCOLOGY INC
1184 Corner Ketch Rd (19711-2324)
PHONE..................610 274-0188
EMP: 6
SALES (est): 80.5K **Privately Held**
SIC: 8011 Oncologist

(G-7155)
OPEN DOOR INC (PA)
254 E Main St (19711-7390)
PHONE..................302 731-1504
Martin S Lampner, *CEO*
Arlene Tayloe, *Vice Pres*
Enrique Alcaraz, *Opers Staff*
Susanna Jessup, *Treasurer*
Justin McKee, *Director*
EMP: 13 EST: 1997
SALES (est): 1MM **Privately Held**
WEB: www.opendoor.com
SIC: 8322 Rehabilitation services

(G-7156)
OPERATA LLC
2035 Sunset Lake Rd B2 (19702-2600)
PHONE..................302 525-0190
Andrew Scott,
EMP: 6
SALES (est): 123.5K **Privately Held**
SIC: 7371 Software programming applications

(G-7157)
OPPENHEIMER GROUP INC
200 Continental Dr # 301 (19713-4336)
PHONE..................302 533-0779
Brett Libke, *Vice Pres*
EMP: 12 EST: 1986
SALES (est): 8.9MM **Privately Held**
SIC: 5141 Food brokers
HQ: Oppenheimer, David And Company I, Llc
11 Burbidge St Suite 101
Coquitlam BC V3K 7
604 461-6779

(G-7158)
OPTION CARE ENTERPRISES INC
604 White Clay Center Dr (19711-5455)
PHONE..................302 355-6100
John Hopkins, *Branch Mgr*
EMP: 41 **Publicly Held**
SIC: 8082 Home health care services
HQ: Option Care Enterprises, Inc.
3000 Lakeside Dr Ste 300n
Bannockburn IL 60015

(G-7159)
ORTHOPEDIC PROPERTIES LLC
1096 Old Churchmans Rd (19713-2102)
PHONE..................302 998-2310
EMP: 5
SALES (est): 399K **Privately Held**
SIC: 8011 Orthopedic physician

(G-7160)
ORTHOPEDIC SPECIALISTS
Also Called: Mohammad Kamali, MD
1096 Old Churchmans Rd (19713-2102)
PHONE..................302 351-4848
Mohammad Kamali, *Principal*
Joshua Vaught, *Executive*
EMP: 33
SALES (est): 3.4MM **Privately Held**
SIC: 8011 Orthopedic physician

(G-7161)
OSG AMERICA LP
111 Continental Dr # 402 (19713-4306)
PHONE..................212 578-1922
EMP: 4
SALES (corp-wide): 366.1MM **Publicly Held**
SIC: 4424 Intercoastal transportation, freight
HQ: Osg America L.P.
302 Knights Run Ave
Tampa FL 33602

(G-7162)
OSSKIN USA INC
2915 Ogletown Rd (19713-1927)
PHONE..................302 266-8200
Randy Wyrofsky, *President*
Jean-Philippe Carmona, *Vice Pres*
Pierre Coutu, *Treasurer*
Julien Arnaud, *Admin Sec*
EMP: 4
SALES (est): 105K **Privately Held**
SIC: 5047 Medical & hospital equipment

(G-7163)
OTO GLOBAL INC
2035 Sunset Lake Rd B2 (19702-2600)
PHONE..................966 597-9694
Muhammed Al Razaz, *CEO*
EMP: 2
SALES (est): 100K **Privately Held**
SIC: 7372 Application computer software

(G-7164)
OUTCOME ASSOCIATES LLC
8 Linette Ct (19702-6815)
PHONE..................302 368-3637
EMP: 2
SALES (est): 95.4K **Privately Held**
SIC: 7372 Application Service Provider

(G-7165)
OUTDOOR DESIGN GROUP LLC
935 Rahway Dr (19711-2687)
P.O. Box 670, Bear (19701-0670)
PHONE..................302 743-2363
Tim Boresen,
EMP: 10
SALES (est): 500K **Privately Held**
SIC: 0782 Lawn & garden services

(G-7166)
P A WOMENCARE
4745 Ogletown Stanton Rd # 231 (19713-2074)
PHONE..................302 731-2900
Fax: 302 731-1306
EMP: 4 EST: 1993
SALES (est): 420K **Privately Held**
SIC: 8031 Osteopathic Physician's Office

(G-7167)
P B INVESTMENT CORP
Also Called: Pb Reit
256 Chapman Rd Ste 100 (19702-5417)
PHONE..................302 266-7920
Peter Georgopoulus, *President*
Linda McFaul, *Vice Pres*
EMP: 6
SQ FT: 1,200
SALES (est): 358.4K **Privately Held**
SIC: 6162 Mortgage bankers

(G-7168)
P&P HORSE TRANSPORTATION
1101 Millstone Dr (19711-1811)
PHONE..................302 388-7687
Howard Peyton, *Principal*
EMP: 4
SALES (est): 269.8K **Privately Held**
SIC: 4789 Transportation services

(G-7169)
PACE LOCAL 2 898
25 S Old Baltimore Pike # 202 (19702-1540)
PHONE..................302 737-8898
Ken Gouneringer, *President*
Dave Chanthony, *Chairman*
Ken Herbine, *Vice Pres*
Maykay Nickle, *Admin Sec*
EMP: 4
SALES (est): 159.7K **Privately Held**
SIC: 8631 Labor unions & similar labor organizations

(G-7170)
PACIFICO INDUSTRIAL LTD
113 Barksdale Pro Ctr (19711-3258)
PHONE..................213 435-1181
Michael Pun, *President*
EMP: 30
SALES (est): 1.8MM **Privately Held**
SIC: 3089 Plastic kitchenware, tableware & houseware

(G-7171)
PALERMO FRANCIS A MD FACC PA
Also Called: Palermo, Francis A MD PA
620 Stanton Christiana Rd (19713-2133)
PHONE..................302 994-1100
Francis Palermo MD, *President*
EMP: 8
SALES (est): 417.7K **Privately Held**
SIC: 8011 Cardiologist & cardio-vascular specialist

(G-7172)
PALLADIAN MANAGEMENT LLC
Also Called: Hunters Crossing
41 Fairway Rd Ofc 2c (19711-5660)
PHONE..................302 737-1971
Cherry Haro, *Branch Mgr*
EMP: 15
SALES (corp-wide): 1.9MM **Privately Held**
SIC: 6531 Cooperative apartment manager
PA: Palladian Management Llc
1071 Post Rd E Ste 1a
Westport CT 06880
203 557-3526

(G-7173)
PANCO MANAGEMENT CORPORATION
Also Called: English Village
15 Fox Hall 15 # 15 (19711-5941)
PHONE..................302 366-1875
Esther Lesieur, *Manager*
EMP: 11
SALES (corp-wide): 14MM **Privately Held**
WEB: www.homesteadgardensapts.com
SIC: 6531 6513 Real estate managers; apartment building operators
PA: Panco Management Corporation
395 W Passaic St Ste 251
Rochelle Park NJ 07662
201 556-0900

(G-7174)
PANZER DERMATOLOGY ASSOC PA
537 Stanton Christiana Rd # 207 (19713-2148)
PHONE..................302 633-7550
Peter B Panzer, *President*
Helen Mashek, *Med Doctor*
Tess Seal, *Manager*
Nancy L Melvin, *Executive*
Mary Kwoka, *Administration*
EMP: 4
SALES (est): 1.9MM **Privately Held**
SIC: 8011 Dermatologist

(G-7175)
PARAGON DESIGN INC
77 E Main St Ste 2 (19711-5000)
P.O. Box 4526 (19715-4526)
PHONE..................302 292-1523
Robert Paraskewich, *President*
Bev Duff, *Controller*
Emilee Hembury, *Creative Dir*
EMP: 6
SQ FT: 3,500
SALES (est): 987.2K **Privately Held**
WEB: www.paragon-design.net
SIC: 7311 Advertising consultant

(G-7176)
PARAGS GLASS COMPANY
107 Albe Dr Ste D (19702-1300)
PHONE..................302 737-0101
William Parag, *Owner*
EMP: 6
SQ FT: 2,500
SALES (est): 645.9K **Privately Held**
SIC: 1793 7536 Glass & glazing work; automotive glass replacement shops

(G-7177)
PARK PLACE DENTAL
210 W Park Pl (19711-4519)
PHONE..................302 455-0333
Michael C Duffy, *President*
EMP: 4
SALES (est): 67.6K **Privately Held**
SIC: 8021 Prosthodontist

(G-7178)
PARKWAY DRY CLEANERS INC (PA)
Also Called: Parkway Cleaners
13 Chestnut Hill Plz (19713-2701)
PHONE..................302 737-2406
Donald Ciccarone, *President*
EMP: 5 EST: 1956
SALES (est): 243.7K **Privately Held**
SIC: 7216 7251 Drycleaning collecting & distributing agency; shoe repair shop

(G-7179)
PARVIZ SOROURI MD PA
Also Called: Bijan Sorouri
10 Darwin Dr Ste C (19711-6658)
PHONE..................302 453-9171
Parviz Sorouri, *Owner*
EMP: 4
SALES (est): 480.3K **Privately Held**
SIC: 8011 Gastronomist; physicians' office, including specialists

(G-7180)
PATHS LLC
1352 Marrows Rd Ste 110 (19711-5476)
PHONE..................302 294-1494
EMP: 25
SALES (corp-wide): 10.9MM **Privately Held**
SIC: 8721 Billing & bookkeeping service
PA: Paths Llc
9 Executive Campus
Cherry Hill NJ 08002
856 671-6000

(G-7181)
PATRICIA AYERS
20 Capano Dr Apt C3 (19702-1718)
PHONE..................609 335-8923
Patricia Ayers, *Principal*
EMP: 4
SALES (est): 46.7K **Privately Held**
SIC: 8322 Individual & family services

(G-7182)
PATRICIA DISARIO DAY CARE
4 Cottonwood Ct (19702-2893)
PHONE..................302 737-8889
James Disario, *Principal*
EMP: 5
SALES (est): 68.6K **Privately Held**
SIC: 8351 Group day care center

(G-7183)
PATRICK J MCCABE
Also Called: State Farm Insurance
262 Chapman Rd Ste 109 (19702-5412)
PHONE..................302 368-3711
Patrick J McCabe, *Owner*
EMP: 4
SALES (est): 474.5K **Privately Held**
WEB: www.patrickmccabe.com
SIC: 6411 Insurance agents & brokers

(G-7184)
PATTERSON PRICE RE LLC
1101 Millstone Dr (19711-1811)
PHONE..................302 366-0200
A John Price, *President*
EMP: 8
SALES (est): 437.3K
SALES (corp-wide): 1.3MM **Privately Held**
WEB: www.pattersonprice.com
SIC: 6531 6552 Real estate agent, residential; subdividers & developers
PA: Patterson Price Real Estate Llc
5 E Green St
Middletown DE 19709
302 378-9550

Newark - New Castle County (G-7185) — GEOGRAPHIC SECTION

(G-7185)
PATTERSON-SCHWARTZ & ASSOC INC
680 S College Ave (19713-1396)
PHONE...................302 733-7000
Christopher Cashman, *Manager*
EMP: 90
SALES (est): 2.2MM
SALES (corp-wide): 32.2MM **Privately Held**
WEB: www.pacinihomes.com
SIC: 6531 Real estate agent, residential
PA: Patterson-Schwartz And Associates, Inc.
7234 Lancaster Pike
Hockessin DE 19707
302 234-5250

(G-7186)
PAUL WOERNER
Also Called: Sign Guys The
610 Banyan Rd (19713-1703)
PHONE...................302 266-6282
EMP: 1 EST: 2011
SALES (est): 80K **Privately Held**
SIC: 3993 Mfg Signs/Advertising Specialties

(G-7187)
PAYPERGIGS INC
2035 Sunset Lake Rd B2 (19702-2600)
PHONE...................917 336-2162
Zahidul Islam Khan, *Director*
EMP: 612
SALES: 1MM **Privately Held**
SIC: 7372 Application computer software

(G-7188)
PAYROLL MANAGEMENT ASSISTANTS
409 White Clay Center Dr (19711-5468)
PHONE...................302 456-6816
James Paoli, *President*
Peggy Smith, *Vice Pres*
Alisha Coen, *Manager*
Anna Kline, *Manager*
Joanna Donovan, *Administration*
EMP: 6
SALES (est): 614.6K **Privately Held**
WEB: www.pmapayroll.com
SIC: 8721 Payroll accounting service

(G-7189)
PC SUPPLIES INC
1003 S Chapel St Ste A (19702-1357)
PHONE...................302 368-4800
R Scott Martin, *President*
Judy Larosch, *Vice Pres*
Charlie Rudewick, *Vice Pres*
EMP: 8
SQ FT: 1,400
SALES: 3.5MM **Privately Held**
WEB: www.pcsupplies.com
SIC: 5045 7378 5734 Computer peripheral equipment; computer software; computers & accessories, personal & home entertainment; computer & data processing equipment repair/maintenance; computer peripheral equipment repair & maintenance; computer peripheral equipment; software, business & non-game; personal computers

(G-7190)
PEDIATRIC ASSOCIATES PA
4735 Ogltn Stntn Rd # 1116 (19713-7006)
PHONE...................302 368-8612
Victoria A Levin, *President*
Neal B Cohn, *Vice Pres*
Barbara L Light, *Vice Pres*
Joseph A Vitale, *Vice Pres*
Sharon Mirto, *Finance*
EMP: 38
SQ FT: 4,000
SALES (est): 3.8MM **Privately Held**
WEB: www.pediatricassociates.org
SIC: 8011 Pediatrician

(G-7191)
PELSA COMPANY INC
610 Peoples Plz (19702-5600)
PHONE...................302 834-3771
Michael Paraskewich, *President*
EMP: 9

SALES: 500K **Privately Held**
SIC: 8711 8732 Civil engineering; survey service: marketing, location, etc.

(G-7192)
PENACHE BEAUTY SALON
16 Polly Drmmond Shpg Ctr (19711-4861)
PHONE...................302 731-5912
Ronald Wilkinson, *Owner*
EMP: 5
SQ FT: 1,800
SALES (est): 98.2K **Privately Held**
SIC: 7231 Unisex hair salons

(G-7193)
PENCADER ASSOCIATES
560 Peoples Plz (19702-4798)
PHONE...................302 838-7838
Douglas Bennett, *Mng Member*
Michael McGavisk,
EMP: 4
SALES: 1.5MM **Privately Held**
SIC: 6531 Appraiser, real estate

(G-7194)
PENCADER MECHANICAL CONTRS
2038 Sunset Lake Rd # 2040 (19702-2630)
PHONE...................302 368-9144
William Cain, *Controller*
Rick Adams, *Manager*
EMP: 6 EST: 1961
SQ FT: 5,000
SALES (est): 884.3K **Privately Held**
WEB: www.penmech.com
SIC: 1761 Sheet metalwork

(G-7195)
PENCO CORPORATION
121 Sandy Dr (19713-1148)
PHONE...................302 738-3212
Rick Peterson, *Manager*
EMP: 8
SALES (corp-wide): 18.8MM **Privately Held**
WEB: www.pencocorp.com
SIC: 5074 Plumbing fittings & supplies
PA: Penco Corporation
1503 W Stein Hwy
Seaford DE 19973
302 629-7911

(G-7196)
PENNONI
121 Continental Dr # 207 (19713-4341)
PHONE...................302 234-4600
Robert Hayden, *President*
Sharon Hayden, *President*
Michael Ellis, *Division Mgr*
John Haupt, *Assoc VP*
John Suender, *Associate*
EMP: 33
SQ FT: 6,000
SALES (est): 3.5MM **Privately Held**
WEB: www.bdabel.com
SIC: 8711 Consulting engineer

(G-7197)
PENNONI ASSOCIATES INC
121 Continental Dr # 207 (19713-4341)
PHONE...................302 655-4451
Peter Nikolov, *Division Mgr*
Charles Perry, *Vice Pres*
Cecil Whitlock, *Assoc VP*
Thomas Craig, *Engineer*
Norman Dixon, *Engineer*
EMP: 50
SALES (corp-wide): 191.8MM **Privately Held**
WEB: www.pennoni.com
SIC: 8711 Consulting engineer
PA: Pennoni Associates Inc.
1900 Market St Fl 3
Philadelphia PA 19103
215 222-3000

(G-7198)
PEOPLE BUILDERS INC
38 Hempstead Dr (19702-7711)
PHONE...................302 250-0716
Velva Rainey, *Principal*
EMP: 4 EST: 2017
SALES (est): 65K **Privately Held**
SIC: 8322 Temporary relief service

(G-7199)
PEPCO HOLDINGS LLC
401 Eagle Run Rd (19702-1602)
P.O. Box 9239 (19714-9239)
PHONE...................202 872-2000
Todd Richardson, *Marketing Staff*
Rhonda Bonvetti, *Branch Mgr*
Mark Krason, *Manager*
EMP: 32
SALES (corp-wide): 35.9B **Publicly Held**
SIC: 4911 Generation, electric power
HQ: Pepco Holdings Llc
701 9th St Nw Ste 3
Washington DC 20001
202 872-2000

(G-7200)
PERA TRADING INC
711 Interchange Blvd (19711-3594)
PHONE...................302 292-1750
Mustafa Tuncer, *President*
◆ EMP: 4 EST: 2012
SALES (est): 845.2K **Privately Held**
SIC: 5032 Granite building stone

(G-7201)
PERFECT NAILS
210 University Plz (19702-1550)
PHONE...................302 731-1964
Larry Truong, *Owner*
Peter Bo, *Owner*
EMP: 5
SALES (est): 173.5K **Privately Held**
SIC: 7231 Manicurist, pedicurist

(G-7202)
PERFORMANCE CONS GROUP INC
1 Innovation Way Ste 304c (19711-5442)
PHONE...................302 738-7532
EMP: 22
SQ FT: 2,200
SALES: 145K **Privately Held**
SIC: 8999 Scientific Consulting

(G-7203)
PERIOPERATIVE SERVICES LLC (PA)
111 Continental Dr # 412 (19713-4306)
PHONE...................302 733-0806
Alan Morales, *Vice Pres*
Lorraine Torres, *Opers Staff*
Bill Payment, *Human Resources*
Kimberly Fell, *Sales Staff*
Linda Larimore, *Supervisor*
EMP: 57
SQ FT: 16,000
SALES (est): 6.2MM **Privately Held**
WEB: www.periop.com
SIC: 8721 Billing & bookkeeping service

(G-7204)
PERISTALSIS PRODUCTIONS INC
6 Newside Ct (19711-4807)
PHONE...................302 366-1106
Cheryl Swift, *Principal*
EMP: 9
SALES (est): 212.2K **Privately Held**
SIC: 7822 Motion picture & tape distribution

(G-7205)
PESSAGNO EQUIPMENT INC
109 Sandy Dr (19713-1148)
PHONE...................302 738-7001
Robert Pessagino, *Principal*
EMP: 4
SALES (est): 460.4K **Privately Held**
SIC: 3799 Trailers & trailer equipment

(G-7206)
PETES GARAGE INC
78 Albe Dr Ste 8 (19702-1393)
PHONE...................302 286-6069
Peter Waldrush, *Principal*
EMP: 4
SALES (est): 339.4K **Privately Held**
SIC: 7538 General automotive repair shops

(G-7207)
PETTINARO CONSTRUCTION CO INC
100 Cindy Dr (19702-8132)
PHONE...................302 832-8823
Gregory Pettinaro, *Branch Mgr*
EMP: 38
SALES (corp-wide): 59.6MM **Privately Held**
SIC: 6531 Real estate brokers & agents
PA: Pettinaro Construction Co Inc
234 N James St
Wilmington DE 19804
302 999-0708

(G-7208)
PETTITT CONSTRUCTION LLC
12 Carlisle Rd (19713-2525)
PHONE...................302 690-0831
William Pettitt, *Partner*
Blythe Pettitt, *Partner*
EMP: 5
SQ FT: 3,000
SALES (est): 549.6K **Privately Held**
SIC: 1542 Nonresidential construction

(G-7209)
PHARMERICA LONG-TERM CARE LLC
Also Called: Ltc Pharmacy
111 Ruthar Dr (19711-8025)
PHONE...................302 454-8234
Victor Manuel, *Branch Mgr*
EMP: 60
SALES (corp-wide): 2B **Privately Held**
WEB: www.pharmerica.com
SIC: 5122 Pharmaceuticals
HQ: Pharmerica Long-Term Care, Llc
3625 Queen Palm Dr
Tampa FL 33619
877 975-2273

(G-7210)
PHASE SNSITIVE INNOVATIONS INC
116 Sandy Dr (19713-1187)
PHONE...................302 456-9003
Dennis W Prather, *CEO*
Kevin Shreve, *Research*
Charles Harrity, *Engineer*
Dan Mackrides, *Electrical Engi*
Christopher Schuetz, *CTO*
EMP: 14
SALES (est): 1.5MM **Privately Held**
SIC: 8711 Engineering services

(G-7211)
PHD TECHNOLOGY SOLUTIONS LLC
111 Continental Dr # 309 (19713-4317)
PHONE...................410 961-7895
Ed Hollyday, *Business Mgr*
Gary Spadaccino, *Engineer*
Donnell Friend, *Mng Member*
Chris Carlucci,
Derek Smith,
EMP: 30
SALES: 1.8MM **Privately Held**
SIC: 7373 Office computer automation systems integration

(G-7212)
PHI SERVICE CO
P.O. Box 6066 (19714-6066)
PHONE...................302 451-5224
EMP: 12
SALES (est): 746.3K **Privately Held**
SIC: 8641 Civic social & fraternal associations

(G-7213)
PHILIPS B ERIC DMD PA
Also Called: Omega Endodontics
Omega Prof Ctr Ste J31 (19713)
PHONE...................302 738-7303
B Eric Phillips, *President*
EMP: 10
SALES (est): 1.4MM **Privately Held**
SIC: 8011 Cardiologist & cardio-vascular specialist

(G-7214)
PHILLIPS & COHEN ASSOC LTD
258 Chapman Rd Ste 205 (19702-5444)
PHONE...................302 355-3500

Christy Nicholson, *Branch Mgr*
EMP: 60
SALES (corp-wide): 27.2MM **Privately Held**
WEB: www.phillips-cohen.com
SIC: 7322 Adjustment & collection services
PA: Phillips & Cohen Associates, Ltd.
1002 Justison St
Wilmington DE 19801
609 518-9000

(G-7215)
PIKE CREEK ANIMAL HOSPITAL
297 Polly Drummond Hl Rd (19711-4834)
PHONE.................................302 454-7780
Laura Richardson, *CEO*
Dr Alan McKersie, *President*
EMP: 20
SALES (est): 997.4K **Privately Held**
SIC: 0742 Animal hospital services, pets & other animal specialties

(G-7216)
PIKE CREEK MORTGAGE SERVICES (PA)
Also Called: Pike Creek Mortgage Group
2100 Drummond Plz Bldg 2 (19711-5743)
PHONE.................................302 892-2811
Wayne Moses, *President*
EMP: 15
SALES (est): 2.1MM **Privately Held**
WEB: www.de-loans.com
SIC: 6163 Mortgage brokers arranging for loans, using money of others

(G-7217)
PIKE CREEK PSYCHLOGICAL CTR PA (PA)
8 Polly Drummond Hill Rd (19711-5703)
PHONE.................................302 738-6859
J D Willetts, *President*
EMP: 13
SALES (est): 818.6K **Privately Held**
SIC: 8322 8049 General counseling services; psychologist, psychotherapist & hypnotist

(G-7218)
PINEAL CONSULTING GROUP LLC
40 E Main St 181 (19711-4639)
PHONE.................................302 219-4822
Jon Brown,
EMP: 10
SALES (est): 215.3K **Privately Held**
SIC: 8742 Management consulting services

(G-7219)
PIONEER HOUSE
413 Salem Church Rd (19702-1452)
PHONE.................................302 286-0892
Cinthia Guy, *Director*
EMP: 20
SALES (est): 238.7K **Privately Held**
SIC: 8322 Social services for the handicapped

(G-7220)
PIRULOS CHILD CARE CENTER LLC
799 Salem Church Rd (19702-3612)
PHONE.................................302 836-3520
Joseph Hurst, *Manager*
EMP: 5 **EST:** 2006
SALES (est): 174.7K **Privately Held**
SIC: 8351 Group day care center

(G-7221)
PLACERS INC OF DELAWARE
1501 Casho Mill Rd Ste 9 (19711-3500)
PHONE.................................302 709-0973
Chris Burkhard, *President*
EMP: 10 **EST:** 2011
SALES: 508.9K
SALES (corp-wide): 7.6MM **Privately Held**
SIC: 7363 Temporary help service
PA: C.B.I. Group, L.L.C
1501 Casho Mill Rd Ste 9
Newark DE 19711
302 266-0860

(G-7222)
PLANNED PARENTHOOD OF DELAWARE
140 E Delaware Ave (19711-4649)
PHONE.................................302 731-7801
Brenda Peirce, *Manager*
EMP: 6
SALES (corp-wide): 4.9MM **Privately Held**
WEB: www.ppde.org
SIC: 8093 Family planning clinic
PA: Planned Parenthood Of Delaware Inc
625 N Shipley St
Wilmington DE 19801
302 655-7293

(G-7223)
PLUMBERS PIPEFITTERS LOCAL 74
201 Executive Dr (19702-3316)
PHONE.................................302 636-7400
Anthony M Papili, *Owner*
EMP: 5
SALES (est): 2.4MM **Privately Held**
SIC: 8631 Labor union

(G-7224)
PMC PUBLICATIONS LLC
201 Michelle Ct (19711-6769)
PHONE.................................302 268-4480
Sachin Karnik, *Principal*
EMP: 1 **EST:** 2018
SALES (est): 37.5K **Privately Held**
SIC: 2741 Miscellaneous publishing

(G-7225)
PNC BANK NATIONAL ASSOCIATION
201 Newark Shopping Ctr (19711-7301)
PHONE.................................302 733-7150
P N Trahan, *Manager*
EMP: 15
SALES (corp-wide): 19.9B **Publicly Held**
WEB: www.pncfunds.com
SIC: 6021 National trust companies with deposits, commercial
HQ: Pnc Bank, National Association
222 Delaware Ave
Wilmington DE 19801
877 762-2000

(G-7226)
PNC BANK NATIONAL ASSOCIATION
25 Castle Mall (19713-3477)
PHONE.................................302 733-7170
Wanda Godwin, *Manager*
EMP: 8
SALES (corp-wide): 19.9B **Publicly Held**
WEB: www.pncfunds.com
SIC: 6021 National trust companies with deposits, commercial
HQ: Pnc Bank, National Association
222 Delaware Ave
Wilmington DE 19801
877 762-2000

(G-7227)
PNC BANK NATIONAL ASSOCIATION
84 University Plz (19702-1549)
PHONE.................................302 733-7160
Sam Barresi, *Manager*
EMP: 12
SALES (corp-wide): 19.9B **Publicly Held**
SIC: 6022 State trust companies accepting deposits, commercial
HQ: Pnc Bank, National Association
222 Delaware Ave
Wilmington DE 19801
877 762-2000

(G-7228)
PNC BANK NATIONAL ASSOCIATION
4643 Stanton Ogletown Rd (19713-2006)
PHONE.................................302 733-7190
Jason Wallace, *Site Mgr*
Sterling Doughty, *Manager*
EMP: 12
SALES (corp-wide): 19.9B **Publicly Held**
SIC: 6021 National commercial banks
HQ: Pnc Bank, National Association
222 Delaware Ave
Wilmington DE 19801
877 762-2000

(G-7229)
POLAND & SULLIVAN INSURANCE
Also Called: Nationwide Insurance
106 Haines St Ste A (19711-5362)
P.O. Box 418 (19715-0418)
PHONE.................................302 738-3535
Andre Hoeschel, *President*
John Yasik, *Vice Pres*
Cindy Serrano, *Administration*
EMP: 11
SALES (est): 2.1MM **Privately Held**
WEB: www.poland-sullivan.com
SIC: 6411 Insurance agents

(G-7230)
POLARSTAR ENGINEERING & MCH
5 Garfield Way Ste B (19713-3457)
PHONE.................................302 368-4639
Stephen Hague, *Owner*
▲ **EMP:** 4
SQ FT: 2,500
SALES (est): 419.5K **Privately Held**
SIC: 3599 Machine shop, jobbing & repair

(G-7231)
POLYMER TECHNOLOGIES INC (PA)
420 Corporate Blvd (19702-3330)
PHONE.................................302 738-9001
Robert Prybutok, *CEO*
Erik Larson, *Vice Pres*
Carl Wolaver, *Vice Pres*
Brian Rollo, *Production*
Benjamin Resine, *Engineer*
▲ **EMP:** 90
SQ FT: 86,000
SALES (est): 31.3MM **Privately Held**
WEB: www.polytechinc.com
SIC: 2821 Polyurethane resins

(G-7232)
POND INC
Also Called: Pond The Ice Arena
101 John F Campbell Rd (19711-5457)
PHONE.................................302 266-0777
Robert Campbell, *President*
Joanne Stella, *Principal*
EMP: 25
SALES (est): 1.2MM **Privately Held**
WEB: www.thepondicearena.com
SIC: 7999 Ice skating rink operation

(G-7233)
PORTER NISSAN BUICK NEWARK
600 Ogletown Rd (19711-5406)
PHONE.................................302 368-6300
Douglas Cameron, *CFO*
Doug Cameron, *CFO*
EMP: 75
SALES: 81.7MM **Privately Held**
SIC: 5511 5012 Automobiles, new & used; automobiles

(G-7234)
POTTS WLDG BOILER REPR CO INC (HQ)
1901 Ogletown Rd (19711-5437)
PHONE.................................302 453-2550
Dennis Dakin, *President*
▼ **EMP:** 189
SQ FT: 200,000
SALES (est): 30.8MM
SALES (corp-wide): 141.5MM **Privately Held**
WEB: www.pottswelding.com
SIC: 3441 3491 Fabricated structural metal; industrial valves
PA: St. John Holdings, Inc.
320 King Of Prussia Rd
Radnor PA 19087
610 964-8702

(G-7235)
POURED FOUNDATIONS OF DE INC
409 Capitol Trl (19711-3864)
PHONE.................................302 234-2050
Richard Sexton, *Principal*
EMP: 5
SALES (est): 331.1K **Privately Held**
SIC: 1771 Concrete work

(G-7236)
POWER DELIVERY SOLUTIONS LLC
100 Commerce Dr Ste 201 (19713-2850)
PHONE.................................302 260-3114
Frank Cascino, *President*
Richard Conlin, *Vice Pres*
Dean Sevy, *Vice Pres*
Eric Whalen, *Vice Pres*
Paige Cresci, *Engineer*
EMP: 30
SQ FT: 10,000
SALES: 3.8MM **Privately Held**
SIC: 8711 Consulting engineer

(G-7237)
POWERTRAIN TECHNOLOGY INC
Also Called: Benchmark Transmissions
2101 Ogletown Rd (19711-5433)
PHONE.................................302 368-4900
Dante Principe, *President*
EMP: 5
SALES (est): 560K **Privately Held**
SIC: 7538 7537 General automotive repair shops; automotive transmission repair shops

(G-7238)
PRECIOUS KNWLDG ERLY LRNG CTR
1000 Village Cir (19713-2952)
PHONE.................................302 293-2588
Lozetta Hayden, *Principal*
EMP: 5 **EST:** 2011
SALES (est): 77.2K **Privately Held**
SIC: 8351 Child day care services

(G-7239)
PRECISE ALIGNMENT MCH TL CO
59 Avignon Dr (19702-5553)
PHONE.................................302 832-2922
Alfred A Lance Sr, *Owner*
EMP: 6
SALES (est): 294.1K **Privately Held**
SIC: 8711 Engineering services

(G-7240)
PRECISE TECHNOLOGY INC
220 Lake Dr Ste 4 (19702-3353)
PHONE.................................302 737-4638
Fax: 302 737-5635
EMP: 30
SALES (corp-wide): 6B **Privately Held**
SIC: 3089 Mfr Plastic Products
PA: Rexam Plc
4 Millbank
London
207 227-4100

(G-7241)
PRECISION AIRCONVEY CORP (PA)
465 Corporate Blvd (19702-3331)
PHONE.................................302 999-8000
Tom Embley, *CEO*
Lawrence Green, *President*
Chris Gillespie, *Project Engr*
Kevin Bock, *Technical Staff*
Joel Bartelt, *Representative*
EMP: 18
SQ FT: 10,000
SALES: 5.3MM **Privately Held**
WEB: www.airconvey.com
SIC: 3569 Filters

(G-7242)
PREIT-RUBIN INC
Also Called: Christiana Mall
715 Christiana Mall (19702)
PHONE.................................302 731-9815
Bob Wahlquist, *Regional Mgr*
EMP: 75

Newark - New Castle County (G-7243)

SALES (corp-wide): 362.4MM **Privately Held**
SIC: 6512 Shopping center, property operation only
HQ: Preit-Rubin, Inc.
200 S Broad St Fl 3
Philadelphia PA 19102
215 875-0700

(G-7243) PREMIER DENTISTRY CHRISTIANA
4745 Ogltn Stntn Rd # 110 (19713-2070)
PHONE.................302 366-7636
Hung V Le, *Principal*
EMP: 4
SALES (est): 476.6K **Privately Held**
SIC: 8021 Dental clinics & offices

(G-7244) PREMIER HEALTHCARE INC
Also Called: Newark Manor
254 W Main St (19711-3235)
PHONE.................302 731-5576
Bruce Boyer, *President*
Nicole Savage, *Counsel*
Paulette Dolbow, *Food Svc Dir*
David Boyer, *Administration*
Gail Boyer, *Admin Sec*
EMP: 48
SQ FT: 24,000
SALES (est): 3.8MM **Privately Held**
SIC: 8052 Intermediate care facilities

(G-7245) PREMIERE HAIR DESIGN
1450 Capitol Trl Ste 109 (19711-5700)
PHONE.................302 368-7711
Barbie Mooney, *Partner*
EMP: 6
SALES (est): 158.4K **Privately Held**
SIC: 7231 Cosmetology & personal hygiene salons

(G-7246) PREMIERE PHYSICIANS PA
314 E Main St Ste 103 (19711-7180)
PHONE.................302 762-6675
Neal Kalin, *Principal*
EMP: 7
SALES (est): 859.9K **Privately Held**
WEB: www.gonnabuyahome.com
SIC: 8011 General & family practice, physician/surgeon

(G-7247) PRESTEGE LLC
16 N Bellwoode Dr (19702-3415)
P.O. Box 724, Bear (19701-0724)
PHONE.................302 312-8548
Willa Lee,
EMP: 7
SALES: 700K **Privately Held**
SIC: 8999 Actuarial consultant

(G-7248) PRESTIGE POWDER INC
13 Tyler Way (19713-3449)
PHONE.................302 737-7086
Allen Boyle, *Principal*
EMP: 5
SALES (est): 619.1K **Privately Held**
WEB: www.americraftawning.com
SIC: 3993 5099 5999 Signs & advertising specialties; signs, except electric; awnings

(G-7249) PRESTIGE POWDER FINISHING INC
13 Tyler Way (19713-3449)
PHONE.................302 737-7500
Allen Boyle, *President*
EMP: 10 **EST:** 1998
SQ FT: 18,500
SALES (est): 1.1MM **Privately Held**
WEB: www.prestigepowder.com
SIC: 3479 Painting of metal products; coating of metals & formed products

(G-7250) PRIDE OF DELAW
57 W Cleveland Ave (19711-7004)
PHONE.................302 861-6857
EMP: 7
SALES (est): 80K **Privately Held**
SIC: 8641 Civic/Social Association

(G-7251) PRIDE OF DELAWARE LODGE
57 W Cleveland Ave (19711-7004)
PHONE.................215 453-9236
William Cornish, *President*
EMP: 5
SQ FT: 1,400
SALES: 150K **Privately Held**
SIC: 8611 Community affairs & services

(G-7252) PRIDES COURT APARTMENTS
Also Called: West Minister Management
6 Sussex Rd Ofc F (19713-3119)
PHONE.................302 737-2085
Jonathan Cohen, *Manager*
EMP: 7
SALES (est): 645.8K **Privately Held**
SIC: 6513 Apartment building operators

(G-7253) PRINCETON COML HOLDINGS LLC
113 Barksdale Pro Ctr (19711-3258)
PHONE.................302 449-4836
Ola Osman,
EMP: 5
SALES: 100K **Privately Held**
SIC: 8748 6531 Business consulting; real estate agents & managers

(G-7254) PRINT ON THIS
3 Green Ct (19702-1355)
PHONE.................302 235-9475
Ivan Meikle, *Principal*
EMP: 2
SALES (est): 83.9K **Privately Held**
SIC: 2752 Commercial printing, lithographic

(G-7255) PRINTED SOLID INC
2860 Ogletown Rd Bldg 6-8 (19713-1820)
PHONE.................302 439-0098
David Randolph, *CEO*
▲ **EMP:** 12
SALES: 700K **Privately Held**
SIC: 2752 Commercial printing, lithographic

(G-7256) PRINTS AND PRINCESSES
202 Hanover Pl (19711-2755)
PHONE.................703 881-1057
Mary L Anest, *Owner*
EMP: 2
SALES (est): 83.9K **Privately Held**
SIC: 2752 Commercial printing, lithographic

(G-7257) PRIORITY RADIO INC
179 Stanton Christiana Rd (19702-1619)
P.O. Box 372, Wilmington (19899-0372)
PHONE.................302 540-5690
Steve Hare, *Principal*
EMP: 6
SALES (est): 311K **Privately Held**
SIC: 4832 Radio broadcasting stations

(G-7258) PRIORITY SERVICES LLC
70 Albe Dr (19702-1322)
PHONE.................302 918-3070
Joseph A Cunane,
EMP: 35
SALES (est): 1.3MM **Privately Held**
SIC: 7349 Building maintenance services

(G-7259) PRISM EVENTS INC
2035 Sunset Lake Rd B2 (19702-2600)
PHONE.................424 252-1070
Imran Ali, *Principal*
Faisal Abbas, *Principal*
Raghib Khan, *Principal*
EMP: 5
SALES (est): 104.7K **Privately Held**
SIC: 7389

(G-7260) PRISON MINISTRIES DELAWARE INC
1 Hartford Pl (19711-2756)
P.O. Box 1055 (19715-1055)
PHONE.................302 737-2792
Fay Whittle, *Exec Dir*
Patricia Mae,
EMP: 15
SALES: 45K **Privately Held**
SIC: 8322 Individual & family services

(G-7261) PRIYA REALTY CORP
Also Called: Super 8 Motel
268 E Main St (19711-7390)
PHONE.................302 737-5050
Jagdish Patel, *President*
EMP: 4
SALES (est): 313.5K **Privately Held**
SIC: 7011 Hotels & motels

(G-7262) PRO AUTOMATED INC
100 Lake Dr Ste 205 (19702-3361)
PHONE.................302 294-6121
John Webb, *CEO*
Stephen James, *Analyst*
Megan Migioia, *Relations*
EMP: 92 **EST:** 2017
SALES (est): 2.8MM **Privately Held**
SIC: 8742 Automation & robotics consultant

(G-7263) PRO WEIGHT LOSS
550 Stanton Christiana Rd (19713-2198)
PHONE.................302 220-9555
EMP: 8
SALES (est): 73.3K **Privately Held**
SIC: 8093 Weight loss clinic, with medical staff

(G-7264) PROACTIVE PRFMCE SOLUTIONS INC (PA)
560 Peoples Plz Ste 139 (19702-4798)
PHONE.................302 375-0451
Andrew Thompson, *President*
EMP: 11 **EST:** 1993
SALES (est): 2.5MM **Privately Held**
SIC: 7379 Computer related consulting services

(G-7265) PRODUCE MARKETING ASSN INC
Also Called: Pma
1500 Casho Mill Rd (19711-3547)
P.O. Box 6036 (19714-6036)
PHONE.................302 738-7100
Bryan Silbermann, *CEO*
Cathy Burns, *President*
Linda F Delaney, *Principal*
Kim Coker, *Business Mgr*
Vicki Bonvetti, *COO*
EMP: 90
SQ FT: 15,000
SALES: 25.6MM **Privately Held**
WEB: www.pma.com
SIC: 1799 Antenna installation

(G-7266) PROFESSIONAL ROOF SERVICES INC (HQ)
229 Lake Dr (19702-3320)
PHONE.................302 731-5770
Blaine Chipola, *President*
EMP: 6
SALES (est): 699.1K
SALES (corp-wide): 10.3MM **Privately Held**
WEB: www.proroofservices.com
SIC: 8744 8748 8713 Facilities support services; systems analysis & engineering consulting services; surveying services
PA: Bluefin, Llc
6312 S Fiddlers Green Cir
Greenwood Village CO 80111
303 847-0190

(G-7267) PROFESSIONAL WINDOW TINTING
9 Albe Dr Ste A (19702-1380)
PHONE.................302 456-3456
Gail Bluestein, *President*
Steven Bluestein, *Vice Pres*
EMP: 5
SALES: 550K **Privately Held**
SIC: 1799 Glass tinting, architectural or automotive

(G-7268) PROGRESIVE DENTAL ARTS
685 E Chestnut Hill Rd (19713-1827)
PHONE.................302 455-9569
Bruce Fay, *President*
EMP: 14
SQ FT: 2,800
SALES: 1.5MM **Privately Held**
SIC: 8021 Dentists' office

(G-7269) PROMOTION ZONE LLC
50 Albe Dr Ste A (19702-1322)
PHONE.................302 832-8565
Givvel Marrero,
EMP: 1
SALES (est): 110.4K **Privately Held**
WEB: www.promotionzone.biz
SIC: 7336 2759 5199 2754 Commercial art & graphic design; decals: printing; advertising specialties; commercial printing, gravure

(G-7270) PROMOTIONS PLUS INC
700 Peoples Plz (19702-5601)
PHONE.................302 836-2820
George Kaufmann, *President*
Sam Onessi, *Vice Pres*
EMP: 9
SQ FT: 2,000
SALES (est): 1MM **Privately Held**
SIC: 7336 Silk screen design

(G-7271) PROTOTEK MACHINING & DEV
307 Markus Ct (19713-1151)
PHONE.................302 368-1226
Jeff Coffman, *President*
EMP: 3
SALES (est): 378K **Privately Held**
WEB: www.prototekde.com
SIC: 3599 Machine shop, jobbing & repair

(G-7272) PURE WELLNESS LLC (PA)
Also Called: Pure Wellness Chiropractic
550 Stanton Christiana Rd # 302 (19713-2132)
PHONE.................302 365-5470
Holly J Corbett, *Principal*
EMP: 15
SALES (est): 1.9MM **Privately Held**
SIC: 8041 Offices & clinics of chiropractors

(G-7273) PURPOSE MINISTRIES INC (PA)
225 Old Baltimore Pike (19702-8409)
PHONE.................302 753-0435
John Paintsil, *Principal*
Clement Owusu - Donkor, *Administration*
EMP: 8
SALES: 70K **Privately Held**
SIC: 8661 7371 Religious organizations; computer software development & applications

(G-7274) PUZS BODY SHOP INC
97 Peoples Dr (19702-1323)
PHONE.................302 368-8265
Francis Walls, *President*
EMP: 6
SALES (est): 741.2K **Privately Held**
SIC: 7532 Body shop, automotive

(G-7275) PYRAMID GROUP MGT SVCS CORP
227 E Delaware Ave (19711-4606)
PHONE.................302 737-1770
Andrew Bondy, *President*
EMP: 5

SALES (est): 443K **Privately Held**
SIC: 8742 Business consultant

(G-7276)
Q AND R ELECTRIC LLC
701 Brook Dr (19713-1308)
PHONE..................302 670-1817
Charito Runge, *Mng Member*
Cary Runge,
EMP: 4
SALES (est): 426.8K **Privately Held**
SIC: 1731 General electrical contractor

(G-7277)
QBECK INSPECTION GROUP
242 Chapman Rd (19702-5405)
PHONE..................302 452-9257
Larry Macnallen, *Manager*
EMP: 20
SALES (est): 856.6K **Publicly Held**
WEB: www.bek.com
SIC: 8711 Construction & civil engineering
HQ: B E & K, Inc.
  2000 International Pk Dr
  Birmingham AL 35243
  205 972-6000

(G-7278)
QIENNA WEALTH MANAGEMENT INC
112 Capitol Trl (19711-3716)
PHONE..................610 765-6008
Nicolas Galarza, *President*
EMP: 2
SALES (est): 195.5K **Privately Held**
SIC: 6282 Investment advice

(G-7279)
QOE INC
955 Dawson Dr Ste 3 (19713-5814)
P.O. Box 7717 (19714-7717)
PHONE..................302 455-1234
Alan D Chambers, *President*
Veda Chambers, *Owner*
EMP: 6
SQ FT: 2,500
SALES (est): 597.6K **Privately Held**
WEB: www.qoeinc.com
SIC: 5999 7629 Business machines & equipment; electrical repair shops

(G-7280)
QPS LLC
Also Called: Quest Pharmaceutical Services
110 Executive Dr Ste 7 (19702-3352)
PHONE..................302 369-3753
EMP: 127 **Privately Held**
SIC: 5122 Pharmaceuticals
PA: Qps, Llc
  3 Innovation Way Ste 240
  Newark DE 19711

(G-7281)
QPS HOLDINGS LLC (PA)
3 Innovation Way Ste 240 (19713-5456)
PHONE..................302 369-5601
T Ben Hsu, *CFO*
Suzanne Canfield, *Marketing Staff*
Benjamin Chien, *Mng Member*
Dale Bourg,
Yisheng Lee,
EMP: 10
SALES (est): 90.9MM **Privately Held**
SIC: 6719 Personal holding companies, except banks

(G-7282)
QUALITY APPLIANCE SERVICES
202 Nathaniel Rd (19713-3061)
PHONE..................302 766-4808
EMP: 8
SALES (est): 95.8K **Privately Held**
SIC: 7629 Electrical household appliance repair

(G-7283)
QUALITY INN
48 Geoffrey Dr (19713-3603)
PHONE..................302 292-1500
Wendy Lee, *General Mgr*
Fred Acosta, *Principal*
Stephanie Walker, *Sales Staff*
EMP: 14
SALES (est): 723.2K **Privately Held**
SIC: 7011 Hotels & motels

(G-7284)
QUANTUM CORPORATION
211 Executive Dr Ste 1 (19702-3358)
PHONE..................302 737-7012
Donald Drew, *Branch Mgr*
EMP: 9
SALES (corp-wide): 402.6MM **Publicly Held**
WEB: www.quantum.com
SIC: 3572 Computer storage devices
PA: Quantum Corporation
  224 Airport Pkwy Ste 550
  San Jose CA 95110
  408 944-4000

(G-7285)
QUANTUM POLYMERS CORPORATION
211 Executive Dr Ste 1 (19702-3358)
PHONE..................302 737-7012
Hemant Bheda, *CEO*
Ellen Witherspoon, *Sales Staff*
EMP: 11
SQ FT: 22,000
SALES (est): 2.2MM **Privately Held**
SIC: 3089 Stock shapes, plastic

(G-7286)
QUERYLOOP INC
Also Called: Publica.la
2035 Sunset Lake Rd B2 (19702-2600)
PHONE..................412 253-6265
Pablo Laurino, *CEO*
EMP: 2
SALES (est): 56.5K **Privately Held**
SIC: 7372 Publishers' computer software

(G-7287)
QUEST DIAGNOSTICS INCORPORATED
A98 100 Omega Dr (19713)
PHONE..................302 455-0720
EMP: 5
SALES (corp-wide): 7.5B **Publicly Held**
SIC: 8071 Medical laboratories
PA: Quest Diagnostics Incorporated
  500 Plaza Dr Ste G
  Secaucus NJ 07094
  973 520-2700

(G-7288)
QWINTRY LLC
825 Dawson Dr (19713-3438)
PHONE..................858 633-6353
Victor Prodi, *Principal*
EMP: 4
SALES (est): 398.1K **Privately Held**
SIC: 4212 Delivery service, vehicular

(G-7289)
R & J TAYLOR INC
Also Called: Master Shower Doors
1712 Ogletown Rd (19711-5428)
PHONE..................302 368-7888
Jean Taylor, *President*
Ron Taylor, *Vice Pres*
EMP: 6
SALES (est): 500K **Privately Held**
WEB: www.mrshowerdoorde.com
SIC: 1799 1751 Home/office interiors finishing, furnishing & remodeling; window & door (prefabricated) installation

(G-7290)
R & K MOTORS & MACHINE SHOP
60 Aleph Dr (19702-1319)
PHONE..................302 737-4596
Peter Kopalovick, *President*
EMP: 3 EST: 1972
SQ FT: 2,200
SALES (est): 449.3K **Privately Held**
SIC: 7538 3599 Diesel engine repair: automotive; machine shop, jobbing & repair

(G-7291)
R A CHANCE PLUMBING INC
11 Fern Ct (19702-2886)
PHONE..................302 292-1315
Richard A Chance, *President*
EMP: 9
SQ FT: 1,600
SALES (est): 1.1MM **Privately Held**
WEB: www.rachance.com
SIC: 1711 Plumbing contractors

(G-7292)
R E MICHEL COMPANY LLC
904 Interchange Blvd (19711-3563)
PHONE..................302 368-9410
Jim Smithson, *Branch Mgr*
EMP: 6
SALES (corp-wide): 898.2MM **Privately Held**
WEB: www.remichel.com
SIC: 5075 Warm air heating equipment & supplies
PA: R. E. Michel Company, Llc
  1 Re Michel Dr
  Glen Burnie MD 21060
  410 760-4000

(G-7293)
RAAD360 LLC
550 S College Ave 107ofc (19716-1307)
PHONE..................855 722-3360
Michael Loveless, *Principal*
Vamsi Godavarthi, *Vice Pres*
Youyu He, *Vice Pres*
Dieter Hotz, *Vice Pres*
Vijay Nidumolu, *Vice Pres*
EMP: 14
SQ FT: 307
SALES (est): 415.5K **Privately Held**
SIC: 7372 Business oriented computer software; data processing & preparation; ; computer software development & applications; business consultant; systems engineering consultant, ex. computer or professional

(G-7294)
RAAS INFOTEK LLC
262 Chapman Rd Ste 105a (19702-5418)
PHONE..................302 894-3184
S Kankanala, *Mng Member*
Seetharamaiah Kankanala, *Mng Member*
Fathe Singh, *Technology*
EMP: 40
SALES: 4MM **Privately Held**
WEB: www.raasinfotek.com
SIC: 7379 7371 Computer related consulting services; computer software development

(G-7295)
RADIATION ONCOLOGY
4755 Stanton Ogeltown Rd (19718-0001)
PHONE..................302 733-1830
Christopher Koprowski, *President*
EMP: 30
SALES (est): 644.2K **Privately Held**
SIC: 8011 Radiologist

(G-7296)
RAIN OF LIGHT INC
28 Tyre Ave (19711-7142)
PHONE..................302 312-7642
Natoyah Swift, *CEO*
EMP: 7
SALES (est): 280K **Privately Held**
SIC: 8322 Individual & family services

(G-7297)
RAPE OF THE LOCKE INC
700 Barksdale Rd Ste 5 (19711-3260)
PHONE..................302 368-5370
Susan Annone, *President*
EMP: 6
SQ FT: 2,000
SALES (est): 152K **Privately Held**
SIC: 7231 7241 Hairdressers; barber shops

(G-7298)
RATH INCORPORATED (DH)
Also Called: Rath Performance Fibers
300 Ruthar Dr Ste 1 (19711-8017)
PHONE..................302 294-4446
Les Crippenton, *President*
Ralph T Grizzel, *Vice Pres*
David Grube, *Controller*
▲ EMP: 63
SQ FT: 30,000
SALES (est): 13MM
SALES (corp-wide): 355.8K **Privately Held**
WEB: www.rath-usa.com
SIC: 5169 Manmade fibers
HQ: Chamottewaren- Und Thonofenfabrik
  Aug. Rath Jun. Gmbh
  HafnerstraBe 3
  KrumnnuBbaum 3375
  275 724-010

(G-7299)
RATNER COMPANIES LC
Also Called: Creative Hairdressers
591 College Sq (19711-8603)
PHONE..................302 366-9032
Alice Kelly, *Manager*
EMP: 24 **Privately Held**
WEB: www.haircuttery.com
SIC: 7231 Unisex hair salons
HQ: Ratner Companies, L.C.
  1577 Spring Hill Rd # 500
  Vienna VA 22182
  703 269-5400

(G-7300)
RAYMOND ENTRMT GROUP LLC
62 N Chapel St Ste 4 (19711-2284)
PHONE..................302 731-2000
David Raymond,
Chris Raymond,
Richard Tapia, *Associate*
EMP: 5
SQ FT: 1,200
SALES (est): 166.1K **Privately Held**
WEB: www.raymondeg.com
SIC: 7929 Musical entertainers; entertainment service

(G-7301)
RAYMOND HARNER
Also Called: Accent Coatings
317 Jaymar Blvd (19702-2881)
PHONE..................302 737-0755
Raymond Harner, *Principal*
EMP: 2
SALES (est): 186.2K **Privately Held**
SIC: 3479 Metal coating & allied service

(G-7302)
RAYMOND V FEEHERY JR DPM
Also Called: New Castle Assoc & Podiatry
620 Stanton Christiana Rd # 303 (19713-2135)
PHONE..................302 999-8511
Raymond V Feehery Jr, *Owner*
EMP: 9
SALES (est): 820.8K **Privately Held**
SIC: 8043 Offices & clinics of podiatrists

(G-7303)
RAYMOND W PETRUNICH
1400 Peoples Plz Ste 124 (19702-5706)
PHONE..................302 836-3565
Raymond W Petrunich, *Principal*
EMP: 5
SALES (est): 326.8K **Privately Held**
SIC: 8021 Dental surgeon

(G-7304)
REAL LIFE ENTERTAINMENT
Northway Dr (19713)
PHONE..................516 413-2782
Alton Williams, *Owner*
EMP: 4
SALES (est): 95K **Privately Held**
SIC: 7929 Entertainers & entertainment groups

(G-7305)
RECOVERYIP INNOVATIONS LLC
200 Continental Dr # 401 (19713-4334)
PHONE..................617 901-3414
Bildad Stlouis,
EMP: 5
SALES: 139.4K **Privately Held**
SIC: 7373 Systems software development services

(G-7306)
RED LION MEDICAL SAFETY INC
123a Sandy Dr (19713-1148)
PHONE..................302 731-8600
Jess A McBride, *CEO*
Dave Cox, *General Mgr*
EMP: 6
SALES (est): 550.3K **Privately Held**
WEB: www.redlionmedical.com
SIC: 8734 Product certification, safety or performance

Newark - New Castle County (G-7307)

(G-7307)
RED RHINO LABS LLC
2035 Sunset Lake Rd B2 (19702-2600)
PHONE..................650 275-2464
Ryan Lee, *Mng Member*
EMP: 2
SALES: 5K **Privately Held**
SIC: 7372 Application computer software

(G-7308)
RED ROOF
1119 S College Ave (19713-2307)
PHONE..................302 368-8521
EMP: 7
SALES (est): 167.1K **Privately Held**
SIC: 7011 Hotels & motels

(G-7309)
RED ROOF INNS INC
415 Stanton Christiana Rd (19713-2119)
PHONE..................302 292-2870
Ben Cummins, *Branch Mgr*
EMP: 12 **Privately Held**
WEB: www.redroof.com
SIC: 7011 Hotels & motels
HQ: Red Roof Inns, Inc.
  7815 Walton Pkwy
  New Albany OH 43054
  614 744-2600

(G-7310)
REDMILL AUTO REPAIR
1209 Capitol Trl (19711-3923)
PHONE..................302 292-2155
Marty Krajawski, *Owner*
EMP: 5
SALES (est): 472.7K **Privately Held**
SIC: 7538 General automotive repair shops

(G-7311)
REGIS CORPORATION
Also Called: Essentially Hair
105 Christiana Mall (19702-3201)
PHONE..................302 454-2800
EMP: 17
SALES (corp-wide): 1.6B **Publicly Held**
SIC: 7231 Beauty Shop
PA: Regis Corporation
  7201 Metro Blvd
  Minneapolis MN 55439
  952 947-7777

(G-7312)
REGUS CORPORATION
200 Continental Dr # 401 (19713-4337)
PHONE..................302 318-1300
Jason Heller, *Area Mgr*
EMP: 4
SALES (corp-wide): 3.1B **Privately Held**
SIC: 7389 Office facilities & secretarial service rental
HQ: Regus Corporation
  15305 Dallas Pkwy Ste 400
  Addison TX 75001
  972 361-8100

(G-7313)
REHABILITATION ASSOCIATES
Also Called: Kennedy, Debra DC
87 Omega Dr Bldg B (19713-2065)
PHONE..................302 529-8783
Fax: 302 733-7495
EMP: 9
SALES (est): 1MM **Privately Held**
SIC: 8011 Medical Doctor's Office

(G-7314)
REHABILITATION ASSOCIATES PA (PA)
2600 Glasgow Ave Ste 210 (19702-5704)
PHONE..................302 832-8894
Barry Bakst, *President*
Arnold Glassman, *Principal*
Craig D Sternberg, *Principal*
Stephen Beneck, *Med Doctor*
EMP: 9
SALES (est): 2.9MM **Privately Held**
SIC: 8011 Physical medicine, physician/surgeon

(G-7315)
REILLY SWEEPING INC
10 Albe Dr (19702-1334)
PHONE..................302 738-8961
EMP: 20
SALES (corp-wide): 229.5MM **Privately Held**
SIC: 4959 Sweeping service: road, airport, parking lot, etc.
HQ: Reilly Sweeping, Inc.
  10 Kresge Rd
  Fairless Hills PA 19030
  215 736-1556

(G-7316)
REMLINE CORP
456 Corporate Blvd (19702-3330)
PHONE..................302 737-7228
Stephanie Petrella, *President*
Linda Moreland, *Vice Pres*
Lesli Leath, *Project Mgr*
Danielle Lloyd, *Project Mgr*
June Dalecki, *Purch Mgr*
EMP: 25
SQ FT: 22,500
SALES (est): 5.9MM **Privately Held**
WEB: www.remline.com
SIC: 7311 8732 5199 8743 Advertising agencies; market analysis or research; advertising specialties; promotion service; screen printing

(G-7317)
RENT-A-CENTER INC
19 Chestnut Hill Plz (19713-2701)
PHONE..................302 731-7900
Ronda Rawlings, *Branch Mgr*
EMP: 5
SALES (corp-wide): 2.6B **Publicly Held**
WEB: www.rentacenter.com
SIC: 7359 Appliance rental; furniture rental; home entertainment equipment rental; television rental
PA: Rent-A-Center, Inc.
  5501 Headquarters Dr
  Plano TX 75024
  972 801-1100

(G-7318)
RENTOKIL NORTH AMERICA INC
1712 Ogletown Rd (19711-5428)
P.O. Box 7959 (19714-7959)
PHONE..................302 733-0851
Charlie Huth, *Branch Mgr*
EMP: 20
SALES (corp-wide): 3.2B **Privately Held**
SIC: 0782 7342 Lawn & garden services; bird proofing
HQ: Rentokil North America, Inc.
  1125 Berkshire Blvd # 15
  Wyomissing PA 19610
  610 372-9700

(G-7319)
RENTOKIL NORTH AMERICA INC
701 Dawson Dr (19713-3413)
PHONE..................302 325-2687
James Harrison, *Manager*
EMP: 14
SALES (corp-wide): 3.2B **Privately Held**
WEB: www.ehrlichdistribution.com
SIC: 7342 Pest control services
HQ: Rentokil North America, Inc.
  1125 Berkshire Blvd # 15
  Wyomissing PA 19610
  610 372-9700

(G-7320)
RENU CHIROPRACTIC WELLNESS
907 S College Ave (19713-2303)
PHONE..................302 368-0124
Doris Leach, *COO*
EMP: 8
SALES (est): 396.3K **Privately Held**
SIC: 8041 Offices & clinics of chiropractors

(G-7321)
REPORTING SOLUTIONS LLC
102 Cannonball Ln (19702-3097)
PHONE..................857 284-3583
Bildad St Louis, *Mng Member*
EMP: 6
SALES (corp-wide): 150K **Privately Held**
SIC: 7371 Computer software development & applications
PA: Reporting Solutions, Llc
  745 Atlantic Ave
  Boston MA 02111
  857 284-3583

(G-7322)
REPRODUCTIVE ASSOCIATES DEL PA (PA)
Also Called: Reproductive Associates Del
4735 Ogletown Stanton Rd (19713-2072)
PHONE..................302 623-4242
Barbara A McGuirk MD, *President*
EMP: 25
SALES (est): 3.9MM **Privately Held**
WEB: www.reproassoc-de.com
SIC: 8011 Obstetrician

(G-7323)
RESCUE PRINTIG
17 Lynch Farm Dr (19713-2823)
PHONE..................302 286-7266
Joan Poirier, *Principal*
EMP: 2 **EST:** 2017
SALES (est): 83.9K **Privately Held**
SIC: 2752 Commercial printing, lithographic

(G-7324)
RESCUE SURGICAL SOLUTIONS LLC
1305 Whittaker Rd (19702-1024)
PHONE..................302 722-5877
Kafui Gbewonyo, *Principal*
EMP: 4 **EST:** 2017
SALES (est): 90.1K **Privately Held**
SIC: 8011 Medical centers

(G-7325)
RESIDENCE INN BY MARRIOTT LLC
240 Chapman Rd (19702-5421)
PHONE..................302 453-9200
Sean Snyder, *Engineer*
Aaron Smith, *Manager*
John Dowell, *Manager*
EMP: 33
SALES (corp-wide): 20.7B **Publicly Held**
SIC: 7011 Hotels & motels
HQ: Residence Inn By Marriott, Llc
  10400 Fernwood Rd
  Bethesda MD 20817
  301 380-3000

(G-7326)
RESOURCES FOR HUMAN DEV INC
12 Montrose Dr (19713-2757)
PHONE..................302 731-5283
EMP: 43
SALES (corp-wide): 255.8MM **Privately Held**
SIC: 8742 Business planning & organizing services
PA: Resources For Human Development, Inc.
  4700 Wissahickon Ave # 126
  Philadelphia PA 19144
  215 951-0300

(G-7327)
RESOURCES FOR HUMAN DEV INC
262 Chatman Rd Ste 102 (19702)
PHONE..................215 951-0300
EMP: 58
SALES (corp-wide): 255.8MM **Privately Held**
SIC: 8322 Individual & family services
PA: Resources For Human Development, Inc.
  4700 Wissahickon Ave # 126
  Philadelphia PA 19144
  215 951-0300

(G-7328)
RETROCODE INC
2035 Sunset Lake Rd B2 (19702-2600)
PHONE..................302 570-0002
Sasa Slavnic, *CEO*
EMP: 1
SALES: 100K **Privately Held**
SIC: 7372 Business oriented computer software

(G-7329)
RETROSHEET INC
20 Sunset Rd (19711-5236)
PHONE..................302 731-1570
David Smith, *President*
EMP: 5
SALES (est): 150.6K **Privately Held**
WEB: www.retrosheet.org
SIC: 8699 Personal interest organization

(G-7330)
REVIEW
325 Academy St Rm 201 (19716-6199)
PHONE..................302 831-2771
Sandy Iverson, *President*
Matt Bittle, *Editor*
Lauren Cappelloni, *Editor*
Adem Cemerlic, *Editor*
Sarah Eller, *Editor*
EMP: 50
SALES (est): 1.7MM **Privately Held**
WEB: www.thereview.com
SIC: 2711 2741 Newspapers, publishing & printing; miscellaneous publishing

(G-7331)
REX AUTO BODY INC
27 North St (19711-2250)
PHONE..................302 731-4707
William R Cockerham, *President*
Joe Cockerham, *General Mgr*
Betty Cockerham, *Corp Secy*
EMP: 9 **EST:** 1971
SQ FT: 3,000
SALES (est): 437.1K **Privately Held**
SIC: 7532 Body shop, automotive

(G-7332)
REYBOLD HOMES INC
2350 Pulaski Hwy (19702-3408)
PHONE..................302 834-3000
Lex Burkett, *Manager*
EMP: 118
SALES (corp-wide): 2.8MM **Privately Held**
SIC: 1521 Single-family housing construction
PA: Reybold Homes, Inc.
  116 E Scotland Dr
  Bear DE 19701
  302 832-7100

(G-7333)
REYNOLDS METALS COMPANY LLC
Also Called: Alcoa
700 Pencader Dr (19702-3310)
PHONE..................302 366-0555
Mike M Burk, *General Mgr*
EMP: 50
SALES (corp-wide): 13.4B **Publicly Held**
SIC: 3411 Aluminum cans
HQ: Reynolds Metals Company, Llc
  390 Park Ave
  New York NY 10022
  212 518-5400

(G-7334)
RHINO CABLING GROUP INC
528 Sepia Ct (19702-3669)
PHONE..................302 312-1033
Kevin Harris, *President*
EMP: 10
SALES: 750K **Privately Held**
WEB: www.rhinocabling.com
SIC: 1731 Fiber optic cable installation

(G-7335)
RHINO LNNGS DEL AUTO STYLE INC
841 Old Baltimore Pike (19702-1317)
PHONE..................302 368-4660
Guy Campbell, *President*
EMP: 10
SQ FT: 13,000
SALES (est): 1.3MM **Privately Held**
WEB: www.rhiноliningsde.com
SIC: 5531 5085 Truck equipment & parts; industrial supplies

(G-7336)
RHINO SMART PUBLICATIONS
55 Shull Dr (19711-7716)
PHONE..................302 737-3422
Weldon Burge, *Principal*

GEOGRAPHIC SECTION

Newark - New Castle County (G-7367)

EMP: 2
SALES (est): 123.8K **Privately Held**
SIC: 2741 Miscellaneous publishing

(G-7337)
RICHARD C MCKAY DC PA
Also Called: Advanced Back & Neck Pain Ctr
54 Omega Dr Bldg F54 (19713-2062)
PHONE.................................302 368-1300
Richard C McKay DC, *President*
EMP: 6
SQ FT: 1,350
SALES (est): 498.4K **Privately Held**
SIC: 8041 Offices & clinics of chiropractors

(G-7338)
RICHARD L SHERRY MD
Also Called: Brandy Wine
2600 Glasgow Ave Ste 206 (19702-5704)
PHONE.................................302 836-3937
Richard L Sherry, *President*
EMP: 10 **Privately Held**
SIC: 8011 General & family practice, physician/surgeon
PA: Richard L Sherry Md
    2500 Grubb Rd Ste 234
    Wilmington DE 19810

(G-7339)
RICOH USA INC
131 Continental Dr # 109 (19713-4305)
PHONE.................................302 737-8000
Lee McArthur, *Branch Mgr*
EMP: 66 **Privately Held**
SIC: 5044 Photocopy machines
HQ: Ricoh Usa, Inc.
    300 Eagleview Blvd # 200
    Exton PA 19341
    610 296-8000

(G-7340)
RILEY ELECTRIC
1235 Old Coochs Bridge Rd (19713-2334)
PHONE.................................302 533-5918
Ron Kellett, *Principal*
EMP: 8
SALES (est): 1.1MM **Privately Held**
SIC: 1731 Electrical work

(G-7341)
RILEY ELECTRIC INC
1235 Old Coochs Bridge Rd (19713-2334)
PHONE.................................302 276-3581
John Riley, *President*
Gene Grady, *Vice Pres*
Lisa Kellett, *Office Mgr*
EMP: 5
SALES (est): 408.2K **Privately Held**
SIC: 1731 Banking machine installation & service

(G-7342)
RINEHIMER BODY SHOP INC
Also Called: Rinehimer Auto Works
6 Mill Park Ct (19713-1986)
PHONE.................................302 737-7350
Richie Rinehimer, *President*
Donna Rinehimer, *Treasurer*
EMP: 15
SALES (est): 1.4MM **Privately Held**
SIC: 7538 General automotive repair shops

(G-7343)
RISING SUNSET PUBLISHING LLC
200 Continental Dr # 401 (19713-4334)
PHONE.................................877 231-5425
Ronald Henderson,
Shevaughn Henderson,
EMP: 5
SALES: 150K **Privately Held**
SIC: 8699 Literary, film or cultural club

(G-7344)
RISINGPLATFORMPRODUCTIONS LLC
2035 Sunset Lake Rd B2 (19702-2600)
PHONE.................................660 283-0183
Salim Grant, *Principal*
EMP: 5
SALES (est): 96.5K **Privately Held**
SIC: 7819 Developing & laboratory services, motion picture

(G-7345)
RITTENHOUSE MOTOR CO INC
217 Hullihen Dr (19711-3650)
PHONE.................................302 731-5059
Fax: 302 368-3879
EMP: 31
SQ FT: 10,000
SALES (est): 4.6MM **Privately Held**
SIC: 5511 7538 Ret & Repair Automobiles

(G-7346)
RIVAS ULISES
Also Called: Rivas Ironworks
31 Albe Dr Ste 3 (19702-1360)
PHONE.................................302 454-8595
Ulises Rivas, *Owner*
EMP: 3
SALES (est): 190K **Privately Held**
SIC: 3441 Fabricated structural metal

(G-7347)
RNH INSTALLATION
42 Albe Dr Ste E (19702-1358)
PHONE.................................302 731-8900
Chris Wilberg, *Principal*
EMP: 6 EST: 2007
SALES (est): 383.2K **Privately Held**
SIC: 1799 Service station equipment installation, maintenance & repair

(G-7348)
ROAD & RAIL SERVICES INC
502 S College Ave Ste C (19713-1327)
PHONE.................................302 731-2552
Robert Arnrine, *Manager*
EMP: 455
SALES (corp-wide): 200.8MM **Privately Held**
SIC: 4789 4741 Railroad maintenance & repair services; rental of railroad cars
PA: Road & Rail Services, Inc.
    4233 Bardstown Rd Ste 200
    Louisville KY 40218
    502 495-6688

(G-7349)
ROBERT A PENNA DMD
4735 Ogletown Stanton Rd # 1104 (19713-2089)
PHONE.................................302 623-4060
Robert A Penna DMD, *Owner*
EMP: 5
SALES (est): 201.8K **Privately Held**
SIC: 8021 Offices & clinics of dentists

(G-7350)
ROBERT ELGART AUTOMOTIVE
698 Pencader Dr (19702-3348)
PHONE.................................800 220-7777
Robert Elgart, *Principal*
EMP: 4
SALES (est): 132.8K **Privately Held**
SIC: 2992 Lubricating oils

(G-7351)
ROBERT S CALLAHAN MD PA
32 Omega Dr J (19713-2058)
PHONE.................................302 731-0942
Robert S Callahan, *Principal*
EMP: 5
SALES (est): 330.6K **Privately Held**
SIC: 8031 8011 Offices & clinics of osteopathic physicians; physicians' office, including specialists

(G-7352)
ROBERT T JONES & FOARD INC
Also Called: Foard R T & Jones Funeral Home
122 W Main St (19711-3241)
PHONE.................................302 731-4627
Robert T Foard Jr, *President*
Louis A Fiorucci Jr, *Director*
EMP: 6
SQ FT: 4,500
SALES (est): 806.8K **Privately Held**
SIC: 7261 Funeral home; funeral director

(G-7353)
ROBERTO A URIBE PHD
300 Creek View Rd Ste 101 (19711-8547)
PHONE.................................302 524-0814
Roberto A Uribe PHD, *Owner*
EMP: 8
SALES (est): 65.7K **Privately Held**
SIC: 8049 Offices of health practitioner

(G-7354)
ROCKFORD CENTER
100 Rockford Dr (19713-2121)
PHONE.................................302 996-5480
Virginia Robichaud, *CEO*
Michelle Preston, *Ch Nursing Ofcr*
Jackie Tomasetti, *Social Dir*
John Shaw, *Food Svc Dir*
EMP: 100
SALES (est): 31.1MM
SALES (corp-wide): 10.7B **Publicly Held**
WEB: www.rockfordcenter.com
SIC: 8062 8063 General medical & surgical hospitals; psychiatric hospitals
PA: Universal Health Services, Inc.
    367 S Gulph Rd
    King Of Prussia PA 19406
    610 768-3300

(G-7355)
ROCKWOOD APARTMENTS
100 Cindy Dr (19702-8132)
PHONE.................................302 832-8823
Stephanie Woodruff, *Manager*
EMP: 12
SALES (est): 447.2K **Privately Held**
SIC: 6513 Apartment building operators

(G-7356)
RODNEY TRUST CO
121 Continental Dr # 107 (19713-4326)
PHONE.................................302 737-1205
Gregory Belcher, *President*
Jessica Bogia, *Officer*
EMP: 5
SALES (est): 320.1K **Privately Held**
WEB: www.rodneytrust.com
SIC: 6733 Trusts

(G-7357)
ROHM AND HAAS ELECTRONIC (DH)
451 Bellevue Rd (19713-3431)
PHONE.................................302 366-0500
Mario Stanghellini, *President*
EMP: 14
SALES (est): 4.3MM
SALES (corp-wide): 61B **Publicly Held**
SIC: 3471 Polishing, metals or formed products
HQ: The Dow Chemical Company
    2211 H H Dow Way
    Midland MI 48642
    989 636-1000

(G-7358)
ROHM HAAS ELECTRONIC MTLS LLC
Also Called: Dow Electronic Materials
451 Bellevue Rd (19713-3431)
PHONE.................................302 366-0500
Tony Khouri, *Manager*
EMP: 8
SALES (corp-wide): 61B **Publicly Held**
SIC: 2819 2869 Industrial inorganic chemicals; industrial organic chemicals
HQ: Rohm And Haas Electronic Materials Llc
    455 Forest St
    Marlborough MA 01752
    508 481-7950

(G-7359)
ROHM HAAS ELECTRONIC MTLS LLC
Also Called: Rohm and Haas Co
231 Lake Dr (19702-3320)
PHONE.................................302 366-0500
EMP: 6
SALES (corp-wide): 61B **Publicly Held**
SIC: 2819 Industrial inorganic chemicals
HQ: Rohm And Haas Electronic Materials Llc
    455 Forest St
    Marlborough MA 01752
    508 481-7950

(G-7360)
ROHMA INC
2035 Sunset Lake Rd B2 (19702-2600)
PHONE.................................909 234-5381
Raymond Dai, *President*
Terry Giang, *President*
EMP: 6

SALES (est): 120.8K **Privately Held**
SIC: 7389

(G-7361)
ROLLER SERVICE CORPORATION (PA)
Also Called: R S C
23 Mcmillan Way (19713-3400)
PHONE.................................302 737-5000
James R Veacock Sr, *President*
John Dempsey, *Vice Pres*
John Gentile, *Treasurer*
John Veacock, *Admin Sec*
EMP: 35
SQ FT: 12,800
SALES (est): 6.8MM **Privately Held**
WEB: www.rollerservice.com
SIC: 3555 3562 Printing trade parts & attachments; roller bearings & parts

(G-7362)
ROMANO MASONRY INC
322 Markus Ct Ste A (19713-1192)
PHONE.................................302 368-4155
D Barry Romano, *President*
Greg Romano, *Vice Pres*
Tim Carter, *Project Mgr*
EMP: 50
SQ FT: 4,400
SALES: 7MM **Privately Held**
WEB: www.romanomasonry.com
SIC: 1741 Masonry & other stonework

(G-7363)
ROMER LABS TECHNOLOGY INC
130 Sandy Dr (19713-1147)
P.O. Box 66971, Saint Louis MO (63166-6971)
PHONE.................................855 337-6637
Michael Prinster, *CEO*
EMP: 25
SALES (est): 4.9MM
SALES (corp-wide): 22.5MM **Privately Held**
SIC: 3823 Analyzers, industrial process type
HQ: Romer Labs Division Holding Gmbh
    Erber Campus 1
    Getzersdorf 3131
    278 280-3

(G-7364)
RONALD S POGACH OD RES
6 Ironwood Dr (19711-2313)
PHONE.................................302 994-3300
Ronald S Pogach, *Principal*
EMP: 4
SALES (est): 249.1K **Privately Held**
SIC: 8042 Offices & clinics of optometrists

(G-7365)
ROSS W BURNAM CPA PA
625 Barksdale Rd Ste 107 (19711-4535)
PHONE.................................302 453-8161
Ross W Burnam, *Owner*
EMP: 4
SALES (est): 302.7K **Privately Held**
SIC: 8721 Certified public accountant

(G-7366)
ROTARY INTERNATIONAL
307 Stamford Dr (19711-2723)
PHONE.................................302 738-0827
Brian Maloney, *Branch Mgr*
EMP: 17
SALES (corp-wide): 503.3MM **Privately Held**
WEB: www.rotary5340.org
SIC: 8699 Charitable organization
PA: Rotary International
    1 Rotary Ctr
    Evanston IL 60201
    847 866-3000

(G-7367)
ROTO-ROOTER SERVICES COMPANY
1001 Dawson Dr Ste 3 (19713-5804)
PHONE.................................302 659-7637
Marty Smith, *Manager*
EMP: 40

Newark - New Castle County (G-7368)

SALES (corp-wide): 1.7B **Publicly Held**
SIC: 7699 1711 7623 Sewer cleaning & rodding; plumbing, heating, air-conditioning contractors; heating systems repair & maintenance; refrigeration repair service
HQ: Roto-Rooter Services Company
255 E 5th St Ste 2500
Cincinnati OH 45202
513 762-6690

(G-7368)
ROVIER LLC
3 Dublin Dr (19702-7709)
PHONE..................302 832-6726
Elias Kourpas, *CEO*
EMP: 4
SALES (est): 148.3K **Privately Held**
SIC: 7371 Computer software development

(G-7369)
ROYAL ERA LLC
406 Suburban Dr 188 (19711-3566)
PHONE..................484 574-0260
Nathaniel Mason,
EMP: 2
SALES (est): 52.5K **Privately Held**
SIC: 2731 7371 Books: publishing only; computer software development & applications

(G-7370)
RUSSELL ASSOCIATES INC
Also Called: Pall Aerospace
560 Peoples Plz 125 (19702-4798)
PHONE..................443 992-5777
Ruby R Chandy, *Principal*
EMP: 3
SALES (corp-wide): 19.8B **Publicly Held**
SIC: 3812 Acceleration indicators & systems components, aerospace
HQ: Russell Associates Inc
10540 Ridge Rd Ste 300
New Port Richey FL 34654
727 815-3100

(G-7371)
RYDER TRUCK RENTAL INC
750 Christiana Stanton Rd (19713-2028)
PHONE..................302 995-9607
Joy Miller, *Manager*
EMP: 15
SALES (corp-wide): 8.4B **Publicly Held**
SIC: 7513 Truck rental, without drivers
HQ: Ryder Truck Rental, Inc.
11690 Nw 105th St
Medley FL 33178
305 500-3726

(G-7372)
S & F MONUMENTS
635 Churchmans Rd (19702-1917)
PHONE..................302 722-8045
EMP: 2
SALES (est): 91.3K **Privately Held**
SIC: 3272 Mfg Concrete Products

(G-7373)
S & K ENTERPRISES INC
Also Called: Interstate Battery First State
205 Gabor Dr (19702-6630)
PHONE..................302 292-1250
Stan Kirk, *President*
Sandy Hruska, *Vice Pres*
EMP: 8
SQ FT: 4,500
SALES (est): 1.8MM **Privately Held**
SIC: 5013 Automotive supplies & parts

(G-7374)
S T GOOD INSURANCE INC (HQ)
Also Called: Nationwide
875 Aaa Blvd Ste A (19713-3624)
PHONE..................215 969-8385
Joseph L Tatum, *CEO*
Jeffrey Good, *Vice Pres*
EMP: 20
SQ FT: 5,000
SALES (est): 5.1MM
SALES (corp-wide): 146MM **Privately Held**
WEB: www.thegoodagency.com
SIC: 6411 Insurance agents; insurance brokers; life insurance agents

PA: Relation Insurance, Inc.
1277 Treat Blvd Ste 400
Walnut Creek CA 94597
800 404-4969

(G-7375)
SAENGER PORCELAIN
18 Mimosa Dr (19711-7510)
PHONE..................302 738-5349
Peter Saenger, *Owner*
EMP: 2
SALES (est): 76K **Privately Held**
WEB: www.saengerporcelain.com
SIC: 3262 Tableware, vitreous china

(G-7376)
SAGE HOSPITALITY RESOURCES LLC
Also Called: Fairfield Inn
65 Geoffrey Dr (19713-3603)
PHONE..................302 292-1500
Danielle Brown, *Manager*
EMP: 27
SALES (corp-wide): 336.9MM **Privately Held**
WEB: www.21chotel.com
SIC: 7011 Hotels & motels
PA: Sage Hospitality Resources L.L.C.
1575 Welton St Ste 300
Denver CO 80202
303 595-7200

(G-7377)
SAIENNI STAIRS LLC
120 Sandy Dr Ste E (19713-1135)
PHONE..................302 292-2699
Michael Saienni, *President*
Jeremy Noblitt, *Vice Pres*
Angie Dean, *Controller*
EMP: 8
SQ FT: 2,000
SALES: 968K **Privately Held**
SIC: 1799 Home/office interiors finishing, furnishing & remodeling

(G-7378)
SALLY BEAUTY SUPPLY LLC
Also Called: Cosmoprof
2665 Capitol Trl (19711-7242)
PHONE..................302 731-0285
Sherry Letnainzyn, *Manager*
EMP: 5 **Publicly Held**
WEB: www.schoeneman.com
SIC: 5087 Beauty parlor equipment & supplies
HQ: Sally Beauty Supply Llc
3001 Colorado Blvd
Denton TX 76210
940 898-7500

(G-7379)
SALLY BEAUTY SUPPLY LLC
220 College Sq (19711-5451)
PHONE..................302 737-8837
Christine Quinn, *Manager*
EMP: 5 **Publicly Held**
WEB: www.sallybeauty.com
SIC: 5087 Beauty parlor equipment & supplies
HQ: Sally Beauty Supply Llc
3001 Colorado Blvd
Denton TX 76210
940 898-7500

(G-7380)
SALON RISPOLI INC
1115 Churchmans Rd (19713-2112)
PHONE..................302 731-9202
Mario Rispoli, *Owner*
EMP: 5
SALES (est): 225.1K **Privately Held**
SIC: 7231 Hairdressers

(G-7381)
SANDLER OCCPTNAL MDICINE ASSOC
168 S Main St Ste 206 (19711-7962)
PHONE..................302 369-0171
Howard Sandler, *President*
EMP: 25
SALES (est): 1.3MM **Privately Held**
SIC: 8748 Business consulting

(G-7382)
SANDY BRAE LABORATORIES INC
119a Sandy Dr (19713-1148)
PHONE..................302 456-0446
Robert Spring, *President*
EMP: 4
SALES (est): 987.9K **Privately Held**
WEB: www.sandybrae.com
SIC: 5172 Lubricating oils & greases

(G-7383)
SANDY ROSE INC
Also Called: Salem Village Child Care
1000 Village Cir (19713-2952)
PHONE..................302 454-1649
Sandy Henry, *President*
EMP: 10
SALES: 135K **Privately Held**
SIC: 8351 Group day care center

(G-7384)
SANTO STUCCO
13 Metten Rd (19713-1565)
PHONE..................302 453-0901
Rayma Vreeland, *Principal*
EMP: 3
SALES (est): 170.8K **Privately Held**
SIC: 1771 3299 Exterior concrete stucco contractor; stucco

(G-7385)
SANTORA CPA GROUP PA
220 Continental Dr # 112 (19713-4304)
PHONE..................302 737-6200
Heath Kahrs, *Managing Dir*
Theresa Hughes, *Exec VP*
Meghann Felice, *Accountant*
Lynn Smiddy, *Accountant*
Kathie Skinner, *Office Mgr*
EMP: 41
SQ FT: 9,000
SALES (est): 3.2MM **Privately Held**
WEB: www.santoracpa.com
SIC: 8721 8748 Certified public accountant; business consulting

(G-7386)
SARAH K SMITH DDS
83 Beech Hill Dr (19711-2945)
PHONE..................302 442-3233
Sarah K Smith DDS, *Owner*
EMP: 4 **EST**: 2018
SALES (est): 61.5K **Privately Held**
SIC: 8021 Offices & clinics of dentists

(G-7387)
SARDO & SONS WAREHOUSING INC (PA)
111 Lake Dr Ste E (19702-3334)
PHONE..................302 369-2100
Angelo Sardo, *President*
Laurie Pietruczenia, *Accounting Mgr*
▲ EMP: 5 **EST**: 1952
SQ FT: 3,000
SALES (est): 23.2MM **Privately Held**
SIC: 4225 4212 General warehousing; local trucking, without storage

(G-7388)
SARDO & SONS WAREHOUSING INC
401 Pencader Dr Ste A (19702-3339)
PHONE..................302 737-3000
Gary Zicarelli, *Manager*
EMP: 25
SALES (corp-wide): 23.2MM **Privately Held**
SIC: 4225 General warehousing
PA: Sardo & Sons Warehousing, Inc.
111 Lake Dr Ste E
Newark DE 19702
302 369-2100

(G-7389)
SARDO & SONS WAREHOUSING INC
300 White Clay Center Dr (19711-5467)
PHONE..................302 369-0852
Dave Sardo, *Manager*
EMP: 18
SALES (corp-wide): 23.2MM **Privately Held**
SIC: 4225 General warehousing

PA: Sardo & Sons Warehousing, Inc.
111 Lake Dr Ste E
Newark DE 19702
302 369-2100

(G-7390)
SAREGAMA INDIA LIMITED
200 Continental Dr # 401 (19713-4334)
PHONE..................859 490-0156
Jai Mitwa, *Director*
EMP: 7 **Privately Held**
SIC: 3652 Compact laser discs, prerecorded
HQ: Saregama India Limited
The Studios Dum Dum
Kolkata WB 70009

(G-7391)
SAS NANOTECHNOLOGIES LLC
550 S College Ave Ste 110 (19713-1324)
PHONE..................214 235-1008
Sumedh Surwade, *Mng Member*
EMP: 1
SALES (est): 58.9K **Privately Held**
SIC: 2869 Industrial organic chemicals

(G-7392)
SCALIAS DAY CARE CENTER INC
701 Old Harmony Rd (19711-6919)
PHONE..................302 366-1430
Esther Scalia, *President*
Louis P Scalia Sr, *Corp Secy*
EMP: 14
SALES (est): 553.5K **Privately Held**
SIC: 8351 Group day care center; preschool center

(G-7393)
SCHLOSSER ASSOC MECH CNTRS INC
2047 Sunset Lake Rd (19702-2629)
P.O. Box 7984 (19714-7984)
PHONE..................302 738-7333
Paul Schlosser Jr, *President*
Mary Clark, *General Mgr*
Joanne Schlosser, *Corp Secy*
Steve Dennis, *Vice Pres*
Paul Schlosser Sr, *Shareholder*
EMP: 25
SQ FT: 7,000
SALES (est): 4.4MM **Privately Held**
SIC: 1711 5983 Plumbing contractors; fuel oil dealers

(G-7394)
SCHOON INC
Also Called: System4 of Delaware
200 Continental Dr # 401 (19713-4334)
PHONE..................302 894-7574
Alex Wilson, *President*
Susan Canale, *Officer*
EMP: 5
SALES (est): 159.7K **Privately Held**
SIC: 7349 Cleaning service, industrial or commercial; building & office cleaning services; building cleaning service

(G-7395)
SCIENTIFIC GAMES CORPORATION
220 Continental Dr # 407 (19713-4311)
PHONE..................302 737-4300
Dwayne Laird, *Controller*
EMP: 19
SALES (corp-wide): 3.3B **Publicly Held**
WEB: www.scientificgames.com
SIC: 7373 7999 2754 4813 Computer integrated systems design; lottery operation; commercial printing, gravure; telephone communication, except radio; electronic computers
PA: Scientific Games Corporation
6601 Bermuda Rd
Las Vegas NV 89119
702 897-7150

(G-7396)
SCORELOGIX LLC
1 Innovation Way Ste 300 (19711-5490)
PHONE..................302 294-6532
Sureh Annappindi, *CEO*
Vince Leusner, *Principal*
EMP: 25

▲ = Import ▼=Export
◆ =Import/Export

GEOGRAPHIC SECTION
Newark - New Castle County (G-7426)

SALES (est): 1.2MM **Privately Held**
WEB: www.scorelogix.com
SIC: 7371 Computer software development

(G-7397)
SCOTTRADE INC
1257 Churchmans Rd (19713-2149)
PHONE..................302 658-6511
Fax: 302 658-6516
EMP: 5
SALES (corp-wide): 934.5MM **Privately Held**
SIC: 6211 Security Brokers And Dealers, Nsk
PA: Scottrade, Inc.
  12800 Corporate Hill Dr
  Saint Louis MO 63131
  314 965-1555

(G-7398)
SDIX LLC
111 Pencader Dr (19702-3322)
PHONE..................302 456-6789
WEI-Wu He PHD, *President*
EMP: 100
SALES: 22.5MM **Privately Held**
SIC: 8731 Biotechnical research, commercial
PA: Origene Technologies, Inc.
  9620 Med Ctr Dr Ste 200
  Rockville MD 20850

(G-7399)
SEASONS HSPICE PLLTIVE CARE DE
220 Continental Dr # 407 (19713-4311)
PHONE..................847 692-1000
Todd Stern,
David Schlesinger,
EMP: 50
SALES (est): 1MM **Privately Held**
SIC: 8052 Personal care facility
PA: Seasons Hospice, Inc.
  6400 Shafer Ct Ste 700
  Rosemont IL 60018

(G-7400)
SECURITY QUALITY
930 Old Harmony Rd Ste H (19713-4161)
PHONE..................302 286-1200
G Dipasquale, *Vice Pres*
Gaetano Dipasquale, *Vice Pres*
EMP: 7
SALES: 160K **Privately Held**
SIC: 7382 Burglar alarm maintenance & monitoring

(G-7401)
SECURITY WATCH CORP
260 Chapman Rd Ste 100c (19713-5410)
PHONE..................302 286-6728
Fred Roper, *Manager*
EMP: 15
SALES (corp-wide): 2MM **Privately Held**
SIC: 7381 Security guard service
PA: Security Watch Corp
  1254 W Chester Pike # 206
  Havertown PA
  610 924-0110

(G-7402)
SEI ROBOTICS CORPORATION
12 Timber Creek Ln (19711-2606)
PHONE..................858 752-8675
Sha A Banayan, *CEO*
Yin Jishen, *President*
EMP: 234
SALES: 26MM **Privately Held**
SIC: 7372 Application computer software

(G-7403)
SELECT HEALTH SERVICES LLC
560 Peoples Plz (19702-4798)
PHONE..................504 737-4300
EMP: 4
SALES (est): 132.9K **Privately Held**
SIC: 8099 Health & allied services

(G-7404)
SELWOR ENTERPRISES INC
Also Called: Goddard Early Learning Center
50 Polly Drummond Hill Rd (19711-5703)
PHONE..................302 454-9454
Edd Rolls, *President*
Ed Rolls, *President*
Cindy Rolls, *Corp Secy*
EMP: 18
SQ FT: 6,500
SALES (est): 818.8K **Privately Held**
SIC: 8351 7299 Preschool center; house & babysitting services

(G-7405)
SEMICONDUCTOR TECHNOLOGIES
231 Lake Dr (19702-3320)
PHONE..................302 420-1432
EMP: 1
SALES (est): 46.5K **Privately Held**
SIC: 2299 Polishing felts

(G-7406)
SEMP WELLNESS LLC
173 Rhythm Ct (19713-1946)
PHONE..................302 525-9612
EMP: 4 EST: 2016
SALES (est): 36.5K **Privately Held**
SIC: 7991 Physical fitness facilities

(G-7407)
SENDSAFELY LLC
40 E Main St Ste 897 (19711-4639)
PHONE..................917 375-5891
Brian Holyfield, *Mng Member*
Joseph Hamler,
Carey Narin,
EMP: 10
SALES: 500K **Privately Held**
SIC: 7379

(G-7408)
SEPARATION METHODS TECH INC
31 Blue Hen Dr (19713-3405)
PHONE..................302 368-0610
Hafeez Fatunmbi PHD, *President*
Carl Davis, *Sales Staff*
Kemi Fatunmbi, *Administration*
EMP: 14
SQ FT: 10,000
SALES (est): 2MM **Privately Held**
WEB: www.separationmethods.com
SIC: 3826 8731 Analytical instruments; biotechnical research, commercial

(G-7409)
SEPAX TECHNOLOGIES INC (PA)
5 Innovation Way Ste 100 (19711-5459)
PHONE..................302 366-1101
Xueying Huang, *President*
Helen Gu, *Vice Pres*
Randy Litteral, *Sales Staff*
▲ EMP: 13
SALES (est): 7.4MM **Privately Held**
WEB: www.sepax-tech.com
SIC: 5169 3829 Chemicals & allied products; measuring & controlling devices

(G-7410)
SERVICEMASTER OF NEWARK
116 Cann Rd (19702-4714)
PHONE..................302 834-8006
George Crossland, *President*
Linda Crossland, *Vice Pres*
EMP: 12
SALES (est): 370K **Privately Held**
SIC: 7349 Building maintenance services

(G-7411)
SETH IVINS DR MD
620 Stanton Christn Rd # 305 (19713-2135)
PHONE..................302 824-7280
Seth Ivins, *Principal*
EMP: 5
SALES (est): 350.2K **Privately Held**
SIC: 8011 Internal medicine, physician/surgeon

(G-7412)
SEVONE INC
Also Called: Sev One Technology Center
550 S College Ave (19716-1307)
PHONE..................302 319-5400
Scarlett Hutton, *Manager*
Bobby Kunz, *Manager*
Michael Fisher, *Software Engr*
Sean Lafferty, *Software Engr*
Dave Hegenbarth, *Director*
EMP: 34
SALES (corp-wide): 42.9MM **Privately Held**
SIC: 7373 Systems integration services
HQ: Sevone Inc.
  800 Boylston St Spc 29
  Boston MA 02199
  617 982-7700

(G-7413)
SHASHIKALA PATEL MD
314 E Main St Ste 404 (19711-7182)
PHONE..................302 737-5074
Shashikala Patel MD, *Owner*
EMP: 4
SALES (est): 105.2K **Privately Held**
SIC: 8011 Offices & clinics of medical doctors

(G-7414)
SHELDON LIMITED PARTNERSHIP
Also Called: Bluffs, The
810 Sheldon Dr (19711-4319)
PHONE..................302 738-3048
Donna Clementoni, *Manager*
EMP: 6
SALES (corp-wide): 968.4K **Privately Held**
SIC: 6513 Apartment building operators
PA: Sheldon Limited Partnership
  8120 Woodmont Ave Ste 900
  Bethesda MD 20814
  301 951-0500

(G-7415)
SHELTER DEVELOPMENT LLC
Also Called: Vinings At Christiana
200 Vinings Way (19702-7602)
PHONE..................302 737-4999
Anita Robinson, *Manager*
EMP: 5 **Privately Held**
WEB: www.shelterproperties.com
SIC: 6513 Apartment building operators
HQ: Shelter Development, Llc
  218 N Charles St Ste 220
  Baltimore MD 21201
  410 962-0595

(G-7416)
SHERWEB INC
2915 Ogletown Rd 1073 (19713-1927)
PHONE..................888 567-6610
Catherine Castonguay, *Principal*
Rodrigo Vasconcelos, *Business Mgr*
Mark Newnam, *Administration*
EMP: 8
SALES (est): 173.3K **Privately Held**
SIC: 7379 7371 Computer related consulting services; computer software development & applications

(G-7417)
SHORE CONSULTANTS LTD
Also Called: Software Plus
179 W Chestnut Hill Rd # 7 (19713-2210)
PHONE..................302 737-3375
Richard Bruno, *President*
Nathan V Plafker, *Treasurer*
Paul M Wisniewski, *Manager*
EMP: 10
SQ FT: 2,400
SALES (est): 980K **Privately Held**
WEB: www.shorecon.com
SIC: 5734 7371 7372 Modems, monitors, terminals & disk drives: computers; computer software systems analysis & design, custom; prepackaged software

(G-7418)
SHRI SWAMI NARAYAN LLC
Also Called: Howard Johnson
1119 S College Ave (19713-2307)
PHONE..................302 738-3198
Peter Bhai, *Partner*
EMP: 20
SALES (est): 1.5MM **Privately Held**
SIC: 7011 Hotels & motels

(G-7419)
SHUTTERCASE INC
2035 Sunset Lake Rd B2 (19702-2600)
PHONE..................347 480-1614
EMP: 2
SALES (est): 88.9K **Privately Held**
SIC: 3442 Shutters, door or window: metal

(G-7420)
SI360 INC
2035 Sunset Lake Rd B2 (19702-2600)
PHONE..................800 849-6058
Craig Etkin, *President*
EMP: 10
SALES (est): 261K **Privately Held**
SIC: 2741

(G-7421)
SIC BIOMETRICS INC
2915 Ogletown Rd Ste 1737 (19713-1927)
PHONE..................866 499-8377
Eric Talbot, *CEO*
Robert Williams, *President*
EMP: 5
SALES (est): 114.5K **Privately Held**
SIC: 3699 Security devices

(G-7422)
SIEGFRIED J SCHULZE INC
Also Called: Schulze, S J
12 Mill Park Ct (19713-1986)
PHONE..................302 737-0403
Lutz S Schulze, *President*
Elke Mackiewicz, *Corp Secy*
Mark M Mackiewicz, *Vice Pres*
EMP: 13 EST: 1976
SQ FT: 1,000
SALES (est): 1.4MM **Privately Held**
SIC: 1711 Plumbing contractors

(G-7423)
SIEMANOWSKI CONSULTING INC
13 Covered Bridge Ln (19711-2062)
PHONE..................302 368-1081
Aaron Siemanowski, *Principal*
EMP: 4
SALES (est): 303.6K **Privately Held**
SIC: 8748 Business consulting

(G-7424)
SIEMENS CORPORATION
100 Gbc Dr (19702-2461)
PHONE..................302 690-2046
Juan Lopez, *Engineer*
William Diienno, *IT/INT Sup*
George Plummer, *Director*
Frank Southwell, *Director*
EMP: 18
SALES (corp-wide): 96.9B **Privately Held**
SIC: 5063 Electrical apparatus & equipment
HQ: Siemens Corporation
  300 New Jersey Ave Nw # 10
  Washington DC 20001
  202 434-4800

(G-7425)
SIEMENS HLTHCARE DGNOSTICS INC
500 Gbc Dr (19702-2466)
P.O. Box 6101 (19714-6101)
PHONE..................302 631-7357
Cathy Knutsen, *Manager*
EMP: 65
SALES (corp-wide): 96.9B **Privately Held**
WEB: www.dpcweb.com
SIC: 5047 2835 Medical & hospital equipment; in vitro & in vivo diagnostic substances
HQ: Siemens Healthcare Diagnostics Inc.
  511 Benedict Ave
  Tarrytown NY 10591
  914 631-8000

(G-7426)
SIGMA DATA SYSTEMS INC
197 Possum Park Rd (19711-3817)
P.O. Box 9767 (19714-9767)
PHONE..................302 453-8812
H Dean Spears, *President*
Michael Poirier, *Vice Pres*
Jack Feldhaus, *Manager*
Keith Chisarik, *Info Tech Dir*
Meri Spears, *IT/INT Sup*
EMP: 9
SQ FT: 5,000
SALES (est): 1.4MM **Privately Held**
WEB: www.vac4.com
SIC: 7379 Computer related consulting services

Newark - New Castle County (G-7427)

(G-7427)
SIGNATURE SELECTIONS LLC (PA)
110 Executive Dr Ste 5 (19702-3352)
PHONE.................................631 256-6900
Zubin Mehta,
Lori Dalton Massie,
EMP: 2
SQ FT: 30,000
SALES (est): 3.1MM Privately Held
SIC: 2084 Wines

(G-7428)
SIGNS RITE
Also Called: Signs-Rite Lettering Graphics
11 Kings Bridge Ct (19702-4249)
PHONE.................................302 836-6144
Bob Quinn, Owner
EMP: 5
SALES (est): 268K Privately Held
SIC: 3993 Signs, not made in custom sign painting shops

(G-7429)
SILLY SMILES LLC
200 Biddle Ave Ste 201 (19702-3966)
PHONE.................................302 838-1865
Eric R Copes, Mng Member
EMP: 4
SALES (est): 488K Privately Held
SIC: 8021 Dentists' office

(G-7430)
SIMM ASSOCIATES INC
800 Pencader Dr (19702-3354)
P.O. Box 7526 (19714-7526)
PHONE.................................302 283-2800
Gregory Simendinger, President
Gregory L Simendinger, President
Jeff Simendinger, Vice Pres
Stephen Iorii, Manager
EMP: 170
SQ FT: 32,000
SALES (est): 16.9MM Privately Held
WEB: www.simmassociates.com
SIC: 7322 Collection agency, except real estate

(G-7431)
SIMON MSTR & SIDLOW ASSOC INC
750 Prides Xing Ste 100 (19713-6108)
PHONE.................................302 652-3480
Bill Master, President
Susan Fisher, Principal
EMP: 30
SALES (est): 194.7K Privately Held
SIC: 8721 Certified public accountant

(G-7432)
SIMPLYMIDDLE
26 Auckland Dr (19702-4299)
PHONE.................................302 200-0102
Akinyemi Famakinwa, Owner
Johnson Boyd, Officer
Tammy Shore, Officer
EMP: 10 EST: 2014
SALES (est): 151.6K Privately Held
SIC: 8399 Social service information exchange

(G-7433)
SIRIUSIQ MOBILE LLC
200 Continental Dr (19713-4334)
PHONE.................................888 414-2047
Heather Field,
EMP: 12
SALES (est): 90.5K Privately Held
SIC: 8742 7372 General management consultant; business oriented computer software

(G-7434)
SKANSKA USA BUILDING INC
313 Wyoming Rd (19711-5311)
PHONE.................................215 495-8790
EMP: 41
SALES (corp-wide): 18B Privately Held
SIC: 1541 Industrial buildings & warehouses
HQ: Skanska Usa Building Inc.
   389 Interpace Pkwy Ste 5
   Parsippany NJ 07054
   973 753-3500

(G-7435)
SKETCHES AND PIXELS LLC
2035 Sunset Lake Rd B2 (19702-2600)
PHONE.................................312 834-4402
Quinn Smith,
EMP: 5
SALES: 100K Privately Held
SIC: 7371 Computer software development & applications

(G-7436)
SKIPLIST INC
2035 Sunset Lake Rd B2 (19702-2600)
PHONE.................................440 855-0319
Andrew Wolfe, CEO
EMP: 6
SALES (est): 144.4K Privately Held
SIC: 7379

(G-7437)
SKS ENTERPRISE
200 Continental Dr (19713-4334)
PHONE.................................302 310-2511
Kenneth Walker Jr, Principal
EMP: 65
SQ FT: 40,000
SALES (est): 3.2MM Privately Held
SIC: 6211 6531 Syndicate shares (real estate, entertainment, equip.) sales; auction, real estate

(G-7438)
SKYLINE SUPPLY INC
62 Albe Dr Ste C (19702-1370)
PHONE.................................302 894-9190
Dave Malatesta, CEO
Dennis M Ludwig, Treasurer
EMP: 5 EST: 2001
SQ FT: 4,000
SALES: 2MM Privately Held
SIC: 5085 Fasteners, industrial: nuts, bolts, screws, etc.

(G-7439)
SLEEP DISORDER CENTER DEL INC
4735 Ogltn Stntn Rd # 1225 (19713-2072)
PHONE.................................302 224-6000
Rochelle D Thawley, Manager
EMP: 4
SALES (est): 463.2K Privately Held
SIC: 8011 Clinic, operated by physicians

(G-7440)
SLEEP DISORDERS CTR-CHRISTIANA
774 Christiana Rd Ste 103 (19713-4248)
PHONE.................................302 623-0650
Mary Hancock, Principal
EMP: 4
SALES (est): 116.7K Privately Held
SIC: 8093 Drug clinic, outpatient

(G-7441)
SLM CORPORATION (PA)
Also Called: Sallie Mae
300 Continental Dr (19713-4322)
PHONE.................................302 451-0200
Raymond J Quinlan, Ch of Bd
Jonathan R Boyles, Senior VP
Kelly Christiano, Senior VP
Jeffrey F Dale, Senior VP
Nicolas Jafarieh, Senior VP
EMP: 65
SQ FT: 160,000
SALES: 1.8B Publicly Held
WEB: www.salliemae.com
SIC: 6111 6141 7322 Student Loan Marketing Association; personal credit institutions; adjustment & collection services

(G-7442)
SLM FINANCIAL CORPORATION (HQ)
Also Called: Sallie Mae Financial
300 Continental Dr Fl 1 (19713-4322)
P.O. Box 3409, Wilmington (19804-0249)
PHONE.................................856 642-8300
Joanne Jackson, President
Michael Yurko, Treasurer
Carol Rymal, Admin Sec
EMP: 15
SQ FT: 30,000
SALES (est): 4MM
SALES (corp-wide): 1.8B Publicly Held
WEB: www.slma.com
SIC: 6111 6162 Student Loan Marketing Association; mortgage bankers & correspondents
PA: Slm Corporation
   300 Continental Dr
   Newark DE 19713
   302 451-0200

(G-7443)
SMALL WONDER DENTAL
715 Nottingham Rd (19711-7406)
PHONE.................................302 525-6463
David J Gaz, Owner
EMP: 4
SALES (est): 232.6K Privately Held
SIC: 8021 Dentists' office

(G-7444)
SMART ARMOR PROTECTED LLC
19 Kris Ct (19702-6843)
PHONE.................................480 823-8122
Justin Zastrow, Mng Member
EMP: 40
SALES (est): 735.1K Privately Held
SIC: 7379

(G-7445)
SMART INTERNATIONAL INC
2035 Sunset Lake Rd B2 (19702-2600)
PHONE.................................302 451-9517
Maria Agustina Lacava,
EMP: 1
SALES (est): 53.2K Privately Held
SIC: 2752 Commercial printing, lithographic

(G-7446)
SMART PLUS TRANSPORT LLC
624 N Barrett Ln (19702-2999)
PHONE.................................347 963-0980
Linford Kumador, Owner
EMP: 4
SQ FT: 800
SALES: 100K Privately Held
SIC: 4212 Local trucking, without storage

(G-7447)
SMART PRINTING MGT LLC
560 Peoples Plz Ste 301 (19702-4798)
PHONE.................................855 549-4900
Jane Stevens, Principal
EMP: 4
SALES (est): 189.1K Privately Held
SIC: 8741 Management services

(G-7448)
SMB LIGHTING
36 Anthony Dr (19702-8429)
PHONE.................................302 733-0664
Shawn Butcher, Principal
EMP: 2
SALES (est): 128.8K Privately Held
SIC: 3648 Lighting equipment

(G-7449)
SMILE BRITE DENTAL CARE LLC (PA)
300 Biddle Ave Ste 204 (19702-3972)
PHONE.................................302 838-8306
Taurance N Bishop, President
Taurance Bishop, Fmly & Gen Dent
EMP: 13
SALES (est): 1.6MM Privately Held
SIC: 8021 Dentists' office

(G-7450)
SMITH BROTHERS COMMUNICATION
27 Harkfort Rd (19702-6307)
P.O. Box 2901, Wilmington (19805-0901)
PHONE.................................302 293-5224
Terry Smith, CEO
EMP: 6
SALES (est): 320K Privately Held
SIC: 7629 Telecommunication equipment repair (except telephones)

(G-7451)
SOBIESKI LIFE SAFETY
1325 Old Coochs Bridge Rd (19713-2311)
PHONE.................................800 321-1332
Walter Telford, Principal
EMP: 5
SALES (est): 528.6K Privately Held
SIC: 7382 Security systems services

(G-7452)
SOCIETY FOR WHOLE-BODY AUTORAD
110 Executive Dr Ste 7 (19702-3352)
PHONE.................................302 369-5240
Dr Eric Solon, President
EMP: 6
SALES (est): 118.1K Privately Held
SIC: 8621 Scientific membership association

(G-7453)
SOFTWARE BANANAS LLC
2915 Ogletown Rd Ste 2304 (19713-1927)
PHONE.................................302 348-8488
EMP: 2 EST: 2015
SALES (est): 68.4K Privately Held
SIC: 7372 Prepackaged software

(G-7454)
SOLAR FOUNDATIONS USA INC
206 Mcfarland Dr (19702-3680)
PHONE.................................518 935-3360
Michael Zuritis, President
Paul Lapinski, Vice Pres
EMP: 6 EST: 2009
SALES (est): 534.6K Privately Held
SIC: 3433 7389 Solar heaters & collectors;

(G-7455)
SOLAVITEK ENGINEERING INC
2915 Ogletown Rd Ste 2823 (19713-1927)
PHONE.................................514 949-6981
Alain Lussier, President
EMP: 1
SALES (est): 61.6K Privately Held
SIC: 3694 Generators, automotive & aircraft

(G-7456)
SOLUTIONS OF ADVANT-EDGE
1 Shea Way (19713-3421)
PHONE.................................302 533-6858
Jacqueline Ogborne, President
Don Holland, Vice Pres
Laurie Holland, Vice Pres
EMP: 5
SQ FT: 1,200
SALES (est): 1.4MM Privately Held
WEB: www.medtrace.com
SIC: 4953 Recycling, waste materials

(G-7457)
SOLVAY SPCLTY POLYMERS USA LLC
100 Interchange Blvd (19711-3549)
PHONE.................................302 452-6609
EMP: 7
SALES (corp-wide): 12.4MM Privately Held
SIC: 2819 Industrial inorganic chemicals
HQ: Solvay Specialty Polymers Usa, L.L.C.
   4500 Mcginnis Ferry Rd
   Alpharetta GA 30005
   770 772-8200

(G-7458)
SONESTA
240 Chapman Rd (19702-5405)
PHONE.................................302 453-9200
Michael Fruin, VP Opers
EMP: 29
SALES (corp-wide): 340.3K Privately Held
SIC: 7011 Hotels & motels
PA: Sonesta
   255 Washington St Ste 230
   Newton MA
   617 421-5400

(G-7459)
SONSHINE DENTAL LABS INC
300 Creek View Rd Ste 105 (19711-8547)
PHONE.................................302 731-5582
John J Ryan, President
Elizabeth A Ryan, Vice Pres
EMP: 13
SQ FT: 1,600

GEOGRAPHIC SECTION
Newark - New Castle County (G-7494)

SALES: 1.5MM **Privately Held**
SIC: 8072 Dental laboratories

(G-7460)
SOPO-360 LLC
1 Innovation Way Ste 400 (19711-5463)
PHONE....................703 585-3706
EMP: 4
SALES (est): 152.6K **Privately Held**
SIC: 8742 Management Consulting Services

(G-7461)
SOUTH FORKS INC
Also Called: Party Restaurant Outlet
136 Sandy Dr (19713-1147)
PHONE....................302 731-0344
Anthony Over, *President*
Tom Grant, *Vice Pres*
Elizabeth A Over, *Admin Sec*
EMP: 6
SALES (est): 1.9MM **Privately Held**
WEB: www.profoods.net
SIC: 5046 5087 5149 5147 Restaurant equipment & supplies; janitors' supplies; dried or canned foods; meats, fresh

(G-7462)
SPA AT COROLLA INC
271 W Main St (19711-3237)
PHONE....................302 292-2858
EMP: 17
SALES (est): 620K **Privately Held**
SIC: 7991 Physical Fitness Facility

(G-7463)
SPALLCO ENTERPRISES INC
Also Called: Spallco Car & Truck Rental
915 S Chapel St (19713-3419)
PHONE....................302 368-5950
Mike Parkowski, *Manager*
EMP: 5 **Privately Held**
SIC: 7514 Rent-a-car service
PA: Spallco Enterprises, Inc
    702 Philadelphia Pike
    Wilmington DE 19809

(G-7464)
SPARKLEAN LAUNDROMAT
750 Peoples Plz (19702-5601)
PHONE....................302 838-2226
EMP: 4
SALES (est): 41.8K **Privately Held**
SIC: 7215 Coin-operated laundries & cleaning

(G-7465)
SPCA
455 Stanton Christiana Rd (19713-2119)
P.O. Box 398, Georgetown (19947-0398)
PHONE....................302 698-3006
Pamela C Biddle, *President*
EMP: 4
SALES (est): 152.5K **Privately Held**
SIC: 8699 Animal humane society

(G-7466)
SPECIAL OLYMPICS INC
Also Called: Special Olympics of Deleware
619 S College Ave (19716-1901)
PHONE....................302 831-4653
Corinne Plummer, *Manager*
Ann Grunert, *Exec Dir*
EMP: 11
SALES (corp-wide): 104.6MM **Privately Held**
WEB: www.sonh.org
SIC: 8322 Social services for the handicapped
PA: Special Olympics, Inc.
    1133 19th St Nw
    Washington DC 20036
    202 628-3630

(G-7467)
SPECIAL OLYMPICS DELAWARE INC
Univer Of De 619 S Collge St Univer Of (19716)
PHONE....................302 831-4653
Ann Grunert, *Exec Dir*
EMP: 10
SALES: 1.7MM **Privately Held**
SIC: 8322 Association for the handicapped

(G-7468)
SPECIALTY REHABILITATION INC
4701 Ogltn Stntn Rd # 4100 (19713-2075)
PHONE....................302 709-0440
Lisa Marshall, *Director*
EMP: 10
SALES (est): 375.1K **Privately Held**
WEB: www.specialtyrehabilitation.com
SIC: 8049 Physical therapist

(G-7469)
SPECTRUM HONE & LACE LLC
310 Haines St Ste 116 (19717-5226)
PHONE....................313 268-5455
Jessica Cornwell, *Principal*
EMP: 2 EST: 2016
SALES (est): 62.6K **Privately Held**
SIC: 3291 Hones

(G-7470)
SPEEDY PUBLISHING LLC
40 E Main St 1156 (19711-4639)
PHONE....................888 248-4521
Colin Scott,
EMP: 7
SALES: 1.3MM **Privately Held**
SIC: 2741 Miscellaneous publishing

(G-7471)
SPICER MULLIKIN FUNERAL HOMES
121 W Park Pl (19711-4567)
PHONE....................302 368-9500
Harvey C Smith Jr, *President*
EMP: 16
SALES (corp-wide): 2.5MM **Privately Held**
SIC: 7261 Funeral home
PA: Spicer Mullikin Funeral Homes Inc
    1000 N Dupont Hwy
    New Castle DE 19720
    302 368-9500

(G-7472)
SPINE & ORTHOPEDIC SPECIALIST
1101 Twin C Ln Ste 203 (19713-2159)
PHONE....................302 633-1280
Julie Marley, *Principal*
EMP: 5
SALES (est): 268.4K **Privately Held**
SIC: 8049 Physical therapist

(G-7473)
SPINE CARE OF DELAWARE
4102b Ogletown Stanton Rd (19713-4183)
PHONE....................302 894-1900
Bruce Rudin, *CEO*
Manish Shah, *Manager*
Rachel Magner, *Director*
EMP: 7
SQ FT: 1,000
SALES (est): 1.6MM **Privately Held**
WEB: www.spinecareofmanassas.com
SIC: 8011 Physicians' office, including specialists

(G-7474)
SPRINGSIDE LLC
200 Biddle Ave Ste 205 (19702-3966)
PHONE....................302 838-7223
Jell Rule, *Mng Member*
EMP: 5
SALES (est): 536.3K **Privately Held**
SIC: 6531 Real estate leasing & rentals

(G-7475)
SPRINT
710 Peoples Plz (19702-5601)
PHONE....................302 261-8500
EMP: 5
SALES (est): 48.5K **Privately Held**
SIC: 4812 Cellular telephone services

(G-7476)
ST FRANCIS BARIATRIC CENTER
537 Stanton Christiana Rd (19713-2146)
PHONE....................302 421-4721
Jamie Powell, *Vice Pres*
Beth Schwenk, *Executive*
EMP: 6

SALES (est): 80.5K **Privately Held**
SIC: 8011 Surgeon

(G-7477)
ST FRANCIS HOSPITAL
1220 Capitol Trl (19711-3924)
PHONE....................302 369-9370
EMP: 8 EST: 2016
SALES (est): 82.2K **Privately Held**
SIC: 8062 General medical & surgical hospitals

(G-7478)
STACY K GATES
Also Called: State Farm Insurance
33 Possum Park Mall (19711-5591)
PHONE....................302 368-1968
Stacy Gates, *Owner*
EMP: 4
SQ FT: 900
SALES (est): 509.3K **Privately Held**
SIC: 6411 Insurance agents & brokers

(G-7479)
STALLARD CHASSIS CO
123 Sandy Dr (19713-1148)
PHONE....................302 292-1800
Mark Stallard Sr, *President*
EMP: 12
SQ FT: 30,000
SALES (est): 1.7MM **Privately Held**
WEB: www.stallardchassis.com
SIC: 3799 Midget autos, power driven

(G-7480)
STANDARD PIPE SERVICES LLC
567 Walther Rd (19702-2903)
PHONE....................302 286-0701
Frank Impagliazzo, *President*
Mark Schneider, *COO*
Bert Andrus, *Vice Pres*
Robin Quinn, *CFO*
EMP: 52 EST: 2016
SALES (est): 7.5MM **Privately Held**
SIC: 1623 Water, sewer & utility lines

(G-7481)
STANDLEE HAY FEED LLC
1800 Ogletown Rd Ste B (19711-5474)
PHONE....................302 737-5117
Mike Standlee, *Principal*
EMP: 7
SALES (est): 1.1MM **Privately Held**
SIC: 5191 Feed

(G-7482)
STANLEY GOLEBURN DDS
1290 Peoples Plz (19702-5701)
PHONE....................302 297-3750
EMP: 4
SALES (est): 61.5K **Privately Held**
SIC: 8021 Offices & clinics of dentists

(G-7483)
STAR CAMPUS II
550 S College Ave Ste 107 (19716-1308)
PHONE....................302 514-7586
EMP: 2
SALES (est): 143.9K **Privately Held**
SIC: 3711 Motor vehicles & car bodies

(G-7484)
STAR STATES LEASING CORP
Also Called: Wsfs Credit
30 Blue Hen Dr Ste 200 (19713-3445)
PHONE....................302 283-4500
John Hricik, *President*
Mike Muller, *Vice Pres*
EMP: 35
SALES (est): 4.4MM
SALES (corp-wide): 455.5MM **Publicly Held**
WEB: www.wsfsbank.com
SIC: 6159 7515 Automobile finance leasing; passenger car leasing
HQ: Wilmington Savings Fund Society
    500 Delaware Ave Ste 500 # 500
    Wilmington DE 19801
    302 792-6000

(G-7485)
STATE FARM INSURANCE
1250 Peoples Plz (19702-5701)
PHONE....................302 832-0344
David R Palmer, *Owner*
Bill Bamonto, *Owner*

EMP: 4 EST: 1989
SALES (est): 574.5K **Privately Held**
SIC: 6411 Insurance agents & brokers

(G-7486)
STATE WIDE PLUMBING INC
Also Called: Statewide Plumbing
27 Albe Dr Ste J (19702-1325)
P.O. Box 77, Middletown (19709-0077)
PHONE....................302 292-0924
Tom Pulgini, *President*
EMP: 11
SQ FT: 2,000
SALES (est): 1.3MM **Privately Held**
SIC: 1711 Plumbing contractors

(G-7487)
STB MANAGEMENT
2202 Drummond Plz (19711-5711)
PHONE....................302 737-5105
Peter Fulwiler, *CEO*
EMP: 4
SALES (est): 491.1K **Privately Held**
SIC: 6211 Security brokers & dealers

(G-7488)
STEP BY STEP FURN INSTALLATION
246 Ingram St (19702-4116)
P.O. Box 302, Bear (19701-0302)
PHONE....................302 834-8257
EMP: 8 EST: 1999
SALES (est): 610K **Privately Held**
SIC: 1799 Trade Contractor

(G-7489)
STEPHEN A NIEMOELLER DMD PA
523 Capitol Trl (19711-3859)
PHONE....................302 737-3320
Stephen A Niemoeller, *Owner*
EMP: 5
SALES (est): 225.9K **Privately Held**
SIC: 8021 Dentists' office

(G-7490)
STEREOCHEMICAL INC
667 Dawson Dr Ste E (19713-3437)
PHONE....................302 266-0700
Lawrence D Kwart, *President*
Edward J Gaffney, *CFO*
EMP: 3
SQ FT: 3,800
SALES: 120K **Privately Held**
SIC: 8731 8734 2869 Chemical laboratory, except testing; testing laboratories; industrial organic chemicals

(G-7491)
STILL INDUSTRIES INC
287 S Main St (19711-4564)
PHONE....................302 368-8832
EMP: 1
SALES (est): 39.6K **Privately Held**
SIC: 3999 Manufacturing industries

(G-7492)
STRACKE ENTERPRISES INC
5 Beacon Ln (19711-1904)
PHONE....................302 743-6515
Kathy Stracke, *President*
EMP: 4
SALES: 720K **Privately Held**
SIC: 1799 Paint & wallpaper stripping

(G-7493)
STRATEGIC SOLUTIONS INTL INC
700 Barksdale Rd Ste 6 (19711-3260)
PHONE....................302 525-6313
Connie R Charles, *CEO*
EMP: 5
SALES (est): 625.7K **Privately Held**
WEB: www.ssizone.com
SIC: 8742 Business consultant

(G-7494)
STRATEGY HOUSE INC
231 Executive Dr Ste 15 (19702-3324)
PHONE....................302 658-1500
Paul Bastianelli, *President*
Kristin Scully, *Principal*
EMP: 6
SALES (est): 431.3K **Privately Held**
SIC: 8748 Business consulting

Newark - New Castle County (G-7495) GEOGRAPHIC SECTION

(G-7495)
STRATIS VISUALS LLC
20 Tyler Way (19713-3464)
PHONE 860 482-1208
EMP: 1
SALES (corp-wide): 13.3MM **Privately Held**
SIC: 2752 Commercial printing, lithographic
PA: Stratis Visuals Llc
129 Industrial Ln
Torrington CT 06790
860 482-1208

(G-7496)
STUDENT MEDIA GROUP
500 Creek View Rd Ste 3e (19711-8549)
PHONE 302 607-2580
Paul Alford, *Owner*
Katy Gorschboth, *Opers-Prdtn-Mfg*
▲ EMP: 10
SALES (est): 911.9K **Privately Held**
SIC: 2721 Magazines: publishing & printing

(G-7497)
STUDENTUP INC
2035 Sunset Lake Rd (19702-2600)
PHONE 951 427-7563
Robin Salimans, *CEO*
EMP: 4
SALES: 400K **Privately Held**
SIC: 4813

(G-7498)
STUMP B GONE INC
17 Red Mill Rd (19711-6665)
PHONE 302 737-7779
David Moore, *Owner*
EMP: 4
SALES (est): 145.9K **Privately Held**
SIC: 0782 0783 5989 Landscape contractors; removal services, bush & tree; fuel dealers

(G-7499)
SUCCULENTS SOAP SAND SCENTS
103 Rockrose Dr (19711-6825)
PHONE 302 757-0697
Jay Lynch, *Principal*
EMP: 2
SALES (est): 192.2K **Privately Held**
SIC: 2844 Toilet preparations

(G-7500)
SUJO MUSIC PUBLISHING
402 Longfield Rd (19713-2710)
PHONE 302 731-8575
Joseph Campbell, *Owner*
EMP: 1
SALES (est): 48.6K **Privately Held**
SIC: 2741 Miscellaneous publishing

(G-7501)
SULLIVAN ANNA MARIE DO
2 Polly Drummond Hill Rd (19711-5703)
PHONE 302 454-1680
Anna Sullivan, *Principal*
EMP: 4 EST: 2008
SALES (est): 174.1K **Privately Held**
SIC: 8031 Offices & clinics of osteopathic physicians

(G-7502)
SUMMER CONSULTANTS INC
131 Continental Dr # 302 (19713-4323)
PHONE 484 493-4150
Edward Kroman, *Finance*
James Hoffman, *Branch Mgr*
EMP: 10
SALES (corp-wide): 5.2MM **Privately Held**
SIC: 8711 Engineering services
PA: Summer Consultants Inc
7900 Westpark Dr Ste A405
Mc Lean VA 22102
703 556-8320

(G-7503)
SUMMIT BRIDGE INV PRPTS LLC
912 Westerly Ct (19702-4823)
PHONE 410 499-1456
Stephen Berkeridge,
EMP: 5

SQ FT: 7,200
SALES (est): 129.6K **Privately Held**
SIC: 6531 Real estate leasing & rentals

(G-7504)
SUMMIT INDUSTRIAL CORPORATION
1109 Elkton Rd (19711-3508)
PHONE 302 368-2718
Sandra Patnovic, *President*
Robert Patnovic, *Admin Sec*
EMP: 5
SQ FT: 6,000
SALES (est): 550K **Privately Held**
SIC: 3599 Machine shop, jobbing & repair

(G-7505)
SUMMIT PROPERTIES INC
Also Called: Summit Pike Creek
100 Red Fox Ln Bldg 100 # 100 (19711-5999)
PHONE 302 737-3747
Christina Hunt, *Manager*
EMP: 8 **Privately Held**
WEB: www.summitproperties.com
SIC: 6513 Apartment building operators
HQ: Summit Properties Inc.
309 E Morehead St Ste 200
Charlotte NC 28202
704 334-3000

(G-7506)
SUNCO SALON
67 Marrows Rd (19713-3701)
PHONE 302 456-0240
Billy Phan, *Owner*
EMP: 5
SALES (est): 87.3K **Privately Held**
SIC: 7231 Beauty shops

(G-7507)
SUNLIGHT SALON LLC
610 Plaza Dr (19702-6368)
PHONE 302 456-1799
Ben Ho, *Partner*
Binh Ho,
EMP: 9
SALES: 950K **Privately Held**
SIC: 7231 Manicurist, pedicurist

(G-7508)
SUNSHINE KIDS ACADEMY
924 Old Harmony Rd # 104 (19713-4185)
PHONE 302 444-4270
Gladys Nuahma, *Owner*
EMP: 15 EST: 2009
SALES (est): 175.1K **Privately Held**
SIC: 8351 Child day care services

(G-7509)
SUNTRUST MORTGAGE INC
200 Continental Dr # 207 (19713-4334)
PHONE 302 453-2350
EMP: 14
SALES (corp-wide): 9.1B **Publicly Held**
SIC: 6162 Mortgage Banker/Correspondent
HQ: Suntrust Mortgage, Inc.
901 Semmes Ave
Richmond VA 23224
804 291-0740

(G-7510)
SUPER C INC
1352 Marrows Rd Ste 104 (19711-5476)
PHONE 302 533-6024
Fei Deng, *President*
EMP: 4 EST: 2016
SALES (est): 529K **Privately Held**
SIC: 7389

(G-7511)
SUPERCRITICAL FLUID TECH (PA)
Also Called: Sft
1 Innovation Way (19711-5442)
PHONE 302 738-3420
Robert James, *President*
Kenneth Krewson, *General Mgr*
Melinda Basilio, *Sales Staff*
Heather Cloud, *Sales Staff*
Kenneth James, *Med Doctor*
▲ EMP: 4
SQ FT: 7,000

SALES (est): 1.2MM **Privately Held**
WEB: www.supercriticalfluid.com
SIC: 3826 5084 Analytical instruments; industrial machinery & equipment

(G-7512)
SUPERCRITICAL FLUID TECH
120 Sandy Dr Ste 2b (19713-1135)
PHONE 302 738-3420
Robert James, *President*
EMP: 8 **Privately Held**
WEB: www.supercriticalfluid.com
SIC: 3826 Analytical instruments
PA: Supercritical Fluid Technologies, Inc
1 Innovation Way
Newark DE 19711

(G-7513)
SUPERIOR COMMERCIAL CLEANING
446 Douglas D Alley Dr (19713-2324)
PHONE 302 897-2544
EMP: 4 EST: 2011
SALES (est): 61.1K **Privately Held**
SIC: 7349 Building Maintenance Services

(G-7514)
SURE GOOD FOODS USA LLC
40 E Main St Ste 1187 (19711-4639)
PHONE 905 288-1136
Troy Warren, *President*
EMP: 45 EST: 2017
SALES: 100MM
SALES (corp-wide): 329.1MM **Privately Held**
SIC: 5147 Meats & meat products
PA: Sure Good Foods Ltd
2333 North Sheridan Way Suite 100
Mississauga ON L5K 1
905 286-1619

(G-7515)
SURGE NETWORKS INC
2035 Sunset Lake Rd B2 (19702-2600)
PHONE 206 432-5047
Yachen Liu, *Principal*
EMP: 8
SALES (est): 182.5K **Privately Held**
SIC: 7371 Computer software development & applications

(G-7516)
SURGICAL CRITICAL ASSOC
4735 Ogletown Stanton Rd # 3301 (19713-7021)
PHONE 302 623-4370
EMP: 6
SALES (est): 80.5K **Privately Held**
SIC: 8011 Offices & clinics of medical doctors

(G-7517)
SUSAN T FISCHER
Also Called: Let's Have Fun Daycare
57 Avignon Dr (19702-5553)
PHONE 302 832-2570
Susan T Fischer, *Principal*
EMP: 5 EST: 2011
SALES (est): 170K **Privately Held**
SIC: 8351 Group day care center

(G-7518)
SWAROVSKI US HOLDING LIMITED
715 Christiana Mall (19702)
PHONE 302 737-4811
Alice Andree, *Branch Mgr*
EMP: 4
SALES (corp-wide): 4.7B **Privately Held**
SIC: 3961 Costume jewelry
HQ: Swarovski U.S. Holding Limited
1 Kenney Dr
Cranston RI 02920
401 463-6400

(G-7519)
SWEENY AND ASSOCIATES
112 Possum Hollow Rd (19711-3910)
PHONE 302 453-1645
Ron Sweeny, *Principal*
EMP: 4
SALES (est): 326.8K **Privately Held**
SIC: 8742 Real estate consultant

(G-7520)
SWEETEN COMPANIES INC
Also Called: Sweeten Solar
149 Salem Church Rd (19713-2941)
PHONE 302 737-6161
Michael Sweeten, *President*
EMP: 3
SALES: 150K **Privately Held**
SIC: 5074 3448 1611 Heating equipment & panels, solar; sunrooms, prefabricated metal; general contractor, highway & street construction

(G-7521)
SWEETS BY SAMANTHA LLC
Also Called: Sweet Luci
3 Linette Ct (19702-6815)
PHONE 302 740-2218
Samantha Zebrowski, *Managing Prtnr*
EMP: 11
SALES (est): 250K **Privately Held**
SIC: 2051 Cakes, bakery: except frozen

(G-7522)
SWIFT POOLS INC
1123 Capitol Trl (19711-3921)
PHONE 302 738-9800
John E Swift Sr, *President*
John E Swift IV, *Treasurer*
Bonnie Swift, *Admin Sec*
EMP: 28
SQ FT: 3,500
SALES (est): 2.8MM **Privately Held**
WEB: www.swiftpools.com
SIC: 1799 5999 Swimming pool construction; spa or hot tub installation or construction; swimming pools, hot tubs & sauna equipment & supplies

(G-7523)
SWITCH INC
Also Called: Switch Skates & Snowboards
54 E Main St (19711-4639)
PHONE 302 738-7499
James Tunis, *CEO*
EMP: 5
SALES (est): 580K **Privately Held**
WEB: www.micromedicinc.net
SIC: 5091 Sporting & recreation goods

(G-7524)
SYGUL INC
Also Called: Edufar
2035 Sunset Lake Rd B2 (19702-2600)
PHONE 315 384-1848
Sudesh Famesh, *Principal*
EMP: 20
SALES: 25K **Privately Held**
SIC: 7371 Computer software development & applications

(G-7525)
SYNERGY MEDICAL USA INC
2915 Ogletown Rd Ste 2565 (19713-1927)
PHONE 302 444-0163
Jean Boutin, *President*
EMP: 10 EST: 2016
SALES (est): 1.1MM **Privately Held**
SIC: 5047 Medical & hospital equipment

(G-7526)
SYSTEMS APPROACH LTD
309 Palomino Dr (19711-8310)
PHONE 302 743-6331
Roger Voyce, *President*
Roger Boyce, *President*
Susan Reeves, *General Mgr*
EMP: 7
SALES (est): 554.2K **Privately Held**
WEB: www.systemsapproachltd.com
SIC: 7389 Drafting service, except temporary help

(G-7527)
T B PAINTING RESTORATION
162 Madison Dr (19711-4406)
PHONE 610 283-4100
EMP: 2
SALES (est): 68K **Privately Held**
SIC: 5198 2851 Paints, varnishes & supplies; wood fillers or sealers

(G-7528)
TABELLA INC
2035 Sunset Lake Rd (19702-2600)
PHONE 415 799-2389

GEOGRAPHIC SECTION   Newark - New Castle County (G-7558)

EMP: 7
SALES (est): 164.3K **Privately Held**
SIC: 7371 Computer software development & applications

(G-7529)
TADE INFO TECH SOLUTIONS
60 Avignon Dr (19702-5518)
PHONE..................................302 832-1449
Thomas Kitchen, *President*
EMP: 5
SALES (est): 192.3K **Privately Held**
SIC: 8748 Business consulting

(G-7530)
TAGHLEEF INDUSTRIES LLC
500 Creek View Rd Ste 300 (19711-8549)
PHONE..................................302 326-5500
▲ EMP: 5
SALES (est): 696.5K
SALES (corp-wide): 117MM **Privately Held**
SIC: 5199 Whol Nondurable Goods
PA: Taghleef Industries Llc
    Near Dutco Tanant Taghleef Industries
    Llc Building, Jebel Ali In
    Dubai
    488 011-00

(G-7531)
TAGHLEEF INDUSTRIES INC
500 Creek View Rd Ste 300 (19711-8549)
PHONE..................................302 326-5500
EMP: 320
SALES (corp-wide): 660.5MM **Privately Held**
SIC: 3081 Polypropylene film & sheet
HQ: Taghleef Industries Inc.
    500 Creek View Rd Ste 301
    Newark DE 19711
    302 326-5500

(G-7532)
TAGHLEEF INDUSTRIES INC (HQ)
Also Called: Aet Films
500 Creek View Rd Ste 301 (19711-8549)
PHONE..................................302 326-5500
Detlef Schuhmann, *CEO*
Rashed Al Ghurair, *Chairman*
Wolfgang Meyer, *COO*
◆ EMP: 92
SQ FT: 50,000
SALES (est): 300MM
SALES (corp-wide): 660.5MM **Privately Held**
WEB: www.appliedextrusion.com
SIC: 3081 Polypropylene film & sheet
PA: Taghleef Industries Llc
    Near Dutco Tanant Taghleef Industries
    Llc Building, Jebel Ali In
    Dubai
    488 011-00

(G-7533)
TAI JUN INTERNATIONAL INC
511 Penn Manor Dr (19711-2418)
PHONE..................................302 239-9336
EMP: 5 EST: 1989
SQ FT: 800
SALES: 102.8K **Privately Held**
SIC: 5099 5137 Mfg Representative For Carry Bags & Stationary

(G-7534)
TALENTS PUBLISHING LLC
220 E Delaware Ave (19711-4693)
PHONE..................................302 353-4574
EMP: 1 EST: 2007
SALES (est): 67K **Privately Held**
SIC: 2731 Books-Publishing/Printing

(G-7535)
TALK WITH TWILA MINISTRIES
260 Chapman Rd (19702-5490)
PHONE..................................302 525-6472
EMP: 8
SALES (est): 73.3K **Privately Held**
SIC: 8093 Mental health clinic, outpatient

(G-7536)
TALLEY BROTHERS INC
116 Sandy Dr Ste C (19713-1187)
P.O. Box 5505 (19714-5505)
PHONE..................................302 224-5376
Rscott Killen, *President*

William West, *Vice Pres*
EMP: 28
SQ FT: 3,000
SALES: 8.4MM **Privately Held**
SIC: 1541 1771 1542 Industrial buildings, new construction; renovation, remodeling & repairs: industrial buildings; prefabricated building erection, industrial; concrete work; commercial & office building, new construction; commercial & office buildings, renovation & repair; commercial & office buildings, prefabricated erection

(G-7537)
TANDEM HOSTED RESOURCES INC
Also Called: Qnectus
300 Creek View Rd Ste 202 (19711-8548)
PHONE..................................302 740-7099
Peter Danby, *President*
Anthony George, *COO*
Andrew Kulp, *Vice Pres*
Dustin Sterkenburg, *Vice Pres*
EMP: 10
SALES (est): 950K **Privately Held**
SIC: 7373 7371 Computer integrated systems design; computer software writing services

(G-7538)
TANTINI LLC
136 S Main St (19711-7900)
PHONE..................................302 444-4024
Sonya Bright, *Branch Mgr*
EMP: 4
SALES (corp-wide): 764.6K **Privately Held**
SIC: 7299 Tanning salon
PA: Tantini, L.L.C.
    172 William L Dalton Dr
    Glassboro NJ 08028
    856 582-0826

(G-7539)
TAPP NETWORKS LLC
136 Woodland Rd (19702-1474)
PHONE..................................302 222-3384
Kyle Barkins,
EMP: 6
SALES (est): 141K **Privately Held**
SIC: 7379

(G-7540)
TARPON STRATEGIES LLC
64 Thompson Cir (19711-7129)
PHONE..................................215 806-2723
Zeb Congdon, *President*
EMP: 1
SALES (est): 125.1K **Privately Held**
SIC: 5199 7389 8748 5047 General merchandise, non-durable; ; business consulting; instruments, surgical & medical; hospital furniture, except beds

(G-7541)
TD AMERITRADE INC
1257 Churchmans Rd (19713-2149)
PHONE..................................302 368-1050
Richard Thompson, *Manager*
EMP: 5
SALES (corp-wide): 6B **Publicly Held**
SIC: 6211 Stock brokers & dealers
HQ: Td Ameritrade, Inc.
    12800 Corporate Hill Dr
    Saint Louis MO 63131
    314 965-1555

(G-7542)
TD BANK NA
230 E Delaware Ave (19711-4607)
PHONE..................................302 455-1781
Matt Lintangne, *Manager*
EMP: 13
SALES (corp-wide): 22.8B **Privately Held**
SIC: 6022 State commercial banks
HQ: Td Bank, N.A.
    1701 Route 70 E Ste 200
    Cherry Hill NJ 08003
    856 751-2739

(G-7543)
TDM PHARMACEUTICAL RES LLC
100 Biddle Ave Ste 202 (19702-3983)
PHONE..................................302 832-1008
Daphen Shum,

EMP: 9
SALES (est): 1MM **Privately Held**
SIC: 8733 Noncommercial research organizations

(G-7544)
TECHNCAL STFFING RESOURCES LLC
Also Called: Allstates Technical Services
262 Chapman Rd (19702-5448)
P.O. Box 8255 (19714-8255)
PHONE..................................302 452-9933
Robert Pinson, *General Mgr*
EMP: 4 **Publicly Held**
WEB: www.asts.net
SIC: 8711 Construction & civil engineering
HQ: Technical Staffing Resources, Llc
    10 Inverness Center Pkwy
    Birmingham AL 35242
    205 437-7100

(G-7545)
TECHNICARE INC
39 Lakewood Cir (19711-2349)
PHONE..................................302 322-7766
Denise M Cairo, *President*
Denise Cairo, *President*
Robert A Cairo, *Vice Pres*
EMP: 7
SQ FT: 5,700
SALES (est): 1.2MM **Privately Held**
SIC: 5084 1731 7378 Recycling machinery & equipment; safety & security specialization; computer peripheral equipment repair & maintenance

(G-7546)
TECHNIQUES INC
Also Called: Techniques Inc Borden E Smith
20 Lenape Ln (19713-1311)
PHONE..................................302 422-7760
Borden E Smith, *President*
EMP: 5
SQ FT: 6,000
SALES (est): 350K **Privately Held**
SIC: 7532 Body shop, automotive

(G-7547)
TECHNOLOGY TRANSFERS INC
16 Anderson Ln (19711-3064)
PHONE..................................302 234-4718
Godwin Igwe, *President*
EMP: 5
SALES (est): 231.5K **Privately Held**
SIC: 8711 Consulting engineer

(G-7548)
TECHXPONENT INC
131 Arielle Dr (19702-2678)
PHONE..................................410 701-0089
Muhammad Baqir, *Principal*
Naveed Baqir, *Principal*
Amna Latif, *Principal*
Salsabila Mouiz, *Principal*
Mark Quinn, *Principal*
EMP: 10
SALES (est): 180.6K **Privately Held**
SIC: 7389

(G-7549)
TECOT ELECTRIC SUPPLY CO
501 Interchange Blvd (19711-3558)
PHONE..................................302 368-9161
Chuck Cannon, *Branch Mgr*
EMP: 4
SALES (corp-wide): 220.5MM **Privately Held**
SIC: 5063 Electrical supplies
HQ: Tecot Electric Supply Co (Inc)
    55 Lukens Dr
    New Castle DE
    302 429-9100

(G-7550)
TECS PLUS
260 Chapman Rd Ste 104a (19702-5410)
PHONE..................................302 437-6890
Amanda Pokhan, *Principal*
EMP: 4
SALES (est): 412.8K **Privately Held**
SIC: 7379 Computer related consulting services

(G-7551)
TEK TREE LLC (PA)
1106 Drummond Plz (19711-5705)
PHONE..................................302 368-2730
Prasad Valla, *Sales Staff*
Raghuveer Bandi, *Mng Member*
EMP: 18
SALES (est): 3.9MM **Privately Held**
SIC: 8748 Systems engineering consultant, ex. computer or professional

(G-7552)
TEKSOLV USD INC
100 Lake Dr (19702-3340)
PHONE..................................302 738-1050
Chris Bonson, *Branch Mgr*
EMP: 6
SALES (corp-wide): 39.7MM **Privately Held**
SIC: 3531 Construction machinery
PA: Teksolv Usd, Inc.
    130 Executive Dr Ste 5
    Newark DE 19702
    302 738-1050

(G-7553)
TEKSOLV USD INC (PA)
130 Executive Dr Ste 5 (19702-3349)
PHONE..................................302 738-1050
John Mouser, *President*
Ricky Reams, *General Mgr*
Aaron Stewart, *Superintendent*
Steve Smith, *Engineer*
William Blechinger, *Consultant*
EMP: 83
SALES (est): 39.7MM **Privately Held**
SIC: 8741 Business management

(G-7554)
TELL LAB
540 S College Ave (19713-1302)
PHONE..................................302 831-7121
EMP: 5
SALES (est): 250.5K **Privately Held**
SIC: 8734 Testing laboratories

(G-7555)
TEMP-AIR INC
Also Called: Tempair
200 Happy Ln (19711-8006)
PHONE..................................302 369-3880
Michael Schmib, *Manager*
EMP: 10
SALES (corp-wide): 5.9B **Privately Held**
SIC: 7359 Equipment rental & leasing
HQ: Temp-Air, Inc.
    3700 W Preserve Blvd
    Burnsville MN 55337
    800 836-7432

(G-7556)
TEN BEARS ENVIRONMENTAL LLC
1080 S Chapel St Ste 200 (19702-1379)
PHONE..................................302 731-8633
J McAndrew, *Mng Member*
Joe McAndrew, *Mng Member*
John Gurski, *Manager*
EMP: 9
SALES (est): 694.7K **Privately Held**
WEB: www.tenbears.us
SIC: 8748 8711 Environmental consultant; engineering services

(G-7557)
TERRY WHITE
Also Called: State Farm Insurance
200 Continental Dr # 109 (19713-4303)
PHONE..................................302 652-4969
Terry White, *Owner*
Eric Blondin, *Sales Associate*
Rob Mullen, *Manager*
EMP: 6
SALES (est): 968K **Privately Held**
SIC: 6411 Insurance agents & brokers

(G-7558)
TESTEX INC
8 Fox Ln (19711-2071)
P.O. Box 867 (19715-0867)
PHONE..................................302 731-5693
Mary Ellen Stachnik, *President*
Ray Behe, *General Mgr*
Robert Stachnik, *Director*
EMP: 6 EST: 1964

(PA)=Parent Co (HQ)=Headquarters (DH)=Div Headquarters
✪ = New Business established in last 2 years

2020 Harris Directory of Delaware Businesses

Newark - New Castle County (G-7559)   GEOGRAPHIC SECTION

SALES (est): 407K **Privately Held**
SIC: 3829 Measuring & controlling devices

(G-7559)
TETRA TECH INC
240 Continental Dr # 200 (19713-4360)
PHONE.................................302 738-7551
Andy Mazzeo, *Manager*
EMP: 13
SALES (corp-wide): 3.1B **Publicly Held**
SIC: 8711 Consulting engineer
PA: Tetra Tech, Inc.
   3475 E Foothill Blvd
   Pasadena CA 91107
   626 351-4664

(G-7560)
TETRA TECH INC
Also Called: Tetra Tech Engrg & Arch Svcs
240 Continental Dr # 200 (19713-4360)
PHONE.................................302 738-7551
Robert Maffia, *Branch Mgr*
EMP: 23
SALES (corp-wide): 3.1B **Publicly Held**
WEB: www.tetratech.com
SIC: 8711 Engineering services
PA: Tetra Tech, Inc.
   3475 E Foothill Blvd
   Pasadena CA 91107
   626 351-4664

(G-7561)
THE ASCENDANT GROUP INC
2035 Sunset Lake Rd B2 (19702-2600)
PHONE.................................302 450-4494
Kimberly Reed, *Senior Partner*
Raoul Davis, *Partner*
EMP: 13
SALES (est): 1.6MM **Privately Held**
SIC: 8743 Public relations services

(G-7562)
THOMAS BROTHERS LLC
12 Oak Ave (19711-4728)
PHONE.................................302 366-1316
Stuart Thomas, *Mng Member*
Howard Thomas,
Sheldon Thomas,
Steve Thomas,
EMP: 7
SALES (est): 610K **Privately Held**
SIC: 1522 Residential construction

(G-7563)
THOMAS BUILDING GROUP INC
35 Albe Dr (19702-1321)
PHONE.................................302 283-0600
Lori Loller, *President*
EMP: 50
SQ FT: 2,500
SALES (est): 2MM **Privately Held**
SIC: 1795 Demolition, buildings & other structures

(G-7564)
THOMCO INC
314 E Main St Ste 401 (19711-7182)
PHONE.................................302 454-0361
Jeffrey Thomas, *President*
Suzanne Thomas, *Corp Secy*
Joe Lazorick, *Sales Staff*
Andrew Waterman, *Agent*
EMP: 4
SALES (est): 484K **Privately Held**
WEB: www.thomco1.com
SIC: 5033 Insulation materials

(G-7565)
THORNLEY COMPANY INC
1 Innovation Way Ste 100 (19711-5462)
P.O. Box 269, Conshohocken PA (19428-0269)
PHONE.................................302 224-8300
H Douglas Thornley, *President*
▲ EMP: 8 EST: 1954
SQ FT: 2,000
SALES (est): 1.9MM **Privately Held**
WEB: www.thornleycompany.com
SIC: 5169 Chemicals & allied products

(G-7566)
TIMTEC INC
301 Ruthar Dr Ste A (19711-8031)
P.O. Box 8941 (19714-8941)
PHONE.................................302 292-8500
Murat Niyazymbetov, *President*
EMP: 10
SALES (est): 1MM **Privately Held**
SIC: 2819 Ammonium compounds, except fertilizers

(G-7567)
TIMTEC LLC
301 Ruthar Dr Ste A (19711-8031)
P.O. Box 8941 (19714-8941)
PHONE.................................302 292-8500
Murat Niyazymbetov, *Mng Member*
EMP: 10
SALES (est): 784.9K **Privately Held**
SIC: 8731 8742 Biotechnical research, commercial; management consulting services

(G-7568)
TIPTON COMMUNICATIONS GROUP
323 E Main St (19711-7152)
PHONE.................................302 454-7901
Daniel R Tipton, *President*
Laura B Tipton, *Corp Secy*
EMP: 8
SALES (est): 872.8K **Privately Held**
SIC: 8743 8249 8742 Public relations services; business training services; hospital & health services consultant

(G-7569)
TJ CUSTOM WOODWORKS INC
4 Mistweave Ct (19711-2980)
PHONE.................................302 563-8535
Thomas Jenkins, *Principal*
EMP: 1
SALES (est): 54.1K **Privately Held**
SIC: 2431 Millwork

(G-7570)
TNT WINDOW CLEANING
35 Salem Church Rd (19713-4928)
PHONE.................................302 326-2411
Tom Robinson, *Owner*
EMP: 5
SALES (est): 122.2K **Privately Held**
SIC: 7349 Window cleaning

(G-7571)
TO A TEE PRINTING
2860 Ogletown Rd (19713-1857)
PHONE.................................302 525-6336
EMP: 2
SALES (est): 117K **Privately Held**
SIC: 2759 Commercial printing

(G-7572)
TODAY NAILS
1129 Churchmans Rd (19713-2112)
PHONE.................................302 286-7937
Joel Dao, *Owner*
EMP: 4
SALES (est): 73.8K **Privately Held**
SIC: 7231 Manicurist, pedicurist

(G-7573)
TODAYS KID INC (NOT INC)
10 Songsmith Dr (19702-4405)
P.O. Box 283, Bear (19701-0283)
PHONE.................................302 834-5620
Dee Worley, *Owner*
EMP: 8
SALES (est): 142K **Privately Held**
SIC: 8351 Child day care services

(G-7574)
TOM WISELEY INSURANCE AGENCY
Also Called: Allstate
1400 Peoples Plz Ste 228 (19702-5708)
PHONE.................................302 832-7700
Tom Wiseley, *Owner*
Kevin Hamill, *COO*
EMP: 8
SALES (est): 1.1MM **Privately Held**
SIC: 6411 Insurance agents, brokers & service

(G-7575)
TOPAZ & ASSOCIATES LLC
3 Francis Cir Ste 1 (19711-2625)
PHONE.................................302 448-8914
Robert Smith,
EMP: 10

SALES: 1.5MM **Privately Held**
SIC: 6531 Real estate agents & managers

(G-7576)
TOPS INTERNATIONAL CORP
707 Interchange Blvd (19711-3594)
PHONE.................................302 738-8889
Jean Shih, *President*
EMP: 5
SALES (est): 330.9K **Privately Held**
SIC: 5045 5159 4225 Computers & accessories, personal & home entertainment; printers, computer; cotton merchants; cotton or cotton linters, country buyers; general warehousing & storage

(G-7577)
TOTAL CARE PHYSICIANS
Also Called: Glasgow Medical Center
2600 Glasgow Ave Ste 124 (19702-4776)
PHONE.................................302 836-4200
Maricar Belicena-Badillo, *Principal*
EMP: 4
SALES (corp-wide): 6.9MM **Privately Held**
SIC: 8031 8011 Offices & clinics of osteopathic physicians; internal medicine practitioners
PA: Total Care Physicians
   405 Silverside Rd Ste 111
   Wilmington DE 19809
   302 798-0666

(G-7578)
TOTAL CLIMATE CONTROL INC
Also Called: Honeywell Authorized Dealer
2694 Frazer Rd (19702-4503)
PHONE.................................302 836-6240
Carl Chopack, *President*
Janet Chopack, *Vice Pres*
EMP: 5
SQ FT: 3,000
SALES (est): 565.5K **Privately Held**
WEB: www.totalclimatecontrolinc.com
SIC: 1711 Warm air heating & air conditioning contractor; refrigeration contractor

(G-7579)
TOWN AND COUNTRY SALON INC
1923 Kirkwood Hwy (19711-5725)
PHONE.................................302 737-1855
Carrie Rutt, *President*
Thomas Rutt, *Vice Pres*
EMP: 50
SQ FT: 1,500
SALES (est): 2.5MM **Privately Held**
WEB: www.townncountrysalon.com
SIC: 7231 Unisex hair salons

(G-7580)
TOWNE PLACE SUITES BY MARRIOTT
Also Called: Nab Hospitality
410 Eagle Run Rd (19702-1603)
PHONE.................................302 369-6212
Joan Payne, *General Mgr*
EMP: 18 EST: 2005
SALES (est): 1.5MM **Privately Held**
SIC: 7011 Hotel, franchised

(G-7581)
TRANQUILITY COUNSELING INC
314 E Main St Ste 402 (19711-7182)
PHONE.................................302 636-0700
Kimberley Colgan, *Principal*
EMP: 6 EST: 2008
SALES (est): 153.5K **Privately Held**
SIC: 8322 Social worker; general counseling services

(G-7582)
TRAVEL TRAVEL NEWARK INC
760 Peoples Plz (19702-5601)
PHONE.................................302 737-5555
Joan Simmons, *President*
EMP: 4
SQ FT: 2,000
SALES (est): 698.8K **Privately Held**
SIC: 4724 Travel agencies

(G-7583)
TRELLTEX INC
211 Executive Dr Ste 9 (19702-3358)
PHONE.................................302 738-4313
EMP: 15
SALES (corp-wide): 27MM **Privately Held**
SIC: 5085 Rubber goods, mechanical
PA: Trelltex, Inc.
   4444 Homestead Rd
   Houston TX 77028
   713 675-8590

(G-7584)
TRI STATE BATTERY AND AUTO ELC (PA)
107 Albe Dr Ste H (19702-1300)
P.O. Box 5808 (19714-5808)
PHONE.................................302 292-2330
Gary Emory Sutch II, *President*
Debbie Davis, *Vice Pres*
Tim Sutch, *Sales Mgr*
▲ EMP: 14
SQ FT: 6,000
SALES (est): 5.2MM **Privately Held**
SIC: 5013 5063 Automotive batteries; electrical supplies

(G-7585)
TRI STATE TERMITE & PEST CTRL
1170 Corner Ketch Rd (19711-2324)
PHONE.................................302 239-0512
Don Klenotiz, *President*
Lori Christina, *Admin Sec*
EMP: 5
SALES (est): 413.3K **Privately Held**
SIC: 7342 Pest control in structures; pest control services

(G-7586)
TRI-STATE BIRD RESCUE RES INC
170 Possum Hollow Rd (19711-3910)
PHONE.................................302 737-9543
Michelle Carrera, *Manager*
Lisa Smith, *Exec Dir*
EMP: 20
SALES (est): 1.5MM **Privately Held**
WEB: www.tristatebird.org
SIC: 0752 Shelters, animal

(G-7587)
TRI-STATE GROUTING LLC
567 Walther Rd (19702-2903)
P.O. Box 99, Bear (19701-0099)
PHONE.................................302 286-0701
Mark H Schneider,
Bert Andrus,
EMP: 20 EST: 1977
SQ FT: 4,000
SALES (est): 2.7MM
SALES (corp-wide): 838MM **Publicly Held**
SIC: 1623 Sewer line construction
HQ: Aqua Resources, Inc.
   762 W Lancaster Ave
   Bryn Mawr PA 19010
   610 525-1400

(G-7588)
TRI-STATE HEALTH
266 S College Ave (19711-5235)
PHONE.................................302 368-2563
Muhammad A Niaz MD, *Owner*
Azhar Akhlaq, *Manager*
EMP: 4
SALES (est): 450K **Privately Held**
SIC: 8011 General & family practice, physician/surgeon

(G-7589)
TRI-STATE SEC & CONTRLS LLC
2860 Ogletown Rd 23 (19713-1857)
PHONE.................................302 299-2175
Marc Bobik, *Mng Member*
EMP: 13
SALES (est): 707.6K **Privately Held**
SIC: 1731 General electrical contractor

(G-7590)
TRICOMM SERVICES CORPORATION
604 Interchange Blvd (19711-3560)
PHONE.................................302 454-2975

2020 Harris Directory of Delaware Businesses

▲ = Import ▼=Export
◆ =Import/Export

Joe Kirkner, *Principal*
EMP: 9
SALES (est): 921.7K **Privately Held**
SIC: 1731 Cable television installation

(G-7591)
TRILOGY SALON AND DAY SPA INC
1200 Capitol Trl (19711-3924)
PHONE..................................302 292-3511
Randy Richardson, *President*
EMP: 30
SQ FT: 5,700
SALES (est): 942K **Privately Held**
SIC: 7231 Cosmetology & personal hygiene salons

(G-7592)
TRIM WASTE MANAGEMENT LLC (PA)
Also Called: Twm
667 Dawson Dr Ste C (19713-3437)
PHONE..................................302 738-2500
Kevin McCloskey, *Mng Member*
EMP: 2
SALES (est): 415.3K **Privately Held**
SIC: 8711 3599 Engineering services; custom machinery

(G-7593)
TRIMBLE NAVIGATION LIMITED
Also Called: Eastern Percision
107c Albe Dr Ste C (19702-1336)
PHONE..................................302 368-2434
Gay Carter, *Manager*
EMP: 5
SALES (corp-wide): 3.1B **Publicly Held**
WEB: www.trimble.com
SIC: 5049 Surveyors' instruments
PA: Trimble Inc.
935 Stewart Dr
Sunnyvale CA 94085
408 481-8000

(G-7594)
TRINITY HOME HEALTH CARE CORP (PA)
1400 Peoples Plz Ste 215 (19702-5708)
PHONE..................................302 838-2710
Colleen Curtis, *CEO*
EMP: 28
SQ FT: 1,383
SALES (est): 825K **Privately Held**
SIC: 8082 Home health care services

(G-7595)
TRINITY HOME HEALTH CARE LLC
1400 Peoples Plz Ste 215 (19702-5708)
PHONE..................................410 620-9366
Colleen Curtis, *CEO*
EMP: 7
SQ FT: 1,383
SALES (est): 97K **Privately Held**
SIC: 8082 Home health care services
PA: Trinity Home Health Care Corp.
1400 Peoples Plz Ste 215
Newark DE 19702

(G-7596)
TROY GRANITE INC (PA)
711 Interchange Blvd (19711-3594)
PHONE..................................302 292-1750
Mustafa Tuncer, *President*
▲ **EMP:** 20
SALES (est): 3MM **Privately Held**
SIC: 1799 Counter top installation

(G-7597)
TRUE RELIGION APPAREL INC
132 Christiana Mall (19702-3202)
PHONE..................................302 894-9425
EMP: 5
SALES (corp-wide): 350MM **Privately Held**
SIC: 2369 2325 2339 Jeans: girls', children's & infants'; jeans: men's, youths' & boys'; jeans: women's, misses' & juniors'
HQ: True Religion Apparel, Inc.
1888 Rosecrans Ave # 1000
Manhattan Beach CA 90266
323 266-3072

(G-7598)
TS AIR ENTERPRISES LLC
700 Barksdale Rd Ste 3 (19711-3260)
PHONE..................................302 533-7458
Timothy Hamb, *President*
EMP: 1 **EST:** 2009
SALES (est): 137K **Privately Held**
SIC: 3564 Air purification equipment

(G-7599)
TT LUXURY GROUP LLC
Also Called: Tickle Toes
46 Vansant Rd (19711-4839)
PHONE..................................732 242-9795
Nicole Fiorina, *Mng Member*
EMP: 9
SALES (est): 790.5K **Privately Held**
SIC: 2361 Dresses: girls', children's & infants'

(G-7600)
TURF PRO INC
103 Sandy Dr Ste 100 (19713-1193)
PHONE..................................302 218-3530
John K Heitzender, *President*
EMP: 29
SALES (est): 1.1MM **Privately Held**
SIC: 0782 Landscape contractors

(G-7601)
TURQUOISE SHOP INC
Also Called: Janvier Jewelers
543 Christiana Mall (19702-3209)
PHONE..................................302 366-7448
Edward Janvier, *President*
Harvey Lee Janvier, *Treasurer*
EMP: 15
SQ FT: 960
SALES (est): 1.9MM **Privately Held**
WEB: www.turquoiseshop.com
SIC: 5944 7631 Jewelry, precious stones & precious metals; clocks; watches; jewelry repair services

(G-7602)
TUSI AND SON MECHANICAL INC
675a Dawson Dr (19713-3411)
PHONE..................................302 731-8228
Vincent Tusi, *President*
EMP: 5
SALES (est): 623.4K **Privately Held**
SIC: 1711 Heating & air conditioning contractors; refrigeration contractor

(G-7603)
TYLAUR INC
Also Called: Signs By Tomorrow
2659 Kirkwood Hwy (19711-7242)
PHONE..................................302 894-9330
Sharon L Rizzo, *President*
Clement Rizzo, *Admin Sec*
EMP: 5 **EST:** 2001
SQ FT: 1,200
SALES: 417K **Privately Held**
SIC: 3993 Signs & advertising specialties

(G-7604)
U A G INC
841 Old Baltimore Pike (19702-1317)
PHONE..................................302 731-2747
Michael D Lattomus, *President*
EMP: 14
SALES (est): 756.4K **Privately Held**
SIC: 7536 Automotive glass replacement shops

(G-7605)
U HAUL COMPANY INDEPENDENT DLR
Also Called: U-Haul
8 Mill Park Ct (19713-1986)
PHONE..................................302 369-8230
Greg Keresty, *Owner*
EMP: 5
SALES (est): 149.3K **Privately Held**
SIC: 7513 Truck rental & leasing, no drivers

(G-7606)
UAW-GM LEGAL SERVICES PLAN
Also Called: U A W Legal Services
4051 Ogletown Rd Ste 201 (19713-3101)
PHONE..................................302 562-8212
Sandra E Messick, *Manager*
EMP: 13
SALES (corp-wide): 24.6MM **Privately Held**
SIC: 8111 Legal aid service
PA: Uaw-Gm Legal Services Plan
200 Walker St
Detroit MI

(G-7607)
UDEL HOLDINGS LLC
91 Thorn Ln Ofc 2 (19711-4446)
PHONE..................................877 833-8737
EMP: 49
SALES (est): 2.3MM **Privately Held**
SIC: 6513 Apartment building operators
HQ: Century Campus Housing Management Lp
1001 Fannin St Ste 1350
Houston TX 77002
713 871-5100

(G-7608)
UMA CHATTERJEE MD
620 Stanton Christiana Rd (19713-2133)
PHONE..................................302 995-7500
Uma Chatterjee MD, *Owner*
EMP: 4
SALES (est): 311K **Privately Held**
SIC: 8011 Gynecologist

(G-7609)
UMBRELLA TRANSPORT GROUP INC
39 Glennwood Dr (19702-3769)
PHONE..................................301 919-1623
Virginia Navarro, *President*
William Hawkins, *COO*
EMP: 6
SALES (est): 515.1K **Privately Held**
SIC: 4731 Brokers, shipping

(G-7610)
UNDER WHISTLE
49 N Bellwoode Dr (19702-3409)
PHONE..................................302 250-8400
EMP: 1
SALES (est): 75.4K **Privately Held**
SIC: 3999 Whistles

(G-7611)
UNITED AUTO WORKERS LOCAL 435
698 Old Baltimore Pike (19702-1312)
PHONE..................................302 995-6001
Dave Myers, *Principal*
James G Brown, *Admin Sec*
William Wosik, *Admin Sec*
EMP: 10
SALES (est): 211.4K **Privately Held**
SIC: 8631 Collective bargaining unit

(G-7612)
UNITED BROKERAGE PACKAGING
110 Executive Dr Ste 5 (19702-3352)
PHONE..................................302 294-6782
EMP: 4 **EST:** 2015
SALES (est): 190.3K **Privately Held**
SIC: 6282 Investment advisory service

(G-7613)
UNITED COCOA PROCESSOR INC
Also Called: Ucp
701 Pencader Dr Ste F (19702-3360)
PHONE..................................302 731-0825
Peter Liu, *CEO*
Jonathan Liu, *President*
James Liu, *Vice Pres*
Adriana Cherundolo, *Human Res Mgr*
◆ **EMP:** 42
SQ FT: 93,000
SALES (est): 9.2MM **Privately Held**
WEB: www.ucpco.com
SIC: 2066 Chocolate; cocoa butter

(G-7614)
UNITED PARCEL SERVICE INC
Also Called: UPS
211 Lake Dr (19702-3320)
PHONE..................................302 453-7462
EMP: 8
SALES (corp-wide): 71.8B **Publicly Held**
SIC: 4512 Air cargo carrier, scheduled
HQ: United Parcel Service, Inc.
55 Glenlake Pkwy
Atlanta GA 30328
404 828-6000

(G-7615)
UNITED STATES MLE MNS HAIR CRE (PA)
Also Called: American Male Hair Care
169 E Main St (19711-7313)
PHONE..................................302 368-1273
Cris Arnold, *Owner*
EMP: 4
SALES (est): 304.5K **Privately Held**
SIC: 7241 Barber shops

(G-7616)
UNITED TELE WKRS LOCAL 13101
Also Called: United Tele Wkrs Delaware-C W
350 Gooding Dr (19702-1906)
PHONE..................................302 737-0400
Walter Speakman, *President*
Sandy Taylor, *Admin Sec*
EMP: 6
SALES (est): 19.7K **Privately Held**
SIC: 8631 8641 Labor union; civic social & fraternal associations

(G-7617)
UNIVERSITY GARDEN ASSOCIATES
Also Called: University Garden Apts
281 Beverly Rd Apt H5 (19711-7926)
PHONE..................................302 368-3823
Ralph V Watts, *Owner*
James Watts, *Co-Owner*
EMP: 8
SALES (est): 374.2K **Privately Held**
SIC: 6513 Apartment hotel operation

(G-7618)
UNIVERSITY OF DE PRINTING
222 Suth Chapel St Rm 124 (19702)
PHONE..................................302 831-2153
Rodney Brown, *Manager*
EMP: 20
SALES: 3MM **Privately Held**
SIC: 7389 Printing broker

(G-7619)
UNIVERSITY OF DELAWARE
Also Called: Protermant Services
222 S Chapel St Rm 133 (19716-5600)
PHONE..................................302 831-2792
John Brennan, *Pub Rel Dir*
George Walueff, *Office Mgr*
Joe Lapalombara, *Program Mgr*
Melody Phillips, *Admin Asst*
EMP: 15
SALES (corp-wide): 1B **Privately Held**
WEB: www.udel.edu
SIC: 7299 8221 Visa procurement service; university
PA: University Of Delaware
220 Hullihen Hall
Newark DE 19716
302 831-2107

(G-7620)
UNIVERSITY OF DELAWARE
Also Called: Bartol Research Institute
104 The Grn Rm 217 (19716-2593)
PHONE..................................302 831-4811
Stuart Pittel, *Director*
EMP: 35
SALES (corp-wide): 1B **Privately Held**
WEB: www.udel.edu
SIC: 8733 8221 Noncommercial research organizations; university
PA: University Of Delaware
220 Hullihen Hall
Newark DE 19716
302 831-2107

(G-7621)
UNIVERSITY OF DELAWARE
Also Called: Computing & Network Service
192 S Chapel St (19716-4320)
PHONE..................................302 831-6041
Susan J Foster, *Vice Pres*
Walt Babich, *Instructor*
EMP: 150

Newark - New Castle County (G-7622)   GEOGRAPHIC SECTION

SALES (corp-wide): 1B Privately Held
WEB: www.udel.edu
SIC: 7379 8221 Computer related maintenance services; university
PA: University Of Delaware
  220 Hullihen Hall
  Newark DE 19716
  302 831-2107

(G-7622)
UNIVERSITY OF DELAWARE
Also Called: Univ of Del
363 New London Rd (19711-7044)
PHONE..................302 831-2501
Marvin Friger, Manager
EMP: 50
SALES (corp-wide): 1B Privately Held
WEB: www.udel.edu
SIC: 8322 8221 Multi-service center; university
PA: University Of Delaware
  220 Hullihen Hall
  Newark DE 19716
  302 831-2107

(G-7623)
UNIVERSITY OF DELAWARE
Also Called: Accounting Dept
42 Amstel Ave Rm 206 (19716-2799)
PHONE..................302 831-2961
Virgil E Alexander, Research
Paul Laux, Finance
Jeff Gillestie, Administration
EMP: 29
SALES (corp-wide): 1B Privately Held
WEB: www.udel.edu
SIC: 8721 8221 Accounting services, except auditing; university
PA: University Of Delaware
  220 Hullihen Hall
  Newark DE 19716
  302 831-2107

(G-7624)
UNIVERSITY OF DELAWARE
Also Called: Delaware Geological Survey
257 Academy St (19716-7500)
PHONE..................302 831-2833
David Wunsch, Director
Tatyana Polenova, Professor
EMP: 17
SALES (corp-wide): 1B Privately Held
WEB: www.udel.edu
SIC: 8733 8221 Research institute; university
PA: University Of Delaware
  220 Hullihen Hall
  Newark DE 19716
  302 831-2107

(G-7625)
UNIVERSITY OF DELAWARE
200 Academy St (19716-5899)
PHONE..................302 831-1141
Bob Stozek, Assoc VP
Zach Platsis, Manager
Ken Grablewski, Director
EMP: 125
SALES (corp-wide): 1B Privately Held
WEB: www.udel.edu
SIC: 7349 8221 Building maintenance services; university
PA: University Of Delaware
  220 Hullihen Hall
  Newark DE 19716
  302 831-2107

(G-7626)
UNIVERSITY OF DELAWARE
Also Called: Research Office Vice Provost
162 The Grn Rm 210 (19716-0099)
PHONE..................302 831-2136
Mark Barteau, Director
William Wentz, Officer
Elizabeth Higley, Training Spec
Arthi Jayaraman, Assoc Prof
EMP: 25
SALES (corp-wide): 1B Privately Held
WEB: www.udel.edu
SIC: 8732 8221 Educational research; university
PA: University Of Delaware
  220 Hullihen Hall
  Newark DE 19716
  302 831-2107

(G-7627)
UNIVERSITY OF DELAWARE
Center For Composite Materials
101 Academy St Ste 202 (19716-3143)
PHONE..................302 831-8149
John W Gillespie Jr, Director
EMP: 300
SALES (corp-wide): 1B Privately Held
WEB: www.udel.edu
SIC: 8731 8221 Natural resource research; university
PA: University Of Delaware
  220 Hullihen Hall
  Newark DE 19716
  302 831-2107

(G-7628)
UNIVERSITY OF DELAWARE
Also Called: Center For Composite Material
7 Mcmillan Way Ste 3 (19713-3459)
PHONE..................302 831-6300
John Gillespie, Branch Mgr
EMP: 80
SALES (corp-wide): 1B Privately Held
SIC: 8731 8221 Natural resource research; university
PA: University Of Delaware
  220 Hullihen Hall
  Newark DE 19716
  302 831-2107

(G-7629)
UNIVERSITY OF DELAWARE
Also Called: Dept of Anthropology
135 Monroe Hl (19716)
PHONE..................302 831-2802
Karen Rosenberg, Ch of Bd
EMP: 15
SALES (corp-wide): 1B Privately Held
WEB: www.udel.edu
SIC: 8221 8733 University; archeological expeditions
PA: University Of Delaware
  220 Hullihen Hall
  Newark DE 19716
  302 831-2107

(G-7630)
UNIVERSITY VILLAGE APARTMENT
Also Called: Kushner Companies
207 Mederia Cir (19702-1544)
PHONE..................302 731-5972
Andrea Rich, Manager
EMP: 4
SALES (est): 601.1K
SALES (corp-wide): 214.2MM Privately Held
WEB: www.kushnercompanies.com
SIC: 6513 Apartment building operators
PA: The Kushner Companies Inc
  666 5th Ave Fl 15
  New York NY 10103
  212 527-5000

(G-7631)
UPS SUPPLY CHAIN SOLUTIONS INC
220 Lake Dr Ste 1 (19702-3353)
PHONE..................302 631-5259
Addison Paul, Branch Mgr
EMP: 10
SALES (corp-wide): 71.8B Publicly Held
SIC: 4731 Freight transportation arrangement
HQ: Ups Supply Chain Solutions, Inc.
  12380 Morris Rd
  Alpharetta GA 30005
  800 742-5727

(G-7632)
URGENT AMBULANCE SERVICE INC (PA)
8 Tyler Way (19713-3449)
PHONE..................302 454-1821
Edward L Mac Chione, President
Dan Macchione, Exec VP
EMP: 32
SQ FT: 3,500
SALES (est): 5.1MM Privately Held
SIC: 4119 Ambulance service

(G-7633)
URGENT AMBULANCE SERVICE INC
Also Called: Urgent Ambulance Svc Newark
8 Tyler Way (19713-3449)
PHONE..................302 454-1821
Dan Macchoine, Manager
EMP: 25
SALES (corp-wide): 5.1MM Privately Held
SIC: 4119 Ambulance service
PA: Urgent Ambulance Service, Inc.
  8 Tyler Way
  Newark DE 19713
  302 454-1821

(G-7634)
URS GROUP INC
4051 Ogletown Rd Ste 300 (19713-3101)
PHONE..................302 731-7824
Lee Anne Simmar, Manager
EMP: 65
SALES (corp-wide): 20.1B Publicly Held
SIC: 8711 Consulting engineer
HQ: Urs Group, Inc.
  300 S Grand Ave Ste 1100
  Los Angeles CA 90071
  213 593-8000

(G-7635)
V & A TRUCKING LLC
10 Malvern Ave (19713-2603)
PHONE..................302 276-5548
Victor Hernandez, Mng Member
EMP: 4
SALES (est): 200.3K Privately Held
SIC: 4212 Local trucking, without storage

(G-7636)
V E GUERRAZZI INC
122 Sandy Dr Ste D (19713-1188)
PHONE..................302 369-5557
Vernon Guerrazi, President
EMP: 10 EST: 1998
SQ FT: 3,000
SALES (est): 1.5MM Privately Held
SIC: 3444 Sheet metalwork

(G-7637)
V F W POST HOME
Also Called: VFW Post 475
100 Veterans Dr (19711-4515)
PHONE..................302 366-8438
William Schaen, Vice Pres
EMP: 7
SQ FT: 5,500
SALES: 148.4K Privately Held
SIC: 8641 Veterans' organization

(G-7638)
VAL-TECH INC
Also Called: V T I
24 Mcmillan Way (19713-3492)
PHONE..................302 738-0500
Roger Beam, President
Joanna Beam, Vice Pres
Susan Haupt, Vice Pres
EMP: 20 EST: 1970
SQ FT: 15,000
SALES (est): 3.5MM Privately Held
WEB: www.vt-inc.com
SIC: 3625 3679 3822 Control equipment, electric; electronic switches; auto controls regulating residntl & coml environmt & applncs

(G-7639)
VALASSIS DIRECT MAIL INC
300 Mcintire Dr (19711-1800)
PHONE..................302 861-3567
Mark Wise, Director
EMP: 125 Privately Held
WEB: www.advo.com
SIC: 7331 Direct mail advertising services
HQ: Valassis Direct Mail, Inc.
  235 Great Pond Dr
  Windsor CT 06095
  800 437-0479

(G-7640)
VALCO ENTERPRISES LLC
4142 Ogletown Stanton Rd (19713-4169)
PHONE..................514 938-8474
Calus Brueckner, Mng Member
Gabriel Desjardins, Manager

▲ EMP: 4
SALES (est): 1.1MM Privately Held
SIC: 5141 Food brokers

(G-7641)
VALENTINA LIQUORS
430 Old Baltimore Pike (19702-8410)
PHONE..................302 368-3264
Dean Grisco, Owner
EMP: 8
SALES (est): 398.6K Privately Held
SIC: 5149 Soft drinks

(G-7642)
VALLEY STREAM VILLAGE APTS
500 Valley Stream Dr (19702-2934)
PHONE..................302 733-0844
Luis Capano, Owner
Doreen Piacitelli, General Mgr
EMP: 4
SALES (est): 373K Privately Held
SIC: 6531 Real estate brokers & agents

(G-7643)
VANCE A FUNK III
273 E Main St Ste 100 (19711-7331)
PHONE..................302 368-2561
Vance A Funk III, Owner
EMP: 6
SALES (est): 569.7K Privately Held
WEB: www.vancefunk.com
SIC: 8111 General practice attorney, lawyer

(G-7644)
VAPE ESCAPE
1834 Capitol Trl (19711-5722)
PHONE..................302 737-8273
Terrence Gail, General Mgr
EMP: 4
SALES (est): 249K Privately Held
SIC: 5194 Smokeless tobacco

(G-7645)
VASCULAR SPECIALISTS DEL PA
1 Centurian Dr Ste 307 (19713-2127)
PHONE..................302 733-5700
Rhonda Disabatino, Principal
EMP: 6
SALES (est): 392.1K Privately Held
SIC: 8011 Cardiologist & cardio-vascular specialist

(G-7646)
VASSALLO MICHAEL ELEC CONTR
4 Mill Park Ct (19713-1901)
PHONE..................302 455-9405
Michael Vassallo, President
Roberta A Vassallo, Corp Secy
EMP: 13
SQ FT: 3,964
SALES (est): 1.3MM Privately Held
SIC: 1731 General electrical contractor

(G-7647)
VCA ANIMAL HOSPITALS INC
Also Called: VCA Glasglow
650 Peoples Plz (19702-5600)
PHONE..................302 834-1118
Robert Flanagan, Owner
EMP: 7
SALES (est): 249.3K
SALES (corp-wide): 37.6B Privately Held
WEB: www.vcawoodlands.com
SIC: 0742 Veterinarian, animal specialties
HQ: Vca Inc.
  12401 W Olympic Blvd
  Los Angeles CA 90064
  310 571-6500

(G-7648)
VCA INC
1501 Kirkwood Hwy (19711-5715)
PHONE..................302 737-1098
Heather Pappas, Office Mgr
Linda Simione, Manager
Kim Herrman, Director
EMP: 24

GEOGRAPHIC SECTION

Newark - New Castle County (G-7680)

SALES (corp-wide): 37.6B **Privately Held**
WEB: www.vcawoodlands.com
SIC: 0742 Veterinarian, animal specialties; animal hospital services, pets & other animal specialties
HQ: Vca Inc.
12401 W Olympic Blvd
Los Angeles CA 90064
310 571-6500

(G-7649)
VELO AMIS
24 Nightingale Cir (19711-3776)
PHONE.................................302 757-2783
EMP: 6 EST: 2017
SALES (est): 126.7K **Privately Held**
SIC: 7997 Membership sports & recreation clubs

(G-7650)
VERA BRADLEY DESIGNS INC
510 Christiana Mall (19702-3210)
PHONE.................................302 733-0880
Vera Bradley, *Branch Mgr*
EMP: 4
SALES (corp-wide): 416.1MM **Publicly Held**
SIC: 7389 Design services
HQ: Vera Bradley Designs, Inc.
12420 Stonebridge Rd
Roanoke IN 46783
260 482-4673

(G-7651)
VERIZON WIRELESS INC
1209 Churchmans Rd (19713-2149)
PHONE.................................302 737-5028
Ramsey Moorman, *Manager*
EMP: 4
SALES (corp-wide): 130.8B **Publicly Held**
WEB: www.verizonwireless.com
SIC: 5999 4813 4812 Telephone & communication equipment; telephone communication, except radio; cellular telephone services
HQ: Verizon Wireless, Inc.
1 Verizon Way
Basking Ridge NJ 07920

(G-7652)
VERSATILE IMPEX INC
Also Called: American Sports
74 Albe Dr Ste 3 (19702-1350)
PHONE.................................302 369-9480
Mohammed A Iqbal, *President*
Michael Iqbal, *Vice Pres*
▲ EMP: 5
SALES (est): 815.3K **Privately Held**
WEB: www.americansports.com
SIC: 5091 Sporting & recreation goods

(G-7653)
VERSITRON INC
83 Albe Dr Ste C (19702-1374)
PHONE.................................302 894-0699
Richard Tull, *President*
Nadine Tull, *Corp Secy*
Greg Massott, *Sales Mgr*
Mark Legutko, *Graphic Designe*
EMP: 75
SQ FT: 7,500
SALES (est): 13.4MM **Privately Held**
WEB: www.versitron.com
SIC: 3661 3669 Fiber optics communications equipment; visual communication systems

(G-7654)
VESTA WASH LLC
146 Woodland Rd (19702-1474)
PHONE.................................302 559-7533
Timothy Tim, *Mng Member*
EMP: 5 EST: 2013
SALES (est): 500K **Privately Held**
SIC: 7699 Cleaning services

(G-7655)
VETCON INDUSTRIES LLC
2035 Sunset Lake Rd B2 (19702-2600)
PHONE.................................850 207-6723
Michael Blakeslee, *Principal*
Phillip Warner,
EMP: 1
SALES (est): 39.6K **Privately Held**
SIC: 3999 Manufacturing industries

(G-7656)
VICTOR COLBERT CONSTRUCTION
1612 Pulaski Hwy (19702-4105)
PHONE.................................302 834-1174
Victor Colbert, *Owner*
EMP: 20
SALES (est): 775.8K **Privately Held**
SIC: 1771 Blacktop (asphalt) work

(G-7657)
VICTOR COLBERT CONSTRUCTION
723 Old Baltimore Pike (19702-1316)
PHONE.................................302 368-7270
Victor Colbert, *Owner*
EMP: 21
SALES (est): 2MM **Privately Held**
SIC: 1771 Concrete work

(G-7658)
VILLAGE WINDHOVER APARTMENTS
Also Called: Village Wndhver Rent Aprtments
104 Sandburg Pl (19702-4426)
PHONE.................................302 834-1168
Paul Burger, *Owner*
Carolyn Esterling, *Manager*
EMP: 12
SALES (est): 795.3K **Privately Held**
SIC: 6513 Apartment building operators

(G-7659)
VINCES SPORTS CENTER INC
14 Gender Rd (19713-2899)
PHONE.................................302 738-4859
Vince Santucci, *President*
EMP: 5
SQ FT: 16,800
SALES (est): 370K **Privately Held**
SIC: 7999 7992 Miniature golf course operation; baseball batting cage; public golf courses

(G-7660)
VIRION THERAPEUTICS LLC
7 Creek Bend Ct (19711-3763)
PHONE.................................800 841-9303
Bernard Rudnick, *Principal*
Andrew Luber, *Principal*
Neal Murakami, *Principal*
EMP: 4
SALES (est): 92.1K **Privately Held**
SIC: 7389

(G-7661)
VITAS HEALTHCARE CORPORATION
100 Cmmrce Dr Chrstina (19713)
PHONE.................................302 451-4000
Hugh Westbrook, *Branch Mgr*
Debra Vermette, *Director*
EMP: 95
SALES (corp-wide): 1.7B **Publicly Held**
WEB: www.vitasinnovativehospicecare.com
SIC: 8082 Home health care services
HQ: Vitas Healthcare Corporation
201 S Biscayne Blvd # 400
Miami FL 33131
305 374-4143

(G-7662)
VLS IT CONSULTING INC
260 Chapman Rd Ste 104a (19702-5410)
PHONE.................................302 368-5656
Lilma Jagnanan, *President*
EMP: 12
SALES (est): 1.6MM **Privately Held**
SIC: 7379

(G-7663)
VNA OF DELAWARE
Also Called: Christiana High Sch Wellness
190 Salem Church Rd (19713-2938)
PHONE.................................302 454-5422
Lynn Jones, *Director*
EMP: 6 EST: 2000
SALES (est): 127.7K **Privately Held**
SIC: 8082 Home health care services

(G-7664)
VOLTVAULT INC
134 Sandy Dr (19713-1147)
PHONE.................................302 981-5339
Ken Laubsch, *President*
Brian Waibel, *Vice Pres*
EMP: 4
SALES (est): 100K **Privately Held**
SIC: 3629 Electrical industrial apparatus

(G-7665)
VOYYP INC
2035 Sunset Lake Rd B2 (19702-2600)
PHONE.................................833 342-5667
EMP: 4
SALES (est): 100K **Privately Held**
SIC: 4812 Cellular telephone services

(G-7666)
VP RACING FUELS INC
16 Brookhill Dr (19702-1301)
PHONE.................................302 368-1500
James J Kelly, *Branch Mgr*
EMP: 8 **Privately Held**
SIC: 5172 Lubricating oils & greases
HQ: Vp Racing Fuels, Inc
7124 Richter Rd
Elmendorf TX 78112
210 635-7744

(G-7667)
W B MASON CO INC
100 Interchange Blvd (19711-3549)
PHONE.................................888 926-2766
Sara Jester, *President*
EMP: 124
SALES (corp-wide): 773MM **Privately Held**
SIC: 5712 2752 Office furniture; commercial printing, lithographic
PA: W. B. Mason Co., Inc.
59 Center St
Brockton MA 02301
781 794-8800

(G-7668)
W C UNGERER INSURANCE AGENCY
124 Autumn Horseshoe (19702-2397)
PHONE.................................302 368-8505
William Ungerer, *Owner*
EMP: 4
SALES (est): 352K **Privately Held**
SIC: 6411 Insurance agents

(G-7669)
W F CONSTRUCTION INC
74 Albe Dr Ste 8 (19702-1350)
P.O. Box 9817 (19714-4917)
PHONE.................................302 420-6747
William W Finch Jr, *President*
EMP: 4
SALES (est): 200K **Privately Held**
SIC: 1791 Structural steel erection

(G-7670)
W GIFFORD INC
807 Chesapeake Ct (19702-4825)
PHONE.................................302 420-6112
Warren Gifford, *Principal*
EMP: 4 EST: 2012
SALES (est): 411.6K **Privately Held**
SIC: 4212 Local trucking, without storage

(G-7671)
W L GORE & ASSOCIATES INC
555 Paper Mill Rd (19711-7513)
P.O. Box 9329 (19714-9329)
PHONE.................................410 506-7787
Fax: 410 996-8585
EMP: 74 EST: 1959
SALES (est): 8.3MM **Privately Held**
SIC: 3999 Mfg Misc Products

(G-7672)
W L GORE & ASSOCIATES INC
1901 Barksdale Rd (19711-2542)
PHONE.................................302 368-3700
Bill Schroder, *Sales Staff*
Jackie Boatwright, *Associate*
Rainer WA Rla Nder, *Associate*
EMP: 134

SALES (corp-wide): 3.4B **Privately Held**
WEB: www.gore.com
SIC: 3357 2821 5131 3841 Communication wire; polytetrafluoroethylene resins (teflon); synthetic fabrics; medical instruments & equipment, blood & bone work; industrial inorganic chemicals; medical & laboratory rubber sundries & related products
PA: W. L. Gore & Associates, Inc.
555 Paper Mill Rd
Newark DE 19711
302 738-4880

(G-7673)
WABISABI DESIGN INC
2035 Sunset Lake Rd B2 (19702-2600)
PHONE.................................650 451-8501
EMP: 8 EST: 2018
SALES: 300K **Privately Held**
SIC: 7371 Computer software development & applications

(G-7674)
WALLACE MONTGOMERY & ASSOC LLP
111 Continental Dr # 104 (19713-4306)
PHONE.................................302 510-1080
Matthew Allen, *Partner*
EMP: 39
SALES (corp-wide): 33.5MM **Privately Held**
SIC: 8711 Civil engineering; structural engineering
PA: Wallace Montgomery & Assoc Llp
10150 York Rd Ste 200
Hunt Valley MD
410 494-9093

(G-7675)
WALLFLOWERS PRESS
503 Windsor Dr (19711-7428)
PHONE.................................302 454-1411
Raymond Nichols, *Principal*
EMP: 1
SALES (est): 58.9K **Privately Held**
SIC: 2741 Miscellaneous publishing

(G-7676)
WARREN TRUSS CO (PA)
10 Aleph Dr (19702-1398)
PHONE.................................302 368-8566
Doug Warren, *President*
EMP: 11 EST: 1967
SQ FT: 18,000
SALES (est): 2.1MM **Privately Held**
SIC: 2439 2426 Trusses, wooden roof; hardwood dimension & flooring mills

(G-7677)
WARWICK FUNERAL HOME
121 W Park Pl (19711-4567)
PHONE.................................302 368-9500
Frank Mayer, *President*
EMP: 4
SQ FT: 3,000
SALES (est): 126.8K **Privately Held**
SIC: 7261 Funeral home

(G-7678)
WATER IS LIFE KENYA INC
314 E Main St Ste 2 (19711-7195)
PHONE.................................302 894-7335
Francis Tannian, *President*
Colleen Leithren, *Director*
Margaret J Tannian, *Officer*
EMP: 9
SALES: 278.6K **Privately Held**
SIC: 8699 Charitable organization

(G-7679)
WAY TO GO LED LIGHTING COMPANY
702 Interchange Blvd (19711-3595)
PHONE.................................844 312-4574
Limin Su, *President*
▲ EMP: 10
SALES: 1.1MM **Privately Held**
SIC: 3646 Commercial indusl & institutional electric lighting fixtures

(G-7680)
WEB APPLICATIONS INC
2604 Cindy Dr Ste 4 (19702-5180)
PHONE.................................302 834-0282

Newark - New Castle County (G-7681) — GEOGRAPHIC SECTION

Sunita Alladi, *President*
EMP: 4
SALES (est): 206.7K **Privately Held**
SIC: 7371 Computer software development

(G-7681)
WEGMAN BROS INC
2612 Ogletown Rd (19713-1824)
P.O. Box 7625 (19714-7625)
PHONE.....................302 738-4328
Danny Wegman, *CEO*
Chuck Wegman, *President*
Colleen Wegman, *President*
Ray Wegman, *Vice Pres*
Randall L Wegman, *Treasurer*
EMP: 10 EST: 1959
SALES (est): 1.4MM **Privately Held**
SIC: 1711 Plumbing contractors; warm air heating & air conditioning contractor

(G-7682)
WEITRON INC (PA)
801 Pencader Dr (19702-3337)
PHONE.....................800 398-3816
Deborah W Dayton, *President*
Ryan Gerber, *Controller*
◆ EMP: 47
SQ FT: 40,000
SALES: 50MM **Privately Held**
WEB: www.weitron.com
SIC: 5169 Gases, compressed & liquefied

(G-7683)
WELLS FARGO BANK NATIONAL ASSN
2624 Capitol Trl (19711-7252)
PHONE.....................302 631-1500
Phyllis Maher, *Manager*
EMP: 8
SALES (corp-wide): 101B **Publicly Held**
SIC: 6021 National commercial banks
HQ: Wells Fargo Bank, National Association
    101 N Phillips Ave
    Sioux Falls SD 57104
    605 575-6900

(G-7684)
WELLS FARGO BANK NATIONAL ASSN
2450 Glasgow Ave (19702-4700)
PHONE.....................302 832-6100
Sue Robinson, *Manager*
EMP: 11
SALES (corp-wide): 101B **Publicly Held**
SIC: 6021 National commercial banks
HQ: Wells Fargo Bank, National Association
    101 N Phillips Ave
    Sioux Falls SD 57104
    605 575-6900

(G-7685)
WELLS FARGO CLEARING SVCS LLC
Also Called: Wells Fargo Advisors
4 Creek Bend Ct (19711-3763)
PHONE.....................302 428-5969
EMP: 24
SALES (corp-wide): 101B **Publicly Held**
SIC: 6211 Security brokers & dealers
HQ: Wells Fargo Clearing Services, Llc
    1 N Jefferson Ave Fl 7
    Saint Louis MO 63103
    314 955-3000

(G-7686)
WELLS FARGO CLEARING SVCS LLC
Also Called: Wells Fargo Advisors
131 Continental Dr # 102 (19713-4305)
P.O. Box 8096 (19714-8096)
PHONE.....................302 731-2131
Paul Lu, *Senior VP*
Frank Alteri, *Systems Mgr*
EMP: 30
SALES (corp-wide): 101B **Publicly Held**
SIC: 6282 Investment advice
HQ: Wells Fargo Clearing Services, Llc
    1 N Jefferson Ave Fl 7
    Saint Louis MO 63103
    314 955-3000

(G-7687)
WESTOVER MANAGEMENT COMPANY LP
Also Called: Allandale Village Apartments
1 Allandale Dr (19713-3167)
PHONE.....................302 738-5775
Janet Yanneuzzi, *Manager*
EMP: 6
SALES (corp-wide): 12.6MM **Privately Held**
WEB: www.westovercompanies.com
SIC: 6513 Apartment hotel operation
PA: Westover Management Company, L.P.
    550 American Ave Ste 1
    King Of Prussia PA 19406
    610 494-6430

(G-7688)
WESTOVER MANAGEMENT COMPANY LP
Also Called: Glen Eagle Villiage
24 Sandalwood Dr Ofc 5 (19713-3541)
PHONE.....................302 731-1638
Michelle Carre, *Manager*
EMP: 10
SALES (corp-wide): 12.6MM **Privately Held**
WEB: www.westovercompanies.com
SIC: 6513 Apartment hotel operation
PA: Westover Management Company, L.P.
    550 American Ave Ste 1
    King Of Prussia PA 19406
    610 494-6430

(G-7689)
WESTSIDE FAMILY HEALTHCARE INC
27 Marrows Rd (19713-3701)
PHONE.....................302 455-0900
Janell Williams, *Manager*
Marsha V Reynolds, *Nurse Practr*
EMP: 17
SALES (corp-wide): 22.8MM **Privately Held**
SIC: 8011 8021 Clinic, operated by physicians; offices & clinics of dentists
PA: Westside Family Healthcare, Inc.
    300 Water St Ste 200
    Wilmington DE 19801
    302 656-8292

(G-7690)
WHET INDUSTRIES INC
560 Peoples Plz Ste 144 (19702-4798)
PHONE.....................302 236-2182
EMP: 1
SALES (est): 59.7K **Privately Held**
SIC: 3999 Manufacturing industries

(G-7691)
WHITE CLAY CREEK VTRINARY HOSP
Also Called: Spencer, Richard N Jr Vmd
107 Albe Dr Ste A (19702-1300)
PHONE.....................302 738-9611
Richard Spencer, *President*
EMP: 15
SALES (est): 527.3K **Privately Held**
SIC: 0742 Veterinarian, animal specialties; animal hospital services, pets & other animal specialties

(G-7692)
WHITE MINK BEAUTY SALON
330 College Sq (19711-8601)
PHONE.....................302 737-2081
Don Bettner, *Owner*
EMP: 13
SALES (est): 245.4K **Privately Held**
SIC: 7231 Beauty shops

(G-7693)
WHITING-TURNER CONTRACTING CO
131 Continental Dr # 404 (19713-4358)
PHONE.....................302 292-0676
Chris Mitchell, *Superintendent*
James Martini, *Senior VP*
Scott Breig, *Vice Pres*
Dan Maniscalco, *Project Mgr*
Jeff Chapin, *Manager*
EMP: 40
SALES (corp-wide): 8.6B **Privately Held**
WEB: www.whiting-turner.com
SIC: 1541 1542 Industrial buildings & warehouses; nonresidential construction
PA: The Whiting-Turner Contracting Company
    300 E Joppa Rd Ste 800
    Baltimore MD 21286
    410 821-1100

(G-7694)
WIK ASSOCIATES INC
10 Donaldson Dr (19713-1783)
PHONE.....................302 322-2558
Beverly J Wik, *President*
Marian Young, *Vice Pres*
EMP: 15
SQ FT: 12,000
SALES (est): 839.3K **Privately Held**
WEB: www.wik.net
SIC: 8748 Environmental consultant

(G-7695)
WILL C & WILL FUELS
1218 Grayrock Rd (19713-3325)
PHONE.....................302 366-1915
Clay Will, *Owner*
EMP: 4
SALES (est): 162.5K **Privately Held**
SIC: 1711 5983 Plumbing, heating, air-conditioning contractors; fuel oil dealers

(G-7696)
WILLIAM A ELLERT MD
Also Called: Center of Hope
620 Stanton Christiana Rd (19713-2133)
PHONE.....................302 369-9370
Melissa Tribuiani MD, *Director*
EMP: 8
SALES (est): 256.9K **Privately Held**
SIC: 8011 General & family practice, physician/surgeon

(G-7697)
WILLIAM B FUNK MD
665 Churchmans Rd (19702-1918)
PHONE.....................302 731-0900
William B Funk MD, *Owner*
EMP: 18
SALES (est): 1.3MM **Privately Held**
SIC: 8011 Physicians' office, including specialists

(G-7698)
WILLIAM GONCE
410 Smith Mill Rd (19711-4203)
PHONE.....................302 235-2400
William Gonce, *Principal*
EMP: 4
SALES (est): 185.4K **Privately Held**
SIC: 8021 Dentists' office

(G-7699)
WILLIAM P SMITH DDS
29 Meadowood Dr (19711-7202)
PHONE.....................302 737-7274
William P Smith DDS, *Owner*
EMP: 6
SALES (est): 239.6K **Privately Held**
SIC: 8021 Dentists' office

(G-7700)
WILLIAMS-SONOMA STORES INC
178 Christiana Mall (19702-3202)
PHONE.....................302 368-7707
Melissa Maletsky, *Manager*
EMP: 25
SALES (corp-wide): 5.6B **Publicly Held**
SIC: 5023 Decorative home furnishings & supplies
HQ: Williams-Sonoma Stores, Inc.
    3250 Van Ness Ave
    San Francisco CA 94109
    415 421-7900

(G-7701)
WILMINGTON CHRISTIANA COU
48 Geoffrey Dr (19713-3603)
PHONE.....................302 456-3800
Bill Holper, *Owner*
Jason Abbey, *Manager*
Debbie Sawicki, *Technology*
EMP: 11
SALES (est): 422.5K **Privately Held**
SIC: 7011 Hotel, franchised

(G-7702)
WILMINGTON METROPOLITAN AREA P
Also Called: Wilmapco
100 Discovery Blvd # 800 (19713-1325)
PHONE.....................302 737-6205
Tigist Zegeye, *Exec Dir*
Alexander Caft, *Director*
Charls L Backer, *Asst Director*
EMP: 10 EST: 1964
SALES (est): 953.2K **Privately Held**
WEB: www.wilmapco.org
SIC: 8748 Urban planning & consulting services

(G-7703)
WILMINGTON PHARMATECH CO LLC (PA)
229 Lake Dr (19702-3320)
PHONE.....................302 737-9916
Hui-Yin Harry LI, *President*
Carl Behrens, *Vice Pres*
Yong Chen, *Vice Pres*
Helen Hu, *Vice Pres*
Juliet Wu, *Marketing Mgr*
EMP: 25
SQ FT: 4,000
SALES (est): 4.6MM **Privately Held**
SIC: 8731 Biotechnical research, commercial

(G-7704)
WILMINGTON PSYCHIATRIC SVCS
71 Omega Dr D (19713-2063)
PHONE.....................302 999-8602
Ramnik K Singh, *Principal*
EMP: 4
SALES (est): 560.4K **Privately Held**
SIC: 8049 Clinical psychologist

(G-7705)
WILMINGTON SAVINGS FUND SOC
Also Called: Glasgo Plaza Shopping Center
2400 Peoples Plz (19702-5700)
PHONE.....................302 832-7842
Tracy Stegemeier, *Principal*
EMP: 8
SALES (corp-wide): 455.5MM **Publicly Held**
WEB: www.wsfsbank.com
SIC: 6022 State commercial banks
HQ: Wilmington Savings Fund Society
    500 Delaware Ave Ste 500 # 500
    Wilmington DE 19801
    302 792-6000

(G-7706)
WILMINGTON SAVINGS FUND SOC
500 Creek View Rd Ste 100 (19711-8549)
PHONE.....................302 571-7242
EMP: 4
SALES (corp-wide): 455.5MM **Publicly Held**
SIC: 6022 State commercial banks
HQ: Wilmington Savings Fund Society
    500 Delaware Ave Ste 500 # 500
    Wilmington DE 19801
    302 792-6000

(G-7707)
WILMINGTON SAVINGS FUND SOC
Also Called: University Plaza Branch
21 University Plz (19702)
PHONE.....................302 456-6404
Karen Harris, *Manager*
EMP: 10
SALES (corp-wide): 455.5MM **Publicly Held**
WEB: www.wsfsbank.com
SIC: 6022 State commercial banks
HQ: Wilmington Savings Fund Society
    500 Delaware Ave Ste 500 # 500
    Wilmington DE 19801
    302 792-6000

▲ = Import ▼=Export
◆ =Import/Export

GEOGRAPHIC SECTION

Newark - New Castle County (G-7741)

(G-7708)
WILMINGTON TRAP ASSOCIATION
Also Called: Wta
2828 Pulaski Hwy (19702-3913)
P.O. Box 203 (19715-0203)
PHONE..................302 834-9320
Allan Brown, *President*
William Trone, *Vice Pres*
Steve Hastings, *Admin Sec*
EMP: 25
SALES (est): 235.1K Privately Held
SIC: 8641 Recreation association

(G-7709)
WILSON CARE WILSON CO
5 William Davis Ct (19702-1160)
PHONE..................302 897-5059
Henry Wilson, *Principal*
EMP: 5
SALES (est): 115.1K Privately Held
SIC: 8351 Child day care services

(G-7710)
WINNER FORD OF NEWARK INC
303 E Cleveland Ave (19711-3793)
PHONE..................302 731-2415
Mike Hynansky, *President*
John Hynansky, *Vice Pres*
▼ EMP: 135
SQ FT: 24,000
SALES: 67.3MM Privately Held
SIC: 5511 7513 7515 5531 Automobiles, new & used; truck leasing, without drivers; passenger car leasing; automotive & home supply stores; used car dealers; automobiles & other motor vehicles

(G-7711)
WINNER GROUP INC
Also Called: Saturn
1801 Ogletown Rd (19711-5429)
PHONE..................302 292-8200
Wayne Weir, *Manager*
EMP: 27
SALES (corp-wide): 71.8MM Privately Held
SIC: 5012 7538 7515 5531 Automobiles; general automotive repair shops; passenger car leasing; automotive & home supply stores; automobiles, new & used
PA: Winner Group, Inc
911 N Tatnall St
Wilmington DE 19801
302 764-5900

(G-7712)
WIREGATEIT LLC
1 Latour Ln (19702-4543)
PHONE..................302 538-1304
Dan Akeme,
EMP: 2
SALES: 160K Privately Held
SIC: 3674 Integrated circuits, semiconductor networks, etc.

(G-7713)
WOLFE BACKHOE SERVICE
8 Springlake Dr (19711-6742)
PHONE..................302 737-2628
EMP: 1
SALES (est): 60K Privately Held
SIC: 3531 Backhoes

(G-7714)
WOMEN FIRST LLC
4745 Ogltn Stntn Rd # 106 (19713-2070)
PHONE..................302 368-3257
EMP: 4
SALES (est): 268.3K Privately Held
SIC: 8011 Gynecologist

(G-7715)
WOMENS IMAGING CENTER DELAWARE
46 Omega Dr Ste J24 (19713-2060)
PHONE..................302 738-9494
Steven Edell MD, *President*
EMP: 40
SALES (est): 697.6K Privately Held
SIC: 8099 Physical examination & testing services

(G-7716)
WOMENS WELLNESS CTR & MED SPA
1400 Peoples Plz Ste 301 (19702-5708)
PHONE..................302 643-2500
J Michael Knapp Do, *Owner*
EMP: 6
SALES: 14.1MM Privately Held
SIC: 8011 7231 Gynecologist; obstetrician; cosmetology & personal hygiene salons

(G-7717)
WOOD EXPRESSIONS INCORPORATED
2 Savoy Rd (19702-8610)
PHONE..................302 738-6189
Patricia A Veney, *Principal*
EMP: 2
SALES (est): 167.2K Privately Held
SIC: 2491 Wood products, creosoted

(G-7718)
WOODLYN PHYSICAL THERAPY INC
1082 Old Churchmans Rd # 101 (19713-2143)
PHONE..................610 583-1133
James Brennon, *President*
EMP: 7
SALES (est): 265K Privately Held
SIC: 8049 Physical therapist

(G-7719)
WOOLARD PROPERTIES
42 Vansant Rd (19711-4839)
PHONE..................302 731-1944
James Woolard, *Owner*
EMP: 4
SALES: 150K Privately Held
SIC: 6513 Apartment building operators

(G-7720)
WORLD CLASS PRODUCTS LLC
Also Called: World Class Supply
375 Wedgewood Rd (19711-2041)
PHONE..................302 737-1441
Reid Rowlands,
EMP: 3
SALES (est): 344.7K Privately Held
SIC: 3433 Room & wall heaters, including radiators

(G-7721)
WORLD WIDE COM CORPORATION
40 E Main St Ste 614 (19711-4639)
PHONE..................646 810-8624
EMP: 10
SALES (est): 337.2K Privately Held
SIC: 7389 Business Services

(G-7722)
WORLD WIDE TRADING BROKERS
606 Benham Ct (19711-6015)
PHONE..................302 368-7041
Nader Ramadan, *President*
EMP: 8
SALES: 100K Privately Held
SIC: 5084 5047 Industrial machinery & equipment; medical & hospital equipment

(G-7723)
WORLDS BEST MASSAGE THERAPY
412 Capitol Trl (19711-3865)
PHONE..................302 366-8777
Carrie Nelson, *Owner*
EMP: 5
SALES (est): 123.1K Privately Held
SIC: 8093 Rehabilitation center, outpatient treatment

(G-7724)
WOWDESK INC
2035 Sunset Lake Rd Be (19702-2600)
PHONE..................310 871-5251
Ahmed Soliman, *Principal*
EMP: 6
SALES (est): 120.8K Privately Held
SIC: 7389 Business services

(G-7725)
WUTAP LLC
6 Savoy Rd (19702-8610)
PHONE..................610 457-3559
Gurwinder Singh,
EMP: 1
SALES (est): 32.7K Privately Held
SIC: 7372 7371 7389 Application computer software; computer software development & applications;

(G-7726)
XROSSWATER USA LLC
40 E Main St Ste 118 (19711-4639)
PHONE..................917 310-1344
Malcolm Harrison, *Mng Member*
EMP: 2 EST: 2008
SQ FT: 5,000
SALES (est): 460.4K Privately Held
SIC: 3625 Marine & navy auxiliary controls

(G-7727)
YESLIBERIA INC
10 W Christina Pl (19702-2965)
PHONE..................302 898-6338
Zilabeteh Jallah, *President*
EMP: 1 EST: 2010
SALES: 12.1K Privately Held
SIC: 3999 Education aids, devices & supplies

(G-7728)
YOGO FACTORY
2610 Kirkwood Hwy (19711-7252)
PHONE..................302 266-4506
EMP: 6 EST: 2014
SALES (est): 79.4K Privately Held
SIC: 7999 5143 Yoga instruction; yogurt

(G-7729)
YOGURT CITY
157 E Main St (19711-7313)
PHONE..................302 292-8881
EMP: 5
SALES (est): 476.2K Privately Held
SIC: 5143 Yogurt

(G-7730)
YOKO TRADING
Also Called: Yokodanadotcom
4 Medill Ln (19711-6617)
PHONE..................302 353-4506
Dana Lewis, *Partner*
Yoko Lewis, *Partner*
▲ EMP: 4
SALES (est): 348K Privately Held
SIC: 5131 Textiles, woven

(G-7731)
YOROKOBI INC
2035 Sunset Lake Rd B2 (19702-2600)
PHONE..................323 591-3466
Martin Caetano, *Director*
EMP: 1
SALES (est): 32.7K Privately Held
SIC: 7372 Prepackaged software

(G-7732)
YOUVE BEEN FRAMED
211 E Cobblefield Ct (19713-2267)
PHONE..................302 366-8029
Richard Hanel, *Owner*
EMP: 4
SALES: 135K Privately Held
SIC: 7699 5999 Picture framing, custom; art dealers

(G-7733)
YWCA DELAWARE
153 E Chestnut Hill Rd # 102 (19713-4046)
PHONE..................302 224-4060
Frank Boyko, *Principal*
Robin Mandell, *CFO*
EMP: 10
SALES (corp-wide): 3.9MM Privately Held
SIC: 8641 7991 8351 7032 Youth organizations; physical fitness facilities; child day care services; youth camps; individual & family services
PA: Ywca Delaware
100 W 10th St Ste 515
Wilmington DE 19801
302 655-0039

(G-7734)
Z DATA INC
Also Called: Zdata Mt
40 E Main St Ste 610 (19711-4639)
PHONE..................302 566-5351
Dan Feldhusen, *President*
EMP: 5
SALES: 4.2MM
SALES (corp-wide): 161.4MM Privately Held
SIC: 7371 Custom computer programming services
PA: Atos Se
River Ouest
Bezons 95870
964 450-614

(G-7735)
Z DATA INC
40 E Main St 610 (19711-4639)
PHONE..................302 566-5351
Dan Feldhusen, *President*
Dan Began, *President*
EMP: 5 EST: 2011
SALES (est): 172.3K
SALES (corp-wide): 161.4MM Privately Held
SIC: 7371 7379 Computer software development & applications; computer related consulting services
HQ: Atos It Solutions And Services Inc.
4851 Regent Blvd
Irving TX 75063
682 978-8622

(G-7736)
ZABEL PLSTC&RECNSTRCTVE SURGRY
550 Stanton Christiana Rd (19713-2198)
PHONE..................302 996-6400
David Zabel, *Principal*
EMP: 5
SALES (est): 270K Privately Held
SIC: 8011 Surgeon

(G-7737)
ZACROS AMERICA INC
Also Called: Zacros America Hedwin Division
220 Lake Dr Ste 1 (19702-3353)
PHONE..................302 368-7354
Richard Broo, *President*
EMP: 200
SALES (est): 30.7MM Privately Held
SIC: 2671 Plastic film, coated or laminated for packaging
PA: Fujimori Kogyo Co., Ltd.
1-23-7, Nishishinjuku
Shinjuku-Ku TKY 160-0

(G-7738)
ZAX MOBILE LLC
152 W Main St (19711-3241)
PHONE..................302 261-3232
EMP: 5
SALES (est): 310K Privately Held
SIC: 7371 Custom Computer Programing

(G-7739)
ZEN HEALTH TECHNOLOGY INC
2035 Sunset Lake Rd B2 (19702-2600)
PHONE..................551 194-2345
Daniel Torres, *CEO*
EMP: 5
SALES (est): 104.7K Privately Held
SIC: 7389 Business services

(G-7740)
ZIGGYS INC
Also Called: Ziggy's Wood Floor Mechanics
885 New London Rd (19711-2111)
PHONE..................302 453-1285
Zigmund M Mielnikiewicz, *President*
Barbara Hearne, *Corp Secy*
EMP: 11
SALES: 769.3K Privately Held
WEB: www.ziggysinc.com
SIC: 1752 Wood floor installation & refinishing

(G-7741)
ZIRAS TECHNOLOGIES INC
260 Chapman Rd Ste 200 (19702-5491)
PHONE..................302 286-7303
Dharmendra Kalakota, *Principal*
Shiva Babu, *Business Anlyst*

Haritha Jaggabarapu, *Director*
Vikas Kumar, *Recruiter*
EMP: 10
SALES (est): 425.8K **Privately Held**
SIC: 7379 Computer related consulting services

(G-7742)
ZIZO TAXI CAB LLC
69 Northfield Rd (19713-2714)
PHONE 302 528-5663
Mahmoud Abdou, *Principal*
EMP: 6
SALES (est): 174.2K **Privately Held**
SIC: 4121 Taxicabs

(G-7743)
ZOGO INC
2035 Sunset Lake Rd (19702-2600)
PHONE 978 810-8895
David Neyhart, *Admin Sec*
EMP: 5
SALES (est): 104.7K **Privately Held**
SIC: 7389 Business services

Newport
New Castle County

(G-7744)
A-1 AIR CONDITIONING HEATING
Also Called: A-1 Air Cndtning Htg Refrigera
3 Gregg Ave (19804-3203)
PHONE 302 998-5634
William Hensel, *President*
Joan Hensel, *Vice Pres*
EMP: 4
SALES: 107.3K **Privately Held**
SIC: 1711 Warm air heating & air conditioning contractor

(G-7745)
AIR LQIDE ADVANCED SEPARATIONS
305 Water St (19804-2410)
PHONE 302 225-1100
EMP: 3
SALES (est): 123.2K **Privately Held**
SIC: 2813 Industrial gases

(G-7746)
CUTTING OF PRECISION CONCRETE
213 Maryland Ave (19804-3040)
PHONE 302 543-5833
Gary Tucker, *President*
EMP: 5 **EST:** 2011
SALES (est): 400K **Privately Held**
WEB: www.safesidewalks.com
SIC: 1771 Concrete work

(G-7747)
DIAMOND STATE HOME AUXILIARY
Also Called: VFW Post 2863
8 S Dupont Rd (19804-1323)
PHONE 302 652-9331
Paul Philipps, *President*
Allen Lynch, *President*
Mike Clouthier, *Manager*
EMP: 5
SALES (est): 210K **Privately Held**
SIC: 8641 Veterans' organization

(G-7748)
ELECTRO SOUND SYSTEMS INC
330 Water St Ste 108 (19804-2433)
PHONE 302 543-2292
Thomas Manchester, *CEO*
Sara Bristol, *Principal*
EMP: 10
SALES: 600K **Privately Held**
SIC: 7812 Motion picture & video production

(G-7749)
FB DOOR-DELAWARE LLC
330 Water St (19804-2433)
PHONE 302 995-1000
Stephen Freitas, *CEO*
Nicholas Stonerook, *CFO*

Adam Schultz, *Manager*
EMP: 10 **EST:** 2015
SALES (est): 370.5K
SALES (corp-wide): 13.2MM **Privately Held**
SIC: 1751 Garage door, installation or erection
PA: Foris Solutions Llc
  12131 Wormer
  Redford MI 48239
  269 492-4320

(G-7750)
HARVEY HANNA & ASSOCIATES INC
405 Marsh Ln Ste 1 (19804-2445)
PHONE 302 323-9300
E Thomas Harvey III, *President*
Michael Kinnard, *Vice Pres*
Ryan Kennedy, *Marketing Staff*
Bill Lower, *Director*
EMP: 7
SALES (est): 1.7MM **Privately Held**
SIC: 8742 Real estate consultant

(G-7751)
NATIONAL ASSN LTR CARRIERS
Also Called: N A L C
8 S Dupont Rd Fl 2 (19804-1323)
PHONE 302 652-2933
Bob Wilkerson, *Administration*
EMP: 8
SALES (corp-wide): 1B **Privately Held**
WEB: www.nalc.org
SIC: 8631 Labor union
PA: National Association Of Letter Carriers
  100 Indana Ave Nw Ste 709
  Washington DC 20001
  202 393-4695

(G-7752)
ROBERT B GREGG
301 S Dupont Rd (19804-1082)
PHONE 302 994-9300
Robert B Gregg, *Owner*
EMP: 9
SALES (est): 426K **Privately Held**
SIC: 8721 Accounting, auditing & bookkeeping

Ocean View
Sussex County

(G-7753)
ACADEMY EXPRESS
52 Atlantic Ave (19970-9180)
P.O. Box 400, Bethany Beach (19930-0400)
PHONE 302 537-4805
Arnold Brown, *Branch Mgr*
EMP: 4 **Privately Held**
WEB: www.newworldtours.com
SIC: 4131 Intercity & rural bus transportation
PA: Academy Express
  7920 Gainsford Ct
  Bristow VA 20136

(G-7754)
ADVANCED PROTECTION LLC
Also Called: Signature Alert
9 Briarcliffe Ct (19970-9013)
PHONE 302 539-6041
Andrea Barnes, *Administration*
EMP: 7 **EST:** 2009
SALES (est): 300.8K **Privately Held**
SIC: 7382 Security systems services

(G-7755)
ASHCRAFT MASONRY INC
30171 Jump Ln (19970-2787)
PHONE 302 539-4298
David S Ashcraft, *Owner*
James Ashcraft, *Vice Pres*
Regina Ashcraft, *Treasurer*
EMP: 10
SALES: 1MM **Privately Held**
SIC: 1741 Masonry & other stonework

(G-7756)
ATLANTIC RESOURCE MANAGEMENT
37448 Club House Rd (19970-3638)
P.O. Box 869 (19970-0869)
PHONE 302 539-2029
Lisa Wood, *Owner*
EMP: 10
SALES (est): 615.5K **Privately Held**
SIC: 8748 Environmental consultant

(G-7757)
BAY FOREST HOMEOWNERS ASSN
36115 Bay Forest Dr (19970-8017)
PHONE 302 537-6580
Anise Murray, *Principal*
EMP: 5
SALES (est): 201.7K **Privately Held**
SIC: 8641 Homeowners' association

(G-7758)
BAYSHORE INC
Also Called: Vine Creek Mobile Home Park
Rr 1 Box 252 (19970)
PHONE 302 539-7200
Elmer Cox, *President*
Brett Cox, *Treasurer*
EMP: 6
SALES (est): 288K **Privately Held**
SIC: 7033 6515 5271 4493 Campsite; mobile home site operators; mobile homes; marinas

(G-7759)
BAYSIDE AT BTHANY LKES CLBHUSE
38335 Old Mill Way (19970-3707)
PHONE 302 539-4378
Nancy Lowe, *Principal*
EMP: 10
SALES (est): 295.8K **Privately Held**
SIC: 7997 Membership sports & recreation clubs

(G-7760)
BAYSIDE GOLF LLC DBA BEAR TRAP
7 Clubhouse Dr (19970-3235)
P.O. Box 577 (19970-0577)
PHONE 302 537-5600
Jack Stone, *Manager*
EMP: 12
SALES (est): 519.7K **Privately Held**
SIC: 7992 Public golf courses

(G-7761)
BEAR TRAP PARTNERS
Also Called: Bear Trap Dunes
County Rte 84 (19970)
PHONE 302 537-5600
Joshua Freeman, *Partner*
Michael Moyer, *Superintendent*
Kelly Raab, *Accountant*
Chelsea Johnson, *Director*
EMP: 17
SALES (est): 879.5K **Privately Held**
SIC: 7992 Public golf courses

(G-7762)
BEAR TRAP SALES
21 Vil Grn Dr 101 (19970)
PHONE 302 541-5454
Marc Grimes, *Principal*
EMP: 6
SALES (est): 113.8K **Privately Held**
SIC: 7997 Golf club, membership

(G-7763)
BECKLEY ASSOCIATES LLC
32615 Widgeon Rd (19970-8104)
PHONE 301 943-7343
William Beckley, *President*
EMP: 4
SALES (est): 292.4K **Privately Held**
SIC: 8711 Engineering services

(G-7764)
BENJAMIN B SMITH BUILDERS INC
54 Central Ave (19970)
P.O. Box 762, Bethany Beach (19930-0762)
PHONE 302 537-1916

Benjamin B Smith, *President*
EMP: 5
SALES (est): 575.4K **Privately Held**
SIC: 1542 1521 Commercial & office buildings, renovation & repair; new construction, single-family houses

(G-7765)
BETHANY AUTO PARTS INC (PA)
Also Called: Carquest Auto Parts
13 Atlantic Ave (19970-9115)
P.O. Box 735, Bethany Beach (19930-0735)
PHONE 302 539-0555
John P Roberts, *President*
EMP: 4
SQ FT: 4,000
SALES (est): 1.1MM **Privately Held**
WEB: www.bethanyautoparts.com
SIC: 5013 5531 5088 Automotive supplies & parts; automotive parts; marine supplies

(G-7766)
BETHANY CLUB TENNIS LLC
Also Called: Bethany Tennis Ctr,
30078 Cedar Neck Rd (19970-2758)
PHONE 302 539-5111
EMP: 4
SQ FT: 2,200
SALES (est): 220K **Privately Held**
SIC: 7997 Tennis Club

(G-7767)
BIRELEY & KORTVELESY PA
53 Atlantic Ave Ste 2 (19970-9101)
P.O. Box 1660, Bethany Beach (19930-1660)
PHONE 302 539-0311
Rich Kortvelesy,
EMP: 4
SALES (est): 240K **Privately Held**
SIC: 8721 Certified public accountant

(G-7768)
BKI ENTERPRISES LLC
Also Called: Kalbrosky Associates
23 Willow Oak Ave (19970-3211)
PHONE 302 541-5317
Ira Kalbrosky, *President*
Beverly Kalbrosky, *Shareholder*
EMP: 4
SALES: 250K **Privately Held**
SIC: 7389 Lecture bureau;

(G-7769)
BOBS MARINE SERVICE INC
Routes 17 & 26 (19970)
P.O. Box 306 (19970-0306)
PHONE 302 539-3711
Helen Littleton, *President*
Tracy Littleton, *Manager*
Carl Littleton, *Administration*
Robert Littleton III, *Administration*
EMP: 18 **EST:** 1962
SQ FT: 8,600
SALES (est): 1.9MM **Privately Held**
WEB: www.bobsmarineservice.com
SIC: 7699 5551 Boat repair; boat dealers

(G-7770)
BRUCE MEARS DESIGNER-BUILDER
31370 Railway Rd 2 (19970-3443)
PHONE 302 539-2355
Bruce Mears, *President*
EMP: 13
SALES: 2MM **Privately Held**
WEB: www.brucemears.com
SIC: 1521 New construction, single-family houses

(G-7771)
C M L MANAGEMENT
Also Called: Layton Associates
35837 Atlantic Ave (19967-6908)
P.O. Box 987 (19970-0987)
PHONE 302 537-5599
Mearl Layton, *Principal*
EMP: 4
SALES (est): 272.3K **Privately Held**
SIC: 6531 Real estate agent, residential

GEOGRAPHIC SECTION
Ocean View - Sussex County (G-7803)

(G-7772)
CALVIN B TAYLOR BNKG BERLIN MD
50 Atlantic Ave (19970-9180)
PHONE................302 541-0500
Lynne A Nicodemus, *Site Mgr*
Sally Goodrich, *Manager*
EMP: 4
SALES (corp-wide): 18.9MM **Publicly Held**
WEB: www.taylorbank.com
SIC: 6022 State trust companies accepting deposits, commercial
HQ: Calvin B. Taylor Banking Co. Of Berlin, Maryland
24 N Main St
Berlin MD 21811
410 641-1700

(G-7773)
CAP TITLE OF DELAWARE LLC
29 Atlantic Ave Ste E (19970-9155)
PHONE................302 537-3788
Stephen P Norman,
EMP: 7
SALES (est): 301.2K **Privately Held**
SIC: 6531 Real estate listing services

(G-7774)
CARDIOVASCULAR CONSULTANTS OF
609 Atlantic Ave (19967)
PHONE................302 541-8138
EMP: 4 **EST:** 2011
SALES (est): 170K **Privately Held**
SIC: 8748 Business Consulting Services

(G-7775)
CARL M FREEMAN ASSOCIATES INC
21 Village Green Dr # 101 (19970-3251)
PHONE................302 436-3000
Josh Freeman, *President*
EMP: 90
SALES (est): 8.1MM **Privately Held**
WEB: www.carlmfreemancommunities.com
SIC: 1522 Residential construction

(G-7776)
CESN PARTNERS INC
Also Called: Charles Moon Plumbing & Htg
34541 Atlantic Ave (19970-3547)
PHONE................302 537-1814
Charles Moon, *CEO*
Sheila Neff, *President*
Karen Neff, *Manager*
EMP: 10
SALES (est): 859.6K **Privately Held**
SIC: 1711 Plumbing contractors

(G-7777)
CLARKSVILLE AUTO SERVICE CTR (PA)
Also Called: Clarksville Parts Plus
34461 Atlantic Ave (19970-3546)
PHONE................302 539-1700
David Hamm, *President*
Glenn Phillips, *Vice Pres*
Veronica Hamm, *Treasurer*
Kelly Phillips, *Admin Sec*
EMP: 31
SALES (est): 11.8MM **Privately Held**
SIC: 5531 7534 5013 Automotive tires; tire retreading & repair shops; automotive supplies & parts

(G-7778)
CLOVER FARMS MEATS
Also Called: A & D Enterprises
15 William Ave (19970-9293)
P.O. Box 142, Lehighton PA (18235-0142)
PHONE................610 428-8066
Steven Jzaortis, *President*
Charles Aberchinski, *President*
Robert Ronyack, *Vice Pres*
EMP: 6
SALES: 400K **Privately Held**
SIC: 0191 General farms, primarily crop

(G-7779)
COASTAL POINT
111 Atlantic Ave Ste 2 (19970-9166)
P.O. Box 1324 (19970-1324)
PHONE................302 539-1788
Susan Lyons, *Owner*
EMP: 15
SALES (est): 938.3K **Privately Held**
SIC: 2711 Newspapers, publishing & printing

(G-7780)
COASTAL PRINTING COMPANY
Shops Of Millville Rr 26 (19970)
P.O. Box 1340 (19970-1340)
PHONE................302 537-1700
Willis Fargo, *CEO*
Lance Fargo, *President*
EMP: 8
SQ FT: 9,000
SALES (est): 929.7K **Privately Held**
WEB: www.coastprint.com
SIC: 2752 Commercial printing, offset

(G-7781)
CRAZY LADYZ LLC
9 Atlantic Ave (19970-9115)
PHONE................302 541-4040
Louis Reardon, *Owner*
EMP: 12
SALES (est): 1MM **Privately Held**
SIC: 5137 Women's & children's clothing

(G-7782)
DANDY SIGNS
37384 Club House Rd (19970-3637)
PHONE................301 399-8746
Danny Davis, *Owner*
EMP: 7
SALES (est): 445.1K **Privately Held**
SIC: 3993 Signs & advertising specialties

(G-7783)
DENISE BEAM
Also Called: State Farm Insurance
112 Atlantic Ave (19970-9152)
PHONE................302 539-1900
Denise Beam, *Owner*
EMP: 5
SALES (est): 558.1K **Privately Held**
SIC: 6411 Insurance agents & brokers

(G-7784)
DODD HEALTH INNOVATION LLC
Also Called: Bdc-Healthit
31027 Scissorbill Rd (19970-8027)
PHONE................410 598-7266
John C Dodd, *President*
Phillip Cooke, *COO*
EMP: 8
SALES (est): 186.1K **Privately Held**
SIC: 7372 7373 Prepackaged software; computer integrated systems design

(G-7785)
FORTRESS HOME MAINTENANCE SERV
111 Atlantic Ave Ste 7 (19970-9166)
PHONE................302 539-3446
John Cullen, *Principal*
EMP: 5
SALES (est): 174.2K **Privately Held**
SIC: 7349 Building maintenance services

(G-7786)
FRATERNAL ORDER OF EAGLES BR
35083 Atlantic Ave (19970-3522)
P.O. Box 1074 (19970-1074)
PHONE................302 616-2935
Francis W Culbert, *President*
EMP: 7
SALES (corp-wide): 5.7MM **Privately Held**
SIC: 8641 Fraternal associations
PA: Fraternal Order Of Eagles, Bryan Aerie
2233 Of Bryan, Ohio
221 S Walnut St
Bryan OH 43506
419 636-7812

(G-7787)
FULTON BANK NATIONAL ASSN
Also Called: Fulton Financial Advisors
60 Atlantic Ave (19970)
PHONE................302 539-8031
Sherry Huovinen, *Branch Mgr*
EMP: 9
SALES (corp-wide): 954MM **Publicly Held**
SIC: 6022 State commercial banks
HQ: Fulton Bank, National Association
1 Penn Sq Ste 1 # 1
Lancaster PA 17602
717 581-3166

(G-7788)
G A HASTINGS & ASSOCIATES
102 Central Ave Ste 1 (19970-9019)
PHONE................302 537-5760
Gregory A Hastings, *Owner*
Charlotte Hastings, *Treasurer*
EMP: 6
SQ FT: 750
SALES (est): 829.8K **Privately Held**
SIC: 8712 House designer

(G-7789)
GALE FORCE CLEANING & RESTORE
14 Atlantic Ave (19970-9108)
PHONE................302 539-4683
Leslie Gale, *Principal*
EMP: 11
SALES (est): 1MM **Privately Held**
SIC: 7699 Cleaning services

(G-7790)
GALLERY ONE
125 Atlantic Ave (19967-6741)
P.O. Box 302 (19970-0302)
PHONE................302 537-5055
Cheryl Wisbrock, *Owner*
EMP: 6 **EST:** 2010
SALES (est): 207.3K **Privately Held**
SIC: 8412 Art gallery

(G-7791)
GEORGE K RICKARDS INC
26 Central Ave (19970-9226)
PHONE................302 539-7550
EMP: 6 **EST:** 1960
SALES (est): 530K **Privately Held**
SIC: 1521 General Contractor Of Single Family Homes

(G-7792)
GULFSTREAM DEVELOPMENT CORP
27 Atlantic Ave Ste 101 (19970-9169)
PHONE................302 539-6178
Robert Harris Jr, *President*
Mark Zduriencik, *Chairman*
EMP: 5
SALES (est): 891.3K **Privately Held**
SIC: 1521 6552 New construction, single-family houses; land subdividers & developers, residential

(G-7793)
INDIAN RIVER SOCCER CLUB
32221 Gum Rd (19970)
P.O. Box 1366 (19970-1366)
PHONE................302 542-6397
Rebecca Mais, *President*
EMP: 5
SALES: 141.4K **Privately Held**
SIC: 7997 Soccer club, except professional & semi-professional

(G-7794)
INTERIORS BY KIM INC
33 Central Ave (19970-9315)
PHONE................302 537-2480
Kim Bennett, *President*
Jeff Bennett, *Vice Pres*
Christine Miller, *Admin Sec*
EMP: 7
SQ FT: 5,000
SALES (est): 1.1MM **Privately Held**
SIC: 5713 1799 5231 5722 Floor covering stores; window treatment installation; wallcoverings; electric household appliances, major

(G-7795)
JEFFERSON URIAN DANE STRNER PA
92 Atlantic Ave Ste D (19970-9178)
P.O. Box 477 (19970-0477)
PHONE................302 539-5543
David Doane, *Manager*
EMP: 10
SALES (est): 587.7K
SALES (corp-wide): 5.8MM **Privately Held**
SIC: 8721 Certified public accountant
PA: Jefferson, Urian, Doane & Sterner, P.A.
651 N Bedford St
Georgetown DE 19947
302 856-3900

(G-7796)
JG WENTWORTH HM LENDING INC
37901 Island Dr (19970-3471)
PHONE................302 725-0723
Hayden Evans, *Branch Mgr*
EMP: 27 **Privately Held**
SIC: 6163 Mortgage brokers arranging for loans, using money of others
HQ: J.G. Wentworth Home Lending, Inc.
3350 Commission Ct
Woodbridge VA 22192
888 349-3773

(G-7797)
KELLY MAINTENANCE LTD INC
4 New Castle Ct (19970-9775)
P.O. Box 361 (19970-0361)
PHONE................302 539-3956
Fax: 302 539-5582
EMP: 5
SALES (est): 440K **Privately Held**
SIC: 1521 Single-Family House Construction

(G-7798)
LANDTECH LLC
Also Called: Landtech Land Survey
118 Atlantic Ave (19970-9163)
PHONE................302 539-2366
Jeffery Clark,
Elton Murray,
EMP: 7
SALES (est): 701.9K **Privately Held**
SIC: 8713 Surveying services

(G-7799)
LELA CAPITAL LLC
37259 Fox Dr (19970-3845)
PHONE................917 428-0304
Eqerem Zeka,
EMP: 12 **Privately Held**
SIC: 6719 Investment holding companies, except banks

(G-7800)
LOIS JAMES DDS
17 Atlantic Ave Ste 4 (19970-9102)
PHONE................302 537-4500
Lois James, *Owner*
EMP: 7
SALES (est): 453.9K **Privately Held**
SIC: 8021 Dentists' office

(G-7801)
LULLA WOODWORKING
1 New Castle Ct (19970-9777)
PHONE................302 841-8800
Joel Antonioli, *Principal*
EMP: 2
SALES (est): 93K **Privately Held**
SIC: 2431 Millwork

(G-7802)
MASTER KLEAN COMPANY
P.O. Box 1198, Bethany Beach (19930-1198)
PHONE................302 539-4290
James G Martin, *Owner*
EMP: 5
SALES (est): 86K **Privately Held**
SIC: 7349 5722 7629 Janitorial service, contract basis; vacuum cleaners; vacuum cleaner repair

(G-7803)
MR NATURAL BOTTLED WATER INC
31919 Christine Ln (19970-4114)
P.O. Box 490 (19970-0490)
PHONE................302 436-7700
Rodney J Short, *President*
Eileen Short, *Treasurer*
EMP: 12
SALES (est): 2MM **Privately Held**
SIC: 5149 Mineral or spring water bottling

Ocean View - Sussex County (G-7804)

(G-7804)
NEW IMAGE LASER AND SKIN CARE
118 Atlantic Ave (19970-9163)
PHONE 302 537-4336
Burn Quist, *Owner*
EMP: 4
SALES (est): 315.2K Privately Held
SIC: 8011 7231 Dermatologist; beauty shops

(G-7805)
NOVACARE REHABILITATION
118 Atlantic Ave Ste 302 (19970-9163)
PHONE 302 537-7762
EMP: 8 EST: 2018
SALES (est): 73.3K Privately Held
SIC: 8093 Rehabilitation center, outpatient treatment

(G-7806)
OCEAN PINES AUTO SERVICE CTR
Also Called: Ocean Pines Parts
34461 Atlantic Ave (19970-3546)
PHONE 410 641-7800
David R Hamm, *President*
Glenn R Phillips, *Corp Secy*
Dr Andreas Goldner, *Vice Pres*
EMP: 50
SALES (est): 3.1MM Privately Held
SIC: 7538 5531 General automotive repair shops; automotive parts

(G-7807)
OCEAN VIEW ANIMAL HOSPITAL
118 Atlantic Ave Ste 101 (19970-9163)
PHONE 302 539-2273
Nathan Sheldon, *Principal*
EMP: 6
SALES (est): 355.9K Privately Held
SIC: 0742 Veterinary services, specialties

(G-7808)
OCEAN VIEW FARMS INC (PA)
Also Called: Timmons, Bake Jr
76 West Ave (19970-9793)
PHONE 302 537-4042
Bake Timmons, *President*
EMP: 4
SALES (est): 64.2K Privately Held
SIC: 6531 Real estate agents & managers

(G-7809)
PRECIOUS PAWS ANIMAL HOSPITAL
118 Atlantic Ave Ste 101 (19970-9163)
PHONE 302 539-2273
John Maniatty, *Principal*
Kelly Krivitski, *Office Mgr*
EMP: 12 EST: 2011
SALES (est): 130.2K Privately Held
SIC: 0742 Animal hospital services, pets & other animal specialties

(G-7810)
R W HOME SERVICES INC
Also Called: Gale Force Clg & Restoration
14 Atlantic Ave (19970-9108)
PHONE 302 539-4683
William McCreary, *President*
EMP: 18
SALES (est): 1.6MM Privately Held
SIC: 1799 7342 1541 4959 Cleaning new buildings after construction; disinfecting & deodorizing; renovation, remodeling & repairs: industrial buildings; environmental cleanup services; cleaning service, industrial or commercial

(G-7811)
SCHMIDT & ASSOC
30213 Jump Ln (19970-2788)
PHONE 610 255-3540
EMP: 2
SALES (est): 62.6K Privately Held
SIC: 3296 Mfg Mineral Wool

(G-7812)
SCHRIDER ENTERPRISES INC
Also Called: Fabri-Zone Cleaning Systems
327 Atlantic Ave (19967-6702)
P.O. Box 850, Bethany Beach (19930-0850)
PHONE 302 539-1036
Wendy J Schrider, *President*
Stephen J Schrider, *Vice Pres*
William J Schrider, *Vice Pres*
Isabelle M Schrider, *Admin Sec*
EMP: 5
SALES (est): 240.6K Privately Held
SIC: 7217 Carpet & furniture cleaning on location

(G-7813)
SILVERBACK GYMS LLC
2 Town Rd (19970-9136)
PHONE 302 539-8282
EMP: 4
SALES (est): 36.5K Privately Held
SIC: 7991 Physical fitness facilities

(G-7814)
STEEN WAEHLER SCHRIDER FOX LLC
92 Atlantic Ave Ste B (19970-9178)
P.O. Box 1398 (19970-1398)
PHONE 302 539-7900
Wendy Herman, *Office Mgr*
Brian Riggin, *Office Mgr*
Mary S Fox, *Mng Member*
Mary R Schrider-Fox,
EMP: 9
SALES (est): 855.7K Privately Held
SIC: 8111 General practice attorney, lawyer

(G-7815)
SUMMER HILL CUSTOM HOME BLDR
68 Atlantic Ave (19970-9170)
PHONE 302 462-5853
Steve Smith, *Owner*
EMP: 6
SALES (est): 399.3K Privately Held
SIC: 1799 Special trade contractors

(G-7816)
SUPERIOR SCREEN & GLASS
1 Town Rd (19970-9132)
PHONE 302 541-5399
Joel Antonioli, *Owner*
EMP: 15
SQ FT: 6,000
SALES (est): 922.1K Privately Held
SIC: 1799 1793 1751 Screening contractor: window, door, etc.; glass & glazing work; store fixture installation

(G-7817)
SUSSEX COUNTY SENIOR CTR SVCS
Cedar Neck Rd (19970)
P.O. Box 637 (19970-0637)
PHONE 302 539-2671
Sherrie Stephens, *Director*
EMP: 4
SALES (est): 83.7K Privately Held
SIC: 8322 Old age assistance

(G-7818)
SUSSEX COUNTY WOMAN
23 Daisey Ave (19970-9130)
P.O. Box 1267, Bethany Beach (19930-1267)
PHONE 302 539-2612
Robert Kapke, *Owner*
EMP: 11
SALES (est): 1MM Privately Held
SIC: 5192 Books, periodicals & newspapers

(G-7819)
SWEDISH MASSAGE THERAPY
38227 Muddy Neck Rd (19970-2837)
PHONE 302 841-3166
Geradine Finiello, *Principal*
EMP: 5
SALES (est): 97.7K Privately Held
SIC: 8093 Rehabilitation center, outpatient treatment

(G-7820)
THOMAS BALDWIN DDS
Also Called: Baldwin, Thomas E
31028 Waterthrush Ln (19970-8034)
PHONE 302 829-1243
Thomas Baldwin DDS, *Owner*
EMP: 4
SALES (est): 170K Privately Held
SIC: 8021 Dentists' office

(G-7821)
TIDEWATER PHYSCL THRPY AND REB
63 Atlantic Ave (19970-9167)
PHONE 302 537-7260
Dawn Belanger, *Manager*
EMP: 5
SALES (corp-wide): 2.6MM Privately Held
WEB: www.tidewaterpt.com
SIC: 8049 Physical therapist
PA: Tidewater Physical Therapy And Rehabilitation Associates Pa
406 Marvel Ct
Easton MD 21601
410 822-3116

(G-7822)
TIMOTHY B OHARE CUSTOM BLDR
31494 Railway Rd (19970-3452)
PHONE 302 537-9559
Timothy B O'Hare, *President*
EMP: 12
SALES (est): 1.6MM Privately Held
SIC: 1521 New construction, single-family houses; general remodeling, single-family houses

(G-7823)
VILLAGE SQ ACDEMY LRNG CTR LLC
30792 Whites Neck Rd (19970-3510)
PHONE 302 539-5000
Tecola G Hernandez, *Director*
Tecola Gibbs-Hernandez, *Director*
EMP: 8
SALES (est): 213.2K Privately Held
SIC: 8351 Preschool center

(G-7824)
WILMINGTON SAVINGS FUND SOC
69 Atlantic Ave (19970-9167)
PHONE 302 360-0004
EMP: 4
SALES (corp-wide): 455.5MM Publicly Held
SIC: 6022 State commercial banks
HQ: Wilmington Savings Fund Society
500 Delaware Ave Ste 500 # 500
Wilmington DE 19801
302 792-6000

Odessa
New Castle County

(G-7825)
DELAWARE WILD LANDS INC
315 Main St (19730-2009)
P.O. Box 505 (19730-0505)
PHONE 302 378-2736
Debbie Turner, *General Mgr*
Ronald Haas, *Project Mgr*
Kate Hackett, *Exec Dir*
EMP: 5 EST: 1961
SQ FT: 500
SALES: 2MM Privately Held
SIC: 8641 Environmental protection organization

(G-7826)
DUNKLEY ENTERPRISES LLC
Also Called: Hungry Student Athletes
139 Wallace Rd (19730-2055)
P.O. Box 222 (19730-0222)
PHONE 302 275-0100
Spencer Dunkley,
Denise Dunkley,
Kingsley Dunkley,
EMP: 5
SALES (est): 281.4K Privately Held
SIC: 4214 Furniture moving & storage, local

(G-7827)
GREEN ACRES PRE SCHOOL
411 N 6th St (19730-2045)
P.O. Box 221 (19730-0221)
PHONE 302 378-9250
Marlene Green, *Owner*
EMP: 12
SALES: 250K Privately Held
SIC: 8351 Preschool center

(G-7828)
JADE ENTERPRISES INC
Also Called: Lawn Doctor Dover-Middletown
103 S Dupont Hwy (19730)
P.O. Box 464 (19730-0464)
PHONE 302 378-3435
Dennis Faust, *President*
Janice Faust, *Admin Sec*
EMP: 4
SQ FT: 1,600
SALES (est): 569.9K Privately Held
SIC: 0782 Lawn care services

(G-7829)
M & M CONSTRUCTION INC
101 Main St (19730-2005)
P.O. Box 101 (19730-0101)
PHONE 410 758-1071
EMP: 6
SALES (est): 500K Privately Held
SIC: 1771 1791 Concrete Work

(G-7830)
MIDDLETOWN WELL DRILLING CO (PA)
115 S 6th St (19730)
PHONE 302 378-9396
Joseph Borrell, *Owner*
Christine Newland, *Co-Owner*
EMP: 5 EST: 1946
SALES (est): 550K Privately Held
SIC: 1781 Water well drilling

(G-7831)
NUCAR CONSULTING INC
313 N Dupont Hwy Ste 100 (19730)
P.O. Box 5000 (19730-5000)
PHONE 302 696-6000
Jim Capron, *President*
Chris Blum, *Vice Pres*
EMP: 20 EST: 1997
SALES (est): 1.9MM Privately Held
WEB: www.nucarconsulting.com
SIC: 8748 Business consulting

(G-7832)
ODESSA HISTORIC FOUNDATION
201 Main St (19730-2007)
P.O. Box 697 (19730-0697)
PHONE 302 378-4119
H Donnan Sharp, *President*
William Gotwals, *Treasurer*
Debbie Buckson, *Exec Dir*
EMP: 26
SALES: 811.4K Privately Held
SIC: 8412 Historical society

(G-7833)
WHITTINGTON & AULGUR
313 N Dupont Hwy Ste 110 (19730)
P.O. Box 617 (19730-0617)
PHONE 302 378-1661
Robert Aulgur, *Partner*
EMP: 10
SALES (corp-wide): 2.5MM Privately Held
SIC: 8111 Legal services
PA: Whittington & Aulgur
2979 Barley Mill Rd
Yorklyn DE 19736
302 235-5800

Port Penn
New Castle County

(G-7834)
GJ CHALFANT WELDING LLC ◆
119 S Congress St (19731-3105)
PHONE 302 983-0822
Greg Chalfant, *Principal*
EMP: 1 EST: 2019

GEOGRAPHIC SECTION

Rehoboth Beach - Sussex County (G-7863)

SALES (est): 25K **Privately Held**
SIC: 7692 Welding repair

Rehoboth Beach
Sussex County

(G-7835)
A V C INC
Also Called: Audio Visual Communications
20807 Coastal Hwy Ste 4 (19971-8013)
PHONE...................................302 227-2549
Joseph P Wastler, *President*
EMP: 7
SQ FT: 600
SALES (est): 879.1K
SALES (corp-wide): 337.3MM **Publicly Held**
SIC: 5999 5065 Telephone & communication equipment; closed circuit television; telephone equipment; security control equipment & systems; sound equipment, electronic
PA: Ceco Environmental Corp.
  14651 Dallas Pkwy Ste 50
  Dallas TX 75254
  214 357-6181

(G-7836)
A WOMANS TOUCH MOVING & PKG
109 Shady Ridge Dr (19971-9661)
PHONE...................................302 265-4729
Mary Nicholson, *Principal*
EMP: 4
SALES (est): 339.5K **Privately Held**
SIC: 5199 Packaging materials

(G-7837)
ADMIRAL HOTEL
2 Baltimore Ave (19971-2104)
PHONE...................................302 227-2103
Walter Brett, *Owner*
Karen Brown, *Manager*
EMP: 5
SQ FT: 17,500
SALES (est): 399.9K **Privately Held**
WEB: www.admiralrehoboth.com
SIC: 7011 Motels

(G-7838)
AIDS DELAWARE INC
37201 Rehoboth Avenue Ext # 1 (19971-3192)
PHONE...................................302 226-3519
Maureen Leary, *Branch Mgr*
EMP: 4 **Privately Held**
SIC: 8399 Advocacy group
PA: Aids Delaware, Inc.
  100 W 10th St Ste 315
  Wilmington DE 19801

(G-7839)
ALEX AND ANI LLC
36494 Seaside Outlet Dr # 1420 (19971-1232)
PHONE...................................302 227-7360
EMP: 7 **Privately Held**
SIC: 5944 3911 Jewelry, precious stones & precious metals; jewelry, precious metal
PA: Alex And Ani, Llc
  2000 Chapel View Blvd # 360
  Cranston RI 02920

(G-7840)
AMS OF DELAWARE
20576 Coastal Hwy (19971-8062)
PHONE...................................302 227-1320
Michael Errico, *Principal*
EMP: 6 EST: 2011
SALES (est): 216K **Privately Held**
SIC: 8322 Alcoholism counseling, nontreatment

(G-7841)
ANCHORAGE MOTEL INC
18809 Coastal Hwy (19971-6153)
PHONE...................................302 645-8320
Cleburn Johnston III, *President*
Melissa Jones, *Corp Secy*
EMP: 6
SQ FT: 17,000
SALES (est): 300K **Privately Held**
WEB: www.anchoragemotelinc.com
SIC: 7011 Motels

(G-7842)
ANDERSON FLOOR COVERINGS INC
4286 Highway One (19971)
PHONE...................................302 227-3244
Stephen Anderson, *President*
Mark Matushik, *Corp Secy*
John Fleming, *Vice Pres*
EMP: 10 EST: 1976
SQ FT: 10,500
SALES (est): 1.5MM **Privately Held**
SIC: 1752 5713 Floor laying & floor work; carpet laying; linoleum installation; carpets

(G-7843)
ANDREI S REMO
35948 Haven Dr Unit 305 (19971-8787)
PHONE...................................302 569-4555
Dzmitry McCusker, *Owner*
EMP: 4
SALES: 250K **Privately Held**
SIC: 1542 1611 Nonresidential construction; highway & street construction

(G-7844)
ANS CORPORATION (PA)
Also Called: Accent On Travel
37156 Rehoboth Avenue Ext (19971-3104)
PHONE...................................410 296-8330
Annette Stellhorn, *CEO*
Richard Stellhorn, *CFO*
EMP: 9
SQ FT: 14,000
SALES: 6MM **Privately Held**
WEB: www.accentontravelinc.com
SIC: 4724 Travel agencies

(G-7845)
APPLE ELECTRIC INC
18854 John J Williams Hwy (19971-4402)
PHONE...................................302 645-5105
Lisa M Prestipino, *President*
Steve Prestipino, *Vice Pres*
EMP: 25
SQ FT: 1,500
SALES (est): 3.3MM **Privately Held**
SIC: 1731 General electrical contractor

(G-7846)
APPLIED BANK
37012 Country Club Rd (19971-1099)
PHONE...................................302 227-3044
John Schroeder, *Vice Pres*
EMP: 18 **Privately Held**
SIC: 6021 National commercial banks
PA: Applied Bank
  2200 Concord Pike Ste 102
  Wilmington DE 19803

(G-7847)
ARTISANS BANK INC
19358 Miller Rd (19971-6118)
PHONE...................................302 296-0155
Tiffany Walter, *Manager*
EMP: 7
SALES (corp-wide): 22.8MM **Privately Held**
SIC: 6036 State savings banks, not federally chartered
PA: Artisans Bank Inc
  2961 Centerville Rd # 101
  Wilmington DE 19808
  302 658-6881

(G-7848)
AT&T CORP
19354 Miller Rd Ste A (19971-6122)
PHONE...................................302 644-4529
Michael Spaccarelli, *Branch Mgr*
EMP: 94
SALES (corp-wide): 170.7B **Publicly Held**
SIC: 4812 Cellular telephone services
HQ: At&T Corp.
  1 At&T Way
  Bedminster NJ 07921
  800 403-3302

(G-7849)
ATI HOLDINGS LLC
Also Called: ATI Physical Therapy
19266 Coastal Hwy Unit 9 (19971-6117)
PHONE...................................302 226-2230
Philip Allen, *Principal*
EMP: 21
SALES (corp-wide): 338.3MM **Privately Held**
SIC: 8049 Physical therapist
PA: Ati Holdings, Llc
  790 Remington Blvd
  Bolingbrook IL 60440
  630 296-2222

(G-7850)
ATLANTIC MANAGEMENT
34821 Derrickson Dr (19971-6144)
PHONE...................................302 222-3919
Chris Burg, *Principal*
EMP: 5 EST: 2012
SALES (est): 804.8K **Privately Held**
SIC: 8741 Management services

(G-7851)
ATLANTIC MANAGEMENT LTD
29 Midway Shopping Ctr (19971)
PHONE...................................302 645-9511
Richard H Derrickson, *President*
Norma Lee Derrickson, *Corp Secy*
EMP: 15
SALES (est): 1.5MM **Privately Held**
WEB: www.rehobothlodging.com
SIC: 8741 6512 Hotel or motel management; shopping center, property operation only

(G-7852)
AVENUE DAY SPA
Also Called: Avenue Apothecary and Spa
110 Rehoboth Ave Ste A (19971-2108)
PHONE...................................302 227-5649
Victoria Fry, *President*
Tin Desilver, *Vice Pres*
Jessica Fry, *Manager*
Tim De Silver, *Executive*
EMP: 15
SALES: 320K **Privately Held**
WEB: www.avenuedayspa.com
SIC: 7991 Spas

(G-7853)
BAD HAIR DAY INC
20 Lake Ave (19971-2110)
PHONE...................................302 226-4247
Drexel Davison, *President*
EMP: 34
SALES (est): 922.4K **Privately Held**
WEB: www.badhairdaysalon.com
SIC: 7231 Hairdressers

(G-7854)
BANK OF DELMARVA
4575 Highway One (19971-6215)
PHONE...................................302 226-8900
June Betts, *Manager*
Paul Mylander, *Director*
EMP: 5
SALES (corp-wide): 24.7MM **Publicly Held**
WEB: www.bankofdelmarvahb.com
SIC: 6022 6029 State trust companies accepting deposits, commercial; commercial banks
HQ: The Bank Of Delmarva
  2245 Northwood Dr
  Salisbury MD 21801
  410 548-1100

(G-7855)
BASIC BLOCK CORP
Also Called: H & R Block
4590 Highway One Ste 118 (19971)
PHONE...................................302 645-2000
Ernest Deangelis Jr, *President*
EMP: 15
SQ FT: 2,200
SALES: 483K **Privately Held**
SIC: 7291 Tax return preparation services

(G-7856)
BATESCAINELLI LLC
319 Byview Ave Rhboth Bch Rehoboth Beach (19971)
PHONE...................................202 618-2040
Stephen Bates, *Info Tech Mgr*

EMP: 2 EST: 2012
SALES (est): 141.8K **Privately Held**
SIC: 8748 7372 7373 7389 Systems engineering consultant, ex. computer or professional; business oriented computer software; office computer automation systems integration; ; compensation & benefits planning consultant; commercial physical research

(G-7857)
BEACH BUTLER SERVICES LLC
28 Manor Dr (19971-1923)
PHONE...................................302 227-0114
Sharon S Roy, *Principal*
EMP: 10
SALES (est): 192.7K **Privately Held**
SIC: 8999 Services

(G-7858)
BEACH TANS AND HAIR DESIGN
Also Called: Beach Tans & Hair Designs
23 Midway Shopping Ctr (19971)
PHONE...................................302 645-8267
Robert Heath, *Owner*
EMP: 7
SALES (est): 240K **Privately Held**
WEB: www.beachtan.us
SIC: 7299 Tanning salon

(G-7859)
BEACON MEDICAL GROUP PA
18947 John J Williams Hwy # 303 (19971-4477)
PHONE...................................302 947-9767
EMP: 5
SALES (est): 368.5K **Privately Held**
SIC: 8011 Offices & clinics of medical doctors

(G-7860)
BEACON PEDIATRICS LLC
18947 J J Williams Hwy311 (19971)
PHONE...................................302 645-8212
Nancy M Gideon, *Principal*
EMP: 11
SALES (est): 1.2MM **Privately Held**
SIC: 8011 Pediatrician

(G-7861)
BEAVER TREE SERVICE INC
108 2nd St (19971-2281)
PHONE...................................302 226-3564
James Beaver, *Branch Mgr*
EMP: 6
SALES (corp-wide): 1.2MM **Privately Held**
SIC: 0783 Planting, pruning & trimming services
PA: Beaver Tree Service, Inc
  1301 S Division St
  Salisbury MD 21804
  410 651-0779

(G-7862)
BEEBE MEDICAL CENTER INC
18947 John J Williams Hwy # 201 (19971-4476)
PHONE...................................302 645-3100
Douglas Rahn, *Director*
EMP: 112
SALES (corp-wide): 447.8MM **Privately Held**
SIC: 8062 General medical & surgical hospitals
PA: Beebe Medical Center, Inc.
  424 Savannah Rd
  Lewes DE 19958
  302 645-3300

(G-7863)
BEEBE MEDICAL CENTER INC
38149 Terrace Rd (19971-2074)
PHONE...................................302 645-3289
EMP: 62
SALES (corp-wide): 447.8MM **Privately Held**
SIC: 8011 Medical centers
PA: Beebe Medical Center, Inc.
  424 Savannah Rd
  Lewes DE 19958
  302 645-3300

Rehoboth Beach - Sussex County (G-7864) — GEOGRAPHIC SECTION

(G-7864)
BEEBE MEDICAL CENTER INC
Also Called: Women's Imaging Center
18941 John J Williams Hwy (19971-4404)
Rural Route 24 (19971)
PHONE.............................302 645-3010
Graham Robbins, Branch Mgr
EMP: 211
SALES (corp-wide): 447.8MM **Privately Held**
SIC: 8011 Medical centers
PA: Beebe Medical Center, Inc.
424 Savannah Rd
Lewes DE 19958
302 645-3300

(G-7865)
BELL ROCK CAPITAL LLC (PA)
35568 Airport Rd (19971-4620)
PHONE.............................302 227-7607
Jacqueline Reeves, Managing Dir
Jacquelyn Blue, CFO
Cassandra Toroian,
EMP: 10
SALES (est): 9MM **Privately Held**
SIC: 6799 Investors

(G-7866)
BELLINGERS JEWELERS
20747 Coastal Hwy (19971-8004)
PHONE.............................302 227-6410
Dale Bellinger, President
Nancy Morris Bellinger, Vice Pres
EMP: 4
SALES (est): 370K **Privately Held**
WEB: www.bellingersjewelers.com
SIC: 5944 7631 Jewelry, precious stones & precious metals; jewelry repair services

(G-7867)
BEST WESTERN GOLDLEAF HT LLC
1400 Hwy 1 (19971)
PHONE.............................302 226-1100
Maha Awayes, President
EMP: 15
SALES (est): 1MM **Privately Held**
SIC: 7011 Hotels & motels

(G-7868)
BIG CHILL INC
19406 Coastal Hwy (19971-6126)
PHONE.............................302 727-5568
EMP: 6
SALES (est): 22K **Privately Held**
SIC: 2024 Ice cream, bulk

(G-7869)
BIN 66 FINE WINE & SPIRIT
20729 Coastal Hwy (19971-8000)
PHONE.............................302 227-6966
EMP: 5
SALES (est): 508.5K **Privately Held**
SIC: 5182 Wine

(G-7870)
BIZ TEC INC
Also Called: TP Computing
18806 John J Williams Hwy (19971-4402)
PHONE.............................302 227-1967
EMP: 9 **EST:** 1995
SQ FT: 2,500
SALES: 1.1MM **Privately Held**
SIC: 7378 5734 Computer Maintenance/Repair Ret Computers/Software

(G-7871)
BOARDWALK BUILDERS INC
37395 Martin St (19971-8046)
PHONE.............................302 227-5754
Patricia McDaniel, President
Patricia Mc Daniel, President
Eric Engelhart, Production
Kelsey Hamilton, Marketing Staff
EMP: 19
SALES (est): 2.7MM **Privately Held**
SIC: 1521 New construction, single-family houses; general remodeling, single-family houses

(G-7872)
BOARDWALK PLAZA INCORPORATED (PA)
2 Olive Ave (19971-2806)
PHONE.............................302 227-0441
Jeffrey E Zerby, CEO
L Orme Meade, Vice Pres
Ruth Ann Zerby, Treasurer
Kathryn E Meade, Admin Sec
EMP: 59
SALES (est): 3.9MM **Privately Held**
SIC: 7011 5812 Hotels; eating places

(G-7873)
BOYS GIRLS CLUBS
19285 Holland Glade Rd (19971-4180)
PHONE.............................302 260-9864
Millie Tronic, Principal
Demaris Miller, Director
EMP: 5
SALES: 120K **Privately Held**
SIC: 8641 Youth organizations

(G-7874)
BRANDYWINE SNIOR LVING MGT LLC
36101 Seaside Blvd (19971-6165)
PHONE.............................302 226-8750
Donna Winegar, Exec Dir
EMP: 85
SALES (corp-wide): 174.7MM **Privately Held**
WEB: www.brandycare.com
SIC: 8051 Skilled nursing care facilities
PA: Brandywine Senior Living Management Llc
525 Fellowship Rd Ste 360
Mount Laurel NJ 08054
856 778-6100

(G-7875)
BREAKERS ASSOCIATES
Also Called: Breakers Hotel, The
105 2nd St (19971-2283)
PHONE.............................302 227-6688
Ronald Lankford, Owner
Shawney Banks, Facilities Dir
EMP: 20
SALES (est): 1.1MM **Privately Held**
WEB: www.thebreakershotel.com
SIC: 7011 Resort hotel; hotels

(G-7876)
BRIAN COSTLEIGH LLC
1 Beach Ave (19971-2501)
PHONE.............................302 645-3775
Brian Costleigh, Principal
EMP: 6 **EST:** 2012
SALES (est): 143.9K **Privately Held**
SIC: 8062 General medical & surgical hospitals

(G-7877)
BRIGHTON HOTELS LLC
Also Called: Brighton Suites Hotel
34 Wilmington Ave (19971-2217)
PHONE.............................302 227-5780
Lisa Murdock, General Mgr
Robert Pomeranz,
EMP: 50
SALES (est): 2MM **Privately Held**
WEB: www.brightonsuites.com
SIC: 7011 Hotels

(G-7878)
BROADPOINT CONSTRUCTION LLC
Also Called: Broadpoint Custom Homes
37251 Rehoboth Avenue Ext (19971-3192)
PHONE.............................302 567-2100
John Schneider Jr, Partner
Nicholas Hammonds, Partner
Douglas Motley, Partner
EMP: 6
SALES (est): 720.2K **Privately Held**
SIC: 1541 1542 1531 Industrial buildings, new construction; nonresidential construction; shopping center construction; commercial & office building, new construction; operative builders

(G-7879)
BROADWATER OYSTER COMPANY LLC
4 S Lake Ter (19971-4155)
PHONE.............................610 220-7776
Ted Nowakowski, Owner
EMP: 2 **EST:** 2015
SALES (est): 72.7K **Privately Held**
SIC: 3732 Fishing boats: lobster, crab, oyster, etc.: small

(G-7880)
BUDGET TRUCK RENTAL LLC
Also Called: Ryder
18744 John J Williams Hwy (19971-4400)
PHONE.............................302 644-0132
Tony Street, Manager
EMP: 11
SALES (corp-wide): 9.1B **Publicly Held**
SIC: 7513 Truck rental, without drivers
HQ: Budget Truck Rental Llc
6 Sylvan Way Ste 1
Parsippany NJ 07054

(G-7881)
BURKE DERMATOLOGY
18947 John J Williams Hwy (19971-4474)
PHONE.............................302 703-6585
EMP: 15
SALES (corp-wide): 1.7MM **Privately Held**
SIC: 8011 Dermatologist
PA: Burke Dermatology
774 Christiana Rd Ste 107
Newark DE 19713
302 230-3376

(G-7882)
CAMELS HUMP INC
63 Fields End (19971-1611)
PHONE.............................302 227-5719
Mohammad Shihadeh, President
Marcia W Shihadeh, Treasurer
EMP: 15 **EST:** 1975
SQ FT: 5,000
SALES (est): 590K **Privately Held**
SIC: 5812 5813 5141 Eating places; bar (drinking places); groceries, general line

(G-7883)
CAPE HENLOPEN SENIOR CENTER
11 Christian St (19971-3001)
PHONE.............................302 227-2055
Linda Vonvillle, Administration
EMP: 6
SALES: 466.9K **Privately Held**
WEB: www.capehenlopenseniorcenter.org
SIC: 8322 8699 Senior citizens' center or association; charitable organization

(G-7884)
CAPITAL ONE NATIONAL ASSN
19268 Old Landing Rd (19971-4621)
PHONE.............................302 645-1360
Greg Hazzard, Branch Mgr
EMP: 5 **Publicly Held**
WEB: www.chevychasebank.com
SIC: 6035 Savings institutions, federally chartered
HQ: Capital One, National Association
1680 Capital One Dr
Mc Lean VA 22102
800 655-2265

(G-7885)
CENTER FOR INLAND BAYS INC
39375 Inlet Rd (19971-2600)
PHONE.............................302 226-8105
Pat Campbell White, Chairman
Bob Collins, Manager
Victoria Spice, Manager
Chris Bason, Exec Dir
Ken P Oyster, Assistant
EMP: 7
SALES: 1.1MM **Privately Held**
WEB: www.inlandbays.org
SIC: 8641 Environmental protection organization

(G-7886)
CENTURY 21 MANN & SONS
Also Called: Mann & Moore Associates
19606 Coastal Hwy # 205 (19971-8596)
PHONE.............................302 227-9477
Betty Mann, President
Bob McVai, Principal
Bob McVey, Vice Pres
Bill Mann, Broker
EMP: 53
SALES: 3.2MM **Privately Held**
WEB: www.mannandsons.com
SIC: 6531 Real estate agent, residential

(G-7887)
CHESAPEAKEMAINE TREY
316 Rehoboth Ave (19971-3108)
PHONE.............................302 226-3600
EMP: 4 **EST:** 2016
SALES (est): 314.6K **Privately Held**
SIC: 2082 Malt beverages

(G-7888)
CHRISTIAN SCIENCE READING ROOM
Also Called: First Church of Christ
801 Bayard Ave (19971-2213)
PHONE.............................302 227-7650
Roseann Shores, Owner
Christian Science Church, Owner
EMP: 18
SALES (est): 159.4K **Privately Held**
SIC: 8699 Christian Science reading room

(G-7889)
CHURCH STREET ASSOCIATES
33 Baltimore Ave Ste H (19971-2156)
PHONE.............................302 227-1599
Norman Sugrue, Partner
Stephen Chase, Partner
William Clark, Partner
EMP: 4
SQ FT: 1,000
SALES (est): 361.7K **Privately Held**
SIC: 6512 Commercial & industrial building operation

(G-7890)
CITY CAB OF DELWARE INC
164 Henlopen Ave (19971-1633)
PHONE.............................302 227-8294
Tom Antonio, President
Bill Howarth, Manager
EMP: 12 **Privately Held**
SIC: 4121 Taxicabs
PA: City Cab Of Delware Inc
1203 State College Rd
Dover DE 19904

(G-7891)
CLEAN ENERGY USA LLC (PA)
20184 Phillips St (19971-8049)
PHONE.............................302 227-1337
Dave Preston, CEO
Chris Schell,
EMP: 8
SQ FT: 3,000
SALES (est): 2MM **Privately Held**
SIC: 1711 Solar energy contractor

(G-7892)
CLEAR SPACE THEATRE COMPANY
20 Baltimore Ave (19971-2104)
PHONE.............................302 227-2270
Chris Berg, Ch of Bd
Wesley Paulson, Exec Dir
EMP: 4 **EST:** 2010
SQ FT: 6,500
SALES: 841.1K **Privately Held**
SIC: 7922 Legitimate live theater producers

(G-7893)
COASTAL IT CONSULTING
4 Tall Oaks Ct (19971-8602)
PHONE.............................302 226-9395
Norman Blackwood, Owner
EMP: 7
SALES (est): 217.4K **Privately Held**
SIC: 7378 Computer maintenance & repair

(G-7894)
COASTAL KIDS PEDIATRIC DNTSTRY
18947 John J Williams Hwy (19971-4474)
PHONE.............................302 644-4460
EMP: 4 **EST:** 2013

GEOGRAPHIC SECTION
Rehoboth Beach - Sussex County (G-7924)

SALES (est): 188.5K **Privately Held**
SIC: 8021 8011 Pedodontist; offices & clinics of medical doctors

(G-7895)
COASTAL PROPERTIES I LLC
Also Called: Bellmoor, The
6 Christian St (19971-3002)
P.O. Box 1 (19971-0001)
PHONE.................302 227-5800
Robert H Moore, *President*
Robert Chadwick, *Vice Pres*
JB Moore, *Vice Pres*
Marion W Moore, *Vice Pres*
Todd W Moore, *Vice Pres*
EMP: 25 EST: 1974
SALES (est): 3.5MM **Privately Held**
WEB: www.thebellmoor.com
SIC: 7011 5812 Motels; eating places

(G-7896)
COLDWELL BANKER REHOBOTH RESRT
20184 Coastal Hwy (19971-8020)
PHONE.................302 227-5000
Rick Bennett, *Vice Pres*
Jeffrey Zerby, *Vice Pres*
Veronica Kiernan, *Treasurer*
Francis Pipczynski, *Accountant*
Dennis Barnes, *Sales Staff*
EMP: 50
SQ FT: 3,500
SALES (est): 2.9MM **Privately Held**
WEB: www.cbanker.com
SIC: 6531 Real estate agent, residential

(G-7897)
COLLIERS TRIM SHOP INC
2206 Hwy One (19971)
PHONE.................302 227-8398
Michael Sockriter, *President*
EMP: 5 EST: 1949
SALES (est): 310K **Privately Held**
SIC: 7641 7532 Furniture upholstery repair; interior repair services

(G-7898)
COLONIAL OAKS HOTEL LLC
Also Called: Fairfield Inn Suites Rehoboth
19113 Coastal Hwy (19971-6125)
PHONE.................302 645-7766
Toni Coverdale, *Bookkeeper*
Christian Hudson, *Manager*
EMP: 20
SQ FT: 90,000
SALES (est): 1.1MM **Privately Held**
SIC: 7011 Hotels & motels

(G-7899)
CONCH ISLAND
211 Rehoboth Ave (19971-2137)
PHONE.................302 226-9378
Bryan Derrickson, *Principal*
EMP: 7
SALES (est): 377.6K **Privately Held**
SIC: 7374 Data processing service

(G-7900)
CONLEY & WRIGHT DDS
Also Called: Maplewood Dental Associates
18913 John J Williams Hwy (19971-4404)
PHONE.................302 645-6671
T E Conley DDS, *Partner*
Bruce Wright, *Partner*
Steve Wright, *Partner*
Steve B Wright, *Fmly & Gen Dent*
EMP: 5
SALES (est): 830.2K **Privately Held**
SIC: 8021 Dentists' office

(G-7901)
COOPER SIMPLER ASSOCIATES INC
Also Called: Beach View Motel
6 Wilmington Ave (19971-2926)
PHONE.................302 227-2999
Samuel Cooper, *President*
Karen Simpler, *Partner*
Kenneth Simpler, *Partner*
EMP: 9
SQ FT: 12,000
SALES (est): 672.8K **Privately Held**
WEB: www.beachviewmotel.com
SIC: 7011 Motels

(G-7902)
COUNTY BANK (PA)
19927 Shuttle Rd (19971-4215)
PHONE.................302 226-9800
Wayne Dukes, *CEO*
Harold Slatcher, *President*
David Gillan, *COO*
Shrubb Deborah Kay, *Assistant VP*
Karen Mumford, *Assistant VP*
EMP: 19
SQ FT: 15,000
SALES (est): 17MM **Privately Held**
WEB: www.countybankdel.com
SIC: 6021 National commercial banks

(G-7903)
CREATIVE COURTYARDS
20184 Phillips St (19971-8049)
PHONE.................302 226-1994
John Glenn, *Principal*
EMP: 6
SALES (est): 76.2K **Privately Held**
SIC: 7011 Hotels & motels

(G-7904)
CROWLEY AND ASSOC RLTY INC
20250 Coastal Hwy (19971-8021)
P.O. Box 465 (19971-0465)
PHONE.................302 227-6131
Wanda M Crowley, *Principal*
EMP: 12
SALES (corp-wide): 1.7MM **Privately Held**
WEB: www.crowleyrealestate.com
SIC: 6531 Selling agent, real estate; rental agent, real estate
PA: Crowley And Associates Realty, Inc.
     1000 N Pennsylvania Ave
     Bethany Beach DE
     302 539-4013

(G-7905)
CURTIS J LECIEJEWSKI DDS PA
19643 Blue Bird Ln Unit 1 (19971-6129)
PHONE.................302 226-7960
Curtis Leciejewski, *Principal*
Michael D Keller, *Principal*
EMP: 4
SALES (est): 199.1K **Privately Held**
SIC: 8021 Dentists' office

(G-7906)
D F QUILLEN & SONS INC (PA)
Also Called: True Value
803 Rehoboth Ave Ste F (19971)
PHONE.................302 227-2531
Dennard F Quillen Jr, *CEO*
Dennard F Quillen III, *President*
Charlotte Quillen, *Corp Secy*
Christopher Quillen, *Vice Pres*
Frederick Ward, *Vice Pres*
EMP: 20
SQ FT: 20,000
SALES: 2MM **Privately Held**
WEB: www.rentgrs.com
SIC: 5251 5211 1521 Hardware; lumber & other building materials; single-family home remodeling, additions & repairs

(G-7907)
DACK TRADING LLC
18585 Cstl Hwy Unt10 Ofc (19971)
PHONE.................917 576-4432
AMR Elewa, *Mng Member*
EMP: 5
SALES (est): 273.7K **Privately Held**
SIC: 5153 5031 Grains; pallets, wood

(G-7908)
DCOR
37545 Atlantic Ave (19971-1199)
PHONE.................302 227-9341
Ed Albers, *Principal*
EMP: 5
SALES (est): 420.7K **Privately Held**
SIC: 8621 Professional membership organizations

(G-7909)
DEBBIE REED
Also Called: Re/Max
319 Rehoboth Ave (19971-3127)
PHONE.................302 227-3818
Debbie Reed, *Owner*
Sandra Jefferson, *Buyer*
Dianne Deming, *Real Est Agnt*
Tiffany Omalley, *Real Est Agnt*
EMP: 13
SALES (est): 790.9K **Privately Held**
WEB: www.debbiereed.com
SIC: 6531 Real estate agent, residential

(G-7910)
DEJA VU RECORD ALBUM COVER ART
35982 Bay Dr (19971-8448)
PHONE.................302 227-8909
Robert Weymouth, *Principal*
EMP: 1
SALES (est): 56K **Privately Held**
SIC: 2782 Record albums

(G-7911)
DELAWARE COUNCL ON GMBLNG PRBL
37201 Rehoboth Avenue Ext (19971-3192)
PHONE.................302 226-5041
Lemont Dupont, *Branch Mgr*
EMP: 7 **Privately Held**
WEB: www.dcgp.org
SIC: 8322 General counseling services
PA: Delaware Council On Gambling Problems
     100 W 10th St Ste 303
     Wilmington DE 19801

(G-7912)
DELAWARE EYE INSTITUTE PA
Also Called: Delaware Eye Optical
18791 J J Williams Hwy (19971)
PHONE.................302 645-2300
David Robinson, *Med Doctor*
Robert Uffelman,
Rosemarie Berardinelli,
EMP: 27
SALES (est): 4MM **Privately Held**
SIC: 8011 Eyes, ears, nose & throat specialist: physician/surgeon; ophthalmologist

(G-7913)
DELAWARE EYE SURGERY CENTER
18791 John J Williams Hwy (19971-4487)
PHONE.................302 645-2300
Art Belson, *Med Doctor*
Robert Uffelman, *Administration*
EMP: 5
SALES (est): 734.2K **Privately Held**
WEB: www.delawareeye.com
SIC: 8011 Eyes, ears, nose & throat specialist: physician/surgeon; ophthalmologist

(G-7914)
DELAWARE REALTY GROUP INC
Also Called: Re/Max
317 Rehoboth Ave (19971-3127)
PHONE.................302 227-4800
Joseph Reed, *President*
Schaefer Gabrielle, *Accounts Exec*
Cyndi Marsh, *Director*
Robert M Reed, *Real Est Agnt*
Robert Burton, *Associate*
EMP: 7
SALES (est): 1MM **Privately Held**
WEB: www.jackdaggett.com
SIC: 6531 Real estate agent, residential

(G-7915)
DEWEY ARTIST COLLABORATION INC
19817 Hebron Rd (19971)
P.O. Box 42 (19971-0042)
PHONE.................302 212-9798
Leah Beach, *Principal*
EMP: 4
SALES (est): 100.1K **Privately Held**
SIC: 8699 Charitable organization

(G-7916)
DICK PALMER WOODWORKING
Near Midway Rd 1 (19971)
PHONE.................302 227-8419
Richard Palmer, *Owner*
EMP: 1
SALES (est): 54.9K **Privately Held**
SIC: 2499 Decorative wood & woodwork

(G-7917)
DILLON DISTRIBUTORS LLC
35584 Airport Rd (19971-4620)
PHONE.................302 226-9700
Michael Dillon, *Principal*
EMP: 4
SALES (est): 395.7K **Privately Held**
SIC: 5199 Nondurable goods

(G-7918)
DOGFISH HEAD INC
Also Called: Dogfish Head Brewings & Eats
320 Rehoboth Ave (19971-3108)
PHONE.................302 226-2739
Sam Calagione, *President*
Mariah Calagione, *Treasurer*
Timothy Parrott, *Graphic Designe*
EMP: 14
SALES (est): 800K **Privately Held**
SIC: 5812 2082 Seafood restaurants; malt beverages

(G-7919)
DOMINRING BLGCAL RES GROUP LLC
19266 Coastal Hwy (19971-6117)
PHONE.................951 327-8062
Garviea Freeny, *Principal*
EMP: 10
SALES: 200K **Privately Held**
SIC: 8742 Business consultant

(G-7920)
DOVER ELECTRIC SUPPLY CO INC
18585 Curstol Hwy Ste 15 (19971)
PHONE.................302 645-0555
Joyce Wooters, *Manager*
EMP: 4
SALES (corp-wide): 10.9MM **Privately Held**
WEB: www.doverelectric.com
SIC: 5063 Electrical supplies
PA: Dover Electric Supply Co Inc
     1631 S Dupont Hwy
     Dover DE 19901
     302 674-0115

(G-7921)
DREAM WEAVER INTERIORS INC
34 Midway Shopping Ctr (19971)
PHONE.................302 644-0800
Susan Johnson, *President*
Cynthia Oronzio, *Vice Pres*
Maggie Stevenson, *Admin Sec*
EMP: 4
SQ FT: 3,000
SALES: 600K **Privately Held**
WEB: www.dreamweaverinteriors.com
SIC: 7389 5714 Interior decorating; draperies

(G-7922)
DUSTNTIME
36181 Field Ln (19971-8655)
PHONE.................302 858-7876
Jennifer Kellog, *Managing Prtnr*
Jimi Kellog, *Partner*
EMP: 14
SALES (est): 363.3K **Privately Held**
SIC: 7699 7389 Cleaning services;

(G-7923)
EAST SUSSEX PUBLIC BRDCSTG
Also Called: Radio Sussex
13 Breakwater Dr (19971-9573)
PHONE.................302 644-7385
Winfield Standiford, *President*
Winfield S Standiford III, *President*
Craig W Abbott, *Bd of Directors*
Tom Dooley, *Bd of Directors*
Richard M McReynolds, *Bd of Directors*
EMP: 4
SALES: 25K **Privately Held**
SIC: 4832 Educational

(G-7924)
ECHELON INTERIORS LLC
55 Cascade Ln Ste A (19971-8528)
PHONE.................302 519-9151
Jason Exline, *Opers Mgr*
Beth Remington, *Mng Member*
Maxine Lewis, *Agent*

Rehoboth Beach - Sussex County (G-7925)

GEOGRAPHIC SECTION

Chris Schell,
EMP: 5
SALES: 500K **Privately Held**
SIC: 7389 Interior designer

(G-7925)
ECONO LODGE INN SUITES RESORT
19540 Coastal Hwy (19971-6120)
PHONE..................302 227-0500
Sal Gallo, *President*
Terry Bartley, *General Mgr*
EMP: 19
SQ FT: 13,500
SALES (est): 1.5MM **Privately Held**
WEB: www.econolodgerehoboth.com
SIC: 7011 Hotels & motels

(G-7926)
EMMERT AUCTION ASSOCIATES
4270d Rehoboth Svc Ctr (19971)
PHONE..................302 227-1433
William Emmert, *Owner*
EMP: 11
SALES (est): 752.7K **Privately Held**
WEB: www.emmertauction.com
SIC: 7389 Auctioneers, fee basis; auction, appraisal & exchange services

(G-7927)
ENHANCED DENTAL CARE
18947 John J Williams Hwy (19971-4474)
PHONE..................302 645-7200
EMP: 4
SALES (est): 126.3K **Privately Held**
SIC: 8021 Offices & clinics of dentists

(G-7928)
ERNIE DEANGELIS (PA)
Also Called: Tomato Sunshine
19791 Coastal Hwy (19971-6157)
PHONE..................302 226-9533
Ernie Deangelis, *Owner*
EMP: 10
SALES: 1.3MM **Privately Held**
SIC: 5148 0782 Fresh fruits & vegetables; garden centers

(G-7929)
EXPRESS HOTEL INC
19953 Shuttle Rd (19971-4214)
PHONE..................302 227-4030
EMP: 8
SALES (est): 341.3K **Privately Held**
SIC: 7011 Hotels & motels

(G-7930)
FAE MCKENZIE
54 Baltimore Ave (19971-2130)
PHONE..................302 227-6700
EMP: 1 **EST:** 2011
SALES (est): 59K **Privately Held**
SIC: 3421 Mfg Cutlery

(G-7931)
FANNON COLOR PRINTING LLC
20 Harbor Rd (19971-1204)
PHONE..................302 227-2164
James Fannon, *Principal*
EMP: 2 **EST:** 2010
SALES (est): 140.7K **Privately Held**
SIC: 2752 Commercial printing, lithographic

(G-7932)
FAW CASSON
20376 Coastal Hwy Ste 204 (19971-8015)
PHONE..................302 226-1919
Alison Houck, *Managing Prtnr*
EMP: 6
SALES (est): 153.9K **Privately Held**
SIC: 8721 Accounting, auditing & bookkeeping

(G-7933)
FIRST STATE HEALTH & WELLNESS (PA)
Also Called: Midway Chiropractic
18585 Coastal Hwy Unit 26 (19971-6147)
PHONE..................302 645-6681
Stacey Cohen, *Owner*
EMP: 10 **EST:** 2007
SALES (est): 757.1K **Privately Held**
SIC: 8041 Offices & clinics of chiropractors

(G-7934)
FISHTAIL PRINT COMPANY
18585 Coastal Hwy (19971-6147)
PHONE..................302 408-4800
EMP: 2 **EST:** 2018
SALES (est): 89.6K **Privately Held**
SIC: 2752 Commercial printing, lithographic

(G-7935)
FISHTAIL PRINT COMPANY
125 Cornwall Rd (19971-1423)
PHONE..................302 682-3053
Connor Ghabra, *Principal*
EMP: 2 **EST:** 2018
SALES (est): 83.9K **Privately Held**
SIC: 2752 Commercial printing, lithographic

(G-7936)
FME LIGHTING LLC
21019 Rogers Ave (19971-1971)
P.O. Box 488, Hockessin (19707-0488)
PHONE..................877 234-8460
Patrick McKeefery, *Mng Member*
Colin McKeefery,
EMP: 2
SALES (est): 1.5MM **Privately Held**
SIC: 3645 Residential lighting fixtures; fluorescent lighting fixtures, residential

(G-7937)
FRESH INDUSTRIES LTD
Also Called: Juicefresh
37385 Henlopen Jct (19971-1685)
PHONE..................205 737-3747
David Harrison, *Principal*
EMP: 3 **EST:** 2012
SALES (est): 162.1K **Privately Held**
SIC: 2033 Vegetable juices; fresh

(G-7938)
FULTON BANK NATIONAL ASSN
Also Called: Fulton Financial Advisors
20281 Coastal Hwy (19971-8028)
PHONE..................302 227-0330
Kathy ARA, *Manager*
EMP: 9
SALES (corp-wide): 954MM **Publicly Held**
SIC: 6021 National commercial banks
HQ: Fulton Bank, National Association
1 Penn Sq Ste 1 # 1
Lancaster PA 17602
717 581-3166

(G-7939)
FUN SPORT INC
Also Called: Midway Speedway
Rr 1 (19971)
P.O. Box 960 (19971-0960)
PHONE..................302 644-2042
Jim Loomis, *President*
EMP: 6
SALES (est): 1.2MM **Privately Held**
SIC: 7996 Amusement parks

(G-7940)
G K ASSOCIATES INC
19 Eagles Lndg Unit 2 (19971-2788)
PHONE..................302 381-2824
Kathryn Withrow, *President*
EMP: 1
SALES: 75K **Privately Held**
SIC: 3669 3647 Emergency alarms; vehicular lighting equipment

(G-7941)
G REHOBOTH
234 Rehoboth Ave (19971-2134)
PHONE..................302 278-7677
EMP: 4
SALES (est): 46.4K **Privately Held**
SIC: 7999 Recreation services

(G-7942)
GALLO REALTY INC (PA)
Also Called: Prudential Gallo Realtor
37230 Rehoboth Avenue Ext (19971-3198)
PHONE..................302 945-7368
Elizabeth D Gallo, *President*
Bette Gallo, *Broker*
Kim Lawson, *Agent*
EMP: 6 **EST:** 1979
SQ FT: 2,000
SALES (est): 1.9MM **Privately Held**
WEB: www.prugallo.com
SIC: 6531 Real estate agent, residential

(G-7943)
GARAGE
18791 Coastal Hwy (19971-6152)
PHONE..................302 645-7288
Robert Wyatt, *Owner*
EMP: 5
SALES (est): 384K **Privately Held**
SIC: 5013 7539 Radiators; automotive repair shops

(G-7944)
GEORGE H BUNTING JR
Also Called: State Farm Insurance
19716 Sea Air Ave 1 (19971-3800)
P.O. Box 377 (19971-0377)
PHONE..................302 227-3891
George H Bunting Jr, *Owner*
George Bunting, *Agent*
EMP: 5
SALES (est): 661.7K **Privately Held**
SIC: 6411 Insurance agents & brokers

(G-7945)
GEORGE M HOWARD & SONS INC
18682 Munchy Branch Rd (19971-8753)
PHONE..................302 645-9655
John Howard, *President*
EMP: 4
SALES (est): 354K **Privately Held**
SIC: 1711 1629 Septic system construction; land preparation construction

(G-7946)
GEORGE METZ
Also Called: Sea Esta Motel III
37385 Rehoboth Avenue Ext (19971)
PHONE..................302 227-4343
George Metz, *Owner*
Cynthia Metz, *Co-Owner*
EMP: 7
SALES (est): 230K **Privately Held**
SIC: 7011 Motels

(G-7947)
GGE AMUSEMENTS
34974 Oyster House Rd (19971)
P.O. Box 622 (19971-0622)
PHONE..................302 227-0661
Rita Falcone, *President*
EMP: 7
SALES (est): 363.9K **Privately Held**
SIC: 7359 7929 Vending machine rental; entertainment service

(G-7948)
GIF NORTH AMERICA LLC
18227 Shockley Dr (19971-1337)
PHONE..................703 969-9243
Peter G Hartmann, *President*
EMP: 500
SALES (est): 58.3MM **Privately Held**
SIC: 8711 3714 Engineering services; motor vehicle parts & accessories

(G-7949)
GLOBAL FINANCIAL ADVISORS NETW
38291 Blackstone Ave (19971-2076)
PHONE..................302 697-3565
Brad Barrows, *Owner*
EMP: 4
SALES (est): 414.3K **Privately Held**
SIC: 6282 Investment advisory service

(G-7950)
GLOBAL MERCHANT PARTNERS LLC
38131 West Dr Unit 730 (19971-1772)
PHONE..................302 425-3567
Toby Guinn,
EMP: 1
SALES (est): 48.3K **Privately Held**
SIC: 7389 3578 8721 Purchasing service; point-of-sale devices; payroll accounting service

(G-7951)
GOLDS GYM
3712 Highway One (19971)
PHONE..................302 226-4653
Lisa Lawson, *President*
EMP: 9
SQ FT: 11,000
SALES (est): 174.5K **Privately Held**
SIC: 7991 Physical fitness facilities

(G-7952)
GOVERNMENT PORTFOLIO LLC
35546 Hatteras Ct (19971-4820)
PHONE..................301 718-9742
Lise S Haupt,
Dennis Berlin,
EMP: 10
SQ FT: 1,000
SALES: 1.3MM **Privately Held**
SIC: 6722 Money market mutual funds

(G-7953)
GRAMONOLI ENTERPRISES INC
Also Called: Yesteryars Phtgraphic Emporium
21 Rehoboth Ave (19971-2119)
PHONE..................302 227-1288
James Miller, *President*
EMP: 6
SALES: 250K **Privately Held**
SIC: 7221 Photographer, still or video

(G-7954)
GRAND RENTAL STATION
19897 Hebron Rd Unit G (19971-1253)
PHONE..................302 227-7368
Chris Quillen, *Owner*
Don Mitchell, *Technical Staff*
EMP: 4
SALES (est): 771.4K **Privately Held**
SIC: 7359 Equipment rental & leasing

(G-7955)
GREENLEA LLC
31 Rolling Rd (19971-1628)
PHONE..................302 227-7868
John Jones,
EMP: 4
SALES (est): 120.8K **Privately Held**
SIC: 6531 7389 Multiple listing service, real estate;

(G-7956)
GULCH GROUP LLC
Also Called: Bittenpixel
38 Olive Ave 1 (19971-2816)
PHONE..................202 697-1756
Christopher Tallia,
EMP: 1
SALES (est): 46.3K **Privately Held**
SIC: 7336 7372 7389 7371 Graphic arts & related design; application computer software; business oriented computer software; ; computer software systems analysis & design, custom

(G-7957)
HABIB BOLOURCHI MD FACC
Also Called: Henlopen Cardiology
4503 Hwy 1 (19971)
PHONE..................302 645-7672
Habib Bolourchi MD, *Owner*
EMP: 6
SALES (est): 336.5K **Privately Held**
SIC: 8011 Offices & clinics of medical doctors

(G-7958)
HEALTHY AT HOME CARE LLC
7 Kendal Ln (19971-2721)
PHONE..................571 228-5935
EMP: 7
SALES (est): 62.7K **Privately Held**
SIC: 8082 Home health care services

(G-7959)
HELOPEN CONDOMINIUM COUNCIL
Also Called: Henlopen Condominiums
527 N Boardwalk (19971-2831)
PHONE..................302 227-6409
Anthony Casale, *President*
Ellen Daleiao, *President*
Jerry Liguori, *Manager*
EMP: 7
SALES (est): 570.4K **Privately Held**
WEB: www.henlopen.com
SIC: 8641 Condominium association

GEOGRAPHIC SECTION

Rehoboth Beach - Sussex County (G-7992)

(G-7960)
HENLOPEN ACRES BEACH CLUB INC
28 Dune Way (19971)
P.O. Box 184 (19971-0184)
PHONE.................................302 227-9919
Joni Reich, *President*
EMP: 5
SALES: 283.1K **Privately Held**
SIC: 7997 Country club, membership

(G-7961)
HENLOPEN CARDIOLOGY PA (PA)
18959 Coastal Hwy Ste A (19971)
PHONE.................................302 645-7671
Nasi Bollurchi, *Manager*
EMP: 6
SALES (est): 683.2K **Privately Held**
SIC: 8011 Cardiologist & cardio-vascular specialist

(G-7962)
HENLOPEN HOTEL INC
511 N Boardwalk (19971-2162)
PHONE.................................302 227-2551
Louis J Capano, *President*
Steve Collins, *General Mgr*
EMP: 15
SQ FT: 90,000
SALES (est): 1.1MM **Privately Held**
WEB: www.henlopenhotel.com
SIC: 7011 Resort hotel; hotels

(G-7963)
HETE TECH SUPPORT
45 Kings Creek Cir (19971-1058)
PHONE.................................302 226-1892
Samuel Hete, *Principal*
EMP: 4
SALES (est): 83.6K **Privately Held**
SIC: 8399 Advocacy group

(G-7964)
HIGH SEAS MOTEL
12 Christian St (19971-3002)
PHONE.................................302 227-2022
Nick Chiartas, *Owner*
EMP: 4
SQ FT: 10,000
SALES (est): 140K **Privately Held**
WEB: www.highseasde.com
SIC: 7011 Motels

(G-7965)
HOLIDAY INN EXPRESS
19953 Shuttle Rd (19971-4214)
PHONE.................................302 227-4030
Sharleen Norris, *Owner*
Diana Huebler, *General Mgr*
Isac Henry, *Manager*
Gretchen Howk, *Manager*
Stephanie McHenry, *Manager*
EMP: 15
SALES (est): 700.1K **Privately Held**
WEB: www.holiday-rehoboth.com
SIC: 7011 Hotels & motels

(G-7966)
HUDSON JNES JAYWORK FISHER LLC
309 Rehoboth Ave (19971-3127)
PHONE.................................302 227-9441
Bill Becker, *Manager*
EMP: 10
SALES (corp-wide): 3.8MM **Privately Held**
WEB: www.delawarelaw.com
SIC: 8111 General practice law office
PA: Hudson Jones Jaywork & Fisher Llc
    225 S State St
    Dover DE 19901
    302 734-7401

(G-7967)
INDIAN RIVER CAPTAINS ASSOC
39415 Inlet Rd (19971-2600)
PHONE.................................302 227-3071
EMP: 4
SALES (est): 191.8K **Privately Held**
SIC: 4493 Marinas

(G-7968)
INNS OF REHOBOTH BEACH LLC
18826 Coastal Hwy (19971-6150)
PHONE.................................302 645-8003
Renei Thompson, *Branch Mgr*
EMP: 9 EST: 2013
SALES (est): 227.9K **Privately Held**
SIC: 7011 Inns

(G-7969)
J&J CONTRACTING CO INC
19287 Miller Rd Unit 4 (19971-6124)
PHONE.................................302 227-0800
James J Raymond Jr, *Principal*
EMP: 4
SALES (est): 785.1K **Privately Held**
SIC: 5194 1521 Tobacco & tobacco products; patio & deck construction & repair

(G-7970)
JACK LINGO INC REALTOR (PA)
246 Rehoboth Ave (19971-2134)
P.O. Box 605 (19971-0605)
PHONE.................................302 227-3883
Jack Lingo, *President*
Jack Ling0, *President*
Diane Dempsey, *Accountant*
Tjark Bateman, *Sales Staff*
Jeanmarie Clavier, *Sales Staff*
EMP: 37
SQ FT: 2,200
SALES (est): 4.6MM **Privately Held**
WEB: www.jacklingo.com
SIC: 6531 Real estate agent, residential

(G-7971)
JENNIFER M D HUNG
18947 John J Williams Hwy (19971-4474)
PHONE.................................302 644-0690
Jennifer Hung, *Manager*
EMP: 6 EST: 2017
SALES (est): 80.5K **Privately Held**
SIC: 8011 Offices & clinics of medical doctors

(G-7972)
JESSICA S DICERBO DDS
18947 John J Williams Hwy (19971-4474)
PHONE.................................302 644-4460
Jessica Dicerbo, *Principal*
EMP: 4
SALES (est): 61.5K **Privately Held**
SIC: 8021 Offices & clinics of dentists

(G-7973)
JOHNSON ORTHODONTICS
18947 John J Williams Hwy # 310 (19971-4477)
PHONE.................................302 645-5554
Jonathan Johnson, *Owner*
EMP: 5
SALES (est): 378.3K **Privately Held**
SIC: 8021 Orthodontist

(G-7974)
JOSEPH SCHWARTZ PSYD
19606 Coastal Hwy # 102 (19971-8596)
PHONE.................................302 213-3287
EMP: 6
SALES (est): 80.5K **Privately Held**
SIC: 8011 Offices & clinics of medical doctors

(G-7975)
JUDY V
39401 Inlet Rd (19971-2600)
PHONE.................................302 226-2214
Albert Adams, *Owner*
EMP: 6
SALES (est): 161.9K **Privately Held**
SIC: 7999 Fishing boats, party: operation

(G-7976)
KARL J ZEREN DDS
18947 John J Williams Hwy (19971-4474)
PHONE.................................302 644-2773
Karl J Zeren, *Principal*
EMP: 4 EST: 2016
SALES (est): 121.5K **Privately Held**
SIC: 8021 Offices & clinics of dentists

(G-7977)
KEEFER MOUNTAIN ENTERPRISE
56 Delaware Ave (19971-2219)
PHONE.................................814 657-3998
Edward Keefer, *President*
EMP: 4 EST: 2011
SALES (est): 223K **Privately Held**
SIC: 7389 Business services

(G-7978)
KENNY SIMPLER
Also Called: Avenue Inn
33 Wilmington Ave (19971-2218)
PHONE.................................302 226-2900
Kenny Simpler, *Owner*
EMP: 7
SALES (est): 421.3K **Privately Held**
SIC: 7011 Hotels

(G-7979)
KENSINGTON CROSS LTD (PA)
18585 Coastal Hwy (19971-6147)
PHONE.................................888 999-9360
Frederick S Gnesin, *President*
Michael J Piazza, *Vice Pres*
EMP: 12
SQ FT: 3,000
SALES (est): 3.8MM **Privately Held**
WEB: www.kensingtoncross.com
SIC: 6211 Investment bankers

(G-7980)
KEVIN FLEMING
Also Called: Kevin Fleming Photography
37021 Rehobth Ave Ext (19971-6159)
PHONE.................................302 227-4994
Kevin Fleming, *Owner*
▲ EMP: 3 EST: 2002
SALES (est): 136.8K **Privately Held**
WEB: www.theamericabook.com
SIC: 2731 Book publishing

(G-7981)
KIDS COTTAGE LLC
35448 Wolfe Neck Rd (19971-8788)
PHONE.................................302 644-7690
Lori Schell,
Taryn Burris,
EMP: 30
SALES (est): 750K **Privately Held**
SIC: 8351 Preschool center

(G-7982)
KINGS CREEK COUNTRY CLUB INC
1 Kings Creek Cir (19971-1034)
PHONE.................................302 227-8951
Stephen R Lett, *President*
Kenneth H Diggs, *Vice Pres*
Gail Petren, *Treasurer*
John Hardin Young, *Admin Sec*
EMP: 10
SALES: 3.2MM **Privately Held**
SIC: 7997 Country club, membership

(G-7983)
KOHR BROTHERS INC
5 Rehoboth Ave (19971-2119)
PHONE.................................302 227-9354
Sean Martin, *Manager*
EMP: 15
SALES (est): 310K
SALES (corp-wide): 14MM **Privately Held**
SIC: 5812 6794 Frozen yogurt stand; franchises, selling or licensing
PA: Kohr Brothers, Inc.
    2151 Richmond Rd Ste 200
    Charlottesville VA 22911
    434 975-1500

(G-7984)
LACOSTE USA INC
Also Called: Devanlay
36470 Seaside Outlet Dr (19971-1212)
PHONE.................................302 227-9575
Mark Gaskins, *General Mgr*
EMP: 7
SALES (corp-wide): 6B **Privately Held**
SIC: 5137 Women's & children's clothing
HQ: Lacoste Usa, Inc.
    551 Madison Ave Ste 1300
    New York NY 10022

(G-7985)
LEGGS HANES BALI PLAYTEX OTLT
36454 Seaside Outlet Dr (19971-1222)
PHONE.................................302 227-8943
Sarah Lee, *Owner*
EMP: 5
SALES (est): 302.4K **Privately Held**
SIC: 3643 Outlets, electric: convenience

(G-7986)
LIDS CORPORATION
Also Called: Lids / Hatworld
35706 Byside Outl Dr S440 (19971)
PHONE.................................302 226-8580
Lane Aldridge, *Branch Mgr*
EMP: 7
SALES (corp-wide): 2.1B **Publicly Held**
WEB: www.hatworld.com
SIC: 5136 Hats, men's & boys'
HQ: Lids Corporation
    7555 Woodland Dr
    Indianapolis IN 46278

(G-7987)
LITTLE LEAGUE BASEBALL INC
125 Beachfield Dr (19971-9674)
PHONE.................................302 227-0888
Mike Simpler, *Principal*
EMP: 4
SALES (est): 38.1K **Privately Held**
SIC: 7997 Baseball club, except professional & semi-professional

(G-7988)
LLC SCHELL BROTHERS
55 Cascade Ln B (19971-8528)
PHONE.................................302 226-1994
Adam Pettengell, *Sales Staff*
Michelle Capaldi, *Branch Mgr*
EMP: 10
SALES (corp-wide): 15.8MM **Privately Held**
SIC: 1799 Building board-up contractor
PA: Schell Brothers Llc
    20184 Phillips St
    Rehoboth Beach DE 19971
    302 226-1994

(G-7989)
LOGO MOTIVE INC
35576 Airport Rd (19971-4620)
PHONE.................................302 645-2959
Jeff Vernon, *Manager*
EMP: 3
SALES (est): 378.9K **Privately Held**
SIC: 2759 Screen printing

(G-7990)
LOMAS PROPERTIES LLC
Also Called: Crosswinds Motel
312 Rehoboth Ave (19971-3108)
PHONE.................................302 260-9245
Dale Lomes, *Owner*
EMP: 4
SALES (est): 132.1K **Privately Held**
SIC: 7011 Motel, franchised

(G-7991)
LONG & FOSTER REAL ESTATE INC
37156 Rehoboth Avenue Ext # 5 (19971-3104)
PHONE.................................302 227-3821
Carol Mapderniak, *General Mgr*
Susannah Griffin, *Real Est Agnt*
EMP: 5
SALES (corp-wide): 225.3B **Publicly Held**
WEB: www.longandfoster.com
SIC: 6531 6519 Real estate agent, residential; real property lessors
HQ: Long & Foster Real Estate Inc
    11225 Nuckols Rd Ste A
    Glen Allen VA 23059
    804 346-4411

(G-7992)
M C TEK LLC
Also Called: Geekytek
19122 Coastal Hwy Unit B (19971-6136)
PHONE.................................302 644-9695
Chanh Ly,
EMP: 8

(PA)=Parent Co (HQ)=Headquarters (DH)=Div Headquarters
✪ = New Business established in last 2 years

2020 Harris Directory of Delaware Businesses

Rehoboth Beach - Sussex County (G-7993)   GEOGRAPHIC SECTION

SALES (est): 730.7K **Privately Held**
SIC: **7373** 8741 Computer integrated systems design; business management

(G-7993)
M&J SERVICES LLC
307 Bayview Ave (19971-1909)
PHONE.....................................302 227-8725
Jack Phillip, *Owner*
EMP: 5
SALES (est): 138.1K **Privately Held**
SIC: **7699** Cleaning services

(G-7994)
MAGGIO/SHIELDS TEAMS
70 Rehoboth Ave Ste 101 (19971-2127)
PHONE.....................................302 226-3770
Betty Mann, *Principal*
Joe Maggio, *Broker*
EMP: 10
SALES (est): 634.8K **Privately Held**
SIC: **6531** Real estate agent, residential; real estate brokers & agents

(G-7995)
MAN MAID CLEANING INC
29 Fox Creek Dr (19971-8615)
PHONE.....................................302 226-5050
Joe Biliski, *President*
EMP: 6
SALES: 96K **Privately Held**
SIC: **7699** Cleaning services

(G-7996)
MANUFACTURERS & TRADERS TR CO
Also Called: M&T
302 Rehoboth Ave (19971-3108)
PHONE.....................................302 855-2227
Patricia Hastings, *Manager*
EMP: 7
SALES (corp-wide): 6.4B **Publicly Held**
WEB: www.binghamlegg.com
SIC: **6022** State commercial banks
HQ: Manufacturers And Traders Trust Company
1 M&T Plz Fl 3
Buffalo NY 14203
716 842-4200

(G-7997)
MAPLEWOOD HOME OWNERS CLUBHOUS
12 Vassar Dr (19971-9421)
PHONE.....................................302 645-9925
EMP: 5
SALES (est): 64.3K **Privately Held**
SIC: **8641** Civic/Social Association

(G-7998)
MARINERS COURT CONDO ASSN
4 Laurel St (19971-2948)
P.O. Box 514 (19971-0514)
PHONE.....................................443 742-7812
Donald Oconner, *President*
EMP: 36
SALES (est): 428.7K **Privately Held**
SIC: **8641** Condominium association

(G-7999)
MARK SHOWELL INTERIORS LTD
59 Baltimore Ave (19971-2131)
PHONE.....................................302 227-2272
Mark Showell, *President*
EMP: 10
SQ FT: 20,000
SALES (est): 1.1MM **Privately Held**
SIC: **7389** Interior design services

(G-8000)
MARSHALL HOTELS & RESORTS INC
Also Called: Marina Suites
1115 Hwy One (19971)
PHONE.....................................302 227-1700
Chris Wilk, *Manager*
EMP: 24
SALES (corp-wide): 5.5MM **Privately Held**
WEB: www.fenwickinn.com
SIC: **4493** Marine basins

PA: Marshall Hotels & Resorts, Inc.
1315 S Division St
Salisbury MD 21804
410 749-8464

(G-8001)
MARSHALL WAGNER & ASSOCIATES
19643 Blue Bird Ln Unit 2 (19971-6129)
PHONE.....................................302 227-2537
Doug Marshall, *Partner*
EMP: 7
SALES (est): 599K **Privately Held**
SIC: **8721** Certified public accountant

(G-8002)
MARY COSTAS WOODWORKING
527 School Ln (19971-1807)
PHONE.....................................302 227-6255
Mary Costa, *Principal*
EMP: 2 EST: 2011
SALES (est): 176.1K **Privately Held**
SIC: **2431** Millwork

(G-8003)
MERRILL LYNCH PIERCE FENNER
19535 Carmelot Dr (19971)
P.O. Box 390 (19971-0390)
PHONE.....................................302 227-5159
Jonathan Lokken, *Manager*
EMP: 20
SALES (corp-wide): 110.5B **Publicly Held**
WEB: www.merlyn.com
SIC: **6211** Security brokers & dealers
HQ: Merrill Lynch, Pierce, Fenner & Smith Incorporated
111 8th Ave
New York NY 10011
800 637-7455

(G-8004)
METERPRO SERVICES INC
112 Stockley St (19971-2272)
PHONE.....................................302 227-8596
Nelson Shugart, *President*
EMP: 1
SQ FT: 2,500
SALES (est): 248.4K **Privately Held**
SIC: **3824** Water meters

(G-8005)
MICROCOM TECH LLC
18971 Goldfinch Cv (19971-4462)
PHONE.....................................858 775-5559
Hung Nguyen, *CEO*
EMP: 5
SALES: 200K **Privately Held**
SIC: **7371** 7389 Computer software development & applications;

(G-8006)
MICROLOG CORPORATION MARYLAND
17027 Taramac Dr (19971-9644)
PHONE.....................................301 540-5501
Richard E Meccarielli, *President*
Sandy Comni, *Principal*
EMP: 8 EST: 1977
SQ FT: 25,000
SALES: 1.5MM **Privately Held**
WEB: www.mlog.com
SIC: **7371** Computer software development

(G-8007)
MIDWAY FITNESS CENTER
Also Called: Midway Fitnes Racquetball CLB
28b Midway Shopping Ctr (19971)
PHONE.....................................302 645-0407
Rich Garett, *Owner*
EMP: 7
SALES (est): 293.9K **Privately Held**
WEB: www.midwayfitness.com
SIC: **7991** 5941 Athletic club & gymnasiums, membership; sporting goods & bicycle shops

(G-8008)
MIDWAY REALTY INC
29 Midway Shopping Ctr (19971)
PHONE.....................................302 645-9511
Richard H Derrickson, *President*
Donald L Derrickson, *Corp Secy*

Ethel Derrickson, *Vice Pres*
EMP: 4 EST: 1953
SQ FT: 60,000
SALES (est): 438.2K **Privately Held**
SIC: **6512** Shopping center, property operation only

(G-8009)
MIDWAY VENTURES LLC
Also Called: Hampton Inn
18826 Coastal Hwy (19971-6150)
PHONE.....................................302 645-8003
Michael A Meoli, *Mng Member*
Anthony J Meoli, *Mng Member*
EMP: 35
SALES (est): 1.9MM **Privately Held**
SIC: **7011** Hotels & motels

(G-8010)
MOORES ENTERPRISES INC
Also Called: Oceanus Motel
6 2nd St (19971-2118)
P.O. Box 324 (19971-0324)
PHONE.....................................302 227-8200
Robert H Moore, *President*
EMP: 10
SQ FT: 12,000
SALES (est): 714.9K **Privately Held**
SIC: **7011** Motels

(G-8011)
MORANS REFRIGERATION SERVICE
146 Glade Cir W (19971-4106)
PHONE.....................................703 642-1200
Charles H Moran III, *President*
Fortney Joseph M, *Vice Pres*
Frances Moran, *Treasurer*
Barbara Moran, *Admin Sec*
EMP: 18 EST: 1971
SALES (est): 2.3MM **Privately Held**
SIC: **1711** 7623 Warm air heating & air conditioning contractor; refrigeration repair service

(G-8012)
MORGAN STANLEY
55 Cascade Ln (19971-8528)
PHONE.....................................302 644-6600
C W Mitchell, *Manager*
EMP: 26
SALES (corp-wide): 50.1B **Publicly Held**
SIC: **6411** Insurance agents, brokers & service
PA: Morgan Stanley
1585 Broadway
New York NY 10036
212 761-4000

(G-8013)
MORGAN STNLEY SMITH BARNEY LLC
55 Cascade Ln (19971-8528)
PHONE.....................................302 644-6600
Ed Duffy, *Branch Mgr*
EMP: 4
SALES (corp-wide): 50.1B **Publicly Held**
SIC: **6282** Investment advice
HQ: Morgan Stanley Smith Barney, Llc
2000 Westchester Ave
Purchase NY 10577

(G-8014)
MORRIS JAMES LLP
19339 Coastal Hwy # 300 (19971-6213)
PHONE.....................................302 260-7290
EMP: 21
SALES (corp-wide): 21.2MM **Privately Held**
SIC: **8111** General practice attorney, lawyer
PA: Morris James Llp
500 Delaware Ave Ste 1500
Wilmington DE 19801
302 888-6863

(G-8015)
MR COPY INC
20200 Coastal Hwy Ste A (19971-8057)
PHONE.....................................302 227-4666
George Banashak, *President*
EMP: 5
SQ FT: 1,800

SALES (est): 474.2K **Privately Held**
SIC: **7334** 3993 Photocopying & duplicating services; signs & advertising specialties

(G-8016)
NETTEL PARTNERS LLC
8 Venetian Dr (19971-1937)
PHONE.....................................215 290-7383
John Neff, *Branch Mgr*
EMP: 11
SALES (corp-wide): 1.9MM **Privately Held**
SIC: **7389** Telemarketing services
PA: Nettel Partners, Llc
101 N Synnott Ave
Wenonah NJ 08090
215 964-9345

(G-8017)
NICOLA PIZZA INC
Also Called: Nic-O-Boli
8 N 1st St (19971-2116)
PHONE.....................................302 227-6211
Nicholas S Caggiano Jr, *President*
Joan Caggiano, *Corp Secy*
EMP: 30
SQ FT: 6,000
SALES (est): 1.4MM **Privately Held**
WEB: www.nicolapizza.com
SIC: **5812** 2038 Pizza restaurants; frozen specialties

(G-8018)
OCEAN ATLANTIC AGENCY INC
330 Rehoboth Ave (19971-3108)
PHONE.....................................302 227-6767
Ronald Lankford, *Owner*
Justin Healy, *Partner*
Mariya Oldfather, *Real Est Agnt*
EMP: 11
SALES (est): 743.5K **Privately Held**
SIC: **6531** Real estate agent, residential; real estate brokers & agents

(G-8019)
OCEAN ATLANTIC ASSOCIATES LLC
Also Called: Ocean Atlantic Companies
18949 Coastal Hwy # 301 (19971-6219)
PHONE.....................................302 227-3573
Preston Schell, *Partner*
Jennifer Nagle, *Partner*
Erin Scharp, *Partner*
Tom Tipton, *COO*
Jaime Zolper, *Vice Pres*
EMP: 10
SALES (est): 1.2MM **Privately Held**
WEB: www.oceanatlantic.net
SIC: **6531** Real estate brokers & agents; real estate agent, residential

(G-8020)
OCEAN ATLANTIC MANAGEMENT LLC
Also Called: Ocean Atlantic Companies
18949 Coastal Hwy # 301 (19971-6219)
PHONE.....................................302 227-3573
Preston Schell, *President*
EMP: 13
SALES (est): 464.2K **Privately Held**
SIC: **6552** Land subdividers & developers, residential

(G-8021)
OCEAN TRAVEL
19478 Coastal Hwy Unit 7 (19971-6126)
P.O. Box 999 (19971-0999)
PHONE.....................................302 227-1607
Genevieve Wilson, *Owner*
EMP: 4
SALES (est): 437.7K **Privately Held**
SIC: **4724** Travel agencies

(G-8022)
OLD INLET BAIT AND TACKLE INC (PA)
Also Called: Wetsu Tackle Distributors
25012 Coastal Hwy (19971-8009)
P.O. Box 129 (19971-0129)
PHONE.....................................302 227-7974
Amos Evans, *President*
Linda Evans, *Corp Secy*
EMP: 15
SQ FT: 3,200

GEOGRAPHIC SECTION
Rehoboth Beach - Sussex County (G-8054)

SALES: 941.4K **Privately Held**
WEB: www.oldinlet.com
SIC: **5941** 5091 Bait & tackle; fishing equipment & supplies

(G-8023)
ONE VIRGINIA
Also Called: Avenue Condominium
1 Virginia Ave Ste 1 # 1 (19971-2886)
PHONE..................................302 227-9533
Robert Adams, *President*
EMP: 4
SALES (est): 261.6K **Privately Held**
SIC: **8641** Condominium association

(G-8024)
OUTLET LIQUORS
19724 Coastal Hwy Unit 1 (19971-6198)
PHONE..................................302 227-7700
Sue Cassidy, *Manager*
EMP: 5
SALES (est): 480K **Privately Held**
SIC: **5182** Liquor

(G-8025)
OVERTURE LLC
20660 Coastal Hwy Unit 1 (19971-8053)
PHONE..................................302 226-1940
Terry Menacker, *Branch Mgr*
EMP: 5
SALES (est): 223.7K **Privately Held**
SIC: **7622** Television repair shop
PA: Overture L.L.C.
2423 Concord Pike
Wilmington DE 19803

(G-8026)
P C BOHLER ENGINEERING
18958 Coastal Hwy (19971-6196)
PHONE..................................302 644-1155
Dave Kuklish, *Manager*
EMP: 42
SALES (corp-wide): 58.7MM **Privately Held**
SIC: **8711** Engineering services
PA: P C Bohler Engineering
35 Technology Dr Ste 5
Warren NJ 07059
908 222-0023

(G-8027)
PACKEM ASSOCIATES PARTNERSHIP
Also Called: Brighton Suites
34 Wilmington Ave (19971-2217)
PHONE..................................302 227-5780
Joe Callahan, *Branch Mgr*
EMP: 9
SALES (est): 327.2K
SALES (corp-wide): 1.5MM **Privately Held**
WEB: www.caymansuites.com
SIC: **7011** Hotels
PA: Packem Associates Ltd Partnership
4750 Owings Mills Blvd
Owings Mills MD 21117
410 356-9900

(G-8028)
PAR 4 GOLF INC
38 Glade Cir E (19971-4140)
PHONE..................................302 227-5663
James Jones, *Owner*
EMP: 1 EST: 2015
SALES (est): 51.6K **Privately Held**
SIC: **3949** Sporting & athletic goods

(G-8029)
PENCO CORPORATION
Rr 1 (19971-9801)
PHONE..................................302 227-9188
Brad Jester, *Manager*
EMP: 7
SALES (corp-wide): 18.4MM **Privately Held**
WEB: www.pencocorp.com
SIC: **5074** Plumbing fittings & supplies
PA: Penco Corporation
1503 W Stein Hwy
Seaford DE 19973
302 629-7911

(G-8030)
PENSKE TRUCK LEASING CORP
19659 Blue Bird Ln (19971-8599)
PHONE..................................302 260-7039
EMP: 6
SALES (corp-wide): 9.6B **Privately Held**
SIC: **7513** Truck rental & leasing, no drivers
HQ: Penske Truck Leasing Corporation
2675 Morgantown Rd
Reading PA 19607
610 775-6000

(G-8031)
PEP-UP INC
Also Called: Pep-Up 11
18979 Coastal Hwy (19971)
PHONE..................................302 645-2600
Dawn Baldwin, *Manager*
EMP: 5
SALES (corp-wide): 38.2MM **Privately Held**
WEB: www.pep-up.com
SIC: **5172** 5984 Service station supplies, petroleum; liquefied petroleum gas, delivered to customers' premises
PA: Pep-Up, Inc.
24987 Dupont Blvd
Georgetown DE 19947
302 856-2555

(G-8032)
PHIPPINS CABINETRY
20807 Coastal Hwy Apt 1 (19971-8013)
PHONE..................................302 212-2189
George Phippin, *Principal*
EMP: 4
SALES (est): 387.6K **Privately Held**
SIC: **2434** Wood kitchen cabinets

(G-8033)
POINT COFFEE SHOP AND BAKERY
37140 Rehoboth Avenue Ext (19971-3196)
PHONE..................................302 260-9734
Anne Tillig, *Principal*
EMP: 8
SALES (est): 155.1K **Privately Held**
SIC: **5812** 5149 Coffee shop; bakery products

(G-8034)
PORT DEL-MAR-VA INC
260 Port Delmarva (19971-9501)
PHONE..................................302 227-7409
EMP: 9
SQ FT: 2,000
SALES (est): 115.2K **Privately Held**
SIC: **7033** Trailer Park/Campsites

(G-8035)
PRECISION MARINE CONSTRUCTION
125 Blackpool Rd (19971-3516)
PHONE..................................302 227-2711
Charles Hopkins, *Principal*
EMP: 8 EST: 2009
SALES (est): 728.3K **Privately Held**
SIC: **1629** Marine construction

(G-8036)
PRESICSON PAIN RHBLTATION SVCS
18958 Coastal Hwy (19971-6196)
PHONE..................................302 827-2321
Jeffrey Conly, *Principal*
EMP: 4 EST: 2010
SALES (est): 142.2K **Privately Held**
SIC: **8093** Rehabilitation center, outpatient treatment

(G-8037)
PYNE CHIROPRACTIC PA
18977 Munchy Branch Rd # 3 (19971-8763)
PHONE..................................302 644-1792
David M Pyne, *President*
EMP: 4
SALES (est): 290K **Privately Held**
SIC: **8041** Offices & clinics of chiropractors

(G-8038)
QLEAN IMPLANTS INC
19266 Coastal Hwy Unit 4 (19971-6117)
PHONE..................................302 613-0804
EMP: 4
SALES (est): 61.5K **Privately Held**
SIC: **8021** Specialized dental practitioners

(G-8039)
QUILLENS RENT ALL INC
Also Called: Grand Rental Station
803 Rehoboth Ave Ste G (19971)
PHONE..................................302 227-3151
Chris Quillen, *President*
EMP: 8
SQ FT: 3,600
SALES (est): 860K **Privately Held**
SIC: **7359** Equipment rental & leasing

(G-8040)
RATNER COMPANIES LC
Also Called: Creative Hairdressers
19323 Lighthouse Plaza Bl (19971-6162)
PHONE..................................302 226-9822
Melanie Windgate, *Branch Mgr*
EMP: 12 **Privately Held**
WEB: www.haircuttery.com
SIC: **7231** Unisex hair salons
HQ: Ratner Companies, L.C.
1577 Spring Hill Rd # 500
Vienna VA 22182
703 269-5400

(G-8041)
RAYMOND JAMES FINCL SVCS INC
20281 Coastal Hwy (19971-8028)
PHONE..................................302 227-0330
Liz Petrutcelli, *Branch Mgr*
EMP: 7
SALES (corp-wide): 8B **Publicly Held**
SIC: **6399** Bank deposit insurance
HQ: Raymond James Financial Services, Inc.
880 Carillon Pkwy
Saint Petersburg FL 33716
727 567-1000

(G-8042)
RBAH INC
20259 Coastal Hwy (19971-8028)
PHONE..................................302 227-2009
Timothy Dabkowski, *Principal*
EMP: 6 EST: 2010
SALES (est): 338.5K **Privately Held**
SIC: **0742** Animal hospital services, pets & other animal specialties

(G-8043)
RCK SOLIATIRE LLC
19266 Cstl Hwy Unit 4108 (19971)
PHONE..................................551 358-8400
Ripin C Khatroja,
EMP: 10
SALES (est): 369.4K **Privately Held**
SIC: **3911** Jewelry, precious metal

(G-8044)
RE/MAX REALTY GROUP-RENTALS
323 Rehoboth Ave Ste A (19971-2178)
PHONE..................................302 227-4800
Tyler Fleck, *Director*
EMP: 10
SALES (est): 85.1K **Privately Held**
SIC: **7011** Vacation lodges

(G-8045)
READY SET TEXTILES INC
19266 Coastal Hwy (19971-6117)
PHONE..................................302 518-6583
Iain Scorgie, *President*
▲ EMP: 6
SQ FT: 500
SALES: 6.5MM **Privately Held**
SIC: **5023** Sheets, textile

(G-8046)
REGIS CORPORATION
Also Called: Holiday Hair 141
19330 Coastal Hwy (19971)
PHONE..................................302 227-9730
Mary Ann Gardheir, *Manager*
EMP: 7
SALES (corp-wide): 1B **Publicly Held**
WEB: www.regiscorp.com
SIC: **7231** Unisex hair salons
PA: Regis Corporation
7201 Metro Blvd
Edina MN 55439
952 947-7777

(G-8047)
REHOBOTH ART LEAGUE INC
12 Dodds Ln (19971-1668)
PHONE..................................302 227-8408
Diana Beebe, *President*
James O Marshall III, *Vice Pres*
Janet Menard, *Bookkeeper*
Sheila Bravo, *Exec Dir*
Jay Pastore, *Director*
EMP: 4
SALES: 1MM **Privately Held**
WEB: www.rehobothartleague.org
SIC: **8412** Museum

(G-8048)
REHOBOTH BAY SAILING ASSN
Highway One (19971)
P.O. Box 483 (19971-0483)
PHONE..................................302 227-9008
Harold Dukes, *Principal*
EMP: 4
SALES: 193.2K **Privately Held**
SIC: **7997** Membership sports & recreation clubs

(G-8049)
REHOBOTH BEACH COUNTRY CLUB
221 W Side Dr (19971-1308)
P.O. Box 291 (19971-0291)
PHONE..................................302 227-3811
Michael Stattler, *President*
EMP: 60 EST: 1925
SQ FT: 43,000
SALES: 5MM **Privately Held**
WEB: www.rehobothbeachpatrol.com
SIC: **7997** Country club, membership; golf club, membership; tennis club, membership

(G-8050)
REHOBOTH BEACH DENT
19643 Blue Bird Ln (19971-6129)
PHONE..................................302 226-7960
Curtis Leciejewski, *Owner*
Michael Keller, *Principal*
EMP: 8 EST: 2013
SALES (est): 253.7K **Privately Held**
SIC: **8021** Dentists' office

(G-8051)
REHOBOTH BEACH DEWEY BEACH CHA
501 Rehoboth Ave (19971-3126)
PHONE..................................302 227-2233
Carol Everhart, *Exec Dir*
EMP: 10
SALES: 751.5K **Privately Held**
WEB: www.beach-fun.com
SIC: **8611** Chamber of Commerce

(G-8052)
REHOBOTH BEACH HISTORICAL SOC (PA)
Also Called: Rehoboth Beach Museum
17 Christian St (19971-3001)
PHONE..................................302 227-7310
Bill Bahan, *President*
Nancy Alexander, *Director*
EMP: 7
SALES (est): 393.9K **Privately Held**
SIC: **8412** Historical society

(G-8053)
REHOBOTH CAR WASH INC
37053 Rehoboth Avenue Ext (19971-7141)
PHONE..................................302 227-6177
Christopher Dispoto, *Owner*
EMP: 25
SALES (est): 957.3K **Privately Held**
SIC: **7542** Carwash, automatic

(G-8054)
REHOBOTH INN LLC
20494 Coastal Hwy (19971-8030)
P.O. Box 737 (19971-0737)
PHONE..................................302 226-2410
Rodney Wilson, *Owner*
EMP: 6
SALES (est): 564.7K **Privately Held**
WEB: www.rehobothinn.com
SIC: **7011** Motels

Rehoboth Beach - Sussex County (G-8055)   GEOGRAPHIC SECTION

(G-8055)
REHOBOTH REALTY INC
Also Called: Coldwell Banker
4157 Highway One (19971)
PHONE..................302 227-5000
James Kiernan, *President*
Ruth Ann Zerby, *Principal*
Veronica Kiernan, *Vice Pres*
EMP: 50
SALES (est): 2.2MM **Privately Held**
WEB: www.rehobothbythesea.com
SIC: 6531 Real estate agent, residential

(G-8056)
REHOBOTH SUMMER CHLD THEATRE
20 Baltimore Ave (19971-2104)
P.O. Box 871 (19971-0871)
PHONE..................302 227-6766
EMP: 14
SALES: 50.7K **Privately Held**
SIC: 7922 Theatrical Producers/Services

(G-8057)
RESORT HOTEL LLC
Also Called: Comfort Inn
19210 Coastal Hwy (19971-6116)
PHONE..................302 226-1515
Ronald Schaffer, *CEO*
Jennifer Coverdale, *General Mgr*
Jessica Kresge, *General Mgr*
Stephen Silver, *Principal*
EMP: 20
SALES (est): 1.6MM **Privately Held**
WEB: www.ahrinc.com
SIC: 7011 Hotels & motels

(G-8058)
RICHMAN WEALTH MANAGEMENT
19468 Manchester Dr (19971-4019)
PHONE..................443 536-6936
EMP: 5
SALES (est): 248.8K **Privately Held**
SIC: 8741 Management services

(G-8059)
RIGHT PROPERTY MGT CO LLC (PA)
20245 Bay Vista Rd # 205 (19971-8024)
PHONE..................302 227-1155
EMP: 11
SALES (est): 1.6MM **Privately Held**
SIC: 8741 Business management

(G-8060)
ROBINSON & COOK EYES SURGICAL
18791 John J Williams Hwy (19971-4401)
PHONE..................302 645-2300
David Robinson MD, *President*
EMP: 30
SALES (est): 1.2MM **Privately Held**
SIC: 8011 Ophthalmologist

(G-8061)
RODEWAY INN
19604 Blue Bird Ln (19971-8597)
PHONE..................302 227-0401
Terrance Bartley,
EMP: 30 **EST:** 1998
SALES: 1MM **Privately Held**
SIC: 7011 Hotels & motels

(G-8062)
RONALD L BARROWS
Also Called: Rehoboth Country Club
184 E Side Dr (19971-1300)
PHONE..................302 227-3616
Ronald L Barrows, *Owner*
EMP: 12
SALES: 250K **Privately Held**
SIC: 7997 Country club, membership

(G-8063)
ROTARY INTERNATIONAL
58 Rolling Rd (19971-1661)
PHONE..................302 227-5862
Elizabeth Grieb, *Branch Mgr*
EMP: 12
SALES (corp-wide): 503.3MM **Privately Held**
WEB: www.rotary5340.org
SIC: 8641 Civic associations

PA: Rotary International
1 Rotary Ctr
Evanston IL 60201
847 866-3000

(G-8064)
S F F ART INC (PA)
Also Called: Creative Impressions
200 Rehoboth Ave Ste A (19971-2134)
PHONE..................302 226-9410
Scott Frohman, *President*
Patricia Frohman, *Admin Sec*
EMP: 4
SQ FT: 3,000
SALES (est): 666.4K **Privately Held**
WEB: www.sffaudio.com
SIC: 7999 Art gallery, commercial

(G-8065)
SAFEGUARD
20 Cavendish Ct (19971-8642)
PHONE..................301 299-8806
Brenda Poole, *Manager*
EMP: 1
SALES (est): 46.4K **Privately Held**
SIC: 2761 Manifold business forms

(G-8066)
SANDCASTLE MOTEL
123 2nd St (19971-2283)
PHONE..................302 227-0400
Donald L Derrickson, *Owner*
EMP: 9
SQ FT: 32,000
SALES (est): 387.7K **Privately Held**
WEB: www.thesandcastlemotel.com
SIC: 7011 Motels

(G-8067)
SANDS INC
Also Called: Atlantic Sands Hotel
101 N Boardwalk (19971-2160)
PHONE..................302 227-2511
Ronald E Lankford, *President*
Rick Perez, *General Mgr*
Herbert Flickinger, *Vice Pres*
Ramune Stupuraite, *Controller*
Regina Moore, *Human Resources*
EMP: 65
SQ FT: 80,000
SALES (est): 5.3MM **Privately Held**
WEB: www.atlanticsandshotel.com
SIC: 7011 Resort hotel; hotels

(G-8068)
SCHELL BROTHERS LLC (PA)
20184 Phillips St (19971-8049)
PHONE..................302 226-1994
Kathy Cottingham, *QC Mgr*
Kaylie Austin, *Sales Staff*
Andrew Rogan, *Sales Staff*
Joni Von Vorys, *Sales Staff*
Joni Vorys, *Sales Staff*
EMP: 10
SALES (est): 15.8MM **Privately Held**
SIC: 1521 New construction, single-family houses

(G-8069)
SEA WITCH INC
Also Called: Sea Witch Inn & Spa
65 Lake Ave (19971-2107)
PHONE..................302 226-3900
Inez Conover, *President*
Holly Moore, *Vice Pres*
Samuel Handwerger, *CFO*
EMP: 4
SALES (est): 450K **Privately Held**
SIC: 7011 Bed & breakfast inn

(G-8070)
SEAGREEN BICYCLE LLP
54 Baltimore Ave (19971-2130)
PHONE..................302 226-2323
Eric Lowe, *Partner*
EMP: 5 **EST:** 2014
SALES (est): 109.7K **Privately Held**
SIC: 5091 6531 7699 Bicycles; real estate leasing & rentals; bicycle repair shop

(G-8071)
SEASIDE AMUSEMENTS INC
Also Called: Funland
6 Delaware Ave (19971-2904)
PHONE..................302 227-1921
EMP: 7

SALES (corp-wide): 2.3MM **Privately Held**
SIC: 7993 Amusement Device Operator
PA: Seaside Amusements Inc
359 E Granada Ave
Hershey PA
717 227-2785

(G-8072)
SEASIDE POINTE
36101 Seaside Blvd (19971-6165)
PHONE..................302 226-8750
EMP: 4
SALES (est): 88.2K **Privately Held**
SIC: 8052 Intermediate care facilities

(G-8073)
SHELL WE BOUNCE
20699 Coastal Hwy (19971-8064)
PHONE..................302 727-5411
Julie Derick, *Owner*
EMP: 6
SALES (est): 427.6K **Privately Held**
SIC: 7359 Equipment rental & leasing

(G-8074)
SHORE COMMUNITY MEDICAL
18947 John J Williams Hwy # 215 (19971-4476)
PHONE..................302 827-4365
Ahmed Elmanan, *Director*
Leslie N Sinclair, *Associate*
EMP: 5 **EST:** 2011
SALES (est): 312.4K **Privately Held**
SIC: 8011 Clinic, operated by physicians

(G-8075)
SHORE PROPERTY MAINTENANCE LLC
4 S Lake Ter (19971-4155)
PHONE..................302 227-7786
Ted Nowakowski, *Owner*
EMP: 30
SALES (est): 623.5K **Privately Held**
SIC: 0782 Landscape contractors

(G-8076)
SILVER WORKS INC
149 Rehoboth Ave (19971-2148)
PHONE..................302 227-1707
Max White, *President*
EMP: 12
SQ FT: 6,300
SALES: 798.9K **Privately Held**
SIC: 5944 3911 Jewelry, precious stones & precious metals; jewelry, precious metal

(G-8077)
SIMPLER AND SONS LLC
37139 Rehoboth Avenue Ext (19971-3194)
PHONE..................302 296-4400
Alex Moore, *CEO*
Patrick Staib, *COO*
EMP: 7
SALES (est): 334.2K **Privately Held**
SIC: 7011 Resort hotel

(G-8078)
SKIM USA
1904 Highway One (19971)
PHONE..................302 227-4011
Harry Wilson R, *Principal*
EMP: 13
SALES: 23.5K **Privately Held**
SIC: 8699 7997 Amateur sports promotion; membership sports & recreation clubs

(G-8079)
SKINIFY LLC
Also Called: Decalgirl.com
35770 Airport Rd (19971-4663)
PHONE..................302 212-5689
Ryan Peters, *CEO*
Amanda Peters, *COO*
Matt Hoopes, *Production*
EMP: 18
SQ FT: 19,100
SALES (est): 1.8MM **Privately Held**
SIC: 2752 Decals, lithographed

(G-8080)
SODEL CONCEPTS II LLC
220 Rehoboth Ave Unit A (19971-2134)
P.O. Box 49 (19971-0049)
PHONE..................302 228-3786
EMP: 6
SALES (est): 124.8K **Privately Held**
SIC: 8741 Restaurant management

(G-8081)
SOLUTIONS PROPERTY MANAGEMENT
38 Hannah Loop (19971-3149)
P.O. Box 594, Bethany Beach (19930-0594)
PHONE..................302 581-9060
Cathy McCallister, *Principal*
EMP: 5
SALES (est): 145.9K **Privately Held**
SIC: 8641 Condominium association

(G-8082)
SOUTHERN DEL ASSOC DNTL SPC
Also Called: Sdads
20398 Silver Lake Dr # 2 (19971-2090)
PHONE..................302 226-1606
Otto Tidwell, *Owner*
EMP: 4
SALES (est): 387.2K **Privately Held**
SIC: 8021 Maxillofacial specialist

(G-8083)
SOUTHERN DEL PHYSCL THERAPY
70 Rehoboth Ave 37155 (19971-2171)
PHONE..................302 227-2008
Julie Knowles, *Principal*
EMP: 4 **Privately Held**
SIC: 8049 Physical therapist
PA: Southern Delaware Physical Therapy Inc
701 Savannah Rd Ste A
Lewes DE 19958

(G-8084)
SOUTHERN DELAWARE SURGERY CTR
18941 John J Williams Hwy (19971-4404)
PHONE..................302 644-6992
Susan Fausett, *Mng Member*
Denise P Ritchard, *Manager*
Eric Cancoski, *Director*
EMP: 12
SQ FT: 13,137
SALES: 1.2MM **Privately Held**
SIC: 8062 General medical & surgical hospitals

(G-8085)
SPRING LAKE BATH & TENNIS CLUB
323 Rehoboth Ave (19971-2177)
P.O. Box 625 (19971-0625)
PHONE..................302 227-6136
Daniel Anderson, *Partner*
Stanley Thompson, *Partner*
Phyllis Donovan, *Admin Sec*
EMP: 4 **EST:** 1985
SALES (est): 83K **Privately Held**
SIC: 7997 Membership sports & recreation clubs

(G-8086)
STAR OF THE SEA ASSOC OF OWNRS
Also Called: Star of Sea Condominium
307 S Boardwalk Ste L2 (19971-2273)
PHONE..................302 227-6006
Roger Applegate, *President*
Donald Alexander, *Treasurer*
EMP: 7
SALES (est): 389.5K **Privately Held**
WEB: www.starofthesea-de.com
SIC: 8641 Condominium association

(G-8087)
STAUFFER FAMILY LLC
Also Called: Rodney's Animal Crackers
36 Glade Cir E (19971-4140)
P.O. Box 1393 (19971-5393)
PHONE..................302 227-5820
Rodney Stauffer, *President*
Scott Stauffer, *CFO*

GEOGRAPHIC SECTION

Rehoboth Beach - Sussex County (G-8116)

EMP: 2 EST: 2010
SALES (est): 1MM Privately Held
SIC: 2052 7389 Cookies;

(G-8088)
STONE HARBOR SQUARE LLC
42 Rehoboth Ave Ste 23 (19971-2122)
PHONE.................302 227-5227
Clinton Bunting, *Principal*
EMP: 7
SALES (est): 120.7K Privately Held
SIC: 8011 Offices & clinics of medical doctors

(G-8089)
STRIDE RITE CORPORATION
36474 Seaside Outlet Dr # 1570 (19971-0027)
PHONE.................302 226-2288
EMP: 8
SALES (corp-wide): 2.4B Publicly Held
SIC: 5139 Whol Footwear
HQ: The Stride Rite Corporation
500 Totten Pond Rd Ste 1
Waltham MA 02451
617 824-6000

(G-8090)
STUART KINGSTON INC (PA)
1 Grenoble Pl (19971-2847)
PHONE.................302 227-2524
Joseph Stein, *President*
Diane Stein, *Corp Secy*
▲ EMP: 13 EST: 1930
SQ FT: 15,000
SALES (est): 1.5MM Privately Held
SIC: 5331 5713 5999 5094 Variety stores; carpets; art dealers; precious stones (gems)

(G-8091)
SUN COMMUNITIES INC
Also Called: Sea Air Village
19837 Sea Air Ave (19971-3806)
PHONE.................302 227-8118
Mark Adams, *District Mgr*
EMP: 4
SALES (corp-wide): 1.1B Publicly Held
WEB: www.suncommunities.com
SIC: 6515 Mobile home site operators
PA: Sun Communities, Inc.
27777 Franklin Rd Ste 200
Southfield MI 48034
248 208-2500

(G-8092)
SUNNY HOSPITALITY LLC
Also Called: AmericInn
36012 Airport Rd (19971-4645)
PHONE.................302 226-0700
Ted Watkins,
Anne Watkins,
EMP: 15
SALES (est): 1MM Privately Held
SIC: 7011 Hotels & motels

(G-8093)
SWORD PARTS LLC
19266 Coastal Hwy 4-37 (19971-6117)
PHONE.................302 246-1346
Mehmet Karatokus,
Sultan Karatokus,
EMP: 2
SALES (est): 146.7K Privately Held
SIC: 3714 Transmissions, motor vehicle; motor vehicle body components & frame; shock absorbers, motor vehicle; steering mechanisms, motor vehicle

(G-8094)
T-MOBILE USA INC
18585 Coastal Hwy Unit 12 (19971-6147)
PHONE.................302 644-7222
EMP: 6
SALES (corp-wide): 83.9B Publicly Held
SIC: 4812 Cellular telephone services
HQ: T-Mobile Usa, Inc.
12920 Se 38th St
Bellevue WA 98006
425 378-4000

(G-8095)
TD BANK NA
Also Called: Rehoboth Beach, De Branch
34980 Midway Outlet Dr (19971-8585)
PHONE.................302 644-0952
EMP: 9
SALES (corp-wide): 22.8B Privately Held
SIC: 6029 6021 Commercial banks; national commercial banks
HQ: Td Bank, N.A.
1701 Route 70 E Ste 200
Cherry Hill NJ 08003
856 751-2739

(G-8096)
THETA VEST INC
Also Called: Rehoboth Bay Mobile Home Cmnty
21707 B St (19971-8410)
PHONE.................302 227-3745
Craig Hudson, *President*
Joseph R Hudson Sr, *Vice Pres*
Caron Thompson, *Director*
EMP: 14
SQ FT: 3,000
SALES (est): 46.2MM Privately Held
WEB: www.hudmgt.com
SIC: 6515 5271 Mobile home site operators; mobile homes

(G-8097)
THREE BS PAINTING CONTRACTORS
37021 Rehoboth Avenue Ext D (19971-6159)
PHONE.................302 227-1497
Raymond G Harp, *President*
William D Emmert, *President*
Raymond Harp, *Corp Secy*
EMP: 5
SQ FT: 2,000
SALES (est): 260.4K Privately Held
SIC: 1721 1742 Painting & paper hanging; drywall

(G-8098)
TIFFANY PINES I CONDO ASSN
20037 Old Landing Rd (19971-4612)
PHONE.................302 227-0913
Christopher Quillen, *Principal*
EMP: 5
SALES (est): 99.3K Privately Held
SIC: 8641 Condominium association

(G-8099)
TROPICAL HARVEST INC
10 Cardiff Rd (19971-3504)
PHONE.................302 682-9463
Prem N Chatani, *President*
EMP: 4
SALES: 150K Privately Held
SIC: 2037 Frozen fruits & vegetables

(G-8100)
TUNNELL & RAYSOR PA
323 Rehoboth Ave Ste E (19971-2182)
PHONE.................302 226-4420
Harold E Dukes, *Partner*
EMP: 4
SALES (corp-wide): 6.4MM Privately Held
WEB: www.tunnellraysor.com
SIC: 8111 General practice attorney, lawyer
PA: Tunnell & Raysor, P.A.
30 E Pine St
Georgetown DE 19947
302 856-7313

(G-8101)
TURNSTONE BUILDERS LLC
37395 Oyster House Rd (19971-8058)
PHONE.................302 227-8876
Donald Stewart, *Managing Dir*
Harvey Ryan, *Managing Dir*
EMP: 13
SALES (est): 1.1MM Privately Held
SIC: 1521 New construction, single-family houses

(G-8102)
U TRANSIT INC
Also Called: Jolly Trolley
12 Hazlett St (19971-2507)
P.O. Box 311 (19971-0311)
PHONE.................302 227-1197
David Hastings, *President*
Christine Hastings, *Vice Pres*
EMP: 8
SALES (est): 893.7K Privately Held
SIC: 2721 7319 4725 4111 Magazines: publishing only, not printed on site; display advertising service; sightseeing tour companies; tours, conducted; trolley operation

(G-8103)
UBIVIS MANAGEMENT LLC
19266 Coastal Hwy 4-1065 (19971-6117)
PHONE.................833 824-8476
Sophia St-Martin,
EMP: 29
SALES: 1.5MM Privately Held
SIC: 8742 Construction project management consultant

(G-8104)
UMBRELLA CORPORATION
Also Called: Intellution
19266 Coastal Hwy 4-73r (19971-6117)
PHONE.................302 603-7100
Steven L Mendez II, *Principal*
Darrell Mayfield, *Principal*
Leticia Mendez, *Principal*
Michel Mendez, *Principal*
Stephanie Mendez, *Principal*
EMP: 20
SALES (est): 329.3K Privately Held
SIC: 8748 Energy conservation consultant

(G-8105)
UNION MORTGAGE GROUP INC
Also Called: Mortgage Capitol
323 Rehoboth Ave Ste D (19971-2181)
PHONE.................302 227-6687
Lee Bandekow, *Branch Mgr*
EMP: 4 Publicly Held
WEB: www.mtgcap.com
SIC: 6162 6163 Mortgage bankers & correspondents; loan brokers
HQ: Union Mortgage Group, Inc.
4355 Innslake Dr Ste 350
Glen Allen VA 23060
703 621-7900

(G-8106)
VICTORIAS SCRET PINK MAIN LINE
35000 Midway Outlet Dr (19971-8515)
PHONE.................302 644-1035
Caroline Murnane, *Assoc VP*
EMP: 3
SALES (est): 78K Privately Held
SIC: 5999 5632 2341 Toiletries, cosmetics & perfumes; lingerie & corsets (underwear); women's & children's underwear

(G-8107)
WALTER DORING
Also Called: Master Movers
35584 Airport Rd (19971-4620)
P.O. Box 635, Ocean View (19970-0635)
PHONE.................302 727-6773
Walter Doring, *Principal*
EMP: 8
SALES (est): 339.2K Privately Held
SIC: 4789 Cargo loading & unloading services

(G-8108)
WARD & TAYLOR LLC
37212 Rehoboth Avenue Ext (19971-3198)
PHONE.................302 227-1403
Ingrid Wilcox, *Branch Mgr*
EMP: 6
SALES (corp-wide): 5.6MM Privately Held
SIC: 8111 Real estate law
PA: Ward & Taylor, Llc
2710 Centerville Rd # 210
Wilmington DE 19808
302 225-3350

(G-8109)
WEBRO HOLDINGS LLC (PA)
19266 Coastal Hwy 4-1049 (19971-6117)
PHONE.................302 314-3334
Charles W Stroman, *CEO*
EMP: 4
SALES (est): 610.8K Privately Held
SIC: 7363 3511 3724 Pilot service, aviation; turbines & turbine generator sets; aircraft; aircraft engines & engine parts; aircraft parts & equipment

(G-8110)
WELLS FARGO BANK NATIONAL ASSN
4600 Hwy 1 (19971)
PHONE.................302 644-6351
Michelle Gallagher, *Manager*
EMP: 10
SALES (corp-wide): 101B Publicly Held
SIC: 6021 National commercial banks
HQ: Wells Fargo Bank, National Association
101 N Phillips Ave
Sioux Falls SD 57104
605 575-6900

(G-8111)
WELLS FARGO HOME MORTGAGE INC
18977 Munchy Branch Rd # 6 (19971-8763)
PHONE.................302 227-5700
Ed Swiatek, *Manager*
EMP: 8
SALES (corp-wide): 101B Publicly Held
WEB: www.wfhm.com
SIC: 6162 Mortgage bankers
HQ: Wells Fargo Home Mortgage Inc
1 Home Campus
Des Moines IA 50328
515 324-3707

(G-8112)
WEST RHOBOTH CMNTY LAND TR INC
19801 Norwood St (19971-1243)
P.O. Box 633 (19971-0633)
PHONE.................302 260-9519
Richard Legatski, *President*
Elizabeth Doty, *Director*
EMP: 4
SALES: 61.5K Privately Held
SIC: 8399 Community development groups

(G-8113)
WESTSIDE N BEGNINGS YTH IMPRVM
19801 Norwood St (19971-1243)
PHONE.................302 227-5442
Eleanor Whaley, *President*
Mary Stervent, *Principal*
Elizabeth Doty, *Manager*
EMP: 4 EST: 1977
SALES: 116.4K Privately Held
SIC: 8069 Drug addiction rehabilitation hospital

(G-8114)
WHARTONS LANDSCAPING GRDN CTR
19385 Old Landing Rd (19971-4686)
PHONE.................302 426-4854
EMP: 4
SALES (est): 186.7K Privately Held
SIC: 0781 Landscape services

(G-8115)
WIEDMAN ENTERPRISES INC
Also Called: Matt's Auto Care
38335 Martins Ln (19971-2078)
PHONE.................302 226-2407
Matthew Wiedman, *President*
EMP: 5
SALES (est): 145K Privately Held
SIC: 7538 General automotive repair shops

(G-8116)
WILLIAMS INSURANCE AGENCY INC (PA)
20220 Coastal Hwy (19971-8021)
P.O. Box 1174 (19971-0814)
PHONE.................302 227-2501
Joseph T Moore, *President*
Seth Costello, *Exec VP*
Michael V Buchler, *Vice Pres*
Bud Clark, *Vice Pres*
Patty Walker, *Vice Pres*
EMP: 27
SQ FT: 4,000
SALES (est): 11.1MM Privately Held
WEB: www.paulgallagher.com
SIC: 6411 Insurance agents; insurance brokers

Rehoboth Beach - Sussex County (G-8117)

(G-8117)
WILMINGTON SAVINGS FUND SOC
19335 Coastal Hwy (19971-6100)
PHONE...................302 226-5648
Carolyn Neisser, *Branch Mgr*
Michele Hysock, *Manager*
EMP: 21
SALES (corp-wide): 455.5MM **Publicly Held**
SIC: 6035 Savings institutions, federally chartered
HQ: Wilmington Savings Fund Society
500 Delaware Ave Ste 500 # 500
Wilmington DE 19801
302 792-6000

(G-8118)
WOLFE NECK TREATMENT PLANT
36160 Wolfe Neck Rd (19971-8719)
PHONE...................302 644-2761
Gordon German, *Manager*
Kay Dewson, *Manager*
EMP: 19
SALES (est): 577.2K **Privately Held**
SIC: 4952 Sewerage systems

(G-8119)
WRIGHT BRUCE B DDS OFFICE RES
15 Venetian Dr (19971-1937)
PHONE...................302 227-8707
Bruce Wright, *Principal*
EMP: 4
SALES (est): 100.6K **Privately Held**
SIC: 8021 Offices & clinics of dentists

(G-8120)
YACHT ANYTHING LTD
Also Called: Alarm Cmmncations Sytems Group
20913 Coastal Hwy (19971-8001)
PHONE...................302 226-3335
William L Delle Donne, *President*
EMP: 5
SALES (est): 736.2K **Privately Held**
SIC: 1623 1731 Telephone & communication line construction; communications specialization

(G-8121)
YOUNG MENS CHRISTIAN ASSOCIAT
Also Called: YMCA
20080 Church St (19971-3195)
PHONE...................302 296-9622
Terry Rasberry, *Director*
Suzette Chambers-Marrin, *Admin Sec*
EMP: 85
SALES (corp-wide): 35MM **Privately Held**
WEB: www.ymcade.org
SIC: 7997 7991 8351 7032 Membership sports & recreation clubs; physical fitness facilities; child day care services; youth camps; individual & family services; youth organizations
PA: Young Men's Christian Association Of Wilmington, Delaware
100 W 10th St Ste 1100
Wilmington DE 19801
302 221-9622

Rockland
New Castle County

(G-8122)
BREAKWATER ACCOUNTING ADVISORY
100 S Rockland Falls Rd (19732-2917)
PHONE...................302 543-4564
Kim Dolan, *Opers Staff*
Lisa McFadden, *Advisor*
Suzanne Shahan, *Associate*
Kristine Woodruff, *Associate*
EMP: 4
SALES (est): 56.9K **Privately Held**
SIC: 8721 Accounting, auditing & bookkeeping

(G-8123)
DELAWARE COUNSEL GROUP LLP
100 S Rockland Falls Rd (19732-2917)
PHONE...................302 543-4870
Ellisa Habbart, *Owner*
EMP: 4
SALES (est): 294K
SALES (corp-wide): 807.3K **Privately Held**
SIC: 8111 General practice attorney, lawyer
PA: The Delaware Counsel Group Llp
2 Mill Rd Ste 108
Wilmington DE 19806
302 576-9600

(G-8124)
PATTERNS
2 Rockland Meadows Rd (19732-2909)
PHONE...................302 654-9075
EMP: 2
SALES (est): 170.6K **Privately Held**
SIC: 3543 Industrial patterns

Saint Georges
New Castle County

(G-8125)
F SARTIN TYSON INC
4376 Krkwood St Gorges Rd (19733-2027)
P.O. Box 97 (19733-0097)
PHONE...................302 834-4571
Paul Fisher, *President*
Ann Fisher, *Admin Sec*
EMP: 15
SQ FT: 5,000
SALES (est): 2.4MM **Privately Held**
SIC: 3272 Concrete products

(G-8126)
INTEGRATED WIRG SOLUTIONS LLC
1695 S Dupont Hwy (19733-2031)
PHONE...................302 999-8448
EMP: 20
SALES (est): 115.6K **Privately Held**
SIC: 1731 General electrical contractor

(G-8127)
KENCREST SERVICES
240 Clarks Corner Rd (19733-2012)
P.O. Box 245 (19733-0245)
PHONE...................302 834-3365
Barbara Cephas, *Branch Mgr*
EMP: 7 **Privately Held**
SIC: 8361 Residential care
PA: Kencrest Services
960a Harvest Dr Ste 100
Blue Bell PA 19422

(G-8128)
MARTOM LANDSCAPING CO INC
1699 St Georges Bus Ctr (19733)
P.O. Box 6 (19733-0006)
PHONE...................302 322-1920
Mark Thompson, *President*
EMP: 20
SQ FT: 3,000
SALES (est): 1.4MM **Privately Held**
SIC: 0782 Landscape contractors

(G-8129)
SAINT GEORGES CULTR & ARTS REV
1 Delaware St (19733-2013)
PHONE...................302 836-8202
Lawrence Fontana, *President*
Benjamin Rizzo, *Treasurer*
Russell Rozanski, *Director*
Howard Isenberg, *Bd of Directors*
EMP: 7
SALES (est): 86.9K **Privately Held**
SIC: 8399 Social services

(G-8130)
STAPLEFORDS SALES AND SERVICE
Also Called: Stapleford's Oldsmobile
1402 S Dupont Hwy (19733-2030)
P.O. Box 68 (19733-0068)
PHONE...................302 834-4568
Charles E Stapleford Jr, *President*
Richard B Stapleford, *Vice Pres*
EMP: 35 **EST:** 1913
SQ FT: 5,000
SALES (est): 7.4MM **Privately Held**
WEB: www.staplefordschevrolet.com
SIC: 5012 7539 4141 Automobiles; automotive repair shops; local bus charter service

(G-8131)
UNITED TRANSIT COMPANY L L C
1 Main St (19733-2017)
P.O. Box 302 (19733-0302)
PHONE...................302 838-3575
EMP: 4 **EST:** 2008
SALES (est): 140K **Privately Held**
SIC: 4111 Local/Suburban Transportation

Seaford
Sussex County

(G-8132)
1 A LIFESAFER INC
1300 Rd 535 (19973)
PHONE...................800 634-3077
EMP: 1
SALES (corp-wide): 4.3MM **Privately Held**
SIC: 3829 Measuring & controlling devices
PA: 1 A Lifesafer, Inc.
4290 Glendale Milford Rd
Blue Ash OH 45242
513 651-9560

(G-8133)
1995 PROPERTY MANAGEMENT INC
25309 Church Rd (19973-8666)
P.O. Box 1295 (19973-5295)
PHONE...................302 745-1187
Shawn Sylvia, *Principal*
EMP: 5 **EST:** 2009
SALES (est): 387K **Privately Held**
SIC: 8741 Management services

(G-8134)
715 EAST KING ST OPRATIONS LLC
Also Called: Lofland Park Center
715 E King St (19973-3505)
PHONE...................302 628-3000
Wanda Thornton, *Purch Agent*
Vanessa Adams, *Human Res Dir*
Tesha Horsey, *Director*
Dolores Timmons, *Director*
Onna Outten, *Social Dir*
EMP: 125
SALES (est): 2.4MM **Publicly Held**
SIC: 8051 Skilled nursing care facilities
HQ: Skilled Healthcare, Llc
27442 Portola Pkwy # 200
Foothill Ranch CA 92610
949 282-5800

(G-8135)
A S I CONTROLS
221 High St (19973-3950)
PHONE...................302 629-7730
Bill Messick, *Principal*
EMP: 2
SALES (est): 189.8K **Privately Held**
WEB: www.asicontrols.com
SIC: 3829 Measuring & controlling devices

(G-8136)
AARONS SALES & LEASING
Also Called: Aaron's F244
850 Norman Eskridge Hwy (19973-1718)
PHONE...................302 628-8870
Jay Richards, *Owner*
EMP: 7
SALES (est): 368.4K **Privately Held**
SIC: 7359 Furniture rental; home appliance, furniture & entertainment rental services

(G-8137)
ACE CASH EXPRESS INC
22978 Sussex Hwy (19973-5861)
P.O. Box 1677, Salisbury MD (21802-1677)
PHONE...................302 628-0422
Fax: 302 628-0425
EMP: 4
SALES (corp-wide): 2.3B **Privately Held**
SIC: 6099 Check Clearing Services
HQ: Ace Cash Express, Inc.
1231 Greenway Dr Ste 600
Irving TX 75038
817 689-9384

(G-8138)
ADAMS OIL CO INC
Pine St Extd (19973)
P.O. Box 532 (19973-0532)
PHONE...................302 629-4531
Wayne Adams, *President*
Delores Lloyd, *Corp Secy*
Marvin Adams, *Vice Pres*
EMP: 7
SQ FT: 1,000
SALES (est): 2.1MM **Privately Held**
SIC: 5172 Fuel oil; gasoline

(G-8139)
ADVANCED MOTORSPORTS
8734 Concord Rd (19973-8423)
PHONE...................302 629-3301
Rick Elliott, *Owner*
EMP: 4
SALES (est): 480K **Privately Held**
SIC: 7948 Motor vehicle racing & drivers

(G-8140)
ADVANCED OFFICE SYSTEMS & SUPS
9683 Tharp Rd (19973-7707)
PHONE...................302 629-7505
James Brace, *Owner*
EMP: 1
SALES: 75K **Privately Held**
SIC: 2759 Business forms: printing

(G-8141)
AERO-MARINE LAMINATES INC
Also Called: Aero Marine Laminates
22762 Sussex Hwy (19973-5837)
PHONE...................302 628-3944
Remsen Haynes, *President*
Peter Calimano, *Vice Pres*
Troy Zelo, *Manager*
▼**EMP:** 10
SALES (est): 1.1MM **Privately Held**
WEB: www.aeromarinerc.com
SIC: 3944 5945 Boat & ship models, toy & hobby; models, toy & hobby

(G-8142)
ALASKAWILD SEAFOODS
8589 Cannon Rd (19973-5654)
PHONE...................302 337-0710
Jon Clucas, *Principal*
EMP: 4
SALES (est): 391.5K **Privately Held**
SIC: 5146 Seafoods

(G-8143)
ALLEN HARIM FOODS LLC (DH)
126 N Shipley St (19973-3100)
PHONE...................302 629-9136
Joe Moran, *CEO*
Tim Thomas, *Transptn Dir*
Dennis Cross, *Purch Agent*
Brian Hildreth, *CFO*
Henry Johnson, *Manager*
EMP: 40 **EST:** 2011
SALES (est): 285.3MM **Privately Held**
SIC: 0251 Broiler, fryer & roaster chickens
HQ: Harim Usa, Ltd
126 N Shipley St
Seaford DE 19973
302 629-9136

(G-8144)
ALLEN HARIM FOODS LLC
Also Called: Seaford Feed Mill
20799 Allen Rd (19973)
PHONE...................302 629-9460

▲ = Import ▼=Export
◆ =Import/Export

Chad Allen, *Branch Mgr*
EMP: 30 **Privately Held**
SIC: 5153 Grains
HQ: Allen Harim Foods, Llc
126 N Shipley St
Seaford DE 19973
302 629-9136

(G-8145)
AMBIENT MEDICAL CARE
24459 Sussex Hwy Ste 2 (19973-4433)
P.O. Box 1827 (19973-8827)
PHONE..................................302 629-3099
Robert A Henry, *Principal*
EMP: 5 **EST:** 2008
SALES (est): 527.9K **Privately Held**
SIC: 8099 Blood related health services

(G-8146)
AMERICAN DIAGNOSTIC SVCS INC
1109 Middleford Rd (19973-3607)
PHONE..................................302 628-4209
EMP: 4
SALES (corp-wide): 149.4MM **Privately Held**
SIC: 8999 Actuarial consultant
HQ: American Diagnostic Services, Inc.
101 Rock Rd
Horsham PA

(G-8147)
AMERICAN LEGION (PA)
601 Bridgeville Hwy # 213 (19973-1523)
P.O. Box 930 (19973-0930)
PHONE..................................302 628-5221
Richard Santos, *Director*
EMP: 8
SALES: 93.3K **Privately Held**
SIC: 8641 Veterans' organization

(G-8148)
AMERICAN LEGION LOG CABIN
230 N Front St Unit 6 (19973-2717)
P.O. Box 781 (19973-0781)
PHONE..................................302 629-9915
Bruce McBride, *Principal*
EMP: 4
SALES (est): 210K **Privately Held**
SIC: 8641 Veterans' organization

(G-8149)
AMERICAN PRECAST INC
301 Nanticoke Ave (19973-4005)
PHONE..................................302 629-6688
Johnnie Dane, *Principal*
EMP: 5
SALES (est): 475.7K **Privately Held**
SIC: 3272 Concrete products

(G-8150)
AMERICAN WATER WELL SYSTEM
1129 A Brickyard Rd (19973)
P.O. Box 300 (19973-0300)
PHONE..................................302 629-3796
John A Mc Farland Sr, *Ch of Bd*
John A McFarland Sr, *President*
John A Mc Farland Jr, *President*
Paul S McCreary Sr, *Corp Secy*
Paul S McReary Sr, *Corp Secy*
EMP: 10
SALES (est): 1MM **Privately Held**
SIC: 1781 Water well servicing

(G-8151)
ANCHOR ENTERPRISES
22 W High St (19973-4147)
PHONE..................................302 629-7969
EMP: 2
SALES (est): 86.6K **Privately Held**
SIC: 3441 Fabricated structural metal

(G-8152)
ANDOVER COMPANIES INC
207 S Paula Lynne Dr (19973-9460)
P.O. Box 479 (19973-0479)
PHONE..................................410 705-1503
Steven Frame, *Principal*
EMP: 4
SALES (est): 255.3K **Privately Held**
SIC: 5013 Automotive supplies & parts

(G-8153)
ANDREWS CONSTRUCTION LLC
25489 Janice Dr (19973-6379)
PHONE..................................302 604-8166
Kevin Andrews, *Mng Member*
EMP: 6
SALES (est): 120.8K **Privately Held**
SIC: 7389

(G-8154)
ARRAY OF MONOGRAMS
300 Megan Ave (19973-9404)
PHONE..................................302 998-2381
William Wockenfuss, *President*
EMP: 1
SALES (est): 106.4K **Privately Held**
WEB: www.arrayof.com
SIC: 2395 Embroidery & art needlework

(G-8155)
ARTHRITIS AND OSTEOPOROSIS LLC (PA)
1350 Middleford Rd # 502 (19973-3664)
PHONE..................................302 628-8300
Ivonne Herrera, *Principal*
EMP: 5
SALES (est): 739.1K **Privately Held**
SIC: 8011 General & family practice, physician/surgeon

(G-8156)
ASA V PEUGH INC
22 W High St (19973-4147)
PHONE..................................302 629-7969
Asa V Peugh, *President*
Michael Peugh, *Treasurer*
Mike Peugh, *Director*
EMP: 11 **EST:** 1977
SQ FT: 8,000
SALES (est): 4MM **Privately Held**
WEB: www.anchor-enterprises.com
SIC: 3441 3446 Fabricated structural metal; ornamental metalwork

(G-8157)
ATI HOLDINGS LLC
Also Called: ATI Physical Therapy
22832 Sussex Hwy (19973-5862)
PHONE..................................302 536-5562
Ryan Kardos, *Director*
EMP: 21
SALES (corp-wide): 338.3MM **Privately Held**
SIC: 8049 Physical therapist
PA: Ati Holdings, Llc
790 Remington Blvd
Bolingbrook IL 60440
630 296-2222

(G-8158)
ATLANTIC REALTY MANAGEMENT
Also Called: Village of Cool Branch Homes
100 Hitch Pond Cir (19973-6221)
PHONE..................................302 629-0770
Lary McKinly, *President*
EMP: 4
SALES (est): 411.8K **Privately Held**
WEB: www.coolbranch.com
SIC: 2451 Mobile homes

(G-8159)
B AND C AWNING
709 Washington Ave (19973-1519)
PHONE..................................302 629-4465
Dale Shaffer, *Owner*
EMP: 2
SALES (est): 73.8K **Privately Held**
SIC: 2394 Awnings, fabric: made from purchased materials

(G-8160)
B-LINE PRINTING
22876 Sussex Hwy Unit 7 (19973-5853)
PHONE..................................302 628-1311
William Drylie, *Owner*
EMP: 1
SQ FT: 800
SALES (est): 59K **Privately Held**
SIC: 2759 Commercial printing

(G-8161)
BANK OF DELMARVA
910 Norman Eskridge Hwy (19973-1720)
PHONE..................................302 629-2700
Ingunn Straume, *Branch Mgr*
EMP: 5
SALES (corp-wide): 24.7MM **Publicly Held**
WEB: www.bankofdelmarvahb.com
SIC: 6022 6029 State commercial banks; commercial banks
HQ: The Bank Of Delmarva
2245 Northwood Dr
Salisbury MD 21801
410 548-1100

(G-8162)
BARTONS LANDSCAPING/LAWN INC
20689 Sussex Hwy (19973-5690)
PHONE..................................302 629-2213
Philip C Barton, *President*
Tim Conaway, *Treasurer*
Brenda Ryan, *Office Mgr*
Julie Barton, *Admin Sec*
EMP: 35
SQ FT: 2,225
SALES (est): 1.2MM **Privately Held**
WEB: www.bartonslandscaping.com
SIC: 0782 5261 Landscape contractors; garden maintenance services; garden planting services; nurseries & garden centers

(G-8163)
BAYNUM ENTERPRISES INC (PA)
Also Called: Pizza King
300 W Stein Hwy (19973-1335)
PHONE..................................302 629-6104
Shirley Baynum, *President*
Brad Baynum, *Vice Pres*
EMP: 100
SQ FT: 8,000
SALES: 5MM **Privately Held**
SIC: 5812 6514 Pizza restaurants; dwelling operators, except apartments

(G-8164)
BEACHBALLS COM LLC
112 S Bradford St (19973-3802)
PHONE..................................302 628-8888
David Layton, *Owner*
▲ **EMP:** 5
SALES (est): 287.2K **Privately Held**
SIC: 3949 Balls: baseball, football, basketball, etc.

(G-8165)
BENEVOLENT PROTECTVE ORDR ELKS
Also Called: ELKS LODGE
8846 Elks Rd (19973)
P.O. Box 476 (19973-0476)
PHONE..................................302 629-2458
Arthur League, *President*
EMP: 10
SALES (est): 122.1K **Privately Held**
SIC: 8641 Civic associations

(G-8166)
BENSON ENTERPRISE INC
11676 Park Dr (19973-7200)
PHONE..................................302 344-9183
Jeffrey T Benson Sr, *President*
EMP: 4
SALES (est): 183K **Privately Held**
SIC: 4213 Trucking, except local

(G-8167)
BEST OFFICE PROS
26082 Butler Branch Rd (19973-6971)
P.O. Box 820 (19973-0820)
PHONE..................................302 629-4561
Eva Dupont, *Partner*
EMP: 3
SALES (est): 221.5K **Privately Held**
SIC: 2759 Business forms: printing

(G-8168)
BIG DOG FARM LLC
12 Crossgate Dr (19973-1244)
PHONE..................................302 841-7721
Daryl Tull, *Principal*
EMP: 4
SALES (est): 63.9K **Privately Held**
SIC: 0251 Broiler, fryer & roaster chickens

(G-8169)
BINKLEY HURST LP
22375 Sussex Hwy (19973-5848)
PHONE..................................302 628-3135
Walter Blinky, *Principal*
EMP: 7
SALES (est): 472.1K **Privately Held**
SIC: 5083 Farm equipment parts & supplies

(G-8170)
BIO MEDIC CORPORATION (PA)
742 Sussex Ave (19973-2057)
PHONE..................................302 628-4300
George Gabriel, *Ch of Bd*
Frank Marinaccio, *Vice Pres*
Edmond Silverberg, *Vice Pres*
◆ **EMP:** 13
SALES (est): 90MM **Privately Held**
SIC: 5049 3821 3496 3914 Laboratory equipment, except medical or dental; laboratory apparatus & furniture; cages, wire; cutlery; telephones & telephone apparatus

(G-8171)
BIOMEDIC DATA SYSTEMS INC
1 Silas Rd (19973-2061)
PHONE..................................302 628-4100
Neil Campbell, *President*
Mani Guesfeird, *Vice Pres*
Curt Miller, *Research*
Melissa Jewell, *Manager*
EMP: 550
SQ FT: 20,000
SALES (est): 43MM
SALES (corp-wide): 90MM **Privately Held**
WEB: www.bmds.com
SIC: 7371 Custom computer programming services
PA: Bio Medic Corporation
742 Sussex Ave
Seaford DE 19973
302 628-4300

(G-8172)
BODY AND SOUL FITNESS LLC
1035 W Stein Hwy (19973-1146)
PHONE..................................302 536-1278
EMP: 4
SALES (est): 59.9K **Privately Held**
SIC: 7991 Health club

(G-8173)
BOYS & GIRLS CLUBS DEL INC
Also Called: Boys & Girls Clubs Wstn Sussex
310 Virginia Ave (19973-1516)
PHONE..................................302 628-3789
Chris Couch, *Director*
EMP: 25
SALES (corp-wide): 20.8MM **Privately Held**
SIC: 8641 Youth organizations
PA: Boys & Girls Clubs Of Delaware, Inc.
669 S Union St
Wilmington DE 19805
302 658-1870

(G-8174)
BROAD CREEK MEDICAL SERVICE
Also Called: Broadcreek Medical Service
1601 Middleford Rd (19973-3617)
PHONE..................................302 629-0202
Tod Emeigh, *President*
EMP: 10
SQ FT: 1,800
SALES (est): 1.1MM **Privately Held**
SIC: 7352 5047 Medical equipment rental; medical laboratory equipment; physician equipment & supplies

(G-8175)
BROKER POST
1310 Bridgeville Hwy (19973-1617)
PHONE..................................302 628-8467
John Hannenfeld, *President*
John Hennenfeld, *Owner*
EMP: 5
SALES (est): 282.1K **Privately Held**
WEB: www.brokerpost.com
SIC: 6531 Real estate agent, commercial

Seaford - Sussex County (G-8176)

(G-8176)
BRUCES WELDING INC
21263 Nattell Ln (19973-6560)
PHONE.................................302 629-3891
Bruce Burtelle, *President*
EMP: 3
SQ FT: 7,600
SALES: 450K **Privately Held**
WEB: www.brucehibbsjr.com
SIC: 7692 Welding repair

(G-8177)
BUSYMAMA CUPCAKES
328 E Poplar St (19973-3414)
PHONE.................................302 259-9988
EMP: 4
SALES (est): 149.8K **Privately Held**
SIC: 2051 Bread, cake & related products

(G-8178)
BUTLERS SEWING CENTER INC
1023 W Stein Hwy (19973-1146)
PHONE.................................302 629-9155
Edward H Butler, *President*
Douglas Butler, *Partner*
Shirley Butler, *Treasurer*
EMP: 5
SQ FT: 1,800
SALES (est): 388.9K **Privately Held**
SIC: 5949 2391 5722 Sewing supplies; draperies, plastic & textile: from purchased materials; sewing machines

(G-8179)
C WHITE & SONS LLC
5635 Neals School Rd (19973-6746)
PHONE.................................302 629-4848
Charles White,
EMP: 9
SALES (est): 1.2MM **Privately Held**
SIC: 1711 Septic system construction

(G-8180)
CALLAWAY FARNELL AND MOORE
Also Called: Farnell & Gast Insurance
500 W Stein Hwy (19973-1202)
PHONE.................................302 629-4514
George Farnell, *President*
Kathryn Farnell, *Vice Pres*
Sue Bramhall, *Sales Staff*
EMP: 4
SQ FT: 4,000
SALES (est): 290K **Privately Held**
SIC: 6531 Real estate brokers & agents

(G-8181)
CANNON ENTERPRISES
22719 Bridgeville Hwy (19973-5818)
PHONE.................................302 629-6746
Ray Cannon, *Owner*
EMP: 1
SALES (est): 324.7K **Privately Held**
SIC: 3231 Windshields, glass: made from purchased glass

(G-8182)
CAPITOL BILLIARDS INC
735 Nylon Blvd (19973-1225)
PHONE.................................302 629-0298
Ralph Causey, *President*
EMP: 4
SALES (est): 334.6K **Privately Held**
SIC: 5091 7999 Billiard equipment & supplies; billiard parlor

(G-8183)
CASH ADVANCE PLUS (PA)
N607 N 607 N Dual Hwy Rr (19973)
PHONE.................................302 629-6266
Edward Wilgus, *Owner*
EMP: 4 EST: 1997
SALES (est): 3.4MM **Privately Held**
SIC: 6141 Personal credit institutions

(G-8184)
CDI INC SOFR SYSTEM LLC
1330 Middleford Rd (19973-3648)
PHONE.................................302 536-7397
Jesse Frederick-Conaway, *CEO*
EMP: 4
SALES (est): 356.2K **Privately Held**
SIC: 3535 Conveyors & conveying equipment

(G-8185)
CENTURY SEALS INC
503 Harrington St (19973-3719)
P.O. Box 720 (19973-0720)
PHONE.................................302 629-0324
Terry Phillips, *President*
Lisa Fizer, *Vice Pres*
Donna Lauck, *Vice Pres*
Michael Marchsteiner, *Design Engr*
Joe Favinger, *Sales Engr*
EMP: 30
SQ FT: 6,000
SALES: 5MM **Privately Held**
WEB: www.centuryseals.com
SIC: 3679 Hermetic seals for electronic equipment

(G-8186)
CHALLENGE AUTOMOTIVE SVCS INC
Also Called: AAMCO Transmissions
22598 Sussex Hwy (19973-5835)
PHONE.................................302 629-3058
Carl Schulze, *Owner*
EMP: 4
SALES (est): 129.7K **Privately Held**
SIC: 7537 Automotive transmission repair shops

(G-8187)
CHAMBERS MOTORS INC
20610 Sussex Hwy (19973-5684)
P.O. Box 494 (19973-0494)
PHONE.................................302 629-3553
William Chambers Jr, *President*
Liz Chambers, *Director*
EMP: 28
SQ FT: 7,000
SALES (est): 2.8MM **Privately Held**
SIC: 7549 Towing service, automotive

(G-8188)
CHANDLER HEIGHTS II LP
802 Clementine Ct (19973-2873)
PHONE.................................302 629-8048
William Roupp, *Exec Dir*
William D Roupp, *Exec Dir*
EMP: 11
SALES (est): 339.8K **Privately Held**
SIC: 6514 Dwelling operators, except apartments

(G-8189)
CHANEY ENTERPRISES
22223 Eskridge Rd (19973-8144)
PHONE.................................302 990-5039
EMP: 4
SALES (est): 290.8K **Privately Held**
SIC: 3273 Ready-mixed concrete

(G-8190)
CHAPIS DRAFTING & BLUE PRINT
8057 Hearns Pond Rd (19973-5719)
PHONE.................................302 629-6373
John Chapis, *Principal*
EMP: 4 EST: 2011
SALES (est): 330.8K **Privately Held**
SIC: 2752 Commercial printing, lithographic

(G-8191)
CHARLOTTE WILSON
Also Called: Christian Recovery Spa
629 Rosemary Dr (19973-7627)
PHONE.................................302 500-1440
Charlotte Wilson, *Owner*
Cordelia Hicks, *Exec Sec*
EMP: 5
SALES (est): 32.7K **Privately Held**
SIC: 7231 Cosmetology & personal hygiene salons

(G-8192)
CHESAPEAKECAREGIVERS LLC
10105 Concord Rd (19973-8649)
PHONE.................................302 841-9686
Patrick Murray, *Principal*
EMP: 7 EST: 2017
SALES (est): 64.2K **Privately Held**
SIC: 8082 Home health care services

(G-8193)
CHILDREN YOUTH & THEIR FAM
Also Called: Division of Family Services
350 Virginia Ave (19973-1516)
PHONE.................................302 628-2024
Michelle Warch, *Director*
EMP: 15 **Privately Held**
SIC: 8322 9199 Family counseling services; offender self-help agency;
HQ: Children, Youth & Their Families, Delaware Dept Of Services For
1825 Faulkland Rd
Wilmington DE 19805

(G-8194)
CHILDREN FMILIES FIRST DEL INC
Also Called: Seafood House, The
400 N Market Street Ext (19973-1573)
PHONE.................................302 629-6996
Don Loden, *Branch Mgr*
EMP: 25
SALES (corp-wide): 16.8MM **Privately Held**
SIC: 8322 8361 Child related social services; residential care for children
PA: Children & Families First Delaware Inc.
809 N Washington St
Wilmington DE 19801
302 658-5177

(G-8195)
CITIFINANCIAL CREDIT COMPANY
22974 Sussex Hwy (19973-5861)
PHONE.................................302 628-9253
Kari Paquette, *Manager*
EMP: 5
SALES (corp-wide): 72.8B **Publicly Held**
WEB: www.citifinancial.com
SIC: 6141 Personal credit institutions
HQ: Citifinancial Credit Company
300 Saint Paul St Fl 3
Baltimore MD 21202
410 332-3000

(G-8196)
CITIZENS BANK NATIONAL ASSN
22870 Sussex Hwy (19973-5852)
PHONE.................................302 628-6150
Pamela Jones, *Branch Mgr*
EMP: 10
SALES (corp-wide): 7.3B **Publicly Held**
SIC: 6022 State commercial banks
HQ: Citizens Bank, National Association
1 Citizens Plz Ste 1 # 1
Providence RI 02903
401 282-7000

(G-8197)
CITY OF SEAFORD INC
Also Called: Hooper's Landing
1019 W Locust St (19973-2124)
PHONE.................................302 629-2890
Ed Butler, *Mayor*
EMP: 14 **Privately Held**
SIC: 7992 Public golf courses
PA: City Of Seaford
414 High St
Seaford DE 19973
302 629-9173

(G-8198)
CLARKS SWIMMING POOLS INC
22855 Sussex Hwy (19973)
PHONE.................................302 629-8835
Chad E Clark, *President*
EMP: 9 EST: 1973
SQ FT: 3,200
SALES (est): 970K **Privately Held**
WEB: www.clarksswimmingpools.com
SIC: 1799 5999 Swimming pool construction; swimming pools, above ground; spas & hot tubs

(G-8199)
COASTAL CABINETRY LLC
400 Megan Ave (19973-9405)
PHONE.................................302 542-4155
Rich Doyle,
Frank Delgaudio,
Mark Hubbard,
EMP: 8

SALES (est): 630K **Privately Held**
SIC: 2434 1751 Wood kitchen cabinets; cabinet building & installation

(G-8200)
COASTAL MAINTENANCE LLC
26253 Sussex Hwy (19973-8522)
PHONE.................................302 536-1290
Richard Roop, *Principal*
EMP: 5
SALES (est): 286K **Privately Held**
SIC: 7349 Building maintenance services

(G-8201)
COMCAST CORPORATION
500 High St (19973-3916)
PHONE.................................302 262-8996
EMP: 55
SALES (corp-wide): 94.5B **Publicly Held**
SIC: 4841 Cable television services
PA: Comcast Corporation
1701 Jfk Blvd
Philadelphia PA 19103
215 286-1700

(G-8202)
COMFORT SUITES
23420 Sussex Hwy (19973-5867)
PHONE.................................302 628-5400
Manish Patel, *Owner*
EMP: 15 EST: 2008
SALES (est): 527.3K **Privately Held**
SIC: 7011 Hotel, franchised

(G-8203)
COMPLETE AUTO BODY INC
Also Called: Hertrich's Collision Center
26907 Sussex Hwy (19973-8559)
PHONE.................................302 629-3955
Fred Hertrich, *President*
EMP: 20
SQ FT: 25,000
SALES (est): 1.1MM **Privately Held**
SIC: 7532 Body shop, automotive; paint shop, automotive

(G-8204)
CONNECTIONS COMMUNITY SUPPORT
105 N Front St (19973-2707)
PHONE.................................302 536-1952
EMP: 60 **Privately Held**
SIC: 8322 8093 Individual & family services; detoxification center, outpatient
PA: Connections Community Support Programs, Inc.
3821 Lancaster Pike
Wilmington DE 19805

(G-8205)
CONSOLIDATED CONSTRUCTION SVCS
7450 Rivershore Dr (19973-4328)
PHONE.................................302 629-6070
Chuck Harrison, *President*
Debra Harrison, *Corp Secy*
EMP: 10
SALES (est): 1.4MM **Privately Held**
SIC: 5032 1743 Ceramic wall & floor tile; terrazzo work

(G-8206)
COOL BRANCH ASSOCIATES LLC
100 Hitch Pond Cir (19973-6221)
PHONE.................................302 629-5363
Brian McKinley,
EMP: 4
SALES (est): 499.3K **Privately Held**
SIC: 2452 Modular homes, prefabricated, wood

(G-8207)
COOPEREALTY ASSOCIATES INC (PA)
615 W Stein Hwy (19973-1203)
PHONE.................................302 629-6693
Thomas J Cooper, *President*
EMP: 39
SQ FT: 4,000
SALES (est): 877.2K **Privately Held**
WEB: www.cooperealty.com
SIC: 6531 Real estate brokers & agents

GEOGRAPHIC SECTION
Seaford - Sussex County (G-8238)

(G-8208)
COPART INC
26029 Bethel Concord Rd (19973-6329)
PHONE..................302 628-5412
Denise Johnson, *General Mgr*
Jeffrey Burns, *General Mgr*
David Goslee, *General Mgr*
EMP: 17
SALES (corp-wide): 2B **Publicly Held**
SIC: 5012 Automobile auction
PA: Copart, Inc.
  14185 Dallas Pkwy Ste 300
  Dallas TX 75254
  972 391-5000

(G-8209)
COTTEN ENGINEERING LLC
10087 Concord Rd (19973-8646)
PHONE..................302 628-9164
Michael Cotten, *Principal*
EMP: 5
SALES (est): 412.6K **Privately Held**
SIC: 8711 Engineering services

(G-8210)
COVEYS CAR CARE INC
1300 Middleford Rd (19973-3612)
PHONE..................302 629-2746
C Kenneth Covey, *President*
EMP: 7 **EST:** 1964
SALES (est): 500K **Privately Held**
SIC: 7538 5013 General automotive repair shops; automotive supplies & parts

(G-8211)
COX ELECTRIC INC
10851 Airport Rd Unit 1 (19973-6323)
PHONE..................302 629-5448
Michael Cox, *President*
Eric Cox, *Vice Pres*
Rose Fischer, *Admin Sec*
EMP: 4
SALES: 150K **Privately Held**
SIC: 1731 1711 General electrical contractor; septic system construction

(G-8212)
CRAIG BALL SALES INC
103 Davis Dr (19973-9408)
PHONE..................302 628-9900
Leo F O'Hara, *President*
Leo F O'Hara, *President*
Lee O'Hara, *Sales Staff*
▲ **EMP:** 1
SALES: 250K **Privately Held**
SIC: 3714 Motor vehicle parts & accessories

(G-8213)
CRAIG TECHNOLOGIES INC (PA)
103 Davis Dr (19973-9408)
P.O. Box 180 (19973-0180)
PHONE..................302 628-9900
Donald Hollenbeck, *President*
Paul Hollenbeck, *Vice Pres*
Robert Hollenbeck, *Vice Pres*
Leo O'Hara, *Treasurer*
Phyllis Hollenbeck, *Personnel*
▲ **EMP:** 22
SQ FT: 250,000
SALES (est): 6.2MM **Privately Held**
WEB: www.craigtechnologies.com
SIC: 3089 Injection molding of plastics

(G-8214)
CREATIVE KITCHENS AND FLOORS
Also Called: C K F
507 Hickory Ln (19973-2023)
PHONE..................302 629-3166
Mike Griffith, *President*
Charles Hardesty, *Vice Pres*
Bonnie Griffith, *Treasurer*
Joan Hardesty, *Admin Sec*
EMP: 5
SQ FT: 2,100
SALES (est): 660.5K **Privately Held**
SIC: 1799 1752 Kitchen & bathroom remodeling; floor laying & floor work

(G-8215)
CURIOSITY SERVICE FOUNDATION
2001 Bridgeville Hwy (19973-1728)
P.O. Box 826 (19973-0826)
PHONE..................302 628-4140
Michelle Trocino-Wells, *Principal*
EMP: 4
SALES: 390.6K **Privately Held**
SIC: 8699 Charitable organization

(G-8216)
CUTEM UP TREE CARE DEL INC
10404 Old Furnace Rd (19973-8110)
PHONE..................302 629-4655
Kenna Nethken, *President*
EMP: 5
SALES: 250K **Privately Held**
SIC: 0783 0782 Planting, pruning & trimming services; landscape contractors

(G-8217)
DAVIS WELDING SERVICE LLC ✪
26075 River Rd (19973-5905)
PHONE..................302 465-3004
EMP: 7 **EST:** 2019
SALES (est): 82.1K **Privately Held**
SIC: 7692 Welding repair

(G-8218)
DAYS INN AND SUITES SEAFORD
23450 Sussex Hwy (19973-5867)
PHONE..................302 629-4300
Shaan Christy, *Principal*
EMP: 11
SALES (est): 426.8K **Privately Held**
SIC: 7011 Hotels & motels

(G-8219)
DELAWARE SPINE & REHAB LLC
105 New St Ste 1 (19973-3945)
PHONE..................813 965-0903
Hugueline Brun, *CEO*
EMP: 4
SALES (est): 149.1K **Privately Held**
SIC: 8041 Offices & clinics of chiropractors

(G-8220)
DELAWARE TEEN CHALLENGE INC (PA)
611 3rd St (19973-2723)
P.O. Box 1271 (19973-5271)
PHONE..................302 629-8824
Bob Carey, *Principal*
Diane Pentoney, *Office Mgr*
Susan Bramble, *Exec Dir*
EMP: 11
SALES: 762.7K **Privately Held**
SIC: 8322 Individual & family services

(G-8221)
DELAWARE TITLE LOANS INC
22994 Sussex Hwy (19973-5861)
PHONE..................302 629-8843
EMP: 15
SALES (corp-wide): 7.7MM **Privately Held**
SIC: 6159 Loan institutions, general & industrial
PA: Delaware Title Loans, Inc.
  8601 Dunwoody Pl Ste 406
  Atlanta GA 30350
  770 552-9840

(G-8222)
DENT PRO INC
14470 Baker Mill Rd (19973-8251)
PHONE..................302 628-0978
David Hignutt, *Branch Mgr*
EMP: 5
SALES (corp-wide): 920.4K **Privately Held**
SIC: 7532 Body shop, automotive
PA: Dent Pro Inc
  2205 Winchester Blvd
  Campbell CA 95008
  408 370-9500

(G-8223)
DIANES BUS SERVICE
Rr 2 Box 79 (19973-9802)
PHONE..................302 629-4336
Diane Horne, *Owner*
EMP: 13
SALES: 300K **Privately Held**
SIC: 4151 School buses

(G-8224)
DIXIE LINE FARM INC
9455 Airport Rd (19973-8501)
PHONE..................302 236-7402
John Zoch, *President*
EMP: 4
SALES (est): 147.6K **Privately Held**
SIC: 0251 Broiler, fryer & roaster chickens

(G-8225)
DON-LEE MARGIN CORPORATION
25271 Figgs Rd (19973-6943)
PHONE..................302 629-7567
Denise Dickerson, *President*
Jack Chambers, *Vice Pres*
Crystal L Chambers, *Manager*
EMP: 30
SQ FT: 4,000
SALES (est): 1.5MM **Privately Held**
SIC: 7349 Janitorial service, contract basis; building maintenance, except repairs; maid services, contract or fee basis

(G-8226)
DRH ENTERPRISES LLC
6796 Hearns Pond Rd (19973-5702)
P.O. Box 13 (19973-0013)
PHONE..................302 864-0060
Charles W Hastings, *Principal*
EMP: 4
SALES (est): 242.3K **Privately Held**
SIC: 8748 Business consulting

(G-8227)
DUCK IN CAR WASH
9817 Spotless St (19973-5860)
P.O. Box 1173 (19973-5173)
PHONE..................302 536-7056
Garrett Grier, *President*
EMP: 4
SALES (est): 91.2K **Privately Held**
SIC: 7542 Washing & polishing, automotive

(G-8228)
DUNBAR ARMORED INC
186 Kent Dr (19973-1585)
PHONE..................302 628-5401
Harvey Sourey, *Branch Mgr*
EMP: 45
SALES (corp-wide): 3.4B **Publicly Held**
SIC: 7381 Armored car services
HQ: Dunbar Armored, Inc.
  50 Schilling Rd
  Hunt Valley MD 21031
  410 584-9800

(G-8229)
EAST COAST BUILDERS INC
Rr 1 Box 350 (19973-9801)
P.O. Box 413 (19973-0413)
PHONE..................302 629-3551
Randy Pentoney, *President*
Diane Pentoney, *Corp Secy*
EMP: 10
SQ FT: 2,000
SALES: 500K **Privately Held**
SIC: 1771 Concrete work

(G-8230)
EASTERN SHORE METAL DETECTORS
20380 Wesley Church Rd (19973-6557)
PHONE..................302 628-1985
John Rebman, *Principal*
EMP: 4
SALES (est): 329.5K **Privately Held**
SIC: 3669 Metal detectors

(G-8231)
EASTERN SHORE METALS LLC
102 Park Ave (19973-9479)
PHONE..................302 629-6629
Ralph Perry, *Senior VP*
John Collins, *Sales Staff*
▲ **EMP:** 19 **EST:** 2012
SALES (est): 19.4MM **Privately Held**
SIC: 5084 7389 3542 Sawmill machinery & equipment; metal slitting & shearing; presses: forming, stamping, punching, sizing (machine tools)

(G-8232)
EDWINA C GRANADA MD
9109 Middleford Rd (19973-7830)
P.O. Box 913 (19973-0913)
PHONE..................302 629-7555
Edwina C Granada MD, *Owner*
Mar Granada, *Co-Owner*
Mark Granada, *Co-Owner*
EMP: 4
SALES (est): 280K **Privately Held**
SIC: 8011 Pediatrician

(G-8233)
EFFECTIVE ADVERTISING SEAFORD
511 N Phillips St (19973-2307)
PHONE..................302 628-1946
EMP: 4 **EST:** 2010
SALES (est): 250K **Privately Held**
SIC: 7311 Advertising Agency

(G-8234)
EFFICIENT SERVICES INC
24660 German Rd (19973-7319)
P.O. Box 858 (19973-0858)
PHONE..................302 629-2124
Phillip Grice, *President*
Vernon Grice, *Vice Pres*
Myra Grice, *Admin Sec*
EMP: 7
SALES (est): 208.5K **Privately Held**
SIC: 7349 5812 5962 Janitorial service, contract basis; caterers; merchandising machine operators

(G-8235)
ELKINGTON I KENT DDS
Also Called: Seaford Dental Associates
218 Pennsylvania Ave (19973-3820)
PHONE..................302 629-3008
Kent I Elkington, *Owner*
EMP: 4
SALES (est): 391.9K **Privately Held**
SIC: 8021 Dentists' office

(G-8236)
EMULSION PRODUCTS COMPANY
Also Called: Gardner Asphalt
25938 Nanticoke Ave (19973-4012)
PHONE..................302 629-3505
Raymond T Hyer, *President*
Robert Hickey, *COO*
Shawn Poole, *Treasurer*
▲ **EMP:** 20
SQ FT: 20,000
SALES (est): 3.7MM
SALES (corp-wide): 270.5MM **Privately Held**
WEB: www.sta-kool.com
SIC: 2951 2892 Asphalt & asphaltic paving mixtures (not from refineries); emulsions (explosive)
PA: Gardner-Gibson, Incorporated
  4161 E 7th Ave
  Tampa FL 33605
  813 248-2101

(G-8237)
ENT ALLERGY CENTER
8468 Herring Run Rd (19973-5763)
PHONE..................302 629-3400
Claude Dimarco, *Owner*
Candice Clayton, *Office Mgr*
EMP: 7
SALES (est): 691.8K **Privately Held**
WEB: www.entallergycenter.com
SIC: 8011 Ears, nose & throat specialist: physician/surgeon

(G-8238)
ERIC CLINE
Also Called: State Farm Insurance
22366 Sussex Hwy (19973-5833)
PHONE..................302 629-3984
Eric Cline, *Manager*
EMP: 4

Seaford - Sussex County (G-8239)

SALES: 350K **Privately Held**
SIC: 6411 Insurance agents & brokers

(G-8239)
ESL INC
Also Called: Eastern Shore Leasing
Rr 13 Box South (19973)
P.O. Box 1420 (19973-5420)
PHONE..................302 629-4553
Fred Hertrick III, *President*
E Vernon Ingram, *Vice Pres*
Harriett Hertrick, *Admin Sec*
EMP: 4
SQ FT: 7,500
SALES (est): 450K **Privately Held**
WEB: www.esl.com
SIC: 7515 7513 Passenger car leasing; truck leasing, without drivers

(G-8240)
EVANS
604 S Market St (19973-4540)
PHONE..................302 629-0545
Martin Evans, *Principal*
EMP: 4
SALES (est): 258.5K **Privately Held**
SIC: 8734 Product testing laboratories

(G-8241)
FALCO INDUSTRIES INC
200 Bedford Falls Dr # 1 (19973-1594)
PHONE..................302 628-1170
EMP: 2
SALES (est): 114.5K **Privately Held**
SIC: 3999 Atomizers, toiletry

(G-8242)
FANTASY BEAUTY SALON
224 High St (19973-3932)
PHONE..................302 629-6762
Sara Lee Thomas, *Owner*
EMP: 7
SALES (est): 108.6K **Privately Held**
SIC: 7231 Beauty shops

(G-8243)
FEDEX GROUND PACKAGE SYS INC
161 Venture Dr (19973-1576)
PHONE..................800 463-3339
EMP: 8
SALES (corp-wide): 69.6B **Publicly Held**
WEB: www.fedex.com
SIC: 4212 Delivery service, vehicular
HQ: Fedex Ground Package System, Inc.
1000 Fed Ex Dr
Coraopolis PA 15108
800 463-3339

(G-8244)
FIRST STATE FABRICATION LLC
26546 Seaford Rd (19973-5949)
P.O. Box 763, Laurel (19956-0763)
PHONE..................302 875-2417
Scott Calloway, *Mng Member*
Theresa L Calloway,
EMP: 6
SALES (est): 900K **Privately Held**
WEB: www.firststatefab.com
SIC: 3441 Fabricated structural metal

(G-8245)
FITNESS MTIVATION INST OF AMER
26685 Sussex Hwy (19973-8525)
PHONE..................302 628-3488
Michael A Triglia, *President*
Alyson Triglia, *Vice Pres*
Ken Lipper, *Manager*
Tasha Puffenburger, *Admin Sec*
Tiffany Presley, *Assistant*
EMP: 4
SALES: 750K **Privately Held**
SIC: 7991 Physical fitness facilities

(G-8246)
FOGARTY LLC
5 Coty Ln (19973-8016)
PHONE..................610 731-4804
Josh Fogarty,
EMP: 8
SALES (est): 61.1K **Privately Held**
SIC: 8082 Home health care services

(G-8247)
FREEDOM RIDES AUTO
26831 Sussex Hwy (19973-8529)
P.O. Box 650 (19973-0650)
PHONE..................302 422-4559
David Houston, *General Mgr*
Kelly Gale, *Principal*
Teresa Adkins, *Inv Control Mgr*
EMP: 5 EST: 2012
SALES (est): 746K **Privately Held**
SIC: 7538 General automotive repair shops

(G-8248)
GARDNER ASPHALT CORPORATION
25938 Nanticoke Ave (19973-4012)
PHONE..................302 629-3505
Raymond Hyer, *President*
Rene Lujan, *Sales Mgr*
Jamie Hill, *Sales Staff*
Steven Buchanan, *Manager*
EMP: 27
SALES (est): 1.6MM
SALES (corp-wide): 270.5MM **Privately Held**
WEB: www.sta-kool.com
SIC: 1771 1761 2952 Driveway, parking lot & blacktop contractors; roofing, siding & sheet metal work; asphalt felts & coatings
PA: Gardner-Gibson, Incorporated
4161 E 7th Ave
Tampa FL 33605
813 248-2101

(G-8249)
GARDNER INDUSTRIES INC
25938 Nanticoke Ave (19973-4012)
PHONE..................302 448-9195
EMP: 2
SALES (est): 74.7K **Privately Held**
SIC: 3999 Manufacturing industries

(G-8250)
GARDNER-GIBSON INC
25938 Nanticoke Ave (19973-4012)
PHONE..................302 628-4290
Shawn Poole, *Treasurer*
Steven Buchanan, *Manager*
EMP: 2
SALES (est): 90.7K **Privately Held**
SIC: 2951 Asphalt paving mixtures & blocks

(G-8251)
GENESIS HALTHCARE - MAIN VOICE
1100 Norman Eskridge Hwy (19973-1724)
PHONE..................302 536-6390
Maryann Swift, *Executive*
EMP: 5 EST: 2016
SALES (est): 101.1K **Privately Held**
SIC: 8051 Skilled nursing care facilities

(G-8252)
GENESIS HEALTHCARE SEAFOOD CTR
Also Called: Seaford Center
1100 Norman Eskridge Hwy (19973-1724)
PHONE..................302 629-3575
D Schonbrunner, *Exec Dir*
Marcie Smith, *Director*
Lori Jones, *Social Dir*
Allen Ward, *Social Dir*
Jessica Collins, *Hlthcr Dir*
EMP: 142
SALES (est): 3.2MM **Publicly Held**
WEB: www.pleasantviewretirement.com
SIC: 8051 Skilled nursing care facilities
HQ: Genesis Healthcare Llc
101 E State St
Kennett Square PA 19348

(G-8253)
GEORGE MILES & BUHR LLC
Also Called: Gmb - Seaford
400 High St (19973-3914)
PHONE..................302 628-1421
Terry Gundry, *Engineer*
Judy Schwartz, *Manager*
EMP: 5
SALES (est): 461.1K
SALES (corp-wide): 8MM **Privately Held**
SIC: 8711 Consulting engineer
PA: George, Miles & Buhr Llc
206 W Main St
Salisbury MD 21801
410 742-3115

(G-8254)
GRIFFIN HOME BUILDERS INC
118 N Pine St (19973-3320)
P.O. Box 623 (19973-0623)
PHONE..................302 629-5615
Fax: 302 629-5375
EMP: 11
SALES (est): 1.3MM **Privately Held**
SIC: 1521 Single-Family House Construction

(G-8255)
H&L CONSTRUCTION CORP
5673 Woodland Ferry Rd (19973-3016)
PHONE..................302 875-5634
EMP: 7
SALES: 720K **Privately Held**
SIC: 1521 Contractor Of Single Family Homes

(G-8256)
HALPERN EYE ASSOCIATES INC
Also Called: Halpern Opthamology
1301 Bridgeville Hwy (19973-1616)
P.O. Box 488 (19973-0488)
PHONE..................302 629-6816
Janet Surts, *Principal*
EMP: 13
SALES (corp-wide): 4.3MM **Privately Held**
WEB: www.halperneye.com
SIC: 8042 Offices & clinics of optometrists
PA: Halpern Eye Associates, Inc.
885 S Governors Ave
Dover DE 19904
302 734-5861

(G-8257)
HAMILTON ASSOCIATES
413 High St (19973-3923)
P.O. Box 1431 (19973-5431)
PHONE..................302 629-4949
Herbert Quick, *Owner*
EMP: 4
SALES: 100K **Privately Held**
SIC: 7336 Graphic arts & related design

(G-8258)
HAMPTON INN
22871 Sussex Hwy (19973-5851)
PHONE..................302 629-4500
EMP: 12
SALES (est): 552.5K **Privately Held**
SIC: 7011 Hotels And Motels

(G-8259)
HAMPTON INN SEAFORD
799 N Dual Hwy (19973)
PHONE..................302 629-4500
Theresa Horseman, *Principal*
EMP: 8
SALES (est): 272.4K **Privately Held**
SIC: 7011 Hotels & motels

(G-8260)
HARBOR HOUSE SEAFOOD INC (PA)
504 Bridgeville Hwy (19973-1522)
PHONE..................302 629-0444
Gary Colbourne, *President*
Mark Bryan, *Vice Pres*
Lance Massey, *Transptn Dir*
Gary Hill, *Sales Staff*
Jill Bryan, *Mktg Dir*
▲ EMP: 71
SQ FT: 6,600
SALES (est): 54MM **Privately Held**
WEB: www.harborhouseseafood.com
SIC: 5146 Seafoods

(G-8261)
HARIM USA LTD (HQ)
126 N Shipley St (19973-3100)
P.O. Box 1380, Millsboro (19966-5380)
PHONE..................302 629-9136
Paula Gray, *Safety Mgr*
Barbara Watkins, *Buyer*
Jessie Lane, *Purchasing*
Shelley Workman, *Executive*
EMP: 6 EST: 2011
SALES (est): 285.3MM **Privately Held**
SIC: 2015 Poultry, processed

(G-8262)
HARROLD & SON INC
27129 Woodland Rd (19973-6961)
PHONE..................302 629-9504
Joe Harrold, *President*
Evelyn Harrold, *Corp Secy*
EMP: 6
SALES (est): 460K **Privately Held**
SIC: 1796 Millwright

(G-8263)
HENDERSON MECHANICAL INC
105 New St Ste 2seaford (19973-3945)
PHONE..................302 629-3753
Dan Henderson, *President*
Karen S Henderson, *Vice Pres*
EMP: 6 EST: 1996
SALES (est): 1MM **Privately Held**
SIC: 1711 Mechanical contractor

(G-8264)
HERR FOODS INCORPORATED
22706 Sussex Hwy (19973-5837)
PHONE..................302 628-9161
Kevin Johnson, *Manager*
EMP: 40
SALES (corp-wide): 392.5MM **Privately Held**
WEB: www.herrs.com
SIC: 5145 Snack foods
PA: Herr Foods Incorporated
20 Herr Dr
Nottingham PA 19362
610 932-9330

(G-8265)
HOLLYWOOD GRILL RESTAURANT
Also Called: Hampton Inn
22871 Sussex Hwy (19973-5851)
PHONE..................302 629-4500
Shalin Patel, *General Mgr*
EMP: 15
SALES (corp-wide): 15.5MM **Privately Held**
SIC: 7011 Hotels & motels
PA: Hollywood Grill Restaurant Inc
1811 Concord Pike
Wilmington DE 19803
302 655-1348

(G-8266)
HOLTS METAL WORKS INC
3325 Horseshoe Rd (19973-5017)
PHONE..................302 628-1609
EMP: 2 EST: 2002
SALES: 292K **Privately Held**
SIC: 3535 Mfg Conveyors/Equipment

(G-8267)
HOME TEAM REALTY
959 Norman Eskridge Hwy (19973-1719)
PHONE..................302 629-7711
Frank Parks, *CEO*
EMP: 15
SALES (est): 1.2MM **Privately Held**
WEB: www.frankparks.com
SIC: 6531 Real estate agent, residential

(G-8268)
HOMELESS CAT HELPERS INC
550 N Pine St (19973-2518)
P.O. Box 1234 (19973-5234)
PHONE..................302 344-3015
D C Brown, *President*
EMP: 10
SALES: 20K **Privately Held**
SIC: 0752 Shelters, animal

(G-8269)
IG BURTON & COMPANY INC
24799 Sussex Hwy (19973-8463)
PHONE..................302 629-2800
Rick Astarita, *General Mgr*
Daniel Hall, *General Mgr*
I G Burton, *Manager*
Benjamin Didonato, *Advisor*
EMP: 50

GEOGRAPHIC SECTION

Seaford - Sussex County (G-8300)

SALES (corp-wide): 225MM **Privately Held**
WEB: www.igburton.com
SIC: 5511 5013 Automobiles, new & used; motor vehicle supplies & new parts
PA: I.G. Burton & Company, Inc.
   793 Bay Rd
   Milford DE 19963
   302 422-3041

(G-8270)
IMPACT GRAPHIX
415 Harrington St (19973-3721)
PHONE.................................302 337-7076
Thomas Weaver, *President*
EMP: 3 EST: 2015
SALES (est): 80.2K **Privately Held**
SIC: 3993 Signs & advertising specialties

(G-8271)
INTEGRA ADM GROUP INC (PA)
Also Called: F & S Property Management Co
110 S Shipley St (19973-3714)
PHONE.................................800 959-3518
David Smith, *President*
EMP: 13
SQ FT: 2,000
SALES (est): 20.7MM **Privately Held**
WEB: www.integratpa.com
SIC: 6411 Insurance claim processing, except medical; insurance brokers

(G-8272)
INVISTA CAPITAL MANAGEMENT LLC
25876 Dupont Rd (19973-4387)
PHONE.................................302 629-1100
Kent Smith, *Vice Pres*
EMP: 25
SALES (corp-wide): 40.6B **Privately Held**
WEB: www.invista.com
SIC: 2869 2221 2282 Laboratory chemicals, organic; broadwoven fabric mills, manmade; nylon yarn: throwing, twisting, winding or spooling
HQ: Invista Capital Management, Llc
   2801 Centerville Rd
   Wilmington DE 19808
   302 683-3000

(G-8273)
IRON LION ENTERPRISES INC
22319 Dixie Ln (19973-6661)
PHONE.................................302 628-8320
Edward Prongay, *President*
EMP: 2
SALES (est): 166.1K **Privately Held**
SIC: 3965 Fasteners, hooks & eyes

(G-8274)
J & L SERVICES INC
5670 Glestown Reliance Rd (19973-6044)
PHONE.................................410 943-3355
James A Burt, *President*
Hazel Burt, *Treasurer*
EMP: 15
SALES (est): 1.6MM **Privately Held**
SIC: 1799 1751 1521 Building site preparation; carpentry work; single-family housing construction; single-family home remodeling, additions & repairs

(G-8275)
J AND J DISPLAY
101 Park Ave Unit 2 (19973-5798)
P.O. Box 237 (19973-0237)
PHONE.................................302 628-4190
Robert Hemmen,
▲ EMP: 3
SALES (est): 561.9K **Privately Held**
WEB: www.jjdisplay.com
SIC: 2542 Partitions & fixtures, except wood

(G-8276)
JACKSON HEWITT TAX SERVICE (PA)
1004 W Stein Hwy (19973-1145)
PHONE.................................302 629-4548
Don Short, *Manager*
EMP: 6
SQ FT: 1,800
SALES (est): 427.6K **Privately Held**
SIC: 7291 Tax return preparation services

(G-8277)
JAMES F PALMER (PA)
8857 Riverside Dr (19973-3654)
PHONE.................................302 629-6162
James F Palmer, *Owner*
EMP: 5
SALES (est): 454.9K **Privately Held**
SIC: 8043 Offices & clinics of podiatrists

(G-8278)
JBS SOUDERTON INC
Also Called: Mopak
4957 Stein Hwy (19973)
PHONE.................................302 629-0725
Donnie Kerr, *Manager*
EMP: 3 **Publicly Held**
SIC: 2048 Livestock feeds
HQ: Jbs Souderton, Inc
   249 Allentown Rd
   Souderton PA 18964
   215 723-5555

(G-8279)
JCR ENTERPRISES INC
126 N Shipley St (19973-3100)
PHONE.................................302 629-9163
Pat Cawley, *President*
Warren R Allen Jr, *Vice Pres*
EMP: 34
SQ FT: 80,000
SALES (est): 3.6MM **Privately Held**
SIC: 2015 Turkey processing & slaughtering

(G-8280)
JOAQUIN CABRERA MD
8472 Herring Run Rd (19973-5763)
PHONE.................................302 629-8977
Joaquin Cabrera MD, *Owner*
EMP: 7
SALES (est): 347.7K **Privately Held**
SIC: 8011 Obstetrician

(G-8281)
JOHN C LEVERAGE
Also Called: State Farm Insurance
26876 Sussex Hwy (19973-8599)
P.O. Box 567 (19973-0567)
PHONE.................................302 629-3525
John C Leverage, *Owner*
EMP: 4
SALES (est): 509.7K **Privately Held**
SIC: 6411 Insurance agents & brokers

(G-8282)
JOHN C LYNCH DDS PA
543 N Shipley St Ste E (19973-2339)
PHONE.................................302 629-7115
John Lynch DDS, *President*
EMP: 8
SALES (est): 728.8K **Privately Held**
SIC: 8021 Dentists' office

(G-8283)
KAPA INC LLC (PA)
Also Called: Peninsula Dry Cleaners
815 Norman Eskridge Hwy (19973-1717)
PHONE.................................302 740-1235
Neoklis Kypreos,
John Alloway,
Matthew Parks,
EMP: 4
SQ FT: 5,000
SALES (est): 526.1K **Privately Held**
SIC: 7216 Cleaning & dyeing, except rugs

(G-8284)
KAREN SCHREIBER
Also Called: Little Sprouts Learning Academ
425 E Stein Hwy (19973)
PHONE.................................302 628-3007
Karen Schreiber, *Owner*
EMP: 8
SQ FT: 4,300
SALES (est): 127.4K **Privately Held**
SIC: 8351 Preschool center

(G-8285)
KAYE CONSTRUCTION
22223 Eskridge Rd (19973-8144)
PHONE.................................302 628-6962
Edward J Kaye, *Owner*
EMP: 23
SALES (est): 2.2MM **Privately Held**
SIC: 1521 1794 4953 New construction, single-family houses; excavation work; recycling, waste materials

(G-8286)
KELLY APPLIANCE SERVICE
22251 Conrail Rd (19973-5729)
PHONE.................................302 628-5396
Steve Kelly, *President*
Christina Flaming, *Corp Secy*
Gale Kelly, *Vice Pres*
EMP: 6
SALES (est): 360K **Privately Held**
SIC: 7699 5722 Household appliance repair services; household appliance stores

(G-8287)
KENCO GROUP INC
1700 Dulany St (19973-1906)
PHONE.................................302 629-4295
Donald Colburn, *Branch Mgr*
EMP: 39
SALES (corp-wide): 1.6B **Privately Held**
WEB: www.kencogroup.com
SIC: 4225 6512 General warehousing; nonresidential building operators
PA: Kenco Group, Inc.
   2001 Riverside Dr Ste 3100
   Chattanooga TN 37406
   423 622-1113

(G-8288)
LAB PRODUCTS INC
Also Called: Metal Systems Div
742 Sussex Ave (19973-2057)
P.O. Box 639 (19973-0639)
PHONE.................................302 628-4300
George Gabriel, *President*
Marc Willis, *Vice Pres*
Phil Lastowski, *Engineer*
Shannon Shelton, *Sales Executive*
Bob Voigt, *Technical Staff*
▲ EMP: 18
SQ FT: 2,000
SALES (est): 2.6MM
SALES (corp-wide): 90MM **Privately Held**
WEB: www.labproductsinc.com
SIC: 0971 Animal hunting & trapping, commercial
PA: Bio Medic Corporation
   742 Sussex Ave
   Seaford DE 19973
   302 628-4300

(G-8289)
LABORATORY CORPORATION AMERICA
Also Called: Labcorp of America
701 Health Services Dr (19973-5784)
PHONE.................................302 629-3182
Kim Merritt, *Manager*
EMP: 5 **Publicly Held**
SIC: 8071 Testing laboratories
HQ: Laboratory Corporation Of America
   358 S Main St Ste 458
   Burlington NC 27215
   336 229-1127

(G-8290)
LAMBDEN BUS SERVICE
10174 Airport Rd (19973-8508)
PHONE.................................302 629-4358
Beverly Lambden, *Owner*
EMP: 5
SALES (est): 248.1K **Privately Held**
SIC: 4151 School buses

(G-8291)
LANK JOHNSON AND TULL
521 N Market Street Ext (19973-1574)
P.O. Box 418 (19973-0418)
PHONE.................................302 629-9543
Richard Tull, *General Mgr*
EMP: 5
SALES (corp-wide): 2.3MM **Privately Held**
SIC: 8721 Certified public accountant
PA: Lank, Johnson And Tull
   268 Milford Harrington Hw
   Milford DE 19963
   302 422-3308

(G-8292)
LEGACY VULCAN LLC
14208 County Seat Hwy (19973-8314)
PHONE.................................302 875-5733
EMP: 2 **Publicly Held**
SIC: 1442 Construction sand & gravel
HQ: Legacy Vulcan, Llc
   1200 Urban Center Dr
   Vestavia AL 35242
   205 298-3000

(G-8293)
LEWIS MILLER INC
Also Called: Miller Lewis Surveyors
8957 Middleford Rd (19973)
PHONE.................................302 629-9895
Don Miller, *President*
EMP: 8
SALES (est): 540K **Privately Held**
WEB: www.millerlewis.net
SIC: 8713 Surveying services

(G-8294)
LIGHTED PATHWAY DAY CARE CTR
425 W Stein Hwy (19973)
PHONE.................................302 629-8583
Evelyn R Stanley, *CEO*
EMP: 15 EST: 2010
SALES (est): 160.4K **Privately Held**
SIC: 8351 Child day care services

(G-8295)
LISA RYAN HOBBS DPM
543 N Shipley St Ste C (19973-2339)
PHONE.................................302 629-3000
Lisa Hobbs, *Principal*
EMP: 8
SALES (est): 87K **Privately Held**
SIC: 8043 Offices & clinics of podiatrists

(G-8296)
LOWES HOME CENTERS LLC
22880 Sussex Hwy (19973-5852)
PHONE.................................302 536-4000
EMP: 150
SALES (corp-wide): 71.3B **Publicly Held**
SIC: 5211 5031 5722 5064 Home centers; building materials, exterior; building materials, interior; household appliance stores; electrical appliances, television & radio
HQ: Lowe's Home Centers, Llc
   1605 Curtis Bridge Rd
   Wilkesboro NC 28697
   336 658-4000

(G-8297)
LRK DENTAL
543 N Shipley St (19973-2339)
PHONE.................................302 629-7115
EMP: 4
SALES (est): 92.4K **Privately Held**
SIC: 8021 Offices & clinics of dentists

(G-8298)
LYNNE BETTS
Also Called: Michaelynne
28 N Pine Street Ext (19973-1426)
PHONE.................................302 265-5602
EMP: 5
SALES (est): 80.6K **Privately Held**
SIC: 8082 Home Health Care Services

(G-8299)
MAF INDUSTRIES
27797 Oneals Rd (19973-6301)
PHONE.................................302 249-1254
Nicholas Disalvo, *Principal*
EMP: 2 EST: 2015
SALES (est): 96.7K **Privately Held**
SIC: 3999 Manufacturing industries

(G-8300)
MAIL ROOMS LTD
500 Arbutus Ave (19973-1302)
PHONE.................................302 629-4838
Fax: 302 628-9325
EMP: 2
SQ FT: 2,000
SALES: 118K **Privately Held**
SIC: 7389 5943 2752 Business Services Ret Stationery Lithographic Commercial Printing

Seaford - Sussex County (G-8301)

(G-8301)
MANOR HOUSE
1001 Middleford Rd (19973-3638)
PHONE..............................302 629-4368
Connie Spencer, *Info Tech Dir*
Dennis Shaffer, *Food Svc Dir*
EMP: 15
SALES (est): 792.9K Privately Held
SIC: 8051 Skilled nursing care facilities

(G-8302)
MANUFACTURERS & TRADERS TR CO
Also Called: M&T
509 W Stein Hwy (19973-1201)
PHONE..............................302 856-4470
Dennis Kinnel, *Branch Mgr*
EMP: 16
SALES (corp-wide): 6.4B Publicly Held
WEB: www.binghamlegg.com
SIC: 6022 State commercial banks
HQ: Manufacturers And Traders Trust Company
    1 M&T Plz Fl 3
    Buffalo NY 14203
    716 842-4200

(G-8303)
MANUFACTURERS & TRADERS TR CO
Also Called: M&T
670 N Dual Hwy (19973)
PHONE..............................302 855-2283
Lora Schuler, *Site Mgr*
EMP: 8
SALES (corp-wide): 6.4B Publicly Held
WEB: www.binghamlegg.com
SIC: 6022 State commercial banks
HQ: Manufacturers And Traders Trust Company
    1 M&T Plz Fl 3
    Buffalo NY 14203
    716 842-4200

(G-8304)
MARINER FINANCE LLC
22826 Sussex Hwy (19973-5862)
PHONE..............................302 628-3970
Shelly Pusey, *Manager*
EMP: 4
SALES (corp-wide): 23.9MM Privately Held
SIC: 6141 Consumer finance companies
PA: Mariner Finance, Llc
    8211 Town Center Dr
    Nottingham MD 21236
    410 882-5200

(G-8305)
MC MULLEN SEPTIC SERVICE INC
22593 Bridgeville Hwy (19973-5822)
PHONE..............................302 629-6221
Mike McMullen, *President*
Brian McMullen, *Vice Pres*
EMP: 5
SALES (est): 627K Privately Held
SIC: 7699 Septic tank cleaning service

(G-8306)
MEADE INC
22536 Sussex Hwy (19973-5835)
PHONE..............................302 262-3394
Darryl Meade, *Branch Mgr*
EMP: 7
SALES (est): 534.8K Privately Held
SIC: 2759 Screen printing
PA: Meade, Inc
    8207 Cloverleaf Dr Frnt
    Millersville MD 21108

(G-8307)
MERNIES MARKET
4610 Woodland Church Rd (19973-4777)
PHONE..............................302 629-9877
John Gundry, *Partner*
Anthony Gundry, *Partner*
EMP: 9
SALES (est): 426.8K Privately Held
SIC: 0161 Market garden

(G-8308)
MESSICK AND JOHNSON LLC
955 Norman Eskridge Hwy (19973-1719)
P.O. Box 505 (19973-0505)
PHONE..............................302 628-3111
Dave Johnson,
EMP: 5
SALES (est): 308.3K Privately Held
SIC: 1611 General contractor, highway & street construction

(G-8309)
MESSICK SIGNS & SERVICE
7684 Gum Branch Rd (19973-4356)
PHONE..............................302 629-6999
Eric Messick, *Owner*
EMP: 1
SALES (est): 78.1K Privately Held
SIC: 3993 Signs & advertising specialties

(G-8310)
MID-ATLANTIC SERVICES A-TEAM (PA)
8558 Elks Rd (19973-5643)
P.O. Box 708 (19973-0708)
PHONE..............................302 628-3403
Rosemary Everton, *President*
Michael R Everton, *Treasurer*
Mary Baker, *Shareholder*
Theresa Everton, *Shareholder*
EMP: 28
SQ FT: 3,000
SALES (est): 6MM Privately Held
SIC: 7349 Janitorial service, contract basis

(G-8311)
MORNING STAR PUBLICATIONS INC
Also Called: Seaford Star
951 Norman Eskridge Hwy D (19973-1719)
P.O. Box 1000 (19973-1000)
PHONE..............................302 629-9788
Bryant Richardson, *President*
Carol Richardson, *Treasurer*
EMP: 10
SALES (est): 1MM Privately Held
WEB: www.msbusinessreport.com
SIC: 2711 Newspapers: publishing only, not printed on site

(G-8312)
MULLEN THOMAS R DMD PA
8466 Herring Run Rd D (19973-5763)
PHONE..............................302 629-3588
Thomas Mullen, *Principal*
EMP: 5
SALES (est): 420K Privately Held
SIC: 8021 Dental surgeon; maxillofacial specialist

(G-8313)
MUNCIE INSURANCE SERVICES (PA)
Also Called: Nationwide
1011 Norman Eskridge Hwy (19973-1721)
PHONE..............................302 629-9414
Marvin Muncie, *Owner*
EMP: 7
SALES (est): 1.1MM Privately Held
SIC: 6411 Insurance information & consulting services

(G-8314)
MUNDY INDUSTRIAL CONTRS INC
25876 Dupont Rd (19973-4387)
PHONE..............................302 629-1100
EMP: 4
SALES (est): 409K Privately Held
SIC: 1542 Commercial & office building contractors

(G-8315)
MURRAYS MOTORS
Also Called: Murray Motors
26029 Bethel Concord Rd (19973-6329)
PHONE..............................302 628-0500
Jesse Eskridge, *Manager*
EMP: 7
SALES (corp-wide): 802.6K Privately Held
SIC: 5093 5015 Junk & scrap; automotive parts & supplies, used
PA: Murray's Motors
    Rr 26
    Dagsboro DE

(G-8316)
NANTICOKE CARDIOLOGY
200 Federal St (19973-5764)
PHONE..............................302 629-9099
Richard Simons, *Partner*
Angel Alicea, *Partner*
Richard Simons, *Partner*
Alvaro I Buenano, *Med Doctor*
EMP: 23
SALES (est): 2.2MM Privately Held
SIC: 8011 Cardiologist & cardio-vascular specialist; general & family practice, physician/surgeon

(G-8317)
NANTICOKE EAR NOSE AND THROAT
900 Middleford Rd (19973-3604)
PHONE..............................302 629-9067
Joseph Olekszyk, *President*
EMP: 7
SQ FT: 2,500
SALES (est): 777.7K Privately Held
SIC: 8011 Ears, nose & throat specialist: physician/surgeon

(G-8318)
NANTICOKE FENCE LLC
23464 Sussex Hwy (19973-5869)
PHONE..............................302 628-7808
Mary Thresa Allen,
EMP: 5
SALES (est): 247.4K Privately Held
SIC: 1799 Fence construction

(G-8319)
NANTICOKE GASTROENTEROLOGY
Also Called: Dr Mackler
924 Middleford Rd (19973-3604)
PHONE..............................302 629-2229
Bradley P Mackler, *President*
Lin McFarland, *Office Mgr*
EMP: 8
SALES (est): 919.2K Privately Held
SIC: 8011 Gastronomist

(G-8320)
NANTICOKE HEALTH SERVICES INC
1320 Middleford Rd (19973-3649)
PHONE..............................302 629-4240
EMP: 42 Privately Held
SIC: 8011 General & family practice, physician/surgeon
PA: Nanticoke Health Services, Inc.
    801 Middleford Rd
    Seaford DE 19973

(G-8321)
NANTICOKE HEALTH SERVICES INC
701 Middleford Rd (19973-3600)
PHONE..............................302 628-6344
Holly Camper, *Branch Mgr*
EMP: 30 Privately Held
SIC: 8011 Oncologist
PA: Nanticoke Health Services, Inc.
    801 Middleford Rd
    Seaford DE 19973

(G-8322)
NANTICOKE HEALTH SERVICES INC
1309 Bridgeville Hwy (19973-1616)
PHONE..............................302 629-3923
Waheed Aziz, *Branch Mgr*
EMP: 84 Privately Held
SIC: 8011 General & family practice, physician/surgeon
PA: Nanticoke Health Services, Inc.
    801 Middleford Rd
    Seaford DE 19973

(G-8323)
NANTICOKE HEALTH SERVICES INC (PA)
801 Middleford Rd (19973-3636)
PHONE..............................302 629-6611
E Hancock, *Principal*
Mary Diedrich, *Business Mgr*
Anthony Policastro, *Vice Pres*
Annedreea Webber, *Vice Pres*
James Watson, *Engineer*
EMP: 45
SALES: 164.2MM Privately Held
SIC: 8099 Medical services organization

(G-8324)
NANTICOKE INDUSTRIES LLC
28986 Cannon Dr (19973-3025)
PHONE..............................302 245-8825
Grace Whitaker, *Mng Member*
Roy Whitaker, *Mng Member*
EMP: 4
SQ FT: 3,000
SALES: 100K Privately Held
SIC: 2499 3732 Applicators, wood; yachts, building & repairing

(G-8325)
NANTICOKE MEMORIAL HOSP INC
Also Called: Nanticoke Occptional Hlth Svcs
543 N Shipley St Ste F (19973-2339)
PHONE..............................302 629-6875
Janet Bennett, *Vice Pres*
Jeck Dilts MD, *Manager*
Bonnie Kendall, *Executive*
EMP: 4 Privately Held
WEB: www.nanticoke.org
SIC: 8049 Occupational therapist
HQ: Nanticoke Memorial Hospital, Inc.
    801 Middleford Rd
    Seaford DE 19973
    302 629-6611

(G-8326)
NANTICOKE OBGYN ASSOCIATES P A
10 Tidewater Dr (19973-9768)
PHONE..............................302 629-2434
James Rupp, *President*
EMP: 10
SALES (est): 764K Privately Held
SIC: 8011 Gynecologist

(G-8327)
NATIONAL HVAC SERVICE
Also Called: Comfort Service Company
N Usa Rt 13 (19973)
P.O. Box 1500 (19973-5500)
PHONE..............................570 825-2894
Joe Aurillo, *Manager*
EMP: 25
SALES (est): 5.5MM Privately Held
WEB: www.nationalhvacservice.com
SIC: 1711 Heating & air conditioning contractors
PA: National H.V.A.C. Service, Ltd
    100 Bradford Rd Ste 120
    Wexford PA 15090

(G-8328)
NEMOURS FOUNDATION
Also Called: Nemours Dpont Pdatrics Seaford
49 Fallon Ave (19973-1577)
PHONE..............................302 629-5030
EMP: 127
SALES (corp-wide): 1.3B Privately Held
SIC: 8011 Primary care medical clinic
PA: Nemours Foundation
    10140 Centurion Pkwy N
    Jacksonville FL 32256
    904 697-4100

(G-8329)
NEMOURS FUNDATION PENSION PLAN
49 Fallon Ave (19973-1577)
PHONE..............................302 629-5030
EMP: 40
SALES (corp-wide): 77.3MM Privately Held
SIC: 8011 Pediatrician
PA: The Nemours Foundation Pension Plan
    10140 Centurion Pkwy N
    Jacksonville FL 32256
    904 697-4100

GEOGRAPHIC SECTION
Seaford - Sussex County (G-8357)

(G-8330)
NOUVIR LIGHTING CORPORATION
Also Called: Nouvir Research
20915 Sussex Hwy (19973-5692)
PHONE.................302 628-9933
Rugh Ellen Miller, *President*
Jack Miller, *Vice Pres*
Matthew Miller, *Vice Pres*
Bernice Miller, *Shareholder*
EMP: 10
SALES: 1MM **Privately Held**
WEB: www.nouvir.com
SIC: 3357 Fiber optic cable (insulated)

(G-8331)
NOUVIR LIGHTNING CORPORATION
Also Called: Design Technology
20915 Sussex Hwy (19973-5692)
PHONE.................302 628-9888
Ruth E Miller, *President*
EMP: 2
SALES (est): 187.7K **Privately Held**
SIC: 3357 3643 7389 Fiber optic cable (insulated); lightning arrestors & coils; design services

(G-8332)
NOVACARE REHABILITATION SEAFOR
300 Hlth Svcs Dr Ste 301 (19973)
PHONE.................302 990-2951
EMP: 8
SALES (est): 73.3K **Privately Held**
SIC: 8093 Rehabilitation center, outpatient treatment

(G-8333)
NUTRIEN AG SOLUTIONS INC
8518 Potts Ln (19973-5975)
PHONE.................302 629-2780
Barry Harris, *Manager*
EMP: 3 **Privately Held**
WEB: www.cropproductionservices.com
SIC: 2875 5191 2048 Fertilizers, mixing only; pesticides; insecticides; chemicals, agricultural; prepared feeds; bird food, prepared
HQ: Nutrien Ag Solutions, Inc.
  3005 Rocky Mountain Ave
  Loveland CO 80538
  970 685-3300

(G-8334)
NUTRIEN AG SOLUTIONS INC
8562 Elks Rd (19973-5643)
PHONE.................302 629-3047
Robert Herring, *General Mgr*
EMP: 12 **Privately Held**
WEB: www.cropproductionservices.com
SIC: 5191 Chemicals, agricultural; fertilizer & fertilizer materials
HQ: Nutrien Ag Solutions, Inc.
  3005 Rocky Mountain Ave
  Loveland CO 80538
  970 685-3300

(G-8335)
OIL SPOT EXPRESS LUBE CENTER
915 Norman Eskridge Hwy (19973-1719)
PHONE.................302 628-9866
Jeff Larrimore, *Manager*
EMP: 8
SALES (est): 235.6K **Privately Held**
SIC: 7538 General automotive repair shops

(G-8336)
ONEMAIN FINANCIAL GROUP LLC
22974 Sussex Hwy (19973-5861)
PHONE.................302 628-9253
Linda Birch, *Manager*
EMP: 4
SALES (corp-wide): 4.2B **Publicly Held**
SIC: 6282 Investment advice
HQ: Onemain Financial Group, Llc
  100 International Dr # 150
  Baltimore MD 21202
  855 663-6246

(G-8337)
ONSITE CONSTRUCTION INC
9654 Brickyard Rd Unit 2 (19973-8434)
PHONE.................302 628-4244
Kevin Pritchett, *President*
Kimberly George, *CFO*
EMP: 20
SALES (est): 2.9MM **Privately Held**
SIC: 1521 Single-family housing construction

(G-8338)
OPEN DOOR INC
107 Pennsylvania Ave (19973-3817)
PHONE.................302 629-7900
Susan Berryman, *Branch Mgr*
EMP: 4
SALES (corp-wide): 1MM **Privately Held**
SIC: 8322 Individual & family services
PA: Open Door, Inc.
  254 E Main St
  Newark DE 19711
  302 731-1504

(G-8339)
ORIENT CORPORATION OF AMERICA
Also Called: Orient Corp of America
111 Park Ave (19973-9478)
PHONE.................302 628-1300
Dave Curry, *Manager*
EMP: 20
SQ FT: 8,000 **Privately Held**
WEB: www.orient-usa.com
SIC: 2865 2899 Dyes & pigments; chemical preparations
HQ: Orient Corporation Of America
  6 Commerce Dr Ste 301
  Cranford NJ 07016
  908 298-0990

(G-8340)
PANZEEA
225 High St (19973-3926)
PHONE.................770 573-3672
Anbu Pandian, *Principal*
Arivudainambi Jaganathan, *Principal*
Maharajan Manickam, *Principal*
EMP: 10
SALES (est): 102.2K **Privately Held**
SIC: 8099 7373 Medical services organization; systems software development services

(G-8341)
PATIENT FIRST MEDICAL LLC
1330 Middleford Rd # 301 (19973-3648)
PHONE.................302 536-7740
Victorino Dejesus, *Principal*
EMP: 5
SALES (est): 380.6K **Privately Held**
SIC: 8099 Health & allied services

(G-8342)
PAUL H AGUILLON MD
Also Called: Sussex Medical Center
401 Concord Rd (19973-4274)
PHONE.................302 629-6664
H P Aguillon MD, *Owner*
Manesh Patel MD,
EMP: 6
SALES (est): 435.7K **Privately Held**
SIC: 8011 General & family practice, physician/surgeon

(G-8343)
PENCO CORPORATION (PA)
1503 W Stein Hwy (19973-1198)
P.O. Box 690 (19973-0690)
PHONE.................302 629-7911
Kent T Peterson, *President*
George H Sapna II, *Corp Secy*
Mike Hignutt, *Finance Mgr*
Emily Willis, *Human Resources*
Scott Sapna, *VP Sales*
EMP: 58
SQ FT: 63,000
SALES (est): 18.4MM **Privately Held**
WEB: www.pencocorp.com
SIC: 4225 5074 General warehousing; plumbing fittings & supplies

(G-8344)
PENCO CORPORATION
1800 Dulany St 6 (19973-1908)
PHONE.................302 629-3061
Steve Milligan, *Manager*
EMP: 5
SALES (corp-wide): 18.4MM **Privately Held**
SIC: 4225 General warehousing & storage
PA: Penco Corporation
  1503 W Stein Hwy
  Seaford DE 19973
  302 629-7911

(G-8345)
PENCO CORPORATION
1503 W Stein Hwy (19973-1198)
PHONE.................302 629-7911
Steve Milligan, *Manager*
EMP: 4
SALES (corp-wide): 18.4MM **Privately Held**
WEB: www.pencocorp.com
SIC: 1541 2611 Industrial buildings & warehouses; pulp mills
PA: Penco Corporation
  1503 W Stein Hwy
  Seaford DE 19973
  302 629-7911

(G-8346)
PENINSULA CHIROPRACTIC CENTER
26685 Sussex Hwy (19973-8525)
PHONE.................302 629-4344
Michael Triglia, *President*
EMP: 7 **EST:** 1979
SALES (est): 632.8K **Privately Held**
WEB: www.peninsulachiropracticcenter.com
SIC: 8041 Offices & clinics of chiropractors

(G-8347)
PENINSULA HOME CARE LLC
8466 Herring Run Rd (19973-5763)
PHONE.................302 629-4914
Todd Wiebusch, *Principal*
Jenna Hare, *Manager*
EMP: 6
SALES (est): 190.4K **Privately Held**
SIC: 8059 Personal care home, with health care

(G-8348)
PENINSULA HOME HEALTH CARE
514 W Stein Hwy (19973-1202)
PHONE.................302 629-5672
Chuck Kelly, *President*
Mark Obier, *Vice Pres*
Karen Kelly, *Treasurer*
Chris Obier, *Admin Sec*
EMP: 10
SQ FT: 3,200
SALES (est): 3.1MM **Privately Held**
SIC: 5047 Medical equipment & supplies

(G-8349)
PENINSULA OIL CO INC (PA)
Also Called: Peninsula Oil & Propane
40 S Market St (19973)
PHONE.................302 422-6691
Geraud Damis, *CEO*
Virginia E Willey, *Admin Sec*
EMP: 25
SQ FT: 4,000
SALES (est): 27.7MM **Privately Held**
SIC: 5171 5411 Petroleum bulk stations; convenience stores, independent

(G-8350)
PENNEY ENTERPRISES INC
Also Called: Print Shack
9203 Brickyard Rd (19973-8468)
PHONE.................302 629-4430
William Whaley, *President*
Martha E Whaley, *Vice Pres*
EMP: 4
SALES (est): 444.8K **Privately Held**
WEB: www.progunstuff.com
SIC: 2752 3993 Commercial printing, offset; advertising novelties

(G-8351)
PENNSULA HOME CARE LLC
501 Health Services Dr (19973-5782)
PHONE.................302 629-4914
Robyn Coughenour, *Principal*
Tisha Donovan, *Lic Prac Nurse*
EMP: 7
SALES (est): 315.4K **Privately Held**
SIC: 8082 Home health care services

(G-8352)
PENSKE TRUCK LEASING CORP
24799 Sussex Hwy (19973-8463)
PHONE.................302 629-5373
Sean Mullins, *Branch Mgr*
EMP: 12
SALES (corp-wide): 9.6B **Privately Held**
SIC: 7513 Truck rental & leasing, no drivers
HQ: Penske Truck Leasing Corporation
  2675 Morgantown Rd
  Reading PA 19607
  610 775-6000

(G-8353)
PERDUE FARMS INC
1000 Nanticoke Ave (19973-4009)
PHONE.................302 629-3216
Roger Lipinski, *Research*
Den Smith, *Manager*
EMP: 7
SALES (corp-wide): 5.9B **Privately Held**
WEB: www.perdue.com
SIC: 2015 Poultry slaughtering & processing
PA: Perdue Farms Inc.
  31149 Old Ocean City Rd
  Salisbury MD 21804
  410 543-3000

(G-8354)
PERDUE FARMS INC
Also Called: Seaford Grain North
300 New St (19973-3918)
PHONE.................410 543-3424
Martin Stewart, *Branch Mgr*
EMP: 4
SALES (corp-wide): 5.9B **Privately Held**
SIC: 2015 Poultry slaughtering & processing
PA: Perdue Farms Inc.
  31149 Old Ocean City Rd
  Salisbury MD 21804
  410 543-3000

(G-8355)
PERDUE-AGRIRECYCLE LLC
28338 Enviro Way (19973-5964)
PHONE.................302 628-2360
Cathy Kline, *Mng Member*
Patti Vega,
EMP: 20 **EST:** 2000
SQ FT: 68,000
SALES (est): 3.4MM
SALES (corp-wide): 5.9B **Privately Held**
WEB: www.perdueagrirecycle.com
SIC: 4953 Recycling, waste materials
PA: Perdue Farms Inc.
  31149 Old Ocean City Rd
  Salisbury MD 21804
  410 543-3000

(G-8356)
PHILLIPS SIGNS INC
20874 Sussex Hwy (19973-5686)
PHONE.................302 629-3550
Benjamin Phillips, *President*
Ben Phillips, *President*
Matt Phillips, *General Mgr*
Robin Ruggiero, *Admin Sec*
EMP: 15
SQ FT: 2,596
SALES: 1.2MM **Privately Held**
WEB: www.phillipssigns.net
SIC: 3993 Signs, not made in custom sign painting shops; neon signs

(G-8357)
PHYSIOTHERAPY CORPORATION
300 Hlth Svcs Dr Unit 301 (19973)
PHONE.................302 628-8568
Ryan Fleming, *Branch Mgr*
EMP: 4 **Privately Held**
SIC: 8049 Physical therapist

Seaford - Sussex County (G-8358)

PA: Physiotherapy Corporation
680 American Ave Ste 200
King Of Prussia PA 19406

(G-8358)
PNC BANK NATIONAL ASSOCIATION
1200 W Stein Hwy (19973-1150)
PHONE..................302 629-5000
Paula Coulbourn, *Manager*
EMP: 14
SALES (corp-wide): 19.9B **Publicly Held**
SIC: 6022 State trust companies accepting deposits, commercial
HQ: Pnc Bank, National Association
222 Delaware Ave
Wilmington DE 19801
877 762-2000

(G-8359)
POLYTECHNIC RESOURCES INC
185 Kent Dr (19973-1585)
P.O. Box 1557 (19973-5557)
PHONE..................302 629-4221
Amitabh Sharma, *Principal*
Alan Wuertenberg, *Manager*
EMP: 8
SALES (est): 1MM **Privately Held**
SIC: 3999 Manufacturing industries

(G-8360)
POWERHOUSE GYM
620 W Stein Hwy (19973-1204)
PHONE..................302 262-0262
Tony Taglipour, *Owner*
EMP: 5
SALES (est): 123.7K **Privately Held**
SIC: 7991 Athletic club & gymnasiums, membership

(G-8361)
PREMIER SPINE AND REHAB
8470 Herring Run Rd (19973-5763)
PHONE..................302 404-5293
EMP: 7
SALES (est): 76.3K **Privately Held**
SIC: 8093 Rehabilitation center, outpatient treatment

(G-8362)
PREMIER STAFFING SOLUTIONS INC
809 Norman Eskridge Hwy (19973-1717)
PHONE..................302 628-7700
EMP: 73
SALES (corp-wide): 3.6MM **Privately Held**
SIC: 7361 Employment agencies
PA: Premier Staffing Solutions, Inc.
123 W Market St
Georgetown DE 19947
302 344-5996

(G-8363)
PRETTY NAILS
22986 Sussex Hwy (19973-5861)
PHONE..................302 628-3937
Hong Tom, *Owner*
EMP: 5
SALES (est): 75K **Privately Held**
SIC: 7231 Manicurist, pedicurist

(G-8364)
PRINT SHACK INC
9203 Brickyard Rd (19973-8468)
PHONE..................302 629-4430
William Whaley, *President*
EMP: 9
SALES (est): 1MM **Privately Held**
SIC: 2732 Book printing

(G-8365)
PROFESSIONAL LEASING INC
Also Called: Plp Financial
740 Sussex Ave (19973-2057)
P.O. Box 149 (19973-0149)
PHONE..................302 629-4350
George S Gabriel, *President*
Frank Anderson, *Corp Secy*
Hunter Hopkins, *Sales Staff*
EMP: 9
SQ FT: 4,500
SALES (est): 1.2MM **Privately Held**
WEB: www.professionalease.com
SIC: 7359 7515 Equipment rental & leasing; passenger car leasing

(G-8366)
QUEST DIAGNOSTICS INCORPORATED
808 Middleford Rd Ste 4 (19973-3650)
PHONE..................302 628-3078
EMP: 4
SALES (corp-wide): 7.5B **Publicly Held**
SIC: 8071 Testing laboratories
PA: Quest Diagnostics Incorporated
500 Plaza Dr Ste G
Secaucus NJ 07094
973 520-2700

(G-8367)
R J FARMS INC
2864 Long Acre Ln (19973-5088)
PHONE..................302 629-2520
Randall C Willin Jr, *President*
John C Willin, *Treasurer*
EMP: 4
SQ FT: 4,000
SALES (est): 467.9K **Privately Held**
SIC: 6531 Real estate leasing & rentals

(G-8368)
R M VILLASENOR MD
9726 N Shore Dr (19973-7818)
PHONE..................302 629-4078
R M Villasenor MD, *Owner*
Roberto Villasenor MD, *Owner*
EMP: 4
SALES (est): 200K **Privately Held**
SIC: 8011 Offices & clinics of medical doctors

(G-8369)
R&R LOGISTICS INC
29299 Hearns Ln (19973-3096)
PHONE..................302 629-4255
Philip E Roberts, *President*
EMP: 4
SALES (est): 320.9K **Privately Held**
SIC: 4212 Local trucking, without storage

(G-8370)
RAINBOW DAY CARE & PRE-SCH
26630 Sussex Hwy (19973-8526)
PHONE..................302 628-1020
EMP: 9
SALES (est): 128.4K **Privately Held**
SIC: 8351 Child Day Care Services

(G-8371)
RALPH H GIVENS
27545 Johnson Rd (19973-4375)
PHONE..................302 629-4319
Ralph H Givens, *Principal*
EMP: 4
SALES (est): 390.5K **Privately Held**
SIC: 0161 0119 Vegetables & melons; cash grains

(G-8372)
RAYS AND SONS MECHANICAL LLC
307 S Winding Brooke Dr (19973-4813)
P.O. Box 288, Woodside (19980-0288)
PHONE..................302 697-2100
Sharon Andrews, *Mng Member*
EMP: 8
SALES: 550K **Privately Held**
SIC: 1711 7389 Warm air heating & air conditioning contractor; plumbing contractors;

(G-8373)
REDDISH WALTON
11 Fallon Ave (19973-1577)
PHONE..................302 629-4787
Walton Reddish, *Executive*
EMP: 8 **EST:** 2017
SALES (est): 65.7K **Privately Held**
SIC: 8049 Offices of health practitioner

(G-8374)
REGIONAL BUILDERS INC
100 Park Ave (19973-9479)
P.O. Box 769 (19973-0769)
PHONE..................302 628-8660
Robert S Boyd, *CEO*
Alan Dail, *Superintendent*
Joan E Neal, *Vice Pres*
Joan D Neal, *CPA*
Barry Neal, *Associate*
EMP: 23
SQ FT: 7,700
SALES: 3.3MM **Privately Held**
WEB: www.regionalbuilders.com
SIC: 1542 3448 Commercial & office building, new construction; prefabricated metal buildings

(G-8375)
REGIS CORPORATION
Also Called: Holiday Hair
632 N Dual Hwy (19973)
PHONE..................302 629-2916
Candice Conklin, *Branch Mgr*
EMP: 7
SALES (corp-wide): 1B **Publicly Held**
WEB: www.regiscorp.com
SIC: 7231 Unisex hair salons
PA: Regis Corporation
7201 Metro Blvd
Edina MN 55439
952 947-7777

(G-8376)
REGIS CORPORATION
22899 Sussex Hwy (19973-5851)
PHONE..................302 628-0484
Sharon Luke, *Branch Mgr*
EMP: 8
SALES (corp-wide): 1B **Publicly Held**
SIC: 7231 Unisex hair salons
PA: Regis Corporation
7201 Metro Blvd
Edina MN 55439
952 947-7777

(G-8377)
RENT-A-CENTER INC
23002 Sussex Hwy (19973-5866)
PHONE..................302 629-8925
Catherine Nelson, *Office Mgr*
EMP: 5
SALES (corp-wide): 2.6B **Publicly Held**
WEB: www.rentacenter.com
SIC: 7359 Appliance rental; furniture rental; home entertainment equipment rental; television rental
PA: Rent-A-Center, Inc.
5501 Headquarters Dr
Plano TX 75024
972 801-1100

(G-8378)
RESTORATION GUYS LLC
10971 Pit Rd (19973-7461)
PHONE..................302 542-4045
Josh Muncy, *Mng Member*
EMP: 7
SALES: 1.2MM **Privately Held**
SIC: 1521 New construction, single-family houses

(G-8379)
RISING STAR COMMUNICATION
14830 Josephs Rd (19973-8231)
PHONE..................302 462-5474
William E Webb, *Principal*
EMP: 5 **EST:** 2010
SALES (est): 186.2K **Privately Held**
SIC: 4899 Communication services

(G-8380)
ROBERTS OXYGEN COMPANY INC
Also Called: Robert Oxygen Company 33
22785 Sussex Hwy 102 (19973)
PHONE..................302 337-9666
Dave Garner, *Manager*
EMP: 7
SALES (corp-wide): 139.2MM **Privately Held**
WEB: www.robertsoxygen.com
SIC: 5085 5169 Welding supplies; compressed gas
PA: Roberts Oxygen Company, Inc.
15830 Redland Rd
Rockville MD 20855
301 315-9090

(G-8381)
ROBINSON REALESTATE
Also Called: Robinson Insurance Agency
605 N Hall St (19973-2437)
P.O. Box 571 (19973-0571)
PHONE..................302 629-4574
Geraldine P Thomas, *Owner*
EMP: 6 **EST:** 1960
SQ FT: 2,500
SALES (est): 568.9K **Privately Held**
SIC: 6531 Real estate agent, residential

(G-8382)
ROSALINA DEJESUS-JILOCA MD
9835 Warrens Way (19973-7954)
PHONE..................302 629-4238
R Dejesus-Jiloca MD, *Owner*
EMP: 10
SALES (est): 234.9K **Privately Held**
SIC: 8011 Offices & clinics of medical doctors

(G-8383)
SALLY BEAUTY SUPPLY LLC
22883 Sussex Hwy (19973-5851)
PHONE..................302 629-5160
Tiffany Thomas, *Manager*
EMP: 5 **Publicly Held**
WEB: www.sallybeauty.com
SIC: 5999 5122 Cosmetics; cosmetics
HQ: Sally Beauty Supply Llc
3001 Colorado Blvd
Denton TX 76210
940 898-7500

(G-8384)
SALVATION ARMY
22943 Sussex Hwy (19973-5871)
PHONE..................302 628-2020
Joyce Tull, *Manager*
EMP: 19
SALES (corp-wide): 2.2B **Privately Held**
SIC: 8322 Social service center
HQ: The Salvation Army
440 W Nyack Rd Ofc
West Nyack NY 10994
845 620-7200

(G-8385)
SCOTTYS TRUCKING INC
11667 Park Dr (19973-7237)
PHONE..................302 629-5156
EMP: 4 **EST:** 2009
SALES (est): 210K **Privately Held**
SIC: 4212 Local Trucking Operator

(G-8386)
SEAFORD ANIMAL HOSPITAL INC
22661 Atlanta Rd (19973-6625)
PHONE..................302 629-7325
William C Wade, *President*
Jaime Ober, *Manager*
Suzanne Wade, *Admin Sec*
EMP: 10
SALES (est): 993.1K **Privately Held**
WEB: www.seafordah.com
SIC: 0742 Animal hospital services, pets & other animal specialties

(G-8387)
SEAFORD CONCRETE PRODUCTS LLC
22288 Coverdale Rd (19973-7036)
PHONE..................302 628-6964
Edward J Kaye, *Principal*
EMP: 5 **EST:** 2010
SALES (est): 355.9K **Privately Held**
SIC: 1771 Foundation & footing contractor

(G-8388)
SEAFORD ENDOSCOPY CENTER
13 Fallon Ave (19973-1577)
PHONE..................302 629-7177
Bradley Mackler, *Owner*
Joyce Miller, *Principal*
EMP: 9
SALES (est): 641.9K **Privately Held**
SIC: 8011 Endocrinologist

GEOGRAPHIC SECTION
Seaford - Sussex County (G-8420)

(G-8389)
SEAFORD FEDERAL CREDIT UNION (PA)
24488 Sussex Hwy Ste 1 (19973-8470)
PHONE.................................302 629-7852
Kathy Greenwood, *Manager*
EMP: 7
SALES (est): 1.3MM Privately Held
WEB: www.seafordfcu.com
SIC: 6062 State credit unions, not federally chartered

(G-8390)
SEAFORD ICE
504 Bridgeville Hwy (19973-1522)
PHONE.................................302 629-2562
EMP: 5
SALES (est): 372.2K Privately Held
SIC: 2097 Mfg Ice

(G-8391)
SEAFORD ICE INC
Also Called: Seaford Ice & Cold Storage
111 S Dual Hwy (19973)
PHONE.................................302 629-2562
EMP: 9
SQ FT: 3,572
SALES (est): 590K Privately Held
SIC: 2097 Manufactures Ice

(G-8392)
SEAFORD MACHINE WORKS INC
1451 Middleford Rd (19973-3613)
P.O. Box 621 (19973-0621)
PHONE.................................302 629-6034
John La Prad, *President*
Philip La Prad, *Vice Pres*
EMP: 18
SQ FT: 6,000
SALES (est): 2.2MM Privately Held
WEB: www.seafordmachshop.com
SIC: 3599 3541 7692 Machine shop, jobbing & repair; machine tool replacement & repair parts, metal cutting types; welding repair

(G-8393)
SEAFORD MISSION INC
611 3rd St (19973-2723)
P.O. Box 1271 (19973-5271)
PHONE.................................302 629-2559
Pat Jones, *President*
Richard Houston, *Vice Pres*
Paul Alexander, *Administration*
EMP: 17
SALES: 240K Privately Held
SIC: 8661 8744 Methodist Church; facilities support services

(G-8394)
SEAFORD POLICE DEPT
300 Virginia Ave (19973-1516)
PHONE.................................302 629-6644
Gary W Morris, *Chief*
EMP: 22
SALES (est): 386.9K Privately Held
SIC: 8641 Youth organizations

(G-8395)
SEAFORD PRESERVATION ASSOC LLC
Also Called: Seaford Meadows Apartments
122 Seaford Meadows Dr (19973-1633)
PHONE.................................302 629-6416
William Demarco, *Vice Pres*
EMP: 13
SALES: 950K Privately Held
SIC: 6513 Apartment building operators

(G-8396)
SENIOR NANTICOKE CENTER INC
310 Virginia Ave Ste B (19973-1516)
PHONE.................................302 629-4939
Susan Franckowiak, *Director*
EMP: 12
SALES: 615.1K Privately Held
SIC: 8322 Senior citizens' center or association

(G-8397)
SERVICE GLASS INC
Rr 20 Box W (19973)
P.O. Box 373 (19973-0373)
PHONE.................................302 629-9139
Bob Booth, *President*
Michelle Booth, *Shareholder*
EMP: 12
SQ FT: 7,200
SALES (est): 2MM Privately Held
SIC: 1793 Glass & glazing work

(G-8398)
SERVICE TIRE TRUCK CENTER INC
24873 Sussex Hwy (19973-8464)
PHONE.................................302 629-5533
Gregory Foskey, *Sales Staff*
Glen High, *Branch Mgr*
John Brown, *Info Tech Dir*
EMP: 12
SALES (corp-wide): 131.1MM Privately Held
WEB: www.sttc.com
SIC: 7534 5531 Tire recapping; truck equipment & parts
PA: Service Tire Truck Center, Inc.
2255 Avenue A
Bethlehem PA 18017
610 954-8473

(G-8399)
SERVICEXPRESS CORPORATION
809 Norman Eskridge Hwy (19973-1717)
PHONE.................................302 854-9118
Bamdad Bahar, *Branch Mgr*
EMP: 554
SIC: 7361 Labor contractors (employment agency)
PA: Servicexpress Corporation
120 N Ray St
Georgetown DE 19947

(G-8400)
SHAMROCK GLASS CO INC
200 N Delaware Ave (19973-2429)
P.O. Box 686 (19973-0686)
PHONE.................................302 629-5500
Al Williams, *President*
Bunnie Gallagher, *Admin Sec*
EMP: 10
SALES (est): 1.3MM Privately Held
WEB: www.shamrockglass.net
SIC: 3231 Medical & laboratory glassware: made from purchased glass

(G-8401)
SHORT INSURANCE ASSOCIATES
106 N Pine St (19973-3320)
PHONE.................................302 629-0999
Daniel Short, *Owner*
EMP: 4
SALES (est): 239.4K Privately Held
SIC: 6411 Insurance agents, brokers & service

(G-8402)
SKATEWORLD INC (PA)
23601 Dove Rd (19973-7263)
PHONE.................................302 875-2121
Richard Slatcher, *President*
Deborah Slatcher, *Corp Secy*
EMP: 26
SQ FT: 12,000
SALES (est): 180K Privately Held
SIC: 7999 Roller skating rink operation

(G-8403)
SMITH FIRM LLC
8866 Riverside Dr (19973-3655)
PHONE.................................302 875-5595
Mike Smith, *Principal*
EMP: 5
SALES (est): 405.6K Privately Held
SIC: 8111 General practice law office

(G-8404)
SOIL SERVICE INC
117 New St (19973-3901)
PHONE.................................302 629-7054
Ralph Byron Palmer Sr, *President*
Ralph Byron Palmer Jr, *Corp Secy*
Charles E Palmer, *Vice Pres*
EMP: 7 EST: 1934
SQ FT: 1,500
SALES (est): 3.4MM Privately Held
SIC: 5191 5261 Fertilizer & fertilizer materials; limestone, agricultural; fertilizer

(G-8405)
SOUTHERN DELAWARE FOOT
543 N Shipley St Ste C (19973-2339)
PHONE.................................302 404-5915
Bradley T Lemon DPM, *Owner*
EMP: 5
SALES (est): 421.3K Privately Held
SIC: 8043 Offices & clinics of podiatrists

(G-8406)
SOUTHERN DENTAL LLC
703 Health Services Dr (19973-5784)
PHONE.................................302 536-7589
Paul Edwin Brown, *Owner*
EMP: 4
SALES (est): 175.3K Privately Held
SIC: 8021 Dentists' office

(G-8407)
SPI PHARMA INC
1800 Dulany St (19973-1908)
PHONE.................................302 262-3223
Paul Lopresto, *Manager*
EMP: 38
SALES (corp-wide): 20B Privately Held
WEB: www.spipharma.com
SIC: 5122 Pharmaceuticals
HQ: Spi Pharma, Inc.
503 Carr Rd Ste 210
Wilmington DE 19809

(G-8408)
STATE LINE FARMS LLC
26394 Old Carriage Rd (19973-4664)
PHONE.................................302 628-4506
Randall Willin III,
Brent Willin,
EMP: 5
SALES: 400K Privately Held
SIC: 0251 Broiler, fryer & roaster chickens

(G-8409)
STEPHENS MANAGEMENT CORP
321 E Stein Hwy (19973-1415)
P.O. Box 594 (19973-0594)
PHONE.................................302 629-4393
Darlene Warner, *President*
June Woodward, *Vice Pres*
EMP: 7
SALES (est): 730.1K Privately Held
SIC: 6531 Real estate managers

(G-8410)
STYLES BY US
324 E Stein Hwy (19973-1416)
PHONE.................................302 629-3244
Angie Collins, *Owner*
EMP: 7
SALES (est): 134K Privately Held
SIC: 7231 Hairdressers

(G-8411)
SURGICAL NANTICOKE ASSOC PA
543 N Shipley St Ste A (19973-2339)
PHONE.................................302 629-8662
Steven Carey, *President*
Samuel Miller MD, *Vice Pres*
EMP: 7
SALES (est): 858.2K Privately Held
SIC: 8011 Cardiologist & cardio-vascular specialist

(G-8412)
SUSAN J BETTS OD
8500 Herring Run Rd (19973-5795)
PHONE.................................302 629-6691
Susan J Betts, *Owner*
EMP: 8
SALES (est): 237K Privately Held
SIC: 8042 Specialized optometrists

(G-8413)
SUSSEX COUNTY ANIMAL ASSN
4503 Briarhook Rd (19973-6604)
P.O. Box 1697 (19973-8997)
PHONE.................................302 628-5198
Kathleen Braza, *Owner*
EMP: 4
SALES: 33.8K Privately Held
SIC: 0742 Veterinary services, specialties

(G-8414)
SUSSEX COUNTY FEDERAL CR UN (PA)
1941 Bridgeville Hwy (19973-1614)
P.O. Box 1800 (19973-8800)
PHONE.................................302 629-0100
Amy Shea, *Personnel*
Richard Stoops, *Manager*
▲ EMP: 21
SALES: 9.7MM Privately Held
SIC: 6061 Federal credit unions

(G-8415)
SUSSEX FLOOR
10271 Old Furnace Rd (19973-8122)
PHONE.................................302 629-5620
Brian Gillis, *Owner*
Shirley Gillis, *Owner*
EMP: 4 EST: 1995
SALES (est): 75.7K Privately Held
SIC: 7349 Floor waxing

(G-8416)
SUSSEX PRINTING CORP
Also Called: Sussex Guide
24904 Sussex Hwy (19973-8466)
P.O. Box 1210 (19973-5210)
PHONE.................................302 629-9303
Layton Ayres, *President*
Elizabeth Ayres, *Vice Pres*
Timothy Ayres, *Vice Pres*
Dixie Judy, *Comptroller*
Chuck Fryling, *Sales Mgr*
EMP: 60 EST: 1957
SQ FT: 3,000
SALES (est): 5.4MM Privately Held
SIC: 2741 2791 2771 2759 Guides: publishing & printing; typesetting; greeting cards; commercial printing; commercial printing, lithographic

(G-8417)
SUSSEX PRSCHOOL ERLY CARE CTRS
Also Called: Discovery Island Preschool
126 N Shipley St (19973-3100)
P.O. Box 14 (19973-0014)
PHONE.................................302 732-7529
Margaret Clark, *Owner*
Karen Schreiber, *Partner*
EMP: 7
SALES (est): 250.4K Privately Held
SIC: 8351 Preschool center

(G-8418)
SUSSEX SAND & GRAVEL INC
22223 Eskridge Rd (19973-8144)
PHONE.................................302 628-6962
Eddie J Kaye, *Principal*
EMP: 3
SALES (est): 179.7K Privately Held
SIC: 1442 Gravel mining

(G-8419)
TEAGLE AND SONS
6 N Street Ext (19973-1510)
PHONE.................................302 682-8639
Henry M Teagle, *Owner*
EMP: 6
SALES (est): 78.7K Privately Held
SIC: 7349 Building maintenance services

(G-8420)
TELAMON CORPORATION
517 Bridgeville Hwy (19973-1521)
PHONE.................................302 629-5557
Margaret Antel, *Branch Mgr*
Laura Galvan, *Manager*
Karla Steward, *Manager*
EMP: 8
SALES (corp-wide): 70.5MM Privately Held
SIC: 8331 Job training services
PA: Telamon Corporation
5560 Munford Rd Ste 201
Raleigh NC 27612
919 851-7611

Seaford - Sussex County (G-8421) — GEOGRAPHIC SECTION

(G-8421)
THOMAS ROOFING SUPPLY COMPANY
1164 Airport Rd Ste 13 (19973)
P.O. Box 374 (19973-0374)
PHONE.................302 629-4521
Daniel Thomas, *Owner*
John Thomas, *Co-Owner*
EMP: 24 EST: 1947
SALES: 1.5MM **Privately Held**
SIC: 5033 Roofing, asphalt & sheet metal

(G-8422)
TIDEWATER PHYSCL THRPY AND REB
Also Called: Tidewater Electricmyology
808 Middleford Rd Ste 7 (19973-3650)
P.O. Box 1564, Easton MD (21601-8932)
PHONE.................302 629-4024
Carmen Carey, *Manager*
EMP: 9
SALES (corp-wide): 2.6MM **Privately Held**
WEB: www.tidewaterpt.com
SIC: 8049 8093 Physical therapist; rehabilitation center, outpatient treatment
PA: Tidewater Physical Therapy And Rehabilitation Associates Pa
406 Marvel Ct
Easton MD 21601
410 822-3116

(G-8423)
TIMOTHY WESTGATE
1415 W Stein Hwy (19973-1156)
PHONE.................302 629-9197
Timothy Westgate, *Executive*
EMP: 8
SALES (est): 87K **Privately Held**
SIC: 8042 Offices & clinics of optometrists

(G-8424)
TINAS TINY TOTS DAYCARE
8779 Concord Rd (19973-8422)
PHONE.................302 536-7077
Christina L Mummert, *Principal*
EMP: 5
SALES (est): 84K **Privately Held**
SIC: 8351 Group day care center

(G-8425)
TRINITY LOGISTICS INC (HQ)
50 Fallon Ave (19973-1578)
P.O. Box 1620 (19973-8920)
PHONE.................302 253-3900
Donnan R Burris, *President*
Douglas Heilesen, *General Mgr*
Richard Clair, *COO*
Sarah Russtorn, *COO*
William Banning, *Senior VP*
EMP: 165
SQ FT: 50,000
SALES (est): 1.3B
SALES (corp-wide): 1.4B **Privately Held**
SIC: 4731 Truck transportation brokers
PA: Burris Logistics
501 Se 5th St
Milford DE 19963
302 839-4531

(G-8426)
TUCKER MECHANICAL SERVICE INC
8185 Bethel Rd (19973-3063)
P.O. Box 295, Bethel (19931-0295)
PHONE.................302 536-7730
Douglas Tucker, *President*
EMP: 4
SALES (est): 556.7K **Privately Held**
SIC: 5083 7699 Irrigation equipment; agricultural equipment repair services

(G-8427)
TULL BROTHERS INC
24960 Dairy Ln (19973-6997)
PHONE.................302 629-3071
Cecil B Tull, *Ch of Bd*
Earl B Tull, *President*
Karen Johnson, *Vice Pres*
Benjaman Tull, *Vice Pres*
Gary Johnson, *Admin Sec*
EMP: 35
SQ FT: 12,000
SALES (est): 5MM **Privately Held**
WEB: www.tullbrothers.com
SIC: 5083 5261 Farm equipment parts & supplies; lawn & garden equipment

(G-8428)
V F W VIRGIL WILSON POST
Also Called: V F W Virgil Wilson Post 4961
Middleford Rd (19973)
PHONE.................302 629-3092
Sam Atkins, *President*
Rick Norman, *Principal*
EMP: 4
SALES (est): 205.1K **Privately Held**
SIC: 8641 Veterans' organization

(G-8429)
VACATION CLUB
9290 River Vista Dr (19973-8600)
P.O. Box 1396 (19973-5396)
PHONE.................302 628-1144
EMP: 5
SALES (est): 105.1K **Privately Held**
SIC: 7997 Membership sports & recreation clubs

(G-8430)
VERIZON DELAWARE LLC
8722 Concord Rd (19973-8423)
PHONE.................302 629-4502
Gary Allison, *Manager*
EMP: 16
SALES (corp-wide): 130.8B **Publicly Held**
SIC: 4813 Telephone cable service, land or submarine
HQ: Verizon Delaware Llc
901 N Tatnall St Fl 2
Wilmington DE 19801
302 571-1571

(G-8431)
VIDEO DEN
27180 Williams Ave (19973-5921)
PHONE.................302 628-9835
James Horne, *Owner*
EMP: 5
SQ FT: 1,600
SALES (est): 50K **Privately Held**
SIC: 7841 7359 5735 5731 Video disk/tape rental to the general public; video cassette recorder & accessory rental; video tapes, prerecorded; tape recorders & players; antennas, satellite dish; television sets

(G-8432)
WALKERS MARINE CORPORATION
26912 Walker Rd (19973-4771)
P.O. Box 247 (19973-0247)
PHONE.................302 629-8666
Chris Walker, *President*
Debbie Walker, *Vice Pres*
Sylvia Walker, *Treasurer*
EMP: 4
SALES: 696K **Privately Held**
WEB: www.walkersmarine.com
SIC: 5551 4493 Motor boat dealers; marine supplies & equipment; marinas

(G-8433)
WARREN ELECTRIC CO INC
21621 Sussex Hwy (19973)
P.O. Box 557 (19973-0557)
PHONE.................302 629-9134
David Mc Natt Sr, *President*
Ness McNatt, *Treasurer*
EMP: 6
SALES (est): 798.6K **Privately Held**
SIC: 7694 5063 Electric motor repair; motors, electric

(G-8434)
WATSON-MARLOW FLOW SMART INC
213 Nesbitt Dr (19973-9401)
PHONE.................302 536-6388
Steve Lavargna, *CEO*
Pamela Patrick, *General Mgr*
Tasha McMahan, *Controller*
Mark Lovallo, *Sales Engr*
▲ EMP: 45
SQ FT: 27,800
SALES: 6MM
SALES (corp-wide): 1.5B **Privately Held**
SIC: 3053 Gaskets & sealing devices
HQ: Watson-Marlow Limited
Bickland Water Road
Falmouth TR11
132 637-0370

(G-8435)
WATSON-YATES FUNERAL HOME INC
609 E King St (19973-3502)
P.O. Box 356 (19973-0356)
PHONE.................302 629-8561
Gary W Yates, *President*
EMP: 4
SALES (est): 320.3K **Privately Held**
SIC: 7261 Funeral home; funeral director

(G-8436)
WENTWORTH INC
Also Called: H & R Block
22946 Sussex Hwy (19973-5861)
PHONE.................302 629-6284
Elizabeth Wentworth, *President*
EMP: 18
SALES (est): 642.5K **Privately Held**
SIC: 7291 Tax return preparation services

(G-8437)
WHOLESALE MILLWORK INC (PA)
107 Park Ave (19973-9478)
PHONE.................888 964-8746
Joseph Stephan Palencar, *President*
Patrick Evans, *Sales Staff*
Chris Gardner, *Sales Staff*
Jim Henneman, *Sales Staff*
Sabrina Johnson, *Sales Staff*
▲ EMP: 10
SQ FT: 40,000
SALES (est): 15.9MM **Privately Held**
SIC: 5031 Millwork

(G-8438)
WILLIAM A ODAY
Also Called: William A O'Day Ands Son
4148 Woodland Ferry Rd (19973-4651)
PHONE.................302 629-7854
William A Oday, *Mng Member*
EMP: 5
SALES (est): 334.9K **Privately Held**
SIC: 0191 General farms, primarily crop

(G-8439)
WILLIAM A ODAY & SON LLC
4148 Woodland Ferry Rd (19973-4651)
PHONE.................302 629-7854
William O'Day, *Partner*
EMP: 4
SALES (est): 238.1K **Privately Held**
SIC: 0191 General farms, primarily crop

(G-8440)
WILLIN FARMS LLC
2864 Long Acre Ln (19973-5088)
PHONE.................302 629-2520
Randall C Willin Jr,
Faith Willin,
John Willin,
John C Willin,
EMP: 8
SQ FT: 1,200
SALES (est): 596.1K **Privately Held**
SIC: 0191 General farms, primarily crop

(G-8441)
WILMINGTON SAVINGS FUND SOC
22820 Sussex Hwy (19973-5862)
PHONE.................302 360-0440
Paul B Hughes, *Vice Pres*
EMP: 9
SALES (corp-wide): 455.5MM **Publicly Held**
SIC: 6022 State commercial banks
HQ: Wilmington Savings Fund Society
500 Delaware Ave Ste 500 # 500
Wilmington DE 19801
302 792-6000

(G-8442)
WOMENS MEDICAL CENTER INC
Also Called: Women's Medical Center PA
1301 Middleford Rd (19973-3611)
PHONE.................302 629-5409
Patrick Tierno, *President*
EMP: 9
SALES (est): 823.3K **Privately Held**
SIC: 8011 Gynecologist; obstetrician

(G-8443)
WORMS QUALITY CARPET CARE
21729 Maple Dr (19973-5674)
PHONE.................302 629-3114
Matthew H Spence Jr,
EMP: 8
SALES (est): 177.8K **Privately Held**
SIC: 7217 Carpet & furniture cleaning on location

(G-8444)
XPO LOGISTICS FREIGHT INC
104 Park Ave (19973-9479)
PHONE.................302 629-5228
John Secoist, *Manager*
EMP: 30
SALES (corp-wide): 17.2B **Publicly Held**
WEB: www.con-way.com
SIC: 4213 Trucking, except local
HQ: Xpo Logistics Freight, Inc.
2211 Old Earhart Rd # 100
Ann Arbor MI 48105
800 755-2728

(G-8445)
YELLOW TRANS
26902 Bethel Concord Rd (19973-6304)
PHONE.................302 628-2805
Mark Collins, *Principal*
Jeff Marine, *Principal*
Tom Wooden, *Manager*
EMP: 16
SALES (est): 549.6K **Privately Held**
SIC: 4789 Transportation services

Selbyville
Sussex County

(G-8446)
ABLE WHELLING AND MACHINE
Also Called: Able Welding & Machine
45 Railroad Ave (19975-9675)
P.O. Box 1075 (19975-1075)
PHONE.................302 436-1929
Debra Behney, *Owner*
Lloyd Behney, *Co-Owner*
EMP: 4
SQ FT: 2,400
SALES (est): 316.4K **Privately Held**
SIC: 5712 7349 3599 Mattresses; building maintenance services; cleaning service, industrial or commercial; machine shop, jobbing & repair

(G-8447)
ALUTECH UNITED INC (PA)
Also Called: Alutech Awnings
117 Dixon St (19975-3022)
P.O. Box 329 (19975-0329)
PHONE.................302 436-6005
Joachim Schanz, *President*
George Pfaller, *Vice Pres*
Wes Hines, *Natl Sales Mgr*
Jason Killen, *Sales Staff*
Russell Pfaller, *Manager*
◆ EMP: 5
SQ FT: 25,000
SALES: 6MM **Privately Held**
WEB: www.ALUTECH.com
SIC: 3442 Shutters, door or window: metal

(G-8448)
ANIMAL HEALTH SALES INC
Also Called: Selbyville Pet and Garden Ctr
44 Rte 113 (19975)
PHONE.................302 436-8286
Donald J Lynch, *President*
Jean Lynch, *President*
Kevin Lynch, *Treasurer*
EMP: 18
SQ FT: 14,400

GEOGRAPHIC SECTION

Selbyville - Sussex County (G-8477)

SALES (est): 3MM **Privately Held**
WEB: www.amazingpetfoods.com
SIC: 5122 5199 Animal medicines; biologicals & allied products; pharmaceuticals; pet supplies

(G-8449)
ANTEBELLUM HOSPITALITY INC
118 W Church St (19975-2010)
P.O. Box 519 (19975-0519)
PHONE...................302 436-4375
Bill Shoemaker, *President*
Ray Gindroz, *Principal*
Mark Nickita, *Principal*
Donald Powers, *Principal*
Dhiru Thadani, *Principal*
EMP: 7
SALES: 1MM **Privately Held**
WEB: www.ahi-services.com
SIC: 8741 Business management

(G-8450)
ARROW SAFETY DEVICE CO
123 Dixon St (19975-3022)
PHONE...................302 856-2516
Alfred Hopkin, *CEO*
David T Steier, *President*
Set Mostaglin, *Vice Pres*
Leah Hudson, *Sales Staff*
Penny Johnson, *Sales Staff*
▲ EMP: 16
SQ FT: 7,800
SALES: 4.5MM **Privately Held**
SIC: 3647 Vehicular lighting equipment

(G-8451)
ATLANTIC GENERAL HOSPITAL CORP
38394 Dupont Blvd Unit 6 (19975-3049)
PHONE...................302 524-5007
Brandi Musselman, *Branch Mgr*
EMP: 15 **Privately Held**
SIC: 8062 General medical & surgical hospitals
PA: Atlantic General Hospital Corporation
9733 Healthway Dr
Berlin MD 21811

(G-8452)
AVALANCHE STRATEGIES LLC
Also Called: Think Fast Toys.com
144 Dixon St (19975-3053)
PHONE...................302 436-7060
William Spraul, *CEO*
Stu Eisenman, *President*
Cyrus Jiroir, *Vice Pres*
James Fishinger, *Controller*
Emma Prettyman, *Cust Mgr*
▲ EMP: 180 EST: 2015
SQ FT: 100,000
SALES (est): 23.1MM **Privately Held**
SIC: 7384 8742 Photographic services; marketing consulting services

(G-8453)
BAYSIDE RESORT GOLF CLUB
Also Called: Golf Bayside
31806 Lakeview Dr (19975-3700)
PHONE...................302 436-3400
Robert C Crowther, *Director*
EMP: 25
SALES (est): 1.6MM **Privately Held**
SIC: 7997 7992 Golf club, membership; public golf courses

(G-8454)
BAYSIDE SPORTS CLUB LLC
31381 Sorsyphia (19975)
PHONE...................302 436-3550
Jack Nicklaus, *Principal*
EMP: 16
SALES (est): 669K **Privately Held**
SIC: 7997 Membership sports & recreation clubs

(G-8455)
BAYVILLE POSTAL SVC
37232 Lighthouse Rd (19975-3981)
PHONE...................302 436-2715
Andrew Adkins, *Mng Member*
EMP: 5
SALES (est): 451.6K **Privately Held**
SIC: 7389 Post office contract stations

(G-8456)
BETHANY RESORT FURN WHSE
145 Dixon St (19975-3022)
PHONE...................302 251-4101
Bill Timmons, *Controller*
▲ EMP: 4
SALES (est): 124.4K **Privately Held**
SIC: 2392 Household furnishings

(G-8457)
BILL CANNONS GARAGE INC
Rr 2 Box 125 (19975)
PHONE...................302 436-4200
William D Cannon, *President*
Becky Cannon, *Vice Pres*
EMP: 10
SQ FT: 12,200
SALES (est): 950K **Privately Held**
SIC: 7538 5531 General automotive repair shops; automotive parts

(G-8458)
BODY DOUBLE SWIMWEAR
1007 Coastal Hwy (19944)
PHONE...................302 537-1444
Nancy Rupert, *Owner*
EMP: 6
SQ FT: 1,700
SALES (est): 450.9K **Privately Held**
SIC: 5699 2339 Bathing suits; bathing suits: women's, misses' & juniors'

(G-8459)
BRANDON TATUM
Also Called: Vogue On 54
36666 Bluewater Run W # 7 (19975-4392)
PHONE...................302 564-7428
Brandon Tatum, *Owner*
EMP: 7
SALES (est): 56.9K **Privately Held**
SIC: 7231 Unisex hair salons

(G-8460)
BRANDYWINE ASSISTED LIVING
Also Called: Brandywine Sr Care
21111 Arrington Dr # 101 (19975-3608)
PHONE...................302 436-0808
Brenda Bacon,
EMP: 476
SALES (est): 7.6MM
SALES (corp-wide): 174.7MM **Privately Held**
WEB: www.brandycare.com
SIC: 8322 Senior citizens' center or association
PA: Brandywine Senior Living Management Llc
525 Fellowship Rd Ste 360
Mount Laurel NJ 08054
856 778-6100

(G-8461)
BRASURES CARPET CARE INC (PA)
35131 Lighthouse Rd (19975-4048)
P.O. Box 114 (19975-0114)
PHONE...................302 436-5652
David L Brasure, *President*
Peggy L Brasure, *Vice Pres*
EMP: 9
SQ FT: 6,000
SALES (est): 886.8K **Privately Held**
WEB: www.brasurescarpetcare.com
SIC: 7217 7216 5713 Carpet & furniture cleaning on location; curtain cleaning & repair; rugs

(G-8462)
BRASURES PEST CONTROL INC
38187 Dickerson Rd (19975-3527)
P.O. Box 1100 (19975-1100)
PHONE...................302 436-8140
Carroll W Brasure, *President*
Christopher Brasure, *Vice Pres*
Tammy Collins, *Vice Pres*
EMP: 25
SALES (est): 1MM **Privately Held**
WEB: www.brasures.com
SIC: 7342 5713 Exterminating & fumigating; floor covering stores

(G-8463)
BUNTING & MURRAY CNSTR CORP
32996 Lighthouse Rd (19975-4024)
PHONE...................302 436-5144
Jay C Murray, *President*
C Coleman Bunting Jr, *President*
Susan Ross, *CFO*
Carlton Murray, *Director*
Clifton Murray, *Director*
EMP: 55
SQ FT: 4,000
SALES (est): 11.6MM **Privately Held**
WEB: www.buntingandmurray.com
SIC: 1623 1794 Water, sewer & utility lines; excavation work; excavation & grading, building construction

(G-8464)
BUNTING CONSTRUCTION CORP
32996 Lighthouse Rd (19975-4024)
PHONE...................302 436-5124
C Coleman Bunting, *President*
Michael Sasada, *Vice Pres*
Steven Yoder, *Vice Pres*
Dawn Zibragos, *Purch Agent*
Susan W Ross, *Treasurer*
EMP: 18
SQ FT: 4,000
SALES: 17MM **Privately Held**
WEB: www.buntingconstruction.com
SIC: 1521 1542 New construction, single-family houses; general remodeling, single-family houses; townhouse construction; commercial & office building, new construction

(G-8465)
CABINETRY UNLIMITED LLC
7 Hosier St (19975-9300)
P.O. Box 687 (19975-0687)
PHONE...................302 436-5030
Dieter Baier, *President*
Joseph A Dougherty, *President*
Mary Ellen Dougherty, *Corp Secy*
Steve Graham, *Plant Mgr*
EMP: 30
SQ FT: 22,000
SALES (est): 11.8MM **Privately Held**
WEB: www.cabinetryunlimited.com
SIC: 5031 2541 5211 Kitchen cabinets; table or counter tops, plastic laminated; counter tops

(G-8466)
CHARLES A KLEIN & SONS INC
3 Mason Dr (19975-9617)
PHONE...................410 549-6960
Paul Burfoot, *Production*
Harry Shriver, *Production*
Ro Downey, *Accountant*
Tim Brown, *Manager*
EMP: 8
SALES (corp-wide): 30.7MM **Privately Held**
SIC: 1711 Plumbing contractors
PA: Charles A. Klein & Sons, Inc.
5220 Klee Mill Rd S
Sykesville MD 21784
410 781-4946

(G-8467)
CHARLES A ZONKO BUILDERS INC
37116 Lighthouse Rd (19975-3909)
PHONE...................302 436-0222
Charles A Zonko, *President*
Bonnie Zonko, *Corp Secy*
EMP: 35 EST: 1973
SQ FT: 1,500
SALES: 20MM **Privately Held**
SIC: 1521 New construction, single-family houses; general remodeling, single-family houses

(G-8468)
CHESAPEAKE SEAGLASS JEWELRY
11505 W Sand Cove Rd (19975-3796)
PHONE...................410 778-4999
EMP: 1
SALES (est): 37.5K **Privately Held**
SIC: 2741 Miscellaneous publishing

(G-8469)
COASTAL CARE PHYSICAL THERAPY
37197 E Stoney Run (19975-4325)
PHONE...................480 236-3863
Maricryst Birao, *Agent*
EMP: 8
SALES (est): 65.7K **Privately Held**
SIC: 8049 Physical therapist

(G-8470)
COASTAL VETERINARY
33053 Lighthouse Rd (19975-4017)
PHONE...................302 524-8550
Mary Helen Staruch, *Owner*
EMP: 7 EST: 2016
SALES (est): 274.6K **Privately Held**
SIC: 0742 Animal hospital services, pets & other animal specialties

(G-8471)
CORE FUNCTIONS LLC
21142 Arrington Dr (19975-3600)
PHONE...................443 956-9626
Mary Grimm, *Owner*
Maureen Kitchelt, *Owner*
EMP: 5
SALES (est): 298.6K **Privately Held**
SIC: 7389 8742 ; management engineering

(G-8472)
CRAFTSMAN CBNTRY WOODWORKS INC
37357 Tree Top Ln (19975-3350)
PHONE...................302 841-5274
Richard Jensen, *Principal*
EMP: 4
SQ FT: 2,000
SALES (est): 195.6K **Privately Held**
SIC: 8741 Construction management

(G-8473)
CROOSROADS AUTO REPAIR INC
32469 Lighthouse Rd (19975-3410)
PHONE...................302 436-9100
Lloyd Bare, *Owner*
EMP: 5
SALES (est): 572.5K **Privately Held**
SIC: 7699 Repair services

(G-8474)
CROSSROADS VETERINARY CLINIC
36774 Dupont Blvd (19975-3008)
PHONE...................302 436-5984
Christian Brandt, *Principal*
EMP: 6
SALES (est): 290K **Privately Held**
SIC: 0742 Animal hospital services, pets & other animal specialties

(G-8475)
CYGNET CONSTRUCTION CORP
50 Saw Mill Ln (19975)
PHONE...................302 436-5212
Gladys Swann, *President*
James E Swann III, *Treasurer*
Nancy Swann, *Admin Sec*
EMP: 6
SALES (est): 567K **Privately Held**
SIC: 1794 Excavation work

(G-8476)
D A JONES INC
Also Called: Champion Window Cleaners
37479 Leisure Dr (19975-3841)
PHONE...................302 836-9238
David A Jones, *President*
EMP: 5
SALES: 108K **Privately Held**
SIC: 7349 Maid services, contract or fee basis

(G-8477)
DANNYS CUSTOM UPHOLSTERY
34799 Lighthouse Rd (19975-4002)
PHONE...................302 436-8200
EMP: 1
SALES (est): 46.5K **Privately Held**
SIC: 2211 Canvas

Selbyville - Sussex County (G-8478)

(G-8478)
DATATECH ENTERPRISES INC (PA)
Also Called: Acolyst
36322 Sunflower Blvd (19975-3751)
PHONE.................................540 370-0010
Ellie Nazemoff, *President*
Kaveh Nazemoff, *Vice Pres*
Valeh Nazemoff, *Executive*
EMP: 14
SALES (est): 5MM **Privately Held**
WEB: www.acolyst.com
SIC: 7379 7373 7371 7372 Computer related consulting services; computer integrated systems design; custom computer programming services; prepackaged software; data processing & preparation; computer facilities management

(G-8479)
DAVES CONTRACTING INC
37172 Brickman Ln (19975-3338)
PHONE.................................302 436-5129
David Brickman, *President*
EMP: 4
SALES (est): 371.7K **Privately Held**
SIC: 1711 Plumbing contractors

(G-8480)
DEAD ON CONSTRUCTION
P.O. Box 1092 (19975-1092)
PHONE.................................302 462-5023
Lazaro Agustin, *Principal*
EMP: 6
SALES (est): 356.8K **Privately Held**
SIC: 1521 Single-family housing construction

(G-8481)
DELTA SALES CORP
5 W Church St (19975-2003)
P.O. Box 681 (19975-0681)
PHONE.................................302 436-6063
David Speier, *President*
John Ashman, *Vice Pres*
EMP: 65
SALES (est): 10.2MM **Privately Held**
SIC: 5051 Steel

(G-8482)
DONNAS FAMILY CUT & CURL INC
106 Bayville Shopping Ctr (19975)
PHONE.................................302 436-8999
Donna Emm, *President*
EMP: 8
SALES (est): 198.6K **Privately Held**
SIC: 7231 Beauty shops

(G-8483)
DR JAMES KRAMER
13 S Main St 348 (19975-9664)
PHONE.................................302 436-5133
James Kenneth Kramer, *Principal*
EMP: 5
SALES (est): 336.9K **Privately Held**
SIC: 8021 Dentists' office

(G-8484)
EAST COAST ELASTOMERICS INC
Also Called: Ece Weatherguard
38298 London Ave Unit 4 (19975-4080)
PHONE.................................302 524-8004
Daniel Ash, *President*
EMP: 18
SQ FT: 1,500
SALES (est): 1.6MM **Privately Held**
WEB: www.eceweatherguard.com
SIC: 1799 Waterproofing

(G-8485)
EASTERN SHORE PORCH PATIO INC
17 Mason Dr (19975-3057)
P.O. Box 168 (19975-0168)
PHONE.................................302 436-9520
Robert C Douglas, *President*
EMP: 20
SQ FT: 9,000
SALES (est): 3.6MM **Privately Held**
WEB: www.esvinylproducts.com
SIC: 1799 1521 5712 Fence construction; general remodeling, single-family houses; outdoor & garden furniture

(G-8486)
ED HILEMAN DRYWALL INC
36722 Roxana Rd (19975-3305)
PHONE.................................302 436-6277
Ed Hileman, *President*
EMP: 7
SALES (est): 500K **Privately Held**
SIC: 1742 Drywall

(G-8487)
ELIZABETH C PARBERRY DR
37600 Bearhole Rd (19975)
PHONE.................................302 436-1803
Elizabeth Parberry, *Principal*
EMP: 4
SALES (est): 188.4K **Privately Held**
SIC: 8041 Offices & clinics of chiropractors

(G-8488)
ENERGY GYM
36666 Bluewater Run W # 1 (19975-4392)
PHONE.................................302 436-9001
Tony Hall, *Principal*
EMP: 11 **EST:** 2010
SALES (est): 343.6K **Privately Held**
SIC: 7991 Health club

(G-8489)
ENVIRONMENTAL RESOURCES INC
38173 Dupont Blvd (19975-3033)
P.O. Box 169 (19975-0169)
PHONE.................................302 436-9637
Thomas Nobile, *Principal*
EMP: 5
SALES: 950K **Privately Held**
SIC: 8748 Environmental consultant

(G-8490)
FARLOW-TAYLOR CONSTRUCTION
Also Called: Farlow-Taylor Woodworks
7 Discovery Ln (19975-9642)
PHONE.................................302 436-9660
Chris Farlow, *President*
Tom Taylor, *Vice Pres*
EMP: 2
SQ FT: 2,750
SALES (est): 140K **Privately Held**
SIC: 2499 Decorative wood & woodwork

(G-8491)
FENWICK ISLAND MARINE LLC
Rr 1 (19975)
PHONE.................................302 436-4702
Tim Joy,
EMP: 4
SALES: 370K **Privately Held**
SIC: 4493 Marinas

(G-8492)
FERRELL COOLING & HEATING INC
32971 Lighthouse Rd (19975-4088)
PHONE.................................302 436-2922
Sally Ferrell, *Principal*
EMP: 6
SALES (est): 747.8K **Privately Held**
SIC: 1711 Warm air heating & air conditioning contractor; heating & air conditioning contractors

(G-8493)
FIREPLACE SPECIALITIES LLC
44 Rte 113 (19975)
PHONE.................................302 436-9250
Kevin Lynch, *Manager*
Les Evans,
EMP: 4
SALES (est): 230.3K **Privately Held**
SIC: 1741 Masonry & other stonework

(G-8494)
FREEDOM LANDSCAPE & IRRIGATION
38488 Dupont Blvd (19975-3041)
P.O. Box 439 (19975-0439)
PHONE.................................302 436-7100
Craig Morris, *President*
EMP: 4
SALES (est): 126.3K **Privately Held**
SIC: 0781 Landscape services

(G-8495)
FUNCTIONALIT INC
31454 Forsythia Dr (19975-3710)
PHONE.................................703 566-6624
Nancy Green, *President*
EMP: 5
SALES (est): 1.5MM **Privately Held**
WEB: www.functionali-t.com
SIC: 8742 Human resource consulting services

(G-8496)
GPM INVESTMENTS LLC
Also Called: Shore Stop 294
36345 Lighthouse Rd # 301 (19975-3985)
PHONE.................................302 436-6330
L Leatherbury, *General Mgr*
EMP: 10
SALES (corp-wide): 3.7B **Privately Held**
SIC: 6799 Investors
HQ: Gpm Investments, Llc
8565 Magellan Pkwy # 400
Richmond VA 23227
276 328-3669

(G-8497)
HAINES FABRICATION & MCH LLC
45 Railroad Ave (19975-9675)
PHONE.................................302 436-1929
Donald Haines, *Mng Member*
Donald H Haines, *Mng Member*
EMP: 15
SALES (est): 3.8MM **Privately Held**
SIC: 7692 Welding repair

(G-8498)
HAIRS TO YOU
Also Called: Expressions Hair Salon
61 S Dupont Hwy (19975)
PHONE.................................302 436-1728
Tammy Fidderman, *Owner*
Josephine Adams, *Owner*
EMP: 4
SALES (est): 93.1K **Privately Held**
SIC: 7231 Beauty shops

(G-8499)
HARDY DEVELOPMENT
Also Called: Hardy's Development
32984 Lighthouse Rd (19975-4024)
PHONE.................................302 436-4496
Bonnie Hardy, *Branch Mgr*
EMP: 6 **Privately Held**
WEB: www.hardysselfstorage.com
SIC: 4225 Warehousing, self-storage
PA: Hardy Development
328 S Main St
Bel Air MD 21014

(G-8500)
HEAVENLY HOUND HOTEL
33049 Lighthouse Rd (19975-4017)
P.O. Box 54 (19975-0054)
PHONE.................................302 436-2926
Janice Baker, *President*
Joseph Baker, *Admin Sec*
EMP: 5
SALES (est): 204.4K **Privately Held**
SIC: 0752 Boarding services, kennels

(G-8501)
HIGH TIDE NEWS
11243 Signature Blvd (19975-3703)
PHONE.................................302 727-0390
Samuel Clayland, *Division Mgr*
Judy Layman, *Principal*
EMP: 3
SALES (est): 154.8K **Privately Held**
SIC: 2711 Newspapers

(G-8502)
HOBAN AUTO & MACHINESHOP INC
Also Called: Hoban Service Center
19 N Main St (19975-9697)
P.O. Box 43 (19975-0043)
PHONE.................................302 436-8013
John Hoban, *Owner*
Pamela Hoban, *Vice Pres*
EMP: 6
SALES (est): 832.2K **Privately Held**
SIC: 7538 General automotive repair shops

(G-8503)
HOLLAND CORP
33357 Deer Run Rd (19975-3531)
PHONE.................................302 245-5645
G Shoemaker, *President*
EMP: 5 **EST:** 2010
SALES (est): 133.8K **Privately Held**
SIC: 7389 Interior design services

(G-8504)
HOST NATION PERSPECTIVES LLC
36970 Old Mill Bridge Rd (19975-3935)
PHONE.................................443 292-6702
John Hagerty,
EMP: 6
SALES (est): 294.2K **Privately Held**
SIC: 8742 Human resource consulting services

(G-8505)
IACCHETTA BUILDERS INC
Rr 1 Box 79 (19975)
PHONE.................................302 436-4525
Dino Iacchetta, *President*
Lori Iacchetta, *Admin Sec*
EMP: 4
SALES (est): 1.2MM **Privately Held**
SIC: 1521 1542 New construction, single-family houses; general remodeling, single-family houses; commercial & office building, new construction; commercial & office buildings, renovation & repair

(G-8506)
INDEPENDENT STUDIO INC
36666 Bluewater Run W # 3 (19975-4392)
PHONE.................................302 436-5581
Matthew Amey, *President*
Jay Cooper, *Vice Pres*
Jerome G Denk III, *Vice Pres*
Todd Noble Holloway, *Vice Pres*
EMP: 4
SQ FT: 1,750
SALES: 300K **Privately Held**
WEB: www.independenttattoo.com
SIC: 7299 Tattoo parlor

(G-8507)
J & J BULKHEADING
Snow Goose Ln Unit 3c (19975)
P.O. Box 600 (19975-0600)
PHONE.................................302 436-2800
Jerry Kenney,
EMP: 8 **EST:** 2003
SALES (est): 761.4K **Privately Held**
SIC: 1629 Dock construction

(G-8508)
JERIS LLC
37427 Kingfisher Dr (19975-4150)
PHONE.................................443 745-9023
Kathleen Bromley, *Accountant*
Chrisjeris Minor,
EMP: 12
SALES (est): 280.8K **Privately Held**
SIC: 8748 Business consulting

(G-8509)
JOHNSON JR HENRY & SON FARM
37047 Johnson Rd (19975-3524)
PHONE.................................302 436-8501
Henry Johnson IV, *Partner*
Glenn Johnson, *Partner*
Keith Johnson, *Partner*
EMP: 7
SALES (est): 1MM **Privately Held**
SIC: 5153 Grains

(G-8510)
JOSHUA M FREEMAN FOUNDATION
31556 Winterberry Pkwy (19975-3707)
PHONE.................................302 436-3003
Patti Grimes, *Exec Dir*
EMP: 11
SALES: 4.3MM **Privately Held**
SIC: 7922 Performing arts center production

GEOGRAPHIC SECTION

Selbyville - Sussex County (G-8540)

(G-8511)
KB COLDIRON INC
36546 Dupont Blvd (19975-3006)
P.O. Box 297, Frankford (19945-0297)
PHONE....................302 436-4224
Kerry Coldiron, *President*
EMP: 60
SQ FT: 20,000
SALES (est): 13.3MM **Privately Held**
WEB: www.kbcoldiron.com
SIC: **1542** Commercial & office building, new construction; commercial & office buildings, renovation & repair

(G-8512)
KIMBERLY A LEAMAN PA
38178 Dockside Dr # 1262 (19975-2858)
PHONE....................301 261-4115
Kimberly A Leaman, *Owner*
EMP: 4
SALES (est): 274.1K **Privately Held**
SIC: **8111** General practice attorney, lawyer

(G-8513)
M & L CONTRACTORS INC
13354 Blueberry Rd (19975)
P.O. Box 512 (19975-0512)
PHONE....................302 436-9303
Carlton Murray, *President*
Jay Murray, *Vice Pres*
Clifton Murray, *Treasurer*
EMP: 10
SQ FT: 1,500
SALES (est): 755K **Privately Held**
SIC: **1741** Concrete block masonry laying

(G-8514)
MALLERD LAKES
37976 Pelican Ln (19975-4604)
PHONE....................443 783-2993
Stacey Seldy, *Administration*
EMP: 10 EST: 2014
SALES (est): 99.6K **Privately Held**
SIC: **8641** Condominium association

(G-8515)
MARYLAND AGENCY FINANCIAL GROU
38781 Wilson Ave (19975-4417)
PHONE....................410 420-8866
EMP: 4
SALES (est): 621.4K **Privately Held**
SIC: **6029** Commercial Bank

(G-8516)
MARYS LITTLE LAMBS DAYCARE
31730 Phillips Rd (19975-3321)
PHONE....................302 436-5796
Mary Atkins, *Principal*
EMP: 5 EST: 2009
SALES (est): 67.9K **Privately Held**
SIC: **8351** Child day care services

(G-8517)
MAXIM HAIR & NAILS LLC
31225 Americana Pkwy # 7 (19975-3793)
PHONE....................410 920-8656
Ramona Sterca, *Mng Member*
EMP: 5
SALES (est): 81.6K **Privately Held**
SIC: **7231** Hairdressers; manicurist, pedicurist

(G-8518)
MC CABE ENTERPRISES INC
30175 Rabbit Naw Rd (19975-3032)
PHONE....................302 436-5176
EMP: 6
SQ FT: 400
SALES: 2.1MM **Privately Held**
SIC: **0191** 0254 General Crop Farm Poultry Hatchery

(G-8519)
MERRITT MARINE CNSTR INC
32992 Lighthouse Rd (19975-4024)
PHONE....................302 436-2881
Demmy Merritt, *President*
Janice Merritt, *Admin Sec*
EMP: 6 EST: 1964
SALES (est): 617.1K **Privately Held**
SIC: **1629** Marine construction

(G-8520)
MIDCOAST GYMNSTICS DNCE STUDIO
Also Called: Mid-Coast Gymnastic Studio
15 Duke Street Ext (19975-9319)
P.O. Box 50 (19975-0050)
PHONE....................302 436-6007
Kimberly Wickham, *Owner*
EMP: 8 EST: 1995
SALES (est): 395.5K **Privately Held**
SIC: **7933** Bowling centers

(G-8521)
MIDLANTIC MARINE CENTER INC
36624 Dupont Blvd (19975-3007)
PHONE....................302 436-2628
Robert K Rosenberg, *President*
EMP: 11
SALES (est): 1.2MM **Privately Held**
SIC: **7699** 4493 Nautical repair services; boat repair; boat yards, storage & incidental repair

(G-8522)
MIDNIGHT BLUE INC
Also Called: McGraphix Advertising Products
37091 E White Tail Dr (19975-3536)
PHONE....................302 436-9665
Steve McDonald, *President*
Steve Mc Donald, *Sr Corp Ofcr*
Al McDonald, *Vice Pres*
EMP: 12
SALES (est): 1.6MM **Privately Held**
WEB: www.mcgraphixinc.com
SIC: **2759** 7389 Screen printing; embroidering of advertising on shirts, etc.; printing broker

(G-8523)
MOUNTAIRE FARMS INC
35 Railroad Ave (19975-9675)
P.O. Box 710 (19975-0710)
PHONE....................302 988-6200
Michael Steele, *Plant Mgr*
Mark Houston, *Sales Staff*
Owen Phillip, *Branch Mgr*
Mark Ondo, *Planning Mgr*
Bill Grimes, *Manager*
EMP: 17
SALES (corp-wide): 1.4B **Privately Held**
SIC: **2015** Poultry slaughtering & processing
HQ: Mountaire Farms Inc.
1901 Napa Valley Dr
Little Rock AR 72212
501 372-6524

(G-8524)
MOUNTAIRE FARMS INC
37 Railroad Ave (19975-9675)
PHONE....................302 988-6289
Michelle Gonzalez, *Export Mgr*
Scott Burton, *Regl Sales Mgr*
Fred Bowen, *Director*
◆ EMP: 4 EST: 2014
SALES (est): 334.7K **Privately Held**
SIC: **0751** Livestock services, except veterinary

(G-8525)
MOUNTAIRE FARMS INC
Hoosier St (19975)
P.O. Box 710 (19975-0710)
PHONE....................302 436-8241
Michael Tirrell, *Vice Pres*
Thom Heckman, *Purch Mgr*
Keni Joy Walters Clark, *Purch Agent*
James Cates, *Controller*
James Le Cates, *Controller*
EMP: 1600
SALES (corp-wide): 1.4B **Privately Held**
SIC: **0191** General farms, primarily crop
HQ: Mountaire Farms Inc.
1901 Napa Valley Dr
Little Rock AR 72212
501 372-6524

(G-8526)
MOUNTAIRE OF DELMARVA INC
55 Hosier St (19975-9300)
P.O. Box 710 (19975-0710)
PHONE....................302 988-6207
William Reeves, *Director*
EMP: 6
SALES (est): 864.3K **Privately Held**
SIC: **5144** Poultry products

(G-8527)
MUMFORD SHEET METAL WORKS INC
101 Cemetery Rd (19975-9312)
P.O. Box 170 (19975-0170)
PHONE....................302 436-8251
John Mumford, *President*
Dale Mumford Jr, *Vice Pres*
Stewart Mumford, *Vice Pres*
EMP: 20 EST: 1932
SQ FT: 40,000
SALES (est): 7MM **Privately Held**
SIC: **5074** 5031 5072 1761 Plumbing fittings & supplies; lumber, plywood & millwork; hardware; hand tools; sheet metalwork

(G-8528)
NORTH BAY MARINA INCORPORATED
36543 Lighthouse Rd (19975-3977)
PHONE....................302 436-4211
J Scott McCurdy, *President*
Mary M Mc Curdy, *Vice Pres*
Roy F Moore, *Treasurer*
Bernadine K Mc Curdy, *Admin Sec*
EMP: 17
SQ FT: 8,500
SALES (est): 3.9MM **Privately Held**
SIC: **5551** 4493 Motor boat dealers; boat yards, storage & incidental repair

(G-8529)
PENINSULA REGIONAL MEDICAL CTR
Also Called: Peninsula Regional Prmry Care
15 N Williams St (19975-7514)
PHONE....................302 436-8004
Carolanne Erker, *Manager*
EMP: 6
SALES (corp-wide): 411.6MM **Privately Held**
WEB: www.abilityrehab.com
SIC: **8062** 8011 General medical & surgical hospitals; offices & clinics of medical doctors
PA: Peninsula Regional Medical Center
100 E Carroll St
Salisbury MD 21801
410 546-6400

(G-8530)
PERRONE ENTERPRISES INC
36829 W Pond Cir (19975-4307)
PHONE....................302 436-8031
Raymond Perrone, *Principal*
EMP: 4
SALES (est): 277K **Privately Held**
SIC: **8748** Business consulting

(G-8531)
PMB ASSOCIATES LLC
37816 Eagle Ln Unit 325 (19975-4644)
PHONE....................302 436-0111
Patty Bowers,
Patricia Bowers,
EMP: 2
SALES (est): 191.3K **Privately Held**
SIC: **2732** Book printing

(G-8532)
PNC BANK NATIONAL ASSOCIATION
31231 Americana Pkwy (19975-3785)
PHONE....................302 436-5400
Kathy Castrovillo, *Branch Mgr*
EMP: 9
SALES (corp-wide): 19.9B **Publicly Held**
WEB: www.pncfunds.com
SIC: **6021** National commercial banks
HQ: Pnc Bank, National Association
222 Delaware Ave
Wilmington DE 19801
877 762-2000

(G-8533)
POOLSIDE CNSTR & RENOVATION
Rr 54 (19975)
PHONE....................302 436-9711
Julius Oairey III, *President*
EMP: 5 EST: 2001
SALES (est): 526.1K **Privately Held**
SIC: **1521** 8111 General remodeling, single-family houses; legal services

(G-8534)
PROPER PITCH LLC
131 Dixon St (19975-3022)
P.O. Box 314 (19975-0314)
PHONE....................302 436-5442
Scott Stewart,
▼ EMP: 1
SQ FT: 5,000
SALES (est): 177.8K **Privately Held**
WEB: www.properpitch.com
SIC: **3599** 5551 Propellers, ship & boat: machined; boat dealers

(G-8535)
QUAKER CITY AUTO PARTS INC
Also Called: Selbyville Auto Parts
12 N Main St (19975-9688)
P.O. Box 717 (19975-0717)
PHONE....................302 436-5114
Darryl Wharton, *Manager*
EMP: 4
SALES (corp-wide): 3.2MM **Privately Held**
SIC: **5013** Automotive supplies & parts
PA: Quaker City Auto Parts Inc
508 E King St
Seaford DE 19973
302 629-3557

(G-8536)
QUINTECCENT INC
37808 Salty Way W (19975-3918)
PHONE....................443 838-5447
Ken G Limparis, *President*
Ronna Limparis, *CFO*
EMP: 2
SALES (est): 311.4K **Privately Held**
SIC: **3663** 8711 8734 8742 Radio & TV communications equipment; engineering services; testing laboratories; management consulting services; business consulting

(G-8537)
RED DOG PLUMBING AND HEATING
37058 Roxana Rd (19975-3308)
PHONE....................302 436-5024
Sally Berger, *Principal*
EMP: 6
SALES (est): 111K **Privately Held**
SIC: **1711** Plumbing contractors

(G-8538)
RED SUN CUSTOM APPAREL INC
1 Mason Dr (19975-9617)
PHONE....................302 988-8230
William E Regan, *President*
EMP: 40
SQ FT: 5,000
SALES (est): 3.3MM **Privately Held**
WEB: www.redsuncustom.com
SIC: **7389** 2396 Embroidering of advertising on shirts, etc.; screen printing on fabric articles

(G-8539)
RESORT POKER LEAGUE
38291 Osprey Ct Apt 1168 (19975-2846)
PHONE....................302 604-8706
EMP: 4 EST: 2011
SALES (est): 75.6K **Privately Held**
SIC: **7997** Membership sports & recreation clubs

(G-8540)
RESORTQUEST DELAWARE RE LLC
37458 Lion Dr Unit 7 (19975-3887)
PHONE....................302 436-1100
Carl Freeman, *Branch Mgr*
EMP: 5 **Publicly Held**
SIC: **6531** Real estate leasing & rentals
HQ: Resortquest Delaware Real Estate Llc
33546 Market Pl
Bethany Beach DE 19930
302 541-8999

Selbyville - Sussex County (G-8541) — GEOGRAPHIC SECTION

(G-8541)
RICH HEBERT & ASSOCIATES
38027 Fenwick Shoals Blvd (19975-9102)
PHONE...................................202 255-3474
Richard Hebert, *Owner*
EMP: 6
SALES (est): 132.8K **Privately Held**
SIC: 7832 Motion picture theaters, except drive-in

(G-8542)
SAFE HARBOR PROPERTY MGT LLC
11 Polly Branch Rd (19975-7504)
P.O. Box 589 (19975-0589)
PHONE...................................302 436-9882
Jeff Bowden,
EMP: 5
SALES (est): 334.7K **Privately Held**
SIC: 8741 Management services

(G-8543)
SEASIDE GRAPHICS CORP
1 Mason Dr (19975-9617)
PHONE...................................302 436-9460
Debbie Maxfield, *President*
Steven Hershey, *Vice Pres*
EMP: 11
SQ FT: 10,000
SALES (est): 1MM **Privately Held**
WEB: www.sgtees.com
SIC: 7336 Silk screen design

(G-8544)
SELBYVILLE CLEANERS INC (PA)
Also Called: Wilgus Glamorama
68 Hosier St (19975)
P.O. Box 1010 (19975-1010)
PHONE...................................302 249-3444
Jeff Wilgus, *President*
EMP: 45 **EST:** 1939
SQ FT: 26,000
SALES (est): 998.1K **Privately Held**
WEB: www.jwilgus.com
SIC: 7211 7213 Power laundries, family & commercial; linen supply

(G-8545)
SHADY PARK INC
36773 Lighthouse Rd (19975-3957)
P.O. Box 1 (19975-0001)
PHONE...................................302 436-8441
Anna Lee Gray, *President*
Annette Ferrell, *Treasurer*
Carolyn Smith, *Admin Sec*
EMP: 4
SALES (est): 346.2K **Privately Held**
SIC: 6515 Mobile home site operators

(G-8546)
SOUTH SHORE PROVISIONS LLC
18 Ruth St (19975-9619)
PHONE...................................443 614-2442
Debra Behney, *Mng Member*
EMP: 5 **EST:** 2015
SALES (est): 162.9K **Privately Held**
SIC: 5941 4493 Fishing equipment; marinas

(G-8547)
SPACEPORT SUPPORT SERVICES
6 Dixon St (19975)
P.O. Box 681 (19975-0681)
PHONE...................................302 524-4020
Sep Mostaghim, *Principal*
EMP: 6
SALES (est): 1.2MM **Privately Held**
SIC: 8711 Engineering services

(G-8548)
SPARK PRODUCTIONS LLC
Also Called: Oc Car Shows
38025 Fenwick Shoals Blvd (19975-9102)
PHONE...................................302 436-0183
EMP: 4
SALES (est): 320K **Privately Held**
SIC: 8743 Public Relations Services

(G-8549)
STATE LINE BUILDING SUPPLY
Rr 113 (19975)
P.O. Box 792 (19975-0792)
PHONE...................................302 436-8624
Ronald Crook, *President*
EMP: 17
SALES (est): 6.4MM
SALES (corp-wide): 3.1B **Publicly Held**
WEB: www.cmifay.com
SIC: 5031 Building materials, exterior
HQ: Gypsum Management And Supply, Inc.
100 Crescent Center Pkwy
Tucker GA 30084
770 939-1711

(G-8550)
STUCCO SMITH SYSTEMS
31912 Phillips Rd (19975-3323)
PHONE...................................302 245-8179
EMP: 5
SALES (est): 301.9K **Privately Held**
SIC: 1742 Stucco work, interior

(G-8551)
SUSSEX EYE CENTER PA
17 Lighthouse Rd (19975-7500)
P.O. Box 1009 (19975-1009)
PHONE...................................302 436-2020
Dr Carl Maschauer, *Manager*
EMP: 4
SALES (est): 433.4K
SALES (corp-wide): 1.5MM **Privately Held**
SIC: 8042 Specialized optometrists
PA: Sussex Eye Center Pa
502 W Market St
Georgetown DE 19947
302 856-2020

(G-8552)
ULTIMATE EXPRESS INC
37976 Bayview Cir E (19975-2871)
PHONE...................................443 523-0800
Nikolajs Litvinenkovs, *President*
EMP: 10
SQ FT: 13,000
SALES (est): 302.8K **Privately Held**
SIC: 4213 Trucking, except local

(G-8553)
WEATHER OR NOT INC
38294 London Ave Unit 3 (19975-4079)
PHONE...................................302 436-7533
Bryan Warner, *Branch Mgr*
EMP: 16
SALES (corp-wide): 1.7MM **Privately Held**
WEB: www.weatherornot.com
SIC: 1522 Condominium construction
PA: Weather Or Not Inc
660 S Coastal Hwy
Bethany Beach DE
302 539-2533

(G-8554)
WILLIAM J WINKLER
Also Called: Roots Landscaping
36226 Dupont Blvd (19975-3004)
PHONE...................................302 732-0866
Bill Winkler, *Principal*
EMP: 4
SALES (est): 182.1K **Privately Held**
SIC: 0781 Landscape services

(G-8555)
WILMINGTON SAVINGS FUND SOC
38394 Dupont Blvd (19975-3049)
PHONE...................................302 436-4179
Cristine Debruyn, *Manager*
EMP: 21
SALES (corp-wide): 455.5MM **Publicly Held**
SIC: 6022 State commercial banks
HQ: Wilmington Savings Fund Society
500 Delaware Ave Ste 500 # 500
Wilmington DE 19801
302 792-6000

(G-8556)
XENITH SOLUTIONS LLC
26211 Crosswinds Lndg (19975-4475)
PHONE...................................703 963-3523
Rowdy Adams,
Jack Gustafson,
Rodney Hite,
Lee Shabe,
EMP: 4
SALES (est): 148.7K **Privately Held**
SIC: 8741 Business management

(G-8557)
ZICHERHEIT LLC
38824 Wilson Ave (19975-4415)
PHONE...................................302 510-3718
Chuck Ziethen,
Celia Ziethen,
EMP: 11
SALES: 30K **Privately Held**
SIC: 7381 7389 Security guard service; notary publics

Smyrna
Kent County

(G-8558)
190 STADIUM LLC
Also Called: Best Western Smyrna Inn
190 Stadium St (19977-2813)
PHONE...................................302 659-3635
EMP: 11 **EST:** 2008
SALES (est): 646.6K **Privately Held**
SIC: 7011 Hotels & motels

(G-8559)
A1 SANITATION SERVICE INC
27 E Chestnut St (19977)
PHONE...................................302 653-9591
Anthony Smertka, *President*
Michael Rosco, *President*
EMP: 15
SALES: 200K **Privately Held**
SIC: 7699 5099 Septic tank cleaning service; toilets, portable

(G-8560)
ACADEMY OF EARLY LEARNING
310 N Main St Bldg A (19977-1078)
PHONE...................................302 659-0750
Eftihia Zerefos, *President*
EMP: 8 **EST:** 2010
SALES (est): 173.8K **Privately Held**
SIC: 8351 Preschool center

(G-8561)
ACORN BOOKS INC
727 Lexington Ave (19977-1254)
PHONE...................................302 508-2219
Ginny M Jewell, *President*
Ginny Jewell, *President*
Glynda Marie Shane, *Vice Pres*
EMP: 7
SALES (est): 1.2MM **Privately Held**
SIC: 5192 Books, periodicals & newspapers

(G-8562)
AG & G SHEET METAL INC
129 N Union St (19977-1148)
PHONE...................................302 653-4111
Ronald Grantland, *President*
EMP: 9
SQ FT: 4,500
SALES (est): 1.6MM **Privately Held**
SIC: 3444 Sheet metalwork

(G-8563)
ALEXANDER RV SERVICE CENTER (PA)
5710 Dupont Pkwy (19977-9601)
PHONE...................................302 653-3250
EMP: 4
SALES (est): 514.6K **Privately Held**
SIC: 8743 Public Relations Services

(G-8564)
ALFRED MOORE
1057 Wheatleys Pond Rd (19977-3819)
PHONE...................................302 653-7600
Alfred Moore, *Principal*
EMP: 5
SALES (est): 277.9K **Privately Held**
SIC: 0191 General farms, primarily crop

(G-8565)
ALL PETS MEDICAL CENTER
Also Called: Dover Animal Hospital
10 Artisan Dr (19977-3711)
PHONE...................................302 653-2300
Patricia Woody, *Owner*
Patricia A Woodie,
EMP: 9
SALES (est): 514.1K **Privately Held**
SIC: 0742 Animal hospital services, pets & other animal specialties

(G-8566)
ALLURE SALON
599 Jimmy Dr Ste 15 (19977-5811)
PHONE...................................302 653-6125
Shannon McGalillard, *Owner*
EMP: 8
SALES (est): 75K **Privately Held**
SIC: 7231 Manicurist, pedicurist

(G-8567)
ALS TV SERVICE
1200 Wheatleys Pond Rd (19977-3804)
P.O. Box 188, Cheswold (19936-0188)
PHONE...................................302 653-3711
Albert Moses, *Owner*
EMP: 7
SQ FT: 2,000
SALES (est): 813K **Privately Held**
SIC: 7622 Television repair shop

(G-8568)
AMDISVET LLC
230 Ashton Ct Ste 100 (19977-1855)
PHONE...................................302 514-9130
EMP: 4
SALES (est): 233.2K **Privately Held**
SIC: 5734 7372 7389 Ret Computers/Software Prepackaged Software Svc

(G-8569)
AMERICAN LGION AMBLANCE STN 64
Also Called: HARRISON, DAVID C POST #14 AME
900 Smyrna Clayton Blvd (19977-2230)
P.O. Box 345 (19977-0345)
PHONE...................................302 653-6465
Owen Cole, *Principal*
EMP: 5
SALES: 1.3MM **Privately Held**
SIC: 8641 Veterans' organization

(G-8570)
ANDERSON LANDSCAPING
95 Jump Dr (19977-4633)
PHONE...................................302 423-3904
Brian Anderson, *Principal*
EMP: 4
SALES (est): 40.9K **Privately Held**
SIC: 0781 Landscape services

(G-8571)
ANN JACKSON VMD
Also Called: Sassafras Veterinary Hospital
310 N Main St Bldg N (19977-1078)
PHONE...................................302 659-3624
Ann Jackson, *Owner*
▲ **EMP:** 4
SALES (est): 222.7K **Privately Held**
SIC: 0742 Animal hospital services, pets & other animal specialties

(G-8572)
ANYTIME FITNESS
599 Jimmy Dr Ste 18 (19977-5811)
PHONE...................................302 653-4496
Daniel Fonedless, *Principal*
EMP: 6
SALES (est): 189.1K **Privately Held**
SIC: 7991 Physical fitness clubs with training equipment

(G-8573)
AOD SMYMA 43
222 N Dupont Blvd (19977-1511)
PHONE...................................302 659-5060
Amy Fibelkorn, *Principal*
EMP: 4
SALES (est): 80.9K **Privately Held**
SIC: 8093 Mental health clinic, outpatient

GEOGRAPHIC SECTION
Smyrna - Kent County (G-8605)

(G-8574)
APGAR TURF FARM INC
1381 Smyrna Leipsic Rd (19977-3446)
P.O. Box 587 (19977-0587)
PHONE..................302 653-9389
Arnold Apgar, *President*
Florence Apgar, *Corp Secy*
John Apgar, *Vice Pres*
EMP: 5
SQ FT: 3,600
SALES (est): 400K **Privately Held**
SIC: 0181 Sod farms

(G-8575)
AQUA PRO INC
Also Called: API
104 Big Woods Rd (19977-3500)
P.O. Box 329, Townsend (19734-0329)
PHONE..................302 659-6593
Robert Metzgar, *President*
EMP: 8 **EST:** 1998
SALES (est): 469.8K **Privately Held**
SIC: 7349 1711 Cleaning service, industrial or commercial; plumbing, heating, air-conditioning contractors

(G-8576)
ASCENSION INDUSTRIES LLC
104 Needham Dr (19977-4472)
PHONE..................302 659-1778
Jeffrey Warner, *CEO*
EMP: 5
SALES (est): 248.5K **Privately Held**
SIC: 8742 7389 New products & services consultants;

(G-8577)
ATI HOLDINGS LLC
Also Called: ATI Physical Therapy
1000 Smyrna Clayton Blvd # 4 (19977-2228)
PHONE..................302 659-3102
Shawn Schlegel, *Branch Mgr*
EMP: 21
SALES (corp-wide): 338.3MM **Privately Held**
SIC: 8049 Physical therapist
PA: Ati Holdings, Llc
790 Remington Blvd
Bolingbrook IL 60440
630 296-2222

(G-8578)
ATTENTION TO DETAIL IN SMYRNA
5702 Dupont Pkwy (19977-9601)
PHONE..................302 388-1267
Samuel Bane, *Principal*
EMP: 4
SALES (est): 94.2K **Privately Held**
SIC: 7542 Washing & polishing, automotive

(G-8579)
B&P TRANSIT
979 Mount Friendship Rd (19977-3879)
P.O. Box 293 (19977-0293)
PHONE..................302 653-8466
Pearl Cole, *Partner*
Jacqueline Painter, *Partner*
EMP: 14
SALES (est): 352.3K **Privately Held**
SIC: 4151 School buses

(G-8580)
BARKER BENCHARK THERPY & REHAB
208 N Dupont Blvd (19977-1511)
PHONE..................302 659-7552
Julie Marrs, *Principal*
EMP: 5
SALES (est): 139.8K **Privately Held**
SIC: 8093 Rehabilitation center, outpatient treatment

(G-8581)
BLANCA O LIM MD
38 Deak Dr (19977-1268)
PHONE..................302 653-1669
Blanca Lim, *Owner*
EMP: 20
SALES (est): 323.1K **Privately Held**
SIC: 8011 Internal medicine, physician/surgeon

(G-8582)
BLUE HEN DENTAL LLC
231 S Dupont Blvd (19977-1550)
PHONE..................302 538-0448
EMP: 4
SALES (est): 61.5K **Privately Held**
SIC: 8021 Dental clinic

(G-8583)
BMA OF SMYRNA
Also Called: Fresenius Medical Services
Gateway Shopping Ctr N (19977)
PHONE..................302 659-5220
Brenda Richards, *Manager*
EMP: 5
SALES (corp-wide): 37.1B **Privately Held**
SIC: 8011 Offices & clinics of medical doctors
PA: Fresenius Se & Co. Kgaa
Else-Kroner-Str. 1
Bad Homburg 61352
617 260-80

(G-8584)
BOYS & GIRLS CLUBS OF AMERICA
240 E Commerce St (19977-1506)
PHONE..................302 659-5610
Trisha Moses, *Director*
EMP: 10
SALES (corp-wide): 141.3MM **Privately Held**
WEB: www.careerlaunch.net
SIC: 8641 Youth organizations
PA: Boys & Girls Clubs Of America
1275 Peachtree St Ne # 500
Atlanta GA 30309
404 487-5700

(G-8585)
BRIAN A WISK
17 W Glenwood Ave (19977-1106)
PHONE..................302 653-5011
Brian A Wisk, *Principal*
EMP: 4
SALES (est): 104.1K **Privately Held**
SIC: 8021 Dentists' office

(G-8586)
BRIGHT FINISH LLC
56 Arrowood Dr (19977-4436)
PHONE..................888 974-4747
Kosta Papanicolas, *Mng Member*
EMP: 7
SALES (est): 407.5K **Privately Held**
SIC: 1799 1522 Exterior cleaning, including sandblasting; hotel/motel & multi-family home renovation & remodeling

(G-8587)
BRITTONS WISE COMPUTERS INC
Also Called: Bwci Animal Hospital MGT Sys
777 Paddock Rd (19977-9687)
PHONE..................302 659-0343
Dustin Britton, *President*
Cynthia Baker, *Principal*
EMP: 7
SALES (est): 210K **Privately Held**
WEB: www.bwci.com
SIC: 7371 7373 Computer software development; computer integrated systems design

(G-8588)
C & C TECHNOLOGIES INC
P.O. Box 1081, Clayton (19938-1081)
PHONE..................302 653-7623
David O Czetli, *President*
Ute Czetli, *Treasurer*
EMP: 4
SALES (est): 530.8K **Privately Held**
SIC: 3599 Machine shop, jobbing & repair

(G-8589)
CAIMAR CORPORATION
Also Called: Di Sabatino, M P DDS
17 W Glenwood Ave (19977-1106)
PHONE..................302 653-5011
Mario Di Sabatino DDS, *President*
Carol Di Sabatino, *Treasurer*
EMP: 9 **EST:** 1970
SQ FT: 2,800
SALES (est): 475.8K **Privately Held**
SIC: 8021 Dentists' office

(G-8590)
CANDLELIGHT CLEANING
379 Lake Dr (19977-1320)
PHONE..................302 270-1218
Christy Willis, *Partner*
Nicki Shirey, *Partner*
EMP: 6
SALES (est): 350K **Privately Held**
SIC: 7699 Cleaning services

(G-8591)
CARIDAD ROSAL MA MD
Also Called: SMA Pediatrics
38 Deak Dr (19977-1268)
PHONE..................302 653-6174
Rosal Caridad, *Owner*
Jennifer Liquido, *Med Doctor*
EMP: 20
SALES (est): 1MM **Privately Held**
SIC: 8011 Pediatrician

(G-8592)
CELLCO PARTNERSHIP
Also Called: Verizon Wireless
239 N Dupont Blvd (19977-1546)
PHONE..................302 653-8183
EMP: 25
SALES (corp-wide): 130.8B **Publicly Held**
SIC: 4813 4812 Telephone communication, except radio; cellular telephone services
HQ: Cellco Partnership
1 Verizon Way
Basking Ridge NJ 07920

(G-8593)
CHRIS KISSELL
Also Called: First State Twr & Antenna Svc
1474 Big Woods Rd (19977-3518)
PHONE..................302 547-4800
Lorraine Kissell, *Ch of Bd*
Chris Kissell, *Owner*
EMP: 4 **EST:** 2010
SALES (est): 258.3K **Privately Held**
SIC: 1623 Communication line & transmission tower construction

(G-8594)
CHRISTIANA CARE HEALTH SYS INC
100 S Main St Ste 105 (19977-1478)
PHONE..................302 659-4401
Kevin Schultz, *Manager*
John Savage, *Technician*
Paula Smallwood, *Nurse*
EMP: 11
SALES (corp-wide): 1.5B **Privately Held**
SIC: 8011 8031 Offices & clinics of medical doctors; offices & clinics of osteopathic physicians
HQ: Christiana Care Health System, Inc.
200 Hygeia Dr
Newark DE 19713
302 733-1000

(G-8595)
CIPOLLONI BROTHERS LLC
879 Black Diamond Rd (19977-9663)
PHONE..................302 449-0960
Brande Cipolloni, *President*
EMP: 5
SALES (est): 359.1K **Privately Held**
SIC: 1771 Concrete work

(G-8596)
CITIZENS BANK NATIONAL ASSN
7 W Glenwood Ave (19977-1106)
PHONE..................302 653-9245
Sharon Wright, *Manager*
EMP: 6
SALES (corp-wide): 7.3B **Publicly Held**
SIC: 6022 State trust companies accepting deposits, commercial
HQ: Citizens Bank, National Association
1 Citizens Plz Ste # 1
Providence RI 02903
401 282-7000

(G-8597)
CLASS LIMOUSINE SERVICE
1271 S Dupont Blvd (19977-2892)
PHONE..................302 653-1166
Kevin Alexander, *President*
EMP: 5
SALES (est): 257.6K **Privately Held**
SIC: 4119 Limousine rental, with driver

(G-8598)
CLEAN HANDS LLC
60 Markham Ct (19977-3915)
PHONE..................215 681-1435
Zakia Walker,
EMP: 10
SALES (est): 147.9K **Privately Held**
SIC: 7349 1721 Building & office cleaning services; commercial painting

(G-8599)
CLEAVER
246 Nursery Ln (19977-5214)
PHONE..................302 659-1707
Kenneth Cleaver, *Owner*
Roxanne Cleaver, *Co-Owner*
EMP: 4
SALES (est): 200K **Privately Held**
SIC: 8748 Business consulting

(G-8600)
CNJ CONTRACTING LLC
1189 Alabam Rd (19977-9311)
PHONE..................302 659-3750
Mary Middleton, *President*
EMP: 6
SALES (est): 553.2K **Privately Held**
WEB: www.cnjs.com
SIC: 1771 1741 1794 1623 Concrete work; masonry & other stonework; excavation work; water, sewer & utility lines

(G-8601)
COLLETT AND SONS WELDING
370 N Main St (19977-1011)
P.O. Box 321, Middletown (19709-0321)
PHONE..................302 223-6525
John V Collett, *President*
Peggy Bowman, *Office Mgr*
EMP: 6 **EST:** 2013
SALES (est): 597.5K **Privately Held**
SIC: 1799 Welding on site

(G-8602)
COLUMBIA CARE NEW YORK LLC
200 S Dupont Blvd (19977-1552)
PHONE..................302 297-8614
EMP: 9
SALES (corp-wide): 5.4MM **Privately Held**
SIC: 8011 Dispensary, operated by physicians
PA: Columbia Care Ny Llc
100 Latona Rd
Rochester NY 14615
585 732-7112

(G-8603)
CONNECTIONS COMMUNITY SUPPORT
676 Black Diamond Rd (19977-9670)
PHONE..................302 389-1118
Michael Pearson, *Manager*
Beanie Cunningham, *Manager*
EMP: 90 **Privately Held**
SIC: 8361 Geriatric residential care
PA: Connections Community Support Programs, Inc.
3821 Lancaster Pike
Wilmington DE 19805

(G-8604)
CONNECTIONS COMMUNITY SUPPORT
222 N Dupont Blvd (19977-1511)
PHONE..................302 653-1505
EMP: 66
SALES (corp-wide): 45.1MM **Privately Held**
SIC: 8093 Specialty Outpatient Clinic
PA: Connections Community Support Programs, Inc.
3821 Lancaster Pike
Wilmington DE 19805
302 984-2302

(G-8605)
CORE CONSTRUCTION LLC
115 E Glenwood Ave (19977-1424)
PHONE..................302 449-4186

Smyrna - Kent County (G-8606)

Dwayne L Bull,
Dwayne Bull,
EMP: 5
SQ FT: 1,200
SALES (est): 192.9K **Privately Held**
SIC: 8748 Business consulting

(G-8606)
COUNTRY GREEN LANDSCAPING
949 S Dupont Blvd (19977-1749)
PHONE..................302 653-1600
Joseph R Haas, *Owner*
EMP: 4 **EST:** 2012
SALES (est): 128K **Privately Held**
SIC: 0781 Landscape services

(G-8607)
CREATIVE FLOORING CONTRS INC
100c E Glenwood Ave (19977-1003)
P.O. Box 350 (19977-0350)
PHONE..................302 653-7521
Lisa M Rose, *President*
Lorraine M Rose, *Vice Pres*
EMP: 15
SQ FT: 8,000
SALES (est): 2.5MM **Privately Held**
SIC: 1752 Floor laying & floor work

(G-8608)
CURBS ETC INC
3528 S Dupont Blvd (19977-2857)
PHONE..................302 653-3511
Carol Ewing, *President*
Charles Ewing III, *Vice Pres*
EMP: 8
SQ FT: 1,800
SALES (est): 743.4K **Privately Held**
SIC: 0782 1771 Highway lawn & garden maintenance services; landscape contractors; concrete work; curb construction

(G-8609)
D & D CONTRACTORS INC
206 Blckbird Grnspring Rd (19977-9494)
PHONE..................302 378-9724
Daniel Keeler, *President*
EMP: 12
SALES (est): 1.8MM **Privately Held**
SIC: 6552 1795 Land subdividers & developers, commercial; land subdividers & developers, residential; wrecking & demolition work

(G-8610)
D R DEAKYNE DDS
231 N New St (19977-1133)
PHONE..................302 653-6661
David R Deakyne DDS, *President*
EMP: 8
SQ FT: 3,458
SALES (est): 287K **Privately Held**
SIC: 8021 Dentists' office

(G-8611)
DAVID L TOWNSEND CO INC
Also Called: Townsend Fitness Equipment
1041 Clyton Grenspring Rd (19977-9414)
PHONE..................302 378-7967
David Townsend, *President*
Maryann Townsend, *Treasurer*
Melissa Caldwell, *Admin Sec*
EMP: 8
SALES (est): 856.5K **Privately Held**
SIC: 7991 Physical fitness facilities

(G-8612)
DEAKYNE DENTAL ASSOCIATES PA
27 Deak Dr (19977-1268)
PHONE..................302 653-6661
David Deakyne, *Principal*
EMP: 4
SALES (est): 391.9K **Privately Held**
SIC: 8021 Dentists' office

(G-8613)
DEBORAH KIRK
100 S Main St Ste 205 (19977-1479)
PHONE..................302 653-6022
Deborah T Kirk, *Principal*
EMP: 5 **EST:** 2007
SALES (est): 555.3K **Privately Held**
SIC: 8011 Physicians' office, including specialists

(G-8614)
DEL-ONE FEDERAL CREDIT UNION
201 Pharmacy Dr (19977-5813)
PHONE..................302 739-4496
EMP: 5 **Privately Held**
SIC: 6061 Federal credit unions
PA: Del-One Federal Credit Union
270 Beiser Blvd
Dover DE 19904

(G-8615)
DELAWARE GENTLE DENTAL GROUP
17 N Main St (19977-1111)
PHONE..................302 514-6200
Clyde A Maxwell, *Principal*
EMP: 4
SALES (est): 210.2K **Privately Held**
SIC: 8021 Dentists' office

(G-8616)
DELAWARE HOMES INC
200 S Dupont Blvd Ste 105 (19977-1552)
P.O. Box 38, Townsend (19734-0038)
PHONE..................302 223-6258
Michael Selvattil, *Branch Mgr*
EMP: 14
SALES (corp-wide): 1.6MM **Privately Held**
SIC: 1521 Single-family housing construction
PA: Delaware Homes, Inc.
401 Main St
Townsend DE 19734
302 378-9510

(G-8617)
DELAWARE MUNICIPAL ELC CORP
22 Artisan Dr (19977-3711)
P.O. Box 310 (19977-0310)
PHONE..................302 653-2733
Kimberly Schlichcing, *Branch Mgr*
EMP: 6
SALES (corp-wide): 4.8MM **Privately Held**
SIC: 4911 Electric services
PA: The Delaware Municipal Electric Corporation
860 Buttner Pl
Dover DE 19904
302 659-0200

(G-8618)
DELAWARE ORTHOPEDIC AND SPORTS
208 N Dupont Blvd (19977-1511)
PHONE..................302 653-8389
EMP: 22
SALES (est): 500K **Privately Held**
SIC: 8049 Physical therapist

(G-8619)
DELAWARE PHARMACIST SOCIETY
27 N Main St (19977-1111)
PHONE..................302 659-3088
Pat Grant, *Director*
EMP: 5
SALES: 45.6K **Privately Held**
SIC: 5122 Pharmaceuticals

(G-8620)
DELAWARE PUBLIC HEALTH LAB
30 Sunnyside Rd (19977-1707)
PHONE..................302 223-1520
EMP: 5
SALES (est): 267.4K **Privately Held**
SIC: 8071 Medical laboratories

(G-8621)
DELAWARE TITLE LOANS INC
202 N Dupont Blvd (19977-1511)
PHONE..................302 653-8315
EMP: 7
SALES (corp-wide): 7.7MM **Privately Held**
SIC: 6159 Loan institutions, general & industrial
PA: Delaware Title Loans, Inc.
8601 Dunwoody Pl Ste 406
Atlanta GA 30350
770 552-9840

(G-8622)
DELP TRUCKING
71 Lenora Dr (19977-3867)
PHONE..................302 275-6541
Brian Delp, *Principal*
EMP: 4
SALES (est): 265.6K **Privately Held**
SIC: 4212 Local trucking, without storage

(G-8623)
DELVINA I WILLSON
Also Called: Sew Right 4 You Embroidery
300 Garrisons Cir (19977-2861)
PHONE..................302 659-3672
Delvina I Willson, *Principal*
EMP: 1
SALES (est): 40K **Privately Held**
SIC: 2395 Embroidery & art needlework

(G-8624)
DOMIAN INTERNATIONAL SVC LLC
22 Zion Dr (19977-6800)
PHONE..................804 837-3616
Hans Lewis, *Partner*
Dakaque Lewis, *Mng Member*
EMP: 4
SALES (est): 62.9K **Privately Held**
SIC: 7299 7389 5199 5399 Consumer purchasing services; personal service agents, brokers & bureaus; exhibit construction by industrial contractors; ; general merchandise, non-durable; Army-Navy goods; ; pasteurized & mineral waters, bottled & canned

(G-8625)
DOVER AUTOMOTIVE INC
Also Called: NAPA Auto Parts
5 E Glenwood Ave (19977-1423)
PHONE..................302 653-9234
Wayne Grimes, *Manager*
EMP: 7
SALES (corp-wide): 4.5MM **Privately Held**
SIC: 5531 5013 Automobile & truck equipment & parts; motor vehicle supplies & new parts
PA: Dover Automotive Inc
29 S West St
Dover DE
302 674-0211

(G-8626)
DRAIN KINGS LLC
3867 Wheatleys Pond Rd (19977-3739)
PHONE..................302 399-8980
Mike Ferrell, *Principal*
EMP: 5
SALES (est): 350K **Privately Held**
SIC: 7699 Sewer cleaning & rodding

(G-8627)
DUCK CREEK PRINTING LLC
228 E Glenwood Ave (19977-1080)
P.O. Box 404 (19977-0404)
PHONE..................302 653-5121
Donald Beamer, *Owner*
EMP: 6
SALES (est): 856.1K **Privately Held**
SIC: 2752 Commercial printing, offset

(G-8628)
DUCTS UNLIMITED INC
339 W Mount Vernon St (19977-1128)
PHONE..................302 378-4125
Cheryl Sparco, *President*
Michael Sparco, *Opers Staff*
EMP: 8
SALES: 700K **Privately Held**
SIC: 1711 1761 3444 5039 Heating & air conditioning contractors; sheet metalwork; ducts, sheet metal; air ducts, sheet metal

(G-8629)
ENTERPRISE RENT-A-CAR
119 N Dupont Blvd Ste F (19977-1597)
PHONE..................302 653-4330
Mike Penes, *Branch Mgr*
EMP: 7
SALES (corp-wide): 4.5B **Privately Held**
SIC: 7514 Passenger car rental
HQ: Enterprise Rent-A-Car Company Of Los Angeles, Llc
333 City Blvd W Ste 1000
Orange CA 92868
657 221-4400

(G-8630)
EXPANDING OUR KIDS WORLD
3460 S Dupont Blvd (19977-2856)
PHONE..................302 659-0293
Marlena George, *Director*
EMP: 22
SALES (est): 401.7K **Privately Held**
SIC: 8351 Preschool center

(G-8631)
FAMILY MEDICINE SMYRNA CLAYTON
319 N Carter Rd (19977-1282)
PHONE..................302 653-1050
A Douglas Chervenak, *President*
Georgia Vansant, *Office Mgr*
EMP: 7
SALES (est): 330K **Privately Held**
SIC: 8031 Offices & clinics of osteopathic physicians

(G-8632)
FAMILY RESPIRATORY & MED SUPL
5609 Dupont Pkwy Ste 15 (19977-9211)
PHONE..................302 653-3602
Sue Murphy, *Manager*
EMP: 2 **EST:** 2018
SALES (est): 86.6K **Privately Held**
SIC: 3842 Surgical appliances & supplies

(G-8633)
FARIES FUNERAL DIRECTORS INC (PA)
29 S Main St (19977-1430)
PHONE..................302 653-8816
Wells A Faries Jr, *President*
W C Faries, *Director*
EMP: 4
SALES (est): 608.7K **Privately Held**
WEB: www.fariesfuneralhome.com
SIC: 7261 Funeral home; funeral director

(G-8634)
FIRST LINE DEFENSE LLC
885 Mount Friendship Rd (19977-3880)
PHONE..................302 287-2764
Nathaniel Johnson, *Principal*
EMP: 4
SALES (est): 267.4K **Privately Held**
SIC: 3812 Defense systems & equipment

(G-8635)
FISHER AUTO PARTS INC
Also Called: Manlove Auto Parts
5736 Dupont Pkwy (19977-9601)
PHONE..................302 653-9241
Robert Solloway, *Branch Mgr*
EMP: 7
SALES (corp-wide): 891.9MM **Privately Held**
WEB: www.fisherautoparts.com
SIC: 5013 Automotive supplies & parts
PA: Fisher Auto Parts, Inc.
512 Greenville Ave
Staunton VA 24401
540 885-8901

(G-8636)
FLETCHER PLUMBING HTG & AC INC (PA)
18 Myrtle St (19977-1075)
PHONE..................302 653-6277
Edward Fletcher, *President*
Brian Fletcher, *Vice Pres*
EMP: 15
SALES (est): 2.4MM **Privately Held**
SIC: 1711 Heating & air conditioning contractors; warm air heating & air conditioning contractor; plumbing contractors

GEOGRAPHIC SECTION
Smyrna - Kent County (G-8671)

(G-8637)
FROGGYS INDUSTRIAL SUPPLY INC
370 N Main St (19977-1011)
P.O. Box 450 (19977-0450)
PHONE..................................302 508-2340
Chris Sanders, *General Mgr*
Lauren Collett, *Treasurer*
EMP: 4
SALES (est): 217.6K **Privately Held**
SIC: 5085 Fasteners, industrial: nuts, bolts, screws, etc.

(G-8638)
FUTURE LEADERS
906 Boxwood Dr (19977-1265)
PHONE..................................862 262-7312
Althea Parrish, *Principal*
EMP: 5
SALES (est): 42K **Privately Held**
SIC: 8351 Child day care services

(G-8639)
GARRISONS LAKE GOLF CLUB
101 W Fairways Cir (19977-1829)
PHONE..................................302 659-1206
Carol Russell, *Principal*
EMP: 7
SALES (est): 153K **Privately Held**
SIC: 7992 Public golf courses

(G-8640)
GEORGE STAATS
Also Called: Imperial Farm
1570 Vndyke Grenspring Rd (19977-9416)
PHONE..................................302 653-9729
George Staats, *Owner*
EMP: 4
SALES (est): 368.5K **Privately Held**
SIC: 0213 Hogs

(G-8641)
GIFT LOVE EARLY LEARNING CTR
115 E North St (19977-1444)
PHONE..................................302 659-1984
Mark Bell, *Partner*
EMP: 5
SALES (est): 106.6K **Privately Held**
SIC: 8351 Group day care center

(G-8642)
GLENWOOD DENTAL ASSOCIATES LLP
17 W Glenwood Ave (19977-1106)
PHONE..................................302 653-5011
Tina M Shane, *Principal*
EMP: 5
SALES (est): 297.6K **Privately Held**
SIC: 8021 Dentists' office

(G-8643)
GOLD MEDAL GYMNASTICS INC
56 Artisan Dr Ste 1 (19977-3775)
PHONE..................................302 659-5569
Brenda Luft, *Owner*
EMP: 6
SALES (est): 172.9K **Privately Held**
SIC: 7991 Athletic club & gymnasiums, membership

(G-8644)
GOLF COURSE AT GARRISONS LAKE
101 W Fairways Cir (19977-1829)
PHONE..................................302 659-1206
Carol Russell, *Executive Asst*
EMP: 9
SALES: 492K **Privately Held**
SIC: 7992 Public golf courses

(G-8645)
GOVERNORS PLACE TOWNHOMES
17 Providence Dr (19977-1052)
PHONE..................................302 653-6655
Ronald Cantor, *Owner*
EMP: 5
SALES (est): 276.1K **Privately Held**
SIC: 6513 Apartment building operators

(G-8646)
GREEN VALLEY PAVILION
3034 S Dupont Blvd (19977-1898)
PHONE..................................302 653-5085
Joyce Winters, *Principal*
EMP: 25
SALES (est): 565.1K **Privately Held**
SIC: 8361 8059 8051 Geriatric residential care; nursing home, except skilled & intermediate care facility; skilled nursing care facilities

(G-8647)
GUNN SHOT PHOTOGRAPHY
154 Cathleen Dr (19977-8208)
PHONE..................................302 399-3094
EMP: 4
SALES (est): 46K **Privately Held**
SIC: 7221 Photographer, still or video

(G-8648)
H & H TRUCK AND TRAILER REPAIR
738 Paddock Rd (19977-9686)
P.O. Box 151, Middletown (19709-0151)
PHONE..................................302 653-1446
Danny Hitchens, *Owner*
EMP: 4
SALES (est): 309.2K **Privately Held**
SIC: 7539 7538 Trailer repair; general truck repair

(G-8649)
HALPERN EYE ASSOCIATES INC
201 Stadium St (19977-2899)
PHONE..................................302 653-3400
Sherri Taylor, *Manager*
EMP: 7
SALES (corp-wide): 4.3MM **Privately Held**
WEB: www.halperneye.com
SIC: 8042 Specialized optometrists
PA: Halpern Eye Associates, Inc.
  885 S Governors Ave
  Dover DE 19904
  302 734-5861

(G-8650)
HEALTH & SOCIAL SVCS DEL DEPT
Also Called: Delaware Hosp For Chrnclly Ill
100 Sunnyside Rd (19977-1752)
PHONE..................................302 223-1000
Jack Askin, *Training Dir*
Kerrie Gebhart, *Executive*
Rodney Holderbaum, *Fmly & Gen Dent*
EMP: 750 **Privately Held**
SIC: 8069 9431 8051 Chronic disease hospital; administration of public health programs; skilled nursing care facilities
HQ: Delaware Dept Of Health And Social Services
  1901 N Dupont Hwy
  New Castle DE 19720

(G-8651)
HEIRLOOM CREATIONS
5899 Underwoods Corner Rd (19977-3759)
P.O. Box 471, Clayton (19938-0471)
PHONE..................................302 659-1817
Deborah Perrine, *Owner*
EMP: 2
SALES (est): 27K **Privately Held**
SIC: 2521 Wood office furniture

(G-8652)
HIGH HORSE PERFORMANCE INC
93 Artisan Dr Ste 6 (19977-3765)
PHONE..................................302 894-1115
Joshua Schwartz, *President*
EMP: 6
SALES (est): 530.3K **Privately Held**
SIC: 7538 General automotive repair shops

(G-8653)
HOLLY HILL ESTATES
271 Berry Dr (19977-2726)
PHONE..................................302 653-7503
Holly Malone, *Owner*
EMP: 6

SALES (est): 431.5K **Privately Held**
SIC: 6515 Mobile home site operators

(G-8654)
HORNS MACHINE SHOP INC
3652 Big Woods Rd (19977-2935)
P.O. Box 810, Clayton (19938-0810)
PHONE..................................302 653-6663
Ricky Nash, *President*
Tricia Nash, *Vice Pres*
EMP: 6 **EST:** 1966
SQ FT: 2,840
SALES: 550K **Privately Held**
SIC: 3599 Machine shop, jobbing & repair

(G-8655)
HOUND DOG RECOVERY LLC
2151 S Dupont Blvd (19977-2882)
P.O. Box 28 (19977-0028)
PHONE..................................302 836-3806
Crystal Grelock, *Mng Member*
Ryan Grelock,
EMP: 7
SALES (est): 103.6K **Privately Held**
SIC: 7549 Towing services

(G-8656)
I 3 A LLC
5819 Underwoods Corner Rd (19977-3759)
PHONE..................................302 659-0909
EMP: 8 **EST:** 2009
SALES (est): 1.2MM **Privately Held**
SIC: 8711 Engineering Services

(G-8657)
ICONIC TSUNAMI LLC
57 Pier Head Blvd Ste 2 (19977-8202)
PHONE..................................302 223-3411
▼ **EMP:** 4
SQ FT: 3,600
SALES (est): 432.8K **Privately Held**
SIC: 5045 Whol Computers/Peripherals

(G-8658)
INTERIM HEALTHCARE DEL LLC
100 S Main St Ste 203 (19977-1479)
PHONE..................................302 322-2743
Anna Maria Mannino,
Nicholas Manninok,
EMP: 150
SALES (est): 3.6MM **Privately Held**
SIC: 7363 8082 Temporary help service; visiting nurse service

(G-8659)
INTERNTNAL AGRCLTURE PROD GROU
22 Zion Dr (19977-6800)
PHONE..................................302 450-2008
Dorothy Lewis,
EMP: 1
SALES (est): 39.5K **Privately Held**
SIC: 2066 Cocoa & cocoa products

(G-8660)
J A BANKS & ASSOCIATES LLC
486 Joseph Wick Dr (19977-4659)
PHONE..................................914 260-2003
Verna Banks,
EMP: 10
SALES (est): 289.1K **Privately Held**
SIC: 6799 6531 Investors; real estate leasing & rentals

(G-8661)
JAIDEN JEWELS SHOES AND ACC
533 Brenford Station Rd (19977-4609)
PHONE..................................302 659-2473
Jacquelyn Jackson-Douglas, *Principal*
Jacquelyn Douglas, *Principal*
EMP: 2
SALES (est): 257K **Privately Held**
SIC: 5139 Shoes

(G-8662)
JAMES POOLE
215 Hawkey Branch Rd (19977-3127)
PHONE..................................215 407-4046
James Poole, *Principal*
EMP: 4
SALES (est): 217.5K **Privately Held**
SIC: 4212 Local trucking, without storage

(G-8663)
JAMES T VAUGHN
1181 Paddock Rd (19977-9679)
PHONE..................................302 653-9261
James T Vaughn, *Principal*
EMP: 7
SALES (est): 558K **Privately Held**
SIC: 7389 Personal service agents, brokers & bureaus

(G-8664)
JIAO JUNFANG MD
315 N Carter Rd (19977-1282)
PHONE..................................302 453-1342
Junfang Jiao, *President*
EMP: 5
SALES (est): 78.5K **Privately Held**
SIC: 8011 Ears, nose & throat specialist: physician/surgeon

(G-8665)
JUST LIKE HOME
314 W Mount Vernon St (19977-1129)
PHONE..................................302 653-0605
D Laub, *Principal*
EMP: 7
SALES (est): 100.8K **Privately Held**
SIC: 8051 Skilled nursing care facilities

(G-8666)
KENT CONSTRUCTION CO (PA)
2 Big Oak Rd (19977-3501)
PHONE..................................302 653-6469
Ernest C Davison III, *President*
Patricia Hibbert, *General Mgr*
EMP: 26
SQ FT: 7,000
SALES (est): 12.3MM **Privately Held**
SIC: 1542 1541 Commercial & office building, new construction; industrial buildings, new construction

(G-8667)
KENT GENERAL HOSPITAL
401 N Carter Rd (19977-1281)
PHONE..................................302 653-2010
Deanna Rigby, *Director*
EMP: 5 **Privately Held**
SIC: 8062 General medical & surgical hospitals
HQ: Kent General Hospital
  640 S State St
  Dover DE 19901
  302 674-4700

(G-8668)
KREAM PUFF CLEAN
49 Trala St (19977-2216)
PHONE..................................251 509-1639
Thomas Bell, *Principal*
EMP: 10
SALES (est): 124.8K **Privately Held**
SIC: 7699 Cleaning services

(G-8669)
LABORATORY CORPORATION AMERICA
100 S Main St (19977-1477)
PHONE..................................302 653-5119
Ron Weakley, *Branch Mgr*
EMP: 4 **Publicly Held**
SIC: 8071 Medical laboratories
HQ: Laboratory Corporation Of America
  358 S Main St Ste 458
  Burlington NC 27215
  336 229-1127

(G-8670)
LAST TANGLE SALON AND SPA
76 E Glenwood Ave (19977-1002)
PHONE..................................302 653-6638
Denise Janeka, *President*
EMP: 6
SALES (est): 118.3K **Privately Held**
SIC: 7991 Spas

(G-8671)
LEAGER CONSTRUCTION INC
732 Smyrna Landing Rd (19977-9631)
P.O. Box 146 (19977-0146)
PHONE..................................302 653-8021
Joseph M Leager, *President*
Kim Leager, *Admin Sec*
EMP: 6

SALES (est): 436.3K **Privately Held**
SIC: 1771 1711 Concrete work; septic system construction

(G-8672)
LEGACY DISTILLING LLC
106 W Commerce St (19977-1119)
PHONE.................................302 983-1269
Ron Gomes Jr, *Principal*
EMP: 8
SALES (est): 904.2K **Privately Held**
SIC: 2085 Distilled & blended liquors

(G-8673)
LISA A FAGIOLETTI DMD LLC
25 W Commerce St (19977-1463)
PHONE.................................302 514-9064
Lisa A Fagioletti, *Principal*
Lisa Fagioletti, *Principal*
EMP: 5
SALES (est): 307.1K **Privately Held**
SIC: 8021 Offices & clinics of dentists

(G-8674)
LISA TRABAUDO DAY CARE
316 Lisa Ct (19977-9407)
PHONE.................................302 653-3529
John Trabaudo, *Principal*
Lisa Trabaudo, *Director*
EMP: 5
SALES (est): 63.3K **Privately Held**
SIC: 8351 Child day care services

(G-8675)
LITTLE KIDS SWAGG LRNG CTR LLC
433 S Dupont Blvd (19977-1701)
PHONE.................................302 480-4404
Shakiah Davis, *Principal*
EMP: 5
SALES (est): 83.8K **Privately Held**
SIC: 8351 Child day care services

(G-8676)
LOVING CARE NURSERY SCHOOL
22 Dwight Ave (19977-1482)
PHONE.................................302 653-6990
Bettielou Wagner, *Owner*
William Wagner, *Co-Owner*
EMP: 7 **EST:** 1964
SALES: 135K **Privately Held**
SIC: 8351 Nursery school

(G-8677)
LUBE DEPOT
205 W Glenwood Ave (19977-1108)
PHONE.................................302 659-3329
Gary Register, *Owner*
EMP: 9
SALES (est): 561.1K **Privately Held**
SIC: 7538 General automotive repair shops

(G-8678)
MAC CONTRACTORS INC
131 Dodge Dr (19977-1880)
PHONE.................................302 653-5765
Amrut Patel, *President*
Nila Patel, *Treasurer*
EMP: 4
SALES (est): 650.4K **Privately Held**
SIC: 1542 Commercial & office building, new construction

(G-8679)
MARKSMAN EMBROIDERY
1312 Twin Willows Rd (19977-3546)
PHONE.................................302 223-6740
Bruce Caballero, *Principal*
EMP: 1
SALES (est): 44.5K **Privately Held**
SIC: 2395 Embroidery products, except schiffli machine; embroidery & art needlework

(G-8680)
MATTHEWS TOWING & RECOVERY
710 Black Diamond Rd (19977-9672)
PHONE.................................302 463-1108
Lucas Matthews, *President*
EMP: 4

SALES (est): 105.5K **Privately Held**
SIC: 7549 Towing service, automotive; towing services

(G-8681)
MISSION BRACELETS
1201 Woodland Beach Rd (19977-3456)
PHONE.................................302 528-5065
Katie Brobst, *Principal*
EMP: 2
SALES (est): 102.7K **Privately Held**
SIC: 3961 Bracelets, except precious metal

(G-8682)
MORRIS CT TRUCKING INC
803 Masseys Church Rd (19977-9451)
PHONE.................................302 653-2396
Carol Morris, *President*
EMP: 5
SALES (est): 577K **Privately Held**
SIC: 4212 Local trucking, without storage

(G-8683)
MURRY TRUCKING LLC
568 Blckbird Grnspring Rd (19977-9476)
PHONE.................................302 653-4811
John J Murry, *Principal*
Carol Murry, *Admin Sec*
Ashley Murry,
James C Murry,
EMP: 12
SALES: 1.4MM **Privately Held**
SIC: 4212 7389 Local trucking, without storage;

(G-8684)
NAOMI RUTH HOWARD
654 Brenford Station Rd (19977-4618)
PHONE.................................828 284-8721
Naomi Howard, *CEO*
EMP: 8
SALES (est): 65.7K **Privately Held**
SIC: 8049 Offices of health practitioner

(G-8685)
NATIONAL AUTO MOVERS LLC
46 Bluegrass Blvd (19977-3938)
PHONE.................................302 229-9256
EMP: 8
SALES (est): 510.1K **Privately Held**
SIC: 4789 Cargo loading & unloading services

(G-8686)
OERIGO CONSULTING LLC
82 E Cayhill Ln (19977-3923)
PHONE.................................302 353-4719
Regis L Williams, *Owner*
EMP: 5
SALES (est): 40K **Privately Held**
SIC: 7231 7389 Beauty shops;

(G-8687)
PENINSULA ACOUSTICAL CO INC
441 Pier Head Blvd (19977-8205)
PHONE.................................302 653-3551
Dana Stonesifer, *President*
EMP: 7
SALES: 500K **Privately Held**
SIC: 1742 1743 Acoustical & ceiling work; tile installation, ceramic

(G-8688)
PERSANTE SLEEP CENTER
100 S Main St Ste 201 (19977-1479)
PHONE.................................302 508-2130
EMP: 5
SALES (est): 78.5K **Privately Held**
SIC: 8011 Offices & clinics of medical doctors

(G-8689)
PINNACLE RHBILITATION HLTH CTR
3034 S Dupont Blvd (19977-1898)
PHONE.................................302 653-5085
Karen Hickman, *Director*
EMP: 14
SALES (est): 18.7MM **Privately Held**
SIC: 8099 Blood related health services

(G-8690)
PNC BANK NATIONAL ASSOCIATION
7 S Main St (19977-1430)
PHONE.................................302 653-2475
Rose Mary Mast, *Manager*
EMP: 12
SALES (corp-wide): 19.9B **Publicly Held**
SIC: 6021 National commercial banks
HQ: Pnc Bank, National Association
222 Delaware Ave
Wilmington DE 19801
877 762-2000

(G-8691)
PREMIER PHYSICAL THERAPY &
100 S Main St Ste 300 (19977-1495)
PHONE.................................302 389-7855
Richard Binstein, *Principal*
EMP: 5
SALES (est): 24.4K
SALES (corp-wide): 453.9MM **Publicly Held**
SIC: 8049 Physical therapist
PA: U.S. Physical Therapy, Inc.
1300 W Sam Houston Pkwy S # 300
Houston TX 77042
713 297-7000

(G-8692)
PRESTWICK HOUSE INC
58 Artisan Dr (19977-3711)
P.O. Box 658, Clayton (19938-0658)
PHONE.................................302 659-2070
James Scott, *President*
Kendra Scott, *Corp Secy*
Patricia Scott, *Vice Pres*
Samantha Clark, *Manager*
EMP: 30
SQ FT: 15,000
SALES: 6MM **Privately Held**
WEB: www.prestwickhouse.com
SIC: 2741 5942 Miscellaneous publishing; book stores

(G-8693)
PRO 2 RESPIRATORY SERVICES
56 Artisan Dr Ste 5 (19977-3775)
PHONE.................................302 514-9843
EMP: 8
SALES (est): 61.1K **Privately Held**
SIC: 8082 Home health care services

(G-8694)
PROFESSIONAL IMAGING
97 Nita Dr (19977-4838)
PHONE.................................302 653-3522
EMP: 4 **EST:** 2011
SALES (est): 62.7K **Privately Held**
SIC: 8071 Medical laboratories

(G-8695)
PURE WELLNESS LLC
699 S Carter Rd Unit 5 (19977-7754)
PHONE.................................302 389-8915
EMP: 9
SALES (corp-wide): 1.9MM **Privately Held**
SIC: 8099 Childbirth preparation clinic
PA: Pure Wellness, Llc
550 Stanton Christiana Rd # 302
Newark DE 19713
302 365-5470

(G-8696)
RALPH CAHALL & SON PAVING
2284 Bryn Zion Rd (19977-3895)
PHONE.................................302 653-4220
R Steven Cahall, *President*
Diane Cahall, *Corp Secy*
EMP: 80
SALES (est): 5MM **Privately Held**
SIC: 1794 1611 1771 Excavation work; surfacing & paving; concrete work

(G-8697)
RAYMOND A STACHECKI
3157 Big Oak Rd (19977-3108)
PHONE.................................302 653-6004
Raymond Stachecki, *Owner*
EMP: 4
SALES (est): 300K **Privately Held**
SIC: 0191 General farms, primarily crop

(G-8698)
RECORDS GEBHART AGENCY INC
Also Called: Records-Gebhart Insurance
2 N Market St (19977-1115)
PHONE.................................302 653-9211
Kyle Gebhart, *President*
EMP: 6 **EST:** 1959
SQ FT: 2,100
SALES (est): 1MM **Privately Held**
SIC: 6411 Insurance agents

(G-8699)
REHRIG PENN LOGISTICS INC
171 Hemlock Way (19977-2729)
PHONE.................................302 659-3337
Terry Fenwick, *Principal*
EMP: 4 **Privately Held**
SIC: 5031 Pallets, wood
HQ: Rehrig Penn Logistics, Inc.
7800 100th St
Pleasant Prairie WI 53158

(G-8700)
RENT-A-CENTER INC
120 E Glenwood Ave (19977-1003)
PHONE.................................302 653-3701
Selix Wilson, *Manager*
EMP: 5
SALES (corp-wide): 2.6B **Publicly Held**
WEB: www.rentacenter.com
SIC: 7359 Appliance rental
PA: Rent-A-Center, Inc.
5501 Headquarters Dr
Plano TX 75024
972 801-1100

(G-8701)
RICHARDS INVESTMENT GROUP CORP
381 Grayton Dr (19977-4461)
PHONE.................................302 399-0450
Sean Richards, *Officer*
EMP: 6
SALES (est): 78.6K **Privately Held**
SIC: 7699 Industrial equipment cleaning

(G-8702)
ROBERT DONLICK MD
16 Garrisons Cir (19977-2858)
PHONE.................................302 653-8916
Robert Donlick MD, *Owner*
EMP: 6
SQ FT: 1,516
SALES (est): 476.2K **Privately Held**
SIC: 8011 General & family practice, physician/surgeon

(G-8703)
ROMMEL CYCLES LLC (PA)
Also Called: Harley-Davidson
450 Stadium St (19977-2839)
PHONE.................................302 658-8800
Donna Marvel, *Office Mgr*
Jason Hartke, *Manager*
Dave Rommel,
EMP: 80
SALES (est): 9.5MM **Privately Held**
WEB: www.annapolishd.com
SIC: 7699 5571 Motorcycle repair service; motorcycle parts & accessories

(G-8704)
ROYAL HAIR DESIGN LLC
129 E Glenwood Ave (19977-1424)
PHONE.................................302 312-4569
Dwayne Bull,
EMP: 4
SALES (est): 76K **Privately Held**
SIC: 7231 Unisex hair salons

(G-8705)
ROYAL TREATMENTS
14 S Main St (19977-1431)
PHONE.................................302 722-6733
Karen Gill, *Owner*
EMP: 1
SALES (est): 67.5K **Privately Held**
SIC: 2391 1799 Curtains & draperies; window treatment installation

(G-8706)
RPJ WASTE SERVICES INC
453 Pier Head Blvd (19977-8205)
PHONE.................................302 653-9999

GEOGRAPHIC SECTION — Smyrna - Kent County (G-8739)

Julie E Davidson, *President*
Earnest Davidson, *Vice Pres*
James Davidson, *Vice Pres*
EMP: 14
SQ FT: 6,000
SALES: 3.5MM **Privately Held**
WEB: www.rpjwaste.com
SIC: 1795 Wrecking & demolition work

(G-8707)
RUSH REALTY LLC
395 Southern View Dr (19977-4088)
PHONE 302 219-6707
Demarcus Rush,
EMP: 6
SALES: 256K **Privately Held**
SIC: 6531 Real estate agents & managers

(G-8708)
RUTHIE FRANCZEK
6827 Underwoods Corner Rd (19977-3758)
PHONE 302 659-1000
Ruthie Franczek, *Owner*
EMP: 4
SALES (est): 195.5K **Privately Held**
SIC: 0742 Veterinarian, animal specialties

(G-8709)
RWM EMBROIDERY & MORE LLC
19 Village Sq (19977-1852)
PHONE 302 653-8384
Bob McGinnis, *Owner*
EMP: 12
SALES (est): 884K **Privately Held**
SIC: 2395 Embroidery products, except schiffli machine; embroidery & art needlework

(G-8710)
SAGGIO MANAGEMENT GROUP INC
350 N High St Ext (19977-1183)
PHONE 302 659-6560
Ralph Estep, *Principal*
EMP: 5
SALES (est): 385.9K **Privately Held**
SIC: 8741 Management services

(G-8711)
SAGGIO MANAGEMENT GROUP INC
665 S Carter Rd Unit 2 (19977-7728)
PHONE 302 659-6560
Ralph Estep, *Principal*
EMP: 4
SALES (est): 614.4K **Privately Held**
SIC: 6282 Investment advice

(G-8712)
SCHREPPLER CHROPRACTIC OFFS PA
892 S Dupont Blvd (19977-1723)
PHONE 302 653-5525
George Schreppler DC, *President*
EMP: 5
SALES (est): 318K **Privately Held**
SIC: 8041 Offices & clinics of chiropractors

(G-8713)
SHAMROCK CONSTRUCTION INC
380 Lake Dr (19977-1358)
PHONE 302 376-0320
Terry Kelly, *Partner*
EMP: 4
SALES (est): 244.9K **Privately Held**
SIC: 1522 Residential construction

(G-8714)
SHARLAY COMPUTER SYSTEMS
15 Delhi Ct (19977-4854)
PHONE 302 588-3170
Al Ballard, *President*
Sylvia Snow-Ballard, *Corp Secy*
EMP: 8
SALES: 200K **Privately Held**
SIC: 7373 Systems engineering, computer related

(G-8715)
SHURE-LINE ELECTRICAL INC
100 Artisan Dr (19977-3711)
PHONE 302 389-1114
Edgar L Hitch Jr, *President*
Connie Meyers, *Director*
EMP: 60
SALES (est): 11.6MM **Privately Held**
SIC: 1731 General electrical contractor

(G-8716)
SIMAR FUEL INC
126 S Dupont Blvd (19977-1514)
PHONE 302 304-1969
EMP: 3
SALES (est): 169K **Privately Held**
SIC: 2869 Fuels

(G-8717)
SMILE PLACE
17 N Main St (19977-1111)
P.O. Box 659 (19977-0659)
PHONE 302 514-6200
Lewis Yu, *Principal*
EMP: 5
SALES (est): 397.7K **Privately Held**
SIC: 8021 Dentists' office

(G-8718)
SMYRNA DENTAL CENTER PA
679 S Carter Rd Unit 5 (19977-7755)
PHONE 302 223-6194
Rama Lakshmi Yerneni, *President*
EMP: 4 **EST:** 2008
SALES (est): 308.5K **Privately Held**
SIC: 8021 Dentists' office

(G-8719)
SMYRNA MEDICAL ASSOCIATES PA
38 Deak Dr (19977-1268)
PHONE 302 653-6174
Rufino V Rosal MD, *Principal*
EMP: 23
SQ FT: 3,908
SALES (est): 2.3MM **Privately Held**
SIC: 8011 Internal medicine, physician/surgeon

(G-8720)
SMYRNA NEWS & TOBACCO
456 W Glenwood Ave Ste B2 (19977-1087)
PHONE 302 653-9620
Randy Dawson, *Owner*
EMP: 5
SALES (est): 254.5K **Privately Held**
SIC: 2711 Newspapers, publishing & printing

(G-8721)
SMYRNA SCHOOL DISTRICT
Also Called: Special Services Center
80 Monrovia Ave (19977-1530)
PHONE 302 653-3135
Donald Bates, *Director*
EMP: 25
SALES (corp-wide): 33.7MM **Privately Held**
WEB: www.smyrnaschooldistrict.com
SIC: 8211 8351 Public elementary & secondary schools; public elementary school; child day care services
PA: Smyrna School District
82 Monrovia Ave
Smyrna DE 19977
302 653-8585

(G-8722)
SNOW FARMS INC
249 Raymond Neck Rd (19977-2928)
PHONE 302 653-7534
Bruce Snow, *President*
EMP: 5
SALES (est): 441.7K **Privately Held**
SIC: 0191 General farms, primarily crop

(G-8723)
SOUTHERN DEL PHYSCL THERAPY
207 Stadium St (19977-2899)
PHONE 302 659-0173
Julie Moyerknowles, *CEO*
EMP: 5 **Privately Held**
WEB: www.southerndelawarept.com
SIC: 8049 Physical therapist
PA: Southern Delaware Physical Therapy Inc
701 Savannah Rd Ste A
Lewes DE 19958

(G-8724)
STERLING NURSERY INC
1575 Vndyke Grenspring Rd (19977-9489)
PHONE 302 653-7060
Richard W Sterling, *President*
Barbara E Sterling, *Treasurer*
EMP: 5
SALES (est): 350K **Privately Held**
SIC: 0181 5193 Nursery stock, growing of; nursery stock

(G-8725)
STL & ASSOCIATES LLC
198 Greens Branch Ln (19977-1097)
P.O. Box 126 (19977-0126)
PHONE 302 359-2801
Shawn Barbour, *President*
Teresa Barbour, *Vice Pres*
EMP: 8
SALES (est): 214.3K **Privately Held**
SIC: 7349 7389 Janitorial service, contract basis;

(G-8726)
STONE MEDIC
73 Kristin Ct (19977-8207)
PHONE 302 233-6039
Howard Pyle, *Owner*
EMP: 1
SALES (est): 57.5K **Privately Held**
SIC: 2542 Cabinets: show, display or storage: except wood

(G-8727)
SURPLUS & EXCESS LINE LTD
4 Village Sq Ste 900 (19977-1852)
PHONE 302 653-5016
Howell Wallace, *President*
Mike Mercer, *Vice Pres*
Teresa Boole, *Admin Sec*
EMP: 5
SQ FT: 1,500
SALES (est): 778K **Privately Held**
WEB: www.surplus-excesslines.com
SIC: 6411 Insurance brokers

(G-8728)
T A H FIRST INC
571 Kates Way (19977-1623)
P.O. Box 432 (19977-0432)
PHONE 302 653-6114
Harold Horan III, *President*
EMP: 5
SALES (est): 386.3K **Privately Held**
SIC: 4213 Automobiles, transport & delivery

(G-8729)
TELAMON CORP HEAD START PRGRAM
204 Georges Aly Fl 2 (19977-2540)
PHONE 302 653-3766
Renita Spultz, *Director*
EMP: 88
SALES (est): 86.1K **Privately Held**
SIC: 8351 8741 Head start center, except in conjunction with school; management services

(G-8730)
TENDER LOVING KARE CHILD CARE
Also Called: Alibel
649 S Carter Rd (19977-7727)
PHONE 302 653-5677
Melissa Schulte, *Director*
EMP: 35
SALES (est): 714.2K **Privately Held**
SIC: 8351 Child day care services

(G-8731)
THORN ELECTRIC INC
405 W Commerce St (19977-1216)
PHONE 302 653-4300
Joseph Thorn III, *President*
EMP: 13
SQ FT: 1,650
SALES: 1.1MM **Privately Held**
SIC: 1731 General electrical contractor

(G-8732)
TREVOR ENNIS DC
29 N East St (19977-1413)
PHONE 302 389-2225
Trevor Ennis, *Executive*
EMP: 7
SALES (est): 79.5K **Privately Held**
SIC: 8041 Offices & clinics of chiropractors

(G-8733)
TWO FARMS INC
304 N Dupont Blvd (19977-1512)
PHONE 302 653-8345
Diana Cunningham, *Branch Mgr*
EMP: 19
SALES (corp-wide): 171.3MM **Privately Held**
SIC: 0191 General farms, primarily crop
PA: Two Farms, Inc.
3611 Roland Ave
Baltimore MD 21211
410 889-0200

(G-8734)
UNCORKED CANVAS PARTIES LLC
1477 Sunnyside Rd (19977-3615)
PHONE 302 659-1396
EMP: 2
SALES (est): 95.4K **Privately Held**
SIC: 2211 Canvas

(G-8735)
VALOUR ARABIANS
1950 Vndyke Grenspring Rd (19977-9448)
PHONE 302 653-4066
Margo Wallace, *Owner*
Lee Bonini, *Vice Pres*
Beth Hammelbacher, *Office Admin*
EMP: 8
SALES (est): 311.8K **Privately Held**
SIC: 0272 Horse farm

(G-8736)
VETERANS OF FOREIGN WARS NEWMN
Also Called: Veterans Fgn Wars Nwman L-Urba
4941 Wheatleys Pond Rd (19977-3731)
PHONE 302 653-8801
Jack Achenbach, *Quartermaster*
EMP: 6
SALES (est): 130.5K **Privately Held**
SIC: 8641 Veterans' organization

(G-8737)
W D PRESSLEY INC
5779 Dupont Pkwy (19977-9635)
P.O. Box 477 (19977-0477)
PHONE 302 653-4381
William Pressley Sr, *CEO*
Brenda Pressley, *Vice Pres*
EMP: 8
SALES (est): 1.1MM **Privately Held**
WEB: www.wdpressley.com
SIC: 1521 1542 General remodeling, single-family houses; commercial & office buildings, renovation & repair

(G-8738)
WALKER & SONS INC
838 Sunnyside Rd (19977-3606)
PHONE 302 653-5635
EMP: 10
SALES (est): 440.7K **Privately Held**
SIC: 7363 Truck driver services

(G-8739)
WALLS & DAVENPORT INC
Also Called: H & R Block
94 E Glenwood Ave (19977)
PHONE 302 653-4779
David Walls, *President*
EMP: 4
SALES (corp-wide): 853.9K **Privately Held**
SIC: 7291 Tax return preparation services
PA: Walls & Davenport Inc
2137 S Dupont Hwy
Dover DE 19901
302 697-2786

Smyrna - Kent County (G-8740)

(G-8740)
WEAVER SANITATION
6 Manor Dr (19977-1730)
PHONE..........................302 653-8777
Richard Weaver, *Owner*
Martha Weaver, *Owner*
EMP: 5
SALES (est): 422.5K **Privately Held**
SIC: 7699 Septic tank cleaning service

(G-8741)
WEB N APP LLC
58 Burnside Dr (19977-4028)
PHONE..........................810 309-8242
Taha Abbasi, *President*
EMP: 4 EST: 2016
SALES (est): 76.5K **Privately Held**
SIC: 7374 Computer graphics service

(G-8742)
WELLSPRING COUNSELING SERVICES
115 E Glenwood Ave (19977-1424)
PHONE..........................302 373-8904
Michael N Bryson, *Owner*
EMP: 4
SALES (est): 42.4K **Privately Held**
SIC: 8322 Individual & family services

(G-8743)
WENTZEL TRANSPORTATION
33 Brenford Station Rd (19977-4600)
PHONE..........................302 355-9465
Maryjane Wentzel, *Principal*
EMP: 6
SALES (est): 850K **Privately Held**
SIC: 4731 Freight transportation arrangement

(G-8744)
WHITEHOOK SOLUTIONS LLC
219 Garrisons Cir (19977-1832)
PHONE..........................302 222-5177
Cherylann Borrelli,
Richard Borrelli,
EMP: 4
SALES: 200K **Privately Held**
SIC: 7361 Employment agencies

(G-8745)
WILLIAM H RDFORD NURSERIES INC
Also Called: William H Radford Ldscp Contrs
853 Black Diamond Rd (19977-9663)
PHONE..........................302 659-3130
Bill Radford, *President*
Karla Radford, *Vice Pres*
William H Radford, *Sales Executive*
Karla J Radford, *Executive*
EMP: 20
SALES (est): 2.7MM **Privately Held**
SIC: 0782 Landscape contractors

(G-8746)
WILLIS FORD INC
15 N Dupont Blvd (19977-1544)
PHONE..........................302 653-5900
William H Willis Jr, *President*
Harry D Willis, *Vice Pres*
Nicholas Onufrovich, *Sales Mgr*
Frank Lauro, *Sales Staff*
Lisa Fletcher, *Consultant*
EMP: 38
SALES (est): 14.9MM **Privately Held**
WEB: www.willisford.com
SIC: 5511 5531 7538 7532 Automobiles, new & used; automotive parts; general automotive repair shops; top & body repair & paint shops

(G-8747)
WILMINGTON SAVINGS FUND SOC
400 Jimmy Dr (19977-5801)
PHONE..........................302 389-3151
Tim Sparrow, *Manager*
EMP: 4
SALES (corp-wide): 455.5MM **Publicly Held**
SIC: 6022 State commercial banks
HQ: Wilmington Savings Fund Society
500 Delaware Ave Ste 500 # 500
Wilmington DE 19801
302 792-6000

(G-8748)
XBOS
456 W Glenwood Ave Ste D (19977-1087)
PHONE..........................302 653-1800
Sheik Shah, *Principal*
EMP: 4
SALES (est): 230K **Privately Held**
SIC: 7999 Recreation center

Talleyville
New Castle County

(G-8749)
ATTENTION DFICIT DISORDER ASSN
101 Brandywine Blvd A (19803-1838)
PHONE..........................302 478-0255
Linda Anderson, *President*
EMP: 8 EST: 2008
SALES: 322.6K **Privately Held**
SIC: 8699 Membership organizations

(G-8750)
PERFORMANCE BASED RESULTS
Also Called: P B R
400 Delaware Ave (19803-5232)
PHONE..........................302 478-4443
Paul Cherry, *Owner*
Patrick Connor, *Managing Prtnr*
EMP: 8
SALES: 250K **Privately Held**
WEB: www.pbresults.com
SIC: 8742 Sales (including sales management) consultant

(G-8751)
SILVERSIDE CLUB INC
418 Brandywine Blvd (19803-1806)
P.O. Box 7206, Wilmington (19803-0206)
PHONE..........................302 478-4568
Alfred Burke Jr, *Principal*
EMP: 14
SALES (est): 236.1K **Privately Held**
SIC: 7997 Golf club, membership

(G-8752)
STEVEN SACHS APPRAISAL ACCESS
19 Brandywine Blvd (19803-1838)
PHONE..........................302 477-9676
Steven Sachs, *Owner*
EMP: 5 EST: 2001
SALES (est): 389.1K **Privately Held**
WEB: www.stevensachsappraisal.com
SIC: 6531 Appraiser, real estate

Townsend
New Castle County

(G-8753)
ADVANCED BIZZ INNOVATIONS LLC
405 South St (19734-3017)
P.O. Box 122, Middletown (19709-0122)
PHONE..........................302 397-1162
Joques Mhloyi, *Principal*
EMP: 5
SALES: 30K **Privately Held**
SIC: 7349 Janitorial service, contract basis

(G-8754)
AERO ENTERPRISES INC
1270 Caldwell Corner Rd (19734-9255)
PHONE..........................302 378-1396
David Cannavo, *President*
EMP: 6
SALES (est): 750K **Privately Held**
SIC: 4581 Aircraft maintenance & repair services

(G-8755)
AIR QUALITY REMEDIATION LLC
1274 Caldwell Corner Rd (19734-9255)
P.O. Box 337 (19734-0337)
PHONE..........................302 464-1050
David Brenton, *Mng Member*
Connie Haymond, *Mng Member*
EMP: 10
SALES (est): 415K **Privately Held**
SIC: 7342 Disinfecting services

(G-8756)
ALL CLEAN SERVICES
859 Union Church Rd (19734-9121)
PHONE..........................302 378-7376
Frank Lorusso, *Owner*
EMP: 7
SALES (est): 180.7K **Privately Held**
SIC: 7349 Janitorial service, contract basis

(G-8757)
ALPHA TECHNOLOGIES CONSULTING
1405 Gibraltar Ct (19734-2887)
PHONE..........................302 898-2862
Olajide Balogun, *Mng Member*
EMP: 15
SALES (est): 205.9K **Privately Held**
SIC: 7361 Placement agencies

(G-8758)
ARMORED FIRE PROTECTION LLC
33 Mailly Dr (19734-2207)
PHONE..........................302 563-3516
William Mrovowski, *General Mgr*
Dan Sullivan, *Opers Mgr*
Shey Mrovowski, *Office Mgr*
EMP: 5
SALES (est): 168.8K **Privately Held**
SIC: 1711 Fire sprinkler system installation

(G-8759)
ARROWSMITH CLEANING SOLUTIONS
34 Dornoch Way (19734-2863)
PHONE..........................302 377-5614
EMP: 5
SALES (est): 140.5K **Privately Held**
SIC: 7349 Janitorial service, contract basis

(G-8760)
ATLANTIC OIL & GAS LLC
1405 Gibraltar Ct (19734-2887)
PHONE..........................302 898-2862
EMP: 2
SALES (est): 65.5K **Privately Held**
SIC: 1389 Oil & gas field services

(G-8761)
ATTIC AWAY FROM HOME
893 Noxontown Rd (19734-9363)
PHONE..........................302 378-2600
Don McKeown, *Owner*
EMP: 5
SALES (est): 96.7K **Privately Held**
SIC: 8351 Child day care services

(G-8762)
BAY ANIMAL HOSPITAL LLC
3891 Dupont Pkwy (19734-9389)
PHONE..........................302 279-1082
Howard Maguire Jr, *Executive Asst*
EMP: 4
SALES (est): 390.5K **Privately Held**
SIC: 0742 Animal hospital services, pets & other animal specialties

(G-8763)
BEACH BABIES CHILD CARE
6020 Summit Bridge Rd (19734-9614)
PHONE..........................302 378-4778
Deborah Toner, *Branch Mgr*
EMP: 14
SALES (corp-wide): 2.5MM **Privately Held**
SIC: 8351 Group day care center
PA: Beach Babies Child Care
31169 Learning Ln
Lewes DE 19958
302 644-1585

(G-8764)
BENJAMIN TANEI
Also Called: Tee's Kitchen
404 Sitka Spruce Ln (19734-9442)
PHONE..........................302 521-2033
Tanei Benjamin, *Owner*
EMP: 1
SALES (est): 34.2K **Privately Held**
SIC: 2759 Screen printing

(G-8765)
BRANDX HEIRLOOM TOMATOES
103 Ashley Ann Ct (19734-2030)
PHONE..........................302 287-1782
Xiomara Lozano, *Principal*
EMP: 8 EST: 2017
SALES (est): 76K **Privately Held**
SIC: 8099 Health & allied services

(G-8766)
BREEZE CONSTRUCTION LLC
39 Basalt St (19734-2013)
PHONE..........................302 522-9201
Sommer Flynn, *Mng Member*
EMP: 5
SALES: 125K **Privately Held**
SIC: 1542 1522 1521 Commercial & office building contractors; multi-family dwellings, new construction; new construction, single-family houses

(G-8767)
BUBBA GAME CALLS
158 Blackbird Station Rd (19734-9506)
PHONE..........................302 332-2004
Timothy Seward, *Principal*
EMP: 1
SALES (est): 47K **Privately Held**
SIC: 3949 Game calls

(G-8768)
CARLISLE MACHINE SHOP INC
970 Blackbird Landing Rd (19734-9141)
PHONE..........................302 653-2584
Bob Carlisle, *President*
Sheila Carlisle, *Treasurer*
EMP: 1
SALES (est): 139.6K **Privately Held**
SIC: 3599 Machine shop, jobbing & repair

(G-8769)
CHARLES ANDREWS
Also Called: Charles Andrews Upholstery
3305 Harris Rd (19734-9735)
PHONE..........................302 378-7116
Charles Andrews, *Owner*
EMP: 1
SQ FT: 4,000
SALES (est): 71.5K **Privately Held**
SIC: 7641 2512 Reupholstery; upholstered household furniture

(G-8770)
COLLETT & SON WELDING INC
550 Green Giant Rd (19734-9322)
P.O. Box 321, Middletown (19709-0321)
PHONE..........................302 376-1830
John V Collett, *President*
Margaret Bowman, *Admin Sec*
John Collet, *Admin Sec*
Kimberly J Collet, *Admin Sec*
EMP: 9 EST: 1984
SALES (est): 1.7MM **Privately Held**
SIC: 1799 Welding on site

(G-8771)
COMFORT KEEPERS
6303 Summit Bridge Rd (19734-9617)
PHONE..........................302 378-0994
EMP: 8
SALES (est): 61.1K **Privately Held**
SIC: 8082 Visiting nurse service

(G-8772)
COMMERCIAL WATERMAN
518 Flemings Landing Rd (19734-9756)
PHONE..........................302 659-3031
Paul L Mc Ginnis, *Owner*
EMP: 11
SALES (est): 161.3K **Privately Held**
SIC: 0913 Crabs, catching of

(G-8773)
CONNECTIONS COMMUNITY SUPPORT
994 Blackbird Landing Rd (19734-9141)
PHONE..........................302 659-0512
Catherine D McKay, *Principal*
EMP: 45 **Privately Held**
SIC: 8322 Community center
PA: Connections Community Support Programs, Inc.
3821 Lancaster Pike
Wilmington DE 19805

GEOGRAPHIC SECTION

Townsend - New Castle County (G-8808)

(G-8774)
COUNTRY KIDS HOME DAY CARE
1069 Vndyke Grenspring Rd (19734-9231)
PHONE..................302 653-4134
Dawn Carden, *Principal*
EMP: 5 EST: 2010
SALES (est): 69.4K Privately Held
SIC: 8351 Child day care services

(G-8775)
CREATIVE MINDS DAYCARE
2 Mica St (19734-2027)
PHONE..................302 378-0741
Michelle Craig, *Principal*
EMP: 5
SALES (est): 59.4K Privately Held
SIC: 8351 Group day care center

(G-8776)
CROKER OARS USA INC
212 Karins Blvd (19734-3029)
PHONE..................302 897-6705
Darren Croker, *President*
Gregory Doyle, *Director*
EMP: 2
SALES (est): 309.8K Privately Held
SIC: 3732 Boat building & repairing

(G-8777)
CUSTOM PORCELAIN INC
54 Cart Rd (19734-9685)
PHONE..................302 659-6590
Patricia Wyatt, *President*
EMP: 5
SALES (est): 440K Privately Held
SIC: 1799 Bathtub refinishing

(G-8778)
D&G INC
4195 Dupont Pkwy (19734-9728)
PHONE..................302 378-4877
Fredrick Drake, *President*
EMP: 6
SALES (est): 350.8K Privately Held
SIC: 7549 Towing services

(G-8779)
DELAWARE HOMES INC (PA)
401 Main St (19734-9022)
P.O. Box 38 (19734-0038)
PHONE..................302 378-9510
Michael C Selvaggio, *President*
EMP: 7 EST: 1986
SALES (est): 1.6MM Privately Held
SIC: 1521 New construction, single-family houses

(G-8780)
DELAWARE SEPTIC SERVICE LLC
893 Noxontown Rd (19734-9363)
PHONE..................302 376-6412
Fax: 302 376-5903
EMP: 4
SALES (est): 360K Privately Held
SIC: 7699 Repair Services

(G-8781)
DELAWARE SOLID WASTE AUTHORITY
276 Pine Tree Rd (19734-9104)
PHONE..................302 378-1407
Ann M Dykes, *Branch Mgr*
EMP: 26
SALES (corp-wide): 85.8MM Privately Held
SIC: 4953 Refuse collection & disposal services
PA: Delaware Solid Waste Authority
1128 S Bradford St
Dover DE 19904
302 739-5361

(G-8782)
DELCARM LLC (PA)
1482 Levels Rd (19734)
PHONE..................610 345-9001
Tim McCardell, *Mng Member*
EMP: 10
SALES (est): 5.1MM Privately Held
SIC: 0721 Crop spraying services

(G-8783)
DEPRO-SERICAL USA INC
Also Called: Depro Serical
4676 Dupont Pkwy (19734-9100)
PHONE..................302 368-8040
Ute Lehming, *President*
Guenter Lehming, *Chairman*
Bertha Lawler, *Manager*
EMP: 6
SQ FT: 20,000
SALES (est): 650K Privately Held
SIC: 5032 2752 Brick, stone & related material; commercial printing, lithographic

(G-8784)
DIBIASOS CLG RSTRATION SVC INC
690 Blackbird Station Rd (19734-9304)
P.O. Box 43 (19734-0043)
PHONE..................302 376-7111
Alfred Dibiaso, *President*
Denese Dibiaso, *Treasurer*
EMP: 7
SALES (est): 445K Privately Held
SIC: 7217 7389 8744 Carpet & upholstery cleaning; water softener service;

(G-8785)
EVERGREEN LED
29 Dornoch Way (19734-2863)
PHONE..................302 218-7819
Sam Scherwitz, *Principal*
Bob Aellis, *Vice Pres*
EMP: 6
SALES (est): 950K Privately Held
SIC: 3648 Lighting equipment

(G-8786)
EVOLUTION RX LLC
512 Aviemore Dr (19734-2818)
PHONE..................614 344-4600
Sajid Inayat, *Principal*
EMP: 4
SALES (est): 250K Privately Held
SIC: 7371 Software programming applications

(G-8787)
FRANK BARTSCH SAW MILL
186 Mckays Corner Rd (19734-9282)
PHONE..................302 653-9721
Franklin Bartsch, *Owner*
EMP: 4
SALES (est): 298.9K Privately Held
SIC: 2421 Custom sawmill

(G-8788)
FRED DRAKE AUTOMOTIVE INC
Also Called: Fred Drake Salvage
4195 Dupont Pkwy (19734-9728)
PHONE..................302 378-4877
Fred Drake Jr, *President*
Bob Hill, *Clerk*
EMP: 7
SQ FT: 2,500
SALES (est): 692.2K Privately Held
SIC: 7549 5015 5932 Towing service, automotive; motor vehicle parts, used; used merchandise stores

(G-8789)
GLORY CONTRACTING
231 Ratledge Rd (19734-9547)
PHONE..................302 275-5430
Daniel Moody, *Owner*
EMP: 5
SALES (est): 149.1K Privately Held
SIC: 2491 Wood preserving

(G-8790)
GREGG & SONS MECHANICAL LLC
256 Gum Bush Rd (19734-9769)
PHONE..................302 223-8145
Beverly Bartlett, *Principal*
Gregg Uhde, *Mng Member*
Myriam Uhde, *Mng Member*
EMP: 5
SALES (est): 500K Privately Held
SIC: 1799 1711 Food service equipment installation; refrigeration contractor

(G-8791)
H&S CLEANING SERVICE INC
684 Southerness Dr (19734-3802)
PHONE..................302 449-2928
Fax: 856 241-1063
EMP: 35
SQ FT: 10,000
SALES (est): 854K Privately Held
SIC: 7349 Building Maintenance Services

(G-8792)
HALLIES HELPING HANDS HOME
616 Brittany Cir (19734-9057)
PHONE..................844 277-8911
Hallie Gibson, *Agent*
EMP: 8
SALES (est): 61.1K Privately Held
SIC: 8082 Home health care services

(G-8793)
HAMPTON ENTERPRISES DELAWARE
413 Prestwick Pl (19734-2838)
PHONE..................302 378-7365
Lamont Hampton, *CEO*
EMP: 7
SALES (est): 391.7K Privately Held
SIC: 7217 Carpet & upholstery cleaning

(G-8794)
INC CHIMES
409 Zamora Ct (19734-3054)
PHONE..................302 449-1926
EMP: 2 EST: 2011
SALES (est): 129.7K Privately Held
SIC: 3699 Chimes, electric

(G-8795)
INDEPENDENT DISPOSAL SERVICES
604 Cannery Ln (19734-9409)
P.O. Box 490 (19734-0490)
PHONE..................302 378-5400
Bruce Georgov, *Owner*
EMP: 75
SALES (est): 2.6MM Privately Held
SIC: 4953 Recycling, waste materials

(G-8796)
INFORMED TOUCH MASSAGE THERAPY
905 Ibiza Ct (19734-3052)
PHONE..................302 229-8239
Jodi Collins, *Principal*
EMP: 7
SALES (est): 81.3K Privately Held
SIC: 8093 Rehabilitation center, outpatient treatment

(G-8797)
INSIGHT ENGINEERING SOLUTIONS
Also Called: Ies
640 Ravenglass Dr (19734-2829)
PHONE..................302 378-4842
Devanand M Prasad, *CEO*
Michael Robertson, *President*
Devanand Prasad, *Manager*
EMP: 9
SALES (est): 40K Privately Held
SIC: 7376 8748 7371 7373 Computer facilities management; systems engineering consultant, ex. computer or professional; computer software systems analysis & design, custom; local area network (LAN) systems integrator

(G-8798)
INSTRUMENTS & THERMAL PRODUCTS
8 Millburn Ct (19734-2865)
PHONE..................302 378-6290
Robert D Long, *President*
John Lowery, *Treasurer*
Paula Long, *Admin Sec*
EMP: 4
SQ FT: 1,000
SALES (est): 1MM Privately Held
WEB: www.itp4temp.com
SIC: 5084 Controlling instruments & accessories

(G-8799)
J & B CAULKERS CO
1414 Dexter Corner Rd (19734-9238)
PHONE..................302 653-7325
James Frazier, *Owner*
EMP: 4
SQ FT: 2,000
SALES (est): 283.1K Privately Held
SIC: 1799 Caulking (construction); waterproofing

(G-8800)
JANETTE REDROW LTD
Also Called: Jr
635 Cannery Ln (19734-9420)
P.O. Box 296 (19734-0296)
PHONE..................302 659-3534
Janette H Redrow, *President*
▲ EMP: 5
SALES (est): 2MM Privately Held
SIC: 5088 1629 1541 Transportation equipment & supplies; drainage system construction; steel building construction

(G-8801)
JEFF BARTSCH TRCKG EXCVTG INC
299 Saw Mill Rd (19734-9640)
PHONE..................302 653-9329
Jeff Bartsch, *President*
Vickie Bartsch, *Vice Pres*
EMP: 4
SALES (est): 705.7K Privately Held
SIC: 4213 1794 Trucking, except local; excavation work

(G-8802)
JORDAN MARKETING
678 Southerness Dr (19734-3802)
PHONE..................302 428-0147
Charles Jordan, *President*
EMP: 4
SALES (est): 491.1K Privately Held
WEB: www.jordanmarketing.com
SIC: 5199 Advertising specialties

(G-8803)
JUNIOR ANDERSON DOVER
3920 Dupont Pkwy Ste B (19734-9390)
PHONE..................302 376-7979
EMP: 4
SALES (est): 61.5K Privately Held
SIC: 8021 Offices & clinics of dentists

(G-8804)
KARI HEVERIN PHOTOGRAPHY
582 Union Church Rd (19734-9111)
PHONE..................302 943-0176
Kari Heverin, *Principal*
EMP: 4 EST: 2017
SALES (est): 46K Privately Held
SIC: 7221 Photographer, still or video

(G-8805)
LEMAY ENTERPRISES INC
480 Oak Hill School Rd (19734-9204)
PHONE..................302 659-3278
Ron Lemay, *President*
EMP: 2
SALES (est): 166.2K Privately Held
SIC: 3452 Washers

(G-8806)
LEVI CALLING
858 Green Giant Rd (19734-9330)
PHONE..................302 449-0017
Sheri Spurgeon, *Principal*
EMP: 6
SALES: 406.8K Privately Held
SIC: 7929 Musical entertainers

(G-8807)
MACKMETTS AUTO BODY
Also Called: Macknett's Body Shop
300 Saw Mill Branch Rd (19734-9014)
PHONE..................302 366-8107
Howard Mackmetts, *Owner*
EMP: 4
SALES (est): 249.2K Privately Held
SIC: 7532 Body shop, automotive

(G-8808)
MAKK-O INDUSTRIES INC
4640 Dupont Pkwy (19734-9100)
PHONE..................302 376-0160

Townsend - New Castle County (G-8809)

Vincent Passalacqua, *President*
EMP: 5
SQ FT: 5,000
SALES: 300K **Privately Held**
WEB: www.makk-o.com
SIC: 5072 Miscellaneous fasteners; nuts (hardware); bolts

(G-8809)
MICHAEL A BEECHER
Also Called: Swamp Machine Shop
1122 Dexter Corner Rd (19734-9671)
PHONE..................302 285-3357
Michael Beecher, *Principal*
EMP: 3
SALES (est): 212.3K **Privately Held**
SIC: 3599 Machine shop, jobbing & repair

(G-8810)
MICHAEL LO SAPIO
900 Grears Corner Rd (19734-9672)
PHONE..................201 919-2643
Michael Lo Sapio, *Principal*
EMP: 5
SALES (est): 94.9K **Privately Held**
SIC: 7997 Membership sports & recreation clubs

(G-8811)
ML WHITEMAN AND SONS INC
261 Gum Bush Rd (19734-9768)
P.O. Box 34 (19734-0034)
PHONE..................302 659-1001
EMP: 5
SALES (est): 410.8K **Privately Held**
SIC: 7389

(G-8812)
NANCY DUFRESNE
Also Called: Guap International Enterprise
4 Denny Lynn Dr (19734-2022)
PHONE..................302 378-7236
Nancy Dufresne, *Principal*
EMP: 5
SALES (est): 104.7K **Privately Held**
SIC: 7389

(G-8813)
ODESSA EARLY EDUCATION CENTER
27 Mailly Dr (19734-2207)
PHONE..................302 376-5254
Cristine Aguilar, *Owner*
EMP: 8
SALES (est): 81.6K **Privately Held**
SIC: 8351 Nursery school

(G-8814)
ODESSA NATIONAL GOLF CRSE LLC
1131 Fieldsboro Rd (19734-9188)
PHONE..................302 464-1007
Dale Loeslein, *Manager*
EMP: 13
SALES (est): 836K **Privately Held**
SIC: 7992 Public golf courses

(G-8815)
PARKWAY LAW LLC
3171 Dupont Pkwy (19734-9780)
P.O. Box 1016, Middletown (19709-7016)
PHONE..................302 449-0400
Dominic Dalascio, *Mng Member*
Lisa Witcher, *Admin Sec*
EMP: 8
SALES (est): 301.3K **Privately Held**
SIC: 8111 General practice law office

(G-8816)
POWELL LIFE SKILLS INC
209 Glenshee Dr (19734-3814)
P.O. Box 338 (19734-0338)
PHONE..................302 378-2706
Rita Powell, *President*
EMP: 170
SALES: 3MM **Privately Held**
SIC: 8399 Council for social agency

(G-8817)
PRECIOUS LITTLE ANGELS DAYCARE
123 Edgar Rd (19734-2416)
PHONE..................302 378-2912
Ivonne Romero, *Principal*
EMP: 5
SALES (est): 103.8K **Privately Held**
SIC: 8351 Group day care center

(G-8818)
RENTZS SIGN SERVICE
4676 Dupont Pkwy (19734-9100)
PHONE..................302 378-9607
Robert Rentz, *Principal*
EMP: 1
SALES (est): 46K **Privately Held**
SIC: 3993 Signs & advertising specialties

(G-8819)
RHODES CUSTOM AUTO WORKS INC
Also Called: Rhodes Custom Auto Works & Col
3445 Harris Rd (19734-9383)
PHONE..................302 378-1701
Larry Rhodes, *President*
EMP: 4 **EST:** 1991
SALES (est): 760.6K **Privately Held**
WEB: www.rhodescustomauto.com
SIC: 7532 Customizing services, non-factory basis

(G-8820)
ROBERT J SEWARD AND SON
Also Called: Seward, R J & Son
134 Ebenezer Church Rd (19734-9633)
PHONE..................302 378-9414
Timothy Seward, *Owner*
EMP: 2
SALES (est): 320.1K **Privately Held**
SIC: 1381 1711 Drilling water intake wells; plumbing contractors

(G-8821)
SEW THERE EMBROIDERY
188 Green Giant Rd (19734-9674)
PHONE..................302 545-0127
Becky Cronin, *Principal*
EMP: 1
SALES (est): 53K **Privately Held**
SIC: 2395 Embroidery products, except schiffli machine; embroidery & art needlework

(G-8822)
SOUTH DELAWARE MASONRY INC
319 Main St (19734-7703)
P.O. Box 72 (19734-0072)
PHONE..................302 378-1998
Joseph Mandes, *President*
EMP: 9
SQ FT: 2,760
SALES (est): 763.4K **Privately Held**
SIC: 1741 Masonry & other stonework

(G-8823)
STATEWIDE MECHANICAL INC
3295 Harris Rd (19734-9735)
P.O. Box 170, Port Penn (19731-0170)
PHONE..................302 376-6117
Paige Stewart, *President*
Robert Stewart, *Vice Pres*
EMP: 6
SALES (est): 1.3MM **Privately Held**
WEB: www.statewidemechanical.com
SIC: 1711 Mechanical contractor

(G-8824)
SUMMIT HEATING AND AC LLC (PA)
4361 Dupont Pkwy (19734-9397)
PHONE..................302 378-1203
Jeanette Burns, *Principal*
EMP: 9
SALES (est): 1.8MM **Privately Held**
SIC: 1711 Heating systems repair & maintenance; warm air heating & air conditioning contractor

(G-8825)
TANNER OPERATIONS INC
39 Anchor Inn Rd (19734-9733)
PHONE..................302 464-2194
Wendy L Tanner, *President*
EMP: 10
SALES: 25K **Privately Held**
SIC: 5064 Electrical appliances, television & radio

(G-8826)
TC DENTAL EQUIPMENT SERVICES
262 Dogtown Rd (19734-9632)
PHONE..................302 740-9049
EMP: 2
SALES (est): 146.2K **Privately Held**
SIC: 3843 Dental equipment

(G-8827)
TOWNSEND FMLY COSMTC DENTISTRY
3920 Dupont Pkwy (19734-9390)
PHONE..................302 376-7979
Venetia A Dover, *Principal*
EMP: 4 **EST:** 2013
SALES (est): 131.5K **Privately Held**
SIC: 8021 Dentists' office

(G-8828)
TOWNSEND KITCHENS CABINETS &
1028 Blackbird Landing Rd (19734-9142)
PHONE..................302 659-1007
Dan Parks, *Owner*
EMP: 1
SALES (est): 61.5K **Privately Held**
SIC: 2434 Wood kitchen cabinets

(G-8829)
TRI-STATE UNDERGROUND INC
4369 Dupont Pkwy (19734-9397)
PHONE..................302 836-8030
Rick Hess, *President*
EMP: 11
SALES (est): 289.1K **Privately Held**
SIC: 1623 Underground utilities contractor

(G-8830)
V & P CUSTOM FINISHERS INC
139 Ratledge Rd (19734-9615)
PHONE..................302 376-6367
Barbara Velazquez, *President*
EMP: 7
SALES: 800K **Privately Held**
SIC: 1751 Finish & trim carpentry

(G-8831)
WACO LID FILMS INC
467 Blackbird Station Rd (19734-9668)
PHONE..................302 378-7053
EMP: 4
SALES (est): 550K **Privately Held**
SIC: 5043 7812 Photographic Equipment And Supplies, Nsk

(G-8832)
WHITEMANS PAVING INC
501 Toledo Ct (19734-2879)
PHONE..................302 378-1828
Daniel M Whiteman, *President*
Tina Whiteman, *Vice Pres*
EMP: 5 **EST:** 2000
SALES (est): 408.3K **Privately Held**
SIC: 1611 Surfacing & paving

(G-8833)
WILLEY FARMS INC
4092 Dupont Pkwy (19734-9392)
PHONE..................302 378-8441
Christopher Willey, *President*
Irene Willey, *Principal*
Sarah Willey, *Admin Sec*
EMP: 65
SQ FT: 30,000
SALES: 10.4MM **Privately Held**
WEB: www.willeyfarmsde.com
SIC: 5148 5431 5261 5023 Fruits; fruit & vegetable markets; nursery stock, seeds & bulbs; home furnishings, wicker, rattan or reed; nursery stock; plants, potted

Viola
Kent County

(G-8834)
CHAMBERS BUS SERVICE INC
8964 S Dupont Hwy (19979)
P.O. Box 47 (19979-0047)
PHONE..................302 284-9655
Betty Chambers, *President*
William Chambers Jr, *Vice Pres*
EMP: 22
SALES (est): 852K **Privately Held**
SIC: 4131 Intercity bus line

(G-8835)
ERIC HOBBS TRUCKING INC
3292 Turkey Point Rd (19979-2009)
P.O. Box 60 (19979-0060)
PHONE..................302 697-2090
Eric Hobbs, *President*
Pamela Hobbs, *Vice Pres*
EMP: 26
SQ FT: 1,500
SALES: 1.2MM **Privately Held**
SIC: 4213 Trucking, except local

(G-8836)
GSM SYSTEMS INC
215 E Evens Rd (19979-9700)
PHONE..................302 284-8304
Patricia A Mayer, *President*
EMP: 10
SALES (est): 700K **Privately Held**
SIC: 7363 7389 Engineering help service;

(G-8837)
HOBBS ENTERPRISES INC
4398 Turkey Point Rd (19979-9712)
PHONE..................302 697-2090
Greg N Hobbs, *Principal*
EMP: 5 **EST:** 2008
SALES (est): 707.3K **Privately Held**
SIC: 4213 Trucking, except local

(G-8838)
WILLIAM CHAMBERS AND SON
8964 S Dupont Hwy (19979)
PHONE..................302 284-9655
William Chambers Jr, *President*
Betty L Chambers, *Corp Secy*
EMP: 6 **EST:** 1915
SQ FT: 7,000
SALES (est): 485.4K **Privately Held**
SIC: 1799 7538 Welding on site; truck engine repair, except industrial

(G-8839)
WILMINGTON SAVINGS FUND SOC
Also Called: First National Bank
105 Irish Hl Rd (19979)
PHONE..................302 284-3201
Vicki Ebaugh, *Manager*
EMP: 17
SALES (corp-wide): 455.5MM **Publicly Held**
WEB: www.fnbwyomingde.com
SIC: 6022 State commercial banks
HQ: Wilmington Savings Fund Society
500 Delaware Ave Ste 500 # 500
Wilmington DE 19801
302 792-6000

Wilmington
New Castle County

(G-8840)
1 FAIR CHIROPRACTIC & MED INC
811 Windsor St (19801-1445)
PHONE..................302 528-1068
Travis Pearson, *Corp Secy*
EMP: 4 **EST:** 2013
SALES (est): 119.2K **Privately Held**
SIC: 8041 7389 Offices & clinics of chiropractors;

(G-8841)
1000 DEGREES PIZZERIA
4500 New Linden Rd (19808)
PHONE..................609 382-3022
EMP: 8
SALES (est): 105.5K **Privately Held**
SIC: 5812 6794 Pizza restaurants; franchises, selling or licensing

(G-8842)
1102 WEST STREET LTD PARTNR
Also Called: Courtyard By Marriott
1102 N West St (19801-1006)
PHONE..................302 429-7600

GEOGRAPHIC SECTION

Wilmington - New Castle County (G-8873)

Christina Vanzandt, *Partner*
EMP: 35
SALES (est): 1.4MM **Privately Held**
WEB: www.1102westculverst.com
SIC: 7011 Hotels & motels

(G-8843)
1110 ON PARKWAY NEDI SPA
1110 N Bancroft Pkwy # 2 (19805-2669)
PHONE.................................302 576-1110
Lauren Michaels,
EMP: 12
SALES (est): 409.4K **Privately Held**
SIC: 7991 Spas

(G-8844)
1212 CORPORATION
2700 N Washington St (19802-3536)
PHONE.................................302 764-4048
Steven Burns, *CEO*
William J Harrison, *President*
EMP: 6
SALES: 55.6K **Privately Held**
SIC: 8069 Alcoholism rehabilitation hospital

(G-8845)
1300 PUBLISHING COMPANY LLC
1306 W 6th St (19805-3216)
PHONE.................................302 268-2684
EMP: 1
SALES (est): 37.5K **Privately Held**
SIC: 2741 Miscellaneous publishing

(G-8846)
1313 INNOVATION
1313 N Market St 1150nw (19801-6101)
PHONE.................................302 407-0420
Paul McConnell, *President*
EMP: 5
SALES (est): 554.3K **Privately Held**
SIC: 7389 Office facilities & secretarial service rental

(G-8847)
1401 CONDOMINIUM ASSOCIATION
1401 Pennsylvania Ave # 108 (19806-4125)
PHONE.................................302 656-8171
Chris Bell, *President*
Stephen Sfida, *Manager*
EMP: 20
SALES (est): 1MM **Privately Held**
SIC: 8641 Condominium association

(G-8848)
1401 HAIR DESIGNS LTD
1401 Penns Ave Ste 102 (19806-4125)
PHONE.................................302 655-1401
Joyce Bell, *President*
EMP: 4
SALES: 80K **Privately Held**
WEB: www.1401bell.com
SIC: 7231 Unisex hair salons

(G-8849)
1ST CLASS GLASS LLC
108 A St (19801-5219)
PHONE.................................302 229-9203
Josh White,
EMP: 6
SALES (est): 609.6K **Privately Held**
SIC: 1793 Glass & glazing work

(G-8850)
1ST STATE ACCESSIBILITY LLC
105 Brookside Dr (19804-1103)
PHONE.................................844 663-4396
Teal Connell,
EMP: 4 **EST:** 2015
SALES (est): 179.5K **Privately Held**
SIC: 7389 1799 Bathroom fixture reglazing; kitchen & bathroom remodeling

(G-8851)
2 DAYS BATH LLC
6603 Governor Printz Blvd (19809-2027)
PHONE.................................302 798-0103
Andrew Wahlund,
EMP: 15
SQ FT: 3,606
SALES: 3.4MM **Privately Held**
WEB: www.2daysbath.com
SIC: 1799 Kitchen & bathroom remodeling

(G-8852)
20 20 FINCL ADVISORS OF DEL
100 S Dupont Rd (19804-1324)
PHONE.................................302 777-2020
Howard Buck, *President*
Samir Thakkar, *Managing Prtnr*
EMP: 4
SALES (est): 468.3K **Privately Held**
WEB: www.2020fa.com
SIC: 6282 Investment advice

(G-8853)
20DOLLAR CLUB ASSOCIATION
2716 Jacqueline Dr K23 (19810-2037)
PHONE.................................978 908-6047
EMP: 4
SALES (est): 38.1K **Privately Held**
SIC: 7997 Membership sports & recreation clubs

(G-8854)
21ST CENTURY INSURANCE COMPANY
3 Beaver Valley Rd # 100 (19803-1125)
PHONE.................................302 252-2000
William D Loucks Jr, *Branch Mgr*
EMP: 5
SALES (corp-wide): 48.2B **Privately Held**
SIC: 6411 Insurance agents, brokers & service
HQ: 21st Century Insurance Company
6301 Owensmouth Ave
Woodland Hills CA 91367
877 310-5687

(G-8855)
21ST CENTURY N AMER INSUR CO (DH)
3 Beaver Valley Rd (19803-1124)
PHONE.................................877 310-5687
Bruce W Marlow, *President*
Richard A Andre, *Senior VP*
Michael J Cassanego, *Senior VP*
John M Lorentz, *Vice Pres*
Jes S C Zaragoza, *Vice Pres*
EMP: 1500
SQ FT: 406,000
SALES (est): 1B
SALES (corp-wide): 48.2B **Privately Held**
WEB: www.i21.com
SIC: 6411 Fire insurance underwriters' laboratories
HQ: Farmers Group, Inc.
6301 Owensmouth Ave
Woodland Hills CA 91367
323 932-3200

(G-8856)
2NDQUADRANT INC
1000 N West St Ste 1200 (19801-1058)
PHONE.................................650 378-1218
Faiz S Husain, *President*
EMP: 4
SALES (est): 338K **Privately Held**
SIC: 7379 Computer related consulting services

(G-8857)
302 SPORTS
116 Winston Ave (19804-1755)
PHONE.................................302 650-8479
Nicholas Halliday, *Owner*
EMP: 5
SALES (est): 137.6K **Privately Held**
SIC: 4832 Sports

(G-8858)
3RD STATE WELDING SUPPLY LLC
32 Germay Dr Ste C (19804-1118)
PHONE.................................302 777-1088
Joe Belahanty, *Principal*
EMP: 3
SALES: 58K **Privately Held**
SIC: 7692 Welding repair

(G-8859)
3SIGMA LABS INC
300 Delaware Ave Ste 210 (19801-6601)
PHONE.................................925 236-2618
Ravi Prakash, *Vice Pres*
EMP: 6
SALES (est): 137.2K **Privately Held**
SIC: 8734 Testing laboratories

(G-8860)
4 CORNERS LLC
511 W 37th St (19802-2018)
P.O. Box 9075 (19809-0075)
PHONE.................................302 723-2264
EMP: 7 **EST:** 2005
SALES (est): 430K **Privately Held**
SIC: 6531 Real Estate - General Contractor

(G-8861)
422 HOTEL LLC
Also Called: Sheraton Suites Wilmington
422 Delaware Ave (19801-1508)
PHONE.................................401 946-4600
Elizabeth Procaccianti,
Michelle Joyal,
EMP: 92
SQ FT: 189,940
SALES (est): 262.6K **Privately Held**
SIC: 7011 Resort hotel, franchised

(G-8862)
44 NEW ENGLAND MANAGEMENT CO
Also Called: Inn At Wilmington
300 Rocky Run Pkwy (19803-1515)
PHONE.................................302 479-7900
Christine Campanella, *Branch Mgr*
EMP: 28
SALES (corp-wide): 158.7MM **Privately Held**
WEB: www.hersha.com
SIC: 7011 Hotels
HQ: 44 New England Management Co
450 Friendship Rd
Harrisburg PA 17111
717 412-5500

(G-8863)
44 NEW ENGLAND MANAGEMENT CO
Also Called: Courtyard By Marriott
320 Rocky Run Pkwy (19803-1515)
PHONE.................................302 477-9500
Laura Farrell, *Manager*
EMP: 50
SALES (corp-wide): 158.7MM **Privately Held**
WEB: www.hersha.com
SIC: 7011 Hotels & motels
HQ: 44 New England Management Co
450 Friendship Rd
Harrisburg PA 17111
717 412-5500

(G-8864)
4SIGHT GROUP LLC
4023 Knnett Pike Wlmngton Wilmington (19807)
PHONE.................................800 490-2131
Linda M Dickey, *Partner*
Robert Bowden,
Kevin Hammond,
Paul F McCarthy,
William Willis,
EMP: 5
SALES (est): 482.1K **Privately Held**
WEB: www.4sightgroup.com
SIC: 7379

(G-8865)
700 NRTH KING ST WLMINGTON LLC
Also Called: Doubletree Downtown Wilmington
700 N King St (19801-3504)
PHONE.................................302 655-0400
Alan Filer, *General Mgr*
EMP: 110
SALES (est): 2.4MM
SALES (corp-wide): 52.2MM **Privately Held**
SIC: 7011 Hotels & motels
PA: Crestline Hotels & Resorts, Llc
3950 University Dr # 301
Fairfax VA 22030
571 529-6100

(G-8866)
7C INFOTECH INC (PA)
108 W 13th St (19801)
PHONE.................................717 288-8686
Zhen Zhu, *CEO*
EMP: 2
SALES (est): 146K **Privately Held**
SIC: 5961 7372 7389 ; application computer software;

(G-8867)
7DAY FARMERS MARKET LLC
3901 Lancaster Pike (19805-1514)
PHONE.................................302 476-8924
EMP: 4
SALES (est): 177.1K **Privately Held**
SIC: 5148 Fresh fruits & vegetables

(G-8868)
810 SUTH BROOM ST OPRTIONS LLC
Also Called: Genesis Health Care
810 S Broom St (19805-4245)
PHONE.................................302 655-1375
Fax: 302 652-1483
EMP: 120
SALES (est): 1MM **Publicly Held**
SIC: 8051 Skilled Nursing Care Facility
HQ: Genesis Healthcare Llc
101 E State St
Kennett Square PA 19348

(G-8869)
900 F STREET OWNER LLC
251 Little Falls Dr (19808-1674)
PHONE.................................212 355-1500
Wendy Mosler, *President*
Peter Allen, *Vice Pres*
Billy Cohen, *Vice Pres*
Len Goldberg, *Treasurer*
EMP: 55
SALES (est): 195.3K **Privately Held**
SIC: 7011 Hotels

(G-8870)
924 INC
Also Called: Brandywine Technology
4550 Linden Hill Rd # 100 (19808-2930)
PHONE.................................302 656-6100
Joel Pierson, *President*
Anne Keehan, *Vice Pres*
Kim McColgan, *Vice Pres*
Sean Palat, *Director*
Derek Kilby, *Recruiter*
EMP: 27
SQ FT: 2,600
SALES (est): 3.6MM **Privately Held**
WEB: www.brandywinetechnology.com
SIC: 8742 7373 7361 Business consultant; computer integrated systems design; employment agencies

(G-8871)
A B C LENDING CORP
1944 Maryland Ave (19805-4605)
PHONE.................................302 655-5313
EMP: 4
SALES (est): 256.3K **Privately Held**
SIC: 6163 Loan brokers

(G-8872)
A C ELECTRIC COMPANY
Also Called: AC Electric
3406 Broom Pl (19802-2512)
PHONE.................................302 764-7429
Arnold Brown, *Owner*
EMP: 4
SALES (est): 231.3K **Privately Held**
SIC: 1731 Electrical work

(G-8873)
A C EMSLEY & ASSOCIATES
12 S Union St (19805-3828)
PHONE.................................302 429-9191
Allen C Emsley, *Partner*
EMP: 8
SALES: 120K **Privately Held**
SIC: 6531 Real estate agent, residential

Wilmington - New Castle County (G-8874)   GEOGRAPHIC SECTION

(G-8874)
A CARING DOCTOR MINNESOTA PA
Also Called: Banfield Pet Hospital 1103
3010 Brandywine Pkwy (19803-1498)
P.O. Box 7138 (19803-0138)
PHONE.................................302 478-3910
S Tyson, *Branch Mgr*
EMP: 20
SALES (corp-wide): 37.6B **Privately Held**
WEB: www.banfield.net
SIC: 0742 Animal hospital services, pets & other animal specialties
HQ: A Caring Doctor Minnesota Pa
8000 Ne Tillamook St
Portland OR 97213
503 922-5000

(G-8875)
A D ALPINE DMD
Also Called: Rafetto, Ray S DMD
4901 Limestone Rd (19808-1271)
PHONE.................................302 239-4600
A D Alpine DMD, *Partner*
EMP: 18
SALES (est): 724.6K **Privately Held**
SIC: 8021 Orthodontist

(G-8876)
A DOOR OF HOPE INC (PA)
Also Called: NEW CASTLE COUNTY CRISIS PREGN
3407 Lancaster Pike Ste B (19805-5543)
PHONE.................................302 998-9000
Kathleen Coleman, *Supervisor*
Carol Doherty, *Exec Dir*
Ginny Geiger, *Director*
EMP: 6 **EST:** 1997
SALES: 415.9K **Privately Held**
SIC: 8322 Crisis center

(G-8877)
A FELIX DUPONT JR CO
3120 Kennett Pike (19807-3052)
PHONE.................................302 658-5244
EMP: 2
SALES (est): 145.6K **Privately Held**
SIC: 2879 Agricultural Chemicals, Nec

(G-8878)
A GENTLEMANS TOUCH INC
Also Called: Wibsc
1321 Lancaster Ave Ste A (19805-3901)
PHONE.................................302 655-7015
R Scott Rollins Sr, *President*
Tiny L Lewis, *Vice Pres*
Theo A Rollins, *Asst Mgr*
EMP: 10
SALES: 65K **Privately Held**
SIC: 8231 7231 7241 Documentation center; beauty shops; barber shops

(G-8879)
A I DUPONT HOSPITAL FOR CHILD
24 Hurst Rd (19803-3717)
PHONE.................................302 651-4186
Ai Dupont, *Executive*
EMP: 5 **EST:** 2016
SALES (est): 79.2K **Privately Held**
SIC: 8011 Offices & clinics of medical doctors

(G-8880)
A J DAUPHIN & SON INC
3313 Elizabeth Ave (19808-6106)
PHONE.................................302 994-1454
Daniel J Dauphin, *President*
A John Dauphin III, *Vice Pres*
Karen Dauphin, *Treasurer*
EMP: 9
SQ FT: 3,000
SALES (est): 292.8K **Privately Held**
SIC: 1711 Plumbing contractors

(G-8881)
A LEAP OF FAITH INC
Also Called: A Leap Faith Child Dev Ctr
1715 W 4th St (19805-3547)
PHONE.................................302 543-2056
Melanie T Price, *Exec Dir*
EMP: 10
SQ FT: 12,000
SALES (est): 321.3K **Privately Held**
SIC: 8351 Group day care center

(G-8882)
A R MYERS CORPORATION
Also Called: A R Myers Auto Body
1300 E 18th St (19801)
PHONE.................................302 652-3164
Aubrey R Myers, *President*
Donna Myers, *Vice Pres*
Tim Chambers, *Project Mgr*
EMP: 25
SQ FT: 20,000
SALES (est): 3.2MM **Privately Held**
SIC: 7532 7536 Paint shop, automotive; automotive glass replacement shops

(G-8883)
A SEED HOPE COUNSELING CTR LLC
1601 Milltown Rd Ste 1 (19808-4047)
PHONE.................................302 605-6702
Kelly Hatton, *Principal*
EMP: 6
SALES (est): 111K **Privately Held**
SIC: 8322 General counseling services

(G-8884)
A T I FUNDING CORPORATION (HQ)
Also Called: ATI Funding
801 N West St Fl 2 (19801-1525)
PHONE.................................302 656-8937
Mary W Snyder, *President*
Dale Reid, *Principal*
Peter C Fulweilber, *Vice Pres*
Kenneth J Kubacki, *Treasurer*
EMP: 15
SALES (est): 4.5B **Publicly Held**
WEB: www.alleghenytechnologies.com
SIC: 3462 Iron & steel forgings

(G-8885)
A TO Z LANDSCAPING SERVICES
11 Lewis Cir (19804-1618)
PHONE.................................302 994-1552
Joe McKee, *President*
EMP: 4
SALES (est): 280K **Privately Held**
SIC: 0782 Landscape contractors

(G-8886)
A V RESOURCES INC
240 N James St Ste B2 (19804-3172)
P.O. Box 5548 (19808-0548)
PHONE.................................302 994-1488
Kathleen Yacucci, *President*
Rob Yacucci, *Vice Pres*
EMP: 5
SQ FT: 3,000
SALES: 500K **Privately Held**
WEB: www.avresourcesonline.com
SIC: 5999 7359 Audio-visual equipment & supplies; audio-visual equipment & supply rental

(G-8887)
A&F GROUP LLC
750 Shipyard Dr Ste 300 (19801-5159)
PHONE.................................302 504-9937
Michael Flickinger, *Area Mgr*
Emily Alaimo, *Opers Staff*
Jeannette Blake, *VP Sales*
Mindy Gulledge, *Sales Staff*
Todd Bavol,
EMP: 4
SALES (est): 376K **Privately Held**
SIC: 7361 Placement agencies

(G-8888)
A+ PRINTING
501 Birmingham Ave (19804-1907)
PHONE.................................302 273-3147
EMP: 2
SALES (est): 83.9K **Privately Held**
SIC: 2752 Commercial printing, lithographic

(G-8889)
A1 NATIONWIDE LLC
1201 N Orange St Ste 7037 (19801-1189)
PHONE.................................302 327-9302
Joey McAbee, *Principal*
Renee McAbee, *Principal*
EMP: 9
SALES (est): 312K **Privately Held**
SIC: 7389 Repossession service

(G-8890)
A2B AUTO GROUP
1211 E 15th St (19802-5214)
P.O. Box 9526 (19809-0526)
PHONE.................................302 786-2331
EMP: 5
SALES (est): 252.9K **Privately Held**
SIC: 7538 General automotive repair shops

(G-8891)
A2PS CONSULTING AND SFTWR LLC
2711 Centerville Rd # 120 (19808-1676)
PHONE.................................331 201-6101
EMP: 15
SALES: 2MM **Privately Held**
SIC: 7371 7389 Custom Computer Programing Business Serv Non-Commercial Site

(G-8892)
A66 INC
2711 Centerville Rd # 400 (19808-1660)
PHONE.................................800 444-0446
George Davey, *President*
Michael Pieper, *Vice Pres*
EMP: 2
SALES (est): 200K **Privately Held**
SIC: 8733 2834 5122 Noncommercial research organizations; pharmaceutical preparations; pharmaceuticals

(G-8893)
AAA CLUB ALLIANCE INC (PA)
Also Called: AAA Keystone
1 River Pl (19801-5125)
PHONE.................................302 299-4700
Thomas C Wiedemann, *CEO*
Allen J Dewalle, *Ch of Bd*
Debra Bromson, *Counsel*
Robyn Thompson, *Counsel*
Thomas McManus, *Vice Pres*
EMP: 300
SQ FT: 160,000
SALES (est): 528.9MM **Privately Held**
WEB: www.aaamidatlantic.net
SIC: 4724 6331 6351 6512 Travel agencies; property damage insurance; fire, marine & casualty insurance & carriers; liability insurance; commercial & industrial building operation

(G-8894)
AARON S CHIDEKEL M D
1600 Rockland Rd (19803-3607)
PHONE.................................302 651-6400
Aaron Chidekel, *Chairman*
EMP: 5
SALES (est): 78.5K **Privately Held**
SIC: 8011 Offices & clinics of medical doctors

(G-8895)
AARP
Also Called: AARP Delaware
222 Delaware Ave Ste 1610 (19801-1675)
PHONE.................................202 434-2277
John Barnes, *Exec Dir*
EMP: 10
SALES (corp-wide): 1.6B **Privately Held**
WEB: www.aarppharmacyservices.com
SIC: 8399 Health systems agency
PA: Aarp
601 E St Nw
Washington DC 20049
202 434-2277

(G-8896)
AB CREATIVE PUBLISHING LLC
1104 Philadelphia Pike (19809-2031)
PHONE.................................202 802-6909
EMP: 2
SALES (est): 73.1K **Privately Held**
SIC: 2721 Magazines: publishing & printing

(G-8897)
ABAD & SALAMEDA PA
Also Called: Brandy Bine Medical Associates
1508 Penns Ave Ste 1c (19806-4347)
PHONE.................................302 652-4705
Aileen Abad, *President*
Remedios Abad MD, *Principal*
Lolita Salameda MD, *Principal*
EMP: 6
SALES (est): 301.4K **Privately Held**
SIC: 8011 General & family practice, physician/surgeon

(G-8898)
ABC INC
500 W 2nd St (19801-2312)
PHONE.................................302 429-0189
Johnnie Braxton, *Branch Mgr*
EMP: 4
SALES (corp-wide): 69.5B **Publicly Held**
WEB: www.abc.com
SIC: 4833 Television broadcasting stations
HQ: Abc, Inc.
77 W 66th St Rm 100
New York NY 10023
212 456-7777

(G-8899)
ABC SALES & SERVICE INC
2520 W 6th St (19805-2909)
PHONE.................................302 652-3683
George Skomorucha, *President*
Matthew Skomorucha, *Vice Pres*
Stephen Skomorucha, *Vice Pres*
Bill Davis, *Sales Staff*
Joan Skomorucha, *Admin Sec*
EMP: 21
SALES (est): 3.6MM **Privately Held**
SIC: 5722 7629 5064 Electric household appliances, major; electrical household appliance repair; electrical appliances, major

(G-8900)
ABCWARE LLC
Also Called: Match Software
2207 Concord Pike 816 (19803-2908)
PHONE.................................888 755-1485
Michel Bujardet, *President*
EMP: 1
SALES (est): 70.9K **Privately Held**
SIC: 7372 7389 Application computer software;

(G-8901)
ABEL CENTER FOR OCULOFACIAL
1941 Limestone Rd Ste 201 (19808-5400)
PHONE.................................302 998-3220
ARI Abel, *President*
EMP: 5
SALES (est): 466.6K **Privately Held**
SIC: 8011 Plastic surgeon

(G-8902)
ABHA ARCHITECTS INC
1621 N Lincoln St (19806-2521)
PHONE.................................302 658-6426
Chandra Nilekani, *Vice Pres*
Michael Deptula, *Vice Pres*
Stephanie Forman, *Marketing Mgr*
Sherry Sweetman, *Office Mgr*
Bryan Williams, *Associate*
EMP: 25
SQ FT: 4,000
SALES (est): 3.5MM **Privately Held**
WEB: www.abha.com
SIC: 8712 7389 Architectural engineering; interior design services

(G-8903)
ABIGAIL E MARTIN M D
1600 Rockland Rd (19803-3607)
PHONE.................................302 651-4000
Abigail Martin, *Executive*
EMP: 4
SALES (est): 72.2K **Privately Held**
SIC: 8011 Pediatrician

(G-8904)
ABLE RECYCLING INC
3711 Valley Brook Dr (19808-1342)
PHONE.................................302 324-1760
Betty Davidson, *President*
Laurie Hess, *Vice Pres*
William Davidson, *Treasurer*
Lisa Lewandowski, *Admin Sec*
EMP: 10
SALES (est): 847.5K **Privately Held**
SIC: 4953 Recycling, waste materials

GEOGRAPHIC SECTION

Wilmington - New Castle County (G-8934)

(G-8905)
ABM INDUSTRIES INCORPORATED
2110 Duncan Rd (19808-4602)
PHONE..................302 999-1898
EMP: 47
SALES (corp-wide): 6.5B Publicly Held
SIC: 7349 Janitorial service, contract basis
PA: Abm Industries Incorporated
   1 Liberty Plz Fl 7
   New York NY 10006
   212 297-0200

(G-8906)
ABM JANITORIAL SERVICES INC
2110 Duncan Rd (19808-4602)
PHONE..................302 571-9900
Polly Shweiger, Manager
EMP: 700
SALES (corp-wide): 6.5B Publicly Held
SIC: 7349 7217 Janitorial service, contract basis; carpet & upholstery cleaning
HQ: Abm Janitorial Services, Inc.
   1111 Fannin St Ste 1500
   Houston TX 77002
   866 624-1520

(G-8907)
ABOVE AND BEYOND COVERAGE LLC
3616 Kirkwood Hwy (19808-5124)
PHONE..................201 417-5189
Walter Jarvis,
EMP: 50
SALES (est): 764.1K Privately Held
SIC: 8742 Management consulting services

(G-8908)
ABRAMS & BAYLISS LLP
20 Montchanin Rd Ste 200 (19807-2174)
PHONE..................302 778-1000
Kevin G Abrams, Partner
Thompson Bayliss, Partner
John M Seaman, Partner
EMP: 14
SALES (est): 1.6MM Privately Held
SIC: 8111 Corporate, partnership & business law

(G-8909)
ABSALOM JONES SENIOR CENTER
310 Kiamensi Rd Ste B (19804-2958)
PHONE..................302 998-0363
Joan Budrow, Director
Lynn Balfour, Director
Diana Zanning, Director
EMP: 5
SALES (est): 240K Privately Held
SIC: 8322 Senior citizens' center or association

(G-8910)
AC GROUP INC
Also Called: Accelcomm
3422 Old Capitol Trl # 163 (19808-6124)
PHONE..................201 840-5566
James Kontolios, Partner
EMP: 3
SALES: 500K Privately Held
WEB: www.accelcommgroup.com
SIC: 8711 8748 3679 3825 Electrical or electronic engineering; systems analysis & engineering consulting services; microwave components; digital test equipment, electronic & electrical circuits; microwave test equipment

(G-8911)
ACA MORTGAGE CO INC
3202 Kirkwood Hwy Ste 205 (19808-6154)
PHONE..................302 225-1390
Clare Crossan, President
EMP: 20
SALES (est): 2MM Privately Held
SIC: 6163 Mortgage brokers arranging for loans, using money of others

(G-8912)
ACADEMY BUSINESS MCH & PRTG CO
Also Called: Academy Printing
12 S Maryland Ave (19804-1340)
PHONE..................302 654-3200
Edward Purzycki, President
EMP: 6
SQ FT: 3,000
SALES (est): 846K Privately Held
SIC: 2752 Commercial printing, offset

(G-8913)
ACADIA REALTY TRUST
3001 Brandywine Pkwy (19803-1464)
PHONE..................302 479-5510
John Dowling, Manager
EMP: 4 Publicly Held
WEB: www.acadiarealty.com
SIC: 6798 Real estate investment trusts
PA: Acadia Realty Trust
   411 Theodore Fremd Ave # 30
   Rye NY 10580

(G-8914)
ACCESS VERSALIGN INC (PA)
701 Cornell Dr Ste 13 (19801-5782)
PHONE..................302 225-7800
Marc Greenberg, CEO
EMP: 4
SALES (est): 4.2MM Privately Held
SIC: 5045 7378 7373 Computers, peripherals & software; computer maintenance & repair; computer integrated systems design

(G-8915)
ACCESSQUINT LLC
300 Delaware Ave Ste 200 (19801-6601)
PHONE..................302 351-4064
Veera Sandiparthi,
EMP: 10
SALES (est): 221.8K Privately Held
SIC: 7372 Prepackaged software

(G-8916)
ACCLAIM ACADEMY LLC
1521 Concord Pike Ste 301 (19803-3644)
PHONE..................215 848-7827
Joseph R Martin, CEO
EMP: 25
SALES (est): 687.9K Privately Held
SIC: 8351 Preschool center

(G-8917)
ACCU PERSONNEL INC
1707 Concord Pike (19803-3603)
PHONE..................302 384-8777
EMP: 14
SALES (corp-wide): 13.9MM Privately Held
SIC: 7361 Employment agencies
PA: Accu Personnel Inc.
   911 Kings Hwy N Ste 100
   Cherry Hill NJ 08034
   856 482-2222

(G-8918)
ACCURATE MACHINE INC
Also Called: Accurate Power
304 Falco Dr (19804-2401)
PHONE..................302 992-9606
James M Rowe Jr, President
EMP: 4 EST: 1996
SQ FT: 5,000
SALES: 250K Privately Held
WEB: www.accuratepower.com
SIC: 7539 Machine shop, automotive

(G-8919)
ACE AMERICAN INSURANCE COMPANY
1 Beaver Valley Rd (19803-1115)
PHONE..................302 476-6000
James Duffy, Consultant
Eric Justice, Director
EMP: 13
SALES (corp-wide): 32.7B Privately Held
WEB: www.aceamericaninsurancecompany.com
SIC: 6321 Accident & health insurance
HQ: Ace American Insurance Company
   436 Walnut St
   Philadelphia PA 19106
   215 640-1000

(G-8920)
ACENTIUM INC
251 Little Falls Dr (19808-1674)
PHONE..................617 938-3938
Amine Hamdi, CEO
EMP: 10
SALES (est): 180.6K Privately Held
SIC: 7389 Business services

(G-8921)
ACHIEVE LOGISTIC SYSTEMS
510 A St (19801-5328)
PHONE..................302 654-4701
Darral Mosley, Mng Member
EMP: 4
SALES (est): 130.2K Privately Held
SIC: 4731 4151 Freight transportation arrangement; school buses

(G-8922)
ACI ENERGY INC
1105 N Market St Ste 650 (19801-1216)
PHONE..................302 588-3024
Rob McLeese, President
Willis McLeese, Chairman
Greg Lawyer, Exec VP
Colin T Brown, Admin Sec
EMP: 69
SALES (est): 8.3MM Privately Held
SIC: 4911 Electric services

(G-8923)
ACORN ENERGY INC (PA)
1000 N West St Ste 1200 (19801-1058)
PHONE..................302 656-1708
Jan H Loeb, President
Walter Czarnecki, President
Tracy Clifford, CFO
Mannie Jackson, Bd of Directors
EMP: 2
SALES: 5MM Publicly Held
WEB: www.dssiinc.com
SIC: 7372 8711 3823 Prepackaged software; engineering services; industrial process control instruments

(G-8924)
ACOUSTIC AUDIO TEK LLC
1000 N West St Ste 1200 (19801-1058)
PHONE..................302 685-2113
Ningning Wang, President
EMP: 3 EST: 2014
SALES (est): 242.7K Privately Held
SIC: 3651 Household audio & video equipment

(G-8925)
ACTION AUTOMOTIVE INC
Also Called: Brandywine Auto Parts
2200 Rodman Rd (19805-4132)
PHONE..................302 429-0643
Bruce Hansel, General Mgr
EMP: 5
SALES (corp-wide): 8.4MM Privately Held
SIC: 5013 5531 Automotive supplies & parts; automotive parts
PA: Action Automotive, Inc.
   8 E 9th St
   Chester PA 19013
   610 876-7271

(G-8926)
ACTION ENVIRONMENTAL SERVICE
501 Silverside Rd Ste 114 (19809-1376)
PHONE..................302 798-3100
Charlotte Baldwin, President
William C Baldwin, Manager
EMP: 7
SQ FT: 400
SALES (est): 332.7K Privately Held
SIC: 8748 Environmental consultant

(G-8927)
ACTIVE CRANE RENTALS INC
103 Water St (19804-2492)
PHONE..................302 998-1000
Steven Schmeusser, President
Rebecca Kendall, Vice Pres
Richard Randall, Opers Mgr
Karen Schmeusser, Treasurer
EMP: 20
SQ FT: 5,000
SALES (est): 4.5MM Privately Held
SIC: 7353 Cranes & aerial lift equipment, rental or leasing

(G-8928)
ACTS RTRMNT-LIFE CMMNITIES INC
Also Called: Country House
4830 Kennett Pike (19807-1866)
PHONE..................302 654-5101
Carmen McKim, Marketing Staff
Sarah Jariwala, Office Mgr
Marylou Dellafera, Branch Mgr
Gerry Treese, Food Svc Dir
Jane Rigg, Hlthcr Dir
EMP: 556
SALES (corp-wide): 107MM Privately Held
SIC: 8082 Home health care services
PA: Acts Retirement-Life Communities, Inc.
   375 Morris Rd
   West Point PA 19486
   215 661-8330

(G-8929)
ACUITIVE INC
4001 Kennett Pike Ste 134 (19807-2000)
PHONE..................214 738-1099
Mark Hoover, President
Judith H Boyle, Corp Secy
David E Danielson, Exec VP
John M Jaeger, Exec VP
Thomas C Garland, Vice Pres
EMP: 5
SALES (est): 1.2MM Privately Held
WEB: www.acuitive.com
SIC: 8748 Business consulting

(G-8930)
ACUMEN HEALTH TECHNOLOGIES LLC
2207 Concord Pike 224 (19803-2908)
PHONE..................800 941-0356
Irfan Hisamuddin,
EMP: 10
SALES (est): 487.4K Privately Held
SIC: 7372 Educational computer software

(G-8931)
ACURIO LLC
108 W 13th St (19801)
P.O. Box 175, Jersey City NJ (07303-0175)
PHONE..................201 932-8160
Jason Ritchwood, CEO
EMP: 1
SALES (est): 54.6K Privately Held
SIC: 3724 5072 3069 Lubricating systems, aircraft; nonelectric starters, aircraft; nuts (hardware); rubber hardware

(G-8932)
ADAMLOUIS LTD LIABILITY CO
427 N Tatnall St (19801-2230)
PHONE..................973 937-7524
Adam Marre, CEO
EMP: 4
SALES (est): 213.4K Privately Held
SIC: 8742 Marketing consulting services

(G-8933)
ADAMS AUTO PARTS INC (PA)
1601 Northeast Blvd (19802-5119)
PHONE..................302 655-9693
William King, President
William R King Jr, President
Jeffrey A Adams, Vice Pres
EMP: 15 EST: 1945
SQ FT: 7,100
SALES (est): 4.3MM Privately Held
WEB: www.adamsautoparts.com
SIC: 5013 5531 Automotive supplies & parts; automobile & truck equipment & parts; automotive accessories; automotive parts

(G-8934)
ADAMS BAKERY CORPORATION
2711 Centerville Rd # 400 (19808-1660)
PHONE..................802 863-2696
Andrew Matthews, Principal
EMP: 1 EST: 2005
SALES (est): 66.6K Privately Held
SIC: 2051 Bakery: wholesale or wholesale/retail combined

Wilmington - New Castle County (G-8935)

(G-8935)
ADDITIVE MFG TECH INC
919 N Market St Ste 950 (19801-3036)
PHONE.................540 577-9260
Luis Folgar, *Principal*
EMP: 5
SALES (est): 130.5K **Privately Held**
SIC: 2741

(G-8936)
ADDUS HEALTHCARE INC
3521 Silverside Rd (19810-4900)
PHONE.................302 995-9010
Sheila Zwook, *Manager*
EMP: 6 **Publicly Held**
WEB: www.addus.com
SIC: 8082 Home health care services
HQ: Addus Healthcare, Inc.
2300 Warrenville Rd # 100
Downers Grove IL 60515
630 296-3400

(G-8937)
ADH HOLDINGS LLC
908 E 17th St (19802-5111)
PHONE.................302 482-4138
EMP: 5 EST: 2013
SALES (est): 250K **Privately Held**
SIC: 6719 Holding Company

(G-8938)
ADKINS & ASSOC CPA
Also Called: Adkins & Associates CPA
2615 E Riding Dr (19808-3640)
PHONE.................302 737-2390
Frank Adkins, *Owner*
EMP: 5
SALES (est): 140K **Privately Held**
SIC: 7291 Tax return preparation services

(G-8939)
ADMIRAL WEST INC
Also Called: Admiral Motel
726 Greenwood Rd (19807-2986)
PHONE.................609 729-0031
Margaret C Hill, *President*
EMP: 45
SQ FT: 140,000
SALES (est): 1.2MM **Privately Held**
WEB: www.admiralresort.com
SIC: 7011 Motels

(G-8940)
ADOPTIONS FROM HEART INC
18a Trolley Sq (19806-3334)
PHONE.................302 658-8883
Kimberly Dotts, *Principal*
EMP: 4
SALES (corp-wide): 5.4MM **Privately Held**
WEB: www.adoptionsfromtheheart.org
SIC: 8322 Adoption services
PA: Adoptions From The Heart, Inc.
30 Hampstead Cir Ste 31
Wynnewood PA 19096
610 642-7200

(G-8941)
ADP CAPITAL MANAGEMENT INC
800 Delaware Ave Ste 601 (19801-1365)
PHONE.................302 657-4060
John Daly, *Finance*
EMP: 5
SALES (est): 517.9K
SALES (corp-wide): 14.1B **Publicly Held**
SIC: 6722 Management investment, open-end
PA: Automatic Data Processing, Inc.
1 Adp Blvd Ste 1 # 1
Roseland NJ 07068
973 974-5000

(G-8942)
ADP PACIFIC INC
800 Delaware Ave Ste 601 (19801-1365)
PHONE.................302 657-4060
Carlos A Rodriguez, *CEO*
Steve J Anenen, *President*
Mark D Benjamin, *President*
John C Ayala, *Vice Pres*
Michael A Bonarti, *Vice Pres*
EMP: 6

SALES (est): 342.1K
SALES (corp-wide): 14.1B **Publicly Held**
SIC: 8742 Human resource consulting services
PA: Automatic Data Processing, Inc.
1 Adp Blvd Ste 1 # 1
Roseland NJ 07068
973 974-5000

(G-8943)
ADPESE LLC
3616 Kirkwood Hwy (19808-5124)
PHONE.................302 223-5411
Davida Harris, *CEO*
Allene Harris, *President*
Araina Moon, *Admin Sec*
EMP: 7 EST: 2017
SALES (est): 39.9K **Privately Held**
SIC: 7299 Personal document & information services

(G-8944)
ADVACARE LLC
3601 Old Capitol Trl A5a6 (19808-6042)
PHONE.................302 448-5045
David Botha, *Mng Member*
EMP: 4
SALES (est): 323.2K **Privately Held**
SIC: 2389 5023 Apparel for handicapped; blankets

(G-8945)
ADVANCE CENTRAL SERVICES INC (PA)
1313 N Market St Fl 10 (19801-6107)
PHONE.................302 830-9732
Jeff Hively, *President*
Jeffrey Leyton, *Senior Engr*
Erich Walburn, *CFO*
Peter Barash, *Senior Mgr*
Michael Kelly, *Exec Dir*
EMP: 30
SQ FT: 100,000
SALES (est): 12.4MM **Privately Held**
WEB: www.newspapersupport.com
SIC: 8741 Administrative management

(G-8946)
ADVANCE MAGAZINE PUBLS INC
Also Called: Advance Magazine Group
1201 N Market St Ste 600 (19801-1160)
PHONE.................302 830-4630
Bill Cauffman, *Manager*
Steve Diangelo, *Manager*
Sheryl Jeffries, *Manager*
Nancy Luongo, *Manager*
Gabe Hernandez, *Information Mgr*
EMP: 64
SALES (corp-wide): 5.4B **Privately Held**
WEB: www.condenast.com
SIC: 2721 Magazines: publishing & printing
HQ: Advance Magazine Publishers Inc.
1 World Trade Ctr Fl 43
New York NY 10007
212 286-2860

(G-8947)
ADVANCE MARINE LLC
900 Smiths Bridge Rd (19807-1330)
PHONE.................302 656-2111
Jacob M Dupont, *President*
▲ EMP: 3 EST: 2011
SALES (est): 400K **Privately Held**
SIC: 0919 3531 5084 4491 Whale fishing & whale products; construction machinery; industrial machinery & equipment; marine cargo handling

(G-8948)
ADVANCE NANOTECH INC
1000 N West St Fl 10 (19801-1059)
PHONE.................212 583-0080
Joe Parkinson, *Chairman*
EMP: 2
SALES (est): 104.2K **Privately Held**
SIC: 3825 Instruments to measure electricity

(G-8949)
ADVANCED ANESTHESIOLOGY & PAIN
5307 Limestone Rd Ste 103 (19808-1275)
PHONE.................302 283-3300
Paul Hannan, *Principal*

EMP: 7
SALES (est): 539.6K **Privately Held**
SIC: 8011 Anesthesiologist

(G-8950)
ADVANCED CARE CENTERS DELAWARE
3910 Concord Pike (19803-1716)
PHONE.................302 472-4878
Timothy A Martin, *Principal*
EMP: 5
SALES (est): 94.3K **Privately Held**
SIC: 8351 Child day care services

(G-8951)
ADVANCED CNSTR TECHNIQUES INC (HQ)
Also Called: Advanced Cnstr Techniques
1000 N West St Ste 1200 (19801-1058)
PHONE.................302 295-4868
Douglas Heenan, *President*
Stephen Howe, *Treasurer*
EMP: 85
SALES (est): 10MM
SALES (corp-wide): 9.4MM **Privately Held**
SIC: 1771 Stucco, gunite & grouting contractors; grouting work
PA: Advanced Construction Techniques Ltd
3935 Lloydtown-Aurora Rd
King City ON L7B 0
905 939-7755

(G-8952)
ADVANCED INTERNET SOLUTIONS
14 Ashley Pl (19804-1314)
PHONE.................302 584-4641
Matt Doyle, *President*
EMP: 4
SQ FT: 300
SALES (est): 45.2K **Privately Held**
SIC: 8742 Marketing consulting services

(G-8953)
ADVANCED MATERIALS TECHNOLOGY
3521 Silvr Rd Ste 1k Qui (19810)
PHONE.................302 477-2510
Joseph Destefano, *President*
Joseph Kirkland AB, *Vice Pres*
Timothy Langlois, *Vice Pres*
John P Larmann, *Vice Pres*
Timothy J Langlois Bs, *Vice Pres*
EMP: 5
SQ FT: 2,000
SALES (est): 784.8K **Privately Held**
WEB: www.advanced-materials-tech.com
SIC: 8731 Biotechnical research, commercial

(G-8954)
ADVANCED NETWORKING INC
1316 Philadelphia Pike (19809-1855)
PHONE.................302 442-6199
Richard B Raphael, *President*
Lori A Raphael, *Vice Pres*
Joe Eigenbrot, *Opers Mgr*
Karen Bredbenner, *Technology*
EMP: 12
SQ FT: 1,500
SALES (est): 1.3MM **Privately Held**
WEB: www.advnetwork.com
SIC: 1731 Telephone & telephone equipment installation; computer installation

(G-8955)
ADVANCED RCVABLE SOLUTIONS INC
1300 First State Blvd (19804-3548)
PHONE.................302 225-6001
Jeff Kucharski, *CEO*
Thomas Nusspickle, *Vice Pres*
EMP: 30
SALES (est): 956.7K **Privately Held**
SIC: 7322 Collection agency, except real estate

(G-8956)
ADVANCED SECURITY SYSTEMS INC
1800 Milltown Rd (19808-4012)
PHONE.................302 998-7222
Gary S Ellis, *President*

Deloris M Ellis, *Corp Secy*
Jeffrey U Ellis, *Vice Pres*
EMP: 4 EST: 1978
SALES (est): 588.7K **Privately Held**
SIC: 1731 7382 Fire detection & burglar alarm systems specialization; security systems services

(G-8957)
ADVANCED SURGICAL SPECIALISTS
1401 Foulk Rd Ste 207 (19803-2764)
PHONE.................302 475-4900
Katherine A Sahm, *Principal*
EMP: 6
SALES (est): 443.4K **Privately Held**
SIC: 8011 Surgeon

(G-8958)
ADVANGELISTS LLC
919 N Market St Ste 425 (19801-3014)
PHONE.................734 546-4989
Deepankr Katyal, *Mng Member*
EMP: 1
SALES (corp-wide): 1.4MM **Publicly Held**
SIC: 7336 7372 Creative services to advertisers, except writers; utility computer software
HQ: Advangelists, Llc
61 Broadway Rm 1105
Seattle WA 10006
516 246-9422

(G-8959)
ADVANTAGE DELAWARE LLC
3524 Silverside Rd (19810-4929)
PHONE.................302 479-7764
Susan Barrowman, *Sales Staff*
Stephen Wolf, *Mktg Dir*
EMP: 4
SALES (est): 124.2K **Privately Held**
SIC: 7291 Tax return preparation services

(G-8960)
ADVANTAGE SECURITY INC
802 First State Blvd (19804-3573)
PHONE.................302 652-3060
Carl Ottosen, *Principal*
Joseph Allen, *Principal*
EMP: 10
SALES (est): 247.8K
SALES (corp-wide): 1.4MM **Privately Held**
SIC: 7381 Guard services
PA: Sonitrol Security Of Delaware Valley
802 First State Blvd
Wilmington DE 19804
302 652-3060

(G-8961)
ADVICE WALLET INC
1811 Silverside Rd (19810-4345)
PHONE.................510 280-2475
EMP: 15 EST: 2013
SALES (est): 860K **Privately Held**
SIC: 7372 Prepackaged Software Services

(G-8962)
AECOM TECHNOLOGY CORPORATION
1013 Centre Rd Ste 222 (19805-1273)
PHONE.................302 468-5878
Bruce Kay, *Branch Mgr*
EMP: 35
SALES (corp-wide): 20.1B **Publicly Held**
SIC: 8712 7389 Architectural engineering; building inspection service
PA: Aecom
1999 Avenue Of The Stars # 2600
Los Angeles CA 90067
213 593-8000

(G-8963)
AECOM USA INC
1013 Centre Rd Ste 222 (19805-1273)
PHONE.................302 781-5963
William Marshall, *Manager*
Peggy Pendergast, *Manager*
EMP: 40
SALES (corp-wide): 20.1B **Publicly Held**
SIC: 8748 8711 Business consulting; construction & civil engineering
HQ: Aecom Usa, Inc.
605 3rd Ave
New York NY 10158
212 973-2900

GEOGRAPHIC SECTION   Wilmington - New Castle County (G-8993)

(G-8964)
AEOLUS PHARMACEUTICALS INC (PA)
824 N Market St Ste 1000 (19801-4941)
PHONE..................................949 481-9825
David Cavalier, *Ch of Bd*
John L McManus, *President*
EMP: 4
SALES: 2MM **Publicly Held**
WEB: www.aeoluspharma.com
SIC: 2834 Pharmaceutical preparations

(G-8965)
AERO TAXI INC
1315 Chadwick Rd (19803-4115)
PHONE..................................302 328-3430
Dirk Dinkeloo, *President*
Erin Jacob, *Vice Pres*
EMP: 14 EST: 1960
SALES (est): 1.9MM **Privately Held**
WEB: www.aerotaxi.com
SIC: 4522 Flying charter service

(G-8966)
AESTHTIC PLSTIC SURGERY DEL PA
1600 Penns Ave Ste A (19806-4048)
PHONE..................................302 656-0214
Ian Lonergan, *President*
Dawn Micun, *Manager*
EMP: 10
SALES (est): 1.7MM **Privately Held**
SIC: 8011 Surgeon; plastic surgeon

(G-8967)
AESTHTIC SPECIAL CARE ASSOC PA
Also Called: Nguyen, Keith C/O Aesthetic
2323 Penns Ave Ste Ll (19806-1332)
PHONE..................................302 482-4444
Chane Poum, *Principal*
EMP: 19
SALES (est): 1.6MM **Privately Held**
SIC: 8742 Management consulting services

(G-8968)
AFFILATE MARKS INVESTMENTS INC
3411 Silverside Rd (19810-4812)
PHONE..................................302 478-7451
David Apostiloco, *President*
EMP: 5
SALES (est): 407.1K
SALES (corp-wide): 94.5B **Publicly Held**
SIC: 6794 Patent buying, licensing, leasing
HQ: Comcast Holdings Corporation
    1 Comcast Ctr
    Philadelphia PA 19103
    215 665-1700

(G-8969)
AFFILIATE VENTURE GROUP
2419 Kirkwood Hwy (19805-4906)
PHONE..................................302 379-6961
Cathie Terry, *Principal*
EMP: 2
SALES (est): 107.8K **Privately Held**
SIC: 3944 Banks, toy

(G-8970)
AFFINITY RESEARCH CHEMICALS
406 Meco Dr (19804-1112)
PHONE..................................302 525-4060
Peng WEI, *President*
Yaxi Shen, *Vice Pres*
Peipei LI, *Treasurer*
Yuanyuan Huang, *Admin Sec*
EMP: 4
SQ FT: 3,300
SALES (est): 485K **Privately Held**
SIC: 2819 Industrial inorganic chemicals

(G-8971)
AFFINITY WEALTH MANAGEMENT
2961 Centerville Rd # 310 (19808-1663)
PHONE..................................302 652-6767
Donald Kalil, *President*
James Kalil Jr, *Vice Pres*
James Kalil Sr, *Treasurer*
Michael Sicuranza, *Advisor*
Abigail McCloskey, *Associate*
EMP: 12 EST: 1969
SALES (est): 1.4MM **Privately Held**
WEB: www.affinitywealth.com
SIC: 8741 Financial management for business

(G-8972)
AFGCEAA CORPORATION
1521 Concord Pike Ste 303 (19803-3644)
PHONE..................................617 314-0814
Nnaemeka Osakwe, *President*
Ruby Opara, *Admin Sec*
EMP: 8
SQ FT: 500
SALES (est): 50.2K **Privately Held**
SIC: 8699 Charitable organization

(G-8973)
AFRICAN WOOD INC
Also Called: Afrwood
1201 N Orange St Ste 902 (19801-1177)
PHONE..................................302 884-6738
David Amakobe, *CEO*
EMP: 5
SQ FT: 200
SALES (est): 700.5K **Privately Held**
WEB: www.afrwood.com
SIC: 5149 5159 5211 8748 Coffee & tea; oil nuts, kernels, seeds; peanuts (bulk), unroasted; solar heating equipment; business consulting

(G-8974)
AFRIKELIST CORPORATION
1201 N Orange St Ste 700 (19801-1186)
PHONE..................................800 767-1744
Abdoulaye Sene, *President*
EMP: 12 EST: 2016
SQ FT: 25,000
SALES (est): 500.7K **Privately Held**
SIC: 5015 7371 Automotive supplies, used; computer software systems analysis & design, custom

(G-8975)
AGERA LABORATORIES
2 Mill Rd (19806-2175)
PHONE..................................302 888-1500
David Pernock, *CEO*
EMP: 4
SALES (est): 287.4K **Privately Held**
SIC: 8734 Testing laboratories
PA: Fibrocell Science, Inc.
    405 Eagleview Blvd
    Exton PA 19341

(G-8976)
AGH PARENT LLC
1209 N Orange St (19801-1120)
PHONE..................................919 298-2267
Greg Lindberg, *Manager*
EMP: 5000
SALES (est): 3.9MM **Privately Held**
SIC: 8399 Advocacy group

(G-8977)
AGILE 1
Also Called: Act One
1013 Centre Rd Ste 200 (19805-1265)
PHONE..................................302 791-6900
Jennifer Painter, *Partner*
Evan Oconnor, *Sales Engr*
Sam Barnes, *Manager*
Jenn Blazer, *Manager*
Pamela Caughman, *Manager*
EMP: 12
SALES (est): 1.4MM **Privately Held**
SIC: 8741 Management services

(G-8978)
AGILENT TECHNOLOGIES INC
300 Century Blvd (19808-6270)
PHONE..................................408 345-8886
Linda Johnson, *Branch Mgr*
George Saienni, *Manager*
EMP: 3275
SALES (corp-wide): 5.1B **Publicly Held**
WEB: www.agilent.com
SIC: 3825 Instruments to measure electricity
PA: Agilent Technologies, Inc.
    5301 Stevens Creek Blvd
    Santa Clara CA 95051
    408 345-8886

(G-8979)
AGILENT TECHNOLOGIES INC
2850 Centerville Rd (19808-1610)
PHONE..................................877 424-4536
Jeff Langan, *Principal*
Barbara Sekel, *Vice Pres*
Shridhar Dighe, *Research*
Raj Nath, *VP Bus Dvlpt*
David Steinberg, *Sales Staff*
EMP: 1500
SALES (corp-wide): 5.1B **Publicly Held**
WEB: www.agilent.com
SIC: 3825 Instruments to measure electricity
PA: Agilent Technologies, Inc.
    5301 Stevens Creek Blvd
    Santa Clara CA 95051
    408 345-8886

(G-8980)
AGREE ARLINGTON TX LLC
2801 Centerville Rd # 300 (19808-1609)
PHONE..................................302 683-3008
Dean Williams, *Vice Pres*
EMP: 1
SALES (est): 3.9MM
SALES (corp-wide): 148.2MM **Publicly Held**
SIC: 2221 Broadwoven fabric mills, man-made
PA: Agree Realty Corporation
    70 E Long Lake Rd
    Bloomfield Hills MI 48304
    248 737-4190

(G-8981)
AH (UK) INC (HQ)
1011 Centre Rd Ste 322 (19805-1266)
PHONE..................................302 288-0115
Roger K Newport, *CEO*
Amy K Donacher, *Admin Sec*
EMP: 2
SALES (est): 236.2K **Publicly Held**
SIC: 3312 Sheet or strip, steel, hot-rolled

(G-8982)
AH THERAPY SERVICES LLC
725 Halstead Rd (19803-2227)
PHONE..................................302 379-0528
EMP: 7
SALES (est): 81K **Privately Held**
SIC: 8093 Rehabilitation center, outpatient treatment

(G-8983)
AI DUPONT
2200 Concord Pike (19803-2909)
PHONE..................................302 528-6520
Ai Dupont, *Principal*
EMP: 2
SALES (est): 94.4K **Privately Held**
SIC: 2879 Agricultural chemicals

(G-8984)
AI DUPONT HOSP FOR CHILDREN
1600 Rockland Rd (19803-3607)
PHONE..................................302 651-4620
David Bailey MD, *President*
Steven R Sparks, *Senior VP*
Gina Altieri, *Vice Pres*
R Jay Cummings, *Vice Pres*
Debbie I Chang, *Vice Pres*
EMP: 4000
SALES (est): 32.2MM **Privately Held**
SIC: 8062 General medical & surgical hospitals

(G-8985)
AI ENTERPRISES
234 Philadelphia Pike # 10 (19809-3126)
PHONE..................................302 764-2342
Abraham Ini, *President*
EMP: 4
SALES (est): 320K **Privately Held**
SIC: 6513 6514 6512 Apartment building operators; residential building, four or fewer units: operation; commercial & industrial building operation

(G-8986)
AIDS DELAWARE INC (PA)
100 W 10th St Ste 315 (19801-1642)
PHONE..................................302 652-6776
John Gardner, *Exec Dir*
Elise Mora, *Director*
EMP: 24
SQ FT: 55,000
SALES: 3MM **Privately Held**
SIC: 8322 7389 Aid to families with dependent children (AFDC); outreach program; fund raising organizations

(G-8987)
AIG AIG
3 Beaver Valley Rd (19803-1124)
PHONE..................................302 252-4683
EMP: 5
SALES (est): 194.5K **Privately Held**
SIC: 6411 Insurance Agent/Broker

(G-8988)
AIG FEDERAL SAVINGS BANK
503 Carr Rd 130 (19809-2863)
PHONE..................................302 661-8992
Robert W Pierce, *CEO*
William Hespe, *Ch of Bd*
Robert Rossiter, *COO*
Peter Molendyke, *Senior VP*
Melissa Robins, *Senior VP*
EMP: 34
SQ FT: 5,500
SALES: 5.9MM
SALES (corp-wide): 47.3B **Publicly Held**
WEB: www.aig.com
SIC: 6411 Insurance agents, brokers & service
PA: American International Group, Inc.
    80 Pine St Fl 4
    New York NY 10005
    212 770-7000

(G-8989)
AIM METALS & ALLOYS USA INC (PA)
1209 N Orange St (19801-1120)
PHONE..................................212 450-4519
Elaine Hegler, *Manager*
EMP: 5
SALES (est): 1.4MM **Privately Held**
SIC: 1389 Oil & gas field services

(G-8990)
AIMCO/BETHESDA GP LLC
2711 Centerville Rd (19808-1660)
PHONE..................................303 757-8101
Aimee Reynolds, *Manager*
EMP: 50 EST: 2000
SALES (est): 2.6MM **Publicly Held**
SIC: 6799 Real estate investors, except property operators
HQ: Aimco Properties, L.P.
    4582 S Ulster St Ste 1100
    Denver CO 80237

(G-8991)
AIR INTRNATIONAL US SBUSID INC (PA)
2711 Centerville Rd # 300 (19808-1660)
PHONE..................................248 819-1602
Todd Sheppelman, *President*
Michael Repetto, *Director*
EMP: 90
SALES (est): 10.2MM **Privately Held**
SIC: 3585 Air conditioning, motor vehicle

(G-8992)
AIR LIQUIDE AMERICA LP
Also Called: Air Liquide Medal Div
305 Water St (19804-2410)
PHONE..................................302 225-2132
Michael Bailey, *Manager*
EMP: 7
SALES (corp-wide): 121.9MM **Privately Held**
SIC: 2813 3443 3564 3822 Industrial gases; fabricated plate work (boiler shop); blowers & fans; auto controls regulating residntl & coml environmt & applncs
HQ: Air Liquide America L.P.
    9811 Katy Fwy Ste 100
    Houston TX 77024
    713 624-8000

(G-8993)
AIR LQIDE ADVANCED TECH US LLC
305 Water St (19804-2410)
PHONE..................................302 225-1100
EMP: 24

Wilmington - New Castle County (G-8994)

SALES (corp-wide): 121.9MM **Privately Held**
SIC: **2813** Industrial gases
HQ: Air Liquide Advanced Technologies Us Llc
9807 Katy Fwy
Houston TX 77024

(G-8994)
AIRBNB INC
2711 Centerville Rd (19808-1660)
PHONE..................................415 800-5959
EMP: 7
SALES (corp-wide): 2.5B **Privately Held**
SIC: **7041** Membership-basis organization hotels
PA: Airbnb, Inc.
888 Brannan St
San Francisco CA 94103
415 800-5959

(G-8995)
AIRCRAFT SPECIALTIES
106 Baynard Blvd (19803-4239)
PHONE..................................302 762-0816
George Haak, *Principal*
EMP: 3
SALES (est): 242.5K **Privately Held**
SIC: **3721** Aircraft

(G-8996)
AIRGAS INC
1521 Concord Pike Ste 101 (19803-3614)
PHONE..................................302 575-1822
Boyce Fagioli, *President*
EMP: 5
SALES (corp-wide): 121.9MM **Privately Held**
WEB: www.airgas.com
SIC: **5084** Welding machinery & equipment
HQ: Airgas, Inc.
259 N Radnor Chester Rd # 100
Radnor PA 19087
610 687-5253

(G-8997)
AL JUSANT TRAVEL
1801 W 4th St Frnt Ste (19805-3498)
PHONE..................................302 427-2594
Anil Abraham, *President*
Mark Osborne, *Vice Pres*
EMP: 4
SQ FT: 1,200
SALES (est): 687.2K **Privately Held**
WEB: www.ajtravelinc.com
SIC: **4724** Travel agencies

(G-8998)
ALAN M BILLINGSLEY JR
Also Called: B & B Contracting
2502 Tigani Dr (19808-2519)
PHONE..................................302 998-7907
Alan M Billingsley Jr, *Principal*
EMP: 6
SALES (est): 351.9K **Privately Held**
SIC: **1799** Kitchen & bathroom remodeling

(G-8999)
ALAN R LEVINE DDS
Also Called: Sirkin Levine Dental Assoc
2018 Naamans Rd Ste A2 (19810-2660)
PHONE..................................302 475-3743
Alan R Levine DDS, *Owner*
EMP: 12
SALES (est): 652.5K **Privately Held**
SIC: **8021** Dentists' office

(G-9000)
ALAN WARRINGTON DO
5307 Limestone Rd Ste 202 (19808-1283)
PHONE..................................302 239-9399
Alan Warrington, *Owner*
EMP: 4
SALES (est): 457.7K **Privately Held**
SIC: **8031** Offices & clinics of osteopathic physicians

(G-9001)
ALBAN ASSOCIATES
Also Called: Canby Park Apartments
1600 Bonwood Rd (19805-4634)
P.O. Box 10723 (19850-0723)
PHONE..................................302 656-1827
Paul Boerger, *Owner*
EMP: 7

SALES (est): 378.2K **Privately Held**
SIC: **6513** Apartment building operators

(G-9002)
ALC FUNDING CORPORATION
1403 Foulk Rd Ste 200 (19803-2788)
PHONE..................................302 656-8923
Dale Reid, *Principal*
EMP: 6 **Publicly Held**
WEB: www.alleghenyludlum.com
SIC: **6719** Investment holding companies, except banks
HQ: Ati Operating Holdings, Llc
1000 Six Ppg Pl
Pittsburgh PA 15222
412 394-2800

(G-9003)
ALCATEL-LUCENT USA INC
1415 Foulk Rd Ste 104 (19803-2748)
PHONE..................................302 529-3900
Jeff Sandler, *Regional VP*
EMP: 50
SQ FT: 12,000
SALES (corp-wide): 25B **Privately Held**
WEB: www.lucent.com
SIC: **4813** Voice telephone communications
HQ: Nokia Of America Corporation
600 Mountain Ave Ste 700
New Providence NJ 07974

(G-9004)
ALDER ASSOCIATES LLC
1209 N Orange St (19801-1120)
PHONE..................................360 833-0988
Laura Pedro,
Jackie Eiting,
Jill Irvin,
Maggie Larkin,
Quentin Prideaux,
EMP: 5
SALES: 1.3MM **Privately Held**
SIC: **8742** Training & development consultant

(G-9005)
ALEXIS WIRT
Also Called: Petal Pushers Flowers
610 Harrington St (19805-3723)
PHONE..................................302 654-4236
Alexis Wirt, *Principal*
EMP: 2
SALES (est): 158.7K **Privately Held**
SIC: **3545** Pushers

(G-9006)
ALFA-ORDER LLC
3422 Old Capitol Trl # 1824 (19808-6124)
PHONE..................................302 319-2663
EMP: 1 EST: 2012
SALES (est): 79K **Privately Held**
SIC: **7372** Prepackaged Software Services

(G-9007)
ALFIERI ANTHONY D DO FACC
701 Foulk Rd Ste 2b (19803-3733)
PHONE..................................302 397-8199
Anthony Alfieri, *Principal*
EMP: 4
SALES (est): 108.1K **Privately Held**
SIC: **8031** 8011 Offices & clinics of osteopathic physicians; specialized medical practitioners, except internal

(G-9008)
ALFRED IDPONT HOSP FOR CHLDREN (HQ)
Also Called: A I Dupont Hosp For Children
1600 Rockland Rd (19803-3607)
P.O. Box 269 (19899-0269)
PHONE..................................302 651-4000
Thomas Ferry, *CEO*
Dustin Samples, *Editor*
Stephen T Lawless, *Vice Pres*
William Britton, *CFO*
Stephen Shaffer, *Med Doctor*
EMP: 2568
SALES: 553.2MM
SALES (corp-wide): 1.3B **Privately Held**
WEB: www.kidshealth.org
SIC: **8011** Pediatrician
PA: Nemours Foundation
10140 Centurion Pkwy N
Jacksonville FL 32256
904 697-4100

(G-9009)
ALGORITHM SCIENCES LLC
702 N West St Ste 101 (19801-1524)
PHONE..................................734 904-9491
Matthew Duffy, *Vice Pres*
Jamal Mubarak, *Vice Pres*
Kamal Mubarak MD,
EMP: 4
SQ FT: 50
SALES (est): 180K **Privately Held**
SIC: **8731** Biotechnical research, commercial

(G-9010)
ALIAS INC
913 N Market St (19801-3019)
PHONE..................................302 481-5556
Ali Salazar, *Principal*
EMP: 9
SALES (est): 256.1K **Privately Held**
SIC: **5199** 7389 8611 Gifts & novelties; ; business associations

(G-9011)
ALL AMERICAN TRUCK BROKERS
2205 E Huntington Dr (19808-4952)
PHONE..................................302 654-6101
Joseph B Walther, *President*
William Patterson, *Vice Pres*
EMP: 5
SQ FT: 14,000
SALES: 250K **Privately Held**
SIC: **4212** 5013 7538 Dump truck haulage; truck parts & accessories; general truck repair

(G-9012)
ALL AROUND MOVERZ
314 W 35th St (19802-2639)
PHONE..................................302 494-9925
Diandre Polk, *Principal*
EMP: 6
SALES (est): 360.7K **Privately Held**
SIC: **4789** Cargo loading & unloading services

(G-9013)
ALL DENTURE CENTER
1 Winston Ave (19804-1760)
PHONE..................................302 656-8202
Donald Jones, *President*
EMP: 12
SALES (est): 182.7K **Privately Held**
SIC: **8072** Dental laboratories

(G-9014)
ALL IN ONE TRANSPORTATION LLC
32 Brookside Dr (19894-9000)
PHONE..................................302 482-3222
Anthony Swift, *Mng Member*
EMP: 65
SALES (est): 496.5K **Privately Held**
SIC: **4789** Cargo loading & unloading services

(G-9015)
ALL MY CHILDREN INC
Also Called: All My Children Elsmere
8 Walnut Ave (19805-1144)
PHONE..................................302 995-9191
Nichole Tarentino, *Owner*
EMP: 18
SALES: 100K **Privately Held**
SIC: **8351** Group day care center

(G-9016)
ALL STAR LINEN AND UNIFORM CO
3217 Heathwood Rd (19810-3427)
PHONE..................................302 897-9003
James Giardinelli, *Opers Mgr*
EMP: 9 EST: 2010
SALES (est): 265.8K **Privately Held**
SIC: **7213** Linen supply

(G-9017)
ALLAN C GOLDFEDER DMD
2415 Milltown Rd (19808-3903)
PHONE..................................302 994-1782
Allan C Goldfeder MD, *Owner*
EMP: 8
SALES (est): 359K **Privately Held**
SIC: **8021** Dental clinic

(G-9018)
ALLAN S TOCKER OD
5151 W Woodmill Dr (19808-4067)
PHONE..................................302 995-9060
Allan Tocker, *Principal*
EMP: 4
SALES (est): 244.6K **Privately Held**
SIC: **8042** 5995 Specialized optometrists; optical goods stores

(G-9019)
ALLEN INSURANCE GROUP (PA)
Also Called: Smith & Allen Insurance
410 Delaware Ave (19801-1508)
PHONE..................................302 654-8823
W Bradley Allen, *President*
Jacklyn Allen, *Vice Pres*
John Allen, *Vice Pres*
Barbara Oneal, *Vice Pres*
Chanel Jobes, *Agent*
EMP: 11
SALES (est): 2MM **Privately Held**
WEB: www.alleninsurance.com
SIC: **6411** Insurance agents

(G-9020)
ALLERGY ASSOCIATES PA INC
1400 Philadelphia Pike A6 (19809-1856)
PHONE..................................302 798-8070
Michael Wydila, *President*
EMP: 12
SQ FT: 1,000
SALES (est): 1MM **Privately Held**
SIC: **8011** Allergist

(G-9021)
ALLIED DIAGNSTC PATHOLOGY CONS
Also Called: Pathology Dept
701 N Clayton St (19805-3165)
PHONE..................................302 575-8103
Sophia Kotliar, *Director*
EMP: 4
SALES (est): 445.3K **Privately Held**
WEB: www.allieddiagnostic.com
SIC: **8071** Medical laboratories

(G-9022)
ALLIED ELEC SOLUTIONS LTD
4661 Malden Dr (19803-4817)
PHONE..................................302 893-0257
Edward Shaughnessy, *President*
Donald Todd, *Vice Pres*
EMP: 15
SALES (est): 884.4K **Privately Held**
SIC: **1731** 1711 General electrical contractor; solar energy contractor

(G-9023)
ALLIED LOCK & SAFE COMPANY
709 N Shipley St (19801-1728)
PHONE..................................302 658-3172
Joseph Blansfield, *Partner*
Donna Blansfield, *Partner*
EMP: 8
SQ FT: 6,000
SALES: 800K **Privately Held**
SIC: **5072** 5251 7699 Security devices, locks; door locks & lock sets; locksmith shop

(G-9024)
ALLIEDBARTON SECURITY SVCS LLC
Also Called: Allied Barton Security Svcs
824 N Market St Ste 102 (19801-4937)
PHONE..................................302 498-0450
Gordon Sebree, *Manager*
EMP: 6
SALES (corp-wide): 4.8B **Privately Held**
WEB: www.alliedsg.com
SIC: **7381** Security guard service
HQ: Alliedbarton Security Services Llc
8 Tower Bridge 161 Wshgtn
Conshohocken PA 19428
610 239-1100

(G-9025)
ALLMOND & EASTBURN
Also Called: Allmond, Charles M III
409 Glenside Ave (19803-4325)
PHONE..................................302 764-2193
Thomas Eastburn, *Partner*
EMP: 5

SALES (est): 454.5K **Privately Held**
SIC: **8111** General practice attorney, lawyer

(G-9026)
ALMM VENTURES LLC
Also Called: Alive
117 N Market St Ste 300 (19801-2538)
PHONE..................................302 778-1300
David Atadan, *Mng Member*
EMP: 4 **EST**: 2016
SALES (est): 87.5K **Privately Held**
SIC: **7379** 7311 ; advertising consultant

(G-9027)
ALMOND TOC INC
1209 N Orange St (19801-1120)
PHONE..................................347 756-2318
EMP: 3
SALES (est): 160K **Privately Held**
SIC: **7372** Prepackaged Software Services

(G-9028)
ALOHA MOVERS
4306 Miller Rd (19802-1949)
PHONE..................................302 559-4310
Fadi Takla, *Principal*
EMP: 10
SALES (est): 390.3K **Privately Held**
SIC: **4789** Cargo loading & unloading services

(G-9029)
ALOYSIUS BUTLR CLARK ASSOC INC
Also Called: AB&c
819 N Washington St (19801-1595)
PHONE..................................302 655-1552
Michael Gallagher, *Principal*
Thomas McGivney, *Principal*
Paul Pomeroy, *Principal*
David Brond, *Vice Pres*
John Orr, *Vice Pres*
EMP: 75 **EST**: 1972
SALES (est): 12.3MM **Privately Held**
WEB: www.a-b-c.com
SIC: **7311** 8743 Advertising consultant; public relations services

(G-9030)
ALPHAGRAPHICS FRANCHISING INC
248 Weldin Ridge Rd (19803-3974)
PHONE..................................302 559-8369
EMP: 2
SALES (est): 83.9K **Privately Held**
SIC: **2752** Commercial printing, lithographic

(G-9031)
ALPHASENSE INC
470 Century Blvd (19808-6271)
PHONE..................................302 998-1116
EMP: 4 **EST**: 2009
SALES (est): 323.1K **Privately Held**
SIC: **3674** 3699 Mfg Semiconductors/Related Devices Mfg Electrical Equipment/Supplies

(G-9032)
ALPHASURE TECHNOLOGIES
5909 Old Capitol Trl (19808-4836)
PHONE..................................302 992-0900
Mark Garfinkel, *President*
EMP: 4
SALES (est): 251.1K **Privately Held**
WEB: www.alpha-sure.com
SIC: **4813** Data telephone communications

(G-9033)
ALPINE RAFETTO ORTHODONTICS
4901 Limestone Rd Ste 4 (19808-1271)
PHONE..................................302 239-2304
Vickie Dobroski, *Principal*
EMP: 8
SALES (est): 99K **Privately Held**
SIC: **8021** Orthodontist

(G-9034)
ALTRA CARGO INC
4004 N Market St (19802-2220)
PHONE..................................302 256-0748
Sampson Opoku, *President*
EMP: 4 **EST**: 2014

SALES (est): 200.9K **Privately Held**
SIC: **4789** Cargo loading & unloading services

(G-9035)
ALTSCHULER MICKI DESIGNS
4001 Montchanin Rd (19807-1342)
PHONE..................................302 655-6867
Micki Altschuler, *Owner*
EMP: 1
SALES (est): 81.5K **Privately Held**
SIC: **3961** Costume jewelry, ex. precious metal & semiprecious stones

(G-9036)
ALVATEK ELECTRONICS LLC
1200 Penns Ave Ste 101 (19806-4350)
P.O. Box 7847 (19803-0847)
PHONE..................................302 655-5870
Enrique E Koenig, *CEO*
▲ EMP: 10
SQ FT: 1,600
SALES (est): 1.2MM **Privately Held**
SIC: **5065** Electronic parts

(G-9037)
ALYVANT THERAPEUTICS INC
251 Little Falls Dr (19808-1674)
PHONE..................................646 767-5878
Gillian Cannon, *President*
EMP: 8
SALES (est): 95K **Privately Held**
SIC: **8011** 2834 Offices & clinics of medical doctors; pharmaceutical preparations

(G-9038)
ALZHEIMERS ASSN DEL CHAPTER
2306 Kirkwood Hwy (19805-4927)
PHONE..................................302 633-4420
Edna Ellett, *Director*
EMP: 200
SALES (est): 1.4MM **Privately Held**
SIC: **8322** Individual & family services

(G-9039)
AMER INC
Also Called: Sir Speedy
1010 N Union St Ste D (19805-2731)
PHONE..................................302 654-2498
Dan Nester, *President*
Karen Marshall, *Principal*
Dan Nestor, *VP Opers*
◆ EMP: 7
SQ FT: 5,000
SALES (est): 1MM **Privately Held**
SIC: **2759** 7334 2791 2789 Commercial printing; photocopying & duplicating services; typesetting; bookbinding & related work; commercial printing, offset

(G-9040)
AMER INDUSTRIAL TECH INC
Also Called: A I T
100 Amer Rd Ste 200 (19809-3564)
P.O. Box 293, Yorklyn (19736-0293)
PHONE..................................302 765-3318
Ahmad E Amer, *President*
Ralph Lecky, *Vice Pres*
EMP: 50
SQ FT: 200,000
SALES (est): 10.2MM **Privately Held**
WEB: www.amerindustrial.com
SIC: **3443** Industrial vessels, tanks & containers

(G-9041)
AMERICA GROUP
2036 Foulk Rd Ste 104 (19810-3649)
PHONE..................................302 529-1320
Ken Rudzinski, *Owner*
EMP: 6
SALES (est): 526.9K **Privately Held**
WEB: www.americagroup.com
SIC: **8742** Financial consultant

(G-9042)
AMERICAN BLDRS CONTRS SUP INC
Also Called: ABC Supply 31
1550 First State Blvd (19804-3564)
PHONE..................................302 994-1166
Mike Balay, *Branch Mgr*
EMP: 13

SALES (corp-wide): 3.5B **Privately Held**
WEB: www.abcsupply.com
SIC: **5033** 5031 Roofing, asphalt & sheet metal; siding, except wood; windows
HQ: American Builders & Contractors Supply Co., Inc.
1 Abc Pkwy
Beloit WI 53511
608 362-7777

(G-9043)
AMERICAN CABINETRY LLC
307 Commercial Dr (19805-1906)
PHONE..................................302 655-4064
Jess Rushie, *Mng Member*
EMP: 4
SALES (est): 577.4K **Privately Held**
SIC: **5211** 1799 Cabinets, kitchen; counter top installation

(G-9044)
AMERICAN DOMAIN NAMES LLC
3422 Old Capitol Trl (19808-6124)
PHONE..................................253 785-0332
Christopher Mettin, *Mng Member*
EMP: 12
SALES (est): 619.9K **Privately Held**
SIC: **7375** Information retrieval services

(G-9045)
AMERICAN FRNDS OF THE RYAL SOC
1000 N West St Ste 1200 (19801-1058)
PHONE..................................302 295-4959
EMP: 8
SALES (est): 23.7K **Privately Held**
SIC: **8699** Membership organizations

(G-9046)
AMERICAN GEN LF INSUR CO DEL
Also Called: Aiu North America
503 Carr Rd (19809-2863)
Rural Route 23 7a (19809)
PHONE..................................302 575-5200
James French, *Manager*
EMP: 15
SALES (corp-wide): 47.3B **Publicly Held**
WEB: www.aiglifeinsurancecompany.com
SIC: **6331** Fire, marine & casualty insurance
HQ: American General Life Insurance Company Of Delaware
2727 Allen Pkwy Ste A
Houston TX 77019
713 522-1111

(G-9047)
AMERICAN GENERAL
405 N King St (19801-3700)
PHONE..................................302 575-5200
EMP: 8
SALES (est): 425.9K **Privately Held**
SIC: **6371** Pension/Health/Welfare Fund

(G-9048)
AMERICAN INCOME LIFE INSURANCE
1521 Concord Pike Ste 301 (19803-3644)
PHONE..................................610 277-9499
Matt Malehorn, *Manager*
EMP: 24
SALES (corp-wide): 4.3B **Publicly Held**
SIC: **6311** Life insurance
HQ: American Income Life Insurance Hernandez Agency
3333 N Mayfair Rd Ste 302
Wauwatosa WI 53222
254 741-5701

(G-9049)
AMERICAN INCORPORATORS LTD
Also Called: Registered Agents
1013 Centre Rd Ste 403a (19805-1270)
PHONE..................................302 421-5752
Ann Chilton, *President*
H Murray Sawyer Jr, *Chairman*
Ann G Sawyer, *Admin Sec*
EMP: 15
SALES (est): 1.1MM **Privately Held**
SIC: **8111** Legal services

(G-9050)
AMERICAN INSERT FLANGE CO INC
1603 Jessup St Ste 6 (19802-4255)
P.O. Box 7187 (19803-0187)
PHONE..................................302 777-7464
Bill Yanchulis, *General Mgr*
EMP: 12
SALES (est): 1.6MM **Privately Held**
SIC: **3494** Pipe fittings

(G-9051)
AMERICAN INSTITUTE FOR PUB SVC
Also Called: Jefferson Awards
100 W 10th St Ste 1005 (19801-1652)
PHONE..................................302 622-9101
Sam Beard, *President*
Jayme Mitchell, *Office Mgr*
Heather Tedesco, *Exec Dir*
Jodi Klebick, *Director*
EMP: 8
SALES: 2.8MM **Privately Held**
SIC: **8742** 8322 Incentive or award program consultant; social worker

(G-9052)
AMERICAN KARATE STUDIO
1812 Marsh Rd Ste 421 (19810-4522)
PHONE..................................302 529-7800
Pat Caputo, *Owner*
EMP: 10
SALES (est): 329K **Privately Held**
WEB: www.delawarekarate.com
SIC: **7999** Karate instruction; martial arts school

(G-9053)
AMERICAN LIFE INSURANCE CO (HQ)
Also Called: MetLife
1 Alico Plz (19801-3784)
P.O. Box 2226 (19899-2226)
PHONE..................................302 594-2000
Marlene Debel, *CEO*
Frank Chan, *Vice Pres*
Lisa Lee, *Tax Mgr*
Neil Denton, *Marketing Staff*
Tami Cooper, *Info Tech Dir*
EMP: 100 **EST**: 1921
SALES (est): 382.2MM
SALES (corp-wide): 67.9B **Publicly Held**
WEB: www.alico.com
SIC: **6411** 6321 6324 Insurance agents & brokers; accident & health insurance; group hospitalization plans
PA: Metlife, Inc.
200 Park Ave
New York NY 10166
212 578-9500

(G-9054)
AMERICAN METER HOLDINGS CORP (DH)
1105 N Market St Ste 1300 (19801-1241)
PHONE..................................302 477-0208
Frederick Janssen, *President*
Michael W Cunningham, *CFO*
▲ EMP: 1
SALES (est): 69.3MM
SALES (corp-wide): 41.8B **Publicly Held**
SIC: **3824** 3823 Gas meters, domestic & large capacity; industrial; on-stream gas/liquid analysis instruments, industrial
HQ: Elster Gmbh
SteinernstraBe 19-21
Mainz-Kastel 55252
613 460-50

(G-9055)
AMERICAN SEABOARD EXTERIORS
14 Ashley Pl (19804-1314)
PHONE..................................302 571-9896
Brian Blair, *President*
Michael Gallo, *Partner*
Howard J Cresswell Jr, *Corp Secy*
EMP: 50
SQ FT: 5,000
SALES (est): 6MM **Privately Held**
WEB: www.amsb.net
SIC: **1799** Cleaning building exteriors; caulking (construction); waterproofing

Wilmington - New Castle County (G-9056) GEOGRAPHIC SECTION

(G-9056)
AMERICAN SOC CYTOPATHOLOGY INC
Also Called: A S C
100 W 10th St Ste 605 (19801-6604)
PHONE..................302 543-6583
Andrew Renshaw, *President*
Elizabeth Jenkins, *Exec Dir*
EMP: 5
SALES (est): 1.3MM **Privately Held**
SIC: 8699 Charitable organization

(G-9057)
AMERICAN SPORTS LICENSING (PA)
1011 Centre Rd Ste 310 (19805-1266)
PHONE..................302 288-0122
Michael Hines, *President*
EMP: 86
SALES (est): 1.2MM **Privately Held**
SIC: 7997 Membership sports & recreation clubs

(G-9058)
AMERICAN TIMBER BROKERAGE
Also Called: J&J Quality Wood
1305 N Dupont St B (19806-4093)
PHONE..................302 655-8471
James Winfield, *President*
EMP: 1
SALES (est): 66.2K **Privately Held**
SIC: 2411 Logging camps & contractors

(G-9059)
AMERICAN-AMICABLE HOLDING INC (DH)
1105 N Market St Ste 1300 (19801-1241)
P.O. Box 8985 (19899-8985)
PHONE..................302 427-0355
Charles B Cooper, *President*
EMP: 4
SQ FT: 58,200
SALES (est): 39.2MM
SALES (corp-wide): 5.9B **Privately Held**
SIC: 6311 6321 Life insurance; accident & health insurance
HQ: Ia American Life Insurance Company
425 Austin Ave
Waco TX 76701
480 473-5540

(G-9060)
AMERICAN-EURASIAN EXCH CO LLC
Also Called: Aeec
4023 Kennett Pike 267 (19807-2018)
PHONE..................202 701-4009
Dan Little,
EMP: 5
SALES (est): 186.1K **Privately Held**
SIC: 7389 Personal service agents, brokers & bureaus

(G-9061)
AMERIPRISE FINANCIAL SERVICES
2 Righter Pkwy (19803-1532)
PHONE..................302 476-8000
James Miller, *Manager*
EMP: 4
SALES (est): 151.9K **Privately Held**
SIC: 6282 Investment advice

(G-9062)
AMERIPRISE FINANCIAL SVCS INC
5195 W Woodmill Dr 27 (19808-4067)
PHONE..................302 543-5784
Robert Allen, *Branch Mgr*
EMP: 10
SALES (corp-wide): 12.8B **Publicly Held**
WEB: www.amps.com
SIC: 6282 Investment advice
HQ: Ameriprise Financial Services Inc.
707 2nd Ave S
Minneapolis MN 55402
612 671-2733

(G-9063)
AMERIPRISE FINANCIAL SVCS INC
1805 Foulk Rd Ste A (19810-3700)
PHONE..................302 475-5105
Harry Orth, *Branch Mgr*
William Carter, *Advisor*
Clarence Sabatino, *Advisor*
EMP: 10
SALES (corp-wide): 12.8B **Publicly Held**
SIC: 6282 Investment advice
HQ: Ameriprise Financial Services Inc.
707 2nd Ave S
Minneapolis MN 55402
612 671-2733

(G-9064)
AMERIPRISE FINANCIAL SVCS INC
1011 Centre Rd Ste 100 (19805-1270)
PHONE..................302 468-8200
Jason Salinsky, *Manager*
Michelle Hand, *Advisor*
De Forest Johnson, *Advisor*
Jay Meister, *Advisor*
David Sacker, *Advisor*
EMP: 30
SALES (corp-wide): 12.8B **Publicly Held**
WEB: www.amps.com
SIC: 6282 Investment advisory service
HQ: Ameriprise Financial Services Inc.
707 2nd Ave S
Minneapolis MN 55402
612 671-2733

(G-9065)
AMERIPRISE FINANCIAL SVCS INC
2106 Silverside Rd # 201 (19810-4162)
PHONE..................302 475-2357
James Hayes, *Branch Mgr*
Matthew Boatmon, *Advisor*
EMP: 10
SALES (corp-wide): 12.8B **Publicly Held**
WEB: www.amps.com
SIC: 6282 Investment advisory service
HQ: Ameriprise Financial Services Inc.
707 2nd Ave S
Minneapolis MN 55402
612 671-2733

(G-9066)
AMERIRPISE
1 Righter Pkwy Ste 250 (19803-1555)
PHONE..................302 656-7773
Joseph Amodei, *Principal*
John Garniewski, *Principal*
Terry Pruitt, *Manager*
Andre Duffie, *Advisor*
John Stella, *Advisor*
EMP: 9
SALES (est): 1.2MM **Privately Held**
SIC: 6282 Investment advice

(G-9067)
AMES ENGINEERING CORP
805 E 13th St (19802-5000)
PHONE..................302 658-6945
Steve Ames, *President*
Spencer Beckett, *General Mgr*
Richard Gotwals, *Vice Pres*
EMP: 25
SQ FT: 32,000
SALES (est): 1.6MM **Privately Held**
SIC: 8711 3565 Electrical or electronic engineering; designing; ship, boat, machine & product; packaging machinery

(G-9068)
AMF BOWLING CENTERS INC
3215 Kirkwood Hwy (19808-6129)
PHONE..................302 998-5316
Kevin Sass, *Manager*
EMP: 30
SALES (corp-wide): 342.2MM **Privately Held**
WEB: www.kidsports.org
SIC: 7933 Ten pin center
HQ: Amf Bowling Centers, Inc.
7313 Bell Creek Rd
Mechanicsville VA 23111

(G-9069)
AMICK MART J MD
3105 Limestone Rd Ste 301 (19808-2156)
PHONE..................302 633-1700
Mart J Amick MD, *Owner*
EMP: 12
SALES (est): 239.3K **Privately Held**
SIC: 8011 Pulmonary specialist, physician/surgeon

(G-9070)
AMPCO UES SUB INC
103 Foulk Rd Ste 202 (19803-3742)
PHONE..................302 691-6420
John S Stanik, *CEO*
Rose Hoover, *Vice Pres*
Dee Ann Johnson, *CFO*
EMP: 6
SALES (corp-wide): 419.4MM **Publicly Held**
SIC: 6719 Investment holding companies, except banks
PA: Ampco-Pittsburgh Corporation
726 Bell Ave Ste 301
Carnegie PA 15106
412 456-4400

(G-9071)
AMPLE BUSINESS SOLUTIONS INC
501 Silverside Rd (19809-1374)
PHONE..................302 752-4270
Anil Rajasekhar Chunduru, *Director*
EMP: 22 EST: 2012
SQ FT: 1,000
SALES (est): 1.1MM **Privately Held**
SIC: 7374 Data processing & preparation

(G-9072)
AMY WACHTER MD
3506 Kennett Pike (19807-3019)
PHONE..................302 661-3070
Amy Wachter, *President*
EMP: 4 EST: 2017
SALES (est): 70.6K **Privately Held**
SIC: 8011 Offices & clinics of medical doctors

(G-9073)
ANALYTICAL BIOLOGICAL SVCS INC
Also Called: ABS
701 Cornell Dr Ste 4 (19801-5782)
PHONE..................302 654-4492
Charles Saller, *President*
EMP: 20
SQ FT: 10,000
SALES (est): 4.4MM **Privately Held**
WEB: www.absbio.com
SIC: 2836 8733 Biological products, except diagnostic; medical research

(G-9074)
ANALYTTICA DATALAB INC
1007 N Orange St Fl 4 (19801-1242)
PHONE..................917 300-3325
Rajiv Baphna, *CEO*
Shilpi Jain, *Vice Pres*
Gregory Tylek, *Accountant*
Cindy Ellers, *Manager*
Rupal Baphna,
EMP: 45 EST: 2014
SALES: 1MM **Privately Held**
SIC: 7374 Data processing & preparation

(G-9075)
ANCAR ENTERPRISES LLC (PA)
Also Called: AlphaGraphics
3411 Silverside Rd 103 (19810-4812)
PHONE..................302 477-1884
Atul Chugh, *President*
EMP: 3
SALES (est): 1.2MM **Privately Held**
SIC: 2752 2754 Commercial printing, lithographic; offset & photolithographic printing; labels: gravure printing

(G-9076)
ANCHOR APP INC
222 Delaware Ave Ste 1200 (19801-1611)
PHONE..................302 421-6890
Elias Jureidini, *CEO*
EMP: 1
SQ FT: 150

SALES (est): 67K **Privately Held**
SIC: 7372 Application computer software

(G-9077)
ANDERSEN FORD ARCHITECTS LLC
611 Haverhill Rd (19803-2402)
PHONE..................302 388-7862
EMP: 4
SALES (est): 215.7K **Privately Held**
SIC: 8712 Architectural engineering

(G-9078)
ANDERSON GROUP INC
3411 Silverside Rd # 103 (19810-4812)
PHONE..................302 478-6160
Herbert F Gerhard, *President*
Mark F Fornari, *Treasurer*
Howard L Nelson, *Treasurer*
George P Warren Jr, *Admin Sec*
◆ **EMP:** 3
SALES (est): 277.2MM
SALES (corp-wide): 3.6B **Publicly Held**
SIC: 5047 5063 5099 7699 Industrial safety devices: first aid kits & masks; electrical apparatus & equipment; lifesaving & survival equipment (non-medical); hydraulic equipment repair; cylinders, pressure: metal plate
HQ: Charter Consolidated Limited
322 High Holborn
London

(G-9079)
ANDREW J GLICK MD
2000 Foulk Rd Ste F (19810-3642)
PHONE..................302 652-8990
Andrew Glick MD, *Partner*
Dr Bruce Benge, *Partner*
Michael Lovis, *Partner*
EMP: 20
SALES (est): 592K **Privately Held**
SIC: 8011 Urologist

(G-9080)
ANDREW SIMOFF HORSE TRNSP
3719 Old Capitol Trl (19808-6001)
PHONE..................302 994-1433
Andrew Simoff, *President*
EMP: 5
SQ FT: 1,500
SALES: 500K **Privately Held**
SIC: 4212 Animal transport

(G-9081)
ANDREW W DONOHUE D O
34 Harlech Dr (19807-2508)
PHONE..................302 999-7386
Andrew W Donohue, *Principal*
EMP: 4
SALES (est): 157K **Privately Held**
SIC: 8031 Offices & clinics of osteopathic physicians

(G-9082)
ANDREW WEINSTEIN MD INC
Also Called: Asthma Allergy Care Delaware
111 Walnut Ridge Rd (19807-1635)
PHONE..................302 428-1675
Andrew G Weinstein, *President*
EMP: 7
SALES (est): 259K **Privately Held**
SIC: 8011 General & family practice, physician/surgeon

(G-9083)
ANGEE INC (PA)
1201 N Orange St Ste 7419 (19801-1286)
PHONE..................650 320-1775
Maxwell Rattmer, *Vice Pres*
EMP: 20
SALES (est): 777.3K **Privately Held**
SIC: 7371 Computer software development & applications

(G-9084)
ANGELA SALDARRIAGA
5578 Kirkwood Hwy (19808-5002)
PHONE..................302 633-1182
Angela Saldarriaga, *Owner*
EMP: 7
SALES (est): 592.1K **Privately Held**
SIC: 8011 Offices & clinics of medical doctors

GEOGRAPHIC SECTION
Wilmington - New Castle County (G-9117)

(G-9085)
ANGELS VISITING
3101 Limestone Rd Ste E (19808-2148)
PHONE................................302 691-8700
Justin Smith, *Manager*
EMP: 6
SALES (est): 90K **Privately Held**
SIC: 8082 Home health care services

(G-9086)
ANNA MARIE MAZOCH DDS PA
2601 Annand Dr Ste 18 (19808-3719)
PHONE................................302 998-9594
Anna Marie Mazoch, *Principal*
EMP: 5 EST: 2008
SALES (est): 298.4K **Privately Held**
SIC: 8021 Dentists' office

(G-9087)
ANNEXUS HEALTH LLC
1105 N Market St Fl 11 (19801-1216)
PHONE................................302 547-4154
Dominick Joseph Baffone III,
Bradley Frazier,
EMP: 14
SALES (est): 283.5K **Privately Held**
SIC: 7371 Computer software development & applications

(G-9088)
ANNIEMAC HOME MORTGAGE LLC
4839 Limestone Rd (19808-1902)
PHONE................................302 234-2956
Vincent Ingui, *President*
EMP: 25
SALES (corp-wide): 26.5MM **Privately Held**
SIC: 6162 Mortgage bankers
PA: Anniemac Home Mortgage Llc
     700 E Gate Dr Ste 400
     Mount Laurel NJ 08054
     856 252-1506

(G-9089)
ANQ LLC
3422 Old Capitol Trl # 510 (19808-6124)
PHONE................................408 837-3678
EMP: 4
SALES: 600K **Privately Held**
SIC: 8742 Management consulting services

(G-9090)
ANTHONY A VASILE DO
700 W Lea Blvd Ste 301 (19802-2546)
PHONE................................302 764-2072
Anthony Vasile Do, *Owner*
EMP: 5
SALES (est): 387.6K **Privately Held**
SIC: 8031 Offices & clinics of osteopathic physicians

(G-9091)
ANVIL ENTERPRISES LLC
300 Delaware Ave Ste 210a (19801-6601)
PHONE................................323 230-9376
Marc Kamyab, *CEO*
EMP: 2
SALES (est): 56.5K **Privately Held**
SIC: 7372 Application computer software

(G-9092)
ANYTIME FITNESS
1851 Marsh Rd (19810-4505)
PHONE................................302 475-2404
Valesta Tejan-Kamara, *Owner*
EMP: 7
SALES (est): 210.1K **Privately Held**
SIC: 7991 Physical fitness clubs with training equipment

(G-9093)
ANZILOTTI ORTHODONTICS
203 Montchanin Rd (19807-2101)
PHONE................................302 750-0117
EMP: 4
SALES (est): 112.7K **Privately Held**
SIC: 8021 Orthodontist

(G-9094)
APARTMENT COMMUNITIES CORP
Also Called: Town Court Apartments
402 Foulk Rd Apt 1a9 (19803-3813)
P.O. Box 7189 (19803-0189)
PHONE................................302 656-7781
Frank E Acierno, *President*
Patty Fredricks, *General Mgr*
EMP: 80
SALES (est): 3.8MM **Privately Held**
SIC: 6513 8741 Apartment hotel operation; management services

(G-9095)
APEX ENGINEERING INC
27 W Market St (19804-3138)
PHONE................................302 994-1900
Stephen Davies, *President*
Jim Chandler, *Vice Pres*
Meredith Wickersham, *Design Engr*
Stephen Woodin, *Design Engr*
Cindy Depace, *Executive Asst*
EMP: 12
SALES (est): 1.5MM **Privately Held**
WEB: www.apexengineeringinc.com
SIC: 8711 Civil engineering

(G-9096)
APEX PIPING SYSTEMS INC
Also Called: N. Barton Sheet Metal & Hvac
3629 Old Capitol Trl (19808-6025)
PHONE................................302 998-5272
Jim Schneckenburger, *Manager*
EMP: 24
SALES (corp-wide): 19.4MM **Privately Held**
SIC: 1761 Roofing contractor; sheet metalwork; siding contractor
PA: Apex Piping Systems, Inc.
     302 Falco Dr
     Wilmington DE 19804
     302 995-6136

(G-9097)
APEX PIPING SYSTEMS INC (PA)
302 Falco Dr (19804-2401)
PHONE................................302 995-6136
Pat Oakes, *President*
Kirk Gerhart, *General Mgr*
Patrick Oakes, *General Mgr*
Francis Winnington, *General Mgr*
Steve Onley, *Vice Pres*
EMP: 81
SQ FT: 35,000
SALES (est): 19.4MM **Privately Held**
WEB: www.apexpiping.com
SIC: 3498 3443 3317 3312 Piping systems for pulp paper & chemical industries; coils, pipe: fabricated from purchased pipe; process vessels, industrial: metal plate; welded pipe & tubes; pipes & tubes

(G-9098)
APP PROS LLC
2404 Jacqueline Dr Apt A9 (19810-2006)
PHONE................................646 441-0788
Huzaifa Kapadia, *Principal*
EMP: 2
SALES (est): 77.5K **Privately Held**
SIC: 7372 Prepackaged software

(G-9099)
APPLIED BANK
2200 Concord Pike (19803-2909)
PHONE................................302 326-4200
Rocco A Abessinio, *President*
EMP: 18 **Privately Held**
SIC: 6021 National commercial banks
PA: Applied Bank
     2200 Concord Pike Ste 102
     Wilmington DE 19803

(G-9100)
APPLIED BANK (PA)
2200 Concord Pike Ste 102 (19803-2909)
P.O. Box P.O. Box 15060 (19885-0001)
PHONE................................302 326-4200
Rocco Abessinio, *President*
Carl Kruelle, *Senior VP*
Robert J Smith, *Vice Pres*
James Dougherty, *Executive*
Diane Witiak, *Admin Sec*
EMP: 20
SQ FT: 10,000
SALES: 11.3MM **Privately Held**
WEB: www.appliedbank.com
SIC: 6021 National commercial banks

(G-9101)
APPLIED CARD HOLDINGS INC
601 Delaware Ave Ste 100 (19801-1463)
P.O. Box 17125 (19850-7125)
PHONE................................302 326-4200
Rocco A Abessinio, *Ch of Bd*
EMP: 7
SALES (est): 910.8K **Privately Held**
SIC: 7389 Credit card service

(G-9102)
APPLIED DIAMOND INC
3825 Lancaster Pike # 200 (19805-1559)
PHONE................................302 999-1132
Joseph W Tabeling, *President*
EMP: 1
SALES (est): 150K **Privately Held**
WEB: www.usapplieddiamond.com
SIC: 3545 Diamond cutting tools for turning, boring, burnishing, etc.

(G-9103)
APPMOTION INC
1000 N West St Ste 1200 (19801-1058)
PHONE................................347 513-6333
Mhd-Ammar Aboulnasr, *Director*
EMP: 3 EST: 2014
SQ FT: 100
SALES (est): 145.5K **Privately Held**
SIC: 7372 Publishers' computer software

(G-9104)
APPRAISAL ASSOCIATES INC
2101 N Tatnall St (19802-4109)
PHONE................................302 652-0710
Robert H Mc Kennon, *President*
EMP: 4
SQ FT: 1,700
SALES (est): 270K **Privately Held**
SIC: 6531 Appraiser, real estate

(G-9105)
APTUSTECH LLC
1209 Ornge St Corp Tr Ctr (19801)
PHONE................................347 254-5619
Asher Baum, *CEO*
EMP: 3
SALES (est): 250K **Privately Held**
SIC: 2323 7389 Men's & boys' neckwear;

(G-9106)
AQUATIC MANAGEMENT
4905 Mermaid Blvd (19808-1004)
PHONE................................302 235-1818
Michael Ramon, *Owner*
EMP: 5
SALES (est): 429.3K **Privately Held**
SIC: 8741 Business management

(G-9107)
AQUILA OF DELAWARE INC (PA)
1812 Newport Gap Pike (19808-6179)
PHONE................................302 999-1106
Joan Chatterton, *President*
Mandell Much, *Director*
Lauren Rhoades, *Director*
EMP: 15
SALES (est): 3MM **Privately Held**
SIC: 8748 Business consulting

(G-9108)
AQUION INC
2711 Centerville Rd Ste 4 (19808-1660)
PHONE................................847 725-3000
Michael Madsen, *President*
EMP: 2 EST: 2005
SALES (est): 123.3K **Privately Held**
SIC: 3589 Water treatment equipment, industrial

(G-9109)
ARA TECHNOLOGIES INC
7703 Pleasant Ct (19802-1775)
PHONE................................215 605-5707
Aaron Astillero, *President*
EMP: 4 EST: 2002
SALES (est): 252K **Privately Held**
SIC: 8711 7371 Consulting engineer; computer software development

(G-9110)
ARACENT HEALTHCARE LLC
3411 Silve Road Bayna Bui (19810)
PHONE................................302 478-8865
Bill Skinner, *General Mgr*
Tom Ritchie, *CFO*
Allan Sawyer,
Thomas Ritchie,
EMP: 6
SQ FT: 2,000
SALES (est): 950.4K **Privately Held**
WEB: www.aracent.com
SIC: 5047 Medical & hospital equipment
PA: Ritchie Sawyer Corporation
     2502 Pin Oak Dr
     Wilmington DE 19810

(G-9111)
ARANGODB INC
251 Little Falls Dr (19808-1674)
PHONE................................415 659-5938
Claudius Weinberger, *Principal*
Frank Celler, *Principal*
Lars Fink, *Principal*
Donlad Reinke, *Principal*
Andreas Weinberger, *Principal*
EMP: 6
SALES (est): 155.3K **Privately Held**
SIC: 7389

(G-9112)
ARBOR MANAGEMENT LLC
4 Denny Rd Ste 1 (19809-3445)
PHONE................................302 764-6450
Kevin P Kelly, *President*
David Curtis, *President*
EMP: 170
SALES (est): 12.1MM **Privately Held**
SIC: 6531 Real estate managers

(G-9113)
ARC A RESOURCE CTR FOR YOUTH
2005 Baynard Blvd (19802-3917)
PHONE................................302 658-6134
Stella Guest, *Manager*
EMP: 4
SALES (est): 144.6K **Privately Held**
SIC: 8322 Individual & family services

(G-9114)
ARC DOCUMENT SOLUTIONS INC
110 S Poplar St (19801-5050)
PHONE................................302 654-2365
Fax: 302 655-2970
EMP: 24
SALES (corp-wide): 423.7MM **Publicly Held**
SIC: 7334 Photocopying Services
PA: Arc Document Solutions, Inc.
     1981 N Broadway Ste 385
     Walnut Creek CA 94583
     925 949-5100

(G-9115)
ARC FINANCE LTD
251 Little Falls Dr (19808-1674)
PHONE................................914 478-3851
Nicola Armacost, *Exec Dir*
EMP: 5
SALES (est): 89.3K **Privately Held**
SIC: 8399 Social services

(G-9116)
ARC HUD I INC
2 S Augustine St (19804-2504)
PHONE................................302 996-9400
Vanessa Corbin, *Accounting Mgr*
Patricia Kelleher, *Administration*
EMP: 7
SALES (est): 203.1K **Privately Held**
SIC: 8748 Urban planning & consulting services

(G-9117)
ARC HUD VII INC
2 S Augustine St (19804-2504)
PHONE................................302 996-9400
Terry Olson, *Principal*
Vanessa Corbin, *Manager*
EMP: 7
SALES (est): 144.1K **Privately Held**
SIC: 8748 City planning

Wilmington - New Castle County (G-9118) GEOGRAPHIC SECTION

(G-9118)
ARC OF DELAWARE
2 S Augustine St Ste B (19804-2504)
PHONE....................302 996-9400
John Dimeglio, *Controller*
Terry Olson, *Exec Dir*
Judy Govatos, *Exec Dir*
Susannah Eaton-Ryan, *Director*
Steven Knox, *Director*
EMP: 20
SALES: 509.2K **Privately Held**
SIC: 8322 Social services for the handicapped; family service agency

(G-9119)
ARC OFFSHORE INVESTMENTS INC
3511 Silverside Rd # 105 (19810-4902)
PHONE....................561 670-9938
Lawrence Pirritino, *Principal*
EMP: 2
SALES (est): 65.5K **Privately Held**
SIC: 1389 Oil consultants

(G-9120)
ARCADIS US INC
824 N Market St Ste 820 (19801-4939)
PHONE....................302 658-1718
Robert Daoust, *Manager*
EMP: 25
SALES (corp-wide): 6.4MM **Privately Held**
WEB: www.pirnie.com
SIC: 8711 Consulting engineer
HQ: Arcadis U.S., Inc.
   630 Plaza Dr Sté 200
   Highlands Ranch CO 80129
   720 344-3500

(G-9121)
ARCANGEL INC
Also Called: Catherine Deane
1013 Centre Rd Ste 403 (19805-1270)
PHONE....................347 771-0789
Catherine Deane, *CEO*
EMP: 2
SALES: 1MM **Privately Held**
SIC: 2335 Wedding gowns & dresses
HQ: Atelier Arcangel Limited
   1st Floor
   London
   207 680-9716

(G-9122)
ARCHER & GREINER PC
300 Delaware Ave Ste 1100 (19801-1670)
PHONE....................302 777-4350
L Peter, *Principal*
EMP: 5
SALES (est): 429.2K
SALES (corp-wide): 57.5MM **Privately Held**
SIC: 8111 General practice law office
PA: Archer & Greiner, P.C.
   33 E Euclid Ave
   Haddonfield NJ 08033
   856 795-2121

(G-9123)
ARCHITECT ENGINEER INS CO RISK
Also Called: Architects Engineers Loss Ctrl
4001 Kennett Pike Ste 318 (19807-2039)
PHONE....................302 658-2342
Harold A Dombeck, *President*
George X Cannon, *President*
John J Gain, *Principal*
Jason Peterson, *Principal*
Mitch Sellett, *Vice Pres*
EMP: 7
SQ FT: 1,800
SALES (est): 365K **Privately Held**
SIC: 6321 Reinsurance carriers, accident & health

(G-9124)
ARCHITECTURE PLUS PA
234 N James St (19804-3132)
PHONE....................302 999-1614
Mark Hitchcock, *President*
EMP: 6
SALES (est): 480K **Privately Held**
SIC: 8712 Architectural services

(G-9125)
ARCPOINT LABS
222 Philadelphia Pike # 5 (19809-3166)
P.O. Box 9534 (19809-0534)
PHONE....................302 268-6560
EMP: 4
SALES (est): 144.1K **Privately Held**
SIC: 8071 Medical laboratories

(G-9126)
AREX HOLDING INC
501 Silverside Rd Ste 105 (19809-1376)
PHONE....................646 216-2091
EMP: 1
SALES (est): 95.9K **Privately Held**
SIC: 3621 Mfg Motors/Generators

(G-9127)
ARHC MCNWDNY01 LLC
2711 Centerville Rd # 400 (19808-1660)
PHONE....................518 213-1000
EMP: 20
SALES (est): 750K **Privately Held**
SIC: 6531 Fiduciary, real estate

(G-9128)
ARIES SECURITY LLC
1226 N King St (19801-3232)
PHONE....................302 365-0026
Brian Markus, *CEO*
Orv Varner, *CFO*
Susan Markus, *Office Mgr*
Joseph Mlodzianowski, *Office Mgr*
EMP: 6 **EST:** 2008
SALES: 1.2MM **Privately Held**
SIC: 5045 8711 8731 7371 Computers, peripherals & software; consulting engineer; computer (hardware) development; computer software systems analysis & design, custom

(G-9129)
ARINC CTRL & INFO SYSTEMS LLC (PA)
1209 N Orange St (19801-1120)
PHONE....................302 658-7581
Robert Bowen,
EMP: 4
SALES (est): 971.5K **Privately Held**
SIC: 4899 Data communication services

(G-9130)
ARM CHAIR SCOUTS LLC
427 N Tatnall St 24852 (19801-2230)
PHONE....................315 360-8692
Aaron Sanford, *President*
EMP: 10
SALES (est): 215.3K **Privately Held**
SIC: 8742 Management consulting services

(G-9131)
ARMAND DE MD SANCTIC
2101 Foulk Rd (19810-4710)
PHONE....................302 475-2535
Armand De Sanctic MD, *Owner*
EMP: 10
SALES (est): 326.5K **Privately Held**
SIC: 8011 Offices & clinics of medical doctors

(G-9132)
ARMINIO JOSEPH A MD & ASSOC PA
Also Called: Warsal, Nabil F MD
1701 Augustine Cut Off (19803-4415)
PHONE....................302 654-6245
Dr Joseph A Arminio, *President*
Nabil F Warsal MD, *Owner*
Dr Augusto Amurao, *Corp Secy*
Dr Nabil Warsol, *Vice Pres*
EMP: 12
SQ FT: 2,000
SALES (est): 939.2K **Privately Held**
SIC: 8011 Surgeon

(G-9133)
ARMSTRONG CORK FINANCE LLC (HQ)
818 N Washington St (19801-1510)
PHONE....................302 652-1520
George A Lorch, *President*
William J Wimer, *Exec VP*
Louis L Davenport, *Vice Pres*
Robert A Sills, *Vice Pres*
EMP: 4
SALES (est): 11.9MM
SALES (corp-wide): 975.3MM **Publicly Held**
SIC: 6153 Short-term business credit
PA: Armstrong World Industries, Inc.
   2500 Columbia Ave
   Lancaster PA 17603
   717 397-0611

(G-9134)
ARRIM LLC (PA)
919 N Market St Ste 950 (19801-3036)
PHONE....................617 697-7914
Xingjie Zhu,
EMP: 2 **EST:** 2018
SALES: 10K **Privately Held**
SIC: 3829 7389 Measuring & controlling devices;

(G-9135)
ART FLOOR INC
9 Jefferson Ave (19805-1322)
P.O. Box 1299, Hockessin (19707-5299)
PHONE....................302 636-9201
William Bartoshesky, *President*
Cynthia Bartoshesky, *Vice Pres*
EMP: 38
SALES (est): 7.7MM **Privately Held**
WEB: www.artfloorinc.com
SIC: 5023 5713 Floor coverings; floor covering stores

(G-9136)
ARTEAGA PROPERTIES LLC
2711 Centerville Rd # 200 (19808-1660)
PHONE....................808 339-6906
Frank Artega,
EMP: 5 **EST:** 2016
SQ FT: 5,000
SALES: 9MM **Privately Held**
SIC: 7699 5088 Aircraft & heavy equipment repair services; aircraft engines & engine parts

(G-9137)
ARTEVET LLC
1000 N West St Ste 1200 (19801-1058)
PHONE....................443 255-0016
Aniket Parikh, *Mng Member*
EMP: 25
SALES (est): 79.7K **Privately Held**
SIC: 2836 Veterinary biological products

(G-9138)
ARTICLE 19 INC
1000 N West St Ste 1200 (19801-1058)
PHONE....................302 295-4959
John M Barker, *Exec Dir*
EMP: 5
SALES: 734.9K **Privately Held**
SIC: 8399 Social services

(G-9139)
ARTISANS BANK INC
223 W 9th St (19801-1631)
PHONE....................302 656-8188
Katie Wroten, *COO*
EMP: 7
SALES (corp-wide): 22.8MM **Privately Held**
SIC: 6036 State savings banks, not federally chartered
PA: Artisans Bank Inc
   2961 Centerville Rd # 101
   Wilmington DE 19808
   302 658-6881

(G-9140)
ARTISANS BANK INC (PA)
2961 Centerville Rd # 101 (19808-1672)
PHONE....................302 658-6881
Stephen C Nelson, *President*
Mark E Huntley, *President*
Charles Brown, *Senior VP*
James Flanders, *Senior VP*
Michele Speary, *Vice Pres*
EMP: 100
SQ FT: 15,000
SALES: 22.8MM **Privately Held**
WEB: www.artisansbank.com
SIC: 6036 State savings banks, not federally chartered

(G-9141)
ARTISANS BANK INC
3631 Silverside Rd (19810-5101)
PHONE....................302 479-2553
Janice Zebley, *Manager*
EMP: 6
SALES (corp-wide): 22.8MM **Privately Held**
WEB: www.artisansbank.com
SIC: 6036 State savings banks, not federally chartered
PA: Artisans Bank Inc
   2961 Centerville Rd # 101
   Wilmington DE 19808
   302 658-6881

(G-9142)
ARTISANS BANK INC
1706 Marsh Rd (19810-4606)
PHONE....................302 479-2550
Florence Miller, *Manager*
EMP: 5
SALES (corp-wide): 22.8MM **Privately Held**
WEB: www.artisansbank.com
SIC: 6036 State savings banks, not federally chartered
PA: Artisans Bank Inc
   2961 Centerville Rd # 101
   Wilmington DE 19808
   302 658-6881

(G-9143)
ARTISANS BANK INC
Also Called: Artisans Wilmington Bank
4901 Kirkwood Hwy (19808-5011)
PHONE....................302 993-8220
Maira Carillo, *Manager*
EMP: 8
SALES (corp-wide): 22.8MM **Privately Held**
WEB: www.artisansbank.com
SIC: 6036 State savings banks, not federally chartered
PA: Artisans Bank Inc
   2961 Centerville Rd # 101
   Wilmington DE 19808
   302 658-6881

(G-9144)
ARTISANS BANK INC
4551 New Linden Hill Rd (19808)
PHONE....................302 738-3744
Ken Beaudean, *Manager*
EMP: 7
SALES (corp-wide): 22.8MM **Privately Held**
WEB: www.artisansbank.com
SIC: 6036 8231 6029 State savings banks, not federally chartered; libraries; commercial banks
PA: Artisans Bank Inc
   2961 Centerville Rd # 101
   Wilmington DE 19808
   302 658-6881

(G-9145)
ARUGIE ENTERPRISES CORP
Also Called: Arg Communications
612 S Colonial Ave Ste A (19805-1956)
PHONE....................302 225-2000
Joseph Ruggieri, *President*
Angel Jernoska, *Principal*
EMP: 7
SALES (est): 590K **Privately Held**
SIC: 1731 Electrical work

(G-9146)
ASBURY CARBONS INC
103 Foulk Rd Ste 202 (19803-3742)
PHONE....................302 652-0266
Michael Ball, *Branch Mgr*
EMP: 2
SALES (corp-wide): 126.7MM **Privately Held**
SIC: 1499 Gemstone & industrial diamond mining
PA: Asbury Carbons, Inc.
   405 Old Main St
   Asbury NJ 08802
   908 537-2155

(G-9147)
ASFERIK LLC
717 W Oakmeade Dr (19810-1455)
PHONE....................302 981-6519

GEOGRAPHIC SECTION
Wilmington - New Castle County (G-9175)

EMP: 2
SALES (est): 88.5K Privately Held
SIC: 3949 Sporting & athletic goods

(G-9148)
ASHBY & GEDDES
500 Delaware Ave Ste 8 (19801-7400)
P.O. Box 1150 (19899-1150)
PHONE.................................302 654-1888
James Mc C Geddes, *President*
Tiffany Lydon, *Research*
Steven Balick, *Director*
Richard Heins, *Director*
F Mickler, *Director*
EMP: 40
SALES (est): 5.5MM Privately Held
WEB: www.ashby-geddes.com
SIC: 8111 General practice attorney, lawyer

(G-9149)
ASHFORD CAPITAL MANAGEMENT
1 Walkers Mill Rd (19807-2134)
P.O. Box 4172 (19807-0172)
PHONE.................................302 655-1750
Theodore H Ashford, *President*
Gregory Falcon, *Vice Pres*
Anthony Petrucci, *CFO*
Jeff Rollins, *Sr Invest Ofcr*
Cliff J Short, *Sr Invest Ofcr*
EMP: 10
SALES (est): 2.8MM Privately Held
SIC: 6282 Investment advisory service

(G-9150)
ASHLAND LLC
Also Called: Ashland Credit Union
500 Hercules Rd (19808-1513)
PHONE.................................302 995-4180
Logan Sturgill, *Marketing Mgr*
John Hoffman, *Manager*
Sharonann Steward, *Manager*
Ricardo De Genova, *Director*
EMP: 32
SALES (corp-wide): 2.4B Publicly Held
SIC: 5169 Chemicals & allied products
HQ: Ashland Llc
  50 E Rivercenter Blvd # 1600
  Covington KY 41011
  859 815-3333

(G-9151)
ASHLAND LLC
Ashlands Aqualon
1313 N Market St Fl 8 (19801-6107)
PHONE.................................302 594-5000
Vera Holmes, *Counsel*
Roger Willstein, *Manager*
EMP: 25
SALES (corp-wide): 2.4B Publicly Held
SIC: 5169 1611 1622 2821 Alkalines & chlorine; alcohols & anti-freeze compounds; highway & street construction; surfacing & paving; concrete construction: roads, highways, sidewalks, etc.; general contractor, highway & street construction; bridge construction; plastics materials & resins; polyesters; ester gum; thermoplastic materials; heavy distillates; oils, lubricating; paving mixtures
HQ: Ashland Llc
  50 E Rivercenter Blvd # 1600
  Covington KY 41011
  859 815-3333

(G-9152)
ASHLAND SPCALTY INGREDIENTS GP
8145 Blazer Dr (19808)
PHONE.................................302 995-3000
EMP: 68
SALES (corp-wide): 2.4B Publicly Held
SIC: 2869 Industrial organic chemicals
HQ: Ashland Specialty Ingredients G.P.
  5200 Laser Pkwy
  Dublin OH 43017
  302 594-5000

(G-9153)
ASPENOLOGIES LLC
106 Belmont Dr (19808-4329)
PHONE.................................302 234-4346
Bonnie Staves, *Mng Member*
Lorraine Scott,
Thomas Scott,

Thomas Staves,
◆ EMP: 4
SALES (est): 367K Privately Held
SIC: 5734 7389 Computer software & accessories;

(G-9154)
ASPHALT STRIPING SVCS DEL LLC
12 Hosta Ct (19808-1953)
PHONE.................................302 456-9820
Thomas Donovan,
EMP: 4
SALES (est): 146.7K Privately Held
SIC: 1721 7389 Pavement marking contractor;

(G-9155)
ASSET MANAGEMENT ALLIANCE
222 Delaware Ave Ste 109 (19801-1681)
PHONE.................................302 656-5238
Dave Casey, *Partner*
Sarah Ruane, *Office Admin*
EMP: 14
SALES (est): 2.3MM Privately Held
WEB: www.assetmanagementalliance.com
SIC: 6531 Real estate managers

(G-9156)
ASSOCIATES IN HLTH PSYCHOLOGY (PA)
Also Called: AHP
1521 Concord Pike Ste 103 (19803-3614)
PHONE.................................302 428-0205
Sharon Jacobs, *Director*
EMP: 10
SALES (est): 879.4K Privately Held
SIC: 8049 Clinical psychologist

(G-9157)
ASSOCIATES INTERNATIONAL INC
100 Rogers Rd (19801-5704)
PHONE.................................302 656-4500
Lammot Copeland, *CEO*
Joe Farley Jr, *CEO*
Charles Copeland, *President*
William Englehart, *Vice Pres*
Bryan Taylor, *Vice Pres*
▲ EMP: 60 EST: 1973
SQ FT: 29,214
SALES (est): 12.3MM Privately Held
SIC: 2752 2791 2741 Commercial printing, lithographic; typesetting; miscellaneous publishing

(G-9158)
ASSOCIATION EDUCTIONAL PUBLR
300 Mrtin Lther King Blvd (19801-2437)
PHONE.................................302 295-8350
Charlene Gaynor, *CEO*
EMP: 10
SALES: 1.6MM Privately Held
WEB: www.aepweb.org
SIC: 8699 Charitable organization

(G-9159)
ASSOCIATION FOR THE RIGHTS (PA)
Also Called: ARC of Delaware
1016 Centre Rd Ste 1 (19805-1234)
PHONE.................................302 996-9400
Eliane Raign, *Principal*
John Dimeglio, *Controller*
Tina Simpkins, *Accountant*
Susannah E Ryan, *Manager*
EMP: 12
SALES: 647.4K Privately Held
SIC: 8621 Professional membership organizations

(G-9160)
ASSOCTION BRDS THLGCAL EDUCATN
Also Called: IN TRUST
100 W 10th St Ste 703 (19801-6605)
PHONE.................................302 654-7770
Anne Anderson, *Chairman*
Amy Kardash, *Director*
Julia A Jones, *Executive Asst*
Theresa Griffith, *Assistant*
EMP: 8

SALES: 7.8MM Privately Held
SIC: 8748 Business consulting

(G-9161)
ASSOCTION PATHOLOGY CHAIRS INC
100 W 10th St 603 (19801-6604)
PHONE.................................301 634-7880
Fred Becker, *President*
Kenneth Endicott, *Exec Dir*
EMP: 7
SQ FT: 400
SALES: 1MM Privately Held
SIC: 8621 8011 Medical field-related associations; pathologist

(G-9162)
ASSURANCE MEDIA LLC
590 Century Blvd Ste B (19808-6272)
P.O. Box 5087 (19808-0087)
PHONE.................................302 892-3540
Jennifer McKenzie, *President*
James Bowe, *Principal*
Tom Diorrio, *Principal*
Chris Honeycutt, *Principal*
Brian Jester, *Principal*
EMP: 20
SQ FT: 20,000
SALES (est): 5.5MM Privately Held
SIC: 1731 Computer installation

(G-9163)
ASSURANCE PARTNERS INTL
1201 N Market St Ste 1600 (19801-1147)
PHONE.................................302 478-0173
Franco Maglione, *President*
EMP: 10
SALES (est): 810.8K Privately Held
SIC: 6411 6211 Insurance agents & brokers; investment firm, general brokerage

(G-9164)
ASTHMA AND ALLERGY CARE DEL (PA)
1941 Limestone Rd Ste 209 (19808-5400)
PHONE.................................302 995-2952
Richard Kim, *Partner*
Richard H Kim, *Med Doctor*
EMP: 8
SALES (est): 1MM Privately Held
SIC: 8011 Allergist

(G-9165)
ASTON HOME HEALTH
1021 Gilpin Ave Ste 100 (19806-3271)
PHONE.................................302 421-3686
Maria Consuelo V Singson, *Principal*
EMP: 13
SALES: 1.3MM Privately Held
SIC: 8049 Nurses & other medical assistants

(G-9166)
ASTRAL PLANE WOODWORKS INC
28 Germay Dr Ste 28b (19804-1105)
PHONE.................................302 654-8666
Pete Steele, *President*
EMP: 1
SALES (est): 120K Privately Held
SIC: 2511 Wood household furniture

(G-9167)
ASTRAZENECA FOUNDATION
1800 Concord Pike (19850)
P.O. Box 15437 (19850-5437)
PHONE.................................302 886-3000
Paul Hudson, *President*
EMP: 4
SALES (est): 171.9K Privately Held
SIC: 8699 Charitable organization

(G-9168)
ASTRAZENECA LP (DH)
1800 Concord Pike (19803-2910)
P.O. Box 15437 (19850-5437)
PHONE.................................302 886-3000
Antony Zook, *CEO*
Lynn Hester, *Partner*
Larry Specht, *Principal*
John McCarthy, *Vice Pres*
Kenneth Murtha, *Vice Pres*
▲ EMP: 2500
SQ FT: 1,200,000

SALES (est): 2.3B
SALES (corp-wide): 22B Privately Held
WEB: www.newpurplepill.com
SIC: 2834 Pharmaceutical preparations

(G-9169)
ASTUTE GENERAL CONTRACTING LLC
306 Stanton Rd (19804-3630)
PHONE.................................302 383-4942
Brian M Jones,
EMP: 4
SALES (est): 172.9K Privately Held
SIC: 1521 Single-family home remodeling, additions & repairs

(G-9170)
AT SYSTEMS ATLANTIC INC
4200 Governor Printz Blvd (19802-2315)
PHONE.................................302 762-5444
Marvin Woods, *President*
Jim Purcell, *Vice Pres*
Paul Balcer, *Branch Mgr*
Pete Dickson, *Consultant*
Eddie Shanks, *Admin Sec*
EMP: 14
SALES (est): 966.5K Privately Held
SIC: 7389 Personal service agents, brokers & bureaus

(G-9171)
ATECHNOLOGIE LLC
1521 Concord Pike Ste 301 (19803-3644)
PHONE.................................781 325-5230
Tony Harb, *President*
EMP: 8
SALES (est): 7.2MM Privately Held
SIC: 5065 1799 Electronic parts; antenna installation

(G-9172)
ATG TRADING LLC
1013 Centre Rd Ste 403b (19805-1270)
PHONE.................................909 348-0620
Aileen Wang,
EMP: 5 EST: 2017
SALES (est): 125.7K Privately Held
SIC: 5199 Variety store merchandise

(G-9173)
ATI HOLDINGS LLC
Also Called: ATI Physical Therapy
1208 Kirkwood Hwy (19805-2120)
PHONE.................................302 993-1450
Timothy McHugh, *Branch Mgr*
EMP: 21
SALES (corp-wide): 338.3MM Privately Held
SIC: 8049 Physical therapist
PA: Ati Holdings, Llc
  790 Remington Blvd
  Bolingbrook IL 60440
  630 296-2222

(G-9174)
ATI HOLDINGS LLC
Also Called: ATI Physical Therapy
100 Valley Center Rd (19808-2950)
PHONE.................................302 994-1200
Brian Larue, *Branch Mgr*
EMP: 21
SALES (corp-wide): 338.3MM Privately Held
SIC: 8049 Physical therapist
PA: Ati Holdings, Llc
  790 Remington Blvd
  Bolingbrook IL 60440
  630 296-2222

(G-9175)
ATI HOLDINGS LLC
Also Called: North Orthopedic and Hand Ctr
1812 Marsh Rd Ste 505 (19810-4515)
PHONE.................................302 475-7500
EMP: 21
SALES (corp-wide): 338.3MM Privately Held
SIC: 8049 Physical therapist
PA: Ati Holdings, Llc
  790 Remington Blvd
  Bolingbrook IL 60440
  630 296-2222

Wilmington - New Castle County (G-9176)   GEOGRAPHIC SECTION

(G-9176)
ATI HOLDINGS LLC
Also Called: ATI Physical Therapy
914 Justison St (19801-5150)
PHONE..................302 351-0302
EMP: 21
SALES (corp-wide): 338.3MM **Privately Held**
SIC: 8049 Physical therapist
PA: Ati Holdings, Llc
  790 Remington Blvd
  Bolingbrook IL 60440
  630 296-2222

(G-9177)
ATI HOLDINGS LLC
Also Called: ATI Physical Therapy
1600 N Washington St (19802-4722)
PHONE..................302 656-2521
Edward R Miersch, Owner
EMP: 21
SALES (corp-wide): 338.3MM **Privately Held**
SIC: 8049 Physical therapist
PA: Ati Holdings, Llc
  790 Remington Blvd
  Bolingbrook IL 60440
  630 296-2222

(G-9178)
ATI HOLDINGS LLC
Also Called: ATI Physical Therapy
213 Greenhill Ave Ste C (19805-1800)
PHONE..................302 658-7800
Jason Mafabolta, Director
EMP: 10
SALES (corp-wide): 338.3MM **Privately Held**
SIC: 8049 Physical therapist
PA: Ati Holdings, Llc
  790 Remington Blvd
  Bolingbrook IL 60440
  630 296-2222

(G-9179)
ATLANTIC LANDSCAPE CO
800 A St (19801-5334)
PHONE..................302 661-1950
Bill Gioffre, President
EMP: 8
SALES (est): 1.5MM **Privately Held**
WEB: www.atlantic-companies.net
SIC: 0781 Landscape services

(G-9180)
ATLAS MANAGEMENT INC (DH)
103 Foulk Rd (19803-3742)
PHONE..................302 576-2749
Brian J Duffy, President
Andrew Panaccione, Vice Pres
Timothy Gifford, Admin Sec
EMP: 8
SALES (est): 636MM
SALES (corp-wide): 9B **Privately Held**
SIC: 6726 Management investment funds, closed-end
HQ: Skf Usa Inc.
  890 Forty Foot Rd
  Lansdale PA 19446
  267 436-6000

(G-9181)
ATOM ALLOYS LLC
Also Called: Atom Solutions United States
3411 Silverside Rd Ste (19810-4812)
PHONE..................786 975-3771
John Fillmon, Exec VP
EMP: 4 EST: 2011
SALES (est): 309.3K **Privately Held**
SIC: 3443 Fuel tanks (oil, gas, etc.): metal plate

(G-9182)
AUM LLC
Also Called: Leadsrain
20c Trolley Sq (19806-3355)
PHONE..................302 385-6767
Jaydeep Thakkar, CEO
Steve Robinson, Sales Staff
Mak Patel, Marketing Mgr
Nick Peter, Marketing Mgr
EMP: 10
SALES: 200K **Privately Held**
SIC: 7371 Computer software development

(G-9183)
AURAGIN LLC
427 N Tatnall St (19801-2230)
PHONE..................800 383-5109
Chris J Chung,
James Martin Duffy,
EMP: 2
SALES (est): 88.7K **Privately Held**
SIC: 2834 Pharmaceutical preparations

(G-9184)
AUSTIN ALLIANCE ELECTRIC INC
300 Delaware Ave Ste 210a (19801-6601)
PHONE..................843 297-8078
Cristina Davenport, Manager
EMP: 42
SALES (corp-wide): 18MM **Privately Held**
SIC: 8742 Construction project management consultant
PA: Austin Alliance Electric, Inc.
  1807 Unit 104 Capitl Blvd
  Raleigh NC 27604
  843 297-8078

(G-9185)
AUSTRLIAN PHYSTHERAPY CTRS LTD
Also Called: Maitland Australian
300 Delaware Ave Ste 1014 (19801-1671)
P.O. Box 1244, Cutchogue NY (11935-0883)
PHONE..................631 298-5367
Christopher Showalter, President
Joanne Showalter, CFO
EMP: 5
SQ FT: 2,600
SALES (est): 132K **Privately Held**
SIC: 8049 8299 Physiotherapist; educational service, nondegree granting: continuing educ.

(G-9186)
AUTO EQUITY LOANS
4701 Kirkwood Hwy (19808-5007)
PHONE..................302 998-3009
S Lambardo, Branch Mgr
EMP: 4
SALES (corp-wide): 3.1MM **Privately Held**
SIC: 6141 Automobile loans, including insurance
PA: Auto Equity Loans
  15231 N 87th St Ste 115b
  Scottsdale AZ 85260
  480 307-6388

(G-9187)
AUTOMATION INC
408 Harvey Dr (19804-2493)
P.O. Box 3016 (19804-0016)
PHONE..................302 999-0971
Donald Sheldrake Jr, President
Mary J Sheldrake, Vice Pres
EMP: 19
SQ FT: 20,000
SALES (est): 2.3MM **Privately Held**
WEB: www.automationinc.net
SIC: 3599 3625 Machine shop, jobbing & repair; relays & industrial controls

(G-9188)
AUTOMATION PARTNERSHIP
Also Called: Tap
502 First State Blvd (19804-3746)
PHONE..................302 478-9060
Richard Archer, CEO
Dr Michael Shore, Manager
EMP: 5
SALES (est): 1.6MM **Privately Held**
WEB: www.automationpartnership.com
SIC: 5084 Robots, industrial

(G-9189)
AUTOMATION SOLUTIONS INC
20 Montchanin Rd Ste 200 (19807-2174)
PHONE..................302 478-9060
Andrew Parrott, Manager
EMP: 6
SALES (corp-wide): 8MM **Privately Held**
WEB: www.automationsolutionsinc.com
SIC: 5021 Office & public building furniture
PA: Automation Solutions, Inc.
  38 3rd Ave Ste 100w
  Boston MA 02129
  617 681-6700

(G-9190)
AUTOMOTIVE SERVICES INC
Also Called: Northeast Body Shop
2510 Northeast Blvd (19802-4511)
PHONE..................302 762-0100
Charles A Allen, President
Bonnie Allen, Admin Sec
EMP: 19
SQ FT: 5,000
SALES (est): 2MM **Privately Held**
SIC: 7532 5521 Body shop, automotive; automobiles, used cars only

(G-9191)
AUTOPART INTERNATIONAL INC
401 Marsh Ln Ste 5 (19804-2491)
PHONE..................302 998-2920
Bill Wolf, Branch Mgr
EMP: 11
SALES (corp-wide): 9.5B **Publicly Held**
SIC: 5013 Automotive supplies & parts
HQ: Autopart International, Inc.
  192 Mansfield Ave
  Norton MA 02766
  781 784-1111

(G-9192)
AUTOWEB TECHNOLOGIES INC
2801 Cntrvlle Rd Fl 1 Flr 1 (19808)
PHONE..................443 485-4200
Ben Vaughn, CEO
EMP: 5
SALES (est): 296.6K **Privately Held**
SIC: 7371 Computer software development

(G-9193)
AUTUMN HILL PATIO & LANDSCAPE
242 Barberry Dr (19808-1950)
PHONE..................302 293-1183
Ryan Coyne, Owner
EMP: 4
SALES (est): 197.8K **Privately Held**
SIC: 0781 Landscape services

(G-9194)
AV AUTO WORX LLC
124 Middleboro Rd (19804-1660)
PHONE..................302 384-7646
James Birli,
EMP: 10
SALES (est): 257.7K **Privately Held**
SIC: 7538 General automotive repair shops

(G-9195)
AVALON DENTAL
34 Kiamensi Rd (19804-2908)
PHONE..................302 999-8822
Parham Farhi, President
EMP: 4 EST: 2008
SALES (est): 270.7K **Privately Held**
SIC: 8021 Dentists' office

(G-9196)
AVANTYS HEALTH LLC
1000 N West St Ste 1200 (19801-1058)
PHONE..................302 521-2848
Olivier Hemandez,
EMP: 5
SALES (est): 122.7K **Privately Held**
SIC: 8741 Management services

(G-9197)
AVENUE CUTS INC
1700 N Scott St Lowr Lowr (19806-2356)
PHONE..................302 655-1718
Kelly Hughes, President
EMP: 7
SALES (est): 91.9K **Privately Held**
SIC: 7231 Beauty shops

(G-9198)
AVEREST INC
2201 Valley Ave (19810-2510)
PHONE..................302 281-2062
Manan Thacker, President
EMP: 4
SALES (est): 131.6K **Privately Held**
SIC: 7373 5015 Systems engineering, computer related; automotive supplies, used

(G-9199)
AVIMAN MANAGEMENT LLC
910 Gilpin Ave (19806-3211)
PHONE..................302 377-5788
Wallace Levi Coleman,
EMP: 26
SALES: 7MM **Privately Held**
SIC: 1542 1622 7389 Commercial & office building contractors; bridge, tunnel & elevated highway;

(G-9200)
AWL MACHINE
Also Called: Aw Layman Machine
327 7th Ave (19805-4763)
PHONE..................302 888-0440
Allen Layman, Owner
EMP: 1
SQ FT: 1,800
SALES (est): 101.4K **Privately Held**
SIC: 3599 Machine shop, jobbing & repair

(G-9201)
AXA EQUITABLE LIFE INSUR CO
Also Called: Equitable Life Assurance
200 Bellevue Pkwy Ste 200 # 200 (19809-3727)
PHONE..................302 655-7231
Mark Mackey, Branch Mgr
Michael Brewer, Advisor
EMP: 15
SALES (corp-wide): 12B **Publicly Held**
WEB: www.equitable.com
SIC: 6411 Insurance agents, brokers & service
HQ: Axa Equitable Life Insurance Company
  1290 Avenue Of The Americ
  New York NY 10104
  212 554-1234

(G-9202)
AYALA PHARMACEUTICALS INC
1313 N Market St Ste 51 (19801-6101)
PHONE..................857 444-0553
Roni Mamluk, CEO
Gary Gordon, Chief Mktg Ofcr
EMP: 10
SALES (est): 371.7K **Privately Held**
SIC: 8732 2834 Research services, except laboratory; druggists' preparations (pharmaceuticals)

(G-9203)
AYON LANDSCAPING
313 Orinda Dr (19804-1115)
P.O. Box 30312 (19805-7312)
PHONE..................302 275-0205
Bill Ayon, Owner
EMP: 4 EST: 2012
SALES (est): 96.9K **Privately Held**
SIC: 0781 Landscape services

(G-9204)
AZTEC COPIES LLC
Also Called: Aztec Printing and Design
3636 Silverside Rd (19810-5191)
PHONE..................302 575-1993
Jeffrey Durham, President
Edward Dwornik, Vice Pres
Drake Dwornik, Technology
EMP: 14
SQ FT: 7,500
SALES: 2MM **Privately Held**
WEB: www.azteccopies.com
SIC: 7336 Commercial art & graphic design

(G-9205)
AZUR GCS INC
1201 N Orange St Ste 7293 (19801-1271)
PHONE..................302 884-6713
Andrew Thompson, CEO
EMP: 6
SALES (est): 67.1K **Privately Held**
SIC: 4813 Telephone communication, except radio

GEOGRAPHIC SECTION

Wilmington - New Castle County (G-9233)

(G-9206)
AZURITE03 INC
1104 Philadelphia Pike (19809-2031)
PHONE 866 667-5119
Stewart Anderson, *President*
▲ EMP: 4
SALES (est): 1.7MM **Privately Held**
SIC: 5032 Brick, stone & related material

(G-9207)
B & B INDUSTRIES INC
1507 A St (19801-5499)
PHONE 302 655-6156
Michael A Bloom, *President*
David Bloom, *President*
Daniel Bloom, *Vice Pres*
EMP: 17
SQ FT: 55,000
SALES (est): 5.5MM **Privately Held**
SIC: 5051 Steel

(G-9208)
B & B TICKETTOWN INC
1601 Concord Pike Ste 61 (19803-3623)
PHONE 302 656-9797
EMP: 5
SQ FT: 400
SALES (est): 263.4K **Privately Held**
SIC: 7999 7922 Ticket sales office for sporting events, contract; ticket agency, theatrical

(G-9209)
B & F CERAMICS
2644 Boxwood Dr (19810-1608)
PHONE 302 475-4721
EMP: 1
SALES (est): 44.8K **Privately Held**
SIC: 3269 Pottery products

(G-9210)
B & M MEATS INC
21 Commerce St (19801-5425)
P.O. Box 491 (19899-0491)
PHONE 302 655-5521
Yossi Baruch, *President*
Annette Baruch, *Corp Secy*
Tony Tagliafierro, *VP Opers*
Tim Power, *Sales Mgr*
Sandy Veo-Gale, *Supervisor*
EMP: 12
SQ FT: 3,000
SALES (est): 5.4MM **Privately Held**
SIC: 5147 Meats & meat products

(G-9211)
B DOHERTY INC
5301 Limestone Rd Ste 100 (19808-1251)
P.O. Box 7543, Newark (19714-7543)
PHONE 302 239-3500
Bernard Doherty, *President*
EMP: 7 EST: 1999
SALES: 500K **Privately Held**
SIC: 1522 1542 Residential construction; commercial & office building contractors

(G-9212)
B F SHIN OF SALISBURY INC
1715 Lovering Ave (19806-2119)
PHONE 302 652-3521
James Shinn, *President*
EMP: 7
SALES (est): 853.2K **Privately Held**
SIC: 5198 Paints

(G-9213)
B SAFE INC (PA)
Also Called: Honeywell Authorized Dealer
109 Baltimore Ave (19805-2554)
PHONE 302 633-1833
Philip H Gardner, *President*
Joseph Gallagher, *Exec VP*
Joe Gallagher, *Vice Pres*
Susan Grear, *Credit Mgr*
Jessica Lee, *Sales Staff*
EMP: 25
SALES (est): 6.9MM **Privately Held**
SIC: 7382 Burglar alarm maintenance & monitoring; fire alarm maintenance & monitoring; protective devices, security

(G-9214)
B WILLIAMS HOLDING CORP (HQ)
1403 Foulk Rd Ste 200 (19803-2788)
PHONE 302 656-8596
Kenneth Kubacki, *President*
EMP: 10
SALES (est): 1.3B
SALES (corp-wide): 3.5B **Publicly Held**
SIC: 3579 3661 3861 7359 Mailing machines; facsimile equipment; photocopy machines; business machine & electronic equipment rental services; business machine repair, electric; machinery & equipment finance leasing
PA: Pitney Bowes Inc.
 3001 Summer St Ste 3
 Stamford CT 06905
 203 356-5000

(G-9215)
BA CREDIT CARD TRUST
1100 N King St (19884-0011)
PHONE 704 386-5681
EMP: 9
SALES (est): 752.2K
SALES (corp-wide): 110.5B **Publicly Held**
WEB: www.bankofamerica.com
SIC: 6733 Trusts
PA: Bank Of America Corporation
 100 N Tryon St Ste 170
 Charlotte NC 28202
 704 386-5681

(G-9216)
BAABAO INC
300 Delaware Ave Ste 210a (19801-6601)
PHONE 415 990-6767
Jennifer Chao, *CEO*
Pei-Pei Ni, *President*
EMP: 2
SALES (est): 68.4K **Privately Held**
SIC: 7372 Application computer software

(G-9217)
BABE STYLING STUDIO INC
213 N Market St (19801-2527)
PHONE 302 543-7738
Ebon Flagg, *President*
EMP: 8 EST: 2009
SALES (est): 37.2K **Privately Held**
SIC: 7231 Unisex hair salons

(G-9218)
BABEL INC
1 Commerce St (19801)
PHONE 866 327-3465
Nathan Johnson, *President*
EMP: 5
SALES (est): 117.2K **Privately Held**
SIC: 7372 Business oriented computer software

(G-9219)
BABES ON SQUARE
1411 Foulk Rd Ste A (19803-2773)
PHONE 302 477-9190
Andrea Keating, *Owner*
EMP: 6
SALES (est): 232.5K **Privately Held**
SIC: 8351 Preschool center

(G-9220)
BACK CLINIC INC
5550 Kirkwood Hwy (19808-5000)
PHONE 302 995-2100
Ellen H Levine, *Director*
EMP: 15
SALES (est): 1.2MM **Privately Held**
WEB: www.backclinicinc.com
SIC: 8049 Physical therapist

(G-9221)
BAFFONE & ASSOCIATES LLC
1211 N King St Fl 1 (19801-3217)
PHONE 302 655-1544
Mike Baffone, *Mng Member*
EMP: 4
SALES (est): 219.7K **Privately Held**
SIC: 8721 Certified public accountant

(G-9222)
BAKER JAMES CCJR DDS
1304 N Broom St Uppr (19806-4239)
PHONE 302 658-9511
James C Baker Jr DDS, *Owner*
EMP: 6
SALES (est): 234.9K **Privately Held**
SIC: 8021 Dentists' office

(G-9223)
BAKER TILLY VIRCHOW KRAUSE LLP
1105 N Market St Ste 700 (19801-1270)
PHONE 302 442-4600
Janet Nieves, *Office Mgr*
Brandy Evans, *Manager*
Donn Rocco, *Administration*
EMP: 5
SALES (corp-wide): 522MM **Privately Held**
WEB: www.parentenet.com
SIC: 8721 Certified public accountant
PA: Baker Tilly Virchow Krause, Llp
 205 N Michigan Ave # 2800
 Chicago IL 60601
 312 729-8000

(G-9224)
BALANCECO2 INC
103 Ascension Dr (19808-7901)
PHONE 302 494-9476
Natarajan Kumaresan, *CEO*
Selva Kumar, *Exec Dir*
EMP: 15
SALES: 950K **Privately Held**
SIC: 4931 Electric & other services combined

(G-9225)
BALFOUR BEATTY LLC (HQ)
1011 Centre Rd Ste 322 (19805-1266)
PHONE 302 573-3873
Mark Crouser, *President*
Joanne Bonfiglio, *Vice Pres*
Leslie Cohn, *Vice Pres*
Ed Prendergast, *Vice Pres*
Peter Zinkin, *Vice Pres*
◆ EMP: 5
SQ FT: 150,000
SALES: 4.6B
SALES (corp-wide): 8.7B **Privately Held**
SIC: 1542 8712 8741 Commercial & office building, new construction; architectural engineering; management services
PA: Balfour Beatty Plc
 5 Churchill Place
 London E14 5
 800 030-4127

(G-9226)
BALICK & BALICK PLLC
711 N King St (19801-3503)
PHONE 302 658-4265
Adam Balick, *Partner*
Autum Schneider, *Admin Sec*
EMP: 7
SQ FT: 2,000
SALES (est): 813.2K **Privately Held**
WEB: www.balick.com
SIC: 8111 General practice attorney, lawyer

(G-9227)
BALLARD SPAHR LLP
919 N Market St Ste 1201 (19801-3062)
PHONE 302 252-4465
Tobby Daluz, *Partner*
Jenna Millman, *Counsel*
Michelle Dawson, *Legal Staff*
Monica Patanian, *Legal Staff*
Claire Volpe, *Legal Staff*
EMP: 7
SALES (corp-wide): 224.2MM **Privately Held**
SIC: 8111 General practice attorney, lawyer
PA: Ballard Spahr Llp
 1735 Market St Fl 51
 Philadelphia PA 19103
 215 665-8500

(G-9228)
BALLISTICS TECHNOLOGY INTL LTD (PA)
2207 Concord Pike 657 (19803-2908)
PHONE 877 291-1111
James Sigurdson, *President*
John Sutton, *Director*
▲ EMP: 2
SQ FT: 13,000
SALES: 1.2MM **Privately Held**
SIC: 3272 Concrete products

(G-9229)
BALLY HOLDING COMPANY DELAWARE (HQ)
3411 Silverside Rd 108wb (19810-4812)
PHONE 610 845-7511
John J Dau, *Ch of Bd*
James P Reichart, *President*
Ann D Conway, *Vice Pres*
Carol L Beadencup, *Treasurer*
Mary Alice Avery, *Director*
EMP: 4 EST: 1981
SALES: 14.8MM **Privately Held**
SIC: 2499 Kitchen, bathroom & household ware: wood
PA: Bally Holding Company Of Pennsylvania
 30 S 7th St
 Bally PA 19503
 610 845-7511

(G-9230)
BANACOM SIGNS INC
3201 Miller Rd Ste A (19802-2542)
PHONE 302 429-6243
Hector Delfabro, *President*
Adrian Del Fabro, *Research*
Gabriel Delfabro, *Treasurer*
Gabriel Del Fabro, *MIS Dir*
EMP: 4
SALES: 200K **Privately Held**
SIC: 3993 Signs & advertising specialties

(G-9231)
BANCORP INC (PA)
409 Silverside Rd Ste 105 (19809-1771)
PHONE 302 385-5000
Damian M Kozlowski, *CEO*
Daniel G Cohen, *Ch of Bd*
Jonathan Kohan, *Managing Dir*
Jennifer Terry, *Managing Dir*
Gregor Garry, *COO*
EMP: 42
SQ FT: 62,136
SALES: 301.7MM **Publicly Held**
SIC: 6021 National commercial banks

(G-9232)
BANCORP BANK (HQ)
Also Called: BANCORP.COM
409 Silverside Rd Ste 105 (19809-1771)
PHONE 302 385-5000
Betsy Z Cohen, *CEO*
Daniel G Cohen, *Ch of Bd*
Frank M Mastrangelo, *President*
Cleveanna Young, *President*
Gregor Garry, *COO*
EMP: 40
SALES: 301.1MM
SALES (corp-wide): 301.7MM **Publicly Held**
WEB: www.thebancorp.com
SIC: 6029 Commercial banks
PA: The Bancorp Inc
 409 Silverside Rd Ste 105
 Wilmington DE 19809
 302 385-5000

(G-9233)
BANCROFT CARPENTRY COMPANY (HQ)
44 Bancroft Mills Rd (19806-2028)
PHONE 302 655-3434
Stephen M Mockbee, *President*
Nash Childs, *Vice Pres*
John Barr, *Treasurer*
Don Stow, *Finance Mgr*
EMP: 4
SQ FT: 4,000

(PA)=Parent Co (HQ)=Headquarters (DH)=Div Headquarters
✪ = New Business established in last 2 years

2020 Harris Directory of Delaware Businesses

Wilmington - New Castle County (G-9234)   GEOGRAPHIC SECTION

SALES (est): 2.4MM
SALES (corp-wide): 34.6MM **Privately Held**
WEB: www.bc-const.com
SIC: **2431** 2434 Millwork; wood kitchen cabinets
PA: Bancroft Construction Company
1300 N Grant Ave Ste 101
Wilmington DE 19806
302 655-3434

(G-9234)
BANCROFT CONSTRUCTION COMPANY (PA)
1300 N Grant Ave Ste 101 (19806-2456)
PHONE.................................302 655-3434
Stephen M Mockbee, *President*
Nash Childs, *Exec VP*
Tiffany Brownie, *Project Mgr*
Kaitlin Cliver, *Project Mgr*
John Falini, *Project Mgr*
▲ EMP: 70
SALES (est): 34.6MM **Privately Held**
SIC: **1542** 1541 Commercial & office building, new construction; industrial buildings & warehouses

(G-9235)
BANCROFT HOMES INC
1300 N Grant Ave Ste 204 (19806-2456)
PHONE.................................302 655-5461
Steven Mockbee, *President*
Mike N Christopher, *Project Mgr*
EMP: 8
SALES (est): 926.7K **Privately Held**
SIC: **1521** New construction, single-family houses

(G-9236)
BANCROFT NEUROHEALTH
321 E 11th St (19801-3422)
PHONE.................................302 691-8531
Carol Chapin, *Exec Dir*
EMP: 22
SALES (corp-wide): 149.3MM **Privately Held**
SIC: **8099** Blood related health services
PA: Bancroft Neurohealth, A New Jersey Nonprofit Corporation
1255 Caldwell Rd
Cherry Hill NJ 08034
844 234-8387

(G-9237)
BANK AMERICA NATIONAL ASSN
5215 Concord Pike (19803-1416)
PHONE.................................302 478-1005
EMP: 19
SALES (corp-wide): 110.5B **Publicly Held**
SIC: **6021** National commercial banks
HQ: Bank Of America, National Association
100 S Tryon St
Charlotte NC 28202
704 386-5681

(G-9238)
BANK AMERICA NATIONAL ASSN
3816 Kennett Pike (19807-2302)
PHONE.................................302 656-5399
EMP: 19
SALES (corp-wide): 110.5B **Publicly Held**
SIC: **6021** National commercial banks
HQ: Bank Of America, National Association
100 S Tryon St
Charlotte NC 28202
704 386-5681

(G-9239)
BANK AMERICA NATIONAL ASSN
1100 N King St (19884-0011)
PHONE.................................302 765-2108
Jason Donovan, *Principal*
Nathan Dankenbring, *Senior VP*
Mark Bishop, *Vice Pres*
Victoria McGarvey, *Vice Pres*
Jeffrey Snavely, *Vice Pres*
EMP: 19

SALES (corp-wide): 110.5B **Publicly Held**
WEB: www.bofa.com
SIC: **6021** National commercial banks
HQ: Bank Of America, National Association
100 S Tryon St
Charlotte NC 28202
704 386-5681

(G-9240)
BANK OF AMERICA CORPORATION
1100 N Market St (19890-1100)
PHONE.................................302 432-0407
Bank Delaware, *President*
Shanon Passmore, *Executive Asst*
EMP: 14
SALES (corp-wide): 110.5B **Publicly Held**
SIC: **6021** National commercial banks
PA: Bank Of America Corporation
100 N Tryon St Ste 170
Charlotte NC 28202
704 386-5681

(G-9241)
BANK OF NEW YORK MELLON
4005 Kennett Pike (19807-2018)
PHONE.................................302 421-2207
Gregg Landis, *President*
EMP: 8 **Privately Held**
SIC: **6712** Bank holding companies

(G-9242)
BANK OF NEW YORK MELLON CORP
4005 Kennett Pike Fl 1 (19807-2018)
PHONE.................................302 416-6283
EMP: 8
SALES (corp-wide): 12.8B **Publicly Held**
SIC: **6712** Bank holding companies
PA: The Bank Of New York Mellon Corporation
240 E Greenwich St
New York NY 10007
212 495-1784

(G-9243)
BANK OF NEW YORK MELLON CORP
Also Called: Bny Mellon
3801 Kennett Pike E155 (19807-2321)
PHONE.................................302 421-2335
Jeffrey Dillman, *Branch Mgr*
EMP: 4
SALES (corp-wide): 12.8B **Publicly Held**
SIC: **6733** Personal investment trust management
PA: The Bank Of New York Mellon Corporation
240 E Greenwich St
New York NY 10007
212 495-1784

(G-9244)
BANK OF NEW YORK MELLON CORP
301 Bellevue Pkwy (19809-3705)
PHONE.................................302 791-1700
Timothy G Shack, *CEO*
EMP: 4
SALES (corp-wide): 12.8B **Publicly Held**
SIC: **6099** 8721 6282 Electronic funds transfer network, including switching; accounting services, except auditing; investment advice
PA: The Bank Of New York Mellon Corporation
240 E Greenwich St
New York NY 10007
212 495-1784

(G-9245)
BANTAM TECHNOLOGIES LLC
1201 N Orange St 700-7019 (19801-1155)
PHONE.................................302 256-5823
Kasey Turner,
EMP: 4
SQ FT: 250
SALES: 4.7MM **Privately Held**
SIC: **7382** 7371 Security systems services; computer software development & applications

(G-9246)
BAR & ASSOCIATES LTD
Also Called: Bar & Associates Intr Design
3410 Old Capitol Trl # 2 (19808-6152)
PHONE.................................302 999-9233
Humberto Humes, *President*
EMP: 7
SALES (est): 368.6K **Privately Held**
SIC: **7389** Interior design services

(G-9247)
BARBACANE THORNTON & COMPANY
3411 Silverside Rd 200s (19810-4811)
PHONE.................................302 478-8940
Robert M Barbacane, *Partner*
Pamela Baker, *Partner*
Frank Defroda, *Partner*
Al Pisanelli, *Partner*
Robert Yemola, *Accountant*
EMP: 25
SALES (est): 2.5MM **Privately Held**
WEB: www.btcpa.com
SIC: **8721** Certified public accountant

(G-9248)
BARBARA GRAPHICS INC
Also Called: Signs Now
506 First State Blvd (19804-3746)
PHONE.................................302 636-9040
Barbara Carlson, *President*
Mark Carlson, *Vice Pres*
EMP: 3
SALES (est): 326.2K **Privately Held**
SIC: **3993** Signs & advertising specialties

(G-9249)
BARBIZON OF DELAWARE INC
Also Called: Barbizon School of Modeling
17 Trolley Sq Ste B (19806)
PHONE.................................302 658-6666
Joan S Bernard, *President*
EMP: 27
SALES (est): 795.8K **Privately Held**
SIC: **8299** 7361 Finishing school, charm & modeling; model registry

(G-9250)
BARCLAYS BANK DELAWARE (DH)
Also Called: BARCLAYCARD US
100 S West St (19801-5015)
P.O. Box 8801 (19899-8801)
PHONE.................................302 255-8000
Barry Rodrigues, *CEO*
James Stewart, *President*
Glenn Watson, *Assistant VP*
EMP: 260
SALES: 3.9B
SALES (corp-wide): 37.8B **Privately Held**
WEB: www.juniperbank.com
SIC: **6035** Federal savings banks
HQ: Barclays Financial Corporation
125 S West St
Wilmington DE 19801
302 622-8990

(G-9251)
BARCLAYS FINANCIAL CORPORATION
100 S West St (19801-5015)
PHONE.................................302 652-6201
EMP: 4
SALES (corp-wide): 37.8B **Privately Held**
WEB: www.juniperfinancial.com
SIC: **6282** Investment advice
HQ: Barclays Financial Corporation
125 S West St
Wilmington DE 19801
302 622-8990

(G-9252)
BARCLAYS PLC
125 S West St (19801-5014)
PHONE.................................302 622-8990
Caitlin Brizee, *Vice Pres*
Evette Saldana, *Vice Pres*
John Porter, *Treasurer*
Lisa Johnson, *Branch Mgr*
Lisa Herberger, *Director*
EMP: 31
SALES (corp-wide): 37.8B **Privately Held**
SIC: **7371** Computer software development & applications

PA: Barclays Plc
1 Churchill Place
London E14 5
207 623-2323

(G-9253)
BARDON U S CORPORATION (DH)
300 Delaware Ave Fl 9 (19801-1607)
PHONE.................................302 552-3136
Bill Bolsover, *President*
Al Stone, *Treasurer*
Darryl E Smith, *Admin Sec*
Linda S Bubacz, *Asst Sec*
EMP: 5
SALES (est): 201.6MM
SALES (corp-wide): 4.5B **Privately Held**
SIC: **3273** 2951 1442 Ready-mixed concrete; asphalt & asphaltic paving mixtures (not from refineries); concrete, bituminous; common sand mining; gravel mining
HQ: Aggregate Industries - Mwr, Inc.
2815 Dodd Rd
Eagan MN 55121
651 683-0600

(G-9254)
BARGAIN TIRE & SERVICE INC
3415 N Market St Ste 17 (19802-2731)
PHONE.................................302 764-8900
Mario Ferroni, *President*
Christopher Russ, *Manager*
EMP: 10
SQ FT: 5,000
SALES (est): 1.3MM **Privately Held**
SIC: **5531** 5014 7539 Automotive tires; tires & tubes; shock absorber replacement

(G-9255)
BARLOWS UPHOLSTERY INC
Also Called: Barlow Upholstery
1002 W 28th St (19802-2999)
PHONE.................................302 655-3955
David Barlow, *President*
Barbara Pfarner, *Corp Secy*
Jay Barlow, *Vice Pres*
EMP: 4
SQ FT: 16,000
SALES: 230K **Privately Held**
SIC: **2512** 7641 2391 Upholstered household furniture; reupholstery; draperies, plastic & textile: from purchased materials

(G-9256)
BARRY KLASSMAN DDS RES
706 Bristol Rd (19803-2224)
PHONE.................................302 478-0475
Barry Klassman, *Principal*
EMP: 4 EST: 2010
SALES (est): 89.4K **Privately Held**
SIC: **8021** Offices & clinics of dentists

(G-9257)
BASELL CAPITAL CORPORATION
2 Righter Pkwy Ste 300 (19803-1551)
PHONE.................................302 683-8000
Tammy Coughlin, *Business Mgr*
Giuseppe Saggese, *Vice Pres*
EMP: 9
SALES (est): 941.5K **Privately Held**
SIC: **2869** Industrial organic chemicals

(G-9258)
BASF CORPORATION
Also Called: Coating Effects Div
205 S James St (19804-2424)
PHONE.................................302 992-5600
Bruce Ciancio, *Info Tech Mgr*
EMP: 200
SALES (corp-wide): 69.5B **Privately Held**
WEB: www.cibasc.com
SIC: **2869** 2865 Industrial organic chemicals; cyclic crudes & intermediates
HQ: Basf Corporation
100 Park Ave
Florham Park NJ 07932
973 245-6000

(G-9259)
BAT ELECTRONICS INC
Also Called: Balanced Audio Technology
1300 First State Blvd (19804-3548)
PHONE.................................302 999-8855

GEOGRAPHIC SECTION

Wilmington - New Castle County (G-9289)

James Davis, *President*
EMP: 6
SALES (est): 642K **Privately Held**
SIC: 3651 Audio electronic systems
PA: Audiophile Music Direct Inc.
1811 W Bryn Mawr Ave
Chicago IL 60660

(G-9260)
BATTA RAMESH C ASSOCIATES PA (PA)
4600 New Linden Hill Rd (19808)
PHONE..................302 998-9463
Ramesh C Batta, *President*
Mary Batta, *Vice Pres*
John Chittick, *Info Tech Mgr*
Michelle Batta, *Admin Sec*
EMP: 25 **EST:** 1978
SQ FT: 2,400
SALES (est): 2.9MM **Privately Held**
WEB: www.rcbatta.com
SIC: 8711 8713 Civil engineering; surveying services

(G-9261)
BATTAGLIA JOSEPH A & DIAMOND
900 Foulk Rd Ste 200 (19803-3155)
PHONE..................302 655-8868
Steven Diamond, *Owner*
EMP: 5
SALES (est): 389.5K **Privately Held**
SIC: 8031 Offices & clinics of osteopathic physicians

(G-9262)
BAUMANN INDUSTRIES INC
2412 W Heather Rd Ste 200 (19803-2720)
PHONE..................302 593-1049
Bruce Ritterson, *Principal*
EMP: 3
SALES (est): 249.3K **Privately Held**
SIC: 3999 Barber & beauty shop equipment

(G-9263)
BAYADA HOME HEALTH CARE INC
750 S Madison St (19801)
PHONE..................302 655-1333
Laura Workman, *Branch Mgr*
EMP: 84
SALES (corp-wide): 672.5MM **Privately Held**
SIC: 8082 Visiting nurse service
PA: Bayada Home Health Care, Inc.
1 W Main St
Moorestown NJ 08057
856 231-1000

(G-9264)
BAYADA HOME HEALTH CARE INC
750 Shipyard Dr Ste 101 (19801-5161)
PHONE..................302 655-1333
Jean Mullin, *Branch Mgr*
EMP: 4
SALES (corp-wide): 672.5MM **Privately Held**
SIC: 8049 8082 Nurses & other medical assistants; home health care services
PA: Bayada Home Health Care, Inc.
1 W Main St
Moorestown NJ 08057
856 231-1000

(G-9265)
BAYESIAN HEALTH INC
251 Little Falls Dr (19808-1674)
PHONE..................408 205-8035
Suchi Saria, *CEO*
EMP: 8
SALES (est): 79.4K **Privately Held**
SIC: 7372 Utility computer software; application computer software

(G-9266)
BAYNARD HOUSE CONDOMINIUMS
2400 Baynard Blvd (19802-3948)
PHONE..................302 319-3740
Morgan Conner, *President*
Brian Lamborn, *Vice Pres*
William Donnelly, *Treasurer*
Stephen Crary, *Admin Sec*
EMP: 6
SALES (est): 130.3K **Privately Held**
SIC: 8641 Condominium association

(G-9267)
BAYTOWN SYSTEMS INC
2711 Centerville Rd # 400 (19808-1660)
PHONE..................302 689-3421
Alit Suryadi, *Business Mgr*
EMP: 5 **EST:** 2013
SQ FT: 500
SALES (est): 310K **Privately Held**
SIC: 5045 Printers, computer

(G-9268)
BB TECHNOLOGIES INC
801 N West St Fl 2 (19801-1525)
PHONE..................302 652-2300
Kenneth J Kubacki, *President*
Anna M Baird, *Vice Pres*
Clara Paschitti, *Treasurer*
EMP: 7
SALES (est): 937.6K **Privately Held**
WEB: www.blackbox.com
SIC: 5045 Computer peripheral equipment
HQ: Black Box Corporation Of Pennsylvania
1000 Park Dr
Lawrence PA 15055
724 746-5500

(G-9269)
BBEST LLC
Also Called: E-Commerce
1232 N King St (19801-3226)
PHONE..................302 581-9963
EMP: 12
SALES (est): 251.1K **Privately Held**
SIC: 7371 Computer software development & applications

(G-9270)
BBHOTEL CORP (PA)
Also Called: Be Better Hotels
108 W 13th St (19801)
PHONE..................939 272-3953
EMP: 2
SALES (est): 168.4K **Privately Held**
SIC: 7372 Prepackaged Software Services

(G-9271)
BC CONSULTING INC
4905 Mermaid Blvd (19808-1004)
PHONE..................302 234-7710
Kathleen Boylan, *Principal*
Thomas E Cahill, *Vice Pres*
EMP: 7
SQ FT: 1,800
SALES (est): 319K **Privately Held**
WEB: www.bcconsulting.com
SIC: 6531 Real estate managers

(G-9272)
BDO USA LLP
4250 Lancaster Pike # 120 (19805-1520)
P.O. Box 3566 (19807-0566)
PHONE..................302 656-5500
James Doyle, *Managing Prtnr*
Jennifer Spooner, *Managing Prtnr*
John Barkmeyer, *Partner*
Gregory Falk, *Partner*
Louis Gomes, *Partner*
EMP: 71
SALES (corp-wide): 1.6B **Privately Held**
SIC: 8721 Certified public accountant
PA: Bdo Usa, Llp
330 N Wabash Ave Ste 3200
Chicago IL 60611
312 240-1236

(G-9273)
BEANSTOCK MEDIA INC (PA)
300 Delaware Ave Ste 1100 (19801-1670)
PHONE..................415 912-1530
James Waltz, *CEO*
Jim Waltz, *CEO*
Ryan Maynard, *COO*
Audrey Agustine-Kirk, *Vice Pres*
Joe Lyons, *Risk Mgmt Dir*
EMP: 26
SALES (est): 2.1MM **Privately Held**
SIC: 7311 Advertising consultant

(G-9274)
BEAR ALIGNMENT CENTER
1317 N Scott St (19806-4023)
PHONE..................302 655-9219
Robert Gregg, *Owner*
EMP: 5
SALES (est): 260K **Privately Held**
SIC: 7539 Wheel alignment, automotive; brake services

(G-9275)
BEASLEY BROADCAST GROUP INC
812 Philadelphia Pike # 2 (19809-2372)
PHONE..................302 765-1160
Jane Bartsch, *Principal*
EMP: 20
SALES (corp-wide): 257.4MM **Publicly Held**
WEB: www.bbgi.com
SIC: 4832 Radio broadcasting stations
PA: Beasley Broadcast Group, Inc.
3033 Riviera Dr Ste 200
Naples FL 34103
239 263-5000

(G-9276)
BEASLEY FM ACQUISITION CORP
812 Philadelphia Pike (19809-2372)
PHONE..................302 765-1160
Dan Sultzbach, *General Mgr*
EMP: 9
SALES (est): 284.7K **Privately Held**
SIC: 4832 Radio broadcasting stations

(G-9277)
BEAUTIFUL GATE OUTREACH CENTER
604 N Walnut St (19801-3808)
PHONE..................302 472-3002
Janet Bivins, *President*
Renee Beaman, *Exec Dir*
EMP: 14
SQ FT: 3,000
SALES: 428.1K **Privately Held**
SIC: 8322 Outreach program

(G-9278)
BEAUTIFUL LASHES
2513 N Tatnall St (19802-4153)
PHONE..................302 983-9521
Brandi Roy, *Principal*
EMP: 4
SALES (est): 33.3K **Privately Held**
SIC: 7231 Cosmetology & personal hygiene salons

(G-9279)
BEAUTIFUL SMILES OF DELAWARE
4901 Limestone Rd Ste 1 (19808-1271)
PHONE..................302 656-0558
Victor Venturena, *Principal*
EMP: 4
SALES (est): 361.3K **Privately Held**
SIC: 8021 Offices & clinics of dentists

(G-9280)
BECKERS CHIMNEY AND ROOFG LLC
209 Main St (19804-3904)
PHONE..................302 463-8294
Brandon Becker,
EMP: 25 **EST:** 2013
SALES (est): 271.2K **Privately Held**
SIC: 1761 Roofing contractor

(G-9281)
BEESON FUNERAL HOME (PA)
412 Philadelphia Pike (19809-2182)
PHONE..................302 764-2900
Matt Grieco, *Owner*
EMP: 6 **EST:** 1939
SALES (est): 675.7K **Privately Held**
WEB: www.griecofuneralhomes.com
SIC: 7261 Funeral home

(G-9282)
BEHAVIORAL HEALTH ASSOC
1303 Del Ave Apt 1216 (19806)
PHONE..................302 429-6200
Sandra Taub, *Owner*
EMP: 8

SALES (est): 73.3K **Privately Held**
SIC: 8093 Specialty outpatient clinics

(G-9283)
BEKART HOLDING LLC
1201 N Orange St Ste 7524 (19801-1298)
PHONE..................302 600-7000
Art Bekian, *Mng Member*
EMP: 10
SALES: 3MM **Privately Held**
SIC: 1522 Hotel/motel & multi-family home construction

(G-9284)
BELCHIM CROP PRTECTION US CORP (DH)
2751 Centerville Rd # 100 (19808-1627)
P.O. Box 1347 (19899-1347)
PHONE..................302 407-3590
Thomas Wood, *President*
EMP: 12
SQ FT: 5,000
SALES (corp-wide): 1.9MM **Privately Held**
SIC: 6719 Investment holding companies, except banks
HQ: Belchim Crop Protection
Technologielaan 7
Londerzeel 1840
523 009-06

(G-9285)
BELCHIM CROP PRTECTION USA LLC
2751 Centerville Rd # 100 (19808-1600)
PHONE..................302 407-3590
Thomas Wood, *Manager*
▲ **EMP:** 12
SQ FT: 5,000
SALES: 6.2MM
SALES (corp-wide): 1.9MM **Privately Held**
SIC: 2879 Agricultural chemicals
HQ: Belchim Crop Protection Us Corporation
2751 Centerville Rd # 100
Wilmington DE 19808
302 407-3590

(G-9286)
BELCO INC
909 Delaware Ave (19806-4701)
P.O. Box 1909 (19899-1909)
PHONE..................302 655-1561
James D Carota, *Vice Pres*
Jill Cantera, *Vice Pres*
Richard D Cantera, *Vice Pres*
Steven C Cantera, *Vice Pres*
Arthur A Carota Jr, *Vice Pres*
EMP: 4
SQ FT: 15,000
SALES (est): 495.6K **Privately Held**
SIC: 6512 Commercial & industrial building operation

(G-9287)
BELFINT LYONS & SHUMAN P A
1011 Centre Rd Ste 310 (19805-1266)
PHONE..................302 225-0600
Norman J Shuman, *President*
Joanne Beach, *Accountant*
Steven Blahut, *Accountant*
Tini Graff, *Accountant*
Cindy Jones-Taddei, *Accountant*
EMP: 60
SALES (est): 5.9MM **Privately Held**
SIC: 8721 Accounting services, except auditing; billing & bookkeeping service; certified public accountant

(G-9288)
BELLEVUE COMMUNITY CENTER
500 Duncan Rd Ofc A (19809-2369)
PHONE..................302 429-5859
EMP: 4 **EST:** 2017
SALES (est): 46.7K **Privately Held**
SIC: 8322 Community center

(G-9289)
BELLEVUE CONTRACTORS LLC
909 Delaware Ave (19806-4701)
P.O. Box 8909 (19899-8909)
PHONE..................302 655-1522

Wilmington - New Castle County (G-9290) GEOGRAPHIC SECTION

Jill Cantera, *Vice Pres*
Dick Canter, *Vice Pres*
Arthur Carota, *Vice Pres*
Larry Gehrke, *Vice Pres*
Sharon Swankoski, *Project Mgr*
EMP: 15
SQ FT: 8,000
SALES (est): 1.5MM **Privately Held**
WEB: www.bellevuecontractors.com
SIC: 1521 Single-family housing construction

(G-9290)
BELLEVUE HEART GROUP LLC
1016 Delaware Ave (19806-4704)
PHONE.............................302 468-4500
Hamid Deliri, *Mng Member*
EMP: 5
SALES (est): 284.4K **Privately Held**
SIC: 8011 Cardiologist & cardio-vascular specialist

(G-9291)
BELLEVUE HOLDING COMPANY (PA)
909 Delaware Ave (19806-4701)
P.O. Box 1909 (19899-1909)
PHONE.............................302 655-1561
Larry Gehrke, *President*
Jill Cantera, *Vice Pres*
Richard D Cantera, *Vice Pres*
Arthur A Carota Jr, *Vice Pres*
James D Carota, *Vice Pres*
EMP: 25
SQ FT: 5,000
SALES (est): 2MM **Privately Held**
SIC: 8741 1542 Construction management; commercial & office building, new construction

(G-9292)
BELLEVUE REALTY CO
909 Delaware Ave (19806-4701)
P.O. Box 1909 (19899-1909)
PHONE.............................302 655-1818
Marvin Sachs, *Vice Pres*
Matthew Gehrke, *Manager*
EMP: 10
SALES (est): 924.3K **Privately Held**
WEB: www.bellevuerealtyco.com
SIC: 6531 Real estate brokers & agents

(G-9293)
BELLEVUE REMODEL & DESIGN LLC
222 Philadelphia Pike # 9 (19809-3166)
PHONE.............................302 482-7200
Brian Sorg,
Victoria Sorg,
EMP: 6
SQ FT: 1,360
SALES (est): 455.5K **Privately Held**
SIC: 1521 Single-family housing construction

(G-9294)
BELLEX INTERNATIONAL CORP (PA)
200 Bellevue Pkwy Ste 180 (19809-3747)
PHONE.............................302 791-5180
Osamu Mihama, *President*
Hiroko Komatsu, *General Mgr*
Andrea Kornbluth, *Bd of Directors*
▲ **EMP:** 4
SALES (est): 1.3MM **Privately Held**
WEB: www.bellexinternational.com
SIC: 5169 5065 Chemicals & allied products; electronic parts & equipment

(G-9295)
BENCHMARK BUILDERS INC (PA)
818 First State Blvd (19804-3573)
P.O. Box 3246 (19804-0346)
PHONE.............................302 995-6945
Matt Egan, *President*
Francis Julian, *Vice Pres*
Richard Julian, *Admin Sec*
EMP: 34
SQ FT: 7,500
SALES (est): 7.8MM **Privately Held**
WEB: www.benchmarkbuilders.com
SIC: 1531 Speculative builder, single-family houses

(G-9296)
BENCHMARK TRANSMISSIONS INC
1301 Centerville Rd (19808-6219)
PHONE.............................302 999-9400
Joseph Principe, *Manager*
EMP: 5
SALES (est): 370K **Privately Held**
SIC: 7537 Automotive transmission repair shops

(G-9297)
BENEFICIAL CONSUMER DISC CO (DH)
301 N Walnut St (19801-3964)
PHONE.............................302 425-2500
Daniel E Rosequist, *President*
Ross Longfield, *Exec VP*
Bradford Harrison, *Vice Pres*
Janice Lewis, *Vice Pres*
Elizabeth A Dawson, *Treasurer*
EMP: 5 **EST:** 1976
SALES (est): 12.6MM
SALES (corp-wide): 87.7B **Privately Held**
SIC: 6141 Consumer finance companies
HQ: Hsbc Finance Corporation
1421 W Shure Dr Ste 100
Arlington Heights IL 60004
224 880-7000

(G-9298)
BENEFICIAL OKLAHOMA INC (DH)
301 N Walnut St (19801-3964)
PHONE.............................302 529-8701
David Greenwood, *Principal*
EMP: 15
SALES (est): 11.1MM
SALES (corp-wide): 87.7B **Privately Held**
SIC: 6035 Federal savings & loan associations
HQ: Hsbc Finance Corporation
1421 W Shure Dr Ste 100
Arlington Heights IL 60004
224 880-7000

(G-9299)
BENEFIT ADMINISTRATORS DEL
5708 Limestone Rd (19808-1216)
PHONE.............................302 234-1978
EMP: 4
SALES: 282.4K **Privately Held**
SIC: 6411 Insurance Agent/Broker

(G-9300)
BENEFIT SERVICES UNLIMITED
2500 Grubb Rd Ste 140 (19810-4711)
PHONE.............................302 479-5696
Jacqueline Gunther, *President*
EMP: 46
SQ FT: 11,000
SALES (est): 15MM **Privately Held**
SIC: 6371 Pension funds

(G-9301)
BENESCH FRIEDLANDER COPLAN &
Also Called: Attorney Rymond H Lemischs Off
222 Delaware Ave Ste 801 (19801-1611)
PHONE.............................216 363-4500
Raymond H Lemisch, *Manager*
Arlicia Payne, *Office Admin*
EMP: 10
SALES (corp-wide): 57.2MM **Privately Held**
SIC: 8111 General practice attorney, lawyer
PA: Benesch, Friedlander, Coplan & Aronoff Llp
200 Public Sq Ste 2300
Cleveland OH 44114
216 363-4500

(G-9302)
BENITIME SOLUTIONS INC
Also Called: Pridestaff
701 Foulk Rd Ste 2f (19803-3733)
PHONE.............................302 476-8097
Monica Eboda, *Principal*
EMP: 4
SQ FT: 1,268
SALES (est): 202.4K **Privately Held**
SIC: 7363 Temporary help service

(G-9303)
BENTLEY MILLS INC
2711 Centerville Rd # 400 (19808-1660)
PHONE.............................800 423-4709
EMP: 2
SALES (corp-wide): 222.2MM **Privately Held**
SIC: 2273 Carpets, textile fiber
PA: Bentley Mills, Inc.
14641 Don Julian Rd
City Of Industry CA 91746
626 333-4585

(G-9304)
BERKSHIRE AT LIMESTONE
1526 Braken Ave (19808-4388)
PHONE.............................302 635-7495
Jean Simpson, *Office Mgr*
EMP: 4 **EST:** 2012
SALES (est): 250.1K **Privately Held**
SIC: 5032 Limestone

(G-9305)
BERLEY SECURITY SYSTEMS INC
6701 Governor Printz Blvd (19809-1809)
PHONE.............................302 791-9056
Tom Hagenback, *President*
EMP: 10
SALES (est): 983.9K **Privately Held**
SIC: 7382 Burglar alarm maintenance & monitoring

(G-9306)
BERNARD AND BERNARD INC
Also Called: Delaware Temp System
5187 W Woodmill Dr Ste 1 (19808-4067)
PHONE.............................302 999-7213
Barney Barnard, *Manager*
Sheila Skilling, *Consultant*
EMP: 4
SALES (corp-wide): 1.2MM **Privately Held**
WEB: www.bernardpersonnel.com
SIC: 7361 Placement agencies
PA: Bernard And Bernard Incorporated
540 Greenhill Ave
Wilmington DE

(G-9307)
BERNARD ND RUTH SIEGEL JCC
101 Garden Of Eden Rd (19803-1511)
PHONE.............................302 478-5660
Stacey Colton, *Marketing Staff*
Ivy Harlev, *Exec Dir*
Adam Cook, *Director*
Kristina Beard, *Administration*
Debra Steinberg, *Professor*
EMP: 100
SALES: 5.5MM **Privately Held**
SIC: 8322 Community center

(G-9308)
BERNARDO ANTHONY J JR DR DDS
301 S Dupont Rd (19805-1416)
PHONE.............................302 998-9244
EMP: 4
SALES (est): 61.5K **Privately Held**
SIC: 8021 Offices & clinics of dentists

(G-9309)
BERNARDON PC
123 S Justison St Ste 101 (19801-5364)
PHONE.............................302 622-9550
William E Halloway, *President*
Christina Marconi, *Project Dir*
Michael Welz, *QA Dir*
Neil Liebman, *Admin Mgr*
EMP: 10
SALES (corp-wide): 6.2MM **Privately Held**
SIC: 8712 0781 7389 Architectural engineering; landscape planning services; interior decorating
PA: Bernardon Pc
10 N High St Fl 3
West Chester PA 19380
610 444-2900

(G-9310)
BERNICES EDTL SCL AG CTR INC
2516 W 4th St (19805-3308)
PHONE.............................302 651-0286
Bernice Thomas, *President*
EMP: 5
SALES: 307.1K **Privately Held**
SIC: 8351 Child day care services

(G-9311)
BESSEMER TRUST COMPANY
1007 N Orange St Ste 1450 (19801-1273)
PHONE.............................302 230-2675
George Kern, *Branch Mgr*
EMP: 11
SALES (corp-wide): 724.8MM **Privately Held**
SIC: 6733 Trusts
HQ: Bessemer Trust Company, N.A
630 5th Ave
New York NY 10111
212 708-9100

(G-9312)
BESSEMER TRUST COMPANY DEL NA
1007 N Orange St Ste 1450 (19801-1273)
PHONE.............................212 708-9182
John A Hilton Jr,
EMP: 20 **EST:** 2015
SALES (est): 129.2K **Privately Held**
SIC: 6021 National commercial banks

(G-9313)
BEST BUDDIES INTERNATIONAL INC
1401 Penns Ave Ste 104 (19806-4125)
PHONE.............................302 691-3187
Leslie Kosek, *Branch Mgr*
EMP: 6
SALES (corp-wide): 21.6MM **Privately Held**
SIC: 8641 Civic social & fraternal associations
PA: Best Buddies International, Inc.
100 Se 2nd St Ste 2200
Miami FL 33131

(G-9314)
BEST STONEWORKS OF DELAWARE
3015 Bellevue Ave (19802-2401)
PHONE.............................302 765-3497
Howard Garfinkel, *President*
EMP: 8
SALES: 500K **Privately Held**
WEB: www.beststoneworks.com
SIC: 3272 Building stone, artificial: concrete

(G-9315)
BESTFIELD ASSOCIATES INC
Also Called: Bestfield Homes
200 Mary Ella Dr (19805-1542)
PHONE.............................302 633-6361
Anthony Di Egidio Sr, *President*
EMP: 18
SQ FT: 1,500
SALES (est): 2.9MM **Privately Held**
WEB: www.bestfieldhomes.com
SIC: 1521 New construction, single-family houses

(G-9316)
BETHEL VILLA ASSOCIATES LP
506 E 5th St Fl 2 (19801-4706)
PHONE.............................302 426-9688
Alfred Good, *Manager*
EMP: 7
SALES (corp-wide): 25.1MM **Privately Held**
SIC: 6513 Apartment building operators
HQ: Bethel Villa Associates Lp
832 Germantown Pike Ste 5
Plymouth Meeting PA 19462

(G-9317)
BETHEL VILLAS 2009 ASSOC LP
506 E 5th St (19801-4706)
PHONE.............................610 278-1733
Isreal Roizman, *Partner*
EMP: 7
SALES: 950K **Privately Held**
SIC: 6513 Apartment building operators

GEOGRAPHIC SECTION
Wilmington - New Castle County (G-9350)

(G-9318)
BETZ&BETZ ENTERPRISES LLC
528 W 3rd St (19801-2320)
PHONE...................302 602-0613
Craig Betz,
Neil Betz,
EMP: 2
SALES (est): 90.7K Privately Held
SIC: 2676 7389 Towels, napkins & tissue paper products;

(G-9319)
BEVER MOBILITY PRODUCTS INC
2711 Centerville Rd (19808-1660)
PHONE...................312 375-0300
Jeroen Van Den Broek, President
Thomas Thorelli, Treasurer
EMP: 1 Privately Held
SIC: 3714 7389 Motor vehicle parts & accessories;

(G-9320)
BEVERLY L BOVE PA
Also Called: Beverly Bove Attorney At Law
1020 W 18th St Ste 2 (19802-3892)
P.O. Box 1607 (19899-1607)
PHONE...................302 777-3500
Beverly L Bove PA, Owner
EMP: 8
SALES (est): 890.4K Privately Held
SIC: 8111 General practice attorney, lawyer

(G-9321)
BEVERLYS HELP IN HAND
2520 W 4th St (19805-3308)
PHONE...................302 651-9304
Beverly Winward, Owner
EMP: 5
SALES (est): 205.7K Privately Held
SIC: 8351 Group day care center

(G-9322)
BEW PRODUCTIONS
Also Called: Entertainment Production Svcs
1004 Berkeley Rd (19807-2814)
PHONE...................302 547-8661
Robert Hendry, Principal
EMP: 6
SALES (est): 76.1K Privately Held
SIC: 7822 Motion picture & tape distribution

(G-9323)
BF DISC INC
103 Foulk Rd (19803-3742)
PHONE...................302 691-6351
EMP: 2
SALES (est): 104.7K Privately Held
SIC: 3011 Tires & inner tubes

(G-9324)
BFI WASTE SERVICES LLC
Also Called: Site 321
1420 New York Ave (19801-5826)
PHONE...................302 658-4097
Michael Stang, Manager
EMP: 34
SALES (corp-wide): 10B Publicly Held
WEB: www.sunsetwaste.com
SIC: 4953 4212 Refuse systems; local trucking, without storage
HQ: Bfi Waste Services, Llc
18500 N Allied Way # 100
Phoenix AZ 85054
480 627-2700

(G-9325)
BGDEDGE INC
Also Called: Instant Imprints of Delaware
3652 Silverside Rd (19810-5191)
PHONE...................302 477-1734
Brian Drysdale, President
EMP: 2
SALES: 130K Privately Held
SIC: 2752 Commercial printing, lithographic

(G-9326)
BIA SEPARATIONS INC
1000 N West St Ste 1200 (19801-1058)
PHONE...................510 740-4045
Darryl G Glover, CEO
EMP: 3

SALES: 60K Privately Held
SIC: 3826 Analytical instruments

(G-9327)
BIEHL & CO LP
1 Hausel Rd (19801-5800)
PHONE...................302 594-9700
Paul Cruz, Manager
Taylor Arnold, Agent
EMP: 4
SALES (corp-wide): 1.1MM Privately Held
SIC: 8711 Marine engineering
HQ: Biehl & Co., L.P.
5200 Hollister St Ste 300
Houston TX 77040
713 690-7200

(G-9328)
BIF III HOLTWOOD LLC
2711 Centerville Rd # 400 (19808-1660)
PHONE...................819 561-2722
Felipe Pinel, CEO
Thomas Deedy, COO
Kimball A Osmars, COO
Valerie Hannah, CFO
EMP: 20 EST: 2016
SALES: 20MM Privately Held
SIC: 3569 Gas generators

(G-9329)
BIFFERATO GENTILOTTI LLC (PA)
4250 Lancaster Pike Ste 1 (19805-1520)
P.O. Box 2165 (19899-2165)
PHONE...................302 429-1900
Jeffrey M Gentilotti, Partner
Amy Kiefer, Manager
Vincent A Bifferato,
Ian Connor Bifferato,
Jeffery M Gentilotti,
EMP: 5
SALES (est): 3.8MM Privately Held
WEB: www.bgbde.com
SIC: 8111 Specialized law offices, attorneys

(G-9330)
BIFFERATO GENTILOTTI LLC
4250 Lancaster Pike (19805-1520)
PHONE...................302 429-1900
Missy Thomas, Branch Mgr
Deanna Dominelli, Legal Staff
EMP: 4
SALES (est): 401.5K
SALES (corp-wide): 3.8MM Privately Held
WEB: www.bgbde.com
SIC: 8111 Specialized law offices, attorneys
PA: Bifferato Gentilotti Llc
4250 Lancaster Pike Ste 1
Wilmington DE 19805
302 429-1900

(G-9331)
BIG BRTHERS BIG SISTERS OF DEL
413 Larch Cir (19804-2370)
PHONE...................302 998-3577
Mary Fox, President
Tiyona McCollister, Manager
Onita Wells, Manager
EMP: 19
SALES: 722.1K Privately Held
WEB: www.bbbsde.org
SIC: 8322 Youth center

(G-9332)
BIG TIME TOWING LLC
913 N Market St Ste 200 (19801-3097)
PHONE...................302 510-1160
EMP: 8
SALES (est): 82.5K Privately Held
SIC: 7549 Towing services

(G-9333)
BIG TOMORROW LLC
800 Delaware Ave (19801-1322)
PHONE...................650 714-3912
Peter Presley,
Aric Cheston,
Nick Delamare,
Alicia Graham,
EMP: 10 EST: 2013

SALES (est): 380K Privately Held
SIC: 8742 7389 Management consulting services;

(G-9334)
BIG TOY CUSTOM CAR CARE INC
1806 Tulip St (19805-3824)
PHONE...................302 668-6729
Chevy L Anderson Sr, Principal
EMP: 4 EST: 2016
SALES (est): 34.1K Privately Held
SIC: 7542 Carwashes

(G-9335)
BIGGS & BATTAGLIA
921 N Orange St (19801-1603)
P.O. Box 1489 (19899-1489)
PHONE...................302 655-9677
Victor F Battaglia, Partner
Philip Bartoshesky, Partner
Robert K Beste Jr, Partner
John Biggs III, Partner
Paul A Bradley, Partner
EMP: 15
SALES (est): 1.4MM Privately Held
WEB: www.batlaw.com
SIC: 8111 General practice law office

(G-9336)
BIJOTI INC
1808 N Washington St (19802-4730)
PHONE...................908 916-7764
Joshua Marpet, CEO
EMP: 10
SQ FT: 9,300
SALES (est): 570K Privately Held
SIC: 7372 Application computer software

(G-9337)
BILL WARD INC
1010 Philadelphia Pike (19809-2000)
PHONE...................302 762-6600
Bill Ward, President
William F Ward Sr, Vice Pres
▲ EMP: 5
SQ FT: 6,000
SALES (est): 535.9K Privately Held
WEB: www.billward.com
SIC: 5199 Advertising specialties

(G-9338)
BILLOWS ELECTRIC SUPPLY CO INC
480 First State Blvd (19804-3745)
PHONE...................302 996-9133
Jeff Billows, CEO
EMP: 8 Privately Held
SIC: 5063 Electrical supplies
PA: Billows Electric Supply Company, Inc.
1813 Underwood Blvd
Delran NJ 08075

(G-9339)
BINKLEY HORTICULTURE SERVICES
1524 Clinton St (19806-1315)
PHONE...................484 459-2391
Erica Boston, Owner
EMP: 4 EST: 2011
SALES (est): 93.3K Privately Held
SIC: 0781 Horticulture services

(G-9340)
BIOMATIK USA LLC
105 Silverside Rd 501 (19809-1727)
PHONE...................416 273-4858
Michael He,
EMP: 15
SALES (est): 697.7K Privately Held
SIC: 8731 Biotechnical research, commercial

(G-9341)
BIRTHDAYBOXIO INC
251 Little Falls Dr (19808-1674)
PHONE...................302 990-2616
William Benjamin Young, Principal
EMP: 1
SALES (est): 37.5K Privately Held
SIC: 2741

(G-9342)
BISHOP ENTERPRISES CORPORATION
2207 Concord Pike Ste 412 (19803-2908)
PHONE...................302 379-2884
Patsy G Bishop, President
EMP: 22
SALES (est): 849.3K Privately Held
SIC: 8748 Business consulting

(G-9343)
BIZBOOST INC
4023 Kennett Pike 50297 (19807-2018)
PHONE...................732 865-8050
Charles Betta, Managing Dir
EMP: 4
SALES: 380K Privately Held
SIC: 6153 Working capital financing

(G-9344)
BK 2 SI LLC
1201 N Orange St Ste 600 (19801-1171)
PHONE...................800 246-2677
Andre Anderson, CEO
EMP: 1
SALES (est): 59.1K Privately Held
SIC: 7372 7389 Publishers' computer software;

(G-9345)
BK TEMP HOME CARE
2101 N Tatnall St (19802-4109)
PHONE...................302 575-1400
EMP: 6
SALES (est): 143.5K Privately Held
SIC: 8059 Personal care home, with health care

(G-9346)
BLACK & VEATCH CORPORATION
200 Bellevue Pkwy Ste 430 (19809-3712)
PHONE...................302 798-0200
Callixtus Aulisio, Branch Mgr
EMP: 30
SALES (corp-wide): 2.8B Privately Held
SIC: 8711 Consulting engineer
HQ: Black & Veatch Corporation
11401 Lamar Ave
Overland Park KS 66211
913 458-2000

(G-9347)
BLACK ROCK INC
400 Bellevue Pkwy (19809-3723)
PHONE...................302 797-2009
Praveenkumar Jagannathan, Vice Pres
Mike Weintel, Vice Pres
Anitha Pai, Database Admin
Emily Dansereau, Analyst
Ellen Bockius, Associate
EMP: 12
SALES (est): 2.5MM Privately Held
SIC: 6722 Money market mutual funds

(G-9348)
BLACKGRID CONSULTING LLC
2711 Centerville Rd (19808-1660)
PHONE...................302 319-2013
Steven W Ashton,
EMP: 5
SALES (est): 211.6K Privately Held
SIC: 8742 Management consulting services

(G-9349)
BLACKROCK ENHNCED GLOBL DVDEND
100 Bellevue Pkwy (19809-3716)
PHONE...................800 441-7762
Richard E Cavanagh, Ch of Bd
Karen P Robards, Ch of Bd
John M Perlowski, President
Charles Park, COO
Jonathan Diorio, Vice Pres
EMP: 8
SALES: 29.1MM Privately Held
SIC: 6733 Trusts

(G-9350)
BLACKROCK FINANCIAL MANAGEMENT
400 Bellevue Pkwy (19809-3723)
PHONE...................302 797-2000

Wilmington - New Castle County (G-9351)

EMP: 4
SALES (est): 257.9K **Publicly Held**
SIC: 6282 Investment advice
PA: Blackrock, Inc.
55 E 52nd St
New York NY 10055

(G-9351)
BLACKROCK FUNDS II
Also Called: Blackrock Total
100 Bellevue Pkwy (19809-3716)
PHONE.................302 797-2000
Helen Marie Sheehan, *Manager*
EMP: 12
SALES (est): 1.9MM **Privately Held**
SIC: 6722 Money market mutual funds

(G-9352)
BLACKROCK GLOBAL LONG
100 Bellevue Pkwy (19809-3716)
PHONE.................302 797-2000
Scott Bowers, *Vice Pres*
William Fagan, *Vice Pres*
Leinee Hornbeck, *Vice Pres*
Matt Luongo, *Vice Pres*
Amy Whitelaw, *Portfolio Mgr*
EMP: 4
SALES (est): 322.9K **Privately Held**
SIC: 6722 Money market mutual funds

(G-9353)
BLACKROCK INCOME TRUST INC
100 Bellevue Pkwy (19809-3716)
PHONE.................800 441-7762
Richard E Cavanagh, *Ch of Bd*
Karen P Robards, *Ch of Bd*
John M Perlowski, *President*
Jonathan Diorio, *Vice Pres*
Neal J Andrews, *CFO*
EMP: 8
SALES (est): 36.5MM **Privately Held**
SIC: 6726 Management investment funds, closed-end

(G-9354)
BLACKROCK INSTNL MGT CORP
Also Called: Pimc
100 Bellevue Pkwy (19809-3716)
PHONE.................302 797-2000
Ralph L Schlosstein, *Principal*
Susan L Wagner, *Principal*
EMP: 88 **EST:** 1977
SQ FT: 10,000
SALES (est): 9MM **Publicly Held**
WEB: www.blackrock.com
SIC: 6282 Investment advisory service
HQ: Blackrock Holdco 2, Inc.
40 E 52nd St
New York NY 10022
212 754-5300

(G-9355)
BLACKROCK INTERMEDIATE
100 Bellevue Pkwy (19809-3716)
PHONE.................302 797-2000
John Abella, *Principal*
EMP: 17
SALES (est): 4.1MM **Privately Held**
SIC: 6722 Money market mutual funds

(G-9356)
BLACKROCK LNG-HRZON EQITY FUND
100 Bellevue Pkwy (19809-3716)
PHONE.................800 441-7762
EMP: 4
SALES (est): 333.1K **Publicly Held**
WEB: www.ml.com
SIC: 6722 Money market mutual funds
PA: Blackrock, Inc.
55 E 52nd St
New York NY 10055

(G-9357)
BLACKROCK MNCPL 2030 TRGET TER
100 Bellevue Pkwy (19809-3716)
PHONE.................800 882-0052
Richard E Cavanagh, *Ch of Bd*
Karen P Robards, *Ch of Bd*
John M Perlowski, *President*
Jonathan Diorio, *Vice Pres*
Neal J Andrews, *CFO*
EMP: 8
SALES: 91.3MM **Privately Held**
SIC: 6726 Management investment funds, closed-end

(G-9358)
BLACKROCK MNCPL INCOME INV QLT
100 Bellevue Pkwy (19809-3716)
PHONE.................800 441-7762
Richard E Cavanagh, *Ch of Bd*
Karen P Robards, *Ch of Bd*
John M Perlowski, *President*
Jonathan Diorio, *Vice Pres*
Neal J Andrews, *CFO*
EMP: 8
SALES: 9.3MM **Privately Held**
SIC: 6722 Management investment, open-end

(G-9359)
BLACKROCK MNHLDNGS CAL QLTY FU
100 Bellevue Pkwy (19809-3716)
PHONE.................800 441-7762
Richard E Cavanagh, *Ch of Bd*
Karen P Robards, *Ch of Bd*
John M Perlowski, *President*
Neal J Andrews, *CFO*
Jay M Fife, *Treasurer*
EMP: 8
SALES: 38.7MM **Privately Held**
SIC: 6726 Management investment funds, closed-end

(G-9360)
BLACKROCK MNHLDNGS NJ QLTY FUN
100 Bellevue Pkwy (19809-3716)
PHONE.................800 441-7762
Richard E Cavanagh, *Ch of Bd*
Karen P Robards, *Ch of Bd*
John M Perlowski, *President*
Jonathan Diorio, *Vice Pres*
Neal J Andrews, *CFO*
EMP: 8
SALES: 31.2MM **Privately Held**
SIC: 6726 Management investment funds, closed-end

(G-9361)
BLACKROCK NY MNCPL INCOME QLTY
100 Bellevue Pkwy (19809-3716)
PHONE.................800 441-7762
Richard E Cavanagh, *Ch of Bd*
Karen P Robards, *Ch of Bd*
John M Perlowski, *President*
Jonathan Diorio, *Vice Pres*
Neal J Andrews, *CFO*
EMP: 8
SALES: 5.8MM **Privately Held**
SIC: 6726 Management investment funds, closed-end

(G-9362)
BLACKROCK NY MNCPL INCOME TR I
100 Bellevue Pkwy (19809-3716)
PHONE.................800 441-7762
Richard E Cavanagh, *Ch of Bd*
Karen P Robards, *Ch of Bd*
John M Perlowski, *President*
Jonathan Diorio, *Vice Pres*
Neal J Andrews, *CFO*
EMP: 8
SALES: 5.1MM **Privately Held**
SIC: 6733 Trusts

(G-9363)
BLACKROCK NY MUNICPL INCOME TR
100 Bellevue Pkwy (19809-3716)
PHONE.................800 441-7762
Richard E Cavanagh, *Ch of Bd*
Karen P Robards, *Ch of Bd*
John M Perlowski, *President*
Jonathan Diorio, *Vice Pres*
Neal J Andrews, *CFO*
EMP: 8
SALES: 12.6MM **Privately Held**
SIC: 6733 Trusts

(G-9364)
BLACKSTONE BUILDING GROUP LLC
3310 Coachman Rd (19803-1945)
PHONE.................302 824-4632
Benjamin Bell,
EMP: 5
SALES (est): 190.2K **Privately Held**
SIC: 1542 Nonresidential construction

(G-9365)
BLACKTHORN ADVISORY GROUP LLC
750 Shipyard Dr Ste 200 (19801-5160)
PHONE.................302 442-6484
EMP: 7 **EST:** 2012
SALES (est): 851.9K **Privately Held**
SIC: 7379

(G-9366)
BLADE PLATFORMS LLC
1000 N West St (19801-1050)
PHONE.................646 431-1666
Vlad Sidoren, *Manager*
▲ **EMP:** 4
SALES (est): 439.4K **Privately Held**
SIC: 7353 Heavy construction equipment rental

(G-9367)
BLAKE AND VAUGHAN ENGRG INC
800 Woodlawn Ave (19805-2815)
PHONE.................302 888-1780
Daniel Blake, *President*
Jeff Vaughan, *Principal*
EMP: 12
SQ FT: 3,000
SALES (est): 1.9MM **Privately Held**
SIC: 8711 Civil engineering

(G-9368)
BLANK ROME LLP
1201 N Market St Ste 800 (19801-1807)
PHONE.................302 425-6400
Tom Preston,
Lisa Oriente, *Assistant*
Adam V Orlacchio, *Associate*
EMP: 40
SALES (corp-wide): 152.9MM **Privately Held**
WEB: www.blankrome.com
SIC: 8111 General practice attorney, lawyer
PA: Blank Rome Llp
1 Logan Sq
Philadelphia PA 19103
215 569-5500

(G-9369)
BLIND FACTORY
3316 Kirkwood Hwy (19808-6132)
PHONE.................302 838-1211
Richard Keith Sr, *President*
Denice Baker, *Site Mgr*
EMP: 1
SALES (est): 12.4K **Privately Held**
SIC: 2591 Blinds vertical

(G-9370)
BLINDSIGHT DELAWARE LLC
2915 Newport Gap Pike (19808-2376)
PHONE.................302 998-5913
Loretta Harper-Brown, *Exec Dir*
L Hrper-Brown, *Director*
EMP: 30 **EST:** 2015
SALES (est): 414.5K **Privately Held**
SIC: 8699 Charitable organization

(G-9371)
BLOOD BANK OF DELMARVA INC
913 N Market St Ste 905 (19801-4926)
PHONE.................302 737-8400
Helen Graham, *Director*
EMP: 8
SALES (corp-wide): 22.7MM **Privately Held**
SIC: 8099 Blood bank
PA: Blood Bank Of Delmarva, Inc.
100 Hygeia Dr
Newark DE 19713
302 737-1151

(G-9372)
BLOOM CONSULTING
2812 Landon Dr (19810-2213)
PHONE.................302 584-1592
Seth Bloom, *President*
EMP: 6
SALES: 200K **Privately Held**
WEB: www.bloomconsultinginc.com
SIC: 8742 Financial consultant

(G-9373)
BLOSSOM PHILADELPHIA
3518 Silverside Rd Ste 22 (19810-4907)
PHONE.................215 242-4200
Michele Toy, *President*
Deb Wolf, *Director*
EMP: 11
SALES (est): 585.8K **Privately Held**
SIC: 8322 Social services for the handicapped

(G-9374)
BLUE CHIP SERVICES LTD
501 Silverside Rd Ste 90 (19809-1376)
PHONE.................302 798-5010
EMP: 5 **EST:** 1985
SALES (est): 94K **Privately Held**
SIC: 7349 Building Maintenance Services

(G-9375)
BLUE DIAMOND DENTAL PA
Also Called: Vincent J Daniels DMD
2300 Penns Ave Ste 2c (19806-1379)
PHONE.................302 655-8387
Vincent Daniels DMD, *President*
Vincent Daniels DMD, *President*
Melanie Daniels, *Shareholder*
Vincent Daniels, *Fmly & Gen Dent*
EMP: 9
SQ FT: 4,000
SALES (est): 948.6K **Privately Held**
SIC: 8021 Dentists' office

(G-9376)
BLUE ENERGY INTERNATIONAL LLC
1209 N Orange St (19801-1120)
PHONE.................480 941-5100
Jim Ameduri,
EMP: 4
SALES (est): 243.2K **Privately Held**
SIC: 4931 Electric & other services combined

(G-9377)
BLUE ENERGY PARTNERS LLC
1209 N Orange St (19801-1120)
PHONE.................480 941-5100
Jim Ameduri,
EMP: 10
SALES (est): 727.4K **Privately Held**
SIC: 4931 Electric & other services combined

(G-9378)
BLUE MARBLE LOGISTICS LLC (PA)
800 N King St Ste 102 (19801-3544)
P.O. Box 147 (19899-0147)
PHONE.................302 661-4390
Dan Boylan, *President*
Jeff Berryman, *Vice Pres*
Dennis Schofield, *Vice Pres*
Andrew Thompson, *Vice Pres*
EMP: 15
SQ FT: 3,000
SALES (est): 4.5MM **Privately Held**
SIC: 5044 Copying equipment

(G-9379)
BLUE OCEAN SYSTEMS LLC
3511 Silverside Rd # 204 (19810-4902)
PHONE.................866 355-5989
Rajendra Mittal, *Project Mgr*
Karen Musselman, *Marketing Staff*
Pam Lidowski, *Office Mgr*
Rong Zhang, *Consultant*
Ashutosh Bhatnagar, *Director*
EMP: 9
SALES (est): 1.3MM **Privately Held**
SIC: 7373 Value-added resellers, computer systems

GEOGRAPHIC SECTION
Wilmington - New Castle County (G-9410)

(G-9380)
BLUE PIE PRODUCTIONS USA LLC
3 Germay Dr Ste 44002 (19804-1127)
PHONE..................917 817-7174
Damien Reilly,
EMP: 12
SALES (est): 394.6K Privately Held
SIC: 7389 Music recording producer

(G-9381)
BLUE SKY CLEAN
293 Carlow Dr (19808-3683)
PHONE..................302 584-5800
Gary Ventresca, *Principal*
EMP: 2
SALES (est): 155.4K Privately Held
WEB: www.blueskyclean.net
SIC: 7699 2899 5087 Cleaning services; chemical supplies for foundries; laundry equipment & supplies; cleaning & maintenance equipment & supplies; janitors' supplies

(G-9382)
BLUE SWAN CLEANERS INC (PA)
Also Called: Swan Cleaners
2001 Delaware Ave (19806-2207)
P.O. Box 3722 (19807-0722)
PHONE..................302 652-7607
Ronald Olivere, *President*
Kathleen Dent, *Admin Sec*
EMP: 16
SQ FT: 3,500
SALES (est): 420.4K Privately Held
SIC: 7216 7212 Drycleaning plants, except rugs; garment pressing

(G-9383)
BLUESTONE AM LLC
728 Westcliff Rd (19803-1712)
P.O. Box 7281 (19803-0281)
PHONE..................302 477-0370
EMP: 11
SALES (est): 911.7K Privately Held
SIC: 8748 Systems engineering consultant, ex. computer or professional

(G-9384)
BLUESTONE COMMUNICATION
3600 Silverside Rd (19810-5100)
P.O. Box 7499 (19803-0499)
PHONE..................302 478-4200
EMP: 8
SALES (est): 53.8MM Privately Held
SIC: 4899 Communication services

(G-9385)
BLUEVAULT LLC
Also Called: CMS
1300 N Broom St (19806-4206)
P.O. Box 288 (19899-0288)
PHONE..................302 425-4367
Don Garvey, *Opers Staff*
Javon Simons, *Senior Engr*
Joe Grieco, *CFO*
Michelle Davis, *Manager*
Matt Rainville, *Director*
EMP: 12
SQ FT: 2,400
SALES (est): 1.3MM Privately Held
WEB: www.claimantsystems.com
SIC: 7372 Prepackaged software

(G-9386)
BML APP DEVELOPMENT
123 Berry Dr (19808-3617)
PHONE..................302 528-7381
Bruce Morris, *CEO*
EMP: 4 EST: 2013
SALES (est): 240K Privately Held
SIC: 7371 7389 Computer software development & applications;

(G-9387)
BMO DELAWARE TRUST COMPANY
20 Montchanin Rd Ste 240 (19807-2174)
PHONE..................302 652-1660
Douglas Lundblad, *Administration*
Douglas N Lundblad, *Administration*
EMP: 6 EST: 2012
SALES (est): 1MM Privately Held
SIC: 6022 State commercial banks

(G-9388)
BMP SUNSTONE CORPORATION
3711 Kennett Pike Ste 200 (19807-2161)
PHONE..................610 940-1675
David Gao, *CEO*
Zhijun Tong, *President*
Yanping Zhao, *COO*
Fred M Powell, *CFO*
EMP: 1198
SALES (est): 66.6MM Privately Held
WEB: www.beijingmedpharm.com
SIC: 5122 Drugs, proprietaries & sundries
PA: Sanofi
54 Rue La Boetie
Paris 8e Arrondissement 75008

(G-9389)
BOB LAFAZIA
Also Called: Bob's Custom Clubs
2635 Grendon Dr (19808-3828)
PHONE..................302 633-1456
Bob Lafazia, *Principal*
EMP: 5 EST: 2009
SALES (est): 79.1K Privately Held
SIC: 7997 Membership sports & recreation clubs

(G-9390)
BODELL BOVE LLC
1225 N King St Ste 1000 (19801-3250)
PHONE..................302 655-6749
Joseph Bodell Jr, *Partner*
Jeri Craw, *Legal Staff*
Adam Lazarow, *Associate*
EMP: 13 Privately Held
SIC: 8111 Specialized law offices, attorneys
PA: Bodell Bove, Llc
1845 Walnut St Ste 1100
Philadelphia PA 19103

(G-9391)
BOMBAY HOOK LTD
1105 N Market St (19801-1216)
PHONE..................302 571-8644
EMP: 4
SALES (est): 209.8K
SALES (corp-wide): 25.9B Publicly Held
SIC: 6726 Investment offices
HQ: Viacomcbs Inc.
1515 Broadway
New York NY 10036
212 258-6000

(G-9392)
BOMBSHELL BEAUTY INC
331 Rockmeade Dr (19810-1423)
PHONE..................302 559-3011
Suzanne Martinelli, *CEO*
EMP: 5 EST: 2011
SQ FT: 2,500
SALES (est): 207.3K Privately Held
SIC: 3999 Hair, dressing of, for the trade

(G-9393)
BOOKS & TOBACCOS INC
4555 Kirkwood Hwy (19808-5117)
PHONE..................302 994-3156
Andy Summer, *President*
Donna R Summer, *Vice Pres*
EMP: 12
SALES (est): 462.8K Privately Held
SIC: 7999 5199 5192 Lottery tickets, sale of; lighters, cigarette & cigar; books, periodicals & newspapers

(G-9394)
BOOST LEARNING LLC
721 Ambleside Dr (19808-1502)
PHONE..................302 691-5821
Eric Randolph, *Principal*
EMP: 5
SALES (est): 98.4K Privately Held
SIC: 8351 Preschool center

(G-9395)
BOSTON LAND CO MGT SVCS INC
Also Called: Quaker Hill Place Co
200 N Washington St Ofc 1 (19801-2300)
PHONE..................302 571-0100
Judith Vansice, *Principal*
EMP: 9
SALES (corp-wide): 4.1MM Privately Held
WEB: www.bostonlandcompany.com
SIC: 6531 6513 Real estate managers; apartment building operators
PA: The Boston Land Company Management Services Inc
411 Waverley Oaks Rd # 313
Waltham MA 02452
781 547-4280

(G-9396)
BOTICA CBD INC
300 Delaware Ave Ste 210 (19801-6601)
PHONE..................619 800-5857
Tayde Aburto, *President*
EMP: 1
SALES (est): 39.5K Privately Held
SIC: 2023 Dietary supplements, dairy & non-dairy based

(G-9397)
BOUDART & MENSINGER LLP
2710 Centerville Rd # 101 (19808-1652)
PHONE..................302 428-0100
Thomas Jenkins, *Principal*
EMP: 6
SALES (est): 755.1K Privately Held
SIC: 8111 General practice law office

(G-9398)
BOULDEN BUSES INC
32 Honeysuckle Ln (19804-3992)
PHONE..................302 998-5463
Kenneth Darsney, *President*
Charlene Fanny, *Vice Pres*
EMP: 35
SALES (est): 1.3MM Privately Held
SIC: 4151 School buses

(G-9399)
BOULOS MAGDY I MD PA
1306 N Broom St Ofc 1 (19806-4238)
PHONE..................302 571-9750
Boulos Magdy I, *President*
EMP: 4
SQ FT: 1,200
SALES (est): 199.8K Privately Held
SIC: 8011 Neurologist

(G-9400)
BOVE PSYCHOLOGICAL SVCS LLC
108 Peirce Rd (19803-3728)
PHONE..................302 299-5193
Kathryn Bove-Yocum,
EMP: 8 EST: 2017
SALES (est): 64K Privately Held
SIC: 8059 Personal care home, with health care

(G-9401)
BOVELL LOWINGER BAIL BONDS
1900 W 4th St (19805-3422)
PHONE..................302 427-9000
Shirley Pruitt, *Owner*
Robert Bovell, *Owner*
EMP: 4
SALES (est): 346.8K Privately Held
WEB: www.fastbailbonds.com
SIC: 7389 Bail bonding

(G-9402)
BOXWOOD PLANING MILL INC
2 Meco Cir (19804-1109)
PHONE..................302 999-0249
Phillip O'Connell, *President*
Timothy O'Connell Jr, *Vice Pres*
EMP: 2
SQ FT: 14,000
SALES (est): 179.8K Privately Held
SIC: 2431 Planing mill, millwork; moldings, wood: unfinished & prefinished; doors, wood

(G-9403)
BOYER & BOYER (PA)
Also Called: BOPyer& Boyer CPA
2392 Limestone Rd (19808-4127)
PHONE..................302 998-3700
Donald L Boyer, *Owner*
Carrie Haddick, *Accountant*
Katherine Hikins, *Accountant*
Brandon Hunter, *Accountant*
Jennifer Stover, *Accountant*
EMP: 9
SQ FT: 3,500
SALES: 500K Privately Held
SIC: 8721 Certified public accountant

(G-9404)
BOYS & GIRLS CLUBS DEL INC (PA)
669 S Union St (19805-3852)
PHONE..................302 658-1870
Stuart Sharkey, *Ch of Bd*
George Krupanski Jr, *President*
Christopher Basher, *Vice Pres*
Janice Bates, *Vice Pres*
James C Logullo, *Vice Pres*
EMP: 305
SQ FT: 10,000
SALES: 20.8MM Privately Held
SIC: 8641 Youth organizations

(G-9405)
BOYS & GIRLS CLUBS DEL INC
Also Called: H. Fletcher Brown
1601 N Spruce St (19802-5026)
PHONE..................302 656-1386
Joe Riley, *Director*
EMP: 18
SALES (corp-wide): 20.8MM Privately Held
SIC: 8641 Youth organizations
PA: Boys & Girls Clubs Of Delaware, Inc.
669 S Union St
Wilmington DE 19805
302 658-1870

(G-9406)
BOYS & GIRLS CLUBS DEL INC
Also Called: Clarence Fraim
669 S Union St (19805-3852)
PHONE..................302 655-4591
Tyrone Perry, *Exec Dir*
Rachel Kane, *Director*
EMP: 25
SALES (corp-wide): 20.8MM Privately Held
SIC: 8641 Youth organizations
PA: Boys & Girls Clubs Of Delaware, Inc.
669 S Union St
Wilmington DE 19805
302 658-1870

(G-9407)
BP STAFFING INC
Also Called: Bernard Personnel
5187 W Woodmill Dr Ste 1 (19808-4067)
PHONE..................302 999-7213
Al Collins, *President*
EMP: 4 EST: 2005
SALES (est): 265.8K Privately Held
SIC: 7363 8742 Help supply services; personnel management consultant

(G-9408)
BPG OFFICE INVSTORS III/IV LLC
1000 N West St Ste 900 (19801-1050)
PHONE..................302 691-2100
C F Buccini, *Mng Member*
Chris Buccini, *Mng Member*
Christopher F Buccini, *Mng Member*
EMP: 10
SQ FT: 4,000
SALES (est): 1.2MM Privately Held
SIC: 6531 Real estate agents & managers

(G-9409)
BPG OFFICE PARTNERS VIII LLC
1000 N West St Ste 900 (19801-1050)
PHONE..................302 250-3065
Christopher Buccini, *Principal*
EMP: 50
SALES (est): 517.6K Privately Held
SIC: 6798 Real estate investment trusts

(G-9410)
BPG REAL ESTATE SERVICES LLC
3505 Silverside Rd # 105 (19810-4905)
PHONE..................302 478-1190
Chris Derasmo, *Principal*
EMP: 5

Wilmington - New Castle County (G-9411)

GEOGRAPHIC SECTION

SALES (est): 334.5K
SALES (corp-wide): 4.7MM **Privately Held**
SIC: 6531 Real estate brokers & agents
PA: Bpg Real Estate Services Llc
1000 N West St Ste 1000 # 1000
Wilmington DE 19801
302 777-2000

(G-9412)
BPG REAL ESTATE SERVICES LLC (PA)
1000 N West St Ste 1000 # 1000 (19801-1000)
PHONE..................302 777-2000
Christopher Buccini,
Robert Buccini,
Dave Pollin,
EMP: 25
SALES (est): 4.7MM **Privately Held**
SIC: 6531 Real estate leasing & rentals

(G-9412)
BPGS CONSTRUCTION LLC
1000 N West St (19801-1050)
PHONE..................302 691-2111
Bryan Haldeman, *Project Engr*
H Wesley Schwandt,
EMP: 55
SALES (est): 9MM **Privately Held**
SIC: 8741 Construction management

(G-9413)
BRADLEYS AUTO CENTER INC
5 E 41st St (19802-2338)
PHONE..................302 762-2247
Robert Bradley, *President*
EMP: 5
SQ FT: 5,000
SALES (est): 638.5K **Privately Held**
SIC: 7538 Engine rebuilding: automotive

(G-9414)
BRAINBASE INC (PA)
1000 N West St Ste 1200 (19801-1058)
PHONE..................412 515-9000
Nate Cavanaugh, *Principal*
EMP: 7
SALES (est): 876.3K **Privately Held**
SIC: 4813 ;

(G-9415)
BRAKES ENGINE & TRACKS LLC
501 Silverside Rd Pmb 29 (19809-1374)
PHONE..................302 476-9450
EMP: 5
SALES (est): 157.1K **Privately Held**
SIC: 5088 Whol Transportation Equipment

(G-9416)
BRANDI WINE PEDIATRIC INC
Also Called: Disanto, Joseph MD
3521 Silverside Rd Ste 1f (19810-4900)
PHONE..................302 478-7805
Rob Walter, *President*
Joseph Di Santo, *Principal*
Joseph Disanto, *Med Doctor*
EMP: 30
SALES (est): 1.6MM **Privately Held**
SIC: 8011 Pediatrician

(G-9417)
BRANDYWINE APARTMENT ASSOC LP
2702 Jacqueline Dr H19 (19810-2032)
PHONE..................302 475-8600
Paul Gravenhorst, *Partner*
EMP: 13
SQ FT: 3,000
SALES (est): 702.7K **Privately Held**
SIC: 6513 Apartment hotel operation

(G-9418)
BRANDYWINE BODY SHOP INC
1325 Newport Gap Pike (19804-2845)
PHONE..................302 998-0424
Gary Louth, *CEO*
Lisa Louth, *Vice Pres*
EMP: 9
SQ FT: 10,000
SALES (est): 917.1K **Privately Held**
SIC: 7532 Body shop, automotive

(G-9419)
BRANDYWINE BOTANICALS LLC
318 Tindall Rd (19805-1305)
PHONE..................302 354-4650
Robin Kielkowski, *Principal*
EMP: 2
SALES (est): 160.7K **Privately Held**
SIC: 2844 Toilet preparations

(G-9420)
BRANDYWINE CAD DESIGN INC
3204 Concord Pike (19803-5015)
PHONE..................302 478-8334
Donald Lloyd, *President*
Joe Kozlowski, *Manager*
William Deckman, *Info Tech Mgr*
Laura Cooke, *Executive Asst*
Patricia Lloyd, *Admin Sec*
EMP: 24
SQ FT: 7,000
SALES (est): 2.1MM **Privately Held**
WEB: www.bcad.com
SIC: 7374 8711 8712 Data processing & preparation; engineering services; architectural services

(G-9421)
BRANDYWINE CARE L L C
Also Called: Charles E Hill MD
1300 Delaware Ave Ste 1 (19806-4727)
PHONE..................302 658-5822
Sue Hill, *Manager*
Charles E Hill MD,
EMP: 10
SALES (est): 297.5K **Privately Held**
SIC: 8011 General & family practice, physician/surgeon

(G-9422)
BRANDYWINE CENTER FOR AUTISM
210 Bellefonte Ave (19809-2502)
PHONE..................302 762-2636
Marcus A Henry, *CEO*
Valpresious Ham, *Opers Staff*
EMP: 7
SALES (est): 99.4K **Privately Held**
SIC: 8322 Social service center

(G-9423)
BRANDYWINE CENTER FOR DANCE &
2700 Ebright Rd (19810-1129)
PHONE..................302 798-0124
Bonnie Castagna, *Principal*
EMP: 4
SALES (est): 81.8K **Privately Held**
WEB: www.brandywinecenterfordance.com
SIC: 7911 Dance instructor & school services

(G-9424)
BRANDYWINE CHRYSLER JEEP DODGE (PA)
3807 Kirkwood Hwy (19808-5107)
PHONE..................302 998-0458
Robert T Jones Jr, *President*
Francine Young, *Corp Secy*
EMP: 81 EST: 1968
SQ FT: 20,000
SALES (est): 28.6MM **Privately Held**
SIC: 5511 7539 Automobiles, new & used; automotive repair shops

(G-9425)
BRANDYWINE COSMETIC SURGERY (PA)
410 Foulk Rd Ste 201 (19803-3802)
PHONE..................302 652-3331
Christopher Whitney, *Principal*
EMP: 5
SALES (est): 763.3K **Privately Held**
SIC: 8011 Plastic surgeon

(G-9426)
BRANDYWINE COUNSELING
500 Duncan Rd Ofc 1 (19809-2369)
PHONE..................302 762-7120
Lynn M Fahey, *Manager*
EMP: 31
SALES (corp-wide): 12.4MM **Privately Held**
SIC: 8322 General counseling services

PA: Brandywine Counseling & Community Services, Inc.
2713 Lancaster Ave
Wilmington DE 19805
302 655-9880

(G-9427)
BRANDYWINE COUNSELING (PA)
2713 Lancaster Ave (19805-5220)
PHONE..................302 655-9880
Lynn M Fahey, *Exec Dir*
EMP: 60
SALES: 12.4MM **Privately Held**
SIC: 8093 Alcohol clinic, outpatient

(G-9428)
BRANDYWINE COUNTRY CLUB
302 River Rd Apt D2 (19809-2749)
PHONE..................302 478-4604
Ronald Rottmann, *Exec Dir*
EMP: 75 EST: 1945
SQ FT: 3,500
SALES: 1.3MM **Privately Held**
SIC: 7997 Golf club, membership; tennis club, membership; swimming club, membership

(G-9429)
BRANDYWINE DENTAL CARE
707 Foulk Rd Ste 201 (19803-3737)
PHONE..................302 421-9960
Shefali Pandya, *Principal*
EMP: 4 EST: 2012
SALES (est): 404.1K **Privately Held**
SIC: 8021 Dentists' office

(G-9430)
BRANDYWINE ELEVATOR CO INC (PA)
300 B And O Ln (19804-1448)
PHONE..................866 636-0102
Michael Sanfrancesco, *President*
Lorrie Sonsini, *Consultant*
EMP: 8
SQ FT: 1,800
SALES: 5.6MM **Privately Held**
SIC: 5084 1796 Elevators; elevator installation & conversion

(G-9431)
BRANDYWINE EXTERIORS CORP
221 Valley Rd (19804-1356)
PHONE..................302 746-7134
Joshua Boesen, *President*
EMP: 25
SALES: 4MM **Privately Held**
SIC: 1522 Residential construction

(G-9432)
BRANDYWINE FAMILY MEDICINE
2500 Grubb Rd Ste 212 (19810-4796)
PHONE..................302 475-5000
Valerie Elener, *Principal*
EMP: 4
SALES (est): 280K **Privately Held**
SIC: 8031 8011 Offices & clinics of osteopathic physicians; general & family practice, physician/surgeon

(G-9433)
BRANDYWINE FINE PROPERTIES
5701 Kennett Pike (19807-1311)
PHONE..................302 691-3052
George Hobbs, *Owner*
Michael Kelczewski, *Agent*
Linda Chase, *Real Est Agnt*
EMP: 10
SALES (est): 678.7K **Privately Held**
SIC: 6531 Real estate agents & managers

(G-9434)
BRANDYWINE FUND INC
3711 Kennett Pike Ste 100 (19807-2156)
P.O. Box 4166 (19807-0166)
PHONE..................302 656-3017
Bill D Alonzo, *President*
EMP: 35
SALES (est): 2.4MM **Privately Held**
SIC: 6722 Money market mutual funds

(G-9435)
BRANDYWINE GRAPHICS INC
Also Called: CNW Enterprise
500 S Colonial Ave (19805-1900)
PHONE..................302 655-7571
Robert R Shaw Jr, *President*
Aida Shaw, *President*
Craig Shaw, *Vice Pres*
EMP: 7
SQ FT: 18,500
SALES (est): 1MM **Privately Held**
WEB: www.brandywinegraphicsinc.com
SIC: 2761 2752 5112 Strip forms (manifold business forms); unit sets (manifold business forms); commercial printing, offset; business forms

(G-9436)
BRANDYWINE HILLS APARTMENTS
Also Called: Evergreen Reallty
4310 Miller Rd Apt 106 (19802-1919)
PHONE..................302 764-3242
Steven Woolfgang, *Owner*
EMP: 25 EST: 1965
SALES (est): 814.7K **Privately Held**
SIC: 6513 Apartment building operators

(G-9437)
BRANDYWINE HNDRED VTRNARY HOSP
806 Silverside Rd (19809-1324)
PHONE..................302 792-2777
Steven Hardy, *Owner*
EMP: 10 EST: 1974
SALES (est): 556.5K **Privately Held**
SIC: 0742 Animal hospital services, pets & other animal specialties

(G-9438)
BRANDYWINE HUNDRED FIRE CO 1
Also Called: BRANDYWINE HUNDRED FIRE CO NO
1006 Brandywine Blvd (19809-2530)
PHONE..................302 764-4901
Thomas Finlechiro, *Chief*
EMP: 80
SQ FT: 9,900
SALES: 1.7MM **Privately Held**
SIC: 7389 8322 Fire protection service other than forestry or public; emergency shelters

(G-9439)
BRANDYWINE I & 2 APTS
2702 Jacqueline Dr H19 (19810-2093)
PHONE..................302 475-8600
Wanda Hirchy, *Owner*
EMP: 10
SALES (est): 267.1K **Privately Held**
SIC: 6513 Apartment building operators

(G-9440)
BRANDYWINE IMAGING LLC
Also Called: Diagnostic Imaging Associates
3206 Concord Pike (19803-5015)
PHONE..................302 654-5300
Joseph Peacock,
Valerie J Gilliam, *Radiology*
EMP: 23
SALES: 950K
SALES (corp-wide): 4.2MM **Privately Held**
SIC: 8071 Medical laboratories
PA: Omega Imaging Associates, L.L.C.
6 Omega Dr
Newark DE 19713
302 738-9300

(G-9441)
BRANDYWINE LACROSSE CLUB
2403 W Heather Rd (19803-2719)
PHONE..................302 249-1840
Kenneth Rittenhouse, *Principal*
EMP: 4
SALES (est): 38.1K **Privately Held**
SIC: 7997 Membership sports & recreation clubs

(G-9442)
BRANDYWINE MILL WORK
1907 N Market St (19802-4812)
PHONE..................302 652-3008
EMP: 2

GEOGRAPHIC SECTION
Wilmington - New Castle County (G-9474)

SALES (est): 171.1K **Privately Held**
SIC: 2431 Millwork

(G-9443)
BRANDYWINE NURSERIES INC
4 James Ct (19801-5250)
P.O. Box 9333 (19809-0333)
PHONE.................................302 429-0865
Brien H Jamison, *President*
Joseph F Jamison Jr, *Vice Pres*
EMP: 48
SQ FT: 5,000
SALES (est): 2MM **Privately Held**
WEB: www.brandywinenurseries.com
SIC: 0781 0782 Landscape planning services; landscape contractors

(G-9444)
BRANDYWINE NURSING & REHAB
505 Greenbank Rd (19808-3164)
PHONE.................................302 683-0444
Harry Tractman, *President*
Fred Dibartolo, *Administration*
EMP: 200
SQ FT: 22,000
SALES (est): 10.9MM **Privately Held**
WEB: www.brandywinenursing.org
SIC: 8051 Convalescent home with continuous nursing care

(G-9445)
BRANDYWINE OB GYN
3520 Silverside Rd 2l1 (19810-4933)
PHONE.................................302 477-1375
Joseph Espinosa, *Manager*
EMP: 5 EST: 2010
SALES (est): 565.3K **Privately Held**
SIC: 8011 Gynecologist

(G-9446)
BRANDYWINE OCCPATIONAL THERAPY
800 Carr Rd (19809-2163)
PHONE.................................302 740-4798
Lauren Janusz, *Principal*
EMP: 4
SALES (est): 104.9K **Privately Held**
SIC: 8093 Rehabilitation center, outpatient treatment

(G-9447)
BRANDYWINE PAIN CENTER
4512 Kirkwood Hwy Ste 200 (19808-5122)
PHONE.................................302 998-2585
Emmanuel Devotta, *Principal*
EMP: 15
SALES (est): 733.4K **Privately Held**
SIC: 8049 Offices of health practitioner

(G-9448)
BRANDYWINE PARK CONDOS
Also Called: Brandywine Park Condominiums
1704 N Park Dr Apt 115 (19806-2167)
PHONE.................................302 655-2262
Thomas Kraph, *Partner*
Louis Capano, *Partner*
Ann Lemay, *Partner*
EMP: 5
SALES (est): 343.1K **Privately Held**
SIC: 8641 Condominium association

(G-9449)
BRANDYWINE PDT GROUP INTL INC
Also Called: Bpg International
3 Mill Rd Ste 202 (19806-2147)
PHONE.................................302 472-1463
Frank Lesniak, *CEO*
Rob Heflin, *President*
▲ EMP: 46
SALES (est): 800.5K **Privately Held**
SIC: 3999 Atomizers, toiletry

(G-9450)
BRANDYWINE PODIATRY PA (PA)
1010 N Bancroft Pkwy # 12 (19805-2668)
PHONE.................................302 658-1129
Christopher L Savage, *President*
EMP: 5
SALES (est): 600.2K **Privately Held**
SIC: 8043 Offices & clinics of podiatrists

(G-9451)
BRANDYWINE PROCESS SERVERS
2500 Delaware Ave (19806-1220)
P.O. Box 1360 (19899-1360)
PHONE.................................302 475-2600
Kevin Dunn, *President*
EMP: 5
SALES (est): 395.9K **Privately Held**
SIC: 7389 Process serving service

(G-9452)
BRANDYWINE REALTY MANAGEMENT
Also Called: Brandywine Management
3200 Lancaster Ave (19805-1463)
PHONE.................................302 656-1058
Harold F Thomas, *President*
Bud Thomas, *President*
Deborah Brumbaugh, *Vice Pres*
EMP: 12
SALES (est): 1.1MM **Privately Held**
WEB: www.renthome.org
SIC: 6531 Real estate managers

(G-9453)
BRANDYWINE REALTY TRUST
300 Delaware Ave Ste 1630 (19801-1626)
PHONE.................................302 655-5900
Esther Wyatt, *Branch Mgr*
EMP: 4
SALES (corp-wide): 544.3MM **Privately Held**
SIC: 6531 Real estate agent, commercial
PA: Brandywine Realty Trust
2929 Walnut St Ste 1700
Philadelphia PA 19104
610 325-5600

(G-9454)
BRANDYWINE RUBBER MILLS LLC
1704 N Park Dr Apt 508 (19806-2171)
PHONE.................................267 499-3993
EMP: 2
SALES (est): 90.2K **Privately Held**
SIC: 3069 Fabricated rubber products

(G-9455)
BRANDYWINE TOTAL HEALTH CARE
3214 Naamans Rd (19810-1004)
PHONE.................................302 478-3028
Donald F Feeney, *President*
Deborah Forney, *Office Mgr*
EMP: 5
SALES (est): 516.1K **Privately Held**
WEB: www.bw-totalhealth.com
SIC: 8041 Offices & clinics of chiropractors

(G-9456)
BRANDYWINE TREE AND SHRUB LLC
214 Alders Dr (19803-5304)
PHONE.................................302 475-7594
John Florentino, *Mng Member*
EMP: 8
SALES (est): 664.5K **Privately Held**
SIC: 0783 Planting, pruning & trimming services

(G-9457)
BRANDYWINE UROLOGY CONS PA (PA)
2000 Foulk Rd Ste F (19810-3642)
PHONE.................................302 652-8990
David J Cozzolino, *Partner*
EMP: 25
SALES (est): 3MM **Privately Held**
WEB: www.brandywineurology.com
SIC: 8011 Urologist

(G-9458)
BRANDYWINE VALLEY PROPERTIES
1806 Breen Ln (19810-4507)
P.O. Box 7368 (19803-0368)
PHONE.................................302 475-7660
David L Sibert, *President*
EMP: 6
SALES (est): 250K **Privately Held**
SIC: 6531 Condominium manager

(G-9459)
BRANDYWINE VALLEY WOODWORKING
1212 Bruce Rd (19803-4202)
PHONE.................................302 743-5640
Richard Blaylock, *Owner*
EMP: 2
SQ FT: 1,200
SALES: 98K **Privately Held**
SIC: 2511 Children's wood furniture

(G-9460)
BRANDYWINE VETERINARY HOSPITAL
3848 Kennett Pike (19807-2302)
PHONE.................................302 476-8779
EMP: 8
SALES (est): 82.2K **Privately Held**
SIC: 8062 0742 General medical & surgical hospitals; animal hospital services, pets & other animal specialties

(G-9461)
BRANDYWINE VOLLEYBALL CLUB
3023 Maple Shade Ln (19810-3423)
PHONE.................................302 898-6452
Gina Trinsey, *Director*
Barbara Trinsey, *Athletic Dir*
EMP: 5 EST: 2011
SALES (est): 89.2K **Privately Held**
SIC: 7997 Membership sports & recreation clubs

(G-9462)
BRANDYWINE ZOO
1001 N Park Dr (19802-3801)
PHONE.................................302 571-7747
Larry Gurrkie, *Vice Pres*
Nancy Salscolaski, *Director*
EMP: 30
SALES: 550.1K **Privately Held**
SIC: 8744 Facilities support services

(G-9463)
BRANDYWOOD PLAZA ASSOC LLC
2126 W Newport Pike (19804-3742)
PHONE.................................302 633-9134
Wendi Mulhern, *General Mgr*
Robert M Stella, *Mng Member*
Robert Stella, *Real Est Agnt*
EMP: 4
SALES (est): 468.1K **Privately Held**
SIC: 6531 Real estate agent, commercial

(G-9464)
BRECKENRIDGE SOFTWARE TECH (PA)
2514 Eaton Rd (19810-3504)
PHONE.................................302 656-8460
Bradley Strobel, *President*
Tim Reid, *Technical Staff*
EMP: 5
SALES (est): 300.2K **Privately Held**
WEB: www.breckenridgesoftware.com
SIC: 7371 8742 Computer software development; marketing consulting services

(G-9465)
BRECKSTONE GROUP INC
Also Called: Breckstone Architecture
2417 Lancaster Ave (19805-3736)
P.O. Box 65, Montchanin (19710-0065)
PHONE.................................302 654-3646
Todd Breck, *President*
Deborah Breck, *Treasurer*
EMP: 8
SQ FT: 2,500
SALES: 600K **Privately Held**
SIC: 8712 Architectural services

(G-9466)
BREEDING & DAY INC (PA)
3316 Silverside Rd (19810-3307)
PHONE.................................302 478-4585
Clifford Breeding, *President*
EMP: 30
SQ FT: 1,500
SALES (est): 3.1MM **Privately Held**
WEB: www.breedingandday.com
SIC: 1711 Plumbing contractors

(G-9467)
BREES HOME DAY CARE
915 E 26th St (19802-4433)
PHONE.................................302 762-0876
Brenda Villanueva, *Principal*
EMP: 5
SALES (est): 60.3K **Privately Held**
SIC: 8351 Child day care services

(G-9468)
BREWSTER PRODUCTS INC
2305 Swynford Rd (19810-1229)
PHONE.................................302 798-1988
Bart Brewster, *Owner*
EMP: 6
SQ FT: 2,500
SALES (est): 846.5K **Privately Held**
SIC: 5169 7359 Detergents; appliance rental

(G-9469)
BREWSTER PRODUCTS INC
3607 Downing Dr Ste E (19802-2409)
PHONE.................................302 764-4463
Bart Brewster, *President*
Riva J Brewster, *Vice Pres*
EMP: 5
SQ FT: 2,000
SALES (est): 383.8K **Privately Held**
SIC: 5046 Restaurant equipment & supplies

(G-9470)
BRICE DARLA M DDS MS
3512 Silverside Rd Ste 3 (19810-4941)
PHONE.................................302 478-4700
Darla Brice, *Principal*
EMP: 4 EST: 2007
SALES (est): 220K **Privately Held**
SIC: 8021 Dentists' office

(G-9471)
BRIDGE STUDIO OF DELAWARE
1409 Foulk Rd Ste 101 (19803-2755)
PHONE.................................302 479-5431
▲ EMP: 4
SALES (est): 148.7K **Privately Held**
SIC: 7999 Amusement/Recreation Services

(G-9472)
BRIDGESTONE RET OPERATIONS LLC
Also Called: Firestone
3301 Old Capitol Trl (19808-6209)
PHONE.................................302 995-2487
Britton Merritt, *Manager*
EMP: 11 **Privately Held**
WEB: www.bfis.com
SIC: 5531 7534 Automotive tires; automotive accessories; rebuilding & retreading tires
HQ: Bridgestone Retail Operations, Llc
333 E Lake St 300
Bloomingdale IL 60108
630 259-9000

(G-9473)
BRIGHT BGNNNGS LRNG ACDEMY LLC
111 N Cleveland Ave (19805-1714)
PHONE.................................302 655-1346
EMP: 5 EST: 2016
SQ FT: 8,500
SALES (est): 48.9K **Privately Held**
SIC: 8351 Child Day Care Services

(G-9474)
BRIGHT HORIZONS CHLD CTRS LLC
Also Called: Eagle's Nest
201 N Walnut St (19801-2920)
PHONE.................................302 282-6378
Jen Solwik, *Director*
Lynn Saracino, *Director*
EMP: 8
SALES (corp-wide): 1.9B **Publicly Held**
WEB: www.atlantaga.ncr.com
SIC: 8351 Group day care center
HQ: Bright Horizons Children's Centers Llc
200 Talcott Ave
Watertown MA 02472
617 673-8000

Wilmington - New Castle County (G-9475)   GEOGRAPHIC SECTION

(G-9475)
BRIGHT HORIZONS CHLD CTRS LLC
Also Called: Bright Horizons Child Care Ctr
3515 Silverside Rd # 102 (19810-4906)
PHONE..................................302 477-1023
Meg Panner, *Director*
Diane Soliwoda, *Director*
EMP: 20
SALES (corp-wide): 1.9B **Publicly Held**
WEB: www.atlantaga.ncr.com
SIC: 8351 Group day care center
HQ: Bright Horizons Children's Centers Llc
200 Talcott Ave
Watertown MA 02472
617 673-8000

(G-9476)
BRIGHT NEW BEGINNINGS
8 W Holly Oak Rd (19809-1343)
PHONE..................................610 637-9809
Beverly Gray, *Principal*
EMP: 5
SALES (est): 74.7K **Privately Held**
SIC: 8351 Child day care services

(G-9477)
BRIGHTFIELDS INC (PA)
801 Industrial St (19801-4368)
PHONE..................................302 656-9600
Marian Young, *President*
Jenna Harwanko, *Vice Pres*
Craig Olsen, *Project Mgr*
Margaret Callahan, *Opers Mgr*
Lisa Davis, *Finance Mgr*
EMP: 44
SQ FT: 5,000
SALES (est): 12.1MM **Privately Held**
WEB: www.brightfieldsinc.com
SIC: 8748 8711 8999 8744 Environmental consultant; engineering services; earth science services; geological consultant; facilities support services; ; hazardous waste collection & disposal

(G-9478)
BRISCOES ONSITE DETAILING
100 Greenhill Ave Ste C (19805-1863)
PHONE..................................302 420-1629
EMP: 7
SALES (est): 61.2K **Privately Held**
SIC: 7542 Washing & polishing, automotive

(G-9479)
BRISTOL-MYERS SQUIBB COMPANY
1209 N Orange St (19801-1120)
PHONE..................................800 321-1335
James M Cornelius, *Chairman*
EMP: 40
SALES (corp-wide): 22.5B **Publicly Held**
SIC: 2834 Pharmaceutical preparations
PA: Bristol-Myers Squibb Company
430 E 29th St Fl 14
New York NY 10016
212 546-4000

(G-9480)
BRITTINGHAM INC
5809 Kennett Pike (19807-1115)
PHONE..................................302 656-8173
William A Wolhar, *President*
George Herman, *President*
Baird C Brittingham, *Exec VP*
Lavelle Arnold, *Treasurer*
EMP: 5
SQ FT: 2,500
SALES (est): 574.1K **Privately Held**
WEB: www.brittingham.com
SIC: 6211 Stock brokers & dealers

(G-9481)
BROADBERRY DATA SYSTEMS LLC
1308 Delaware Ave (19806-4740)
PHONE..................................302 295-1086
Mark Ray, *Branch Mgr*
EMP: 47 **Privately Held**
SIC: 3571 5045 Electronic computers; computer peripheral equipment
PA: Broadberry Data Systems Llc
501 Silverside Rd Ste 119
Wilmington DE 19809

(G-9482)
BROADBERRY DATA SYSTEMS LLC (PA)
501 Silverside Rd Ste 119 (19809-1376)
PHONE..................................800 496-9918
Mark Ray, *President*
Pam Poler, *Partner*
EMP: 5
SALES (est): 4MM **Privately Held**
SIC: 3571 5045 Electronic computers; computer peripheral equipment

(G-9483)
BRODIE INVITATIONS
229 Linden Ave (19805-2515)
PHONE..................................302 999-7889
Mary Brodie, *Owner*
EMP: 1
SALES (est): 81.7K **Privately Held**
SIC: 2759 Invitation & stationery printing & engraving

(G-9484)
BRONCO MANUFACTURING INC
1605 Forrest Rd (19810-4316)
PHONE..................................302 475-1210
Dennis Fahey, *President*
David Barlow, *Vice Pres*
EMP: 4
SQ FT: 8,000
SALES (est): 293.3K **Privately Held**
SIC: 3429 3599 Manufactured hardware (general); machine shop, jobbing & repair

(G-9485)
BROOKS COURIER SERVICE INC
831 E 28th St (19802-3606)
P.O. Box 9560 (19809-0560)
PHONE..................................302 762-4661
William F Brooks, *President*
Michael D Boyle, *Vice Pres*
EMP: 140
SQ FT: 22,000
SALES (est): 12.4MM **Privately Held**
WEB: www.brookscourier.com
SIC: 7389 4215 Courier or messenger service; courier services, except by air

(G-9486)
BROUSSEAU & BROUSSEAU C P A
5708 Limestone Rd (19808-1216)
PHONE..................................302 234-1976
Daniel Brousseau, *President*
EMP: 4
SALES (est): 271.9K **Privately Held**
SIC: 8721 Certified public accountant

(G-9487)
BROWN ADVISORY INCORPORATED
5701 Kennett Pike 100 (19807-1311)
PHONE..................................302 351-7600
David Nichols, *Portfolio Mgr*
Dominic Difebo, *Analyst*
EMP: 7 **Privately Held**
SIC: 6282 Investment advisory service
PA: Brown Advisory Incorporated
901 S Bond St Ste 400
Baltimore MD 21231

(G-9488)
BROWN BROTHERS HARRIMAN & CO
919 N Market St Ste 710 (19801-3065)
PHONE..................................302 552-4040
Glenn Morley, *Vice Pres*
Harry Martin, *Manager*
EMP: 13
SALES (corp-wide): 1.7B **Privately Held**
WEB: www.bbh.com
SIC: 6091 6211 6282 Nondeposit trust facilities; dealers, security; investment advisory service
PA: Brown Brothers Harriman & Co.
140 Brdwy
New York NY 10005
212 483-1818

(G-9489)
BROWN EAGLE INC
1000 N West St Ste 1200 (19801-1058)
PHONE..................................302 295-3816
Badih Chaarani, *CEO*
Chawki Charani, *Director*
EMP: 35
SALES (est): 1.4MM **Privately Held**
SIC: 5961 7371 Catalog & mail-order houses; computer software development & applications

(G-9490)
BROWN STONE NIMEROFF LLC
901 N Market St (19801-3022)
PHONE..................................302 428-8142
Robert Munsell, *Branch Mgr*
EMP: 28 **Privately Held**
SIC: 8111 Administrative & government law
PA: Brown Stone Nimeroff Llc
1500 John F Kennedy Blvd # 610
Philadelphia PA 19102

(G-9491)
BROWNSTEIN MERYL MED LPCMH
3526 Silverside Rd Ste 36 (19810-4901)
PHONE..................................302 479-5060
EMP: 4
SALES (est): 150.2K **Privately Held**
SIC: 8322 Family counseling services

(G-9492)
BRUCE E KATZ M D
1401 Foulk Rd Ste 101 (19803-2764)
PHONE..................................302 478-5500
Bruce Katz, *Med Doctor*
EMP: 5
SALES (est): 88K **Privately Held**
SIC: 8011 Orthopedic physician

(G-9493)
BRUCE E MATTHEWS DDS PA (PA)
1403 Silverside Rd Ste A (19810-4434)
PHONE..................................302 475-9220
Bruce Matthews DDS, *Owner*
EMP: 10
SALES (est): 962.5K **Privately Held**
SIC: 8021 Dentists' office

(G-9494)
BRUCE G FAY DMD PA
900 Foulk Rd Ste 203 (19803-3155)
PHONE..................................302 778-3822
Bruce Fay, *President*
EMP: 7 **EST:** 1994
SALES (est): 689.3K **Privately Held**
SIC: 8021 Dental surgeon

(G-9495)
BRYN MAWR TRUST COMPANY
5301 Limestone Rd Ste 106 (19808-1251)
PHONE..................................302 529-5984
Mark Kane, *Senior VP*
Ron Dankanich, *Vice Pres*
Ron Tennant, *Vice Pres*
Genia Samson, *Branch Mgr*
EMP: 13
SALES (corp-wide): 188.6MM **Privately Held**
WEB: www.fbdel.com
SIC: 6029 Commercial banks
HQ: Bryn Mawr Trust Company
801 W Lancaster Ave
Bryn Mawr PA 19010
610 581-4819

(G-9496)
BTS ENTERPRISES INC
Also Called: Beyond The Studs
2702 Lancaster Ave (19805-5221)
PHONE..................................302 428-6080
Greta Colgan, *President*
EMP: 4
SALES (est): 391K **Privately Held**
WEB: www.beyond-the-studs.com
SIC: 7382 Security systems services

(G-9497)
BUCCINI/POLLIN GROUP INC (PA)
Also Called: Bpg
1000 N West St Ste 1000 # 1000 (19801-1000)
PHONE..................................302 691-2100
Dave Pollin, *President*
Greg J Miller, *President*
Christopher Buccini, *Principal*
David B Pollin, *Chairman*
Darren Anzelone, *Vice Pres*
EMP: 112
SQ FT: 5,000
SALES (est): 28MM **Privately Held**
SIC: 7011 Hotels & motels

(G-9498)
BUCK SIMPERS ARCHT + ASSOC INC
954 Justison St (19801-5149)
PHONE..................................302 658-9300
Buck Simpers, *President*
Kelly Lucas, *Admin Asst*
EMP: 10
SALES (est): 2MM **Privately Held**
WEB: www.simpers.com
SIC: 8712 8741 7389 Architectural engineering; construction management; interior design services

(G-9499)
BUCKLEYS INC
Also Called: Buckley's Autocare
1604 E Newport Pike (19804-2529)
PHONE..................................302 999-8285
Greg Buckley, *President*
Susan Sherman, *Teacher*
EMP: 8
SQ FT: 5,500
SALES: 1MM **Privately Held**
SIC: 7539 Automotive repair shops

(G-9500)
BUDGET RENT A CAR SYSTEM INC
100 S Front St (19801)
PHONE..................................302 652-0629
Lisa Spano, *Manager*
EMP: 5
SALES (corp-wide): 9.1B **Publicly Held**
WEB: www.blackdogventures.com
SIC: 7514 Rent-a-car service
HQ: Budget Rent A Car System, Inc.
6 Sylvan Way Ste 1
Parsippany NJ 07054
973 496-3500

(G-9501)
BUFFALO CONCRETE CO INC
307 A St Ste A (19801-5345)
PHONE..................................302 378-4421
William Dimondi, *President*
EMP: 2
SALES (est): 286.8K **Privately Held**
SIC: 3531 Concrete plants

(G-9502)
BUG RITE EXTREMINATOR COMP
303 Portland Ave (19804-2211)
PHONE..................................302 738-4373
EMP: 4
SALES (est): 140K **Privately Held**
SIC: 7342 Pest control in structures

(G-9503)
BUILDING SYSTEMS AND SVCS INC
Also Called: Honeywell Authorized Dealer
1504 Kirkwood Hwy (19805-4916)
PHONE..................................302 996-0900
Kevin D Haskins, *President*
Sam Coniglio, *Sales Staff*
Jeffrey Hayes, *Manager*
▲ **EMP:** 22
SQ FT: 5,000
SALES (est): 11.7MM **Privately Held**
WEB: www.bssinc.net
SIC: 5075 Warm air heating & air conditioning

(G-9504)
BULLENS BUCKTAILS INC
3906 Chestnut St (19808-5708)
PHONE..................................302 998-6288
Chieck Bullen, *Owner*
EMP: 1
SALES (est): 56.9K **Privately Held**
SIC: 3949 Fishing equipment

(G-9505)
BUMPERS & COMPANY
1104 Philadelphia Pike (19809-2031)
PHONE..................................302 798-3300

▲ = Import ▼ =Export
◆ =Import/Export

GEOGRAPHIC SECTION
Wilmington - New Castle County (G-9537)

John Mager, *Owner*
Ann Dean, *Bookkeeper*
Laura J Linderman, *Human Resources*
EMP: 12
SALES (est): 1.1MM **Privately Held**
SIC: 8721 Accounting services, except auditing

(G-9506)
BURGEON IT SERVICES LLC
1601 Concord Pike Ste 36e (19803-3635)
PHONE 302 613-0999
Alekhya Chodavarapu, *CFO*
Nandakishore Umar Lakakuna,
Raja Burgeon, *Recruiter*
EMP: 15 **EST:** 2010
SALES (est): 1MM **Privately Held**
SIC: 7379 Computer related consulting services

(G-9507)
BURKE PAINTING CO INC
25 Brookside Dr (19804-1101)
PHONE 302 998-8500
Robert Burke, *President*
EMP: 15
SALES (est): 980K **Privately Held**
SIC: 1721 Exterior commercial painting contractor; exterior residential painting contractor; interior commercial painting contractor; interior residential painting contractor

(G-9508)
BURLINGTON MANOR ASSOCIATES
Also Called: Burlington Manor Apartments
4 Denny Rd (19809-3445)
PHONE 609 387-3184
William Demarco, *Managing Prtnr*
Jacqueline Edmanson, *Mng Member*
EMP: 13
SALES (est): 1.2MM **Privately Held**
SIC: 6513 Apartment building operators

(G-9509)
BUSINESS CENTRIC SVCS GROUP
1000 N West St Ste 1000 # 1000 (19801-1000)
PHONE 302 984-3800
John Davis, *Director*
EMP: 4
SALES (est): 344.7K **Privately Held**
SIC: 8111 Specialized law offices, attorneys

(G-9510)
BUSINESS HISTORY CONFERENCE
298 Buck Rd (19807-2106)
P.O. Box 3630 (19807-0630)
PHONE 302 658-2400
Edward Dupont, *President*
EMP: 2
SALES: 214.6K **Privately Held**
SIC: 2721 Periodicals

(G-9511)
BUSINESS INSURANCE SERVICES
Also Called: Nationwide Insurance
109 N Dupont Rd (19807-3105)
P.O. Box 4380 (19807-0380)
PHONE 302 655-5300
Joe Chambers, *President*
Janet Hess, *Treasurer*
Linda Josephson, *Manager*
John Chrzanowski, *Producer*
Dave Clark, *Producer*
EMP: 7
SALES (est): 1MM **Privately Held**
SIC: 6411 Insurance brokers

(G-9512)
BUSINESS SLIP LLC
201 E 39th St Ste 201 # 201 (19802-2332)
PHONE 302 563-3660
Mr Samuel Pipkin,
EMP: 1
SALES (est): 91.5K **Privately Held**
SIC: 2522 Office furniture, except wood

(G-9513)
BUTAMAX ADVANCED BIOFUELS LLC
200 Powder Mill Rd (19803-2907)
PHONE 302 695-3617
Mark Buse, *Branch Mgr*
Sharon Templeton, *Executive Asst*
EMP: 2 **Privately Held**
SIC: 1382 Oil & gas exploration services
PA: Butamax Advanced Biofuels, Llc
  Henry Clay Rr 141
  Wilmington DE 19880

(G-9514)
BUTAMAX ADVANCED BIOFUELS LLC (PA)
Henry Clay Rr 141 (19880)
PHONE 302 695-6787
Stuart Thomas, *CEO*
EMP: 11
SALES (est): 16.7MM **Privately Held**
SIC: 2869 Industrial organic chemicals

(G-9515)
BUTLER FINANCIAL LTD
900 Foulk Rd Ste 201 (19803-3155)
PHONE 302 778-2170
Bob Campbell, *President*
EMP: 4
SALES (est): 540.5K **Privately Held**
SIC: 6282 Investment advice

(G-9516)
BUTLER WOODCRAFTERS
1204 Brook Dr (19803-4110)
PHONE 302 764-0744
Bill Levine, *Manager*
EMP: 1
SALES (est): 72.8K **Privately Held**
SIC: 2499 2511 2521 2531 Wood products; wood household furniture; wood office furniture; public building & related furniture

(G-9517)
BYRON & DAVIS CCCC
601 Philadelphia Pike (19809-2549)
P.O. Box 9049 (19809-0049)
PHONE 302 792-2334
Glenn Davis, *President*
EMP: 9
SALES (est): 621K **Privately Held**
WEB: www.byrondavis.com
SIC: 7322 8742 Collection agency, except real estate; financial consultant

(G-9518)
BYSNESS INC
1521 Concord Pike Ste 303 (19803-3644)
PHONE 937 687-8701
EMP: 10
SALES (est): 217.5K **Privately Held**
SIC: 7371 Computer software development & applications

(G-9519)
BZ CONSTRUCTION SERVICES INC
120 E Ayre St (19804-2507)
PHONE 302 999-7505
Brian Zych, *President*
Diane Leblanc, *Assistant*
EMP: 9
SALES: 2.5MM **Privately Held**
SIC: 8741 Construction management

(G-9520)
C & B INTERNET SERVICES LLC
704 N King St Ste 500 (19801-3584)
PHONE 302 384-9804
Ben Wilber,
EMP: 5
SALES: 47K **Privately Held**
SIC: 4813

(G-9521)
C & D CONTRACTORS INC
14 E 40th St Lowr (19802-2300)
P.O. Box 9236 (19809-0236)
PHONE 302 764-2020
Kathy Ryan, *President*
William M Mahon, *Vice Pres*
William Mc Mahon, *Vice Pres*
EMP: 32
SQ FT: 10,000
SALES (est): 4.2MM **Privately Held**
SIC: 1711 Mechanical contractor

(G-9522)
C AND L BRADFORD AND ASSOC
1604 Trevalley Rd (19810-4330)
PHONE 302 529-8566
Carol B Holt, *President*
Laura Durojaiye, *Vice Pres*
EMP: 9
SALES: 250K **Privately Held**
SIC: 8741 8748 Management services; business consulting

(G-9523)
C P M INDUSTRIES INC
3511 Silverside Rd # 210 (19810-4902)
P.O. Box 6006 (19804-0606)
PHONE 302 478-8200
Leonard L Yowell, *President*
Bruce Warner, *Sales Mgr*
▲ **EMP:** 7
SQ FT: 2,500
SALES (est): 1.7MM **Privately Held**
WEB: www.cpmindustries.com
SIC: 5169 Industrial chemicals

(G-9524)
C S C CORPORATION TEXAS INC
2711 Centerville Rd # 400 (19808-1660)
PHONE 302 636-5440
John Fortunado, *CFO*
Maya Turner, *Sales Staff*
Edward Kavanagh, *Manager*
Joe Panchisin, *Manager*
Brian Fitzgerald, *Admin Mgr*
EMP: 74
SALES (est): 2MM **Privately Held**
SIC: 8611 Business associations

(G-9525)
C V INTERNATIONAL INC
603 Christiana Ave (19801-5834)
PHONE 302 427-0440
EMP: 8
SALES (corp-wide): 8.9MM **Privately Held**
SIC: 4731 Brokers, shipping
PA: C V International, Inc.
  1128 W Olney Rd
  Norfolk VA 23507
  757 466-1170

(G-9526)
CA CASSIDY VMD
3705 Lancaster Pike (19805-1510)
PHONE 302 998-2995
C A Cassidy, *Owner*
EMP: 4
SALES (est): 150K **Privately Held**
SIC: 0742 Veterinarian, animal specialties

(G-9527)
CABLICONS LLC
1201 N Orange St Ste 600 (19801-1171)
PHONE 843 458-7702
Shane Holley,
Buddy Holley,
Karl St George,
EMP: 3 **EST:** 2015
SQ FT: 1,200
SALES (est): 173.8K **Privately Held**
SIC: 2298 Cable, fiber

(G-9528)
CACTUS ANNIES RESTAURANT & BAR
211 W 9th St (19801-1619)
PHONE 302 655-9004
Ann Ackerson, *Owner*
EMP: 10
SALES (est): 402.2K **Privately Held**
SIC: 8741 Restaurant management

(G-9529)
CADIA RHABILITATION PIKE CREEK
Also Called: Cadia Rhabilitation Pike Creek
3540 Three Little Bkrs Bl (19808-1754)
PHONE 302 455-0808
Karen Litwa, *Principal*
EMP: 36

(G-9530)
CADIA RHABILITATION SILVERSIDE
3322 Silverside Rd (19810-3307)
PHONE 302 478-8889
EMP: 21
SALES (est): 1.1MM **Privately Held**
SIC: 8051 Skilled nursing care facilities

(G-9531)
CADIA RVERSIDE HEALTHCARE SVCS
3540 Three Little Bakers (19808-1754)
PHONE 302 455-0808
Paul Schweiger, *Human Res Dir*
EMP: 9
SALES (est): 224.7K **Privately Held**
SIC: 8051 Skilled nursing care facilities

(G-9532)
CADRENDER LLC
716 N Tatnall St (19801-1716)
PHONE 302 657-0700
Andrew Burkert, *Mng Member*
Tina Burkert,
EMP: 7
SALES (est): 583.3K **Privately Held**
WEB: www.cadrender.com
SIC: 7374 8712 Computer graphics service; architectural services

(G-9533)
CAE(US) INC (HQ)
1011 Ct Rd Ste 322 (19805)
PHONE 813 885-7481
Stephane Lefebvre, *President*
Darrel Lane, *Treasurer*
Anne Mari Hicks, *Controller*
Hartland Paterson, *Admin Sec*
◆ **EMP:** 2
SALES (est): 395.6MM
SALES (corp-wide): 2.2B **Privately Held**
SIC: 3559 Cryogenic machinery, industrial
PA: Cae Inc
  8585 Ch De La Cote-De-Liesse
  Saint-Laurent QC H4T 1
  514 341-6780

(G-9534)
CAFE MANAGEMENT ASSOCIATES
1428 N Clayton St (19806-4006)
PHONE 302 655-4959
Jonas Miller, *Manager*
EMP: 5
SALES (est): 225K **Privately Held**
SIC: 8741 Management services

(G-9535)
CAIN HOME HEALTH SERVICES
913 N Market St Ste 200 (19801-3097)
PHONE 302 268-6919
Stacey Cain, *Principal*
EMP: 16
SALES (est): 178.9K **Privately Held**
SIC: 8082 Home health care services

(G-9536)
CALFO & HAIGHT INC
21 Glover Cir (19804-3201)
PHONE 302 998-3852
Augustine J Calfo, *President*
Nick Calfo, *Vice Pres*
Geraldine Calfo, *Admin Sec*
EMP: 20
SQ FT: 2,500
SALES (est): 2.9MM **Privately Held**
SIC: 1711 Plumbing contractors; heating & air conditioning contractors

(G-9537)
CALIFORNIA VIDEO 2
1716 Marsh Rd (19810-4606)
PHONE 302 477-6944
Jeff Stalter, *Owner*
EMP: 8
SALES (est): 90.8K **Privately Held**
SIC: 7841 Video tape rental

Wilmington - New Castle County (G-9538)

(G-9538)
CALLOWAYS CUSTOM INTERIORS CO
Also Called: Calloway's Interiors
211 Brookland Ave (19805-1112)
PHONE................................302 994-7931
Jesse T Calloway, *President*
Bernice Calloway, *Vice Pres*
EMP: 1
SQ FT: 3,500
SALES (est): 85.1K **Privately Held**
SIC: 2391 7641 2392 Draperies, plastic & textile: from purchased materials; re-upholstery; slipcovers: made of fabric, plastic etc.

(G-9539)
CALMET CORPORATION
717 N Union St Ste 100 (19805-3031)
PHONE................................714 505-6765
Anupam Thakur, *President*
▲ EMP: 25
SQ FT: 500
SALES (est): 4MM **Privately Held**
SIC: 5051 Castings, rough: iron or steel

(G-9540)
CALPINE CORPORATION
Also Called: Hay Road Power Complex
198 Hay Rd (19809-3511)
P.O. Box 231 (19899-0231)
PHONE................................302 764-4478
D Lawson, *Opers Mgr*
Dave Knotts, *Plant Engr*
Roy Killgore, *Branch Mgr*
EMP: 28
SALES (corp-wide): 9.5B **Privately Held**
WEB: www.conectiv.com
SIC: 4911 Generation, electric power
HQ: Calpine Corporation
   717 Texas St Ste 1000
   Houston TX 77002
   713 830-2000

(G-9541)
CALPINE CORPORATION
200 Hay Rd (19809-3558)
PHONE................................302 824-4779
EMP: 9
SALES (corp-wide): 9.5B **Privately Held**
SIC: 4911 Electric services
HQ: Calpine Corporation
   717 Texas St Ste 1000
   Houston TX 77002
   713 830-2000

(G-9542)
CALPINE OPERATING SVCS CO INC
500 Delaware Ave Ste 600 (19801-7406)
PHONE................................302 468-5400
EMP: 6
SALES (corp-wide): 9.5B **Privately Held**
SIC: 4911 Generation, electric power
HQ: Calpine Operating Services Company, Inc.
   717 Texas St Ste 1000
   Houston TX 77002
   713 830-2000

(G-9543)
CALVERT MECHANICAL SYSTEMS INC
Also Called: Calvert Comfort Cooling & Htg
410 Meco Dr (19804-1112)
PHONE................................302 998-0460
Christopher Lenhard, *President*
David Murray, *Vice Pres*
Dave Murray, *Sales Executive*
EMP: 30
SQ FT: 9,200
SALES (est): 6.8MM **Privately Held**
WEB: www.calvertcomfort.com
SIC: 1711 Warm air heating & air conditioning contractor

(G-9544)
CAMECK PUBLISHING
3306 Coachman Rd (19803-1946)
PHONE................................302 598-4799
Jessica Sinarski, *Principal*
EMP: 1
SALES (est): 37.5K **Privately Held**
SIC: 2741 Miscellaneous publishing

(G-9545)
CAMERAS ETC INC (PA)
Also Called: Cameras Etc T V & Video
2303 Baynard Blvd (19802-3943)
PHONE................................302 764-9400
James F Cycyk, *President*
Paul Beacher, *Vice Pres*
Susan A Cycyk, *Admin Sec*
EMP: 10 EST: 1977
SQ FT: 3,500
SALES (est): 1.3MM **Privately Held**
WEB: www.camerasetcinc.com
SIC: 5946 5043 5731 Cameras; photographic supplies; photographic cameras, projectors, equipment & supplies; video cameras, recorders & accessories

(G-9546)
CAMP ARROWHEAD BUSINE
913 Wilson Rd (19803-4012)
PHONE................................302 448-6919
Judith Gregory, *Business Mgr*
Dina Hollingsworth, *Office Mgr*
Walt Lafontaine, *Director*
EMP: 4
SALES (est): 173.2K **Privately Held**
SIC: 7032 Sporting & recreational camps

(G-9547)
CAN COLLECTING CLUB
1524 Seton Dr (19809-2239)
PHONE................................302 420-5768
Sal Pantano, *Principal*
EMP: 4 EST: 2015
SALES (est): 38.1K **Privately Held**
SIC: 7997 Membership sports & recreation clubs

(G-9548)
CANAL NEW ORLEANS HOTEL LLC (PA)
1209 N Orange St (19801-1120)
PHONE................................504 962-0500
Jon F Leyens Jr,
EMP: 50
SALES (est): 1.1MM **Privately Held**
SIC: 7011 Hotels

(G-9549)
CANCER SUPPORT CMNTY DEL INC
4810 Lancaster Pike (19807-2516)
PHONE................................302 995-2850
Nicole Pickles, *Exec Dir*
Cynthia Dwyer, *Exec Dir*
Jan Shallcross, *Director*
Sean Hebbel, *Program Dir*
EMP: 7
SALES: 773K **Privately Held**
WEB: www.wellnessdelaware.org
SIC: 8322 Community center

(G-9550)
CANN-ERIKSON BINDERY INC
1 Meco Cir (19804-1108)
P.O. Box 3171 (19804-0171)
PHONE................................302 995-6636
Joseph Vanloon, *President*
Steve Lillard, *Corp Secy*
Joseph Van Loon, *Vice Pres*
EMP: 12 EST: 1935
SQ FT: 10,000
SALES (est): 1.3MM **Privately Held**
WEB: www.cann-erikson.com
SIC: 2675 2782 Die-cut paper & board; looseleaf binders & devices

(G-9551)
CANON SOLUTIONS AMERICA INC
300 Bellevue Pkwy Ste 135 (19809-3704)
PHONE................................302 792-8700
Michael Ciaccio, *Opers Mgr*
James Holte, *Sales Staff*
Jeff V Tiem, *Manager*
Jeff Tiem, *Manager*
EMP: 35 **Privately Held**
SIC: 5044 Photocopy machines
HQ: Canon Solutions America, Inc.
   1 Canon Park
   Melville NY 11747
   631 330-5000

(G-9552)
CANSURROUND PBC
1815 W 13th St Ste 5 (19806-4054)
PHONE................................302 540-2270
Margaret Maley, *CEO*
Jill Teixeira, *Vice Pres*
EMP: 3 EST: 2013
SALES (est): 114.5K **Privately Held**
SIC: 7372 Application computer software

(G-9553)
CAPANO HOMES INC
Also Called: Capano Management
4120 Concord Pike Ste D (19803-5401)
PHONE................................302 384-7980
Louis Capano, *President*
Joe Capano, *Vice Pres*
Christie Haupt, *Manager*
EMP: 25
SALES (est): 7MM **Privately Held**
WEB: www.capanohomes.com
SIC: 1521 Single-family housing construction

(G-9554)
CAPANO MANAGEMENT COMPANY
105 Foulk Rd (19803-3740)
PHONE................................302 429-8700
Louis Capano III, *President*
Bill Krapf, *Vice Pres*
Matthew Plourde, *CFO*
EMP: 99
SALES (est): 3MM **Privately Held**
SIC: 8741 Management services

(G-9555)
CAPGEMINI AMERICA INC
405 N King St (19801-3773)
PHONE................................302 656-7491
Matthew Bernardini, *Branch Mgr*
EMP: 4
SALES (corp-wide): 343.9MM **Privately Held**
SIC: 7379 Computer related consulting services
HQ: Capgemini America, Inc.
   79 5th Ave Fl 3
   New York NY 10003
   212 314-8000

(G-9556)
CAPITAL COMMERCIAL REALTY LLC
5307 Limestone Rd Ste 102 (19808-1275)
PHONE................................302 734-4400
Steve Montague, *Exec.VP*
Christopher Whitfield,
EMP: 5
SALES: 300K **Privately Held**
SIC: 6531 Real estate agent, commercial

(G-9557)
CAPITAL GAINES LLC
4023 Kennett Pike 2082 (19807-2018)
PHONE................................302 433-6777
EMP: 1
SALES (est): 39.4K **Privately Held**
SIC: 2741 Misc Publishing

(G-9558)
CAPITAL ONE NATIONAL ASSN
1 S Orange St (19801-5006)
PHONE................................302 658-3302
Mike Norris, *Vice Pres*
Ryan LI, *Manager*
Jeffrey D'Amato, *Senior Mgr*
EMP: 14 **Publicly Held**
SIC: 6021 National trust companies with deposits, commercial
HQ: Capital One, National Association
   1680 Capital One Dr
   Mc Lean VA 22102
   800 655-2265

(G-9559)
CAPTURE TECHNOLOGIES INC
1013 Centre Rd Ste 403b (19805-1270)
PHONE................................650 772-8006
EMP: 6
SALES (est): 123.5K **Privately Held**
SIC: 7371 Computer software development & applications

(G-9560)
CAR CLINIC INC
59 Germay Dr (19804-1104)
PHONE................................302 421-9100
John Lardear, *President*
EMP: 4
SALES (est): 341.9K **Privately Held**
SIC: 7538 7549 General automotive repair shops; towing service, automotive

(G-9561)
CAR WASH OF PRICES CORNER
Also Called: Prices Corner Car Wash
3213 Kirkwood Hwy (19808-6129)
PHONE................................302 994-9274
John Medek, *President*
William Kincaid, *Business Mgr*
Sharon Medek, *Treasurer*
EMP: 30
SALES (est): 1.3MM **Privately Held**
SIC: 7542 Carwashes

(G-9562)
CARA GUITARS MANUFACTURING
112 Water St (19804-2407)
PHONE................................302 521-0119
Jim Cara, *President*
EMP: 40
SALES (est): 2.3MM **Privately Held**
SIC: 3931 Guitars & parts, electric & non-electric

(G-9563)
CARA PLASTICS INC
1201 N Market St Ste 2100 (19801-1165)
PHONE................................302 622-7070
Richard Wool, *CEO*
EMP: 3
SALES (est): 320K **Privately Held**
SIC: 3089 Carafes, plastic

(G-9564)
CARBOCYCLE CO
919 N Market St Ste 425 (19801-3014)
PHONE................................212 214-4068
Andrew Roe, *Owner*
Shashwat Vajpeyi, *Co-Owner*
Melanie Valencia, *Co-Owner*
EMP: 1
SALES (est): 49.5K **Privately Held**
SIC: 2899 Oils & essential oils

(G-9565)
CARDIOLOGY SPECIALISTS
106 Saint Moritz Dr (19807-1054)
PHONE................................302 453-0624
Rahman Ehsanur MD, *President*
EMP: 4
SALES (est): 310K **Privately Held**
SIC: 8011 Cardiologist & cardio-vascular specialist

(G-9566)
CARDIOMO CARE INC
919 N Market St Ste 425 (19801-3014)
PHONE................................929 360-5107
Roman Bielkin, *Principal*
EMP: 17
SALES (est): 346.3K **Privately Held**
SIC: 5047 Medical & hospital equipment

(G-9567)
CAREPORTMD LLC
4365 Kirkwood Hwy (19808-5113)
PHONE................................302 202-3020
EMP: 12
SALES (corp-wide): 5K **Privately Held**
SIC: 8082 Home health care services
PA: Careportmd, Llc
   1 Innovation Way Ste 400
   Newark DE 19711
   302 283-9001

(G-9568)
CARGO CUBE LICENSING LLC
2711 Centerville Rd # 400 (19808-1660)
PHONE................................844 200-2823
Aldo Disorbo,
EMP: 5
SALES (est): 104.7K **Privately Held**
SIC: 7389 Business services

GEOGRAPHIC SECTION   Wilmington - New Castle County (G-9596)

(G-9569)
CARGOEX INC
1208 First State Blvd (19804-3561)
PHONE.....................800 850-9493
Roman Kelly, *CEO*
EMP: 5
SALES (est): 152.1K Privately Held
SIC: 4731 Freight forwarding

(G-9570)
CARIBB TRANSPORT INC
Also Called: Caribb Moto Cars
2800 Governor Printz Blvd # 3 (19802-3734)
PHONE.....................302 274-2112
Garfield G Cammock, *President*
Laressia Ann Wright, *Shareholder*
EMP: 5
SALES (est): 91.6K Privately Held
SIC: 7538 General automotive repair shops

(G-9571)
CARLETON COURT ASSOCIATES LP
Also Called: Carleton Court Apartments
4 Denny Rd (19809-3445)
PHONE.....................302 454-1800
Leon Weiner, *Owner*
William Demarco, *Vice Pres*
Lori Miller, *Manager*
EMP: 13
SALES: 950K Privately Held
SIC: 6513 Apartment building operators

(G-9572)
CARLISLE GROUP
Also Called: Winterset Farms
2801 Ebright Rd (19810-1130)
PHONE.....................302 475-3010
Mary Ellen Brooks, *Manager*
Susan Merchant, *Shareholder*
EMP: 7
SALES (est): 418.1K Privately Held
SIC: 6515 0752 Mobile home site operators; training services, horses (except racing horses)

(G-9573)
CARMINE POTTER & ASSOCIATES (PA)
840 N Union St (19805-5329)
P.O. Box 30409 (19805-7409)
PHONE.....................302 658-8940
Stephen B Potter, *Partner*
Kenneth Carmine, *Partner*
Tiffany Anders, *Manager*
Baker H Garrett,
EMP: 12
SALES (est): 1.5MM Privately Held
SIC: 8111 General practice attorney, lawyer

(G-9574)
CARNEY MACHINERY CO (PA)
500 E Front St (19801-5020)
P.O. Box 1106 (19899-1106)
PHONE.....................302 571-8382
Michael Carney, *President*
▲ EMP: 6
SQ FT: 65,000
SALES (est): 1.2MM Privately Held
WEB: www.carneymachinery.com
SIC: 5085 Industrial tools

(G-9575)
CAROLINE M WIESNER
Also Called: Family Benefit Home Care
3322 Englewood Rd (19810-3302)
PHONE.....................877 220-9755
Caroline M Wiesner, *Principal*
EMP: 1
SALES (est): 108.6K Privately Held
SIC: 8082 Home health care services

(G-9576)
CARPE VITA HOME CARE
240 N James St (19804-3169)
PHONE.....................302 482-4305
Richard Desimone, *Administration*
EMP: 6
SALES (est): 67.2K Privately Held
SIC: 8082 Home health care services

(G-9577)
CARPENTER INVESTMENTS INC
1105 N Market St Fl 1 (19801-1237)
PHONE.....................302 656-5664
EMP: 4
SALES (est): 230.7K
SALES (corp-wide): 2.3B Publicly Held
SIC: 6799 Investors
PA: Carpenter Technology Corporation
    1735 Market St Fl 15
    Philadelphia PA 19103
    610 208-2000

(G-9578)
CARR PARIS
Also Called: Paris Carr US
511 N Union St Apt 2f (19805-3060)
PHONE.....................302 401-1203
Paris Carr, *Owner*
Alexandria Carr, *Chairman*
Courtney Carr, *Corp Secy*
Karen Carr, *Vice Pres*
Marquita Robinson, *Human Resources*
EMP: 13
SALES (est): 315K Privately Held
SIC: 8742 7349 8999 7389 Management consulting services; building & office cleaning services; commercial & literary writings; technical writing; search & rescue service;

(G-9579)
CARRICK CHIROPRACTIC CENTRE PA
1309 Veale Rd Ste 12 (19810-4609)
PHONE.....................302 478-1443
Thomas Ulrich, *President*
EMP: 7
SALES (est): 390K Privately Held
WEB: www.carrickwellness.com
SIC: 8041 Offices & clinics of chiropractors

(G-9580)
CARSPECKEN-SCOTT INC (PA)
1707 N Lincoln St (19806-2309)
PHONE.....................302 655-7173
Frederick J Carspecken, *President*
Laura Cristy, *Manager*
Don Strabley, *Manager*
Fred Carspecken, *Administration*
EMP: 5
SQ FT: 2,000
SALES (est): 452.3K Privately Held
WEB: www.carspeckenscott.com
SIC: 7699 Picture framing, custom

(G-9581)
CARSPECKEN-SCOTT INC
Also Called: Fcw
3007 Rosemont Ave (19802-2423)
PHONE.....................302 762-7955
Dennis Schafer, *Manager*
EMP: 2
SALES (corp-wide): 452.3K Privately Held
WEB: www.carspeckenscott.com
SIC: 2499 Picture & mirror frames, wood
PA: Carspecken-Scott Inc
    1707 N Lincoln St
    Wilmington DE 19806
    302 655-7173

(G-9582)
CARTER FIRM LLC
2600 N Van Buren St (19802-3456)
PHONE.....................267 420-0717
Armani Carter, *CEO*
Devona Carter, *CFO*
EMP: 1
SALES (est): 23.5K Privately Held
SIC: 8243 3571 8748 Repair training, computer; electronic computers; systems engineering consultant, ex. computer or professional

(G-9583)
CARVERTISE INC
319 6th Ave (19805)
PHONE.....................302 273-1889
Mac Nagaswami, *CEO*
Rose Breyla, *Director*
EMP: 4
SALES (est): 121K Privately Held
SIC: 7312 Outdoor advertising services

(G-9584)
CARZO & ASSOCIATES INC
Also Called: Triad Enterprises
3401 Montchanin Rd (19807-1319)
P.O. Box 279, Montchanin (19710-0279)
PHONE.....................302 575-0336
Pat Carzo, *President*
EMP: 4
SQ FT: 300
SALES: 93K Privately Held
SIC: 8711 1731 Aviation &/or aeronautical engineering; closed circuit television installation; fire detection & burglar alarm systems specialization

(G-9585)
CASALE MARBLE IMPORTS INC
Also Called: Distribution Headquarters
3518 Silverside Rd Ste 22 (19810-4907)
PHONE.....................561 404-4213
Donato W Casale, *President*
◆ EMP: 95
SQ FT: 67,000
SALES (est): 3.9MM Privately Held
WEB: www.casalemarble.net
SIC: 1743 5211 5032 Terrazzo, tile, marble, mosaic work; marble installation, interior; masonry materials & supplies; granite building stone

(G-9586)
CASARINO CHRISTMAN SHALK
1007 N Orange St (19801-1239)
P.O. Box 1276 (19899-1276)
PHONE.....................302 594-4500
Beth H Christman, *Principal*
Stacey L Cummings,
Kenneth M Doss,
Diane Willette,
Colin Shalk,
EMP: 30 EST: 1999
SALES (est): 3.4MM Privately Held
WEB: www.casarino.com
SIC: 8111 General practice attorney, lawyer

(G-9587)
CASE MANAGEMENT SERVICES
234 Philadelphia Pike # 6 (19809-3126)
PHONE.....................302 354-3711
Cheri L Pfeiffer, *Principal*
EMP: 5
SALES (est): 302K Privately Held
SIC: 8741 Business management

(G-9588)
CASSIDY PAINTING INC
20 Germay Dr (19804-1105)
PHONE.....................302 683-0710
Michael Cassidy, *President*
Jim Gray, *Project Mgr*
EMP: 40
SQ FT: 8,000
SALES (est): 3.3MM Privately Held
SIC: 1721 1799 Residential painting; wallcovering contractors; sandblasting of building exteriors

(G-9589)
CASTLE BAG COMPANY
115 Valley Rd (19804-1310)
PHONE.....................302 656-1001
Christine Ditzler, *President*
Harry B Russell, *President*
Christine Russell Ditzler, *Vice Pres*
EMP: 2
SQ FT: 6,000
SALES (est): 750K Privately Held
SIC: 2673 Plastic bags: made from purchased materials

(G-9590)
CATHOLIC CEMETARIES INC (PA)
Also Called: Cathedral Cemetary
2400 Lancaster Ave (19805-3737)
PHONE.....................302 254-4701
Mark Christian, *Director*
Joseph F Redman, *Director*
EMP: 10 EST: 1876
SALES (est): 3.5MM Privately Held
WEB: www.cathcemde.com
SIC: 6553 Cemeteries, real estate operation

(G-9591)
CATHOLIC CEMETARIES INC
Also Called: Saints Cemetary
6001 Kirkwood Hwy (19808-4816)
PHONE.....................302 737-2524
Tom Kane, *Superintendent*
EMP: 20
SALES (est): 732.6K
SALES (corp-wide): 3.5MM Privately Held
WEB: www.cathcemde.com
SIC: 6553 Cemeteries, real estate operation
PA: Catholic Cemetaries Inc
    2400 Lancaster Ave
    Wilmington DE 19805
    302 254-4701

(G-9592)
CATHOLIC CHARITIES INC
Also Called: Siena Hall
2307 Kentmere Pkwy (19806-2019)
PHONE.....................302 573-3122
Alan J Daul, *Exec Dir*
EMP: 25
SALES (corp-wide): 6.8MM Privately Held
WEB: www.ccwilm.org
SIC: 8322 Social service center
PA: Catholic Charities Inc
    2601 W 4th St
    Wilmington DE 19805
    302 655-9624

(G-9593)
CATHOLIC CHARITIES INC
300 Bayard Ave (19805-3345)
PHONE.....................302 654-1184
Kimberly Ellis, *Principal*
EMP: 15
SALES (corp-wide): 6.8MM Privately Held
SIC: 8322 Social service center; adoption services; emergency shelters; substance abuse counseling
PA: Catholic Charities Inc
    2601 W 4th St
    Wilmington DE 19805
    302 655-9624

(G-9594)
CATHOLIC CHARITIES INC (PA)
2601 W 4th St (19805-3309)
PHONE.....................302 655-9624
Melissa Jenkins, *Manager*
Kay Klein, *Manager*
Valerie Twanmoh, *Director*
Richelle Vible, *Executive*
EMP: 50
SQ FT: 20,000
SALES (est): 6.8MM Privately Held
WEB: www.ccwilm.org
SIC: 8322 Social service center; adoption services; emergency shelters; substance abuse counseling

(G-9595)
CATHOLIC DOCESE WILMINGTON INC
Also Called: Catholic Charities Thrift Ctr
1320 E 23rd St (19802-4603)
PHONE.....................302 764-2717
Jennifer Murphy, *Manager*
EMP: 4
SALES (corp-wide): 26.1MM Privately Held
SIC: 8699 7389 Charitable organization; flea market
PA: Catholic Diocese Of Wilmington, Inc.
    1925 Delaware Ave
    Wilmington DE 19806
    302 573-3100

(G-9596)
CAVALIER GROUP (PA)
Also Called: Cavalier Apartments
105 Foulk Rd (19803-3740)
PHONE.....................302 429-8700
Louis J Capano Jr, *General Ptnr*
Joseph M Capano, *General Ptnr*
Louis Capano, *General Ptnr*
EMP: 6
SQ FT: 1,000
SALES: 7MM Privately Held
WEB: www.thecavaliergroup.com
SIC: 6513 Apartment building operators

Wilmington - New Castle County (G-9597) GEOGRAPHIC SECTION

(G-9597)
CAWSL ENTERPRISES INC (HQ)
3411 Silverside Rd (19810-4812)
PHONE..................302 478-6160
Thomas L Sandor, *President*
John A Sanders, *Corp Secy*
William G Warden III, *Vice Pres*
William G Warden IV, *Vice Pres*
EMP: 6
SALES (est): 100.1MM
SALES (corp-wide): 179MM **Privately Held**
SIC: 6211 Investment firm, general brokerage
PA: Superior Group, Inc.
100 Front St Ste 525
Conshohocken PA 19428
610 397-2040

(G-9598)
CB RICHARD ELLIS RE SVCS LLC
1007 N Orange St Ste 100 (19801-1256)
PHONE..................302 661-6700
Bob Rogers, *Branch Mgr*
EMP: 11
SALES (corp-wide): 21.3B **Publicly Held**
WEB: www.insigniafinancial.com
SIC: 6531 Real estate agent, commercial
HQ: Cb Richard Ellis Real Estate Services, Llc
200 Park Ave Fl 19
New York NY 10166
212 984-8000

(G-9599)
CBBC OPCO LLC (PA)
200 Bellevue Pkwy Ste 210 (19809-3709)
PHONE..................863 967-0636
EMP: 2
SALES (est): 210.7K **Privately Held**
SIC: 2011 Boxed beef from meat slaughtered on site

(G-9600)
CBC HOLDING INC
1201 N Market St Fl 9 (19801-1147)
PHONE..................302 254-2000
Richard J Nolan Jr, *Exec VP*
Matthew J Trachtenberg, *Vice Pres*
Peter F Tobin, *CFO*
David S Barrell, *Admin Sec*
EMP: 140
SQ FT: 180,000
SALES (est): 440.8MM
SALES (corp-wide): 131.4B **Publicly Held**
SIC: 6712 6022 Bank holding companies; state commercial banks
PA: Jpmorgan Chase & Co.
383 Madison Ave
New York NY 10179
212 270-6000

(G-9601)
CBRE INC
1007 N Orange St Ste 100 (19801-1256)
PHONE..................302 661-6700
Robert Walters, *Manager*
EMP: 9
SALES (corp-wide): 21.3B **Publicly Held**
SIC: 6531 Real estate agent, commercial
HQ: Cbre, Inc.
400 S Hope St Ste 25
Los Angeles CA 90071
213 613-3333

(G-9602)
CCMC INC
Also Called: Center For Women's Health
2106 Silverside Rd # 202 (19810-4162)
PHONE..................302 477-9660
Natalie Blagowidow, *Branch Mgr*
Theresa Burcher, *Obstetrician*
EMP: 8
SALES (corp-wide): 1.2B **Privately Held**
SIC: 8011 General & family practice, physician/surgeon
HQ: Ccmc, Inc.
1 Medical Center Blvd
Chester PA 19013
610 447-2000

(G-9603)
CD CLEAN ENERGY AND INFRASTRUC (PA)
251 Little Falls Dr (19808-1674)
PHONE..................480 653-8450
Jon Faltis, *Principal*
Benoit Allehaut, *Principal*
John Breckenridge, *Principal*
Tim Short, *Principal*
EMP: 4
SALES (est): 306.9K **Privately Held**
SIC: 6531 Buying agent, real estate

(G-9604)
CDA ENGINEERING INC
6 Larch Ave Ste 401 (19804-2366)
PHONE..................302 998-9202
Colmcille Deascanis, *Owner*
Jennifer Murphy, *Sr Project Mgr*
EMP: 5
SALES (est): 470.9K **Privately Held**
SIC: 8711 Civil engineering

(G-9605)
CDO USA INC
1013 Centre Rd Ste 403a (19805-1270)
PHONE..................347 429-5110
Camille Obadia, *Vice Pres*
EMP: 1
SALES: 20K **Privately Held**
SIC: 2844 Toilet preparations

(G-9606)
CECIL VAULT & MEMORIAL CO INC
5701 Kirkwood Hwy (19808-4810)
PHONE..................302 994-3806
Toll Free:..................877 -
Dan Cecil, *President*
Constance Cecil, *Vice Pres*
EMP: 8 **EST:** 1920
SQ FT: 7,000
SALES: 739.2K **Privately Held**
SIC: 3272 5999 Burial vaults, concrete or precast terrazzo; tombstones

(G-9607)
CECILIA WILLIAMS
3710 N Market St (19802-2214)
PHONE..................302 250-6269
Cecilia Williams, *Principal*
EMP: 4
SALES (est): 31.6K **Privately Held**
SIC: 7231 Beauty shops

(G-9608)
CECON GROUP LLC
242 N James St Ste 202 (19804-3168)
PHONE..................302 994-8000
Michael C Fisher, *President*
Stanley Tocker, *President*
Barry E Bowen, *Vice Pres*
Mike Fisher, *Project Mgr*
Boyd Sorenson, *Treasurer*
EMP: 7
SQ FT: 1,600
SALES (est): 640.5K
SALES (corp-wide): 41MM **Privately Held**
WEB: www.cecon.com
SIC: 8711 8748 Consulting engineer; business consulting
PA: Becht Engineering Co. Inc.
20 Church St
Liberty Corner NJ 07938
908 580-1119

(G-9609)
CELANESE INTERNATIONAL CORP
Silverside Rd Rodney 34 (19810)
PHONE..................972 443-4000
EMP: 4
SALES (est): 3.7MM
SALES (corp-wide): 7.1B **Publicly Held**
SIC: 2819 2821 2869 Industrial inorganic chemicals; polyethylene resins; acetates: amyl, butyl & ethyl; acetic & chloroacetic acid & metallic salts
PA: Celanese Corporation
222 Las Colinas Blvd W # 900
Irving TX 75039
972 443-4000

(G-9610)
CELL POINT LLC
1201 N Market St (19801-1147)
PHONE..................302 658-9200
David Rollo, *President*
Terry Colip, *Mng Member*
Jerry Bryant,
EMP: 65
SALES (est): 5.1MM **Privately Held**
SIC: 7371 Computer software writers, free-lance

(G-9611)
CELLCO PARTNERSHIP
Also Called: Verizon
4407 Concord Pike (19803-1489)
PHONE..................302 530-4620
Chuck Linsdrom, *Branch Mgr*
EMP: 8
SALES (corp-wide): 130.8B **Publicly Held**
SIC: 4812 Cellular telephone services
HQ: Cellco Partnership
1 Verizon Way
Basking Ridge NJ 07920

(G-9612)
CENTER FOR INTRVNTNAL PAIN SPI
405 Silverside Rd Ste 100 (19809-1768)
PHONE..................302 792-1370
EMP: 6
SALES (est): 80.5K **Privately Held**
SIC: 8011 Orthopedic physician

(G-9613)
CENTERVILLE COMPANY CONTRS
5714 Kennett Pike (19807-1331)
PHONE..................302 656-8666
EMP: 4
SALES (est): 200.9K **Privately Held**
SIC: 0782 1794 Landscape contractors; excavation work

(G-9614)
CENTERVILLE VETERINARY HOSP
5804 Kennett Pike (19807-1197)
PHONE..................302 655-3315
Don Coats, *Manager*
EMP: 17 **EST:** 1958
SALES (est): 519.1K **Privately Held**
WEB: www.cvh1.com
SIC: 0742 Animal hospital services, pets & other animal specialties; veterinarian, animal specialties

(G-9615)
CENTRAL FIRM LLC
1201 N Orange St Ste 7016 (19801-1188)
PHONE..................610 470-9836
Margaret Loftus, *CEO*
A Robert Gallagher, *President*
EMP: 2
SQ FT: 138
SALES (est): 88.3K **Privately Held**
SIC: 3661 4841 7373 8111 Telephone central office equipment, dial or manual; direct broadcast satellite services (DBS); value-added resellers, computer systems; specialized legal services; administrative services consultant

(G-9616)
CENTRIX HR
213 W 4th St (19801-2204)
PHONE..................302 777-7818
Bill Black, *Owner*
EMP: 5
SALES (est): 253.5K **Privately Held**
SIC: 7361 Employment agencies

(G-9617)
CERTIFIED ASSETS MGT INTL LLC
100 Todds Ln (19802-3212)
PHONE..................302 765-3352
Alberto Washington, *Manager*
EMP: 9 **EST:** 2012
SALES (est): 869K **Privately Held**
SIC: 5094 Coins

(G-9618)
CERTIFIED LOCK & ACCESS LLC
3 Germay Dr Ste 7 (19804-1127)
PHONE..................302 383-7507
Stephen Miller, *Vice Pres*
EMP: 5 **EST:** 2009
SALES (est): 717.9K **Privately Held**
SIC: 7699 1731 Locksmith shop; access control systems specialization

(G-9619)
CERTIFIED MECHANICAL CONTRS
117 David Rd (19804-2648)
PHONE..................302 559-3727
Kenneth R Silva, *Owner*
EMP: 6
SALES (est): 494.8K **Privately Held**
SIC: 1711 Mechanical contractor

(G-9620)
CFD GROUP INC
919 N Market St Ste 950 (19801-3036)
PHONE..................242 698-1039
David Drake, *President*
EMP: 20
SALES (est): 817.4K **Privately Held**
SIC: 6211 Investment firm, general brokerage

(G-9621)
CFG LAB INC
1521 Concord Pike Ste 301 (19803-3644)
PHONE..................302 261-3403
Aleksandr Goldshtadt, *Principal*
EMP: 2
SALES (est): 861.6K **Privately Held**
SIC: 5169 2869 Chemicals & allied products; laboratory chemicals, organic

(G-9622)
CGC CONSULTING LLC
5400 Limestone Rd Ste 200 (19808-1232)
PHONE..................302 489-2280
Terry Tucker,
Deirdre S Smith,
Stacy B Ziegler,
EMP: 6
SQ FT: 20,000
SALES (est): 553.6K
SALES (corp-wide): 26.1MM **Privately Held**
SIC: 8711 Civil engineering
PA: Duffield Associates, Inc.
5400 Limestone Rd
Wilmington DE 19808
302 239-6634

(G-9623)
CGS INFOTECH INC
501 Silverside Rd Ste 105 (19809-1376)
PHONE..................302 351-2434
Cgsl Anjali, *Vice Pres*
AMI Shah, *Director*
EMP: 42
SALES (est): 1.4MM **Privately Held**
WEB: www.cgsinfotech.com
SIC: 7374 Computer graphics service

(G-9624)
CHALLENGE PROGRAM
1124 E 7th St (19801-4502)
PHONE..................302 655-0945
Andrew McKnight, *President*
Kim Slocomb, *Program Mgr*
Alden Gibbs, *Business Dir*
EMP: 8
SALES: 1.6MM **Privately Held**
WEB: www.challengeprogram.org
SIC: 8699 Charitable organization

(G-9625)
CHAMBERS INSURANCE AGENCY INC
109 N Dupont Rd (19807-3105)
P.O. Box 4380 (19807-0380)
PHONE..................302 655-5300
Joe Chambers, *President*
EMP: 9 **EST:** 1972
SALES (est): 870K **Privately Held**
SIC: 6411 Insurance agents

GEOGRAPHIC SECTION
Wilmington - New Castle County (G-9656)

(G-9626)
CHAMBERS OPTOMETRIST
2323 Pennsylvania Ave (19806-1332)
PHONE..................302 543-6492
EMP: 8
SALES (est): 87K Privately Held
SIC: 8042 Offices & clinics of optometrists

(G-9627)
CHAMPIONS + LEGENDS CORP
251 Little Falls Dr (19808-1674)
PHONE..................702 605-2522
Shahin Mottahed, CEO
EMP: 2
SALES (est): 74.4K Privately Held
SIC: 2834 Tinctures, pharmaceutical

(G-9628)
CHANCERY COURT REPORTERS
500 N King St Ste 11400 (19801-3768)
PHONE..................302 255-0515
Lorraine Marino, Principal
EMP: 5
SALES (est): 170K Privately Held
SIC: 7338 Court reporting service

(G-9629)
CHANDLER AND LYNCH CPA
3510 Silverside Rd Ste 4 (19810-4937)
PHONE..................302 478-9800
Ed Lynch, Partner
Jay Chandler, Principal
EMP: 10
SALES (est): 707.5K Privately Held
SIC: 8721 Accounting, auditing & bookkeeping

(G-9630)
CHARLES ALLEN LTD
9 W Greenbriar Rd (19810-4105)
PHONE..................302 475-5048
Cheryl Rifon, Owner
EMP: 1
SALES (est): 67.8K Privately Held
SIC: 3911 5944 Jewelry, precious metal; jewelry stores

(G-9631)
CHARLES D CALHOON DDS P
4600 New Linden HI 102 (19808)
PHONE..................302 731-0202
Charles D Calhoon, Principal
EMP: 4
SALES (est): 287.2K Privately Held
SIC: 8021 Dental clinic

(G-9632)
CHARLES J VEITH DMD
2300 Penns Ave Ste 5c (19806-1305)
PHONE..................302 658-7354
Charles J Veith DMD, Owner
EMP: 4
SALES (est): 421.1K Privately Held
SIC: 8021 Offices & clinics of dentists

(G-9633)
CHARLES M WALLACE
1906 Newport Gap Pike (19808-6136)
PHONE..................302 998-1412
Charles Wallace, Owner
EMP: 8
SALES (est): 854.2K Privately Held
SIC: 6411 Insurance agents

(G-9634)
CHARLES OGDEN
Also Called: Thumbs Only
2205 Jones Ln (19810-2710)
PHONE..................305 606-4512
Charles Ogden, Owner
EMP: 1
SALES (est): 59.1K Privately Held
WEB: www.thumbsonly.com
SIC: 2499 3231 Novelties, wood fiber; stained glass; made from purchased glass

(G-9635)
CHARLES P ARCARO FUNERAL HOME
2309 Lancaster Ave (19805-3735)
PHONE..................302 658-9095
Charles P Arcaro, Owner
EMP: 4 EST: 1963
SQ FT: 2,400
SALES (est): 220K Privately Held
SIC: 7261 Funeral home

(G-9636)
CHARLES S KNOTHE INC
3516 Silverside Rd Ste 14 (19810-4931)
PHONE..................302 478-8800
Charles Knothe, President
EMP: 4
SALES (est): 316K Privately Held
SIC: 8111 General practice attorney, lawyer

(G-9637)
CHARLES S RESKOVITZ INC
1018 Liberty Rd (19804-2857)
P.O. Box 5068 (19808-0068)
PHONE..................302 999-9455
Charles Stephan, President
Daniel Stephan, Vice Pres
Joanne Stephan, Treasurer
EMP: 9
SQ FT: 2,400
SALES (est): 1.3MM Privately Held
SIC: 1711 Plumbing contractors

(G-9638)
CHARLES SCHWAB & CO INC
602 Delaware Ave (19801-1430)
PHONE..................302 622-3600
Rich Hepp, Branch Mgr
EMP: 18
SALES (corp-wide): 10.1B Publicly Held
SIC: 6211 Brokers, security; dealers, security; investment firm, general brokerage
HQ: Charles Schwab & Co., Inc.
211 Main St Fl 17
San Francisco CA 94105
415 636-7000

(G-9639)
CHARLES WANG MD PA
1700 Wawaset St Ste 200 (19806-2142)
PHONE..................302 655-1500
Charles Wang, Owner
EMP: 6
SALES (est): 486.6K Privately Held
SIC: 8011 Ophthalmologist

(G-9640)
CHARTER DYNAMICS LLC
Also Called: Enteraxion
427 N Ttnall St Ste 70775 (19802)
PHONE..................888 260-4579
Nathalie Brinkley, CFO
Julian Brinkley, Mng Member
EMP: 4
SALES: 360K Privately Held
SIC: 7372 Prepackaged software

(G-9641)
CHASE CENTER ON RIVER
815 Justison St Ste B (19801-5156)
PHONE..................302 655-2187
Richard Encao, President
EMP: 6 EST: 2009
SALES (est): 299.2K Privately Held
SIC: 8322 Geriatric social service

(G-9642)
CHATNGO CORPORATION
901 N Market St (19801-3022)
PHONE..................302 504-4291
EMP: 7 EST: 2016
SALES (est): 152.8K Privately Held
SIC: 7372 Prepackaged Software Services

(G-9643)
CHELTEN APARTMENTS ASSOC LP
4 Denny Rd (19809-3445)
PHONE..................302 322-6323
Jackie Edmanson, Principal
Tom Perkins, Principal
EMP: 13
SALES (est): 775.6K Privately Held
SIC: 6513 Apartment hotel operation

(G-9644)
CHEM TECH INC
6725 Governor Prntz Blvd (19809-1800)
P.O. Box 9658 (19809-0658)
PHONE..................302 798-9675
C R Donovan Jr, President
EMP: 3 EST: 1963
SQ FT: 4,000
SALES (est): 335.7K Privately Held
SIC: 2992 2842 Lubricating oils & greases; cleaning or polishing preparations

(G-9645)
CHEMAXON LLC
3511 Silverside Rd # 105 (19810-4902)
P.O. Box 1026, Salem MA (01970-6026)
PHONE..................281 528-0485
Bahram Manavi, Sales Staff
Richard Johnson,
Valeria Kortvelyesi,
EMP: 7
SQ FT: 1,000
SALES (est): 833.4K Privately Held
SIC: 7371 Computer software development

(G-9646)
CHEMFIRST INC (HQ)
1007 Market St (19898-1100)
P.O. Box 7005, Pascagoula MS (39568-7005)
PHONE..................302 774-1000
Jeff Coe, President
Daniel P Anderson, Vice Pres
Max P Bowman, Vice Pres
Chet Webb, Vice Pres
Kenneth Porter, Treasurer
◆ EMP: 59
SALES (est): 34.9MM
SALES (corp-wide): 6.6B Publicly Held
WEB: www.chemfirst.com
SIC: 2865 3567 3312 Cyclic crudes & intermediates; aniline, nitrobenzene; benzene; toluene; incinerators; metal; domestic or commercial; induction & dielectric heating equipment; ingots, steel; billets, steel
PA: The Chemours Company
1007 Market St
Wilmington DE 19898
302 773-1000

(G-9647)
CHEMOURS CO FC LLC ✪
200 Powder Mill Rd (19803-2907)
PHONE..................302 353-5003
EMP: 7 EST: 2019
SALES (est): 984.6K
SALES (corp-wide): 6.6B Publicly Held
SIC: 2899 Chemical preparations
PA: The Chemours Company
1007 Market St
Wilmington DE 19898
302 773-1000

(G-9648)
CHEMOURS COMPANY (PA)
1007 Market St (19898-1100)
P.O. Box 2047 (19899-2047)
PHONE..................302 773-1000
Richard H Brown, Ch of Bd
Mark P Vergnano, President
Edwin Sparks, President
Mark E Newman, COO
Susan M Kelliher, Senior VP
▲ EMP: 277
SALES: 6.6B Publicly Held
SIC: 2879 Agricultural chemicals

(G-9649)
CHEMOURS COMPANY FC LLC (HQ)
1007 Market St (19898-1100)
P.O. Box 2915 (19805-0915)
PHONE..................302 773-1000
Mark Vergnano,
◆ EMP: 277
SALES (est): 1B
SALES (corp-wide): 6.6B Publicly Held
SIC: 2879 2816 Agricultural chemicals; titanium dioxide, anatase or rutile (pigments)
PA: The Chemours Company
1007 Market St
Wilmington DE 19898
302 773-1000

(G-9650)
CHEMOURS COMPANY FC LLC
Also Called: Performance Lubricants
1007 Market St (19898-1100)
PHONE..................302 773-1267
Mark Gullo, Manager
EMP: 17
SALES (corp-wide): 6.6B Publicly Held
WEB: www.dupont.com
SIC: 5172 Lubricating oils & greases
HQ: The Chemours Company Fc Llc
1007 Market St
Wilmington DE 19898
302 773-1000

(G-9651)
CHEMOURS COMPANY FC LLC
Animal Health Solutions
4301 Lncaster Pike Barley (19805)
PHONE..................678 427-1530
Gabriel Pardo, Manager
EMP: 182
SALES (corp-wide): 6.6B Publicly Held
WEB: www.dupont.com
SIC: 2879 Agricultural chemicals
HQ: The Chemours Company Fc Llc
1007 Market St
Wilmington DE 19898
302 773-1000

(G-9652)
CHEMOURS COMPANY FC LLC
Also Called: Fluoroproducts
Chestnut Run (19880)
PHONE..................302 540-5423
Simone Genna, Manager
EMP: 51
SALES (corp-wide): 6.6B Publicly Held
WEB: www.dupont.com
SIC: 2899 Chemical preparations
HQ: The Chemours Company Fc Llc
1007 Market St
Wilmington DE 19898
302 773-1000

(G-9653)
CHEMOURS COMPANY FC LLC
Also Called: Surface Protection
1007 Market St (19898-1100)
PHONE..................302 545-0072
Warren Hoy, Plant Mgr
Thomas Band, Manager
EMP: 50
SALES (corp-wide): 6.6B Publicly Held
WEB: www.dupont.com
SIC: 2819 Industrial inorganic chemicals
HQ: The Chemours Company Fc Llc
1007 Market St
Wilmington DE 19898
302 773-1000

(G-9654)
CHEMRING NORTH AMER GROUP INC (DH)
1105 N Market St (19801-1216)
PHONE..................302 658-5687
Daniel McKenrick, President
Jane Janosko, Executive Asst
EMP: 5 EST: 2008
SALES (est): 6.4MM
SALES (corp-wide): 390.3MM Privately Held
SIC: 3479 Coating of metals & formed products

(G-9655)
CHESAPEAKE NEUROLOGY SERVICE
12 Stable Ln (19803-1935)
PHONE..................302 563-7253
EMP: 4
SALES (est): 64.7K Privately Held
SIC: 8011 Neurologist

(G-9656)
CHESTER BETHEL UNITED METHODIS
Also Called: Chester Bethel Preschool
2619 Foulk Rd (19810-1421)
PHONE..................302 475-3549
Vicky Anignani, Director
Diane Anonaratl, Director
EMP: 12
SQ FT: 130,000

Wilmington - New Castle County (G-9657)

GEOGRAPHIC SECTION

SALES (est): 550.8K **Privately Held**
SIC: **8661** 8351 Methodist Church; child day care services

(G-9657)
CHESTNUT INVESTORS II INC
Also Called: Delphi Capital
590 Madison Ave Fl 30 (19899)
PHONE.....................................302 478-5142
EMP: 25
SALES (corp-wide): 40.6B **Privately Held**
SIC: **6719** Investment Holding Company
HQ: Delphi Financial Group, Inc.
1105 N Market St Ste 1230
Wilmington DE 19801
302 478-5142

(G-9658)
CHESTNUT RUN FEDERAL CR UN (PA)
974 Centre Rd (19805-1269)
P.O. Box 5037 (19808-0037)
PHONE.....................................302 999-2967
John G Ingram, *Principal*
John Poore, *Principal*
Peter Sonne, *Principal*
David Trefsger, *Principal*
Cheryl Chilcutt, *Manager*
EMP: 14
SQ FT: 4,100
SALES: 1.6MM **Privately Held**
WEB: www.chestnutrunfcu.org
SIC: **6061** Federal credit unions

(G-9659)
CHEZ NICHOLE HAIR & NAIL SALON
Also Called: Chez Nichole Beauty Salon
1901 W 11th St Ste B (19805-2740)
PHONE.....................................302 654-8888
Madelyn Magglin, *President*
Joseph Cannatelli, *President*
EMP: 25
SALES (est): 320.1K **Privately Held**
SIC: **7231** 5051 Unisex hair salons; nails

(G-9660)
CHICHESTER BUSINESS PARK LLC
1940 Rising Sun Ln (19807-3033)
PHONE.....................................302 379-3140
Henry Didonato,
EMP: 5
SALES: 100.4K **Privately Held**
SIC: **6531** Real estate leasing & rentals

(G-9661)
CHILD INC (PA)
507 Philadelphia Pike (19809-2177)
PHONE.....................................302 762-8989
Martha V Dupont, *President*
Timothy Brandau, *Med Doctor*
Tim Brandau, *Exec Dir*
Anne Undorf, *Administration*
Ginette Malone, *Receptionist*
EMP: 30
SQ FT: 6,000
SALES: 5.2MM **Privately Held**
WEB: www.childinc.com
SIC: **8322** 8699 Outreach program; charitable organization

(G-9662)
CHILDREN YOUTH & THEIR FAM
321 E 11th St Fl 1 (19801-3417)
PHONE.....................................302 577-6011
EMP: 5 **Privately Held**
SIC: **8322** 9441 Child related social services;
HQ: Children, Youth & Their Families, Delaware Dept Of Services For
1825 Faulkland Rd
Wilmington DE 19805

(G-9663)
CHILDREN YOUTH & THEIR FAM
Division Child Mntal Hlth Svcs
1825 Faulkland Rd (19805-1121)
PHONE.....................................302 633-2600
Carol De Santis, *Manager*
Darbar Gorezowerk, *Admin Sec*
EMP: 35 **Privately Held**

SIC: **8011** 9431 Occupational & industrial specialist, physician/surgeon; administration of public health programs;
HQ: Children, Youth & Their Families, Delaware Dept Of Services For
1825 Faulkland Rd
Wilmington DE 19805

(G-9664)
CHILDREN FMILIES FIRST DEL INC (PA)
809 N Washington St (19801-1509)
PHONE.....................................302 658-5177
Jennifer B Jonach, *Ch of Bd*
Katy Connolly, *Ch of Bd*
Peter Hazen, *Treasurer*
Paul McCommons, *Asst Treas*
Mike McHugh, *Supervisor*
EMP: 54
SALES: 16.8MM **Privately Held**
SIC: **8322** Child related social services

(G-9665)
CHILDRENS BEACH HOUSE INC (PA)
100 W 10th St Ste 411 (19801-1643)
PHONE.....................................302 655-4288
Thomas Sturgis, *President*
Nicholas Imhoff, *Business Mgr*
Charles Sterner, *Treasurer*
Richard Garrett, *Exec Dir*
Jennifer Clement, *Director*
EMP: 45
SALES: 2.4MM **Privately Held**
WEB: www.cbhinc.org
SIC: **8322** Children's aid society; family location service

(G-9666)
CHIME INC
Also Called: Wave
1013 Centre Rd Ste 403 (19805-1270)
PHONE.....................................978 844-1162
EMP: 40
SALES: 200K **Privately Held**
SIC: **7389** Money Transfer

(G-9667)
CHINA MONITOR INC
134 Chatenay Ln (19807-1429)
PHONE.....................................302 351-2324
Joseph Kasputys, *CEO*
EMP: 13
SALES: 950K **Privately Held**
SIC: **8732** Commercial nonphysical research

(G-9668)
CHIQUITA BRANDS LLC
101 River Rd (19801-5886)
PHONE.....................................302 571-9781
Phil Colgate, *Manager*
EMP: 17
SALES (corp-wide): 3B **Privately Held**
SIC: **5148** Fruits
HQ: Chiquita Brands L.L.C.
Dcota Bldg 1855 Griffin
Dania FL 33004
954 924-5801

(G-9669)
CHIROPRACTIC SERVICES PA
536 Greenhill Ave (19805-1851)
PHONE.....................................302 654-0404
Douglas Fazzick, *Owner*
EMP: 4
SALES (est): 169.1K **Privately Held**
SIC: **8041** Offices & clinics of chiropractors

(G-9670)
CHOCOLATE SWIRL LLC
401 Justison St Apt 312 (19801-5293)
PHONE.....................................718 407-0034
Lisa Bracigliano,
EMP: 1
SALES (est): 97.9K **Privately Held**
SIC: **2064** Candy & other confectionery products

(G-9671)
CHOUDHARY ARABINDA K MD
1600 Rockland Rd (19803-3607)
PHONE.....................................302 651-4000
Arabinda Choudhary, *Executive*
EMP: 4

SALES (est): 81.1K **Privately Held**
SIC: **8011** Pediatrician

(G-9672)
CHRISSINGER AND BAUMBERGER
Also Called: Liberty Mutual
3 Mill Rd Ste 301 (19806-2164)
PHONE.....................................302 777-0100
Ted Kelley, *Owner*
EMP: 17
SALES (est): 3.7MM **Privately Held**
SIC: **6331** Automobile insurance

(G-9673)
CHRIST CH EPISCPAL PRESCHOOL
505 E Buck Rd (19807-2167)
P.O. Box 3510 (19807-0510)
PHONE.....................................302 472-0021
Jo Harney, *Director*
EMP: 25
SALES: 710.6K **Privately Held**
SIC: **8661** 8351 Religious organizations; preschool center

(G-9674)
CHRISTIANA BODY SHOP INC
96 Germay Dr (19804-1105)
PHONE.....................................302 655-1085
Christine D Cox, *President*
Ernie Cox, *Vice Pres*
Ernest Cox, *Treasurer*
Megan Cox, *Manager*
EMP: 7 EST: 1962
SALES (est): 1.1MM **Privately Held**
WEB: www.christianabody.com
SIC: **7532** Body shop, automotive

(G-9675)
CHRISTIANA CARE
601 Delaware Ave Ste 300 (19801-1461)
PHONE.....................................302 654-4925
EMP: 8
SALES (est): 82.2K **Privately Held**
SIC: **8062** 8031 General medical & surgical hospitals; offices & clinics of osteopathic physicians

(G-9676)
CHRISTIANA CARE
1941 Limestone Rd Ste 204 (19808-5400)
PHONE.....................................302 633-3750
Estelle H Whitney, *Principal*
Damian Andrisani, *Med Doctor*
Brian Galinat, *Med Doctor*
EMP: 10
SALES (est): 438.4K **Privately Held**
SIC: **8062** 8011 General medical & surgical hospitals; offices & clinics of medical doctors

(G-9677)
CHRISTIANA CARE HEALTH SYS INC
Also Called: Asari, Julie Y MD
4512 Kirkwood Hwy Ste 300 (19808-5129)
PHONE.....................................302 623-7500
James E Damour MD, *President*
Nancy Lasson, *Executive*
EMP: 15
SALES (corp-wide): 1.5B **Privately Held**
SIC: **8062** General medical & surgical hospitals
HQ: Christiana Care Health System, Inc.
200 Hygeia Dr
Newark DE 19713
302 733-1000

(G-9678)
CHRISTIANA CARE HEALTH SYS INC
2002 Foulk Rd Ste C (19810-3643)
PHONE.....................................302 529-1975
EMP: 4
SALES (corp-wide): 1.5B **Privately Held**
SIC: **8011** Internal medicine, physician/surgeon
HQ: Christiana Care Health System, Inc.
200 Hygeia Dr
Newark DE 19713
302 733-1000

(G-9679)
CHRISTIANA CARE HEALTH SYS INC
Also Called: Center For Rehabilitation
501 W 14th St (19801-1013)
PHONE.....................................302 733-1000
Charles Smith, *President*
Robert Mulrooney, *Vice Pres*
Judy Townsley, *Vice Pres*
Thomas Zeidman, *Opers Mgr*
Sharon Urban, *Opers Staff*
EMP: 139
SALES (corp-wide): 1.5B **Privately Held**
SIC: **8741** 8062 Hospital management; general medical & surgical hospitals
HQ: Christiana Care Health System, Inc.
200 Hygeia Dr
Newark DE 19713
302 733-1000

(G-9680)
CHRISTIANA CARE HEALTH SYS INC
Also Called: Cardiac Diagnostic Center
3521 Silverside Rd Ste 1a (19810-4900)
PHONE.....................................302 477-6500
Ann Marie Nessick, *Manager*
Marc Grobman, *Family Practiti*
EMP: 8
SALES (corp-wide): 1.5B **Privately Held**
WEB: www.cardiologyconsultantspa.com
SIC: **8011** 8734 Cardiologist & cardio-vascular specialist; testing laboratories
HQ: Christiana Care Health System, Inc.
200 Hygeia Dr
Newark DE 19713
302 733-1000

(G-9681)
CHRISTIANA CARE HLTH SVCS INC
501 W 14th St Ste 8 (19801-1013)
PHONE.....................................302 428-6662
Paul Schweizer, *President*
EMP: 17
SALES (corp-wide): 1.5B **Privately Held**
SIC: **8049** Physical therapist
PA: Christiana Care Health Services, Inc.
4755 Ogletown Stanton Rd
Newark DE 19718
302 733-1000

(G-9682)
CHRISTIANA CARE HLTH SVCS INC
Also Called: Christiana Physcl Therapy Plus
1401 Foulk Rd Ste 100 (19803-2764)
PHONE.....................................302 477-3300
Paul Schweizer, *President*
EMP: 10
SALES (corp-wide): 1.5B **Privately Held**
SIC: **8049** Physical therapist
PA: Christiana Care Health Services, Inc.
4755 Ogletown Stanton Rd
Newark DE 19718
302 733-1000

(G-9683)
CHRISTIANA CARE HLTH SVCS INC
Also Called: Wellness Centers
2501 Ebright Rd (19810-1125)
PHONE.....................................302 477-3960
Jody Pezzner, *Director*
EMP: 7
SALES (corp-wide): 1.5B **Privately Held**
SIC: **8011** Primary care medical clinic
PA: Christiana Care Health Services, Inc.
4755 Ogletown Stanton Rd
Newark DE 19718
302 733-1000

(G-9684)
CHRISTIANA CARE HLTH SVCS INC
Also Called: Alan B Evantash
2302 W 16th St (19806-1307)
PHONE.....................................302 733-1805
Alan B Evantash, *Director*
EMP: 6
SALES (corp-wide): 1.5B **Privately Held**
SIC: **8062** General medical & surgical hospitals

GEOGRAPHIC SECTION

Wilmington - New Castle County (G-9713)

PA: Christiana Care Health Services, Inc.
4755 Ogletown Stanton Rd
Newark DE 19718
302 733-1000

(G-9685)
CHRISTIANA CARE HOME HEALTH
Also Called: Evergreen Center Alzheimer
3000 Newport Gap Pike (19808-2378)
PHONE...................302 995-8448
Lynn Williams-Spencer, *Manager*
EMP: 13
SALES (corp-wide): 1.5B **Privately Held**
WEB: www.christianacare.com
SIC: 8082 8322 Visiting nurse service; adult day care center
HQ: Christiana Care Home Health And Community Services Inc
1 Reads Way Ste 100
New Castle DE 19720
302 327-5583

(G-9686)
CHRISTIANA COUNSELING
5235 W Woodmill Dr Ste 47 (19808-4068)
PHONE...................302 995-1680
Robert Blaine Morris, *President*
Kris Fowler, *Corp Secy*
Adam Morris, *Vice Pres*
EMP: 5
SALES (est): 828.7K **Privately Held**
WEB: www.christianacounseling.com
SIC: 8011 Psychiatrists & psychoanalysts

(G-9687)
CHRISTIANA INCORPORATORS INC
508 Main St (19804-3911)
PHONE...................302 998-2008
Ralph V Estep, *President*
EMP: 7
SALES (est): 799.9K **Privately Held**
WEB: www.taxesbyestep.com
SIC: 8721 Certified public accountant

(G-9688)
CHRISTIANA MATERIALS INC
305 W Newport Pike (19804-3154)
PHONE...................302 633-5600
William Saienni Jr, *President*
Barry Baker, *Vice Pres*
Harry Johnson, *Admin Sec*
EMP: 12
SALES: 8.2MM **Privately Held**
SIC: 2951 5032 Asphalt paving mixtures & blocks; building stone

(G-9689)
CHRISTIANA VILLAGE APTS
225 W 4th St Apt 3a (19801-2270)
PHONE...................302 427-0403
Delores Martin, *Manager*
EMP: 4
SALES (est): 288.4K **Privately Held**
SIC: 6513 Apartment building operators

(G-9690)
CHRISTINA CULTURAL ARTS CENTER
Also Called: EARLY CHILDHOOD EDUCATION ARTS
705 N Market St (19801-3008)
PHONE...................302 652-0101
Steven Werbey, *President*
Yvonne Smith, *Opers Staff*
Jo A Jackson, *Finance*
H Ray Jones Avery, *Director*
Kim Graham, *Director*
EMP: 41
SQ FT: 170
SALES: 1.4MM **Privately Held**
WEB: www.ccac-de.org
SIC: 8699 Art council

(G-9691)
CHRISTINE W MAYNARD MD
4600 New Lndn Hll Rd 20 (19808)
PHONE...................302 995-7073
Christine Maynard MD, *Owner*
EMP: 4
SALES (est): 105.1K **Privately Held**
SIC: 8049 Offices of health practitioner

(G-9692)
CHRISTOPHER BARAN DDS
1601 Milltown Rd Ste 19 (19808-4084)
PHONE...................903 968-7467
Christopher Baran, *Principal*
EMP: 4
SALES (est): 67.6K **Privately Held**
SIC: 8021 Offices & clinics of dentists

(G-9693)
CHRYSTAL HOLDINGS
Also Called: E D I S Interiors
222 Delaware Ave (19801-1621)
PHONE...................302 655-2398
Andy Disabatinol, *CEO*
Richard Disabatinol, *Vice Pres*
EMP: 4
SALES (est): 391.8K **Privately Held**
SIC: 1542 Commercial & office building, new construction

(G-9694)
CHUBB INA OVRSEAS HOLDINGS INC (HQ)
1 Beaver Valley Rd (19803-1115)
PHONE...................302 476-6000
Bob Jacobs, *Principal*
Mary Simons, *Financial Analy*
Eugene Delmonico, *Underwriter*
Kathleen McCreary, *Manager*
Mario Scorzetti, *Consultant*
EMP: 10
SALES (est): 9.4MM
SALES (corp-wide): 32.7B **Privately Held**
SIC: 8741 Management services
PA: Chubb Limited
Barengasse 32
ZUrich ZH 8001
434 567-600

(G-9695)
CHUBB INSURANCE COMPANY
1 Beaver Valley Rd (19803-1115)
PHONE...................302 477-1892
Cindy Battiste, *Underwriter*
Luke Menser, *Manager*
Laurie Tumulty, *Producer*
William Jefferys, *Analyst*
EMP: 4
SALES (corp-wide): 32.7B **Privately Held**
SIC: 6351 Credit & other financial responsibility insurance
HQ: Chubb Insurance Company
11133 Ave Of The Americas
New York NY 10019
212 642-7800

(G-9696)
CHUBB US HOLDING INC
Also Called: Ace Global Solution
1 Beaver Valley Rd 4e (19803-1115)
PHONE...................215 640-1000
Steven Snyder, *President*
Lucienne Hardy, *Assistant VP*
Joseph Kelly, *Assistant VP*
Lisa Linder, *Assistant VP*
Shirley Madden, *Finance Mgr*
EMP: 800
SALES (corp-wide): 32.7B **Privately Held**
WEB: www.ace.bm
SIC: 6411 Property & casualty insurance agent
HQ: Chubb Us Holding Inc.
1601 Chestnut St
Philadelphia PA 19192

(G-9697)
CHUCK GEORGE INC
Also Called: Delaware Metals
400 Water St (19804-2421)
PHONE...................302 994-7444
Chuck George, *President*
Karen George, *Admin Sec*
EMP: 30 EST: 1953
SQ FT: 16,000
SALES (est): 4.6MM **Privately Held**
SIC: 8731 7692 Industrial laboratory, except testing; welding repair

(G-9698)
CHURCHMENS MACHINE COMPANY
401 Brookside Ave (19805-2490)
PHONE...................302 994-8660
Edward Hook, *President*
Robert Hook, *Exec VP*
Todd Springer, *Purchasing*
Nadine Hook, *Admin Sec*
EMP: 19
SQ FT: 10,000
SALES (est): 3.8MM **Privately Held**
WEB: www.churchmens.com
SIC: 3599 Machine shop, jobbing & repair

(G-9699)
CIANCON GLOBAL LLC
Also Called: Castle Consultants
501 Silverside Rd Ste 105 (19809-1376)
PHONE...................302 365-0956
Vishal Jain, *Principal*
EMP: 22
SQ FT: 1,200
SALES (est): 2.6MM **Privately Held**
SIC: 4953 Recycling, waste materials

(G-9700)
CIBA SPECIALTY CHEM N AMER
205 S James St (19804-2424)
PHONE...................302 992-5600
John Shaphly, *Principal*
EMP: 11 EST: 2014
SALES (est): 990.9K **Privately Held**
SIC: 5169 Chemicals & allied products

(G-9701)
CICONTE ROSEMAN & WASSERMAN
1300 N King St (19801-3220)
P.O. Box 1126 (19899-1126)
PHONE...................302 658-7101
EMP: 16
SALES (est): 1.9MM **Privately Held**
SIC: 8111 Legal Services Office

(G-9702)
CIELO SALON & SPA INC
600 Delaware Ave (19801-1430)
PHONE...................302 575-0400
Laron Thomas, *President*
EMP: 17
SALES (est): 373.4K **Privately Held**
SIC: 7231 Beauty shops

(G-9703)
CIGNA CORPORATE SERVICES LLC
300 Bellevue Pkwy Ste 101 (19809-3704)
PHONE...................302 792-4906
Regina Campbell, *Sales Staff*
Megan Francione, *Administration*
EMP: 76
SALES (est): 25.3MM
SALES (corp-wide): 141.6B **Publicly Held**
SIC: 6311 Life insurance
HQ: Cigna Health And Life Insurance Company
900 Cottage Grove Rd
Bloomfield CT 06002

(G-9704)
CIGNA CORPORATION
300 Bellevue Pkwy (19809-3704)
PHONE...................302 792-4906
EMP: 169
SALES (corp-wide): 34.9B **Publicly Held**
SIC: 6311 6321 Life Insurance Carrier Accident/Health Insurance Carrier
PA: Cigna Corporation
900 Cottage Grove Rd
Bloomfield CT 06002
860 226-6000

(G-9705)
CIGNA CORPORATION
300 Bellevue Pkwy (19809-3704)
PHONE...................302 792-4906
Maryann Najmola, *Administration*
EMP: 8
SALES (corp-wide): 141.6B **Publicly Held**
SIC: 6799 Investors
HQ: Cigna Holding Company
900 Cottage Grove Rd
Bloomfield CT 06002
860 226-6000

(G-9706)
CIGNA REAL ESTATE INC (DH)
1 Beaver Valley Rd (19803-1115)
P.O. Box 15050 (19850-5050)
PHONE...................302 476-3337
William C Hartman, *President*
EMP: 7
SALES (est): 722.8K
SALES (corp-wide): 32.7B **Privately Held**
SIC: 6531 6512 6799 6519 Real estate agents & managers; nonresidential building operators; investors; real property lessors
HQ: Ace Property And Casualty Insurance Company
2 Liberty Pl 2 Liberty Place
Philadelphia PA 19102
215 761-1000

(G-9707)
CINEMARK USA INC
Also Called: Cinemark Movies 10
1796 W Newport Pike (19804-3540)
PHONE...................302 994-7280
Ron Landry, *Branch Mgr*
EMP: 35 **Publicly Held**
SIC: 7832 Motion picture theaters, except drive-in
HQ: Cinemark Usa, Inc.
3900 Dallas Pkwy Ste 500
Plano TX 75093
972 665-1000

(G-9708)
CINEMAVERICKS MEDIA LLC
2433 Hammond Pl (19808-4263)
PHONE...................302 438-1144
EMP: 5 EST: 2012
SALES (est): 113.8K **Privately Held**
SIC: 4899 Communication services,

(G-9709)
CINTAS CORPORATION NO 2
Also Called: Cintas J98
2925 Northeast Blvd (19802-3705)
PHONE...................302 765-6460
Jim Scanler, *General Mgr*
EMP: 8
SALES (corp-wide): 6.8B **Publicly Held**
SIC: 5084 Safety equipment
HQ: Cintas Corporation No. 2
6800 Cintas Blvd
Mason OH 45040

(G-9710)
CIO STORY LLC
19c Trolley Sq (19806-3355)
PHONE...................408 915-5559
Vijay Karthik Udayakumar, *Principal*
EMP: 2
SALES (est): 107.4K **Privately Held**
SIC: 2721 Magazines: publishing & printing

(G-9711)
CIRCLE TIME LEARNING CENTER
1002 S Grant Ave (19805-4110)
PHONE...................302 384-7193
Serritta Jeffers, *Principal*
EMP: 5
SALES (est): 52.9K **Privately Held**
SIC: 8351 Child day care services

(G-9712)
CIRCLE VETERINARY CLINIC
Also Called: McCracken M Jill
1212 E Newport Pike (19804-1941)
PHONE...................302 652-6587
David Wilkins, *President*
EMP: 15
SQ FT: 1,350
SALES (est): 720K **Privately Held**
SIC: 0742 Animal hospital services, pets & other animal specialties

(G-9713)
CITIGROUP GLOBAL MARKETS INC
Also Called: Smith Barney Consulting Group
222 Delaware Ave Fl 7 (19801-1663)
PHONE...................302 888-4100
James Tracy, *Branch Mgr*
James J Tracy, *Director*
John Kramer, *Admin Asst*
EMP: 100

Wilmington - New Castle County (G-9714)

SALES (corp-wide): 72.8B **Publicly Held**
WEB: www.salomonsmithbarney.com
SIC: 6211 Security brokers & dealers
HQ: Citigroup Global Markets Inc.
388 Greenwich St Fl 18
New York NY 10013
212 816-6000

(G-9714)
CITIZENS BANK NATIONAL ASSN
4435 Kirkwood Hwy (19808-5115)
PHONE..................302 633-4503
Dennis Eaton, *Manager*
EMP: 6
SALES (corp-wide): 7.3B **Publicly Held**
SIC: 6022 State commercial banks
HQ: Citizens Bank, National Association
1 Citizens Plz Ste 1 # 1
Providence RI 02903
401 282-7000

(G-9715)
CITIZENS BANK NATIONAL ASSN
1620 Marsh Rd (19803-3598)
PHONE..................302 477-1205
Mary A Gallagher, *Manager*
EMP: 5
SALES (corp-wide): 7.3B **Publicly Held**
SIC: 6022 State trust companies accepting deposits, commercial
HQ: Citizens Bank, National Association
1 Citizens Plz Ste 1 # 1
Providence RI 02903
401 282-7000

(G-9716)
CITIZENS BANK NATIONAL ASSN
4720 Limestone Rd (19808-1928)
PHONE..................302 633-3080
Stephanie Quill, *Branch Mgr*
EMP: 10
SALES (corp-wide): 7.3B **Publicly Held**
SIC: 6022 State commercial banks
HQ: Citizens Bank, National Association
1 Citizens Plz Ste 1 # 1
Providence RI 02903
401 282-7000

(G-9717)
CITIZENS BANK NATIONAL ASSN
2084 Naamans Rd (19810-2655)
PHONE..................302 529-6100
Tom Minto, *Manager*
EMP: 5
SALES (corp-wide): 7.3B **Publicly Held**
SIC: 6022 State commercial banks
HQ: Citizens Bank, National Association
1 Citizens Plz Ste 1 # 1
Providence RI 02903
401 282-7000

(G-9718)
CITIZENS BANK NATIONAL ASSN
919 N Market St Ste 200 (19801-3068)
PHONE..................302 421-2229
Warner S Waters Jr, *Branch Mgr*
EMP: 13
SALES (corp-wide): 7.3B **Publicly Held**
SIC: 6022 State commercial banks
HQ: Citizens Bank, National Association
1 Citizens Plz Ste 1 # 1
Providence RI 02903
401 282-7000

(G-9719)
CITIZENS BANK NATIONAL ASSN
1422 N Dupont St (19806-4030)
PHONE..................302 421-2240
John Alioto, *Branch Mgr*
EMP: 6
SALES (corp-wide): 7.3B **Publicly Held**
WEB: www.ccoinvest.com
SIC: 6022 State commercial banks
HQ: Citizens Bank, National Association
1 Citizens Plz Ste 1 # 1
Providence RI 02903
401 282-7000

(G-9720)
CITROSUCO NORTH AMERICA INC
1000 Ferry Rd (19801-5862)
PHONE..................302 652-8763
Phill Spears, *Branch Mgr*
EMP: 10
SALES (corp-wide): 595.1MM **Privately Held**
SIC: 4222 Warehousing, cold storage or refrigerated
HQ: Citrosuco North America, Inc.
5937 State Road 60 E
Lake Wales FL 33898
863 696-7400

(G-9721)
CITY ELECTRIC CONTRACTING CO
204 Channel Rd (19809-3595)
PHONE..................302 764-0775
Denise Widdoes, *President*
Dan Mitchell, *Vice Pres*
Albina Baraba, *Admin Sec*
EMP: 10
SQ FT: 4,800
SALES: 1.2MM **Privately Held**
WEB: www.cityelectriccontracting.com
SIC: 1731 General electrical contractor

(G-9722)
CITY ELECTRIC SUPPLY COMPANY
6 Medori Blvd (19801-5781)
PHONE..................302 777-5300
Jimmy Resh, *Branch Mgr*
EMP: 5
SALES (corp-wide): 1.6B **Privately Held**
SIC: 5063 Electrical construction materials
PA: City Electric Supply Company
11675 Sw Tom Mackie Blvrd
Port Saint Lucie FL 34987
214 865-6801

(G-9723)
CITY OF WILMINGTON
Also Called: Utility Billing
800 N French St Fl 1 (19801-3537)
PHONE..................302 576-2584
Mike Marinelli, *Manager*
EMP: 20 **Privately Held**
SIC: 4941 Water supply
PA: City Of Wilmington
800 N French St Fl 5
Wilmington DE 19801
302 576-2415

(G-9724)
CITY ONE HOUR CLEANERS
615 N King St (19801-3775)
PHONE..................302 658-0001
Yong H Cha, *Owner*
EMP: 6
SQ FT: 1,000
SALES (est): 190.2K **Privately Held**
WEB: www.citycleaners.net
SIC: 7216 Drycleaning plants, except rugs

(G-9725)
CITY SYSTEMS INC
13 Gale Ln (19807-2264)
PHONE..................302 655-9914
Fax: 302 655-9994
EMP: 5
SALES (est): 320K **Privately Held**
SIC: 6513 Real Estate Agents And Managers

(G-9726)
CITY WINDOW CLEANING OF DEL
130b Middleboro Rd (19804-1621)
P.O. Box 53 (19899-0053)
PHONE..................302 633-0633
H Herbert Hirzel, *President*
Susie Pope, *Office Mgr*
EMP: 25
SQ FT: 3,200
SALES: 800K **Privately Held**
SIC: 7349 Window cleaning

(G-9727)
CITYWIDE TRANSPORTATION INC
6705 Governor Printz Blvd (19809-1800)
PHONE..................302 792-0159
Vincent Strmel, *President*
EMP: 15 EST: 2003
SALES (est): 939.9K **Privately Held**
SIC: 4119 Limousine rental, with driver

(G-9728)
CLAIRVYANT TECHNOSOLUTIONS INC
Also Called: Mentoris
5700 Kirkwood Hwy Ste 107 (19808-4883)
PHONE..................302 999-7172
Sundar Seth, *CEO*
Aho Bilam, *COO*
EMP: 30
SQ FT: 1,700
SALES (est): 12.4MM **Privately Held**
SIC: 7372 Business oriented computer software

(G-9729)
CLAREMONT SCHOOL LLC
1501 Marsh Rd (19803-3546)
PHONE..................302 478-4531
Victoria Boone, *President*
Stephani Richardson, *Principal*
Mark Boone, *Vice Pres*
EMP: 5
SQ FT: 3,000
SALES (est): 196.3K **Privately Held**
SIC: 8351 Montessori child development center

(G-9730)
CLARIOS
Also Called: Johnson Controls
812 First State Blvd (19804-3573)
PHONE..................302 996-0309
EMP: 7 **Privately Held**
SIC: 2531 Seats, automobile
HQ: Johnson Controls Inc
5757 N Green Bay Ave
Milwaukee WI 53209
414 524-1200

(G-9731)
CLARK & SONS INC (PA)
314 E Ayre St (19804-2587)
PHONE..................302 998-7552
Paul T Clark Sr, *President*
Clifford H Clark, *Vice Pres*
James K Clark, *Vice Pres*
William W Clark, *Vice Pres*
Rick Dehoyos, *Broker*
EMP: 25 EST: 1963
SQ FT: 21,000
SALES (est): 9.5MM **Privately Held**
WEB: www.clarkandsonsdoors.com
SIC: 1751 Garage door, installation or erection

(G-9732)
CLARK & SONS OVERHEAD DOORS
314 E Ayre St (19804-2587)
PHONE..................302 998-7552
James Clark, *President*
EMP: 50 EST: 1976
SALES (est): 4.3MM **Privately Held**
SIC: 1751 5072 Garage door, installation or erection; window & door (prefabricated) installation; hardware

(G-9733)
CLASSIC AUTO BODY INC
Also Called: Classic Auto Body Wilmington
103 Brookside Dr (19804-1103)
PHONE..................302 655-4044
Earl V Nichols Jr, *President*
Cathryne D Nichols, *Vice Pres*
Kathryne Nichols, *Vice Pres*
EMP: 5
SALES (est): 350K **Privately Held**
SIC: 7532 Body shop, automotive

(G-9734)
CLASSIC COOKIES OF DOWINGTOWN
2628 Longwood Dr (19810-3704)
PHONE..................302 494-9662
Jeffrey A Schoch, *Principal*
EMP: 5
SALES (est): 280.5K **Privately Held**
SIC: 5149 Cookies

(G-9735)
CLAYMORE SENIOR CENTER INC
504 S Clayton St (19805-4211)
PHONE..................302 428-3170
Donna McPoland, *Exec Dir*
EMP: 5
SQ FT: 20,000
SALES: 277.4K **Privately Held**
SIC: 8322 Senior citizens' center or association

(G-9736)
CLEAMOL LLC
330 Water St Ste 105 (19804-2433)
PHONE..................513 885-3462
Rongyu Yuan, *Chairman*
EMP: 4
SALES (est): 209.1K **Privately Held**
SIC: 2836 Biological products, except diagnostic

(G-9737)
CLEAN-A-TANK INC
207 S Ogle Ave (19805-1422)
P.O. Box 329, Royersford PA (19468-0329)
PHONE..................302 250-4229
Brent L Evans, *President*
EMP: 5
SALES: 204.6K **Privately Held**
SIC: 0279 Animal specialties

(G-9738)
CLEANTECH ENERGY SOLUTIONS LLC
300 Delaware Ave Ste 210a (19801-6601)
P.O. Box 60125, Potomac MD (20859-0125)
PHONE..................301 704-2831
Robert H Edwards Jr, *Mng Member*
Helen Edwards,
Lisa Wilson Edwards,
Robert H Edwards III,
EMP: 4 EST: 2017
SQ FT: 6,000
SALES: 1MM **Privately Held**
SIC: 8748 6282 Energy conservation consultant; investment counselors

(G-9739)
CLEAR CHANNEL OUTDOOR INC
24 Germay Dr (19804-1105)
PHONE..................302 658-5520
Paul Bozentka, *Manager*
EMP: 30
SALES (corp-wide): 2.7B **Privately Held**
WEB: www.clearchanneloutdoor.com
SIC: 7312 3993 Billboard advertising; signs & advertising specialties
HQ: Clear Channel Outdoor, Llc
4830 N Loop 160 W Ste 111
San Antonio TX 78249

(G-9740)
CLEARWATER ENRGY RESOURCES LLC
2711 Centerville Rd (19808-1660)
PHONE..................510 267-8921
Lisa Van Velsor, *Principal*
EMP: 4
SALES (est): 102.9K **Privately Held**
SIC: 8741 4931 Administrative management;

(G-9741)
CLIFFORD L ANZILOTTI DDS PC (PA)
2101 Foulk Rd (19810-4710)
PHONE..................302 475-2050
Clifford L Anzilotti DDS, *President*
George Davis, *Med Doctor*
DEA Zufelt, *Manager*
EMP: 15
SQ FT: 2,000
SALES (est): 976.7K **Privately Held**
SIC: 8021 Orthodontist

GEOGRAPHIC SECTION — Wilmington - New Castle County (G-9772)

(G-9742)
CLIMATE SOLUTIONS SERVICES
2426 Calf Run Dr (19808-4265)
PHONE................302 275-9919
EMP: 5
SALES (est): 272.8K **Privately Held**
SIC: 1711 Heating & air conditioning contractors

(G-9743)
CLINICAL BREAST IMAGING
2401 Penns Ave Ste 115 (19806-1432)
PHONE................302 658-4800
Virgina Clemmer, *Director*
EMP: 7
SALES (est): 364.6K **Privately Held**
SIC: 8071 X-ray laboratory, including dental

(G-9744)
CLINPHARMA CLINICAL RES LLC
1000 N West St Ste 1200 (19801-1058)
PHONE................646 961-3437
Mike Xie, *Manager*
EMP: 4 EST: 2007
SALES (est): 447.3K **Privately Held**
SIC: 8071 7371 Medical laboratories; computer software development & applications

(G-9745)
CLIPPER ADVISOR LLC
2711 Centerville Rd # 400 (19808-1660)
PHONE................203 428-5251
Zhen Liu,
EMP: 30 EST: 2015
SALES (est): 1.6MM **Privately Held**
SIC: 6282 Investment advice

(G-9746)
CLOUD SERVICES SOLUTIONS INC
1521 Concord Pike Ste 301 (19803-3644)
PHONE................888 335-3132
Stephen Roche, *CEO*
EMP: 5
SALES (est): 208K **Privately Held**
SIC: 8741 8742 Business management; management consulting services

(G-9747)
CLOUD SOFTWARE DEVELOPMENT LLC
3411 Silverside Rd # 104 (19810-4812)
PHONE................703 957-9847
Tom Parker, *CEO*
Shawn Duffy, *President*
EMP: 5 EST: 2017
SALES (est): 107K **Privately Held**
SIC: 7371 Custom computer programming services

(G-9748)
CLOUDCOFFER LLC
1201 N Orange St Ste 600 (19801-1171)
PHONE................412 620-3203
EMP: 20
SALES (est): 444.9K **Privately Held**
SIC: 7373 8748 Computer Systems Design Business Consulting Svcs

(G-9749)
CMH CAPITAL INC (DH)
1105 N Market St Ste 1300 (19801-1241)
P.O. Box 9790, Maryville TN (37802-9790)
PHONE................302 651-7947
Kevin Clayton, *President*
EMP: 1
SQ FT: 25,000
SALES (est): 2.7B
SALES (corp-wide): 225.3B **Publicly Held**
SIC: 2451 Mobile homes, except recreational
HQ: Clayton Homes, Inc.
5000 Clayton Rd
Maryville TN 37804
865 380-3000

(G-9750)
CNH CPTAL OPRTING LASE EQP RCV
1209 N Orange St (19801-1120)
PHONE................262 636-6011
EMP: 432
SALES (est): 10.5K
SALES (corp-wide): 29.7B **Privately Held**
SIC: 3523 3531 Tractors, farm; tractors, construction
HQ: Case Construction Equipment, Inc.
700 State St
Racine WI 53404

(G-9751)
COASTAL
1201 N Orange St Ste 700 (19801-1186)
PHONE................302 319-4061
Margaret Greene, *Administration*
EMP: 4
SALES (est): 459.8K **Privately Held**
SIC: 6282 Investment advice

(G-9752)
COASTAL HOSPITALITY LLC
1000 N West St Ste 1200 (19801-1058)
PHONE................302 304-3156
Ronald Frisbee, *Branch Mgr*
EMP: 4
SALES (corp-wide): 3.2MM **Privately Held**
SIC: 7361 Employment agencies
PA: Coastal Hospitality Llc
101 W Ridgely Rd Ste 6a
Lutherville Timonium MD 21093
443 621-4331

(G-9753)
COASTAL MARINE AVI SVC LLC
Also Called: Cmas
3422 Old Capitol Trl # 1388 (19808-6124)
PHONE................904 200-2749
EMP: 5
SALES: 15K **Privately Held**
SIC: 7389 Marine Aviation Service

(G-9754)
COASTAL MECHANICAL
Also Called: Tristate Mechanical
1 Carsdale Ct (19808-2141)
PHONE................302 994-9100
Damian A Nardo, *President*
EMP: 80
SALES (est): 5MM **Privately Held**
SIC: 1711 Warm air heating & air conditioning contractor; plumbing contractors

(G-9755)
COATINGS INC
30 Commerce St (19801-5426)
PHONE................302 661-1962
Stephen Chicosky Jr, *President*
▲ EMP: 4 EST: 1949
SQ FT: 22,000
SALES (est): 360K **Privately Held**
SIC: 1799 1721 Sandblasting of building exteriors; industrial painting; commercial painting

(G-9756)
COBRA RAZORS
4007 Montchanin Rd (19807-1342)
PHONE................302 540-0464
Chris, *Principal*
EMP: 3
SALES (est): 128.1K **Privately Held**
SIC: 3421 Razor blades & razors

(G-9757)
COD LIFT TRUCK INC
1240 E 16th St (19802-5217)
PHONE................302 656-7731
Bernie Barczak, *President*
Morris Lornell, *Treasurer*
EMP: 6
SQ FT: 8,500
SALES: 401.4K **Privately Held**
SIC: 5084 7539 Lift trucks & parts; automotive repair shops

(G-9758)
COGENTRIX DELAWARE HOLDINGS (DH)
1105 N Market St Ste 1108 (19801-1216)
PHONE................847 908-2800
Bruce Mc Millen, *President*
Tom Schwartz, *Treasurer*
Lori Hladik, *Admin Sec*
EMP: 392
SALES (est): 267.1MM
SALES (corp-wide): 2.4B **Publicly Held**
SIC: 4911 Electric services
HQ: Cogentrix Energy Power Management Llc
13860 Balntyn Corp Pl # 300
Charlotte NC 28277
704 525-3800

(G-9759)
COGHAN-HAES LLC
101 S Mary St (19804-3112)
PHONE................302 325-4210
Coghan Richard Jr, *Mng Member*
Richard Coghan Jr, *Mng Member*
EMP: 20
SALES (est): 1.2MM **Privately Held**
SIC: 1761 Gutter & downspout contractor

(G-9760)
COGNITION GROUP INC
2055 Limestone Rd Ste 200 (19808-5536)
PHONE................302 454-1265
Tonmoy Sharma, *Principal*
EMP: 4
SALES (est): 430.3K **Privately Held**
SIC: 8742 Business consultant

(G-9761)
COHEN SEGLIAS PALLAS
1007 N Orange St Ste 1130 (19801-1236)
PHONE................302 425-5089
Mark Stadler, *Branch Mgr*
EMP: 22
SALES (corp-wide): 13.9MM **Privately Held**
SIC: 8111 General practice attorney, lawyer
PA: Cohen Seglias Pallas Greenhall & Furman, P.C.
30 S 17th St Fl 19
Philadelphia PA 19103
215 564-1700

(G-9762)
COHESIVE STRATEGIES INC
Also Called: Archer Group, The
600 N King St Ste 2 (19801-3784)
PHONE................302 429-9120
Todd Miller, *President*
Patrick Callahan, *President*
Michael Derins, *Principal*
April Biddle, *Sr Project Mgr*
Le'rhone Walker, *Info Tech Dir*
EMP: 35
SALES (est): 6.6MM **Privately Held**
WEB: www.cohesive-strategies.com
SIC: 7311 Advertising consultant

(G-9763)
COIFFURE LTD (PA)
2401 Penns.Ave Ste 104 (19806-1430)
PHONE................302 652-3443
Samuel C Terranova, *President*
EMP: 5
SQ FT: 1,250
SALES (est): 377.5K **Privately Held**
SIC: 7231 5947 Hairdressers; gift shop

(G-9764)
COIFFURE LTD
4031 Kennett Pike (19807-2047)
PHONE................302 652-3463
Sam Terranova, *Branch Mgr*
EMP: 5
SALES (corp-wide): 377.5K **Privately Held**
SIC: 7231 Beauty shops
PA: Coiffure Ltd
2401 Penns Ave Ste 104
Wilmington DE 19806
302 652-3443

(G-9765)
COKO PRINTS
3 Doe Run Ct Apt 1b (19808-2046)
PHONE................302 507-1683
Oscar O Dominguez, *Principal*
EMP: 2 EST: 2016
SALES (est): 96.7K **Privately Held**
SIC: 2752 Commercial printing, lithographic

(G-9766)
COLE REALTY INC
Also Called: ERA
705 Philadelphia Pike (19809-2539)
PHONE................302 764-4700
Margaret Cole, *President*
EMP: 17
SALES (est): 1MM **Privately Held**
WEB: www.eracolerealty.com
SIC: 6531 Real estate agent, residential

(G-9767)
COLE SCHOTZ PC
500 Delaware Ave Ste 1410 (19801-1496)
PHONE................302 984-9541
Marion M Quirk, *Manager*
Patrick J Reilley, *Associate*
EMP: 25
SALES (corp-wide): 18.1MM **Privately Held**
SIC: 8111 General practice attorney, lawyer
PA: Cole Schotz P.C.
25 Main St Ste 300
Hackensack NJ 07601
201 489-3000

(G-9768)
COLGATE-PALMOLIVE COMPANY
1105 N Market St Ste 1300 (19801-1241)
PHONE................302 428-1554
Alex Santiago, *Purchasing*
Jairo Garcia, *Regl Sales Mgr*
Shanahan William, *Manager*
Webb Jim, *Manager*
Ellen Hancock, *Bd of Directors*
EMP: 279
SALES (corp-wide): 15.5B **Publicly Held**
WEB: www.colgate.com
SIC: 2834 Pharmaceutical preparations
PA: Colgate-Palmolive Company
300 Park Ave Fl 3
New York NY 10022
212 310-2000

(G-9769)
COLLECTIONS MARKETING CENTER (PA)
Also Called: C M C
112 S French St Ste 500 (19801-5035)
PHONE................302 830-9262
Vytas Kisielius, *CEO*
Ray Peloso, *CEO*
Don Willey, *Ch of Bd*
Gregory J Bell, *CFO*
Alicia Eggers, *Accountant*
EMP: 38
SALES (est): 9.5MM **Privately Held**
SIC: 7371 Computer software development

(G-9770)
COLLEGE AVENUE STUDENT LN LLC
Also Called: College Ave Student Loans
233 N King St Ste 400 (19801-2545)
PHONE................302 684-6070
Joseph A Depaulo, *CEO*
Timothy Staley, *COO*
James Keller, *CFO*
Debra Weiss, *Controller*
Michael Rosica, *Ch Credit Ofcr*
EMP: 56 EST: 2014
SALES (est): 4MM **Privately Held**
SIC: 6141 Licensed loan companies, small

(G-9771)
COLLEGIATE NETWORK INC
3901 Centerville Rd (19807-1938)
PHONE................302 652-4600
Jacob Lane, *President*
EMP: 5
SALES: 825K **Privately Held**
SIC: 8699 Charitable organization

(G-9772)
COLLENDER GRIFFITH CHANG INC
1601 Milltown Rd Ste 9 (19808-4084)
PHONE................302 992-0600
Gerard P Viars, *Treasurer*
Victor Chang, *Treasurer*
EMP: 4

Wilmington - New Castle County (G-9773)

SALES (est): 400K **Privately Held**
SIC: **6411** Insurance agents

(G-9774)
COLONIAL CLEANING SERVICES INC
126b Middleboro Rd (19804-1621)
P.O. Box 6546 (19804-0546)
PHONE..................................302 660-2067
Bobby Friant, *President*
EMP: 5
SALES (est): 66K **Privately Held**
SIC: **7217** 7349 Carpet & upholstery cleaning; air duct cleaning; building & office cleaning services

(G-9774)
COLONIAL CONSTRUCTION COMPANY
Also Called: Colonial Cleaning
126 Middleboro Rd (19804-1621)
PHONE..................................302 994-5705
Joseph L Fragomele, *President*
EMP: 19
SQ FT: 10,000
SALES (est): 3.4MM **Privately Held**
WEB: www.colonialconst.com
SIC: **1521** 1541 1542 General remodeling, single-family houses; prefabricated building erection, industrial; commercial & office buildings, renovation & repair

(G-9775)
COLONIAL PARKING INC (HQ)
715 N Orange St Fl 1 (19801-1755)
PHONE..................................302 651-3600
John Hatfield, *President*
Chris Hankins, *Vice Pres*
Joseph Nadel, *Vice Pres*
Jeff Browne, *Project Mgr*
Essayas Weldegioris, *Project Mgr*
EMP: 20 EST: 1965
SQ FT: 10,000
SALES (est): 5.9MM
SALES (corp-wide): 76MM **Privately Held**
WEB: www.colonialparking.com
SIC: **7521** Parking lots; parking garage
PA: Forge Company
1050 Thmas Jfferson St Nw
Washington DC 20007
202 295-8100

(G-9776)
COLONIAL PARKING INC
800 N French St (19801-3594)
PHONE..................................302 651-3618
Jeff Garrison, *Manager*
EMP: 7
SALES (corp-wide): 76MM **Privately Held**
WEB: www.colonialparking.com
SIC: **7521** Parking garage; parking lots
HQ: Colonial Parking Inc
715 N Orange St Fl 1
Wilmington DE 19801
302 651-3600

(G-9777)
COLONY NORTH APARTMENTS
319 E Lea Blvd (19802-2353)
PHONE..................................302 762-0405
Ralph Paul, *Partner*
Douglas Paul, *Partner*
Roslaie Paul, *Partner*
EMP: 10
SQ FT: 750,000
SALES (est): 933.2K **Privately Held**
SIC: **6513** Apartment building operators

(G-9778)
COLOURWORKS PHOTOGRAPHIC SVCS
1902 Superfine Ln (19802-4922)
PHONE..................................302 428-0222
Eric Russell, *President*
Gerard E Piotrowski, *Admin Sec*
EMP: 8
SQ FT: 5,000
SALES (est): 740K **Privately Held**
WEB: www.colourworks.com
SIC: **7384** 7335 Film processing & finishing laboratory; photographic studio, commercial

(G-9779)
COLUMBUS INN MANAGEMENT I
105 Foulk Rd (19803-3740)
PHONE..................................302 429-8700
Joseph Capano, *Principal*
EMP: 5 EST: 2010
SALES (est): 360K **Privately Held**
SIC: **8741** Management services

(G-9780)
COMCAST MO INVESTMENTS LLC
1201 N Market St Ste 1000 (19801-1807)
PHONE..................................302 594-8705
Mark Mossman, *Principal*
EMP: 8
SALES (est): 273.1K
SALES (corp-wide): 94.5B **Publicly Held**
SIC: **4841** Cable & other pay television services
PA: Comcast Corporation
1701 Jfk Blvd
Philadelphia PA 19103
215 286-1700

(G-9781)
COMENITY BANK (HQ)
1 Righter Pkwy Ste 100 (19803-1533)
P.O. Box 182127, Columbus OH (43218-2127)
PHONE..................................614 729-4000
Timothy King, *President*
EMP: 8
SALES: 3.1B **Publicly Held**
WEB: www.worldfinancialnetworknationalbank.com
SIC: **6022** State commercial banks

(G-9782)
COMMAND SECURITY CORPORATION
3511 Silverside Rd (19810-4902)
PHONE..................................302 478-7003
EMP: 168
SALES (corp-wide): 156.7MM **Publicly Held**
SIC: **7381** Detective/Armored Car Services
PA: Command Security Corporation
512 Herndon Pkwy Ste A
Herndon VA 20170
703 464-4735

(G-9783)
COMMERCE ASSOCIATES LP
1201 N Orange St Ste 700 (19801-1186)
PHONE..................................302 573-2500
Richard Stat, *President*
EMP: 4
SALES (est): 352.9K **Privately Held**
SIC: **6512** Commercial & industrial building operation

(G-9784)
COMMERCE GLOBAL INC
2419 Dorval Rd (19810-3528)
PHONE..................................302 478-0853
Thomas Boettcher, *President*
EMP: 5
SALES (est): 220.9K **Privately Held**
SIC: **8711** Engineering services

(G-9785)
COMMERCIAL CLEANING SERVICES
814 Philadelphia Pike A (19809-2357)
PHONE..................................302 764-3424
Diane Arthur, *Principal*
EMP: 5
SALES (est): 275.9K **Privately Held**
SIC: **7349** Building maintenance services

(G-9786)
COMMERCIAL EQUIPMENT SERVICE
1411 Windybush Rd (19810-4419)
P.O. Box 428, Claymont (19703-0428)
PHONE..................................302 475-6682
James Valentine, *President*
Nancy Valentine, *Corp Secy*
EMP: 5 EST: 1985
SALES (est): 450K **Privately Held**
SIC: **7623** Air conditioning repair

(G-9787)
COMMERCIAL GROUND CARE INC
852 Cranbrook Dr (19803-4802)
PHONE..................................302 762-5410
Thomas Kilman, *Manager*
EMP: 8
SALES (est): 224.1K **Privately Held**
SIC: **0782** Landscape contractors

(G-9788)
COMMONWEALTH CONSTRUCTION
2317 Pennsylvania Ave (19806-1318)
P.O. Box 918 (19899-0918)
PHONE..................................302 654-6611
Benjamin Vinton III, *President*
Michael Rosaio, *Sr Project Mgr*
Frank Rosaio, *Supervisor*
EMP: 4
SALES (est): 391.1K **Privately Held**
SIC: **1521** Single-family housing construction

(G-9789)
COMMONWEALTH CONTRUCTION CO
2317 Pennsylvania Ave (19806-1318)
P.O. Box 918 (19899-0918)
PHONE..................................302 654-6611
Benjamin Vinton III, *President*
EMP: 24
SQ FT: 3,000
SALES (est): 6.1MM **Privately Held**
WEB: www.itscommonwealth.com
SIC: **1542** 1521 Commercial & office building, new construction; commercial & office buildings, renovation & repair; new construction, single-family houses

(G-9790)
COMMONWEALTH GROUP
4550 New Linden Hill Rd (19808)
PHONE..................................302 995-6400
EMP: 4
SALES (est): 165.5K **Privately Held**
SIC: **8748** Business consulting

(G-9791)
COMMONWEALTH GROUP LLC (PA)
300 Water St Ste 300 # 300 (19801-5046)
PHONE..................................302 472-7200
Brock J Vinton, *President*
Natalie Freeman, *Controller*
Nancy Rife, *Controller*
Tom Cassel, *Sales Mgr*
EMP: 24 EST: 1972
SALES (est): 3.2MM **Privately Held**
WEB: www.commonwealthltd.net
SIC: **6531** 6552 Real estate managers; real estate leasing & rentals; land subdividers & developers, commercial

(G-9792)
COMMONWEALTH TRUST CO
29 Bancroft Mills Rd (19806-2039)
P.O. Box 350 (19899-0350)
PHONE..................................302 658-7214
Caroline Horty Dickerson, *CEO*
Cynthia D M Brown, *President*
Peter A Horty, *Chairman*
James A Horty, *Vice Pres*
Sharon Abrams, *Human Res Mgr*
EMP: 10
SQ FT: 6,500
SALES (est): 1.8MM **Privately Held**
WEB: www.comtrst.com
SIC: **6733** 6531 Trusts; real estate agents & managers

(G-9793)
COMMUNITY HOUSING INC (PA)
613 N Washington St (19801-2135)
PHONE..................................302 652-3991
Gary Pollio, *Director*
EMP: 6
SQ FT: 5,000
SALES (est): 2MM **Privately Held**
SIC: **6513** Apartment building operators

(G-9794)
COMMUNITY INTERACTIONS INC
625 W Newport Pike (19804-3259)
PHONE..................................302 993-7846
Morris Gibbs, *Financial Exec*
Tonya Richardson, *Branch Mgr*
EMP: 7
SALES (est): 306.4K
SALES (corp-wide): 23.8MM **Privately Held**
SIC: **8399** Advocacy group
PA: Community Interactions, Inc
740 S Chester Rd Ste A
Swarthmore PA 19081
610 328-9008

(G-9795)
COMMUNITY LEGAL AID SOCIETY (PA)
100 W 10th St Ste 801 (19801-6605)
PHONE..................................302 757-7001
Gottschalk E Deborah I, *Project Dir*
Amy Desmond, *Accountant*
Daniel G Atkins, *Exec Dir*
James G McGiffin Jr, *Exec Dir*
William Dunn, *Director*
EMP: 100
SALES: 5.2MM **Privately Held**
SIC: **8111** Legal aid service

(G-9796)
COMMUNITY TWERED FEDERAL CR UN
3670 Kirkwood Hwy (19808-5104)
PHONE..................................302 994-3617
Carl Bliey, *Branch Mgr*
EMP: 9
SALES (corp-wide): 3.4MM **Privately Held**
SIC: **6061** Federal credit unions
PA: Community Towered Federal Credit Union
401 Eagle Run Rd
Newark DE 19702
302 368-2396

(G-9797)
COMPACT MEMBRANE SYSTEMS INC
335 Water St (19804-2410)
PHONE..................................302 999-7996
Dr Stuart Nemser, *CEO*
John Bowser, *President*
Andrew Feiring, *Research*
Ken Pennisi, *Engineer*
Ryan Cook, *Finance*
EMP: 22
SQ FT: 6,000
SALES (est): 4.7MM **Privately Held**
WEB: www.compactmembrane.com
SIC: **8734** Testing laboratories

(G-9798)
COMPANY CORPORATION (HQ)
Also Called: CSC
2711 Centerville Rd # 400 (19808-1660)
PHONE..................................302 636-5440
Bruce Wynn, *CEO*
David Straub, *President*
Brett Davis, *Vice Pres*
David Dohar, *Accounts Mgr*
Maureen Cogan, *Technology*
▲ EMP: 100 EST: 1973
SALES: 11.5MM
SALES (corp-wide): 394.6MM **Privately Held**
WEB: www.corporate.com
SIC: **8742** Corporation organizing
PA: Corporation Service Company Inc
251 Little Falls Dr
Wilmington DE 19808
302 636-5400

(G-9799)
COMPASSIONATE CARE
405 Marsh Ln Ste 4 (19804-2445)
PHONE..................................302 654-5401
EMP: 5
SALES (est): 114.1K **Privately Held**
SIC: **8052** Personal care facility

GEOGRAPHIC SECTION

Wilmington - New Castle County (G-9827)

(G-9800)
COMPASSIONATE CARE HOSPI OF CE
702 Wilmington Ave B (19805-5111)
PHONE.....................302 993-9090
Cathy Stauffer, *Senior VP*
EMP: 7 **Publicly Held**
SIC: 8052 Personal care facility
HQ: Compassionate Care Hospice Of Central New Jersey Llc
261 Connecticut Dr Ste 1
Burlington NJ 08016
609 267-1178

(G-9801)
COMPASSIONATE CARE HOSPICE OF
405 Marsh Ln Ste 4 (19804-2445)
PHONE.....................302 994-1704
Judith Grey,
EMP: 61
SALES (est): 1MM **Publicly Held**
SIC: 8051 Skilled nursing care facilities
PA: Amedisys, Inc.
3854 American Way Ste A
Baton Rouge LA 70816

(G-9802)
COMPASSIONATE CARE TRNSPT LLC
510 Howard St (19804-1222)
PHONE.....................215 847-9836
Hamza Oshomah,
EMP: 5
SALES (est): 115K **Privately Held**
SIC: 4789 Transportation services

(G-9803)
COMPASSRED INC
605 N Market St Fl 2 (19801-3167)
PHONE.....................302 383-2856
Patrick Callahan, *CEO*
Darren Mahoney, *Managing Prtnr*
EMP: 5
SALES (est): 156.6K **Privately Held**
SIC: 7371 Custom computer programming services

(G-9804)
COMPETITION GAME CALLS
208 Brookland Ave (19805-1113)
PHONE.....................302 345-7463
EMP: 2
SALES (est): 74.1K **Privately Held**
SIC: 3949 Game calls

(G-9805)
COMPLEX SYSTEMS INC
1105 N Market St Ste 1300 (19801-1241)
PHONE.....................302 651-8300
EMP: 5 **Privately Held**
SIC: 6719 Holding Company

(G-9806)
COMPTON PK PRSRVTION ASSOC LLC
Also Called: Compton Apartments
4 Denny Rd (19809-3445)
PHONE.....................302 654-4369
Fern Moore, *Manager*
William Demarco,
EMP: 13
SALES: 1.9MM **Privately Held**
SIC: 6513 Apartment building operators

(G-9807)
COMPUTERS FIXED TODAY
301 E Lea Blvd (19802-2353)
PHONE.....................302 724-6411
Theo Morgan, *Owner*
Juanita Rodriguez, *Owner*
EMP: 4
SALES: 135K **Privately Held**
SIC: 5734 7622 Computer software & accessories; television repair shop

(G-9808)
CONCI LLC
1013 Centre Rd (19805-1265)
PHONE.....................847 665-9285
David Persiko, *Mng Member*
EMP: 55
SALES (est): 832.1K **Privately Held**
SIC: 7371 Custom computer programming services

(G-9809)
CONCORD AGENCY INC
3520 Silverside Rd Ste 28 (19810-4933)
PHONE.....................302 478-4000
Donald Balick, *President*
Loretta Rivera, *Vice Pres*
Jean Balick, *Admin Sec*
EMP: 5 **EST:** 1970
SQ FT: 3,800
SALES (est): 510K **Privately Held**
WEB: www.concordagency.com
SIC: 6411 Insurance agents

(G-9810)
CONCORD CORPORATE SERVICES INC (DH)
1100 Carr Rd (19809-1610)
PHONE.....................302 791-8200
Edward T Haslam, *President*
EMP: 500
SQ FT: 110,000
SALES (est): 63.1MM
SALES (corp-wide): 5.8B **Publicly Held**
SIC: 6099 Electronic funds transfer network, including switching
HQ: Concord Efs, Inc
7000 Goodlett Farms Pkwy
Cordova TN 38016
901 371-8000

(G-9811)
CONCORD DENTAL
2304 Concord Pike (19803-2912)
PHONE.....................302 836-3750
EMP: 4
SALES (est): 61.5K **Privately Held**
SIC: 8021 Offices & clinics of dentists

(G-9812)
CONCORD MALL LLC
4737 Concord Pike Fl 3 (19803-1442)
PHONE.....................302 478-9271
Janet Lambert,
Frank E Acierno,
EMP: 30
SQ FT: 900,000
SALES (est): 4MM **Privately Held**
SIC: 6512 Shopping center, regional (300,000 - 1,000,000 sq ft); shopping center, property operation only

(G-9813)
CONCORD MED SPINE & PAIN CTR
6 Sharpley Rd (19803-2941)
PHONE.....................302 652-1107
Trent Ryan DC, *Principal*
EMP: 5
SALES (est): 323.5K **Privately Held**
SIC: 8011 8041 Medical centers; offices & clinics of chiropractors

(G-9814)
CONCRETE CO INC
101 Brookside Dr (19804-1103)
PHONE.....................302 652-1101
Eugene F Gentile, *President*
Dennis Gerace, *Vice Pres*
Judy Gerace, *Admin Sec*
EMP: 6 **EST:** 1971
SQ FT: 2,500
SALES: 800K **Privately Held**
WEB: www.theconcreteco.com
SIC: 3273 Ready-mixed concrete

(G-9815)
CONDE NAST INTERNATIONAL INC (HQ)
Also Called: Cond Nast's
1313 N Market St Fl 11 (19801-1151)
PHONE.....................515 243-3273
Charles H Townsend, *CEO*
Robert A Sauerberg Jr, *CEO*
Edward Menicheschi, *President*
Gina Sanders, *President*
Fred Santarpia, *Exec VP*
EMP: 36
SALES (est): 419MM
SALES (corp-wide): 5.4B **Privately Held**
SIC: 2721 Magazines: publishing & printing
PA: Advance Publications, Inc.
1 World Trade Ctr Fl 43
New York NY 10007
718 981-1234

(G-9816)
CONDUCERENT INCORPORATED
1011 Centre Rd Ste 104 (19805-1266)
P.O. Box 237, Rockland (19732-0237)
PHONE.....................302 543-8525
Kim Paternoster, *Ch of Bd*
Magdalena Keenan, *President*
Angela Foley, *Vice Pres*
EMP: 5
SALES (est): 176.8K **Privately Held**
SIC: 8742 7389 7361 Management consulting services; human resource consulting services; ; executive placement

(G-9817)
CONECTIV LLC (DH)
800 N King St Ste 400 (19801-3543)
P.O. Box 231 (19899-0231)
PHONE.....................202 872-2680
John M Derrick Jr, *CEO*
Dennis R Wraase, *President*
Gary Stockbritge, *Principal*
Donna Parsons, *Supervisor*
Diana Deangelis, *Admin Sec*
EMP: 123
SQ FT: 130,000
SALES (est): 2.8B
SALES (corp-wide): 35.9B **Publicly Held**
WEB: www.conectiv.com
SIC: 4911 4924 1731 5172 Generation, electric power; natural gas distribution; electrical work; crude oil
HQ: Pepco Holdings Llc
701 9th St Nw Ste 3
Washington DC 20001
202 872-2000

(G-9818)
CONECTIV LLC
630 Mrtin Lther King Blvd (19801-2306)
PHONE.....................800 375-7117
Vonda Ellerbe, *Principal*
EMP: 10
SALES (corp-wide): 35.9B **Publicly Held**
WEB: www.conectiv.com
SIC: 4911 Generation, electric power
HQ: Conectiv, Llc
800 N King St Ste 400
Wilmington DE 19801
202 872-2680

(G-9819)
CONFAB INC
1216 D St (19801-5628)
P.O. Box 574, Claymont (19703-0574)
PHONE.....................302 429-0140
Andrew J Szinai, *President*
EMP: 2
SALES (est): 215.3K **Privately Held**
SIC: 3449 Bars, concrete reinforcing: fabricated steel

(G-9820)
CONGO CAPITAL MANAGEMENT LLC (HQ)
3911 Concord Pike (19803-1736)
PHONE.....................732 337-6643
Dale A Congo, *President*
Randall Burkert, *Managing Dir*
Derek Desouza, *Managing Dir*
Tony C Banks,
Ali Boz,
EMP: 12
SQ FT: 2,500
SALES (est): 611.2K
SALES (corp-wide): 1.1MM **Privately Held**
SIC: 1711 8999 Solar energy contractor; weather related services
PA: Congo Industries Inc.
3911 Concord Pike
Wilmington DE 19803
732 337-6643

(G-9821)
CONGO CAPITAL MANAGEMENT LLC
3911 Concord Pike (19803-1736)
PHONE.....................732 337-6643
Dale Congo, *Branch Mgr*
EMP: 5
SALES (corp-wide): 1.1MM **Privately Held**
SIC: 4911 Electric services
HQ: Congo Capital Management, Llc
3911 Concord Pike
Wilmington DE 19803
732 337-6643

(G-9822)
CONGO FUNERAL HOME (PA)
2317 N Market St (19802-4297)
P.O. Box 2593 (19805-0593)
PHONE.....................302 652-6640
Ernest M Congo, *President*
Cheris D Congo, *Vice Pres*
Nedra Ashley, *Accountant*
Brittainey Houi, *Office Mgr*
EMP: 17
SQ FT: 2,500
SALES (est): 2MM **Privately Held**
WEB: www.congofuneralhome.com
SIC: 7261 Funeral home

(G-9823)
CONLIN CORPORATION
Also Called: Delaware Tool Cleaning
737 Ambleside Dr (19808-1541)
PHONE.....................302 633-9174
Douglas C Conlin, *President*
Joann Christian, *Vice Pres*
EMP: 20
SALES: 425.1K **Privately Held**
SIC: 2241 Rubber thread & yarns, fabric covered

(G-9824)
CONMAC SECURITY SYSTEMS INC
205 Beau Tree Dr (19810-1177)
PHONE.....................302 529-9286
Michael Connelly, *President*
EMP: 46
SQ FT: 800
SALES: 1.3MM **Privately Held**
SIC: 7381 Security guard service

(G-9825)
CONNECTING GENERATIONS INC
100 W 10th St Ste 1115 (19801-1653)
PHONE.....................302 656-2122
Darryl Simms, *Chairman*
Joanna Carty, *Manager*
Richard Kapolka, *Exec Dir*
EMP: 10
SALES: 597.1K **Privately Held**
SIC: 8742 Human resource consulting services

(G-9826)
CONNECTIONS COMMUNITY SUPPORT (PA)
3821 Lancaster Pike (19805-1512)
PHONE.....................302 984-2302
Catherine Devaney McKay, *CEO*
Joseph Connor, *Editor*
Diane Berger, *Business Mgr*
Chris De Vaney, *COO*
Chris Devaney, *COO*
EMP: 70
SQ FT: 20,000
SALES: 102MM **Privately Held**
SIC: 8322 8361 8049 Rehabilitation services; general counseling services; substance abuse rehabilitation; home for the mentally handicapped; geriatric residential care; home for destitute men & women; rehabilitation center, residential; health care incidental; psychiatric social worker

(G-9827)
CONNECTIONS COMMUNITY SUPPORT
604 N West St (19801-2103)
PHONE.....................302 654-7120
Margaret Bowers, *Branch Mgr*
EMP: 45 **Privately Held**
SIC: 8399 Community development groups
PA: Connections Community Support Programs, Inc.
3821 Lancaster Pike
Wilmington DE 19805

Wilmington - New Castle County (G-9828)

(G-9828)
CONNECTIONS COMMUNITY SUPPORT
Also Called: CSP Supervised Apartments
500 W 10th St (19801-1422)
PHONE...................302 654-9289
EMP: 11
SALES (corp-wide): 45.1MM Privately Held
SIC: 8322 Individual/Family Services
PA: Connections Community Support Programs, Inc.
500 W 10th St
Wilmington DE 19805
302 984-2302

(G-9829)
CONNECTIONS DEVELOPMENT CORP (PA)
3821 Lancaster Pike (19805-1512)
PHONE...................302 984-3380
Catherine D McKay, Principal
EMP: 11
SALES (est): 3.2MM Privately Held
SIC: 8011 General & family practice, physician/surgeon

(G-9830)
CONNIE F CICORELLI DDS PA
1401 Silverside Rd Ste 2a (19810-4400)
PHONE...................302 798-5797
Connie F Cicorelli DDS, President
EMP: 5
SALES (est): 366.1K Privately Held
SIC: 8021 Dentists' office

(G-9831)
CONNOLLY FLOORING INC
315 Water St (19804-2410)
PHONE...................302 996-9470
Mike Connolly, President
Wendy Connolly, Vice Pres
Jackie Campbell, Manager
Will Satterfield, Supervisor
EMP: 30
SALES (est): 5.4MM Privately Held
WEB: www.connollyflooring.com
SIC: 1752 5713 Carpet laying; floor covering stores

(G-9832)
CONSOLDTED FABRICATION CONSTRS
1216 D St (19801-5628)
PHONE...................302 654-9001
Tor Larson, Manager
EMP: 50
SALES (corp-wide): 148MM Privately Held
SIC: 3324 Steel investment foundries
PA: Consolidated Fabrication And Constructors Inc
3851 Ellsworth St
Gary IN 46408
219 884-6150

(G-9833)
CONSOLIDATED LLC
1216 D St (19801-5600)
PHONE...................302 654-9001
Tor Larson, Mng Member
EMP: 28
SALES (est): 9.3MM Privately Held
SIC: 1542 Nonresidential construction

(G-9834)
CONSTRUCT APP INC
2711 Centerville Rd # 400 (19808-1660)
PHONE...................415 702-0634
Drew Beaurline, CEO
Patrick Albert, Engineer
EMP: 18
SALES (est): 345.5K Privately Held
SIC: 7371 Computer software development & applications

(G-9835)
CONSTRUCTION MGT SVCS INC (PA)
3600 Silverside Rd (19810-5100)
P.O. Box 7499 (19803-0499)
PHONE...................302 478-4200
William A Goeller, President
Regina M Camponelli, VP Admin
Michael C Goeller, Vice Pres

Gerard J Herr, Treasurer
EMP: 650
SQ FT: 10,000
SALES: 362.4MM Privately Held
SIC: 1731 8741 General electrical contractor; construction management

(G-9836)
CONSULT DYNAMICS INC
Also Called: D C A Net
1204 N West St (19801-1026)
PHONE...................302 295-4700
Irwin Duncan, Manager
EMP: 20 Privately Held
WEB: www.dcanet.net
SIC: 8721 Billing & bookkeeping service
PA: Consult Dynamics Inc
1016 Delaware Ave
Wilmington DE 19806

(G-9837)
CONSULT DYNAMICS INC (PA)
Also Called: D C A Net
1016 Delaware Ave (19806-4704)
PHONE...................302 654-1019
Keith Duncan, President
Irwin Duncan, Senior VP
J David Duncan, CFO
EMP: 24
SQ FT: 3,300
SALES (est): 4.8MM Privately Held
WEB: www.dcanet.net
SIC: 7373 4813 Value-added resellers, computer systems; telephone communication, except radio

(G-9838)
CONTACTLIFELINE INC (PA)
314 Brandywine Blvd (19809-3242)
P.O. Box 9525 (19809-0525)
PHONE...................302 761-9800
Patricia Tedford, Exec Dir
EMP: 10
SALES (est): 657.4K Privately Held
WEB: www.contactdelaware.org
SIC: 8322 Crisis intervention center

(G-9839)
CONTI ELECTRIC OF N J INC
2633 Skylark Rd (19808-1633)
PHONE...................302 996-3905
John Conti, President
EMP: 7
SALES (est): 436.6K Privately Held
SIC: 1731 General electrical contractor

(G-9840)
CONTINENTAL FINANCE CO LLC (PA)
4550 Linden Hill Rd # 400 (19808-2952)
P.O. Box 8099, Newark (19714-8099)
PHONE...................302 456-1930
Steve McSorley,
EMP: 30
SALES (est): 9.2MM Privately Held
SIC: 7389 Credit card service

(G-9841)
CONTINENTAL JEWELERS INC
2209 Silverside Rd (19810-4501)
PHONE...................302 475-2000
Paul Cohen, Owner
Chrysa Cohen, Owner
EMP: 16
SQ FT: 2,500
SALES (est): 1.8MM Privately Held
WEB: www.continentaljewelers.com
SIC: 5944 7631 Jewelry, precious stones & precious metals; watches; jewelry repair services; watch repair

(G-9842)
CONTINENTAL MORTGAGE CORP
3422 Old Capitol Trl (19808-6124)
PHONE...................302 996-5807
Russell Murray, President
EMP: 6
SQ FT: 168
SALES (est): 565.3K Privately Held
SIC: 6162 Mortgage brokers, using own money

(G-9843)
CONTRACT ENVIRONMENTS INC
1020 W 18th St Ste 1 (19802-3892)
PHONE...................302 658-0668
Beverly Thomes, President
Nick Dargenio, Project Mgr
Michelle Bellafore-Dough, Bookkeeper
Beverly D Thomes II, Manager
EMP: 7
SQ FT: 2,500
SALES (est): 674.4K Privately Held
WEB: www.contractenvironments.net
SIC: 7389 Interior design services; interior designer

(G-9844)
CONTRACTORS MATERIALS LLC
925 S Heald St (19801-5732)
PHONE...................302 656-6066
Bonnie Tipton, Principal
EMP: 2
SALES (est): 96K Privately Held
SIC: 1429 Crushed & broken stone

(G-9845)
CONVERGENCE GROUP INC
1011 Centre Rd Ste 104 (19805-1266)
PHONE...................302 234-7400
Kevin Foley, President
EMP: 10
SALES (est): 228K
SALES (corp-wide): 6.4MM Privately Held
WEB: www.denovocorp.com
SIC: 8742 Marketing consulting services
PA: De Novo Corporation
1011 Centre Rd Ste 104
Wilmington DE 19805
302 234-7407

(G-9846)
CONVERGONE GVRNMENT SLTONS LLC
242 N James St Ste 201 (19804-3168)
PHONE...................302 999-7020
Drew Waldrin, Manager
EMP: 6
SALES (corp-wide): 96.1MM Privately Held
SIC: 8748 Telecommunications consultant
HQ: Convergeone Government Solutions, Llc
350 Clark Dr Ste 120
Budd Lake NJ 07828

(G-9847)
COOCH & TAYLOR ATTYS
1000 N West St Fl 10 (19801-1059)
PHONE...................302 652-3641
Fax: 302 652-5379
EMP: 13
SALES (est): 1.4MM Privately Held
SIC: 8111 Legal Services Office

(G-9848)
COOCH AND TAYLOR A PROF ASSN (PA)
Also Called: Cooch and Taylor Attys At Law
1007 N Orange St Ste 1120 (19801-1236)
P.O. Box 1680 (19899-1680)
PHONE...................302 984-3800
Thomas Shellenberger, President
Christopher H Lee, Managing Dir
Matthew Emilio, Editor
Susan Whalley, Accounting Mgr
Edward W Cooch Jr, Council Mbr
EMP: 50
SALES (est): 6.7MM Privately Held
SIC: 8111 General practice attorney, lawyer

(G-9849)
COOK & COOK LTD PARTNERSHIP
304 Centennial Cir (19807-2130)
PHONE...................302 428-0109
G Leigh Cook, Partner
EMP: 20
SALES (est): 330.9K Privately Held
SIC: 8021 Dentists' office

(G-9850)
COOK AWESOME FOOD LLC
1308 W 13th St Apt 2 (19806-4247)
P.O. Box 631, Montchanin (19710-0631)
PHONE...................302 990-2665
Blair Stubbs,
EMP: 1
SQ FT: 162
SALES (est): 42.7K Privately Held
SIC: 2099 Seasonings & spices

(G-9851)
COOL NERDS MARKETING INC
300 N Market St Ste 208 (19801-2530)
PHONE...................302 304-3440
Bruce Gunacti, CEO
EMP: 15
SQ FT: 3,000
SALES: 1MM Privately Held
SIC: 8742 Marketing consulting services

(G-9852)
COOLPOP NATION
2418 Rambler Rd (19810-3828)
PHONE...................302 584-8833
EMP: 2
SALES (est): 107.5K Privately Held
SIC: 2211 7389 Sheets, bedding & table cloths: cotton;

(G-9853)
COOPERSON ASSOCIATES LLC
1504 N French St (19801-3118)
PHONE...................302 655-1105
Jay Cooperson, Mng Member
Stevern Kosluk,
Qiao Liang,
Michael Lukshides,
Robert Spring,
EMP: 9
SALES (est): 993.5K Privately Held
SIC: 8712 Architectural engineering

(G-9854)
COOPERSON ASSOCIATES INC
2417 Lancaster Ave 2 (19805-3736)
PHONE...................302 655-1105
Jay Norman Cooperson, President
EMP: 4
SALES (est): 158.3K Privately Held
SIC: 8712 Architectural engineering

(G-9855)
COPRA INC
1000 N West St Ste 1501 (19801-1001)
PHONE...................917 224-1727
Den Minges, President
EMP: 5
SALES (est): 204K Privately Held
SIC: 5142 Fruit juices, frozen

(G-9856)
COPY CRAFT INC
707 Kirkwood Hwy (19805-5110)
PHONE...................302 633-1313
EMP: 25 EST: 1981
SQ FT: 9,000
SALES (est): 1.5MM Privately Held
SIC: 7334 7331 2752 Duplicating Service Commercial Offset Printing & Mail Handling

(G-9857)
COQONUT INC (PA)
251 Little Falls Dr (19808-1674)
PHONE...................347 419-7709
Patrick Bucquet, CEO
EMP: 2
SALES: 50K Privately Held
SIC: 7389 7372 Financial services; application computer software

(G-9858)
CORCORAN & ASSOCIATES PA CPA
Also Called: Corcoran & Company PA CPA
3801 Kennett Pike C100 (19807-2319)
PHONE...................302 478-9515
Thomas J Corcoran, President
EMP: 5
SALES (est): 406.3K Privately Held
WEB: www.corcorancpa.com
SIC: 8721 Certified public accountant

GEOGRAPHIC SECTION
Wilmington - New Castle County (G-9890)

(G-9859)
CORE PURCHASE LLC
910 Foulk Rd Ste 201 (19803-3159)
PHONE..................................616 328-5715
EMP: 2
SALES (est): 66.2K Privately Held
SIC: 7372 Publishers' computer software

(G-9860)
CORE VALUE GLOBAL LLC
1209 N Orange St (19801-1120)
PHONE..................................908 312-4070
Igor Kruglyak,
EMP: 5
SALES (est): 124.8K Privately Held
SIC: 8742 Management consulting services

(G-9861)
CORELINK MINISTRIES
Also Called: Corelink Solution, The
2207 Concord Pike (19803-2908)
P.O. Box 396 (19899-0396)
PHONE..................................610 505-6043
James Bernard Rosseau, CEO
EMP: 4
SALES (est): 23.1K Privately Held
SIC: 8331 Job training services

(G-9862)
CORIZON LLC
Also Called: Key West Program
200 Greenbank Rd (19808-4760)
PHONE..................................302 998-3958
Harry Coyle, Principal
EMP: 10
SALES (corp-wide): 1.2B Privately Held
SIC: 8093 Substance abuse clinics (outpatient)
HQ: Corizon, Llc
    103 Powell Ct
    Brentwood TN 37027
    615 373-3100

(G-9863)
CORNERSTONE WEST CMNTY DEV CO
710 N Lincoln St (19805-3016)
PHONE..................................302 658-4171
Paul F Calistro Jr, President
EMP: 9
SALES: 1MM Privately Held
WEB: www.westendnh.org
SIC: 8399 Community development groups

(G-9864)
CORPORATE ARCFT TECHNICAL SVCS
415 Riblett Ln (19808-1303)
PHONE..................................302 383-9400
Gary Fender, President
Terry Fender, Vice Pres
EMP: 7
SQ FT: 1,200
SALES (est): 324.7K Privately Held
SIC: 7622 8711 Aircraft radio equipment repair; structural engineering

(G-9865)
CORPORATE HOLDING SERVICES (PA)
818 N Washington St (19801-1510)
PHONE..................................302 428-0515
Henry Beckler, President
Jeannette Grzybowski, Vice Pres
EMP: 4
SALES (est): 407.1K Privately Held
SIC: 8742 Corporation organizing

(G-9866)
CORPORATION SERVICE COMPANY (PA)
Also Called: C S C
251 Little Falls Dr (19808-1674)
PHONE..................................302 636-5400
Rodman Ward III, CEO
Deborah Atta-Fynn, Partner
Angelika Rodriguez, Partner
Shannon Strickland, Partner
Ej Dealy, Vice Pres
▲ EMP: 450
SALES (est): 394.6MM Privately Held
WEB: www.incspot.com
SIC: 7349 Building maintenance services

(G-9867)
CORPORATIONS & COMPANIES INC
910 Foulk Rd Ste 201 (19803-3159)
PHONE..................................302 652-4800
Stephen Robinson, President
EMP: 4
SALES (est): 516.4K Privately Held
WEB: www.corpco.com
SIC: 8748 Business consulting

(G-9868)
CORRIN TREE LANDSCAPE
1307 N Rodney St (19806-4226)
PHONE..................................302 521-8333
Philip A Cornell, Principal
EMP: 9
SALES (est): 665.1K Privately Held
SIC: 0781 Landscape planning services

(G-9869)
CORTEVA INC (PA)
Also Called: Corteva Agriscience
974 Centre Rd Bldg 735 (19805-1269)
PHONE..................................302 485-3000
James C Collins Jr, CEO
Gregory Page, Ch of Bd
Rajan Gajaria, Exec VP
Cornel B Fuerer, Senior VP
Neal Gutterson, Senior VP
EMP: 31
SALES (est): 30.6B Publicly Held
SIC: 0721 2879 7342 Crop protecting services; fungicides, herbicides; pest control in structures

(G-9870)
COSMETIC INNOVATORS LLC
1201 N Orange St Ste 7198 (19801-1214)
PHONE..................................310 310-9784
Paul Drake, Comptroller
EMP: 5
SALES (est): 448.8K Privately Held
SIC: 5999 2844 Toiletries, cosmetics & perfumes; depilatories (cosmetic)

(G-9871)
COSMIC STRANDS LLC
913 N Market St Ste 200 (19801-3097)
PHONE..................................302 660-3268
EMP: 1
SALES (est): 61.8K Privately Held
SIC: 2731 Book publishing

(G-9872)
COSMODOG SOFTWARE INC
309 Grandview Ave (19809-3040)
PHONE..................................302 762-2437
Robert Curl, Principal
EMP: 2
SALES (est): 111.1K Privately Held
SIC: 7372 Prepackaged software

(G-9873)
COUNCIL OF DEVON
2401 Penns Ave Apt 606 (19806-1409)
PHONE..................................302 658-5366
Lawernce O'Brien, Manager
EMP: 15
SALES (est): 816.5K Privately Held
SIC: 8641 Condominium association

(G-9874)
COUNSELING SERVICES INC
18c Trolley Sq (19806-3355)
PHONE..................................302 894-1477
Ron Wolskee, President
EMP: 1
SALES (est): 201.6K Privately Held
SIC: 8322 General counseling services

(G-9875)
COUNTERPOINT SOFTWARE INC
1901 N Lincoln St (19806-2313)
PHONE..................................302 426-6500
Alan Yandziak, President
Athena Vekkos, Treasurer
Scott Vanosten, Manager
EMP: 6
SALES (est): 650K Privately Held
WEB: www.counterpointsoftwareinc.com
SIC: 7379 Computer related consulting services

(G-9876)
COUNTRY SWIM CLUB INC
2700 Centerville Rd (19808-1608)
P.O. Box 4546 (19807-4546)
PHONE..................................302 420-5043
Sonia Allen, President
EMP: 4
SALES: 56K Privately Held
SIC: 7997 Swimming club, membership

(G-9877)
COURT RECORD & DATA MGT SVCS
Also Called: Crds
1300 First State Blvd H (19804-3548)
PHONE..................................732 955-6567
Antoinette Ruocchio, CEO
Krista Pilichowski, Vice Pres
EMP: 5 EST: 2013
SQ FT: 2,000
SALES (est): 745.7K Privately Held
SIC: 7374 Optical scanning data service

(G-9878)
COURTYARD MANAGEMENT CORP
Also Called: Marriott
1102 N West St (19801-1006)
PHONE..................................302 429-7600
Barbara Dell, Branch Mgr
EMP: 167
SALES (corp-wide): 20.7B Publicly Held
SIC: 7011 Hotels & motels
HQ: Courtyard Management Corporation
    10400 Fernwood Rd
    Bethesda MD 20817

(G-9879)
COVENANT PRESCHOOL
503 Duncan Rd (19809-2333)
PHONE..................................302 764-8503
Ginny Jones, Pastor
Ellen Tyrawski, Director
Nancy Long, Admin Sec
EMP: 14
SALES (est): 317.8K Privately Held
SIC: 8351 Preschool center

(G-9880)
COVENANT PROPERTIES I
15 Middleton Dr (19808-4320)
PHONE..................................302 234-5655
EMP: 7
SALES (est): 308.3K Privately Held
SIC: 6512 Nonresidential building operators

(G-9881)
COVENTRY HEALTH CARE DEL INC
2751 Centerville Rd # 400 (19808-1627)
PHONE..................................302 995-6100
Mark Malloy, CEO
EMP: 100
SALES (est): 23.4MM
SALES (corp-wide): 194.5B Publicly Held
WEB: www.chcde.com
SIC: 6324 Health maintenance organization (HMO), insurance only
HQ: Coventry Health Care, Inc.
    6720 Rockledge Dr 700b
    Bethesda MD 20817
    301 581-0600

(G-9882)
COVER & ROSSITER PA
2711 Centerville Rd # 100 (19808-1668)
PHONE..................................302 656-6632
Geoff Langdon, President
Karen Bradshaw, Finance Mgr
Peter Hopkins, Tax Mgr
Jennifer Pacilli, Tax Mgr
Michael Beraud, Accountant
EMP: 30
SALES (est): 2.4MM Privately Held
WEB: www.coverrossiter.com
SIC: 8721 Certified public accountant

(G-9883)
COVERDECK SYSTEMS INC
408 Meco Dr A (19804-1112)
PHONE..................................302 427-7578
Mary Betty, President
▲ EMP: 30

SALES: 1MM Privately Held
WEB: www.coverdeck.com
SIC: 5023 Floor coverings

(G-9884)
COWCHOK TF INC
2615 Kimbrough Dr (19810-1404)
PHONE..................................302 475-4510
T F Cowchok, Principal
EMP: 4 EST: 1970
SALES (est): 407.9K Privately Held
SIC: 6331 Fire, marine & casualty insurance & carriers; property damage insurance

(G-9885)
COWIE TECHNOLOGY CORP
510 1st Blvd State (19804)
PHONE..................................302 998-7037
Goerge Cowie, Owner
EMP: 9
SALES (est): 694.1K Privately Held
WEB: www.cowie.com
SIC: 8731 Commercial physical research

(G-9886)
COZEN OCONNOR
1201 N Market St Ste 1001 (19801-1166)
PHONE..................................302 295-2000
Joe Lepo, Manager
EMP: 17
SALES (corp-wide): 285.6MM Privately Held
WEB: www.cozen.com
SIC: 8111 General practice attorney, lawyer; taxation law; real estate law; corporate, partnership & business law
PA: Cozen O'connor
    1650 Market St Ste 2800
    Philadelphia PA 19103
    215 665-2053

(G-9887)
CPEX PHARMACEUTICALS INC
1105 N Market St Ste 1300 (19801-1241)
PHONE..................................302 651-8300
John A Sedor, President
Lance Berman, Senior VP
Nils Bergenhem, Vice Pres
Robert P Hebert, CFO
EMP: 17
SQ FT: 15,700
SALES (est): 1.4MM
SALES (corp-wide): 9.8MM Privately Held
WEB: www.bentleypharm.com
SIC: 2834 Drugs acting on the cardiovascular system, except diagnostic
HQ: I Fcb Holdings Inc
    933 Macarthur Blvd
    Mahwah NJ

(G-9888)
CPMG INC
Also Called: My Mailbox Store
2207 Concord Pike (19803-2908)
PHONE..................................302 429-8688
Jeffrey Cragg, President
Terry Cragg, Executive
▲ EMP: 4
SQ FT: 680
SALES (est): 354K Privately Held
SIC: 7389 4783 4731 Packaging & labeling services; packing goods for shipping; agents, shipping

(G-9889)
CPR SOLUTIONS INC
2502 Silverside Rd Ste 6 (19810-3740)
PHONE..................................302 477-1114
Kimberly Hodge, CEO
EMP: 6 EST: 2017
SQ FT: 1,000
SALES (est): 70.8K Privately Held
SIC: 8099 Medical services organization

(G-9890)
CR24 LLC
221 W 9th St Ste 224 (19801-1619)
PHONE..................................888 427-9357
Josh Kelso,
EMP: 15
SALES (est): 325.9K Privately Held
SIC: 8742 Marketing consulting services

Wilmington - New Castle County (G-9891)

(G-9891)
CRAFTS REPORT PUBLISHING CO
100 Rogers Rd (19801-5704)
P.O. Box 1992 (19899-1992)
PHONE.................................302 656-2209
Lammot Copeland Jr, *President*
Fredk S Kessler,
EMP: 11
SQ FT: 10,000
SALES (est): 943.1K Privately Held
SIC: 2721 Magazines: publishing & printing

(G-9892)
CRAIGS WOODWORKS LLC ◆
2017 S Woodmill Dr (19808-4989)
PHONE.................................302 998-4201
Craig T Lamey, *Principal*
EMP: 1 **EST:** 2019
SALES (est): 54.1K Privately Held
SIC: 2431 Millwork

(G-9893)
CRAMER & DIMICHELE PA
1801 W Newport Pike (19804-3529)
PHONE.................................302 293-1230
EMP: 5
SALES (est): 165.5K Privately Held
SIC: 8621 Professional membership organizations

(G-9894)
CRANSTON HALL APARTMENTS
3314 Old Capitol Trl # 2 (19808-6276)
PHONE.................................302 999-7001
Donald Mc Kay, *President*
Steve Lendz, *Superintendent*
EMP: 9
SQ FT: 1,500
SALES (est): 941.4K Privately Held
SIC: 6513 Apartment hotel operation

(G-9895)
CREATIVE LEARNING CHILD CARE
1220 Apple St (19801-5414)
PHONE.................................302 691-3167
Tina Flowers, *Owner*
EMP: 5
SALES (est): 83.3K Privately Held
SIC: 8351 Child day care services

(G-9896)
CREDITSHOP LLC
123 S Justison St Ste 602 (19801-5360)
PHONE.................................302 588-0107
Kathleen Leonik, *Manager*
EMP: 10
SALES (corp-wide): 13MM Privately Held
SIC: 6163 Loan agents
PA: Creditshop Llc
    504 Lavaca St Ste 930
    Austin TX 78701
    800 317-9240

(G-9897)
CRESCENT DENTAL ASSOCIATES
129 S West St (19801-5014)
PHONE.................................302 230-0000
Syamack Ganjavian, *Principal*
EMP: 4
SALES (est): 447.3K Privately Held
SIC: 8021 Dentists' office

(G-9898)
CRESTLINE HOTELS & RESORTS LLC
700 N King St (19801-3504)
PHONE.................................302 655-0400
Alan Filer, *Manager*
EMP: 110
SALES (corp-wide): 52.2MM Privately Held
SIC: 8741 Hotel or motel management
PA: Crestline Hotels & Resorts, Llc
    3950 University Dr # 301
    Fairfax VA 22030
    571 529-6100

(G-9899)
CRITERIUM JAGIASI ENGINEERS
1500 Shallcross Ave (19806-3037)
PHONE.................................302 498-5600
Janis Edwards, *Principal*
EMP: 5
SALES (est): 469.1K Privately Held
SIC: 8711 Structural engineering

(G-9900)
CRITICAL CARE SYSTEMS INTL INC
Also Called: Christiana Care Wound Care Ctr
700 W Lea Blvd Ste 300 (19802-2546)
PHONE.................................302 765-4132
EMP: 9
SALES (corp-wide): 43.6MM Privately Held
SIC: 8011 Medical centers
PA: Critical Care Systems International, Inc.
    61 Spit Brook Rd Ste 505
    Nashua NH 03060
    603 888-1500

(G-9901)
CROCHET CREATIONS BY DEBBIE
1219 Mckennans Church Rd (19808-2130)
PHONE.................................302 287-2462
Debra Tomchick, *Principal*
EMP: 1
SALES (est): 49.8K Privately Held
SIC: 2399 Hand woven & crocheted products

(G-9902)
CROESUS INC
1007 N Orange St (19801-1239)
PHONE.................................302 472-9260
EMP: 2
SALES (est): 130K Privately Held
SIC: 3599 Industrial machinery

(G-9903)
CROSS & SIMON LLC
913 N Market St Ste 1100 (19801-3029)
P.O. Box 1380 (19899-1380)
PHONE.................................302 777-4200
Christopher Simon, *COO*
Richard H Cross Jr, *Mng Member*
Tara Dirocco, *Mng Member*
Michael Joyce,
Chris Simon,
EMP: 20
SALES (est): 1.9MM Privately Held
WEB: www.crosslaw.com
SIC: 8111 Specialized law offices, attorneys

(G-9904)
CROSSFIT DIAMOND STATE LLC
1801 Lincoln Ave (19809-1428)
PHONE.................................201 803-1159
EMP: 6
SALES (est): 201.2K Privately Held
SIC: 7991 Health club

(G-9905)
CROSSROADS WIRELESS HOLDG LLC
919 N Market St Ste 600 (19801-3037)
PHONE.................................405 946-1200
Tom Riley,
EMP: 25
SQ FT: 6,000
SALES (est): 2.5MM Privately Held
SIC: 4812 5999 Cellular telephone services; mobile telephones & equipment

(G-9906)
CROWN CORK & SEAL RECEIVABLES (HQ)
Also Called: Crown Cork Seal Receivables De
5301 Limestone Rd Ste 221 (19808-1265)
PHONE.................................215 698-5100
Timothy J Donahue, *President*
Thomas Kelly, *CFO*
Kevin Clothier, *Treasurer*
▼ **EMP:** 7

SALES (est): 1.7MM
SALES (corp-wide): 11.1B Publicly Held
WEB: www.crownholdings.net
SIC: 3411 Metal cans
PA: Crown Holdings Inc.
    770 Township Line Rd # 100
    Yardley PA 19067
    215 698-5100

(G-9907)
CRW PARTS INC
3 James Ct (19801-5251)
PHONE.................................302 651-9300
Anna Rusk, *Branch Mgr*
EMP: 10
SALES (corp-wide): 37.7MM Privately Held
WEB: www.crwparts.com
SIC: 5013 Automotive supplies & parts; automotive supplies
PA: Crw Parts Inc.
    1211 68th St
    Baltimore MD 21237
    410 866-3307

(G-9908)
CRYPTOMARKET INC (PA)
Also Called: Cryptomkt
1209 N Orange St (19801-1120)
PHONE.................................860 222-0318
Martin Jofre, *CEO*
EMP: 2
SALES (est): 912.4K Privately Held
SIC: 7372 Application computer software

(G-9909)
CRYSTAL HOLDINGS INC (PA)
110 S Poplar St Ste 400 (19801-5044)
P.O. Box 726, Lewes (19958-0726)
PHONE.................................302 421-5700
Brian Disabatino, *Principal*
Danielle Skipski, *Accounting Mgr*
Allison Balch, *Marketing Staff*
EMP: 55
SQ FT: 17,000
SALES (est): 13.6MM Privately Held
SIC: 8741 6531 1541 1542 Administrative management; construction management; real estate managers; industrial buildings, new construction; renovation, remodeling & repairs: industrial buildings; commercial & office building, new construction; commercial & office buildings, renovation & repair

(G-9910)
CSC CORPORATE DOMAINS INC
251 Little Falls Dr (19808-1674)
PHONE.................................902 746-5201
Mark Calandra, *President*
Kristen Jones, *Partner*
Quinn Taggart, *Partner*
Sandra Horwitz, *Managing Dir*
Alan Halpern, *Vice Pres*
EMP: 19
SALES (est): 1.8MM
SALES (corp-wide): 394.6MM Privately Held
WEB: www.incspot.com
SIC: 8111 Legal services
PA: Corporation Service Company Inc
    251 Little Falls Dr
    Wilmington DE 19808
    302 636-5400

(G-9911)
CSC ENTITY SERVICES LLC
103 Foulk Rd Ste 200 (19803-3742)
PHONE.................................302 654-7584
David Epps, *President*
Robert C Campbell, *Vice Pres*
James P Lisa, *Admin Sec*
EMP: 4
SALES (est): 487.5K
SALES (corp-wide): 394.6MM Privately Held
WEB: www.incspot.com
SIC: 8741 Business management
PA: Corporation Service Company Inc
    251 Little Falls Dr
    Wilmington DE 19808
    302 636-5400

(G-9912)
CSC TEM INGERSOLL RAND
4899 Limestone Rd (19808-1902)
PHONE.................................302 765-3208
Steve Hornyak, *General Mgr*
EMP: 1
SALES (est): 90.3K Privately Held
SIC: 3131 Rands

(G-9913)
CSX TRANSPORTATION INC
1155 Centerville Rd (19804-2005)
PHONE.................................302 998-8613
Ken Hall, *General Mgr*
Larry Koster,
EMP: 36
SALES (corp-wide): 12.2B Publicly Held
WEB: www.csxt.com
SIC: 4011 Railroads, line-haul operating
HQ: Csx Transportation, Inc.
    500 Water St
    Jacksonville FL 32202
    904 359-3100

(G-9914)
CT CORPORATION SYSTEM (PA)
1209 N Orange St (19801-1120)
PHONE.................................302 658-4968
CT Raynes, *Principal*
EMP: 24
SALES (est): 3.7MM Privately Held
SIC: 7372 Business oriented computer software

(G-9915)
CUBE MEDIA L L C
501 Silverside Rd 345 (19809-1374)
PHONE.................................716 239-2789
Mateo Ramirez,
EMP: 7 **EST:** 2018
SALES (est): 37.9K Privately Held
SIC: 7929 Entertainment service

(G-9916)
CUBIC PRODUCTS LLC
2711 Centerville Rd # 300 (19808-1665)
PHONE.................................781 990-3886
Nicola Sloan, *Mng Member*
EMP: 20 **EST:** 2014
SALES (est): 1.3MM Privately Held
SIC: 2599 Cabinets, factory

(G-9917)
CULIQUIP LLC
20 Germay Dr (19804-1105)
PHONE.................................302 654-4974
Angelo Bizzarro, *Principal*
EMP: 66 **EST:** 2008
SALES (est): 331.1K
SALES (corp-wide): 29.4MM Privately Held
SIC: 2434 Wood kitchen cabinets
PA: Fsph, Inc.
    20010 Fisher Ave Ste E
    Poolesville MD 20837
    301 349-2001

(G-9918)
CUMMINS POWER GENERATION INC
1706 E 12th St (19809-3562)
PHONE.................................302 762-2027
Dave Santarosa, *Manager*
EMP: 446
SALES (corp-wide): 23.7B Publicly Held
SIC: 3621 3519 Generators & sets, electric; internal combustion engines
HQ: Cummins Power Generation Inc.
    1400 73rd Ave Ne
    Minneapolis MN 55432
    763 574-5000

(G-9919)
CURRENCY TECHNICS METRICS INC
4200 Governor Printz Blvd (19802-2315)
PHONE.................................302 482-4846
Bill Brooks, *President*
Pat Balcer, *Vice Pres*
Robert Dickerson, *Vice Pres*
Peter J Rushie III, *Vice Pres*
Mark Denio, *Software Engr*
EMP: 20
SQ FT: 8,000

SALES (est): 3.7MM **Privately Held**
SIC: **3695** Computer software tape & disks: blank, rigid & floppy

(G-9920)
CURRIE HAIR SKIN NAILSS
317 Justison St (19801-5164)
PHONE................................302 777-7755
Randy Currie, *Principal*
EMP: 7
SALES (corp-wide): 2.6MM **Privately Held**
SIC: **7231** Manicurist, pedicurist
PA: Currie Hair Skin And Nails Of Wayne, Llc
605 W Lancaster Ave
Wayne PA 19087
610 558-4247

(G-9921)
CURVES FOR WOMEN
2001 Concord Pike 202 (19803-2904)
PHONE................................302 477-9400
EMP: 12
SALES (est): 131.2K **Privately Held**
SIC: **7991** Exercise Salon

(G-9922)
CURZON CORP
Also Called: Seymour's Cleaners
900 N Union St (19805-5326)
PHONE................................302 655-5551
Andrew Berger, *Owner*
Sally Berger, *Corp Secy*
EMP: 25
SQ FT: 4,500
SALES (est): 875.3K **Privately Held**
SIC: **7216** 7219 7251 Cleaning & dyeing, except rugs; garment making, alteration & repair; shoe repair shop

(G-9923)
CUSHMAN & WAKEFIELD DEL INC
1 Commerce St Ste 782 (19801)
PHONE................................302 655-9621
Glenn Rufrano, *Branch Mgr*
EMP: 6
SALES (corp-wide): 8.2B **Privately Held**
SIC: **6531** Real estate agent, commercial
HQ: Cushman & Wakefield Of Delaware, Inc.
1290 Ave Of The Americas
New York NY 10104

(G-9924)
CUSTOM AMERICA
173 Edgemoor Rd (19809-3153)
PHONE................................856 516-1103
▲ EMP: 4
SALES (est): 388.5K **Privately Held**
SIC: **3089** Injection molding of plastics

(G-9925)
CUSTOM CREATIONS BY DESIGN
1 Murphy Rd (19803-3044)
PHONE................................302 482-2267
Scott Gillespie, *Owner*
EMP: 4
SALES (est): 432.5K **Privately Held**
SIC: **7389** Design services

(G-9926)
CUSTOM SHEET METAL OF DELAWARE
464 E Ayre St (19804-2513)
PHONE................................302 998-6865
Bill Wilson, *President*
EMP: 5
SALES (est): 693.3K **Privately Held**
SIC: **3599** 3444 Machine shop, jobbing & repair; sheet metalwork

(G-9927)
CUSTOMS BENEFITS
501 Silverside Rd Ste 120 (19809-1377)
PHONE................................302 798-2884
Leon Champagne, *Owner*
James W Kelly, *Corp Secy*
EMP: 5
SQ FT: 1,000
SALES (est): 305.2K **Privately Held**
SIC: **7389** Packaging & labeling services

(G-9928)
CUTLER INDUSTRIES INC
2711 Centerville Rd # 400 (19808-1660)
PHONE................................302 689-3779
Alit Suryadi, *Business Mgr*
EMP: 5
SQ FT: 500
SALES (est): 440K **Privately Held**
SIC: **5045** Printers, computer

(G-9929)
CUTS & STYLES BARLEY MILL INC
4300 Lancaster Pike (19805)
PHONE................................302 999-8059
EMP: 5 EST: 1983
SALES (est): 170K **Privately Held**
SIC: **7241** 7231 Barber Shop Beauty Shop

(G-9930)
CUTTING EDGE OF DELAWARE INC
511 E 5th St (19801-4705)
P.O. Box 104, Port Penn (19731-0104)
PHONE................................302 834-8723
Sean P Johnston, *President*
EMP: 11
SALES (est): 591.7K **Privately Held**
SIC: **7241** 0782 0781 Barber shops; landscape contractors; bermuda sprigging services; landscape planning services

(G-9931)
CYBELE SOFTWARE INC
3422 Old Capitol Trl (19808-6124)
PHONE................................302 892-9625
Gustavo Ricardi, *President*
EMP: 9
SALES (est): 575K **Privately Held**
WEB: www.cybelesoft.com
SIC: **7372** Prepackaged software

(G-9932)
CYNTHIA A MUMMA DDS
1304 N Broom St Ste 1 (19806-4248)
PHONE................................302 652-2451
Cynthia Mumma, *Principal*
EMP: 7
SALES (est): 514.7K **Privately Held**
SIC: **8021** Dentists' office

(G-9933)
CYNTHIA CROSSER DC FIAMA
3101 Limestone Rd Ste B (19808-2148)
PHONE................................302 239-5014
EMP: 8
SALES (est): 82.2K **Privately Held**
SIC: **8062** General medical & surgical hospitals

(G-9934)
CYPRESS CAPITAL MANAGEMENT LLC
3801 Kennett Pike C304 (19807-2321)
PHONE................................302 429-8436
Richard Arvedlund, *President*
EMP: 10
SALES (est): 1MM
SALES (corp-wide): 455.5MM **Publicly Held**
SIC: **8742** Financial consultant
PA: Wsfs Financial Corporation
500 Delaware Ave
Wilmington DE 19801
302 792-6000

(G-9935)
CYTEC INDUSTRIES INC
3 Weldin Park Dr (19803-4708)
PHONE................................302 530-7665
Bryant Ries, *Principal*
EMP: 3
SALES (corp-wide): 12.4MM **Privately Held**
SIC: **3999** Barber & beauty shop equipment
HQ: Cytec Industries Inc.
4500 Mcginnis Ferry Rd
Alpharetta GA 30005

(G-9936)
D & H AUTOMOTIVE & TOWING INC
4016th Ave Ste B (19805)
PHONE................................302 655-7611
Dave Hudson, *President*
EMP: 7
SQ FT: 1,500
SALES (est): 572.3K **Privately Held**
SIC: **7539** 7549 Automotive repair shops; towing service, automotive

(G-9937)
D B NIBOUAR DDS
5317 Limestone Rd (19808-1252)
PHONE................................302 239-0502
D B Nibouar DDS, *Owner*
EMP: 15
SALES (est): 226.2K **Privately Held**
SIC: **8021** Dentists' office

(G-9938)
D C MITCHELL LLC
8 Hadco Rd Ste B (19804-1003)
PHONE................................302 998-1181
Dave Mitchell, *Mng Member*
EMP: 2
SQ FT: 3,000
SALES (est): 181.5K **Privately Held**
SIC: **3429** Manufactured hardware (general)

(G-9939)
D E LEAGER CONSTRUCTION
3725 Washington Ave (19808-6034)
PHONE................................302 994-1060
David.E Leager, *Owner*
EMP: 4
SALES (est): 412.5K **Privately Held**
SIC: **1611** 1794 7513 Surfacing & paving; excavation work; truck rental & leasing, no drivers

(G-9940)
D F DISTRIBUTION INC
Also Called: Cloudburst Lawn Sprink
6603 Gov Prince Blvd Stea (19809)
PHONE................................302 798-5999
Brett Forrest, *President*
EMP: 22
SALES (est): 3.2MM **Privately Held**
SIC: **1711** Irrigation sprinkler system installation

(G-9941)
D P INVESTMENT L L C
400 B And O Ln Ste A (19804-1458)
PHONE................................302 998-7031
EMP: 4
SALES (est): 226.4K **Privately Held**
SIC: **1521** Single-Family House Construction

(G-9942)
D S WILLIAMS DMD PA
5317 Limestone Rd (19808-1252)
PHONE................................302 239-5272
David S Williams, *Owner*
David Williams, *Fmly & Gen Dent*
EMP: 10
SALES (est): 624.6K **Privately Held**
SIC: **8021** Dentists' office

(G-9943)
D SHINN INC
1409 Haines Ave (19809-2716)
PHONE................................302 792-2033
Don Shinn, *President*
EMP: 15
SALES (est): 2.3MM **Privately Held**
SIC: **1761** Roofing contractor

(G-9944)
D&F JOINT VENTURES DE LLC
2002 N Bancroft Pkwy (19806-2204)
PHONE................................302 652-5151
EMP: 5
SALES (est): 255K **Privately Held**
SIC: **7389** Business services

(G-9945)
DA VINCI EBUSINESS LTD
2207 Concord Pike Ste 181 (19803-2908)
PHONE................................610 399-3988
Tim Brien, *CEO*
EMP: 5 EST: 2000
SALES (est): 500K **Privately Held**
SIC: **8742** Management consulting services

(G-9946)
DABVASAN INC
Also Called: Pak Mail
1812 Marsh Rd Ste 6 (19810-4533)
PHONE................................302 529-1100
Carol Holt, *President*
EMP: 9
SALES (est): 497.4K **Privately Held**
SIC: **7389** Mailbox rental & related service

(G-9947)
DAISY CONSTRUCTION COMPANY
102 Larch Cir Ste 301 (19804-2371)
PHONE................................302 658-4417
Leonard Iacono, *President*
Verino Pettinaro, *Treasurer*
EMP: 100
SQ FT: 10,000
SALES (est): 20.6MM **Privately Held**
SIC: **1771** 1611 Concrete work; surfacing & paving

(G-9948)
DALE HAWKINS
Also Called: Hawkins Reporting Service
715 N King St Ste 200 (19801-3551)
PHONE................................302 658-6697
Dale C Hawkins, *Owner*
EMP: 8
SQ FT: 1,200
SALES (est): 444.4K **Privately Held**
SIC: **7338** Court reporting service

(G-9949)
DALSTRONG AMERICA INC
3411 Silverside Rd (19810-4812)
PHONE................................716 380-4998
Gizem Gulec, *CFO*
EMP: 2
SALES (est): 73.4K **Privately Held**
SIC: **3421** Knife blades & blanks

(G-9950)
DALTON & ASSOCIATES PA
1106 W 10th St (19806-4522)
PHONE................................302 652-2050
Bartholomew Dalton, *President*
EMP: 9
SALES (est): 1MM **Privately Held**
WEB: www.daltonandassociatespa.com
SIC: **8111** General practice attorney, lawyer

(G-9951)
DANA CONTAINER INC
Also Called: Dana Railcare
1280 Railcar Ave (19802-4614)
PHONE................................302 652-8550
Ron Dana, *President*
EMP: 42
SALES (corp-wide): 30.3MM **Privately Held**
WEB: www.danacontainer.com
SIC: **4741** Railroad car cleaning, icing, ventilating & heating
PA: Dana Container, Inc.
210 Essex Ave E
Avenel NJ 07001
732 750-9100

(G-9952)
DANA RAILCARE INC
1280 Railcar Ave (19802-4614)
PHONE................................302 652-8550
Golden Workman, *Vice Pres*
EMP: 35
SALES (est): 2.9MM **Privately Held**
SIC: **4789** 4741 Railroad car repair; railroad car cleaning, icing, ventilating & heating

(G-9953)
DANAHER CORPORATION
501 Silverside Rd Ste 105 (19809-1376)
PHONE................................302 798-5741
George Sherman, *Branch Mgr*
EMP: 1
SALES (corp-wide): 19.8B **Publicly Held**
SIC: **3423** Hand & edge tools

Wilmington - New Castle County (G-9954)

PA: Danaher Corporation
2200 Penn Ave Nw Ste 800w
Washington DC 20037
202 828-0850

(G-9954)
DANCEDELAWARE
2005 Concord Pike Ste 204 (19803-2982)
PHONE 302 998-1222
Valerie Smith Byron, *Owner*
Sam Farley, *Director*
Charlotte Jenkins, *Director*
Elizabeth Peled, *Director*
Erica Schmidt, *Director*
EMP: 4 **EST:** 2009
SALES (est): 130.1K **Privately Held**
SIC: 7911 Dance studio & school

(G-9955)
DANIEL D RAPPA INC
1624 E Ayre St (19804-2542)
PHONE 302 994-1199
Daniel D Rappa Sr, *President*
Daniel D Rappa Jr, *Corp Secy*
EMP: 44
SALES (est): 4.5MM **Privately Held**
SIC: 1711 Warm air heating & air conditioning contractor; plumbing contractors

(G-9956)
DANIEL M MCDERMOTT CHFC CFP
Also Called: Topkis, William M Chfc
3520 Silverside Rd Ste 25 (19810-4933)
PHONE 302 778-5677
William M Topkis, *Principal*
EMP: 4
SALES (est): 470.1K **Privately Held**
SIC: 8742 Financial consultant

(G-9957)
DANIELS + TANSEY LLP
1013 Centre Rd Ste 220 (19805-1265)
PHONE 302 594-1070
Ann Tansey, *Principal*
Sarah Bolen, *Sr Associate*
EMP: 4
SALES (est): 680.1K **Privately Held**
SIC: 6722 Management investment, open-end

(G-9958)
DANIELS LAWN CARE
1211 Gary Ave (19808-5715)
PHONE 302 218-0173
EMP: 4 **EST:** 2010
SALES (est): 146.5K **Privately Held**
SIC: 0782 Lawn care services

(G-9959)
DANN J GLADNICK DMD PA
1104 N Broom St (19806-4315)
PHONE 302 654-7243
Dann J Gladnick, *Principal*
EMP: 5
SALES (est): 305.4K **Privately Held**
SIC: 8021 Dental surgeon

(G-9960)
DARBY LEASING LLC
3411 Silverside Rd # 104 (19810-4812)
PHONE 302 477-0500
Jaimee Griffin,
EMP: 5
SALES (est): 153.4K **Privately Held**
SIC: 7359 Equipment rental & leasing

(G-9961)
DATA AGE INTERNATIONAL LLC
2701 Centerville Rd (19808-1607)
PHONE 302 760-9222
Martn Quintana Mathieu, *CEO*
EMP: 45
SALES: 1MM **Privately Held**
SIC: 7371 Computer software development & applications

(G-9962)
DATA-BI LLC
601 Entwisle Ct (19808-1512)
PHONE 302 290-3138
Terry Foreman, *Exec Dir*
Yiqun Wang,
EMP: 5

SALES (est): 258.8K **Privately Held**
SIC: 7371 7373 7374 7379 Computer software development & applications; systems integration services; data processing & preparation; tabulating service; data processing consultant

(G-9963)
DAVE ARLETTA
Also Called: Sanford Day Camp
2621 Epping Rd (19810-1166)
PHONE 302 475-8013
Dave Arletta, *Director*
EMP: 35
SALES (est): 254.7K **Privately Held**
SIC: 7032 Sporting & recreational camps

(G-9964)
DAVID A DOREY ESQ
1201 N Market St Ste 800 (19801-1807)
PHONE 302 425-6400
Steven Caponi,
EMP: 14 **EST:** 2011
SALES (est): 510.2K **Privately Held**
SIC: 8111 General practice attorney, lawyer

(G-9965)
DAVID A KING DDS
2601 Annand Dr Ste 10 (19808-3719)
PHONE 302 998-0331
David A King, *Principal*
EMP: 4
SALES (est): 67.3K **Privately Held**
SIC: 8021 Offices & clinics of dentists

(G-9966)
DAVID BROWN GEAR SYSTEMS USA (PA)
300 Delaware Ave Ste 1370 (19801-1658)
P.O. Box 5040, Glen Allen VA (23058-5040)
PHONE 540 416-2062
Marcelo Zatatero, *President*
▲ **EMP:** 9
SQ FT: 1,600
SALES (est): 1.8MM **Privately Held**
SIC: 3566 Gears, power transmission, except automotive

(G-9967)
DAVID BROWN GEAR SYSTEMS USA
300 Delaware Ave Ste 1370 (19801-1658)
PHONE 540 943-8375
EMP: 7
SALES (corp-wide): 2MM **Privately Held**
SIC: 3566 Mfg Gear Box/ Transmission
PA: David Brown Gear Systems Usa Inc.
300 Delaware Ave Ste 1370
Wilmington DE 19801
540 416-2062

(G-9968)
DAVID C LARNED MD
2300 Penns Ave Ste 3a (19806-1379)
PHONE 302 655-7600
David C Larned MD, *Principal*
David Larned, *Med Doctor*
EMP: 4
SALES (est): 260K **Privately Held**
SIC: 8011 Ophthalmologist

(G-9969)
DAVID E MASTROTA DMD PA
Also Called: Great Whites Dental
2215 Pennsylvania Ave (19806-2443)
PHONE 302 654-0100
David Mastrota DMD, *Owner*
David Mastrota, *Owner*
EMP: 4
SALES (est): 321.6K **Privately Held**
SIC: 8021 Dentists' office

(G-9970)
DAVID L ISAACS DDS
707 Foulk Rd Ste 103 (19803-3737)
PHONE 302 654-2904
David L Isaacs DDS, *President*
EMP: 15
SALES (est): 377.9K **Privately Held**
SIC: 8021 Dentists' office

(G-9971)
DAVID POPOVICH LLC
Also Called: Wolvesuff
19c Trolley Sq Ste 20c (19806-3355)
PHONE 855 464-9653
David Popovich,
EMP: 6 **EST:** 2017
SALES: 1MM **Privately Held**
SIC: 5961 7389

(G-9972)
DAVID ROCKWELL & ASSOCIATES
208 W Pembrey Dr (19803-2008)
PHONE 302 478-9900
David Rockwell, *President*
EMP: 7
SALES: 1MM **Privately Held**
SIC: 0782 Landscape contractors

(G-9973)
DAVID SAUNDERS GENERAL CONTRS
1204 E Willow Run Dr (19805-1254)
PHONE 302 998-0056
Dave Saunders, *President*
Mike Pirk, *Manager*
EMP: 5 **EST:** 1998
SALES (est): 341K **Privately Held**
SIC: 1761 Roofing contractor; gutter & downspout contractor; siding contractor

(G-9974)
DAX-WAVE CONSULTING LLC
1000 N West St Ste 1200 (19801-1058)
PHONE 424 543-6662
Luis Fernando,
EMP: 5
SALES (est): 300K **Privately Held**
SIC: 7379 7371 8741 Computer related consulting services; computer software development & applications; management services

(G-9975)
DBD WHOLESALE LLC
213 Sunset Dr (19809)
PHONE 215 301-6277
Zhi Huang, *Principal*
EMP: 4
SALES (est): 107.5K **Privately Held**
SIC: 5999 7389 Miscellaneous retail stores;

(G-9976)
DC CONSULTING SERVICE LLC
3422 Old Capitol Trl (19808-6124)
PHONE 617 594-9780
Rinkesh Nigam, *Mng Member*
EMP: 10
SALES (est): 615.3K **Privately Held**
SIC: 7371 7389 Computer software development & applications;

(G-9977)
DC PRINTING INC
2305 Pennsylvania Ave (19806-1318)
PHONE 302 545-6666
EMP: 2 **EST:** 2011
SALES (est): 116.3K **Privately Held**
SIC: 2752 Commercial printing, lithographic

(G-9978)
DCC DESIGN GROUP LLC
2 Mill Rd Ste 103 (19806-2175)
PHONE 302 777-2100
Nicole Cocolin,
EMP: 6
SALES (est): 173.2K **Privately Held**
SIC: 7389 Interior design services

(G-9979)
DCC INC
2639 Grendon Dr (19808-3828)
PHONE 302 750-1207
EMP: 8
SALES (est): 162.3K **Privately Held**
SIC: 8351 Child day care services

(G-9980)
DCH AUTO GROUP (USA) INC
3411 Silverside Rd 108 (19810-4812)
PHONE 302 478-4600
EMP: 6

SALES (est): 73K
SALES (corp-wide): 11.8B **Publicly Held**
SIC: 8742 Banking & finance consultant
PA: Lithia Motors, Inc.
150 N Bartlett St
Medford OR 97501
541 776-6401

(G-9981)
DCRAC
600 S Harrison St (19805-4306)
PHONE 302 298-3289
Lillian Harrison, *Principal*
Rashmi Rangan, *Exec Dir*
EMP: 4
SALES (est): 96.8K **Privately Held**
SIC: 8699 Charitable organization

(G-9982)
DD & E INVESTMENT GROUP INC
1000 N St (19801)
PHONE 302 319-2780
David Davis, *President*
EMP: 5
SALES (est): 516.6K **Privately Held**
SIC: 6799 Investors

(G-9983)
DD SNACKS LLC
230 Alban Dr (19805-4630)
PHONE 302 652-3850
Donald Downs, *Principal*
EMP: 4 **EST:** 2017
SALES (est): 61.5K **Privately Held**
SIC: 8021 Offices & clinics of dentists

(G-9984)
DDK
3825 Lancaster Pike (19805-1559)
PHONE 302 999-1132
Joseph Tabeling, *Owner*
EMP: 17
SALES (est): 1.2MM **Privately Held**
SIC: 3545 Diamond cutting tools for turning, boring, burnishing, etc.

(G-9985)
DE CATERING INC
Also Called: Sherm's Catering
913 Brandywine Blvd (19809-2545)
P.O. Box 11983 (19850-1983)
PHONE 302 607-7200
Michael Porter, *President*
EMP: 25
SALES (est): 744.4K **Privately Held**
SIC: 5812 8742 Contract food services; restaurant & food services consultants

(G-9986)
DE NISIO GENERAL CONSTRUCTION
1306 N Bancroft Pkwy (19806-2426)
PHONE 302 656-9460
Lawrence De Nisio, *Owner*
EMP: 4
SALES (est): 198.4K **Privately Held**
SIC: 1771 1751 Concrete work; carpentry work

(G-9987)
DE NOVO CORPORATION (PA)
Also Called: Creative Solutions Intl
1011 Centre Rd Ste 104 (19805-1266)
PHONE 302 234-7407
Kevin Foley, *President*
William Keenan, *President*
Kim Paternoster, *Exec VP*
Lisa McKenny, *Recruiter*
EMP: 20
SALES (est): 6.4MM **Privately Held**
WEB: www.denovocorp.com
SIC: 7336 8748 Creative services to advertisers, except writers; business consulting

(G-9988)
DEALS ON WHEELS INC (PA)
Also Called: Deals On Wheels Used Cars
1220 Centerville Rd (19808-6237)
PHONE 302 999-9955
Vincent Avallone, *President*
EMP: 31

GEOGRAPHIC SECTION
Wilmington - New Castle County (G-10016)

SALES (est): 3.1MM **Privately Held**
SIC: **7538** 5521 General automotive repair shops; automobiles, used cars only

(G-9989)
DEAN DIGITAL IMAGING INC
2 S Poplar St Ste B (19801-5052)
PHONE..................302 655-6992
Floyd Dean, *President*
Vicky Yelton, *Treasurer*
EMP: 7
SALES: 500K **Privately Held**
WEB: www.deandigital.com
SIC: **7335** Commercial photography

(G-9990)
DEATON MCCUE & CO INC
62 Rockford Rd Ste 10a (19806-1052)
PHONE..................302 658-7789
Sean McCue, *President*
Stephen Deaton, *CFO*
Mitch Berkowitz, *Broker*
EMP: 8
SQ FT: 3,000
SALES (est): 1.1MM **Privately Held**
WEB: www.deatonmccue.com
SIC: **6531** Real estate managers

(G-9991)
DEAVEN DEVELOPMENT CORP
1615 E Ayre St (19804-2514)
PHONE..................302 994-5793
Donald F Deaven, *President*
Lori Deaven, *Treasurer*
EMP: 2
SQ FT: 2,000
SALES (est): 180K **Privately Held**
SIC: **3441** 1791 3446 Fabricated structural metal; structural steel erection; ornamental metalwork

(G-9992)
DEEP MUSCLE THERAPY CENTER DEL
Also Called: Deeps On Massage
5700 Kirkwood Hwy Ste 206 (19808-4884)
PHONE..................302 397-8073
Debbi Jedlicka, *President*
EMP: 18
SALES (est): 667.2K **Privately Held**
WEB: www.dmtcmassage.com
SIC: **7299** Massage parlor

(G-9993)
DEFENSE COMMUNICATION LLC
Also Called: Def Com
3422 Old Capitol Trl # 700 (19808-6124)
PHONE..................850 348-0708
EMP: 10
SALES: 345.4K **Privately Held**
SIC: **1731** Electrical Contractor

(G-9994)
DEFENSE SHIELD TRUST
504 N Broom St (19805-3115)
PHONE..................540 815-8248
EMP: 25 EST: 2015
SALES (est): 980.4K **Privately Held**
SIC: **6211** Security Broker/Dealer

(G-9995)
DEFY THERAPY SERVICES LLC
2213 Beaumont Rd (19803-3016)
PHONE..................302 290-9562
Mary McCormick, *Principal*
EMP: 8
SALES (est): 73.3K **Privately Held**
SIC: **8093** Rehabilitation center, outpatient treatment

(G-9996)
DEKADU INC
2711 Centerville Rd # 400 (19808-1660)
PHONE..................763 390-3266
John Paul Deneut, *President*
Roland Kaehler,
EMP: 5
SALES (est): 87.9K **Privately Held**
SIC: **7371** 7389 Computer software development;

(G-9997)
DEL CAMPO PLUMBING & HEATING
2429 Hartley Pl (19808-4258)
PHONE..................302 998-3648
Michael A Delcampo, *President*
EMP: 5
SALES (est): 420K **Privately Held**
SIC: **1711** Plumbing contractors; warm air heating & air conditioning contractor

(G-9998)
DEL-MR-VA CNCIL INC BOY SCUTS (PA)
100 W 10th St Ste 915 (19801-1652)
PHONE..................302 622-3300
Frances M West, *President*
Jeena Abraham, *Controller*
Patrick Sterrett, *Exec Dir*
Justin Rodstrom, *Director*
Carol Swank, *Admin Asst*
EMP: 24
SQ FT: 13,000
SALES: 5MM **Privately Held**
WEB: www.delmarvacouncil.com
SIC: **8641** Boy Scout organization

(G-9999)
DEL-ONE FEDERAL CREDIT UNION
Also Called: Delaware Fedral Credit Union
824 N Market St Ste 104 (19801-4937)
PHONE..................302 577-2667
Ruby Harrington, *Branch Mgr*
EMP: 5 **Privately Held**
WEB: www.del-one.org
SIC: **6061** Federal credit unions
PA: Del-One Federal Credit Union
270 Beiser Blvd
Dover DE 19904

(G-10000)
DELAWARE 87ERS LLC
300 Martin L King Blvd # 200 (19801-2437)
PHONE..................302 351-5385
Sandra Kemmel, *Office Mgr*
Tyler Hutson, *Director*
Alex Yoh, *Director*
EMP: 20
SALES (est): 1.1MM **Privately Held**
SIC: **7389** Convention & show services

(G-10001)
DELAWARE ART MUSEUM INC
2301 Kentmere Pkwy (19806-2019)
PHONE..................302 571-9590
Danielle Rice, *President*
Lauren McMahon, *Sales Staff*
Molly Giordano, *Marketing Staff*
Tricia Mongan, *Assistant*
EMP: 45
SQ FT: 100,000
SALES (est): 2.2MM **Privately Held**
WEB: www.delart.org
SIC: **8412** Museum

(G-10002)
DELAWARE ASSOCIATION
100 W 10th St Ste 103 (19801-1632)
PHONE..................302 622-9177
Thomas Cook, *Director*
EMP: 4
SALES: 9.6MM **Privately Held**
WEB: www.delawarenonprofit.org
SIC: **8621** Professional membership organizations

(G-10003)
DELAWARE ASSOCIATION FOR BLIND (PA)
2915 Newport Gap Pike (19808-2376)
PHONE..................302 998-5913
Sharon Sutlic, *Principal*
Linda S Lauria, *Director*
Janet Berry, *Director*
EMP: 14
SALES: 507.9K **Privately Held**
WEB: www.dabdel.org
SIC: **8621** Professional membership organizations

(G-10004)
DELAWARE BACKPAN RHBLTTN ASSOC
2006 Foulk Rd Ste B (19810-3644)
PHONE..................302 529-8783
EMP: 50
SALES (est): 1.7MM **Privately Held**
SIC: **8041** Offices And Clinics Of Chiropractors Medical Doctors

(G-10005)
DELAWARE BD TRADE HOLDINGS INC
Also Called: Dbot
1313 N Market St Fl 8 (19801-6107)
PHONE..................302 298-0600
John F Wallace, *CEO*
Joseph L Valenza, *President*
Dennis J Boylan, *COO*
Joseph Jennings, *CFO*
EMP: 15
SQ FT: 11,000
SALES (est): 1.2MM **Publicly Held**
SIC: **6231** Security & commodity exchanges
PA: Ideanomics, Inc.
1 Exchange Plz Fl 19
New York NY 10006

(G-10006)
DELAWARE BEACON NETWORK LLC
1201 N Market St Fl 1 (19801-1147)
PHONE..................302 218-2755
Michelle Wojciechowski, *CEO*
EMP: 4 EST: 2016
SALES (est): 108.6K **Privately Held**
SIC: **7371** Computer software development & applications

(G-10007)
DELAWARE BREAST CANCER COALIT (PA)
100 W 10th St Ste 209 (19801-1641)
PHONE..................302 778-1102
Rachelle Schindler, *Bookkeeper*
Victoria Cooke, *Exec Dir*
Connie Holdridge, *Education*
EMP: 17
SALES: 1.2MM **Privately Held**
WEB: www.debreastcancer.org
SIC: **8322** Social service center

(G-10008)
DELAWARE BRICK COMPANY (PA)
1114 Centerville Rd (19804-2097)
PHONE..................302 994-0948
Margaret Hinton, *President*
Kenneth B Barnes Jr, *Principal*
Sean C Callaghan, *Principal*
Michael Hinton, *Principal*
Charles Schauber, *Corp Secy*
EMP: 26 EST: 1946
SQ FT: 3,500
SALES (est): 10.3MM **Privately Held**
SIC: **5211** 5032 Brick; brick, except refractory

(G-10009)
DELAWARE BUS INCORPORATORS INC
3422 Old Capitol Trl (19808-6124)
P.O. Box 5722 (19808-0722)
PHONE..................302 996-5819
Douglas Murray, *President*
Russell Murray, *Vice Pres*
EMP: 5
SQ FT: 3,000
SALES (est): 653.9K **Privately Held**
WEB: www.eincorporate.com
SIC: **8111** Specialized legal services

(G-10010)
DELAWARE CAPITAL FORMATION INC (HQ)
501 Silverside Rd Ste 5 (19809-1375)
PHONE..................302 793-4921
Amy Ward, *President*
Lloyd Martin, *Vice Pres*
Alfred Suesser, *Vice Pres*
Jeremiah Mulligan, *Treasurer*
Robert Whoriskey, *Asst Treas*
EMP: 7
SALES (est): 1.5B
SALES (corp-wide): 6.9B **Publicly Held**
SIC: **5084** 3463 3542 3823 Food product manufacturing machinery; bearing & bearing race forgings, nonferrous; machine tools, metal forming type; flow instruments, industrial process type
PA: Dover Corporation
3005 Highland Pkwy # 200
Downers Grove IL 60515
630 541-1540

(G-10011)
DELAWARE CAPITAL HOLDINGS INC (DH)
501 Silverside Rd Ste 5 (19809-1375)
PHONE..................302 793-4921
John F Mc Niff, *President*
Alfred Suesser, *Treasurer*
Robert Kuhbach, *Admin Sec*
◆ EMP: 6
SALES (est): 1.5B
SALES (corp-wide): 6.9B **Publicly Held**
SIC: **5084** 3533 7699 Food product manufacturing machinery; oil field machinery & equipment; elevators: inspection, service & repair
HQ: Delaware Capital Formation, Inc.
501 Silverside Rd Ste 5
Wilmington DE 19809
302 793-4921

(G-10012)
DELAWARE CAR COMPANY
Second & Lombard St (19801)
P.O. Box 233 (19899-0233)
PHONE..................302 655-6665
Harry E Hill, *Managing Prtnr*
Thomas J Crowley, *General Ptnr*
EMP: 50
SQ FT: 133,000
SALES (est): 3.8MM **Privately Held**
SIC: **4789** 3743 Railroad car repair; railroad equipment

(G-10013)
DELAWARE CENTER FOR JUSTICE
100 W 10th St Ste 905 (19801-6605)
PHONE..................302 658-7174
Janet A Leban, *Exec Dir*
EMP: 17
SALES: 1.3MM **Privately Held**
WEB: www.dcjustice.org
SIC: **8399** Community development groups; advocacy group

(G-10014)
DELAWARE CHEMICAL CORPORATION
1105 N Market St Ste 1300 (19801-1241)
P.O. Box 8985 (19899-8985)
PHONE..................302 234-1463
Edward J Jones, *President*
Mary Irons, *Vice Pres*
EMP: 7
SALES (est): 614.7K
SALES (corp-wide): 95.3MM **Privately Held**
SIC: **2819** Industrial inorganic chemicals
PA: Arkema
420 Rue D Estienne D Orves
Colombes 92700
149 008-080

(G-10015)
DELAWARE CHILDREN S MUSEUM
550 Justison St (19801-5142)
PHONE..................302 654-2340
Karen Rose, *Principal*
EMP: 7
SALES (est): 186.3K **Privately Held**
SIC: **8412** Museum

(G-10016)
DELAWARE CHILDRENS MUSEUM INC
550 Justison St (19801-5142)
PHONE..................302 654-2340
Heather Warren, *Manager*
Julie Van Blarcom, *Director*
Julie Blarcom, *Executive*
EMP: 4

Wilmington - New Castle County (G-10017) GEOGRAPHIC SECTION

SALES: 1.2MM **Privately Held**
SIC: **8412** Museum

(G-10017)
DELAWARE CLAIMS AGENCY LLC
230 N Market St (19801-2528)
P.O. Box 515 (19899-0515)
PHONE..................212 957-2180
EMP: 5
SALES (est): 340K **Privately Held**
SIC: **8111** Legal Support Services

(G-10018)
DELAWARE CLAIMS PROC FCILTY
1007 N Orange St (19801-1239)
PHONE..................302 427-8913
John Mekus, *Exec Dir*
EMP: 93
SALES (est): 8.8MM **Privately Held**
WEB: www.celotextrust.com
SIC: **6733** Trusts

(G-10019)
DELAWARE CLINICAL & LABORTRY
Also Called: Hematology/Oncology Office
4512 Kirkwood Hwy Ste 200 (19808-5122)
PHONE..................302 999-8095
Lisa Michaels, *Branch Mgr*
EMP: 6
SALES (corp-wide): 1.3MM **Privately Held**
WEB: www.delawarephysicianscare.com
SIC: **8071** Pathological laboratory
PA: Delaware Clinical & Laboratory Physicians Pa
  4701 Ogletown Stanton Rd
  Newark DE 19713
  302 737-7700

(G-10020)
DELAWARE CLITN AGNST DMSTC VLN
100 W 10th St Ste 903 (19801-6605)
PHONE..................302 658-2958
Carol Post, *Director*
Erin Curry, *Administration*
EMP: 6
SALES: 1.7MM **Privately Held**
WEB: www.dcadv.org
SIC: **8322** Individual & family services

(G-10021)
DELAWARE COLOR LAB
Also Called: Foschi Fine Photography
2107 Naamans Rd (19810-1326)
PHONE..................302 529-1339
Rudy Foschi, *Partner*
Ted Foschi, *Partner*
EMP: 7
SALES (est): 460.4K **Privately Held**
WEB: www.foschifinephotography.com
SIC: **7384** Film processing & finishing laboratory; photofinishing laboratory

(G-10022)
DELAWARE COMM REINVSTMNT ACTN
600 S Harrison St (19805-4306)
PHONE..................302 298-3250
Carol Davis, *Ch of Bd*
Marisela Tovar-Rangel, *Program Mgr*
Rashmi Rangan, *Manager*
EMP: 7
SALES: 616.3K **Privately Held**
WEB: www.dcrac.org
SIC: **8611** 8699 Business associations; charitable organization

(G-10023)
DELAWARE COMMUNITY FOUNDATION (PA)
100 W 10th St Ste 115 (19801-1660)
PHONE..................302 571-8004
Fred Spears, *President*
Richard Gentsch, *Exec VP*
Marie Stewart, *Client Mgr*
EMP: 11
SALES: 24MM **Privately Held**
SIC: **6732** 8733 Charitable trust management; noncommercial research organizations

(G-10024)
DELAWARE COMMUNITY INV CORP
100 W 10th St Ste 303 (19801-1642)
PHONE..................302 655-1420
Doris Schnider, *President*
Christina Stanley, *Vice Pres*
Dee Johnson, *CFO*
Dionna Sargent, *Officer*
EMP: 6
SALES: 949.2K **Privately Held**
SIC: **6162** Mortgage bankers & correspondents

(G-10025)
DELAWARE CONTRACT TESTING LLC
4517 Verona Dr (19808-5623)
P.O. Box 887, Bear (19701-0887)
PHONE..................302 650-4030
Ryan Holzbaur,
EMP: 1
SALES: 20K **Privately Held**
SIC: **3564** Blowers & fans

(G-10026)
DELAWARE CORPORATE AGENTS INC
4406 Tennyson Rd (19802-1240)
PHONE..................302 762-8637
Steven D Goldberg, *President*
Jane Goldberg, *Vice Pres*
EMP: 4
SALES (est): 209K **Privately Held**
WEB: www.delcorp.com
SIC: **6531** Escrow agent, real estate

(G-10027)
DELAWARE COUNCL ON GMBLNG PRBL (PA)
100 W 10th St Ste 303 (19801-1642)
PHONE..................302 655-3261
Elizabeth B Pertzoff, *Director*
EMP: 8
SALES: 1.4MM **Privately Held**
SIC: **8093** Substance abuse clinics (outpatient)

(G-10028)
DELAWARE COUNSEL GROUP LLP (PA)
Also Called: Decg
2 Mill Rd Ste 108 (19806-2175)
PHONE..................302 576-9600
Ellisa Opstbaum Habbart, *Partner*
EMP: 9
SALES (est): 807.3K **Privately Held**
WEB: www.delawarecounselgroup.com
SIC: **8111** General practice law office

(G-10029)
DELAWARE COUNTY PAIN MGT
208 N Union St (19805-3430)
PHONE..................302 575-1145
EMP: 5
SALES (est): 123K
SALES (corp-wide): 1.6MM **Privately Held**
SIC: **8011** 8041 Physicians' office, including specialists; offices & clinics of chiropractors
PA: Delaware County Pain Management
  1308 Macdade Blvd
  Folsom PA 19033
  610 532-0657

(G-10030)
DELAWARE CRDOVASCULAR ASSOC PA
1403 Foulk Rd Ste 101 (19803-2788)
PHONE..................302 543-4800
Stephen M Blumberg, *Principal*
EMP: 12 **Privately Held**
SIC: **8011** Cardiologist & cardio-vascular specialist
PA: Delaware Cardiovascular Associates, P.A.
  1403 Foulk Rd Ste 101a
  Wilmington DE 19803

(G-10031)
DELAWARE CTR FOR HMLESS VTRANS
1405 Veale Rd (19810-4331)
PHONE..................302 898-2647
David Mosley, *Vice Pres*
EMP: 14
SALES: 199.3K **Privately Held**
SIC: **8322** Individual & family services

(G-10032)
DELAWARE CTR FOR HRTCLTURE INC
Also Called: DCH
1810 N Dupont St (19806-3308)
PHONE..................302 658-6262
Pamela Sapko, *Exec Dir*
EMP: 15 EST: 1977
SQ FT: 12,000
SALES: 1.4MM **Privately Held**
WEB: www.dehort.org
SIC: **8699** Personal interest organization

(G-10033)
DELAWARE CURATIVE WORKSHOP (PA)
1600 N Washington St (19802-4722)
P.O. Box 4453 (19807-0453)
PHONE..................302 656-2521
Mike Walls, *Director*
EMP: 88
SQ FT: 40,000
SALES: 287.8K **Privately Held**
WEB: www.delawarecurative.com
SIC: **8093** 8049 Rehabilitation center, outpatient treatment; physical therapist; occupational therapist; psychologist, psychotherapist & hypnotist

(G-10034)
DELAWARE DAGNSTC REHABILITATIO
P.O. Box 4056 (19807-0056)
PHONE..................302 777-3955
W King, *Principal*
EMP: 5
SALES (est): 155.7K **Privately Held**
SIC: **8322** Rehabilitation services

(G-10035)
DELAWARE DANCE CENTER INC
4751 Shopp Of Lndnhill Rd (19808)
PHONE..................302 454-1440
Jane Griffin, *President*
EMP: 9
SALES (est): 151.1K **Privately Held**
SIC: **7911** Dance studio & school

(G-10036)
DELAWARE DENTISTRY
2505 Silverside Rd (19810-3707)
PHONE..................302 475-6900
Daniel Fink, *Owner*
EMP: 4 EST: 2007
SALES (est): 302.3K **Privately Held**
SIC: **8021** Dentists' office

(G-10037)
DELAWARE DEPOSITORY SVC CO LLC
3601 N Market St (19802-2736)
PHONE..................302 762-2635
Jon Potts,
Simon Schatz,
EMP: 8
SQ FT: 20,000
SALES (est): 1MM
SALES (corp-wide): 8.8MM **Privately Held**
WEB: www.delawaredepository.com
SIC: **6141** Installment sales finance, other than banks
PA: Fidelitrade Incorporated
  3601 N Market St
  Wilmington DE 19802
  302 762-6200

(G-10038)
DELAWARE DERMATOLOGIC
14 Alders Ln (19807-3050)
PHONE..................302 593-8625
Ben Bansal, *Principal*
EMP: 4

SALES (est): 354.8K **Privately Held**
SIC: **2834** Dermatologicals

(G-10039)
DELAWARE DIAGNOSTIC & REHAB
Also Called: Delaware Dgnstc Rhbltation Cen
131 S West St (19801-5014)
PHONE..................302 777-3955
William Atkins, *Owner*
EMP: 9
SALES (est): 482K **Privately Held**
SIC: **8322** Rehabilitation services

(G-10040)
DELAWARE DIAGNOSTIC GROUP LLC
2060 Limestone Rd (19808-5500)
PHONE..................302 472-5555
Muhammad Haq, *Principal*
EMP: 5
SALES (est): 567.2K **Privately Held**
SIC: **8011** Radiologist

(G-10041)
DELAWARE DIAMOND KNIVES INC
3825 Lancaster Pike # 200 (19805-1559)
PHONE..................302 999-7476
Joseph Tabeling, *President*
Linda Tabeling, *Vice Pres*
Bill Tabeling, *Prdtn Mgr*
Victor Tabeling, *Sales Staff*
Martha Burgess, *Marketing Staff*
EMP: 25
SALES (est): 4.1MM **Privately Held**
WEB: www.ddk.com
SIC: **3421** Knife blades & blanks

(G-10042)
DELAWARE DIRECT INC
220 Valley Rd (19804-1312)
PHONE..................302 658-8223
Jeffrey Gooding, *President*
Kim Coyle, *Marketing Mgr*
EMP: 7
SQ FT: 7,600
SALES (est): 973.3K **Privately Held**
WEB: www.delawaredirect.com
SIC: **4226** Special warehousing & storage

(G-10043)
DELAWARE ECUMENICAL COUNCIL
240 N James St Ste 111 (19804-3167)
PHONE..................302 225-1040
Debra Lewis, *Technology*
Robert P Hall, *Director*
EMP: 9
SALES: 223.8K **Privately Held**
WEB: www.deccf.org
SIC: **7389** Personal service agents, brokers & bureaus

(G-10044)
DELAWARE EQUITY FUND IV
Also Called: Cynwyd Club Apartments
100 W 10th St Ste 303 (19801-1642)
PHONE..................302 655-1420
Doris Schnider, *Partner*
EMP: 6
SALES (est): 384.4K **Privately Held**
SIC: **6513** Apartment building operators

(G-10045)
DELAWARE EYE SURGEONS
2710 Centerville Rd # 102 (19808-1652)
PHONE..................302 956-0285
S G Smith MD, *Owner*
Amanda Fichter Do, *Principal*
EMP: 8
SALES (est): 348.7K **Privately Held**
SIC: **8011** Ophthalmologist

(G-10046)
DELAWARE FAMILY VOICES INC
Also Called: FAMILY TO FAMILY
3301 Englewood Rd (19810-3323)
PHONE..................302 588-4908
Ann Phillips, *Exec Dir*
EMP: 10
SALES: 115.8K **Privately Held**
SIC: **8748** Urban planning & consulting services

GEOGRAPHIC SECTION

Wilmington - New Castle County (G-10075)

(G-10047)
DELAWARE FIRST FEDERAL CR UN (PA)
1815 Newport Gap Pike # 1 (19808-6241)
PHONE................................302 998-0665
Sharon Shaper, *President*
James Brown, *Treasurer*
Michael Matweychuk, *Admin Sec*
EMP: 12
SQ FT: 3,000
SALES: 670K **Privately Held**
WEB: www.delawarefirstfederalcreditunion.com
SIC: 6061 6163 Federal credit unions; loan brokers

(G-10048)
DELAWARE GUIDANCE SERVICES FOR (PA)
1213 Delaware Ave (19806-4707)
PHONE................................302 652-3948
Steve Walczak, *President*
Bruce Kelsey, *Exec Dir*
Robert Miller, *Director*
EMP: 15
SALES: 10.1MM **Privately Held**
WEB: www.delawareguidance.org
SIC: 8322 Family counseling services

(G-10049)
DELAWARE HARDSCAPE SUPPLY LLC
4701 B And O Ln (19804)
PHONE................................302 996-6464
Chris Disabatino,
EMP: 6 EST: 2011
SALES (est): 574.6K **Privately Held**
SIC: 5261 5083 Lawn & garden equipment; landscaping equipment

(G-10050)
DELAWARE HEALTH NET INC
601 New Castle Ave (19801-5821)
PHONE................................410 788-9715
Craig Law, *CEO*
EMP: 6 EST: 2008
SALES: 796.3K **Privately Held**
SIC: 8099 Medical services organization

(G-10051)
DELAWARE HEARING AIDS
1601 Concord Pike Ste 65 (19803-3623)
PHONE................................302 652-3558
Robert Hanrahan, *Owner*
Barbara Madora, *Admin Sec*
EMP: 4
SALES (est): 315.4K **Privately Held**
WEB: www.delawarehearingaids.com
SIC: 5999 7629 Hearing aids; hearing aid repair

(G-10052)
DELAWARE HELPLINE INC
625 N Orange St Fl 3 (19801-2250)
PHONE................................302 255-1810
EMP: 10
SALES: 587.6K **Privately Held**
SIC: 8621 Non Profit Organization

(G-10053)
DELAWARE HIV SERVICES INC
100 W 10th St Ste 415 (19801-1643)
PHONE................................302 654-5471
Robert Raup, *Finance Dir*
Bob Rauk, *Finance*
George Lincoln, *Case Mgr*
Kristine Loller, *Case Mgr*
Raphia Noumbissi, *Manager*
EMP: 11
SQ FT: 3,000
SALES: 2.5MM **Privately Held**
WEB: www.delawarehiv.org
SIC: 8322 Social service center

(G-10054)
DELAWARE HMANITIES COUNCIL INC
100 W 10th St Ste 509 (19801-6612)
PHONE................................302 657-0650
Bob Bercaw, *Finance Dir*
Michele Anstine, *Exec Dir*
Lisa Dill, *Officer*
Ciera Fisher, *Officer*
Erin Obrien, *Officer*
EMP: 5
SALES: 744.2K **Privately Held**
SIC: 8399 Council for social agency

(G-10055)
DELAWARE HUMANE ASSOCIATION
701 A St (19801-5331)
PHONE................................302 571-0111
Calvin Stewart, *President*
Debra Grandizio, *Vice Pres*
Robert Kalik, *Treasurer*
Kevin Usilton, *Exec Dir*
Patrick Carroll, *Exec Dir*
EMP: 35
SQ FT: 3,000
SALES: 3.5MM **Privately Held**
WEB: www.dehumane.org
SIC: 8699 Animal humane society

(G-10056)
DELAWARE IMAGING NETWORK
Also Called: Silverside Mall
2700 Silverside Rd Ste 1b (19810-3724)
PHONE................................302 478-1100
Nancy Chambers, *Manager*
EMP: 10 **Publicly Held**
SIC: 8011 Radiologist
HQ: Delaware Imaging Network
  40 Polly Drmmnd Hl Rd 4
  Newark DE 19711
  302 652-3016

(G-10057)
DELAWARE INCORPORATION SVCS
704 N King St Ste 500 (19801-3584)
P.O. Box 1031 (19899-1031)
PHONE................................302 658-1733
Paul Cotrell, *President*
EMP: 10
SALES (est): 463.8K **Privately Held**
SIC: 8742 Financial consultant

(G-10058)
DELAWARE INNOVATION SPACE INC
200 Powder Mill Rd E500 (19803-2907)
PHONE................................302 695-2201
William Provine, *CEO*
Charles Riordan, *Ch of Bd*
Tim Mueller, *Vice Pres*
Jeff Bullock, *Treasurer*
Mike Rinkunas, *Director*
EMP: 8
SQ FT: 100,000
SALES (est): 193.7K **Privately Held**
SIC: 8748 7389 8741 8731 Business consulting; ; management services; biological research

(G-10059)
DELAWARE INTERCORP INC
3511 Silverside Rd # 105 (19810-4902)
PHONE................................302 266-9367
Russell P Rozanski, *President*
Larry D Sullivan, *Comptroller*
EMP: 8
SQ FT: 2,500
SALES (est): 1MM **Privately Held**
WEB: www.delawareintercorp.com
SIC: 8742 Corporation organizing

(G-10060)
DELAWARE ITALIAN-AMERICAN
2208 Highland Pl (19805-2619)
PHONE................................302 545-6406
Eva Peterson, *Principal*
EMP: 1
SALES (est): 71.7K **Privately Held**
SIC: 2721 Magazines: publishing only, not printed on site

(G-10061)
DELAWARE LACROSSE FOUNDATION
P.O. Box 5066 (19808-0066)
PHONE................................302 831-8661
Robert F Shillinglaw, *President*
EMP: 15
SQ FT: 2,207
SALES: 14.8K **Privately Held**
SIC: 8699 7997 Charitable organization; membership sports & recreation clubs

(G-10062)
DELAWARE MARKETING PARTNERS
Also Called: Delaware Marketing Group
3801 Kennett Pike D301 (19807-2328)
PHONE................................302 575-1610
Kenneth Scott, *President*
Christie Bleach, *Vice Pres*
Susan Hanway Scott, *Vice Pres*
Megan Rassman, *Accounts Exec*
Andrew Scott, *Internal Med*
EMP: 7
SQ FT: 1,000
SALES (est): 595.5K **Privately Held**
WEB: www.delawaremarketinggroup.com
SIC: 8742 Financial consultant

(G-10063)
DELAWARE MEAT COMPANY LLC
Also Called: Lab
28 Brookside Dr (19804-1102)
PHONE................................302 438-0252
Terri Sorantino, *Mng Member*
EMP: 2
SALES (est): 80K **Privately Held**
SIC: 2084 Wines

(G-10064)
DELAWARE MEDICAL ASSOCIATES PA
Also Called: Dr. Armand Neal Dsanctis Jr MD
2101 Foulk Rd Ste 2 (19810-4710)
PHONE................................302 475-2535
Armand N Desanctis, *Principal*
EMP: 14 EST: 2009
SALES (est): 1.1MM **Privately Held**
SIC: 8099 Physical examination & testing services

(G-10065)
DELAWARE MEDICAL CARE INC
Also Called: Delaware Family Care Assoc
2700 Silverside Rd Ste 2 (19810-3724)
PHONE................................302 225-6868
Nancy Chambers, *Manager*
EMP: 20
SQ FT: 32,000
SALES (est): 1.5MM **Privately Held**
WEB: www.delawarefamilycare.com
SIC: 8011 Primary care medical clinic

(G-10066)
DELAWARE MERCHANT SERVICES
Also Called: Metro Merchant Services
510 Century Blvd (19808-6272)
PHONE................................302 838-9100
Mark S Landis, *President*
Karen Landis, *Vice Pres*
EMP: 6
SALES (est): 901K **Privately Held**
WEB: www.demerchantservices.com
SIC: 7389 Credit card service

(G-10067)
DELAWARE MOTOR SALES INC (PA)
Also Called: Autoteam Delaware
1606 Pennsylvania Ave (19806-4089)
PHONE................................302 656-3100
Michael Uffner, *President*
Lee Asher, *General Mgr*
Matthew Kersey, *General Mgr*
Marilyn Uffner, *Vice Pres*
Bill Blythe, *Info Tech Dir*
EMP: 120 EST: 1982
SQ FT: 39,000
SALES (est): 52.9MM **Privately Held**
WEB: www.autoteamdelaware.com
SIC: 5511 7515 Automobiles, new & used; passenger car leasing

(G-10068)
DELAWARE MUSEUM OF NATURAL
4840 Kennett Pike (19807-1827)
P.O. Box 3937 (19807-0937)
PHONE................................302 658-9111
William D Zantzinger, *President*
Gregory A Inskip, *Vice Pres*
John J Kirby, *Treasurer*
W Halsey Spruance, *Exec Dir*
Halsey Spruance, *Exec Dir*
EMP: 26
SQ FT: 66,000
SALES: 1.8MM **Privately Held**
WEB: www.delmnh.org
SIC: 8412 Museum

(G-10069)
DELAWARE OPEN M R I
3211a Concord Pike (19803-5014)
PHONE................................302 479-5400
Steven Edil, *Manager*
EMP: 4
SALES (est): 172.1K **Privately Held**
SIC: 8011 Radiologist

(G-10070)
DELAWARE OPHTHALMOLOGY CONS PA (PA)
3501 Silverside Rd (19810-4910)
PHONE................................302 479-3937
Robert Abel Jr, *President*
Edward F Becker MD, *Vice Pres*
Gordon A Bussard MD, *Vice Pres*
Harry A Lebowitz MD, *Vice Pres*
Sandy Fasano, *CFO*
EMP: 50
SQ FT: 12,086
SALES (est): 9.4MM **Privately Held**
SIC: 8011 Ophthalmologist

(G-10071)
DELAWARE ORTHOPAEDIC SPECIALIS
1941 Limestone Rd Ste 101 (19808-5413)
PHONE................................302 633-3555
Joshua D Vaught, *Principal*
Amy Milhorn, *Director*
Joshua Vaught, *Officer*
EMP: 21
SALES (est): 2.3MM **Privately Held**
SIC: 8011 Orthopedic physician

(G-10072)
DELAWARE PAIN & SPINE CENTER
2055 Limestone Rd Ste 201 (19808-5536)
P.O. Box 8252, Newark (19714-8252)
PHONE................................302 737-0800
Uday Uthaman, *President*
EMP: 4
SALES (est): 409.2K **Privately Held**
SIC: 8011 Orthopedic physician

(G-10073)
DELAWARE PARK RACING LLC
777 Delaware Park Blvd (19804-4122)
PHONE................................302 994-6700
James Hashimoto, *Principal*
Robin Metz, *Exec Dir*
EMP: 5
SALES (est): 175.8K **Privately Held**
SIC: 7992 Public golf courses

(G-10074)
DELAWARE PERIODONTICS
1110 N Bancroft Pkwy # 1 (19805-2669)
PHONE................................302 658-7871
Bradford Klassman, *Principal*
Bradford L Klassman, *Principal*
Holly Titus, *Sr Project Mgr*
Kim Gallagher, *Manager*
Barry Klassman, *Fmly & Gen Dent*
EMP: 7 EST: 2011
SALES (est): 849.6K **Privately Held**
SIC: 8021 Periodontist

(G-10075)
DELAWARE RACING ASSOCIATION
777 Delaware Park Blvd (19804-4122)
PHONE................................302 994-6700
William M Rickman Jr, *Branch Mgr*
EMP: 97
SALES (corp-wide): 79.8MM **Privately Held**
SIC: 8611 Merchants' association
PA: Delaware Racing Association
  777 Delaware Park Blvd
  Wilmington DE 19804
  302 994-2521

Wilmington - New Castle County (G-10076) GEOGRAPHIC SECTION

(G-10076)
DELAWARE RACING ASSOCIATION (PA)
Also Called: Delaware Park
777 Delaware Park Blvd (19804-4122)
PHONE 302 994-2521
William M Rickman Jr, *CEO*
William Fasy, *President*
Terry Smith, *Vice Pres*
John Bell, *Senior Engr*
Sheryl Cartwright, *Human Res Mgr*
▲ **EMP:** 1000
SQ FT: 580,000
SALES (est): 79.8MM **Privately Held**
WEB: www.delawarepark.com
SIC: 7948 7993 Horse race track operation; slot machines

(G-10077)
DELAWARE RE ADVISORS LLC
Also Called: Integra Realty Resources
1013 Centre Rd Ste 201 (19805-1265)
PHONE 302 998-4030
Douglas Nickel,
EMP: 5
SALES: 900K **Privately Held**
SIC: 6531 Real estate agent, commercial; appraiser, real estate

(G-10078)
DELAWARE REGISTRY LTD
3511 Silverside Rd # 105 (19810-4902)
PHONE 302 477-9800
Barbara Stargatt, *President*
Daniel Stargatt, *Vice Pres*
EMP: 8
SALES (est): 657.6K
SALES (corp-wide): 2.2MM **Privately Held**
WEB: www.delawareregistry.com
SIC: 7361 Registries
HQ: Yacht Delaware Registry, Ltd
3511 Silverside Rd # 105
Wilmington DE 19810
302 477-9800

(G-10079)
DELAWARE RETIRED SCHL PRSNL
100 Galewood Ct (19803-3977)
P.O. Box 7262 (19803-0262)
PHONE 302 674-8252
Everett Toomey, *President*
Wayne Emsley, *Exec Dir*
EMP: 20
SALES (est): 38.7K **Privately Held**
SIC: 8641 7389 Civic social & fraternal associations;

(G-10080)
DELAWARE RIDERS BASBAL CLB INC
2214 Nassau Dr (19810-2831)
PHONE 302 475-1915
Michael D Bannon, *Principal*
EMP: 4
SALES (est): 61.4K **Privately Held**
SIC: 7997 Membership sports & recreation clubs

(G-10081)
DELAWARE RIVER STEVEDORES INC
1 Hausel Rd Ste 115 (19801-5876)
PHONE 302 657-0472
Robert Palaima, *President*
Bob Mulholland, *Terminal Mgr*
Patti Leatherman, *Opers Staff*
Dave Norbut, *Manager*
Michael Billups, *Director*
EMP: 9
SALES (corp-wide): 9.2MM **Privately Held**
SIC: 4491 Stevedoring
PA: Delaware River Stevedores Inc
441 N 5th St Ste 210
Philadelphia PA 19123
215 440-4100

(G-10082)
DELAWARE RUG CO INC
5 Forrest Ave (19805-5016)
PHONE 302 998-8881
Nick Michael, *President*
Maria V Michael, *Vice Pres*
EMP: 5
SQ FT: 5,000
SALES (est): 740K **Privately Held**
SIC: 5713 7217 Carpets; rugs; carpet & furniture cleaning on location

(G-10083)
DELAWARE SECRETARY OF STATE
Also Called: Port of Wilmington
1 Hausel Rd Lbby (19801-5882)
PHONE 302 472-7678
Gene Bailey, *Branch Mgr*
EMP: 20 **Privately Held**
SIC: 8711 9621 Engineering services; port authority or district: government, non-operating;
HQ: Delaware Secretary Of State
401 Federal St Ste 3
Dover DE 19901
302 739-4111

(G-10084)
DELAWARE SLEEP DSRDER CTRS LLC (PA)
701 Foulk Rd Ste 1g (19803-3733)
PHONE 302 669-6141
Steven D Conley,
EMP: 38 **EST:** 2006
SQ FT: 2,500
SALES (est): 4.4MM **Privately Held**
SIC: 8011 Clinic, operated by physicians

(G-10085)
DELAWARE STAR DENTAL
5507 Kirkwood Hwy (19808-5001)
PHONE 302 994-3093
Syed Shetar, *President*
EMP: 4
SALES (est): 156.1K **Privately Held**
SIC: 8021 Offices & clinics of dentists

(G-10086)
DELAWARE STATE BAR ASSOCIATION
405 N King St Ste 100 (19801-3700)
PHONE 302 658-5279
Rina Marks, *Exec Dir*
Mark S Vavala,
EMP: 6
SALES: 2MM **Privately Held**
WEB: www.dsba.org
SIC: 8621 Bar association

(G-10087)
DELAWARE STATE CHAMBER
1201 N Orange St Ste 200 (19801-1167)
P.O. Box 671 (19899-0671)
PHONE 302 655-7221
Joan Verplanck, *President*
James Wolfe, *President*
Anthony Richard Heffron, *Principal*
Mark Branard, *Exec VP*
Thomas McCarthy, *Exec VP*
EMP: 15 **EST:** 1836
SALES: 1.5MM **Privately Held**
SIC: 8611 Chamber of Commerce

(G-10088)
DELAWARE SURGICAL GROUP PA (PA)
1941 Limestone Rd Ste 213 (19808-5434)
PHONE 302 892-2100
Michael K Conway MD, *President*
EMP: 9
SALES (est): 914.2K **Privately Held**
SIC: 8011 Surgeon

(G-10089)
DELAWARE SYMPHONY ASSOCIATION
Also Called: DELAWARE SYMPHONY ORCHESTRA
100 W 10th St Ste 1003 (19801-1652)
PHONE 302 656-7442
Charles Babcock, *President*
Stephen A Manocchio, *Partner*
I David Plaza, *Treasurer*
Libby Burgazli, *Finance Mgr*
Stephanie Wilson, *Persnl Mgr*
EMP: 85
SALES: 1.7MM **Privately Held**
WEB: www.delawaresymphony.org
SIC: 7929 Symphony orchestras

(G-10090)
DELAWARE THEATRE COMPANY
200 Water St (19801-5030)
PHONE 302 594-1100
Nathan Renner-Johnson, *General Mgr*
Jillian Farley, *Business Mgr*
Bud Martin, *Exec Dir*
Amery Camerido, *Director*
Jeremy Toy, *Technician*
EMP: 31
SALES: 2.8MM **Privately Held**
WEB: www.delawaretheatre.com
SIC: 7922 Theatrical companies

(G-10091)
DELAWARE TITLE LOANS INC
3300 Concord Pike Ste 2 (19803-5038)
PHONE 302 478-8505
Patricia Lewis, *Manager*
EMP: 13
SALES (corp-wide): 7.7MM **Privately Held**
SIC: 6163 Loan brokers
PA: Delaware Title Loans, Inc.
8601 Dunwoody Pl Ste 406
Atlanta GA 30350
770 552-9840

(G-10092)
DELAWARE VALLEY BROKERAGE INC
1415 Foulk Rd Ste 103 (19803-2748)
PHONE 302 477-9700
Frank Kesselman, *President*
Ashley Hughes, *Broker*
EMP: 9
SALES (est): 850K **Privately Held**
SIC: 6211 Investment firm, general brokerage

(G-10093)
DELAWARE VALLEY ENT INC
1508 Penns Ave Ste 1a (19806-4348)
P.O. Box 9557 (19809-0557)
PHONE 302 427-2444
EMP: 5
SALES (est): 208.8K **Privately Held**
SIC: 8043 Podiatrist's Office

(G-10094)
DELAWARE VALLEY FIELD SVCS LLC
321 Robinson Ln (19805-4690)
PHONE 302 384-8617
Ray Saccomandi,
Allyson Saccomandi,
EMP: 6
SALES (est): 320.3K **Privately Held**
SIC: 7389 Interior decorating

(G-10095)
DELAWARE VALLEY GROUP LLC
Also Called: Dynamic Recycling Enterprise
1720 Gilpin Ave (19806-2304)
PHONE 302 777-7007
Richard Collins,
EMP: 5
SALES (est): 394.5K **Privately Held**
SIC: 7361 Employment agencies

(G-10096)
DELAWARE VALLEY ORTHODONTICS
5500 Skyline Dr Ste 1 (19808-1772)
PHONE 302 239-3531
Ronald B Rawlins, *Principal*
EMP: 4
SALES (est): 159.5K **Privately Held**
SIC: 8021 Orthodontist

(G-10097)
DELCASTLE GOLF CLUB
801 Mckennans Church Rd (19808-2124)
PHONE 302 995-1990
EMP: 4
SALES (est): 54.7K **Privately Held**
SIC: 7992 Public golf courses

(G-10098)
DELCASTLE GOLF CLUB MANAGEMENT
3800 Valley Brook Dr (19808-1345)
PHONE 302 998-9505
William Hackett, *President*
Margaret Hackett, *Corp Secy*
Darrell Mc Cabe, *Vice Pres*
Matt Storck, *Manager*
EMP: 50
SALES (est): 1.5MM **Privately Held**
SIC: 7992 7299 5812 5813 Public golf courses; banquet hall facilities; eating places; drinking places; golf goods & equipment

(G-10099)
DELCHEM INC
1318 E 12th St Ste 1 (19802-5301)
P.O. Box 10703 (19850-0703)
PHONE 302 426-1800
Richard Fagioli, *President*
Mike Fagioli, *Vice Pres*
John Matukaitis, *Sales Executive*
EMP: 12 **EST:** 1980
SQ FT: 35,000
SALES (est): 3.4MM **Privately Held**
WEB: www.delchem.com
SIC: 2891 Sealants; adhesives

(G-10100)
DELCOLLO SECURITY TECHNOLOGIES
226 Brookside Dr (19804-1319)
PHONE 302 994-5400
Daniel Delcollo, *Principal*
Donna Mahoney, *Office Mgr*
Jim Street, *Manager*
EMP: 8
SALES (est): 845.1K **Privately Held**
SIC: 1731 Electrical work

(G-10101)
DELMAR TERMITE & PEST CONTROL
700 Cornell Dr (19801-5762)
P.O. Box 3836 (19807-0836)
PHONE 302 658-5010
Darnell Drummond, *Principal*
EMP: 6
SALES (est): 490.1K **Privately Held**
SIC: 7342 Pest control in structures

(G-10102)
DELMARVA BROADCASTING CO INC (PA)
Also Called: Radio Station Wdel-AM
2727 Shipley Rd (19810-3210)
PHONE 302 478-2700
Julian H Booker, *President*
Heather Szarka, *General Mgr*
Jonathan Haith, *Vice Pres*
Bill Grant, *Accounts Mgr*
Mark Vanderhaar, *Accounts Mgr*
EMP: 70 **EST:** 1922
SQ FT: 9,000
SALES (est): 30.4MM **Privately Held**
WEB: www.delmarvabroadcasting.com
SIC: 4832 Contemporary

(G-10103)
DELMARVA POWER & LIGHT COMPANY
Also Called: Gas Div
630 Mrtin Lther King Blvd (19801-2306)
P.O. Box 231 (19899-0231)
PHONE 302 429-3376
Don Bridge, *Project Mgr*
Jack Urban, *Manager*
Lisa D Alvino, *Manager*
EMP: 21
SALES (corp-wide): 35.9B **Publicly Held**
SIC: 4911 Distribution, electric power
HQ: Delmarva Power & Light Company
500 N Wakefield Dr Fl 2
Newark DE 19702
302 454-0300

(G-10104)
DELMARVA POWER & LIGHT COMPANY
200 Hay Rd (19809-3560)
P.O. Box 231 (19899-0231)
PHONE 302 454-0300

▲ = Import ▼ = Export
◆ = Import/Export

John Kutys, *Manager*
EMP: 115
SALES (corp-wide): 35.9B **Publicly Held**
SIC: 4911 4924 Generation, electric power; natural gas distribution
HQ: Delmarva Power & Light Company
500 N Wakefield Dr Fl 2
Newark DE 19702
302 454-0300

(G-10105)
DELPHI FINANCIAL GROUP INC (HQ)
1105 N Market St Ste 1230 (19801-1216)
P.O. Box 8985 (19899-8985)
PHONE...................................302 478-5142
Robert Rosenkranz, *CEO*
Donald A Sherman, *President*
Harold F Ilg, *Exec VP*
Chad W Coulter, *Senior VP*
Thomas W Burghart, *Treasurer*
EMP: 40
SALES (est): 966.9MM **Privately Held**
WEB: www.delphifin.com
SIC: 6321 Disability health insurance

(G-10106)
DELTA FORMS INC
5 Germay Dr (19804-1104)
PHONE...................................302 652-3266
David Disabatino, *President*
EMP: 11 **EST:** 1970
SALES (est): 2.3MM **Privately Held**
SIC: 2752 Color lithography; commercial printing, offset

(G-10107)
DELTA RISK LLC
108 W 13th St (19801-1145)
PHONE...................................312 203-8307
EMP: 15
SALES (est): 860K **Privately Held**
SIC: 7382 Security Systems Services

(G-10108)
DENCO INC
501 Silverside Rd Ste 132 (19809-1386)
PHONE...................................302 798-4200
Dudley Spencer PHD, *President*
Ivars Ivansons, *Engineer*
EMP: 7
SQ FT: 7,000
SALES (est): 881.3K **Privately Held**
SIC: 3841 Surgical & medical instruments

(G-10109)
DENNEK LLC
7 Rockford Rd Apt C5 (19806-1010)
PHONE...................................302 703-0790
John Kennedy,
EMP: 4
SALES (est): 108.8K **Privately Held**
SIC: 7373 7389 Systems engineering, computer related; office computer automation systems integration;

(G-10110)
DENOVIX INC
Also Called: Denovix Inc.
3411 Silverside Rd (19810-4812)
PHONE...................................302 442-6911
Fernando Kielhorn, *CEO*
Kevin Kelley, *Business Mgr*
Teresa Clarke-Myers, *Office Mgr*
Dave Ash, *Manager*
Thom Loring, *Software Engr*
◆ **EMP:** 25
SQ FT: 5,400
SALES (est): 1.4MM **Privately Held**
SIC: 3826 Spectroscopic & other optical properties measuring equipment

(G-10111)
DENTAL ASSOCIATES PA
2300 Penns Ave Ste 6cd (19806-1392)
PHONE...................................302 571-0878
Daniel Truono, *President*
EMP: 7
SALES (est): 722.8K **Privately Held**
SIC: 8021 Dentists' office

(G-10112)
DENTAL ASSOCIATES DELAWARE PA (PA)
Also Called: Group Investments Associates
1415 Foulk Rd Ste 200 (19803-2748)
PHONE...................................302 477-4900
William A Friz DDS, *President*
K F Anzilotti DDS, *Treasurer*
Sharon Urbanchuck, *Office Mgr*
Lynn Murray, *Executive Asst*
Erik Bradley, *Fmly & Gen Dent*
EMP: 40
SQ FT: 5,000
SALES (est): 5.9MM **Privately Held**
SIC: 8021 Dentists' office

(G-10113)
DENTAL ASSOCIATES DELAWARE PA
Also Called: Dental Management Strategies
1415 Foulk Rd Ste 200 (19803-2748)
PHONE...................................302 477-4900
Howard C Giles, *Principal*
EMP: 19
SALES (corp-wide): 5.9MM **Privately Held**
SIC: 8021 Dentists' office
PA: Dental Associates Of Delaware Pa
1415 Foulk Rd Ste 200
Wilmington DE 19803
302 477-4900

(G-10114)
DENTAL ASSOCIATES HOCKESSIN
1415 Foulk Rd Ste 201 (19803-2748)
PHONE...................................302 239-5917
Richard D Bond, *Principal*
EMP: 4
SALES (est): 142.4K **Privately Held**
SIC: 8021 Dentists' office

(G-10115)
DENTAL DIAGNOSTICS & SERVICES
217 W 9th St (19801-1619)
PHONE...................................302 655-2626
Janice Miller, *Manager*
EMP: 4
SALES (est): 140.7K **Privately Held**
SIC: 8021 Offices & clinics of dentists

(G-10116)
DENTAL SLEEP SOLUTION
4901 Limestone Rd (19808-1271)
PHONE...................................302 235-8249
EMP: 4 **EST:** 2017
SALES (est): 67.6K **Privately Held**
SIC: 8021 8299 Offices & clinics of dentists; meditation therapy

(G-10117)
DENTISTRY FOR CHILDREN
2036 Foulk Rd Ste 200 (19810-3650)
PHONE...................................302 475-7640
Rachel Maher, *Office Mgr*
EMP: 10
SALES (corp-wide): 767.9K **Privately Held**
SIC: 8021 Dentists' office
PA: Dentistry For Children
1450 E Chestnut Ave 6c
Vineland NJ 08361
856 696-5400

(G-10118)
DEPOSITORY TRUST CO DEL LLC
3601 N Market St (19802-2736)
PHONE...................................302 762-2635
Scott Schwartz, *General Counsel*
Jonathan E Potts,
EMP: 40
SALES (est): 3.2MM
SALES (corp-wide): 8.8MM **Privately Held**
SIC: 6091 Nondeposit trust facilities
PA: Fidelitrade Incorporated
3601 N Market St
Wilmington DE 19802
302 762-6200

(G-10119)
DESANGOSSE US INC
103 Foulk Rd (19803-3742)
PHONE...................................302 691-6137
EMP: 1
SALES (est): 62.3K **Privately Held**
SIC: 3999 Mfg Misc Products

(G-10120)
DESIGN COLLABORATIVE INC
Also Called: D C I
1211 Delaware Ave Ste Dc1 (19806-4719)
PHONE...................................302 652-4221
Lee Sparks, *President*
Joseph Chickadel, *Vice Pres*
Brian Thomas, *Project Mgr*
John Dobraniecki, *Associate*
EMP: 10
SQ FT: 2,200
SALES (est): 1.6MM **Privately Held**
WEB: www.dciarchitects.com
SIC: 8712 Architectural engineering; house designer

(G-10121)
DESIGN CONTRACTING INC
1000 N Heald St (19802-5237)
P.O. Box 25125 (19899-5125)
PHONE...................................302 429-6900
Andrew Diffley, *President*
EMP: 5
SQ FT: 6,200
SALES (est): 882.7K **Privately Held**
SIC: 1795 Demolition, buildings & other structures

(G-10122)
DESIGN SERVICES LTD
1403 Silverside Rd Ste C (19810-4434)
PHONE...................................302 475-5663
Rita Wilkins, *President*
EMP: 4
SQ FT: 2,200
SALES (est): 476.4K **Privately Held**
WEB: www.dsltdonline.com
SIC: 7389 Interior designer

(G-10123)
DESIGN SPECIFIC US INC
501 Silverside Rd Ste 105 (19809-1376)
PHONE...................................650 318-6473
Richard Fletcher, *President*
▲ **EMP:** 2
SALES (est): 103.2K **Privately Held**
SIC: 3999 2515 Wheelchair lifts; foundations & platforms
PA: Design Specific Limited
Unit 1-5, Parkside Farm
Lewes E SUSSEX

(G-10124)
DESIGN TRIBE REPUBLIC LLC
300 Delaware Ave Ste 210a (19801-6601)
PHONE...................................302 918-5279
Nicholas McGinnis,
EMP: 5
SALES (est): 166.1K **Privately Held**
SIC: 8742 8748 Marketing consulting services; business consulting

(G-10125)
DETROIT DESL RMNFACTURING CORP
1105 N Market St Ste 1300 (19801-1241)
PHONE...................................302 427-3564
Roger Pols, *Branch Mgr*
EMP: 4
SALES (corp-wide): 185.6B **Privately Held**
SIC: 6211 Investment firm, general brokerage
HQ: Detroit Diesel Remanufacturing Llc
100 Lodestone Way
Tooele UT 84074

(G-10126)
DEUTSCHE BANK TR CO AMERICAS
1011 Centre Rd Ste 200 (19805-1266)
PHONE...................................302 636-3301
Edward Reznick, *President*
EMP: 40
SALES (corp-wide): 13.2B **Privately Held**
WEB: www.db.com
SIC: 6021 6211 National commercial banks; security brokers & dealers
HQ: Deutsche Bank Trust Company Americas
60 Wall St Bsmt 1
New York NY 10005
212 250-2500

(G-10127)
DEUTSCHE BANK TRUST CO DEL
1011 Centre Rd Ste 200 (19805-1266)
PHONE...................................302 636-3300
Donna Mitchell, *President*
Jrgen Fitschen, *Co-CEO*
Edward A Reznick, *COO*
Henry Ritchotte, *COO*
Nic Devine, *Vice Pres*
EMP: 151
SQ FT: 43,000
SALES: 31.2MM
SALES (corp-wide): 13.2B **Privately Held**
WEB: www.bankerstrust.com
SIC: 6021 National commercial banks
HQ: Deutsche Bank Trust Corporation
60 Wall St Bsmt
New York NY 10005
212 250-2500

(G-10128)
DEUTSCHE BNK US FNCL MKTS HLDG
1011 Centre Rd Ste 200 (19805-1266)
PHONE...................................302 636-3301
EMP: 8
SALES (corp-wide): 13.2B **Privately Held**
SIC: 6733 Trusts
HQ: Deutsche Bank Us Financial Markets Holding Corp
60 Wall St Bsmt 1
New York NY 10005

(G-10129)
DEVELOPING MINDS PRESCHOOL
2106 Saint James Ch Rd (19808-5225)
PHONE...................................302 995-9611
Tracy McCraken, *Partner*
Dianne Sogarty, *Partner*
EMP: 8
SALES (est): 137.8K **Privately Held**
SIC: 8351 Preschool center

(G-10130)
DEWBERRY INSURANCE AGENCY INC
5700 Kirkwood Hwy Ste 103 (19808-4871)
P.O. Box 5286 (19808-0286)
PHONE...................................302 995-9550
Steve Dewberry, *President*
EMP: 6
SALES (est): 1.3MM **Privately Held**
SIC: 6411 Insurance agents, brokers & service

(G-10131)
DEWSON CONSTRUCTION COMPANY
7 S Lincoln St (19805-3809)
PHONE...................................302 427-2250
Timothy J Dewson, *President*
John McMahon, *Vice Pres*
Scott Kaeppler, *Project Mgr*
EMP: 42
SQ FT: 1,000
SALES: 5MM **Privately Held**
WEB: www.dewsonconstruction.com
SIC: 1521 New construction, single-family houses; general remodeling, single-family houses

(G-10132)
DEXSTA FEDERAL CREDIT UNION
300 Foulk Rd Ste 100 (19803-3819)
PHONE...................................302 996-4893
Carman Chrysler, *Partner*
Patrick Rhoades, *Vice Pres*
Sherry Sawicki, *Mktg Coord*
Tara Merwin, *Branch Mgr*
Shobha Patel, *Branch Mgr*
EMP: 10

Wilmington - New Castle County (G-10133)   GEOGRAPHIC SECTION

SALES (corp-wide): 10.6MM **Privately Held**
SIC: **6061** Federal credit unions
PA: Dexsta Federal Credit Union
1310 Centerville Rd
Wilmington DE 19808
302 996-4893

(G-10133)
DEXSTA FEDERAL CREDIT UNION (PA)
1310 Centerville Rd (19808-6220)
PHONE..................302 996-4893
Christine M Kaczmarczyk, *President*
Keith Parsons, *Exec VP*
Jerry King, *Vice Pres*
EMP: 21
SALES: 10.6MM **Privately Held**
SIC: **6061** Federal credit unions

(G-10134)
DEXSTA FEDERAL CREDIT UNION
E444-108 (19880)
PHONE..................302 695-3888
Keith Parsons, *Manager*
EMP: 10
SALES (corp-wide): 10.6MM **Privately Held**
SIC: **6061 6062** Federal credit unions; state credit unions
PA: Dexsta Federal Credit Union
1310 Centerville Rd
Wilmington DE 19808
302 996-4893

(G-10135)
DEZINS UNLIMITED INC
323 Clubhouse Ln (19810-2263)
PHONE..................302 652-4545
Ellen Sarafian, *Owner*
EMP: 6
SALES (est): 350K **Privately Held**
SIC: **1799** Window treatment installation

(G-10136)
DH TECH WILMINGTON DE
1 Limousine Dr (19803-4363)
PHONE..................215 680-9194
Timothy Lillard, *Principal*
Kris Kimmey, *Technician*
EMP: 2
SALES (est): 118.3K **Privately Held**
SIC: **1389** Construction, repair & dismantling services

(G-10137)
DHM WILMINGTON LLC
Also Called: Doubletree Hotel Wilmington
700 N King St (19801-3504)
PHONE..................302 656-8952
Andrew Jarrett, *Principal*
Eric Jolikko, *Mng Member*
EMP: 99
SALES: 950K **Privately Held**
SIC: **7011** Hotels & motels

(G-10138)
DIALOG NEWS PAPER INC
1925 Delaware Ave Fl 3 (19806-2301)
P.O. Box 2208 (19899-2208)
PHONE..................302 573-3109
Jim Grant, *General Mgr*
Christine Scarpa, *Advt Staff*
Ingrid Thomas, *Advt Staff*
EMP: 8
SALES (est): 338.4K
SALES (corp-wide): 26.1MM **Privately Held**
WEB: www.thedialog.org
SIC: **8999** Editorial service
PA: Catholic Diocese Of Wilmington, Inc.
1925 Delaware Ave
Wilmington DE 19806
302 573-3100

(G-10139)
DIAMOND CHEMICAL & SUPPLY CO
Also Called: Airwick/Delaware
524 S Walnut St Ste B (19801-5243)
PHONE..................302 656-7786
Richard L Ventresca Sr, *President*
Richard G Ventresca, *Vice Pres*
Sandy Murr, *Sales Staff*
Amy Streaker, *Sales Staff*
Susan Hartzel, *Office Mgr*
EMP: 25 EST: 1923
SQ FT: 24,040
SALES (est): 8.2MM **Privately Held**
WEB: www.diamondchemical.com
SIC: **5087** 5113 5169 7359 Janitors' supplies; paper & products, wrapping or coarse; industrial chemicals; equipment rental & leasing

(G-10140)
DIAMOND MATERIALS LLC
242 N James St Ste 102 (19804-3183)
PHONE..................302 658-6524
Jason Norman, *QC Mgr*
Christy Mahan, *Asst Controller*
Joshua Crane, *Manager*
Todd Lester, *Manager*
Chris Vogel, *Manager*
EMP: 100
SALES (est): 38.3MM **Privately Held**
WEB: www.diamondmaterials.com
SIC: **2951** Paving mixtures

(G-10141)
DIAMOND PEST CONTROL
6 Weldin Park Dr (19803-4708)
PHONE..................302 654-2300
Frank Krzanowski, *Owner*
EMP: 6
SALES (est): 494.8K **Privately Held**
WEB: www.dpca.net
SIC: **7342** Pest control in structures; pest control services

(G-10142)
DIAMOND STATE DOOR
2107 Othoson Ave (19804-4840)
PHONE..................302 743-4667
Chuck Bradford, *Owner*
EMP: 4
SALES (est): 234.3K **Privately Held**
SIC: **1751** 7389 Garage door, installation or erection;

(G-10143)
DIAMOND STATE EXPRESS LLC
1610 E Newport Pike Spc 5 (19804-2529)
PHONE..................302 563-3514
EMP: 4
SALES (est): 193.4K **Privately Held**
SIC: **4212** Local trucking, without storage

(G-10144)
DIAMOND STATE PORT CORPORATION
Also Called: Port of Wilmington
1 Hausel Rd Lbby (19801-5882)
PHONE..................302 472-7678
David Krygier, *Project Engr*
Victor Farkas, *Controller*
Sylvia Floyd-Kennard, *Human Res Dir*
Jerry Custis, *Security Mgr*
Bill Stansbury, *Manager*
EMP: 55
SALES (est): 9.2MM **Privately Held**
SIC: **4491** Waterfront terminal operation

(G-10145)
DIAMOND STATE PROMOTIONS
5231 W Woodmill Dr (19808-4068)
PHONE..................302 999-1900
Louis Nicastro, *Owner*
EMP: 5
SALES (est): 817.3K **Privately Held**
SIC: **7311** Advertising agencies

(G-10146)
DIAMOND STATE PTY RENTL & SLS
53 Germay Dr (19804-1104)
PHONE..................302 777-6677
Mary Beth Jones, *President*
Susanne Jones, *Vice Pres*
Anne Cecilia Jones, *Treasurer*
EMP: 25
SQ FT: 18,000
SALES (est): 2.4MM **Privately Held**
SIC: **7359** 5812 Party supplies rental services; dishes, silverware, tables & banquet accessories rental; eating places

(G-10147)
DIAMOND STATE RECYCLING CORP
1600 Bowers St (19802-4699)
P.O. Box 9798 (19809-0798)
PHONE..................302 655-1501
Scott Sherr, *CEO*
EMP: 22
SQ FT: 22,000
SALES (est): 6.9MM **Privately Held**
SIC: **5093** 4953 3341 Metal scrap & waste materials; recycling, waste materials; secondary nonferrous metals

(G-10148)
DIAMOND STATE TELE COML UN
Also Called: LOCAL 13100 CWA
1819 Newport Rd Ste A (19808-6039)
PHONE..................302 999-1100
Diana Markowski, *President*
Patrice Swift, *Vice Pres*
Debrah Wright, *Treasurer*
Rosemary Delong, *Admin Sec*
EMP: 11
SALES: 54K **Privately Held**
SIC: **8631** Labor union

(G-10149)
DIAMOND TECHNOLOGIES INC
221 W 9th St 200 (19801-1619)
PHONE..................302 421-8252
Gregory L Ballance, *President*
Jason Ballance, *Director*
EMP: 45
SQ FT: 10,000
SALES (est): 5.3MM **Privately Held**
WEB: www.diamondtechnologies.com
SIC: **7379** Computer related consulting services

(G-10150)
DICK BROADBENT INSURANCE
715 Greenbank Rd (19808-3167)
P.O. Box 5284 (19808-0284)
PHONE..................302 998-0137
Dick Broadbent, *President*
Charles Wallace, *Manager*
EMP: 4
SALES (est): 448K **Privately Held**
SIC: **6411** Insurance agents, brokers & service

(G-10151)
DIGITAL BROADCAST CORPORATION
2207 Concord Pike 619 (19803-2908)
PHONE..................215 285-0912
EMP: 10
SQ FT: 2,500
SALES (est): 381.5K **Privately Held**
SIC: **7389** Music & broadcasting services

(G-10152)
DIGITAL INK SCIENCES LLC
3 Germay Dr Ste 4 (19804-1127)
PHONE..................951 757-0027
Scott Colman, *Mng Member*
Grant French,
EMP: 3
SQ FT: 2,500
SALES: 1MM **Privately Held**
SIC: **2893** Printing ink

(G-10153)
DIGITAL TECHNOLOGY
1201 N Orange St Ste 71 (19801-1155)
PHONE..................416 829-8400
Zameer Mulla, *CEO*
EMP: 10
SALES (est): 215.9K **Privately Held**
SIC: **7379** Computer related services

(G-10154)
DILIGENT DETAIL
2203 Mitch Rd (19804-3917)
PHONE..................302 482-2836
Doug Breakiron, *Owner*
EMP: 2
SALES (est): 167.5K **Privately Held**
SIC: **2842** Automobile polish

(G-10155)
DIMA II INC
2400 W 4th St (19805-3306)
PHONE..................302 427-0787
Milt Misogianes, *President*
Josh Thomas-Acker, *Exec Dir*
Doug McGregor, *Director*
Caroline Molter, *Director*
Simon Shute, *Director*
EMP: 7
SALES: 64K **Privately Held**
SIC: **8093** Mental health clinic, outpatient

(G-10156)
DIMENSIONAL INSIGHT INC
501 Silverside Rd Ste 2 (19809-1375)
PHONE..................302 791-0687
Jon Bumbaugh, *Manager*
EMP: 2
SALES (corp-wide): 18.2MM **Privately Held**
WEB: www.dimins.com
SIC: **7372** Prepackaged software
PA: Dimensional Insight Incorporated
60 Mall Rd Ste 210
Burlington MA 01803
781 229-9111

(G-10157)
DIOCESAN COUNCIL INC
Also Called: St David's Episcopal Day Sch
2320 Grubb Rd (19810-2702)
PHONE..................302 475-4688
Janet Leishman, *Director*
EMP: 20
SALES (corp-wide): 3.7MM **Privately Held**
WEB: www.stdavidsde.org
SIC: **8661** 8351 Episcopal Church; child day care services
PA: The Council Diocesan Inc
913 Wilson Rd
Wilmington DE

(G-10158)
DIOCESE OF WILMINGTON
Also Called: Resurrection Parish
3000 Videre Dr (19808-3647)
PHONE..................302 368-0146
Bill Graney, *Principal*
Annabelle Capritta, *Branch Mgr*
EMP: 28
SALES (corp-wide): 26.1MM **Privately Held**
SIC: **8661** 8099 Catholic Church; medical services organization
HQ: Diocese Of Wilmington
809 S Broom St
Wilmington DE 19805

(G-10159)
DIPNA INC
Also Called: Days Inn Wilmington
5209 Concord Pike (19803-1416)
PHONE..................302 478-0300
Dipak Shah, *President*
Pierson Carter, *Manager*
Pragna Shah, *Admin Sec*
EMP: 26
SQ FT: 35,000
SALES (est): 2.2MM **Privately Held**
SIC: **7011** Hotels & motels

(G-10160)
DIRECT CREMATION SERVICES DEL
1900 Delaware Ave (19806-2302)
PHONE..................302 656-6873
William Doherty, *President*
EMP: 10
SALES (est): 160.9K **Privately Held**
SIC: **7261** Funeral director

(G-10161)
DIRECT MOBILE TRANSIT INC
2110 Duncan Rd 3 (19808-4602)
PHONE..................302 218-5106
Michael Dana Bantum, *President*
EMP: 11
SALES (est): 139.6K **Privately Held**
SIC: **4111** Local & suburban transit

Wilmington - New Castle County (G-10191)

(G-10162)
DIS DAYCARE
1725 W 7th St (19805-3168)
PHONE..................302 888-0350
Diane R Fitzgerald, *Principal*
EMP: 11
SALES (est): 295.4K **Privately Held**
SIC: 8351 Group day care center

(G-10163)
DIS MANAGEMENT
713 Greenbank Rd (19808-3167)
PHONE..................302 543-4481
Brent Applebaum, *Principal*
EMP: 5
SALES (est): 468.2K **Privately Held**
SIC: 8741 Business management

(G-10164)
DISABATINO CONSTRUCTION CO
1 S Cleveland Ave (19805-1400)
PHONE..................302 652-3838
Lawrence J Disabatino, *President*
Kevin Disabatino, *Business Mgr*
Steve Cael, *Vice Pres*
Michael Di Sabatino, *Vice Pres*
Jeffrey Disabatino, *Project Mgr*
EMP: 250
SQ FT: 11,000
SALES (est): 42.3MM **Privately Held**
WEB: www.disabatino.com
SIC: 1542 1541 1522 1521 Commercial & office building, new construction; industrial buildings & warehouses; residential construction; single-family housing construction

(G-10165)
DISABATINO ENTERPRISES LLC
1 S Cleveland Ave (19805-1400)
PHONE..................302 652-3838
Lawrence Disabatino, *Mng Member*
EMP: 75
SALES (est): 1.8MM **Privately Held**
SIC: 1611 General contractor, highway & street construction

(G-10166)
DISABATINO LANDSCAPING INC
471 B And O Ln (19804-1450)
PHONE..................302 764-0408
Chris Disabatino, *CEO*
Jessica Doran, *Office Mgr*
Ivan Mazur, *Consultant*
Tessa Marks, *Executive*
EMP: 100
SALES: 6MM **Privately Held**
SIC: 0781 Landscape services

(G-10167)
DISABATINO LDSCPG TREE SVC INC
471 B And O Ln (19804-1450)
PHONE..................302 764-0408
Christopher Disabatino, *President*
Thomas W Wiechecki, *Vice Pres*
EMP: 10
SQ FT: 4,000
SALES (est): 1.7MM **Privately Held**
WEB: www.disabatinoinc.com
SIC: 0781 Landscape services

(G-10168)
DISTRIBUTION MARKETING OF DEL
818 S Heald St Ste A (19801-5790)
PHONE..................302 658-6397
Robert Rebock, *President*
Herb Stant, *Corp Secy*
Stanley Budner, *Shareholder*
EMP: 6
SALES (est): 810K **Privately Held**
SIC: 5192 Newspapers

(G-10169)
DIVERSIFIED CHEMICAL PDTS INC
60 Germay Dr (19804-1105)
PHONE..................302 656-5293
James Longo Jr, *President*
David Longo, *Vice Pres*
Doug Carroccia, *QC Mgr*
EMP: 9
SQ FT: 4,000
SALES (est): 1MM **Privately Held**
WEB: www.diversifiedchemical.com
SIC: 8731 2899 Commercial research laboratory; chemical preparations

(G-10170)
DIVERSIFIED FINANCIAL CONS
2200 Concord Pike 104 (19803-2909)
PHONE..................302 765-3500
Frank M Levy, *Owner*
Stephanie Levy, *Opers Staff*
David Levy, *Advisor*
EMP: 4
SALES (est): 585.4K **Privately Held**
WEB: www.dfc-de.com
SIC: 6282 8721 Investment advisory service; accounting, auditing & bookkeeping

(G-10171)
DIVERSIFIED LIGHTING ASSOC INC
5466 Fairmont Dr (19808-3432)
PHONE..................302 286-6370
Bob Minutella, *Principal*
EMP: 6
SALES (corp-wide): 18.4MM **Privately Held**
WEB: www.diversifiedlighting.com
SIC: 5063 Lighting fixtures
PA: Diversified Lighting Associates, Inc.
1 Ivybrook Blvd Ste 100
Warminster PA 18974
215 442-0700

(G-10172)
DJONT/JPM WILMINGTON LSG LLC
Also Called: Doubltree By Hilton Wilmington
4727 Concord Pike (19803-1408)
PHONE..................302 478-6000
Evelyn Montalvo, *General Mgr*
EMP: 100
SALES (est): 2.9MM **Privately Held**
WEB: www.doubletreewilmington.com
SIC: 7011 5812 Hotels & motels; eating places
PA: The Buccini/Pollin Group Inc
1000 N West St Ste 1000 # 1000
Wilmington DE 19801

(G-10173)
DKMRBH INC
704 N King St Ste 500 (19801-3584)
PHONE..................302 250-4428
Akhilesh Kandhari, *President*
EMP: 12
SALES (est): 810K **Privately Held**
SIC: 7361 Employment agencies

(G-10174)
DLA PIPER LLP (US)
919 N Market St (19801-3023)
PHONE..................302 654-3025
Lee I Miller, *Branch Mgr*
Kaitlin McKenzie, *Associate*
EMP: 300 **Privately Held**
SIC: 8111 Corporate, partnership & business law
HQ: Dla Piper Llp (Us)
6225 Smith Ave Ste 200
Baltimore MD 21209
410 580-3000

(G-10175)
DLS DISCOVERY
824 N Market St (19801-3024)
PHONE..................302 654-3345
Reese Hitchens, *Principal*
EMP: 1
SALES (est): 226.5K **Privately Held**
SIC: 3823 Digital displays of process variables

(G-10176)
DLS DISCOVERY LLC
Also Called: Digital Legal
1007 N Orange St Ste 510 (19801-1248)
PHONE..................302 888-2060
James Luckey, *Accounts Mgr*
Reese Hitchens, *Consultant*
Rebecca Simeone, *Executive*
Bruce Duff,
Edward Carp,
▲ **EMP:** 55
SALES (est): 4.4MM **Privately Held**
SIC: 7389 Document embossing

(G-10177)
DMD BUSINESS FORMS & PRTG CO
204 S Maryland Ave (19804-1344)
PHONE..................302 998-8200
Kathy A Doyle, *President*
Dave Doyle, *Treasurer*
Colleen Doyle, *Sales Staff*
EMP: 4
SQ FT: 800
SALES: 350K **Privately Held**
SIC: 2752 Commercial printing, offset

(G-10178)
DND LIMOUSINE SERVICE
104c S John St (19804-3109)
PHONE..................302 998-5856
Dan Merry, *President*
EMP: 30
SALES (est): 1.1MM **Privately Held**
SIC: 4119 Limousine rental, with driver

(G-10179)
DO IT WISER LLC (PA)
3422 Old Capitol Trl (19808-6124)
PHONE..................800 816-0944
Alejandro Lopez, *Mng Member*
EMP: 1
SALES (est): 282.4K **Privately Held**
SIC: 2893 Printing ink

(G-10180)
DOE LEGAL LLC
1200 Philadelphia Pike # 1 (19809-2040)
PHONE..................302 798-7500
Thomas J Russo, *President*
John C Russo, *President*
Joe Timlin, *CFO*
Robert Bachmann, *Accounts Exec*
Jack M Sheekey, *Accounts Exec*
EMP: 45 **EST:** 1971
SQ FT: 10,000
SALES (est): 3.5MM **Privately Held**
WEB: www.doetech.com
SIC: 5045 Computers, peripherals & software

(G-10181)
DOE TECHNOLOGIES INC
Also Called: DOE Legal
1200 Philadelphia Pike # 1 (19809-2040)
PHONE..................302 792-1285
Joe Timlin, *CEO*
Thomas J Russo, *President*
Jim Beck, *Senior VP*
John Russo, *Vice Pres*
Scott Miller, *Mktg Dir*
EMP: 42
SQ FT: 30,000
SALES (est): 6.6MM **Privately Held**
SIC: 7371 7389 Computer software development; software programming applications; recording studio, noncommercial records

(G-10182)
DOG DAYZ DOG DAY CARE CENTER
3000 W 2nd St (19805-1744)
PHONE..................302 655-5506
Michelle Latham, *Owner*
EMP: 4
SALES: 100K **Privately Held**
SIC: 8351 Child day care services

(G-10183)
DOHERTY & ASSOCIATES INC
5301 Limestone Rd Ste 100 (19808-1251)
PHONE..................302 239-3500
Debbie Doherty, *President*
EMP: 15
SALES (est): 1MM **Privately Held**
SIC: 8721 Billing & bookkeeping service

(G-10184)
DOHERY FUNERAL HOMES INC
3200 Limestone Rd (19808-2199)
PHONE..................302 999-8277
James Mullin, *President*
Jim Mullin, *General Mgr*
Bill Doherty III, *Vice Pres*
Chris Gillis, *Director*
Michele G Linder, *Director*
EMP: 12
SALES (est): 484.8K **Privately Held**
SIC: 7261 Funeral director; funeral home

(G-10185)
DOJUPA LLC
Also Called: Dxl
5586 Kirkwood Hwy (19808-5002)
PHONE..................302 300-2009
Jean Paul Libert, *CEO*
Emmanuel Galichon, *CFO*
EMP: 5
SALES (est): 470K **Privately Held**
WEB: www.dxlus.com
SIC: 8742 Marketing consulting services

(G-10186)
DOLE FOOD COMPANY INC
Port Of Wilmington Lbr Rd (19899)
PHONE..................302 652-6060
Juan Soto, *Warehouse Mgr*
Sean Clancy, *Manager*
EMP: 20
SQ FT: 200
SALES (corp-wide): 1.1B **Privately Held**
WEB: www.dole.com
SIC: 0161 Vegetables & melons
PA: Dole Food Company, Inc.
1 Dole Dr
Westlake Village CA 91362
818 874-4000

(G-10187)
DOLE FRESH FRUIT COMPANY
70 Gist Rd (19801-5880)
PHONE..................302 652-6484
Sean Clancy, *Terminal Mgr*
EMP: 97
SALES (corp-wide): 1.1B **Privately Held**
SIC: 5148 Fruits, fresh; banana ripening
HQ: Dole Fresh Fruit Company
1 Dole Dr
Westlake Village CA 91362
818 874-4000

(G-10188)
DOLE FRESH FRUIT COMPANY
1 Hausel Rd (19801-5800)
PHONE..................302 652-2215
Joseph Dakey, *Branch Mgr*
EMP: 10
SALES (corp-wide): 1.1B **Privately Held**
SIC: 5148 Fruits, fresh
HQ: Dole Fresh Fruit Company
1 Dole Dr
Westlake Village CA 91362
818 874-4000

(G-10189)
DOMENIC DI DONATO PLBG HTG INC
128 Shrewsbury Dr (19810-1410)
PHONE..................856 207-4919
Domenic Didonato, *President*
EMP: 8
SALES (est): 1MM **Privately Held**
SIC: 1711 Plumbing contractors

(G-10190)
DOMINIC A DI FEBO & SONS
812 Rose St (19805-2818)
PHONE..................302 425-5054
Dominic A Di Febo, *President*
Joseph Di Febo, *Vice Pres*
John Di Febo, *Treasurer*
Angela Crowl, *Admin Sec*
EMP: 15 **EST:** 1936
SALES: 900K **Privately Held**
WEB: www.difebohardwoodfloors.com
SIC: 1752 Wood floor installation & refinishing

(G-10191)
DOMINIC GIOFFRE DDS PA
4901 Limestone Rd Ste 1 (19808-1271)
PHONE..................302 239-0410
Dominic Gioffre DDS, *President*
EMP: 15
SALES (est): 592.9K **Privately Held**
SIC: 8021 Dentists' office

Wilmington - New Castle County (G-10192)

GEOGRAPHIC SECTION

(G-10192)
DON D CORP
1615 E Ayre St (19804-2514)
PHONE.................302 994-5793
Don Deaven, *President*
Lori Deaven, *Admin Sec*
EMP: 25
SQ FT: 2,000
SALES (est): 1.5MM **Privately Held**
SIC: 7353 Cranes & aerial lift equipment, rental or leasing

(G-10193)
DON ROGERS INC (PA)
242 N James St Ste 102 (19804-3183)
PHONE.................302 658-6524
Don Rogers, *Principal*
Dennis Robinson, *Principal*
EMP: 22 **EST:** 1953
SQ FT: 10,000
SALES (est): 2.7MM **Privately Held**
WEB: www.donrogersinc.com
SIC: 1611 1794 Highway & street paving contractor; excavation & grading, building construction

(G-10194)
DONALD A GIRARD MD
2601 Annand Dr Ste 19 (19808-3719)
PHONE.................302 633-5755
Donald Girard, *Owner*
EMP: 7
SALES (est): 348.1K **Privately Held**
SIC: 8011 Gastronomist

(G-10195)
DONALD EICHHOLZ
Also Called: Eichholz Services
210 Cordon Rd (19803-5315)
PHONE.................302 792-1236
Donald A Eichholz, *Owner*
EMP: 4
SALES (est): 290.4K **Privately Held**
WEB: www.eichholzservices.com
SIC: 1731 1711 General electrical contractor; warm air heating & air conditioning contractor

(G-10196)
DONALD F DEAVEN INC
1615 E Ayre St (19804-2514)
PHONE.................302 994-5793
Donald D Deaven, *President*
Lori Deaven, *Treasurer*
Lisa Deaven, *Admin Sec*
EMP: 22
SQ FT: 2,000
SALES (est): 5MM **Privately Held**
SIC: 3441 1791 3446 Fabricated structural metal; structural steel erection; ornamental metalwork

(G-10197)
DONALDSON ELECTRIC
124 Middleboro Rd (19804-1660)
PHONE.................302 660-7534
Kim Donaldson, *President*
Michael Donaldson, *Vice Pres*
EMP: 8 **EST:** 2013
SALES (est): 853.6K **Privately Held**
SIC: 1731 General electrical contractor

(G-10198)
DONGJIN USA INC
Also Called: Big Centric
175 Edgemoor Rd (19809-9002)
PHONE.................302 691-8510
Jay Rehee, *President*
Stephan Rhee, *President*
EMP: 11
SALES (est): 1.2MM **Privately Held**
SIC: 3089 Coloring & finishing of plastic products

(G-10199)
DONNER CORPORATION
919 N Market St Ste 601 (19801-3043)
PHONE.................302 778-0844
Christopher Bell, *President*
Christine Welch, *President*
EMP: 1
SALES (est): 96.5K **Privately Held**
SIC: 2297 Nonwoven fabrics

(G-10200)
DONR LLC
251 Little Falls Dr (19808-1674)
PHONE.................857 400-8679
William Zeb Couch,
EMP: 2
SQ FT: 990
SALES (est): 56.5K **Privately Held**
SIC: 7372 Business oriented computer software

(G-10201)
DOOR OF SECOND CHANCES INC
604 W 32nd St (19802-2633)
PHONE.................302 898-3959
EMP: 20
SALES (est): 770K **Privately Held**
SIC: 8322 Individual/Family Services

(G-10202)
DORILYN ENGLISH PHD
18c Trolley Sq (19806-3355)
PHONE.................302 655-6506
Dorilyn English, *Executive*
EMP: 7 **EST:** 2017
SALES (est): 109.3K **Privately Held**
SIC: 8049 Offices of health practitioner

(G-10203)
DORINDA F DOVE
1508 W 7th St (19805-3110)
PHONE.................302 658-2229
Dorinda Dove, *Executive*
EMP: 7 **EST:** 2017
SALES (est): 64.5K **Privately Held**
SIC: 8049 Offices of health practitioner

(G-10204)
DOROSHOW PASQUALE KARWITZ SIEG (PA)
Also Called: Doroshow Pasquale Law Offices
1202 Kirkwood Hwy (19805-2120)
PHONE.................302 998-2397
Robert Pasquale, *Partner*
Shaku Bhaya, *Partner*
Eric M Doroshow, *Partner*
Arthur Krawitz, *Partner*
Arthur M Krawitz,
EMP: 45 **EST:** 1977
SQ FT: 1,500
SALES (est): 10.6MM **Privately Held**
SIC: 8111 General practice attorney, lawyer

(G-10205)
DOROSHOW PASQUALE KARWITZ SIEG
1208 Kirkwood Hwy (19805-2120)
PHONE.................302 998-0100
Jacqueline Lammeree, *Principal*
Kristine Wallace, *Manager*
Wendy Lang, *Executive*
EMP: 19
SALES (corp-wide): 10.6MM **Privately Held**
SIC: 8111 Bankruptcy law
PA: Doroshow Pasquale Krawitz Siegel Bhaya
1202 Kirkwood Hwy
Wilmington DE 19805
302 998-2397

(G-10206)
DORSEY AND WHITNEY DEL LLP
300 Delaware Ave Ste 1010 (19801-1671)
PHONE.................302 425-7171
William Lasher, *Managing Prtnr*
Eric Schnabel, *Managing Prtnr*
EMP: 5
SALES (est): 268.7K **Privately Held**
SIC: 8111 General practice attorney, lawyer

(G-10207)
DORSIA ALLIANCE LTD
Also Called: Spacetime Engineering
717 N Union St Ste 125 (19805-3031)
PHONE.................302 492-5052
Hans Spieleder, *President*
Tom Funk, *Vice Pres*
Robert Hoferer, *Vice Pres*
Ruben Baltazar, *Manager*
EMP: 3 **EST:** 2013
SALES (est): 241.8K **Privately Held**
SIC: 3663 Satellites, communications

(G-10208)
DOT POP INC
Also Called: Sign and Graphics
1010 N Union St Ste D (19805-2731)
PHONE.................302 691-3160
Dan Nestor, *Principal*
EMP: 5
SALES (est): 377.1K **Privately Held**
SIC: 3993 Electric signs

(G-10209)
DOUBLEUDIAMOND LLC
1209 N Orange St (19801-1120)
PHONE.................206 502-0144
Kyle Kim, *CEO*
Michael Murawski, *Finance*
EMP: 4
SALES (est): 46.4K **Privately Held**
SIC: 7999 Card & game services

(G-10210)
DOUBLTREE HTELS SUITES RESORTS
4727 Concord Pike (19803-1408)
PHONE.................302 478-6000
Terry Augusta, *General Mgr*
EMP: 29 **EST:** 2009
SALES (est): 1.7MM **Privately Held**
SIC: 7011 5812 Hotels & motels; eating places

(G-10211)
DOUG GREEN WOODWORKING
330 N Maryland Ave (19804-1302)
PHONE.................302 652-6522
Douglas G Green, *Owner*
EMP: 3
SALES (est): 319.5K **Privately Held**
SIC: 2431 Millwork

(G-10212)
DOUGHERTY DENTAL SOLUTIONS LLC
1805 Foulk Rd (19810-3700)
PHONE.................302 475-3270
EMP: 4
SALES (est): 61.5K **Privately Held**
SIC: 8021 Offices & clinics of dentists

(G-10213)
DOUGLAS MORROW
Also Called: Emergency Medical Mgmnt
211 Beau Tree Dr Ste 100 (19810-1177)
PHONE.................302 750-9161
Douglas Morrow, *Principal*
EMP: 5
SALES (est): 148.9K **Privately Held**
SIC: 8099 Health & allied services

(G-10214)
DOUGLAS R JOHNSTON M D
1600 Rockland Rd (19803-3607)
PHONE.................302 651-4000
Douglas Johnston, *Manager*
EMP: 5
SALES (est): 85.3K **Privately Held**
SIC: 8011 Offices & clinics of medical doctors

(G-10215)
DOYJUL APARTMENTS
Also Called: Doyjul Center
3403 Lancaster Pike (19805-5533)
PHONE.................302 998-0088
Harry A Simeone, *Owner*
EMP: 10
SALES (est): 742.2K **Privately Held**
SIC: 6513 6512 Apartment building operators; shopping center, property operation only

(G-10216)
DOZR LTD
3411 Silverside Rd (19810-4812)
PHONE.................844 218-3697
Kevin Forestell, *CEO*
EMP: 27 **EST:** 2016
SALES (est): 633.7K **Privately Held**
SIC: 7353 Heavy construction equipment rental

(G-10217)
DP FIRE & SAFETY INC
411 Orinda Dr (19804-1113)
PHONE.................302 998-5430
Deborah C Pruitt, *President*
David Pruitt, *Admin Sec*
Vicki Loney, *Admin Asst*
EMP: 10
SALES (est): 900K **Privately Held**
WEB: www.dpfire.com
SIC: 5999 3699 Fire extinguishers; safety supplies & equipment; fire control or bombing equipment, electronic

(G-10218)
DR AZARCON & ASSOC
3411 Silverside Rd 107r (19810-4812)
PHONE.................302 478-2969
Constantine Azarcon, *Principal*
EMP: 5
SALES (est): 419.9K **Privately Held**
SIC: 8011 Physicians' office, including specialists

(G-10219)
DR CLYDE A MAXWELL JR
Also Called: Thesmilezone.com
4201 Miller Rd (19802-1914)
PHONE.................302 765-3373
Clyde A Maxwell, *Principal*
Kathy Wilson, *Manager*
EMP: 5
SALES (est): 485.3K **Privately Held**
SIC: 8021 Dentists' office

(G-10220)
DR DUNNER USA INC
103 Foulk Rd (19803-3742)
PHONE.................302 656-1950
Robert Bastong, *Vice Pres*
EMP: 1 **EST:** 2017
SALES (est): 39.5K **Privately Held**
SIC: 2099 Food preparations

(G-10221)
DR FANNY BERG P C
Also Called: Berg, Fanny J MD
2000 Foulk Rd Ste A (19810-3642)
PHONE.................302 475-8000
Fanny Berg MD, *Principal*
Patti F Walters, *Office Mgr*
EMP: 4
SALES (est): 501.3K **Privately Held**
SIC: 8011 Dermatologist

(G-10222)
DR FAY MINTZ-GUTTIN DMD
623 Kilburn Rd (19803-1721)
PHONE.................302 356-0392
EMP: 4 **EST:** 2011
SALES (est): 116.7K **Privately Held**
SIC: 8021 Dentist's Office

(G-10223)
DR HOWARD GILES - WILMINGTON
1415 Foulk Rd Ste 200 (19803-2748)
PHONE.................302 477-4900
EMP: 7
SALES (est): 93K **Privately Held**
SIC: 8021 Dentists' office

(G-10224)
DR JASON PARKER DO
1600 Rockland Rd (19803-3607)
PHONE.................302 651-5874
Jason Parker, *Principal*
EMP: 4 **EST:** 2011
SALES (est): 96.7K **Privately Held**
SIC: 8031 Offices & clinics of osteopathic physicians

(G-10225)
DR JEFFREY E FELZER DMD PC
3105 Limestone Rd Ste 203 (19808-2151)
PHONE.................302 995-6979
Jeffrey Felzer, *Principal*
EMP: 5 **EST:** 2011
SALES (est): 296.2K **Privately Held**
SIC: 8021 Offices & clinics of dentists

(G-10226)
DR JILLIAN G STEVENS DO
812 Bezel Rd (19803-4824)
PHONE.................302 762-7332

Jillian G Stevens, *Principal*
EMP: 4 **EST:** 2011
SALES (est): 80.1K **Privately Held**
SIC: 8031 Offices & clinics of osteopathic physicians

(G-10227)
DR MEHDI BALAKHANI
2319 Pennsylvania Ave (19806-1318)
PHONE..................302 368-8900
Dr Mehdi Balakhani, *Owner*
EMP: 4
SALES (est): 116.8K **Privately Held**
SIC: 8011 Plastic surgeon

(G-10228)
DR ROBERT M COLLINS
5500 Skyline Dr Ste 3 (19808-1772)
PHONE..................302 239-3655
Robert M Collins, *Principal*
EMP: 7
SALES (est): 353.3K **Privately Held**
SIC: 8021 Dentists' office

(G-10229)
DR SHEFALI PANDYA
707 Foulk Rd (19803-3737)
PHONE..................302 421-9960
Shefali Pandya, *Principal*
EMP: 6 **EST:** 2010
SALES (est): 295.7K **Privately Held**
SIC: 8021 Offices & clinics of dentists

(G-10230)
DRAGON CLOUD INC
1 Commerce St (19801)
PHONE..................702 508-2676
Srinu Gedela, *Director*
EMP: 1200
SALES (est): 15.8MM **Privately Held**
SIC: 2731 Books: publishing & printing

(G-10231)
DRASS INSURANCE AGENCY INC
205 N James St (19804-3155)
PHONE..................302 998-1331
Louis M Leoni Jr, *President*
Laurie Denfee, *Vice Pres*
Martha Drass, *Treasurer*
EMP: 4
SQ FT: 2,400
SALES: 4.4MM **Privately Held**
WEB: www.drassinsurance.com
SIC: 6411 Insurance agents

(G-10232)
DREAM WEAVER LLC
1521 Concord Pike Ste 301 (19803-3644)
PHONE..................302 352-9473
Trinanjan Gupta, *Mng Member*
Manish Gupta, *Manager*
EMP: 7 **EST:** 2012
SALES (est): 359K **Privately Held**
SIC: 7371 7372 Custom computer programming services; business oriented computer software

(G-10233)
DREAM WEAVERS EMBROIDERY
8 Whitehall Cir (19808-5626)
PHONE..................302 998-4264
Kevin Keating, *Owner*
EMP: 1
SALES (est): 44K **Privately Held**
SIC: 2395 Embroidery & art needlework

(G-10234)
DRG HOLDCO INC
2711 Centerville Rd (19808-1660)
PHONE..................610 974-9760
Jonathan M Sandler, *President*
EMP: 1
SALES (est): 47.2K **Privately Held**
SIC: 2834 Drugs acting on the central nervous system & sense organs
HQ: Piramal Critical Care, Inc.
3950 Schelden Cir
Bethlehem PA 18017
800 414-1901

(G-10235)
DRIFTWOOD HOSPITALITY MGT LLC
Also Called: Double Tree By Hilton
700 N King St (19801-3504)
PHONE..................302 655-0400
Alan Filer, *Principal*
EMP: 100
SALES (est): 2.5MM
SALES (corp-wide): 232.9MM **Privately Held**
SIC: 7011 Hotels & motels
PA: Driftwood Hospitality Management Llc
11770 Us Highway 1 # 202
North Palm Beach FL 33408
561 207-2700

(G-10236)
DRINKER BIDDLE & REATH LLP
222 Delaware Ave Ste 1400 (19801-1633)
PHONE..................302 467-4200
Willie Martinez, *Facilities Mgr*
Beth Coyder, *Branch Mgr*
Brian McCauley, *Director*
Yodi Hailemariam, *Associate*
EMP: 10
SALES (corp-wide): 235.9MM **Privately Held**
WEB: www.drinkerbiddle.com
SIC: 8111 General practice law office
PA: Drinker, Biddle & Reath Llp
1 Logan Sq Ste 2000
Philadelphia PA 19103
215 988-2700

(G-10237)
DROP TABLE LLC
Also Called: Clickloot
Trolley Sq Ste 20c (19806)
PHONE..................650 669-8753
Andrei Boghiu, *Mng Member*
Andrei Diaconu,
Bogdan Popa,
EMP: 4
SALES: 500K **Privately Held**
SIC: 7371 Computer software development & applications

(G-10238)
DT INVESTMENT PARTNERS LLC
1013 Centre Rd (19805-1265)
PHONE..................302 442-6203
Jonathan Smith, *Branch Mgr*
EMP: 4 **Privately Held**
SIC: 6799 Investors
PA: Dt Investment Partners Llc
1 Dickinson Dr Ste 103
Chadds Ford PA 19317

(G-10239)
DTG GENERAL CONTRACTOR
220 East Ct (19810-2529)
PHONE..................321 439-0893
Alex Ocasio, *Partner*
Felix Amparo, *Partner*
Uriel Peres, *Partner*
Angel Santana, *Partner*
EMP: 4
SALES (est): 118.3K **Privately Held**
SIC: 8611 Contractors' association

(G-10240)
DU PONT LYNNE M MD
910 Foulk Rd (19803-3158)
PHONE..................302 777-7966
Margaret L Dupont, *Principal*
James Ritter, *Executive*
EMP: 5
SALES (est): 149.9K **Privately Held**
SIC: 8011 Physicians' office, including specialists

(G-10241)
DU PONT CHEM ENRGY OPRTONS INC (DH)
Also Called: Dupont
974 Centre Rd (19805-1269)
PHONE..................302 774-1000
Charles Holiday, *CEO*
Kraig Struglia, *Top Exec*
Lori Knauer, *Counsel*
Linda West, *Vice Pres*
Edgar Woolard, *Vice Pres*
▼ **EMP:** 5
SALES (est): 10.2MM
SALES (corp-wide): 30.6B **Publicly Held**
SIC: 2819 3482 Industrial inorganic chemicals; small arms ammunition
HQ: E. I. Du Pont De Nemours And Company
974 Centre Rd Bldg 735
Wilmington DE 19805
302 485-3000

(G-10242)
DU PONT DELAWARE INC (DH)
Also Called: Dupont
974 Centre Rd Chestnut (19805)
P.O. Box 2915 (19805-0915)
PHONE..................302 774-1000
Ellen Kullman, *Ch of Bd*
Chad Holliday, *Ch of Bd*
Doug Muzyka, *Vice Pres*
Jeffrey Chen, *Research*
Eydie Triplett, *Research*
EMP: 4
SALES (est): 2.8MM
SALES (corp-wide): 30.6B **Publicly Held**
SIC: 8999 Actuarial consultant
HQ: E. I. Du Pont De Nemours And Company
974 Centre Rd Bldg 735
Wilmington DE 19805
302 485-3000

(G-10243)
DU PONT ELASTOMERS LP
974 Centre Rd (19805-1269)
PHONE..................302 774-1000
Charles Holliday, *President*
Kathy Rees, *Business Mgr*
Andreas Krueger, *Counsel*
Peter Mester, *Counsel*
Ryan Bedgood, *Vice Pres*
EMP: 100
SALES (est): 17.5MM
SALES (corp-wide): 30.6B **Publicly Held**
SIC: 5171 Petroleum bulk stations & terminals
HQ: E. I. Du Pont De Nemours And Company
974 Centre Rd Bldg 735
Wilmington DE 19805
302 485-3000

(G-10244)
DU PONT FOREIGN SALES CORP
974 Centre Rd (19805-1269)
PHONE..................302 774-1000
Charles Holliday, *CEO*
EMP: 2000
SALES (est): 22.6MM
SALES (corp-wide): 30.6B **Publicly Held**
WEB: www.dupont.com
SIC: 7389 Personal service agents, brokers & bureaus
HQ: E. I. Du Pont De Nemours And Company
974 Centre Rd Bldg 735
Wilmington DE 19805
302 485-3000

(G-10245)
DUFFIELD ASSOCIATES INC (PA)
5400 Limestone Rd (19808-1284)
PHONE..................302 239-6634
Stacy Ziegler, *CEO*
Guy Marcozzi, *President*
Deirdre Smith, *COO*
Scott Hoffman, *Project Mgr*
Jordan Morrison, *Project Mgr*
EMP: 94
SQ FT: 20,000
SALES (est): 26.1MM **Privately Held**
WEB: www.duffnet.com
SIC: 8711 Consulting engineer

(G-10246)
DUGAN DT ROOFING INC
Also Called: Dugan, Dt Roofing Co
20 S Woodward Ave (19805-2355)
PHONE..................302 636-9300
Dan T Dugan, *Owner*
EMP: 6
SQ FT: 3,000
SALES (est): 400K **Privately Held**
WEB: www.commercialroofers.org
SIC: 1521 Single-family home remodeling, additions & repairs

(G-10247)
DUNBAR ARMORED INC
320 Water St Ste A (19804-2434)
PHONE..................302 892-4950
Kris Nonnenmacher, *Manager*
EMP: 42
SALES (corp-wide): 3.4B **Publicly Held**
SIC: 7381 Armored car services
HQ: Dunbar Armored, Inc.
50 Schilling Rd
Hunt Valley MD 21031
410 584-9800

(G-10248)
DUPONT ASIA PACIFIC LIMITED (HQ)
974 Centre Rd (19805-1269)
PHONE..................302 774-1000
Charles O Holliday Jr, *Ch of Bd*
▼ **EMP:** 3
SALES (est): 2.2MM
SALES (corp-wide): 61B **Publicly Held**
SIC: 2879 Agricultural chemicals
PA: Dow Inc.
2211 H H Dow Way
Midland MI 48642
989 636-1000

(G-10249)
DUPONT ATHNTCATION SYSTEMS LLC
4417 Lancaster Pike (19805-1523)
PHONE..................800 345-9999
EMP: 3
SALES (est): 154.9K **Privately Held**
SIC: 2819 Industrial inorganic chemicals

(G-10250)
DUPONT CAPITAL MANAGEMENT CORP
1 Righter Pkwy Ste 3200 (19803-1510)
PHONE..................302 477-6000
Valerie J Sill, *President*
Ming Shao, *Manager*
Erik Zipf, *Manager*
Rick Dumont, *Info Tech Mgr*
EMP: 7
SALES (est): 2MM
SALES (corp-wide): 30.6B **Publicly Held**
WEB: www.dupontcapital.com
SIC: 6722 Money market mutual funds
HQ: E. I. Du Pont De Nemours And Company
974 Centre Rd Bldg 735
Wilmington DE 19805
302 485-3000

(G-10251)
DUPONT DE NEMOURS INC (PA)
974 Centre Rd (19805-1269)
PHONE..................302 774-1000
C Marc Doyle, *CEO*
Edward D Breen, *Ch of Bd*
Gregory R Friedman, *Vice Pres*
Jeanmarie F Desmond, *CFO*
Michael Goss, *Controller*
EMP: 277
SALES: 85.9B **Publicly Held**
SIC: 2821 3081 3086 3674 Thermoplastic materials; thermosetting materials; plasticizer/additive based plastic materials; molding compounds, plastics; plastic film & sheet; plastics foam products; insulation or cushioning material, foamed plastic; solar cells; integrated circuits, semiconductor networks, etc.; nutrition services

(G-10252)
DUPONT DE NEMOURS INC
4250 Lancaster Pike (19805-1520)
PHONE..................302 999-7932
EMP: 6
SALES (corp-wide): 85.9B **Publicly Held**
SIC: 2879 Agricultural chemicals
PA: Dupont De Nemours, Inc.
974 Centre Rd
Wilmington DE 19805
302 774-1000

Wilmington - New Castle County (G-10253)

GEOGRAPHIC SECTION

(G-10253)
DUPONT DISPLAYS INC (DH)
974 Centre Rd (19805-1269)
PHONE.................805 562-9293
Ellen J Kullman, *CEO*
Johns S Richard, *CEO*
Steve Quindlen, *President*
Steve Gallow, *Vice Pres*
Frank Ferro, *Analyst*
EMP: 35
SALES (est): 16.3MM
SALES (corp-wide): 30.6B **Publicly Held**
WEB: www.dupontdisplays.com
SIC: 3674 8731 Light emitting diodes; commercial research laboratory
HQ: E. I. Du Pont De Nemours And Company
974 Centre Rd Bldg 735
Wilmington DE 19805
302 485-3000

(G-10254)
DUPONT ESL SECURITY
200 Powder Mill Rd (19803-2907)
PHONE.................302 695-1657
EMP: 27
SALES (est): 1.1MM **Privately Held**
SIC: 7381 Guard services

(G-10255)
DUPONT FLAMENTS - AMERICAS LLC
974 Centre Rd (19805-1269)
PHONE.................302 774-1000
Russel Brezler, *Senior Engr*
John Locklear, *Mng Member*
▼ **EMP:** 7
SALES (est): 704.5K
SALES (corp-wide): 30.6B **Publicly Held**
WEB: www.dupont.com
SIC: 3991 Brushes, household or industrial; brushes, except paint & varnish
HQ: E. I. Du Pont De Nemours And Company
974 Centre Rd Bldg 735
Wilmington DE 19805
302 485-3000

(G-10256)
DUPONT NORTH AMERICA INC
1007 N Market St (19801-1227)
PHONE.................302 774-1000
Max E Burnham, *President*
John A Mc Ateer, *Treasurer*
Gary Murray, *Accountant*
G F Maccormack, *Director*
David Hellmann, *Admin Sec*
EMP: 300
SQ FT: 8,000
SALES (est): 305.5K
SALES (corp-wide): 30.6B **Publicly Held**
WEB: www.dupont.com
SIC: 4959 Environmental cleanup services
HQ: E. I. Du Pont De Nemours And Company
974 Centre Rd Bldg 735
Wilmington DE 19805
302 485-3000

(G-10257)
DUPONT NUTRITION USA INC
974 Centre Rd (19805-1269)
PHONE.................302 774-1000
Matthias Heinzel, *President*
EMP: 8
SALES (est): 1.1MM
SALES (corp-wide): 30.6B **Publicly Held**
SIC: 2869 Industrial organic chemicals
HQ: Specialty Products N&H, Inc.
200 Powder Mill Rd
Wilmington DE 19803
302 774-1000

(G-10258)
DUPONT PRFMCE COATINGS INC
4417 Lncaster Pike Barley (19805)
PHONE.................302 892-1064
Ellen Kullman, *CEO*
Leslie Love, *Business Mgr*
Shelley Stewart, *Vice Pres*
Susan Powell, *Project Mgr*
Robert Shaul, *Mfg Mgr*
EMP: 1304 **EST:** 1998

SALES (est): 98.4MM **Privately Held**
SIC: 8711 Engineering services

(G-10259)
DUPONT PRFMCE ELASTOMERS LLC (DH)
4417 Lancaster Pike # 72 (19805-1523)
PHONE.................302 774-1000
Diane Gulias, *Mng Member*
◆ **EMP:** 450
SALES (est): 230.6MM
SALES (corp-wide): 30.6B **Publicly Held**
SIC: 2821 Plastics materials & resins
HQ: E. I. Du Pont De Nemours And Company
974 Centre Rd Bldg 735
Wilmington DE 19805
302 485-3000

(G-10260)
DUPONT SPECIALTY PDTS USA LLC (HQ)
974 Centre Rd (19805-1269)
PHONE.................302 774-1000
Edward Breen, *CEO*
EMP: 14
SALES (est): 249.1MM
SALES (corp-wide): 85.9B **Publicly Held**
SIC: 0721 Crop planting & protection
PA: Dupont De Nemours, Inc.
974 Centre Rd
Wilmington DE 19805
302 774-1000

(G-10261)
DUPONT SPECIALTY PDTS USA LLC
Dupont Engrg Polymers Div
974 Centre Rd Chestnu Chestnut Run (19805)
PHONE.................302 774-1000
Michael Gill, *Engineer*
Brandon Nutter, *Engineer*
Toni Butler, *Sales Staff*
Klayton Diorio, *Sales Staff*
Don Brizzolara, *Branch Mgr*
EMP: 50
SALES (corp-wide): 85.9B **Publicly Held**
WEB: www.dupont.com
SIC: 2819 Industrial inorganic chemicals
HQ: Dupont Specialty Products Usa, Llc
974 Centre Rd
Wilmington DE 19805
302 774-1000

(G-10262)
DUPONT SPECIALTY PDTS USA LLC
Rising Sun Ln Rr 141 (19803)
PHONE.................302 695-3295
Armando Byrne, *Technical Mgr*
EMP: 26
SALES (corp-wide): 85.9B **Publicly Held**
WEB: www.dupont.com
SIC: 8731 Commercial physical research
HQ: Dupont Specialty Products Usa, Llc
974 Centre Rd
Wilmington DE 19805
302 774-1000

(G-10263)
DUPONT SPECIALTY PDTS USA LLC
Also Called: Dupont Personal Protection
974 Centre Rd Ches Chestnut Run (19805)
P.O. Box 2915 (19805-0915)
PHONE.................302 774-1000
Jeffrey C Jung, *Branch Mgr*
EMP: 6
SALES (corp-wide): 85.9B **Publicly Held**
WEB: www.dupont.com
SIC: 2297 Nonwoven fabrics
HQ: Dupont Specialty Products Usa, Llc
974 Centre Rd
Wilmington DE 19805
302 774-1000

(G-10264)
DUPONT TATE LYLE BIO PDTS LLC
1007 Market St Fl 2 (19898-1100)
P.O. Box 1039 (19899-1039)
PHONE.................865 408-1962
John D Halberstadt, *President*

Pete Weader, *Officer*
EMP: 2
SALES (est): 15.8K **Privately Held**
SIC: 2869 Polyhydric alcohol esters, aminos, etc.

(G-10265)
DUPONT TXTLES INTRIORS DEL INC (DH)
974 Centre Rd (19805-1269)
PHONE.................302 774-1000
Ellen Kullman, *President*
Richard Goodmanson, *Exec VP*
Michael Walker, *Vice Pres*
Linda West, *Vice Pres*
Jeff Keefer, *CFO*
▼ **EMP:** 8
SALES (est): 6.4MM
SALES (corp-wide): 30.6B **Publicly Held**
SIC: 2789 Bookbinding & related work
HQ: E. I. Du Pont De Nemours And Company
974 Centre Rd Bldg 735
Wilmington DE 19805
302 485-3000

(G-10266)
DUQUE NIEVA MD PA (PA)
1010 N Bancroft Pkwy L3 (19805-2690)
PHONE.................302 655-2048
Nieva Duque MD, *Owner*
EMP: 8
SALES (est): 944.5K **Privately Held**
SIC: 8011 Obstetrician

(G-10267)
DUQUE NIEVA MD PA
12 Trolley Sq Ste B (19806)
PHONE.................302 655-5661
N Duque, *Principal*
EMP: 4
SALES (corp-wide): 944.5K **Privately Held**
SIC: 8011 General & family practice, physician/surgeon
PA: Duque Nieva Md Pa
1010 N Bancroft Pkwy L3
Wilmington DE 19805
302 655-2048

(G-10268)
DURAFIBER TECH DFT ENTPS INC (HQ)
300 Delaware Ave Ste 1100 (19801-1670)
PHONE.................704 912-3770
Frank Papa, *CEO*
Rick Spurlock, *Vice Pres*
Erwin Bette, *CFO*
David Ascher, *Council Mbr*
◆ **EMP:** 75
SALES (est): 417.3MM
SALES (corp-wide): 16.4B **Privately Held**
SIC: 2824 Nylon fibers
PA: Sun Capital Partners, Inc.
5200 Town Center Cir # 600
Boca Raton FL 33486
561 962-3400

(G-10269)
DUST AWAY CLEANING SVCS INC
700 Cornell Dr Ste E1 (19801-5762)
P.O. Box 346 (19899-0346)
PHONE.................302 658-8803
Carrie Myer, *President*
EMP: 20
SQ FT: 1,500
SALES (est): 447.5K **Privately Held**
SIC: 7349 Janitorial service, contract basis; cleaning service, industrial or commercial

(G-10270)
DVHD INC
Also Called: Delaware Valley Housing Dev
1716 Shallcross Ave Ste 2 (19806-2322)
P.O. Box 9083 (19809-0083)
PHONE.................302 584-3547
Allexea Blackwell, *CEO*
Sharon Copeland, *Director*
EMP: 5
SALES (est): 184.7K **Privately Held**
SIC: 8748 Urban planning & consulting services

(G-10271)
DYNAMIC DEVICES LLC
8 Lewis Cir (19804-1618)
PHONE.................302 994-2401
John Fernau, *Manager*
Kelly Kreitlow,
EMP: 10
SALES (est): 1.9MM **Privately Held**
WEB: www.dynamicdevices.com
SIC: 8742 Management consulting services

(G-10272)
DYNAMIC SUPPORT SERVICES INC
1209 N Orange St (19801-1120)
PHONE.................202 820-3113
Sifatullah Muradi, *Principal*
Nathan Ertel, *Principal*
Salim Shirzai, *Principal*
EMP: 5
SALES (est): 104.7K **Privately Held**
SIC: 7389

(G-10273)
DYNAMIC THERAPY SERVICES LLC
305 N Union St 101 (19805-3453)
PHONE.................302 778-0810
David Griffith, *Manager*
EMP: 15
SALES (corp-wide): 12.9MM **Privately Held**
WEB: www.dynamicpt.com
SIC: 8049 Physical therapist
PA: Dynamic Therapy Services Llc
1501 Blueball Ave
Linwood PA 19061
610 859-8850

(G-10274)
DYNAMIC THERAPY SERVICES LLC
4709 Kirkwood Hwy (19808-5007)
PHONE.................302 998-9880
Greg Robinson, *Branch Mgr*
Annabelle Magno-Odell,
EMP: 16
SALES (corp-wide): 12.9MM **Privately Held**
SIC: 8049 Physical therapist
PA: Dynamic Therapy Services Llc
1501 Blueball Ave
Linwood PA 19061
610 859-8850

(G-10275)
E B D MANAGEMENT INC
Also Called: Edward B De Seta & Associates
4001 Kennett Pike Ste 10 (19807-2000)
P.O. Box 4549 (19807-4549)
PHONE.................302 428-1313
Edward B De Seta, *President*
EMP: 7
SALES (est): 590K **Privately Held**
WEB: www.ebdmanagement.com
SIC: 6531 Real estate agents & managers

(G-10276)
E E ROSSER INC
5109 Governor Printz Blvd (19809-2743)
PHONE.................302 762-9643
Gary Rosser, *President*
EMP: 6 **EST:** 1964
SALES: 800K **Privately Held**
SIC: 5084 5169 Welding machinery & equipment; compressed gas

(G-10277)
E EARLE DOWNING INC
1221 Bowers St Ste 5 (19802-4637)
P.O. Box 1151 (19899-1151)
PHONE.................302 656-9908
Bruce Downing, *President*
Mary Anne Downing, *Vice Pres*
Heather Slemmer, *Office Mgr*
EMP: 20 **EST:** 1938
SQ FT: 2,000
SALES (est): 4.7MM **Privately Held**
SIC: 1611 Highway & street paving contractor; surfacing & paving

▲ = Import ▼=Export
◆ =Import/Export

GEOGRAPHIC SECTION
Wilmington - New Castle County (G-10300)

(G-10278)
E I DU PONT DE NEMOURS & CO (HQ)
Also Called: Dupont
974 Centre Rd Bldg 735 (19805-1269)
PHONE.................................302 485-3000
Edward D Breen, *Ch of Bd*
Justin Mayer, *Business Mgr*
Evelyn Brantney, *Counsel*
Brad Lance, *Vice Pres*
Timothy McCann, *Vice Pres*
◆ **EMP:** 6000 **EST:** 1802
SALES: 26.2B
SALES (corp-wide): 30.6B **Publicly Held**
WEB: www.dupont.com
SIC: 2879 2824 2865 2821 Agricultural chemicals; nylon fibers; polyester fibers; dyes & pigments; thermoplastic materials; pharmaceutical preparations
PA: Corteva, Inc.
974 Centre Rd Bldg 735
Wilmington DE 19805
302 485-3000

(G-10279)
E I DU PONT DE NEMOURS & CO
Also Called: Dupont
702 Canter Rd (19810)
PHONE.................................302 999-3301
Donald Dunn, *Manager*
EMP: 50
SALES (corp-wide): 30.6B **Publicly Held**
WEB: www.dupont.com
SIC: 2819 Industrial inorganic chemicals
HQ: E. I. Du Pont De Nemours And Company
974 Centre Rd Bldg 735
Wilmington DE 19805
302 485-3000

(G-10280)
E I DU PONT DE NEMOURS & CO
Also Called: Dupont
970 Centre Rd 709 (19805-1269)
PHONE.................................302 774-1000
T W Boaz, *Manager*
EMP: 9
SALES (corp-wide): 30.6B **Publicly Held**
WEB: www.dupont.com
SIC: 2819 Industrial inorganic chemicals
HQ: E. I. Du Pont De Nemours And Company
974 Centre Rd Bldg 735
Wilmington DE 19805
302 485-3000

(G-10281)
E I DU PONT DE NEMOURS & CO
Also Called: Dupont
4417 Lancaster Pike (19805-1523)
PHONE.................................302 892-8832
David Dean, *Technical Mgr*
Bill Gibson, *Engineer*
Grant Vincent, *Engineer*
Theresa McGinn, *Finance*
Nathan King, *Manager*
EMP: 410
SALES (corp-wide): 30.6B **Publicly Held**
WEB: www.dupont.com
SIC: 2819 Industrial inorganic chemicals
HQ: E. I. Du Pont De Nemours And Company
974 Centre Rd Bldg 735
Wilmington DE 19805
302 485-3000

(G-10282)
E I DU PONT DE NEMOURS & CO
Also Called: Dupont
4117 Lancaster Pike (19805)
PHONE.................................302 774-1000
EMP: 10
SALES (corp-wide): 30.6B **Publicly Held**
WEB: www.dupont.com
SIC: 3081 Unsupported plastics film & sheet
HQ: E. I. Du Pont De Nemours And Company
974 Centre Rd Bldg 735
Wilmington DE 19805
302 485-3000

(G-10283)
E I DU PONT DE NEMOURS & CO
Also Called: Dupont
974 Centre Rd Bldg 730 (19805-1269)
PHONE.................................302 999-2826
EMP: 343
SALES (corp-wide): 30.6B **Publicly Held**
SIC: 2879 2865 2821 Agricultural chemicals; dyes & pigments; thermoplastic materials
HQ: E. I. Du Pont De Nemours And Company
974 Centre Rd Bldg 735
Wilmington DE 19805
302 485-3000

(G-10284)
E I DU PONT DE NEMOURS & CO
Also Called: Dupont Building Innovations
4417 Lancaster Pike 735 (19805-1523)
PHONE.................................302 892-8832
EMP: 410
SALES (corp-wide): 30.6B **Publicly Held**
SIC: 7389 Purchasing service
HQ: E. I. Du Pont De Nemours And Company
974 Centre Rd Bldg 735
Wilmington DE 19805
302 485-3000

(G-10285)
E I DU PONT DE NEMOURS & CO
Also Called: Dupont Accounts Payable
P.O. Box 80040 (19880-0040)
PHONE.................................615 847-6920
Edward D Breen, *Ch of Bd*
EMP: 56
SALES (corp-wide): 30.6B **Publicly Held**
SIC: 2819 Industrial inorganic chemicals
HQ: E. I. Du Pont De Nemours And Company
974 Centre Rd Bldg 735
Wilmington DE 19805
302 485-3000

(G-10286)
E I DU PONT DE NEMOURS & CO
Also Called: Dupont Industrial Biosciences
200 Power Mill Rd (19803)
PHONE.................................302 695-7228
EMP: 7
SALES (corp-wide): 30.6B **Publicly Held**
SIC: 2879 Agricultural chemicals
HQ: E. I. Du Pont De Nemours And Company
974 Centre Rd Bldg 735
Wilmington DE 19805
302 485-3000

(G-10287)
E I DU PONT DE NEMOURS & CO
1 Righter Pkwy (19803-1534)
PHONE.................................843 335-5934
Valerie J Sill Cfa, *CEO*
EMP: 13
SALES (est): 1.6MM **Privately Held**
SIC: 2899 Chemical preparations

(G-10288)
E I DU PONT DE NEMOURS & CO
Dupont Industrial Biosciences
Chestnut Run Plz Bldg 7 (19805)
PHONE.................................302 774-1000
William F Feehery, *President*
EMP: 8
SALES (corp-wide): 30.6B **Publicly Held**
SIC: 8731 Biotechnical research, commercial
HQ: E. I. Du Pont De Nemours And Company
974 Centre Rd Bldg 735
Wilmington DE 19805
302 485-3000

(G-10289)
E I DU PONT DE NEMOURS & CO
1007 Market St (19898-1100)
PHONE.................................844 773-2436
Mark Sagrans, *Counsel*
Luis Concepcion, *Senior Buyer*
George Mashack, *Research*
Mark Mason, *Engineer*
Darin Sloan, *Marketing Mgr*
EMP: 6
SALES (corp-wide): 30.6B **Publicly Held**
SIC: 2879 Agricultural chemicals
HQ: E. I. Du Pont De Nemours And Company
974 Centre Rd Bldg 735
Wilmington DE 19805
302 485-3000

(G-10290)
E I DU PONT DE NEMOURS & CO
974 Chestnut Run Plz B (19805-1269)
PHONE.................................800 441-7515
EMP: 2
SALES (corp-wide): 30.6B **Publicly Held**
SIC: 2879 2824 2865 2821 Agricultural chemicals; nylon fibers; polyester fibers; dyes & pigments; thermoplastic materials; pharmaceutical preparations
HQ: E. I. Du Pont De Nemours And Company
974 Centre Rd Bldg 735
Wilmington DE 19805
302 485-3000

(G-10291)
E I DU PONT DE NEMOURS & CO
Also Called: Dupont
Chestnt Run Plz 708 141 (19805)
PHONE.................................302 999-4356
Ram Ratnagiri, *Research*
Jamie Chance, *Engineer*
Rong Jiao, *Engineer*
Gabriel Schumacher, *Engineer*
Ryan-Paul Milano, *Credit Staff*
EMP: 50
SALES (corp-wide): 30.6B **Publicly Held**
SIC: 8711 Engineering services
HQ: E. I. Du Pont De Nemours And Company
974 Centre Rd Bldg 735
Wilmington DE 19805
302 485-3000

(G-10292)
E I DU PONT DE NEMOURS & CO
Also Called: Dupont
300 Delaware Ave (19801-1607)
PHONE.................................302 792-4371
H L Kelley, *Principal*
Nathan W Love, *Purch Mgr*
EMP: 51
SALES (corp-wide): 30.6B **Publicly Held**
WEB: www.dupont.com
SIC: 2819 Industrial inorganic chemicals
HQ: E. I. Du Pont De Nemours And Company
974 Centre Rd Bldg 735
Wilmington DE 19805
302 485-3000

(G-10293)
E I DU PONT DE NEMOURS & CO
Also Called: Dupont
Barley Mill Plaza (19898-0001)
PHONE.................................302 996-4000
Barry Day, *Principal*
EMP: 50
SALES (corp-wide): 30.6B **Publicly Held**
WEB: www.dupont.com
SIC: 3844 3841 X-ray apparatus & tubes; surgical & medical instruments
HQ: E. I. Du Pont De Nemours And Company
974 Centre Rd Bldg 735
Wilmington DE 19805
302 485-3000

(G-10294)
E I DU PONT DE NEMOURS & CO
Also Called: Dupont
974 Centre Rd (19805-1269)
PHONE.................................302 774-1000
Gary Pfeiffer, *Vice Pres*
Michael Elder, *Engineer*
Bhuma Rajagopalan, *Engineer*
Alexander Benchev, *Marketing Staff*
Zachary Mendiz, *Manager*
EMP: 14
SALES (corp-wide): 30.6B **Publicly Held**
WEB: www.dupont.com
SIC: 1382 Oil & gas exploration services
HQ: E. I. Du Pont De Nemours And Company
974 Centre Rd Bldg 735
Wilmington DE 19805
302 485-3000

(G-10295)
E I DU PONT DE NEMOURS & CO
Also Called: Dupont
Rt 141 Lancaster Pike (19898-0001)
PHONE.................................302 774-1000
John Krol, *President*
EMP: 51
SALES (corp-wide): 30.6B **Publicly Held**
WEB: www.dupont.com
SIC: 2819 Industrial inorganic chemicals
HQ: E. I. Du Pont De Nemours And Company
974 Centre Rd Bldg 735
Wilmington DE 19805
302 485-3000

(G-10296)
E I DU PONT DE NEMOURS & CO
Also Called: Playhouse On Rodney Square
901 N Market St (19801-3022)
PHONE.................................302 888-0200
Shekhar Subramoney, *Research*
John Gardner, *Manager*
Olga Grushin, *Consultant*
Veronique Vallee, *Technology*
EMP: 15
SALES (corp-wide): 30.6B **Publicly Held**
WEB: www.dupont.com
SIC: 7929 Entertainers & entertainment groups
HQ: E. I. Du Pont De Nemours And Company
974 Centre Rd Bldg 735
Wilmington DE 19805
302 485-3000

(G-10297)
E I DU PONT DE NEMOURS & CO
Also Called: Dupont
1011 Centre Rd Ste 200 (19805-1266)
PHONE.................................302 654-8198
Elliott Golinkoff, *Exec VP*
EMP: 333
SALES (corp-wide): 30.6B **Publicly Held**
WEB: www.dupont.com
SIC: 2821 Thermoplastic materials
HQ: E. I. Du Pont De Nemours And Company
974 Centre Rd Bldg 735
Wilmington DE 19805
302 485-3000

(G-10298)
E I DU PONT DE NEMOURS & CO
Also Called: Dupont
22 Barley Mill Dr (19807)
PHONE.................................302 774-1000
Rosanne T Danner, *Branch Mgr*
Linda Bankston, *Info Tech Dir*
Gil Choi, *IT/INT Sup*
Vicki Garrison, *Planning*
EMP: 50
SALES (corp-wide): 30.6B **Publicly Held**
WEB: www.dupont.com
SIC: 2819 Industrial inorganic chemicals
HQ: E. I. Du Pont De Nemours And Company
974 Centre Rd Bldg 735
Wilmington DE 19805
302 485-3000

(G-10299)
E I DU PONT DE NEMOURS & CO
Also Called: Dupont
Corporate Data Ctr (19899)
P.O. Box 2909 (19805-0909)
PHONE.................................302 774-1000
Bill Kirkey, *Manager*
EMP: 50
SALES (corp-wide): 30.6B **Publicly Held**
WEB: www.dupont.com
SIC: 2819 Industrial inorganic chemicals
HQ: E. I. Du Pont De Nemours And Company
974 Centre Rd Bldg 735
Wilmington DE 19805
302 485-3000

(G-10300)
E I DU PONT DE NEMOURS & CO
Also Called: Dupont
Faulkland Rd & Centre Rd (19808)
PHONE.................................302 999-4329
Frank Stillburn, *Principal*
EMP: 17

Wilmington - New Castle County (G-10301)

SALES (corp-wide): 30.6B **Publicly Held**
WEB: www.dupont.com
SIC: **2819** Industrial inorganic chemicals
HQ: E. I. Du Pont De Nemours And Company
974 Centre Rd Bldg 735
Wilmington DE 19805
302 485-3000

(G-10301)
E I DU PONT DE NEMOURS & CO
4417 Lancaster Pike (19805-1523)
PHONE.....................................302 892-5655
EMP: 339
SALES (corp-wide): 30.6B **Publicly Held**
WEB: www.dupont.com
SIC: **2879** 2824 2834 2865 Agricultural chemicals; nylon fibers; pharmaceutical preparations; dyes & pigments; thermoplastic materials
HQ: E. I. Du Pont De Nemours And Company
974 Centre Rd Bldg 735
Wilmington DE 19805
302 485-3000

(G-10302)
E I DU PONT DE NEMOURS & CO
Also Called: Dupont Experimental Station
200 Powder Mill Rd (19803-2907)
PHONE.....................................302 695-3742
Robert Scott, *Branch Mgr*
EMP: 51
SALES (corp-wide): 30.6B **Publicly Held**
WEB: www.dupont.com
SIC: **2819** Industrial inorganic chemicals
HQ: E. I. Du Pont De Nemours And Company
974 Centre Rd Bldg 735
Wilmington DE 19805
302 485-3000

(G-10303)
E I DU PONT DE NEMOURS & CO
Also Called: Nonwovens Indus & Active Packg
4417 Lancaster Pike (19805-1523)
P.O. Box 2915 (19805-0915)
PHONE.....................................302 999-5072
Otto Fernandez, *Manager*
EMP: 709
SALES (corp-wide): 30.6B **Publicly Held**
WEB: www.dupont.com
SIC: **7389** Packaging & labeling services
HQ: E. I. Du Pont De Nemours And Company
974 Centre Rd Bldg 735
Wilmington DE 19805
302 485-3000

(G-10304)
E I DU PONT DE NEMOURS & CO
Dupont Displays
4417 Lancaster Pike (19805-1523)
PHONE.....................................805 562-5307
William F Feehery, *Branch Mgr*
EMP: 50
SALES (corp-wide): 30.6B **Publicly Held**
WEB: www.dupont.com
SIC: **3555** 8731 Printing trades machinery; commercial physical research
HQ: E. I. Du Pont De Nemours And Company
974 Centre Rd Bldg 735
Wilmington DE 19805
302 485-3000

(G-10305)
E I DU PONT DE NEMOURS & CO
4417 Lancaster Pike Ste 2 (19805-1523)
PHONE.....................................302 774-1000
Barry Day, *Manager*
EMP: 182
SALES (corp-wide): 30.6B **Publicly Held**
WEB: www.dupont.com
SIC: **2879** Agricultural chemicals
HQ: E. I. Du Pont De Nemours And Company
974 Centre Rd Bldg 735
Wilmington DE 19805
302 485-3000

(G-10306)
E I DU PONT DE NEMOURS & CO
Dupont Qualicon
Experimentl Statn Bdg 400 (19880)
PHONE.....................................302 695-5300
Beth A Peck, *CFO*
EMP: 75
SALES (corp-wide): 30.6B **Publicly Held**
WEB: www.dupont.com
SIC: **8734** 3556 2835 Food testing service; food products machinery; in vitro & in vivo diagnostic substances
HQ: E. I. Du Pont De Nemours And Company
974 Centre Rd Bldg 735
Wilmington DE 19805
302 485-3000

(G-10307)
E I DU PONT DE NEMOURS & CO
4417 Lancaster Pike (19805-1523)
P.O. Box 263, Rockland (19732-0263)
PHONE.....................................302 658-7796
William F Feehery, *CEO*
EMP: 182
SALES (corp-wide): 30.6B **Publicly Held**
SIC: **2879** Agricultural chemicals
HQ: E. I. Du Pont De Nemours And Company
974 Centre Rd Bldg 735
Wilmington DE 19805
302 485-3000

(G-10308)
E I DU PONT DE NEMOURS & CO
Dupont Engineering RES & Tech
Chestnut Run Plz Bldg 722 (19805)
PHONE.....................................302 774-1000
Ted Diehl, *Branch Mgr*
EMP: 97
SALES (corp-wide): 30.6B **Publicly Held**
SIC: **8731** Biological research; agricultural research
HQ: E. I. Du Pont De Nemours And Company
974 Centre Rd Bldg 735
Wilmington DE 19805
302 485-3000

(G-10309)
E M C PROCESS COMPANY INC
1663 E Ayre St (19804-2514)
P.O. Box 3035 (19804-0035)
PHONE.....................................302 999-9204
George F Baumeister, *President*
EMP: 5
SQ FT: 4,000
SALES (est): 544.8K **Privately Held**
WEB: www.emcprocess.com
SIC: **3479** Coating of metals & formed products; painting, coating & hot dipping

(G-10310)
E W BROWN INC
1202 E 16th St (19802-5217)
P.O. Box 1680, Hockessin (19707-5680)
PHONE.....................................302 652-6612
Charles E Brown Jr, *President*
Albert Brown, *Vice Pres*
EMP: 4
SQ FT: 3,400
SALES (est): 371.7K **Privately Held**
WEB: www.ewbrown.com
SIC: **2394** 1799 Awnings, fabric: made from purchased materials; awning installation

(G-10311)
E&N SURGICAL LLC
251 Little Falls Dr (19808-1674)
PHONE.....................................860 471-0786
David Ford,
EMP: 1
SALES (est): 55K **Privately Held**
SIC: **3842** Surgical appliances & supplies

(G-10312)
E-DMZ SECURITY LLC
501 Silverside Rd Ste 143 (19809-1372)
PHONE.....................................302 791-9370
EMP: 22
SALES (est): 2.8MM **Privately Held**
SIC: **7373** 7379 Computer Systems Design Computer Related Services

(G-10313)
E-INDUSTRIAL SUPPLIERS LLC
2207 Concord Pike Ste 648 (19803-2908)
PHONE.....................................302 251-6210
William M Agal,
Wafa Agal,
EMP: 7
SALES: 1MM **Privately Held**
WEB: www.eindustrialsuppliers.com
SIC: **5085** 5082 Industrial supplies; general construction machinery & equipment

(G-10314)
EAGLE PLAZA ASSOCIATES INC
234 N James St (19804-3132)
PHONE.....................................302 999-0708
Verino Pettinaro, *President*
Tracy Crowley, *Partner*
Cindy Pettinaro, *Partner*
Gregory Pettinaro, *Partner*
Victoria Pettinaro, *Partner*
EMP: 14 **EST:** 1981
SQ FT: 2,000
SALES (est): 609.3K **Privately Held**
SIC: **6512** Shopping center, property operation only

(G-10315)
EAGLE US INC
1105 N Market St Ste 1300 (19801-1241)
PHONE.....................................484 913-0300
John C Stipa, *President*
Mark R B Pearson, *Vice Pres*
Joanne Della Valle, *Treasurer*
Roy A Burrows, *Admin Sec*
William K Langan, *Asst Sec*
EMP: 1580
SALES (est): 358.4MM
SALES (corp-wide): 724.5MM **Privately Held**
SIC: **8748** Environmental consultant
HQ: Erm Emerald Us Inc.
1150 N Market St Ste 1300
Wilmington DE 19801
302 651-8300

(G-10316)
EARLY FOUNDATIONS THERAPEUTIC
Also Called: Early Foundation Preschool
2814 W 2nd St (19805-1807)
PHONE.....................................302 384-6905
Joan D Fletcher, *Principal*
EMP: 5
SALES (est): 126K **Privately Held**
SIC: **8641** Civic social & fraternal associations

(G-10317)
EARLY LEARNING CENTER
1218 B St (19801-5844)
PHONE.....................................302 831-0584
Heidi Beck, *Principal*
EMP: 5 **EST:** 2015
SALES (est): 52.9K **Privately Held**
SIC: **8351** Child day care services

(G-10318)
EAST COAST CLEANING CO LLC
528 Ruxton Dr (19809-2830)
P.O. Box 7588 (19803-0588)
PHONE.....................................302 762-6820
Curtis Jackson, *Owner*
Michelle Jackson, *Partner*
EMP: 11
SALES (est): 100K **Privately Held**
WEB: www.eastcoastcleaningco.com
SIC: **5087** Cleaning & maintenance equipment & supplies

(G-10319)
EAST COAST ELECTRIC INC
824 Kiamensi Rd (19804-3420)
PHONE.....................................302 998-1577
Robert C Race, *President*
EMP: 10
SALES (est): 1.5MM **Privately Held**
SIC: **1731** General electrical contractor

(G-10320)
EAST COAST MINORITY SUPPLIER
610 W 8th St (19801-1450)
PHONE.....................................302 656-3337

Rock Brown, *President*
EMP: 25
SALES (est): 1.4MM **Privately Held**
SIC: **5231** 5211 1522 1541 Wallpaper; lumber & other building materials; residential construction; industrial buildings & warehouses; nonresidential construction

(G-10321)
EAST SIDE CMMTY LRNG CNTR FNDT
3000 N Claymont St (19802-2807)
P.O. Box 951 (19899-0951)
PHONE.....................................302 762-5834
Charles McDowell, *President*
Will Robinson, *Exec Dir*
EMP: 6
SALES: 770.3K **Privately Held**
SIC: **6732** Trusts: educational, religious, etc.

(G-10322)
EASTERN HOME IMPROVEMENTS INC (PA)
Also Called: Four Seasons Sunrooms
3112 Lancaster Ave (19805-1461)
PHONE.....................................302 655-9920
Ken Quinn, *President*
Eric Quinn, *Vice Pres*
EMP: 8
SQ FT: 2,200
SALES (est): 3.2MM **Privately Held**
SIC: **1521** 1793 1542 Single-family home remodeling, additions & repairs; glass & glazing work; commercial & office buildings, renovation & repair

(G-10323)
EASTERN HWY SPECIALISTS INC
920 N Church St (19801-4343)
P.O. Box 129, Montchanin (19710-0129)
PHONE.....................................302 777-7673
Robert Field, *President*
Clairemarie Field, *Shareholder*
EMP: 37
SQ FT: 800
SALES (est): 8.4MM **Privately Held**
SIC: **1622** Bridge construction; highway construction, elevated

(G-10324)
EASTERN PROPERTY GROUP INC
Also Called: Pebble Hill Apartments
3408 Miller Rd C7 (19802-2529)
PHONE.....................................302 764-7112
Marene Riser, *Branch Mgr*
EMP: 5
SALES (est): 442.5K
SALES (corp-wide): 3.4MM **Privately Held**
SIC: **6513** Apartment building operators
PA: Eastern Property Group, Inc
28 S Waterloo Rd Ste 201
Devon PA 19333
610 293-1400

(G-10325)
EASTERN PROSPERITY GROUP
Also Called: Pebble Hill Assoc A Partnr
3408 Miller Rd (19802-2529)
PHONE.....................................302 764-7112
Nancy Huston, *Manager*
EMP: 5
SQ FT: 125,000
SALES (est): 326.1K **Privately Held**
SIC: **6513** Apartment building operators

(G-10326)
EASTERN STATES CNSTR SVC INC
702 First State Blvd (19804-3558)
PHONE.....................................302 995-2259
Richard J Julian, *President*
Terence T Gleason, *Vice Pres*
Eugene Julian, *Vice Pres*
Patricia M Falgowski, *Admin Sec*
EMP: 80
SQ FT: 6,500
SALES (est): 17.4MM **Privately Held**
SIC: **1799** 1623 1611 Building site preparation; underground utilities contractor; general contractor, highway & street construction

GEOGRAPHIC SECTION
Wilmington - New Castle County (G-10359)

(G-10327)
EASTERN STATES DEVELPMENT INC
702 First State Blvd (19804-3558)
PHONE..................302 998-0683
Eugene M Julian, *President*
Francis R Julian, *Vice Pres*
Richard J Julian, *Treasurer*
EMP: 5
SQ FT: 1,000
SALES (est): 1.6MM **Privately Held**
SIC: 6552 Land subdividers & developers, commercial

(G-10328)
EASTLAKE APARTMENTS LLC
Also Called: Eastlake Village
2412 Thatcher St (19802-4512)
PHONE..................302 764-0215
David Curtis,
EMP: 13
SALES (est): 606.2K **Privately Held**
SIC: 6513 Apartment building operators

(G-10329)
EASTSIDE BLUPRT CMNTY DEV CORP
121 N Poplar St (19801-3955)
PHONE..................302 384-2350
David Mosley, *Exec Dir*
EMP: 10
SALES (est): 390K **Privately Held**
SIC: 8399 Community development groups

(G-10330)
EASY ANALYTIC SOFTWARE INC
21 Paladin Dr (19802-1701)
PHONE..................302 762-4271
Gregory Gergen, *Branch Mgr*
EMP: 2 **Privately Held**
SIC: 7372 Prepackaged software
PA: Easy Analytic Software Inc
7359 196th St
Flushing NY 11366

(G-10331)
EASY CORP LTD
3422 Old Capitol Trl (19808-6124)
PHONE..................302 824-0109
EMP: 14
SALES (est): 950K **Privately Held**
SIC: 8741 Management Services

(G-10332)
EBC CARPET SERVICES CORP
1300 First State Blvd 1 (19804-3548)
PHONE..................302 995-7461
Christopher Rankin, *President*
Gerald Denhof, *Vice Pres*
Christine Rankin, *Admin Sec*
EMP: 30
SALES (est): 2.5MM **Privately Held**
WEB: www.ebcusa.com
SIC: 7217 Carpet & rug cleaning & repairing plant

(G-10333)
EBC NATIONAL INC
1300 First State Blvd (19804-3548)
PHONE..................302 995-7461
Christopher R Rankin, *Principal*
EMP: 7
SALES (est): 216K **Privately Held**
SIC: 7217 Carpet & upholstery cleaning

(G-10334)
EBC SYSTEMS LLC
1 Ave Of The Arts (19801-5047)
PHONE..................302 472-1896
Bill Endicott,
EMP: 8
SALES (est): 511.7K **Privately Held**
SIC: 7373 Systems integration services

(G-10335)
ECHELON STUDIOS INC (PA)
19c Trolley Sq (19806-3355)
PHONE..................800 208-9052
Eric Louzil, *President*
EMP: 1
SALES (est): 328.2K **Privately Held**
SIC: 7822 Motion picture distribution

(G-10336)
ECKERT SMANS CHRIN MELLOTT LLC
222 Delaware Ave Fl 7 (19801-1663)
PHONE..................302 574-7400
Francis Pileggi, *Branch Mgr*
EMP: 51
SALES (corp-wide): 132.1MM **Privately Held**
SIC: 8111 General practice attorney, lawyer
PA: Eckert, Seamans, Cherin & Mellott, L.L.C.
600 Grant St Fl 44
Pittsburgh PA 15219
412 566-6000

(G-10337)
ECLIPES ERECTION INC
330 Water St (19804-2433)
PHONE..................302 633-1421
David N Sills IV, *President*
EMP: 40
SALES (est): 1.3MM **Privately Held**
WEB: www.daystarsills.com
SIC: 1799 Erection & dismantling of forms for poured concrete

(G-10338)
ECLIPSE SOFTWARE INC
908 Greenhill Ave (19805-2640)
PHONE..................212 727-1136
Andrew Weigel, *President*
EMP: 2
SALES (est): 78.9K **Privately Held**
SIC: 7372 Business oriented computer software

(G-10339)
ECO PLASTIC PRODUCTS DEL INC
18 Germay Dr (19804-1105)
PHONE..................302 575-9227
Jim Kelley, *CEO*
EMP: 2
SALES (est): 90.7K **Privately Held**
SIC: 2611 Pulp manufactured from waste or recycled paper

(G-10340)
ECO SBC 2015-1 REO 167061 LLC
Also Called: Elison Db 2015-1
824 N Market St (19801-3024)
PHONE..................302 652-8013
Katherine Meagher, *Principal*
EMP: 20 **EST:** 2017
SALES (est): 371.5K **Privately Held**
SIC: 8742 Real estate consultant

(G-10341)
ECSQUARED INC
1801 Forrest Rd (19810-4318)
PHONE..................302 750-8554
Edward Crowder, *President*
Eric Christy, *Vice Pres*
Erik Christie, *Sales Mgr*
EMP: 5
SQ FT: 1,750
SALES (est): 1MM **Privately Held**
SIC: 8742 Hospital & health services consultant

(G-10342)
ED TURULSKI CUSTOM WOODWORKING
1020 Liberty Rd (19804-2857)
P.O. Box 5935 (19808-0935)
PHONE..................302 658-2221
Edward Turulski, *President*
EMP: 9
SALES (est): 400K **Privately Held**
SIC: 1751 Cabinet & finish carpentry

(G-10343)
EDAURA INC
1209 N Orange St (19801-1120)
PHONE..................707 330-9836
Nidal Khalifeh, *CEO*
EMP: 8 **EST:** 2015
SALES (est): 186.1K **Privately Held**
SIC: 7372 Educational computer software

(G-10344)
EDEN GREEN LLC
300 Delaware Ave Ste 210a (19801-6601)
PHONE..................817 999-1570
Jaco Booyens, *Principal*
EMP: 10
SALES (est): 190.8K **Privately Held**
SIC: 8748 Agricultural consultant

(G-10345)
EDEN LAND CARE
202 New Rd Unit 7 (19805-4141)
P.O. Box 1581, Hockessin (19707-5581)
PHONE..................302 379-2405
EMP: 5
SALES (est): 140.7K **Privately Held**
SIC: 8351 Child day care services

(G-10346)
EDGE CONSTRUCTION CORP
300 M L King Blvd 300 (19801)
PHONE..................302 778-5200
Dan Bachtle, *CEO*
EMP: 6
SALES (est): 966K **Privately Held**
WEB: www.edgeconstructioncorp.com
SIC: 1521 1542 New construction, single-family houses; commercial & office building, new construction

(G-10347)
EDGE MOOR DUPONT EMPLOYEES
104 Hay Rd (19809-3509)
PHONE..................302 761-2282
Michael Stasio, *President*
EMP: 4
SALES (est): 94.8K **Privately Held**
SIC: 6061 Federal credit unions

(G-10348)
EDGEMOOR COMMUNITY CENTER INC
500 Duncan Rd Ofc A (19809-2360)
PHONE..................302 762-1391
Scott Borino, *Exec Dir*
Joe Wisniewski, *Exec Dir*
Christine Grosso, *Admin Asst*
EMP: 35
SQ FT: 48,000
SALES: 1MM **Privately Held**
SIC: 8351 Child day care services

(G-10349)
EDIS BUILDING SYSTEMS INC
110 S Poplar St Ste 400 (19801-5053)
PHONE..................302 421-5700
E Andrew Disabatino, *President*
Richard P Di Sabatino Jr, *Vice Pres*
Michael Miller, *Treasurer*
Frances F Williams, *Admin Sec*
EMP: 5
SQ FT: 17,000
SALES (est): 1.3MM
SALES (corp-wide): 13.6MM **Privately Held**
SIC: 5039 Prefabricated buildings
PA: Crystal Holdings, Inc.
110 S Poplar St Ste 400
Wilmington DE 19801
302 421-5700

(G-10350)
EDIS COMPANY
110 S Poplar St Ste 400 (19801-5053)
P.O. Box 2697 (19805-0697)
PHONE..................302 421-5700
A Andrew Di Sabatino Jr, *President*
Richard P Di Sabatino Jr, *Vice Pres*
Meredith Christian, *Project Mgr*
Leon Thompson, *Project Mgr*
Frances F Williams, *Treasurer*
EMP: 45
SQ FT: 17,000
SALES (est): 12.2MM
SALES (corp-wide): 13.6MM **Privately Held**
WEB: www.ediscompany.com
SIC: 1541 1542 Industrial buildings, new construction; commercial & office building, new construction
PA: Crystal Holdings, Inc.
110 S Poplar St Ste 400
Wilmington DE 19801
302 421-5700

(G-10351)
EDIT INC
1026 Sedwick Dr (19803-3331)
PHONE..................302 478-7069
Richard B Tippett, *President*
Judith Tippett, *Vice Pres*
EMP: 2
SALES (est): 130.9K **Privately Held**
SIC: 2741 Business service newsletters: publishing & printing

(G-10352)
EDUCATION SVCS UNLIMITED LLC
Also Called: Lifespan Development Centers
500 Mckennans Church Rd (19808-1360)
PHONE..................302 650-4210
Tricia Howarth,
EMP: 10
SALES (est): 108.3K **Privately Held**
SIC: 8351 Preschool center

(G-10353)
EDUCATIONAL ASSETS CORP
1011 Centre Rd Ste 320 (19805-1266)
PHONE..................302 288-0149
EMP: 5 **EST:** 2001
SALES (est): 470K **Privately Held**
SIC: 6719 Holding Company

(G-10354)
EDUCATIONAL ENRICHMENT CENTER
Also Called: Eec
730 Halstead Rd (19803-2228)
PHONE..................302 478-8697
Nancy McConnell, *President*
EMP: 30
SALES (est): 1MM **Privately Held**
WEB: www.eecinc.org
SIC: 8351 Group day care center

(G-10355)
EDWARD B BAYLEY DMD
1610 Sunset Ln (19810-4149)
PHONE..................302 766-4633
EMP: 4
SALES (est): 82.3K **Privately Held**
SIC: 8021 Offices & clinics of dentists

(G-10356)
EDWARD B DE SETA & ASSOCIATES
Also Called: Dbd Maangment
4001 Kennett Pike Ste 10 (19807-2000)
P.O. Box 4549 (19807-4549)
PHONE..................302 428-1313
Edward B De Seta, *President*
Wanda L De Seta, *Vice Pres*
EMP: 5
SALES (est): 500K **Privately Held**
SIC: 6552 Subdividers & developers

(G-10357)
EDWARD J HENRY & SONS INC
Also Called: Henry Auto Body Shop
2300 W 4th St (19805-3325)
PHONE..................302 658-4324
Edward J Henry III, *President*
Charles D Thomas, *Vice Pres*
Ann Marie Henry-Thomas, *Treasurer*
Catherine H May, *Admin Sec*
EMP: 15
SQ FT: 18,900
SALES (est): 1.1MM **Privately Held**
SIC: 7532 Body shop, automotive

(G-10358)
EDWARD R BELL
909 Clifford Brown Walk (19801-3619)
PHONE..................302 658-1555
Fax: 302 764-6421
EMP: 8
SALES (est): 340K **Privately Held**
SIC: 7261 Funeral Service/Crematory

(G-10359)
EDWARD S YALISOVE DDS PA
1111 N Franklin St (19806-4327)
PHONE..................302 658-4124
Edward Yalisove DDS, *Owner*
EMP: 5
SALES (est): 233.9K **Privately Held**
SIC: 8021 Dentists' office

Wilmington - New Castle County (G-10360)

GEOGRAPHIC SECTION

(G-10360)
EDWIN S KUIPERS DDS
300 Foulk Rd Ste 101 (19803-3819)
PHONE....................302 652-3775
Edwin Kuipers, *Executive*
EMP: 4 SALES (est): 105.6K **Privately Held**
SIC: 8021 Dentists' office

(G-10361)
EFOTOLABCOM INC
1900 Superfine Ln (19802-4920)
PHONE....................302 984-0807
Joel Plotkin, *Principal*
EMP: 4
SALES (est): 278.3K **Privately Held**
SIC: 7379

(G-10362)
EGG HARBOR CITY APARTMENTS LLC
Also Called: Summit Chase Apartments, The
9 Courtyard Ln (19802-1470)
PHONE....................302 543-6514
Yvonne Bernubez, *Principal*
EMP: 4 EST: 2015
SALES (est): 250K **Privately Held**
SIC: 6513 Apartment building operators

(G-10363)
EGS FINANCIAL CARE INC
P.O. Box 15110 (19850-5110)
PHONE....................800 227-4000
EMP: 10
SALES (corp-wide): 5.4B **Privately Held**
SIC: 6282 Investment advice
HQ: Egs Financial Care, Inc.
5 Park Plz Ste 1100
Irvine CA 92614
877 217-4423

(G-10364)
EITV USA INC
501 Silverside Rd Ste 105 (19809-1376)
PHONE....................305 517-7715
Rodrigo Araugo, *Director*
EMP: 3
SALES (est): 71.1K **Privately Held**
SIC: 7372 Application computer software

(G-10365)
EKALT LLC
20c Trolley Sq (19806-3355)
PHONE....................302 300-4853
EMP: 8
SALES: 100K **Privately Held**
SIC: 7371 7389 Custom Computer Programing Business Serv Non-Commercial Site

(G-10366)
ELCOACH INC
251 Little Falls Dr (19808-1674)
PHONE....................302 261-3794
Assem Emam, *President*
EMP: 4
SALES (est): 46.4K **Privately Held**
SIC: 7999 Physical fitness instruction

(G-10367)
ELDERLY COMFORT CORPORATION
800 N West St Fl 3 (19801-1565)
P.O. Box 1570 (19899-1570)
PHONE....................302 530-6680
Tina Larose, *Ch of Bd*
EMP: 12 EST: 2011
SALES (est): 355K **Privately Held**
SIC: 8052 Personal care facility

(G-10368)
ELEMENT MTLS TECH WLMNGTON INC
Also Called: S L Pharma Labs, Inc.
1300 First State Blvd (19804-3548)
PHONE....................302 636-0202
Waheed Sheikh, *President*
EMP: 14
SALES (est): 2.5MM
SALES (corp-wide): 825.4MM **Privately Held**
WEB: www.slpharmalabs.com
SIC: 8734 Water testing laboratory

HQ: Exova Group Limited
Lochend Industrial Estate
Newbridge
131 333-4360

(G-10369)
ELEMENTARY WORKSHOP INC
Also Called: Montessori Teachers Association
502 N Pine St (19801-4433)
PHONE....................302 656-1498
Fax: 302 656-1905
EMP: 19
SALES: 100.7K **Privately Held**
SIC: 8211 8351 Elementary/Secondary School Child Day Care Services

(G-10370)
ELEUTHRIAN MLLS-HGLEY FNDTION
Also Called: HAGLEY MUSEUM AND LIBRARY
200 Hagley Rd (19807)
P.O. Box 3630 (19807-0630)
PHONE....................302 658-2400
Jeanne Belk, *Treasurer*
Erik Rau, *Director*
Marjorie Kelly, *Asst Sec*
EMP: 160 EST: 1952
SQ FT: 53,500
SALES: 15.9MM **Privately Held**
SIC: 8412 Museum

(G-10371)
ELEVATE DVM INC
3 Penny Lane Ct (19803-4023)
PHONE....................302 761-9650
Kathy Gloyd Dvm, *Principal*
Bonnie Gamble, *Project Mgr*
Lisa Scott, *Manager*
Robin Hipple, *Technical Staff*
EMP: 8
SALES (est): 154.2K **Privately Held**
SIC: 0742 Veterinary services, specialties

(G-10372)
ELEVATED STUDIOS HQ
34a Trolley Sq (19806-3334)
PHONE....................302 407-3229
EMP: 4
SALES (est): 144.3K **Privately Held**
SIC: 7999 Martial arts school

(G-10373)
ELEVATIONTV
108 W 13th St (19801)
PHONE....................978 317-9285
Eric Diaz, *CEO*
EMP: 4
SALES (est): 37.7K **Privately Held**
SIC: 8999 8748 Inventor; communications consulting

(G-10374)
ELF HOMES INC
Also Called: Green Stay CA
3616 Kirkwood Hwy Ste A (19808-5124)
PHONE....................650 918-7829
EMP: 9
SALES: 1MM **Privately Held**
SIC: 6531 Real Estate Agent/Manager

(G-10375)
ELIAS MAMBERG MD
1301 N Harrison St # 104 (19806-3128)
PHONE....................302 428-0337
Elias Mamberg, *Owner*
EMP: 4
SALES (est): 261.5K **Privately Held**
SIC: 8011 Obstetrician

(G-10376)
ELITE LANDSCAPE
414 Meco Dr (19804-1112)
PHONE....................302 543-7305
Carl Berny, *Owner*
EMP: 9
SALES (est): 353.3K **Privately Held**
SIC: 0781 Landscape services

(G-10377)
ELITE TAX SERVICES LLC
30b Trolley Sq (19806-3352)
PHONE....................302 256-0401
Tilquainta Cox,
EMP: 5

SALES (est): 181.4K **Privately Held**
SIC: 7291 8721 Tax return preparation services; accounting, auditing & bookkeeping

(G-10378)
ELITE TRNSPT & LOGISTICS INC
300 Delaware Ave Ste 210 (19801-6601)
PHONE....................302 348-8480
Amanda Perez, *Principal*
Shaun Shells, *Principal*
EMP: 13
SALES (est): 637K **Privately Held**
SIC: 4789 Freight car loading & unloading

(G-10379)
ELLIS FALL SFETY SOLUTIONS LLC
306 Country Club Dr (19803-2920)
PHONE....................302 571-8470
Nigel Ellia,
Cheryl Scanlon-Zinner, *Training Spec*
EMP: 4
SALES: 500K **Privately Held**
SIC: 8748 Safety training service

(G-10380)
ELLIS LADDER IMPROVEMENTS
306 Country Club Dr (19803-2920)
PHONE....................302 571-8470
J Nigel Ellis, *CEO*
Andrew Durney, *Accountant*
Anna Pancoast, *Info Tech Mgr*
EMP: 4
SALES (est): 25K **Privately Held**
SIC: 5084 Safety equipment

(G-10381)
ELLMORE AUTO COLLISION
Also Called: Frank Smiths Twing Atobody Repr
4921 Governor Printz Blvd (19809-3501)
PHONE....................302 762-2301
Frank Smith, *CEO*
EMP: 7
SQ FT: 3,000
SALES (est): 548.1K **Privately Held**
SIC: 7549 7532 Towing service, automotive; body shop, automotive; body shop, trucks

(G-10382)
ELMER SCHULTZ SERVICES INC
Also Called: Commercial Food Equipment Repr
36 Belmont Ave (19804-1538)
PHONE....................302 655-8900
Roger McGuire, *Branch Mgr*
EMP: 7
SALES (corp-wide): 8.6MM **Privately Held**
SIC: 5046 Restaurant equipment & supplies
PA: Elmer Schultz Services, Inc.
540 N 3rd St
Philadelphia PA 19123
215 627-5400

(G-10383)
ELSMERE FIRE CO 1 INC
1107 Kirkwood Hwy (19805-2117)
PHONE....................302 999-0183
Warren F Jones, *President*
John Bolin, *Chief*
Mark Facciolo, *Chief*
Kenneth Dunn, *Vice Pres*
Jack Parisi, *Vice Pres*
EMP: 5
SQ FT: 6,000
SALES: 1.4MM **Privately Held**
SIC: 7389 Fire protection service other than forestry or public

(G-10384)
ELSMERE PRESBYTERIAN CHURCH
606 New Rd (19805-5125)
PHONE....................302 998-6365
Tom Stouk, *Pastor*
EMP: 13
SALES (est): 590.7K **Privately Held**
SIC: 8661 8351 Presbyterian Church; child day care services

(G-10385)
ELWYN
Also Called: Delaware Elwyn
321 E 11th St Fl 1 (19801-3417)
PHONE....................302 658-8860
Sara Beckary, *Opers Staff*
Donna Skinner, *Human Res Dir*
Rhonda Williams, *Marketing Staff*
Yvette Grier, *Psychologist*
Vernay Lewis, *Case Mgr*
EMP: 87
SALES (corp-wide): 314.5MM **Privately Held**
WEB: www.caelwyn.org
SIC: 8093 8331 2441 2396 Rehabilitation center, outpatient treatment; job counseling; job training services; nailed wood boxes & shook; automotive & apparel trimmings
PA: Elwyn Of Pennsylvania And Delaware
111 Elwyn Rd
Media PA 19063
610 662-7372

(G-10386)
ELZUFON AUSTIN REARDON TARLOV (PA)
300 Delaware Ave Ste 1700 (19801-1612)
P.O. Box 1630 (19899-1630)
PHONE....................302 428-3181
John Elzufon, *Partner*
William F Taylor Jr, *Director*
Vicki Spangler, *Officer*
H G Baker, *Associate*
Peter McGivney, *Associate*
EMP: 40
SALES (est): 4.9MM **Privately Held**
WEB: www.elzufon.com
SIC: 8111 General practice attorney, lawyer

(G-10387)
EMBRACE HOME LOANS INC
5341 Limestone Rd Ste 101 (19808-1222)
PHONE....................302 635-7998
Joseph Beacher, *Branch Mgr*
EMP: 9
SALES (corp-wide): 221MM **Privately Held**
SIC: 6162 Mortgage bankers & correspondents
PA: Embrace Home Loans, Inc.
25 Enterprise Ctr # 200
Middletown RI 02842
401 846-3100

(G-10388)
EMBROID ME LLC
4385 Kirkwood Hwy (19808-5113)
PHONE....................302 993-0204
EMP: 1
SALES (est): 33.7K **Privately Held**
SIC: 2395 Embroidery & art needlework

(G-10389)
EMENDO BIO INC
1811 Silverside Rd (19810-4345)
PHONE....................516 595-1849
Todd Wider, *Principal*
Julie Amar, *Principal*
David Baram, *Principal*
EMP: 5
SALES (est): 104.7K **Privately Held**
SIC: 7389

(G-10390)
EMERALD INDUSTRIES LLC
4157 Concord Pike (19803-1487)
PHONE....................302 450-1416
EMP: 3 EST: 2004
SQ FT: 400
SALES (est): 148.1K **Privately Held**
SIC: 2111 Mfg Cigarettes

(G-10391)
EMERGNCY RESPONSE PROTOCOL LLC
101 W Ayre St (19804-3103)
PHONE....................302 994-2600
Angela Tiberi, *CEO*
Dave Tiberi, *President*
Al Abuasi, *Vice Pres*
EMP: 8

GEOGRAPHIC SECTION
Wilmington - New Castle County (G-10422)

SALES (est): 284.2K **Privately Held**
SIC: 7382 1731 Protective devices, security; fiber optic cable installation; voice, data & video wiring contractor; safety & security specialization

(G-10392)
EMMA JEFFERIES DAY CARE
603 W 39th St (19802-2034)
PHONE.................302 762-3235
Lewis V Jefferies, *Principal*
EMP: 5
SALES (est): 54.7K **Privately Held**
SIC: 8351 Group day care center

(G-10393)
EMMENT A OAT CONTRACTOR INC
501 W Newport Pike (19804-3233)
PHONE.................302 999-1567
Robert E Oat, *President*
Emment A Oat, *Vice Pres*
Donna R Oat, *Admin Sec*
EMP: 5
SALES: 500K **Privately Held**
SIC: 1541 Renovation, remodeling & repairs: industrial buildings

(G-10394)
EMPIRE FLIPPERS LLC
427 N Tatnall St 34425 (19801-2230)
PHONE.................323 638-0438
Joseph Magnotti, *CEO*
Justin Cooke, *CFO*
Andrew Voda, *Business Anlyst*
EMP: 17
SALES: 10MM **Privately Held**
SIC: 7389 Brokers, business: buying & selling business enterprises

(G-10395)
ENCORE DESIGNS INC
1607 Walton Rd (19803-3416)
PHONE.................302 798-5678
EMP: 2
SALES (est): 120K **Privately Held**
SIC: 2759 Commercial Printing

(G-10396)
ENCROSS LLC
1521 Concord Pike Ste 301 (19803-3644)
PHONE.................302 351-2593
Randall Hirt, *Principal*
EMP: 12
SALES (est): 676.2K **Privately Held**
SIC: 7373 7379 7371 8748 Systems software development services; computer related consulting services; computer software systems analysis & design, custom; business consulting

(G-10397)
ENDEVOR LLC
3844 Kennett Pike Ste 210 (19807-2305)
PHONE.................302 543-5055
Timothy Johnson, *Mng Member*
Richard Gilbert,
EMP: 6
SQ FT: 1,300
SALES: 651K **Privately Held**
SIC: 7371 Computer software development

(G-10398)
ENDOVASCULAR CONSULTANTS LLC
701 N Clayton St 601 (19805-3165)
PHONE.................302 482-1333
EMP: 7
SALES (est): 470.4K **Privately Held**
SIC: 8748 Business consulting

(G-10399)
ENDURNCE REINSURANCE CORP AMER
1209 N Orange St (19801-1120)
PHONE.................973 898-9575
Perry Roderick, *Principal*
EMP: 15 EST: 2008
SALES (est): 3.3MM **Privately Held**
SIC: 6411 Insurance agents, brokers & service

(G-10400)
ENER-G GROUP INC
3422 Old Capitol Trl (19808-6124)
PHONE.................917 281-0020
Samina Sadiq, *Principal*
EMP: 10
SALES (est): 304.8K **Privately Held**
SIC: 8731 Energy research

(G-10401)
ENERKEM MISS BIOFUELS LLC
222 Delaware Ave Fl 9 (19801-1621)
PHONE.................514 875-0284
Vincent Chornet, *CEO*
Dino Mili, *Principal*
Stephanie Issacs, *Director*
EMP: 1
SALES (est): 130K **Privately Held**
SIC: 2869 Industrial organic chemicals

(G-10402)
ENGINEERED SYSTEMS & DESIGNS
Also Called: Esd
3 S Tatnall St (19801-2457)
PHONE.................302 456-0446
Robert Spring, *President*
William Spring, *Vice Pres*
EMP: 4 EST: 1975
SQ FT: 5,000
SALES: 280K **Privately Held**
WEB: www.esdinc.com
SIC: 3823 3825 Water quality monitoring & control systems; instruments to measure electricity

(G-10403)
ENGINEERING INCORPORATED
6 Lewis Cir (19804-1618)
PHONE.................302 995-6862
Karl M Mruz, *President*
EMP: 7 EST: 1962
SQ FT: 9,000
SALES (est): 570K **Privately Held**
SIC: 3441 Joists, open web steel: long-span series

(G-10404)
ENSYN GA BIOREFINERY I LLC
1521 Concord Pike Ste 205 (19803-3645)
PHONE.................303 425-3740
Rick Tallman,
EMP: 1
SALES (est): 110K **Privately Held**
SIC: 2869 Industrial organic chemicals

(G-10405)
ENT AND ALLERGY DELAWARE LLC (PA)
Also Called: Silverside Medical Center
1401 Foulk Rd Ste 205 (19803-2764)
PHONE.................302 478-8467
Rob Goss, *Principal*
Nurse Practitioner, *Principal*
EMP: 23 EST: 2010
SALES (est): 5.7MM **Privately Held**
SIC: 8011 Allergist

(G-10406)
ENT AND ALLERGY DELAWARE LLC
1941 Limestone Rd (19808-5408)
PHONE.................302 998-0300
Kieran Connolly, *Owner*
Rob Goss, *COO*
Michelle Diteodoro, *Marketing Staff*
William Geimeier, *Med Doctor*
Gregg Goldstein, *Med Doctor*
EMP: 15
SALES (corp-wide): 5.7MM **Privately Held**
SIC: 8011 Ears, nose & throat specialist: physician/surgeon
PA: Ent And Allergy Of Delaware, Llc
1401 Foulk Rd Ste 205
Wilmington DE 19803
302 478-8467

(G-10407)
ENTERPRISE FLASHER CO INC
4 Hadco Rd (19804-1085)
PHONE.................302 999-0856
Anne Builderback, *President*
Courtney Roehm, *Vice Pres*
Mary Mauk, *Cust Mgr*
Mike Peco, *Cust Mgr*
EMP: 17
SQ FT: 8,000
SALES (est): 2.7MM **Privately Held**
WEB: www.enterpriseflasher.com
SIC: 7359 5999 Work zone traffic equipment (flags, cones, barrels, etc.); safety supplies & equipment

(G-10408)
ENTERPRISE LEARNING SOLUTIONS
236 Weldin Ridge Rd (19803-3974)
PHONE.................302 762-6595
EMP: 5
SALES (est): 59.9K **Privately Held**
SIC: 8351 Child day care services

(G-10409)
ENTERPRISE LSG PHLADELPHIA LLC
Also Called: Alamo
100 S French St Unit 115a (19801-5019)
PHONE.................302 425-4404
EMP: 6
SALES (corp-wide): 4.5B **Privately Held**
SIC: 7514 Rent-a-car service
HQ: Enterprise Leasing Company Of Philadelphia, Llc
2434 W Main St 2436
Norristown PA 19403

(G-10410)
ENTERPRISE LSG PHLADELPHIA LLC
Also Called: Enterprise Rent-A-Car
4727 Concord Pike (19803-1408)
PHONE.................302 479-7829
EMP: 6
SALES (corp-wide): 4.5B **Privately Held**
SIC: 7514 Rent-a-car service
HQ: Enterprise Leasing Company Of Philadelphia, Llc
2434 W Main St 2436
Norristown PA 19403

(G-10411)
ENTERPRISE LSG PHLADELPHIA LLC
Also Called: Enterprise Rent-A-Car
520 S Walnut St (19801-5230)
PHONE.................302 656-5464
Steve Burns, *Manager*
EMP: 6
SALES (corp-wide): 4.5B **Privately Held**
SIC: 7514 Passenger car rental
HQ: Enterprise Leasing Company Of Philadelphia, Llc
2434 W Main St 2436
Norristown PA 19403

(G-10412)
ENTERPRISE LSG PHLADELPHIA LLC
Also Called: Enterprise Rent-A-Car
100 Philadelphia Pike (19809-3180)
PHONE.................302 761-4545
EMP: 6
SALES (corp-wide): 4.5B **Privately Held**
SIC: 7514 Passenger car rental
HQ: Enterprise Leasing Company Of Philadelphia, Llc
2434 W Main St 2436
Norristown PA 19403

(G-10413)
ENTERPRISE MASONRY CORPORATION
3010 Bellevue Ave (19802-2402)
PHONE.................302 764-6858
Gregory Furtaw, *President*
Patrick Riely, *Vice Pres*
Kyle Furtaw, *Project Mgr*
Rhonda Malatesta, *Treasurer*
EMP: 45
SQ FT: 12,500
SALES (est): 9.1MM **Privately Held**
SIC: 1741 Masonry & other stonework

(G-10414)
ENTERPRISE RENT-A-CAR
2415 Lancaster Ave (19805-3736)
PHONE.................302 575-1021
EMP: 7
SALES (corp-wide): 4.5B **Privately Held**
SIC: 7514 Passenger car rental
HQ: Enterprise Rent-A-Car Company Of Los Angeles, Llc
333 City Blvd W Ste 1000
Orange CA 92868
657 221-4400

(G-10415)
ENTERPRISE RSURCE PLANNERS INC (PA)
4023 Kennett Pike 312 (19807-2018)
PHONE.................800 716-3660
Stephen Roche, *President*
Robert McLaughlin, *Exec VP*
EMP: 4
SALES (est): 6.8MM **Privately Held**
WEB: www.erplanners.com
SIC: 8742 Management consulting services

(G-10416)
ENTH INC
3422 Old Capitol Trl # 2096 (19808-6124)
PHONE.................630 986-8700
EMP: 4
SALES (est): 191.7K **Privately Held**
SIC: 7372 Prepackaged Software Services

(G-10417)
ENTOURAGE FINANCIAL GROUP LLC
1703 N Pine St (19802-5008)
PHONE.................302 352-9473
Brandon Tate,
EMP: 4
SALES: 45K **Privately Held**
SIC: 6311 6411 Life insurance; education services, insurance

(G-10418)
ENVIRONICS ANALYTICS INC
1000 N West St Ste 1200 (19801-1058)
PHONE.................302 600-0304
EMP: 50
SALES (est): 1.1MM **Privately Held**
SIC: 8732 Commercial Nonphysical Research

(G-10419)
ENVIRONMENTAL ALLIANCE INC (PA)
5341 Limestone Rd (19808-1222)
PHONE.................302 995-7544
William Smith, *President*
Dori S Smith, *Corp Secy*
Paul C Miller, *Vice Pres*
Tom Murphy, *Project Mgr*
Daniela Pava, *Accounts Mgr*
EMP: 29
SQ FT: 8,500
SALES: 8.7MM **Privately Held**
WEB: www.envalliance.com
SIC: 8748 Environmental consultant

(G-10420)
ENVIRONMENTAL VERSACORP (PA)
501 Silverside Rd Ste 98 (19809-1376)
PHONE.................302 798-1839
Angela Haghler, *President*
David Wayson, *Vice Pres*
Clifford Kraus, *Treasurer*
EMP: 4
SALES: 3MM **Privately Held**
SIC: 8744

(G-10421)
ENVISION CONSULTING LLC
2008 Woodlawn Ave (19806-2234)
PHONE.................302 658-9027
Sally C Coonin, *Principal*
EMP: 4
SALES (est): 194K **Privately Held**
SIC: 8748 Business consulting

(G-10422)
ENVISION SOLUTION LLC
3422 Old Capitol Trl # 714 (19808-6124)
PHONE.................302 442-7329
Ryan Phillips,
EMP: 15 EST: 2013
SALES (est): 648.7K **Privately Held**
SIC: 8748 Business consulting

Wilmington - New Castle County (G-10423)   GEOGRAPHIC SECTION

(G-10423)
ENVOLVE INC (PA)
1209 N Orange St (19801-1120)
PHONE.................................314 349-3571
Michael Neidorff, *President*
EMP: 430 EST: 2015
SALES: 32MM **Privately Held**
SIC: 8082 Home health care services

(G-10424)
EPB ASSOCIATES INC
107 W Sutton Pl (19810-4115)
P.O. Box 7397 (19803-0397)
PHONE.................................302 475-7301
Frank A Bush Jr, *President*
Lydia White, *Corp Secy*
Edwin Bush, *Vice Pres*
EMP: 13
SALES: 1.5MM **Privately Held**
WEB: www.epbassociates.com
SIC: 1629 1623 Earthmoving contractor; sewer line construction; water main construction

(G-10425)
EPIC RESEARCH LLC
1105 N Market St Ste 1600 (19801-1201)
PHONE.................................703 297-8121
EMP: 5
SALES (est): 1MM **Privately Held**
SIC: 8733 Research institute

(G-10426)
EPIQ SYSTEMS INC
824 N Market St (19801-3024)
PHONE.................................302 574-2600
Jennifer Meyerowitz, *Vice Pres*
EMP: 30
SALES (corp-wide): 589.6MM **Privately Held**
SIC: 7371 Computer software development
HQ: Epiq Systems, Inc.
2 Ravinia Dr Ste 850
Atlanta GA 30346
913 621-9500

(G-10427)
EPOTEC INC
62 Rockford Rd (19806-1047)
PHONE.................................302 654-3090
J Hayes Batson, *President*
Richard D Flanagan PHD, *Ch Credit Ofcr*
Catherine Gross, *CIO*
EMP: 110 EST: 1997
SALES (est): 3.2MM **Privately Held**
SIC: 7371 Computer software development

(G-10428)
EPRINTIT USA INC
1000 N West St (19801-1050)
PHONE.................................613 299-7105
Tony Gagliano, *President*
Mark Patenaude, *Vice Pres*
EMP: 10
SQ FT: 1,200
SALES: 400K
SALES (corp-wide): 387.5MM **Privately Held**
SIC: 8741 Management services
HQ: 1772887 Ontario Limited
15 Benton Rd
North York ON M6M 3
416 364-3333

(G-10429)
EPTHI INC
300 Delaware Ave (19801-1607)
PHONE.................................917 821-1935
Tommeso Pernici, *President*
EMP: 4
SALES (corp-wide): 269.8K **Privately Held**
SIC: 4899 Data communication services
PA: Epthi Inc.
77 W 55th St Apt 9h
New York NY 10019
917 821-1935

(G-10430)
EQUITY CONTRACTING LLC
102 Robino Ct Ste 203 (19804-2360)
PHONE.................................302 504-1468
EMP: 7

SALES: 950K **Privately Held**
SIC: 1522 Residential Construction

(G-10431)
ERCO CEILINGS INC
2 S Dupont Rd (19805-1446)
PHONE.................................302 994-6200
Stanley Sykora, *Manager*
EMP: 10
SALES (corp-wide): 32.5MM **Privately Held**
SIC: 5039 Ceiling systems & products
PA: Erco Ceilings, Inc.
32 Delsea Dr N
Glassboro NJ 08028
856 881-4200

(G-10432)
ERCO CEILINGS & INTERIORS INC (HQ)
2 S Dupont Rd (19805-1446)
PHONE.................................302 994-6200
Richard Sykora, *President*
Randy Otto, *Vice Pres*
EMP: 15
SALES: 4.3MM
SALES (corp-wide): 32.5MM **Privately Held**
WEB: www.ercoonline.com
SIC: 1742 5211 Acoustical & ceiling work; lumber & other building materials
PA: Erco Ceilings, Inc.
32 Delsea Dr N
Glassboro NJ 08028
856 881-4200

(G-10433)
ERGOS CONSULTORES LLC
3411 Silverside Rd # 104 (19810-4812)
PHONE.................................549 404-6360
Pablo Calatroni,
EMP: 10
SALES (est): 180.6K **Privately Held**
SIC: 7389

(G-10434)
ERI INVESTMENTS INC
801 N West St Fl 2 (19801-1525)
PHONE.................................302 656-8089
John Bergonzi, *President*
Philip Conti, *President*
Kenneth Kubacki, *Vice Pres*
Claire A Paschitti, *Treasurer*
EMP: 10
SALES: 569.2MM
SALES (corp-wide): 4.5B **Publicly Held**
WEB: www.eqt.com
SIC: 6719 Investment holding companies, except banks
PA: Eqt Corporation
625 Liberty Ave Ste 1700
Pittsburgh PA 15222
412 553-5700

(G-10435)
ERIK S BRADLEY DDS
1415 Foulk Rd Ste 200 (19803-2748)
PHONE.................................302 239-5917
Erik Bradley, *Fmly & Gen Dent*
EMP: 4
SALES (est): 61.5K **Privately Held**
SIC: 8021 Offices & clinics of dentists

(G-10436)
ESIS INC
P.O. Box 15054 (19850-5054)
PHONE.................................215 640-1000
Joe Vasquez, *CEO*
EMP: 4
SALES (corp-wide): 32.7B **Privately Held**
SIC: 8742 Management consulting services
HQ: Esis, Inc.
436 Walnut St
Philadelphia PA 19106
215 640-1000

(G-10437)
ESPOSITO MANSORY LLC
471 B And O Ln (19804-1450)
PHONE.................................302 996-4961
Vincent Esposito,
EMP: 10
SALES (est): 422K **Privately Held**
SIC: 1741 Concrete block masonry laying

(G-10438)
ESSENTIAL HEALTH BRANDS LLC
1000 N West St Ste 1200 (19801-1058)
PHONE.................................302 322-1249
Sean C Mulrooney,
EMP: 5
SALES (est): 399.1K **Privately Held**
SIC: 7311 Advertising agencies

(G-10439)
ESSILOR AMERICA HOLDING CO INC (HQ)
1209 N Orange St (19801-1120)
PHONE.................................214 496-4000
EMP: 10 EST: 1996
SALES (est): 2.6B
SALES (corp-wide): 1.4MM **Privately Held**
SIC: 3851 5048 Ophthalmic goods; ophthalmic goods
PA: Essilorluxottica
147 Rue De Paris
Charenton-Le-Pont 94220
149 774-224

(G-10440)
ETECHBOYS INC
3616 Kirkwood Hwy Ste A (19808-5124)
PHONE.................................800 549-4208
Raymond Brunner, *CEO*
EMP: 5
SALES (est): 207.7K **Privately Held**
SIC: 4911 Electric services

(G-10441)
ETERNAL HEALTH LLC
4837 Limestone Rd (19808-1902)
PHONE.................................302 635-7421
Megan E Richardson, *President*
EMP: 5
SALES (est): 100.5K **Privately Held**
SIC: 8099 Health & allied services

(G-10442)
EUROPEAN PERFORMANCE INC
806 Wilmington Ave (19805-5113)
PHONE.................................302 633-1122
John Lengyel, *President*
Laura Lengyel, *Vice Pres*
Susan Wiley, *Admin Sec*
EMP: 8
SALES (est): 1.1MM **Privately Held**
SIC: 7538 Engine rebuilding: automotive

(G-10443)
EVEN & ODD MINDS LLC (PA)
1521 Concord Pike Ste 301 (19803-3644)
PHONE.................................619 663-7284
Ravi Goel, *Managing Prtnr*
Lisa Davis, *Human Res Mgr*
Tasha Abay, *Recruiter*
EMP: 15
SQ FT: 1,000
SALES (est): 2.5MM **Privately Held**
SIC: 8742 7379 Human resource consulting services; computer related consulting services

(G-10444)
EVENTZILLA CORPORATION
19c Trolley Sq (19806-3355)
PHONE.................................888 817-2837
M Rambacthavachalam, *President*
EMP: 13
SALES: 460K **Privately Held**
SIC: 7371 Computer software development & applications

(G-10445)
EVEREST GRANITE LLC
3410 Old Capitol Trl (19808-6152)
PHONE.................................302 229-4733
Alberto Jaldez, *Mng Member*
EMP: 1
SALES: 400K **Privately Held**
SIC: 1799 1411 Counter top installation; granite, dimension-quarrying

(G-10446)
EVERETT ROBINSON
Also Called: C-West Entertainment
1 Margit Ln (19810-2048)
PHONE.................................302 530-6574
Everett Robinson, *Principal*

EMP: 15
SALES (est): 63.8K **Privately Held**
SIC: 7929 7221 7812 7922 Entertainers & entertainment groups; photographer, still or video; television film production; performing arts center production; business management

(G-10447)
EVERGREEN REALTY
100 Ethan Ct Apt H (19804-3163)
PHONE.................................302 999-8805
Lauren J Wolfgang, *General Counsel*
Kevin Wolfgang,
Gregory Wolfgang,
Lauren Wolfgang,
EMP: 20
SALES (est): 1.2MM **Privately Held**
SIC: 6513 Apartment building operators

(G-10448)
EVERGREEN REALTY INC
Also Called: Driftwood Club Apartments
125 Greenbank Rd Apt A4 (19808-4746)
PHONE.................................302 998-0354
Kevin Wolfegang, *President*
EMP: 5
SALES (est): 585K **Privately Held**
SIC: 6513 Apartment building operators

(G-10449)
EVERGREEN RESOURCES GROUP LLC
2 Righter Pkwy Ste 120 (19803-1528)
PHONE.................................302 477-0189
Scott Cullinan, *President*
EMP: 7
SALES (est): 76.3K
SALES (corp-wide): 54B **Publicly Held**
SIC: 8999 Earth science services
HQ: Etp Legacy Lp
8111 Westchester Dr # 600
Dallas TX 75225
214 981-0700

(G-10450)
EVERYBODY NEEDS INK
209 Lister Dr (19808-2329)
PHONE.................................302 633-0866
Charles W Crile, *Partner*
Richard Couch, *Partner*
EMP: 4
SALES (est): 148.7K **Privately Held**
SIC: 7299 Tattoo parlor

(G-10451)
EVONSYS LLC
4550 New Lnden Hl Rd Ste (19808)
PHONE.................................302 544-2156
Arunkumar M Subramanian, *CEO*
EMP: 8 EST: 2015
SQ FT: 2,000
SALES: 450.2K **Privately Held**
SIC: 7379

(G-10452)
EVOQUA WATER TECHNOLOGIES LLC
1020 Christiana Ave Ste 1 (19801-5884)
PHONE.................................302 654-3712
Glenn Culler, *Manager*
EMP: 9
SALES (corp-wide): 1.4B **Publicly Held**
SIC: 5149 Mineral or spring water bottling
HQ: Evoqua Water Technologies Llc
210 6th Ave Ste 3300
Pittsburgh PA 15222
724 772-0044

(G-10453)
EVS LAWN SERVICE INC
2609 Ebright Rd (19810-1146)
PHONE.................................302 475-9222
Christopher Evens, *President*
EMP: 5
SALES (est): 124K **Privately Held**
SIC: 0782 Lawn & garden services

(G-10454)
EWASTE EXPRESS
6 Rosetree Ct (19810-3209)
PHONE.................................302 691-8052
Rebecca Deshetler, *President*
EMP: 5 EST: 2013
SQ FT: 7,000

GEOGRAPHIC SECTION
Wilmington - New Castle County (G-10486)

SALES (est): 651.6K **Privately Held**
SIC: 5093 Scrap & waste materials

(G-10455)
EWEBVALET CO INC
22 Center Meeting Rd (19807-1302)
PHONE.....................302 893-0903
Charles Beattie, *President*
EMP: 6
SALES (est): 127.7K **Privately Held**
SIC: 4813

(G-10456)
EXALENZ BIOSCIENCE INC
1313 N Market St (19801-6101)
PHONE.....................888 392-5369
Denise Biol, *Vice Pres*
EMP: 8
SALES (est): 504.8K
SALES (corp-wide): 3.7MM **Privately Held**
SIC: 8071 Biological laboratory
PA: Exalenz Bioscience Ltd
    4 Hamaayan
    Modiin-Maccabim-Reut 71778
    897 375-38

(G-10457)
EXCAPE ENTERTAINMENT US LTD
704 N King St Ste 500 (19801-3584)
PHONE.....................949 943-9219
James Fiorillo Ortega, *CEO*
Steven Teear, *COO*
EMP: 7
SALES (est): 530.7K **Privately Held**
SIC: 7359 3699 Home entertainment equipment rental; automotive driving simulators (training aids), electronic

(G-10458)
EXCO INC (HQ)
1007 N Orange St (19801-1239)
PHONE.....................905 477-3065
Brian Robbins, *CEO*
Paul Riganelli, *President*
Drew Knight, *Vice Pres*
EMP: 100
SALES (est): 66.9MM
SALES (corp-wide): 376.2MM **Privately Held**
SIC: 6719 3111 Public utility holding companies; industrial leather products
PA: Exco Technologies Limited
    130 Spy Crt
    Markham ON L3R 5
    905 477-3065

(G-10459)
EXECUTIVE AUTO REPAIRS INC
480 B And O Ln (19804-1452)
PHONE.....................302 995-6220
Michael Groome, *President*
Vincent Colasante, *Vice Pres*
Diane Groome, *Treasurer*
EMP: 6
SQ FT: 6,000
SALES (est): 677.5K **Privately Held**
SIC: 7532 Body shop, automotive

(G-10460)
EXPECTING MIRACLES LLC
2506 Teal Rd (19805-1055)
PHONE.....................302 893-3220
Adrienne Talabisco, *Principal*
EMP: 4
SALES (est): 28.8K **Privately Held**
SIC: 7231 Beauty shops

(G-10461)
EXPLORATION SYSTEMS & TECH
Also Called: Est
1209 N Orange St (19801-1120)
PHONE.....................302 335-3911
Robert Poisson, *Owner*
Lynn Rollins, *Principal*
▼ EMP: 6
SALES (est): 413.2K **Privately Held**
SIC: 3728 Aircraft parts & equipment

(G-10462)
EXPLORER NEW BUILD LLC
2711 Centerville Rd # 120 (19808-1676)
PHONE.....................305 436-4000

EMP: 4
SALES (est): 4.5MM
SALES (corp-wide): 6B **Publicly Held**
SIC: 4731 Brokers, shipping
PA: Norwegian Cruise Line Holdings Ltd.
    7665 Corp Ctr Dr
    Miami FL 33126
    305 436-4000

(G-10463)
EXPRESS LEGAL DOCUMENTS LLC (HQ)
Also Called: Eld
1201 N Orange St (19801-1155)
PHONE.....................212 710-1374
Tanya Guinevere Hunte,
EMP: 20
SALES (est): 873.9K
SALES (corp-wide): 2.1MM **Privately Held**
SIC: 8742 8111 Industry specialist consultants; specialized legal services
PA: Hunte Corporate Enterprise, Llc
    1201 N Orange St Ste 7377
    Wilmington DE 19801
    212 710-1341

(G-10464)
EYE CONSULTANTS LLC
1941 Limestone Rd Ste 200 (19808-5400)
PHONE.....................302 998-2333
Heather L Dealy, *Principal*
EMP: 6
SALES (est): 273.5K **Privately Held**
SIC: 8011 Ophthalmologist

(G-10465)
EYE PHYSICIANS AND SURGEONS PA
Also Called: Wahl, John MD
1207 N Scott St Ste 1 (19806-4059)
PHONE.....................302 225-1018
S H Franklin MD, *President*
Jeffrey Minkovitz, *Partner*
Dennis Mirra Od, *Principal*
Tom Cocoran, *Administration*
EMP: 30
SALES (est): 5.1MM **Privately Held**
SIC: 8011 Ophthalmologist

(G-10466)
EZION FAIR COMMUNITY ACADEMY
1400 B St (19801-5837)
PHONE.....................302 652-9114
Dr Christopher Curry, *Pastor*
EMP: 10
SALES (est): 301K **Privately Held**
SIC: 8351 Child day care services

(G-10467)
EZY BIOTECH LLC
3513 Concord Pike # 3100 (19803-5027)
PHONE.....................212 247-4261
Hua Gu, *Principal*
Yongrui Zou, *Principal*
Gann Xu, *Chairman*
EMP: 4
SALES (est): 134.8K **Privately Held**
SIC: 8731 Biotechnological research, commercial

(G-10468)
F & G CONSTRUCTION CO INC
25 Maple Ave (19804-1434)
PHONE.....................302 994-1406
Anthony Fontana, *President*
EMP: 5
SQ FT: 2,400
SALES (est): 483.8K **Privately Held**
SIC: 1611 Concrete construction: roads, highways, sidewalks, etc.; highway & street paving contractor

(G-10469)
F P T & W MEDICAL ASSOCIATES
1508 Penns Ave Ste 2b (19806-4339)
PHONE.....................800 421-2368
Dr Dennis L Farr, *Partner*
Dr Patricia H Purcell, *Partner*
Dr Carl E Turner, *Partner*
Dr Marc A Woolley, *Partner*
EMP: 17
SQ FT: 1,500

SALES (est): 503.6K **Privately Held**
SIC: 8071 X-ray laboratory, including dental

(G-10470)
FABBY INC
1013 Centre Rd Ste 403b (19805-1270)
PHONE.....................408 891-7991
Andrei Kulik, *CEO*
EMP: 10
SALES (est): 217.5K **Privately Held**
SIC: 7371 Computer software development & applications

(G-10471)
FABIT CORP
1201 N Orange St Ste 775 (19801-1173)
PHONE.....................832 217-0864
Badruddin Pitter, *Admin Sec*
EMP: 5
SALES (est): 1.6MM **Privately Held**
SIC: 7371 Computer software systems analysis & design, custom

(G-10472)
FABMANIANET
2834 W Oakland Dr (19808-2409)
PHONE.....................302 994-5801
Robert Fitch, *Owner*
EMP: 1 EST: 2000
SALES (est): 46.9K **Privately Held**
SIC: 7372 Home entertainment computer software

(G-10473)
FABRIZIO SALON
Also Called: Fabrizio Salon & Spa
1604 W 16th St (19806-4026)
PHONE.....................302 254-3432
Fabrizio Galieti, *Owner*
EMP: 13
SALES (est): 340.1K **Privately Held**
WEB: www.fabriziosalonspa.com
SIC: 7231 Hairdressers

(G-10474)
FACILITY SERVICES GROUP INC
300 Cornell Dr Ste A1 (19801-5768)
PHONE.....................302 317-3029
Albert Grimes, *President*
▲ EMP: 5 EST: 2012
SALES (est): 501.5K **Privately Held**
SIC: 1752 Carpet laying

(G-10475)
FAIR SQUARE FINANCIAL LLC
1000 N West St Ste 1100 (19801-1050)
PHONE.....................571 205-0305
Jennifer Lee Taylor, *Manager*
EMP: 4
SALES (est): 98.4K **Privately Held**
SIC: 8742 Financial consultant

(G-10476)
FAIRCHILD DAY SCHOOL
103 Lyndhurst Ave (19803-2343)
PHONE.....................302 478-4646
Rosemary Penrod, *Director*
EMP: 4
SALES (est): 81.2K **Privately Held**
SIC: 8351 Preschool center

(G-10477)
FAIRVILLE PRODUCTS INC
41 Germay Dr Ste 1 (19804-1100)
PHONE.....................302 425-4400
Robert Tatnall, *CEO*
Sandra Tatnall, *Vice Pres*
Deb McGhee, *Buyer*
Bob Gatchel, *Engineer*
Smitty Smith, *Sales Staff*
EMP: 2
SQ FT: 2,400
SALES: 200K **Privately Held**
WEB: www.fuelright.com
SIC: 2911 Fuel additives

(G-10478)
FAITH PRESBYTERIAN CHURCH
Also Called: Faith Day Care and Preschool
720 Marsh Rd (19803-4334)
PHONE.....................302 764-8615
Rev James O Brown Jr, *Pastor*
Nancy Rowels, *Treasurer*

Pauline Jennings, *Admin Sec*
Cindy Naylor, *Admin Sec*
EMP: 10
SALES (est): 592.1K **Privately Held**
SIC: 8661 8351 Presbyterian Church; child day care services

(G-10479)
FAITHFUL FRIENDS INC
Also Called: Faithful Friends Animal Soc
12 Germay Dr (19804-1105)
PHONE.....................302 427-8514
Jeannie Disabatino, *Opers Staff*
Kevin Rentz, *Marketing Staff*
Phyllis Frank, *Office Mgr*
Brittany Anthony, *Manager*
Jaime Lay, *Manager*
EMP: 60
SALES: 4.1MM **Privately Held**
SIC: 8699 Animal humane society; charitable organization

(G-10480)
FALCIDIAN LLC
270 Presidential Dr (19807-3302)
P.O. Box 3569 (19807-0569)
PHONE.....................302 656-5500
Ronald E Derr, *Executive*
EMP: 4 EST: 2005
SALES (est): 639.9K **Privately Held**
SIC: 6141 Financing: automobiles, furniture, etc., not a deposit bank

(G-10481)
FALCON CREST INV INTL INC
1201 N Orange St Ste 600 (19801-1171)
PHONE.....................240 701-1746
Samuel K Diame, *President*
EMP: 5
SALES (est): 950K **Privately Held**
SIC: 1522 Residential construction

(G-10482)
FALCON STEEL CO
811 S Market St (19801-5223)
PHONE.....................302 571-0890
William E Obrien, *President*
Helen O'Brien, *Corp Secy*
John O'Brien, *CFO*
Al N Katz, *Human Res Dir*
▲ EMP: 100
SQ FT: 10,000
SALES (est): 8.1MM **Privately Held**
WEB: www.falconsteel.com
SIC: 1791 Structural steel erection

(G-10483)
FALCONS MEDIA GROUP INC
251 Little Falls Dr (19808-1674)
P.O. Box 1346, Montclair NJ (07042-1346)
PHONE.....................201 247-6489
Eyad Bajes, *CEO*
EMP: 4
SALES (est): 89.7K **Privately Held**
SIC: 7371 Software programming applications

(G-10484)
FAMILY & FRIENDS CARING PEROLA
14 Oxford Way (19807-2571)
PHONE.....................302 683-0611
EMP: 15 EST: 1999
SALES (est): 570K **Privately Held**
SIC: 8699 Membership Organization

(G-10485)
FAMILY CHIROPRACTIC OFFICE PA
3105 Limestone Rd Ste 303 (19808-2156)
PHONE.....................302 993-9113
Tim Ciolkosz, *Owner*
Andrea Moses, *Co-Owner*
EMP: 5
SALES (est): 450.7K **Privately Held**
SIC: 8041 Offices & clinics of chiropractors

(G-10486)
FAMILY CNSLING CTR ST PULS INC
301 N Van Buren St (19805-3615)
P.O. Box 3803 (19807-0803)
PHONE.....................302 576-4136
Theresa Marie Elitz, *Principal*
Rob McCreary, *Exec Dir*

Wilmington - New Castle County (G-10487)   GEOGRAPHIC SECTION

Marie Redfield, *Admin Asst*
EMP: 11
SALES: 486K **Privately Held**
SIC: 8322 Individual & family services

(G-10487)
FAMILY DENTAL CARE
1601 Milltown Rd Ste 19 (19808-4084)
PHONE.................302 999-7600
Alfred B Brown DDS, *Managing Prtnr*
Mark Brown, *Principal*
EMP: 9
SALES (est): 299.1K **Privately Held**
SIC: 8021 Dentists' office

(G-10488)
FAMILY DENTAL CENTER
1 Winston Ave (19804-1760)
PHONE.................302 656-8266
Donald Jones, *Owner*
EMP: 15
SALES (est): 925.2K **Privately Held**
WEB: www.famdentdel.com
SIC: 8021 Dentists' office

(G-10489)
FAMILY DENTISTRY WILMINGTON
1708 Lovering Ave Ste 101 (19806-2141)
PHONE.................302 656-2434
Stacy Slocomb, *Principal*
EMP: 8
SALES (est): 84.5K **Privately Held**
SIC: 8021 Offices & clinics of dentists

(G-10490)
FAMILY EAR NOSE & THROAT
1941 Limestone Rd Ste 210 (19808-5400)
PHONE.................302 998-0300
Gerald Suh, *President*
Dr Kuwon Suh, *President*
Dr Mike Teixido, *Corp Secy*
Dr Tim Oto Gabriel, *Vice Pres*
EMP: 25
SALES (est): 713.4K **Privately Held**
SIC: 8011 Ears, nose & throat specialist; physician/surgeon

(G-10491)
FAMILY ENT PHYSICIANS INC (PA)
1941 Limestone Rd Ste 210 (19808-5400)
PHONE.................302 998-0300
Timoteo R Gabriel, *President*
Kuwon Suh, *Treasurer*
EMP: 28
SALES (est): 713.4K **Privately Held**
SIC: 8011 Ears, nose & throat specialist; physician/surgeon

(G-10492)
FAMILY MEDICINE AT GREENVILLE
213 Greenhill Ave Ste B (19805-1800)
PHONE.................302 429-5870
Stephanie Malleus, *President*
James M Gill, *Med Doctor*
EMP: 10
SALES (est): 1.1MM **Privately Held**
SIC: 8011 Ophthalmologist

(G-10493)
FAMILY MEDICINE CTR NATICCHIA
1400 N Washington St (19801-1024)
PHONE.................302 477-3300
Jennifer Naticchia, *Executive*
David Simpson, *Family Practiti*
EMP: 9 EST: 2013
SALES (est): 495.4K **Privately Held**
SIC: 8011 Medical centers

(G-10494)
FAMILY PRACTICE ASSOCIATION PA
2701 Kirkwood Hwy (19805-4911)
PHONE.................302 656-5416
Edward Sobel, *President*
John Moore MD, *Vice Pres*
EMP: 30
SQ FT: 5,000
SALES (est): 3.1MM **Privately Held**
SIC: 8621 Professional membership organizations

(G-10495)
FAMILY PROMISE OF NORTHERN NEW
2104 St James Church Rd (19808-5225)
PHONE.................302 998-2222
Denison Hatch, *President*
Patrick V Downes, *Principal*
Cathy Hatton, *Office Mgr*
Carolyn Gordon, *Exec Dir*
Greg Munson, *Exec Dir*
EMP: 6
SALES: 535.4K **Privately Held**
SIC: 8322 Individual & family services

(G-10496)
FAMILY WRKPLACE CONNECTION INC (PA)
2005 Baynard Blvd (19802-3917)
PHONE.................302 479-1660
Ralph Klesius, *Exec Dir*
EMP: 54
SQ FT: 10,000
SALES (est): 1.6MM **Privately Held**
WEB: www.familyandworkplace.org
SIC: 8322 8351 Child related social services; child day care services

(G-10497)
FAR FLUNG BUNGY LLC
4405 Whittier Rd (19802-1231)
PHONE.................302 421-8226
Erik Knudsen, *Owner*
EMP: 11
SALES (est): 122.8K **Privately Held**
SIC: 7822 Motion picture & tape distribution

(G-10498)
FARE4AIR LLC
500 Delaware Ave (19899-0009)
PHONE.................844 663-4040
EMP: 15
SALES: 1.2MM **Privately Held**
SIC: 4724 4725 Travel Agency Tour Operator

(G-10499)
FAREED SERVICES
9202 Westview Rd (19802-7704)
PHONE.................302 559-8594
Jason Rodriguez, *Owner*
EMP: 4
SALES: 275K **Privately Held**
SIC: 8748 7389 Business consulting;

(G-10500)
FARNAM HALL VENTURES LLC
3422 Old Capitol Trl (19808-6124)
PHONE.................347 687-2152
David Solin, *Partner*
David Ries,
EMP: 2
SALES: 500K **Privately Held**
SIC: 7372 Application computer software

(G-10501)
FARRAND VILLAGE APARTMENTS
16 Deville Cir (19808-4516)
PHONE.................302 998-5796
Margi Mc Lean, *Manager*
EMP: 4
SALES (est): 319.8K **Privately Held**
SIC: 6513 Apartment building operators

(G-10502)
FAST BAILBONDS LLC
1224 N King St (19801-3232)
PHONE.................302 778-4400
Wendy Condo,
EMP: 6
SALES (est): 195.1K **Privately Held**
SIC: 7389 Bail bonding; notary publics

(G-10503)
FAST FEET INC
Also Called: Fast Feet Shoe Repair
4737 Concord Pike Ste 415 (19803-1448)
PHONE.................302 478-5300
Mariah Verbruggen, *Owner*
EMP: 4
SALES (est): 146.3K **Privately Held**
SIC: 7251 Shoe repair shop

PA: Fast Feet Inc
69 Grissom Dr
Bear DE 19701

(G-10504)
FAST4WRD TOWING & REPAIR LLC
10 Meco Cir (19804-1109)
PHONE.................302 331-5157
Christopher Gedney, *Principal*
EMP: 4
SALES (est): 246.7K **Privately Held**
SIC: 7549 Towing services

(G-10505)
FASTSIGNS
1300 Frst State Blvd Ste (19804)
PHONE.................302 998-6755
EMP: 1
SALES (est): 52.1K **Privately Held**
SIC: 3993 Signs & advertising specialties

(G-10506)
FASTTRAK
1500 Eastlawn Ave (19802-2403)
PHONE.................302 761-5454
Charles McClure, *Principal*
EMP: 30
SALES (est): 1.6MM **Privately Held**
WEB: www.fasttrak.net
SIC: 1752 Floor laying & floor work

(G-10507)
FATHERS DAY GALA INC
436 S Buttonwood St (19801-5306)
PHONE.................302 981-4117
Karen Y Burton, *CEO*
EMP: 5
SALES: 3K **Privately Held**
SIC: 8399 Social services

(G-10508)
FAUSTIN ENTERPRISES LLC
1224 N King St (19801-3232)
PHONE.................302 543-2687
Mikel Faustino,
EMP: 4
SALES (est): 483K **Privately Held**
SIC: 4731 Domestic freight forwarding

(G-10509)
FBK GRAPHICO INC
2207 Concord Pike (19803-2908)
PHONE.................302 743-4784
Jim Fagan, *President*
EMP: 2
SALES (est): 96.1K **Privately Held**
SIC: 2759 Commercial printing

(G-10510)
FEARN-CLNDANIEL ARCHITECTS INC
6 Larch Ave Ste 398 (19804-2356)
PHONE.................302 998-7615
Kenneth Fearn, *President*
Wade Clendaniel, *Vice Pres*
Ken Fearn, *Associate*
EMP: 4
SALES (est): 320.7K **Privately Held**
SIC: 8712 Architectural engineering

(G-10511)
FEBYS FISHERY INC
3701 Lancaster Pike (19805-1510)
PHONE.................302 998-9501
Phillip Di Febo, *President*
Mary Di Febo, *Corp Secy*
EMP: 29
SQ FT: 7,000
SALES (est): 1MM **Privately Held**
WEB: www.febysfishery.com
SIC: 5812 5421 5146 Seafood restaurants; seafood markets; seafoods

(G-10512)
FEDERAL COURT REPORTERS
844 N King St Unit 24 (19801-3519)
PHONE.................302 573-6195
Leonard Dibbs, *Owner*
EMP: 7
SALES: 800K **Privately Held**
SIC: 7338 Court reporting service

(G-10513)
FEDERAL ENERGY INF
251 Little Falls Dr (19808-1674)
PHONE.................858 521-3300
Gerard Nolan,
Robert Miller,
Angel Mojica,
EMP: 10 EST: 2018
SALES (est): 512.1K **Privately Held**
SIC: 1731 Energy management controls

(G-10514)
FEDERAL EXPRESS CORPORATION
Also Called: Fedex
1209 N Orange St (19801-1120)
PHONE.................800 463-3339
EMP: 5
SALES (corp-wide): 69.6B **Publicly Held**
SIC: 4513 Air courier services
HQ: Federal Express Corporation
3610 Hacks Cross Rd
Memphis TN 38125
901 369-3600

(G-10515)
FEDERAL EXPRESS CORPORATION
Also Called: Fedex
827 N King St (19801-3517)
PHONE.................302 577-2667
EMP: 100
SALES (corp-wide): 47.4B **Publicly Held**
SIC: 4513 Air Courier Service
HQ: Federal Express Corporation
3610 Hacks Cross Rd
Memphis TN 38125
901 369-3600

(G-10516)
FEDERAL HOME LOAN ADM INC
1201 N Orange St Ste 600 (19801-1171)
P.O. Box 11141, Newport Beach CA (92658-5020)
PHONE.................855 345-2669
Nicholas Krakana, *CEO*
EMP: 55 EST: 2013
SQ FT: 4,500
SALES: 750MM **Privately Held**
SIC: 6162 Bond & mortgage companies

(G-10517)
FEDEX OFFICE & PRINT SVCS INC
4120 Concord Pike (19803-5401)
PHONE.................302 475-9501
EMP: 20
SALES (corp-wide): 69.6B **Publicly Held**
WEB: www.kinkos.com
SIC: 7334 Photocopying & duplicating services
HQ: Fedex Office And Print Services, Inc.
7900 Legacy Dr
Plano TX 75024
800 463-3339

(G-10518)
FEDEX OFFICE & PRINT SVCS INC
1201 N Market St Ste 1200 (19801-1163)
PHONE.................302 652-2151
EMP: 5
SALES (corp-wide): 69.6B **Publicly Held**
WEB: www.kinkos.com
SIC: 7334 Photocopying & duplicating services
HQ: Fedex Office And Print Services, Inc.
7900 Legacy Dr
Plano TX 75024
800 463-3339

(G-10519)
FEDEX OFFICE & PRINT SVCS INC
4721a Kirkwood Hwy (19808-5007)
PHONE.................302 996-0264
Sean Naughton, *Director*
EMP: 4
SALES (corp-wide): 69.6B **Publicly Held**
WEB: www.fedex.com
SIC: 2752 2759 5099 7334 Commercial printing, lithographic; commercial printing; signs, except electric; photocopying & duplicating services

GEOGRAPHIC SECTION

Wilmington - New Castle County (G-10547)

HQ: Fedex Office And Print Services, Inc.
7900 Legacy Dr
Plano TX 75024
800 463-3339

(G-10520)
FERGUSON ENTERPRISES LLC
2000 Maryland Ave (19805-4606)
PHONE.................................302 656-4421
John McGillen, *Sales Staff*
Brad Smith, *Branch Mgr*
Don Newsome, *Branch Mgr*
Don Newsone, *Manager*
EMP: 23
SALES (corp-wide): 20.7B **Privately Held**
WEB: www.ferguson.com
SIC: 5074 Plumbing fittings & supplies
HQ: Ferguson Enterprises, Llc
12500 Jefferson Ave
Newport News VA 23602
757 874-7795

(G-10521)
FERM DEVELOPMENT LLC
501 Silverside Rd (19809-1374)
PHONE.................................302 792-1102
Jack Ferm,
EMP: 7
SALES (est): 1.7MM **Privately Held**
SIC: 6552 Subdividers & developers

(G-10522)
FERRANTE & ASSOCIATES INC
175 Fairhill Dr (19808-4312)
PHONE.................................781 891-4328
Audrey Ferrante, *President*
Nancy Pakenham-Walsh, *Finance Dir*
Catherine M Conneely, *Administration*
EMP: 2 EST: 1988
SALES: 1MM **Privately Held**
SIC: 3555 Printing presses

(G-10523)
FERRARA ASSET MANAGEMENT INC
2711 Centerville Rd # 120 (19808-1660)
PHONE.................................401 286-8464
William Ferrara, *CEO*
EMP: 7 EST: 2014
SALES (est): 1.4MM **Privately Held**
SIC: 6722 7389 ;

(G-10524)
FERRARA HALEY & BEVIS
1716 Wawaset St (19806-2131)
PHONE.................................302 656-7247
Louis Ferrara, *Owner*
EMP: 11
SALES (est): 912.6K **Privately Held**
SIC: 8111 General practice attorney, lawyer

(G-10525)
FERRARI HAIR STUDIO LTD
4559 New Linden Hill Rd (19808)
PHONE.................................302 731-7505
Angelo V Ferrari, *President*
Ronald F Ferrari, *Vice Pres*
EMP: 25
SQ FT: 2,000
SALES (est): 642.3K **Privately Held**
SIC: 7231 Hairdressers

(G-10526)
FERRY JOSEPH & PEARCE PA (PA)
824 N Market St Ste 1000 (19801-4941)
P.O. Box 1351 (19899-1351)
PHONE.................................302 575-1555
David J Ferry Jr, *President*
Michael B Joseph, *Vice Pres*
Tammy Markey, *Legal Staff*
Robert Pearce,
Teresa Thomas, *Assistant*
EMP: 28
SALES (est): 2.9MM **Privately Held**
WEB: www.ferryjoseph.com
SIC: 8111 General practice attorney, lawyer

(G-10527)
FFI GENERAL CONTRACTOR IN
13 Perth Dr (19803-2612)
PHONE.................................302 420-1242
Hope Townsend, *Manager*

EMP: 5
SALES (est): 538.8K **Privately Held**
SIC: 1611 General contractor, highway & street construction

(G-10528)
FIA CARD SERVICES NAT ASSN
11 King St (19884-0001)
PHONE.................................302 457-0517
Richard Proctor, *Branch Mgr*
EMP: 200
SALES (corp-wide): 110.5B **Publicly Held**
WEB: www.mbna.com
SIC: 6021 National commercial banks
HQ: Fia Card Services, National Association
1100 N King St
Wilmington DE 19884
800 362-6255

(G-10529)
FIA CARD SERVICES NAT ASSN (HQ)
1100 N King St (19884-0011)
PHONE.................................800 362-6255
Brian T Moynihan, *President*
Linsz Mark D, *Treasurer*
Mogensen Lauren A, *Admin Sec*
EMP: 51
SALES (est): 467.8MM
SALES (corp-wide): 110.5B **Publicly Held**
WEB: www.mbna.com
SIC: 7389 Credit card service
PA: Bank Of America Corporation
100 N Tryon St Ste 170
Charlotte NC 28202
704 386-5681

(G-10530)
FIA CARD SERVICES NAT ASSN
1200 N French St (19884-0012)
PHONE.................................302 432-1573
Ceil Sculthorpe, *Manager*
EMP: 267
SALES (corp-wide): 110.5B **Publicly Held**
WEB: www.mbna.com
SIC: 6021 National commercial banks
HQ: Fia Card Services, National Association
1100 N King St
Wilmington DE 19884
800 362-6255

(G-10531)
FIBRE PROCESSING CORPORATION
701 Garasches Ln (19801-5528)
PHONE.................................302 654-3659
Anthony J Di Ottavio, *President*
Jacquelyne Di Ottavio, *Corp Secy*
▼ EMP: 68 EST: 1887
SQ FT: 100,000
SALES (est): 12MM **Privately Held**
WEB: www.fibrep.com
SIC: 2299 Batting, wadding, padding & fillings; batts & batting: cotton mill waste & related material

(G-10532)
FIDELITRADE INCORPORATED (PA)
3601 N Market St (19802-2736)
PHONE.................................302 762-6200
Jonathan E Potts, *President*
Simon Schatz, *Vice Pres*
Nathan Masten, *IT/INT Sup*
EMP: 17
SQ FT: 20,404
SALES (est): 8.8MM **Privately Held**
WEB: www.fidelitrade.com
SIC: 5094 Bullion, precious metals

(G-10533)
FIDELITY INCOME ADVISORS CO
3911 Concord Pike # 8030 (19803-6044)
P.O. Box 91, Mansfield TX (76063-0091)
PHONE.................................302 223-9444
Kw Booker II, *Principal*
Kayden Booker, *Principal*
Clarissa Price, *Principal*
Nikki Rhodes, *Principal*

EMP: 33
SALES (est): 1.1MM **Privately Held**
SIC: 6282 Investment advisory service

(G-10534)
FIDELITY NATIONAL FINCL INC
1220 N Market St Ste 201 (19801-2540)
PHONE.................................302 658-2102
Frank Kristan, *Branch Mgr*
EMP: 60
SALES (corp-wide): 7.5B **Publicly Held**
WEB: www.goldleaf-tech.com
SIC: 7389 Credit card service
PA: Fidelity National Financial, Inc.
601 Riverside Ave Fl 4
Jacksonville FL 32204
904 854-8100

(G-10535)
FIDELITY NATIONAL INFO SVCS (PA)
600 N King St Fl 10 (19801-3783)
PHONE.................................302 658-2102
Christina Gray, *President*
Dean M Lusky, *President*
Michael Zuckerman, *Vice Pres*
Peggy Issel, *Finance Mgr*
EMP: 17
SALES (est): 3.8MM **Privately Held**
SIC: 6411 Insurance agents

(G-10536)
FIDUKS INDUSTRIAL SERVICES INC (PA)
7 Meco Cir (19804-1193)
PHONE.................................302 994-2534
Gerald H Wybranski, *President*
Harold J Kuhn, *Principal*
EMP: 17
SQ FT: 10,000
SALES (est): 3MM **Privately Held**
WEB: www.fiduks.com
SIC: 7699 5084 Industrial machinery & equipment repair; machine tools & accessories

(G-10537)
FIDUKS INDUSTRIAL SERVICES INC
7 Meco Cir (19804-1193)
PHONE.................................302 994-2534
Karen Kershaw, *Branch Mgr*
EMP: 10
SALES (corp-wide): 3MM **Privately Held**
WEB: www.fiduks.com
SIC: 5084 Hydraulic systems equipment & supplies
PA: Fiduk's Industrial Services, Inc.
7 Meco Cir
Wilmington DE 19804
302 994-2534

(G-10538)
FIELDSTONE GOLF CLUB LP
1000 Dean Rd (19807-1648)
PHONE.................................302 254-4569
Mike Sanders, *General Mgr*
▲ EMP: 75
SALES (est): 4.7MM **Privately Held**
WEB: www.fieldstonegolf.com
SIC: 7997 Golf club, membership

(G-10539)
FINAL FINISHES INC
708 Woodtop Rd (19804-2628)
PHONE.................................302 995-1850
Wayne Gravell, *President*
Mickey Gravell, *Admin Sec*
EMP: 5
SALES (est): 300.6K **Privately Held**
SIC: 1721 Interior residential painting contractor

(G-10540)
FINANCIAL HOUSE INC
5818 Kennett Pike (19807-1116)
PHONE.................................302 654-5451
Joseph E Biloon, *Partner*
Mary Ann Blair, *Partner*
A Duer Pierce Jr, *Partner*
Emily R Woodson, *Partner*
Leo Strine, *CIO*
EMP: 14
SQ FT: 4,500

SALES (est): 1.9MM **Privately Held**
WEB: www.financialhouse.com
SIC: 8742 Financial consultant

(G-10541)
FINANCIAL SERVICES
Also Called: Rmch
1000 N West St Ste 1200 (19801-1058)
P.O. Box 132, Yorklyn (19736-0132)
PHONE.................................302 478-4707
Randi Dorante, *CEO*
Jim Chu, *Vice Ch Bd*
Randy Vaughn, *Vice Chairman*
R Natashi, *CFO*
EMP: 20
SQ FT: 500
SALES (est): 1MM **Privately Held**
SIC: 8742 Management consulting services

(G-10542)
FINOCCHIARO LANDSCAPE INC
41 N Cliffe Dr (19809-1623)
PHONE.................................302 792-2201
Robert M Finocchiaro, *President*
Kathleen Finocchiaro, *Treasurer*
EMP: 4
SALES (est): 193.8K **Privately Held**
SIC: 0782 Lawn care services

(G-10543)
FIREFLY DRONE OPERATIONS LLC
Also Called: Firefly Drone Ops
2643 Bittersweet Dr (19810-1643)
PHONE.................................305 206-6955
Marlene Garcia,
Humberto Hoyos,
EMP: 2 EST: 2017
SALES (est): 69.8K **Privately Held**
SIC: 7335 7389 8713 3728 Aerial photography, except mapmaking; ; surveying services; ; photogrammetric engineering; target drones; target drones, for use by ships: metal

(G-10544)
FIRST ACCESS INC
427 N Tatnall St (19801-2230)
PHONE.................................949 455-4027
Kimberly Darling, *CEO*
Tiffany Lombardo, *Director*
EMP: 10
SALES: 12K **Privately Held**
SIC: 6411 Insurance agents, brokers & service

(G-10545)
FIRST AMERICAN TITLE INSUR CO
704 N King St (19801-3583)
PHONE.................................302 421-9440
Donna Penge, *Manager*
EMP: 5 **Publicly Held**
WEB: www.fatc.com
SIC: 6361 Real estate title insurance
HQ: First American Title Insurance Company
1 First American Way
Santa Ana CA 92707
800 854-3643

(G-10546)
FIRST LINCOLN HOLDINGS INC
1219 N West St (19801-1044)
P.O. Box 249 (19899-0249)
PHONE.................................302 429-4900
Martin Oliner, *Ch of Bd*
Dave Taylor, *Treasurer*
EMP: 20
SALES (est): 3.6MM **Privately Held**
SIC: 6311 Life insurance carriers; life reinsurance

(G-10547)
FIRST POWER LLC
22 Peirce Rd (19803-3726)
PHONE.................................610 247-5750
Jeffrey Macel, *Mng Member*
EMP: 9
SALES (est): 670K **Privately Held**
SIC: 6552 Subdividers & developers

Wilmington - New Castle County (G-10548)

(G-10548)
FIRST REPUBLIC BANK
1201 N Market St Ste 1002 (19801-1807)
PHONE.....................302 777-2699
Anton Bodor, *Branch Mgr*
Paul Larosa, *Manager*
EMP: 156
SALES (corp-wide): 3.5B **Publicly Held**
SIC: 6022 State commercial banks
PA: First Republic Bank
111 Pine St Fl 2
San Francisco CA 94111
415 392-1400

(G-10549)
FIRST STATE BUILDING LLC
720 Stanton Christiana Rd (19804)
P.O. Box 1049, Newark (19715-1049)
PHONE.....................302 803-5082
Eric Carst, *President*
EMP: 6
SALES (est): 312.9K **Privately Held**
SIC: 1542 Nonresidential construction

(G-10550)
FIRST STATE CONTROLS INC
2207 Concord Pike 220 (19803-2908)
PHONE.....................302 559-7822
Christopher Cullen, *President*
EMP: 12
SQ FT: 1,500
SALES: 600K **Privately Held**
SIC: 3357 Communication wire

(G-10551)
FIRST STATE DISTRIBUTORS INC
222a 7th Ave (19805-4762)
PHONE.....................302 655-8266
Mike Catts, *President*
Dan Mumford, *Vice Pres*
EMP: 7
SALES (est): 956.9K **Privately Held**
SIC: 5084 5198 Safety equipment; paint spray equipment, industrial; paints

(G-10552)
FIRST STATE MEDICAL ASSOC LLC
2055 Limestone Rd Ste 111 (19808-5536)
PHONE.....................302 999-8169
Jose Caspero,
Marcia Gina C Castro, *Internal Med*
Franklin Ampadu,
Marcia Caspero,
EMP: 7
SQ FT: 1,900
SALES (est): 266.2K **Privately Held**
SIC: 8011 Clinic, operated by physicians

(G-10553)
FIRST STATE REHAB HOME LLC
111 Oxford Pl (19803-4517)
PHONE.....................443 252-7367
Anthony Gangemi, *Principal*
EMP: 4
SALES (est): 93.2K **Privately Held**
SIC: 8093 Rehabilitation center, outpatient treatment

(G-10554)
FIRST STATE SERVICES
205 Admiral Dr (19804-3403)
PHONE.....................302 985-1560
Lee Wilt, *Owner*
EMP: 4
SALES: 100K **Privately Held**
SIC: 1521 Mobile home repair, on site

(G-10555)
FIRST STATE TRUST COMPANY
1 Righter Pkwy Ste 120 (19803-1533)
PHONE.....................302 573-5967
Marianne Quinn, *President*
Ken Pisani, *Vice Pres*
Kelly Torello, *Opers Staff*
Richard J Gelinas, *CFO*
Jane Bowerman, *Manager*
EMP: 12
SALES (est): 2.6MM **Privately Held**
SIC: 6091 Nondeposit trust facilities

(G-10556)
FIRST STATE VEIN AND LASER CTR
1300 N Franklin St (19806-4212)
PHONE.....................302 294-0700
Lynn Shapira, *President*
EMP: 5
SALES (est): 257.7K **Privately Held**
SIC: 8011 General & family practice, physician/surgeon

(G-10557)
FIRST TECH
700 Cornell Dr Ste E5 (19801-5762)
PHONE.....................302 421-3650
Bill Florio, *President*
Sandeep Reddy, *Manager*
EMP: 20
SALES (est): 938.6K **Privately Held**
SIC: 7378 Computer maintenance & repair

(G-10558)
FIRST UN FINCL INVESTMENTS INC
2711 Centerville Rd # 400 (19808-1660)
PHONE.....................646 652-6580
Bill Hill, *Owner*
EMP: 4
SALES (est): 249K
SALES (corp-wide): 101B **Publicly Held**
SIC: 6282 Investment advice
PA: Wells Fargo & Company
420 Montgomery St Frnt
San Francisco CA 94104
866 249-3302

(G-10559)
FISH & MONKEY PRODUCTIONS LLC
1612 W 16th St (19806-4026)
PHONE.....................302 897-4318
Dan Healy, *Principal*
EMP: 10
SALES (est): 205.8K **Privately Held**
SIC: 7822 Motion picture & tape distribution

(G-10560)
FISH & RICHARDSON PC
222 Delaware Ave (19801-1621)
PHONE.....................302 652-5070
Fax: 302 652-0607
EMP: 45
SALES (est): 702.9K **Privately Held**
SIC: 8111 Legal Services Office

(G-10561)
FISH & RICHARDSON PC
222 Delaware Ave Ste 1700 (19801-1675)
P.O. Box 1114 (19899-1114)
PHONE.....................302 652-5070
William J Marsden Jr, *Principal*
Donna Wunsch, *Office Mgr*
Fran Glover, *Manager*
Jean Manis, *Admin Sec*
Kelly A Del Dotto, *Associate*
EMP: 37
SALES (corp-wide): 88.5MM **Privately Held**
WEB: www.fr.com
SIC: 8111 Patent solicitor
PA: Fish & Richardson P.C.
1 Marina Park Dr Ste 1700
Boston MA 02210
617 542-5070

(G-10562)
FISHER AUTO PARTS INC
Also Called: Manlove Auto Parts
1600 E Newport Pike Ste C (19804-2541)
PHONE.....................302 998-3111
Bradley Eaton, *Branch Mgr*
EMP: 9
SALES (corp-wide): 891.9MM **Privately Held**
WEB: www.fisherautoparts.com
SIC: 5013 5531 Automotive supplies & parts; automotive parts
PA: Fisher Auto Parts, Inc.
512 Greenville Ave
Staunton VA 24401
540 885-8901

(G-10563)
FISHING INC
503 Windsor Ave (19804-3261)
PHONE.....................302 999-9961
Morili Folarin, *CEO*
Fola Folarin, *President*
EMP: 6
SALES (est): 1.2MM **Privately Held**
SIC: 3556 Smokers, food processing equipment

(G-10564)
FISONS US INVESTMENT HOLDINGS (DH)
3711 Kennett Pike Ste 334 (19807-2155)
PHONE.....................302 777-7222
Phil Ridolfi, *President*
Joan Hanlon, *Vice Pres*
EMP: 4
SALES (est): 343.2K **Privately Held**
SIC: 2834 Drugs acting on the cardiovascular system, except diagnostic; drugs affecting parasitic & infective diseases; drugs acting on the central nervous system & sense organs

(G-10565)
FITOVATE LLC
2702 E Landsdowne Dr (19810-3432)
PHONE.....................302 463-9790
Clayton Minott, *CEO*
EMP: 1 **EST:** 2014
SALES (est): 57K **Privately Held**
SIC: 7372 Application computer software

(G-10566)
FIVE SIXTY ENTERPRISE LLC
501 Silverside Rd Ste 505 (19809-1374)
PHONE.....................302 268-6530
Steven Johnson, *Mng Member*
EMP: 20
SALES: 7MM **Privately Held**
SIC: 8742 Management consulting services

(G-10567)
FIVE STAR FRANCHISING LLC (HQ)
Also Called: Five-Star Basketball
1209 N Orange St (19801-1120)
PHONE.....................646 838-3992
Joseph Samberg,
EMP: 6
SALES (est): 74.1K
SALES (corp-wide): 367.5K **Privately Held**
SIC: 7941 Sports clubs, managers & promoters

(G-10568)
FIVE STAR QUALITY CARE INC
Also Called: Foulk Manor South
407 Foulk Rd (19803-3809)
PHONE.....................302 655-6249
Mike Salitsky, *Branch Mgr*
EMP: 60 **Publicly Held**
WEB: www.fivestarqualitycare.com
SIC: 8051 Skilled nursing care facilities
PA: Five Star Senior Living Inc.
400 Centre St
Newton MA 02458

(G-10569)
FIVE STAR QUALITY CARE INC
Also Called: Forwood Manor
1912 Marsh Rd (19810-3954)
PHONE.....................302 792-5115
Gail Martinez, *Manager*
EMP: 5 **Publicly Held**
WEB: www.fivestarqualitycare.com
SIC: 8051 Skilled nursing care facilities
PA: Five Star Senior Living Inc.
400 Centre St
Newton MA 02458

(G-10570)
FIVE STAR SENIOR LIVING INC
Also Called: Foulk Manor North
1212 Foulk Rd Ste 1 (19803-2765)
PHONE.....................302 478-4296
Virginia Gray, *Manager*
EMP: 63 **Publicly Held**
WEB: www.fivestarqualitycare.com
SIC: 8051 Convalescent home with continuous nursing care
PA: Five Star Senior Living Inc.
400 Centre St
Newton MA 02458

(G-10571)
FLAVORS & MORE INC
2711 Centerville Rd # 400 (19808-1660)
PHONE.....................917 887-9241
Arnab Ghosh, *Vice Pres*
EMP: 4
SQ FT: 400
SALES (est): 127.5K **Privately Held**
SIC: 5194 Smokeless tobacco

(G-10572)
FLEEK INC
Also Called: Fleek Fleet
3616 Kirkwood Hwy A1470 (19808-5124)
PHONE.....................888 870-1291
Joel Kasr, *CEO*
EMP: 6
SALES: 500K **Privately Held**
SIC: 4729 7371 Carpool/vanpool arrangement

(G-10573)
FLEX IP SOLUTIONS INC
2313 Shipley Rd (19803-1849)
PHONE.....................610 359-5812
EMP: 4 **EST:** 2012
SALES (est): 299.4K **Privately Held**
SIC: 8748 Telecommunications consultant

(G-10574)
FLIGHT CENTRE TRAVEL GROUP USA
3616 Kirkwood Hwy Ste B (19808-5124)
PHONE.....................302 633-1996
Denise D'Amora, *Manager*
EMP: 7 **Privately Held**
WEB: www.libertytravel.com
SIC: 4724 Tourist agency arranging transport, lodging & car rental
HQ: Flight Centre Travel Group (Usa) Inc
5 Paragon Dr Ste 200
Montvale NJ 07645
201 934-3500

(G-10575)
FLIGHT CENTRE TRAVEL GROUP USA
4737 Concord Pike Ste 835 (19803-1494)
PHONE.....................302 479-7581
Patricia Booth, *Branch Mgr*
EMP: 7 **Privately Held**
WEB: www.libertytravel.com
SIC: 4724 Tourist agency arranging transport, lodging & car rental
HQ: Flight Centre Travel Group (Usa) Inc
5 Paragon Dr Ste 200
Montvale NJ 07645
201 934-3500

(G-10576)
FLOORING SOLUTIONS INC
500 A St (19801-5328)
P.O. Box 30000 (19805-7000)
PHONE.....................302 655-8001
Dominic A Marra, *President*
Lesie Marra, *Vice Pres*
EMP: 10
SQ FT: 5,000
SALES (est): 2.7MM **Privately Held**
SIC: 1752 Floor laying & floor work

(G-10577)
FLORISTWARE INC
19c Trolley Sq (19806-3355)
PHONE.....................888 531-3012
EMP: 8
SALES (est): 456.4K **Privately Held**
SIC: 7372 Prepackaged Software Services

(G-10578)
FLOWERS COUNSEL GROUP LLC (PA)
1105 N Market St Ste 800 (19801-1202)
P.O. Box 580 (19899-0580)
PHONE.....................302 656-7370
Chipman Flowers,
EMP: 5
SALES (est): 512.8K **Privately Held**
SIC: 8111 General practice law office

GEOGRAPHIC SECTION
Wilmington - New Castle County (G-10607)

(G-10579)
FLOWLINE TECHNOLOGIES INC
1201 N Orange St Ste 600 (19801-1171)
PHONE..................................302 256-5825
Kim Lavery, *President*
Christopher Larson, *Manager*
Mr R Matarajan, *Manager*
EMP: 7
SALES: 1.7MM **Privately Held**
SIC: 8711 Industrial engineers

(G-10580)
FLOWPAY CORPORATION
221 W 9th St Ste 300 (19801-1619)
PHONE..................................720 425-3244
Robert Steiger, *President*
James Jones, *COO*
EMP: 2
SQ FT: 4,000
SALES (est): 110K **Privately Held**
SIC: 7372 7371 Business oriented computer software; computer software development & applications

(G-10581)
FLOYD DEAN INC
2 S Poplar St Ste B (19801-5052)
PHONE..................................302 655-7193
Floyd Dean, *President*
Victoria M Yelton, *Vice Pres*
EMP: 8
SQ FT: 4,500
SALES (est): 216.9K **Privately Held**
WEB: www.floyddean.com
SIC: 7335 Commercial photography

(G-10582)
FLUOROGISTX LLC
Also Called: Delaware Specialty Dist
3704 Kennett Pike Ste 100 (19807-2173)
PHONE..................................302 479-7614
David Jones, *President*
Eric Long, *Regl Sales Mgr*
John Rivers, *Regl Sales Mgr*
Kevin Bauler, *Sales Staff*
Karen Bullen, *Manager*
EMP: 12
SALES (est): 5.4MM **Privately Held**
SIC: 3086 Plastics foam products

(G-10583)
FLUTE PRO SHOP INC
4023 Kennett Pike Ste 30 (19807-2018)
P.O. Box 4023 (19807-0023)
PHONE..................................302 479-5000
Joan Sparks, *President*
EMP: 5
SALES (est): 572K **Privately Held**
SIC: 5736 7699 7389 Pianos; musical instrument repair services; business services

(G-10584)
FOCUS BEHAVIORAL HEALTH
410 Foulk Rd Ste 105 (19803-3835)
PHONE..................................302 762-2285
Diane Carrado, *Principal*
EMP: 13
SALES (est): 429.7K **Privately Held**
SIC: 8093 Mental health clinic, outpatient

(G-10585)
FOLDFAST GOALS LLC
1211 Stony Run Dr (19803-3539)
PHONE..................................302 478-7881
Richard Raber, *President*
Lisa Townsend, *Vice Pres*
▲ EMP: 2
SQ FT: 3,500
SALES (est): 170K **Privately Held**
SIC: 3949 Lacrosse equipment & supplies, general; soccer equipment & supplies

(G-10586)
FOOD EQUIPMENT SERVICE INC
3316a Old Capitol Trl (19808-6210)
PHONE..................................302 996-9363
George Fox, *President*
EMP: 14
SALES: 1.5MM **Privately Held**
WEB: www.foodequipmentservice.com
SIC: 7389 7629 Industrial & commercial equipment inspection service; electrical equipment repair services

(G-10587)
FOOT & ANKLE ASSOCIATES
3801 Kennett Pike A102 (19807-2307)
PHONE..................................302 652-5767
Victor Nippert, *Manager*
EMP: 10 **Privately Held**
WEB: www.footandanklellp.com
SIC: 8043 Offices & clinics of podiatrists
PA: Foot & Ankle Associates
    692 Unionville Rd
    Kennett Square PA 19348

(G-10588)
FOOT CARE GROUP INC (PA)
Also Called: Haley, David
1601 Milltown Rd Ste 24 (19808-4084)
PHONE..................................302 998-0178
Dr David Haley, *Owner*
Chris Bailey, *Office Mgr*
▲ EMP: 20
SALES (est): 1.9MM **Privately Held**
WEB: www.footcaregroup.org
SIC: 8043 Offices & clinics of podiatrists

(G-10589)
FOR DELAWARE CENTER
Also Called: Dcca
200 S Madison St (19801-5110)
PHONE..................................302 656-6466
Jay Miller, *President*
Leslie Shaffer, *Exec Dir*
David M Keller, *Director*
EMP: 17
SALES: 901.1K **Privately Held**
WEB: www.thedcca.org
SIC: 8412 Museum

(G-10590)
FORCEBEYOND INC
Also Called: Wholesale
1521 Concord Pike Ste 301 (19803-3644)
PHONE..................................302 995-6588
Steve Bai, *President*
Nicholas Lintner, *Vice Pres*
Sunny Chen, *CFO*
▲ EMP: 35
SALES (est): 3.7MM **Privately Held**
SIC: 3324 3089 3544 3069 Commercial investment castings, ferrous; injection molding of plastics; dies & die holders for metal cutting, forming, die casting; rubber automotive products

(G-10591)
FOREST PARK APARTMENTS
5501 Limeric Cir Ofc 33 (19808-3431)
PHONE..................................302 737-6151
Doug Kelley, *Director*
EMP: 7
SALES (est): 490K **Privately Held**
SIC: 6513 Apartment building operators

(G-10592)
FOREVER INC (PA)
Also Called: Fulton Paper & Party Supply
1006 W 27th St (19802-2946)
PHONE..................................302 594-0400
Michael D Gavetti, *President*
Dorothy L Quigley, *Vice Pres*
Dorothy Quigley, *Vice Pres*
Jenny Martinez, *Manager*
EMP: 35
SQ FT: 30,000
SALES (est): 2.8MM **Privately Held**
SIC: 5947 5199 5113 Balloon shops; party favors; party favors, balloons, hats, etc.; bags, paper & disposable plastic

(G-10593)
FOREVER FRESH LLC
Also Called: 4ever Fresh
6 Denny Rd Ste 303 (19809-3444)
PHONE..................................302 510-8538
Evan Myers, *General Mgr*
Cristian Tagle,
Hernan Garces,
Pablo Garces,
◆ EMP: 8
SQ FT: 1,200
SALES: 22MM **Privately Held**
SIC: 5148 Fruits, fresh

(G-10594)
FORGOTTEN FEW FOUNDATION INC
1927 W 4th St (19805-3421)
PHONE..................................302 494-6212
Brunilda Luna-Mercado, *Exec Dir*
EMP: 8
SQ FT: 1,500
SALES (est): 62.6K **Privately Held**
SIC: 8322 Emergency social services

(G-10595)
FORUM TO ADVNCE MNRTIES IN ENG
Also Called: Fame
2005 Baynard Blvd (19802-3917)
PHONE..................................302 777-3254
Don Baker, *Exec Dir*
EMP: 40
SQ FT: 900
SALES: 711.4K **Privately Held**
WEB: www.famedelaware.org
SIC: 7389 Personal service agents, brokers & bureaus

(G-10596)
FORWARD MOTION INC
735 S Market St Ste D (19801-5246)
P.O. Box 30700 (19805-7700)
PHONE..................................302 658-2829
Michael Demoss, *President*
EMP: 1
SALES: 50K **Privately Held**
WEB: www.forwardmotioninc.com
SIC: 3714 5531 Motor vehicle parts & accessories; automotive parts; automotive accessories

(G-10597)
FOSCHI STUDIO
2107 Naamans Rd (19810-1326)
PHONE..................................302 439-4457
Rudy Foschi, *Partner*
Theodore Foschi, *Partner*
EMP: 4
SALES (est): 269.7K **Privately Held**
SIC: 7221 Photographer, still or video

(G-10598)
FOSS-BROWN INC (PA)
3411 Silverside Rd 100wb (19810-4812)
PHONE..................................610 940-6040
Lance Charen, *President*
EMP: 15 EST: 1958
SQ FT: 2,200
SALES (est): 1.6MM **Privately Held**
SIC: 5072 Builders' hardware

(G-10599)
FOULK LAWN & EQUIPMENT CO INC
Also Called: John Deere Authorized Dealer
2018 Foulk Rd (19810-3624)
PHONE..................................302 475-3233
Anthony J Socorso Sr, *President*
A Joseph Socorso Jr, *Corp Secy*
EMP: 5 EST: 1954
SQ FT: 3,000
SALES (est): 673.3K **Privately Held**
SIC: 5261 7699 5082 Lawnmowers & tractors; lawn mower repair shop; tractor repair; construction & mining machinery

(G-10600)
FOULK PRE-SCHL & DAY CRE CNTR
2711 Carpenter Station Rd (19810-2057)
PHONE..................................302 529-1580
Judy Crawford, *Director*
EMP: 7
SALES (est): 163.2K
SALES (corp-wide): 778.3K **Privately Held**
SIC: 8351 Preschool center
PA: Foulk Pre-School And Day Care Center Incorporated
    2 Tenby Dr
    Wilmington DE 19803
    302 478-3047

(G-10601)
FOULK PRE-SCHL & DAY CRE CNTR (PA)
2 Tenby Dr (19803-2619)
PHONE..................................302 478-3047
Benjamin S Crawford, *President*
Judith J Crawford, *Vice Pres*
Keith Crawford, *Admin Sec*
EMP: 9
SQ FT: 3,000
SALES (est): 778.3K **Privately Held**
SIC: 8351 Preschool center; group day care center

(G-10602)
FOULK ROAD DENTAL & ASSOCIATES
300 Foulk Rd Ste 101 (19803-3819)
PHONE..................................302 652-3775
Andrea Boffa, *Manager*
John Russo, *Director*
Nicholas J Russo, *Director*
Edwin S Kuipers, *Fmly & Gen Dent*
EMP: 12
SALES (est): 1.5MM **Privately Held**
SIC: 8021 Dentists' office

(G-10603)
FOUNDATION SOURCE PHILANTHROPI
501 Silverside Rd (19809-1374)
PHONE..................................800 839-1754
EMP: 28
SALES (est): 1.1MM
SALES (corp-wide): 11.9MM **Privately Held**
SIC: 8699 Charitable organization
PA: Foundation Source Philanthropi
    55 Walls Dr
    Fairfield CT 06824
    203 319-3700

(G-10604)
FOUR BROTHERS AUTO SERVICE
101 N Union St (19805-3427)
PHONE..................................302 482-2932
Wilfredo Rosa, *Owner*
EMP: 5
SALES (est): 474.5K **Privately Held**
SIC: 7538 General automotive repair shops

(G-10605)
FOUR POINT SOLUTIONS LTD
3422 Old Capitol Trl (19808-6124)
PHONE..................................613 907-6400
Barrie Ellis, *President*
Jason Gunning, *Vice Pres*
EMP: 50 EST: 2015
SQ FT: 8,000
SALES (est): 1.6MM **Privately Held**
SIC: 7371 7372 Computer software systems analysis & design, custom; business oriented computer software

(G-10606)
FOURTH FLOOR
1205 N Orange St (19801-1120)
PHONE..................................302 472-8416
Patrick Ashley, *Manager*
EMP: 6
SALES (est): 381.9K **Privately Held**
WEB: www.thefourthfloor.com
SIC: 7389 Financial services

(G-10607)
FOX & ROACH LP
Also Called: Prudential Fox Roach Realtors
2200 Concord Pike 1 (19803-2909)
PHONE..................................302 477-5500
Mathews Didomencio, *Principal*
Charles Ingersoll, *General Ptnr*
Kim Gamaitoni, *Sales Staff*
Michael Wilson, *Agent*
Genevia Weston, *Real Est Agnt*
EMP: 50
SALES (corp-wide): 16.3MM **Privately Held**
WEB: www.prufoxroach.com
SIC: 6531 Real estate agent, residential
PA: Fox & Roach Lp
    431 W Lancaster Ave
    Devon PA 19333
    610 722-7851

Wilmington - New Castle County (G-10608)

(G-10608)
FOX ROTHSCHILD LLP
919 N Market St Ste 1300 (19801-3092)
P.O. Box 2323 (19899-2323)
PHONE..................................302 654-7444
Michael Isaacs, *Partner*
Neal Levitsky, *Principal*
Kimberlee Knopf, *Counsel*
Deborah Somerville, *Advt Staff*
Marlys Hickman, *Office Admin*
EMP: 15
SALES (est): 1.2MM Privately Held
SIC: 8111 General practice attorney, lawyer

(G-10609)
FPL ENERGY AMERICAN WIND LLC
3801 Kennett Pike C200 (19807-2324)
PHONE..................................302 655-0632
EMP: 6
SALES (est): 465.8K
SALES (corp-wide): 16.7B Publicly Held
SIC: 4911 Generation, electric power
HQ: Nextera Energy Resources, Llc
700 Universe Blvd
Juno Beach FL 33408
561 691-7171

(G-10610)
FRANCIS KELLY SONS INC
8 Meco Cir (19804-1109)
PHONE..................................302 999-7400
Daniel K Kelly, *President*
Daniel J Kelly, *President*
EMP: 9
SQ FT: 2,000
SALES: 500K Privately Held
SIC: 1771 Concrete work

(G-10611)
FRANCIS MASE PEDIATRICS
700 W Lea Blvd Ste 209 (19802-2545)
PHONE..................................302 762-5656
Francis Mase, *Principal*
EMP: 10
SALES (est): 201K Privately Held
SIC: 8011 Pediatrician

(G-10612)
FRANCIS POLLINGER & SON INC
57 Germay Dr (19804-1104)
PHONE..................................302 655-8097
Francis Pollinger Sr, *President*
Kay Pollinger, *Corp Secy*
Francis Pollinger Jr, *Vice Pres*
Colleen Pollinger, *Admin Sec*
EMP: 25
SQ FT: 4,800
SALES (est): 2.9MM Privately Held
SIC: 1761 1751 1521 Roofing contractor; gutter & downspout contractor; siding contractor; roof repair; window & door installation & erection; general remodeling, single-family houses

(G-10613)
FRANK R YOCUM SONS WLPR BLIND (PA)
5716 Kennett Pike (19807-1329)
PHONE..................................302 888-2000
Frank Yocum Jr, *President*
James Yocum, *Treasurer*
EMP: 3
SQ FT: 1,000
SALES: 800K Privately Held
SIC: 3442 Shutters, door or window: metal; jalousies, metal

(G-10614)
FRANKE USA HOLDING INC (DH)
1105 N Market St Ste 1300 (19801-1241)
PHONE..................................615 462-4000
Hans J Ott, *President*
Roger D Schlatter, *Principal*
Roy John, *Vice Pres*
Stefan Lindqvist, *Vice Pres*
Lauren Cummins, *Project Mgr*
◆ **EMP:** 11
SALES (est): 473.3MM
SALES (corp-wide): 355.8K Privately Held
SIC: 3589 5023 5084 Commercial cooking & foodwarming equipment; kitchenware; food industry machinery
HQ: Franke Holding Ag
Franke-Strasse 2
Aarburg AG 4663
627 873-131

(G-10615)
FRANKEL ENTERPRISES INC
Also Called: Mayfair Apartments
1300 N Harrison St A100 (19806-3267)
PHONE..................................302 652-6364
Kathleen S McManus, *Manager*
EMP: 6
SALES (corp-wide): 4.1MM Privately Held
SIC: 6513 Apartment building operators
PA: Frankel Enterprises Inc
1845 Walnut St Ste 1610
Philadelphia PA 19103
215 751-0900

(G-10616)
FRANKLIN FIBRE-LAMITEX CORP
903 E 13th St (19802-5102)
P.O. Box 1768 (19899-1768)
PHONE..................................302 652-3621
James E Vachris Jr, *President*
Virginia Carr, *CFO*
Rich Rathell, *Sales Mgr*
▲ **EMP:** 26
SQ FT: 56,000
SALES (est): 6.7MM Privately Held
WEB: www.franklinfibre.com
SIC: 3083 Laminated plastics plate & sheet

(G-10617)
FRANKLIN KENNET LLC
1113 N Franklin St (19806-4301)
PHONE..................................302 655-6536
Tom H Delporte, *Partner*
EMP: 15
SALES (est): 450.7K Privately Held
SIC: 8742 Human resource consulting services

(G-10618)
FRANKLIN RUBBER STAMP CO INC
301 W 8th St Frnt Ste (19801-1553)
PHONE..................................302 654-8841
Tom Tanzilli, *President*
Susan Stoltz, *Treasurer*
EMP: 13 **EST:** 1930
SALES (est): 1.7MM Privately Held
WEB: www.franklinstamps.com
SIC: 3953 Marking devices

(G-10619)
FRANKLIN T VARONE INC
Also Called: Varone Insurance Offices
1403 Silverside Rd Ste A (19810-4434)
PHONE..................................302 475-6200
Franklin T Varone, *President*
EMP: 4
SQ FT: 2,700
SALES: 1.5MM Privately Held
SIC: 6411 Insurance agents, brokers & service

(G-10620)
FRANTA RCHARD E ATTRNEY AT LAW
1301 N Harrison St # 102 (19806-3142)
PHONE..................................302 428-1800
Richard E Franta, *Owner*
EMP: 4
SALES (est): 425.3K Privately Held
SIC: 8111 General practice attorney, lawyer

(G-10621)
FRATERNAL ORDER EAGLES INC
Also Called: Foe 74
415 Philadelphia Pike (19809-2152)
PHONE..................................302 764-6100
Dave Winchester, *Manager*
EMP: 4
SALES (est): 473.3MM
SALES (corp-wide): 5.7MM Privately Held
WEB: www.fraternalorderofeagles.tribe.net
SIC: 8641 Fraternal associations
PA: Fraternal Order Of Eagles, Bryan Aerie
2233 Of Bryan, Ohio
221 S Walnut St
Bryan OH 43506
419 636-7812

(G-10622)
FRAZZBERRY
4734 Limestone Rd (19808-1928)
PHONE..................................302 543-7791
Charles Frasso, *Principal*
EMP: 8
SALES (est): 495.3K Privately Held
SIC: 2024 Ice cream, bulk

(G-10623)
FREAKIN FRESH SALSA INC
2 Biltmore Ct (19808-1378)
P.O. Box 863, Hockessin (19707-0863)
PHONE..................................302 750-9789
Cecilia Andrzejewski, *President*
Michael Andrzejewski, *Vice Pres*
EMP: 2 **EST:** 2009
SALES (est): 217.2K Privately Held
SIC: 5149 2032 Condiments; Mexican foods: packaged in cans, jars, etc.

(G-10624)
FRED L WRIGHT DDS
5309 Limestone Rd A (19808-1222)
PHONE..................................302 239-1641
Fred Wright DDS, *Owner*
EMP: 7
SALES (est): 152.5K Privately Held
SIC: 8021 Dentists' office

(G-10625)
FRED S FINK ORTHODONTIST
23 The Commons (19810-4907)
PHONE..................................302 478-6930
Fred Fink, *Executive*
EMP: 4
SALES (est): 92.3K Privately Held
SIC: 8021 Orthodontist

(G-10626)
FRED S SMALLS INSURANCE (PA)
5227 W Woodmill Dr Ste 43 (19808-4068)
PHONE..................................302 633-1980
Fred Small, *Owner*
Harriett Watson, *Manager*
Fernando Hurtado, *Producer*
EMP: 15
SQ FT: 3,200
SALES (est): 2.5MM Privately Held
SIC: 6411 Insurance brokers

(G-10627)
FREDERICK ENTERPRISES INC
Also Called: Joseph Frederick & Sons
810 Stanton Rd (19804-3640)
PHONE..................................302 994-5786
Brian Frederick, *President*
Rayan Frederick, *Vice Pres*
John Ratcliffe, *Treasurer*
Rosie Eubanks, *Technology*
EMP: 39
SQ FT: 8,800
SALES (est): 6MM Privately Held
WEB: www.jfrederickandsons.com
SIC: 1711 Boiler & furnace contractors

(G-10628)
FREDERICK N HARTMAN
1410 Jan Dr (19803-3409)
PHONE..................................302 479-5068
Frederick N Hartman, *Principal*
EMP: 4 **EST:** 2009
SALES (est): 117.6K Privately Held
SIC: 8021 Offices & clinics of dentists

(G-10629)
FREEDOM PAPER COMPANY LLC
1201 N Orange St Ste 700 (19801-1186)
PHONE..................................443 542-5845
Kamose Muhammad, *CEO*
Setu Muhammad, *General Mgr*
EMP: 8
SQ FT: 1,500
SALES (est): 1.4MM Privately Held
SIC: 5113 Industrial & personal service paper

(G-10630)
FREEMARKETS INVESTMENT CO INC
1105 N Market St Ste 1300 (19801-1241)
PHONE..................................302 427-2089
Sean Breiner, *Director*
EMP: 6
SALES (est): 10MM Privately Held
WEB: www.freemarket.com
SIC: 6211 Security brokers & dealers

(G-10631)
FREIBOTT LAW FIRM
1711 E Newport Pike (19804-2530)
P.O. Box 6168 (19804-0768)
PHONE..................................302 633-9000
Frederick Freibott, *Owner*
EMP: 11
SALES (est): 745.7K Privately Held
WEB: www.freibottlaw.com
SIC: 8111 General practice attorney, lawyer

(G-10632)
FRENCH STREET MANAGEMENT
1105 N Market St Ste 1300 (19801-1241)
PHONE..................................302 571-8597
EMP: 18
SALES (est): 364K Privately Held
SIC: 6531 Real estate managers

(G-10633)
FRENIUS MEDICAL CARE
7 S Clayton St (19805-3948)
PHONE..................................302 421-9177
Betty Babb, *Manager*
EMP: 8
SALES (est): 232K Privately Held
SIC: 8062 General medical & surgical hospitals

(G-10634)
FRENSENIUS MEDICAL CTR
4000 N Washington St (19802-2136)
PHONE..................................302 762-2903
Alica Vogleson, *Office Mgr*
EMP: 6
SALES (est): 80.5K Privately Held
SIC: 8011 Medical centers

(G-10635)
FRESENIUS MEDICAL CARE N AMER
605 W Newport Pike (19804-3235)
PHONE..................................302 633-6228
EMP: 7
SALES (corp-wide): 18.3B Privately Held
SIC: 8092 Kidney dialysis centers
HQ: Fresenius Usa Manufacturing, Inc.
920 Winter St
Waltham MA 02451

(G-10636)
FRESENIUS USA INC
303 A St (19801-5324)
PHONE..................................302 658-7469
Donyale Showers, *Manager*
EMP: 27
SALES (corp-wide): 18.3B Privately Held
WEB: www.fresenius.org
SIC: 8092 Kidney dialysis centers
HQ: Fresenius Usa, Inc.
4040 Nelson Ave
Concord CA 94520
925 288-4218

(G-10637)
FRESHBOOKS USA INC
2711 Centerville Rd # 300 (19808-1665)
PHONE..................................416 525-5384
Levi Cooperman, *Ch of Bd*
EMP: 2
SALES (est): 131.6K Privately Held
SIC: 7372 7389 Business oriented computer software;

(G-10638)
FRIEDLANDER AND GORRIS
1201 N Market St Ste 2200 (19801-1165)
PHONE..................................302 573-3500

Joel Friedlander, *Principal*
EMP: 7
SALES (est): 1.3MM **Privately Held**
WEB: www.bmf-law.com
SIC: 8111 Corporate, partnership & business law

(G-10639)
FRIENDS OF UNIVERSITY SUSSEX
1000 N West St Ste 1200 (19801-1058)
PHONE.................................302 295-4959
Bank Schwab, *Principal*
EMP: 10
SALES: 448.2K **Privately Held**
SIC: 8699 Membership organizations

(G-10640)
FRIENDSHIP HOUSE INCORPORATED
720 N Orange St (19801-1708)
PHONE.................................302 652-8033
Marcy Perkins, *Branch Mgr*
EMP: 10 **Privately Held**
SIC: 8322 Emergency shelters
PA: Friendship House Incorporated
226 N Walnut St
Wilmington DE 19801

(G-10641)
FRIENDSHIP HOUSE INCORPORATED (PA)
226 N Walnut St (19801-3934)
P.O. Box 1517 (19899-1517)
PHONE.................................302 652-8133
William Perkins, *CEO*
Donald Drane, *President*
Curt Johnson, *President*
EMP: 19
SQ FT: 10,000
SALES: 1.3MM **Privately Held**
SIC: 8322 Social service center

(G-10642)
FRIESS ASSOCIATES LLC
3711 Kennett Pike Ste 100 (19807-2156)
P.O. Box 4166 (19807-0166)
PHONE.................................302 656-3017
Gordon Kaiser, *Manager*
EMP: 35 **Publicly Held**
SIC: 6282 Investment advisory service
HQ: Friess Associates, Llc
115 E Snow King Ave
Jackson WY 83001
307 733-3938

(G-10643)
FRIZBEE MEDICAL INC
1013 Centre Rd (19805-1265)
PHONE.................................424 901-1534
Dan Gazit, *Director*
David Kulber, *Director*
EMP: 1 **EST:** 2017
SALES (est): 55K **Privately Held**
SIC: 3842 7389 Implants, surgical; grafts, artificial: for surgery;

(G-10644)
FRONTIER TECHNOLOGIES INC (PA)
1521 Concord Pike Ste 302 (19803-3645)
PHONE.................................302 225-2530
Jayshree Moorthy, *CEO*
Krish Moorthy, *COO*
EMP: 4
SQ FT: 2,000
SALES (est): 9.8MM **Privately Held**
WEB: www.ftiusa.com
SIC: 7379 Computer related consulting services

(G-10645)
FULCRUM PHARMACY MGT INC
501 N Shipley St (19801-2226)
P.O. Box 2695 (19805-0695)
PHONE.................................302 658-8020
Cristy Crkvenac, *Owner*
Michelle Oxenford, *Human Resources*
EMP: 4
SALES (est): 430K **Privately Held**
SIC: 5122 2834 Pharmaceuticals: pharmaceutical preparations; tranquilizers or mental drug preparations

(G-10646)
FULL GAME AHEAD USA LLC
Trolley Sq Ste 20c (19806)
PHONE.................................302 281-0102
Yvelain Mazade, *Director*
EMP: 2
SALES: 120K **Privately Held**
SIC: 7372 Application computer software

(G-10647)
FULTON BANK NATIONAL ASSN
Also Called: Fulton Financial Advisors
800 Foulk Rd (19803-3109)
PHONE.................................302 407-3291
Sara Defrancis, *Branch Mgr*
EMP: 9
SALES (corp-wide): 954MM **Publicly Held**
SIC: 6022 State commercial banks
HQ: Fulton Bank, National Association
1 Penn Sq Ste 1 # 1
Lancaster PA 17602
717 581-3166

(G-10648)
FULTON PAPER COMPANY
1006 W 27th St (19802-2990)
PHONE.................................302 594-0400
Michael D Gavetti, *President*
Dorothy L Quigley, *Corp Secy*
EMP: 17 **EST:** 1934
SQ FT: 30,000
SALES (est): 1.9MM **Privately Held**
SIC: 5943 5947 5113 Stationery stores; party favors; bags, paper & disposable plastic

(G-10649)
FUR BABY TRACKER LLC
302 Taft Ave (19805-1303)
PHONE.................................610 563-3294
Amanda Hoffmeyer, *Principal*
EMP: 5
SALES (est): 104.7K **Privately Held**
SIC: 7389

(G-10650)
FUSION
3444 Naamans Rd Fl 1 (19810-1064)
PHONE.................................302 479-9444
Lorri Czarnota, *Owner*
EMP: 25
SALES (est): 362.3K **Privately Held**
SIC: 7231 Beauty shops

(G-10651)
FUSION HEALTH WORKS
829 N Harrison St (19806-4628)
PHONE.................................302 543-4714
EMP: 5 **EST:** 2008
SALES (est): 177.9K **Privately Held**
SIC: 8099 Health/Allied Services

(G-10652)
FUSURA LLC
800 Delaware Ave Ste 500 (19801-1366)
P.O. Box 70, Montchanin (19710-0070)
PHONE.................................302 397-2200
Mark A Parsells, *President*
EMP: 65 **EST:** 2000
SALES (est): 7MM **Privately Held**
WEB: www.fusura.com
SIC: 6411 Insurance agents

(G-10653)
FUTURE DEVELOPMENT LEARNING
500 Maryland Ave (19805-4427)
PHONE.................................302 652-7500
Haneefah Allen, *President*
Yusuf Allen, *CFO*
EMP: 5 **EST:** 2007
SALES (est): 140.3K **Privately Held**
SIC: 8351 Child day care services

(G-10654)
FUTURE FORD SALES INC (PA)
Also Called: Sheridan Ford Sales
4001 Kirkwood Hwy (19808-5111)
PHONE.................................302 999-0261
Joseph E Sheridan, *President*
Duane Hill, *Principal*
Roy Chapman, *Vice Pres*
Bob Faulkner, *Foreman/Supr*
Scott Perry, *Finance Mgr*
EMP: 85
SQ FT: 33,000
SALES: 45.2MM **Privately Held**
WEB: www.sheridanfordsales.com
SIC: 7515 5511 5013 5521 Passenger car leasing; automobiles, new & used; pickups, new & used; automotive supplies & parts; used car dealers; automobiles & other motor vehicles; top & body repair & paint shops

(G-10655)
FYRBEACON INC
2711 Centerville Rd # 400 (19808-1660)
PHONE.................................562 569-0547
Ruupak N Omar,
EMP: 25
SALES (est): 371.6K **Privately Held**
SIC: 7389 Business services

(G-10656)
G & D COLLECTION GROUP INC
234 Philadelphia Pike # 9 (19809-3126)
PHONE.................................302 482-2512
Edward J Gavin, *CEO*
Brian Dunphy, *President*
EMP: 10 **EST:** 2007
SQ FT: 2,000
SALES: 2MM **Privately Held**
SIC: 7322 Collection agency, except real estate

(G-10657)
G B LYONS DDS
100 W Rockwind Rd (19801)
P.O. Box 295, Montchanin (19710-0295)
PHONE.................................302 654-1765
Garett B Lyons DDS, *Owner*
G B Lyons Jr DDS, *Owner*
EMP: 16
SALES (est): 480.2K **Privately Held**
SIC: 8021 Maxillofacial specialist

(G-10658)
G FEDALE ROOFING AND SIDING
101 S Mary St (19804-3112)
PHONE.................................302 225-7663
Glen Fedale, *Owner*
Adam Fedale, *Co-Owner*
Allan Fedale, *Co-Owner*
Allen Fedale, *Vice Pres*
Jacob Domanski, *Project Mgr*
EMP: 11 **EST:** 2014
SALES (est): 181.5K **Privately Held**
SIC: 1761 Roofing contractor

(G-10659)
G W KELLER DDS
1110 N Bancroft Pkwy # 2 (19805-2669)
PHONE.................................302 652-3586
George Keller DDS, *Owner*
EMP: 15
SALES (est): 719.6K **Privately Held**
SIC: 8021 Periodontist

(G-10660)
G2 PERFORMANCE BAND ACC
2207 Concord Pike Ste 220 (19803-2908)
PHONE.................................800 554-8523
EMP: 1
SALES (est): 45.9K **Privately Held**
SIC: 2389 Band uniforms

(G-10661)
GABRIEL JR TIMOTEO R MD
Also Called: Family Ear Nose/Throat Physcn
1941 Limestone Rd Ste 210 (19808-5400)
PHONE.................................302 998-0300
Timoteo R Gabriel Jr, *President*
EMP: 5
SALES (est): 296K **Privately Held**
SIC: 8011 Eyes, ears, nose & throat specialist: physician/surgeon

(G-10662)
GAHAGAN & BRYANT ASSOC INC
Also Called: GBA
3801 Kennett Pike C302 (19807-2321)
PHONE.................................302 652-4948
Peter Steel, *Manager*
EMP: 11
SALES (corp-wide): 11.5MM **Privately Held**
SIC: 8711 Consulting engineer
PA: Gahagan & Bryant Associates, Inc.
3802 W Bay To Bay Blvd # 22
Tampa FL 33629
813 831-4408

(G-10663)
GAINOR AWNINGS INC
1 Elm Ave (19805-1199)
PHONE.................................302 998-8611
Woodward Eastburn, *President*
EMP: 8
SQ FT: 2,400
SALES (est): 700K **Privately Held**
SIC: 2394 1799 Awnings, fabric: made from purchased materials; awning installation

(G-10664)
GALAXY SIGN & LIGHTING
2117 Armour Dr (19808-5303)
PHONE.................................302 757-5349
David Gail, *Principal*
EMP: 1
SALES (est): 46K **Privately Held**
SIC: 3993 Signs & advertising specialties

(G-10665)
GALLAGHER & ASSOCIATES PA
5500 Skyline Dr Ste 6 (19808-1772)
PHONE.................................302 239-5501
Michael Gallagher, *President*
EMP: 5
SALES (est): 294.7K **Privately Held**
SIC: 8721 Certified public accountant

(G-10666)
GALLEYWARE COMPANY INC
330 Water St Ste 107 (19804-2433)
PHONE.................................302 996-9480
Kris Nonnenmacher, *President*
Melinda Nonnenmacher, *Corp Secy*
◆ **EMP:** 3
SQ FT: 5,500
SALES (est): 493.4K **Privately Held**
WEB: www.galleyware.com
SIC: 3089 Dishes, plastic, except foam

(G-10667)
GAME CHANGING INDUSTRIES LLC (PA)
3422 Old Capitol Trl (19808-6124)
PHONE.................................302 498-8321
Alexander Tonkov,
EMP: 4
SALES (est): 735.7K **Privately Held**
SIC: 8711 Electrical or electronic engineering

(G-10668)
GAMUT COLOR INC
1600 N Scott St (19806-2528)
PHONE.................................302 652-7171
Shawn Mc Clafferty, *President*
EMP: 9
SQ FT: 500
SALES (est): 333.4K **Privately Held**
SIC: 8748 Publishing consultant

(G-10669)
GARCIA PODIATRY GROUP
Also Called: Garcia, Luis M Jr DPM
1941 Limestone Rd Ste 208 (19808-5432)
PHONE.................................302 994-5956
Luis Garcia, *Owner*
EMP: 5
SALES (est): 782.2K **Privately Held**
SIC: 8043 Offices & clinics of podiatrists

(G-10670)
GARDA CL ATLANTIC INC (DH)
Also Called: Gcl A
4200 Governor Printz Blvd (19802-2315)
PHONE.................................302 762-5444
Stephan Cretier, *President*
Chris W Jamroz, *President*
Patrick Prince, *Senior VP*
Paul Balcer, *Executive*
EMP: 35 **EST:** 1951
SALES (est): 27.8MM
SALES (corp-wide): 44.8MM **Privately Held**
WEB: www.atsystems.com
SIC: 7381 Armored car services

Wilmington - New Castle County (G-10671)

(G-10671)
GARRETT MOTION INC
251 Little Falls Dr (19808-1674)
PHONE...................................973 867-7017
Olivier Rabiller, *CEO*
EMP: 3
SALES (est): 170.9K
SALES (corp-wide): 3.3B **Privately Held**
SIC: 3511 Turbines & turbine generator sets
PA: Garrett Motion Sarl
Zone D'activites La Piece 16
Rolle VD 1180
787 242-346

(G-10672)
GARRETT TRANSPORTATION I INC (HQ)
251 Little Falls Dr (19808-1674)
PHONE...................................973 455-2000
Darius Adamczyk, *CEO*
EMP: 5
SALES (est): 114.5K
SALES (corp-wide): 22.6MM **Privately Held**
SIC: 3724 Aircraft engines & engine parts
PA: Garrett Motion Inc.
89 Hedqrters Plz N Ste 14
Morristown NJ 07960
973 867-7016

(G-10673)
GARY L WAITE DMD
5500 Skyline Dr Ste 2 (19808-1772)
PHONE...................................302 239-8586
Gary Waite DMD, *Owner*
Gary Waite, *Owner*
EMP: 5
SALES (est): 348.9K **Privately Held**
SIC: 8021 Dentists' office

(G-10674)
GARY R COLLINS DDS
5500 Skyline Dr Ste 1 (19808-1772)
PHONE...................................302 239-3531
Gary R Collins, *Principal*
EMP: 5
SALES (est): 192.2K **Privately Held**
SIC: 8021 Offices & clinics of dentists

(G-10675)
GATES AND COMPANY LLC
4001 Kennett Pike Ste 206 (19807-2029)
PHONE...................................302 428-1338
Kelly Gates, *Managing Dir*
David Gates, *Mng Member*
EMP: 10 **EST:** 1999
SALES (est): 930K **Privately Held**
SIC: 6211 Security brokers & dealers

(G-10676)
GATESAIR INC
2711 Centerville Rd (19808-1660)
PHONE...................................513 459-3400
EMP: 2
SALES (corp-wide): 3.8B **Privately Held**
SIC: 1731 3663 7371 Communications specialization; radio & TV communications equipment; computer software development & applications
HQ: Gatesair, Inc.
5300 Kings Island Dr
Mason OH 45040
513 459-3400

(G-10677)
GATEWAY HOUSE INC
121 N Poplar St Apt A11 (19801-3955)
PHONE...................................302 571-8885
Lottie Lee, *President*
Sherrie Johnson, *Exec Dir*
EMP: 14
SQ FT: 2,500
SALES: 306.9K **Privately Held**
WEB: www.gatewayhouse.ws
SIC: 8361 Residential care

(G-10678)
GATTO GRAPHIX LLC
2412 Greenleaf Dr (19810-2414)
PHONE...................................302 598-5377
James Mills, *Owner*
EMP: 1
SALES (est): 77.2K **Privately Held**
SIC: 3993 Signs & advertising specialties

(G-10679)
GAUDENZIA INC
Also Called: Gaudenzia Fresh Start
604 W 10th St (19801-1424)
PHONE...................................302 421-9945
Macolm Ennel, *Principal*
EMP: 5
SALES (est): 146.8K **Privately Held**
SIC: 8351 Child day care services

(G-10680)
GAVINSOLMONESE
919 N Market St (19801-3023)
PHONE...................................302 655-8997
Joe Solmonese, *Managing Dir*
Judy Sacher, *Vice Pres*
Amy Gavin, *Manager*
Tom Hays, *Director*
Stanley Mastil, *Director*
EMP: 14
SALES (est): 990.9K **Privately Held**
SIC: 8742 Business consultant

(G-10681)
GB HOME IMPROVEMENT
100 Greenhill Ave Ste F (19805-1863)
PHONE...................................302 654-5411
Kenneth Moses, *Principal*
EMP: 6 **EST:** 2008
SALES (est): 119K **Privately Held**
SIC: 7299 Home improvement & renovation contractor agency

(G-10682)
GBC INTERNATIONAL CORP (PA)
Also Called: Smart Shoppers
2711 Centerville Rd # 400 (19808-1660)
PHONE...................................404 860-2533
Benjamin Lau, *CEO*
EMP: 7
SALES (est): 8.5MM **Privately Held**
SIC: 8732 Market analysis, business & economic research

(G-10683)
GBG USA INC
1209 N Orange St (19801-1120)
PHONE...................................888 342-7243
Lori Baxter, *Principal*
EMP: 8 **Privately Held**
SIC: 5139 5137 5136 Footwear; sportswear, women's & children's; sportswear, men's & boys'
HQ: Gbg Usa Inc.
350 5th Ave Lbby 11
New York NY 10118
646 839-7000

(G-10684)
GE CAPITAL INTL HOLDINGS CORP (HQ)
1209 N Orange St (19801-1120)
PHONE...................................302 658-7581
EMP: 14
SALES (est): 9.3MM
SALES (corp-wide): 117.3B **Publicly Held**
SIC: 7389 Business Services
PA: General Electric Company
3135 Easton Tpke
Fairfield CT 02210
203 373-2211

(G-10685)
GE TF TRUST
Rodney Sq N 1100 N Mkt St (19890-0001)
PHONE...................................302 636-6196
EMP: 44
SALES (est): 124.4K
SALES (corp-wide): 1.3B **Publicly Held**
SIC: 6733 Trusts
PA: Pacwest Bancorp
9701 Wilshire Blvd # 700
Beverly Hills CA 90212
310 887-8500

(G-10686)
GEICO CORPORATION
4541 Kirkwood Hwy (19806-5117)
PHONE...................................302 998-9192
Anne Scharp, *Agent*
EMP: 8
SALES (corp-wide): 225.3B **Publicly Held**
SIC: 6411 Insurance agents, brokers & service
HQ: Geico Corporation
5260 Western Ave
Chevy Chase MD 20815
301 986-3000

(G-10687)
GEM GROUP LP
501 Carr Rd (19809-2866)
PHONE...................................302 762-2008
Scott Ernsberger, *Branch Mgr*
EMP: 5
SALES (corp-wide): 6.7MM **Privately Held**
SIC: 6399 Deposit insurance
HQ: The Gem Group L P
3 Gateway Ctr 401 Liberty
Pittsburgh PA 15222
412 471-2885

(G-10688)
GEMINI BUILDING SYSTEMS LLC
Also Called: Janitorial Services and Sups
1607 E Newport Pike (19804-2528)
P.O. Box 6444 (19804-0444)
PHONE...................................302 654-5310
Janet Killian-Welte,
EMP: 94 **EST:** 1998
SQ FT: 10,000
SALES: 1.5MM **Privately Held**
WEB: www.geminillc.net
SIC: 1799 7349 Construction site cleanup; building & office cleaning services; janitorial service, contract basis; floor waxing; cleaning service, industrial or commercial

(G-10689)
GEMINI HAIR DESIGNS
22a Trolley Sq (19806-3367)
PHONE...................................302 654-9371
Erna Bollock, *Owner*
EMP: 7
SALES (est): 160.8K **Privately Held**
SIC: 7231 Manicurist, pedicurist

(G-10690)
GENE AND TAFFIN A RAY FAMILY
501 Silverside Rd Ste 123 (19809-1377)
PHONE...................................800 839-1754
Gene W Ray, *Principal*
EMP: 19
SALES (est): 157K **Privately Held**
SIC: 8699 Charitable organization

(G-10691)
GENERAL HLTHCARE RESOURCES LLC
5700 Kirkwood Hwy Ste 203 (19808-4884)
PHONE...................................302 998-0469
John Quirk, *Director*
EMP: 243
SALES (corp-wide): 41.8MM **Privately Held**
SIC: 8082 Home health care services
HQ: General Healthcare Resources, Llc
2250 Hickory Rd Ste 240
Plymouth Meeting PA 19462

(G-10692)
GENERATIONS HOME CARE INC
5211 W Woodmill Dr (19808-4068)
PHONE...................................302 322-3100
Paulette Austin, *Principal*
Lawrence Markman, *Director*
EMP: 21
SALES: 7.3MM **Privately Held**
SIC: 8082 Home health care services

(G-10693)
GENESIS LABORATORIES INC (PA)
11 Middleton Dr (19808-4320)
PHONE...................................832 217-8585
Fabian Maclaren, *CEO*
EMP: 3
SQ FT: 17,000
SALES: 2MM **Privately Held**
SIC: 2834 Pharmaceutical preparations

(G-10694)
GENOESE MILLER & ASSOCIATES
615 W 18th St (19802-4707)
PHONE...................................302 655-9505
EMP: 11
SALES (est): 660K **Privately Held**
SIC: 8721 Certified Public Accountants

(G-10695)
GENSOURCE FINCL ASRN CO LLC
3422 Old Capitol Trl (19808-6124)
PHONE...................................302 415-3030
Hayley Reitz, *Vice Pres*
EMP: 10
SQ FT: 20,000
SALES (est): 458.4K **Privately Held**
SIC: 7389 Financial services

(G-10696)
GENTLE TOUCH DENTISTRY
303 E Lea Blvd (19802-2353)
PHONE...................................302 765-3373
EMP: 4
SALES (est): 61.5K **Privately Held**
SIC: 8021 Offices & clinics of dentists

(G-10697)
GEORGE E FRATTALI DDS
1801 Rockland Rd Ste 100 (19803-3650)
PHONE...................................302 651-4408
George Frattali, *Owner*
EMP: 4 **EST:** 2018
SALES (est): 61.5K **Privately Held**
SIC: 8021 Offices & clinics of dentists

(G-10698)
GEORGE F KEMPF SUPPLY CO INC
1101 E 7th St (19801-4501)
PHONE...................................302 658-3760
EMP: 7 **Privately Held**
SIC: 5039 Whol Construction Materials

(G-10699)
GEORGE H BURNS INC
Also Called: Honeywell Authorized Dealer
200 N Ford Ave (19805-1834)
P.O. Box 2524 (19805-0524)
PHONE...................................302 658-0752
Philip Burns, *President*
Norman Williamson Sr, *Vice Pres*
Allan Koch, *Treasurer*
Norman Williamson Jr, *Admin Sec*
EMP: 25
SQ FT: 5,000
SALES (est): 3.1MM **Privately Held**
WEB: www.george-h-burns.com
SIC: 1711 Warm air heating & air conditioning contractor

(G-10700)
GEORGE HARDCASTLE & SONS INC (PA)
Also Called: Hardcastle Gallery
5714 Kennett Pike (19807-1331)
PHONE...................................302 655-5230
Mike Brock, *President*
David Berndt, *President*
J Berndt, *Corp Secy*
Lynn Brock, *Corp Secy*
EMP: 4
SALES (est): 596.8K **Privately Held**
WEB: www.hardcastlegallery.com
SIC: 5999 7699 Art dealers; picture framing, custom

(G-10701)
GEORGE J WEINER ASSOCIATES
2961 Centerville Rd # 300 (19808-1671)
PHONE...................................302 658-0218
Terrence L Wolf, *President*
Xavier F Decaire, *Vice Pres*
Donald T Fulton, *Treasurer*
Karen Skipicki, *Admin Sec*
EMP: 13
SQ FT: 5,000
SALES (est): 1.5MM **Privately Held**
SIC: 6411 Insurance agents

GEOGRAPHIC SECTION
Wilmington - New Castle County (G-10732)

(G-10702)
GEORGE MARCUS SALON INC
3629 Silverside Rd Ste 1 (19810-5106)
PHONE..................................302 475-7530
George Marcus, *President*
EMP: 15
SALES (est): 136.1K **Privately Held**
SIC: 7231 Hairdressers

(G-10703)
GEORGE MTSTSOS MD CRDIOLGY LLC
3521 Silverside Rd Ste 2k (19810-4900)
PHONE..................................302 482-2035
George D Moutsatsos, *Principal*
EMP: 5
SALES (est): 205.3K **Privately Held**
SIC: 8011 Offices & clinics of medical doctors

(G-10704)
GEORGTOWN PRSRVATION ASSOC LLC
Also Called: Georgetown Apartments
4 Denny Rd (19809-3445)
PHONE..................................302 856-1557
Jackie Edmanson, *CEO*
EMP: 4
SALES (est): 333.8K **Privately Held**
SIC: 6513 Apartment hotel operation

(G-10705)
GETRESPONSE INC
1011 Centre Rd Ste 322 (19805-1266)
PHONE..................................302 573-3895
Ireneusz Rybinski, *Manager*
Filip Szyler, *Manager*
EMP: 4
SALES (corp-wide): 982.5K **Privately Held**
SIC: 7371 Computer software development & applications
PA: Getresponse Inc.
  71 Summer St Fl 5
  Boston MA 02110
  617 778-2422

(G-10706)
GETTIER STAFFING SERVICES INC
2 Centerville Rd (19808-4708)
P.O. Box 5251 (19808-0251)
PHONE..................................302 478-0911
James Gettier, *CEO*
Louis Manerchia, *President*
Ronald Phillips, *Senior VP*
EMP: 12
SALES (est): 1.2MM **Privately Held**
SIC: 1541 1542 Industrial buildings, new construction; warehouse construction; nonresidential construction

(G-10707)
GF MCLAUGHLIN LLC
800 W 20th St (19802-3815)
PHONE..................................302 279-6018
Eugene F McLaughlin, *Principal*
EMP: 5
SALES (est): 410.6K **Privately Held**
SIC: 1611 General contractor, highway & street construction

(G-10708)
GFP CEMENT CONTRACTORS LLC
14 Hadco Rd (19804-1014)
PHONE..................................302 998-7687
Stacy Papa,
Laura Fedal,
EMP: 15 **EST:** 2012
SALES (est): 3.9MM **Privately Held**
SIC: 1541 Industrial buildings, new construction

(G-10709)
GHG ENTERPRISES LLC
Also Called: Golden Horse Shoe Gaming
1209 N Orange St (19801-1120)
PHONE..................................817 705-0313
Philip Guitar, *Principal*
EMP: 5
SALES (est): 107K **Privately Held**
SIC: 7371 Computer software development & applications

(G-10710)
GILANI MALIK JAVED MD
1309 Veale Rd Ste 11 (19810-4609)
PHONE..................................302 737-8116
Malik J Gilani MD, *Owner*
EMP: 4 **EST:** 1997
SALES (est): 170.6K **Privately Held**
SIC: 8011 Offices & clinics of medical doctors

(G-10711)
GILDEA ENTERPRISES INC
2100 Willow Way (19810-4154)
PHONE..................................302 475-1184
Robert Gildea Jr, *President*
Susan Gildea, *Treasurer*
EMP: 5
SALES: 300K **Privately Held**
SIC: 0782 Landscape contractors

(G-10712)
GILPIN MORTGAGE
1400 N Dupont St (19806-4030)
PHONE..................................302 656-5400
Anne Riley, *Owner*
EMP: 12
SALES (est): 946.9K **Privately Held**
SIC: 6162 Mortgage bankers

(G-10713)
GINA MADALINE MS CCC/SLP
2504 Pennington Dr (19810-4704)
PHONE..................................302 220-0931
Gina Madaline, *Principal*
EMP: 5 **EST:** 2012
SALES (est): 90.5K **Privately Held**
SIC: 8069 Eye, ear, nose & throat hospital

(G-10714)
GIORDANO DELCOLLO & WERB LLC
Also Called: Giordano, Delcollo Werb Gdw
5315 Limestone Rd (19808-1222)
PHONE..................................302 234-6855
Joseph A Giordano,
Dean C Delcollo,
Dade D Werb,
EMP: 6
SALES (est): 709.4K **Privately Held**
SIC: 8111 General practice attorney, lawyer

(G-10715)
GIORGI KITCHENS INC
4 Meco Cir (19804-1109)
PHONE..................................302 762-1121
Pete Giorgi Sr, *Manager*
EMP: 10
SALES (corp-wide): 1.8MM **Privately Held**
WEB: www.giorgikitchens.com
SIC: 1799 Kitchen & bathroom remodeling
PA: Giorgi Kitchens Inc
  218 Philadelphia Pike
  Wilmington DE
  302 762-1121

(G-10716)
GIRLS INCORPORATED OF DELAWARE (PA)
1019 Brown St (19805-4812)
PHONE..................................302 575-1041
Suzzette Schultz, *President*
EMP: 20 **EST:** 1955
SALES (est): 669.2K **Privately Held**
SIC: 8641 Youth organizations

(G-10717)
GIUMARRA INTERNATIONAL MKTG
11 Gist Rd Ste 101 (19801-5879)
PHONE..................................302 652-4009
Greg Murray, *Principal*
Mike Rodgers, *Manager*
EMP: 5 **Privately Held**
SIC: 7389 Brokers' services
PA: Giumarra International Marketing
  11220 Edison Hwy
  Bakersfield CA 93301

(G-10718)
GKUA INC
1000 N West St Ste 1200 (19801-1058)
PHONE..................................415 971-5341
Beau Golob, *Principal*

EMP: 12
SALES (est): 262.3K **Privately Held**
SIC: 7319 8742 Advertising; marketing consulting services

(G-10719)
GLAXOSMITHKLINE CAPITAL INC
1105 N Market St Ste 622 (19801-1216)
P.O. Box 8985 (19899-8985)
PHONE..................................302 656-5280
Richard Miller, *Vice Pres*
Linda Earland, *Manager*
Richard Overton, *Consultant*
Janet Lewis, *Exec Dir*
William K Langan, *Admin Sec*
EMP: 4
SALES (est): 14.6K
SALES (corp-wide): 40.6B **Privately Held**
SIC: 2834 Pharmaceutical preparations
PA: Glaxosmithkline Plc
  G S K House
  Brentford MIDDX TW8 9
  208 047-5000

(G-10720)
GLAXOSMITHKLINE HOLDINGS (DH)
Also Called: Glaxosmithkline Svcs Unlimited
1105 N Market St (19801-1216)
P.O. Box 8985 (19899-8985)
PHONE..................................302 984-6932
Deirdre Connelly, *President*
Julian S Heslop, *CFO*
Brenda Stephens, *Executive*
Shirley Reilly, *Executive Asst*
◆ **EMP:** 250 **EST:** 1830
SQ FT: 500,000
SALES (est): 6.8B
SALES (corp-wide): 40.6B **Privately Held**
WEB: www.gsk.com
SIC: 2834 2836 2833 2844 Cough medicines; vaccines & other immunizing products; vaccines; antibiotics; face creams or lotions; suntan lotions & oils; oral preparations; toothpastes or powders, dentifrices; medical laboratories
HQ: Glaxosmithkline Finance Plc
  G S K House
  Brentford MIDDX TW8 9
  208 047-5000

(G-10721)
GLENMEDE TRUST CO NAT ASSN
1201 N Market St Ste 1501 (19801-1163)
PHONE..................................302 661-2900
Jeffrey Rogers, *Principal*
EMP: 5 **Privately Held**
SIC: 6282 Investment advisory service
HQ: The Glenmede Trust Company National Association
  1 Liberty Pl Ste 1200
  Philadelphia PA 19103
  215 419-6000

(G-10722)
GLOBAL CURRENTS INV MGT LLC
2 Righter Pkwy (19803-1532)
PHONE..................................302 476-3800
Peter Sundman, *CEO*
EMP: 15
SALES (est): 1.7MM
SALES (corp-wide): 2.9B **Publicly Held**
SIC: 6722 Management investment, open-end
PA: Legg Mason Inc
  100 International Dr
  Baltimore MD 21202
  410 539-0000

(G-10723)
GLOBAL DEV PARTNERS INC
2711 Centerville Rd # 400 (19808-1660)
PHONE..................................480 330-7931
Faisal Naveed, *CEO*
EMP: 5 **EST:** 2016
SALES (est): 110.6K **Privately Held**
SIC: 8748 Business consulting

(G-10724)
GLOBAL ENTP WORLDWIDE LLC (PA)
1201 N Orange St Ste 700 (19801-1186)
PHONE..................................713 260-9687
Muhammad Iqbal,
▼ **EMP:** 70
SQ FT: 20,000
SALES (est): 6.3MM **Privately Held**
SIC: 5099 Wood chips

(G-10725)
GLOBAL GAMING BUSINESS
2413 Horace Dr (19808-3356)
PHONE..................................302 994-3898
Roger Gros, *Principal*
EMP: 2
SALES (est): 92.1K **Privately Held**
SIC: 7372 Publishers' computer software

(G-10726)
GLOBAL GARMENTS (USA) LLC
1 Commerce St (19801)
PHONE..................................617 340-3329
EMP: 1
SALES (est): 46.5K **Privately Held**
SIC: 2253 Blouses, shirts, pants & suits

(G-10727)
GLOBAL INNOVATION HOLDING LLC
Also Called: Global Innovation Institute
191 N Market St 425 (19801)
PHONE..................................877 276-7701
Charles Anthony Mills,
EMP: 4
SALES: 200K **Privately Held**
SIC: 6719 Holding companies

(G-10728)
GLOBAL NETWORK EXECUTIVE INC
Also Called: G E N
702 N West St Ste 101 (19801-1524)
PHONE..................................302 251-8940
Martin Hegi, *President*
Christina Pereira, *Manager*
EMP: 10
SALES (est): 1MM **Privately Held**
SIC: 7361 Executive placement

(G-10729)
GLOBAL PROTECTION MGT LLC
1105 N Market St Ste 400 (19801-1389)
PHONE..................................302 425-4190
Anthony Gentile, *President*
EMP: 100
SALES (est): 1.2MM
SALES (corp-wide): 4.8B **Privately Held**
SIC: 7381 Protective services, guard; detective agency
HQ: Sos Security Llc
  1915 Us Highway 46 Ste 2
  Parsippany NJ 07054
  973 402-6600

(G-10730)
GLOBAL SCIENTIFIC GLASS INC
3 S Tatnall St (19801-2457)
PHONE..................................302 429-9330
Ed Diviney, *President*
▲ **EMP:** 1
SALES: 43K **Privately Held**
SIC: 3229 Pressed & blown glass

(G-10731)
GLOBAL SHOPAHOLICS LLC
601 Cornell Dr Unit G11 (19801-5789)
PHONE..................................703 608-7108
EMP: 10
SALES (est): 30.7K **Privately Held**
SIC: 7389 Business services

(G-10732)
GLOBALTEC NETWORKS INC
1013 Centre Rd (19805-1265)
PHONE..................................646 321-8627
Graeme Savill, *Director*
Barry Chalmers, *Director*
EMP: 5
SALES (est): 260K **Privately Held**
SIC: 4813 Telephone communications broker

Wilmington - New Castle County (G-10733)

(G-10733)
GLOSSGIRL INC
1320 N Union St (19806-2534)
PHONE..................302 888-4520
EMP: 6
SALES (est): 140.1K
SALES (corp-wide): 167.8K **Privately Held**
SIC: 7231 Hairdressers
PA: Glossgirl, Inc.
   276 E Main St
   Newark DE 19711
   302 737-8080

(G-10734)
GMG SOLUTIONS LLC
Also Called: Mysherpa
4550 Linden Hill Rd # 301 (19808-2955)
PHONE..................302 781-3008
Erick McCue, *Engineer*
Ashley Webb, *Technical Staff*
Chris Raymond, *IT/INT Sup*
Greg Gurev,
EMP: 20
SQ FT: 3,500
SALES (est): 1.3MM **Privately Held**
WEB: www.mysherpa.com
SIC: 7379 Computer related maintenance services

(G-10735)
GO4SPIN
251 Little Falls Dr (19808-1674)
PHONE..................310 400-2588
Mikhail Khrushch, *CEO*
EMP: 5
SALES (est): 81.7K **Privately Held**
SIC: 7514 Passenger car rental

(G-10736)
GOLD LEAF SERVICES LLC
1591 Letitia Ln (19809-1528)
PHONE..................302 373-3333
Joseph F Gold, *Mng Member*
EMP: 4
SALES (est): 235.9K **Privately Held**
SIC: 0782 Lawn & garden services

(G-10737)
GOLDEN GLOBE INTL SVCS LTD
913 N Market St Ste 200 (19801-3097)
PHONE..................302 487-0022
Sukaina Manji, *President*
Mehbub Manji, *Principal*
EMP: 130
SALES (est): 1.8MM **Privately Held**
SIC: 7389

(G-10738)
GOLDEN RUBBER STAMP CO
841 N Tatnall St (19801-1717)
P.O. Box 365 (19899-0365)
PHONE..................302 658-7343
Stan Golden, *Owner*
EMP: 1
SALES (est): 85.1K **Privately Held**
SIC: 5099 3953 Rubber stamps; marking devices

(G-10739)
GOLDFEIN & HOSMER PC
3513 Concord Pike # 2000 (19803-5027)
PHONE..................302 656-3301
Bill Preston, *Branch Mgr*
EMP: 4
SALES (corp-wide): 8.1MM **Privately Held**
WEB: www.goldfeinlaw.com
SIC: 8111 General practice attorney, lawyer
PA: Goldfein & Hosmer Pc
   1880 Jfk Blvd Fl 20
   Philadelphia PA 19103
   215 979-8200

(G-10740)
GOLDIS ENTERPRISES INC (PA)
Also Called: I K O
120 Hay Rd (19809-3509)
PHONE..................302 764-3100
Henry Koschitzky, *President*
Saul Koschitzky, *Vice Pres*
Tim Wrigley, *Technical Mgr*
Steven Grier, *Engineer*
Michael Pinder, *Chief Acct*
EMP: 1

SQ FT: 100,000
SALES (est): 54.8MM **Privately Held**
WEB: www.iko.com
SIC: 2952 5033 Roofing materials; roofing, asphalt & sheet metal

(G-10741)
GOLDIS HOLDINGS INC (PA)
Also Called: I K O Productions
120 Hay Rd (19809-3509)
PHONE..................302 764-3100
Sarena Koschitzky, *President*
Hayden Williams, *Sales Staff*
EMP: 66
SQ FT: 100,000
SALES (est): 42.2MM **Privately Held**
SIC: 2952 5033 Roofing materials; roofing & siding materials

(G-10742)
GOLDSTAR- CASH LLC (PA)
Also Called: Goldstar Cash
711 N Market St (19801-3008)
P.O. Box 18524, Philadelphia PA (19129-0524)
PHONE..................302 427-2535
EMP: 4 EST: 2003
SQ FT: 2,500
SALES (est): 410K **Privately Held**
SIC: 6099 6163 5999 Check Cashing Payday Loans & Retail Electronic

(G-10743)
GOLFCLUB LLC
1209 Orange St Wilmington (19801)
PHONE..................908 770-7892
Christopher Silano, *CEO*
George Taskos, *Chief Engr*
EMP: 2
SALES (est): 89.7K **Privately Held**
SIC: 3949 Driving ranges, golf, electronic

(G-10744)
GOLT ADJ SERVICE INC
3516 Silverside Rd Ste 16 (19810-4932)
PHONE..................302 798-5500
EMP: 20
SALES (est): 776.9K **Privately Held**
SIC: 7389 Business Services

(G-10745)
GONSER AND GONSER P A
3411 Silverside Rd 203hg (19810-4812)
PHONE..................302 478-4445
Andrew Gonser, *President*
Zachary Berl, *Admin Sec*
EMP: 8
SALES (est): 760.8K **Privately Held**
SIC: 8111 Divorce & family law

(G-10746)
GOOD HOME SOLUTIONS LLC
20 North Ave (19804-1842)
PHONE..................302 540-3190
Nancy Good, *Principal*
EMP: 4 EST: 2011
SALES (est): 282.4K **Privately Held**
SIC: 8748 Business consulting

(G-10747)
GOOD TO GO DELIVERY LLC
831 N Union St (19805-5323)
PHONE..................302 893-2734
Seth Goldkrantz, *CEO*
Lisa Guariano, *President*
EMP: 15
SALES (est): 562.6K **Privately Held**
WEB: www.goodtogodelivery.com
SIC: 4212 Delivery service, vehicular

(G-10748)
GOODEALS INC
537 Main St (19804-3910)
PHONE..................302 999-1737
John Baker, *Principal*
EMP: 8
SALES (est): 275.7K **Privately Held**
SIC: 4953 5932 Refuse collection & disposal services; furniture, secondhand

(G-10749)
GOODWILL INDS DEL DEL CNTY INC (PA)
Also Called: Goodwill Center
300 E Lea Blvd (19802-2354)
PHONE..................302 761-4640
Chris Quintanilla, *Ch of Bd*
Ted Van Name, *President*
Trudy Spence-Parker, *Vice Pres*
EMP: 40
SALES (est): 36.4MM **Privately Held**
SIC: 5932 8331 Used merchandise stores; vocational training agency

(G-10750)
GOODWORLD INC
2711 Centerville Rd # 400 (19808-1660)
PHONE..................845 325-2232
John Gossart, *CEO*
EMP: 6
SALES (est): 310K **Privately Held**
SIC: 7379 7389 ;

(G-10751)
GOODYEAR TIRE & RUBBER COMPANY
3217 Kirkwood Hwy (19808-6129)
PHONE..................302 998-0428
Partick Leach, *Manager*
EMP: 12
SALES (corp-wide): 15.4B **Publicly Held**
WEB: www.goodyear.com
SIC: 5531 5014 Automotive tires; automobile tires & tubes
PA: The Goodyear Tire & Rubber Company
   200 E Innovation Way
   Akron OH 44316
   786 796-2121

(G-10752)
GOORLAND AND MANN INC
825 N Union St (19805-5398)
PHONE..................302 655-1514
Suzanne Goorland, *CEO*
Rachel Goorland, *Vice Pres*
EMP: 9 EST: 1965
SQ FT: 20,000
SALES: 2.1MM **Privately Held**
SIC: 5087 Janitors' supplies

(G-10753)
GOORLAND ENTERPRISES LLC
800b Plant St (19801-4362)
P.O. Box 9460 (19809-0460)
PHONE..................302 229-4573
EMP: 5 EST: 2011
SQ FT: 2,000
SALES (est): 310K **Privately Held**
SIC: 5087 5999 Whol Service Establishment Equipment

(G-10754)
GORDON FOURNARIS MAMMARELLA PA
1925 Lovering Ave (19806-2157)
PHONE..................302 652-2900
Peter Gordon, *Partner*
Emanuel Fournaris, *Partner*
Thomas Mammarella, *Partner*
Daniel Hayward, *Director*
Bryan Keenan, *Director*
EMP: 28
SALES (est): 3.9MM **Privately Held**
WEB: www.gfmlaw.com
SIC: 8111 General practice law office

(G-10755)
GOT HEALTH-E LLC
3616 Kirkwood Hwy Ste A (19808-5124)
PHONE..................203 583-5447
Kayode Olufowobi, *President*
EMP: 5
SQ FT: 1,200
SALES (est): 107K **Privately Held**
SIC: 7371 Computer software development

(G-10756)
GOULD MOTOR TECHNOLOGIES INC
100 S West St (19801-5015)
PHONE..................618 932-8446
EMP: 5
SALES (est): 300K **Privately Held**
SIC: 7539 Automotive Repair

(G-10757)
GRABOWSKI SPRANO VNCLETTE CPAS
Also Called: Sparano, Joseph C CPA
1814 Newport Gap Pike (19808-6148)
PHONE..................302 999-7300
CJ Vincelette, *Partner*
Alex Patseliev, *Accountant*
Glenn Davis, *CPA*
Evelyn Joiner, *CPA*
Thomas Grabowski,
EMP: 6
SALES (est): 477.1K **Privately Held**
SIC: 8721 Certified public accountant

(G-10758)
GRAND NATIONAL USA INC
2711 Centerville Rd # 400 (19808-1660)
PHONE..................416 746-3511
Jeff Otis, *President*
Charles Cheung, *CFO*
▲ EMP: 4
SALES (est): 542.2K **Privately Held**
SIC: 5136 Men's & boys' clothing

(G-10759)
GRAND OPERA HOUSE INC
818 N Market St Fl 2 (19801-3087)
PHONE..................302 652-5577
Kenneth Wesler, *President*
Robert VA Harra Jr, *Chairman*
Julia Dougherty, *Opers Staff*
Nancy Powel, *Finance*
Terry Cruz, *Marketing Staff*
EMP: 50
SQ FT: 200,000
SALES: 7.5MM **Privately Held**
SIC: 7922 Performing arts center production

(G-10760)
GRANT & EISENHOFER PA (PA)
123 S Justison St Ste 700 (19801-5360)
P.O. Box 752 (19899-0752)
PHONE..................302 622-7000
Jay W Eisenhofer, *President*
Thomas Ayala, *Counsel*
Carrie Vine, *Counsel*
Mary P Debus, *Controller*
Heather Lytwynec, *Marketing Staff*
EMP: 70 EST: 1997
SALES (est): 12.5MM **Privately Held**
WEB: www.gelaw.com
SIC: 8111 General practice attorney, lawyer

(G-10761)
GRAPE SOLUTIONS
3210 Wilson Ave (19808-6212)
PHONE..................201 784-9797
EMP: 4
SALES (est): 139K **Privately Held**
SIC: 8748 Business consulting

(G-10762)
GRAPETREE INC
901 Mount Lebanon Rd (19803-1612)
PHONE..................302 655-1950
EMP: 5 EST: 1970
SALES (est): 300K **Privately Held**
SIC: 6531 Real Estate Agent/Manager

(G-10763)
GRASSWORKS LAWN CARE SERVICE
Also Called: Grass Works Lawn Care Service
809a Kiamensi Rd (19804-3419)
P.O. Box 5480 (19804-0480)
PHONE..................302 683-0833
Jon Sibol, *President*
Tracey Sibol, *Vice Pres*
EMP: 4 EST: 1994
SQ FT: 2,000
SALES (est): 198.4K **Privately Held**
SIC: 0782 Lawn care services

(G-10764)
GRAYDIE WELDING LLC
42 W Reamer Ave (19804-1716)
PHONE..................302 753-0695
Harry B Bachman, *Principal*
EMP: 1
SALES (est): 47.4K **Privately Held**
SIC: 7692 Welding repair

GEOGRAPHIC SECTION
Wilmington - New Castle County (G-10796)

(G-10765)
GRAYDON HURST & SON INC
2901 Baynard Blvd Ste 4 (19802-2973)
PHONE..................................302 762-2444
Walter A Belczyk Jr, *President*
Cathy Belczyk, *Treasurer*
EMP: 6 **EST:** 1932
SALES: 550K **Privately Held**
SIC: 1771 1711 Concrete work; plumbing contractors

(G-10766)
GRAYLYN CREST III SWIM CLUB
2015 Kynwyd Rd (19810-3843)
PHONE..................................302 547-5809
Sandra Huelong, *Principal*
EMP: 6
SALES: 115.4K **Privately Held**
SIC: 7997 Swimming club, membership

(G-10767)
GRAYLYN DENTAL
2205 Silverside Rd Ste 2 (19810-4534)
PHONE..................................302 475-5555
Joseph Kelly, *President*
EMP: 7
SALES (est): 699K **Privately Held**
SIC: 8021 Dental clinic

(G-10768)
GREAT CLIPS
4235 Concord Pike (19803-1403)
PHONE..................................302 478-2022
Bill Keeporth, *Owner*
EMP: 8 **EST:** 2012
SALES (est): 37.3K **Privately Held**
SIC: 7231 Unisex hair salons

(G-10769)
GREATER WILMINGTON CONVENTION (PA)
100 W 10th St Ste 20 (19801-1632)
PHONE..................................302 652-4088
Mary Simpson, *Finance*
Gaby Indellini, *Marketing Staff*
Sarah Willoughby, *Exec Dir*
J Harry Feldman, *Exec Dir*
Rose Roberts, *Director*
EMP: 8
SALES: 1.7MM **Privately Held**
SIC: 7389 Convention & show services

(G-10770)
GREELEY & NISTA ORTHODONTICS
1405 Silverside Rd Ste A (19810-4445)
PHONE..................................302 475-4102
John M Nista, *Partner*
M C Greeley, *Partner*
EMP: 18
SALES (est): 1.2MM **Privately Held**
SIC: 8021 Orthodontist

(G-10771)
GREEN EARTH TECH GROUP LLC
1000 N West St (19801-1050)
PHONE..................................302 257-5617
Bn Hameed, *CEO*
EMP: 20
SALES (est): 1MM **Privately Held**
SIC: 1795 Wrecking & demolition work

(G-10772)
GREEN OAK REAL ESTATE LP
1209 N Orange St (19801-1120)
PHONE..................................212 359-7800
Andrew Yoon, *COO*
EMP: 100 **EST:** 2010
SQ FT: 10,000
SALES: 70MM **Privately Held**
SIC: 6531 Real estate brokers & agents

(G-10773)
GREEN ROOM RESTAURANT
Also Called: Hotel Dupont Company
100 W 11th St (19801)
PHONE..................................302 594-3100
Jacques Amblard, *Principal*
EMP: 30
SALES (est): 3.1MM **Privately Held**
SIC: 7011 Hotels

(G-10774)
GREENAMOYER CONSTRUCTION
212 S Woodward Ave (19805-2359)
PHONE..................................302 999-8235
EMP: 1 **EST:** 1975
SALES: 90K **Privately Held**
SIC: 1389 Oil/Gas Field Services

(G-10775)
GREENBANK CHILD DEV CTR
708 Greenbank Rd (19808-3168)
PHONE..................................302 994-8574
Ginger Bright, *President*
Anthony Bright, *Treasurer*
EMP: 9 **EST:** 1979
SQ FT: 2,100
SALES (est): 116.7K **Privately Held**
SIC: 8351 Group day care center

(G-10776)
GREENBERG PRAURIG LLC
1007 N Orange St Ste 1200 (19801-1236)
PHONE..................................302 661-7000
Brian Colborn, *Principal*
Justin E Mann, *Associate*
EMP: 37 **EST:** 2007
SALES (est): 245.8K **Privately Held**
SIC: 8111 Specialized law offices, attorneys

(G-10777)
GREENBERG SUPPLY CO INC
809 E 5th St (19801-4899)
P.O. Box 9248 (19809-0248)
PHONE..................................302 656-4496
Gary W Greenberg, *President*
Alvin Hall Jr, *Vice Pres*
Pat Beckman, *Admin Sec*
EMP: 35 **EST:** 1946
SQ FT: 45,000
SALES (est): 21.9MM **Privately Held**
WEB: www.greenbergsupply.com
SIC: 5075 5074 5085 5078 Air conditioning & ventilation equipment & supplies; plumbing & hydronic heating supplies; industrial supplies; refrigeration equipment & supplies

(G-10778)
GREENE TWEED OF DELAWARE INC
1105 N Market St Ste 1300 (19801-1241)
PHONE..................................302 888-2560
Bruce Rhoades, *Project Mgr*
William P Maher, *Treasurer*
Frank Dicostanza, *Analyst*
EMP: 7
SALES (est): 13.5MM
SALES (corp-wide): 280.7MM **Privately Held**
SIC: 3053 Gaskets & sealing devices
PA: Tweed Greene & Co Inc
2075 Detwiler Rd
Kulpsville PA 19443
215 256-9521

(G-10779)
GREENVILLE COUNTRY CLUB INC
201 Owls Nest Rd (19807-1129)
P.O. Box 3920 (19807-0920)
PHONE..................................302 652-3255
Eric Holloway, *President*
Donald Taylor, *President*
Steven Griffin, *General Mgr*
Carol Munsch, *Controller*
Brian Daley, *Office Mgr*
EMP: 35
SALES: 2.8MM **Privately Held**
WEB: www.greenvillecc.com
SIC: 7997 5812 Country club, membership; eating places

(G-10780)
GREENVILLE TRAVEL AGENCY INC
3926 Kennett Pike (19807-2304)
PHONE..................................302 658-3585
Frank Martinez Jr, *President*
Glen Hey, *Principal*
Debbie Hoy, *Agent*
Jean Martinez, *Admin Sec*
EMP: 8
SQ FT: 1,300
SALES (est): 1.1MM **Privately Held**
WEB: www.greenvilletravel.com
SIC: 4724 Tourist agency arranging transport, lodging & car rental

(G-10781)
GREENVLLE RETIREMENT CMNTY LLC
Also Called: STONEGATES
4031 Kennett Pike (19807-2047)
PHONE..................................302 658-6200
Bruce Hendricks, *Director*
Cathline Neylan,
Charles Cantera,
Pierce Crompton,
EMP: 125
SALES: 14.4MM **Privately Held**
WEB: www.stonegates.com
SIC: 8051 Convalescent home with continuous nursing care

(G-10782)
GREENWING SOLUTIONS INC
1201 N Orange St Ste 700 (19801-1186)
PHONE..................................302 295-5690
EMP: 5
SALES (est): 365.8K **Privately Held**
SIC: 8748 Business consulting
PA: Greenwing Solutions, Inc.
5508 Limeric Cir Apt 25
Wilmington DE 19808

(G-10783)
GRIFFEN CORPORATE SERVICES
300 Delaware Ave Fl 9 (19801-1607)
PHONE..................................302 576-2890
EMP: 15 **Privately Held**
SIC: 6719 Investment holding companies, except banks

(G-10784)
GRIFFS SIGNS LLC
101 Westmoreland Ave (19804-1752)
PHONE..................................302 784-5596
Matt Griffith, *Principal*
EMP: 1
SALES (est): 46K **Privately Held**
SIC: 3993 Signs & advertising specialties

(G-10785)
GRILLO HOLDINGS INC
2711 Centerville Rd # 400 (19808-1660)
PHONE..................................302 261-9668
Andres Meira, *CEO*
Federico Meira, *MIS Mgr*
EMP: 1
SQ FT: 900
SALES (est): 89K **Privately Held**
SIC: 3669 Emergency alarms

(G-10786)
GRIND OR STARVE LLC
608 W Lea Blvd Apt C4 (19802-2049)
PHONE..................................302 322-1679
Jai Howard, *President*
EMP: 5
SALES (est): 676.8K **Privately Held**
SIC: 7311 8742 Advertising consultant; marketing consulting services

(G-10787)
GRISWOLD HOME CARE
115 Christina Landing Dr # 708 (19801-5401)
PHONE..................................302 750-4564
Anne Eidschun, *Principal*
EMP: 6 **EST:** 2015
SALES (est): 72.3K **Privately Held**
SIC: 8082 Home health care services

(G-10788)
GRM PRO IMAGING LLC
Also Called: Speed Pro Imiging
401 Marsh Ln Ste 3 (19804-2491)
PHONE..................................302 999-8162
Gary Meltz, *Mng Member*
EMP: 2 **EST:** 2012
SQ FT: 3,000
SALES (est): 222.8K **Privately Held**
SIC: 2752 Commercial printing, offset

(G-10789)
GROUP THREE INC (PA)
Also Called: Gti Millwork
1100 Duncan St Ste A (19805-4782)
PHONE..................................302 658-4158
Jeff Moore, *President*
Elliott Colton, *Admin Sec*
EMP: 7
SQ FT: 10,000
SALES (est): 768.6K **Privately Held**
WEB: www.groupthree.com
SIC: 2511 5712 2431 Wood household furniture; customized furniture & cabinets; millwork

(G-10790)
GROUPE VICTOIRE LLC
800 Delaware Ave (19801-1322)
PHONE..................................302 384-5355
EMP: 5
SALES (est): 189.2K **Privately Held**
SIC: 7323 Credit Reporting Services

(G-10791)
GRUBB LUMBER COMPANY INC
200 A St (19801-5221)
P.O. Box 627 (19899-0627)
PHONE..................................302 652-2800
David Arronson, *President*
EMP: 45
SQ FT: 65,000
SALES: 29.6MM **Privately Held**
SIC: 2431 5031 2426 2421 Millwork; lumber: rough, dressed & finished; hardwood dimension & flooring mills; sawmills & planing mills, general

(G-10792)
GRUPO ACOSTA ECUADOR LIMITED
501 Silverside Rd (19809-1374)
PHONE..................................302 231-2981
Jang F Acosta, *President*
Jang Acosta, *President*
Paolo Morocho, *Vice Pres*
Daniel Peters, *CFO*
EMP: 219
SALES: 25.7MM **Privately Held**
SIC: 5199 General merchandise, nondurable

(G-10793)
GSB&B LLC
Also Called: Gellert Scali Busenkell Brown
1201 N Orange St Ste 300 (19801-1167)
PHONE..................................302 425-5800
Margaret England, *Counsel*
Angie Poulin, *Office Mgr*
Ronald Gellert,
Michael Scali,
EMP: 8 **EST:** 2013
SALES (est): 525.1K **Privately Held**
SIC: 8111 General practice attorney, lawyer

(G-10794)
GT USA WILMINGTON LLC
1 Hausel Rd (19801-5800)
PHONE..................................302 472-7679
John Haroldson, *Marketing Staff*
Eric Casey,
EMP: 4
SALES (est): 122.6K **Privately Held**
SIC: 7389

(G-10795)
GTS TECHNICAL SALES LLC
122 Middleboro Rd (19804-1621)
PHONE..................................302 778-1362
Steve Shellem,
Gary Peters,
EMP: 7 **EST:** 2001
SALES (est): 4.2MM **Privately Held**
SIC: 5085 Valves & fittings

(G-10796)
GUARDIAN ANGEL CHILD CARE
1000 Wilson St (19801-3432)
PHONE..................................302 428-3620
Janet Chandler, *Director*
EMP: 5
SALES (est): 106.7K **Privately Held**
SIC: 8351 Preschool center

Wilmington - New Castle County (G-10797)

(G-10797)
GUEDON CO
Also Called: Guco
1106 Cypress Rd (19810-1908)
PHONE.................................302 375-6151
Rudolph J Ovecka Jr, *Owner*
EMP: 2 **EST:** 1967
SALES (est): 92K **Privately Held**
WEB: www.gucoline.com
SIC: 3993 Signs & advertising specialties

(G-10798)
GUIDE IDLER AND CONVEYOR BELT
8 S Stuyvesant Dr (19809-3432)
PHONE.................................302 762-7564
Russell Knapp, *President*
EMP: 1
SALES (est): 63.3K **Privately Held**
SIC: 3496 Conveyor belts

(G-10799)
GUINEVERE ASSOCIATES INC
2 Nob Hill Rd (19808-1206)
PHONE.................................302 635-7798
David Jonocha, *President*
EMP: 7
SALES (est): 892.3K **Privately Held**
SIC: 5199 Gifts & novelties

(G-10800)
GULF DEVELOPMENT PARTNERS LLC
910 Foulk Rd Ste 201 (19803-3159)
PHONE.................................646 334-1245
Irwin Menken,
EMP: 7
SALES (est): 162.6K **Privately Held**
SIC: 8742 Management consulting services

(G-10801)
GUND SECURITIES CORPORATION
1105 N Market St Ste 1300 (19801-1241)
P.O. Box 8985 (19899-8985)
PHONE.................................302 479-9210
Hilton Young, *CEO*
EMP: 15
SALES (est): 798.6K **Privately Held**
SIC: 6211 Security brokers & dealers

(G-10802)
GUNNIP & COMPANY
Also Called: Gunnip Employment Services
2751 Centerville Rd # 300 (19808-1627)
PHONE.................................302 225-5000
Charles L Robertson, *Partner*
Don Bromley, *Partner*
William Brower, *Partner*
John Enderle, *Partner*
John P Garniewski, *Partner*
EMP: 70
SQ FT: 16,000
SALES (est): 8.6MM **Privately Held**
WEB: www.gunnip.com
SIC: 8721 Certified public accountant; accounting services, except auditing

(G-10803)
GUNTON CORPORATION
Also Called: Pella Window and Door
3617 Kirkwood Hwy (19808-5103)
PHONE.................................302 999-0535
Fax: 302 999-9932
EMP: 6
SALES (corp-wide): 15.2MM **Privately Held**
SIC: 5031 Ret Windows & Doors
PA: Gunton Corporation
  26150 Richmond Rd
  Cleveland OH 44146
  216 831-2420

(G-10804)
GYM SOURCE
3901 Concord Pike (19803-1715)
PHONE.................................302 478-4069
EMP: 1
SALES (est): 33K **Privately Held**
SIC: 5941 3949 Exercise equipment; snowshoes

(G-10805)
H CLEMONS CONSULTING INC
Also Called: Hcnrg Solutions
1000 N West St Ste 1200 (19801-1058)
PHONE.................................302 295-5097
Deborah L Hunt-Clemons, *President*
EMP: 25
SQ FT: 1,600
SALES (est): 150K **Privately Held**
SIC: 8748 Business consulting

(G-10806)
H D C INC
Also Called: Harvey Development Company
405 Marsh Ln Ste 1 (19804-2445)
PHONE.................................302 323-9300
Thomas Harvey, *President*
Thomas Hanna, *COO*
Stacey McIlvaine, *Controller*
EMP: 9
SQ FT: 3,000
SALES (est): 895.4K **Privately Held**
SIC: 6531 Appraiser, real estate

(G-10807)
H D LEE COMPANY INC (HQ)
3411 Silverside Rd 200hb (19810-4817)
PHONE.................................302 477-3930
Laura Meagher, *President*
Helen L Winslow, *Vice Pres*
Jacquelyn A Pellegrino, *Asst Sec*
EMP: 12
SQ FT: 47,000
SALES (est): 915.3K
SALES (corp-wide): 13.8B **Publicly Held**
SIC: 2211 5136 5137 Jean fabrics; men's & boys' clothing; women's & children's clothing
PA: V.F. Corporation
  105 Corporate Center Blvd
  Greensboro NC 27408
  336 424-6000

(G-10808)
H DEAN MCSPADDEN DDS
Also Called: Rockland Dental Associates
11 Old Barley Mill Rd (19807-3000)
PHONE.................................302 571-0680
H Dean Mc Spadden DDS, *Owner*
EMP: 7
SALES (est): 135.3K **Privately Held**
SIC: 8021 Dentists' office

(G-10809)
H JUAREZ TRANSPORT INC
3314 Old Capitol Trl L5 (19808-6235)
PHONE.................................302 407-5102
Walter Zoel Juarez Reyes, *President*
EMP: 4
SALES (est): 89K **Privately Held**
SIC: 4789 Transportation services

(G-10810)
H S B C OVERSEAS CORP DE
300 Delaware Ave Ste 1400 (19801-1650)
PHONE.................................302 657-8400
Richard Leigh, *President*
EMP: 17 **EST:** 1987
SALES (est): 77.9K
SALES (corp-wide): 87.7B **Privately Held**
WEB: www.us.hsbc.com
SIC: 6722 Mutual fund sales, on own account
HQ: Hsbc Usa, Inc.
  107 Iris Glen Dr Se
  Conyers GA 30013
  212 525-5000

(G-10811)
H&H TRADING INTERNATIONAL LLC
1201 N Orange St Ste 600 (19801-1171)
PHONE.................................480 580-3911
Sabrina Hayouna,
◆ **EMP:** 5
SALES (est): 275K **Privately Held**
WEB: www.hhtradingintl.com
SIC: 2038 7389 Ethnic foods, frozen;

(G-10812)
H&R BLOCK INC
Also Called: H & R Block
4711 Kirkwood Hwy (19808-5007)
PHONE.................................302 999-7488
John Rudick, *Manager*
EMP: 16
SALES (corp-wide): 3B **Publicly Held**
WEB: www.hrblock.com
SIC: 7291 8721 Tax return preparation services; accounting, auditing & bookkeeping
PA: H&R Block, Inc.
  1 H&R Block Way
  Kansas City MO 64105
  816 854-3000

(G-10813)
H&R BLOCK INC
Also Called: H & R Block
1720 Marsh Rd (19810-4606)
PHONE.................................302 478-9140
Marilyn Morgan, *Manager*
EMP: 10
SALES (corp-wide): 3B **Publicly Held**
WEB: www.hrblock.com
SIC: 7291 Tax return preparation services
PA: H&R Block, Inc.
  1 H&R Block Way
  Kansas City MO 64105
  816 854-3000

(G-10814)
H&R BLOCK INC
Also Called: H & R Block
3629b Silverside Rd (19810-5101)
PHONE.................................302 478-6300
Stanley Lamar, *President*
EMP: 12
SALES (corp-wide): 3B **Publicly Held**
WEB: www.hrblock.com
SIC: 7291 Tax return preparation services
PA: H&R Block, Inc.
  1 H&R Block Way
  Kansas City MO 64105
  816 854-3000

(G-10815)
HABITAT FOR HUMANITY (PA)
1920 Hutton St (19802-4905)
PHONE.................................302 652-0365
Kevin Smith, *CEO*
Beverly Ward, *Director*
EMP: 12
SQ FT: 13,000
SALES: 4.6MM **Privately Held**
WEB: www.habitatncc.org
SIC: 1521 8322 Single-family housing construction; individual & family services

(G-10816)
HACKETT INDUSTRIES LLC
701 S Franklin St (19805-4330)
PHONE.................................302 357-2539
Ismaaeel H Hackett, *Principal*
EMP: 6
SALES (est): 210.4K **Privately Held**
SIC: 3999 Manufacturing industries

(G-10817)
HAGERTY DRIVERS CLUB LLC
2711 Centerville Rd # 400 (19808-1660)
PHONE.................................302 504-6086
Brian Clymer, *Principal*
EMP: 4 **EST:** 2018
SALES (est): 38.1K **Privately Held**
SIC: 7997 Membership sports & recreation clubs

(G-10818)
HAIR DESIGNS BY LINDA INC
704 W Matson Run Pkwy (19802-1912)
PHONE.................................302 478-7080
Linda Travers, *CEO*
EMP: 4
SALES (est): 62.1K **Privately Held**
SIC: 7231 Beauty shops

(G-10819)
HAIR DESIGNS BY REGINA
Also Called: A Cut Above
1920 Lancaster Ave (19805-3808)
PHONE.................................302 652-8089
Regina Claggett, *Owner*
EMP: 4
SALES (est): 98.8K **Privately Held**
SIC: 7231 Hairdressers

(G-10820)
HAIR GALLERY
Also Called: Head Masters Salon
2080 Naamans Rd (19810-2655)
PHONE.................................302 475-6714
Mary Dziekan, *Owner*
EMP: 14
SALES (est): 680.7K **Privately Held**
SIC: 5087 Beauty salon & barber shop equipment & supplies

(G-10821)
HAIR LEVELS
4737 Concord Pike (19803-1442)
PHONE.................................302 212-0842
EMP: 4
SALES (est): 28.8K **Privately Held**
SIC: 7231 Hairdressers

(G-10822)
HAIRWORKS INC
1601 Concord Pike Ste 21 (19803-3613)
PHONE.................................302 656-0566
Patricia M Palandrani, *President*
Teresa Koval, *Owner*
Janet Milam, *Owner*
EMP: 17
SQ FT: 1,350
SALES (est): 890K **Privately Held**
SIC: 7231 Unisex hair salons

(G-10823)
HAJOCA CORPORATION
Also Called: Weinstein Supply Div
303 E 30th St (19802-3201)
PHONE.................................302 764-6000
Donald Elliott, *Manager*
EMP: 10
SALES (corp-wide): 2.3B **Privately Held**
WEB: www.hajoca.com
SIC: 5074 Plumbing & hydronic heating supplies
PA: Hajoca Corporation
  2001 Joshua Rd
  Lafayette Hill PA 19444
  610 649-1430

(G-10824)
HALL BURKE VFW POST 5447 INC
1605 Philadelphia Pike (19809-1540)
PHONE.................................302 798-2052
Edward Edwards, *President*
EMP: 10
SQ FT: 10,000
SALES (est): 261.9K **Privately Held**
SIC: 8641 Civic associations; community membership club

(G-10825)
HALL INTERNATIONAL IND CORP
1000 N West St Ste 1200 (19801-1058)
PHONE.................................302 777-2290
EMP: 16 **Privately Held**
SIC: 6719 Holding Company

(G-10826)
HALO MEDICAL TECHNOLOGIES LLC
1805 Foulk Rd Ste G (19810-3700)
PHONE.................................302 475-2300
Clare Rosa,
EMP: 5 **EST:** 2013
SALES (est): 451.7K **Privately Held**
SIC: 8099 Physical examination & testing services

(G-10827)
HAMILTON HOUSE CONDOMINIUM
1403 Shallcross Ave # 304 (19806-3034)
PHONE.................................302 658-7787
Louis Wiley, *President*
Ralph Gilby, *Treasurer*
EMP: 5 **EST:** 1973
SALES (est): 314.6K **Privately Held**
WEB: www.hamiltonhousecondos.com
SIC: 8641 Condominium association

GEOGRAPHIC SECTION
Wilmington - New Castle County (G-10857)

(G-10828)
HAMILTON PEPPER LLP
1313 N Market St Ste 5100 (19801-6111)
P.O. Box 1709 (19899-1709)
PHONE..................302 777-6500
David Straton, *Managing Prtnr*
Steve McVey,
Ashleigh K Reibach, *Associate*
EMP: 40
SALES (corp-wide): 171.7MM **Privately Held**
WEB: www.pepperlaw.com
SIC: 8111 General practice law office; general practice attorney, lawyer
PA: Pepper Hamilton Llp
  3000 Two Lgan Sq 18th Rnc
  Philadelphia PA 19103
  215 981-4000

(G-10829)
HAMPSHIRE GROUP LIMITED
Hampshire Brands
919 N Market St Ste 600 (19801-3037)
PHONE..................212 840-5666
EMP: 60
SALES (corp-wide): 91.4MM **Publicly Held**
SIC: 2329 Mfg Men's/Boy's Clothing
PA: Hampshire Group, Limited
  1924 Pearman Dairy Rd
  Anderson SC 29625
  212 540-5666

(G-10830)
HAND & SPA
3654 Concord Pike (19803-5022)
PHONE..................302 478-1700
Jerry Le Reux, *Owner*
EMP: 5
SALES (est): 91.2K **Privately Held**
SIC: 7299 Massage parlor

(G-10831)
HANDLER BUILDERS INC
Also Called: Deerborne Woods Sales Center
5169 W Woodmill Dr (19808-4067)
PHONE..................302 999-9200
Mark Handler, *President*
EMP: 50
SALES (est): 2.3MM **Privately Held**
SIC: 1521 New construction, single-family houses

(G-10832)
HANDLER CORPORATION
5169 W Woodmill Dr Ste 10 (19808-4015)
PHONE..................302 999-9200
Mark Handler, *President*
Ruth Handler, *Corp Secy*
Rob Allen, *Vice Pres*
Paul Handler, *Vice Pres*
Dave Macey, *Sales Associate*
EMP: 34
SQ FT: 4,000
SALES (est): 5.3MM **Privately Held**
WEB: www.handlerhomes.com
SIC: 1521 New construction, single-family houses

(G-10833)
HANGSTER INC
1201 N Orange St Ste 600 (19801-1171)
P.O. Box 18038, Stanford CA (94309-8038)
PHONE..................619 871-8086
Julio Buendia, *CEO*
Vincent Becerra, *COO*
Juan Posadas-Castillo, *Chief Engr*
Oscar Barillas, *CFO*
EMP: 4
SALES (est): 150K **Privately Held**
SIC: 7374 Computer processing services

(G-10834)
HANNAS PHRM SUP CO INC
2505 W 6th St (19805-2908)
PHONE..................302 571-8761
Mark Hanna, *President*
Matthew Hanna, *Vice Pres*
EMP: 13
SQ FT: 7,600
SALES (est): 4MM **Privately Held**
SIC: 5047 5122 Medical equipment & supplies; pharmaceuticals

(G-10835)
HAR-LEX LLC (PA)
105 Chandler Ave (19807-1107)
PHONE..................302 476-2322
Priit Porila,
EMP: 5
SALES: 500K **Privately Held**
SIC: 7371 8748 7389 Computer software development & applications; business consulting; business services

(G-10836)
HARDIN & ASSOCIATES INC
1300 N Grant Ave Ste 204 (19806-2456)
P.O. Box 7943 (19803-0943)
PHONE..................302 654-9923
Vaughn Hardin, *President*
Ann Mattingly, *Manager*
EMP: 6
SALES (est): 560.6K **Privately Held**
SIC: 8742 Business planning & organizing services

(G-10837)
HARMON INVESTMENTS LLC
Also Called: Meticulous Maids, The
2626 Drayton Dr (19808-3804)
PHONE..................302 383-2176
John Harmon,
EMP: 4
SALES (est): 43.3K **Privately Held**
SIC: 7349 Janitorial service, contract basis

(G-10838)
HARMONIOUS MIND LLC
5189 W Woodmill Dr 30a (19808-4009)
PHONE..................302 668-1059
Fawzia Hasan, *Med Doctor*
Manisha Wadhwa, *Manager*
Sanjay Wadhwa, *Manager*
EMP: 9
SALES (est): 555.3K **Privately Held**
SIC: 8011 Psychiatrist

(G-10839)
HARMONIOUSLY PBC
3 Germay Dr Ste 4-1696 (19804-1127)
PHONE..................302 291-1106
Sean Carr, *CEO*
EMP: 1 **EST:** 2018
SALES (est): 71.1K **Privately Held**
SIC: 2741 Miscellaneous publishing

(G-10840)
HARMONY TRUCKING INC
305 W Newport Pike (19804-3154)
PHONE..................302 633-5600
William Saienni Jr, *President*
Carolyn Hamby, *Admin Sec*
EMP: 9
SQ FT: 10,000
SALES (est): 740K **Privately Held**
SIC: 4212 Light haulage & cartage, local

(G-10841)
HARRIET TUBMAN SAFE HOUSE INC
914 E 7th St (19801-4415)
P.O. Box 4551 (19807-4551)
PHONE..................302 351-4434
Earl W Woodlen Jr, *President*
EMP: 7
SQ FT: 1,200
SALES (est): 26.6K **Privately Held**
SIC: 7389 Bail bonding

(G-10842)
HARRIS BERGER LLC (PA)
1105 N Market St Ste 1100 (19801-1209)
PHONE..................302 665-1140
Peter McGivney, *Counsel*
Benjamin Berger, *Mng Member*
Michelle Quinn, *Director*
Marsha Nicholls, *Admin Sec*
Brian Gottesman,
EMP: 6
SALES (est): 904.4K **Privately Held**
SIC: 8111 General practice law office

(G-10843)
HARRISON PROPERTIES LTD INC
1311 N Rodney St Ste A (19806-4259)
PHONE..................302 888-2650
Janis Harrison, *Partner*
Robert C Harrison, *Vice Pres*
EMP: 4
SALES (est): 479.6K **Privately Held**
WEB: www.harrisonpropertiesltd.com
SIC: 6531 Real estate managers

(G-10844)
HARRY J LAWALL & SON INC
Also Called: Lawall Prosthetics & Orthotics
1822 Augustine Cut Off (19803-4405)
PHONE..................302 429-7630
Ed Moran, *Branch Mgr*
EMP: 15
SALES (corp-wide): 16.8MM **Privately Held**
SIC: 3842 Limbs, artificial; orthopedic appliances
PA: Harry J. Lawall & Son, Inc.
  8028 Frankford Ave
  Philadelphia PA 19136
  215 338-6611

(G-10845)
HARTING GRAPHICS LTD
305 Brandywine Blvd (19809-3241)
PHONE..................302 762-6397
Theodore Harting, *President*
Helen Rolph, *Manager*
EMP: 9
SQ FT: 9,500
SALES (est): 1.1MM **Privately Held**
WEB: www.hartinggraphics.com
SIC: 7336 3993 Silk screen design; signs & advertising specialties

(G-10846)
HARTNETT ACCOUNTING & TAX SERV
1202 Foulk Rd Ste 5 (19803-2796)
PHONE..................302 477-0660
John Hartnett, *Principal*
EMP: 4
SALES (est): 344.7K **Privately Held**
SIC: 8721 Accounting services, except auditing

(G-10847)
HARVEST COMMUNITY DEV CORP
2205 Lancaster Ave (19805-3733)
PHONE..................302 654-2613
EMP: 30
SQ FT: 20,000
SALES: 1MM **Privately Held**
SIC: 8299 8351 School/Educational Services Child Day Care Services

(G-10848)
HARVEY MACELREE LTD
5721 Kennett Pike (19807-1311)
PHONE..................302 654-4454
Christophe Curtin, *Branch Mgr*
EMP: 18
SALES (corp-wide): 11.4MM **Privately Held**
SIC: 8111 General practice attorney, lawyer
PA: Harvey Macelree Ltd
  17 W Miner St
  West Chester PA 19382
  610 436-0100

(G-10849)
HARVEY ROAD AUTOMOTIVE INC
1004 W 25th St (19802-3312)
PHONE..................302 654-7500
Joe Scanlon, *President*
EMP: 6
SALES (est): 708.8K **Privately Held**
SIC: 7538 General automotive repair shops

(G-10850)
HARVEY ROAD AUTOMOTIVE INC
1503 Harvey Rd (19810-4211)
PHONE..................302 475-0369
Joe Scanlon, *President*
EMP: 5
SQ FT: 1,200
SALES (est): 320.2K **Privately Held**
SIC: 7539 Automotive repair shops

(G-10851)
HASTIN-KARIN INC
704 N King St (19801-3583)
PHONE..................347 377-8415
EMP: 5
SALES (est): 146.1K **Privately Held**
SIC: 7361 Labor contractors (employment agency)

(G-10852)
HATHWORTH INC
913 N Market St Ste 200 (19801-3097)
PHONE..................302 884-7616
Robert Smith, *Manager*
EMP: 8
SALES: 1.5MM **Privately Held**
SIC: 5031 Lumber, plywood & millwork; lumber: rough, dressed & finished

(G-10853)
HATZEL & BUEHLER INC (HQ)
3600 Silverside Rd Ste A (19810-5116)
P.O. Box 7499 (19803-0499)
PHONE..................302 478-4200
William A Goeller, *President*
Michael C Goeller, *Vice Pres*
Nick Howard, *Vice Pres*
James Ivey, *Vice Pres*
Gerard J Herr, *Treasurer*
EMP: 23 **EST:** 1884
SQ FT: 10,000
SALES: 362.4MM **Privately Held**
WEB: www.hatzelandbuehler.com
SIC: 1731 General electrical contractor
PA: Construction Management Services, Inc.
  3600 Silverside Rd
  Wilmington DE 19810
  302 478-4200

(G-10854)
HATZEL & BUEHLER INC
1 Righter Pkwy Ste 110 (19803-1510)
P.O. Box 610, Claymont (19703-0610)
PHONE..................302 798-5422
John Condi, *Branch Mgr*
EMP: 150
SALES (corp-wide): 362.4MM **Privately Held**
WEB: www.hatzelandbuehler.com
SIC: 1731 General electrical contractor
HQ: Hatzel & Buehler, Inc.
  3600 Silverside Rd Ste A
  Wilmington DE 19810
  302 478-4200

(G-10855)
HAUS OF LACQUER LLC (PA)
300 N Market St (19801-2530)
PHONE..................302 690-0309
Natasha Redden, *Mng Member*
Tiffany Alwan,
EMP: 35
SQ FT: 1,800
SALES: 350K **Privately Held**
SIC: 7991 Spas

(G-10856)
HAYES SEWING MACHINE COMPANY
4425 Concord Pike (19803-1489)
PHONE..................302 764-9033
Trevor D Hayes, *President*
Phyllis Mary Hayes, *Corp Secy*
EMP: 10
SQ FT: 5,000
SALES (est): 1.4MM **Privately Held**
WEB: www.trevhayes.com
SIC: 5722 7699 5949 Sewing machines; gas appliance repair service; sewing, needlework & piece goods

(G-10857)
HAYLOFT ENTERPRISES INC
3 Mill Rd (19806-2146)
PHONE..................302 656-7600
Rob Heflin, *Principal*
▼ **EMP:** 2
SALES (est): 160K **Privately Held**
SIC: 3714 Filters: oil, fuel & air, motor vehicle

Wilmington - New Castle County (G-10858)

(G-10858)
HB DUPONT PLAZA
422 Delaware Ave (19801-1508)
PHONE..................................302 998-7271
EMP: 2
SALES (est): 74.4K Privately Held
SIC: 2879 Agricultural chemicals

(G-10859)
HB FITNESS DELAWARE INC
Also Called: Retro Fitness
5810 Kirkwood Hwy Ste B (19808-4868)
PHONE..................................302 384-7245
Bryant Aivalotis, *Principal*
EMP: 11 EST: 2008
SALES (est): 390.1K Privately Held
SIC: 7991 Physical fitness facilities

(G-10860)
HCC CORPORATION LLC
FCC Enviromental
505 S Market St Dept 2610 (19801-5208)
PHONE..................................302 421-9306
Lea Miller, *Manager*
EMP: 8 Publicly Held
SIC: 7699 Waste cleaning services
HQ: Hcc Corporation, Llc
    2175 Point Blvd Ste 375
    Elgin IL 60123

(G-10861)
HCHC UK HOLDINGS INC
2751 Centerville Rd # 342 (19808-1627)
PHONE..................................302 225-5007
John P Garniewski Jr, *President*
Christopher Jones, *Treasurer*
EMP: 10 Privately Held
SIC: 6719 Personal holding companies, except banks
HQ: Joy Global Underground Mining Llc
    117 Thorn Hill Rd
    Warrendale PA 15086
    724 779-4500

(G-10862)
HCR MANOR CARE SVC FLA III INC
Also Called: Heartland
700 Foulk Rd (19803-3708)
PHONE..................................302 764-0181
Christina Conaway, *Branch Mgr*
EMP: 7
SALES (corp-wide): 8.2B Privately Held
SIC: 8049 Nutrition specialist
HQ: Hcr Manor Care Service Of Florida Iii, Inc.
    333 N Summit St
    Toledo OH 43604

(G-10863)
HCR MANORCARE MED SVCS FLA LLC
Also Called: Manorcare Hlth Svcs Pike Creek
5651 Limestone Rd (19808-1217)
PHONE..................................302 239-8583
Amy Hansell, *Human Res Dir*
Donald Boger, *Branch Mgr*
Troy Brown, *Director*
EMP: 125
SALES (corp-wide): 8.2B Privately Held
WEB: www.manorcare.com
SIC: 8051 Convalescent home with continuous nursing care
HQ: Hcr Manorcare Medical Services Of Florida, Llc
    333 N Summit St Ste 100
    Toledo OH 43604
    419 252-5500

(G-10864)
HEAD QUARTERS
1400 Philadelphia Pike A5 (19809-1856)
PHONE..................................302 798-1639
Cindy Erickson, *President*
Brent Erickson, *Vice Pres*
EMP: 8
SALES (est): 420K Privately Held
SIC: 7231 Unisex hair salons

(G-10865)
HEADSTREAM INC
5301 Limestone Rd Ste 204 (19808-1265)
PHONE..................................302 356-0156
Prathapagirhi Aravind, *President*
Thirupathi Reddy, *Opers Mgr*
Jay Selim, *Human Resources*
EMP: 65
SQ FT: 2,000
SALES (est): 6.5MM Privately Held
SIC: 7379 Computer related consulting services

(G-10866)
HEALEX SYSTEMS LTD
11 Middleton Dr (19808-4320)
PHONE..................................302 235-5750
Nicolas Place, *President*
Nicholas Place, *Principal*
Pamela Place, *Corp Secy*
Jeffrey Place, *Vice Pres*
Jack Chang, *IT/INT Sup*
EMP: 20
SALES (est): 994.4K Privately Held
WEB: www.healex.com
SIC: 7371 Computer software development

(G-10867)
HEALTH & SOCIAL SVCS DEL DEPT
Also Called: Office of Chief Med Examiner
200 S Adams St (19801-5104)
PHONE..................................302 577-3420
Richard Callery, *Chief*
Adrienne S Perlman, *Med Doctor*
EMP: 4 Privately Held
SIC: 8011 9431 Specialized medical practitioners, except internal; administration of public health programs;
HQ: Delaware Dept Of Health And Social Services
    1901 N Dupont Hwy
    New Castle DE 19720

(G-10868)
HEALTH & SOCIAL SVCS DEL DEPT
Also Called: Division of Social Services
1624 Jessup St (19802-4210)
PHONE..................................302 552-3530
Donna Realer, *Manager*
EMP: 40 Privately Held
SIC: 8399 9431 8322 Community development groups; administration of public health programs; ; individual & family services
HQ: Delaware Dept Of Health And Social Services
    1901 N Dupont Hwy
    New Castle DE 19720

(G-10869)
HEALTH CARE CONSULTANTS INC
Also Called: New Behavorial Network
240 N James St Ste 111 (19804-3167)
PHONE..................................302 892-9210
Linda Bagley, *Branch Mgr*
EMP: 144
SALES (corp-wide): 9.5MM Privately Held
WEB: www.nbngroup.com
SIC: 8082 Visiting nurse service
PA: Health Care Consultants, Inc
    2 Pin Oak Ln Ste 250
    Cherry Hill NJ 08003
    856 235-9111

(G-10870)
HEALTH SUPPORT SERVICES
512 W 22nd St Apt 2 (19802-4086)
PHONE..................................302 287-4952
Sandra Jackson, *Principal*
EMP: 5
SALES (est): 67.7K Privately Held
SIC: 8099 Health & allied services

(G-10871)
HEALTHY HOMES DE INC
2421 Kirkwood Hwy (19805-4906)
PHONE..................................302 998-1001
Tom Walsh, *President*
EMP: 1
SALES (est): 110.1K Privately Held
SIC: 3635 Household vacuum cleaners

(G-10872)
HEALTHY SMILES OF DELAWARE PA
1700 Shallcross Ave Ste 2 (19806-2344)
PHONE..................................302 658-7200
EMP: 8
SALES (est): 600K Privately Held
SIC: 3843 Mfg Dental Equipment/Supplies

(G-10873)
HEALY & LONG INC
2000 Rodman Rd (19805-4135)
P.O. Box 30278 (19805-7278)
PHONE..................................302 654-8039
John E Healy III, *CEO*
Michael A Jevin, *President*
EMP: 4
SALES (est): 267.3K Privately Held
SIC: 1771 Concrete work
PA: Healy & Long Holdings, Inc.
    2000 Rodman Rd
    Wilmington DE 19805

(G-10874)
HEALY LONG & JEVIN INC
2000 Rodman Rd (19805-4135)
P.O. Box 30278 (19805-7278)
PHONE..................................302 654-8039
John E Healy III, *CEO*
Michael A Jevin, *President*
John E Healy IV, *Corp Secy*
Cathy Clark, *COO*
Jay P Goldacker, *Project Mgr*
EMP: 10
SQ FT: 7,000
SALES (est): 1.3MM Privately Held
WEB: www.healylongjevin.com
SIC: 1771 Exterior concrete stucco contractor
PA: Healy & Long Holdings, Inc.
    2000 Rodman Rd
    Wilmington DE 19805

(G-10875)
HEARST MEDIA SERVICES CONN LLC
1209 N Orange St (19801-1120)
PHONE..................................203 330-6231
Edward Tyles,
EMP: 50
SALES (est): 160.8K Privately Held
SIC: 2711 Newspapers, publishing & printing

(G-10876)
HEART START ER TRAINING INC
2724 Jacqueline Dr M33 (19810-2043)
PHONE..................................302 420-1917
Clarence Pearsall III, *Principal*
EMP: 5
SALES (est): 70.9K Privately Held
SIC: 8351 Head start center, except in conjunction with school

(G-10877)
HEARTFELT BOOKS PUBLISHING
1000 N West St Ste 1200 (19801-1058)
PHONE..................................866 557-6522
Regina Lee, *CEO*
EMP: 1
SALES (est): 54.7K Privately Held
SIC: 2731 Books: publishing & printing

(G-10878)
HEATED WEAR LLC
427 N Ttnall St Ste 16278 (19801)
PHONE..................................347 510-7965
Steve Wuebker,
EMP: 8
SALES: 1.7MM Privately Held
SIC: 2252 2329 Socks; hunting coats & vests, men's; sweaters & sweater jackets: men's & boys'

(G-10879)
HECKLER & FRABIZZIO PA
800 Delaware Ave Ste 200 (19801-1367)
P.O. Box 128 (19899-0128)
PHONE..................................302 573-4800
George B Heckler Jr, *President*
Patrick Rock, *Partner*
Denise Anderson, *Finance Mgr*
Lisa David, *Supervisor*
William Rimmer, *Director*
EMP: 12
SALES (est): 1.9MM Privately Held
WEB: www.hfddel.com
SIC: 8111 General practice attorney, lawyer

(G-10880)
HEIMAN GOUGE & KAUFMAN LLP
800 N King St Ste 303 (19801-3549)
PHONE..................................302 658-1800
Henry Heiman, *Partner*
Donald Gouge, *Partner*
Susan Kaufman, *Partner*
EMP: 5
SALES (est): 428.2K Privately Held
WEB: www.hgkde.com
SIC: 8111 General practice attorney, lawyer

(G-10881)
HEIMAN ABER GOLDLUST & BAKER
Also Called: Heiman, Henry A
800 N King St Ste 303 (19801-3549)
P.O. Box 1675 (19899-1675)
PHONE..................................302 658-1800
Henry A Heiman, *Partner*
Gary Aber, *Partner*
Darrell Baker, *Partner*
Perry F Goldlust, *Partner*
EMP: 20
SQ FT: 7,000
SALES (est): 1.1MM Privately Held
SIC: 8111 General practice law office

(G-10882)
HELENA SCHROYER MD
Also Called: Bancroft Family Care
1010 N Bancroft Pkwy (19805-2690)
PHONE..................................302 429-5870
Helena Schroyer, *Principal*
EMP: 4
SALES (est): 137.7K Privately Held
SIC: 8011 Offices & clinics of medical doctors

(G-10883)
HELLENIC UNIV CLB WILMINGTON
1407 Foulk Rd Ste 100 (19803-2700)
PHONE..................................302 479-8811
Theodore Nannas, *Principal*
EMP: 4
SALES (est): 84.5K Privately Held
SIC: 7997 Membership sports & recreation clubs

(G-10884)
HENDERSON SOFTWARE
5 Citation Ct (19808-4331)
PHONE..................................302 239-7573
EMP: 2
SALES (est): 123.6K Privately Held
SIC: 7372 Prepackaged Software Services

(G-10885)
HENRY BROS AUTOBODY & PNT SP
Also Called: Henry Bros
2013 W Newport Pike (19804-3793)
PHONE..................................302 994-4438
James J Henry Sr, *Partner*
Robert J Henry Sr, *Partner*
EMP: 12
SQ FT: 16,500
SALES (est): 1.2MM Privately Held
SIC: 7532 Body shop, automotive; paint shop, automotive

(G-10886)
HENRYS CAR CARE INC
2207 Saint James Dr (19808-5218)
PHONE..................................302 994-5766
Henry J Donato Jr, *President*
Garett Vallone, *Vice Pres*
EMP: 8
SQ FT: 1,800
SALES (est): 850K Privately Held
SIC: 7538 General automotive repair shops

GEOGRAPHIC SECTION
Wilmington - New Castle County (G-10915)

(G-10887)
HENTKOWSKI INC
Also Called: Honeywell Authorized Dealer
3420 Old Capitol Trl (19808-6199)
PHONE..................................302 998-2257
Barbara Hentkowski-Roberts, *Principal*
Brian Roberts, *Sales Mgr*
EMP: 17 EST: 1968
SQ FT: 10,500
SALES: 2.5MM **Privately Held**
WEB: www.hentkowski.com
SIC: 1711 Warm air heating & air conditioning contractor

(G-10888)
HERBERT T CASALENA DDS
2300 Penns Ave Ste 6a (19806-1301)
PHONE..................................302 984-1712
EMP: 11
SALES (est): 700K **Privately Held**
SIC: 8021 Dentist's Office

(G-10889)
HERCULES INTERNATIONAL LTD LLC
1313 N Market St Ste A (19801-1150)
PHONE..................................302 594-5000
Bruce Jester, *Vice Pres*
Allen A Spizzo, *CFO*
EMP: 5
SALES (est): 391.6K
SALES (corp-wide): 2.4B **Publicly Held**
SIC: 2869 Olefins
HQ: Hercules Llc
    500 Hercules Rd
    Wilmington DE 19808
    302 594-5000

(G-10890)
HERCULES LLC (DH)
500 Hercules Rd (19808-1513)
PHONE..................................302 594-5000
Allen A Spizzo, *CEO*
Stephen M Butz, *Principal*
John Hoffman, *Project Mgr*
Stuart C Shears, *Treasurer*
◆ EMP: 212 EST: 1912
SQ FT: 679,000
SALES (est): 663.8MM
SALES (corp-wide): 2.4B **Publicly Held**
WEB: www.herc.com
SIC: 2869 2891 Olefins; adhesives

(G-10891)
HERDEG DUPONT DALLE PAZZE LLP
15 Center Meeting Rd (19807-1301)
PHONE..................................302 655-6500
John A Herdeg, *Partner*
William B Dupont Jr, *Partner*
James P Dalle Pazze, *Partner*
EMP: 5
SALES (est): 557.9K **Privately Held**
SIC: 8111 General practice attorney, lawyer

(G-10892)
HERITAGE MACHINE SHOP LLC
2 James Ct (19801-5250)
PHONE..................................302 656-3313
Gary Allanson, *Mng Member*
Christy Allanson,
EMP: 7
SQ FT: 3,000
SALES: 800K **Privately Held**
WEB: www.heritagemachineshop.com
SIC: 3599 Machine shop, jobbing & repair

(G-10893)
HERITAGE MEDICAL ASSOCIATES PA
2601 Annand Dr Ste 4 (19808-3719)
PHONE..................................302 998-3334
Amini Manouchehr, *President*
EMP: 5
SALES (est): 585.7K **Privately Held**
SIC: 8011 Clinic, operated by physicians

(G-10894)
HEROX PBC
3 Germay Dr Unit 4-402 (19804-1127)
PHONE..................................604 681-3651
Christian Cotichini, *CEO*
Kal Sahota, *Vice Pres*
EMP: 10

SALES (est): 421.3K **Privately Held**
SIC: 7374 Data processing & preparation

(G-10895)
HERTZ CORPORATION
100 S French St Ste D (19801-5016)
PHONE..................................302 654-8312
John Moore, *Branch Mgr*
EMP: 23
SALES (corp-wide): 9.5B **Publicly Held**
SIC: 7514 Rent-a-car service
HQ: The Hertz Corporation
    8501 Williams Rd
    Estero FL 33928
    239 301-7000

(G-10896)
HERTZ CORPORATION
500 Hercules Rd (19808-1513)
PHONE..................................302 428-0637
John Moore, *President*
EMP: 23
SALES (corp-wide): 9.5B **Publicly Held**
SIC: 7514 Rent-a-car service
HQ: The Hertz Corporation
    8501 Williams Rd
    Estero FL 33928
    239 301-7000

(G-10897)
HETRICK-DRAKE ASSOCIATES INC
Also Called: Hetrick, C H Associates
2018 Duncan Rd (19808-5932)
PHONE..................................302 998-7500
Peter Drake, *President*
Dennis Dorsey, *Shareholder*
John Walsh, *Admin Sec*
EMP: 9 EST: 1948
SQ FT: 2,000
SALES (est): 910K **Privately Held**
WEB: www.chhetrick.com
SIC: 6411 Insurance adjusters

(G-10898)
HEWLETT-PACKARD WORLD TRADE (PA)
Also Called: HP
2850 Centerville Rd (19808-1610)
PHONE..................................877 424-4536
Christopher R Guarino, *President*
Michael R McMullen, *Vice Pres*
Steven Clark, *CFO*
D Craig Nordlund, *Admin Sec*
EMP: 22
SALES (est): 6.3B **Privately Held**
SIC: 3571 3577 3572 3575 Electronic computers; computer peripheral equipment; plotters, computer; printers, computer; optical scanning devices; computer storage devices; computer disk & drum drives & components; computer tape drives & components; computer terminals

(G-10899)
HEXAGON METROLOGY INC
800 First State Blvd (19804-3573)
PHONE..................................302 351-3580
EMP: 3
SALES (corp-wide): 4.1B **Privately Held**
SIC: 3823 Industrial instrmnts msrmnt display/control process variable
HQ: Hexagon Metrology, Inc.
    250 Circuit Dr
    North Kingstown RI 02852
    401 886-2000

(G-10900)
HH PROPERTY MANAGEMENT
6 Larch Ave (19804-2300)
PHONE..................................302 999-1414
Hugh McLaughin, *Owner*
EMP: 8 EST: 2007
SALES (est): 738K **Privately Held**
SIC: 6531 Real estate managers

(G-10901)
HI LINE AUTO DETAILING
1618 Newport Gap Pike (19808-6208)
PHONE..................................302 420-5368
Colette Barbour, *Principal*
EMP: 4
SALES (est): 72K **Privately Held**
SIC: 7542 Washing & polishing, automotive

(G-10902)
HIFU SERVICES INC
3411 Silverside Rd (19810-4812)
PHONE..................................650 867-4972
EMP: 9
SALES (est): 440K **Privately Held**
SIC: 7389 Business Services At Non-Commercial Site

(G-10903)
HIGH-TECH MACHINE COMPANY INC
Also Called: Htm Management
10 Lewis Cir (19804-1618)
PHONE..................................302 636-0267
Neal Crosley, *President*
Don Piegalski, *Vice Pres*
Tom Marra, *Opers Mgr*
Mary Moore, *Production*
Larry Parks, *QC Mgr*
EMP: 14
SQ FT: 6,500
SALES (est): 2.6MM **Privately Held**
WEB: www.hightechmachineinc.com
SIC: 3599 Machine shop, jobbing & repair

(G-10904)
HIGHLAND ORCHARDS (PA)
4 Clyth Dr (19803-2610)
PHONE..................................302 478-1392
Mathew Linton, *Partner*
EMP: 5
SALES (est): 505.2K **Privately Held**
SIC: 0175 Deciduous tree fruits

(G-10905)
HIGHMARKS INC (PA)
Also Called: Highmark Blue Cross
800 Delaware Ave Ste 900 (19801-1368)
P.O. Box 1991 (19899-1991)
PHONE..................................302 421-3000
Timothy J Constantine, *President*
Phillip A Carter, *Assoc VP*
Dianne Coates, *Executive Asst*
William E Kirk III, *Admin Sec*
EMP: 370 EST: 1935
SQ FT: 30,000
SALES: 468.7MM **Privately Held**
WEB: www.bcbsde.com
SIC: 6321 Health insurance carriers

(G-10906)
HIGHMARKS INC
Also Called: Blue Cross
800 W Delaware Ave (19809-1132)
P.O. Box 8868 (19899-8868)
PHONE..................................302 421-3000
Tim Constantine, *Vice Pres*
EMP: 8
SALES (corp-wide): 468.7MM **Privately Held**
WEB: www.bcbsde.com
SIC: 6324 6311 6331 6351 Dental insurance; health maintenance organization (HMO), insurance only; life insurance; fire, marine & casualty insurance; liability insurance; business management
PA: Highmarks, Inc.
    800 Delaware Ave Ste 900
    Wilmington DE 19801
    302 421-3000

(G-10907)
HILL BANCSHARES DELAWARE INC (PA)
1105 N Market St Ste 1300 (19801-1241)
P.O. Box 8985 (19899-8985)
PHONE..................................302 651-8389
EMP: 5
SALES (est): 5.5MM **Privately Held**
SIC: 6022 State commercial banks

(G-10908)
HILL LUTH DAY CARE CENTER
1018 W 6th St (19805-3210)
PHONE..................................302 656-3224
Jea Street, *Owner*
EMP: 50
SALES (est): 431.9K **Privately Held**
SIC: 8351 Child day care services

(G-10909)
HILLSIDE CENTER
Also Called: GENESIS HEALTH CARE
810 S Broom St (19805-4245)
PHONE..................................302 652-1181
Kathleen Duca, *Administration*
EMP: 12
SALES: 12MM **Privately Held**
SIC: 8322 8059 8051 8049 Rehabilitation services; nursing home, except skilled & intermediate care facility; skilled nursing care facilities; physical therapist

(G-10910)
HILLTOP LUTHERAN NEIGHBORHD
Also Called: EARLY CHILDHOOD ASSISTANCE PRO
1018 W 6th St (19805-3210)
PHONE..................................302 656-3224
Jea Street, *Exec Dir*
Matthew Johnson, *Director*
EMP: 50
SQ FT: 2,500
SALES: 2MM **Privately Held**
SIC: 8351 8661 Group day care center; Lutheran Church

(G-10911)
HILTON CORP (PA)
Also Called: Hilton Marine
1900 Kirkwood Hwy (19805-4923)
PHONE..................................302 994-3365
Hilton Wright, *President*
Andrew Hilton, *Vice Pres*
Samuel S Wright, *Vice Pres*
Laura Wright, *Admin Sec*
EMP: 4
SQ FT: 3,000
SALES (est): 1.3MM **Privately Held**
WEB: www.hiltoncorp.com
SIC: 5088 5551 Marine crafts & supplies; marine supplies & equipment

(G-10912)
HILTON MARINE SUPPLY COMPANY
1900 Kirkwood Hwy (19805-4930)
PHONE..................................302 994-3365
Andrew Hilton, *President*
Laura Wright, *Corp Secy*
Hilton A Wright, *Vice Pres*
Samuel Wright, *Vice Pres*
EMP: 4 EST: 1941
SQ FT: 12,000
SALES: 1MM
SALES (corp-wide): 1.3MM **Privately Held**
WEB: www.hiltoncorp.com
SIC: 5088 5551 Marine propulsion machinery & equipment; marine supplies
PA: Hilton Corp
    1900 Kirkwood Hwy
    Wilmington DE 19805
    302 994-3365

(G-10913)
HILYARDS INC (PA)
Also Called: Hilyard's Business Solutions
1616 Newport Gap Pike (19808-6294)
PHONE..................................302 995-2201
Robert H Hilyard, *CEO*
Susan Hilyard, *President*
Greg Altemus, *Vice Pres*
Gregory Altemus, *Vice Pres*
EMP: 40 EST: 1959
SQ FT: 18,100
SALES (est): 21.6MM **Privately Held**
WEB: www.hilyards.com
SIC: 5044 Copying equipment

(G-10914)
HIMONT INC
2801 Centerville Rd (19808-1609)
PHONE..................................302 996-6000
Robert Herzog, *Principal*
EMP: 3
SALES (est): 232.6K **Privately Held**
SIC: 2821 Plastics materials & resins

(G-10915)
HINDIN MEDIA LLC (PA)
1116 Webster Dr (19803-3421)
PHONE..................................302 463-4612
David Hindin, *Mng Member*

Wilmington - New Castle County (G-10916)

GEOGRAPHIC SECTION

EMP: 1
SALES (est): 129.4K **Privately Held**
SIC: 2741 7389 Miscellaneous publishing;

(G-10916)
HIS IMAGE BARBERSHOP
505 N Lincoln St (19805-3011)
PHONE 302 256-2792
EMP: 4
SALES (est): 26.6K **Privately Held**
SIC: 7241 Barber shops

(G-10917)
HISTORIC RED CLAY VALLEY INC (PA)
Also Called: WILMINGTON & WESTERN RAILROAD
1601 Railroad Ave (19808-6027)
P.O. Box 5787 (19808-0787)
PHONE 302 998-1930
Peter Lane, *President*
Carole Wells, *Principal*
David Ludlow, *Exec Dir*
EMP: 4
SQ FT: 23,250
SALES: 1.1MM **Privately Held**
WEB: www.wwrr.org
SIC: 7999 Scenic railroads for amusement

(G-10918)
HISTORICAL SOCIETY OF DEL INC
505 N Market St (19801-3091)
PHONE 302 295-2400
EMP: 26
SALES (corp-wide): 1.5MM **Privately Held**
SIC: 8412 Museum/Art Gallery
PA: The Historical Society Of Delaware Inc
505 N Market St
Wilmington DE 19801
302 655-7161

(G-10919)
HISTORICAL SOCIETY OF DELWARE (PA)
505 N Market St (19801-3091)
PHONE 302 655-7161
Richard Poole, *President*
Daniel F Wolcott Jr, *Treasurer*
Sarah Dougherty, *Manager*
Siri Nesheim, *Manager*
Joan Reynolds Hoge, *Director*
◆ **EMP:** 26
SALES: 1.3MM **Privately Held**
WEB: www.hsd.org
SIC: 8412 8231 5331 Historical society; museum; public library; variety stores

(G-10920)
HLH CONSTRUCTION MGT SVCS INC
2000 Rodman Rd (19805-4135)
PHONE 302 654-7508
John E Healy III, *Principal*
EMP: 11
SALES (est): 1.6MM **Privately Held**
SIC: 8741 Management services

(G-10921)
HMA CONCRETE LLC
Also Called: Heritage Concrete
307 A St (19801-5345)
PHONE 302 777-1235
Derek S Vanderslice, *Mng Member*
EMP: 17 **EST:** 2012
SALES (est): 2.2MM **Privately Held**
SIC: 3273 Ready-mixed concrete

(G-10922)
HOARD INC
251 Little Falls Dr (19808-1674)
PHONE 980 333-1703
Jason Davis, *CEO*
EMP: 15 **Privately Held**
SIC: 7372 Application computer software

(G-10923)
HOERNER INC
602 Elizabeth Ave (19809-2666)
PHONE 302 762-4406
Kristopher Hoerner, *Owner*
EMP: 10

SALES (est): 456.4K **Privately Held**
SIC: 0781 Landscape counseling & planning

(G-10924)
HOGAN & VEITH PA
Also Called: Hogan McDaniel
1311 Delaware Ave Ste 1 (19806-4717)
PHONE 302 656-7540
Daniel Hogan, *President*
EMP: 7
SALES (est): 597K **Privately Held**
WEB: www.dkhogan.com
SIC: 8111 General practice attorney, lawyer

(G-10925)
HOGAR CREA INT OF DELAWARE
1126 Brandywine St (19802-5219)
PHONE 302 762-2875
EMP: 5
SALES (est): 362.9K **Privately Held**
SIC: 8093 Specialty Outpatient Clinic

(G-10926)
HOLLAND MULCH INC
135 Hay Rd (19809-3508)
PHONE 302 765-3100
John Duffy Jr, *President*
EMP: 10
SQ FT: 1,200
SALES (est): 2.2MM **Privately Held**
SIC: 4953 Recycling, waste materials

(G-10927)
HOLLIE ENTERPRISES LLC
1201 N Orange St Ste 600 (19801-1171)
PHONE 903 721-1904
Michael Hollie, *President*
Thelma Hollie, *Vice Pres*
EMP: 5
SALES (est): 295K **Privately Held**
SIC: 5015 6211 5087 4731 Automotive supplies, used; syndicate shares (real estate, entertainment, equip.) sales; concrete burial vaults & boxes; truck transportation brokers; local trucking with storage

(G-10928)
HOLLY OAK TOWING AND SERVICE
Also Called: Alycia
6521 Governor Printz Blvd (19809-2037)
PHONE 302 792-1500
Craig Mummert, *President*
EMP: 8
SQ FT: 2,000
SALES (est): 832.2K **Privately Held**
SIC: 7549 Towing service, automotive

(G-10929)
HOLLYWELL LOGISTICS LLC
Also Called: Railway Logistics
802 N West St Ste 105 (19801-1526)
PHONE 267 901-4272
Akmal Khaydarov, *President*
Bob Kurban, *Managing Prtnr*
EMP: 68
SALES (est): 9.7MM **Privately Held**
SIC: 4731 Transportation agents & brokers

(G-10930)
HOLLYWOOD GRILL RESTAURANT (PA)
Also Called: Hampton Inn
1811 Concord Pike (19803-2901)
PHONE 302 655-1348
Phil Haslett, *Shareholder*
EMP: 70
SQ FT: 3,000
SALES (est): 15.5MM **Privately Held**
SIC: 7011 5812 5813 6531 Hotels & motels; restaurant, family: independent; restaurant, family: chain; drinking places; cocktail lounge; real estate agents & managers

(G-10931)
HOLLYWOOD GRILL RESTAURANT
Also Called: Homewood Suites
350 Rocky Run Pkwy (19803-1515)
PHONE 302 479-2000

Denis Dowse, *Manager*
EMP: 93
SALES (corp-wide): 15.5MM **Privately Held**
SIC: 7011 Hotels & motels
PA: Hollywood Grill Restaurant Inc
1811 Concord Pike
Wilmington DE 19803
302 655-1348

(G-10932)
HOLLYWOOD TAN (PA)
4575 Kirkwood Hwy (19808-5117)
PHONE 302 995-2692
Dolly McShane, *Owner*
EMP: 5
SALES (est): 340.6K **Privately Held**
SIC: 7299 Tanning salon

(G-10933)
HOLLYWOOD TANS
3100 Naamans Rd Ste 34 (19810-2100)
PHONE 302 478-8267
Renee Milner, *Owner*
EMP: 7
SALES (est): 254.3K **Privately Held**
SIC: 7299 Tanning salon

(G-10934)
HOME FINDERS REAL ESTATE CO
31 Trolley Sq Ste C (19806)
PHONE 302 655-8091
Barry G Godfrey, *President*
EMP: 5
SALES: 300K **Privately Held**
WEB: www.exclusivebuyer.com
SIC: 6531 Real estate agent, residential; real estate brokers & agents

(G-10935)
HOME FOR AGED WMN-MNQUADALE HM
Also Called: GILPIN HALL
1101 Gilpin Ave (19806-3214)
PHONE 302 654-1810
Harvey Smith, *President*
Jeffrey Jones, *Controller*
Cathy Conner, *Mktg Dir*
Vicki Roberts, *Payroll Mgr*
Paul Smiley, *Technology*
EMP: 170
SQ FT: 90,000
SALES: 12.5MM **Privately Held**
SIC: 8361 8322 8051 Home for the aged; individual & family services; skilled nursing care facilities

(G-10936)
HOME HEALTH HEARTFEL
5179 W Woodmill Dr (19808-4067)
PHONE 302 660-2686
Michelle Fiore, *President*
EMP: 4 **EST:** 2015
SALES (est): 90.7K **Privately Held**
SIC: 8082 Home health care services

(G-10937)
HOME HEALTH SERVICES BY TLC
287 Christiana Ave Ste 24 (19801)
PHONE 302 322-5510
Ruel G Harriott, *President*
Louise Harriott, *Vice Pres*
EMP: 50
SALES (est): 978.6K **Privately Held**
WEB: www.homehealthservicesbytlc.com
SIC: 8082 Home health care services

(G-10938)
HOME OF DIVINE PROVIDENCE INC
Also Called: Bayard House
300 Bayard Ave (19805-3345)
PHONE 302 654-1184
Shavenne Hines, *Director*
EMP: 6 **EST:** 1979
SALES (est): 298K **Privately Held**
SIC: 8069 Maternity hospital

(G-10939)
HOME OF MERCIFUL REST SOCIETY
Also Called: KENTMERE NURSING CARE CENTER
1900 Lovering Ave (19806-2123)
PHONE 302 652-3311
Eileen Mahler, *Exec Dir*
Mark Meister,
EMP: 120
SALES: 12.7MM **Privately Held**
WEB: www.kentmerenursing.com
SIC: 8051 8052 Convalescent home with continuous nursing care; intermediate care facilities

(G-10940)
HOME SERVICES LLC
3410 Old Capitol Trl # 2 (19808-6152)
PHONE 302 510-4580
Wayne Salvadori, *Owner*
EMP: 6
SALES (est): 402.7K **Privately Held**
SIC: 1521 General remodeling, single-family houses

(G-10941)
HOMELAND SEC VERIFICATION LLC
Also Called: I9 Directcom
4001 Kennett Pike (19807-2315)
PHONE 888 791-4614
Michael D Brown, *CTO*
James H Sills III,
EMP: 5
SALES (est): 263.2K **Privately Held**
SIC: 7375 Information retrieval services

(G-10942)
HOMES FOR LIFE FOUNDATION
1106 Berkeley Rd (19807-2816)
PHONE 302 571-1217
Lanny Edelsohn, *President*
EMP: 11
SALES: 110.9K **Privately Held**
SIC: 8399 Fund raising organization, non-fee basis

(G-10943)
HOMESTAR REMODELING LLC
405 Silverside Rd Ste 250 (19809-1773)
PHONE 302 528-5898
Anton Ladden, *Exec Dir*
Brandon Nieves,
EMP: 37 **EST:** 2015
SALES (est): 177.8K **Privately Held**
SIC: 1521 General remodeling, single-family houses

(G-10944)
HOMEWATCH CAREGIVERS LLC
5560 Kirkwood Hwy (19808-5002)
PHONE 302 691-5358
James Nacchia, *Branch Mgr*
EMP: 11
SALES (corp-wide): 30.9MM **Privately Held**
SIC: 8082 Home health care services
HQ: Homewatch Caregivers, Llc
6251 Greenwood Plaza Blvd # 250
Greenwood Village CO 80111
303 758-5111

(G-10945)
HOMEWOOD SUITES
820 Justison St (19801-5152)
PHONE 302 565-2100
Loren Forland, *General Mgr*
EMP: 30
SALES (est): 137.8K **Privately Held**
SIC: 7011 Hotels

(G-10946)
HOMSEY ARCHITECTS INC
2003 N Scott St (19806-2191)
PHONE 302 656-4491
Eldon Homsey, *President*
Charles Ryan, *Vice Pres*
Ryan C Al, *Architect*
Shannon M Al, *Architect*
EMP: 10 **EST:** 1935
SQ FT: 1,300

GEOGRAPHIC SECTION
Wilmington - New Castle County (G-10975)

SALES (est): 1.3MM **Privately Held**
WEB: www.homsey.com
SIC: 8712 Architectural engineering

(G-10947)
HONEY BEE SEASONAL KIT & MKT
11a Trolley Sq (19806-3334)
PHONE..................302 407-5579
EMP: 4
SALES (est): 281.3K **Privately Held**
SIC: 8742 Marketing consulting services

(G-10948)
HONEYWELL SAFETY PDTS USA INC (HQ)
2711 Centerville Rd (19808-1660)
PHONE..................302 636-5401
David M Cote, CEO
Roger Fradin, President
Terrence Hahn, President
Alex Ismail, President
Andreas Kramvis, President
▼ EMP: 15
SALES (est): 420MM
SALES (corp-wide): 41.8B **Publicly Held**
SIC: 5099 Lifesaving & survival equipment (non-medical)
PA: Honeywell International Inc.
300 S Tryon St
Charlotte NC 28202
973 455-2000

(G-10949)
HOOPS FOR HOPE DELAWARE
1204 B St (19801-5606)
PHONE..................302 229-7600
Alonzo Redden, Owner
EMP: 15
SALES (est): 79.2K **Privately Held**
SIC: 7032 7389 Summer camp, except day & sports instructional;

(G-10950)
HOOVER COMPUTER SERVICES INC
4611 Bedford Blvd (19803-3901)
PHONE..................302 529-7050
John Hoover, President
Susan Hoover, Vice Pres
EMP: 6
SALES (est): 610K **Privately Held**
WEB: www.hoovercs.com
SIC: 7371 7379 5045 Custom computer programming services; computer related consulting services; computer peripheral equipment

(G-10951)
HOPE HOUSE DAYCARE
2814 W 2nd St (19805-1807)
PHONE..................302 407-3404
Eden Coleman, Owner
EMP: 13 EST: 2014
SALES (est): 130.8K **Privately Held**
SIC: 8351 7032 Child day care services; summer camp, except day & sports instructional

(G-10952)
HORIZON AERONAUTICS INC
300 Delaware Ave Ste 300 # 300 (19801-1607)
PHONE..................409 504-2645
Thomas Wright, CEO
EMP: 4
SALES (est): 146.3K **Privately Held**
SIC: 2752 Schedules, transportation: lithographed

(G-10953)
HORIZON HOUSE OF DELAWARE INC
1902 Maryland Ave (19805-4605)
PHONE..................302 658-2392
Wayne Chiodo, President
EMP: 30
SQ FT: 5,000
SALES (est): 2MM **Privately Held**
SIC: 8322 Social services for the handicapped

(G-10954)
HORIZON INTL HOLDINGS LLC (HQ)
251 Little Falls Dr (19808-1674)
PHONE..................302 636-5401
EMP: 2613
SALES (est): 45.7MM
SALES (corp-wide): 849.9MM **Publicly Held**
SIC: 3714 Trailer hitches, motor vehicle
PA: Horizon Global Corporation
2600 W Big Beavr Rd # 55
Troy MI 48084
248 593-8820

(G-10955)
HORIZON SERVICES INC (PA)
320 Century Blvd (19808-6270)
PHONE..................302 762-1200
David Geiger, President
Beth Carlin, General Mgr
David Dworsky, Business Mgr
Troy Rainsberg, Vice Pres
Frank M Madormo, Controller
EMP: 151
SQ FT: 8,000
SALES (est): 194MM **Privately Held**
SIC: 1711 Plumbing contractors

(G-10956)
HORNBERGER MANAGEMENT COMPANY (PA)
1 Commerce St Fl 7 (19801)
PHONE..................302 573-2541
Frederick Hornberger CPC, President
EMP: 6
SQ FT: 1,000
SALES (est): 855.2K **Privately Held**
WEB: www.hmc.com
SIC: 7361 Executive placement

(G-10957)
HORTY & HORTY PA (PA)
503 Carr Rd Ste 120 (19809-2863)
PHONE..................302 652-4194
Douglas Philips, President
EMP: 20
SQ FT: 15,000
SALES (est): 3.4MM **Privately Held**
WEB: www.horty.com
SIC: 8721 Certified public accountant

(G-10958)
HOSPITALISTS OF DELAWARE
701 Foulk Rd Ste 2f (19803-3733)
PHONE..................302 984-2577
Shaunak Patel, Principal
EMP: 8
SALES (est): 263.4K **Privately Held**
SIC: 8062 General medical & surgical hospitals

(G-10959)
HOUNSELL DENTAL LLC
2300 Pennsylvania Ave (19806-1392)
PHONE..................302 691-8132
EMP: 4
SALES (est): 231.4K **Privately Held**
SIC: 8021 Dental clinic

(G-10960)
HOUSE OF WRIGHT MORTUARY (PA)
208 E 35th St (19802-2812)
P.O. Box 447 (19899-0447)
PHONE..................302 762-8448
Robert O Wright II, President
Justin A Wribht, Vice Pres
Justin A Wright, Vice Pres
EMP: 16
SALES (est): 1.6MM **Privately Held**
SIC: 7261 Funeral home

(G-10961)
HOUSING ALLIANCE DELAWARE INC
100 W 10th St Ste 611 (19801-6604)
PHONE..................302 654-0126
Jim Peffley, Ch of Bd
Sara Weimer, Vice Pres
Christina Showalter, Exec Dir
Benjamin Grossberg, Associate
Benjamin Schladweiler, Associate
EMP: 11

SALES (est): 956.3K **Privately Held**
SIC: 8322 Self-help organization

(G-10962)
HOWMEDICA OSTEONICS CORP
Also Called: Stryker Chiropractic
2118 Kirkwood Hwy Ste A (19805-4933)
PHONE..................302 655-3239
Robert Stryker, Branch Mgr
EMP: 4
SALES (corp-wide): 13.6B **Publicly Held**
SIC: 8041 Offices & clinics of chiropractors
HQ: Howmedica Osteonics Corp.
325 Corporate Dr
Mahwah NJ 07430
201 831-5000

(G-10963)
HQ GLOBAL WORKPLACES INC
1000 N West St Ste 1200 (19801-1058)
PHONE..................302 295-4800
EMP: 5
SALES (corp-wide): 3.1B **Privately Held**
SIC: 7389 Office facilities & secretarial service rental
HQ: Hq Global Workplaces, Inc.
15305 Dallas Pkwy Ste 400
Addison TX 75001
972 361-8100

(G-10964)
HS CAPITAL LLC
Also Called: Bay Area Market Place
847 Cranbrook Dr (19803-4801)
PHONE..................302 598-2961
Paul Stortini, Vice Pres
Eric Herrera,
EMP: 5
SQ FT: 5,000
SALES (est): 302.1K **Privately Held**
SIC: 5411 4731 Co-operative food stores; agents, shipping

(G-10965)
HS CAPITAL LLC
300 Delaware Ave Ste 1370 (19801-1658)
PHONE..................302 317-3614
EMP: 4
SALES (est): 106.6K **Privately Held**
SIC: 6799 Investors

(G-10966)
HSBC BANK USA (DH)
300 Delaware Ave Ste 1400 (19801-1650)
PHONE..................302 778-0169
Irene Dorner, President
David Goeden, President
Andy Ireland, President
Martin J G Glynn, Principal
Vincent J Mancuso, Senior VP
◆ EMP: 1079
SALES (est): 189.3MM
SALES (corp-wide): 87.7B **Publicly Held**
WEB: www.joinhousehold.com
SIC: 6021 National commercial banks
HQ: Hsbc Usa, Inc.
107 Iris Glen Dr Se
Conyers GA 30013
212 525-5000

(G-10967)
HSBC NORTH AMERICA INC
1105 N Market St Fl 1 (19801-1237)
PHONE..................302 652-4673
Jorge Garcia, Assoc VP
Louis Clay, Manager
Rachna Shah, Manager
Richard Davis, Consultant
EMP: 10
SALES (corp-wide): 87.7B **Publicly Held**
SIC: 6021 National commercial banks
HQ: Hsbc North America Inc.
1 Seneca Tower 1 # 1
Buffalo NY 14203
716 841-2424

(G-10968)
HTK AUTOMOTIVE USA CORP
Also Called: Decoded USA
3422 Old Capitol Trl (19808-6124)
PHONE..................888 998-9366
Karim Boumajdi, President
EMP: 25
SQ FT: 7,000
SALES: 45.3MM **Privately Held**
SIC: 3694 Automotive electrical equipment

(G-10969)
HTK AUTOMOTIVE USA CORPORATION
Also Called: Advanced Automotive Tech
3422 Old Capitol Trl # 1851 (19808-6124)
PHONE..................310 504-2283
EMP: 25 EST: 2011
SALES (est): 1.7MM **Privately Held**
SIC: 5999 5015 Ret Misc Merchandise Whol Used Auto Parts

(G-10970)
HUBGETS INC
4250 Lancaster Pike # 120 (19805-1520)
PHONE..................239 206-2995
Bogdan Carstoiu, CEO
Elena Carstoiu, COO
EMP: 5 EST: 2014
SALES (est): 150K **Privately Held**
SIC: 7371 Computer software development

(G-10971)
HUDSON VALLEY INVESTMENT CORP
Also Called: Hudson Valley Magazine
3301 Lancaster Pike 5c (19805-1436)
PHONE..................302 656-1825
Robert Martinelli, President
EMP: 1
SALES (est): 126.5K
SALES (corp-wide): 1.3B **Publicly Held**
WEB: www.hudsonvalleybank.com
SIC: 6211 2721 Flotation companies; periodicals
HQ: Sterling National Bank
400 Rella Blvd Fl 3
Montebello NY 10901
845 369-8040

(G-10972)
HUNGROSITY LLC
1201 N Orange St Ste 600 (19801-1171)
PHONE..................401 527-1133
EMP: 2
SALES (est): 65.5K **Privately Held**
SIC: 7372 Prepackaged Software Services

(G-10973)
HUNT VICMEAD CLUB
Also Called: Bidermann Golf Course
601 Adams Dam Rd (19807-1410)
PHONE..................302 655-3336
Joe McCarron, Controller
Christopher Patterson, Branch Mgr
Amanda Parent, Manager
Alex Treptow, Manager
EMP: 8
SALES (est): 262.9K
SALES (corp-wide): 4.8MM **Privately Held**
SIC: 7997 Golf club, membership
PA: Hunt Vicmead Club
903 Owls Nest Rd
Wilmington DE 19807
302 655-9601

(G-10974)
HUNT VICMEAD CLUB (PA)
Also Called: Biderman Golf Club
903 Owls Nest Rd (19807-1613)
P.O. Box 3501 (19807-0501)
PHONE..................302 655-9601
Rodney Scott, Ch of Bd
Christopher Patterson, Chairman
Richard Cairns, Treasurer
Nancy Brown, Manager
EMP: 45
SALES: 4.8MM **Privately Held**
WEB: www.vicmead.com
SIC: 7997 Golf club, membership

(G-10975)
HUNTE CORPORATE ENTERPRISE LLC (PA)
Also Called: Hce
1201 N Orange St Ste 7377 (19801-1283)
PHONE..................212 710-1341
Tanya Guinevere Hunte,
EMP: 9
SALES (est): 2.1MM **Privately Held**
SIC: 6719 Personal holding companies, except banks

Wilmington - New Castle County (G-10976)   GEOGRAPHIC SECTION

(G-10976)
HUNTINGTON AUTO TRUST 2012-1
Rodney Sq N 1100 N Mkt St (19890-0001)
PHONE..................302 636-5401
EMP: 139
SALES (est): 219.2K
SALES (corp-wide): 5.2B Publicly Held
SIC: 6733 Trusts
PA: Huntington Bancshares Incorporated
41 S High St
Columbus OH 43215
614 480-8300

(G-10977)
HUNTINGTON AUTO TRUST 2012-2
Rodney Sq N 1100 N Mkt St (19890-0001)
PHONE..................302 636-5401
EMP: 186 EST: 2012
SALES (est): 51.3K
SALES (corp-wide): 5.2B Publicly Held
SIC: 6733 Trusts
PA: Huntington Bancshares Incorporated
41 S High St
Columbus OH 43215
614 480-8300

(G-10978)
HURLOCK ROOFING COMPANY
26 Brookside Dr (19804-1189)
PHONE..................302 654-2783
Alfred J Hurlock III, *President*
Marie V Speakman, *Corp Secy*
John D Speakman Jr, *Vice Pres*
EMP: 20
SQ FT: 6,200
SALES (est): 1.9MM Privately Held
WEB: www.hurlockroofing.com
SIC: 1761 Roofing contractor; gutter & downspout contractor; siding contractor

(G-10979)
HY-POINT DAIRY FARMS INC
425 Beaver Valley Rd (19803-1103)
PHONE..................302 478-1414
William Meany, *President*
James L Meany, *Shareholder*
EMP: 105
SQ FT: 200,000
SALES: 16MM Privately Held
SIC: 5143 2026 Ice cream & ices; milk & cream, except fermented, cultured & flavored

(G-10980)
HY-POINT EQUIPMENT CO
425 Beaver Valley Rd (19803-1103)
PHONE..................302 478-0388
John C Meany, *President*
Rosemarie Lee, *Corp Secy*
Robert Meany, *Vice Pres*
EMP: 10
SQ FT: 25,000
SALES (est): 3.4MM Privately Held
WEB: www.hypointequipment.com
SIC: 5046 Restaurant equipment & supplies

(G-10981)
HYAS US INC
251 Little Falls Dr (19808-1674)
PHONE..................250 327-9743
David Ratner, *CEO*
EMP: 5
SALES: 1MM Privately Held
SIC: 8741 Administrative management

(G-10982)
HYPERGAMES INC
919 N Market St Ste 950 (19801-3036)
PHONE..................424 343-6370
Maxim Aoehurem, *Co-Founder*
Sereei Araeoeim, *Co-Founder*
Arsen Ivecisov, *Co-Founder*
Evgenii Kan, *Co-Founder*
Dmitry Radchenko, *Director*
EMP: 5
SALES: 5MM Privately Held
SIC: 7371 7389 Computer software development;

(G-10983)
HYSIOTHERAPY ASSOCIATES INC
Also Called: Chester Cnty Ortho Sprts Physc
3411 Silverside Rd # 105 (19810-4812)
PHONE..................610 444-1270
Roger Collins, *Director*
Phillip Donley, *Director*
EMP: 20
SALES (est): 1.7MM Privately Held
SIC: 5047 8093 Therapy equipment; rehabilitation center, outpatient treatment

(G-10984)
I-PULSE INC
2711 Centerville Rd # 400 (19808-1660)
PHONE..................604 689-8765
Laurent Frescaline, *CEO*
Robert Friedland, *Chairman*
Hirofumi Katase, *Exec VP*
Philippe Boisseau, *Director*
Ian Cockerill, *Director*
EMP: 2
SALES (est): 81.9K Privately Held
SIC: 1382 1731 1311 Oil & gas exploration services; general electrical contractor; crude petroleum & natural gas

(G-10985)
IACONO - SUMMER CHASE
Also Called: Village of Canterbury
102 Robino Ct Ste 101 (19804)
PHONE..................302 994-2505
Charles Robino, *Partner*
Paul Robino, *Partner*
Michael Stortini, *Partner*
Leonard Iacono, *General Ptnr*
EMP: 10
SALES: 2.8MM Privately Held
SIC: 6513 Apartment building operators

(G-10986)
IBI GROUP (DELAWARE) INC
501 Silverside Rd # 307 (19809-1374)
PHONE..................614 818-4900
Scott Stewart, *CEO*
EMP: 104
SALES (corp-wide): 278.3MM Privately Held
SIC: 6719 Holding companies
PA: Ibi Group Inc
55 St Clair Ave W Suite 700
Toronto ON M4V 2
416 596-1930

(G-10987)
IBI GROUP (US) INC (HQ)
501 Silverside Rd # 307 (19809-1374)
PHONE..................949 833-5588
Scott Stewart, *CEO*
Lynne Hansen, *Human Resources*
Darlene Sneed, *Admin Asst*
Anthony Nouanesengsy, *Administration*
Angad Singh, *Analyst*
EMP: 119
SALES (est): 18.5MM
SALES (corp-wide): 278.3MM Privately Held
SIC: 8711 Civil engineering
PA: Ibi Group Inc
55 St Clair Ave W Suite 700
Toronto ON M4V 2
416 596-1930

(G-10988)
ICETECCOM INC (PA)
3411 Silverside Rd # 201 (19810-4812)
PHONE..................302 477-1792
Mike Wester, *President*
EMP: 4
SALES (est): 375.4K Privately Held
SIC: 8742 Business consultant

(G-10989)
ICONIC SKUS LLC
4023 Kennett Pike Ste 226 (19807-2018)
PHONE..................302 722-4547
EMP: 5
SALES (est): 266.1K Privately Held
SIC: 8742 Marketing consulting services

(G-10990)
ICS AMERICA INC
1209 N Orange St (19801-1120)
PHONE..................215 979-1620
Scott Key, *President*
EMP: 4 EST: 2000
SALES (est): 476.5K Privately Held
SIC: 7389 Personal service agents, brokers & bureaus

(G-10991)
ID GRIFFITH INC
735 S Market St Frnt (19801-5246)
PHONE..................302 656-8253
David L Zarrilli, *President*
Michael H Treml, *Vice Pres*
Richard A Murphy, *Treasurer*
Louis Guerrina, *Chief Mktg Ofcr*
Christine M Loncki, *Admin Sec*
EMP: 85
SQ FT: 10,000
SALES (est): 31.1MM Privately Held
WEB: www.idgriffith.com
SIC: 1711 Mechanical contractor; warm air heating & air conditioning contractor; process piping contractor

(G-10992)
IDF CONNECT INC
2207 Concord Pike 359 (19803-2908)
PHONE..................888 765-1611
Richard Sand, *CEO*
EMP: 3 EST: 2012
SALES (est): 98.4K Privately Held
SIC: 7372 Application computer software

(G-10993)
IDPA HOLDINGS INC
200 Bellevue Pkwy Ste 300 (19809-3727)
PHONE..................302 281-3600
EMP: 9
SALES (est): 753.2K
SALES (corp-wide): 307.4MM Publicly Held
SIC: 6794 Patent owners & lessors
HQ: Interdigital Wireless, Inc.
200 Bellevue Pkwy Ste 300
Wilmington DE 19809

(G-10994)
IDTP HOLDINGS INC
200 Bellevue Pkwy Ste 300 (19809-3727)
PHONE..................302 281-3600
EMP: 6
SALES (est): 504K
SALES (corp-wide): 307.4MM Publicly Held
SIC: 6794 Patent owners & lessors
HQ: Interdigital Wireless, Inc.
200 Bellevue Pkwy Ste 300
Wilmington DE 19809

(G-10995)
IDYLC HOMES LLC
103 Cambridge Dr (19803-2605)
PHONE..................302 295-3719
Jason Decena, *Mng Member*
Jenaida Abella,
EMP: 3
SALES: 250K Privately Held
SIC: 3634 2674 3469 Coffee makers, electric; household; grocers' bags: made from purchased materials; household cooking & kitchen utensils, metal

(G-10996)
IEH AUTO PARTS LLC
3315 Old Capitol Trl (19808-6209)
PHONE..................302 994-7171
Greg Price, *Manager*
EMP: 29
SALES (corp-wide): 11.7B Publicly Held
SIC: 5013 Automotive supplies & parts
HQ: Ieh Auto Parts Llc
108 Townpark Dr Nw
Kennesaw GA 30144
770 701-5000

(G-10997)
IJI INC
2711 Centerville Rd # 400 (19808-1660)
PHONE..................732 485-9427
Vin Foresta, *President*
EMP: 20 EST: 2017
SALES (est): 372.5K Privately Held
SIC: 7379

(G-10998)
IKO INDUSTRIES INC
6 Denny Rd Ste 200 (19809-3444)
PHONE..................302 764-3100
Ron Healey, *CEO*
Robert Parsons, *Plant Supt*
Nick Nachbar, *Plant Mgr*
Aubrey Ellis, *Mfg Staff*
Dan Redmond, *Mfg Staff*
EMP: 6
SALES (corp-wide): 54.8MM Privately Held
SIC: 2952 Roofing materials
HQ: Iko Industries Inc.
120 Hay Rd
Wilmington DE 19809
302 764-3100

(G-10999)
IKO MANUFACTURING INC
120 Hay Rd (19809-3599)
PHONE..................302 764-3100
David Koschitzky, *President*
EMP: 80
SQ FT: 100,000
SALES (est): 8.5MM Privately Held
SIC: 2952 5033 Asphalt felts & coatings; roofing & siding materials
PA: Goldis Holdings, Inc
120 Hay Rd
Wilmington DE 19809

(G-11000)
IKO PRODUCTION INC (HQ)
Also Called: Iko Manufacturing
120 Hay Rd (19809-3509)
PHONE..................302 764-3100
David Koschitzky, *President*
Roy Baumer, *Plant Mgr*
Bobby Carboni, *Production*
Jehosafat Sanchez, *Production*
Marcus Vera, *Plant Engr*
▲ EMP: 87
SQ FT: 100,000
SALES (est): 33.6MM Privately Held
SIC: 2952 Roofing materials

(G-11001)
IKO SALES INC
Also Called: Iko Productions
120 Hay Rd (19809-3509)
PHONE..................302 764-3100
David Koschitzky, *President*
Henry Fear, *Vice Pres*
Chad Bing, *Sales Staff*
Lora Manning, *Sales Staff*
Michael Valeri, *Sales Staff*
EMP: 75
SQ FT: 100,000
SALES (est): 16.3MM Privately Held
WEB: www.ikoproductions.com
SIC: 5033 Roofing & siding materials

(G-11002)
IKO SALES LTD
120 Hay Rd (19809-3509)
PHONE..................302 764-3100
Brad Harges, *Manager*
EMP: 100
SALES (corp-wide): 54.8MM Privately Held
SIC: 3317 Steel pipe & tubes
HQ: Iko Sales Limited
1600 42 Ave Se
Calgary AB
403 265-6022

(G-11003)
IKO SOUTHEAST INC (HQ)
6 Denny Rd Ste 200 (19809-3444)
PHONE..................815 936-9600
David Koschitzky, *President*
Raymond Hatfield, *Maint Spvr*
Chris Isbell, *Purchasing*
Bob Orledge, *Engineer*
Jim Olowniuk, *Regl Sales Mgr*
EMP: 33
SALES (est): 17.6MM
SALES (corp-wide): 54.8MM Privately Held
SIC: 3295 Roofing granules
PA: Goldis Enterprises, Inc.
120 Hay Rd
Wilmington DE 19809
302 764-3100

GEOGRAPHIC SECTION
Wilmington - New Castle County (G-11033)

(G-11004)
ILGEN INC
3422 Old Capitol Trl (19808-6124)
PHONE.....................518 369-0069
Ilya Tsimafeyeu, *CEO*
EMP: 2
SALES (est): 74.4K **Privately Held**
SIC: 2834 Medicines, capsuled or ampuled

(G-11005)
IMAGING GROUP DELAWARE PA
St Francis Hospital Depa (19805)
PHONE.....................302 421-4300
EMP: 5 **EST:** 2017
SALES (est): 72.5K **Privately Held**
SIC: 8011 Radiologist

(G-11006)
IMNA SOLUTIONS INC
704 N King St Ste 500 (19801-3584)
P.O. Box 1031 (19899-1031)
PHONE.....................347 821-8238
Israel Haikin, *President*
EMP: 16
SALES (est): 273.5K **Privately Held**
SIC: 7382 Security systems services
PA: I.M.N.A Solutions Ltd
31 Hayam Rd.
Havazzelet Hash
524 234-239

(G-11007)
IMPACT IRRGATION SOLUTIONS INC
3213 Heathwood Rd (19810-3427)
PHONE.....................484 723-3600
EMP: 4
SALES (est): 108.1K **Privately Held**
SIC: 4971 Irrigation systems

(G-11008)
IMPERIAL DYNASTY ARTS PROGRAM
1008 S Broom St (19805-4566)
PHONE.....................302 521-8551
Devin Fletcher, *President*
Tyree Miller, *Vice Pres*
EMP: 10
SALES (est): 510K **Privately Held**
SIC: 3931 Percussion instruments & parts

(G-11009)
IN THE DRIVERS SEAT
1811 Gravers Ln (19810-4516)
PHONE.....................302 475-3361
Thomas Whetham, *Principal*
EMP: 7
SALES (est): 233K **Privately Held**
SIC: 4119 Automobile rental, with driver

(G-11010)
IN VISION EYE CARE
Also Called: Fairfax Eye Works
2205 Concord Pike (19803-2908)
PHONE.....................302 655-1952
Roger Ammon, *Owner*
EMP: 12
SALES (est): 987.6K **Privately Held**
SIC: 8042 Offices & clinics of optometrists

(G-11011)
INC PLAN (USA)
Also Called: Plan USA
26c Trolley Sq (19806-3356)
PHONE.....................302 428-1200
Henry Beckler, *President*
Caroline Quigley, *Exec VP*
EMP: 6
SALES (est): 715K **Privately Held**
WEB: www.incplan.net
SIC: 7389 Authors' agents & brokers

(G-11012)
INCENCO INTERNATIONAL
1806 Jaybee Rd (19803-3323)
PHONE.....................302 478-8400
Jyo Patel, *Owner*
EMP: 13
SALES (est): 427.7K **Privately Held**
SIC: 8732 8742 Commercial nonphysical research; business consultant

(G-11013)
INCITE SOLUTIONS INC
5714 Kennett Pike Ofc 3 (19807-1331)
PHONE.....................302 655-8952
Thomas Scott, *President*
EMP: 6 **EST:** 2000
SALES (est): 828.3K **Privately Held**
WEB: www.incitesolutions.com
SIC: 5045 Computers, peripherals & software

(G-11014)
INCOLOR INC
1401 Todds Ln (19802-2417)
PHONE.....................302 984-2695
Bob McClean, *President*
Robert Krischbaum, *Graphic Designe*
EMP: 5
SALES (est): 457.6K **Privately Held**
WEB: www.incolor.com
SIC: 7389 Personal service agents, brokers & bureaus

(G-11015)
INCORPORATORS USA LLC
Also Called: American Incorporators
1013 Centre Rd Ste 403a (19805-1270)
PHONE.....................800 441-5940
Ann Chilton, *CEO*
Laura Bryda, *Vice Pres*
Kerry Jester, *CPA*
EMP: 13
SALES (est): 609K **Privately Held**
SIC: 8748 Business consulting

(G-11016)
INCYTE CORPORATION (PA)
1801 Augustine Cut Off (19803-4404)
PHONE.....................302 498-6700
Herve Hoppenot, *Ch of Bd*
Dashyant Dhanak, *Exec VP*
Barry P Flannelly, *Exec VP*
Vijay Iyengar, *Exec VP*
Maria E Pasquale, *Exec VP*
EMP: 207
SQ FT: 344,000
SALES: 1.8B **Publicly Held**
WEB: www.incyte.com
SIC: 2834 Pharmaceutical preparations

(G-11017)
INDEPENDENT RESOURCES INC (PA)
6 Denny Rd Ste 101 (19809-3444)
PHONE.....................302 765-0191
Phyllis Farrare-Henders, *General Mgr*
Joseph Derex, *Principal*
Larry D Henderson, *Exec Dir*
Phyllis Ferrer, *Director*
▲ **EMP:** 15
SQ FT: 1,600
SALES (est): 653.7K **Privately Held**
SIC: 8699 Charitable organization

(G-11018)
INDEPENDENT SCHOOL MGT INC (PA)
1316 N Union St (19806-2594)
PHONE.....................302 656-4944
Roxanne Elliott, *President*
Weldon Burge, *Editor*
W Rodman Snelling, *Chairman*
Scott Medina, *Marketing Staff*
Marshall Miele, *Manager*
EMP: 39
SQ FT: 6,500
SALES (est): 10.4MM **Privately Held**
WEB: www.isminc.com
SIC: 6411 8742 2741 Insurance agents, brokers & service; management consulting services; miscellaneous publishing

(G-11019)
INDO AMINES AMERICAS LLC
5301 Limestone Rd Ste 100 (19808-1251)
PHONE.....................301 466-9902
Vijay Bhalchandra Palkar, *CEO*
EMP: 3 **EST:** 2014
SALES (est): 81.8K **Privately Held**
SIC: 2819 Chemicals, high purity: refined from technical grade

(G-11020)
INDUSTRAPLATE CORP
5 James Ct (19801-5251)
P.O. Box 10812 (19850-0812)
PHONE.....................302 654-5210
Stephen Orr, *President*
David Orr Jr, *Vice Pres*
Joann Glanden, *Admin Sec*
EMP: 10 **EST:** 1961
SALES: 900K **Privately Held**
SIC: 3471 Plating of metals or formed products; finishing, metals or formed products

(G-11021)
INDUSTRIAL METAL TREATING CORP
Also Called: Atlantic Heat Treat
402 E Front St (19801-3956)
PHONE.....................302 656-1677
Chris Schopfer, *President*
Rich Cooper, *Plant Mgr*
David Skinner, *Office Mgr*
EMP: 10
SQ FT: 42,000
SALES (est): 3.1MM **Privately Held**
WEB: www.treatmetal.com
SIC: 3398 3471 Metal heat treating; sand blasting of metal parts

(G-11022)
INDUSTRIAL RESOURCE NETWRK INC
Also Called: Irn
707 S Church St (19801-5540)
PHONE.....................302 888-2905
William J Ries, *President*
EMP: 11
SQ FT: 22,000
SALES (est): 1.3MM **Privately Held**
SIC: 7699 5085 5162 Industrial equipment services; drums, new or reconditioned; plastics products

(G-11023)
INDUSTRY ARC
251 Little Falls Dr (19808-1674)
PHONE.....................614 588-8538
EMP: 10
SALES (est): 750K **Privately Held**
SIC: 8748 Business consulting

(G-11024)
INEOS CHLOR AMERICAS INC
2036 Foulk Rd Ste 204 (19810-3650)
P.O. Box 761, Plaquemine LA (70765-0761)
PHONE.....................302 529-9601
▲ **EMP:** 4
SALES (est): 575.4K
SALES (corp-wide): 17.9B **Privately Held**
SIC: 2821 Mfg Plastic Materials/Resins
HQ: Inovyn Chlorvinyls Limited
38 Hans Crescent
London WA7 4
192 851-6948

(G-11025)
INFLUENCERS LAB MEDIA LLC
300 Martin Luther King (19801-2437)
PHONE.....................302 444-6990
Kenyon Wilson,
EMP: 4
SALES (est): 22.8K **Privately Held**
SIC: 4899 Communication services

(G-11026)
INFO SYSTEMS LLC (DH)
Also Called: ISI Connect
590 Century Blvd (19808-6273)
PHONE.....................302 633-9800
Mark Stellini,
EMP: 125 **EST:** 1982
SQ FT: 18,000
SALES (est): 26MM **Privately Held**
SIC: 5045 7373 Computers; computer integrated systems design
HQ: Mtm Technologies, Inc.
4 Manhattanville Rd # 106
Purchase NY 10577
866 383-2867

(G-11027)
INFORMATION SAFEGUARD INC (PA)
1201 N Orange St Ste 700 (19801-1186)
PHONE.....................410 604-2660
Vance Stone, *President*
EMP: 4
SALES (est): 289K **Privately Held**
WEB: www.informationsafeguard.com
SIC: 7376 Computer facilities management

(G-11028)
INFUSION CARE DELAWARE HOME
9 N Hampshire Ct (19807-2535)
PHONE.....................302 423-2511
Sharon Burtonyoung, *Principal*
EMP: 4
SALES (est): 81.1K **Privately Held**
SIC: 8059 Nursing & personal care

(G-11029)
ING BANK FSB
Also Called: Ing Direct Wilmington Cafe
802 Delaware Ave Fl 1 (19801-1300)
PHONE.....................302 255-3750
Bryan Nook, *Manager*
EMP: 4 **Publicly Held**
SIC: 4813
HQ: Ing Bank Fsb
802 Delaware Ave
Wilmington DE 19801

(G-11030)
ING BANK FSB (HQ)
Also Called: Ing Direct
802 Delaware Ave (19801-1377)
PHONE.....................302 658-2200
Ralph Hamers, *CEO*
Jim Kelly, *COO*
Roel Louwhoff, *COO*
Pg Flynn, *CFO*
Patrick Flynn, *CFO*
EMP: 47
SQ FT: 39,000
SALES (est): 155.7MM **Publicly Held**
SIC: 6035 6211 Savings institutions, federally chartered; security brokers & dealers

(G-11031)
INGLESIDE HOMES INC (PA)
Also Called: Ingleside Rtirement Apartments
1005 N Franklin St (19806-4553)
PHONE.....................302 575-0250
Lawrence R Cessna, *President*
Susan Jonas, *Bookkeeper*
Keith Ropka, *Administration*
EMP: 85
SQ FT: 25,000
SALES: 6.4MM **Privately Held**
WEB: www.inglesidehomes.org
SIC: 8082 8322 8361 Home health care services; geriatric social service; geriatric residential care

(G-11032)
INGLESIDE HOMES INC
Also Called: Ingleside Assisted Living
1605 N Broom St (19806-3009)
PHONE.....................302 984-0950
Keith Ropka, *Principal*
Patsy McNichol, *Hlthcr Dir*
EMP: 30
SALES (corp-wide): 6.4MM **Privately Held**
WEB: www.inglesidehomes.org
SIC: 8051 8052 6513 Skilled nursing care facilities; intermediate care facilities; retirement hotel operation
PA: Ingleside Homes, Inc.
1005 N Franklin St
Wilmington DE 19806
302 575-0250

(G-11033)
INGLESIDE RTRMENT APRTMNTS LLC
1005 N Franklin St (19806-4553)
PHONE.....................302 575-0250
Lawrence Cessna,
EMP: 80
SALES: 4.3MM **Privately Held**
SIC: 6513 Retirement hotel operation

Wilmington - New Castle County (G-11034)

(G-11034)
INITIAL TRADING CO
5716 Kennett Pike Ste D (19807-1328)
PHONE..................302 428-1132
Dona Hazzard, *President*
EMP: 1
SQ FT: 1,800
SALES: 59K **Privately Held**
SIC: 2511 5719 7389 Wood household furniture; linens; lettering service

(G-11035)
INITIALLY YOURS INC
1412 Kirkwood Hwy (19805-2124)
PHONE..................302 999-0562
Therese Moore, *President*
Mary Ruoff, *Corp Secy*
EMP: 4
SQ FT: 1,400
SALES (est): 332.7K **Privately Held**
SIC: 2395 7336 Emblems, embroidered; embroidery products, except schiffli machine; decorative & novelty stitching, for the trade; silk screen design

(G-11036)
INN AT WILMINGTON
300 Rocky Run Pkwy (19803-1515)
PHONE..................302 479-7900
Colleen Owens, *President*
EMP: 30
SALES (est): 1.1MM **Privately Held**
SIC: 7011 Inns

(G-11037)
INNCLUDE LLC
3511 Silverside Rd # 105 (19810-4902)
PHONE..................310 430-6552
Eric Kaya, *Mng Member*
EMP: 4
SALES: 250K **Privately Held**
SIC: 7371 7372 Computer software development & applications; application computer software

(G-11038)
INNOVATION VENTURES LP
1601 Concord Pike Ste 82 (19803-3630)
PHONE..................302 777-1616
David J Freschman, *Principal*
EMP: 4
SALES (est): 550.1K **Privately Held**
SIC: 6163 Loan agents

(G-11039)
INSIGNIA GLOBAL CORPORATION
913 N Market St Ste 200 (19801-3097)
PHONE..................302 310-4107
Simon Borgawkar, *President*
EMP: 5
SALES: 100K **Privately Held**
SIC: 7361 Placement agencies

(G-11040)
INSITE CONSTRUCTORS INC
3201 Tanya Dr (19803-1936)
PHONE..................302 479-5555
Joseph Gallo, *President*
EMP: 5
SQ FT: 1,800
SALES (est): 782.2K **Privately Held**
SIC: 1542 Commercial & office building contractors

(G-11041)
INSPECTWARE
123 E Ayre St (19804-2506)
PHONE..................302 999-9601
John Kerrigan,
EMP: 6
SQ FT: 2,347
SALES (est): 354.6K **Privately Held**
WEB: www.reliablehomeinspection.org
SIC: 7372 Business oriented computer software

(G-11042)
INSTANODE INC
501 Silverside Rd Ste 105 (19809-1376)
PHONE..................352 327-8872
Anand Sridharan, *CEO*
EMP: 4
SALES (est): 47.4K **Privately Held**
SIC: 7375 4813 Information retrieval services;

(G-11043)
INSURANCE & FINANCIAL SVCS INC
Also Called: Nationwide
1523 Concord Pike Ste 400 (19803-3654)
PHONE..................302 239-5895
Richard H Lapenta, *CEO*
John R Davis, *Vice Pres*
EMP: 20
SQ FT: 3,000
SALES (est): 6MM **Privately Held**
WEB: www.ifs-de.com
SIC: 6411 Insurance agents

(G-11044)
INSURANCE & FINCL SVCS LTD DEL
Also Called: Ifs
1523 Concord Pike Ste 400 (19803-3654)
PHONE..................302 234-1200
John Davis, *Owner*
Stephen Burnett, *Exec VP*
Dylan Furlano, *Accounts Mgr*
Darlene Wilkins, *Accounts Mgr*
Linda Thomas, *Manager*
EMP: 4
SALES (est): 629.5K **Privately Held**
SIC: 6411 8742 Insurance agents; financial consultant

(G-11045)
INSURANCE NETWORKS ALIANCE LLC
3411 Silverside Rd Bynardb (19810-4812)
PHONE..................302 268-1010
Ray Scotto,
EMP: 5
SALES: 150K **Privately Held**
SIC: 8611 Trade associations

(G-11046)
INSURANCE OFFICE AMERICA INC
Also Called: Nationwide
900 Philadelphia Pike (19809-2280)
PHONE..................302 764-1000
Diana Handy, *Principal*
Thomas Hornung, *Accounts Exec*
EMP: 7
SALES (corp-wide): 199MM **Privately Held**
SIC: 6411 Insurance agents
HQ: Insurance Office Of America, Inc.
1855 W State Road 434
Longwood FL 32750
407 788-3000

(G-11047)
INTEGRATED AVI SOLUTIONS LLC
3700 Centerville Rd (19807-1935)
PHONE..................302 351-3427
John W Bragger Jr, *President*
EMP: 4
SALES (est): 266K **Privately Held**
SIC: 8742 Transportation consultant

(G-11048)
INTEGRATED DATA CORP (PA)
1000 N West St Ste 1200 (19801-1058)
PHONE..................302 295-5057
David C Bryan, *President*
Walter T Bristow III, *Vice Pres*
Stuart W Settle Jr, *Admin Sec*
▲ **EMP:** 2
SQ FT: 5,000
SALES (est): 371.3K **Privately Held**
WEB: www.integrateddatacorp.com
SIC: 3663 Pagers (one-way)

(G-11049)
INTEGRATED GREEN PARTNERS LLC
1209 N Orange St (19801-1120)
PHONE..................402 871-8347
Stuart Clark,
EMP: 4 **Privately Held**
SIC: 6719 Holding companies

(G-11050)
INTEGRATED TECHNOLOGY SYSTEMS
1401 Penns Ave Apt 310 (19806-4123)
P.O. Box 2514, Wilkes Barre PA (18703-2514)
PHONE..................302 429-0560
Arna Silbergeld-Bleckman, *President*
EMP: 2
SALES (est): 133K **Privately Held**
SIC: 3861 Tripods, camera & projector

(G-11051)
INTEGRATED WEALTH MGT LLC (PA)
5511 Kirkwood Hwy (19808-5001)
PHONE..................302 442-4233
Burt Hutchinson, *Mng Member*
EMP: 4
SQ FT: 2,500
SALES (est): 886.5K **Privately Held**
SIC: 6282 Investment advisory service

(G-11052)
INTELLIGENT SIGNAGE INC (PA)
4006 Coleridge Rd (19802-1906)
PHONE..................302 762-4100
Francis J Coughan, *Owner*
Jeffery Chaet, *Vice Pres*
Bill Turkel, *Treasurer*
EMP: 5
SALES: 750K **Privately Held**
WEB: www.intelligentsignage.net
SIC: 8748 Business consulting

(G-11053)
INTERCOASTAL TITLE AGENCY INC
10 Cohee Cir (19803-1114)
PHONE..................302 478-7752
Charlotte E Wick, *Manager*
EMP: 5
SALES (est): 470K **Privately Held**
WEB: www.intercoastaltitle.com
SIC: 6361 Title insurance

(G-11054)
INTERCOLLEGIATE STUDIES INST
3901 Centerville Rd (19807-1938)
P.O. Box 4431 (19807-0431)
PHONE..................302 656-3292
Christopher Long, *President*
T Kenneth Cribb Jr, *President*
Elaine Pinder, *CFO*
EMP: 65 **EST:** 1953
SALES: 7.8MM **Privately Held**
WEB: www.isi.org
SIC: 8641 Educator's association

(G-11055)
INTERCONTINENTAL CHEM SVCS INC
Also Called: I C S
1020 Christiana Ave Ste B (19801-5884)
PHONE..................302 654-6800
Rick Ryan, *CEO*
John Vitale, *President*
John C Foreman, *Vice Pres*
Doris Smith, *Admin Sec*
EMP: 20
SQ FT: 270,000
SALES (est): 4.1MM **Privately Held**
SIC: 4225 General warehousing

(G-11056)
INTERCONTINENTAL MARKETING
Also Called: Global Institute, The
807 Essex Rd (19807-2931)
PHONE..................302 429-7555
Terry Schuster, *President*
Ron Davis, *CFO*
William T Grubb, *Director*
Frank Hewitt, *Administration*
EMP: 7
SALES (est): 297.4K **Privately Held**
SIC: 8742 Financial consultant

(G-11057)
INTERCONTINENTAL TECH LLC
Also Called: Ict
3106 Centerville Rd (19807-2502)
PHONE..................302 984-2111

Richard Paverd, *President*
EMP: 4
SALES (est): 292K **Privately Held**
WEB: www.inttec.com
SIC: 7379 8742 ; management information systems consultant

(G-11058)
INTERDGITAL COMMUNICATIONS INC (DH)
Also Called: Interdgital Communications LLC
200 Bellevue Pkwy Ste 300 (19809-3727)
PHONE..................610 878-7800
Steven T Clontz, *Ch of Bd*
William J Merritt, *President*
Daniel Mullarkey, *Principal*
Bruce G Bernstein, *Counsel*
Brian G Kiernan, *Exec VP*
EMP: 80
SQ FT: 52,000
SALES (est): 39.6MM
SALES (corp-wide): 307.4MM **Publicly Held**
WEB: www.interdigital.com
SIC: 3663 5999 Mobile communication equipment; mobile telephones & equipment

(G-11059)
INTERDIGITAL INC (PA)
200 Bellevue Pkwy Ste 300 (19809-3727)
PHONE..................302 281-3600
S Douglas Hutcheson, *Ch of Bd*
William J Merritt, *President*
Kai Oistamo, *COO*
Richard J Brezski, *CFO*
Jannie K Lau,
EMP: 3
SQ FT: 36,200
SALES: 307.4MM **Publicly Held**
SIC: 3663 5999 Mobile communication equipment; mobile telephones & equipment

(G-11060)
INTERDIGITAL BELGIUM LLC
200 Bellevue Pkwy (19809-3727)
PHONE..................302 281-3600
EMP: 5 **EST:** 2018
SALES (est): 117.1K
SALES (corp-wide): 307.4MM **Publicly Held**
SIC: 6794 Patent owners & lessors
HQ: Interdigital Wireless, Inc.
200 Bellevue Pkwy Ste 300
Wilmington DE 19809

(G-11061)
INTERDIGITAL WIRELESS INC (HQ)
200 Bellevue Pkwy Ste 300 (19809-3727)
PHONE..................302 281-3600
S Douglas Hutcheson, *Ch of Bd*
William J Merritt, *President*
Kai Oistamo, *COO*
Richard J Brezski, *CFO*
Jannie K Lau,
EMP: 71
SQ FT: 36,200
SALES: 307.4MM **Publicly Held**
SIC: 3663 5999 Mobile communication equipment; mobile telephones & equipment
PA: Interdigital, Inc.
200 Bellevue Pkwy Ste 300
Wilmington DE 19809
302 281-3600

(G-11062)
INTERFAITH CMNTY HSING OF DEL
Also Called: ICHDE
613 N Washington St (19801-2135)
PHONE..................302 652-3991
Gary Pollio, *President*
Bpb Rawlinson, *CFO*
Darlene Sample, *CFO*
EMP: 18
SALES: 2MM **Privately Held**
SIC: 6552 1521 6514 Land subdividers & developers, residential; single-family housing construction; townhouse construction; single-family home remodeling, additions & repairs; new construction, single-family houses; dwelling operators, except apartments

GEOGRAPHIC SECTION   Wilmington - New Castle County (G-11095)

(G-11063)
INTERJET WEST INC
1013 Centre Rd Ste 403a (19805-1270)
PHONE....................209 848-0290
Justin Barnes, *Vice Pres*
EMP: 12
SALES (est): 360.6K **Privately Held**
SIC: 4522 Air transportation, nonscheduled

(G-11064)
INTERNAL MEDICINE ASSOCIATES
3105 Limestone Rd Ste 301 (19808-2179)
PHONE....................302 633-1700
Mart Amick, *Principal*
Robert Kopecki, *Principal*
Ana Rutkowski, *Office Mgr*
EMP: 13
SALES (est): 2.7MM **Privately Held**
SIC: 8011 Internal medicine, physician/surgeon

(G-11065)
INTERNATIONAL ELECTRICAL SVCS
15 Atkins Ave (19805-1405)
P.O. Box 30137 (19805-7137)
PHONE....................302 438-6096
Joseph Fazekas, *President*
EMP: 1
SALES (est): 53.3K **Privately Held**
SIC: 7699 3449 Industrial machinery & equipment repair; miscellaneous metalwork

(G-11066)
INTERNATIONAL PETRO CORP DEL
Also Called: International Petro Corp Del
505 S Market St (19801-5287)
PHONE....................302 421-9306
Lea Miller, *President*
Ed Flake, *Vice Pres*
EMP: 58
SQ FT: 7,500
SALES (est): 19MM **Publicly Held**
SIC: 4953 Non-hazardous waste disposal sites
PA: Heritage-Crystal Clean, Inc.
2175 Point Blvd Ste 375
Elgin IL 60123

(G-11067)
INTERNATIONAL SPINE PAIN
3411 Silverside Rd 103r (19810-4805)
PHONE....................302 478-7001
Peter M Witherell, *Principal*
James E Downing, *Med Doctor*
EMP: 5
SALES (est): 369.8K **Privately Held**
SIC: 8011 8031 8748 Specialized medical practitioners, except internal; offices & clinics of osteopathic physicians; business consulting

(G-11068)
INTERNATIONAL STD ELC CORP (DH)
1105 N Market St Ste 1217 (19801-1216)
PHONE....................302 427-3769
Daniel P Weadock, *Ch of Bd*
Marvin R Sambur, *Principal*
Louis J Giuliani, *Exec VP*
Bertil T Nilsson, *Exec VP*
Roger W Langsdorf, *Vice Pres*
EMP: 11
SALES (est): 2.1MM
SALES (corp-wide): 2.7B **Publicly Held**
WEB: www.ittind.com
SIC: 3711 Motor vehicles & car bodies
HQ: Itt Llc
1133 Westchester Ave N-100
White Plains NY 10604
914 641-2000

(G-11069)
INTERNATIONAL TRAVEL NETWORK
Also Called: ASAP Tickets
1000 N West St Ste 1200 (19801-1058)
PHONE....................415 840-0207
Peter Vazan, *CEO*
Alex Weinstein, *President*
EMP: 9 EST: 2004

SALES (est): 1.7MM **Privately Held**
SIC: 4724 Travel agencies

(G-11070)
INTOHOST INC
501 Silverside Rd Ste 105 (19809-1376)
PHONE....................888 567-2607
Israr Ul Haq, *President*
EMP: 10 EST: 2018
SALES: 3.6K **Privately Held**
SIC: 4813

(G-11071)
INTRINSIC PARTNERS LLC
4001 Kennett Pike Ste 134 (19807-2000)
PHONE....................610 388-0853
Dennis Sheehy, *Mng Member*
EMP: 100
SALES (est): 2.8MM **Privately Held**
SIC: 7379 8742 Computer related consulting services; management consulting services

(G-11072)
INVENSIS INC
1000 N West St Ste 1200 (19801-1058)
PHONE....................302 351-3509
Vara Prasad Rongala, *President*
Samanth Srikantan, *Manager*
EMP: 200 EST: 2010
SALES (est): 24.1MM **Privately Held**
SIC: 7374 Data processing & preparation
PA: Invensis Technology Private Limited
1st Floor Upkar Chambers
Bengaluru KA 56000

(G-11073)
INVESTMENT PROPERTY SERVICES L
102 Robino Ct Ste 101 (19804)
PHONE....................302 994-3907
Leonard Iacono, *Principal*
EMP: 4
SALES (est): 531.6K **Privately Held**
SIC: 6282 Investment advisory service

(G-11074)
INVISIBLE HAND LABS LLC
2711 Centerville Rd # 400 (19808-1660)
PHONE....................434 989-9642
Karl Quist,
EMP: 3
SALES (est): 83.9K **Privately Held**
SIC: 3999 Manufacturing industries

(G-11075)
INVISTA CAPITAL MANAGEMENT LLC (HQ)
2801 Centerville Rd (19808-1609)
PHONE....................302 683-3000
Steve R McCracken,
Morris L Cranor,
William C Pickett,
▲ EMP: 8
SALES (est): 2.4B
SALES (corp-wide): 40.6B **Privately Held**
WEB: www.invista.com
SIC: 2821 Plastics materials & resins
PA: Koch Industries, Inc.
4111 E 37th St N
Wichita KS 67220
316 828-5500

(G-11076)
INVISTA CAPITAL MANAGEMENT LLC
4417 Lancaster Pike (19805-1523)
PHONE....................877 446-8478
Steve R McCracken, *Manager*
EMP: 44
SALES (corp-wide): 40.6B **Privately Held**
WEB: www.invista.com
SIC: 2821 Plastics materials & resins
HQ: Invista Capital Management, Llc
2801 Centerville Rd
Wilmington DE 19808
302 683-3000

(G-11077)
INVISTA SARL
3 Little Leaf Ct (19810-3702)
PHONE....................302 683-3001
Teresa Miller, *Marketing Staff*
EMP: 4

SALES (est): 359K **Privately Held**
SIC: 2821 Plastics materials & resins

(G-11078)
IOVATE HEALTH SCIENCES USA INC (HQ)
1105 N Market St Ste 1330 (19801-1207)
PHONE....................888 334-4448
Paul Gardiner, *President*
Norm Vanderee, *CFO*
EMP: 32
SALES (est): 13.4MM
SALES (corp-wide): 109.6MM **Privately Held**
WEB: www.iovate.com
SIC: 4225 General warehousing & storage
PA: Kerr Investment Holding Corp
381 North Service Rd W
Oakville ON L6M 0
905 678-3119

(G-11079)
IP CAMERA WAREHOUSE LLC
Also Called: National Supply Contractors
3422 Old Capitol Trl (19808-6124)
PHONE....................302 358-2690
EMP: 5
SALES (est): 211.2K **Privately Held**
SIC: 7382 Confinement surveillance systems maintenance & monitoring

(G-11080)
IPR INTERNATIONAL LLC (PA)
1201 N Market St Ste 201 (19801-1160)
PHONE....................302 304-8774
Tami Fratis, *CEO*
Michael J Emmi, *Ch of Bd*
Kirk Horton, *Partner*
Robert J Bray Jr, *Exec VP*
Bruce Carlson, *Senior VP*
EMP: 50
SQ FT: 8,800
SALES (est): 15.2MM **Privately Held**
WEB: www.iprintl.com
SIC: 7374 Service bureau, computer; data processing service

(G-11081)
IQARUS AMERICAS INC
1209 N Orange St (19801-1120)
PHONE....................407 222-5726
Jetlir Bajrami, *CFO*
EMP: 37
SALES (est): 11MM **Privately Held**
SIC: 8062 General medical & surgical hospitals

(G-11082)
IRON WORKERS LOCAL 451
203 Old Dupont Rd (19804-1099)
PHONE....................302 994-0946
Jeff Hendrickson, *President*
EMP: 4
SQ FT: 1,500
SALES: 867.3K **Privately Held**
SIC: 8631 Labor union

(G-11083)
IRONDT CORP
3411 Silverside Rd (19810-4812)
PHONE....................347 539-6471
Sergii Tkachenko, *Director*
EMP: 5
SALES (est): 318.1K **Privately Held**
SIC: 5013 Automotive supplies & parts

(G-11084)
IRVING IA EXTRACT DIET PILLS
3717 Valley Brook Dr (19808-1342)
PHONE....................302 218-0472
EMP: 2
SALES (est): 120K **Privately Held**
SIC: 2836 Mfg Biological Products

(G-11085)
IRWIN L LIFRAK MD PC
1010 N Union St Ste 5 (19805-2731)
PHONE....................302 654-7317
Irwin L Lifrak MD, *Owner*
James Sheehan, *Contractor*
EMP: 4
SALES (est): 467.7K **Privately Held**
SIC: 8011 Internal medicine, physician/surgeon

(G-11086)
ISA PROFESSIONAL LTD
919 N Market St Ste 425 (19801-3014)
PHONE....................647 869-1552
Alexander Caban, *President*
EMP: 5
SALES (est): 165.7K **Privately Held**
SIC: 3999 Barber & beauty shop equipment

(G-11087)
ISAACS AUTOMOTIVE INC
15 W Ayre St (19804-3101)
PHONE....................302 995-2519
Steve Isaac, *President*
EMP: 4
SALES (est): 343.3K **Privately Held**
SIC: 7538 General truck repair

(G-11088)
ISAACS ISACS FMLY DENTISTRY PA
707 Foulk Rd Ste 103 (19803-3737)
PHONE....................302 654-1328
David Isaac, *Partner*
EMP: 11
SQ FT: 1,700
SALES (est): 754.6K **Privately Held**
SIC: 8021 Dentists' office

(G-11089)
ISLAND GENIUS LLC
1201 N Market St Ste 2300 (19801-1165)
PHONE....................888 529-5506
David Follett,
EMP: 3
SALES (est): 83.9K **Privately Held**
SIC: 3999 Manufacturing industries

(G-11090)
ISM
15 Sharpley Rd (19803-2940)
PHONE....................302 656-2376
EMP: 5
SALES (est): 219.5K **Privately Held**
SIC: 5149 Canned goods: fruit, vegetables, seafood, meats, etc.

(G-11091)
ITANGO INC
1201 N Orange St Ste 600 (19801-1171)
PHONE....................302 648-2646
Adrian Le Pera, *Principal*
EMP: 2
SALES (est): 120K **Privately Held**
SIC: 7371 7372 Custom computer programming services; application computer software

(G-11092)
ITHACA HOLDCO 2 LLC
1209 N Orange St (19801-1120)
PHONE....................650 385-5000
Anal Chakravarthy,
EMP: 1
SALES (est): 32.7K **Privately Held**
SIC: 7372 Prepackaged software

(G-11093)
ITIYAM LLC
1000 N West St Ste 1200 (19801-1058)
PHONE....................703 291-1600
Raj Yallapragada, *President*
EMP: 10
SALES (est): 729K **Privately Held**
SIC: 7373 Computer integrated systems design

(G-11094)
IVEEAPP CORP (PA)
251 Little Falls Dr (19808-1674)
PHONE....................610 999-6290
Louis Troilo, *Principal*
Alex Zacney, *Principal*
EMP: 4
SALES: 2MM **Privately Held**
SIC: 8093 7371 Specialty outpatient clinics; computer software development & applications

(G-11095)
IVY GABLES LLC
2210 Swiss Ln (19810-4241)
PHONE....................302 475-9400
Tammy Loudon, *Owner*

Wilmington - New Castle County (G-11096) GEOGRAPHIC SECTION

George Loudon, *Co-Owner*
Rebecca White, *Exec Dir*
EMP: 15
SALES (est): 281.9K **Privately Held**
SIC: 8051 Skilled nursing care facilities

(G-11096)
IZZYS LAWN SERVICE INC
1936 Seneca Rd (19805-4129)
PHONE.................302 293-9221
Ismael Romero, *Owner*
EMP: 4
SALES (est): 127.3K **Privately Held**
SIC: 0782 Lawn care services

(G-11097)
J & M INDUSTRIES INC
1014 S Market St (19801-5228)
PHONE.................302 575-0200
James Maddox, *President*
Nancy Maddox, *Vice Pres*
EMP: 5
SQ FT: 5,000
SALES (est): 542.9K **Privately Held**
SIC: 1794 Excavation work

(G-11098)
J & S GENERAL CONTRACTORS
1815 Williamson St (19806-2327)
PHONE.................302 658-4499
John W Piazza Sr, *Owner*
EMP: 11
SQ FT: 3,000
SALES (est): 717.4K **Privately Held**
SIC: 1521 1542 6513 6514 Single-family home remodeling, additions & repairs; commercial & office buildings, renovation & repair; apartment building operators; dwelling operators, except apartments

(G-11099)
J & W MC CORMICK LTD
Also Called: Maids
508 First State Blvd (19804-3746)
PHONE.................302 798-0336
Wayne Mc Cormick, *President*
Jean Mc Cormick, *Vice Pres*
EMP: 38
SQ FT: 2,500
SALES (est): 635.6K **Privately Held**
SIC: 7349 Maid services, contract or fee basis

(G-11100)
J A E SEAFOOD
403 Philadelphia Pike # 1 (19809-2170)
PHONE.................302 765-2546
Jay Lee, *Owner*
EMP: 40
SALES (est): 2.4MM **Privately Held**
SIC: 5146 Fish & seafoods

(G-11101)
J A MOORE & SONS INC
Also Called: Moore, J A Construction Co
3201 Miller Rd (19802-2542)
PHONE.................302 765-0110
Tom Cekine, *Manager*
EMP: 6
SALES (corp-wide): 1.4MM **Privately Held**
WEB: www.jamooredevelopment.com
SIC: 1542 Nonresidential construction
PA: J A Moore & Sons Inc
20408 Silver Lake Dr A
Rehoboth Beach DE 19971
302 226-8080

(G-11102)
J A PYNE JR DDS PA
4925 Old Capitol Trl (19808-5211)
PHONE.................302 994-7730
J A Pyne Jr DDS, *President*
EMP: 7
SALES (est): 477.8K **Privately Held**
SIC: 8021 Offices & clinics of dentists

(G-11103)
J ALEXANDER PRODUCTIONS LLC
2208 Van Buren Pl (19802-3931)
PHONE.................302 559-6667
J Alexander, *Principal*
EMP: 11

SALES (est): 205.4K **Privately Held**
SIC: 7822 Motion picture & tape distribution

(G-11104)
J E PELLEGRINO & ASSOCIATES
301 Robinson Ln Bldg 1 (19805-4688)
PHONE.................302 655-2565
James E Pellegrino, *President*
Jean L Pellegrino, *Vice Pres*
EMP: 8
SQ FT: 2,500
SALES (est): 870K **Privately Held**
SIC: 1711 Warm air heating & air conditioning contractor

(G-11105)
J E RISPOLI CONTRACTOR INC
402 Hillside Ave (19805-1010)
PHONE.................302 999-1310
Joseph A Rispoli, *President*
Joann Medori, *Corp Secy*
EMP: 25 **EST:** 1964
SQ FT: 5,000
SALES: 1MM **Privately Held**
SIC: 1771 Curb & sidewalk contractors

(G-11106)
J F SOBIESKI MECH CONTRS INC (PA)
Also Called: Sobieski J F Mechanical Contrs
14 Hadco Rd (19804-1014)
PHONE.................302 993-0103
John F Sobieski III, *CEO*
Richard H Steele, *President*
Robert Sobieski, *Vice Pres*
Kim Sobieski, *Purchasing*
Emily Santivasci, *Accountant*
EMP: 123
SQ FT: 25,000
SALES (est): 69.1MM **Privately Held**
WEB: www.sobieskiinc.com
SIC: 1711 Mechanical contractor; fire sprinkler system installation

(G-11107)
J M AJA TRANSPORTATION LLC
524 W Holly Oak Rd (19809-1306)
PHONE.................302 562-6028
Mutasem Ajaj, *President*
EMP: 8
SALES (est): 230.3K **Privately Held**
SIC: 4789 Pipeline terminal facilities, independently operated

(G-11108)
J MICHAEL FAY DDS PA
3105 Limestone Rd Ste 304 (19808-2156)
PHONE.................302 998-2244
Robert G Hahn, *Principal*
Robert Hahn, *Associate*
EMP: 11
SALES (est): 1.3MM **Privately Held**
SIC: 8021 Dentists' office

(G-11109)
J RIHL INC
Also Called: Costa and Rihl Mech Contrs
3518 Silverside Rd Ste 22 (19810-4907)
PHONE.................856 778-5899
John Rihl, *President*
EMP: 6
SALES (est): 649.5K **Privately Held**
SIC: 1711 Plumbing, heating, air-conditioning contractors

(G-11110)
J S MCKELVEY DDS
Also Called: Dental Health Assoc Pike Creek
4901 Limestone Rd (19808-1271)
PHONE.................302 239-0303
J S McKelvey DDS, *Owner*
Tj Hammer, *COO*
EMP: 15
SALES (est): 1.1MM **Privately Held**
SIC: 8021 Dentists' office

(G-11111)
J STACHON PLUMBING LLC
1311 Hillside Blvd (19803-4234)
PHONE.................302 998-0938
EMP: 4
SALES (est): 253.1K **Privately Held**
SIC: 1711 Plumbing contractors

(G-11112)
J V AUTO SERVICE INC
1500 W Newport Pike (19804-3546)
PHONE.................302 999-0786
Joseph Van Sant, *President*
Cheryl Vansant, *Corp Secy*
EMP: 10
SQ FT: 1,600
SALES (est): 1.2MM **Privately Held**
WEB: www.jvautoservice.com
SIC: 7538 General automotive repair shops

(G-11113)
JABEZ CORP
Also Called: Haldas Brothers
2201 Silverside Rd (19810-4501)
PHONE.................302 475-7600
John Eleutheriou, *President*
EMP: 12 **EST:** 1959
SQ FT: 2,000
SALES (est): 1MM **Privately Held**
SIC: 5421 5144 Meat markets, including freezer provisioners; poultry & poultry products

(G-11114)
JACK LEWIS
Also Called: State Farm Insurance
2018 Naamans Rd Ste A4 (19810-2660)
P.O. Box 1517 (19899-1517)
PHONE.................302 475-2010
EMP: 6
SALES (est): 731.8K **Privately Held**
SIC: 6411 Insurance agents & brokers

(G-11115)
JACK PARISI TILE CO INC
2319 Frederick Ave (19805-2257)
PHONE.................302 892-2455
Jack Parisi, *President*
EMP: 4 **EST:** 2009
SALES (est): 373.6K **Privately Held**
SIC: 5211 5032 1743 Tile, ceramic; tile & clay products; tile installation, ceramic

(G-11116)
JACK SAXTON CONSTRUCTION CO
1228 Evergreen Rd (19803-3514)
PHONE.................302 764-5683
John Saxton, *President*
EMP: 4
SALES (est): 414.7K **Privately Held**
SIC: 1521 General remodeling, single-family houses

(G-11117)
JACOBS & CRUMPLAR PA
750 Shipyard Dr Ste 200 (19801-5160)
PHONE.................302 656-5445
Robert Jacobs, *President*
Thomas C Crumplar, *Vice Pres*
Thomas Crumplar, *Vice Pres*
Marla R Eskin,
EMP: 25 **EST:** 1981
SQ FT: 1,000
SALES (est): 3.1MM **Privately Held**
SIC: 8111 General practice law office; specialized law offices, attorneys

(G-11118)
JAMARK ENTERPRISES INC
Also Called: Natural Lawn of America
40 Germay Dr (19804-1105)
PHONE.................302 652-2000
Katherine Yates, *President*
Rick Yates, *Principal*
EMP: 10
SALES: 500K **Privately Held**
SIC: 0782 Lawn care services

(G-11119)
JAMES & JESSES BARBR & BUTY SP
Also Called: James Jesses Barbr Maudes Buty
931 Bennett St Ste 933 (19801-4309)
PHONE.................302 658-9617
Jesse Dandy, *Owner*
EMP: 5
SQ FT: 1,500
SALES (est): 168.1K **Privately Held**
SIC: 7231 Cosmetologist

(G-11120)
JAMES FIERRO DO PA
1805 Foulk Rd Ste F (19810-3700)
PHONE.................302 529-2255
James D Fierro, *Owner*
EMP: 5
SALES (est): 726.8K **Privately Held**
SIC: 8011 General & family practice, physician/surgeon

(G-11121)
JAMES H HAYS MD
4512 Kirkwood Hwy Ste 302 (19808-5122)
PHONE.................302 633-1212
James H Hays MD, *Owner*
Pramod Yadhati, *Partner*
EMP: 4
SALES (est): 239.8K **Privately Held**
SIC: 8011 Endocrinologist

(G-11122)
JAMES L HOLZMAN
Also Called: Prickett Jones & Elliott
1310 N King St (19801-3220)
P.O. Box 1328 (19899-1328)
PHONE.................302 888-6500
James Holzman, *Partner*
Paul Fioravanti, *Director*
EMP: 45
SALES (est): 2.9MM **Privately Held**
SIC: 8111 General practice attorney, lawyer

(G-11123)
JAMES STEWART ROSTOCKI
14 Westover Cir (19807-2975)
PHONE.................302 250-5541
Jennifer M Murphy, *CEO*
EMP: 5
SALES (est): 265K **Privately Held**
SIC: 7389

(G-11124)
JAMES T CHANDLER & SON INC (PA)
Also Called: Chandler Funeral Homes
2506 Concord Pike (19803-5003)
PHONE.................302 478-7100
James T Chandler IV, *President*
Duwayne Casini, *Principal*
Chad H Chandler, *Treasurer*
Vivienne Delano, *Accountant*
Debbie Wesselman, *Manager*
EMP: 15
SQ FT: 7,500
SALES (est): 2.1MM **Privately Held**
WEB: www.chandlerfuneralhome.com
SIC: 7261 Funeral home; crematory

(G-11125)
JAMES TIGANI III DDS
1021 Gilpin Ave Ste 205 (19806-3272)
PHONE.................302 571-8740
James Tigani III DMD, *Owner*
Clark Edrianne, *Manager*
EMP: 13
SALES (est): 810K **Privately Held**
SIC: 8021 Dentists' office

(G-11126)
JAMIE H KESKENY
1600 Rockland Rd (19803-3607)
PHONE.................302 651-6060
Jamie H Keskeny, *Principal*
EMP: 4 **EST:** 2013
SALES (est): 124.3K **Privately Held**
SIC: 8069 Eye, ear, nose & throat hospital

(G-11127)
JAN STERN EQINE ASSSTED THRAPY
112 Shinn Cir (19808-1114)
PHONE.................302 234-9835
James Stern, *Principal*
EMP: 5
SALES (est): 110.7K **Privately Held**
SIC: 8093 Rehabilitation center, outpatient treatment

(G-11128)
JANET HUGHES AND ASSOCIATES
Also Called: Hughes & Associates
203 Plymouth Rd (19803-3116)
PHONE.................302 656-5252

GEOGRAPHIC SECTION

Wilmington - New Castle County (G-11161)

Janet Hughes, *President*
Kent Devries, *Office Mgr*
EMP: 10
SQ FT: 3,800
SALES (est): 1.3MM **Privately Held**
WEB: www.janethughes.com
SIC: 7311 Advertising consultant

(G-11129)
JANIS DICRISTOFARO DAY CARE
1104 Arundel Dr (19808-2135)
PHONE 302 998-6630
Janis Dichristofaro, *Principal*
EMP: 6
SALES (est): 73.4K **Privately Held**
SIC: 8351 Child day care services

(G-11130)
JAVED GILANI MD
1309 Veale Rd Ste 11 (19810-4609)
PHONE 302 478-7160
Javed Gilani MD, *Principal*
EMP: 4
SALES (est): 271.9K **Privately Held**
SIC: 8049 8099 Offices of health practitioner; health & allied services

(G-11131)
JAY D LUFTY MD
2300 Penns Ave Ste 2a (19806-1379)
PHONE 302 658-0404
William Medford, *Partner*
Jay Lufty, *Principal*
EMP: 10
SALES (est): 560K **Privately Held**
SIC: 8011 Offices & clinics of medical doctors

(G-11132)
JAY GUNDEL AND ASSOCIATES INC
2502 Silverside Rd Ste 8 (19810-3740)
PHONE 302 658-1674
Jay Gundel, *President*
Susan Gundel, *Treasurer*
EMP: 5
SALES (est): 895.6K **Privately Held**
WEB: www.jaygundel.com
SIC: 7311 Advertising consultant

(G-11133)
JAYSONS LLC
Also Called: Surestay
1807 Concord Pike (19803-2901)
PHONE 302 656-9436
Mary Taylor, *General Mgr*
Mike Khatiwala,
Dilip Ghandi,
Minesh Patel,
Prerna Patel,
EMP: 30
SQ FT: 44,400
SALES (est): 1.2MM **Privately Held**
SIC: 7011 Hotels & motels

(G-11134)
JAYU LLC
501 Silverside Rd 345 (19809-1374)
PHONE 888 534-3018
Benjamin Sena, *Principal*
Ronald Joven, *Principal*
Soojae Jung, *Principal*
EMP: 10
SALES (est): 180.6K **Privately Held**
SIC: 7389

(G-11135)
JBS CONTRACTING
2211 Bradmoor Rd (19803-3018)
PHONE 302 543-7264
EMP: 5
SALES (est): 240K **Privately Held**
SIC: 1799 Special trade contractors

(G-11136)
JC ZIMNY ROD CO
106 Whitekirk Dr (19808-1349)
PHONE 302 998-9187
John Zimny, *Owner*
EMP: 1 EST: 2001
SALES (est): 12.5K **Privately Held**
WEB: www.bamboorods.com
SIC: 3949 Rods & rod parts, fishing

(G-11137)
JEANDAR MASONRY CONSTRUCTION
5905 Old Capitol Trl (19808-4836)
PHONE 302 994-2616
Darryl Remedio, *President*
EMP: 4
SALES (est): 290K **Privately Held**
SIC: 1741 Masonry & other stonework

(G-11138)
JEANETTE Y SON DENTIST
2601 Annand Dr Ste 8 (19808-3719)
PHONE 302 998-8283
Jeanette Y Son, *Owner*
EMP: 5
SALES (est): 322.2K **Privately Held**
SIC: 8021 Dentists' office

(G-11139)
JEB PLASTICS INC
3521 Silverside Rd 2i-1 (19810-4900)
PHONE 302 479-9223
Robert Rosini, *President*
Kathryn Rosini, *Treasurer*
EMP: 3
SQ FT: 720
SALES: 500K **Privately Held**
WEB: www.jebplastics.com
SIC: 2673 2759 Bags: plastic, laminated & coated; plastic & pliofilm bags; plastic bags: made from purchased materials; bags, plastic: printing

(G-11140)
JEDI INC (PA)
Also Called: Lawn Doctor Aston-Middletown
409 Nichols Ave (19803-5233)
P.O. Box 901, Concordville PA (19331-0901)
PHONE 610 459-4477
Jesse Wooleyhan, *President*
Diane L Wooleyhan, *Corp Secy*
EMP: 5 EST: 1978
SALES (est): 674.7K **Privately Held**
SIC: 0782 Lawn care services

(G-11141)
JEENA M JOLLY DDS
217 W 9th St (19801-1619)
PHONE 302 655-2626
Jeena Jolly, *Principal*
EMP: 4
SALES (est): 84.9K **Privately Held**
SIC: 8021 Dentists' office

(G-11142)
JEFF EZELL DR
20 Westover Cir (19807-2975)
PHONE 302 654-5955
Jeff Ezell, *Principal*
EMP: 5
SALES (est): 153.6K **Privately Held**
SIC: 8011 Offices & clinics of medical doctors

(G-11143)
JEFF THOMAS
Also Called: Texaco
4201 N Market St (19802-2223)
PHONE 302 762-9154
Fax: 302 762-8431
EMP: 7
SALES (est): 800K **Privately Held**
SIC: 5541 5411 3589 Gasoline Service Station Ret Groceries Mfg Service Industry Machinery

(G-11144)
JEFFREY K MARTIN PC
1508 Penns Ave Ste 1c (19806-4347)
PHONE 302 777-4681
EMP: 4
SALES (est): 340K **Privately Held**
SIC: 8111 Legal Services Office

(G-11145)
JENNER ENTERPRISES INC (PA)
Also Called: JENNER ENTERPRISES/DBA FASTSIGNS
1300 First State Blvd (19804-3548)
P.O. Box 5471 (19808-0471)
PHONE 302 998-6755
Michael P Levitsky, *President*
Michael Levitsky, *President*
Janet Levitsky, *Corp Secy*
EMP: 17
SQ FT: 1,500
SALES (est): 2.2MM **Privately Held**
SIC: 3993 Signs & advertising specialties

(G-11146)
JENNER ENTERPRISES INC
Also Called: Fastsigns
3203 Concord Pike (19803-5036)
PHONE 302 479-5686
Robert Bartow, *Manager*
EMP: 2
SALES (corp-wide): 2.2MM **Privately Held**
SIC: 3993 Signs & advertising specialties
PA: Jenner Enterprises Inc
1300 First State Blvd
Wilmington DE 19804
302 998-6755

(G-11147)
JENNIFER L JOSEPH DDS
5317 Limestone Rd Ste 2 (19808-1252)
PHONE 302 239-6677
Jennifer Joseph, *Executive*
EMP: 4 EST: 2015
SALES (est): 92.4K **Privately Held**
SIC: 8021 Dentists' office

(G-11148)
JENNS TAIL WAGGERS
8 Carpenter Plz (19810-2049)
PHONE 302 475-9621
Jenn Schmidt, *Owner*
EMP: 10
SALES (est): 340.8K **Privately Held**
SIC: 0752 Grooming services, pet & animal specialties

(G-11149)
JENNY CRAIG WGHT LOSS CTRS INC
4447 Concord Pike (19803-1489)
PHONE 302 477-9202
Camille Nuccio, *Director*
EMP: 5
SALES (corp-wide): 127MM **Privately Held**
SIC: 7299 Diet center, without medical staff
HQ: Jenny Craig Weight Loss Centers, Inc.
5770 Fleet St
Carlsbad CA 92008

(G-11150)
JENRIN DISCOVERY LLC
2515 Lori Ln N (19810-3445)
PHONE 302 379-1679
John F McElroy, *Branch Mgr*
EMP: 5
SALES (est): 362K
SALES (corp-wide): 1.2MM **Privately Held**
SIC: 8731 Biotechnical research, commercial
PA: Jenrin Discovery, Llc
1193 Killarney Ln
West Chester PA 19382
302 379-1679

(G-11151)
JET PRODUCTS LLC (PA)
2207 Concord Pike 640 (19803-2908)
PHONE 877 453-8868
Jim Wambaugh,
▲ **EMP:** 8
SQ FT: 25,000
SALES: 2.5MM **Privately Held**
SIC: 5032 Cement

(G-11152)
JEWISH COMMUNITY CENTER INC
Also Called: J C C Fitness Center
101 Grde Of Eden Rd 102 (19803)
PHONE 302 478-5660
Connie Sugarman, *President*
Amy Levtion, *President*
Robert Davis, *Vice Pres*
Nan Lipstein, *Vice Pres*
Martin Lubaroff, *Vice Pres*
EMP: 35
SQ FT: 15,000
SALES: 5.1MM **Privately Held**
SIC: 8322 Community center

(G-11153)
JEWISH FEDERATION OF DELAWARE
101 Garden Of Eden Rd (19803-1511)
PHONE 302 478-5660
Barry Kayne, *President*
Sam Asher, *Vice Pres*
EMP: 13
SALES (est): 4.8MM **Privately Held**
WEB: www.shalomdel.org
SIC: 8399 8661 Advocacy group; religious organizations

(G-11154)
JGARVEY ENTERPRISES INC
Also Called: Certapro Painters of Delaware
405 Old Dupont Rd (19804-1258)
P.O. Box 3365 (19804-4365)
PHONE 302 562-7282
Jeff Garvey, *President*
EMP: 4
SQ FT: 1,200
SALES: 1.1MM **Privately Held**
SIC: 1721 Interior residential painting contractor; interior commercial painting contractor

(G-11155)
JI DCI JOINT VENTURE 1
1211 Delaware Ave (19806-4716)
PHONE 302 652-4221
Paul Johnstone, *Co-Venturer*
Joseph Chickadel, *Co-Venturer*
EMP: 8 EST: 2013
SALES (est): 368.3K **Privately Held**
SIC: 8712 Architectural services

(G-11156)
JI DCI JV-II
1211 Delaware Ave (19806-4716)
PHONE 302 652-4221
Paul Johnstone, *Partner*
Leigh P Johnstone, *Principal*
Joseph Chickadel, *Principal*
EMP: 12 EST: 2015
SALES (est): 462.9K **Privately Held**
SIC: 8712 8711 0781 7389 Architectural services; engineering services; landscape counseling & planning; building inspection service; interior design services

(G-11157)
JILL DUSAK
1815 W 13th St Ste 1 (19806-4054)
PHONE 302 652-4705
Jill Dusak, *Manager*
EMP: 8 EST: 2017
SALES (est): 65.7K **Privately Held**
SIC: 8049 Offices of health practitioner

(G-11158)
JILL GARRIDO DDS
2000 Foulk Rd Ste C (19810-3642)
PHONE 302 475-3110
Jill Garrido, *Principal*
EMP: 4
SALES (est): 67.6K **Privately Held**
SIC: 8021 Offices & clinics of dentists

(G-11159)
JILLANN I HOUNSELL DDS
2300 Penns Ave Ste 6a (19806-1301)
PHONE 302 691-3000
Jillann Hounsell, *Executive*
EMP: 4 EST: 2017
SALES (est): 61.5K **Privately Held**
SIC: 8021 Offices & clinics of dentists

(G-11160)
JIM KOUNNAS OPTOMETRISTS (PA)
501 Silverside Rd (19809-1374)
PHONE 302 722-6197
Jim Kounnas, *President*
EMP: 7 EST: 2001
SQ FT: 2,500
SALES: 2.2MM **Privately Held**
SIC: 3851 5995 5048 Frames, lenses & parts, eyeglass & spectacle; eyeglasses, prescription; frames, ophthalmic

(G-11161)
JJS INDUSTRIES LP
2424 E Parris Dr (19808-4508)
PHONE 302 690-2957

Wilmington - New Castle County (G-11162)   GEOGRAPHIC SECTION

EMP: 2
SALES (est): 110.8K Privately Held
SIC: 3999 Manufacturing industries

(G-11162)
JNI CCC JV1
2317 Pennsylvania Ave (19806-1318)
PHONE.................................302 654-6611
Angela Ilis, *Principal*
Paul L Johnstone,
Ben Vinton,
Benjamin Vinton,
EMP: 4
SALES (est): 950K Privately Held
SIC: 1542 7389 Nonresidential construction;

(G-11163)
JOBS FOR DELAWARE GRADUATES (PA)
5157 W Woodmill Dr Ste 16 (19808-4067)
PHONE.................................302 995-7175
Sue Lee, *President*
EMP: 4
SALES: 3.9MM Privately Held
WEB: www.jobsfordelawaregraduates.org
SIC: 8331 Job training services

(G-11164)
JOE FALCO PORTABLE WELDING
4517 Roslyn Dr (19804-4016)
PHONE.................................302 998-1115
Joe Falco, *President*
EMP: 1
SALES (est): 135.6K Privately Held
SIC: 7692 Welding repair

(G-11165)
JOE GERACE
Also Called: Gerace Signs
3315 Elizabeth Ave (19808-6106)
PHONE.................................302 994-3114
Joe Gerace, *Owner*
EMP: 1
SALES (est): 72.4K Privately Held
SIC: 3993 Signs & advertising specialties

(G-11166)
JOES BARBER SHOP
2505 Concord Pike Ste 1 (19803-5029)
PHONE.................................302 478-2837
Joseph Gioggre, *Owner*
EMP: 4
SALES (est): 49.1K Privately Held
SIC: 7241 Barber shops

(G-11167)
JOHN B FONTANA JR DDS
1708 Lovering Ave Ste 101 (19806-2141)
PHONE.................................302 656-2434
John B Fontana Jr DDS, *Owner*
EMP: 4
SALES (est): 315K Privately Held
SIC: 8021 Endodontist

(G-11168)
JOHN E SULLIVAN
5305 Limestone Rd Ste 200 (19808-1247)
PHONE.................................302 234-6855
John E Sullivan, *Owner*
EMP: 4
SALES (est): 317.6K Privately Held
SIC: 8111 General practice attorney, lawyer

(G-11169)
JOHN F YASIK FUNERAL SERVICES
1900 Delaware Ave (19806-2302)
PHONE.................................302 428-9986
EMP: 4 EST: 2017
SALES (est): 61.4K Privately Held
SIC: 7261 Funeral home

(G-11170)
JOHN F YASIK INC
Also Called: Yasik, John F & Son
607 S Harrison St (19805-4305)
P.O. Box 5133 (19808-0133)
PHONE.................................302 652-5114
Stephanie A Yasik, *President*
John F Yasik Jr, *Corp Secy*
John F Yasik III, *Vice Pres*
EMP: 4

SALES (est): 447.4K Privately Held
SIC: 7261 Funeral home

(G-11171)
JOHN HOCUTT JR MD
3521 Silverside Rd Ste 2b (19810-4900)
PHONE.................................302 475-7800
John Hocutt Jr, *Owner*
EMP: 6
SALES (est): 430K Privately Held
SIC: 8011 8043 General & family practice, physician/surgeon; offices & clinics of podiatrists

(G-11172)
JOHN J BUCKLEY ASSOCIATES INC
105 Farm Ave (19810-2926)
PHONE.................................302 475-5443
John J Buckley, *President*
Sheila B Buckley, *Corp Secy*
EMP: 2
SALES: 600K Privately Held
SIC: 2819 5084 Industrial inorganic chemicals; cleaning equipment, high pressure, sand or steam

(G-11173)
JOHN J THALER II DDS
3512 Silverside Rd Ste 13 (19810-4913)
PHONE.................................302 478-9000
EMP: 4
SALES (est): 61.5K Privately Held
SIC: 8021 Offices And Clinics Of Dentists

(G-11174)
JOHN JOHNSON DR
325 S Dupont St (19805-3916)
PHONE.................................302 999-7104
John Johnson, *Principal*
EMP: 4
SALES (est): 95K Privately Held
SIC: 8011 8049 Physicians' office, including specialists; offices of health practitioner

(G-11175)
JOHN N RUSSO DDS
300 Foulk Rd Ste 101 (19803-3819)
PHONE.................................302 652-3775
John Russo, *Owner*
Mary C Russo, *Agent*
EMP: 14
SALES (est): 481.9K Privately Held
SIC: 8021 Dentists' office

(G-11176)
JOHN WILLIAMS PA
1225 N King St Ste 700 (19801-3246)
PHONE.................................302 571-4780
John Williams, *President*
EMP: 4
SALES (est): 388.3K Privately Held
SIC: 8111 General practice attorney, lawyer

(G-11177)
JOHNS BODY SHOP INC
2302 W 3rd St (19805)
PHONE.................................302 658-5133
Guy De Bonaventura, *President*
Neal De Bonaventura, *Principal*
Amelia De Bonaventura, *Corp Secy*
EMP: 17
SQ FT: 10,000
SALES: 1.7MM Privately Held
SIC: 7532 Body shop, automotive

(G-11178)
JOHNS LANDSCAPING
2306 W Newport Pike C (19804-3851)
PHONE.................................302 507-4773
John Ginder, *Owner*
EMP: 4
SALES: 48K Privately Held
SIC: 0782 Landscape contractors

(G-11179)
JOHNSON & JOHNSON
500 Swedes Landing Rd (19801-4417)
PHONE.................................302 652-3840
Kenneth Cook, *President*
EMP: 48

SALES (corp-wide): 81.5B Publicly Held
WEB: www.jnj.com
SIC: 3842 Dressings, surgical
PA: Johnson & Johnson
1 Johnson And Johnson Plz
New Brunswick NJ 08933
732 524-0400

(G-11180)
JON IRBY III
204 W 21st St (19802-4006)
PHONE.................................302 652-0564
Jon Irby III, *Owner*
EMP: 4
SALES (est): 121.3K Privately Held
SIC: 7389 Business services

(G-11181)
JONES ENTERPRISES INCORPORATED
1521 Concord Pike Ste 301 (19803-3644)
PHONE.................................888 639-1194
Joe Jones, *CEO*
EMP: 6 EST: 2014
SALES (est): 384K Privately Held
SIC: 6531 Real estate brokers & agents

(G-11182)
JONMOR INVESTMENTS INC
3411 Silverside Rd 103 (19810-4812)
PHONE.................................302 477-1380
Tom Ottinger, *Controller*
EMP: 4 EST: 2011
SALES (est): 162K Privately Held
SIC: 8111 Patent, trademark & copyright law

(G-11183)
JOSE D MANALO MD PA INC
Also Called: Family Medical Associates
2300 Penns Ave Ste 1a (19806-1333)
PHONE.................................302 655-0355
Fax: 302 651-9462
EMP: 7 EST: 1984
SALES (est): 480K Privately Held
SIC: 8011 Medical Doctor's Office

(G-11184)
JOSEPH A HURLEY PA
1215 N King St (19801-3285)
PHONE.................................302 658-8980
Joseph Hurley, *Owner*
EMP: 7
SALES (est): 552.5K Privately Held
SIC: 8111 General practice attorney, lawyer

(G-11185)
JOSEPH A KUHN MD LLC
102 Haywood Rd (19807-1114)
PHONE.................................302 656-3801
Joseph A Kuhn MD, *Owner*
EMP: 5
SALES (est): 92.5K Privately Held
SIC: 8011 Offices & clinics of medical doctors

(G-11186)
JOSEPH A SANTILLO INC
2403 E Parris Dr (19808-4507)
PHONE.................................302 661-7313
Carmilla R Santillo, *President*
Carmella S Santillo, *President*
Joseph A Santillo, *Vice Pres*
EMP: 6
SALES (est): 860K Privately Held
SIC: 1542 Commercial & office buildings, renovation & repair

(G-11187)
JOSEPH BRYER MD
2300 Penns Ave Ste 3b (19806-1333)
PHONE.................................302 426-9440
Joseph Bryer, *Owner*
EMP: 4
SALES (est): 176.8K Privately Held
WEB: www.josephbryer.com
SIC: 8011 Internal medicine, physician/surgeon

(G-11188)
JOSEPH C KELLY DDS
2205 Silverside Rd Ste 2 (19810-4534)
PHONE.................................302 475-5555
Joe Creazzo, *Manager*

EMP: 7 EST: 2017
SALES (est): 93K Privately Held
SIC: 8021 Offices & clinics of dentists

(G-11189)
JOSEPH E STEVENS & FATHER
715 Melrose Ave (19809-2659)
PHONE.................................302 654-8556
Joseph E Stevens, *President*
Joseph Stevens Sr, *Vice Pres*
Denise Stevens, *Admin Sec*
EMP: 6
SALES (est): 451.1K Privately Held
SIC: 1751 1521 1522 Carpentry work; new construction, single-family houses; multi-family dwellings, new construction

(G-11190)
JOSEPH F SPERA DMD PA
2101 Foulk Rd (19810-4710)
PHONE.................................302 475-1122
Dr Joseph F Spera, *Owner*
EMP: 6
SQ FT: 1,600
SALES (est): 400K Privately Held
SIC: 8021 Dental surgeon; maxillofacial specialist

(G-11191)
JOSEPH G GOLDBERG OD
801 E Newport Pike (19804-1920)
PHONE.................................302 999-1286
Joseph G Goldberg Od, *Owner*
EMP: 7
SALES (est): 415.4K Privately Held
SIC: 8011 8042 Offices & clinics of medical doctors; offices & clinics of optometrists

(G-11192)
JOSEPH J DANYO MD
3701 Kennett Pike 400b (19807-2162)
PHONE.................................302 888-0508
Joseph Danyo, *Owner*
EMP: 6
SALES (est): 727.9K Privately Held
WEB: www.danyoplasticsurgery.com
SIC: 8011 Plastic surgeon

(G-11193)
JOSEPH LONGOBARDI ATTY
1303 Delaware Ave Ste 115 (19806-3421)
PHONE.................................302 575-1502
Joseph Longobardi, *Owner*
EMP: 4
SALES (est): 450.2K Privately Held
SIC: 8111 General practice attorney, lawyer

(G-11194)
JOSEPH MOORE
Also Called: Jobs By Joe
1412 Athens Rd (19803-5112)
PHONE.................................302 478-5659
Joseph Moore, *Principal*
EMP: 5
SALES (est): 456.7K Privately Held
SIC: 7361 Employment agencies

(G-11195)
JOSEPH W BENSON PA
1701 N Market St (19802-4808)
P.O. Box 248 (19899-0248)
PHONE.................................302 656-8811
Joseph W Benson, *President*
EMP: 7
SALES (est): 713.3K Privately Held
WEB: www.jwbpa.com
SIC: 8111 General practice attorney, lawyer

(G-11196)
JOSHUA A BECK
2205 Rvera Ln Hlliday Hls Holliday Hls (19810)
PHONE.................................302 529-9426
Joshua A Beck, *Principal*
EMP: 6 EST: 2010
SALES (est): 312K Privately Held
SIC: 8999 Services

(G-11197)
JOTO INC
1209 N Orange St (19801-1120)
PHONE.................................260 337-3362
Danny Freeman, *CEO*

GEOGRAPHIC SECTION   Wilmington - New Castle County (G-11228)

EMP: 1
SALES (est): 67K **Privately Held**
SIC: 7372 Application computer software

(G-11198)
JOURNEYS LLC
5201 W Wdmill Dr Ste 31ll (19808)
PHONE.................................302 384-7843
Rebecca Trent, *Principal*
EMP: 6
SALES (est): 386.8K **Privately Held**
SIC: 4724 Travel agencies

(G-11199)
JOY CLEANERS INC
301 Greenhill Ave (19805-1846)
PHONE.................................302 656-3537
Harry Amey, *Owner*
EMP: 8
SALES: 559.4K **Privately Held**
SIC: 7216 7219 Drycleaning plants, except rugs; fur garment cleaning, repairing & storage

(G-11200)
JOYCE CO
3 Mill Rd (19806-2146)
PHONE.................................302 353-4011
EMP: 50
SALES: 50MM **Privately Held**
SIC: 6799 Investor

(G-11201)
JPMORGAN CHASE BANK NAT ASSN
300 N King St (19801-2524)
PHONE.................................302 282-1624
Willam Garner, *Branch Mgr*
EMP: 26
SALES (corp-wide): 131.4B **Publicly Held**
WEB: www.chase.com
SIC: 6022 State commercial banks
HQ: Jpmorgan Chase Bank, National Association
    1111 Polaris Pkwy
    Columbus OH 43240
    614 436-3055

(G-11202)
JR GETTIER & ASSOCIATES INC
Also Called: Gettier Security
2 Centerville Rd (19808-4708)
P.O. Box 5251 (19808-0251)
PHONE.................................302 478-0911
Jim Gettier, *CEO*
Lou Manerchia, *President*
John Dillon, *Vice Pres*
Lou Manchier, *Financial Exec*
Donavon Davis, *Manager*
EMP: 500
SQ FT: 4,500
SALES (est): 11.2MM **Privately Held**
WEB: www.gettier.com
SIC: 7381 8748 Private investigator; guard services; business consulting

(G-11203)
JRW CLEANING SOLUTIONS LLC
2405 N Madison St (19802-3437)
PHONE.................................484 942-9995
Whitney Gillis, *Owner*
EMP: 5
SALES (est): 47K **Privately Held**
SIC: 7349 Building & office cleaning services

(G-11204)
JSF CONSTRUCTION CO INC
316 Main St (19804-3907)
PHONE.................................302 999-9573
James Fulghum, *President*
Morine Fulghum, *Vice Pres*
EMP: 6
SQ FT: 1,500
SALES: 1.5MM **Privately Held**
SIC: 1521 1761 1731 1711 New construction, single-family houses; patio & deck construction & repair; roofing contractor; siding contractor; general electrical contractor; warm air heating & air conditioning contractor; ventilation & duct work contractor

(G-11205)
JSTANLEY SALON
204 N Union St (19805-3430)
PHONE.................................302 778-1885
EMP: 4
SALES (est): 26.6K **Privately Held**
SIC: 7241 Barber shops

(G-11206)
JTHAN LLC
7 Meco Cir (19804-1108)
PHONE.................................302 994-2534
Joseph Nitsche,
EMP: 9
SALES (est): 182.9K **Privately Held**
SIC: 7389 Business services

(G-11207)
JUMPIN JACKS
508 E 35th St (19802-2818)
PHONE.................................302 762-7604
Jackie Bowers, *Owner*
Jackie Locket, *Owner*
EMP: 5
SALES (est): 78.5K **Privately Held**
SIC: 8351 Child day care services

(G-11208)
JUNEBUGS LITTLE RUBIES LLC
1104-1106 D St (19801)
PHONE.................................302 494-7552
Cher-Ron Truitt,
EMP: 7 EST: 2017 **Privately Held**
SIC: 8351 Child day care services

(G-11209)
JUNI HOLDINGS INC
251 Little Falls Dr (19808-1674)
PHONE.................................415 949-4860
Robert Lamptey, *Principal*
EMP: 12
SALES: 200K **Privately Held**
SIC: 6099 7371 Money order issuance; computer software development & applications

(G-11210)
JUNIPER BANK
100 S West St (19801-5015)
PHONE.................................302 255-8000
Erik Toivonen, *Principal*
Bill Spurlock, *Manager*
Jim Stewart, *Executive*
EMP: 11
SALES (est): 1.9MM **Privately Held**
SIC: 6099 Functions related to deposit banking

(G-11211)
JUWELO USA INC
1000 N West St Ste 1200 (19801-1058)
PHONE.................................888 471-7614
EMP: 7
SALES (est): 667.3K
SALES (corp-wide): 56.6MM **Privately Held**
SIC: 3911 Jewelry, precious metal
PA: Elumeo Se
    Erkelenzdamm 59-61
    Berlin 10999
    306 959-790

(G-11212)
JW TULL CONTRACTING SVCS LLC
1203 Philadelphia Pike (19809-2032)
PHONE.................................302 494-8179
William Tull,
EMP: 10
SALES: 1.5MM **Privately Held**
SIC: 1799 1761 1542 Antenna installation; roofing, siding & sheet metal work; commercial & office buildings, renovation & repair

(G-11213)
K AND L GATES
600 N King St Ste 901 (19801-3777)
P.O. Box 2899, Martinsburg WV (25402-2899)
PHONE.................................302 416-7000
Steven L Caponi, *Partner*
Eric N Feldman, *Partner*
Nicholas I Froio, *Partner*
Andrew Skouvakis, *Partner*
Lisa R Stark, *Partner*
EMP: 5 EST: 2017
SALES (est): 474.5K **Privately Held**
SIC: 8742 8111 Corporate objectives & policies consultant; corporation organizing; business consultant; financial consultant; corporate, partnership & business law

(G-11214)
K C WEAVER AND SONS INC
108 E Keystone Ave (19804-2026)
PHONE.................................302 994-8399
Kenneth Weaver Sr, *Owner*
Jennifer Weaver, *Treasurer*
EMP: 6
SALES (est): 407K **Privately Held**
SIC: 1711 Plumbing contractors

(G-11215)
K F DUNN & ASSOCIATES
819 N Washington St (19801-1509)
PHONE.................................302 328-3347
Kathleen F Dunn, *President*
EMP: 11
SALES (est): 805.2K **Privately Held**
WEB: www.kfdunn.com
SIC: 7311 Advertising agencies

(G-11216)
K&B INVESTORS LLC
Also Called: Lawfully Yours
1908 Oak Lane Rd (19803-5215)
P.O. Box 7346 (19803-0346)
PHONE.................................302 357-9723
Brian K Harris, *Mng Member*
K'June Evans-Harris, *Manager*
EMP: 2
SALES (est): 140K **Privately Held**
SIC: 6798 2679 7929 Real estate investment trusts; gift wrap & novelties, paper; entertainment service

(G-11217)
K-TRON INVESTMENT CO (DH)
300 Delaware Ave Ste 900 (19801-1671)
PHONE.................................856 589-0500
Kenneth Camp, *President*
Dorit Bannett, *Treasurer*
Barry Wallace, *Technical Staff*
Pamela Jasinski, *Admin Sec*
▼ EMP: 45
SQ FT: 1,200
SALES (est): 102.2MM **Publicly Held**
SIC: 3823 Industrial process control instruments
HQ: K-Tron International, Inc.
    590 Woodbury Glassboro Rd
    Sewell NJ 08080
    856 589-0500

(G-11218)
K2 ADVANCED MEDIA LLC (PA)
108 W 13th St (19802)
PHONE.................................408 305-7007
Aaron C Huber, *Principal*
EMP: 3
SALES (est): 15.7MM **Privately Held**
SIC: 2711 Newspapers, publishing & printing

(G-11219)
K9 NATURAL FOODS USA LLC
108 W 13th St (19801)
PHONE.................................855 596-2887
Audry Henniger,
EMP: 27
SALES (est): 648.1K **Privately Held**
SIC: 3999 Pet supplies

(G-11220)
KAHL COMPANY INC
3526 Silverside Rd Ste 38 (19810-4901)
PHONE.................................302 478-8450
Louis R Kahl, *President*
EMP: 6
SQ FT: 2,000
SALES (est): 1.1MM **Privately Held**
SIC: 5084 Chemical process equipment

(G-11221)
KALEIDO HEALTH SOLUTIONS INC
2810 N Church St (19802-4447)
P.O. Box 21789, Charleston SC (29413-1789)
PHONE.................................908 721-7020
Jill Balderson, *CEO*
EMP: 5 EST: 2017
SALES (est): 142.4K **Privately Held**
SIC: 7371 Computer software development & applications

(G-11222)
KALMAR INVESTMENTS INC
3701 Kennett Pike Ste 100 (19807-2163)
P.O. Box 4157 (19807-0157)
PHONE.................................302 658-7575
Ford B Draper Jr, *President*
Brian D Draper, *Corp Secy*
James E Gowen, *Portfolio Mgr*
Steffen J Torres, *Portfolio Mgr*
Marjorie L McMenamin, *Sales Executive*
EMP: 27
SQ FT: 5,000
SALES (est): 8.1MM **Privately Held**
WEB: www.kalmarinvestments.com
SIC: 6282 Investment advisory service

(G-11223)
KALMAR NYCKEL FOUNDATION
1124 E 7th St (19801-4509)
PHONE.................................302 429-7447
Richard Julian, *President*
George C Hering III, *Chairman*
Sharon Litcofsky, *Port Captain*
Martin B McDonough, *Treasurer*
C Parsells, *Exec Dir*
EMP: 6
SALES: 1.3MM **Privately Held**
WEB: www.kalmarnyckel.org
SIC: 8412 Museums & art galleries

(G-11224)
KANKANA LLC
1201 N Orange St Ste 600 (19801-1171)
PHONE.................................302 597-6998
EMP: 1
SALES (est): 35K **Privately Held**
SIC: 7372 Prepackaged Software Services

(G-11225)
KARDMASTER GRAPHICS
24 Colony Blvd (19802-1402)
PHONE.................................610 434-5262
William Snyder, *President*
EMP: 25
SQ FT: 1,200
SALES (est): 2MM **Privately Held**
SIC: 2741 2731 2752 Miscellaneous publishing; pamphlets: publishing only, not printed on site; commercial printing, lithographic

(G-11226)
KAREN KIM ZOGHEIB LCSW
2110 Dunhill Dr (19810-4702)
PHONE.................................786 897-3022
Karen Kim Zogheib, *Principal*
EMP: 6 EST: 2011
SALES (est): 152.9K **Privately Held**
SIC: 8322 Social worker

(G-11227)
KATHARINE L MAYER ATTY
Also Called: McCarter English
919 N Market St (19801-3023)
PHONE.................................302 984-6312
Katharine Mayer, *Principal*
Cynthia Betz, *Manager*
Susan Newton, *Admin Sec*
Maria Saravia, *Admin Sec*
Daniel J Brown, *Associate*
EMP: 15
SALES (est): 1.1MM **Privately Held**
SIC: 8111 General practice attorney, lawyer

(G-11228)
KATHERINE LAFFEY
Also Called: Family Mediation Services
1509 Gilpin Ave (19806-3015)
PHONE.................................302 651-7999
Katherine Laffey, *Owner*
EMP: 5

SALES (est): 487.7K **Privately Held**
SIC: 8111 General practice attorney, lawyer

(G-11229)
KATHLEEN M CRONAN MD
Also Called: Emergency Room
1600 Rockland Rd (19803-3607)
P.O. Box 269 (19899-0269)
PHONE........................302 651-5860
Kathleen Cronan, *Director*
EMP: 23
SALES (est): 596.7K **Privately Held**
SIC: 8011 Pediatrician

(G-11230)
KB ELECTRICAL SERVICES
1 S Clayton St (19805-3948)
PHONE........................302 276-5733
EMP: 5
SALES (est): 110.7K **Privately Held**
SIC: 4911 Electric services

(G-11231)
KC & ASSOCIATES INC
155 Oldbury Dr (19808-1433)
PHONE........................302 633-3300
Carolyn Warawa, *President*
EMP: 8
SALES (est): 656.1K **Privately Held**
WEB: www.kcassociatesinc.com
SIC: 8742 8732 Marketing consulting services; market analysis or research

(G-11232)
KEEN COMPRESSED GAS CO (PA)
101 Rogers Rd Ste 200 (19801-5797)
P.O. Box 15146 (19850-5146)
PHONE........................302 594-4545
J Merrill Keen, *CEO*
Bryan Keen, *President*
Jon Keen, *Vice Pres*
Will Keen, *Vice Pres*
David Haas, *CFO*
EMP: 11
SQ FT: 30,000
SALES: 28.8MM **Privately Held**
WEB: www.keengas.com
SIC: 5085 5169 Welding supplies; gases, compressed & liquefied

(G-11233)
KEEP IN TOUCH SYSTEMS INC
19c Trolley Sq (19806-3355)
PHONE........................510 868-8088
Gal Oren, *President*
EMP: 5
SALES (est): 475.3K **Privately Held**
SIC: 4813

(G-11234)
KEITH D STOLTZ FOUNDATION
20 Montchanin Rd Ste 250 (19807-2181)
PHONE........................302 654-3600
Keith Stoltz, *Principal*
EMP: 14
SALES: 1.9K **Privately Held**
SIC: 8699 Charitable organization

(G-11235)
KELLER TRUCK PARTS INC
5 Medori Blvd (19801-5781)
PHONE........................302 658-5107
Robert Glassman, *Manager*
EMP: 5 **Privately Held**
SIC: 5013 Truck parts & accessories
HQ: Keller Truck Parts, Inc.
  3530 S Hanover St
  Baltimore MD 21225
  410 355-8686

(G-11236)
KELLY & ASSOC INSUR GROUP INC
Also Called: Kelly Benefit Strategy
1201 N Orange St Ste 1100 (19801-1191)
PHONE........................302 661-6324
Jason Danner, *Branch Mgr*
EMP: 8
SALES (corp-wide): 293MM **Privately Held**
WEB: www.kaig.com
SIC: 6411 Insurance brokers

PA: Kelly & Associates Insurance Group, Inc.
  1 Kelly Way
  Sparks Glencoe MD 21152
  410 527-3400

(G-11237)
KELLY ANN HATTON
1601 Milltown Rd Ste 1 (19808-4047)
PHONE........................484 571-5369
Kelly Hatton, *Manager*
EMP: 4
SALES (est): 61.5K **Privately Held**
SIC: 8021 Offices & clinics of dentists

(G-11238)
KELMAR ASSOCIATES LLC
2200 Concord Pike 12 (19803-2909)
PHONE........................781 213-6926
EMP: 57
SALES (corp-wide): 8.1MM **Privately Held**
SIC: 8742 Management consulting services
PA: Kelmar Associates, Llc
  500 Edgewater Dr Ste 525
  Wakefield MA 01880

(G-11239)
KEN-DEL PRODUCTIONS INC
Also Called: Delaware Film & Tape Vault Co
1500 First State Blvd (19804-3596)
PHONE........................302 999-1111
H Edwin Kennedy, *President*
Shirley Lotz, *Corp Secy*
Marjorie L Kennedy, *Vice Pres*
EMP: 12 **EST:** 1950
SQ FT: 25,000
SALES (est): 880K **Privately Held**
SIC: 7812 Video production

(G-11240)
KENNETH DE GROUT DC
1401 Silverside Rd Ste 1 (19810-4400)
PHONE........................302 475-5600
Kenneth De Grout, *President*
EMP: 7
SALES (est): 414.9K **Privately Held**
SIC: 8041 Offices & clinics of chiropractors

(G-11241)
KENNETH R SCHUSTER
712 N West St (19801-1524)
PHONE........................302 984-1000
Kenneth Schuster, *Branch Mgr*
EMP: 4
SALES (est): 241.6K
SALES (corp-wide): 2.3MM **Privately Held**
SIC: 8111 General practice attorney, lawyer
PA: Kenneth R Schuster
  334 W Front St
  Media PA 19063
  610 892-9200

(G-11242)
KENS LAWN SERVICE INC
732 Westcliff Rd (19803-1712)
PHONE........................302 478-2714
Ken Takvorian, *President*
EMP: 8
SQ FT: 4,000
SALES (est): 310K **Privately Held**
SIC: 0782 Lawn care services

(G-11243)
KENSINGTON TOURS LTD
Also Called: Horizon and Co
2207 Concord Pike 645 (19803-2908)
PHONE........................888 903-2001
Jeff Willner, *CEO*
Dave Volman, *President*
Marc Moore, *Vice Pres*
EMP: 100
SQ FT: 17,000
SALES (est): 1.8MM **Privately Held**
SIC: 7999 Tour & guide services

(G-11244)
KENT COUNTY PAINTING INC
1700 First State Blvd (19804-3566)
P.O. Box 3042 (19804-0042)
PHONE........................302 994-9628
Anthony Maccari, *President*
EMP: 15

SQ FT: 18,000
SALES: 719.6K
SALES (corp-wide): 3.8MM **Privately Held**
SIC: 1721 Commercial painting
PA: Maccari Companies Inc
  1700 First State Blvd
  Wilmington DE 19804
  302 994-9628

(G-11245)
KENTMERE HEALTHCARE CNSLTNG
3511 Silverside Rd # 202 (19810-4902)
PHONE........................302 478-7600
Jeffrey Petrizzi, *Principal*
Jennifer May, *Controller*
Russel E Kaufman, *Chief Mktg Ofcr*
Danielle Ellis, *Office Mgr*
EMP: 7 **EST:** 2007
SALES (est): 966.3K **Privately Held**
SIC: 8011 Clinic, operated by physicians

(G-11246)
KENTMERE VETERINARY HOSPITAL
Also Called: Coogan, Kevin P Vmd
1710 Lovering Ave (19806-2120)
PHONE........................302 655-6610
Kevin Coogan, *Owner*
EMP: 4
SALES (est): 173.8K **Privately Held**
SIC: 0742 Animal hospital services, pets & other animal specialties

(G-11247)
KERRY & G INC
1621 Willow Ave (19804-3531)
PHONE........................302 999-0022
Kerry Elliot, *Manager*
EMP: 5
SALES (est): 68.3K **Privately Held**
WEB: www.gilpinhall.org
SIC: 8351 Child day care services

(G-11248)
KEY NATIONAL TRUST COMPANY DEL
1105 N Market St Ste 500 (19801-1253)
PHONE........................302 574-4702
EMP: 4
SALES: 886K **Privately Held**
SIC: 6091 Nondeposit trust facilities

(G-11249)
KEY-TEL COMMUNICATIONS INC
2642 Foulk Rd (19810-1422)
PHONE........................302 475-3066
Kenneth Donahoe, *President*
Lawrence Donahoe, *Vice Pres*
EMP: 5
SALES (est): 440K **Privately Held**
SIC: 4813 5999 Telephone communication, except radio; telephone equipment & systems

(G-11250)
KEYBOARDERS LLC
501 Silverside Rd Ste 54 (19809-1388)
PHONE........................302 438-8055
EMP: 5
SALES: 400K **Privately Held**
SIC: 7379 7371 Computer Related Consulting Software Development Or Applications

(G-11251)
KEYLENT INC
1000 N West St Ste 1200 (19801-1058)
PHONE........................401 864-6498
Ravi Mudunuri, *President*
Murali Singampalli, *Technical Staff*
EMP: 50
SQ FT: 700
SALES (est): 71.4K **Privately Held**
SIC: 7371 Computer software development & applications

(G-11252)
KEYROCK LLC
3524 Silverside Rd 35b (19810-4929)
PHONE........................818 605-7772
Wayman Crosby,
EMP: 2

SALES: 100K **Privately Held**
SIC: 1389 Construction, repair & dismantling services

(G-11253)
KEYSTATE CORPORATE MGT LLC
824 N Market St Ste 210 (19801-4909)
PHONE........................302 425-5158
Monte Miller, *CEO*
Joshua Miller, *President*
EMP: 4
SALES (est): 265.8K **Privately Held**
SIC: 8741 Business management

(G-11254)
KEYSTONE FINISHING INC
1800 Lovering Ave (19806-2122)
PHONE........................925 825-2498
Patrick Keen, *President*
EMP: 12
SALES (est): 62.4K **Privately Held**
SIC: 1721 Painting & paper hanging

(G-11255)
KGC ENTERPRISES INC
Also Called: Kc Sign Wilmington
3617 Kirkwood Hwy (19806-5103)
PHONE........................302 668-1835
Eric Watkins, *Branch Mgr*
EMP: 4 **Privately Held**
SIC: 1799 3993 Sign installation & maintenance; signs & advertising specialties
PA: Kgc Enterprises, Inc.
  142 Conchester Hwy
  Aston PA 19014

(G-11256)
KHAN FAMILY FOUNDATION INC
501 Silverside Rd (19809-1374)
PHONE........................800 839-1754
T Khan, *Principal*
EMP: 7
SALES (est): 1.3MM **Privately Held**
SIC: 8699 Charitable organization

(G-11257)
KHANYI MEDIA CORPORATION
105 Silverside Rd Ste 501 (19809-1727)
PHONE........................302 482-8142
EMP: 5
SALES (est): 441.4K **Privately Held**
SIC: 8322 Individual/Family Services

(G-11258)
KIDDOCS
4600 New Linden Hl 204 (19808)
PHONE........................302 892-3300
Ephigena Giannoukos, *President*
EMP: 5
SALES (est): 427.7K **Privately Held**
WEB: www.kiddocs.info
SIC: 8011 Pediatrician

(G-11259)
KIDS KORNER DAY CARE
706 W Newport Pike (19804-3238)
PHONE........................302 998-4606
Karen Ness, *Director*
Joan Lameeth, *Director*
EMP: 5
SALES (est): 92.1K **Privately Held**
SIC: 8351 Child day care services

(G-11260)
KIDZ KLUB
200 N Union St (19805-3457)
PHONE........................302 652-5439
Mona Sampson, *Owner*
EMP: 5
SALES (est): 88.4K **Privately Held**
SIC: 8351 Child day care services

(G-11261)
KIMOS HAWAIIAN SHAVE ICE
2628 Newell Dr (19808-3332)
PHONE........................302 998-1763
Fred Lathim, *President*
EMP: 1
SALES (est): 64.1K **Privately Held**
SIC: 2097 5999 8743 Manufactured ice; ice; public relations services

GEOGRAPHIC SECTION

Wilmington - New Castle County (G-11294)

(G-11262)
KIMS CLEANERS
3 Murphy Rd (19803-3044)
PHONE.................................302 656-2397
Kim, *Principal*
EMP: 4 **EST:** 1999
SALES (est): 68.9K **Privately Held**
SIC: 7216 Drycleaning plants, except rugs

(G-11263)
KIND MIND KIDS
111 Lands End Rd (19807-2519)
P.O. Box 3682 (19807-0682)
PHONE.................................302 545-0380
Valerie Martin, *Principal*
EMP: 7
SALES (est): 133.7K **Privately Held**
SIC: 8351 Child day care services

(G-11264)
KIND TO KIDS FOUNDATION
100 W 10th St Ste 606 (19801-6604)
PHONE.................................302 654-5440
Tom Stevenson, *Ch of Bd*
Caroline Jones, *President*
EMP: 4
SQ FT: 800
SALES: 385.6K **Privately Held**
SIC: 8699 8299 Charitable organization; educational services

(G-11265)
KINDERCARE LEARNING CTRS LLC
Also Called: Kindercare Center 1006
2018 Naamans Rd C (19810-2659)
PHONE.................................302 475-2212
Michelle France, *Director*
EMP: 20
SALES (corp-wide): 963.9MM **Privately Held**
WEB: www.kindercare.com
SIC: 8351 Group day care center
HQ: Kindercare Learning Centers, Llc
    650 Ne Holladay St # 1400
    Portland OR 97232
    503 872-1300

(G-11266)
KINDERCARE LEARNING CTRS LLC
Also Called: Kindercare Center 45
3449 Hillock Ln (19808-1711)
PHONE.................................302 731-7138
Kimberly Dahlberg, *Director*
EMP: 12
SALES (corp-wide): 963.9MM **Privately Held**
WEB: www.kindercare.com
SIC: 8351 Group day care center
HQ: Kindercare Learning Centers, Llc
    650 Ne Holladay St # 1400
    Portland OR 97232
    503 872-1300

(G-11267)
KINETIC SKATEBOARDING
5319 Concord Pike (19803-1418)
PHONE.................................856 375-2236
EMP: 1
SALES (est): 110.4K **Privately Held**
SIC: 3949 Skateboards

(G-11268)
KING & MINSK PA INC
1805 Foulk Rd Ste D (19810-3700)
PHONE.................................302 475-3270
Paige King DMD, *President*
Cynthia Minsk DMD, *Vice Pres*
EMP: 14 **EST:** 1964
SALES (est): 775K **Privately Held**
SIC: 8021 Dentists' office

(G-11269)
KINTYRE SOLUTIONS LLC
2817 Kennedy Rd (19810-3447)
PHONE.................................888 636-0010
Brian Kennedy, *Mng Member*
Jennifer Kennedy, *Director*
EMP: 9
SALES: 2.8MM **Privately Held**
SIC: 8742 7389 5961 Management information systems consultant; ; computer software, mail order

(G-11270)
KIOSKED CORPORATION
2711 Centerville Rd # 400 (19808-1660)
PHONE.................................803 993-8463
EMP: 8
SALES (est): 600K **Privately Held**
SIC: 7311 Advertising Agency

(G-11271)
KIRK CABINETRY LLC
Also Called: Kirk Custom Furniture
601 Cornell Dr Ste 11-G (19801-5789)
PHONE.................................302 220-3377
Richard Kirk, *Owner*
EMP: 1
SALES: 75K **Privately Held**
SIC: 5712 2511 Furniture stores; wood household furniture

(G-11272)
KIRK FAMILY PRACTICE
5 Courtney Rd (19807-2505)
PHONE.................................302 423-2049
EMP: 6
SALES (est): 80.5K **Privately Held**
SIC: 8011 General & family practice, physician/surgeon

(G-11273)
KIRKWOOD AUTO CENTER LLC
4913 Kirkwood Hwy (19808-5011)
PHONE.................................302 995-6179
Norman Jones, *Administration*
EMP: 16
SQ FT: 20,000
SALES (est): 2.9MM **Privately Held**
WEB: www.kirkwoodautocenter.com
SIC: 7538 General automotive repair shops

(G-11274)
KIRKWOOD DENTAL ASSOCIATES PA (PA)
710 Greenbank Rd Ste A (19808-3196)
PHONE.................................302 994-2582
Arthur Young, *President*
Eric Esbitt, *Treasurer*
Nicholas Punturieri, *Admin Sec*
EMP: 19
SALES: 2.9MM **Privately Held**
WEB: www.kdental.com
SIC: 8021 Dentists' office

(G-11275)
KIRKWOOD FTNES RACQUETBALL CLB (PA)
1800 Naamans Rd (19810-2600)
PHONE.................................302 529-1865
Steven Qualls, *President*
EMP: 13
SALES (est): 681.3K **Privately Held**
SIC: 7997 7991 Racquetball club, membership; physical fitness clubs with training equipment; athletic club & gymnasiums, membership; health club

(G-11276)
KISSFLOW INC
1000 N West St Ste 1200 (19801-1058)
PHONE.................................650 396-7692
Suresh Sambandam, *Principal*
EMP: 200 **EST:** 2012
SALES (est): 6.5MM **Privately Held**
SIC: 7371 Custom computer programming services

(G-11277)
KLAUS DR ROBERT MD
1100 Lovering Ave Apt 810 (19806-3289)
PHONE.................................302 422-3500
Robert Klaus, *Owner*
Phyllis Ingram, *Office Mgr*
Tadele Desalew, *Endocrinology*
David S Bargnesi, *Urology*
Merry D Carde, *Nurse*
EMP: 4
SALES (est): 190.1K **Privately Held**
SIC: 8011 Physical medicine, physician/surgeon

(G-11278)
KM KLACKO & ASSOCIATE
509 Redfern Ave (19807-3121)
PHONE.................................302 652-1482
Kathrene Klacko, *Owner*
EMP: 5
SALES (est): 92.1K **Privately Held**
SIC: 7299 Party planning service

(G-11279)
KNEPPER & STRATTON (PA)
1228 N King St (19801-3236)
PHONE.................................302 658-1717
Martin Knepper, *Managing Prtnr*
Barbara H Stratton, *Partner*
E M Knepper,
EMP: 6
SALES (est): 660.1K **Privately Held**
WEB: www.knepperstratton.com
SIC: 8111 General practice law office

(G-11280)
KNIGHT CONSTRUCTION
2508 Dorval Rd (19810-2222)
PHONE.................................610 496-6879
Richard H Knight, *Owner*
EMP: 4
SALES: 100K **Privately Held**
SIC: 1751 Carpentry work

(G-11281)
KNIGHT HAULING INC
2508 Dorval Rd (19810-2222)
PHONE.................................610 494-6800
Richard H Knight, *President*
Martin T Knight, *Treasurer*
EMP: 4
SALES (est): 602.6K **Privately Held**
SIC: 7353 7389 Heavy construction equipment rental;

(G-11282)
KNIGHTS OF COLUMBUS
1801 Lancaster Ave (19805-3805)
P.O. Box 1449, Hockessin (19707-5449)
PHONE.................................302 559-9959
Herbert T Casalena, *President*
EMP: 13
SALES (corp-wide): 2.3B **Privately Held**
SIC: 8641 Fraternal associations
PA: Knights Of Columbus
    1 Columbus Plz Ste 1700
    New Haven CT 06510
    203 752-4000

(G-11283)
KNOTTS CONSTRUCTION INC
1504 Upsan Downs Ln (19810-4444)
PHONE.................................302 475-7074
Wayne Knotts, *President*
EMP: 7
SALES (est): 801.5K **Privately Held**
SIC: 1521 Single-family housing construction

(G-11284)
KNOWPRO LLC
1013 Centre Rd Ste 403 (19805-1270)
PHONE.................................772 538-6477
Charles Krivan, *Mng Member*
EMP: 8
SALES (est): 216.3K **Privately Held**
SIC: 7373 Systems software development services

(G-11285)
KOA TECHNOLOGIES LLC
108 W 13th St (19801-1145)
PHONE.................................760 471-5726
Cameron Matthews,
EMP: 1
SALES (est): 85K **Privately Held**
SIC: 7372 Prepackaged software

(G-11286)
KOCH ACCOUNTING SERVICES LLC
2801 Centerville Rd (19808-1609)
PHONE.................................877 446-8478
Ric Steele, *President*
EMP: 22
SALES (est): 1.4MM
SALES (corp-wide): 40.6B **Privately Held**
SIC: 8711 1629 Engineering services; industrial plant construction; chemical plant & refinery construction; oil refinery construction
HQ: Koch Engineered Solutions, Llc
    4111 E 37th St N
    Wichita KS 67220
    316 828-8515

(G-11287)
KOCH METHANOL INVESTMENTS LLC (PA)
1209 N Orange St (19801-1120)
PHONE.................................302 658-7581
Jim Sorlie, *Vice Pres*
EMP: 2
SALES (est): 5.9MM **Privately Held**
SIC: 2899 Chemical preparations

(G-11288)
KONCORDIA GROUP LLC
1201 N Market St Ste 401 (19801-1160)
PHONE.................................302 427-1350
Julie Knox, *Project Mgr*
Fred Freestone, *Marketing Staff*
Amy Dicampli, *Office Mgr*
Alissa Bye, *Manager*
Emily Webb, *Manager*
EMP: 15
SALES (est): 2.5MM **Privately Held**
SIC: 7311 Advertising consultant

(G-11289)
KOREAN MARTIAL ARTS INSTITUTE (PA)
2419 W Newport Pike (19804-3846)
PHONE.................................302 992-7999
John L Godwin, *President*
Michele Godwin, *Vice Pres*
EMP: 10
SALES (est): 539.8K **Privately Held**
SIC: 7999 Karate instruction; martial arts school

(G-11290)
KOTY INC
850 N Church St (19801-4341)
PHONE.................................302 654-2665
EMP: 20
SALES: 1.5MM **Privately Held**
SIC: 2431 Architectural Millwork

(G-11291)
KRAMER GROUP LLC
2116 Peachtree Dr (19805-1050)
PHONE.................................717 368-2117
Marcus Kramer,
EMP: 8 **EST:** 2012
SALES (est): 140.8K **Privately Held**
SIC: 8748 Business consulting

(G-11292)
KRAPFS COACHES INC
Also Called: Gregg Bus Service
1400 First State Blvd (19804-3563)
PHONE.................................302 993-7855
Don Kane, *Opers Mgr*
Bradley Krapf, *Branch Mgr*
EMP: 30
SALES (corp-wide): 49.1MM **Privately Held**
WEB: www.krapfbus.com
SIC: 4142 4141 Bus charter service, except local; local bus charter service
PA: Krapf's Coaches, Inc.
    1060 Saunders Ln
    West Chester PA 19380
    610 431-1500

(G-11293)
KRAVE LIKE LLC
7 Deer Run Dr (19807-2403)
PHONE.................................302 482-4550
Nicholas D'Alonzo, *Mng Member*
Jonathan Samchez,
Dan Stanton,
Douglas Weaver,
EMP: 5
SALES (est): 350K **Privately Held**
SIC: 2086 Soft drinks: packaged in cans, bottles, etc.

(G-11294)
KRC WASTE MANAGEMENT INC
P.O. Box 3115 (19804-0115)
PHONE.................................302 999-9276
Karen Randolph, *President*
EMP: 4
SQ FT: 1,200
SALES (est): 350K **Privately Held**
SIC: 4953 Refuse collection & disposal services; rubbish collection & disposal

Wilmington - New Castle County (G-11295)

(G-11295)
KRIENEN-GRIFFITH INC (PA)
Also Called: Krienen-Griffith Funeral Home
1400 Kirkwood Hwy (19805-2124)
PHONE.................................302 994-9614
William J Krienen III, *President*
EMP: 5
SALES (est): 726.8K **Privately Held**
WEB: www.delawarefuneral.com
SIC: 7261 Funeral home

(G-11296)
KRISTEN SMITH
3706 Kennett Pike (19807-2157)
PHONE.................................302 623-6320
Kristen Smith, *Principal*
EMP: 13
SALES (est): 80.1K **Privately Held**
SIC: 8011 General & family practice, physician/surgeon

(G-11297)
KST LAND DESIGN INC
2627 Skylark Rd (19808-1633)
P.O. Box 169, New Castle (19720-0169)
PHONE.................................302 328-1879
Kevin S Thomas, *President*
EMP: 7
SALES (est): 222.2K **Privately Held**
SIC: 0782 Lawn care services

(G-11298)
KT&D INC
1013 Centre Rd Ste 200 (19805-1265)
P.O. Box 2048 (19899-2048)
PHONE.................................302 429-8500
Scott P Yerkes, *CEO*
Ronald C Dickens, *President*
Kelly A McGovern, *Vice Pres*
Bruce E Smith, *Vice Pres*
Rose Ann Jordan, *Treasurer*
EMP: 18 **EST:** 1929
SQ FT: 7,000
SALES (est): 4MM **Privately Held**
WEB: www.ktd-ins.com
SIC: 6411 Insurance agents

(G-11299)
KUBERA GLOBAL SOLUTIONS LLC
1521 Concord Pike Ste 301 (19803-3644)
PHONE.................................480 241-5124
Robert Hilton, *President*
EMP: 12 **EST:** 2012
SALES (est): 373.4K **Privately Held**
SIC: 8741 Financial management for business

(G-11300)
KUPFERMAN & ASSOCIATES LLC
1701 Shallcross Ave Ste D (19806-2347)
PHONE.................................302 656-7566
Karen Long, *CPA*
Ira Kupferman, *Mng Member*
Tom Wallace, *Manager*
EMP: 6
SALES (est): 464.5K **Privately Held**
WEB: www.kupfermancpa.com
SIC: 8721 Certified public accountant

(G-11301)
KURARAY AMERICA INC
Also Called: Kuraray Intrlyer Solutions Off
2200 Concord Pike # 1101 (19803-2909)
PHONE.................................302 992-4204
EMP: 14 **Privately Held**
SIC: 2821 3081 3843 Vinyl resins; polyvinyl film & sheet; glue, dental
HQ: Kuraray America, Inc.
2625 Bay Area Blvd # 600
Houston TX 77058

(G-11302)
KURTZ COLLECTION
1010 N Union St (19805-2731)
PHONE.................................302 654-0442
Josephine Kurtz, *Principal*
EMP: 7
SALES (est): 370K **Privately Held**
SIC: 2273 Carpets & rugs

(G-11303)
KVM DEPOT INC
1007 N Orange St (19801-1239)
PHONE.................................302 472-9190
David Miller, *President*
EMP: 12
SALES (est): 1.1MM **Privately Held**
SIC: 5045 Computers, peripherals & software

(G-11304)
KW COMMERCIAL
1521 Concord Pike (19803-3642)
PHONE.................................302 299-1123
EMP: 8 **EST:** 2012
SALES (est): 355.9K **Privately Held**
SIC: 6531 Real estate agent, commercial

(G-11305)
KWIKBUCK INC
Trolley Sq Ste 20c (19806)
PHONE.................................774 517-8959
Jean Pierre Duvenhage, *President*
EMP: 6
SALES: 100K **Privately Held**
SIC: 7371 7389 Computer software development & applications;

(G-11306)
L & M SERVICES INC
617 Lafayette Blvd (19801-2365)
P.O. Box 30661 (19805-7661)
PHONE.................................302 658-3735
Delores R Lake, *President*
Lonnie Lake, *Corp Secy*
Anthony V Mason, *Vice Pres*
EMP: 12
SALES (est): 260.4K **Privately Held**
SIC: 7217 7349 Carpet & upholstery cleaning on customer premises; floor waxing

(G-11307)
L A S TRUCKING LLC
5 W Holly Oak Rd (19809-1342)
PHONE.................................302 439-4433
Lawrence Sheridan, *Principal*
EMP: 4
SALES (est): 199.3K **Privately Held**
SIC: 4212 Local trucking, without storage

(G-11308)
L E STANSELL INC
Also Called: Craft Bookbinding Co
2525 Ebright Rd (19810-1125)
PHONE.................................302 475-1534
L Edward Stansell, *President*
Sandra L Stansell, *Corp Secy*
EMP: 2
SALES (est): 189.6K **Privately Held**
WEB: www.bookrestoration.net
SIC: 2789 2782 5112 Bookbinding & related work; looseleaf binders & devices; looseleaf binders

(G-11309)
L E YORK LAW LLC
182 Belmont Dr (19808-4329)
PHONE.................................302 234-8338
Lydia York, *Principal*
EMP: 3
SALES (est): 95.7K **Privately Held**
SIC: 2711 Newspapers, publishing & printing

(G-11310)
L F CONLIN DDS
1202 Foulk Rd (19803-2796)
PHONE.................................302 764-0930
L F Conlin Jr, *Owner*
EMP: 5
SALES (est): 353.7K **Privately Held**
SIC: 8021 Dentists' office

(G-11311)
LA FLORESTA PERDIDA INC (PA)
3411 Silverside Rd 101wd (19810-4870)
PHONE.................................302 478-8900
Phillip G Rust Jr, *President*
Joseph Harrison, *Corp Secy*
Richard C Rust, *Vice Pres*
EMP: 10
SALES (est): 2MM **Privately Held**
SIC: 5031 Lumber, plywood & millwork

(G-11312)
LA JOLLA FINCL PARTNERS LLC
2711 Centerville Rd # 400 (19808-1660)
PHONE.................................858 864-0146
EMP: 6 **EST:** 2006
SALES: 150K **Privately Held**
SIC: 8748 Business Consulting Services

(G-11313)
LABATON SUCHAROW LLP
300 Delaware Ave Ste 1340 (19801-1658)
PHONE.................................302 573-6938
Christine Azar, *Partner*
Thomas Curry, *Associate*
EMP: 13
SALES (est): 653.4K
SALES (corp-wide): 27.5MM **Privately Held**
SIC: 8111 General practice law office
PA: Labaton Sucharow Llp
140 Broadway Ste 2300
New York NY 10005
212 907-0700

(G-11314)
LABORATOIRES ESTHEDERM USA INC
2711 Centerville Rd # 300 (19808-1665)
PHONE.................................514 270-3763
David Durand, *CEO*
EMP: 5 **EST:** 1988
SALES: 2MM **Privately Held**
SIC: 2844 Face creams or lotions

(G-11315)
LABORATORY CORPORATION AMERICA
2123 Concord Pike (19803-2906)
PHONE.................................302 651-9502
Candance Willoby, *Manager*
EMP: 25 **Publicly Held**
SIC: 8071 Testing laboratories
HQ: Laboratory Corporation Of America
358 S Main St Ste 458
Burlington NC 27215
336 229-1127

(G-11316)
LABORATORY CORPORATION AMERICA
1400 Philadelphia Pike (19809-1856)
PHONE.................................302 798-2520
Clarence Lever, *Manager*
EMP: 25 **Publicly Held**
WEB: www.labcorp.com
SIC: 8071 Testing laboratories
HQ: Laboratory Corporation Of America
358 S Main St Ste 458
Burlington NC 27215
336 229-1127

(G-11317)
LABORATORY CORPORATION AMERICA
3105 Limestone Rd Ste 105 (19808-2156)
PHONE.................................302 998-7340
Rosemary Stokes, *Manager*
EMP: 25 **Publicly Held**
WEB: www.labcorp.com
SIC: 8071 Medical laboratories
HQ: Laboratory Corporation Of America
358 S Main St Ste 458
Burlington NC 27215
336 229-1127

(G-11318)
LABORATORY CORPORATION AMERICA
1941 Limestone Rd Ste 109 (19808-5413)
PHONE.................................302 994-8575
Clifton Hunt, *Branch Mgr*
EMP: 25 **Publicly Held**
WEB: www.labcorp.com
SIC: 8071 Testing laboratories
HQ: Laboratory Corporation Of America
358 S Main St Ste 458
Burlington NC 27215
336 229-1127

(G-11319)
LABWARE INC (HQ)
3 Mill Rd Ste 102 (19806-2154)
PHONE.................................302 658-8444
Vance Kershner, *President*
Eric Vest, *Vice Pres*
Doug Judge, *QC Mgr*
Clem Padin, *CFO*
Dave Ferrell, *Controller*
EMP: 50
SQ FT: 14,000
SALES (est): 24.5MM **Privately Held**
SIC: 7371 Computer software development

(G-11320)
LABWARE INC
400 Burnt Mill Rd (19807-1010)
PHONE.................................302 658-8444
Debra Adelman, *Principal*
EMP: 4 **Privately Held**
SIC: 7372 Prepackaged software
HQ: Labware, Inc.
3 Mill Rd Ste 102
Wilmington DE 19806

(G-11321)
LABWARE GLOBAL SERVICES INC
3 Mill Rd Ste 102 (19806-2154)
PHONE.................................302 658-8444
Vance Kersner, *President*
David Ferrell, *Vice Pres*
David Nixon, *Vice Pres*
Carlisle Peet, *Vice Pres*
Michael Greene, *Project Mgr*
EMP: 14
SALES (est): 1MM **Privately Held**
SIC: 7371 7372 6719 Computer software development & applications; business oriented computer software; personal holding companies, except banks
PA: Labware Holdings, Inc.
3 Mill Rd Ste 102
Wilmington DE 19806

(G-11322)
LABWARE HOLDINGS INC (PA)
3 Mill Rd Ste 102 (19806-2154)
PHONE.................................302 658-8444
Vance Kershner, *President*
David Nixon, *Vice Pres*
Shannon Beyl, *Finance Mgr*
Jeff Loudon, *Practice Mgr*
John Carlisle Peet, *Admin Sec*
EMP: 32
SQ FT: 14,000
SALES: 110MM **Privately Held**
WEB: www.labware.com
SIC: 7371 7372 6719 Computer software development & applications; business oriented computer software; personal holding companies, except banks

(G-11323)
LAFAZIA CONSTRUCTION
149 Belmont Dr (19808-4330)
PHONE.................................302 234-1300
Robert Lafazia, *Owner*
EMP: 8
SALES (est): 580K **Privately Held**
SIC: 1771 Concrete work

(G-11324)
LAFFEY KATHRYN J THE LAW OFF
1500 Shallcross Ave 2b (19806-3037)
PHONE.................................302 651-7999
Kathryn Laffey, *Partner*
Kerr F Glennon,
EMP: 4
SALES (est): 224.1K **Privately Held**
WEB: www.laffeylaw.com
SIC: 8111 General practice attorney, lawyer

(G-11325)
LAMBRO TECHNOLOGIES LLC
206 Kirk Ave (19803-4920)
PHONE.................................302 351-2559
Shannon Watson, *Director*
Byron Burpulis, *Director*
John Jurewicz, *Director*
EMP: 8
SALES (est): 560K **Privately Held**
WEB: www.lambrotech.com
SIC: 7379 Computer related consulting services

GEOGRAPHIC SECTION

Wilmington - New Castle County (G-11357)

(G-11326)
LANDIS LTD
420 B And O Ln (19804-1451)
PHONE..................302 656-9024
Timothy S Skirvin, *President*
▲ EMP: 5 EST: 1975
SQ FT: 20,000
SALES (est): 883.8K **Privately Held**
SIC: 5032 Marble building stone

(G-11327)
LANDIS RATH & COBB LLP
919 N Market St Ste 1800 (19801-3033)
PHONE..................302 467-4400
Adam Landis, *Partner*
Richard Cobb, *Partner*
Daniel Rath, *Partner*
Melissa Ramirez, *Legal Staff*
Matthew McGuire, *Associate*
EMP: 15
SALES (est): 1.4MM **Privately Held**
SIC: 8111 General practice law office

(G-11328)
LANDMARK PARKING INC (DH)
1205 N Orange St (19801-1120)
PHONE..................302 651-3610
Richard G Hatfield, *President*
John Lyon, *Vice Pres*
Gregory S Hatfield, *Treasurer*
EMP: 12
SQ FT: 10,000
SALES (est): 713.5K
SALES (corp-wide): 76MM **Privately Held**
WEB: www.landmarkparking.com
SIC: 7521 Parking garage
HQ: Colonial Parking Inc
715 N Orange St Fl 1
Wilmington DE 19801
302 651-3600

(G-11329)
LANE HOME SERVICES INC
Also Called: Lane Roofing
45 Germay Dr Ste A (19804-1126)
PHONE..................302 652-7663
Christopher Lane, *President*
EMP: 12
SALES (est): 1.2MM **Privately Held**
SIC: 1761 Roofing contractor

(G-11330)
LANNING WOODWORKS
2404 Overlook Dr (19810-2533)
PHONE..................302 353-4726
Harry Lanning, *Principal*
EMP: 1
SALES (est): 54.1K **Privately Held**
SIC: 2431 Millwork

(G-11331)
LARRY WALLIS
20 Kentshire Ct (19807-2583)
PHONE..................856 456-3925
Larry Wallis, *Principal*
EMP: 4
SALES (est): 205.4K **Privately Held**
SIC: 8042 Offices & clinics of optometrists

(G-11332)
LASER MANAGEMENT GROUP LLC
Also Called: First Sight Laser Center
5590 Kirkwood Hwy (19808-5002)
PHONE..................302 992-9030
Mike Frost,
EMP: 3
SALES (est): 274.2K **Privately Held**
SIC: 3674 Photoelectric cells, solid state (electronic eye)

(G-11333)
LASER MARKING WORKS LLC
3511 Silverside Rd # 105 (19810-4902)
PHONE..................786 307-6203
Jose R Vigil, *Admin Sec*
EMP: 3
SQ FT: 1,400
SALES (est): 270K **Privately Held**
SIC: 3555 Engraving machinery & equipment, except plates

(G-11334)
LASER ONLINE LLC
801 N King St (19801)
PHONE..................302 261-5225
Antonio Garley, *CEO*
EMP: 15
SALES (est): 337K **Privately Held**
SIC: 5045 Computers, peripherals & software

(G-11335)
LASTING IMPRESSION INC A
504 Philadelphia Pike (19809-2155)
PHONE..................302 762-9200
Al Mayne, *President*
Gretchen Mayne, *Treasurer*
EMP: 4
SQ FT: 1,700
SALES (est): 622.4K **Privately Held**
SIC: 2759 2396 Screen printing; screen printing on fabric articles

(G-11336)
LATIN AMERICAN CMNTY CTR CORP
Also Called: Latin American Community Ctr
403 N Van Buren St (19805-3243)
PHONE..................302 655-7338
Melissa Browne, *Vice Pres*
Steve Villanueva, *Vice Pres*
Laura Adarve, *Manager*
Wanda Burgos, *Manager*
Maria Matos, *Exec Dir*
EMP: 70
SQ FT: 28,000
SALES: 4.7MM **Privately Held**
WEB: www.laccweb.com
SIC: 8322 Community center

(G-11337)
LAU & ASSOC LTD
20 Montchanin Rd (19807-2160)
PHONE..................302 792-5955
Judith Lau, *President*
Tom Weary, *Ch Invest Ofcr*
EMP: 11
SALES (est): 790K **Privately Held**
SIC: 8741 Financial management for business

(G-11338)
LAVOND MACKEY
Also Called: Mackeys Complete Cnstr Co
2808 N Jefferson St Apt 1 (19802-3020)
PHONE..................484 466-8055
Lavond Mackey, *Owner*
EMP: 25
SALES (est): 1MM **Privately Held**
SIC: 1629 Heavy construction

(G-11339)
LAW DEBENTURE TRUST COMPANY
901 N Market St (19801-3022)
PHONE..................302 655-3505
Larry Nicholls, *President*
EMP: 4
SALES (est): 702.6K **Privately Held**
SIC: 6021 National commercial banks

(G-11340)
LAW FIRM
702 N King St Ste 600 (19801)
P.O. Box 1675 (19899-1675)
PHONE..................302 472-4900
Gary Aber, *Owner*
Saagar Shah, *Principal*
Darrell Baker, *Director*
EMP: 18
SALES (est): 1.6MM **Privately Held**
SIC: 8111 Specialized law offices, attorneys

(G-11341)
LAWALL PROSTHETICS - ORTHOTICS (PA)
1822 Augustine Cut Off (19803-4405)
PHONE..................302 427-3668
Harry J Lawall Jr, *President*
Edward F Moran, *Vice Pres*
EMP: 10
SALES (est): 6.3MM **Privately Held**
SIC: 8011 5999 Specialized medical practitioners, except internal; orthopedic & prosthesis applications

(G-11342)
LAWALL PROSTHETICS - ORTHOTICS
1600 Rockland Rd (19803-3607)
PHONE..................302 429-7625
Ed Moran, *Manager*
Stephen Simmons, *Info Tech Dir*
EMP: 50 **Privately Held**
SIC: 8011 Specialized medical practitioners, except internal
PA: Lawall Prosthetics - Orthotics Inc.
1822 Augustine Cut Off
Wilmington DE 19803

(G-11343)
LAWN DOCTOR OF WILMINGTON INC
203 N Dupont Rd (19804-1207)
P.O. Box 3049 (19804-0049)
PHONE..................302 656-4900
Fax: 302 656-5896
EMP: 12
SALES (est): 616.6K **Privately Held**
SIC: 0782 Lawn Care

(G-11344)
LAWRENCE AGENCIES INC
113 Kirkwood Sq (19808-4859)
PHONE..................302 995-6936
Abdul Salaam Lawrence, *President*
EMP: 6
SALES (est): 206.1K **Privately Held**
SIC: 6411 Insurance agents & brokers

(G-11345)
LAWRENCE JP & ASSOCIATES
3012 N Heald St (19802-2831)
PHONE..................313 293-2692
EMP: 12 EST: 2008
SALES: 950K **Privately Held**
SIC: 7389 Business Services

(G-11346)
LAWRENCE LEVINSON ATTORNEY
1326 N King St (19801-3220)
PHONE..................302 656-3393
Lawrence Levinson, *Owner*
EMP: 4
SALES (est): 338.1K **Privately Held**
SIC: 8111 General practice attorney, lawyer

(G-11347)
LC HOMES INC
105 Foulk Rd (19803-3740)
PHONE..................302 429-8700
Louis Capano, *Principal*
EMP: 5 EST: 1947
SALES (est): 1MM **Privately Held**
SIC: 6531 Real estate brokers & agents

(G-11348)
LE HERBE LLC (PA)
1209 N Orange St (19801-1120)
PHONE..................949 317-1100
Jay Grillo, *Mng Member*
EMP: 4
SQ FT: 1,200
SALES: 1MM **Privately Held**
SIC: 2087 Powders, drink

(G-11349)
LEAGUE OF WMEN VTERS NEW CSTLE
2400 W 17th St R (19806-1343)
PHONE..................302 571-8948
Marjorie Johnson, *President*
Christine L Stillson, *President*
Anita Puglisi, *Director*
EMP: 15
SALES (est): 698.4K **Privately Held**
SIC: 8641 Civic associations

(G-11350)
LEARNING CARE GROUP INC
5305 Limestone Rd (19808-1255)
PHONE..................302 235-5702
EMP: 23
SALES (corp-wide): 164MM **Privately Held**
SIC: 8351 Preschool center
HQ: Learning Care Group, Inc.
21333 Haggerty Rd Ste 300
Novi MI 48375

(G-11351)
LEARNING CTR AT MADISON ST LLC
600 N Madison St (19801-2023)
PHONE..................302 543-7588
Joseph Kirueya, *Principal*
EMP: 10
SALES (est): 126.2K **Privately Held**
SIC: 8351 Child day care services

(G-11352)
LEARNING4 LRNG PROFESSIONALS
317 E Christian St (19804-2213)
P.O. Box 6431 (19804-0431)
PHONE..................302 994-0451
Catherine Lombardozzi, *Principal*
EMP: 5 EST: 2012
SALES (est): 75.3K **Privately Held**
SIC: 8351 Child day care services

(G-11353)
LED SIGN CITY
3422 Old Capitol Trl (19808-6124)
PHONE..................866 343-4011
EMP: 1
SALES (est): 50.6K **Privately Held**
SIC: 3993 Signs & advertising specialties

(G-11354)
LEDTOLIGHT (PA)
Trolley Sq Ste 20c (19806)
PHONE..................941 323-6664
Allai Boicoune, *President*
Cynthia Boicoune, *Owner*
EMP: 4 EST: 2012
SQ FT: 350
SALES: 240K **Privately Held**
SIC: 5063 3648 Lighting fittings & accessories; lighting equipment

(G-11355)
LEE BELL INC (HQ)
3411 Silverside Rd (19810-4812)
PHONE..................302 477-3930
Helen Winslow, *Vice Pres*
EMP: 4
SALES (est): 1.3MM
SALES (corp-wide): 13.8B **Publicly Held**
SIC: 2325 2321 2329 2339 Jeans: men's, youths' & boys'; slacks, dress: men's, youths' & boys'; trousers, dress (separate): men's, youths' & boys'; men's & boys' dress shirts; jackets (suede, leatherette, etc.), sport: men's & boys'; sweaters & sweater jackets: men's & boys'; jeans: women's, misses' & juniors'; slacks: women's, misses' & juniors'; women's & misses' blouses & shirts; jeans: girls', children's & infants'; slacks: girls' & children's; warm-up, jogging & sweat suits: girls' & children's; bathing suits & swimwear: girls', children's & infants'
PA: V.F. Corporation
105 Corporate Center Blvd
Greensboro NC 27408
336 424-6000

(G-11356)
LEE MC NEILL ASSOCIATES
1302 Grinnell Rd (19803-5106)
P.O. Box 7022 (19803-0022)
PHONE..................302 593-6172
Lee H McNeill, *Owner*
EMP: 5
SALES: 700K **Privately Held**
SIC: 7513 5012 5511 Truck leasing, without drivers; truck rental, without drivers; trucks, commercial; truck tractors; pickups, new & used

(G-11357)
LEECH TSHMAN FSCALDO LAMPL LLC
1007 N Orange St Fl 4 (19801-1242)
PHONE..................302 421-9379
Te Fuscaldo, *Manager*
EMP: 7

Wilmington - New Castle County (G-11358)

SALES (corp-wide): 15.1MM **Privately Held**
SIC: 8111 General practice attorney, lawyer; general practice law office
PA: Leech Tishman Fuscaldo & Lampl, Llc.
525 William Penn Pl Fl 28
Pittsburgh PA 15219
412 261-1600

(G-11358)
LEEDS WEST INV GROUP LLC
Also Called: Midas Muffler
3425 Kirkwood Hwy (19808-6133)
PHONE...................302 998-0533
Judd Shader, *Principal*
EMP: 42
SALES (corp-wide): 13.8MM **Privately Held**
SIC: 7533 Muffler shop, sale or repair & installation
PA: Leeds West Investment Group, Llc
7450 E Progress Pl
Greenwood Village CO 80111
303 980-8748

(G-11359)
LEES LAWN CARE
224 S Cleveland Ave (19805-1431)
PHONE...................302 658-2546
Kim Lee, *Principal*
EMP: 4 EST: 2011
SALES (est): 141.9K **Privately Held**
SIC: 0782 Lawn care services

(G-11360)
LEGACY FOODS LLC
915 S Heald St (19801-5732)
PHONE...................302 656-5540
EMP: 4
SALES (est): 699.5K
SALES (corp-wide): 548.6K **Privately Held**
SIC: 5149 Groceries & related products
PA: Legacy Foods, Llc
704 Pulaski Hwy
Joppa MD 21085
410 671-9005

(G-11361)
LEGAL SERVICES CORP DELAWARE
100 W 10th St Ste 203 (19801-1632)
PHONE...................302 575-0408
Katherine Castano, *Sr Project Mgr*
Douglas Canfield, *Exec Dir*
Michael Lynch, *Representative*
EMP: 7
SALES: 1.6MM **Privately Held**
SIC: 8111 Legal aid service

(G-11362)
LEGAL SERVICES OF DELAWARE (PA)
100 W 10th St Ste 203 (19801-1632)
PHONE...................302 575-0408
Douglas B Canfield, *Exec Dir*
EMP: 10
SQ FT: 4,200
SALES (est): 1.2MM **Privately Held**
SIC: 8111 General practice attorney, lawyer

(G-11363)
LEGION TRANSFORMATION CTR LLC
97 Galewood Rd (19803-3962)
PHONE...................302 543-4922
Robert Thompson, *Principal*
EMP: 6
SALES (est): 90.1K **Privately Held**
SIC: 7991 Physical fitness facilities

(G-11364)
LEGIST MEDIA LTD
605 N Market St Fl 2 (19801-3167)
P.O. Box 26098 (19899-6098)
PHONE...................302 655-2730
Sharon Bradley, *Vice Pres*
EMP: 5
SALES (est): 129.5K **Privately Held**
SIC: 4899 Communication services

(G-11365)
LEHMAN BROTHERS/GP INC
919 N Market St Ste 506 (19801-3065)
PHONE...................877 740-0108
David Herrmann, *Branch Mgr*
EMP: 16
SALES (corp-wide): 28.1MM **Privately Held**
WEB: www.lehmanbrothers.com
SIC: 6211 Security brokers & dealers
HQ: Lehman Brothers/Gp Inc.
1301 Avenue Of The Americ
New York NY 10019
212 526-0836

(G-11366)
LEILUNA LLC
4023 Kennett Pike # 5830 (19807-2018)
PHONE...................888 201-6444
Aaron Samia, *Director*
Brandon Middleton,
EMP: 15 EST: 2015
SALES (est): 1.9MM **Privately Held**
SIC: 2834 Vitamin, nutrient & hematinic preparations for human use

(G-11367)
LEINY SNACKS
3 Germay Dr Ste 7 (19804-1127)
PHONE...................302 494-2499
Marleny Poline, *Manager*
EMP: 10
SALES (est): 684.9K **Privately Held**
SIC: 2064 Candy & other confectionery products

(G-11368)
LENAPE PROPERTIES MGT INC
903 N French St Ste 106 (19801-3355)
PHONE...................302 426-0200
Louis Ramunno, *President*
EMP: 6
SALES (est): 878.5K **Privately Held**
SIC: 6531 Real estate managers

(G-11369)
LENAR DETECTIVE AGENCY INC
Also Called: Colonial Secrity Service
411 S Dupont St (19805-3917)
PHONE...................302 994-3011
Sam Chickadel, *Manager*
EMP: 225
SALES (corp-wide): 8.5MM **Privately Held**
SIC: 7381 Detective agency; security guard service
PA: Lenar Detective Agency Inc
170 Us Highway 206
Hillsborough NJ 08844
908 298-0012

(G-11370)
LEO J KITUSKIE DDS
1941 Limestone Rd Ste 120 (19808-5424)
PHONE...................302 479-3937
Leo Kituskie, *Manager*
EMP: 4 EST: 2015
SALES (est): 104.5K **Privately Held**
SIC: 8021 Dentists' office

(G-11371)
LEON N WEINER & ASSOCIATES INC (PA)
1 Fox Pt Ctr 4 Denny Rd (19809)
PHONE...................302 656-1354
Kevin P Kelly, *President*
David Curtis, *Exec VP*
Glenn Brooks, *Senior VP*
William Demarco, *Vice Pres*
John Gorlich, *Vice Pres*
EMP: 75 EST: 1961
SQ FT: 14,000
SALES (est): 54MM **Privately Held**
SIC: 6552 1521 1542 Subdividers & developers; new construction, single-family houses; general remodeling, single-family houses; nonresidential construction; commercial & office buildings, renovation & repair

(G-11372)
LEON N WEINER & ASSOCIATES INC
Also Called: Huntington Towers
4 Denny Rd Ste 1 (19809-3445)
PHONE...................860 447-2282
Marisol Rodriguez, *Branch Mgr*
EMP: 4
SALES (corp-wide): 54MM **Privately Held**
SIC: 6513 Apartment building operators
PA: Leon N. Weiner & Associates, Inc.
1 Fox Pt Ctr 4 Denny Rd
Wilmington DE 19809
302 656-1354

(G-11373)
LEONARD L WILLIAMS
1214 N King St (19801-3218)
PHONE...................302 652-3141
Leonard L Williams, *Owner*
EMP: 4
SALES (est): 234.7K **Privately Held**
SIC: 8111 General practice attorney, lawyer

(G-11374)
LEOUNES CATERED AFFAIRS
511 Saint George Dr (19809-2831)
PHONE...................302 547-3233
Leslie Noji, *Principal*
EMP: 6
SALES: 80K **Privately Held**
SIC: 0782 5812 Landscape contractors; caterers

(G-11375)
LESSONS LEARND DY CARE /PRESCH
207 N Union St (19805-3429)
PHONE...................302 777-2200
Dayna Moore, *Owner*
EMP: 25
SALES (est): 676.7K **Privately Held**
SIC: 8351 Child day care services

(G-11376)
LET US LIFT IT INC
Also Called: Bafundo & Associates
802 W 20th St (19802-3815)
PHONE...................302 654-2221
Leonard Bafundo, *CEO*
Jamie Bafundo, *President*
EMP: 6
SALES: 1MM **Privately Held**
SIC: 1761 Roofing contractor

(G-11377)
LEUKEMIA & LYMPHOMA SOC INC
100 W 10th St Ste 209 (19801-1641)
PHONE...................302 661-7300
EMP: 5
SALES (corp-wide): 281.6MM **Privately Held**
SIC: 8699 8399 Membership Organization Social Services
PA: The Leukemia & Lymphoma Society Inc
3 International Dr # 200
Rye Brook NY 10573
914 949-5213

(G-11378)
LEXISNEXIS RISK ASSETS INC (DH)
Also Called: Choicepoint
1105 N Market St Ste 501 (19801-1253)
PHONE...................800 458-9410
Derek V Smith, *Ch of Bd*
Deidre Collins, *President*
Douglas C Curling, *President*
David T Lee, *Exec VP*
Steven W Surbaugh, *Exec VP*
EMP: 700
SQ FT: 206,000
SALES (est): 2.5B
SALES (corp-wide): 9.8B **Privately Held**
WEB: www.choicepointinc.com
SIC: 6411 7375 8721 7323 Information bureaus, insurance; information retrieval services; accounting, auditing & bookkeeping; credit reporting services

(G-11379)
LIBERTY DALYSIS WILMINGTON LLC
Also Called: DSI Wilmington Dialysis
913 Delaware Ave (19806-4701)
P.O. Box 10282, Uniondale NY (11555-0282)
PHONE...................302 429-0142
EMP: 18
SALES (est): 807.6K **Privately Held**
SIC: 8092 Kidney Dialysis Centers
PA: Dialysis Newco, Inc.
424 Church St Ste 1900
Nashville TN 37219

(G-11380)
LIBERTY MECHANICAL LLC
2032 Duncan Rd (19808-5932)
PHONE...................302 397-8863
Joanna Blounts,
EMP: 6
SALES (est): 445.4K **Privately Held**
SIC: 1711 Mechanical contractor

(G-11381)
LIBERTY MUTUAL FIRE INSUR CO
1011 Centre Rd Ste 400 (19805-1200)
PHONE...................302 993-0500
Donald Burns, *Vice Pres*
EMP: 25
SALES (corp-wide): 38.3B **Privately Held**
SIC: 6331 Automobile insurance
HQ: Liberty Mutual Fire Insurance Co Inc
175 Berkeley St
Boston MA 02116
617 357-9500

(G-11382)
LIBERTY MUTUAL INSURANCE CO
1011 Centre Rd Ste 400 (19805-1200)
PHONE...................302 993-0500
Lou Knecht, *President*
Jacqui Whalley, *Business Anlyst*
Eric Kriczky, *Manager*
Marilyn Schumm, *Manager*
EMP: 35
SALES (corp-wide): 38.3B **Privately Held**
WEB: www.libertymutual.com
SIC: 6331 Fire, marine & casualty insurance
HQ: Liberty Mutual Insurance Company
175 Berkeley St
Boston MA 02116
617 357-9500

(G-11383)
LIFE AT ST FRNCIS HLTHCARE INC
Also Called: St. Francis Life
1072 Justison St (19801-5162)
PHONE...................302 660-3297
Amy L Milligan, *Administration*
EMP: 5
SALES (est): 4.4MM **Privately Held**
SIC: 8099 Health & allied services

(G-11384)
LIFE BEFORE US LLC
2711 Centerville Rd (19808-1660)
PHONE...................917 690-3380
EMP: 2
SALES (est): 70.1K **Privately Held**
SIC: 7372 Prepackaged Software Services

(G-11385)
LIFE SCIENCES INTL LLC
1209 N Orange St (19801-1120)
PHONE...................603 436-9444
Seth Hoogasian, *President*
Ken Apicerno, *Treasurer*
Maura Spellman, *Asst Treas*
EMP: 3
SALES (est): 33.7K
SALES (corp-wide): 24.3B **Publicly Held**
SIC: 3821 Laboratory apparatus & furniture
HQ: Helmet Securities Limited
93-96 Chadwick Road
Runcorn

GEOGRAPHIC SECTION
Wilmington - New Castle County (G-11420)

(G-11386)
LIGHTS OUT SCREEN PRINTING CO
1805 Beech St (19805-3838)
PHONE..................302 409-0560
EMP: 2
SALES (est): 83.9K Privately Held
SIC: 2752 Lithographic Commercial Printing

(G-11387)
LIGHTSCAPES INC
Also Called: Cloudburst Sprinkler Systems
6603a Gvernor Printz Blvd (19809)
PHONE..................302 798-5451
Brett Forest, *President*
EMP: 8
SALES (est): 1.2MM Privately Held
SIC: 5087 1731 Sprinkler systems; lighting contractor

(G-11388)
LIMESTONE COUNTRY DAY SCHOOL
Also Called: Limestone Hills Day School
5671 Ocheltree Ln (19808-1285)
PHONE..................302 239-9041
Linda Griffin, *Manager*
EMP: 11
SALES (corp-wide): 434.3K Privately Held
WEB: www.limestonehillsdayschool.net
SIC: 8351 8211 Preschool center; kindergarten
PA: Limestone Country Day School
    411 Paloni Ln
    Hockessin DE

(G-11389)
LIMESTONE MEDICAL CENTER INC
Also Called: Limestone Medical Aid Unit
1941 Limestone Rd Ste 113 (19808-5413)
P.O. Box 5040 (19808-0040)
PHONE..................302 992-0500
Tom Mulhern, *Director*
EMP: 80
SQ FT: 76,000
SALES (est): 12.4MM Privately Held
SIC: 8011 Medical centers

(G-11390)
LIMESTONE OPEN MRI LLC (PA)
2060 Limestone Rd (19808-5500)
PHONE..................302 246-2001
Teriq Quraishi,
EMP: 11 EST: 2008
SALES (est): 1.3MM Privately Held
SIC: 8011 Radiologist

(G-11391)
LIMEWOOD INVESTMENTS DEL INC
801 N West St Fl 2 (19801-1525)
PHONE..................302 656-8915
Ken J Kubacki, *Treasurer*
EMP: 4 Privately Held
SIC: 6719 Investment holding companies, except banks

(G-11392)
LINDA MCCORMICK
Also Called: Locust Cnstr & Contg Svcs
200 Tyrone Ave (19804-1929)
PHONE..................443 987-2099
Linda McCormick, *Owner*
EMP: 1
SALES (est): 250K Privately Held
SIC: 1542 5047 8742 1799 Commercial & office building contractors; medical equipment & supplies; management consulting services; home/office interiors finishing, furnishing & remodeling

(G-11393)
LINDCO
Also Called: Lindco Packaging
122 Alapocas Dr (19803-4503)
PHONE..................302 652-0708
EMP: 6 EST: 1994
SALES (est): 440K Privately Held
SIC: 8748 Business Consulting Services

(G-11394)
LINDEN HILL CLEANERS INC
4561 New Linden Hill Rd (19808)
PHONE..................302 368-9795
Won Lee, *President*
Yount Lee, *Vice Pres*
EMP: 7
SALES (est): 180.1K Privately Held
SIC: 7216 Cleaning & dyeing, except rugs

(G-11395)
LINDEN HILL ELEMENTARY PTA
3415 Skyline Dr (19808-1701)
PHONE..................302 454-3406
Mary Bradley, *Principal*
EMP: 26
SALES (est): 46K Privately Held
SIC: 8641 Parent-teachers' association

(G-11396)
LINK METALS LLC (PA)
3524 Silverside Rd 35b (19810-4929)
PHONE..................302 295-5066
Cindy Verlinich,
▲ EMP: 2
SALES (est): 306.4K Privately Held
SIC: 3312 Tool & die steel & alloys

(G-11397)
LINKEDIN PROFILE SERVICES LLC
108 W 13th St (19801)
PHONE..................703 679-7719
Karl Berkoben,
EMP: 12
SQ FT: 1,000
SALES (est): 240K Privately Held
SIC: 7338 7373 Resume writing service; computer integrated systems design

(G-11398)
LION TOTALCARE INC
9 Germay Dr Ste 200a (19804-1143)
PHONE..................610 444-1700
Jeff Boles, *President*
EMP: 45
SALES: 950K
SALES (corp-wide): 2.4MM Privately Held
WEB: www.lionprotectivesystems.com
SIC: 7699 Repair services
HQ: Lion Apparel, Inc.
    7200 Poe Ave Ste 400
    Dayton OH 45414
    937 898-1949

(G-11399)
LIP BALM LAND LLC
19c Trolley Sq (19806-3355)
PHONE..................302 319-9919
EMP: 2
SALES (est): 74.4K Privately Held
SIC: 2834 Lip balms

(G-11400)
LITCHARTS LLC
2711 Centerville Rd # 400 (19808-1660)
P.O. Box 1162, Madison NJ (07940-8162)
PHONE..................646 481-4807
Justin Kestler, *Mng Member*
Ben Florman,
EMP: 2
SALES (est): 76.8K Privately Held
SIC: 2741 7389 Miscellaneous publishing;

(G-11401)
LITTLE BLESSINGS DAYCARE
2010 N Market St (19802-4815)
PHONE..................302 655-8962
Malcolm Dawson, *President*
EMP: 10
SALES (est): 313.4K Privately Held
SIC: 8351 Group day care center

(G-11402)
LITTLE FOLKS TOO DAY CARE
1318 N Market St (19801-1133)
PHONE..................302 652-3420
Heike Parodi, *Manager*
EMP: 6
SALES (corp-wide): 721K Privately Held
SIC: 8351 Group day care center
PA: Little Folks Too Day Care
    1320 N Market St
    Wilmington DE 19801
    302 652-1238

(G-11403)
LITTLE FOLKS TOO DAY CARE (PA)
1320 N Market St (19801-1179)
PHONE..................302 652-1238
Cleonice Decherney, *President*
EMP: 38
SQ FT: 5,000
SALES: 721K Privately Held
SIC: 8351 Group day care center

(G-11404)
LITTLE GYM OF NCC
Also Called: Little Gym, The
4758 Limestone Rd Ste A (19808-4389)
PHONE..................302 543-5524
Amy Lancer, *Owner*
EMP: 6
SALES (est): 180K Privately Held
SIC: 7999 Gymnastic instruction, non-membership

(G-11405)
LITTLE NESTS PORTRAITS (PA)
2100 N Bancroft Pkwy (19806-2206)
PHONE..................610 459-8622
Laura Novak, *Owner*
EMP: 10
SALES (est): 2.2MM Privately Held
SIC: 5099 7221 7336 Portraits; photographic studios, portrait; art design services

(G-11406)
LITTLE PEOPLES COLLEGE
3507 Old Capitol Trl (19808-6125)
PHONE..................302 998-4929
Ann Ebaugh, *Director*
EMP: 4
SALES (est): 146.8K Privately Held
SIC: 8351 Child day care services

(G-11407)
LITTLE SCHOLARS LEARNING CTR
2511 W 4th St Ste A (19805-3350)
PHONE..................302 656-8785
Lisa Mosley, *Owner*
EMP: 16
SALES (est): 460.9K Privately Held
SIC: 8351 Preschool center

(G-11408)
LITTLE STAR INC
5702 Kirkwood Hwy (19808-4811)
PHONE..................302 995-2920
Elizabeth Cahill, *President*
EMP: 10
SALES (est): 303.5K Privately Held
SIC: 8351 Group day care center

(G-11409)
LITTLE STEPS DAYCARE
212 W 21st St (19802-4006)
PHONE..................302 654-4867
Julia Woulard, *Principal*
EMP: 5
SALES (est): 68.4K Privately Held
SIC: 8351 Group day care center

(G-11410)
LITUATION CREATIVE DESIGNS INC
3201 N Jefferson St (19802-2614)
PHONE..................302 494-4399
Xavier Cole, *President*
EMP: 15
SALES (est): 72.1K Privately Held
SIC: 8699 Charitable organization

(G-11411)
LITYX LLC
1000 N West St Ste 1200 (19801-1058)
PHONE..................888 548-9947
Paul Maiste, *President*
Gary Robinson, *COO*
Simon Poole, *Vice Pres*
EMP: 9
SALES: 2.2MM Privately Held
SIC: 8748 7372 Business consulting; business oriented computer software

(G-11412)
LIVE TYPING INC
1521 Concord Pike Ste 303 (19803-3644)
PHONE..................415 670-9601
Vladislav Korobov, *CEO*
EMP: 30 EST: 2013
SALES (est): 1.8MM Privately Held
SIC: 7371 7389 Computer software development;

(G-11413)
LIVING HARVEST INTERNTL MINST
Also Called: House of Deborah
701 N Clnl Ave Apt 202 (19805)
PHONE..................302 757-4273
Stephanie Jackson, *Chairman*
EMP: 4
SALES: 10K Privately Held
SIC: 8361 Residential care

(G-11414)
LLB ACQUISITION LLC
1209 N Orange St (19801-1120)
PHONE..................212 750-8300
Joseph Henderson, *Principal*
EMP: 8 EST: 2007
SALES (est): 604.1K Privately Held
SIC: 6799 Investors

(G-11415)
LLC LEVY WILSON
3801 Kennett Pike D204 (19807-2321)
PHONE..................302 888-1088
EMP: 14 EST: 2010
SALES (est): 937.2K Privately Held
SIC: 8621 Professional Organization

(G-11416)
LLOYDS WLDG & FABRICATION LLC
1101 E 8th St (19801-4356)
PHONE..................302 384-7662
EMP: 1
SALES (est): 42.6K Privately Held
SIC: 7692 Welding repair

(G-11417)
LNBE LLC
Also Called: E-Commerce
1226 N King St (19801-3232)
PHONE..................302 393-2201
EMP: 20
SALES (est): 375.4K Privately Held
SIC: 7371 Computer software development & applications

(G-11418)
LOADBALANCERORGINC
4550 Linden Hill Rd # 201 (19808-2930)
P.O. Box 3569 (19807-0569)
PHONE..................888 867-9504
Malcolm Turnbull, *President*
Jake Borman, *Principal*
EMP: 2
SALES (est): 208.8K Privately Held
SIC: 7372 5961 Prepackaged software; computer equipment & electronics, mail order

(G-11419)
LOCAL INVESTMENTS LLC
215 Sunset Dr (19809)
PHONE..................302 422-0731
Ronald Mendoza,
Carlos Herrerra,
EMP: 4 EST: 2016
SALES (est): 109.8K Privately Held
SIC: 6531 Real estate agents & managers

(G-11420)
LOCAL TV FINANCE LLC
2711 Centerville Rd # 400 (19808-1660)
PHONE..................302 636-5401
Kevin G Levy, *Principal*
EMP: 20
SALES (est): 43.6K
SALES (corp-wide): 2.7B Publicly Held
SIC: 7389 Financial services

Wilmington - New Castle County (G-11421)

HQ: Tribune Media Company
515 N State St Ste 2400
Chicago IL 60654
312 222-3394

(G-11421)
LOCALSPIN LLC
1521 Concord Pike Ste 301 (19803-3644)
P.O. Box 754, Franklin Lakes NJ (07417-0754)
PHONE..................917 232-7203
John Myers,
EMP: 2
SALES (est): 119.1K **Privately Held**
SIC: 7372 Application computer software

(G-11422)
LOCKHEED MARTIN OVERSEAS LLC
251 Little Falls Dr (19808-1674)
PHONE..................301 897-6923
EMP: 3 **Publicly Held**
SIC: 8742 3761 Management information systems consultant; guided missiles & space vehicles
HQ: Lockheed Martin Overseas, Llc
6801 Rockledge Dr
Bethesda MD 20817
301 897-6000

(G-11423)
LODES CHIROPRACTIC CENTER PA
3411 Silverside Rd 102hb (19810-4879)
PHONE..................302 477-1565
Michael R Lodes, President
EMP: 5
SALES (est): 455.3K **Privately Held**
SIC: 8041 Offices & clinics of chiropractors

(G-11424)
LODGE LANE ASSISTED LIVING
1221 Lodge Ln (19809-2766)
PHONE..................302 757-8100
K Freidman, Exec Dir
Karen Freidman, Exec Dir
EMP: 30 EST: 2013
SALES (est): 548K **Privately Held**
SIC: 8059 8699 Nursing & personal care; charitable organization

(G-11425)
LOFTCOM INC
1000 N West St Fl 12 (19801-1050)
PHONE..................800 563-6900
Carlos Lopez, President
EMP: 7
SALES (est): 136.4K **Privately Held**
SIC: 7389 Business services

(G-11426)
LOGNEX INC
1000 N West St Ste 1200 (19801-1058)
PHONE..................786 650-7755
EMP: 1
SALES: 50K **Privately Held**
SIC: 7372 Business oriented computer software

(G-11427)
LOGUE BROTHERS INC
Also Called: Texaco
3507 Miller Rd (19802-2521)
PHONE..................302 762-1896
Robert C Logue, President
EMP: 10
SQ FT: 22,500
SALES (est): 1.1MM **Privately Held**
SIC: 5541 7542 Gasoline service stations; carwash, automatic

(G-11428)
LOIZIDES & ASSOCIATES PC
1225 N King St Ste 800 (19801-3246)
PHONE..................302 654-0248
Chris Loizides, President
EMP: 8
SQ FT: 800
SALES (est): 694.8K **Privately Held**
SIC: 8111 General practice attorney, lawyer

(G-11429)
LOLAHSOUL JEWELRY INC
P.O. Box 2576 (19805-0576)
PHONE..................888 771-7087
Kamysha Martin, CEO
EMP: 2
SALES (est): 124.1K **Privately Held**
SIC: 3911 Jewelry, precious metal

(G-11430)
LONG & TANN & D ONOFRIO INC (PA)
3906 Concord Pike Ste F (19803-1733)
PHONE..................302 477-1970
Peter D' Onofrio, President
Richard Tann, Principal
EMP: 5
SQ FT: 1,250
SALES (est): 746.9K **Privately Held**
WEB: www.ltdeng.com
SIC: 8711 Structural engineering

(G-11431)
LONGO AND ASSOCIATES LLP
2010 Limestone Rd (19808-5506)
PHONE..................302 477-7500
Carolyn Gillespie, Partner
EMP: 7
SALES (est): 281.7K **Privately Held**
SIC: 8742 Management consulting services

(G-11432)
LONGVIEW FARMS CIVIC ASSN
1107 S Overhill Ct (19810-3109)
PHONE..................302 475-6684
Bart Smith, President
Roger Lee, Vice Pres
Lorraine Bisignani, Director
EMP: 5
SALES (est): 77.3K **Privately Held**
SIC: 8641 Dwelling-related associations

(G-11433)
LOOKSIEBIN LLC
4708 Weatherhill Dr (19808-1995)
PHONE..................410 869-2192
Christopher Wells, Principal
Nicholas Goble, Principal
EMP: 5
SALES (est): 104.7K **Privately Held**
SIC: 7389

(G-11434)
LOOM NETWORK INC
427 N Tatnall St 38768 (19801-2230)
PHONE..................404 939-1294
Matthew Campbell, CEO
EMP: 11
SALES: 3MM **Privately Held**
SIC: 7371 Computer software development & applications

(G-11435)
LORD PRINTING LLC
Also Called: Minuteman Press
1812 Marsh Rd Ste 411 (19810-4522)
PHONE..................302 439-3253
James Lord, Principal
Thomas Lord, Principal
Martha Landrigan, Vice Pres
EMP: 4
SQ FT: 1,364
SALES (est): 375K **Privately Held**
SIC: 2752 Commercial printing, lithographic

(G-11436)
LORELTON
2200 W 4th St Apt 229 (19805-3359)
PHONE..................302 573-3580
Jenniffer McFall, Sales Dir
Kenneth Carson, Exec Dir
Michael Comegys, Exec Dir
David Parkinson, Director
Tim Swann, Director
EMP: 45
SALES (est): 3.3MM **Privately Held**
WEB: www.lorelton.com
SIC: 6513 Retirement hotel operation

(G-11437)
LOSCO AND MARCONI PA
1813 N Franklin St (19802-3828)
P.O. Box 1677 (19899-1677)
PHONE..................302 656-7776
Daniel R Losco, President
Denise Losco, Office Mgr
William P Brady,
Thomas C Marconi,
EMP: 9
SALES (est): 974K **Privately Held**
WEB: www.delaw.org
SIC: 8111 Specialized law offices, attorneys

(G-11438)
LOSEMYNUMBERCOM LLC
427 N Tatnall St # 10885 (19801-2230)
PHONE..................302 778-9741
Panayiotis Stamus,
EMP: 4
SALES: 500K **Privately Held**
SIC: 4899 Data communication services

(G-11439)
LOUGHRAN MEDICAL GROUP PA
3411 Silverside Rd 103wb (19810-4848)
PHONE..................302 479-8464
Joseph Loughran MD, President
Timothy Hennesy, Partner
James Loughran MD, Vice Pres
EMP: 7
SALES (est): 789.6K **Privately Held**
SIC: 8011 Internal medicine, physician/surgeon; internal medicine practitioners

(G-11440)
LOUIS K RAFETTO DMD
3512 Silverside Rd Ste 12 (19810-4913)
PHONE..................302 477-1800
Louis K Rafetto DMD, Owner
EMP: 5
SALES (est): 433.6K **Privately Held**
SIC: 8021 Dental surgeon

(G-11441)
LOUIS P MARTIN DDS
1941 Limestone Rd Ste 105 (19808-5413)
PHONE..................302 994-4900
Louis P Martin DDS, Principal
EMP: 7
SALES (est): 185.6K **Privately Held**
SIC: 8021 Dentists' office

(G-11442)
LOUVIERS FEDERAL CREDIT UNION
1007 N Market St (19801-1227)
PHONE..................302 571-9513
EMP: 30 **Privately Held**
SIC: 6061 Federal credit unions
PA: Louviers Federal Credit Union
185 S Main St
Newark DE 19711

(G-11443)
LOUVIERS MORTGAGE CORPORATION
4839 Limestone Rd (19808-1902)
PHONE..................302 234-4129
Vincent Ingui, President
EMP: 15
SALES (est): 1.1MM **Privately Held**
SIC: 6163 Mortgage brokers arranging for loans, using money of others

(G-11444)
LOWES HOME CENTERS LLC
3100 Brandywine Pkwy Fl 1 (19803-1496)
PHONE..................302 479-7799
Frank Ancos, Manager
EMP: 150
SALES (corp-wide): 71.3B **Publicly Held**
SIC: 5211 5031 5722 5064 Lumber & other building materials; building materials, exterior; building materials, interior; household appliance stores; electrical appliances, television & radio
HQ: Lowe's Home Centers, Llc
1605 Curtis Bridge Rd
Wilkesboro NC 28697
336 658-4000

(G-11445)
LOYALTY IS EARNED INC (PA)
Also Called: Lie
3616 Kirkwood Hwy Ste A (19805-5124)
PHONE..................347 606-6383
Reginald A Brown Jr, President
EMP: 1
SALES (est): 50K **Privately Held**
SIC: 7549 3999 Towing services; advertising display products

(G-11446)
LRC NORTH AMERICA INC
1105 N Market St (19801-1216)
PHONE..................302 427-2845
Andrew Slater, President
Robert Kaiser, Vice Pres
◆ EMP: 20
SALES (est): 1.4MM
SALES (corp-wide): 16.6B **Privately Held**
SIC: 2834 3069 3421 Proprietary drug products; medical sundries, rubber; clippers, fingernail & toenail
HQ: London International Group Limited
35 New Bridge Street
London

(G-11447)
LSF NETWORKS LLC
300 Delaware Ave Ste 210a (19801-6601)
PHONE..................213 537-2402
Kenneth Hsu,
EMP: 3
SALES (est): 86.5K **Privately Held**
SIC: 2741

(G-11448)
LUMBER INDUSTRIES INC
5809 Kennett Pike (19807-1115)
PHONE..................302 655-9651
George D Herman, President
Baird Brittingham, Chairman
Steve Sweeny, Vice Pres
Bill Wolhar, Vice Pres
John Brittingham, Treasurer
EMP: 7
SQ FT: 1,000
SALES (est): 554.9K **Privately Held**
WEB: www.lumberindustries.com
SIC: 7389 Financial services

(G-11449)
LUMENTY TECHNOLOGIES INC
3411 Silverside Rd # 104 (19810-4812)
PHONE..................971 331-3113
Alexander Ulanovskiy, CEO
Andrey Veremeev, Manager
▲ EMP: 14
SALES (est): 390.6K **Privately Held**
SIC: 5065 Mobile telephone equipment

(G-11450)
LUMHAA LLC
108 W 13th St (19801)
PHONE..................916 517-9972
Shriya Sekhsaria,
EMP: 7
SALES (est): 193.9K **Privately Held**
SIC: 2741

(G-11451)
LUNE ROUGE ENTRMT USA INC
251 Little Falls Dr (19808-1674)
PHONE..................514 556-2101
Stphane Mongeau, President
EMP: 25
SALES (est): 78.8K **Privately Held**
SIC: 7929 Entertainment service

(G-11452)
LUSOTRADING CORP
1521 Concord Pike Ste 303 (19803-3644)
PHONE..................302 288-0670
EMP: 2
SALES (est): 140K **Privately Held**
SIC: 5149 2079 2091 Whol Groceries Mfg Edible Fats/Oils Mfg Canned/Cured Fish/Seafood

(G-11453)
LUTHERAN COMMUNITY SERVICES
2809 Baynard Blvd (19802-2967)
PHONE..................302 654-8886
Jean Warren, General Mgr

▲ = Import ▼=Export
◆ =Import/Export

GEOGRAPHIC SECTION

Wilmington - New Castle County

Greg Moore, *Director*
Sandy Betley, *Program Dir*
Steve Tindall, *Executive*
EMP: 6
SALES: 1.4MM **Privately Held**
WEB: www.lcsde.org
SIC: 8322 8741 Social service center; financial management for business

(G-11454)
LUTHERAN SENIOR SERVICES INC (PA)
1201 N Harrison St # 1204 (19806-3534)
PHONE 302 654-4490
Linda Dugan, *Manager*
John Teoli, *Exec Dir*
EMP: 41 **EST:** 1967
SALES: 3.7MM **Privately Held**
WEB: www.luthertowers.com
SIC: 8052 Intermediate care facilities

(G-11455)
LUTHERAN SENIOR SERVICES INC
Also Called: Luther Towers II
1420 N Franklin St Ste 1 (19806-3122)
PHONE 302 654-4490
Linda Dugan, *Manager*
EMP: 5
SALES (corp-wide): 3.7MM **Privately Held**
WEB: www.luthertowers.com
SIC: 6513 Retirement hotel operation
PA: Lutheran Senior Services, Inc.
1201 N Harrison St # 1204
Wilmington DE 19806
302 654-4490

(G-11456)
LUTZ ENGINEERING INC
3324 Hermitage Rd (19810-2108)
PHONE 302 479-9017
Maria Masington, *President*
Robert Lutz, *Vice Pres*
David Davenport, *Engineer*
EMP: 5 **EST:** 1997
SALES: 834.6K **Privately Held**
WEB: www.lutz-engr.com
SIC: 8711 Consulting engineer

(G-11457)
LUXCORE LLC
300 Delaware Ave Ste 210a (19801-6601)
PHONE 302 777-0538
John McAfee,
EMP: 19
SALES: 100K **Privately Held**
SIC: 7379 Computer related consulting services

(G-11458)
LUXIASUITES LLC
Also Called: Justison Landing
331 Justison St (19801-5181)
PHONE 302 654-8527
EMP: 7
SALES (corp-wide): 2.4MM **Privately Held**
SIC: 6513 Apartment building operators
PA: Luxiasuites Llc
322 A St Ste 300
Wilmington DE 19801
302 778-2900

(G-11459)
LUXIASUITES LLC (PA)
322 A St Ste 300 (19801-5354)
PHONE 302 778-2900
Liz Allman, *Sales Staff*
Robert E Buccini, *Mng Member*
EMP: 27
SALES (est): 2.4MM **Privately Held**
SIC: 7011 Hotels

(G-11460)
LUXIASUITES LLC
Also Called: Residences At City Center
1007 N Orange St (19801-1239)
PHONE 302 778-3000
Dan Jasinski, *Manager*
EMP: 9
SALES (corp-wide): 2.4MM **Privately Held**
SIC: 7299 Apartment locating service
PA: Luxiasuites Llc
322 A St Ste 300
Wilmington DE 19801
302 778-2900

(G-11461)
LUXIASUITES LLC
Also Called: Christina Landing
115 Christina Landing Dr (19801-5401)
PHONE 302 426-1200
Lenox Lauren, *Branch Mgr*
EMP: 5
SALES (corp-wide): 2.4MM **Privately Held**
SIC: 7011 Hotels
PA: Luxiasuites Llc
322 A St Ste 300
Wilmington DE 19801
302 778-2900

(G-11462)
LYCRA COMPANY LLC (DH)
Also Called: Apparel & Advanced Textiles
2711 Centerville Rd # 300 (19808-1660)
PHONE 316 226-9361
David Trerotola, *CEO*
Toby Harrison, *Vice Pres*
◆ **EMP:** 600
SQ FT: 1,500
SALES (est): 200.3MM
SALES (corp-wide): 40.6B **Privately Held**
SIC: 2221 Textile mills, broadwoven: silk & manmade, also glass
HQ: Invista Equities, Llc
4111 E 37th St N
Wichita KS 67220
770 792-4221

(G-11463)
LYNNANNE KASARDA MD
1802 W 4th St (19805-3420)
PHONE 302 655-5822
Lynnanne Kasarda, *Principal*
EMP: 4
SALES (est): 72.3K **Privately Held**
SIC: 8011 Offices & clinics of medical doctors

(G-11464)
LYONS DAVID J LAW OFFICE
1526 Gilpin Ave (19806-3016)
PHONE 302 777-5698
David J Lyons, *Owner*
EMP: 5
SALES (est): 402K **Privately Held**
SIC: 8111 General practice attorney, lawyer

(G-11465)
LYONS DOUGHTY & VELDHUIS
15 Ashley Pl Ste 2b (19804-1396)
PHONE 302 428-1670
Stephen Doughtry, *Owner*
George Scafidi, *Supervisor*
Brian Todd, *Supervisor*
Stephen Doughty, *Shareholder*
EMP: 65
SALES (est): 2.4MM **Privately Held**
SIC: 8111 General practice law office

(G-11466)
LYONS INSURANCE AGENCY INC (PA)
Also Called: Nationwide
501 Carr Rd Ste 301 (19809-2866)
PHONE 302 227-7100
David F Lyons, *President*
Harry Garrett, *Vice Pres*
Martin Maureen, *Accounts Mgr*
Robert Applegate, *Accounts Exec*
Chris Anderson, *Manager*
EMP: 25
SALES (est): 5.1MM **Privately Held**
SIC: 6411 Insurance agents; property & casualty insurance agent; life insurance agents

(G-11467)
M & M MARKETING GROUP LLC
1521 Concord Pike (19803-3642)
PHONE 321 274-5352
EMP: 5
SALES: 500K **Privately Held**
SIC: 5099 Market Beauty Products To Salons And Spas

(G-11468)
M AND J INDUSTRIES
105 Hayman Pl (19803-3400)
PHONE 302 559-5005
Peter Bilous, *Principal*
EMP: 1
SALES (est): 50K **Privately Held**
SIC: 3999 Manufacturing industries

(G-11469)
M AND R
2909 Lancaster Ave (19805-5226)
PHONE 302 421-9838
Pedro Marrero, *Owner*
EMP: 3
SALES (est): 208.2K **Privately Held**
SIC: 3341 Gold smelting & refining (secondary)

(G-11470)
M AUGER ENTERPRISE INC
Also Called: Badger Electric
101 Cassidy Dr (19804)
PHONE 302 992-9922
Marc Auger, *President*
◆ **EMP:** 29
SALES (est): 4.2MM **Privately Held**
WEB: www.badgerde.com
SIC: 1731 General electrical contractor

(G-11471)
M DAVIS & SONS INC (PA)
19 Germay Dr (19804-1104)
PHONE 302 998-3385
Margaret D Del Fabbro, *CEO*
Charles R Davis, *Ch of Bd*
John S Bonk, *President*
▲ **EMP:** 134 **EST:** 1870
SQ FT: 20,000
SALES (est): 64.7MM **Privately Held**
WEB: www.mdavisinc.com
SIC: 1711 1731 1791 Plumbing contractors; mechanical contractor; ventilation & duct work contractor; general electrical contractor; iron work, structural

(G-11472)
M DAVIS & SONS INC
200 Hadco Rd (19804-1074)
PHONE 302 998-3385
Charles Davis, *Principal*
EMP: 6
SALES (corp-wide): 64.7MM **Privately Held**
SIC: 1711 Mechanical contractor
PA: M. Davis & Sons, Inc.
19 Germay Dr
Wilmington DE 19804
302 998-3385

(G-11473)
M TECH EUROPEAN AUTOHOUSE INC
2517 W 6th St (19805-2908)
PHONE 302 472-6813
Omid Tammar, *President*
EMP: 4
SALES (est): 370.9K **Privately Held**
SIC: 7538 General automotive repair shops

(G-11474)
M-CAP TECHNOLOGIES INTL (PA)
3521 Silverside Rd (19810-4900)
PHONE 302 695-5329
Ernie Porta, *President*
Rick Stejskal, *Finance Dir*
EMP: 5
SALES (est): 203.6K **Privately Held**
SIC: 8731 Commercial physical research

(G-11475)
MAACO COLLISION REPR AUTO PNTG
2400 Northeast Blvd (19802-4509)
PHONE 610 628-3867
Craig Schlott, *Owner*
EMP: 5
SALES (est): 45.4K **Privately Held**
SIC: 7542 7532 Carwash, automatic; body shop, automotive

(G-11476)
MACCARI COMPANIES INC (PA)
1700 First State Blvd (19804-3566)
P.O. Box 6468 (19804-0468)
PHONE 302 994-9628
Anthony Maccari, *President*
Jean M Maccari, *Corp Secy*
EMP: 5
SQ FT: 20,000
SALES (est): 3.8MM **Privately Held**
SIC: 1721 1799 Industrial painting; sandblasting of building exteriors

(G-11477)
MACELREE & HARVEY LTD
5721 Kennett Pike (19807-1311)
PHONE 302 654-4454
Felice Glennon Kerr, *Principal*
Carolyn Van Fleet, *Human Res Dir*
Annette Odonnell, *Receptionist*
Patrick Boyer, *Associate*
Kristen Matthews, *Associate*
EMP: 9
SALES (est): 611.8K **Privately Held**
SIC: 8111 General practice attorney, lawyer

(G-11478)
MACFARLANE A RADFORD MD PA
Also Called: Millcreek Pediatrics
203 W Pembrey Dr (19803-2008)
PHONE 302 633-6338
A Radford Macfarland, *President*
EMP: 10
SALES (est): 965.3K **Privately Held**
SIC: 8011 Pediatrician

(G-11479)
MACHINE LEARNING SYSTEMS LLC
123 Odyssey Dr (19808-1558)
PHONE 302 299-2621
Gautam Mukherjee,
EMP: 1
SALES (est): 51.6K **Privately Held**
SIC: 7372 Business oriented computer software

(G-11480)
MACINTOSH ENGINEERING INC
2 Mill Rd Ste 100 (19806-2175)
PHONE 302 252-9200
Robert Macintosh, *President*
Eric Heller, *Project Mgr*
Mark Nauman, *Engineer*
Chelsea Collins, *Project Engr*
Richard Savona, *Design Engr*
EMP: 17
SALES (est): 2.6MM **Privately Held**
WEB: www.onmac.com
SIC: 8711 Structural engineering

(G-11481)
MACKLYN HOME CARE
5179 W Woodmill Dr (19808-4067)
PHONE 302 690-9397
Krista Gaul, *Owner*
Donna Durnan, *Director*
EMP: 8
SALES: 1.3MM **Privately Held**
SIC: 8082 4119 Home health care services; local passenger transportation

(G-11482)
MADDOX CONCRETE CO INC (PA)
11 Millside Dr (19801-5596)
PHONE 302 656-2000
James R Maddox, *President*
EMP: 1
SQ FT: 2,000
SALES (est): 330.1K **Privately Held**
WEB: www.maddoxconcrete.com
SIC: 3273 5032 Ready-mixed concrete; concrete mixtures

(G-11483)
MADRONA LABS INC
1209 N Orange St (19801-1120)
PHONE 216 375-1978
Greg Gottisman, *Branch Mgr*
EMP: 4

(PA)=Parent Co (HQ)=Headquarters (DH)=Div Headquarters
✪ = New Business established in last 2 years

Wilmington - New Castle County (G-11484) GEOGRAPHIC SECTION

SALES (corp-wide): 616.1K **Privately Held**
SIC: 7371 Computer software development & applications
PA: Madrona Labs, Inc.
999 3rd Ave Ste 3400
Seattle WA 98104
216 375-1978

(G-11484)
MAGELLAN MIDSTREAM PARTNERS LP
Also Called: Megellan Terminal
1050 Christiana Ave Ste A (19801-5867)
PHONE 302 654-3717
Carlos Cockburn, *General Mgr*
John Weaver, *Manager*
Paul Hafner, *Supervisor*
EMP: 17
SALES (corp-wide): 2.8B **Publicly Held**
WEB: www.twc.com
SIC: 4226 Oil & gasoline storage caverns for hire
PA: Magellan Midstream Partners, Lp
1 Williams Ctr Bsmt 2
Tulsa OK 74172
918 574-7000

(G-11485)
MAGETTI GORUP LLC
2711 Centerville Rd # 120 (19808-1660)
PHONE 302 355-5540
Tom Jones,
Shaun Tucker,
EMP: 99
SALES (est): 2.4MM **Privately Held**
SIC: 8741 Management services

(G-11486)
MAGIC CAR WASH INC
3221 Naamans Rd (19810-1003)
PHONE 302 479-5911
Dave Emerson, *President*
Eve Emerson, *President*
EMP: 30
SALES: 100K **Privately Held**
SIC: 7542 Washing & polishing, automotive

(G-11487)
MAGNECO LLC
19c Trolley Sq (19806-3355)
PHONE 302 613-0080
EMP: 1
SALES: 0 **Privately Held**
SIC: 5961 7372 General merchandise, mail order; application computer software

(G-11488)
MAGUIRE & SONS INC
Also Called: Maguire Pest Control
1035 Philadelphia Pike C (19809-2039)
P.O. Box 684, Claymont (19703-0684)
PHONE 302 798-1200
Allan Maguire, *President*
EMP: 8
SALES: 490K **Privately Held**
SIC: 7342 Pest control in structures

(G-11489)
MAHAVIR LLC
Also Called: Goddard School, The
111 S West St (19801-5014)
PHONE 302 651-7995
Kenur Talsania,
EMP: 35
SALES (est): 242K **Privately Held**
SIC: 8351 Preschool center

(G-11490)
MAIN GATE LAUNDRY
123 Kirkwood Sq (19808-4859)
PHONE 302 998-9949
Linda Burns, *Owner*
EMP: 5
SALES (est): 139.4K **Privately Held**
SIC: 7216 7211 Drycleaning plants, except rugs; power laundries, family & commercial

(G-11491)
MAIN LIGHT INDUSTRIES INC
1614 Newport Gap Pike (19808-6208)
P.O. Box 1352 (19899-1352)
PHONE 302 998-8017
Aidas Gimbutas, *President*

Mark Schock, *Mfg Mgr*
Ryan Searles, *Warehouse Mgr*
Bob Weir, *Sales Mgr*
Robert Cox, *Manager*
EMP: 119
SQ FT: 16,000
SALES (est): 17.9MM **Privately Held**
WEB: www.mainlight.com
SIC: 3648 5049 7922 Stage lighting equipment; theatrical equipment & supplies; equipment rental, theatrical

(G-11492)
MAIN TOWERS ASSOICATES LP
Also Called: Main Towers Apartments
4 Denny Rd (19809-3445)
PHONE 302 761-7327
Jackie Edmanson, *Principal*
EMP: 4
SALES (est): 477.7K **Privately Held**
SIC: 6513 Retirement hotel operation

(G-11493)
MAINTENANCE TROUBLESHOOTI
2917 Cheshire Rd (19810-3202)
PHONE 302 477-1045
Thomas B Davis, *Principal*
EMP: 5
SALES (est): 181.5K **Privately Held**
SIC: 7349 Building maintenance services

(G-11494)
MAJALCO LLC
1013 Centre Rd Ste 403a (19805-1270)
PHONE 703 507-5298
Marc Jacques-Louis,
EMP: 1 **EST:** 2013
SALES (est): 35K **Privately Held**
SIC: 2844 7373 8243 8361 Cosmetic preparations; office computer automation systems integration; operator training, computer; residential care; management services;

(G-11495)
MAJESTIQUE VENTURES & HLTH CRE
Also Called: Saheed Rufai
4708 Kirkwood Hwy Ste D (19808-5022)
PHONE 302 633-4010
Magie Akben, *President*
Saheed Rufai, *Exec Dir*
EMP: 50
SALES: 500K **Privately Held**
WEB: www.majestiqueventures.com
SIC: 7361 Nurses' registry

(G-11496)
MALIK JOHN S ATTY AT LAW
100 E 14th St (19801-3210)
PHONE 302 427-2247
John Malik, *Owner*
EMP: 4
SALES (est): 364.2K **Privately Held**
SIC: 8111 Criminal law

(G-11497)
MAMMELES INC (PA)
Also Called: Mammele's Paint Stores
2300 Kirkwood Hwy (19805-4905)
P.O. Box 4458 (19807-0458)
PHONE 302 998-0541
Robert Alan Peoples, *President*
Andrew M Peoples, *Vice Pres*
John E Peoples, *Treasurer*
EMP: 5
SQ FT: 12,000
SALES (est): 2.2MM **Privately Held**
WEB: www.mammeles.com
SIC: 5198 5231 Paints; varnishes; paint brushes, rollers, sprayers; wallcoverings; paint; paint brushes, rollers, sprayers & other supplies

(G-11498)
MANAGEMENT ASSOCIATES INC
Also Called: Interfaith Community Housing
613 N Washington St (19801-2135)
PHONE 302 652-3991
Gary Polil, *President*
EMP: 15
SALES: 2MM **Privately Held**
SIC: 6513 Apartment building operators

PA: Community Housing Inc
613 N Washington St
Wilmington DE 19801
302 652-3991

(G-11499)
MANAGEMENT PAIN LLC
5231 W Woodmill Dr Ste 45 (19808-4068)
PHONE 302 543-5180
Liana Lera Ayotte, *Principal*
EMP: 6
SALES (est): 326K **Privately Held**
SIC: 8093 Specialty outpatient clinics

(G-11500)
MANCOR US INC
1011 Centre Rd Ste 322 (19805-1266)
PHONE 302 573-3858
Mike Andrews, *CEO*
EMP: 5
SALES (est): 446.7K
SALES (corp-wide): 156.6MM **Privately Held**
SIC: 3441 Building components, structural steel
PA: Mancor Canada Inc
2485 Speers Rd
Oakville ON L6L 2
905 827-3737

(G-11501)
MANETO INC (HQ)
103 Foulk Rd (19803-3742)
PHONE 302 656-4285
EMP: 6
SALES (est): 6.9MM
SALES (corp-wide): 720.5MM **Privately Held**
SIC: 3996 3253 2273 2435 Hard surface floor coverings; wall tile, ceramic; floor tile, ceramic; rugs, tufted; carpets, hand & machine made; veneer stock, hardwood; hardwood plywood, prefinished; panels, hardwood plywood; plywood, hardwood or hardwood faced
PA: Mannington Mills Inc.
75 Mannington Mills Rd
Salem NJ 08079
856 935-3000

(G-11502)
MANGROVE HOLDINGS LLC
Also Called: Telaris Communication Group
1000 N West St Ste 1200 (19801-1058)
PHONE 305 587-2950
EMP: 17
SQ FT: 2,000 **Privately Held**
SIC: 6719 Holding Company

(G-11503)
MANLEY HVAC INC
3705 Wild Cherry Ln (19808-4611)
PHONE 302 998-4654
Manley Husfelt, *President*
EMP: 5
SALES (est): 430K **Privately Held**
SIC: 1711 Heating & air conditioning contractors

(G-11504)
MANNING GROSS + MASSENBURG LLP
1007 N Orange St Apt 1051 (19801-1250)
PHONE 302 657-2100
Harry L Manion, *Branch Mgr*
Tece Behl, *Legal Staff*
Nathan Barillo, *Associate*
Dustin Beckley, *Associate*
Lindsay Weiss, *Associate*
EMP: 16
SALES (corp-wide): 30.9MM **Privately Held**
SIC: 8111 General practice law office
PA: Manning Gross + Massenburg Llp
125 High St Fl 6
Boston MA 02110
617 670-8800

(G-11505)
MANUFACTURERS & TRADERS TR CO
Also Called: M&T
3801 Kennett Pike (19807-2321)
PHONE 302 651-8738
Amy Sterkenburg, *Vice Pres*
Christina Bennefield, *Portfolio Mgr*

Patricia Clark, *Branch Mgr*
EMP: 14
SALES (corp-wide): 6.4B **Publicly Held**
WEB: www.binghamlegg.com
SIC: 6022 State commercial banks
HQ: Manufacturers And Traders Trust Company
1 M&T Plz Fl 3
Buffalo NY 14203
716 842-4200

(G-11506)
MANUFACTURERS & TRADERS TR CO
Also Called: M&T
2301 Concord Pike (19803-2911)
PHONE 302 472-3233
David Collins, *Engineer*
Charles Emory, *Branch Mgr*
EMP: 9
SALES (corp-wide): 6.4B **Publicly Held**
WEB: www.binghamlegg.com
SIC: 6022 State trust companies accepting deposits, commercial
HQ: Manufacturers And Traders Trust Company
1 M&T Plz Fl 3
Buffalo NY 14203
716 842-4200

(G-11507)
MANUFACTURERS & TRADERS TR CO
Also Called: M&T
1309 Kirkwood Hwy (19805-2121)
PHONE 302 472-3141
Mary Ann Askan, *Branch Mgr*
EMP: 8
SALES (corp-wide): 6.4B **Publicly Held**
WEB: www.binghamlegg.com
SIC: 6022 State commercial banks
HQ: Manufacturers And Traders Trust Company
1 M&T Plz Fl 3
Buffalo NY 14203
716 842-4200

(G-11508)
MANUFACTURERS & TRADERS TR CO
Also Called: M&T
2371 Limestone Rd (19808-4103)
PHONE 302 651-1757
Brandon Smith, *Vice Pres*
Porche Johnson, *Manager*
Rory Maher, *Manager*
EMP: 13
SALES (corp-wide): 6.4B **Publicly Held**
WEB: www.binghamlegg.com
SIC: 6022 State trust companies accepting deposits, commercial
HQ: Manufacturers And Traders Trust Company
1 M&T Plz Fl 3
Buffalo NY 14203
716 842-4200

(G-11509)
MANUFACTURERS & TRADERS TR CO
Also Called: M&T
1812 Marsh Rd (19810-4581)
PHONE 302 651-1803
Cynthia Corliss, *Vice Pres*
Kendrall Elder, *Branch Mgr*
William Lundstrom, *Agent*
EMP: 13
SALES (corp-wide): 6.4B **Publicly Held**
WEB: www.binghamlegg.com
SIC: 6022 State trust companies accepting deposits, commercial
HQ: Manufacturers And Traders Trust Company
1 M&T Plz Fl 3
Buffalo NY 14203
716 842-4200

(G-11510)
MANUFACTURERS & TRADERS TR CO
Also Called: M&T
100 N James St (19804-3123)
PHONE 302 651-1544
Dianne Franehitti, *Manager*
EMP: 12

▲ = Import ▼=Export
◆ =Import/Export

GEOGRAPHIC SECTION
Wilmington - New Castle County (G-11540)

SALES (corp-wide): 6.4B **Publicly Held**
WEB: www.binghamlegg.com
SIC: **6022** State trust companies accepting deposits, commercial
HQ: Manufacturers And Traders Trust Company
1 M&T Plz Fl 3
Buffalo NY 14203
716 842-4200

(G-11511)
MANUFACTURERS & TRADERS TR CO
Also Called: M&T
1207 N Union St (19806-2531)
PHONE.................................302 656-1260
Shirley Hawk, *Manager*
EMP: 10
SALES (corp-wide): 6.4B **Publicly Held**
WEB: www.binghamlegg.com
SIC: **6022** State trust companies accepting deposits, commercial
HQ: Manufacturers And Traders Trust Company
1 M&T Plz Fl 3
Buffalo NY 14203
716 842-4200

(G-11512)
MANUFACTURERS & TRADERS TR CO
Also Called: M&T
15 W Lea Blvd (19802-1324)
PHONE.................................302 472-3161
Sandra Ortiz, *Vice Pres*
Jane Smith, *Manager*
EMP: 5
SALES (corp-wide): 6.4B **Publicly Held**
WEB: www.binghamlegg.com
SIC: **6022** State commercial banks
HQ: Manufacturers And Traders Trust Company
1 M&T Plz Fl 3
Buffalo NY 14203
716 842-4200

(G-11513)
MANUFACTURERS & TRADERS TR CO
Also Called: M&T
5107 Concord Pike (19803-1414)
PHONE.................................302 477-1761
Fax: 302 472-3323
EMP: 6
SALES (corp-wide): 5.7B **Publicly Held**
SIC: **6022** State Commercial Bank
HQ: Manufacturers And Traders Trust Company
1 M And T Plz
Buffalo NY 14203
716 842-4200

(G-11514)
MANUFACTURERS & TRADERS TR CO
Also Called: M&T
301 W 11th St (19801-1519)
PHONE.................................302 651-1000
Sarah Barsky, *Vice Pres*
Delores Cribb, *Manager*
Yatish Brar, *Executive*
Bill Bergen,
EMP: 8
SALES (corp-wide): 6.4B **Publicly Held**
WEB: www.binghamlegg.com
SIC: **6022** State commercial banks
HQ: Manufacturers And Traders Trust Company
1 M&T Plz Fl 3
Buffalo NY 14203
716 842-4200

(G-11515)
MANUFACTURERS & TRADERS TR CO
Also Called: M&T
1100 N Market St (19801-1243)
PHONE.................................302 636-6000
Paul Desaro, *President*
Beryl Barmore, *Vice Pres*
Sharon Owens, *Vice Pres*
Don Byrom, *Loan Officer*
Olga Negoreva, *Manager*
EMP: 15

SALES (corp-wide): 6.4B **Publicly Held**
WEB: www.binghamlegg.com
SIC: **6022** State commercial banks
HQ: Manufacturers And Traders Trust Company
1 M&T Plz Fl 3
Buffalo NY 14203
716 842-4200

(G-11516)
MANUFACTURERS & TRADERS TR CO
Also Called: M&T
4899 Limestone Rd (19808-1902)
PHONE.................................302 472-3309
Jim Whittaker, *Manager*
EMP: 11
SALES (corp-wide): 6.4B **Publicly Held**
WEB: www.binghamlegg.com
SIC: **6022** State commercial banks
HQ: Manufacturers And Traders Trust Company
1 M&T Plz Fl 3
Buffalo NY 14203
716 842-4200

(G-11517)
MAPLES FIDUCIARY SVCS DEL INC
4001 Kennett Pike Ste 302 (19807-2039)
PHONE.................................302 338-9130
Robyn Joe, *COO*
Abali Hoilett, *Senior VP*
Cleveland Stewart, *Senior VP*
Angel Fu, *Assistant VP*
Michael Hackett, *Assistant VP*
EMP: 6
SALES (est): 203K **Privately Held**
SIC: **7338** Secretarial & typing service

(G-11518)
MARA LABS INC
1013 Centre Rd Ste 403b (19805-1270)
PHONE.................................650 564-4971
Nishith Rastogi, *CEO*
EMP: 47
SALES: 1MM **Privately Held**
SIC: **7371** Computer software development & applications

(G-11519)
MARBLE CITY SOFTWARE INC
1900 Gilpin Ave (19806-2308)
PHONE.................................302 658-2583
Michael Power, *CEO*
Ruth Power, *Treasurer*
EMP: 2
SALES (est): 106K **Privately Held**
SIC: **7372** Prepackaged software

(G-11520)
MARC WSBURG LPCMH MNTAL HLTH C
1201 Philadelphia Pike (19809-2042)
PHONE.................................302 798-4400
EMP: 8
SALES (est): 73.3K **Privately Held**
SIC: **8093** Mental health clinic, outpatient

(G-11521)
MARCH OF DIMES INC
Also Called: Delaware Chapter
236 N James St Ste C (19804-3165)
PHONE.................................302 225-1020
Leslie Kosck, *Exec Dir*
EMP: 6
SALES (corp-wide): 111MM **Privately Held**
SIC: **8399** Fund raising organization, non-fee basis
PA: March Of Dimes Inc.
1550 Crystal Dr Ste 1300
Arlington VA 22202
571 257-2324

(G-11522)
MARGARET HARRIS-NEMTUDA
3513 Concord Pike # 1000 (19803-5027)
PHONE.................................302 477-5500
Walter Keiper, *Owner*
EMP: 4
SALES (est): 139K **Privately Held**
SIC: **6531** Real estate agents & managers

(G-11523)
MARGARET M MUNLEY DDS
2004 Foulk Rd Ste 2 (19810-3641)
PHONE.................................302 475-2626
Margaret M Munley DDS, *Owner*
EMP: 4
SALES (est): 199.3K **Privately Held**
SIC: **8021** Periodontist

(G-11524)
MARGOLIS EDELSTEIN
300 Delaware Ave Ste 800 (19801-1697)
PHONE.................................302 888-1112
Edelstein Margolis, *Branch Mgr*
EMP: 43
SALES (corp-wide): 35.8MM **Privately Held**
SIC: **8111** General practice law office
PA: Margolis Edelstein
170 S Indepe Mall W Ste W
Philadelphia PA 19106
215 922-1100

(G-11525)
MARIN BAYARD
521 N West St (19801-2139)
PHONE.................................302 658-4200
Bayard Marin, *Owner*
EMP: 5
SALES (est): 444.9K **Privately Held**
SIC: **8111** Malpractice & negligence law

(G-11526)
MARINE LUBRICANTS INC
1130 E 7th St (19801-4502)
P.O. Box 389, New Castle (19720-0389)
PHONE.................................302 429-7570
Joseph K Mc Cammon, *President*
H Hickman Rowland, *Corp Secy*
EMP: 8
SQ FT: 15,000
SALES (est): 1.3MM **Privately Held**
WEB: www.marinelubricants.com
SIC: **4213** Liquid petroleum transport, non-local

(G-11527)
MARINER FINANCE LLC
3616 Kirkwood Hwy (19808-5124)
PHONE.................................302 384-6047
Kevin Gamble, *Manager*
EMP: 6
SALES (corp-wide): 23.9MM **Privately Held**
SIC: **6141** Consumer finance companies
PA: Mariner Finance, Llc
8211 Town Center Dr
Nottingham MD 21236
410 882-5200

(G-11528)
MARIO F MEDORI INC
20 Millside Dr (19801-5542)
PHONE.................................302 239-4550
Mark Medori, *President*
Mary A Medori, *Corp Secy*
Mario F Medori, *Vice Pres*
EMP: 8
SALES: 200K **Privately Held**
SIC: **1741** 1541 Stone masonry; industrial buildings & warehouses

(G-11529)
MARIO MEDORI INC
20 Millside Dr (19801-5542)
PHONE.................................302 656-8432
Mario Medori, *CEO*
EMP: 11
SALES (est): 783.4K **Privately Held**
SIC: **1741** Masonry & other stonework

(G-11530)
MARK A FORTUNATO
1415 Foulk Rd (19803-2748)
PHONE.................................302 477-4900
Mark A Fortunato, *Principal*
EMP: 50
SALES (est): 185K **Privately Held**
SIC: **8021** Dentists' office

(G-11531)
MARK C GLADNICK DDS
5513 Kirkwood Hwy (19808-5001)
PHONE.................................302 994-2660
Mark Gladnick DDS, *Owner*
Mark C Gladnick DDS, *Owner*

EMP: 7
SALES (est): 430.3K **Privately Held**
SIC: **8021** Dentists' office

(G-11532)
MARKATOS SERVICES INC
Also Called: Markatos Cleaning Services
1411 Philadelphia Pike B (19809-1823)
PHONE.................................302 792-0606
Harry Markatos, *President*
Susan Markatos, *Vice Pres*
EMP: 35
SQ FT: 4,000
SALES (est): 938.3K **Privately Held**
SIC: **7349** Maid services, contract or fee basis; building & office cleaning services

(G-11533)
MARKES INTERNATIONAL INC
270 Presidential Dr (19807-3302)
PHONE.................................302 656-5500
Charles H Elter, *Principal*
EMP: 3
SALES (est): 237.9K **Privately Held**
SIC: **3826** Analytical instruments

(G-11534)
MARKET EDGE LLC (PA)
1003 Park Pl (19806-4304)
PHONE.................................302 442-6800
Paul Drees, *President*
Jeffrey Healy, *Business Mgr*
David Anshen, *Project Mgr*
Meera Gandhi, *Marketing Staff*
Tony Rademaker, *Manager*
EMP: 20
SALES (est): 2.9MM **Privately Held**
WEB: www.mkt-edge.com
SIC: **8742** Management consulting services

(G-11535)
MARKET KEYS LLC
Also Called: Tspkeycom
108 W 13th St (19801)
PHONE.................................205 800-0285
John Pope,
EMP: 1
SALES (est): 20K **Privately Held**
SIC: **2741**

(G-11536)
MARKETING CREATORS INC
802 N West St (19801-1526)
PHONE.................................302 409-0344
Paul Dukes, *President*
EMP: 99
SALES (est): 3.7MM **Privately Held**
SIC: **8742** Marketing consulting services

(G-11537)
MARKETING ENTERPRISE CAPYURING
Also Called: M E C C Ad
1600 Desmond Rd (19805-4670)
PHONE.................................302 293-9250
EMP: 1
SALES (est): 50.3K **Privately Held**
WEB: www.meccad.com
SIC: **3993** 8742 Signs & advertising specialties; marketing consulting services

(G-11538)
MARKING SERVICES INC
3505 Silverside Rd # 101 (19810-4905)
PHONE.................................302 478-0381
Jeff Dickinson, *President*
EMP: 6
SALES (est): 658.1K **Privately Held**
SIC: **3531** Line markers, self-propelled

(G-11539)
MARKIZON PRINTING
111 Nevada Ave (19803-3231)
PHONE.................................610 715-7989
EMP: 2 EST: 2018
SALES (est): 83.9K **Privately Held**
SIC: **2752** Commercial printing, lithographic

(G-11540)
MARKS ONEILL OBRIEN DOHER
300 Delaware Ave Ste 900 (19801-1671)
PHONE.................................302 658-6538

Wilmington - New Castle County (G-11541)   GEOGRAPHIC SECTION

K Simmons, *Principal*
Michael F Duggan, *Associate*
EMP: 33
SALES (corp-wide): 21.8MM **Privately Held**
SIC: 8111 General practice attorney, lawyer
PA: Marks, O'neill, O'brien, Doherty & Kelly, P.C.
1617 John F Kennedy Blvd
Philadelphia PA 19103
215 564-6688

(G-11541)
MARLETTE FUNDING LLC
1523 Concord Pike Ste 201 (19803-3656)
PHONE 302 358-2730
Jeffrey Meiler, *CEO*
Josh Tonderys, *President*
Jason Swift, *COO*
Ron Czyzyk, *Credit Staff*
Doug Mihalow, *Credit Staff*
EMP: 9
SALES (est): 1.4MM **Privately Held**
SIC: 6141 Consumer finance companies

(G-11542)
MARON MRVEL BRDLEY ANDERSON PA (PA)
1201 N Market St Ste 900 (19801-1100)
P.O. Box 288 (19899-0288)
PHONE 302 425-5177
Jennifer Parks, *President*
Tom Tardy, *Counsel*
Rachel Nuzzi, *Human Res Dir*
Gilbert Pinkett, *Info Tech Mgr*
James J Maron, *Director*
EMP: 51
SALES (est): 12MM **Privately Held**
SIC: 8111 General practice attorney, lawyer

(G-11543)
MARSH USA INC
1201 N Market St Ste 500 (19801-1160)
PHONE 302 888-4300
James Griffith, *Regional Mgr*
Mark Mossman, *Manager*
John A Edgar, *Systems Dir*
Elizabeth Phillips, *Representative*
EMP: 20
SALES (corp-wide): 14.9B **Publicly Held**
WEB: www.marsh.com
SIC: 6411 Insurance brokers
HQ: Marsh Usa Inc.
1166 Ave Of The Americas
New York NY 10036
212 345-6000

(G-11544)
MARSHA S EDDORLOV
Also Called: Orlov Counseling
Heritage Prosessional Plz (19808-3719)
PHONE 302 994-4014
Leland Orlov, *Owner*
Marsha Edd Orlov,
Marsha E Orlov,
EMP: 5
SALES (est): 87.8K **Privately Held**
SIC: 8049 Clinical psychologist

(G-11545)
MARSHALL DENNEHEY
1220 N Market St Ste 201 (19801-2540)
PHONE 302 552-4300
Lori Forsythe, *Manager*
EMP: 26
SALES (corp-wide): 153.4MM **Privately Held**
WEB: www.mdwcg.com
SIC: 8111 General practice law office
PA: Marshall Dennehey Warner Coleman & Goggin P.C.
2000 Market St Ste 2300
Philadelphia PA 19103
215 575-2600

(G-11546)
MARSICO & WEINSTIEN DDS
Also Called: Marsico Weinstien
2390 Limestone Rd (19808-4104)
PHONE 302 998-8474
Edward Weinstien DDS, *Partner*
Edward Weinstien, *Fmly & Gen Dent*
EMP: 7

SALES (est): 873.1K **Privately Held**
SIC: 8021 Maxillofacial specialist

(G-11547)
MARTA BISKUP DDS
3522 Silverside Rd (19810-4916)
PHONE 302 478-0000
EMP: 4
SALES (est): 67.6K **Privately Held**
SIC: 8021 Dentists' office

(G-11548)
MARTA BLACKHURST DMD
3522 Silverside Rd (19810-4916)
PHONE 302 478-1504
Marta Blackhurst DMD, *Principal*
EMP: 4
SALES (est): 206.5K **Privately Held**
SIC: 8021 Dental surgeon

(G-11549)
MARTIN DANIEL D & ASSOC LLC
1301 N Harrison St (19806-3128)
PHONE 302 658-2884
Daniel D Martin,
EMP: 6
SALES (est): 381.3K **Privately Held**
SIC: 8111 General practice law office

(G-11550)
MARTIN LUTHER HOMES EAST INC
Also Called: Grubb Road Neighborhood Home
2412 Grubb Rd (19810-2704)
PHONE 302 475-4920
Ben Satchel, *Manager*
EMP: 6
SALES (est): 208.2K **Privately Held**
SIC: 8052 8322 Intermediate care facilities; individual & family services
PA: Martin Luther Homes East, Inc.
4980 S 18th St
Omaha NE

(G-11551)
MARTINELLI HOLDINGS LLC (PA)
Also Called: Today Media
3301 Lancaster Pike 5c (19805-1436)
PHONE 302 656-1809
R Martinelli, *President*
Lisa Fleetwood, *Accounts Exec*
Avie Silver, *Adv Dir*
Leeanne Rocheleau, *Executive Asst*
EMP: 50
SALES: 15K **Privately Held**
SIC: 2721 Magazines: publishing only, not printed on site

(G-11552)
MARTINS LANDSCAPING LLC
703 Wilson Rd (19803-3955)
PHONE 302 984-2887
Rick Martin, *Principal*
EMP: 4
SALES (est): 183.5K **Privately Held**
SIC: 0781 Landscape services

(G-11553)
MARVI CLEANERS LIMITED INC
309 Philadelphia Pike (19809-2150)
PHONE 302 764-3077
Mario Marconi, *President*
Christine Marconi, *Vice Pres*
EMP: 7
SQ FT: 1,250
SALES (est): 380K **Privately Held**
SIC: 7216 7212 7219 Cleaning & dyeing, except rugs; garment pressing; garment alteration & repair shop

(G-11554)
MARVIN & PALMER ASSOCIATES
200 Bellevue Pkwy Ste 220 (19809-3727)
PHONE 302 573-3570
Dave Marvin, *Chairman*
Stan Palmer, *Vice Pres*
C P Schutt, *Vice Pres*
Karen Buckley, *CFO*
EMP: 50
SQ FT: 12,000

SALES (est): 13.6MM **Privately Held**
SIC: 6282 Investment counselors

(G-11555)
MARY CAMPBELL CENTER INC
4641 Weldin Rd (19803-4829)
PHONE 302 762-6025
Tarah Pappas, *Business Mgr*
Heather Colantuono, *Program Mgr*
Lyndsay Hawk, *Manager*
Kelley Franklin, *Info Tech Mgr*
Bradley Gaudioso, *Technology*
EMP: 170
SQ FT: 60,000
SALES: 15.2MM **Privately Held**
WEB: www.marycampbellcenter.org
SIC: 8052 8361 Intermediate care facilities; children's home; home for the physically handicapped

(G-11556)
MARY DODSON
1403 Foulk Rd Ste 105 (19803-2788)
PHONE 302 479-0100
Mary Dodson, *Executive*
EMP: 8
SALES (est): 65.7K **Privately Held**
SIC: 8049 Offices of health practitioner

(G-11557)
MARY E HERRING DAYCARE CENTER
2450 N Market St (19802-4200)
PHONE 302 652-5978
Juanita P Matthews, *Director*
Juanita Lyles, *Director*
EMP: 6
SALES: 145.5K **Privately Held**
SIC: 8351 Group day care center

(G-11558)
MARY SWEENEY-LEHR
3209 Coachman Rd (19803-1902)
PHONE 302 764-0589
Mary Sweeney-Lehr, *Principal*
Christian J Lehr, *Fmly & Gen Dent*
EMP: 4
SALES (est): 210K **Privately Held**
SIC: 8021 Offices & clinics of dentists

(G-11559)
MARY ZIEKEN
Also Called: Headmasters Beauty Salon
2080 Naamans Rd (19810-2655)
PHONE 302 475-6714
Mary Zieken, *Owner*
EMP: 14
SQ FT: 2,000
SALES (est): 67.6K **Privately Held**
SIC: 7231 Beauty shops

(G-11560)
MARYANN K BAILEY DDS
1802 W 4th St (19805-3420)
PHONE 302 655-5822
Maryann Bailey, *Fmly & Gen Dent*
EMP: 4 **EST:** 2017
SALES (est): 61.5K **Privately Held**
SIC: 8021 Offices & clinics of dentists

(G-11561)
MASLEY ENTERPRISES INC
1601 Jessup St (19802-4209)
PHONE 302 427-9885
Francis J Masley, *CEO*
Donna Masley, *President*
EMP: 50
SQ FT: 20,000
SALES (est): 4.9MM **Privately Held**
WEB: www.militarygloves.com
SIC: 2381 3151 5199 3949 Fabric dress & work gloves; welders' gloves; leather goods, except footwear, gloves, luggage, belting; mitts & gloves, baseball

(G-11562)
MASS FOR THE HOMELESS INC
2817 Ambler Ct (19808-2802)
PHONE 302 368-1030
Susan Booker, *President*
Wilson G Somers, *Principal*
EMP: 6
SALES (est): 108.2K **Privately Held**
SIC: 8699 Charitable organization

(G-11563)
MASSAGE BY ALICIA
700 Garnet Rd (19804-2614)
PHONE 352 401-4328
EMP: 8
SALES (est): 65.7K **Privately Held**
SIC: 8049

(G-11564)
MASTER-HALCO INC
P.O. Box 1791 (19899-1791)
PHONE 302 475-6714
EMP: 12 **Privately Held**
WEB: www.fenceonline.com
SIC: 5039 Wire fence, gates & accessories
HQ: Master-Halco, Inc.
3010 Lbj Fwy Ste 800
Dallas TX 75234
972 714-7300

(G-11565)
MASTRIANA PROPERTY MANAGEMENT
5500 Skyline Dr Ste 6 (19808-1772)
PHONE 302 234-4860
John Mastriana, *CEO*
EMP: 4
SALES (est): 438K **Privately Held**
SIC: 6531 Real estate managers

(G-11566)
MATERIAL SUPPLY INC
924 S Heald St (19801-5733)
PHONE 302 658-6524
Quentin Saienni, *President*
EMP: 20
SALES (est): 2.6MM **Privately Held**
SIC: 1611 2951 General contractor, highway & street construction; asphalt paving mixtures & blocks

(G-11567)
MATERNITY ASSOCIATES PA
Also Called: Carlson, John C MD
3524 Silverside Rd Ste 33 (19810-4929)
PHONE 302 478-7973
John C Carlson MD, *President*
Jane E Carlson, *Office Mgr*
Nancy L Branciaroli, *Assistant*
EMP: 6
SALES (est): 538.8K **Privately Held**
SIC: 8011 Gynecologist

(G-11568)
MATTER MUSIC INC
427 N Tatnall St 25426 (19801-2230)
PHONE 650 793-7749
Paul Meed, *CEO*
EMP: 15
SALES (est): 305.2K **Privately Held**
SIC: 7372 7389 Prepackaged software;

(G-11569)
MATTHEW GOTTHOLD DR
1403 Foulk Rd Ste 103 (19803-2788)
PHONE 302 762-6222
Diana Lambeth, *Branch Mgr*
EMP: 4 **Privately Held**
SIC: 8011 Pediatrician
PA: Matthew Gotthold Dr
1409 Foulk Rd Ste 100
Wilmington DE 19803

(G-11570)
MATTHEW GOTTHOLD DR (PA)
Also Called: Scott, Patricia A L MD
1409 Foulk Rd Ste 100 (19803-2755)
PHONE 302 762-6222
Matthew Gotthold, *Owner*
Diana Lambeth, *Principal*
EMP: 6
SALES (est): 1.2MM **Privately Held**
SIC: 8011 Pediatrician

(G-11571)
MATTHEW J MCILRATH DC
1201 Philadelphia Pike (19809-2042)
PHONE 302 798-7033
Matthew J Mc Ilrath DC, *Owner*
EMP: 5
SALES (est): 117.1K **Privately Held**
SIC: 8041 Offices & clinics of chiropractors

GEOGRAPHIC SECTION
Wilmington - New Castle County (G-11601)

(G-11572)
MATTHEW SMITH
Also Called: Matthew's Formal Wear
1810 W 4th St (19805-3420)
PHONE.................................302 654-4853
Matthew Smith, *Owner*
EMP: 4
SQ FT: 6,000
SALES (est): 275.2K **Privately Held**
WEB: www.matthewsformalwear.com
SIC: 5699 7299 Custom tailor; tuxedo rental

(G-11573)
MATTHEW W LAWRENCE DO
1500 Shallcross Ave (19806-3037)
PHONE.................................302 652-6050
Matthew Lawrence, *Owner*
EMP: 10
SALES (est): 209K **Privately Held**
SIC: 8011 Surgeon

(G-11574)
MATTIES CLEANING SERVICE
5 Sunset Ct (19810-4137)
PHONE.................................302 229-3585
Gloria Grantham, *Owner*
EMP: 10
SALES (est): 171.4K **Privately Held**
SIC: 7699 Cleaning services

(G-11575)
MAUREEN FREEBERY
Also Called: Maureens Beauty Salon
4801 Limestone Rd (19808-1902)
PHONE.................................302 234-7800
Maureen Freebery, *Owner*
EMP: 30
SALES (est): 394.2K **Privately Held**
SIC: 7231 Beauty shops

(G-11576)
MAUREENS FOR MEN & WOMEN
4813 Limestone Rd (19808-1902)
PHONE.................................302 234-7800
Maureen Freebery, *Owner*
EMP: 14
SALES (est): 340K **Privately Held**
SIC: 7231 Beauty shops

(G-11577)
MAURTEN US CORPORATION
1000 N West St Ste 1200 (19801-1058)
PHONE.................................302 669-9085
Olof Skold, *CEO*
EMP: 2
SALES: 675K
SALES (corp-wide): 47.3K **Privately Held**
SIC: 2086 Carbonated beverages, nonalcoholic: bottled & canned
HQ: Maurten Ab
   Arvid Wallgrens Backe 20
   Goteborg 413 4
   733 989-528

(G-11578)
MAX RE ASSOCIATES INC (PA)
Also Called: Re/Max
3302 Concord Pike (19803-5017)
PHONE.................................302 477-3900
John W Ford, *CEO*
John Ford, *President*
Robert Shadduck, *Principal*
Paul Faust, *Vice Pres*
Jim Welch, *Vice Pres*
EMP: 85
SALES (est): 5.6MM **Privately Held**
WEB: www.donash.com
SIC: 6531 Real estate agent, residential

(G-11579)
MAXIM HEALTHCARE SERVICES INC
Also Called: De Homecare
1523 Concord Pike Ste 100 (19803-3653)
PHONE.................................302 478-3434
Bryan Wade, *Branch Mgr*
EMP: 11
SALES (corp-wide): 1.5B **Privately Held**
WEB: www.maximstaffing.com
SIC: 8082 Home health care services
PA: Maxim Healthcare Services, Inc.
   7227 Lee Deforest Dr
   Columbia MD 21046
   410 910-1500

(G-11580)
MAXINES DAYCARE
1027 Lancaster Ave (19805-4006)
PHONE.................................302 652-7242
Maxine Williams, *Principal*
EMP: 5 EST: 2010
SALES (est): 55.1K **Privately Held**
SIC: 8351 Group day care center

(G-11581)
MB AEROSPACE ACP (PA)
2711 Centerville Rd # 400 (19808-1660)
PHONE.................................586 772-2500
Craig Gallagher, *CEO*
Gregor Goodwin, *CFO*
Tabatha Darichuk, *Controller*
Anthony Brenz, *Finance*
EMP: 9
SALES (est): 81.6MM **Privately Held**
SIC: 3724 Aircraft engines & engine parts

(G-11582)
MB VETERANS CENTER LLC
1405 Veale Rd (19810-4331)
PHONE.................................302 384-2350
David Mosley, *CEO*
EMP: 4 EST: 2017
SQ FT: 2,000
SALES (est): 50.6K **Privately Held**
SIC: 8322 Emergency social services

(G-11583)
MBNA MARKETING SYSTEMS INC
1100 N King St (19884-0011)
PHONE.................................302 456-8588
Bruce Hammonds, *CEO*
Vernon Wright, *Treasurer*
John Scheflen, *Admin Sec*
EMP: 1484
SALES (est): 68.8MM
SALES (corp-wide): 110.5B **Publicly Held**
SIC: 7389 Telemarketing services
HQ: Fia Card Services, National Association
   1100 N King St
   Wilmington DE 19884
   800 362-6255

(G-11584)
MCB LANDSCAPING LLC
1020 Darley Rd (19810-2910)
P.O. Box 354, Ridley Park PA (19078-0354)
PHONE.................................215 421-1083
Sabrina Rumpeltin, *Principal*
Jared Rumpeltin, *Principal*
EMP: 5 EST: 2016
SALES (est): 134K **Privately Held**
SIC: 0781 Landscape services

(G-11585)
MCCALL BROOKS INSURANCE AGENCY
Also Called: Nationwide
1805 Foulk Rd Ste H (19810-3700)
PHONE.................................302 475-8200
Brooks M Mc Caull, *Owner*
Brooks M McCaull, *Principal*
EMP: 7
SALES (est): 908.2K **Privately Held**
SIC: 6411 Insurance agents, brokers & service

(G-11586)
MCCARTER & ENGLISH LLP
405 N King St Ste 800 (19801-3715)
PHONE.................................302 984-6300
Deborah McCraw, *President*
Laurence Rubinow, *Counsel*
Cecilia Beirne, *Manager*
Bobbi Mortimer, *Executive*
Elizabeth Ferguson, *Admin Sec*
EMP: 53
SALES (corp-wide): 149MM **Privately Held**
SIC: 8111 General practice attorney, lawyer
PA: Mccarter & English Llp
   4 Gatway Ctr 100 Mlbrry S 4 Gateway Ctr
   Newark NJ 07102
   973 622-4444

(G-11587)
MCCLAFFERTY PRINTING COMPANY
1600 N Scott St (19806-2599)
PHONE.................................302 652-8112
Mary Beth McClafferty, *President*
Michael Naughton, *Vice Pres*
EMP: 46
SQ FT: 12,500
SALES (est): 10.9MM **Privately Held**
WEB: www.mcclaffertyprinting.com
SIC: 2752 Commercial printing, offset

(G-11588)
MCCONNELL BROS INC
400 E Ayre St (19804-2513)
PHONE.................................302 218-4240
Dan Mc Connell, *President*
EMP: 6
SALES (est): 481.4K **Privately Held**
SIC: 1761 7389 Roofing contractor; building inspection service

(G-11589)
MCCONNELL DEVELOPMENT INC (PA)
1201 N Market St Ste 400 (19801-1164)
PHONE.................................302 428-0712
Paul M Mc Connell, *President*
Linda R Mc Connell, *Vice Pres*
EMP: 5
SALES (est): 2.9MM **Privately Held**
SIC: 6552 Land subdividers & developers, commercial

(G-11590)
MCCONNELL JOHNSON RE CO LLC
1201 N Market St Ste 1605 (19801-1164)
PHONE.................................302 421-2000
Eileen G Moran, *Engineer*
Scott Johnson, *Mng Member*
Paul McConnell,
EMP: 12
SALES (est): 1.6MM **Privately Held**
WEB: www.mcconnelldevelopment.com
SIC: 6531 Real estate agent, commercial

(G-11591)
MCCORMICK CONTRACTING & SUPPOR
200 Tyrone Ave (19804-1929)
PHONE.................................443 987-2099
Linda McCormick, *Principal*
EMP: 4
SALES (est): 92.1K **Privately Held**
SIC: 7389

(G-11592)
MCCRERY FUNERAL HOMES INC
3924 Concord Pike (19803-1782)
PHONE.................................302 478-2204
Albert J McCrery III, *CEO*
Dorothy McCrery, *Treasurer*
EMP: 8 EST: 1912
SQ FT: 4,000
SALES (est): 825.3K **Privately Held**
WEB: www.mccreryfuneralhome.com
SIC: 7261 Funeral home

(G-11593)
MCDANIEL PLUMBING & HEATING
106 Rowland Park Blvd (19803-4231)
PHONE.................................302 322-3075
EMP: 50
SALES (est): 3.5MM **Privately Held**
SIC: 1711 Plumbing Heating & Air Conditioning Contractor

(G-11594)
MCDONALD SAFETY EQUIPMENT INC
Also Called: Brandywine Vly Fire Safety Div
581 Copper Dr (19804-2409)
P.O. Box 6008 (19804-0608)
PHONE.................................302 999-0151
Brian Mc Donald, *President*
Brian McDonald, *President*
Thomas Jones, *Vice Pres*
Bernadette Krajewski, *Vice Pres*
Susan McDonald, *Office Mgr*
EMP: 12
SALES (est): 3.4MM **Privately Held**
WEB: www.mcdonaldsafety.com
SIC: 5099 Safety equipment & supplies

(G-11595)
MCELROY & SON INC
15 E Edmont Rd (19804)
PHONE.................................302 995-2623
Sandra McElroy, *President*
James Mc Elroy Jr, *Vice Pres*
Christopher Mc Elroy, *Admin Sec*
EMP: 18
SALES: 466.5K **Privately Held**
SIC: 1721 Painting & paper hanging

(G-11596)
MCGIVNEY KLUGER & COOK PC
1201 N Orange St Ste 504 (19801-1119)
PHONE.................................302 656-1200
Paul Sunshine, *Branch Mgr*
EMP: 18 **Privately Held**
SIC: 8111 General practice attorney, lawyer
PA: Mcgivney, Kluger & Cook, P.C.
   18 Columbia Tpke Ste 300
   Florham Park NJ 07932

(G-11597)
MCHUGH ELECTRIC INC
100 Cassidy Dr Ste 105 (19804-2440)
P.O. Box 259, Middletown (19709-0259)
PHONE.................................302 995-9091
EMP: 5 EST: 2007
SALES (est): 440K **Privately Held**
SIC: 7539 Automotive Repair

(G-11598)
MCI COMMUNICATIONS CORPORATION
Also Called: Verizon Business
200 Bellevue Pkwy Ste 500 (19809-3741)
PHONE.................................302 791-4900
Leo Hussey, *Director*
EMP: 10
SALES (corp-wide): 130.8B **Publicly Held**
SIC: 4813 Local & long distance telephone communications
HQ: Mci Communications Corporation
   22001 Loudoun County Pkwy
   Ashburn VA 20147
   703 886-5600

(G-11599)
MCI LLC
Also Called: Verizon Business
452 E Ayre St (19804-2513)
PHONE.................................302 407-5034
EMP: 11
SALES (corp-wide): 2.4MM **Privately Held**
SIC: 4813 Telephone communication, except radio
PA: Mci Llc
   2102 Kirkwood Hwy
   Wilmington DE 19805
   302 293-0028

(G-11600)
MCI LLC (PA)
Also Called: Verizon Business
2102 Kirkwood Hwy (19805-4902)
PHONE.................................302 293-0028
EMP: 8
SALES (est): 2.4MM **Privately Held**
SIC: 4813 Telephone communication, except radio

(G-11601)
MCKELVEY HIRES DRY CLEANING
Also Called: 1 Hour Martinizing
808 First State Blvd (19804-3573)
PHONE.................................302 998-9191
Barbara Hires, *President*
Connie McKelvey, *Admin Sec*
EMP: 10
SQ FT: 2,500
SALES (est): 174.2K **Privately Held**
SIC: 7212 7216 Pickup station, laundry & drycleaning; cleaning & dyeing, except rugs

Wilmington - New Castle County (G-11602)

GEOGRAPHIC SECTION

(G-11602)
MCLAUGHLIN GORDON L LAW OFFICE
1203 N Orange St (19801-1120)
PHONE.....................302 651-7979
Gordon L McLaughlin, *Owner*
EMP: 5
SALES (est): 427.8K Privately Held
SIC: 8111 General practice attorney, lawyer

(G-11603)
MCLAUGHLIN MORTON HOLDG CO LLC
1203 N Orange St Fl 2 (19801-1120)
PHONE.....................302 426-1313
Michael P Morton,
Gordon McLaughlin,
EMP: 10
SALES (est): 527K Privately Held
SIC: 8111 General practice attorney, lawyer

(G-11604)
MCLEEN PROPERTIES
240 N James St Ste 100c (19804-3167)
PHONE.....................302 482-1486
Michael Donovan, *Partner*
EMP: 7
SALES (est): 1.1MM Privately Held
SIC: 6512 Nonresidential building operators

(G-11605)
MCNEIL AND FMLY MGT GROUP LLC
2 White Oak Rd (19809-3265)
PHONE.....................302 830-3267
Zannie McNeil,
EMP: 10
SALES (est): 2MM Privately Held
SIC: 8741 Management services

(G-11606)
MCNICHOL ENTERPRISES INC (PA)
1106 Elderon Dr (19808-1908)
PHONE.....................302 633-9348
Hugh J McNichol IV, *President*
Catherine R McNichol, *Vice Pres*
Kathryn E McNichol, *Vice Pres*
EMP: 17
SALES: 200K Privately Held
WEB: www.trinettc.com
SIC: 8748 8742 Telecommunications consultant; educational consultant; publishing consultant; corporate objectives & policies consultant

(G-11607)
MCSGLOBAL INC
1220 N Market St (19801-2535)
PHONE.....................302 427-6970
Sridhar Chimaladinne, *Branch Mgr*
EMP: 4
SALES (corp-wide): 5.7MM Privately Held
WEB: www.mcsglobal.com
SIC: 7379 Computer related consulting services
PA: Mcsg Wind-Down Incorporated
    3190 Frview Pk Dr Ste 800
    Falls Church VA 22042
    732 640-2360

(G-11608)
MCSHARES INC
Also Called: Brandywine Ingredient Tech
2207 Concord Pike 407 (19803-2908)
PHONE.....................302 656-3168
John De Campo, *Branch Mgr*
EMP: 1
SALES (corp-wide): 27.5MM Privately Held
SIC: 2041 Flour; wheat germ
PA: Mcshares, Inc.
    1835 E North St
    Salina KS 67401
    785 825-2181

(G-11609)
MDA LENDING SOLUTIONS INC
5300 Brandywine Pkwy # 100 (19803-1470)
PHONE.....................302 433-8006
EMP: 18
SALES (est): 3.7MM Privately Held
SIC: 6163 Loan Broker

(G-11610)
MDM MCHNCAL INSTLLTION USA LLC
1201 N Orange St Ste 700 (19801-1186)
PHONE.....................617 938-9634
Cezary Sadlinski, *Administration*
EMP: 6
SALES (est): 111K Privately Held
SIC: 1711 Mechanical contractor

(G-11611)
MEADOWBROOK GOLF GROUP INC
Also Called: Ed Oliver Golf Club
800 N Dupont Rd (19807-2920)
PHONE.....................302 571-9041
Chris Bloss, *Branch Mgr*
EMP: 30 Privately Held
WEB: www.birkdalegolf.com
SIC: 7992 Public golf courses
PA: Meadowbrook Golf Group, Inc.
    5385 Gateway Blvd Ste 12
    Lakeland FL 33811

(G-11612)
MEALS ON WHEELS DELAWARE INC
100 W 10th St Ste 207 (19801-1625)
PHONE.....................302 656-6451
Elizabeth Dougherty, *President*
Ashley Gliniak, *Marketing Staff*
Mari Considine, *Exec Dir*
Regina Dodds, *Director*
Tricia Bovell, *Admin Asst*
EMP: 4
SALES (est): 592.3K Privately Held
WEB: www.mealsonwheelsde.com
SIC: 8322 Meal delivery program

(G-11613)
MEBRO INC
Also Called: SERVPRO
225 N James St (19804-3124)
PHONE.....................302 992-0104
Drew Mehan Sr, *CEO*
Linda Mehan, *Vice Pres*
Tara Brown, *Treasurer*
EMP: 20
SQ FT: 50,000
SALES (est): 730K Privately Held
SIC: 7349 1521 1799 1542 Building maintenance services; repairing fire damage, single-family houses; construction site cleanup; exterior cleaning, including sandblasting; commercial & office buildings, renovation & repair; renovation, remodeling & repairs: industrial buildings

(G-11614)
MED TRANSPORT LLC
3524 Silverside Rd 35b (19810-4929)
PHONE.....................513 257-7626
Mattie James, *Principal*
EMP: 24
SALES (est): 408.6K Privately Held
SIC: 4789 Transportation services

(G-11615)
MEDIBID
2711 Centerville Rd (19808-1660)
PHONE.....................888 855-6334
EMP: 8
SALES (est): 420K Privately Held
SIC: 7372 Prepackaged Software Services

(G-11616)
MEDICAL COPY SERVICES
Also Called: MCS
901 N Market St Ste 460 (19801-3013)
PHONE.....................302 654-4741
David Bean, *Owner*
EMP: 4
SALES (est): 236.7K Privately Held
SIC: 7334 Photocopying & duplicating services

(G-11617)
MEDICI VENTURES INC
1209 N Orange St (19801-1120)
PHONE.....................801 319-7029
Jonathan Johnson, *President*
Steve Hopkins, *COO*
Jeremy Smith, *CTO*
Joel Weight, *CTO*
EMP: 35
SALES (est): 641.4K
SALES (corp-wide): 1.8B Publicly Held
SIC: 7371 6799 Computer software development & applications; venture capital companies
PA: Overstock.Com, Inc.
    799 W Coliseum Way
    Midvale UT 84047
    801 947-3100

(G-11618)
MEDICTEK INC
902 N Market St Apt 805 (19801-3051)
PHONE.....................302 351-4924
G B Hendrickson, *President*
EMP: 17
SQ FT: 1,500
SALES (est): 1.1MM Privately Held
SIC: 7373 Office computer automation systems integration

(G-11619)
MEDIGUIDE AMERICA LLC (PA)
4001 Kennett Pike Ste 218 (19807-2029)
PHONE.....................302 425-5900
Kara Connor, *Vice Pres*
Kevin Thomas, *Vice Pres*
Michael T Marquardt,
John M Burris,
Manuel Juarez,
EMP: 20
SQ FT: 5,000
SALES: 2.8MM Privately Held
WEB: www.mediguideamerica.com
SIC: 8742 Hospital & health services consultant

(G-11620)
MEDIMMUNE LLC
1800 Concord Pike (19897-0001)
PHONE.....................301 398-1200
EMP: 5
SALES (corp-wide): 22B Privately Held
SIC: 2834 Pharmaceutical preparations
HQ: Medimmune, Llc
    1 Medimmune Way
    Gaithersburg MD 20878
    301 398-0000

(G-11621)
MEDREP INC
903 Berkeley Rd (19807-2811)
PHONE.....................302 571-0263
Robert M Sommerlatte, *President*
Jamie Williams, *Products*
EMP: 5
SALES: 3MM Privately Held
WEB: www.medrep-inc.com
SIC: 5047 Medical equipment & supplies

(G-11622)
MEFTA LLC
Also Called: Middle East Free Trade Assoc
1220 N Market St (19801-2535)
PHONE.....................804 433-3566
EMP: 12
SQ FT: 1,200
SALES: 950K Privately Held
WEB: www.mefta.com
SIC: 8748 6221 Business consulting; commodity traders, contracts

(G-11623)
MEGAN HEGENBARTH
Also Called: Earth Wind and Expedition
6 Onyx Ct (19810-2227)
PHONE.....................302 477-9872
Megan Hegenbarth, *President*
EMP: 4
SALES (est): 92K Privately Held
SIC: 7999 Tour & guide services

(G-11624)
MEHAR INVESTMENT GROUP LLC (PA)
Also Called: Mig Environmental
1624 Newport Gap Pike (19808-6208)
P.O. Box 5674 (19808-5674)
PHONE.....................302 999-1888
Inderpreet Singh,
EMP: 6
SALES (est): 529.7K Privately Held
WEB: www.migenvironmental.com
SIC: 8748 Environmental consultant

(G-11625)
MEINEKE CAR CARE CENTER
Also Called: Meineke Discount Mufflers
1512 Kirkwood Hwy (19805-4916)
PHONE.....................302 995-2020
Maris Handerson, *Owner*
EMP: 4
SALES (est): 205.5K Privately Held
SIC: 7533 Muffler shop, sale or repair & installation

(G-11626)
MELLON PRIVATE WEALTH MGT
4005 Kennett Pike (19807-2018)
PHONE.....................302 421-2306
EMP: 6
SALES (est): 285.4K
SALES (corp-wide): 12.8B Publicly Held
WEB: www.bankofny.com
SIC: 7389 Financial services
PA: The Bank Of New York Mellon Corporation
    240 E Greenwich St
    New York NY 10007
    212 495-1784

(G-11627)
MELODY ENTERTAINMENT USA INC
717 N Union St Apt 68 (19805-3031)
PHONE.....................305 505-7659
Gamal Marwan, *CEO*
EMP: 6
SALES (est): 187.6K Privately Held
SIC: 7812 2741 7313 Television film production; music book & sheet music publishing; radio, television, publisher representatives

(G-11628)
MELTRONE INC
Also Called: Captain's Catch
5828 Kirkwood Hwy (19808-4813)
PHONE.....................302 998-3457
Richard S Melson, *President*
Barbara Melson, *Vice Pres*
EMP: 16
SALES (est): 1.3MM Privately Held
SIC: 5421 5146 Seafood markets; seafoods

(G-11629)
MENCHACA BUILDING CORP
4 Lloyd Pl (19810-1325)
PHONE.....................302 475-4581
Richard Menchaca, *President*
Sherry Menchaca, *Corp Secy*
EMP: 6
SALES (est): 329.9K Privately Held
SIC: 1751 Framing contractor

(G-11630)
MEND ME MASSAGE THERAPY INC
6 W Salisbury Dr (19809-3416)
PHONE.....................302 229-1250
Peihua Luo Yaschur, *Agent*
EMP: 8
SALES (est): 73.3K Privately Held
SIC: 8093 Rehabilitation center, outpatient treatment

(G-11631)
MENNO FREIGHT LOGISTICS LLC
504 E Boxborough Dr (19810-1460)
PHONE.....................302 229-8137
Martin S Rosenberger, *Principal*
EMP: 4 EST: 2010
SALES (est): 207.4K Privately Held
SIC: 4789 Cargo loading & unloading services

(G-11632)
MENTAL HEALTH ASSN IN DEL
100 W 10th St Ste 600 (19801-6604)
PHONE.....................302 654-6833
Michael F Gallagher, *President*
Amy Milligan, *President*
James Lafferty, *Exec Dir*
EMP: 8

GEOGRAPHIC SECTION
Wilmington - New Castle County (G-11662)

SQ FT: 2,500
SALES: 1.3MM **Privately Held**
SIC: 8093 Mental health clinic, outpatient

(G-11633)
MENTOR CONSULTANTS INC
3200 Concord Pike (19803-5015)
P.O. Box 489, Concordville PA (19331-0489)
PHONE..................................610 566-4004
Sheldon D Barnett, *President*
Sue Barnett, *Corp Secy*
EMP: 6
SALES: 500K **Privately Held**
WEB: www.mentormail.com
SIC: 8748 7371 8742 Systems analysis or design; computer software development; management information systems consultant

(G-11634)
MERA RD 2 LLC
251 Little Falls Dr (19808-1674)
PHONE..................................305 577-3443
Rafael Aguirre, *President*
Sagrario Diaz, *Principal*
Natalie Jacobs, *Principal*
Gabriel Marquez, *Regional Mgr*
EMP: 4
SALES: 3.5MM **Privately Held**
SIC: 8741 Restaurant management

(G-11635)
MERA USA LLC
251 Little Falls Dr (19808-1674)
PHONE..................................305 577-3443
Rafael Aguirre, *Manager*
Gabriel Marquez, *Manager*
EMP: 5
SALES: 3.5MM **Privately Held**
SIC: 6719 Investment holding companies, except banks

(G-11636)
MERCANTILE PRESS INC
3007 Bellevue Ave (19802-2428)
PHONE..................................302 764-6884
Coleman E Bye III, *President*
Coleman E Bye Jr, *Chairman*
Jane S Bye, *Corp Secy*
EMP: 18 EST: 1884
SQ FT: 20,000
SALES: 1.9MM **Privately Held**
WEB: www.mercantilepress.com
SIC: 2752 2671 2672 Commercial printing, offset; packaging paper & plastics film, coated & laminated; coated & laminated paper

(G-11637)
MERCK HOLDINGS LLC
Also Called: Merck Holdings Inc.
5307 Limestone Rd Ste 200 (19808-1283)
PHONE..................................302 234-1401
Kurt Landgraf, *Principal*
EMP: 3
SALES (est): 234.1K
SALES (corp-wide): 42.2B **Publicly Held**
SIC: 8731 2834 Medical research, commercial; pharmaceutical preparations
PA: Merck & Co., Inc.
2000 Galloping Hill Rd
Kenilworth NJ 07033
908 740-4000

(G-11638)
MERCY INC
218 W 35th St (19802-2613)
PHONE..................................302 764-7781
EMP: 4
SALES (est): 187.6K **Privately Held**
SIC: 2323 Mfg Men's/Boy's Neckwear

(G-11639)
MERESTONE CONSULTANTS INC (PA)
5215 W Woodmill Dr Ste 38 (19808-4068)
PHONE..................................302 992-7900
Michael Early, *President*
Grant Gregor, *Project Mgr*
Roger Gross, *Engineer*
Kellie Dillon, *Assistant*
EMP: 15
SALES (est): 1.4MM **Privately Held**
WEB: www.merestoneconsultants.com
SIC: 8713 8711 Surveying services; construction & civil engineering

(G-11640)
MERGERS ACQSTONS STRTEGIES LLC (PA)
Also Called: Rls Associates
5183 W Woodmill Dr Ste 3 (19808-4067)
PHONE..................................302 992-0400
David Bernstein, *Mng Member*
Douglas Karan, *Director*
Michael Zoglio, *Director*
Neil J Abitabilo, *Sr Associate*
Neil Abitabilo, *Sr Associate*
EMP: 8
SQ FT: 1,600
SALES (est): 2MM **Privately Held**
WEB: www.rlsassociates.com
SIC: 7389 Brokers, business: buying & selling business enterprises

(G-11641)
MERIDIAN BANK
1601 Concord Pike Ste 45 (19803-3634)
PHONE..................................302 477-9449
Joan Fitzgerald, *Vice Pres*
Sam Frisoli, *Branch Mgr*
Treg Adams, *Manager*
EMP: 20
SALES (est): 553.2K **Privately Held**
SIC: 6021 National commercial banks

(G-11642)
MERION REALTY SERVICES LLC
1303 Delaware Ave (19806-3419)
PHONE..................................302 656-8543
EMP: 4 EST: 2011
SALES (est): 315.7K **Privately Held**
SIC: 8742 Real estate consultant

(G-11643)
MERIT CONSTRUCTION ENGINEERS
5700 Kirkwood Hwy Ste 201 (19808-4884)
PHONE..................................302 992-9810
Ronald Dills, *President*
EMP: 18
SALES (est): 3.2MM **Privately Held**
SIC: 8711 Civil engineering

(G-11644)
MERIT CONSTRUCTION ENGINEERS
1605 E Ayre St (19804-2514)
P.O. Box 651, New Castle (19720-0651)
PHONE..................................302 992-9810
Ron Dills, *President*
Matt Ballintyn, *Vice Pres*
EMP: 18
SQ FT: 650
SALES (est): 1.4MM **Privately Held**
SIC: 1794 1623 1771 Excavation & grading, building construction; water main construction; concrete work

(G-11645)
MERMAN MANAGEMENT INC
5145 W Woodmill Dr 22 (19808-4067)
PHONE..................................302 456-9904
Maryanne Murray, *Principal*
EMP: 5
SALES (est): 343.7K **Privately Held**
SIC: 8741 Management services

(G-11646)
MERRILL LYNCH PIERCE FENNER
1201 N Market St Ste 2000 (19801-1165)
P.O. Box 10922 (19850-0922)
PHONE..................................302 571-5100
Angela Contini, *Assistant VP*
Christopher Chatfield, *Research*
Scot Armstrong, *Manager*
Lisa Primack, *Director*
EMP: 75
SALES (corp-wide): 110.5B **Publicly Held**
WEB: www.merlyn.com
SIC: 6211 6726 Security brokers & dealers; investment offices
HQ: Merrill Lynch, Pierce, Fenner & Smith Incorporated
111 8th Ave
New York NY 10011
800 637-7455

(G-11647)
META GALAXIC PUBLISHING INC
2711 Centerville Rd # 1205323 (19808-1660)
PHONE..................................302 245-7939
Bea Lloyd, *President*
EMP: 1
SALES (est): 50.8K **Privately Held**
WEB: www.meta-corp.com
SIC: 2731 Book publishing

(G-11648)
METAQUOTES SOFTWARE CORP
602 Rockwood Rd (19802-1121)
PHONE..................................657 859-6918
Yvaine Yang, *Principal*
EMP: 50
SALES: 5MM **Privately Held**
SIC: 7371 7389 Computer software development & applications;

(G-11649)
METHODIST MISSION AND CHURCH E
Also Called: Methodist Action Program
1218 B St (19801-5844)
PHONE..................................302 225-5862
Kathryn Cooper-Nicholas, *Director*
EMP: 6
SALES (est): 290K **Privately Held**
SIC: 8322 Temporary relief service; social service center

(G-11650)
METROPLTAN WLMNGTON URBAN LEAG
Also Called: M W U L
100 W 10th St Ste 710 (19801-6605)
PHONE..................................302 778-8300
Fax: 302 622-4303
EMP: 6
SALES: 714.2K **Privately Held**
SIC: 8322 Individual/Family Services

(G-11651)
MEYER & MEYER INC
Also Called: Meyer & Meyer Reatly
2706 Kirkwood Hwy (19805-4912)
PHONE..................................302 994-9600
Peter Meyers, *President*
Justin Meyer, *Vice Pres*
EMP: 20
SQ FT: 4,000
SALES (est): 5MM **Privately Held**
WEB: www.meyerrealty.net
SIC: 6211 Mortgages, buying & selling

(G-11652)
MGJ ENTERPRISES INC
Also Called: lrg
4023 Kennett Pike 624 (19807-2018)
PHONE..................................866 525-8529
Michael Luzio, *President*
Kevin Christensen, *Senior Engr*
Ernie Perez, *Technology*
Beth Cox, *Network Enginr*
Melissa Winder, *Administration*
EMP: 30
SALES (corp-wide): 444.1MM **Privately Held**
SIC: 4813 ;
HQ: Mgj Enterprises, Inc.
2000 Ericsson Dr
Warrendale PA 15086
866 525-8529

(G-11653)
MICHAEL A MC CULLOCH MD
1600 Rockland Rd (19803-3607)
PHONE..................................302 651-6600
Michael McCulloch, *Executive*
EMP: 4
SALES (est): 77.2K **Privately Held**
SIC: 8011 Pediatrician

(G-11654)
MICHAEL A MEALEY & SONS INC (PA)
Also Called: Mealey Funeral Homes
703 N Broom St (19805-3117)
P.O. Box 2866 (19805-0866)
PHONE..................................302 652-5913
Charles F Mealey Jr, *President*
EMP: 12 EST: 1912
SALES (est): 739.9K **Privately Held**
WEB: www.mealeyfuneralhome.com
SIC: 7261 Funeral home

(G-11655)
MICHAEL A MEALEY & SONS INC
Also Called: Mealey Fnrl Homes & Crematory
2509 Limestone Rd (19805-4107)
P.O. Box 2866 (19805-0866)
PHONE..................................302 654-3005
Laura Mealey, *Manager*
EMP: 17
SALES (corp-wide): 739.9K **Privately Held**
WEB: www.mealeyfuneralhome.com
SIC: 7261 Funeral home
PA: Michael A Mealey & Sons Inc
703 N Broom St
Wilmington DE 19805
302 652-5913

(G-11656)
MICHAEL A OBRIEN & SONS
405 E Ayre St (19804-2512)
PHONE..................................302 994-2894
Michael A O'Brien Sr, *Owner*
EMP: 2 EST: 1963
SALES (est): 203.8K **Privately Held**
SIC: 2541 2434 1751 Table or counter tops, plastic laminated; wood kitchen cabinets; cabinet building & installation

(G-11657)
MICHAEL A POLECK DDS PA
5501 Kirkwood Hwy (19808-5001)
PHONE..................................302 994-7730
Michael A Poleck DDS, *President*
EMP: 8
SALES (est): 470.9K **Privately Held**
SIC: 8021 Dentists' office

(G-11658)
MICHAEL B JOSEPH
824 N Market St Fl 10 (19801-3024)
P.O. Box 1350 (19899-1350)
PHONE..................................302 656-0123
Michael B Joseph, *Owner*
EMP: 15
SALES (est): 824.5K **Privately Held**
SIC: 8111 General practice attorney, lawyer

(G-11659)
MICHAEL ELLER INCOME TAX SVC
724 N Union St (19805-3032)
PHONE..................................302 652-5916
Michael Eller, *President*
EMP: 5
SALES (est): 159.6K **Privately Held**
SIC: 7291 Tax return preparation services

(G-11660)
MICHAEL GIOIA
3520 Silverside Rd Ste 27 (19810-4933)
PHONE..................................302 479-7780
Michael Gioia, *Owner*
EMP: 4
SALES: 190K **Privately Held**
SIC: 6282 Investment advice

(G-11661)
MICHAEL K ROSENTHAL
2300 Penns Ave Ste 3c (19806-1379)
PHONE..................................302 652-3469
Michael Rosenthal, *Principal*
EMP: 5
SALES (est): 411.1K **Privately Held**
SIC: 8011 Dermatologist

(G-11662)
MICHAEL MATTHIAS
3801 Kennett Pike E207 (19807-2321)
PHONE..................................302 575-0100
Michael Matthias, *Owner*

Wilmington - New Castle County (G-11663) GEOGRAPHIC SECTION

EMP: 5
SALES (est): 93.4K **Privately Held**
SIC: 8011 8021 Offices & clinics of medical doctors; offices & clinics of dentists

(G-11663)
MICHAEL P MORTON PA
3704 Kennett Pike Ste 200 (19807-2173)
PHONE..................................302 426-1313
Michael P Morton, *Owner*
EMP: 9
SALES (est): 1MM **Privately Held**
SIC: 8111 General practice attorney, lawyer

(G-11664)
MICHAEL PDMNCZKY CNSRVATOR LLC
1715 N Rodney St (19806-3021)
PHONE..................................302 388-0656
Michael Podmaniczky,
EMP: 1
SALES: 35K **Privately Held**
SIC: 2519 8999 7389 Household furniture; art related services;

(G-11665)
MICHAEL S WIROSLOFF DMD
5185 W Woodmill Dr Ste 2 (19808-4067)
PHONE..................................302 998-8588
Dr Michael Wirosloff, *Owner*
EMP: 5
SALES (est): 197.9K **Privately Held**
SIC: 8021 Orthodontist

(G-11666)
MICHAEL SCHWARTZ
Also Called: A B C Ticket Co
1400 Philadelphia Pike (19809-1856)
PHONE..................................302 791-9999
EMP: 17
SQ FT: 2,000
SALES (est): 202.1K **Privately Held**
SIC: 7922 7999 Ticket agency, theatrical; ticket sales office for sporting events, contract

(G-11667)
MICHAEL T ROSEN DDS PA
2601 Annand Dr Ste 2 (19808-3719)
PHONE..................................866 561-5067
Michael T Rosen DDS, *Principal*
EMP: 4
SALES (est): 126.2K **Privately Held**
SIC: 8021 Dentists' office

(G-11668)
MICHAEL T TEIXIDO MD
1941 Limestone Rd Ste 210 (19808-5400)
PHONE..................................302 998-0300
Michael T Teixido MD, *Principal*
EMP: 4
SALES (est): 158.3K **Privately Held**
SIC: 8011 Ears, nose & throat specialist; physician/surgeon

(G-11669)
MICHAEL-BRUNO LLC (PA)
2711 Centerville Rd # 120 (19808-1676)
PHONE..................................315 941-8514
Michael Sedge, *Mng Member*
Daniele Sedge,
EMP: 4
SALES (est): 2.1MM **Privately Held**
SIC: 8711 1542 Engineering services; commercial & office building contractors

(G-11670)
MICHELE BRODER
2300 Penns Ave Ste 5c (19806-1305)
PHONE..................................302 652-1533
Michele Broder, *Owner*
EMP: 4
SALES (est): 241.6K **Privately Held**
SIC: 8021 Prosthodontist

(G-11671)
MICHELET FINANCE INC
1105 N Market St Ste 1300 (19801-1241)
PHONE..................................302 427-8571
EMP: 4
SALES (est): 172.1K
SALES (corp-wide): 95.3MM **Privately Held**
SIC: 5044 Office equipment

PA: Arkema
420 Rue D Estienne D Orves
Colombes 92700
149 008-080

(G-11672)
MICHELLE E PAPA DO
1100 S Broom St Ste 1 (19805-4585)
PHONE..................................302 656-5424
Michelle E Papa, *Principal*
EMP: 5
SALES (est): 78.5K **Privately Held**
SIC: 8011 Offices & clinics of medical doctors

(G-11673)
MICHELLE S JONES
1600 Rockland Rd (19803-3607)
PHONE..................................302 651-4801
Michele Morrow, *Principal*
EMP: 9 **EST:** 2013
SALES (est): 188.3K **Privately Held**
SIC: 8049 Nurses, registered & practical

(G-11674)
MICRO OVENS OF DELAWARE
Also Called: All Appliance Repair
309 Main St (19804-3906)
PHONE..................................302 998-8444
James Keating, *Owner*
Marie Keating, *Owner*
EMP: 4 **EST:** 1976
SQ FT: 2,000
SALES: 250K **Privately Held**
WEB: www.allappliancerepair.com
SIC: 7629 Electrical household appliance repair

(G-11675)
MICRODRY INC
913 N Market St Ste 200 (19801-3097)
PHONE..................................302 416-3021
Iain Scorgie, *President*
Paul Cuthberson, *COO*
EMP: 8
SQ FT: 2,700
SALES (est): 91.3MM **Privately Held**
SIC: 5023 Sheets, textile

(G-11676)
MICRON INCORPORATED
3815 Lancaster Pike (19805-1599)
PHONE..................................302 998-1184
James F Ficca Jr, *President*
James M Ficca, *Vice Pres*
Katherine Melody, *Vice Pres*
EMP: 7
SQ FT: 12,000
SALES (est): 1MM **Privately Held**
WEB: www.micronanalytical.com
SIC: 8734 Testing laboratories

(G-11677)
MICROTUNE LP LLC
103 Foulk Rd Ste 202 (19803-3742)
PHONE..................................302 691-6037
Everett Rogers, *COO*
EMP: 83
SALES (est): 2.7MM
SALES (corp-wide): 24.2B **Publicly Held**
WEB: www.microtune.com
SIC: 5065 Communication equipment
HQ: Microtune, Inc.
2201 10th St
Plano TX 75074

(G-11678)
MID ATLANTIC CARE LLC (PA)
520 Robinson Ln (19805-4616)
P.O. Box 6511 (19804-0511)
PHONE..................................302 266-8306
Yousif Omer, *CEO*
Amy Yonko,
EMP: 7
SALES (est): 1.3MM **Privately Held**
SIC: 4119 Ambulance service

(G-11679)
MID ATLANTIC SURGICAL PRACTICE
701 N Clayton St (19805-3165)
PHONE..................................302 652-6050
Nora Truscello, *Manager*
EMP: 12
SALES (est): 1MM **Privately Held**
SIC: 8011 Surgeon

(G-11680)
MID STATES SALES & MARKETING
3411 Silverside Rd # 104 (19810-4809)
PHONE..................................302 888-2475
Chris Quinlan, *President*
Joseph Quinlan, *Shareholder*
EMP: 50
SALES (est): 6.3MM **Privately Held**
WEB: www.midstatesales.com
SIC: 5122 8742 Toiletries; management consulting services

(G-11681)
MID-ATLANTIC SERVICES A-TEAM
700 Cornell Dr (19801-5762)
PHONE..................................302 984-9559
Rosemary Everton, *Branch Mgr*
EMP: 91
SALES (corp-wide): 6MM **Privately Held**
SIC: 7349 Janitorial service, contract basis
PA: Mid-Atlantic Services A-Team Corp
8558 Elks Rd
Seaford DE 19973
302 628-3403

(G-11682)
MIDDLE DEPT INSPTN AGCY INC
2024 Duncan Rd Fl 2 (19808-5932)
PHONE..................................302 999-0243
Kim Whatchel, *Manager*
EMP: 4
SALES (corp-wide): 9MM **Privately Held**
WEB: www.mdia.net
SIC: 7389 Building inspection service
PA: Middle Department Inspection Agency, Inc.
1337 W Chester Pike
West Chester PA 19382
610 696-3900

(G-11683)
MIDDLEWARE INC
1000 N West St Ste 1200 (19801-1058)
PHONE..................................415 213-2625
Oleksandr Vityaz, *President*
Erina Serbina, *Director*
EMP: 50
SQ FT: 1,000
SALES: 5.5MM **Privately Held**
SIC: 7371 Computer software development & applications

(G-11684)
MIG CONSULTING LLC (PA)
1624 Newport Gap Pike (19808-6208)
PHONE..................................302 999-1888
Inderpreet Singh, *Engineer*
EMP: 7
SALES (est): 2.5MM **Privately Held**
SIC: 8711 Engineering services

(G-11685)
MIKE FAELLA INC
2208 Sconset Rd (19810-4235)
PHONE..................................302 475-2116
Michael Faella, *President*
EMP: 4
SALES (est): 191K **Privately Held**
SIC: 1741 Masonry & other stonework

(G-11686)
MIKES GLASS SERVICE INC
108 A St (19801-5239)
PHONE..................................302 658-7936
Lee R Tibbett Jr, *President*
Shirley Tibbett, *Corp Secy*
EMP: 13
SQ FT: 10,000
SALES (est): 1.4MM **Privately Held**
SIC: 1793 7536 Glass & glazing work; automotive glass replacement shops

(G-11687)
MIL INTERNATIONAL INCORPORATED
203 Alisons Way (19807-1759)
PHONE..................................302 234-7501
Mohan Iyer, *President*
▲ **EMP:** 6
SQ FT: 800
SALES: 4.5MM **Privately Held**
WEB: www.milinternational.com
SIC: 5169 Chemical additives

(G-11688)
MILL CREEK SELECT
2006 Limestone Rd (19808-5553)
PHONE..................................302 995-2090
EMP: 4 **EST:** 2018
SALES (est): 67.6K **Privately Held**
SIC: 8021 Offices & clinics of dentists

(G-11689)
MILLCREEK BARBER SHOP
Also Called: Milcreek Barber Shop
4573 Kirkwood Hwy (19808-5117)
PHONE..................................302 998-2174
William Delancey, *Owner*
EMP: 14
SQ FT: 1,200
SALES (est): 191.8K **Privately Held**
SIC: 7241 Barber shops

(G-11690)
MILLCREEK MOBILE HM PK LAND CO
Also Called: Murray Manor
5600 Old Capitol Trl (19808-4951)
PHONE..................................302 998-3045
Lee Murray, *President*
Bernice Murray, *Vice Pres*
Bill Ferguson, *Manager*
EMP: 12
SALES (est): 1.1MM **Privately Held**
WEB: www.murraymanor.com
SIC: 6515 Mobile home site operators

(G-11691)
MILLCREEK TEXACO STATION
109 Bellant Cir (19807-2219)
PHONE..................................302 571-8489
John Lamgrell, *Owner*
EMP: 8
SQ FT: 1,500
SALES (est): 568.9K **Privately Held**
SIC: 5541 7538 Filling stations, gasoline; general automotive repair shops

(G-11692)
MILLENIUM COUNSELING
1601 Milltown Rd Ste 14 (19808-4084)
PHONE..................................302 995-9188
Trish Hillstone, *Principal*
EMP: 4
SALES (est): 154.5K **Privately Held**
SIC: 8322 General counseling services

(G-11693)
MILLER & ASSOCIATES PA
Also Called: Miller & Associates Cpas
5500 Skyline Dr Ste 5 (19808-1717)
PHONE..................................302 234-0678
David M Miller, *President*
EMP: 6
SALES (est): 314.8K **Privately Held**
SIC: 8721 7291 Certified public accountant; tax return preparation services

(G-11694)
MILLER MAURO GROUP INC
3512 Silverside Rd Ste 9 (19810-4941)
PHONE..................................302 426-6565
Joseph Mauro, *CEO*
Ruthy Miller, *Creative Dir*
EMP: 5
SQ FT: 1,635
SALES (est): 360K **Privately Held**
WEB: www.mmg.com
SIC: 7336 Creative services to advertisers, except writers; graphic arts & related design

(G-11695)
MILLER PUBLISHING INC
5 Servan Ct (19805-2995)
PHONE..................................302 576-6579
Frederick Miller, *President*
EMP: 1
SALES (est): 96K **Privately Held**
WEB: www.millerpublishinginc.com
SIC: 2731 Book publishing

(G-11696)
MILLION GROUP
100 South Rd (19809-3033)
PHONE..................................302 543-8354
Ali Hayes, *Client Mgr*
Carliss Illion,
EMP: 4

GEOGRAPHIC SECTION
Wilmington - New Castle County (G-11727)

SALES (est): 314K **Privately Held**
SIC: 7331 Direct mail advertising services

(G-11697)
MILLTOWN DENTAL LLC
2601 Annand Dr Ste 18 (19808-3719)
PHONE.....................302 998-3332
EMP: 4 EST: 2016
SALES (est): 174.3K **Privately Held**
SIC: 8021 Dentist's Office

(G-11698)
MILLWRIGHTS LOCAL UNION 1548
1013 Centre Rd Ste 201 (19805-1265)
PHONE.....................410 355-0011
Jack L Johns, *President*
Patrick Williams, *Vice Pres*
David Morris, *Treasurer*
Robert Lipscomb, *Admin Sec*
Michael Schmidt, *Admin Sec*
EMP: 10
SALES: 88.4K **Privately Held**
SIC: 8631 Labor union

(G-11699)
MILTON & HATTIE KUTZ FOUNDATON
101 Garden Of Eden Rd (19803-1511)
PHONE.....................302 427-2100
Gina Kozizki, *Office Mgr*
EMP: 11
SALES: 105.5K **Privately Held**
SIC: 6732 Charitable trust management; educational trust management

(G-11700)
MILTON & HATTIE KUTZ HOME INC
704 River Rd (19809-2746)
PHONE.....................302 764-7000
Karen Freeman, *President*
Dave Bacher, *CFO*
Robin Collison, *Bookkeeper*
Karen Friedman, *Director*
EMP: 140
SQ FT: 49,500
SALES: 14.6MM **Privately Held**
WEB: www.kutzhome.org
SIC: 8051 8052 Convalescent home with continuous nursing care; personal care facility

(G-11701)
MILUNSKY FAMILY DENTISTRY
103 Danforth Pl (19810-4405)
PHONE.....................610 566-5322
Jacob Milunsky DMD, *Principal*
EMP: 4
SALES (est): 317.5K **Privately Held**
SIC: 8021 Dental clinics & offices

(G-11702)
MILUNSKY FAMILY DENTISTRY PC
103 Danforth Pl (19810-4405)
PHONE.....................610 872-8042
EMP: 4
SALES (est): 61.5K **Privately Held**
SIC: 8021 Dental clinics & offices

(G-11703)
MINATEE BUSINESS GROUP
114 Lloyd St (19804-2822)
PHONE.....................302 543-5092
EMP: 5
SALES (est): 248.6K **Privately Held**
SIC: 8741 Business management

(G-11704)
MINISTRY OF CARING INC
830 N Spruce St Lowr (19801-4239)
PHONE.....................302 652-8947
Dr Gary Isaacs, *Director*
EMP: 155
SALES (corp-wide): 11.6MM **Privately Held**
SIC: 8399 Health & welfare council
PA: Ministry Of Caring, Inc
 115 E 14th St
 Wilmington DE 19801
 302 428-3702

(G-11705)
MINISTRY OF CARING INC (PA)
115 E 14th St (19801-3209)
PHONE.....................302 428-3702
Rhonda Miller, *Hum Res Coord*
Ronald Giannone, *Exec Dir*
John Bates, *Deputy Dir*
Chaz Enerio, *Deputy Dir*
Marie Keefer, *Deputy Dir*
EMP: 7
SQ FT: 4,500
SALES: 11.6MM **Privately Held**
WEB: www.ministryofcaring.org
SIC: 8699 8661 Charitable organization; non-church religious organizations

(G-11706)
MINISTRY OF CARING INC
Also Called: House of Joseph
1328 W 3rd St (19805-3662)
PHONE.....................302 652-0904
Willy Newfon, *Director*
EMP: 6
SALES (corp-wide): 11.6MM **Privately Held**
WEB: www.ministryofcaring.org
SIC: 8322 7021 Temporary relief service; rooming & boarding houses
PA: Ministry Of Caring, Inc
 115 E 14th St
 Wilmington DE 19801
 302 428-3702

(G-11707)
MINISTRY OF CARING INC
Also Called: Emmanuel Diningroom
121 N Jackson St (19805-3670)
PHONE.....................302 658-6123
Bro Miguel Ramirez, *Director*
EMP: 8
SALES (corp-wide): 11.6MM **Privately Held**
WEB: www.ministryofcaring.org
SIC: 8322 Meal delivery program
PA: Ministry Of Caring, Inc
 115 E 14th St
 Wilmington DE 19801
 302 428-3702

(G-11708)
MINISTRY OF CARING INC
Also Called: Job Placement Center
1100 Lancaster Ave (19805-4009)
PHONE.....................302 652-5522
Myra Holmes, *Director*
EMP: 4
SALES (corp-wide): 11.6MM **Privately Held**
WEB: www.ministryofcaring.org
SIC: 8322 Crisis intervention center
PA: Ministry Of Caring, Inc
 115 E 14th St
 Wilmington DE 19801
 302 428-3702

(G-11709)
MINISTRY OF CARING INC
Also Called: Mary Mother of Hope House III
515 N Broom St (19805-3114)
PHONE.....................302 652-0970
Renee Mosley, *Deputy Dir*
EMP: 7
SALES (corp-wide): 11.6MM **Privately Held**
WEB: www.ministryofcaring.org
SIC: 8322 Crisis intervention center
PA: Ministry Of Caring, Inc
 115 E 14th St
 Wilmington DE 19801
 302 428-3702

(G-11710)
MINISTRY OF CARING INC
Also Called: Ministry Caring Distribution
1410 N Claymont St (19802-5227)
PHONE.....................302 652-0969
Myra Holmes, *Director*
EMP: 9
SALES (corp-wide): 11.6MM **Privately Held**
WEB: www.ministryofcaring.org
SIC: 8322 Outreach program
PA: Ministry Of Caring, Inc
 115 E 14th St
 Wilmington DE 19801
 302 428-3702

(G-11711)
MINUTE LOAN CENTER
3210 Kirkwood Hwy (19808-6130)
PHONE.....................302 994-6588
EMP: 4
SALES (est): 480.2K **Privately Held**
SIC: 6141 Personal credit institutions

(G-11712)
MISS KITTYS KIDDIES
441 Anderson Dr (19801-5718)
PHONE.....................302 571-1547
EMP: 7
SALES (est): 65.8K **Privately Held**
SIC: 8059 Nursing & personal care

(G-11713)
MISS MAFIA LLC
919 N Market St Ste 950 (19801-3036)
PHONE.....................800 246-2677
Kirsty Whitaker,
EMP: 11
SALES: 200K **Privately Held**
SIC: 7389 7371 Styling of fashions, apparel, furniture, textiles, etc.; ; computer software development & applications

(G-11714)
MITCHELL ASSOCIATES INC (PA)
1 Ave Of The Arts Ste B (19801-5094)
PHONE.....................302 594-9400
Louis B Rosenberg, *President*
Sheree L Jones, *Vice Pres*
Kim Leborys, *Treasurer*
William Endicott, *Admin Sec*
EMP: 38
SQ FT: 16,500
SALES (est): 5.3MM **Privately Held**
WEB: www.mitchellai.com
SIC: 7389 7336 Interior designer; graphic arts & related design

(G-11715)
MITEK HOLDINGS INC (DH)
802 N West St (19801-1526)
PHONE.....................302 429-1816
Susan Besley, *Administration*
EMP: 5
SALES (est): 5MM
SALES (corp-wide): 225.3B **Publicly Held**
SIC: 7389 Financial services
HQ: Mitek Industries, Inc.
 16023 Swinly Rdg
 Chesterfield MO 63017
 314 434-1200

(G-11716)
MJM FABRICATIONS INC
506 Crest Rd (19803-4322)
PHONE.....................302 764-0163
Michael Molder, *President*
EMP: 6
SALES (est): 859K **Privately Held**
SIC: 3441 Fabricated structural metal

(G-11717)
MMR INDUSTRIES INC
7 Dartmouth Rd (19808-4633)
PHONE.....................302 999-9561
Michael S Brenner, *Principal*
EMP: 2
SALES (est): 101.6K **Privately Held**
SIC: 3999 Manufacturing industries

(G-11718)
MOBILE MUZIC INC
2517 Nicholby Dr (19808-4212)
PHONE.....................302 998-5951
Tony Lewis, *President*
EMP: 6
SALES (est): 78.1K **Privately Held**
SIC: 7929 Disc jockey service

(G-11719)
MOBIUS NEW MEDIA INC
818 N Market St Fl 2r (19801-3087)
PHONE.....................302 475-9880
Matt Urban, *President*
Luis Lopez, *Engineer*
Barry Crell, *Treasurer*
Jim Davis, *Software Dev*
Joe Del Tufo, *Admin Sec*
EMP: 8

SALES (est): 710K **Privately Held**
SIC: 7374 Computer graphics service

(G-11720)
MODERN DENTAL
2 Righter Pkwy Ste 110 (19803-1528)
PHONE.....................302 478-1748
EMP: 4 EST: 2015
SALES (est): 150.2K **Privately Held**
SIC: 8021 Dental clinic

(G-11721)
MODERNTHINK LLC
2 Mill Rd Ste 102 (19806-2175)
PHONE.....................302 764-4477
Suzi Schmittlein, *Project Mgr*
Karen Kukulka, *Opers Staff*
Scott Cawwood,
Richard Boyer,
Eileen Edmunds,
EMP: 10
SALES (est): 1.1MM **Privately Held**
WEB: www.modernthink.com
SIC: 8742 Human resource consulting services

(G-11722)
MODIFIED THERMOSET RESINS INC
Also Called: Ppc Coatings
2 Pixie Rd (19810-1314)
PHONE.....................302 235-3710
Merav Narunsky, *President*
Cliff Narunsky, *General Mgr*
EMP: 9
SQ FT: 1,000
SALES (est): 981.2K **Privately Held**
SIC: 2851 Paints & allied products

(G-11723)
MODULATION THERAPEUTICS INC
2711 Centerville Rd # 400 (19808-1660)
PHONE.....................813 784-0033
Dr Lori Hazlehurst, *President*
EMP: 3
SALES (est): 171.1K **Privately Held**
SIC: 2834 Pharmaceutical preparations

(G-11724)
MOGHUL LIFE INC
1201 N Orange St Ste 600 (19801-1171)
PHONE.....................347 560-9124
Monica Humes, *CEO*
Kristine Bolt, *Vice Pres*
James Burke, *Marketing Staff*
EMP: 1
SALES (est): 28.2K **Privately Held**
SIC: 8748 7822 8742 2731 Publishing consultant; distribution, exclusive of production: motion picture; distribution channels consultant; books: publishing & printing; books: printing & binding;

(G-11725)
MOHAWK TILE MBL DISTRS OF DEL
2700 W 3rd St (19805-1811)
PHONE.....................302 655-7164
Robert M Klinges, *President*
Micheal J Klinges, *Treasurer*
Edward F Klinges, *Admin Sec*
EMP: 5 EST: 1968
SQ FT: 7,000
SALES (est): 629.2K **Privately Held**
SIC: 5032 Ceramic wall & floor tile; marble building stone

(G-11726)
MOLD MEDICS GLOBAL LLC
300 Water St Ste 300 # 300 (19801-5046)
PHONE.....................301 943-9428
Roger Berwanger, *Principal*
Tom Cassel, *CFO*
Brock Vinton, *Mng Member*
Don Holler, *Director*
EMP: 4
SALES (est): 133.4K **Privately Held**
SIC: 1799 Decontamination services

(G-11727)
MOLDED COMPONENTS INC
3817 Katherine Ave (19808-4638)
PHONE.....................302 588-2240
Ryan Rebecca Carpenter, *Principal*

Wilmington - New Castle County (G-11728)

EMP: 4 **EST:** 2013
SALES (est): 414.9K **Privately Held**
SIC: 3089 Molding primary plastic

(G-11728)
MOMENTUM MANAGEMENT GROUP INC
Also Called: Corexcel
3411 Silverside Rd 201w (19810-4806)
PHONE 302 477-9730
Susan Bowlby, *President*
EMP: 6
SQ FT: 1,500
SALES (est): 847.3K **Privately Held**
WEB: www.corexcel.com
SIC: 8742 Training & development consultant

(G-11729)
MOMS CLUB
5447 Crestline Rd (19808-3659)
PHONE 302 738-8822
Dawn Briggs, *Principal*
EMP: 4
SALES (est): 89.4K **Privately Held**
SIC: 8699 Personal interest organization

(G-11730)
MOMS HOUSE INC
Also Called: MOM'S HOUSE OF WILMINGTON
1718 Howland St (19805-5315)
PHONE 302 658-3433
Mary Kay Wilson, *Director*
EMP: 4
SALES: 172.7K **Privately Held**
SIC: 8351 Child day care services

(G-11731)
MONEY GALAXY INC
1000 N West St Ste 1200 (19801-1058)
PHONE 302 319-2008
EMP: 12 **EST:** 2011
SALES (est): 720K **Privately Held**
SIC: 7372 8742 Prepackaged Software Services Management Consulting Services

(G-11732)
MONEYKEY - TX INC
3422 Old Capitol Trl (19808-6124)
PHONE 866 255-1668
Clive Kinross, *President*
EMP: 4
SALES (est): 469.5K **Privately Held**
SIC: 6141 Personal credit institutions

(G-11733)
MONRO INC
Also Called: Monro Mufflers
600 Kirkwood Hwy (19805)
PHONE 302 999-0237
Drew Thompson, *Manager*
EMP: 4
SALES (corp-wide): 1.2B **Publicly Held**
WEB: www.monro.com
SIC: 7533 Muffler shop, sale or repair & installation
PA: Monro, Inc.
    200 Holleder Pkwy
    Rochester NY 14615
    585 647-6400

(G-11734)
MONROE IKO INC
120 Hay Rd (19809-3509)
PHONE 302 764-3100
Henry Koschitzky, *President*
EMP: 100
SALES (est): 7.8MM **Privately Held**
SIC: 2952 Roofing materials

(G-11735)
MONTCHANIN DESIGN GROUP INC
1907 N Market St (19802-4812)
PHONE 302 652-3008
Michael Looney, *President*
Zachary Davis, *Vice Pres*
EMP: 12
SQ FT: 2,500
SALES (est): 2MM **Privately Held**
WEB: www.montchanindesign.com
SIC: 8712 8741 Architectural engineering; construction management

(G-11736)
MONTESINO ASSOCIATES
1719 Delaware Ave 3 (19806-2362)
PHONE 302 888-2355
Peter J Schmitt, *Owner*
EMP: 7
SALES (est): 574.4K **Privately Held**
SIC: 8742 Marketing consulting services

(G-11737)
MONTESINO TECHNOLOGIES INC
1719 Delaware Ave 3 (19806-2362)
PHONE 302 888-2355
Peter Schmitt, *President*
EMP: 5 **EST:** 1999
SALES (est): 390K **Privately Held**
SIC: 7389 Packaging & labeling services

(G-11738)
MONTESSORI LEARNING CENTRE
2313 Concord Pike (19803-2911)
PHONE 302 478-2575
Vienna Broadbelt, *Owner*
Vienna Boroadbelt, *Owner*
EMP: 9
SQ FT: 2,100
SALES (est): 260K **Privately Held**
WEB: www.montessorilc.com
SIC: 8351 Child day care services; Montessori child development center

(G-11739)
MONTGOMERY MCCRACKEN
300 Delaware Ave Ste 750 (19801-6600)
PHONE 302 504-7800
John M Bloxom, *Branch Mgr*
EMP: 30
SALES (corp-wide): 46.2MM **Privately Held**
WEB: www.mmwr.com
SIC: 8111 General practice attorney, lawyer
PA: Montgomery, Mccracken, Walker & Rhoads, Llp
    123 S Broad St Fl 24
    Philadelphia PA 19109
    215 772-1500

(G-11740)
MONTGOMERY KENNETH JOHN
610 Ohio Ave (19805-1023)
PHONE 302 992-0484
Kenneth J Montgomery, *Owner*
EMP: 6
SALES (est): 300K **Privately Held**
SIC: 4213 Trucking, except local

(G-11741)
MONZACK MERSKY MCLAUGHLIN
1201 N Orange St Ste 400 (19801-1167)
P.O. Box 2031 (19899-2031)
PHONE 302 656-8162
Melvin Monzack, *Principal*
Francis Monaco Jr, *Principal*
Frederick B Rosner,
EMP: 28
SALES (est): 3.1MM **Privately Held**
WEB: www.monlaw.com
SIC: 8111 General practice law office

(G-11742)
MOONY AND ZEAGER INC
Also Called: Quality Family Construction
2518 Pennington Way (19810-1238)
PHONE 302 593-8166
Harry Moony, *President*
Emerson Zeager, *Principal*
EMP: 4
SALES (est): 600K **Privately Held**
SIC: 1521 1542 Single-family housing construction; commercial & office building contractors

(G-11743)
MOOR INSTRUMENTS INC
501 Silverside Rd Ste 66 (19809-1394)
PHONE 302 798-7470
David Boggett, *President*
Linda Wade, *Office Mgr*
EMP: 2 **EST:** 1994
SQ FT: 220
SALES (est): 372.6K **Privately Held**
WEB: www.moorinstruments.com
SIC: 3841 Surgical & medical instruments

(G-11744)
MOORE INSURANCE & FINANCIAL
1702 Kirkwood Hwy Ste 101 (19805-4939)
PHONE 302 999-9101
Darren Moore, *Manager*
EMP: 6
SALES: 500K **Privately Held**
SIC: 6411 Insurance agents & brokers

(G-11745)
MOORE INTERNATIONAL LLC
913 N Market St Ste 200 (19801-3097)
PHONE 302 603-7262
Shoneika Moore,
EMP: 4
SQ FT: 200
SALES: 25K **Privately Held**
SIC: 8742 Marketing consulting services

(G-11746)
MOORE PHYSCIAL THERAPY
1806 N Van Buren St # 110 (19802-3851)
PHONE 302 654-8142
Robert Altschuler, *Principal*
EMP: 4
SALES (est): 92.8K **Privately Held**
SIC: 8093 Rehabilitation center, outpatient treatment

(G-11747)
MOORWAY PAINTING MANAGEMENT
1 Hayden Ave (19804-1742)
PHONE 302 764-5002
Rahim El, *Owner*
Kamira El, *Manager*
EMP: 8
SALES: 170K **Privately Held**
SIC: 8741 5231 Business management; paint & painting supplies

(G-11748)
MORE THAN FITNESS INC
718 Grandview Ave (19809-2627)
PHONE 302 690-5655
Jeremy Moore, *Principal*
Robyn Howton, *Principal*
Brandon Pratta, *Principal*
Stacey Richardson, *Principal*
Charley Ward, *Principal*
EMP: 6
SALES (est): 130.9K **Privately Held**
SIC: 7991 Physical fitness facilities

(G-11749)
MORGAN KALMAN CLINIC PA
2501 Silverside Rd Ste 1 (19810-3726)
PHONE 302 529-5500
Craig D Morgan MD, *Partner*
Victor R Kalman, *Partner*
Jill Garzia, *Manager*
EMP: 15 **EST:** 1998
SQ FT: 3,000
SALES (est): 2.1MM **Privately Held**
WEB: www.morgankalman.com
SIC: 8011 Orthopedic physician; surgeon

(G-11750)
MORGAN KALMAN CLINIC
2701 Kirkwood Hwy (19805-4911)
PHONE 610 869-5757
Morgan Kalman, *Branch Mgr*
EMP: 17 **Privately Held**
SIC: 8011 Clinic, operated by physicians
PA: Kalman Morgan Clinic
    900 W Baltimore Pike # 103
    West Grove PA 19390

(G-11751)
MORGAN LEWIS INTERNATIONAL LLC (PA)
1007 N Orange St Ste 500 (19801-1254)
PHONE 302 574-3000
Lewis Morgan, *Principal*
EMP: 9
SALES (est): 2.8MM **Privately Held**
SIC: 8111 General practice attorney, lawyer

(G-11752)
MORGAN STANLEY & CO LLC
2751 Centerville Rd # 104 (19808-1600)
PHONE 302 573-4000
Thomas Grenda, *Financial Analy*
Donald Didoeato, *Manager*
EMP: 20
SALES (corp-wide): 50.1B **Publicly Held**
WEB: www.msvp.com
SIC: 6211 Brokers, security
HQ: Morgan Stanley & Co. Llc
    1585 Broadway
    New York NY 10036
    212 761-4000

(G-11753)
MORGAN STNLEY INTL HLDINGS INC
2751 Centerville Rd # 104 (19808-1627)
PHONE 302 657-2000
Sean Farrell, *Manager*
EMP: 100
SALES (corp-wide): 50.1B **Publicly Held**
SIC: 6719 Investment holding companies, except banks
HQ: Stanley Morgan International Holdings Inc
    1585 Broadway
    New York NY 10036

(G-11754)
MORGAN STNLEY SMITH BARNEY LLC
2751 Centerville Rd # 104 (19808-1600)
PHONE 302 636-5500
Gerald Laudicina, *Branch Mgr*
EMP: 4
SALES (corp-wide): 50.1B **Publicly Held**
SIC: 7389 Financial services
HQ: Morgan Stanley Smith Barney, Llc
    2000 Westchester Ave
    Purchase NY 10577

(G-11755)
MORRIS AND MORRIS
4001 Kennett Pike Ste 300 (19807-2039)
PHONE 302 426-0400
Karen Morris, *Partner*
Patrick Morris, *Partner*
EMP: 4
SALES (est): 431.4K **Privately Held**
WEB: www.morrisandmorrislaw.com
SIC: 8111 General practice attorney, lawyer

(G-11756)
MORRIS JAMES LLP
803 N Broom St (19806-4624)
PHONE 302 655-2599
Francis J Jones Jr, *Partner*
EMP: 15
SALES (est): 112.5K **Privately Held**
SIC: 8111 General practice attorney, lawyer

(G-11757)
MORRIS JAMES LLP
500 Delaware Ave Ste 500 # 500 (19801-7405)
P.O. Box 2328 (19899-2328)
PHONE 302 888-6800
Susan Ament, *Principal*
Sherry A Perna, *Controller*
Helen Phillips, *Admin Asst*
Gail Collins, *Administration*
EMP: 16
SALES (corp-wide): 21.2MM **Privately Held**
SIC: 8111 General practice attorney, lawyer
PA: Morris James Llp
    500 Delaware Ave Ste 1500
    Wilmington DE 19801
    302 888-6863

(G-11758)
MORRIS JAMES LLP (PA)
Also Called: Mars James Hitchens & Williams
500 Delaware Ave Ste 1500 (19801-1494)
P.O. Box 2306 (19899-2306)
PHONE 302 888-6863
Richard Gallperin, *Partner*
Morris James, *Partner*
Edward M McNally, *Partner*
Stepeh M Miller, *Partner*

GEOGRAPHIC SECTION
Wilmington - New Castle County (G-11788)

D P Mucollough, *Partner*
EMP: 97 **EST:** 1932
SALES (est): 21.2MM **Privately Held**
WEB: www.morrisjames.com
SIC: 8111 General practice attorney, lawyer

(G-11759)
MORRIS NCHOLS ARSHT TNNELL LLP
1201 N Market St Fl 16 (19801-1147)
P.O. Box 1347 (19899-1347)
PHONE.................................302 658-9200
Walter C Tuthill, *Partner*
Jack Blumenfeld, *Partner*
Donna Culver, *Partner*
Rob Dehney, *Partner*
Andrew Johnston, *Partner*
EMP: 200 **EST:** 1932
SQ FT: 67,000
SALES (est): 35.1MM **Privately Held**
WEB: www.mnat.com
SIC: 8111 General practice attorney, lawyer

(G-11760)
MORTGAGE AMERICA INC
5315 Limestone Rd (19808-1222)
PHONE.................................302 239-0600
Damian Gallagher, *Manager*
EMP: 7 **Privately Held**
SIC: 6162 Mortgage bankers
PA: Mortgage America, Inc.
1425 Grape St
Whitehall PA 18052

(G-11761)
MORTGAGE NETWORK SOLUTIONS LLC
223 Pine Cliff Dr (19810-1312)
PHONE.................................302 252-0100
Michael Kushner, *Branch Mgr*
Cheryl Rappucci,
EMP: 49 **Privately Held**
SIC: 6162 Mortgage bankers
PA: Mortgage Network Solutions, Llc
2036 Foulk Rd Ste 102
Wilmington DE

(G-11762)
MOSSAIC
Also Called: Fairfax Neighborhood Home
219 Potomac Rd (19803-3120)
PHONE.................................302 428-1680
Jill Turner, *Manager*
EMP: 4
SALES (est): 113.3K **Privately Held**
SIC: 8052 Home for the mentally retarded, with health care

(G-11763)
MOTTO COMPUTER INC
3317 Old Capitol Trl C (19808-6275)
PHONE.................................302 633-6783
Simon Lo, *President*
EMP: 4
SALES (est): 600K **Privately Held**
WEB: www.mottocomputer.com
SIC: 7378 Computer & data processing equipment repair/maintenance

(G-11764)
MOVING SCIENCES LLC
1201 N Orange St Ste 600 (19801-1171)
PHONE.................................617 871-9892
Yz Lee, *CEO*
EMP: 2
SALES (est): 97.4K **Privately Held**
SIC: 7372 7371 7389 Application computer software; computer software development;

(G-11765)
MP AXLE INC
1329 Tulane Rd (19803-5141)
PHONE.................................302 478-6442
Ahron Augenbraum, *Principal*
EMP: 2 **EST:** 2010
SALES (est): 137.3K **Privately Held**
SIC: 2391 Curtains & draperies

(G-11766)
MR CHRIS HAIR DESIGN
Also Called: Mr Chris Beauty Salon
209 W 9th St (19801-1619)
PHONE.................................302 658-2121
Chris Sarmousakis, *President*
Marika Sarmousakis, *Principal*
EMP: 4
SALES (est): 183.9K **Privately Held**
SIC: 7231 Hairdressers

(G-11767)
MR ROYAL TOUCH MBL DETAILING
230 Paynter Dr (19804-1304)
PHONE.................................302 229-0161
Nathan Johnson, *Principal*
EMP: 5
SALES (est): 77.6K **Privately Held**
SIC: 7542 Washing & polishing, automotive

(G-11768)
MRESOURCE LLC (PA)
1220 N Market St Ste 808 (19801-2595)
P.O. Box 5370, Chicago IL (60680-5370)
PHONE.................................312 608-4789
John Hancock, *CEO*
Mark Mergler, *COO*
EMP: 3 **EST:** 2009
SALES (est): 1MM **Privately Held**
SIC: 7372 Application computer software

(G-11769)
MS FINANCING LLC
Also Called: Morgan Stanley
1209 N Orange St (19801-1120)
PHONE.................................212 276-1206
Ethan Schiffman, *Manager*
Ethan J Schiffman, *Manager*
EMP: 15
SALES (est): 3.3MM
SALES (corp-wide): 50.1B **Publicly Held**
SIC: 6282 Investment advice
PA: Morgan Stanley
1585 Broadway
New York NY 10036
212 761-4000

(G-11770)
MS HATHERS LRNG CTR CHILDCARE
205 Brookland Ave (19805-1112)
PHONE.................................302 994-2448
Heather Wiktorwizz, *Owner*
EMP: 5 **EST:** 2012
SALES (est): 101K **Privately Held**
SIC: 8351 Child day care services

(G-11771)
MSC INDUSTRIAL DIRECT CO INC
401 Marsh Ln Ste 2 (19804-2491)
PHONE.................................302 998-1214
Michael James, *Owner*
EMP: 15 **Publicly Held**
SIC: 5085 Industrial supplies
PA: Msc Industrial Direct Co., Inc.
75 Maxess Rd
Melville NY 11747

(G-11772)
MTB ARTISANS LLC
2205 Kentmere Pkwy (19806-2017)
PHONE.................................303 475-9024
Chris Squier, *Mng Member*
EMP: 3
SALES (est): 99.4K **Privately Held**
SIC: 2511 Wood household furniture

(G-11773)
MULLICO GENERAL CONSTRUCTION
510 Foulkstone Rd (19803-2414)
PHONE.................................302 475-4400
Eugene D Mulligan III, *President*
Rosalie A Mulligan, *Corp Secy*
Dennis W Mulligan, *Treasurer*
EMP: 10
SALES: 1.3MM **Privately Held**
WEB: www.mullicoconstruction.com
SIC: 1521 General remodeling, single-family houses

(G-11774)
MULTI-CBLE ADV SEC SLTNS INC
19c Trolley Sq (19806-3355)
PHONE.................................703 909-6239
David Cosnotti, *CEO*
Travis Johnston, *COO*
Peter Karlewicz, *CFO*
EMP: 4 **EST:** 2012
SALES (est): 83.7K **Privately Held**
SIC: 7381 Guard services

(G-11775)
MUMFORD-BJORKMAN ASSOCIATES
Also Called: M B A
222a 7th Ave (19805-4762)
P.O. Box 733, New Castle (19720-0733)
PHONE.................................302 655-8234
Mike Catts, *President*
Daniel Mumford, *President*
Linda Mumford, *Corp Secy*
Michael Catts, *Vice Pres*
Andrew Mumford, *Vice Pres*
EMP: 15
SQ FT: 800
SALES (est): 919.1K **Privately Held**
SIC: 7389 Inspection & testing services

(G-11776)
MURPHY & LANDON PC
Also Called: Murphy Spadaro & Landon
1011 Centre Rd Ste 210 (19805-1266)
PHONE.................................302 472-8100
Frank Murphy, *President*
Phillip Edwards, *Partner*
Jonathan Parshall, *Partner*
Roger Landon, *Vice Pres*
Carl N Kunz III,
EMP: 15
SQ FT: 11,000
SALES (est): 1.6MM **Privately Held**
WEB: www.msllaw.com
SIC: 8111 General practice law office; general practice attorney, lawyer

(G-11777)
MURPHY MARINE SERVICES INC
701 Christiana Ave (19801-5842)
PHONE.................................302 571-4700
John Coulahan, *President*
Mark Murphy, *President*
Timothy Creedon, *Superintendent*
Ed Heinlein, *VP Opers*
Malone Stephanie, *HR Admin*
EMP: 300
SALES (est): 26.6MM **Privately Held**
WEB: www.murphymarine.com
SIC: 4491 Stevedoring

(G-11778)
MUSI COMMERCIAL PROPERTIES INC
5700 Kennett Pike (19807-1312)
PHONE.................................302 594-1000
Ken J Musi, *President*
EMP: 6
SQ FT: 2,000
SALES (est): 502.1K **Privately Held**
WEB: www.musicommercial.com
SIC: 6531 Real estate agent, commercial

(G-11779)
MUST APP CORP
1013 Centre Rd Ste 403b (19805-1270)
PHONE.................................905 537-5522
Evgeny Muravjev, *CEO*
EMP: 10
SALES (est): 217.5K **Privately Held**
SIC: 7371 Computer software development & applications

(G-11780)
MUVERS INC
427 N Tatnall St (19801-2230)
PHONE.................................888 508-4849
Mark Daniels, *President*
EMP: 7
SQ FT: 920
SALES: 1.2MM **Privately Held**
SIC: 4212 Moving services

(G-11781)
MV FARINOLA INC
4023 Kennett Pike Ste 219 (19807-2018)
PHONE.................................302 545-8492
Michael V Farinola, *President*
Veronica Farinola, *Vice Pres*
EMP: 2 **EST:** 1992
SALES: 550K **Privately Held**
SIC: 8742 3534 Administrative services consultant; elevators & equipment

(G-11782)
MVL STRUCTURES GROUP LLC
1000 N West St Ste 1501 (19801-1001)
PHONE.................................302 652-7580
Jamil Oudeif, *Principal*
EMP: 35
SALES (est): 645.2K **Privately Held**
SIC: 8711 1542 Building construction consultant; commercial & office building, new construction

(G-11783)
MVL-AL OTHMAN AL ZAMEL JV LLC
1000 N West St Ste 1501 (19801-1001)
PHONE.................................832 302-2757
Marty Muller, *Project Mgr*
Ibrahim Musa, *Manager*
EMP: 50
SALES (est): 1.7MM **Privately Held**
SIC: 1542 Commercial & office building, new construction

(G-11784)
MVL-SAQA JV LLC
1000 N West St Ste 1501 (19801-1001)
PHONE.................................832 302-2757
Marty Muller, *Project Mgr*
Ibrahim Musa, *Manager*
EMP: 50
SALES (est): 1.7MM **Privately Held**
SIC: 1542 Commercial & office building, new construction

(G-11785)
MWIDM INC (PA)
913 N Market St Ste 200 (19801-3097)
PHONE.................................302 298-0101
Amrinder Romana, *President*
EMP: 46
SQ FT: 4,000
SALES: 69.1MM **Privately Held**
SIC: 8742 7372 7361 Management consulting services; personnel management consultant; prepackaged software; application computer software; business oriented computer software; executive placement

(G-11786)
MY BENEFIT ADVISOR LLC
2207 Concord Pike Ste 152 (19803-2908)
PHONE.................................302 588-7242
Brian McLaughlin, *Vice Pres*
Ana Espaillat, *Accounts Mgr*
Dawn Lucchi, *Manager*
Ron Clark,
EMP: 7
SQ FT: 1,800
SALES (est): 351.3K **Privately Held**
SIC: 8748 Business consulting

(G-11787)
MY DIGITAL SHIELD
300 Delaware Ave Ste 210 (19801-6601)
PHONE.................................423 310-8977
Tim Pazda, *President*
Zhanna Brown, *Vice Pres*
EMP: 7
SALES (est): 680.4K **Privately Held**
SIC: 7379 Computer related consulting services

(G-11788)
MY MARKET QUEST INC
501 Silverside Rd Ste 105 (19809-1376)
PHONE.................................213 265-9767
Linda Jacob, *CEO*
EMP: 15
SALES (est): 468.5K **Privately Held**
SIC: 8742 Management consulting services

Wilmington - New Castle County (G-11789)

GEOGRAPHIC SECTION

(G-11789)
MY QME INC
1000 Kirk Ave Ste 1000 # 1000 (19806-4633)
PHONE 302 218-8730
Bentley Charlemagne, *CEO*
Fred Barnett, *Vice Pres*
Tom Bergey, *Vice Pres*
EMP: 40
SALES (est): 1.2MM **Privately Held**
SIC: **8742** 3555 7374 Marketing consulting services; printing trades machinery; computer graphics service

(G-11790)
MYSCHEDULE INC
2711 Centerville Rd # 400 (19808-1660)
PHONE 877 235-6825
Christopher Tallia, *CEO*
Stephen Tallia, *Principal*
EMP: 4
SALES (est): 89.7K **Privately Held**
SIC: **7371** Custom computer programming services

(G-11791)
MYSERVE INC
129 Jade Dr (19810-2258)
P.O. Box 7192 (19803-0192)
PHONE 302 528-4822
Adam Goldstein, *Principal*
EMP: 7
SALES (est): 185.9K **Privately Held**
SIC: **4832** Sports

(G-11792)
NAAMANS CREEK WATERSHED
2204 Hillside Rd (19810-4018)
PHONE 302 475-3037
Maryann Cinaglia, *President*
EMP: 7
SALES (est): 343.8K **Privately Held**
SIC: **4941** Water supply

(G-11793)
NAB MOTEL INC
Also Called: Fairview Inn
1051 S Market St (19801-5227)
PHONE 302 656-9431
Bob Patel, *President*
Nalini Patel, *Admin Sec*
EMP: 10
SALES (est): 718.9K **Privately Held**
SIC: **7011** Motel, franchised

(G-11794)
NAGENGAST JANET DAY CARE
602 Ashford Rd (19803-2406)
PHONE 302 656-6898
Janet Nagengast, *Director*
EMP: 5
SALES (est): 108K **Privately Held**
SIC: **8351** Child day care services

(G-11795)
NALLYS AUTO PLAZA INC (PA)
2412 W Newport Pike (19804-3831)
PHONE 302 543-8126
Michael Nally, *President*
EMP: 9
SALES (est): 1MM **Privately Held**
SIC: **7538** General automotive repair shops

(G-11796)
NANCY CONKLIN INTERIORS
3220 Swarthmore Rd (19807-3126)
P.O. Box 4408 (19807-0408)
PHONE 302 655-0877
William Gilcrest, *Principal*
EMP: 5
SALES (est): 394.9K **Privately Held**
SIC: **7389** Interior designer; interior design services

(G-11797)
NANNAS HAINES & SCHIAVO PA
Also Called: Nannas & Schiavo
1407 Foulk Rd Ste 100 (19803-2700)
PHONE 302 479-8800
Theodore Nannas, *President*
David Haines, *Treasurer*
Michael Forwood, *CPA*
Charles A Schiavo, *Admin Sec*
EMP: 20
SQ FT: 2,700
SALES (est): 1.9MM **Privately Held**
WEB: www.nhspa.com
SIC: **8721** Accounting services, except auditing

(G-11798)
NANODROP TECHNOLOGIES LLC
3411 Silverside Rd 100bc (19810-4893)
PHONE 302 479-7707
Chris Petty, *Manager*
EMP: 45
SALES (est): 4.7MM
SALES (corp-wide): 24.3B **Publicly Held**
WEB: www.thermo.com
SIC: **3821** Laboratory apparatus & furniture
PA: Thermo Fisher Scientific Inc.
   168 3rd Ave
   Waltham MA 02451
   781 622-1000

(G-11799)
NANOSHEL LLC
3422 Old Capitol Trl (19808-6124)
PHONE 302 268-6163
EMP: 2
SALES (est): 86.2K **Privately Held**
SIC: **1081** Metal mining services

(G-11800)
NAPA M3 INC
1521 Concord Pike Ste 301 (19803-3644)
PHONE 719 660-6263
JC Newburn, *CEO*
Jason Newburn, *President*
EMP: 1
SALES (est): 90.2K **Privately Held**
SIC: **3714** 5511 5571 Motor vehicle parts & accessories; automobiles, new & used; motorcycle dealers

(G-11801)
NAPIGEN INC
200 Powder Mill Rd E4003431 (19803-2907)
PHONE 302 419-8117
Hajime Sakai, *CEO*
Byung Chun Yoo, *Director*
EMP: 7
SALES (est): 166.2K **Privately Held**
SIC: **8731** Biotechnical research, commercial

(G-11802)
NASH OMNISCAPING LLC
118 Valley Rd (19804-1300)
P.O. Box 40, Montchanin (19710-0040)
PHONE 302 654-4000
Michael Nash, *Mng Member*
EMP: 7
SALES: 1MM **Privately Held**
SIC: **0782** Landscape contractors

(G-11803)
NASON CONSTRUCTION INC (PA)
3411 Silverside Rd # 200 (19810-4803)
PHONE 302 529-2510
Thomas W Nason II, *Ch of Bd*
Julie Topkis-Nason, *Vice Pres*
Matthew Hussion, *Controller*
Susan Peck, *Controller*
Janet Diamond, *Accountant*
EMP: 31
SQ FT: 6,500
SALES (est): 21.2MM **Privately Held**
WEB: www.nasonconstruction.com
SIC: **1542** 1541 Commercial & office building, new construction; industrial buildings & warehouses

(G-11804)
NATIO ASSOC FOR THE ADVAN OF
Also Called: N A A C P
408 E 8th St (19801-3608)
P.O. Box 998 (19899-0998)
PHONE 302 655-0998
Charles Brittingham, *Principal*
EMP: 12
SALES (corp-wide): 26.6MM **Privately Held**
WEB: www.detroitnaacp.org
SIC: **8641** Social associations
PA: National Association For The Advancement Of Colored People
   4805 Mount Hope Dr
   Baltimore MD 21215
   410 580-5777

(G-11805)
NATIONAL APPLIANCE WHSE INC
2101 Concord Pike (19803-2906)
PHONE 302 543-7636
Mark Stomachin, *Principal*
EMP: 4
SALES (est): 499.4K **Privately Held**
SIC: **5064** Electrical appliances, major

(G-11806)
NATIONAL HOLDING INVESTMENT CO (HQ)
1011 Centre Rd (19805-1267)
PHONE 302 573-3887
Steve Moores, *Principal*
Glenn Burns, *Exec VP*
John Atkinson, *Vice Pres*
Joanne Bonfiglio, *Vice Pres*
Peter Zinkin, *Vice Pres*
EMP: 12
SALES (est): 6.5MM
SALES (corp-wide): 323.3MM **Publicly Held**
WEB: www.belfint.com
SIC: **6726** Investment offices
PA: National Presto Industries, Inc.
   3925 N Hastings Way
   Eau Claire WI 54703
   715 839-2121

(G-11807)
NATIONAL INDUSTRIES FOR THE BL
3314 Tunison Dr (19810-3230)
PHONE 302 477-0860
EMP: 2
SALES (est): 84.2K **Privately Held**
SIC: **3999** Manufacturing industries

(G-11808)
NATIONAL MEDICAL CARE INC
Also Called: Fresenius Med Care Brandywine
303 A St (19801-5324)
PHONE 302 658-7469
Allison Jenks, *Manager*
EMP: 19
SALES (corp-wide): 18.3B **Privately Held**
WEB: www.bamap.com
SIC: **8092** Kidney dialysis centers
HQ: National Medical Care, Inc.
   920 Winter St Ste A
   Waltham MA 02451

(G-11809)
NATIONAL RESTORTN & FACLTY SVC
1800 Walnut St (19809-1551)
PHONE 856 401-0100
John Marroni, *President*
Dorian Evans, *Vice Pres*
EMP: 25 EST: 2008
SQ FT: 6,000
SALES (est): 3.8MM **Privately Held**
SIC: **1521** 1542 Repairing fire damage, single-family houses; commercial & office buildings, renovation & repair

(G-11810)
NATIONAL SIGNING SOURCE LLC
1521 Concord Pike Ste 300 (19803-3645)
PHONE 773 885-3285
EMP: 50
SALES (est): 1.7MM **Privately Held**
SIC: **7389**

(G-11811)
NATIONAL SOCIETY INC
Also Called: Delaware Soc Rdlgy Profession
1538 Cleland Crse (19805-4517)
PHONE 302 656-9572
Carla Lafferty, *President*
EMP: 5
SALES (est): 146.6K **Privately Held**
SIC: **8621** Health association

(G-11812)
NATIONAL STRESS CLINIC LLC
1201 N Orange St Ste 600 (19801-1171)
PHONE 646 571-8627
Tim Jackson,
EMP: 7
SALES: 250K **Privately Held**
SIC: **8093** Specialty outpatient clinics

(G-11813)
NATIONAL TAPE DUPLICATORS
1500 First State Blvd (19804-3564)
PHONE 302 999-1110
Bill Burges, *Office Mgr*
EMP: 3 EST: 2001
SALES (est): 148.3K **Privately Held**
WEB: www.ken-del.com
SIC: **3695** Optical disks & tape, blank

(G-11814)
NATIONS EQUITY INVESTMENTS INC
1201 N Orange St Ste 700 (19801-1186)
PHONE 302 257-9287
Jason Rodriguez, *President*
EMP: 5
SALES: 980K **Privately Held**
SIC: **8748** Business consulting

(G-11815)
NATIONWIDE HLTH INFO TECH INC
1000 N West St Ste 1200 (19801-1058)
PHONE 302 295-5033
EMP: 8
SALES: 800K **Privately Held**
SIC: **7371** Custom Computer Programing

(G-11816)
NATIONWIDE MUTUAL INSURANCE CO
501 Silverside Rd Ste 28 (19809-1375)
PHONE 302 479-5560
Richard Finney, *Manager*
EMP: 4
SALES (corp-wide): 13.2B **Privately Held**
WEB: www.nirassn.com
SIC: **6411** Insurance agents, brokers & service
PA: Nationwide Mutual Insurance Company
   1 Nationwide Plz
   Columbus OH 43215
   614 249-7111

(G-11817)
NATIVE COMMUNICATIONS LLC
4023 Kennett Pike 176 (19807-2018)
PHONE 302 439-0640
Donald Holloway,
EMP: 4 EST: 2010
SALES (est): 121.7K **Privately Held**
SIC: **7374** Data processing & preparation

(G-11818)
NATURALAWN OF AMERICA INC
40 Germay Dr (19804-1105)
PHONE 302 652-2000
Cathy Yates, *Owner*
EMP: 10
SALES (corp-wide): 8.5MM **Privately Held**
WEB: www.icemelter.com
SIC: **0782** Lawn care services
PA: Naturalawn Of America, Inc.
   1 E Church St
   Frederick MD 21701
   301 694-5440

(G-11819)
NATURES CALL LLC
601 Philadelphia Pike (19809-2549)
PHONE 302 777-7767
Kevin Cleaver,
EMP: 5
SQ FT: 10,000
SALES (est): 750K **Privately Held**
SIC: **0781** Landscape architects; landscape services

(G-11820)
NAUGHTY APPLE
4209 Birch Cir (19808-2964)
PHONE 954 300-7158

GEOGRAPHIC SECTION
Wilmington - New Castle County (G-11850)

EMP: 2
SALES (est): 104K **Privately Held**
SIC: 3571 Mfg Electronic Computers

(G-11821)
NAVIENT CORPORATION (PA)
123 S Justison St Ste 300 (19801-5363)
PHONE.................................302 283-8000
William M Diefenderfer III, *Ch of Bd*
John F Remondi, *President*
Nicole Stolba, *Counsel*
Brian Burgess, *Vice Pres*
Richard Jackson, *Vice Pres*
EMP: 71
SQ FT: 46,000
SALES: 5.6B **Publicly Held**
SIC: 6211 6163 Security brokers & dealers; loan brokers

(G-11822)
NAVIENT CORPORATION
123 S Justison St Ste 300 (19801-5363)
PHONE.................................302 283-8000
John Remondi,
EMP: 99
SALES (est): 3MM **Privately Held**
SIC: 6211 Security brokers & dealers

(G-11823)
NAVIENT CORPORATION
Also Called: Navient Dept Edcatn Ln Srvcing
123 S Justison St Ste 300 (19801-5363)
PHONE.................................302 283-8000
John Remondi,
EMP: 99
SALES (corp-wide): 5.6B **Publicly Held**
SIC: 6211 Security brokers & dealers
PA: Navient Corporation
123 S Justison St Ste 300
Wilmington DE 19801
302 283-8000

(G-11824)
NAVY LEAGUE OF UNITED STATES
2205 Glen Avon Rd (19808-5209)
PHONE.................................302 456-4410
Matthew McCartney, *Branch Mgr*
EMP: 6
SALES (corp-wide): 9.2MM **Privately Held**
WEB: www.navyleague-richmond.com
SIC: 8621 Education & teacher association
PA: Navy League Of The United States
2300 Wilson Blvd Ste 300
Arlington VA 22201
703 528-1775

(G-11825)
NAVY OPERATIONAL SUPPORT CTR W
3920 Kirkwood Hwy (19808-5110)
PHONE.................................312 998-3328
EMP: 4
SALES (est): 58K **Privately Held**
SIC: 8399 Advocacy group

(G-11826)
NCF SUPPORTING ORGANIZATION
15 Center Meeting Rd (19807-1301)
PHONE.................................850 776-2789
EMP: 4
SALES (est): 77K **Privately Held**
SIC: 8399 Advocacy group

(G-11827)
NECESSARY LUXURY
Also Called: Necessary Lxury Mssage Therapy
806 Woodsdale Rd (19809-2245)
PHONE.................................302 764-4032
Susan Rissolo, *Principal*
EMP: 5
SALES (est): 107.9K **Privately Held**
SIC: 8093 Rehabilitation center, outpatient treatment

(G-11828)
NEFSC INC
Also Called: National Educatn Finical Svcs
405 Silverside Rd Ste 200 (19809-1768)
PHONE.................................302 746-1771
Joseph Gano, *President*
Johanna Liadis, *Vice Pres*

EMP: 9
SALES: 1.2MM **Privately Held**
WEB: www.nationaleducation.com
SIC: 6163 Mortgage brokers arranging for loans, using money of others

(G-11829)
NEHEMIAH GTWY CMNTY DEV CORP
201 W 23rd St (19802-4125)
PHONE.................................302 655-0803
Victor Valentine, *CEO*
Carol Davis, *Finance*
Joan Chandler, *Director*
EMP: 8
SALES: 214.4K **Privately Held**
WEB: www.nehemiahgateway.org
SIC: 8699 8322 Charitable organization; individual & family services

(G-11830)
NEIGHBORHOOD HOUSE INC (PA)
1218 B St (19801-5898)
PHONE.................................302 658-5404
Alison Windle, *Exec Dir*
Judy Morton, *Admin Sec*
EMP: 13
SALES: 785.6K **Privately Held**
SIC: 8322 1521 8299 8351 Community center; crisis intervention center; single-family housing construction; tutoring school; child day care services

(G-11831)
NEIGHBORLY HOME CARE
2101 W 2nd St (19805-3322)
PHONE.................................610 420-1868
Rod Rhen, *Principal*
EMP: 4 **EST:** 2013
SALES (est): 89.4K **Privately Held**
SIC: 8082 Home health care services

(G-11832)
NEMOURS ENERGY (PA)
400 W 9th St Ste 200 (19801-1504)
PHONE.................................302 655-4838
J S Dean Jr, *Partner*
EMP: 3 **EST:** 1984
SALES (est): 617.2K **Privately Held**
SIC: 1311 Crude petroleum production; natural gas production

(G-11833)
NEMOURS FOUNDATION
Alfred I Dupont
1600 Rockland Rd (19803-3607)
P.O. Box 269 (19899-0269)
PHONE.................................302 651-4000
Steven M Selbst, *Vice Chairman*
Tara Collins, *Area Mgr*
Linda D Norman, *Dean*
Dana N Bledsoe, *Vice Pres*
Catherine Brown-Butler, *Vice Pres*
EMP: 1800
SALES (corp-wide): 1.3B **Privately Held**
SIC: 6733 8062 Trusts; general medical & surgical hospitals
PA: Nemours Foundation
10140 Centurion Pkwy N
Jacksonville FL 32256
904 697-4100

(G-11834)
NEMOURS FOUNDATION
Also Called: Nemours Research Institute
1600 Rockland Rd (19803-3607)
PHONE.................................302 651-6811
Jennifer Pendley, *Managing Dir*
Martha McGill, *Vice Pres*
Rachelle Ciarrocchi, *Opers Mgr*
Kirsten Most, *Opers Mgr*
Raeanna Bonetti, *Opers Staff*
EMP: 40
SALES (corp-wide): 1.3B **Privately Held**
SIC: 8011 Pediatrician
PA: Nemours Foundation
10140 Centurion Pkwy N
Jacksonville FL 32256
904 697-4100

(G-11835)
NEMOURS FOUNDATION
Also Called: Nemours Senior Care Wilmington
1801 Rockland Rd (19803-3648)
PHONE.................................302 651-4400
Gina Altieri, *Vice Pres*
John Zhao, *Supervisor*
Andy Maphis, *Technical Staff*
Jeffrey Santoro, *Director*
Thomas Ferry PHD, *Administration*
EMP: 40
SALES (corp-wide): 1.3B **Privately Held**
SIC: 8011 Pediatrician
PA: Nemours Foundation
10140 Centurion Pkwy N
Jacksonville FL 32256
904 697-4100

(G-11836)
NEMOURS FOUNDATION
Also Called: Alfred I Dupont Hospital
1600 Rockland Rd (19803-3607)
PHONE.................................302 651-4000
Keith Drago, *Branch Mgr*
Ann Hurst, *Executive*
EMP: 1025
SALES (corp-wide): 1.3B **Privately Held**
SIC: 6733 8093 Trusts; specialty outpatient clinics
PA: Nemours Foundation
10140 Centurion Pkwy N
Jacksonville FL 32256
904 697-4100

(G-11837)
NET MONARCH
5161 W Woodmill Dr (19808-4067)
PHONE.................................302 994-9407
EMP: 5
SALES: 400K **Privately Held**
SIC: 3699 7379 Security Control Sytems And Equipment

(G-11838)
NETINSTINCTS INC
501 Silverside Rd Ste 105 (19809-1376)
PHONE.................................302 521-9478
Kiran Chepyala, *CEO*
EMP: 11
SQ FT: 2,000
SALES (est): 476.1K **Privately Held**
SIC: 8748 Telecommunications consultant

(G-11839)
NETWORK DESIGN TECHNOLOGIES
Also Called: NDT
1000 N West St Ste 1200 (19801-1058)
P.O. Box 332, Bala Cynwyd PA (19004-0332)
PHONE.................................610 991-2929
Joseph D Ruffin Jr, *CEO*
EMP: 5
SALES (est): 420.5K **Privately Held**
SIC: 7379 Computer related consulting services;

(G-11840)
NETWORK MAPPING INC
1013 Centre Rd Ste 403a (19805-1270)
PHONE.................................310 560-4142
Kevin Jacobs, *CEO*
Paul Richardson, *President*
David Langworth, *Vice Pres*
EMP: 5
SALES (est): 315.4K
SALES (corp-wide): 3.1B **Publicly Held**
SIC: 8711 Engineering services
PA: Trimble Inc.
935 Stewart Dr
Sunnyvale CA 94085
408 481-8000

(G-11841)
NETWORK SCRAP METAL CORP (PA)
Also Called: Nsmc
1000 N West St Ste 1501 (19801-1001)
PHONE.................................910 202-0655
Samuel Miller, *Ch of Bd*
Miles Kath, *Vice Pres*
EMP: 7

SALES (est): 1.8MM **Privately Held**
SIC: 5052 5093 Iron ore; metal scrap & waste materials

(G-11842)
NEUBERGER & BERMAN TRUST CO
919 N Market St Ste 506 (19801-3065)
PHONE.................................302 658-8522
Albert C Bellas, *Ch of Bd*
Stephen Brent Wells, *President*
John Mac, *Vice Pres*
EMP: 5
SALES: 9.2MM **Privately Held**
SIC: 6733 Trusts

(G-11843)
NEURACON BIOTECH INC
1313 N Market St Ste 5100 (19801-6111)
PHONE.................................813 966-3129
EMP: 5
SALES (est): 339.2K **Privately Held**
SIC: 2834 Pharmaceutical preparations

(G-11844)
NEURO FITNESS THERAPY
3300 Concord Pike Ste 4 (19803-5038)
PHONE.................................302 753-2700
EMP: 7
SALES (est): 80.6K **Privately Held**
SIC: 7991 Physical fitness facilities

(G-11845)
NEUROLIXIS INC (PA)
251 Little Falls Dr (19808-1674)
PHONE.................................215 910-2261
Adrian Newman-Tancredi, *CEO*
Mark Varney, *Principal*
EMP: 4
SALES (est): 231.8K **Privately Held**
SIC: 2834 Pharmaceutical preparations

(G-11846)
NEURORX INC
913 N Market St Ste 200 (19801-3097)
PHONE.................................202 340-1352
Jonathan Javitt, *CEO*
Chaim Hurvitz, *Director*
Daniel Javitt, *Director*
James Lawrence, *Director*
EMP: 11
SALES (est): 347.3K **Privately Held**
SIC: 8731 Biotechnical research, commercial

(G-11847)
NEVRON SOFTWARE LLC
501 Silverside Rd Ste 105 (19809-1376)
PHONE.................................302 792-0175
Blagovest Milanov,
Christo Bahchevanov,
EMP: 10
SQ FT: 150
SALES (est): 664.4K **Privately Held**
SIC: 7372 Prepackaged software

(G-11848)
NEW ALDEN-BERKLEY ASSOC LLC
Also Called: New Alden-Berkley Apartments
4 Denny Rd (19809-3445)
PHONE.................................207 774-5341
William Demarco,
EMP: 13
SALES: 1MM **Privately Held**
SIC: 6513 Apartment building operators

(G-11849)
NEW B & M MEATS INC
21 Commerce St (19801-5425)
P.O. Box 491 (19899-0491)
PHONE.................................302 655-5331
Yossi Baruch, *President*
EMP: 3 **EST:** 2016
SALES (est): 75.4K **Privately Held**
SIC: 2013 2015 Prepared beef products from purchased beef; chicken, processed: frozen

(G-11850)
NEW BALANCE RETAIL MANAGEMENT
5300 Brandywine Pkwy (19803-1470)
PHONE.................................302 230-3062
John Strojny, *Manager*

Wilmington - New Castle County (G-11851)   GEOGRAPHIC SECTION

EMP: 5
SALES (est): 354.7K **Privately Held**
SIC: 8741 Management services

(G-11851)
NEW CASTLE CNTY BD OF REALTORS
3615 Miller Rd (19802-2523)
PHONE..................................302 762-4800
Susan Helm, *Exec VP*
EMP: 7
SALES: 934.2K **Privately Held**
WEB: www.nccbor.com
SIC: 6531 Real estate brokers & agents

(G-11852)
NEW CASTLE COUNTY HEAD START
310 Kiamensi Rd Ste A (19804-2958)
PHONE..................................302 999-8480
Melissa Earl, *General Mgr*
EMP: 38
SALES (corp-wide): 6.1MM **Privately Held**
SIC: 8351 Head start center, except in conjunction with school
PA: New Castle County Head Start Inc
256 Chapman Rd Ste 103
Newark DE 19702
302 452-1500

(G-11853)
NEW CASTLE HOT MIX INC
Also Called: Minquadale Plant
925 S Heald St (19801-5732)
PHONE..................................302 655-2119
Nick Ferrarra, *President*
EMP: 5
SALES (est): 217.1K
SALES (corp-wide): 3MM **Privately Held**
SIC: 1771 Blacktop (asphalt) work
PA: Bear Materials Llc
4048 New Castle Ave
New Castle DE 19720
302 658-5241

(G-11854)
NEW CINGULAR WIRELESS SVCS INC
Also Called: AT&T Wireless
3401 Kirkwood Hwy (19808-6133)
PHONE..................................302 999-0055
Jeff Gingrich, *Sales Staff*
MAI Storey, *Branch Mgr*
EMP: 10
SALES (corp-wide): 170.7B **Publicly Held**
WEB: www.attws.com
SIC: 4812 Cellular telephone services
HQ: New Cingular Wireless Services, Inc.
7277 164th Ave Ne
Redmond WA 98052

(G-11855)
NEW CINGULAR WIRELESS SVCS INC
Also Called: AT&T
4120 Concord Pike Ste 2 (19803-5401)
PHONE..................................302 762-1366
Mark Turulski, *Branch Mgr*
EMP: 19
SALES (corp-wide): 170.7B **Publicly Held**
WEB: www.attws.com
SIC: 4812 Cellular telephone services
HQ: New Cingular Wireless Services, Inc.
7277 164th Ave Ne
Redmond WA 98052

(G-11856)
NEW CNDLELIGHT PRODUCTIONS INC
2208 Millers Rd (19810-4000)
PHONE..................................302 475-2313
Maureen T Cotellese, *Manager*
EMP: 30
SALES: 1.1MM **Privately Held**
SIC: 7822 Motion picture & tape distribution

(G-11857)
NEW COLONY NORTH ENTERPRISES
319 E Lea Blvd (19802-2353)
PHONE..................................302 762-0405
Ralph Paul, *Owner*
Douglas Paul, *Office Mgr*
EMP: 8 EST: 1967
SALES (est): 305.8K **Privately Held**
SIC: 6513 Apartment building operators

(G-11858)
NEW COMPTON TOWNE ASSOC LP
Also Called: Compton Towne House Apartments
4 Denny Rd (19809-3445)
PHONE..................................302 571-0217
Jackie Edmanson, *Partner*
EMP: 4
SALES (est): 330.2K **Privately Held**
SIC: 6513 Apartment building operators

(G-11859)
NEW CONCEPT DENTAL
2004 Foulk Rd Ste 1 (19810-3641)
PHONE..................................302 778-3822
Kristie Kaufman, *Manager*
Bruce Fay, *Fmly & Gen Dent*
EMP: 5
SALES (est): 367.2K **Privately Held**
WEB: www.newconceptdental.com
SIC: 8021 Dental clinic

(G-11860)
NEW CONCEPT TECHNOLOGIES LLC
3422 Old Capitol Trl (19808-6124)
PHONE..................................518 533-5367
Dickson Simeon,
EMP: 40 EST: 2013
SALES (est): 1.1MM **Privately Held**
SIC: 7371 4813 Computer software development & applications;

(G-11861)
NEW CSTLE CNTY CHMBER COMMERCE
920 Justison St (19801-5150)
PHONE..................................302 737-4343
Ron Walker, *President*
Dora Cheatham, *Director*
Joanna Staib, *Assistant*
EMP: 14
SQ FT: 5,000
SALES: 1.3MM **Privately Held**
WEB: www.nccccc.com
SIC: 8611 Chamber of Commerce; community affairs & services

(G-11862)
NEW DAY MONTESSORI
1 Middleton Dr (19808-4320)
PHONE..................................302 235-2554
Kim McColgan, *Director*
EMP: 6
SALES (est): 168.9K **Privately Held**
SIC: 8351 Montessori child development center

(G-11863)
NEW HOPE VEHICLE EXPORTS LLC
1000 S Market St (19801-5244)
PHONE..................................302 275-6482
Javier Marmol,
William Donato,
EMP: 6 EST: 2012
SALES (est): 483.9K **Privately Held**
SIC: 4731 4412 Freight transportation arrangement; deep sea foreign transportation of freight

(G-11864)
NEW LIFE FURNITURE SYSTEMS
1675 E Ayre St (19804-2514)
PHONE..................................302 994-9054
Scott Alexander, *Owner*
Robert Trent, *Co-Owner*
EMP: 8
SALES (est): 260.1K **Privately Held**
SIC: 7641 Antique furniture repair & restoration

(G-11865)
NEW LIFE MEDICALS LLC
3524 Silverside Rd 35b (19810-4929)
PHONE..................................302 478-7973
EMP: 2
SALES (est): 74.4K **Privately Held**
SIC: 2834 Pharmaceutical preparations

(G-11866)
NEW LOOK HOME INC
100 Bestfield Rd (19804-2722)
PHONE..................................302 994-4397
George L Callahan, *President*
EMP: 2
SALES (est): 40K **Privately Held**
SIC: 2431 Millwork

(G-11867)
NEW NORDIC US INC
Also Called: New Nordic USA
1000 N West St (19801-1050)
PHONE..................................514 390-2316
Marinus Blaabjerg, *President*
EMP: 1
SALES (est): 129.1K **Privately Held**
SIC: 2834 Pharmaceutical preparations
PA: New Nordic Healthbrands Ab
Sodra Forstadsgatan 3
Malmo 211 4

(G-11868)
NEW ORLEANS HOTEL EQUITY LLC
1000 N West St Ste 1400 (19801-1054)
PHONE..................................302 757-7300
Lisa Besescheck,
David Buffam,
EMP: 8
SALES (est): 154.4K **Privately Held**
SIC: 7011 Hotels

(G-11869)
NEW PERSPECTIVES INC
2055 Limestone Rd Ste 109 (19808-5536)
PHONE..................................302 489-0220
Dennis Karridan, *President*
Dennis Carradin, *Exec Dir*
Holly Osters, *Regional*
EMP: 7
SALES (est): 468.6K **Privately Held**
WEB: www.newperspectivesinc.com
SIC: 8999 8049 Psychological consultant; clinical psychologist

(G-11870)
NEW TEMPLE CORP
Also Called: Delaware Consistory, The
818 N Market St Fl 3 (19801-3087)
PHONE..................................302 998-6475
J A Pletz, *Chairman*
EMP: 5
SALES (est): 158.5K **Privately Held**
SIC: 8641 Fraternal associations

(G-11871)
NEW TREND HAIR SALON
4569 Kirkwood Hwy (19808-5117)
PHONE..................................302 998-3331
Mike Keaten, *Principal*
EMP: 5
SALES (est): 158.7K **Privately Held**
SIC: 7231 Hairdressers

(G-11872)
NEW U NUTRITION INC
2801 Lancaster Ave (19805-5232)
PHONE..................................302 543-4555
Romeo Riley, *Principal*
EMP: 5
SALES (est): 190.5K **Privately Held**
SIC: 8099 Nutrition services

(G-11873)
NEW WINDSOR ASSOCIATES LLC
4 Denny Rd (19809-3445)
PHONE..................................207 774-5341
EMP: 6
SALES (est): 185.7K **Privately Held**
SIC: 6798 Real estate investment trusts

(G-11874)
NEW WNDSOR APARTMENTS ASSOC LP
4 Denny Rd (19809-3445)
PHONE..................................302 656-1354
Kevin Kelly, *Partner*
Mike Stahler, *Controller*
William Demarco, *Director*
EMP: 5
SALES: 490K **Privately Held**
SIC: 6513 Apartment building operators

(G-11875)
NEWARC WELDING & FABRICATING
30 Commerce St (19801-5426)
PHONE..................................302 658-5214
Bruce Blair, *President*
Tracy Blair, *Shareholder*
EMP: 9 EST: 1949
SQ FT: 22,000
SALES (est): 1.9MM **Privately Held**
SIC: 3443 Process vessels, industrial: metal plate; vessels, process or storage (from boiler shops): metal plate; jackets, industrial: metal plate

(G-11876)
NEWMARKKFSM
Also Called: GBA
1105 N Market St Ste 1610 (19801-1201)
PHONE..................................302 655-0600
William Elliman, *Director*
Neal Dangello, *Director*
Wills Elliman, *Director*
EMP: 4
SALES (est): 367.8K **Privately Held**
WEB: www.gba.com
SIC: 6531 Appraiser, real estate

(G-11877)
NEWPORT
22 W Market St (19804-3139)
PHONE..................................302 995-2840
Richars Wojcik, *Principal*
EMP: 2
SALES (est): 111.3K **Privately Held**
SIC: 3648 Lighting equipment

(G-11878)
NEWPORT BUILDERS & WINDOWLAND
2 E Ayre St (19804-2537)
PHONE..................................302 994-3537
Marshall Lombardi Jr, *President*
Judy Lombardi, *Vice Pres*
EMP: 12 EST: 1963
SQ FT: 15,000
SALES: 1.2MM **Privately Held**
SIC: 5211 1751 1799 Windows, storm: wood or metal; screens, door & window; window & door installation & erection; screening contractor: window, door, etc.; awning installation

(G-11879)
NEWPORT VENTURES INC
Also Called: Exxon
20 N James St (19804-3121)
PHONE..................................302 998-1693
Robert Weber, *CEO*
Joseph Fitzgerald, *President*
Richard Kemske, *Vice Pres*
Jeanne Fitzgerald, *Shareholder*
Bonnie Kemske, *Shareholder*
EMP: 12
SQ FT: 1,100
SALES (est): 1.2MM **Privately Held**
SIC: 5541 7542 5411 Filling stations, gasoline; carwash, self-service; convenience stores, independent

(G-11880)
NEXT GENERATION PLANT SVCS INC
103 Foulk Rd Ste 202 (19803-3742)
PHONE..................................302 654-7584
EMP: 2
SALES (est): 101K **Privately Held**
SIC: 7372 Application computer software

(G-11881)
NEXT MUSIC INC
1811 Silverside Rd (19810-4345)
PHONE..................................650 300-4881

GEOGRAPHIC SECTION
Wilmington - New Castle County (G-11912)

EMP: 5
SALES (est): 290K Privately Held
SIC: 7371 Custom Computer Programing

(G-11882)
NEXT TRUCKING INC
1209 N Orange St (19801-1120)
PHONE..................213 568-0388
Hanbing Yan, *President*
Kwong CHI Chung, *Shareholder*
EMP: 50
SALES: 25MM Privately Held
SIC: 7371 Computer software development & applications

(G-11883)
NEXUS SERVICES AMERICA LLC (PA)
2711 Centerville Rd # 400 (19808-1660)
PHONE..................800 946-4626
EMP: 4
SALES (est): 3.1MM Privately Held
SIC: 4789 Space flight operations, except government

(G-11884)
NGK NORTH AMERICA INC (HQ)
1105 N Market St Ste 1300 (19801-1241)
P.O. Box 8985 (19899-8985)
PHONE..................302 654-1344
Susumu Sakabe, *President*
◆ EMP: 8
SALES (est): 116.9MM Privately Held
SIC: 3714 5013 3264 5063 Motor vehicle parts & accessories; automotive supplies & parts; insulators, electrical: porcelain; insulators, electrical

(G-11885)
NGK SPARK PLUGS USA HOLDG INC (HQ)
1011 Centre Rd (19805-1267)
PHONE..................302 288-0131
Shin Odo, *President*
◆ EMP: 7
SALES (est): 147.5MM Privately Held
SIC: 3643 3264 Current-carrying wiring devices; porcelain parts for electrical devices, molded; spark plugs, porcelain

(G-11886)
NHB ADVISORS INC
919 N Market St Ste 600 (19801-3037)
PHONE..................610 660-0060
Harvey L Nachman, *President*
Thomas D Hays III, *Vice Pres*
Howard B Brownstein, *Admin Sec*
EMP: 8
SQ FT: 1,500
SALES (est): 710K Privately Held
WEB: www.nhbteam.com
SIC: 8742 Management consulting services

(G-11887)
NICHINO AMERICA INC
4550 Linden Hill Rd # 501 (19808-2941)
PHONE..................302 636-9001
Jeffrey Johnson, *President*
Francis Winslow, *Vice Pres*
Nancy Hoagland, *Accountant*
Sam Monroe, *Sales Dir*
Wayne Brown, *Sales Staff*
▲ EMP: 48
SQ FT: 11,000
SALES: 80MM Privately Held
WEB: www.nichino.net
SIC: 8731 Agricultural research
HQ: Nihon Nohyaku Co., Ltd.
1-19-8, Kyobashi
Chuo-Ku TKY 104-0

(G-11888)
NICKLE INSURANCE
Also Called: Nationwide
3920 Kennett Pike (19807-2304)
PHONE..................302 654-0347
Henry Nickle, *Owner*
EMP: 8
SALES (est): 642.7K Privately Held
SIC: 6411 Insurance agents

(G-11889)
NICKS WELDING REPAIR LLC
3705 Oak Ridge Rd (19808-1338)
PHONE..................302 545-1494
Nicholas Pisklak, *Principal*
Camila Pisklak, *Principal*
Stephen Pisklak, *Principal*
EMP: 3
SALES (est): 62.9K Privately Held
SIC: 7692 Welding repair

(G-11890)
NITRO IMPACT INC
3422 Old Capitol Trl 68 (19808-6124)
PHONE..................347 694-7000
Mark Louie Apao, *Ch of Bd*
Louis Uretsky, *Consultant*
EMP: 10
SALES (est): 993.6K Privately Held
SIC: 5112 Stationery & office supplies

(G-11891)
NK CONSULTING INC
Also Called: Nk News
427 N Ttnall St Ste 83747 (19801)
PHONE..................330 269-5775
Chad Ocarroll, *CEO*
Hamish Macdonald, *COO*
EMP: 14
SALES (est): 62.6K Privately Held
SIC: 7383 7389 News reporting services for newspapers & periodicals; subscription fulfillment services: magazine, newspaper, etc.

(G-11892)
NNN 824 NORTH MARKET ST LLC
824 N Market St Ste 111 (19801-3024)
PHONE..................302 652-8013
Anthony W Thompson, *CEO*
EMP: 15
SALES (est): 1MM Privately Held
SIC: 6531 Real estate agent, commercial

(G-11893)
NOLTE & BRODOWAY PA
1013 Centre Rd (19805-1265)
PHONE..................302 777-1700
Stokes Nolte, *Partner*
Barbara Brodoway, *Partner*
EMP: 6
SALES (est): 440K Privately Held
WEB: www.nb-de.com
SIC: 8111 General practice attorney, lawyer

(G-11894)
NONPROFIT BUS SOLUTIONS LLC
2701 Centerville Rd (19808-1607)
PHONE..................302 353-4606
Sarah Houghton, *Vice Pres*
Khawar Khan,
EMP: 15
SQ FT: 2,300
SALES (est): 1.2MM Privately Held
SIC: 8621 Professional membership organizations

(G-11895)
NORAMCO INC
500 Swedes Landing Rd (19801-4596)
PHONE..................302 761-2923
Jim Mish, *President*
Fari Azad, *Vice Pres*
Jonathan Laskos, *Facilities Mgr*
Adam Gaulding, *QC Mgr*
Stanley Ramski, *Engineer*
EMP: 50 Privately Held
WEB: www.jnj.com
SIC: 2834 Pharmaceutical preparations
HQ: Noramco, Inc.
1550 Olympic Dr
Athens GA 30601
706 286-8247

(G-11896)
NORMAN S BROUDY M D
Also Called: Norman Broudy MD and Assoc
825 N Washington St (19801-1509)
PHONE..................302 655-7100
Norman S Broudy, *Owner*
EMP: 4

SALES (est): 577.4K Privately Held
SIC: 8049 Clinical psychologist

(G-11897)
NORTH AMERICAN BRANDS INC
501 Silverside Rd (19809-1374)
PHONE..................519 680-0385
Michael Crowley, *CEO*
Devon Park, *CFO*
▲ EMP: 28
SQ FT: 5,000
SALES: 350K
SALES (corp-wide): 6.2MM Privately Held
SIC: 3699 Electrical equipment & supplies
PA: North American Brands Inc
3 Buchanan Crt
London ON N5Z 4
519 680-1550

(G-11898)
NORTH AMERICAN HARDWOODS LTD
2711 Centerville Rd (19808-1660)
PHONE..................516 848-7729
Eva Wilson, *Principal*
EMP: 11
SALES (est): 1.7MM Privately Held
SIC: 5031 Pallets, wood

(G-11899)
NORTH FACE APPAREL CORP
3411 Silverside Rd (19810-4812)
PHONE..................336 424-7755
Christine Hernandez, *General Counsel*
EMP: 20 Privately Held
SIC: 6719 Investment holding companies, except banks

(G-11900)
NORTH HILLS CLEANERS INC
211 Philadelphia Pike (19809-3159)
PHONE..................302 764-1234
Mark Peters, *President*
Amy L Peters, *Vice Pres*
EMP: 12 EST: 1947
SQ FT: 8,000
SALES (est): 805.5K Privately Held
SIC: 7216 7219 Cleaning & dyeing, except rugs; laundry, except power & coin-operated

(G-11901)
NORTH QUARTER CREOLE
837 N Union St (19805-5323)
PHONE..................302 691-7890
EMP: 3
SALES (est): 87K Privately Held
SIC: 3131 Quarters

(G-11902)
NORTH WILMINGTON WOMENS CENTER
2002 Foulk Rd Ste A (19810-3643)
PHONE..................302 529-7900
James Cosgrove, *Principal*
EMP: 6
SALES (est): 253.6K Privately Held
SIC: 8062 General medical & surgical hospitals

(G-11903)
NORTHEAST EARLY LEARNING CTR
3014 Governor Printz Blvd (19802-2829)
PHONE..................302 762-5803
Gladys Benson, *President*
EMP: 11
SALES (est): 201.3K Privately Held
SIC: 8299 8351 Arts & crafts schools; child day care services

(G-11904)
NORTHEAST TREATMENT CTRS INC
Also Called: Kirkwood Detox
3315 Kirkwood Hwy (19808-6131)
PHONE..................302 691-0140
Mark Kraus, *Branch Mgr*
EMP: 50
SALES (corp-wide): 40.7MM Privately Held
SIC: 8093 Mental health clinic, outpatient

PA: Northeast Treatment Centers, Inc.
499 N 5th St Ste A
Philadelphia PA 19123
215 451-7000

(G-11905)
NORTHEASTERN COATING SYSTEMS
140 Belmont Dr (19808-4329)
PHONE..................302 328-6545
Vincent Falconi, *Principal*
EMP: 5 EST: 2011
SALES (est): 383.7K Privately Held
SIC: 1752 Floor laying & floor work

(G-11906)
NORTHERN DEL YOUTH FOR CHRST
310 Kiamensi Rd Ste A (19804-2958)
P.O. Box 5070 (19808-0070)
PHONE..................302 995-6937
EMP: 6
SQ FT: 1,700
SALES: 255.6K Privately Held
SIC: 8661 8399 Organization Working With Young People & Neighborhood Development Organization

(G-11907)
NORTHERN TRUST COMPANY
1313 N Market St Ste 5100 (19801-6111)
PHONE..................302 428-8700
EMP: 31
SALES (corp-wide): 6.6B Publicly Held
WEB: www.trustrite.com
SIC: 6021 National commercial banks
HQ: The Northern Trust Company
50 S La Salle St
Chicago IL 60603
312 630-6000

(G-11908)
NORTHERNSIGS MFG LLC
809 Taylor St (19801-4335)
PHONE..................302 383-9270
EMP: 1
SALES (est): 59.7K Privately Held
SIC: 3999 Manufacturing industries

(G-11909)
NORTONLIFELOCK INC
1209 N Orange St (19801-1120)
PHONE..................650 527-8000
EMP: 2
SALES (corp-wide): 4.7B Publicly Held
SIC: 7372 Prepackaged software
PA: Nortonlifelock Inc.
60 E Rio Salado Pkwy # 1
Tempe AZ 85281
650 527-8000

(G-11910)
NOVAEO LLC
4023 Kennett Pike # 5823 (19807-2018)
PHONE..................832 643-2153
Aaron Samia,
EMP: 20
SALES (est): 750K Privately Held
SIC: 2834 Vitamin, nutrient & hematinic preparations for human use

(G-11911)
NOVAK DRUCE CNNLLY BV+QIGG LLP (PA)
1007 N Orange St (19801-1239)
PHONE..................302 252-9922
Collins J Seitz Jr, *Managing Prtnr*
Rudolph E Hutz, *Partner*
Richard M Beck, *Partner*
Jeffrey Bove, *Partner*
Paul E Crawford, *Partner*
EMP: 130
SQ FT: 100,000
SALES (est): 21.3MM Privately Held
WEB: www.cbhlaw.com
SIC: 8111 General practice law office

(G-11912)
NOVARTIS CORPORATION
205 S James St (19804-2424)
PHONE..................302 992-5610
Phil King, *Manager*
EMP: 350

Wilmington - New Castle County (G-11913)

SALES (corp-wide): 51.9B **Privately Held**
WEB: www.novartis.com
SIC: 2834 Pharmaceutical preparations
HQ: Novartis Corporation
1 S Ridgedale Ave Ste 1 # 1
East Hanover NJ 07936
212 307-1122

(G-11913)
NOVIN LLC
919 N Market St Ste 425 (19801-3014)
PHONE..............................315 670-7979
Agshin Rzayev, *President*
EMP: 5
SALES (est): 164.3K **Privately Held**
SIC: 6799 Commodity contract trading companies

(G-11914)
NOVO NORDISK PHARMA INC
103 Foulk Rd Ste 282 (19803-3742)
PHONE..............................302 691-6181
Ulrich Otte, *President*
Craig Bleifer, *Admin Sec*
EMP: 1
SALES (est): 47.2K
SALES (corp-wide): 19.5B **Privately Held**
SIC: 2834 Pharmaceutical preparations
HQ: Novo Nordisk U.S. Commercial Holdings, Inc.
103 Foulk Rd Ste 282
Wilmington DE 19803
302 691-6181

(G-11915)
NOVO NRDISK US COML HLDNGS INC (DH)
103 Foulk Rd Ste 282 (19803-3742)
PHONE..............................302 691-6181
Ulrich Otte, *President*
Craig Bleifer, *Admin Sec*
EMP: 2
SALES (est): 280.3K
SALES (corp-wide): 19.5B **Privately Held**
SIC: 2834 Pharmaceutical preparations
HQ: Novo Nordisk Us Holdings, Inc.
103 Foulk Rd Ste 282
Wilmington DE 19803
302 691-6181

(G-11916)
NOWCARE LLC (PA)
1010 Concord Ave (19802-3367)
PHONE..............................302 777-5551
Todd Bogos,
EMP: 8
SALES (est): 1.1MM **Privately Held**
SIC: 8041 Offices & clinics of chiropractors

(G-11917)
NSPIRE AUTOMATION LLC
251 Little Falls Dr (19808-1674)
PHONE..............................404 545-0821
Prateek Garg,
EMP: 5
SALES (est): 104.3K **Privately Held**
SIC: 7379 Computer related maintenance services

(G-11918)
NT EZLINQ HOLDINGS LLC
251 Little Falls Dr (19808-1674)
PHONE..............................302 351-3051
Angela Ilisie,
EMP: 1
SALES (est): 56K **Privately Held**
SIC: 3669 Communications equipment

(G-11919)
NT PHILADELPHIA LLC
3705 Concord Pike Ste 2 (19803-5071)
PHONE..............................302 384-8967
Brent Applebaum, *Branch Mgr*
EMP: 4 **Publicly Held**
SIC: 6531 Real estate agent, residential
HQ: Nt Philadelphia Llc
1207 Fayette St
Conshohocken PA 19428
610 828-9558

(G-11920)
NTL (TRIANGLE) LLC (DH)
2711 Centerville Rd (19808-1660)
PHONE..............................302 525-0027
Robert Mackenzie, *President*
EMP: 12

SALES (est): 4.2MM
SALES (corp-wide): 11.9B **Privately Held**
SIC: 4841 Cable television services

(G-11921)
NUCLEAR ELECTRIC INSURANCE LTD (PA)
Also Called: Neil
1201 N Market St Ste 1100 (19801-1805)
PHONE..............................302 888-3000
Bruce A Sassi, *President*
Gregory J Blackburn, *Vice Pres*
Michael W Kolodner, *Vice Pres*
Kenneth C Manne, *Vice Pres*
R Benjamin Mays, *Vice Pres*
EMP: 60
SQ FT: 19,000
SALES: 215.9MM **Privately Held**
WEB: www.nmlneil.com
SIC: 6331 Property damage insurance

(G-11922)
NUCLEAR SERVICE ORGANIZATION (PA)
Also Called: Nucelectric Insurance Limited
1201 N Market St Ste 1100 (19801-1807)
PHONE..............................302 888-3000
Gregory G Wilks, *President*
EMP: 6
SALES (est): 1.9MM **Privately Held**
SIC: 4911

(G-11923)
NURSES CONNECTION
1021 Gilpin Ave (19806-3270)
PHONE..............................302 421-3687
Marylou Singson, *President*
EMP: 5
SALES (est): 227K **Privately Held**
SIC: 7361 Nurses' registry

(G-11924)
NVCOMPUTERS INC
300 Delaware Ave Ste 210 (19801-6601)
PHONE..............................860 878-0525
Nathan Varghese, *CEO*
EMP: 5
SALES (est): 179.1K **Privately Held**
SIC: 7371 7389 Computer software development & applications;

(G-11925)
O KELLY ERNST BELLI WALLEN LLC
901 N Market St Ste 1000 (19801-3070)
PHONE..............................302 778-4001
Sean T Okelly, *Principal*
Eva Devincentis, *Office Admin*
EMP: 6
SALES (est): 662.6K **Privately Held**
SIC: 8111 General practice attorney, lawyer

(G-11926)
O&G KNWLDGE SHRING PLTFORM LLC
Also Called: O&G Knwldge Sharing Consortium
808 W Boxborough Dr (19810-1457)
PHONE..............................303 872-0533
Mohammad Mian, *Mng Member*
EMP: 3
SQ FT: 100
SALES: 150K **Privately Held**
SIC: 1389 Oil consultants

(G-11927)
OAK GROVE SENIOR CENTER INC
11 Poplar Ave (19805-2134)
PHONE..............................302 998-3319
Kathleen Gland, *Exec Dir*
EMP: 6
SQ FT: 2,800
SALES: 177.7K **Privately Held**
SIC: 8322 Senior citizens' center or association

(G-11928)
OAKWOOD FUNDING CORPORATION
913 N Market St Ste 410 (19801-3019)
PHONE..............................336 855-2400
EMP: 6

SALES (est): 291.7K
SALES (corp-wide): 225.3B **Publicly Held**
SIC: 6162 Mortgage bankers & correspondents
HQ: Vanderbilt Mortgage And Finance, Inc.
500 Alcoa Trl
Maryville TN 37804
865 380-3000

(G-11929)
OATES CONSULTANTS LLC
234 Philadelphia Pike # 9 (19809-3126)
PHONE..............................302 477-0109
Phadrea Oates, *Principal*
EMP: 5
SALES: 40K **Privately Held**
SIC: 7291 Tax return preparation services

(G-11930)
OBJECTIVE ZERO FOUNDATION
919 N Market St Ste 425 (19801-3014)
PHONE..............................202 573-9660
Kayla Bailey, *Principal*
Blake Bassett, *Exec Dir*
EMP: 17
SALES: 82K **Privately Held**
SIC: 8641 Civic social & fraternal associations

(G-11931)
OBJECTS WORLDWIDE INC
Also Called: Owi
910 Foulk Rd Ste 201 (19803-3159)
P.O. Box 642, Merrifield VA (22116-0642)
PHONE..............................703 623-7861
Tamilmaran Arulmozhidurai, *President*
Arunachalam S Babu, *Vice Pres*
EMP: 7
SALES (est): 539.6K **Privately Held**
WEB: www.owiusa.com
SIC: 7371 7389 Computer software development & applications;

(G-11932)
OCCIDENTAL L TRANSAMERICA
Also Called: Estate Planning Delaware Vly
1415 Foulk Rd Ste 103 (19803-2748)
PHONE..............................302 477-9700
Frank Kesselman, *CEO*
EMP: 15
SQ FT: 2,000
SALES (est): 1.9MM **Privately Held**
WEB: www.epdv.com
SIC: 6411 Insurance agents

(G-11933)
OCEAN FIRST ENTERPRISES LLC
501 Silverside Rd Ste 507 (19809-1374)
PHONE..............................302 232-8547
Roger Davis, *Mng Member*
EMP: 15
SALES: 2.5MM **Privately Held**
SIC: 8748 Business consulting

(G-11934)
OCI MELAMINE AMERICAS INC (DH)
1209 N Orange St (19801-1120)
PHONE..............................800 615-8284
Tim Scheerhoorn, *President*
▲ **EMP:** 1
SALES (est): 261K
SALES (corp-wide): 3.2B **Privately Held**
SIC: 2821 Melamine resins, melamine-formaldehyde
HQ: Oci Nitrogen B.V.
Mijnweg 1
Geleen
467 020-111

(G-11935)
OCONNELL SPEEDY PRINTING INC
Also Called: American Speedy Printing
715 N King St (19801-3540)
PHONE..............................302 656-1475
Ellen Oconnell, *President*
David Oconnell, *Vice Pres*
EMP: 5
SALES (est): 400K **Privately Held**
SIC: 2752 Commercial printing, offset

(G-11936)
ODYSSEY HEALTHCARE INC
1407 Foulk Rd Ste 200 (19803-2754)
PHONE..............................302 478-1297
Nora Satalino, *Branch Mgr*
EMP: 33
SALES (corp-wide): 1.4B **Privately Held**
SIC: 8051 Skilled nursing care facilities
HQ: Odyssey Healthcare, Inc.
7801 Mesquite Bend Dr # 105
Irving TX 75063

(G-11937)
OFC PARTNERS XIV BELLEVUE
300 Bellevue Pkwy (19809-3704)
PHONE..............................302 439-3345
EMP: 4
SALES (est): 61.5K **Privately Held**
SIC: 8021 Dentist's Office

(G-11938)
OFFICE BPO LLC
1201 N Orange St Ste 600 (19801-1171)
PHONE..............................248 716-5136
Sheila Konanur, *Mng Member*
EMP: 1
SALES (est): 32.7K **Privately Held**
SIC: 7372 Application computer software

(G-11939)
OFFICE JOHN M LAW
100 E 14th St (19801-3210)
PHONE..............................302 427-2369
John Malik, *Owner*
EMP: 4 EST: 2011
SALES (est): 205.4K **Privately Held**
SIC: 8111 General practice law office

(G-11940)
OFFICE PARTNERS XIV BELLEVUE
322 A St Ste 300 (19801-5354)
PHONE..............................302 691-2100
Robert E Buccini, *Mng Member*
EMP: 4
SALES (est): 238K **Privately Held**
SIC: 8748 Business consulting

(G-11941)
OHANA COMPANIES INC
1405 Foulk Rd Ste 200 (19803-2769)
P.O. Box 7330 (19803-0330)
PHONE..............................302 225-5505
Eric Rubino, *CEO*
Michele Barbaccio, *Opers Staff*
Brad Newsom, *VP Finance*
Alex Giacco, *Officer*
EMP: 12
SQ FT: 4,000
SALES (est): 2MM
SALES (corp-wide): 1.8MM **Privately Held**
SIC: 8742 Marketing consulting services
PA: 360incentives.Com Canada Inc
300 King St
Whitby ON L1N 4
866 684-2308

(G-11942)
OK VIDEO
406 Philadelphia Pike (19809-2153)
PHONE..............................302 762-2333
David Klein, *Partner*
Susan Olvenburg, *Partner*
EMP: 11
SALES (est): 901.4K **Privately Held**
WEB: www.okvideode.com
SIC: 7812 Video tape production; video production

(G-11943)
OLD COUNTRY GARDEN CENTER INC
414 Wilson Rd (19803-3950)
PHONE..............................302 652-3317
Stephen Keulman, *President*
Chris Keulman, *Vice Pres*
Erika Keulman, *Admin Sec*
EMP: 30
SQ FT: 3,000

GEOGRAPHIC SECTION
Wilmington - New Castle County (G-11976)

SALES (est): 1.7MM **Privately Held**
SIC: 0181 5947 5261 0782 Nursery stock, growing of; flowers: grown under cover (e.g. greenhouse production); flowers grown in field nurseries; bedding plants, growing of; gift shop; nurseries & garden centers; landscape contractors

(G-11944)
OLD REPUBLIC NAT TITLE INSUR
600 N King St 100 (19801-3776)
PHONE..................302 661-1997
John Gilbert, *Assistant VP*
William Schlitte, *Vice Pres*
Patricia Cook, *Production*
Brandi Cashdan, *Auditor*
Renee Grajewski, *Director*
EMP: 11
SALES (corp-wide): 6B **Publicly Held**
SIC: 6541 Title abstract offices
HQ: Old Republic National Title Insurance Company
400 2nd Ave S
Minneapolis MN 55401
612 371-1111

(G-11945)
OLGA N GANOUDIS JEWELRY
1313 N Scott St (19806-4072)
PHONE..................302 421-9820
Olga Ganoudis, *Owner*
▲ **EMP:** 1
SALES: 99K **Privately Held**
WEB: www.olgaganoudis.com
SIC: 3911 Jewelry, precious metal

(G-11946)
OLYMPIAD SCHOOLS INC
Also Called: Olympiad Gymnastic
380 Water St (19804-2411)
PHONE..................302 636-0606
Edger M Knepper, *President*
Patsy Knepper, *Corp Secy*
EMP: 15
SALES (est): 576.1K **Privately Held**
SIC: 7999 Gymnastic instruction, nonmembership

(G-11947)
OMEGA IMAGING ASSOCIATES LLC
Also Called: Wilmington Mri Center
1020 N Union St Ste C (19805-2736)
PHONE..................302 654-5245
Tze Kakhy, *Owner*
EMP: 5
SALES (corp-wide): 4.2MM **Privately Held**
SIC: 8071 8011 X-ray laboratory, including dental; radiologist
PA: Omega Imaging Associates, L.L.C.
6 Omega Dr
Newark DE 19713
302 738-9300

(G-11948)
OMEGA IMAGING ASSOCIATES LLC
3105 Limestone Rd Ste 106 (19808-2147)
PHONE..................302 995-2037
Michael Fay, *Manager*
EMP: 11
SALES (corp-wide): 4.2MM **Privately Held**
SIC: 8071 Medical laboratories
PA: Omega Imaging Associates, L.L.C.
6 Omega Dr
Newark DE 19713
302 738-9300

(G-11949)
OMNI GAMES INC
910 Foulk Rd Ste 201 (19803-3159)
PHONE..................302 652-4800
Maksym Petkov, *CEO*
Ruslan Babych, *Principal*
Alexandr Pyatkov, *Principal*
Borys Shulyayev, *Principal*
EMP: 18
SALES (est): 345.5K **Privately Held**
SIC: 7371 Computer software development & applications

(G-11950)
OMNINET INTERNATIONAL INC (PA)
427 N Tatnall St (19801-2230)
PHONE..................208 246-5022
Jose Lopez, *President*
EMP: 27
SQ FT: 1,000
SALES (est): 2.3MM **Privately Held**
SIC: 8742 7371 Management consulting services; computer software development

(G-11951)
ON NATIONAL ALLIANCE
2400 W 4th St (19805-3306)
PHONE..................302 427-0787
J Thomas-Acker, *Exec Dir*
Joshua Thomas, *Exec Dir*
Josh Thomas-Acker, *Exec Dir*
EMP: 25
SQ FT: 1,700
SALES: 731K **Privately Held**
SIC: 8093 Mental health clinic, outpatient

(G-11952)
ON POINT PARTNERS LLC
18 Germay Dr 2a (19804-1105)
PHONE..................302 655-5606
Gary Fredericks,
EMP: 6 **EST:** 2011
SALES (est): 231.3K **Privately Held**
SIC: 8742 General management consultant

(G-11953)
ONE COMMERCE CTR CONDO COUNCIL
1 Commerce St Ste 700 (19801)
PHONE..................302 573-2513
Richard Stat, *President*
EMP: 6
SALES (est): 154.2K **Privately Held**
SIC: 8641 Condominium association

(G-11954)
ONE EDM LLC
3524 Silverside Rd (19810-4929)
PHONE..................908 399-0536
Tom Cozzens,
EMP: 30
SALES (est): 1.1MM **Privately Held**
SIC: 2836 Culture media

(G-11955)
ONE HUNDRED WEST TENTH ST
1100 N Market St (19899)
PHONE..................302 651-1469
Bob Hara, *President*
EMP: 15
SALES (est): 636.8K **Privately Held**
SIC: 6531 6733 Real estate managers; trusts

(G-11956)
ONE SYSTEM INCORPORATED
4023 Kennett Pike Ste 645 (19807-2018)
PHONE..................888 311-1110
Stan McCade, *CEO*
Rony Varghese, *General Mgr*
Tim Walters, *Development*
Stan McCabe, *Sales Staff*
David Morris, *Services*
EMP: 18
SALES: 500K **Privately Held**
SIC: 7371 8743 Software programming applications; computer software development & applications; public relations services

(G-11957)
ONE VILLAGE ALLIANCE INC
1401 A St (19801-5409)
P.O. Box 363 (19899-0363)
PHONE..................302 275-1715
Chandra Pitts, *Exec Dir*
EMP: 7 **EST:** 2010
SALES (est): 164K **Privately Held**
SIC: 8322 9532 Outreach program; urban & community development

(G-11958)
ONEMAIN FINANCIAL GROUP LLC
4325 Concord Pike (19803-1461)
PHONE..................302 478-8070
Larry Le, *Branch Mgr*
EMP: 5
SALES (corp-wide): 4.2B **Publicly Held**
SIC: 6282 Investment advice
HQ: Onemain Financial Group, Llc
100 International Dr # 150
Baltimore MD 21202
855 663-6246

(G-11959)
ONI ACQUISITION CORP
2711 Centerville Rd (19808-1660)
PHONE..................212 271-3800
Calvin Shintani, *Asst Sec*
EMP: 6 **Privately Held**
SIC: 6719 Investment holding companies, except banks

(G-11960)
ONIX SILVERSIDE LLC
3322 Silverside Rd (19810-3307)
PHONE..................484 731-2500
Jennifer Coverdale, *General Mgr*
Ronald Schafer, *Manager*
EMP: 90
SALES (est): 2.1MM **Privately Held**
SIC: 8051 Skilled nursing care facilities

(G-11961)
OPEN MRI AT TROLLEY SQUARE LLC
1010 N Bancroft Pkwy (19805-2690)
PHONE..................302 472-5555
Kristin Mills, *Principal*
David Schluck, *Mng Member*
EMP: 10
SALES (est): 426.6K **Privately Held**
SIC: 8011 Radiologist

(G-11962)
OPERADELAWARE INC
Also Called: Opera Studios
4 S Poplar St (19801-5009)
PHONE..................302 658-8063
Brendan Cooke, *Director*
Mary Wilcosky, *Social Dir*
EMP: 6
SALES: 988.8K **Privately Held**
SIC: 7922 Opera company

(G-11963)
OPTIMA CLEANING SYSTEMS INC
110 Valley Rd (19804-1311)
P.O. Box 3117 (19804-0117)
PHONE..................302 652-3979
Thomas Delle Donne, *President*
EMP: 80
SALES (est): 1.2MM **Privately Held**
SIC: 7349 Cleaning service, industrial or commercial

(G-11964)
OPTOMETRY ASSOCIATES PC
419 S Market St (19801)
PHONE..................302 654-6490
Dr P Lench, *President*
EMP: 4
SALES (est): 441.1K **Privately Held**
SIC: 3841 Optometers

(G-11965)
OPUS DESIGN BUILD LLC
1000 N West St Fl 10 (19801-1059)
PHONE..................952 656-4444
Jeff Walker,
EMP: 95
SALES (est): 12.5MM **Privately Held**
SIC: 1542 Commercial & office building, new construction

(G-11966)
OPUS FINANCIAL SVCS USA INC
19c Trolley Sq (19806-3355)
PHONE..................646 435-5616
Fred Davis, *CEO*
EMP: 5 **EST:** 2015
SALES (est): 146.1K **Privately Held**
SIC: 7361 Employment agencies

(G-11967)
ORAL & MAXILLOFACIAL SURGERY
2601 Annand Dr Ste 10 (19808-3719)
PHONE..................302 998-0331
Judy Norcross, *Manager*
EMP: 6
SALES (est): 120.2K **Privately Held**
SIC: 8021 Offices & clinics of dentists

(G-11968)
ORAL MXLLFCIAL SRGERY ASSOC PA
1304 N Broom St (19806-4266)
PHONE..................302 655-6183
James Goodwill, *President*
Michael Kremer, *Manager*
EMP: 10
SALES (est): 1.1MM **Privately Held**
SIC: 8021 Maxillofacial specialist; dental surgeon

(G-11969)
ORANGE POWER ELECTRIC INC
300 Delaware Ave (19801-1607)
PHONE..................205 886-5815
Lynette Horton, *President*
Ishan Jaithwa, *Partner*
Shuhui LI, *Vice Pres*
EMP: 6
SALES (est): 251.5K **Privately Held**
SIC: 3629 Inverters, nonrotating: electrical

(G-11970)
ORBEEX TRADING INC
3411 Silverside Rd (19810-4812)
PHONE..................786 403-9124
Jessica Lovera, *President*
EMP: 10
SALES: 50K **Privately Held**
SIC: 7371 7389 Computer software development & applications;

(G-11971)
ORBIT RESEARCH LLC (PA)
3422 Old Capitol Trl # 25 (19808-6124)
PHONE..................302 683-1063
Carla Morris,
EMP: 5
SALES: 500K **Privately Held**
SIC: 7993 Coin-operated amusement devices

(G-11972)
ORDERING INC
2711 Centerville Rd # 400 (19808-1660)
PHONE..................888 443-6203
EMP: 15
SALES: 500K **Privately Held**
SIC: 7372 Prepackaged Software Services

(G-11973)
ORION GROUP LLC
2801 Centerville Rd (19808-1609)
PHONE..................302 357-9137
Seth Spiller, *President*
EMP: 6
SALES (est): 171.4K **Privately Held**
SIC: 8741 Business management

(G-11974)
ORJAM LTD
3602 Squirrel Hill Ct (19808-3116)
PHONE..................302 482-5016
Damian J Davis, *President*
EMP: 10
SALES (est): 182.1K **Privately Held**
SIC: 1521 Single-family housing construction

(G-11975)
ORLANDO J CAMP & ASSOCIATES
1808 Pan Rd (19803-3343)
PHONE..................302 478-3720
Orlando J Camp, *President*
EMP: 6
SQ FT: 18,000
SALES (est): 750K **Privately Held**
SIC: 5113 Towels, paper

(G-11976)
OROS COMMUNICATIONS LLC
2711 Centerville Rd # 400 (19808-1660)
PHONE..................954 228-7399
Richard Godfrey,
EMP: 2
SALES (est): 88.3K **Privately Held**
SIC: 3663 Space satellite communications equipment

Wilmington - New Castle County (G-11977) GEOGRAPHIC SECTION

(G-11977)
ORTHOPAEDIC & SPORTS PHYS
617 W Newport Pike (19804-3235)
PHONE..................302 683-0782
Nalini Advani, *Principal*
EMP: 5
SALES (est): 349.4K **Privately Held**
SIC: 8049 Physical therapist

(G-11978)
ORTHOPAEDIC SPECIALISTS PA
7 S Clayton St Ste 600 (19805-3948)
PHONE..................302 655-9494
Errol Ger, *Partner*
Andrew J Gelman, *Partner*
Beth Williamson, *Assistant*
EMP: 35
SALES (est): 749K **Privately Held**
SIC: 8011 Pathologist; orthopedic physician

(G-11979)
OSAKA GAS USA CORPORATION
Also Called: Osaka Gas Freedom Energy Corp
1209 N Orange St (19801-1120)
PHONE..................302 658-7581
Claude Leglise, *Managing Dir*
Matt Carroll, *Human Res Dir*
David Cocanower, *Manager*
Ricardo Aldana, *Director*
EMP: 7
SALES (est): 150.1K **Privately Held**
SIC: 4925 Gas production and/or distribution
PA: Osaka Gas Co., Ltd.
4-1-2, Hiranomachi, Chuo-Ku
Osaka OSK 541-0

(G-11980)
OSFS WLMNGTON PHLDLPHIA PRVNCE
2200 Kentmere Pkwy (19806-2018)
PHONE..................302 656-8529
William Guerin, *Principal*
EMP: 4
SALES (est): 251.1K **Privately Held**
SIC: 6733 Trusts

(G-11981)
OSO GRANDE HV LLC
251 Little Falls Dr (19808-1674)
PHONE..................858 521-3300
Tristan Grimbert, *CEO*
EMP: 4
SQ FT: 2,000
SALES (est): 103K **Privately Held**
SIC: 4911

(G-11982)
OTHG INC
1708 Tulip St (19805-3933)
PHONE..................302 421-9187
Kedrin Henson, *President*
EMP: 7
SALES (est): 257.7K **Privately Held**
SIC: 1521 Single-family housing construction

(G-11983)
OUR FUTURE CHILD CARE CTR LLC
3400 N Market St (19802-2732)
PHONE..................302 762-8645
Thelma C Jamison,
EMP: 5
SALES (est): 145.3K **Privately Held**
SIC: 8351 Child day care services

(G-11984)
OUTPATENT ANSTHSIA SPCLISTS PA
2006 Limestone Rd Ste 5 (19808-5553)
PHONE..................302 995-1860
David Blumberg, *President*
EMP: 10
SALES (est): 1.8MM **Privately Held**
SIC: 8011 Anesthesiologist

(G-11985)
OVATION HEALTH INTL LLC
515 Giada Dr (19808-1430)
PHONE..................302 765-7595
Yi Zhu, *CEO*
EMP: 4 EST: 2014
SALES (est): 63.8K **Privately Held**
SIC: 8011 General & family practice, physician/surgeon

(G-11986)
OVO DIGITAL SERVICES LLC
Also Called: Ovocrm
3616 Kirkwood Hwy 1547 (19808-5124)
PHONE..................415 741-1615
Erhan Tezakar, *CEO*
EMP: 6
SALES: 100K **Privately Held**
SIC: 7371 7389 Computer software development & applications;

(G-11987)
OWENS CORNINGFIBREBOARD
1105 N Market St Ste 1300 (19801-1241)
PHONE..................302 654-4250
Joseph Rhein, *Owner*
EMP: 3
SALES (est): 211.9K **Privately Held**
SIC: 2677 Envelopes

(G-11988)
OWLS NEST HORTICULTURAL SVCS
Also Called: Owl's Nest Horticultural
805 Owls Nest Rd (19807-1611)
P.O. Box 3651 (19807-0651)
PHONE..................302 654-6989
Eric Bross, *President*
Mark Goldfogel, *Master*
EMP: 7
SQ FT: 4,000
SALES: 350K **Privately Held**
SIC: 0782 Garden maintenance services; lawn care services

(G-11989)
OXFORD PLASTIC SYSTEMS LLC
1011 Centre Rd Ste 312 (19805-1266)
PHONE..................800 567-9182
EMP: 2
SALES (est): 88.9K **Privately Held**
SIC: 3089 Fences, gates & accessories: plastic

(G-11990)
P A ALFIERI CARDIOLOGY (PA)
701 Foulk Rd Ste 2b (19803-3733)
PHONE..................302 731-0001
Anthony D Alfieri, *Principal*
Paul J Alfieri, *Med Doctor*
Anthony Alfieri, *Osteopathy*
EMP: 29
SALES (est): 3.9MM **Privately Held**
SIC: 8011 Cardiologist & cardio-vascular specialist

(G-11991)
P A BAYARD
600 N King St Ste 400 (19801-3779)
P.O. Box 25130 (19899-5130)
PHONE..................302 429-4212
Charlene Davis, *Director*
Curtis Bounds, *Director*
Scott Cousins, *Director*
Erin Fay, *Director*
Jason Jowers, *Director*
EMP: 54 EST: 1966
SALES (est): 9.2MM **Privately Held**
SIC: 8111 General practice law office

(G-11992)
P A BRANDYWINE PEDIATRICS
3521 Silverside Rd Ste 1f (19810-4900)
PHONE..................302 479-9610
Kate Chaplinski, *Principal*
EMP: 14 EST: 2012
SALES (est): 1.4MM **Privately Held**
SIC: 8011 Pediatrician

(G-11993)
P A ORTHO-SURG
Also Called: Ortho-Surg P.A. Pension Plan
2401 Penns Ave Ste 115 (19806-1432)
PHONE..................302 658-4800
Virginia B Clemmer MD, *Principal*
EMP: 4
SALES (est): 342.1K **Privately Held**
SIC: 8011 Surgeon

(G-11994)
P D SUPPLY INC
Also Called: Pleasant Distributors
307 Commercial Dr (19805-1906)
PHONE..................302 655-3358
Jeff Rushie, *President*
EMP: 6 EST: 1947
SQ FT: 10,400
SALES (est): 1.4MM **Privately Held**
SIC: 5031 5211 Building materials, interior; lumber & other building materials

(G-11995)
P M O ADVISORS L L C
700 Hopeton Rd (19807-2944)
PHONE..................302 545-1159
Michael Desch, *President*
EMP: 1
SALES (est): 107.8K **Privately Held**
SIC: 3571 Electronic computers

(G-11996)
P R C MANAGEMENT CO INC
2601 Carpenter Station Rd (19810-2050)
PHONE..................302 475-7643
Robert Kaye, *President*
EMP: 9
SALES (est): 540K **Privately Held**
SIC: 6531 Real estate managers

(G-11997)
P&L TRANSPORTATION INC (PA)
Also Called: Paducah & Louisville Railway
301 N Market St Ste 1414 (19801-2529)
PHONE..................800 444-2580
J Thomas Garrett, *President*
Anthony V Reck, *Principal*
Thomas A Greene, *Vice Pres*
EMP: 8
SQ FT: 22,000
SALES (est): 63.5K **Privately Held**
SIC: 6719 Public utility holding companies

(G-11998)
P-KS WHOLESALE GROCER INC
Also Called: Pks Food
915 S Heald St (19801-5732)
PHONE..................302 656-5540
Pete Kirtses, *President*
Athy Kirtses, *Treasurer*
EMP: 10
SQ FT: 15,000
SALES (est): 4.6MM **Privately Held**
SIC: 5149 Groceries & related products

(G-11999)
PABIAN VENTURES LLC
101 N Maryland Ave (19804-1335)
PHONE..................302 762-1992
Edward N Pabian, *Mng Member*
EMP: 6
SALES (est): 1.1MM **Privately Held**
SIC: 8742 Real estate consultant

(G-12000)
PACE ELECTRIC
3603 Old Capitol Trl B4 (19808-6045)
PHONE..................302 328-2600
Ken Adams, *Owner*
EMP: 4
SALES (est): 219.4K **Privately Held**
SIC: 1731 General electrical contractor

(G-12001)
PACE ENTERPRISES LLC
1405 Silverside Rd Ste B (19810-4445)
PHONE..................302 529-2500
Debra J Pace, *Principal*
EMP: 5 EST: 2000
SALES (est): 346.2K **Privately Held**
SIC: 8021 Dental clinic

(G-12002)
PACE INC
5171 W Woodmill Dr Ste 9 (19808-4067)
PHONE..................302 999-9812
Bruce Johnson, *President*
Doreen Benson, *Business Mgr*
EMP: 24
SALES (est): 1.3MM **Privately Held**
WEB: www.paceinconline.com
SIC: 8093 Rehabilitation center, outpatient treatment

(G-12003)
PACER INTERNATIONAL ONE LLC
16 Taylors Mill Ln (19808-3668)
P.O. Box 5015 (19808-0015)
PHONE..................302 588-9500
Luke A Bernhardt, *Mng Member*
EMP: 17
SALES: 5MM **Privately Held**
SIC: 6531 7389 6799 6211 Real estate agents & managers; ; real estate investors, except property operators; syndicate shares (real estate, entertainment, equip.) sales; general contractor, highway & street construction

(G-12004)
PACIFIC CARGO LLC
11 Gist Rd Ste 201 (19801-5879)
PHONE..................302 521-6317
Harold Cohen, *Mng Member*
EMP: 4
SQ FT: 500
SALES: 380K **Privately Held**
SIC: 4731 Freight transportation arrangement

(G-12005)
PAIN & SLEEP THERAPY CENTER
4901 Limestone Rd (19808-1271)
PHONE..................302 314-1409
EMP: 8
SALES (est): 73.3K **Privately Held**
SIC: 8093 Rehabilitation center, outpatient treatment

(G-12006)
PAINTERS LOCAL UNION 277
Also Called: District Council 21
922 New Rd Ste 1 (19805-5199)
PHONE..................302 994-7835
Stacey Reynolds, *General Mgr*
EMP: 5
SALES (corp-wide): 1.1MM **Privately Held**
SIC: 1721 Painting & paper hanging
PA: Painters Local Union 277
2116 Ocean Heights Ave
Egg Harbor Township NJ 08234
609 653-4433

(G-12007)
PALA TILE & CARPET CONTRS INC
600 S Colonial Ave (19805-1956)
PHONE..................302 652-4500
Richard Zambanini, *President*
William N Pala Sr, *Vice Pres*
EMP: 20
SALES (est): 4.5MM **Privately Held**
SIC: 5713 1743 Floor tile; carpets; vinyl floor covering; tile installation, ceramic

(G-12008)
PALADIN SPORTS CLUB INC
Also Called: Paladin Sports & Social Club
500 Paladin Dr (19802-1745)
PHONE..................302 764-5335
Verino Pettinaro, *President*
EMP: 10
SALES (est): 247.5K **Privately Held**
SIC: 7991 7997 Athletic club & gymnasiums, membership; indoor/outdoor court clubs

(G-12009)
PALMETTO MGT & ENGRG LLC
4550 Linden Hill Rd # 400 (19808-2952)
PHONE..................302 993-2766
J Alexander,
Frank Harty,
EMP: 150
SALES (est): 5.5MM **Privately Held**
SIC: 8741 Construction management

(G-12010)
PAM PIPES & PUPPETS
18 Wordsworth Dr (19808-2339)
PHONE..................302 999-0078
EMP: 1
SALES (est): 52K **Privately Held**
SIC: 3999 Mfg Misc Products

GEOGRAPHIC SECTION
Wilmington - New Castle County (G-12040)

(G-12011)
PANCO MANAGEMENT CORPORATION
Also Called: Cynwood Apartments
1302 Cynwyd Club Dr (19808-3047)
PHONE 302 995-6152
Chris Elswick, *Manager*
EMP: 9
SALES (corp-wide): 14MM **Privately Held**
WEB: www.homesteadgardensapts.com
SIC: 6531 6513 Real estate managers; apartment building operators
PA: Panco Management Corporation
395 W Passaic St Ste 251
Rochelle Park NJ 07662
201 556-0900

(G-12012)
PANCO MANAGEMENT CORPORATION
Also Called: Cedar Tree Apartments
2512 Cedar Tree Dr Ofc 2d (19810-1437)
PHONE 302 475-9337
Gina Giovenella, *Manager*
EMP: 9
SALES (corp-wide): 14MM **Privately Held**
WEB: www.homesteadgardensapts.com
SIC: 6531 6513 Real estate managers; apartment building operators
PA: Panco Management Corporation
395 W Passaic St Ste 251
Rochelle Park NJ 07662
201 556-0900

(G-12013)
PANDOL BROS INC
Christiana Ctr (19884-0001)
PHONE 302 571-8923
Joe Rull, *Manager*
EMP: 40
SALES (corp-wide): 29.7MM **Privately Held**
WEB: www.pandol.com
SIC: 5148 Fruits, fresh; vegetables, fresh
PA: Pandol Bros., Inc.
33150 Pond Rd
Delano CA 93215
661 725-3755

(G-12014)
PANO DEVELOPMENT INC
1701 Augustine Cut Off # 15 (19803-4494)
PHONE 302 428-1062
Mario B Capano, *President*
Frank Capano, *Corp Secy*
EMP: 9
SQ FT: 17,000
SALES (est): 743.9K **Privately Held**
SIC: 1521 Single-family housing construction

(G-12015)
PAOLI SERVICES INC
400 B And O Ln (19804-1458)
PHONE 302 998-7031
Domenick Paoli, *President*
Todd Jorgensen, *Division Mgr*
EMP: 30
SQ FT: 8,700
SALES (est): 4.6MM **Privately Held**
SIC: 1521 Single-family housing construction

(G-12016)
PARAGON ENGINEERING CORP
708 Philadelphia Pike # 1 (19809-2500)
PHONE 302 762-6010
Dave Bobiak, *President*
Stephen W Bobiak Jr, *Vice Pres*
Lawrence Ellis, *Vice Pres*
EMP: 36
SALES (est): 4.9MM **Privately Held**
WEB: www.paragon-eng.com
SIC: 8711 Consulting engineer

(G-12017)
PARAGON MASONRY CORPORATION
501 Silverside Rd Ste 1 (19809-1375)
PHONE 302 798-7314
Frank Gordano, *President*
EMP: 22
SQ FT: 350
SALES (est): 1MM **Privately Held**
SIC: 1741 Concrete block masonry laying

(G-12018)
PARCELS INC (PA)
Also Called: Delaware Document Retrieval
230 N Market St (19801-2528)
P.O. Box 646, New Castle (19720-0646)
PHONE 302 888-1718
Maureen C Johnson, *CEO*
James A Johnson, *President*
Spencer Anspach, *Production*
Anthony Casale, *Manager*
Bryan Davis, *Manager*
EMP: 135
SQ FT: 35,000
SALES (est): 15MM **Privately Held**
WEB: www.parcelsinc.com
SIC: 4215 Package delivery, vehicular

(G-12019)
PARENT INFORMATION CTR DEL INC (PA)
6 Larch Ave Ste 404 (19804-2366)
PHONE 302 999-7394
Marie Aghazadian, *Exec Dir*
EMP: 5
SALES (est): 496.8K **Privately Held**
SIC: 8742 Training & development consultant

(G-12020)
PARK PLACE DENTAL
300 Foulk Rd (19803-3886)
PHONE 302 652-3775
EMP: 4
SALES (est): 88.9K **Privately Held**
SIC: 8021 Offices & clinics of dentists

(G-12021)
PARK PLAZA CONDO ASSOCIATION
Also Called: Park Plaza Condominiums
1100 Lovering Ave Ste 15 (19806-3265)
PHONE 302 658-3526
Charles Griffith, *President*
EMP: 6
SQ FT: 4,000
SALES (est): 220K **Privately Held**
SIC: 8641 Condominium association

(G-12022)
PARK VIEW
1800 N Broom St (19802-3809)
PHONE 302 429-7288
Denise Miller, *Principal*
EMP: 5
SALES (est): 360K **Privately Held**
WEB: www.whadelaware.org
SIC: 6513 Apartment building operators

(G-12023)
PARKS & RECREATION DEL DIV
Also Called: Bellevue State Park
800 Carr Rd (19809-2163)
PHONE 302 761-6963
Paul Nicholson, *Supervisor*
EMP: 11 **Privately Held**
SIC: 8611 9512 Business associations; land, mineral & wildlife conservation;
HQ: Delaware Division Of Parks & Recreation
89 Kings Hwy
Dover DE 19901
302 739-9220

(G-12024)
PARKS & RECREATION DEL DIV
Also Called: Brandywine Zoo
1001 N Park Dr (19802-3801)
PHONE 302 571-7788
Nancy Falasco, *Director*
EMP: 10 **Privately Held**
SIC: 7999 9512 Zoological garden, commercial; ping pong parlor; land, mineral & wildlife conservation;
HQ: Delaware Division Of Parks & Recreation
89 Kings Hwy
Dover DE 19901
302 739-9220

(G-12025)
PARKVIEW COVALESCENT CENTER
2801 W 6th St (19805-1828)
PHONE 302 655-0955
Ronald Schafer, *Principal*
EMP: 8
SALES (est): 162.5K **Privately Held**
SIC: 8051 Skilled nursing care facilities

(G-12026)
PARKWOOD TRUST COMPANY
919 N Market St Ste 429 (19801-3014)
PHONE 302 426-1220
Morton L Mandel, *Ch of Bd*
EMP: 7
SQ FT: 1,100
SALES (est): 307.7K **Privately Held**
SIC: 6282 Investment advice
PA: Parkwood Corporation
1000 Lakeside Ave E
Cleveland OH 44114

(G-12027)
PARTNERSHIP FOR DE ESTUARY
110 S Poplar St Ste 202 (19801-5034)
PHONE 302 655-4990
Jennifer Adkins, *Partner*
Kathy Klein, *Exec Dir*
Emily Baumbach, *Planning*
Kaitlin Tucker, *Planning*
EMP: 6
SALES (est): 2.9MM **Privately Held**
WEB: www.delawareestuary.org
SIC: 8731 Commercial physical research

(G-12028)
PARTNRRE CPITL INVSTMENTS CORP
1209 N Orange St (19801-1120)
PHONE 608 347-5824
Adam Stuart, *Principal*
EMP: 11
SALES (est): 1.3MM **Privately Held**
SIC: 6799 Investors

(G-12029)
PARTSQUARRY-AVIATION DIV
110 W 9th St (19801-1618)
PHONE 302 703-7195
EMP: 7
SALES: 950K **Privately Held**
SIC: 7363 Pilot service, aviation

(G-12030)
PASQUALE FUCCI MD
1508 Penns Ave Ste 1c (19806-4347)
PHONE 302 652-4705
Pasquale Fucci, *Med Doctor*
EMP: 4
SALES (est): 79.7K **Privately Held**
SIC: 8011 Internal medicine, physician/surgeon

(G-12031)
PATHSCALE INC
427 N Tatnall St 16370 (19801-2230)
PHONE 408 520-0811
Christopher Bergman, *CEO*
EMP: 50
SQ FT: 16,500
SALES (est): 4.2MM **Privately Held**
WEB: www.pathscale.com
SIC: 7371 7379 Computer software development & applications; computer related consulting services

(G-12032)
PATHWAYS OF DELAWARE INC
101 Rogers Rd Ste 102 (19801-5778)
PHONE 302 573-5073
Jonathan McAllister, *Principal*
Terri Bradley, *Principal*
Coley Harris, *Principal*
EMP: 99
SALES (est): 842.1K
SALES (corp-wide): 122.4MM **Privately Held**
SIC: 8399 Community action agency
PA: Pathways Health And Community Support Llc
10304 Spotsylvania Ave
Fredericksburg VA 22408
540 710-6085

(G-12033)
PATRICIA H PURCELL MD
601 Cheltenham Rd (19808-1504)
PHONE 302 428-1142
Patricia Purcell MD, *Owner*
EMP: 7
SALES (est): 527.8K **Privately Held**
SIC: 8011 General & family practice, physician/surgeon

(G-12034)
PATRICIA P MCGONIGLE
222 Delaware Ave Ste 1500 (19801-1682)
P.O. Box 68 (19899-0068)
PHONE 302 888-7605
Patricia McGonigle, *Owner*
EMP: 14
SALES (est): 456.7K **Privately Held**
SIC: 8111 General practice attorney, lawyer

(G-12035)
PATRIOT GOVERNMENT SVCS INC
44 Bancroft Mills Rd (19806-2028)
PHONE 302 655-3434
Stephen Mockbee, *President*
Betsy Eitel, *Manager*
EMP: 5
SQ FT: 5,000
SALES (est): 470K **Privately Held**
SIC: 1521 Single-family housing construction

(G-12036)
PATRIOT SYSTEMS INC
1204 First State Blvd (19804-3561)
PHONE 302 472-9727
Peter M Harmon, *President*
EMP: 8
SALES (est): 1.2MM **Privately Held**
SIC: 7389 Fire protection service other than forestry or public

(G-12037)
PATTERSON PRICE
5 E Green St (19801)
PHONE 302 378-9852
Price Patterson, *Partner*
EMP: 15 EST: 2010
SALES (est): 537.2K **Privately Held**
SIC: 6531 Real estate managers

(G-12038)
PATTERSON-SCHWARTZ & ASSOC INC
Also Called: Patterson Schwartz Real Estate
3705 Kennett Pike (19807-2135)
PHONE 302 429-4500
Ann Belmonte, *Branch Mgr*
Marcus Du Phily, *Real Est Agnt*
EMP: 50
SALES (est): 2MM
SALES (corp-wide): 32.2MM **Privately Held**
WEB: www.pacinihomes.com
SIC: 6531 Real estate agent, residential
PA: Patterson-Schwartz And Associates, Inc.
7234 Lancaster Pike
Hockessin DE 19707
302 234-5250

(G-12039)
PAUL ASSOCIATES
304 Country Club Dr (19803-2920)
PHONE 302 584-0064
Paula Paul, *Principal*
EMP: 4
SALES (est): 247.1K **Privately Held**
SIC: 8742 Management consulting services

(G-12040)
PAUL C ANISMAN M D
1600 Rockland Rd (19803-3607)
PHONE 302 651-6600
Paul C Anisman MD, *Principal*
EMP: 4
SALES (est): 80.7K **Privately Held**
SIC: 8011 Pediatrician

Wilmington - New Castle County (G-12041)

(G-12041)
PAUL F CAMPANELLA INC
Also Called: Paul F Campanella Auto Service
1703 Augustine Cut Off (19803-4402)
PHONE...................................302 777-7170
Paul F Campanella, *President*
EMP: 10
SALES: 2MM **Privately Held**
SIC: 7538 General automotive repair shops

(G-12042)
PAUL IMBER DO
2700 Silverside Rd Ste 3a (19810-3724)
PHONE...................................302 478-5647
Paul Imber Do, *Owner*
EMP: 7
SALES (est): 321.1K **Privately Held**
SIC: 8031 8011 Offices & clinics of osteopathic physicians; ears, nose & throat specialist; physician/surgeon

(G-12043)
PAUL RENZI
Also Called: Paul J Renzi Masonary
6 Brookside Dr (19804-1102)
PHONE...................................302 478-3166
Paul Renzi, *Principal*
EMP: 4
SALES (est): 157.9K **Privately Held**
SIC: 8071 Medical laboratories

(G-12044)
PAUL SICA MD
Also Called: 2300 PA Ave Condo Assoc
2300 Penns Ave Ste 5b (19806-1305)
PHONE...................................302 652-3469
EMP: 7
SALES (est): 595.3K **Privately Held**
SIC: 8011 Dermatologist

(G-12045)
PAUL SORVINO FOODS INC
4001 Kennett Pike Ste 134 (19807-2000)
PHONE...................................302 547-1977
Paul Sorvino, *President*
Ronnie Robinson, *Vice Pres*
EMP: 7
SALES (est): 1.1MM **Privately Held**
WEB: www.supermarket-associates.com
SIC: 5146 Seafoods

(G-12046)
PAULS HOUSE INC
1405 Veale Rd (19810-4331)
PHONE...................................302 384-2350
Paul Dougherty, *President*
David Mosley, *Vice Pres*
EMP: 12
SALES: 199.3K **Privately Held**
SIC: 8322 Individual & family services

(G-12047)
PAXFUL INC
3422 Old Capitol Trl (19808-6124)
PHONE...................................865 272-9385
Ray Youseff, *CEO*
EMP: 10
SQ FT: 500
SALES (est): 101.2K **Privately Held**
SIC: 7299 Personal financial services

(G-12048)
PAYMENEX INC
501 Silverside Rd Ste 105 (19809-1376)
PHONE...................................302 504-6044
Kingsley Aguoru, *President*
Jennifer Aguoru, *Director*
EMP: 67
SQ FT: 72
SALES: 3.4MM **Privately Held**
SIC: 7379

(G-12049)
PBE COMPANIES LLC
2711 Centerville Rd (19808-1660)
PHONE...................................617 346-7459
Scott Dow, *President*
EMP: 25
SALES (est): 892K
SALES (corp-wide): 1.4B **Publicly Held**
SIC: 6512 Nonresidential building operators
HQ: Santander Holdings Usa, Inc.
75 State St
Boston MA 02109
617 346-7200

(G-12050)
PBTV GLOBAL INC
2105a W Newport Pike (19804-3719)
PHONE...................................302 292-1400
Et Jackson, *CEO*
Mark Johnson, *Vice Pres*
EMP: 10 EST: 2014
SALES (est): 3MM **Privately Held**
SIC: 3679 7372 Electronic components; application computer software

(G-12051)
PCMH SUPPORT TEAM - PRIVACY
2607 N Harrison St (19802-2922)
PHONE...................................267 254-2111
EMP: 4
SALES (est): 44.6K **Privately Held**
SIC: 8399 Advocacy group

(G-12052)
PCMS HOLDINGS INC
200 Bellevue Pkwy Ste 300 (19809-3727)
PHONE...................................302 281-3600
EMP: 6
SALES (est): 329.3K
SALES (corp-wide): 307.4MM **Publicly Held**
SIC: 6799 Investors
HQ: Interdigital Wireless, Inc.
200 Bellevue Pkwy Ste 300
Wilmington DE 19809

(G-12053)
PCU SYSTEMS LLC
3524 Silverside Rd 35b (19810-4929)
PHONE...................................888 780-9728
Raghu Varma Kizhakkemadhom, *Owner*
EMP: 1
SALES (est): 64.3K **Privately Held**
SIC: 3825 3544 7389 Engine electrical test equipment; digital test equipment, electronic & electrical circuits; jigs & fixtures;

(G-12054)
PDE I LLC
Also Called: Sheraton Suites Wilmington
422 Delaware Ave (19801-1508)
PHONE...................................302 654-8300
Elizabeth Procaccianti, *Manager*
Michelle Joyal, *Administration*
EMP: 92 EST: 1992
SQ FT: 199,000
SALES (est): 8.3MM **Privately Held**
SIC: 7011 Hotels & motels

(G-12055)
PDM INCORPORATED
Also Called: Pine Derivatives Marketing
3411 Silverside Rd 104wb (19810-4851)
PHONE...................................302 478-0768
Walter L Cleaver Jr, *President*
Bob Wherry, *Sales Staff*
Joann Murray, *Admin Mgr*
▲ **EMP:** 5
SQ FT: 2,000
SALES (est): 1.2MM **Privately Held**
WEB: www.pdmchemicals.com
SIC: 5169 Chemicals & allied products

(G-12056)
PDR VC LTD LIABILITY COMPANY
427 N Tatnall St 92059 (19801-2230)
PHONE...................................424 281-4669
Pedram Rostami,
EMP: 5
SALES (est): 107K **Privately Held**
SIC: 7371 8322 7929 Computer software development & applications; travelers' aid; entertainment service

(G-12057)
PEAK CRYOTHERAPY
3105 Limestone Rd (19808-2147)
PHONE...................................302 502-3160
John Distefano, *Principal*
EMP: 4
SALES (est): 137.5K **Privately Held**
SIC: 8049 Physical therapist

(G-12058)
PEAS AND LOVE CORPORATION
1209 N Orange St (19801-1120)
PHONE...................................301 537-3593
Michael Bruch, *CEO*
EMP: 1
SALES (est): 43.6K **Privately Held**
SIC: 7372 Application computer software

(G-12059)
PEEK PERFORMANCE GROUP LLC
300 Delaware Ave (19801-1607)
PHONE...................................480 242-6087
EMP: 25
SALES: 250K **Privately Held**
SIC: 8741 Management Services

(G-12060)
PEIRCE-PHELPS INC
360 Water St (19804-2411)
PHONE...................................302 633-9352
Robin Hinds, *Manager*
EMP: 4
SALES (corp-wide): 35.5MM **Privately Held**
SIC: 5075 Air conditioning & ventilation equipment & supplies
PA: Peirce Enterprises, Inc.
516 Township Line Rd
Blue Bell PA 19422
215 879-7235

(G-12061)
PEMCO LIGHTING PRODUCTS INC
150 Pemco Way (19804-3542)
PHONE...................................302 892-9000
John W Bowers, *President*
Toby Boyd, *General Mgr*
Donna Logan, *Corp Secy*
Donna Payne, *Vice Pres*
Vance Grosso, *Sales Associate*
▲ **EMP:** 1
SQ FT: 40,000
SALES (est): 4.1MM **Privately Held**
SIC: 3646 3645 Commercial indusl & institutional electric lighting fixtures; residential lighting fixtures

(G-12062)
PEMCO LIGHTING PRODUCTS LLC
150 Pemco Way (19804-3542)
PHONE...................................302 892-9000
John W Bowers, *President*
EMP: 4
SALES (est): 153K **Privately Held**
SIC: 3646 Commercial indusl & institutional electric lighting fixtures

(G-12063)
PENFLEX III LLC
702 First State Blvd (19804-3572)
PHONE...................................302 998-0683
Francis Julian, *Mng Member*
EMP: 5
SALES (est): 218.5K **Privately Held**
SIC: 6531 Real estate leasing & rentals

(G-12064)
PENINSULA UNTD MTHDST HMES INC
Also Called: Country House, The
4830 Kennett Pike (19807-1866)
PHONE...................................302 654-5101
Perri White, *Exec Dir*
EMP: 215
SALES (corp-wide): 24.6MM **Privately Held**
SIC: 8361 8051 Home for the aged; convalescent home with continuous nursing care
PA: Peninsula United Methodist Homes, Inc.
726 Loveville Rd Ste 3000
Hockessin DE 19707
302 235-6800

(G-12065)
PENN LABS INC
Also Called: Glaxosmithkline Company
2711 Centerville Rd # 400 (19808-1660)
PHONE...................................215 751-4000
Christopher Gent, *Chairman*
EMP: 15
SALES (est): 1.6MM
SALES (corp-wide): 40.6B **Privately Held**
SIC: 8731 Biological research
HQ: Glaxosmithkline Llc
5 Crescent Dr
Philadelphia PA 19112
215 751-4000

(G-12066)
PENN MUTUAL LIFE INSURANCE CO
1521 Concord Pike Ste 305 (19803-3644)
PHONE...................................302 655-7151
EMP: 13
SALES (corp-wide): 1.8B **Privately Held**
SIC: 6311 Life Insurance Carrier
PA: The Penn Mutual Life Insurance Co
600 Dresher Rd
Horsham PA 19044
215 956-8000

(G-12067)
PENN VIRGINIA HOLDING CORP
1011 Centre Rd Ste 310 (19805-1266)
PHONE...................................302 288-0158
Jim Dearlove, *Principal*
EMP: 110
SALES (est): 4.2MM
SALES (corp-wide): 440.8MM **Publicly Held**
SIC: 1382 Oil & gas exploration services
PA: Penn Virginia Corporation
16285 Park Ten Pl Ste 500
Houston TX 77084
713 722-6500

(G-12068)
PENNA ORTHODONTICS
2710 Centerville Rd (19808-1644)
PHONE...................................302 998-8783
Robert Penna, *Principal*
EMP: 7 EST: 2009
SALES (est): 358.2K **Privately Held**
SIC: 8021 Orthodontist

(G-12069)
PENNENGINEERING HOLDINGS LLC (DH)
Also Called: Pennengineering Holdings, Inc.
103 Foulk Rd Ste 108 (19803-3742)
PHONE...................................302 576-2746
William M Shockley, *President*
Joseph R Coluzzi, *Vice Pres*
Richard F Davies, *Treasurer*
Scott Kelley, *Admin Sec*
EMP: 143
SALES (est): 13.9MM
SALES (corp-wide): 483.7MM **Privately Held**
WEB: www.penn-eng.com
SIC: 3429 3549 Metal fasteners; metal-working machinery
HQ: Penn Engineering & Manufacturing Corp.
5190 Old Easton Rd
Danboro PA 18916
215 766-8853

(G-12070)
PENNROSE MANAGEMENT COMPANY
Also Called: Clayton Court Apartments
502 N Dupont St (19805-3149)
PHONE...................................302 571-8295
Monica Barley, *Manager*
EMP: 4
SALES (corp-wide): 73.3MM **Privately Held**
SIC: 6513 Apartment building operators
PA: Pennrose Management Company Inc
1301 N 31st St
Philadelphia PA 19121
267 386-8600

GEOGRAPHIC SECTION
Wilmington - New Castle County (G-12099)

(G-12071)
PENNSYLVANIA INC
Also Called: Wash Depot, The
1420 Lancaster Ave (19805-3905)
PHONE..................................302 498-0904
EMP: 5
SALES (est): 220K Privately Held
SIC: 7215 Coin-Operated Laundry

(G-12072)
PENNY EXPRESS INC
1202 E 13th St (19802-5036)
PHONE..................................302 571-0544
G Chernekoff, *President*
Polly Chernekoff, *Corp Secy*
EMP: 4
SQ FT: 15,000
SALES (est): 1MM Privately Held
SIC: 4213 4212 Contract haulers; local trucking, without storage

(G-12073)
PENNY HILL LAWN & LANDSCAPING
602 Elizabeth Ave (19809-2666)
PHONE..................................302 762-4406
Christopher Hoerner, *Owner*
EMP: 4 EST: 2007
SALES (est): 140.4K Privately Held
SIC: 0781 Landscape services

(G-12074)
PENNZOIL-QUAKER STATE COMPANY
Also Called: Jiffy Lube 312
3725 Kirkwood Hwy (19808-5105)
PHONE..................................302 999-7323
Mike Dunter, *Manager*
EMP: 20
SALES (corp-wide): 388.3B Privately Held
SIC: 7549 Lubrication service, automotive
HQ: Pennzoil-Quaker State Company
150 N Dairy Ashford Rd
Houston TX 77079
713 245-4800

(G-12075)
PENSKE PERFORMANCE INC (HQ)
1105 N Market St (19801-1216)
PHONE..................................302 656-2082
Roger Penske, *President*
Lawrence Bluth, *Vice Pres*
Soloman Cohen, *Vice Pres*
Walter Czarnecki, *Vice Pres*
Richard J Peters, *Treasurer*
EMP: 60
SALES (est): 2.7MM
SALES (corp-wide): 9.6B Privately Held
SIC: 7948 3711 Motor vehicle racing & drivers; race car owners; race car drivers; stock car racing; automobile assembly, including specialty automobiles
PA: Penske Corporation
2555 S Telegraph Rd
Bloomfield Hills MI 48302
248 648-2000

(G-12076)
PENSKE TRUCK LEASING CO LP
3625 Kirkwood Hwy (19808-5103)
PHONE..................................302 994-7899
Henry Kuratle, *Branch Mgr*
EMP: 14
SALES (corp-wide): 9.6B Privately Held
WEB: www.pensketruckleasing.com
SIC: 7513 Truck rental & leasing, no drivers
HQ: Penske Truck Leasing Co., L.P.
2675 Morgantown Rd
Reading PA 19607
610 775-6000

(G-12077)
PENSKE TRUCK LEASING CORP
4709 Ferris Dr (19808-1103)
PHONE..................................302 658-3255
Henry Kuratle, *Branch Mgr*
EMP: 12
SALES (corp-wide): 9.6B Privately Held
SIC: 7513 Truck rental & leasing, no drivers
HQ: Penske Truck Leasing Corporation
2675 Morgantown Rd
Reading PA 19607
610 775-6000

(G-12078)
PENTIUS INC
1201 N Orange St Ste 7382 (19801-1286)
PHONE..................................855 825-3778
Theodore Hissey IV, *President*
EMP: 45
SQ FT: 2,200
SALES: 55MM Privately Held
SIC: 7373 Systems software development services

(G-12079)
PEOPLES SETTLEMENT ASSC OF WL
Also Called: People's Settlement Day Care
408 E 8th St (19801-3699)
PHONE..................................302 658-4133
Enid Wallace-Simms, *President*
Patrica Allen, *Vice Pres*
Barbara Crowell, *Vice Pres*
John Buckley, *Treasurer*
Dimberu Merriam, *Treasurer*
EMP: 35
SALES: 216.3K Privately Held
WEB: www.psassociation.com
SIC: 8351 8322 Child day care services; individual & family services

(G-12080)
PEPCO HOLDINGS LLC
630 Mrtin Lthar King Blvd (19801-2306)
P.O. Box 231 (19899-0231)
PHONE..................................202 872-2000
Joseph Riding, *Principal*
Rich Aiello, *Manager*
John Colicchio, *Supervisor*
Matthew Kiel, *Supervisor*
Christopher Smack, *Supervisor*
EMP: 22
SALES (corp-wide): 35.9B Publicly Held
SIC: 4911 4924 Generation, electric power; natural gas distribution
HQ: Pepco Holdings Llc
701 9th St Nw Ste 3
Washington DC 20001
202 872-2000

(G-12081)
PEPSI-COLA BTLG OF WILMINGTON
3501 Governor Printz Blvd (19802-2804)
PHONE..................................302 761-4848
Roger Coale, *Plant Mgr*
Mark W Robinson, *CFO*
Bob Coleman, *Sales Mgr*
Ben Petosa, *Sales Staff*
Rick Palmer, *Manager*
EMP: 110 EST: 1935
SQ FT: 90,000
SALES (est): 14.4MM
SALES (corp-wide): 64.6B Publicly Held
SIC: 2086 5149 Carbonated soft drinks, bottled & canned; soft drinks
PA: Pepsico, Inc.
700 Anderson Hill Rd
Purchase NY 10577
914 253-2000

(G-12082)
PEPSI-COLA METRO BTLG CO INC
3501 Governor Printz Blvd (19802-2804)
PHONE..................................302 764-6770
Pete Kraus, *Manager*
EMP: 150
SALES (corp-wide): 64.6B Publicly Held
WEB: www.joy-of-cola.com
SIC: 2086 5149 Soft drinks: packaged in cans, bottles, etc.; soft drinks
HQ: Pepsi-Cola Metropolitan Bottling Company, Inc.
1111 Westchester Ave
White Plains NY 10604
914 767-5000

(G-12083)
PERASTIC LLC
1704 N Park Dr Apt 508 (19806-2171)
PHONE..................................917 592-4219
Gregory Whitman Field, *President*

John Gicker, *Principal*
EMP: 5
SALES (est): 219.4K Privately Held
SIC: 7389

(G-12084)
PERFORMANCE AUTO BODY & PAINT
200 Bradford St (19801-5402)
PHONE..................................302 655-6170
Blaine Bailey, *Owner*
EMP: 4 EST: 2007
SALES (est): 194.5K Privately Held
SIC: 7532 Paint shop, automotive

(G-12085)
PERFORMANCE MATERIALS NA INC
974 Chestnut Run Plz (19805-1269)
PHONE..................................302 892-7009
EMP: 5000
SALES (est): 44.3MM
SALES (corp-wide): 61B Publicly Held
SIC: 8748 Business consulting
PA: Dow Inc.
2211 H H Dow Way
Midland MI 48642
989 636-1000

(G-12086)
PERINATAL ASSOCATION DELAWARE
715 N Tatnall St (19801-1715)
PHONE..................................302 654-1088
EMP: 21
SALES (est): 914.2K Privately Held
SIC: 8742 Management Consulting Services

(G-12087)
PERPETUAL INVSTMENTS GROUP LLC
251 Little Falls Dr (19808-1674)
PHONE..................................718 795-3394
Tanveer Sajid,
EMP: 50
SALES: 500K Privately Held
SIC: 7389 Business services

(G-12088)
PERRY & ASSOC
6 Larch Ave Ste 397 (19804-2356)
PHONE..................................302 472-8701
EMP: 4
SALES (est): 181K Privately Held
SIC: 8082 Home health care services

(G-12089)
PERRY AND ASSOCIATES SERVICES
300 Delaware Ave Ste 210 (19801-6601)
PHONE..................................302 581-3092
Perry Veney Sr, *Principal*
Dakeisha Watson, *Principal*
EMP: 5
SALES (est): 1MM Privately Held
SIC: 6411 Insurance claim adjusters, not employed by insurance company

(G-12090)
PERSEPHONE JONES MD
1600 Rockland Rd (19803-3607)
PHONE..................................302 651-4000
Persephone Jones, *Executive*
EMP: 4 EST: 2017
SALES (est): 70.6K Privately Held
SIC: 8011 Pediatrician

(G-12091)
PERSONAL HEALTH PDT DEV LLC
Also Called: Phresh Products
4023 Kennett Pike Ste 622 (19807-2018)
PHONE..................................888 901-6150
Paul Lepore, *Officer*
Harold Hoffman,
EMP: 20
SALES: 1.6MM Privately Held
SIC: 2833 5047 Medicinals & botanicals; medical equipment & supplies

(G-12092)
PERTEH
1800 Naamans Rd (19810-2600)
PHONE..................................302 200-0912
EMP: 2
SALES (est): 67K Privately Held
SIC: 2341 Women's & children's underwear

(G-12093)
PETCUBE INC
2711 Centerville Rd # 400 (19808-1660)
PHONE..................................786 375-9065
EMP: 31
SALES (corp-wide): 3.6MM Privately Held
SIC: 7379 7371 Computer Related Services Custom Computer Programing
PA: Petcube, Inc.
555 De Haro St Ste 280a
San Francisco CA 94107
424 302-6107

(G-12094)
PETER D FURNESS ELC CO INC
1604 Todds Ln (19802-2422)
P.O. Box 1186 (19899-1186)
PHONE..................................302 764-6030
Dan Hahn, *President*
Lisa Barker, *President*
Tom Hoffman, *President*
Daniel J Hahn Sr, *Exec VP*
Thomas Hoffman, *Vice Pres*
EMP: 150
SQ FT: 12,000
SALES: 34.2MM Privately Held
WEB: www.furnesselectric.com
SIC: 1731 General electrical contractor

(G-12095)
PETER F SUBACH
Also Called: Giordano, Lawrence S
1601 Milltown Rd Ste 17 (19808-4084)
PHONE..................................302 995-1870
Lawrence S Giordano DDS, *President*
Peter Subach, *Vice Pres*
Peter F Subach, *Frmly & Gen Dent*
EMP: 9
SALES (est): 576.9K Privately Held
SIC: 8021 Maxillofacial specialist

(G-12096)
PETER F TOWNSEND MD
3519 Silverside Rd # 101 (19810-4909)
PHONE..................................302 633-3555
Jana Siwek MD, *Manager*
EMP: 40
SALES (est): 625.5K Privately Held
SIC: 8011 Orthopedic physician

(G-12097)
PETER R COGGINS MD
Also Called: Aesthetic Surgical Associates
5811 Kennett Pike (19807-1137)
PHONE..................................302 655-1115
Peter R Coggins MD, *Owner*
Kristine Di Biasa, *Manager*
EMP: 4
SALES (est): 431.6K Privately Held
SIC: 8011 Plastic surgeon

(G-12098)
PETER SHIN (PA)
Also Called: Wholesale Asgard
805 W 21st St (19802-3818)
PHONE..................................302 498-0977
Peter Shin, *Owner*
Peter Shinn, *Owner*
▲ EMP: 1
SALES (est): 81.4K Privately Held
WEB: www.asgardpress.com
SIC: 2711 Newspapers, publishing & printing

(G-12099)
PETERS ALAN E PETERS & ASSOC
1200 Penns Ave Ste 202 (19806-4350)
PHONE..................................302 656-1007
Alan E Peters, *President*
EMP: 5
SALES (est): 549.4K Privately Held
WEB: www.petersfinancialplanning.com
SIC: 6211 Investment firm, general brokerage

Wilmington - New Castle County (G-12100)   GEOGRAPHIC SECTION

(G-12100)
PETERS JOHN DVM
136 Hitching Post Dr (19803-1913)
PHONE..................................302 478-5981
Peters Dvm, *Manager*
EMP: 6
SALES (est): 178.6K **Privately Held**
SIC: 0742 Veterinarian, animal specialties

(G-12101)
PETRUCON CONSTRUCTION INC
100 N Cleveland Ave (19805-1715)
P.O. Box 2593 (19805-0593)
PHONE..................................302 571-5781
Ernest Congo, *President*
James Petruccelli, *Vice Pres*
EMP: 12
SQ FT: 800
SALES (est): 4.8MM **Privately Held**
SIC: 1522 1542 Renovation, hotel/motel; hotel/motel & multi-family home renovation & remodeling; remodeling, multi-family dwellings; commercial & office building contractors

(G-12102)
PETTINARO CONSTRUCTION CO INC (PA)
234 N James St (19804-3197)
PHONE..................................302 999-0708
Gregory Pettinaro, *CEO*
Verino Pettinaro, *CEO*
Michael R Walsh, *COO*
EMP: 89 EST: 1965
SQ FT: 25,000
SALES (est): 59.6MM **Privately Held**
WEB: www.pettinarorelocation.com
SIC: 1541 1542 6531 6519 Industrial buildings, new construction; renovation, remodeling & repairs; industrial buildings; commercial & office buildings, new construction; commercial & office buildings, renovation & repair; real estate agents & managers; real property lessors; single-family housing construction

(G-12103)
PETTINARO ENTERPRISES LLC
234 N James St (19804-3132)
PHONE..................................302 999-0708
Verino Pettinaro,
Tracey Crowley,
Cindy Pettinaro,
Gregory Pettinaro,
Victoria Pettinaro,
EMP: 30
SQ FT: 25,000
SALES (est): 2MM **Privately Held**
SIC: 6513 Apartment building operators

(G-12104)
PFPC TRUST COMPANY
301 Bellevue Pkwy Fl 4 (19809-3705)
PHONE..................................302 791-2000
EMP: 159
SALES (est): 586K
SALES (corp-wide): 18B **Publicly Held**
SIC: 6091 Nondeposit Trust Facility
HQ: Pfpc Worldwide Inc
    301 Bellevue Pkwy
    Wilmington DE 19809
    302 791-1700

(G-12105)
PFPC WORLDWIDE INC (DH)
301 Bellevue Pkwy (19809-3705)
PHONE..................................302 791-1700
Timothy G Shack, *CEO*
Stephen M Wynne, *President*
John Fulgoney, *Vice Pres*
Nancy B Wolcott, *Vice Pres*
EMP: 11
SALES (est): 29.6MM
SALES (corp-wide): 19.9B **Publicly Held**
SIC: 6099 8721 6282 7372 Electronic funds transfer network, including switching; accounting services, except auditing; investment advice; application computer software

(G-12106)
PGA ACQUISITIONS V LLC
1002 Justison St (19801-5148)
PHONE..................................302 355-3500
Howard A Enders, *Principal*
EMP: 5
SALES (est): 466.5K **Privately Held**
SIC: 6799 Investors

(G-12107)
PHALCO INC
10 Germay Dr (19804-1158)
PHONE..................................302 654-2620
J Patrick Phalan Jr, *President*
David Marko,
EMP: 5
SQ FT: 5,000
SALES: 750K **Privately Held**
WEB: www.phalco.com
SIC: 1623 7389 5084 Water, sewer & utility lines; industrial & commercial equipment inspection service; industrial machine parts

(G-12108)
PHARMUNION LLC
3524 Silverside Rd 35b (19810-4929)
PHONE..................................415 307-5128
Richard Zakchia, *CEO*
EMP: 3
SALES (est): 81.8K **Privately Held**
SIC: 2834 Pharmaceutical preparations

(G-12109)
PHASE FLATS II L P
601 N Union St (19805-3029)
PHONE..................................717 291-1911
Rodney Lambert, *President*
Stephanie Brown, *Manager*
EMP: 5
SALES (est): 129K **Privately Held**
SIC: 6513 Apartment building operators

(G-12110)
PHASE I FLATS L P
401-535 N Union St (19805)
PHONE..................................717 291-1911
Rodney Lambert, *Partner*
Stephanie Brown, *Manager*
EMP: 5
SALES (est): 359.7K **Privately Held**
SIC: 6513 Apartment building operators

(G-12111)
PHAZEBREAK COATINGS LLC
1105 N Market St Ste 1300 (19801-1241)
PHONE..................................844 467-4293
Maria Cantu-Browning,
Karen Kraus,
EMP: 5
SALES (est): 126.7K **Privately Held**
SIC: 7389

(G-12112)
PHILADELPH FT ANKL ASSCTS
503 E 35th St (19802-2817)
PHONE..................................215 465-5342
Sean McCants, *Mng Member*
EMP: 6
SALES (est): 360K **Privately Held**
SIC: 8082 Home health care services

(G-12113)
PHILADLPHIA BALL RLLER BEARING
701 Cornell Dr Ste 12 (19801-5782)
PHONE..................................215 727-0982
James Reys, *Manager*
EMP: 4
SALES (corp-wide): 11.7MM **Privately Held**
SIC: 5085 5084 Bearings; metal refining machinery & equipment
PA: Philadelphia Ball & Roller Bearing Co
    400 N 6th St
    Philadelphia PA 19123
    215 574-0900

(G-12114)
PHILIP M FINESTRAUSS PA
1404 N King St (19801-3122)
P.O. Box 1409 (19899-1409)
PHONE..................................302 984-1600
Philip M Finestrauss, *President*
Andrea J Finestrauss, *Admin Sec*
EMP: 4
SQ FT: 2,200
SALES (est): 320K **Privately Held**
SIC: 8111 General practice law office

(G-12115)
PHILLIP E WEIR
Also Called: Greenhill Auto Service
600 Greenhill Ave (19805-1853)
PHONE..................................302 652-1312
Phillip E Weir, *Owner*
EMP: 4
SQ FT: 3,500
SALES (est): 286.9K **Privately Held**
SIC: 7538 General automotive repair shops

(G-12116)
PHILLIPS GLDMN MCLGHLN & HLL
1200 N Broom St (19806-4204)
PHONE..................................302 655-4200
John Phillips Jr, *President*
Stephen W Spence, *Corp Secy*
Robert S Goldman, *Vice Pres*
James P Hall,
EMP: 31
SQ FT: 7,000
SALES (est): 3.8MM **Privately Held**
SIC: 8111 General practice attorney, lawyer

(G-12117)
PHILLIPS & COHEN ASSOC LTD (PA)
1002 Justison St (19801-5148)
PHONE..................................609 518-9000
Matthew M Phillips, *Ch of Bd*
Adam S Cohen, *Ch of Bd*
Howard Enders, *President*
John Miller, *CFO*
EMP: 80 EST: 1997
SQ FT: 10,000
SALES (est): 26.9MM **Privately Held**
WEB: www.phillips-cohen.com
SIC: 7322 Adjustment & collection services

(G-12118)
PHILLIPS INSULATION INC
8 Brookside Dr (19804-1102)
PHONE..................................302 655-6523
Michael D Phillips, *President*
Ruth Anne Phillips, *Vice Pres*
EMP: 7 EST: 1977
SQ FT: 1,600
SALES (est): 685.2K **Privately Held**
SIC: 1742 Insulation, buildings

(G-12119)
PHILLY PLASTICS CORP
1201 N Orange St (19801-1155)
PHONE..................................718 435-4808
Jacob Kryman, *Principal*
EMP: 1
SALES (est): 72.4K **Privately Held**
SIC: 3089 Plastic processing

(G-12120)
PHILLY PRETZEL
4737 Concord Pike (19803-1442)
PHONE..................................302 478-5658
Stan Alten, *Owner*
EMP: 7
SALES (est): 252.1K **Privately Held**
SIC: 2052 Cookies & crackers

(G-12121)
PHILYMACK GAMES LLC
1209 N Orange St (19801-1120)
PHONE..................................302 658-7581
Phillip McIntyre, *Principal*
EMP: 4
SALES (est): 139.8K **Privately Held**
SIC: 3944 Electronic games & toys

(G-12122)
PHLY LLC
500 Delaware Ave Unit 1 (19899-7101)
P.O. Box 1960 (19899-1960)
PHONE..................................778 882-2391
Adel Elmouassarani, *CEO*
Adel Alzebeir, *CTO*
Adam Verity, *Officer*
EMP: 8
SALES (est): 182.5K **Privately Held**
SIC: 7371 Computer software development & applications

(G-12123)
PHOENIX FILTRATION INC
403 Marsh Ln Ste 2-4 (19804-2402)
PHONE..................................302 998-8805
Henry E Potts Jr, *President*
▲ EMP: 4
SALES (est): 1.4MM **Privately Held**
SIC: 5085 Filters, industrial

(G-12124)
PHOENIX HOME THEATER INC
Also Called: Phoenix Restoration
403 Marsh Ln 3 (19804-2402)
PHONE..................................302 295-1390
Brian Potts, *President*
EMP: 15
SQ FT: 12,500
SALES (est): 2.8MM **Privately Held**
WEB: www.phoenixrestores.com
SIC: 1799 Post-disaster renovations

(G-12125)
PHOENIX RHBILITATION HLTH SVCS
4001 Miller Rd Ste 2 (19802-1961)
PHONE..................................302 764-2008
Kim Dare, *Branch Mgr*
EMP: 4
SALES (corp-wide): 14.8MM **Privately Held**
SIC: 8049 Physical therapist
PA: Phoenix Rehabilitation And Health
    Services, Inc.
    430 Innovation Dr
    Blairsville PA 15717
    724 463-7478

(G-12126)
PHOENIX TRNSP & LOGISTICS INC (HQ)
1000 N West St Ste 1200 (19801-1058)
PHONE..................................302 348-8814
Joel Brown, *President*
Chloe G Ayala, *Principal*
Tameka Y Brown, *Principal*
Lisa A Johnson, *Principal*
EMP: 4
SALES (est): 2.8MM **Privately Held**
SIC: 4213 Trucking, except local

(G-12127)
PHOENIX VITAE HOLDINGS LLC
251 Little Falls Dr (19808-1674)
PHONE..................................302 351-3047
Anastasios Kyriakides,
EMP: 1
SALES (est): 56K **Privately Held**
SIC: 3669 Communications equipment

(G-12128)
PHS CORPORATE SERVICES INC
1313 N Market St (19801-6101)
P.O. Box 1709 (19899-1709)
PHONE..................................302 571-1128
Richard Eckman, *President*
Andrew Logan, *Vice Pres*
Benjamin Strauss, *Vice Pres*
EMP: 5
SALES (est): 366.4K **Privately Held**
SIC: 8742 Corporation organizing

(G-12129)
PHYSICIAN DSPNSNG SOLUTIONS
390 Mitch Rd (19804-3943)
PHONE..................................302 734-7246
Ganesh R Balu, *Principal*
EMP: 20
SALES (est): 197.1K **Privately Held**
SIC: 8011 General & family practice, physician/surgeon

(G-12130)
PHYSIOTHERAPY ASSOCIATES INC
2401 Penns Ave Ste 112 (19806-1432)
PHONE..................................302 655-8989
Kenneth Dill, *Branch Mgr*
EMP: 6 **Privately Held**
SIC: 8049 Physical therapist

GEOGRAPHIC SECTION
Wilmington - New Castle County (G-12160)

HQ: Physiotherapy Associates, Inc.
680 American Ave Ste 200
King Of Prussia PA 19406
610 644-7824

(G-12131)
PHYSIOTHERAPY ASSOCIATES INC
Also Called: Physio Therapy Association
3411 Silverside Rd # 105 (19810-4812)
PHONE.....................610 444-1270
Phil Donnely, *President*
EMP: 8 **Privately Held**
WEB: www.myphysio.com
SIC: 8049 Physical therapist
HQ: Physiotherapy Associates, Inc.
680 American Ave Ste 200
King Of Prussia PA 19406
610 644-7824

(G-12132)
PIECES OF A DREAM INC
2404 W 7th St (19805-2819)
P.O. Box 7022 (19803-0022)
PHONE.....................302 593-6172
Ashley Sullivan-Kirsey, *Director*
EMP: 4
SALES (est): 183.6K **Privately Held**
SIC: 7922 Theatrical producers & services

(G-12133)
PIERPONT INDUSTRIES
11 Harlech Dr (19807-2507)
PHONE.....................302 998-9220
Charles Christy, *President*
EMP: 1
SALES (est): 56.1K **Privately Held**
SIC: 3999 Atomizers, toiletry

(G-12134)
PIKE CREEK ASSOC IN WNS CARE (PA)
Also Called: Pike Creek Assoc In Wmncare PA
4600 New Lndn Hill Rd 1 (19808)
PHONE.....................302 995-7062
Susan Gorondy MD, *Owner*
EMP: 14
SALES (est): 1.1MM **Privately Held**
SIC: 8011 Gynecologist

(G-12135)
PIKE CREEK AUTOMOTIVE INC
2379 Limestone Rd (19808-4103)
PHONE.....................302 998-2234
Paul Campanella, *President*
EMP: 6 **EST:** 2015
SALES (est): 49.9K **Privately Held**
SIC: 7539 Automotive repair shops

(G-12136)
PIKE CREEK BIKE LINE INC
4768 Limestone Rd (19808-1928)
PHONE.....................610 747-1200
Thomas Casadevall, *Ch of Bd*
John Waddell, *President*
Mary Lou Keller, *Corp Secy*
EMP: 5
SALES (est): 240K **Privately Held**
SIC: 5941 7699 Bicycle & bicycle parts; bicycle repair shop

(G-12137)
PIKE CREEK COMPUTER COMPANY
Also Called: Pike Creek Software
2206 Milltown Rd (19808-4019)
PHONE.....................302 239-5113
John Knupp, *President*
Gloria Knupp, *Vice Pres*
Steve Knupp, *Treasurer*
Ellen Kelley, *Admin Sec*
EMP: 12
SALES (est): 930K **Privately Held**
SIC: 7371 Computer software systems analysis & design, custom

(G-12138)
PIKE CREEK COURT CLUB INC
Also Called: Pike Creek Fitness Club
4905 Mermaid Blvd Ste B (19808-1004)
PHONE.....................302 239-6688
Ruly Carpenter, *President*
David H C Carpenter, *Vice Pres*
EMP: 100

SQ FT: 36,000
SALES (est): 1MM **Privately Held**
SIC: 7997 7991 Membership sports & recreation clubs; physical fitness facilities

(G-12139)
PIKE CREEK IMAGING CENTER
Also Called: Diagnostic Imaging Assoc
3105 Limestone Rd Ste 106 (19808-2147)
PHONE.....................302 995-2037
Joseph Peacock, *Partner*
EMP: 14
SALES (est): 728.3K
SALES (corp-wide): 4.2MM **Privately Held**
SIC: 8011 Radiologist
PA: Omega Imaging Associates, L.L.C.
6 Omega Dr
Newark DE 19713
302 738-9300

(G-12140)
PIKE CREEK PEDIATRIC ASSOC
Also Called: Feick, Judith MD
100 S Riding Blvd (19808-3692)
PHONE.....................302 239-7755
Marilyn K Lynam MD, *Partner*
Cynthia Gabrielli, *Vice Pres*
Judith N Feick, *Med Doctor*
EMP: 16
SALES (est): 1.4MM **Privately Held**
SIC: 8011 Pediatrician

(G-12141)
PINCKNEY WDNGER URBAN JYCE LLC
3711 Kennett Pike Ste 210 (19807-2161)
PHONE.....................302 504-1497
Joanne P Pinckney,
Elizabeth W Joyce,
Patricia Urban,
Micheal A Weidinger,
EMP: 8
SALES (est): 841.3K **Privately Held**
SIC: 8111 Corporate, partnership & business law; bankruptcy law

(G-12142)
PINNACLE FUNDING INC
2002 Baynard Blvd (19802-3918)
PHONE.....................302 657-0160
Thomas G Hodgson, *President*
EMP: 4 **EST:** 1998
SALES (est): 5MM **Privately Held**
WEB: www.pinnaclefunding.com
SIC: 6159 Machinery & equipment finance leasing; equipment & vehicle finance leasing companies

(G-12143)
PIONEER FENCE CO INC
109 S John St (19804-3157)
PHONE.....................302 998-2892
H Robert Chambers Jr, *President*
Richard Chambers, *Vice Pres*
Scott Chambers, *Vice Pres*
EMP: 12 **EST:** 1939
SQ FT: 4,500
SALES (est): 1.5MM **Privately Held**
SIC: 1799 Fence construction

(G-12144)
PITNEY BOWES INTL HOLDINGS (DH)
801 N West St Fl 2 (19801-1525)
PHONE.....................302 656-8595
Bruce Nolop, *President*
Kennith Kubacki, *Vice Pres*
Clara Paschitti, *Asst Sec*
EMP: 12
SALES: 1.3B
SALES (corp-wide): 3.5B **Publicly Held**
SIC: 6719 Investment holding companies, except banks
HQ: B. Williams Holding Corp.
1403 Foulk Rd Ste 200
Wilmington DE 19803
302 656-8596

(G-12145)
PIXORIZE INC
251 Little Falls Dr (19808-1674)
P.O. Box 1190, New York NY (10021-0037)
PHONE.....................737 529-4404
David Westfall, *CEO*
Nathan Liu, *COO*

EMP: 2
SALES: 90K **Privately Held**
SIC: 2741 Miscellaneous publishing

(G-12146)
PIZAZZ BEAUTY STUDIO
4001 N Market St (19802-2219)
PHONE.....................302 761-9820
Beverly Monroe, *President*
EMP: 5
SALES: 2MM **Privately Held**
SIC: 7231 Hairdressers

(G-12147)
PKG LLC
251 Little Falls Dr (19808-1674)
PHONE.....................269 651-8640
Jamie Lego,
Lynn Lego,
EMP: 2
SALES (est): 73.4K **Privately Held**
SIC: 3423 Tools or equipment for use with sporting arms

(G-12148)
PLAIN & FANCY INC
Also Called: Plain & Fancy Interiors
5716 Kennett Pike Ste E (19807-1328)
PHONE.....................302 656-9901
Molly Wiley, *President*
EMP: 5 **EST:** 1959
SQ FT: 1,500
SALES (est): 327.8K **Privately Held**
WEB: www.plainfancy.com
SIC: 7389 Interior design services

(G-12149)
PLANET X SKATEBOARDS
2400 Shellpot Dr (19803-2548)
PHONE.....................484 886-9287
Angel Acevedo, *Principal*
EMP: 2
SALES (est): 126K **Privately Held**
SIC: 3949 Skateboards

(G-12150)
PLANNED PARENTHOOD OF DELAWARE (PA)
625 N Shipley St (19801-2249)
PHONE.....................302 655-7293
Nanci Hoffman, *President*
Ruth Lytle-Barnaby, *General Mgr*
Linda Scott, *CFO*
Lori Magno, *Office Mgr*
EMP: 20
SQ FT: 10,000
SALES: 4.9MM **Privately Held**
WEB: www.ppde.org
SIC: 8093 Family planning clinic

(G-12151)
PLANNED RESIDENTIAL COMMUNITES
Also Called: Valley Run Apartments
2601 Carpenter Station Rd (19810-2056)
PHONE.....................302 475-4621
John Bristol, *General Mgr*
Garry Gribble, *Sr Project Mgr*
Anthony Santaularia, *Director*
EMP: 12
SALES (corp-wide): 10.1MM **Privately Held**
SIC: 6531 Real estate agents & managers
PA: Planned Residential Communities Management Co (Inc)
40 State Route 36 Ste 1
West Long Branch NJ 07764
732 222-5062

(G-12152)
PLATENGER LLC
1201 N Orange St Ste 7126 (19801-1195)
PHONE.....................302 298-0896
Manuel Garcia,
EMP: 1
SALES: 20K **Privately Held**
SIC: 7372 Prepackaged software

(G-12153)
PLATINUM US DISTRIBUTION INC
Also Called: Wellnx Life Sciences USA
1201 N Orange St Ste 741 (19801-1175)
PHONE.....................905 364-8713
Dana Johnson, *President*

Brad Woodgate, *Principal*
EMP: 5
SQ FT: 7,000
SALES (est): 39.6MM
SALES (corp-wide): 5.7MM **Privately Held**
SIC: 2834 Pharmaceutical preparations
PA: Global Health Technologies Inc
6335 Edwards Blvd
Mississauga ON
905 364-8690

(G-12154)
PLAY FOR GOOD INC
3411 Silverside Rd 104r (19810-4812)
PHONE.....................312 520-9788
Amee Kamdar, *Principal*
Janet Moehring, *Principal*
EMP: 6
SALES (est): 190K **Privately Held**
SIC: 6732 Charitable trust management

(G-12155)
PLAYFIT EDUCATION INC
3575 Silverside Rd # 404 (19810-4944)
PHONE.....................302 438-3257
Curtis Hinson, *President*
Curt Hinson, *President*
EMP: 4
SALES (est): 290.1K **Privately Held**
SIC: 7999 Physical fitness instruction

(G-12156)
PLAYSIGHT INTERACTIVE USA INC
1201 N Orange St Ste 600 (19801-1171)
PHONE.....................800 246-2677
Chen Shachar, *CEO*
Yuval Bar Yosef, *Vice Pres*
EMP: 15
SQ FT: 4,000
SALES (est): 740K **Privately Held**
SIC: 7371 Computer software development & applications

(G-12157)
PLAZA FUEL
2213 Concord Pike (19803-2908)
PHONE.....................302 275-6242
Steven Henck, *Principal*
EMP: 3
SALES (est): 163.3K **Privately Held**
SIC: 2869 Fuels

(G-12158)
PLEASANT HILL LANES INC
Also Called: Pleasant Hill Bowling Alley
1001 W Newport Pike (19804-3335)
PHONE.....................302 998-8811
Cheryl Woodward, *President*
Charles Woodward, *Manager*
EMP: 30
SALES (est): 1.8MM **Privately Held**
WEB: www.pleasanthilllanes.com
SIC: 7933 5941 Ten pin center; bowling equipment & supplies

(G-12159)
PLEXUS FITNESS
20 Montchanin Rd Ste 60 (19807-2179)
PHONE.....................302 654-9642
Jennifer Collison, *Principal*
EMP: 15
SALES (est): 874.5K **Privately Held**
SIC: 7991 Physical fitness facilities

(G-12160)
PLM CONSULTING INC
828 N Jefferson St (19801-1432)
PHONE.....................302 984-2698
Philip Winkler, *President*
Graham Smith, *Vice Pres*
Deborah A Winkler, *Treasurer*
EMP: 10
SQ FT: 3,000
SALES: 1MM **Privately Held**
WEB: www.plmconsulting.com
SIC: 7379 7371 Computer related consulting services; custom computer programming services

Wilmington - New Castle County (G-12161)   GEOGRAPHIC SECTION

(G-12161)
PLOENERS AUTOMOTIVE PDTS CO
510 S Market St (19801-5209)
P.O. Box 1408 (19899-1408)
PHONE.................................302 655-4418
Mark Ploener, *President*
Randall Ploener, *Corp Secy*
EMP: 9 **EST:** 1947
SQ FT: 3,000
SALES (est): 2.1MM **Privately Held**
SIC: 5013 5063 Truck parts & accessories; storage batteries, industrial

(G-12162)
PLUSHBEDS INC (PA)
1201 N Orange St Ste 7058 (19801-1190)
PHONE.................................888 758-7423
Michael Hughes, *Principal*
Dawn Hughes, *Vice Pres*
John Vasey, *Sales Mgr*
Patrick Gunther, *Relations*
EMP: 9 **EST:** 2010
SALES (est): 1.1MM **Privately Held**
SIC: 5712 2515 Mattresses; mattresses & bedsprings

(G-12163)
PMCAA INC
913 N Market St Ste 200 (19801-3097)
PHONE.................................302 439-6028
Time Cotten, *President*
EMP: 4
SALES (est): 91.3K **Privately Held**
SIC: 8748 Business consulting

(G-12164)
PNC BANCORP INC (HQ)
300 Delaware Ave (19801-1607)
PHONE.................................302 427-5896
James E Rohr, *Ch of Bd*
Maria Schaffer, *Exec VP*
Louis Caputo, *Vice Pres*
Linda Heckert, *Vice Pres*
Joe Randazzo, *Vice Pres*
EMP: 36
SQ FT: 650,000
SALES (est): 9.8B
SALES (corp-wide): 19.9B **Publicly Held**
WEB: www.pncbank.com
SIC: 6021 National trust companies with deposits, commercial
PA: The Pnc Financial Services Group Inc
  300 5th Ave
  Pittsburgh PA 15222
  888 762-2265

(G-12165)
PNC BANK NATIONAL ASSOCIATION
2751 Centerville Rd # 101 (19808-1600)
PHONE.................................302 994-6337
EMP: 9
SALES (corp-wide): 19.9B **Publicly Held**
SIC: 6211 Securities flotation companies
HQ: Pnc Bank, National Association
  222 Delaware Ave
  Wilmington DE 19801
  877 762-2000

(G-12166)
PNC BANK NATIONAL ASSOCIATION (DH)
Also Called: National City Bank
222 Delaware Ave (19801-1637)
PHONE.................................877 762-2000
Peter Raskind, *Principal*
Gregory M Jelinek, *Principal*
William Lulis, *Vice Pres*
▲ **EMP:** 240 **EST:** 1845
SQ FT: 420,000
SALES: 9.8B
SALES (corp-wide): 19.9B **Publicly Held**
WEB: www.allegiantbank.com
SIC: 6021 National commercial banks

(G-12167)
PNC BANK NATIONAL ASSOCIATION
1009 N Union St (19805-2752)
PHONE.................................302 429-1761
Linda Broadway, *Principal*
Jose Henao, *Manager*
EMP: 12

SALES (corp-wide): 19.9B **Publicly Held**
WEB: www.pncfunds.com
SIC: 6021 National trust companies with deposits, commercial
HQ: Pnc Bank, National Association
  222 Delaware Ave
  Wilmington DE 19801
  877 762-2000

(G-12168)
PNC BANK NATIONAL ASSOCIATION
1704 Marsh Rd (19810-4606)
PHONE.................................302 479-4529
Alice Belcher, *Manager*
EMP: 10
SALES (corp-wide): 19.9B **Publicly Held**
SIC: 6021 National commercial banks
HQ: Pnc Bank, National Association
  222 Delaware Ave
  Wilmington DE 19801
  877 762-2000

(G-12169)
PNC BANK NATIONAL ASSOCIATION
4111 Concord Pike (19803-1401)
PHONE.................................302 479-4520
Mark Digiacomo, *Manager*
EMP: 10
SALES (corp-wide): 19.9B **Publicly Held**
SIC: 6021 National commercial banks
HQ: Pnc Bank, National Association
  222 Delaware Ave
  Wilmington DE 19801
  877 762-2000

(G-12170)
PNC BANK NATIONAL ASSOCIATION
4725 Kirkwood Hwy (19808-5097)
PHONE.................................302 993-3013
Pamela Jamison, *Branch Mgr*
EMP: 17
SALES (corp-wide): 19.9B **Publicly Held**
SIC: 6021 National commercial banks
HQ: Pnc Bank, National Association
  222 Delaware Ave
  Wilmington DE 19801
  877 762-2000

(G-12171)
PNC BANK NATIONAL ASSOCIATION
4301 Concord Pike (19803-1461)
PHONE.................................302 478-7822
Patrick Carson, *Branch Mgr*
EMP: 12
SALES (corp-wide): 19.9B **Publicly Held**
WEB: www.pncfunds.com
SIC: 6021 National trust companies with deposits, commercial
HQ: Pnc Bank, National Association
  222 Delaware Ave
  Wilmington DE 19801
  877 762-2000

(G-12172)
PNC BANK NATIONAL ASSOCIATION
5325 Limestone Rd (19808-1222)
PHONE.................................302 235-4010
Karen Pingley, *Manager*
EMP: 6
SALES (corp-wide): 19.9B **Publicly Held**
WEB: www.pncfunds.com
SIC: 6021 National trust companies with deposits, commercial
HQ: Pnc Bank, National Association
  222 Delaware Ave
  Wilmington DE 19801
  877 762-2000

(G-12173)
PNC BANK NATIONAL ASSOCIATION
2203 Kirkwood Hwy (19805-4903)
PHONE.................................302 993-3000
Shirley Dowdy, *Branch Mgr*
EMP: 6
SALES (corp-wide): 19.9B **Publicly Held**
WEB: www.pncfunds.com
SIC: 6021 National trust companies with deposits, commercial

HQ: Pnc Bank, National Association
  222 Delaware Ave
  Wilmington DE 19801
  877 762-2000

(G-12174)
PNC BANK NATIONAL ASSOCIATION
3840 Kennett Pike (19807-2389)
PHONE.................................302 429-1167
Todd Hutchison, *Branch Mgr*
EMP: 12
SALES (corp-wide): 19.9B **Publicly Held**
SIC: 6021 National commercial banks
HQ: Pnc Bank, National Association
  222 Delaware Ave
  Wilmington DE 19801
  877 762-2000

(G-12175)
PNC FINANCIAL SVCS GROUP INC
300 Delaware Ave (19801-1607)
PHONE.................................302 429-1364
Morgan Calvert, *Chairman*
Bonnie Kost, *Vice Pres*
Charles Hutson, *Administration*
EMP: 10
SALES (corp-wide): 19.9B **Publicly Held**
SIC: 6021 National commercial banks
PA: The Pnc Financial Services Group Inc
  300 5th Ave
  Pittsburgh PA 15222
  888 762-2265

(G-12176)
PNC NATIONAL BANK OF DELAWARE (DH)
300 Bellevue Pkwy Ste 200 (19809-3704)
PHONE.................................302 479-4529
James Gorman, *President*
Karen Blair, *Senior VP*
Chaonei Chan, *Senior VP*
David Tomlinson, *Senior VP*
Don Catsadimas, *Vice Pres*
EMP: 90
SALES: 157.5MM
SALES (corp-wide): 19.9B **Publicly Held**
WEB: www.pncbank.com
SIC: 6022 State commercial banks
HQ: Pnc Bank, National Association
  222 Delaware Ave
  Wilmington DE 19801
  877 762-2000

(G-12177)
POINT EGHT THIRD PRDCTIONS LLC (PA)
913 N Market St Ste 200 (19801-3097)
PHONE.................................302 317-9419
Paul Bogan,
Gary Bogan,
EMP: 6
SQ FT: 600
SALES: 100K **Privately Held**
SIC: 7812 Video production

(G-12178)
POINTE SNAPS
1000 Marsh Rd (19803-4340)
PHONE.................................260 602-0898
EMP: 2
SALES (est): 85K **Privately Held**
SIC: 2211 Shoe fabrics

(G-12179)
POINTLOOK CORPORATION
717 N Union St (19805-3031)
PHONE.................................415 448-6002
Haley Jones, *Treasurer*
EMP: 8
SALES (corp-wide): 90K **Privately Held**
SIC: 7374 7371 Data processing & preparation; computer software development & applications
PA: Pointlook Corporation
  280 Lee Ave
  San Francisco CA 94112
  415 598-8551

(G-12180)
POLAR MECHANICAL INC
330 Water St (19804-2433)
PHONE.................................302 994-9566
EMP: 30

SQ FT: 10,000
SALES: 5.5MM **Privately Held**
SIC: 8711 Mechanical Services

(G-12181)
POLICE ATHC LEAG WLMINGTON INC
3707 N Market St (19802-2213)
PHONE.................................302 764-6170
Wilbert Miller, *Exec Dir*
EMP: 8 **EST:** 1998
SALES: 1.1MM **Privately Held**
SIC: 8641 Recreation association

(G-12182)
POLISH AMERICAN CIVIC ASSN
618 S Franklin St (19805-4302)
PHONE.................................302 652-9324
Joseph Kaminski, *President*
Bob Wilson, *Owner*
EMP: 4
SALES (est): 94.2K **Privately Held**
SIC: 7997 Membership sports & recreation clubs

(G-12183)
POLISH LIBRARY ASSOCIATION
433 S Van Buren St (19805-4065)
PHONE.................................302 652-9555
Tom Olexsky, *President*
John Bartkowski, *Treasurer*
John Lafferty, *Director*
Walter Przybylek, *Admin Sec*
EMP: 5
SALES (est): 133.8K **Privately Held**
SIC: 8641 Bars & restaurants, members only

(G-12184)
POLYDEL CORPORATION
820 N Buttonwood St (19801-4328)
P.O. Box 7234 (19803-0234)
PHONE.................................302 655-8200
Claude Beaudoin, *President*
Gregory Beaudoin, *Vice Pres*
▲ **EMP:** 16
SQ FT: 24,000
SALES (est): 2.2MM **Privately Held**
SIC: 2899 Chemical preparations

(G-12185)
POLYMORPHIC SOFTWARE INC (PA)
Also Called: Mindqube
1521 Concord Pike Ste 301 (19803-3644)
PHONE.................................786 612-0257
Jaime Mena, *CEO*
Carlo Mazini, *President*
EMP: 4
SALES (est): 151.2K **Privately Held**
SIC: 7371 Computer software development

(G-12186)
POPPITI SIGNS INC
Also Called: Anthony J Poppiti Signs
2513 Dean Dr (19808-3313)
PHONE.................................302 999-8003
Kevin Poppiti, *President*
EMP: 2
SALES (est): 102.5K **Privately Held**
WEB: www.poppiti.net
SIC: 3993 Signs, not made in custom sign painting shops

(G-12187)
POPPYCOCK TATTOO
800 N Orange St (19801-1710)
PHONE.................................302 543-7973
Tina Maridito, *Owner*
EMP: 4 **EST:** 2009
SALES (est): 124K **Privately Held**
SIC: 7299 Tattoo parlor

(G-12188)
PORTRAIT INNOVATIONS INC
5601 Concord Pike Ste D (19803-6421)
PHONE.................................302 477-1696
EMP: 8 **Privately Held**
SIC: 7221 Photographer, still or video
HQ: Portrait Innovations, Inc.
  2016 Ayrsley Town Blvd # 200
  Charlotte NC 28273
  704 499-9300

GEOGRAPHIC SECTION
Wilmington - New Castle County (G-12221)

(G-12189)
POSH SALON
1017 N Lincoln St (19805-2741)
PHONE..................302 655-7000
Michelle Ziegler, *Partner*
Christa Rich, *Principal*
EMP: 12
SALES (est): 293K **Privately Held**
SIC: 7231 Cosmetology & personal hygiene salons

(G-12190)
POSIDON ADVENTURE INC
3301 Lancaster Pike 5a (19805-1436)
PHONE..................302 543-5024
Scott Jenkins, *President*
Sandra Jenkins, *Vice Pres*
EMP: 10
SALES (est): 959.2K **Privately Held**
SIC: 5091 7999 4725 Diving equipment & supplies; diving instruction, underwater; tours, conducted

(G-12191)
POSITIONEERING LLC
19c Trolley Sq (19806-3355)
PHONE..................302 415-3200
Antony Leary,
EMP: 5
SALES (est): 186.8K **Privately Held**
SIC: 8742 7389 Business consultant;

(G-12192)
POSITIVE RESULTS CLEANING INC
338 B And O Ln (19804-1448)
PHONE..................302 575-1146
Daniel Rodriguez, *Owner*
EMP: 7
SALES (est): 381.9K **Privately Held**
SIC: 7217 Carpet & upholstery cleaning

(G-12193)
POSTAL ASSOCIATES INC
110 Hoiland Dr (19803-3228)
PHONE..................302 584-1244
Anthony E Simone, *Principal*
EMP: 4
SALES (est): 266.1K **Privately Held**
SIC: 8742 Management consulting services

(G-12194)
POSTIMPRESSIONS INCORPORATED
1400 Maryland Ave (19805-4700)
PHONE..................302 656-2271
John P Grabowski, *President*
Pam Grabowski, *Vice Pres*
EMP: 5
SQ FT: 10,000
SALES (est): 417.6K **Privately Held**
SIC: 2741 Miscellaneous publishing

(G-12195)
POTTER ANDERSON & CORROON LLP
1313 N Market St Fl 6 (19801-6108)
P.O. Box 951 (19899-0951)
PHONE..................302 984-6000
Donald J Wolfe Jr, *Managing Prtnr*
EMP: 176
SQ FT: 7,500
SALES (est): 18.6MM **Privately Held**
WEB: www.potteranderson.com
SIC: 8111 General practice attorney, lawyer

(G-12196)
POWER FINANCIAL GROUP INC
Also Called: Power Options
494 First State Blvd (19804-3745)
P.O. Box 1461, Hockessin (19707-5461)
PHONE..................302 992-7971
Ernest Zerenner, *President*
Greg Zerenner, *Vice Pres*
Rose Marie Zerenner, *Admin Sec*
Rose Zerenner, *Admin Sec*
Mike Chupka, *Education*
EMP: 4 EST: 1997
SALES: 1.2MM **Privately Held**
WEB: www.poweropt.com
SIC: 7389 Financial services

(G-12197)
PRATCHER KRAYER LLC
1000 N West St Fl 10 (19801-1059)
P.O. Box 591 (19899-0591)
PHONE..................302 803-5291
Samuel Pratcher, *Vice Pres*
Samuel D Pratcher III,
Nicholas Krayer,
EMP: 6 EST: 2017
SALES (est): 158.4K **Privately Held**
SIC: 8111 Specialized law offices, attorneys

(G-12198)
PRAXAIR DISTRIBUTION INC
2 Medori Blvd (19801-5781)
PHONE..................302 654-8755
David Stroble, *Principal*
EMP: 8 **Privately Held**
SIC: 5084 Welding machinery & equipment
HQ: Praxair Distribution, Inc.
10 Riverview Dr
Danbury CT 06810
203 837-2000

(G-12199)
PRECIOUS LITTLE HANDS CHILDCAR
702b Kirkwood Hwy (19805-5111)
PHONE..................302 298-5027
Tazeema Bourne, *Principal*
Derrick Loatman, *Principal*
EMP: 8
SQ FT: 3,000
SALES (est): 68.3K **Privately Held**
SIC: 8351 Child day care services

(G-12200)
PRECIOUS NAILS
2607 Kirkwood Hwy (19805-4909)
PHONE..................302 292-1690
Anh Nguyen, *Owner*
EMP: 4
SALES (est): 28.8K **Privately Held**
SIC: 7231 Manicurist, pedicurist

(G-12201)
PRECISION CARE & WELLNESS LLC
Also Called: Wilmington 1st Walk-In
4001 Miller Rd Ste 1 (19802-1961)
PHONE..................302 407-5222
Mbwidiffu Dibal, *Principal*
Taylor Burge, *Principal*
EMP: 7
SALES (est): 105.5K **Privately Held**
SIC: 8099 Health & allied services

(G-12202)
PRECISION COLOR GRAPHICS LLC
1401 Todds Ln (19802-2417)
PHONE..................302 661-2595
Simon Cranny,
EMP: 6
SALES (est): 213.1K **Privately Held**
SIC: 7336 Graphic arts & related design

(G-12203)
PRECISION DENTAL LABORATORY
1403 Foulk Rd Ste 107 (19803-2788)
PHONE..................302 478-5608
Debra Zerbe, *President*
EMP: 4
SALES (est): 382.5K **Privately Held**
WEB: www.precision-dental.com
SIC: 8072 Crown & bridge production

(G-12204)
PRECISION DOOR SERVICE
330 Water St Ste 109 (19804-2789)
PHONE..................302 343-6394
Dean Wilkinson, *President*
Michelle Overway, *Office Mgr*
EMP: 4
SALES (est): 311.2K **Privately Held**
SIC: 7699 5211 Garage door repair; garage doors, sale & installation

(G-12205)
PRECISION DRYWALL INC
Also Called: Precision Drywall Construction
2711 Centerville Rd # 400 (19808-1645)
PHONE..................415 550-8880
Nehemiah Brown Jr, *President*
EMP: 39
SALES (est): 1.3MM **Privately Held**
SIC: 1742 Acoustical & ceiling work

(G-12206)
PRECISION POLYOLEFINS LLC
2711 Centerville Rd # 400 (19808-1660)
PHONE..................301 588-3709
Lawrence Sita,
EMP: 1
SALES (est): 63.1K **Privately Held**
SIC: 2821 Plastics materials & resins

(G-12207)
PRECISION SYSTEMS INDS LLC
2711 Centerville Rd # 400 (19808-1660)
PHONE..................224 388-9837
George Hines, *Partner*
EMP: 5
SALES: 5K **Privately Held**
SIC: 3699 Electrical equipment & supplies

(G-12208)
PRECISIONCURE LLC
2207 Concord Pike 301 (19803-2908)
PHONE..................302 622-9119
Jeff Thommes,
EMP: 8
SALES (est): 331.4K **Privately Held**
SIC: 7371 Computer software development & applications

(G-12209)
PRECISIONISTS INC
Also Called: Tpi
1 Righter Pkwy Ste 150 (19803-1510)
PHONE..................610 241-5354
Ernest Dianastasis, *CEO*
Kendal Reynolds, *Director*
EMP: 4
SQ FT: 3,600
SALES (est): 105.9K **Privately Held**
SIC: 7379 8742 Computer related consulting services; management consulting services

(G-12210)
PREFERED TAX SERVICE INC
Also Called: Preferred Business Services
2201 N Market St Ste A (19802-4227)
PHONE..................302 654-4388
Ann Swan, *President*
Eddie Swan, *Vice Pres*
EMP: 6
SALES (est): 340K **Privately Held**
WEB: www.preferredtax.com
SIC: 7291 Tax return preparation services

(G-12211)
PREFERRED CONTRACTORS INC
204 S Park Dr (19809-1362)
PHONE..................302 798-5457
Michael Feil, *President*
Robin Feil, *Treasurer*
EMP: 7
SQ FT: 200
SALES (est): 398.4K **Privately Held**
WEB: www.preferredcontractors.com
SIC: 1521 Single-family home remodeling, additions & repairs

(G-12212)
PREFERRED FIRE PROTECTION
4321 Miller Rd (19802-1901)
PHONE..................302 256-0607
Earl Hood, *Principal*
EMP: 10
SALES (est): 1.5MM **Privately Held**
SIC: 1711 Fire sprinkler system installation

(G-12213)
PREFFERED MECHANICAL SERVICES
330 Water St Ste 107 (19804-2433)
PHONE..................302 993-1122
EMP: 7 EST: 1999

SALES (est): 620K **Privately Held**
SIC: 1711 Heating And Air-Conditioning Contractor

(G-12214)
PRELUDE THERAPEUTICS INC
200 Powder Mill Rd (19803-2907)
PHONE..................302 644-5427
Victoria Tait, *Principal*
EMP: 20
SALES (est): 82.6K **Privately Held**
SIC: 8049 Physical therapist

(G-12215)
PREMIER BUILDERS INC
2601 Annand Dr Ste 21 (19808-3719)
PHONE..................302 999-8500
Ken Ralsten, *President*
EMP: 5
SALES (est): 774K **Privately Held**
WEB: www.premierbuilders-inc.com
SIC: 1542 Commercial & office building, new construction

(G-12216)
PREMIER NAT LN & LSG GROUP LLC
504 N Broom St (19805-3115)
PHONE..................302 295-2194
EMP: 50 EST: 2017
SALES (est): 641.1K **Privately Held**
SIC: 7389 Business Services

(G-12217)
PREMIER SALONS INTL INC
Also Called: Premier Salon 22920
4737 Concord Pike (19803-1442)
PHONE..................302 477-3459
Michelle Mc Culley, *Manager*
EMP: 7
SALES (corp-wide): 161.4MM **Privately Held**
WEB: www.premiersalons.com
SIC: 7231 Beauty shops
HQ: Premier Salons International, Inc.
8341 10th Ave N
Minneapolis MN 55427

(G-12218)
PREMIER SOLUTIONS INTL
Also Called: Premier Salon
4737 Concord Pike Ste 100 (19803-1476)
PHONE..................302 477-1334
Tim Plighton, *Owner*
EMP: 6
SALES (corp-wide): 161.4MM **Privately Held**
WEB: www.premiermeeting.com
SIC: 7231 Unisex hair salons
HQ: Beauty Express Canada Inc
170 Duffield Dr Suite 200
Markham ON L6G 1
905 258-0684

(G-12219)
PREMIERE ORAL AND FACIAL SURG
1202 Foulk Rd (19803-2796)
PHONE..................302 273-8300
EMP: 5 EST: 2016
SALES (est): 149.9K **Privately Held**
SIC: 8011 Surgeon

(G-12220)
PRENTICE-HALL CORP SYSTEM INC (PA)
Also Called: Prentice Hall Legal Fincl Svcs
2711 Centerville Rd # 120 (19808-1676)
PHONE..................302 636-5440
Daniel R Butler, *President*
Bruce R Winn, *President*
William H Freeborn Jr, *Vice Pres*
William Freeborn, *Vice Pres*
Mark A Rosser, *Vice Pres*
EMP: 10
SALES (est): 6.3MM **Privately Held**
WEB: www.rdgcocab.com
SIC: 8111 Legal services

(G-12221)
PRESCRIPTION CENTER INC
Also Called: Richard Margolin Apothecary
4616 Sylvans Dr (19803-4814)
PHONE..................302 764-8564
Richard H Margolin, *President*

Wilmington - New Castle County (G-12222)   GEOGRAPHIC SECTION

Marcia A Margolin, *Admin Sec*
EMP: 4
SQ FT: 1,000
SALES (est): 710K **Privately Held**
SIC: 5912 5047 Drug stores; medical equipment & supplies

(G-12222)
PRESSAIR INTERNATIONAL
3501 Silverside Rd (19810-4910)
PHONE..................................302 636-5440
Karl-Heinz Trondle, *Principal*
EMP: 2
SALES (est): 114.2K **Privately Held**
SIC: 3714 Motor vehicle parts & accessories

(G-12223)
PRESTIGE CONTRACTORS INC
2615 N Tatnall St (19802-3525)
P.O. Box 14 (19899-0014)
PHONE..................................302 722-1032
Zachary Jackson, *CEO*
EMP: 6
SALES (est): 641K **Privately Held**
SIC: 1542 1522 Nonresidential construction; residential construction

(G-12224)
PRICE IS RIGHT CONTRACTING LLC
919 N Market St Ste 950 (19801-3036)
PHONE..................................215 760-1416
James Price,
EMP: 10
SALES (est): 317K **Privately Held**
SIC: 5082 Contractors' materials

(G-12225)
PRIDE KLEAN INC
Also Called: Pride Klean Service
301 S Maryland Ave Apt 2 (19804-1360)
PHONE..................................302 994-8500
Peter Chakonas, *CEO*
Daniel Cult, *COO*
EMP: 32
SALES (est): 800K **Privately Held**
SIC: 7349 Janitorial service, contract basis

(G-12226)
PRIME PRODUCTS USA INC
15 Germay Dr Ste 100 (19804-1138)
PHONE..................................302 528-3866
Stewart Modell, *President*
▲ EMP: 9
SALES (est): 76K **Privately Held**
SIC: 2911 Oils, fuel

(G-12227)
PRIMETIME LIMOUSINE
1812 Marsh Rd Ste 6 (19810-4533)
PHONE..................................302 425-5599
William Maher, *Owner*
EMP: 10
SALES (est): 204.4K **Privately Held**
WEB: www.primetimelimos.com
SIC: 4119 Limousine rental, with driver

(G-12228)
PRINCIPAL FINANCIAL GROUP INC
1013 Centre Rd Ste 100 (19805-1265)
PHONE..................................302 993-8045
Barry Griswell, *CEO*
EMP: 74 **Publicly Held**
SIC: 6311 Life insurance
PA: Principal Financial Group, Inc.
711 High St
Des Moines IA 50392

(G-12229)
PRINT-N-PRESS INC
300 Cassidy Dr Ste 301 (19804-2442)
PHONE..................................302 994-6665
Thomas Mc Cartney, *President*
EMP: 7
SQ FT: 2,700
SALES (est): 976.2K **Privately Held**
SIC: 2752 Commercial printing, offset

(G-12230)
PRINTIFY LLC (PA)
108 W 13th St (19801)
PHONE..................................415 968-6351
EMP: 6 EST: 2018

SALES (est): 1.9MM **Privately Held**
SIC: 8742 Business consultant

(G-12231)
PRIORITY PLUS FEDERAL CR UN
6 Lynam St (19804-3135)
PHONE..................................302 633-6480
Susan Winward, *President*
Annette Garofalo, *VP Opers*
EMP: 4
SALES: 654.6K **Privately Held**
SIC: 6061 Federal credit unions

(G-12232)
PRIVATE DUTY HOME CARE
109 Clyde St (19804-2803)
PHONE..................................302 482-3502
EMP: 4
SALES (est): 51.5K **Privately Held**
SIC: 8082 Home Health Care Services

(G-12233)
PRO PEST MANAGEMENT OF DE INC
200 Cassidy Dr Ste 201 (19804-2441)
PHONE..................................302 994-2847
Jack Vickers, *Principal*
EMP: 14
SALES (est): 1.4MM **Privately Held**
SIC: 8741 Business management

(G-12234)
PRO PHYSL THERAPY FTNS ACCT
Also Called: Pro Physical Therapy
1812 Marsh Rd Ste 505 (19810-4515)
PHONE..................................302 658-7800
Franklin Rooks, *Owner*
EMP: 16
SALES (est): 389.7K **Privately Held**
WEB: www.propt.com
SIC: 8049 Physical therapist

(G-12235)
PRO REHAB CHIROPRACTORS
215 Peirce Rd (19803-3729)
PHONE..................................302 652-2225
EMP: 7
SALES (est): 82.1K **Privately Held**
SIC: 8041 Offices & clinics of chiropractors

(G-12236)
PRO-TECH ENGINEERING INC
1200 First State Blvd (19804-3561)
P.O. Box 673, Delaware City (19706-0673)
PHONE..................................302 998-1717
James W McCaa Sr, *President*
Paul Roath, *Vice Pres*
EMP: 25 EST: 1996
SQ FT: 1,200
SALES (est): 1.7MM **Privately Held**
SIC: 8711 Consulting engineer

(G-12237)
PROCACCIANTI GROUP LLC
Also Called: Sheraton Suites Wilmington
422 Delaware Ave (19801-1508)
PHONE..................................401 946-4600
Elizabeth Procaccianti,
EMP: 28
SALES (corp-wide): 31.7MM **Privately Held**
SIC: 8741 Hotel or motel management
PA: The Procaccianti Group Llc
1140 Reservoir Ave
Cranston RI 02920
401 946-4600

(G-12238)
PROCESS ACADEMY LLC
4023 Kennett Pike (19807-2018)
PHONE..................................302 415-3104
Robert Costa,
EMP: 3
SALES (est): 75.2K **Privately Held**
SIC: 7372 8243 7389 Business oriented computer software; educational computer software; operator training, computer; software training, computer;

(G-12239)
PROFESSIONAL RECRUITING CONS
Also Called: PRC
3617a Silverside Rd (19810)
PHONE..................................302 479-9550
Roger Malatesta, *President*
EMP: 5
SQ FT: 1,200
SALES: 500K **Privately Held**
WEB: www.prcstaffing.com
SIC: 7361 Executive placement

(G-12240)
PROFESSIONALS LLC
1000 N West St Ste 1283 (19801-1050)
PHONE..................................302 295-2330
Shoban Pattam, *President*
Hari Pattam, *Officer*
EMP: 6 EST: 2005
SALES (est): 247K **Privately Held**
SIC: 7371 Computer software systems analysis & design, custom

(G-12241)
PROGRESSIVE DENTAL ARTS
5301 Limestone Rd Ste 212 (19808-1265)
PHONE..................................302 234-2222
EMP: 4
SALES (est): 99K **Privately Held**
SIC: 8021 Dentists' office

(G-12242)
PROGRESSIVE INVESTMENT CO INC
801 N West St Fl 2 (19801-1525)
PHONE..................................302 656-8597
S Patricia Griffith, *CEO*
Susan Patricia Griffith, *CEO*
EMP: 10
SQ FT: 75,000
SALES (corp-wide): 31.9B **Publicly Held**
SIC: 6719 Investment holding companies, except banks
PA: The Progressive Corporation
6300 Wilson Mills Rd
Mayfield Village OH 44143
440 461-5000

(G-12243)
PROGRESSIVE SERVICES INC
300 Commercial Dr (19805-1907)
PHONE..................................302 658-7260
Michael Hirst, *President*
EMP: 50
SQ FT: 7,000
SALES (est): 6.2MM **Privately Held**
SIC: 1731 Electrical work

(G-12244)
PROGRESSIVE SOFTWARE CMPT INC
1 Righter Pkwy Ste 280 (19803-1555)
PHONE..................................302 479-9700
Chris J O'Neill, *President*
Richard Lash, *CFO*
Jim Martin, *Technology*
EMP: 125
SQ FT: 8,000
SALES: 10MM **Privately Held**
WEB: www.psci.com
SIC: 7373 7371 Computer integrated systems design; custom computer programming services

(G-12245)
PROGRESSIVE TELECOM LLC
3422 Old Capitol Trl # 1483 (19808-6124)
PHONE..................................302 883-8883
Varun Anand, *CEO*
Amanjyot Singh, *COO*
Ryan Green, *Info Tech Mgr*
EMP: 25
SQ FT: 1,500
SALES: 62.8MM **Privately Held**
SIC: 4813 Voice telephone communications

(G-12246)
PROJECT ASSISTANTS INC
1521 Concord Pike Ste 301 (19803-3644)
PHONE..................................302 477-9711
Augustus Cicala, *CEO*
Lisa Houser, *Office Mgr*
EMP: 25

SQ FT: 6,000
SALES (est): 2MM **Privately Held**
WEB: www.projectassistants.com
SIC: 7371 Computer software development & applications

(G-12247)
PROJECT OF PROVIDENCE LLC
1007 Park Pl Apt A (19806-4304)
PHONE..................................302 438-8970
Tamara Williams, *Principal*
EMP: 5
SALES (est): 155.4K **Privately Held**
SIC: 8244 8742 Business college or school; marketing consulting services

(G-12248)
PROJECT OTR LLC
1209 N Orange St (19801-1120)
PHONE..................................404 964-2244
Vang Wong, *CEO*
EMP: 9
SALES (est): 198.2K **Privately Held**
SIC: 8742 Marketing consulting services

(G-12249)
PROJECT WIDGETS INC
501 Silverside Rd Ste 29 (19809-1388)
PHONE..................................302 439-3414
Ira Brown, *President*
Erica Truono, *Office Mgr*
EMP: 6
SALES: 1.4MM **Privately Held**
SIC: 8748 Business consulting

(G-12250)
PROMENTA LLC
3422 Old Capitol Trl (19808-6124)
PHONE..................................302 552-2922
Paul Feenan,
EMP: 1 EST: 2009
SALES (est): 35.8K **Privately Held**
SIC: 7372 Business oriented computer software

(G-12251)
PROMINENT INSURANCE SVCS INC
1201 N Orange St Ste 700 (19801-1186)
PHONE..................................302 351-3368
Jason Rodriguez, *CEO*
Montanez Reed, *President*
EMP: 5
SALES (est): 603.4K **Privately Held**
SIC: 6411 Insurance agents

(G-12252)
PROMOTORA SYSTEMS INC
1224 N King St (19801-3232)
PHONE..................................302 304-3147
Adrianne Phillips, *Principal*
EMP: 4 EST: 2011
SQ FT: 700
SALES (est): 384.1K **Privately Held**
SIC: 4725 Arrangement of travel tour packages, wholesale

(G-12253)
PRORANK BUSINESS SOLUTIONS LLC
1515 W 6th St (19805-3105)
PHONE..................................302 256-0642
Kyron Robinson, *Owner*
EMP: 6 EST: 2013
SALES (est): 238.9K **Privately Held**
SIC: 8741 Business management

(G-12254)
PROTECH SOLUTIONS GROUP LLC
1000 N West St Ste 1200 (19801-1058)
PHONE..................................844 744-2418
Luis Armando Contreras, *Principal*
EMP: 5
SALES: 5MM **Privately Held**
SIC: 7371 Computer software development & applications

(G-12255)
PROTECT AMERICA INC
234 N James St (19804-3132)
PHONE..................................302 999-9045
EMP: 4

GEOGRAPHIC SECTION   Wilmington - New Castle County (G-12287)

SALES (est): 229.1K **Privately Held**
SIC: 7382 Burglar alarm maintenance & monitoring
HQ: Protect America, Inc.
3800 Quick Hill Rd 1-100
Austin TX 78728

(G-12256)
PROTOCOL LABS INC
427 N Tatnall St 51207 (19801-2230)
PHONE..................................302 703-7194
Juan Batiz-Benet, *CEO*
Jesse Clayburgh, *Vice Pres*
EMP: 10
SALES (est): 89.9K **Privately Held**
SIC: 7371 Computer software development & applications

(G-12257)
PROVIDENCE HALL ASSOCIATES LP
Also Called: Providence Hall Apartments
4 Denny Rd (19809-3445)
PHONE..................................518 828-4700
William Demarco, *Vice Pres*
EMP: 36
SALES: 744.3K **Privately Held**
SIC: 6513 Apartment building operators

(G-12258)
PRUDENT ENDODONTICS
2036 Foulk Rd (19810-3648)
PHONE..................................302 475-3803
Rinku Parmar, *Principal*
EMP: 4 EST: 2013
SALES (est): 228.7K **Privately Held**
SIC: 8021 Endodontist

(G-12259)
PSI-TEC CORPORATION (PA)
Also Called: Physicchmcal Scences Inst Tech
2320 Lighthouse Ln (19810-2531)
PHONE..................................425 943-9493
Ron Genova, *CEO*
Frederick Goetz, *President*
Mary T Goetz, *Vice Pres*
EMP: 4
SQ FT: 2,000
SALES (est): 266.8K **Privately Held**
WEB: www.psiteccorp.com
SIC: 8999 Scientific consulting

(G-12260)
PSP CORP
203 Churchill Dr (19803-4203)
P.O. Box 608, New Castle (19720-0608)
PHONE..................................302 764-7730
Philip Penrose, *President*
Jay Penrose, *Vice Pres*
Fran Brousseau, *Treasurer*
Wayne Hawkins, *Manager*
Linda Chamblee, *Admin Sec*
EMP: 3
SALES (est): 336.9K **Privately Held**
WEB: www.psp.state.pa.us
SIC: 3317 3699 3229 Steel pipe & tubes; security devices; glass fiber products

(G-12261)
PSYCHOANALYTIC ELECTRONIC
1013 Centre Rd (19805-1265)
PHONE..................................949 495-3332
EMP: 1
SALES (est): 37.5K **Privately Held**
SIC: 2741 Miscellaneous publishing

(G-12262)
PSYCHOLOGICAL SERVICES
422 Woodstock Ln (19808-4413)
PHONE..................................302 489-0213
Maria Ana, *Principal*
EMP: 4
SALES (est): 71.8K **Privately Held**
SIC: 8049 Psychologist, psychotherapist & hypnotist

(G-12263)
PTA DELAWARE MILITARY ACADEMY
12 Middleboro Rd (19804)
PHONE..................................302 998-0745
Anthony Tullela, *Principal*
EMP: 40

SALES (est): 15.8K **Privately Held**
SIC: 8641 Parent-teachers' association

(G-12264)
PTA LOMBARDY ELEMENTARY
442 Foulk Rd (19803)
PHONE..................................302 478-6054
Howard Zucker, *Principal*
EMP: 6
SALES: 35K **Privately Held**
SIC: 8641 Parent-teachers' association

(G-12265)
PUBLIC ALLIES DELEWARE INC
100 W 10th St Ste 812 (19801-6605)
PHONE..................................302 573-4438
Pamela Leland, *President*
EMP: 4
SALES (est): 122.4K **Privately Held**
SIC: 8641 Youth organizations

(G-12266)
PUBLICATION PRINT
3846 Kennett Pike (19807-2302)
PHONE..................................302 992-2040
Morgan Sherry, *Principal*
EMP: 1 EST: 2012
SALES (est): 60.3K **Privately Held**
SIC: 2741 Miscellaneous publishing

(G-12267)
PULMONARY & SLEEP CONS LLC
4512 Kirkwood Hwy (19808-5123)
PHONE..................................302 994-4060
EMP: 5 EST: 2009
SALES (est): 347.5K **Privately Held**
SIC: 8031 8011 Offices & clinics of osteopathic physicians; pulmonary specialist, physician/surgeon

(G-12268)
PULMONARY ASSOCIATES PA (PA)
7 S Clayton St 500 (19805-3948)
PHONE..................................302 656-2213
Joseph F Kestner Jr, *President*
EMP: 7
SALES (est): 703.7K **Privately Held**
SIC: 8011 Pulmonary specialist, physician/surgeon

(G-12269)
PUMP AND CORROSION TECH INC
310 Cornell Dr Ste B5 (19801-5769)
P.O. Box 9555 (19809-0555)
PHONE..................................302 655-3490
Dan Scott, *President*
Greg Conroy, *President*
Pete Longmire, *President*
Gary Gooden, *Vice Pres*
EMP: 4
SQ FT: 8,000
SALES (est): 1.4MM **Privately Held**
WEB: www.pumpandcorrosion.com
SIC: 5084 Pumps & pumping equipment

(G-12270)
PURE AIR HOLDINGS CORP (HQ)
1105 N Market St Ste 1300 (19801-1241)
PHONE..................................302 655-7130
Jessica Holliday, *President*
Jessica J Holliday, *President*
EMP: 5
SALES (est): 1.8MM
SALES (corp-wide): 8.9B **Publicly Held**
SIC: 2813 Industrial gases
PA: Air Products And Chemicals, Inc.
7201 Hamilton Blvd
Allentown PA 18195
610 481-4911

(G-12271)
PURE WELLNESS LLC
1010 N Bancroft Pkwy (19805-2690)
PHONE..................................302 543-5679
Holly J Corbett, *Branch Mgr*
EMP: 6
SALES (corp-wide): 1.9MM **Privately Held**
SIC: 8041 Offices & clinics of chiropractors

PA: Pure Wellness, Llc
550 Stanton Christiana Rd # 302
Newark DE 19713
302 365-5470

(G-12272)
PUZZLES OF LIFE
831 N Market St (19801-4931)
PHONE..................................302 339-0327
Francis Brantley, *CEO*
EMP: 5
SALES (est): 170K **Privately Held**
SIC: 8322 Rehabilitation services

(G-12273)
Q VANDENBERG & SONS INC
Also Called: Totalgreen Holland
3422 Old Capitol Trl (19808-6124)
PHONE..................................800 242-2852
Q Vandenberg, *President*
Edwin Van Aarle, *Manager*
▲ EMP: 20
SALES: 4.5MM
SALES (corp-wide): 484.2K **Privately Held**
SIC: 5191 Garden supplies
HQ: Q. Van Den Berg En Zonen N.V.
Bennebroekerdijk 150
Zwaanshoek 2136
235 484-848

(G-12274)
QBR TELECOM INC
913 N Market St Ste 200 (19801-3097)
PHONE..................................302 510-1155
EMP: 10 EST: 2016
SALES (est): 20.7K **Privately Held**
SIC: 8999 Communication services

(G-12275)
QMOBI INC
919 N Market St Ste 425 (19801-3014)
PHONE..................................800 246-2677
Dmitry Radchenko, *Director*
EMP: 40
SALES (est): 647.7K **Privately Held**
SIC: 7371 Computer software development & applications

(G-12276)
QSR GROUP LLC
913 N Market St Ste 200 (19801-3097)
PHONE..................................302 268-6909
Jamil Ahmed Quazi, *CEO*
EMP: 5 EST: 2014
SQ FT: 900
SALES: 96.1K **Privately Held**
SIC: 7371 4813 8748 Computer software development & applications; telephone communication, except radio; telecommunications consultant

(G-12277)
QUALITY ASSURED INC
Also Called: ServiceMaster
223 Valley Rd (19804-1356)
P.O. Box 3309 (19804-4309)
PHONE..................................302 652-4151
John N De Loretto, *President*
EMP: 20
SQ FT: 7,200
SALES: 1.1MM **Privately Held**
SIC: 7349 Building maintenance services

(G-12278)
QUALITY AUTO CARE CENTERS
Also Called: Quality Automotive
4325 Kirkwood Hwy (19808-5113)
P.O. Box 452, Westtown PA (19395-0452)
PHONE..................................302 992-7978
Denny Greenfield, *President*
Lynn Greenfield, *Vice Pres*
EMP: 9
SALES (est): 590K **Privately Held**
SIC: 7549 7539 Lubrication service, automotive; brake repair, automotive

(G-12279)
QUALITY DISTRIBUTORS INC
244 Steeplechase Cir (19808-1977)
PHONE..................................917 335-6662
Sahir Saiyad, *President*
EMP: 5
SALES (est): 652.4K **Privately Held**
SIC: 5065 7389 Sound equipment, electronic; video equipment, electronic;

(G-12280)
QUALITY HTG AR-CNDITIONING INC
Also Called: QH&a
31 Brookside Dr (19804-1101)
PHONE..................................302 654-5247
Horace A Wahl Jr, *President*
Horace A Wahl III, *Senior VP*
Janice Wahl, *Admin Sec*
EMP: 66
SQ FT: 13,040
SALES (est): 18MM **Privately Held**
SIC: 1711 3444 1761 Warm air heating & air conditioning contractor; sheet metalwork; roofing, siding & sheet metal work

(G-12281)
QUALITY III FIRE PROTECTION
1607 Todds Ln (19802-2421)
P.O. Box 9667 (19809-0667)
PHONE..................................302 762-8262
Michael Woodie, *President*
Grishka Woodie, *Vice Pres*
EMP: 7
SALES (est): 741.4K **Privately Held**
SIC: 7389 Fire protection service other than forestry or public

(G-12282)
QUANTUS INNOVATIONS LLC
136 Fairhill Dr (19808-4309)
PHONE..................................302 356-1661
Parayali Jayesh,
Reena Jayesh,
EMP: 2
SALES (est): 177.3K **Privately Held**
SIC: 7372 Business oriented computer software

(G-12283)
QUARTA-RAD INC
1201 N Orange St Ste 7234 (19801-1233)
PHONE..................................201 877-2002
Victor Shvetsky, *President*
EMP: 2 EST: 2012
SALES (est): 648K **Privately Held**
SIC: 3829 3674 Count rate meters, nuclear radiation; fire detector systems, nonelectric; gas detectors; scintillation detectors; nuclear detectors, solid state

(G-12284)
QUAVO INC
1201 N Orange St Ste 7115 (19801-1194)
PHONE..................................484 802-4693
Richard Jefferson, *CEO*
David Chmielewski, *Co-Owner*
Kevin Mayes, *Co-Owner*
Joseph McLean, *Co-Owner*
Daniel Penne, *Co-Owner*
EMP: 21
SALES (est): 354.7K **Privately Held**
SIC: 7371 Computer software development & applications

(G-12285)
QUBOAI CORPORATION
3524 Silverside Rd (19810-4929)
PHONE..................................484 889-5789
Konstantin Perederiy, *CEO*
EMP: 2
SALES (est): 104.2K **Privately Held**
SIC: 3823 Digital displays of process variables

(G-12286)
QUEST DIAGNOSTICS INCORPORATED
2700 Slverstone Rd Ste 1b (19810)
PHONE..................................302 478-1100
Annmarie Carlozzi, *Manager*
EMP: 4
SALES (corp-wide): 7.5B **Publicly Held**
WEB: www.questdiagnostics.com
SIC: 8071 Medical laboratories
PA: Quest Diagnostics Incorporated
500 Plaza Dr Ste G
Secaucus NJ 07094
973 520-2700

(G-12287)
QUEST DIAGNOSTICS INCORPORATED
1941 Limestone Rd Ste 108 (19808-5424)
PHONE..................................302 239-5273

Wilmington - New Castle County (G-12288)   GEOGRAPHIC SECTION

Clifton Hunt, *Owner*
EMP: 17
SALES (corp-wide): 7.5B **Publicly Held**
WEB: www.questdiagnostics.com
SIC: 8071 Testing laboratories
PA: Quest Diagnostics Incorporated
500 Plaza Dr Ste G
Secaucus NJ 07094
973 520-2700

(G-12288)
QUICKBORN CONSULTING LLC (PA)
501 Silverside Rd Ste 105 (19809-1376)
PHONE 302 407-0922
Mr Gbor Tozsr, *CEO*
EMP: 5
SALES (est): 559.5K **Privately Held**
SIC: 7379

(G-12289)
QUINN DATA CORPORATION
922 New Rd Ste 1 (19805-5199)
PHONE 302 429-7450
Michael Quinn, *President*
Catherine Hazzard, *Vice Pres*
EMP: 6
SQ FT: 1,500
SALES (est): 828.3K **Privately Held**
WEB: www.quinndata.com
SIC: 5734 5045 Personal computers; computer peripheral equipment; computers; computer peripheral equipment

(G-12290)
QUINN-MILLER GROUP INC
34 Germay Dr (19804-1105)
PHONE 302 738-9742
Robert Quinn, *President*
Sue Ann Strickland, *Manager*
Nancy Quinn, *Director*
EMP: 4
SALES (est): 682.6K **Privately Held**
SIC: 7352 5047 5999 8399 Medical equipment rental; medical equipment & supplies; medical apparatus & supplies; health systems agency

(G-12291)
QUIP LABORATORIES INCORPORATED
1500 Eastlawn Ave (19802-2403)
PHONE 302 761-2600
Tim Hidell, *President*
Patty Kanzer, *Finance*
Kyle Debruhl, *Marketing Staff*
Tim McHugh, *Manager*
Donna Monroe, *Director*
EMP: 30 **EST:** 1981
SQ FT: 30,000
SALES (est): 8.8MM **Privately Held**
WEB: www.quiplabs.com
SIC: 2842 Cleaning or polishing preparations

(G-12292)
R & W TRANSPORTATION CORP
201 N Walnut St (19801-2920)
PHONE 703 670-5483
Brown Rebecca J, *President*
James M West, *President*
EMP: 9
SALES (est): 387.7K **Privately Held**
SIC: 4212 Local trucking, without storage

(G-12293)
R C FABRICATORS INC
824 N Locust St (19801-4352)
PHONE 302 573-8989
Rebecca Suppe, *CEO*
Danny Reatter, *President*
Robert C Suppe, *Vice Pres*
Marc Klair, *Safety Dir*
Jason Suppe, *Project Mgr*
EMP: 89 **EST:** 1981
SQ FT: 50,000
SALES (est): 30.4MM **Privately Held**
WEB: www.rcfabricators.com
SIC: 3441 1791 1799 7692 Fabricated structural metal; structural steel erection; welding on site; welding repair

(G-12294)
R E WILLIAMS PROF ACCTG FRM TAX
3628 Silverside Rd (19810-5190)
P.O. Box 7448 (19803-0448)
PHONE 302 598-7171
Ronnie E Williams, *Principal*
EMP: 5
SALES (est): 107.4K **Privately Held**
SIC: 7291 Tax return preparation services

(G-12295)
R G ALTSCHULER MD
Also Called: Bancroft Internal Medicine
1806 N Van Buren St # 200 (19802-3851)
PHONE 302 652-3771
Robert G Altschuler, *Owner*
Eric Underhill MD, *Co-Owner*
EMP: 4
SALES (est): 364.6K **Privately Held**
SIC: 8011 Internal medicine, physician/surgeon

(G-12296)
R H D BRANDYWINE HILLS
710 W Matson Run Pkwy (19802-1912)
PHONE 302 764-3660
Cynthia Guy, *Manager*
EMP: 20
SALES (est): 412.7K **Privately Held**
SIC: 8093 Mental health clinic, outpatient

(G-12297)
R R ROOFING INC 2
4807 Lancaster Pike (19807-2515)
P.O. Box 1597, Hockessin (19707-5597)
PHONE 302 218-7474
Jon Kelcy, *Principal*
EMP: 8
SALES (est): 649.8K **Privately Held**
SIC: 1761 Roof repair; roofing contractor

(G-12298)
R STOKES NOLTE ESQUIRE &
Also Called: Nolte & Associates
1010 N Bancroft Pkwy # 21 (19805-2690)
PHONE 302 777-1700
Stokes Nolte, *Owner*
EMP: 4
SALES (est): 289K **Privately Held**
SIC: 8111 General practice law office

(G-12299)
R&R HOMECARE
100 Beauregard Ct (19810-1181)
PHONE 302 478-3448
Robbert Rebman, *Principal*
EMP: 4 **EST:** 2011
SALES (est): 77.8K **Privately Held**
SIC: 8082 Home health care services

(G-12300)
RAAFAT Z ABDEL-MISIH MD
1021 Gilpin Ave Ste 203 (19806-3272)
PHONE 302 658-7533
Raafat Z Abdel-Misih, *Owner*
EMP: 8
SALES (est): 305.4K **Privately Held**
SIC: 8011 Surgeon

(G-12301)
RADIOCUT INC
251 Little Falls Dr (19808-1674)
PHONE 302 613-1280
Guillermo Mario Narvaja, *CEO*
EMP: 9
SALES: 80K **Privately Held**
SIC: 7371 Computer software development & applications

(G-12302)
RADIOLOGY ASSOCIATES INC (PA)
1701 Augustine Cut Off # 100 (19803-4425)
PHONE 302 832-5590
Magid Mansoory MD, *President*
Thomas Fiss MD, *Vice Pres*
Garth Koniver MD, *Treasurer*
EMP: 50
SQ FT: 3,000
SALES (est): 4.6MM **Privately Held**
SIC: 8011 Radiologist

(G-12303)
RADIUS RX DIRECT INC
501 N Shipley St Unit 2 (19801-2226)
P.O. Box 1159 (19899-1159)
PHONE 302 658-9196
Christy Crkvenac, *President*
Todd Crkvenac, *Vice Pres*
EMP: 9
SALES (est): 2.3MM **Privately Held**
SIC: 5122 Pharmaceuticals

(G-12304)
RADIUS SERVICES LLC (PA)
16 Hadco Rd (19804-1014)
PHONE 302 993-0600
Walter E Telford,
Ben Biggs,
EMP: 57
SQ FT: 30,000
SALES (est): 3.6MM **Privately Held**
SIC: 1711 Fire sprinkler system installation; heating & air conditioning contractors

(G-12305)
RAFI SOOFI MD
1941 Limestone Rd Ste 216 (19808-5400)
PHONE 302 999-1644
Fax: 302 999-1686
EMP: 4
SALES (est): 258.1K **Privately Held**
SIC: 8011 Medical Doctor's Office

(G-12306)
RAHAIM & SAINTS ATTYS AT LAW (PA)
2055 Limestone Rd Ste 211 (19808-5536)
PHONE 302 892-9200
Andrew D Rahaim, *Partner*
Sheldon Saints, *Partner*
Mayo Jennefer,
EMP: 15
SALES (est): 2.1MM **Privately Held**
WEB: www.rahaimsaints.com
SIC: 8111 General practice attorney, lawyer

(G-12307)
RAINMAKER SOFTWARE GROUP LLC
1925 Lovering Ave (19806-2157)
PHONE 800 616-6701
Ricardo Garcia,
EMP: 5
SALES: 100K **Privately Held**
SIC: 7371 Computer software development

(G-12308)
RALLYPOINT SOLUTIONS LLC
3411 Silverside Rd (19810-4812)
PHONE 302 543-8087
Kris Zupan, *CEO*
EMP: 15
SALES (est): 206.5K **Privately Held**
SIC: 8748 Business consulting

(G-12309)
RALPH PAUL INC
319 E Lea Blvd (19802-2353)
PHONE 302 764-9162
Ralph Paul, *Principal*
EMP: 5
SALES (est): 170.7K **Privately Held**
SIC: 7389 Business services

(G-12310)
RALPH TOMASES DDS PA
Also Called: Safian, Gary D DDS
707 Foulk Rd Ste 203 (19803-3737)
PHONE 302 652-8656
Gary D Safan DDS, *President*
Dr Ralph Tomases, *Vice Pres*
EMP: 5
SALES (est): 452.1K **Privately Held**
SIC: 8021 Dentists' office

(G-12311)
RALPHS SCISSORS SENSATIONS
511 Philadelphia Pike A (19809-2190)
PHONE 302 764-2744
Ralph Jioffre, *Owner*
EMP: 4
SALES (est): 119.6K **Privately Held**
SIC: 7231 Hairdressers

(G-12312)
RAMA LLC
300 Delaware Ave Ste 210a (19801-6601)
PHONE 202 596-9547
Alexander Titus,
Anne Barnard,
Reza Hosseini Ghomi,
Margaret McDonell,
EMP: 4
SALES (est): 37.7K **Privately Held**
SIC: 8999 Scientific consulting

(G-12313)
RAMON GALVAN
814 W Boxborough Dr (19810-1457)
PHONE 201 797-7172
EMP: 4
SALES (est): 150.9K **Privately Held**
SIC: 8021 Dentist's Office

(G-12314)
RAMONA CLAY
Also Called: Boomers Staffing USA
1313 Innovation 1313 N (19801)
PHONE 866 448-0834
Ramona Clay, *Owner*
EMP: 5
SALES (est): 146.1K **Privately Held**
SIC: 7361 Executive placement

(G-12315)
RAMUNNO & RAMUNNO & SCERBA PA
903 N French St Ste 106 (19801-3355)
PHONE 302 656-9400
L Vincent Ramunno, *President*
Vincent Ramunno, *President*
Lawrence Ramunno, *Vice Pres*
Ward Glenn,
EMP: 10 **EST:** 1969
SALES (est): 1.1MM **Privately Held**
WEB: www.ramunnolaw.com
SIC: 8111 General practice law office

(G-12316)
RANDSTAD PROFESSIONALS US LLC
Also Called: Randstad Finance & Accounting
2 Mill Rd Ste 200 (19806-2184)
PHONE 302 658-6181
Dom Vacca, *Branch Mgr*
Monica Hassler, *Director*
EMP: 10
SALES (corp-wide): 26.4B **Privately Held**
SIC: 7361 Executive placement
HQ: Randstad Professionals Us, Llc
150 Presidential Way Fl 4
Woburn MA 01801

(G-12317)
RAPUANO IRON WORKS INC
14 Whitekirk Dr (19808-1347)
PHONE 302 571-1809
Kathrine Rapuano, *President*
Leon Raprano, *Vice Pres*
EMP: 5
SQ FT: 7,000
SALES: 200K **Privately Held**
WEB: www.rapuanoironworks.com
SIC: 1791 Iron work, structural

(G-12318)
RAS ADDIS & ASSOCIATES INC
460 Robinson Dr (19801-5745)
PHONE 302 571-1683
Sylvia Scott, *President*
Andrew T Scott, *Vice Pres*
Crystal L Scott, *Vice Pres*
Richard Scott, *Vice Pres*
EMP: 15
SALES: 190K **Privately Held**
SIC: 0781 7349 Landscape services; janitorial service, contract basis

(G-12319)
RASKOB FOUNDATION FOR CATHOLIC
10 Montchanin Rd (19807-2166)
PHONE 302 655-4440
Frederick Perella, *Exec VP*
EMP: 10
SQ FT: 30,000

GEOGRAPHIC SECTION — Wilmington - New Castle County (G-12347)

(G-12319) (continued)
SALES: 11.1MM **Privately Held**
WEB: www.rfca.org
SIC: 8641 Civic social & fraternal associations

(G-12320)
RATNER & PRESTIA PC
1007 N Orange St Ste 205 (19801-1255)
P.O. Box 1596 (19899-1596)
PHONE.................302 778-2500
Ling Zhong, *Counsel*
Costas S Krikelis, *Manager*
Rex Donnelly, *Manager*
John McGlynn, *Shareholder*
EMP: 11
SALES (corp-wide): 10.7MM **Privately Held**
WEB: www.ratnerprestia.com
SIC: 8111 Patent, trademark & copyright law
PA: Ratner & Prestia, P.C.
    2200 Renaissance Blvd # 350
    King Of Prussia PA 19406
    610 407-0700

(G-12321)
RATNER COMPANIES LC
Also Called: Creative Hairdressers
3218 Kirkwood Hwy (19808-6130)
PHONE.................302 999-7724
Shelly Russell, *Manager*
EMP: 9 **Privately Held**
WEB: www.haircuttery.com
SIC: 7231 Unisex hair salons
HQ: Ratner Companies, L.C.
    1577 Spring Hill Rd # 500
    Vienna VA 22182
    703 269-5400

(G-12322)
RATNER COMPANIES LC
Also Called: Creative Hairdressers
5607 Concord Pike (19803-1428)
PHONE.................302 478-9978
Tina McCain, *Branch Mgr*
EMP: 10 **Privately Held**
WEB: www.haircuttery.com
SIC: 7231 Unisex hair salons
HQ: Ratner Companies, L.C.
    1577 Spring Hill Rd # 500
    Vienna VA 22182
    703 269-5400

(G-12323)
RAUMA SURVIVORS FOUNDATION
2055 Limestone Rd Ste 109 (19808-5536)
PHONE.................302 275-9705
Dennis Carradin, *President*
EMP: 6
SALES: 34.9K **Privately Held**
SIC: 8322 Social service center

(G-12324)
RAWLINS ORTHODONTICS
5500 Skyline Dr Ste 1 (19808-1772)
PHONE.................302 239-3533
Valley Delaware, *Principal*
EMP: 7 EST: 2011
SALES (est): 472.7K **Privately Held**
SIC: 8021 Orthodontist

(G-12325)
RAYMOND CHUNG INDUSTRIES CORP
12 Sharons Way (19808-5236)
PHONE.................302 384-9796
Raymond Chung, *Principal*
EMP: 2
SALES (est): 243.7K **Privately Held**
SIC: 3999 Barber & beauty shop equipment

(G-12326)
RAYMOND E TOMASSETTI ESQ
14 W Market St (19804-3139)
P.O. Box 3058 (19804-0058)
PHONE.................302 995-2840
Raymond E Tomassetti Jr, *Manager*
EMP: 4 **Privately Held**
SIC: 8111 General practice attorney, lawyer
PA: Raymond E Tomassetti Esq
    1209 Coastal Hwy Fl 2
    Fenwick Island DE 19944

(G-12327)
RAYMOND JAMES & ASSOCIATES INC
20 Montchanin Rd Ste 280 (19807-2174)
PHONE.................302 656-1534
EMP: 5
SALES (corp-wide): 8B **Publicly Held**
SIC: 6211 Brokers, security
HQ: Raymond James & Associates Inc
    880 Carillon Pkwy
    Saint Petersburg FL 33716
    727 567-1000

(G-12328)
RAYMOND JAMES & ASSOCIATES INC
Also Called: Raymond James
200 Bellevue Pkwy Ste 425 (19809-3713)
PHONE.................302 798-9113
John Schoff, *Manager*
Alex McLachlan, *Exec Dir*
EMP: 4
SALES (corp-wide): 8B **Publicly Held**
WEB: www.krgg.com
SIC: 6211 Brokers, security
HQ: Raymond James & Associates Inc
    880 Carillon Pkwy
    Saint Petersburg FL 33716
    727 567-1000

(G-12329)
RAYMOND JAMES FINANCIAL SVC
Also Called: Raymon James Financial Service
900 Foulk Rd Ste 201 (19803-3155)
PHONE.................302 778-2170
Mark McGreevy, *President*
Bradley J Foy, *Sales Associate*
EMP: 7
SALES (est): 882.7K **Privately Held**
SIC: 6211 Brokers, security

(G-12330)
RAYMOND JAMES FINCL SVCS INC
900 Foulk Rd Ste 201 (19803-3155)
PHONE.................302 778-2170
Mark McGreevy, *President*
Daniel Butler, *Manager*
EMP: 11
SALES (corp-wide): 8B **Publicly Held**
WEB: www.rjf.com
SIC: 6211 Brokers, security
HQ: Raymond James Financial Services, Inc.
    880 Carillon Pkwy
    Saint Petersburg FL 33716
    727 567-1000

(G-12331)
RAYMOND JAMES FINCL SVCS INC
20 Montchanin Rd Ste 280 (19807-2174)
PHONE.................302 656-1534
William C Thompson Sr Vp, *Branch Mgr*
EMP: 5
SALES (corp-wide): 8B **Publicly Held**
SIC: 6211 Brokers, security
HQ: Raymond James Financial Services, Inc.
    880 Carillon Pkwy
    Saint Petersburg FL 33716
    727 567-1000

(G-12332)
RAYTHEON COMPANY
100 W 10th St (19801-6603)
PHONE.................302 656-1339
Dennis J Picard, *President*
John Fritz, *Opers Staff*
Meredith McNeely, *Manager*
Julian Zottl, *Director*
EMP: 132
SALES (corp-wide): 27B **Publicly Held**
SIC: 3812 Defense systems & equipment
PA: Raytheon Company
    870 Winter St
    Waltham MA 02451
    781 522-3000

(G-12333)
RBC
2751 Centerville Rd # 212 (19808-1627)
PHONE.................302 892-5901
Alex Graham, *Managing Dir*
Michael Lexton, *Managing Dir*
David McFadzean, *Managing Dir*
Victoria Turnbull, *Managing Dir*
Catie Tobin, *Top Exec*
EMP: 4
SALES (est): 341.3K **Privately Held**
SIC: 6211 Security brokers & dealers

(G-12334)
RBC CAPITAL MARKETS LLC
Also Called: Rbc Wealth Management
1000 N West St Ste 110 (19801-1050)
PHONE.................302 252-9444
EMP: 5
SALES (corp-wide): 21.4B **Privately Held**
SIC: 7389 6282 Finishing services; investment advice
HQ: Rbc Capital Markets, Llc
    60 S 6th St Ste 700
    Minneapolis MN 55402
    612 371-2711

(G-12335)
RBC TRUST COMPANY DELAWARE LTD
4550 New Linden Hill Rd (19808)
PHONE.................302 892-6900
Michael Reed, *President*
Edward D Deverell, *Vice Pres*
Catherine E Milner, *Vice Pres*
Linda E Durso, *CFO*
Thomas Nagle, *Consultant*
EMP: 40
SALES: 10.2MM
SALES (corp-wide): 21.4B **Privately Held**
WEB: www.royalbank.com
SIC: 6733 Trusts
PA: Royal Bank Of Canada
    200 Bay St
    Toronto ON M5J 2
    416 974-3940

(G-12336)
RCT STUDIO INC
251 Little Falls Dr (19808-1674)
PHONE.................669 255-1562
Cheng Lyu, *CEO*
EMP: 7
SALES (est): 164.3K **Privately Held**
SIC: 7371 Computer software development & applications

(G-12337)
RE MAX OF WILMINGTON (PA)
Also Called: Re/Max
5307 Limestone Rd Ste 100 (19808-1282)
PHONE.................302 234-2500
Bruce White, *Principal*
John Keating, *Broker*
Sandra Smyth, *Broker*
Temy Swinford, *Broker*
Paul Webster, *Broker*
EMP: 40
SQ FT: 3,000
SALES (est): 4.1MM **Privately Held**
SIC: 6531 Real estate agent, residential

(G-12338)
RE MAX OF WILMINGTON
Also Called: Re/Max
2323 Pennsylvania Ave (19806-1332)
PHONE.................302 657-8000
James Barone, *Manager*
EMP: 20 **Privately Held**
SIC: 6531 Real estate agent, residential
PA: Re Max Of Wilmington
    5307 Limestone Rd Ste 100
    Wilmington DE 19808

(G-12339)
RE-UP APP INC
8603 Park Ct (19802-7702)
PHONE.................267 972-1183
Opeyemi Oyekanmi, *CEO*
EMP: 3
SALES (est): 71.1K **Privately Held**
SIC: 7372 Prepackaged software

(G-12340)
REACH RIVERSIDE DEV CORP
2300 Bowers St (19802-4610)
PHONE.................302 540-1698
Logan Herring, *CEO*
David Ford, *Principal*
Kenyetta McCurdy-Byrd, *Principal*
EMP: 8
SALES (est): 62.6K **Privately Held**
SIC: 8322 Individual & family services

(G-12341)
READ-ALOUDDELAWARE INC (PA)
Also Called: READ ALOUD DELAWARE
100 W 10th St Ste 309 (19801-1683)
PHONE.................302 656-5256
Mary W Hirschbiel, *Exec Dir*
Kristin Peyton, *Admin Asst*
EMP: 6
SQ FT: 2,329
SALES: 525.2K **Privately Held**
WEB: www.readalouddelaware.org
SIC: 8699 Charitable organization

(G-12342)
READING ASSIST INSTITUTE (PA)
100 W 10th St Ste 910 (19801-6605)
PHONE.................302 425-4080
Kathleen Traskos, *President*
Heath Kahrs, *Treasurer*
Rebecca Combs, *Exec Dir*
Vickie Innes, *Exec Dir*
Donna Fierro, *Director*
EMP: 10
SALES: 1.1MM **Privately Held**
WEB: www.readingassist.org
SIC: 8299 8748 Reading school, including speed reading; business consulting

(G-12343)
REAL ESTATE PARTNERS LLC
Also Called: Bill Luke Team
2800 Lancaster Ave Ste 8 (19805-5200)
PHONE.................302 656-0251
William Luke, *General Mgr*
EMP: 7
SALES (est): 782.5K **Privately Held**
WEB: www.lansol.net
SIC: 6531 Real estate agent, residential

(G-12344)
REBECCA JAFFEE MD
Also Called: Desai, Parul M
3105 Limestone Rd Ste 300 (19808-2156)
PHONE.................302 992-0200
Rebecca Jaffee MD, *Owner*
Karen L Hill, *Supervisor*
EMP: 10
SALES (est): 927.3K **Privately Held**
SIC: 8011 General & family practice, physician/surgeon

(G-12345)
REBEKAH FEDELE DMD PA
3101 Limestone Rd Ste C (19808-2148)
PHONE.................302 994-9555
Rebekah Fedele, *Owner*
EMP: 5
SALES (est): 290K **Privately Held**
SIC: 8021 Dentists' office

(G-12346)
RED CARPET TRAVEL AGENCY INC (PA)
Also Called: Uniglobe
1812 Marsh Rd Ste 413 (19810-4522)
PHONE.................302 475-1220
Mark Rachko, *President*
Steven Rachko, *Vice Pres*
Helen S Whitson, *Treasurer*
EMP: 20 EST: 1970
SQ FT: 1,600
SALES (est): 3.4MM **Privately Held**
SIC: 4724 Travel agencies

(G-12347)
RED CLAY CONSOLIDATED SCHL DST
Also Called: Nutrition Dept Supervisor
1798 Limestone Rd (19804-4106)
PHONE.................302 992-5580
Michael Lewindowski, *Manager*
Rob Pritchard, *Technology*

Wilmington - New Castle County (G-12348)   GEOGRAPHIC SECTION

EMP: 6
SALES (corp-wide): 130.5MM **Privately Held**
WEB: www.aiduponths.com
SIC: 8742 Food & beverage consultant
PA: Red Clay Consolidated School District
1502 Spruce Ave
Wilmington DE 19805
302 552-3700

(G-12348)
REDLEO SOFTWARE INC
1201 N Orange St Ste 7495 (19801-1298)
PHONE..................................302 691-9072
Love Kumar, *President*
EMP: 15
SALES (est): 359.5K **Privately Held**
SIC: 8742 7361 Management consulting services; employment agencies

(G-12349)
REDZUN LLC
108 W 13th St (19801)
PHONE..................................512 657-4100
Enrique Ferraro, *Principal*
EMP: 4 EST: 2013
SALES (est): 200K **Privately Held**
SIC: 5963 7389 Direct sales, telemarketing;

(G-12350)
REED ELSEVIER CAPITAL INC
1105 N Market St Ste 501 (19801-1253)
PHONE..................................302 427-9299
Renee Simonton, *President*
EMP: 10
SALES (est): 543K
SALES (corp-wide): 9.8B **Privately Held**
WEB: www.reed-elsevier.com
SIC: 2741 Miscellaneous publishing
HQ: Relx Group Plc
Grand Buildings
London
207 166-5500

(G-12351)
REEDS REFUGE CENTER INC
1601 N Pine St (19802-5007)
PHONE..................................302 428-1830
Cora Reed, *President*
EMP: 57
SALES: 188.8K **Privately Held**
SIC: 8322 Social service center

(G-12352)
REFLECTION BIOTECHNOLOGIES INC
1013 Centre Rd Ste 403b (19805-1270)
PHONE..................................212 765-2200
Juliana Xu, *President*
EMP: 2
SALES (est): 74.4K **Privately Held**
SIC: 2836 Biological products, except diagnostic

(G-12353)
REGAL CINEMAS INC
Also Called: Brandywine Town Center 16
3300 Brandywine Pkwy (19803-1463)
PHONE..................................302 479-0753
EMP: 35 **Privately Held**
WEB: www.regalcinemas.com
SIC: 7832 Motion picture theaters, except drive-in
HQ: Regal Cinemas, Inc.
101 E Blount Ave Ste 100
Knoxville TN 37920
865 922-1123

(G-12354)
REGAL PAINTING & DECORATING
209 S Woodward Ave (19805-2358)
P.O. Box 2509 (19805-0509)
PHONE..................................302 994-8943
Ronald Ciafre, *President*
Robert Jeffery, *Vice Pres*
Debra Jeffery, *Admin Sec*
EMP: 13
SQ FT: 1,500
SALES (est): 806.4K **Privately Held**
SIC: 1721 7389 Residential painting; interior decorating

(G-12355)
REGENCY HLTHCARE REHAB CTR LLC
Also Called: ST. FRANCIS CARE CENTER AT WIL
801 N Broom St (19806-4624)
PHONE..................................302 654-8400
Meir Gelley,
EMP: 110 EST: 2007
SALES: 11.1MM **Privately Held**
SIC: 8051 Convalescent home with continuous nursing care

(G-12356)
REGER RIZZO & DARNALL LLP
1001 N Jefferson St # 202 (19801-1493)
PHONE..................................302 652-3611
Louis Rizzo, *Branch Mgr*
Tracy Hughes, *Legal Staff*
Jennifer L Zegel, *Associate*
EMP: 14
SALES (corp-wide): 6.3MM **Privately Held**
WEB: www.rrkdlaw.com
SIC: 8111 General practice attorney, lawyer
PA: Reger Rizzo & Darnall Llp
2929 Arch St Ste 1300
Philadelphia PA 19104
215 387-1080

(G-12357)
REGINA COLEMAN
Also Called: Creative Children
2720 Chinchilla Dr (19810-1509)
PHONE..................................215 476-4682
Regina Coleman, *Owner*
EMP: 6
SQ FT: 27,000
SALES (est): 133.2K **Privately Held**
SIC: 8351 Group day care center

(G-12358)
REGIONAL HMATOLOGY ONCOLOGY PA (PA)
1010 N Bancroft Pkwy # 21 (19805-2690)
PHONE..................................302 731-7782
Timothy Wozniak MD, *President*
Martha Hosfordskapof, *Admin Sec*
EMP: 20
SALES (est): 5.3MM **Privately Held**
SIC: 8011 Oncologist

(G-12359)
REGIONAL MEDICAL GROUP LLC
4512 Kirkwood Hwy Ste 202 (19808-5122)
P.O. Box 5930 (19808-0930)
PHONE..................................302 993-7890
Susan A Cassidy, *Administration*
Andra Popescu, *Cardiology*
EMP: 5
SALES (est): 289K **Privately Held**
SIC: 8099 Health & allied services

(G-12360)
REGIONAL ORTHOPAEDIC ASSOC (PA)
1941 Limestone Rd Ste 101 (19808-5413)
PHONE..................................302 633-3555
David L Axon MD, *Partner*
Brian J Galinat MD, *Partner*
Paul C Lupcha MD, *Partner*
Peter F Townsend MD, *Partner*
Mark Eskander, *Surgeon*
EMP: 28
SALES (est): 2.9MM **Privately Held**
WEB: www.delawareorthopaediccenter.com
SIC: 8011 Orthopedic physician; surgeon

(G-12361)
REGIS CORPORATION
1406 N Du Pont St (19806)
PHONE..................................302 654-4477
EMP: 8
SALES (corp-wide): 1B **Publicly Held**
SIC: 7231 Unisex hair salons
PA: Regis Corporation
7201 Metro Blvd
Edina MN 55439
952 947-7777

(G-12362)
REGIS CORPORATION
Also Called: Supercuts
1732 Marsh Rd (19810-4606)
PHONE..................................302 478-5065
Rick Fuller, *Branch Mgr*
EMP: 8
SALES (corp-wide): 1B **Publicly Held**
SIC: 7231 Unisex hair salons
PA: Regis Corporation
7201 Metro Blvd
Edina MN 55439
952 947-7777

(G-12363)
REGISTERED AGENTS LTD
Also Called: Registered Agents Limited
1013 Centre Rd Ste 403a (19805-1270)
PHONE..................................302 421-5750
H Murray Sawyer, *President*
Laura Bryda, *Vice Pres*
Sid S Garnett, *Vice Pres*
Michelle Stallings, *Legal Staff*
EMP: 23
SALES (est): 1.4MM **Privately Held**
WEB: www.inclegal.com
SIC: 7389 Automobile recovery service

(G-12364)
REGISTRED AGNTS LEGAL SVCS LLC
1013 Centre Rd Ste 403s (19805-1270)
PHONE..................................302 427-6970
Michael Ashley, *Mng Member*
Murray Sawyer, *Mng Member*
EMP: 5
SALES (est): 535.4K **Privately Held**
SIC: 8741 Business management

(G-12365)
REGISTRY FURNITURE INC
1000 N West St Ste 1200 (19801-1058)
PHONE..................................626 297-9508
Nansan Lai, *Treasurer*
EMP: 2
SALES (est): 125.4K **Privately Held**
SIC: 2521 Wood office furniture

(G-12366)
REGUS CORPORATION
1000 N West St Ste 1200 (19801-1058)
PHONE..................................302 295-4800
Jeanine Losino, *Branch Mgr*
EMP: 4
SALES (corp-wide): 3.1B **Privately Held**
SIC: 7389 Office facilities & secretarial service rental
HQ: Regus Corporation
15305 Dallas Pkwy Ste 400
Addison TX 75001
972 361-8100

(G-12367)
REHABILITATION CONSULTANTS INC
Also Called: Novacare Rehabilitation
3411 Silverside Rd 105s (19810-4867)
PHONE..................................302 478-5240
Robert Catalano, *President*
EMP: 23
SALES (est): 1MM **Privately Held**
SIC: 8049 Physiotherapist
HQ: Physiotherapy Associates, Inc.
680 American Ave Ste 200
King Of Prussia PA 19406
610 644-7824

(G-12368)
REHABITATION CONSULTANTS
3411 Silverside Rd # 105 (19810-4812)
PHONE..................................302 478-2131
Robert M Catalano, *Owner*
EMP: 20
SALES (est): 253.1K **Privately Held**
WEB: www.rehabconsultantsinc.com
SIC: 8093 Rehabilitation center, outpatient treatment

(G-12369)
REIL MACHINES USA INC
Also Called: Electro Temp Technology
3511 Silverside Rd # 105 (19810-4902)
PHONE..................................905 488-9263
Larissa Yui, *CFO*
Sascha Yui, *Director*

EMP: 10
SALES (est): 916.4K **Privately Held**
SIC: 5078 5064 Drinking water coolers, mechanical; electric household appliances

(G-12370)
REILLY JANICZEK & MCDEVITT PC
1013 Centre Rd Ste 210 (19805-1265)
PHONE..................................302 777-1700
R Stokes Nolte, *Partner*
EMP: 12
SALES (est): 659.8K
SALES (corp-wide): 12MM **Privately Held**
SIC: 8111 General practice law office
PA: Reilly Janiczek & Mcdevitt P.C.
2500 Mcclellan Ave # 240
Pennsauken NJ 08109
856 317-7180

(G-12371)
REIVER HYMAN & CO INC
4104 N Market St (19802-2222)
PHONE..................................302 764-2040
Alan T Reiver, *President*
EMP: 5
SQ FT: 5,000
SALES: 1MM **Privately Held**
SIC: 5713 5023 Carpets; floor coverings; window covering parts & accessories

(G-12372)
REKINDLE FAMILY MEDICINE
5590 Kirkwood Hwy (19808-5002)
PHONE..................................302 565-4799
Kimberly Nalda, *Principal*
EMP: 4
SALES (est): 91.6K **Privately Held**
SIC: 8099 Health & allied services

(G-12373)
RELIABLE COPY SERVICE INC
1007 N Orange St Ste 110 (19801-1256)
PHONE..................................302 654-8080
David Hernan, *General Mgr*
David Disanto, *Graphic Designe*
EMP: 12
SALES (est): 1.5MM
SALES (corp-wide): 50.4MM **Privately Held**
SIC: 7334 Blueprinting service
PA: Reliable Copy Service Inc.
1650 Arch St Ste 2210
Philadelphia PA 19103
215 563-3363

(G-12374)
RELIABLE HOME INSPECTION (PA)
100 Old Kennett Rd (19807-1726)
PHONE..................................302 455-1200
John Kerrigan, *President*
Tammy Kerrigan, *Vice Pres*
EMP: 11
SALES (est): 1.5MM **Privately Held**
WEB: www.reliablehomeinspection.com
SIC: 7389 Building inspection service

(G-12375)
RELIABLE HOME SERVICES LLC
1821 Marsh Rd (19810-4505)
PHONE..................................302 246-6000
EMP: 6 EST: 2009
SALES (est): 250K **Privately Held**
SIC: 8322 Individual/Family Services

(G-12376)
RELIANCE EGLEFORD UPSTREAM LLC
1007 N Orange St (19801-1239)
PHONE..................................302 472-7437
EMP: 5
SALES (est): 234.2K
SALES (corp-wide): 52.2B **Privately Held**
SIC: 1481 2911 Mine exploration, non-metallic minerals; petroleum refining
PA: Reliance Industries Limited
3rd Floor, Maker Chambers-Iv,
Mumbai MH 40002
222 204-2268

GEOGRAPHIC SECTION — Wilmington - New Castle County

(G-12377)
RELIANCE TRUST COMPANY LLC
200 Bellevue Pkwy Ste 220 (19809-3727)
PHONE................302 246-5400
Christopher M Teevan, *Principal*
EMP: 6
SALES (est): 1MM **Privately Held**
SIC: 6021 National commercial banks

(G-12378)
REMAX SUNVEST REALTY CORP (PA)
Also Called: Re/Max
2103a W Newport Pike (19804-3719)
PHONE................302 995-1589
Carl Chen, *President*
Pauline Chin, *Corp Secy*
Kenneth Mayhew, *Vice Pres*
EMP: 41
SALES (est): 2MM **Privately Held**
WEB: www.carlchenhomes.com
SIC: 6531 Real estate agent, residential

(G-12379)
REMOTE INC
Also Called: Remote Apps
2711 Centerville Rd # 400 (19808-1645)
PHONE................302 636-5440
Kathryn Wlliams, *Manager*
Katie Williams, *Manager*
EMP: 1
SALES (est): 36K **Privately Held**
SIC: 7372 Application computer software

(G-12380)
RENT-A-CENTER INC
1932 Maryland Ave (19805-4605)
PHONE................302 654-7700
Anabell Enciso, *Manager*
EMP: 5
SALES (corp-wide): 2.6B **Publicly Held**
WEB: www.rentacenter.com
SIC: 7359 Appliance rental; furniture rental; home entertainment equipment rental; television rental
PA: Rent-A-Center, Inc.
     5501 Headquarters Dr
     Plano TX 75024
     972 801-1100

(G-12381)
RENZI GROUP INC
Also Called: Romantic Gardens
109 Mcdaniel Ave (19803-2529)
PHONE................302 588-2603
Chris Renzi, *President*
EMP: 4
SQ FT: 2,200
SALES: 120K **Privately Held**
SIC: 1542 1521 Commercial & office buildings, renovation & repair; general remodeling, single-family houses

(G-12382)
REPRODUCTIVE ASSOCIATES DEL PA
2700 Silverside Rd Ste 2a (19810-3724)
PHONE................302 478-8000
Ronald F Feinberg, *Principal*
Keith Stalker, *Engineer*
Leigh Uyeda, *Finance Mgr*
Gina Racine, *Mktg Coord*
Mikey Kopyna, *Marketing Staff*
EMP: 7
SALES (est): 401.2K **Privately Held**
SIC: 8011 Gynecologist
PA: Reproductive Associates Of Delaware, P.A.
     4735 Ogletown Stanton Rd
     Newark DE 19713

(G-12383)
REPUBLIC SERVICES INC
1420 New York Ave (19801-5826)
PHONE................302 658-4097
Bob Ziegler, *Manager*
EMP: 34
SALES (corp-wide): 10B **Publicly Held**
SIC: 4953 Refuse collection & disposal services
PA: Republic Services, Inc.
     18500 N Allied Way # 100
     Phoenix AZ 85054
     480 627-2700

(G-12384)
REPUBLICAN STATE COMMITTEE DEL
3301 Lancaster Pike 4b (19805-1436)
PHONE................302 668-1954
Thomas Ross, *Chairman*
Paula Manolakos, *Manager*
Seth Wimer, *Director*
EMP: 4
SALES (est): 244.2K **Privately Held**
SIC: 8651 Political fundraising

(G-12385)
RESEARCH & INNOVATION CO
200 Bellevue Pkwy Ste 300 (19809-3727)
PHONE................302 281-3600
William J Merritt, *CEO*
EMP: 4
SALES (est): 76.5K
SALES (corp-wide): 307.4MM **Publicly Held**
SIC: 8731 Computer (hardware) development
HQ: Interdigital Wireless, Inc.
     200 Bellevue Pkwy Ste 300
     Wilmington DE 19809

(G-12386)
RESOURCE MORTGAGE CORP
3301 Lancaster Pike Ste 9 (19805-1436)
PHONE................302 657-0181
Michelle Slack, *President*
Joe Beacher, *Vice Pres*
EMP: 10
SALES (est): 760K **Privately Held**
SIC: 6163 Mortgage brokers arranging for loans, using money of others

(G-12387)
RESOURCES FOR HUMAN DEV INC
2804 Grubb Rd (19810-2319)
PHONE................302 691-7574
EMP: 43
SALES (corp-wide): 255.8MM **Privately Held**
SIC: 8742 Business planning & organizing services
PA: Resources For Human Development, Inc.
     4700 Wissahickon Ave # 126
     Philadelphia PA 19144
     215 951-0300

(G-12388)
RESPONSIBLE PUBLISHING
301 Snuff Mill Rd (19807-1025)
PHONE................609 412-9621
Brooke Mufferi, *Principal*
EMP: 1
SALES (est): 38.1K **Privately Held**
SIC: 2741 Miscellaneous publishing

(G-12389)
RESTORATION DYNAMICS LLC (PA)
215 Rodman St (19805-3321)
PHONE................302 378-3729
Nathaniel Kadle,
EMP: 8
SQ FT: 1,350
SALES: 803K **Privately Held**
SIC: 1611 1741 Highway & street paving contractor; masonry & other stonework

(G-12390)
RESTORE INCORPORATED
3411 Silverside Rd # 104 (19810-4809)
PHONE................302 655-6257
Cathy Murray, *Branch Mgr*
EMP: 14
SALES (corp-wide): 1.9MM **Privately Held**
WEB: www.restoreusa.com
SIC: 2992 Lubricating oils & greases
PA: Restore Incorporated
     3000 Ne 30th Pl Ste 201
     Fort Lauderdale FL 33306
     954 563-7001

(G-12391)
RESURRECTION CENTER (PA)
Also Called: 8th Baptist Church
3301 N Market St Ste 1 (19802-2738)
PHONE................302 762-8311
Dr Cleo V Townsend, *Pastor*
Dr S Todd Townsend Sr, *Bishop*
EMP: 7
SALES (est): 2.3MM **Privately Held**
SIC: 6732 Trusts: educational, religious, etc.

(G-12392)
RETAIL SERVICES WIS CORP
3411 Silverside Rd # 205 (19810-4812)
PHONE................302 477-0667
Patrick Boyle, *Branch Mgr*
EMP: 62
SQ FT: 1,200
SALES (corp-wide): 69.5MM **Privately Held**
WEB: www.wisusa.com
SIC: 7389 Inventory computing service
HQ: Retail Services Wis Corporation
     9265 Sky Park Ct Ste 100
     San Diego CA 92123
     858 565-8111

(G-12393)
RETINOVITREOUS ASSOCIATES LTD
1523 Concord Pike Ste 100 (19803-3653)
PHONE................302 351-1087
EMP: 12
SALES (est): 145.6K **Privately Held**
SIC: 8011 Medical Doctor's Office

(G-12394)
RETINOVITREOUS ASSOCIATES LTD
Also Called: Mid Atlantic Retina
1523 Concord Pike Ste 101 (19803-3653)
PHONE................302 351-1085
EMP: 5
SALES (corp-wide): 4.8MM **Privately Held**
SIC: 8011 Ophthalmologist
PA: Retinovitreous Associates Ltd
     4060 Butler Pike Ste 200
     Plymouth Meeting PA
     800 331-6634

(G-12395)
RETIRED SENIOR VOLUNTEER
12 Yellow Pine Ct (19808-1028)
PHONE................610 565-5563
EMP: 6 EST: 1975
SALES: 220.8K **Privately Held**
SIC: 8322 Individual/Family Services

(G-12396)
REVOD CORPORATION (HQ)
1403 Foulk Rd (19803-2788)
PHONE................302 477-1795
Amy Ward, *Vice Pres*
▼ EMP: 4
SALES (est): 27.2MM
SALES (corp-wide): 6.9B **Publicly Held**
SIC: 6726 7699 Investment offices; elevators: inspection, service & repair
PA: Dover Corporation
     3005 Highland Pkwy # 200
     Downers Grove IL 60515
     630 541-1540

(G-12397)
RFPC & WABTEC
1011 Centre Rd Ste 310 (19805-1266)
PHONE................302 573-3977
EMP: 7 **Privately Held**
SIC: 6719 Holding Company

(G-12398)
RFS ENTERPRISES INC
202 New Rd Unit 2 (19805-4140)
PHONE................302 888-0143
Robert Smulski, *President*
EMP: 4 EST: 2013
SALES (est): 240K **Privately Held**
SIC: 8748 Business consulting

(G-12399)
RGP HOLDING INC (PA)
1105 N Market St (19801-1216)
PHONE................302 661-0117
Raymond G Perelman, *President*
◆ EMP: 8

SALES (est): 57.9MM **Privately Held**
SIC: 3255 1499 1741 Firebrick, clay; castable refractories, clay; foundry refractories, clay; diatomaceous earth mining; perlite mining; refractory or acid brick masonry

(G-12400)
RHI REFRACTORIES HOLDING CO (DH)
1105 N Market St Ste 1300 (19801-1241)
PHONE................302 655-6497
Norbert Wittmann, *President*
Peggy Groover, *Principal*
◆ EMP: 1
SALES (est): 144.9MM
SALES (corp-wide): 3.4B **Privately Held**
SIC: 3255 1459 3546 3272 Clay refractories; magnesite mining; power-driven handtools; solid containing units, concrete; shredders, industrial & commercial; crucibles: graphite, magnesite, chrome, silica, etc.
HQ: Vrd Americas B.V.
     Hofplein 19 3e Verdiepin
     Arnhem
     263 635-763

(G-12401)
RHOADES & MORROW LLC
1225 N King St Ste 1200 (19801-3254)
P.O. Box 874 (19899-0874)
PHONE................302 427-9500
Joseph J Rhoades, *Owner*
EMP: 12
SQ FT: 1,300
SALES (est): 1.2MM **Privately Held**
SIC: 8111 Specialized law offices, attorneys

(G-12402)
RHODESIDE INC
322 Compton Ct (19801-3616)
PHONE................505 261-4568
Ronald Rhodes, *President*
Tyshawn Moreland, *Principal*
Sherkiera Rhodes, *Principal*
EMP: 5
SALES (est): 91.5K **Privately Held**
SIC: 7922 Entertainment promotion

(G-12403)
RHONDIUM CORPORATION
Also Called: Triodent
35a The Commons (19810-4929)
PHONE................800 771-4364
Dr Simon McDonald, *CEO*
Manfred Pahlen, *Director*
EMP: 10
SALES (est): 1.6MM **Privately Held**
SIC: 5047 Dentists' professional supplies

(G-12404)
RI HERITAGE INN TOPEKA INC
Also Called: Topeka Residence Inn
1209 N Orange St (19801-1120)
PHONE................785 271-8903
Fax: 785 271-8903
EMP: 20 **Privately Held**
SIC: 7011 Hotel/Motel Operation
HQ: R.I. Heritage Inn Of Topeka, Inc.
     4850 32nd Ave S
     Fargo ND

(G-12405)
RIBODYNAMICS LLC
2711 Centerville Rd # 400 (19808-1660)
PHONE................518 339-6605
Daniele Fabris,
EMP: 2
SALES (est): 104.2K **Privately Held**
SIC: 3826 8999 Analytical instruments; scientific consulting

(G-12406)
RICHARD E CHODROFF DMD
3105 Limestone Rd Ste 203 (19808-2151)
PHONE................302 995-6979
Richard Chodroff, *Owner*
EMP: 5
SALES (est): 192.1K **Privately Held**
SIC: 8021 Dentists' office

Wilmington - New Castle County (G-12407)

(G-12407)
RICHARD EARL FISHER
820 Kiamensi Rd (19804-3420)
PHONE..................302 598-1957
Richard E Fisher, *Owner*
EMP: 2
SALES (est): 93.9K **Privately Held**
SIC: 2673 2843 3089 2844 Bags: plastic, laminated & coated; oils & greases; blister or bubble formed packaging, plastic; suntan lotions & oils

(G-12408)
RICHARD HRRMANN STRBILDERS INC
500 Robinson Ln (19805-4616)
PHONE..................302 654-4329
Richard Herrmann Jr, *President*
Keith Herrmann, *Vice Pres*
EMP: 5 **EST:** 1956
SQ FT: 6,000
SALES (est): 1.2MM **Privately Held**
SIC: 2431 Staircases & stairs, wood

(G-12409)
RICHARD J LEACH UPHOLSTERY
506 Grove Rd (19807)
PHONE..................302 764-2067
Richardj Leach, *Principal*
EMP: 4
SALES (est): 192.7K **Privately Held**
SIC: 5087 Service establishment equipment

(G-12410)
RICHARD L SHERRY MD (PA)
Also Called: Brandywine Eye Center
2500 Grubb Rd Ste 234 (19810-4796)
PHONE..................302 475-1880
Roxann Briggs, *President*
Richard L Sherry MD, *Owner*
Nan Schiowitz, *Partner*
Marna Sherry, *Administration*
EMP: 10
SALES (est): 2.1MM **Privately Held**
SIC: 8011 General & family practice, physician/surgeon

(G-12411)
RICHARD S COBB ESQUIRE
919 N Market St Ste 600 (19801-3037)
P.O. Box 2087 (19899-2087)
PHONE..................302 467-4430
Richard S Cobb, *Partner*
Adam Landis, *Partner*
Daniel Rath, *Partner*
EMP: 15
SALES (est): 657.8K **Privately Held**
SIC: 8111 Bankruptcy law

(G-12412)
RICHARDS LAYTON & FINGER P A
Uknown (19801)
P.O. Box 551 (19899-0551)
PHONE..................302 651-7700
Monica Ayres, *Principal*
Daniel Klein, *Director*
EMP: 21
SALES (est): 2MM **Privately Held**
SIC: 8111 General practice attorney, lawyer

(G-12413)
RICHARDS LAYTON & FINGER P A
1 Rodney Sq 920 N King St (19801)
PHONE..................302 651-7700
William J Wade, *President*
C Stephen Bigler, *President*
Doneene K Damon, *President*
Lorraine Robitzski, *President*
Fred Cottrell, *Partner*
EMP: 320 **EST:** 1900
SQ FT: 100,000
SALES (est): 56MM **Privately Held**
WEB: www.rlf.com
SIC: 8111 General practice attorney, lawyer; general practice law office

(G-12414)
RICHARDSON PARK COMMUNITY
Also Called: CAP
701 S Maryland Ave (19804-1633)
PHONE..................302 428-1247
Robert Broesler, *Exec Dir*
Debrah Steinbrunner, *Admin Sec*
EMP: 23
SQ FT: 1,700
SALES: 89.2K **Privately Held**
SIC: 8641 Civic social & fraternal associations

(G-12415)
RICOH USA INC
Nightrider Overnite Copy Svc
1 Commerce St Ste 850 (19801)
PHONE..................302 573-3562
Connally Brown, *Branch Mgr*
EMP: 15 **Privately Held**
WEB: www.ikon.com
SIC: 5044 Office equipment
HQ: Ricoh Usa, Inc.
300 Eagleview Blvd # 200
Exton PA 19341
610 296-8000

(G-12416)
RIDERS APP INC
1 Commerce St 1 # 1 (19801)
PHONE..................347 484-4344
Igor Debantur, *CEO*
Anatoly Chernyakov, *Vice Pres*
EMP: 7
SQ FT: 500
SALES (est): 430K **Privately Held**
SIC: 7373 Systems software development services

(G-12417)
RIDGEWOOD ELECTRIC POWER TR V
1314 N King St (19801-3220)
PHONE..................302 888-7444
Kathleen P McSherry, *Principal*
EMP: 6
SALES (est): 430.1K **Privately Held**
SIC: 4911 Electric services

(G-12418)
RIDGEWOOD ELECTRIC PWR TR III
1314 N King St (19801-3220)
PHONE..................302 888-7444
Kathleen P McSherry, *Principal*
EMP: 13
SALES (est): 1MM **Privately Held**
SIC: 4911 Electric services

(G-12419)
RIDRODSKY & LONG PA (PA)
300 Delaware Ave Ste LI (19801-1634)
PHONE..................302 691-8822
Diane Moore, *Office Mgr*
EMP: 10
SALES (est): 1MM **Privately Held**
SIC: 8111 General practice attorney, lawyer

(G-12420)
RIEMEL OF DELAWARE LLC
460 B And O Ln (19804-1452)
PHONE..................302 998-5806
Giacomo Stella, *President*
EMP: 6
SQ FT: 3,200
SALES: 250K **Privately Held**
SIC: 3599 Machine shop, jobbing & repair

(G-12421)
RIGEL ENERGY GROUP LLC
300 Delaware Ave (19801-1607)
PHONE..................888 624-9844
EMP: 10
SALES (est): 570K **Privately Held**
SIC: 3646 3612 5063 Commercial Lighting Fixtures, Nsk

(G-12422)
RIGHT AT HOME
1500 N French St (19801-3118)
PHONE..................302 652-1550
Joe Bakey, *Owner*
EMP: 7
SALES (est): 173.1K **Privately Held**
SIC: 8082 Home health care services

(G-12423)
RIPPL LABS INC (PA)
2711 Centerville Rd # 400 (19808-1645)
PHONE..................551 427-1997
Vikas Sapra, *CEO*
EMP: 10
SALES (est): 111.9K **Privately Held**
SIC: 4813

(G-12424)
RISING STARS CHILD CARE INC
Also Called: Rising Star Preschool
415 Milmar Rd (19804-1129)
PHONE..................302 998-7682
Kathleen Hughes, *President*
EMP: 12
SALES (est): 136.6K **Privately Held**
SIC: 8351 Group day care center

(G-12425)
RISK CONSULTAN
720 Nottingham Rd (19805-2839)
PHONE..................302 655-3350
B F Cloud, *President*
EMP: 4
SALES (est): 299.4K **Privately Held**
SIC: 6411 Pension & retirement plan consultants

(G-12426)
RITCHIE SAWYER CORPORATION (PA)
2502 Pin Oak Dr (19810-1635)
P.O. Box 30558 (19805-7558)
PHONE..................302 475-1971
Tom Ritchie, *Ch of Bd*
Allen Sawyer, *President*
EMP: 10
SALES (est): 717.5K **Privately Held**
WEB: www.ritchiesawyer.com
SIC: 8721 7371 Accounting, auditing & bookkeeping; computer software development

(G-12427)
RIVERFRONT DEV CORP DEL
815 Justison St Ste D (19801-5156)
PHONE..................302 425-4890
Sherman Lewis, *Supervisor*
Megan McGoinchey, *Exec Dir*
Michael S Purzycki, *Exec Dir*
EMP: 15
SQ FT: 125,000
SALES: 3.9MM **Privately Held**
WEB: www.riverfrontwilm.com
SIC: 6552 Land subdividers & developers, commercial; land subdividers & developers, residential

(G-12428)
RIVERFRONT DEVELOPMENT CORP
815 Justison St Ste D (19801-5156)
PHONE..................302 425-4890
Joe Valenti, *Marketing Mgr*
EMP: 12
SALES: 3.5MM **Privately Held**
SIC: 6552 Subdividers & developers

(G-12429)
RIVERSIDE HEALTHCARE CENTER
700 W Lea Blvd Ste 102 (19802-2541)
PHONE..................302 764-2615
Nigel Veater, *Administration*
EMP: 200
SALES (est): 3.1MM
SALES (corp-wide): 1.5B **Privately Held**
SIC: 8051 Skilled nursing care facilities
PA: Christiana Care Health Services, Inc.
4755 Ogletown Stanton Rd
Newark DE 19718
302 733-1000

(G-12430)
RIVERSTONE FINANCIAL II LLC
901 N Market St Ste 463 (19801-3022)
PHONE..................302 295-5310
Sabetay Palatchi, *Principal*
EMP: 4
SALES (est): 185.1K **Privately Held**
SIC: 6282 Investment advice

(G-12431)
RKJ CONSTRUCTION INC
2252 Saint James Dr (19808-5219)
PHONE..................302 690-0959
Kirti Joshi, *President*
EMP: 5 **EST:** 2014
SALES (est): 308.4K **Privately Held**
SIC: 1521 Single-family housing construction

(G-12432)
RLK PRESS INC
3511 Silverside Rd (19810-4902)
PHONE..................267 565-5138
Davey Dunn, *President*
EMP: 2
SALES (est): 61.1K **Privately Held**
SIC: 2741 Miscellaneous publishing

(G-12433)
ROADRUNNER EXPRESS INC
21 Millside Dr (19801-5541)
PHONE..................302 426-9551
Mary Anne Baker, *President*
EMP: 46
SALES (est): 1.5MM **Privately Held**
WEB: www.roadrunnerexp.com
SIC: 4119 Limousine rental, with driver

(G-12434)
ROBERT A HEINLE M D
1600 Rockland Rd (19803-3607)
PHONE..................302 651-6400
Robert Heinle, *Owner*
EMP: 4
SALES (est): 80.7K **Privately Held**
SIC: 8011 Pediatrician

(G-12435)
ROBERT BIRD
Also Called: Home Instead Senior Care
1701 Shallcross Ave Ste A (19806-2347)
PHONE..................302 654-4003
Robert Bird, *Owner*
EMP: 15
SALES (est): 777.7K **Privately Held**
SIC: 8082 Home health care services

(G-12436)
ROBERT C DIRECTOR DDS
1110 N Bancroft Pkwy # 2 (19805-2669)
PHONE..................302 658-7358
Director C Robert, *Owner*
Marlene Michaels, *Principal*
EMP: 4
SALES (est): 149.3K **Privately Held**
SIC: 8021 Dental clinics & offices

(G-12437)
ROBERT FICKLING
Also Called: Directfit
2307 Paulwynn Rd (19810-2727)
PHONE..................980 422-4754
Robert Fickling, *Owner*
EMP: 1 **EST:** 2014
SALES (est): 50.6K **Privately Held**
SIC: 3949 Gymnasium equipment

(G-12438)
ROBERT G BURKE PAINTING CO
1614 E Ayre St (19804-2515)
PHONE..................302 998-2200
Robert G Burke, *President*
EMP: 10
SALES (est): 450K **Privately Held**
SIC: 1721 Painting & paper hanging

(G-12439)
ROBERT HALF INTERNATIONAL INC
Also Called: Accountemps
500 Delaware Ave Ste 700 (19801-7407)
PHONE..................302 252-3162
Erin Steele, *Director*
Patrice Childress, *Administration*
EMP: 22
SALES (corp-wide): 5.8B **Publicly Held**
WEB: www.rhii.com
SIC: 7361 Placement agencies
PA: Robert Half International Inc.
2884 Sand Hill Rd Ste 200
Menlo Park CA 94025
650 234-6000

GEOGRAPHIC SECTION
Wilmington - New Castle County (G-12471)

(G-12440)
ROBERT J PEOPLES INC
1 Westmoreland Ave Apt A (19804-1763)
P.O. Box 65, New Castle (19720-0065)
PHONE..................302 322-0595
Steve Pedrick, *President*
Steven Pedrick, *President*
Sandra Pedrick, *Admin Sec*
EMP: 10
SQ FT: 3,000
SALES (est): 626.7K **Privately Held**
SIC: 1721 Exterior commercial painting contractor; interior commercial painting contractor

(G-12441)
ROBERT MULLIN
208 N Spring Valley Rd (19807-2427)
PHONE..................302 322-9002
Robert Mullin, *Owner*
Denise Mullin, *Owner*
Patrick Mullin, *Office Mgr*
EMP: 5
SQ FT: 18,000
SALES (est): 455.9K **Privately Held**
SIC: 1711 Warm air heating & air conditioning contractor

(G-12442)
ROBINO MANAGEMENT GROUP INC
5189 W Woodmill Dr 30a (19808-4009)
PHONE..................302 633-6001
Paul A Robino, *President*
EMP: 38
SQ FT: 2,300
SALES (est): 2MM **Privately Held**
SIC: 6531 Real estate managers

(G-12443)
ROBINS HAIR & TANNING
2716 Naamans Rd (19810-1139)
PHONE..................302 529-9000
Robin Bilone, *Owner*
EMP: 5
SALES (est): 117.9K **Privately Held**
SIC: 7231 7299 Hairdressers; tanning salon

(G-12444)
ROBINSON GRAYSON AND WARD PA
Also Called: Robinson and Grayson
910 Foulk Rd Ste 200 (19803-3159)
PHONE..................302 655-6262
Stephen Robinson, *Partner*
Rosemarie Morris, *Manager*
EMP: 5
SALES (est): 461.7K **Privately Held**
WEB: www.robgraylaw.com
SIC: 8111 General practice attorney, lawyer

(G-12445)
ROCCOS AUTOMOTIVE SERVICE
Also Called: Rocco Automotive
2379 Limestone Rd (19808-8010)
PHONE..................302 998-2234
Tony Rocco, *President*
Suzan J Langston, *Corp Secy*
Barbara A Rocco, *Vice Pres*
EMP: 13
SQ FT: 11,000
SALES (est): 750K **Privately Held**
SIC: 7538 Engine repair; truck engine repair, except industrial

(G-12446)
ROCHELLE E HAAS M D
1600 Rockland Rd (19803-3607)
PHONE..................302 651-5600
Rochelle Haas, *Principal*
EMP: 5
SALES (est): 83.1K **Privately Held**
SIC: 8011 Offices & clinics of medical doctors

(G-12447)
ROCK MANOR GOLF COURSE
1319 Carruthers Ln (19803-4601)
PHONE..................302 295-1400
Kyle Dalton, *General Mgr*
EMP: 5 EST: 2011
SALES (est): 426.1K **Privately Held**
SIC: 7992 Public golf courses

(G-12448)
ROCK SOLID CONTRACTING AND DEV
1213 B St (19801-5605)
PHONE..................302 655-8250
Norman Oliver, *Partner*
EMP: 6
SALES (est): 437.4K **Privately Held**
SIC: 1541 Industrial buildings & warehouses

(G-12449)
ROCKFORD ICE
1218 Glenside Ave (19803-3304)
PHONE..................302 478-7280
James Gardner, *Owner*
EMP: 1 EST: 1995
SALES (est): 74K **Privately Held**
SIC: 2097 5999 Manufactured ice; miscellaneous retail stores

(G-12450)
ROCKFORD MAP GALLERY LLC
1800 Lovering Ave (19806-2122)
PHONE..................302 740-1851
Patrik Keen,
EMP: 4
SALES (est): 357.1K **Privately Held**
SIC: 2752 Maps, lithographed

(G-12451)
ROCKFORD PARK CONDOMINIUM HOME
2302 Riddle Ave Ofc (19806-2139)
PHONE..................302 658-7842
Barbara Worrell, *Manager*
EMP: 6
SQ FT: 5,000
SALES (est): 118.4K **Privately Held**
SIC: 8641 Condominium association

(G-12452)
ROCKLAND BUILDERS INC
1605 E Ayre St (19804-2514)
PHONE..................302 995-6800
David T Heaney, *President*
EMP: 15
SALES (est): 1.3MM **Privately Held**
SIC: 1521 New construction, single-family houses

(G-12453)
ROCKLAND PLACE
1519 Rockland Rd (19803-3611)
PHONE..................302 777-3099
EMP: 23 EST: 2008
SALES (est): 1.6MM **Privately Held**
SIC: 8051 Skilled nursing care facilities

(G-12454)
ROCKLAND SPORTS LLC
Also Called: Dupont Country Club
1001 Rockland Rd (19803-2923)
PHONE..................302 654-4435
Robert Wirth, *CEO*
EMP: 55
SALES (est): 47.7K **Privately Held**
SIC: 7997 Membership sports & recreation clubs

(G-12455)
ROCKLAND SURGERY CENTER LP
Also Called: Center For Advnced Srgcal Arts
2710 Centerville Rd # 100 (19808-1652)
PHONE..................302 999-0200
Lorraine Troutner, *Manager*
Stewart G Smith, *Director*
Bernadette Odum, *Director*
EMP: 20
SQ FT: 8,100
SALES: 3.5MM **Privately Held**
SIC: 8011 Surgeon

(G-12456)
ROCKLEDGE GLOBAL PARTNERS LTD
1000 N West St Ste 1200 (19801-1058)
PHONE..................800 659-1102
Manuel Celaya, *Director*
EMP: 12

SALES: 1,000K **Privately Held**
SIC: 8748 Business consulting

(G-12457)
ROCKWOOD FINANCIAL GROUP INC
228 Philadelphia Pike A (19809-3125)
PHONE..................302 791-0237
Tom Shumosic, *President*
EMP: 4
SALES: 450K **Privately Held**
WEB: www.rockwoodfinancial.com
SIC: 7389 Financial services

(G-12458)
ROCKWOOD MUSEUM
610 Shipley Rd (19809-3609)
PHONE..................302 761-4340
Michael Clark, *President*
Phillip Nord, *Director*
Philip Nord, *Director*
EMP: 6
SALES (est): 117K **Privately Held**
SIC: 8412 Museum

(G-12459)
ROD-AES SURVERYORS CO
Also Called: AES Surveyors
3913 Old Capitol Trl (19808-5723)
PHONE..................302 993-1059
Donald A Elrod, *President*
EMP: 5
SQ FT: 900
SALES (est): 380.7K **Privately Held**
WEB: www.aessurveyors.com
SIC: 8713 Photogrammetric engineering

(G-12460)
RODNEY RBNSN LDSCP ARCHTS INC
30 Hill Rd (19806)
PHONE..................302 888-1544
Rodney Robinson, *President*
EMP: 7
SQ FT: 1,000
SALES: 950K **Privately Held**
WEB: www.rrla.com
SIC: 0781 Landscape architects

(G-12461)
RODNEY SQUARE ASSOCIATES
1 Rodney Sq (19801)
PHONE..................302 652-1536
Barbara Paxson, *Manager*
EMP: 6
SALES (corp-wide): 1.8MM **Privately Held**
SIC: 6512 Commercial & industrial building operation
PA: Rodney Square Associates
2005 Market St Ste 4100
Philadelphia PA 19103
215 563-3558

(G-12462)
RODRIGUEZ MARIEVE O DMD PA
Also Called: Gentle Care Family Dentistry
1407 Foulk Rd (19803-2762)
PHONE..................302 655-5862
Marieve O Rodriguez, *Principal*
EMP: 5
SALES (est): 380K **Privately Held**
SIC: 8021 Dentists' office

(G-12463)
ROEBERG MOORE & ASSOCIATES PA
Also Called: Moore, William X Jr
910 Gilpin Ave (19806-3211)
PHONE..................302 658-4757
David Roeberg, *Partner*
William Moore, *Vice Pres*
Curtis J Crowther,
EMP: 10
SQ FT: 7,000
SALES (est): 1.3MM **Privately Held**
SIC: 8111 General practice law office

(G-12464)
ROGER D ANDERSON
Also Called: Smith, Katzenscein and Jenkins
800 Delaware Ave Ste 1000 (19801-1354)
P.O. Box 410 (19899-0410)
PHONE..................302 652-8400
Roger Anderson, *Partner*
Kelly Green, *Counsel*
EMP: 23
SALES (est): 1.7MM **Privately Held**
SIC: 8111 General practice attorney, lawyer

(G-12465)
ROIZMAN & ASSOCIATES INC
Also Called: Bethel Villa Apartments
506 E 5th St (19801-4706)
PHONE..................302 426-9688
Camilla Grave, *Manager*
EMP: 5
SALES (corp-wide): 25.1MM **Privately Held**
WEB: www.roizman.com
SIC: 6513 6552 Apartment building operators; subdividers & developers
PA: Roizman & Associates, Inc.
832 Germantown Pike Ste 5
Plymouth Meeting PA 19462
610 278-1733

(G-12466)
ROLLINS LEASING LLC (DH)
2200 Concord Pike (19803-2909)
P.O. Box 563, Reading PA (19603-0563)
PHONE..................302 426-2700
I Larry Brown, *CEO*
David Burr, *Ch of Bd*
Gerard F Griesser, *Vice Chairman*
Barbara Griest, *COO*
Terry Scott, *Exec VP*
▲ **EMP:** 214
SQ FT: 65,000
SALES (est): 108.2MM
SALES (corp-wide): 9.6B **Privately Held**
SIC: 7513 Truck rental, without drivers
HQ: Penske Truck Leasing Co., L.P.
2675 Morgantown Rd
Reading PA 19607
610 775-6000

(G-12467)
ROMAN INDUSTRIES INC
2421 E Heather Rd (19803-2717)
PHONE..................302 420-9420
Tom Mc Glothlin, *Principal*
EMP: 2 EST: 2010
SALES (est): 166.2K **Privately Held**
SIC: 3999 Manufacturing industries

(G-12468)
ROMIE LLC
300 Delaware Ave Ste 210a (19801-6601)
PHONE..................866 698-0052
Rajnarine Brigmohan, *President*
EMP: 1
SALES (est): 26K **Privately Held**
SIC: 8731 7372 Computer (hardware) development; operating systems computer software

(G-12469)
RONALD MCDONALD HOUSE DELAWARE
1901 Rockland Rd (19803-3629)
PHONE..................302 428-5299
Margaret Aument, *Opers Staff*
Erin McGrath, *Marketing Staff*
Sara Funaiock, *Manager*
Pam Cornforth, *Director*
Carol Sayles, *Executive Asst*
EMP: 11
SQ FT: 60,000
SALES: 2.9MM **Privately Held**
WEB: www.rmhde.org
SIC: 8322 Individual & family services

(G-12470)
RONALD W PEACOCK INC
110 Matthes Ave (19804-1534)
PHONE..................302 571-9313
Ronald W Peacock, *President*
Michelle Peacock, *Principal*
EMP: 11
SQ FT: 1,200
SALES (est): 618.7K **Privately Held**
SIC: 1721 Painting & paper hanging

(G-12471)
RONAN GILL LLC
717 N Union St Pmb 6 (19805-3031)
PHONE..................877 549-7712
Ronan Gill,

Wilmington - New Castle County (G-12472)

EMP: 10
SALES: 500K Privately Held
SIC: 2759 5699 Screen printing; sports apparel

(G-12472)
RONNIES AUTO REPAIRS INC (PA)
4 S Mary St (19804-3111)
PHONE.................302 994-4703
Ronald Roberts Jr, *Owner*
EMP: 5
SQ FT: 1,200
SALES (est): 658.7K Privately Held
SIC: 7538 General automotive repair shops

(G-12473)
ROOFERS INC
Also Called: Tri State Roofers
404 Meco Dr (19804-1112)
PHONE.................302 995-7027
Francis Sanna, *President*
Janice Sanna, *Corp Secy*
Charles High, *Vice Pres*
Ron Sanna, *Vice Pres*
EMP: 35
SQ FT: 12,000
SALES (est): 4.7MM Privately Held
SIC: 1761 Roofing contractor; gutter & downspout contractor; roof repair; sheet metalwork

(G-12474)
ROPE-IT GOLF LLC
3 River Rd (19809-3205)
PHONE.................305 767-3481
Louis Girifalco,
Marc Reda,
EMP: 3
SALES (est): 216.6K Privately Held
SIC: 3949 Golf equipment

(G-12475)
ROSEN MOSS SNYDER BLEEFELD
501 Silverside Rd Ste 33 (19809-1388)
PHONE.................302 475-8060
Alan N Frank, *Branch Mgr*
EMP: 4
SALES (corp-wide): 2.1MM Privately Held
SIC: 8111 General practice attorney, lawyer
PA: Rosen Moss Snyder Bleefeld
   101 Greenwood Ave Ste 410
   Jenkintown PA 19046
   215 935-0315

(G-12476)
ROSENTHAL CHIROPRACTIC OFFS PA (PA)
507 S Maryland Ave (19804-1665)
PHONE.................302 999-0633
Scott Rosenthal, *President*
EMP: 4
SALES (est): 286.3K Privately Held
WEB: www.rosenthalchiropractic.com
SIC: 8041 Offices & clinics of chiropractors

(G-12477)
ROSENTHAL MONHAIT GODDESS PA
919 N Market St Ste 1401 (19801-3046)
P.O. Box 1070 (19899-1070)
PHONE.................302 656-4433
Joseph Rosenthal, *Managing Prtnr*
Carmella Kenne, *Managing Prtnr*
Edward Rosenthal, *VP Finance*
Jeffrey Goddess, *Mng Member*
Carmella Keener,
EMP: 16 EST: 1960
SALES (est): 1.5MM Privately Held
WEB: www.rmglaw.com
SIC: 8111 General practice law office; corporate, partnership & business law; real estate law

(G-12478)
ROSNER LAW GROUP LLC
824 N Market St Ste 810 (19801-4939)
PHONE.................302 295-4877
Frederick B Rosner, *Principal*
Scott Leonhardt, *Associate*
EMP: 4

SALES (est): 345.6K Privately Held
SIC: 8111 General practice attorney, lawyer

(G-12479)
ROSS ARONSTAM & MORITZ LLP
100 S West St (19801-5015)
PHONE.................302 576-1600
Bradley R Aronstam, *Partner*
Garrett B Moritz, *Partner*
David E Ross, *Partner*
Collins J Seitz Jr, *Partner*
Jennifer Lano, *Legal Staff*
EMP: 18
SALES (est): 489K Privately Held
SIC: 8111 General practice attorney, lawyer

(G-12480)
ROSSI AUTO BODY INC
512 Belmont Ave (19804-1449)
PHONE.................302 999-7707
Gary Rossi, *President*
Frank Rossi, *Corp Secy*
John J Rossi, *Vice Pres*
EMP: 7
SQ FT: 2,500
SALES (est): 560.8K Privately Held
SIC: 7532 7549 Body shop, automotive; paint shop, automotive; towing service, automotive

(G-12481)
ROXLOR LLC
1013 Centre Rd Ste 106 (19805-1265)
PHONE.................302 778-4166
Gary Shap, *VP Bus Dvlpt*
Roger Dodd, *VP Sales*
Robert Veghte,
▲ **EMP:** 5
SALES (est): 490.9K Privately Held
WEB: www.roxlor.com
SIC: 2023 Dietary supplements, dairy & non-dairy based

(G-12482)
ROY COVEY
Also Called: Midway Muffler Shop
701 Kirkwood Hwy (19805-5110)
PHONE.................302 995-2900
Roy Covey, *Owner*
EMP: 4
SQ FT: 2,500
SALES (est): 271.1K Privately Held
SIC: 7533 7539 Muffler shop, sale or repair & installation; shock absorber replacement; brake repair, automotive

(G-12483)
ROYAL BANK AMERICA LEASING LLC
1000 Rocky Run Pkwy (19803-1455)
PHONE.................302 529-5984
Frederick Peters, *President*
EMP: 6
SALES (corp-wide): 188.6MM Privately Held
SIC: 6029 Commercial banks
HQ: Royal Bank Amercia Leasing, Llc
   915 Montgomery Ave # 401
   Penn Valley PA 19072
   610 668-4700

(G-12484)
ROYAL BANK AMERICA LEASING LLC
20 Montchanin Rd Ste 100 (19807-2179)
PHONE.................302 798-1790
Robert W Eaddy, *President*
EMP: 12
SALES (corp-wide): 188.6MM Privately Held
SIC: 6022 State commercial banks
HQ: Royal Bank Amercia Leasing, Llc
   915 Montgomery Ave # 401
   Penn Valley PA 19072
   610 668-4700

(G-12485)
ROYAL CLEANERS
3914 Concord Pike (19803-1716)
PHONE.................302 478-0955
Steve Kim, *Owner*
EMP: 8

SALES (est): 330K Privately Held
SIC: 7216 Cleaning & dyeing, except rugs

(G-12486)
RS WIDDOES AND SON INC
204 Channel Rd (19809-3505)
PHONE.................302 764-7455
Richard S Widdoes, *President*
Mike Widdoes, *Vice Pres*
EMP: 7
SQ FT: 1,500
SALES: 500K Privately Held
SIC: 1771 1611 Concrete work; general contractor, highway & street construction

(G-12487)
RSL INVESTORS INC
1105 Market Ste 1230 (19899)
P.O. Box 8985 (19899-8985)
PHONE.................302 478-5142
Robert Rosekranz, *President*
EMP: 25
SALES (est): 1.3MM Privately Held
WEB: www.delphifin.com
SIC: 6211 Investment bankers
HQ: Delphi Financial Group, Inc.
   1105 N Market St Ste 1230
   Wilmington DE 19801
   302 478-5142

(G-12488)
RU INC
2711 Centerville Rd (19808-1660)
PHONE.................917 346-0285
Ryan Finnesey, *President*
EMP: 140 EST: 2002
SALES: 12MM Privately Held
SIC: 7379 7372 Computer related consulting services; business oriented computer software

(G-12489)
RUBIO CONSTRUCTION LLC
6 E 40th St (19802-2335)
PHONE.................302 377-0353
Tabither P Madden,
EMP: 4
SALES: 100K Privately Held
SIC: 1521 General remodeling, single-family houses

(G-12490)
RUDLYN INC
Also Called: Rudy Auto Body
3900 Governor Printz Blvd (19802-2308)
PHONE.................302 764-5677
Rudy Di Bonaventura, *President*
Linda Di Bonaventura, *Vice Pres*
EMP: 17
SQ FT: 17,000
SALES: 740K Privately Held
SIC: 7532 Body shop, automotive

(G-12491)
RUDY MARINE INC (PA)
Also Called: Rudy's Outboard Service
411 S Maryland Ave (19804-1627)
PHONE.................302 999-8735
Thomas Rudloff, *President*
EMP: 12
SALES (est): 3.2MM Privately Held
WEB: www.rudymarine.com
SIC: 5551 7699 Motor boat dealers; marine supplies; marine engine repair

(G-12492)
RUKKET LLC
Also Called: Rukket Sports
5006 Kennett Pike (19807-1818)
PHONE.................855 478-5538
Jana Skrabalkova, *Mng Member*
Ryan Dickerson,
Samuel Hyland,
◆ **EMP:** 6
SALES: 697.8K Privately Held
SIC: 5941 3949 Sporting goods & bicycle shops; sporting & athletic goods

(G-12493)
RUMMEL KLEPPER & KAHL LLP
Also Called: RK&k
1 Riverwal Ctr 110 S Po (19801)
PHONE.................302 468-4880
Mark M Dumler, *Branch Mgr*
EMP: 22

SALES (corp-wide): 210.8MM Privately Held
SIC: 8711 Civil engineering
PA: Rummel, Klepper & Kahl, Llp
   700 E Pratt St Ste 500
   Baltimore MD 21202
   410 728-2900

(G-12494)
RUNWAY LIQUIDATION LLC
Also Called: Bcbg
2500 Grubb Rd Ste 234 (19810-4796)
PHONE.................305 451-1481
EMP: 3
SALES (corp-wide): 570.1MM Privately Held
SIC: 2335 Women's, juniors' & misses' dresses
HQ: Runway Liquidation, Llc
   2761 Fruitland Ave
   Vernon CA 90058
   323 589-2224

(G-12495)
RUSSELL A PAULUS & SON INC
193 Christina Landing Dr (19801-5253)
PHONE.................302 998-4494
Russell Paulus, *President*
Donna Paulus, *Vice Pres*
EMP: 9
SALES (est): 630.7K Privately Held
SIC: 1761 Roofing, siding & sheet metal work

(G-12496)
RUSSELL J TIBBETTS DDS PA
Also Called: Thomas, Irving O DDS
3516 Silverside Rd Ste 17 (19810-4932)
PHONE.................302 479-5959
Russell J Tibbetts, *Owner*
Lisa Brown, *Manager*
EMP: 7
SQ FT: 2,000
SALES (est): 440K Privately Held
SIC: 8021 Dentists' office

(G-12497)
RUSSO BROTHERS INC
16 White Oak Rd (19809-3265)
PHONE.................302 764-5562
Steven J Russo, *President*
Kathleen Russo, *Treasurer*
EMP: 4 EST: 1920
SQ FT: 2,000
SALES (est): 423.5K Privately Held
SIC: 1711 Warm air heating & air conditioning contractor; plumbing contractors

(G-12498)
RUSSO MARY CLAIRE REAL ESTATE
3211 Cardiff Dr (19810-3425)
PHONE.................302 529-2653
John Russo, *Principal*
EMP: 4
SALES (est): 107.9K Privately Held
SIC: 8021 Offices & clinics of dentists

(G-12499)
RW GREER INC
203 Philadelphia Pike (19809-3159)
PHONE.................302 764-0376
David Greer, *President*
Erin Daniels, *Office Mgr*
EMP: 9 EST: 1973
SQ FT: 1,000
SALES (est): 1MM Privately Held
WEB: www.greerrw.com
SIC: 1711 Plumbing contractors; warm air heating & air conditioning contractor

(G-12500)
RYDER TRUCK RENTAL INC
300 S Madison St (19801)
PHONE.................302 571-4210
Doug Thompson, *Branch Mgr*
EMP: 12
SALES (corp-wide): 8.4B Publicly Held
SIC: 7513 Truck rental, without drivers
HQ: Ryder Truck Rental, Inc.
   11690 Nw 105th St
   Medley FL 33178
   305 500-3726

GEOGRAPHIC SECTION
Wilmington - New Castle County (G-12533)

(G-12501)
RYDER TRUCK RENTAL INC
6605 Governor Printz Blvd (19809-2027)
PHONE..................302 798-1472
Gary Guillen, *Manager*
EMP: 20
SALES (corp-wide): 8.4B **Publicly Held**
SIC: 7513 7359 Truck rental, without drivers; equipment rental & leasing
HQ: Ryder Truck Rental, Inc.
11690 Nw 105th St
Medley FL 33178
305 500-3726

(G-12502)
RYERSON GERALYN
1601 Milltown Rd Ste 8 (19808-4073)
PHONE..................302 547-3060
Geralyn Ryerson, *President*
EMP: 4
SALES (est): 42.4K **Privately Held**
SIC: 8322 Individual & family services

(G-12503)
RYLAND FUNERAL HOME INC
9 W 30th St Lowr Ste (19802-3135)
PHONE..................302 764-7711
Julius Ryland Jr, *President*
EMP: 7
SALES (est): 430K **Privately Held**
SIC: 7261 Funeral home

(G-12504)
S & A HOLDING ASSOCIATES INC
4737 Concord Pike Ste 261 (19803-1477)
P.O. Box 7189 (19803-0189)
PHONE..................302 479-8314
Franch Aciero, *Vice Pres*
EMP: 5
SALES (est): 280.4K **Privately Held**
SIC: 6512 Shopping center, property operation only

(G-12505)
S & H ENTERPRISES INC
Also Called: S&H Investigative Services
112 Water St (19804-2407)
P.O. Box 12245 (19850-2245)
PHONE..................302 999-9911
John Slogowski, *President*
Caryn Gloyd, *Vice Pres*
EMP: 12
SALES (est): 231.7K **Privately Held**
WEB: www.snh.net
SIC: 7381 Private investigator

(G-12506)
S G WILLIAMS & BROS CO (PA)
301 N Tatnall St (19801-2446)
PHONE..................302 656-8167
John D Griffith, *President*
Helen Griffith, *Corp Secy*
EMP: 15 EST: 1910
SQ FT: 15,000
SALES (est): 15MM **Privately Held**
SIC: 5082 5051 1761 3444 General construction machinery & equipment; aluminum bars, rods, ingots, sheets, pipes, plates, etc.; roofing, siding & sheet metal work; gutters, sheet metal

(G-12507)
S J DESMOND INC
22 Lloyd Pl (19810-1325)
P.O. Box 9511 (19809-0511)
PHONE..................302 475-6520
Stephen J Desmond, *President*
Susan Desmond, *Admin Sec*
▲ EMP: 6 EST: 1997
SALES: 250K **Privately Held**
SIC: 1731 Electrical work

(G-12508)
S P S INTERNATIONAL INV CO (DH)
1105 N Market St Ste 1300 (19801-1241)
PHONE..................302 478-9055
EMP: 7
SALES (est): 8.4MM
SALES (corp-wide): 225.3B **Publicly Held**
SIC: 3324 Steel investment foundries
HQ: Sps Technologies, Llc
301 Highland Ave
Jenkintown PA 19046
215 572-3000

(G-12509)
S WALLACE HOLDINGS LLC
251 Little Falls Dr (19808-1674)
PHONE..................917 304-1164
Sherene A Wallace,
EMP: 5
SALES: 100K **Privately Held**
SIC: 7323 Credit reporting services

(G-12510)
S&D INDUSTRIES LLC
2711 Centerville Rd # 400 (19808-1660)
PHONE..................703 801-3643
Robert Shaver, *Principal*
EMP: 5
SALES (est): 150.7K **Privately Held**
SIC: 3999 Manufacturing industries

(G-12511)
SABION SOUND REINFORCEMENT CO
15 W Reamer Ave (19804-1715)
PHONE..................302 427-0551
Guy D Cartelli, *Owner*
EMP: 2
SALES (est): 161.5K **Privately Held**
SIC: 3993 Signs & advertising specialties

(G-12512)
SACHE SOCIAL CLUB
317 Townsend St (19801-5315)
PHONE..................302 287-4813
EMP: 4
SALES (est): 41.9K **Privately Held**
SIC: 7997 Membership sports & recreation clubs

(G-12513)
SACRED HEART VILLAGE I INC
920 N Monroe St (19801-1383)
PHONE..................302 428-0801
Ronald Giannone, *Director*
Christa Rowe, *Administration*
EMP: 20
SALES: 952.8K **Privately Held**
SIC: 8361 Home for the aged

(G-12514)
SACRED HEART VILLAGE II INC
625 E 10th St (19801-4039)
PHONE..................302 428-3702
Jean Forlano, *Accountant*
Ronald Giannone, *Director*
EMP: 6
SALES (est): 147.1K **Privately Held**
SIC: 8361 Home for the aged

(G-12515)
SAFE HOME CONTROL INC
1000 N West St (19801-1050)
PHONE..................302 504-6300
EMP: 4 EST: 2015
SALES (est): 93.4K **Privately Held**
SIC: 7382 Security systems services

(G-12516)
SAFE SPACE DELAWARE INC
500 W 2nd St (19801-2312)
PHONE..................302 691-7946
Allen Conover, *CEO*
EMP: 18
SALES: 1.9MM **Privately Held**
SIC: 8093 Mental health clinic, outpatient

(G-12517)
SAFEGUARD DX LABORATORY
110 S Poplar St Ste 200 (19801-5034)
PHONE..................888 919-8275
John Distefano, *Principal*
EMP: 2
SALES (est): 104.2K **Privately Held**
SIC: 3821 Clinical laboratory instruments, except medical & dental

(G-12518)
SAFELITE FULFILLMENT INC
Also Called: Safelite Autoglass 363
4722 Kirkwood Hwy (19808-5008)
PHONE..................302 999-9908
Laraine Peel, *Manager*
EMP: 11
SALES (corp-wide): 177.9K **Privately Held**
WEB: www.belronus.com
SIC: 7536 Automotive glass replacement shops
HQ: Safelite Fulfillment, Inc.
7400 Safelite Way
Columbus OH 43235
614 210-9000

(G-12519)
SAFELITE GLASS CORP
Also Called: Safelite Autoglass
109 Rogers Rd Ste 4 (19801-5779)
PHONE..................302 656-4640
Danny Beiseigel, *Manager*
EMP: 12
SALES (corp-wide): 177.9K **Privately Held**
SIC: 7536 5013 Automotive glass replacement shops; automobile glass
HQ: Safelite Glass Corp.
7400 Safelite Way
Columbus OH 43235
614 210-9000

(G-12520)
SAFEPLACE CORPORATION
4 Chaville Way (19807-1422)
P.O. Box 4119 (19807-4119)
PHONE..................302 479-9000
John Fannin, *CEO*
EMP: 4
SALES (est): 297.9K **Privately Held**
SIC: 7389 Building inspection service

(G-12521)
SAFER TECHNOLOGIES LLC
427 N Tatnall St (19801-2230)
PHONE..................302 497-0333
Joseph Carlucci, *Director*
EMP: 5 EST: 2013
SALES (est): 107K **Privately Held**
SIC: 7371 Computer software development

(G-12522)
SAHAVE INC
919 N Market St Ste 950 (19801-3036)
PHONE..................630 401-5211
EMP: 10
SALES (est): 257.8K **Privately Held**
SIC: 7373 Systems software development services

(G-12523)
SAIN COSMOS LLC
3524 Silverside Rd 35b (19810-4929)
PHONE..................936 244-7017
EMP: 10
SALES (est): 217.5K **Privately Held**
SIC: 7371 Computer software systems analysis & design, custom

(G-12524)
SALEM COUNTY AMATEUR RADIO CLB
2015 Bentwood Ct (19804-3937)
PHONE..................302 689-8127
Robert Slippey, *Principal*
EMP: 4
SALES (est): 38.1K **Privately Held**
SIC: 7997 Membership sports & recreation clubs

(G-12525)
SALLY BEAUTY SUPPLY LLC
Also Called: Sally Beauty Supply 1497
4395 Kirkwood Hwy (19808-5113)
PHONE..................302 995-6197
Kathy Monger, *Manager*
EMP: 4 **Publicly Held**
WEB: www.sallybeauty.com
SIC: 5087 Beauty parlor equipment & supplies
HQ: Sally Beauty Supply Llc
3001 Colorado Blvd
Denton TX 76210
940 898-7500

(G-12526)
SALS AUTO SERVICES INC
Also Called: Mobil
3000 Lancaster Ave (19805-1459)
PHONE..................302 654-1168
Sal Panarello, *President*
EMP: 5
SQ FT: 2,500
SALES: 600K **Privately Held**
SIC: 5541 7549 Filling stations, gasoline; do-it-yourself garages

(G-12527)
SALS GARAGE INC
705 N Lincoln St Ste 1 (19805-3043)
PHONE..................302 655-4981
Salvatore Vassallo, *President*
John Vassallo, *Vice Pres*
EMP: 5
SQ FT: 5,000
SALES (est): 322.4K **Privately Held**
WEB: www.salsgaragede.com
SIC: 7538 General automotive repair shops

(G-12528)
SALVATION ARMY
2 S Augustine St (19804-2504)
PHONE..................302 996-9400
Terry Reilly, *President*
EMP: 20
SALES (corp-wide): 2.2B **Privately Held**
SIC: 8322 Individual & family services
HQ: The Salvation Army
440 W Nyack Rd Ofc
West Nyack NY 10994
845 620-7200

(G-12529)
SALVATION ARMY
400 N Orange St (19801-2219)
P.O. Box 308 (19899-0308)
PHONE..................302 656-1696
Tim Duperree, *Manager*
EMP: 100
SALES (corp-wide): 2.2B **Privately Held**
WEB: www.salvationarmy-usaeast.org
SIC: 8322 8351 Senior citizens' center or association; family service agency; child day care services
HQ: The Salvation Army
440 W Nyack Rd Ofc
West Nyack NY 10994
845 620-7200

(G-12530)
SALVATION ARMY
107 S Market St (19801-5235)
PHONE..................302 654-8808
John Swires, *Administration*
EMP: 25
SALES (corp-wide): 2.2B **Privately Held**
WEB: www.salvationarmy-usaeast.org
SIC: 8399 8641 Advocacy group; civic social & fraternal associations
HQ: The Salvation Army
440 W Nyack Rd Ofc
West Nyack NY 10994
845 620-7200

(G-12531)
SAM WALTS & ASSOCIATES
Also Called: Sam Waltz & Associates Counsel
11 Downs Dr (19807-2555)
P.O. Box 3798 (19807-0798)
PHONE..................302 777-2211
Sam Waltz, *Owner*
EMP: 7
SQ FT: 3,000
SALES (est): 523.3K **Privately Held**
WEB: www.samwaltz.com
SIC: 8742 Management consulting services

(G-12532)
SAMARITAN OUTREACH
1410 N Claymont St (19802-5227)
PHONE..................302 594-9476
Karen Lienau, *Principal*
EMP: 6
SALES (est): 120.3K **Privately Held**
SIC: 8322 Outreach program

(G-12533)
SAMS CONSTRUCTION LLC
1405 Haines Ave (19809-2716)
P.O. Box 9827 (19809-0827)
PHONE..................302 654-6542
Sam Matinez,
EMP: 25 EST: 1992

Wilmington - New Castle County (G-12534)   GEOGRAPHIC SECTION

SALES (est): 2.5MM **Privately Held**
SIC: **1521** Single-family housing construction

(G-12534)
SAMS CONSTRUCTION LLC
1227 E 15th St (19802-5214)
P.O. Box 9827 (19809-0827)
PHONE..................................302 654-6542
Samuel Martinez,
EMP: 25
SQ FT: 5,000
SALES (est): 1.6MM **Privately Held**
SIC: **1611** Highway & street construction

(G-12535)
SAMUEL BLUMBERG PHD
2300 Pennsylvania Ave (19806-1392)
PHONE..................................302 652-7733
Samuel Blumberg, *Principal*
EMP: 4
SALES (est): 89K **Privately Held**
SIC: **8049** Clinical psychologist

(G-12536)
SANCO CONSTRUCTION CO INC
24 Brookside Dr (19804-1102)
PHONE..................................302 633-4156
Christopher Marcozzi, *President*
Ralph Marcozzi, *Admin Sec*
EMP: 9
SQ FT: 1,200
SALES (est): 1.4MM **Privately Held**
SIC: **1611 1771** Highway & street paving contractor; parking lot construction

(G-12537)
SANCTUARY SPA AND SALOON
1847 Marsh Rd (19810-4505)
PHONE..................................302 475-1469
Joan Grave, *Partner*
Barbara Hafner, *Manager*
EMP: 10
SALES (est): 629.5K **Privately Held**
SIC: **7299 7991** Massage parlor & steam bath services; spas

(G-12538)
SANDEBBARNANRICWAY CORP
Also Called: Lewis Educational Games
2221 Inwood Rd (19810-2807)
PHONE..................................302 475-2705
Richard W Lewis, *President*
EMP: 2
SALES: 30K **Privately Held**
SIC: **3999 3944** Education aids, devices & supplies; games, toys & children's vehicles

(G-12539)
SANDERSON ALBIDRESS AGENCY
1211b Milltown Rd (19808-3003)
PHONE..................................302 368-3010
Albidress Sanderson, *Owner*
EMP: 5
SALES (est): 607.1K **Privately Held**
SIC: **6411** Insurance agents & brokers

(G-12540)
SANJABAN CORP
4023 Kennett Pike # 701 (19807-2018)
PHONE..................................612 805-5971
Mashfiqul Alam, *President*
EMP: 5
SALES: 500K **Privately Held**
SIC: **7379** Computer related consulting services

(G-12541)
SANTANDER BANK NA
824 N Market St Ste 100 (19801-3374)
PHONE..................................302 654-5182
Marie Sherlock, *Branch Mgr*
EMP: 10
SALES (corp-wide): 1.4B **Publicly Held**
SIC: **6022** State commercial banks
HQ: Santander Bank, N.A.
75 State St
Boston MA 02109
617 757-3410

(G-12542)
SARGENT & LUNDY LLC
500 Delaware Ave Ste 400 (19801-7404)
PHONE..................................302 622-7200
Matthew Thibodeau, *Vice Pres*
Carol Newhard, *Human Resources*
Paul Kish, *Sr Project Mgr*
David Miller, *Manager*
Thomas Cavalcante, *Consultant*
EMP: 170
SALES (corp-wide): 332.5MM **Privately Held**
WEB: www.sargentlundy.com
SIC: **8711** Consulting engineer
PA: Sargent & Lundy, L.L.C.
55 E Monroe St Ste 2700
Chicago IL 60603
312 269-2000

(G-12543)
SATELLITE CONNECTION INC
4001 Kennett Pike Ste 134 (19807-2000)
PHONE..................................302 328-2462
Neeshard Ahamad, *Principal*
EMP: 5
SALES (est): 191.1K **Privately Held**
SIC: **4841** Direct broadcast satellite services (DBS)

(G-12544)
SATTAR A SYED DMD PA
5507 Kirkwood Hwy (19808-5001)
PHONE..................................302 994-3093
Sattar A Syed, *Principal*
EMP: 7 EST: 2007
SALES (est): 429K **Privately Held**
SIC: **8021** Dentists' office

(G-12545)
SAUER HOLDINGS INC
1403 Foulk Rd Ste 200 (19803-2788)
PHONE..................................302 656-8989
William N Steitz, *President*
Kenneth Kubacki, *Treasurer*
EMP: 47
SALES (est): 1.3MM
SALES (corp-wide): 2.8MM **Privately Held**
SIC: **8711** Engineering services
PA: Sauer Industries, Inc.
30 51st St
Pittsburgh PA 15201
412 687-4100

(G-12546)
SAUL EWING ARNSTEIN & LEHR LLP
1201 N Market St Ste 2300 (19801-1165)
P.O. Box 1266 (19899-1266)
PHONE..................................302 654-1413
William Manning, *Managing Prtnr*
Daniel H Krapf, *Vice Chairman*
Denise Frawley, *Executive*
Carl B Everett,
Norman Pernick,
EMP: 50
SALES (corp-wide): 138.6MM **Privately Held**
WEB: www.saul.com
SIC: **8111** General practice attorney, lawyer
PA: Saul Ewing Arnstein & Lehr Llp
1500 Market St Fl 38
Philadelphia PA 19102
215 972-7777

(G-12547)
SAYHI LLC
1521 Concord Pike Ste 301 (19803-3644)
PHONE..................................860 631-7725
Lee Bossio,
EMP: 4
SALES (est): 132.7K **Privately Held**
SIC: **7389** Translation services;

(G-12548)
SC FOSTER LLC
43 Stonewold Way (19807-2566)
PHONE..................................302 383-0201
Scott Foster, *Mng Member*
EMP: 15
SQ FT: 5,000
SALES (est): 1.1MM **Privately Held**
WEB: www.scfoster.com
SIC: **7379** Computer related consulting services

(G-12549)
SC MARKETING US INC
2711 Centerville Rd # 120 (19808-1660)
PHONE..................................714 352-4992
Peer Dohrn, *Ch of Bd*
James A Estep Jr, *Manager*
EMP: 5
SQ FT: 250
SALES (est): 483.7K **Privately Held**
SIC: **8743** Sales promotion

(G-12550)
SC&A CONSTRUCTION INC
3411 Silverside Rd 202hg (19810-4836)
P.O. Box 7202 (19803-0202)
PHONE..................................302 478-6030
C David Murtagh, *CEO*
Lee Weersing, *President*
Thomas L Cover, *Vice Pres*
Caroline Cover, *Marketing Staff*
Tamara Curran, *Admin Sec*
EMP: 26
SQ FT: 4,500
SALES: 9MM **Privately Held**
WEB: www.scaconstructs.com
SIC: **1542 1521** Commercial & office building, new construction; shopping center construction; new construction, single-family houses

(G-12551)
SCALIA S LANDSCAPING
504 N Dupont Rd (19804-1214)
PHONE..................................302 651-9822
Anthony Scalia, *Owner*
EMP: 4
SALES (est): 146.8K **Privately Held**
SIC: **0781** Landscape services

(G-12552)
SCANPOINT INC
5700 Kirkwood Hwy Ste 202 (19808-4884)
PHONE..................................603 429-0777
Bill Cross, *President*
EMP: 8
SALES: 1.2MM **Privately Held**
WEB: www.scanpoint.com
SIC: **7371** Software programming applications

(G-12553)
SCHLEGEL ASSOCIATES INC
6 Palomino Ct Ste 101 (19803-1920)
PHONE..................................302 477-1810
Louis T Schlegel, *President*
EMP: 4
SALES: 800K **Privately Held**
SIC: **5084** Chemical process equipment

(G-12554)
SCHNADER HRRSON SGAL LEWIS LLP
824 N Market St Ste 800 (19801-4939)
PHONE..................................302 888-4554
Joan Kluger, *Managing Prtnr*
EMP: 58
SALES (corp-wide): 50MM **Privately Held**
SIC: **8111** General practice attorney, lawyer
PA: Schnader Harrison Segal & Lewis L.L.P.
1600 Market St Ste 3600
Philadelphia PA 19103
215 751-2000

(G-12555)
SCHOENBECK & SCHOENBECK PA
1211 Milltown Rd A (19808-3003)
PHONE..................................302 239-9316
Donna Schoenbeck, *President*
Janell S Ostroski, *Associate*
EMP: 4
SQ FT: 1,250
SALES (est): 200K **Privately Held**
WEB: www.schoenbeck.com
SIC: **8111** General practice attorney, lawyer

(G-12556)
SCHROEDL COMPANY
Also Called: Schroedl Cleaning Svcs Sup Co
422 B And O Ln (19804-1445)
PHONE..................................410 358-5500
John P Gallon, *President*
EMP: 58
SQ FT: 6,500
SALES (est): 1.6MM **Privately Held**
SIC: **7216** Curtain cleaning & repair

(G-12557)
SCHWEIZER CLEANING SERVICE
317 Brookside Dr (19804-1358)
PHONE..................................302 995-2816
Oscar Schweizer, *Owner*
EMP: 6
SALES (est): 93.4K **Privately Held**
SIC: **7349** Cleaning service, industrial or commercial

(G-12558)
SCICOM SCNTIFIC COMMUNICATIONS
Also Called: Scicom Systems
101 Beauregard Ct (19810-1181)
PHONE..................................302 475-2694
Paul Sienkiewicz, *President*
EMP: 4
SALES: 500K **Privately Held**
SIC: **7379** Computer related consulting services

(G-12559)
SCIENTIFIC USA INC
2711 Centerville Rd # 120 (19808-1660)
PHONE..................................425 681-9462
Michael Sweaney, *CEO*
Jacqui Budd, *Director*
Tricia Stevens, *Advisor*
EMP: 5 EST: 2011
SALES (est): 240.2K **Privately Held**
SIC: **7389** Cosmetic kits, assembling & packaging

(G-12560)
SCINORX TECHNOLOGIES INC
1521 Concord Pike (19803-3642)
PHONE..................................302 268-5447
Khushbu Agrawal, *President*
EMP: 5
SALES (est): 114.8K **Privately Held**
SIC: **7379**

(G-12561)
SCIO RISK GROUP LLC
808 N Lincoln St Ste 1 (19805-5320)
PHONE..................................302 897-1534
Erin Bickley,
EMP: 12
SALES (est): 489.6K **Privately Held**
SIC: **8748** Business consulting

(G-12562)
SCISSOR WIZARDS INC
1402 Harrison Ave (19809-1705)
PHONE..................................302 475-9575
Debbie Swayngim, *President*
George Swayngim, *Vice Pres*
EMP: 8
SQ FT: 1,400
SALES (est): 100.7K **Privately Held**
SIC: **7231** Hairdressers

(G-12563)
SCITUATE SOLAR I LLC
2711 Centerville Rd # 400 (19808-1660)
PHONE..................................212 419-4843
Richard Turnure, *Partner*
EMP: 8 EST: 2012
SALES (est): 517.8K
SALES (corp-wide): 10.7B **Publicly Held**
SIC: **4911** Generation, electric power
PA: The Aes Corporation
4300 Wilson Blvd Ste 1100
Arlington VA 22203
703 522-1315

(G-12564)
SCOTTS CO
100 W 10th St Lbby (19801-1647)
PHONE..................................302 777-4779
Scott Hines, *President*
EMP: 5
SALES (est): 392K **Privately Held**
SIC: **5149** Sandwiches

GEOGRAPHIC SECTION
Wilmington - New Castle County (G-12594)

(G-12565)
SEAMENS CENTER WILMINGTON INC
Port Of Wilmington (19899)
P.O. Box 405 (19899-0405)
PHONE.................302 575-1300
Joan Lyons, *Director*
EMP: 15
SALES: 309.7K **Privately Held**
SIC: 8621 Professional membership organizations

(G-12566)
SEARS ROEBUCK AND CO
4737 Concord Pike Ste 410 (19803-1431)
PHONE.................302 995-9295
Frank Cordomeyer, *Manager*
EMP: 73
SALES (corp-wide): 26.9B **Publicly Held**
SIC: 7549 Automotive maintenance services
HQ: Sears, Roebuck And Co.
3333 Beverly Rd
Hoffman Estates IL 60179
847 286-2500

(G-12567)
SECOND CHANCE SOLUTIONS LLC
913 N Market St Ste 200 (19801-3097)
PHONE.................302 204-0551
Atu Kyeison, *CEO*
EMP: 7
SALES (est): 183.7K **Privately Held**
SIC: 8742 Management consulting services

(G-12568)
SECURITAS ELECTRONIC SEC INC
1100 First State Blvd (19804-3550)
PHONE.................302 992-7950
Dave Shakespeare, *Branch Mgr*
Fred Goss, *Technical Staff*
EMP: 23
SALES (corp-wide): 10.6B **Privately Held**
SIC: 7382 Security systems services
HQ: Securitas Electronic Security Inc.
3800 Tabs Dr
Uniontown OH 44685
855 331-0359

(G-12569)
SECURITAS SEC SVCS USA INC
Also Called: Mid-Atlantic Region
1220 N Market St Ste 800 (19801-2540)
PHONE.................302 573-6802
EMP: 195
SALES (corp-wide): 10.6B **Privately Held**
WEB: www.securitasinc.com
SIC: 7381 Security guard service
HQ: Securitas Security Services Usa, Inc.
9 Campus Dr
Parsippany NJ 07054
973 267-5300

(G-12570)
SECURITECH INC
205 N Marshall St (19804-2713)
PHONE.................302 996-9230
M Scott Wilson, *President*
EMP: 10
SALES: 264K **Privately Held**
WEB: www.securitech.net
SIC: 3699 5065 Security control equipment & systems; security control equipment & systems

(G-12571)
SECURITY INSTRUMENT CORP DEL (PA)
309 W Newport Pike (19804-3148)
PHONE.................302 998-2261
Arthur Mattei Sr, *President*
Gary Mattei, *Corp Secy*
Arthur Mattei Jr, *Vice Pres*
EMP: 77 EST: 1962
SQ FT: 5,000
SALES (est): 17MM **Privately Held**
WEB: www.securityinstrument.com
SIC: 1731 7382 Fire detection & burglar alarm systems specialization; burglar alarm maintenance & monitoring

(G-12572)
SEEDS OF JESUS DAY CARE LLC
12 Mary Ella Dr (19805-1548)
PHONE.................302 494-6568
Sarah Reyes, *Principal*
EMP: 5
SALES (est): 105.6K **Privately Held**
SIC: 8351 Child day care services

(G-12573)
SEITZ VANOGTROP & GREEN
222 Delaware Ave Ste 1500 (19801-1682)
P.O. Box 68 (19899-0068)
PHONE.................302 888-0600
Bernard Vanogtrop, *Partner*
James S Green, *Principal*
George Seitz, *Principal*
Cheryl Walters, *Corp Counsel*
Joanna Fichter, *Manager*
EMP: 13
SALES (est): 1.3MM **Privately Held**
WEB: www.svglaw.com
SIC: 8111 General practice attorney, lawyer

(G-12574)
SELECT MEDICAL CORPORATION
Also Called: Select Spclty Hsptal- Wlmngton
701 N Clayton St Fl 5 (19805-3165)
PHONE.................302 421-4545
Marsha Edwards, *Branch Mgr*
EMP: 94
SALES (corp-wide): 5B **Publicly Held**
SIC: 8062 General medical & surgical hospitals
HQ: Select Medical Corporation
4714 Gettysburg Rd
Mechanicsburg PA 17055
717 972-1100

(G-12575)
SELECT SPECIALTY HOSPITAL
701 N Clayton St Fl 5 (19805-3165)
PHONE.................302 421-4590
Carol Charisman, *CEO*
Donna Garris, *Officer*
EMP: 93
SALES (est): 5.5MM
SALES (corp-wide): 5B **Publicly Held**
WEB: www.selectmedicalcorp.com
SIC: 8069 Specialty hospitals, except psychiatric
HQ: Select Medical Corporation
4714 Gettysburg Rd
Mechanicsburg PA 17055
717 972-1100

(G-12576)
SELLERS SENIOR CENTER INC
2800 Silverside Rd (19810-3710)
PHONE.................302 762-2050
Linda Murphy, *President*
Caroyln Ciccarona, *Director*
EMP: 5
SQ FT: 10,000
SALES: 201.6K **Privately Held**
SIC: 8322 Senior citizens' center or association

(G-12577)
SEMICONDUCTORPLUS INC
913 N Market St Ste 200 (19801-3097)
PHONE.................302 330-7533
Km Rashid, *President*
Mohamed Karim, *Vice Pres*
Jack Burton, *Sales Staff*
EMP: 4
SALES (est): 547.9K **Privately Held**
SIC: 5063 5065 Switches, except electronic; capacitors, electronic; connectors, electronic; rectifiers, electronic; resistors, electronic

(G-12578)
SENTINEL SELF STORAGE (PA)
200 First State Blvd (19804-3538)
PHONE.................302 999-0704
Francis Julian, *President*
EMP: 4
SALES (est): 409.2K **Privately Held**
WEB: www.storeatsentinel.com
SIC: 4225 Warehousing, self-storage

(G-12579)
SENTINEL TRANSPORTATION LLC (DH)
3521 Silverside Rd Ste 2a (19810-4914)
PHONE.................302 477-1640
Ralph Benson,
Ramona Rameruiz,
Orville White,
EMP: 14
SQ FT: 3,100
SALES (est): 178.8MM
SALES (corp-wide): 30.6B **Publicly Held**
WEB: www.sentineltransport.com
SIC: 4212 Local trucking, without storage
HQ: E. I. Du Pont De Nemours And Company
974 Centre Rd Bldg 735
Wilmington DE 19805
302 485-3000

(G-12580)
SENTINEL-SG LLC
919 N Market St Ste 425 (19801-3014)
PHONE.................580 458-9184
Dean E Young, *Mng Member*
John G Mays,
EMP: 5 EST: 2016
SALES (est): 121.6K **Privately Held**
SIC: 8748 Business consulting

(G-12581)
SEPIA CLEANERS
336 S Heald St (19801-5478)
PHONE.................302 656-0700
Charles Smith, *Owner*
Naomi Smith, *Co-Owner*
EMP: 4
SQ FT: 800
SALES: 60K **Privately Held**
SIC: 7212 7216 Garment pressing & cleaners' agents; cleaning & dyeing, except rugs

(G-12582)
SEREDUKE DESIGN CONS LLC
408 Concord Ave (19803-2316)
PHONE.................302 478-3468
Christian Sereduke, *Principal*
EMP: 4 EST: 2009
SALES (est): 254.8K **Privately Held**
SIC: 8748 Business consulting

(G-12583)
SERENE MINDS
410 Foulk Rd Ste 102 (19803-3835)
PHONE.................302 478-6199
Christine Maccord, *Principal*
EMP: 5
SALES (est): 351.2K **Privately Held**
SIC: 8011 Psychiatrist

(G-12584)
SERVER MANAGEMENT LLC
1201 N Orange St (19801-1155)
PHONE.................302 300-1745
Adrian Crismaru, *CEO*
EMP: 4
SALES: 314.3K **Privately Held**
SIC: 7371 7389 Custom computer programming services;

(G-12585)
SERVICE CORPS RETIRED EXECS
Also Called: S C O R E 42
1105 N Market St Lbby 2 (19801-1237)
PHONE.................302 573-6552
Thomas Doughty, *Chairman*
EMP: 47
SALES (corp-wide): 13.1MM **Privately Held**
WEB: www.score199.mv.com
SIC: 8611 Business associations
PA: Service Corps Of Retired Executives Association
1175 Herndon Pkwy Ste 900
Herndon VA 20170
703 487-3612

(G-12586)
SERVO2GOCOM LTD
4023 Kennett Pike Ste 583 (19807-2018)
PHONE.................877 378-0240
Warren Osak, *President*
▼ EMP: 25

SALES (est): 2.5MM **Privately Held**
SIC: 5065 Electronic parts & equipment

(G-12587)
SETH RAL & ASSOCIATES INC
2308 Ruthwynn Dr (19803-1923)
PHONE.................302 478-9020
Ken Griffith, *President*
EMP: 7
SQ FT: 1,400
SALES (est): 480K **Privately Held**
SIC: 8611 5065 5023 Manufacturers' institute; electronic parts & equipment; home furnishings

(G-12588)
SEVERN TRENT INC (DH)
1011 Centre Rd Ste 320 (19805-1266)
PHONE.................302 427-5990
Ken Kelly, *CEO*
Leonard F Graziano, *President*
David L Chester, *CFO*
Peter Winnington, *Treasurer*
Adele A Stevens, *Asst Sec*
◆ EMP: 26
SALES: 233.9MM
SALES (corp-wide): 2.2B **Privately Held**
WEB: www.severntrent.com
SIC: 3589 7371 8741 Sewage & water treatment equipment; computer software writing services; management services
HQ: Severn Trent Overseas Holdings Limited
2 St. Johns Street
Coventry W MIDLANDS
800 783-4444

(G-12589)
SEWICKLEY CAPITAL INC (PA)
501 Silverside Rd Ste 67 (19809-1394)
PHONE.................302 793-4964
G Watts Humphrey, *CEO*
EMP: 1 EST: 1999
SALES (est): 229.1MM **Privately Held**
SIC: 3559 3822 Plastics working machinery; temperature controls, automatic

(G-12590)
SFE SOLAR ENERGY INC
2711 Centerville Rd # 400 (19808-1660)
PHONE.................905 366-7037
Gerald Haggarty, *President*
Shelley Lewis, *CFO*
EMP: 10
SQ FT: 1,500
SALES (est): 354.1K **Privately Held**
SIC: 4911 Generation, electric power

(G-12591)
SFIN 3 INC (PA)
1007 N Orange St (19801-1239)
PHONE.................302 472-9276
James Provo, *Associate*
EMP: 4
SALES (est): 750.9K **Privately Held**
SIC: 8742 Business consultant

(G-12592)
SHALLCROSS MORTGAGE CO INC (PA)
410 Century Blvd (19808-6271)
PHONE.................302 999-9800
Jay Pierce Sr, *Ch of Bd*
Eleanor Pierce, *Treasurer*
Beatrice White, *Admin Sec*
EMP: 7
SQ FT: 3,500
SALES (est): 1.2MM **Privately Held**
SIC: 6162 Mortgage brokers, using own money

(G-12593)
SHARON CONSTRUCTION INC
4932 Old Capitol Trl (19808-5212)
PHONE.................302 999-1345
Sharon Landry, *President*
Virginia Batzel, *Admin Sec*
EMP: 4
SALES (est): 299.8K **Privately Held**
SIC: 4212 Local trucking, without storage

(G-12594)
SHARP FARM (PA)
5727 Kennett Pike (19807-1311)
P.O. Box 3779 (19807-0779)
PHONE.................302 652-7729

Wilmington - New Castle County (G-12595)

Bayard Sharp, *Owner*
EMP: 4
SALES (est): 532.9K **Privately Held**
SIC: 7948 Horses, racing

(G-12595)
SHAUNA SULLIVAN LCSW
3100 Naamans Rd (19810-2100)
PHONE...........................302 383-6826
EMP: 6
SALES (est): 129K **Privately Held**
SIC: 8093 Specialty Outpatient Clinic

(G-12596)
SHEKINAH GLORY SIGN COMPANY
2608 Kirkwood Hwy (19805-4910)
PHONE...........................302 256-0426
EMP: 1
SALES (est): 46K **Privately Held**
SIC: 3993 Signs & advertising specialties

(G-12597)
SHELIAS CHILDCARE CENTER
1621 N Heald St (19802-5146)
PHONE...........................302 472-9648
Mary Guy, *Principal*
EMP: 5
SALES (est): 67.2K **Privately Held**
SIC: 8351 Group day care center

(G-12598)
SHELLCREST SWIM CLUB
916 Wilson Rd (19803-4018)
PHONE...........................302 529-1464
EMP: 5
SALES (est): 41.9K **Privately Held**
SIC: 7997 Swimming club, membership

(G-12599)
SHELLHORN & HILL INC (PA)
501 S Market St (19801-5229)
P.O. Box 2569 (19805-0569)
PHONE...........................302 654-4200
Michael D Hill, *President*
Larry Dugan, *Vice Pres*
Dave Edinger, *Manager*
Wayne Peace, *Admin Sec*
EMP: 60
SQ FT: 1,500
SALES (est): 18.3MM **Privately Held**
WEB: www.shellhornbarandgrill.com
SIC: 5172 5983 5541 Petroleum products; fuel oil dealers; gasoline service stations

(G-12600)
SHELLYS OF DELAWARE INC
Also Called: Shelly's We Do Everything
610 W 8th St (19801-1450)
PHONE...........................302 656-3337
R W Brown, *President*
Sarah Johnson, *Corp Secy*
EMP: 13
SQ FT: 3,780
SALES (est): 1.6MM **Privately Held**
WEB: www.shellysheroes.org
SIC: 1542 1521 1541 Commercial & office building, new construction; new construction, single-family houses; industrial buildings, new construction

(G-12601)
SHIELDS BROTHERS
315 1st Ave (19804-2225)
PHONE...........................302 999-1094
EMP: 1 **EST:** 1997
SALES (est): 34.6K **Privately Held**
SIC: 2395 Pleating/Stitching Services

(G-12602)
SHILOH INDUSTRIES INC
103 Foulk Rd Ste 202 (19803-3742)
PHONE...........................302 656-1950
Theodore Zampetis, *CEO*
EMP: 6 **Publicly Held**
SIC: 3465 Automotive stampings
PA: Shiloh Industries, Inc.
880 Steel Dr
Valley City OH 44280

(G-12603)
SHINY AGENCY LLC
1800 Wawaset St (19806-2133)
PHONE...........................302 384-6494
Katherine Thorbahn, *Managing Prtnr*
EMP: 4
SALES (est): 281K **Privately Held**
SIC: 7311 Advertising agencies

(G-12604)
SHIPLEY ASSOCIATES INC
135 S West St (19801-5014)
PHONE...........................302 652-1766
EMP: 2
SALES (est): 130K **Privately Held**
SIC: 3537 Mfg Industrial Trucks/Tractors

(G-12605)
SHIPYARD CENTER LLC
234 N James St (19804-3132)
PHONE...........................302 999-0708
Gregory Pettinaro,
Tim Decola,
EMP: 5
SALES (est): 950K **Privately Held**
SIC: 6519 Real property lessors

(G-12606)
SHIRE NORTH AMERICAN GROUP INC (HQ)
103 Foulk Rd Ste 202 (19803-3742)
PHONE...........................484 595-8800
John Miller, *Treasurer*
Caroline West, *Officer*
Ellen Rosenberg, *Admin Sec*
EMP: 5
SALES (est): 1.3MM
SALES (corp-wide): 15.1B **Privately Held**
SIC: 2834 Pharmaceutical preparations
PA: Shire Plc
1 Kingdom Street
London W2 6B
125 689-4003

(G-12607)
SHOPIFY PAYMENTS (USA) INC
1209 N Orange St (19801-1120)
PHONE...........................613 241-2828
Tobias Lutke, *President*
Mathew Paciga, *Partner*
Louis Kearns, *Director*
EMP: 4
SALES: 60.6MM
SALES (corp-wide): 1B **Privately Held**
SIC: 7389 Financial services
PA: Shopify Inc
150 Elgin St 8th Floor
Ottawa ON K2P 1
613 241-2828

(G-12608)
SHOR ASSOCIATES INC
240 Philadelphia Pike (19809-3125)
PHONE...........................302 764-1701
Craig Shor, *President*
Catherine Lynch, *Vice Pres*
EMP: 5
SQ FT: 600
SALES (est): 660.1K **Privately Held**
SIC: 7311 Advertising consultant

(G-12609)
SHORT WARS PRODUCTIONS LLC
1907 N Franklin St (19802-3830)
PHONE...........................302 932-0707
Sean Gardner, *Principal*
EMP: 13
SALES: 5K **Privately Held**
SIC: 7822 Motion picture & tape distribution

(G-12610)
SIEGFRIED GROUP LLP (PA)
Also Called: Siegfried Resources
1201 N Market St Ste 700 (19801-1153)
PHONE...........................302 984-1800
Joan Davidson, *President*
Robert L Siegfried Jr, *Partner*
Blake Kolo, *Managing Dir*
Karen Campbell, *Vice Pres*
Cynthia Gee, *Vice Pres*
EMP: 150
SALES (est): 170MM **Privately Held**
WEB: www.siegfriedgroup.com
SIC: 8721 Certified public accountant

(G-12611)
SIEMENS
4001 Vandever Ave (19802-4609)
PHONE...........................302 220-1544
EMP: 3
SALES (est): 175.4K **Privately Held**
SIC: 3661 Telephones & telephone apparatus

(G-12612)
SIGMA TELECOM LLC
501 Silverside Rd Ste 105 (19809-1376)
PHONE...........................347 741-8397
Musa RAD, *Mng Member*
EMP: 28
SALES (est): 8MM
SALES (corp-wide): 12.8MM **Privately Held**
SIC: 4813 Long distance telephone communications
PA: Sigma Isletim Ve Ulastirma Sanayi Ve Ticaret Limited Sirketi
N:3a/120 Barbaros Mahallesi
Istanbul (Anatolia) 34746
216 999-3586

(G-12613)
SIGN EXPRESS
Also Called: Dmi
103 S Augustine St (19804-2505)
PHONE...........................302 999-0893
Chris Iannone, *Owner*
EMP: 7
SALES (est): 420K **Privately Held**
WEB: www.signsdelaware.com
SIC: 3993 Signs & advertising specialties

(G-12614)
SIGN SHOP
146 Bungalow Ave (19805-5010)
PHONE...........................302 998-2443
James Booker, *Owner*
EMP: 1
SALES (est): 48.7K **Privately Held**
SIC: 3993 Signs, not made in custom sign painting shops

(G-12615)
SIGNSCAPE DESIGNS & SIGNS
1709 Philadelphia Pike # 1 (19809-1560)
PHONE...........................302 798-2926
Robert Lesperance, *Partner*
Mildred Winslow, *Partner*
EMP: 2
SQ FT: 1,050
SALES: 150K **Privately Held**
WEB: www.302signs.com
SIC: 3993 Signs & advertising specialties

(G-12616)
SILVER LINING SOLUTIONS LLC
49 Bancroft Mills Rd P8 (19806-2030)
PHONE...........................302 691-7100
Toni Beltz, *President*
Mark Beltz, *Vice Pres*
EMP: 5
SALES (est): 688.4K **Privately Held**
SIC: 6512 Nonresidential building operators

(G-12617)
SILVER SPRINGS APARTMENTS
12 Mary Ella Dr Ste E (19805-1548)
PHONE...........................302 992-0800
Archie Simmons, *Manager*
Lewis Riviera, *Manager*
EMP: 4
SALES (est): 283.1K **Privately Held**
SIC: 6513 Apartment building operators

(G-12618)
SILVERBROOK CEMETERY CO
3300 Lancaster Pike (19805-1435)
PHONE...........................302 658-0953
Paul L White Jr, *President*
Brenda White, *Treasurer*
Ronald Fox, *Admin Sec*
EMP: 6 **EST:** 1895
SQ FT: 3,000
SALES: 500K **Privately Held**
SIC: 6553 Cemeteries, real estate operation

(G-12619)
SILVERSIDE CONTRACTING INC
2801 N Broom St (19802-2913)
PHONE...........................302 798-1907
Richard W Hartnett, *President*
Daniel J Hartnett, *Vice Pres*
Mary V Hartnett, *Treasurer*
Mary Hartnett, *Treasurer*
EMP: 6
SALES: 1MM **Privately Held**
SIC: 1521 1542 General remodeling, single-family houses; commercial & office building, new construction

(G-12620)
SILVERSIDE DENTAL ASSOCIATES
3512 Silverside Rd Ste 6 (19810-4941)
PHONE...........................302 478-4700
Anna Drasher, *Manager*
EMP: 4
SALES (est): 217.9K **Privately Held**
SIC: 8021 Dentists' office

(G-12621)
SILVERSIDE OPEN MRI IMAGING
2501 Silverside Rd Ste A (19810-3722)
PHONE...........................302 246-2000
Edward White, *Principal*
EMP: 4 **EST:** 2007
SALES (est): 296.1K **Privately Held**
SIC: 8011 3845 Radiologist; magnetic resonance imaging device, nuclear

(G-12622)
SILVIEW AUTO CARE
806 W Newport Pike (19804-3252)
PHONE...........................302 994-1617
Keith Conard, *Owner*
EMP: 4
SALES (est): 310.8K **Privately Held**
SIC: 7538 General automotive repair shops

(G-12623)
SIMON EYE ASSOCIATES PA
912 N Union St (19805-5326)
PHONE...........................302 655-8180
Carey McNeill, *Branch Mgr*
EMP: 5
SALES (corp-wide): 4.7MM **Privately Held**
WEB: www.simoneye.com
SIC: 8042 Specialized optometrists
PA: Simon Eye Associates, P.A.
5301 Limestone Rd Ste 128
Wilmington DE 19808
302 239-1389

(G-12624)
SIMON EYE ASSOCIATES PA (PA)
5301 Limestone Rd Ste 128 (19808-1253)
PHONE...........................302 239-1389
Charles Simon Od, *President*
EMP: 10
SALES (est): 4.7MM **Privately Held**
WEB: www.simoneye.com
SIC: 8042 Specialized optometrists

(G-12625)
SIMPLE SPACE LLC
300 Delaware Ave Ste 210a (19801-6601)
PHONE...........................801 520-3680
Jacob Longhurst,
Ammon Lewis,
Riley Schaad,
EMP: 5
SALES (est): 104.7K **Privately Held**
SIC: 7389

(G-12626)
SIMPLER LOGISTICS LLC
300 Delaware Ave Ste 210 (19801-6601)
PHONE...........................800 619-8321
Christopher Phillips,
EMP: 5
SALES: 140K **Privately Held**
SIC: 8742 Transportation consultant

(G-12627)
SIMPLY GREEN
216 S Maryland Ave (19804-1344)
PHONE...........................302 256-0822
EMP: 7

GEOGRAPHIC SECTION   Wilmington - New Castle County (G-12658)

SALES (est): 287.2K **Privately Held**
SIC: 0782 Lawn care services

(G-12628)
SIMPLY STYLNG-SCHL OF CSMTLGY
204 N Union St (19805-3430)
PHONE.................................302 778-1885
Jerome Stanley, *CEO*
EMP: 3 EST: 1997
SALES: 53K **Privately Held**
SIC: 5087 6732 2721 Beauty salon & barber shop equipment & supplies; educational trust management; magazines: publishing only, not printed on site

(G-12629)
SIMPLYMIDDLE LLC
901 N Market St Ste 719 (19801-3098)
PHONE.................................302 217-3460
Sanni Ibrahim, *Principal*
Akinyemi Famakinwa, *Mng Member*
Israel Deray,
EMP: 12
SQ FT: 508
SALES: 200K **Privately Held**
SIC: 8399 7311 Social service information exchange; advertising agencies

(G-12630)
SINC BUSINESS CORPORATION (PA)
Also Called: Sinc Time Clock
251 Little Falls Dr (19808-1674)
PHONE.................................480 210-1798
Samuel Philip Dolbel, *CEO*
EMP: 2
SALES: 100K **Privately Held**
SIC: 7372 Application computer software

(G-12631)
SINGULAR KEY INC
251 Little Falls Dr (19808-1674)
PHONE.................................408 753-5848
Justin Maniar, *CEO*
Hitesh Kalra, *Officer*
EMP: 10
SALES (est): 247K **Privately Held**
SIC: 5045 5734 7372 7371 Computer software; software, business & non-game; business oriented computer software; application computer software; utility computer software; computer software development & applications

(G-12632)
SINNOTT EXC CONSULTING LLC
319 Hampton Rd (19803-2425)
PHONE.................................302 656-2898
Dan Sinnott, *Principal*
EMP: 4
SALES (est): 248.3K **Privately Held**
SIC: 8748 8711 Business consulting; consulting engineer

(G-12633)
SINUSWARS LLC
501 Silverside Rd Ste 105 (19809-1376)
PHONE.................................212 901-0805
Treveshen Padayachee,
▼ EMP: 10
SALES (est): 1.4MM **Privately Held**
SIC: 5122 Patent medicines

(G-12634)
SIP INC OF DELAWARE (HQ)
1101 E 8th St (19801-4356)
P.O. Box 1770, Manassas VA (20108-1770)
PHONE.................................302 654-4533
Frank E Williams III, *CEO*
Danny C Danlup, *Vice Pres*
Scott Mc Kellar, *Sales Mgr*
EMP: 7
SQ FT: 2,000
SALES (est): 5.6MM
SALES (corp-wide): 79.5MM **Publicly Held**
SIC: 3441 Fabricated structural metal for bridges
PA: Williams Industries Incorporated
   1128 Tyler Farms Dr
   Raleigh NC 27603
   919 604-1746

(G-12635)
SISUAQ SCIENTIFIC
1 Commerce St (19801)
PHONE.................................302 739-3073
Liguo Su, *Owner*
EMP: 1
SALES (est): 77K **Privately Held**
SIC: 3826 Analytical instruments

(G-12636)
SITWA GROUP LLC (PA)
1925 Lovering Ave (19806-2157)
PHONE.................................786 802-4155
Juan Santana, *Vice Pres*
Andres Perez, *Admin Sec*
EMP: 2
SALES (est): 56.5K **Privately Held**
SIC: 7372 Prepackaged software

(G-12637)
SIX ANGELS DEVELOPMENT INC
7 Medori Blvd (19801-5781)
PHONE.................................302 218-1548
Michael Miles, *President*
EMP: 8
SALES: 600K **Privately Held**
SIC: 8748 7389 Environmental consultant;

(G-12638)
SIX PLUS INC
5714 Kennett Pike (19807-1331)
PHONE.................................302 652-3296
George A Weymouth, *President*
Cary Lambert, *Corp Secy*
EMP: 7
SQ FT: 1,200
SALES (est): 616.8K **Privately Held**
SIC: 8741 Management services

(G-12639)
SKADDEN ARPS SLATE MEAGHER
920 N King St Ste 700 (19801-3365)
PHONE.................................302 651-3000
Robert S Sanders, *Managing Prtnr*
Lara Zaitzeff, *Counsel*
Gail S Disanto, *Manager*
Andrew Good, *Associate*
EMP: 130
SALES (est): 65.2K **Privately Held**
SIC: 8111 General practice attorney, lawyer

(G-12640)
SKADDEN ARPS SLATE MEAGHER & F
1 Rodney Sq (19801)
P.O. Box 636 (19899-0636)
PHONE.................................302 651-3000
Edward P Welch, *Partner*
Thomas J Allingham II, *Partner*
Mark S Chehi, *Partner*
Anthony W Clark, *Partner*
Brian Krause, *Partner*
EMP: 317
SALES (corp-wide): 461.9MM **Privately Held**
WEB: www.skadden.com
SIC: 8111 General practice attorney, lawyer
PA: Skadden, Arps, Slate, Meagher & Flom Llp
   4 Times Sq Fl 24
   New York NY 10036
   212 735-3000

(G-12641)
SKAJAQUODA CAPITAL LLC
717 N Union St Ste 5 (19805-3031)
PHONE.................................302 504-4448
Einar Agustsson,
EMP: 19
SALES (est): 8.8MM **Privately Held**
SIC: 6211 Investment bankers

(G-12642)
SKATING CLUB OF WILMINGTON INC
1301 Carruthers Ln (19803-4601)
PHONE.................................302 656-5005
Peter A Bilous, *President*
DOT Gualtieri, *Manager*
EMP: 17
SQ FT: 35,000
SALES: 804.1K **Privately Held**
WEB: www.wilmicesk8.com
SIC: 7997 Ice sports

(G-12643)
SKY WORLD TRAVELER
1013 Centre Rd Ste 403s (19805-1270)
PHONE.................................844 591-9060
Antonio Parker, *Owner*
EMP: 10
SALES (est): 180.6K **Privately Held**
SIC: 7389 Business services

(G-12644)
SKYNETHOSTINGNET INC
501 Silverside Rd (19809-1374)
PHONE.................................302 384-1784
Sagara Kelaniya, *Vice Pres*
EMP: 15
SALES (est): 164.2K **Privately Held**
SIC: 4813

(G-12645)
SLATER FIREPLACES INC
Also Called: Fireplace Shoppe
1726 Newport Gap Pike (19808-6120)
PHONE.................................302 999-1200
Kenneth R Slater, *President*
Christine Lashley, *Vice Pres*
Colleen Slater, *Treasurer*
Steven Slater, *Shareholder*
Gloria Slater, *Admin Sec*
EMP: 7
SALES (est): 933.4K **Privately Held**
SIC: 5719 7349 5699 Fireplace equipment & accessories; janitorial service, contract basis; T-shirts, custom printed

(G-12646)
SLIMSTIM INC
1209 N Orange St (19801-1120)
PHONE.................................310 560-4950
Jeff Brennan, *President*
EMP: 3
SALES (est): 170.9K **Privately Held**
SIC: 3845 Electromedical equipment

(G-12647)
SM TECHNOMINE INC (PA)
802 N West St (19801-1526)
PHONE.................................312 492-4386
Sanket Modi, *CEO*
EMP: 10
SALES (est): 3.4MM **Privately Held**
SIC: 8732 7389 7371 7379 Market analysis or research; telemarketing services; software programming applications; ; computer graphics service

(G-12648)
SM TECHNOMINE INC
19c Trolley Sq (19806-3355)
PHONE.................................312 492-4386
Dave Pise, *Manager*
EMP: 10
SALES (corp-wide): 3.4MM **Privately Held**
SIC: 7389 Telemarketing services
PA: Sm Technomine Inc.
   802 N West St
   Wilmington DE 19801
   312 492-4386

(G-12649)
SMAKKFITNESS LLC
401 N Market St (19801-3002)
PHONE.................................213 280-7569
La'marqus Collins,
EMP: 5
SALES: 25K **Privately Held**
SIC: 7991 Physical fitness facilities

(G-12650)
SMALL BUSINESS DEVELOPMENT CTR
Also Called: Small Bus Resource Info Cebter
1318 N Market St (19801-1133)
PHONE.................................302 571-1555
Clinton Tymes, *Director*
EMP: 11
SALES (est): 710K **Privately Held**
SIC: 8611 Business associations

(G-12651)
SMALL WONDER DAY CARE INC
100 Greenhill Ave Ste A (19805-1863)
PHONE.................................302 654-2269
Kim Markooni, *Director*
EMP: 20
SALES (est): 371.1K **Privately Held**
SIC: 8351 Group day care center

(G-12652)
SMALLS REAL ESTATE COMPANY
5227 W Woodmill Dr Ste 42 (19808-4068)
PHONE.................................302 633-1985
Fred Small, *President*
EMP: 10
SALES (est): 146.4K **Privately Held**
SIC: 6531 Real estate brokers & agents

(G-12653)
SMALLS STEPPING STONE
1408 Clifford Brown Walk (19801-3128)
PHONE.................................302 652-3011
Clara Smalls, *Owner*
EMP: 45
SQ FT: 5,300
SALES (est): 669.1K **Privately Held**
SIC: 8351 Preschool center

(G-12654)
SMART HOSPITALITY & MGT LLC
3411 Silverside Rd (19810-4812)
PHONE.................................212 444-1989
David Friedland, *President*
EMP: 23
SQ FT: 1,100
SALES: 3.6MM **Privately Held**
SIC: 7389 Hotel & motel reservation service

(G-12655)
SMARTSTUDENTS LLC
4701 Limestone Rd Ste 182 (19808-1927)
P.O. Box 182 (19899-0182)
PHONE.................................302 597-6586
Chahin Aghrim,
Artur Zvinchuk,
EMP: 9
SALES: 750K **Privately Held**
SIC: 7371 7389 Computer software development & applications;

(G-12656)
SMARTWHEEL INC
1521 Concord Pike Ste 303 (19803-3644)
PHONE.................................617 542-7400
Richard Strauss, *Branch Mgr*
EMP: 1
SALES (corp-wide): 452.1K **Privately Held**
SIC: 3714 Instrument board assemblies, motor vehicle
PA: Smartwheel Inc.
   5 Faye Ln
   Londonderry NH

(G-12657)
SMILE BRITE DENTAL CARE LLC
1401 Pennsylvania Ave # 106 (19806-4125)
PHONE.................................302 384-8448
Taurance N Bishop, *Branch Mgr*
EMP: 5
SALES (est): 256.1K **Privately Held**
SIC: 8021 Dentists' office
PA: Smile Brite Dental Care, Llc
   300 Biddle Ave Ste 204
   Newark DE 19702

(G-12658)
SMILE SOLUTIONS BY EMMI DENTAL
1601 Milltown Rd Ste 25 (19808-4084)
PHONE.................................302 999-8113
Jeffrey Emmi, *Principal*
Irene Caldwell, *Office Mgr*
EMP: 7
SALES (est): 677.8K **Privately Held**
SIC: 8021 Dentists' office

Wilmington - New Castle County (G-12659)   GEOGRAPHIC SECTION

(G-12659)
SMITH & NEPHEW HOLDINGS INC (DH)
1201 N Orange St Ste 788 (19801-1173)
PHONE..................................302 884-6720
Cliff Lomax, *President*
Laura Whitsitt, *Vice Pres*
Henry Faber, *Project Mgr*
Paul Renick, *Research*
Eric Roche, *Research*
▲ **EMP:** 8
SALES (est): 637.6MM
SALES (corp-wide): 4.9B **Privately Held**
SIC: 5047 3841 Medical equipment & supplies; surgical & medical instruments
HQ: Smith & Nephew (Overseas) Limited
  15 Adam Street
  London WC2N
  207 401-7646

(G-12660)
SMITH KATZENSTEIN & FURLOW LLP
1000 N West St Ste 1500 (19801-1054)
P.O. Box 410 (19899-0410)
PHONE..................................302 652-8400
Craig B Smith, *Partner*
Laurence V Cronin, *Partner*
Clark W Furlow, *Partner*
Vicki A Hagel, *Partner*
David A Jenkins, *Partner*
EMP: 22
SALES (est): 2.3MM **Privately Held**
WEB: www.skfdelaware.com
SIC: 8111 General practice attorney, lawyer; corporate, partnership & business law; securities law; bankruptcy law

(G-12661)
SMITH SUPERIOR PNTG REPR SVCS
Also Called: Smith Superior Home Services
2911 N Franklin St (19802-2932)
PHONE..................................302 384-6575
EMP: 4
SALES (est): 125.6K **Privately Held**
SIC: 1721 Painting/Paper Hanging Contractor

(G-12662)
SMITHFELD INTL INVESTMENTS INC
3411 Silverside Rd (19810-4812)
PHONE..................................302 477-1358
Charles McArrick, *President*
Gordon Stewart, *Admin Sec*
EMP: 5
SALES (est): 402.1K **Privately Held**
SIC: 6282 Investment advice

(G-12663)
SMITHS JACK TOWING & SVC CTR
Also Called: Jack Smith Towing
1806 Philadelphia Pike (19809-1545)
PHONE..................................302 798-6667
Thomas Smith, *President*
Jim Smith, *Vice Pres*
EMP: 7 **EST:** 1927
SQ FT: 1,500
SALES (est): 590K **Privately Held**
SIC: 7538 7549 General automotive repair shops; towing services

(G-12664)
SMRC SMART AUTOMOTIVE
1209 Ornge St Corp Tr Ctr R Ation Trust Ct (19801)
PHONE..................................317 941-7257
Kevin Lauwick,
EMP: 1
SALES (est): 62.1K
SALES (corp-wide): 1B **Privately Held**
SIC: 3089 Automotive parts, plastic
HQ: Samvardhana Motherson Automotive Systems Group B.V.
  Hoogoorddreef 15
  Amsterdam
  205 222-555

(G-12665)
SNTC HOLDING INC (DH)
919 N Market St Ste 200 (19801-3068)
PHONE..................................302 777-5261
Martin J Wygod, *Principal*
EMP: 6
SALES (est): 72.5MM
SALES (corp-wide): 705MM **Privately Held**
SIC: 6371 Union welfare, benefit & health funds
HQ: Webmd Health Corp.
  395 Hudson St Fl 3
  New York NY 10014
  212 624-3700

(G-12666)
SNYDER & COMPANY PA
Also Called: Dennis H Snyder Assoc
1405 Silverside Rd (19810-4445)
P.O. Box 9506 (19809-0506)
PHONE..................................302 475-1600
Dennis H Snyder, *Owner*
EMP: 10
SALES (est): 876K **Privately Held**
WEB: www.snydercpa.com
SIC: 8721 Certified public accountant

(G-12667)
SNYDER ASSOCIATES PA
Also Called: Snyder & Associates
300 Delaware Ave Ste 1014 (19801-1671)
P.O. Box 90 (19899-0090)
PHONE..................................302 657-8300
Bayard J Snyder, *President*
Allen Richd,
EMP: 5
SALES (est): 410.3K **Privately Held**
SIC: 8111 General practice law office

(G-12668)
SOCIETY OF ST VINCENT DE PAUL
1414 N King St (19801-3122)
PHONE..................................302 328-5166
Paul Collins, *President*
Richard Day, *Treasurer*
Andrea Starr, *Admin Sec*
EMP: 4
SQ FT: 300
SALES: 500K **Privately Held**
SIC: 8699 Charitable organization

(G-12669)
SOCRATICLAW CO INC
3900 Centerville Rd (19807-1939)
PHONE..................................302 654-9191
Wade Scott, *President*
Shrew Dury, *Principal*
EMP: 2
SALES (est): 59.3K **Privately Held**
SIC: 2741 Miscellaneous publishing

(G-12670)
SODAT OF DELAWARE INC (PA)
625 N Orange St Fl 2 (19801-2296)
PHONE..................................302 656-2810
Aron Shapiro, *President*
Delisa A Lusby, *Psychologist*
Eric Saul, *Director*
Stephanie Stachoni, *Director*
EMP: 17
SALES (est): 534.6K **Privately Held*
WEB: www.sodatdelaware.org
SIC: 8093 Alcohol clinic, outpatient; drug clinic, outpatient

(G-12671)
SOFTMOGUL INC
2711 Centerville Rd # 400 (19808-1660)
PHONE..................................414 426-1650
Albi Zhulali, *CEO*
EMP: 7
SALES (est): 175.7K **Privately Held**
SIC: 7371 Computer software development & applications

(G-12672)
SOFTWARE SERVICES OF DE INC (PA)
Also Called: Ssd Technology Partners
1024 Justison St (19801-5148)
PHONE..................................302 654-3172
Barbara Hines, *President*
Nick Ewen, *Vice Pres*
Nancy Froome, *Vice Pres*
Mike O'Brien, *Engineer*
Terry Tucker, *CFO*
EMP: 34
SQ FT: 10,000
SALES (est): 6.4MM **Privately Held**
WEB: www.ssdel.com
SIC: 5734 7378 7371 Modems, monitors, terminals & disk drives: computers; computer maintenance & repair; custom computer programming services

(G-12673)
SOJOURNERS PLACE INC
2901 Northeast Blvd (19802-3705)
P.O. Box 2845 (19805-0845)
PHONE..................................302 764-4592
Pat Kennerly, *Bookkeeper*
Eric Harris, *Exec Dir*
EMP: 20
SALES: 516.3K **Privately Held**
SIC: 8322 Emergency shelters

(G-12674)
SOLACE LIFESCIENCES INC
501 Silverside Rd Ste 7 (19809-1375)
PHONE..................................302 275-4195
Christopher Gross, *COO*
Chris Gross, *COO*
Michelle Weakland, *Vice Pres*
Ashley Blanke, *VP Bus Dvlpt*
EMP: 7
SALES: 2MM **Privately Held**
SIC: 5087 5731 8742 Stress reducing equipment, electric; consumer electronic equipment; marketing consulting services

(G-12675)
SOLENIS HOLDINGS 3 LLC (DH)
3 Beaver Valley Rd # 500 (19803-1124)
PHONE..................................866 337-1533
EMP: 5
SALES (est): 695.5MM
SALES (corp-wide): 767.2MM **Privately Held**
SIC: 2899 Sizes

(G-12676)
SOLENIS INTERNATIONAL LLC (PA)
3 Beaver Valley Rd # 500 (19803-1124)
PHONE..................................302 994-1698
Dave Nocek, *Vice Pres*
Dwight Emerich, *Manager*
Matt Wangerin, *Manager*
John Panichella, *Manager*
EMP: 27
SALES (est): 767.2MM **Privately Held**
SIC: 2899 Water treating compounds

(G-12677)
SOLENIS LLC (DH)
2475 Pinnacle Dr (19803-3700)
PHONE..................................866 337-1533
John Panichella, *CEO*
John Cavanaugh, *Area Mgr*
Roger Ladewig, *Plant Mgr*
Erin Loew, *Plant Mgr*
Gordon Johnson, *Site Mgr*
▼ **EMP:** 350 **EST:** 2014
SQ FT: 40,000
SALES (est): 841.6MM
SALES (corp-wide): 767.2MM **Privately Held**
SIC: 2899 Sizes
HQ: Solenis Holdings 3 Llc
  3 Beaver Valley Rd # 500
  Wilmington DE 19803
  866 337-1533

(G-12678)
SOLENIS LLC
Also Called: Ashland Water Technologies
500 Hercules Rd (19808-1513)
PHONE..................................302 594-5000
Paul Raymond, *Branch Mgr*
EMP: 5
SALES (corp-wide): 767.2MM **Privately Held**
SIC: 5169 Chemicals & allied products
HQ: Solenis Llc
  2475 Pinnacle Dr
  Wilmington DE 19803
  866 337-1533

(G-12679)
SOLUFY CORP
1201 N Orange St Ste 7228 (19801-1233)
PHONE..................................877 476-5839
Mario Boileau, *Principal*
Gerry Lamarche, *Principal*
Matthew Midas, *Principal*
EMP: 26 **EST:** 2017
SALES (est): 886.4K **Privately Held**
SIC: 7372 Prepackaged software

(G-12680)
SOLVETECH INC
1711 Philadelphia Pike (19809-1542)
P.O. Box 9245 (19809-0245)
PHONE..................................302 798-5400
Douglas C Lawrence, *President*
EMP: 9
SQ FT: 2,000
SALES (est): 1.7MM **Privately Held**
WEB: www.gauging.com
SIC: 3829 Gauging instruments, thickness ultrasonic

(G-12681)
SOMERVILLE MANNING GALLERY
101 Stone Block Row (19807-3038)
PHONE..................................302 652-0271
Vickie Manning, *President*
Sadie Somerville, *Vice Pres*
Rebecca Moore, *Director*
EMP: 4
SQ FT: 1,600
SALES (est): 317.2K **Privately Held**
WEB: www.somervillemanning.com
SIC: 7999 8412 Art gallery, commercial; museums & art galleries

(G-12682)
SORBENT GREEN LLC (PA)
Also Called: Greensorb
1209 N Orange St (19801-1120)
P.O. Box 2229, Aiken SC (29802-2229)
PHONE..................................800 259-3577
Tom Uskup, *Mng Member*
▼ **EMP:** 1
SQ FT: 1,000
SALES (est): 907.5K **Privately Held**
SIC: 3295 2869 Clay, ground or otherwise treated; industrial organic chemicals

(G-12683)
SOS SECURITY INCORPORATED
1000 N West St Ste 200 (19801-1052)
PHONE..................................302 425-4755
Michael Wieland, *Manager*
EMP: 8
SALES (corp-wide): 103.4MM **Privately Held**
WEB: www.sossecurity.com
SIC: 7381 Security guard service
PA: Sos Security Incorporated
  1915 Us Highway 46 Ste 1
  Parsippany NJ 07054
  973 402-6600

(G-12684)
SOUNDBOKS INC (PA)
2711 Centerville Rd # 400 (19808-1660)
PHONE..................................213 436-5888
Jesper Theil Thomsen, *CEO*
Hjalte Wieth, *Managing Dir*
Christoffer Nyvold, *COO*
EMP: 9
SQ FT: 300
SALES (est): 352.6K **Privately Held**
SIC: 3651 Speaker systems

(G-12685)
SOURCING TIME LLC
3422 Old Capitol Trl (19808-6124)
PHONE..................................302 409-0890
George Karavasilis, *Principal*
EMP: 1
SALES (est): 57.7K **Privately Held**
SIC: 2741

(G-12686)
SOUTHBRDGE MED ADVSORY COUNCIL (PA)
Also Called: HENRIETTA JOHNSON MEDICAL CENT
601 New Castle Ave (19801-5821)
PHONE..................................302 655-6187
Rosa Rivera-Prado, *CEO*
Ephraim Kaba, *CFO*
Allie Sethman, *CFO*
Charles Case, *Chief Mktg Ofcr*
Terry A Reed, *Office Mgr*
EMP: 39
SQ FT: 15,000

GEOGRAPHIC SECTION
Wilmington - New Castle County (G-12716)

SALES: 4.8MM **Privately Held**
WEB: www.hjmc.org
SIC: 8011 Primary care medical clinic

(G-12687)
SOUTHERN CRAB COMPANY
2831 Kennedy Rd (19810-3446)
PHONE..................302 478-0181
Barry Lamb, *Partner*
Patrick O'Sullivan, *Vice Pres*
Vincent MAI, *Treasurer*
EMP: 210
SQ FT: 200,000
SALES: 38MM **Privately Held**
SIC: 5146 Seafoods

(G-12688)
SOUTHWEST AMERICAN CORP
Also Called: Sun West Homes
2200 N Grant Ave (19806-2240)
PHONE..................302 652-7003
Edward Bauer, *President*
EMP: 6
SALES (est): 535.9K **Privately Held**
SIC: 6798 Real estate investment trusts

(G-12689)
SOVEREIGN CAPITL MGT GROUP INC
Also Called: Sovereign Capital MGT Group
1000 N West St Ste 1200 (19801-1058)
PHONE..................619 294-8989
Todd A Mikles, *CEO*
William White, *President*
James Payne, *Chief Engr*
Jonathon Reeser, *VP Finance*
Chad Wardwell, *VP Finance*
EMP: 619
SALES (est): 4.4MM **Privately Held**
SIC: 6531 7389 Real estate agents & managers; financial services

(G-12690)
SP PLUS CORPORATION
111 W 11th St Lowr (19801-1225)
PHONE..................302 652-1410
Tim Meyer, *Manager*
EMP: 6
SALES (corp-wide): 1.4B **Publicly Held**
SIC: 7521 Parking lots
PA: Sp Plus Corporation
    200 E Randolph St # 7700
    Chicago IL 60601
    312 274-2000

(G-12691)
SPAIN MAGIC ROSE LLC (PA)
3411 Silverside Rd (19810-4812)
PHONE..................941 312-2051
Antonio Sosa,
EMP: 4
SALES (est): 516.5K **Privately Held**
SIC: 5149 Spices & seasonings

(G-12692)
SPALLCO ENTERPRISES INC (PA)
Also Called: Spallco Car & Truck Rentals
702 Philadelphia Pike (19809-2540)
P.O. Box 9628 (19809-0628)
PHONE..................302 762-3825
Joe Spall, *President*
Barbara Spall, *Treasurer*
EMP: 4
SALES (est): 844K **Privately Held**
SIC: 7514 7513 Rent-a-car service; truck rental & leasing, no drivers

(G-12693)
SPARKIA INC
2711 Centerville Rd # 400 (19808-1660)
PHONE..................302 636-5440
Pablo Martinez, *CEO*
Karlo Rodriguez, *Principal*
EMP: 5
SALES (est): 300K **Privately Held**
SIC: 8732 Business analysis

(G-12694)
SPARKLE MOBILE DENTAL SERVICES
718 W 38th St (19802-2033)
PHONE..................302 762-4322
Ramona Ryle, *Principal*
EMP: 4

SALES (est): 162.4K **Privately Held**
SIC: 8021 Dental clinic

(G-12695)
SPECIAL CARE INC
Also Called: Griswold Special Care
5145 W Woodmill Dr 22 (19808-4067)
PHONE..................302 456-9904
Mary Ann Murray, *Branch Mgr*
EMP: 7
SALES (corp-wide): 7.4MM **Privately Held**
WEB: www.home-care.com
SIC: 8082 Home health care services
PA: Special Care, Inc.
    800 Bethlehem Pike
    Glenside PA 19038
    215 402-0200

(G-12696)
SPECIALTY MACHINE WORKS
319 Robinson Ln (19805-4690)
PHONE..................302 429-8970
Andreas Nesemann, *Owner*
EMP: 1
SQ FT: 1,400
SALES (est): 85.7K **Privately Held**
SIC: 3599 Machine shop, jobbing & repair

(G-12697)
SPECIALTY PRODUCTS N&H INC (DH)
Also Called: Specialty Products N&H, LLC
200 Powder Mill Rd (19803-2907)
PHONE..................302 774-1000
Micheal P Heffernan, *President*
Michael P Heffernan, *President*
Calissa W Brown, *Vice Pres*
James P Donaghey, *Vice Pres*
Sharon E Smith, *Vice Pres*
EMP: 7
SALES (est): 1.6MM
SALES (corp-wide): 30.6B **Publicly Held**
SIC: 2879 2824 Agricultural chemicals; nylon fibers; polyester fibers

(G-12698)
SPECTR-PHYSICS HLDINGS USA INC
3411 Silverside Rd Ste 10 (19810-4812)
PHONE..................302 478-4600
EMP: 5
SQ FT: 1,456
SALES (est): 358.8K **Privately Held**
SIC: 3827 3596 3825 3812 Mfg Optical Instr/Lens Mfg Scale/Balance-Nonlab Mfg Elec Measuring Instr Mfg Search/Navgatn Equip
HQ: Spectra-Physics Ab
    Pyramidbacken 3
    Kungens Kurva
    855 646-800

(G-12699)
SPECTRUM MAGNETICS LLC (PA)
1210 First State Blvd (19804-3561)
PHONE..................302 993-1070
Jianrong Lin,
John Q Xiao, *Administration*
▲ EMP: 2
SALES (est): 373.7K **Privately Held**
SIC: 3498 Piping systems for pulp paper & chemical industries

(G-12700)
SPECTRUM TAX CONSULTANTS USA
800 Delaware Ave Fl 10 (19801-1322)
PHONE..................866 544-1408
EMP: 4 EST: 2002
SALES: 425K **Privately Held**
SIC: 8748 Tax Recovery Services

(G-12701)
SPEECH CLINIC
5147 W Woodmill Dr Ste 21 (19808-4067)
PHONE..................302 999-0702
John Azzara, *Director*
EMP: 25
SALES (est): 1.1MM **Privately Held**
SIC: 8049 Speech pathologist

(G-12702)
SPEKCITON BIOSCIENCES LLC
2509 Berwyn Rd (19810-3526)
PHONE..................302 353-2694
Andy Ragone, *Principal*
EMP: 1
SALES (est): 60.2K **Privately Held**
SIC: 3829 Thermometers & temperature sensors

(G-12703)
SPI HOLDING COMPANY
Also Called: SPI Pharma
503 Carr Rd Ste 210 (19809-2864)
PHONE..................800 789-9755
Rana Kayal, *President*
Dan Antonelli, *President*
Carmen Sciackitano, *Senior VP*
Paul Lopresto, *Vice Pres*
Quentis Rogers, *Vice Pres*
EMP: 368
SALES (est): 45.8MM
SALES (corp-wide): 20B **Privately Held**
SIC: 2869 Sweeteners, synthetic
PA: Associated British Foods Plc
    Fourth Floor
    London W1K 4
    207 399-6500

(G-12704)
SPI PHARMA INC (HQ)
503 Carr Rd Ste 210 (19809-2864)
PHONE..................302 576-8500
Rana Kayal, *President*
Harry Maclacklin, *Controller*
Ernesto Giannoni, *CPA*
Lynne Webb, *Cust Mgr*
Beth Morrison, *Technology*
▼ EMP: 50
SALES (est): 135.6MM
SALES (corp-wide): 20B **Privately Held**
SIC: 5122 Pharmaceuticals
PA: Associated British Foods Plc
    Fourth Floor
    London W1K 4
    207 399-6500

(G-12705)
SPIKES COACH LINES
34 Vining Ln (19807-3128)
PHONE..................302 438-3644
EMP: 4
SALES (est): 102.5K **Privately Held**
SIC: 4111 Bus transportation

(G-12706)
SPINE GROUP LLC
1426 N Clayton St (19806-4006)
PHONE..................302 595-3030
Damon Cary, *Osteopathy*
EMP: 9
SALES (est): 559.8K **Privately Held**
SIC: 8748 8011 Business consulting; offices & clinics of medical doctors

(G-12707)
SPIRITS PATH TO WELLNESS LLC
1405 Greenhill Ave (19806-1124)
PHONE..................302 998-0074
Diana Bozzo, *Principal*
EMP: 7
SALES (est): 83.6K **Privately Held**
SIC: 8099 Health & allied services

(G-12708)
SPORTING GOODS PROPERTIES
974 Centre Rd (19805-1269)
PHONE..................302 774-1000
Robert M Reardon, *President*
Richard H Heath, *Treasurer*
Andrew T O'Neill, *Comptroller*
Ann L Douglas, *Admin Sec*
EMP: 8
SALES (est): 922.8K
SALES (corp-wide): 30.6B **Publicly Held**
SIC: 5091 Sporting & recreation goods
HQ: E. I. Du Pont De Nemours And Company
    974 Centre Rd Bldg 735
    Wilmington DE 19805
    302 485-3000

(G-12709)
SPORTS CAR SERVICE INC
3901 N Market St (19802-2217)
PHONE..................302 764-7439
John W Jacobson, *Owner*
Carol Ann Pampuch, *Office Mgr*
EMP: 15
SQ FT: 30,100
SALES (est): 1.1MM **Privately Held**
WEB: www.sportscarservice.com
SIC: 7538 5521 General automotive repair shops; automobiles, used cars only

(G-12710)
SPORTS CAR TIRE INC
1203 E 13th St (19802-5210)
P.O. Box 9295 (19809-0295)
PHONE..................302 571-8473
Tom Cresswell, *President*
Les Tronzo, *Vice Pres*
Chris Misero, *Opers Mgr*
Pat Walsh, *Sales Associate*
EMP: 23
SQ FT: 17,000
SALES (est): 3.2MM **Privately Held**
WEB: www.sportscartire.com
SIC: 5531 5013 Automotive tires; wheels, motor vehicle

(G-12711)
SPOTLIGHT PUBLICATIONS LLC
3301 Lancaster Pike 5c (19805-1436)
PHONE..................302 504-1329
Angelo Martinelli, *Principal*
EMP: 2
SALES (est): 147.2K **Privately Held**
SIC: 2741 Miscellaneous publishing

(G-12712)
SPRATLEY PUBLISHING
Also Called: Spratley Publishing Co
1203 Apple St (19801-5413)
PHONE..................267 779-7353
Jeffrey Spratley, *Owner*
EMP: 2
SALES: 10K **Privately Held**
SIC: 3555 Printing trades machinery

(G-12713)
SPRING COMMUNICATIONS INC
Also Called: AT&T Authorized Retailer
2090 Naamans Rd (19810-2655)
PHONE..................302 475-1052
EMP: 7
SALES (corp-wide): 280MM **Privately Held**
SIC: 4813 Local & long distance telephone communications
HQ: Spring Communications, Inc.
    12550 Reed Rd Ste 100
    Sugar Land TX 77478
    801 277-7777

(G-12714)
SPRINGHAUS LLC
251 Little Falls Dr (19808-1674)
PHONE..................302 397-5261
Jorge Huck, *Principal*
EMP: 2
SALES (est): 85.7K **Privately Held**
SIC: 2048 Feed premixes

(G-12715)
SPRINGLEAF FINCL HOLDINGS LLC
1 Righter Pkwy (19803-1534)
PHONE..................302 543-6767
EMP: 335
SALES (corp-wide): 2.1B **Privately Held**
SIC: 7389 Financial services
PA: Springleaf Financial Holdings, Llc
    601 Nw 2nd St
    Evansville IN 47708
    800 961-5577

(G-12716)
SPRINT QUALITY PRINTING INC
3609 Silverside Rd (19810-5109)
PHONE..................302 478-0720
Carson Dempsey, *President*
Kathleen Dempsey, *Vice Pres*
EMP: 5
SQ FT: 3,700
SALES (est): 710.2K **Privately Held**
SIC: 2752 Commercial printing, offset

(PA)=Parent Co (HQ)=Headquarters (DH)=Div Headquarters
✪ = New Business established in last 2 years

Wilmington - New Castle County (G-12717) — GEOGRAPHIC SECTION

(G-12717)
SPRINT SPECTRUM LP
4511 Kirkwood Hwy (19808-5117)
PHONE..................302 993-3700
Mark Kline, *Branch Mgr*
EMP: 20 **Publicly Held**
WEB: www.sprintpcs.com
SIC: 4812 Cellular telephone services
HQ: Sprint Spectrum L.P.
6800 Sprint Pkwy
Overland Park KS 66251

(G-12718)
SQS GLOBAL SOLUTIONS LLC
1201 N Orange St Ste 7383 (19801-1286)
PHONE..................302 691-9682
Abdullah Alamgir,
EMP: 10
SALES (est): 281.1K **Privately Held**
SIC: 5961 6799 8748 ; commodity contract trading companies; business consulting

(G-12719)
SRS DISTRIBUTION INC
1204 E 12th St Ste 5 (19802-5317)
PHONE..................240 965-8350
EMP: 18 **Privately Held**
SIC: 5033 Roofing & siding materials
PA: Srs Distribution Inc.
5900 S Lk Frest Dr Ste 40
Mckinney TX 75070

(G-12720)
ST ANTHONYS COMMUNITY CENTER
1703 W 10th St (19805-2709)
PHONE..................302 421-3721
Herschel Quillen, *President*
Rev Roberto Balducelli, *Vice Pres*
Steven Mockbee, *Vice Pres*
Debra A Wirt, *Exec Dir*
Richard Bacon, *Admin Sec*
EMP: 50
SQ FT: 18,000
SALES: 4.7MM **Privately Held**
SIC: 8322 Social service center

(G-12721)
ST ANTHONYS HOUSING MGT CORP
1701 W 10th St Ste 200 (19805-2700)
PHONE..................302 421-3756
Tori Adams, *Manager*
Domenick Peronti, *Director*
EMP: 6
SALES: 169K **Privately Held**
SIC: 8741 Management services

(G-12722)
ST FRANCIS HOSPITAL INC
701 N Clayton St (19805-3155)
P.O. Box 2500 (19805-0500)
PHONE..................616 685-3538
Brian Dietz, *CEO*
Margaret M Lewis, *President*
Dennis Gagliardo, *Principal*
Joseph Desantis, *Vice Chairman*
Mary Finn, *Vice Pres*
EMP: 1000
SQ FT: 400,000
SALES: 133.4MM
SALES (corp-wide): 18.3B **Privately Held**
SIC: 8062 General medical & surgical hospitals
PA: Trinity Health Corporation
20555 Victor Pkwy
Livonia MI 48152
734 343-1000

(G-12723)
ST JAMES PLACE ASSOCIATES
4 Denny Rd (19809-3445)
PHONE..................302 764-6450
William Demarco, *Partner*
EMP: 13
SALES (est): 538.9K **Privately Held**
SIC: 6513 Apartment building operators

(G-12724)
ST LAWRENCE GRANT AVE TRUST
2010 Pennsylvania Ave (19806-2430)
PHONE..................302 652-7978
James Stein, *Partner*
Joseph Stein, *Partner*
Richard Stein, *Partner*
EMP: 5
SQ FT: 7,000
SALES (est): 436.6K **Privately Held**
SIC: 6798 Real estate investment trusts

(G-12725)
ST LOGISTICS
812 Philadelphia Pike (19809-2372)
PHONE..................302 407-5931
Dakota A Carr, *President*
EMP: 7
SALES (est): 107.7K **Privately Held**
SIC: 4789 Transportation services

(G-12726)
ST MARKS UNITED METHODIST CH
Also Called: St Mark's Pre-School
1700 Limestone Rd (19804-4100)
PHONE..................302 994-0400
Nancy Mayhew, *Exec Dir*
EMP: 27
SALES (est): 875.2K **Privately Held**
SIC: 8661 8351 Methodist Church; preschool center

(G-12727)
ST MICHAELS SCHOOL INC
305 E 7th St (19801-3800)
PHONE..................302 656-3389
Helen Raleigh, *Director*
EMP: 40
SALES: 2.3MM **Privately Held**
WEB: www.smsliv.org
SIC: 8351 Preschool center

(G-12728)
ST PATRICK CENTER INC
Also Called: SAINT PATRICK'S CENTER
107 E 14th St (19801-3209)
PHONE..................302 652-6219
Joseph Hickey, *President*
EMP: 8
SALES (est): 994.1K **Privately Held**
SIC: 8322 Senior citizens' center or association

(G-12729)
ST STEPHENS EVANG LUTHERAN CH
Also Called: St Stephens Lutheran Church
1301 N Broom St (19806-4205)
PHONE..................302 652-7623
Matthew Hummel, *Pastor*
Jason Churchill, *Pastor*
EMP: 4
SALES: 375K **Privately Held**
SIC: 8661 8641 Lutheran Church; civic social & fraternal associations

(G-12730)
STAIKOS ASSOCIATES ARCHITECTS (PA)
502 Dell Hill Rd (19809)
PHONE..................302 764-1678
Nicholas Staikos, *Owner*
EMP: 8
SALES (est): 952.4K **Privately Held**
WEB: www.staikos.com
SIC: 8712 7389 Architectural engineering;

(G-12731)
STAINLESS ALLOYS INC
103 Foulk Rd Ste 202 (19803-3742)
PHONE..................800 499-7833
Cristobal Fuentes, *President*
Miguel Ferrandis, *Vice Pres*
Mary J Riley, *Admin Sec*
EMP: 4
SALES (est): 250.9K
SALES (corp-wide): 81.9MM **Privately Held**
SIC: 3316 Cold finishing of steel shapes
HQ: North American Stainless, Inc.
6870 Us Highway 42 E
Ghent KY 41045
502 347-6000

(G-12732)
STAINLESS STEEL INVEST INC
103 Foulk Rd Ste 202 (19803-3742)
PHONE..................800 499-7833
Cristobal Fuentes, *President*
Mary Jean Riley, *Vice Pres*
Anil Yadav, *Vice Pres*
Pat Feeley, *Commercial*
EMP: 4
SALES (est): 283.2K
SALES (corp-wide): 81.9MM **Privately Held**
SIC: 3316 3312 Cold finishing of steel shapes; blast furnaces & steel mills
HQ: North American Stainless, Inc.
6870 Us Highway 42 E
Ghent KY 41045
502 347-6000

(G-12733)
STAMFORD SCREEN PRINTING INC
3801 Kennett Pike C107 (19807-2326)
PHONE..................302 654-2442
Cynthia A Prendergast, *President*
EMP: 5
SQ FT: 1,500
SALES (est): 450K **Privately Held**
WEB: www.verycoolproducts.com
SIC: 5199 2759 2395 Advertising specialties; screen printing; embroidery products, except schiffli machine

(G-12734)
STAN PERKOSKIS PLUMBING & HTG
1818 Marsh Rd (19810-4539)
PHONE..................302 529-1220
Stanley Perkoski Jr, *President*
EMP: 15
SALES (est): 2.7MM **Privately Held**
SIC: 1711 Plumbing contractors

(G-12735)
STANDARD INDUSTRIAL SUPPLY CO
1625 N Heald St (19802-5146)
P.O. Box 98, Montchanin (19710-0098)
PHONE..................302 656-1631
Andrew Gold, *President*
EMP: 5 EST: 1949
SQ FT: 10,000
SALES (est): 784.9K **Privately Held**
SIC: 5085 5072 Industrial supplies; hardware

(G-12736)
STANLEY GOLDEN
Also Called: Grays Fine Printing
841 N Tatnall St (19801-1717)
P.O. Box 365 (19899-0365)
PHONE..................302 652-5626
Stanley Golden, *Owner*
EMP: 3
SALES (est): 231.1K **Privately Held**
SIC: 2752 2759 2791 Commercial printing, offset; letterpress printing; typesetting

(G-12737)
STANLEY H GOLOSKOV DDS PA
2500 Grubb Rd Ste 130 (19810-4711)
PHONE..................302 475-0600
Stanley H Goloskov DDS, *President*
Joan Garone, *Executive Asst*
EMP: 9
SALES (est): 582.3K **Privately Held**
SIC: 8021 Dentists' office

(G-12738)
STAPEN CONSTRUCTION INC
9 Harlech Dr (19807-2507)
PHONE..................302 218-2190
Jeff Stapen, *President*
Aaron Stapen, *Vice Pres*
EMP: 4
SALES: 4.5MM **Privately Held**
SIC: 1521 Single-family housing construction

(G-12739)
STAPLEFORDS AT WILMINGTON INC
315 Springhill Ave (19809-3143)
PHONE..................302 762-0637
Maurice Stapleford, *President*
Stephanie Fuhr, *Corp Secy*
Bruce Stapleford, *Vice Pres*
EMP: 4
SALES (est): 404.7K **Privately Held**
SIC: 1711 Heating & air conditioning contractors

(G-12740)
STAPLER ATHLETIC ASSOCIATION
1900 N Scott St (19806-2320)
PHONE..................302 652-9769
Frank Farren, *President*
EMP: 6
SALES: 46.1K **Privately Held**
SIC: 8611 Merchants' association

(G-12741)
STAR NAIL SALON
16a Trolley Sq (19806-3334)
PHONE..................302 498-0702
Van Tran, *Owner*
EMP: 4
SALES (est): 88.3K **Privately Held**
SIC: 7231 Manicurist, pedicurist

(G-12742)
STAR NAILS & SPA
1518 Philadelphia Pike (19809-1826)
PHONE..................302 798-6245
EMP: 4 EST: 2008
SALES (est): 113.5K **Privately Held**
SIC: 7231 Manicurist, pedicurist

(G-12743)
STARR WRIGHT INSUR AGCY INC
Also Called: Starr Wright USA
405 Silverside Rd 102b (19809-1774)
PHONE..................302 483-0190
Walter Wilson, *Ch of Bd*
Bryan Lewis, *President*
Cynthia Wilson, *Asst Controller*
Suzanne Skibicki, *Supervisor*
John D Huntley, *Director*
EMP: 30
SQ FT: 10,000
SALES: 17MM
SALES (corp-wide): 286.5MM **Privately Held**
SIC: 6411 Insurance agents & brokers
PA: Special Agents Mutual Benefit Association Inc
11301 Old Georgetown Rd
Rockville MD 20852
301 984-1440

(G-12744)
STATE FARM MUTL AUTO INSUR CO
Also Called: State Farm Insurance
1601 Concord Pike Ste 88 (19803-3623)
PHONE..................302 434-3333
Abby Pubusky, *Principal*
Nicholas Demaio, *Manager*
David Soleye, *Manager*
EMP: 71
SALES (corp-wide): 39.5B **Privately Held**
SIC: 6411 Insurance agents & brokers
PA: State Farm Mutual Automobile Insurance Company
1 State Farm Plz
Bloomington IL 61710
309 766-2311

(G-12745)
STATE LINE MACHINE INC
200 State Line Rd (19803-1439)
P.O. Box 7617 (19803-0617)
PHONE..................302 478-0285
Fulton S Owensby Sr, *President*
Pam Owensby, *Corp Secy*
EMP: 12
SQ FT: 7,000
SALES (est): 3.5MM **Privately Held**
WEB: www.statelinemachine.com
SIC: 7699 5085 Construction equipment repair; industrial supplies

(G-12746)
STATWHIZ VENTURES LLC
1201 N Orange St Ste 600 (19801-1171)
PHONE..................310 819-5427
Siva Moturi, *Partner*
EMP: 2
SALES (est): 120K **Privately Held**
SIC: 7372 7389 Application computer software;

GEOGRAPHIC SECTION
Wilmington - New Castle County (G-12776)

(G-12747)
STAY PRIME INC
1201 N Orange St Ste 600 (19801-1171)
PHONE.................................612 770-6753
Tyler Hayes, *CEO*
Will Imholte, *COO*
Owen Imholte, *CFO*
EMP: 3 **EST:** 2013
SALES (est): 169K **Privately Held**
SIC: 7372 Application computer software

(G-12748)
STEEL SUPPLIERS INC
Also Called: Steel Suppliers Erectors
701 E Front St (19801-5040)
P.O. Box 2662 (19805-0662)
PHONE.................................302 654-5243
Michael A Bloom, *President*
David Bloom, *CFO*
EMP: 110 **EST:** 1945
SQ FT: 75,000
SALES (est): 70.4MM **Privately Held**
SIC: 5051 1791 3441 Steel; structural shapes, iron or steel; reinforcement mesh, wire; building front installation metal; exterior wall system installation; concrete reinforcement, placing of; building components, structural steel

(G-12749)
STEERING SLTIONS IP HOLDG CORP
1209 N Orange St (19801-1120)
PHONE.................................313 556-5000
William Gerald Quigley III, *Vice Pres*
Andrew Thurston Perry, *Treasurer*
Yi Fan, *Admin Sec*
Peter Michael Ziparo, *Asst Sec*
EMP: 6
SALES (est): 13.1K **Privately Held**
SIC: 3714 Motor vehicle parts & accessories
HQ: Steering Solutions Corporation
3900 E Holland Rd
Saginaw MI 48601

(G-12750)
STEIN TREE SERVICE INC
17 Austin Rd (19810-2202)
P.O. Box 367, Rockland (19732-0367)
PHONE.................................302 731-1718
Jeff Stein, *President*
EMP: 12
SALES: 850K **Privately Held**
SIC: 0783 Planting, pruning & trimming services

(G-12751)
STELLA ABG ACQUISITION INC
1105 N Market St Ste 1300 (19801-1241)
PHONE.................................302 654-6682
Jean-Luc Belingard, *Chairman*
EMP: 4
SALES (est): 210.7K
SALES (corp-wide): 7.5MM **Privately Held**
SIC: 6726 Investment offices
HQ: Biomerieux Sa
376 Chemin De L Orme
Marcy-L'Etoile 69280
478 872-000

(G-12752)
STEP UP DAYCARE
Also Called: Step-Up Daycare
2715 N Tatnall St (19802-3527)
PHONE.................................302 762-3183
Janice Brooks, *Principal*
EMP: 5
SALES (est): 54.8K **Privately Held**
SIC: 8351 Group day care center

(G-12753)
STEPHANIE GALBRAITH
Also Called: Healthy Kneads
1429 Stapler Pl (19806-2529)
PHONE.................................302 290-2235
Stephanie Galbraith, *Principal*
EMP: 4
SALES (est): 215.8K **Privately Held**
SIC: 7299 Massage parlor

(G-12754)
STEPHANO SLACK LLC
1700 W 14th St (19806-4012)
PHONE.................................302 777-7400
Willie Mays, *Accountant*
Jennifer Crawford, *Manager*
Richard Skinner, *Manager*
Nora Hallett, *Executive Asst*
EMP: 6
SALES (corp-wide): 2.3MM **Privately Held**
SIC: 8721 Certified public accountant
PA: Stephano Slack, Llc
125 Strafford Ave Ste 200
Wayne PA 19087
610 687-1600

(G-12755)
STEPHEN F WETHERILL MD
133 Montchan Dr (19807-2125)
PHONE.................................302 478-3700
EMP: 4
SQ FT: 1,100
SALES (est): 339.8K **Privately Held**
SIC: 8011 Medical Doctor's Office

(G-12756)
STEPHEN JANKOVIC CHIROPRACTOR
1309 Beale Rd Ste 12 (19810)
PHONE.................................302 384-8540
Stephen Jankovic, *Owner*
EMP: 6 **EST:** 2011
SALES (est): 138K **Privately Held**
SIC: 8041 Offices & clinics of chiropractors

(G-12757)
STERICYCLE COMM SOLUTIONS INC
1521 Concord Pike Ste 202 (19803-3645)
PHONE.................................302 656-0630
Bradley Bishop, *Accounts Mgr*
EMP: 18
SALES (corp-wide): 3.4B **Publicly Held**
SIC: 7389 Telephone answering service
HQ: Stericycle Communication Solutions, Inc.
4010 Commercial Ave
Northbrook IL 60062
866 783-9820

(G-12758)
STEVEN ABDILL
Also Called: Golegik Technologies
24a Trolley Sq Ste 101 (19806-3334)
P.O. Box 101 (19899-0101)
PHONE.................................443 243-6864
Steven Abdill, *Owner*
EMP: 1
SALES (est): 35K **Privately Held**
SIC: 3825 3569 7378 5044 Network analyzers; liquid automation machinery & equipment; computer & data processing equipment repair/maintenance; copying equipment; photocopy machines

(G-12759)
STEVEN BROWN & ASSOCIATES INC
9 S Cleveland Ave (19805-1426)
PHONE.................................302 652-4722
Steven D Brown, *President*
Gina M Klempa, *Bookkeeper*
EMP: 5
SQ FT: 2,200
SALES: 3.1MM **Privately Held**
WEB: www.stevenbrownassociates.com
SIC: 5087 5084 1711 Sprinkler systems; pumps & pumping equipment; fire sprinkler system installation

(G-12760)
STEVEN E DIAMOND M D
900 Foulk Rd Ste 200 (19803-3155)
PHONE.................................302 655-8868
Steven Diamond, *Owner*
EMP: 8
SALES (est): 75.4K **Privately Held**
SIC: 8051 Skilled nursing care facilities

(G-12761)
STEVEN J STIRPARO
3622 Silverside Rd (19810-5190)
PHONE.................................302 479-9555
Steven J Stirparo, *Owner*

Drew Kelly, *Principal*
Drew Sikorski, *Principal*
Judy Sikroski, *Admin Sec*
EMP: 4
SALES (est): 339.3K **Privately Held**
SIC: 8111 General practice attorney, lawyer

(G-12762)
STEVENS & LEE PC
919 N Market St Ste 1300 (19801-3092)
PHONE.................................302 654-5180
Walter McEvilly, *Partner*
EMP: 24
SALES (corp-wide): 40.9MM **Privately Held**
SIC: 8111 General practice attorney, lawyer
PA: Stevens & Lee P.C.
111 N 6th St
Reading PA 19601
610 478-2000

(G-12763)
STEWART LAW FIRM
Also Called: Stewart and Martin
301 N Market St (19801-2529)
PHONE.................................302 652-5200
Gordon Stewart, *Managing Prtnr*
Dawn Kilcreasc, *Director*
Leanne C McGrory, *Director*
Tanya Murray, *Director*
EMP: 36
SALES (est): 3.2MM **Privately Held**
WEB: www.delawarecorporatelaw.com
SIC: 8111 6719 Specialized law offices, attorneys; investment holding companies, except banks

(G-12764)
STEWART SEPTIMUS MD
2055 Limestone Rd Ste 117 (19808-5536)
PHONE.................................302 992-9940
Stewart Septimus, *Owner*
EMP: 4
SALES (est): 290K **Privately Held**
SIC: 8011 Physicians' office, including specialists

(G-12765)
STEWART TITLE COMPANY
Also Called: Pmh Financial
5300 Brandywine Pkwy (19803-1470)
PHONE.................................302 433-8766
Tatyana Raisova, *Administration*
EMP: 4
SALES (corp-wide): 1.9B **Publicly Held**
SIC: 6163 Loan brokers
HQ: Stewart Title Company
1360 Post Oak Blvd # 100
Houston TX 77056
713 625-8100

(G-12766)
STEWART TITLE GUARANTY COMPANY
1 Righter Pkwy Ste 160 (19803-1550)
PHONE.................................302 651-9201
Dick Yerger, *Principal*
EMP: 11
SALES (corp-wide): 1.9B **Publicly Held**
SIC: 6361 Title insurance
HQ: Stewart Title Guaranty Company
1360 Post Oak Blvd # 100
Houston TX 77056
713 625-8100

(G-12767)
STIFEL BANK AND TRUST
1413 Foulk Rd Ste 204 (19803-2758)
PHONE.................................302 478-8880
Rick Tremblay, *Manager*
EMP: 6
SALES (corp-wide): 3.2B **Publicly Held**
SIC: 6162 Mortgage bankers & correspondents
HQ: Stifel Bank And Trust
12655 Olive Blvd Ste 250
Saint Louis MO 63141

(G-12768)
STOKES GARAGE INC
101 Old Dupont Rd (19805)
PHONE.................................302 994-0613
Andrei Cratty, *President*
Robert Stokes Jr, *President*

EMP: 5
SALES: 500K **Privately Held**
WEB: www.stokesgarage.com
SIC: 7538 7532 General automotive repair shops; body shop, trucks

(G-12769)
STOLTZ REALTY CO
Also Called: Plaza Apartments
1303 Delaware Ave Ste 101 (19806-3416)
PHONE.................................302 656-8543
Diana Hamel, *Manager*
EMP: 25
SALES (corp-wide): 7.4MM **Privately Held**
WEB: www.stoltzusa.com
SIC: 6531 6513 Real estate brokers & agents; apartment building operators
PA: Stoltz Realty Co
3704 Kennett Pike Ste 200
Wilmington DE
302 656-2852

(G-12770)
STONEY BATTER FAMILY MEDICINE
5311 Limestone Rd Ste 201 (19808-1258)
PHONE.................................302 234-9109
Hal Kramer, *President*
EMP: 22
SALES (est): 3.1MM **Privately Held**
SIC: 8011 General & family practice, physician/surgeon

(G-12771)
STONEYBROOK ASSOCIATES LP
Also Called: Stoneybrook Apartments
4 Denny Rd (19809-3445)
PHONE.................................302 764-6450
William Demarco, *Vice Pres*
EMP: 13
SALES: 2MM **Privately Held**
SIC: 6513 Retirement hotel operation

(G-12772)
STONEYBROOK PRESVTN ASSOC LLC
Also Called: Stoneybrook Apartments
4 Denny Rd (19809-3445)
PHONE.................................302 764-9430
Cathy Thomas, *Office Mgr*
William Demarco,
EMP: 13
SALES (est): 980K **Privately Held**
SIC: 6513 Apartment building operators

(G-12773)
STORK ELECTRIC INC
9 Germay Dr Ste 100 (19804-1156)
PHONE.................................302 654-9427
Richard S Deptula, *President*
EMP: 8
SALES (est): 690K **Privately Held**
SIC: 1731 Electrical work

(G-12774)
STRATEGIC FUND RAISING INC (PA)
300 Delaware Ave Ste 1370 (19801-1658)
PHONE.................................651 649-0404
Michael Bills, *CEO*
EMP: 20
SALES (est): 17MM **Privately Held**
WEB: www.strategicfundraising.com
SIC: 7389 Telemarketing services

(G-12775)
STREAM APP LLC
1500 Lancaster Ave (19805-3995)
PHONE.................................610 420-5864
David Polykoff, *CEO*
EMP: 7
SALES (est): 184.8K **Privately Held**
SIC: 7372 7389 Prepackaged software;

(G-12776)
STRIDE SERVICES INC
200 Powder Mill Rd (19803-2907)
PHONE.................................302 540-4713
Seetha Coleman-Kammula, *President*
James Dinnage, *Admin Sec*
EMP: 16

Wilmington - New Castle County (G-12777) — GEOGRAPHIC SECTION

SALES: 400K **Privately Held**
SIC: 8731 8999 Commercial physical research; scientific consulting

(G-12777)
STRIPE-A-LOT INC
Also Called: Advance Paving Services
55 Germay Dr (19804-1104)
PHONE 302 654-9175
Rick Romero, *President*
Kaushik V Shah, *Accountant*
EMP: 20
SQ FT: 1,500
SALES (est): 2.6MM **Privately Held**
SIC: 1771 Blacktop (asphalt) work

(G-12778)
STROBERT TREE SERVICES
1506 A St (19801-5412)
PHONE 302 633-3478
Jon Auer, *Director*
EMP: 4 EST: 2010
SALES (est): 481.8K **Privately Held**
SIC: 0783 Planting, pruning & trimming services

(G-12779)
STROBERT TREE SERVICES INC
1806 Zebley Rd (19810-1502)
PHONE 302 475-7089
Andrew Strobert, *President*
Sam Strobert, *Manager*
▲ EMP: 45
SALES (est): 5.2MM **Privately Held**
SIC: 0783 Planting, pruning & trimming services

(G-12780)
STUART KINGSTON GALLERIES INC
Also Called: Stuart Kingston Jewelers
3704 Kennett Pike Ste 100 (19807-2173)
PHONE 302 652-7978
Joseph Stein, *President*
James Stein, *Vice Pres*
EMP: 16
SQ FT: 7,000
SALES (est): 1.1MM **Privately Held**
WEB: www.stuartkingstonjewelers.com
SIC: 5963 5947 5944 7389 Furnishings, including furniture, house-to-house; gift shop; jewelry, precious stones & precious metals; interior design services

(G-12781)
STUDIO 11
2301 Penns Ave Apt D (19806-1341)
PHONE 302 622-9959
Carolann Leone, *Principal*
EMP: 12
SALES (est): 119.7K **Privately Held**
SIC: 7997 Membership sports & recreation clubs

(G-12782)
STYLELABS INC
108 W 13th St (19801)
PHONE 347 674-7993
Tom De Ridder, *Principal*
Tim Pashuysen, *Principal*
Dagbert Sansen, *Sales Mgr*
EMP: 45
SALES (est): 710.6K **Privately Held**
SIC: 7371 Computer software development & applications; computer software development

(G-12783)
STYLES MILLENIUM
1923 W 4th St (19805-3421)
PHONE 302 472-3427
Johns Lamotte, *Owner*
EMP: 8
SALES (est): 170K **Privately Held**
SIC: 7241 Barber shops

(G-12784)
SUBCODEVS INC
919 N Market St (19801-3023)
PHONE 704 234-6780
Subodh Srivastava, *CEO*
Prince Srivastava, *Business Mgr*
EMP: 6

SALES (est): 123.5K **Privately Held**
SIC: 7371 Computer software development & applications

(G-12785)
SUBURBAN LAWN & EQUIPMENT INC (PA)
1601 Naamans Rd (19810-3020)
PHONE 302 475-4300
Anthony J Petruccelli, *President*
Mike J Petruccelli, *Corp Secy*
EMP: 9
SQ FT: 2,600
SALES (est): 2.9MM **Privately Held**
WEB: www.sublawneq.com
SIC: 5261 5251 7699 Lawnmowers & tractors; garden tractors & tillers; chainsaws; snowblowers; tools, power; lawn mower repair shop; power tool repair

(G-12786)
SUBURBAN MARKETING ASSOCIATES (PA)
3301 Lancaster Pike 5c (19805-1436)
PHONE 302 656-8440
Robert F Martinelli, *President*
EMP: 53
SQ FT: 8,000
SALES (est): 5.2MM **Privately Held**
WEB: www.visionstoday.com
SIC: 5192 Magazines

(G-12787)
SUBURBAN PSYCHIATRIC SVCS LLC
5177 W Woodmill Dr Ste 6 (19808-4067)
PHONE 302 999-9834
Inderpreet Singh, *Principal*
EMP: 12
SALES (est): 204.1K **Privately Held**
SIC: 8322 General counseling services

(G-12788)
SUBURBAN PUBLISHING INC (PA)
Also Called: Mainline Today
3301 Lancaster Pike 5c (19805-1436)
PHONE 302 656-1809
Angelo Martinelli, *Ch of Bd*
Robert F Martinelli, *President*
Mark Nardone, *Editor*
Monica Weber, *Vice Pres*
Drew Ostroski, *Manager*
EMP: 44
SQ FT: 10,000
SALES (est): 4MM **Privately Held**
WEB: www.delawaretoday.com
SIC: 2721 Magazines: publishing only, not printed on site

(G-12789)
SUEZ NORTH AMERICA INC (DH)
Also Called: United Water Delaware
2000 First State Blvd (19804-3569)
P.O. Box 6508 (19804-0508)
PHONE 302 633-5670
Axel Vayssiere, *President*
Susan Skomorucha, *General Mgr*
Deborah Butler, *Superintendent*
Larry Finnicum, *Vice Pres*
Jim Glozzy, *Vice Pres*
EMP: 10
SQ FT: 28,000
SALES (est): 665MM
SALES (corp-wide): 91.7MM **Privately Held**
SIC: 4941 3569 3589 Water supply; generators: steam, liquid oxygen or nitrogen; water treatment equipment, industrial
HQ: Suez International
    Tour Cb 21
    Courbevoie 92400
    146 256-000

(G-12790)
SUEZ WATER DELAWARE INC
Also Called: United Water Delaware Inc.
2000 First State Blvd (19804-3569)
P.O. Box 6508 (19804-0508)
PHONE 302 633-5905
David Cherdaeoyne, *President*
Victor Mercado, *Vice Pres*
EMP: 68
SQ FT: 8,000

SALES (est): 17.1MM
SALES (corp-wide): 91.7MM **Privately Held**
SIC: 4941 Water supply
HQ: Suez North America Inc.
    2000 First State Blvd
    Wilmington DE 19804
    302 633-5670

(G-12791)
SUMMER LRNG COLLABORATIVE INC
1313 N Market St 1150nw (19801-6101)
PHONE 860 751-9887
Catherine Lindroth, *Exec Dir*
EMP: 4
SALES: 1MM **Privately Held**
SIC: 8699 Charitable organization

(G-12792)
SUN COAL & COKE LLC
2401 Penns Ave Ste 111 (19806-1432)
PHONE 630 824-1000
Frederick Henderson, *CEO*
Michael Thomson, *COO*
Matthew Mc Grath, *Senior VP*
Steven R Morey, *Vice Pres*
Richard W Westbrook, *Vice Pres*
EMP: 749
SALES (est): 16.5MM
SALES (corp-wide): 1.4B **Publicly Held**
SIC: 8731 Energy research
PA: Suncoke Energy, Inc.
    1011 Warrenville Rd # 600
    Lisle IL 60532
    630 824-1000

(G-12793)
SUN GABON OIL COMPANY
201 N Walnut St Ste 1300t (19801-2920)
PHONE 302 293-6000
EMP: 1
SALES (est): 59.8K
SALES (corp-wide): 54B **Publicly Held**
WEB: www.sunocoinc.com
SIC: 1311 Crude petroleum production
HQ: Etc Sunoco Holdings Llc
    3801 West Chester Pike
    Newtown Square PA 19073
    215 977-3000

(G-12794)
SUN MALAYSIA PETROLEUM COMPANY
201 N Walnut St Ste 1300t (19801-2920)
PHONE 302 293-6000
Scott Leonhard, *Principal*
EMP: 1
SALES (est): 14.9K
SALES (corp-wide): 54B **Publicly Held**
WEB: www.sunocoinc.com
SIC: 2911 Petroleum refining
HQ: Etc Sunoco Holdings Llc
    3801 West Chester Pike
    Newtown Square PA 19073
    215 977-3000

(G-12795)
SUN NATIONAL BANK
4401 Concord Pike (19803-1489)
PHONE 302 334-4091
Tom Holiday, *Manager*
EMP: 5 **Publicly Held**
WEB: www.citynatbank.com
SIC: 6021 National commercial banks
HQ: Sun National Bank
    975 Hooper Ave
    Toms River NJ 08753
    800 786-9066

(G-12796)
SUN NOORDZEE OIL COMPANY
201 N Walnut St Ste 1300 (19801-2920)
PHONE 302 293-6000
EMP: 1
SALES (est): 15.8K
SALES (corp-wide): 54B **Publicly Held**
WEB: www.sunocoinc.com
SIC: 2911 Petroleum refining
HQ: Etc Sunoco Holdings Llc
    3801 West Chester Pike
    Newtown Square PA 19073
    215 977-3000

(G-12797)
SUN ORIENT EXPLORATION COMPANY
201 N Walnut St Ste 1300 (19801-2920)
PHONE 302 293-6000
EMP: 1
SALES (est): 63.5K
SALES (corp-wide): 54B **Publicly Held**
WEB: www.sunocoinc.com
SIC: 1382 Oil & gas exploration services
HQ: Etc Sunoco Holdings Llc
    3801 West Chester Pike
    Newtown Square PA 19073
    215 977-3000

(G-12798)
SUN-IN-ONE INC
500 Philadelphia Pike # 1 (19809-2146)
PHONE 302 762-3100
Tom Bird, *Engineer*
William Rawheiser, *Consultant*
EMP: 2 EST: 2012
SQ FT: 2,000
SALES (est): 622.3K **Privately Held**
SIC: 5074 3648 4911 Heating equipment & panels, solar; outdoor lighting equipment;

(G-12799)
SUNDAY BREAKFAST MISSION
600 E 5th St Apt C1 (19801-4712)
P.O. Box 342 (19899-0342)
PHONE 302 656-8542
Roger Todd, *Finance Dir*
Gerald A Foster, *Commissioner*
Thomas Laymon, *Exec Dir*
Mark Doherty, *Director*
Janice Laymon, *Director*
EMP: 10
SALES: 6.2MM **Privately Held**
WEB: www.sundaybreakfastmission.org
SIC: 8361 Home for destitute men & women

(G-12800)
SUNDEW PAINTING INC
500 S Colonial Ave (19805-1900)
PHONE 302 994-7004
Nicholas J Nardo Sr, *President*
Shirley Nardo, *Corp Secy*
Joseph Dino Nardo, *Vice Pres*
EMP: 25
SQ FT: 5,000
SALES (est): 2.5MM **Privately Held**
SIC: 1721 Exterior residential painting contractor; interior residential painting contractor; exterior commercial painting contractor; interior commercial painting contractor

(G-12801)
SUNRISE SENIOR LIVING LLC
Also Called: Sunrise of Wilmington
2215 Shipley Rd (19803-2305)
PHONE 302 475-9163
Michael Friedel, *Manager*
Sheri Parsons, *Director*
Nancy Curran, *Hlthcr Dir*
EMP: 100
SALES (corp-wide): 4.7B **Publicly Held**
WEB: www.sunrise.com
SIC: 8051 8361 Skilled nursing care facilities; residential care
HQ: Sunrise Senior Living, Llc
    7902 Westpark Dr
    Mc Lean VA 22102

(G-12802)
SUNWORKS CORPORATION
30 Evergreen Dr (19850)
PHONE 302 655-5772
John Klein, *Vice Pres*
EMP: 4
SALES: 300K **Privately Held**
SIC: 1542 Greenhouse construction

(G-12803)
SUPER PERFECTION CLG SVCS LLC
7 Colony Blvd Apt 302 (19802-1433)
PHONE 267 619-4441
Denise Brown,
EMP: 7 EST: 2017
SALES (est): 102.5K **Privately Held**
SIC: 7699 Cleaning services

GEOGRAPHIC SECTION
Wilmington - New Castle County (G-12834)

(G-12804)
SUPER SUPPERS
3619 Silverside Rd (19810-5101)
PHONE...................302 478-5935
Cathy Hagan, *Executive*
EMP: 3 EST: 2010
SALES (est): 192.4K **Privately Held**
SIC: 2099 Food preparations

(G-12805)
SUPERCUTS INC
2504 Foulk Rd (19810-1420)
PHONE...................302 475-5001
Ester Dougherty, *Branch Mgr*
EMP: 9
SALES (corp-wide): 1B **Publicly Held**
WEB: www.supercuts.com
SIC: 7231 Unisex hair salons
HQ: Supercuts, Inc.
  7201 Metro Blvd
  Minneapolis MN 55439
  952 947-7777

(G-12806)
SUPERIOR CLR OF WILMINGTON INC
Also Called: Superior Cleaners Wilmington
808 First State Blvd (19804-3573)
PHONE...................302 633-3323
Michael Strauss, *President*
EMP: 7
SALES (est): 369.2K **Privately Held**
WEB: www.thesuperiorcleaner.com
SIC: 7216 Cleaning & dyeing, except rugs

(G-12807)
SUPERIOR ELECTRIC SERVICE CO (PA)
36 Germay Dr (19804-1105)
PHONE...................302 658-5949
Jane Fitzsimmons, *President*
James Fitzsimmons, *Vice Pres*
Steve Zoladkiewicz, *Purch Agent*
Joelle Cordrey, *Comptroller*
EMP: 34
SQ FT: 27,000
SALES (est): 7.3MM **Privately Held**
WEB: www.superiorelectric.biz
SIC: 1731 General electrical contractor

(G-12808)
SUPERIOR GRAPHIC & PRINTING
1432 Governor House Cir (19809-2485)
PHONE...................302 290-3475
Adnan Hussain, *Owner*
EMP: 1
SALES (est): 94.6K **Privately Held**
SIC: 2759 Screen printing

(G-12809)
SUPERLODGE
1213 N West St (19801-1044)
PHONE...................302 654-5544
Anup Patel, *Principal*
EMP: 9
SALES (est): 384.7K **Privately Held**
SIC: 7011 Motels

(G-12810)
SUPERMARKET ASSOCIATES INC
4001 Kennett Pike (19807-2315)
PHONE...................302 547-1977
Ronnie Robinson, *President*
Kristin Robinson, *Vice Pres*
EMP: 7
SALES (est): 1.4MM **Privately Held**
SIC: 5141 Food brokers

(G-12811)
SUPERSTORE LLC
1000 N West St Ste 1200 (19801-1058)
PHONE...................302 200-4933
Joshua Kiprop Kisorio,
EMP: 10
SALES (est): 271.K **Privately Held**
SIC: 5045 Computer software

(G-12812)
SUPPLY CHAIN CONSULTANTS INC
Also Called: Arkieva
5460 Fairmont Dr (19808-3432)
PHONE...................302 738-9215
Harpal Singh, *CEO*
Bibi I Singh, *President*
Walter Cisneros, *Superintendent*
Kenneth Fordyce, *Director*
Barbara Berry, *Executive Asst*
EMP: 40
SQ FT: 14,160
SALES (est): 6.1MM **Privately Held**
WEB: www.arkieva.com
SIC: 8742 7371 Business consultant; computer software development

(G-12813)
SUPPORTIVE CARE SOLUTIONS LLC
1606 Newport Gap Pike (19808-6208)
P.O. Box 5463 (19808-0463)
PHONE...................302 598-4797
David Simkins, *Principal*
EMP: 4
SALES (est): 104.3K **Privately Held**
SIC: 8399 Advocacy group

(G-12814)
SUPREME COURT UNITED STATES
Also Called: US Probation Pretrial
824 N Market St (19801-3024)
PHONE...................302 252-2950
John McDonough, *Branch Mgr*
EMP: 27 **Publicly Held**
SIC: 8322 9211 Probation office; courts;
HQ: Supreme Court, United States
  1 1st St Ne
  Washington DC 20543
  202 479-3000

(G-12815)
SUPREME COURT OF THE STATE DEL
Also Called: Register In Chancery
500 N King St Ste 11600 (19801-3734)
PHONE...................302 255-0544
EMP: 4
SQ FT: 1,500 **Privately Held**
SIC: 8111 Securities law
HQ: Supreme Court Of The State Of Delaware
  55 The Grn
  Dover DE 19901
  302 739-4155

(G-12816)
SUPREME GRAND LODGE OF U S A
Also Called: Loyal Orange Institution
1315 Biggs Rd (19805-1345)
PHONE...................302 998-3549
Samuel Stewart, *President*
Frederick E Stewart, *Treasurer*
EMP: 4
SALES (est): 124.6K **Privately Held**
SIC: 8641 Social club, membership

(G-12817)
SURETRONIX SOLUTIONS LLC
111 Brookside Dr (19804-1103)
PHONE...................302 407-3146
Maged Zamzam,
EMP: 3 EST: 2016
SALES (est): 96.7K **Privately Held**
SIC: 8711 3825 3679 3672 Electrical or electronic engineering; digital test equipment, electronic & electrical circuits; electronic circuits; printed circuit boards; integrated circuits, semiconductor networks, etc.

(G-12818)
SURVIVORS ABUSE IN RCOVERY INC
Also Called: S.O.A.R
405 Foulk Rd (19803-3809)
PHONE...................302 651-0181
Stephen R Brodt, *President*
Valerie Marek, *Marketing Staff*
EMP: 5
SALES: 866K **Privately Held**
SIC: 8322 General counseling services

(G-12819)
SUSTAINABLE ENERGY UTILITY
1011 Centre Rd Ste 210 (19805-1266)
PHONE...................302 504-3071
EMP: 5
SALES (est): 84.7K **Privately Held**
SIC: 4911 Electric services

(G-12820)
SUSTAINABLE-GENERATION LLC
Also Called: Sustainable Generation
110 S Poplar St Ste 400 (19801-5044)
PHONE...................917 678-6947
Scott Woods, *CEO*
Straud Ben Fredregill, *Principal*
Ben Fredregill, *Vice Pres*
EMP: 5 EST: 2012
SALES (est): 437.5K **Privately Held**
SIC: 8748 Environmental consultant

(G-12821)
SUTTON BUS & TRUCK CO INC
5609 Old Capitol Trl Frnt (19808-4932)
PHONE...................302 995-7444
Ronald Sutton, *President*
David Sutton, *Vice Pres*
EMP: 55
SQ FT: 1,500
SALES (est): 3.5MM **Privately Held**
SIC: 4151 4212 School buses; dump truck haulage

(G-12822)
SWAMI ENTERPRISES INC
Also Called: Dunkin' Donuts
1702 Faulkland Rd (19805-1160)
PHONE...................302 999-8077
Nick Baden, *President*
EMP: 5
SALES (est): 136.6K **Privately Held**
SIC: 5461 5812 7389 Doughnuts; eating places; business services

(G-12823)
SWEET VENOM EFFECT LLC
1004 Kirkwood St Ste 1 (19801-4024)
PHONE...................302 674-5831
James May,
EMP: 25
SALES (est): 809.2K **Privately Held**
SIC: 2051 Bakery: wholesale or wholesale/retail combined

(G-12824)
SWIATOWICZ DENTAL ASSOCIATES
1211 Milltown Rd (19808-3003)
PHONE...................302 476-8185
Andrew Swiatowicz, *Principal*
EMP: 5
SALES (est): 108.9K **Privately Held**
SIC: 8021 Dental clinic

(G-12825)
SWIFT FINANCIAL LLC (HQ)
Also Called: Swift Capital
3505 Silverside Rd (19810-4905)
PHONE...................302 374-7019
Ed Harycki, *CEO*
Doug Bland, *President*
Paul Sveen, *CFO*
Al Natali, *Ch Credit Ofcr*
John Klose, *CTO*
EMP: 42
SALES (est): 43.6MM
SALES (corp-wide): 15.4B **Publicly Held**
SIC: 6153 7389 Working capital financing; financial services
PA: Paypal Holdings, Inc.
  2211 N 1st St
  San Jose CA 95131
  408 967-1000

(G-12826)
SWIT INC
Also Called: Corporation
501 Silverside Rd Ste 105 (19809-1376)
PHONE...................302 792-0175
WEI Hua, *CEO*
EMP: 200
SALES (est): 2.3MM **Privately Held**
SIC: 7371 7379 Computer software development & applications; computer related services

(G-12827)
SYBOUNHEUANG GROUP INC
514 Centerville Rd (19808-4718)
PHONE...................302 999-9339
Long Sybounheuang, *President*
Bounmy Sybounheuang, *Vice Pres*
EMP: 4
SQ FT: 1,000 **Privately Held**
SIC: 6719 6552 Investment holding companies, except banks; land subdividers & developers, commercial

(G-12828)
SYF INDUSTRIES
1410 Prospect Dr (19809-2429)
PHONE...................302 384-6214
EMP: 1
SALES (est): 40.4K **Privately Held**
SIC: 3999 Manufacturing industries

(G-12829)
SYLVIA SAIENNA
Also Called: Majo Hair Studio
100 Westgate Dr (19808-1428)
PHONE...................302 683-9082
Sylvia Saienna, *Owner*
EMP: 20
SQ FT: 2,400
SALES (est): 195.3K **Privately Held**
SIC: 7231 Unisex hair salons

(G-12830)
SYMBIOSYS CONSULTING LLC
920 Justison St (19801-5150)
PHONE...................302 507-7649
Stewart Belsham,
EMP: 10
SALES (est): 594.3K **Privately Held**
SIC: 7379 Computer related maintenance services

(G-12831)
SYMMETRY DIMENSIONS INC
108 W 13th St (19801)
PHONE...................302 918-5536
Ryan Neil, *President*
EMP: 12
SALES: 3MM **Privately Held**
SIC: 7372 Prepackaged software

(G-12832)
SYNC IT LLC
1314 Oberlin Rd (19803-5110)
P.O. Box 8118 (19803-8118)
PHONE...................904 697-1132
Christopher Abili, *CEO*
Lucia Abili, *COO*
Linda Abili, *Administration*
EMP: 4
SALES (est): 131.6K **Privately Held**
SIC: 7373 Computer integrated systems design

(G-12833)
SYNCHRGNIX INFO STRATEGIES LLC (HQ)
2 Righter Pkwy Ste 205 (19803-1529)
PHONE...................302 892-4800
Kelley Kendle, *CEO*
Frank Garafalo, *VP Finance*
Rahul Mankad, *Accounts Mgr*
Kirra Sponenberg, *Corp Comm Staff*
Lauren Sobocinski, *Marketing Staff*
EMP: 42
SALES (est): 13.1MM **Privately Held**
WEB: www.synchrogenix.com
SIC: 8731 Commercial physical research

(G-12834)
SYNCRETIC PRESS
1137 Webster Dr (19803-3459)
PHONE...................443 723-8355
Enrique Moras, *Principal*
EMP: 1
SALES (est): 37.5K **Privately Held**
SIC: 2741 Miscellaneous publishing

Wilmington - New Castle County (G-12835)   GEOGRAPHIC SECTION

(G-12835)
SYNCRETIC SOFTWARE INC
228 Philadelphia Pike (19809-3125)
PHONE...................................302 762-2600
Seth Rosenberg, *President*
Timothy Brennan, *Vice Pres*
EMP: 12
SQ FT: 4,000
SALES (est): 1.3MM **Privately Held**
WEB: www.syncretic.com
SIC: 7379 7371 Computer related consulting services; software programming applications

(G-12836)
SYNGENTA CORPORATION (DH)
3411 Silverside Rd # 100 (19810-4811)
PHONE...................................302 425-2000
Mark Brazinski, *General Mgr*
Rick Mitchell, *Business Mgr*
Todd Grauel, *Counsel*
Jason Fogden, *Vice Pres*
Tim Primus, *Vice Pres*
▼ **EMP:** 25 EST: 2000
SALES (est): 1.4B
SALES (corp-wide): 63.3B **Privately Held**
SIC: 2879 5191 8741 Agricultural chemicals; seeds: field, garden & flower; management services
HQ: Syngenta Ag
Rosentalstrasse 67
Basel BS 4058
613 231-111

(G-12837)
SYNTEC CORPORATION (PA)
109 Rogers Rd Ste 5 (19801-5779)
PHONE...................................302 421-8393
Robert Di Stefano, *President*
EMP: 16
SQ FT: 13,000
SALES (est): 4MM **Privately Held**
WEB: www.synteccorp.com
SIC: 5169 2869 Chemicals, industrial & heavy; industrial organic chemicals

(G-12838)
SYSOD INC
300 Delaware Ave Ste 210a (19801-6601)
PHONE...................................973 333-4848
EMP: 5 EST: 2017
SALES: 120K **Privately Held**
SIC: 7372 Application computer software

(G-12839)
SYSTEMATIC ACHIEVEMENT INC
2404 Dorval Rd (19810-3529)
PHONE...................................302 479-5829
Charles Paslay, *President*
EMP: 1
SALES (est): 85.2K **Privately Held**
SIC: 3999 Education aids, devices & supplies

(G-12840)
SZEWCZYK COMPANY P A
Also Called: Szewczyk and Company
3403 Lancaster Pike Ste 4 (19805-5533)
PHONE...................................302 998-1117
Joseph Szewczyk, *President*
EMP: 5
SALES (est): 349.5K **Privately Held**
SIC: 8721 Certified public accountant

(G-12841)
T & H BAIL BOND INC (PA)
625 N King St Apt 1 (19801-3752)
PHONE...................................302 777-7982
Virginia Pridgen, *President*
EMP: 5
SALES (est): 506.6K **Privately Held**
SIC: 7389 Bail bonding

(G-12842)
T & H BAIL BONDS AGENCY LLC
625 N King St Frnt (19801-3751)
PHONE...................................302 777-7982
Latrisha Seward,
EMP: 6
SALES (est): 132.9K **Privately Held**
SIC: 7389 Bail bonding

(G-12843)
T & L CONSULTING SERVICES LLC
222 Philadelphia Pike # 4 (19809-3166)
PHONE...................................302 573-1585
Alberta Crowley,
EMP: 8 EST: 2017
SALES (est): 61.1K **Privately Held**
SIC: 8082 Home health care services

(G-12844)
T A RIETDORF & SONS INC
735 S Market St Ste D (19801-5246)
P.O. Box 1528 (19899-1528)
PHONE...................................302 429-0341
Timothy Rietdorf, *President*
June Rietdorf, *Corp Secy*
Karl Rietdorf, *Vice Pres*
EMP: 6
SQ FT: 1,000
SALES: 220K **Privately Held**
SIC: 1731 General electrical contractor

(G-12845)
T S N PUBLISHING CO INC
Also Called: Out & About
307 A St Ste C (19801-5345)
PHONE...................................302 655-6483
Gerald Duphily, *President*
EMP: 7
SALES (est): 949.7K **Privately Held**
WEB: www.out-and-about.com
SIC: 2721 2741 Magazines: publishing only, not printed on site; newsletter publishing

(G-12846)
T-MOBILE
Also Called: T-Mobile Preferred Retailer
724 N Market St (19801-3009)
PHONE...................................302 652-7738
Dave Chung, *President*
EMP: 5
SALES (est): 154K **Privately Held**
SIC: 4812 Cellular telephone services

(G-12847)
TABLEART LLC
3616 Kirkwood Hwy (19808-5124)
P.O. Box 678, Avon CT (06001-0678)
PHONE...................................650 587-8769
Sudhakar Gorti, *Mng Member*
EMP: 6
SALES: 1.8MM **Privately Held**
SIC: 7372 7389 Application computer software;

(G-12848)
TADPOLE ACADEMY LLC
1238 N Walnut St (19801-3222)
PHONE...................................302 658-2141
Crystal Smith, *Principal*
EMP: 7
SALES (est): 153.1K **Privately Held**
SIC: 8351 Preschool center

(G-12849)
TAG SALE BY CHANGEOVER
2501 Bryn Mawr Ave (19803-5308)
PHONE...................................302 478-2450
Kay Riley, *Owner*
EMP: 10
SALES (est): 370K **Privately Held**
SIC: 7389 Appraisers, except real estate

(G-12850)
TALLEYS GARAGE INC
416 Roseanna Ave (19803-1831)
PHONE...................................302 652-0463
James Talley, *President*
James Talley Jr, *Vice Pres*
Leonard N Talley, *Treasurer*
EMP: 5
SALES (est): 605K **Privately Held**
SIC: 5261 7699 Garden supplies & tools; lawn mower repair shop

(G-12851)
TANGENT CABLE SYSTEMS INC
3700 Washington Ave (19808-6034)
PHONE...................................302 994-4104
Lee A Burkey, *President*
Susan E Burkey, *Vice Pres*
Ray Burton, *Vice Pres*
Cary Johnson, *Treasurer*
Suellen Burkey, *Admin Sec*
EMP: 30
SQ FT: 780
SALES (est): 5.1MM **Privately Held**
WEB: www.tangentcable.com
SIC: 1731 General electrical contractor

(G-12852)
TANSLEY ASSOCIATES (USA) INC
1209 N Orange St (19801-1120)
PHONE...................................403 569-8566
EMP: 11
SALES (est): 246.9K **Privately Held**
SIC: 5199 General merchandise, nondurable

(G-12853)
TAP 99 LLC
1521 Concord Pike (19803-3642)
PHONE...................................301 541-7395
EMP: 1
SALES (est): 36.7K **Privately Held**
SIC: 7372 Prepackaged Software Services

(G-12854)
TATSAPOD-AAME
1112 Newport Gap Pike (19804-2865)
PHONE...................................302 897-8963
Janet M Harmon, *Principal*
EMP: 13
SALES (est): 161K **Privately Held**
SIC: 8322 Individual & family services

(G-12855)
TBC RETAIL GROUP INC
Also Called: Tire Kingdom
5508 Concord Pike (19803-1426)
PHONE...................................302 478-8013
Robert Simmons, *Manager*
EMP: 25
SALES (corp-wide): 2.7B **Privately Held**
SIC: 5014 5531 7538 Automobile tires & tubes; automotive tires; general automotive repair shops
HQ: Tbc Retail Group, Inc.
4280 Prof Ctr Dr Ste 400
Palm Beach Gardens FL 33410
561 383-3000

(G-12856)
TC ELECTRIC COMPANY INC
6701 Governor Printz Blvd (19809-1809)
PHONE...................................302 791-0378
Thomas Curley, *President*
EMP: 30
SALES (est): 4.2MM **Privately Held**
SIC: 1731 General electrical contractor

(G-12857)
TCAR HOLDINGS LLC
1209 N Orange St (19801-1120)
PHONE...................................720 328-0944
Rich Montgomery, *Mng Member*
EMP: 5
SALES (est): 150.6K
SALES (corp-wide): 10MM **Privately Held**
SIC: 4013 Railroad terminals
PA: Alpenglow Rail Services Corp
383 Inverness Pkwy # 325
Englewood CO 80112
720 328-0944

(G-12858)
TCI INSPECTIONS USA LLC
2711 Centerville Rd # 120 (19808-1676)
PHONE...................................302 261-5208
EMP: 2
SALES (est): 82.7K **Privately Held**
SIC: 1389 Oil & gas field services

(G-12859)
TD BANK NA
300 Delaware Ave Ste 110 (19801-1638)
PHONE...................................302 655-5031
Donna Stone, *Manager*
EMP: 9
SALES (corp-wide): 22.8B **Privately Held**
SIC: 6021 National commercial banks
HQ: Td Bank, N.A.
1701 Route 70 E Ste 200
Cherry Hill NJ 08003
856 751-2739

(G-12860)
TD BANK NA
1803 Marsh Rd (19810-4505)
PHONE...................................302 529-8727
Bob Edelman, *Branch Mgr*
EMP: 13
SALES (corp-wide): 22.8B **Privately Held**
SIC: 6021 National commercial banks
HQ: Td Bank, N.A.
1701 Route 70 E Ste 200
Cherry Hill NJ 08003
856 751-2739

(G-12861)
TD BANK NA
Also Called: Collateral Department
2035 Limestone Rd (19808-5529)
PHONE...................................302 351-4560
Bharat Masrani, *CEO*
Rochelle Ragin, *President*
Mok Choe, *Chief*
Chris Giamo, *Exec VP*
Maria Friedman, *Assistant VP*
EMP: 4
SALES (corp-wide): 22.8B **Privately Held**
SIC: 6021 National commercial banks
HQ: Td Bank, N.A.
1701 Route 70 E Ste 200
Cherry Hill NJ 08003
856 751-2739

(G-12862)
TD BANK NA
Also Called: Banknorth Massachusetts
2035 Limestone Rd (19808-5529)
PHONE...................................508 793-4188
Kevin Haley, *Branch Mgr*
EMP: 8
SALES (corp-wide): 22.8B **Privately Held**
WEB: www.tdbank.com
SIC: 6021 National commercial banks
HQ: Td Bank, N.A.
1701 Route 70 E Ste 200
Cherry Hill NJ 08003
856 751-2739

(G-12863)
TDY HOLDINGS LLC (DH)
1403 Foulk Rd Ste 200 (19803-2788)
PHONE...................................302 254-4172
Ken Kubacki, *Principal*
EMP: 9
SALES (est): 1.6B **Publicly Held**
SIC: 3462 Iron & steel forgings
HQ: Ati Operating Holdings, Llc
1000 Six Ppg Pl
Pittsburgh PA 15222
412 394-2800

(G-12864)
TE CONNECTIVITY
4550 New Linden Hill Rd (19808)
PHONE...................................302 633-2740
Driscoll A Nina, *Vice Pres*
EMP: 1
SALES (est): 43K **Privately Held**
SIC: 3229 Fiber optics strands

(G-12865)
TEAM WILSON
3838 Kennett Pike (19807-2302)
PHONE...................................302 888-1088
EMP: 7 EST: 1983
SALES (est): 400K **Privately Held**
SIC: 6531 Real Estate Agent/Manager

(G-12866)
TECH CENTRAL LLC
501 Silverside Rd Ste 110 (19809-1376)
PHONE...................................717 273-3301
Douglas Fava, *Mng Member*
EMP: 18
SALES (est): 864.4K **Privately Held**
SIC: 7371 Computer software development

(G-12867)
TECH IMPACT
100 W 10th St Ste 1007 (19801-1652)
PHONE...................................302 256-5015
Patrick Callihan, *Exec Dir*
EMP: 50 EST: 2013
SQ FT: 750
SALES (est): 701K **Privately Held**
SIC: 7378 Computer maintenance & repair

GEOGRAPHIC SECTION
Wilmington - New Castle County (G-12899)

(G-12868)
TECH INTERNATIONAL CORP (PA)
3411 Silverside Rd 102w (19810-4806)
P.O. Box 417 (19899-0417)
PHONE..................302 478-2301
Chux Amobi, *President*
Eugene J Amobi, *Senior VP*
EMP: 5
SALES (est): 1.2MM **Privately Held**
WEB: www.techinternationalcorp.com
SIC: 7379 8711 Computer related consulting services; engineering services

(G-12869)
TECHNICAL WRITERS INC
3511 Silverside Rd # 201 (19810-4902)
PHONE..................302 477-1972
Janice Tate, *President*
John Tate, *Vice Pres*
Mary Feeley, *Manager*
EMP: 25
SALES (est): 744.5K **Privately Held**
WEB: www.technicalwriters.com
SIC: 8999 Technical writing

(G-12870)
TECHNO RELIEF LIMITED
3511 Silverside Rd # 105 (19810-4902)
PHONE..................416 453-9393
Anand Mohan, *COO*
Rajeev Agarwal, *Sales Dir*
EMP: 8
SALES (est): 89.9K **Privately Held**
SIC: 8322 Temporary relief service

(G-12871)
TECHNO SOFT INC (PA)
Also Called: Technosoft Inc
4001 Knneth Pike Ste 250b (19807)
PHONE..................302 392-5200
Ravi Mandalapu, *President*
EMP: 12
SQ FT: 1,500
SALES (est): 4.2MM **Privately Held**
WEB: www.globaltechnosoft.com
SIC: 7379 Computer related consulting services

(G-12872)
TECHSOLUTIONS INC
5630 Kirkwood Hwy (19808-5004)
PHONE..................302 656-8324
Richard Monnig, *President*
Tricia Monnig, *Corp Secy*
Richard Kenney, *Vice Pres*
EMP: 15
SALES (est): 2.7MM **Privately Held**
WEB: www.techsolutionsinc.com
SIC: 5045 Computers, peripherals & software

(G-12873)
TECNATOM USA CORPORATION
1209 N Orange St (19801-1120)
P.O. Box 474, Ballentine SC (29002-0474)
PHONE..................412 265-7226
EMP: 5
SALES (est): 104.7K **Privately Held**
SIC: 7389 Business Serv Non-Commercial Site

(G-12874)
TECNOLOGIKA USA INC
501 Silverside Rd (19809-1374)
PHONE..................302 597-7611
Joseph Castle, *Director*
EMP: 8
SALES (est): 4MM **Privately Held**
SIC: 8742 Marketing consulting services
HQ: Tecnologika Limited
91 Brick Lane
London
203 432-5120

(G-12875)
TEE PEES FROM RATTLESNKS
2001 Rockford Rd (19806-1241)
PHONE..................302 654-0709
Linda Vinton, *Owner*
EMP: 2
SALES (est): 103.6K **Privately Held**
SIC: 2394 5999 Tents: made from purchased materials; tents

(G-12876)
TEKSTROM INC
1301 Milltown Rd (19808-3005)
PHONE..................302 709-5900
Charanjeet Minhas, *President*
Surender Kadam, *Administration*
EMP: 40
SQ FT: 2,000
SALES (est): 4MM **Privately Held**
WEB: www.tekstrom.com
SIC: 7379

(G-12877)
TELEDUCTION ASSOCIATES INC
1 Weldin Park Dr (19803-4708)
PHONE..................302 429-0303
Sharon Baker, *CEO*
Franklin Baker, *Vice Pres*
EMP: 6 EST: 1976
SALES (est): 453.2K **Privately Held**
WEB: www.teleduction.com
SIC: 7812 Television film production

(G-12878)
TELESONIC PC INC (PA)
805 E 13th St (19802-5000)
PHONE..................302 658-6945
Bernard Katz, *President*
Etta Eckrich, *Executive Asst*
EMP: 7
SQ FT: 30,000
SALES: 2MM **Privately Held**
SIC: 3565 Packaging machinery

(G-12879)
TELESONIC PC INC
1330 E 12th St (19802-5316)
PHONE..................302 658-6945
Etta Eckrich, *Executive Asst*
EMP: 2
SALES (corp-wide): 2MM **Privately Held**
SIC: 3565 Packaging machinery
PA: Telesonic Pc Inc.
805 E 13th St
Wilmington DE 19802
302 658-6945

(G-12880)
TELGIAN CORPORATION
4001 Kennett Pike Ste 308 (19807-2039)
PHONE..................480 753-5444
John Sannin, *Exec VP*
EMP: 34 **Privately Held**
SIC: 1711 8711 1731 8748 Fire sprinkler system installation; fire protection engineering; fire detection & burglar alarm systems specialization; systems analysis & engineering consulting services
PA: Telgian Corporation
10230 S 50th Pl Ste 100
Phoenix AZ 85044

(G-12881)
TELGIAN ENGRG & CONSULTING LLC
4001 Kennett Pike Ste 308 (19807-2039)
PHONE..................480 282-5392
Drew Gerard, *Branch Mgr*
EMP: 17
SALES (corp-wide): 65MM **Privately Held**
SIC: 8711 Engineering services
PA: Telgian Engineering & Consulting, Llc
10230 S 50th Pl Ste 100
Phoenix AZ 85044
480 753-5444

(G-12882)
TEN BLADE ENTERPRISES LLC
800 Industrial St (19801-4367)
PHONE..................484 843-4811
Carl Fagel,
EMP: 8
SALES (est): 64K **Privately Held**
SIC: 8059 Personal care home, with health care

(G-12883)
TENMAT INC
23 Copper Dr Ste 5 (19804-2443)
PHONE..................302 633-6600
Roberto Casini, *General Mgr*
Jim Sutcliffe, *Controller*
Marco Kristen, *Marketing Mgr*
◆ EMP: 5
SALES (est): 1.6MM **Privately Held**
WEB: www.tenmat.com
SIC: 5169 Chemicals & allied products

(G-12884)
TERRY L HORTON
501 W 14th St (19801-1013)
PHONE..................302 320-4900
Terry Horton, *Principal*
EMP: 5 EST: 2017
SALES (est): 78.5K **Privately Held**
SIC: 8011 Offices & clinics of medical doctors

(G-12885)
TESTEK AEROSPACE HOLDINGS LLC
1209 N Orange St (19801-1120)
PHONE..................302 658-7581
Shilpa Patel, *Finance Dir*
EMP: 1
SALES (est): 64.3K **Privately Held**
SIC: 3823 Industrial process control instruments

(G-12886)
TETRIS COMPANY LLC
103 Foulk Rd Ste 202 (19803-3742)
PHONE..................302 656-1950
EMP: 1
SALES (est): 51.5K **Privately Held**
SIC: 3944 Board games, children's & adults'

(G-12887)
TEVEBAUGH ASSOCIATES INC (PA)
2 Mill Rd Ste 210 (19806-2184)
PHONE..................302 984-1400
James Tevebaugh, *President*
Robert J Reid, *Principal*
Richard Stratford, *Vice Pres*
Shawn Crowley, *Manager*
EMP: 10
SALES (est): 1.9MM **Privately Held**
WEB: www.tevebaugh.com
SIC: 8712 Architectural services

(G-12888)
TEXAVINO LLC
3422 Old Capitol Trl # 1444 (19808-6124)
PHONE..................302 295-0829
Boghdan Carstoiu,
EMP: 2
SALES (est): 98.7K **Privately Held**
SIC: 2084 Wines

(G-12889)
TEXTRONICS INC
3825 Lancaster Pike # 201 (19805-1559)
PHONE..................302 351-2109
Stacey Burr, *CEO*
EMP: 15
SALES (est): 665.2K
SALES (corp-wide): 24.3B **Privately Held**
WEB: www.textronicsinc.com
SIC: 8011 Health maintenance organization
HQ: Adidas North America, Inc.
3449 N Anchor St Ste 500
Portland OR 97217
971 234-2300

(G-12890)
TGX HOLDINGS LLC
1201 N Market St (19801-1147)
PHONE..................212 260-6300
Yehuda Fulda, *Mng Member*
EMP: 150 EST: 2009
SQ FT: 8,500
SALES (est): 348.3K **Privately Held**
SIC: 8741 Management services

(G-12891)
THE NATURE CONSERVANCY
Also Called: Delaware Field Office
100 W 10th St Ste 1107 (19801-1653)
PHONE..................302 654-4707
Roger Jones, *Director*
EMP: 20
SALES (corp-wide): 992.1MM **Privately Held**
WEB: www.nature.org
SIC: 8641 Environmental protection organization
PA: The Nature Conservancy
4245 Fairfax Dr Ste 100
Arlington VA 22203
703 841-5300

(G-12892)
THE PROFESSIONALS
3812 Governor Printz Blvd (19802-2306)
PHONE..................302 764-5501
George Leach, *Partner*
Brandon Mayfield, *Partner*
EMP: 6
SALES (est): 129.6K **Privately Held**
SIC: 7241 Barber shops

(G-12893)
THEDIGITALSUPPORT
5301 Limestone Rd Ste 100 (19808-1251)
PHONE..................347 305-4006
Joaquin Burgos, *Principal*
EMP: 5 EST: 2016
SALES (est): 152.2K **Privately Held**
SIC: 8399 Advocacy group

(G-12894)
THERAPY ARCHITECTS
2700 Silverside Rd Ste 4a (19810-3724)
PHONE..................610 246-5705
Ayyappan Rajasekaran, *President*
EMP: 1
SALES (est): 81K **Privately Held**
SIC: 2834 Druggists' preparations (pharmaceuticals)

(G-12895)
THERMAL PIPE SYSTEMS INC (PA)
5205 W Woodmill Dr Ste 33 (19808-4068)
PHONE..................302 999-1588
Samuel A Cousins, *President*
Elizabeth Cousins, *General Mgr*
Judith F Cousins, *Corp Secy*
Elizabeth G Korrell, *Vice Pres*
◆ EMP: 5
SQ FT: 2,200
SALES: 2MM **Privately Held**
WEB: www.thermalpipesystems.com
SIC: 3498 Fabricated pipe & fittings

(G-12896)
THERMOELECTRICS UNLIMITED INC
5109 Governor Printz Blvd (19809-2743)
PHONE..................302 764-6618
Jean P Paris, *President*
Albert Fonda, *Vice Pres*
EMP: 6
SQ FT: 2,400
SALES (est): 746K **Privately Held**
SIC: 3674 Thermoelectric devices, solid state

(G-12897)
THIRD FDRAL SAV LN ASSN CLVLAN (PA)
103 Foulk Rd Ste 101 (19803-3742)
PHONE..................302 661-2009
Marc Stefanski, *Ch of Bd*
Stephen Fowle, *CFO*
EMP: 4
SALES (est): 894.9MM **Publicly Held**
SIC: 6035 Federal savings & loan associations

(G-12898)
THIRST 2 LEARN LLC
802 Naamans Rd (19810-2005)
PHONE..................302 475-7080
Kimberly Smithe,
EMP: 6
SALES (est): 101.2K **Privately Held**
SIC: 8351 Child day care services

(G-12899)
THOMAS DOUGHERTY DDS
5317 Limestone Rd Ste 5 (19808-1252)
PHONE..................302 239-2500
Thomas Dougherty, *President*
EMP: 9
SALES (est): 846.7K **Privately Held**
SIC: 8021 Dental surgeon; maxillofacial specialist

Wilmington - New Castle County (G-12900)

(G-12900)
THOMAS F CAVANAUGH
Also Called: On Time Construction
123 Hawthorne Ave (19805-2327)
PHONE..................................302 995-2859
Karen Cavanaugh, *Principal*
EMP: 5
SALES (est): 381.7K **Privately Held**
SIC: 1521 Single-family housing construction

(G-12901)
THOMAS J ALLINGHAM II
1 Rodney Sq (19801)
PHONE..................................302 651-3000
Thomas J Allingham II, *Partner*
EMP: 50
SALES (est): 134.2K **Privately Held**
SIC: 8111 General practice attorney, lawyer

(G-12902)
THOMAS JENKINS DMD
Also Called: Aesthetis Special Care Assoc
2323 Penns Ave Ste LI (19806-1332)
PHONE..................................302 426-0526
Thomas Jenkins DMD, *Owner*
Keith Nguin DMD, *Co-Owner*
EMP: 16
SALES (est): 566.7K **Privately Held**
SIC: 8021 Dental surgeon

(G-12903)
THOMPSON CLEANERS
4746 Limestone Rd Ste A (19808-1928)
PHONE..................................302 998-0935
Oscar Son, *Owner*
EMP: 5
SALES (est): 159.7K **Privately Held**
SIC: 7216 Drycleaning collecting & distributing agency

(G-12904)
THOMSON REUTERS (GRC) INC
2711 Centerville Rd # 400 (19808-1660)
PHONE..................................212 227-7357
Thomson Reuters, *Principal*
Victoria Kummer, *Editor*
Jane Lippmann, *Manager*
Sharon Reich, *Producer*
Ryan Ulivi, *Consultant*
EMP: 3000
SALES (est): 9.4MM **Privately Held**
SIC: 7291 8111 8721 8733 Tax return preparation services; legal services; accounting services, except auditing; research institute; scientific research agency; management services

(G-12905)
THOROUGHTHREADS
3605 Old Capitol Trl C3 (19808-6043)
PHONE..................................302 356-0502
EMP: 2
SALES (est): 83.9K **Privately Held**
SIC: 2752 Commercial printing, lithographic

(G-12906)
THREE JS DISC TIRE & AUTO SVC
Also Called: J Star
3724 Kirkwood Hwy (19808-5106)
PHONE..................................302 995-6141
Hank Glnnelli, *Owner*
Rosemary Gunillie, *Co-Owner*
EMP: 25
SALES (est): 1.1MM **Privately Held**
SIC: 7538 General automotive repair shops

(G-12907)
TIEDEMANN TRUST COMPANY (PA)
200 Bellevue Pkwy Ste 525 (19809-3739)
PHONE..................................302 656-5644
Carl Tiedemann, *President*
Robert Nayden, *Assistant VP*
Michael Brady, *Vice Pres*
Theresa Dolan, *Vice Pres*
Kimberly Evans, *Vice Pres*
EMP: 7
SALES (est): 1MM **Privately Held**
WEB: www.tiedemanntrust.com
SIC: 6733 Trusts

(G-12908)
TIGANI FAMILY DENTISTRY PA
1021 Gilpin Ave Ste 205 (19806-3272)
PHONE..................................302 571-8740
EMP: 4
SALES (est): 61.5K **Privately Held**
SIC: 8021 Dental clinics & offices

(G-12909)
TIGHE AND COTTRELL PA (PA)
704 N King St Fl 5005 (19801-3583)
P.O. Box 1031 (19899-1031)
PHONE..................................302 658-6400
Paul Cottrell, *Partner*
EMP: 10
SALES (est): 1.3MM **Privately Held**
WEB: www.delaware-incorporation.com
SIC: 8111 General practice attorney, lawyer

(G-12910)
TILE MARKET OF DELAWARE INC (PA)
Also Called: Stone Shop, The
405 Marsh Ln Ste 3 (19804-2445)
PHONE..................................302 777-4663
John Watson, *President*
Paul Anderson, *General Mgr*
Tim Watson, *Treasurer*
Terry Bennett, *Sales Staff*
Megan Desantis, *Sales Staff*
▲ **EMP:** 85
SQ FT: 50,000
SALES (est): 12MM **Privately Held**
SIC: 1743 Tile installation, ceramic

(G-12911)
TILE SHOP LLC
1200 Rocky Run Pkwy (19803-1456)
PHONE..................................302 250-4889
EMP: 4
SALES (corp-wide): 357.2MM **Publicly Held**
SIC: 1743 Tile installation, ceramic
HQ: The Tile Shop Llc
14000 Carlson Pkwy
Plymouth MN 55441
763 541-1444

(G-12912)
TIMOTHY AND ROSEMARY CLAY DMD
533 Main St (19804-3910)
PHONE..................................302 998-0500
Timothy Clay, *Partner*
Rosemary K Clay, *Fmly & Gen Dent*
EMP: 16
SALES (est): 1.4MM **Privately Held**
SIC: 8021 Dentists' office

(G-12913)
TIMOTHY D HUMPHREYS
1831 Delaware Ave (19806-2357)
PHONE..................................302 225-3000
Timothy Humphreys, *Founder*
Peggy Vavala, *Accountant*
Eric Maccollum, *CPA*
Robert Houck, *Senior Mgr*
Joanne Wyness, *Assistant*
EMP: 15
SALES (est): 1.1MM **Privately Held**
SIC: 8721 Certified public accountant

(G-12914)
TIMOTHY LIVERIGHT MD
625 N Shipley St (19801-2228)
PHONE..................................302 655-7293
Timothy Liveright, *Executive*
EMP: 5
SALES (est): 72.5K **Privately Held**
SIC: 8011 Offices & clinics of medical doctors

(G-12915)
TINY TOTS CHILDCARE AND LEARNI
1014 W 24th St (19802-3308)
PHONE..................................302 651-9060
Yvonne Brown, *Owner*
EMP: 5
SALES (est): 156.4K **Privately Held**
SIC: 8351 Child day care services

(G-12916)
TIRE SALES & SERVICE INC
600 First State Blvd (19804-3559)
PHONE..................................302 658-8955
Eugene M Julian, *President*
Frank Julian, *Vice Pres*
Joseph R Julian, *Vice Pres*
Thomas Jarrell, *Treasurer*
Richard Julian, *Admin Sec*
EMP: 20
SQ FT: 7,000
SALES (est): 5.4MM **Privately Held**
SIC: 5014 5531 Truck tires & tubes; automotive tires

(G-12917)
TLC HOME CARE
2055 Melson Rd (19808-5933)
PHONE..................................302 983-5720
Harold Bozeman, *Principal*
EMP: 4 **EST:** 2008
SALES (est): 66.5K **Privately Held**
SIC: 8082 Home health care services

(G-12918)
TLC PERSONAL ASSISTANTS
1214 Linden St (19805-4056)
PHONE..................................302 290-9902
Tilquainta Cox, *Owner*
EMP: 4
SALES (est): 150.8K **Privately Held**
SIC: 8721 8742 Billing & bookkeeping service; administrative services consultant

(G-12919)
TM MANAGEMENT LLC
30 Hill Rd (19806)
PHONE..................................302 654-4940
Tracie Farnan, *Principal*
EMP: 4
SALES (est): 480.7K **Privately Held**
SIC: 8741 Business management

(G-12920)
TMI COMPANY STORE HOLDING CORP
Also Called: Maids
508 First State Blvd (19804-3746)
PHONE..................................302 992-0220
Joanne Withers, *Manager*
EMP: 40
SALES (corp-wide): 17.8MM **Privately Held**
WEB: www.maids.com
SIC: 7349 Maid services, contract or fee basis
HQ: Tmi Company Store Holding Corp.
9394 W Dodge Rd Ste 140
Omaha NE 68114
402 359-4444

(G-12921)
TODAYS ENERGY SOLUTIONS LLC
608 Beaver Falls Pl (19808-1648)
PHONE..................................302 438-0285
Sean Regan,
EMP: 4
SALES: 250K **Privately Held**
SIC: 5063 Electrical apparatus & equipment

(G-12922)
TODD ROWEN DMD
25 Milltown Rd Ste A (19808-3107)
PHONE..................................302 994-5887
Todd Rowen, *Owner*
EMP: 8
SALES (est): 361.3K **Privately Held**
SIC: 8021 Dentists' office

(G-12923)
TODDLERS TECH INC
2704 W 4th St (19805-1817)
PHONE..................................302 655-4487
Carlton Carter, *Vice Pres*
Alice Carter, *Director*
EMP: 13
SQ FT: 3,000
SALES (est): 452.8K **Privately Held**
SIC: 8351 Group day care center

(G-12924)
TODDS
1601 Concord Pike Ste 49 (19803-3623)
PHONE..................................302 658-0387
Todd Appleton, *Owner*
Carlos Herrera, *Plant Mgr*
EMP: 10
SALES (est): 358K **Privately Held**
SIC: 7231 Hairdressers

(G-12925)
TOMS BARBER SHOP
3317 Old Capitol Trl A (19808-6239)
PHONE..................................302 992-9635
Jerry Gouge, *Owner*
EMP: 5
SALES (est): 86.3K **Privately Held**
SIC: 7241 Hair stylist, men

(G-12926)
TOOLOOK INC
500 Delaware Ave Unit 1 (19899-7101)
PHONE..................................240 330-3307
Fedor Karmanov, *President*
EMP: 10 **EST:** 2016
SALES: 1MM **Privately Held**
SIC: 7371 Computer software development

(G-12927)
TOP DOG BEST GAMES LLC
3422 Old Capitol Trl (19808-6124)
PHONE..................................949 859-8869
Ted Cheron, *CEO*
Loretta Cheron, *CFO*
Ted P Cheron,
Greg Furlong,
EMP: 4
SQ FT: 5,000
SALES (est): 258K **Privately Held**
SIC: 3944 Electronic games & toys

(G-12928)
TOP OF HLLBRNDYWINE APARTMENTS
Also Called: Top of The Hill-Brandwine Apts
2101 Prior Rd (19809-1127)
PHONE..................................302 798-9971
Susan Carson, *Manager*
EMP: 9 **EST:** 1999
SALES (est): 712.1K **Privately Held**
SIC: 6513 Apartment building operators

(G-12929)
TOP QALITY INDUS FINISHERS INC
1204 E 12th St Ste 1 (19802-5317)
P.O. Box 9625 (19809-0625)
PHONE..................................302 778-5005
Edward Camacho, *President*
Oscar Camacho, *Co-Owner*
Kevin Walto, *Co-Owner*
EMP: 6
SALES (est): 1.1MM **Privately Held**
SIC: 1721 3479 Residential painting; hot dip coating of metals or formed products

(G-12930)
TOP RATED MEDIA INC
1000 N West St Ste 1200 (19801-1058)
PHONE..................................888 550-9273
Steve Simons, *CFO*
EMP: 30
SQ FT: 5,000
SALES (est): 580K **Privately Held**
SIC: 7311 Advertising agencies

(G-12931)
TOPIARY TECH LLC
2711 Centerville Rd # 400 (19808-1660)
PHONE..................................302 636-5440
D Saliga,
EMP: 5
SALES (est): 270K **Privately Held**
SIC: 7372 Application computer software

(G-12932)
TOPKIS FINANCIAL ADVISORS LLC
910 Foulk Rd Ste 200 (19803-3159)
PHONE..................................302 654-4444
William Topkis, *Manager*
EMP: 9
SALES (est): 1.1MM **Privately Held**
SIC: 6282 Investment advisory service

GEOGRAPHIC SECTION
Wilmington - New Castle County (G-12964)

(G-12933)
TOPTAL LLC (PA)
2810 N Church St # 36879 (19802-4447)
P.O. Box 1299, Palo Alto CA (94302-1299)
PHONE..................................650 843-9206
Taso Duval, *CEO*
Taso D Val, *Principal*
Toby Clarence-Smith, *Chief*
Carlos Aguirre, *Vice Pres*
Mike Dowhan, *Vice Pres*
EMP: 52
SALES (est): 46.6MM **Privately Held**
SIC: 7379 Computer related consulting services

(G-12934)
TOPTRACKER LLC
2810 N Church St # 36879 (19802-4447)
PHONE..................................415 230-0131
Taso Duval,
EMP: 500
SQ FT: 150
SALES (est): 55.8K **Privately Held**
SIC: 7371 Computer software development & applications

(G-12935)
TORC YOGA LLC
4 Caleb Ter (19805-1159)
PHONE..................................856 408-9118
Tia Wright,
EMP: 4
SALES (est): 66.8K **Privately Held**
SIC: 7999 Yoga instruction

(G-12936)
TOTAL BEAUTY SUPPLY INC
2320 Sconset Rd (19810-4237)
PHONE..................................302 798-4647
Robert Custer, *President*
Vicki Schwam, *Corp Secy*
EMP: 5
SALES (est): 655.2K **Privately Held**
SIC: 5087 5999 Beauty parlor equipment & supplies; hair care products; cosmetics

(G-12937)
TOTAL CARE PHYSICIANS
2601 Annand Dr Ste 4 (19808-3719)
PHONE..................................302 998-2977
Constantin Michell, *Principal*
EMP: 25
SALES (corp-wide): 6.9MM **Privately Held**
SIC: 8011 General & family practice, physician/surgeon
PA: Total Care Physicians
405 Silverside Rd Ste 111
Wilmington DE 19809
302 798-0666

(G-12938)
TOTAL CARE PHYSICIANS (PA)
405 Silverside Rd Ste 111 (19809-1768)
PHONE..................................302 798-0666
Theodore Michell MD, *President*
Robert Palandjian, *Family Practiti*
EMP: 30
SALES (est): 6.9MM **Privately Held**
SIC: 8011 General & family practice, physician/surgeon

(G-12939)
TOTAL HEALTH & REHABILITATION
2060 Limestone Rd Ste 202 (19808-5500)
PHONE..................................302 999-9202
Craig Filippone, *Principal*
EMP: 4
SALES (est): 129.5K **Privately Held**
SIC: 8093 8049 8011 Rehabilitation center, outpatient treatment; physical therapist; physical medicine, physician/surgeon

(G-12940)
TOTAL RISC TECHNOLOGY USA LLC
3411 Silverside Rd (19810-4812)
PHONE..................................972 422-9375
EMP: 90 **EST:** 2009
SALES (est): 1.2MM **Privately Held**
SIC: 7379 Computer Related Services

(G-12941)
TOTAL TURF & LANDSCAPING
852 Cranbrook Dr (19803-4802)
PHONE..................................302 762-5410
Terry Hannig, *Principal*
EMP: 4
SALES (est): 170.5K **Privately Held**
SIC: 0781 Landscape services

(G-12942)
TOUBASAM INC
710 N Market St Ste 2b (19801-4922)
P.O. Box 692 (19899-0692)
PHONE..................................302 299-2954
Madior Khoussa, *Opers Staff*
EMP: 5
SALES (est): 100.7K **Privately Held**
SIC: 0711 Fertilizer application services

(G-12943)
TOWLE INSTITUTE
4210 Limestone Rd (19808-2009)
PHONE..................................302 993-1408
Sylvia Shows, *Branch Mgr*
EMP: 5 **Privately Held**
SIC: 8733 Noncommercial research organizations
PA: Towle Institute
505 Schoolhouse Rd
Hockessin DE 19707

(G-12944)
TOWNE & COUNTRY CLEANERS INC
3301 Concord Pike Ste B (19803-5093)
PHONE..................................302 478-8911
Gary Greenberg, *President*
EMP: 8 **EST:** 1950
SQ FT: 3,000
SALES: 500K **Privately Held**
SIC: 7216 Drycleaning collecting & distributing agency

(G-12945)
TOYO FIBRE USA INC
2706 Alexander Dr (19810-1104)
PHONE..................................302 475-3699
Minoru Sano, *President*
EMP: 2
SALES (est): 153.6K **Privately Held**
SIC: 2673 Bags: plastic, laminated & coated

(G-12946)
TRACTION WHOLESALE CENTER INC
600 S Heald St (19801-5636)
PHONE..................................302 743-8473
Lance Elwood, *Manager*
EMP: 6
SALES (corp-wide): 23.7MM **Privately Held**
SIC: 5014 5084 Automobile tires & tubes; tractors, industrial
PA: Traction Wholesale Center, Inc.
3100 Marwin Rd
Bensalem PA 19020
215 642-3170

(G-12947)
TRADEMARK PRODUCTIONS INC
2711 Cntrvlle Rd Pmb 7051 7051 Pmb (19808)
PHONE..................................416 787-0365
EMP: 11 **EST:** 1999
SQ FT: 42,000
SALES: 1.4MM **Privately Held**
SIC: 2273 Mfg Carpets/Rugs

(G-12948)
TRADEMARK SIGNS
2621 Boxwood Dr (19810-1607)
PHONE..................................484 832-5770
EMP: 1
SALES (est): 46K **Privately Held**
SIC: 3993 Signs & advertising specialties

(G-12949)
TRAFFIC SIGN SOLUTIONS INC
1000 N West St Ste 1200 (19801-1058)
PHONE..................................302 295-4836
EMP: 1
SALES (est): 47.5K **Privately Held**
SIC: 3993 Signs & advertising specialties

(G-12950)
TRAINOR CONSULTING LLC
9 Carillon Ct (19803-2900)
PHONE..................................302 428-1677
EMP: 4 **EST:** 2012
SALES (est): 251.1K **Privately Held**
SIC: 8748 Business consulting

(G-12951)
TRAITEL TELECOM CORP
3422 Old Capitol Trl (19808-6124)
P.O. Box 26065, San Diego CA (92196-0065)
PHONE..................................619 331-1913
Eli Traitel, *CEO*
EMP: 23
SQ FT: 2,000
SALES (est): 546.9K **Privately Held**
SIC: 4813 Telephone communication, except radio

(G-12952)
TRANS LOGISTICS LLC
4000 N Market St (19802-2220)
PHONE..................................267 244-6550
Lawrence Amankwah, *Principal*
EMP: 12
SALES (est): 243.3K **Privately Held**
SIC: 4789 Transportation services

(G-12953)
TRANS UN STTLMENT SLUTIONS INC (DH)
5300 Brandywine Pkwy # 100 (19803-1470)
PHONE..................................800 916-8800
Rick Lynch, *President*
EMP: 100
SALES (est): 5.6MM
SALES (corp-wide): 2.3B **Publicly Held**
SIC: 6531 6541 Real estate brokers & agents; title abstract offices
HQ: Trans Union Llc
555 W Adams St Fl 1
Chicago IL 60661
312 985-2000

(G-12954)
TRANSACTIONAL WEB INC
8 W 13th St (19801)
PHONE..................................908 216-5054
Earle West, *CEO*
EMP: 5
SALES (est): 259.3K **Privately Held**
WEB: www.transactionalweb.com
SIC: 7371 Computer software development

(G-12955)
TRANSCONTINENTAL AIRWAYS CORP
1000 N West St Ste 1200 (19801-1058)
PHONE..................................202 817-2020
Andrew Blong, *Chairman*
Hiwa Merani, *Director*
EMP: 14
SALES (est): 779.7K **Privately Held**
SIC: 4522 Air passenger carriers, nonscheduled

(G-12956)
TRANSFLO TERMINAL SERVICES INC
1205 Centerville Rd (19808-6217)
PHONE..................................302 994-3853
Neil Brown, *Manager*
E Brown, *Manager*
EMP: 10
SALES (corp-wide): 12.2B **Publicly Held**
SIC: 4011 Railroads, line-haul operating
HQ: Transflo Terminal Services, Inc.
500 Water St J975
Jacksonville FL 32202

(G-12957)
TRANSPORT WKRS UN AMER INTL UN
Also Called: Transport Wkrs Un O Local 2015
1524 Bonwood Rd (19805-4632)
PHONE..................................302 652-1503
James Riley, *President*
John Carlton, *Vice Pres*
EMP: 7
SALES: 120K **Privately Held**
SIC: 8631 Labor union

(G-12958)
TRANSPORTATION DELAWARE DEPT
Also Called: Delaware Transit
119 Lwer Beech St Ste 100 (19805)
PHONE..................................302 658-8960
Stephen Kingsberry, *Manager*
Mary Wahl, *Manager*
EMP: 5 **Privately Held**
WEB: www.dartfirststate.com
SIC: 4141 9621 Local bus charter service; regulation, administration of transportation;
HQ: Delaware Department Of Transportation
800 S Bay Rd
Dover DE 19901

(G-12959)
TRANSWORLD DIVERSFD SVCS INC
100 Sico Rd (19801-5865)
PHONE..................................302 777-5902
Liu Rittenhouse, *Branch Mgr*
EMP: 13 **Privately Held**
WEB: www.twds-usa.com
SIC: 7363 7389 Help supply services; artists' agents & brokers
PA: Transworld Diversified Services, Inc.
4115 W Spruce St
Tampa FL

(G-12960)
TRAVEL CO INC
1700 Augustine Cut Off (19803-4403)
PHONE..................................302 652-6263
Sheila Batty, *President*
Norman Batty, *Corp Secy*
EMP: 5
SQ FT: 1,800
SALES: 2MM **Privately Held**
SIC: 6411 Insurance agents, brokers & service

(G-12961)
TRAVELWAY GROUP USA INC
251 Little Falls Dr (19808-1674)
PHONE..................................514 331-3130
EMP: 2
SALES (corp-wide): 64.8MM **Privately Held**
SIC: 3161 Luggage
PA: Travelway Group International Inc
4600 Ch Du Bois-Franc
Saint-Laurent QC H4S 1
514 331-3130

(G-12962)
TRAVIS CHROPRACTIC
Also Called: Travis, Dr Arthur W
1911 Foulk Rd (19810-3634)
PHONE..................................610 485-9800
Arthur W Travis, *Owner*
Judith Travis, *Co-Owner*
EMP: 4
SALES (est): 211.4K **Privately Held**
SIC: 8041 Offices & clinics of chiropractors

(G-12963)
TREEHOUSE WELLNESS CENTER LLC
714 W 11th St (19801-1315)
P.O. Box 25171 (19899-5171)
PHONE..................................302 893-1001
Diane Moss, *CEO*
EMP: 17
SALES (est): 546.2K **Privately Held**
SIC: 8249 8748 Business training services; business consulting

(G-12964)
TRELLIST INC (PA)
117 N Market St Ste 300 (19801-2538)
PHONE..................................302 778-1300
David Atadan, *CEO*
Patrick Toman, *President*
John Emerick, *COO*
Holly Wolfe, *Marketing Staff*
EMP: 42
SQ FT: 15,000
SALES (est): 9.1MM **Privately Held**
WEB: www.trellist.com
SIC: 8742 Marketing consulting services

Wilmington - New Castle County (G-12965)

(G-12965)
TRELLIST INC
Also Called: Forthright Consulting
2317 Macdonough Rd # 100 (19805-2620)
PHONE..................................302 593-1432
David Atadan, *CEO*
EMP: 4
SALES (corp-wide): 9.1MM **Privately Held**
SIC: 8748 Business consulting
PA: Trellist, Inc.
    117 N Market St Ste 300
    Wilmington DE 19801
    302 778-1300

(G-12966)
TRI STATE FOOT & ANKLE CTR LLC
2018 Naamans Rd Bldg 1 (19810-2634)
PHONE..................................302 475-1299
Harold Gruber, *Owner*
EMP: 4
SALES (est): 546.2K **Privately Held**
WEB: www.tristatefootandankle.com
SIC: 8043 Offices & clinics of podiatrists

(G-12967)
TRI-STATE TECHNOLOGIES INC
701 Cornell Dr Ste 13 (19801-5782)
PHONE..................................302 658-5400
Edward Mendez, *President*
Connie Mendez, *Vice Pres*
EMP: 45
SQ FT: 4,000
SALES (est): 2.9MM **Privately Held**
WEB: www.tri-statetechnologies.com
SIC: 1711 1731 Mechanical contractor; general electrical contractor

(G-12968)
TRIAL TRANSPORT LOGISTICS
400 Wyoming Ave (19809-1304)
PHONE..................................302 383-5907
Patricia A Schierbaum, *President*
EMP: 6
SALES (est): 331.3K **Privately Held**
SIC: 4789 Transportation services

(G-12969)
TRIALOGICS LLC
3 Mill Rd Ste 306a (19806-2164)
PHONE..................................302 313-9000
Christopher Gropp,
EMP: 10
SQ FT: 2,500
SALES (est): 524.3K **Privately Held**
SIC: 7371 Computer software development

(G-12970)
TRICKLESTAR INC
251 Little Falls Dr (19808-1674)
PHONE..................................888 700-1098
Bernard Emby, *CEO*
EMP: 2
SALES (est): 88.3K **Privately Held**
SIC: 3625 Switches, electronic applications

(G-12971)
TRICKY MINUTE GAMES INC
108 W 13th St (19801)
PHONE..................................302 319-5137
Andrew Prizer, *President*
EMP: 1 EST: 2014
SALES (est): 67K **Privately Held**
SIC: 7372 Application computer software

(G-12972)
TRIHOLD INC
110 Hackney Cir (19803-1909)
PHONE..................................302 475-4517
Brian Weisberg, *Owner*
EMP: 1
SALES (est): 77.2K **Privately Held**
SIC: 3172 Wallets

(G-12973)
TRINET CONSULTANTS INC (HQ)
1106 Elderon Dr (19808-1908)
PHONE..................................302 633-9348
Hugh McNichol IV, *President*
Katherine E McNichol, *Corp Secy*
EMP: 13
SQ FT: 3,000
SALES (est): 300K **Privately Held**
SIC: 8748 Telecommunications consultant

(G-12974)
TRINITY CLOUD COMPANY
1013 Centre Rd Ste 403s (19805-1270)
PHONE..................................973 494-8190
Ansela Joseph Peter, *President*
Sumit Kapoor, *Marketing Staff*
Mukesh Tallam, *Technical Staff*
EMP: 50 EST: 2012
SQ FT: 1,500
SALES: 1.8MM **Privately Held**
SIC: 7361 Employment agencies

(G-12975)
TRINITY GOLD CONSULTING LLC
807 Brown St (19805-4808)
P.O. Box 30551 (19805-7551)
PHONE..................................302 476-9774
John Word, *Principal*
EMP: 7
SALES (est): 45.5K **Privately Held**
SIC: 8748 Business consulting

(G-12976)
TRINITY HEALTH CORPORATION
701 N Clayton St (19805-3165)
PHONE..................................302 421-4100
Richard Long, *CEO*
EMP: 12
SALES (corp-wide): 18.3B **Privately Held**
SIC: 8062 General medical & surgical hospitals
PA: Trinity Health Corporation
    20555 Victor Pkwy
    Livonia MI 48152
    734 343-1000

(G-12977)
TRINITY MEDICAL ASSOC
410 Foulk Rd Ste 200b (19803-3802)
PHONE..................................302 762-6675
Deann Lake, *Manager*
Baldev Lamba, *Professor*
EMP: 5
SALES (est): 184.7K **Privately Held**
SIC: 8011 Offices & clinics of medical doctors

(G-12978)
TRISCO FOODS LLC
2711 Centerville Rd # 400 (19808-1660)
PHONE..................................719 352-3218
Mike Tristram,
EMP: 65
SALES (est): 1.8MM **Privately Held**
SIC: 2033 2087 2099 Barbecue sauce: packaged in cans, jars, etc.; jams, including imitation: packaged in cans, jars, etc.; beverage bases, concentrates, syrups, powders & mixes; syrups, drink; pastes, flavoring; dessert mixes & fillings

(G-12979)
TRISTAR SOLAR FARM LLC
1521 Concord Pike (19803-3642)
PHONE..................................626 457-1381
EMP: 5
SQ FT: 80,000
SALES (est): 126.2K **Privately Held**
SIC: 4931 Electric And Other Services Combined

(G-12980)
TRISTATE COURIER & CARRIAGE
1001 N Jefferson St # 100 (19801-1493)
PHONE..................................302 654-3245
Patricia Ritchie, *President*
Allen N Duff, *Corp Secy*
Bruce Duff, *Vice Pres*
Edward Earp, *Vice Pres*
Jeffrey Low, *CFO*
EMP: 25
SQ FT: 3,000
SALES: 1.6MM **Privately Held**
WEB: www.delawareinjuryattorney.com
SIC: 7389 Courier or messenger service

(G-12981)
TRITEK TECHNOLOGIES INC
1 Medori Blvd Ste B (19801-5777)
PHONE..................................302 573-5096
Ed Cohen, *VP Engrg*
James Malatesta, *Branch Mgr*
EMP: 5
SALES (est): 378.1K
SALES (corp-wide): 1.2MM **Privately Held**
SIC: 3579 Mailing, letter handling & addressing machines
PA: Tritek Technologies, Inc.
    103 E Bridle Path
    Hockessin DE 19707
    302 239-1638

(G-12982)
TROLLEY LAUNDRY
Also Called: Zucchini Brothers
33a Trolley Sq (19806-3371)
PHONE..................................302 654-3538
Tom Guidl, *President*
EMP: 5
SQ FT: 1,000
SALES (est): 218.3K **Privately Held**
WEB: www.zucchinibrothers.com
SIC: 7215 Laundry, coin-operated

(G-12983)
TROLLEY SQ OPN MRI & IMGNG CTR
Also Called: Bancroft Pkwy Open Mri & Imgng
1010 N Bancroft Pkwy # 101 (19805-2690)
PHONE..................................302 472-5555
John W Rollins, *Mng Member*
EMP: 10
SALES (est): 536.6K **Privately Held**
SIC: 8011 Radiologist

(G-12984)
TROPHY SHOP
303 W 8th St (19801-1730)
PHONE..................................302 656-4438
Thomas Tanzilli, *President*
EMP: 15
SQ FT: 18,000
SALES: 1.1MM **Privately Held**
SIC: 3993 Signs & advertising specialties

(G-12985)
TRU GENERAL CONTRACTOR INC
3307 Faulkland Rd (19808-2428)
PHONE..................................302 354-0553
Mustafa Kilincarslan, *President*
Lisa Celik-Kilincarslan, *Corp Secy*
Onur Zaim, *Vice Pres*
EMP: 5
SALES: 200K **Privately Held**
SIC: 1521 New construction, single-family houses

(G-12986)
TRUE ACCESS CAPITAL CORP
100 W 10th St Ste 300 (19801-1642)
PHONE..................................302 652-6774
Vandell Hampton Jr, *President*
Richard Campbell, *Banking Exec*
Thomas Hanson, *Banking Exec*
Paul Hughes, *Banking Exec*
Pedro Viera, *Banking Exec*
EMP: 10
SQ FT: 4,000
SALES (est): 1.8MM **Privately Held**
WEB: www.firststateloan.org
SIC: 6162 Loan correspondents

(G-12987)
TRUE INTELLIGENCE TECH INC
2711 Centerville Rd # 400 (19808-1660)
PHONE..................................979 209-0335
EMP: 8
SALES (est): 349.2K **Privately Held**
SIC: 7371 Custom Computer Programing

(G-12988)
TRUGREEN LIMITED PARTNERSHIP
Also Called: Tru Green-Chemlawn
1350 First State Blvd (19804-3562)
P.O. Box 6209 (19804-0809)
PHONE..................................302 724-6620
EMP: 60
SALES (corp-wide): 3.2B **Privately Held**
SIC: 0782 Lawn care services
HQ: Trugreen Limited Partnership
    1790 Kirby Pkwy
    Memphis TN 38138
    866 417-7866

(G-12989)
TRUTRAC LLC
1201 N Orange St Ste 700 (19801-1186)
PHONE..................................833 878-8722
Marc Nault,
EMP: 8 EST: 2016
SALES: 500K **Privately Held**
SIC: 5045 Computer software

(G-12990)
TTNA ENERGY SYSTEMS LLC
3422 Old Capitol Trl # 1468 (19808-6124)
P.O. Box 4287, Glen Allen VA (23058-4287)
PHONE..................................302 384-9147
Sekar Veerappan,
EMP: 3
SALES (est): 216.7K **Privately Held**
SIC: 3826 Differential thermal analysis instruments

(G-12991)
TUCSON HOTELS LP (PA)
Also Called: John Q Hammons Hotels
2711 Centerville Rd # 400 (19808-1660)
PHONE..................................678 830-2438
Ron Brown, *Partner*
Jonathan Eilian, *Partner*
Chris Pawelko, *Vice Pres*
EMP: 65
SQ FT: 10,226
SALES: 593MM **Privately Held**
WEB: www.holidayinnportland.com
SIC: 7011 Hotels & motels

(G-12992)
TURFHOUND INC
5500 Skyline Dr Ste 6 (19808-1772)
PHONE..................................215 783-8143
Richard Reynolds, *President*
Catherine De Marco, *Vice Pres*
EMP: 3
SQ FT: 22,000
SALES: 2.9MM **Privately Held**
SIC: 3523 Turf & grounds equipment

(G-12993)
TURNING POINT COLLECTION LLC
1020 W 18th St (19802-3892)
P.O. Box 4451 (19807-0451)
PHONE..................................302 416-0092
Beverly Thomes, *Managing Prtnr*
EMP: 2
SALES: 2MM **Privately Held**
SIC: 2531 7389 Public building & related furniture; brokers' services

(G-12994)
TUSI BROTHERS INC
1 Copper Dr Ste 1 # 1 (19804-2446)
P.O. Box 6057 (19804-0657)
PHONE..................................302 998-6383
Francis Tusi, *President*
Donna Tusi, *Treasurer*
EMP: 23
SQ FT: 5,000
SALES: 2.5MM **Privately Held**
SIC: 1731 General electrical contractor

(G-12995)
TUTOR TIME LEARNING CTRS LLC
5305 Limestone Rd (19808-1256)
PHONE..................................302 235-5701
Jennifer Netta, *Director*
EMP: 30
SALES (corp-wide): 164MM **Privately Held**
SIC: 8351 Preschool center
HQ: Tutor Time Learning Centers, Llc
    21333 Haggerty Rd Ste 300
    Novi MI 48375
    248 697-9000

(G-12996)
TUTOR TIME LRNG SYSTEMS INC
2001 Brandywine Pkwy (19803-5403)
PHONE..................................302 478-7366

Wilmington - New Castle County (G-13026)

EMP: 25
SALES (corp-wide): 340.2MM **Privately Held**
SIC: 8351 Child Day Care Services
HQ: Tutor Time Learning Systems, Inc.
621 Nw 53rd St Ste 450
Boca Raton FL

(G-12997)
TWADDELL PLUMBING AND HEATING
1907 Zebley Rd (19810-1503)
PHONE 302 475-5577
Willard Twaddell, *President*
Roberta Twaddell, *Corp Secy*
Jamie Twaddell, *Vice Pres*
Kim Twaddell, *Admin Sec*
EMP: 4
SALES (est): 400.2K **Privately Held**
SIC: 1711 1521 Warm air heating & air conditioning contractor; plumbing contractors; general remodeling, single-family houses

(G-12998)
TWINCO ROMAX LLC
1 Crowell Rd (19804-3556)
PHONE 302 998-3019
EMP: 6
SALES (est): 1MM **Privately Held**
SIC: 2899 Chemical preparations

(G-12999)
TWO ROSES UNITED LLC
543 E 35th St (19802-2817)
PHONE 302 593-2453
Rosalie Dendy, *Mng Member*
EMP: 4
SALES: 500K **Privately Held**
SIC: 5961 7389 Catalog & mail-order houses;

(G-13000)
TY JENNIFER MD
1600 Rockland Rd (19803-3607)
PHONE 302 651-4459
M Jennifer, *Executive*
EMP: 4
SALES (est): 111.7K **Privately Held**
SIC: 8011 Internal medicine, physician/surgeon

(G-13001)
TYBOUT REDFEARN & PELL PA
750 Shipyard Dr Ste 400 (19801-5158)
P.O. Box 2092 (19899-2092)
PHONE 302 658-6901
David Culley, *Partner*
Danielle Yearick, *Partner*
Joanna McLaughlin, *Asst Office Mgr*
Andrew Lukashunas, *Director*
Anne L Naczi,
EMP: 53
SALES (est): 6.1MM **Privately Held**
SIC: 8111 General practice attorney, lawyer

(G-13002)
TYCOS GENERAL CONTRACTORS INC
2112 Silverside Rd (19810)
PHONE 302 478-9267
Sergio Solis, *President*
EMP: 6 **EST:** 2016
SALES (est): 230.2K **Privately Held**
SIC: 1542 Commercial & office building contractors

(G-13003)
U SCOPE SOLUTIONS LLC
2711 Centerville Rd # 400 (19808-1660)
PHONE 844 872-6372
Earl Randolph, *Mng Member*
EMP: 12 **EST:** 2014
SALES: 1.1MM **Privately Held**
SIC: 7371 Computer software development & applications

(G-13004)
U-HAUL INTERNATIONAL INC
2920 Governor Printz Blvd (19802-3706)
PHONE 302 762-6445
Mohamed Moustafa, *Branch Mgr*
EMP: 7
SALES (corp-wide): 3.7B **Publicly Held**
SIC: 7513 Truck rental & leasing, no drivers
HQ: U-Haul International, Inc.
2727 N Central Ave
Phoenix AZ 85004
602 263-6011

(G-13005)
UACJ TRADING AMERICA CO LTD (PA)
1209 N Orange St (19801-1120)
PHONE 312 636-5941
Michinori Morikawa, *President*
Yohei Hasegawa, *Vice Pres*
EMP: 10 **EST:** 2014
SQ FT: 700
SALES (est): 2MM **Privately Held**
SIC: 8611 3353 5015 3354 Business associations; aluminum sheet, plate & foil; aluminum sheet & strip; automotive supplies, used; aluminum extruded products

(G-13006)
UBINET INC
831 N Tatnall St (19801-1717)
PHONE 302 722-6015
Karl Smith, *CEO*
EMP: 5
SALES: 500K **Privately Held**
SIC: 8733 Research institute

(G-13007)
UBS FINANCIAL SERVICES INC
500 Delaware Ave Ste 901 (19801-7409)
PHONE 302 657-5331
Robert Rittereiser, *Manager*
EMP: 13
SALES (corp-wide): 29.9B **Privately Held**
SIC: 7389 Financial services
HQ: Ubs Financial Services Inc.
1285 Ave Of The Americas
New York NY 10019
212 713-2000

(G-13008)
ULTIMATE IMAGES INC
3100 Naamans Rd Ste 8 (19810-2100)
PHONE 302 479-0292
Beth Laplante, *President*
EMP: 13
SALES (est): 246.5K **Privately Held**
SIC: 7231 Unisex hair salons

(G-13009)
ULTRAFINE TECHNOLOGIES INC
405 Derby Way (19810-2265)
PHONE 302 384-6513
Berhan Tecle, *President*
Omar A Kekia, *Development*
EMP: 3
SQ FT: 1,500
SALES: 1MM **Privately Held**
WEB: www.ultrafinetechnologies.com
SIC: 5169 3625 8731 Chemicals & allied products; electric controls & control accessories, industrial; electronic research

(G-13010)
UNIDEL FOUNDATION INC
3801 Kennett Pike C303 (19807-2325)
PHONE 302 658-9200
G Loessner, *Admin Sec*
EMP: 9
SALES: 22.8MM **Privately Held**
SIC: 8699 Charitable organization

(G-13011)
UNIFIED COMPANIES INC
Also Called: Unified Biz Club
1201 N Orange St Ste 600 (19801-1171)
P.O. Box 8189, Waukegan IL (60079-8189)
PHONE 866 936-0515
Ronald Clark, *CEO*
Deshon Wynn, *Director*
Sheila Lantigua Clark, *Admin Sec*
EMP: 8
SQ FT: 500
SALES: 475K **Privately Held**
SIC: 7311 Advertising consultant

(G-13012)
UNIFOREST WOOD PRODUCTS INC
501 Silverside Rd Ste 105 (19809-1376)
PHONE 302 450-4541
George Villanueva, *President*
▼ **EMP:** 12
SALES: 1.3MM **Privately Held**
SIC: 5031 Lumber, plywood & millwork

(G-13013)
UNION PRESS PRINTING INC
1723 W 8th St (19805-3153)
PHONE 302 652-0496
Chrissy Grimes, *President*
John Bove, *Vice Pres*
EMP: 6 **EST:** 1935
SQ FT: 2,000
SALES (est): 949.5K **Privately Held**
WEB: www.unionpress.com
SIC: 2752 2796 Commercial printing, offset; letterpress plates, preparation of

(G-13014)
UNION WHL ACOUSTICAL SUP CO
Also Called: Union Whl Acoustical Sup Co
500 E Front St Ste 1 (19801-5017)
PHONE 302 656-4462
James F McLaughlin Jr, *President*
William Stackhouse, *Corp Secy*
Chad Morris, *Vice Pres*
EMP: 7
SQ FT: 13,000
SALES: 2MM
SALES (corp-wide): 4MM **Privately Held**
SIC: 5039 Ceiling systems & products
PA: J & P Holding Co Inc
500 E Front St Ste 1
Wilmington DE 19801
302 656-4462

(G-13015)
UNION WHOLESALE CO (HQ)
500 E Front St Ste 1 (19801-5017)
PHONE 302 656-4462
James L McLaughlin, *President*
James F McLaughlin, *President*
Christopher Milyo, *Vice Pres*
Chad Morris, *Vice Pres*
Dave Poplos, *Project Mgr*
EMP: 20
SQ FT: 13,000
SALES (est): 1.8MM
SALES (corp-wide): 4MM **Privately Held**
WEB: www.uwco.net
SIC: 1742 Acoustical & ceiling work
PA: J & P Holding Co Inc
500 E Front St Ste 1
Wilmington DE 19801
302 656-4462

(G-13016)
UNIQUE CREATIONS BY CHLOE LLC
501 Silverside Rd (19809-1374)
PHONE 855 942-0477
Todd Davis,
EMP: 25
SALES (est): 442.8K **Privately Held**
SIC: 8742 Management consulting services

(G-13017)
UNIQUE IMAGE LLC
Also Called: Unique Image T-Shirts Company
4577 Kirkwood Hwy (19808-5117)
PHONE 302 658-2266
Bob Gleber,
EMP: 26
SQ FT: 2,500
SALES (est): 3.3MM **Privately Held**
WEB: www.uniquetees.net
SIC: 2396 7389 2759 Screen printing on fabric articles; embroidering of advertising on shirts, etc.; promotional printing

(G-13018)
UNIQUE PRO-CO LLC
1301 Birch Ln (19809-2464)
PHONE 302 723-2365
Gene Grady, *Director*
EMP: 5
SALES (est): 194.1K **Privately Held**
SIC: 4212 Local trucking, without storage

(G-13019)
UNIQUE TRACKING LLC
1013 Centre Rd Ste 403a (19805-1270)
PHONE 912 220-3522
Johnnie Henderson, *Mng Member*
Robert Clarke,
EMP: 3
SALES (est): 106K **Privately Held**
SIC: 2759 Commercial printing

(G-13020)
UNITE USA INC (PA)
2207 Concord Pike Ste 301 (19803-2908)
PHONE 609 915-9130
Daniel Brillman, *CEO*
Taylor Justice, *President*
Rachel McMillan, *Accounts Mgr*
Ally Pratt, *Marketing Staff*
Molly Blumgart, *Manager*
EMP: 27
SQ FT: 2,400
SALES (est): 2.3MM **Privately Held**
SIC: 7371 Computer software writing services

(G-13021)
UNITED AIR LINES INC (HQ)
Also Called: United Airlines, Inc.
2711 Centerville Rd # 120 (19808-1676)
PHONE 872 825-1911
Fred Abbott, *Senior VP*
EMP: 15
SALES: 14.7MM
SALES (corp-wide): 41.3B **Publicly Held**
SIC: 4512 Air passenger carrier, scheduled
PA: United Airlines Holdings, Inc.
233 S Wacker Dr Ste 710
Chicago IL 60606
872 825-4000

(G-13022)
UNITED CEREBRAL PALSY OF DE
700 River Rd (19809-2704)
PHONE 302 764-6216
EMP: 15
SALES (corp-wide): 1.6MM **Privately Held**
SIC: 8322 Social service center
PA: United Cerebral Palsy Of De, Inc
700 River Rd Apt A
Wilmington DE 19809
302 764-2400

(G-13023)
UNITED CEREBRAL PALSY OF DE (PA)
700 River Rd Apt A (19809-2765)
PHONE 302 764-2400
William J Mc Cool III, *Exec Dir*
William McCool, *Director*
EMP: 25
SQ FT: 3,000
SALES: 1.6MM **Privately Held**
SIC: 8322 Association for the handicapped

(G-13024)
UNITED DISTRIBUTION INC
1000 N West St Ste 1200 (19801-1058)
PHONE 302 429-0400
EMP: 10 **EST:** 2002
SALES (est): 790K **Privately Held**
SIC: 4214 Local Trucking-With Storage

(G-13025)
UNITED OUTDOOR ADVERTISING
2502 W 6th St (19805-2909)
PHONE 302 652-3177
Thomas Finn, *President*
Kevin Finn, *Vice Pres*
EMP: 5
SQ FT: 10,000
SALES: 400K **Privately Held**
SIC: 7312 6512 Billboard advertising; commercial & industrial building operation

(G-13026)
UNITED STEELWORKERS
Also Called: Uswa
3847 Evelyn Dr (19808-4618)
PHONE 302 999-0412
M Stapleford, *Branch Mgr*
EMP: 50

Wilmington - New Castle County (G-13027)

SALES (corp-wide): 4.9MM **Privately Held**
WEB: www.uswa.org
SIC: 8631 Labor union
PA: United Steelworkers
60 Bolevard Of The Allies
Pittsburgh PA 15222
412 562-2400

(G-13027)
UNITED TELECOMMUNICATIONS
103 Foulk Rd Ste 226 (19803-3742)
PHONE.....................302 654-6108
EMP: 24
SALES (est): 1.8MM **Privately Held**
SIC: 6211 Security Broker/Dealer

(G-13028)
UNITED WAY OF DELAWARE INC (PA)
625 N Orange St Fl 3 (19801-2247)
PHONE.....................302 573-3700
Michelle A Taylor, *President*
Jerry Hunter, *Vice Pres*
Elaine Mercier, *Vice Pres*
John Moore, *Vice Pres*
Natalie Washington, *Manager*
EMP: 44 EST: 1946
SQ FT: 18,000
SALES: 15.5MM **Privately Held**
SIC: 8322 Individual & family services

(G-13029)
UNITED WORLDWIDE EXPRESS LLC
1202 E 16th St (19802-5217)
PHONE.....................347 651-5111
EMP: 8
SALES (est): 1MM **Privately Held**
SIC: 8742 Franchising consultant

(G-13030)
UNITY CONSTRUCTION INC
Also Called: Unity Development
3403 Lancaster Pike Ste 2 (19805-5533)
PHONE.....................302 998-0531
Michael Simeone, *President*
Harry Simeone, *Vice Pres*
Mary Ann Mihaly, *Admin Asst*
EMP: 21
SQ FT: 2,500
SALES (est): 1.7MM **Privately Held**
SIC: 6512 8741 Nonresidential building operators; construction management

(G-13031)
UNIVERSTY & WHIST CLUB WLMGTON
805 N Broom St (19806-4624)
PHONE.....................302 658-5125
Ted Dwyer, *President*
Stacey Inglis, *Marketing Staff*
Sharon Dawson, *Manager*
Gloria Fountain, *Manager*
EMP: 15
SALES (est): 2.4MM **Privately Held**
WEB: www.universityandwhistclub.com
SIC: 8641 5812 Social club, membership; eating places

(G-13032)
UNIVITA OF FLORIDA INC
Also Called: All-Med Services of Florida,
1000 N King St (19801-3335)
PHONE.....................239 936-4449
EMP: 20
SALES (corp-wide): 66.6MM **Privately Held**
SIC: 7352 Medical Equipment Rental
HQ: Univita Of Florida, Inc.
3700 Commerce Pkwy
Miramar FL 33025
305 826-0244

(G-13033)
UNO MESSENGER LLC
300 Delaware Ave Ste 210a (19801-6601)
PHONE.....................513 703-8091
James Pinelli,
Zac Demarco,
Jeff Morales,
Aaron Peters,
EMP: 4

SALES (est): 89.7K **Privately Held**
SIC: 7371 Computer software development & applications

(G-13034)
URBAN RETAIL PROPERTIES LLC
Also Called: Urban Retail Properties Co
4737 Concord Pike (19803-1442)
PHONE.....................302 479-8314
James Oeste, *Manager*
EMP: 8
SALES (corp-wide): 49.2MM **Privately Held**
SIC: 6512 Shopping center, property operation only
HQ: Urban Retail Properties, Llc
111 E Wacker Dr Ste 2400
Chicago IL 60601

(G-13035)
URBAN SVCS FCILITIES MAINT LLC
2707 N Market St (19802-3626)
PHONE.....................302 993-6363
William Howard, *President*
EMP: 4 EST: 2016
SALES (est): 121.6K **Privately Held**
SIC: 1752 1751 1721 Wood floor installation & refinishing; finish & trim carpentry; commercial painting

(G-13036)
URBANPROMISE WILMINGTON INC
2401 Thatcher St (19802-4539)
P.O. Box 326 (19899-0326)
PHONE.....................302 425-5502
Emily Kennedy, *Mfg Dir*
Larissa Bergen, *Info Tech Dir*
Robert Prestowitz, *Director*
Vanessa Church, *Director*
Deborah Holcombe, *Director*
EMP: 12
SALES: 1.7MM **Privately Held**
SIC: 8322 Youth center

(G-13037)
URIE & BLANTON INC
510 A St (19801-5397)
PHONE.....................302 658-8604
Donald Urie, *President*
Robert Urie, *Vice Pres*
John M Urie Jr, *Admin Sec*
EMP: 9 EST: 1951
SQ FT: 20,000
SALES (est): 1.4MM **Privately Held**
SIC: 5084 5085 Welding machinery & equipment; industrial supplies

(G-13038)
URIGEN PHARMACEUTICALS INC (PA)
501 Silverside Rd Pmb 95 (19809-1374)
PHONE.....................732 640-0160
Dan Vickery, *Ch of Bd*
William J Garner MD, *President*
H Denny Liggitt, *Vice Pres*
Martin E Shmagin, *CFO*
▲ EMP: 7
SALES (est): 740K **Privately Held**
WEB: www.geneswitch.com
SIC: 2834 Pharmaceutical preparations

(G-13039)
US INSTALLATION GROUP INC
355 Water St (19804-2410)
PHONE.....................302 994-1644
Manuel Gonzalez, *Manager*
EMP: 16
SALES (corp-wide): 53.5MM **Privately Held**
SIC: 1799 Antenna installation
PA: U.S. Installation Group Inc.
5030 Champion Blvd
Boca Raton FL 33496
561 962-0452

(G-13040)
US TELEX CORPORATION
4001 Kennett Pike Ste 300 (19807-2039)
PHONE.....................302 652-2707
Robert L Larson, *President*
EMP: 20

SALES (est): 311.4K **Privately Held**
SIC: 7539 7371 Electrical services; custom computer programming services

(G-13041)
USI INC
Also Called: Nationwide
1007 N Orange St Ste 1115 (19801-1211)
PHONE.....................302 658-8000
Ken Evans, *Manager*
EMP: 75 **Privately Held**
SIC: 6411 Insurance information & consulting services; insurance agents; insurance brokers
PA: Usi, Inc.
100 Summit Lake Dr # 400
Valhalla NY 10595

(G-13042)
V2S CORPORATION
1013 Centre Rd Ste 403a (19805-1270)
PHONE.....................302 384-9947
Ms Ann Chilton, *CEO*
Mr H Murray Sawyer, *President*
EMP: 100
SALES (est): 1.3MM **Privately Held**
SIC: 8742 Business consultant

(G-13043)
VA MEDICAL CENTER
1601 Kirkwood Hwy (19805-4917)
PHONE.....................302 994-2511
Charles Dorman, *Manager*
Paul Schuele, *Nursing Dir*
Celita Rivera, *Records Dir*
Jean Stipe, *Nurse*
Lisa Stottlemyer,
EMP: 16
SALES (est): 1.5MM **Privately Held**
SIC: 8011 Medical centers; psychiatric clinic

(G-13044)
VALLEN DISTRIBUTION INC
205 S James St (19804-2424)
PHONE.....................302 992-5604
Derrick Clayton, *Director*
EMP: 5
SALES (corp-wide): 11.3MM **Privately Held**
WEB: www.tilsonmachine.com
SIC: 5084 Industrial machinery & equipment
HQ: Vallen Distribution, Inc.
2100 The Oaks Pkwy
Belmont NC 28012

(G-13045)
VALUE RATE CLEANERS
4405 Concord Pike (19803-1489)
PHONE.....................302 477-9191
EMP: 4
SALES (est): 44.6K **Privately Held**
SIC: 7216 Drycleaning Plant

(G-13046)
VAM APPS CO
1013 Centre Rd Ste 403b (19805-1270)
PHONE.....................786 220-4826
Victor Belogub, *Principal*
EMP: 7
SALES (est): 164.3K **Privately Held**
SIC: 7371 Computer software development & applications

(G-13047)
VAN BUREN MEDICAL ASSOCIATES
1941 Limestone Rd Ste 211 (19808-5433)
PHONE.....................302 998-1151
Kent Sallea, *President*
Sandy Sallee, *Manager*
EMP: 21
SALES (est): 1.6MM **Privately Held**
SIC: 8011 General & family practice, physician/surgeon

(G-13048)
VANDEMARK & LYNCH INC
4305 Miller Rd (19802-1901)
PHONE.....................302 764-7635
Stephan Lehm, *President*
John S Bianco, *Vice Pres*
Stephen L Johns, *Vice Pres*
Stephen Johns, *Vice Pres*
Christopher M O'Keefe, *Vice Pres*

EMP: 35
SQ FT: 12,335
SALES: 3.2MM **Privately Held**
WEB: www.vandemarklynch.com
SIC: 8711 Consulting engineer

(G-13049)
VANGUARD MANUFACTURING INC
11 Lewis Cir (19804-1618)
P.O. Box 6376 (19804-0976)
PHONE.....................302 994-9302
David S Miller, *President*
▲ EMP: 9
SQ FT: 5,000
SALES (est): 980.2K **Privately Held**
SIC: 2393 7389 Bags & containers, except sleeping bags: textile; sewing contractor

(G-13050)
VARI DEVELOPMENT CORP
Also Called: Vari Builders
1309 Veale Rd Ste 20 (19810-4609)
PHONE.....................302 479-5571
Anthony Vari, *President*
Joan Vari, *Corp Secy*
EMP: 8
SQ FT: 18,000
SALES (est): 954.3K **Privately Held**
SIC: 1542 1521 Commercial & office building, new construction; new construction, single-family houses

(G-13051)
VAUGHAN BCKLEY MODULAR SLS INC
1521 Concord Pike Ste 301 (19803-3644)
PHONE.....................215 259-7509
Vaughan Buckley, *President*
EMP: 1 EST: 2017
SALES (est): 114K **Privately Held**
SIC: 5211 3448 Modular homes; prefabricated metal buildings

(G-13052)
VD&L HOLDINGS INC
4305 Miller Rd (19802-1901)
PHONE.....................302 764-7635
Stephan Lehm, *President*
EMP: 58
SALES (est): 4.8MM **Privately Held**
SIC: 8711 Civil engineering

(G-13053)
VECTOR MARKETING CORP
5301 Limestone Rd Ste 105 (19808-1251)
PHONE.....................716 373-6141
Renee Heigel, *Principal*
Jeff Bry, *Manager*
EMP: 4
SALES (est): 508.9K **Privately Held**
SIC: 8742 Marketing consulting services

(G-13054)
VECTORVANCE LLC (PA)
1201 N Orange St Ste 600 (19801-1171)
PHONE.....................347 779-9932
Yien Lung, *General Mgr*
EMP: 4 EST: 2015
SALES: 15MM **Privately Held**
SIC: 5065 Electronic parts & equipment

(G-13055)
VEDAHAM INC
2711 Centerville Rd # 400 (19808-1660)
PHONE.....................302 250-4594
Bhulakshmi Sathyasai, *Director*
EMP: 18
SALES: 440K **Privately Held**
SIC: 7371 Custom computer programming services

(G-13056)
VELOCITY POINTE LLC
20 Whitekirk Dr (19808-1347)
PHONE.....................302 351-8305
Regis Betsch,
EMP: 4
SALES: 20K **Privately Held**
SIC: 8742 Management consulting services

GEOGRAPHIC SECTION
Wilmington - New Castle County (G-13088)

(G-13057)
VENSOFT LLC
Also Called: Sunglobal Technologies
4001 Kennett Pike Ste 250 (19807-2029)
PHONE.................................302 392-9000
Ravi Mandalapu, *President*
EMP: 45
SALES: 5.8MM **Privately Held**
SIC: 7379 7371 Computer related consulting services; ; custom computer programming services; software programming applications

(G-13058)
VERAMORPH LLC
Also Called: Veramorph Materials
200 Powder Mill Rd E50 (19803-2907)
PHONE.................................401 473-1318
Paul Godfrin,
EMP: 1 **EST:** 2017
SALES (est): 54.4K **Privately Held**
SIC: 2869 2834 High purity grade chemicals, organic; powders, pharmaceutical

(G-13059)
VERDE ADVANTAGE GROUP LLC
1000 N West St Ste 1200 (19801-1058)
PHONE.................................302 333-5701
Jose Almeida, *CEO*
EMP: 1
SALES: 250K **Privately Held**
SIC: 7372 Prepackaged software

(G-13060)
VERISTUFFCOM INC
1313 N Market St Ste 5100 (19801-6111)
PHONE.................................972 545-2434
EMP: 4
SALES (est): 200K **Privately Held**
SIC: 7371 Custom Computer Programing

(G-13061)
VERITO TECHNOLOGIES LLC
251 Little Falls Dr (19808-1674)
PHONE.................................855 583-7486
Jatin Narang, *CEO*
EMP: 10 **EST:** 2016
SALES (est): 261.2K **Privately Held**
SIC: 7379 Computer related maintenance services

(G-13062)
VERIZON DELAWARE LLC (HQ)
901 N Tatnall St Fl 2 (19801-1644)
PHONE.................................302 571-1571
William R Allan,
William F Heitmann,
Bonnie L Metz,
EMP: 225
SALES (est): 138.5MM
SALES (corp-wide): 130.8B **Publicly Held**
SIC: 4812 7373 2741 4813 Cellular telephone services; computer integrated systems design; directories, telephone: publishing only, not printed on site; local telephone communications
PA: Verizon Communications Inc.
1095 Ave Of The Americas
New York NY 10036
212 395-1000

(G-13063)
VERIZON DELAWARE LLC
3900 N Washington St Fl 1 (19802-2126)
P.O. Box 5 (19899-0005)
PHONE.................................302 761-6079
Debbie Melvin, *Manager*
EMP: 27
SALES (corp-wide): 130.8B **Publicly Held**
SIC: 4813 Telephone communication, except radio
HQ: Verizon Delaware Llc
901 N Tatnall St Fl 2
Wilmington DE 19801
302 571-1571

(G-13064)
VERSATUS CORP
919 N Market St Ste 425 (19801-3014)
PHONE.................................203 293-3597
Pavel Degtyarev, *President*
EMP: 5

SALES (est): 129.7K **Privately Held**
SIC: 7373 Systems software development services; computer systems analysis & design; systems engineering, computer related

(G-13065)
VERSCOM LLC (PA)
Also Called: VERSCOM CARRIER
501 Silverside Rd Ste 105 (19809-1376)
PHONE.................................866 238-9189
Gokce Bilyay, *CEO*
Aydin Pirinccioglu, *CTO*
Emir Nil,
▼ **EMP:** 24
SQ FT: 1,200
SALES: 101.5MM **Privately Held**
WEB: www.verscom.com
SIC: 8748 Telecommunications consultant

(G-13066)
VERTEX INDUSTRIES INC
Also Called: Austenitex
818 S Heald St Ste C (19801-5790)
PHONE.................................302 472-0601
Alexander Conforti, *President*
Adrienne Conforti, *Vice Pres*
Brian Beverin, *Sls & Mktg Exec*
Susan Conforti, *Treasurer*
◆ **EMP:** 6
SQ FT: 10,000
SALES: 2.5MM **Privately Held**
WEB: www.vertexindustries.com
SIC: 5051 5074 5085 Pipe & tubing, steel; iron or steel flat products; cable, wire; plumbing fittings & supplies; industrial fittings; valves & fittings

(G-13067)
VERTICAL BLIND FACTORY INC (PA)
Also Called: Margaret Keith's Draperies
3 Meco Cir (19804-1108)
PHONE.................................302 998-9616
Margaret Keith, *President*
Richard W Keith, *Vice Pres*
EMP: 15
SQ FT: 10,000
SALES (est): 1.4MM **Privately Held**
SIC: 2591 2211 7699 Window blinds; blinds vertical; mini blinds; window shades; draperies & drapery fabrics, cotton; window blind repair services; venetian blind repair shop

(G-13068)
VERTIGO GROUP INC
200 N Market St (19801-2528)
PHONE.................................302 298-0825
EMP: 15 **EST:** 2014
SALES (est): 299.3K **Privately Held**
SIC: 7371 Custom Computer Programing

(G-13069)
VETDIET USA INC
Also Called: Vetdiet International
1209 N Orange St (19801-1120)
PHONE.................................514 622-7313
EMP: 6
SALES (est): 120.8K **Privately Held**
SIC: 7389 Business Serv Non-Commercial Site

(G-13070)
VETERANS HEALTH ADMINISTRATION
Also Called: Wilmington VAM&roc
1601 Kirkwood Hwy (19805-4917)
PHONE.................................302 994-2511
Lori Barbanel, *Branch Mgr*
Catherine Welde, *Director*
EMP: 500 **Publicly Held**
WEB: www.veterans-ru.org
SIC: 8011 9451 Clinic, operated by physicians; psychiatric clinic;
HQ: Veterans Health Administration
810 Vermont Ave Nw
Washington DC 20420

(G-13071)
VETERANS HEALTH ADMINISTRATION
Also Called: Wilmington Vet Center
2710 Centerville Rd (19808-1644)
PHONE.................................302 994-1660

Jones Sp Encer, *Manager*
EMP: 7 **Publicly Held**
WEB: www.veterans-ru.org
SIC: 8011 9451 Medical centers; psychiatric clinic;
HQ: Veterans Health Administration
810 Vermont Ave Nw
Washington DC 20420

(G-13072)
VETERANS RE-ENTRY RESOURCES
1405 Veale Rd (19810-4331)
PHONE.................................302 384-2350
EMP: 10
SALES (est): 176.3K **Privately Held**
SIC: 6514 8399 8322 Dwelling Operator Individual/Family Svcs Social Service

(G-13073)
VEW TECHNOLOGIES INC
3422 Old Capitol Trl (19808-6124)
PHONE.................................310 560-3814
Shapour Sanaie, *CEO*
EMP: 4
SALES (est): 89.7K **Privately Held**
SIC: 7371 Computer software development & applications

(G-13074)
VIA MDICAL DAY SPA PASCA SALON
3212 Brookline Rd (19808-2613)
PHONE.................................302 757-2830
Toni Toomey, *Principal*
EMP: 4 **EST:** 2008
SALES (est): 118.2K **Privately Held**
SIC: 7991 Spas

(G-13075)
VIA NETWORKS INC
2711 Centerville Rd # 400 (19808-1660)
PHONE.................................314 727-2087
Vijay Reddy, *Principal*
EMP: 6
SALES (est): 569.9K **Privately Held**
WEB: www.viasystems.com
SIC: 3672 Circuit boards, television & radio printed

(G-13076)
VICTOR J VENTURENA DDS
1117 N Franklin St (19806-4331)
PHONE.................................302 656-0558
Victor J Venturena DDS, *Owner*
EMP: 7
SALES (est): 398.7K **Privately Held**
SIC: 8021 Dentists' office

(G-13077)
VICTOR L GREGORY JR DMD
5301 Limestone Rd Ste 211 (19801-1265)
PHONE.................................302 239-1827
Victor Gregory, *Owner*
EMP: 7
SALES (est): 466K **Privately Held**
SIC: 8021 Dentists' office

(G-13078)
VICTORIAN GLASSWORKS
1800 Harrison Ave (19809-1340)
PHONE.................................302 798-4847
Dawn Queripel, *Owner*
EMP: 1
SALES (est): 54K **Privately Held**
SIC: 3231 Stained glass: made from purchased glass

(G-13079)
VICTORY RACING CHASSIS INC
12 Hadco Rd (19804-1014)
PHONE.................................302 593-2255
Richard Byron, *President*
EMP: 1
SALES: 20K **Privately Held**
SIC: 3711 Chassis, motor vehicle

(G-13080)
VIDEO TECH CENTER INC (PA)
Also Called: Your Service
2400 Kingman Dr (19810-3508)
PHONE.................................302 691-7213
Mitchell Poist, *President*
EMP: 27

SALES (est): 775.2K **Privately Held**
WEB: www.videotechcenter.com
SIC: 7622 7629 Communication equipment repair; radio repair & installation; home entertainment repair services; electrical household appliance repair

(G-13081)
VILLAGE AT FOX POINT
1436 Kynlyn Dr (19809-2423)
PHONE.................................302 762-7480
Rosemarie Upchurch, *Owner*
Chris Crampton, *Manager*
EMP: 8
SALES (est): 610K **Privately Held**
SIC: 6513 Apartment building operators

(G-13082)
VILLAGE GREEN INC
Also Called: Tropic Wholesale
4303 Miller Rd (19802-1901)
PHONE.................................302 764-2234
Scott Weiler, *President*
Sharon Weiler, *Vice Pres*
Lois Robinson, *Office Mgr*
Phil Krula, *Technology*
EMP: 26
SQ FT: 8,400
SALES (est): 2.7MM **Privately Held**
SIC: 7389 5992 5193 Plant care service; florists; plants, potted

(G-13083)
VINCENZA & MARGHERITA BISTRO
1717 Marsh Rd (19810-4607)
PHONE.................................302 479-7999
Margherita Carrieri-Russo, *Owner*
EMP: 9
SALES (est): 225.6K **Privately Held**
SIC: 5812 2032 American restaurant; Italian foods: packaged in cans, jars, etc.

(G-13084)
VINTAGE PROPERTIES LLC
Also Called: Arbor Pointe
4000 Dawnbrook Dr (19804-3925)
PHONE.................................302 994-4442
Judy Stewart, *Manager*
EMP: 8
SALES (corp-wide): 546.5K **Privately Held**
SIC: 6513 Apartment building operators
PA: Vintage Properties, Llc
102 Robino Ct Ste 101
Wilmington DE 19804
302 994-2505

(G-13085)
VINTAGE PROPERTIES LLC (PA)
102 Robino Ct Ste 101 (19804)
PHONE.................................302 994-2505
Nate Sorenson, *Director*
Linda Smith,
EMP: 7
SALES (est): 546.5K **Privately Held**
SIC: 6512 Nonresidential building operators

(G-13086)
VIOLET AURA INC
5412 Delray Dr (19808-2607)
PHONE.................................302 654-4008
Robert Galster, *President*
EMP: 15
SALES (est): 430.1K **Privately Held**
SIC: 7389

(G-13087)
VIRONEX INC (PA)
3 Owls Nest Rd (19807-1136)
PHONE.................................302 661-1400
Alan Livadas, *President*
Kevin Daney, *CFO*
EMP: 60
SALES (est): 4.1MM **Privately Held**
WEB: www.vironex.com
SIC: 0711 Soil chemical treatment services; soil testing services

(G-13088)
VIRONEX ENVMTL FIELD SVCS INC
3 Owls Nest Rd (19807-1136)
PHONE.................................302 661-1400

Wilmington - New Castle County (G-13089)   GEOGRAPHIC SECTION

EMP: 50
SQ FT: 3,000
SALES (est): 1.9MM **Privately Held**
SIC: 8742 Management Consulting Services

(G-13089)
VIRTUAL BUSINESS ENTPS LLC
Also Called: Stewart Management Company
Farmers Bank Bldg 301ste (19801)
PHONE.................................302 472-9100
Charles Anthony Shippam, *CEO*
Joan L Yori, *Vice Pres*
Gregory S Harrison, *CFO*
EMP: 8
SQ FT: 10,000
SALES (est): 2.5MM **Privately Held**
SIC: 8748 Business consulting

(G-13090)
VISHVA INC
Also Called: Sids Liquor
1104 Maryland Ave (19805-4838)
PHONE.................................302 425-3801
EMP: 4
SALES (est): 342.1K **Privately Held**
SIC: 5182 Liquor

(G-13091)
VISION & HEARING INC
Also Called: Dr Stanley Strauss
1809 Marsh Rd (19810-4505)
PHONE.................................302 475-8897
Stanley Strauss, *President*
EMP: 4
SALES (est): 262.6K **Privately Held**
SIC: 8099 Hearing testing service

(G-13092)
VISION CENTER OF DELAWARE INC (PA)
Also Called: Eye Center of Delaware
213 Greenhill Ave Ste A (19805-1800)
PHONE.................................302 656-8867
George Popel MD, *President*
EMP: 15
SALES (est): 2.3MM **Privately Held**
SIC: 8011 Ophthalmologist

(G-13093)
VISIONS HAIR DESIGN
2807 Concord Pike (19803-5008)
PHONE.................................302 477-0820
Margie Hartnett, *Owner*
EMP: 8
SALES (est): 122K **Privately Held**
WEB: www.visions-hair.com
SIC: 7231 7241 Hairdressers; barber shops

(G-13094)
VISUAL ARTS STUDIO INC
4 Forest Creek Ln (19809-1373)
PHONE.................................302 652-0925
Christine Steele, *President*
Dennis Steele, *Vice Pres*
EMP: 4
SALES: 500K **Privately Held**
WEB: www.vastudio.net
SIC: 7336 Commercial art & illustration

(G-13095)
VITAL RENEWABLE ENERGY COMPANY (PA)
2711 Centerville Rd (19808-1660)
PHONE.................................202 595-2944
Ricardo Roccia, *CEO*
Douglas Costa, *Controller*
EMP: 2
SALES: 775.7K **Privately Held**
SIC: 6722 2869 Management investment, open-end; fuels

(G-13096)
VITELLUS LLC (PA)
Also Called: Happynest
1209 N Orange St (19801-1120)
PHONE.................................718 782-3539
Jesse Prince, *CEO*
EMP: 2
SALES (est): 203.5K **Privately Held**
SIC: 6531 7389 7372 Real estate agents & managers; financial services; application computer software

(G-13097)
VIVIAN A HOUGHTON ESQUIRE
800 N West St Fl 2 (19801-1565)
PHONE.................................302 658-0518
Vivian A Houghton, *Owner*
EMP: 5
SALES (est): 531.6K **Privately Held**
WEB: www.vivianhoughton.com
SIC: 8111 General practice attorney, lawyer

(G-13098)
VIVIG SHOES
3801 Kennett Pike C103 (19807-2321)
PHONE.................................302 427-2700
EMP: 11
SALES (est): 820K **Privately Held**
SIC: 5139 5137 Whol Footwear Whol Women's/Child's Clothing

(G-13099)
VOICE 4 IMPACT INC
515 Lennox Rd (19809-2116)
PHONE.................................484 410-0111
Jennifer L Peters,
EMP: 1 EST: 2016
SALES (est): 59.4K **Privately Held**
SIC: 7372 7389 Business oriented computer software;

(G-13100)
VOITURE NATIONALE LA SOCIETY
1017 Faun Rd (19803-3312)
PHONE.................................302 478-7591
Chip Rossen, *Director*
EMP: 7
SALES (corp-wide): 625.6K **Privately Held**
SIC: 8641 Fraternal associations
PA: Voiture Nationale La Society
   250 E 38th St
   Indianapolis IN 46205
   317 634-1804

(G-13101)
VOLUME MOB INC
3616 Kirkwood Hwy Ste A (19808-5124)
PHONE.................................302 433-6629
Ains Prasad, *President*
EMP: 4
SQ FT: 800 **Privately Held**
SIC: 8621 Professional membership organizations

(G-13102)
VOLUNTEERS FOR ADOLESCENT
Also Called: Vapp
611 W 18th St (19802-4707)
PHONE.................................302 658-3331
Yvonne Gordon, *President*
Lisa Oglesby, *Administration*
EMP: 8 EST: 2015
SALES (est): 166.4K **Privately Held**
SIC: 8399 Social services

(G-13103)
VOLVANT INC (PA)
919 N Market St Ste 950 (19801-3036)
PHONE.................................805 456-6464
Walter Gonzalez, *CEO*
EMP: 7
SALES: 1MM **Privately Held**
SIC: 7371 Computer software development

(G-13104)
VORTEX LABS LLC
1209 N Orange St (19801-1120)
PHONE.................................302 231-1294
Pierre Cazettes, *Mng Member*
EMP: 5
SALES: 500K **Privately Held**
SIC: 7371 Computer software development

(G-13105)
VOXX ELECTRONICS CORP
2302 Concord Pike (19803-2912)
PHONE.................................302 656-5303
Allan Henderson, *Branch Mgr*
EMP: 12

SALES (corp-wide): 446.8MM **Publicly Held**
SIC: 5065 Mobile telephone equipment
HQ: Voxx Electronics Corp.
   150 Marcus Blvd
   Hauppauge NY 11788
   631 231-7750

(G-13106)
VPN EXPRESS INCORPORATED
427 N Ttnail St Ste 99229 (19801)
PHONE.................................302 351-8029
Monsef Chakir, *President*
EMP: 20
SALES (est): 300.5K **Privately Held**
SIC: 7374 Data processing & preparation

(G-13107)
VULCAN INTERNATIONAL CORP (PA)
300 Delaware Ave Ste 1704 (19801-1612)
PHONE.................................302 428-3181
Benjamin Gettler, *Ch of Bd*
Vernon E Bachman, *Vice Pres*
Warren C Falberg, *Director*
Thomas D Gettler, *Director*
Edward B Kerin, *Director*
◆ EMP: 12 EST: 1928
SQ FT: 88,000
SALES (est): 9.7MM **Publicly Held**
WEB: www.vulcorp.com
SIC: 3069 2499 3949 Heels, boot or shoe; rubber, composition or fiber; soles, boot or shoe: rubber, composition or fiber; top lift sheets, rubber; lasts, boot & shoe; bowling pins

(G-13108)
VULCRAFT SALES CORP (HQ)
300 Delaware Ave Ste 210 (19801-6601)
PHONE.................................302 427-5832
F Kenneth Iverson, *President*
▼ EMP: 11
SALES: 16MM
SALES (corp-wide): 25B **Publicly Held**
SIC: 5051 Metals service centers & offices
PA: Nucor Corporation
   1915 Rexford Rd Ste 400
   Charlotte NC 28211
   704 366-7000

(G-13109)
W R GRACE & CO
1521 Concord Pike Ste 341 (19803-3642)
PHONE.................................410 531-4000
Walter Raquet, *Branch Mgr*
EMP: 164
SALES (corp-wide): 1.9B **Publicly Held**
SIC: 2819 Catalysts, chemical
PA: W. R. Grace & Co.
   7500 Grace Dr
   Columbia MD 21044
   410 531-4000

(G-13110)
W23 S12 HOLDINGS LLC
Also Called: Hilo House
2000 Pnsylvnia Ave Ste 10 (19806)
PHONE.................................610 348-3825
EMP: 4
SALES (est): 36.5K **Privately Held**
SIC: 7991 7371 Physical fitness facilities; computer software development & applications

(G-13111)
W7ENERGY LLC
200 Powder Mill Rd E400-3 (19803-2907)
PHONE.................................302 897-1653
Yushan Yan, *Principal*
Santiago Rojas, *COO*
EMP: 4
SALES (est): 175.6K **Privately Held**
SIC: 8731 Commercial physical research

(G-13112)
WAGSTAFF DAY CARE CENTER INC
310 Kiamensi Rd Rm 301 (19804-2959)
PHONE.................................302 998-7818
Freddie Anderson, *President*
EMP: 11
SALES (est): 138.6K **Privately Held**
SIC: 8351 Group day care center

(G-13113)
WAHL FAMILY DENTISTRY
2003 Concord Pike (19803-2904)
PHONE.................................302 655-1228
Michael Whal, *Owner*
EMP: 25
SALES (est): 1.6MM **Privately Held**
SIC: 8021 Dentists' office

(G-13114)
WALAN SPECIALTY CNSTR PDTS LLC
501 Christiana Ave (19801)
PHONE.................................724 545-2300
Lisa Dharwadkar,
Anil Bhadsavle,
EMP: 4
SALES (est): 216.3K **Privately Held**
SIC: 1521 Single-family housing construction

(G-13115)
WALDEN LLC
Also Called: Walden Townhomes
1 Henry Ct (19808-2017)
PHONE.................................302 998-8112
Louis Capano,
EMP: 5
SALES (est): 444.7K **Privately Held**
SIC: 6513 Apartment building operators

(G-13116)
WALNUT GREEN ASSET MGT LL
1301 Walnut Green Rd (19807-1649)
P.O. Box 4016 (19807-0016)
PHONE.................................302 689-3798
Anthony Hitschler, *Principal*
Samuel Hyland, *Manager*
EMP: 6
SALES (est): 231.1K **Privately Held**
SIC: 8741 Financial management for business

(G-13117)
WANG CONSULTANTS INC
4023 Kennett Pike Ste 603 (19807-2018)
PHONE.................................626 483-0265
Jay Wang, *President*
EMP: 5 EST: 2013
SQ FT: 300
SALES (est): 264.2K **Privately Held**
SIC: 8742 Business planning & organizing services

(G-13118)
WARAIN CORP
P.O. Box 13133 (19850-3133)
PHONE.................................762 670-3452
EMP: 5
SALES (est): 104.3K **Privately Held**
SIC: 7379 Computer Related Services

(G-13119)
WARD & TAYLOR LLC (PA)
2710 Centerville Rd # 210 (19808-1664)
PHONE.................................302 225-3350
William E Ward, *Mng Member*
Carol Strouth, *Manager*
Wendy Martin, *Admin Asst*
Tracy Pritt, *Admin Asst*
Nina Davis, *Legal Staff*
EMP: 33
SQ FT: 17,000
SALES (est): 5.6MM **Privately Held**
WEB: www.wardtaylor.com
SIC: 8111 Real estate law

(G-13120)
WARTRUDE SERVICES INC
1601 Milltown Rd (19808-4027)
PHONE.................................302 213-3944
Holly Hamilton, *President*
Randy Cain, *Director*
EMP: 14
SQ FT: 200
SALES (est): 980K **Privately Held**
SIC: 8742 Real estate consultant

(G-13121)
WASTE MANAGEMENT DELAWARE INC
300 Harvey Dr (19804-2430)
PHONE.................................302 994-0944
Jim Fish, *CEO*
David Steiner, *CEO*

▲ = Import ▼=Export
◆ =Import/Export

Kevin Shegog, *Division Mgr*
Carly Fitzpatrick, *Manager*
EMP: 175
SALES (corp-wide): 14.9B **Publicly Held**
WEB: www.wm.com
SIC: 4953 Refuse systems
HQ: Waste Management Of Delaware Inc.
1001 Fannin St Ste 4000
Houston TX 77002
713 512-6200

(G-13122)
WATERCRAFT LLC
801 Owls Nest Rd (19807-1611)
PHONE..................................302 757-0786
Nick Ganc, *Owner*
EMP: 2
SALES (est): 168.7K **Privately Held**
SIC: 3589 5999 7389 Water treatment equipment, industrial; water purification equipment; water softener service

(G-13123)
WATTS ELECTRIC COMPANY
2027 Harwyn Rd (19810-3870)
PHONE..................................302 529-1183
Michael Watts, *Owner*
EMP: 5
SALES (est): 373K **Privately Held**
SIC: 1731 General electrical contractor

(G-13124)
WAVERTECH LLC
Also Called: Wavertise
913 N Market St Ste 200 (19801-3097)
PHONE..................................877 735-0897
EMP: 5 **EST:** 2016
SQ FT: 1,500
SALES: 3MM **Privately Held**
SIC: 7372 Prepackaged Software Services

(G-13125)
WAYMAN FIRE PROTECTION INC
403 Meco Dr (19804-1110)
PHONE..................................302 994-5757
Duane Wayman, *President*
Bob McGonigle, *General Mgr*
Joe Plunkett, *General Mgr*
Bob Weitzel, *General Mgr*
Alisha Bryson, *Vice Pres*
EMP: 160 **EST:** 1974
SQ FT: 12,000
SALES: 16MM **Privately Held**
WEB: www.waymanfireprotection.com
SIC: 3669 Fire alarm apparatus, electric

(G-13126)
WAYNE INDUSTRIES INC (PA)
1105 N Market St Ste 1300 (19801-1241)
P.O. Box 8985 (19899-8985)
PHONE..................................302 478-6160
Robert A Milnes, *President*
Franklin A Milnes, *Exec VP*
Harry E Evans, *Vice Pres*
Martha Heil, *Treasurer*
EMP: 5
SQ FT: 143,000
SALES: 20.5MM **Privately Held**
WEB: www.ebsco.com
SIC: 2241 5131 Bindings, textile; piece goods & other fabrics

(G-13127)
WBI CAPITAL ADVISORS LLC (PA)
251 Little Falls Dr (19808-1674)
PHONE..................................856 361-6362
San Zhang, *Mng Member*
EMP: 2
SALES (est): 1.3MM **Privately Held**
SIC: 6282 7372 Investment advisory service; application computer software

(G-13128)
WDBID DBA DOWNTOWN VISIONS
409 N Orange St (19801-2218)
PHONE..................................302 425-5374
Martin Hageman, *Exec Dir*
EMP: 50
SALES (est): 520.5K **Privately Held**
SIC: 8999 Services

(G-13129)
WDBID MANAGEMENT COMPANY
Also Called: DOWNTOWN VISIONS
409 N Orange St (19801-2218)
PHONE..................................302 425-5374
Martin P Hageman, *Director*
EMP: 52
SALES: 2.9MM **Privately Held**
WEB: www.downtownvisions.com
SIC: 8641 Civic social & fraternal associations

(G-13130)
WE COBBLE LLC
4023 Kennett Pike # 50098 (19807-2018)
PHONE..................................302 504-4294
Philip Moore, *CEO*
EMP: 15
SALES (est): 448.5K **Privately Held**
SIC: 5045 7371 Computer software; computer software development

(G-13131)
WEATHER OR NOT DOG WALKERS
1300 Tulane Rd (19803-5140)
PHONE..................................302 304-8399
Lisa McGrath, *Principal*
EMP: 7
SALES (est): 57.3K **Privately Held**
SIC: 7299 Pet sitting, in-home

(G-13132)
WEATHERHILL DENTAL
5317 Limestone Rd Ste 2 (19808-1252)
PHONE..................................302 239-6677
Erika Williams, *Principal*
EMP: 8 **EST:** 2014
SALES (est): 228.9K **Privately Held**
SIC: 8021 Dentists' office; dental clinic

(G-13133)
WEB ADVANTAGE INC
216 Paddock Ln (19803-1919)
PHONE..................................302 479-7634
Hollis Thomases, *President*
David Cease, *Vice Pres*
EMP: 10
SALES (est): 660K **Privately Held**
SIC: 2741

(G-13134)
WEBBROWSER MEDIA INC
Also Called: Quick Browser
3422 Old Capitol Trl (19808-6124)
PHONE..................................302 830-3664
Tobyn Sowden, *CEO*
EMP: 7
SALES (est): 164.3K **Privately Held**
SIC: 7371 Computer software development & applications

(G-13135)
WEBBS CLEANERS CORP (PA)
1403 Philadelphia Pike A (19809-1899)
PHONE..................................302 798-0655
Taisoo Yum, *President*
Kyong Shik Yum, *Vice Pres*
EMP: 6
SALES (est): 192.9K **Privately Held**
SIC: 7216 Cleaning & dyeing, except rugs

(G-13136)
WEE CARE DAY CARE SALV ARMY
400 N Orange St (19801-2219)
P.O. Box 308 (19899-0308)
PHONE..................................302 472-0712
Ann Jeuell, *Director*
EMP: 15
SALES (est): 200.1K **Privately Held**
SIC: 8351 Child day care services

(G-13137)
WEEPOR COMPANY INC
103 Foulk Rd Ste 202 (19803-3742)
PHONE..................................302 575-9945
John S Moore, *President*
Sandra Keller, *Vice Pres*
A P Waterman Jr, *Vice Pres*
Marian Wagner, *Admin Sec*
Samuel A Gilliland, *Asst Sec*
EMP: 5

SALES (est): 402.7K **Privately Held**
SIC: 6799 Investors

(G-13138)
WEIK NITSCHE & DOUGHERTY
305 N Union St Unit 2 (19805-3454)
P.O. Box 2324 (19899-2324)
PHONE..................................302 655-4040
Garry Nitsche, *Managing Prtnr*
Shawn Dougherty, *Partner*
Michael Galbraith, *Partner*
Joseph Weik, *Partner*
EMP: 30
SALES (est): 3.2MM **Privately Held**
WEB: www.weiknitsche.com
SIC: 8111 General practice attorney, lawyer

(G-13139)
WEINER DEVELOPMENT LLC
4 Denny Rd Ste 1 (19809-3445)
PHONE..................................302 764-9430
Leon Weiner, *Principal*
Kevin Kelly,
EMP: 50
SALES (est): 400K **Privately Held**
WEB: www.lnwa.com
SIC: 1521 Single-family housing construction

(G-13140)
WEISS & SAVILLE PA
1105 N Market St Ste 200 (19801-1276)
P.O. Box 370 (19899-0370)
PHONE..................................302 656-0400
Michael Weiss, *President*
Yvonne Saville, *Admin Sec*
Jeanne Burge, *Clerk*
EMP: 5
SALES (est): 607K **Privately Held**
WEB: www.mweissesq.com
SIC: 8111 General practice law office

(G-13141)
WELFARE FOUNDATION INC
100 W 10th St Ste 1109 (19801-1653)
PHONE..................................302 683-8200
Robert H Bolling Jr, *President*
J Simpson Dean Jr, *Vice Pres*
Edward B Dupont, *Treasurer*
Steve Martinenda, *Treasurer*
W Laird Stabler Jr, *Admin Sec*
EMP: 4
SQ FT: 6,056
SALES (est): 15.6MM **Privately Held**
SIC: 8699 Charitable organization

(G-13142)
WELL DONE CLEANING SERVICES
401 S Broom St (19805-3943)
PHONE..................................443 407-3064
EMP: 7
SALES (est): 162.6K **Privately Held**
SIC: 8742 Management Consulting Services

(G-13143)
WELLINGTON MANAGEMENT GROUP
300 Delaware Ave Ste 1380 (19801-1658)
PHONE..................................215 569-8900
Carol Attwood Kleiman, *President*
Robert Scott Campbell, *Owner*
Craig C Cole, *Director*
EMP: 7
SALES (est): 614.5K **Privately Held**
SIC: 8741 Business management

(G-13144)
WELLS FARGO BANK NATIONAL ASSN
505 Carr Rd Ste 200 (19809-2870)
PHONE..................................302 765-5534
EMP: 16
SALES (corp-wide): 101B **Publicly Held**
SIC: 6021 National commercial banks
HQ: Wells Fargo Bank, National Association
101 N Phillips Ave
Sioux Falls SD 57104
605 575-6900

(G-13145)
WELLS FARGO BANK NATIONAL ASSN
3801 Kennett Pike (19807-2321)
PHONE..................................302 428-8600
Richard Batty, *Office Mgr*
EMP: 17
SALES (corp-wide): 101B **Publicly Held**
SIC: 6021 National commercial banks
HQ: Wells Fargo Bank, National Association
101 N Phillips Ave
Sioux Falls SD 57104
605 575-6900

(G-13146)
WELLS FARGO BANK NATIONAL ASSN
2024 Naamans Rd (19810-2655)
PHONE..................................302 529-2550
Rhonda Bishop, *Manager*
EMP: 12
SALES (corp-wide): 101B **Publicly Held**
SIC: 6021 National commercial banks
HQ: Wells Fargo Bank, National Association
101 N Phillips Ave
Sioux Falls SD 57104
605 575-6900

(G-13147)
WELLS FARGO BANK NATIONAL ASSN
2011 Concord Pike (19803-2904)
PHONE..................................302 421-7508
Barbara Parag, *Manager*
EMP: 20
SALES (corp-wide): 101B **Publicly Held**
SIC: 6021 National commercial banks
HQ: Wells Fargo Bank, National Association
101 N Phillips Ave
Sioux Falls SD 57104
605 575-6900

(G-13148)
WELLS FARGO BANK NATIONAL ASSN
3215 Old Capitol Trl (19808-6215)
PHONE..................................302 636-4306
Dorothy Defebro, *Manager*
EMP: 16
SALES (corp-wide): 101B **Publicly Held**
SIC: 6021 National commercial banks
HQ: Wells Fargo Bank, National Association
101 N Phillips Ave
Sioux Falls SD 57104
605 575-6900

(G-13149)
WELLS FARGO BANK NATIONAL ASSN
814 Philadelphia Pike (19809-2357)
PHONE..................................302 761-1300
Joe Piccirelli, *Manager*
EMP: 8
SALES (corp-wide): 101B **Publicly Held**
SIC: 6021 National commercial banks
HQ: Wells Fargo Bank, National Association
101 N Phillips Ave
Sioux Falls SD 57104
605 575-6900

(G-13150)
WELLS FARGO BANK NATIONAL ASSN
100 W 10th St Lbby 1 (19801-1645)
PHONE..................................302 622-3350
Ruthine Ruth, *Branch Mgr*
EMP: 8
SALES (corp-wide): 101B **Publicly Held**
SIC: 6021 National commercial banks
HQ: Wells Fargo Bank, National Association
101 N Phillips Ave
Sioux Falls SD 57104
605 575-6900

Wilmington - New Castle County (G-13151) GEOGRAPHIC SECTION

(G-13151)
WELLS FARGO BANK NATIONAL ASSN
4015 Kennett Pike (19807-2018)
PHONE.................302 421-7820
Shaakira Marton, *Manager*
EMP: 8
SALES (corp-wide): 101B **Publicly Held**
SIC: 6021 National commercial banks
HQ: Wells Fargo Bank, National Association
   101 N Phillips Ave
   Sioux Falls SD 57104
   605 575-6900

(G-13152)
WELLS FARGO CLEARING SVCS LLC
Also Called: Wells Fargo Advisors
3801 Kennett Pike (19807-2321)
P.O. Box 3740 (19807-0740)
PHONE.................302 428-8600
Gary Gittings Jr, *Manager*
Lisa Littles, *Consultant*
Don Dewees, *Director*
EMP: 36
SALES (corp-wide): 101B **Publicly Held**
WEB: www.wachoviasec.com
SIC: 6211 Brokers, security
HQ: Wells Fargo Clearing Services, Llc
   1 N Jefferson Ave Fl 7
   Saint Louis MO 63103
   314 955-3000

(G-13153)
WELLS FARGO DELAWARE TRUST CO
919 N Market St Ste 1600 (19801-3046)
PHONE.................302 575-2002
Sandra Carreker, *President*
Ann Dukart, *Vice Pres*
Rosemary Kennard, *Vice Pres*
EMP: 7
SALES: 18.4MM
SALES (corp-wide): 101B **Publicly Held**
SIC: 6733 Trusts, except educational, religious, charity: management
HQ: Wells Fargo Bank, National Association
   101 N Phillips Ave
   Sioux Falls SD 57104
   605 575-6900

(G-13154)
WELLSPRING FARM INC
Also Called: Wellspring Tack Shop
800 Carr Rd (19809-2163)
PHONE.................302 798-2407
Katherine C Van Dyke, *President*
EMP: 6
SALES (est): 195.9K **Privately Held**
SIC: 7999 Riding stable

(G-13155)
WEN INTERNATIONAL INC
101 Wayland Rd (19807-2529)
PHONE.................845 354-1773
Sharon Chang, *President*
Frank Zimdhal, *Vice Pres*
▲ EMP: 6
SQ FT: 8,000
SALES (est): 1.1MM **Privately Held**
SIC: 5149 Flavourings & fragrances

(G-13156)
WENTWORTH GROUP
4100 Dawnbrook Dr (19804-3932)
P.O. Box 767, Bel Air MD (21014-0767)
PHONE.................302 998-2115
EMP: 4
SALES (est): 169.9K **Privately Held**
SIC: 6331 Fire/Casualty Insurance Carrier

(G-13157)
WEPRO LLC (PA)
901 N Market St Ste 705 (19801-3098)
PHONE.................310 650-8622
Lan Saadatnejadi, *President*
EMP: 2
SALES (est): 118K **Privately Held**
SIC: 7372 Application computer software

(G-13158)
WER WIRELESS INC
Also Called: Verizon Wreless Authorized Ret
4737 Concord Pike Ste 416 (19803-1448)
PHONE.................302 478-7748
EMP: 26 **Privately Held**
SIC: 5065 4812 Whol Electronic Parts/Equipment Radiotelephone Communication
PA: We R Wireless Inc.
   520 Fellowship Rd E508
   Mount Laurel NJ 08054

(G-13159)
WER WIRELESS OF CONCORD INC
Also Called: Veze Wireless of Concord Inc
4737 Concord Pike Ste 416 (19803-1448)
PHONE.................302 478-7748
EMP: 16
SALES (est): 728.4K **Privately Held**
SIC: 5999 4812 Ret Misc Merchandise Radiotelephone Communication
PA: We R Wireless Inc.
   520 Fellowship Rd E508
   Mount Laurel NJ 08054

(G-13160)
WERB & SULLIVAN
300 Delaware Ave Ste 1300 (19801-1658)
P.O. Box 25046 (19899-5046)
PHONE.................302 652-1100
Duane W Werb, *Managing Prtnr*
Brian A Sullivan, *Partner*
William Aukamp, *Counsel*
Isaac Stemler, *Legal Staff*
EMP: 10
SALES (est): 757.3K **Privately Held**
SIC: 8111 General practice law office

(G-13161)
WERTZ & CO
116 Valley Rd (19804-1300)
PHONE.................302 658-5186
Robin L Becker, *President*
EMP: 23
SALES (est): 5MM **Privately Held**
SIC: 1521 1761 General remodeling, single-family houses; roofing contractor

(G-13162)
WESCO DISTRIBUTION INC
11 Brookside Dr (19804-1101)
PHONE.................302 655-9611
Mike Justice, *Manager*
EMP: 10 **Publicly Held**
SIC: 5063 5085 Electrical apparatus & equipment; industrial supplies
HQ: Wesco Distribution, Inc.
   225 W Station Square Dr # 700
   Pittsburgh PA 15219

(G-13163)
WEST CENTER CY EARLY LRNG CTR
600 N Madison St (19801-2023)
PHONE.................302 656-0485
Fax: 302 656-6116
EMP: 25
SALES: 1MM **Privately Held**
SIC: 8351 Child Day Care Services, Nsk

(G-13164)
WEST END MACHINE SHOP INC
1405 Brown St (19805-4777)
PHONE.................302 654-8436
William Betley, *President*
EMP: 4 EST: 1936
SQ FT: 3,700
SALES (est): 619.4K **Privately Held**
SIC: 3599 Machine shop, jobbing & repair

(G-13165)
WEST END NEIGHBORHOOD HSE INC
Also Called: West End Nghbrhd Chld Care
1725 W 8th St (19805-3153)
PHONE.................302 654-2731
Victoria Mells, *Director*
EMP: 8
SALES (corp-wide): 4.5MM **Privately Held**
SIC: 8322 Multi-service center

PA: The West End Neighborhood House Incorporated
   710 N Lincoln St
   Wilmington DE 19805
   302 658-4171

(G-13166)
WEST END NEIGHBORHOOD HSE INC (PA)
710 N Lincoln St (19805-3016)
PHONE.................302 658-4171
Joseph Johnson, *CFO*
Meghann Felice, *Accountant*
Amanda August, *Case Mgr*
Tasha Warren, *Supervisor*
Paul F Calistro Jr, *Exec Dir*
EMP: 68
SALES: 4.5MM **Privately Held**
SIC: 8322 Multi-service center

(G-13167)
WEST ORANGE OFFICE EXEC PK LLC
2711 Centerville Rd # 400 (19808-1660)
PHONE.................973 320-3227
Moses Berger,
EMP: 15 EST: 2017
SALES (est): 229.1K **Privately Held**
SIC: 6519 Sub-lessors of real estate

(G-13168)
WEST WILMINGTON SVNTH DAY ADV
Also Called: Wilmington Junior Academy
3003 Mill Creek Rd (19808-1335)
PHONE.................302 998-3961
Mike Marinkovic, *Principal*
Renee Fegley, *Director*
EMP: 9
SALES (est): 444.1K **Privately Held**
SIC: 8351 8211 Preschool center; academy; private elementary school
PA: West Wilmington Seventh Day Adventist Church
   3003 Mill Creek Rd
   Wilmington DE 19808

(G-13169)
WESTLAKE CHEMICAL PRODUCTS
103 Foulk Rd (19803-3742)
PHONE.................302 691-6028
John Moore, *Principal*
EMP: 3
SALES (est): 134.2K **Publicly Held**
SIC: 3999 Manufacturing industries
PA: Westlake Chemical Corporation
   2801 Post Oak Blvd Ste 60
   Houston TX 77056

(G-13170)
WESTON SENIOR LIVING CENTER
Also Called: Weston Sr Living Ctr
4800 Lancaster Pike (19807-2559)
PHONE.................302 994-4434
Mitzi Montz, *Vice Pres*
EMP: 15 EST: 2014
SALES (est): 869.3K **Privately Held**
SIC: 8051 Convalescent home with continuous nursing care

(G-13171)
WESTSIDE FAMILY HEALTHCARE INC
908 E 16th St Ste B (19802-5145)
PHONE.................302 575-1414
Pori Cobb, *Branch Mgr*
EMP: 17
SALES (corp-wide): 22.8MM **Privately Held**
SIC: 8011 8021 Clinic, operated by physicians; offices & clinics of dentists
PA: Westside Family Healthcare, Inc.
   300 Water St Ste 200
   Wilmington DE 19801
   302 656-8292

(G-13172)
WESTSIDE FAMILY HEALTHCARE INC (PA)
300 Water St Ste 200 (19801-5043)
PHONE.................302 656-8292
Lolita A Lopez, *President*

Nakishia Bailey, *Principal*
Beryl Barmore, *Principal*
Leslie Bastienelli, *Principal*
Richard Carroll, *Principal*
EMP: 17
SQ FT: 23,000
SALES: 22.8MM **Privately Held**
SIC: 8011 8021 Clinic, operated by physicians; offices & clinics of dentists

(G-13173)
WESTSIDE FAMILY HEALTHCARE INC
1802 W 4th St (19805-3420)
PHONE.................302 656-8292
Lolita A Lopez, *Branch Mgr*
Lydia De Leon, *Manager*
EMP: 17
SALES (corp-wide): 22.8MM **Privately Held**
SIC: 8011 8021 Clinic, operated by physicians; offices & clinics of dentists
PA: Westside Family Healthcare, Inc.
   300 Water St Ste 200
   Wilmington DE 19801
   302 656-8292

(G-13174)
WESTWOOD PROPERTIES LTD
Also Called: Maryland Park Apartments
699 Robinson Ln (19805-4617)
P.O. Box 7228, Newark (19714-7228)
PHONE.................302 655-0274
Mike Purzycki, *Partner*
EMP: 8
SALES (est): 600K **Privately Held**
SIC: 6513 Apartment building operators

(G-13175)
WETZEL & ASSOCIATES PA
2201 W 11th St (19805-2603)
PHONE.................302 652-1200
Benjamin Wetzel, *Owner*
EMP: 5
SALES (est): 435.8K **Privately Held**
WEB: www.wetzellaw.com
SIC: 7389 Accomodation locating services

(G-13176)
WEYL ENTERPRISES INC
Also Called: Custom Satellite and Sound
1206 Kirkwood Hwy (19805-2120)
PHONE.................302 993-1248
David Weyl, *President*
EMP: 5
SALES (est): 779.8K **Privately Held**
SIC: 3571 Electronic computers

(G-13177)
WEYMOUTH SWYZE CRROON INSUR IN
Also Called: Nationwide
5710 Kennett Pike (19807-1312)
P.O. Box 3939 (19807-0939)
PHONE.................302 655-3705
R Bruce Swayze, *President*
EMP: 10
SQ FT: 2,000
SALES: 1.7MM **Privately Held**
SIC: 6411 Insurance agents, brokers & service

(G-13178)
WGAMES INCORPORATED
1209 N Orange St (19801-1120)
PHONE.................206 618-3699
Daniel Kajouie, *President*
Erik Fisher, *Vice Pres*
EMP: 8
SALES (est): 282.8K **Privately Held**
SIC: 7371 Computer software development

(G-13179)
WH NUTRITIONALS LLC
1000 N West St Fl 17 (19801-1053)
PHONE.................302 357-3611
Jennifer Hatcher,
EMP: 5
SALES (est): 254.1K **Privately Held**
SIC: 5122 Pharmaceuticals

GEOGRAPHIC SECTION
Wilmington - New Castle County (G-13210)

(G-13180)
WH2P INC
3704 Kennett Pike Ste 400 (19807-2176)
P.O. Box 22, Yorklyn (19736-0022)
PHONE.................................302 530-6555
Brian Havertine, *President*
Greg Williamson, *Vice Pres*
Joseph Harris, *Treasurer*
Roger Poole, *Admin Sec*
EMP: 6
SQ FT: 1,800
SALES: 800K **Privately Held**
WEB: www.wh2p.com
SIC: 7311 Advertising agencies

(G-13181)
WHARTON LEVIN EHRMANTRAUT
300 Delaware Ave Ste 1704 (19801-1612)
PHONE.................................302 252-0090
Andrew Vernick, *Branch Mgr*
EMP: 6
SALES (est): 254.9K **Privately Held**
SIC: 8111 General practice attorney, lawyer

(G-13182)
WHEELCHAIR MECHANIX
2110 Shipley Rd (19803-2357)
PHONE.................................302 478-0858
Laura Boscola, *President*
EMP: 2
SALES: 70K **Privately Held**
SIC: 3842 Wheelchairs

(G-13183)
WHEELER WOLFENDEN & DWARES CPA
4550 New Linden Hl Rd # 201 (19808-2915)
PHONE.................................302 254-8240
John Wheeler, *President*
David Wolfenden, *Director*
EMP: 15
SALES (est): 920K **Privately Held**
SIC: 8721 Certified public accountant

(G-13184)
WHEELER WOLFENDEN & DWARES PA
824 N Market St Ste 720 (19801-4940)
PHONE.................................302 254-8240
John Wheeler, *Partner*
Leonard Dwares, *Partner*
Dave Wolfenden, *Partner*
Erica Poore, *Accountant*
EMP: 35
SALES (est): 1.8MM **Privately Held**
SIC: 8748 Business consulting

(G-13185)
WHISMAN JOHN
Also Called: Motorsport Series
5201 W Woodmill Dr Ste 31 (19808-4068)
PHONE.................................302 530-1676
John Whisman, *Owner*
EMP: 2
SALES: 10K **Privately Held**
SIC: 2396 2395 Screen printing on fabric articles; emblems, embroidered

(G-13186)
WHITAKER CORPORATION
4550 New Lndn Hll Rd 14 (19808)
PHONE.................................302 633-2740
Mark Young, *President*
Driscoll Nina, *Director*
EMP: 12
SQ FT: 6,000
SALES (est): 1MM
SALES (corp-wide): 13.9B **Privately Held**
WEB: www.raychem.com
SIC: 8111 Legal services
HQ: Te Connectivity Corporation
1050 Westlakes Dr
Berwyn PA 19312
610 893-9800

(G-13187)
WHITAKER LLC
Also Called: AMP-In
4550 New Linden (19808)
PHONE.................................302 633-2740
Mark Young, *President*
EMP: 6

SALES (est): 129.4K **Privately Held**
SIC: 3643 7371 Electric connectors; computer software development & applications

(G-13188)
WHITE & ASSOCIATES
114 W 40th St Ste A (19802-2120)
PHONE.................................302 765-3736
Vincent White, *Owner*
EMP: 4 EST: 1985
SALES (est): 256.8K **Privately Held**
SIC: 8742 Human resource consulting services

(G-13189)
WHITE AND WILLIAMS LLP
Also Called: White & Williams
600 N King St Ste 800 (19801-3778)
PHONE.................................302 654-0424
John Balaguer, *Manager*
EMP: 18
SALES (corp-wide): 81.2MM **Privately Held**
SIC: 8111 General practice attorney, lawyer
PA: White And Williams, Llp
1650 Marke St One Liber P
Philadelphia PA 19103
215 864-7000

(G-13190)
WHITE HORSE WINERY
15 Guyencourt Rd (19807-1415)
PHONE.................................302 388-4850
Brock Vinton, *Principal*
EMP: 2
SALES (est): 62.3K **Privately Held**
SIC: 2084 Wines

(G-13191)
WHITE OAK LANDSCAPE MGT INC
17 Owls Nest Rd (19807-1125)
PHONE.................................302 652-7533
William Duncan, *President*
EMP: 9
SALES (est): 641.5K **Privately Held**
SIC: 0782 Landscape contractors

(G-13192)
WHITE ROBBINS COMPANY
Also Called: White Robbins Condo & Assn
3513 Concord Pike # 2100 (19803-5027)
PHONE.................................302 478-5555
Tucker Robbins, *Owner*
Peter Dietz, *Property Mgr*
Megan Staats, *Property Mgr*
Moira D Pando, *Manager*
Susan Short, *Admin Sec*
EMP: 5
SALES (est): 250K **Privately Held**
SIC: 6531 Real estate managers

(G-13193)
WHITECROW RESEARCH INC
2711 Centerville Rd # 300 (19808-1665)
PHONE.................................908 752-4200
Neel Majithia, *Principal*
EMP: 10
SALES (est): 335.6K **Privately Held**
SIC: 7361 Employment agencies

(G-13194)
WHITES BODY SHOP
Also Called: Whites Auto Repair & Body Shop
436 S Buttonwood St (19801-5306)
PHONE.................................302 655-4369
Clarence White, *Owner*
EMP: 5
SALES (est): 277.3K **Privately Held**
SIC: 7532 Body shop, automotive

(G-13195)
WHITMAN REQUARDT AND ASSOC LLP
Also Called: Whitman Requardt and Assoc
1013 Centre Rd Ste 302 (19805-1265)
PHONE.................................302 571-9001
Jeff Riegner, *Branch Mgr*
EMP: 14
SALES (corp-wide): 107.7MM **Privately Held**
WEB: www.wrallp.com
SIC: 8711 Consulting engineer

PA: Whitman, Requardt And Associates, Llp
801 S Caroline St
Baltimore MD 21231
410 235-3450

(G-13196)
WHITTENS FINE JEWELRY
Also Called: Wholesale Jewelry Outlet
4719 Kirkwood Hwy (19808-5007)
PHONE.................................302 995-7464
Craig Whitten, *Owner*
EMP: 5
SALES (est): 396.5K **Privately Held**
WEB: www.whittensfinejewelry.com
SIC: 7631 5944 Jewelry repair services; jewelry stores

(G-13197)
WHOLESALE JANITOR SUPPLY CO
Also Called: Dominick P Ferrari, President
26 Germay Dr (19804-1105)
PHONE.................................302 655-5722
Dominick P Ferrari, *President*
EMP: 4
SQ FT: 7,300
SALES: 3MM **Privately Held**
SIC: 5087 Janitors' supplies

(G-13198)
WHOLESALE JEWELRY OUTLET INC
3616 Kirkwood Hwy (19808-5124)
PHONE.................................302 994-5114
Craig Whitten, *Owner*
EMP: 5
SALES: 270K **Privately Held**
SIC: 5094 5944 Jewelry; jewelry, precious stones & precious metals

(G-13199)
WILBRAHAM LAWLER & BUBA PC
901 N Market St Ste 800 (19801-3090)
PHONE.................................302 421-9922
Edward Wilbraham, *President*
EMP: 5 **Privately Held**
SIC: 8111 General practice attorney, lawyer
PA: Wilbraham Lawler & Buba Pc
1818 Market St Ste 3100
Philadelphia PA 19103

(G-13200)
WILCOX & FETZER LTD
1330 N King St (19801-3230)
PHONE.................................302 655-0477
Kurt A Fetzer, *President*
Robert W Wilcox Sr, *Vice Pres*
Rebecca Laurenzi, *Manager*
Jerry Searfass, *Litigation*
EMP: 20 EST: 1976
SQ FT: 2,500
SALES: 470K **Privately Held**
WEB: www.wilfet.com
SIC: 7338 Court reporting service

(G-13201)
WILDERMAN PHYSICAL THERAPY LLC
2626 Belaire Dr (19808-3835)
PHONE.................................717 873-6836
David Wilderman, *Principal*
EMP: 8
SALES (est): 65.7K **Privately Held**
SIC: 8049 Physical therapist

(G-13202)
WILEY-LISS INC
1105 N Market St Ste 1300 (19801-1241)
PHONE.................................302 429-8627
Robert Wilder, *President*
EMP: 3
SALES (est): 146.3K
SALES (corp-wide): 1.8B **Publicly Held**
WEB: www.wiley.com
SIC: 2731 Books: publishing only; textbooks: publishing only, not printed on site
PA: John Wiley & Sons, Inc.
111 River St Ste 2000
Hoboken NJ 07030
201 748-6000

(G-13203)
WILKINSON ROOFING & SIDING INC
1000 First State Blvd (19804-3575)
P.O. Box 1236, Chadds Ford PA (19317-0670)
PHONE.................................302 998-0176
Kenneth Balagur, *President*
Joseph Adams, *Manager*
EMP: 21
SQ FT: 18,000
SALES (est): 3.6MM **Privately Held**
SIC: 1761 Roofing contractor; roof repair; siding contractor; gutter & downspout contractor

(G-13204)
WILKINSON TECHNOLOGY SVCS LLC
4 Squirrel Run (19807-2030)
PHONE.................................302 384-7770
John Wilkinson,
EMP: 5
SALES (est): 233.5K **Privately Held**
SIC: 7374 Service bureau, computer

(G-13205)
WILKS LUKOFF & BRACEGIRDLE LLC
1300 N Grant Ave Ste 100 (19806-2458)
PHONE.................................302 225-0850
David E Wilks,
Thad J Bracegirdle,
Thad Bracegirdle,
Paul M Lukoff,
Joseph Weik,
EMP: 9
SALES (est): 780K **Privately Held**
SIC: 8111 Specialized law offices, attorneys

(G-13206)
WILLIAM D SHELLADY INC
112 A St (19801-5219)
P.O. Box 1588 (19899-1588)
PHONE.................................302 652-3106
Eugene A Matlusky, *President*
James Wahl, *Vice Pres*
EMP: 75 EST: 1909
SQ FT: 5,000
SALES (est): 3.1MM **Privately Held**
SIC: 1711 Plumbing contractors; warm air heating & air conditioning contractor

(G-13207)
WILLIAM DELCAMPO MECHANICAL SE
2429 Hartley Pl (19804-4258)
PHONE.................................302 992-9748
Williams Del Campo, *Owner*
EMP: 6
SALES (est): 594.5K **Privately Held**
SIC: 1711 Mechanical contractor

(G-13208)
WILLIAM E WARD PA
2710 Centerville Rd # 200 (19808-1644)
P.O. Box 4360 (19807-0360)
PHONE.................................302 225-3350
William E Ward, *President*
EMP: 11
SALES (est): 419.5K **Privately Held**
SIC: 8111 General practice attorney, lawyer

(G-13209)
WILLIAM G DAY COMPANY
1603 Jessup St Ste 4 (19802-4255)
P.O. Box 7548 (19803-0548)
PHONE.................................302 427-3700
EMP: 12 EST: 1997
SQ FT: 2,000
SALES: 2MM **Privately Held**
SIC: 1711 Plumbing/Heating/Air Cond Contractor

(G-13210)
WILLIAM G ROBELEN INC
3110 Lancaster Ave (19805-1461)
PHONE.................................302 656-8726
William Masciantonio Jr, *President*
Phillip Masciantonio, *Vice Pres*
EMP: 6
SQ FT: 2,500

Wilmington - New Castle County (G-13211) — GEOGRAPHIC SECTION

SALES (est): 610K **Privately Held**
SIC: 1711 Plumbing contractors; warm air heating & air conditioning contractor

(G-13211)
WILLIAM GRANT & SONS USA CORP
1011 Centre Rd Ste 310 (19805-1266)
PHONE..................302 573-3880
Vickie Sivemore, *Manager*
◆ EMP: 2
SALES (est): 351.6K
SALES (corp-wide): 1.7B **Privately Held**
SIC: 5182 2085 Bottling wines & liquors; distilled & blended liquors
HQ: William Grant & Sons Limited
    Phoenix Crescent
    Bellshill

(G-13212)
WILLIAM H MCDANIEL INC
14 E 40th St Lowr (19802-2300)
PHONE..................302 764-2020
William H McDaniel Jr, *President*
EMP: 10
SQ FT: 15,000
SALES (est): 843.2K **Privately Held**
SIC: 1711 Mechanical contractor

(G-13213)
WILLIAM HCKS ANDRSON CMNTY CTR
501 N Madison St (19801-2060)
PHONE..................302 571-4266
Romain Alexander, *Director*
Herbert W White, *Administration*
EMP: 30
SALES (est): 403.4K **Privately Held**
SIC: 8322 Community center

(G-13214)
WILLIAM HUMPHREYS & CO LLC
1701 Shallcross Ave (19806-2347)
PHONE..................302 225-3904
Thomas J Williams, *Principal*
Rob Diton, *Associate*
Robert Houck, *Associate*
EMP: 4
SALES (est): 363K **Privately Held**
SIC: 8721 Certified public accountant

(G-13215)
WILLIAM N CANN INC
Also Called: Cann Printing
1 Meco Cir (19804-1108)
PHONE..................302 995-0820
William Cann Jr, *CEO*
Frank T Griffin, *President*
Jerry Price, *Vice Pres*
Celeste Sheehan, *Treasurer*
Price Jerry, *Accounts Mgr*
EMP: 23 EST: 1932
SQ FT: 18,000
SALES (est): 2.9MM **Privately Held**
WEB: www.cannprinting.com
SIC: 2752 2791 2789 Commercial printing, offset; typesetting; bookbinding & related work

(G-13216)
WILLIAM W ERHART PA
2961 Centerville Rd (19808-1666)
PHONE..................302 651-0113
William Erhart, *Partner*
EMP: 4
SALES (est): 280K **Privately Held**
SIC: 8111 General practice attorney, lawyer

(G-13217)
WILLIAMS INSURANCE AGENCY INC
Also Called: G N G Insurance
5301 Limestone Rd Ste 100 (19808-1251)
PHONE..................302 239-5500
Paul Gallagher, *Manager*
EMP: 8
SALES (corp-wide): 11.1MM **Privately Held**
WEB: www.paulgallagher.com
SIC: 6411 Insurance agents

PA: Williams Insurance Agency Inc
    20220 Coastal Hwy
    Rehoboth Beach DE 19971
    302 227-2501

(G-13218)
WILLIAMS LAW FIRM PA
1201 N Orange St Ste 600 (19801-1171)
P.O. Box 511 (19899-0511)
PHONE..................302 575-0873
David N Williams, *Partner*
Brian Crawford, *General Counsel*
Williams D Nicol,
John Williams,
EMP: 5
SALES (est): 654.4K **Privately Held**
SIC: 8111 General practice attorney, lawyer

(G-13219)
WILLOW RUN CIVIC ASSOCIATION
1504 Bondridge Rd (19805-1230)
P.O. Box 5686 (19808-5686)
PHONE..................302 994-2250
Theresa Riddleberger, *Treasurer*
EMP: 4
SALES (est): 85.2K **Privately Held**
SIC: 8641 Civic associations

(G-13220)
WILM OTOLARNGOLOGY
2300 Penns Ave Ste 2a (19806-1379)
PHONE..................302 658-0404
William Medford, *Partner*
Jay Luft, *Partner*
EMP: 10
SALES (est): 206.4K **Privately Held**
SIC: 8011 Eyes, ears, nose & throat specialist: physician/surgeon

(G-13221)
WILMINGTON
1201 N Orange St Ste 7463 (19801-1293)
PHONE..................302 357-4509
Vincent Cooper, *Bd of Directors*
Kelsey Bacon, *Bd of Directors*
Malcolm Coley, *Bd of Directors*
Shawn Davis, *Bd of Directors*
Jonathon Farmer, *Bd of Directors*
EMP: 7
SALES (est): 279.3K **Privately Held**
SIC: 3523 5084 1542 2833 Irrigation equipment, self-propelled; brewery products manufacturing machinery, commercial; greenhouse construction; organic medicinal chemicals: bulk, uncompounded; botanical products, medicinal: ground, graded or milled

(G-13222)
WILMINGTON & NEWARK DENTAL
2300 Penns Ave Ste LI (19806-1396)
PHONE..................302 571-0526
Richard Dettro, *President*
Jack Leyh Cdt, *Vice Pres*
EMP: 7
SQ FT: 2,500
SALES (est): 617.9K **Privately Held**
SIC: 8072 Dental laboratories

(G-13223)
WILMINGTON ANIMAL HOSPITAL
828 Philadelphia Pike (19809-2332)
PHONE..................302 762-2694
Dr Shelly Epstein, *Owner*
Stephanie Connell, *Admin Asst*
EMP: 20
SQ FT: 5,000
SALES (est): 942.8K **Privately Held**
WEB: www.wilmingtonanimalhospital.com
SIC: 0742 Animal hospital services, pets & other animal specialties

(G-13224)
WILMINGTON BLUE ROCKS BASEBALL
801 Shipyard Dr (19801-5154)
PHONE..................302 888-2015
Christopher Kemple, *General Mgr*
Matt Minker, *General Ptnr*
Joseph McCarthy, *Sales Staff*
Erin Del, *Office Mgr*

Zach Chatman, *Assistant*
EMP: 12
SALES (est): 1.3MM **Privately Held**
WEB: www.bluerocks.com
SIC: 7941 Baseball club, professional & semi-professional

(G-13225)
WILMINGTON BREW WORKS LLC
3201 Miller Rd (19802-2542)
PHONE..................302 757-4971
Craig Wensell, *Principal*
Keith Hughes, *CFO*
EMP: 3
SALES (est): 131.7K **Privately Held**
SIC: 2082 Beer (alcoholic beverage)

(G-13226)
WILMINGTON CLUB INC
1103 N Market St (19801-1223)
P.O. Box 433 (19899-0433)
PHONE..................302 658-4287
John E Riteel, *President*
Marcus Meyer, *General Mgr*
Charles Cummy, *Vice Pres*
Christopher Patterson, *Treasurer*
Michael Ledyard, *Admin Sec*
EMP: 20
SQ FT: 20,000
SALES (est): 765.4K **Privately Held**
WEB: www.wilmingtonrotaryclub.org
SIC: 8641 Bars & restaurants, members only; social club, membership

(G-13227)
WILMINGTON COLLISION CTR LLC
214 E Lea Blvd (19802-2301)
PHONE..................302 764-3520
Michael Lucas, *President*
EMP: 4
SALES (est): 379.4K **Privately Held**
SIC: 7532 Collision shops, automotive; body shop, automotive

(G-13228)
WILMINGTON COUNTRY CLUB
4825 Kennett Pike (19807-1813)
PHONE..................302 655-6171
Philip Lannelli, *General Mgr*
S Daniel Pierson, *Superintendent*
Stephen Buenaga, *Human Res Dir*
Chris Annone, *Manager*
Zac Woods, *Manager*
EMP: 150
SALES: 15.7MM **Privately Held**
WEB: www.wilmingtoncc.com
SIC: 7997 5941 5813 5812 Country club, membership; sporting goods & bicycle shops; drinking places; eating places

(G-13229)
WILMINGTON DENTAL ASSOC PA
2309 Pennsylvania Ave (19806-1318)
PHONE..................302 654-6915
John J Lenz, *Partner*
Anthony Vattilana, *Partner*
EMP: 13
SQ FT: 4,000
SALES (est): 968.6K **Privately Held**
WEB: www.wilmingtondentalcare.com/index.html
SIC: 8021 Dentists' office

(G-13230)
WILMINGTON ELKS HOME INC
Also Called: Elks Lodge 307
1310 Carruthers Ln (19803-4604)
PHONE..................302 652-0313
Charles Burns, *President*
Joe Heller, *Principal*
Lori Mason, *Treasurer*
Joe Mazur, *Treasurer*
Kelly Burns, *Admin Sec*
EMP: 4
SALES: 95K **Privately Held**
SIC: 8641 Social club, membership; civic associations

(G-13231)
WILMINGTON HEAD START
Also Called: Leslie Johnson Center
2401 Northeast Blvd (19802-4508)
PHONE..................302 762-8038
Kimberly Winder, *Manager*
EMP: 5
SALES (est): 192.3K **Privately Held**
SIC: 8351 Head start center, except in conjunction with school

(G-13232)
WILMINGTON HEADSTART INC
Also Called: Inf Head Start Center
1238 N Walnut St (19801-3222)
PHONE..................302 421-3620
Deboarh Thomas, *Director*
EMP: 4
SALES (est): 51.1K
SALES (corp-wide): 4.7MM **Privately Held**
SIC: 8351 Head start center, except in conjunction with school
PA: Wilmington Headstart Incorporated
    100 W 10th St Ste 1016
    Wilmington DE 19801
    302 762-8038

(G-13233)
WILMINGTON HEADSTART INC (PA)
100 W 10th St Ste 1016 (19801-6607)
PHONE..................302 762-8038
Susan Frederick, *Comptroller*
Kellen Anderson, *Human Res Mgr*
Deborah Thomas, *Director*
Maryann Mieczkowski, *Director*
Dawn Guyer, *Admin Sec*
EMP: 42
SALES: 4.7MM **Privately Held**
SIC: 8351 Head start center, except in conjunction with school

(G-13234)
WILMINGTON HOTEL VENTURE
Also Called: Doubletree Hotel
700 N King St (19801-3504)
PHONE..................302 655-0400
James Riley, *President*
Ann Riley, *Vice Pres*
EMP: 150 EST: 1979
SALES: 5.4MM **Privately Held**
SIC: 7011 Hotels & motels

(G-13235)
WILMINGTON HOUSING PARTNR CORP
800 N French St Fl 7 (19801-3590)
PHONE..................302 576-3000
Steven Martin, *Accountant*
Gerard Cain, *Exec Dir*
EMP: 4
SALES: 135.6K **Privately Held**
SIC: 1521 Single-family housing construction

(G-13236)
WILMINGTON INFRARED TECH
108 Shinn Cir (19808-1114)
PHONE..................302 234-6761
MEI-WEI Tsao, *Owner*
Marshall Gary, *Engineer*
EMP: 5
SQ FT: 800
SALES: 170K **Privately Held**
SIC: 3826 Infrared analytical instruments

(G-13237)
WILMINGTON MEDICAL ASSOCIATES
Also Called: Sokoloff, Bruce H MD
2700 Silverside Rd Ste 3 (19810-3724)
PHONE..................302 478-0400
Bruce Slkollff, *Partner*
EMP: 13
SALES (est): 1.6MM **Privately Held**
SIC: 8011 Pulmonary specialist, physician/surgeon

(G-13238)
WILMINGTON MONTESSORI SCHOOL
1400 Harvey Rd (19810-4210)
PHONE..................302 475-0555
Lisa Lalama, *Director*

▲ = Import ▼ = Export
◆ = Import/Export

GEOGRAPHIC SECTION
Wilmington - New Castle County (G-13263)

EMP: 75
SALES: 4.4MM **Privately Held**
WEB: www.wilmingtonmontessori.com
SIC: 8351 8211 Preschool center; private elementary school

(G-13239)
WILMINGTON OTOLRYNGLGY ASSC
Also Called: Medford, William L Jr MD
2300 Penns Ave Ste 2a (19806-1379)
PHONE...................302 658-0404
W L Medford Jr, *President*
Jay D Luft MD, *Principal*
EMP: 8
SALES (est): 1MM **Privately Held**
SIC: 8011 Physicians' office, including specialists; surgeon

(G-13240)
WILMINGTON PAIN/REHAB CNTR PA
1021 Gilpin Ave Ste 101 (19806-3271)
PHONE...................302 575-1776
Ross Ufberg, *President*
EMP: 6
SALES (est): 511K **Privately Held**
SIC: 8093 Rehabilitation center, outpatient treatment

(G-13241)
WILMINGTON PARKING AUTHORITY (PA)
625 N Orange St Ste 2c (19801-2250)
PHONE...................302 655-4442
Drew Horseman, *Finance*
Chris Jones, *Finance*
Lucy Clemens, *Manager*
Stanley Soja, *Exec Dir*
Karla Britt, *Director*
EMP: 48
SQ FT: 5,000
SALES: 8.2MM **Privately Held**
WEB: www.wilmingtonparking.com
SIC: 7521 Parking garage; parking lots

(G-13242)
WILMINGTON POLICE AND FIRE FED
1701 Shallcross Ave Ste B (19806-2347)
PHONE...................302 654-0818
Evelyn Vega, *Principal*
Amanda Basciano, *Accountant*
Stephanie Bupp, *Accountant*
Teresa Hirs, *Accountant*
Sandy Huff, *Accountant*
EMP: 9
SALES: 367.6K **Privately Held**
SIC: 6061 Federal credit unions

(G-13243)
WILMINGTON RENAISSANCE CORP
100 W 10th St Ste 206 (19801-1632)
PHONE...................302 425-5500
Carrie Gray, *Director*
EMP: 5
SALES: 1.6MM **Privately Held**
SIC: 8399 Community development groups

(G-13244)
WILMINGTON RESOURCES
106 Clifton Park Cir (19802-1796)
P.O. Box 9385 (19809-0385)
PHONE...................302 746-7162
Alison Etinoff, *Principal*
EMP: 10
SALES (est): 144.2K **Privately Held**
SIC: 1623 5015 5063 7389 Water, sewer & utility lines; automotive supplies, used; signaling equipment, electrical;

(G-13245)
WILMINGTON SAVINGS FUND SOC (HQ)
Also Called: WSFS
500 Delaware Ave Ste 500 # 500 (19801-7405)
PHONE...................302 792-6000
Mark A Turner, *CEO*
Marvin N Schoenhals, *Ch of Bd*
Calvert Morgan Jr, *Vice Ch Bd*
Danielle Conway, *President*
Cheryl Emory, *President*
EMP: 150
SQ FT: 20,000
SALES: 426.9MM
SALES (corp-wide): 455.5MM **Publicly Held**
WEB: www.wsfsbank.com
SIC: 6022 State commercial banks
PA: Wsfs Financial Corporation
500 Delaware Ave
Wilmington DE 19801
302 792-6000

(G-13246)
WILMINGTON SAVINGS FUND SOC
Also Called: First State Plaza
1600 W Newport Pike (19804-3500)
PHONE...................302 999-1227
Randy Stolberg, *Manager*
EMP: 8
SALES (corp-wide): 455.5MM **Publicly Held**
WEB: www.wsfsbank.com
SIC: 6022 State commercial banks
HQ: Wilmington Savings Fund Society
500 Delaware Ave Ste 500 # 500
Wilmington DE 19801
302 792-6000

(G-13247)
WILMINGTON SAVINGS FUND SOC
3801 Kennett Pike (19807-2321)
PHONE...................888 665-9609
John Bailey, *Engineer*
EMP: 5
SALES (corp-wide): 455.5MM **Publicly Held**
SIC: 6029 Commercial banks
HQ: Wilmington Savings Fund Society
500 Delaware Ave Ste 500 # 500
Wilmington DE 19801
302 792-6000

(G-13248)
WILMINGTON SAVINGS FUND SOC
211 N Union St (19805-3429)
PHONE...................302 571-6508
Meg Thomas, *Branch Mgr*
EMP: 6
SALES (corp-wide): 455.5MM **Publicly Held**
SIC: 6029 Commercial banks
HQ: Wilmington Savings Fund Society
500 Delaware Ave Ste 500 # 500
Wilmington DE 19801
302 792-6000

(G-13249)
WILMINGTON SAVINGS FUND SOC
Also Called: Pike Creek Branch
4730 Limestone Rd (19808-1928)
PHONE...................302 633-5700
Mel Personti, *Manager*
EMP: 9
SALES (corp-wide): 455.5MM **Publicly Held**
WEB: www.wsfsbank.com
SIC: 6022 State commercial banks
HQ: Wilmington Savings Fund Society
500 Delaware Ave Ste 500 # 500
Wilmington DE 19801
302 792-6000

(G-13250)
WILMINGTON SAVINGS FUND SOC
Also Called: Trolley Square Branch 307
1711 Delaware Ave (19806-2329)
PHONE...................302 571-6516
Lauren Wilson, *Manager*
EMP: 7
SALES (corp-wide): 455.5MM **Publicly Held**
WEB: www.wsfsbank.com
SIC: 6035 Federal savings banks
HQ: Wilmington Savings Fund Society
500 Delaware Ave Ste 500 # 500
Wilmington DE 19801
302 792-6000

(G-13251)
WILMINGTON SAVINGS FUND SOC
Also Called: Prices Corner Branch
3202 Kirkwood Hwy Frnt (19808-6154)
PHONE...................302 633-5704
Jane Matyger, *Manager*
EMP: 14
SALES (corp-wide): 455.5MM **Publicly Held**
WEB: www.wsfsbank.com
SIC: 6022 State commercial banks
HQ: Wilmington Savings Fund Society
500 Delaware Ave Ste 500 # 500
Wilmington DE 19801
302 792-6000

(G-13252)
WILMINGTON SAVINGS FUND SOC
2005 Concord Pike (19803-2983)
PHONE...................302 571-6500
Steven Agabides, *Branch Mgr*
EMP: 5
SALES (corp-wide): 455.5MM **Publicly Held**
WEB: www.wsfsbank.com
SIC: 6035 Savings institutions, federally chartered
HQ: Wilmington Savings Fund Society
500 Delaware Ave Ste 500 # 500
Wilmington DE 19801
302 792-6000

(G-13253)
WILMINGTON SAVINGS FUND SOC
2522 Foulk Rd (19810-1420)
PHONE...................302 529-9300
Dan Moran, *Manager*
EMP: 4
SALES (corp-wide): 455.5MM **Publicly Held**
SIC: 6029 Commercial banks
HQ: Wilmington Savings Fund Society
500 Delaware Ave Ste 500 # 500
Wilmington DE 19801
302 792-6000

(G-13254)
WILMINGTON SAVINGS FUND SOC
Wsfs Bank Ctr 500 Del Ave Wsfs Bank Center (19801)
PHONE...................302 792-6000
Paul Greenplate, *Vice Pres*
Kathleen Burke, *Marketing Staff*
Sharon Croft, *Asst Sec*
EMP: 12
SALES (corp-wide): 455.5MM **Publicly Held**
SIC: 6029 Commercial banks
HQ: Wilmington Savings Fund Society
500 Delaware Ave Ste 500 # 500
Wilmington DE 19801
302 792-6000

(G-13255)
WILMINGTON SAVINGS FUND SOC
500 Delaware Ave Ste 3 (19801-7400)
PHONE...................302 571-7090
EMP: 9
SALES (corp-wide): 455.5MM **Publicly Held**
SIC: 6035 Federal savings & loan associations
HQ: Wilmington Savings Fund Society
500 Delaware Ave Ste 500 # 500
Wilmington DE 19801
302 792-6000

(G-13256)
WILMINGTON SENIOR CENTER INC
Also Called: Wilmington Senior Center
1909 N Market St (19802-4812)
PHONE...................302 651-3440
Sandria Burton, *Director*
EMP: 15
SALES (corp-wide): 848.3K **Privately Held**
WEB: www.wilmingtonseniorcenter.org
SIC: 7361 Employment agencies
PA: Senior Wilmington Center Inc
1901 N Market St
Wilmington DE 19802
302 651-3400

(G-13257)
WILMINGTON SENIOR CENTER INC (PA)
1901 N Market St (19802-4897)
PHONE...................302 651-3400
Cynthia Stewart, *Finance Dir*
Kathleen Purcell, *Exec Dir*
EMP: 40
SQ FT: 15,000
SALES: 848.3K **Privately Held**
WEB: www.wilmingtonseniorcenter.org
SIC: 8322 Senior citizens' center or association

(G-13258)
WILMINGTON STRING ENSEMBLE
1310 Hillside Blvd (19803-4214)
PHONE...................302 764-1201
Karen Ahramjian, *Owner*
EMP: 21
SALES (est): 220.9K **Privately Held**
SIC: 7929 7922 Orchestras or bands; theatrical producers & services

(G-13259)
WILMINGTON TRANSPORTATION CTR
Also Called: Greyhound 5511
101 N French St (19801-2505)
PHONE...................302 655-6111
Gail Mssengill, *President*
EMP: 7
SALES: 200K **Privately Held**
SIC: 4142 Bus charter service, except local

(G-13260)
WILMINGTON TRUST
Rodney Sq N 1100 N Mkt St (19890-0001)
PHONE...................302 651-1000
EMP: 37 **EST:** 2015
SALES (est): 3.6MM **Privately Held**
SIC: 6733 Trusts

(G-13261)
WILMINGTON TRUST COMPANY (DH)
Also Called: M&T
1100 N Market St (19890-0001)
PHONE...................302 651-1000
Robert V A Harra Jr, *President*
Jennifer Anderson, *President*
William Buccella, *President*
William J Farrell, *President*
Mary Fisher, *President*
EMP: 118
SQ FT: 200,000
SALES: 282.8MM
SALES (corp-wide): 6.4B **Publicly Held**
WEB: www.binghamlegg.com
SIC: 6733 Trusts
HQ: Manufacturers And Traders Trust Company
1 M&T Plz Fl 3
Buffalo NY 14203
716 842-4200

(G-13262)
WILMINGTON TRUST COMPANY TT
1100 N Market St (19890-0001)
PHONE...................302 427-4812
EMP: 6
SALES: 1.1MM **Privately Held**
SIC: 6022 State commercial banks

(G-13263)
WILMINGTON TRUST CORPORATION
Rodney Sq N 1100 N Mkt St (19890-0001)
PHONE...................302 651-8378
Donald E Foley, *CEO*
Mark J Czarnecki, *President*
Robert V A Harra Jr, *President*
Robert G Wilmers, *Chairman*
Michael A Digregorio, *Exec VP*
EMP: 34 **EST:** 1985

SALES (est): 5.6MM **Privately Held**
SIC: 6282 7389 8741 Investment advisory service; financial services; management services

(G-13264)
WILMINGTON TRUST SP SERVICES (HQ)
1105 N Market St Ste 1300 (19801-1241)
PHONE...................302 427-7650
Sania Beven, *President*
Charles Hanlon, *Vice Pres*
EMP: 975
SALES (est): 135.3MM
SALES (corp-wide): 361.4MM **Privately Held**
SIC: 2711 Newspapers
PA: Abarta, Inc.
200 Alpha Dr
Pittsburgh PA 15238
412 963-6226

(G-13265)
WILMINGTON TUG INC (PA)
11 Gist Rd Ste 200 (19801-5879)
P.O. Box 389, New Castle (19720-0389)
PHONE...................302 652-1666
H Hickman Rowland Jr, *President*
David Walters, *Vice Pres*
Bill Martin, *Engineer*
Christopher Rowland, *Treasurer*
EMP: 45 EST: 1965
SQ FT: 1,600
SALES (est): 7.1MM **Privately Held**
WEB: www.wilmingtontug.com
SIC: 4492 Marine towing services; tugboat service

(G-13266)
WILMINGTON TURNERS CLUB
701 S Clayton St (19805-4214)
PHONE...................302 658-9011
Thomas Frick, *Owner*
EMP: 10
SALES (est): 166.1K **Privately Held**
SIC: 7997 Membership sports & recreation clubs

(G-13267)
WILMINGTON YOUTH ORGANIZATION
615 W 37th St (19802-2028)
PHONE...................302 761-9030
Keith Leke, *President*
EMP: 5
SALES (est): 43.6K **Privately Held**
SIC: 8641 Youth organizations

(G-13268)
WILMINGTON YOUTH ROWING ASSN
500 E Front St Frnt Frnt (19801-5017)
PHONE...................302 777-4533
Faith Pizor, *Director*
EMP: 15
SALES: 236.7K **Privately Held**
WEB: www.wyra.org
SIC: 8699 Athletic organizations

(G-13269)
WIN FROM WTHIN XC CAMP/TATNALL
10 Courtney Rd (19807-2548)
PHONE...................302 494-5312
Patrick Castagno, *Principal*
EMP: 20 EST: 2014
SALES (est): 168.9K **Privately Held**
SIC: 7032 7389 Summer camp, except day & sports instructional;

(G-13270)
WINDCREST ANIMAL HOSPITAL
3705 Lancaster Pike (19805-1510)
PHONE...................302 239-9464
Bruce Damme, *Owner*
Lidia Epps, *General Mgr*
Ian Frey, *Practice Mgr*
Harold Patchell, *Practice Mgr*
Karen Gustafson, *Technology*
EMP: 30
SALES (est): 2.8MM **Privately Held**
WEB: www.windcrestanimal.com
SIC: 0742 Animal hospital services, pets & other animal specialties; veterinarian, animal specialties

(G-13271)
WINKER LABS LLC
2711 Centerville Rd # 400 (19808-1660)
PHONE...................630 449-8130
Philip Jenkins, *General Mgr*
EMP: 1 EST: 2015
SALES (est): 57K **Privately Held**
SIC: 7372 7389 Application computer software;

(G-13272)
WINNER GROUP INC (PA)
911 N Tatnall St (19801-1605)
P.O. Box 954 (19899-0954)
PHONE...................302 764-5900
John Hynansky, *President*
EMP: 400
SQ FT: 10,000
SALES (est): 71.8MM **Privately Held**
SIC: 5511 7514 Automobiles, new & used; rent-a-car service

(G-13273)
WINNER GROUP MANAGEMENT INC (PA)
Also Called: Winner Automotive Group
520 S Walnut St (19801-5230)
PHONE...................302 571-5200
John Hynansky, *President*
Thomas Mihok, *General Mgr*
Jerome Raphael, *General Mgr*
Patrick Shuey, *General Mgr*
Frank Costa, *Parts Mgr*
EMP: 25
SQ FT: 10,000
SALES (est): 3.1MM **Privately Held**
SIC: 8742 Business consultant; training & development consultant

(G-13274)
WINNER INFINITI INC
Also Called: Winner Porsche
1300 N Union St (19806-2534)
PHONE...................302 764-5900
John Hynansky, *President*
Darin Pile, *Sales Staff*
EMP: 21
SALES (est): 7.4MM **Privately Held**
WEB: www.winneraudi.com
SIC: 5511 5531 7538 Automobiles, new & used; automotive parts; general automotive repair shops

(G-13275)
WINNER PREMIER COLLISION CTR
520 S Walnut St (19801-5230)
PHONE...................302 571-5200
John Hynansky, *CEO*
EMP: 50
SQ FT: 30,000
SALES (est): 1.9MM **Privately Held**
WEB: www.winnerauto.com
SIC: 7532 Collision shops, automotive

(G-13276)
WINNERS CIRCLE INC
Also Called: Audi Wilmington
1300 N Union St (19806-2534)
PHONE...................302 661-2100
Michael Hynansky, *President*
EMP: 50
SALES (est): 2.1MM **Privately Held**
SIC: 5511 7549 Automobiles, new & used; automotive maintenance services

(G-13277)
WINTERTHUR MUSEUM
1520 N Rodney St (19806-3008)
PHONE...................302 740-9771
Lyn Lewis, *Comms Dir*
EMP: 4 EST: 2018
SALES (est): 38.5K **Privately Held**
SIC: 8412 Museum

(G-13278)
WIRELESS ELECTRONICS INC
32 Germay Dr Ste C (19804-1118)
PHONE...................302 652-1301
EMP: 5 **Privately Held**
SIC: 7622 Radio/Television Repair
PA: Wireless Electronics Inc
2905 Southampton Rd
Philadelphia PA 19154

(G-13279)
WISE POWER SYSTEMS INC
500 Philadelphia Pike # 100 (19809-2146)
PHONE...................302 351-4613
William Rawheiser, *President*
EMP: 10
SALES (est): 1.4MM **Privately Held**
SIC: 8748 Energy conservation consultant

(G-13280)
WIT SERVICES LLC
Also Called: Whatever It Takes Services
1174 Elderon Dr (19808-1924)
PHONE...................302 995-2983
William Robinson,
EMP: 6
SALES: 500K **Privately Held**
SIC: 1522 Hotel/motel & multi-family home renovation & remodeling

(G-13281)
WITHYOUWITHME INC
1209 N Orange St (19801-1120)
PHONE...................202 377-9743
Sam Baynes, *President*
EMP: 4
SALES (est): 154.1K **Privately Held**
SIC: 3699 Security devices

(G-13282)
WM SYSTEMS INC
2711 Centerville Rd # 120 (19808-1676)
PHONE...................302 450-4482
Raul F Russian, *President*
Guillermo Halmoguera, *Exec VP*
EMP: 5
SQ FT: 1,000
SALES (est): 981.6K **Privately Held**
SIC: 5082 8734 Oil field equipment; food testing service

(G-13283)
WMK FINANCING INC
300 Delaware Ave (19801-1607)
PHONE...................302 576-2697
EMP: 34
SALES (est): 37.2K
SALES (corp-wide): 3.5B **Publicly Held**
SIC: 7389 Financial services
PA: Weis Markets, Inc.
1000 S 2nd St
Sunbury PA 17801
570 286-4571

(G-13284)
WOHLSEN CONSTRUCTION COMPANY
501 Carr Rd Ste 100 (19809-2866)
PHONE...................302 324-9900
David B Brodie, *Sales & Mktg St*
Dana A Buttorff, *Executive*
EMP: 20
SALES (corp-wide): 199.5MM **Privately Held**
WEB: www.wohlsen.com
SIC: 1542 1541 8741 School building construction; commercial & office building, new construction; hospital construction; industrial buildings, new construction; warehouse construction; construction management
PA: Wohlsen Construction Company Inc
548 Steel Way
Lancaster PA 17601
717 299-2500

(G-13285)
WOLANSKI & SONS ELECTRIC INC
22 Main Ave (19804-1829)
PHONE...................302 999-0838
Walter W Wolanski, *President*
Mark Wolanski, *Vice Pres*
EMP: 4 EST: 1979
SALES (est): 349.8K **Privately Held**
WEB: www.wolanski.net
SIC: 1731 General electrical contractor

(G-13286)
WOLF WOOD WORKS LLC
4 Star Pine Cir (19808-1012)
PHONE...................302 275-7227
Kevin Creswell, *Principal*
EMP: 1

SALES (est): 64.2K **Privately Held**
SIC: 2431 Millwork

(G-13287)
WOLFS ELITE AUTOS
2130 W Newport Pike (19804-3721)
PHONE...................302 999-9199
Ryan D Wolf, *Owner*
EMP: 5
SALES (est): 288.5K **Privately Held**
SIC: 7538 5521 General automotive repair shops; used car dealers

(G-13288)
WOLOSHIN AND LYNCH ASSOCIATES (PA)
3200 Concord Pike (19803-5015)
P.O. Box 7329 (19803-0329)
PHONE...................302 477-3200
Melvyn Woloshin, *Owner*
David Gagne, *Director*
James Natalie, *Director*
William O'Day, *Associate*
EMP: 15
SQ FT: 6,000
SALES (est): 2.8MM **Privately Held**
SIC: 8111 Bankruptcy referee; general practice law office

(G-13289)
WOMBLE BOND DICKINSON (US) LLP
1313 N Market St Fl 12 (19801-1151)
PHONE...................302 252-4320
Frank Monaco, *Partner*
EMP: 65
SALES (corp-wide): 239.4MM **Privately Held**
SIC: 8111 General practice attorney, lawyer
PA: Womble Bond Dickinson (Us) Llp
1 W 4th St
Winston Salem NC 27101
336 721-3600

(G-13290)
WOMEN TO WOMEN OB/GYN ASSOC PA
1100 N Grant Ave Ste C (19805-2670)
PHONE...................302 778-2229
Nancy Fan, *President*
Arthur A Dermen, *Med Doctor*
Audrey A Sernyak, *Med Doctor*
Tanika Long, *Anesthesiology*
Dennis Reilly, *Anesthesiology*
EMP: 8
SALES (est): 712.6K **Privately Held**
SIC: 8011 Obstetrician; gynecologist

(G-13291)
WOMENS FITNESS
4811 Limestone Rd (19808-1902)
PHONE...................302 239-5088
Bain Margareth, *Owner*
EMP: 6
SALES (est): 140.3K **Privately Held**
SIC: 7991 Health club

(G-13292)
WOMENS HEALTH CTR CHRISTN CARE
501 W 14th St (19801-1013)
PHONE...................302 428-5810
Mary T Lednum, *Director*
EMP: 15
SALES (est): 272.8K **Privately Held**
SIC: 8062 General medical & surgical hospitals

(G-13293)
WOMENS TENNIS C N C C
507 Rockwood Rd (19802-1118)
P.O. Box 535, Hockessin (19707-0535)
PHONE...................302 762-2078
EMP: 8
SALES: 2.6K **Privately Held**
SIC: 7997 Membership Sport/Recreation Club

(G-13294)
WOOD CREATIONS BY BILL
26 Windsor Rd (19809-2145)
PHONE...................302 764-6497
Gertrude Holland, *Principal*
EMP: 3

GEOGRAPHIC SECTION
Wilmington - New Castle County (G-13327)

SALES (est): 210K **Privately Held**
SIC: 3993 Signs & advertising specialties

(G-13295)
WOODLAND APARTMENTS LP
1201 Centre Rd (19805-1202)
PHONE...................302 994-9003
Timothy O Fanning, *Partner*
Michael Bonner, *Vice Pres*
Florence Teofilak,
EMP: 7
SALES (est): 541.9K **Privately Held**
SIC: 6513 Apartment hotel operation

(G-13296)
WOODLAND HILL PRESERVATION
4 Denny Rd (19809-3445)
PHONE...................302 764-6450
William Demarco,
EMP: 13 EST: 2012
SALES (est): 534.6K **Privately Held**
SIC: 6513 Apartment building operators

(G-13297)
WOODLAWN TRUSTEES INC
2201 W 11th St (19805-2699)
PHONE...................302 655-6215
Lynn Williams, *President*
Stephen Clark, *Vice Pres*
Newlin E Wood Jr, *Treasurer*
Elke Mc Ginley, *Asst Sec*
EMP: 40
SQ FT: 2,500
SALES (est): 2.6MM **Privately Held**
WEB: www.woodlawntrustees.com
SIC: 6531 6552 Real estate managers; subdividers & developers

(G-13298)
WOODMILL DENTAL
5185 W Woodmill Dr Ste 2 (19808-4067)
PHONE...................302 998-8588
John Eum, *Principal*
EMP: 4
SALES (est): 61.5K **Privately Held**
SIC: 8021 Offices & clinics of dentists

(G-13299)
WOODMILL DENTAL
5185 W Woodmill Dr Ste 2 (19808-4067)
PHONE...................302 998-8588
EMP: 4
SALES (est): 61.5K **Privately Held**
SIC: 8021 Dentist's Office

(G-13300)
WOODS EDGE APARTMENTS
Also Called: Apartment Communities
1204 Terra Hill Dr Apt 3b (19809-3538)
PHONE...................302 762-8300
Joetta Keys, *Manager*
EMP: 5
SALES (est): 393.3K **Privately Held**
SIC: 6513 Apartment building operators

(G-13301)
WOODWORKS
550 Copper Dr (19804-2418)
PHONE...................302 995-0800
R Heck, *Principal*
EMP: 4
SALES (est): 240K **Privately Held**
SIC: 2431 Millwork

(G-13302)
WORK FIRST CASUALTY COMPANY (PA)
501 Silverside Rd Ste 39 (19809-1388)
PHONE...................302 477-1710
Jamie Madden, *President*
Debbie Nowak, *Vice Pres*
Bruce Winterrowd, *Vice Pres*
Blaine Moon, *CFO*
EMP: 12
SALES (est): 5MM **Privately Held**
SIC: 6411 Insurance agents

(G-13303)
WORKAWAY VENTURES INC
1521 Concord Pike Ste 303 (19803-3644)
PHONE...................843 608-9108
Kerrana Williamson, *President*
EMP: 2

SALES (est): 96K **Privately Held**
SIC: 2741

(G-13304)
WORKROOM ENTERPRISES LLC
300 Delaware Ave Ste 210a (19801-6601)
PHONE...................417 621-5577
Murphy Mastin, *Mng Member*
EMP: 7
SALES: 40K **Privately Held**
SIC: 2834 Dermatologicals

(G-13305)
WORLDWIND INC (PA)
Also Called: Craig Joyner Entertainment
202 E 29th St (19802-3632)
PHONE...................302 762-0556
EMP: 5
SALES (est): 380.9K **Privately Held**
SIC: 7922 Theatrical Producers/Services

(G-13306)
WOW TECH USA LTD
103 Foulk Rd Ste 200 (19803-3742)
PHONE...................613 828-6678
Bruce Murison, *CEO*
▲ EMP: 4
SALES (est): 54.6K **Privately Held**
SIC: 8082 Home health care services

(G-13307)
WSFS FINANCIAL CORPORATION (PA)
500 Delaware Ave (19801-1490)
PHONE...................302 792-6000
Mark A Turner, *Ch of Bd*
Rodger Levenson, *President*
Marcedes Carter, *President*
Thomas Stevenson, *President*
Arthur J Bacci, *Exec VP*
EMP: 51
SQ FT: 78,432
SALES: 455.5MM **Publicly Held**
SIC: 6021 National commercial banks

(G-13308)
WSFS INVESTMENT GROUP INC
838 N Market St (19801-3154)
PHONE...................302 573-3258
Robert Mack, *Executive*
EMP: 5
SALES (est): 628.4K
SALES (corp-wide): 455.5MM **Publicly Held**
SIC: 6799 Investors
PA: Wsfs Financial Corporation
500 Delaware Ave
Wilmington DE 19801
302 792-6000

(G-13309)
WTA INC
Also Called: Altitude Trampoline Park
510 Justison St (19801-5142)
PHONE...................302 397-8142
Coner Smith, *Manager*
EMP: 32
SALES (est): 643.7K
SALES (corp-wide): 1.8MM **Privately Held**
SIC: 7999 Trampoline operation
PA: Wta Inc.
30174 Foskey Ln
Delmar MD 21875
410 896-2219

(G-13310)
WWD INC
Also Called: Miller's Beverage Center
5998 Kirkwood Hwy (19808-4815)
PHONE...................302 994-4553
William Dickhart, *President*
EMP: 6
SALES (corp-wide): 1.2MM **Privately Held**
SIC: 6512 Nonresidential building operators
PA: Wwd Inc
31 Wakefield Dr
Newark DE 19711
302 994-4553

(G-13311)
WYATT RIDLEY CORP
Also Called: Sheer Expressions
109 Kirkwood Sq (19808-4859)
PHONE...................302 998-8860
Dina Wyatt, *President*
EMP: 9
SALES (est): 231.5K **Privately Held**
WEB: www.shear-expressions.com
SIC: 7231 Beauty shops

(G-13312)
WYNDHAM GROUP INC
2207 Concord Pike 696 (19803-2908)
PHONE...................704 905-9750
Adam James, *President*
Roger Kerr, *Manager*
EMP: 9
SALES (est): 642.5K **Privately Held**
SIC: 7379 8742 Computer related consulting services; management consulting services

(G-13313)
XAPIX INC (PA)
1209 N Orange St (19801-1120)
PHONE...................408 508-4324
Ralph Klingmann, *CEO*
EMP: 3
SALES (est): 82.4K **Privately Held**
SIC: 7372 Prepackaged software

(G-13314)
XAVIER INC
Also Called: School For Young Children
1315 N Union St (19806-2533)
PHONE...................302 655-1962
Colleen Conaty, *President*
EMP: 9
SALES (est): 234K **Privately Held**
SIC: 8351 Child day care services

(G-13315)
XCMG MACHINERY US LLC
901 N Market St Ste 705 (19801-3098)
PHONE...................786 796-1094
EMP: 1
SALES (est): 60K **Privately Held**
SIC: 3531 Construction machinery

(G-13316)
XCS CORPORATION
Also Called: Sky Trax
500 Water St (19804-2423)
P.O. Box 184, New Castle (19720-0184)
PHONE...................302 514-0600
Richard Ungerbuehler, *President*
David C Emanuel, *Vice Pres*
Larry G Mahan, *Vice Pres*
EMP: 7
SQ FT: 3,300
SALES: 362K **Privately Held**
WEB: www.xcscorp.com
SIC: 8711 7336 7373 7375 Engineering services; graphic arts & related design; computer systems analysis & design; data base information retrieval; software programming applications

(G-13317)
XERAFY INC
3511 Silverside Rd Ste 10 (19810-4902)
PHONE...................817 938-4197
EMP: 2
SALES (est): 88.3K **Privately Held**
SIC: 3629 7371 Electrical industrial apparatus; computer software development & applications

(G-13318)
XEROX CORPORATION
2711 Centerville Rd # 400 (19808-1660)
PHONE...................585 422-0272
EMP: 3 EST: 2016
SALES (est): 94.5K **Privately Held**
SIC: 3577 Computer peripheral equipment
PA: Fujifilm Holdings Corporation
9-7-3, Akasaka
Minato-Ku TKY 107-0

(G-13319)
XEROX CORPORATION
200 Bellevue Pkwy Ste 300 (19809-3727)
PHONE...................302 792-5100
George Jeng, *Manager*
Kecia Burpulis, *Manager*

EMP: 24
SALES (corp-wide): 9.8B **Publicly Held**
WEB: www.xerox.com
SIC: 5044 7699 Duplicating machines; industrial machinery & equipment repair
HQ: Xerox Corporation
201 Merritt 7
Norwalk CT 06851
203 968-3000

(G-13320)
XGATE DENTAL INC
913 N Market St Ste 200 (19801-3097)
PHONE...................302 613-2142
EMP: 4
SALES (est): 61.5K **Privately Held**
SIC: 8021 Offices & clinics of dentists

(G-13321)
XINNIX TICKETING INC
3 W 4th St (19801-2285)
PHONE...................302 778-1818
EMP: 4 EST: 2012
SALES (est): 90.9K **Privately Held**
SIC: 4111 Bus transportation

(G-13322)
XSC IP LLC
1201 N Market St Ste 2300 (19801-1165)
PHONE...................305 384-6700
Ryan Shear, *CEO*
Noah Gottlieb, *President*
Dan Kaplan, *COO*
Brian Koles, *Director*
EMP: 20
SALES (est): 268.9K **Privately Held**
SIC: 6513 Apartment building operators

(G-13323)
XTIUM LLC
2207 Concord Pike 242 (19803-2908)
PHONE...................302 351-6177
Timothy W Vogel, *Mng Member*
Shawn Carey,
Peter B Ritz,
Andrea Vogel,
EMP: 20
SQ FT: 600
SALES (est): 2.3MM **Privately Held**
WEB: www.xtium.com
SIC: 7379

(G-13324)
XXL CLOUD INC
913 N Market St Ste 200 (19801-3097)
PHONE...................302 298-0050
EMP: 4
SALES (est): 115.4K **Privately Held**
SIC: 7371 Custom Computer Programing

(G-13325)
YANEZ & DE YANEZ MD PC
Also Called: Yanez & Associates
2401 Penns Ave Ste 110 (19806-1432)
PHONE...................302 655-2991
Jose R De Yanez MD, *President*
Nedia De Yanez, *Treasurer*
EMP: 5 EST: 1972
SQ FT: 2,500
SALES (est): 259.4K **Privately Held**
WEB: www.yanezlazcano.com
SIC: 8049 Clinical psychologist; hypnotist

(G-13326)
YELLOW PINE ASSOCIATES INC (PA)
Also Called: Davidson Associates
18 Yellow Pine Ct (19808-1028)
PHONE...................302 994-9500
James Davidson, *President*
EMP: 4
SALES (est): 467.8K **Privately Held**
SIC: 8711 8748 Fire protection engineering; safety training service

(G-13327)
YHP HOLDINGS LLC
251 Little Falls Dr (19808-1674)
PHONE...................302 636-5401
Eli Hopson, *Principal*
Dewight Flinch, *Principal*
EMP: 5 EST: 2017 **Privately Held**
SIC: 6719 Holding companies

Wilmington - New Castle County (G-13328)

(G-13328)
YMCA CENTRAL BRANCH LLC
501 W 11th St Ste 100 (19801-6408)
PHONE..................302 571-6950
Jonathan Gershen, *Vice Pres*
EMP: 10 **EST:** 2015
SALES (est): 266K **Privately Held**
SIC: 7997 Membership sports & recreation clubs

(G-13329)
YOTTA GAMES LLC
1013 Centre Rd Ste 403s (19805-1270)
PHONE..................425 247-0756
EMP: 1 **EST:** 2018
SALES (est): 41K **Privately Held**
SIC: 3944 Electronic games & toys

(G-13330)
YOUNG CNWAY STRGATT TAYLOR LLP (PA)
Also Called: Young, Conaway & Associates
1000 N King St (19801-3335)
P.O. Box 391 (19899-0391)
PHONE..................302 571-6600
William D Johnston, *President*
Sheldon A Weinstein, *Managing Prtnr*
Bruce M Stargatt, *Partner*
C Vincent Alexander, *Partner*
William W Bowser, *Partner*
▲ **EMP:** 225
SQ FT: 20,000
SALES (est): 38.8MM **Privately Held**
WEB: www.ycst.com
SIC: 8111 General practice law office

(G-13331)
YOUNG MENS CHRISTIAN ASSOCIAT
Also Called: Walnut Street Y M C A
1000 N Walnut St (19801-3339)
PHONE..................302 571-6935
Jack Booker, *Exec Dir*
Brenda Overton, *Director*
EMP: 60
SALES (corp-wide): 35MM **Privately Held**
WEB: www.ymcade.org
SIC: 7997 7991 Membership sports & recreation clubs; physical fitness facilities
PA: Young Men's Christian Association Of
Wilmington, Delaware
100 W 10th St Ste 1100
Wilmington DE 19801
302 221-9622

(G-13332)
YOUNG MENS CHRISTIAN ASSOCIAT
Also Called: YMCA
501 W 11th St Ste 100 (19801-6408)
PHONE..................302 571-6900
Michael Graves, *President*
EMP: 207
SALES (corp-wide): 35MM **Privately Held**
WEB: www.ymcade.org
SIC: 7011 8361 8351 8322 YMCA/YMHA hotel; residential care; child day care services; individual & family services; membership sports & recreation clubs; physical fitness facilities
PA: Young Men's Christian Association Of
Wilmington, Delaware
100 W 10th St Ste 1100
Wilmington DE 19801
302 221-9622

(G-13333)
YOUNG MENS CHRISTIAN ASSOCIAT
Also Called: Resource Center YMCA
1000 N Walnut St (19801-3339)
PHONE..................302 472-9622
Stewart Fretz, *Supervisor*
Krystina Schneider, *Director*
EMP: 10
SALES (corp-wide): 35MM **Privately Held**
WEB: www.ymcade.org
SIC: 7999 7991 Recreation services; physical fitness facilities

PA: Young Men's Christian Association Of
Wilmington, Delaware
100 W 10th St Ste 1100
Wilmington DE 19801
302 221-9622

(G-13334)
YOUNG MNS CHRSTN ASSN WLMNGTON (PA)
Also Called: YMCA of Delaware
100 W 10th St Ste 1100 (19801-6607)
PHONE..................302 221-9622
William Farrell II, *Vice Ch Bd*
Joseph E Johnson, *Vice Ch Bd*
Michael P Graves, *President*
Lynn Jones, *Chairman*
Vince Jordan, *Facilities Dir*
EMP: 21
SQ FT: 123,000
SALES: 35MM **Privately Held**
WEB: www.ymcade.org
SIC: 7997 7011 Membership sports & recreation clubs; YMCA/YMHA hotel

(G-13335)
YOUR DENTISTRY TODAY INC
3801 Kennett Pike E207 (19807-2340)
PHONE..................302 575-0100
Michael Matthias, *Principal*
EMP: 5
SALES (est): 485.3K **Privately Held**
SIC: 8021 Dental clinics & offices

(G-13336)
YOUYU HOME TECHNOLOGY LLC
108 W 13th St (19801)
PHONE..................347 796-4305
EMP: 15
SALES: 50K **Privately Held**
SIC: 7371 Computer software development & applications

(G-13337)
YWCA DELAWARE (PA)
100 W 10th St Ste 515 (19801-6610)
PHONE..................302 655-0039
Stacey Johnson, *Program Mgr*
Genevieve Marino, *Exec Dir*
Cindy Larock, *Director*
EMP: 98
SALES: 3.9MM **Privately Held**
SIC: 7991 8641 Physical fitness facilities; civic social & fraternal associations

(G-13338)
ZACHARY CHIPMAN DMD PA
5505 Kirkwood Hwy (19808-5001)
PHONE..................302 994-8696
Zachary Chipman, *Principal*
EMP: 5
SALES (est): 355.8K **Privately Held**
SIC: 8021 Dental surgeon

(G-13339)
ZAHN INCORPORATED
Also Called: Mgza
110 S Poplar St Ste 200 (19801-5034)
PHONE..................302 425-3700
Mary G Severino, *President*
EMP: 8
SALES (est): 1MM **Privately Held**
WEB: www.mgza.com
SIC: 8712 7389 8748 Architectural services; interior design services; business consulting

(G-13340)
ZAREK DONOHUE LLC
Also Called: Progressive Health of Delaware
3521 Silverside Rd Ste 2j (19810-4900)
PHONE..................302 543-5454
David Donohue, *Principal*
EMP: 21 **EST:** 2005
SALES (est): 471.9K **Privately Held**
SIC: 8011 Internal medicine practitioners

(G-13341)
ZAVIER J DECAIRE
Also Called: New York Life
300 Delaware Ave Fl 8 (19801-1607)
PHONE..................302 658-0218
Zavier J Decaire, *Partner*
Donald Fulton, *Partner*
Terry Wolf, *Partner*

Xavier Decaire, *Agent*
EMP: 16
SALES (est): 810.8K **Privately Held**
SIC: 6411 Insurance agents & brokers

(G-13342)
ZEAL PRINT CO LLC
129 S Cleveland Ave (19805-1428)
PHONE..................302 407-5745
Rodney Jordan, *Principal*
EMP: 2
SALES (est): 121.7K **Privately Held**
SIC: 2752 Commercial printing, lithographic

(G-13343)
ZEN THERAPY & BODY WORK
201 S Maryland Ave (19804-1343)
PHONE..................302 252-1733
Yuezhen Zhang, *Agent*
EMP: 8
SALES (est): 73.3K **Privately Held**
SIC: 8093 Rehabilitation center, outpatient treatment

(G-13344)
ZENECA HOLDINGS INC (HQ)
Also Called: Astra Zeneca Pharmaceuticals
1800 Concord Pike (19897-0001)
P.O. Box 15437 (19850-5437)
PHONE..................302 886-3000
Jonathan R Symonds, *Ch of Bd*
David R Brennan, *President*
Johnny Chowoe, *Opers Dir*
Klaus Fister, *Opers Dir*
Dave Trapani, *Opers Staff*
▲ **EMP:** 31
SQ FT: 1,200,000
SALES (est): 3.5MM
SALES (corp-wide): 22B **Privately Held**
SIC: 2899 2834 Chemical preparations; druggists' preparations (pharmaceuticals)
PA: Astrazeneca Plc
1 Francis Crick Avenue Cambridge Biomedical Campus
Cambridge CAMBS CB2 0
203 749-5000

(G-13345)
ZENECA INC (DH)
1800 Concord Pike (19897-0001)
PHONE..................302 886-3000
Steven Mohr, *Chairman*
Mark Uhle, *CFO*
David E White, *Treasurer*
EMP: 5 **EST:** 1971
SQ FT: 1,200,000
SALES (est): 1.4MM
SALES (corp-wide): 22B **Privately Held**
WEB: www.zeneaagproducts.com
SIC: 2834 Pharmaceutical preparations
HQ: Zeneca Holdings Inc.
1800 Concord Pike
Wilmington DE 19897
302 886-3000

(G-13346)
ZENKER AND STYER PA
Also Called: Zenker & Styer
1202 Foulk Rd Ste 5 (19803-2796)
PHONE..................302 475-9006
Malcom Styer, *President*
EMP: 4 **EST:** 1968
SQ FT: 1,200
SALES (est): 240K **Privately Held**
SIC: 8721 Certified public accountant

(G-13347)
ZENPAY INC
200 Belview Pkwy Ste 420 (19808)
PHONE..................650 336-6512
EMP: 5 **EST:** 2013
SALES (est): 265.4K **Privately Held**
SIC: 6099 Depository Banking Services

(G-13348)
ZEPHYR ALUMINUM LLC
50 Germay Dr Ste 2 (19804-1187)
PHONE..................302 571-0585
Lori Baum, *Bookkeeper*
Tom Tankersley, *Manager*
EMP: 5
SALES (corp-wide): 17MM **Privately Held**
SIC: 1793 Glass & glazing work

PA: Zephyr Aluminum, Llc
625 2nd St
Lancaster PA 17603
717 397-3618

(G-13349)
ZEROWAIT CORPORATION
707 Kirkwood Hwy (19805-5110)
PHONE..................302 996-9408
Mike Linett, *President*
July Linett, *Vice Pres*
Robert Robinson, *Vice Pres*
Scott Fritsch, *Engineer*
Chris Mire, *Engineer*
EMP: 15
SQ FT: 7,000
SALES (est): 1.6MM **Privately Held**
WEB: www.zerowait.com
SIC: 7378 3572 Computer maintenance & repair; computer storage devices

(G-13350)
ZIETA TECHNOLOGIES LLC (PA)
501 Silverside Rd Ste 39 (19809-1388)
PHONE..................302 252-5249
Rajeev Sinha, *Accounts Exec*
Cnida Barat,
Shivaji Singh,
Ashok Bezawada, *Associate*
EMP: 14
SALES (est): 5.2MM **Privately Held**
SIC: 8748 Business consulting

(G-13351)
ZILPA LTD
300 Delaware Ave Ste 210 (19801-6601)
PHONE..................800 504-5368
Kent Charugundla, *CEO*
EMP: 4 **EST:** 2016
SALES: 2MM **Privately Held**
SIC: 7371 Computer software development & applications

(G-13352)
ZIV INVESTMENTS CO
4001 Kennett Pike Ste 316 (19807-2039)
P.O. Box 198 (19899-0198)
PHONE..................302 573-5080
Peter Ziv, *Principal*
EMP: 14
SALES (est): 1.4MM **Privately Held**
SIC: 6211 Securities flotation companies

(G-13353)
ZUBER & ASSOCIATES INC
Also Called: Omega Physical Therapy
16 Burnett Dr (19810-2205)
PHONE..................302 478-1618
Peter Zuber, *President*
EMP: 5
SQ FT: 1,300
SALES (est): 132.1K **Privately Held**
SIC: 8049 Physiotherapist

(G-13354)
ZUMIDIAN
501 Silverside Rd (19809-1374)
PHONE..................302 219-3500
Nicolas Zumbiehl, *Owner*
EMP: 2
SALES (est): 130.1K **Privately Held**
SIC: 7372 Application computer software

(G-13355)
ZUTZ RISK MANAGEMENT
300 Delaware Ave Ste 1600 (19801-1612)
PHONE..................302 658-8000
Harry Zutz, *Owner*
EMP: 70 **EST:** 1999
SALES (est): 2.8MM **Privately Held**
WEB: www.zutzgroup.com
SIC: 8742 Management consulting services

Winterthur
New Castle County

(G-13356)
ARQITECTURE LLC
5105 Kennett Pike (19735-1819)
PHONE..................302 777-5666
Todd Danner,
EMP: 5

SALES (est): 416K **Privately Held**
SIC: 7389 8712 Interior design services; architectural services

(G-13357)
WINTERTHUR MUSEUM GARDEN & LIB
5105 Kennett Pike (19735-0002)
PHONE 302 888-4600
Carol B Cadou, *CEO*
Rick Medlock, *Maint Spvr*
Daisy McCarter, *Bookkeeper*
Kris Demesse, *Senior Mgr*
Leslie Bowman, *Director*
▲ **EMP:** 40
SALES (est): 2MM **Privately Held**
SIC: 8412 Museum

Wyoming
Kent County

(G-13358)
A NOD TO STELLA EMBROIDERY
120 Pine St (19934-1142)
PHONE 302 697-6308
Barbara Menden, *Principal*
EMP: 1
SALES (est): 38.2K **Privately Held**
SIC: 2395 Embroidery & art needlework

(G-13359)
CAMDEN DRYWALL INC
203 Harrison Ave (19934-1175)
PHONE 302 697-9653
Richard C Greene Sr, *President*
Florence Greene, *Admin Sec*
EMP: 6
SALES: 600K **Privately Held**
SIC: 1742 Drywall

(G-13360)
DELAWARE GUITAR SCHOOL
200 Southern Blvd (19934-1028)
PHONE 302 697-2341
James Rezac, *Principal*
EMP: 1
SALES (est): 40.1K **Privately Held**
SIC: 2741 Miscellaneous publishing

(G-13361)
DELMARVA POLE BUILDING SUP INC
317 N Layton Ave (19934-1235)
PHONE 302 698-3636
Frederick Ruhe, *Principal*
EMP: 9
SALES (est): 2.6MM **Privately Held**
SIC: 1521 Single-family housing construction

(G-13362)
DELMARVA TRUSS AND PANEL LLC
317 N Layton Ave (19934-1235)
PHONE 302 270-8888
Vernon Beachy, *Principal*
EMP: 4
SALES (est): 222.7K **Privately Held**
SIC: 2439 Structural wood members

(G-13363)
IMPARTS INC
Also Called: Avenue Imparts
100 N Railroad Ave (19934-1024)
PHONE 302 697-0990
Kevin Maier, *President*
EMP: 6
SQ FT: 4,000
SALES (est): 869.9K **Privately Held**
WEB: www.avenueimparts.com
SIC: 5013 Automotive supplies & parts

Yorklyn
New Castle County

(G-13364)
BRAND DESIGN CO INC
Also Called: House Industries
1145 York Lane Rd (19736)
P.O. Box 166 (19736-0166)
PHONE 302 234-2356
Andrew Cruz, *President*
Ronald Roat Jr, *CFO*
Brian Awitan, *Sales Staff*
Brazo Fuerte, *CIO*
Andy Cruzowner, *Art Dir*
EMP: 8
SQ FT: 2,500
SALES (est): 1MM **Privately Held**
WEB: www.houseindustries.com
SIC: 7336 Graphic arts & related design

(G-13365)
DAVIS YOUNG ASSOCIATES INC (PA)
2896 Creek Rd (19736)
P.O. Box 451, Montchanin (19710-0451)
PHONE 610 388-0932
Zachary Davis, *President*
EMP: 15
SQ FT: 1,000
SALES (est): 880K **Privately Held**
SIC: 0782 1741 Landscape contractors; masonry & other stonework

(G-13366)
GENTLEMAN DOOR COMPANY INC
506 Dawson Tract Rd (19736)
P.O. Box 77 (19736-0077)
PHONE 302 239-4045
Ann Strab, *President*
Thomas Strab, *Vice Pres*
Tom Strab, *Vice Pres*
EMP: 2
SALES: 50K **Privately Held**
SIC: 3699 Door opening & closing devices, electrical

(G-13367)
SUNHAVEN AWNING CO
2870 Creek Rd (19736-9714)
PHONE 302 239-7990
Cliff Cooke, *President*
EMP: 4
SALES: 500K **Privately Held**
SIC: 3444 Awnings & canopies

(G-13368)
WHITTINGTON & AULGUR (PA)
2979 Barley Mill Rd (19736-9702)
PHONE 302 235-5800
Thomas D Whittington Jr, *Partner*
Robert Aulgar, *Partner*
EMP: 8
SALES (est): 2.5MM **Privately Held**
SIC: 8111 General practice attorney, lawyer

SIC INDEX

Standard Industrial Classification Alphabetical Index

SIC NO	PRODUCT

A

3291 Abrasive Prdts
6321 Accident & Health Insurance
8721 Accounting, Auditing & Bookkeeping Svcs
2891 Adhesives & Sealants
7322 Adjustment & Collection Svcs
7311 Advertising Agencies
7319 Advertising, NEC
3563 Air & Gas Compressors
3585 Air Conditioning & Heating Eqpt
4513 Air Courier Svcs
4522 Air Transportation, Nonscheduled
4512 Air Transportation, Scheduled
3721 Aircraft
3724 Aircraft Engines & Engine Parts
3728 Aircraft Parts & Eqpt, NEC
4581 Airports, Flying Fields & Terminal Svcs
2812 Alkalies & Chlorine
3354 Aluminum Extruded Prdts
3355 Aluminum Rolling & Drawing, NEC
3353 Aluminum Sheet, Plate & Foil
7999 Amusement & Recreation Svcs, NEC
7996 Amusement Parks
3826 Analytical Instruments
0291 Animal Production, NEC
0279 Animal Specialties, NEC
0752 Animal Specialty Svcs, Exc Veterinary
2389 Apparel & Accessories, NEC
3446 Architectural & Ornamental Metal Work
8712 Architectural Services
7694 Armature Rewinding Shops
2952 Asphalt Felts & Coatings
3822 Automatic Temperature Controls
3581 Automatic Vending Machines
7521 Automobile Parking Lots & Garages
5012 Automobiles & Other Motor Vehicles Wholesale
7533 Automotive Exhaust System Repair Shops
7536 Automotive Glass Replacement Shops
7539 Automotive Repair Shops, NEC
3465 Automotive Stampings
7549 Automotive Svcs, Except Repair & Car Washes
7537 Automotive Transmission Repair Shops
2396 Automotive Trimmings, Apparel Findings, Related Prdts

B

2673 Bags: Plastics, Laminated & Coated
2674 Bags: Uncoated Paper & Multiwall
3562 Ball & Roller Bearings
7929 Bands, Orchestras, Actors & Entertainers
7241 Barber Shops
7231 Beauty Shops
0211 Beef Cattle Feedlots
0212 Beef Cattle, Except Feedlots
5181 Beer & Ale Wholesale
0171 Berry Crops
2836 Biological Prdts, Exc Diagnostic Substances
2782 Blankbooks & Looseleaf Binders
3312 Blast Furnaces, Coke Ovens, Steel & Rolling Mills
3564 Blowers & Fans
3732 Boat Building & Repairing
3452 Bolts, Nuts, Screws, Rivets & Washers
2732 Book Printing, Not Publishing
2789 Bookbinding
5192 Books, Periodicals & Newspapers Wholesale
2731 Books: Publishing & Printing
3131 Boot & Shoe Cut Stock & Findings
7933 Bowling Centers
2051 Bread, Bakery Prdts Exc Cookies & Crackers
5032 Brick, Stone & Related Construction Mtrls Wholesale
1622 Bridge, Tunnel & Elevated Hwy Construction
3991 Brooms & Brushes
7349 Building Cleaning & Maintenance Svcs, NEC
4142 Bus Charter Service, Except Local
8611 Business Associations
8748 Business Consulting Svcs, NEC
7389 Business Svcs, NEC
2021 Butter

C

4841 Cable & Other Pay TV Svcs
3578 Calculating & Accounting Eqpt
2064 Candy & Confectionery Prdts
2033 Canned Fruits, Vegetables & Preserves
2032 Canned Specialties
2394 Canvas Prdts
7542 Car Washes
3955 Carbon Paper & Inked Ribbons
3592 Carburetors, Pistons, Rings & Valves
1751 Carpentry Work
7217 Carpet & Upholstery Cleaning
2273 Carpets & Rugs
0119 Cash Grains, NEC
2823 Cellulosic Man-Made Fibers
3241 Cement, Hydraulic
6553 Cemetery Subdividers & Developers
3253 Ceramic Tile
2022 Cheese
1479 Chemical & Fertilizer Mining
2899 Chemical Preparations, NEC
5169 Chemicals & Allied Prdts, NEC Wholesale
0251 Chicken & Poultry Farms
0252 Chicken Egg Farms
8351 Child Day Care Svcs
2361 Children's & Infants' Dresses & Blouses
3261 China Plumbing Fixtures & Fittings
3262 China, Table & Kitchen Articles
2066 Chocolate & Cocoa Prdts
2111 Cigarettes
8641 Civic, Social & Fraternal Associations
3255 Clay Refractories
1459 Clay, Ceramic & Refractory Minerals, NEC
5052 Coal & Other Minerals & Ores Wholesale
3479 Coating & Engraving, NEC
2095 Coffee
7215 Coin Operated Laundries & Cleaning
7993 Coin-Operated Amusement Devices & Arcades
3316 Cold Rolled Steel Sheet, Strip & Bars
7336 Commercial Art & Graphic Design
6029 Commercial Banks, NEC
8732 Commercial Economic, Sociological & Educational Research
5046 Commercial Eqpt, NEC Wholesale
3582 Commercial Laundry, Dry Clean & Pressing Mchs
7335 Commercial Photography
8731 Commercial Physical & Biological Research
2759 Commercial Printing
2754 Commercial Printing: Gravure
2752 Commercial Printing: Lithographic
3646 Commercial, Indl & Institutional Lighting Fixtures
6221 Commodity Contracts Brokers & Dealers
4899 Communication Svcs, NEC
3669 Communications Eqpt, NEC
7376 Computer Facilities Management Svcs
7373 Computer Integrated Systems Design
7378 Computer Maintenance & Repair
3577 Computer Peripheral Eqpt, NEC
7379 Computer Related Svcs, NEC
7377 Computer Rental & Leasing
3572 Computer Storage Devices
3575 Computer Terminals
5045 Computers & Peripheral Eqpt & Software Wholesale
3271 Concrete Block & Brick
3272 Concrete Prdts
1771 Concrete Work
5145 Confectionery Wholesale
5082 Construction & Mining Mach & Eqpt Wholesale
3531 Construction Machinery & Eqpt
5039 Construction Materials, NEC Wholesale
1442 Construction Sand & Gravel
2679 Converted Paper Prdts, NEC
3535 Conveyors & Eqpt
2052 Cookies & Crackers
1021 Copper Ores
2298 Cordage & Twine
0115 Corn
2653 Corrugated & Solid Fiber Boxes
3961 Costume Jewelry & Novelties
2261 Cotton Fabric Finishers
2211 Cotton, Woven Fabric
4215 Courier Svcs, Except Air
6159 Credit Institutions, Misc Business
6153 Credit Institutions, Short-Term Business
7323 Credit Reporting Svcs
0191 Crop Farming, Misc
0722 Crop Harvesting By Machine
1311 Crude Petroleum & Natural Gas
1429 Crushed & Broken Stone, NEC
3643 Current-Carrying Wiring Devices
2391 Curtains & Draperies
7371 Custom Computer Programming Svcs
3281 Cut Stone Prdts
3421 Cutlery
2865 Cyclic-Crudes, Intermediates, Dyes & Org Pigments

D

0241 Dairy Farms
5143 Dairy Prdts, Except Dried Or Canned Wholesale
7911 Dance Studios, Schools & Halls
7374 Data & Computer Processing & Preparation
0175 Deciduous Tree Fruits
4424 Deep Sea Domestic Transportation Of Freight
4412 Deep Sea Foreign Transportation Of Freight
4481 Deep Sea Transportation Of Passengers
3843 Dental Eqpt & Splys
8072 Dental Laboratories
7381 Detective & Armored Car Svcs
2835 Diagnostic Substances
2675 Die-Cut Paper & Board
3544 Dies, Tools, Jigs, Fixtures & Indl Molds
1411 Dimension Stone
7331 Direct Mail Advertising Svcs
7342 Disinfecting & Pest Control Svcs
3942 Dolls & Stuffed Toys
2591 Drapery Hardware, Window Blinds & Shades
2381 Dress & Work Gloves
2034 Dried Fruits, Vegetables & Soup
1381 Drilling Oil & Gas Wells
5122 Drugs, Drug Proprietaries & Sundries Wholesale
7216 Dry Cleaning Plants, Except Rug Cleaning
5099 Durable Goods: NEC Wholesale

E

3263 Earthenware, Whiteware, Table & Kitchen Articles
6732 Education, Religious & Charitable Trusts
4931 Electric & Other Svcs Combined
3634 Electric Household Appliances
3641 Electric Lamps
4911 Electric Svcs
7629 Electrical & Elex Repair Shop, NEC
5064 Electrical Appliances, TV & Radios Wholesale
3694 Electrical Eqpt For Internal Combustion Engines
3629 Electrical Indl Apparatus, NEC
3699 Electrical Machinery, Eqpt & Splys, NEC
1731 Electrical Work
5063 Electrl Apparatus, Eqpt, Wiring Splys Wholesale
3313 Electrometallurgical Prdts
3845 Electromedical & Electrotherapeutic Apparatus
3677 Electronic Coils & Transformers
3679 Electronic Components, NEC
3571 Electronic Computers
5065 Electronic Parts & Eqpt Wholesale
3471 Electroplating, Plating, Polishing, Anodizing & Coloring
3534 Elevators & Moving Stairways
7361 Employment Agencies
3431 Enameled Iron & Metal Sanitary Ware
8711 Engineering Services
2677 Envelopes
7359 Equipment Rental & Leasing, NEC
1794 Excavating & Grading Work
2892 Explosives

F

2241 Fabric Mills, Cotton, Wool, Silk & Man-Made
3499 Fabricated Metal Prdts, NEC
3498 Fabricated Pipe & Pipe Fittings
3443 Fabricated Plate Work
3069 Fabricated Rubber Prdts, NEC
3441 Fabricated Structural Steel
2399 Fabricated Textile Prdts, NEC
2297 Fabrics, Nonwoven
8744 Facilities Support Mgmt Svcs
5083 Farm & Garden Mach & Eqpt Wholesale
3523 Farm Machinery & Eqpt
0762 Farm Management Svcs
4221 Farm Product Warehousing & Storage
5191 Farm Splys Wholesale
5159 Farm-Prdt Raw Mtrls, NEC Wholesale
3965 Fasteners, Buttons, Needles & Pins
6111 Federal Credit Agencies
6061 Federal Credit Unions

SIC INDEX

SIC NO	PRODUCT
6035	Federal Savings Institutions
4482	Ferries
1061	Ferroalloy Ores, Except Vanadium
2875	Fertilizers, Mixing Only
0139	Field Crops, Except Cash Grains, NEC
6331	Fire, Marine & Casualty Insurance
5146	Fish & Seafood Wholesale
2091	Fish & Seafoods, Canned & Cured
2092	Fish & Seafoods, Fresh & Frozen
4785	Fixed Facilities, Inspection, Weighing Svcs Transptn
2087	Flavoring Extracts & Syrups
1752	Floor Laying & Other Floor Work, NEC
2041	Flour, Grain Milling
5193	Flowers, Nursery Stock & Florists' Splys Wholesale
3824	Fluid Meters & Counters
3594	Fluid Power Pumps & Motors
3492	Fluid Power Valves & Hose Fittings
0182	Food Crops Grown Under Cover
3556	Food Prdts Machinery
2099	Food Preparations, NEC
5139	Footwear Wholesale
0851	Forestry Svcs
4731	Freight Forwarding & Arrangement
5148	Fresh Fruits & Vegetables Wholesale
2037	Frozen Fruits, Juices & Vegetables
2038	Frozen Specialties
6099	Functions Related To Deposit Banking, NEC
7261	Funeral Svcs & Crematories
2599	Furniture & Fixtures, NEC
5021	Furniture Wholesale

G

SIC NO	PRODUCT
3944	Games, Toys & Children's Vehicles
3524	Garden, Lawn Tractors & Eqpt
7212	Garment Pressing & Cleaners' Agents
4932	Gas & Other Svcs Combined
4925	Gas Production &/Or Distribution
3053	Gaskets, Packing & Sealing Devices
7538	General Automotive Repair Shop
1541	General Contractors, Indl Bldgs & Warehouses
1542	General Contractors, Nonresidential & Non-indl Bldgs
1522	General Contractors, Residential Other Than Single Family
1521	General Contractors, Single Family Houses
8062	General Medical & Surgical Hospitals
4225	General Warehousing & Storage
2369	Girls' & Infants' Outerwear, NEC
1793	Glass & Glazing Work
3221	Glass Containers
3231	Glass Prdts Made Of Purchased Glass
5153	Grain & Field Beans Wholesale
3321	Gray Iron Foundries
2771	Greeting Card Publishing
5149	Groceries & Related Prdts, NEC Wholesale
5141	Groceries, General Line Wholesale
3761	Guided Missiles & Space Vehicles

H

SIC NO	PRODUCT
3423	Hand & Edge Tools
3171	Handbags & Purses
5072	Hardware Wholesale
3429	Hardware, NEC
2426	Hardwood Dimension & Flooring Mills
2435	Hardwood Veneer & Plywood
2353	Hats, Caps & Millinery
8099	Health & Allied Svcs, NEC
5075	Heating & Air Conditioning Eqpt & Splys Wholesale
3433	Heating Eqpt
7353	Heavy Construction Eqpt Rental & Leasing
1629	Heavy Construction, NEC
7363	Help Supply Svcs
1611	Highway & Street Construction
0213	Hogs
5023	Home Furnishings Wholesale
8082	Home Health Care Svcs
0272	Horse & Other Equine Production
2252	Hosiery, Except Women's
6324	Hospital & Medical Svc Plans Carriers
7011	Hotels, Motels & Tourist Courts
2392	House furnishings: Textile
3651	Household Audio & Video Eqpt
3631	Household Cooking Eqpt
2519	Household Furniture, NEC
3635	Household Vacuum Cleaners
0971	Hunting & Trapping

I

SIC NO	PRODUCT
2097	Ice
2024	Ice Cream
8322	Individual & Family Social Svcs
5113	Indl & Personal Svc Paper Wholesale
2819	Indl Inorganic Chemicals, NEC
3823	Indl Instruments For Meas, Display & Control
3569	Indl Machinery & Eqpt, NEC
3567	Indl Process Furnaces & Ovens
3537	Indl Trucks, Tractors, Trailers & Stackers
2813	Industrial Gases
7218	Industrial Launderers
5084	Industrial Mach & Eqpt Wholesale
2869	Industrial Organic Chemicals, NEC
3543	Industrial Patterns
1446	Industrial Sand
5085	Industrial Splys Wholesale
3491	Industrial Valves
7375	Information Retrieval Svcs
2816	Inorganic Pigments
1796	Installation Or Erection Of Bldg Eqpt & Machinery, NEC
3825	Instrs For Measuring & Testing Electricity
6411	Insurance Agents, Brokers & Svc
6399	Insurance Carriers, NEC
4131	Intercity & Rural Bus Transportation
8052	Intermediate Care Facilities
3519	Internal Combustion Engines, NEC
6282	Investment Advice
6799	Investors, NEC
0134	Irish Potatoes
3462	Iron & Steel Forgings
1011	Iron Ores
4971	Irrigation Systems

J

SIC NO	PRODUCT
3915	Jewelers Findings & Lapidary Work
5094	Jewelry, Watches, Precious Stones Wholesale
3911	Jewelry: Precious Metal
8331	Job Training & Vocational Rehabilitation Svcs

K

SIC NO	PRODUCT
8092	Kidney Dialysis Centers
2253	Knit Outerwear Mills
2254	Knit Underwear Mills

L

SIC NO	PRODUCT
8631	Labor Unions & Similar Organizations
3821	Laboratory Apparatus & Furniture
6552	Land Subdividers & Developers
0781	Landscape Counseling & Planning
7219	Laundry & Garment Svcs, NEC
0782	Lawn & Garden Svcs
3952	Lead Pencils, Crayons & Artist's Mtrls
3151	Leather Gloves & Mittens
3199	Leather Goods, NEC
3111	Leather Tanning & Finishing
8111	Legal Svcs
6519	Lessors Of Real Estate, NEC
6311	Life Insurance Carriers
3648	Lighting Eqpt, NEC
7213	Linen Sply
3996	Linoleum & Hard Surface Floor Coverings, NEC
2085	Liquors, Distilled, Rectified & Blended
0751	Livestock Svcs, Except Veterinary
6163	Loan Brokers
4111	Local & Suburban Transit
4141	Local Bus Charter Svc
4119	Local Passenger Transportation: NEC
4214	Local Trucking With Storage
4212	Local Trucking Without Storage
2411	Logging
2992	Lubricating Oils & Greases
3161	Luggage
5031	Lumber, Plywood & Millwork Wholesale

M

SIC NO	PRODUCT
3545	Machine Tool Access
3541	Machine Tools: Cutting
3542	Machine Tools: Forming
3599	Machinery & Eqpt, Indl & Commercial, NEC
2083	Malt
2082	Malt Beverages
8742	Management Consulting Services
6722	Management Investment Offices
8741	Management Services
2761	Manifold Business Forms
3999	Manufacturing Industries, NEC
4493	Marinas
4491	Marine Cargo Handling
0919	Marine Fishing, Misc
3953	Marking Devices
1741	Masonry & Other Stonework
2515	Mattresses & Bedsprings
3829	Measuring & Controlling Devices, NEC
2011	Meat Packing Plants
5147	Meats & Meat Prdts Wholesale
3568	Mechanical Power Transmission Eqpt, NEC
7352	Medical Eqpt Rental & Leasing
8071	Medical Laboratories
5047	Medical, Dental & Hospital Eqpt & Splys Wholesale
2833	Medicinal Chemicals & Botanical Prdts
8699	Membership Organizations, NEC
7997	Membership Sports & Recreation Clubs
7041	Membership-Basis Hotels
5136	Men's & Boys' Clothing & Furnishings Wholesale
2329	Men's & Boys' Clothing, NEC
2323	Men's & Boys' Neckwear
2325	Men's & Boys' Separate Trousers & Casual Slacks
2321	Men's & Boys' Shirts
2311	Men's & Boys' Suits, Coats & Overcoats
2326	Men's & Boys' Work Clothing
3412	Metal Barrels, Drums, Kegs & Pails
3411	Metal Cans
3442	Metal Doors, Sash, Frames, Molding & Trim
3398	Metal Heat Treating
2514	Metal Household Furniture
1081	Metal Mining Svcs
1099	Metal Ores, NEC
3469	Metal Stampings, NEC
5051	Metals Service Centers
3549	Metalworking Machinery, NEC
2026	Milk
2023	Milk, Condensed & Evaporated
2431	Millwork
3296	Mineral Wool
3295	Minerals & Earths: Ground Or Treated
3496	Misc Fabricated Wire Prdts
2741	Misc Publishing
3449	Misc Structural Metal Work
1499	Miscellaneous Nonmetallic Mining
7299	Miscellaneous Personal Svcs, NEC
2451	Mobile Homes
3061	Molded, Extruded & Lathe-Cut Rubber Mechanical Goods
6162	Mortgage Bankers & Loan Correspondents
7822	Motion Picture & Video Tape Distribution
7812	Motion Picture & Video Tape Production
7832	Motion Picture Theaters, Except Drive-In
3714	Motor Vehicle Parts & Access
5015	Motor Vehicle Parts, Used Wholesale
5013	Motor Vehicle Splys & New Parts Wholesale
3711	Motor Vehicles & Car Bodies
3751	Motorcycles, Bicycles & Parts
3621	Motors & Generators
8412	Museums & Art Galleries
3931	Musical Instruments

N

SIC NO	PRODUCT
6021	National Commercial Banks
4924	Natural Gas Distribution
1321	Natural Gas Liquids
4922	Natural Gas Transmission
4923	Natural Gas Transmission & Distribution
7383	News Syndicates
2711	Newspapers: Publishing & Printing
2873	Nitrogenous Fertilizers
3297	Nonclay Refractories
8733	Noncommercial Research Organizations
3644	Noncurrent-Carrying Wiring Devices
6091	Nondeposit Trust Facilities
5199	Nondurable Goods, NEC Wholesale
3463	Nonferrous Forgings
3369	Nonferrous Foundries: Castings, NEC
3357	Nonferrous Wire Drawing
3299	Nonmetallic Mineral Prdts, NEC
1481	Nonmetallic Minerals Svcs, Except Fuels
8059	Nursing & Personal Care Facilities, NEC

O

SIC NO	PRODUCT
5044	Office Eqpt Wholesale
2522	Office Furniture, Except Wood
3579	Office Machines, NEC
8041	Offices & Clinics Of Chiropractors
8021	Offices & Clinics Of Dentists
8011	Offices & Clinics Of Doctors Of Medicine
8031	Offices & Clinics Of Doctors Of Osteopathy
8049	Offices & Clinics Of Health Practitioners, NEC
8042	Offices & Clinics Of Optometrists
8043	Offices & Clinics Of Podiatrists
6712	Offices Of Bank Holding Co's
6719	Offices Of Holding Co's, NEC
1382	Oil & Gas Field Exploration Svcs
1389	Oil & Gas Field Svcs, NEC
3533	Oil Field Machinery & Eqpt

SIC INDEX

SIC NO	PRODUCT
1531	Operative Builders
6513	Operators Of Apartment Buildings
6514	Operators Of Dwellings, Except Apartments
6512	Operators Of Nonresidential Bldgs
6515	Operators of Residential Mobile Home Sites
3851	Ophthalmic Goods
5048	Ophthalmic Goods Wholesale
3827	Optical Instruments
0181	Ornamental Floriculture & Nursery Prdts
0783	Ornamental Shrub & Tree Svc
3842	Orthopedic, Prosthetic & Surgical Appliances/Splys
7312	Outdoor Advertising Svcs

P

SIC NO	PRODUCT
5142	Packaged Frozen Foods Wholesale
3565	Packaging Machinery
4783	Packing & Crating Svcs
1721	Painting & Paper Hanging Contractors
5198	Paints, Varnishes & Splys Wholesale
2851	Paints, Varnishes, Lacquers, Enamels
2671	Paper Coating & Laminating for Packaging
2672	Paper Coating & Laminating, Exc for Packaging
2621	Paper Mills
2542	Partitions & Fixtures, Except Wood
7515	Passenger Car Leasing
7514	Passenger Car Rental
4729	Passenger Transportation Arrangement, NEC
6794	Patent Owners & Lessors
2951	Paving Mixtures & Blocks
6371	Pension, Health & Welfare Funds
2844	Perfumes, Cosmetics & Toilet Preparations
2721	Periodicals: Publishing & Printing
6141	Personal Credit Institutions
3172	Personal Leather Goods
2879	Pesticides & Agricultural Chemicals, NEC
5172	Petroleum & Petroleum Prdts Wholesale
5171	Petroleum Bulk Stations & Terminals
2911	Petroleum Refining
2834	Pharmaceuticals
3652	Phonograph Records & Magnetic Tape
2874	Phosphatic Fertilizers
7334	Photocopying & Duplicating Svcs
7384	Photofinishing Labs
3861	Photographic Eqpt & Splys
5043	Photographic Eqpt & Splys Wholesale
7221	Photographic Studios, Portrait
7991	Physical Fitness Facilities
2035	Pickled Fruits, Vegetables, Sauces & Dressings
5131	Piece Goods, Notions & Dry Goods Wholesale
1742	Plastering, Drywall, Acoustical & Insulation Work
3085	Plastic Bottles
3086	Plastic Foam Prdts
3083	Plastic Laminated Plate & Sheet
3088	Plastic Plumbing Fixtures
3089	Plastic Prdts
3082	Plastic Unsupported Profile Shapes
3081	Plastic Unsupported Sheet & Film
5162	Plastics Materials & Basic Shapes Wholesale
2821	Plastics, Mtrls & Nonvulcanizable Elastomers
2796	Platemaking & Related Svcs
2395	Pleating & Stitching For The Trade
5074	Plumbing & Heating Splys Wholesale
3432	Plumbing Fixture Fittings & Trim, Brass
1711	Plumbing, Heating & Air Conditioning Contractors
8651	Political Organizations
3264	Porcelain Electrical Splys
2096	Potato Chips & Similar Prdts
3269	Pottery Prdts, NEC
5144	Poultry & Poultry Prdts Wholesale
0254	Poultry Hatcheries
2015	Poultry Slaughtering, Dressing & Processing
3546	Power Hand Tools
7211	Power Laundries, Family & Commercial
3612	Power, Distribution & Specialty Transformers
3448	Prefabricated Metal Buildings & Cmpnts
2452	Prefabricated Wood Buildings & Cmpnts
7372	Prepackaged Software
2048	Prepared Feeds For Animals & Fowls
3229	Pressed & Blown Glassware, NEC
3692	Primary Batteries: Dry & Wet
3399	Primary Metal Prdts, NEC
3672	Printed Circuit Boards
2893	Printing Ink
3555	Printing Trades Machinery & Eqpt
5049	Professional Eqpt & Splys, NEC Wholesale
8621	Professional Membership Organizations
7941	Professional Sports Clubs & Promoters
8063	Psychiatric Hospitals
2531	Public Building & Related Furniture
7992	Public Golf Courses
8743	Public Relations Svcs
2611	Pulp Mills
3561	Pumps & Pumping Eqpt

R

SIC NO	PRODUCT
7948	Racing & Track Operations
3663	Radio & T V Communications, Systs & Eqpt, Broadcast/Studio
7622	Radio & TV Repair Shops
4832	Radio Broadcasting Stations
7313	Radio, TV & Publishers Adv Reps
4812	Radiotelephone Communications
4741	Railroad Car Rental
3743	Railroad Eqpt
4011	Railroads, Line-Hauling Operations
3273	Ready-Mixed Concrete
6531	Real Estate Agents & Managers
6798	Real Estate Investment Trusts
2493	Reconstituted Wood Prdts
3695	Recording Media
4222	Refrigerated Warehousing & Storage
7623	Refrigeration & Air Conditioning Svc & Repair Shop
5078	Refrigeration Eqpt & Splys Wholesale
4953	Refuse Systems
3625	Relays & Indl Controls
7699	Repair Shop & Related Svcs, NEC
8361	Residential Care
3645	Residential Lighting Fixtures
7641	Reupholstery & Furniture Repair
3356	Rolling, Drawing-Extruding Of Nonferrous Metals
5033	Roofing, Siding & Insulation Mtrls Wholesale
1761	Roofing, Siding & Sheet Metal Work
7021	Rooming & Boarding Houses
3052	Rubber & Plastic Hose & Belting

S

SIC NO	PRODUCT
2068	Salted & Roasted Nuts & Seeds
2676	Sanitary Paper Prdts
4959	Sanitary Svcs, NEC
2013	Sausages & Meat Prdts
6036	Savings Institutions, Except Federal
2421	Saw & Planing Mills
3596	Scales & Balances, Exc Laboratory
4151	School Buses
5093	Scrap & Waste Materials Wholesale
3812	Search, Detection, Navigation & Guidance Systs & Instrs
3341	Secondary Smelting & Refining Of Nonferrous Metals
7338	Secretarial & Court Reporting Svcs
6231	Security & Commodity Exchanges
6211	Security Brokers & Dealers
7382	Security Systems Svcs
3674	Semiconductors
5087	Service Establishment Eqpt & Splys Wholesale
3589	Service Ind Machines, NEC
7819	Services Allied To Motion Picture Prdtn
8999	Services Not Elsewhere Classified
4952	Sewerage Systems
3444	Sheet Metal Work
0913	Shellfish Fishing
7251	Shoe Repair & Shoeshine Parlors
2079	Shortening, Oils & Margarine
3993	Signs & Advertising Displays
2221	Silk & Man-Made Fiber
3914	Silverware, Plated & Stainless Steel Ware
8051	Skilled Nursing Facilities
3484	Small Arms
3482	Small Arms Ammunition
2841	Soap & Detergents
8399	Social Services, NEC
2086	Soft Drinks
0711	Soil Preparation Svcs
0721	Soil Preparation, Planting & Cultivating Svc
0116	Soybeans
2842	Spec Cleaning, Polishing & Sanitation Preparations
3559	Special Ind Machinery, NEC
1799	Special Trade Contractors, NEC
4226	Special Warehousing & Storage, NEC
8069	Specialty Hospitals, Except Psychiatric
8093	Specialty Outpatient Facilities, NEC
3566	Speed Changers, Drives & Gears
3949	Sporting & Athletic Goods, NEC
7032	Sporting & Recreational Camps
5091	Sporting & Recreational Goods & Splys Wholesale
6022	State Commercial Banks
6062	State Credit Unions
5112	Stationery & Office Splys Wholesale
3511	Steam, Gas & Hydraulic Turbines & Engines
3324	Steel Investment Foundries
3317	Steel Pipe & Tubes
3315	Steel Wire Drawing & Nails & Spikes
3691	Storage Batteries
1791	Structural Steel Erection
2439	Structural Wood Members, NEC
6351	Surety Insurance Carriers
2843	Surface Active & Finishing Agents, Sulfonated Oils
3841	Surgical & Medical Instrs & Apparatus
8713	Surveying Services
3613	Switchgear & Switchboard Apparatus
4013	Switching & Terminal Svcs
2824	Synthetic Organic Fibers, Exc Cellulosic
2822	Synthetic Rubber (Vulcanizable Elastomers)

T

SIC NO	PRODUCT
3795	Tanks & Tank Components
7291	Tax Return Preparation Svcs
4121	Taxi Cabs
4822	Telegraph & Other Message Communications
3661	Telephone & Telegraph Apparatus
4813	Telephone Communications, Except Radio
4833	Television Broadcasting Stations
4231	Terminal & Joint Terminal Maint Facilities
1743	Terrazzo, Tile, Marble & Mosaic Work
8734	Testing Laboratories
2393	Textile Bags
2269	Textile Finishers, NEC
2299	Textile Goods, NEC
7922	Theatrical Producers & Misc Theatrical Svcs
0811	Timber Tracts
7534	Tire Retreading & Repair Shops
3011	Tires & Inner Tubes
5014	Tires & Tubes Wholesale
6541	Title Abstract Offices
6361	Title Insurance
0132	Tobacco
5194	Tobacco & Tobacco Prdts Wholesale
7532	Top, Body & Upholstery Repair & Paint Shops
4725	Tour Operators
4492	Towing & Tugboat Svcs
5092	Toys & Hobby Goods & Splys Wholesale
7033	Trailer Parks & Camp Sites
5088	Transportation Eqpt & Splys, Except Motor Vehicles Wholesale
3799	Transportation Eqpt, NEC
4789	Transportation Svcs, NEC
4724	Travel Agencies
3713	Truck & Bus Bodies
7513	Truck Rental & Leasing, Without Drivers
3715	Truck Trailers
4213	Trucking, Except Local
6733	Trusts Except Educational, Religious & Charitable
2791	Typesetting

U

SIC NO	PRODUCT
6726	Unit Investment Trusts, Face-Amount Certificate Offices
7519	Utility Trailers & Recreational Vehicle Rental

V

SIC NO	PRODUCT
3494	Valves & Pipe Fittings, NEC
0161	Vegetables & Melons
3647	Vehicular Lighting Eqpt
0742	Veterinary Animal Specialties
7841	Video Tape Rental

W

SIC NO	PRODUCT
3873	Watch & Clock Devices & Parts
7631	Watch, Clock & Jewelry Repair
4941	Water Sply
4489	Water Transport Of Passengers, NEC
4449	Water Transportation Of Freight, NEC
1781	Water Well Drilling
1623	Water, Sewer & Utility Line Construction
3548	Welding Apparatus
7692	Welding Repair
0111	Wheat
2084	Wine & Brandy
5182	Wine & Distilled Alcoholic Beverages Wholesale
3495	Wire Springs
2331	Women's & Misses' Blouses
2335	Women's & Misses' Dresses
2339	Women's & Misses' Outerwear, NEC
2337	Women's & Misses' Suits, Coats & Skirts
5137	Women's, Children's & Infants Clothing Wholesale
2341	Women's, Misses' & Children's Underwear & Nightwear
2441	Wood Boxes
2449	Wood Containers, NEC
2511	Wood Household Furniture
2512	Wood Household Furniture, Upholstered
2434	Wood Kitchen Cabinets
2521	Wood Office Furniture
2448	Wood Pallets & Skids

SIC INDEX

SIC NO	PRODUCT
2499	Wood Prdts, NEC
2491	Wood Preserving
2517	Wood T V, Radio, Phono & Sewing Cabinets
2541	Wood, Office & Store Fixtures
2231	Wool, Woven Fabric

SIC NO	PRODUCT
1795	Wrecking & Demolition Work

X

SIC NO	PRODUCT
3844	X-ray Apparatus & Tubes

Y

SIC NO	PRODUCT
2282	Yarn Texturizing, Throwing, Twisting & Winding Mills

SIC INDEX

Standard Industrial Classification Numerical Index

SIC NO	PRODUCT

01 agricultural production-crops
0111 Wheat
0115 Corn
0116 Soybeans
0119 Cash Grains, NEC
0132 Tobacco
0134 Irish Potatoes
0139 Field Crops, Except Cash Grains, NEC
0161 Vegetables & Melons
0171 Berry Crops
0175 Deciduous Tree Fruits
0181 Ornamental Floriculture & Nursery Prdts
0182 Food Crops Grown Under Cover
0191 Crop Farming, Misc

02 agricultural production-livestock and animal specialties
0211 Beef Cattle Feedlots
0212 Beef Cattle, Except Feedlots
0213 Hogs
0241 Dairy Farms
0251 Chicken & Poultry Farms
0252 Chicken Egg Farms
0254 Poultry Hatcheries
0272 Horse & Other Equine Production
0279 Animal Specialties, NEC
0291 Animal Production, NEC

07 agricultural services
0711 Soil Preparation Svcs
0721 Soil Preparation, Planting & Cultivating Svc
0722 Crop Harvesting By Machine
0742 Veterinary Animal Specialties
0751 Livestock Svcs, Except Veterinary
0752 Animal Specialty Svcs, Exc Veterinary
0762 Farm Management Svcs
0781 Landscape Counseling & Planning
0782 Lawn & Garden Svcs
0783 Ornamental Shrub & Tree Svc

08 forestry
0811 Timber Tracts
0851 Forestry Svcs

09 fishing, hunting, and trapping
0913 Shellfish Fishing
0919 Marine Fishing, Misc
0971 Hunting & Trapping

10 metal mining
1011 Iron Ores
1021 Copper Ores
1061 Ferroalloy Ores, Except Vanadium
1081 Metal Mining Svcs
1099 Metal Ores, NEC

13 oil and gas extraction
1311 Crude Petroleum & Natural Gas
1321 Natural Gas Liquids
1381 Drilling Oil & Gas Wells
1382 Oil & Gas Field Exploration Svcs
1389 Oil & Gas Field Svcs, NEC

14 mining and quarrying of nonmetallic minerals, except fuels
1411 Dimension Stone
1429 Crushed & Broken Stone, NEC
1442 Construction Sand & Gravel
1446 Industrial Sand
1459 Clay, Ceramic & Refractory Minerals, NEC
1479 Chemical & Fertilizer Mining
1481 Nonmetallic Minerals Svcs, Except Fuels
1499 Miscellaneous Nonmetallic Mining

15 building construction-general contractors and operative builders
1521 General Contractors, Single Family Houses
1522 General Contractors, Residential Other Than Single Family
1531 Operative Builders
1541 General Contractors, Indl Bldgs & Warehouses
1542 General Contractors, Nonresidential & Non-indl Bldgs

16 heavy construction other than building construction-contractors
1611 Highway & Street Construction
1622 Bridge, Tunnel & Elevated Hwy Construction
1623 Water, Sewer & Utility Line Construction
1629 Heavy Construction, NEC

17 construction-special trade contractors
1711 Plumbing, Heating & Air Conditioning Contractors
1721 Painting & Paper Hanging Contractors
1731 Electrical Work
1741 Masonry & Other Stonework
1742 Plastering, Drywall, Acoustical & Insulation Work
1743 Terrazzo, Tile, Marble & Mosaic Work
1751 Carpentry Work
1752 Floor Laying & Other Floor Work, NEC
1761 Roofing, Siding & Sheet Metal Work
1771 Concrete Work
1781 Water Well Drilling
1791 Structural Steel Erection
1793 Glass & Glazing Work
1794 Excavating & Grading Work
1795 Wrecking & Demolition Work
1796 Installation Or Erection Of Bldg Eqpt & Machinery, NEC
1799 Special Trade Contractors, NEC

20 food and kindred products
2011 Meat Packing Plants
2013 Sausages & Meat Prdts
2015 Poultry Slaughtering, Dressing & Processing
2021 Butter
2022 Cheese
2023 Milk, Condensed & Evaporated
2024 Ice Cream
2026 Milk
2032 Canned Specialties
2033 Canned Fruits, Vegetables & Preserves
2034 Dried Fruits, Vegetables & Soup
2035 Pickled Fruits, Vegetables, Sauces & Dressings
2037 Frozen Fruits, Juices & Vegetables
2038 Frozen Specialties
2041 Flour, Grain Milling
2048 Prepared Feeds For Animals & Fowls
2051 Bread, Bakery Prdts Exc Cookies & Crackers
2052 Cookies & Crackers
2064 Candy & Confectionery Prdts
2066 Chocolate & Cocoa Prdts
2068 Salted & Roasted Nuts & Seeds
2079 Shortening, Oils & Margarine
2082 Malt Beverages
2083 Malt
2084 Wine & Brandy
2085 Liquors, Distilled, Rectified & Blended
2086 Soft Drinks
2087 Flavoring Extracts & Syrups
2091 Fish & Seafoods, Canned & Cured
2092 Fish & Seafoods, Fresh & Frozen
2095 Coffee
2096 Potato Chips & Similar Prdts
2097 Ice
2099 Food Preparations, NEC

21 tobacco products
2111 Cigarettes

22 textile mill products
2211 Cotton, Woven Fabric
2221 Silk & Man-Made Fiber
2231 Wool, Woven Fabric
2241 Fabric Mills, Cotton, Wool, Silk & Man-Made
2252 Hosiery, Except Women's
2253 Knit Outerwear Mills
2254 Knit Underwear Mills
2261 Cotton Fabric Finishers
2269 Textile Finishers, NEC
2273 Carpets & Rugs
2282 Yarn Texturizing, Throwing, Twisting & Winding Mills
2297 Fabrics, Nonwoven
2298 Cordage & Twine
2299 Textile Goods, NEC

23 apparel and other finished products made from fabrics and similar material
2311 Men's & Boys' Suits, Coats & Overcoats
2321 Men's & Boys' Shirts
2323 Men's & Boys' Neckwear
2325 Men's & Boys' Separate Trousers & Casual Slacks
2326 Men's & Boys' Work Clothing
2329 Men's & Boys' Clothing, NEC
2331 Women's & Misses' Blouses
2335 Women's & Misses' Dresses
2337 Women's & Misses' Suits, Coats & Skirts
2339 Women's & Misses' Outerwear, NEC
2341 Women's, Misses' & Children's Underwear & Nightwear
2353 Hats, Caps & Millinery
2361 Children's & Infants' Dresses & Blouses
2369 Girls' & Infants' Outerwear, NEC
2381 Dress & Work Gloves
2389 Apparel & Accessories, NEC
2391 Curtains & Draperies
2392 House furnishings: Textile
2393 Textile Bags
2394 Canvas Prdts
2395 Pleating & Stitching For The Trade
2396 Automotive Trimmings, Apparel Findings, Related Prdts
2399 Fabricated Textile Prdts, NEC

24 lumber and wood products, except furniture
2411 Logging
2421 Saw & Planing Mills
2426 Hardwood Dimension & Flooring Mills
2431 Millwork
2434 Wood Kitchen Cabinets
2435 Hardwood Veneer & Plywood
2439 Structural Wood Members, NEC
2441 Wood Boxes
2448 Wood Pallets & Skids
2449 Wood Containers, NEC
2451 Mobile Homes
2452 Prefabricated Wood Buildings & Cmpnts
2491 Wood Preserving
2493 Reconstituted Wood Prdts
2499 Wood Prdts, NEC

25 furniture and fixtures
2511 Wood Household Furniture
2512 Wood Household Furniture, Upholstered
2514 Metal Household Furniture
2515 Mattresses & Bedsprings
2517 Wood T V, Radio, Phono & Sewing Cabinets
2519 Household Furniture, NEC
2521 Wood Office Furniture
2522 Office Furniture, Except Wood
2531 Public Building & Related Furniture
2541 Wood, Office & Store Fixtures
2542 Partitions & Fixtures, Except Wood
2591 Drapery Hardware, Window Blinds & Shades
2599 Furniture & Fixtures, NEC

26 paper and allied products
2611 Pulp Mills
2621 Paper Mills
2653 Corrugated & Solid Fiber Boxes
2671 Paper Coating & Laminating for Packaging
2672 Paper Coating & Laminating, Exc for Packaging
2673 Bags: Plastics, Laminated & Coated
2674 Bags: Uncoated Paper & Multiwall
2675 Die-Cut Paper & Board
2676 Sanitary Paper Prdts
2677 Envelopes
2679 Converted Paper Prdts, NEC

27 printing, publishing, and allied industries
2711 Newspapers: Publishing & Printing
2721 Periodicals: Publishing & Printing
2731 Books: Publishing & Printing
2732 Book Printing, Not Publishing
2741 Misc Publishing
2752 Commercial Printing: Lithographic
2754 Commercial Printing: Gravure
2759 Commercial Printing
2761 Manifold Business Forms
2771 Greeting Card Publishing
2782 Blankbooks & Looseleaf Binders

SIC INDEX

SIC NO	PRODUCT
2789	Bookbinding
2791	Typesetting
2796	Platemaking & Related Svcs

28 chemicals and allied products
- 2812 Alkalies & Chlorine
- 2813 Industrial Gases
- 2816 Inorganic Pigments
- 2819 Indl Inorganic Chemicals, NEC
- 2821 Plastics, Mtrls & Nonvulcanizable Elastomers
- 2822 Synthetic Rubber (Vulcanizable Elastomers)
- 2823 Cellulosic Man-Made Fibers
- 2824 Synthetic Organic Fibers, Exc Cellulosic
- 2833 Medicinal Chemicals & Botanical Prdts
- 2834 Pharmaceuticals
- 2835 Diagnostic Substances
- 2836 Biological Prdts, Exc Diagnostic Substances
- 2841 Soap & Detergents
- 2842 Spec Cleaning, Polishing & Sanitation Preparations
- 2843 Surface Active & Finishing Agents, Sulfonated Oils
- 2844 Perfumes, Cosmetics & Toilet Preparations
- 2851 Paints, Varnishes, Lacquers, Enamels
- 2865 Cyclic-Crudes, Intermediates, Dyes & Org Pigments
- 2869 Industrial Organic Chemicals, NEC
- 2873 Nitrogenous Fertilizers
- 2874 Phosphatic Fertilizers
- 2875 Fertilizers, Mixing Only
- 2879 Pesticides & Agricultural Chemicals, NEC
- 2891 Adhesives & Sealants
- 2892 Explosives
- 2893 Printing Ink
- 2899 Chemical Preparations, NEC

29 petroleum refining and related industries
- 2911 Petroleum Refining
- 2951 Paving Mixtures & Blocks
- 2952 Asphalt Felts & Coatings
- 2992 Lubricating Oils & Greases

30 rubber and miscellaneous plastics products
- 3011 Tires & Inner Tubes
- 3052 Rubber & Plastic Hose & Belting
- 3053 Gaskets, Packing & Sealing Devices
- 3061 Molded, Extruded & Lathe-Cut Rubber Mechanical Goods
- 3069 Fabricated Rubber Prdts, NEC
- 3081 Plastic Unsupported Sheet & Film
- 3082 Plastic Unsupported Profile Shapes
- 3083 Plastic Laminated Plate & Sheet
- 3085 Plastic Bottles
- 3086 Plastic Foam Prdts
- 3088 Plastic Plumbing Fixtures
- 3089 Plastic Prdts

31 leather and leather products
- 3111 Leather Tanning & Finishing
- 3131 Boot & Shoe Cut Stock & Findings
- 3151 Leather Gloves & Mittens
- 3161 Luggage
- 3171 Handbags & Purses
- 3172 Personal Leather Goods
- 3199 Leather Goods, NEC

32 stone, clay, glass, and concrete products
- 3221 Glass Containers
- 3229 Pressed & Blown Glassware, NEC
- 3231 Glass Prdts Made Of Purchased Glass
- 3241 Cement, Hydraulic
- 3253 Ceramic Tile
- 3255 Clay Refractories
- 3261 China Plumbing Fixtures & Fittings
- 3262 China, Table & Kitchen Articles
- 3263 Earthenware, Whiteware, Table & Kitchen Articles
- 3264 Porcelain Electrical Splys
- 3269 Pottery Prdts, NEC
- 3271 Concrete Block & Brick
- 3272 Concrete Prdts
- 3273 Ready-Mixed Concrete
- 3281 Cut Stone Prdts
- 3291 Abrasive Prdts
- 3295 Minerals & Earths: Ground Or Treated
- 3296 Mineral Wool
- 3297 Nonclay Refractories
- 3299 Nonmetallic Mineral Prdts, NEC

33 primary metal industries
- 3312 Blast Furnaces, Coke Ovens, Steel & Rolling Mills
- 3313 Electrometallurgical Prdts
- 3315 Steel Wire Drawing & Nails & Spikes
- 3316 Cold Rolled Steel Sheet, Strip & Bars
- 3317 Steel Pipe & Tubes
- 3321 Gray Iron Foundries
- 3324 Steel Investment Foundries
- 3341 Secondary Smelting & Refining Of Nonferrous Metals
- 3353 Aluminum Sheet, Plate & Foil
- 3354 Aluminum Extruded Prdts
- 3355 Aluminum Rolling & Drawing, NEC
- 3356 Rolling, Drawing-Extruding Of Nonferrous Metals
- 3357 Nonferrous Wire Drawing
- 3369 Nonferrous Foundries: Castings, NEC
- 3398 Metal Heat Treating
- 3399 Primary Metal Prdts, NEC

34 fabricated metal products, except machinery and transportation equipment
- 3411 Metal Cans
- 3412 Metal Barrels, Drums, Kegs & Pails
- 3421 Cutlery
- 3423 Hand & Edge Tools
- 3429 Hardware, NEC
- 3431 Enameled Iron & Metal Sanitary Ware
- 3432 Plumbing Fixture Fittings & Trim, Brass
- 3433 Heating Eqpt
- 3441 Fabricated Structural Steel
- 3442 Metal Doors, Sash, Frames, Molding & Trim
- 3443 Fabricated Plate Work
- 3444 Sheet Metal Work
- 3446 Architectural & Ornamental Metal Work
- 3448 Prefabricated Metal Buildings & Cmpnts
- 3449 Misc Structural Metal Work
- 3452 Bolts, Nuts, Screws, Rivets & Washers
- 3462 Iron & Steel Forgings
- 3463 Nonferrous Forgings
- 3465 Automotive Stampings
- 3469 Metal Stampings, NEC
- 3471 Electroplating, Plating, Polishing, Anodizing & Coloring
- 3479 Coating & Engraving, NEC
- 3482 Small Arms Ammunition
- 3484 Small Arms
- 3491 Industrial Valves
- 3492 Fluid Power Valves & Hose Fittings
- 3494 Valves & Pipe Fittings, NEC
- 3495 Wire Springs
- 3496 Misc Fabricated Wire Prdts
- 3498 Fabricated Pipe & Pipe Fittings
- 3499 Fabricated Metal Prdts, NEC

35 industrial and commercial machinery and computer equipment
- 3511 Steam, Gas & Hydraulic Turbines & Engines
- 3519 Internal Combustion Engines, NEC
- 3523 Farm Machinery & Eqpt
- 3524 Garden, Lawn Tractors & Eqpt
- 3531 Construction Machinery & Eqpt
- 3533 Oil Field Machinery & Eqpt
- 3534 Elevators & Moving Stairways
- 3535 Conveyors & Eqpt
- 3537 Indl Trucks, Tractors, Trailers & Stackers
- 3541 Machine Tools: Cutting
- 3542 Machine Tools: Forming
- 3543 Industrial Patterns
- 3544 Dies, Tools, Jigs, Fixtures & Indl Molds
- 3545 Machine Tool Access
- 3546 Power Hand Tools
- 3548 Welding Apparatus
- 3549 Metalworking Machinery, NEC
- 3555 Printing Trades Machinery & Eqpt
- 3556 Food Prdts Machinery
- 3559 Special Ind Machinery, NEC
- 3561 Pumps & Pumping Eqpt
- 3562 Ball & Roller Bearings
- 3563 Air & Gas Compressors
- 3564 Blowers & Fans
- 3565 Packaging Machinery
- 3566 Speed Changers, Drives & Gears
- 3567 Indl Process Furnaces & Ovens
- 3568 Mechanical Power Transmission Eqpt, NEC
- 3569 Indl Machinery & Eqpt, NEC
- 3571 Electronic Computers
- 3572 Computer Storage Devices
- 3575 Computer Terminals
- 3577 Computer Peripheral Eqpt, NEC
- 3578 Calculating & Accounting Eqpt
- 3579 Office Machines, NEC
- 3581 Automatic Vending Machines
- 3582 Commercial Laundry, Dry Clean & Pressing Mchs
- 3585 Air Conditioning & Heating Eqpt
- 3589 Service Ind Machines, NEC
- 3592 Carburetors, Pistons, Rings & Valves
- 3594 Fluid Power Pumps & Motors
- 3596 Scales & Balances, Exc Laboratory
- 3599 Machinery & Eqpt, Indl & Commercial, NEC

36 electronic and other electrical equipment and components, except computer
- 3612 Power, Distribution & Specialty Transformers
- 3613 Switchgear & Switchboard Apparatus
- 3621 Motors & Generators
- 3625 Relays & Indl Controls
- 3629 Electrical Indl Apparatus, NEC
- 3631 Household Cooking Eqpt
- 3634 Electric Household Appliances
- 3635 Household Vacuum Cleaners
- 3641 Electric Lamps
- 3643 Current-Carrying Wiring Devices
- 3644 Noncurrent-Carrying Wiring Devices
- 3645 Residential Lighting Fixtures
- 3646 Commercial, Indl & Institutional Lighting Fixtures
- 3647 Vehicular Lighting Eqpt
- 3648 Lighting Eqpt, NEC
- 3651 Household Audio & Video Eqpt
- 3652 Phonograph Records & Magnetic Tape
- 3661 Telephone & Telegraph Apparatus
- 3663 Radio & T V Communications, Systs & Eqpt, Broadcast/Studio
- 3669 Communications Eqpt, NEC
- 3672 Printed Circuit Boards
- 3674 Semiconductors
- 3677 Electronic Coils & Transformers
- 3679 Electronic Components, NEC
- 3691 Storage Batteries
- 3692 Primary Batteries: Dry & Wet
- 3694 Electrical Eqpt For Internal Combustion Engines
- 3695 Recording Media
- 3699 Electrical Machinery, Eqpt & Splys, NEC

37 transportation equipment
- 3711 Motor Vehicles & Car Bodies
- 3713 Truck & Bus Bodies
- 3714 Motor Vehicle Parts & Access
- 3715 Truck Trailers
- 3721 Aircraft
- 3724 Aircraft Engines & Engine Parts
- 3728 Aircraft Parts & Eqpt, NEC
- 3732 Boat Building & Repairing
- 3743 Railroad Eqpt
- 3751 Motorcycles, Bicycles & Parts
- 3761 Guided Missiles & Space Vehicles
- 3795 Tanks & Tank Components
- 3799 Transportation Eqpt, NEC

38 measuring, analyzing and controlling instruments; photographic, medical an
- 3812 Search, Detection, Navigation & Guidance Systs & Instrs
- 3821 Laboratory Apparatus & Furniture
- 3822 Automatic Temperature Controls
- 3823 Indl Instruments For Meas, Display & Control
- 3824 Fluid Meters & Counters
- 3825 Instrs For Measuring & Testing Electricity
- 3826 Analytical Instruments
- 3827 Optical Instruments
- 3829 Measuring & Controlling Devices, NEC
- 3841 Surgical & Medical Instrs & Apparatus
- 3842 Orthopedic, Prosthetic & Surgical Appliances/Splys
- 3843 Dental Eqpt & Splys
- 3844 X-ray Apparatus & Tubes
- 3845 Electromedical & Electrotherapeutic Apparatus
- 3851 Ophthalmic Goods
- 3861 Photographic Eqpt & Splys
- 3873 Watch & Clock Devices & Parts

39 miscellaneous manufacturing industries
- 3911 Jewelry: Precious Metal
- 3914 Silverware, Plated & Stainless Steel Ware
- 3915 Jewelers Findings & Lapidary Work
- 3931 Musical Instruments
- 3942 Dolls & Stuffed Toys
- 3944 Games, Toys & Children's Vehicles
- 3949 Sporting & Athletic Goods, NEC
- 3952 Lead Pencils, Crayons & Artist's Mtrls
- 3953 Marking Devices
- 3955 Carbon Paper & Inked Ribbons
- 3961 Costume Jewelry & Novelties
- 3965 Fasteners, Buttons, Needles & Pins
- 3991 Brooms & Brushes
- 3993 Signs & Advertising Displays
- 3996 Linoleum & Hard Surface Floor Coverings, NEC
- 3999 Manufacturing Industries, NEC

40 railroad transportation
- 4011 Railroads, Line-Hauling Operations

SIC INDEX

SIC NO	PRODUCT
4013	Switching & Terminal Svcs

41 local and suburban transit and interurban highway passenger transportation

- 4111 Local & Suburban Transit
- 4119 Local Passenger Transportation: NEC
- 4121 Taxi Cabs
- 4131 Intercity & Rural Bus Transportation
- 4141 Local Bus Charter Svc
- 4142 Bus Charter Service, Except Local
- 4151 School Buses

42 motor freight transportation and warehousing

- 4212 Local Trucking Without Storage
- 4213 Trucking, Except Local
- 4214 Local Trucking With Storage
- 4215 Courier Svcs, Except Air
- 4221 Farm Product Warehousing & Storage
- 4222 Refrigerated Warehousing & Storage
- 4225 General Warehousing & Storage
- 4226 Special Warehousing & Storage, NEC
- 4231 Terminal & Joint Terminal Maint Facilities

44 water transportation

- 4412 Deep Sea Foreign Transportation Of Freight
- 4424 Deep Sea Domestic Transportation Of Freight
- 4449 Water Transportation Of Freight, NEC
- 4481 Deep Sea Transportation Of Passengers
- 4482 Ferries
- 4489 Water Transport Of Passengers, NEC
- 4491 Marine Cargo Handling
- 4492 Towing & Tugboat Svcs
- 4493 Marinas

45 transportation by air

- 4512 Air Transportation, Scheduled
- 4513 Air Courier Svcs
- 4522 Air Transportation, Nonscheduled
- 4581 Airports, Flying Fields & Terminal Svcs

47 transportation services

- 4724 Travel Agencies
- 4725 Tour Operators
- 4729 Passenger Transportation Arrangement, NEC
- 4731 Freight Forwarding & Arrangement
- 4741 Railroad Car Rental
- 4783 Packing & Crating Svcs
- 4785 Fixed Facilities, Inspection, Weighing Svcs Transptn
- 4789 Transportation Svcs, NEC

48 communications

- 4812 Radiotelephone Communications
- 4813 Telephone Communications, Except Radio
- 4822 Telegraph & Other Message Communications
- 4832 Radio Broadcasting Stations
- 4833 Television Broadcasting Stations
- 4841 Cable & Other Pay TV Svcs
- 4899 Communication Svcs, NEC

49 electric, gas, and sanitary services

- 4911 Electric Svcs
- 4922 Natural Gas Transmission
- 4923 Natural Gas Transmission & Distribution
- 4924 Natural Gas Distribution
- 4925 Gas Production &/Or Distribution
- 4931 Electric & Other Svcs Combined
- 4932 Gas & Other Svcs Combined
- 4941 Water Sply
- 4952 Sewerage Systems
- 4953 Refuse Systems
- 4959 Sanitary Svcs, NEC
- 4971 Irrigation Systems

50 wholesale trade¨durable goods

- 5012 Automobiles & Other Motor Vehicles Wholesale
- 5013 Motor Vehicle Splys & New Parts Wholesale
- 5014 Tires & Tubes Wholesale
- 5015 Motor Vehicle Parts, Used Wholesale
- 5021 Furniture Wholesale
- 5023 Home Furnishings Wholesale
- 5031 Lumber, Plywood & Millwork Wholesale
- 5032 Brick, Stone & Related Construction Mtrls Wholesale
- 5033 Roofing, Siding & Insulation Mtrls Wholesale
- 5039 Construction Materials, NEC Wholesale
- 5043 Photographic Eqpt & Splys Wholesale
- 5044 Office Eqpt Wholesale
- 5045 Computers & Peripheral Eqpt & Software Wholesale
- 5046 Commercial Eqpt, NEC Wholesale
- 5047 Medical, Dental & Hospital Eqpt & Splys Wholesale
- 5048 Ophthalmic Goods Wholesale
- 5049 Professional Eqpt & Splys, NEC Wholesale
- 5051 Metals Service Centers
- 5052 Coal & Other Minerals & Ores Wholesale
- 5063 Electrl Apparatus, Eqpt, Wiring Splys Wholesale
- 5064 Electrical Appliances, TV & Radios Wholesale
- 5065 Electronic Parts & Eqpt Wholesale
- 5072 Hardware Wholesale
- 5074 Plumbing & Heating Splys Wholesale
- 5075 Heating & Air Conditioning Eqpt & Splys Wholesale
- 5078 Refrigeration Eqpt & Splys Wholesale
- 5082 Construction & Mining Mach & Eqpt Wholesale
- 5083 Farm & Garden Mach & Eqpt Wholesale
- 5084 Industrial Mach & Eqpt Wholesale
- 5085 Industrial Splys Wholesale
- 5087 Service Establishment Eqpt & Splys Wholesale
- 5088 Transportation Eqpt & Splys, Except Motor Vehicles Wholesale
- 5091 Sporting & Recreational Goods & Splys Wholesale
- 5092 Toys & Hobby Goods & Splys Wholesale
- 5093 Scrap & Waste Materials Wholesale
- 5094 Jewelry, Watches, Precious Stones Wholesale
- 5099 Durable Goods: NEC Wholesale

51 wholesale trade¨nondurable goods

- 5112 Stationery & Office Splys Wholesale
- 5113 Indl & Personal Svc Paper Wholesale
- 5122 Drugs, Drug Proprietaries & Sundries Wholesale
- 5131 Piece Goods, Notions & Dry Goods Wholesale
- 5136 Men's & Boys' Clothing & Furnishings Wholesale
- 5137 Women's, Children's & Infants Clothing Wholesale
- 5139 Footwear Wholesale
- 5141 Groceries, General Line Wholesale
- 5142 Packaged Frozen Foods Wholesale
- 5143 Dairy Prdts, Except Dried Or Canned Wholesale
- 5144 Poultry & Poultry Prdts Wholesale
- 5145 Confectionery Wholesale
- 5146 Fish & Seafood Wholesale
- 5147 Meats & Meat Prdts Wholesale
- 5148 Fresh Fruits & Vegetables Wholesale
- 5149 Groceries & Related Prdts, NEC Wholesale
- 5153 Grain & Field Beans Wholesale
- 5159 Farm-Prdt Raw Mtrls, NEC Wholesale
- 5162 Plastics Materials & Basic Shapes Wholesale
- 5169 Chemicals & Allied Prdts, NEC Wholesale
- 5171 Petroleum Bulk Stations & Terminals
- 5172 Petroleum & Petroleum Prdts Wholesale
- 5181 Beer & Ale Wholesale
- 5182 Wine & Distilled Alcoholic Beverages Wholesale
- 5191 Farm Splys Wholesale
- 5192 Books, Periodicals & Newspapers Wholesale
- 5193 Flowers, Nursery Stock & Florists' Splys Wholesale
- 5194 Tobacco & Tobacco Prdts Wholesale
- 5198 Paints, Varnishes & Splys Wholesale
- 5199 Nondurable Goods, NEC Wholesale

60 depository institutions

- 6021 National Commercial Banks
- 6022 State Commercial Banks
- 6029 Commercial Banks, NEC
- 6035 Federal Savings Institutions
- 6036 Savings Institutions, Except Federal
- 6061 Federal Credit Unions
- 6062 State Credit Unions
- 6091 Nondeposit Trust Facilities
- 6099 Functions Related To Deposit Banking, NEC

61 nondepository credit institutions

- 6111 Federal Credit Agencies
- 6141 Personal Credit Institutions
- 6153 Credit Institutions, Short-Term Business
- 6159 Credit Institutions, Misc Business
- 6162 Mortgage Bankers & Loan Correspondents
- 6163 Loan Brokers

62 security and commodity brokers, dealers, exchanges, and services

- 6211 Security Brokers & Dealers
- 6221 Commodity Contracts Brokers & Dealers
- 6231 Security & Commodity Exchanges
- 6282 Investment Advice

63 insurance carriers

- 6311 Life Insurance Carriers
- 6321 Accident & Health Insurance
- 6324 Hospital & Medical Svc Plans Carriers
- 6331 Fire, Marine & Casualty Insurance
- 6351 Surety Insurance Carriers
- 6361 Title Insurance
- 6371 Pension, Health & Welfare Funds
- 6399 Insurance Carriers, NEC

64 insurance agents, brokers, and service

- 6411 Insurance Agents, Brokers & Svc

65 real estate

- 6512 Operators Of Nonresidential Bldgs
- 6513 Operators Of Apartment Buildings
- 6514 Operators Of Dwellings, Except Apartments
- 6515 Operators of Residential Mobile Home Sites
- 6519 Lessors Of Real Estate, NEC
- 6531 Real Estate Agents & Managers
- 6541 Title Abstract Offices
- 6552 Land Subdividers & Developers
- 6553 Cemetery Subdividers & Developers

67 holding and other investment offices

- 6712 Offices Of Bank Holding Co's
- 6719 Offices Of Holding Co's, NEC
- 6722 Management Investment Offices
- 6726 Unit Investment Trusts, Face-Amount Certificate Offices
- 6732 Education, Religious & Charitable Trusts
- 6733 Trusts Except Educational, Religious & Charitable
- 6794 Patent Owners & Lessors
- 6798 Real Estate Investment Trusts
- 6799 Investors, NEC

70 hotels, rooming houses, camps, and other lodging places

- 7011 Hotels, Motels & Tourist Courts
- 7021 Rooming & Boarding Houses
- 7032 Sporting & Recreational Camps
- 7033 Trailer Parks & Camp Sites
- 7041 Membership-Basis Hotels

72 personal services

- 7211 Power Laundries, Family & Commercial
- 7212 Garment Pressing & Cleaners' Agents
- 7213 Linen Sply
- 7215 Coin Operated Laundries & Cleaning
- 7216 Dry Cleaning Plants, Except Rug Cleaning
- 7217 Carpet & Upholstery Cleaning
- 7218 Industrial Launderers
- 7219 Laundry & Garment Svcs, NEC
- 7221 Photographic Studios, Portrait
- 7231 Beauty Shops
- 7241 Barber Shops
- 7251 Shoe Repair & Shoeshine Parlors
- 7261 Funeral Svcs & Crematories
- 7291 Tax Return Preparation Svcs
- 7299 Miscellaneous Personal Svcs, NEC

73 business services

- 7311 Advertising Agencies
- 7312 Outdoor Advertising Svcs
- 7313 Radio, TV & Publishers Adv Reps
- 7319 Advertising, NEC
- 7322 Adjustment & Collection Svcs
- 7323 Credit Reporting Svcs
- 7331 Direct Mail Advertising Svcs
- 7334 Photocopying & Duplicating Svcs
- 7335 Commercial Photography
- 7336 Commercial Art & Graphic Design
- 7338 Secretarial & Court Reporting Svcs
- 7342 Disinfecting & Pest Control Svcs
- 7349 Building Cleaning & Maintenance Svcs, NEC
- 7352 Medical Eqpt Rental & Leasing
- 7353 Heavy Construction Eqpt Rental & Leasing
- 7359 Equipment Rental & Leasing, NEC
- 7361 Employment Agencies
- 7363 Help Supply Svcs
- 7371 Custom Computer Programming Svcs
- 7372 Prepackaged Software
- 7373 Computer Integrated Systems Design
- 7374 Data & Computer Processing & Preparation
- 7375 Information Retrieval Svcs
- 7376 Computer Facilities Management Svcs
- 7377 Computer Rental & Leasing
- 7378 Computer Maintenance & Repair
- 7379 Computer Related Svcs, NEC
- 7381 Detective & Armored Car Svcs
- 7382 Security Systems Svcs
- 7383 News Syndicates
- 7384 Photofinishing Labs
- 7389 Business Svcs, NEC

75 automotive repair, services, and parking

- 7513 Truck Rental & Leasing, Without Drivers
- 7514 Passenger Car Rental
- 7515 Passenger Car Leasing
- 7519 Utility Trailers & Recreational Vehicle Rental
- 7521 Automobile Parking Lots & Garages

SIC INDEX

SIC NO	PRODUCT
7532	Top, Body & Upholstery Repair & Paint Shops
7533	Automotive Exhaust System Repair Shops
7534	Tire Retreading & Repair Shops
7536	Automotive Glass Replacement Shops
7537	Automotive Transmission Repair Shops
7538	General Automotive Repair Shop
7539	Automotive Repair Shops, NEC
7542	Car Washes
7549	Automotive Svcs, Except Repair & Car Washes

76 miscellaneous repair services

SIC NO	PRODUCT
7622	Radio & TV Repair Shops
7623	Refrigeration & Air Conditioning Svc & Repair Shop
7629	Electrical & Elex Repair Shop, NEC
7631	Watch, Clock & Jewelry Repair
7641	Reupholstery & Furniture Repair
7692	Welding Repair
7694	Armature Rewinding Shops
7699	Repair Shop & Related Svcs, NEC

78 motion pictures

SIC NO	PRODUCT
7812	Motion Picture & Video Tape Production
7819	Services Allied To Motion Picture Prdtn
7822	Motion Picture & Video Tape Distribution
7832	Motion Picture Theaters, Except Drive-In
7841	Video Tape Rental

79 amusement and recreation services

SIC NO	PRODUCT
7911	Dance Studios, Schools & Halls
7922	Theatrical Producers & Misc Theatrical Svcs
7929	Bands, Orchestras, Actors & Entertainers
7933	Bowling Centers
7941	Professional Sports Clubs & Promoters
7948	Racing & Track Operations
7991	Physical Fitness Facilities
7992	Public Golf Courses
7993	Coin-Operated Amusement Devices & Arcades
7996	Amusement Parks
7997	Membership Sports & Recreation Clubs
7999	Amusement & Recreation Svcs, NEC

80 health services

SIC NO	PRODUCT
8011	Offices & Clinics Of Doctors Of Medicine
8021	Offices & Clinics Of Dentists
8031	Offices & Clinics Of Doctors Of Osteopathy
8041	Offices & Clinics Of Chiropractors
8042	Offices & Clinics Of Optometrists
8043	Offices & Clinics Of Podiatrists
8049	Offices & Clinics Of Health Practitioners, NEC
8051	Skilled Nursing Facilities
8052	Intermediate Care Facilities
8059	Nursing & Personal Care Facilities, NEC
8062	General Medical & Surgical Hospitals
8063	Psychiatric Hospitals
8069	Specialty Hospitals, Except Psychiatric
8071	Medical Laboratories
8072	Dental Laboratories
8082	Home Health Care Svcs
8092	Kidney Dialysis Centers
8093	Specialty Outpatient Facilities, NEC
8099	Health & Allied Svcs, NEC

81 legal services

SIC NO	PRODUCT
8111	Legal Svcs

83 social services

SIC NO	PRODUCT
8322	Individual & Family Social Svcs
8331	Job Training & Vocational Rehabilitation Svcs
8351	Child Day Care Svcs
8361	Residential Care
8399	Social Services, NEC

84 museums, art galleries, and botanical and zoological gardens

SIC NO	PRODUCT
8412	Museums & Art Galleries

86 membership organizations

SIC NO	PRODUCT
8611	Business Associations
8621	Professional Membership Organizations
8631	Labor Unions & Similar Organizations
8641	Civic, Social & Fraternal Associations
8651	Political Organizations
8699	Membership Organizations, NEC

87 engineering, accounting, research, management, and related services

SIC NO	PRODUCT
8711	Engineering Services
8712	Architectural Services
8713	Surveying Services
8721	Accounting, Auditing & Bookkeeping Svcs
8731	Commercial Physical & Biological Research
8732	Commercial Economic, Sociological & Educational Research
8733	Noncommercial Research Organizations
8734	Testing Laboratories
8741	Management Services
8742	Management Consulting Services
8743	Public Relations Svcs
8744	Facilities Support Mgmt Svcs
8748	Business Consulting Svcs, NEC

89 services, not elsewhere classified

SIC NO	PRODUCT
8999	Services Not Elsewhere Classified

SIC SECTION

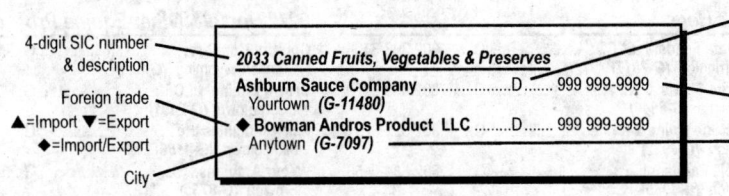

- 4-digit SIC number & description
- Foreign trade
  - ▲ =Import ▼ =Export
  - ◆ =Import/Export
- City
- Indicates approximate employment figure
  - A = Over 500 employees, B = 251-500
  - C = 101-250, D = 51-100, E = 20-50
  - F = 10-19, G = 1-9
- Business phone
- Geographic Section entry number where full company information appears

See footnotes for symbols and codes identification.

- The SIC codes in this section are from the latest Standard Industrial Classification manual published by the U.S. Government's Office of Management and Budget. For more information regarding SICs, see the Explanatory Notes.
- Companies may be listed under multiple classifications.

01 AGRICULTURAL PRODUCTION-CROPS

0111 Wheat

Company	Emp	Phone
Clear Brook Farms Inc	G	302 337-7678
Bridgeville (G-460)		
Elliott John	G	302 846-2487
Delmar (G-997)		
Fa webb & Sons	G	302 335-4548
Milford (G-4408)		
Pettyjohn Farms Inc	G	302 684-4383
Milton (G-4949)		
Schiff Farms Inc	E	302 398-8014
Harrington (G-2884)		
Shadybrook Farms LLC	F	302 734-9966
Dover (G-2074)		
Shawnee Wood Farms Inc	G	302 422-4557
Milford (G-4557)		
T S Smith & Sons Inc	E	302 337-8271
Bridgeville (G-524)		
Westwood Farms Incorporated	F	302 238-7141
Millsboro (G-4826)		
Workmans Inc	G	302 934-9228
Georgetown (G-2709)		

0115 Corn

Company	Emp	Phone
Baker Farms Inc	G	302 378-3750
Middletown (G-3961)		
Elliott John	G	302 846-2487
Delmar (G-997)		
Fa webb & Sons	G	302 335-4548
Milford (G-4408)		
Francis Bergold	G	302 284-8101
Felton (G-2293)		
H & V Farms Inc	G	302 934-1320
Millsboro (G-4701)		
Harry Joseph	G	302 684-3243
Milton (G-4911)		
Hill Farms Inc	G	302 422-0219
Houston (G-3179)		
J L Carpenter Farms LLC	G	302 684-8601
Milton (G-4919)		
Rutkoske Bros Inc	G	302 378-8181
Middletown (G-4227)		
Schiff Farms Inc	E	302 398-8014
Harrington (G-2884)		
Shadybrook Farms LLC	F	302 734-9966
Dover (G-2074)		
Shawnee Wood Farms Inc	G	302 422-4557
Milford (G-4557)		
T S Smith & Sons Inc	E	302 337-8271
Bridgeville (G-524)		
Workmans Inc	G	302 934-9228
Georgetown (G-2709)		

0116 Soybeans

Company	Emp	Phone
Collins Brothers Farms	G	302 238-7822
Millsboro (G-4666)		
Elliott John	G	302 846-2487
Delmar (G-997)		
Fa webb & Sons	G	302 335-4548
Milford (G-4408)		
H & V Farms Inc	G	302 934-1320
Millsboro (G-4701)		
Schiff Farms Inc	E	302 398-8014
Harrington (G-2884)		
Shadybrook Farms LLC	F	302 734-9966
Dover (G-2074)		
Shawnee Wood Farms Inc	G	302 422-3534
Milford (G-4557)		
T S Smith & Sons Inc	E	302 337-8271
Bridgeville (G-524)		
Tantrough Farm	G	302 422-5547
Houston (G-3183)		
Workmans Inc	G	302 934-9228
Georgetown (G-2709)		

0119 Cash Grains, NEC

Company	Emp	Phone
Charles Dempsey Farms	G	302 734-4937
Dover (G-1273)		
Charles H West Farms Inc	E	302 335-3936
Milford (G-4349)		
Clear Brook Farms Inc	G	302 337-7678
Bridgeville (G-460)		
Dulin Brothers	G	302 653-5365
Clayton (G-842)		
Fa webb & Sons	G	302 335-4548
Milford (G-4408)		
Francis Bergold	G	302 284-8101
Felton (G-2293)		
James L Carpenter & Son Inc	G	302 684-8601
Milton (G-4921)		
Kruger Farms Inc	G	302 856-2577
Georgetown (G-2583)		
Ralph H Givens	G	302 629-4319
Seaford (G-8371)		
Shadybrook Farms LLC	F	302 734-9966
Dover (G-2074)		
T S Smith & Sons Inc	E	302 337-8271
Bridgeville (G-524)		
Twin Creek Farms LLC	G	302 249-2294
Milford (G-4581)		
Workmans Inc	G	302 934-9228
Georgetown (G-2709)		

0132 Tobacco

Company	Emp	Phone
Gauri Inc	G	302 731-5300
Newark (G-6642)		

0134 Irish Potatoes

Company	Emp	Phone
Francis Bergold	G	302 284-8101
Felton (G-2293)		
Rutkoske Bros Inc	G	302 378-8181
Middletown (G-4227)		
Shadybrook Farms LLC	F	302 734-9966
Dover (G-2074)		

0139 Field Crops, Except Cash Grains, NEC

Company	Emp	Phone
Barsgr LLC	G	302 645-6665
Lewes (G-3362)		

0161 Vegetables & Melons

Company	Emp	Phone
Baldwin Sayre Inc	G	302 337-0309
Bridgeville (G-451)		
Bobola Farm & Florist	G	302 492-3367
Dover (G-1218)		
Charles H West Farms Inc	E	302 335-3936
Milford (G-4349)		
Dole Food Company Inc	E	302 652-6060
Wilmington (G-10186)		
Evans Farms LLC	G	302 337-8130
Bridgeville (G-469)		
▼ Fifer Orchards Inc	C	302 697-2141
Camden Wyoming (G-637)		
J L Carpenter Farms LLC	G	302 684-8601
Milton (G-4919)		
Shawnee Wood Farms Inc	G	302 422-3534
Milford (G-4557)		
T S Smith & Sons Inc	E	302 337-8271
Bridgeville (G-524)		
Tantrough Farm	G	302 422-5547
Houston (G-3183)		
Workmans Inc	G	302 934-9228
Georgetown (G-2709)		

Company	Emp	Phone
James L Carpenter & Son Inc	G	302 684-8601
Milton (G-4921)		
Mernies Market	G	302 629-9877
Seaford (G-8307)		
Papen Farms Inc	F	302 697-3291
Dover (G-1932)		
Pine Breeze Farms Inc	G	302 337-7717
Bridgeville (G-510)		
Ralph H Givens	G	302 629-4319
Seaford (G-8371)		
Richard Sapp Farms	G	302 684-4727
Milton (G-4960)		
Tantrough Farm	G	302 422-5547
Houston (G-3183)		
V P Produce Inc	G	302 249-0718
Laurel (G-3300)		
Vance Phillips Inc	G	302 542-1501
Laurel (G-3301)		

0171 Berry Crops

Company	Emp	Phone
Blueberry Lne Brry Frm & Orchd	G	302 238-7067
Frankford (G-2347)		
Bobola Farm & Florist	G	302 492-3367
Dover (G-1218)		

0175 Deciduous Tree Fruits

Company	Emp	Phone
Crossings At Oak Orchard	G	302 231-8243
Millsboro (G-4671)		
▼ Fifer Orchards Inc	C	302 697-2141
Camden Wyoming (G-637)		
Highland Orchards	G	302 478-1392
Wilmington (G-10904)		
T S Smith & Sons Inc	E	302 337-8271
Bridgeville (G-524)		

0181 Ornamental Floriculture & Nursery Prdts

Company	Emp	Phone
Affordable Sod Inc	G	302 545-0275
Newark (G-5919)		
Apgar Turf Farm Inc	G	302 653-9389
Smyrna (G-8574)		
Countryside Lawn & Landscape	E	302 832-1320
Newark (G-6304)		
Eggplant Inc	G	302 737-1073
Newark (G-6509)		
Forest View Nursery	E	302 653-7757
Clayton (G-851)		
Lakeside Greenhouses Inc	G	302 875-2457
Laurel (G-3250)		
Old Country Garden Center Inc	E	302 652-3317
Wilmington (G-11943)		
Richard Belotti	F	302 934-7585
Georgetown (G-2639)		
Sandy Hill Greenhouses Inc	F	302 856-2412
Georgetown (G-2647)		
Southern States Coop Inc	F	302 378-9841
Middletown (G-4246)		
Sterling Nursery Inc	G	302 653-7060
Smyrna (G-8724)		

0182 Food Crops Grown Under Cover

Company	Emp	Phone
Clifton Farms Inc	G	302 424-8340
Milford (G-4357)		

0191 Crop Farming, Misc

Company	Emp	Phone
Alfred Moore	G	302 653-7600
Smyrna (G-8564)		

Employee Codes: A=Over 500 employees, B=251-500
C=101-250, D=51-100, E=20-50, F=10-19, G=1-9

2020 Harris Directory of Delaware Businesses

01 AGRICULTURAL PRODUCTION-CROPS

Amick Farms LLC ....D...... 302 846-9511
  Delmar (G-970)
Banks Farm LLC ....G...... 302 542-4100
  Dagsboro (G-881)
Bauer Farms ....G...... 302 284-9722
  Harrington (G-2816)
Bender Farms Llc ....G...... 302 349-5574
  Greenwood (G-2715)
Bennett Farms Inc ....G...... 302 684-1627
  Milford (G-4323)
Broad Acres Inc ....G...... 302 734-2910
  Dover (G-1233)
C&S Farms Inc ....G...... 302 249-0458
  Laurel (G-3206)
Carlisle Farms Inc ....G...... 302 349-5692
  Greenwood (G-2719)
Clover Farms Meats ....G...... 610 428-8066
  Ocean View (G-7778)
Fry Farms Inc ....G...... 302 422-9112
  Milford (G-4418)
Green Acres Farm Inc ....F...... 302 645-8652
  Lewes (G-3521)
H & J Wright Family Farms LLC ...G...... 302 841-9002
  Delmar (G-1000)
Howard Wilkins & Sons Inc .....G...... 302 270-4183
  Lincoln (G-3856)
Hrupsa Farms Ltd Partnership ....G...... 302 270-1817
  Harrington (G-2852)
Jed T James ....G...... 302 875-0101
  Georgetown (G-2572)
M Davis Farms LLC ....G...... 302 856-7018
  Georgetown (G-2593)
Mc Cabe Enterprises Inc ....G...... 302 436-5176
  Selbyville (G-8518)
MJ Webb Farms Inc ....G...... 302 349-4453
  Greenwood (G-2753)
Mount Aire Farms of Delawa ...G...... 302 934-4048
  Millsboro (G-4755)
Mountaire Farms Inc ....A...... 302 436-8241
  Selbyville (G-8525)
O A Newton & Son Co ....E...... 302 337-8211
  Bridgeville (G-503)
Ockels Acres LLC ....G...... 302 684-0456
  Milton (G-4944)
Ockels Farms Inc ....G...... 302 684-0456
  Milton (G-4945)
Raymond A Stachecki ....G...... 302 653-6004
  Smyrna (G-8697)
Richard L Sapp Farms LLC ....F...... 302 684-4727
  Milton (G-4957)
Riverdale Park LLC ....G...... 302 945-2475
  Millsboro (G-4792)
Rtcp Farm Partnership ....G...... 302 584-3584
  Camden Wyoming (G-656)
Snow Farms Inc ....G...... 302 653-7534
  Smyrna (G-8722)
Suburban Farmhouse ....G...... 302 250-6254
  Milton (G-4974)
TA Farms LLC ....G...... 302 492-3030
  Camden Wyoming (G-658)
Thomas Family Farms LLC ......G...... 302 492-3688
  Marydel (G-3923)
Two Farms Inc ....F...... 302 653-8345
  Smyrna (G-8733)
Vincent Farms Inc ....C...... 302 875-5707
  Laurel (G-3302)
Wells Farms Inc ....G...... 302 422-4732
  Milford (G-4603)
Wheatley Farms Inc ....G...... 302 337-7286
  Bridgeville (G-534)
William A ODay ....G...... 302 629-7854
  Seaford (G-8438)
William A ODay & Son LLC .....G...... 302 629-7854
  Seaford (G-8439)
Willin Farms LLC ....G...... 302 629-2520
  Seaford (G-8440)

02 AGRICULTURAL PRODUCTION-LIVESTOCK AND ANIMAL SPECIALTIES

0211 Beef Cattle Feedlots

Tantrough Farm ....G...... 302 422-5547
  Houston (G-3183)

0212 Beef Cattle, Except Feedlots

Rtcp Farm Partnership ....G...... 302 584-3584
  Camden Wyoming (G-656)

Schiff Farms Inc ....E...... 302 398-8014
  Harrington (G-2884)

0213 Hogs

Bi-State Feeders LLC ....G...... 302 398-3408
  Harrington (G-2817)
George Staats ....G...... 302 653-9729
  Smyrna (G-8640)
Keystone Swine Services ....G...... 302 329-9731
  Milton (G-4922)
Ockels Farms Inc ....G...... 302 684-0456
  Milton (G-4945)

0241 Dairy Farms

Charles Dempsey Farms ....G...... 302 734-4937
  Dover (G-1273)
Dempsey Farms LLC ....F...... 302 734-4937
  Dover (G-1413)
Dulin Brothers ....G...... 302 653-5365
  Clayton (G-842)
Howard Wilkins & Sons Inc .....G...... 302 270-4183
  Lincoln (G-3856)
J E Bailey & Sons Inc ....G...... 302 349-4376
  Greenwood (G-2747)
James L Carpenter & Son Inc ...G...... 302 684-8601
  Milton (G-4921)
Lewes Dairy Inc ....E...... 302 645-6281
  Lewes (G-3598)
R Stanley Collier & Son Inc .....G...... 302 398-7855
  Harrington (G-2878)
Robert C Thompson ....G...... 302 492-1053
  Hartly (G-2940)

0251 Chicken & Poultry Farms

Allen Harim Foods LLC ....E...... 302 629-9136
  Seaford (G-8143)
Barsgr LLC ....G...... 302 645-6665
  Lewes (G-3362)
Bg Farms Inc ....G...... 302 875-2167
  Laurel (G-3200)
Big Dog Farm LLC ....G...... 302 841-7721
  Seaford (G-8168)
Bobola Farm & Florist ....G...... 302 492-3367
  Dover (G-1218)
Collins Brothers Farms ....G...... 302 238-7822
  Millsboro (G-4666)
Country Store ....F...... 302 653-5111
  Kenton (G-3184)
Dixie Line Farm Inc ....G...... 302 236-7402
  Seaford (G-8224)
Fa webb & Sons ....G...... 302 335-4548
  Milford (G-4408)
Gerald Brown ....G...... 302 335-5211
  Milford (G-4423)
H & V Farms Inc ....G...... 302 934-1320
  Millsboro (G-4701)
Howard Wilkins & Sons Inc .....G...... 302 270-4183
  Lincoln (G-3856)
Larry Hill Farms LLC ....F...... 302 245-6657
  Delmar (G-1016)
McGinnis Farms LLC ....G...... 302 841-8175
  Dagsboro (G-920)
Perdue Farms Inc ....B...... 302 855-5681
  Dagsboro (G-3271)
Robbins Nest Farm Inc ....G...... 302 422-4722
  Ellendale (G-2263)
State Line Farms LLC ....G...... 302 628-4506
  Seaford (G-8408)
T S Smith & Sons Inc ....E...... 302 337-8271
  Bridgeville (G-524)
Westwood Farms Incorporated ...F...... 302 238-7141
  Millsboro (G-4826)

0252 Chicken Egg Farms

Ockels Farms Inc ....G...... 302 684-0456
  Milton (G-4945)
Puglisi Egg Farms Delaware LLC ...E...... 302 376-1200
  Middletown (G-4202)
Red Bird Egg Farm Inc ....G...... 302 834-2571
  Bear (G-298)

0254 Poultry Hatcheries

Allen Harim Foods LLC ....E...... 302 732-9511
  Dagsboro (G-877)
Barsgr LLC ....G...... 302 645-6665
  Lewes (G-3362)
J E Bailey & Sons Inc ....G...... 302 349-4376
  Greenwood (G-2747)

Mc Cabe Enterprises Inc ....G...... 302 436-5176
  Selbyville (G-8518)

0272 Horse & Other Equine Production

Country Comforts ....G...... 302 242-8527
  Camden Wyoming (G-626)
Crown Equine LLC ....G...... 302 629-2782
  Georgetown (G-2491)
Pck Associates Inc ....G...... 302 378-7192
  Middletown (G-4186)
Valour Arabians ....G...... 302 653-4066
  Smyrna (G-8735)

0279 Animal Specialties, NEC

Clean-A-Tank Inc ....G...... 302 250-4229
  Wilmington (G-9737)

0291 Animal Production, NEC

Harry H Mc Robie ....G...... 302 846-9784
  Delmar (G-1001)

07 AGRICULTURAL SERVICES

0711 Soil Preparation Svcs

Agrolab Inc ....G...... 302 535-6591
  Harrington (G-2806)
Spec Processing Group Inc .....G...... 302 295-2197
  Bear (G-332)
Toubasam Inc ....G...... 302 299-2954
  Wilmington (G-12942)
Vironex Inc ....D...... 302 661-1400
  Wilmington (G-13087)

0721 Soil Preparation, Planting & Cultivating Svc

Air Enterprises Inc ....G...... 302 335-5141
  Magnolia (G-3878)
Allen Chorman Inc ....G...... 302 684-2770
  Milton (G-4861)
Corteva Inc ....E...... 302 485-3000
  Wilmington (G-9869)
Delcarm LLC ....F...... 610 345-9001
  Townsend (G-8782)
Dupont Specialty Pdts USA LLC ...F...... 302 774-1000
  Wilmington (G-10260)
Js Knotts Inc ....G...... 302 284-4888
  Felton (G-2299)

0722 Crop Harvesting By Machine

B Ritter LLC ....G...... 302 945-7294
  Harbeson (G-2774)

0742 Veterinary Animal Specialties

A Caring Doctor Minnesota PA ...E...... 302 478-3910
  Wilmington (G-8874)
A Caring Doctor Minnesota PA ...E...... 302 266-0122
  Newark (G-5865)
A Little Veterinary Clinic PA .....F...... 302 398-3367
  Harrington (G-2804)
All Pets Medical Center ....G...... 302 653-2300
  Smyrna (G-8565)
Animal Haven Veterinary Center ...G...... 302 326-1400
  Bear (G-31)
Animal Veterinary Center LLC ...F...... 302 322-6488
  Bear (G-32)
▲ Ann Jackson Vmd ....G...... 302 659-3624
  Smyrna (G-8571)
Atlantic Veterinary Svcs Inc .....G...... 302 376-7506
  Middletown (G-3952)
Bay Animal Hospital LLC ....G...... 302 279-1082
  Townsend (G-8762)
Brandywine Hndred Vtrnary Hosp ...F...... 302 792-2777
  Wilmington (G-9437)
Brandywine Veterinary Hospital ...G...... 302 476-8779
  Wilmington (G-9460)
Brenford Animal Hospital P A ...E...... 302 678-9418
  Dover (G-1229)
CA Cassidy Vmd ....G...... 302 998-2995
  Wilmington (G-9526)
Centerville Veterinary Hosp .....F...... 302 655-3315
  Wilmington (G-9614)
Circle Veterinary Clinic ....F...... 302 652-6587
  Wilmington (G-9712)
Coastal Veterinary ....G...... 302 524-8550
  Selbyville (G-8470)
Country Roads Veterinary Svc ...G...... 302 514-9087
  Clayton (G-840)

07 AGRICULTURAL SERVICES

Crossroads Veterinary Clinic ....G.. 302 436-5984
 Selbyville *(G-8474)*
Delaware S P C A ....E.. 302 998-2281
 Newark *(G-6409)*
Delmarva Anmal Emrgncy Ctr LLC ...G.. 302 697-0850
 Dover *(G-1408)*
Delmarva Equine Clinic ....G.. 302 735-4735
 Dover *(G-1410)*
Dotty Sweicicki Dvm ....G.. 302 674-1380
 Hartly *(G-2920)*
Dover Animal Hospital ....F.. 302 746-2688
 Dover *(G-1441)*
Eastern Shore Veterinary Hosp ....F.. 302 875-5941
 Laurel *(G-3227)*
Elevate Dvm Inc ....G.. 302 761-9650
 Wilmington *(G-10371)*
Forrest Avenue Animal Hospital ....F.. 302 736-3000
 Dover *(G-1562)*
Four Paws Animal Hospital PA ....F.. 302 629-7297
 Bridgeville *(G-472)*
Georgetown Animal Hospital PA ....G.. 302 856-2623
 Georgetown *(G-2541)*
Golden Merger Corp ....F.. 302 737-8100
 Newark *(G-6672)*
Governors Ave Animal Hospital ....G.. 302 734-5588
 Dover *(G-1605)*
Haven Lake Animal Hospital ....G.. 302 422-8100
 Milford *(G-4436)*
Hockessin Animal Hospital ....G.. 302 239-9464
 Hockessin *(G-3047)*
Karli Flanagan Dvm ....G.. 302 893-7872
 Newark *(G-6868)*
Kentmere Veterinary Hospital ....G.. 302 655-6610
 Wilmington *(G-11246)*
Kirkwood Anmal Brding Grooming .....E.. 302 737-1098
 Newark *(G-6891)*
Lantana Veterinary Center Inc ....F.. 302 234-3275
 Hockessin *(G-3077)*
Limestone Veterinary Hospital ....F.. 302 239-5415
 Hockessin *(G-3082)*
Lums Pond Animal Hospital Inc ....E.. 302 836-5585
 Bear *(G-240)*
Middletown Veterinary Hospital ....G.. 302 378-2342
 Middletown *(G-4161)*
Mmi Holdings Inc ....G.. 302 455-2021
 Newark *(G-7049)*
New London Veterinary Center ....F.. 302 738-5000
 Newark *(G-7107)*
Ocean View Animal Hospital ....G.. 302 539-2273
 Ocean View *(G-7807)*
Peninsula Anmal Hosp Orthpdics ......G.. 302 846-9011
 Delmar *(G-1024)*
Peninsula Veterinary Svcs LLC ....G.. 302 947-0719
 Millsboro *(G-4779)*
Pet Medical Center ....G.. 302 846-2869
 Delmar *(G-1026)*
Peters John Dvm ....G.. 302 478-5981
 Wilmington *(G-12100)*
Pike Creek Animal Hospital ....E.. 302 454-7780
 Newark *(G-7215)*
Precious Paws Animal Hospital ....F.. 302 539-2273
 Ocean View *(G-7809)*
Rbah Inc ....G.. 302 227-2009
 Rehoboth Beach *(G-8042)*
Route 24 Animal Hospital ....G.. 302 945-2330
 Millsboro *(G-4796)*
Ruthie Franczek ....G.. 302 659-1000
 Smyrna *(G-8708)*
Seaford Animal Hospital Inc ....F.. 302 629-7325
 Seaford *(G-8386)*
Sharon Alger-Little Dr ....F.. 302 398-3367
 Harrington *(G-2886)*
Sussex County Animal Assn ....G.. 302 628-5198
 Seaford *(G-8413)*
Sussex Veterinary Hospital ....G.. 302 732-9433
 Dagsboro *(G-936)*
VCA Animal Hospitals Inc ....G.. 302 834-1118
 Newark *(G-7647)*
VCA Inc ....E.. 302 737-1098
 Newark *(G-7648)*
Vet Housecall Service ....G.. 302 656-7291
 Claymont *(G-814)*
Veterinary Specialty Ctr Del PA ....E.. 302 322-6933
 New Castle *(G-5816)*
Western Sussex Animal Hosp Inc .....G.. 302 337-7387
 Bridgeville *(G-532)*
White Clay Creek Vtrinary Hosp ....F.. 302 738-9611
 Newark *(G-7691)*
Wilmington Animal Hospital 302 762-2694
 Wilmington *(G-13223)*

Windcrest Animal Hospital ....E.. 302 239-9464
 Wilmington *(G-13270)*

0751 Livestock Svcs, Except Veterinary

Allen Harim Farms LLC ....E.. 302 629-9136
 Millsboro *(G-4627)*
B & R Boyer Pressure Washing ....G.. 302 875-3603
 Laurel *(G-3194)*
D E I Farms Inc ....G.. 302 684-3415
 Milton *(G-4885)*
M & D Poultry Service ....G.. 302 934-7050
 Millsboro *(G-4729)*
◆ Mountaire Farms Inc ....G.. 302 988-6289
 Selbyville *(G-8524)*

0752 Animal Specialty Svcs, Exc Veterinary

Adandy Farm ....G.. 302 349-5116
 Greenwood *(G-2711)*
American K9 Doggie Daycare & T ....F.. 302 376-9663
 Middletown *(G-3937)*
Animal Inn Inc ....G.. 302 653-5560
 Dover *(G-1127)*
Apex Arabians Inc ....G.. 302 242-6272
 Houston *(G-3176)*
Brenford Animal Hospital P A ....E.. 302 678-9418
 Dover *(G-1229)*
Carlisle Group ....G.. 302 475-3010
 Wilmington *(G-9572)*
Delaware S P C A ....E.. 302 998-2281
 Newark *(G-6409)*
Dog Works South ....G.. 302 366-8161
 Newark *(G-6459)*
Dovington Training Center LLC ....G.. 302 284-2114
 Felton *(G-2287)*
▲ Harrington Raceway Inc ....G.. 302 398-4920
 Harrington *(G-2845)*
Heavenly Hound Hotel ....G.. 302 436-2926
 Selbyville *(G-8500)*
Homeless Cat Helpers Inc ....F.. 302 344-3015
 Seaford *(G-8268)*
Jenns Tail Waggers ....F.. 302 475-9621
 Wilmington *(G-11148)*
Krm Stables ....G.. 302 653-3838
 Clayton *(G-860)*
Marlyn Meadow Arabians ....G.. 302 378-8642
 Middletown *(G-4146)*
Michael Matthew Sponaugle ....G.. 302 566-1010
 Harrington *(G-2868)*
Never Never Lnd Kennel Cattery ......G.. 302 645-6140
 Lewes *(G-3658)*
Paws & People Too ....G.. 302 376-8234
 Middletown *(G-4185)*
RAD Pets Inc ....G.. 302 335-5718
 Felton *(G-2314)*
Sakura Inc ....G.. 302 349-4628
 Greenwood *(G-2761)*
Sharp Farm ....F.. 302 378-9606
 Middletown *(G-4239)*
Tri-State Bird Rescue RES Inc ....E.. 302 737-9543
 Newark *(G-7586)*
Wash-N-Wag ....G.. 302 644-2466
 Lewes *(G-3816)*

0762 Farm Management Svcs

Infarm - Indoor Urban Farming ....C.. 561 809-5183
 Dover *(G-1675)*

0781 Landscape Counseling & Planning

A&V Landscaping ....G.. 302 684-8609
 Milton *(G-4859)*
Addalli Landscaping ....G.. 302 836-2002
 Bear *(G-12)*
Anderson Landscaping ....G.. 302 423-3904
 Smyrna *(G-8570)*
Atlantic Landscape Co ....G.. 302 661-1950
 Wilmington *(G-9179)*
Autumn Hill Patio & Landscape ....G.. 302 293-1183
 Wilmington *(G-9193)*
Ayon Landscaping ....G.. 302 275-0205
 Wilmington *(G-9203)*
Baileys Lawn and Landscape LLC ....G.. 302 376-9113
 Middletown *(G-3959)*
Bas Home and Landscape Svcs ....G.. 302 354-0178
 Hockessin *(G-2961)*
Bernardon PC ....F.. 302 622-9550
 Wilmington *(G-9309)*
Binkley Horticulture Services ....G.. 484 459-2391
 Wilmington *(G-9339)*

Borsello Inc ....E.. 302 472-2600
 Hockessin *(G-2967)*
Brandywine Nurseries Inc ....E.. 302 429-0865
 Wilmington *(G-9443)*
Brightview Landscapes LLC ....D.. 302 731-4162
 Newark *(G-6122)*
Burton Hg & Company Inc ....F.. 302 245-3384
 Dagsboro *(G-887)*
Campbells Landscape Svc Inc ....G.. 302 266-0117
 Newark *(G-6147)*
Cedar Hardscaping L L C 877 569-9859
 Bear *(G-68)*
Cge Landscape Design ....G.. 302 983-4847
 Newark *(G-6181)*
Complete Properties Services ....G.. 302 242-8666
 Camden Wyoming *(G-624)*
Contruction Jones and Ldscpg ....G.. 302 423-6456
 Camden Wyoming *(G-625)*
Corrin Tree & Landscape Co ....G.. 302 753-8733
 Bear *(G-86)*
Corrin Tree Landscape ....G.. 302 521-8333
 Wilmington *(G-9868)*
Country Green Landscaping ....G.. 302 653-1600
 Smyrna *(G-8606)*
Cutting Edge of Delaware Inc ....G.. 302 834-8723
 Wilmington *(G-9930)*
Delaware Lawn & Tree Service ....F.. 302 834-7406
 Bear *(G-109)*
Dick Ennis Inc ....G.. 302 945-2627
 Lewes *(G-3464)*
Disabatino Landscaping Inc ....D.. 302 764-0408
 Wilmington *(G-10166)*
Disabatino Ldscpg Tree Svc Inc ....F.. 302 764-0408
 Wilmington *(G-10167)*
Dreamscape Landscaping ....G.. 302 354-5247
 Claymont *(G-736)*
E A Zando Custom Designs Inc ....F.. 302 684-4601
 Milton *(G-4900)*
Edc LLC ....F.. 302 645-0777
 Lewes *(G-3478)*
Elite Landscape ....G.. 302 543-7305
 Wilmington *(G-10376)*
Emerald Lawn and Ldscpg LLC ....G.. 302 228-1468
 Milford *(G-4404)*
Freedom Landscape & Irrigation ....G.. 302 436-7100
 Selbyville *(G-8494)*
Garden Design Group Inc ....G.. 302 234-3000
 Hockessin *(G-3034)*
Habitat Design Group ....G.. 302 335-4452
 Frederica *(G-2405)*
Hoerner Inc ....F.. 302 762-4406
 Wilmington *(G-10923)*
Integrated Solutions Planning ....G.. 302 297-9215
 Georgetown *(G-2567)*
Irwin Landscaping Inc ....F.. 302 239-9229
 Hockessin *(G-3060)*
J B Landscaping ....E.. 302 645-7202
 Lewes *(G-3566)*
Ji DCI Jv-II ....F.. 302 652-4221
 Wilmington *(G-11156)*
Jobes Landscape Inc ....G.. 302 945-0195
 Lewes *(G-3572)*
Juan Saucedo ....G.. 302 233-4539
 Dover *(G-1714)*
Kent Landscaping Co LLC ....G.. 302 535-4296
 Camden *(G-588)*
Leons Garden World Ej Inc ....F.. 410 392-8630
 New Castle *(G-5480)*
Martins Landscaping LLC ....G.. 302 984-2887
 Wilmington *(G-11552)*
MCB Landscaping LLC ....G.. 215 421-1083
 Wilmington *(G-11584)*
Mf Stoneworks LLC ....G.. 302 265-7732
 Milton *(G-4936)*
Michael A Sinclair Inc ....G.. 302 834-8144
 Bear *(G-253)*
Mitsdrfer Bros Lawn Ldscpg Inc ....G.. 302 633-1150
 Newark *(G-7045)*
Natures Call LLC ....G.. 302 777-7767
 Wilmington *(G-11819)*
Nichols Nursery Inc ....E.. 302 834-2426
 Wilmington *(G-7133)*
Passwaters Landscaping ....G.. 302 542-8077
 Bridgeville *(G-506)*
Penny Hill Lawn & Landscaping ....G.. 302 762-4406
 Wilmington *(G-12073)*
Poof Power Wash & Ldscpg LLC ......G.. 302 595-1576
 Dover *(G-1976)*
Precision Ldscpg & Lawn Care ....G.. 302 492-1583
 Hartly *(G-2938)*

Employee Codes: A=Over 500 employees, B=251-500
C=101-250, D=51-100, E=20-50, F=10-19, G=1-9

2020 Harris Directory of
Delaware Businesses

07 AGRICULTURAL SERVICES

R D Collins & Sons ....F 302 834-3409
  Bear (G-296)
Ras Addis & Associates Inc ....F 302 571-1683
  Wilmington (G-12318)
Rodney Rbnsn Ldscp Archts Inc ....G 302 888-1544
  Wilmington (G-12460)
Scalia S Landscaping ....G 302 651-9822
  Wilmington (G-12551)
Shore Property Maintenance ....F 302 947-4440
  Harbeson (G-2799)
Siteone Landscape Supply LLC ....G 302 836-3903
  Bear (G-324)
Sposato Irrigation Company ....E 302 645-4773
  Milton (G-4971)
Sposato Landscape Company Inc ....G 302 645-4773
  Milton (G-4972)
Superior Yardworks Inc ....G 610 274-2255
  Hockessin (G-3155)
Total Turf & Landscaping ....G 302 762-5410
  Wilmington (G-12941)
Whartons Landscaping LLC ....G 302 947-0913
  Lewes (G-3819)
Whartons Landscaping Grdn Ctr ....G 302 426-4854
  Rehoboth Beach (G-8114)
William J Winkler ....G 302 732-0866
  Selbyville (G-8554)

0782 Lawn & Garden Svcs

1st Impression Inc ....E 302 738-4918
  Newark (G-5852)
A & G Lawn Care LLC ....G 302 584-8719
  Bear (G-2)
A To Z Landscaping Services ....G 302 994-1552
  Wilmington (G-8885)
Above All Gtter Gardening Svcs ....G 302 478-0762
  Newark (G-5885)
Absolutely Green Inc ....F 302 731-1616
  Newark (G-5888)
Antonios Lawn Service LLC ....G 302 293-1200
  New Castle (G-5040)
Baritc Lawn Care LLC ....G 302 420-6072
  New Castle (G-5067)
Bartons Landscaping/Lawn Inc ....E 302 629-2213
  Seaford (G-8162)
Bella Terra Landscapes LLC ....E 302 422-9000
  Lincoln (G-3838)
Borsello Inc ....E 302 472-2600
  Hockessin (G-2967)
Brandywine Nurseries Inc ....E 302 429-0865
  Wilmington (G-9443)
Cedar Hardscaping L L C ....G 877 569-9859
  Bear (G-68)
Centerville Company Contrs ....G 302 656-8666
  Wilmington (G-9613)
Chambers Ldscpg & Lawncare Inc ....G 302 328-1312
  New Castle (G-5141)
Cheap-Scape Inc ....E 302 472-2600
  Hockessin (G-2984)
Christopher T Parsons ....G 302 947-2380
  Millsboro (G-4662)
Commercial Ground Care Inc ....G 302 762-5410
  Wilmington (G-9787)
Common Sense Solutions LLC ....G 302 875-4510
  Laurel (G-3217)
Country Lawn Care & Maint ....G 302 593-3393
  Harbeson (G-2779)
Countryside Lawn & Landscape ....E 302 832-1320
  Newark (G-6304)
Curbs Etc Inc ....G 302 653-3511
  Smyrna (G-8608)
Cutem Up Tree Care Del Inc ....G 302 629-4655
  Seaford (G-8216)
Cutting Edge ....F 302 834-8723
  Delaware City (G-951)
Cutting Edge of Delaware Inc ....F 302 834-8723
  Wilmington (G-9930)
Daniels Lawn Care ....G 302 218-0173
  Wilmington (G-9958)
David M Wagner ....G 302 832-8336
  Bear (G-98)
David Rockwell & Associates ....G 302 478-9900
  Wilmington (G-9972)
Davis Young Associates Inc ....F 610 388-0932
  Yorklyn (G-13365)
Del Lawn Service ....G 302 525-4148
  Newark (G-6362)
Delaware Landscaping Inc ....G 302 698-3001
  Dover (G-1380)
Delaware Secretary of State ....G 302 834-8046
  Bear (G-112)

Dennis Woltemate Lawn Corp ....G 302 738-5266
  Newark (G-6438)
Dependable Lawn Care Inc ....G 302 834-0159
  Middletown (G-4036)
Dick Ennis Inc ....G 302 945-2627
  Lewes (G-3464)
Discovery Solutions Inc ....G 410 929-0025
  Lewes (G-3467)
Eagle Bldg & Grounds Maint LLC ....G 302 264-7058
  Clayton (G-845)
Eagle Building and Grounds ....G 302 508-5403
  Clayton (G-846)
Earthscapes LLC ....G 302 678-0478
  Dover (G-1497)
East Coast Lawn Services Inc ....G 302 453-8400
  Newark (G-6494)
Emerald Green ....G 302 836-6909
  Middletown (G-4057)
Ernie Deangelis ....F 302 226-9533
  Rehoboth Beach (G-7928)
Evan Hurst Property Management ....G 302 375-0398
  Claymont (G-742)
Evs Lawn Service Inc ....G 302 475-9222
  Wilmington (G-10453)
Finocchiaro Landscape Inc ....G 302 792-2201
  Wilmington (G-10542)
Forever Green Landscaping Inc ....F 302 322-9535
  New Castle (G-5324)
Fox Landscaping Corp ....G 302 945-5656
  Millsboro (G-4693)
Gallucios Lawn Care ....G 302 324-8182
  New Castle (G-5342)
Garcia Landscaping Services ....G 302 324-8789
  New Castle (G-5344)
Gildea Enterprises Inc ....G 302 475-1184
  Wilmington (G-10711)
Gold Leaf Services LLC ....G 302 373-3333
  Wilmington (G-10736)
Grass Busters Landscaping Co ....E 302 292-1166
  Newark (G-6682)
Grassworks Lawn Care Service ....G 302 683-0833
  Wilmington (G-10763)
Green Blade Irrigation & Turf ....G 302 736-8873
  Magnolia (G-3893)
Greenleaf Services Inc ....G 302 836-9050
  Lewes (G-3523)
Greenleaf Turf Solutions Inc ....G 302 731-1075
  Newark (G-6687)
Grizzlys Landscape Sup & Svcs ....G 302 644-0654
  Lewes (G-3524)
Horsey Turf Farm LLC ....F 302 875-7299
  Laurel (G-3238)
Integrated Turf Management Sys ....F 302 266-8000
  Newark (G-6789)
Irwin Landscaping Inc ....F 302 239-9229
  Hockessin (G-3060)
Itea Inc ....G 302 328-3716
  Bear (G-193)
Izzys Lawn Service Inc ....G 302 293-9221
  Wilmington (G-11096)
Jack Kellys Ldscpg & Tree Svc ....G 302 239-7185
  Hockessin (G-3064)
Jade Enterprises Inc ....G 302 378-3435
  Odessa (G-7828)
Jamark Enterprises Inc ....F 302 652-2000
  Wilmington (G-11118)
Jason M Bradford ....G 302 236-8236
  Millsboro (G-4713)
Jedi Inc ....G 610 459-4477
  Wilmington (G-11140)
Johns Landscaping ....G 302 507-4773
  Wilmington (G-11178)
Jonny Nichols Ldscp Maint Inc ....G 302 697-2200
  Dover (G-1708)
Keener-Sensenig Co ....F 302 453-8584
  Newark (G-6872)
Kens Lawn Service Inc ....G 302 478-2714
  Wilmington (G-11242)
Kst Land Design Inc ....G 302 328-1879
  Wilmington (G-11297)
Lawn Doctor of Wilmington Inc ....F 302 656-4900
  Wilmington (G-11343)
Lawn Quenchers Inc ....G 302 218-1909
  Bear (G-231)
Lawnworks Inc ....F 302 368-5699
  Wilmington (G-6922)
Lees Lawn Care ....G 302 658-2546
  Wilmington (G-11359)
Leounes Catered Affairs ....G 302 547-3321
  Wilmington (G-11374)

Lords Landscaping Inc ....E 302 539-6119
  Millville (G-4847)
Martom Landscaping Co Inc ....E 302 322-1920
  Saint Georges (G-8128)
Mary Annes Landscaping Inc ....G 302 335-5433
  Felton (G-2306)
Mitsdrfer Bros Lawn Ldscpg Inc ....G 302 633-1150
  Newark (G-7045)
Nash Omniscaping LLC ....G 302 654-4000
  Wilmington (G-11802)
Naturalawn of America Inc ....F 302 652-2000
  Wilmington (G-11818)
Old Country Garden Center Inc ....E 302 652-3317
  Wilmington (G-11943)
Outdoor Design Group LLC ....F 302 743-2363
  Newark (G-7165)
Owls Nest Horticultural Svcs ....G 302 654-6989
  Wilmington (G-11988)
Penwood Property Preservation ....G 302 469-5318
  Felton (G-2308)
Perfection Lawncare Ltd ....G 215 624-7410
  Middletown (G-4189)
Plant Retrievers Whl Nurs ....G 302 337-9833
  Georgetown (G-2620)
Professnal Arfication Svcs Inc ....G 302 752-7003
  Georgetown (G-2629)
R D Collins & Sons ....F 302 834-3409
  Bear (G-296)
Rentokil North America Inc ....E 302 733-0851
  Newark (G-7318)
Richard Belotti ....G 302 934-7585
  Georgetown (G-2639)
S Dorman Lawn Care Inc ....G 302 947-2858
  Georgetown (G-2645)
Shore Property Maintenance LLC ....E 302 227-7786
  Rehoboth Beach (G-8075)
Shubert Enterprises Inc ....E 302 846-3122
  Delmar (G-1029)
Shubert Enterprises Inc ....G 714 595-5762
  Dagsboro (G-933)
Simply Green ....G 302 256-0822
  Wilmington (G-12627)
Sposato Lawn Care ....E 302 645-4773
  Milton (G-4973)
Stump B Gone Inc ....G 302 737-7779
  Newark (G-7498)
Trugreen Limited Partnership ....D 302 724-6620
  Wilmington (G-12988)
Turf Pro Inc ....E 302 218-3530
  Newark (G-7600)
US Lawns Dover ....G 302 703-2818
  Lewes (G-3805)
West Third Enterprises LLC ....G 302 732-3133
  Dagsboro (G-943)
White Oak Landscape MGT Inc ....G 302 652-7533
  Wilmington (G-13191)
Wilcox Landscaping ....E 302 322-3002
  New Castle (G-5834)
William H Rdford Nurseries Inc ....E 302 659-3130
  Smyrna (G-8745)
Wrights Lawn Care Inc ....F 302 684-3058
  Milton (G-4982)

0783 Ornamental Shrub & Tree Svc

Beaver Tree Service Inc ....G 302 226-3564
  Rehoboth Beach (G-7861)
Brandywine Tree and Shrub LLC ....G 302 475-7594
  Wilmington (G-9456)
Complete Tree Care Inc ....G 302 945-8289
  Millsboro (G-4667)
Cutem Up Tree Care Del Inc ....G 302 629-4655
  Seaford (G-8216)
Eastern Ornamentals LLC ....G 302 684-8733
  Milford (G-4402)
Stein Tree Service Inc ....F 302 731-1718
  Wilmington (G-12750)
Strobert Tree Services ....G 302 633-3478
  Wilmington (G-12778)
▲ Strobert Tree Services Inc ....E 302 475-7089
  Wilmington (G-12779)
Stump B Gone Inc ....G 302 737-7779
  Newark (G-7498)
Sussex Tree Inc ....G 302 629-9899
  Bridgeville (G-523)
Tri State Tree Service ....G 302 645-7412
  Milton (G-4978)

SIC SECTION

15 BUILDING CONSTRUCTION-GENERAL CONTRACTORS AND OPERATIVE BUILDERS

08 FORESTRY

0811 Timber Tracts
Whitetail Country Log & Hlg..............G....... 302 846-3982
Delmar *(G-1048)*

0851 Forestry Svcs
Delaware Cy Vlntr Fire Co No 1 ....C....... 302 834-9336
Delaware City *(G-955)*

09 FISHING, HUNTING, AND TRAPPING

0913 Shellfish Fishing
Commercial Waterman ....F....... 302 659-3031
Townsend *(G-8772)*

0919 Marine Fishing, Misc
▲ Advance Marine LLC ....G....... 302 656-2111
Wilmington *(G-8947)*

0971 Hunting & Trapping
▲ Lab Products Inc ....F....... 302 628-4300
Seaford *(G-8288)*
Rocky Mtn Elk Foundation Inc..............E....... 302 697-3621
Camden Wyoming *(G-655)*
Vance Phillips Inc................................G....... 302 542-1501
Laurel *(G-3301)*

10 METAL MINING

1011 Iron Ores
▲ American Minerals Partnership ....C....... 302 652-3301
New Castle *(G-5034)*
Banfield & Temperley Inc ....G....... 347 878-6057
Dover *(G-1169)*

1021 Copper Ores
CC Enterprises LLC.............................G....... 302 265-3677
Newark *(G-6175)*

1061 Ferroalloy Ores, Except Vanadium
African Markets Fund LLC ....G....... 703 944-1514
Dover *(G-1092)*
▲ American Minerals Partnership ....C....... 302 652-3301
New Castle *(G-5034)*

1081 Metal Mining Svcs
Joseph T Ryerson & Son Inc ....E....... 302 366-0555
Newark *(G-6851)*
Nanoshel LLC ....G....... 302 268-6163
Wilmington *(G-11799)*

1099 Metal Ores, NEC
African Markets Fund LLC ....G....... 703 944-1514
Dover *(G-1092)*
▲ American Minerals Partnership ....C....... 302 652-3301
New Castle *(G-5034)*

13 OIL AND GAS EXTRACTION

1311 Crude Petroleum & Natural Gas
I-Pulse Inc..G....... 604 689-8765
Wilmington *(G-10984)*
Nemours Energy ....G....... 302 655-4838
Wilmington *(G-11832)*
Sun Gabon Oil Company ....G....... 302 293-6000
Wilmington *(G-12793)*

1321 Natural Gas Liquids
Party Gas ....G....... 302 730-3880
Dover *(G-1938)*

1381 Drilling Oil & Gas Wells
Robert J Seward and Son ....G....... 302 378-9414
Townsend *(G-8820)*

1382 Oil & Gas Field Exploration Svcs
Butamax Advanced Biofuels LLC ......G....... 302 695-3617
Wilmington *(G-9513)*
E I Du Pont De Nemours & Co ....F....... 302 774-1000
Wilmington *(G-10294)*

I-Pulse Inc..G....... 604 689-8765
Wilmington *(G-10984)*
Penn Virginia Holding Corp ....C....... 302 288-0158
Wilmington *(G-12067)*
Rangeland Nm LLC ....G....... 800 316-6660
Dover *(G-2009)*
Sun Orient Exploration Company ....G....... 302 293-6000
Wilmington *(G-12797)*

1389 Oil & Gas Field Svcs, NEC
Accurate-Energy LLC ....G....... 302 947-9560
Lewes *(G-3323)*
Acuren Inspection Inc ....G....... 302 836-0165
Newark *(G-5897)*
Adv Fuel Polishing Service ....G....... 302 477-1040
Claymont *(G-685)*
Aim Metals & Alloys USA Inc ....G....... 212 450-4519
Wilmington *(G-8989)*
ARC Offshore Investments Inc ....G....... 561 670-9938
Wilmington *(G-9119)*
Atlantic Oil & Gas LLC ....G....... 302 898-2862
Townsend *(G-8760)*
Burton Hg & Company Inc ....F....... 302 245-3384
Dagsboro *(G-887)*
Cunningham Homes LLC ....G....... 267 473-0895
Newark *(G-6326)*
Delaware Storage & Pipeline Co.......G....... 302 736-1774
Dover *(G-1399)*
DH Tech Wilmington De ....G....... 215 680-9194
Wilmington *(G-10136)*
Dick Ennis Inc ....G....... 302 945-2627
Lewes *(G-3464)*
Ecg Industries Inc ....G....... 302 453-0535
Newark *(G-6502)*
Estate Servicing LLC ....G....... 302 731-1119
Newark *(G-6540)*
Greenamoyer Construction ....G....... 302 999-8235
Wilmington *(G-10774)*
Jbm Petroleum Service LLC ....G....... 302 752-6105
Lincoln *(G-3857)*
Keyrock LLC ....G....... 818 605-7772
Wilmington *(G-11252)*
Lone Star Global Services Inc ....G....... 302 744-9800
Dover *(G-1795)*
Mabel R Cole ....G....... 302 378-2792
Middletown *(G-4139)*
O&G Knwldge Shring Pltform LLC....G....... 303 872-0533
Wilmington *(G-11926)*
Property Doctors LLC ....G....... 302 249-7731
Magnolia *(G-3905)*
Rock Solid Servicing LLC ....G....... 302 233-2569
Magnolia *(G-3908)*
TCI Inspections USA LLC ....G....... 302 261-5208
Wilmington *(G-12858)*
Tdw Services Inc ....F....... 302 594-9880
New Castle *(G-5756)*
TEC-Con Inc ....G....... 610 583-8770
New Castle *(G-5757)*
Willey and Co ....G....... 302 629-3327
Laurel *(G-3311)*

14 MINING AND QUARRYING OF NONMETALLIC MINERALS, EXCEPT FUELS

1411 Dimension Stone
Everest Granite LLC ....G....... 302 229-4733
Wilmington *(G-10445)*

1429 Crushed & Broken Stone, NEC
Contractors Materials LLC ....G....... 302 656-6066
Wilmington *(G-9844)*
Pioneer Materials ....G....... 302 284-3580
Felton *(G-2311)*

1442 Construction Sand & Gravel
Bardon U S Corporation ....G....... 302 552-3136
Wilmington *(G-9253)*
Bear Materials LLC ....G....... 302 658-5241
New Castle *(G-5078)*
Cook Hauling LLC ....G....... 302 378-6451
Middletown *(G-4010)*
Goldsboro Sand and Gravel ....G....... 410 310-0402
Camden Wyoming *(G-643)*
Joseph M L Sand & Gravel Co ....F....... 302 856-7396
Georgetown *(G-2578)*

Legacy Vulcan LLC...........................G....... 302 875-5733
Seaford *(G-8292)*
Legacy Vulcan LLC...........................G....... 302 875-0748
Georgetown *(G-2589)*
Lewis Sand and Gravel LLC..............G....... 302 238-0169
Millsboro *(G-4720)*
Material Transit Inc ....F....... 302 395-0556
New Castle *(G-5512)*
Parkway Gravel Inc ....G....... 302 326-0554
New Castle *(G-5604)*
Pkwy Gravel......................................G....... 302 328-5182
New Castle *(G-5624)*
Sussex Sand & Gravel Inc ....G....... 302 628-6962
Seaford *(G-8418)*

1446 Industrial Sand
American Minerals Inc ....G....... 302 652-3301
New Castle *(G-5033)*
Stockley Materials LLC ....G....... 302 856-7601
Georgetown *(G-2666)*

1459 Clay, Ceramic & Refractory Minerals, NEC
◆ Rhi Refractories Holding Co............G....... 302 655-6497
Wilmington *(G-12400)*

1479 Chemical & Fertilizer Mining
▲ Oceanport LLC ....F....... 302 792-2212
Claymont *(G-791)*

1481 Nonmetallic Minerals Svcs, Except Fuels
Reliance Egleford Upstream LLC ....G....... 302 472-7437
Wilmington *(G-12376)*

1499 Miscellaneous Nonmetallic Mining
Asbury Carbons Inc..........................G....... 302 652-0266
Wilmington *(G-9146)*
◆ Rgp Holding Inc ....G....... 302 661-0117
Wilmington *(G-12399)*

15 BUILDING CONSTRUCTION-GENERAL CONTRACTORS AND OPERATIVE BUILDERS

1521 General Contractors, Single Family Houses
36 Builders Inc ....F....... 302 349-9480
Bridgeville *(G-441)*
A Fields Unlimited LLC ....G....... 800 484-2331
Newark *(G-5866)*
Accessible Home Builders Inc..........G....... 302 628-9571
Millsboro *(G-4622)*
Advance Construction Co Del ....F....... 302 697-9444
Camden Wyoming *(G-611)*
Advance Wndw/Sprior Siding Inc.....F....... 302 324-8890
Newark *(G-5903)*
Albert S Lambertson Inc ....G....... 302 734-9649
Dover *(G-1101)*
Aruanno Enterprises Inc ....G....... 302 530-1217
Middletown *(G-3943)*
Aslin Inc ....G....... 302 674-1900
Dover *(G-1145)*
Astute General Contracting LLC ......G....... 302 383-4942
Wilmington *(G-9169)*
Atlantic Enterprises LLC ....G....... 302 542-5427
Lewes *(G-3355)*
Bancroft Homes Inc..........................G....... 302 655-5461
Wilmington *(G-9235)*
Bartlett & Bartlett LLC ....G....... 302 653-7200
Clayton *(G-838)*
Battaglia Mechanical Inc ....E....... 302 325-6100
New Castle *(G-5071)*
Bay Developers Inc..........................F....... 302 736-0924
Dover *(G-1179)*
Bay To Beach Builders Inc ....G....... 302 349-5099
Farmington *(G-2266)*
Beam Construction Inc.....................G....... 302 537-2787
Fenwick Island *(G-2330)*
Beazer Homes Corp..........................G....... 302 378-4161
Middletown *(G-3964)*
Bellevue Contractors LLC ....G....... 302 655-1522
Wilmington *(G-9289)*
Bellevue Remodel & Design LLC.....G....... 302 482-7200
Wilmington *(G-9293)*

Employee Codes: A=Over 500 employees, B=251-500
C=101-250, D=51-100, E=20-50, F=10-19, G=1-9

2020 Harris Directory of
Delaware Businesses

15 BUILDING CONSTRUCTION-GENERAL CONTRACTORS AND OPERATIVE BUILDERS

Benjamin B Smith Builders Inc .... G 302 537-1916
   Ocean View *(G-7764)*
Beracah Homes Inc .... E 302 349-4561
   Greenwood *(G-2716)*
Bestfield Associates Inc .... F 302 633-6361
   Wilmington *(G-9315)*
Black Dog Construction LLC .... G 302 530-4967
   Newark *(G-6088)*
Blenheim Management Company .... E 302 254-0100
   Newark *(G-6093)*
Boardwalk Builders Inc .... F 302 227-5754
   Rehoboth Beach *(G-7871)*
Bradley Arthur & Son Cnstr .... G 302 422-9391
   Milford *(G-4332)*
Brandywine Contractors Inc .... G 302 325-2700
   New Castle *(G-5107)*
Breeze Construction LLC .... G 302 522-9201
   Townsend *(G-8766)*
Brendon T Warfel Construction .... G 302 422-7814
   Milford *(G-4334)*
Bruce Mears Designer-Builder .... F 302 539-2355
   Ocean View *(G-7770)*
Bunting Construction Corp .... F 302 436-5124
   Selbyville *(G-8464)*
C & B Construct .... G 302 378-9862
   Milford *(G-4338)*
C & K Builders LLC .... G 302 324-9811
   Bear *(G-59)*
C Wallace & Associates .... G 302 528-2182
   Hockessin *(G-2973)*
C&M Construction Company LLC .... E 302 663-0936
   Millsboro *(G-4652)*
Capano Homes Inc .... E 302 384-7980
   Wilmington *(G-9553)*
Cape Financial Services Inc .... F 302 645-6274
   Lewes *(G-3400)*
Capstone Homes .... G 302 684-4480
   Milton *(G-4875)*
Carl Deputy & Son Builders LLC .... G 302 284-3041
   Felton *(G-2280)*
Carrie Construction Inc .... G 302 239-5386
   Hockessin *(G-2977)*
Case Hndyman Svcs W Chster LLC .... G 302 234-6558
   Hockessin *(G-2979)*
Charles A Zonko Builders Inc .... E 302 436-0222
   Selbyville *(G-8467)*
Charles R Reed .... G 302 284-3353
   Felton *(G-2282)*
Choice Rmdlg & Restoration Inc .... G 717 917-0601
   Hockessin *(G-2987)*
CK Construction Inc .... G 302 698-3207
   Camden *(G-550)*
Cns Construction Corp .... E 302 224-0450
   Newark *(G-6257)*
Coastal Sun Roms Prch Enclsres .... G 302 537-3679
   Frankford *(G-2355)*
Colonial Construction Company .... F 302 994-5705
   Wilmington *(G-9774)*
Commonwealth Construction .... G 302 654-6611
   Wilmington *(G-9788)*
Commonwealth Contruction Co .... E 302 654-6611
   Wilmington *(G-9789)*
Comstock Custom Cabinets Inc .... G 302 422-2928
   Milford *(G-4364)*
Connell Construction Co .... G 302 738-9428
   Newark *(G-6287)*
Conway Construction LLC .... G 302 453-9260
   Newark *(G-6293)*
Country Life Homes Milford De .... G 302 265-2257
   Milford *(G-4365)*
Cpr Construction Inc .... G 302 322-5770
   New Castle *(G-5207)*
Custom Improvers Inc .... G 302 731-9246
   Newark *(G-6332)*
D F Quillen & Sons Inc .... E 302 227-2531
   Rehoboth Beach *(G-7906)*
D P Investment L L C .... G 302 998-7031
   Wilmington *(G-9941)*
D&S Construction Company .... G 302 650-3209
   Middletown *(G-4018)*
David Waters & Son .... G 302 235-8653
   Hockessin *(G-3001)*
Dead On Construction .... G 302 462-5023
   Selbyville *(G-8480)*
Del Homes Inc .... G 302 697-8204
   Magnolia *(G-3889)*
Del Homes Inc .... E 302 730-1479
   Dover *(G-1351)*
Delaware Homes Inc .... G 302 378-9510
   Townsend *(G-8779)*

Delaware Homes Inc .... F 302 223-6258
   Smyrna *(G-8616)*
Delmarva Builders Inc .... G 302 629-9123
   Bridgeville *(G-465)*
Delmarva Pole Building Sup Inc .... G 302 698-3636
   Wyoming *(G-13361)*
Delpa Builders LLC .... F 302 731-7304
   New Castle *(G-5245)*
Deshong & Sons Contractors .... G 302 453-8500
   Wilmington *(G-6440)*
Dewson Construction Company .... E 302 427-2250
   Wilmington *(G-10131)*
Dimple Construction Inc .... G 302 559-7535
   Bear *(G-119)*
Disabatino Construction Co .... C 302 652-3838
   Wilmington *(G-10164)*
Double Diamone Builders Inc .... F 302 945-2512
   Millsboro *(G-4682)*
Double S Developers Inc .... F 302 838-8880
   Bear *(G-126)*
Dugan Dt Roofing Inc .... G 302 636-9300
   Wilmington *(G-10246)*
E D Custom Contracting Inc .... G 302 653-2646
   Clayton *(G-844)*
Eastern Home Improvements Inc .... G 302 655-9920
   Wilmington *(G-10322)*
Eastern Shore Porch Patio Inc .... E 302 436-9520
   Selbyville *(G-8485)*
Edge Construction Corp .... G 302 778-5200
   Wilmington *(G-10346)*
Empire Investments Inc .... G 302 838-0631
   New Castle *(G-5289)*
First Choice Services Inc .... E 302 648-7877
   Dagsboro *(G-901)*
First State Services .... F 302 985-1560
   Wilmington *(G-10554)*
Francis Pollinger & Son Inc .... E 302 655-8097
   Wilmington *(G-10612)*
G G + A LLC .... G 302 376-6122
   Middletown *(G-4082)*
Garrison Custom Homes .... G 302 644-4008
   Lewes *(G-3508)*
George & Lynch Inc .... G 302 238-7289
   Millsboro *(G-4697)*
George K Rickards Inc .... G 302 539-7550
   Ocean View *(G-7791)*
Gibellino Construction Co .... G 302 455-0500
   Newark *(G-6652)*
Gpe Construction LLC .... G 267 595-8942
   Bear *(G-169)*
Griffin Home Builders Inc .... F 302 629-5615
   Seaford *(G-8254)*
Gulfstream Development Corp .... G 302 539-6178
   Ocean View *(G-7792)*
H H Builders Inc .... G 302 735-9900
   Dover *(G-1622)*
H&L Construction Corp .... G 302 875-5634
   Seaford *(G-8255)*
Habitat For Humanity .... F 302 652-0365
   Wilmington *(G-10815)*
Hanco Inc .... G 302 734-9782
   Dover *(G-1626)*
Handler Builders Inc .... E 302 999-9200
   Wilmington *(G-10831)*
Handler Corporation .... E 302 999-9200
   Wilmington *(G-10832)*
Harvey Miller Construction .... G 302 674-4128
   Dover *(G-1637)*
Henlopen Homes Inc .... G 302 684-0860
   Lewes *(G-3541)*
Herring Creek Builders Inc .... G 302 684-3015
   Milton *(G-4914)*
Hickory Hill Builders Inc .... G 302 934-6109
   Dagsboro *(G-909)*
Hoenen & Mitchell Inc .... G 302 645-6193
   Lewes *(G-3543)*
Home Services LLC .... G 302 510-4580
   Wilmington *(G-10940)*
Homestar Remodeling LLC .... G 302 528-5898
   Wilmington *(G-10943)*
Hugh H Hickman & Sons Inc .... F 302 539-9741
   Bethany Beach *(G-403)*
Humphries Construction Company .... G 302 349-9277
   Greenwood *(G-2744)*
Iacchetta Builders Inc .... G 302 436-4525
   Selbyville *(G-8505)*
Impulse Construction .... G 302 644-0464
   Lewes *(G-3555)*
Integrity MGT Solution Inc .... G 302 270-8976
   Clayton *(G-857)*

Interfaith Cmnty Hsing of Del .... F 302 652-3991
   Wilmington *(G-11062)*
J & L Services Inc .... F 410 943-3355
   Seaford *(G-8274)*
J & S General Contractors .... F 302 658-4499
   Wilmington *(G-11098)*
J B S Construction LLC .... G 302 349-5705
   Greenwood *(G-2746)*
J Culver Construction Inc .... G 302 337-8136
   Bridgeville *(G-485)*
J I Beiler Homes LLC .... G 302 697-1553
   Camden *(G-583)*
J Kenneth Moore & Son Inc .... G 302 736-0563
   Dover *(G-1687)*
J Rocco Construction LLC .... G 302 856-4100
   Georgetown *(G-2570)*
J&J Contracting Co Inc .... G 302 227-0800
   Rehoboth Beach *(G-7969)*
J&J Systems .... G 302 239-2969
   Hockessin *(G-3063)*
Jack Hickman Real Estate .... F 302 539-8000
   Bethany Beach *(G-406)*
Jack Saxton Construction Co .... G 302 764-5683
   Wilmington *(G-11116)*
James A Peel & Sons Inc .... G 302 738-1468
   Newark *(G-6825)*
James Rice Jr Construction Co .... G 302 731-9323
   Newark *(G-6826)*
Jeffrey Hatch .... G 443 496-0449
   Marydel *(G-3919)*
John Campanelli & Sons Inc .... G 302 239-8573
   Hockessin *(G-3067)*
Joseph & Cummings Builder .... G 302 875-4279
   Laurel *(G-3244)*
Joseph Devane Enterprises Inc .... F 302 703-0493
   New Castle *(G-5444)*
Joseph E Stevens & Father .... G 302 654-8556
   Wilmington *(G-11189)*
Jsf Construction Co Inc .... G 302 999-9573
   Wilmington *(G-11204)*
K E Smart & Sons Inc .... G 302 875-7002
   Laurel *(G-3247)*
Kairos Home Pros LLC .... G 302 233-7044
   Dover *(G-1721)*
Kaye Construction .... E 302 628-6962
   Seaford *(G-8285)*
Kelly Maintenance Ltd Inc .... G 302 539-3956
   Ocean View *(G-7797)*
Kersey Homes Inc .... G 302 934-8434
   Millsboro *(G-4717)*
Kings Contracting Inc .... G 302 677-0363
   Dover *(G-1751)*
Knotts Construction Inc .... G 302 475-7074
   Wilmington *(G-11283)*
Kokoszka & Sons Inc .... G 302 328-4807
   New Castle *(G-5468)*
Kristin Konstruction Company .... G 302 791-9670
   Claymont *(G-772)*
Landmark Homes Inc .... G 302 242-1394
   New Castle *(G-5473)*
Lane Builders LLC .... F 302 645-5555
   Lewes *(G-3591)*
Lenape Builders Inc .... F 302 376-3971
   Middletown *(G-4128)*
Leon N Weiner & Associates Inc .... D 302 656-1354
   Wilmington *(G-11371)*
Liberto Development Ltd .... G 302 698-1104
   Dover *(G-1782)*
Lighthouse Construction Inc .... F 302 677-1965
   Magnolia *(G-3898)*
LLC Schell Brothers .... E 302 376-0355
   Middletown *(G-4136)*
Locker Construction Inc .... G 302 239-2859
   Newark *(G-6946)*
Lockwood Design Construction .... G 302 684-4844
   Milton *(G-4925)*
M L Parker Construction Inc .... F 302 798-8530
   Claymont *(G-777)*
M W Fogarty Inc .... G 302 658-5547
   Hockessin *(G-3083)*
Mack Construction & Handy .... G 302 337-3448
   Bridgeville *(G-491)*
Mark Ventresca Associates Inc .... G 302 239-3925
   Hockessin *(G-3089)*
Mazzola Systems Inc .... F 302 738-6808
   Newark *(G-7008)*
Mebro Inc .... E 302 992-0104
   Wilmington *(G-11613)*
Michael W Fogarty Gen Contr .... G 302 658-5547
   Hockessin *(G-3094)*

Miken Builders Inc E 302 537-4444
Millville *(G-4851)*
Minkers Construction Inc E 302 239-9239
Newark *(G-7044)*
Moony and Zeager Inc G 302 593-8166
Wilmington *(G-11742)*
Morning Star Construction LLC F 302 539-0791
Dagsboro *(G-923)*
Mullico General Construction F 302 475-4400
Wilmington *(G-11773)*
Murphy Steel Inc E 302 366-8676
Newark *(G-7073)*
National Restortn & Faclty Svc E 856 401-0100
Wilmington *(G-11809)*
Neighborhood House Inc F 302 658-5404
Wilmington *(G-11830)*
Nvr Inc E 302 732-9900
Dagsboro *(G-926)*
Nvr Inc E 302 731-5770
Newark *(G-7140)*
Oak Construction G 302 703-2013
Lewes *(G-3663)*
Onsite Construction Inc E 302 628-4244
Seaford *(G-8337)*
Orjam Ltd F 302 482-5016
Wilmington *(G-11974)*
Othg Inc G 302 421-9187
Wilmington *(G-11982)*
Pano Development Inc G 302 428-1062
Wilmington *(G-12014)*
Paoli Services Inc E 302 998-7031
Wilmington *(G-12015)*
Paragon Contracting Inc G 302 697-6565
Camden *(G-595)*
Parker Construction Inc G 302 798-8530
Claymont *(G-793)*
Patriot Government Svcs Inc G 302 655-3434
Wilmington *(G-12035)*
Pettinaro Construction Co Inc D 302 999-0708
Wilmington *(G-12102)*
Philadlphia Arms Town Hmes Inc F 302 503-7216
Ellendale *(G-2262)*
Pierson Culver LLC G 302 732-1145
Dagsboro *(G-930)*
PJ Fitzpatrick Inc D 302 325-2360
New Castle *(G-5623)*
Poolside Cnstr & Renovation G 302 436-9711
Selbyville *(G-8533)*
Powell Construction L L C G 302 745-1146
Georgetown *(G-2622)*
Preferred Contractors Inc G 302 798-5457
Wilmington *(G-12211)*
Pulte Home Corporation E 302 999-9525
New Castle *(G-5654)*
Quality Builders Inc G 302 697-0664
Camden *(G-597)*
Quality Construction Cleaning E 302 956-0752
Bridgeville *(G-515)*
Quality Finishers Inc G 302 325-1963
New Castle *(G-5657)*
R D Arnold Construction Inc F 610 255-4739
Middletown *(G-4207)*
Rays Plumbing & Heating Svcs F 302 697-3936
Felton *(G-2315)*
RC Hellings Inc F 302 798-6850
Claymont *(G-799)*
Rcw Renovations Inc G 302 239-3714
Hockessin *(G-3131)*
Renzi Group Inc G 302 588-2603
Wilmington *(G-12381)*
Restoration Guys LLC G 302 542-4045
Seaford *(G-8378)*
Reybold Homes Inc C 302 834-3000
Newark *(G-7332)*
Richard D Whaley Cnstr LLC G 302 934-9525
Millsboro *(G-4789)*
Richard Y Johnson & Son Inc E 302 422-3732
Lincoln *(G-3865)*
Rkj Construction Inc G 302 690-0959
Wilmington *(G-12431)*
Robert C Peoples Inc D 302 834-5268
Bear *(G-308)*
Rockland Builders Inc F 302 995-6800
Wilmington *(G-12452)*
Rons Mobile Home Sales Inc G 302 398-9166
Harrington *(G-2880)*
Rosauri Builders & Remodelers G 302 234-8464
Hockessin *(G-3140)*
Rubio Construction LLC G 302 377-0353
Wilmington *(G-12489)*

S J Passwater General Cnstr G 302 422-1061
Milford *(G-4550)*
Sams Construction LLC E 302 654-6542
Wilmington *(G-12533)*
SC&a Construction Inc E 302 478-6030
Wilmington *(G-12550)*
Schell Brothers LLC F 302 226-1994
Rehoboth Beach *(G-8068)*
Shellys of Delaware Inc F 302 656-3337
Wilmington *(G-12600)*
Shockley Brothers Construction G 302 424-3255
Lincoln *(G-3869)*
Signature Cnstr Svcs LLC F 302 691-1010
New Castle *(G-5711)*
Silverside Contracting Inc G 302 798-1907
Wilmington *(G-12619)*
Space Makers Inc G 302 322-4325
Bear *(G-330)*
Stapen Construction Inc G 302 218-2190
Wilmington *(G-12738)*
State Line Construction Inc F 302 349-4244
Greenwood *(G-2764)*
Steven Schmith F 302 584-8394
Middletown *(G-4248)*
Sussex Cnty Habitat For Humani G 302 855-1153
Georgetown *(G-2674)*
T J Lane Construction Inc G 302 734-1099
Dover *(G-2126)*
Thomas F Cavanaugh G 302 995-2859
Wilmington *(G-12900)*
Timothy B OHare Custom Bldr F 302 537-9559
Ocean View *(G-7822)*
Tlbc LLC G 302 797-8700
Lewes *(G-3787)*
Toll Brothers Inc E 302 832-1700
New Castle *(G-5773)*
Tricon Construction MGT Inc E 302 838-6500
New Castle *(G-5793)*
Tru General Contractor Inc G 302 354-0553
Wilmington *(G-12985)*
Turnstone Builders LLC F 302 227-8876
Rehoboth Beach *(G-8101)*
Twaddell Plumbing and Heating G 302 475-5577
Wilmington *(G-12997)*
U and I Builders Inc G 302 697-1645
Dover *(G-2169)*
Utilicon Solutions Ltd G 302 337-9980
Bridgeville *(G-526)*
Vanguard Construction Inc G 302 697-9187
Dover *(G-2187)*
Vari Development Corp G 302 479-5571
Wilmington *(G-13050)*
W D Pressley Inc G 302 653-4381
Smyrna *(G-8737)*
Wade Kimball Construction Inc F 302 284-4732
Camden Wyoming *(G-661)*
Walan Specialty Cnstr Pdts LLC G 724 545-2300
Wilmington *(G-13114)*
Warfel Construction Co Inc E 302 422-8927
Milford *(G-4598)*
Weiner Development LLC E 302 764-9430
Wilmington *(G-13139)*
Wertz & Co E 302 658-5186
Wilmington *(G-13161)*
Williamson Building Corp G 302 644-0605
Lewes *(G-3825)*
Wilmington Housing Partnr Corp G 302 576-3000
Wilmington *(G-13235)*
Wilson Construction Co Inc G 302 856-3115
Georgetown *(G-2704)*
Woods General Contracting G 302 856-4047
Georgetown *(G-2708)*
Yencer Builders Inc G 302 284-9989
Felton *(G-2327)*

1522 General Contractors, Residential Other Than Single Family

Aruanno Enterprises Inc G 302 530-1217
Middletown *(G-3943)*
Atlantic Homes LLC G 302 947-0223
Lewes *(G-3356)*
B Doherty Inc G 302 239-3500
Wilmington *(G-9211)*
Bekart Holding LLC F 302 600-7000
Wilmington *(G-9283)*
Brandywine Exteriors Corp E 302 746-7134
Wilmington *(G-9431)*
Breeze Construction LLC G 302 522-9201
Townsend *(G-8766)*

Bright Finish LLC G 888 974-4747
Smyrna *(G-8586)*
Capano Management Company G 302 737-8056
Newark *(G-6149)*
Carl M Freeman Associates Inc D 302 436-3000
Ocean View *(G-7775)*
Cirillo Bros Inc E 302 326-1540
New Castle *(G-5162)*
Custom Improvers Inc G 302 731-9246
Newark *(G-6332)*
Deldeo Builders Inc F 302 791-0243
Claymont *(G-733)*
Diamond State Pole Bldings LLC G 302 387-1710
Felton *(G-2286)*
Dieste Mark Design Build LLC F 301 921-9050
Bethany Beach *(G-398)*
Disabatino Construction Co C 302 652-3838
Wilmington *(G-10164)*
E A Zando Custom Designs Inc F 302 684-4601
Milton *(G-4900)*
East Coast Minority Supplier E 302 656-3337
Wilmington *(G-10320)*
Ebanks Construction LLC F 302 420-7584
New Castle *(G-5279)*
▼ **Empire Construction Company** G 302 235-2093
Newark *(G-6524)*
Equity Contracting LLC G 302 504-1468
Wilmington *(G-10430)*
Falcon Crest Inv Intl Inc G 240 701-1746
Wilmington *(G-10481)*
H & M Construction G 302 645-6639
Lewes *(G-3527)*
H & T Builders Inc G 302 422-0745
Milford *(G-4429)*
H B P Inc E 302 378-9693
Middletown *(G-4098)*
Henlopen Homes LLC G 302 684-0860
Milton *(G-4913)*
J Rocco Construction LLC G 302 856-4100
Georgetown *(G-2570)*
John Campanelli & Sons Inc G 302 239-8573
Hockessin *(G-3067)*
Joseph E Stevens & Father G 302 654-8556
Wilmington *(G-11189)*
Kristin Konstruction Company G 302 791-9670
Claymont *(G-772)*
Martin Construction Svcs LLC F 302 200-0885
Newark *(G-6994)*
Mazzola Systems Inc F 302 738-6808
Newark *(G-7008)*
Nail It Down General Contrs G 302 698-3073
Dover *(G-1881)*
Newark Building Services LLC G 302 377-7687
Newark *(G-7111)*
Nvr Inc E 302 731-5770
Newark *(G-7140)*
Petrucon Construction Inc F 302 571-5781
Wilmington *(G-12101)*
Preferred Construction Inc G 302 322-9568
New Castle *(G-5637)*
Prestige Contractors Inc G 302 722-1032
Wilmington *(G-12223)*
Pro Clean Wilmington Inc G 302 836-8080
Delaware City *(G-964)*
Rapid Renovation and Repr LLC F 302 475-5400
Harrington *(G-2879)*
Roberts Wilbert G 215 867-5655
Middletown *(G-4221)*
Scuba World Inc F 302 698-1117
Dover *(G-2064)*
Separe Inc E 302 736-5000
Dover *(G-2069)*
Shamrock Construction Inc G 302 376-0320
Smyrna *(G-8713)*
Thomas Brothers LLC G 302 366-1316
Newark *(G-7562)*
Vvs Inc G 302 827-2525
Lewes *(G-3812)*
Warren Reid E 302 877-0901
Laurel *(G-3304)*
Weather or Not Inc F 302 436-7533
Selbyville *(G-8553)*
Wit Services LLC G 302 995-2983
Wilmington *(G-13280)*

1531 Operative Builders

Benchmark Builders Inc E 302 995-6945
Wilmington *(G-9295)*
Berman Development Corp G 302 323-9522
New Castle *(G-5084)*

Broadpoint Construction LLC ....G....... 302 567-2100
Rehoboth Beach *(G-7878)*
Cape Financial Services Inc............F....... 302 645-6274
Lewes *(G-3400)*
Carl M Freeman Associates Inc............C....... 302 539-6961
Bethany Beach *(G-391)*
Construction Layout Services............G....... 302 998-1800
Newark *(G-6289)*
Creative Builders Inc............G....... 302 228-8153
Harbeson *(G-2780)*
Del Homes Inc............G....... 302 697-8204
Magnolia *(G-3889)*
Gearhart Construction Inc............G....... 302 674-5466
Dover *(G-1587)*
Hudson Management & Entps LLC............G....... 302 645-9464
Milton *(G-4917)*
J D Construction............G....... 302 292-8789
Newark *(G-6815)*
No Joke I LLC............G....... 302 395-0882
New Castle *(G-5573)*
Nvr Inc............E....... 302 731-5770
Newark *(G-7140)*
Pulte Home Corporation............E....... 302 378-9091
Middletown *(G-4203)*

1541 General Contractors, Indl Bldgs & Warehouses

Advance Construction Co Del............F....... 302 697-9444
Camden Wyoming *(G-611)*
▲ **Bancroft Construction Company**............D....... 302 655-3434
Wilmington *(G-9234)*
Breslin Contracting Inc............E....... 302 322-0320
New Castle *(G-5110)*
Bristol Industrial Corporation............F....... 302 322-1100
New Castle *(G-5115)*
Broadpoint Construction LLC............G....... 302 567-2100
Rehoboth Beach *(G-7878)*
Building Concepts America Inc............E....... 302 292-0200
Newark *(G-6131)*
Colonial Construction Company............F....... 302 994-5705
Wilmington *(G-9774)*
Conventional Builders Inc............F....... 302 422-2429
Houston *(G-3177)*
Crystal Holdings Inc............D....... 302 421-5700
Wilmington *(G-9909)*
Dan H Beachy & Sons Inc............G....... 302 492-1493
Hartly *(G-2918)*
Deshong & Sons Contractors............G....... 302 453-8500
Newark *(G-6440)*
Disabatino Construction Co............C....... 302 652-3838
Wilmington *(G-10164)*
East Coast Minority Supplier............E....... 302 656-3337
Wilmington *(G-10320)*
Eastern Metals Inc............F....... 302 454-7886
Newark *(G-6499)*
Edis Company............E....... 302 421-5700
Wilmington *(G-10350)*
Emment A Oat Contractor Inc............G....... 302 999-1567
Wilmington *(G-10393)*
Essies Kitchen LLC............G....... 302 465-2856
Dover *(G-1531)*
Gettier Staffing Services Inc............F....... 302 478-0911
Wilmington *(G-10706)*
Gfp Cement Contractors LLC............F....... 302 998-7687
Wilmington *(G-10708)*
Guardian Envmtl Svcs Co Inc............D....... 302 918-3070
Newark *(G-6695)*
Hart Construction Co Inc............F....... 302 737-7886
Newark *(G-6712)*
▲ **Janette Redrow Ltd**............G....... 302 659-3534
Townsend *(G-8800)*
Jeffrey Hatch............G....... 443 496-0449
Marydel *(G-3919)*
John L Briggs & Co............F....... 302 856-7033
Georgetown *(G-2577)*
Kent Construction Co............E....... 302 653-6469
Smyrna *(G-8666)*
Kristin Konstruction Company............G....... 302 791-9670
Claymont *(G-772)*
Lynx General Contracting............G....... 302 368-9401
Newark *(G-6961)*
Mario F Medori Inc............G....... 302 239-4550
Wilmington *(G-11528)*
Mebro Inc............E....... 302 992-0104
Wilmington *(G-11613)*
Metro Steel Incorporated............E....... 302 778-2288
New Castle *(G-5519)*
Miken Builders Inc............E....... 302 537-4444
Millville *(G-4851)*
Mitten Construction Co............E....... 302 697-2124
Dover *(G-1862)*
Nason Construction Inc............E....... 302 529-2510
Wilmington *(G-11803)*
Penco Corporation............G....... 302 629-7911
Seaford *(G-8345)*
Pettinaro Construction Co Inc............D....... 302 999-0708
Wilmington *(G-12102)*
R W Home Services Inc............F....... 302 539-4683
Ocean View *(G-7810)*
Reybold Construction Corp............E....... 302 832-7100
Bear *(G-304)*
Rock Solid Contracting and Dev............G....... 302 655-8250
Wilmington *(G-12448)*
Shellys of Delaware Inc............F....... 302 656-3337
Wilmington *(G-12600)*
Skanska USA Building Inc............E....... 215 495-8790
Newark *(G-7434)*
Talley Brothers Inc............E....... 302 224-5376
Newark *(G-7536)*
Whayland Company Inc............F....... 302 875-5445
Laurel *(G-3309)*
Whiting-Turner Contracting Co............E....... 302 292-0676
Newark *(G-7693)*
Wohlsen Construction Company............E....... 302 324-9900
Wilmington *(G-13284)*

1542 General Contractors, Nonresidential & Non-indl Bldgs

Absolute Equity............F....... 302 983-2591
Delaware City *(G-945)*
Advance Construction Co Del............F....... 302 697-9444
Camden Wyoming *(G-611)*
Aecom Energy & Cnstr Inc............F....... 302 234-1445
Hockessin *(G-2952)*
Albert S Lambertson Inc............G....... 302 734-9649
Dover *(G-1101)*
Amakor Inc............F....... 302 834-8664
Delaware City *(G-947)*
Andrei S Remo............G....... 302 569-4555
Rehoboth Beach *(G-7843)*
Aviman Management LLC............E....... 302 377-5788
Wilmington *(G-9199)*
B Doherty Inc............G....... 302 239-3500
Wilmington *(G-9211)*
◆ **Balfour Beatty LLC**............G....... 302 573-3873
Wilmington *(G-9225)*
Ballard Builders LLC............F....... 302 363-1677
Clayton *(G-836)*
▲ **Bancroft Construction Company**............D....... 302 655-3434
Wilmington *(G-9234)*
Bay Developers Inc............F....... 302 736-0924
Dover *(G-1179)*
Bellevue Holding Company............E....... 302 655-1561
Wilmington *(G-9291)*
Benjamin B Smith Builders Inc............G....... 302 537-1916
Ocean View *(G-7764)*
Blackstone Building Group LLC............G....... 302 824-4632
Wilmington *(G-9364)*
Brandywine Contractors Inc............E....... 302 325-2700
New Castle *(G-5106)*
Brandywine Contractors Inc............G....... 302 325-2700
New Castle *(G-5107)*
Breeze Construction LLC............G....... 302 522-9201
Townsend *(G-8766)*
Brendon T Warfel Construction............G....... 302 422-7814
Milford *(G-4334)*
Breslin Contracting Inc............E....... 302 322-0320
New Castle *(G-5110)*
Broadpoint Construction LLC............G....... 302 567-2100
Rehoboth Beach *(G-7878)*
Brs Consulting Inc............G....... 302 786-2326
Harrington *(G-2819)*
Bunting Construction Corp............F....... 302 436-5124
Selbyville *(G-8464)*
Cape Financial Services Inc............F....... 302 645-6274
Lewes *(G-3400)*
Carl Deputy & Son Builders LLC............G....... 302 284-3041
Felton *(G-2280)*
Chilimidos LLC............G....... 302 388-1880
Hockessin *(G-2986)*
Choice Builders LLC............G....... 302 856-7234
Georgetown *(G-2470)*
Chrystal Holdings............G....... 302 655-2398
Wilmington *(G-9693)*
Cirillo Bros Inc............E....... 302 326-1540
New Castle *(G-5162)*
Colonial Construction Company............F....... 302 994-5705
Wilmington *(G-9774)*
Commonwealth Contruction Co............E....... 302 654-6611
Wilmington *(G-9789)*
Consolidated LLC............E....... 302 654-9001
Wilmington *(G-9833)*
Construction Unlimited Inc............G....... 302 836-3140
Bear *(G-83)*
Conventional Builders Inc............F....... 302 422-2429
Houston *(G-3177)*
Crystal Holdings Inc............D....... 302 421-5700
Wilmington *(G-9909)*
Dal Construction............E....... 302 538-5310
Camden *(G-555)*
Dan H Beachy & Sons Inc............G....... 302 492-1493
Hartly *(G-2918)*
Deiter Inc............G....... 302 875-9167
Georgetown *(G-2497)*
Del Homes Inc............G....... 302 697-8204
Magnolia *(G-3889)*
Delcon Builders Inc............F....... 609 499-7747
New Castle *(G-5243)*
Deldeo Builders Inc............F....... 302 791-0243
Claymont *(G-733)*
Delmarva Builders Inc............G....... 302 629-9123
Bridgeville *(G-465)*
Deshong & Sons Contractors............G....... 302 453-8500
Newark *(G-6440)*
Diamond Hill Inc............G....... 302 999-0302
New Castle *(G-5251)*
Diamond State Pole Bldings LLC............G....... 302 387-1710
Felton *(G-2286)*
Disabatino Construction Co............C....... 302 652-3838
Wilmington *(G-10164)*
Dry Wall Associates Ltd............D....... 302 737-3220
Newark *(G-6475)*
East Coast Minority Supplier............E....... 302 656-3337
Wilmington *(G-10320)*
Eastern Home Improvements Inc............G....... 302 655-9920
Wilmington *(G-10322)*
Ebanks Construction LLC............F....... 302 420-7584
New Castle *(G-5279)*
Edge Construction Corp............G....... 302 778-5200
Wilmington *(G-10346)*
Edis Company............E....... 302 421-5700
Wilmington *(G-10350)*
Empire Investments Inc............G....... 302 838-0631
New Castle *(G-5289)*
First State Building LLC............G....... 302 803-5082
Wilmington *(G-10549)*
From Ground Up Construction............G....... 302 747-0996
Newark *(G-6625)*
Gettier Staffing Services Inc............F....... 302 478-0911
Wilmington *(G-10706)*
Guardian Construction Co Inc............D....... 302 834-1000
New Castle *(G-5365)*
Hart Construction Co Inc............F....... 302 737-7886
Newark *(G-6712)*
Humphries Construction Company............G....... 302 349-9277
Greenwood *(G-2744)*
Iacchetta Builders Inc............G....... 302 436-4525
Selbyville *(G-8505)*
Insite Constructors Inc............G....... 302 479-5555
Wilmington *(G-11040)*
J & S General Contractors............F....... 302 658-4499
Wilmington *(G-11098)*
J A Moore & Sons Inc............G....... 302 765-0110
Wilmington *(G-11101)*
James Rice Jr Construction Co............G....... 302 731-9323
Newark *(G-6826)*
Jni CCC Jv1............G....... 302 654-6611
Wilmington *(G-11162)*
John Campanelli & Sons Inc............G....... 302 239-8573
Hockessin *(G-3067)*
John L Briggs & Co............F....... 302 856-7033
Georgetown *(G-2577)*
Joseph A Santillo Inc............G....... 302 661-7313
Wilmington *(G-11186)*
JW Tull Contracting Svcs LLC............F....... 302 494-8179
Wilmington *(G-11212)*
KB Coldiron Inc............D....... 302 436-4224
Selbyville *(G-8511)*
Kent Construction Co............E....... 302 653-6469
Smyrna *(G-8666)*
Kristin Konstruction Company............G....... 302 791-9670
Claymont *(G-772)*
Larry Hill Farms Inc............F....... 302 875-0886
Delmar *(G-1015)*
Leon N Weiner & Associates Inc............D....... 302 656-1354
Wilmington *(G-11371)*
Lighthouse Construction Inc............F....... 302 677-1965
Magnolia *(G-3898)*

Linda McCormick ....G.... 443 987-2099
Wilmington *(G-11392)*
Locker Construction Inc ....G.... 302 239-2859
Newark *(G-6946)*
Lockwood Design Construction ....G.... 302 684-4844
Milton *(G-4925)*
M L Parker Construction Inc ....F.... 302 798-8530
Claymont *(G-777)*
M W Fogarty Inc ....G.... 302 658-5547
Hockessin *(G-3083)*
Mac Contractors Inc ....G.... 302 653-5765
Smyrna *(G-8678)*
Martin Construction Svcs LLC ....F.... 302 200-0885
Newark *(G-6994)*
Mason Building Group Inc ....C.... 302 292-0600
Newark *(G-6999)*
Mebro Inc ....E.... 302 992-0104
Wilmington *(G-11613)*
Michael-Bruno LLC ....G.... 315 941-8514
Wilmington *(G-11669)*
Mike Molitor Contractor LLC ....G.... 302 528-6300
Hockessin *(G-3095)*
Miken Builders Inc ....E.... 302 537-4444
Millville *(G-4851)*
Milestone Construction Co Inc ....F.... 302 442-4252
Newark *(G-7040)*
Mind Body & Sole ....G.... 302 537-3668
Bethany Beach *(G-415)*
Mitten Construction Co ....E.... 302 697-2124
Dover *(G-1862)*
Moony and Zeager Inc ....G.... 302 593-8166
Wilmington *(G-11742)*
Moore Farms ....F.... 302 629-4999
Georgetown *(G-2606)*
Mundy Industrial Contrs Inc ....G.... 302 629-1100
Seaford *(G-8314)*
Mvl Structures Group LLC ....E.... 302 652-7580
Wilmington *(G-11782)*
Mvl-Al Othman Al Zamel JV LLC ....E.... 832 302-2757
Wilmington *(G-11783)*
Mvl-Saqa JV LLC ....E.... 832 302-2757
Wilmington *(G-11784)*
Nason Construction Inc ....E.... 302 529-2510
Wilmington *(G-11803)*
National Restortn & Faclty Svc ....E.... 856 401-0100
Wilmington *(G-11809)*
North East Contractors Inc ....E.... 302 286-6324
Newark *(G-7138)*
Opus Design Build LLC ....D.... 952 656-4444
Wilmington *(G-11965)*
Petrucon Construction Inc ....F.... 302 571-5781
Wilmington *(G-12101)*
Pettinaro Construction Co Inc ....D.... 302 999-0708
Wilmington *(G-12102)*
Pettitt Construction LLC ....G.... 302 690-0831
Newark *(G-7208)*
Preferred Construction Inc ....G.... 302 322-9568
New Castle *(G-5637)*
Premier Builders Inc ....G.... 302 999-8500
Wilmington *(G-12215)*
Prestige Contractors Inc ....G.... 302 722-1032
Wilmington *(G-12223)*
Regal Contractors LLC ....G.... 302 736-5000
Dover *(G-2019)*
Regional Builders Inc ....E.... 302 628-8660
Seaford *(G-8374)*
Renovate LLC ....G.... 302 378-1768
Middletown *(G-4218)*
Renzi Group Inc ....G.... 302 588-2603
Wilmington *(G-12381)*
Reybold Construction Corp ....E.... 302 832-7100
Bear *(G-304)*
Richard Y Johnson & Son Inc ....E.... 302 422-3732
Lincoln *(G-3865)*
Robert C Peoples Inc ....D.... 302 834-5268
Bear *(G-308)*
Roberts Wilbert ....G.... 215 867-5655
Middletown *(G-4221)*
Roberts Const Co ....E.... 302 335-4141
Frederica *(G-2411)*
Rosauri Builders & Remodelers ....G.... 302 234-8464
Hockessin *(G-3140)*
SC&a Construction Inc ....E.... 302 478-6030
Wilmington *(G-12550)*
Shellys of Delaware Inc ....F.... 302 656-3337
Wilmington *(G-12600)*
Shure-Line Construction Inc ....E.... 302 653-4610
Kenton *(G-3185)*
Signature Furniture Svcs LLC ....E.... 302 691-1010
New Castle *(G-5712)*
Silverside Contracting Inc ....G.... 302 798-1907
Wilmington *(G-12619)*
Simpson Gary Contracting LLC ....G.... 302 398-7733
Harrington *(G-2889)*
Smarter Home & Office LLC ....G.... 302 723-9313
New Castle *(G-5718)*
Space Makers Inc ....G.... 302 322-4325
Bear *(G-330)*
Sunworks Corporation ....G.... 302 655-5772
Wilmington *(G-12802)*
Talley Brothers Inc ....E.... 302 224-5376
Newark *(G-7536)*
Taylor Kline Inc ....F.... 302 328-8306
New Castle *(G-5754)*
Tolton Builders Inc ....G.... 302 239-5357
Hockessin *(G-3162)*
Tycos General Contractors Inc ....G.... 302 478-9267
Wilmington *(G-13002)*
Vanguard Construction Inc ....G.... 302 697-9187
Dover *(G-2187)*
Vari Development Corp ....G.... 302 479-5571
Wilmington *(G-13050)*
W D Pressley Inc ....G.... 302 653-4381
Smyrna *(G-8737)*
W Enterprises LLC ....G.... 302 875-0430
Laurel *(G-3303)*
Warfel Construction Co Inc ....E.... 302 422-8927
Milford *(G-4598)*
Westwood Farms Incorporated ....F.... 302 238-7141
Millsboro *(G-4826)*
Whayland Company Inc ....F.... 302 875-5445
Laurel *(G-3309)*
Whayland Company LLC ....F.... 302 875-5445
Laurel *(G-3310)*
White Eagle Integrations ....G.... 302 464-0550
Middletown *(G-4285)*
Whiting-Turner Contracting Co ....E.... 302 292-0676
Newark *(G-7693)*
Wilmington ....G.... 302 357-4509
Wilmington *(G-13221)*
Wohlsen Construction Company ....E.... 302 324-9900
Wilmington *(G-13284)*
Woods General Contracting ....G.... 302 856-4047
Georgetown *(G-2708)*
Zacs Inc ....G.... 302 242-4653
Magnolia *(G-3913)*

16 HEAVY CONSTRUCTION OTHER THAN BUILDING CONSTRUCTION-CONTRACTORS

1611 Highway & Street Construction

A P Croll & Son Inc ....D.... 302 856-6177
Georgetown *(G-2419)*
A-Del Construction Company Inc ....D.... 302 453-8286
Newark *(G-5871)*
Allan Myers Md Inc ....C.... 302 883-3501
Dover *(G-1109)*
Amears Contractors Inc ....G.... 302 791-7767
Claymont *(G-690)*
Andrei S Remo ....G.... 302 569-4555
Rehoboth Beach *(G-7843)*
Ashland LLC ....E.... 302 594-5000
Wilmington *(G-9151)*
Austin & Bednash Construction ....E.... 302 376-5590
Newark *(G-6026)*
Baker & Sons Paving ....G.... 302 945-6333
Middletown *(G-3960)*
Bayside Sealcoating Supply ....G.... 302 697-6441
Camden Wyoming *(G-618)*
Bramble Construction Co Inc ....F.... 302 856-6723
Georgetown *(G-2458)*
Brandywine Construction Co ....D.... 302 571-9773
New Castle *(G-5105)*
Brick Doctor Inc ....G.... 302 678-3380
Dover *(G-1231)*
C&J Paving Inc ....F.... 302 684-0211
Milton *(G-4873)*
Concrete Walls Inc ....G.... 302 293-7061
Bear *(G-82)*
D E Leager Construction ....G.... 302 994-1060
Wilmington *(G-9939)*
Daisy Construction Company ....D.... 302 658-4417
Wilmington *(G-9947)*
David G Horsey & Sons Inc ....D.... 302 875-3033
Laurel *(G-3221)*
David M Sartin Sr ....G.... 302 838-1074
Bear *(G-97)*
Disabatino Enterprises LLC ....D.... 302 652-3838
Wilmington *(G-10165)*
Dixie Construction Company Inc ....E.... 302 858-5007
Georgetown *(G-2511)*
Don Rogers Inc ....E.... 302 658-6524
Wilmington *(G-10193)*
Ds Paving ....G.... 302 832-3748
Bear *(G-128)*
E Earle Downing Inc ....E.... 302 656-9908
Wilmington *(G-10277)*
Eastern States Cnstr Svc Inc ....D.... 302 995-2259
Wilmington *(G-10326)*
F & G Construction Co Inc ....G.... 302 994-1406
Wilmington *(G-10468)*
Ffi General Contractor In ....G.... 302 420-1242
Wilmington *(G-10527)*
George & Lynch Inc ....C.... 302 736-3031
Dover *(G-1590)*
George P Stewart ....G.... 302 737-4927
Newark *(G-6648)*
GF McLaughlin LLC ....G.... 302 279-6018
Wilmington *(G-10707)*
Harmony Construction Inc ....F.... 302 737-8700
Newark *(G-6709)*
Harrisons Asphalt Paving ....G.... 302 674-1255
Dover *(G-1633)*
Highland Construction LLC ....F.... 302 286-6990
Bear *(G-185)*
James L Webb Paving Co Inc ....G.... 302 697-2000
Camden *(G-584)*
Jerrys Inc ....F.... 302 422-7676
Milford *(G-4457)*
Jjid Inc ....E.... 302 836-0414
Bear *(G-201)*
Keoghs Contracting Company ....G.... 302 656-0058
New Castle *(G-5460)*
Martys Contracting ....G.... 302 234-8690
Hockessin *(G-3091)*
Material Supply Inc ....E.... 302 658-6524
Wilmington *(G-11566)*
Matts Management Family LLC ....F.... 302 732-3715
Frankford *(G-2372)*
McKenzie Paving Inc ....F.... 302 376-8560
Middletown *(G-4150)*
McNeil Paving ....G.... 302 945-7131
Millsboro *(G-4738)*
Melvin L Joseph Cnstr Co ....E.... 302 856-7396
Georgetown *(G-2602)*
Messick and Johnson LLc ....G.... 302 628-3111
Seaford *(G-8308)*
Mitten Construction Co ....E.... 302 697-2124
Dover *(G-1862)*
Mumford and Miller Con Inc ....C.... 302 378-7736
Middletown *(G-4171)*
Naudain Enterprises LLC ....E.... 302 239-6840
Hockessin *(G-3102)*
New Castle County Flooring ....G.... 302 218-0507
Newark *(G-7100)*
Pacer International One LLC ....F.... 302 588-9500
Wilmington *(G-12003)*
Palmer & Associates Inc ....G.... 302 834-9329
Bear *(G-275)*
Peninsula Pave & Seal LLC ....G.... 302 226-7283
Georgetown *(G-2615)*
Peter Domanski & Sons ....G.... 302 475-3214
Hockessin *(G-3118)*
Ralph Cahall & Son Paving ....D.... 302 653-4220
Smyrna *(G-8696)*
Restoration Dynamics LLC ....G.... 302 378-3729
Wilmington *(G-12389)*
Road Site Construction Inc ....F.... 302 645-1922
Lewes *(G-3720)*
Rock Bottom Paving Inc ....G.... 800 728-3160
Felton *(G-2318)*
Rp Ventures and Holdings Inc ....E.... 410 398-3000
New Castle *(G-5690)*
RS Widdoes and Son Inc ....G.... 302 764-7455
Wilmington *(G-12486)*
Sams Construction LLC ....E.... 302 654-6542
Wilmington *(G-12534)*
Sanco Construction Co Inc ....G.... 302 633-4156
Wilmington *(G-12536)*
South Jersey Paving ....G.... 856 498-8647
Bear *(G-329)*
Straight Line Striping LLC ....G.... 302 228-3335
Georgetown *(G-2668)*
Sweeten Companies Inc ....G.... 302 737-6161
Newark *(G-7520)*
Teal Construction Inc ....D.... 302 276-6034
Dover *(G-2134)*

S I C

16 HEAVY CONSTRUCTION OTHER THAN BUILDING CONSTRUCTION-CONTRACTORS

Transportation Delaware Dept .... B 302 326-8950
  Bear *(G-357)*
Transportation Delaware Dept .... E 302 653-4128
  Middletown *(G-4267)*
Voshell Bros Welding Inc .... E 302 674-1414
  Dover *(G-2199)*
Walo US Holdings Inc .... G 212 691-4537
  Dover *(G-2204)*
Wb Paving LLC .... G 302 838-1886
  Bear *(G-373)*
Whitemans Paving Inc .... G 302 378-1828
  Townsend *(G-8832)*

1622 Bridge, Tunnel & Elevated Hwy Construction

Ashland LLC .... E 302 594-5000
  Wilmington *(G-9151)*
Aviman Management LLC .... E 302 377-5788
  Wilmington *(G-9199)*
Eastern Hwy Specialists Inc .... E 302 777-7673
  Wilmington *(G-10323)*
First State Crane Service .... F 302 398-8885
  Felton *(G-2292)*

1623 Water, Sewer & Utility Line Construction

Asplundh Tree Expert Co .... B 302 678-4702
  Dover *(G-1147)*
Bramble Construction Co Inc .... F 302 856-6723
  Georgetown *(G-2458)*
Brandywine Construction Co .... D 302 571-9773
  New Castle *(G-5105)*
Bunting & Murray Cnstr Corp .... D 302 436-5144
  Selbyville *(G-8463)*
Chris Kissell .... G 302 547-4800
  Smyrna *(G-8593)*
CNJ Contracting LLC .... G 302 659-3750
  Smyrna *(G-8600)*
Core & Main LP .... G 302 737-1500
  Newark *(G-6297)*
Current Solutions .... G 302 724-5243
  Dover *(G-1330)*
David Bridge .... G 302 429-3317
  Bear *(G-95)*
Dixie Construction Company Inc .... E 302 858-5007
  Georgetown *(G-2511)*
Dycom Industries Inc .... G 302 613-0958
  New Castle *(G-5269)*
Eastern States Cnstr Svc Inc .... D 302 995-2259
  Wilmington *(G-10326)*
Epb Associates Inc .... F 302 475-7301
  Wilmington *(G-10424)*
Fast Pipe Lining East Inc .... F 302 368-7414
  Newark *(G-6574)*
George & Lynch Inc .... C 302 736-3031
  Dover *(G-1590)*
H I E Contractors Inc .... F 302 224-3032
  Newark *(G-6697)*
Hopkins Construction Inc .... F 302 337-3366
  Bridgeville *(G-482)*
Joseph T Hardy & Son Inc .... E 302 328-9457
  New Castle *(G-5446)*
Melcar Underground Ltd .... E 484 653-8259
  Lewes *(G-3633)*
Merit Construction Engineers .... F 302 992-9810
  Wilmington *(G-11644)*
Phalco Inc .... G 302 654-2620
  Wilmington *(G-12107)*
Standard Pipe Services LLC .... D 302 286-0701
  Newark *(G-7480)*
Teal Construction Inc .... D 302 276-6034
  Dover *(G-2134)*
Tri-State Grouting LLC .... E 302 286-0701
  Newark *(G-7587)*
Tri-State Underground Inc .... F 302 836-8030
  Townsend *(G-8829)*
Tri-State Underground Inc .... G 302 293-9352
  Bear *(G-358)*
Triton Construction Co Inc .... E 516 780-8100
  New Castle *(G-5795)*
Underground Locating Services .... G 302 856-9626
  Georgetown *(G-2697)*
US Bortek LLC .... F 888 203-7686
  Camden *(G-604)*
Utilicon Solutions Ltd .... G 302 337-9980
  Bridgeville *(G-526)*
Utilisite Inc .... F 302 945-5022
  Lewes *(G-3806)*

Utility Lines Cnstr Svcs LLC .... F 302 337-9980
  Bridgeville *(G-527)*
Voshell Bros Welding Inc .... E 302 674-1414
  Dover *(G-2199)*
Wilmington Resources .... F 302 746-7162
  Wilmington *(G-13244)*
Yacht Anything Ltd .... G 302 226-3335
  Rehoboth Beach *(G-8120)*
Zober Contracting Services Inc .... G 302 270-3078
  Dover *(G-2253)*

1629 Heavy Construction, NEC

Artesian Wastewater MD Inc .... E 302 453-6900
  Newark *(G-6002)*
Artesian Wastewater MGT Inc .... E 302 453-6900
  Newark *(G-6003)*
Asplundh Tree Expert Co .... B 302 678-4702
  Dover *(G-1147)*
Breakwater Construction Envmtl .... E 302 945-5800
  Millsboro *(G-4648)*
CBI Services LLC .... E 302 325-8400
  New Castle *(G-5138)*
Crimson Group LLC .... G 301 252-3779
  Newark *(G-6316)*
▲ Croda Uniqema Inc .... E 302 429-5599
  New Castle *(G-5210)*
Delaware City Refining Co LLC .... C 302 834-6000
  Delaware City *(G-954)*
Epb Associates Inc .... F 302 475-7301
  Wilmington *(G-10424)*
First State Crane Service .... F 302 398-8885
  Felton *(G-2292)*
George & Lynch Inc .... C 302 736-3031
  Dover *(G-1590)*
George M Howard & Sons Inc .... G 302 645-9655
  Rehoboth Beach *(G-7945)*
Interstate Construction Inc .... E 302 369-3590
  Newark *(G-6798)*
J & J Bulkheading .... G 302 436-2800
  Selbyville *(G-8507)*
▲ Janette Redrow Ltd .... G 302 659-3534
  Townsend *(G-8800)*
Jjid Inc .... E 302 836-0414
  Bear *(G-201)*
John T Rogers Jr .... G 302 945-3016
  Millsboro *(G-4715)*
Koch Accounting Services LLC .... E 877 446-8478
  Wilmington *(G-11286)*
Lavond Mackey .... E 484 466-8055
  Wilmington *(G-11338)*
Melvin L Joseph Cnstr Co .... E 302 856-7396
  Georgetown *(G-2602)*
Merritt Marine Cnstr Inc .... G 302 436-2881
  Selbyville *(G-8519)*
Mumford and Miller Con Inc .... C 302 378-7736
  Middletown *(G-4171)*
Pauls Paving Inc .... F 302 539-9123
  Frankford *(G-2379)*
Precision Marine Construction .... G 302 227-2711
  Rehoboth Beach *(G-8035)*
▼ Sun Marine Maintenance Inc .... F 302 539-6756
  Frankford *(G-2391)*
W Sharp Paynter & Sons Inc .... G 302 684-8508
  Milton *(G-4979)*

17 CONSTRUCTION-SPECIAL TRADE CONTRACTORS

1711 Plumbing, Heating & Air Conditioning Contractors

A & A Air Services Inc .... E 302 436-4800
  Frankford *(G-2342)*
A & A Mechanical Service Inc .... G 302 234-9949
  Hockessin *(G-2949)*
A & H Plumbing & Heating Inc .... G 302 223-8027
  Clayton *(G-830)*
A and D Plumbing LLC .... G 302 387-9232
  Magnolia *(G-3877)*
A J Dauphin & Son Inc .... G 302 994-1454
  Wilmington *(G-8880)*
A-1 Air Conditioning Heating .... G 302 998-5634
  Newport *(G-7744)*
Affordable Heating & AC .... G 302 328-9220
  New Castle *(G-5017)*
After Hours Heating & Air .... G 302 945-3310
  Millsboro *(G-4624)*
Air Doctorx Inc .... F 302 492-1333
  Hartly *(G-2912)*

Allied Elec Solutions Ltd .... F 302 893-0257
  Wilmington *(G-9022)*
Amstel Mechanical Contractors .... G 302 836-6469
  New Castle *(G-5036)*
Angler Plumbing LLC .... G 302 293-5691
  Newark *(G-5970)*
Aqua Pro Inc .... G 302 659-6593
  Smyrna *(G-8575)*
Arctec Air Heating & Cooling .... G 302 629-7129
  Bridgeville *(G-447)*
Armored Fire Protection LLC .... G 302 563-3516
  Townsend *(G-8758)*
Around Clock Htg AC Inc .... G 302 856-9306
  Georgetown *(G-2435)*
Associates Contracting Inc .... F 302 734-4311
  Dover *(G-1150)*
Atlantic Refrigeration Inc .... E 302 645-9321
  Lewes *(G-3358)*
B Walls Son Htg & A Conditions .... F 302 856-4045
  Georgetown *(G-2443)*
Back Bay Plumbing .... G 302 945-1210
  Millsboro *(G-4633)*
Battaglia Associates Inc .... C 302 325-6100
  New Castle *(G-5069)*
Battaglia Electric Inc .... C 302 325-6100
  New Castle *(G-5070)*
Bear Industries Inc .... D 302 368-1311
  Newark *(G-6065)*
Bill Rust Plumbing .... G 302 422-6061
  Harrington *(G-2818)*
Bjk Plumbing & Heating LLC .... G 215 828-2556
  Magnolia *(G-3882)*
Blm Industries Inc .... G 302 238-7745
  Millsboro *(G-4645)*
Blue Skies Solar & Wind Power .... E 302 326-0856
  New Castle *(G-5097)*
Booths Services Plbg Htg & AC .... G 302 454-7385
  Newark *(G-6107)*
Brandywine Contractors Inc .... G 302 325-2700
  New Castle *(G-5107)*
Breeding & Day Inc .... E 302 478-4585
  Wilmington *(G-9466)*
Budget Rooter Inc .... F 302 322-3011
  New Castle *(G-5120)*
Burns & McBride Inc .... D 302 656-5110
  New Castle *(G-5121)*
C & D Contractors Inc .... E 302 764-2020
  Wilmington *(G-9521)*
C White & Sons LLC .... G 302 629-4848
  Seaford *(G-8179)*
Cahill Plumbing & Heating Inc .... G 302 894-1802
  Newark *(G-6144)*
Calfo & Haight Inc .... G 302 998-3852
  Wilmington *(G-9536)*
Calvert Mechanical Systems Inc .... E 302 998-0460
  Wilmington *(G-9543)*
Certified Mechanical Contrs .... G 302 559-3727
  Wilmington *(G-9619)*
Cesn Partners Inc .... F 302 537-1814
  Ocean View *(G-7776)*
Charles A Klein & Sons Inc .... G 410 549-6960
  Selbyville *(G-8466)*
Charles Moon Plumbing & Htg .... G 302 798-6666
  Claymont *(G-713)*
Charles S Reskovitz Inc .... G 302 999-9455
  Wilmington *(G-9637)*
Chesapeake Climate Control LLC ... E 302 732-6006
  Frankford *(G-2353)*
Chesapeake Plumbing & Htg Inc ..... E 302 732-6006
  Frankford *(G-2354)*
Christiana Mechanical Inc .... F 302 378-7308
  Middletown *(G-3989)*
Clark Services Inc Delaware .... G 302 834-0556
  Bear *(G-76)*
Clark Services Inc of Del .... F 302 322-1118
  New Castle *(G-5174)*
Clarke Service Groupdotcom LLC ... F 302 875-0300
  Laurel *(G-3216)*
Clean Delaware LLC .... E 302 684-4221
  Lewes *(G-3427)*
Clean Energy Usa LLC .... G 302 227-1337
  Rehoboth Beach *(G-7891)*
Clendaniel Plbg Htg & Coolg .... G 302 684-3152
  Milton *(G-4880)*
Climate Control Heating Inc .... G 302 349-5778
  Greenwood *(G-2720)*
Climate Solutions Services .... G 302 275-9919
  Wilmington *(G-9742)*
CMI Electric Inc .... E 302 731-5556
  Newark *(G-6253)*

17 CONSTRUCTION-SPECIAL TRADE CONTRACTORS

Company	Code	Phone
CMI Electric Inc — Newark (G-6254)	E	302 731-5556
Cmp Fire LLC — Newark (G-6255)	G	410 620-2062
Coastal Mechanical — Wilmington (G-9754)	D	302 994-9100
Collins Mechanical Inc — Harrington (G-2828)	E	302 398-8877
Community Heating & AC — Lincoln (G-3843)	G	302 422-6839
Congo Capital Management LLC — Wilmington (G-9820)	F	732 337-6643
Cooper Bros Inc — New Castle (G-5194)	F	302 323-0717
Cox Electric Inc — Seaford (G-8211)	G	302 629-5448
Cs Webb Daughters & Son Inc — Hockessin (G-2998)	G	302 239-2801
Custom Mechanical Inc — Frankford (G-2358)	E	302 537-1150
D & C Mechanical LLC — Greenwood (G-2726)	G	302 604-9025
D F Distribution Inc — Wilmington (G-9940)	G	302 798-5999
Daniel D Rappa Inc — Wilmington (G-9955)	E	302 994-1199
Daves Contracting Inc — Selbyville (G-8479)	G	302 436-5129
Del Campo Plumbing & Heating — Wilmington (G-9997)	G	302 998-3648
Delaware Heating & AC — Bear (G-108)	F	302 738-4669
Delaware Heating & AC Svcs Inc — Newark (G-6383)	E	302 738-4669
Delmarva Refrigeration Inc — Delmar (G-992)	G	302 846-2727
Dewitt Heating and AC Inc — Bear (G-115)	G	267 228-7355
Domenic Di Donato Plbg Htg Inc — Wilmington (G-10189)	G	856 207-4919
Donald Eichholz — Wilmington (G-10195)		302 792-1236
Ducts Unlimited Inc — Smyrna (G-8628)	E	302 378-4125
Eastern Shore Energy Inc — Camden (G-566)	E	302 697-9230
Elite Mechanical — Dagsboro (G-899)	G	302 321-9215
Elvin Schrock and Sons Inc — Greenwood (G-2737)	G	302 349-4384
Esquire Plumbing & Heating Co — Middletown (G-4062)	G	302 378-7001
Federal Mechanical Contractors — New Castle (G-5305)	F	302 656-2998
Ferrell Cooling & Heating Inc — Selbyville (G-8492)	G	302 436-2922
First Class Heating & AC Inc — Millsboro (G-4690)	F	302 934-8900
First Class Heating AC — Newark (G-6580)	E	302 834-1036
Fletcher Plumbing Htg & AC Inc — Smyrna (G-8636)	F	302 653-6277
Flo Mechanical LLC — Hockessin (G-3030)	G	302 239-7299
Flowrite Inc — Bear (G-156)	G	302 547-5657
Frederick Enterprises Inc — Wilmington (G-10627)	E	302 994-5786
General Refrigeration Company — Delmar (G-999)	E	302 846-3073
George H Burns Inc — Wilmington (G-10699)	E	302 658-0752
George M Howard & Sons Inc — Rehoboth Beach (G-7945)	G	302 645-9655
Gold Star Services — Newark (G-6671)	F	302 376-7677
Graydon Hurst & Son Inc — Wilmington (G-10765)	G	302 762-2444
Gregg & Sons Mechanical LLC — Townsend (G-8790)	G	302 223-8145
H & R Heating & AC — New Castle (G-5367)	E	302 323-9919
Happy Hours — Milford (G-4435)		302 422-9766
Harry Caswell Inc — Millsboro (G-4704)	E	302 945-5322
Harry L Adams Inc — New Castle (G-5377)	G	302 328-5268
Hellens Heating & Air I — Harbeson (G-2784)	G	302 945-1875
Henderson Mechanical Inc — Seaford (G-8263)	G	302 629-3753
Henry Eashum & Son Inc — Camden (G-578)	F	302 697-6164
Hentkowski Inc — Wilmington (G-10887)	F	302 998-2257
Hillside Oil Company Inc — Newark (G-6729)	E	302 738-4144
Hollingsworth Heating & AC — Milford (G-4443)	G	302 422-7525
Horizon Services Inc — Wilmington (G-10955)	C	302 762-1200
Hyett Refrigeration Inc — Harbeson (G-2786)	F	302 684-4600
ID Griffith Inc — Wilmington (G-10991)	D	302 656-8253
J E Pellegrino & Associates — Wilmington (G-11104)	G	302 655-2565
J F Sobieski Mech Contrs Inc — Wilmington (G-11106)	C	302 993-0103
J J White Inc — New Castle (G-5429)	A	215 722-1000
J Rihl Inc — Wilmington (G-11109)		856 778-5899
J Stachon Plumbing LLC — Wilmington (G-11111)	G	302 998-0938
John Hiott Refrigeration & AC — Camden Wyoming (G-648)	F	302 697-3050
Joseph T Richardson Inc — Harrington (G-2859)	F	302 398-8101
Jsf Construction Co Inc — Wilmington (G-11204)	G	302 999-9573
K and B Hvac Svcs LLC — Delmar (G-1012)	G	302 846-3111
K BS Plumbing Incorporated — Dover (G-1717)	G	302 678-2757
K C Weaver and Sons Inc — Wilmington (G-11214)	G	302 994-8399
Kmp Mechanical LLC — Newark (G-6898)		410 392-6126
Kw Solar Solutions Inc — Bear (G-225)	G	302 838-8400
Kw Solar Solutions Inc — Bear (G-226)	G	302 838-8400
Leager Construction Inc — Smyrna (G-8671)	G	302 653-8021
Liberty Mechanical LLC — Wilmington (G-11380)	G	302 397-8863
M D Plumbing Drain Cleaning — Marydel (G-3920)	G	302 492-8880
▲ M Davis & Sons Inc — Wilmington (G-11471)	C	302 998-3385
M Davis & Sons Inc — Wilmington (G-11472)	G	302 998-3385
Maichle S Heating Air — New Castle (G-5499)	F	302 328-4822
Malins Jim E Plumbing & Htg — Hockessin (G-3085)	G	302 239-2755
Manley Hvac Inc — Wilmington (G-11503)	G	302 998-4654
Mary Annes Landscaping Inc — Felton (G-2306)	G	302 335-5433
McCrea Equipment Company Inc — Harbeson (G-2791)	G	302 945-0821
McDaniel Plumbing & Heating — Wilmington (G-11593)	E	302 322-3075
McMahon Heating & AC — Lewes (G-3630)	F	302 945-4300
Mdm McHncal Instltion USA LLC — Wilmington (G-11610)	G	617 938-9634
Megee Plumbing & Heating Co — Georgetown (G-2600)	D	302 856-6311
Merit Mechanical Co Inc — Newark (G-7019)	D	302 366-8601
Merit Services Inc — Newark (G-7020)	D	302 366-8601
Midway Services Inc — Lincoln (G-3861)	G	302 422-8603
Miller John H Plumbing & Htg — Camden (G-591)	F	302 697-1012
Modern Controls Inc — New Castle (G-5532)	E	302 325-6800
Monroe Mechanical Contracting — Clayton (G-865)	G	302 223-6020
Morans Refrigeration Service — Rehoboth Beach (G-8011)	F	703 642-1200
National HVAC Service — New Castle (G-5546)	E	302 323-1776
National HVAC Service — Seaford (G-8327)	E	570 825-2894
North Star Heating & Air Inc — Dagsboro (G-925)	E	302 732-3967
Ocean View Plumbing Inc — Dagsboro (G-927)	F	302 732-9117
Pierce Total Comfort LLC — Middletown (G-4191)	G	302 378-7714
Preferred Fire Protection — Wilmington (G-12212)	F	302 256-0607
Preffered Mechanical Services — Wilmington (G-12213)	G	302 993-1122
Premier Heating & AC — Milton (G-4953)	E	302 684-1888
Quality Htg Ar-Cnditioning Inc — Wilmington (G-12280)	D	302 654-5247
R A Chance Plumbing Inc — Newark (G-7291)	E	302 292-1315
R A Chance Plumbing Inc — New Castle (G-5661)	G	302 324-8200
R S Bauer LLC — Harrington (G-2877)	F	302 398-4668
Rabspan Inc — New Castle (G-5664)	G	302 324-8104
Radius Services LLC — Wilmington (G-12304)	G	302 993-0600
Rays and Sons Mechanical LLC — Seaford (G-8372)	G	302 697-2100
Rays Plumbing & Heating Svcs — Felton (G-2315)	F	302 697-3936
Red Dog Plumbing and Heating — Selbyville (G-8537)	G	302 436-5024
Rigid Builders LLC — Georgetown (G-2640)	F	732 425-3443
Robert Gears — Frankford (G-2383)	G	302 834-7487
Robert J Seward and Son — Townsend (G-8820)	G	302 378-9414
Robert Mullin — Wilmington (G-12441)		302 322-9002
Roto-Rooter Services Company — Newark (G-7367)	E	302 659-7637
Russo Brothers Inc — Wilmington (G-12497)	G	302 764-5562
Rw Greer Inc — Wilmington (G-12499)	G	302 764-0376
Rw Heating & Air Inc — Harbeson (G-2798)	G	302 856-4330
Schlosser Assoc Mech Cntrs Inc — Newark (G-7393)	E	302 738-7333
Scotts Refrigeration & AC — Frankford (G-2386)	G	302 732-3736
Service Unlimited Inc — New Castle (G-5700)	E	302 326-2665
Siegfried J Schulze Inc — Newark (G-7422)		302 737-0403
Solar Heating Inc — Bear (G-327)	E	302 836-3943
Stan Perkoskis Plumbing & Htg — Wilmington (G-12734)	F	302 529-1220
Staplefords At Wilmington Inc — Wilmington (G-12739)	G	302 762-0637
State Wide Plumbing Inc — Newark (G-7486)	F	302 292-0924
Statewide Mechanical Inc — Townsend (G-8823)	G	302 376-6117
Stay True Plumbing — Bear (G-338)	G	302 464-1198
Steven Brown & Associates Inc — Wilmington (G-12759)	G	302 652-4722
Summit Heating and AC LLC — Townsend (G-8824)	G	302 378-1203
Summit Mechanical Inc — Bear (G-340)	E	302 836-8814
Telgian Corporation — Wilmington (G-12880)	E	480 753-5444
Thomas A Cochran & Sons Inc — New Castle (G-5768)	F	302 656-6054
Tj S Plumbing Heating L — Frankford (G-2393)		302 228-7129
Top Notch Htg & A C & Rfrgn — Lewes (G-3789)	G	302 645-7171
Total Climate Control Inc — Newark (G-7578)	G	302 836-6240
Traps Plumbing Heating A/C — Dover (G-2161)	G	302 677-1775
Tri-State Technologies Inc — Wilmington (G-12967)	E	302 658-5400
Tusi and Son Mechanical Inc — Newark (G-7602)	G	302 731-8228
Twaddell Plumbing and Heating — Wilmington (G-12997)	G	302 475-5577

Employee Codes: A=Over 500 employees, B=251-500
C=101-250, D=51-100, E=20-50, F=10-19, G=1-9

17 CONSTRUCTION-SPECIAL TRADE CONTRACTORS

Company	Rating	Phone
Wegman Bros Inc	F	302 738-4328
Newark *(G-7681)*		
Wilkins Fuel Co	G	302 422-5597
Milford *(G-4605)*		
Will C & Will Fuels	G	302 366-1915
Newark *(G-7695)*		
Willey and Co	G	302 629-3327
Laurel *(G-3311)*		
William D Shellady Inc	D	302 652-3106
Wilmington *(G-13206)*		
William Delcampo Mechanical SE	G	302 992-9748
Wilmington *(G-13207)*		
William G Day Company	F	302 427-3700
Wilmington *(G-13209)*		
William G Robelen Inc	G	302 656-8726
Wilmington *(G-13210)*		
William H McDaniel Inc	F	302 764-2020
Wilmington *(G-13212)*		
X/L Mechanical Inc	G	203 233-3329
Camden *(G-608)*		
Yerkie Corp	G	302 653-1321
Clayton *(G-875)*		

1721 Painting & Paper Hanging Contractors

Company	Rating	Phone
A1 Striping Inc	G	302 738-5016
Newark *(G-5872)*		
Asphalt Striping Svcs Del LLC	G	302 456-9820
Wilmington *(G-9154)*		
Bell Painting & Wall Covering	F	302 738-8854
Newark *(G-6069)*		
Burke Painting Co Inc	F	302 998-8500
Wilmington *(G-9507)*		
Cannon Sline LLC	D	302 658-1420
New Castle *(G-5131)*		
Cassidy Painting Inc	E	302 683-0710
Wilmington *(G-9588)*		
Clean Hands LLC	F	215 681-1435
Smyrna *(G-8598)*		
▲ Coatings Inc	G	302 661-1962
Wilmington *(G-9755)*		
Color Works Painting Inc	F	302 324-8411
New Castle *(G-5183)*		
Connor Charles & Sons Painting	G	302 945-1746
Georgetown *(G-2482)*		
D C Painting Corp	G	302 218-1211
Hockessin *(G-2999)*		
DPs Custom Painting LLC	G	302 732-3232
Frankford *(G-2360)*		
Durrell Sandblasting & Pntg Co	G	302 836-1113
Newark *(G-6481)*		
Facepainting	G	302 344-3145
New Castle *(G-5302)*		
Final Finishes Inc	G	302 995-1850
Wilmington *(G-10539)*		
G T Painting Inc	F	302 734-7771
Dover *(G-1577)*		
J G M Associates	G	302 645-2159
Lewes *(G-3567)*		
J Michaels Painting Inc	F	302 738-8465
Newark *(G-6817)*		
J Rocco Construction LLC	G	302 856-4100
Georgetown *(G-2570)*		
James Hughes Company Inc	G	302 239-4529
Hockessin *(G-3065)*		
Jamestown Painting & Dctg Inc	E	302 454-7344
Newark *(G-6827)*		
Jgarvey Enterprises Inc	G	302 562-7282
Wilmington *(G-11154)*		
John Mobile Sndblst & Pain	G	302 270-5627
Hartly *(G-2928)*		
Kent County Painting Inc	F	302 994-9628
Wilmington *(G-11244)*		
Keystone Finishing Inc	F	925 825-2498
Wilmington *(G-11254)*		
Kokoszka & Sons Inc	G	302 328-4807
New Castle *(G-5468)*		
Maccari Companies Inc	G	302 994-9628
Wilmington *(G-11476)*		
Marinis Bros Inc	F	302 322-9663
New Castle *(G-5506)*		
Mayse Painting & Contg LLC	G	443 553-6503
Middletown *(G-4148)*		
McElroy & Son Inc	F	302 995-2623
Wilmington *(G-11595)*		
Nu-Look Painting Contractors	G	302 734-9203
Dover *(G-1910)*		
O B Pntg & Powerwashing Inc	G	302 238-7384
Millsboro *(G-4765)*		
Painters Local Union 277	G	302 994-7835
Wilmington *(G-12006)*		
Quality Finishers Inc	G	302 325-1963
Regal Painting & Decorating	F	302 994-8943
Wilmington *(G-12354)*		
Reis Enterprises LLC	G	302 740-8382
Bear *(G-301)*		
Robert G Burke Painting Co	F	302 998-2200
Wilmington *(G-12438)*		
Robert J Peoples Inc	F	302 984-2017
New Castle *(G-5680)*		
Robert J Peoples Inc	F	302 322-0595
Wilmington *(G-12440)*		
Ronald W Peacock Inc	F	302 571-9313
Wilmington *(G-12470)*		
Smith Superior Pntg Repr Svcs	G	302 384-6575
Wilmington *(G-12661)*		
Sundew Painting Inc	E	302 994-7004
Wilmington *(G-12800)*		
Sundew Painting Inc	E	302 684-5858
Harbeson *(G-2801)*		
Superior Drywall Inc	F	302 732-9800
Dagsboro *(G-935)*		
Taylor & Sons Inc	G	302 856-6962
Georgetown *(G-2686)*		
Three Bs Painting Contractors	G	302 227-1497
Rehoboth Beach *(G-8097)*		
Top Qality Indus Finishers Inc	G	302 778-5005
Wilmington *(G-12929)*		
Urban Svcs Fcilities Maint LLC	G	302 993-6363
Wilmington *(G-13035)*		
Wilkisons Marking Service Inc	G	302 697-3669
Dover *(G-2226)*		

1731 Electrical Work

Company	Rating	Phone
A & A Electrical Inc	F	302 436-4800
Frankford *(G-2343)*		
A & B Electric	G	302 349-4050
Greenwood *(G-2710)*		
A C Electric Company	F	302 764-7429
Wilmington *(G-8872)*		
A Plus Electric & Security	G	302 455-1725
Newark *(G-5869)*		
Advanced Coatings Engrg LLC	E	888 607-0000
Newark *(G-5904)*		
Advanced Networking Inc	F	302 442-6199
Wilmington *(G-8954)*		
Advanced Power Control Inc	D	302 368-0443
Newark *(G-5907)*		
Advanced Power Generation	G	302 375-6145
Claymont *(G-686)*		
Advanced Security Systems Inc	G	302 998-7222
Wilmington *(G-8956)*		
Aezi Electrical Services LLC	G	302 547-5734
Middletown *(G-3932)*		
Airwave Technology	G	302 734-7838
Dover *(G-1098)*		
Alarm Systems Co of Delaware	G	302 239-7754
Hockessin *(G-2954)*		
Alliance Electric Inc	F	302 366-0295
Newark *(G-5940)*		
Allied Elec Solutions Ltd	F	302 893-0257
Wilmington *(G-9022)*		
AMP Electric LLC	G	302 337-8050
Bridgeville *(G-446)*		
Anaconda Prtctive Concepts Inc	F	302 834-1125
Newark *(G-5965)*		
Anchor Electric Inc	G	302 221-6111
New Castle *(G-5037)*		
Apple Electric Inc	E	302 645-5105
Rehoboth Beach *(G-7845)*		
Artisan Electrical Inc	G	302 645-5844
Lewes *(G-3348)*		
Arugie Enterprises Corp	G	302 225-2000
Wilmington *(G-9145)*		
Associates Contracting Inc	F	302 734-4311
Dover *(G-1150)*		
Assurance Media LLC	E	302 892-3540
Wilmington *(G-9162)*		
Atr Electrical Services Inc	G	302 373-7769
Middletown *(G-3954)*		
B & M Electric Inc	G	302 745-3807
Georgetown *(G-2442)*		
B Safe Inc	G	302 422-3916
Dover *(G-1167)*		
Baby Tel Communications Inc	G	302 368-3969
Newark *(G-6040)*		
Battaglia Associates Inc	G	302 325-6100
New Castle *(G-5069)*		
Battaglia Electric Inc	C	302 325-6100
New Castle *(G-5070)*		
Bauguess Electrical Svcs Inc	G	302 737-5614
Newark *(G-6053)*		
Bausum & Duckett Elc Co Inc	G	302 846-0536
Delmar *(G-973)*		
Beacon Air Inc	G	302 323-1688
New Castle *(G-5077)*		
Boxwood Electric Inc	G	302 368-3257
New Castle *(G-5101)*		
Boyces Electrical Service	G	302 875-5877
Laurel *(G-3203)*		
Brandywine Electronics Corp	F	302 324-9992
Bear *(G-56)*		
BW Electric Inc	E	302 566-6248
Harrington *(G-2821)*		
Byers Industrial Services LLC	E	302 836-4790
Bear *(G-58)*		
Cahill Contracting	F	302 378-9650
Middletown *(G-3979)*		
Cardenti Electric	F	302 834-1278
Bear *(G-64)*		
Carzo & Associates Inc	G	302 575-0336
Wilmington *(G-9584)*		
Certified Lock & Access LLC	G	302 383-7507
Wilmington *(G-9618)*		
Chieffo Electric Inc	E	302 292-6813
Middletown *(G-3986)*		
City Electric Contracting Co	F	302 764-0775
Wilmington *(G-9721)*		
Cmy Solutions LLC	G	321 732-1866
Newark *(G-6256)*		
Communications & Wiring Co	G	302 539-0809
Dagsboro *(G-893)*		
Conectiv LLC	C	202 872-2680
Wilmington *(G-9817)*		
Conectiv Communications Inc	G	302 224-1177
Newark *(G-6282)*		
Conectiv Energy Supply Inc	D	302 454-0300
Newark *(G-6283)*		
Construction MGT Svcs Inc	A	302 478-4200
Wilmington *(G-9835)*		
Conti Electric of N J Inc	G	302 996-3905
Wilmington *(G-9839)*		
Cox Electric Inc	G	302 629-5448
Seaford *(G-8211)*		
Current Solutions Inc	G	302 736-5210
Camden Wyoming *(G-629)*		
Daniel George Bebee Inc	G	443 359-1542
Laurel *(G-3220)*		
Dave Smagala	G	302 383-2761
Claymont *(G-729)*		
Defense Communication LLC	F	850 348-0708
Wilmington *(G-9993)*		
Delcollo Security Technologies	G	302 994-5400
Wilmington *(G-10100)*		
Delmarva Communications Inc	F	302 324-1230
New Castle *(G-5244)*		
Devary Electric Inc	G	302 674-4560
Dover *(G-1417)*		
Diamond Electric Inc	E	302 697-3296
Dover *(G-1421)*		
Donald Eichholz	G	302 792-1236
Wilmington *(G-10195)*		
Donaldson Electric	G	302 660-7534
Wilmington *(G-10197)*		
East Coast Electric Inc	F	302 998-1577
Wilmington *(G-10319)*		
Electrical Associates Inc	G	302 678-1068
Hartly *(G-2921)*		
Electrical Power Systems Inc	G	302 325-3502
New Castle *(G-5283)*		
Electronic Systems Specialist	G	302 738-4165
Newark *(G-6510)*		
Emergncy Response Protocol LLC	G	302 994-2600
Wilmington *(G-10391)*		
Erosion Control Services De	G	302 218-8913
Bear *(G-145)*		
Federal Energy Inf	F	858 521-3300
Wilmington *(G-10513)*		
Fiber One Inc	F	302 834-0890
Newark *(G-6577)*		
First State Electric Company	E	302 322-0140
New Castle *(G-5315)*		
FM Electric Inc	G	302 492-3900
Marydel *(G-3916)*		
Galloway Electric Co Inc	F	302 453-8385
Newark *(G-6633)*		
Gatesair Inc	G	513 459-3400
Wilmington *(G-10676)*		
George & Lynch Inc	C	302 736-3031
Dover *(G-1590)*		

Gerone C Hudson Elec Contr ......F 302 539-3332
Frankford *(G-2365)*
Gray Audograph Agency Inc ......E 302 658-1700
New Castle *(G-5359)*
H & A Electric Co ......G 302 678-8252
Dover *(G-1621)*
Hatzel & Buehler Inc ......E 302 478-4200
Wilmington *(G-10853)*
Hatzel & Buehler Inc ......C 302 798-5422
Wilmington *(G-10854)*
Hazzard Electrical Contractors ......G 302 645-8457
Lewes *(G-3538)*
Hockessin Electric Inc ......G 302 239-9332
Hockessin *(G-3052)*
Hts 20 LLP ......G 800 690-2029
Milton *(G-4916)*
I-Pulse Inc ......G 604 689-8765
Wilmington *(G-10984)*
Integrated Wirg Solutions LLC ......E 302 999-8448
Saint Georges *(G-8126)*
Integrity Tech Solutions Inc ......G 302 369-9093
Newark *(G-6793)*
J R Pini Electrical Contrs ......F 302 368-2311
Newark *(G-6819)*
James F Givens Inc ......G 302 875-5436
Laurel *(G-3242)*
Jsf Construction Co Inc ......G 302 999-9573
Wilmington *(G-11204)*
Kokoszka & Sons Inc ......G 302 328-4807
New Castle *(G-5468)*
Kriss Contracting Inc ......E 302 492-3502
Hartly *(G-2932)*
La Vere Electric Inc ......G 302 422-9185
Milford *(G-4469)*
Lee Townsend Electrical Contr ......G 302 697-3432
Dover *(G-1778)*
Liberty Electric LLC ......G 410 275-9200
Bear *(G-234)*
Light Action Inc ......F 302 328-7800
New Castle *(G-5481)*
Lightscapes Inc ......G 302 798-5451
Wilmington *(G-11387)*
◆ M Auger Enterprise Inc ......E 302 992-9922
Wilmington *(G-11470)*
M D Electric LLC ......G 302 838-2852
Bear *(G-242)*
▲ M Davis & Sons Inc ......C 302 998-3385
Wilmington *(G-11471)*
Martel Inc ......F 302 744-9566
Dover *(G-1821)*
Megee Plumbing & Heating Co ......D 302 856-6311
Georgetown *(G-2600)*
Messina Charles Plbg & Elc Co ......D 302 674-5696
Dover *(G-1842)*
Mid-Atlantic Elec Svcs Inc ......E 302 945-2555
Millsboro *(G-4745)*
Mid-County Electric Inc ......F 302 934-8304
Millsboro *(G-4747)*
Midshore Electrical Services ......G 302 945-2555
Harbeson *(G-2792)*
Murphy Electric Inc ......F 302 644-0404
Lewes *(G-3652)*
Nesmith & Company Inc ......E 215 755-4570
Claymont *(G-788)*
Nickle Elec Companies Inc ......E 302 856-1006
Georgetown *(G-2609)*
Nickle Elec Companies Inc ......C 302 453-4000
Newark *(G-7134)*
P S C Contracting Inc ......F 302 838-2998
Delaware City *(G-962)*
P S C Electric Contractor Inc ......F 302 838-2998
Delaware City *(G-963)*
Pace Electric ......G 302 328-2600
Wilmington *(G-12000)*
Peter D Furness Elc Co Inc ......C 302 764-6030
Wilmington *(G-12094)*
Power Plus Electrical Contg ......F 302 736-5070
Dover *(G-1978)*
Preferred Electric Inc ......D 302 322-1217
New Castle *(G-5638)*
Preferred Security Inc ......G 302 834-7800
Bear *(G-288)*
Prince Telecom LLC ......D 302 324-1800
New Castle *(G-5643)*
Pro-Grade Electric LLC ......G 302 258-7745
Georgetown *(G-2628)*
Progressive Services Inc ......E 302 658-7260
Wilmington *(G-12243)*
Q and R Electric LLC ......G 302 670-1817
Newark *(G-7276)*

Ram Electric Inc ......G 302 875-2356
Laurel *(G-3278)*
Rays Plumbing & Heating Svcs ......F 302 697-3936
Felton *(G-2315)*
Remco Electric ......G 302 422-6833
Milford *(G-4536)*
Rhino Cabling Group Inc ......F 302 312-1033
Newark *(G-7334)*
Riley Electric ......G 302 533-5918
Newark *(G-7340)*
Riley Electric Inc ......G 302 276-3581
Newark *(G-7341)*
Roberts Electric Inc ......G 302 233-3017
Magnolia *(G-3907)*
▲ S J Desmond Inc ......G 302 475-6520
Wilmington *(G-12507)*
Satterfield & Ryan Inc ......F 302 422-4919
Milford *(G-4553)*
Security Inc ......F 302 652-5276
Claymont *(G-802)*
Security Instrument Corp Del ......D 302 998-2261
Wilmington *(G-12571)*
Service Unlimited Inc ......E 302 326-2665
New Castle *(G-5700)*
Shore Electric Inc ......G 302 645-4503
Lewes *(G-3740)*
Shure Line Electrical Inc ......G 302 856-3110
Georgetown *(G-2655)*
Shure-Line Electrical Inc ......D 302 389-1114
Smyrna *(G-8715)*
Simmons Electrical Service LLC ......G 410 543-1480
Delmar *(G-1030)*
Simplex Time Recorder LLC ......F 302 325-6300
New Castle *(G-5714)*
Smartis ......G 302 653-8355
Dover *(G-2089)*
Solar Heating Inc ......E 302 836-3943
Bear *(G-327)*
Stork Electric Inc ......G 302 654-9427
Wilmington *(G-12773)*
Superior Electric Service Co ......E 302 658-5949
Wilmington *(G-12807)*
Sure Line Electrical Inc ......E 302 856-3110
Georgetown *(G-2672)*
T A Rietdorf & Sons Inc ......G 302 429-0341
Wilmington *(G-12844)*
Tangent Cable Systems Inc ......E 302 994-4104
Wilmington *(G-12851)*
Taylor Electric Service Inc ......G 302 422-3966
Milford *(G-4576)*
Tc Electric Company Inc ......E 302 791-0378
Wilmington *(G-12856)*
Technicare Inc ......G 302 322-7766
Newark *(G-7545)*
Telgian Corporation ......E 480 753-5444
Wilmington *(G-12880)*
Thorn Electric Inc ......F 302 653-4300
Smyrna *(G-8731)*
Towles Electric Inc ......G 302 674-4985
Dover *(G-2154)*
Transcore LP ......E 302 677-7262
Dover *(G-2159)*
Tri-State SEC & Contrls LLC ......F 302 299-2175
Newark *(G-7589)*
Tri-State Technologies Inc ......E 302 658-5400
Wilmington *(G-12967)*
Tricomm Services Corporation ......G 302 454-2975
Newark *(G-7590)*
Tudor Electric Inc ......E 302 736-1444
Dover *(G-2165)*
Tusi Brothers Inc ......E 302 998-6383
Wilmington *(G-12994)*
Vassallo Michael Elec Contr ......F 302 455-9405
Newark *(G-7646)*
Vector Security Inc ......E 302 422-7031
Milford *(G-4589)*
Wanex Electrical Service LLC ......F 302 326-1700
New Castle *(G-5822)*
Watts Electric Company ......G 302 529-1183
Wilmington *(G-13123)*
Wayne Bennett ......G 302 436-2379
Frankford *(G-2397)*
White Eagle Electrical Contg ......F 302 378-3366
Middletown *(G-4284)*
Wolanski & Sons Electric Inc ......G 302 999-0838
Wilmington *(G-13285)*
Yacht Anything Ltd ......G 302 226-3335
Rehoboth Beach *(G-8120)*

1741 Masonry & Other Stonework

Amer Masonry T A Marino ......G 302 834-1511
New Castle *(G-5030)*
Ashcraft Masonry Inc ......F 302 537-4298
Ocean View *(G-7755)*
Blair Carmean Masonry ......G 302 934-6103
Georgetown *(G-2455)*
Blue Hen Masonry Inc ......G 302 398-8737
Greenwood *(G-2718)*
Brick Doctor Inc ......G 302 678-3380
Dover *(G-1231)*
Clean Sweep ......G 302 422-6085
Milford *(G-4355)*
CNJ Contracting LLC ......G 302 659-3750
Smyrna *(G-8600)*
Colonial Masonry Ltd ......G 302 349-4945
Greenwood *(G-2721)*
Corrado American LLC ......E 302 655-6501
New Castle *(G-5196)*
Davis Young Associates Inc ......F 610 388-0932
Yorklyn *(G-13365)*
Enterprise Masonry Corporation ......E 302 764-6858
Wilmington *(G-10413)*
Esposito Mansory LLC ......F 302 996-4961
Wilmington *(G-10437)*
Falasco Masonry Inc ......G 302 697-8971
Camden Wyoming *(G-636)*
Fireplace Specialities LLC ......G 302 436-9250
Selbyville *(G-8493)*
J D Masonry Inc ......F 302 684-1009
Harbeson *(G-2787)*
J W Humphries Masonary ......G 302 284-0510
Felton *(G-2297)*
Jeandar Masonry Construction ......G 302 994-2616
Wilmington *(G-11137)*
Joseph L Hinks ......G 302 875-2260
Laurel *(G-3245)*
Joseph Rizzo & Sons Cnstr Co ......E 302 656-8116
New Castle *(G-5445)*
L A Masonary Inc ......F 302 239-6833
Newark *(G-6907)*
Lawrence Legates Masnry Co Inc ......G 302 422-8043
Milford *(G-4472)*
Lighthouse Masonry Inc ......G 302 945-1392
Lewes *(G-3609)*
M & L Contractors Inc ......F 302 436-9303
Selbyville *(G-8513)*
Mainline Masonry Inc ......E 302 998-2499
Middletown *(G-4142)*
Mario F Medori Inc ......G 302 239-4550
Wilmington *(G-11528)*
Mario Medori Inc ......F 302 656-8432
Wilmington *(G-11529)*
Mike Faella Inc ......G 302 475-2116
Wilmington *(G-11685)*
Nu-Tech Masonry Inc ......F 302 934-5660
Millsboro *(G-4764)*
Paragon Masonry Corporation ......E 302 798-7314
Wilmington *(G-12017)*
Peninsula Masonry Inc ......E 302 684-3410
Harbeson *(G-2795)*
Premier Restoration Cnstr Inc ......F 302 832-1288
Middletown *(G-4198)*
R F Gentner & Son ......G 302 947-2733
Harbeson *(G-2796)*
Restoration Dynamics LLC ......G 302 378-3729
Wilmington *(G-12389)*
◆ Rgp Holding Inc ......G 302 661-0117
Wilmington *(G-12399)*
Riddles Masonry ......G 302 238-7225
Millsboro *(G-4791)*
Roger Rullo Brick Pointing ......G 302 378-8100
Middletown *(G-4223)*
Romano Masonry Inc ......E 302 368-4155
Newark *(G-7362)*
Shore Masonry Inc ......G 302 945-5933
Millsboro *(G-4800)*
South Delaware Masonry Inc ......G 302 378-1998
Townsend *(G-8822)*
Stonegate Granite ......G 302 500-8081
Georgetown *(G-2667)*
Thomas E OGrady Masonry ......G 302 378-8245
Middletown *(G-4257)*
Trenton Block Delaware Inc ......G 302 684-0112
Milton *(G-4977)*
Vivid Colors Carpet LLC ......G 302 335-3933
Frederica *(G-2415)*
Walter W Snyder ......G 302 378-1817
Middletown *(G-4280)*

S I C

17 CONSTRUCTION-SPECIAL TRADE CONTRACTORS

Wilson Masonry Corp .... F 302 398-8240
  Harrington *(G-2908)*

1742 Plastering, Drywall, Acoustical & Insulation Work

A L N Construction Inc .... D 302 292-1580
  Newark *(G-5868)*
A S A P Insulation Inc .... F 302 836-9040
  Newark *(G-5870)*
Blue Hen Insulation Inc .... G 302 424-4482
  Milford *(G-4327)*
Camden Drywall Inc .... G 302 697-9653
  Wyoming *(G-13359)*
Cook Plastering Inc .... F 302 737-0778
  Newark *(G-6295)*
Custom Drywall Inc .... G 302 369-3266
  Newark *(G-6330)*
D M S Stucco Construction Co .... F 302 368-2618
  Newark *(G-6342)*
Dale Insulation Co of Delaware .... G 302 324-9332
  New Castle *(G-5213)*
Delmarva Spray Foam LLC .... F 302 752-1080
  Georgetown *(G-2509)*
Dry Wall Inc .... E 302 838-6500
  New Castle *(G-5262)*
Eastern Industrial Svcs Inc .... D 302 455-1400
  New Castle *(G-5278)*
Ed Hileman Drywall Inc .... G 302 436-6277
  Selbyville *(G-8486)*
Erco Ceilings & Interiors Inc .... F 302 994-6200
  Wilmington *(G-10432)*
H & C Insulation LLC .... G 302 448-0777
  Greenwood *(G-2743)*
Hensco LLC .... G 302 423-1638
  Harrington *(G-2849)*
Heritage Interiors Inc .... E 302 369-3199
  Newark *(G-6725)*
J & G Acoustical Co .... E 302 285-3630
  Middletown *(G-4112)*
J Michaels Painting Inc .... G 302 738-8465
  Newark *(G-6817)*
Kenco Drywall .... E 302 697-6489
  Felton *(G-2300)*
M3 Contracting LLC .... E 302 781-3143
  Newark *(G-6968)*
Master Interiors Inc .... E 302 368-9361
  Newark *(G-7000)*
Master Interiors Inc .... G 302 368-9361
  Milford *(G-4489)*
Newark Insulation Co Inc .... F 302 731-8970
  Newark *(G-7122)*
O Morales Stucco Plaster Inc .... G 302 834-8891
  Bear *(G-269)*
Pauls Plastering Inc .... E 302 654-5583
  New Castle *(G-5609)*
Peninsula Acoustical Co Inc .... G 302 653-3551
  Smyrna *(G-8687)*
Phillips Insulation Inc .... G 302 655-6523
  Wilmington *(G-12118)*
Precision Drywall Inc .... E 415 550-8880
  Wilmington *(G-12205)*
Rexmex Drywall LLC .... G 302 343-9140
  Hartly *(G-2939)*
Southland Insulators Del LLC .... D 302 854-0344
  Georgetown *(G-2662)*
Spacecon LLC .... G 302 322-9285
  New Castle *(G-5727)*
State Drywall Co Inc .... E 302 239-2843
  Hockessin *(G-3148)*
Stucco Smith Systems .... G 302 245-8179
  Selbyville *(G-8550)*
Superior Drywall Inc .... F 302 732-9800
  Dagsboro *(G-935)*
Three Bs Painting Contractors .... G 302 227-1497
  Rehoboth Beach *(G-8097)*
Tri-State Drywall LLC .... E 302 798-2709
  Claymont *(G-812)*
Union Wholesale Co .... E 302 656-4462
  Wilmington *(G-13015)*

1743 Terrazzo, Tile, Marble & Mosaic Work

◆ Casale Marble Imports Inc .... D 561 404-4213
  Wilmington *(G-9585)*
Ceramic Tile Supply Co .... D 302 737-4968
  Newark *(G-6180)*
Consolidated Construction Svcs .... F 302 629-6070
  Seaford *(G-8205)*
Dippold Marble Granite .... G 302 734-8505
  Dover *(G-1427)*

Jack Parisi Tile Co Inc .... G 302 892-2455
  Wilmington *(G-11115)*
▲ Keystone Granite and Tile Inc .... G 302 323-0200
  New Castle *(G-5462)*
Pala Tile & Carpet Contrs Inc .... E 302 652-4500
  Wilmington *(G-12007)*
Peninsula Acoustical Co Inc .... G 302 653-3551
  Smyrna *(G-8687)*
Tile Market of Delaware Inc .... G 302 644-7100
  Lewes *(G-3786)*
▲ Tile Market of Delaware Inc .... D 302 777-4663
  Wilmington *(G-12910)*
Tile Shop LLC .... G 302 250-4889
  Wilmington *(G-12911)*

1751 Carpentry Work

Beeline Services LLC .... G 302 376-7399
  Middletown *(G-3965)*
Clark & Sons Inc .... E 302 998-7552
  Wilmington *(G-9731)*
Clark & Sons Inc .... G 302 856-3372
  Georgetown *(G-2474)*
Clark & Sons Overhead Doors .... E 302 998-7552
  Wilmington *(G-9732)*
Coastal Cabinetry LLC .... G 302 542-4155
  Seaford *(G-8199)*
Comstock Custom Cabinets Inc .... G 302 422-2928
  Milford *(G-4364)*
Construction Unlimited Inc .... G 302 836-3140
  Bear *(G-83)*
Custom Framers Inc .... E 302 684-5377
  Harbeson *(G-2781)*
De Nisio General Construction .... G 302 656-9460
  Wilmington *(G-9986)*
Del-Mar Door Services Inc .... G 800 492-2392
  Middletown *(G-4025)*
Diamond State Door .... G 302 743-4667
  Wilmington *(G-10142)*
Ed Turulski Custom Woodworking .... G 302 658-2221
  Wilmington *(G-10342)*
FB Door-Delaware LLC .... F 302 995-1000
  Newport *(G-7749)*
First State Carpentry LLC .... G 302 738-8849
  Newark *(G-6582)*
Francis Pollinger & Son Inc .... E 302 655-8097
  Wilmington *(G-10612)*
G2 Group Inc .... G 302 836-4202
  Bear *(G-163)*
H & M Construction .... G 302 645-6639
  Lewes *(G-3527)*
J & A Overhead Door Inc .... G 302 846-9915
  Delmar *(G-1005)*
J & L Services Inc .... F 410 943-3355
  Seaford *(G-8274)*
J R Brooks Custom Framing LLC .... G 302 538-3637
  Felton *(G-2296)*
Jbr Contractors Inc .... E 856 296-9594
  Millsboro *(G-4714)*
Joseph E Stevens & Father .... G 302 654-8556
  Wilmington *(G-11189)*
Kevin Garber .... G 302 834-0639
  Bear *(G-216)*
Knight Construction .... G 610 496-6879
  Wilmington *(G-11280)*
Mark Ventresca Associates Inc .... G 302 239-3925
  Hockessin *(G-3089)*
Mason Building Group Inc .... C 302 292-0600
  Newark *(G-6999)*
Mastercrafters Inc .... E 302 678-1470
  Dover *(G-1825)*
Maxwell World .... G 937 463-3579
  Dagsboro *(G-918)*
Menchaca Building Corp .... G 302 475-4581
  Wilmington *(G-11629)*
Michael A OBrien & Sons .... G 302 994-2894
  Wilmington *(G-11656)*
Newport Builders & Windowland .... F 302 994-3537
  Wilmington *(G-11878)*
Oceanic Ventures Inc .... G 302 645-5872
  Lewes *(G-3664)*
Overhead Door Co Delmar Inc .... E 302 424-4400
  Milford *(G-4520)*
Pinnacle Garage Door Company .... G 302 505-4531
  Felton *(G-2310)*
R & J Taylor Inc .... G 302 368-7888
  Newark *(G-7289)*
Rementer Brothers Inc .... G 302 249-4250
  Milton *(G-4956)*
Superior Screen & Glass .... G 302 541-5399
  Ocean View *(G-7816)*

Urban Svcs Fcilities Maint LLC .... G 302 993-6363
  Wilmington *(G-13035)*
V & P Custom Finishers Inc .... G 302 376-6367
  Townsend *(G-8830)*
Yoder Overhead Door Company .... G 302 875-0663
  Delmar *(G-1050)*

1752 Floor Laying & Other Floor Work, NEC

Airbase Carpet Mart Abct Dist .... G 302 323-8800
  New Castle *(G-5019)*
Anderson Floor Coverings Inc .... F 302 227-3244
  Rehoboth Beach *(G-7842)*
Coffin Hardwood Flooring Inc .... G 302 934-6414
  Millsboro *(G-4665)*
Connolly Flooring Inc .... E 302 996-9470
  Wilmington *(G-9831)*
Creative Flooring Contrs Inc .... G 302 653-7521
  Smyrna *(G-8607)*
Creative Floors Inc .... F 302 455-9045
  Newark *(G-6313)*
Creative Kitchens and Floors .... G 302 629-3166
  Seaford *(G-8214)*
Delawres Fnest Hardwood Floors .... G 302 376-0742
  Middletown *(G-4033)*
Dominic A Di Febo & Sons .... F 302 425-5054
  Wilmington *(G-10190)*
Donald G Varnes & Sons Inc .... G 302 737-5953
  Newark *(G-6461)*
Edward Varnes Hardwood Floors .... F 302 292-0919
  Newark *(G-6503)*
Edwards Paul Crpt Installation .... G 302 672-7847
  Dover *(G-1509)*
▲ Facility Services Group Inc .... G 302 317-3029
  Wilmington *(G-10474)*
Fasttrak .... G 302 761-5454
  Wilmington *(G-10506)*
Flooring Solutions Inc .... F 302 655-8001
  Wilmington *(G-10576)*
Margherita Vincent & Anthony .... G 302 834-9023
  Newark *(G-6985)*
Mikes Ceramic Tile Inc .... G 302 376-5743
  Middletown *(G-4165)*
Modular Carpet Recycling Inc .... F 484 885-5890
  New Castle *(G-5534)*
New Castle County Flooring .... G 302 218-0507
  Newark *(G-7100)*
Northeastern Coating Systems .... G 302 328-6545
  Wilmington *(G-11905)*
Spacecon LLC .... G 302 322-9285
  New Castle *(G-5727)*
Urban Svcs Fcilities Maint LLC .... G 302 993-6363
  Wilmington *(G-13035)*
Ziggys Inc .... F 302 453-1285
  Newark *(G-7740)*

1761 Roofing, Siding & Sheet Metal Work

Apex Piping Systems Inc .... E 302 998-5272
  Wilmington *(G-9096)*
Archer Exteriors Inc .... F 302 877-0650
  Georgetown *(G-2434)*
Bayside Exteriors LLC .... G 302 727-5288
  Lewes *(G-3363)*
Beckers Chimney and Roofg LLC .... E 302 463-8294
  Wilmington *(G-9759)*
Best Roofing and Siding Co .... G 302 678-5700
  Dover *(G-1197)*
Coghan-Haes LLC .... E 302 325-4210
  Wilmington *(G-9759)*
CTA Roofing & Waterproofing .... F 302 454-8551
  Newark *(G-6323)*
D Shinn Inc .... F 302 792-2033
  Wilmington *(G-9943)*
David Saunders General Contrs .... G 302 998-0056
  Wilmington *(G-9973)*
Delaware Siding Company Inc .... G 302 836-6971
  Bear *(G-113)*
Delmarva Roofing & Coating Inc .... E 302 349-5174
  Greenwood *(G-2728)*
Dream View Exteriors Group LLC .... G 302 358-9530
  Georgetown *(G-2515)*
Ducts Unlimited Inc .... G 302 378-4125
  Smyrna *(G-8628)*
E D Custom Contracting Inc .... G 302 653-2646
  Clayton *(G-844)*
Eastern Metals Inc .... F 302 454-7886
  Newark *(G-6499)*
Farrell Roofing Inc .... E 302 378-7663
  Middletown *(G-4069)*
Francis Pollinger & Son Inc .... E 302 655-8097
  Wilmington *(G-10612)*

G Fedale General Contrs LLC ....F 302 225-7663
Hockessin *(G-3033)*
G Fedale Roofing and Siding ....F 302 225-7663
Wilmington *(G-10658)*
Gardner Asphalt Corporation ....E 302 629-3505
Seaford *(G-8248)*
Gearhart Construction Inc ....G....... 302 674-5466
Dover *(G-1587)*
H K Griffith Inc.......................................E 302 368-4635
Newark *(G-6698)*
Hickman Overhead Door Company......F 302 422-4249
Milford *(G-4441)*
Home Services Unlimited......................G....... 302 293-8726
Newark *(G-6740)*
Hurlock Roofing Company......................E 302 654-2783
Wilmington *(G-10978)*
Interstate Steel Co Inc ....E 302 598-5159
Newark *(G-6800)*
Jsf Construction Co Inc ....G....... 302 999-9573
Wilmington *(G-11204)*
JW Tull Contracting Svcs LLC..............F 302 494-8179
Wilmington *(G-11212)*
Kirkin Roofing LLC ....G....... 302 483-7135
New Castle *(G-5466)*
L & J Sheet Metal ....F 302 875-2822
Laurel *(G-3249)*
Lane Home Services Inc........................F 302 652-7663
Wilmington *(G-11329)*
Let US Lift It Inc......................................G....... 302 654-2221
Wilmington *(G-11376)*
M A K Roofing Inc ....G....... 302 737-5380
Newark *(G-6963)*
Martin J Burke Inc...................................G....... 302 741-2638
Dover *(G-1823)*
Mastercraft Welding................................G....... 302 697-3932
Dover *(G-1824)*
McConnell Bros Inc ....G....... 302 218-4240
Wilmington *(G-11588)*
Milford Gutter Guys LLC ....G....... 302 424-1931
Lincoln *(G-3862)*
Mill Creek Metals Inc...............................F 302 529-7020
Claymont *(G-782)*
Mumford Sheet Metal Works Inc ....E 302 436-8251
Selbyville *(G-8527)*
P & C Roofing Inc....................................E 302 322-6767
New Castle *(G-5595)*
Pencader Mechanical Contrs................G....... 302 368-9144
Newark *(G-7194)*
Peter Domanski & Sons ....G....... 302 475-3214
Hockessin *(G-3118)*
PJ Fitzpatrick Inc ....D....... 302 325-2360
New Castle *(G-5623)*
Quality Exteriors Inc...............................F 302 398-9283
Harrington *(G-2876)*
Quality Htg Ar-Cnditioning Inc ....D....... 302 654-5247
Wilmington *(G-12280)*
R R Roofing Inc 2....................................G....... 302 218-7474
Wilmington *(G-12297)*
Robert Grant Inc......................................F 302 422-6090
Milford *(G-4546)*
Roofers Inc ....E 302 995-7027
Wilmington *(G-12473)*
Russell A Paulus & Son Inc ....G....... 302 998-4494
Wilmington *(G-12495)*
S G Williams & Bros Co..........................F 302 656-8167
Wilmington *(G-12506)*
Sharp Raingutters....................................F 302 398-4873
Harrington *(G-2887)*
Tazelaar Roofing Service Inc ....G....... 302 697-2643
Dover *(G-2132)*
Tri-State Fbrction McHning LLC ....E 302 232-3133
New Castle *(G-5788)*
Wertz & Co..E 302 658-5186
Wilmington *(G-13161)*
Wilkinson Roofing & Siding Inc.............E 302 998-0176
Wilmington *(G-13203)*

1771 Concrete Work

A G Concrete Works LLC ....G....... 302 841-2227
Dagsboro *(G-876)*
Advanced Cnstr Techniques Inc ....D....... 302 295-4868
Wilmington *(G-8951)*
Blacktop Sealcoating Inc ....G....... 302 234-2243
Newark *(G-6090)*
Boozer Excavation Co Inc......................G....... 302 542-0290
Milton *(G-4870)*
Bradley & Sons Designer Con...............G....... 302 836-8031
Bear *(G-55)*
Brick Doctor Inc.......................................G....... 302 678-3380
Dover *(G-1231)*
C&J Paving Inc...F 302 684-0211
Milton *(G-4873)*
Cipolloni Brothers LLC...........................G....... 302 449-0960
Smyrna *(G-8595)*
Clarks Glasgow Pools Inc ....F 302 834-0200
New Castle *(G-5175)*
CNJ Contracting LLC..............................G....... 302 659-3750
Smyrna *(G-8600)*
Coastal Concrete Works LLC ....G....... 302 381-5261
Harbeson *(G-2776)*
Concrete Services Inc ....F 302 883-2883
Dover *(G-1310)*
Curbs Etc Inc..G....... 302 653-3511
Smyrna *(G-8608)*
Cutting of Precision Concrete ....G....... 302 543-5833
Newport *(G-7746)*
D Gingerich Concrete & Masnry...........E 302 492-8662
Hartly *(G-2917)*
Daisy Construction Company...............D....... 302 658-4417
Wilmington *(G-9947)*
De Nisio General Construction..............G....... 302 656-9460
Wilmington *(G-9986)*
Delmarva Concrete Pumping Inc...........G....... 302 537-4118
Frankford *(G-2359)*
Duncan S Concrete..................................G....... 302 395-1552
Bear *(G-129)*
East Coast Builders Inc..........................F 302 629-3551
Seaford *(G-8229)*
East Coast Poured Walls Inc ....E 302 430-0630
Milford *(G-4399)*
F & N Vazquez Concrete LLC.................G....... 302 725-5305
Lincoln *(G-3846)*
Floor Coatings Etc Inc............................E 302 322-4177
New Castle *(G-5320)*
Francis Kelly Sons Inc............................G....... 302 999-7400
Wilmington *(G-10610)*
Frank Deramo & Son Inc........................F 302 328-0102
New Castle *(G-5328)*
Gardner Asphalt Corporation ....E 302 629-3505
Seaford *(G-8248)*
Graydon Hurst & Son Inc ....G....... 302 762-2444
Wilmington *(G-10765)*
Healy & Long Inc.....................................G....... 302 654-8039
Wilmington *(G-10873)*
Healy Long & Jevin Inc..........................F 302 654-8039
Wilmington *(G-10874)*
Highland Construction LLC ....F 302 286-6990
Bear *(G-185)*
J & T Concrete Inc ....F 302 368-4949
Newark *(G-6814)*
J E Rispoli Contractor Inc ....E 302 999-1310
Wilmington *(G-11105)*
James L Webb Paving Co Inc ....G....... 302 697-2000
Camden *(G-584)*
JT Hoover Concrete Inc..........................E 302 832-7699
Bear *(G-205)*
Kevins Masonry Concrete Co ....G....... 302 382-7259
Felton *(G-2301)*
Lafazia Construction ....G....... 302 234-1300
Wilmington *(G-11323)*
Leager Construction Inc.........................G....... 302 653-8021
Smyrna *(G-8671)*
M & M Construction Inc..........................G....... 410 758-1071
Odessa *(G-7829)*
Magowi Consulting Group LLC ....F 832 301-9230
Newark *(G-6972)*
Merit Construction Engineers...............F 302 992-9810
Wilmington *(G-11644)*
Mumford and Miller Con Inc..................C....... 302 378-7736
Middletown *(G-4171)*
New Castle Hot Mix Inc..........................G....... 302 655-2119
Wilmington *(G-11853)*
O Morales Stucco Plaster Inc ....G....... 302 834-8891
Bear *(G-269)*
Pauls Paving Inc ....F 302 539-9123
Frankford *(G-2379)*
Peninsula Masonry Inc...........................E 302 684-3410
Harbeson *(G-2795)*
Poured Foundations of De Inc...............G....... 302 234-2050
Newark *(G-7235)*
Ralph Cahall & Son Paving....................D....... 302 653-4220
Smyrna *(G-8696)*
Richard D Whaley Cnstr LLC.................G....... 302 934-9525
Millsboro *(G-4789)*
River Asphalt LLC ....G....... 302 934-0881
Dagsboro *(G-932)*
Rp Ventures and Holdings Inc ....E 410 398-3000
New Castle *(G-5690)*
RS Widdoes and Son Inc........................G....... 302 764-7455
Wilmington *(G-12486)*
Sanco Construction Co Inc....................G....... 302 633-4156
Wilmington *(G-12536)*
Santo Stucco ....G....... 302 453-0901
Newark *(G-7384)*
Seaford Concrete Products LLC ....G....... 302 628-6964
Seaford *(G-8387)*
Shea Concrete Ltd ....E 302 422-7221
Milford *(G-4558)*
Shore Masonry Inc...................................G....... 302 945-5933
Millsboro *(G-4800)*
Smith Concrete Inc ....G....... 302 270-9251
Milford *(G-4562)*
Stripe-A-Lot Inc ....E 302 654-9175
Wilmington *(G-12777)*
Superior Foundations Inc ....E 302 293-7061
Bear *(G-342)*
Superior Sealing Services D ....G....... 610 717-6237
Bear *(G-343)*
Talley Brothers Inc..................................E 302 224-5376
Newark *(G-7536)*
Terra Firma of Delmarva Inc..................F 302 846-3350
Delmar *(G-1037)*
Triad Construction Company LLC.........E 302 652-3339
New Castle *(G-5791)*
Trottys Concrete Pumping Inc...............F 302 732-3100
Frankford *(G-2394)*
Victor Colbert Construction...................E 302 834-1174
Newark *(G-7656)*
Victor Colbert Construction...................E 302 368-7270
Newark *(G-7657)*
Wsd Contracting Inc...............................G....... 302 492-8606
Hartly *(G-2944)*
Yardscape Inc...G....... 302 540-0311
Middletown *(G-4293)*

1781 Water Well Drilling

A C Schultes of Delaware Inc ....F 302 337-0700
Bridgeville *(G-442)*
American Water Well System.................F 302 629-3796
Seaford *(G-8150)*
Delmarva Builders Inc ....G....... 302 629-9123
Bridgeville *(G-465)*
Middletown Well Drilling Co...................G....... 302 378-9396
Odessa *(G-7830)*
White Drilling Corp ....G....... 302 422-4057
Lincoln *(G-3873)*

1791 Structural Steel Erection

▼ Amazon Steel Construction Inc........G....... 302 751-1146
Milford *(G-4305)*
Atlas Wldg & Fabrication Inc ....E 302 326-1900
New Castle *(G-5053)*
Deaven Development Corp ....G....... 302 994-5793
Wilmington *(G-9991)*
Donald F Deaven Inc...............................E 302 994-5793
Wilmington *(G-10196)*
East Coast Erectors Inc..........................E 302 323-1800
New Castle *(G-5275)*
Emlyn Construction Co ....G....... 302 697-8247
Dover *(G-1519)*
▲ Falcon Steel Co....................................D....... 302 571-0890
Wilmington *(G-10482)*
H & T Builders Inc....................................G....... 302 422-0745
Milford *(G-4429)*
M & M Construction Inc...........................G....... 410 758-1071
Odessa *(G-7829)*
▲ M Davis & Sons Inc ....C....... 302 998-3385
Wilmington *(G-11471)*
Mid-Atlantic Steel LLC............................E 302 323-1800
New Castle *(G-5527)*
R C Fabricators Inc..................................D....... 302 573-8989
Wilmington *(G-12293)*
Rapuano Iron Works Inc..........................G....... 302 571-1809
Wilmington *(G-12317)*
Steel Suppliers Inc...................................C....... 302 654-5243
Wilmington *(G-12748)*
Summit Steel Inc......................................D....... 302 325-3220
New Castle *(G-5741)*
Tri-State Fbrction McHning LLC ....E 302 232-3133
New Castle *(G-5788)*
W F Construction Inc...............................G....... 302 420-6747
Newark *(G-7669)*

1793 Glass & Glazing Work

1st Class Glass LLC ....G....... 302 229-9203
Wilmington *(G-8849)*
Atlas Glass & Metal LLC.........................G....... 302 456-5958
Newark *(G-6023)*

S
I
C

Employee Codes: A=Over 500 employees, B=251-500
C=101-250, D=51-100, E=20-50, F=10-19, G=1-9

2020 Harris Directory of
Delaware Businesses

465

17 CONSTRUCTION-SPECIAL TRADE CONTRACTORS

Delaware Storefronts LLC ....G... 302 697-1850
  Dover (G-1400)
Eastern Home Improvements Inc ....G... 302 655-9920
  Wilmington (G-10322)
Go-Glass Corporation ....F... 302 674-3390
  Dover (G-1596)
Gregory D Thacker ....G... 302 239-0879
  Newark (G-6689)
Mikes Glass Service Inc ....F... 302 658-7936
  Wilmington (G-11686)
MMR Associates Inc ....G... 302 883-2984
  Dover (G-1865)
New Castle Glass Inc ....G... 302 322-6164
  New Castle (G-5558)
Newark Glass & Mirror Inc ....F... 302 834-1158
  Bear (G-264)
Parags Glass Company ....G... 302 737-0101
  Newark (G-7176)
Premier Glass & Screen Inc ....F... 302 732-3101
  Frankford (G-2380)
Service Glass Inc ....F... 302 629-9139
  Seaford (G-8397)
Superior Screen & Glass ....F... 302 541-5399
  Ocean View (G-7816)
West Ventures Inc ....G... 307 737-9900
  New Castle (G-5830)
Zephyr Aluminum LLC ....G... 302 571-0585
  Wilmington (G-13348)

1794 Excavating & Grading Work

Bobcat of New Castle LLC ....F... 732 780-6880
  New Castle (G-5098)
Bramble Construction Co Inc ....F... 302 856-6723
  Georgetown (G-2458)
Brandywine Construction Co ....D... 302 571-9773
  New Castle (G-5105)
Bunting & Murray Cnstr Corp ....D... 302 436-5144
  Selbyville (G-8463)
Castle Construction Del Inc ....E... 302 326-3600
  New Castle (G-5136)
Centerville Company Contrs ....G... 302 656-8666
  Wilmington (G-9613)
Central Backhoe Service ....G... 302 398-6420
  Milton (G-4877)
Choptank Excavation ....G... 302 378-8114
  Middletown (G-3987)
Christiana Excavating Company ....E... 302 738-8660
  Newark (G-6223)
Cirillo Bros Inc ....E... 302 326-1540
  New Castle (G-5162)
Clean Delaware Inc ....F... 302 684-4221
  Milton (G-4879)
CNJ Contracting LLC ....G... 302 659-3750
  Smyrna (G-8600)
Corrado American LLC ....E... 302 655-6501
  New Castle (G-5196)
Corrado Construction Co LLC ....D... 302 652-3339
  New Castle (G-5197)
Cygnet Construction Corp ....G... 302 436-5212
  Selbyville (G-8475)
D E Leager Construction ....G... 302 994-1060
  Wilmington (G-9939)
David G Horsey & Sons Inc ....D... 302 875-3033
  Laurel (G-3221)
David P Roser Inc ....E... 302 239-7605
  Hockessin (G-3000)
Dirt Works Inc ....F... 302 947-2429
  Lewes (G-3466)
Dixon Contracting Inc ....G... 302 653-4623
  Dover (G-1434)
Don Rogers Inc ....E... 302 658-6524
  Wilmington (G-10193)
J & M Industries Inc ....G... 302 575-0200
  Wilmington (G-11097)
Jeff Bartsch Trckg Excvtg Inc ....G... 302 653-9329
  Townsend (G-8801)
Jerrys Inc ....F... 302 422-7676
  Milford (G-4457)
Kaye Construction ....E... 302 628-6962
  Seaford (G-8285)
Leroy Betts Construction Inc ....G... 302 284-9193
  Felton (G-2303)
M G Hamex Corporation ....F... 302 832-9072
  New Castle (G-5493)
Magowi Consulting Group LLC ....G... 832 301-9230
  Newark (G-6972)
Merit Construction Engineers ....F... 302 992-9810
  Wilmington (G-11644)
Midway Services Inc ....G... 302 422-8603
  Lincoln (G-3861)

Palmer & Associates Inc ....G... 302 834-9329
  Bear (G-275)
Pearce & Moretto Inc ....E... 302 326-0707
  New Castle (G-5611)
R & E Excavation LLC ....G... 302 750-5226
  New Castle (G-5660)
Ralph Cahall & Son Paving ....D... 302 653-4220
  Smyrna (G-8696)
Robert Keating Excavating ....G... 302 239-4670
  Hockessin (G-3139)
Swain Excavation Inc ....G... 302 422-4349
  Lincoln (G-3872)
Swift Construction Co Inc ....G... 302 855-1011
  Georgetown (G-2685)
Terra Firma of Delmarva Inc ....F... 302 846-3350
  Delmar (G-1037)
W Sharp Paynter & Sons Inc ....G... 302 684-8508
  Milton (G-4979)
Walter W Snyder ....G... 302 378-1817
  Middletown (G-4280)

1795 Wrecking & Demolition Work

Burns & Fiorina Demolition ....G... 732 888-1076
  Newark (G-6137)
D & D Contractors Inc ....F... 302 378-9724
  Smyrna (G-8609)
Design Contracting Inc ....G... 302 429-6900
  Wilmington (G-10121)
Geotech LLC ....G... 302 353-9769
  Newark (G-6649)
Green Earth Tech Group LLC ....G... 302 257-5617
  Wilmington (G-10771)
K & L Renovations LLC ....F... 302 456-0373
  Newark (G-6862)
Mid-Atlntic Dismantlement Corp ....D... 302 678-9300
  Dover (G-1851)
Rpj Waste Services Inc ....F... 302 653-9999
  Smyrna (G-8706)
Steven Augusiewicz Inc ....G... 302 738-1919
  Bear (G-339)
Thomas Building Group Inc ....E... 302 283-0600
  Newark (G-7563)

1796 Installation Or Erection Of Bldg Eqpt & Machinery, NEC

▼ Amazon Steel Construction Inc ....G... 302 751-1146
  Milford (G-4305)
Brandywine Elevator Co Inc ....G... 866 636-0102
  Wilmington (G-9430)
▲ Bruce Industrial Co Inc ....D... 302 655-9616
  New Castle (G-5118)
Greg Elect ....G... 215 651-1477
  Hockessin (G-3040)
Harrold & Son Inc ....G... 302 629-9504
  Seaford (G-8262)
Planned Poultry Renovation ....E... 302 875-4196
  Laurel (G-3273)
Pradhan Energy Projects ....G... 305 428-2123
  Hockessin (G-3124)
R & S Fabrication Inc ....F... 302 629-0377
  Bridgeville (G-516)

1799 Special Trade Contractors, NEC

1st State Accessibility LLC ....G... 844 663-4396
  Wilmington (G-8850)
2 Days Bath LLC ....G... 302 798-0103
  Wilmington (G-8851)
A & R Fence Co Inc ....G... 302 366-8550
  Newark (G-5864)
Adam Basement ....G... 302 983-8446
  Newark (G-5898)
Advance Office Instltions Inc ....E... 302 777-5599
  New Castle (G-5008)
Affordable Delivery Svcs LLC ....G... 302 276-0246
  New Castle (G-5016)
Alan M Billingsley Jr ....G... 302 998-7907
  Selbyville (G-8998)
All Restored Inc ....G... 302 222-3537
  Camden Wyoming (G-613)
Allura Bath & Kitchen Inc ....G... 302 731-2851
  Newark (G-5944)
▼ Amazon Steel Construction Inc ....G... 302 751-1146
  Milford (G-4305)
American Cabinetry LLC ....G... 302 655-4064
  Wilmington (G-9043)
American Seaboard Exteriors ....E... 302 571-9896
  Wilmington (G-9055)
Arcadia Fencing Inc ....G... 302 398-7700
  Harrington (G-2812)

Arnold Powerwash LLC ....G... 302 542-9783
  Lewes (G-3346)
Astec Inc ....F... 302 378-2717
  Middletown (G-3946)
Atechnologie LLC ....G... 781 325-5230
  Wilmington (G-9171)
Atlantic Business Contracting ....G... 302 337-7490
  Bridgeville (G-449)
Atlantic Kitchen & Bath LLC ....G... 302 947-9001
  Lewes (G-3357)
Atlantic Source Contg Inc ....G... 302 645-5207
  Lewes (G-3359)
Aztech Contracting Inc ....G... 302 526-2145
  Felton (G-2273)
B & T Contracting ....F... 302 492-8415
  Camden Wyoming (G-616)
B G Halko & Sons Inc ....G... 302 322-2020
  New Castle (G-5063)
Boyds Trailor Hitches ....G... 302 697-9000
  Camden Wyoming (G-619)
Bright Finish LLC 888 974-4747
  Smyrna (G-8586)
Builders LLC General ....G... 302 533-6528
  Newark (G-6130)
Built-Rite Fence Co Inc ....G... 302 366-8329
  Newark (G-6134)
Cassidy Painting Inc ....E... 302 683-0710
  Wilmington (G-9588)
Chas Pools Inc ....F... 302 737-9224
  Middletown (G-3985)
Clarks Glasgow Pools Inc ....F... 302 834-0200
  New Castle (G-5175)
Clarks Swimming Pools Inc ....G... 302 629-8835
  Seaford (G-8198)
Coastal Pump & Tank Inc ....F... 302 398-3061
  Harrington (G-2826)
▲ Coatings Inc ....G... 302 661-1962
  Wilmington (G-9755)
Collett & Son Welding Inc ....G... 302 376-1830
  Townsend (G-8770)
Collett and Sons Welding ....G... 302 223-6525
  Smyrna (G-8601)
County Environmental Inc ....E... 302 322-8946
  New Castle (G-5201)
County Insulation Co ....D... 302 322-8946
  New Castle (G-5202)
Creative Kitchens and Floors ....G... 302 629-3166
  Seaford (G-8214)
CTA Roofing & Waterproofing ....F... 302 454-8551
  Newark (G-6323)
Custom Framers Inc ....E... 302 684-5377
  Harbeson (G-2781)
Custom Porcelain Inc ....G... 302 659-6590
  Townsend (G-8777)
Delaware Valley Fence & Iron ....G... 302 322-8193
  New Castle (G-5242)
Delmarva Roofing & Coating Inc ....E... 302 349-5174
  Greenwood (G-2728)
Delmarva Spray Foam LLC ....F... 302 752-1080
  Georgetown (G-2509)
Dezins Unlimited Inc ....G... 302 652-4545
  Wilmington (G-10135)
Dickerson Fence Co Inc ....G... 302 846-2227
  Delmar (G-993)
Dover Pool & Patio Center Inc ....E... 302 346-7665
  Dover (G-1465)
Dover Pool & Patio Center Inc ....G... 302 839-3300
  Milford (G-4392)
Durrell Sandblasting & Pntg Co ....G... 302 836-1113
  Newark (G-6481)
E W Brown Inc ....G... 302 652-6612
  Wilmington (G-10310)
East Coast Elastomerics Inc ....F... 302 524-8004
  Selbyville (G-8484)
Eastern Industrial Svcs Inc ....D... 302 455-1400
  New Castle (G-5278)
Eastern Shore Porch Patio Inc ....E... 302 436-9520
  Selbyville (G-8485)
Eastern States Cnstr Svc Inc ....D... 302 995-2259
  Wilmington (G-10326)
Ecg Industries Inc ....G... 302 453-0535
  Newark (G-6502)
Eclipes Erection Inc ....E... 302 633-1421
  Wilmington (G-10337)
Everest Granite LLC ....G... 302 229-4733
  Wilmington (G-10445)
Farrell Roofing Inc ....E... 302 378-7663
  Middletown (G-4069)
First State Petroleum Services ....G... 302 398-9704
  Harrington (G-2841)

Gainor Awnings Inc G 302 998-8611
Wilmington *(G-10663)*

Gateway Construction Inc G 302 653-4400
Clayton *(G-852)*

Gemini Building Systems LLC D 302 654-5310
Wilmington *(G-10688)*

Geotech LLC G 302 353-9769
Newark *(G-6649)*

Giorgi Kitchens Inc F 302 762-1121
Wilmington *(G-10715)*

Gotshadeonline Inc G 302 832-8468
Bear *(G-168)*

Gray Audograph Agency Inc E 302 658-1700
New Castle *(G-5359)*

Gregg & Sons Mechanical LLC G 302 223-8145
Townsend *(G-8790)*

Guardian Fence Co F 302 834-3044
Middletown *(G-4097)*

H2o Pro LLC G 302 321-7077
Frankford *(G-2367)*

Harmony Construction Inc F 302 737-8700
Newark *(G-6709)*

Henderson Services Inc F 302 424-1999
Milford *(G-4438)*

Hertiage Builders & Improvemen G 302 275-8675
Bear *(G-182)*

Interiors By Kim Inc G 302 537-2480
Ocean View *(G-7794)*

Iron Hill Fence G 302 453-9060
Newark *(G-6807)*

J & B Caulkers Co G 302 653-7325
Townsend *(G-8799)*

J & G Acoustical Co E 302 285-3630
Middletown *(G-4112)*

J & L Services Inc F 410 943-3355
Seaford *(G-8274)*

J & M Fencing Inc F 302 284-9674
Felton *(G-2295)*

Jbm Petroleum Service LLC G 302 752-6105
Lincoln *(G-3857)*

Jbs Contracting G 302 543-7264
Wilmington *(G-11135)*

Jeffrey Hatch G 443 496-0449
Marydel *(G-3919)*

JW Tull Contracting Svcs LLC F 302 494-8179
Wilmington *(G-11212)*

K & R Seal Coating LLC G 302 530-3649
Bear *(G-210)*

Keene Enterprises Inc G 302 422-2856
Ellendale *(G-2261)*

Kent Sign Company Inc F 302 697-2181
Dover *(G-1739)*

Kgc Enterprises Inc G 302 668-1835
Wilmington *(G-11255)*

Lacieah Inc G 302 365-5585
Newark *(G-6912)*

Linda McCormick G 443 987-2099
Wilmington *(G-11392)*

Line-X Delaware Inc F 302 672-7005
Dover *(G-1791)*

LLC Schell Brothers F 302 226-1994
Rehoboth Beach *(G-7988)*

Lynx General Contracting G 302 368-9401
Newark *(G-6961)*

Maccari Companies Inc G 302 994-9628
Wilmington *(G-11476)*

Marlings Inc F 302 325-1759
New Castle *(G-5509)*

Mastercrafters Inc E 302 678-1470
Dover *(G-1825)*

Mebro Inc E 302 992-0104
Wilmington *(G-11613)*

Messicks Mobile Homes Inc F 302 398-9166
Harrington *(G-2867)*

Mid-Atlantic Systems Dpn Inc G 301 206-9510
Newark *(G-7032)*

Mid-Atlntic Wtrproofing MD Inc G 855 692-4668
Newark *(G-7033)*

Millennia Contracting Inc F 302 654-6200
New Castle *(G-5529)*

Mold Medics Global LLC G 301 943-9428
Wilmington *(G-11726)*

N Mallari Gc Corp G 302 516-7738
Newark *(G-7078)*

Nanticoke Fence LLC G 302 628-7808
Seaford *(G-8318)*

Newark Fence Co G 302 368-5329
Newark *(G-7120)*

Newport Builders & Windowland F 302 994-3537
Wilmington *(G-11878)*

Patio Systems Inc G 302 644-6540
Lewes *(G-3680)*

Phoenix Home Theater Inc F 302 295-1390
Wilmington *(G-12124)*

Pierce Fence Company Inc F 302 674-1996
Dover *(G-1959)*

Pioneer Fence Co Inc F 302 998-2892
Wilmington *(G-12143)*

Preferred Security Inc G 302 834-7800
Bear *(G-288)*

Proclean Inc E 302 656-8080
Delaware City *(G-965)*

Produce Marketing Assn Inc D 302 738-7100
Newark *(G-7265)*

Professional Window Tinting G 302 456-3456
Newark *(G-7267)*

R & J Taylor Inc G 302 368-7888
Newark *(G-7289)*

R C Fabricators Inc D 302 573-8989
Wilmington *(G-12293)*

R W Home Services Inc F 302 539-4683
Ocean View *(G-7810)*

Rnh Installation G 302 731-8900
Newark *(G-7347)*

Royal Treatments G 302 722-6733
Smyrna *(G-8705)*

RPR Environmental Solutions G 302 362-0687
Lincoln *(G-3866)*

Saienni Stairs LLC G 302 292-2699
Newark *(G-7377)*

Shore Tint & More Inc G 302 947-4624
Harbeson *(G-2800)*

Step By Step Furn Installation G 302 834-8257
Newark *(G-7488)*

Stracke Enterprises Inc G 302 743-6515
Newark *(G-7492)*

Summer Hill Custom Home Bldr G 302 462-5853
Ocean View *(G-7815)*

Sunnyfield Contractors Inc F 302 674-8610
Dover *(G-2114)*

Superior Screen & Glass F 302 541-5399
Ocean View *(G-7816)*

Sussex Fencing G 302 945-7008
Millsboro *(G-4807)*

Sussex Machine Works Inc G 302 875-7958
Laurel *(G-3297)*

Swift Pools Inc E 302 738-9800
Newark *(G-7522)*

That Granite Place LLC G 302 337-7490
Bridgeville *(G-525)*

Tri-State Fbrction McHning LLC E 302 232-3133
New Castle *(G-5788)*

▲ **Troy Granite Inc** E 302 292-1750
Newark *(G-7596)*

US Installation Group Inc F 302 994-1644
Wilmington *(G-13039)*

Weavers Construction Inc G 302 270-8876
Felton *(G-2326)*

White Drilling Corp G 302 422-4057
Lincoln *(G-3873)*

Wilkins Enterprises Inc G 302 945-4142
Lewes *(G-3824)*

William Chambers and Son G 302 284-9655
Viola *(G-8838)*

20 FOOD AND KINDRED PRODUCTS

2011 Meat Packing Plants

Cbbc Opco LLC G 863 967-0636
Wilmington *(G-9599)*

2013 Sausages & Meat Prdts

AES Foods G 302 420-8377
Newark *(G-5914)*

Kirby & Holloway Provisions Co E 302 398-3705
Harrington *(G-2863)*

New B & M Meats Inc G 302 655-5331
Wilmington *(G-11849)*

Ralph and Paul Adams Inc B 800 338-4727
Bridgeville *(G-517)*

2015 Poultry Slaughtering, Dressing & Processing

Allen Biotech LLC A 302 629-9136
Millsboro *(G-4626)*

American Express Shuttle Inc G 302 420-8377
Newark *(G-5950)*

Harim Usa Ltd G 302 629-9136
Seaford *(G-8261)*

Jcr Enterprises Inc E 302 629-9163
Seaford *(G-8279)*

◆ **Mountaire Farms Delaware Inc** F 302 934-1100
Millsboro *(G-4756)*

Mountaire Farms Inc F 302 988-6200
Selbyville *(G-8523)*

New B & M Meats Inc G 302 655-5331
Wilmington *(G-11849)*

Perdue Farms Inc G 302 629-3216
Seaford *(G-8353)*

Perdue Farms Inc E 302 337-2210
Bridgeville *(G-507)*

Perdue Farms Inc G 410 543-3424
Seaford *(G-8354)*

Perdue Farms Inc D 302 424-2600
Milford *(G-4525)*

Perdue Farms Incorporated G 302 855-5635
Georgetown *(G-2618)*

2021 Butter

CD Cream G 302 832-5425
Delaware City *(G-950)*

2022 Cheese

Heather Kraft G 302 927-0072
Dagsboro *(G-908)*

2023 Milk, Condensed & Evaporated

Botica Cbd Inc G 619 800-5857
Wilmington *(G-9396)*

Nestle Usa Inc C 302 325-0300
New Castle *(G-5552)*

Nuvim Inc G 302 827-4052
Lewes *(G-3662)*

▲ **Roxlor LLC** G 302 778-4166
Wilmington *(G-12481)*

Tesla Nootropics Inc G 514 718-2270
Dover *(G-2140)*

2024 Ice Cream

Big Chill Inc G 302 727-5568
Rehoboth Beach *(G-7868)*

Dana E Herbert G 302 721-5798
Bear *(G-93)*

Frazzberry G 302 543-7791
Wilmington *(G-10622)*

Sunshine Crepes G 302 537-1765
Bethany Beach *(G-432)*

2026 Milk

Hy-Point Dairy Farms Inc C 302 478-1414
Wilmington *(G-10979)*

Kraft Heinz Company A 302 734-6100
Dover *(G-1758)*

Tuscan/Lehigh Dairies Inc F 302 398-8321
Harrington *(G-2901)*

2032 Canned Specialties

Freakin Fresh Salsa Inc G 302 750-9789
Wilmington *(G-10623)*

Hanover Foods Corporation C 302 653-9281
Clayton *(G-855)*

Mariachi House G 302 635-7361
Hockessin *(G-3088)*

Vincenza & Margherita Bistro G 302 479-7999
Wilmington *(G-13083)*

2033 Canned Fruits, Vegetables & Preserves

Fresh Industries Ltd G 205 737-3747
Rehoboth Beach *(G-7937)*

Hanover Foods Corporation C 302 653-9281
Clayton *(G-855)*

Kraft Heinz Company A 302 734-6100
Dover *(G-1758)*

◆ **Mushroom Supply & Services Inc** F 302 998-2008
Newark *(G-7074)*

Peppers Inc F 302 644-6900
Lewes *(G-3684)*

Trisco Foods LLC D 719 352-3218
Wilmington *(G-12978)*

2034 Dried Fruits, Vegetables & Soup

Hanover Foods Corporation C 302 653-9281
Clayton *(G-855)*

20 FOOD AND KINDRED PRODUCTS

2035 Pickled Fruits, Vegetables, Sauces & Dressings
Kenny Brothers Produce LLC..............G....... 302 337-3007
Bridgeville (G-488)

2037 Frozen Fruits, Juices & Vegetables
Hanover Foods Corporation ....C....... 302 653-9281
Clayton (G-855)
JG Townsend Jr & Co Inc...................E....... 302 856-2525
Georgetown (G-2574)
Juiceplus+ ....G....... 302 322-2616
New Castle (G-5447)
Smoothies Soup and Sandwiches ......G....... 302 280-6183
Laurel (G-3289)
Tropical Harvest Inc ....G....... 302 682-9463
Rehoboth Beach (G-8099)

2038 Frozen Specialties
◆ H&H Trading International LLC ....G....... 480 580-3911
Wilmington (G-10811)
Hanover Foods Corporation ....C....... 302 653-9281
Clayton (G-855)
Nicola Pizza Inc ....E....... 302 227-6211
Rehoboth Beach (G-8017)
Pictsweet Company ....D....... 302 337-8206
Bridgeville (G-509)

2041 Flour, Grain Milling
Kraft Heinz Company ....A....... 302 734-6100
Dover (G-1758)
McShares Inc ....G....... 302 656-3168
Wilmington (G-11608)

2048 Prepared Feeds For Animals & Fowls
B Diamond Feed Company ....G....... 302 697-7576
Camden Wyoming (G-617)
Bi-State Feeders LLC........................G....... 302 398-3408
Harrington (G-2817)
Green Recovery Tech LLC ....G....... 302 317-0062
New Castle (G-5362)
Jbs Souderton Inc ....G....... 302 629-0725
Seaford (G-8278)
Mountaire Farms Inc ....E....... 302 732-6611
Frankford (G-2375)
Numake-1 LLC ....G....... 302 220-4760
New Castle (G-5582)
Nutrien AG Solutions Inc ....G....... 302 629-2780
Seaford (G-8333)
Southern States Coop Inc ....F....... 302 378-9841
Middletown (G-4246)
Southern States Coop Inc ....F....... 302 732-6651
Dagsboro (G-934)
Springhaus LLC ....G....... 302 397-5261
Wilmington (G-12714)

2051 Bread, Bakery Prdts Exc Cookies & Crackers
Adams Bakery Corporation ....G....... 802 863-2696
Wilmington (G-8934)
Bimbo Bakeries Usa Inc ....E....... 302 328-7970
New Castle (G-5090)
Busymama Cupcakes ....G....... 302 259-9988
Seaford (G-8177)
Cakes By Dee ....G....... 302 934-7483
Millsboro (G-4653)
Cole and Latz Inc ....G....... 702 234-2784
New Castle (G-5180)
Kraft Heinz Company ....A....... 302 734-6100
Dover (G-1758)
Marlenka America LLC ....G....... 502 530-0720
Lewes (G-3620)
Pennsylvania Brand Co ....G....... 302 674-5774
Dover (G-1946)
Posh Cupcake ....G....... 302 234-4451
Hockessin (G-3123)
Smackerals By Michelle LLC ....G....... 302 376-8272
Middletown (G-4243)
Sweet Venom Effect LLC ....E....... 302 674-5831
Wilmington (G-12823)
Sweets By Samantha LLC ....F....... 302 740-2218
Newark (G-7521)

2052 Cookies & Crackers
Philly Pretzel ....G....... 302 478-5658
Wilmington (G-12120)
Stauffer Family LLC ....G....... 302 227-5820
Rehoboth Beach (G-8087)

2064 Candy & Confectionery Prdts
Chocolate Swirl LLC ....G....... 718 407-0034
Wilmington (G-9670)
Leiny Snacks ....F....... 302 494-2499
Wilmington (G-11367)

2066 Chocolate & Cocoa Prdts
Chocolate Editions Inc ....G....... 302 479-8400
Claymont (G-715)
Interntnl Agrclture Prod Grou ....G....... 302 450-2008
Smyrna (G-8659)
Kraft Heinz Company ....A....... 302 734-6100
Dover (G-1758)
◆ United Cocoa Processor Inc ....E....... 302 731-0825
Newark (G-7613)
Witors America LLC ....G....... 646 247-4836
Camden (G-606)

2068 Salted & Roasted Nuts & Seeds
▲ Sunshine Nut Company LLC ....E....... 781 352-7766
Lewes (G-3770)

2079 Shortening, Oils & Margarine
Lusotrading Corp ....G....... 302 288-0670
Wilmington (G-11452)

2082 Malt Beverages
Chesapeakemaine Trey ....G....... 302 226-3600
Rehoboth Beach (G-7887)
Delaware Beer Works Inc ....E....... 302 836-2739
Bear (G-104)
Dewey Beer & Food Company LLC ....G....... 302 227-1182
Dewey Beach (G-1056)
▲ Dogfish Head Craft Brewery LLC ....D....... 302 684-1000
Milton (G-4897)
Dogfish Head Inc................................F....... 302 226-2739
Rehoboth Beach (G-7918)
Mispillion River Brewing LLC ....G....... 302 491-6623
Milford (G-4508)
Volunteer Brewing Company LLC ......G....... 610 721-2836
Middletown (G-4277)
Wilmington Brew Works LLC ....G....... 302 757-4971
Wilmington (G-13225)

2083 Malt
Proximity Malt LLC ....F....... 414 755-8388
Laurel (G-3275)

2084 Wine & Brandy
Delaware Meat Company LLC ....G....... 302 438-0252
Wilmington (G-10063)
Harvest Ridge Winery LLC ....G....... 302 250-6583
Marydel (G-3917)
Nassau Vly Vineyards & Winery ....G....... 302 645-9463
Lewes (G-3655)
Pizzadili Partners LLC ....G....... 302 284-9463
Felton (G-2312)
Signature Selections LLC ....G....... 631 256-6900
Newark (G-7427)
▲ Southern Wine Spirits Del LLC .....F....... 800 292-7890
New Castle (G-5726)
Texavino LLC ....G....... 302 295-0829
Wilmington (G-12888)
Universal Bev Importers LLC ....G....... 302 276-0619
Middletown (G-4273)
White Horse Winery ....G....... 302 388-4850
Wilmington (G-13190)

2085 Liquors, Distilled, Rectified & Blended
Beach Time ....G....... 302 644-2850
Lewes (G-3367)
Breakthru Beverage Group LLC ....C....... 302 356-3500
New Castle (G-5109)
Dogfish Head Companies LLC ....G....... 302 684-1000
Milton (G-4896)
Legacy Distilling LLC ....G....... 302 983-1269
Smyrna (G-8672)
R J Baker Distillery ....G....... 302 745-0967
Laurel (G-3277)
◆ William Grant & Sons USA Corp ....G....... 302 573-3880
Wilmington (G-13211)

2086 Soft Drinks
Canada Dry Dstrg Wilmington De .....E....... 302 322-1856
New Castle (G-5130)
Cole and Latz Inc ....G....... 702 234-2784
New Castle (G-5180)

Domian International Svc LLC............G....... 804 837-3616
Smyrna (G-8624)
Krave Like LLC ....G....... 302 482-4550
Wilmington (G-11293)
Maurten US Corporation ....G....... 302 669-9085
Wilmington (G-11577)
Minor Figures Inc ....G....... 714 875-3449
Camden (G-592)
Moon Shot Energy LLC ....G....... 512 297-2626
Lewes (G-3647)
Mr Natural Bottled Water ....G....... 302 436-7700
Frankford (G-2376)
Pepsi Bottling Ventures LLC ....D....... 302 398-3415
Harrington (G-2871)
Pepsi-Cola Btlg of Wilmington ....C....... 302 761-4848
Wilmington (G-12081)
Pepsi-Cola Metro Btlg Co Inc............C....... 302 764-6770
Wilmington (G-12082)

2087 Flavoring Extracts & Syrups
Bettys ....G....... 302 233-2675
Milford (G-4325)
Le Herbe LLC ....G....... 949 317-1100
Wilmington (G-11348)
Trisco Foods LLC ....D....... 719 352-3218
Wilmington (G-12978)

2091 Fish & Seafoods, Canned & Cured
Lusotrading Corp ....G....... 302 288-0670
Wilmington (G-11452)

2092 Fish & Seafoods, Fresh & Frozen
Steven P Copp ....G....... 302 645-9112
Lewes (G-3765)

2095 Coffee
Mbanza Coffee Inc ....G....... 813 403-8724
Newark (G-7010)

2096 Potato Chips & Similar Prdts
Fishers Popcorn Fenwick LLC ....E....... 302 539-8833
Fenwick Island (G-2336)

2097 Ice
Blue Marlin Ice LLC ....G....... 302 697-7800
Dover (G-1214)
Hanover Foods Corporation ....C....... 302 653-9281
Clayton (G-855)
Kimos Hawaiian Shave Ice ....G....... 302 998-1763
Wilmington (G-11261)
Rockford Ice ....G....... 302 478-7280
Wilmington (G-12449)
Seaford Ice...G....... 302 629-2562
Seaford (G-8390)
Seaford Ice Inc ....G....... 302 629-2562
Seaford (G-8391)

2099 Food Preparations, NEC
▲ All Peoples Food LLC ....G....... 302 690-4881
Newark (G-5935)
Andre Noel Thalia ....G....... 302 747-0813
New Castle (G-5038)
◆ Carlyle Cocoa Co LLC ....F....... 302 428-3800
New Castle (G-5134)
Cook Awesome Food LLC..................G....... 302 990-2665
Wilmington (G-9850)
Dr Dunner Usa Inc ....G....... 302 656-1950
Wilmington (G-10220)
Eldas Kitchen LLC ....G....... 925 260-6156
Dover (G-1510)
▲ Firsd Tea North America LLC ......G....... 302 322-1255
New Castle (G-5310)
Grandma ZS Maple Haus ....G....... 412 297-3324
Claymont (G-757)
Kraft Heinz Company ....A....... 302 734-6100
Dover (G-1758)
Martin Grey LLC ....G....... 302 990-0675
Lewes (G-3621)
Phillip L Hrrs Fd/Cnsltnt ....G....... 302 270-2905
Harrington (G-2874)
Super Suppers ....G....... 302 478-5935
Wilmington (G-12804)
Trisco Foods LLC ....D....... 719 352-3218
Wilmington (G-12978)

2020 Harris Directory of Delaware Businesses

21 TOBACCO PRODUCTS

2111 Cigarettes
Emerald Industries LLC ....G...... 302 450-1416
  Wilmington (G-10390)

22 TEXTILE MILL PRODUCTS

2211 Cotton, Woven Fabric
Aloft Canvas LLC ....G...... 302 893-0144
  New Castle (G-5024)
C and C Alpaca Factory ....G...... 609 752-7894
  Lewes (G-3397)
Classic Canvas LLC ....G...... 443 359-0150
  Delmar (G-984)
Coolpop Nation ....G...... 302 584-8833
  Wilmington (G-9852)
Dannys Custom Upholstery ....G...... 302 436-8200
  Selbyville (G-8477)
Denim Duo-Vers ....G...... 302 632-6943
  Milford (G-4386)
H D Lee Company Inc ....F...... 302 477-3930
  Wilmington (G-10807)
Keiths Boat Canvas ....G...... 302 841-8081
  Georgetown (G-2581)
Magic Canvas ....G...... 302 312-4122
  Middletown (G-4140)
Pointe Snaps ....G...... 260 602-0898
  Wilmington (G-12178)
Threads N Denims ....G...... 302 678-0642
  Dover (G-2145)
Uncorked Canvas Parties ....G...... 302 724-7625
  Dover (G-2175)
Uncorked Canvas Parties LLC .....G...... 302 659-1396
  Smyrna (G-8734)
Vertical Blind Factory Inc ....F...... 302 998-9616
  Wilmington (G-13067)

2221 Silk & Man-Made Fiber
Agree Arlington TX LLC ....G...... 302 683-3008
  Wilmington (G-8980)
Baker Safety Equipment Inc ....G...... 302 376-9302
  Bear (G-44)
Invista Capital Management LLC ....E...... 302 629-1100
  Seaford (G-8272)
◆ Lycra Company LLC ....A...... 316 226-9361
  Wilmington (G-11462)
Lycra Company LLC ....G...... 302 731-6800
  Newark (G-6960)

2231 Wool, Woven Fabric
Krisallis ....G...... 610 522-7273
  Bear (G-224)

2241 Fabric Mills, Cotton, Wool, Silk & Man-Made
Conlin Corporation ....E...... 302 633-9174
  Wilmington (G-9823)
Wayne Industries Inc ....G...... 302 478-6160
  Wilmington (G-13126)

2252 Hosiery, Except Women's
Heated Wear LLC ....G...... 347 510-7965
  Wilmington (G-10878)

2253 Knit Outerwear Mills
Flapdoodles Inc ....D...... 302 731-9793
  Newark (G-6595)
Global Garments (usa) LLC ....G...... 617 340-3329
  Wilmington (G-10726)
Great Graphic Originals Ltd ....G...... 302 734-7600
  Dover (G-1608)

2254 Knit Underwear Mills
Ginch Gonch Corp ....G...... 713 240-9900
  Newark (G-6655)

2261 Cotton Fabric Finishers
Carter Printing and Design ....G...... 302 655-2343
  New Castle (G-5135)
D By D Printing LLC ....G...... 302 659-3373
  Dover (G-1335)
James Thompson & Company Inc ....E...... 302 349-4501
  Greenwood (G-2748)

2269 Textile Finishers, NEC
James Thompson & Company Inc ....E...... 302 349-4501
  Greenwood (G-2748)

2273 Carpets & Rugs
Bentley Mills Inc ....G...... 800 423-4709
  Wilmington (G-9303)
Hardwood Mills Inc ....G...... 302 697-7195
  Dover (G-1627)
Josephine Keir Limited ....G...... 302 422-0270
  Milford (G-4462)
Kurtz Collection ....G...... 302 654-0442
  Wilmington (G-11302)
Maneto Inc ....G...... 302 656-4285
  Wilmington (G-11501)
Trademark Productions Inc ....F...... 416 787-0365
  Wilmington (G-12947)
Vivid Colors Carpet LLC ....G...... 302 335-3933
  Frederica (G-2415)

2282 Yarn Texturizing, Throwing, Twisting & Winding Mills
▲ Clover Yarns Inc ....G...... 302 422-4518
  Milford (G-4359)
Invista Capital Management LLC ....E...... 302 629-1100
  Seaford (G-8272)

2297 Fabrics, Nonwoven
Donner Corporation ....G...... 302 778-0844
  Wilmington (G-10199)
Dow Chemical Company ....B...... 302 368-4169
  Newark (G-6467)
Dupont Specialty Pdts USA LLC ....G...... 302 774-1000
  Wilmington (G-10263)

2298 Cordage & Twine
Barry USA Inc ....G...... 800 305-2673
  Newark (G-6049)
Barry USA Inc ....G...... 800 305-2673
  Dover (G-1175)
Cablicons LLC ....G...... 843 458-7702
  Wilmington (G-9527)

2299 Textile Goods, NEC
Be Blessed Design Group LLC ....G...... 302 561-3793
  Bear (G-45)
▼ Fibre Processing Corporation ....D...... 302 654-3659
  Wilmington (G-10531)
Garage ....G...... 302 453-1930
  Newark (G-6638)
Hodges International Inc ....G...... 310 874-8516
  Dover (G-1651)
Oilminers Cbd LLC ....G...... 484 885-9417
  Wilmington (G-7145)
Semiconductor Technologies ....G...... 302 420-1432
  Newark (G-7405)

23 APPAREL AND OTHER FINISHED PRODUCTS MADE FROM FABRICS AND SIMILAR MATERIAL

2311 Men's & Boys' Suits, Coats & Overcoats
Cross Over Camo LLC ....G...... 302 798-1898
  Claymont (G-725)
Fresh Accents LLC ....G...... 301 717-3757
  Bethany Beach (G-399)
Zuhatrend LLC ....G...... 302 883-2656
  Dover (G-2256)

2321 Men's & Boys' Shirts
Lee Bell Inc ....G...... 302 477-3930
  Wilmington (G-11355)

2323 Men's & Boys' Neckwear
Aptustech LLC ....G...... 347 254-5619
  Wilmington (G-9105)
Mercy Inc ....G...... 302 764-7781
  Wilmington (G-11638)

2325 Men's & Boys' Separate Trousers & Casual Slacks
Blue Mountain Apparel La LLC ....G...... 646 787-5679
  Newark (G-6101)
Lee Bell Inc ....G...... 302 477-3930
  Wilmington (G-11355)
True Religion Apparel Inc ....G...... 302 894-9425
  Newark (G-7597)

2326 Men's & Boys' Work Clothing
Fresh Accents LLC ....G...... 301 717-3757
  Bethany Beach (G-399)
Nixon Uniform Service Inc ....C...... 302 325-2875
  New Castle (G-5571)

2329 Men's & Boys' Clothing, NEC
Carpediem Health LLC ....G...... 347 467-4444
  Dover (G-1257)
Hampshire Group Limited ....D...... 212 840-5666
  Wilmington (G-10829)
Heated Wear LLC ....G...... 347 510-7965
  Wilmington (G-10878)
Huzala Inc ....G...... 313 404-6941
  Newark (G-6756)
Kha-Neke Inc ....G...... 302 440-4728
  Newark (G-6883)
Lee Bell Inc ....G...... 302 477-3930
  Wilmington (G-11355)
▲ Majdell Group USA Inc ....G...... 302 722-8223
  Newark (G-6977)

2331 Women's & Misses' Blouses
Lee Bell Inc ....G...... 302 477-3930
  Wilmington (G-11355)

2335 Women's & Misses' Dresses
Arcangel Inc ....G...... 347 771-0789
  Wilmington (G-9121)
Runway Liquidation LLC ....G...... 305 451-1481
  Wilmington (G-12494)

2337 Women's & Misses' Suits, Coats & Skirts
Fresh Accents LLC ....G...... 301 717-3757
  Bethany Beach (G-399)
Maalika K LLC ....G...... 844 622-5452
  Newark (G-6969)

2339 Women's & Misses' Outerwear, NEC
Body Double Swimwear ....G...... 302 537-1444
  Selbyville (G-8458)
Carpediem Health LLC ....G...... 347 467-4444
  Dover (G-1257)
City Theater Co Inc ....G...... 302 831-2206
  Newark (G-6244)
Fit ME By Crystal ....G...... 302 573-1235
  Newark (G-6589)
Lee Bell Inc ....G...... 302 477-3930
  Wilmington (G-11355)
True Religion Apparel Inc ....G...... 302 894-9425
  Newark (G-7597)

2341 Women's, Misses' & Children's Underwear & Nightwear
Perteh ....G...... 302 200-0912
  Wilmington (G-12092)
Victorias Scret Pink Main Line .....G...... 302 644-1035
  Rehoboth Beach (G-8106)

2353 Hats, Caps & Millinery
Express Electric Inc ....G...... 302 456-1919
  Newark (G-6553)
Vannies Hats ....G...... 302 765-7094
  New Castle (G-5813)

2361 Children's & Infants' Dresses & Blouses
Carters Inc ....G...... 302 731-1432
  Newark (G-6162)
TT Luxury Group LLC ....G...... 732 242-9795
  Newark (G-7599)

2369 Girls' & Infants' Outerwear, NEC
Lee Bell Inc ....G...... 302 477-3930
  Wilmington (G-11355)
True Religion Apparel Inc ....G...... 302 894-9425
  Newark (G-7597)

23 APPAREL AND OTHER FINISHED PRODUCTS MADE FROM FABRICS AND SIMILAR MATERIAL

2381 Dress & Work Gloves
Kaul Glove and Mfg Co .... D 302 292-2660
  New Castle (G-5454)
Masley Enterprises Inc .... E 302 427-9885
  Wilmington (G-11561)

2389 Apparel & Accessories, NEC
Advacare LLC .... G 302 448-5045
  Wilmington (G-8944)
Fantast Costumes Inc .... F 302 455-2006
  Dover (G-1540)
G2 Performance Band ACC .... G 800 554-8523
  Wilmington (G-10660)
John M Cooper Reverand .... G 302 684-8639
  Lewes (G-3573)
Mymoroccanbazar Inc .... G 323 238-5747
  Newark (G-7077)
Nagorka .... G 302 537-2392
  Bethany Beach (G-416)

2391 Curtains & Draperies
Barlows Upholstery Inc .... G 302 655-3955
  Wilmington (G-9255)
Butlers Sewing Center Inc .... G 302 629-9155
  Seaford (G-8178)
Calloways Custom Interiors Co .... G 302 994-7931
  Wilmington (G-9538)
Draperies Etc Inc .... F 302 422-7323
  Milford (G-4395)
Emerson & Klair .... G 302 239-6362
  Hockessin (G-3020)
G L K Inc .... G 302 697-3838
  Dover (G-1576)
Mp Axle Inc .... G 302 478-6442
  Wilmington (G-11765)
Royal Treatments .... G 302 722-6733
  Smyrna (G-8705)

2392 House furnishings: Textile
▲ Bethany Resort Furn Whse .... G 302 251-4101
  Selbyville (G-8456)
Bethrant Industries LLC .... G 484 343-5435
  New Castle (G-5088)
Calloways Custom Interiors Co .... G 302 994-7931
  Wilmington (G-9538)
G L K Inc .... G 302 697-3838
  Dover (G-1576)
Katherine Klyc Intl LLC .... G 917 312-0789
  New Castle (G-5452)

2393 Textile Bags
▲ Firsd Tea North America LLC ...... G 302 322-1255
  New Castle (G-5310)
Great Graphic Originals Ltd .... G 302 734-7600
  Dover (G-1608)
Lori Emory .... G 302 737-7352
  Newark (G-6949)
▲ Vanguard Manufacturing Inc .... G 302 994-9302
  Wilmington (G-13049)

2394 Canvas Prdts
B and C Awning .... G 302 629-4465
  Seaford (G-8159)
Callaway Furniture Inc .... G 302 398-8858
  Harrington (G-2823)
Cape Canvas .... G 302 684-8201
  Milton (G-4874)
E W Brown Inc .... G 302 652-6612
  Wilmington (G-10310)
Gainor Awnings Inc .... G 302 998-8611
  Wilmington (G-10663)
Tee Pees From Rattlesnks .... G 302 654-0709
  Wilmington (G-12875)

2395 Pleating & Stitching For The Trade
A Nod To Stella Embroidery .... G 302 697-6308
  Wyoming (G-13358)
A Stitch In Time .... G 302 395-1306
  New Castle (G-4994)
Actors Attic .... G 302 734-8214
  Dover (G-1084)
Alice M Mehaffey .... G 302 697-1893
  Dover (G-1104)
Andrew Pipon .... G 949 337-2249
  Milford (G-4307)
Array of Monograms .... G 302 998-2381
  Seaford (G-8154)

Championship Apparel Corp .... G 302 731-5917
  Newark (G-6186)
Delvina I Willson .... G 302 659-3672
  Smyrna (G-8623)
Dream Weavers Embroidery .... G 302 998-4264
  Wilmington (G-10233)
Embroid Me LLC .... G 302 993-0204
  Wilmington (G-10388)
Five Stars Embroidery .... G 443 466-9692
  Middletown (G-4074)
Flutterby Stitches & EMB .... G 302 531-7784
  Dover (G-1560)
Grassy Creek Quilting .... G 302 528-1653
  Claymont (G-758)
Hoopin It Up Embroidery .... G 302 945-5511
  Millsboro (G-4706)
In A Stitch .... G 302 678-2260
  Dover (G-1668)
Initially Yours Inc .... G 302 999-0562
  Wilmington (G-11035)
Just One Embroiderer .... G 302 832-9655
  Bear (G-206)
Kitschy Stitch .... G 302 200-9889
  Lewes (G-3582)
Lids Corporation .... G 302 736-8465
  Dover (G-1783)
Marksman Embroidery .... G 302 223-6740
  Smyrna (G-8679)
Patricia Hoffmann .... G 203 247-2635
  Bethany Beach (G-419)
Penny Cooper Sportswear & EMB ... G 302 325-3710
  New Castle (G-5615)
Pineapple Stitchery .... G 302 500-8050
  Georgetown (G-2619)
Rwm Embroidery & More LLC .... F 302 653-8384
  Smyrna (G-8709)
Sew There Embroidery .... G 302 545-0127
  Townsend (G-8821)
Shacraft .... G 302 995-6385
  Marshallton (G-3914)
Shields Brothers .... G 302 999-1094
  Wilmington (G-12601)
Stamford Screen Printing Inc .... G 302 654-2442
  Wilmington (G-12733)
T&T Custom Embroidery Inc .... G 302 420-9454
  Bear (G-344)
Whisman John .... G 302 530-1676
  Wilmington (G-13185)

2396 Automotive Trimmings, Apparel Findings, Related Prdts
Atlantic Sun Screen Prtg Inc .... F 302 731-5100
  Newark (G-6021)
Be Blessed Design Group LLC .... G 302 561-3793
  Bear (G-45)
Delaware Screen Printing Inc .... G 302 378-4231
  Middletown (G-4031)
Dream Graphics .... G 302 328-6264
  New Castle (G-5261)
Elwyn .... D 302 658-8860
  Wilmington (G-10385)
Health & Social Svcs Del Dept .... E 302 255-9800
  New Castle (G-5383)
Health & Social Svcs Del Dept .... E 302 255-9855
  New Castle (G-5385)
Jairus Enterprises Inc .... G 302 834-1625
  Bear (G-197)
Kathy Stabley .... G 302 322-7884
  New Castle (G-5453)
Lasting Impression Inc A .... G 302 762-9200
  Wilmington (G-11335)
Red Sun Custom Apparel Inc .... E 302 988-8230
  Selbyville (G-8538)
Stephen Cropper .... G 302 732-3730
  Frankford (G-2390)
Unique Image LLC .... E 302 658-2266
  Wilmington (G-13017)
Whisman John .... G 302 530-1676
  Wilmington (G-13185)

2399 Fabricated Textile Prdts, NEC
Ajs Crochets .... G 302 257-0381
  Dover (G-1100)
Crochet Creations By Debbie .... G 302 287-2462
  Wilmington (G-9901)
Fairway Manufacturing Company ... G 302 398-4630
  Harrington (G-2839)

24 LUMBER AND WOOD PRODUCTS, EXCEPT FURNITURE

2411 Logging
American Timber Brokerage .... G 302 655-8471
  Wilmington (G-9058)
Aslin Inc .... G 302 674-1900
  Dover (G-1145)
D&C Logging .... G 302 846-3982
  Delmar (G-990)
Delaware Valley Fence & Iron .... G 302 322-8193
  New Castle (G-5242)
High Vue Logging Inc .... G 302 697-3606
  Camden (G-579)
Summers Logging LLC .... G 302 234-8725
  Hockessin (G-3152)
Whitetail Country Log & Hlg .... G 302 846-3982
  Delmar (G-1048)

2421 Saw & Planing Mills
Byler Sawmill .... G 302 730-4208
  Dover (G-1244)
Frank Bartsch Saw Mill .... G 302 653-9721
  Townsend (G-8787)
Gordys Lumber Inc .... F 302 875-3502
  Laurel (G-3234)
Grubb Lumber Company Inc .... E 302 652-2800
  Wilmington (G-10791)
Reserves At Sawmill .... G 302 424-1910
  Milford (G-4539)
Rocla Concrete Tie Inc .... E 302 836-5304
  Bear (G-311)
Swartzentruber Sawmill Co .... G 302 492-1665
  Hartly (G-2942)
Woodchuck Enterprises Inc .... G 302 239-8336
  Hockessin (G-3175)

2426 Hardwood Dimension & Flooring Mills
Delmarva Hardwood Products .... F 302 349-4101
  Laurel (G-3222)
Gordys Lumber Inc .... F 302 875-3502
  Laurel (G-3234)
Grubb Lumber Company Inc .... E 302 652-2800
  Wilmington (G-10791)
Hardwood Direct LLC .... G 302 378-3692
  Middletown (G-4105)
Old Wood & Co LLC .... F 302 684-3600
  Harbeson (G-2794)
Warren Truss Co .... F 302 368-8566
  Newark (G-7676)

2431 Millwork
Aderyn Woodworks .... G 219 229-5070
  New Castle (G-5004)
Aldas Refinishing Company .... G 302 528-5028
  Hockessin (G-2955)
Atlantic Aluminum Products Inc ...... D 302 349-9091
  Greenwood (G-2713)
Bancroft Carpentry Company .... G 302 655-3434
  Wilmington (G-9233)
Boxwood Planing Mill Inc .... G 302 999-0249
  Wilmington (G-9402)
Brandywine Mill Work .... G 302 652-3008
  Wilmington (G-9442)
Craigs Woodworks LLC .... G 302 998-4201
  Wilmington (G-9892)
Daniel A Yoder .... G 302 730-4076
  Dover (G-1340)
Delaware Millwork .... G 302 376-8324
  Middletown (G-4029)
Doug Green Woodworking .... G 302 652-6522
  Wilmington (G-10211)
▲ Dover Millwork Inc .... F 302 349-5070
  Harrington (G-2835)
Espositos Woodworking & Cnstr .... G 302 245-5474
  Milton (G-4904)
Frankford Custom Woodworks Inc .. F 302 732-9570
  Frankford (G-2363)
Georges Custom Woodworking .... G 302 541-4599
  Dagsboro (G-903)
Group Three Inc .... G 302 658-4158
  Wilmington (G-10789)
Grubb Lumber Company Inc .... E 302 652-2800
  Wilmington (G-10791)
Johns Woodworking LLC .... G 302 492-3527
  Hartly (G-2929)
Kauffman Woodworks .... G 302 836-1976
  Bear (G-213)

SIC SECTION

25 FURNITURE AND FIXTURES

Koty Inc .... E 302 654-2665
  Wilmington *(G-11290)*
Lanning Woodworks .... G 302 353-4726
  Wilmington *(G-11330)*
Leroy A Coblentz .... G 302 343-7434
  Hartly *(G-2934)*
Lulla Woodworking .... G 302 841-8800
  Ocean View *(G-7801)*
Mary Costas Woodworking .... G 302 227-6255
  Rehoboth Beach *(G-8002)*
Mastermark Woodworking Inc .... G 302 945-9131
  Millsboro *(G-4737)*
Mennos Woodworks .... G 302 381-5525
  Greenwood *(G-2751)*
Monge Woodworking .... G 302 455-0175
  Newark *(G-7050)*
New Look Home Inc .... G 302 994-4397
  Wilmington *(G-11866)*
OBryan Woodworks .... G 302 398-8202
  Harrington *(G-2870)*
ONeill Woodworking LLC .... G 443 669-3458
  Lewes *(G-3669)*
Peirce James Townsend III .... G 302 449-2279
  Middletown *(G-4187)*
Pinnacle Garage Door Company .... G 302 505-4531
  Felton *(G-2310)*
Richard Hrrmann Strbilders Inc .... G 302 654-4329
  Wilmington *(G-12408)*
Taylor Woodworks .... G 302 697-0155
  Magnolia *(G-3910)*
Tj Custom Woodworks Inc .... G 302 563-8535
  Newark *(G-7569)*
Wolf Wood Works LLC .... G 302 275-7227
  Wilmington *(G-13286)*
Woodworks .... G 302 995-0800
  Wilmington *(G-13301)*
Wyoming Millwork Co .... G 302 684-3150
  Milton *(G-4983)*
Wyoming Millwork Co .... E 302 697-8650
  Camden *(G-607)*

2434 Wood Kitchen Cabinets

Bancroft Carpentry Company .... G 302 655-3434
  Wilmington *(G-9233)*
Bylers Woodworking Shop .... G 302 492-1375
  Hartly *(G-2913)*
Cedar Creek Custom Cabinets .... G 302 542-7794
  Milford *(G-4341)*
Coastal Cabinetry LLC .... G 302 542-4155
  Seaford *(G-8199)*
Culiquip LLC .... D 302 654-4974
  Wilmington *(G-9917)*
Custom Cabinet Shop Inc .... F 302 337-8241
  Greenwood *(G-2725)*
Diamond State Cabinetry .... G 302 250-3531
  Millsboro *(G-4678)*
Driftwood Cabinetry LLC .... G 302 645-4876
  Lewes *(G-3474)*
East Coast Cstm Cabinetry LLC .... G 302 245-3040
  Georgetown *(G-2517)*
Mh Custom Cabinets .... G 302 422-7082
  Milford *(G-4493)*
Michael A OBrien & Sons .... G 302 994-2894
  Wilmington *(G-11656)*
Moores Cabinet Refinishing Inc .... G 302 378-3055
  Middletown *(G-4170)*
Phippins Cabinetry .... G 302 212-2189
  Rehoboth Beach *(G-8032)*
Sylvester Custom Cabinetry .... G 302 398-6050
  Harrington *(G-2896)*
Taylor Woodworks .... G 302 745-2049
  Dover *(G-2131)*
Townsend Kitchens Cabinets & .... G 302 659-1007
  Townsend *(G-8828)*
Walnut Grove Cabinets LLC .... G 302 678-2694
  Dover *(G-2203)*
Zenith Products .... G 302 322-2190
  New Castle *(G-5846)*
◆ Zwd Products Corporation .... B 302 326-8200
  New Castle *(G-5848)*

2435 Hardwood Veneer & Plywood

Maneto Inc .... G 302 656-4285
  Wilmington *(G-11501)*

2439 Structural Wood Members, NEC

Delmarva Truss and Panel LLC .... G 302 270-8888
  Wyoming *(G-13362)*

Sam Yoder and Son LLC .... C 302 398-4711
  Greenwood *(G-2762)*
Universal Forest Products .... G 302 855-1250
  Georgetown *(G-2699)*
Warren Truss Co .... F 302 368-8566
  Newark *(G-7676)*
Warren Truss Co .... G 302 337-9470
  Bridgeville *(G-530)*

2441 Wood Boxes

Elwyn .... D 302 658-8860
  Wilmington *(G-10385)*

2448 Wood Pallets & Skids

Dans Pallets & Services .... G 302 836-4848
  Bear *(G-94)*
Greenwood Pallet Co .... G 302 337-8181
  Bridgeville *(G-476)*
Rcd Timber Products Inc .... G 302 778-5700
  New Castle *(G-5668)*

2449 Wood Containers, NEC

H&H Customs Inc .... G 302 378-0810
  Middletown *(G-4099)*

2451 Mobile Homes

Atlantic Realty Management .... G 302 629-0770
  Seaford *(G-8158)*
CMH Capital Inc .... G 302 651-7947
  Wilmington *(G-9749)*
Hippo Trailer .... G 302 854-6661
  Georgetown *(G-2558)*

2452 Prefabricated Wood Buildings & Cmpnts

Beracah Homes Inc .... E 302 349-4561
  Greenwood *(G-2716)*
Cool Branch Associates LLC .... G 302 629-5363
  Seaford *(G-8206)*
Fox Pointe .... G 302 744-9442
  Dover *(G-1564)*
Henlopen Homes Inc .... G 302 684-0860
  Lewes *(G-3541)*
Howard M Joseph Inc .... G 302 335-1300
  Milford *(G-4446)*

2491 Wood Preserving

Glory Contracting .... G 302 275-5430
  Townsend *(G-8789)*
Wood Expressions Incorporated .... G 302 738-6189
  Newark *(G-7717)*

2493 Reconstituted Wood Prdts

Jcr Systems LLC .... G 302 420-6072
  New Castle *(G-5439)*

2499 Wood Prdts, NEC

Artisan Woodworks LLC .... G 302 841-5182
  Harbeson *(G-2772)*
Bally Holding Company Delaware .... G 610 845-7511
  Wilmington *(G-9229)*
Butler Woodcrafters .... G 302 764-0744
  Wilmington *(G-9516)*
Carol Boyd Heron .... G 302 645-0551
  Lewes *(G-3407)*
Carspecken-Scott Inc .... G 302 762-7955
  Wilmington *(G-9581)*
Cedar Neck Decor LLC .... G 918 497-7179
  Dagsboro *(G-891)*
Charles Ogden .... G 305 606-4512
  Wilmington *(G-9634)*
Coastal Woodcraft .... G 302 856-7947
  Georgetown *(G-2475)*
Delaware Animal Products LLC .... G 302 423-7754
  Milford *(G-4374)*
Dick Palmer Woodworking .... G 302 227-8419
  Rehoboth Beach *(G-7916)*
Farlow-Taylor Construction .... G 302 436-9660
  Selbyville *(G-8490)*
Harvest Consumer Products LLC .... E 302 732-6624
  Dagsboro *(G-907)*
Hillandale Farms Delaware Inc .... E 302 492-3644
  Hartly *(G-2926)*
Kenco Trophy Sales .... G 302 846-3339
  Delmar *(G-1013)*
Nanticoke Industries LLC .... G 302 245-8825
  Seaford *(G-8324)*

Stockley Materials LLC .... G 302 856-7601
  Georgetown *(G-2666)*
◆ Vulcan International Corp .... F 302 428-3181
  Wilmington *(G-13107)*

25 FURNITURE AND FIXTURES

2511 Wood Household Furniture

Astral Plane Woodworks Inc .... G 302 654-8666
  Wilmington *(G-9166)*
Brandywine Valley Woodworking .... G 302 743-5640
  Wilmington *(G-9459)*
Butler Woodcrafters .... G 302 764-0744
  Wilmington *(G-9516)*
Group Three Inc .... G 302 658-4158
  Wilmington *(G-10789)*
Initial Trading Co .... G 302 428-1132
  Wilmington *(G-11034)*
Kenton Chair Shop .... F 302 653-2411
  Clayton *(G-859)*
Kirk Cabinetry LLC .... G 302 220-3377
  Wilmington *(G-11271)*
Mtb Artisans LLC .... G 303 475-9024
  Wilmington *(G-11772)*
Quilted Heirlooms .... G 302 354-6061
  Middletown *(G-4206)*
Slice of Wood LLC .... G 315 335-0917
  Delaware City *(G-967)*

2512 Wood Household Furniture, Upholstered

Barlows Upholstery Inc .... G 302 655-3955
  Wilmington *(G-9255)*
Charles Andrews .... G 302 378-7116
  Townsend *(G-8769)*

2514 Metal Household Furniture

Pony Run Kitchens LLC .... G 302 492-3006
  Hartly *(G-2937)*
Tri-State Fbrction McHning LLC .... E 302 232-3133
  New Castle *(G-5788)*
◆ Zwd Products Corporation .... B 302 326-8200
  New Castle *(G-5848)*

2515 Mattresses & Bedsprings

▲ Design Specific US Inc .... G 650 318-6473
  Wilmington *(G-10123)*
Panda Sleep Inc .... G 302 760-9754
  Dover *(G-1931)*
Plushbeds Inc .... G 888 758-7423
  Wilmington *(G-12162)*

2517 Wood T V, Radio, Phono & Sewing Cabinets

Jordan Cabinetry & WD Turning .... G 302 792-1009
  Claymont *(G-770)*

2519 Household Furniture, NEC

Michael Pdmnczky Cnsrvator LLC .... G 302 388-0656
  Wilmington *(G-11664)*

2521 Wood Office Furniture

Butler Woodcrafters .... G 302 764-0744
  Wilmington *(G-9516)*
▲ Corporate Interiors Inc .... D 302 322-1008
  New Castle *(G-5195)*
Heirloom Creations .... G 302 659-1817
  Smyrna *(G-8651)*
Registry Furniture Inc .... G 626 297-9508
  Wilmington *(G-12365)*

2522 Office Furniture, Except Wood

Business Slip LLC .... G 302 563-3660
  Wilmington *(G-9512)*
Hirsh Industries Inc .... C 302 678-3456
  Dover *(G-1649)*

2531 Public Building & Related Furniture

Acorn Site Furnishings .... G 302 249-4979
  Bridgeville *(G-443)*
Butler Woodcrafters .... G 302 764-0744
  Wilmington *(G-9516)*
Clarios .... G 302 996-0309
  Wilmington *(G-9730)*
First State Manufacturing Inc .... D 302 424-4520
  Milford *(G-4414)*

25 FURNITURE AND FIXTURES

Johnson Controls Inc .... G 302 715-5208
  Delmar *(G-1009)*
Turning Point Collection LLC .... G 302 416-0092
  Wilmington *(G-12993)*

2541 Wood, Office & Store Fixtures

3-D Fabrications Inc .... E 302 292-3501
  Newark *(G-5855)*
Cabinetry Unlimited LLC .... E 302 436-5030
  Selbyville *(G-8465)*
Counterparts LLC .... G 302 349-0400
  Greenwood *(G-2723)*
Michael A OBrien & Sons .... G 302 994-2894
  Wilmington *(G-11656)*
Solid Image Inc .... G 302 877-0901
  Laurel *(G-3291)*

2542 Partitions & Fixtures, Except Wood

▲ J and J Display .... G 302 628-4190
  Seaford *(G-8275)*
Stone Medic .... G 302 233-6039
  Smyrna *(G-8726)*

2591 Drapery Hardware, Window Blinds & Shades

Blind Factory .... G 302 838-1211
  Wilmington *(G-9369)*
Local Vertical .... G 302 242-2552
  Dover *(G-1794)*
Vertical Blind Factory Inc .... F 302 998-9616
  Wilmington *(G-13067)*

2599 Furniture & Fixtures, NEC

Cubic Products LLC .... E 781 990-3886
  Wilmington *(G-9916)*
Tarpon Strategies LLC .... G 215 806-2723
  Newark *(G-7540)*

26 PAPER AND ALLIED PRODUCTS

2611 Pulp Mills

Eco Plastic Products Del Inc .... G 302 575-9227
  Wilmington *(G-10339)*
Penco Corporation .... G 302 629-7911
  Seaford *(G-8345)*
Revolution Recovery Del LLC .... F 302 356-3000
  New Castle *(G-5676)*

2621 Paper Mills

Action Unlimited Resources Inc .... E 302 323-1455
  New Castle *(G-5001)*
Advanced Thermal Packaging .... G 302 326-2222
  New Castle *(G-5010)*
Deadcow Computers .... G 302 239-5974
  Newark *(G-6355)*
Henninger Printing Co Inc .... G 302 934-8119
  Millsboro *(G-4705)*
Norkol Converting Corporation .... E 302 283-1080
  Newark *(G-7136)*

2653 Corrugated & Solid Fiber Boxes

True-Pack Ltd .... E 302 326-2222
  New Castle *(G-5798)*

2671 Paper Coating & Laminating for Packaging

Mercantile Press Inc .... F 302 764-6884
  Wilmington *(G-11636)*
Printpack Inc .... C 302 323-4000
  New Castle *(G-5645)*
Zacros America Inc .... C 302 368-7354
  Newark *(G-7737)*

2672 Paper Coating & Laminating, Exc for Packaging

Mercantile Press Inc .... F 302 764-6884
  Wilmington *(G-11636)*

2673 Bags: Plastics, Laminated & Coated

Castle Bag Company .... G 302 656-1001
  Wilmington *(G-9589)*
▲ Grayling Industries Inc .... E 770 751-9095
  Frederica *(G-2403)*
Jeb Plastics Inc .... G 302 479-9223
  Wilmington *(G-11139)*

Printpack Inc .... C 302 323-4000
  New Castle *(G-5645)*
▲ Printpack Enterprises Inc .... G 302 323-0900
  New Castle *(G-5646)*
Richard Earl Fisher .... C 302 598-1957
  Wilmington *(G-12407)*
Toyo Fibre USA Inc .... G 302 475-3699
  Wilmington *(G-12945)*

2674 Bags: Uncoated Paper & Multiwall

◆ AB Group Packaging Inc .... G 302 607-3281
  Newark *(G-5879)*
Idylc Homes LLC .... G 302 295-3719
  Wilmington *(G-10995)*

2675 Die-Cut Paper & Board

Cann-Erikson Bindery Inc .... F 302 995-6636
  Wilmington *(G-9550)*

2676 Sanitary Paper Prdts

BETz&betz Enterprises LLC .... G 302 602-0613
  Wilmington *(G-9318)*
Docs Medical LLC .... G 301 401-1489
  Bear *(G-122)*
Edgewell Personal Care LLC .... B 302 678-6000
  Dover *(G-1506)*
Edgewell Personal Care Company ..... A 302 678-6191
  Dover *(G-1507)*
Playtex Manufacturing Inc .... D 302 678-6000
  Dover *(G-1969)*
Playtex Products LLC .... F 302 678-6000
  Dover *(G-1971)*
Procter & Gamble Paper Pdts Co .... B 302 678-2600
  Dover *(G-1989)*
Socal Auto Supply Inc .... D 818 717-9982
  Lewes *(G-3751)*

2677 Envelopes

Owens Corningfibreboard .... G 302 654-4250
  Wilmington *(G-11987)*

2679 Converted Paper Prdts, NEC

K&B Investors LLC .... G 302 357-9723
  Wilmington *(G-11216)*

27 PRINTING, PUBLISHING, AND ALLIED INDUSTRIES

2711 Newspapers: Publishing & Printing

Cape Gazette Ltd .... E 302 645-7700
  Lewes *(G-3401)*
Coastal Point .... F 302 539-1788
  Ocean View *(G-7779)*
Communicate U Media LLC .... G 610 453-6501
  Middletown *(G-4001)*
Community Publications Inc .... F 302 239-4644
  Middletown *(G-4002)*
County Women S Journal .... G 302 236-1435
  Lewes *(G-3446)*
Delaware Grapevine LLC .... G 302 731-8400
  Newark *(G-6381)*
Delawareblack Com LLC .... G 302 388-1444
  Newark *(G-6423)*
Dover Post Co Inc .... D 302 653-2083
  Dover *(G-1466)*
Dover Post Co Inc .... G 302 378-9531
  Middletown *(G-4044)*
Dover Post Inc .... G 304 222-6025
  Milford *(G-4393)*
Fifty Plus Monthly .... G 302 645-2938
  Milton *(G-4905)*
First State Press LLC .... G 302 731-9058
  Newark *(G-6585)*
Gannett Co Inc .... D 302 325-6600
  New Castle *(G-5343)*
Gatehouse Media Inc .... D 302 678-3616
  Dover *(G-1583)*
Gatehuse Mdia Del Holdings Inc .... G 302 678-3616
  Dover *(G-1584)*
Get Real On Line Classifieds .... G 302 234-6522
  Hockessin *(G-3038)*
Hearst Media Services Conn LLC ...... E 203 330-6231
  Wilmington *(G-10875)*
High Tide News .... G 302 727-0390
  Selbyville *(G-8501)*
Hola Delaware LLC .... G 302 832-3620
  Newark *(G-6735)*

Hoy En Delaware LLC .... G 302 854-0240
  Georgetown *(G-2562)*
I N I Holdings Inc .... G 302 674-3600
  Dover *(G-1665)*
Independent Newsmedia Inc USA ...... G 302 422-1200
  Milford *(G-4449)*
▲ Independent Newsmedia USA Inc .. D 302 674-3600
  Dover *(G-1672)*
Independent Newsmedia USA Inc ...... C 302 674-3600
  Dover *(G-1673)*
Info Titan LLC .... G 510 495-4117
  Dover *(G-1676)*
K2 Advanced Media LLC .... G 408 305-7007
  Wilmington *(G-11218)*
L E York Law LLC .... G 302 234-8338
  Wilmington *(G-11309)*
Morning Report Research Inc .... G 302 730-3793
  Dover *(G-1872)*
Morning Star Publications Inc .... F 302 629-9788
  Seaford *(G-8311)*
New Castle Weekly Inc .... G 302 328-6005
  New Castle *(G-5567)*
News-Journal Company .... E 302 324-2500
  New Castle *(G-5569)*
▲ Peter Shin .... G 302 498-0977
  Wilmington *(G-12098)*
Review .... E 302 831-2771
  Newark *(G-7330)*
Smyrna News & Tobacco .... G 302 653-9620
  Smyrna *(G-8720)*
Spark .... G 302 324-2203
  New Castle *(G-5728)*
Sussex Countian .... G 302 856-0026
  Dover *(G-2120)*
Sussex Post .... G 302 629-5505
  Milford *(G-4574)*
Wave Newspaper .... F 302 537-1881
  Bethany Beach *(G-437)*
Wilmington Trust Sp Services .... A 302 427-7650
  Wilmington *(G-13264)*

2721 Periodicals: Publishing & Printing

AB Creative Publishing LLC .... G 202 802-6909
  Wilmington *(G-8896)*
Action Enterprise Inc .... E 302 537-7223
  Fenwick Island *(G-2328)*
Advance Magazine Publs Inc .... D 302 830-4630
  Wilmington *(G-8946)*
Burris & Baxter Communications ...... G 302 454-8511
  Newark *(G-6138)*
Business History Conference .... G 302 658-2400
  Wilmington *(G-9510)*
CIO Story LLC .... G 408 915-5559
  Wilmington *(G-9710)*
Conde Nast International Inc .... E 515 243-3273
  Wilmington *(G-9815)*
Crafts Report Publishing Co .... F 302 656-2209
  Wilmington *(G-9891)*
Decoy Magazine .... G 302 644-9001
  Lewes *(G-3450)*
Delaware Italian-American .... G 302 545-6406
  Wilmington *(G-10060)*
Envision It Publications LLC .... G 800 329-9411
  Bear *(G-144)*
Henlopen Design LLC .... G 302 265-4330
  Lewes *(G-3540)*
Hudson Valley Investment Corp .... G 302 656-1825
  Wilmington *(G-10971)*
Hypebeast Inc .... E 714 791-0755
  Dover *(G-1663)*
Living Well Magazine .... G 302 355-0929
  Newark *(G-6943)*
Martinelli Holdings LLC .... E 302 656-1809
  Wilmington *(G-11551)*
Simply Styling-Schl of Csmtlgy .... G 302 778-1885
  Wilmington *(G-12628)*
▲ Student Media Group .... F 302 607-2580
  Newark *(G-7496)*
Suburban Publishing Inc .... G 302 656-1809
  Wilmington *(G-12788)*
T S N Publishing Co Inc .... G 302 655-6483
  Wilmington *(G-12845)*
Todays Latino Magazine .... G 302 981-5131
  Middletown *(G-4260)*
U Transit Inc .... G 302 227-1197
  Rehoboth Beach *(G-8102)*
Wutopia Group US Ltd .... F 302 488-0248
  Dover *(G-2241)*

SIC SECTION 27 PRINTING, PUBLISHING, AND ALLIED INDUSTRIES

2731 Books: Publishing & Printing

A Chance To Write It LLC ....G....... 202 256-4524
Lewes *(G-3318)*
Birdsong Books ....G....... 302 378-7274
Middletown *(G-3968)*
▲ Cedar Lane Inc ....F....... 302 328-7232
New Castle *(G-5139)*
Cosmic Strands LLC ....G....... 302 660-3268
Wilmington *(G-9871)*
Dragon Cloud Inc ....A....... 702 508-2676
Wilmington *(G-10230)*
Heartfelt Books Publishing ....G....... 866 557-6522
Wilmington *(G-10877)*
Kardmaster Graphics ....E....... 610 434-5262
Wilmington *(G-11225)*
▲ Kevin Fleming ....G....... 302 227-4994
Rehoboth Beach *(G-7980)*
Linguatext Ltd ....G....... 302 453-8695
Newark *(G-6936)*
Liveware Inc ....F....... 302 791-9446
Claymont *(G-775)*
Medical Society of Delaware ....E....... 302 366-1400
Newark *(G-7018)*
Meta Galaxic Publishing Inc ....G....... 302 245-7939
Wilmington *(G-11647)*
Miller Publishing Inc ....G....... 302 576-6579
Wilmington *(G-11695)*
Moghul Life Inc ....G....... 347 560-9124
Wilmington *(G-11724)*
Pond Publishing & Productions ....G....... 302 284-0200
Felton *(G-2313)*
Readhowyouwant LLC ....G....... 302 730-4560
Dover *(G-2014)*
Royal Era LLC ....G....... 484 574-0260
Newark *(G-7369)*
Talents Publishing LLC ....G....... 302 353-4574
Newark *(G-7534)*
Thi (us) Inc ....G....... 302 792-1444
Claymont *(G-811)*
When Poets Dream Inc ....G....... 818 738-6954
Dover *(G-2222)*
Wiley-Liss Inc ....G....... 302 429-8627
Wilmington *(G-13202)*

2732 Book Printing, Not Publishing

Aafton Research & Media Inc ....G....... 617 407-6619
Dover *(G-1076)*
Moghul Life Inc ....G....... 347 560-9124
Wilmington *(G-11724)*
Pmb Associates LLC ....G....... 302 436-0111
Selbyville *(G-8531)*
Print Shack Inc ....G....... 302 629-4430
Seaford *(G-8364)*

2741 Misc Publishing

1300 Publishing Company LLC ....G....... 302 268-2684
Wilmington *(G-8845)*
321 Down Street Press Inc ....G....... 302 376-3965
Middletown *(G-3924)*
Aag La LLC ....G....... 305 801-7900
Dover *(G-1077)*
Additive Mfg Tech Inc ....G....... 540 577-9260
Wilmington *(G-8935)*
▲ Associates International Inc ....D....... 302 656-4500
Wilmington *(G-9157)*
Beech Hill Press ....G....... 302 588-0315
Newark *(G-6067)*
Birthdayboxio Inc ....G....... 302 990-2616
Wilmington *(G-9341)*
Bottle of Smoke Press ....G....... 302 399-1856
Dover *(G-1223)*
Buchspot LLC ....G....... 302 715-1253
Lewes *(G-3393)*
Byzantium Sky Press ....G....... 302 258-6116
Milton *(G-4872)*
Cameck Publishing ....G....... 302 598-4799
Wilmington *(G-9544)*
Capital Gaines LLC ....G....... 302 433-6777
Wilmington *(G-9557)*
Cherryrich Publishing ....G....... 302 533-6354
Newark *(G-6192)*
Chesapeake Seaglass Jewelry ....G....... 410 778-4999
Selbyville *(G-8468)*
Chip Vickio ....G....... 302 448-0211
Millsboro *(G-4660)*
Cnwynn Publications ....G....... 484 753-1568
Dover *(G-1299)*
Coastal Images Inc ....G....... 302 539-6001
Fenwick Island *(G-2333)*
Cruz Publishing Group ....G....... 302 287-2938
Dover *(G-1328)*
Crystal Diamond Publishing ....G....... 302 737-2130
Newark *(G-6319)*
Delaware Guitar School ....G....... 302 697-2341
Wyoming *(G-13360)*
Devils Party Press ....G....... 310 904-3660
Milton *(G-4893)*
Distillate Media LLC ....G....... 302 270-7945
Dover *(G-1431)*
Edit Inc ....G....... 302 478-7069
Wilmington *(G-10351)*
Emw Publications ....G....... 302 438-9879
Hockessin *(G-3022)*
Finding A Voice Inc ....G....... 315 333-7567
Lewes *(G-3495)*
Fruitbearer Publishing LLC ....G....... 302 856-6649
Georgetown *(G-2535)*
Glimpse Global Inc ....G....... 305 216-7667
Dover *(G-1593)*
Govbizconnect Inc ....G....... 860 341-1925
Dover *(G-1603)*
Green Pages Technologies Inc ....G....... 626 497-6363
Newark *(G-6686)*
Grow USA Press ....G....... 302 725-5195
Milford *(G-4424)*
Harman Hay Publications Inc ....G....... 302 669-9144
Bear *(G-177)*
Harmoniously Pbc ....G....... 302 291-1106
Wilmington *(G-10839)*
Hill Publishing Inc ....G....... 917 826-3722
Newark *(G-6728)*
Hindin Media LLC ....G....... 302 463-4612
Wilmington *(G-10915)*
Hither Creek Press ....G....... 603 387-3444
Milford *(G-4442)*
Hobo News Press Inc ....G....... 302 235-1066
Newark *(G-6732)*
Hotelrunner Inc ....E....... 302 956-9616
Newark *(G-6749)*
Impress ....G....... 302 645-8411
Lewes *(G-3554)*
Independent School MGT Inc ....E....... 302 656-4944
Wilmington *(G-11018)*
Intouch Inc ....G....... 302 313-2594
Dover *(G-1683)*
Joseph M Press Mr ....G....... 302 378-2053
Middletown *(G-4117)*
Kardmaster Graphics ....E....... 610 434-5262
Wilmington *(G-11225)*
Kitty Jazzy Publishing ....G....... 302 897-8842
Newark *(G-6896)*
L & B Publishing ....G....... 302 743-4061
Newark *(G-6905)*
Litcharts LLC ....G....... 646 481-4807
Wilmington *(G-11400)*
Lsf Networks LLC ....G....... 213 537-2402
Wilmington *(G-11447)*
Lumhaa LLC ....G....... 916 517-9972
Wilmington *(G-11450)*
Market Keys LLC ....G....... 205 800-0285
Wilmington *(G-11535)*
Melody Entertainment USA Inc ....G....... 305 505-7659
Wilmington *(G-11627)*
MJM Publishing ....G....... 302 943-3590
Felton *(G-2307)*
New Castle Cnty Shoppers Guide ....E....... 302 325-6600
New Castle *(G-5554)*
Pagetech ....G....... 845 624-4911
Lewes *(G-3676)*
Pat Press ....G....... 302 836-2955
Bear *(G-279)*
Percebe Music Inc ....G....... 850 341-9594
Dover *(G-1949)*
Pixorize Inc ....G....... 737 529-4404
Wilmington *(G-12145)*
Pixstorm LLC ....G....... 617 365-4949
Dover *(G-1961)*
PMC Publications LLC ....G....... 302 268-4480
Newark *(G-7224)*
Postimpressions Incorporated ....G....... 302 656-2271
Wilmington *(G-12194)*
Powers Publishing Group ....G....... 302 519-8575
Millsboro *(G-4786)*
Prestwick House Inc ....E....... 302 659-2070
Smyrna *(G-8692)*
Psychoanalytic Electronic ....G....... 949 495-3332
Wilmington *(G-12261)*
Publication Print ....G....... 302 992-2040
Wilmington *(G-12266)*
Qoro LLC ....G....... 302 322-5900
New Castle *(G-5656)*
Red Ghost Interactive LLC ....G....... 385 485-9100
Middletown *(G-4213)*
Reed Elsevier Capital Inc ....F....... 302 427-9299
Wilmington *(G-12350)*
Responsible Publishing ....G....... 609 412-9621
Wilmington *(G-12388)*
Review ....E....... 302 831-2771
Newark *(G-7330)*
Rhino Smart Publications ....G....... 302 737-3422
Newark *(G-7336)*
Rlk Press Inc ....G....... 267 565-5138
Wilmington *(G-12432)*
Robotick New Media Network LLC ....G....... 213 219-3083
Dover *(G-2039)*
Russell D Earnest & Assoc ....G....... 302 659-0730
Clayton *(G-870)*
Russell D Earnest Assoc ....G....... 302 659-0730
Hartly *(G-2941)*
Ryan Media Lab Inc ....G....... 302 360-8847
Lewes *(G-3727)*
Si360 Inc ....F....... 800 849-6058
Newark *(G-7420)*
Sociomatry Press ....G....... 302 313-5341
Lewes *(G-3753)*
Socraticlaw Co Inc ....G....... 302 654-9191
Wilmington *(G-12669)*
Sourcing Time LLC ....G....... 302 409-0890
Wilmington *(G-12685)*
Speedy Publishing LLC ....G....... 888 248-4521
Newark *(G-7470)*
Spotlight Publications LLC ....G....... 302 504-1329
Wilmington *(G-12711)*
Sujo Music Publishing ....G....... 302 731-8575
Newark *(G-7500)*
Sussex Printing Corp ....D....... 302 629-9303
Seaford *(G-8416)*
Syncretic Press ....G....... 443 723-8355
Wilmington *(G-12834)*
T S N Publishing Co Inc ....G....... 302 655-6483
Wilmington *(G-12845)*
Verizon Delaware LLC ....C....... 302 571-1571
Wilmington *(G-13062)*
Wallflowers Press ....G....... 302 454-1411
Newark *(G-7675)*
Web Advantage Inc ....F....... 302 479-7634
Wilmington *(G-13133)*
Webcasting Media LLC ....G....... 302 261-5178
Lewes *(G-3817)*
Wherebyus Enterprises Inc ....G....... 305 988-0808
Claymont *(G-819)*
Willow Winters Publishing LLC ....G....... 570 885-2513
Middletown *(G-4287)*
Wilson Publications LLC ....G....... 215 237-2344
Bear *(G-378)*
Wna Infotech LLC ....E....... 302 668-5977
Bear *(G-379)*
Workaway Ventures Inc ....G....... 843 608-9108
Wilmington *(G-13303)*
X Leader LLC ....G....... 800 345-2677
Lewes *(G-3831)*
Yellow Light Publishing LLC ....G....... 302 242-0990
Greenwood *(G-2770)*
Yesllama LLC ....G....... 714 270-8731
Dover *(G-2244)*

2752 Commercial Printing: Lithographic

A+ Printing ....G....... 302 273-3147
Wilmington *(G-8888)*
Academy Business Mch & Prtg Co ....G....... 302 654-3200
Wilmington *(G-8912)*
AlphaGraphics Franchising Inc ....G....... 302 559-8369
Wilmington *(G-9030)*
◆ Amer Inc ....G....... 302 654-2498
Wilmington *(G-9039)*
Ancar Enterprises LLC ....G....... 302 477-1884
Wilmington *(G-9075)*
Ancar Enterprises LLC ....F....... 302 453-2600
Newark *(G-5966)*
Armor Graphics Inc ....G....... 302 737-8790
Newark *(G-5996)*
▲ Associates International Inc ....D....... 302 656-4500
Wilmington *(G-9157)*
Axial Medical Printing Inc ....G....... 518 620-4479
Claymont *(G-697)*
Ben-Dom Printing Company ....F....... 302 737-9144
Newark *(G-6072)*
Bgdedge Inc ....G....... 302 477-1734
Wilmington *(G-9325)*

S I C

Employee Codes: A=Over 500 employees, B=251-500
C=101-250, D=51-100, E=20-50, F=10-19, G=1-9
2020 Harris Directory of
Delaware Businesses
473

27 PRINTING, PUBLISHING, AND ALLIED INDUSTRIES SIC SECTION

Bgi Print Solutions..........G....... 302 234-2825
Newark *(G-6077)*
Bgi Print Solutions..........G....... 302 234-2825
Newark *(G-6078)*
Bills Printers Service..........G....... 302 798-0482
Claymont *(G-702)*
Brandywine Graphics Inc..........G....... 302 655-7571
Wilmington *(G-9435)*
Chapis Drafting & Blue Print..........G....... 302 629-6373
Seaford *(G-8190)*
◆ **Chick Harness & Supply Inc**..........E....... 302 398-4630
Harrington *(G-2824)*
Coastal Printing Company..........G....... 302 537-1700
Ocean View *(G-7780)*
Coko Prints..........G....... 302 507-1683
Wilmington *(G-9765)*
Communications Printing Inc..........G....... 302 229-9369
Newark *(G-6270)*
Conventioneer Pubg Co Inc..........G....... 301 487-3907
Georgetown *(G-2483)*
Copy Craft Inc..........E....... 302 633-1313
Wilmington *(G-9856)*
D & B Printing and Mailing Inc..........G....... 302 838-7111
Newark *(G-6339)*
DC Printing Inc..........G....... 302 545-6666
Wilmington *(G-9977)*
Delaware Screen Printing Inc..........G....... 302 378-4231
Middletown *(G-4031)*
Delaware State Printing..........G....... 302 228-9431
Dover *(G-1397)*
Delta Forms Inc..........F....... 302 652-3266
Wilmington *(G-10106)*
Depro-Serical USA Inc..........G....... 302 368-8040
Townsend *(G-8783)*
DMD Business Forms & Prtg Co..........G....... 302 998-8200
Wilmington *(G-10177)*
Dover Litho Printing Co..........F....... 302 698-5292
Dover *(G-1457)*
Dover Post Co Inc..........D....... 302 653-2083
Dover *(G-1466)*
Dover Post Co Inc..........D....... 302 678-3616
Dover *(G-1467)*
Duck Creek Printing LLC..........G....... 302 653-5121
Smyrna *(G-8627)*
Edythe L Pridgen..........G....... 302 652-8887
Bear *(G-141)*
Factors Etc Inc..........D....... 302 834-1625
Bear *(G-148)*
Fannon Color Printing LLC..........G....... 302 227-2164
Rehoboth Beach *(G-7931)*
Fedex Office & Print Svcs Inc..........G....... 302 996-0264
Wilmington *(G-10519)*
Fishtail Print Company..........G....... 302 408-4800
Rehoboth Beach *(G-7934)*
Fishtail Print Company..........G....... 302 682-3053
Rehoboth Beach *(G-7935)*
Gannett Co Inc..........D....... 302 325-6600
New Castle *(G-5343)*
Garile Inc..........E....... 302 366-0848
Newark *(G-6639)*
Grm Pro Imaging LLC..........G....... 302 999-8162
Wilmington *(G-10788)*
Health & Social Svcs Del Dept..........E....... 302 255-9800
New Castle *(G-5383)*
Health & Social Svcs Del Dept..........E....... 302 255-9855
New Castle *(G-5385)*
Horizon Aeronautics Inc..........G....... 409 504-2645
Wilmington *(G-10952)*
I N I Holdings Inc..........G....... 302 674-3600
Dover *(G-1665)*
▲ **Independent Newsmedia USA Inc**....D....... 302 674-3600
Dover *(G-1672)*
Jerry O Thompson Prntng..........G....... 302 832-1309
Bear *(G-200)*
Job Printing..........G....... 302 907-0416
Delmar *(G-1008)*
Kardmaster Graphics..........E....... 610 434-5262
Wilmington *(G-11225)*
Lights Out Screen Printing Co..........G....... 302 409-0560
Wilmington *(G-11386)*
Lord Printing LLC..........G....... 302 439-3253
Wilmington *(G-11435)*
Luke Destefano Inc..........G....... 302 455-0710
Newark *(G-6955)*
Mail Rooms Ltd..........G....... 302 629-4838
Seaford *(G-8300)*
Markizon Printing..........G....... 610 715-7989
Wilmington *(G-11539)*
Marthann Print Center LLC..........G....... 267 884-8130
Dover *(G-1822)*
McClafferty Printing Company..........E....... 302 652-8112
Wilmington *(G-11587)*
Mercantile Press Inc..........F....... 302 764-6884
Wilmington *(G-11636)*
Mgl Screen Printing..........G....... 302 450-6250
Clayton *(G-864)*
Morales Screen Printing..........G....... 302 465-8179
Dover *(G-1871)*
New Image Inc..........G....... 302 738-6824
Newark *(G-7106)*
Newphoenix Screen Printing..........G....... 302 747-8991
Dover *(G-1897)*
News Print Shop..........G....... 302 337-8283
Bridgeville *(G-502)*
Nexsigns LLC..........G....... 302 508-2615
Clayton *(G-866)*
OConnell Speedy Printing Inc..........G....... 302 656-1475
Wilmington *(G-11935)*
One Hour Printing..........G....... 302 220-1684
Newark *(G-7150)*
Penney Enterprises Inc..........G....... 302 629-4430
Seaford *(G-8350)*
◆ **Prince Manufacturing Co**..........F....... 646 747-4208
New Castle *(G-5641)*
Print Coast 2 Coast..........G....... 302 381-4610
Lewes *(G-3697)*
Print On This..........G....... 302 235-9475
Newark *(G-7254)*
Print-N-Press Inc..........G....... 302 994-6665
Wilmington *(G-12229)*
Printcurement..........G....... 302 249-6100
New Castle *(G-5644)*
▲ **Printed Solid Inc**..........F....... 302 439-0098
Newark *(G-7255)*
Printit Solutions..........G....... 302 380-3838
Dover *(G-1987)*
Prints and Princesses..........G....... 703 881-1057
Newark *(G-7256)*
Pulsar Print LLC..........G....... 302 394-9202
New Castle *(G-5653)*
Rcd Printing..........G....... 302 424-8467
Milford *(G-4533)*
Rescue Printig..........G....... 302 286-7266
Newark *(G-7323)*
Rockford Map Gallery LLC..........G....... 302 740-1851
Wilmington *(G-12450)*
Rogers Graphics Inc..........F....... 302 856-0028
Georgetown *(G-2641)*
Rogers Graphics Inc..........G....... 302 422-6694
Harbeson *(G-2797)*
Skinify LLC..........F....... 302 212-5689
Rehoboth Beach *(G-8079)*
Smart International Inc..........G....... 302 451-9517
Newark *(G-7445)*
Southern Printing..........G....... 302 832-3475
New Castle *(G-5725)*
Sprint Quality Printing Inc..........G....... 302 478-0720
Wilmington *(G-12716)*
Stanley Golden..........G....... 302 652-5626
Wilmington *(G-12736)*
Star Art Inc..........G....... 302 261-6732
Bear *(G-337)*
Stephen Cropper..........G....... 302 732-3730
Frankford *(G-2390)*
Stratis Visuals LLC..........G....... 860 482-1208
Newark *(G-7495)*
Sussex Printing Corp..........D....... 302 629-9303
Seaford *(G-8416)*
Thoroughthreads..........G....... 302 356-0502
Wilmington *(G-12905)*
UNI Printing Solutionsllc..........G....... 631 438-6045
New Castle *(G-5802)*
Union Press Printing Inc..........G....... 302 652-0496
Wilmington *(G-13013)*
W B Mason Co Inc..........C....... 888 926-2766
Newark *(G-7667)*
William N Cann Inc..........E....... 302 995-0820
Wilmington *(G-13215)*
Zeal Print Co LLC..........G....... 302 407-5745
Wilmington *(G-13342)*

2754 Commercial Printing: Gravure

Ancar Enterprises LLC..........G....... 302 477-1884
Wilmington *(G-9075)*
Blue Heron Ent Inc..........G....... 302 834-1521
Bear *(G-54)*
Promotion Zone LLC..........G....... 302 832-8565
Newark *(G-7269)*
Scientific Games Corporation..........F....... 302 737-4300
Newark *(G-7395)*
Stephen Cropper..........G....... 302 732-3730
Frankford *(G-2390)*

2759 Commercial Printing

Abba Monument Co Inc..........G....... 302 738-0272
Newark *(G-5880)*
Advanced Office Systems & Sups..........G....... 302 629-7505
Seaford *(G-8140)*
AIA..........G....... 302 407-2252
New Castle *(G-5018)*
◆ **Amer Inc**..........G....... 302 654-2498
Wilmington *(G-9039)*
B-Line Printing..........G....... 302 628-1311
Seaford *(G-8160)*
Benjamin Tanei..........G....... 302 521-2033
Townsend *(G-8764)*
Best Office Pros..........G....... 302 629-4561
Seaford *(G-8167)*
Brodie Invitations..........G....... 302 999-7889
Wilmington *(G-9483)*
Compass Graphics..........G....... 302 378-1977
Middletown *(G-4003)*
Corlo Services Inc..........G....... 302 737-3207
Newark *(G-6299)*
Cosmic Custom Screen Printing..........G....... 302 933-0920
Millsboro *(G-4668)*
Creative Promotions..........G....... 302 697-7896
Camden *(G-553)*
D & D Screen Printing..........G....... 302 349-4231
Greenwood *(G-2727)*
Delaware Screen Printing Inc..........G....... 302 378-4231
Middletown *(G-4031)*
Design Craft..........G....... 302 834-3720
Delaware City *(G-956)*
Diamond State Graphics Inc..........F....... 302 325-1100
New Castle *(G-5252)*
Dragons Lair Printing LLC..........G....... 302 798-4465
Claymont *(G-735)*
Encore Designs Inc..........G....... 302 798-5678
Wilmington *(G-10395)*
Factors Etc Inc..........D....... 302 834-1625
Bear *(G-148)*
Fbk Graphico Inc..........G....... 302 743-4784
Wilmington *(G-10509)*
Fedex Office & Print Svcs Inc..........G....... 302 996-0264
Wilmington *(G-10519)*
First Class Cards LLC..........G....... 302 653-0111
Clayton *(G-850)*
Go Tees LLC..........G....... 708 703-1788
Middletown *(G-4090)*
Jeb Plastics Inc..........G....... 302 479-9223
Wilmington *(G-11139)*
Lasting Impression Inc A..........G....... 302 762-9200
Wilmington *(G-11335)*
Logo Motive Inc..........G....... 302 645-2959
Rehoboth Beach *(G-7989)*
Max One Printing..........G....... 302 897-9050
Bear *(G-249)*
Meade Inc..........G....... 302 262-3394
Seaford *(G-8306)*
▲ **Middletown Ink LLC**..........G....... 302 725-0705
Middletown *(G-4157)*
Midnight Blue Inc..........F....... 302 436-9665
Selbyville *(G-8522)*
New Image Inc..........G....... 302 738-6824
Newark *(G-7106)*
Patio Printing Co Inc..........G....... 302 328-6881
New Castle *(G-5608)*
Promotion Zone LLC..........G....... 302 832-8565
Newark *(G-7269)*
Remline Corp..........E....... 302 737-7228
Newark *(G-7316)*
Richard J Wadsley..........G....... 302 545-7162
Middletown *(G-4220)*
Ronan Gill LLC..........F....... 877 549-7712
Wilmington *(G-12471)*
Sportz Tees..........G....... 302 280-6076
Laurel *(G-3294)*
Stamford Screen Printing Inc..........G....... 302 654-2442
Wilmington *(G-12733)*
Stanley Golden..........G....... 302 652-5626
Wilmington *(G-12736)*
Sunshine Graphics and Printing..........G....... 302 724-5127
Dover *(G-2115)*
Superior Graphic & Printing..........G....... 302 290-3475
Wilmington *(G-12808)*
Sussex Printing Corp..........D....... 302 629-9303
Seaford *(G-8416)*
◆ **Ten Talents Enterprises Inc**..........G....... 302 409-0718
Middletown *(G-4255)*

SIC SECTION

28 CHEMICALS AND ALLIED PRODUCTS

To A Tee Printing ....G....... 302 525-6336
  Newark *(G-7571)*
Unique Image LLC ....E....... 302 658-2266
  Wilmington *(G-13017)*
Unique Tracking LLC ....G....... 912 220-3522
  Wilmington *(G-13019)*
Village Graphics LLC ....G....... 302 697-9288
  Dover *(G-2193)*
Zzhouse Inc ....G....... 302 354-3474
  New Castle *(G-5849)*

2761 Manifold Business Forms

Brandywine Graphics Inc ....G....... 302 655-7571
  Wilmington *(G-9435)*
Go Mozaic LLC ....G....... 302 438-4141
  Claymont *(G-756)*
Safeguard ....G....... 301 299-8806
  Rehoboth Beach *(G-8065)*

2771 Greeting Card Publishing

Sussex Printing Corp ....D....... 302 629-9303
  Seaford *(G-8416)*

2782 Blankbooks & Looseleaf Binders

Cann-Erikson Bindery Inc ....F....... 302 995-6636
  Wilmington *(G-9550)*
Deja Vu Record Album Cover Art ....G....... 302 227-8909
  Rehoboth Beach *(G-7910)*
L E Stansell Inc ....G....... 302 475-1534
  Wilmington *(G-11308)*

2789 Bookbinding

◆ Amer Inc ....G....... 302 654-2498
  Wilmington *(G-9039)*
Ben-Dom Printing Company ....F....... 302 737-9144
  Newark *(G-6072)*
Dover Post Co Inc ....D....... 302 678-3616
  Dover *(G-1467)*
▼ Dupont Txtles Intriors Del Inc ....G....... 302 774-1000
  Wilmington *(G-10265)*
Fox Specialties Inc ....F....... 302 322-5200
  New Castle *(G-5326)*
Garile Inc ....E....... 302 366-0848
  Newark *(G-6639)*
L E Stansell Inc ....G....... 302 475-1534
  Wilmington *(G-11308)*
William N Cann Inc ....E....... 302 995-0820
  Wilmington *(G-13215)*

2791 Typesetting

◆ Amer Inc ....G....... 302 654-2498
  Wilmington *(G-9039)*
▲ Associates International Inc ....D....... 302 656-4500
  Wilmington *(G-9157)*
Ben-Dom Printing Company ....F....... 302 737-9144
  Newark *(G-6072)*
Dover Post Co Inc ....D....... 302 678-3616
  Dover *(G-1467)*
Garile Inc ....E....... 302 366-0848
  Newark *(G-6639)*
Stanley Golden ....G....... 302 652-5626
  Wilmington *(G-12736)*
Sussex Printing Corp ....D....... 302 629-9303
  Seaford *(G-8416)*
William N Cann Inc ....E....... 302 995-0820
  Wilmington *(G-13215)*

2796 Platemaking & Related Svcs

Union Press Printing Inc ....G....... 302 652-0496
  Wilmington *(G-13013)*

28 CHEMICALS AND ALLIED PRODUCTS

2812 Alkalies & Chlorine

Kuehne Chemical Company Inc ....E....... 302 834-4557
  New Castle *(G-5470)*

2813 Industrial Gases

AAL Drtc ....G....... 302 229-5891
  Newark *(G-5875)*
Air Liquide America LP ....G....... 302 225-2132
  Wilmington *(G-8992)*
Air Lqide Advanced Separations ....G....... 302 225-1100
  Newport *(G-7745)*

Air Lqide Advanced Tech US LLC ....G....... 302 225-1100
  Newark *(G-5925)*
Air Lqide Advanced Tech US LLC ....E....... 302 225-1100
  Wilmington *(G-8993)*
Airgas Usa LLC ....E....... 302 834-7404
  Delaware City *(G-946)*
E I Du Pont De Nemours & Co ....G....... 302 366-5763
  Newark *(G-6491)*
Helium3 Tech and Services LLC ....G....... 302 766-2856
  Newark *(G-6721)*
Keen Compressed Gas Co ....E....... 302 594-4545
  New Castle *(G-5456)*
Messer LLC ....E....... 302 798-9342
  Claymont *(G-781)*
Occidental Chemical Corp ....G....... 302 834-3800
  New Castle *(G-5585)*
Pure Air Holdings Corp ....G....... 302 655-7130
  Wilmington *(G-12270)*

2816 Inorganic Pigments

◆ Chemours Company Fc LLC ....B....... 302 773-1000
  Wilmington *(G-9649)*

2819 Indl Inorganic Chemicals, NEC

Affinity Research Chemicals ....G....... 302 525-4060
  Wilmington *(G-8970)*
▲ Amspec Chemical Corporation ....G....... 302 392-1702
  Bear *(G-28)*
Brandywine Chemical Company ....G....... 302 656-5428
  New Castle *(G-5104)*
Celanese International Corp ....G....... 972 443-4000
  Wilmington *(G-9609)*
Chemours Company Fc LLC ....E....... 302 545-0072
  Wilmington *(G-9653)*
Ddh Advanced Mtls Systems Inc ....G....... 515 441-1313
  Newark *(G-6353)*
Debbie Gill ....G....... 302 547-5182
  Middletown *(G-4023)*
Delaware Chemical Corporation ....G....... 302 234-1463
  Wilmington *(G-10014)*
Divine Element Hbb ....G....... 302 538-5209
  Dover *(G-1433)*
Dow Chemical Company ....C....... 302 366-0500
  Newark *(G-6468)*
▼ Du Pont Chem Enrgy Oprtons Inc ..G....... 302 774-1000
  Wilmington *(G-10241)*
Dupont Athntcation Systems LLC ......G....... 800 345-9999
  Wilmington *(G-10249)*
Dupont Specialty Pdts USA LLC ....E....... 302 774-1000
  Wilmington *(G-10261)*
E I Du Pont De Nemours & Co ....E....... 302 999-3301
  Wilmington *(G-10279)*
E I Du Pont De Nemours & Co ....G....... 302 774-1000
  Wilmington *(G-10280)*
E I Du Pont De Nemours & Co ....B....... 302 892-8832
  Wilmington *(G-10281)*
E I Du Pont De Nemours & Co ....D....... 615 847-6920
  Wilmington *(G-10285)*
E I Du Pont De Nemours & Co ....D....... 302 792-4371
  Wilmington *(G-10292)*
E I Du Pont De Nemours & Co ....G....... 302 774-1000
  Wilmington *(G-10295)*
E I Du Pont De Nemours & Co ....G....... 302 774-1000
  Wilmington *(G-10298)*
E I Du Pont De Nemours & Co ....E....... 302 774-1000
  Wilmington *(G-10299)*
E I Du Pont De Nemours & Co ....F....... 302 999-4329
  Wilmington *(G-10300)*
E I Du Pont De Nemours & Co ....D....... 302 695-3742
  Wilmington *(G-10302)*
Element ....G....... 302 645-0777
  Lewes *(G-3480)*
Honeywell International Inc ....D....... 302 791-6700
  Claymont *(G-763)*
Indo Amines Americas LLC ....G....... 301 466-9902
  Wilmington *(G-11019)*
John J Buckley Associates Inc ....G....... 302 475-5443
  Wilmington *(G-11172)*
Kuehne Chemical Company Inc ....E....... 302 834-4557
  New Castle *(G-5470)*
Rohm Haas Electronic Mtls LLC ....D....... 302 366-0500
  Newark *(G-7358)*
Rohm Haas Electronic Mtls LLC ....G....... 302 366-0500
  Newark *(G-7359)*
Solvay Spclty Polymers USA LLC ......G....... 302 452-6609
  Wilmington *(G-7457)*
Timtec Inc ....F....... 302 292-8500
  Newark *(G-7566)*
W L Gore & Associates Inc ....C....... 302 368-3700
  Newark *(G-7672)*

W R Grace & Co ....C....... 410 531-4000
  Wilmington *(G-13109)*

2821 Plastics, Mtrls & Nonvulcanizable Elastomers

Aearo Technologies LLC ....D....... 302 283-5497
  Newark *(G-5913)*
Ashland LLC ....E....... 302 594-5000
  Wilmington *(G-9151)*
◆ Bilcare Research Inc ....D....... 302 838-3200
  Delaware City *(G-949)*
Celanese International Corp ....G....... 972 443-4000
  Wilmington *(G-9609)*
Delmarva Plastics Co ....G....... 302 398-1000
  Harrington *(G-2832)*
Division-Developmental Dsblts ....G....... 302 836-2110
  Bear *(G-121)*
Dow Chemical Company ....G....... 302 366-0500
  Newark *(G-6468)*
Dupont De Nemours Inc ....B....... 302 774-1000
  Wilmington *(G-10251)*
◆ Dupont Prfmce Elastomers LLC .....B....... 302 774-1000
  Wilmington *(G-10259)*
Dupont Specialty Pdts USA LLC ....E....... 302 774-1000
  Newark *(G-6479)*
E I Du Pont De Nemours & Co ....G....... 302 654-8198
  Wilmington *(G-10297)*
E I Du Pont De Nemours & Co ....G....... 302 999-2826
  Wilmington *(G-10283)*
◆ E I Du Pont De Nemours & Co ....A....... 302 485-3000
  Wilmington *(G-10278)*
E I Du Pont De Nemours & Co ....G....... 800 441-7515
  Wilmington *(G-10290)*
E I Du Pont De Nemours & Co ....B....... 302 892-5655
  Wilmington *(G-10301)*
Formosa Plastics Corp Delaware ....C....... 302 836-2200
  Delaware City *(G-958)*
Himont Inc ....G....... 302 996-6000
  Wilmington *(G-10914)*
▲ Ineos Chlor Americas Inc ....G....... 302 529-9601
  Wilmington *(G-11024)*
▲ Intech Services Inc ....G....... 302 366-8530
  Newark *(G-6788)*
▲ Invista Capital Management LLC ...G....... 302 683-3000
  Wilmington *(G-11075)*
Invista Capital Management LLC ....E....... 877 446-8478
  Wilmington *(G-11076)*
Invista Capital Management LLC ....A....... 302 731-6882
  Newark *(G-6801)*
Invista SARL ....G....... 302 683-3001
  Wilmington *(G-11077)*
Kuraray America Inc ....F....... 302 992-4204
  Wilmington *(G-11301)*
▲ Oci Melamine Americas Inc ....G....... 800 615-8284
  Wilmington *(G-11934)*
▲ Polymer Technologies Inc ....D....... 302 738-9001
  Newark *(G-7231)*
Precision Polyolefins LLC ....G....... 301 588-3709
  Wilmington *(G-12206)*
T P Composites Inc ....G....... 610 358-9001
  New Castle *(G-5749)*
Techmer Engnered Solutions LLC .....D....... 610 548-5032
  New Castle *(G-5759)*
W L Gore & Associates Inc ....C....... 302 368-3700
  Newark *(G-7672)*

2822 Synthetic Rubber (Vulcanizable Elastomers)

▲ Arlon LLC ....C....... 302 834-2100
  Bear *(G-34)*
Cowie Technology Corp ....G....... 856 692-2828
  New Castle *(G-5206)*
Dupont Specialty Pdts USA LLC ....C....... 302 451-0717
  Newark *(G-6480)*
Empower Materials Inc ....F....... 302 225-0100
  New Castle *(G-5290)*
Rogers Corporation ....C....... 302 834-2100
  Bear *(G-312)*

2823 Cellulosic Man-Made Fibers

FMC Corporation ....D....... 302 451-0100
  Newark *(G-6596)*

2824 Synthetic Organic Fibers, Exc Cellulosic

▲ Chesapeake Perl Inc ....F....... 302 533-3540
  Newark *(G-6193)*

28 CHEMICALS AND ALLIED PRODUCTS

◆ Durafiber Tech DFT Entps Inc .... D 704 912-3770
    Wilmington *(G-10268)*
◆ E I Du Pont De Nemours & Co .... A 302 485-3000
    Wilmington *(G-10278)*
E I Du Pont De Nemours & Co .... G 800 441-7515
    Wilmington *(G-10290)*
E I Du Pont De Nemours & Co .... B 302 892-5655
    Wilmington *(G-10301)*
Specialty Products N&H Inc .... G 302 774-1000
    Wilmington *(G-12697)*

2833 Medicinal Chemicals & Botanical Prdts

◆ Glaxosmithkline Holdings .... C 302 984-6932
    Wilmington *(G-10720)*
Jmsp USA LLC .... G 337 254-1451
    Camden Wyoming *(G-647)*
Personal Health PDT Dev LLC .... E 888 901-6150
    Wilmington *(G-12091)*
Phoenix Intl Resources LLC .... G 954 309-0120
    Lewes *(G-3689)*
Wilmington .... G 302 357-4509
    (G-13221)

2834 Pharmaceuticals

A2a Intgrted Phrmceuticals LLC .... G 270 202-2461
    Lewes *(G-3320)*
A66 Inc .... G 800 444-0446
    Wilmington *(G-8892)*
▲ Adesis Inc .... E 302 323-4880
    New Castle *(G-5005)*
Aeolus Pharmaceuticals Inc .... G 949 481-9825
    Wilmington *(G-8964)*
Alyvant Therapeutics Inc .... G 646 767-5878
    Wilmington *(G-9037)*
Angita Pharmard LLC .... G 302 234-6794
    Hockessin *(G-2958)*
▲ Astrazeneca LP .... A 302 886-3000
    Wilmington *(G-9168)*
Astrazeneca Pharmaceuticals LP .... A 302 286-3500
    Newark *(G-6013)*
Auragin LLC .... G 800 383-5109
    Wilmington *(G-9183)*
Ayala Pharmaceuticals Inc .... F 857 444-0553
    Wilmington *(G-9202)*
Bristol-Myers Squibb Company .... E 800 321-1335
    Wilmington *(G-9479)*
Champions + Legends Corp .... G 702 605-2522
    Wilmington *(G-9627)*
Colgate-Palmolive Company .... B 302 428-1554
    Wilmington *(G-9768)*
Cpex Pharmaceuticals Inc .... F 302 651-8300
    Wilmington *(G-9887)*
Delaware Dermatologic .... G 302 593-8625
    Wilmington *(G-10038)*
DRG Holdco Inc .... G 610 974-9760
    Wilmington *(G-10234)*
▲ Drnaturalhealing Inc .... G 302 265-2213
    Milford *(G-4396)*
Dupont Nutrition and Health .... G 302 451-0112
    Newark *(G-6478)*
E I Du Pont De Nemours & Co .... B 302 892-5655
    Wilmington *(G-10301)*
◆ E I Du Pont De Nemours & Co .... A 302 485-3000
    Wilmington *(G-10278)*
E I Du Pont De Nemours & Co .... G 800 441-7515
    Wilmington *(G-10290)*
Fisons US Investment Holdings .... G 302 777-7222
    Wilmington *(G-10564)*
FMC Corporation .... D 302 451-0100
    Newark *(G-6596)*
Fulcrum Pharmacy MGT Inc .... G 302 658-8020
    Wilmington *(G-10645)*
Genesis Laboratories Inc .... G 832 217-8585
    Wilmington *(G-10693)*
Glaxosmithkline Capital Inc .... G 302 656-5280
    Wilmington *(G-10719)*
◆ Glaxosmithkline Holdings .... C 302 984-6932
    Wilmington *(G-10720)*
Glycomira LLC .... G 704 651-9789
    Dover *(G-1595)*
Grant Pharmaceuticals Inc .... G 855 364-7268
    Newark *(G-6681)*
Ilgen Inc .... G 518 369-0069
    Wilmington *(G-11004)*
Incyte Corporation .... C 302 498-6700
    Wilmington *(G-11016)*
Leiluna LLC .... F 888 201-6444
    Wilmington *(G-11366)*

Lip Balm Land LLC .... G 302 319-9919
    Wilmington *(G-11399)*
◆ LRC North America Inc .... E 302 427-2845
    Wilmington *(G-11446)*
Marlex Pharmaceuticals Inc .... E 302 328-3355
    New Castle *(G-5508)*
Medimmune LLC .... G 301 398-1200
    Wilmington *(G-11620)*
Merck & Co Inc .... E 410 860-2227
    Millsboro *(G-4742)*
▲ Merck and Company Inc .... E 302 934-8051
    Millsboro *(G-4743)*
Merck Holdings LLC .... G 302 234-1401
    Wilmington *(G-11637)*
Modulation Therapeutics Inc .... G 813 784-0033
    Wilmington *(G-11723)*
Natural Stacks Inc .... G 855 678-2257
    Lewes *(G-3656)*
Neuracon Biotech Inc .... G 813 966-3129
    Wilmington *(G-11843)*
Neurolixis Inc .... G 215 910-2261
    Wilmington *(G-11845)*
New Life Medicals LLC .... G 302 478-7973
    Wilmington *(G-11865)*
New Nordic US Inc .... G 514 390-2316
    Wilmington *(G-11867)*
Noramco Inc .... G 302 761-2923
    Wilmington *(G-11895)*
Novaeo LLC .... E 832 643-2153
    Wilmington *(G-11910)*
Novartis Corporation .... B 302 992-5610
    Wilmington *(G-11912)*
Novo Nordisk Pharma Inc .... G 302 691-6181
    Wilmington *(G-11914)*
Novo Nrdisk US Coml Hldngs Inc .... G 302 691-6181
    Wilmington *(G-11915)*
Pharma E Market LLC .... F 302 737-3711
    Hockessin *(G-3119)*
Pharmunion LLC .... G 415 307-5128
    Wilmington *(G-12108)*
Platinum US Distribution Inc .... G 905 364-8713
    Wilmington *(G-12153)*
Shire North American Group Inc .... G 484 595-8800
    Wilmington *(G-12606)*
▲ Snow Pharmaceuticals LLC .... G 302 436-8855
    Frankford *(G-2388)*
Therapy Architects .... G 610 246-5705
    Wilmington *(G-12894)*
▲ Urigen Pharmaceuticals Inc .... G 732 640-0160
    Wilmington *(G-13038)*
Veramorph LLC .... G 401 473-1318
    Wilmington *(G-13058)*
Workroom Enterprises LLC .... G 417 621-5577
    Wilmington *(G-13304)*
▲ Zeneca Holdings Inc .... E 302 886-3000
    Wilmington *(G-13344)*
Zeneca Inc .... G 302 886-3000
    Wilmington *(G-13345)*

2835 Diagnostic Substances

Carolyn A Drkowski Ht Ascp LLC .... G 443 831-4854
    Lewes *(G-3408)*
E I Du Pont De Nemours & Co .... D 302 695-5300
    Wilmington *(G-10306)*
Easy Diagnostics .... G 302 674-4089
    Dover *(G-1501)*
Siemens Healthcare Diagnostics .... D 302 631-8006
    New Castle *(G-5710)*
Siemens Hlthcare Dgnostics Inc .... D 302 631-7357
    Newark *(G-7425)*

2836 Biological Prdts, Exc Diagnostic Substances

Analytical Biological Svcs Inc .... E 302 654-4492
    Wilmington *(G-9073)*
Artevet LLC .... E 443 255-0016
    Wilmington *(G-9137)*
Cleamol LLC .... G 513 885-3462
    Wilmington *(G-9736)*
Genalyze LLC .... G 732 917-4893
    Middletown *(G-4085)*
◆ Glaxosmithkline Holdings .... C 302 984-6932
    Wilmington *(G-10720)*
◆ Intervet Inc .... B 302 934-4341
    Millsboro *(G-4710)*
Irving IA Extract Diet Pills .... G 302 218-0472
    Wilmington *(G-11084)*
One EDM LLC .... E 908 399-0536
    Wilmington *(G-11954)*

Plume Serum LLC .... G 302 697-9044
    Magnolia *(G-3904)*
Reflection Biotechnologies Inc .... G 212 765-2200
    Wilmington *(G-12352)*

2841 Soap & Detergents

Capriottis of Milford .... G 302 424-3309
    Milford *(G-4340)*
Suds Bar Soap & Essentials LLC .... G 302 674-1303
    Dover *(G-2111)*

2842 Spec Cleaning, Polishing & Sanitation Preparations

Beauty Max Inc .... G 302 735-1705
    Dover *(G-1186)*
Chem Tech Inc .... G 302 798-9675
    Wilmington *(G-9644)*
Diligent Detail .... G 302 482-2836
    Wilmington *(G-10154)*
Dow Chemical Company .... B 302 368-4169
    Newark *(G-6467)*
Gearhalo Us Inc .... G 780 239-2120
    Dover *(G-1586)*
▼ Halosil International Inc .... G 302 543-8095
    New Castle *(G-5373)*
Jeffs Mobile Power Washing .... G 302 753-4726
    Clayton *(G-858)*
Playtex Manufacturing Inc .... D 302 678-6000
    Dover *(G-1969)*
Quip Laboratories Incorporated .... E 302 761-2600
    Wilmington *(G-12291)*
Sanosil International LLC .... F 302 454-8102
    New Castle *(G-5694)*

2843 Surface Active & Finishing Agents, Sulfonated Oils

James Thompson & Company Inc .... E 302 349-4501
    Greenwood *(G-2748)*
Richard Earl Fisher .... G 302 598-1957
    Wilmington *(G-12407)*

2844 Perfumes, Cosmetics & Toilet Preparations

Brandywine Botanicals LLC .... G 302 354-4650
    Wilmington *(G-9419)*
Cdo USA Inc .... G 347 429-5110
    Wilmington *(G-9605)*
Cosmetic Innovators LLC .... G 310 310-9784
    Wilmington *(G-9870)*
◆ Glaxosmithkline Holdings .... C 302 984-6932
    Wilmington *(G-10720)*
Goodales Naturals .... G 302 743-6455
    Newark *(G-6674)*
Laboratoires Esthederm USA Inc .... G 514 270-3763
    Wilmington *(G-11314)*
Majalco LLC .... G 703 507-5298
    Wilmington *(G-11494)*
My Lip Stuff .... G 302 945-5922
    Lewes *(G-3653)*
N Daisy Jax Inc .... E 302 387-3543
    Dover *(G-1880)*
Playtex Manufacturing Inc .... D 302 678-6000
    Dover *(G-1969)*
Prayon Inc .... G 302 449-0875
    Middletown *(G-4196)*
Remarle .... G 215 245-6448
    Middletown *(G-4216)*
Richard Earl Fisher .... G 302 598-1957
    Wilmington *(G-12407)*
Succulents Soap Sand Scents .... G 302 757-0697
    Newark *(G-7499)*
◆ Sun Pharmaceuticals Corp .... F 302 678-6000
    Dover *(G-2113)*

2851 Paints, Varnishes, Lacquers, Enamels

Coatings With A Purpose Inc .... G 302 462-1465
    Georgetown *(G-2476)*
Modified Thermoset Resins Inc .... G 302 235-3710
    Wilmington *(G-11722)*
Steves Painting Plus .... G 302 684-8938
    Lincoln *(G-3871)*
T B Painting Restoration .... G 610 283-4100
    Newark *(G-7527)*

28 CHEMICALS AND ALLIED PRODUCTS

2865 Cyclic-Crudes, Intermediates, Dyes & Org Pigments

BASF Corporation .... C 302 992-5600
  Wilmington *(G-9258)*
◆ Chemfirst Inc .... D 302 774-1000
  Wilmington *(G-9646)*
E I Du Pont De Nemours & Co .... B 302 999-2826
  Wilmington *(G-10283)*
◆ E I Du Pont De Nemours & Co .... A 302 485-3000
  Wilmington *(G-10278)*
E I Du Pont De Nemours & Co .... G 800 441-7515
  Wilmington *(G-10290)*
E I Du Pont De Nemours & Co .... B 302 892-5655
  Wilmington *(G-10301)*
Honeywell International Inc .... D 302 791-6700
  Claymont *(G-763)*
Orient Corporation of America .... E 302 628-1300
  Seaford *(G-8339)*

2869 Industrial Organic Chemicals, NEC

Advanced Bio-Energy Tech Inc .... G 347 363-9927
  Dover *(G-1088)*
Ashland Spcalty Ingredients GP .... D 302 995-3000
  Wilmington *(G-9152)*
Basell Capital Corporation .... G 302 683-8000
  Wilmington *(G-9257)*
BASF Corporation .... C 302 992-5600
  Wilmington *(G-9258)*
Breakthru Beverage Group LLC .... G 302 356-3500
  New Castle *(G-5109)*
Butamax Advanced Biofuels LLC .... F 302 695-6787
  Wilmington *(G-9514)*
Celanese International Corp .... G 972 443-4000
  Wilmington *(G-9609)*
Cfg Lab Inc .... G 302 261-3403
  Wilmington *(G-9621)*
Dupont Nutrition Usa Inc .... G 302 774-1000
  Wilmington *(G-10257)*
Dupont Tate Lyle Bio Pdts LLC .... G 865 408-1962
  Wilmington *(G-10264)*
Elcriton Inc .... G 864 921-5146
  New Castle *(G-5280)*
Enerkem Miss Biofuels LLC .... G 514 875-0284
  Wilmington *(G-10401)*
Ensyn GA Biorefinery I LLC .... G 303 425-3740
  Wilmington *(G-10404)*
▲ Grayling Industries Inc .... E 770 751-9095
  Frederica *(G-2403)*
Gushen America Inc .... G 630 853-3135
  Dover *(G-1616)*
Hercules International Ltd LLC .... G 302 594-5000
  Wilmington *(G-10889)*
◆ Hercules LLC .... C 302 594-5000
  Wilmington *(G-10890)*
Honeywell International Inc .... D 302 791-6700
  Claymont *(G-763)*
Invista Capital Management LLC .... E 302 629-1100
  Seaford *(G-8272)*
Judy Tim Fuel Inc .... G 302 349-5895
  Greenwood *(G-2749)*
Lynch Heights Fuel Corp .... G 302 422-9195
  Milford *(G-4481)*
Memorial Super Fuel .... G 215 512-1012
  New Castle *(G-5515)*
Nova Pangaea Technologies Inc .... G 612 743-6266
  Dover *(G-1903)*
Plaza Fuel .... G 302 275-6242
  Wilmington *(G-12157)*
Riverside Specialty Chem Inc .... G 212 769-3440
  Bear *(G-307)*
Rohm Haas Electronic Mtls LLC .... G 302 366-0500
  Newark *(G-7358)*
Sas Nanotechnologies LLC .... G 214 235-1008
  Newark *(G-7391)*
Simar Fuel Inc .... G 302 304-1969
  Smyrna *(G-8716)*
▼ Sorbent Green LLC .... G 800 259-3577
  Wilmington *(G-12682)*
SPI Holding Company .... B 800 789-9755
  Wilmington *(G-12703)*
Stereochemical Inc .... G 302 266-0700
  Newark *(G-7490)*
Syntec Corporation .... F 302 421-8393
  Wilmington *(G-12837)*
Urbn Steamlab LLC .... G 267 738-3096
  Lewes *(G-3803)*
Veramorph LLC .... G 401 473-1318
  Wilmington *(G-13058)*

Vital Renewable Energy Company .... G 202 595-2944
  Wilmington *(G-13095)*

2873 Nitrogenous Fertilizers

◆ Growmark Fs LLC .... D 302 422-3002
  Milford *(G-4425)*
Poultry Litter Solutions LLC .... G 302 245-5577
  Millsboro *(G-4784)*
Southern States Coop Inc .... F 302 378-9841
  Middletown *(G-4246)*

2874 Phosphatic Fertilizers

Growmark Fs LLC .... G 302 422-3001
  Milford *(G-4426)*
◆ Growmark Fs LLC .... D 302 422-3002
  Milford *(G-4425)*
Southern States Coop Inc .... F 302 378-9841
  Middletown *(G-4246)*

2875 Fertilizers, Mixing Only

▲ Emerald Bioagriculture Corp .... F 517 882-7370
  Hockessin *(G-3019)*
◆ Growmark Fs LLC .... D 302 422-3002
  Milford *(G-4425)*
Harvest Consumer Products LLC .... E 302 732-6624
  Dagsboro *(G-907)*
Nutrien AG Solutions Inc .... G 302 629-2780
  Seaford *(G-8333)*
Peninsula Compost Company LLC .... G 215 595-4218
  New Castle *(G-5612)*
Southern States Coop Inc .... F 302 732-6651
  Dagsboro *(G-934)*
Southern States Coop Inc .... G 302 875-3635
  Laurel *(G-3293)*
Southern States Coop Inc .... F 302 378-9841
  Middletown *(G-4246)*

2879 Pesticides & Agricultural Chemicals, NEC

A Felix Dupont Jr Co .... G 302 658-5244
  Wilmington *(G-8877)*
Ai Dupont .... G 302 528-6520
  Wilmington *(G-8983)*
▲ Belchim Crop Prtection USA LLC ..... F 302 407-3590
  Wilmington *(G-9285)*
▲ Chemours Company .... B 302 773-1000
  Wilmington *(G-9648)*
◆ Chemours Company Fc LLC .... B 302 773-1000
  Wilmington *(G-9649)*
Chemours Company Fc LLC .... C 678 427-1530
  Wilmington *(G-9651)*
Corteva Inc .... E 302 485-3000
  Wilmington *(G-9869)*
▼ Dupont Asia Pacific Limited .... G 302 774-1000
  Wilmington *(G-10248)*
Dupont De Nemours Inc .... G 302 999-7932
  Wilmington *(G-10252)*
Dupont De Nemours Ei & Co .... G 302 659-1079
  Dover *(G-1487)*
E C I Motorsports Inc .... G 302 239-6376
  Newark *(G-6487)*
◆ E I Du Pont De Nemours & Co .... A 302 485-3000
  Wilmington *(G-10278)*
E I Du Pont De Nemours & Co .... B 302 695-7141
  Bear *(G-132)*
E I Du Pont De Nemours & Co .... G 302 239-9424
  Newark *(G-6488)*
E I Du Pont De Nemours & Co .... B 302 999-2826
  Wilmington *(G-10283)*
E I Du Pont De Nemours & Co .... G 302 695-7228
  Wilmington *(G-10286)*
E I Du Pont De Nemours & Co .... G 844 773-2436
  Wilmington *(G-10289)*
E I Du Pont De Nemours & Co .... G 800 441-7515
  Wilmington *(G-10290)*
E I Du Pont De Nemours & Co .... B 302 892-5655
  Wilmington *(G-10301)*
E I Du Pont De Nemours & Co .... G 302 774-1000
  Wilmington *(G-10305)*
E I Du Pont De Nemours & Co .... C 302 658-7796
  Wilmington *(G-10307)*
Els .... G 302 312-3645
  Bear *(G-143)*
HB Dupont Plaza .... G 302 998-7271
  Wilmington *(G-10858)*
Mark Wilson Diguardi .... G 302 897-6625
  Millsboro *(G-4735)*

Meherrin AG & Chem Co .... G 302 337-0330
  Bridgeville *(G-496)*
North Dupont Shell .... G 301 375-6000
  New Castle *(G-5578)*
◆ Sharda USA LLC .... G 610 350-6930
  Hockessin *(G-3145)*
Specialty Products N&H Inc .... G 302 774-1000
  Wilmington *(G-12697)*
▼ Syngenta Corporation .... E 302 425-2000
  Wilmington *(G-12836)*

2891 Adhesives & Sealants

Delchem Inc .... F 302 426-1800
  Wilmington *(G-10099)*
◆ Hercules LLC .... C 302 594-5000
  Wilmington *(G-10890)*
▼ Max Seal Inc .... F 619 946-2650
  Lewes *(G-3625)*

2892 Explosives

▲ Emulsion Products Company .... E 302 629-3505
  Seaford *(G-8236)*

2893 Printing Ink

C & A Ink .... G 302 565-9866
  Newark *(G-6140)*
Digital Ink Sciences LLC .... G 951 757-0027
  Wilmington *(G-10152)*
Do It Wiser LLC .... G 800 816-0944
  Wilmington *(G-10179)*

2899 Chemical Preparations, NEC

Aquacast Liner LLC .... D 302 535-3728
  Newark *(G-5993)*
Blue Sky Clean .... G 302 584-5800
  Wilmington *(G-9381)*
Carbocycle Co .... G 212 214-4068
  Wilmington *(G-9564)*
Chemours Co Fc LLC .... G 302 353-5003
  Wilmington *(G-9647)*
Chemours Company Fc LLC .... G 302 540-5423
  Wilmington *(G-9652)*
Croda Inc .... F 302 429-5249
  New Castle *(G-5208)*
Croda Inc .... F 302 429-5200
  New Castle *(G-5209)*
Diversified Chemical Pdts Inc .... G 302 656-5293
  Wilmington *(G-10169)*
E I Du Pont De Nemours & Co .... F 843 335-5934
  Wilmington *(G-10287)*
Economic Laundry Solutions .... E 302 234-7627
  Hockessin *(G-3017)*
Franklin Jester PA .... G 302 368-3080
  Newark *(G-6612)*
Frontier Scientific Inc .... G 302 266-6891
  Newark *(G-6626)*
Frontier Scientific Svcs Inc .... G 302 266-6891
  Newark *(G-6627)*
Honeywell International Inc .... D 302 791-6700
  Claymont *(G-763)*
Hrd Products Inc .... G 302 757-3587
  Newark *(G-6754)*
Jcr Systems LLC .... G 302 420-6072
  New Castle *(G-5439)*
Koch Methanol Investments LLC .... G 302 658-7581
  Wilmington *(G-11287)*
Lehvoss North Amer Holdg Inc .... G 302 734-1450
  Dover *(G-1780)*
Nalco Company LLC .... E 856 423-6417
  New Castle *(G-5543)*
Nova Consultants Ltd .... F 302 328-1686
  New Castle *(G-5581)*
Orient Corporation of America .... E 302 628-1300
  Seaford *(G-8339)*
▲ Polydel Corporation .... F 302 655-8200
  Wilmington *(G-12184)*
Solenis Holdings 3 LLC .... G 866 337-1533
  Wilmington *(G-12675)*
Solenis International LLC .... G 302 994-1698
  Wilmington *(G-12676)*
▼ Solenis LLC .... B 866 337-1533
  Wilmington *(G-12677)*
Thrupore Technologies Inc .... G 205 657-0714
  New Castle *(G-5769)*
Twinco Romax LLC .... G 302 998-3019
  Wilmington *(G-12998)*
▲ Zeneca Holdings Inc .... E 302 886-3000
  Wilmington *(G-13344)*

Employee Codes: A=Over 500 employees, B=251-500
C=101-250, D=51-100, E=20-50, F=10-19, G=1-9

29 PETROLEUM REFINING AND RELATED INDUSTRIES

2911 Petroleum Refining

Ashland LLC .... E 302 594-5000
  Wilmington *(G-9151)*
Discount Oil LLC .... G 302 737-6560
  Bear *(G-120)*
E I Du Pont De Nemours & Co .... E 302 452-9000
  Newark *(G-6492)*
E I Du Pont De Nemours & Co .... G 302 772-0016
  New Castle *(G-5271)*
Fairville Products Inc .... G 302 425-4400
  Wilmington *(G-10477)*
Honeywell International Inc .... D 302 791-6700
  Claymont *(G-763)*
Innospec Inc .... F 302 454-8100
  Newark *(G-6782)*
Innospec Inc .... G 302 454-8100
  Newark *(G-6783)*
▲ Prime Products Usa Inc .... G 302 528-3866
  Wilmington *(G-12226)*
Reliance Egleford Upstream LLC .... G 302 472-7437
  Wilmington *(G-12376)*
Sun Malaysia Petroleum Company .... G 302 293-6000
  Wilmington *(G-12794)*
Sun Noordzee Oil Company .... G 302 293-6000
  Wilmington *(G-12796)*
Transstate Jet Service Inc .... G 302 346-3102
  Dover *(G-2160)*

2951 Paving Mixtures & Blocks

Ashland LLC .... E 302 594-5000
  Wilmington *(G-9151)*
Bardon U S Corporation .... G 302 552-3136
  Wilmington *(G-9253)*
Chemstar Corp .... G 302 465-3175
  Milford *(G-4350)*
Christiana Materials Inc .... F 302 633-5600
  Wilmington *(G-9688)*
Diamond Materials LLC .... D 302 658-6524
  Wilmington *(G-10140)*
Driveway Mint Pvng/Slcting LLC .... G 302 228-2644
  Bridgeville *(G-468)*
▲ Emulsion Products Company .... E 302 629-3505
  Seaford *(G-8236)*
Gardner-Gibson Inc .... G 302 628-4290
  Seaford *(G-8250)*
Material Supply Inc .... E 302 658-6524
  Wilmington *(G-11566)*

2952 Asphalt Felts & Coatings

Gardner Asphalt Corporation .... E 302 629-3505
  Seaford *(G-8248)*
Goldis Enterprises Inc .... G 302 764-3100
  Wilmington *(G-10740)*
Goldis Holdings Inc .... D 302 764-3100
  Wilmington *(G-10741)*
Iko Industries Inc .... G 302 764-3100
  Wilmington *(G-10998)*
Iko Manufacturing Inc .... D 302 764-3100
  Wilmington *(G-10999)*
▲ Iko Production Inc .... D 302 764-3100
  Wilmington *(G-11000)*
Ipm Inc .... G 302 328-4030
  New Castle *(G-5424)*
Kings Sealcoating .... G 302 674-1568
  Dover *(G-1752)*
Monroe Iko Inc .... D 302 764-3100
  Wilmington *(G-11734)*

2992 Lubricating Oils & Greases

Castrol Industrial N Amer Inc .... D 302 934-9100
  Millsboro *(G-4657)*
Chem Tech Inc .... G 302 798-9675
  Wilmington *(G-9644)*
Restore Incorporated .... F 302 655-6257
  Wilmington *(G-12390)*
Robert Elgart Automotive .... G 800 220-7777
  Newark *(G-7350)*
▼ Ultrachem Inc .... F 302 325-9880
  New Castle *(G-5801)*

30 RUBBER AND MISCELLANEOUS PLASTICS PRODUCTS

3011 Tires & Inner Tubes

BF Disc Inc .... G 302 691-6351
  Wilmington *(G-9323)*
Michelin Corporation .... G 864 458-4698
  Newark *(G-7024)*

3052 Rubber & Plastic Hose & Belting

Industrial Valves & Fittings .... F 302 326-2494
  New Castle *(G-5417)*

3053 Gaskets, Packing & Sealing Devices

Delaware Thrmplastic Specialty .... G 302 424-4722
  Milford *(G-4381)*
Greene Tweed of Delaware Inc .... G 302 888-2560
  Wilmington *(G-10778)*
▲ Miller Metal Fabrication Inc .... D 302 337-2291
  Bridgeville *(G-501)*
▲ Watson-Marlow Flow Smart Inc .... E 302 536-6388
  Seaford *(G-8434)*

3061 Molded, Extruded & Lathe-Cut Rubber Mechanical Goods

Hat Blue Group LLC .... F 225 288-2962
  Lewes *(G-3535)*

3069 Fabricated Rubber Prdts, NEC

Acurio LLC .... G 201 932-8160
  Wilmington *(G-8931)*
Brandywine Rubber Mills LLC .... G 267 499-3993
  Wilmington *(G-9454)*
Fabreeka Intl Holdings Inc .... F 302 452-2500
  Newark *(G-6562)*
▲ Forcebeyond Inc .... E 302 995-6588
  Wilmington *(G-10590)*
Forte Sports Incorporated .... G 302 731-0776
  Newark *(G-6607)*
◆ LRC North America Inc .... E 302 427-2845
  Wilmington *(G-11446)*
Pascale Industries Inc .... F 302 421-9400
  New Castle *(G-5606)*
◆ Vulcan International Corp .... F 302 428-3181
  Wilmington *(G-13107)*
W L Gore & Associates Inc .... C 302 368-3700
  Newark *(G-7672)*

3081 Plastic Unsupported Sheet & Film

Aearo Technologies LLC .... D 302 283-5497
  Newark *(G-5913)*
▲ Ajedium Film Group LLC .... G 302 452-6609
  Newark *(G-5929)*
Axess Corporation .... G 302 292-8500
  New Castle *(G-5061)*
◆ Delstar Technologies Inc .... C 302 378-8888
  Middletown *(G-4034)*
Dupont De Nemours Inc .... B 302 774-1000
  Wilmington *(G-10251)*
E I Du Pont De Nemours & Co .... F 302 774-1000
  Wilmington *(G-10282)*
Fuji Film .... F 302 477-8000
  New Castle *(G-5333)*
▲ Grayling Industries Inc .... E 770 751-9095
  Frederica *(G-2403)*
Kuraray America Inc .... F 302 992-4204
  Wilmington *(G-11301)*
Printpack Inc .... C 302 323-4000
  New Castle *(G-5645)*
Taghleef Industries Inc .... B 302 326-5500
  Newark *(G-7531)*
◆ Taghleef Industries Inc .... D 302 326-5500
  Newark *(G-7532)*
▲ Wilmington Fibre Specialty Co .... E 302 328-7525
  New Castle *(G-5836)*

3082 Plastic Unsupported Profile Shapes

Fbk Medical Tubing Inc .... E 302 855-0585
  Georgetown *(G-2527)*
Tpi Partners Inc .... D 302 855-0139
  Georgetown *(G-2694)*

3083 Plastic Laminated Plate & Sheet

Fbk Medical Tubing Inc .... E 302 855-0585
  Georgetown *(G-2527)*
▲ Franklin Fibre-Lamitex Corp .... E 302 652-3621
  Wilmington *(G-10616)*
Ipd Technologies LLC .... G 302 533-8850
  Newark *(G-6805)*
New Process Fibre Company Inc .... D 302 349-4535
  Greenwood *(G-2757)*

3085 Plastic Bottles

First State Container LLC .... E 603 888-1315
  Newark *(G-6583)*

3086 Plastic Foam Prdts

Aearo Technologies LLC .... D 302 283-5497
  Newark *(G-5913)*
Baytown Packhouse Inc .... G 936 340-2122
  Newark *(G-6061)*
Dupont De Nemours Inc .... B 302 774-1000
  Wilmington *(G-10251)*
Fluorogistx LLC .... F 302 479-7614
  Wilmington *(G-10582)*
Prezoom LLC .... G 302 414-8204
  New Castle *(G-5640)*

3088 Plastic Plumbing Fixtures

Atlantic Source Contg Inc .... G 302 645-5207
  Lewes *(G-3359)*

3089 Plastic Prdts

Atlantic Aluminum Products Inc .... D 302 349-9091
  Greenwood *(G-2713)*
▲ Atlantis Industries Corp .... E 302 684-8542
  Georgetown *(G-2440)*
Axess Corporation .... G 302 292-8500
  New Castle *(G-5061)*
Cara Plastics Inc .... G 302 622-7070
  Wilmington *(G-9563)*
▲ Craig Technologies Inc .... E 302 628-9900
  Seaford *(G-8213)*
Cramaro Tarpaulin Systems Inc .... F 302 292-2170
  Newark *(G-6311)*
Crown Molding Man .... G 302 455-1204
  Newark *(G-6317)*
▲ Custom America .... G 856 516-1103
  Wilmington *(G-9924)*
Delaware Valley Fence & Iron .... G 302 322-8193
  New Castle *(G-5242)*
Dongjin Usa Inc .... F 302 691-8510
  Wilmington *(G-10198)*
Ensinger Penn Fibre Inc .... E 302 349-4505
  Greenwood *(G-2738)*
▲ Forcebeyond Inc .... E 302 995-6588
  Wilmington *(G-10590)*
◆ Galleyware Company Inc .... G 302 996-9480
  Wilmington *(G-10666)*
Gaudlitz Inc .... G 202 468-3876
  Dover *(G-1585)*
Graham Packaging Co Europe LLC .... E 302 453-9464
  Newark *(G-6680)*
▲ Imcg Global Inc .... G 800 559-6140
  Lewes *(G-3553)*
Justin Tanks LLC .... E 302 856-3521
  Georgetown *(G-2579)*
Letica Corporation .... C 302 378-9853
  Middletown *(G-4130)*
Mohawk Plastic Products Inc .... G 302 424-4324
  Milford *(G-4510)*
Molded Components Inc .... G 302 588-2240
  Wilmington *(G-11727)*
▲ Negri Bossi North America Inc .... G 302 328-8020
  New Castle *(G-5549)*
New Castle Engraving Co .... G 302 652-7551
  New Castle *(G-5557)*
New Process Fibre Company Inc .... D 302 349-4535
  Greenwood *(G-2757)*
Oxford Plastic Systems LLC .... G 800 567-9182
  Wilmington *(G-11989)*
Pacifico Industrial Ltd .... E 213 435-1181
  Newark *(G-7170)*
Philly Plastics Corp .... G 718 435-4808
  Wilmington *(G-12119)*
Plasti Pallets Corp .... G 302 737-1977
  Christiana *(G-676)*
Pony Run Kitchens LLC .... G 302 492-3006
  Hartly *(G-2937)*
Precise Technology Inc .... E 302 737-4638
  Newark *(G-7240)*
Quantum Polymers Corporation .... F 302 737-7012
  Newark *(G-7285)*

▲ Resource Intl Inc .... F 302 762-4501
  New Castle (G-5675)
Richard Earl Fisher .... G 302 598-1957
  Wilmington (G-12407)
Smrc Smart Automotive .... G 317 941-7257
  Wilmington (G-12664)
Viacard Concepts .... G 302 537-4602
  Dagsboro (G-942)
▲ Wilmington Fibre Specialty Co .... E 302 328-7525
  New Castle (G-5836)

31 LEATHER AND LEATHER PRODUCTS

3111 Leather Tanning & Finishing
Exco Inc .... D 905 477-3065
  Wilmington (G-10458)
Fairway Manufacturing Company .... G 302 398-4630
  Harrington (G-2839)

3131 Boot & Shoe Cut Stock & Findings
CSC Tem Ingersoll Rand .... G 302 765-3208
  Wilmington (G-9912)
Nora Lees Frnch Quarter Bistro .... G 302 322-7675
  New Castle (G-5574)
North Quarter Creole .... G 302 691-7890
  Wilmington (G-11901)
Shoolex LLC .... G 866 697-3330
  Lewes (G-3739)

3151 Leather Gloves & Mittens
Kaul Glove and Mfg Co .... D 302 292-2660
  New Castle (G-5454)
Masley Enterprises Inc .... E 302 427-9885
  Wilmington (G-11561)

3161 Luggage
Continental Case .... G 302 322-1765
  Newark (G-6291)
Snickers Ditch Trunk Company .... G 302 325-1762
  New Castle (G-5719)
Travelway Group USA Inc .... G 514 331-3130
  Wilmington (G-12961)

3171 Handbags & Purses
Frontgate LLC .... G 302 245-6654
  Bethany Beach (G-400)
Lamar Bags .... G 302 492-8566
  Hartly (G-2933)
Tradeway Corporation .... G 302 834-1957
  New Castle (G-5782)

3172 Personal Leather Goods
Trihold Inc .... G 302 475-4517
  Wilmington (G-12972)

3199 Leather Goods, NEC
Andy Mast .... G 302 653-5014
  Dover (G-1125)
Fairway Manufacturing Company .... G 302 398-4630
  Harrington (G-2839)
Jarel Industries LLC .... G 336 782-0697
  Camden (G-585)
Tough Luck LLC .... G 302 644-8001
  Lewes (G-3792)

32 STONE, CLAY, GLASS, AND CONCRETE PRODUCTS

3221 Glass Containers
Glass Technologists Inc .... G 240 682-0966
  Middletown (G-4087)

3229 Pressed & Blown Glassware, NEC
▲ Global Scientific Glass Inc .... G 302 429-9330
  Wilmington (G-10730)
Gregory D Thacker .... G 302 239-0879
  Newark (G-6689)
Psp Corp .... G 302 764-7730
  Wilmington (G-12260)
R and H Filter Co Inc .... G 302 856-2129
  Georgetown (G-2632)
Studio On 24 Inc .... G 302 644-4424
  Lewes (G-3767)

Te Connectivity .... G 302 633-2740
  Wilmington (G-12864)

3231 Glass Prdts Made Of Purchased Glass
Cannon Enterprises .... G 302 629-6746
  Seaford (G-8181)
Charles Ogden .... G 305 606-4512
  Wilmington (G-9634)
Glass Technologists Inc .... G 240 682-0966
  Middletown (G-4087)
Gregory D Thacker .... G 302 239-0879
  Newark (G-6689)
Hensco LLC .... G 302 423-1638
  Harrington (G-2849)
◆ Miles Scientific Corporation .... F 302 737-6960
  Newark (G-7039)
Shamrock Glass Co Inc .... F 302 629-5500
  Seaford (G-8400)
Victorian Glassworks .... G 302 798-4847
  Wilmington (G-13078)

3241 Cement, Hydraulic
Cimentum .... G 302 635-7262
  Newark (G-6236)

3253 Ceramic Tile
Intelligent Building Mtls LLC .... G 302 261-9922
  Newark (G-6794)
Maneto Inc .... G 302 656-4285
  Wilmington (G-11501)
Micahs General Contracting .... G 302 437-4068
  Bear (G-251)

3255 Clay Refractories
◆ Rgp Holding Inc .... G 302 661-0117
  Wilmington (G-12399)
◆ Rhi Refractories Holding Co .... G 302 655-6497
  Wilmington (G-12400)

3261 China Plumbing Fixtures & Fittings
Sylvester Custom Cabinetry .... G 302 398-6050
  Harrington (G-2896)

3262 China, Table & Kitchen Articles
Saenger Porcelain .... G 302 738-5349
  Newark (G-7375)

3263 Earthenware, Whiteware, Table & Kitchen Articles
Pony Run Kitchens LLC .... G 302 492-3006
  Hartly (G-2937)

3264 Porcelain Electrical Splys
◆ NGK North America Inc .... G 302 654-1344
  Wilmington (G-11884)
◆ NGK Spark Plugs USA Holdg Inc ...... G 302 288-0131
  Wilmington (G-11885)

3269 Pottery Prdts, NEC
Arttista Accessories .... G 302 455-0195
  Newark (G-6008)
B & F Ceramics .... G 302 475-4721
  Wilmington (G-9209)
Intelligent Building Mtls LLC .... G 302 261-9922
  Newark (G-6794)
Joel Gonzalez .... G 302 562-6878
  Middletown (G-4115)
Katlyn Co Ceramics .... G 302 528-1322
  Bear (G-212)
Robert McMann .... G 302 329-9413
  Milton (G-4964)
Valuewrite .... G 302 593-0694
  Middletown (G-4275)

3271 Concrete Block & Brick
All Rock & Mulch LLC .... G 302 838-7625
  Bear (G-25)
Elegant Stone Veneer LLC .... G 302 547-4780
  Seaford (G-6511)
Valley Landscaping and Con Inc .... G 302 922-5020
  Dover (G-2186)

3272 Concrete Prdts
American Precast Inc .... G 302 629-6688
  Seaford (G-8149)

▲ Ballistics Technology Intl Ltd .... G 877 291-1111
  Wilmington (G-9228)
Best Stoneworks of Delaware .... G 302 765-3497
  Wilmington (G-9314)
Cecil Vault & Memorial Co Inc .... G 302 994-3806
  Wilmington (G-9606)
Concrete Bldg Systems Del Inc .... E 302 846-3645
  Delmar (G-986)
Cooper-Wilbert Vault Co Inc .... G 302 376-1331
  Middletown (G-4011)
Delaware Monument and Vault .... G 302 540-2387
  Hockessin (G-3005)
F Sartin Tyson Inc .... F 302 834-4571
  Saint Georges (G-8125)
Glass Technologists Inc .... G 240 682-0966
  Middletown (G-4087)
National Concrete Products LLC .... E 302 349-5528
  Greenwood (G-2756)
◆ Rhi Refractories Holding Co .... G 302 655-6497
  Wilmington (G-12400)
Rocla Concrete Tie Inc .... E 302 836-5304
  Bear (G-311)
S & F Monuments .... G 302 722-8045
  Newark (G-7372)
Smw Sales LLC .... F 302 875-7958
  Laurel (G-3290)
Wm V Sipple & Son Inc .... G 302 422-4214
  Milford (G-4611)

3273 Ready-Mixed Concrete
Atlantic Concrete Company Inc .... D 302 422-8017
  Milford (G-4312)
Atlantic Concrete Company Inc .... G 302 398-8920
  Harrington (G-2815)
Atlantic Concrete Company Inc .... E 302 856-7847
  Lewes (G-3354)
Bardon U S Corporation .... G 302 552-3136
  Wilmington (G-9253)
Cemex Materials LLC .... E 302 378-8920
  Middletown (G-3984)
Chaney Enterprises .... G 302 990-5039
  Seaford (G-8189)
Concrete Co Inc .... G 302 652-1101
  Wilmington (G-9814)
Greggo & Ferrara Inc .... E 302 834-3333
  Bear (G-173)
HMA Concrete LLC .... F 302 777-1235
  Wilmington (G-10921)
Maddox Concrete Co Inc .... G 302 656-2000
  Wilmington (G-11482)
Material Transit Inc .... F 302 395-0556
  New Castle (G-5512)
Southgate Concrete Company .... F 302 376-5280
  Middletown (G-4247)
Thoro-Goods Concrete Co Inc .... E 302 934-8102
  Dagsboro (G-938)

3281 Cut Stone Prdts
Abba Monument Co Inc .... G 302 738-0272
  Newark (G-5880)
Anta Import/Export LLC .... G 302 653-4542
  Clayton (G-834)
H&K Group Inc .... G 302 934-7635
  Dagsboro (G-906)
▲ Keystone Granite and Tile Inc .... G 302 323-0200
  New Castle (G-5462)
Stone Express .... G 302 376-8876
  Middletown (G-4249)

3291 Abrasive Prdts
Dow Chemical Company .... B 302 368-4169
  Newark (G-6467)
Spectrum Hone & Lace Llc .... G 313 268-5455
  Newark (G-7469)

3295 Minerals & Earths: Ground Or Treated
Iko Southeast Inc .... E 815 936-9600
  Wilmington (G-11003)
Prince Minerals LLC .... F 646 747-4200
  New Castle (G-5642)
▼ Sorbent Green LLC .... G 800 259-3577
  Wilmington (G-12682)

3296 Mineral Wool
Ipm Inc .... G 302 328-4030
  New Castle (G-5424)
Schmidt & Assoc 610 255-3540
  Ocean View (G-7811)

32 STONE, CLAY, GLASS, AND CONCRETE PRODUCTS

3297 Nonclay Refractories
◆ Rhi Refractories Holding Co .... G 302 655-6497
Wilmington *(G-12400)*

3299 Nonmetallic Mineral Prdts, NEC
Atlantic Industrial Optics .... G 302 856-7905
Georgetown *(G-2438)*
Best Stucco LLC .... G 302 650-3620
New Castle *(G-5086)*
Santo Stucco .... G 302 453-0901
Newark *(G-7384)*

33 PRIMARY METAL INDUSTRIES

3312 Blast Furnaces, Coke Ovens, Steel & Rolling Mills
Ah (uk) Inc .... G 302 288-0115
Wilmington *(G-8981)*
Apex Piping Systems Inc .... D 302 995-6136
Wilmington *(G-9097)*
ATI Flat Rlled Pdts Hldngs LLC .... G 302 368-7350
Newark *(G-6015)*
◆ Chemfirst Inc .... D 302 774-1000
Wilmington *(G-9646)*
Delaware Valley Fence & Iron .... G 302 322-8193
New Castle *(G-5242)*
Eagle Erectors Inc .... E 302 832-9586
Bear *(G-133)*
◆ Evraz Clymont Stl Holdings Inc ...... B 302 792-5400
Claymont *(G-743)*
Greenbrook Tms Neurohealth Ctr .... G 302 994-4010
Bear *(G-172)*
▲ Link Metals LLC .... G 302 295-5066
Wilmington *(G-11396)*
Seaside Service LLC .... G 302 827-3775
Lewes *(G-3735)*
Stainless Steel Invest Inc .... G 800 499-7833
Wilmington *(G-12732)*

3313 Electrometallurgical Prdts
American Minerals Inc .... G 302 652-3301
New Castle *(G-5033)*

3315 Steel Wire Drawing & Nails & Spikes
Delaware Valley Fence & Iron .... G 302 322-8193
New Castle *(G-5242)*
Priscilla Lancaster .... G 302 792-8305
Claymont *(G-796)*
Wire Works .... G 302 792-8305
Claymont *(G-824)*

3316 Cold Rolled Steel Sheet, Strip & Bars
Stainless Alloys Inc .... G 800 499-7833
Wilmington *(G-12731)*
Stainless Steel Invest Inc .... G 800 499-7833
Wilmington *(G-12732)*

3317 Steel Pipe & Tubes
Apex Piping Systems Inc .... D 302 995-6136
Wilmington *(G-9097)*
▲ Emeca/Spe Usa LLC .... G 302 875-0760
Laurel *(G-3228)*
Handy & Harman .... G 302 697-9521
Camden *(G-574)*
Handytube Corporation .... D 302 697-9521
Camden *(G-575)*
Handytube Corporation .... D 302 697-9521
Camden *(G-576)*
▲ Handytube Corporation .... D 302 697-9521
Camden *(G-577)*
Iko Sales Ltd .... D 302 764-3100
Wilmington *(G-11002)*
Psp Corp .... G 302 764-7730
Wilmington *(G-12260)*

3321 Gray Iron Foundries
Ej Usa Inc .... F 302 378-1100
Middletown *(G-4051)*

3324 Steel Investment Foundries
Consoldted Fabrication Constrs .... E 302 654-9001
Wilmington *(G-9832)*
▲ Forcebeyond Inc .... E 302 995-6588
Wilmington *(G-10590)*
S P S International Inv Co .... G 302 478-9055
Wilmington *(G-12508)*

Tajan Holdings & Investments .... G 302 300-1183
Middletown *(G-4253)*

3341 Secondary Smelting & Refining Of Nonferrous Metals
Diamond State Recycling Corp .... E 302 655-1501
Wilmington *(G-10147)*
M and R .... G 302 421-9838
Wilmington *(G-11469)*

3353 Aluminum Sheet, Plate & Foil
Uacj Trading America Co Ltd .... F 312 636-5941
Wilmington *(G-13005)*

3354 Aluminum Extruded Prdts
Uacj Trading America Co Ltd .... F 312 636-5941
Wilmington *(G-13005)*

3355 Aluminum Rolling & Drawing, NEC
Gelfand Group Inc .... G 310 666-2362
Camden Wyoming *(G-642)*

3356 Rolling, Drawing-Extruding Of Nonferrous Metals
Titanium Black Exec Sltons LLC .... G 813 785-7842
Dover *(G-2149)*

3357 Nonferrous Wire Drawing
First State Controls Inc .... F 302 559-7822
Wilmington *(G-10550)*
Nouvir Lighting Corporation .... F 302 628-9933
Seaford *(G-8330)*
Nouvir Lightning Corporation .... G 302 628-9888
Seaford *(G-8331)*
W L Gore & Associates Inc .... C 302 368-3700
Newark *(G-7672)*

3369 Nonferrous Foundries: Castings, NEC
Diamond State Props .... G 302 528-7146
Bear *(G-117)*

3398 Metal Heat Treating
Industrial Metal Treating Corp .... F 302 656-1677
Wilmington *(G-11021)*

3399 Primary Metal Prdts, NEC
Ametek Inc .... D 302 456-4400
Newark *(G-5962)*

34 FABRICATED METAL PRODUCTS, EXCEPT MACHINERY AND TRANSPORTATION EQUIPMENT

3411 Metal Cans
▼ Crown Cork & Seal Receivables ...... G 215 698-5100
Wilmington *(G-9906)*
▲ Jmt Inter LLC .... G 302 312-5177
Bear *(G-202)*
Reynolds Metals Company LLC .... E 302 366-0555
Newark *(G-7333)*

3412 Metal Barrels, Drums, Kegs & Pails
Aquila Trading LLC .... G 302 290-5566
Hockessin *(G-2959)*

3421 Cutlery
Cobra Razors .... G 302 540-0464
Wilmington *(G-9756)*
Dalstrong America Inc .... G 716 380-4998
Wilmington *(G-9949)*
Delaware Diamond Knives Inc .... E 302 999-7476
Wilmington *(G-10041)*
Fae McKenzie .... G 302 227-6700
Rehoboth Beach *(G-7930)*
◆ LRC North America Inc .... E 302 427-2845
Wilmington *(G-11446)*
Macknyfe Specialties .... G 302 239-4904
Hockessin *(G-3084)*

3423 Hand & Edge Tools
Black & Decker Inc .... G 860 827-3861
Newark *(G-6087)*

Connor Marketing Inc .... G 302 376-6037
Middletown *(G-4006)*
Danaher Corporation .... G 302 798-5741
Wilmington *(G-9953)*
▼ Easy Lawn Inc .... E 302 815-6500
Greenwood *(G-2736)*
Pkg LLC .... G 269 651-8640
Wilmington *(G-12147)*

3429 Hardware, NEC
Black & Decker Inc .... G 860 827-3861
Newark *(G-6087)*
Bronco Manufacturing Inc .... G 302 475-1210
Wilmington *(G-9484)*
D C Mitchell LLC .... G 302 998-1181
Wilmington *(G-9938)*
Fireside Heart & Home .... G 302 337-3025
Bridgeville *(G-470)*
Gibbons Innovations Inc .... G 302 265-4220
Lincoln *(G-3851)*
Marinhrdwremfg/Forcebeyond Inc ..... G 302 691-4787
Newark *(G-6987)*
Pennengineering Holdings LLC .... C 302 576-2746
Wilmington *(G-12069)*

3431 Enameled Iron & Metal Sanitary Ware
Zenith Home Corp .... B 302 326-8200
New Castle *(G-5845)*

3432 Plumbing Fixture Fittings & Trim, Brass
A and D Plumbing LLC .... G 302 387-9232
Magnolia *(G-3877)*
Aqua Flow Sprinklers .... G 302 369-3629
Newark *(G-5991)*
Ferguson Enterprises LLC .... G 302 747-2032
Dover *(G-1548)*

3433 Heating Eqpt
Solar Foundations Usa Inc .... G 518 935-3360
Newark *(G-7454)*
World Class Products LLC .... G 302 737-1441
Newark *(G-7720)*

3441 Fabricated Structural Steel
▼ Amazon Steel Construction Inc ...... G 302 751-1146
Milford *(G-4305)*
Anchor Enterprises .... G 302 629-7969
Seaford *(G-8151)*
Asa V Peugh Inc .... F 302 629-7969
Seaford *(G-8156)*
Crystal Steel Fabricators Inc .... G 302 846-0277
Delmar *(G-988)*
Crystal Steel Fabricators Inc .... C 302 846-0613
Delmar *(G-989)*
Custom Mechanical Inc .... G 302 537-5611
Bethany Beach *(G-393)*
Deaven Development Corp .... G 302 994-5793
Wilmington *(G-9991)*
Donald F Deaven Inc .... E 302 994-5793
Wilmington *(G-10196)*
Eagle Erectors Inc .... E 302 832-9586
Bear *(G-133)*
East Coast Erectors Inc .... E 302 323-1800
New Castle *(G-5275)*
Engineering Incorporated .... G 302 995-6862
Wilmington *(G-10403)*
First State Fabrication LLC .... G 302 875-2417
Seaford *(G-8244)*
Hardcore Cmpstes Oprations Llc ...... D 302 442-5900
New Castle *(G-5374)*
Industrial Products of Del .... F 302 328-6648
New Castle *(G-5415)*
Iron Works Inc .... F 302 684-1887
Milton *(G-4918)*
K & S Ironworks .... F 302 658-0040
Middletown *(G-4119)*
Mancor US Inc .... G 302 573-3858
Wilmington *(G-11500)*
Messick & Gray Cnstr Inc .... E 302 337-8777
Bridgeville *(G-497)*
Messick & Gray Cnstr Inc .... F 302 337-8445
Bridgeville *(G-498)*
▲ Miller Metal Fabrication Inc .... D 302 337-2291
Bridgeville *(G-501)*
MJM Fabrications Inc .... G 302 764-0163
Wilmington *(G-11716)*
Phillips Fabrication .... G 302 875-4424
Laurel *(G-3272)*

34 FABRICATED METAL PRODUCTS, EXCEPT MACHINERY AND TRANSPORTATION EQUIPMENT

▼ Potts Wldg Boiler Repr Co Inc ....C...... 302 453-2550
Newark *(G-7234)*
R C Fabricators Inc ....D...... 302 573-8989
Wilmington *(G-12293)*
Rivas Ulises ....G...... 302 454-8595
Newark *(G-7346)*
Ronald P Wilson ....G...... 302 539-4139
Frankford *(G-2384)*
SIP Inc of Delaware ....G...... 302 654-4533
Wilmington *(G-12634)*
Spg International LLC ....G...... 404 823-3934
Marydel *(G-3922)*
Steel Suppliers Inc ....C...... 302 654-5243
Wilmington *(G-12748)*
Summit Steel Inc ....D...... 302 325-3220
New Castle *(G-5741)*
Tri-State Fbrction McHning LLC ....E...... 302 232-3133
New Castle *(G-5788)*

3442 Metal Doors, Sash, Frames, Molding & Trim

◆ Alutech United Inc ....G...... 302 436-6005
Selbyville *(G-8447)*
Cheslantic Overhead Door ....G...... 443 880-0378
Delmar *(G-983)*
Delmarvalous ....G...... 302 200-2001
Dagsboro *(G-897)*
Frank R Yocum Sons Wlpr Blind ....G...... 302 888-2000
Wilmington *(G-10613)*
Pinnacle Garage Door Company ....G...... 302 505-4531
Felton *(G-2310)*
Shore Shutters and Shade ....G...... 302 569-1738
Millsboro *(G-4801)*
Shuttercase Inc ....G...... 347 480-1614
Newark *(G-7419)*

3443 Fabricated Plate Work

Air Liquide America LP ....G...... 302 225-2132
Wilmington *(G-8992)*
Amer Industrial Tech Inc ....E...... 302 765-3318
Wilmington *(G-9040)*
◆ Anderson Group Inc ....G...... 302 478-6160
Wilmington *(G-9078)*
Anthony J Nappa ....G...... 716 888-0553
Magnolia *(G-3880)*
Apex Piping Systems Inc ....D...... 302 995-6136
Wilmington *(G-9097)*
Atom Alloys LLC ....G...... 786 975-3771
Wilmington *(G-9181)*
Baltimore Aircoil Company Inc ....C...... 302 424-2583
Milford *(G-4317)*
Contractor Materials LLC ....E...... 302 658-5241
New Castle *(G-5193)*
Creative Assemblies Inc ....F...... 302 956-6194
Bridgeville *(G-462)*
Elanco Inc ....G...... 302 731-8500
Bear *(G-142)*
Newarc Welding & Fabricating ....G...... 302 658-5214
Wilmington *(G-11875)*

3444 Sheet Metal Work

A & H Metals Inc ....E...... 302 366-7540
Newark *(G-5863)*
AG & G Sheet Metal Inc ....G...... 302 653-4111
Smyrna *(G-8562)*
Allied Precision Inc ....G...... 302 376-6844
Middletown *(G-3936)*
Atlantic Screen & Mfg Inc ....G...... 302 684-3197
Milton *(G-4865)*
Atlas Wldg & Fabrication Inc ....E...... 302 326-1900
New Castle *(G-5053)*
Custom Mechanical Inc ....G...... 302 537-5611
Bethany Beach *(G-393)*
Custom Mechanical Inc ....E...... 302 537-1150
Frankford *(G-2358)*
Custom Sheet Metal of Delaware ....G...... 302 998-6865
Wilmington *(G-9926)*
Ducts Unlimited Inc ....G...... 302 378-4125
Smyrna *(G-8628)*
East Coast Machine Works ....G...... 302 349-5180
Greenwood *(G-2734)*
Faust Sheet Metal Works Inc ....G...... 302 645-9509
Lewes *(G-3493)*
L & J Sheet Metal ....F...... 302 875-2822
Laurel *(G-3249)*
M Cubed Technologies Inc ....D...... 302 454-8600
Newark *(G-6964)*
Mastercraft Welding ....G...... 302 697-3932
Dover *(G-1824)*

McCabes Mechanical Service Inc ....F...... 302 854-9001
Georgetown *(G-2599)*
Metal-Tech Inc ....E...... 302 322-7770
New Castle *(G-5518)*
Murphy Steel Inc ....E...... 302 366-8676
Newark *(G-7073)*
Phillips Fabrication ....E...... 302 875-4424
Laurel *(G-3272)*
Power Electronics Inc ....E...... 302 653-4822
Clayton *(G-868)*
Quality Htg Ar-Cnditioning Inc ....D...... 302 654-5247
Wilmington *(G-12280)*
Ronald P Wilson ....G...... 302 539-4139
Frankford *(G-2384)*
S G Williams & Bros Co ....F...... 302 656-8167
Wilmington *(G-12506)*
Seaside Service LLC ....G...... 302 827-3775
Lewes *(G-3735)*
Sheet Metal Contracting Co ....E...... 302 834-3727
Bear *(G-319)*
Sunhaven Awning Co ....G...... 302 239-7990
Yorklyn *(G-13367)*
V E Guerrazzi Inc. ....G...... 302 369-5557
Newark *(G-7636)*

3446 Architectural & Ornamental Metal Work

Access4u Inc ....G...... 800 355-7025
Lewes *(G-3322)*
Asa V Peugh Inc ....F...... 302 629-7969
Seaford *(G-8156)*
Atlantic Aluminum Products Inc ....D...... 302 349-9091
Greenwood *(G-2713)*
Custom Mechanical Inc ....G...... 302 537-5611
Bethany Beach *(G-393)*
Deaven Development Corp ....G...... 302 994-5793
Wilmington *(G-9991)*
Delaware Flooring Supply Inc ....G...... 302 276-0031
New Castle *(G-5230)*
Donald F Deaven Inc. ....E...... 302 994-5793
Wilmington *(G-10196)*
Murphy Steel Inc ....E...... 302 366-8676
Newark *(G-7073)*

3448 Prefabricated Metal Buildings & Cmpnts

▼ All-Span Inc ....E...... 302 349-9460
Bridgeville *(G-444)*
Betterlving Ptio Snroms Dlmrva ....G...... 302 251-0000
Dagsboro *(G-882)*
Coastal Sun Roms Prch Enclsres ....G...... 302 537-3679
Frankford *(G-2355)*
Regional Builders Inc ....G...... 302 628-8660
Seaford *(G-8374)*
Steel Buildings Inc ....G...... 302 644-0444
Lewes *(G-3764)*
Street Core Utility Service ....G...... 302 239-4110
Hockessin *(G-3150)*
Sweeten Companies Inc ....G...... 302 737-6161
Newark *(G-7520)*
Vaughan Bckley Modular Sls Inc ....G...... 215 259-7509
Wilmington *(G-13051)*

3449 Misc Structural Metal Work

Confab Inc ....G...... 302 429-0140
Wilmington *(G-9819)*
Cox Industries Inc ....G...... 302 332-8470
Newark *(G-6310)*
International Electrical Svcs ....G...... 302 438-6096
Wilmington *(G-11065)*
Regen Solutions LLC ....G...... 323 362-4336
Dover *(G-2020)*

3452 Bolts, Nuts, Screws, Rivets & Washers

Anthony J Nappa ....G...... 716 888-0553
Magnolia *(G-3880)*
Black & Decker Inc ....G...... 860 827-3861
Newark *(G-6087)*
Fencemaxcom Inc ....G...... 302 343-9063
Hartly *(G-2922)*
Lemay Enterprises Inc ....G...... 302 659-3278
Townsend *(G-8805)*
Mr Window Washer ....G...... 302 588-3624
Claymont *(G-786)*

3462 Iron & Steel Forgings

A T I Funding Corporation ....F...... 302 656-8937
Wilmington *(G-8884)*

Eager Gear ....G...... 302 727-5831
Lewes *(G-3477)*
Square One Electric Service Co ....F...... 302 678-0400
Dover *(G-2099)*
Tdy Holdings LLC ....G...... 302 254-4172
Wilmington *(G-12863)*
Timken Gears & Services Inc ....F...... 302 633-4600
New Castle *(G-5770)*

3463 Nonferrous Forgings

Delaware Capital Formation Inc ....G...... 302 793-4921
Wilmington *(G-10010)*

3465 Automotive Stampings

Shiloh Industries Inc. ....G...... 302 656-1950
Wilmington *(G-12602)*

3469 Metal Stampings, NEC

Bear Forge and Machine Co Inc ....G...... 302 322-5199
Bear *(G-47)*
George Products Company Inc ....F...... 302 449-0199
Middletown *(G-4086)*
Idylc Homes LLC ....G...... 302 295-3719
Wilmington *(G-10995)*

3471 Electroplating, Plating, Polishing, Anodizing & Coloring

Aurista Technologies Inc ....F...... 302 792-4900
Claymont *(G-696)*
Felixcem Corporation Inc. ....G...... 302 324-9101
New Castle *(G-5308)*
Industraplate Corp ....F...... 302 654-5210
Wilmington *(G-11020)*
Industrial Metal Treating Corp ....F...... 302 656-1677
Wilmington *(G-11021)*
Old School Plating ....G...... 302 345-0350
Bear *(G-271)*
Rohm and Haas Electronic ....F...... 302 366-0500
Newark *(G-7357)*

3479 Coating & Engraving, NEC

Chemring North Amer Group Inc ....G...... 302 658-5687
Wilmington *(G-9654)*
Coastal Coatings Inc ....G...... 302 645-1399
Lewes *(G-3436)*
Crazy Coatings ....G...... 302 378-0888
Middletown *(G-4013)*
E M C Process Company Inc ....G...... 302 999-9204
Wilmington *(G-10309)*
General Coatings LLC ....G...... 302 841-7958
Millsboro *(G-4696)*
Metal-Tech Inc ....E...... 302 322-7770
New Castle *(G-5518)*
Orville Sammons Ardens ....G...... 302 492-8620
Dover *(G-1924)*
Perfect Finish Powder Coating ....G...... 302 566-6189
Harrington *(G-2872)*
Prestige Powder Finishing Inc ....F...... 302 737-7500
Newark *(G-7249)*
Raymond Harner ....G...... 302 737-0755
Newark *(G-7301)*
Top Qality Indus Finishers Inc ....G...... 302 778-5005
Wilmington *(G-12929)*
Voigt & Schweitzer LLC ....F...... 302 322-1420
New Castle *(G-5820)*

3482 Small Arms Ammunition

▼ Du Pont Chem Enrgy Oprtons Inc ....G...... 302 774-1000
Wilmington *(G-10241)*

3484 Small Arms

Stockmarket ....G...... 302 697-8878
Magnolia *(G-3909)*

3491 Industrial Valves

Automation & Controls Tech LLC ....G...... 913 908-4344
Milton *(G-4866)*
Eeco Inc ....G...... 302 456-1448
Newark *(G-6506)*
▼ Potts Wldg Boiler Repr Co Inc ....C...... 302 453-2550
Newark *(G-7234)*

3492 Fluid Power Valves & Hose Fittings

▲ Mto Hose Solutions Inc ....G...... 302 266-6555
Newark *(G-7071)*

34 FABRICATED METAL PRODUCTS, EXCEPT MACHINERY AND TRANSPORTATION EQUIPMENT — SIC SECTION

3494 Valves & Pipe Fittings, NEC
American Insert Flange Co Inc ....F 302 777-7464
  Wilmington *(G-9050)*
Solar Unlimited North Amer LLC ....G 302 542-4580
  Lewes *(G-3754)*

3495 Wire Springs
▼ Delmaco Manufacturing Inc ....F 302 856-6345
  Georgetown *(G-2506)*

3496 Misc Fabricated Wire Prdts
◆ Bio Medic Corporation ....F 302 628-4300
  Seaford *(G-8170)*
Guide Idler and Conveyor Belt ....G 302 762-7564
  Wilmington *(G-10798)*
Mid Atlantic Indus Belting ....G 302 453-7353
  Newark *(G-7026)*
▲ OConnor Belting Intl Inc ....E 302 452-2500
  Newark *(G-7142)*
Wire Works ....G 302 792-8305
  Claymont *(G-824)*

3498 Fabricated Pipe & Pipe Fittings
Apex Piping Systems Inc ....D 302 995-6136
  Wilmington *(G-9097)*
Atlantic Screen & Mfg Inc ....G 302 684-3197
  Milton *(G-4865)*
Baltimore Aircoil Company Inc ....C 302 424-2583
  Milford *(G-4317)*
▲ Spectrum Magnetics LLC ....G 302 993-1070
  Wilmington *(G-12699)*
◆ Thermal Pipe Systems Inc ....G 302 999-1588
  Wilmington *(G-12895)*

3499 Fabricated Metal Prdts, NEC
A B Fab & Machining LLC ....G 302 293-4945
  New Castle *(G-4991)*
▼ Delmaco Manufacturing Inc ....F 302 856-6345
  Georgetown *(G-2506)*
Firefly Drone Operations Llc ....G 305 206-6955
  Wilmington *(G-10543)*
Hickory Hill Metal Fabrication ....G 302 382-6727
  Dover *(G-1643)*
Joseph T Ryerson & Son Inc ....E 302 366-0555
  Newark *(G-6851)*
Visionary Energy Systems Inc ....G 410 739-4342
  Dover *(G-2195)*

35 INDUSTRIAL AND COMMERCIAL MACHINERY AND COMPUTER EQUIPMENT

3511 Steam, Gas & Hydraulic Turbines & Engines
Everlift Wind Technology ....G 240 683-9787
  Lewes *(G-3488)*
Garrett Motion Inc ....G 973 867-7017
  Wilmington *(G-10671)*
Junttan USA Inc ....G 302 500-1274
  Laurel *(G-3246)*
Kissangen Inc ....E 414 446-4182
  Newark *(G-6895)*
Webro Holdings LLC ....G 302 314-3334
  Rehoboth Beach *(G-8109)*
Wing2wind Technology Inc ....G 240 683-9787
  Lewes *(G-3828)*

3519 Internal Combustion Engines, NEC
Cummins Power Generation Inc ....B 302 762-2027
  Wilmington *(G-9918)*

3523 Farm Machinery & Eqpt
Cnh Cptal Oprting Lase Eqp Rcv ....B 262 636-6011
  Wilmington *(G-9750)*
▼ Easy Lawn Inc ....E 302 815-6500
  Greenwood *(G-2736)*
Egolf Forest Harvesting Inc ....G 302 846-0634
  Delmar *(G-996)*
▲ Farmers Harvest Inc ....G 302 734-7708
  Dover *(G-1541)*
James Atkinson ....G 302 236-7499
  Harrington *(G-2854)*
Lumi Cases LLC ....G 302 525-6971
  Newark *(G-6956)*

Macknyfe Specialties ....G 302 239-4904
  Hockessin *(G-3084)*
Redhead Farms LLC 443 235-3990
  Delmar *(G-1027)*
Turfhound Inc ....G 215 783-8143
  Wilmington *(G-12992)*
Wilmington ....G 302 357-4509
  Wilmington *(G-13221)*

3524 Garden, Lawn Tractors & Eqpt
East Coast Perennials Inc ....G 302 945-5853
  Millsboro *(G-4683)*
▼ Easy Lawn Inc ....E 302 815-6500
  Greenwood *(G-2736)*
Erosion Control Products Corp ....F 302 815-6500
  Greenwood *(G-2739)*
Hydroseeding Company LLC ....E 302 815-6500
  Greenwood *(G-2745)*

3531 Construction Machinery & Eqpt
▲ Advance Marine LLC ....G 302 656-2111
  Wilmington *(G-8947)*
Bob Reynolds Backhoe Services ....G 302 239-4711
  Hockessin *(G-2965)*
Bos Construction Company ....G 302 875-9120
  Laurel *(G-3202)*
Buffalo Concrete Co Inc ....G 302 378-4421
  Wilmington *(G-9501)*
Central Backhoe Service ....G 302 398-6420
  Milton *(G-4877)*
Cnh Cptal Oprting Lase Eqp Rcv ....B 262 636-6011
  Wilmington *(G-9750)*
Duane Edward Ruark ....G 302 846-2332
  Delmar *(G-994)*
Longneck Backhoe ....G 302 945-3429
  Millsboro *(G-4725)*
Marking Services Inc ....G 302 478-0381
  Wilmington *(G-11538)*
Meredith Salvage ....G 302 349-4776
  Greenwood *(G-2752)*
Prela S Lynch ....G 302 856-2130
  Georgetown *(G-2624)*
Smw Sales LLC ....F 302 875-7958
  Laurel *(G-3290)*
Stockley Materials LLC ....G 302 856-7601
  Georgetown *(G-2666)*
Teksolv Usd Inc ....G 302 738-1050
  Newark *(G-7552)*
Wolfe Backhoe Service ....G 302 737-2628
  Newark *(G-7713)*
Xcmg Machinery Us LLC ....G 786 796-1094
  Wilmington *(G-13315)*

3533 Oil Field Machinery & Eqpt
◆ Delaware Capital Holdings Inc ....G 302 793-4921
  Wilmington *(G-10011)*
Tdw Delaware Inc ....G 302 594-9880
  New Castle *(G-5755)*
Us Engineering Corporation ....F 302 645-7400
  Lewes *(G-3804)*

3534 Elevators & Moving Stairways
Atlantic Elevators ....G 302 537-8304
  Dagsboro *(G-878)*
Brandywine Balustrades ....G 302 893-1837
  Newark *(G-6114)*
M K Customer Elevator Pads ....G 302 698-3110
  Dover *(G-1810)*
MV Farinola Inc ....G 302 545-8492
  Wilmington *(G-11781)*

3535 Conveyors & Eqpt
Airsled Inc ....G 302 292-8911
  Newark *(G-5928)*
▼ Amazon Steel Construction Inc ....G 302 751-1146
  Milford *(G-4305)*
CDI Inc Sofr System LLC ....G 302 536-7325
  Seaford *(G-8184)*
Holts Metal Works Inc ....G 302 628-1609
  Seaford *(G-8266)*

3537 Indl Trucks, Tractors, Trailers & Stackers
3M Company ....C 302 286-2480
  Newark *(G-5859)*
Airsled Inc ....G 302 292-8911
  Newark *(G-5928)*

Shipley Associates Inc ....G 302 652-1766
  Wilmington *(G-12604)*
Wwc III Trucking LLC ....G 302 238-7778
  Millsboro *(G-4831)*

3541 Machine Tools: Cutting
Diy Tool Supply LLC ....G 302 253-8461
  Georgetown *(G-2512)*
Mazzpac LLC ....G 973 641-9159
  Newark *(G-7009)*
Paul A Lange ....G 302 378-1706
  Middletown *(G-4183)*
Seaford Machine Works Inc ....F 302 629-6034
  Seaford *(G-8392)*

3542 Machine Tools: Forming
Delaware Capital Formation Inc ....G 302 793-4921
  Wilmington *(G-10010)*
▲ Eastern Shore Metals LLC ....F 302 629-6629
  Seaford *(G-8231)*
▲ Miller Metal Fabrication Inc ....D 302 337-2291
  Bridgeville *(G-501)*

3543 Industrial Patterns
Patterns ....G 302 654-9075
  Rockland *(G-8124)*

3544 Dies, Tools, Jigs, Fixtures & Indl Molds
▲ Forcebeyond Inc ....E 302 995-6588
  Wilmington *(G-10590)*
Mold Busters LLC ....G 302 339-2204
  Harbeson *(G-2793)*
Ox Pond Industries ....G 703 608-7769
  Dagsboro *(G-928)*
Pcu Systems LLC 888 780-9728
  (G-12053)

3545 Machine Tool Access
Advanced Metal Concepts Inc ....F 302 421-9905
  Middletown *(G-3931)*
Alexis Wirt ....G 302 654-4236
  Wilmington *(G-9005)*
Applied Diamond Inc ....G 302 999-1132
  Wilmington *(G-9102)*
Ddk ....F 302 999-1132
  Wilmington *(G-9984)*
Mechanical Systems Intl Corp ....F 302 453-8315
  Newark *(G-7014)*
Petal Pushers LLC ....G 302 945-0350
  Lewes *(G-3685)*

3546 Power Hand Tools
Black & Decker Corporation ....G 302 738-0250
  Newark *(G-6086)*
Eeco Inc ....G 302 456-1448
  Newark *(G-6506)*
◆ Rhi Refractories Holding Co ....G 302 655-6497
  Wilmington *(G-12400)*

3548 Welding Apparatus
Ef Technologies Inc ....G 302 451-1088
  Newark *(G-6508)*

3549 Metalworking Machinery, NEC
Junttan USA Inc ....G 302 500-1274
  Laurel *(G-3246)*
Pennengineering Holdings LLC ....C 302 576-2746
  Wilmington *(G-12069)*

3555 Printing Trades Machinery & Eqpt
E I Du Pont De Nemours & Co ....E 805 562-5307
  Wilmington *(G-10304)*
Ferrante & Associates Inc ....G 781 891-4328
  Wilmington *(G-10522)*
Laser Marking Works LLC ....G 786 307-6203
  Wilmington *(G-11333)*
My Qme Inc ....E 302 218-8730
  Wilmington *(G-11789)*
Roller Service Corporation ....E 302 737-5000
  Newark *(G-7361)*
Spratley Publishing ....G 267 779-7353
  Wilmington *(G-12712)*

3556 Food Prdts Machinery
E I Du Pont De Nemours & Co ....D 302 695-5300
  Wilmington *(G-10306)*

35 INDUSTRIAL AND COMMERCIAL MACHINERY AND COMPUTER EQUIPMENT

Fishing Inc .... G 302 999-9961
　Wilmington (G-10563)
▲ Metal Msters Fdservice Eqp Inc .... C 302 653-3000
　Clayton (G-863)

3559 Special Ind Machinery, NEC

◆ Cae(us) Inc 813 885-7481
　Wilmington (G-9533)
▲ Negri Bossi Usa Inc .... F 302 328-8020
　New Castle (G-5550)
Sewickley Capital Inc .... G 302 793-4964
　Wilmington (G-12589)

3561 Pumps & Pumping Eqpt

C H P T Manufacturing Inc .... G 302 856-7660
　Georgetown (G-2461)
▼ Easy Lawn Inc .... E 302 815-6500
　Greenwood (G-2736)
Site Work Safety Supplies Inc .... G 302 672-7011
　Dover (G-2085)

3562 Ball & Roller Bearings

Roller Service Corporation .... E 302 737-5000
　Newark (G-7361)

3563 Air & Gas Compressors

De Sales and Service .... G 302 456-1660
　Newark (G-6354)
▼ Easy Lawn Inc .... E 302 815-6500
　Greenwood (G-2736)
Linne Industries LLC .... G 302 454-1439
　Newark (G-6938)

3564 Blowers & Fans

Air Liquide America LP .... G 302 225-2132
　Wilmington (G-8992)
Air Natures Way Inc .... G 302 738-3063
　Newark (G-5926)
Delaware Contract Testing LLC .... G 302 650-4030
　Wilmington (G-10025)
▲ Ptm Manufacturing LLC .... G 302 455-9733
　New Castle (G-5651)
TS Air Enterprises LLC .... G 302 533-7458
　Newark (G-7598)

3565 Packaging Machinery

Ames Engineering Corp .... E 302 658-6945
　Wilmington (G-9067)
Telesonic PC Inc .... G 302 658-6945
　Wilmington (G-12878)
Telesonic PC Inc .... G 302 658-6945
　Wilmington (G-12879)

3566 Speed Changers, Drives & Gears

▲ David Brown Gear Systems USA .... G 540 416-2062
　Wilmington (G-9966)
David Brown Gear Systems USA .... G 540 943-8375
　Wilmington (G-9967)

3567 Indl Process Furnaces & Ovens

◆ Chemfirst Inc .... D 302 774-1000
　Wilmington (G-9646)
▲ Nabertherm Inc .... G 302 322-3665
　New Castle (G-5541)
Thermo Stack LLC .... G 401 885-7781
　Hockessin (G-3160)

3568 Mechanical Power Transmission Eqpt, NEC

▲ Chiorino Inc .... E 302 292-1906
　Newark (G-6200)
Pierce Design & Tool .... G 302 222-3339
　Dover (G-1958)
▲ SSS Clutch Company Inc .... G 302 322-8080
　New Castle (G-5733)

3569 Indl Machinery & Eqpt, NEC

Atlantic Screen & Mfg Inc .... G 302 684-3197
　Milton (G-4865)
Bif III Holtwood LLC .... E 819 561-2722
　Wilmington (G-9328)
Graver Separations Inc .... G 302 731-1700
　Newark (G-6683)
Kissangen Inc .... G 414 446-4182
　Newark (G-6895)

Precision Airconvey Corp .... F 302 999-8000
　Newark (G-7241)
Steven Abdill .... G 443 243-6864
　Wilmington (G-12758)
Suez North America Inc .... F 302 633-5670
　Wilmington (G-12789)

3571 Electronic Computers

Anatrope Inc .... G 202 507-9441
　Dover (G-1123)
Blake Computers .... G 540 843-0656
　Milton (G-4869)
Broadberry Data Systems LLC .... E 302 295-1086
　Wilmington (G-9481)
Broadberry Data Systems LLC .... G 800 496-9918
　Wilmington (G-9482)
Carter Firm LLC .... G 267 420-0717
　Wilmington (G-9582)
Ecomo Inc .... G 412 567-3867
　Dover (G-1502)
▲ Eluktronics Inc .... F 302 380-3242
　Newark (G-6520)
Hewlett-Packard World Trade .... E 877 424-4536
　Wilmington (G-10898)
It S Apples Oranges In .... G 301 333-3696
　Lewes (G-3564)
Naughty Apple .... G 954 300-7158
　Wilmington (G-11820)
P M O Advisors L L C .... G 302 545-1159
　Wilmington (G-11995)
Radiance Vr Inc .... G 937 818-3988
　Lewes (G-3706)
Scientific Games Corporation .... F 302 737-4300
　Newark (G-7395)
Sumuri LLC .... G 302 570-0015
　Camden (G-601)
Weyl Enterprises Inc .... G 302 993-1248
　Wilmington (G-13176)

3572 Computer Storage Devices

Hewlett-Packard World Trade .... E 877 424-4536
　Wilmington (G-10898)
Quantum Corporation .... G 302 737-7012
　Newark (G-7284)
Zerowait Corporation .... F 302 996-9408
　Wilmington (G-13349)

3575 Computer Terminals

Hewlett-Packard World Trade .... E 877 424-4536
　Wilmington (G-10898)
Isaac Fair Corporation .... E 302 324-8015
　New Castle (G-5426)

3577 Computer Peripheral Eqpt, NEC

Ametek Inc .... D 302 456-4400
　Newark (G-5962)
▲ Audioscience Inc .... F 302 324-5333
　New Castle (G-5054)
Cisco Systems Inc .... G 302 492-1735
　Hartly (G-2916)
Creative Micro Designs Inc .... G 302 456-5800
　Newark (G-6314)
East Coast Games Inc .... F 302 838-0669
　Bear (G-136)
Hewlett-Packard World Trade .... E 877 424-4536
　Wilmington (G-10898)
Ncs Pearson Inc .... D 302 736-8006
　Dover (G-1889)
On Demand Services LLC .... G 302 388-1215
　Newark (G-7148)
Xerox Corporation .... G 585 422-0272
　Wilmington (G-13318)

3578 Calculating & Accounting Eqpt

Global Merchant Partners LLC .... G 302 425-3567
　Rehoboth Beach (G-7950)
Huawei Technologies Svc LLC .... G 888 548-2934
　Dover (G-1659)

3579 Office Machines, NEC

B Williams Holding Corp .... F 302 656-8596
　Wilmington (G-9214)
Black & Decker Inc .... G 860 827-3861
　Newark (G-6087)
Tritek Corporation .... F 302 239-1638
　Hockessin (G-3164)
Tritek Technologies Inc .... F 302 239-1638
　Hockessin (G-3165)

Tritek Technologies Inc .... G 302 573-5096
　Wilmington (G-12981)

3581 Automatic Vending Machines

Vending Solutions LLC .... G 302 674-2222
　Dover (G-2189)

3582 Commercial Laundry, Dry Clean & Pressing Mchs

Service General Corp .... C 302 856-3500
　Georgetown (G-2651)

3585 Air Conditioning & Heating Eqpt

Air Intrnational US Sbusid Inc .... D 248 819-1602
　Wilmington (G-8991)
Baltimore Aircoil Company Inc .... C 302 424-2583
　Milford (G-4317)
Beach Mobile Home Supply .... G 302 945-5611
　Millsboro (G-4640)
Bluchill Inc .... G 302 658-2638
　New Castle (G-5093)
Creative Assemblies Inc .... F 302 956-6194
　Bridgeville (G-462)
Eeco Inc .... G 302 456-1448
　Newark (G-6506)
Munters Corporation .... F 302 798-2455
　Claymont (G-787)
Omega Industries Inc .... G 302 734-3835
　Dover (G-1916)
Trane US Inc .... E 302 395-0200
　New Castle (G-5783)

3589 Service Ind Machines, NEC

Aquion Inc .... G 847 725-3000
　Wilmington (G-9108)
B & R Boyer Pressure Washing .... G 302 875-3603
　Laurel (G-3194)
◆ Coffee Artisan LLC .... G 302 297-8800
　Millsboro (G-4664)
▲ Eagle Mhc Company .... B 302 653-3000
　Clayton (G-847)
Evoqua Water Technologies LLC .... G 302 322-6247
　New Castle (G-5298)
◆ Franke USA Holding Inc .... F 615 462-4000
　Wilmington (G-10614)
◆ Graver Technologies LLC .... G 302 731-1700
　Newark (G-6684)
Jaa Industries LLC .... G 302 332-0388
　New Castle (G-5433)
Jeff Thomas .... G 302 762-9154
　Wilmington (G-11143)
▲ Metal Msters Fdservice Eqp Inc .... C 302 653-3000
　Clayton (G-863)
Powerscape LLC .... G 302 945-4626
　Millsboro (G-4787)
◆ Rhi Refractories Holding Co .... G 302 655-6497
　Wilmington (G-12400)
Sanosil International LLC .... F 302 454-8102
　New Castle (G-5694)
◆ Severn Trent Inc .... E 302 427-5990
　Wilmington (G-12588)
Suez North America Inc .... G 302 633-5670
　Wilmington (G-12789)
Verisoft Inc .... G 602 908-7151
　Dover (G-2190)
Watercraft LLC .... G 302 757-0786
　Wilmington (G-13122)

3592 Carburetors, Pistons, Rings & Valves

Mid Atlantic Industrial Sales .... G 302 698-6356
　Camden (G-590)

3594 Fluid Power Pumps & Motors

Smw Sales LLC .... F 302 875-7958
　Laurel (G-3290)

3596 Scales & Balances, Exc Laboratory

Spectr-Physics Hldings USA Inc .... G 302 478-4600
　Wilmington (G-12698)

3599 Machinery & Eqpt, Indl & Commercial, NEC

Able Whelling and Machiene .... G 302 436-1929
　Selbyville (G-8446)
Airespa Worldwide Whl LLC .... G 908 227-4441
　Dover (G-1097)

35 INDUSTRIAL AND COMMERCIAL MACHINERY AND COMPUTER EQUIPMENT

Allied Precision Inc .... G 302 376-6844
  Middletown (G-3936)
Apex Manufacturing Group Inc .... G 484 888-6252
  Newark (G-5981)
Apex Manufacturing Group Inc .... G 484 888-6252
  Newark (G-5982)
Automation Inc .... F 302 999-0971
  Wilmington (G-9187)
Awl Machine .... G 302 888-0440
  Wilmington (G-9200)
Bronco Manufacturing Inc .... G 302 475-1210
  Wilmington (G-9484)
C & C Technologies Inc .... G 302 653-7623
  Smyrna (G-8588)
Carlisle Machine Shop Inc .... G 302 653-2584
  Townsend (G-8768)
Chpt Mfg Inc .... G 302 645-4314
  Lewes (G-3417)
Churchmens Machine Company .... F 302 994-8660
  Wilmington (G-9698)
Croesus Inc .... G 302 472-9260
  Wilmington (G-9902)
Custom Sheet Metal of Delaware .... G 302 998-6865
  Wilmington (G-9926)
Deangelis & Son Inc .... G 302 337-8699
  Bridgeville (G-464)
Delmarva Precision Grinding .... G 302 393-3008
  Milford (G-4384)
Delta Machine & Tool Company .... G 302 738-1788
  Newark (G-6432)
Dess Machine & Manufacturing .... G 302 736-7457
  Dover (G-1416)
Diamond State Machining Inc .... F 302 398-8437
  Farmington (G-2267)
▲ Duhadaway Tool and Die Sp Inc .... D 302 366-0113
  Newark (G-6477)
East Coast Machine Works .... G 302 349-5180
  Greenwood (G-2734)
Extreme Machining LLC .... F 302 368-7595
  Newark (G-6556)
Hage Tool and Machine Inc .... G 302 836-4850
  Bear (G-175)
Heritage Machine Shop LLC .... G 302 656-3313
  Wilmington (G-10892)
High-Tech Machine Company Inc .... F 302 636-0267
  Wilmington (G-10903)
Horns Machine Shop Inc .... G 302 653-6663
  Smyrna (G-8654)
HP Motors Inc .... G 302 368-4543
  Newark (G-6753)
James Machine Shop Inc .... G 302 798-5679
  Claymont (G-767)
Messick & Gray Cnstr Inc .... F 302 337-8445
  Bridgeville (G-498)
Metal-Tech Inc .... E 302 322-7770
  New Castle (G-5518)
Michael A Beecher .... G 302 285-3357
  Townsend (G-8809)
Nanticoke Consulting Inc .... G 302 424-0570
  Greenwood (G-2755)
New Castle Precision Mch LLC .... G 302 650-7849
  New Castle (G-5563)
▲ O A Newton & Son Company .... E 302 337-3782
  Bridgeville (G-504)
▲ Polarstar Engineering & Mch .... G 302 368-4639
  Newark (G-7230)
▼ Proper Pitch LLC .... G 302 436-5442
  Selbyville (G-8534)
Prototek Machining & Dev .... G 302 368-1226
  Newark (G-7271)
R & K Motors & Machine Shop .... G 302 737-4596
  Newark (G-7290)
Red Clay Inc .... G 302 239-2018
  Hockessin (G-3132)
Riemel of Delaware LLC .... G 302 998-5806
  Wilmington (G-12420)
Rumpstich Machine Works Inc .... G 302 422-4816
  Milford (G-4549)
Sachetta Machine & Development .... F 302 378-5468
  Middletown (G-4229)
Seaford Machine Works Inc .... F 302 629-6034
  Seaford (G-8392)
Sheet Metal Contracting Co .... E 302 834-3727
  Bear (G-319)
Specialty Machine Works .... G 302 429-8970
  Wilmington (G-12696)
State Line Machine Inc .... G 302 875-2248
  Laurel (G-3295)
Summit Industrial Corporation .... G 302 368-2718
  Newark (G-7504)

Tri-State Fbrction McHning LLC .... E 302 232-3133
  New Castle (G-5788)
Trim Waste Management LLC .... G 302 738-2500
  Newark (G-7592)
Troutman Machine Company Inc .... G 302 674-3540
  Dover (G-2164)
West End Machine Shop Inc .... G 302 654-8436
  Wilmington (G-13164)

36 ELECTRONIC AND OTHER ELECTRICAL EQUIPMENT AND COMPONENTS, EXCEPT COMPUTER

3612 Power, Distribution & Specialty Transformers

Rigel Energy Group LLC .... F 888 624-9844
  Wilmington (G-12421)

3613 Switchgear & Switchboard Apparatus

Atlantic Control Systems Inc .... G 302 284-9700
  Felton (G-2272)
Deride Igo .... G 302 234-4121
  Newark (G-6439)
Panelmatic Inc .... G 302 324-9193
  New Castle (G-5600)
▼ Panelmatic East Inc .... F 302 324-9193
  New Castle (G-5601)
Power Electronics Inc .... E 302 653-4822
  Clayton (G-868)

3621 Motors & Generators

AC Engineering .... G 215 873-6482
  Bear (G-9)
All American Electric Svcs LLC .... G 410 479-0277
  Greenwood (G-2712)
Ametek Inc .... D 302 456-4400
  Newark (G-5962)
Arex Holding Inc .... G 646 216-2091
  Wilmington (G-9126)
Cummins Power Generation Inc .... B 302 762-2027
  Wilmington (G-9918)
Eeco Inc .... G 302 456-1448
  Newark (G-6506)
Junttan USA Inc .... G 302 500-1274
  Laurel (G-3246)
Kissangen Inc .... E 414 446-4182
  Newark (G-6895)
Renewable Energy Resources Inc .... G 302 544-0054
  Georgetown (G-2635)
▲ Totaltrax Inc .... D 302 514-0600
  New Castle (G-5778)

3625 Relays & Indl Controls

Automation Inc .... F 302 999-0971
  Wilmington (G-9187)
Tricklestar Inc 888 700-1098
  Wilmington (G-12970)
Ultrafine Technologies Inc .... G 302 384-6513
  Wilmington (G-13009)
Val-Tech Inc .... G 302 738-0500
  Newark (G-7638)
Xrosswater USA LLC .... G 917 310-1344
  Newark (G-7726)

3629 Electrical Indl Apparatus, NEC

Dane Waters .... G 302 377-9999
  Claymont (G-727)
Orange Power Electric Inc .... G 205 886-5815
  Wilmington (G-11969)
Voltvault Inc .... G 302 981-5339
  Newark (G-7664)
Wirelisity Inc .... G 213 816-1957
  Lewes (G-3829)
Xerafy Inc .... G 817 938-4197
  Wilmington (G-13317)

3631 Household Cooking Eqpt

Five In One Oven Inc .... G 888 401-3911
  Newark (G-6591)

3634 Electric Household Appliances

Econat Inc .... G 201 925-5239
  Middletown (G-4048)

Idylc Homes LLC .... G 302 295-3719
  Wilmington (G-10995)
McGinnis Farms LLC 302 841-8175
  Dagsboro (G-920)

3635 Household Vacuum Cleaners

Healthy Homes De Inc .... G 302 998-1001
  Wilmington (G-10871)

3641 Electric Lamps

Acuity Brands Lighting Inc .... E 302 476-2055
  New Castle (G-5002)
Blue Arrow Contract Manufactur .... G 302 738-2583
  Newark (G-6098)
Glass Technologists Inc .... G 240 682-0966
  Middletown (G-4087)

3643 Current-Carrying Wiring Devices

DMC Power Inc .... F 302 276-0303
  New Castle (G-5257)
Leggs Hanes Bali Playtex Otlt .... G 302 227-8943
  Rehoboth Beach (G-7985)
◆ NGK Spark Plugs USA Holdg Inc .... G 302 288-0131
  Wilmington (G-11885)
Nouvir Lightning Corporation .... G 302 628-9888
  Seaford (G-8331)
Security Satellite 302 376-0241
  Middletown (G-4235)
Whitaker LLC .... G 302 633-2740
  Wilmington (G-13187)

3644 Noncurrent-Carrying Wiring Devices

302 Aquatics LLC .... G 302 222-4807
  Dover (G-1068)

3645 Residential Lighting Fixtures

Acuity Brands Lighting Inc .... E 302 476-2055
  New Castle (G-5002)
Fme Lighting LLC 877 234-8460
  Rehoboth Beach (G-7936)
▲ Pemco Lighting Products Inc .... G 302 892-9000
  Wilmington (G-12061)

3646 Commercial, Indl & Institutional Lighting Fixtures

Acuity Brands Lighting Inc .... E 302 476-2055
  New Castle (G-5002)
Illumination Technology Inc .... G 410 430-5349
  Delmar (G-1004)
▲ Pemco Lighting Products Inc .... G 302 892-9000
  Wilmington (G-12061)
Pemco Lighting Products LLC .... G 302 892-9000
  Wilmington (G-12062)
Rigel Energy Group LLC .... F 888 624-9844
  Wilmington (G-12421)
▲ Way To Go Led Lighting Company ...... F 844 312-4574
  Newark (G-7679)

3647 Vehicular Lighting Eqpt

▲ Arrow Safety Device Co .... F 302 856-2516
  Selbyville (G-8450)
G K Associates Inc .... G 302 381-2824
  Rehoboth Beach (G-7940)

3648 Lighting Eqpt, NEC

Detweilers Lighting .... G 302 678-5804
  Hartly (G-2919)
Evergreen Led .... G 302 218-7819
  Townsend (G-8785)
▲ Jaykal Led Solutions Inc .... G 302 295-0015
  Harbeson (G-2788)
Ledtolight 941 323-6664
  Wilmington (G-11354)
Main Light Industries Inc .... C 302 998-8017
  Wilmington (G-11491)
Newport .... G 302 995-2840
  Wilmington (G-11877)
Smb Lighting .... G 302 733-0664
  Newark (G-7448)
Sun-In-One Inc .... G 302 762-3100
  Wilmington (G-12798)

3651 Household Audio & Video Eqpt

Acoustic Audio Tek LLC .... G 302 685-2113
  Wilmington (G-8924)
Bat Electronics Inc .... G 302 999-8855
  Wilmington (G-9259)

SIC SECTION

Brandywine Electronics Corp............F...... 302 324-9992
  Bear (G-56)
Helix Inc Ta Audioworks.................G...... 302 285-0555
  Middletown (G-4107)
Maxbright Inc..................................E...... 281 616-7999
  Lewes (G-3626)
Sound-N-Secure Inc......................G...... 302 424-3670
  Milford (G-4563)
Soundboks Inc................................G...... 213 436-5888
  Wilmington (G-12684)

3652 Phonograph Records & Magnetic Tape

Saregama India Limited..................G...... 859 490-0156
  Newark (G-7390)

3661 Telephone & Telegraph Apparatus

2nu Photonics LLC.........................G...... 302 388-2261
  Newark (G-5854)
B Williams Holding Corp.................F...... 302 656-8596
  Wilmington (G-9214)
◆ Bio Medic Corporation................F...... 302 628-4300
  Seaford (G-8170)
Central Firm LLC............................G...... 610 470-9836
  Wilmington (G-9615)
Photon Programming......................G...... 302 328-2925
  New Castle (G-5622)
Shiv Baba LLC.................................F...... 703 314-1203
  Dover (G-2077)
Siemens..G...... 302 220-1544
  Wilmington (G-12611)
Siemens AG....................................G...... 302 836-2933
  Bear (G-321)
Siemens Corporation......................G...... 302 220-1544
  New Castle (G-5709)
Targus U S A..................................G...... 302 644-2311
  Lewes (G-3778)
Versitron Inc..................................D...... 302 894-0699
  Newark (G-7653)

3663 Radio & T V Communications, Systs & Eqpt, Broadcast/Studio

3d Microwave LLC..........................G...... 302 497-0223
  Laurel (G-3188)
C4-Nvis USA LLC............................G...... 213 465-5089
  Dover (G-1246)
Dorsia Alliance Ltd.........................G...... 302 492-5052
  Wilmington (G-10207)
Executive Broadband......................G...... 302 463-4335
  Newark (G-6552)
Gatesair Inc....................................G...... 513 459-3400
  Wilmington (G-10676)
Geo-Fence Inc................................G...... 763 516-8934
  Dover (G-1589)
▲ Integrated Data Corp................G...... 302 295-5057
  Wilmington (G-11048)
Interdgital Communications Inc.....D...... 610 878-7800
  Wilmington (G-11058)
Interdigital Inc...............................G...... 302 281-3600
  Wilmington (G-11059)
Interdigital Wireless Inc.................D...... 302 281-3600
  Wilmington (G-11061)
Newcosmos LLC.............................G...... 302 838-1935
  Bear (G-265)
Oros Communications LLC.............G...... 954 228-7399
  Wilmington (G-11976)
Quinteccent Inc..............................G...... 443 838-5447
  Selbyville (G-8536)
Ted Johnson Enterprises................G...... 302 349-5925
  Greenwood (G-2765)

3669 Communications Eqpt, NEC

Eastern Shore Metal Detectors......G...... 302 628-1985
  Seaford (G-8230)
G K Associates Inc.........................G...... 302 381-2824
  Rehoboth Beach (G-7940)
Grillo Holdings Inc..........................G...... 302 261-9668
  Wilmington (G-10785)
Hill & Smith Inc..............................E...... 302 328-3220
  New Castle (G-5395)
Nt Ezlinq Holdings LLC..................G...... 302 351-3051
  Wilmington (G-11918)
Phoenix Vitae Holdings LLC..........G...... 302 351-3047
  Wilmington (G-12127)
Versitron Inc..................................D...... 302 894-0699
  Newark (G-7653)
Wayman Fire Protection Inc..........C...... 302 994-5757
  Wilmington (G-13125)

3672 Printed Circuit Boards

Rogers Corporation........................C...... 302 834-2100
  Bear (G-312)
Suretronix Solutions LLC................G...... 302 407-3146
  Wilmington (G-12817)
Via Networks Inc...........................G...... 314 727-2087
  Wilmington (G-13075)

3674 Semiconductors

Alphasense Inc...............................G...... 302 998-1116
  Wilmington (G-9031)
▲ Bloom Energy Corporation.......E...... 302 733-7524
  Newark (G-6096)
Dupont De Nemours Inc................B...... 302 774-1000
  Wilmington (G-10251)
Dupont Displays Inc.......................E...... 805 562-9293
  Wilmington (G-10253)
▲ Jaykal Led Solutions Inc..........G...... 302 295-0015
  Harbeson (G-2788)
Laser Management Group LLC.....G...... 302 992-9030
  Wilmington (G-11332)
Quarta-Rad Inc...............................G...... 201 877-2002
  Wilmington (G-12283)
Solar Unlimited North Amer LLC...G...... 302 542-4580
  Lewes (G-3754)
Suretronix Solutions LLC................G...... 302 407-3146
  Wilmington (G-12817)
Thermoelectrics Unlimited Inc.......G...... 302 764-6618
  Wilmington (G-12896)
Wiregateit LLC...............................G...... 302 538-1304
  Newark (G-7712)

3677 Electronic Coils & Transformers

Xergy Inc.......................................G...... 302 629-5768
  Harrington (G-2911)

3679 Electronic Components, NEC

AC Group Inc.................................G...... 201 840-5566
  Wilmington (G-8910)
Atlantic Industrial Optics................G...... 302 856-7905
  Georgetown (G-2438)
Century Seals Inc..........................E...... 302 629-0324
  Seaford (G-8185)
Eeco Inc..G...... 302 456-1448
  Newark (G-6506)
Hollingsead International LLC.......B...... 302 855-5888
  Georgetown (G-2559)
Intelexmicro Inc.............................G...... 302 907-9545
  Laurel (G-3240)
Lexatys LLC....................................F...... 302 715-5029
  Laurel (G-3259)
Pbtv Global Inc..............................F...... 302 292-1400
  Wilmington (G-12050)
Pierce Design & Tool.....................G...... 302 222-3339
  Dover (G-1958)
Suretronix Solutions LLC................G...... 302 407-3146
  Wilmington (G-12817)
Val-Tech Inc...................................E...... 302 738-0500
  Newark (G-7638)

3691 Storage Batteries

Clarios LLC.....................................B...... 302 378-9885
  Middletown (G-3994)
Clarios LLC.....................................F...... 302 696-3221
  Middletown (G-3995)
Talostech LLC.................................G...... 302 332-9236
  New Castle (G-5752)

3692 Primary Batteries: Dry & Wet

Energizer Holdings Inc..................G...... 302 678-6767
  Dover (G-1522)
Talostech LLC.................................G...... 302 332-9236
  New Castle (G-5752)

3694 Electrical Eqpt For Internal Combustion Engines

Htk Automotive USA Corp............E...... 888 998-9366
  Wilmington (G-10968)
Main Office Inc..............................G...... 302 732-3460
  Dagsboro (G-916)
Solavitek Engineering Inc.............G...... 514 949-6981
  Newark (G-7455)

3695 Recording Media

Currency Technics Metrics Inc......E...... 302 482-4846
  Wilmington (G-9919)

National Tape Duplicators..............G...... 302 999-1110
  Wilmington (G-11813)

3699 Electrical Machinery, Eqpt & Splys, NEC

Alphasense Inc...............................G...... 302 998-1116
  Wilmington (G-9031)
Chimes Metro Inc..........................G...... 302 452-3400
  New Castle (G-5149)
Dave Smagala................................G...... 302 383-2761
  Claymont (G-729)
Dp Fire & Safety Inc......................F...... 302 998-5430
  Wilmington (G-10217)
Electric Beach Tanning Company..G...... 302 730-8266
  Dover (G-1513)
Excape Entertainment US Ltd.......G...... 949 943-9219
  Wilmington (G-10457)
Gentleman Door Company Inc.....G...... 302 239-4045
  Yorklyn (G-13366)
Golage Inc.....................................G...... 302 526-1181
  Dover (G-1597)
Inc Chimes....................................G...... 302 449-1926
  Townsend (G-8794)
Max Virtual LLC.............................G...... 302 525-8112
  Newark (G-7006)
Metatron Inc..................................G...... 619 550-4668
  Dover (G-1843)
Mohawk Electrical Systems Inc....E...... 302 422-2500
  Milford (G-4509)
Net Monarch.................................G...... 302 994-9407
  Wilmington (G-11837)
▲ North American Brands Inc....E...... 519 680-0385
  Wilmington (G-11897)
Precision Systems Inds LLC..........G...... 224 388-9837
  Wilmington (G-12207)
Psp Corp..G...... 302 764-7730
  Wilmington (G-12260)
Resonate Forward LLC...................G...... 302 893-9504
  Hockessin (G-3134)
Securitech Inc................................F...... 302 996-9230
  Wilmington (G-12570)
SIC Biometrics Inc.........................G...... 866 499-8377
  Newark (G-7421)
Thermal Transf Composites LLC...G...... 302 635-7156
  Hockessin (G-3159)
Withyouwithme Inc.......................G...... 202 377-9743
  Wilmington (G-13281)

37 TRANSPORTATION EQUIPMENT

3711 Motor Vehicles & Car Bodies

Aetna Hose Hook and Ladder Co..G...... 302 454-3300
  Newark (G-5917)
International Std Elc Corp.............F...... 302 427-3769
  Wilmington (G-11068)
North ATL Intl Ocean Carier..........G...... 786 275-5352
  New Castle (G-5576)
Penske Performance Inc...............D...... 302 656-2082
  Wilmington (G-12075)
Revnation Ltd Liability Co.............G...... 202 672-4120
  Magnolia (G-3906)
Star Campus II..............................G...... 302 514-7586
  Newark (G-7483)
Victory Racing Chassis Inc............G...... 302 593-2255
  Wilmington (G-13079)

3713 Truck & Bus Bodies

Kruger Trailers Inc........................G...... 302 856-2577
  Georgetown (G-2584)
▼ T & J Murray Worldwide Svcs..F...... 302 736-1790
  Dover (G-2125)

3714 Motor Vehicle Parts & Access

Alternative Eco Energy LLC...........G...... 404 434-0660
  Newark (G-5948)
▼ Autoport Inc............................E...... 302 658-5100
  New Castle (G-5057)
Bever Mobility Products Inc.........G...... 312 375-0300
  Wilmington (G-9319)
▲ Craig Ball Sales Inc.................G...... 302 628-9900
  Seaford (G-8212)
Forward Motion Inc......................G...... 302 658-2829
  Wilmington (G-10596)
Gif North America LLC..................B...... 703 969-9243
  Rehoboth Beach (G-7948)
▼ Hayloft Enterprises Inc............G...... 302 656-7600
  Wilmington (G-10857)
Horizon Intl Holdings LLC............A...... 302 636-5401
  Wilmington (G-10954)

37 TRANSPORTATION EQUIPMENT

Lkq Northeast Inc ....G..... 800 223-0171
  Dover *(G-1793)*
NAPA M3 Inc ....G..... 719 660-6263
  Wilmington *(G-11800)*
◆ NGK North America Inc ....G..... 302 654-1344
  Wilmington *(G-11884)*
Pressair International ....G..... 302 636-5440
  Wilmington *(G-12222)*
Smartwheel Inc ....G..... 617 542-7400
  Wilmington *(G-12656)*
Steering Sltions Ip Holdg Corp ....G..... 313 556-5000
  Wilmington *(G-12749)*
Sword Parts LLC ....G..... 302 246-1346
  Rehoboth Beach *(G-8093)*
▲ Wilmington Fibre Specialty Co ....E..... 302 328-7525
  New Castle *(G-5836)*

3715 Truck Trailers

24 Hr Truck Services LLC ....G..... 609 516-7307
  Newark *(G-5853)*
Kruger Trailers Inc ....G..... 302 856-2577
  Georgetown *(G-2584)*
Utility/Eastern ....E..... 302 337-7400
  Bridgeville *(G-528)*

3721 Aircraft

Aircraft Specialties ....G..... 302 762-0816
  Wilmington *(G-8995)*
Anthony Streett ....G..... 302 528-2861
  Dover *(G-1128)*
Boeing Company ....A..... 302 735-2922
  Dover *(G-1219)*
Central Pacific Helicopters ....G..... 760 786-4163
  Lewes *(G-3411)*
Grindstone Aviation LLC ....G..... 302 324-1993
  New Castle *(G-5363)*
▲ Ilc Dover LP ....B..... 302 335-3911
  Frederica *(G-2407)*
Pats Aircraft LLC ....C..... 855 236-1638
  Georgetown *(G-2613)*
Pegasus Air Inc ....G..... 302 875-3540
  Laurel *(G-3269)*
Webro Holdings LLC ....G..... 302 314-3334
  Rehoboth Beach *(G-8109)*

3724 Aircraft Engines & Engine Parts

Acurio LLC ....G..... 201 932-8160
  Wilmington *(G-8931)*
Garrett Transportation I Inc ....G..... 973 455-2000
  Wilmington *(G-10672)*
General Electric Company ....C..... 302 631-1300
  Newark *(G-6644)*
Greenwich Aerogroup Inc ....G..... 302 834-5400
  Middletown *(G-4093)*
Honeywell International Inc ....A..... 302 322-4071
  New Castle *(G-5402)*
MB Aerospace Acp ....G..... 586 772-2500
  Wilmington *(G-11581)*
S&H Logistics LLC ....G..... 708 548-8982
  Dover *(G-2051)*
▲ Tesla Industries Inc ....E..... 302 324-8910
  New Castle *(G-5763)*
Webro Holdings LLC ....G..... 302 314-3334
  Rehoboth Beach *(G-8109)*

3728 Aircraft Parts & Eqpt, NEC

Decrane Aircraft Systems ....A..... 302 253-0390
  Georgetown *(G-2496)*
Envoy Flight Systems Inc ....G..... 302 738-1788
  Newark *(G-6534)*
▼ Exploration Systems & Tech ....G..... 302 335-3911
  Wilmington *(G-10461)*
Firefly Drone Operations Llc ....G..... 305 206-6955
  Wilmington *(G-10543)*
Global Air Strategy Inc ....G..... 302 229-5889
  Newark *(G-6665)*
Nakuuruq Solutions ....G..... 302 526-2223
  Dover *(G-1883)*
Patrick Aircraft Group LLC ....E..... 302 854-9300
  Georgetown *(G-2612)*
Pats Aircraft LLC ....C..... 855 236-1638
  Georgetown *(G-2613)*
Webro Holdings LLC ....G..... 302 314-3334
  Rehoboth Beach *(G-8109)*

3732 Boat Building & Repairing

Broadwater Oyster Company LLC ....G..... 610 220-7776
  Rehoboth Beach *(G-7879)*

Croker Oars Usa Inc ....G..... 302 897-6705
  Townsend *(G-8776)*
F & S Boat Works ....E..... 302 838-5500
  Bear *(G-147)*
Nanticoke Industries LLC ....G..... 302 245-8825
  Seaford *(G-8324)*
Saxton Maritime Services LLC ....G..... 415 870-3881
  Lewes *(G-3731)*

3743 Railroad Eqpt

Delaware Car Company ....E..... 302 655-6665
  Wilmington *(G-10012)*
Revnation Ltd Liability Co ....G..... 202 672-4120
  Magnolia *(G-3906)*

3751 Motorcycles, Bicycles & Parts

Infinity Choppers ....G..... 302 249-7282
  Georgetown *(G-2565)*
Ross Bicycles LLC ....G..... 888 392-5628
  Lewes *(G-3726)*

3761 Guided Missiles & Space Vehicles

Lockheed Martin Overseas LLC ....G..... 301 897-6923
  Wilmington *(G-11422)*

3795 Tanks & Tank Components

Intech Services ....G..... 302 366-1442
  Newark *(G-6787)*

3799 Transportation Eqpt, NEC

Affordable Recreation LLC ....G..... 603 635-2101
  Lewes *(G-3327)*
Circle C Outfit LLC ....G..... 302 337-8828
  Bridgeville *(G-459)*
Michael C Rapa ....G..... 302 236-4423
  Laurel *(G-3264)*
Pessagno Equipment Inc ....G..... 302 738-7001
  Newark *(G-7205)*
Stallard Chassis Co ....F..... 302 292-1800
  Newark *(G-7479)*

38 MEASURING, ANALYZING AND CONTROLLING INSTRUMENTS; PHOTOGRAPHIC, MEDICAL AN

3812 Search, Detection, Navigation & Guidance Systs & Instrs

Absolute Cyber Defense ....G..... 850 532-0233
  Dover *(G-1078)*
First Line Defense LLC ....G..... 302 287-2764
  Smyrna *(G-8634)*
Magen Tactical Defense ....G..... 484 589-0670
  Claymont *(G-779)*
Pilots Assn For Bay River Del ....E..... 302 645-2229
  Lewes *(G-3690)*
Raytheon Company ....C..... 302 656-1339
  Wilmington *(G-12332)*
Russell Associates Inc ....G..... 443 992-5777
  Newark *(G-7370)*
Spectr-Physics Hldings USA Inc ....G..... 302 478-4600
  Wilmington *(G-12698)*
▲ Tesla Industries Inc ....E..... 302 324-8910
  New Castle *(G-5763)*

3821 Laboratory Apparatus & Furniture

Azzota Corporation ....G..... 877 649-2746
  Claymont *(G-698)*
◆ Bio Medic Corporation ....F..... 302 628-4300
  Seaford *(G-8170)*
Delaware Technology Park Inc ....G..... 302 452-1100
  Newark *(G-6417)*
L F Systems Corp ....F..... 302 322-0460
  New Castle *(G-5471)*
Life Sciences Intl LLC ....G..... 603 436-9444
  Wilmington *(G-11385)*
Nanodrop Technologies LLC ....E..... 302 479-7707
  Wilmington *(G-11798)*
Safeguard Dx Laboratory ....G..... 888 919-8275
  Wilmington *(G-12517)*

3822 Automatic Temperature Controls

Air Liquide America LP ....G..... 302 225-2132
  Wilmington *(G-8992)*
Energy Systems Tech Inc ....G..... 302 368-0443
  Newark *(G-6528)*

Sewickley Capital Inc ....G..... 302 793-4964
  Wilmington *(G-12589)*
▲ Totaltrax Inc ....D..... 302 514-0600
  New Castle *(G-5778)*
Val-Tech Inc ....E..... 302 738-0500
  Newark *(G-7638)*

3823 Indl Instruments For Meas, Display & Control

Acorn Energy Inc ....G..... 302 656-1708
  Wilmington *(G-8923)*
▲ American Meter Holdings Corp ......G..... 302 477-0208
  Wilmington *(G-9054)*
Ametek Inc ....D..... 302 456-4400
  Newark *(G-5962)*
Applied Analytics Inc ....E..... 781 791-5005
  Newark *(G-5985)*
Delaware Capital Formation Inc ....G..... 302 793-4921
  Wilmington *(G-10010)*
DLS Discovery ....G..... 302 654-3345
  Wilmington *(G-10175)*
Ecomo Inc ....G..... 412 567-3867
  Dover *(G-1502)*
Eeco Inc ....G..... 302 456-1448
  Newark *(G-6506)*
Engineered Systems & Designs ....G..... 302 456-0446
  Wilmington *(G-10402)*
Hexagon Metrology Inc ....G..... 302 351-3580
  Wilmington *(G-10899)*
▼ K-Tron Investment Co ....E..... 856 589-0500
  Wilmington *(G-11217)*
McCabes Mechanical Service Inc .....F..... 302 854-9001
  Georgetown *(G-2599)*
Quboai Corporation ....G..... 484 889-5789
  Wilmington *(G-12285)*
Romer Labs Technology Inc ....E..... 855 337-6637
  Newark *(G-7363)*
Testek Aerospace Holdings LLC ......G..... 302 658-7581
  Wilmington *(G-12885)*

3824 Fluid Meters & Counters

▲ American Meter Holdings Corp ......G..... 302 477-0208
  Wilmington *(G-9054)*
Meterpro Services Inc ....G..... 302 227-8596
  Rehoboth Beach *(G-8004)*

3825 Instrs For Measuring & Testing Electricity

AC Group Inc ....G..... 201 840-5566
  Wilmington *(G-8910)*
Advance Nanotech Inc ....G..... 212 583-0080
  Wilmington *(G-8948)*
Agilent Technologies Inc ....A..... 408 345-8886
  Wilmington *(G-8978)*
Agilent Technologies Inc ....A..... 877 424-4536
  Wilmington *(G-8979)*
Aim Research Co ....G..... 302 235-5940
  Hockessin *(G-2953)*
Engineered Systems & Designs ....G..... 302 456-0446
  Wilmington *(G-10402)*
Pcu Systems LLC ....G..... 888 780-9728
  Wilmington *(G-12053)*
Spectr-Physics Hldings USA Inc ....G..... 302 478-4600
  Wilmington *(G-12698)*
Steven Abdill ....G..... 443 243-6864
  Wilmington *(G-12758)*
Suretronix Solutions LLC ....G..... 302 407-3146
  Wilmington *(G-12817)*

3826 Analytical Instruments

Ametek Inc ....D..... 302 456-4400
  Newark *(G-5962)*
Apollo Scitech LLC ....G..... 302 861-6557
  Newark *(G-5983)*
Atlantic Remediation ....F..... 610 444-5513
  Hockessin *(G-2960)*
Axess Corporation ....G..... 302 292-8500
  New Castle *(G-5061)*
▲ B & W Tek Inc ....B..... 302 368-7788
  Wilmington *(G-6032)*
B&W Tek LLC ....D..... 302 368-7824
  Newark *(G-6038)*
Bia Separations Inc ....G..... 510 740-4045
  Wilmington *(G-9326)*
Bonna-Agela Technologies Inc ....D..... 302 438-8798
  Hockessin *(G-2966)*
▲ Creative Devices Inc ....G..... 302 378-5433
  Middletown *(G-4014)*

39 MISCELLANEOUS MANUFACTURING INDUSTRIES

◆ Denovix Inc .... E 302 442-6911
   Wilmington (G-10110)
Joint Anlytcl Systms (amrcs) .... G 302 607-0088
   Newark (G-6849)
M&M Mass Spec Consulting LLC .... G 302 250-4488
   Newark (G-6967)
Markes International Inc .... G 302 656-5500
   Wilmington (G-11533)
◆ Miles Scientific Corporation .... F 302 737-6960
   Newark (G-7039)
Mstm LLC .... G 302 239-4447
   Newark (G-7068)
Ribodynamics LLC .... G 518 339-6605
   Wilmington (G-12405)
Separation Methods Tech Inc .... F 302 368-0610
   Newark (G-7408)
Sisuaq Scientific .... G 302 739-3073
   Wilmington (G-12635)
Spectr-Physics Hldings USA Inc .... G 302 478-4600
   Wilmington (G-12698)
▲ Supercritical Fluid Tech .... G 302 738-3420
   Newark (G-7511)
Supercritical Fluid Tech .... G 302 738-3420
   Newark (G-7512)
▲ Ta Instruments - Waters LLC .... C 302 427-4000
   New Castle (G-5751)
Ttna Energy Systems LLC .... G 302 384-9147
   Wilmington (G-12990)
Wilmington Infrared Tech .... G 302 234-6761
   Wilmington (G-13236)

3827 Optical Instruments

Atlantic Industrial Optics .... G 302 856-7905
   Georgetown (G-2438)
Docs Medical LLC .... G 301 401-1489
   Bear (G-122)
Spectr-Physics Hldings USA Inc .... G 302 478-4600
   Wilmington (G-12698)

3829 Measuring & Controlling Devices, NEC

1 A Lifesafer Inc .... G 800 634-3077
   Harrington (G-2803)
1 A Lifesafer Inc .... G 800 634-3077
   Seaford (G-8132)
1 A Lifesafer Inc .... G 800 634-3077
   Georgetown (G-2416)
1 A Lifesafer Inc .... G 800 634-3077
   Harbeson (G-2771)
1 A Lifesafer Inc .... G 800 634-3077
   Millsboro (G-4617)
1 A Lifesafer Inc .... G 800 634-3077
   Newark (G-5850)
1 A Lifesafer Inc .... G 800 634-3077
   Dover (G-1062)
1 A Lifesafer Inc .... G 800 634-3077
   Milford (G-4296)
1 A Lifesafer Inc .... G 800 634-3077
   Lewes (G-3315)
1 A Lifesafer Inc .... G 800 634-3077
   Claymont (G-683)
A S I Controls .... G 302 629-7730
   Seaford (G-8135)
Arrim LLC .... G 617 697-7914
   Wilmington (G-9134)
Avatar Instruments Inc .... G 302 703-6865
   Lewes (G-3360)
Hanbang Group .... G 626 506-7585
   Newark (G-6705)
Horney Industrial Electronics .... G 302 337-3600
   Bridgeville (G-483)
Industrial Physics Inc .... G 302 613-5600
   New Castle (G-5414)
Maintenance Troubleshooting .... G 302 692-0871
   Newark (G-6976)
Millennium Prcess Contrls Svcs .... F 302 455-1717
   Bear (G-256)
Peeper Vehicle Technology Corp .... G 800 971-4134
   Dover (G-1943)
Quarta-Rad Inc .... G 201 877-2002
   Wilmington (G-12283)
▲ Sepax Technologies Inc .... F 302 366-1101
   Newark (G-7409)
Solvetech Inc .... G 302 798-5400
   Wilmington (G-12680)
Spekciton Biosciences LLC .... G 302 353-2694
   Wilmington (G-12702)
Testex Inc .... G 302 731-5693
   Newark (G-7558)

▲ Testing Machines Inc .... E 302 613-5600
   New Castle (G-5764)
Toxtrap Inc .... G 302 698-1400
   Dover (G-2156)

3841 Surgical & Medical Instrs & Apparatus

Caveman Design Inc .... G 302 234-9969
   Hockessin (G-2980)
Clarius Mobile Health Corp .... G 778 800-9975
   Lewes (G-3425)
Datwyler Pharma Packg USA Inc .... G 302 603-8020
   Middletown (G-4019)
Delamed Supplies Inc .... G 917 517-4492
   Claymont (G-731)
Delaware Instrument Lab LLC .... G 302 737-6250
   Newark (G-6389)
Denco Inc .... G 302 798-4200
   Wilmington (G-10108)
Docs Medical LLC .... G 301 401-1489
   Bear (G-122)
E I Du Pont De Nemours & Co .... E 302 996-4000
   Wilmington (G-10293)
Fbk Medical Tubing Inc .... E 302 855-0585
   Georgetown (G-2527)
Hologic Inc .... E 302 631-2700
   Newark (G-6738)
Moor Instruments Inc .... G 302 798-7470
   Wilmington (G-11743)
Optometry Associates PC .... G 302 654-6490
   Wilmington (G-11964)
▲ Smith & Nephew Holdings Inc .... G 302 884-6720
   Wilmington (G-12659)
W L Gore & Associates Inc .... C 302 368-3700
   Newark (G-7672)

3842 Orthopedic, Prosthetic & Surgical Appliances/Splys

Choy Wilson Cdgn .... G 302 424-4141
   Milford (G-4351)
Christana Ctr For Wns Wellness .... G 302 454-9800
   Newark (G-6204)
Dads Workwear Inc .... G 302 663-0068
   Laurel (G-3219)
Delmarv Orthtcs & Prosthtcs .... G 302 678-8311
   Dover (G-1407)
Delmarva Laboratories Inc .... G 302 645-2226
   Milton (G-4891)
E&N Surgical LLC .... G 860 471-0786
   Wilmington (G-10311)
Family Respiratory & Med Supl .... G 302 653-3602
   Smyrna (G-8632)
Frizbee Medical Inc .... G 424 901-1534
   Wilmington (G-10643)
Harry J Lawall & Son Inc .... F 302 429-7630
   Wilmington (G-10844)
▲ Ilc Dover LP .... B 302 335-3911
   Frederica (G-2407)
Independence Prosthtcs-Ortho .... G 302 369-9476
   Newark (G-6770)
Jarel Industries LLC .... G 336 782-0697
   Camden (G-585)
Johnson & Johnson .... E 302 652-3840
   Wilmington (G-11179)
Mih International LLC .... G 301 908-4233
   Newark (G-7038)
New Ilc Dover Inc .... F 302 335-3911
   Frederica (G-2410)
Roll-A-Bout Corporation .... G 302 736-6151
   Frederica (G-2412)
Thomas E Moore Inc .... G 302 653-2000
   Kenton (G-3186)
Wheelchair Mechanix .... G 302 478-0858
   Wilmington (G-13182)
Zimmer US Inc .... G 617 272-0062
   Camden Wyoming (G-662)

3843 Dental Eqpt & Splys

C&G Dental Studio LLC .... G 302 345-4995
   Bear (G-60)
Delaware Smile Center .... G 302 285-7645
   Middletown (G-4032)
Delmarva 2000 Ltd .... G 302 645-2226
   Milton (G-4889)
Delmarva Laboratories Inc .... G 302 645-2226
   Milton (G-4891)
Dentsply Sirona Inc .... D 302 422-4511
   Milford (G-4388)
Dentsply Sirona Inc .... D 302 422-1043
   Milford (G-4389)

Dentsply Sirona Inc .... C 302 430-7474
   Milford (G-4390)
Healthy Smiles of Delaware PA .... G 302 658-7200
   Wilmington (G-10872)
Kuraray America Inc .... F 302 992-4204
   Wilmington (G-11301)
Phocal Therapy Inc .... G 917 803-7168
   Lewes (G-3688)
Tc Dental Equipment Services .... G 302 740-9049
   Townsend (G-8826)

3844 X-ray Apparatus & Tubes

▲ Direct Radiography Corp .... C 302 631-2700
   Newark (G-6452)
E I Du Pont De Nemours & Co .... E 302 996-4000
   Wilmington (G-10293)
Hologic Inc .... C 302 631-2846
   Newark (G-6737)

3845 Electromedical & Electrotherapeutic Apparatus

▲ Direct Radiography Corp .... C 302 631-2700
   Newark (G-6452)
▲ Litecure LLC .... E 302 709-0408
   New Castle (G-5485)
Silverside Open Mri Imaging .... G 302 246-2000
   Wilmington (G-12621)
Slimstim Inc .... G 310 560-4950
   Wilmington (G-12646)

3851 Ophthalmic Goods

Essilor America Holding Co Inc .... F 214 496-4000
   Wilmington (G-10439)
Jim Kounnas Optometrists .... G 302 722-6197
   Wilmington (G-11160)
Luxottica of America Inc .... C 302 322-4131
   New Castle (G-5491)

3861 Photographic Eqpt & Splys

AM Custom Tackle Inc .... G 302 945-7921
   Millsboro (G-4629)
B Williams Holding Corp .... F 302 656-8596
   Wilmington (G-9214)
Integrated Technology Systems .... G 302 429-0560
   Wilmington (G-11050)
Motopods LLC .... G 818 641-4299
   Dover (G-1875)
RDS Engineering LLC .... G 417 763-3727
   Lewes (G-3710)

3873 Watch & Clock Devices & Parts

Aurista Technologies Inc .... F 302 792-4900
   Claymont (G-696)

39 MISCELLANEOUS MANUFACTURING INDUSTRIES

3911 Jewelry: Precious Metal

Alex and Ani LLC .... G 302 731-1420
   Newark (G-5930)
Alex and Ani LLC .... G 302 227-7360
   Rehoboth Beach (G-7839)
Charles Allen Ltd .... G 302 475-5048
   Wilmington (G-9630)
Juwelo Usa Inc .... G 888 471-7614
   Wilmington (G-11211)
Lolahsoul Jewelry Inc .... G 888 771-7087
   Wilmington (G-11429)
▲ Olga N Ganoudis Jewelry .... G 302 421-9820
   Wilmington (G-11945)
Rck Soliatire LLC .... F 551 358-8400
   Rehoboth Beach (G-8043)
Silver Works Inc .... F 302 227-1707
   Rehoboth Beach (G-8076)

3914 Silverware, Plated & Stainless Steel Ware

◆ Bio Medic Corporation .... F 302 628-4300
   Seaford (G-8170)
◆ Leeber Limited USA .... F 302 733-0991
   Newark (G-6930)
Select Stainless Products LLC .... G 302 653-3062
   Clayton (G-871)

3915 Jewelers Findings & Lapidary Work

Gem Merchant LLC G 734 274-1280
Lewes *(G-3510)*

3931 Musical Instruments

Bb Custom Instruments G 302 339-3826
Georgetown *(G-2449)*

Cara Guitars Manufacturing E 302 521-0119
Wilmington *(G-9562)*

Imperial Dynasty Arts Program F 302 521-8551
Wilmington *(G-11008)*

Victor Kornbluth G 302 791-9777
Claymont *(G-815)*

3942 Dolls & Stuffed Toys

Gelfand Group Inc G 310 666-2362
Camden Wyoming *(G-642)*

Linda & Richard Partnership G 302 697-9758
Dover *(G-1790)*

Susan Straughen G 302 856-7703
Georgetown *(G-2673)*

3944 Games, Toys & Children's Vehicles

▼ Aero-Marine Laminates Inc F 302 628-3944
Seaford *(G-8141)*

Affiliate Venture Group G 302 379-6961
Wilmington *(G-8969)*

East Coast Kite Sports G 302 359-0749
Magnolia *(G-3890)*

▲ Kid Agains Inc G 631 830-5228
Dover *(G-1746)*

Kite G 302 324-9569
Bear *(G-219)*

Philymack Games LLC G 302 658-7581
Wilmington *(G-12121)*

Sandebbarnanricway Corp G 302 475-2705
Wilmington *(G-12538)*

Tetris Company LLC G 302 656-1950
Wilmington *(G-12886)*

Top Dog Best Games LLC G 949 859-8869
Wilmington *(G-12927)*

Yotta Games LLC G 425 247-0756
Wilmington *(G-13329)*

▲ Zone Systems Inc F 302 730-8888
Dover *(G-2255)*

3949 Sporting & Athletic Goods, NEC

Abbey Lein Inc G 302 239-2712
Newark *(G-5881)*

Asferik LLC G 302 981-6519
Wilmington *(G-9147)*

▲ Beachballs Com LLC G 302 628-8888
Seaford *(G-8164)*

Black & Decker Inc G 860 827-3861
Newark *(G-6087)*

Bubba Game Calls G 302 332-2004
Townsend *(G-8767)*

Bullens Bucktails Inc G 302 998-6288
Wilmington *(G-9504)*

Competition Game Calls G 302 345-7463
Wilmington *(G-9804)*

Devastator Game Calls LLC G 302 875-5328
Laurel *(G-3223)*

Disrupt Industries Deleware G 424 229-9300
Dover *(G-1429)*

Fells Point Surf Co LLC G 302 212-2005
Dewey Beach *(G-1057)*

▲ Foldfast Goals LLC G 302 478-7881
Wilmington *(G-10585)*

Golfclub LLC G 908 770-7892
Wilmington *(G-10743)*

Gym Source G 302 478-4069
Wilmington *(G-10804)*

Hague Surfboards G 302 745-9336
Lewes *(G-3528)*

J & V Shooters Supply G 302 422-5417
Milford *(G-4453)*

JC Zimny Rod Co G 302 998-9187
Wilmington *(G-11136)*

Kinetic Skateboarding G 856 375-2236
Wilmington *(G-11267)*

Liberty Parks and Playgrounds G 302 659-5083
Clayton *(G-862)*

Masley Enterprises Inc E 302 427-9885
Wilmington *(G-11561)*

Movetec Fitness Equipment LLC G 302 563-4487
Newark *(G-7064)*

National Cricket Associates G 302 454-7294
Newark *(G-7085)*

Par 4 Golf Inc G 302 227-5663
Rehoboth Beach *(G-8028)*

Planet X Skateboards G 484 886-9287
Wilmington *(G-12149)*

Prouse Enterprises LLC G 302 846-9000
Milford *(G-4531)*

Racqueteer G 302 378-1596
Middletown *(G-4209)*

Robert Fickling G 980 422-4754
Wilmington *(G-12437)*

Rope-It Golf LLC G 305 767-3481
Wilmington *(G-12474)*

◆ Rukket LLC G 855 478-5538
Wilmington *(G-12492)*

Sjm Sales Inc G 302 697-6748
Camden Wyoming *(G-657)*

Sling With ME G 302 424-0111
Milford *(G-4561)*

◆ Vulcan International Corp F 302 428-3181
Wilmington *(G-13107)*

3952 Lead Pencils, Crayons & Artist's Mtrls

Artists At Work Inc G 302 424-4427
Ellendale *(G-2257)*

3953 Marking Devices

Franklin Rubber Stamp Co Inc F 302 654-8841
Wilmington *(G-10618)*

Golden Rubber Stamp Co G 302 658-7343
Wilmington *(G-10738)*

Hot Shot Concepts G 302 947-1808
Harbeson *(G-2785)*

Stamps By Impression G 302 645-7191
Lewes *(G-3762)*

3955 Carbon Paper & Inked Ribbons

Identisource LLC G 888 716-7498
Lewes *(G-3551)*

Kent-Sussex Industries Inc B 302 422-4014
Milford *(G-4466)*

3961 Costume Jewelry & Novelties

Altschuler Micki Designs G 302 655-6867
Wilmington *(G-9035)*

Anya International LLC E 847 850-0920
Newark *(G-5976)*

Go Ahead Make My Ring G 302 235-8172
Newark *(G-6668)*

▲ Goldmine Enterprises Inc G 302 834-4314
Bear *(G-167)*

Mission Bracelets G 302 528-5065
Smyrna *(G-8681)*

Swarovski US Holding Limited G 302 737-4811
Newark *(G-7518)*

T K O Designs Inc G 302 539-6992
Bethany Beach *(G-434)*

3965 Fasteners, Buttons, Needles & Pins

Iron Lion Enterprises Inc G 302 628-8320
Seaford *(G-8273)*

3991 Brooms & Brushes

▼ Dupont Flaments - Americas LLC G 302 774-1000
Wilmington *(G-10255)*

3993 Signs & Advertising Displays

9193 4323 Quebec Inc G 855 824-0795
Newark *(G-5862)*

Ad-Art Signs Georgetown Inc G 302 856-7446
Georgetown *(G-2422)*

Alpha To Omega Signs G 302 846-3865
Delmar *(G-969)*

Arena Signs G 302 644-8300
Lewes *(G-3345)*

Art Beat G 302 834-5700
Newark *(G-5999)*

Art Guild Inc G 302 420-8056
New Castle *(G-5047)*

Austin Signs G 302 697-7321
Camden Wyoming *(G-615)*

Ball Room By Bill G 302 328-4014
New Castle *(G-5065)*

Banacom Signs Inc G 302 429-6243
Wilmington *(G-9230)*

Barbara Graphics Inc G 302 636-9040
Wilmington *(G-9248)*

Beachview Mgmt Inc G 302 227-3280
Georgetown *(G-2450)*

Clear Channel Outdoor Inc E 302 658-5520
Wilmington *(G-9739)*

D By D Printing LLC G 302 659-3373
Dover *(G-1335)*

Da Vinci Painting G 302 229-0644
Newark *(G-6343)*

Dandy Signs G 301 399-8746
Ocean View *(G-7782)*

Delaware Sign Co G 302 469-5656
Felton *(G-2285)*

Delmarva Sign Co G 302 934-6188
Georgetown *(G-2508)*

DOT Pop Inc G 302 691-3160
Wilmington *(G-10208)*

East Coast Signs & Graph G 302 335-5824
Milford *(G-4401)*

Electro-Art Sign Company G 302 322-1108
New Castle *(G-5284)*

Fastsigns G 302 998-6755
Wilmington *(G-10505)*

First State Signs Inc F 302 744-9990
Dover *(G-1559)*

Friends and Sign G 302 368-4794
Newark *(G-6624)*

Galaxy Sign & Lighting G 302 757-5349
Wilmington *(G-10664)*

Gary M Munch Inc G 302 525-8301
Newark *(G-6640)*

Gatto Graphix LLC G 302 598-5377
Wilmington *(G-10678)*

Gotshadeonline Inc G 302 832-8468
Bear *(G-168)*

Grier Signs G 302 737-4823
Newark *(G-6690)*

Griffs Signs LLC G 302 784-5596
Wilmington *(G-10784)*

Guedon Co G 302 375-6151
Wilmington *(G-10797)*

Harting Graphics Ltd G 302 762-6397
Wilmington *(G-10845)*

Health & Social Svcs Del Dept E 302 255-9800
New Castle *(G-5383)*

Health & Social Svcs Del Dept E 302 255-9855
New Castle *(G-5385)*

Henninger Printing Co Inc G 302 934-8119
Millsboro *(G-4705)*

Hes Sign Services LLC G 302 232-2100
New Castle *(G-5393)*

Hoopty Do G 302 324-1742
New Castle *(G-5403)*

Impact Graphix G 302 337-7076
Seaford *(G-8270)*

Insta Signs Plus Inc F 302 324-8800
New Castle *(G-5419)*

JD Sign Company LLC G 302 786-2761
Harrington *(G-2855)*

Jenner Enterprises Inc F 302 998-6755
Wilmington *(G-11145)*

Jenner Enterprises Inc G 302 479-5686
Wilmington *(G-11146)*

Joe Gerace G 302 994-3114
Wilmington *(G-11165)*

JP Signdesign Co G 302 733-7547
Newark *(G-6854)*

Kent Sign Company Inc F 302 697-2181
Dover *(G-1739)*

Kgc Enterprises Inc G 302 668-1835
Wilmington *(G-11255)*

Lambertson Signs G 302 645-6700
Lewes *(G-3589)*

Led Sign City G 866 343-4011
Wilmington *(G-11353)*

Marjano LLC G 302 454-7446
Bear *(G-245)*

Marketing Enterprise Capyuring G 302 293-9250
Wilmington *(G-11537)*

Messick Signs & Service G 302 629-6999
Seaford *(G-8309)*

Mimesis Signs G 302 674-5566
Dover *(G-1858)*

Mr Copy Inc G 302 227-4666
Rehoboth Beach *(G-8015)*

Paul Woerner G 302 266-6282
Newark *(G-7186)*

Penney Enterprises Inc G 302 629-4430
Seaford *(G-8350)*

Penuel Sign Co G 302 856-7265
Georgetown *(G-2616)*

Persona Group LLC ....G.... 302 335-5221
Magnolia *(G-3902)*
Phillips Signs Inc ....F.... 302 629-3550
Seaford *(G-8356)*
Poppiti Signs Inc ....G.... 302 999-8003
Wilmington *(G-12186)*
Positive Signs ....G.... 302 378-9559
Middletown *(G-4195)*
Prestige Powder Inc ....G.... 302 737-7086
Newark *(G-7248)*
Quillen Signs LLC ....G.... 302 684-3661
Milton *(G-4954)*
Rentzs Sign Service ....G.... 302 378-9607
Townsend *(G-8818)*
Rocket Signs ....G.... 302 645-1425
Lewes *(G-3722)*
Sabion Sound Reinforcement Co ....G.... 302 427-0551
Wilmington *(G-12511)*
Sams Sign ....G.... 302 947-8152
Millsboro *(G-4798)*
Shekinah Glory Sign Company ....G.... 302 256-0426
Wilmington *(G-12596)*
Sign Express ....G.... 302 999-0893
Wilmington *(G-12613)*
Sign Lnguage Blitz Pblc Benft ....G.... 928 925-3842
Lewes *(G-3742)*
Sign Shop ....G.... 302 998-2443
Wilmington *(G-12614)*
Signs Rite ....G.... 302 836-6144
Newark *(G-7428)*
Signscape Designs & Signs ....G.... 302 798-2926
Wilmington *(G-12615)*
Southern Delaware Signs ....G.... 302 645-1425
Lewes *(G-3759)*
Stop Traffic ....G.... 302 604-1176
Millsboro *(G-4804)*
Trademark Signs ....G.... 484 832-5770
Wilmington *(G-12948)*
Traffic Sign Solutions Inc ....G.... 302 295-4836
Wilmington *(G-12949)*
Trophy Shop ....F.... 302 656-4438
Wilmington *(G-12984)*
Tylaur Inc ....G.... 302 894-9330
Newark *(G-7603)*
Weber Sign Co ....F.... 302 732-1429
Frankford *(G-2398)*
Wood Creations By Bill ....G.... 302 764-6497
Wilmington *(G-13294)*
X Screen Graphix ....G.... 302 422-4550
Milford *(G-4614)*

3996 Linoleum & Hard Surface Floor Coverings, NEC

Maneto Inc ....G.... 302 656-4285
Wilmington *(G-11501)*

3999 Manufacturing Industries, NEC

Albatross Industries LLC ....G.... 850 447-2150
Lewes *(G-3333)*
American Industries LLC ....G.... 302 585-0129
Milton *(G-4863)*
Anything Under Sun LLC ....G.... 302 292-1023
Newark *(G-5977)*
Avkin Inc ....F.... 302 562-7468
New Castle *(G-5059)*
Bambu Candles LLC ....G.... 917 903-2563
Newark *(G-6042)*
Barbosa Manufacturing ....G.... 302 856-6343
Georgetown *(G-2445)*
Baumann Industries Inc ....G.... 302 593-1049
Wilmington *(G-9262)*
Bell Manufacturing Company Inc ....G.... 302 703-2684
Lewes *(G-3376)*
Bold Industries LLC ....G.... 302 858-7237
Frankford *(G-2348)*
Bombshell Beauty Inc ....G.... 302 559-3011
Wilmington *(G-9392)*
Botts Industries ....G.... 302 934-1628
Millsboro *(G-4647)*
▲ **Brandywine PDT Group Intl Inc** ....E.... 302 472-1463
Wilmington *(G-9449)*
Brocks Soy Candles ....G.... 609 841-5121
Dover *(G-1234)*
Candle Parlour ....G.... 302 408-0890
Claymont *(G-706)*
Cbd Pro LLC ....G.... 443 736-9002
Laurel *(G-3210)*
Chemax Manufacturing Corp ....G.... 302 328-2440
New Castle *(G-5143)*
Chimpark LLC ....G.... 226 219-7771
New Castle *(G-5150)*
Clean As A Whistle ....G.... 302 757-5024
Newark *(G-6246)*
Clean As A Whistle Inc ....G.... 302 376-1388
Middletown *(G-3996)*
Close Cuts Lawn Svc & Ldscpg ....G.... 302 422-2248
Milford *(G-4358)*
Coastal Wood Industries ....G.... 302 398-9601
Harrington *(G-2827)*
Curry Industries LLC ....G.... 732 858-1794
Dover *(G-1331)*
Cytec Industries Inc ....G.... 302 530-7665
Wilmington *(G-9935)*
Denices Ragged Wreath ....G.... 302 220-7377
Newark *(G-6437)*
Desangosse US Inc ....G.... 302 691-6137
Wilmington *(G-10119)*
▲ **Design Specific US Inc** ....G.... 650 318-6473
Wilmington *(G-10123)*
Discount Cigarette Depot ....G.... 302 398-4447
Harrington *(G-2833)*
Dog Anya ....G.... 302 456-0108
Newark *(G-6458)*
Driftwood Candles LLC ....G.... 302 858-1600
Millville *(G-4843)*
Eastern Shore Lite Industries ....G.... 302 653-8687
Clayton *(G-848)*
Falco Industries Inc ....G.... 302 628-1170
Seaford *(G-8241)*
Footcare Technologies Inc ....G.... 704 301-6966
Milton *(G-4907)*
Gardner Industries Inc ....G.... 302 448-9195
Seaford *(G-8249)*
Gibson Industries ....G.... 302 653-7874
Clayton *(G-854)*
Good Manufacturing Practices ....G.... 302 222-6808
Dover *(G-1601)*
Goodwill Industries Delaware ....G.... 302 337-8561
Bridgeville *(G-475)*
Grayling Industries Inc ....G.... 302 629-6860
Frederica *(G-2404)*
Grays Peak LLC ....G.... 302 288-0670
Dover *(G-1607)*
Hackett Industries LLC ....G.... 302 357-2539
Wilmington *(G-10816)*
Haunted Industries ....G.... 302 836-5823
Bear *(G-179)*
▼ **Hirsh Industries Inc** ....G.... 302 678-4990
Dover *(G-1648)*
Icy Pup ....G.... 302 777-1776
Fenwick Island *(G-2337)*
Invisible Hand Labs LLC ....G.... 434 989-9642
Wilmington *(G-11074)*
ISA Professional Ltd ....G.... 647 869-1552
Wilmington *(G-11086)*
Island Genius LLC ....G.... 888 529-5506
Wilmington *(G-11089)*
J M Industries ....G.... 302 893-0363
Hockessin *(G-3061)*
Jjs Industries LP ....G.... 302 690-2957
Wilmington *(G-11161)*
K9 Natural Foods USA LLC ....E.... 855 596-2887
Wilmington *(G-11219)*
Kershaw Industries ....G.... 302 464-1051
Middletown *(G-4121)*
Klh Industries LLC ....G.... 800 348-0758
Lewes *(G-3583)*
Laytons Umbrellas ....G.... 302 249-1958
Laurel *(G-3257)*
Lily Wreaths ....G.... 202 251-6004
Harrington *(G-2865)*
Loyalty Is Earned Inc ....G.... 347 606-6383
Wilmington *(G-11445)*
M and J Industries ....G.... 302 559-5005
Wilmington *(G-11468)*
Macknyfe Specialties ....G.... 302 239-4904
Hockessin *(G-3084)*
Maf Industries ....G.... 302 249-1254
Seaford *(G-8299)*
Martial Industries LLC ....G.... 302 983-5742
Middletown *(G-4147)*
Maws Tails Mfg ....G.... 302 740-7664
Milton *(G-4932)*
Mazindustries ....G.... 302 292-3636
Newark *(G-7007)*
Mia Bellas Candles ....G.... 302 331-7038
Hartly *(G-2935)*
Michael J Munroe ....G.... 804 240-7188
Magnolia *(G-3899)*
Millies Scented Rocks LLC ....G.... 302 331-9232
Magnolia *(G-3900)*
MMR Industries Inc ....G.... 302 999-9561
Wilmington *(G-11717)*
Mnr Industries LLC ....G.... 443 485-6213
Dover *(G-1866)*
Monogram Specialties ....G.... 302 292-2424
Newark *(G-7052)*
Myrle Manufacturing LLC ....G.... 302 249-9408
Greenwood *(G-2754)*
National Industries For The Bl ....G.... 302 477-0860
Wilmington *(G-11807)*
Natures Gourmet Candles ....G.... 302 697-2785
Dover *(G-1885)*
Northernsigs Mfg LLC ....G.... 302 383-9270
Wilmington *(G-11908)*
Nova Industries LLC ....G.... 302 218-4837
Bear *(G-267)*
Pam Pipes & Puppets ....G.... 302 999-0078
Wilmington *(G-12010)*
Pandaciti LLC ....G.... 226 219-7771
New Castle *(G-5599)*
Pierpont Industries ....G.... 302 998-9220
Wilmington *(G-12133)*
Polytechnic Resources Inc ....G.... 302 629-4221
Seaford *(G-8359)*
R M Bell Industries Inc ....G.... 302 542-3747
Lewes *(G-3705)*
Raymond Chung Industries Corp ....G.... 302 384-9796
Wilmington *(G-12325)*
Roman Industries Inc ....G.... 302 420-9420
Wilmington *(G-12467)*
Rosas Greek Btq ....G.... 302 678-2147
Dover *(G-2043)*
Rowe Industries Inc ....G.... 443 458-5569
Georgetown *(G-2644)*
S&D Industries LLC ....G.... 703 801-3643
Wilmington *(G-12510)*
Sandebbarnanricway Corp ....G.... 302 475-2705
Wilmington *(G-12538)*
Sandwich Inc ....G.... 647 360-8300
Lewes *(G-3729)*
Sdg Defense Industry LLC ....G.... 302 526-4800
New Castle *(G-5696)*
Snowden Candles ....G.... 302 398-4373
Harrington *(G-2892)*
Staging Dimensions Inc ....F.... 302 328-4100
New Castle *(G-5735)*
Staging Dimesions Inc ....F.... 302 328-4100
New Castle *(G-5736)*
Still Industries Inc ....G.... 302 368-8832
Newark *(G-7491)*
Syf Industries ....G.... 302 384-6214
Wilmington *(G-12828)*
Systematic Achievement Inc ....G.... 302 479-5829
Wilmington *(G-12839)*
Under Whistle ....G.... 302 250-8400
Newark *(G-7610)*
US Green Battery Inc ....G.... 347 723-5963
New Castle *(G-5812)*
Uzin Utz Manufacturing N Amer ....G.... 336 456-4624
Dover *(G-2184)*
Vetcon Industries LLC ....G.... 850 207-6723
Newark *(G-7655)*
Vintage Candle Company ....G.... 302 643-9343
Bridgeville *(G-529)*
W L Gore & Associates Inc ....D.... 410 506-7787
Newark *(G-7671)*
Warren W Seaver ....G.... 302 674-8969
Dover *(G-2206)*
Westlake Chemical Products ....G.... 302 691-6028
Wilmington *(G-13169)*
Westmor Industries ....G.... 302 398-3253
Harrington *(G-2906)*
Westmor Industries ....G.... 302 956-0243
Bridgeville *(G-533)*
What If Y Not Everything Inc ....G.... 732 898-0241
Dover *(G-2218)*
Whet Industries Inc ....G.... 302 236-2182
Newark *(G-7690)*
Yesliberia Inc ....G.... 302 898-6338
Newark *(G-7727)*

40 RAILROAD TRANSPORTATION

4011 Railroads, Line-Hauling Operations

CSX Transportation Inc ....E.... 302 998-8613
Wilmington *(G-9913)*
Delaware Coast Line RR Co ....G.... 302 422-9200
Milford *(G-4378)*

SIC

40 RAILROAD TRANSPORTATION

Transflo Terminal Services Inc ....F 302 994-3853
  Wilmington (G-12956)

4013 Switching & Terminal Svcs

Tcar Holdings LLC ....G 720 328-0944
  Wilmington (G-12857)

41 LOCAL AND SUBURBAN TRANSIT AND INTERURBAN HIGHWAY PASSENGER TRANSPORTATION

4111 Local & Suburban Transit

Arrow Shuttle Service ....G 302 836-5658
  Bear (G-37)
City Wide Transportation Inc ....F 302 792-1225
  Claymont (G-720)
Dans Taxi & Shuttle ....G 302 383-8826
  Claymont (G-728)
Dcat Transit LLC ....G 302 855-1231
  Georgetown (G-2495)
Delaware Transportation Auth ....F 302 760-2000
  Dover (G-1403)
Delaware Trnsp Svcs Inc ....G 302 981-6562
  Dover (G-1404)
Direct Mobile Transit Inc ....F 302 218-5106
  Wilmington (G-10161)
Dover Leasing Co Inc ....G 302 674-2300
  Dover (G-1456)
Gg Shuttle Service ....G 302 684-8818
  Milton (G-4908)
Gold Label Transportation LLC ....G 302 668-2383
  Newark (G-6670)
Preferred Trnsp Systems LLC ....G 302 323-0828
  Bear (G-290)
Shamrock Services LLC ....G 302 519-7609
  Lewes (G-3738)
Spikes Coach Lines ....G 302 438-3644
  Wilmington (G-12705)
U Transit Inc ....G 302 227-1197
  Rehoboth Beach (G-8102)
United Transit Company L L C ....G 302 838-3575
  Saint Georges (G-8131)
Xinnix Ticketing Inc ....G 302 778-1818
  Wilmington (G-13321)

4119 Local Passenger Transportation: NEC

Bayside Limousine ....F 302 644-6999
  Millsboro (G-4636)
Bill M Douthat Jr ....F 407 977-2273
  Lewes (G-3385)
Buker Limousine & Trnsp Svc ....F 302 234-7600
  Newark (G-6135)
Cft Ambulance Service Inc ....E 302 984-2255
  Bear (G-70)
Christiana Care Health Sys Inc ....F 302 623-3970
  New Castle (G-5153)
Christiana Fire Company ....G 302 834-2433
  Bear (G-71)
Citywide Transportation Inc ....F 302 792-0159
  Wilmington (G-9727)
Class Limousine Service ....G 302 653-1166
  Smyrna (G-8597)
Delaware Cy Vlntr Fire Co No 1 ....C 302 834-9336
  Delaware City (G-955)
Dnd Limousine Service ....E 302 998-5856
  Wilmington (G-10178)
Eagle Limousine Inc ....C 302 325-4200
  New Castle (G-5273)
Executive Transportation Inc ....G 302 337-3455
  Greenwood (G-2740)
Felton Community Fire Co Inc ....C 302 284-9552
  Felton (G-2291)
First Class Limousine ....G 302 836-9500
  New Castle (G-5313)
Genes Limousine Service Inc ....E 410 479-8470
  Bridgeville (G-474)
Harding Limo Bus Cnnection LLC ....G 302 376-1818
  Middletown (G-4104)
In The Drivers Seat ....G 302 475-3361
  Wilmington (G-11009)
Limo Exchange ....G 302 322-1200
  New Castle (G-5482)
Limousine Unlimited LLC ....F 302 284-1100
  Felton (G-2304)
Lisa M Horsey ....G 302 725-5767
  Lincoln (G-3860)

Macklyn Home Care ....G 302 690-9397
  Wilmington (G-11481)
Mid Atlantic Care LLC ....G 302 266-8306
  Wilmington (G-11678)
New Castle Shuttle and Taxi SE ....G 302 326-1855
  New Castle (G-5566)
Preferred Trnsp Systems LLC ....G 302 323-0828
  Bear (G-290)
Primecare Medical Trnspt LLC ....E 302 422-0900
  Milford (G-4530)
Primetime Limousine ....F 302 425-5599
  Wilmington (G-12227)
Roadrunner Express Inc ....E 302 426-9551
  Wilmington (G-12433)
Stars Transportation LLC ....G 770 530-1843
  Harrington (G-2893)
Urgent Ambulance Service Inc ....E 302 454-1821
  Newark (G-7632)
Urgent Ambulance Service Inc ....E 302 454-1821
  Newark (G-7633)

4121 Taxi Cabs

Aryvve Technologies LLC ....G 678 977-1252
  Dover (G-1143)
City Cab of Delware Inc ....G 302 734-5968
  Dover (G-1286)
City Cab of Delware Inc ....F 302 227-8294
  Rehoboth Beach (G-7890)
City Cab of Delware Inc ....G 302 734-5968
  Dover (G-1287)
Delmarva Transportation Inc ....G 302 349-0840
  Greenwood (G-2729)
U S Express Taxi Company LLC ....G 302 357-1908
  New Castle (G-5799)
Zizo Taxi Cab LLC ....G 302 528-5663
  Newark (G-7742)

4131 Intercity & Rural Bus Transportation

Academy Express ....G 302 537-4805
  Ocean View (G-7753)
Chambers Bus Service Inc ....E 302 284-9655
  Viola (G-8834)
Hilton Bus Service ....E 302 697-7676
  Camden (G-580)
Matthew Smith Bus Service ....E 302 734-9311
  Dover (G-1828)
RE Calloway Trnsp Inc ....E 302 422-2471
  Houston (G-3182)

4141 Local Bus Charter Svc

Krapfs Coaches Inc ....E 302 993-7855
  Wilmington (G-11292)
R J K Transportation Inc ....F 302 422-3188
  Houston (G-3181)
Staplefords Sales and Service ....E 302 834-4568
  Saint Georges (G-8130)
Transportation Delaware Dept ....G 302 658-8960
  Wilmington (G-12958)
Triple D Charters LLC ....E 302 934-6837
  Millsboro (G-4814)

4142 Bus Charter Service, Except Local

Dawson Bus Service Inc ....D 302 697-9501
  Camden (G-556)
Dawson Bus Service Inc ....F 302 678-2594
  Dover (G-1345)
First Student Inc. ....C 302 995-9607
  Newark (G-6587)
Harding Limo Bus Cnnection LLC ....G 302 376-1818
  Middletown (G-4104)
Jor-Lin Inc. ....E 302 424-4445
  Milford (G-4461)
Krapfs Coaches Inc ....E 302 993-7855
  Wilmington (G-11292)
Matthew Smith Bus Service ....E 302 734-9311
  Dover (G-1828)
Wilmington Transportation Ctr ....G 302 655-6111
  Wilmington (G-13259)

4151 School Buses

Achieve Logistic Systems ....G 302 654-4701
  Wilmington (G-8921)
B&P Transit ....G 302 653-8466
  Smyrna (G-8579)
Boulden Buses Inc ....E 302 998-5463
  Wilmington (G-9398)
Christina School District ....B 302 454-2281
  Newark (G-6229)

Colonial School District ....C 302 323-2700
  New Castle (G-5182)
D&N Bus Service Inc ....F 302 422-3869
  Milford (G-4369)
Dawson Bus Service Inc ....D 302 697-9501
  Camden (G-556)
Dawson Bus Service Inc ....F 302 678-2594
  Dover (G-1345)
Dianes Bus Service ....F 302 629-4336
  Seaford (G-8223)
E A Slack Bus Service Inc ....G 302 697-2012
  Camden Wyoming (G-632)
First Student Inc. ....C 302 995-9607
  Newark (G-6587)
Knotts Incorporated ....D 302 322-0554
  New Castle (G-5467)
Lambden Bus Service ....G 302 629-4358
  Seaford (G-8290)
Larkins Bus Service LLC ....F 302 653-5855
  Clayton (G-861)
Lehanes Bus Service Inc ....E 302 328-7100
  New Castle (G-5475)
Sutton Bus & Truck Co Inc ....D 302 995-7444
  Wilmington (G-12821)

42 MOTOR FREIGHT TRANSPORTATION AND WAREHOUSING

4212 Local Trucking Without Storage

A Collins Trucking Inc ....G 302 438-8334
  Bear (G-5)
Affordable Delivery Svcs LLC ....E 302 276-0246
  New Castle (G-5016)
All American Truck Brokers ....G 302 654-6101
  Wilmington (G-9011)
Andrew Simoff Horse Trnsp ....G 302 994-1433
  Wilmington (G-9080)
Aoz Food and Gas LLC ....G 302 981-2966
  Newark (G-5979)
Asi Transport LLC ....G 302 349-9460
  Bridgeville (G-448)
Atlas World Express LLC ....G 202 536-5238
  Middletown (G-3953)
Berry International Inc ....G 302 674-1300
  Dover (G-1196)
Beth Trucking Inc ....G 918 814-2970
  Newark (G-6075)
BFI Waste Services LLC ....E 302 658-4097
  Wilmington (G-9324)
Bk Lord Trucking ....G 302 284-7890
  Felton (G-2275)
Bloomfield Trucking Inc ....G 302 834-6922
  Middletown (G-3970)
Buzzards Inc ....G 302 945-3500
  Millsboro (G-4651)
C&J Paving Inc ....F 302 684-0211
  Milton (G-4873)
Connolly Options LLC ....E 302 998-2016
  New Castle (G-5191)
Courtesy Trnsp Svcs Inc ....D 302 322-9722
  New Castle (G-5203)
Cr Newlin Trucking Inc ....G 302 678-9124
  Dover (G-1319)
Dawn Arrow Inc ....E 302 328-9695
  New Castle (G-5217)
Delp Trucking ....G 302 275-6541
  Smyrna (G-8622)
Deo Trucking ....G 302 744-9832
  Dover (G-1414)
Dependable Trucking Inc ....F 302 655-6271
  New Castle (G-5248)
Diamond State Express LLC ....G 302 563-3514
  Wilmington (G-10143)
Drone Delivery Systems Corp ....G 757 903-5006
  Lewes (G-3475)
Eastern Mail Transport Inc ....F 302 838-0500
  Bear (G-139)
Elizabeth Malbert ....G 302 422-9015
  Lincoln (G-3845)
Far Trucking LLC ....G 302 266-8034
  Newark (G-6571)
Fedex Ground Package Sys Inc ....G 800 463-3339
  Seaford (G-8243)
First Chice Auto Trck Mddltown ....G 302 376-6333
  Middletown (G-4071)
Foraker Oil Inc ....G 302 834-7595
  Delaware City (G-957)

Gens Trucking Inc ... G ... 302 421-3522
New Castle *(G-5350)*

Geotech LLC ... G ... 302 353-9769
Newark *(G-6649)*

Good To Go Delivery LLC ... F ... 302 893-2734
Wilmington *(G-10747)*

H G Investments LLC ... E ... 302 734-5017
Magnolia *(G-3894)*

Hab Nab Trucking Inc ... E ... 302 245-6900
Bridgeville *(G-478)*

Harmony Trucking Inc ... G ... 302 633-5600
Wilmington *(G-10840)*

High Tide Trucking Inc ... G ... 302 846-3537
Delmar *(G-1003)*

Highland Construction LLC ... F ... 302 286-6990
Bear *(G-185)*

J & S Moving & Dlvry Svc LLC ... G ... 302 357-5675
Newark *(G-6813)*

James Poole ... G ... 215 407-4046
Smyrna *(G-8662)*

Jkb Corp ... E ... 302 734-5017
Dover *(G-1698)*

John T Brown Inc ... G ... 302 398-8518
Harrington *(G-2858)*

Johnny Walker Enterprises LLC ... G ... 408 500-6439
Lewes *(G-3575)*

L A S Trucking LLC ... G ... 302 439-4433
Wilmington *(G-11307)*

Lns Delivery Inc ... G ... 302 448-6848
Millsboro *(G-4722)*

M & W Trucking Inc ... G ... 302 655-6994
New Castle *(G-5492)*

Michael A Sinclair Inc ... G ... 302 834-8144
Bear *(G-253)*

Morris CT Trucking Inc ... G ... 302 653-2396
Smyrna *(G-8682)*

Morris E Justice Inc ... G ... 302 539-7731
Dagsboro *(G-924)*

Move Crew ... G ... 302 290-4684
New Castle *(G-5537)*

Murry Trucking Llc ... F ... 302 653-4811
Smyrna *(G-8683)*

Muvers Inc ... G ... 888 508-4849
Wilmington *(G-11780)*

N and J Delivery Service LLC ... G ... 302 562-3220
Bear *(G-259)*

On-Demand Services LLC ... G ... 302 388-1215
New Castle *(G-5588)*

PB Trucking Inc ... F ... 302 841-3209
Greenwood *(G-2758)*

Penny Express Inc ... G ... 302 571-0544
Wilmington *(G-12072)*

Qwintry LLC ... G ... 858 633-6353
Newark *(G-7288)*

R & W Transportation Corp ... G ... 703 670-5483
Wilmington *(G-12292)*

R&R Logistics Inc ... G ... 302 629-4255
Seaford *(G-8369)*

Reddix Trucking Inc ... G ... 302 745-1277
Lewes *(G-3713)*

Richard Woinski Trucking ... G ... 302 644-1579
Lewes *(G-3719)*

▲ **Sardo & Sons Warehousing Inc** ... G ... 302 369-2100
Newark *(G-7387)*

Scottys Trucking Inc ... G ... 302 629-5156
Seaford *(G-8385)*

Sentinel Transportation LLC ... F ... 302 477-1640
Wilmington *(G-12579)*

SF Express Corporation ... F ... 302 407-6155
New Castle *(G-5702)*

Sharon Construction Inc ... G ... 302 999-1345
Wilmington *(G-12593)*

Shirkey Trucking Corp ... G ... 302 349-2791
Greenwood *(G-2763)*

Smart Plus Transport LLC ... G ... 347 963-0980
Newark *(G-7446)*

Smf Deliveries LLC ... G ... 302 945-6693
Lewes *(G-3749)*

Specialized Carier Systems Inc ... G ... 302 424-4548
Milford *(G-4567)*

Sutton Bus & Truck Co Inc ... D ... 302 995-7444
Wilmington *(G-12821)*

Tmk Trucking LLC ... G ... 302 449-5131
Middletown *(G-4259)*

Triglias Transportation Co ... E ... 302 846-2141
Delmar *(G-1042)*

Unique Pro-Co LLC ... G ... 302 723-2365
Wilmington *(G-13018)*

V & A Trucking LLC ... G ... 302 276-5548
Newark *(G-7635)*

W Gifford Inc ... G ... 302 420-6112
Newark *(G-7670)*

Wagner N J & Sons Trucking ... F ... 302 242-7731
Felton *(G-2325)*

Walleys Trucking Inc ... G ... 302 893-8652
Bear *(G-369)*

Wasteflo LLC ... G ... 410 202-0802
Laurel *(G-3307)*

Whites Family Trucking LLC ... G ... 302 393-1401
Ellendale *(G-2264)*

Whitetail Country Log & Hlg ... G ... 302 846-3982
Delmar *(G-1048)*

Wwc III ... F ... 302 238-7778
Millsboro *(G-4830)*

4213 Trucking, Except Local

A Duie Pyle Inc ... D ... 302 326-9440
New Castle *(G-4993)*

Adam Hobbs & Son Inc ... F ... 302 697-2090
Felton *(G-2269)*

American Van Storage Corp ... E ... 302 369-0900
Newark *(G-5961)*

Armed Forces Driving School ... G ... 302 981-6903
Newark *(G-5995)*

Armstrong Relocation Co LLC ... G ... 302 323-9000
New Castle *(G-5045)*

Asi Transport LLC ... G ... 302 349-9460
Bridgeville *(G-448)*

Atlantic Bulk Carriers ... F ... 302 378-6300
Middletown *(G-3949)*

Banks Farm LLC ... G ... 302 542-4100
Dagsboro *(G-881)*

Baq Logistics LLC ... G ... 302 401-6466
Dover *(G-1171)*

▲ **Bayshore Trnsp Sys Inc** ... D ... 302 366-0220
Newark *(G-6059)*

Bear Concrete Construction ... E ... 302 834-3333
Newark *(G-6062)*

Benson Enterprise Inc ... G ... 302 344-9183
Seaford *(G-8166)*

Burris Logistics ... E ... 302 221-4100
New Castle *(G-5122)*

Christiana Motor Freight Inc ... F ... 302 655-6271
New Castle *(G-5157)*

City Mist LLC ... G ... 302 342-1377
New Castle *(G-5171)*

Co Fs Holding Company LLC ... G ... 302 894-1244
Newark *(G-6258)*

Contractual Carriers Inc ... E ... 302 453-1420
Newark *(G-6292)*

Delaware Moving & Storage Inc ... D ... 302 322-0311
Bear *(G-110)*

Diamond State Corporation ... D ... 302 674-1300
Dover *(G-1425)*

E & J Trucking Inc ... G ... 302 349-4284
Greenwood *(G-2733)*

Eastern Mail Transport Inc ... F ... 302 838-0500
Bear *(G-139)*

Eric Hobbs Trucking Inc ... E ... 302 697-2090
Viola *(G-8835)*

Fedex Freight Corporation ... E ... 800 218-6570
New Castle *(G-5306)*

Foodliner Inc ... D ... 302 368-4204
Newark *(G-6600)*

Freehold Cartage Inc ... G ... 302 658-2005
New Castle *(G-5329)*

George W Oppel ... G ... 302 398-4433
Houston *(G-3178)*

Hab Nab Trucking Inc ... E ... 302 245-6900
Bridgeville *(G-478)*

Hobbs Enterprises Inc ... G ... 302 697-2090
Viola *(G-8837)*

◆ **Holman Moving Systems LLC** ... B ... 302 323-9000
New Castle *(G-5398)*

Holman Moving Systems LLC ... D ... 302 323-9000
New Castle *(G-5399)*

Jeff Bartsch Trckg Excvtg Inc ... G ... 302 653-9329
Townsend *(G-8801)*

Jz Road & Air Cargo Lines Inc ... G ... 302 468-5988
Newark *(G-6861)*

Marine Lubricants Inc ... G ... 302 429-7570
Wilmington *(G-11526)*

Mark IV Transportation Co Inc ... E ... 302 337-9898
Bridgeville *(G-493)*

Material Transit Inc ... F ... 302 395-0556
New Castle *(G-5512)*

Mawuli Logistics LLC ... G ... 302 544-5129
Newark *(G-7004)*

Messicks Mobile Homes Inc ... F ... 302 398-9166
Harrington *(G-2867)*

Montgomery Kenneth John ... G ... 302 992-0484
Wilmington *(G-11740)*

Old Dominion Freight Line Inc ... E ... 302 337-8793
Bridgeville *(G-505)*

On-Demand Services LLC ... G ... 302 388-1215
New Castle *(G-5588)*

Parker Express Inc ... E ... 302 221-5777
New Castle *(G-5602)*

Penny Express Inc ... G ... 302 571-0544
Wilmington *(G-12072)*

Phoenix Trnsp & Logistics Inc ... G ... 302 348-8814
Wilmington *(G-12126)*

Pierson Culver LLC ... G ... 302 732-1145
Dagsboro *(G-930)*

R W Morgan Farms Inc ... G ... 302 542-7740
Lincoln *(G-3864)*

Reed Trucking Company ... D ... 302 684-8585
Milton *(G-4955)*

Ruan Transport Corporation ... G ... 302 696-3270
Middletown *(G-4226)*

Schwerman Trucking Co ... E ... 302 832-3103
Bear *(G-316)*

T A H First Inc ... G ... 302 653-6114
Smyrna *(G-8728)*

Tc Logistics Incorporated ... F ... 302 470-8557
Bear *(G-349)*

Triglias Transportation Co ... E ... 302 846-2141
Delmar *(G-1042)*

Trinity 3 Enterprises Inc ... G ... 267 973-2666
Bear *(G-359)*

Ultimate Express Inc ... F ... 443 523-0800
Selbyville *(G-8552)*

Warren W Seaver ... G ... 302 674-8969
Dover *(G-2206)*

William R Knotts & Son Inc ... F ... 302 674-3496
Dover *(G-2227)*

Xpo Logistics Freight Inc ... E ... 302 629-5228
Seaford *(G-8444)*

Yrc Inc ... G ... 302 322-5111
New Castle *(G-5844)*

4214 Local Trucking With Storage

Advance Office Instlltions Inc ... E ... 302 777-5599
New Castle *(G-5008)*

Bayshore Trnsp Sys Inc ... F ... 302 366-0220
Newark *(G-6060)*

▲ **Bayshore Trnsp Sys Inc** ... D ... 302 366-0220
Newark *(G-6059)*

Bennett & Bennett Inc ... F ... 302 990-8939
New Castle *(G-5081)*

Buntings Garage Inc ... F ... 302 732-9021
Dagsboro *(G-886)*

Christiana Motor Freight Inc ... F ... 302 655-6271
New Castle *(G-5157)*

Contractual Carriers Inc ... E ... 302 453-1420
Newark *(G-6292)*

Davis Trucking & Family LLC ... F ... 302 381-6358
Millsboro *(G-4674)*

Delaware Moving & Storage Inc ... D ... 302 322-0311
Bear *(G-110)*

Diamond State Corporation ... D ... 302 674-1300
Dover *(G-1425)*

Dunkley Enterprises LLC ... G ... 302 275-0100
Odessa *(G-7826)*

Hollie Enterprises LLC ... G ... 903 721-1904
Wilmington *(G-10927)*

◆ **Holman Moving Systems LLC** ... B ... 302 323-9000
New Castle *(G-5398)*

Holman Moving Systems LLC ... D ... 302 323-9000
New Castle *(G-5399)*

New Creation Logistics Inc ... F ... 302 438-3154
Newark *(G-7103)*

On-Demand Services LLC ... G ... 302 388-1215
New Castle *(G-5588)*

Penske Truck Leasing Corp ... G ... 302 449-9294
Middletown *(G-4188)*

United Distribution Inc ... F ... 302 429-0400
Wilmington *(G-13024)*

Whipper Snapper Transport LLC ... G ... 302 265-2437
Milford *(G-4604)*

4215 Courier Svcs, Except Air

Agrima Postal Solutions LLC ... D ... 302 394-6939
Lewes *(G-3328)*

Brooks Courier Service Inc ... C ... 302 762-4661
Wilmington *(G-9485)*

Carr Courier Service Inc ... G ... 302 846-9826
Delmar *(G-979)*

Charles E Carlson ... G ... 302 284-3184
Camden Wyoming *(G-623)*

Employee Codes: A=Over 500 employees, B=251-500
C=101-250, D=51-100, E=20-50, F=10-19, G=1-9

2020 Harris Directory of
Delaware Businesses

491

42 MOTOR FREIGHT TRANSPORTATION AND WAREHOUSING

Darlington Postal Company LLC .... G 410 917-4147
  Newark *(G-6346)*
Delaware Medical Courier .... G 302 670-1247
  Milton *(G-4888)*
Harrymirimax Logistics .... F 302 784-5578
  New Castle *(G-5378)*
Livingston Healthcare Svcs Inc .... B 302 631-5000
  Newark *(G-6944)*
Parcels Inc .... C 302 888-1718
  Wilmington *(G-12018)*
Parcels Inc .... G 302 736-1777
  Dover *(G-1935)*

4221 Farm Product Warehousing & Storage

Milford Grain Co Inc .... G 302 422-6752
  Milford *(G-4498)*

4222 Refrigerated Warehousing & Storage

Blue Marlin Ice LLC .... G 302 697-7800
  Dover *(G-1214)*
Burris Logistics .... E 302 221-4100
  New Castle *(G-5122)*
Citrosuco North America Inc .... F 302 652-8763
  Wilmington *(G-9720)*
United States Cold Storage Inc .... E 302 422-7536
  Milford *(G-4584)*
United States Cold Storage Inc .... E 302 422-7536
  Milford *(G-4585)*

4225 General Warehousing & Storage

Advance Office Instltions Inc .... E 302 777-5599
  New Castle *(G-5008)*
Allstate Van & Storage Corp .... E 302 369-0230
  Newark *(G-5943)*
American Prtable Mini Stor Inc .... G 302 934-9898
  Millsboro *(G-4630)*
American Van Storage Corp .... E 302 369-0900
  Newark *(G-5961)*
Brandywine Chemical Company .... G 302 656-5428
  New Castle *(G-5104)*
Burris Logistics .... E 302 221-4100
  New Castle *(G-5122)*
Burris Logistics .... D 302 398-5050
  Harrington *(G-2820)*
Cannon Cold Storage LLC .... E 302 337-5500
  Bridgeville *(G-457)*
Ceco Inc .... E 302 732-3919
  Dagsboro *(G-890)*
Central Storage .... G 302 678-1919
  Dover *(G-1269)*
D & S Warehousing Inc .... E 302 731-7440
  Newark *(G-6341)*
Delaware Moving & Storage Inc .... D 302 322-0311
  Bear *(G-110)*
DOT Foods Inc .... D 302 300-4239
  Bear *(G-125)*
First State Warehousing .... D 302 426-0802
  New Castle *(G-5319)*
Hardy Development .... G 302 436-4496
  Selbyville *(G-8499)*
Intercontinental Chem Svcs Inc .... E 302 654-6800
  Wilmington *(G-11055)*
Iovate Health Sciences USA Inc .... E 888 334-4448
  Wilmington *(G-11078)*
Kenco Group Inc .... E 302 629-4295
  Seaford *(G-8287)*
Love Creek Marina MBL Hm Site .... F 302 448-6492
  Lewes *(G-3611)*
Mc Ginnis Commercial RE .... G 302 736-2700
  Dover *(G-1831)*
Mtc Delaware LLC .... G 302 654-3400
  New Castle *(G-5538)*
New Creation Logistics Inc .... F 302 438-3154
  Newark *(G-7103)*
On-Demand Services LLC .... G 302 388-1215
  New Castle *(G-5588)*
Penco Corporation .... D 302 629-7911
  Seaford *(G-8343)*
Penco Corporation .... G 302 629-3061
  Seaford *(G-8344)*
Record Storage Center Inc .... G 302 674-8571
  Dover *(G-2016)*
▲ Sardo & Sons Warehousing Inc .... G 302 369-2100
  Newark *(G-7387)*
Sardo & Sons Warehousing Inc .... E 302 737-3000
  Newark *(G-7388)*
Sardo & Sons Warehousing Inc .... F 302 369-0852
  Newark *(G-7389)*

Secure Self Storage .... G 302 832-0400
  New Castle *(G-5698)*
Sentinel Self Storage .... G 302 999-0704
  Wilmington *(G-12578)*
Standard Distributing Co Inc .... E 302 674-4591
  Dover *(G-2102)*
Tops International Corp .... G 302 738-8889
  Newark *(G-7576)*

4226 Special Warehousing & Storage, NEC

Ardexo Inc .... G 855 617-7500
  Dover *(G-1134)*
Ariio Inc .... G 562 481-8717
  Dover *(G-1136)*
Delaware Direct Inc .... G 302 658-8223
  Wilmington *(G-10042)*
Iron Mountain Incorporated .... G 610 636-1424
  New Castle *(G-5425)*
Lifestyle Document MGT Inc .... G 302 856-6387
  Georgetown *(G-2591)*
Magellan Midstream Partners LP .... F 302 654-3717
  Wilmington *(G-11484)*
Meherrin AG & Chem Co .... G 302 337-0330
  Bridgeville *(G-496)*
Secure Self Storage .... G 302 832-0400
  New Castle *(G-5698)*

4231 Terminal & Joint Terminal Maint Facilities

Kimbles AVI Lgistical Svcs Inc .... G 334 663-4954
  Georgetown *(G-2582)*

44 WATER TRANSPORTATION

4412 Deep Sea Foreign Transportation Of Freight

New Hope Vehicle Exports LLC .... G 302 275-6482
  Wilmington *(G-11863)*

4424 Deep Sea Domestic Transportation Of Freight

OSG America LP .... G 212 578-1922
  Newark *(G-7161)*
Vader LLC .... F 302 565-9684
  Bear *(G-366)*

4449 Water Transportation Of Freight, NEC

Delaware Bay Launch Service .... F 302 422-7604
  Milford *(G-4376)*

4481 Deep Sea Transportation Of Passengers

Cruise One .... G 302 698-6468
  Camden Wyoming *(G-628)*

4482 Ferries

Delaware River & Bay Authority .... E 800 643-3779
  Lewes *(G-3457)*

4489 Water Transport Of Passengers, NEC

Delaware Bay Launch Service .... F 302 422-7604
  Milford *(G-4376)*

4491 Marine Cargo Handling

▲ Advance Marine LLC .... G 302 656-2111
  Wilmington *(G-8947)*
Delaware River Stevedores Inc .... G 302 657-0472
  Wilmington *(G-10081)*
Diamond State Port Corporation .... D 302 472-7678
  Wilmington *(G-10144)*
Murphy Marine Services Inc .... B 302 571-4700
  Wilmington *(G-11777)*

4492 Towing & Tugboat Svcs

Buntings Garage Inc .... F 302 732-9021
  Dagsboro *(G-886)*
Dick Ennis Inc .... G 302 945-2627
  Lewes *(G-3464)*
Wilmington Tug Inc .... G 302 652-1666
  Wilmington *(G-13265)*

4493 Marinas

Barsgr LLC .... G 302 645-6665
  Lewes *(G-3362)*

Bayshore Inc .... G 302 539-7200
  Ocean View *(G-7758)*
Cedar Creek Marina .... G 302 422-2040
  Milford *(G-4342)*
Delaware Bay Launch Service .... F 302 422-7604
  Milford *(G-4376)*
Fenwick Island Marine LLC .... G 302 436-4702
  Selbyville *(G-8491)*
Indian River Captains Assoc .... G 302 227-3071
  Rehoboth Beach *(G-7967)*
Jack Hickman Real Estate .... F 302 539-8000
  Bethany Beach *(G-406)*
Love Creek Marina MBL Hm Site .... F 302 448-6492
  Lewes *(G-3611)*
Marshall Hotels & Resorts Inc .... E 302 227-1700
  Rehoboth Beach *(G-8000)*
Midlantic Marine Center Inc .... F 302 436-2628
  Selbyville *(G-8521)*
North Bay Marina Incorporated .... F 302 436-4211
  Selbyville *(G-8528)*
South Shore Provisions LLC .... G 443 614-2442
  Selbyville *(G-8546)*
Summit North Marina .... F 302 836-1800
  Bear *(G-341)*
Walkers Marine Corporation .... G 302 629-8666
  Seaford *(G-8432)*

45 TRANSPORTATION BY AIR

4512 Air Transportation, Scheduled

Penobscot Properties LLC .... G 302 322-4477
  New Castle *(G-5616)*
Travel Agency .... G 302 381-0205
  Lewes *(G-3794)*
United Air Lines Inc .... F 872 825-1911
  Wilmington *(G-13021)*
United Parcel Service Inc .... G 302 453-7462
  Newark *(G-7614)*

4513 Air Courier Svcs

Federal Express Corporation .... G 800 463-3339
  Wilmington *(G-10514)*
Federal Express Corporation .... D 302 577-2667
  Wilmington *(G-10515)*
Federal Express Corporation .... E 800 463-3339
  New Castle *(G-5304)*
Fedex Ground Package Sys Inc .... G 800 463-3339
  New Castle *(G-5307)*
Jz Road & Air Cargo Lines Inc .... G 302 468-5988
  Newark *(G-6861)*
Livingston Healthcare Svcs Inc .... B 302 631-5000
  Newark *(G-6944)*
Midnite Air Corp .... E 614 296-1678
  Newark *(G-7036)*
Penobscot Properties LLC .... G 302 322-4477
  New Castle *(G-5616)*

4522 Air Transportation, Nonscheduled

Aero Taxi Inc .... F 302 328-3430
  Wilmington *(G-8965)*
Air Methods Corporation .... G 302 363-3168
  Georgetown *(G-2426)*
G & G Flight Service Inc .... G 302 674-3264
  Dover *(G-1575)*
Horizon Helicopters Inc .... G 302 368-5135
  Newark *(G-6745)*
Integrated Dynmc Solutions LLC .... G 818 406-8500
  Camden *(G-582)*
Interjet West Inc .... F 209 848-0290
  Wilmington *(G-11063)*
Jz Road & Air Cargo Lines Inc .... G 302 468-5988
  Newark *(G-6861)*
Livingston Healthcare Svcs Inc .... B 302 631-5000
  Newark *(G-6944)*
Penobscot Properties LLC .... G 302 322-4477
  New Castle *(G-5616)*
Transcontinental Airways Corp .... F 202 817-2020
  Wilmington *(G-12955)*

4581 Airports, Flying Fields & Terminal Svcs

Aero Enterprises Inc .... G 302 378-1396
  Townsend *(G-8754)*
Atlantic Aviation Corporation .... E 302 613-4571
  New Castle *(G-5051)*
Brian Garnsey .... G 302 463-1985
  Dover *(G-1230)*
Dassault Aircraft Svcs Corp .... G 302 322-7000
  New Castle *(G-5214)*

Delaware River & Bay Authority............E....... 302 571-6474
New Castle *(G-5236)*
Dumont Aviation LLC............G....... 302 777-1003
New Castle *(G-5264)*
Flyadvanced LLC............G....... 302 324-9970
New Castle *(G-5321)*
Georgetown Air Services............G....... 302 855-2355
Georgetown *(G-2539)*
Georgetown Air Services LLC............F....... 302 855-2355
Georgetown *(G-2540)*
Pats Aircraft LLC............C....... 855 236-1638
Georgetown *(G-2613)*
Rayco Auto & Marine Uphl Inc............G....... 302 323-8844
Hockessin *(G-3129)*
Summit Aviation Inc............D....... 302 834-5400
Middletown *(G-4250)*

47 TRANSPORTATION SERVICES

4724 Travel Agencies

AAA Club Alliance Inc............B....... 302 299-4700
Wilmington *(G-8893)*
AAA Club Alliance Inc............F....... 302 674-8020
Dover *(G-1075)*
Aba Travl & Ent Inc............G....... 305 374-0838
Lewes *(G-3321)*
Advantage Travel Inc............G....... 302 674-8747
Bear *(G-15)*
Al Jusant Travel............G....... 302 427-2594
Wilmington *(G-8997)*
Ans Corporation............G....... 410 296-8330
Rehoboth Beach *(G-7844)*
Bethany Travel Inc............G....... 302 933-0955
Millsboro *(G-4644)*
Creative Travel Inc............F....... 302 658-2900
Newark *(G-6315)*
Cruise Holidays Brandywine Vly............F....... 302 239-6400
Hockessin *(G-2997)*
Cruise One............G....... 302 698-6468
Camden Wyoming *(G-628)*
Cruise Ship Centers............G....... 302 999-0202
Newark *(G-6318)*
Cruise Shoppe Inc............G....... 302 737-7220
Bear *(G-90)*
Cruiseone............G....... 302 945-4620
Millsboro *(G-4672)*
Fare4air LLC............F....... 844 663-4040
Wilmington *(G-10498)*
Flight Centre Travel Group USA............G....... 302 633-1996
Wilmington *(G-10574)*
Flight Centre Travel Group USA............G....... 302 479-7581
Wilmington *(G-10575)*
Greenville Travel Agency Inc............G....... 302 658-3585
Wilmington *(G-10780)*
International Travel Network............G....... 415 840-0207
Wilmington *(G-11069)*
Jetset Travel Inc............G....... 302 678-5050
Dover *(G-1696)*
Journeys LLC............G....... 302 384-7843
Wilmington *(G-11198)*
Kcs Sensational Vacations............G....... 267 886-0991
Dover *(G-1726)*
Mymoroccanbazar Inc............G....... 323 238-5747
Newark *(G-7077)*
Ocean Travel............G....... 302 227-1607
Rehoboth Beach *(G-8021)*
Preferred Travel............G....... 302 838-8966
Bear *(G-289)*
Red Carpet Travel Agency Inc............E....... 302 475-1220
Wilmington *(G-12346)*
Travel Travel Newark Inc............G....... 302 737-5555
Newark *(G-7582)*
Visamtion LLC............G....... 302 268-2177
New Castle *(G-5819)*
Welcome Aboard Travel Ltd............G....... 302 678-9480
Dover *(G-2210)*
Windham Enterprises Inc............G....... 302 678-5777
Dover *(G-2231)*
Windham Travel Inc............G....... 302 678-5777
Dover *(G-2232)*

4725 Tour Operators

Fare4air LLC............F....... 844 663-4040
Wilmington *(G-10498)*
Posidon Adventure Inc............F....... 302 543-5024
Wilmington *(G-12190)*
Promotora Systems Inc............G....... 302 304-3147
Wilmington *(G-12252)*

U Transit Inc............G....... 302 227-1197
Rehoboth Beach *(G-8102)*

4729 Passenger Transportation Arrangement, NEC

Advantage Travel Inc............G....... 302 674-8747
Bear *(G-15)*
Fleek Inc............G....... 888 870-1291
Wilmington *(G-10572)*
Twyne Inc............G....... 213 675-9518
Camden *(G-603)*

4731 Freight Forwarding & Arrangement

Achieve Logistic Systems............G....... 302 654-4701
Wilmington *(G-8921)*
Agrima Postal Solutions LLC............D....... 302 394-6939
Lewes *(G-3328)*
Aku Transport Inc............G....... 302 500-8127
Georgetown *(G-2427)*
Amh Enterprises LLC............E....... 302 337-0300
Bridgeville *(G-445)*
Bettan Trucking LLC............E....... 302 841-3834
Lewes *(G-3380)*
Blockfreight Inc............F....... 614 350-2252
Lewes *(G-3387)*
Briscoe Trucking Inc............F....... 302 836-1327
Newark *(G-6123)*
Burris Freight Management LLC............D....... 800 805-8135
Milford *(G-4336)*
C V International Inc............G....... 302 427-0440
Wilmington *(G-9525)*
Cargoex Inc............G....... 800 850-9493
Wilmington *(G-9569)*
City Mist LLC............G....... 302 342-1377
New Castle *(G-5171)*
▲ Cpmg Inc............G....... 302 429-8688
Wilmington *(G-9888)*
Delaware Trnsp Svcs Inc............G....... 302 981-6562
Dover *(G-1404)*
Evanix Enterprises LLC............G....... 302 384-1806
Middletown *(G-4064)*
Explorer New Build LLC............G....... 305 436-4000
Wilmington *(G-10462)*
Faustin Enterprises LLC............G....... 302 543-2687
Wilmington *(G-10508)*
Gjv Inc............G....... 302 455-1600
Newark *(G-6659)*
Hollie Enterprises LLC............G....... 903 721-1904
Wilmington *(G-10927)*
Hollywell Logistics LLC............D....... 267 901-4272
Wilmington *(G-10929)*
Hs Capital LLC............G....... 302 598-2961
Wilmington *(G-10964)*
MA Transportation LLC............G....... 302 588-5435
Millsboro *(G-4730)*
Makeshopncompany Inc............F....... 302 999-9961
New Castle *(G-5503)*
MD Freight & Logistics LLC............G....... 804 347-1196
Dover *(G-1833)*
New Creation Logistics Inc............F....... 302 438-3154
Newark *(G-7103)*
New Hope Vehicle Exports LLC............G....... 302 275-6482
Wilmington *(G-11863)*
North American Trnspt Co Inc............G....... 856 696-5483
New Castle *(G-5575)*
Ohmyzip............E....... 302 322-8792
New Castle *(G-5586)*
Pacific Cargo LLC............G....... 302 521-6317
Wilmington *(G-12004)*
Penn Del Carriers LLC............G....... 484 424-3768
New Castle *(G-5614)*
Port To Port Intl Corp............E....... 302 654-2444
New Castle *(G-5633)*
Post Shipper LLC............F....... 302 444-8144
Bear *(G-287)*
Pteris Global (usa) Inc............G....... 516 593-5633
Dover *(G-1998)*
Pyramid Transport Inc............E....... 302 337-9340
Bridgeville *(G-514)*
SF Logistics Limited............E....... 302 317-3954
New Castle *(G-5703)*
Shipshap LLC............G....... 425 298-5215
Middletown *(G-4240)*
Tc Trans Inc............G....... 302 339-7952
Georgetown *(G-2687)*
Transcore LP............E....... 302 838-7429
Middletown *(G-4266)*
Triglia Express Inc............E....... 302 846-2248
Delmar *(G-1040)*

Trinity Logistics Inc............G....... 302 595-2116
New Castle *(G-5794)*
Trinity Logistics Inc............C....... 302 253-3900
Seaford *(G-8425)*
Umbrella Transport Group Inc............G....... 301 919-1623
Newark *(G-7609)*
UPS Supply Chain Solutions Inc............F....... 302 631-5259
Newark *(G-7631)*
Wentzel Transportation............G....... 302 355-9465
Smyrna *(G-8743)*

4741 Railroad Car Rental

Dana Container Inc............E....... 302 652-8550
Wilmington *(G-9951)*
Dana Railcare Inc............E....... 302 652-8550
Wilmington *(G-9952)*
Road & Rail Services Inc............B....... 302 731-2552
Newark *(G-7348)*

4783 Packing & Crating Svcs

Atlas Van Lines Agents............E....... 302 369-0900
Newark *(G-6024)*
▲ Cpmg Inc............G....... 302 429-8688
Wilmington *(G-9888)*
Marlex Pharmaceuticals Inc............E....... 302 328-3355
New Castle *(G-5508)*
On-Demand Services LLC............G....... 302 388-1215
New Castle *(G-5588)*

4785 Fixed Facilities, Inspection, Weighing Svcs Transptn

Delaware River & Bay Authority............E....... 302 571-6474
New Castle *(G-5236)*
Delaware River & Bay Authority............C....... 302 571-6303
New Castle *(G-5237)*
Drba Police Fund............D....... 302 571-6326
New Castle *(G-5260)*
Integrated Dynmc Solutions LLC............G....... 818 406-8500
Camden *(G-582)*
Paybysky Inc............G....... 519 641-1771
Lewes *(G-3682)*

4789 Transportation Svcs, NEC

Adkess Transport Services LLC............G....... 978 235-3924
Bear *(G-13)*
AEG International LLC............G....... 302 750-6411
Laurel *(G-3190)*
Alfreda Hicks LLC............G....... 302 312-8721
New Castle *(G-5022)*
All Around Moverz............G....... 302 494-9925
Wilmington *(G-9012)*
All In One Transportation LLC............D....... 302 482-3222
Wilmington *(G-9014)*
Aloha Movers............F....... 302 559-4310
Wilmington *(G-9028)*
Altra Cargo Inc............G....... 302 256-0748
Wilmington *(G-9034)*
Atlantic Bulk Ltd............F....... 302 378-6300
Middletown *(G-3950)*
AV Logistics LLC............G....... 302 725-5407
Milford *(G-4314)*
Base Line Transports L............G....... 302 438-3092
Middletown *(G-3963)*
Bay Shippers LLC............G....... 302 652-5005
New Castle *(G-5072)*
Bluedot Technologies Inc............G....... 415 800-1890
Newark *(G-6102)*
◆ Burris Logistics............D....... 302 839-4531
Milford *(G-4337)*
Compassionate Care Trnspt LLC............G....... 215 847-9836
Wilmington *(G-9802)*
Crown Shipping............G....... 617 909-3357
Dover *(G-1326)*
Dana Railcare Inc............E....... 302 652-8550
Wilmington *(G-9952)*
Delaware Car Company............E....... 302 655-6665
Wilmington *(G-10012)*
Dixon Brothers LLC............F....... 302 377-8289
Newark *(G-6456)*
Dolphin Ship Services Ltd............G....... 302 832-0410
Bear *(G-123)*
E-Lyte Transportation............G....... 808 269-0283
Dover *(G-1492)*
Ed Hunt Inc............G....... 302 339-8443
Dover *(G-1503)*
Elite Trnspt & Logistics Inc............F....... 302 348-8480
Wilmington *(G-10378)*

S I C

H Juarez Transport Inc .... G 302 407-5102
Wilmington *(G-10809)*
Harrymirimax Logisitics .... F 302 784-5578
New Castle *(G-5378)*
Hodges L Wooten .... G 302 335-5162
Magnolia *(G-3895)*
J & J Bus Service .... F 302 744-9002
Dover *(G-1686)*
J M Aja Transportation LLC .... G 302 562-6028
Wilmington *(G-11107)*
John A Donovan .... G 302 540-7512
Newark *(G-6841)*
Kinoland Logistics LLC .... G 302 565-4505
Newark *(G-6889)*
L&J Transportation LLC .... G 302 234-3366
Hockessin *(G-3074)*
Lantransit Enterprises LLC .... F 302 722-4800
Lewes *(G-3592)*
MED Transport LLC .... E 513 257-7626
Wilmington *(G-11614)*
Menno Freight Logistics LLC .... G 302 229-8137
Wilmington *(G-11631)*
Meridian Limo LLC .... G 800 462-1550
Dover *(G-1839)*
National Auto Movers LLC .... G 302 229-9256
Smyrna *(G-8685)*
Nexus Services America LLC .... G 800 946-4626
Wilmington *(G-11883)*
North Atlantic Ocean Ship .... G 302 652-3782
New Castle *(G-5577)*
P&P Horse Transportation .... G 302 388-7687
Newark *(G-7168)*
PCI of Virginia LLC .... F 302 655-7300
New Castle *(G-5610)*
Port Contractors Inc .... D 302 655-7300
New Castle *(G-5632)*
Reddix Transportation Inc .... F 302 249-9331
Lewes *(G-3712)*
Rivera Transportation Inc .... G 302 258-9023
Laurel *(G-3282)*
Road & Rail Services Inc .... B 302 731-2552
Newark *(G-7348)*
Robert Bryan .... G 302 875-5099
Laurel *(G-3284)*
Ruan T119 .... G 302 376-9300
Middletown *(G-4225)*
Savannah Logistics LLC .... G 302 893-7251
Middletown *(G-4230)*
Schiff Transport LLC .... G 302 398-8014
Harrington *(G-2885)*
Spirit-Trans Inc .... G 302 290-9830
Bear *(G-333)*
St Logistics .... G 302 407-5931
Wilmington *(G-12725)*
Trans Logistics LLC .... F 267 244-6550
Wilmington *(G-12952)*
Trial Transport Logistics .... G 302 383-5907
Wilmington *(G-12968)*
Walter Doring .... G 302 727-6773
Rehoboth Beach *(G-8107)*
Wayman Transportation Svc .... G 302 363-5139
Magnolia *(G-3912)*
Yellow Trans .... F 302 628-2805
Seaford *(G-8445)*

48 COMMUNICATIONS

4812 Radiotelephone Communications

Angle Wireless Wholesale LLC .... G 302 883-7788
Newark *(G-5969)*
Appa Inc .... G 302 440-1448
Dover *(G-1130)*
AT&T Corp .... D 302 644-4529
Rehoboth Beach *(G-7848)*
AT&T Mobility LLC .... F 302 674-4888
Dover *(G-1153)*
Cellco Partnership .... G 302 530-4620
Wilmington *(G-9611)*
Cellco Partnership .... D 302 697-8340
Camden *(G-547)*
Cellco Partnership .... F 302 730-5200
Dover *(G-1262)*
Cellco Partnership .... E 302 653-8183
Smyrna *(G-8592)*
Cellco Partnership .... F 302 376-6049
Middletown *(G-3983)*
Crossroads Wireless Holdg LLC .... E 405 946-1200
Wilmington *(G-9905)*
Grahams Wireless Solutions Inc .... F 717 943-0717
Millsboro *(G-4698)*
New Cingular Wireless Svcs Inc .... F 302 999-0055
Wilmington *(G-11854)*
New Cingular Wireless Svcs Inc .... F 302 762-1366
Wilmington *(G-11855)*
Redi Call Corp .... E 302 856-9000
Georgetown *(G-2633)*
Spring Communications Inc .... G 302 297-2000
Millsboro *(G-4803)*
Sprint .... G 302 261-8500
Newark *(G-7475)*
Sprint Spectrum LP .... E 302 993-3700
Wilmington *(G-12717)*
T-Mobile .... G 302 652-7738
Wilmington *(G-12846)*
T-Mobile Usa Inc .... G 302 644-7222
Rehoboth Beach *(G-8094)*
T-Mobile Usa Inc .... G 302 736-1980
Dover *(G-2128)*
T-Mobile Usa Inc .... F 302 838-4500
Bear *(G-345)*
Tdp Wireless Inc .... F 302 424-1900
Dover *(G-2133)*
Verizon Communications Inc .... F 302 324-1385
New Castle *(G-5815)*
Verizon Delaware LLC .... C 302 571-1571
Wilmington *(G-13062)*
Verizon Wireless Inc .... G 302 737-5028
Newark *(G-7651)*
Voyyp Inc .... G 833 342-5667
Newark *(G-7665)*
WER Wireless Inc .... E 302 478-7748
Wilmington *(G-13158)*
WER Wireless of Concord Inc .... F 302 478-7748
Wilmington *(G-13159)*

4813 Telephone Communications, Except Radio

3d Internet Group Inc .... G 302 376-7900
Middletown *(G-3925)*
7p Networks LLC .... F 938 777-7662
Lewes *(G-3317)*
Alcatel-Lucent USA Inc .... E 302 529-3900
Wilmington *(G-9003)*
Alphasure Technologies .... G 302 992-0900
Wilmington *(G-9032)*
Azur Gcs Inc .... G 302 884-6713
Wilmington *(G-9205)*
Brainbase Inc .... G 412 515-9000
Wilmington *(G-9414)*
C & B Internet Services LLC .... G 302 384-9804
Wilmington *(G-9520)*
C4-Nvis USA LLC .... G 213 465-5089
Dover *(G-1246)*
Cellco Partnership .... E 302 653-8183
Smyrna *(G-8592)*
Cellco Partnership .... F 302 376-6049
Middletown *(G-3983)*
Clouto Inc .... G 302 966-9282
Newark *(G-6252)*
Coastal Images Inc .... G 302 539-6001
Fenwick Island *(G-2333)*
Conectiv Communications Inc .... E 302 224-1177
Newark *(G-6282)*
Consult Dynamics Inc .... E 302 654-1019
Wilmington *(G-9837)*
Ewebvalet Co Inc .... G 302 893-0903
Wilmington *(G-10455)*
Firing Distance .... G 302 337-9094
Bridgeville *(G-471)*
Globaltec Networks Inc .... G 646 321-8627
Wilmington *(G-10732)*
Home Media One LLC .... G 302 644-0307
Georgetown *(G-2560)*
Host Integrado Inc .... G 277 326-6719
Lewes *(G-3547)*
Ing Bank Fsb .... G 302 255-3750
Wilmington *(G-11029)*
Instanode Inc .... G 352 327-8872
Wilmington *(G-11042)*
Intohost Inc .... F 888 567-2607
Wilmington *(G-11070)*
Jsi Group LLC .... G 267 582-5850
Hockessin *(G-3070)*
Keep In Touch Systems Inc .... G 510 868-8088
Wilmington *(G-11233)*
Key-Tel Communications Inc .... G 302 475-3066
Wilmington *(G-11249)*
Lnh Inc .... F 302 731-4948
Newark *(G-6945)*
MCI Communications Corporation .... F 302 791-4900
Wilmington *(G-11598)*
MCI LLC .... F 302 407-5034
Wilmington *(G-11599)*
MCI LLC .... G 302 293-0028
Wilmington *(G-11600)*
Mgj Enterprises Inc .... E 866 525-8529
Wilmington *(G-11652)*
New Concept Technologies LLC .... E 518 533-5367
Wilmington *(G-11860)*
Notify Technology Inc .... G 505 818-5888
Newark *(G-7139)*
Progressive Telecom LLC .... E 302 883-8883
Wilmington *(G-12245)*
Qsr Group LLC .... G 302 268-6909
Wilmington *(G-12276)*
Rippl Labs Inc .... F 551 427-1997
Wilmington *(G-12423)*
Scientific Games Corporation .... F 302 737-4300
Newark *(G-7395)*
Search LLC .... E 858 348-4584
Lewes *(G-3734)*
Sigma Telecom LLC .... E 347 741-8397
Wilmington *(G-12612)*
Siteage LLC .... F 302 380-3709
Lewes *(G-3746)*
Skynethostingnet Inc .... F 302 384-1784
Wilmington *(G-12644)*
Spring Communications Inc .... G 302 475-1052
Wilmington *(G-12713)*
Sprint Communications Inc .... E 302 613-4004
New Castle *(G-5731)*
Sprint Communications Inc .... E 302 604-6125
Georgetown *(G-2664)*
Sprint Spectrum LP .... E 302 393-2060
Milford *(G-4568)*
Sprint Spectrum LP .... E 302 322-1712
New Castle *(G-5732)*
Studentup Inc .... G 951 427-7563
Newark *(G-7497)*
Telco Envirotrols Inc .... F 302 846-9103
Delmar *(G-1036)*
Traitel Telecom Corp .... E 619 331-1913
Wilmington *(G-12951)*
Under/Comm Inc .... F 302 424-1554
Milford *(G-4583)*
Utility Audit Group Inc .... G 302 398-8505
Harrington *(G-2903)*
Verizon Delaware LLC .... E 302 761-6079
Wilmington *(G-13063)*
Verizon Delaware LLC .... F 302 629-4502
Seaford *(G-8430)*
Verizon Delaware LLC .... E 302 422-1430
Milford *(G-4590)*
Verizon Delaware LLC .... C 302 571-1571
Wilmington *(G-13062)*
Verizon Wireless Inc .... G 302 737-5028
Newark *(G-7651)*
Vps International LLC .... F 800 493-9356
Lewes *(G-3811)*

4822 Telegraph & Other Message Communications

Generation Consultants LLC .... G 302 722-4884
Newark *(G-6646)*

4832 Radio Broadcasting Stations

302 Sports .... G 302 650-8479
Wilmington *(G-8857)*
887 The Bridge .... F 302 422-6909
Milford *(G-4299)*
Beasley Broadcast Group Inc .... E 302 765-1160
Wilmington *(G-9275)*
Beasley FM Acquisition Corp .... G 302 765-1160
Wilmington *(G-9276)*
Delmarva Broadcasting Co Inc .... D 302 478-2700
Wilmington *(G-10102)*
Delmarva Broadcasting Co Inc .... E 302 422-7575
Milford *(G-4383)*
East Sussex Public Brdcstg .... G 302 644-7385
Rehoboth Beach *(G-7923)*
Gamma Theta Lambda Ed .... G 302 983-9429
Bear *(G-164)*
Heritage Sports Rdo Netwrk LLC .... G 302 492-1132
Hartly *(G-2925)*
Iheartcommunications Inc .... E 302 674-1410
Dover *(G-1666)*
Iheartmedia Inc .... D 302 395-9800
New Castle *(G-5411)*

Lnp Media Group Inc .... E 302 422-7575
  Milford (G-4475)
Myserve Inc .... G 302 528-4822
  Wilmington (G-11791)
Play Game Sports .... G 302 736-0606
  Dover (G-1964)
Porter Broadcasting .... G 302 535-8809
  Dover (G-1977)
Priority Radio Inc .... G 302 540-5690
  Newark (G-7257)
Resort Broadcasting Co LP .... E 302 945-2050
  Lewes (G-3716)
Samson Communications Inc .... F 302 424-1013
  Lincoln (G-3867)
Voice Radio LLC .... G 302 858-5118
  Georgetown (G-2701)
Wafl Wyus Broadcasting Inc .... G 302 422-7575
  Milford (G-4592)
Wjwk .... G 302 856-2567
  Georgetown (G-2706)
Wrdx .... G 302 395-9739
  New Castle (G-5840)

4833 Television Broadcasting Stations

Abc Inc .... G 302 429-0189
  Wilmington (G-8898)
Draper Communications Inc .... F 302 684-8962
  Milton (G-4898)
Gtv Live Shopping LLC .... G 844 694-8688
  Hockessin (G-3041)
Thales Holding Corporation .... A 302 326-0830
  New Castle (G-5766)
Wboc Inc .... F 302 734-9262
  Dover (G-2207)

4841 Cable & Other Pay TV Svcs

Atlantic Broadband .... G 302 378-0780
  Middletown (G-3948)
Bombonais Cable Tech LLC .... G 302 444-1199
  New Castle (G-5099)
Central Firm LLC .... G 610 470-9836
  Wilmington (G-9615)
Comcast Cablevision of Del .... E 302 661-4465
  New Castle (G-5185)
Comcast Cablevision of Del .... F 302 856-4591
  Georgetown (G-2477)
Comcast Cble Cmmunications LLC .... F 302 323-9200
  New Castle (G-5186)
Comcast Corporation .... D 302 262-8996
  Seaford (G-8201)
Comcast Corporation .... D 302 495-5612
  Greenwood (G-2722)
Comcast MO Investments LLC .... G 302 594-8705
  Wilmington (G-9780)
Comcast of Delmarva LLC .... D 215 286-3345
  Dover (G-1304)
Dish Network LLC .... E 302 387-0341
  Camden (G-564)
Executive Broadband .... G 302 463-4335
  Newark (G-6552)
Mediacom LLC .... D 302 732-9332
  Dagsboro (G-921)
NTL (triangle) LLC .... F 302 525-0027
  Wilmington (G-11920)
Satellite Connection Inc .... G 302 328-2462
  Wilmington (G-12543)

4899 Communication Svcs, NEC

ARINC Ctrl & Info Systems LLC .... G 302 658-7581
  Wilmington (G-9129)
Axxess Marine LLC .... G 954 225-1744
  Lewes (G-3361)
Bluestone Communication .... G 302 478-4200
  Wilmington (G-9384)
Cinemavericks Media LLC .... G 302 438-1144
  Wilmington (G-9708)
Clique Digital Media Mktg LLC .... G 305 704-2128
  Dover (G-1294)
Delaware First Media Corp .... G 302 857-7096
  Dover (G-1370)
Epthi Inc .... G 917 821-1935
  Wilmington (G-10429)
Gai Communications Inc .... G 609 254-1470
  Newark (G-6632)
Influencers Lab Media LLC .... G 302 444-6990
  Wilmington (G-11025)
Jerry A Fletcher .... G 302 875-9057
  Delmar (G-1007)

Legist Media Ltd .... G 302 655-2730
  Wilmington (G-11364)
Losemynumbercom LLC .... G 302 778-9741
  Wilmington (G-11438)
Phonecandiescom .... G 215 385-1818
  Bear (G-282)
Providence Media LLC .... G 302 715-1757
  Laurel (G-3274)
Rising Star Communication .... G 302 462-5474
  Seaford (G-8379)

49 ELECTRIC, GAS, AND SANITARY SERVICES

4911 Electric Svcs

Aci Energy Inc .... D 302 588-3024
  Wilmington (G-8922)
Aspire Energy LLC .... G 330 682-7726
  Dover (G-1146)
Atlantic City Electric Company .... E 202 872-2000
  Newark (G-6018)
Blue Hen Utility Services Inc .... G 302 273-3167
  New Castle (G-5094)
Calpine Corporation .... E 302 764-4478
  Wilmington (G-9540)
Calpine Corporation .... G 302 824-4779
  Wilmington (G-9541)
Calpine Operating Svcs Co Inc .... G 302 468-5400
  Wilmington (G-9542)
Captains Grant Solar 1 Inc .... G 410 375-2092
  Millsboro (G-4655)
Carroll Brothers Electric LLC .... G 302 947-4754
  Millsboro (G-4656)
Chesapeake Utilities Corp .... C 302 734-6799
  Dover (G-1274)
City of Dover .... E 302 736-7070
  Dover (G-1290)
City of Milford .... E 302 422-1110
  Milford (G-4354)
CMI Electric Inc .... G 302 731-5556
  Newark (G-6254)
Cogentrix Delaware Holdings .... B 847 908-2800
  Wilmington (G-9758)
Conectiv LLC .... C 202 872-2680
  Wilmington (G-9817)
Conectiv LLC .... F 800 375-7117
  Wilmington (G-9818)
Conectiv LLC .... E 302 429-3018
  Newark (G-6281)
Congo Capital Management LLC .... G 732 337-6643
  Wilmington (G-9821)
Delaware Municipal Elc Corp .... G 302 653-2733
  Smyrna (G-8617)
Delmarva Power & Light Company .... C 302 454-0300
  Newark (G-6426)
Delmarva Power & Light Company .... C 302 454-4450
  Newark (G-6428)
Delmarva Power & Light Company .... E 302 429-3376
  Wilmington (G-10103)
Delmarva Power & Light Company .... C 302 454-0300
  Wilmington (G-10104)
Domian International Svc LLC .... G 804 837-3616
  Smyrna (G-8624)
Elec Integrity .... F 302 388-3430
  Dover (G-1512)
Electrical Integrity LLC .... G 302 388-3430
  New Castle (G-5282)
Energy Center Dover LLC .... F 302 678-4666
  Dover (G-1523)
Etechboys Inc .... G 800 549-4208
  Wilmington (G-10440)
Flemings Electrical Service .... G 302 258-9386
  Laurel (G-3230)
FPL Energy American Wind LLC .... G 302 655-0632
  Wilmington (G-10609)
Garrison Calpine .... G 302 562-5661
  Dover (G-1579)
J Fredericks & Son Elec C .... G 302 733-0307
  Newark (G-6816)
KB Electrical Services .... G 302 276-5733
  Wilmington (G-11230)
Mid Atlantic Renewable Energy .... G 302 672-0741
  Dover (G-1848)
Municipal Services Commission .... F 302 323-2330
  New Castle (G-5539)
NRG Energy Inc .... C 302 934-3537
  Millsboro (G-4763)
Nuclear Service Organization .... G 302 888-3000
  Wilmington (G-11922)

Oso Grande Hv LLC .... G 858 521-3300
  Wilmington (G-11981)
Pepco Holdings LLC .... E 202 872-2000
  Newark (G-7199)
Pepco Holdings LLC .... E 202 872-2000
  Wilmington (G-12080)
Ridgewood Electric Power Tr V .... G 302 888-7444
  Wilmington (G-12417)
Ridgewood Electric Pwr Tr III .... F 302 888-7444
  Wilmington (G-12418)
Scituate Solar I LLC .... G 212 419-4843
  Wilmington (G-12563)
SFE Solar Energy Inc .... G 905 366-7037
  Wilmington (G-12590)
St Delaware Electrical .... G 302 857-5316
  Dover (G-2100)
Sun-In-One Inc .... G 302 762-3100
  Wilmington (G-12798)
Sustainable Energy Utility .... G 302 504-3071
  Wilmington (G-12819)

4922 Natural Gas Transmission

Eastern Shore Natural Gas Co .... F 302 734-6716
  Dover (G-1500)

4923 Natural Gas Transmission & Distribution

Conectiv Energy Supply Inc .... D 302 454-0300
  Newark (G-6283)
Sandpiper Energy Inc .... E 302 736-7656
  Dover (G-2057)

4924 Natural Gas Distribution

Chesapeake Utilities Corp .... C 302 734-6799
  Dover (G-1274)
Conectiv LLC .... C 202 872-2680
  Wilmington (G-9817)
Conectiv Energy Supply Inc .... D 302 454-0300
  Newark (G-6283)
Delmarva Power & Light Company .... C 302 454-0300
  Wilmington (G-10104)
Pepco Holdings LLC .... E 202 872-2000
  Wilmington (G-12080)

4925 Gas Production &/Or Distribution

Conectiv Energy Supply Inc .... G 302 454-0300
  Newark (G-6283)
Osaka Gas USA Corporation .... G 302 658-7581
  Wilmington (G-11979)

4931 Electric & Other Svcs Combined

Balanceco2 Inc .... F 302 494-9476
  Wilmington (G-9224)
Blue Energy International LLC .... G 480 941-5100
  Wilmington (G-9376)
Blue Energy Partners LLC .... F 480 941-5100
  Wilmington (G-9377)
Clearwater Enrgy Resources LLC .... G 510 267-8921
  Wilmington (G-9740)
Indian River Power LLC .... F 302 934-3527
  Dagsboro (G-911)
Tristar Solar Farm LLC .... G 626 457-1381
  Wilmington (G-12979)

4932 Gas & Other Svcs Combined

Peninsula Energy Svcs Co Inc .... F 302 734-6799
  Dover (G-1945)

4941 Water Sply

Artesian Resources Corporation .... G 302 453-6900
  Newark (G-6000)
Artesian Utility Dev Inc .... E 800 332-5114
  Newark (G-6001)
Artesian Water Company Inc .... E 302 453-6900
  Newark (G-6004)
Artesian Water Maryland Inc .... E 302 453-6900
  Newark (G-6005)
Camdenwyoming Sewer & Wtr Auth ..... F 302 697-6372
  Camden (G-544)
City of Wilmington .... E 302 576-2584
  Wilmington (G-9723)
Core & Main LP .... G 302 684-3452
  Milton (G-4883)
Core & Main LP .... G 302 737-1500
  Newark (G-6297)
J H Wilkerson & Son Inc .... G 302 422-4306
  Milford (G-4456)

49 ELECTRIC, GAS, AND SANITARY SERVICES

Long Neck Water Co .... G 302 947-9600
  Millsboro (G-4724)
Municipal Services Commission .... F 302 323-2330
  New Castle (G-5539)
Naamans Creek Watershed .... G 302 475-3037
  Wilmington (G-11792)
National Waterworks Inc .... G 302 653-9096
  Milton (G-4942)
Suez North America Inc .... F 302 633-5670
  Wilmington (G-12789)
Suez Water Delaware Inc .... D 302 633-5905
  Wilmington (G-12790)
Sussex Shores Water Co Corp .... G 302 539-7611
  Bethany Beach (G-433)
Tidewater Utilities Inc .... D 302 674-8056
  Dover (G-2147)

4952 Sewerage Systems

Byron H Jefferson Engineering .... G 302 422-9568
  Lincoln (G-3839)
Camdenwyoming Sewer & Wtr Auth ..... F 302 697-6372
  Camden (G-544)
Core & Main LP .... G 302 684-3452
  Milton (G-4883)
Core & Main LP .... G 302 737-1500
  Newark (G-6297)
Wolfe Neck Treatment Plant .... F 302 644-2761
  Rehoboth Beach (G-8118)

4953 Refuse Systems

Able Recycling Inc .... F 302 324-1760
  Wilmington (G-8904)
Bestrans Inc .... D 302 824-0909
  New Castle (G-5087)
BFI Waste Services LLC .... D 302 284-4440
  Felton (G-2274)
BFI Waste Services LLC .... E 302 658-4097
  Wilmington (G-9324)
Blue Hen Bzzrds Dspose-All LLC .... F 302 856-0913
  Millsboro (G-4646)
Brightfields Inc .... E 302 656-9600
  Wilmington (G-9477)
Buzzards Inc .... G 302 945-3500
  Millsboro (G-4651)
Carolyn Palmatary .... G 302 239-5744
  Hockessin (G-2976)
Cherry Island LLC .... F 302 658-5241
  New Castle (G-5144)
Choice Medwaste LLC .... G 302 366-1187
  Newark (G-6202)
Ciancon Global LLC .... E 302 365-0956
  Wilmington (G-9699)
Clean Delaware Inc .... F 302 684-4221
  Milton (G-4879)
Clean Earth New Castle Inc .... E 302 427-6633
  New Castle (G-5177)
Commodities Plus Inc .... G 302 376-5219
  Newark (G-6269)
D & J Recycling Inc .... G 302 422-0163
  Milford (G-4368)
Data Guard Recycling Inc .... G 302 337-8870
  Bridgeville (G-463)
Delaware Recyclable Products .... F 302 655-1360
  New Castle (G-5235)
Delaware Solid Waste Authority .... E 302 378-1407
  Townsend (G-8781)
Delaware Solid Waste Authority .... E 302 739-5361
  Dover (G-1392)
Delaware Solid Waste Authority .... E 302 764-2732
  Dover (G-1393)
Diamond State Recycling Corp .... E 302 655-1501
  Wilmington (G-10147)
Draw Incorporated .... G 410 208-9513
  Greenwood (G-2732)
Ecg Industries Inc .... G 302 453-0535
  Newark (G-6502)
Evergreen Waste Services LLC .... E 302 635-7055
  Hockessin (G-3024)
First State Disposal .... F 302 644-3885
  Lewes (G-3498)
Goodeals Inc .... G 302 999-1737
  Wilmington (G-10748)
Holland Mulch Inc .... F 302 765-3100
  Wilmington (G-10926)
Independent Disposal Services .... F 302 378-5400
  Townsend (G-8795)
Independent Transfer Operators .... G 302 420-4289
  Hockessin (G-3059)
International Petro Corp Del .... F 302 421-9306
  Wilmington (G-11066)

James Powell .... G 302 539-2351
  Frankford (G-2369)
Kaye Construction .... E 302 628-6962
  Seaford (G-8285)
KRC Waste Management Inc .... G 302 999-9276
  Wilmington (G-11294)
Kroegers Salvage Inc .... F 302 381-7082
  Bridgeville (G-489)
Magnus Environmental Corp .... E 302 655-4443
  New Castle (G-5497)
Mid Atlantic Waste System .... F 610 497-2405
  New Castle (G-5523)
Mid-Shore Envmtl Svcs Inc .... F 302 736-5504
  Bridgeville (G-500)
Modular Carpet Recycling Inc .... F 484 885-5890
  New Castle (G-5534)
Perdue-Agrirecycle LLC .... E 302 628-2360
  Seaford (G-8355)
Randolphs Refuse Service Inc .... G 302 658-5674
  New Castle (G-5665)
Rapid Recycling Inc .... G 302 324-5360
  New Castle (G-5666)
RE Community Holdings II Inc .... G 302 778-9793
  New Castle (G-5669)
Republic Services Inc .... E 302 658-4097
  Wilmington (G-12383)
Solutions of Advant-Edge .... G 302 533-6858
  Newark (G-7456)
Toss That Junk LLC .... G 302 326-3867
  Bear (G-355)
Trash Tech LLC .... G 302 832-8000
  New Castle (G-5786)
Tri-State Waste Solutions Inc .... E 302 622-8600
  New Castle (G-5790)
Waste Industries LLC .... G 302 934-1364
  Millsboro (G-4823)
Waste Management Delaware Inc .... C 302 994-0944
  Wilmington (G-13121)
Waste Management Delaware Inc .... G 302 854-5301
  Laurel (G-3306)
Waste Management Michigan Inc .... G 302 655-1360
  New Castle (G-5824)
Waste Masters Solutions LLC .... G 302 824-0909
  New Castle (G-5825)
Wasteflo LLC .... G 410 202-0802
  Laurel (G-3307)

4959 Sanitary Svcs, NEC

A1 Striping Inc .... G 302 738-5016
  Newark (G-5872)
C&H Environmental Services .... G 302 376-0178
  Middletown (G-3978)
Connor Sweeping Inc .... G 302 368-2210
  Newark (G-6288)
County Environmental Inc .... E 302 322-8946
  New Castle (G-5201)
Delaware Bay & River .... F 302 645-7861
  Lewes (G-3453)
Dupont North America Inc .... F 302 774-1000
  Wilmington (G-10256)
Guardian Envmtl Svcs Co Inc .... D 302 918-3070
  Newark (G-6695)
Hazardous Waste .... G 302 739-9403
  Dover (G-1638)
Infectious Diseases Cons PA .... F 302 994-9692
  Newark (G-6776)
Preferred Enviromental .... G 610 364-1106
  Clayton (G-869)
R W Home Services Inc .... F 302 539-4683
  Ocean View (G-7810)
Reilly Sweeping Inc .... E 302 738-8961
  Newark (G-7315)
Terra Systems Inc .... F 302 798-9553
  Claymont (G-810)

4971 Irrigation Systems

Atlantic Irrigation Spc Inc .... G 302 846-3527
  Delmar (G-972)
Atlantic Water Products .... E 302 326-1166
  New Castle (G-5052)
County of Sussex .... G 302 947-0864
  Millsboro (G-4670)
First State Landscaping .... G 302 420-8604
  Bear (G-153)
Impact Irrgation Solutions Inc .... G 484 723-3600
  Wilmington (G-11007)
Jobes Landscape Inc .... G 302 945-0195
  Lewes (G-3572)
Vincent Farms Inc .... G 302 875-5707
  Laurel (G-3302)

50 WHOLESALE TRADE¨DURABLE GOODS

5012 Automobiles & Other Motor Vehicles Wholesale

▼ Autoport Inc .... E 302 658-5100
  New Castle (G-5057)
Center Stage Auto Auction .... G 302 325-2277
  New Castle (G-5140)
Copart Inc .... F 302 628-5412
  Seaford (G-8208)
Dd Inc De LLC .... G 302 669-9269
  Claymont (G-730)
Delaware Public Auto Auction .... E 302 656-0500
  New Castle (G-5234)
Delmarva Pump Center Inc .... E 302 492-1245
  Marydel (G-3915)
Diamond Motor Sports Inc .... D 302 697-3222
  Dover (G-1423)
Future Ford Sales Inc .... D 302 999-0261
  Wilmington (G-10654)
Harvey Mack Sales & Svc Inc .... E 302 324-8340
  New Castle (G-5382)
Iaa Inc .... G 302 322-1808
  New Castle (G-5407)
Lee Mc Neill Associates .... G 302 593-6172
  Wilmington (G-11356)
One Off Rod & Custom Inc .... G 302 449-1489
  Middletown (G-4179)
Porter Nissan Buick Newark .... D 302 368-6300
  Newark (G-7233)
Staplefords Sales and Service .... E 302 834-4568
  Saint Georges (G-8130)
Tri-State Truck & Eqp Sls LLC .... G 302 276-1253
  New Castle (G-5789)
Utility/Eastern .... E 302 337-7400
  Bridgeville (G-528)
Walls Farm and Garden Ctr Inc .... G 302 422-4565
  Milford (G-4594)
▼ Winner Ford of Newark Inc .... C 302 731-2415
  Newark (G-7710)
Winner Group Inc .... E 302 292-8200
  Newark (G-7711)

5013 Motor Vehicle Splys & New Parts Wholesale

Action Automotive Inc .... G 302 429-0643
  Wilmington (G-8925)
Adams Auto Parts Inc .... F 302 655-9693
  Wilmington (G-8933)
Advance Auto Parts Inc .... G 302 644-0141
  Lewes (G-3325)
All American Truck Brokers .... G 302 654-6101
  Wilmington (G-9011)
Andover Companies Inc .... G 410 705-1503
  Seaford (G-8152)
Arundel Trailer Sales .... G 302 398-6288
  Harrington (G-2813)
Autopart International Inc .... F 302 998-2920
  Wilmington (G-9191)
Berrodin South Inc .... E 302 575-0500
  New Castle (G-5085)
Bethany Auto Parts Inc .... G 302 539-0555
  Ocean View (G-7765)
Bridgestone Ret Operations LLC .... G 302 422-4508
  Milford (G-4335)
C & W Auto Parts Co Inc .... G 302 697-2684
  Magnolia (G-3883)
Carl King Tire Co Inc .... E 302 697-9506
  Camden (G-546)
Clarksville Auto Service Ctr .... E 302 539-1700
  Ocean View (G-7777)
Cochran-Trivits Inc .... G 302 328-2945
  New Castle (G-5179)
Coveys Car Care Inc .... G 302 629-2746
  Seaford (G-8210)
Crw Parts Inc .... F 302 651-9300
  Wilmington (G-9907)
Delaware Tire Center Inc .... F 302 674-0234
  Dover (G-1402)
Dover Automotive Inc .... G 302 653-9234
  Smyrna (G-8625)
Fisher Auto Parts Inc .... G 302 653-9241
  Smyrna (G-8635)
Fisher Auto Parts Inc .... G 302 856-2507
  Georgetown (G-2533)
Fisher Auto Parts Inc .... G 302 998-3111
  Wilmington (G-10562)

SIC SECTION
50 WHOLESALE TRADE¨DURABLE GOODS

Company	Code	Phone
Fishers Auto Parts Inc	G	302 934-8088
Millsboro *(G-4691)*		
Fitzgerald Auto Salvage Inc	D	302 422-7584
Lincoln *(G-3849)*		
Future Ford Sales Inc	D	302 999-0261
Wilmington *(G-10654)*		
Garage	G	302 645-7288
Rehoboth Beach *(G-7943)*		
Gaudlitz Inc	G	202 468-3876
Dover *(G-1585)*		
Genuine Parts Company	G	610 494-6355
Claymont *(G-752)*		
Greg Smith Equipment Sales	G	302 894-9333
Newark *(G-6688)*		
Harvey Mack Sales & Svc Inc	E	302 324-8340
New Castle *(G-5382)*		
Housers Auto Trim Inc	G	302 422-1290
Milford *(G-4445)*		
Ieh Auto Parts LLC	E	302 994-7171
Wilmington *(G-10996)*		
IG Burton & Company Inc	E	302 629-2800
Seaford *(G-8269)*		
Imparts Inc	G	302 697-0990
Wyoming *(G-13363)*		
Irondt Corp	G	347 539-6471
Wilmington *(G-11083)*		
Johns Auto Parts Inc	F	302 322-3273
Bear *(G-204)*		
Keller Truck Parts Inc	G	302 658-5107
Wilmington *(G-11235)*		
Keystone Automotive Inds Inc	F	302 764-8010
New Castle *(G-5461)*		
▲ Mto Hose Solutions Inc	G	302 266-6555
Newark *(G-7071)*		
◆ NGK North America Inc	G	302 654-1344
Wilmington *(G-11884)*		
Pgw Auto Glass LLC	G	302 793-1486
Claymont *(G-794)*		
Ploeners Automotive Pdts Co	G	302 655-4418
Wilmington *(G-12161)*		
Quaker City Auto Parts Inc	G	302 436-5114
Selbyville *(G-8535)*		
S & K Enterprises Inc	G	302 292-1250
Newark *(G-7373)*		
Safelite Glass Corp	G	877 800-2727
Dover *(G-2053)*		
Safelite Glass Corp	F	302 656-4640
Wilmington *(G-12519)*		
Scott Muffler LLC	G	302 378-9247
Middletown *(G-4233)*		
Sp Auto Parts Inc	G	302 337-8897
Bridgeville *(G-521)*		
Sports Car Tire Inc	E	302 571-8473
Wilmington *(G-12710)*		
▼ T & J Murray Worldwide Svcs	F	302 736-1790
Dover *(G-2125)*		
Townsend Bros Inc	D	302 674-0100
Dover *(G-2155)*		
Transaxle LLC	G	302 322-8300
New Castle *(G-5785)*		
▲ Tri State Battery and Auto Elc	F	302 292-2330
Newark *(G-7584)*		
Utility/Eastern	E	302 337-7400
Bridgeville *(G-528)*		
Wholesale Auto Inc	G	302 322-6190
New Castle *(G-5833)*		
Wrenches	G	302 422-2690
Milford *(G-4612)*		

5014 Tires & Tubes Wholesale

Company	Code	Phone
Admiral Tire	G	302 734-5911
Dover *(G-1087)*		
Bargain Tire & Service Inc	F	302 764-8900
Wilmington *(G-9254)*		
Bridgestone Ret Operations LLC	G	302 422-4508
Milford *(G-4335)*		
Carl King Tire Co Inc	E	302 697-9506
Camden *(G-546)*		
Carl King Tire Co Inc	F	302 644-4070
Lewes *(G-3406)*		
Cochran-Trivits Inc	G	302 328-2945
New Castle *(G-5179)*		
Delaware Tire Center Inc	F	302 674-0234
Dover *(G-1402)*		
Delaware Tire Center Inc	F	302 368-2531
Newark *(G-6418)*		
Els Tire Service Inc	F	302 834-1997
Bridgeville *(G-6518)*		
EZ Manufacturing Company LLC	G	302 653-6567
Clayton *(G-849)*		
Goodyear Tire & Rubber Company	F	302 998-0428
Wilmington *(G-10751)*		
Tbc Retail Group Inc	E	302 478-8013
Wilmington *(G-12855)*		
Tire Rack Inc	D	302 325-8260
New Castle *(G-5771)*		
Tire Sales LLC	E	302 994-2900
New Castle *(G-5772)*		
Tire Sales & Service Inc	G	302 658-8955
Wilmington *(G-12916)*		
Traction Wholesale Center Inc	G	302 743-8473
Wilmington *(G-12946)*		
Wellers Tire Service Inc	F	302 337-8228
Bridgeville *(G-531)*		

5015 Motor Vehicle Parts, Used Wholesale

Company	Code	Phone
Afrikelist Corporation	F	800 767-1744
Wilmington *(G-8974)*		
Arundel Trailer Sales	G	302 398-6288
Harrington *(G-2813)*		
Auto Parts of Greenwood	G	302 349-9601
Farmington *(G-2265)*		
Averest Inc	G	302 281-2062
Wilmington *(G-9198)*		
Bridgeville Auto Center Inc	F	302 337-3100
Bridgeville *(G-454)*		
Delaware Auto Salvage Inc	G	302 322-2328
New Castle *(G-5225)*		
Deltrans Inc	G	302 453-8213
Newark *(G-6433)*		
Fred Drake Automotive Inc	G	302 378-4877
Townsend *(G-8788)*		
Goodchild Inc	G	302 368-1681
Newark *(G-6675)*		
Hammond Enterprises Inc	G	302 934-1700
Milford *(G-4433)*		
Hollie Enterprises LLC	F	903 721-1904
Wilmington *(G-10927)*		
Htk Automotive USA Corporation	E	310 504-2283
Wilmington *(G-10969)*		
Lkq Northeast Inc	G	800 223-0171
Dover *(G-1793)*		
Murrays Motors	G	302 628-0500
Seaford *(G-8315)*		
Parts Plus More LLC	G	302 300-4913
Dover *(G-1937)*		
Pinnacle Garage Door Company	G	302 505-4531
Felton *(G-2310)*		
Uacj Trading America Co Ltd	F	312 636-5941
Wilmington *(G-13005)*		
Vehattire LLC	F	302 221-2000
New Castle *(G-5814)*		
Wilmington Resources	F	302 746-7162
Wilmington *(G-13244)*		

5021 Furniture Wholesale

Company	Code	Phone
Advance Office Instltltions Inc	E	302 777-5599
New Castle *(G-5008)*		
Automation Solutions Inc	G	302 478-9060
Wilmington *(G-9189)*		
▼ Browne USA Inc	E	302 326-4802
New Castle *(G-5116)*		
▲ Corporate Interiors Inc	D	302 322-1008
New Castle *(G-5195)*		
Docs Medical LLC	G	301 401-1489
Bear *(G-122)*		
Furniture Whl Connection Inc	F	302 836-6000
Bear *(G-162)*		
Kenneth Deitch	G	302 838-2808
Bear *(G-215)*		
L F Systems Corp	F	302 322-0460
New Castle *(G-5471)*		
Lan Rack Inc	G	949 587-5168
Dover *(G-1764)*		
Laytons Umbrellas	F	302 249-1958
Laurel *(G-3257)*		
Richert Inc	F	302 684-0696
Milton *(G-4961)*		

5023 Home Furnishings Wholesale

Company	Code	Phone
A + Floor Store Inc	F	302 698-2166
Camden Wyoming *(G-609)*		
Advacare LLC	G	302 448-5045
Wilmington *(G-8944)*		
Art Floor Inc	E	302 636-9201
Wilmington *(G-9135)*		
▲ Avs Industries LLC	G	302 221-1705
New Castle *(G-5060)*		
▲ Coverdeck Systems Inc	E	302 427-7578
Wilmington *(G-9883)*		
▲ Duralex Usa Inc	D	302 326-4804
New Castle *(G-5267)*		
F Schumacher & Co	G	302 454-3200
Newark *(G-6561)*		
Fireside Heart & Home	G	302 337-3025
Bridgeville *(G-470)*		
◆ Franke USA Holding Inc	F	615 462-4000
Wilmington *(G-10614)*		
Gb Shades LLC	G	302 798-3028
Claymont *(G-749)*		
General Crpt-Mech Sply	G	302 322-1847
New Castle *(G-5348)*		
L & L Carpet Discount Ctrs Inc	G	302 292-3712
Newark *(G-6906)*		
▲ Lekue USA Inc	D	302 326-4805
New Castle *(G-5478)*		
Microdry Inc	G	302 416-3021
Wilmington *(G-11675)*		
Middletown Kitchen and Bath	G	302 376-5766
Middletown *(G-4158)*		
▲ Ready Set Textiles Inc	G	302 518-6583
Rehoboth Beach *(G-8045)*		
Reiver Hyman & Co Inc	F	302 764-2040
Wilmington *(G-12371)*		
Rite Way Distributors	G	302 535-8507
Felton *(G-2317)*		
▲ Rosle U S A Corp	E	302 326-4801
New Castle *(G-5685)*		
Selling Dreams LLC	G	302 746-7999
Claymont *(G-803)*		
Seth Ral & Associates Inc	F	302 478-9020
Wilmington *(G-12587)*		
Willey Farms Inc	D	302 378-8441
Townsend *(G-8833)*		
Williams-Sonoma Stores Inc	E	302 368-7707
Newark *(G-7700)*		

5031 Lumber, Plywood & Millwork Wholesale

Company	Code	Phone
Allura Bath & Kitchen Inc	G	302 731-2851
Newark *(G-5944)*		
American Bldrs Contrs Sup Inc	F	302 994-1166
Wilmington *(G-9042)*		
American Cedar & Millwork Inc	D	302 645-9580
Lewes *(G-3335)*		
Builders Firstsource Inc	E	302 731-0678
Newark *(G-6129)*		
Cabinetry Unlimited LLC	E	302 436-5030
Selbyville *(G-8465)*		
Clearview Windows LLC	F	302 491-6768
Milford *(G-4356)*		
Crothers Doors and More I	G	302 678-3667
Camden Wyoming *(G-627)*		
Dack Trading LLC	F	917 576-4432
Rehoboth Beach *(G-7907)*		
Delaware Building Supply Corp	E	302 424-3505
Milford *(G-4377)*		
Delaware Flooring Supply Inc	G	302 276-0031
New Castle *(G-5230)*		
Fessenden Hall Incorporated	F	302 674-4505
Dover *(G-1549)*		
Greenwood Pallet Co	G	302 337-8181
Bridgeville *(G-476)*		
Grubb Lumber Company Inc	E	302 652-2800
Wilmington *(G-10791)*		
Gunton Corporation	G	302 999-0535
Wilmington *(G-10803)*		
Hathworth Inc	G	302 884-7616
Wilmington *(G-10852)*		
Hickman Overhead Door Company	F	302 422-4249
Milford *(G-4441)*		
La Floresta Perdida Inc	F	302 478-8900
Wilmington *(G-11311)*		
Lowes Home Centers LLC	C	302 479-7799
Wilmington *(G-11444)*		
Lowes Home Centers LLC	C	302 934-3740
Millsboro *(G-4727)*		
Lowes Home Centers LLC	C	302 376-3006
Middletown *(G-4137)*		
Lowes Home Centers LLC	C	302 735-7500
Dover *(G-1798)*		
Lowes Home Centers LLC	C	302 645-0900
Lewes *(G-3612)*		
Lowes Home Centers LLC	C	302 834-8508
Bear *(G-238)*		
Lowes Home Centers LLC	C	302 697-0700
Camden *(G-589)*		
Lowes Home Centers LLC	C	302 781-1154
Newark *(G-6953)*		

Employee Codes: A=Over 500 employees, B=251-500
C=101-250, D=51-100, E=20-50, F=10-19, G=1-9

50 WHOLESALE TRADE¨DURABLE GOODS SIC SECTION

Lowes Home Centers LLC ....C.... 302 536-4000
Seaford (G-8296)
Lowes Home Centers LLC ....C.... 302 252-3228
New Castle (G-5488)
M/S Hollow Metal Wholesale LLC ....E.... 302 349-9471
Greenwood (G-2750)
Marjam Supply Co Inc ....F.... 302 283-1020
Newark (G-6988)
Metrie Inc ....G.... 302 337-0269
Bridgeville (G-499)
Mumford Sheet Metal Works Inc ....E.... 302 436-8251
Selbyville (G-8527)
North American Hardwoods Ltd ....F.... 516 848-7729
Wilmington (G-11898)
P D Supply Inc ....G.... 302 655-3358
Wilmington (G-11994)
Rcd Timber Products Inc ....G.... 302 778-5700
New Castle (G-5668)
Rehrig Penn Logistics Inc ....G.... 302 659-3337
Smyrna (G-8699)
Robinson Export & Import Corp ....G.... 410 219-7200
Millsboro (G-4794)
Russell Plywood Inc ....F.... 302 689-0137
New Castle (G-5691)
State Line Building Supply ....F.... 302 436-8624
Selbyville (G-8549)
Sussex Lumber Company Inc ....E.... 302 934-8128
Millsboro (G-4808)
▼ Uniforest Wood Products Inc ....F.... 302 450-4541
Wilmington (G-13012)
▲ Wholesale Millwork Inc ....F.... 888 964-8746
Seaford (G-8437)

5032 Brick, Stone & Related Construction Mtrls Wholesale

Allan Myers Materials Inc ....G.... 302 734-8632
Dover (G-1108)
Asphalt Paving Eqp & Sups ....G.... 302 683-0105
Harbeson (G-2773)
▲ Azurite03 Inc ....G.... 866 667-5119
Wilmington (G-9206)
Berkshire At Limestone ....G.... 302 635-7495
Wilmington (G-9304)
▲ Best Granite LLC ....G.... 302 644-8302
Lewes (G-3378)
◆ Casale Marble Imports Inc ....D.... 561 404-4213
Wilmington (G-9585)
Chemlime NJ Inc ....G.... 302 697-2115
Magnolia (G-3885)
Christiana Materials Inc ....F.... 302 633-5600
Wilmington (G-9688)
Consolidated Construction Svcs ....F.... 302 629-6070
Seaford (G-8205)
Delaware Brick Company ....G.... 302 883-2807
Dover (G-1361)
Delaware Brick Company ....E.... 302 994-0948
Wilmington (G-10008)
Depro-Serical USA Inc ....G.... 302 368-8040
Townsend (G-8783)
Jack Parisi Tile Co Inc ....G.... 302 892-2455
Wilmington (G-11115)
▲ Jet Products LLC ....G.... 877 453-8868
Wilmington (G-11151)
▲ Landis Ltd ....G.... 302 656-9024
Wilmington (G-11326)
Maddox Concrete Co Inc ....G.... 302 656-2000
Wilmington (G-11482)
Marble Source Unlimited Inc ....E.... 302 337-7665
Bridgeville (G-492)
Marcus Materials Co ....G.... 302 731-7519
Newark (G-6984)
Michael McCarthy Stones ....G.... 302 539-8056
Millville (G-4850)
Mohawk Tile MBL Distrs of Del ....G.... 302 655-7164
Wilmington (G-11725)
Parker Block Co Inc ....E.... 302 934-9237
Millsboro (G-4769)
◆ Pera Trading Inc ....G.... 302 292-1750
Newark (G-7200)
Porter Sand & Gravel Inc ....G.... 302 335-5132
Harrington (G-2875)

5033 Roofing, Siding & Insulation Mtrls Wholesale

American Bldrs Contrs Sup Inc ....F.... 302 994-1166
Wilmington (G-9042)
Goldis Enterprises Inc ....G.... 302 764-3100
Wilmington (G-10740)
Goldis Holdings Inc ....D.... 302 764-3100
Wilmington (G-10741)
Iko Manufacturing Inc ....D.... 302 764-3100
Wilmington (G-10999)
Iko Sales Inc ....D.... 302 764-3100
Wilmington (G-11001)
J & L Building Materials Inc ....F.... 302 504-0350
New Castle (G-5427)
Mill Creek Metals Inc ....F.... 302 529-7020
Claymont (G-782)
Quality Rofg Sup Lancaster Inc ....F.... 302 644-4115
Lewes (G-3703)
Quality Rofg Sup Lancaster Inc ....G.... 302 322-8322
New Castle (G-5658)
S G Williams of Dover Inc ....F.... 302 678-1080
Dover (G-2050)
SRS Distribution Inc ....F.... 240 965-8350
Wilmington (G-12719)
Thomas Roofing Supply Company ....E.... 302 629-4521
Seaford (G-8421)
Thomco Inc ....G.... 302 454-0361
Newark (G-7564)

5039 Construction Materials, NEC Wholesale

Aesops Gables Inc ....G.... 302 737-2683
Newark (G-5915)
Building Concepts America Inc ....E.... 302 292-0200
Newark (G-6131)
Door & Gate Co LLC ....G.... 888 505-6962
Claymont (G-734)
Ducts Unlimited Inc ....G.... 302 378-4125
Smyrna (G-8628)
Edis Building Systems Inc ....G.... 302 421-5700
Wilmington (G-10349)
Erco Ceilings Inc ....F.... 302 994-6200
Wilmington (G-10431)
Erco Ceilings & Interiors Inc ....F.... 302 398-3200
Harrington (G-2838)
F and M Equipment Ltd ....G.... 302 715-5382
Laurel (G-3229)
George F Kempf Supply Co Inc ....G.... 302 658-3760
Wilmington (G-10698)
J & M Fencing Inc ....F.... 302 284-9674
Felton (G-2295)
Master-Halco Inc ....F.... 302 475-6714
Wilmington (G-11564)
Rew Material ....G.... 302 424-2125
Milford (G-4541)
T & C Enterprise Incorporated ....G.... 302 934-8080
Millsboro (G-4809)
Union Whl Acoustical Sup Co ....G.... 302 656-4462
Wilmington (G-13014)

5043 Photographic Eqpt & Splys Wholesale

▲ Autotype Holdings (usa) Inc ....C.... 302 378-3100
Middletown (G-3956)
Cameras Etc Inc ....F.... 302 764-9400
Wilmington (G-9545)
◆ Fujifilm Imaging Colorants Inc ....E.... 302 477-8022
New Castle (G-5334)
Waco Lid Films Inc ....G.... 302 378-7053
Townsend (G-8831)

5044 Office Eqpt Wholesale

Autotote Canada Inc ....C.... 302 737-4300
Newark (G-6029)
Blue Marble Logistics LLC ....F.... 302 661-4390
Wilmington (G-9378)
Canon Solutions America Inc ....E.... 302 792-8700
Wilmington (G-9551)
Digital Office Solutions Inc ....F.... 302 286-6706
Newark (G-6447)
Hilyards Inc ....E.... 302 995-2201
Wilmington (G-10913)
Laser Tone Bus Systems LLC ....G.... 302 335-2510
Milford (G-4471)
Michelet Finance Inc ....G.... 302 427-8751
Wilmington (G-11671)
No Nonsense Office Mchs LLC ....G.... 302 856-7381
Georgetown (G-2610)
Ricoh Usa Inc ....D.... 302 737-8000
Newark (G-7339)
Ricoh Usa Inc ....F.... 302 573-3562
Wilmington (G-12415)
Steven Abdill ....G.... 443 243-6864
Wilmington (G-12758)
Xerox Corporation ....E.... 302 792-5100
Wilmington (G-13319)

5045 Computers & Peripheral Eqpt & Software Wholesale

34m LLC ....E.... 302 444-8290
Newark (G-5857)
Access Versalign Inc ....G.... 302 225-7800
Wilmington (G-8914)
AR Solutions Inc ....F.... 609 751-9611
Claymont (G-693)
Aries Security LLC ....G.... 302 365-0026
Wilmington (G-9128)
Atlantic Marketing Inc ....G.... 302 674-7036
Dover (G-1157)
Baytown Systems Inc ....G.... 302 689-3421
Wilmington (G-9267)
Bb Technologies Inc ....G.... 302 652-2300
Wilmington (G-9268)
Bits & Bytes Inc ....G.... 302 674-2999
Dover (G-1207)
Broadberry Data Systems LLC ....E.... 302 295-1086
Wilmington (G-9481)
Broadberry Data Systems LLC ....G.... 800 496-9918
Wilmington (G-9482)
Cadapult Ltd ....F.... 302 733-0477
Newark (G-6143)
Cutler Industries Inc ....G.... 302 689-3779
Wilmington (G-9928)
DOE Legal LLC ....E.... 302 798-7500
Wilmington (G-10180)
Ergosix Corporation ....G.... 844 603-1181
Dover (G-1530)
Express Vpn LLC ....G.... 310 601-8492
Newark (G-6554)
Hoover Computer Services Inc ....G.... 302 529-7050
Wilmington (G-10950)
Horizon Systems Inc ....G.... 302 983-3203
New Castle (G-5404)
Hypertec Usa Inc ....G.... 480 626-9000
Dover (G-1664)
▼ Iconic Tsunami LLC ....G.... 302 223-3411
Smyrna (G-8657)
Incite Solutions Inc ....G.... 302 655-8952
Wilmington (G-11013)
Info Systems LLC ....C.... 302 633-9800
Wilmington (G-11026)
Kvm Depot Inc ....F.... 302 472-9190
Wilmington (G-11303)
Lan Rack Inc ....G.... 949 587-5168
Dover (G-1764)
Laser Online LLC ....F.... 302 261-5225
Wilmington (G-11334)
PC Supplies Inc ....G.... 302 368-4800
Newark (G-7189)
Quinn Data Corporation ....G.... 302 429-7450
Wilmington (G-12289)
Ram Tech Systems Inc ....E.... 302 832-6600
Middletown (G-4210)
Singular Key Inc ....F.... 408 753-5848
Wilmington (G-12631)
Superstore LLC ....F.... 302 200-4933
Wilmington (G-12811)
Techsolutions Inc ....F.... 302 656-8324
Wilmington (G-12872)
Tops International Corp ....G.... 302 738-8889
Newark (G-7576)
Trutrac LLC ....G.... 833 878-8722
Wilmington (G-12989)
We Cobble LLC ....F.... 302 504-4294
Wilmington (G-13130)

5046 Commercial Eqpt, NEC Wholesale

Brewster Products Inc ....G.... 302 764-4463
Wilmington (G-9469)
Burke Equipment Company ....E.... 302 248-7070
Delmar (G-975)
Burke Equipment Company ....G.... 302 248-7070
Delmar (G-976)
Elmer Schultz Services Inc ....G.... 302 655-8900
Wilmington (G-10382)
Hy-Point Equipment Co ....F.... 302 478-0388
Wilmington (G-10980)
Jesco Inc ....G.... 302 376-6946
Middletown (G-4114)
Kent Sign Company Inc ....F.... 302 697-2181
Dover (G-1739)
South Forks Inc ....G.... 302 731-0344
Newark (G-7461)
Vending Solutions LLC ....G.... 302 674-2222
Dover (G-2189)

SIC SECTION
50 WHOLESALE TRADE¨DURABLE GOODS

Widgeon Enterprises Inc .... G 302 846-9763
Delmar *(G-1049)*

5047 Medical, Dental & Hospital Eqpt & Splys Wholesale

◆ Anderson Group Inc .... G 302 478-6160
Wilmington *(G-9078)*
Aracent Healthcare LLC .... G 302 478-8865
Wilmington *(G-9110)*
Baker Safety Equipment Inc .... G 302 376-9302
Bear *(G-44)*
Broad Creek Medical Service .... F 302 629-0202
Seaford *(G-8174)*
Cardiomo Care Inc .... F 929 360-5107
Wilmington *(G-9566)*
Dentsply Sirona Inc .... G 302 422-4511
Milford *(G-4387)*
Dienay Distribution Corp .... G 732 766-0814
Middletown *(G-4039)*
First Choice Home Med Equipt .... E 302 323-8700
New Castle *(G-5312)*
Gaudlitz Inc .... G 202 468-3876
Dover *(G-1585)*
Hannas Phrm Sup Co Inc .... F 302 571-8761
Wilmington *(G-10834)*
Hysiotherapy Associates Inc .... E 610 444-1270
Wilmington *(G-10983)*
Jaco LLC .... G 302 645-8068
Milton *(G-4920)*
Junior Bd of Christiana Care .... G 302 733-1100
Newark *(G-6858)*
Linda McCormick .... G 443 987-2099
Wilmington *(G-11392)*
Marosa Surgical Industries .... F 302 674-0907
New Castle *(G-5510)*
Medical Technologies Intl .... E 760 837-4778
Dover *(G-1836)*
Medrep Inc .... G 302 571-0263
Wilmington *(G-11621)*
Medtix LLC .... E 302 645-8070
Milford *(G-4492)*
Medtix LLC .... F 302 265-4550
Lewes *(G-3632)*
Osskin USA Inc .... G 302 266-8200
Newark *(G-7162)*
Peninsula Home Health Care .... F 302 629-5672
Seaford *(G-8348)*
Personal Health PDT Dev LLC .... E 888 901-6150
Wilmington *(G-12091)*
Prescription Center Inc .... G 302 764-8564
Wilmington *(G-12221)*
Purushas Picks Inc .... G 302 918-7663
Bear *(G-295)*
Quinn-Miller Group Inc .... G 302 738-9742
Wilmington *(G-12290)*
Rhondium Corporation .... F 800 771-4364
Wilmington *(G-12403)*
Siemens Hlthcare Dgnostics Inc .... D 302 631-7357
Newark *(G-7425)*
▲ Smith & Nephew Holdings Inc .... G 302 884-6720
Wilmington *(G-12659)*
Synergy Medical USA Inc .... F 302 444-0163
Newark *(G-7525)*
Tarpon Strategies LLC .... G 215 806-2723
Newark *(G-7540)*
World Wide Trading Brokers .... G 302 368-7041
Newark *(G-7722)*

5048 Ophthalmic Goods Wholesale

Essilor America Holding Co Inc .... F 214 496-4000
Wilmington *(G-10439)*
Jim Kounnas Optometrists .... G 302 722-6197
Wilmington *(G-11160)*

5049 Professional Eqpt & Splys, NEC Wholesale

◆ Bio Medic Corporation .... F 302 628-4300
Seaford *(G-8170)*
▲ Buchi Corporation .... D 302 652-3000
New Castle *(G-5119)*
Elsicon Inc .... F 302 266-7030
Newark *(G-6519)*
Igal Biochemical LLC .... G 302 525-2090
Newark *(G-6765)*
Joint Anlytcl Systms (amrcs) .... G 302 607-0088
Newark *(G-6849)*
K & S Technical Services Inc .... G 302 737-9133
Newark *(G-6864)*

Main Light Industries Inc .... C 302 998-8017
Wilmington *(G-11491)*
◆ Miles Scientific Corporation .... F 302 737-6960
Newark *(G-7039)*
Reprographics Center Inc .... G 302 328-5019
New Castle *(G-5672)*
Survey Supply Inc .... G 302 422-3338
Milford *(G-4572)*
Toxtrap Inc .... G 302 698-1400
Dover *(G-2156)*
Trimble Navigation Limited .... G 302 368-2434
Newark *(G-7593)*

5051 Metals Service Centers

B & B Industries Inc .... F 302 655-6156
Wilmington *(G-9207)*
Boyds Trailor Hitches .... G 302 697-9000
Camden Wyoming *(G-619)*
Bristol Industrial Corporation .... F 302 322-1100
New Castle *(G-5115)*
Bushwick Metals LLC .... G 302 328-0590
New Castle *(G-5123)*
▲ Calmet Corporation .... E 714 505-6765
Wilmington *(G-9539)*
Chez Nichole Hair & Nail Salon .... G 302 654-8888
Wilmington *(G-9659)*
Delta Sales Corp .... D 302 436-6063
Selbyville *(G-8481)*
East Coast Stainless Inc .... G 302 366-0675
Newark *(G-6495)*
East Coast Stainless & Alloys .... F 302 366-0675
Newark *(G-6496)*
Industrial Stl Structures Inc .... E 302 275-8892
New Castle *(G-5416)*
Metal Partners Rebar LLC .... F 215 791-3491
New Castle *(G-5517)*
▲ Miller Metal Fabrication Inc .... D 302 337-2291
Bridgeville *(G-501)*
Petroserv Inc .... G 302 398-3260
Harrington *(G-2873)*
S G Williams & Bros Co .... F 302 656-8167
Wilmington *(G-12506)*
Steel and Metal Service .... G 302 322-9960
New Castle *(G-5739)*
Steel Suppliers Inc .... C 302 654-5243
Wilmington *(G-12748)*
◆ Vertex Industries Inc .... G 302 472-0601
Wilmington *(G-13066)*
▼ Vulcraft Sales Corp .... F 302 427-5832
Wilmington *(G-13108)*

5052 Coal & Other Minerals & Ores Wholesale

Banfield & Temperley Inc .... G 347 878-6057
Dover *(G-1169)*
Network Scrap Metal Corp .... G 910 202-0655
Wilmington *(G-11841)*

5063 Electrl Apparatus, Eqpt, Wiring Splys Wholesale

Allpower Generator Sales & Svc .... G 302 793-1690
Claymont *(G-688)*
American Neon Products Company .... F 302 856-3400
Milford *(G-4306)*
◆ Anderson Group Inc .... G 302 478-6160
Wilmington *(G-9078)*
Billows Electric Supply Co Inc .... G 302 996-9133
Wilmington *(G-9338)*
Bristol Industrial Corporation .... F 302 322-1100
New Castle *(G-5115)*
City Electric Supply Company .... G 302 777-5300
Wilmington *(G-9722)*
Colonial Electric Supply Co .... F 302 998-9993
New Castle *(G-5181)*
Conectiv Energy Supply Inc .... D 302 454-0300
Newark *(G-6283)*
Denney Electric Supply Del Inc .... G 302 934-8885
Millsboro *(G-4677)*
Diversified Lighting Assoc Inc .... G 302 286-6370
Wilmington *(G-10171)*
Dover Electric Supply Co Inc .... E 302 674-0115
Dover *(G-1447)*
Dover Electric Supply Co Inc .... G 302 645-0555
Rehoboth Beach *(G-7920)*
Electric Motor Wholesale Inc .... F 302 653-1844
Camden Wyoming *(G-635)*
Graybar Electric Company Inc .... E 302 322-2200
New Castle *(G-5360)*

Griffith Industrial Supply .... G 302 731-0574
Newark *(G-6691)*
Grossman Electric Supply Inc .... G 302 655-5561
New Castle *(G-5364)*
John R Seiberlich Inc .... G 302 356-2400
New Castle *(G-5441)*
Ledtolight .... G 941 323-6664
Wilmington *(G-11354)*
◆ NGK North America Inc .... G 302 654-1344
Wilmington *(G-11884)*
Ploeners Automotive Pdts Co .... G 302 655-4418
Wilmington *(G-12161)*
Powerback Service LLC .... G 302 934-1901
Millsboro *(G-4785)*
Rigel Energy Group LLC .... F 888 624-9844
Wilmington *(G-12421)*
Select Suppliers Ltd .... G 303 523-1813
Dover *(G-2068)*
Semiconductorplus Inc .... G 302 330-7533
Wilmington *(G-12577)*
Siemens Corporation .... F 302 690-2046
Newark *(G-7424)*
Simplex Time Recorder LLC .... G 302 325-6300
New Castle *(G-5714)*
Tecot Electric Supply Co .... G 302 368-9161
Newark *(G-7549)*
Tecot Electric Supply Co .... G 302 735-3300
Dover *(G-2135)*
Todays Energy Solutions LLC .... G 302 438-0285
Wilmington *(G-12921)*
▲ Tri State Battery and Auto Elc .... F 302 292-2330
Newark *(G-7584)*
United Electric Supply Co Inc .... C 800 322-3374
New Castle *(G-5804)*
United Electric Supply Co Inc .... F 302 674-8351
Dover *(G-2180)*
United Electric Supply Co Inc .... G 302 732-1291
Dagsboro *(G-941)*
Warren Electric Co Inc .... G 302 629-9134
Seaford *(G-8433)*
Wesco Distribution Inc .... G 302 655-9611
Wilmington *(G-13162)*
Wilmington Resources .... F 302 746-7162
Wilmington *(G-13244)*
WW Grainger Inc .... F 302 322-1840
New Castle *(G-5842)*

5064 Electrical Appliances, TV & Radios Wholesale

ABC Sales & Service Inc .... E 302 652-3683
Wilmington *(G-8899)*
Appliances Zone .... G 302 280-6073
Delmar *(G-971)*
Artisan Electrical Inc .... G 302 645-5844
Lewes *(G-3348)*
Brandywine Electronics Corp .... F 302 324-9992
Bear *(G-56)*
Gt World Machineries Usa Inc .... F 800 242-4935
Christiana *(G-669)*
Lowes Home Centers LLC .... C 302 479-7799
Wilmington *(G-11444)*
Lowes Home Centers LLC .... C 302 934-3740
Millsboro *(G-4727)*
Lowes Home Centers LLC .... C 302 376-3006
Middletown *(G-4137)*
Lowes Home Centers LLC .... C 302 735-7500
Dover *(G-1798)*
Lowes Home Centers LLC .... C 302 645-0900
Lewes *(G-3612)*
Lowes Home Centers LLC .... C 302 834-8508
Bear *(G-238)*
Lowes Home Centers LLC .... C 302 697-0700
Camden *(G-589)*
Lowes Home Centers LLC .... C 302 781-1154
Newark *(G-6953)*
Lowes Home Centers LLC .... C 302 536-4000
Seaford *(G-8296)*
Lowes Home Centers LLC .... C 302 252-3228
New Castle *(G-5488)*
National Appliance Whse Inc .... G 302 543-7636
Wilmington *(G-11805)*
Reil Machines USA Inc .... F 905 488-9263
Wilmington *(G-12369)*
Tanner Operations Inc .... F 302 464-2194
Townsend *(G-8825)*

5065 Electronic Parts & Eqpt Wholesale

A Plus Electric & Security .... G 302 455-1725
Newark *(G-5869)*

Employee Codes: A=Over 500 employees, B=251-500
C=101-250, D=51-100, E=20-50, F=10-19, G=1-9

2020 Harris Directory of Delaware Businesses

50 WHOLESALE TRADE—DURABLE GOODS

A V C Inc	G	302 227-2549
Rehoboth Beach *(G-7835)*

Alliance International Elec .... G 302 838-3880
  Bear *(G-26)*
▲ Alvatek Electronics LLC .... F 302 655-5870
  Wilmington *(G-9036)*
Atechnologie LLC .... G 781 325-5230
  Wilmington *(G-9171)*
▲ Bellex International Corp .... G 302 791-5180
  Wilmington *(G-9294)*
Delmarva Communications Inc .... F 302 324-1230
  New Castle *(G-5244)*
Electronics Exchange Inc .... G 302 322-5401
  New Castle *(G-5285)*
John R Seiberlich Inc .... D 302 356-2400
  New Castle *(G-5441)*
▲ Lumenty Technologies Inc .... F 971 331-3113
  Wilmington *(G-11449)*
Maxbright Inc .... E 281 616-7999
  Lewes *(G-3626)*
Microtune LP LLC .... D 302 691-6037
  Wilmington *(G-11677)*
Quality Distributors Inc .... G 917 335-6662
  Wilmington *(G-12279)*
S & B Pro Security LLC .... G 800 841-9907
  Dover *(G-2047)*
Securitech Inc .... F 302 996-9230
  Wilmington *(G-12570)*
Semiconductorplus Inc .... G 302 330-7533
  Wilmington *(G-12577)*
▼ Servo2gocom Ltd .... E 877 378-0240
  Wilmington *(G-12586)*
Seth Ral & Associates Inc .... G 302 478-9020
  Wilmington *(G-12587)*
Vectorvance LLC .... G 347 779-9932
  Wilmington *(G-13054)*
▲ Video Walltronics Inc .... G 302 328-4511
  New Castle *(G-5817)*
Voxx Electronics Corp .... F 302 656-5303
  Wilmington *(G-13105)*
WER Wireless Inc .... E 302 478-7748
  Wilmington *(G-13158)*

5072 Hardware Wholesale

Acurio LLC .... G 201 932-8160
  Wilmington *(G-8931)*
Allied Lock & Safe Company .... G 302 658-3172
  Wilmington *(G-9023)*
Building Fasteners Inc .... G 302 738-0671
  Newark *(G-6132)*
Clark & Sons Overhead Doors .... E 302 998-7552
  Wilmington *(G-9732)*
Foss-Brown Inc .... F 610 940-6040
  Wilmington *(G-10598)*
Integrity Corporation Inc .... F 410 392-8665
  Newark *(G-6790)*
Makk-O Industries Inc .... G 302 376-0160
  Townsend *(G-8808)*
Mumford Sheet Metal Works Inc .... E 302 436-8251
  Selbyville *(G-8527)*
Petroserv Inc .... G 302 398-3260
  Harrington *(G-2873)*
Ron Ell Hardware Inc .... F 302 328-8997
  New Castle *(G-5682)*
Standard Industrial Supply Co .... G 302 656-1631
  Wilmington *(G-12735)*
Sumuri LLC .... G 302 570-0015
  Camden *(G-601)*
T & C Enterprise Incorporated .... G 302 934-8080
  Millsboro *(G-4809)*
Triangle Fastener Corporation .... F 302 322-0600
  New Castle *(G-5792)*
WW Grainger Inc .... F 302 322-1840
  New Castle *(G-5842)*

5074 Plumbing & Heating Splys Wholesale

Briggs Company .... E 302 328-9471
  New Castle *(G-5114)*
Bristol Industrial Corporation .... F 302 322-1100
  New Castle *(G-5115)*
Condor Technologies Inc .... G 302 698-4444
  Camden *(G-551)*
Core & Main LP .... G 302 684-3452
  Milton *(G-4883)*
Delaware Plumbing Supply Co .... F 302 656-5437
  New Castle *(G-5233)*
Delmarva Refrigeration Inc .... G 302 846-2727
  Delmar *(G-992)*
Dover Plumbing Supply Co .... F 302 674-0333
  Dover *(G-1464)*
Ferguson Enterprises LLC .... E 302 656-4421
  Wilmington *(G-10520)*
Ferguson Enterprises LLC .... G 302 747-2032
  Dover *(G-1548)*
Ferguson Enterprises LLC .... G 302 934-6040
  Millsboro *(G-4689)*
Ferguson Enterprises LLC .... G 302 322-2836
  New Castle *(G-5309)*
◆ Graver Technologies LLC .... C 302 731-1700
  Newark *(G-6684)*
Greenberg Supply Co Inc .... E 302 656-4496
  Wilmington *(G-10777)*
Hajoca Corporation .... F 302 764-6000
  Wilmington *(G-10823)*
Mumford Sheet Metal Works Inc .... E 302 436-8251
  Selbyville *(G-8527)*
Northeastern Supply Inc .... G 302 698-1414
  Camden *(G-593)*
Northeastern Supply Inc .... G 302 378-7880
  Middletown *(G-4176)*
Penco Corporation .... G 302 698-3108
  Camden *(G-596)*
Penco Corporation .... G 302 227-9188
  Rehoboth Beach *(G-8029)*
Penco Corporation .... G 302 738-3212
  Newark *(G-7195)*
Penco Corporation .... D 302 629-7911
  Seaford *(G-8343)*
Schagrin Gas Co .... E 302 378-2000
  Middletown *(G-4232)*
Sid Harvey Industries Inc .... G 302 746-7760
  Claymont *(G-805)*
Sun-In-One Inc .... G 302 762-3100
  Wilmington *(G-12798)*
Sweeten Companies Inc .... G 302 737-6161
  Newark *(G-7520)*
◆ Vertex Industries Inc .... G 302 472-0601
  Wilmington *(G-13066)*
Waterlogic Usa Inc .... C 302 323-2100
  New Castle *(G-5826)*

5075 Heating & Air Conditioning Eqpt & Splys Wholesale

A & A Mechanical Service Inc .... G 302 234-9949
  Hockessin *(G-2949)*
Berry Refrigeration Co .... E 302 733-0933
  Newark *(G-6073)*
▲ Building Systems and Svcs Inc ... E 302 996-0900
  Wilmington *(G-9503)*
Delmarva Refrigeration Inc .... G 302 846-2727
  Delmar *(G-992)*
Greenberg Supply Co Inc .... E 302 656-4496
  Wilmington *(G-10777)*
John R Seiberlich Inc .... D 302 356-2400
  New Castle *(G-5441)*
Kompressed Air Delaware Inc .... G 302 275-1985
  New Castle *(G-5469)*
Lycon Investment Company .... G 302 732-0940
  Dagsboro *(G-915)*
Peirce-Phelps Inc .... G 302 633-9352
  Wilmington *(G-12060)*
R E Michel Company LLC .... G 302 678-0250
  Dover *(G-2006)*
R E Michel Company LLC .... G 302 322-7480
  Newark *(G-5662)*
R E Michel Company LLC .... G 302 645-0585
  Lewes *(G-3704)*
R E Michel Company LLC .... G 302 368-9410
  Newark *(G-7292)*
United Refrigeration Inc .... G 302 322-1836
  New Castle *(G-5806)*
WJC of Delaware LLC .... G 302 323-9600
  New Castle *(G-5839)*
WW Grainger Inc .... F 302 322-1840
  New Castle *(G-5842)*

5078 Refrigeration Eqpt & Splys Wholesale

Berry Refrigeration Co .... E 302 733-0933
  Newark *(G-6073)*
Delmarva Refrigeration Inc .... G 302 846-2727
  Delmar *(G-992)*
Greenberg Supply Co Inc .... E 302 656-4496
  Wilmington *(G-10777)*
John R Seiberlich Inc .... D 302 356-2400
  New Castle *(G-5441)*
R E Michel Company LLC .... G 302 678-0250
  Dover *(G-2006)*
R E Michel Company LLC .... G 302 645-0585
  Lewes *(G-3704)*
Reil Machines USA Inc .... F 905 488-9263
  Wilmington *(G-12369)*
Thermo King Corporation .... E 302 907-0345
  Delmar *(G-1038)*
Thermo King Corporation .... E 302 907-0345
  Delmar *(G-1039)*
United Refrigeration Inc .... G 302 322-1836
  New Castle *(G-5806)*
WW Grainger Inc .... F 302 322-1840
  New Castle *(G-5842)*

5082 Construction & Mining Mach & Eqpt Wholesale

Alban Tractor Co Inc .... E 302 284-4100
  Felton *(G-2270)*
Atlantic Tractor LLC .... F 302 834-0114
  Newark *(G-6022)*
Bristol Industrial Corporation .... F 302 322-1100
  New Castle *(G-5115)*
Chesapeake Supply & Eqp Co .... G 302 284-1000
  Felton *(G-2283)*
Delaware Brick Company .... G 302 883-2807
  Dover *(G-1361)*
E-Industrial Suppliers LLC .... G 302 251-6210
  Wilmington *(G-10313)*
Eagle Power and Equipment Corp .. F 302 652-3028
  New Castle *(G-5274)*
Fmj Electrical Contracting .... G 215 669-2085
  Claymont *(G-746)*
Foley Incorporated .... E 302 328-4131
  Bear *(G-157)*
Foulk Lawn & Equipment Co Inc .... G 302 475-3233
  Wilmington *(G-10599)*
Giles & Ransome Inc .... G 302 777-5800
  New Castle *(G-5353)*
Industrial Products of Del .... F 302 328-6648
  New Castle *(G-5415)*
▼ Iron Source LLC .... G 302 856-7545
  Georgetown *(G-2568)*
Jesco Inc .... G 302 376-6946
  Middletown *(G-4114)*
Judd Brook 5 LLC .... G 302 846-3355
  Delmar *(G-1011)*
McClung-Logan Equipment Co Inc . F 302 337-3400
  Bridgeville *(G-495)*
Price Is Right Contracting LLC .... F 215 760-1416
  Wilmington *(G-12224)*
S G Williams & Bros Co .... F 302 656-8167
  Wilmington *(G-12506)*
▲ Sun Piledriving Equipment LLC .. G 302 539-6756
  Frankford *(G-2392)*
Th White General Contract .... G 302 945-1829
  Millsboro *(G-4812)*
Wm Systems Inc .... G 302 450-4482
  Wilmington *(G-13282)*

5083 Farm & Garden Mach & Eqpt Wholesale

All Rock & Mulch LLC .... G 302 838-7625
  Bear *(G-25)*
Atlantic Tractor LLC .... E 302 653-8536
  Clayton *(G-835)*
Baxter Farms Inc .... G 302 856-1818
  Georgetown *(G-2447)*
Binkley Hurst LP .... G 302 628-3135
  Seaford *(G-8169)*
Bluewater Wind LLC .... G 302 731-7020
  Lewes *(G-3389)*
Bunting & Bertrand Inc .... F 302 732-6836
  Frankford *(G-2351)*
Burke Equipment Company .... E 302 248-7070
  Delmar *(G-975)*
Burke Equipment Company .... D 302 697-3200
  Felton *(G-2278)*
Delaware Hardscape Supply LLC ... G 302 996-6464
  Wilmington *(G-10049)*
Farmers First Services Inc .... G 302 424-8340
  Milford *(G-4410)*
Hoober Inc .... D 717 768-8231
  Middletown *(G-4109)*
Judd Brook 5 LLC .... G 302 846-3355
  Delmar *(G-1011)*
Messick & Gray Cnstr Inc .... E 302 337-8777
  Bridgeville *(G-497)*
Messick & Gray Cnstr Inc .... F 302 337-8445
  Bridgeville *(G-498)*
Newark Kubota Inc .... F 302 365-6000
  Newark *(G-7123)*
Northeast Agri Systems Inc .... G 302 875-1886
  Laurel *(G-3266)*

SIC SECTION
50 WHOLESALE TRADE¨DURABLE GOODS

▲ **O A Newton & Son Company** ... E ... 302 337-3782
Bridgeville *(G-504)*
Peninsula Poultry Eqp Co Inc ... F ... 302 875-0889
Laurel *(G-3270)*
Richard Sapp Farms ... G ... 302 684-4727
Milton *(G-4960)*
Taylor and Messick Inc ... F ... 302 398-3729
Harrington *(G-2897)*
Tucker Mechanical Service Inc ... G ... 302 536-7730
Seaford *(G-8426)*
Tull Brothers Inc ... E ... 302 629-3071
Seaford *(G-8427)*
W Enterprises LLC ... G ... 302 875-0430
Laurel *(G-3303)*
Walls Irrigation Inc ... F ... 302 422-2262
Milford *(G-4595)*
Whaleys Seed Store Inc ... G ... 302 875-7833
Laurel *(G-3308)*
Willard Agri Service Greenw ... G ... 302 349-4100
Farmington *(G-2268)*
Woodward Enterprises Inc ... F ... 302 378-2849
Middletown *(G-4291)*

5084 Industrial Mach & Eqpt Wholesale

Accudyne Systems Inc ... E ... 302 369-5390
Newark *(G-5889)*
▲ **Advance Marine LLC** ... G ... 302 656-2111
Wilmington *(G-8947)*
▲ **Advanced Machinery Sales Inc** ... F ... 302 322-2226
New Castle *(G-5009)*
Airgas Inc ... G ... 302 575-1822
Wilmington *(G-8996)*
Airgas Usa LLC ... F ... 302 286-5400
Newark *(G-5927)*
Airsled Inc ... G ... 302 292-8911
Newark *(G-5928)*
Aquaflow Pump & Supply Company ... F ... 302 834-1311
Bear *(G-33)*
▲ **Arnold International Inc** ... G ... 302 266-4441
Newark *(G-5998)*
◆ **Asw Machinery Inc** ... F ... 899 792-5288
New Castle *(G-5049)*
Atlantic Elevators ... G ... 302 537-8304
Dagsboro *(G-878)*
Automation Air Inc ... G ... 973 875-6676
Bridgeville *(G-450)*
Automation Partnership ... G ... 302 478-9060
Wilmington *(G-9188)*
▲ **Autotype Holdings (usa) Inc** ... C ... 302 378-3100
Middletown *(G-3956)*
Barrys Cleaning Service ... G ... 302 653-0110
Clayton *(G-837)*
Benz Hydraulics Inc ... F ... 302 328-6648
New Castle *(G-5082)*
Billy Warren Son ... G ... 302 349-5767
Greenwood *(G-2717)*
Brandywine Elevator Co Inc ... G ... 866 636-0102
Wilmington *(G-9430)*
Brooks Machine Inc ... G ... 302 674-5900
Dover *(G-1235)*
▲ **Bruce Industrial Co Inc** ... D ... 302 655-9616
New Castle *(G-5118)*
◆ **Careys Diesel Inc** ... F ... 302 678-3797
Leipsic *(G-3313)*
Catalyst Handling Resources ... E ... 302 798-2200
Claymont *(G-708)*
Cintas Corporation No 2 ... G ... 302 765-6460
Wilmington *(G-9709)*
Cod Lift Truck Inc ... G ... 302 656-7731
Wilmington *(G-9757)*
Deangelis & Son Inc ... G ... 302 337-8699
Bridgeville *(G-464)*
Delaware Capital Formation Inc ... G ... 302 793-4921
Wilmington *(G-10010)*
◆ **Delaware Capital Holdings Inc** ... G ... 302 793-4921
Wilmington *(G-10011)*
E E Rosser Inc ... G ... 302 762-9643
Wilmington *(G-10276)*
Eastern Lift Truck Co Inc ... E ... 302 286-6660
Newark *(G-6498)*
Eastern Lift Truck Co Inc ... F ... 302 875-4031
Laurel *(G-3226)*
▲ **Eastern Shore Metals LLC** ... F ... 302 629-6629
Seaford *(G-8231)*
Ellis Ladder Improvements ... G ... 302 571-8470
Wilmington *(G-10380)*
Experienced Auto Parts Inc ... G ... 302 322-3344
New Castle *(G-5301)*
Fiduks Industrial Services Inc ... F ... 302 994-2534
Wilmington *(G-10537)*
Fiduks Industrial Services Inc ... F ... 302 994-2534
Wilmington *(G-10536)*
First State Automation LLC ... G ... 302 743-4798
New Castle *(G-5314)*
First State Distributors Inc ... G ... 302 655-8266
Wilmington *(G-10551)*
Firstchoice Group America LLC ... G ... 425 242-8626
Lewes *(G-3499)*
Four States LLC ... F ... 302 655-3400
New Castle *(G-5325)*
◆ **Franke USA Holding Inc** ... F ... 615 462-4000
Wilmington *(G-10614)*
G & E Welding Supply Co ... F ... 302 322-9353
New Castle *(G-5339)*
Groff Tractor & Equipment LLC ... F ... 302 349-5760
Greenwood *(G-2742)*
Instruments & Thermal Products ... G ... 302 378-6290
Townsend *(G-8798)*
Jaa Industries LLC ... G ... 302 332-0388
New Castle *(G-5433)*
▼ **JLJ Enterprises Inc** ... F ... 302 398-0229
Harrington *(G-2857)*
John J Buckley Associates Inc ... G ... 302 475-5443
Wilmington *(G-11172)*
John R Seiberlich Inc ... D ... 302 356-2400
New Castle *(G-5441)*
▲ **Jorc Industrial LLC** ... G ... 302 395-0310
New Castle *(G-5443)*
Kaeser Compressors Inc ... G ... 410 242-8793
New Castle *(G-5449)*
Kahl Company Inc ... G ... 302 478-8450
Wilmington *(G-11220)*
Liberty Elevator Experts LLC ... G ... 302 650-4688
Newark *(G-6934)*
Lundberg Tech Inc - America ... G ... 302 738-2500
Newark *(G-6958)*
Lweco Group LLC ... G ... 302 296-8035
Millsboro *(G-4728)*
Material Handling Supply Inc ... F ... 302 571-0176
New Castle *(G-5511)*
McCabes Mechanical Service Inc ... F ... 302 854-9001
Georgetown *(G-2599)*
McCall Handling Co ... F ... 302 846-2334
Delmar *(G-1019)*
Mechanics Paradise Inc ... F ... 302 652-8863
New Castle *(G-5513)*
Messick & Gray Cnstr Inc ... E ... 302 337-8777
Bridgeville *(G-497)*
▲ **Mitusha International Corp** ... G ... 302 674-2977
Dover *(G-1863)*
▲ **O A Newton & Son Company** ... E ... 302 337-3782
Bridgeville *(G-504)*
Pascale Industries Inc ... F ... 302 421-9400
New Castle *(G-5606)*
Phalco Inc ... G ... 302 654-2620
Wilmington *(G-12107)*
Philadlphia Ball Rller Bearing ... G ... 215 727-0982
Wilmington *(G-12113)*
Power Trans Inc ... F ... 302 337-3016
Bridgeville *(G-512)*
Praxair Distribution Inc ... G ... 302 654-8755
Wilmington *(G-12198)*
Progressive Systems Inc ... G ... 302 732-3321
Frankford *(G-2381)*
Pump and Corrosion Tech Inc ... G ... 302 655-3490
Wilmington *(G-12269)*
Schlegel Associates Inc ... G ... 302 477-1810
Wilmington *(G-12553)*
Skab International Corporation ... G ... 412 475-2221
Dover *(G-2087)*
Square One Electric Service Co ... F ... 302 678-0400
Dover *(G-2099)*
Steven Brown & Associates Inc ... G ... 302 652-4722
Wilmington *(G-12759)*
▲ **Supercritical Fluid Tech** ... G ... 302 738-3420
Newark *(G-7511)*
Sussex Hydraulics Sales & Svcs ... G ... 302 846-9702
Delmar *(G-1033)*
Sussex Protection Service LLC ... F ... 302 337-0209
Bridgeville *(G-522)*
Technicare Inc ... G ... 302 322-7766
Newark *(G-7545)*
▲ **Testing Machines Inc** ... E ... 302 613-5600
New Castle *(G-5764)*
▲ **Totaltrax Inc** ... D ... 302 514-0600
New Castle *(G-5778)*
Traction Wholesale Center Inc ... G ... 302 743-8473
Wilmington *(G-12946)*
▲ **Uet International Inc** ... G ... 302 834-0234
Bear *(G-364)*
United Rentals North Amer Inc ... G ... 302 907-0292
Delmar *(G-1046)*
Urie & Blanton Inc ... G ... 302 658-8604
Wilmington *(G-13037)*
Vallen Distribution Inc ... G ... 302 992-5604
Wilmington *(G-13044)*
Vallen Distribution Inc ... G ... 856 542-1453
Delaware City *(G-968)*
Wilmington ... G ... 302 357-4509
Wilmington *(G-13221)*
World Wide Trading Brokers ... G ... 302 368-7041
Newark *(G-7722)*
WW Grainger Inc ... F ... 302 322-1840
New Castle *(G-5842)*

5085 Industrial Splys Wholesale

Applied Constructal Inc ... G ... 203 606-1656
Bethel *(G-440)*
Arlon Partners Inc ... G ... 302 595-1234
Bear *(G-35)*
Briggs Company ... E ... 302 328-9471
New Castle *(G-5114)*
Bristol Industrial Corporation ... F ... 302 322-1100
New Castle *(G-5115)*
Building Fasteners Inc ... G ... 302 738-0671
Newark *(G-6132)*
▲ **Carney Machinery Co** ... G ... 302 571-8382
Wilmington *(G-9574)*
Case Construction Inc ... E ... 302 737-3800
Newark *(G-6164)*
Delmarva Rubber & Gasket Co ... G ... 302 424-8300
Bridgeville *(G-466)*
Dfc Industries Inc ... G ... 215 292-1572
New Castle *(G-5249)*
E-Industrial Suppliers LLC ... G ... 302 251-6210
Wilmington *(G-10313)*
Eastern Shore Equipment Co ... G ... 302 697-3300
Camden Wyoming *(G-633)*
Electric Motor Wholesale Inc ... F ... 302 653-1844
Camden Wyoming *(G-635)*
Fastenal Company ... G ... 302 424-4149
Milford *(G-4411)*
First State Steel Drum Co ... G ... 302 655-2422
New Castle *(G-5318)*
Froggys Industrial Supply Inc ... G ... 302 508-2340
Smyrna *(G-8637)*
G & E Welding Supply Co ... F ... 302 322-9353
New Castle *(G-5339)*
Greenberg Supply Co Inc ... E ... 302 656-4496
Wilmington *(G-10777)*
Griffith Industrial Supply ... G ... 302 731-0574
Newark *(G-6691)*
GTS Technical Sales LLC ... G ... 302 778-1362
Wilmington *(G-10795)*
Hartzell Industries Inc ... G ... 302 322-4900
New Castle *(G-5380)*
▲ **Independent Metal Strap Co Inc** ... E ... 516 621-0030
Dover *(G-1671)*
Industrial Products of Del ... F ... 302 328-6648
New Castle *(G-5415)*
Industrial Resource Netwrk Inc ... F ... 302 888-2905
Wilmington *(G-11022)*
Industrial Valves & Fittings ... F ... 302 326-2494
New Castle *(G-5417)*
Integra Services Tech Inc ... F ... 302 792-0346
Claymont *(G-765)*
John R Seiberlich Inc ... D ... 302 356-2400
New Castle *(G-5441)*
Keen Compressed Gas Co ... F ... 302 594-4545
Wilmington *(G-11232)*
Keen Compressed Gas Co ... G ... 302 736-6814
Dover *(G-1728)*
Keen Compressed Gas Co ... E ... 302 594-4545
New Castle *(G-5456)*
Keen Compressed Gas Co Inc ... G ... 610 583-8770
New Castle *(G-5457)*
▲ **Mitusha International Corp** ... G ... 302 674-2977
Dover *(G-1863)*
Motion Industries Inc ... F ... 302 462-3130
Delmar *(G-1023)*
MSC Industrial Direct Co Inc ... F ... 302 998-1214
Wilmington *(G-11771)*
Petroserv Inc ... G ... 302 398-3260
Harrington *(G-2873)*
Philadlphia Ball Rller Bearing ... G ... 215 727-0982
Wilmington *(G-12113)*
▲ **Phoenix Filtration Inc** ... G ... 302 998-8805
Wilmington *(G-12123)*
Polymart Inc ... G ... 302 656-1470
Hockessin *(G-3122)*

S I C

50 WHOLESALE TRADE¨DURABLE GOODS

Power Trans Inc .... G 302 322-7110
New Castle (G-5634)
Precision Flow LLC .... F 302 544-4417
New Castle (G-5636)
Rhino Lnngs Del Auto Style Inc .... F 302 368-4660
Newark (G-7335)
Roberts Oxygen Company Inc .... G 302 337-9666
Seaford (G-8380)
Royal Instruments Inc .... G 302 328-5900
New Castle (G-5686)
Ruby Industrial Tech LLC .... G 302 674-2943
Dover (G-2045)
Sid Tool Co Inc .... F 302 322-5441
New Castle (G-5707)
Skyline Supply Inc .... G 302 894-9190
Newark (G-7438)
Standard Industrial Supply Co .... G 302 656-1631
Wilmington (G-12735)
State Line Machine Inc .... F 302 478-0285
Wilmington (G-12745)
Summit Aviation Inc .... D 302 834-5400
Middletown (G-4250)
Trelltex Inc .... F 302 738-4313
Newark (G-7583)
Urie & Blanton Inc .... G 302 658-8604
Wilmington (G-13037)
◆ Vertex Industries Inc .... G 302 472-0601
Wilmington (G-13066)
W T Schrider & Sons Inc .... G 302 934-1900
Millsboro (G-4822)
Wesco Distribution Inc .... G 302 655-9611
Wilmington (G-13162)
WW Grainger Inc .... F 302 322-1840
New Castle (G-5842)

5087 Service Establishment Eqpt & Splys Wholesale

Blue Sky Clean .... G 302 584-5800
Wilmington (G-9381)
▲ Cad Import Inc .... E 302 628-4178
New Castle (G-5128)
Central America Distrs LLC .... F 302 628-4178
Georgetown (G-2465)
Diamond Chemical & Supply Co .... E 302 656-7786
Wilmington (G-10139)
East Coast Cleaning Co LLC .... F 302 762-6820
Wilmington (G-10318)
Eastern Shore Equipment Co .... G 302 697-3300
Camden Wyoming (G-633)
Goorland and Mann Inc .... G 302 655-1514
Wilmington (G-10752)
Goorland Enterprises LLC .... G 302 229-4573
Wilmington (G-10753)
Grime Busters USA Inc .... G 302 834-7006
Newark (G-6692)
Hair Gallery .... F 302 475-6714
Wilmington (G-10820)
Hollie Enterprises LLC .... G 903 721-1904
Wilmington (G-10927)
Hoopes Fire Prevention Inc .... F 302 323-0220
Newark (G-6743)
Lightscapes Inc .... G 302 798-5451
Wilmington (G-11387)
Richard J Leach Upholstery .... G 302 764-2067
Wilmington (G-12409)
Sally Beauty Supply LLC .... G 302 731-0285
Newark (G-7378)
Sally Beauty Supply LLC .... G 302 995-6197
Wilmington (G-12525)
Sally Beauty Supply LLC .... G 302 674-2201
Dover (G-2056)
Sally Beauty Supply LLC .... G 302 737-8837
Newark (G-7379)
Simply Stylng-Schl of Csmtlgy .... G 302 778-1885
Wilmington (G-12628)
Solace Lifesciences Inc .... G 302 275-4195
Wilmington (G-12674)
Source Supply Inc .... F 302 328-5110
New Castle (G-5723)
South Forks Inc .... G 302 731-0440
Newark (G-7461)
State Janitorial Supply Co .... G 302 734-4814
Dover (G-2104)
Steven Brown & Associates Inc .... G 302 652-4722
Wilmington (G-12759)
Total Beauty Supply Inc .... G 302 798-4647
Wilmington (G-12936)
Vending Solutions LLC .... G 302 674-2222
Dover (G-2189)

Wholesale Janitor Supply Co .... G 302 655-5722
Wilmington (G-13197)

5088 Transportation Eqpt & Splys, Except Motor Vehicles Wholesale

Arteaga Properties LLC .... G 808 339-6906
Wilmington (G-9136)
Bethany Auto Parts Inc .... G 302 539-0555
Ocean View (G-7765)
Brakes Engine & Tracks LLC .... G 302 476-9450
Wilmington (G-9415)
Delta Engineering Corporation .... F 302 325-9320
New Castle (G-5247)
Dimo Corp .... E 302 324-8100
Wilmington (G-5254)
▼ Eastern Group Inc .... E 302 737-6603
Newark (G-6497)
Hilton Corp .... G 302 994-3365
Wilmington (G-10911)
Hilton Marine Supply Company .... G 302 994-3365
Wilmington (G-10912)
▲ Janette Redrow Ltd .... G 302 659-3534
Townsend (G-8800)
Summit Aviation Inc .... D 302 834-5400
Middletown (G-4250)

5091 Sporting & Recreational Goods & Splys Wholesale

Capitol Billiards Inc .... G 302 629-0298
Seaford (G-8182)
▼ Eastern Group Inc .... E 302 737-6603
Newark (G-6497)
First State Firearms & ACC LLC .... G 302 322-1126
New Castle (G-5316)
James Sutton .... G 302 328-5438
New Castle (G-5435)
Light My Fire Inc .... G 239 777-0878
Dover (G-1787)
Millers Gun Center Inc .... G 302 328-9747
New Castle (G-5530)
Old Inlet Bait and Tackle Inc .... F 302 227-7974
Rehoboth Beach (G-8022)
Posidon Adventure Inc .... F 302 543-5024
Wilmington (G-12190)
Seagreen Bicycle LLP .... G 302 226-2323
Rehoboth Beach (G-8070)
Shorty USA Inc .... G 302 234-7750
Hockessin (G-3146)
Signature Fitness Eqp LLC .... G 888 657-5357
Lewes (G-3744)
Sporting Goods Properties .... G 302 774-1000
Wilmington (G-12708)
Spring Floor Tech LLC .... G 302 528-3474
New Castle (G-5730)
Switch Inc .... G 302 738-7499
Newark (G-7523)
▲ Versatile Impex Inc .... G 302 369-9480
Newark (G-7652)

5092 Toys & Hobby Goods & Splys Wholesale

Gamestop Inc .... F 302 266-7362
Newark (G-6637)
Guidance Gaming .... F 724 708-2321
Dover (G-1614)
Workplace Rebels LLC .... G 917 771-8286
Dover (G-2237)

5093 Scrap & Waste Materials Wholesale

Billy Warren Son .... G 302 349-5767
Greenwood (G-2717)
Delaware Auto Salvage Inc .... G 302 322-2328
New Castle (G-5225)
Diamond State Recycling Corp .... E 302 655-1501
Wilmington (G-10147)
Ewaste Express .... G 302 691-8052
Wilmington (G-10454)
Joseph Smith & Sons Inc .... G 302 492-8091
Hartly (G-2930)
Lkq Northeast Inc .... G 800 223-0171
Dover (G-1793)
Murrays Motors .... G 302 628-0500
Seaford (G-8315)
Network Scrap Metal Corp .... G 910 202-0655
Wilmington (G-11841)
Newark Recycling Center Inc .... G 302 737-7300
Newark (G-7127)

Steel and Metal Service .... G 302 322-9960
New Castle (G-5739)

5094 Jewelry, Watches, Precious Stones Wholesale

Alamad Investments LLC .... G 833 311-8899
Lewes (G-3332)
Aurista Technologies Inc .... F 302 792-4900
Claymont (G-696)
Certified Assets MGT Intl LLC .... G 302 765-3352
Wilmington (G-9617)
Fidelitrade Incorporated .... F 302 762-6200
Wilmington (G-10532)
First State Coin Co .... G 302 734-7776
Dover (G-1554)
Gem Merchant LLC .... G 734 274-1280
Lewes (G-3510)
▲ Stuart Kingston Inc .... F 302 227-2524
Rehoboth Beach (G-8090)
Wholesale Jewelry Outlet Inc .... G 302 994-5114
Wilmington (G-13198)

5099 Durable Goods: NEC Wholesale

A1 Sanitation Service Inc .... F 302 653-9591
Smyrna (G-8559)
Active Supply LLC .... G 888 843-0243
Bear (G-11)
Airbase Carpet Mart Abct Dist .... G 302 323-8800
New Castle (G-5019)
◆ Anderson Group Inc .... G 302 478-6160
Wilmington (G-9078)
Blu H20 Ltd .... G 302 875-4810
Laurel (G-3201)
Delaware City Fire Co No 1 .... G 302 834-9336
Delaware City (G-952)
Direct Importer LLC .... G 302 838-2183
Newark (G-6451)
Fedex Office & Print Svcs Inc .... G 302 996-0264
Wilmington (G-10519)
Flw Wood Products Inc .... G 410 259-4674
Dagsboro (G-902)
Freedom Materials .... G 302 281-0085
Newark (G-6617)
▼ Global Entp Worldwide LLC .... D 713 260-9687
Wilmington (G-10724)
Golden Rubber Stamp Co .... G 302 658-7343
Wilmington (G-10738)
▼ Honeywell Safety Pdts USA Inc .... F 302 636-5401
Wilmington (G-10948)
International Game Technology .... F 302 674-3177
Dover (G-1682)
JG Townsend Jr & Co Inc .... E 302 856-2525
Georgetown (G-2574)
Kratom Foundation LLC .... G 302 645-7400
Lewes (G-3586)
Little Nests Portraits .... F 610 459-8622
Wilmington (G-11405)
M & M Marketing Group LLC .... G 321 274-5352
Wilmington (G-11467)
Maintenance Troubleshooting .... G 302 692-0871
Newark (G-6976)
McDonald Safety Equipment Inc .... F 302 999-0151
Wilmington (G-11594)
MidatIntic Auto Rstration Sups .... G 302 422-3812
Milford (G-4495)
Paradise Grill .... G 302 945-4500
Millsboro (G-4768)
Prepaid Legal Service Inc .... F 302 836-1985
Bear (G-291)
Prestige Powder Inc .... G 302 737-7086
Newark (G-7248)
Tai Jun International Inc .... G 302 239-9336
Newark (G-7533)

51 WHOLESALE TRADE¨NONDURABLE GOODS

5112 Stationery & Office Splys Wholesale

Brandywine Graphics Inc .... G 302 655-7571
Wilmington (G-9435)
L E Stansell Inc .... G 302 475-1534
Wilmington (G-11308)
Nitro Impact Inc .... F 347 694-7000
Wilmington (G-11890)
Total Services Inc .... G 302 575-1132
New Castle (G-5776)

5113 Indl & Personal Svc Paper Wholesale

A E Moore Incorporated ....F....... 302 934-7055
  Millsboro (G-4620)
Diamond Chemical & Supply Co ....E....... 302 656-7786
  Wilmington (G-10139)
Forever Inc.................................G....... 302 449-2100
  Middletown (G-4076)
Forever Inc.................................E....... 302 594-0400
  Wilmington (G-10592)
Forever Inc.................................G....... 302 368-1440
  Newark (G-6604)
Freedom Paper Company LLC ....G....... 443 542-5845
  Wilmington (G-10629)
Fulton Paper Company ....F....... 302 594-0400
  Wilmington (G-10648)
Orlando J Camp & Associates..............G....... 302 478-3720
  Wilmington (G-11975)
▼ Pet Poultry Products LLC...............E....... 302 337-8223
  Bridgeville (G-508)
Wayden Inc ....G....... 302 798-1642
  Claymont (G-817)

5122 Drugs, Drug Proprietaries & Sundries Wholesale

A2a Intgrted Phrmceuticals LLC ....G....... 270 202-2461
  Lewes (G-3320)
A66 Inc ....G....... 800 444-0446
  Wilmington (G-8892)
Animal Health Sales Inc ....F....... 302 436-8286
  Selbyville (G-8448)
Bmp Sunstone Corporation ....A....... 610 940-1675
  Wilmington (G-9388)
Delaware Pharmacist Society ....G....... 302 659-3088
  Smyrna (G-8619)
Disrupt Pharma Tech Africa Inc...........G....... 312 945-8002
  Dover (G-1430)
Elements Beauty Supply North ....G....... 302 738-7732
  Newark (G-6512)
Foresee Pharmaceuticals Inc ....G....... 302 396-5243
  Newark (G-6602)
Fulcrum Pharmacy MGT Inc ....G....... 302 658-8020
  Wilmington (G-10645)
Hannas Phrm Sup Co Inc ....F....... 302 571-8761
  Wilmington (G-10834)
Hotel Environments Inc ....G....... 302 234-9294
  Hockessin (G-3056)
Makeshopncompany Inc ....F....... 302 999-9961
  New Castle (G-5503)
Mid States Sales & Marketing ....E....... 302 888-2475
  Wilmington (G-11680)
▲ Pharmadel LLC ....F....... 302 322-1329
  New Castle (G-5620)
Pharmerica Long-Term Care LLC ....D....... 302 454-8234
  Newark (G-7209)
Physicians Beauty Group LLC ....E....... 866 270-9290
  Dover (G-1956)
Qps LLC ....C....... 302 369-3753
  Newark (G-7280)
Radius Rx Direct Inc ....G....... 302 658-9196
  Wilmington (G-12303)
Resh LLC ....F....... 302 543-5469
  New Castle (G-5674)
Sally Beauty Supply LLC ....G....... 302 629-5160
  Seaford (G-8383)
▼ Sinuswars LLC ....F....... 212 901-0805
  Wilmington (G-12633)
SPI Pharma Inc ....E....... 302 262-3223
  Seaford (G-8407)
▼ SPI Pharma Inc ....E....... 302 576-8500
  Wilmington (G-12704)
Wh Nutritionals LLC ....G....... 302 357-3611
  Wilmington (G-13179)
Xynomic Pharmaceuticals Inc ....F....... 650 430-7561
  Dover (G-2243)

5131 Piece Goods, Notions & Dry Goods Wholesale

◆ Delaware D G Co LLC ....F....... 302 731-0500
  Newark (G-6373)
F Schumacher & Co........................C....... 302 454-3200
  Newark (G-6561)
Henninger Printing Co Inc ....G....... 302 934-8119
  Millsboro (G-4705)
Loomcraft Textile & Supply Co ....F....... 302 454-3232
  Newark (G-6948)
W L Gore & Associates Inc ....C....... 302 368-3700
  Newark (G-7672)

Wayne Industries Inc ....G....... 302 478-6160
  Wilmington (G-13126)
▲ Yoko Trading ....G....... 302 353-4506
  Newark (G-7730)

5136 Men's & Boys' Clothing & Furnishings Wholesale

Gbg USA Inc ....G....... 888 342-7243
  Wilmington (G-10683)
▲ Grand National USA Inc ....G....... 416 746-3511
  Wilmington (G-10758)
Great Graphic Originals Ltd ....G....... 302 734-7600
  Dover (G-1608)
H D Lee Company Inc ....F....... 302 477-3930
  Wilmington (G-10807)
Kaul Glove and Mfg Co.....................D....... 302 292-2660
  New Castle (G-5454)
Lids Corporation ....G....... 302 226-8580
  Rehoboth Beach (G-7986)
▲ Majdell Group USA Inc ....G....... 302 722-8223
  Newark (G-6977)
Sui Trading Co ....G....... 302 239-2012
  Hockessin (G-3151)

5137 Women's, Children's & Infants Clothing Wholesale

Cato Corporation ....G....... 302 854-9548
  Georgetown (G-2464)
Crazy Ladyz LLC ....F....... 302 541-4040
  Ocean View (G-7781)
Flapdoodles Inc.............................D....... 302 731-9793
  Newark (G-6595)
Gbg USA Inc ....G....... 888 342-7243
  Wilmington (G-10683)
Great Graphic Originals Ltd ....G....... 302 734-7600
  Dover (G-1608)
H D Lee Company Inc ....F....... 302 477-3930
  Wilmington (G-10807)
Huzala Inc ....G....... 313 404-6941
  Newark (G-6756)
Lacoste Usa Inc.............................G....... 302 227-9575
  Rehoboth Beach (G-7984)
Tai Jun International Inc ....G....... 302 239-9336
  Newark (G-7533)
Vivig Shoes ....F....... 302 427-2700
  Wilmington (G-13098)

5139 Footwear Wholesale

Elite Feet LLC ....G....... 302 464-1028
  Middletown (G-4055)
Gbg USA Inc ....G....... 888 342-7243
  Wilmington (G-10683)
Jaiden Jewels Shoes and ACC...........G....... 302 659-2473
  Smyrna (G-8661)
Lehigh Vly Safety Sup Co Inc ....G....... 302 323-9166
  New Castle (G-5477)
Shoolex LLC ....G....... 866 697-3330
  Lewes (G-3739)
Stride Rite Corporation ....G....... 302 226-2288
  Rehoboth Beach (G-8089)
Vivig Shoes ....F....... 302 427-2700
  Wilmington (G-13098)

5141 Groceries, General Line Wholesale

Acm Corp....................................F....... 302 736-3864
  Dover (G-1083)
Camels Hump Inc ....F....... 302 227-5719
  Rehoboth Beach (G-7882)
Hughes Delaware Maid Scrapple.........G....... 302 284-4370
  Felton (G-2294)
Jcholley LLC.................................G....... 302 653-6659
  Bear (G-199)
Moran Foods LLC ....F....... 302 798-5042
  Claymont (G-785)
Oppenheimer Group Inc ....F....... 302 533-0779
  Newark (G-7157)
Supermarket Associates Inc ....G....... 302 547-1977
  Wilmington (G-12810)
Thomas E Moore Inc ....F....... 302 674-1500
  Kenton (G-3187)
▲ Valco Enterprises LLC ....G....... 514 938-8474
  Newark (G-7640)

5142 Packaged Frozen Foods Wholesale

Burris Logistics..............................D....... 302 398-5050
  Harrington (G-2820)
Copra Inc ....G....... 917 224-1727
  Wilmington (G-9855)

DOT Foods Inc ....D....... 302 300-4239
  Bear (G-125)
H C Davis Inc ....G....... 302 337-7001
  Bridgeville (G-477)
JG Townsend Jr & Co Inc ....E....... 302 856-2525
  Georgetown (G-2574)
JG Townsend Jr Frz Foods Inc ....E....... 302 856-2525
  Georgetown (G-2575)
Murrys of Maryland Inc ....G....... 302 328-3361
  New Castle (G-5540)

5143 Dairy Prdts, Except Dried Or Canned Wholesale

Burris Logistics..............................D....... 302 398-5050
  Harrington (G-2820)
H C Davis Inc ....G....... 302 337-7001
  Bridgeville (G-477)
Hillandale Farms of Pa Inc ....G....... 302 492-1537
  Hartly (G-2927)
Hy-Point Dairy Farms Inc ....C....... 302 478-1414
  Wilmington (G-10979)
Natural Dairy Products Corp..............G....... 302 455-1261
  Newark (G-7086)
Tuscan/Lehigh Dairies Inc.................F....... 302 398-8321
  Harrington (G-2901)
Yogo Factory ....G....... 302 266-4506
  Newark (G-7728)
Yogurt City ....G....... 302 292-8881
  Newark (G-7729)

5144 Poultry & Poultry Prdts Wholesale

Eastern Shore Poultry Company ....B....... 302 855-1350
  Georgetown (G-2520)
Hillandale Farms of Pa Inc ....G....... 302 492-1537
  Hartly (G-2927)
Jabez Corp...................................F....... 302 475-7600
  Wilmington (G-11113)
Mountaire of Delmarva Inc ....B....... 302 988-6207
  Selbyville (G-8526)
▼ Pet Poultry Products LLC ....E....... 302 337-8223
  Bridgeville (G-508)

5145 Confectionery Wholesale

A E Moore Incorporated ....F....... 302 934-7055
  Millsboro (G-4620)
Harry Kenyon Incorporated ....E....... 302 762-7776
  New Castle (G-5376)
Herr Foods Incorporated ....E....... 302 628-9161
  Seaford (G-8264)
King of Sweets Inc ....F....... 302 730-8200
  Dover (G-1750)

5146 Fish & Seafood Wholesale

Alaskawild Seafoods ....G....... 302 337-0710
  Seaford (G-8142)
Febys Fishery Inc...........................E....... 302 998-9501
  Wilmington (G-10511)
George and Son Seafood Market ....G....... 302 239-7204
  Hockessin (G-3037)
▲ Harbor House Seafood Inc ....D....... 302 629-0444
  Seaford (G-8260)
J A E Seafood ....E....... 302 765-2546
  Wilmington (G-11100)
Lewes Fishhouse & Produce Inc.........E....... 302 827-4074
  Lewes (G-3600)
Meding & Son Seafood ....G....... 302 335-3944
  Milford (G-4491)
Meltrone Inc ....F....... 302 998-3457
  Wilmington (G-11628)
Oceanside Seafood Mkt Deli LLC ....G....... 302 313-5158
  Lewes (G-3666)
Paul Sorvino Foods Inc ....G....... 302 547-1977
  Wilmington (G-12045)
Seafood City Inc............................E....... 302 284-8486
  Felton (G-2319)
Southern Crab Company ....C....... 302 478-0181
  Wilmington (G-12687)
Venus On Halfshell ....G....... 302 227-9292
  Dewey Beach (G-1061)
Wooley Bully Inc ....G....... 302 542-3613
  Millsboro (G-4829)

5147 Meats & Meat Prdts Wholesale

B & M Meats Inc ....F....... 302 655-5521
  Wilmington (G-9210)
Estia Hospitality Group Inc.................F....... 302 798-5319
  Claymont (G-741)

51 WHOLESALE TRADE¨NONDURABLE GOODS SIC SECTION

H C Davis Inc .... G 302 337-7001
Bridgeville (G-477)
Lewes Fishhouse & Produce Inc .... E 302 827-4074
Lewes (G-3600)
Ralph and Paul Adams Inc .... B 800 338-4727
Bridgeville (G-517)
South Forks Inc .... G 302 731-0344
Newark (G-7461)
Sure Good Foods USA LLC .... E 905 288-1136
Newark (G-7514)
▲ West Dover Butcher Shop Inc .... G 302 734-5447
Dover (G-2214)

5148 Fresh Fruits & Vegetables Wholesale

7day Farmers Market LLC .... G 302 476-8924
Wilmington (G-8867)
Chiquita Brands LLC .... F 302 571-9781
Wilmington (G-9668)
David Oppenheimer and Co I LLC .... E 302 533-0779
Newark (G-6349)
Dole Fresh Fruit Company .... D 302 652-6484
Wilmington (G-10187)
Dole Fresh Fruit Company .... F 302 652-2215
Wilmington (G-10188)
Ernie Deangelis .... F 302 226-9533
Rehoboth Beach (G-7928)
Estia Hospitality Group Inc .... F 302 798-5319
Claymont (G-741)
◆ Forever Fresh LLC .... G 302 510-8538
Wilmington (G-10593)
Pandol Bros Inc .... E 302 571-8923
Wilmington (G-12013)
Robert T Minner Jr .... G 302 422-9206
Greenwood (G-2760)
Thomas E Moore Inc .... F 302 674-1500
Kenton (G-3187)
Vinces Produce Inc .... G 302 322-0386
New Castle (G-5818)
Willey Farms Inc .... D 302 378-8441
Townsend (G-8833)

5149 Groceries & Related Prdts, NEC Wholesale

326 Associates LP .... G 302 328-4101
New Castle (G-4990)
African Wood Inc .... G 302 884-6738
Wilmington (G-8973)
Angry 8 LLC .... F 203 304-9256
Newark (G-5971)
Baked LLC .... G 302 212-5202
Dewey Beach (G-1053)
Beach Break & Bakrie .... G 302 537-3800
Bethany Beach (G-383)
Beaverdam Pet Food .... G 302 349-5299
Greenwood (G-2714)
Bimbo Bakeries Usa Inc .... E 302 328-0837
New Castle (G-5091)
Chocolette Distribution LLC .... G 917 547-8905
Lewes (G-3416)
Classic Cookies of Dowingtown .... G 302 494-9662
Wilmington (G-9734)
Elizabeth Beverage Company LLC .... G 302 322-9895
New Castle (G-5286)
Evoqua Water Technologies LLC .... G 302 654-3712
Wilmington (G-10452)
▲ Firsd Tea North America LLC .... G 302 322-1255
New Castle (G-5310)
Food For Pets USA Inc .... G 514 831-4876
Newark (G-6599)
Freakin Fresh Salsa Inc .... G 302 750-9789
Wilmington (G-10623)
Green Roots LLC .... G 516 643-2621
Lewes (G-3522)
Ism .... G 302 656-2376
Wilmington (G-11090)
Jes-Made Bakery .... G 610 558-2131
Newark (G-6836)
Legacy Foods LLC .... G 302 656-5540
Wilmington (G-11360)
Lusotrading Corp .... G 302 288-0670
Wilmington (G-11452)
Mr Natural Bottled Water Inc .... F 302 436-7700
Ocean View (G-7803)
P-Ks Wholesale Grocer Inc .... F 302 656-5540
Wilmington (G-11998)
Peppers Inc .... F 302 645-0812
Lewes (G-3683)
Pepsi-Cola Btlg of Wilmington .... C 302 761-4848
Wilmington (G-12081)
Pepsi-Cola Metro Btlg Co Inc .... C 302 764-6770
Wilmington (G-12082)
Pioneer Distributors Inc .... G 302 644-0791
Milton (G-4952)
Point Coffee Shop and Bakery .... G 302 260-9734
Rehoboth Beach (G-8033)
◆ Rondo Specialty Foods Ltd .... G 800 724-6636
New Castle (G-5683)
Scotts Co .... G 302 777-4779
Wilmington (G-12564)
South Forks Inc .... G 302 731-0344
Newark (G-7461)
Spain Magic Rose LLC .... G 941 312-2051
Wilmington (G-12691)
Tail Bangers Inc .... E 302 947-4900
Millsboro (G-4810)
Tailbangers .... D 302 934-1125
Millsboro (G-4811)
Tasteables .... G 267 777-9143
Claymont (G-809)
Touch of Italy Bakery LLC .... G 302 827-2132
Lewes (G-3791)
Tuscan/Lehigh Dairies Inc .... F 302 398-8321
Harrington (G-2901)
Valentina Liquors .... G 302 368-3264
Newark (G-7641)
▲ Wen International Inc .... G 845 354-1773
Wilmington (G-13155)

5153 Grain & Field Beans Wholesale

Allen Harim Foods LLC .... E 302 629-9460
Seaford (G-8144)
Baldwin Sayre Inc .... G 302 337-0309
Bridgeville (G-451)
Dack Trading LLC .... G 917 576-4432
Rehoboth Beach (G-7907)
Hopkins Granary Inc .... G 302 684-8525
Milton (G-4915)
Johnson Jr Henry & Son Farm .... G 302 436-8501
Selbyville (G-8509)
Laurel Grain Company .... G 302 875-4231
Laurel (G-3253)
Mountaire Farms Delaware Inc .... G 302 398-3296
Harrington (G-2869)

5159 Farm-Prdt Raw Mtrls, NEC Wholesale

African Wood Inc .... G 302 884-6738
Wilmington (G-8973)
Andy Mast .... G 302 653-5014
Dover (G-1125)
Baxter Farms Inc .... G 302 856-1818
Georgetown (G-2447)
Chick/Brook LLC .... G 302 337-7141
Bridgeville (G-458)
Kirkwood Smoke Shop .... G 302 525-6718
Newark (G-6893)
Tops International Corp .... G 302 738-8889
Newark (G-7576)

5162 Plastics Materials & Basic Shapes Wholesale

Industrial Resource Netwrk Inc .... F 302 888-2905
Wilmington (G-11022)
Ion Power Inc .... G 302 832-9550
New Castle (G-5423)
Polymart Inc .... G 302 656-1470
Hockessin (G-3122)

5169 Chemicals & Allied Prdts, NEC Wholesale

A E Moore Incorporated .... F 302 934-7055
Millsboro (G-4620)
Action Unlimited Resources Inc .... E 302 323-1455
New Castle (G-5001)
Airgas Usa LLC .... E 302 834-7404
Delaware City (G-946)
Ashland LLC .... E 302 995-4180
Wilmington (G-9150)
Ashland LLC .... E 302 594-5000
Wilmington (G-9151)
▲ Bellex International Corp .... G 302 791-5180
Wilmington (G-9294)
Blue Ribbon Oil Company Inc .... F 302 832-7601
New Castle (G-5095)
Brewster Products Inc .... G 302 798-1988
Wilmington (G-9468)
▲ C P M Industries Inc .... G 302 478-8200
Wilmington (G-9523)
Cfg Lab Inc .... G 302 261-3403
Wilmington (G-9621)
Ciba Specialty Chem N Amer .... F 302 992-5600
Wilmington (G-9700)
Croda Inc .... F 302 429-5200
New Castle (G-5209)
Degussa International Inc .... G 302 731-9250
Newark (G-6360)
Diamond Chemical & Supply Co .... E 302 656-7786
Wilmington (G-10139)
DSM Desotech Inc .... D 302 328-5435
New Castle (G-5263)
E E Rosser Inc .... G 302 762-9643
Wilmington (G-10276)
▲ Grayling Industries Inc .... E 770 751-9095
Frederica (G-2403)
Interntional Mkt Suppliers Inc .... F 302 392-1840
Bear (G-189)
Keen Compressed Gas Co .... F 302 594-4545
Wilmington (G-11232)
Keen Compressed Gas Co .... E 302 594-4545
New Castle (G-5456)
▲ Mil International Incorporated .... G 302 234-7501
Wilmington (G-11687)
◆ MJL Industrial Inc .... G 302 234-0898
Hockessin (G-3097)
▲ PDM Incorporated .... G 302 478-0768
Wilmington (G-12055)
Progressive Systems Inc .... G 302 732-3321
Frankford (G-2381)
▲ Rath Incorporated .... D 302 294-4446
Newark (G-7298)
Riverside Specialty Chem Inc .... G 212 769-3440
Bear (G-307)
Roberts Oxygen Company Inc .... G 302 337-9666
Seaford (G-8380)
▲ Sepax Technologies Inc .... F 302 366-1101
Newark (G-7409)
Solenis LLC .... G 302 594-5000
Wilmington (G-12678)
Syntec Corporation .... F 302 421-8393
Wilmington (G-12837)
◆ Tenmat Inc .... G 302 633-6600
Wilmington (G-12883)
▲ Thornley Company Inc .... G 302 224-8300
Newark (G-7565)
Ultrafine Technologies Inc .... G 302 384-6513
Wilmington (G-13009)
◆ Weitron Inc .... E 800 398-3816
Newark (G-7682)

5171 Petroleum Bulk Stations & Terminals

Du Pont Elastomers LP .... D 302 774-1000
Wilmington (G-10243)
E I Du Pont De Nemours & Co .... G 302 772-0016
New Castle (G-5271)
Peninsula Oil Co Inc .... E 302 422-6691
Seaford (G-8349)
Service Oil Company .... E 302 734-7433
Dover (G-2072)

5172 Petroleum & Petroleum Prdts Wholesale

Adams Oil Co Inc .... G 302 629-4531
Seaford (G-8138)
C L Burchenal Oil Co Inc .... G 302 697-1517
Camden (G-543)
Chemours Company Fc LLC .... F 302 773-1267
Wilmington (G-9650)
Conectiv LLC .... C 202 872-2680
Wilmington (G-9817)
H R Phillips Inc .... E 302 422-4518
Milford (G-4430)
J William Gordy Fuel Co .... F 302 846-3425
Delmar (G-1006)
Pep-Up Inc .... G 302 645-2600
Rehoboth Beach (G-8031)
Pep-Up Inc .... F 302 856-2555
Georgetown (G-2617)
▲ Petroleum Equipment Inc .... E 302 734-7433
Dover (G-1951)
Petroleum Equipment Inc .... G 302 422-4281
Dover (G-1952)
Sandy Brae Laboratories Inc .... G 302 456-0446
Newark (G-7382)
Service Energy LLC .... G 302 734-7433
New Castle (G-5699)
Service Energy LLC .... D 302 734-7433
Dover (G-2071)

Service Energy LLC	F	302 645-9050
Lewes *(G-3737)*
Shellhorn & Hill Inc	D	302 654-4200
Wilmington *(G-12599)*
Sherman Heating Oils Inc		302 684-4008
Milton *(G-4968)*
Sherman Heating Oils Inc	F	302 684-4008
Milton *(G-4969)*
Smokeys Gulf Service Inc	G	302 378-2451
Middletown *(G-4245)*
Vp Racing Fuels Inc	G	302 368-1500
Newark *(G-7666)*

5181 Beer & Ale Wholesale

Argilla Brewing Company	G	302 731-8200
Newark *(G-5994)*
Carlo Porter Michael	G	267 709-6370
Newark *(G-6156)*
▲ Delaware Importers Inc	D	302 656-4487
New Castle *(G-5231)*
▲ NKS Distributors Inc		302 322-1811
New Castle *(G-5572)*
NKS Distributors Inc	E	302 422-1220
Milford *(G-4513)*
Southern Glazers Wine	E	302 656-4487
New Castle *(G-5724)*
▲ Standard Distributing Co Inc	D	302 655-5511
New Castle *(G-5737)*

5182 Wine & Distilled Alcoholic Beverages Wholesale

Bin 66 Fine Wine & Spirit	G	302 227-6966
Rehoboth Beach *(G-7869)*
▲ Delaware Importers Inc	D	302 656-4487
New Castle *(G-5231)*
Greenwood Liquor Inc	G	302 349-4767
Greenwood *(G-2741)*
▲ NKS Distributors Inc	C	302 322-1811
New Castle *(G-5572)*
Outlet Liquors	G	302 227-7700
Rehoboth Beach *(G-8024)*
Patel Sanjay	G	302 376-0136
Middletown *(G-4180)*
S & S Wines and Spirits	G	302 678-9987
Dover *(G-2048)*
Salted Vines Vineyard Winery	F	302 829-8990
Frankford *(G-2385)*
Sleigh Financial Inc	G	302 684-2929
Milton *(G-4970)*
Southern Glazers Wine	E	302 656-4487
New Castle *(G-5724)*
▲ Standard Distributing Co Inc	D	302 655-5511
New Castle *(G-5737)*
Tax Free Liquors	G	302 846-0410
Delmar *(G-1035)*
Village Wines & Spirits	G	302 376-5583
Middletown *(G-4276)*
Vishva Inc	G	302 425-3801
Wilmington *(G-13090)*
◆ William Grant & Sons USA Corp	G	302 573-3880
Wilmington *(G-13211)*

5191 Farm Splys Wholesale

B Diamond Feed Company	G	302 697-7576
Camden Wyoming *(G-617)*
Bryan & Brittingham Inc	F	302 846-9500
Delmar *(G-974)*
◆ Chick Harness & Supply Inc	E	302 398-4630
Harrington *(G-2824)*
Clark Seed Company Inc	G	302 653-9249
Clayton *(G-839)*
E F AG Products & Service	G	302 945-2415
Harbeson *(G-2782)*
▲ Emerald Bioagriculture Corp	F	517 882-7370
Hockessin *(G-3019)*
Greenview Gardens Inc	G	302 422-8109
Lincoln *(G-3852)*
Growmark Fs LLC	F	302 875-7511
Laurel *(G-3235)*
Growmark Fs LLC	G	302 422-3001
Milford *(G-4426)*
◆ Growmark Fs LLC	D	302 422-3002
Milford *(G-4425)*
Harvest Consumer Products LLC	E	302 732-6624
Dagsboro *(G-907)*
Helena Agri-Enterprises LLC	G	302 337-3881
Bridgeville *(G-481)*
Hudson Farm Supply Co Inc	G	302 398-3654
Harrington *(G-2853)*
Joseph M L Sand & Gravel Co	F	302 856-7396
Georgetown *(G-2578)*
Leons Garden World Ej Inc	F	410 392-8630
New Castle *(G-5480)*
Nutrien AG Solutions Inc	F	302 422-3570
Milford *(G-4516)*
Nutrien AG Solutions Inc	F	302 629-3047
Seaford *(G-8334)*
Nutrien AG Solutions Inc	G	302 629-2780
Seaford *(G-8333)*
Pepper Greenhouses	G	302 684-8092
Milton *(G-4948)*
▲ Q Vandenberg & Sons Inc	E	800 242-2852
Wilmington *(G-12273)*
Soil Service Inc	G	302 629-7054
Seaford *(G-8404)*
Standlee Hay Feed LLC	G	302 737-5117
Newark *(G-7481)*
▼ Syngenta Corporation	F	302 425-2000
Wilmington *(G-12836)*
W Enterprises LLC	G	302 875-0430
Laurel *(G-3303)*
Whaleys Seed Store Inc	G	302 875-7833
Laurel *(G-3308)*

5192 Books, Periodicals & Newspapers Wholesale

Acorn Books Inc	G	302 508-2219
Smyrna *(G-8561)*
Bethany Beach Books	G	302 539-2522
Bethany Beach *(G-386)*
Books & Tobaccos Inc	F	302 994-3156
Wilmington *(G-9393)*
Distribution Marketing of Del	G	302 658-6397
Wilmington *(G-10168)*
Linguatext Ltd	G	302 453-8695
Newark *(G-6936)*
Maintenance Troubleshooting	G	302 692-0871
Newark *(G-6976)*
Suburban Marketing Associates	D	302 656-8440
Wilmington *(G-12786)*
Sussex County Woman	F	302 539-2612
Ocean View *(G-7818)*

5193 Flowers, Nursery Stock & Florists' Splys Wholesale

Harvest Consumer Products LLC	E	302 732-6624
Dagsboro *(G-907)*
Lakeside Greenhouses Inc	G	302 875-2457
Laurel *(G-3250)*
Sieck Wholesale Florist Inc	F	302 356-2000
New Castle *(G-5708)*
Sterling Nursery Inc	G	302 653-7060
Smyrna *(G-8724)*
Village Green Inc	E	302 764-2234
Wilmington *(G-13082)*
Willey Farms Inc	D	302 378-8441
Townsend *(G-8833)*

5194 Tobacco & Tobacco Prdts Wholesale

51 and Prospect	G	443 944-1934
Newark *(G-5860)*
Cigarette City Inc	E	302 836-4889
Newark *(G-6235)*
Delmar Vapor Lounge	G	302 907-0125
Delmar *(G-991)*
Flavors & More Inc	G	917 887-9241
Wilmington *(G-10571)*
Guy & Lady Barrel LLC	G	302 399-3069
Dover *(G-1618)*
Harry Kenyon Incorporated	E	302 762-7776
New Castle *(G-5376)*
J&J Contracting Co Inc	G	302 227-0800
Rehoboth Beach *(G-7969)*
Vape Escape	G	302 737-8273
Newark *(G-7644)*

5198 Paints, Varnishes & Splys Wholesale

B F Shin of Salisbury Inc	G	302 652-3521
Wilmington *(G-9212)*
F Schumacher & Co	C	302 454-3200
Newark *(G-6561)*
First State Distributors Inc	G	302 655-8266
Wilmington *(G-10551)*
Mammeles Inc	G	302 998-0541
Wilmington *(G-11497)*
T B Painting Restoration	F	610 283-4100
Newark *(G-7527)*

5199 Nondurable Goods, NEC Wholesale

A Womans Touch Moving & Pkg	G	302 265-4729
Rehoboth Beach *(G-7836)*
Alias Inc	G	302 481-5556
Wilmington *(G-9010)*
▲ All Classics Ltd	G	302 738-2190
Newark *(G-5933)*
Animal Health Sales Inc	F	302 436-8286
Selbyville *(G-8448)*
Atg Trading LLC	G	909 348-0620
Wilmington *(G-9172)*
▲ Bill Ward Inc	G	302 762-6600
Wilmington *(G-9337)*
Books & Tobaccos Inc	F	302 994-3156
Wilmington *(G-9393)*
Cannons Cake and Candy Sups	G	302 738-3321
Newark *(G-6148)*
Convention Coach	G	302 335-5459
Magnolia *(G-3887)*
Cramaro Tarpaulin Systems Inc	F	302 292-2170
Newark *(G-6311)*
Creative Promotions	G	302 697-7896
Camden *(G-553)*
◆ Custom Decor Inc	E	302 735-7600
Dover *(G-1332)*
Dillon Distributors LLC	G	302 226-9700
Rehoboth Beach *(G-7917)*
Domian International Svc LLC	F	804 837-3616
Smyrna *(G-8624)*
Eecoo LLC		315 503-1477
Newark *(G-6507)*
Forever Inc	E	302 594-0400
Wilmington *(G-10592)*
▲ Francis Enterprises LLC	F	302 276-1316
New Castle *(G-5327)*
Goodman Manufacturing Co LP	G	302 894-1010
Newark *(G-6676)*
Grupo Acosta Ecuador Limited	C	302 231-2981
Wilmington *(G-10792)*
Guinevere Associates Inc	G	302 635-7798
Wilmington *(G-10799)*
Jordan Marketing	G	302 428-0147
Townsend *(G-8802)*
▲ K K American Corporation	G	302 738-8982
Bear *(G-211)*
Masley Enterprises Inc	E	302 427-9885
Wilmington *(G-11561)*
◆ Mid-Atlantic Packaging Company	E	800 284-1332
Dover *(G-1850)*
▲ Monseco Leather LLC	G	302 235-1777
Hockessin *(G-3098)*
Netproteus	G	206 203-2525
Lewes *(G-3657)*
New Image Inc	G	302 738-6824
Newark *(G-7106)*
Promotion Zone LLC	G	302 832-8565
Newark *(G-7269)*
Remline Corp	E	302 737-7228
Newark *(G-7316)*
Site Source Contractor Supply	G	302 322-0444
Bear *(G-323)*
Stamford Screen Printing Inc	G	302 654-2442
Wilmington *(G-12733)*
▲ Taghleef Industries LLC	G	302 326-5500
Newark *(G-7530)*
Tansley Associates (usa) Inc	F	403 569-8566
Wilmington *(G-12852)*
Tarpon Strategies LLC	G	215 806-2723
Newark *(G-7540)*

60 DEPOSITORY INSTITUTIONS

6021 National Commercial Banks

Applied Bank	F	302 326-4200
Wilmington *(G-9099)*
Applied Bank	F	302 227-3044
Rehoboth Beach *(G-7846)*
Applied Bank	F	302 326-4200
Newark *(G-5986)*
Applied Bank	F	302 326-4200
Wilmington *(G-9100)*
Bancorp Inc	E	302 385-5000
Wilmington *(G-9231)*
Bank America National Assn	F	302 478-1005
Wilmington *(G-9237)*
Bank America National Assn	F	302 656-5399
Wilmington *(G-9238)*
Bank America National Assn	F	302 765-2108
Wilmington *(G-9239)*

60 DEPOSITORY INSTITUTIONS SIC SECTION

Bank America National Assn ....F 302 464-1745
Newark (G-6045)
Bank of America Corporation ....F 302 432-0407
Wilmington (G-9240)
Bessemer Trust Company Del NA.........E 212 708-9182
Wilmington (G-9312)
Capital One National Assn ....F 302 658-3302
Wilmington (G-9558)
Citibank National Association ....F 302 477-5418
New Castle (G-5163)
Citicorp Banking Corporation..............C 302 323-3140
New Castle (G-5165)
Citicorp Delaware Services Inc.............F 302 323-3124
New Castle (G-5167)
Citicorp Trust Bank...............................G....... 302 737-7803
New Castle (G-5168)
▲ Citigroup Asia PCF Holdg Corp........G....... 302 323-3100
New Castle (G-5169)
County Bank...G....... 302 947-7300
Millsboro (G-4669)
County Bank...G....... 302 537-0900
Millville (G-4841)
County Bank...G....... 302 855-2000
Georgetown (G-2488)
County Bank...G....... 302 645-8880
Lewes (G-3445)
County Bank...G....... 302 424-2500
Milford (G-4367)
County Bank...F 302 226-9800
Rehoboth Beach (G-7902)
Deutsche Bank Tr Co Americas............E 302 636-3301
Wilmington (G-10126)
Deutsche Bank Trust Co Del.................C 302 636-3300
Wilmington (G-10127)
Fia Card Services Nat Assn ....C 302 457-0517
Wilmington (G-10528)
Fia Card Services Nat Assn ....B 302 432-1573
Wilmington (G-10530)
First National Bnk of Wyoming.............D 302 697-2666
Camden (G-572)
Fulton Bank National Assn ....G....... 302 378-4575
Middletown (G-4080)
Fulton Bank National Assn ....G....... 302 227-0330
Rehoboth Beach (G-7938)
Fulton Bank National Assn ....G....... 302 644-4900
Lewes (G-3506)
◆ Hsbc Bank USA ....A 302 778-0169
Wilmington (G-10966)
Hsbc North America Inc ....F 302 652-4673
Wilmington (G-10967)
JP Morgan Trust Company Del.............F 302 634-3800
Newark (G-6853)
Jpmorgan Chase & Co ....E 312 732-2801
Newark (G-6855)
Jpmorgan Chase Bank Nat Assn ....A 302 634-1000
Newark (G-6856)
Law Debenture Trust Company............G....... 302 655-3505
Wilmington (G-11339)
Manufacturers & Traders Tr Co ....G....... 302 644-9930
Lewes (G-3618)
Meridian Bank..E 302 477-9449
Wilmington (G-11641)
Nessus Investment Corporation...........G....... 302 323-3104
New Castle (G-5551)
Northern Trust Company.......................E 302 428-8700
Wilmington (G-11907)
PNC Bancorp Inc....................................E 302 427-5896
Wilmington (G-12164)
▲ PNC Bank National Association ......C 877 762-2000
Wilmington (G-12166)
PNC Bank National Association ....G....... 302 337-3500
Bridgeville (G-511)
PNC Bank National Association ....E 302 735-3117
Dover (G-1973)
PNC Bank National Association ....E 302 934-3106
Millsboro (G-4783)
PNC Bank National Association ....F 302 733-7150
Newark (G-7225)
PNC Bank National Association ....F 302 653-2475
Smyrna (G-8690)
PNC Bank National Association ....G....... 302 733-7170
Newark (G-7226)
PNC Bank National Association ....E 302 326-4701
New Castle (G-5627)
PNC Bank National Association ....F 302 537-2600
Bethany Beach (G-423)
PNC Bank National Association ....G....... 302 436-5400
Selbyville (G-8532)
PNC Bank National Association ....G....... 302 378-4441
Middletown (G-4194)
PNC Bank National Association...........F 302 733-7190
Newark (G-7228)
PNC Bank National Association...........F 302 429-1761
Wilmington (G-12167)
PNC Bank National Association...........F 302 479-4529
Wilmington (G-12168)
PNC Bank National Association...........F 302 479-4520
Wilmington (G-12169)
PNC Bank National Association...........F 302 993-3013
Wilmington (G-12170)
PNC Bank National Association...........F 302 832-8750
Bear (G-284)
PNC Bank National Association...........F 302 478-7822
Wilmington (G-12171)
PNC Bank National Association...........G....... 302 235-4010
Wilmington (G-12172)
PNC Bank National Association...........F 302 838-6782
Bear (G-285)
PNC Bank National Association...........F 302 422-1015
Milford (G-4527)
PNC Bank National Association...........G....... 302 993-3000
Wilmington (G-12173)
PNC Bank National Association...........F 302 429-1167
Wilmington (G-12174)
PNC Bank National Association...........F 302 735-2160
Dover (G-1974)
PNC Bank National Association...........F 302 832-6180
Bear (G-286)
PNC Bank National Association...........F 302 645-4500
Lewes (G-3694)
PNC Bank National Association...........G....... 302 855-0400
Georgetown (G-2621)
PNC Financial Svcs Group Inc ....F 302 429-1364
Wilmington (G-12175)
Reliance Trust Company LLC...............G....... 302 246-5400
Wilmington (G-12377)
Sun National Bank ....G....... 302 334-4091
Wilmington (G-12795)
Td Bank NA..G....... 302 655-5031
Wilmington (G-12859)
Td Bank NA..F 302 529-8727
Wilmington (G-12860)
Td Bank NA..G....... 302 351-4560
Wilmington (G-12861)
Td Bank NA..G....... 508 793-4188
Wilmington (G-12862)
Td Bank NA..G....... 302 644-0952
Rehoboth Beach (G-8095)
Tracy Peoples LLC.................................G....... 302 927-0280
Dagsboro (G-939)
Wells Fargo Bank National Assn...........G....... 302 631-1500
Newark (G-7683)
Wells Fargo Bank National Assn...........F 302 736-2910
Dover (G-2211)
Wells Fargo Bank National Assn...........G....... 302 449-5485
Middletown (G-4281)
Wells Fargo Bank National Assn...........F 302 541-8660
Millville (G-4858)
Wells Fargo Bank National Assn...........F 302 765-5534
Wilmington (G-13144)
Wells Fargo Bank National Assn...........F 302 428-8600
Wilmington (G-13145)
Wells Fargo Bank National Assn...........F 302 529-2550
Wilmington (G-13146)
Wells Fargo Bank National Assn...........G....... 302 736-2920
Dover (G-2212)
Wells Fargo Bank National Assn...........F 302 235-4300
Hockessin (G-3169)
Wells Fargo Bank National Assn...........F 302 832-6100
Newark (G-7684)
Wells Fargo Bank National Assn...........F 302 644-6351
Rehoboth Beach (G-8110)
Wells Fargo Bank National Assn...........F 302 326-4304
New Castle (G-5828)
Wells Fargo Bank National Assn...........E 302 421-7508
Wilmington (G-13147)
Wells Fargo Bank National Assn...........F 302 636-4306
Wilmington (G-13148)
Wells Fargo Bank National Assn...........G....... 302 761-1300
Wilmington (G-13149)
Wells Fargo Bank National Assn...........G....... 302 622-3350
Wilmington (G-13150)
Wells Fargo Bank National Assn...........G....... 302 421-7820
Wilmington (G-13151)
Wells Fargo Bank National Assn...........G....... 302 832-6104
Bear (G-374)
Wells Fargo Bank National Assn...........G....... 302 235-4304
Hockessin (G-3170)
Wells Fargo Home Mortgage Inc...........G....... 302 239-6300
Hockessin (G-3171)
Wilmington Savings Fund Soc ....F 302 398-3232
Harrington (G-2907)
Wsfs Financial Corporation ....D 302 792-6000
Wilmington (G-13307)

6022 State Commercial Banks

1st State Home Services ....G....... 302 339-5573
Millsboro (G-4618)
1st State PC Training.............................G....... 302 697-0347
Magnolia (G-3876)
Bank of Delmar.......................................G....... 302 732-3610
Dagsboro (G-880)
Bank of Delmar.......................................G....... 302 875-5901
Laurel (G-3195)
Bank of Delmarva...................................G....... 302 226-8900
Rehoboth Beach (G-7854)
Bank of Delmarva...................................G....... 302 629-2700
Seaford (G-8161)
Bank of Ocean City.................................G....... 410 723-4944
Fenwick Island (G-2329)
Bmo Delaware Trust Company.............G....... 302 652-1660
Wilmington (G-9387)
Calvin B Taylor Bnkg Berlin MD ....G....... 302 541-0500
Ocean View (G-7772)
Cbc Holding Inc......................................C 302 254-2000
Wilmington (G-9600)
Citicorp Del-Lease Inc ....D 302 323-3801
New Castle (G-5166)
Citizens Bank National Assn ....F 302 360-6101
Lewes (G-3423)
Citizens Bank National Assn ....F 302 734-0200
Dover (G-1284)
Citizens Bank National Assn ....F 302 292-6401
Newark (G-6238)
Citizens Bank National Assn ....F 302 456-7100
Newark (G-6239)
Citizens Bank National Assn ....G....... 302 856-4231
Georgetown (G-2473)
Citizens Bank National Assn ....G....... 302 645-2024
Lewes (G-3424)
Citizens Bank National Assn ....F 302 283-5600
Newark (G-6240)
Citizens Bank National Assn ....F 302 628-6150
Seaford (G-8196)
Citizens Bank National Assn ....F 302 456-7111
Newark (G-6241)
Citizens Bank National Assn ....F 302 235-4321
Hockessin (G-2989)
Citizens Bank National Assn ....G....... 302 633-4503
Wilmington (G-9714)
Citizens Bank National Assn ....G....... 302 734-0231
Dover (G-1285)
Citizens Bank National Assn ....G....... 302 422-5010
Milford (G-4353)
Citizens Bank National Assn ....G....... 302 653-9245
Smyrna (G-8596)
Citizens Bank National Assn ....G....... 302 477-1205
Wilmington (G-9715)
Citizens Bank National Assn ....F 302 633-3080
Wilmington (G-9716)
Citizens Bank National Assn ....G....... 302 376-3641
Middletown (G-3992)
Citizens Bank National Assn ....G....... 302 529-6100
Wilmington (G-9717)
Citizens Bank National Assn ....F 302 322-0525
New Castle (G-5170)
Citizens Bank National Assn ....F 302 421-2229
Wilmington (G-9718)
Citizens Bank National Assn ....F 302 834-2611
Bear (G-75)
Citizens Bank National Assn ....G....... 302 421-2240
Wilmington (G-9719)
Comenity Bank..G....... 614 729-4000
Wilmington (G-9781)
Community Bank Delaware....................E 302 348-8600
Lewes (G-3444)
County Bank...G....... 302 684-2300
Milton (G-4884)
Discover Bank...E 302 349-4512
Greenwood (G-2731)
First Republic Bank ....C 302 777-2699
Wilmington (G-10548)
First State Motor Sports.........................G....... 302 798-7000
Claymont (G-745)
Fulton Bank National Assn ....G....... 302 407-3291
Wilmington (G-10647)
Fulton Bank National Assn ....G....... 302 737-7766
Newark (G-6628)
Fulton Bank National Assn ....G....... 302 539-8031
Ocean View (G-7787)

60 DEPOSITORY INSTITUTIONS

Fulton Bank National Assn .... G 302 934-5911
  Millsboro (G-4695)
Hill Bancshares Delaware Inc .... G 302 651-8389
  Wilmington (G-10907)
Jpmorgan Chase Bank Nat Assn .... E 302 282-1624
  Wilmington (G-11201)
K Bank .... G 302 645-9700
  Lewes (G-3580)
Manufacturers & Traders Tr Co .... G 302 644-9930
  Lewes (G-3618)
Manufacturers & Traders Tr Co .... D 302 856-4410
  Georgetown (G-2595)
Manufacturers & Traders Tr Co .... G 302 855-2184
  Milton (G-4930)
Manufacturers & Traders Tr Co .... E 302 651-1618
  Newark (G-6981)
Manufacturers & Traders Tr Co .... F 302 856-4470
  Seaford (G-8302)
Manufacturers & Traders Tr Co 302 539-3471
  Bethany Beach (G-412)
Manufacturers & Traders Tr Co 302 651-8738
  Wilmington (G-11505)
Manufacturers & Traders Tr Co 302 285-3277
  Middletown (G-4143)
Manufacturers & Traders Tr Co 302 472-3233
  Wilmington (G-11506)
Manufacturers & Traders Tr Co 302 472-3262
  Claymont (G-780)
Manufacturers & Traders Tr Co .... F 302 735-2010
  Dover (G-1814)
Manufacturers & Traders Tr Co 302 472-3141
  Wilmington (G-11507)
Manufacturers & Traders Tr Co .... F 302 855-2160
  Milford (G-4485)
Manufacturers & Traders Tr Co .... F 302 651-1757
  Wilmington (G-11508)
Manufacturers & Traders Tr Co .... F 302 651-1803
  Wilmington (G-11509)
Manufacturers & Traders Tr Co .... F 302 651-1544
  Wilmington (G-11510)
Manufacturers & Traders Tr Co .... F 302 656-1260
  Wilmington (G-11511)
Manufacturers & Traders Tr Co .... G 302 472-3161
  Wilmington (G-11512)
Manufacturers & Traders Tr Co .... G 302 477-1761
  Wilmington (G-11513)
Manufacturers & Traders Tr Co .... F 302 472-3177
  Hockessin (G-3087)
Manufacturers & Traders Tr Co .... F 302 651-8828
  Bear (G-244)
Manufacturers & Traders Tr Co .... G 302 855-2227
  Rehoboth Beach (G-7996)
Manufacturers & Traders Tr Co .... G 302 651-1000
  Wilmington (G-11514)
Manufacturers & Traders Tr Co .... G 302 855-2873
  Laurel (G-3261)
Manufacturers & Traders Tr Co .... G 302 934-2400
  Millsboro (G-4732)
Manufacturers & Traders Tr Co .... G 302 856-4405
  Georgetown (G-2596)
Manufacturers & Traders Tr Co .... G 302 449-2780
  Middletown (G-4144)
Manufacturers & Traders Tr Co .... G 302 855-2891
  Millsboro (G-4733)
Manufacturers & Traders Tr Co .... G 302 541-8700
  Millville (G-4848)
Manufacturers & Traders Tr Co .... G 302 472-3335
  Newark (G-6982)
Manufacturers & Traders Tr Co .... F 302 292-6060
  Newark (G-6983)
Manufacturers & Traders Tr Co .... G 302 855-2283
  Seaford (G-8303)
Manufacturers & Traders Tr Co .... F 302 735-2075
  Dover (G-1815)
Manufacturers & Traders Tr Co .... E 302 472-3249
  New Castle (G-5505)
Manufacturers & Traders Tr Co .... G 302 855-2297
  Delmar (G-1018)
Manufacturers & Traders Tr Co .... F 302 636-6000
  Wilmington (G-11515)
Manufacturers & Traders Tr Co .... G 302 472-3309
  Wilmington (G-11516)
Manufacturers & Traders Tr Co .... F 302 735-2020
  Dover (G-1816)
PNC Bank National Association .... F 302 733-7160
  Newark (G-7227)
PNC Bank National Association .... F 302 629-5000
  Seaford (G-8358)
PNC Bank National Association .... F 302 235-4000
  Hockessin (G-3121)

PNC Bank National Association .... F 302 733-7192
  New Castle (G-5628)
PNC National Bank of Delaware .... D 302 479-4529
  Wilmington (G-12176)
Royal Bank America Leasing LLC ..... F 302 798-1790
  Wilmington (G-12484)
Santander Bank NA .... F 302 654-5182
  Wilmington (G-12541)
Shore United Bank .... G 302 284-4600
  Felton (G-2322)
Shore United Bank .... F 302 424-4600
  Wilmington (G-4559)
Shore United Bank .... G 302 698-1432
  Camden (G-599)
Td Bank NA .... F 302 455-1781
  Newark (G-7542)
Td Bank NA .... F 302 234-8570
  Hockessin (G-3157)
Wilmington Savings Fund Soc .... C 302 792-6000
  Wilmington (G-13245)
Wilmington Savings Fund Soc .... G 302 360-0020
  Millsboro (G-4828)
Wilmington Savings Fund Soc .... G 302 389-3151
  Smyrna (G-8747)
Wilmington Savings Fund Soc .... E 302 697-8891
  Camden (G-605)
Wilmington Savings Fund Soc .... E 302 436-4179
  Selbyville (G-8555)
Wilmington Savings Fund Soc .... G 302 832-7842
  Newark (G-7705)
Wilmington Savings Fund Soc .... G 302 999-1227
  Wilmington (G-13246)
Wilmington Savings Fund Soc .... G 302 360-0440
  Seaford (G-8441)
Wilmington Savings Fund Soc .... G 302 571-7242
  Newark (G-7706)
Wilmington Savings Fund Soc .... G 302 360-0004
  Ocean View (G-7824)
Wilmington Savings Fund Soc .... F 302 456-6404
  Newark (G-7707)
Wilmington Savings Fund Soc .... G 302 633-5700
  Wilmington (G-13249)
Wilmington Savings Fund Soc .... F 302 633-5704
  Wilmington (G-13251)
Wilmington Savings Fund Soc .... G 302 235-7600
  Hockessin (G-3173)
Wilmington Savings Fund Soc .... F 302 324-5800
  New Castle (G-5837)
Wilmington Savings Fund Soc .... F 302 284-3201
  Viola (G-8839)
Wilmington Savings Fund Soc .... G 302 792-6435
  Claymont (G-822)
Wilmington Trust Company TT .... G 302 427-4812
  Wilmington (G-13262)
Wsfs Financial Corporation .... G 302 346-2930
  Milford (G-4613)

6029 Commercial Banks, NEC

Artisans Bank Inc .... G 302 834-8800
  Bear (G-38)
Artisans Bank Inc .... G 302 430-7681
  Milford (G-4309)
Artisans Bank Inc .... G 302 738-3744
  Wilmington (G-9144)
Bancorp Bank .... E 302 385-5000
  Wilmington (G-9232)
Bank of Delmar .... G 302 875-5901
  Laurel (G-3195)
Bank of Delmarva .... G 302 226-8900
  Rehoboth Beach (G-7854)
Bank of Delmarva .... G 302 629-2700
  Seaford (G-8161)
Bryn Mawr Trust Company .... F 302 529-5984
  Wilmington (G-9495)
County Bank .... G 302 537-0900
  Millville (G-4841)
K Bank .... G 302 645-9700
  Lewes (G-3580)
Manufacturers & Traders Tr Co .... G 302 644-9930
  Lewes (G-3618)
Maryland Agency Financial Grou ..... G 410 420-8866
  Selbyville (G-8515)
Royal Bank America Leasing LLC ..... G 302 529-5984
  Wilmington (G-12483)
Td Bank NA .... G 302 644-0952
  Rehoboth Beach (G-8095)
Wilmington Savings Fund Soc .... G 888 665-9609
  Wilmington (G-13247)
Wilmington Savings Fund Soc .... G 302 838-6300
  Bear (G-377)

Wilmington Savings Fund Soc .... G 302 571-6508
  Wilmington (G-13248)
Wilmington Savings Fund Soc .... G 302 677-1891
  Dover (G-2230)
Wilmington Savings Fund Soc .... G 302 529-9300
  Wilmington (G-13253)
Wilmington Savings Fund Soc .... F 302 792-6000
  Wilmington (G-13254)

6035 Federal Savings Institutions

Artisans Bank Inc .... G 302 674-3214
  Dover (G-1142)
Barclays Bank Delaware .... B 302 255-8000
  Wilmington (G-9250)
Beneficial Oklahoma Inc .... F 302 529-8701
  Wilmington (G-9298)
Capital One National Assn .... G 302 645-1360
  Rehoboth Beach (G-7884)
Ing Bank Fsb .... E 302 658-2200
  Wilmington (G-11030)
Malvern Federal Savings Bank .... G 302 477-7305
  Montchanin (G-4986)
Third Fdral Sav Ln Assn Clvlan .... G 302 661-2009
  Wilmington (G-12897)
Wilmington Savings Fund Soc .... G 302 792-6043
  Claymont (G-821)
Wilmington Savings Fund Soc .... G 302 571-6516
  Wilmington (G-13250)
Wilmington Savings Fund Soc .... G 302 571-6500
  Wilmington (G-13252)
Wilmington Savings Fund Soc .... E 302 226-5648
  Rehoboth Beach (G-8117)
Wilmington Savings Fund Soc .... G 302 571-7090
  Wilmington (G-13255)

6036 Savings Institutions, Except Federal

Artisans Bank Inc .... G 302 656-8188
  Wilmington (G-9139)
Artisans Bank Inc .... D 302 658-6881
  Wilmington (G-9140)
Artisans Bank Inc .... G 302 838-6700
  Newark (G-6007)
Artisans Bank Inc .... G 302 479-2553
  Wilmington (G-9141)
Artisans Bank Inc .... G 302 479-2550
  Wilmington (G-9142)
Artisans Bank Inc .... G 302 674-3214
  Dover (G-1142)
Artisans Bank Inc .... G 302 993-8220
  Wilmington (G-9143)
Artisans Bank Inc .... G 302 738-3744
  Wilmington (G-9144)
Artisans Bank Inc .... G 302 834-8800
  Bear (G-38)
Artisans Bank Inc .... G 302 430-7681
  Milford (G-4309)
Artisans Bank Inc .... G 302 296-0155
  Rehoboth Beach (G-7847)

6061 Federal Credit Unions

American Spirit Federal Cr Un .... F 302 738-4515
  Newark (G-5958)
American Spirit Federal Cr Un .... F 302 738-4515
  Newark (G-5959)
Chestnut Run Federal Cr Un .... F 302 999-2967
  Wilmington (G-9658)
Community Pwered Federal Cr Un ... F 302 392-2930
  Bear (G-80)
Community Pwered Federal Cr Un ... G 302 324-1441
  New Castle (G-5188)
Community Twered Federal Cr Un ... G 302 994-3617
  Wilmington (G-9796)
Community Twered Federal Cr Un ... F 302 368-2396
  Newark (G-6273)
Del-One Federal Credit Union .... F 302 739-2390
  Dover (G-1353)
Del-One Federal Credit Union .... G 302 739-4496
  Dover (G-1354)
Del-One Federal Credit Union .... G 302 739-4496
  Smyrna (G-8614)
Del-One Federal Credit Union .... G 302 424-2969
  Milford (G-4373)
Del-One Federal Credit Union .... E 302 739-4496
  Dover (G-1355)
Del-One Federal Credit Union .... G 302 577-2667
  Wilmington (G-9999)
Del-One Federal Credit Union .... G 302 323-4578
  New Castle (G-5221)

60 DEPOSITORY INSTITUTIONS

Del-One Federal Credit Union .... G 302 739-6389
  Dover *(G-1356)*
Del-One Federal Credit Union .... G 302 856-5100
  Georgetown *(G-2498)*
Delaware Aliance Federal Cr Un .... G 302 429-0404
  New Castle *(G-5224)*
Delaware First Federal Cr Un .... F 302 998-0665
  Wilmington *(G-10047)*
Delaware Rver Bay Auth Emplyee .... G 302 571-6320
  New Castle *(G-5238)*
Delaware State Police Federal .... G 302 324-8141
  New Castle *(G-5240)*
Delaware State Police Federal .... F 302 856-3501
  Georgetown *(G-2503)*
Dexsta Federal Credit Union .... F 302 996-4893
  Wilmington *(G-10132)*
Dexsta Federal Credit Union .... E 302 996-4893
  Wilmington *(G-10133)*
Dexsta Federal Credit Union .... F 302 695-3888
  Wilmington *(G-10134)*
Dfs Corporate Services LLC .... G 302 349-4512
  Greenwood *(G-2730)*
Dover Federal Credit Union .... D 302 678-8000
  Dover *(G-1449)*
Dover Federal Credit Union .... G 302 322-4230
  New Castle *(G-5258)*
Edge Moor Dupont Employees .... G 302 761-2282
  Wilmington *(G-10347)*
First State Federal Credit Un .... F 302 674-5281
  Dover *(G-1556)*
First State Refinery .... G 302 838-8303
  New Castle *(G-5317)*
Louviers Federal Credit Union .... E 302 571-9513
  Wilmington *(G-11442)*
Louviers Federal Credit Union .... F 302 733-0426
  Newark *(G-6952)*
New Castle County School Emplo .... F 302 613-5330
  New Castle *(G-5555)*
New Cstle Cnty Del Em Fdral Cr .... G 302 395-5350
  New Castle *(G-5568)*
Priority Plus Federal Cr Un .... G 302 633-6480
  Wilmington *(G-12231)*
Provident Federal Credit Union .... F 302 734-1133
  Dover *(G-1992)*
▲ Sussex County Federal Cr Un .... E 302 629-0100
  Seaford *(G-8414)*
Sussex County Federal Cr Un .... G 302 422-9110
  Milford *(G-4573)*
Sussex County Federal Cr Un .... G 302 644-7111
  Lewes *(G-3771)*
Sussex County Federal Cr Un .... F 302 322-7777
  New Castle *(G-5745)*
Wilmington Police and Fire Fed .... G 302 654-0818
  Wilmington *(G-13242)*

6062 State Credit Unions

Community Twered Federal Cr Un .... F 302 368-2396
  Newark *(G-6273)*
Dexsta Federal Credit Union .... F 302 695-3888
  Wilmington *(G-10134)*
Dover Federal Credit Union .... D 302 678-8000
  Dover *(G-1449)*
Eagle One Federal Credit Union .... G 302 798-7749
  Claymont *(G-738)*
Seaford Federal Credit Union .... G 302 629-7852
  Seaford *(G-8389)*

6091 Nondeposit Trust Facilities

Brown Brothers Harriman & Co .... F 302 552-4040
  Wilmington *(G-9488)*
Depository Trust Co Del LLC .... E 302 762-2635
  Wilmington *(G-10118)*
First State Trust Company .... F 302 573-5967
  Wilmington *(G-10555)*
Key National Trust Company Del .... G 302 574-4702
  Wilmington *(G-11248)*
Pfpc Trust Company .... C 302 791-2000
  Wilmington *(G-12104)*

6099 Functions Related To Deposit Banking, NEC

Ace Cash Express Inc .... G 302 737-3785
  Newark *(G-5891)*
Ace Cash Express Inc .... G 302 628-0422
  Seaford *(G-8137)*
Argo Financial Services Inc .... G 302 322-7788
  New Castle *(G-5042)*
Bahars Company .... F 302 856-2966
  Georgetown *(G-2444)*

Bank of New York Mellon Corp .... G 302 791-1700
  Wilmington *(G-9244)*
Cash Connect Inc .... E 302 283-4100
  Newark *(G-6165)*
Citigroup Inc .... E 302 631-3530
  Newark *(G-6237)*
Concord Corporate Services Inc .... B 302 791-8200
  Wilmington *(G-9810)*
Custom House Ulc .... F 302 737-4085
  Newark *(G-6331)*
E Z Cash of Delaware Inc .... G 302 846-2920
  Delmar *(G-995)*
EZ Cash of New Hampshire Inc .... G 302 846-0464
  Delmar *(G-998)*
Goldstar- Cash LLC .... G 302 427-2535
  Wilmington *(G-10742)*
Juni Holdings Inc .... F 415 949-4860
  Wilmington *(G-11209)*
Juniper Bank .... F 302 255-8000
  Wilmington *(G-11210)*
Oink Oink LLC .... G 302 924-5034
  Dover *(G-1914)*
Pfpc Worldwide Inc .... F 302 791-1700
  Wilmington *(G-12105)*
Service General Corp .... C 302 856-3500
  Georgetown *(G-2651)*
United Check Cashing .... G 302 792-2545
  Claymont *(G-813)*
Zenpay Inc .... G 650 336-6512
  Wilmington *(G-13347)*

61 NONDEPOSITORY CREDIT INSTITUTIONS

6111 Federal Credit Agencies

Agfirst Farm Credit Bank .... G 302 734-7534
  Dover *(G-1094)*
Agfirst Farm Credit Bank .... G 302 856-9081
  Georgetown *(G-2425)*
Mid Atlantic Farm Credit Aca .... D 302 734-7534
  Dover *(G-1847)*
SLM Corporation .... D 302 451-0200
  Newark *(G-7441)*
SLM Financial Corporation .... F 856 642-8300
  Newark *(G-7442)*

6141 Personal Credit Institutions

Advance America Cash Advance .... F 302 999-0145
  New Castle *(G-5007)*
Auto Equity Loans .... G 302 834-2500
  Bear *(G-43)*
Auto Equity Loans .... G 302 731-0073
  Newark *(G-6028)*
Auto Equity Loans .... G 302 998-3009
  Wilmington *(G-9186)*
Bank of New Castle .... G 800 347-3301
  New Castle *(G-5066)*
Beneficial Consumer Disc Co .... G 302 425-2500
  Wilmington *(G-9297)*
Cash Advance Plus .... G 302 846-3900
  Delmar *(G-980)*
Cash Advance Plus .... G 302 629-6266
  Seaford *(G-8183)*
Citifinancial Inc .... G 302 834-6677
  Bear *(G-73)*
Citifinancial Credit Company .... G 302 628-9253
  Seaford *(G-8195)*
Citifinancial Credit Company .... G 302 834-6677
  Bear *(G-74)*
Citifinancial Credit Company .... G 302 678-8226
  Dover *(G-1283)*
Citifinancial Services Inc .... G 302 875-2813
  Laurel *(G-3214)*
Coastal Credit LLC .... G 302 734-1312
  Dover *(G-1300)*
College Avenue Student Ln LLC .... D 302 684-6070
  Wilmington *(G-9770)*
Delaware Depository Svc Co LLC .... G 302 762-2635
  Wilmington *(G-10037)*
E Z Cash of Delaware Inc .... G 302 424-4013
  Milford *(G-4397)*
EZ Cash of New Hampshire Inc .... G 302 846-0464
  Delmar *(G-998)*
EZ Loans Inc .... F 302 934-5563
  Millsboro *(G-4688)*
Falcidian LLC .... G 302 656-5500
  Wilmington *(G-10480)*

John Lovett Inc .... D 302 455-9460
  Newark *(G-6843)*
Mariner Finance LLC .... G 302 628-3970
  Seaford *(G-8304)*
Mariner Finance LLC .... G 302 384-6047
  Wilmington *(G-11527)*
Marlette Funding LLC .... G 302 358-2730
  Wilmington *(G-11541)*
Minute Loan Center .... G 302 994-6588
  Wilmington *(G-11711)*
Moneykey - TX Inc .... G 866 255-1668
  Wilmington *(G-11732)*
Noble Finance Corp .... G 302 995-2760
  Dover *(G-1899)*
Northeastern Title Loans .... G 302 672-7895
  Dover *(G-1902)*
Northeastern Title Loans .... G 302 326-2210
  New Castle *(G-5579)*
One Main Financial .... G 302 737-9456
  Newark *(G-7151)*
SLM Corporation .... D 302 451-0200
  Newark *(G-7441)*

6153 Credit Institutions, Short-Term Business

Armstrong Cork Finance LLC .... G 302 652-1520
  Wilmington *(G-9133)*
Bizboost Inc .... G 732 865-8050
  Wilmington *(G-9343)*
Citifinancial Credit Company .... G 302 834-6677
  Bear *(G-74)*
Citifinancial Credit Company .... G 302 678-8226
  Dover *(G-1283)*
Dfs Corporate Services LLC .... B 302 735-3902
  Dover *(G-1419)*
John Lovett Inc .... D 302 455-9460
  Newark *(G-6843)*
Oink Oink LLC .... G 302 924-5034
  Dover *(G-1914)*
One Main Financial .... G 302 737-9456
  Newark *(G-7151)*
Swift Financial LLC .... E 302 374-7019
  Wilmington *(G-12825)*

6159 Credit Institutions, Misc Business

American Finance LLC .... D 302 674-0365
  Harrington *(G-2808)*
B Williams Holding Corp .... F 302 656-8596
  Wilmington *(G-9214)*
Delaware Title Loans Inc .... F 302 368-2131
  Newark *(G-6419)*
Delaware Title Loans Inc .... G 302 629-8843
  Seaford *(G-8221)*
Delaware Title Loans Inc .... G 302 328-7482
  New Castle *(G-5241)*
Delaware Title Loans Inc .... G 302 653-8315
  Smyrna *(G-8621)*
Frascella Enterprises Inc .... E 267 467-4496
  Claymont *(G-748)*
Knight Capital Funding LLC .... E 888 523-4363
  Dover *(G-1755)*
Mid Atlantic Farm Credit Aca .... D 302 734-7534
  Dover *(G-1847)*
Midatlantic Farm Credit .... F 302 734-7534
  Dover *(G-1852)*
Midatlantic Farm Credit Aca .... G 302 856-9081
  Georgetown *(G-2604)*
Pinnacle Funding Inc .... G 302 657-0160
  Wilmington *(G-12142)*
Star States Leasing Corp .... E 302 283-4500
  Newark *(G-7484)*

6162 Mortgage Bankers & Loan Correspondents

1st Capitol Mortgage Inc .... G 302 674-5540
  Dover *(G-1066)*
Acre Mortgage & Financial .... G 302 737-5853
  Christiana *(G-664)*
Anniemac Home Mortgage LLC .... E 302 234-2956
  Wilmington *(G-9088)*
Bank America National Assn .... G 302 674-5379
  Dover *(G-1170)*
Bank of Ocean City .... G 410 723-4944
  Fenwick Island *(G-2329)*
Castle Mortgage Services Inc .... F 302 366-0912
  Newark *(G-6167)*
Continental Mortgage Corp .... G 302 996-5807
  Wilmington *(G-9842)*

Delaware Community Inv Corp G 302 655-1420
Wilmington *(G-10024)*
Embrace Home Loans Inc G 302 635-7998
Wilmington *(G-10387)*
Federal Home Loan ADM Inc D 855 345-2669
Wilmington *(G-10516)*
Freedom Mortgage Corporation F 302 368-7100
Newark *(G-6618)*
Gilpin Mortgage F 302 656-5400
Wilmington *(G-10712)*
Mortgage America Inc G 302 239-0600
Wilmington *(G-11760)*
Mortgage Network Solutions LLC E 302 252-0100
Wilmington *(G-11761)*
Movement Mortgage LLC G 302 344-6758
Lewes *(G-3651)*
Oakwood Funding Corporation G 336 855-2400
Wilmington *(G-11928)*
P B Investment Corp G 302 266-7920
Newark *(G-7167)*
Premier Capital Holding G 302 730-1010
Dover *(G-1981)*
Shallcross Mortgage Co Inc G 302 999-9800
Wilmington *(G-12592)*
SLM Financial Corporation F 856 642-8300
Newark *(G-7442)*
Stifel Bank and Trust G 302 478-8880
Wilmington *(G-12767)*
SunTrust Mortgage Inc F 302 453-2350
Newark *(G-7509)*
True Access Capital Corp F 302 652-6774
Wilmington *(G-12986)*
Union Mortgage Group Inc G 302 227-6687
Rehoboth Beach *(G-8105)*
Wells Fargo Home Mortgage Inc G 302 227-5700
Rehoboth Beach *(G-8111)*
Wells Fargo Home Mortgage Inc G 302 239-6300
Hockessin *(G-3171)*

6163 Loan Brokers

A B C Lending Corp G 302 655-5313
Wilmington *(G-8871)*
ABC Payday & Title Lending G 302 322-0233
New Castle *(G-4997)*
Aca Mortgage Co Inc E 302 225-1390
Wilmington *(G-8911)*
American Spirit Federal Cr Un F 302 738-4515
Newark *(G-5958)*
Creditshop LLC F 302 588-0107
Wilmington *(G-9896)*
Del-One Federal Credit Union E 302 739-4496
Dover *(G-1355)*
Delaware Financial Capital F 302 266-9500
Newark *(G-6379)*
Delaware First Federal Cr Un F 302 998-0665
Wilmington *(G-10047)*
Delaware Title Loans Inc F 302 478-8505
Wilmington *(G-10091)*
Delaware Title Loans Inc G 302 644-3640
Lewes *(G-3458)*
First Atlantic Mrtg Svcs LLC G 302 841-8435
Lewes *(G-3497)*
Geris Auto Financial Services G 302 660-9719
Newark *(G-6650)*
Goldstar- Cash LLC G 302 427-2535
Wilmington *(G-10742)*
Innovation Ventures LP G 302 777-1616
Wilmington *(G-11038)*
Interstate Mortgage Corp Inc G 302 733-7620
Newark *(G-6799)*
JG Wentworth HM Lending Inc E 302 725-0723
Ocean View *(G-7796)*
John Lovett Inc D 302 455-9460
Newark *(G-6843)*
Lending Manager Holdings LLC G 888 501-0335
Newark *(G-6931)*
Loan Till Payday LLC E 302 792-5001
Claymont *(G-776)*
Louviers Mortgage Corporation F 302 234-4129
Wilmington *(G-11443)*
Mda Lending Solutions Inc F 302 433-8006
Wilmington *(G-11609)*
Navient Corporation D 302 283-8000
Wilmington *(G-11821)*
Nefsc Inc G 302 746-1771
Wilmington *(G-11828)*
Pike Creek Mortgage Services F 302 892-2811
Newark *(G-7216)*
Provident Federal Credit Union F 302 734-1133
Dover *(G-1992)*
Reliance Mortgage Company Inc G 302 376-7234
Middletown *(G-4215)*
Resource Mortgage Corp F 302 657-0181
Wilmington *(G-12386)*
Stewart Title Company G 302 433-8766
Wilmington *(G-12765)*
Synergy Direct Mortgage F 302 283-0833
Christiana *(G-681)*
Union Mortgage Group Inc G 302 227-6687
Rehoboth Beach *(G-8105)*

62 SECURITY AND COMMODITY BROKERS, DEALERS, EXCHANGES, AND SERVICES

6211 Security Brokers & Dealers

Assurance Partners Intl F 302 478-0173
Wilmington *(G-9163)*
Boothe Investment Group G 302 734-7526
Dover *(G-1221)*
Brittingham Inc G 302 656-8173
Wilmington *(G-9480)*
Brown Brothers Harriman & Co F 302 552-4040
Wilmington *(G-9488)*
Cawsl Enterprises Inc G 302 478-6160
Wilmington *(G-9597)*
Cfd Group Inc E 242 698-1039
Wilmington *(G-9620)*
Charles Schwab & Co Inc F 302 622-3600
Wilmington *(G-9638)*
Citibank Overseas Inv Corp F 302 323-3600
New Castle *(G-5164)*
Citigroup Global Markets Inc D 302 888-4100
Wilmington *(G-9713)*
Defense Shield Trust E 540 815-8248
Wilmington *(G-9994)*
Delaware Valley Brokerage Inc G 302 477-9700
Wilmington *(G-10092)*
Detroit Desl Rmnfacturing Corp G 302 427-3564
Wilmington *(G-10125)*
Deutsche Bank Tr Co Americas E 302 636-3301
Wilmington *(G-10126)*
Freemarkets Investment Co Inc G 302 427-2089
Wilmington *(G-10630)*
Futuretech Inv Group Inc F 302 476-9529
Newark *(G-6630)*
Gates and Company LLC F 302 428-1338
Wilmington *(G-10675)*
Gund Securities Corporation F 302 479-9210
Wilmington *(G-10801)*
Hollie Enterprises LLC G 903 721-1904
Wilmington *(G-10927)*
Hudson Valley Investment Corp G 302 656-1825
Wilmington *(G-10971)*
Ing Bank Fsb E 302 658-2200
Wilmington *(G-11030)*
John Lovett Inc D 302 455-9460
Newark *(G-6843)*
Kensington Cross Ltd F 888 999-9360
Rehoboth Beach *(G-7979)*
Lehman Brothers/Gp Inc F 877 740-0108
Wilmington *(G-11365)*
Merrill Lynch Pierce Fenner E 302 736-7700
Dover *(G-1840)*
Merrill Lynch Pierce Fenner D 302 571-5100
Wilmington *(G-11646)*
Merrill Lynch Pierce Fenner E 302 227-5159
Rehoboth Beach *(G-8003)*
Meyer & Meyer Inc E 302 994-9600
Wilmington *(G-11651)*
Morgan Garanty Intl Fincl Corp E 302 634-1000
Newark *(G-7058)*
Morgan Stanley & Co LLC E 302 573-4000
Wilmington *(G-11752)*
Navient Corporation D 302 283-8000
Wilmington *(G-11821)*
Navient Corporation D 302 283-8000
Wilmington *(G-11822)*
Navient Corporation D 302 283-8000
Wilmington *(G-11823)*
Pacer International One LLC F 302 588-9500
Wilmington *(G-12003)*
Peters Alan E Peters & Assoc G 302 656-1007
Wilmington *(G-12099)*
PNC Bank National Association G 302 994-6337
Wilmington *(G-12165)*
Raymond James & Associates Inc G 302 656-1534
Wilmington *(G-12327)*
Raymond James & Associates Inc G 302 798-9113
Wilmington *(G-12328)*
Raymond James Financial Svc G 302 778-2170
Wilmington *(G-12329)*
Raymond James Fincl Svcs Inc F 302 645-8592
Lewes *(G-3709)*
Raymond James Fincl Svcs Inc G 302 539-3323
Bethany Beach *(G-426)*
Raymond James Fincl Svcs Inc F 302 778-2170
Wilmington *(G-12330)*
Raymond James Fincl Svcs Inc G 302 656-1534
Wilmington *(G-12331)*
Rbc G 302 892-5901
Wilmington *(G-12333)*
Rsl Investors Inc E 302 478-5142
Wilmington *(G-12487)*
Scottrade Inc G 302 658-6511
Newark *(G-7397)*
Skajaquoda Capital LLC F 302 504-4448
Wilmington *(G-12641)*
Sks Enterprise D 302 310-2511
Newark *(G-7437)*
Stb Management G 302 737-5105
Newark *(G-7487)*
Td Ameritrade Inc G 302 368-1050
Newark *(G-7541)*
United Telecommunications E 302 654-6108
Wilmington *(G-13027)*
Wells Fargo Clearing Svcs LLC E 302 428-5969
Newark *(G-7685)*
Wells Fargo Clearing Svcs LLC E 302 428-8600
Wilmington *(G-13152)*
Ziv Investments Co F 302 573-5080
Wilmington *(G-13352)*

6221 Commodity Contracts Brokers & Dealers

DMI Commodities Inc F 877 364-3644
Newark *(G-6457)*
Mefta LLC F 804 433-3566
Wilmington *(G-11622)*
Monterey SW LLC F 302 504-4901
Newark *(G-7054)*
Monterey Swf LLC F 302 504-4901
Newark *(G-7055)*

6231 Security & Commodity Exchanges

Delaware Bd Trade Holdings Inc F 302 298-0600
Wilmington *(G-10005)*

6282 Investment Advice

20 20 Fincl Advisors of Del G 302 777-2020
Wilmington *(G-8852)*
Ameriprise Financial Services G 302 476-8000
Wilmington *(G-9061)*
Ameriprise Financial Svcs Inc F 302 543-5784
Wilmington *(G-9062)*
Ameriprise Financial Svcs Inc F 302 475-5105
Wilmington *(G-9063)*
Ameriprise Financial Svcs Inc E 302 468-8200
Wilmington *(G-9064)*
Ameriprise Financial Svcs Inc F 302 475-2357
Wilmington *(G-9065)*
Amerirpise G 302 656-7773
Wilmington *(G-9066)*
Ashford Capital Management F 302 655-1750
Wilmington *(G-9149)*
Bank of New York Mellon Corp G 302 791-1700
Wilmington *(G-9244)*
Barclays Financial Corporation G 302 652-6201
Wilmington *(G-9251)*
Biddle Capital Management Inc G 302 369-6789
Newark *(G-6079)*
Blackrock Financial Management G 302 797-2000
Wilmington *(G-9350)*
Blackrock Instnl Mgt Corp D 302 797-2000
Wilmington *(G-9354)*
Brown Advisory Incorporated G 302 351-7600
Wilmington *(G-9487)*
Brown Brothers Harriman & Co F 302 552-4040
Wilmington *(G-9488)*
Butler Financial Ltd G 302 778-2170
Wilmington *(G-9515)*
Carey Ins & Fin Services Inc G 302 934-8383
Dagsboro *(G-888)*
Cigna Holdings Inc F 215 761-1000
Claymont *(G-719)*
Cleantech Energy Solutions LLC G 301 704-2831
Wilmington *(G-9738)*

S I C

Employee Codes: A=Over 500 employees, B=251-500
C=101-250, D=51-100, E=20-50, F=10-19, G=1-9
2020 Harris Directory of Delaware Businesses
509

62 SECURITY AND COMMODITY BROKERS, DEALERS, EXCHANGES, AND SERVICES SIC SECTION

Clipper Advisor LLC.......E....... 203 428-5251
Wilmington *(G-9745)*

Coastal.......G....... 302 319-4061
Wilmington *(G-9751)*

Crude Gold Research LLC.......F....... 646 681-7317
Dover *(G-1327)*

Diversified Financial Cons.......G....... 302 765-3500
Wilmington *(G-10170)*

Egs Financial Care Inc.......F....... 800 227-4000
Wilmington *(G-10363)*

Fidelity Income Advisors Co.......E....... 302 223-9444
Wilmington *(G-10533)*

First Command Fincl Plg Inc.......F....... 302 535-8132
Camden Wyoming *(G-638)*

First Un Fincl Investments Inc.......G....... 646 652-6580
Wilmington *(G-10558)*

Friess Associates LLC.......E....... 302 656-3017
Wilmington *(G-10642)*

Glenmede Trust Co Nat Assn.......G....... 302 661-2900
Wilmington *(G-10721)*

Global Financial Advisors Netw.......G....... 302 697-3565
Rehoboth Beach *(G-7949)*

Hcac.......G....... 302 266-8100
Newark *(G-6714)*

Independence Wealth Advisors.......G....... 302 763-1180
Hockessin *(G-3058)*

Integrated Wealth MGT LLC.......G....... 302 442-4233
Wilmington *(G-11051)*

Investment Property Services L.......G....... 302 994-3907
Wilmington *(G-11073)*

John Koziol Inc.......G....... 302 234-5430
Hockessin *(G-3068)*

Kalmar Investments Inc.......E....... 302 658-7575
Wilmington *(G-11222)*

Mallard Advisors LLC.......E....... 302 737-4546
Newark *(G-6979)*

Mallard Advisors LLC.......F....... 302 239-1654
Hockessin *(G-3086)*

Marvin & Palmer Associates.......E....... 302 573-3570
Wilmington *(G-11554)*

Michael Gioia.......G....... 302 479-7780
Wilmington *(G-11660)*

Morgan Stnley Smith Barney LLC.......G....... 302 644-6600
Rehoboth Beach *(G-8013)*

Ms Financing LLC.......F....... 212 276-1206
Wilmington *(G-11769)*

New Visions Inv Group LLC.......G....... 302 299-6234
Newark *(G-7109)*

Onemain Financial Group LLC.......G....... 302 834-6677
Bear *(G-273)*

Onemain Financial Group LLC.......G....... 302 628-9253
Seaford *(G-8336)*

Onemain Financial Group LLC.......G....... 302 674-3900
Dover *(G-1918)*

Onemain Financial Group LLC.......G....... 302 422-9657
Milford *(G-4519)*

Onemain Financial Group LLC.......G....... 302 478-8070
Wilmington *(G-11958)*

Parkwood Trust Company.......G....... 302 426-1220
Wilmington *(G-12026)*

Pfpc Worldwide Inc.......F....... 302 791-1700
Wilmington *(G-12105)*

Playtex Investment Corporation.......G....... 302 678-6000
Dover *(G-1968)*

Qienna Wealth Management Inc.......G....... 610 765-6008
Newark *(G-7278)*

Rbc Capital Markets LLC.......G....... 302 252-9444
Wilmington *(G-12334)*

Riverstone Financial II LLC.......G....... 302 295-5310
Wilmington *(G-12430)*

Rk Advisors LLC.......G....... 302 561-5258
Hockessin *(G-3137)*

Rouse Insurance and Fincl LL.......G....... 302 678-2223
Dover *(G-2044)*

Saggio Management Group Inc.......G....... 302 659-6560
Smyrna *(G-8711)*

Smithfeld Intl Investments Inc.......G....... 302 477-1358
Wilmington *(G-12662)*

Swan Financial Group.......G....... 302 689-6095
Frederica *(G-2414)*

Swarthmore Financial Services.......E....... 302 325-0700
New Castle *(G-5746)*

Topkis Financial Advisors LLC.......G....... 302 654-4444
Wilmington *(G-12932)*

United Brokerage Packaging.......G....... 302 294-6782
Newark *(G-7612)*

Wbi Capital Advisors LLC.......G....... 856 361-6362
Wilmington *(G-13127)*

Wells Fargo Clearing Svcs LLC.......E....... 302 731-2131
Newark *(G-7686)*

Wilmington Trust Corporation.......E....... 302 651-8378
Wilmington *(G-13263)*

63 INSURANCE CARRIERS

6311 Life Insurance Carriers

American Income Life Insurance.......E....... 610 277-9499
Wilmington *(G-9048)*

American-Amicable Holding Inc.......G....... 302 427-0355
Wilmington *(G-9059)*

Cigna Corporate Services LLC.......D....... 302 792-4906
Wilmington *(G-9703)*

Cigna Corporation.......C....... 302 792-4906
Wilmington *(G-9704)*

Cigna Global Holdings Inc.......F....... 302 797-3469
Claymont *(G-718)*

Cigna Holdings Inc.......F....... 215 761-1000
Claymont *(G-719)*

Citicorp Del-Lease Inc.......D....... 302 323-3801
New Castle *(G-5166)*

Donald C Savoy Inc.......G....... 888 992-6755
Newark *(G-6460)*

Entourage Financial Group LLC.......G....... 302 352-9473
Wilmington *(G-10417)*

First Lincoln Holdings Inc.......E....... 302 429-4900
Wilmington *(G-10546)*

Hackney Business Solutions LLC.......G....... 843 496-7236
Newark *(G-6700)*

Highmarks Inc.......G....... 302 421-3000
Wilmington *(G-10906)*

Penn Mutual Life Insurance Co.......F....... 302 655-7151
Wilmington *(G-12066)*

Principal Financial Group Inc.......D....... 302 993-8045
Wilmington *(G-12228)*

6321 Accident & Health Insurance

Ace American Insurance Company.......F....... 302 476-6000
Wilmington *(G-8919)*

American Life Insurance Co.......D....... 302 594-2000
Wilmington *(G-9053)*

American-Amicable Holding Inc.......G....... 302 427-0355
Wilmington *(G-9059)*

Architect Engineer Ins Co Risk.......G....... 302 658-2342
Wilmington *(G-9123)*

Chesapeake Rehab Equipment Inc.......G....... 302 266-6234
Newark *(G-6194)*

Cigna Corporation.......C....... 302 792-4906
Wilmington *(G-9704)*

Cigna Holdings Inc.......F....... 215 761-1000
Claymont *(G-719)*

Citicorp Del-Lease Inc.......D....... 302 323-3801
New Castle *(G-5166)*

Delphi Financial Group Inc.......E....... 302 478-5142
Wilmington *(G-10105)*

Harrington Insurance.......G....... 302 883-5000
Dover *(G-1629)*

Highmarks Inc.......B....... 302 421-3000
Wilmington *(G-10905)*

Highmarks Inc.......G....... 302 674-8492
Dover *(G-1645)*

6324 Hospital & Medical Svc Plans Carriers

Aetna Hose Hook & Ladder Co 9.......E....... 302 454-3305
Newark *(G-5916)*

Aetna Inc.......G....... 860 808-3458
Newark *(G-5918)*

American Life Insurance Co.......D....... 302 594-2000
Wilmington *(G-9053)*

Coventry Health Care Inc.......G....... 302 995-6100
Newark *(G-6308)*

Coventry Health Care Inc.......G....... 800 833-7423
Newark *(G-6309)*

Coventry Health Care Del Inc.......D....... 302 995-6100
Wilmington *(G-9881)*

Highmarks Inc.......G....... 302 421-3000
Wilmington *(G-10906)*

6331 Fire, Marine & Casualty Insurance

AAA Club Alliance Inc.......B....... 302 299-4700
Wilmington *(G-8893)*

AAA Club Alliance Inc.......F....... 302 674-8020
Dover *(G-1075)*

American Gen Lf Insur Co Del.......F....... 302 575-5200
Wilmington *(G-9046)*

Chrissinger and Baumberger.......F....... 302 777-0100
Wilmington *(G-9672)*

Cigna Holdings Inc.......F....... 215 761-1000
Claymont *(G-719)*

Cowchok Tf Inc.......G....... 302 475-4510
Wilmington *(G-9884)*

Highmarks Inc.......G....... 302 421-3000
Wilmington *(G-10906)*

Liberty Mutual Fire Insur Co.......E....... 302 993-0500
Wilmington *(G-11381)*

Liberty Mutual Insurance Co.......E....... 302 993-0500
Wilmington *(G-11382)*

Nuclear Electric Insurance Ltd.......D....... 302 888-3000
Wilmington *(G-11921)*

Progressive Casualty Insur Co.......G....... 302 734-7360
Dover *(G-1990)*

Reese Agency Inc.......G....... 302 678-5656
Dover *(G-2018)*

Steadfast Insurance Company.......G....... 847 605-6000
Dover *(G-2106)*

Wentworth Group.......G....... 302 998-2115
Wilmington *(G-13156)*

6351 Surety Insurance Carriers

AAA Club Alliance Inc.......B....... 302 299-4700
Wilmington *(G-8893)*

Chubb Insurance Company.......G....... 302 477-1892
Wilmington *(G-9695)*

Highmarks Inc.......G....... 302 421-3000
Wilmington *(G-10906)*

6361 Title Insurance

First American Title Insur Co.......F....... 302 855-2120
Georgetown *(G-2531)*

First American Title Insur Co.......G....... 302 421-9440
Wilmington *(G-10545)*

Harrington Insurance.......G....... 302 883-5000
Dover *(G-1629)*

Intercoastal Title Agency Inc.......G....... 302 478-7752
Wilmington *(G-11053)*

Old Republic Nat Title Insur.......G....... 302 734-3570
Dover *(G-1915)*

Stewart Title Guaranty Company.......F....... 302 651-9201
Wilmington *(G-12766)*

6371 Pension, Health & Welfare Funds

American General.......G....... 302 575-5200
Wilmington *(G-9047)*

Benefit Services Unlimited.......E....... 302 479-5696
Wilmington *(G-9300)*

Sntc Holding Inc.......G....... 302 777-5261
Wilmington *(G-12665)*

6399 Insurance Carriers, NEC

Gem Group LP.......G....... 302 762-2008
Wilmington *(G-10687)*

Raymond James Fincl Svcs Inc.......G....... 302 227-0330
Rehoboth Beach *(G-8041)*

64 INSURANCE AGENTS, BROKERS, AND SERVICE

6411 Insurance Agents, Brokers & Svc

21st Century Insurance Company.......G....... 302 252-2000
Wilmington *(G-8854)*

21st Century N Amer Insur Co.......A....... 877 310-5687
Wilmington *(G-8855)*

AAA Club Alliance Inc.......F....... 302 283-4300
Newark *(G-5874)*

Affordable Insur Netwrk Del.......G....... 302 392-4500
Bear *(G-21)*

Affordable Insurance.......G....... 302 834-9641
Bear *(G-22)*

AIG AIG.......G....... 302 252-4683
Wilmington *(G-8987)*

AIG Federal Savings Bank.......E....... 302 661-8992
Wilmington *(G-8988)*

Allen Insurance Group.......F....... 302 654-8823
Wilmington *(G-9019)*

American Life Insurance Co.......D....... 302 594-2000
Wilmington *(G-9053)*

Assurance Partners Intl.......F....... 302 478-0173
Wilmington *(G-9163)*

Axa Equitable Life Insur Co.......F....... 302 655-7231
Wilmington *(G-9201)*

B&H Insurance LLC.......E....... 302 995-2247
Newark *(G-6036)*

Benefit Administrators Del.......G....... 302 234-1978
Wilmington *(G-9299)*

Bishop Associates.......G....... 302 838-1270
Newark *(G-6084)*

SIC SECTION
64 INSURANCE AGENTS, BROKERS, AND SERVICE

Company	Code	Phone
Bob Simmons Agency	G	302 698-1970
Dover (G-1216)		
Bosco Insurance Agency	G	302 678-0647
Dover (G-1222)		
Business Insurance Services	G	302 655-5300
Wilmington (G-9511)		
C Edgar Wood Inc	E	302 674-3500
Dover (G-1245)		
Calvin Sheets	G	302 832-0600
Bear (G-63)		
Carey Jr James E Inc	G	302 934-8383
Dagsboro (G-889)		
Chambers Insurance Agency Inc	G	302 655-5300
Wilmington (G-9625)		
Charles M Wallace	G	302 998-1412
Wilmington (G-9633)		
Chesapeake Insurance Advisors	F	302 544-6900
New Castle (G-5145)		
Chubb US Holding Inc	A	215 640-1000
Wilmington (G-9696)		
Cigna Global Holdings Inc	F	302 797-3469
Claymont (G-718)		
Clark Bffone Mtthews Insur AGC	E	302 322-2261
New Castle (G-5173)		
Cnc Insurance Associates Inc	F	302 678-3860
Dover (G-1296)		
Collender Griffith Chang Inc	G	302 992-0600
Wilmington (G-9772)		
Commercial Insurance Assoc	G	610 436-4608
Newark (G-6268)		
Concord Agency Inc	G	302 478-4000
Wilmington (G-9809)		
Davis Insurance Group Inc	G	302 652-4700
Montchanin (G-4985)		
Delaware Insur Guarantee Assn	G	302 456-3656
Newark (G-6390)		
Denise Beam	G	302 539-1900
Ocean View (G-7783)		
Dewberry Insurance Agency Inc	G	302 995-9550
Wilmington (G-10130)		
Dick Broadbent Insurance	G	302 998-0137
Wilmington (G-10150)		
Donald C Savoy Inc	G	888 992-6755
Newark (G-6460)		
Donald C Savoy Inc	G	302 697-4100
Dover (G-1437)		
Douglas Bennetti Insur Agcy	G	302 724-4490
Dover (G-1440)		
Douglas C Loew & Associates	G	302 453-0550
Newark (G-6464)		
Downs Insurance Associates	G	302 422-8863
Milford (G-4394)		
Drass Insurance Agency Inc	G	302 998-1331
Wilmington (G-10231)		
Emory Agency Inc	G	302 855-2100
Georgetown (G-2522)		
Endurnce Reinsurance Corp Amer	F	973 898-9575
Wilmington (G-10399)		
Entourage Financial Group LLC	G	302 352-9473
Wilmington (G-10417)		
Eric Cline	G	302 629-3984
Seaford (G-8238)		
Farm Financial Services Inc	G	302 854-9760
Georgetown (G-2526)		
Fidelity National Info Svcs	F	302 658-2102
Wilmington (G-10535)		
First Access Inc	F	949 455-4027
Wilmington (G-10544)		
Fox Point Programs Inc	F	800 499-7242
Claymont (G-747)		
Franklin T Varone Inc	G	302 475-6200
Wilmington (G-10619)		
Fred S Smalls Insurance	F	302 633-1980
Wilmington (G-10626)		
Fusura LLC	D	302 397-2200
Wilmington (G-10652)		
Geico Corporation	G	302 998-9192
Wilmington (G-10686)		
George H Bunting Jr	G	302 227-3891
Rehoboth Beach (G-7944)		
George J Weiner Associates	F	302 658-0218
Wilmington (G-10701)		
Harrington Realty Inc	E	302 736-0800
Dover (G-1630)		
Hartle Brian State Farm Agency	G	302 322-1741
New Castle (G-5379)		
Hetrick-Drake Associates Inc	G	302 998-7500
Wilmington (G-10897)		
Hoeschel Inv & Insur Group	F	302 738-3535
Newark (G-6734)		
Independent School MGT Inc	E	302 656-4944
Wilmington (G-11018)		
Insley Insurance & Fincl Svc	G	302 286-0777
Newark (G-6784)		
Insurance & Financial Svcs Inc	G	302 239-5895
Wilmington (G-11043)		
Insurance & Fincl Svcs Ltd Del	G	302 234-1200
Wilmington (G-11044)		
Insurance Associates Inc	F	302 368-0888
Newark (G-6786)		
Insurance Market Inc	E	302 875-7591
Laurel (G-3239)		
Insurance Market Inc	G	302 934-9006
Millsboro (G-4709)		
Insurance Office America Inc	G	302 764-1000
Wilmington (G-11046)		
Integra ADM Group Inc	F	800 959-3518
Seaford (G-8271)		
Jack Lewis	G	302 475-2010
Wilmington (G-11114)		
John Borden	G	302 674-2992
Dover (G-1703)		
John C Leverage	G	302 629-3525
Seaford (G-8281)		
John Koziol Inc	G	302 234-5430
Hockessin (G-3068)		
Kathy Safford	G	302 734-8268
Dover (G-1724)		
Katie Bennett	G	302 697-2650
Camden (G-586)		
Kelly & Assoc Insur Group Inc	G	302 661-6324
Wilmington (G-11236)		
Kevin Lammers Ins	G	302 283-1210
Newark (G-6878)		
KT&d Inc	F	302 429-8500
Wilmington (G-11298)		
L & D Insurance Services LLC	G	302 235-2288
Hockessin (G-3073)		
L & W Insurance Inc	G	302 674-3500
Dover (G-1760)		
Lawrence Agencies Inc	G	302 995-6936
Wilmington (G-11344)		
Lexisnexis Risk Assets Inc	A	800 458-9410
Wilmington (G-11378)		
Lisa Broadbent Insurance Inc	F	302 731-0044
Newark (G-6939)		
Lyons Insurance Agency Inc	E	302 227-7100
Wilmington (G-11466)		
Mark Penuel	G	302 856-7724
Georgetown (G-2597)		
Marsh USA Inc	E	302 888-4300
Wilmington (G-11543)		
Marvel Agency Inc	E	302 422-7844
Milford (G-4488)		
Mary Bryan Inc	F	302 875-5099
Laurel (G-3262)		
McCall Brooks Insurance Agency	G	302 475-8200
Wilmington (G-11585)		
McComrick Insurance Services	G	302 732-6655
Dagsboro (G-919)		
Metropolitan Life Insur Co	E	302 738-0888
Newark (G-7021)		
Metropolitan Life Insur Co	F	302 734-5803
Dover (G-1844)		
Moore Insurance & Financial	G	302 999-9101
Wilmington (G-11744)		
Morgan Stanley	E	302 644-6600
Rehoboth Beach (G-8012)		
Muncie Insurance Services	G	302 678-2800
Dover (G-1879)		
Muncie Insurance Services	G	302 629-9414
Seaford (G-8313)		
Nationwide Corporation	G	302 761-9611
New Castle (G-5548)		
Nationwide Insurance Co	G	302 678-2223
Dover (G-1884)		
Nationwide Mutual Insurance Co	G	302 479-5560
Wilmington (G-11816)		
Nationwide Mutual Insurance Co	F	302 234-5430
Hockessin (G-3101)		
New Castle Insurance Ltd	G	302 328-6111
New Castle (G-5561)		
New York Life Insurance Co	E	302 369-8500
Newark (G-7110)		
Nickle Insurance	G	302 654-0347
Wilmington (G-11888)		
Nickle Insurance Agency Inc	G	302 834-9700
Delaware City (G-961)		
Occidental L Transamerica	F	302 477-9700
Wilmington (G-11932)		
Patrick J McCabe	G	302 368-3711
Newark (G-7183)		
Peninsula Health Alliance Inc	G	302 856-9778
Georgetown (G-2614)		
Penn Del Adjustment Service	G	302 999-0196
Bear (G-281)		
Perry and Associates Services	G	302 581-3092
Wilmington (G-12089)		
Pfister Insurance Inc	G	302 674-3100
Dover (G-1953)		
Phil Hill	G	302 678-0499
Dover (G-1954)		
Planet Payment Solutions Inc	E	516 670-3200
New Castle (G-5625)		
Poland & Sullivan Insurance	F	302 738-3535
Wilmington (G-7229)		
Progressive Casualty Insur Co	G	302 734-7360
Dover (G-1990)		
Prominent Insurance Svcs Inc	G	302 351-3368
Wilmington (G-12251)		
Prudential Insur Co of Amer	E	302 734-7877
Dover (G-1993)		
Prudential Insur Co of Amer	G	302 378-8811
Middletown (G-4201)		
Rawlins Ferguson Jones & Lewis	G	302 337-8231
Bridgeville (G-518)		
Records Gebhart Agency Inc	G	302 653-9211
Smyrna (G-8698)		
Reese Agency Inc	G	302 678-5656
Dover (G-2018)		
Regulatory Insurance Services	G	302 678-2444
Dover (G-2021)		
Rhue & Associates Inc	G	302 422-3058
Milford (G-4542)		
Richard A Parsons Agency Inc	G	302 674-2810
Dover (G-2035)		
Richard E Small Inc	G	302 875-7199
Laurel (G-3280)		
Risk Consultan	G	302 655-3350
Wilmington (G-12425)		
Robert F Mullen Insurance Agcy	G	302 322-5331
Bear (G-309)		
S T Good Insurance Inc	E	215 969-8385
Newark (G-7374)		
Sanderson Albidress Agency	G	302 368-3010
Wilmington (G-12539)		
Schanne Mark State Farm Insur	G	302 422-7231
Milford (G-4554)		
Select Financial Group	G	302 424-7777
Milford (G-4555)		
Sheets Insurance Inc	G	302 832-0441
Bear (G-320)		
Short Insurance Associates	G	302 629-0999
Seaford (G-8401)		
Stacy K Gates	G	302 368-1968
Newark (G-7478)		
Standard Insurance Company	G	302 322-9922
New Castle (G-5738)		
Starr Wright Insur Agcy Inc	E	302 483-0190
Wilmington (G-12743)		
State Farm Insurance	G	302 832-0344
Newark (G-7485)		
State Farm Mutl Auto Insur Co	D	302 434-3333
Wilmington (G-12744)		
Steinebach Robert and Assoc	G	302 328-1212
Christiana (G-680)		
Surplus & Excess Line Ltd	G	302 653-5016
Smyrna (G-8727)		
Terry White	G	302 652-4969
Newark (G-7557)		
Thomas R Wyshock	G	302 645-5070
Lewes (G-3782)		
Tom Wiseley Insurance Agency	G	302 832-7700
Newark (G-7574)		
Travel Co Inc	G	302 652-6263
Wilmington (G-12960)		
Truitt Insurance Agency Inc	G	302 645-9344
Lewes (G-3796)		
Usi Inc	D	302 658-8000
Wilmington (G-13041)		
Virgil P Ellwanger	G	302 934-8083
Millsboro (G-4820)		
W C Ungerer Insurance Agency	G	302 368-8505
Newark (G-7668)		
Weymouth Swyze Crroon Insur In	F	302 655-3705
Wilmington (G-13177)		
Wilgus Associates Inc	E	302 539-7511
Bethany Beach (G-438)		
Wilgus Associates Inc	F	302 644-2960
Lewes (G-3823)		

Employee Codes: A=Over 500 employees, B=251-500
C=101-250, D=51-100, E=20-50, F=10-19, G=1-9

64 INSURANCE AGENTS, BROKERS, AND SERVICE

Williams Insurance Agency Inc ....E........ 302 227-2501
 Rehoboth Beach *(G-8116)*
Williams Insurance Agency Inc ....G........ 302 239-5500
 Wilmington *(G-13217)*
Work First Casualty Company ....F........ 302 477-1710
 Wilmington *(G-13302)*
Zavier J Decaire ....F........ 302 658-0218
 Wilmington *(G-13341)*

65 REAL ESTATE

6512 Operators Of Nonresidential Bldgs

302 Properties LLC ....G........ 302 753-8383
 Newark *(G-5856)*
A-Stover Management Group LLC ....F........ 866 299-0709
 Bear *(G-6)*
AAA Club Alliance Inc ....B........ 302 299-4700
 Wilmington *(G-8893)*
Aftermath Services LLC ....E........ 302 357-3780
 Dover *(G-1093)*
Ai Enterprises ....G........ 302 764-2342
 Wilmington *(G-8985)*
Atlantic Management Ltd ....F........ 302 645-9511
 Rehoboth Beach *(G-7851)*
Belco Inc ....G........ 302 655-1561
 Wilmington *(G-9286)*
Chabbott Ptrosky Coml Realtors ....G........ 302 678-3276
 Dover *(G-1272)*
Church Street Associates ....G........ 302 227-1599
 Rehoboth Beach *(G-7889)*
Cigna Global Holdings Inc ....F........ 302 797-3469
 Claymont *(G-718)*
Cigna Holdings Inc ....F........ 215 761-1000
 Claymont *(G-719)*
Cigna Real Estate Inc ....G........ 302 476-3337
 Wilmington *(G-9706)*
Commerce Associates LP ....G........ 302 573-2500
 Wilmington *(G-9783)*
Concord Mall LLC ....E........ 302 478-9271
 Wilmington *(G-9812)*
Covenant Properties I ....G........ 302 234-5655
 Wilmington *(G-9880)*
Dack Realty Corp ....G........ 302 792-2737
 Claymont *(G-726)*
Delaware Occupational Health S ....E........ 302 368-5100
 Newark *(G-6400)*
Delport Holding Company ....G........ 302 655-7300
 New Castle *(G-5246)*
Dover Mall LLC ....F........ 302 678-4000
 Dover *(G-1459)*
Dover Rent-All Inc ....F........ 302 739-0860
 Dover *(G-1469)*
Doyjul Apartments ....F........ 302 998-0088
 Wilmington *(G-10215)*
Eagle Plaza Associates Inc ....F........ 302 999-0708
 Wilmington *(G-10314)*
Emory Hill RE Svcs Inc ....D........ 302 322-9500
 New Castle *(G-5288)*
Executive Offices Inc ....G........ 302 323-8100
 New Castle *(G-5300)*
Fusco Enterprises ....G........ 302 328-6251
 New Castle *(G-5337)*
Fusco Management Inc ....E........ 302 328-6251
 New Castle *(G-5338)*
Glasgow Shopping Center Corp ....G........ 302 836-1503
 Bear *(G-165)*
Gordy Management Inc ....G........ 302 322-3723
 New Castle *(G-5356)*
H R Phillips Inc ....E........ 302 422-4518
 Milford *(G-4430)*
Habitat America LLC ....E........ 302 875-3525
 Laurel *(G-3236)*
Kenco Group Inc ....E........ 302 629-4295
 Seaford *(G-8287)*
Market Street Center Inc ....G........ 302 856-9024
 Georgetown *(G-2598)*
McLeen Properties ....G........ 302 482-1486
 Wilmington *(G-11604)*
Melchiorre and Melchiorre ....F........ 302 645-6311
 Lewes *(G-3634)*
Midway Realty Inc ....G........ 302 645-9511
 Rehoboth Beach *(G-8008)*
New R V Associates L P ....G........ 302 798-6878
 Claymont *(G-790)*
Parkway Gravel Inc ....D........ 302 658-5241
 New Castle *(G-5603)*
Pbe Companies LLC ....E........ 617 346-7459
 Wilmington *(G-12049)*
Preit-Rubin Inc ....D........ 302 731-9815
 (G-7242)

Property Improvements LLC ....G........ 610 692-5343
 Bethany Beach *(G-424)*
Prudential Gallo Realty ....F........ 302 645-6661
 Lewes *(G-3700)*
Rodney Square Associates ....G........ 302 652-1536
 Wilmington *(G-12461)*
Route 13 Outlet Market ....G........ 302 875-4800
 Laurel *(G-3285)*
S & A Holding Associates Inc ....G........ 302 479-8314
 Wilmington *(G-12504)*
Silver Lining Solutions LLC ....G........ 302 691-7100
 Wilmington *(G-12616)*
Tudor Enterprises L L C ....G........ 302 736-8255
 Dover *(G-2166)*
United Outdoor Advertising ....G........ 302 652-3177
 Wilmington *(G-13025)*
Unity Construction Inc ....E........ 302 998-0531
 Wilmington *(G-13030)*
Urban Retail Properties LLC ....G........ 302 479-8314
 Dover *(G-13034)*
Vintage Properties LLC ....G........ 302 994-2505
 Wilmington *(G-13085)*
Wwd Inc ....G........ 302 994-4553
 Wilmington *(G-13310)*

6513 Operators Of Apartment Buildings

Admirals Club Apts2c ....E........ 302 737-8496
 Newark *(G-5901)*
Ai Enterprises ....G........ 302 764-2342
 Wilmington *(G-8985)*
Aion Prides Court LLC ....G........ 302 737-2085
 Newark *(G-5923)*
Aion University Village LLC ....G........ 302 366-8000
 Newark *(G-5924)*
Alban Associates ....G........ 302 656-1827
 Wilmington *(G-9001)*
Apartment Communities Corp ....D........ 302 656-7781
 Wilmington *(G-9094)*
Apartment Communities Inc ....F........ 302 798-9100
 Claymont *(G-692)*
Appleby Apartments Assoc LP ....G........ 302 219-5014
 New Castle *(G-5041)*
Appoquinimink Development Inc ....G........ 302 378-0878
 Middletown *(G-3942)*
Barrettes Run Apartments ....G........ 302 368-3400
 Newark *(G-6047)*
Belmont Villa Condominiums ....G........ 302 368-1633
 Newark *(G-6071)*
Berman Development Corp ....G........ 302 323-1197
 New Castle *(G-5083)*
Bethel Villa Associates LP ....G........ 302 426-9688
 Wilmington *(G-9316)*
Bethel Villas 2009 Assoc LP ....F........ 610 278-1733
 Wilmington *(G-9317)*
Better Homes of Laurel Inc ....G........ 302 875-4281
 Laurel *(G-3199)*
BNai Brith Snior Ctzens Hsing ....G........ 302 798-6846
 Claymont *(G-703)*
Boston Land Co Mgt Svcs Inc ....G........ 302 571-0100
 Wilmington *(G-9395)*
Brandywine Apartment Assoc LP ....F........ 302 475-8600
 Wilmington *(G-9417)*
Brandywine Hills Apartments ....E........ 302 764-3242
 Wilmington *(G-9436)*
Brandywine I & 2 Apts ....F........ 302 475-8600
 Wilmington *(G-9439)*
Brookside Plaza Apartments LLC ....G........ 302 737-2008
 Newark *(G-6125)*
Buford Manlove Grdns Assoc LP ....E........ 302 652-3991
 Hockessin *(G-2972)*
Burlington Manor Associates ....F........ 609 387-3184
 Wilmington *(G-9508)*
Cabell Corp ....G........ 302 398-8125
 Harrington *(G-2822)*
Capano Management Company ....G........ 302 737-8056
 Newark *(G-6149)*
Carl M Freeman Associates Inc ....C........ 302 539-6961
 Bethany Beach *(G-391)*
Carleton Court Associates LP ....F........ 302 454-1800
 Wilmington *(G-9571)*
Carvel Gardens Associates LP ....G........ 302 875-4281
 Laurel *(G-3208)*
Cavalier Group ....G........ 302 429-8700
 Wilmington *(G-9596)*
Cavalier Group ....G........ 302 368-7437
 Newark *(G-6172)*
Chasemont Apartments ....G........ 302 731-0784
 Newark *(G-6191)*
Chelten Apartments Assoc LP ....F........ 302 322-6323
 Wilmington *(G-9643)*

Christiana Village Apts ....G........ 302 427-0403
 Wilmington *(G-9689)*
Christiana Wood LLC ....G........ 302 322-1172
 New Castle *(G-5158)*
City Systems Inc ....G........ 302 655-9914
 Wilmington *(G-9725)*
Clyde Spinelli ....G........ 302 328-7679
 New Castle *(G-5178)*
Colonial Inv Managment Co ....G........ 302 736-0674
 Dover *(G-1303)*
Colonial Rlty Assoc Ltd Partnr ....F........ 302 737-1254
 Newark *(G-6264)*
Colony North Apartments ....F........ 302 762-0405
 Wilmington *(G-9777)*
Community Housing Inc ....G........ 302 652-3991
 Wilmington *(G-9793)*
Compton Pk Prsrvtion Assoc LLC ....G........ 302 654-4369
 Wilmington *(G-9806)*
Country Village Apartments ....G........ 302 674-0991
 Dover *(G-1316)*
Cranston Hall Apartments ....G........ 302 999-7001
 Wilmington *(G-9894)*
D C J L Partnership ....G........ 302 328-8040
 New Castle *(G-5211)*
Dack Realty Corp ....G........ 302 792-2737
 Claymont *(G-726)*
Delaware Equity Fund IV ....G........ 302 655-1420
 Wilmington *(G-10044)*
Doyjul Apartments ....F........ 302 998-0088
 Wilmington *(G-10215)*
Dunbarton Oaks Associates ....G........ 302 856-7719
 Georgetown *(G-2516)*
East Coast Property MGT Inc ....F........ 302 629-8612
 Milford *(G-4400)*
Eastern Property Group Inc ....G........ 302 764-7112
 Wilmington *(G-10324)*
Eastern Prosperity Group ....G........ 302 764-7112
 Wilmington *(G-10325)*
Eastlake Apartments LLC ....F........ 302 764-0215
 Wilmington *(G-10328)*
Egg Harbor City Apartments LLC ....G........ 302 543-6514
 Wilmington *(G-10362)*
Evergreen Realty ....E........ 302 999-8805
 Wilmington *(G-10447)*
Evergreen Realty Inc ....G........ 302 998-0354
 Wilmington *(G-10448)*
Farrand Village Apartments ....G........ 302 998-5796
 Wilmington *(G-10501)*
First Montgomery Properties ....E........ 302 834-8272
 Bear *(G-152)*
Forest Park Apartments ....G........ 302 737-6151
 Wilmington *(G-10591)*
Foxwood Apts Rehab ....G........ 302 366-8790
 Newark *(G-6610)*
Frankel Enterprises Inc ....G........ 302 652-6364
 Wilmington *(G-10615)*
Galloway Court Apts ....G........ 302 328-0488
 New Castle *(G-5341)*
Galman Group Inc ....G........ 302 737-5550
 Newark *(G-6635)*
Georgetown Manor Apartments ....G........ 302 328-6231
 New Castle *(G-5352)*
Georgetown Prsrvation Assoc LLC ....G........ 302 856-1557
 Wilmington *(G-10704)*
Governors Place Townhomes ....G........ 302 653-6655
 Smyrna *(G-8645)*
Harbor Club Apartments ....E........ 302 738-3561
 Newark *(G-6708)*
Harbour Towne Associates LP ....G........ 302 645-1003
 Lewes *(G-3533)*
Hub Associates ....G........ 302 674-2200
 Dover *(G-1660)*
Iacono - Summer Chase ....F........ 302 994-2505
 Wilmington *(G-10985)*
Ingleside Homes Inc ....E........ 302 984-0950
 Wilmington *(G-11032)*
Ingleside Rtrment Aprtmnts LLC ....D........ 302 575-0250
 Wilmington *(G-11033)*
Iron Hill Apartments Assoc ....G........ 302 366-8228
 Newark *(G-6806)*
J & S General Contractors ....F........ 302 658-4499
 Wilmington *(G-11098)*
Kbf Associates LP ....G........ 302 328-5400
 New Castle *(G-5455)*
Kimberton Apartments Assoc LP ....F........ 302 368-0116
 Newark *(G-6887)*
Leo Ritter & Co ....G........ 302 674-1375
 Dover *(G-1781)*
Leon N Weiner & Associates Inc ....G........ 302 737-9574
 Newark *(G-6932)*

Company	Code	Phone
Leon N Weiner & Associates Inc	G	860 447-2282
Wilmington *(G-11372)*		
Leon N Weiner & Associates Inc	G	302 856-2251
Georgetown *(G-2590)*		
Leon N Weiner & Associates Inc	F	302 322-6323
New Castle *(G-5479)*		
Leon N Weiner & Associates Inc	G	302 422-3343
Milford *(G-4473)*		
Leon N Weiner & Associates Inc	G	302 798-3446
Claymont *(G-773)*		
Lexington Green Apartments	G	302 322-8959
Newark *(G-6933)*		
Lorelton	E	302 573-3580
Wilmington *(G-11436)*		
Louis Capano and Associates	G	302 738-8000
Newark *(G-6951)*		
Lsref4 Lighthouse Corp Acqstn	E	302 737-8500
Newark *(G-6954)*		
Luther Towers III Dover Inc	E	302 674-1408
Dover *(G-1801)*		
Luther Towers IV Dover Inc	E	302 674-1408
Dover *(G-1802)*		
Luther Towers of Dover Inc	E	302 674-1408
Dover *(G-1803)*		
Luther Village I Dover Inc	F	302 674-1408
Dover *(G-1804)*		
Luther Village II Dover Inc	G	302 674-1408
Dover *(G-1805)*		
Luther Village of Dover	G	302 674-3780
Dover *(G-1806)*		
Lutheran Senior Services Inc	G	302 654-4490
Wilmington *(G-11455)*		
Lutheran Snr Srvcs Ssx Cnty	G	302 684-1668
Milton *(G-4927)*		
Luxiasuites LLC	G	302 654-8527
Wilmington *(G-11458)*		
Main Towers Assoicates LP	G	302 761-7327
Wilmington *(G-11492)*		
Main Twers Prsrvtion Assoc LLC	F	302 737-9574
Newark *(G-6975)*		
Management Associates Inc	F	302 652-3991
Wilmington *(G-11498)*		
Market Street Preservation Inc	G	302 422-8255
Milford *(G-4486)*		
Market Street Preservation LP	G	302 422-8255
Milford *(G-4487)*		
Martys Contracting	G	302 234-8690
Hockessin *(G-3091)*		
Mid-Atlantic Realty Co Inc	G	302 322-9500
New Castle *(G-5526)*		
Mid-Atlantic Realty Co Inc	G	302 738-5325
Newark *(G-7030)*		
Mid-Atlantic Realty Co Inc	G	302 737-3110
Newark *(G-7031)*		
Milford Housing Development	E	302 678-0300
Dover *(G-1856)*		
Millsboro Village I LLC	G	302 678-9400
Millsboro *(G-4752)*		
Mispillion III	G	302 422-4429
Milford *(G-4507)*		
ML Newark LLC	F	302 737-2868
Newark *(G-7048)*		
New Alden-Berkley Assoc LLC	F	207 774-5341
Wilmington *(G-11848)*		
New Colony North Enterprises	G	302 762-0405
Wilmington *(G-11857)*		
New Compton Towne Assoc LP	G	302 571-0217
Wilmington *(G-11858)*		
New R V Associates L P	G	302 798-6878
Claymont *(G-790)*		
New Wndsor Apartments Assoc LP	G	302 656-1354
Wilmington *(G-11874)*		
Old Landing II LP	G	302 934-1871
Millsboro *(G-4767)*		
Owners Management Company	G	302 422-0740
Milford *(G-4521)*		
Panco Management Corporation	F	302 366-1875
Newark *(G-7173)*		
Panco Management Corporation	G	302 995-6152
Wilmington *(G-12011)*		
Panco Management Corporation	G	302 475-9337
Wilmington *(G-12012)*		
Park View	G	302 429-7288
Wilmington *(G-12022)*		
Parson Thorne Realty Assoc LP	E	302 422-9367
Milford *(G-4522)*		
Pennrose Management Company	G	302 571-8295
Wilmington *(G-12070)*		
Pettinaro Enterprises LLC	E	302 999-0708
Wilmington *(G-12103)*		
Phase Flats II L P	G	717 291-1911
Wilmington *(G-12109)*		
Phase I Flats L P	G	717 291-1911
Wilmington *(G-12110)*		
Prides Court Apartments		302 737-2085
Newark *(G-7252)*		
Providence Hall Associates LP	E	518 828-4700
Wilmington *(G-12257)*		
Prudential Gallo Realty	F	302 645-6661
Lewes *(G-3700)*		
Robino Management Group Inc	G	302 734-2944
Dover *(G-2038)*		
Rockwood Apartments	F	302 832-8823
Newark *(G-7355)*		
Roizman & Associates Inc	G	302 426-9688
Wilmington *(G-12465)*		
Rp Management Inc	G	302 798-6878
Claymont *(G-801)*		
School Bell Apartments LP	G	302 328-9500
Bear *(G-314)*		
Schoolhouse Trust Inc	G	302 322-6161
Bear *(G-315)*		
Seaford Preservation Assoc LLC	G	302 629-6416
Seaford *(G-8395)*		
Service General Corp	C	302 856-3500
Georgetown *(G-2651)*		
Sheldon Limited Partnership	G	302 738-3048
Newark *(G-7414)*		
Shelter Development LLC	G	302 737-4999
Newark *(G-7415)*		
Silver Springs Apartments	G	302 992-0800
Wilmington *(G-12617)*		
South Gate Realty Assoc LLP	G	302 368-4535
Claymont *(G-806)*		
St James Place Associates	F	302 764-6450
Wilmington *(G-12723)*		
Stoltz Realty Co	G	302 656-8543
Wilmington *(G-12769)*		
Stoltz Realty Co	G	302 798-8500
Claymont *(G-807)*		
Stoneybrook Associates LP	F	302 764-6450
Wilmington *(G-12771)*		
Stoneybrook Presvtn Assoc LLC	F	302 764-9430
Wilmington *(G-12772)*		
Summit Properties Inc	G	302 737-3747
Newark *(G-7505)*		
Top of Hllbrndywine Apartments	G	302 798-9971
Wilmington *(G-12928)*		
Town and Country Trust	F	302 328-8700
Bear *(G-356)*		
Udel Holdings LLC	E	877 833-8737
Newark *(G-7607)*		
Udr Inc	G	302 674-8887
Dover *(G-2172)*		
University Garden Associates	G	302 368-3823
Newark *(G-7617)*		
University Village Apartment	G	302 731-5972
Newark *(G-7630)*		
Vance Phillips Inc	G	302 542-1501
Laurel *(G-3301)*		
Victoria Mews LP Delnware Vall	G	302 489-2000
Hockessin *(G-3168)*		
Victorian Apartments LLC	G	302 678-0968
Dover *(G-2192)*		
Village At Fox Point	G	302 762-7480
Wilmington *(G-13081)*		
Village Windhover Apartments	F	302 834-1168
Newark *(G-7658)*		
Vintage Properties LLC	G	302 994-4442
Wilmington *(G-13084)*		
Walden LLC	G	302 998-8112
Wilmington *(G-13115)*		
West Minister Management	G	302 678-4515
Dover *(G-2215)*		
Westover Management Company LP	G	302 738-5775
Newark *(G-7687)*		
Westover Management Company LP	F	302 731-1638
Newark *(G-7688)*		
Westwood Properties Ltd	G	302 655-0274
Wilmington *(G-13174)*		
Whatcoat Village Assoc LLC	F	856 596-0500
Dover *(G-2221)*		
Windsor Forest Town Homes	G	302 328-1260
New Castle *(G-5838)*		
Woodacres Associates LP	F	302 792-0243
Claymont *(G-826)*		
Woodland Apartments LP	G	302 994-9003
Wilmington *(G-13295)*		
Woodland Hill Preservation	F	302 764-6450
Wilmington *(G-13296)*		
Woods Edge Apartments	G	302 762-8300
Wilmington *(G-13300)*		
Woolard Properties	G	302 731-1944
Newark *(G-7719)*		
Xsc Ip LLC	E	305 384-6700
Wilmington *(G-13322)*		
Zwaanendael LLC	G	302 645-6466
Lewes *(G-3837)*		

6514 Operators Of Dwellings, Except Apartments

Company	Code	Phone
Ai Enterprises	G	302 764-2342
Wilmington *(G-8985)*		
Baynum Enterprises Inc	D	302 629-6104
Seaford *(G-8163)*		
Baynum Enterprises Inc	E	302 875-4477
Laurel *(G-3196)*		
Baynum Enterprises Inc	E	302 934-8699
Millsboro *(G-4635)*		
Chandler Heights II LP	F	302 629-8048
Seaford *(G-8188)*		
Chelten Preservation Assoc LLC	F	302 322-6323
New Castle *(G-5142)*		
Cigna Holdings Inc	F	215 761-1000
Claymont *(G-719)*		
Interfaith Cmnty Hsing of Del	F	302 652-3991
Wilmington *(G-11062)*		
J & S General Contractors	F	302 658-4499
Wilmington *(G-11098)*		
Melchiorre and Melchiorre	F	302 645-6311
Lewes *(G-3634)*		
Prudential Gallo Realty	F	302 645-6661
Lewes *(G-3700)*		
Veterans Re-Entry Resources	F	302 384-2350
Wilmington *(G-13072)*		
Wild Meadows Homes	D	302 730-4700
Dover *(G-2225)*		
Zwaanendael LLC	G	302 645-6466
Lewes *(G-3837)*		

6515 Operators of Residential Mobile Home Sites

Company	Code	Phone
Bayshore Inc	G	302 539-7200
Ocean View *(G-7758)*		
Canterbury Homes Inc	G	302 284-0351
Felton *(G-2279)*		
Carlisle Group	G	302 475-3010
Wilmington *(G-9572)*		
Colonial East LP	F	302 644-4758
Lewes *(G-3442)*		
Dis Inc	F	302 834-1633
Newark *(G-6453)*		
Equity Lifestyle Prpts Inc	G	302 645-5770
Lewes *(G-3486)*		
Equity Lifestyle Prpts Inc	G	302 945-1544
Millsboro *(G-4686)*		
Holly Hill Estates	G	302 653-7503
Smyrna *(G-8653)*		
Hometown America LLC	G	302 945-5186
Lewes *(G-3544)*		
Love Creek Marina MBL Hm Site	F	302 448-6492
Lewes *(G-3611)*		
Millcreek Mobile Hm Pk Land Co	F	302 998-3045
Wilmington *(G-11690)*		
Nanticoke Shores Assoc LLC	G	302 945-1500
Millsboro *(G-4759)*		
Pine Acres Inc	F	302 945-2000
Lewes *(G-3692)*		
Pinewood Acres MBL Hm Pk L L C	G	302 678-1004
Dover *(G-1960)*		
Reybold Group of Companies Inc	G	302 834-2544
Bear *(G-306)*		
Shady Park Inc	G	302 436-8441
Selbyville *(G-8545)*		
Sun Communities Inc	G	302 335-5444
Frederica *(G-2413)*		
Sun Communities Inc	G	302 227-8118
Rehoboth Beach *(G-8091)*		
Theta Vest Inc	F	302 227-3745
Rehoboth Beach *(G-8096)*		
Tunnell Companies LP	F	302 945-9300
Millsboro *(G-4816)*		
Waterford Mhc Inc	G	302 834-9514
Bear *(G-371)*		
White House Beach Inc	G	302 945-3032
Millsboro *(G-4827)*		

Employee Codes: A=Over 500 employees, B=251-500
C=101-250, D=51-100, E=20-50, F=10-19, G=1-9

65 REAL ESTATE

6519 Lessors Of Real Estate, NEC

Carl M Freeman Associates Inc .... C 302 539-6961
 Bethany Beach *(G-391)*
Cigna Real Estate Inc .... G 302 476-3337
 Wilmington *(G-9706)*
Coldwell Bnkr Coml Amato Assoc .... G 302 224-7700
 Newark *(G-6260)*
Double R Holdings Inc .... G 302 645-5555
 Lewes *(G-3470)*
First Class Properties Del LLC .... G 302 677-0770
 Dover *(G-1552)*
Hensco LLC .... G 302 423-1638
 Harrington *(G-2849)*
JG Townsend Jr & Co Inc .... E 302 856-2525
 Georgetown *(G-2574)*
Long & Foster Real Estate Inc .... G 302 227-3821
 Rehoboth Beach *(G-7991)*
Parkway Gravel Inc .... D 302 658-5241
 New Castle *(G-5603)*
Pettinaro Construction Co Inc .... D 302 999-0708
 Wilmington *(G-12102)*
Resortquest Delaware RE LLC .... F 302 541-8999
 Bethany Beach *(G-428)*
Shipyard Center LLC .... G 302 999-0708
 Wilmington *(G-12605)*
Tunnell Companies LP .... E 302 945-9300
 Millsboro *(G-4816)*
Vance Phillips Inc .... G 302 542-1501
 Laurel *(G-3301)*
West Orange Office Exec Pk LLC .... F 973 320-3227
 Wilmington *(G-13167)*
Wilgus Associates Inc .... G 302 644-2960
 Lewes *(G-3823)*

6531 Real Estate Agents & Managers

4 Corners LLC .... G 302 723-2264
 Wilmington *(G-8860)*
A C Emsley & Associates .... G 302 429-9191
 Wilmington *(G-8873)*
A-Stover Management Group LLC .... F 866 299-0709
 Bear *(G-6)*
Agvisory LLC .... G 302 270-5165
 Lewes *(G-3329)*
Appraisal Associates Inc .... G 302 652-0710
 Wilmington *(G-9104)*
Arbor Management LLC .... C 302 764-6450
 Wilmington *(G-9112)*
Arhc McNwdny01 LLC .... E 518 213-1000
 Wilmington *(G-9127)*
Asset Management Alliance .... F 302 656-5238
 Wilmington *(G-9155)*
Babilonia Inc .... G 415 237-3339
 Newark *(G-6039)*
Bc Consulting Inc .... G 302 234-7710
 Wilmington *(G-9271)*
Beimac LLC .... G 302 677-1965
 Magnolia *(G-3881)*
Bellevue Realty Co .... F 302 655-1818
 Wilmington *(G-9292)*
Berkshire Hataway Home Svcs .... F 302 235-6431
 Hockessin *(G-2963)*
Better Homes Laurel II Inc .... E 302 875-4282
 Laurel *(G-3198)*
Boston Land Co Mgt Svcs Inc .... G 302 571-0100
 Wilmington *(G-9395)*
Bpg Office Invstors III/IV LLC .... F 302 691-2100
 Wilmington *(G-9408)*
Bpg Real Estate Services LLC .... G 302 478-1190
 Wilmington *(G-9410)*
Bpg Real Estate Services LLC .... E 302 777-2000
 Wilmington *(G-9411)*
Brandywine Fine Properties .... F 302 691-3052
 Wilmington *(G-9433)*
Brandywine Realty Management .... F 302 656-1058
 Wilmington *(G-9452)*
Brandywine Realty Trust .... G 302 655-5900
 Wilmington *(G-9453)*
Brandywine Valley Properties .... G 302 475-7660
 Wilmington *(G-9458)*
Brandywood Plaza Assoc LLC .... G 302 633-9134
 Wilmington *(G-9463)*
Broker Post .... G 302 628-8467
 Seaford *(G-8175)*
Burns & Ellis Realty Co .... E 302 674-4220
 Dover *(G-1243)*
Burton Realty Inc .... G 302 945-5100
 Millsboro *(G-4650)*
C M L Management .... G 302 537-5599
 Ocean View *(G-7771)*

C21 Gold Key Realty .... G 302 250-6801
 Newark *(G-6142)*
Cabell Corp .... G 302 398-8125
 Harrington *(G-2822)*
Calatlantic Group Inc .... G 302 834-5472
 Bear *(G-62)*
Callaway Farnell and Moore .... G 302 629-4514
 Seaford *(G-8180)*
Cap Title of Delaware LLC .... G 302 537-3788
 Ocean View *(G-7773)*
Capano Management Company .... G 302 737-8056
 Newark *(G-6149)*
Capital Commercial Realty LLC .... G 302 734-4400
 Wilmington *(G-9556)*
Carl M Freeman Associates Inc .... C 302 539-6961
 Bethany Beach *(G-391)*
Carthage Group Inc .... G 610 931-8493
 Newark *(G-6163)*
CB Richard Ellis RE Svcs LLC .... F 302 661-6700
 Wilmington *(G-9598)*
Cbre Inc .... G 302 661-6700
 Wilmington *(G-9601)*
CD Clean Energy and Infrastruc .... G 480 653-8450
 Wilmington *(G-9603)*
Century 21 Fantini Realty .... F 302 798-6688
 Claymont *(G-712)*
Century 21 Mann & Sons .... D 302 227-9477
 Rehoboth Beach *(G-7886)*
Century 21 Tom Livizos Inc .... G 302 737-9000
 Newark *(G-6179)*
Chichester Business Park LLC .... G 302 379-3140
 Wilmington *(G-9660)*
Cigna Real Estate Inc .... G 302 476-3337
 Wilmington *(G-9706)*
Coldwell Banker .... F 302 539-4086
 Bethany Beach *(G-392)*
Coldwell Banker Rehoboth Resrt .... E 302 227-5000
 Rehoboth Beach *(G-7896)*
Coldwell Bnkr Coml Amato Assoc .... G 302 224-7700
 Newark *(G-6260)*
Cole Realty Inc .... G 302 764-4700
 Wilmington *(G-9766)*
Commonwealth Group LLC .... E 302 472-7200
 Wilmington *(G-9791)*
Commonwealth Trust Co .... F 302 658-7214
 Wilmington *(G-9792)*
Cooperealty Associates Inc .... E 302 629-6693
 Seaford *(G-8207)*
Cressona Associates LLC .... F 302 792-2737
 Claymont *(G-724)*
Crowley and Assoc Rlty Inc .... F 302 227-6131
 Rehoboth Beach *(G-7904)*
Crystal Holdings Inc .... D 302 421-5700
 Wilmington *(G-9909)*
Cushman & Wakefield Del Inc .... G 302 655-9621
 Wilmington *(G-9923)*
D M F Associates Inc .... G 302 539-0606
 Bethany Beach *(G-395)*
Dack Realty Corp .... G 302 792-2737
 Claymont *(G-725)*
Deaton McCue & Co Inc .... G 302 658-7789
 Wilmington *(G-9990)*
Debbie Reed .... F 302 227-3818
 Rehoboth Beach *(G-7909)*
Dee & Doreens Team .... F 302 677-0030
 Dover *(G-1349)*
Delaware Corporate Agents Inc .... F 302 762-8637
 Wilmington *(G-10026)*
Delaware RE Advisors LLC .... F 302 998-4030
 Wilmington *(G-10077)*
Delaware Realty Group Inc .... G 302 227-4800
 Rehoboth Beach *(G-7914)*
Delaware Valley Dev LLC .... F 302 235-2500
 Hockessin *(G-3007)*
Dover Consulting Services Inc .... G 302 736-1365
 Dover *(G-1443)*
Dreamville LLC .... G 662 524-0917
 Lewes *(G-3472)*
E B D Management Inc .... G 302 428-1313
 Wilmington *(G-10275)*
Ear Enterprise LLC .... G 302 836-8334
 Bear *(G-135)*
East Coast Property MGT Inc .... F 302 629-8612
 Milford *(G-4400)*
Elf Homes Inc .... G 650 918-7829
 Wilmington *(G-10374)*
ERA Harrington Realty .... E 302 674-4663
 Dover *(G-1527)*
ERA Harrington Realty .... E 302 363-1796
 Dover *(G-1528)*

Excel Property Management LLC .... G 302 541-5312
 Millville *(G-4844)*
Fairville Management Co LLC .... F 302 489-2000
 Hockessin *(G-3026)*
First Class Properties Del LLC .... G 302 677-0770
 Dover *(G-1552)*
First Montgomery Properties .... E 302 834-8272
 Bear *(G-152)*
Fox & Roach LLC .... E 302 239-2343
 Hockessin *(G-3031)*
Fox & Roach LP .... E 302 836-2888
 Bear *(G-158)*
Fox & Roach LP .... E 302 477-5500
 Wilmington *(G-10607)*
French Street Management .... F 302 571-8597
 Wilmington *(G-10632)*
Frontline LLC .... G 302 526-0877
 Lewes *(G-3504)*
Gallo Realty Inc .... G 888 624-6794
 Bethany Beach *(G-401)*
Gallo Realty Inc .... G 302 945-7368
 Rehoboth Beach *(G-7942)*
Galloway Leasing Inc .... F 302 453-8385
 Newark *(G-6634)*
Golden Coastal Realty .... F 302 360-0226
 Lewes *(G-3518)*
Goldenopp RE Solutions .... G 908 565-0510
 Bear *(G-166)*
Grapetree Inc .... G 302 655-1950
 Wilmington *(G-10762)*
Green Oak Real Estate LP .... D 212 359-7800
 Wilmington *(G-10772)*
Greenlea LLC .... G 302 227-7868
 Rehoboth Beach *(G-7955)*
Guardian Property MGT LLC .... E 302 227-7878
 Lewes *(G-3525)*
H D C Inc .... G 302 323-9300
 Wilmington *(G-10806)*
H T G Consulting LLC .... E 302 322-4100
 New Castle *(G-5368)*
Harrington Realty Inc .... E 302 422-2424
 Dover *(G-1631)*
Harrington Realty Inc .... E 302 736-0800
 Dover *(G-1630)*
Harrison Properties Ltd Inc .... F 302 888-2650
 Wilmington *(G-10843)*
Harvey Development Co .... C 302 323-9300
 New Castle *(G-5381)*
Hh Property Management .... F 302 999-1414
 Wilmington *(G-10900)*
Hollywood Grill Restaurant .... D 302 655-1348
 Wilmington *(G-10930)*
Home Finders Real Estate Co .... G 302 655-8091
 Wilmington *(G-10934)*
Home Team Realty .... F 302 629-7711
 Seaford *(G-8267)*
Howard M Joseph Inc .... G 302 335-1300
 Milford *(G-4446)*
Imaging Neuroscience Real Est .... G 302 731-9656
 Newark *(G-6768)*
J A Banks & Associates LLC .... F 914 260-2003
 Smyrna *(G-8660)*
Jack Lingo Inc Realtor .... E 302 227-3883
 Rehoboth Beach *(G-7970)*
Jack Lingo Inc Realtor .... F 302 947-9030
 Lewes *(G-3568)*
Jack Lingo Realtor .... E 302 645-2207
 Lewes *(G-3569)*
JG Townsend Jr & Co Inc .... E 302 856-2525
 Georgetown *(G-2574)*
Joe Maggio Realty .... G 302 539-9300
 Bethany Beach *(G-407)*
Jones Enterprises Incorporated .... G 888 639-1194
 Wilmington *(G-11181)*
Keller Williams Realty Ce .... G 302 653-3624
 Dover *(G-1730)*
Kw Commercial .... G 302 299-1123
 Wilmington *(G-11304)*
L3d LLC .... G 302 677-0031
 Dover *(G-1761)*
Landmark Associates of Del .... G 302 645-7070
 Lewes *(G-3590)*
Lc Homes Inc .... G 302 429-8700
 Wilmington *(G-11347)*
Legum & Norman Mid-West LLC .... G 302 537-9499
 Bethany Beach *(G-408)*
Legum & Norman Mid-West LLC .... G 302 227-8448
 Lewes *(G-3594)*
Lenape Properties MGT Inc .... G 302 426-0200
 Wilmington *(G-11368)*

65 REAL ESTATE

Leslie Kopp Inc .... F 302 541-5207
  Bethany Beach *(G-409)*
Lielles Investments LLC .... E 215 874-0770
  Lewes *(G-3608)*
Local Investments LLC .... G 302 422-0731
  Wilmington *(G-11419)*
Long & Foster Companies Inc .... E 302 539-9040
  Bethany Beach *(G-410)*
Long & Foster Companies Inc .... G 302 539-9767
  Bethany Beach *(G-411)*
Long & Foster Real Estate Inc .... G 302 227-3821
  Rehoboth Beach *(G-7991)*
Luther Martin Foundation Dover .... G 302 674-1408
  Dover *(G-1800)*
Lutheran Senior Svcs of Dover .... F 302 674-1408
  Dover *(G-1807)*
Maggio/Shields Teams .... F 302 226-3770
  Rehoboth Beach *(G-7994)*
Magron Inc .... G 302 324-8094
  New Castle *(G-5498)*
Manufctured Hsing Concepts LLC ..... D 302 934-8848
  Millsboro *(G-4734)*
Margaret Harris-Nemtuda .... G 302 477-5500
  Wilmington *(G-11522)*
Marvel Agency Inc .... E 302 422-7844
  Milford *(G-4488)*
Mastriana Property Management ...... G 302 234-4860
  Wilmington *(G-11565)*
Max RE Associates Inc .... E 302 453-3200
  Newark *(G-7005)*
Max RE Associates Inc .... D 302 477-3900
  Wilmington *(G-11578)*
Max RE Central .... F 302 234-3800
  Hockessin *(G-3092)*
McConnell Johnson RE Co LLC .... F 302 421-2000
  Wilmington *(G-11590)*
Mid-Atlantic Realty Co Inc .... E 302 658-7642
  Newark *(G-7029)*
Mid-Atlantic Realty Co Inc .... G 302 738-5325
  Newark *(G-7030)*
Mid-Atlantic Realty Co Inc .... G 302 737-3110
  Newark *(G-7031)*
Milford Housing Development .... F 302 422-8255
  Milford *(G-4499)*
Moore & Lind Inc .... G 302 934-8818
  Millsboro *(G-4753)*
Musi Commercial Properties Inc .... G 302 594-1000
  Wilmington *(G-11778)*
Nanticoke Shores Assoc LLC .... F 302 945-1500
  Millsboro *(G-4759)*
New Castle Cnty Bd of Realtors .... G 302 762-4800
  Wilmington *(G-11851)*
Newmarkkfsm .... G 302 655-0600
  Wilmington *(G-11876)*
Nickle Insurance Agency Inc .... G 302 834-9700
  Delaware City *(G-961)*
Nnn 824 North Market St LLC .... F 302 652-8013
  Wilmington *(G-11892)*
Nt Philadelphia LLC .... G 302 384-8967
  Wilmington *(G-11919)*
Obsidian Investors LLC .... G 954 560-1499
  Middletown *(G-4177)*
Ocean Atlantic Agency Inc .... F 302 227-6767
  Rehoboth Beach *(G-8018)*
Ocean Atlantic Associates LLC .... F 302 227-3573
  Rehoboth Beach *(G-8019)*
Ocean View Farms Inc .... G 302 537-4042
  Ocean View *(G-7808)*
One Hundred West Tenth St .... F 302 651-1469
  Wilmington *(G-11955)*
P R C Management Co Inc .... G 302 475-7643
  Wilmington *(G-11996)*
Pacer International One LLC .... F 302 588-9500
  Wilmington *(G-12003)*
Palladian Management LLC .... F 302 737-1971
  Newark *(G-7172)*
Panco Management Corporation ...... F 302 366-1875
  Newark *(G-7173)*
Panco Management Corporation ...... G 302 995-6152
  Wilmington *(G-12011)*
Panco Management Corporation ...... G 302 475-9337
  Wilmington *(G-12012)*
Patterson Price .... F 302 378-9852
  Wilmington *(G-12037)*
Patterson Price RE LLC .... G 302 366-0200
  Newark *(G-7184)*
Patterson Price RE LLC .... G 302 378-9550
  Middletown *(G-4181)*
Patterson-Schwartz & Assoc Inc .... B 302 234-5250
  Hockessin *(G-3112)*

Patterson-Schwartz & Assoc Inc .... D 302 733-7000
  Newark *(G-7185)*
Patterson-Schwartz & Assoc Inc .... F 302 285-5100
  Middletown *(G-4182)*
Patterson-Schwartz & Assoc Inc .... G 302 429-4500
  Wilmington *(G-12038)*
Patterson-Schwartz & Assoc Inc .... E 302 672-9400
  Dover *(G-1942)*
Pencader Associates .... G 302 838-7838
  Newark *(G-7193)*
Penflex III LLC .... G 302 998-0683
  Wilmington *(G-12063)*
Pettinaro Construction Co Inc .... E 302 832-8823
  Newark *(G-7207)*
Pettinaro Construction Co Inc .... D 302 999-0708
  Wilmington *(G-12102)*
Planned Residential Communites ..... F 302 475-4621
  Wilmington *(G-12151)*
Princeton Coml Holdings LLC .... G 302 449-4836
  Newark *(G-7253)*
Prudential Fox and Roach Realt .... G 302 378-9500
  Bear *(G-294)*
Prudential Gallo Realty .... G 302 645-6661
  Lewes *(G-3700)*
R J Farms Inc .... G 302 629-2520
  Seaford *(G-8367)*
RE Max of Wilmington .... G 302 234-2500
  Wilmington *(G-12337)*
RE Max of Wilmington .... G 302 657-8000
  Wilmington *(G-12338)*
RE/Max Horizons Inc .... G 302 678-4300
  Dover *(G-2013)*
Real Estate Partners LLC .... G 302 656-0251
  Wilmington *(G-12343)*
Rehoboth Realty Inc .... G 302 227-5000
  Rehoboth Beach *(G-8055)*
Remax 1st Choice LLC .... G 302 378-8700
  Middletown *(G-4217)*
Remax By Sea .... E 302 541-5000
  Bethany Beach *(G-427)*
Remax Coast & Country .... G 302 645-0800
  Lewes *(G-3714)*
Remax Sunvest Realty Corp .... E 302 995-1589
  Wilmington *(G-12378)*
Resortquest Delaware RE LLC .... G 302 436-1100
  Selbyville *(G-8540)*
Resortquest Delaware RE LLC .... F 302 541-8999
  Bethany Beach *(G-428)*
Reybold Group of Companies Inc ..... E 302 832-7100
  Bear *(G-305)*
Richard Bryan .... F 302 645-6100
  Lewes *(G-3718)*
Riggin Group .... G 302 235-2903
  Hockessin *(G-3136)*
Rita Lynn Inc .... G 302 422-3904
  Milford *(G-4544)*
Robino Management Group Inc .... G 302 633-6001
  Wilmington *(G-12442)*
Robinson Realestate .... G 302 629-4574
  Seaford *(G-8381)*
Rocky Lac LLC .... G 302 440-5561
  Bear *(G-310)*
Rush Realty LLC .... G 302 219-6707
  Smyrna *(G-8707)*
Seagreen Bicycle LLP .... G 302 226-2323
  Rehoboth Beach *(G-8070)*
Sks Enterprise .... D 302 310-2511
  Newark *(G-7437)*
Smalls Real Estate Company .... F 302 633-1985
  Wilmington *(G-12652)*
Sovereign Capitl MGT Group Inc ...... A 619 294-8989
  Wilmington *(G-12689)*
Springside LLC .... G 302 838-7223
  Newark *(G-7474)*
St Andrews Apartments .... F 302 834-8600
  Bear *(G-334)*
Stephens Management Corp .... G 302 629-4393
  Seaford *(G-8409)*
Steven Sachs Appraisal Access .... G 302 477-9676
  Talleyville *(G-8752)*
Stoltz Realty Co .... E 302 656-8543
  Wilmington *(G-12769)*
Stoltz Realty Co .... F 302 798-8500
  Claymont *(G-807)*
Stormblade Inc .... G 302 206-1631
  Dover *(G-2109)*
Summit Bridge Inv Prpts LLC .... G 410 499-1456
  Newark *(G-7503)*
Svn Commercial Real Estate .... F 410 543-2440
  Delmar *(G-1034)*

Team Wilson .... G 302 888-1088
  Wilmington *(G-12865)*
Tom Wright Real Estate .... D 302 234-6026
  Hockessin *(G-3163)*
Topaz & Associates LLC .... F 302 448-8914
  Newark *(G-7575)*
Trans Un Sttlment Slutions Inc .... D 800 916-8800
  Wilmington *(G-12953)*
Tunnell Companies LP .... E 302 945-9300
  Millsboro *(G-4816)*
United Group Real Estate LLC .... E 929 999-1277
  New Castle *(G-5805)*
Valley Stream Village Apts .... G 302 733-0844
  Newark *(G-7642)*
Vickie York At Beach Realty .... G 302 539-2145
  Millville *(G-4857)*
Vitellus LLC .... G 718 782-3539
  Wilmington *(G-13096)*
Wanamakers Associates LLC .... G 302 834-3491
  Bear *(G-370)*
Warner Tansey Inc .... G 302 539-3001
  Bethany Beach *(G-436)*
Watsons Auction & Realty Svc .... G 302 422-2392
  Milford *(G-4599)*
Wells Agency Inc .... G 302 422-2121
  Milford *(G-4602)*
White Robbins Company .... G 302 478-5555
  Wilmington *(G-13192)*
Wilgus Associates Inc .... E 302 539-7511
  Bethany Beach *(G-438)*
Wilgus Associates Inc .... F 302 644-2960
  Lewes *(G-3823)*
Wilsons Auction Sales Inc .... G 302 422-3454
  Lincoln *(G-3874)*
Woodlawn Trustees Inc .... E 302 655-6215
  Wilmington *(G-13297)*
Yvonne Hall Inc .... G 302 677-1300
  Dover *(G-2251)*

6541 Title Abstract Offices

Brennan Title Company .... G 302 541-0400
  Frankford *(G-2350)*
Delaware Settlement Services .... G 302 731-2500
  Newark *(G-6411)*
Old Republic Nat Title Insur .... F 302 661-1997
  Wilmington *(G-11944)*
Trans Un Sttlment Slutions Inc .... D 800 916-8800
  Wilmington *(G-12953)*

6552 Land Subdividers & Developers

Barclay Farms .... G 302 697-6939
  Camden *(G-539)*
Commonwealth Group LLC .... E 302 472-7200
  Wilmington *(G-9791)*
D & D Contractors Inc .... F 302 378-9724
  Smyrna *(G-8609)*
Del Homes Inc .... G 302 697-8204
  Magnolia *(G-3889)*
Donne Delle & Associates Inc .... E 302 325-1111
  Newark *(G-6462)*
Eastern States Develpment Inc .... G 302 998-0683
  Wilmington *(G-10327)*
Edward B De Seta & Associates ...... E 302 428-1313
  Wilmington *(G-10356)*
Ferm Development LLC .... E 302 792-1102
  Wilmington *(G-10521)*
First Power LLC .... G 610 247-5750
  Wilmington *(G-10547)*
Glasgow Medical Associates PA ...... G 302 836-8350
  Newark *(G-6662)*
Gulfstream Development Corp .... G 302 539-6178
  Ocean View *(G-7792)*
Interfaith Cmnty Hsing of Del .... F 302 652-3991
  Wilmington *(G-11062)*
Jack Hickman Real Estate .... F 302 539-8000
  Bethany Beach *(G-406)*
Leon N Weiner & Associates Inc ...... D 302 656-1354
  Wilmington *(G-11371)*
McConnell Development Inc .... G 302 428-0712
  Wilmington *(G-11589)*
Ocean Atlantic Management LLC ..... F 302 227-3573
  Rehoboth Beach *(G-8020)*
Parkway Gravel Inc .... D 302 658-5241
  New Castle *(G-5603)*
Patterson Price RE LLC .... G 302 366-0200
  Newark *(G-7184)*
Patterson Price RE LLC .... F 302 378-9550
  Middletown *(G-4181)*
Reybold Construction Corp .... E 302 832-7100
  Bear *(G-304)*

65 REAL ESTATE

Riverfront Dev Corp Del ....F 302 425-4890
  Wilmington (G-12427)
Riverfront Development Corp 302 425-4890
  Wilmington (G-12428)
Roizman & Associates Inc ....G 302 426-9688
  Wilmington (G-12465)
Salt Pond Associates ....F 302 539-2750
  Bethany Beach (G-430)
Sybounheuang Group Inc ....G 302 999-9339
  Wilmington (G-12827)
Tony Ashburn Inc ....G 302 677-1940
  Dover (G-2151)
Woodlawn Trustees Inc ....E 302 655-6215
  Wilmington (G-13297)

6553 Cemetery Subdividers & Developers

Catholic Cemetaries Inc ....F 302 254-4701
  Wilmington (G-9590)
Catholic Cemetaries Inc ....E 302 737-2524
  Wilmington (G-9591)
Odd Fellows Cmtry of Milford ....G 302 422-4619
  Milford (G-4517)
Silverbrook Cemetery Co ....G 302 658-0953
  Wilmington (G-12618)

67 HOLDING AND OTHER INVESTMENT OFFICES

6712 Offices Of Bank Holding Co's

Advantage Delaware ....G 302 365-5398
  Bear (G-14)
Bank of New York Mellon ....G 302 421-2207
  Wilmington (G-9241)
Bank of New York Mellon Corp ....G 302 416-6283
  Wilmington (G-9242)
Cbc Holding Inc ....C 302 254-2000
  Wilmington (G-9600)

6719 Offices Of Holding Co's, NEC

Adh Holdings LLC ....G 302 482-4138
  Wilmington (G-8937)
ALC Funding Corporation ....G 302 656-8923
  Wilmington (G-9002)
Ampco Ues Sub Inc ....G 302 691-6420
  Wilmington (G-9070)
Anglin Associates LLC ....F 302 653-3500
  Clayton (G-833)
Belchim Crop Prtection US Corp ....F 302 407-3590
  Wilmington (G-9284)
Blockweather Holdings LLC ....G 844 644-6837
  Dover (G-1211)
Chestnut Investors II Inc ....E 302 478-5142
  Wilmington (G-9657)
Clyde Bergemann Pwr Group LLC ....D 770 557-3600
  Lewes (G-3432)
Complex Systems Inc ....G 302 651-8300
  Wilmington (G-9805)
Crystal Penn Avenue LP ....D 302 846-0613
  Delmar (G-987)
Educational Assets Corp ....G 302 288-0149
  Wilmington (G-10353)
Eri Investments Inc ....F 302 656-8089
  Wilmington (G-10434)
Exco Inc ....D 905 477-3065
  Wilmington (G-10458)
Faith Fmly Friends Holdg LLC ....F 202 256-4524
  Lewes (G-3490)
Gcg Capital LLC ....B 302 703-7610
  Lewes (G-3509)
Global Innovation Holding LLC ....G 877 276-7701
  Wilmington (G-10727)
Griffen Corporate Services ....F 302 576-2890
  Wilmington (G-10783)
Hall International Ind Corp ....F 302 777-2290
  Wilmington (G-10825)
Hchc Uk Holdings Inc ....F 302 225-5007
  Wilmington (G-10861)
Hsi Service Corp ....G 302 369-3709
  Newark (G-6755)
Hunte Corporate Enterprise LLC ....G 212 710-1341
  Wilmington (G-10975)
Ibi Group (delaware) Inc ....C 614 818-4900
  Wilmington (G-10986)
Instant Global Services Corp ....G 302 514-1047
  Dover (G-1679)
Integrated Green Partners LLC ....G 402 871-8347
  Wilmington (G-11049)

Just Be Holdings LLC ....G 833 454-5273
  Newark (G-6859)
Labware Global Services Inc ....F 302 658-8444
  Wilmington (G-11321)
Labware Holdings Inc ....E 302 658-8444
  Wilmington (G-11322)
Lela Capital LLC ....F 917 428-0304
  Ocean View (G-7799)
Limewood Investments Del Inc ....G 302 656-8915
  Wilmington (G-11391)
Mangrove Holdings LLC ....G 305 587-2950
  Wilmington (G-11502)
Maruko Holdings Usa LLC ....G 917 515-2776
  Lewes (G-3622)
Mera Usa LLC ....G 305 577-3443
  Wilmington (G-11635)
Midway LLC ....G 302 378-9156
  Middletown (G-4164)
Morgan Stnley Intl Hldings Inc ....D 302 657-2000
  Wilmington (G-11753)
Nazhat Enterprises Holdings ....G 415 670-9262
  Dover (G-1887)
North Face Apparel Corp ....E 336 424-7755
  Wilmington (G-11899)
Oni Acquisition Corp ....G 212 271-3800
  Wilmington (G-11959)
P&L Transportation Inc ....G 800 444-2580
  Wilmington (G-11997)
Persona Group LLC ....G 302 335-5221
  Magnolia (G-3902)
Pitney Bowes Intl Holdings ....F 302 656-8595
  Wilmington (G-12144)
Playtex Marketing Corp ....G 302 678-6000
  Dover (G-1970)
Progressive Investment Co Inc ....F 302 656-8597
  Wilmington (G-12242)
Qps Holdings LLC ....F 302 369-5601
  Newark (G-7281)
Rfpc & Wabtec ....G 302 573-3977
  Wilmington (G-12397)
Stewart Law Firm ....E 302 652-5200
  Wilmington (G-12763)
Suthar Holding Corporation ....E 302 291-2490
  Lewes (G-3774)
Sybounheuang Group Inc ....G 302 999-9339
  Wilmington (G-12827)
Thales Holding Corporation ....A 302 326-0830
  New Castle (G-5766)
Willow Tree Equity Holding LLC ....F 213 479-4077
  Lewes (G-3826)
Yhp Holdings LLC ....G 302 636-5401
  Wilmington (G-13327)

6722 Management Investment Offices

ADP Capital Management Inc ....G 302 657-4060
  Wilmington (G-8941)
Black Rock Inc ....F 302 797-2009
  Wilmington (G-9347)
Blackrock Funds II ....F 302 797-2000
  Wilmington (G-9351)
Blackrock Global Long ....G 302 797-2000
  Wilmington (G-9352)
Blackrock Intermediate ....F 302 797-2000
  Wilmington (G-9355)
Blackrock LNG-Hrzon Eqity Fund ....G 800 441-7762
  Wilmington (G-9356)
Blackrock Mncpl Income Inv Qlt ....G 800 441-7762
  Wilmington (G-9358)
Brandywine Fund Inc ....E 302 656-3017
  Wilmington (G-9434)
Daniels + Tansey LLP ....G 302 594-1070
  Wilmington (G-9957)
Dupont Capital Management Corp ....G 302 477-6000
  Wilmington (G-10250)
Elliott Holdings Corporation ....F 650 241-8646
  Middletown (G-4056)
Ferrara Asset Management Inc ....G 401 286-8464
  Wilmington (G-10523)
Global Currents Inv MGT LLC ....F 302 476-3800
  Wilmington (G-10722)
Government Portfolio LLC ....F 301 718-9742
  Rehoboth Beach (G-7952)
H S B C Overseas Corp De ....F 302 657-8400
  Wilmington (G-10810)
Vital Renewable Energy Company ....G 202 595-2944
  Wilmington (G-13095)

6726 Unit Investment Trusts, Face-Amount Certificate Offices

African Markets Fund LLC ....G 703 944-1514
  Dover (G-1092)
Atlas Management Inc ....G 302 576-2749
  Wilmington (G-9180)
Blackrock Income Trust Inc ....G 800 441-7762
  Wilmington (G-9353)
Blackrock Mncpl 2030 Trget Ter ....G 800 882-0052
  Wilmington (G-9357)
Blackrock Mnhldngs Cal Qlty Fu ....G 800 441-7762
  Wilmington (G-9359)
Blackrock Mnhldngs NJ Qlty Fun ....G 800 441-7762
  Wilmington (G-9360)
Blackrock NY Mncpl Income Qlty ....G 800 441-7762
  Wilmington (G-9361)
Bombay Hook Ltd ....G 302 571-8644
  Wilmington (G-9391)
Breakthrugh Cpitl Partners LLC ....G 212 381-4420
  Lewes (G-3391)
Merrill Lynch Pierce Fenner ....D 302 571-5100
  Wilmington (G-11646)
National Holding Investment Co ....F 302 573-3887
  Wilmington (G-11806)
▼ Revod Corporation ....G 302 477-1795
  Wilmington (G-12396)
Stella ABG Acquisition Inc ....G 302 654-6682
  Wilmington (G-12751)
Thales Inc ....G 302 326-0830
  New Castle (G-5765)

6732 Education, Religious & Charitable Trusts

Delaware Community Foundation ....F 302 571-8004
  Wilmington (G-10023)
East Side Cmmty Lrng Cntr Fndt ....G 302 762-5834
  Wilmington (G-10321)
Milton & Hattie Kutz Foundaton ....F 302 427-2100
  Wilmington (G-11699)
Play For Good Inc ....G 312 520-9788
  Wilmington (G-12154)
Resurrection Center ....G 302 762-8311
  Wilmington (G-12391)
Simply Stylng-Schl of Csmtlgy ....G 302 778-1885
  Wilmington (G-12628)
Udaan Inc ....F 267 408-3001
  Bear (G-363)

6733 Trusts Except Educational, Religious & Charitable

Ba Credit Card Trust ....G 704 386-5681
  Wilmington (G-9215)
Bank of New York Mellon Corp ....G 302 421-2335
  Wilmington (G-9243)
Bessemer Trust Company ....F 302 230-2675
  Wilmington (G-9311)
Blackrock Enhnced Globl Dvdend ....G 800 441-7762
  Wilmington (G-9349)
Blackrock NY Mncpl Income Tr I ....G 800 441-7762
  Wilmington (G-9362)
Blackrock NY Municpl Income Tr ....G 800 441-7762
  Wilmington (G-9363)
Boothe Investment Group ....G 302 734-7526
  Dover (G-1221)
Brandywine Trust Co ....E 302 234-5750
  Hockessin (G-2968)
Commonwealth Trust Co ....F 302 658-7214
  Wilmington (G-9792)
Delaware Claims Proc Fcilty ....D 302 427-8913
  Wilmington (G-10018)
Deutsche Bnk US Fncl Mkts Hldg ....G 302 636-3301
  Wilmington (G-10128)
GE Tf Trust ....E 302 636-6196
  Wilmington (G-10685)
Huntington Auto Trust 2012-1 ....C 302 636-5401
  Wilmington (G-10976)
Huntington Auto Trust 2012-2 ....C 302 636-5401
  Wilmington (G-10977)
Indian River Trust ....G 302 661-2320
  Georgetown (G-2564)
Nemours Foundation ....A 302 651-4000
  Wilmington (G-11833)
Nemours Foundation ....A 302 651-4000
  Wilmington (G-11836)
Neuberger & Berman Trust Co ....G 302 658-8522
  Wilmington (G-11842)
One Hundred West Tenth St ....F 302 651-1469
  Wilmington (G-11955)

70 HOTELS, ROOMING HOUSES, CAMPS, AND OTHER LODGING PLACES

Osfs Wlmngton Phldlphia Prvnce ....G....... 302 656-8529
  Wilmington (G-11980)
Rbc Trust Company Delaware Ltd ....E....... 302 892-6900
  Wilmington (G-12335)
Rodney Trust Co ....G....... 302 737-1205
  Newark (G-7356)
Tiedemann Trust Company ....G....... 302 656-5644
  Wilmington (G-12907)
Wells Fargo Delaware Trust Co ....G....... 302 575-2002
  Wilmington (G-13153)
Wilmington Trust ....E....... 302 651-1000
  Wilmington (G-13260)
Wilmington Trust Company ....C....... 302 651-1000
  Wilmington (G-13261)

6794 Patent Owners & Lessors

1000 Degrees Pizzeria ....G....... 609 382-3022
  Wilmington (G-8841)
Affilate Marks Investments Inc ....G....... 302 478-7451
  Wilmington (G-8968)
Idpa Holdings Inc ....G....... 302 281-3600
  Wilmington (G-10993)
Idtp Holdings Inc ....G....... 302 281-3600
  Wilmington (G-10994)
Interdigital Belgium LLC ....G....... 302 281-3600
  Wilmington (G-11060)
Kohr Brothers Inc ....F....... 302 227-9354
  Rehoboth Beach (G-7983)

6798 Real Estate Investment Trusts

Acadia Realty Trust ....G....... 302 479-5510
  Wilmington (G-8913)
All United Prpts Solutions LLC ....F....... 310 853-2223
  Camden (G-535)
Bpg Office Partners Viii LLC ....E....... 302 250-3065
  Wilmington (G-9409)
K&B Investors LLC ....G....... 302 357-9723
  Wilmington (G-11216)
New Windsor Associates LLC ....G....... 207 774-5341
  Wilmington (G-11873)
Southwest American Corp ....G....... 302 652-7003
  Wilmington (G-12688)
St Lawrence Grant Ave Trust ....G....... 302 652-7978
  Wilmington (G-12724)

6799 Investors, NEC

Acopia LLC ....D....... 302 286-5172
  Newark (G-5893)
Aimco/Bethesda GP LLC ....E....... 303 757-8101
  Wilmington (G-8990)
Aurum Capital Ventures Inc ....G....... 877 467-7780
  Dover (G-1160)
Bell Rock Capital LLC ....F....... 302 227-7607
  Rehoboth Beach (G-7865)
Bsr Trade LLC ....G....... 646 250-4409
  Dover (G-1240)
Carpenter Investments Inc ....G....... 302 656-5664
  Wilmington (G-9577)
Cigna Corporation ....G....... 302 792-4906
  Wilmington (G-9705)
Cigna Real Estate Inc ....G....... 302 476-3337
  Wilmington (G-9706)
D M Peoples Investment Corp ....G....... 302 836-1500
  Bear (G-92)
Dd & E Investment Group Inc ....G....... 302 319-2780
  Wilmington (G-9982)
Dt Investment Partners LLC ....G....... 302 442-6203
  Wilmington (G-10238)
Fas Mart / Shore Stop 286 LLC ....G....... 302 366-9694
  Newark (G-6573)
GPM Investments LLC ....G....... 302 436-6330
  Selbyville (G-8496)
Green DOT Capital LLC ....G....... 302 395-0500
  Bear (G-171)
Hs Capital LLC ....G....... 302 317-3614
  Wilmington (G-10965)
J A Banks & Associates LLC ....F....... 914 260-2003
  Smyrna (G-8660)
Joyce Co ....E....... 302 353-4011
  Wilmington (G-11200)
Jsc Ventures LLC ....D....... 302 336-8151
  Dover (G-1712)
Kpv Enterprises Llc ....G....... 302 500-9669
  Bear (G-221)
Landmark Homes ....G....... 302 388-8557
  Dover (G-1765)
Lc Associates LLC ....F....... 302 235-2500
  Hockessin (G-3079)

Lcd Wealth Management LLC ....G....... 302 294-0013
  Hockessin (G-3080)
Llb Acquisition LLC ....G....... 212 750-8300
  Wilmington (G-11414)
McCray Investments ....G....... 302 836-8569
  Newark (G-7012)
Medici Ventures Inc ....E....... 801 319-7029
  Wilmington (G-11617)
Nikko Capital Investments Ltd ....E....... 832 324-5335
  Lewes (G-3659)
Novin LLC ....G....... 315 670-7979
  Wilmington (G-11913)
Obsidian Investors LLC ....G....... 954 560-1499
  Middletown (G-4177)
Pacer International One LLC ....F....... 302 588-9500
  Wilmington (G-12003)
Partnrre Cpitl Invstments Corp ....F....... 608 347-5824
  Wilmington (G-12028)
Pcms Holdings Inc ....G....... 302 281-3600
  Wilmington (G-12052)
Pga Acquisitions V LLC ....G....... 302 355-3500
  Wilmington (G-12106)
PNC Bank National Association ....G....... 302 326-4710
  New Castle (G-5626)
Questar Capital Corporation ....G....... 302 856-9778
  Georgetown (G-2631)
Rite Way Distributors ....G....... 302 535-8507
  Felton (G-2317)
Scottish Ventures LLC ....G....... 302 382-6057
  New Castle (G-5695)
▲ Social Enterprise LLC ....G....... 718 417-4076
  New Castle (G-5720)
Sqs Global Solutions LLC ....G....... 302 691-9682
  Wilmington (G-12718)
Svea Real Estate Group LLC ....F....... 855 262-9665
  Dover (G-2122)
Weepor Company Inc ....G....... 302 575-9945
  Wilmington (G-13137)
Ws One Investment Usa LLC ....F....... 302 317-2610
  New Castle (G-5841)
Wsfs Investment Group Inc ....G....... 302 573-3258
  Wilmington (G-13308)

70 HOTELS, ROOMING HOUSES, CAMPS, AND OTHER LODGING PLACES

7011 Hotels, Motels & Tourist Courts

1102 West Street Ltd Partnr ....E....... 302 429-7600
  Wilmington (G-8842)
190 Stadium LLC ....F....... 302 659-3635
  Smyrna (G-8558)
422 Hotel LLC ....D....... 401 946-4600
  Wilmington (G-8861)
44 Aasha Hospitality Assoc LLC ....E....... 302 674-3784
  Dover (G-1070)
44 New England Management Co ....E....... 302 479-7900
  Wilmington (G-8862)
44 New England Management Co ....E....... 302 477-9500
  Wilmington (G-8863)
700 Nrth King St Wlmington LLC ....C....... 302 655-0400
  Wilmington (G-8865)
764 Dover Leipsic LLC ....F....... 302 736-1204
  Dover (G-1071)
900 F Street Owner LLC ....D....... 212 355-1500
  Wilmington (G-8869)
A & G Kramedas Associates LLC ....F....... 302 674-3300
  Dover (G-1072)
A & G Realty LLC ....F....... 302 674-3300
  Dover (G-1073)
Adams Oceanfront Resort ....F....... 302 227-3030
  Dewey Beach (G-1051)
Addy Sea ....G....... 302 539-3707
  Bethany Beach (G-382)
Admiral Hotel ....G....... 302 227-2103
  Rehoboth Beach (G-7837)
Admiral West Inc ....E....... 609 729-0031
  Wilmington (G-8939)
Amaa Management Corporation ....F....... 302 677-0505
  Dover (G-1115)
AmericInn International LLC ....F....... 302 398-3900
  Harrington (G-2810)
An Inn By Bay ....F....... 302 644-8878
  Lewes (G-3338)
Anchorage Motel Inc ....G....... 302 645-8320
  Rehoboth Beach (G-7841)
Atlantic Budget Inn Millsboro ....E....... 302 934-6711
  Millsboro (G-4632)

Atlantic View Motel ....F....... 302 227-3878
  Dewey Beach (G-1052)
Baymont Inn & Suites Newark ....G....... 302 453-1700
  Newark (G-6056)
Beach House Resources ....G....... 703 980-3336
  Bethany Beach (G-384)
Beach House Services ....G....... 302 645-2554
  Milton (G-4867)
Beacon Hospitality ....G....... 302 249-0502
  Georgetown (G-2452)
Beacon Motel ....E....... 302 645-4888
  Lewes (G-3368)
Bear Hospitality Inc ....G....... 302 326-2500
  Bear (G-48)
Bell Buoy Motel ....G....... 302 227-6000
  Dewey Beach (G-1054)
Best Western Goldleaf Ht LLC ....G....... 302 226-1100
  Rehoboth Beach (G-7867)
Best Western Newark ....G....... 302 738-3400
  Newark (G-6074)
Bethany Beach Bed & Breakfast ....G....... 301 651-2278
  Bethany Beach (G-385)
Bethany Beach Ocean ....G....... 302 539-3201
  Bethany Beach (G-387)
Blue Hen Hotel LLC ....G....... 302 266-0354
  Newark (G-6099)
Boardwalk Plaza Incorporated ....G....... 302 227-0441
  Rehoboth Beach (G-7872)
Bpg Hotel Partners X LLC ....D....... 302 453-9700
  Newark (G-6113)
Breakers Associates ....F....... 302 227-6688
  Rehoboth Beach (G-7875)
Brighton Hotels LLC ....E....... 302 227-5780
  Rehoboth Beach (G-7877)
Buccini/Pollin Group Inc ....C....... 302 691-2100
  Wilmington (G-9497)
Canal New Orleans Hotel LLC ....E....... 504 962-0500
  Wilmington (G-9548)
Chapman Hospitality Inc ....E....... 302 738-3400
  Newark (G-6189)
Chudasama Enterprises LLC ....F....... 302 856-7532
  Georgetown (G-2471)
Coastal Properties I LLC ....F....... 302 227-5800
  Rehoboth Beach (G-7895)
Colonial Oaks Hotel LLC ....E....... 302 645-4766
  Rehoboth Beach (G-7898)
Comfort Inn & Suites ....F....... 302 737-3900
  Newark (G-6267)
Comfort Suites ....F....... 302 628-5400
  Seaford (G-8202)
Comfort Suites Motel ....G....... 302 266-6600
  Hockessin (G-2993)
Concord Towers Inc ....D....... 302 737-2700
  Newark (G-6280)
Cooper Simpler Associates Inc ....G....... 302 227-2999
  Rehoboth Beach (G-7901)
Country Inns Suites ....G....... 302 266-6400
  Newark (G-6303)
Country Villa Motel ....F....... 814 938-8330
  Milford (G-4366)
Courtyard Management Corp ....C....... 302 429-7600
  Wilmington (G-9878)
Courtyard Management Corp ....F....... 302 456-3800
  Newark (G-6305)
Courtyard Newark At Ud ....F....... 302 737-0900
  Newark (G-6306)
Creative Courtyards ....G....... 302 226-1994
  Rehoboth Beach (G-7903)
Dan Licale ....D....... 302 888-2133
  Montchanin (G-4984)
Days Inn and Suites Seaford ....F....... 302 629-4300
  Seaford (G-8218)
Days Inn Dover Downtown ....E....... 302 674-8002
  Dover (G-1346)
Delaware Hotel Associates LP ....D....... 302 792-2700
  Claymont (G-732)
Delaware Motel and Rv Park ....G....... 302 328-3114
  New Castle (G-5232)
Dewey Beach House ....E....... 302 227-4000
  Dewey Beach (G-1055)
Dhm Wilmington LLC ....G....... 302 656-8952
  Wilmington (G-10137)
Dipna Inc ....E....... 302 478-0300
  Wilmington (G-10159)
Djont/Jpm Wilmington Lsg LLC ....F....... 302 478-6000
  Wilmington (G-10172)
Dogfish Inn ....G....... 302 644-8292
  Lewes (G-3468)
Doubltree Htels Suites Resorts ....E....... 302 478-6000
  Wilmington (G-10210)

Dover Hospitality Group LLC .... E 302 677-0900
Dover *(G-1453)*
Dpnl LLC .... F 302 366-8097
Newark *(G-6469)*
Driftwood Hospitality MGT LLC .... D 302 655-0400
Wilmington *(G-10235)*
Dutch Village Motel Inc .... F 302 328-6246
New Castle *(G-5268)*
Eastern Hospitality Management .... F 302 322-9480
New Castle *(G-5277)*
Econo Lodge Inn Suites Resort .... F 302 227-0500
Rehoboth Beach *(G-7925)*
ESA P Portfolio LLC .... F 302 283-0800
Newark *(G-6539)*
Everest Hotel Group LLC .... F 213 272-0088
Camden *(G-569)*
Everest Sonoma Management LLC .... D 213 272-0088
Camden *(G-570)*
Express Hotel Inc .... G 302 227-4030
Rehoboth Beach *(G-7929)*
Four Points By Sheraton .... G 302 266-6600
Newark *(G-6608)*
George Metz .... G 302 227-4343
Rehoboth Beach *(G-7946)*
Gracelawn Memorial Park Inc .... E 302 654-6158
New Castle *(G-5358)*
Green Room Restaurant .... E 302 594-3100
Wilmington *(G-10773)*
Gulab Management Inc .... F 302 422-8089
Milford *(G-4427)*
Gulab Management Inc .... G 302 398-4206
Harrington *(G-2844)*
Gulab Management Inc .... D 302 934-6126
Milford *(G-4428)*
Gulab Management Inc .... E 302 734-4433
Dover *(G-1615)*
Gurukrupa Inc .... G 302 328-6691
New Castle *(G-5366)*
Hampton Inn .... F 302 629-4500
Seaford *(G-8258)*
Hampton Inn .... F 302 422-4320
Milford *(G-4434)*
Hampton Inn Middletown .... F 302 378-5656
Middletown *(G-4103)*
Hampton Inn Seaford .... G 302 629-4500
Seaford *(G-8259)*
Hampton Inn-Dover .... G 302 736-3500
Dover *(G-1625)*
Henlopen Hotel Inc .... F 302 227-2551
Rehoboth Beach *(G-7962)*
Higgins House Victorian B & B .... G 407 324-9238
Dagsboro *(G-910)*
High Seas Motel .... G 302 227-2022
Rehoboth Beach *(G-7964)*
Holiday Inn Express .... F 302 227-4030
Rehoboth Beach *(G-7965)*
Holiday Inn Express .... E 302 398-8800
Harrington *(G-2850)*
Holiday Inn Select .... D 302 792-2700
Claymont *(G-762)*
Hollywood Grill Restaurant .... D 302 655-1348
Wilmington *(G-10930)*
Hollywood Grill Restaurant .... F 302 629-4500
Seaford *(G-8265)*
Hollywood Grill Restaurant .... D 302 479-2000
Wilmington *(G-10931)*
Hollywood Grill Restaurant .... E 302 737-3900
Newark *(G-6736)*
Homewood Suites .... E 302 565-2100
Wilmington *(G-10945)*
Homewood Suites Newark .... G 302 453-9700
Newark *(G-6742)*
Inn At Wilmington .... E 302 479-7900
Wilmington *(G-11036)*
Inn LLC A-1 Dash .... G 302 368-7964
Newark *(G-6781)*
Inns of Rehoboth Beach LLC .... G 302 645-8003
Rehoboth Beach *(G-7968)*
Interstate Hotels Resorts Inc .... E 302 792-2700
Claymont *(G-766)*
J & P Management Inc .... F 302 854-9400
Georgetown *(G-2569)*
Jacks Bstro At Dvid Fnney Inn .... G 302 544-5172
New Castle *(G-5434)*
Jay Ambe Inc .... F 302 654-5400
New Castle *(G-5436)*
Jay Devi Inc .... F 302 777-4700
New Castle *(G-5437)*
Jay Ganesh LLC .... G 302 322-1800
New Castle *(G-5438)*
Jaysons LLC .... E 302 656-9436
Wilmington *(G-11133)*
K W Lands LLC .... E 302 674-2200
Dover *(G-1718)*
K W Lands North LLC .... E 302 678-0600
Dover *(G-1719)*
Kenny Simpler .... G 302 226-2900
Rehoboth Beach *(G-7978)*
Keval Corp .... F 302 453-9100
Newark *(G-6877)*
Khanna Entps Ltd A Ltd Partnr .... E 302 266-6400
Newark *(G-6885)*
Kw Garden .... E 302 735-7770
Dover *(G-1759)*
Lila Keshav Hospitality LLC .... F 302 696-2272
Middletown *(G-4133)*
Lomas Properties LLC .... G 302 260-9245
Rehoboth Beach *(G-7990)*
Luxiasuites LLC .... E 302 778-2900
Wilmington *(G-11459)*
Luxiasuites LLC .... G 302 426-1200
Wilmington *(G-11461)*
MainStay Suites .... F 302 678-8383
Dover *(G-1811)*
Mark One LLC .... F 302 735-4700
Dover *(G-1819)*
Marriott International Inc .... G 800 441-7048
Newark *(G-6991)*
Meris Gardens Bed & Breakfast .... G 302 752-4962
Bethany Beach *(G-414)*
Midway Ventures LLC .... E 302 645-8003
Rehoboth Beach *(G-8009)*
Milford Lodging LLC .... E 302 839-5000
Milford *(G-4500)*
Mj Wilmington Hotel Assoc LP .... E 302 454-1500
Newark *(G-7046)*
Mj Wilmington Hotel Assoc LP .... C 302 454-1500
Newark *(G-7047)*
Moore Partnership .... F 302 227-5253
Dewey Beach *(G-1059)*
Moores Enterprises Inc .... F 302 227-8200
Rehoboth Beach *(G-8010)*
Nab Motel Inc .... F 302 656-9431
Wilmington *(G-11793)*
Nacstar .... E 302 453-1700
Newark *(G-7081)*
Nazar Dover LLC .... E 302 747-5050
Dover *(G-1886)*
New Castle Lodging Corporation .... F 302 654-5544
New Castle *(G-5562)*
New Orleans Hotel Equity LLC .... G 302 757-7300
Wilmington *(G-11868)*
Packem Associates Partnership .... G 302 227-5780
Rehoboth Beach *(G-8027)*
Pagoda Hotel Inc .... A 808 922-1233
New Castle *(G-5597)*
Paul Amos .... F 302 541-9200
Bethany Beach *(G-420)*
Pde I LLC .... D 302 654-8300
Wilmington *(G-12054)*
Pelican Bay Group Inc .... G 302 945-5900
Millsboro *(G-4773)*
Premier Entertainment III LLC .... E 302 674-4600
Dover *(G-1982)*
Priya Realty Corp .... G 302 737-5050
Newark *(G-7261)*
Quality Inn .... F 302 292-1500
Newark *(G-7283)*
Quintasian LLC .... E 302 674-3784
Dover *(G-2005)*
Rama Corporation .... E 302 266-6600
Hockessin *(G-3128)*
Re/Max Realty Group-Rentals .... F 302 227-4800
Rehoboth Beach *(G-8044)*
Red Mill Inn .... G 302 645-9736
Lewes *(G-3711)*
Red Roof .... G 302 368-8521
Newark *(G-7308)*
Red Roof Inns Inc .... F 302 292-2870
Newark *(G-7309)*
Rehoboth Inn LLC .... G 302 226-2410
Rehoboth Beach *(G-8054)*
Relax Inn .... G 302 875-1554
Laurel *(G-3279)*
Residence Inn By Marriott LLC .... E 302 453-9200
Newark *(G-7325)*
Residence Inn Dover .... F 302 677-0777
Dover *(G-2033)*
Resort Custom Homes .... G 302 645-8222
Lewes *(G-3717)*
Resort Hotel LLC .... E 302 226-1515
Rehoboth Beach *(G-8057)*
Rl Heritage Inn Topeka Inc .... E 785 271-8903
Wilmington *(G-12404)*
Riverdale Park LLC .... G 302 945-2475
Millsboro *(G-4792)*
Rodeway Inn .... E 302 227-0401
Rehoboth Beach *(G-8061)*
Routzhan Jessman .... F 302 398-4206
Harrington *(G-2881)*
Sabre Amb LLC .... E 302 299-1400
New Castle *(G-5692)*
Sage Hospitality Resources LLC .... E 302 292-1500
Newark *(G-7376)*
Sandcastle Motel .... G 302 227-0400
Rehoboth Beach *(G-8066)*
Sands Inc .... D 302 227-2511
Rehoboth Beach *(G-8067)*
Savannah Inn .... G 302 645-0330
Lewes *(G-3730)*
Sea Witch Inc .... G 302 226-3900
Rehoboth Beach *(G-8069)*
Seaside Inn .... F 302 251-5000
Fenwick Island *(G-2340)*
Seper 8 Motel .... E 302 734-5701
Dover *(G-2070)*
Shiv Sagar Inc .... F 302 674-3800
Dover *(G-2078)*
Shree Kishna Inc .... F 302 839-5000
Milford *(G-4560)*
Shree Lalji LLC .... G 302 730-8009
Dover *(G-2082)*
Shri SAI Dover LLC .... E 302 747-5050
Dover *(G-2083)*
Shri Swami Narayan LLC .... E 302 738-3198
Newark *(G-7418)*
Shriji Hospitality (not Llc) .... F 302 654-5544
New Castle *(G-5706)*
Simpler and Sons LLC .... G 302 296-4400
Rehoboth Beach *(G-8077)*
Skyways Motor Lodge Corp .... E 302 328-6666
New Castle *(G-5716)*
Sleep Inn & Suites .... E 302 645-6464
Lewes *(G-3748)*
Sonesta .... E 302 453-9200
Newark *(G-7458)*
State Street Inn .... G 302 734-2294
Dover *(G-2105)*
Sun Hotel Inc .... G 302 322-0711
New Castle *(G-5742)*
Sunny Hospitality LLC .... F 302 226-0700
Rehoboth Beach *(G-8092)*
Sunny Hospitality LLC .... F 302 398-3900
Harrington *(G-2895)*
Super Eight Dover .... G 302 734-5701
Dover *(G-2117)*
Superlodge .... G 302 654-5544
Wilmington *(G-12809)*
Surf Club .... G 302 227-7059
Dewey Beach *(G-1060)*
Sussex Sands Inc .... G 302 539-8200
Fenwick Island *(G-2341)*
Towne Place Suites By Marriott .... F 302 369-6212
Newark *(G-7580)*
Tru By Hilton Georgetown LLC .... E 302 515-2100
Georgetown *(G-2695)*
Tucson Hotels LP .... D 678 830-2438
Wilmington *(G-12991)*
Umiya Inc .... G 302 674-4011
Dover *(G-2173)*
Veer Hotels Inc .... G 302 398-3900
Harrington *(G-2904)*
Wilmington Christiana Cou .... F 302 456-3800
Newark *(G-7701)*
Wilmington Hotel Venture .... C 302 655-0400
Wilmington *(G-13234)*
Young Mens Christian Associat .... C 302 571-6900
Wilmington *(G-13332)*
Young MNS Chrstn Assn Wlmngton .... E 302 221-9622
Wilmington *(G-13334)*
Zwaanendael LLC .... G 302 645-6466
Lewes *(G-3837)*

7021 Rooming & Boarding Houses

Beacon Hospitality .... G 302 249-0502
Georgetown *(G-2452)*
DSU Student Housing LLC .... G 302 857-7966
Dover *(G-1485)*
Ministry of Caring Inc .... G 302 652-0904
Wilmington *(G-11706)*

7032 Sporting & Recreational Camps

Bear-Glasgow YMCA ....G...... 302 836-9622
  Newark (G-6066)
Camp Arrowhead Busine ....G...... 302 448-6919
  Wilmington (G-9546)
Dave Arletta ....E...... 302 475-8013
  Wilmington (G-9963)
Ed Hunt Inc ....G...... 302 339-8443
  Dover (G-1503)
Hoops For Hope Delaware ....F...... 302 229-7600
  Wilmington (G-10949)
Hope House Daycare ....F...... 302 407-3404
  Wilmington (G-10951)
Matts Fish Camp Lewes De LLC...................G...... 302 539-4415
  Lewes (G-3624)
Win From Wthin Xc Camp/Tatnall ....E...... 302 494-5312
  Wilmington (G-13269)
Young Mens Christian Associat ....D...... 302 296-9622
  Rehoboth Beach (G-8121)
YWCA Delaware ....F...... 302 224-4060
  Newark (G-7733)

7033 Trailer Parks & Camp Sites

Barsgr LLC ....G...... 302 645-6665
  Lewes (G-3362)
Barsgr LLC ....E...... 302 945-3410
  Millsboro (G-4634)
Bayshore Inc ....G...... 302 539-7200
  Ocean View (G-7758)
Delaware Motel and Rv Park ....G...... 302 328-3114
  New Castle (G-5232)
Gulls Way Campground ....G...... 302 732-6383
  Dagsboro (G-904)
Gulls Way Inc ....G...... 302 732-9629
  Dagsboro (G-905)
Homestead Camping Inc ....G...... 302 684-4278
  Georgetown (G-2561)
Masseys Landing Park Inc ....G...... 302 947-2600
  Millsboro (G-4736)
Pine Acres Inc ....F...... 302 945-2000
  Lewes (G-3692)
Port Del-Mar-Va Inc ....G...... 302 227-7409
  Rehoboth Beach (G-8034)
Steamboat Landing ....G...... 302 645-6500
  Lewes (G-3763)
Tall Pines Associates Llc ....F...... 302 684-0300
  Lewes (G-3777)
Tuckahoe Acres Camping Resort ....G...... 302 539-1841
  Dagsboro (G-940)

7041 Membership-Basis Hotels

Airbnb Inc ....G...... 415 800-5959
  Wilmington (G-8994)
Innpros Inc ....F...... 302 326-2500
  Bear (G-188)

72 PERSONAL SERVICES

7211 Power Laundries, Family & Commercial

AP Linens Inc ....E...... 302 430-0851
  Milford (G-4308)
Harry Louies Laundry & Dry Clg ....F...... 302 734-8195
  Dover (G-1634)
Main Gate Laundry ....G...... 302 998-9949
  Wilmington (G-11490)
Newark Chinese Ldry & Dry Clrs ....G...... 302 368-3305
  Newark (G-7112)
Selbyville Cleaners Inc ....E...... 302 249-3444
  Selbyville (G-8544)

7212 Garment Pressing & Cleaners' Agents

Blue Swan Cleaners Inc ....F...... 302 652-7607
  Wilmington (G-9382)
Capitol Cleaners & Launderers ....G...... 302 378-4744
  Middletown (G-3981)
Capitol Cleaners & Launderers ....D...... 302 674-1511
  Dover (G-1251)
Capitol Cleaners & Launderers ....G...... 302 674-0500
  Dover (G-1252)
Marvi Cleaners Limited Inc ....G...... 302 764-3077
  Wilmington (G-11553)
McKelvey Hires Dry Cleaning ....F...... 302 998-9191
  Wilmington (G-11601)
Sepia Cleaners ....G...... 302 656-0700
  Wilmington (G-12581)

7213 Linen Sply

All Star Linen and Uniform Co ....G...... 302 897-9003
  Wilmington (G-9016)
Alsco Inc ....E...... 302 322-2136
  New Castle (G-5027)
Capitol Cleaners & Launderers ....D...... 302 674-1511
  Dover (G-1251)
Palace Laundry Inc ....E...... 302 322-2136
  New Castle (G-5598)
Selbyville Cleaners Inc ....E...... 302 249-3444
  Selbyville (G-8544)
Socal Auto Supply Inc ....D...... 818 717-9982
  Lewes (G-3751)

7215 Coin Operated Laundries & Cleaning

Brookside Laundromat ....G...... 302 369-3366
  Newark (G-6124)
Classic Image Inc ....G...... 302 658-7281
  New Castle (G-5176)
Emerald City Wash World ....G...... 302 734-1230
  Dover (G-1516)
Om Shiv Groceries Inc ....G...... 302 856-7014
  Georgetown (G-2611)
Pennsylvania Inc ....G...... 302 498-0904
  Wilmington (G-12071)
Sparklean Laundromat ....G...... 302 838-2226
  Newark (G-7464)
Splash Lndrmat LLC - Gorgetown ....G...... 302 249-8231
  Georgetown (G-2663)
Trolley Laundry ....G...... 302 654-3538
  Wilmington (G-12982)
Wolfe Resources Ltd ....F...... 302 798-6397
  Claymont (G-825)

7216 Dry Cleaning Plants, Except Rug Cleaning

Blue Swan Cleaners Inc ....F...... 302 652-7607
  Wilmington (G-9382)
Brasures Carpet Care Inc ....G...... 302 436-5652
  Selbyville (G-8461)
Capitol Cleaners & Launderers ....G...... 302 674-0500
  Dover (G-1252)
City One Hour Cleaners ....G...... 302 658-0001
  Wilmington (G-9724)
Colton Cleaners ....F...... 302 234-9422
  Hockessin (G-2992)
Curzon Corp ....E...... 302 655-5551
  Wilmington (G-9922)
Harry Louies Laundry & Dry Clg ....F...... 302 734-8195
  Dover (G-1634)
Hockessin Cleaners ....G...... 302 239-6071
  Hockessin (G-3049)
Joy Cleaners Inc ....G...... 302 656-3537
  Wilmington (G-11199)
Kapa Inc LLC ....G...... 302 740-1235
  Seaford (G-8283)
Kims Cleaners ....G...... 302 656-2397
  Wilmington (G-11262)
Linden Hill Cleaners Inc ....G...... 302 368-9795
  Wilmington (G-11394)
Main Gate Laundry ....G...... 302 998-9949
  Wilmington (G-11490)
Marvi Cleaners Limited Inc ....G...... 302 764-3077
  Wilmington (G-11553)
McKelvey Hires Dry Cleaning ....G...... 302 998-9191
  Wilmington (G-11601)
Newark Chinese Ldry & Dry Clrs ....G...... 302 368-3305
  Newark (G-7112)
North Hills Cleaners Inc ....F...... 302 764-1234
  Wilmington (G-11900)
Parkway Dry Cleaners Inc ....G...... 302 737-2406
  Wilmington (G-7178)
Proclean Inc ....E...... 302 656-8080
  Delaware City (G-965)
Royal Cleaners ....G...... 302 478-0955
  Wilmington (G-12485)
Schroedl Company ....D...... 410 358-5500
  Wilmington (G-12556)
Sepia Cleaners ....G...... 302 656-0700
  Wilmington (G-12581)
Superior Clr of Wilmington Inc ....G...... 302 633-3323
  Wilmington (G-12806)
Thompson Cleaners ....G...... 302 998-0935
  Wilmington (G-12903)
Towne & Country Cleaners Inc ....G...... 302 478-8911
  Wilmington (G-12944)
Value Rate Cleaners ....G...... 302 477-9191
  Wilmington (G-13045)

Webbs Cleaners Corp ....G...... 302 798-0655
  Wilmington (G-13135)

7217 Carpet & Upholstery Cleaning

ABM Janitorial Services Inc ....A...... 302 571-9900
  Wilmington (G-8906)
Bane Clene Way ....G...... 610 485-1234
  Claymont (G-699)
Brasures Carpet Care Inc ....G...... 302 436-5652
  Selbyville (G-8461)
Colonial Cleaning Services Inc ....G...... 302 660-2067
  Wilmington (G-9773)
Crystal Graham ....F...... 302 669-9318
  Middletown (G-4016)
Delaware Rug Co Inc ....G...... 302 998-8881
  Wilmington (G-10082)
Dibiasos Clg Rstration Svc Inc ....G...... 302 376-7111
  Townsend (G-8784)
EBc Carpet Services Corp ....E...... 302 995-7461
  Wilmington (G-10332)
Ebc National Inc ....G...... 302 995-7461
  Wilmington (G-10333)
Edwards Paul Crpt Installation ....G...... 302 672-7847
  Dover (G-1509)
Grime Busters USA Inc ....G...... 302 834-7006
  Newark (G-6692)
Hampton Enterprises Delaware ....G...... 302 378-7365
  Townsend (G-8793)
L & M Services Inc ....F...... 302 658-3735
  Wilmington (G-11306)
Marlings Inc ....F...... 302 325-1759
  New Castle (G-5509)
Oceanside Elite Clg Bldg Svcs ....E...... 302 339-7777
  Lewes (G-3665)
Positive Results Cleaning Inc ....G...... 302 575-1146
  Wilmington (G-12192)
Proclean Inc ....E...... 302 656-8080
  Delaware City (G-965)
Schrider Enterprises Inc ....G...... 302 539-1036
  Ocean View (G-7812)
Stanley Steemer Intl Inc ....E...... 302 907-0062
  Delmar (G-1031)
Sum Inc ....E...... 302 322-0831
  New Castle (G-5740)
Vivid Colors Carpet LLC ....G...... 302 335-3933
  Frederica (G-2415)
Worms Quality Carpet Care ....G...... 302 629-3114
  Seaford (G-8443)
Worthys Property MGT LLC ....F...... 302 265-8301
  Lincoln (G-3875)

7218 Industrial Launderers

Domain Hr Solutions ....F...... 302 357-9401
  Middletown (G-4041)
Jwr 1 LLC ....G...... 302 379-9951
  Bear (G-209)
Nixon Uniform Service Inc ....C...... 302 325-2875
  New Castle (G-5571)

7219 Laundry & Garment Svcs, NEC

Candlelight Bridal Formal Tlrg ....G...... 302 934-8009
  Millsboro (G-4654)
Curzon Corp ....E...... 302 655-5551
  Wilmington (G-9922)
Harry Louies Laundry & Dry Clg ....F...... 302 734-8195
  Dover (G-1634)
Honey Alteration ....G...... 302 519-2031
  Lewes (G-3546)
Joy Cleaners Inc ....G...... 302 656-3537
  Wilmington (G-11199)
Marvi Cleaners Limited Inc ....G...... 302 764-3077
  Wilmington (G-11553)
North Hills Cleaners Inc ....F...... 302 764-1234
  Wilmington (G-11900)

7221 Photographic Studios, Portrait

Aperture Photography ....G...... 302 377-6590
  Middletown (G-3941)
Belles and Beaus Photography ....G...... 302 368-2468
  Newark (G-6070)
Blue Hen Photography ....G...... 302 690-3259
  Bear (G-53)
Everett Robinson ....F...... 302 530-6574
  Wilmington (G-10446)
Foschi Studio ....G...... 302 439-4457
  Wilmington (G-10597)
Gramonoli Enterprises Inc ....G...... 302 227-1288
  Rehoboth Beach (G-7953)

72 PERSONAL SERVICES

Gs Racing Photos .... G 302 855-1165
  Georgetown (G-2551)
Gunn Shot Photography .... G 302 399-3094
  Smyrna (G-8647)
Joseph A Dudeck .... G 302 559-5552
  Middletown (G-4116)
Kari Heverin Photography .... G 302 943-0176
  Townsend (G-8804)
Lifetouch Portrait Studios Inc .... G 302 453-8080
  Newark (G-6935)
Lifetouch Portrait Studios Inc .... F 302 734-9870
  Dover (G-1786)
Little Nests Portraits .... F 610 459-8622
  Wilmington (G-11405)
Photography By Dennis McD .... G 610 678-0318
  Milton (G-4951)
Portrait Innovations Inc .... G 302 477-1696
  Wilmington (G-12188)
Tpp Acquisition Inc .... F 302 674-4805
  Dover (G-2157)
West Photography .... G 302 858-6003
  Georgetown (G-2703)
Youngs Studio of Photography .... G 302 736-2661
  Dover (G-2248)

7231 Beauty Shops

1401 Hair Designs Ltd .... G 302 655-1401
  Wilmington (G-8848)
4 Seasons Nails & Spa .... G 302 663-9474
  Millsboro (G-4619)
A Gentlemans Touch Inc .... F 302 655-7015
  Wilmington (G-8878)
A R Nails .... G 302 858-4592
  Georgetown (G-2420)
Above Beyond Unisex Hair Salon .... G 302 276-0187
  New Castle (G-4998)
Afterglo Beauty Spa .... G 302 537-7546
  Millville (G-4832)
All About U Evada Concept .... G 302 539-1925
  Millville (G-4833)
Allure Salon .... G 302 653-6125
  Smyrna (G-8566)
Altered Images Hair Studio .... G 302 234-2151
  Newark (G-5947)
Angel Nails .... F 302 449-5067
  Middletown (G-3939)
Army & Air Force Exchange Svc ...... G 302 734-8262
  Dover (G-1140)
Artistic Designs Salon .... G 302 644-2009
  Lewes (G-3349)
Avenue Cuts Inc .... G 302 655-1718
  Wilmington (G-9197)
Babe Styling Studio Inc .... G 302 543-7738
  Wilmington (G-9217)
Bad Hair Day Inc .... E 302 226-4247
  Rehoboth Beach (G-7853)
Beautiful Lashes .... G 302 983-9521
  Wilmington (G-9278)
Beauty Max Inc .... G 302 735-1705
  Dover (G-1186)
Bethany Bch Hair Snippery Inc .... G 302 539-8344
  Millville (G-4837)
Brandon Tatum .... G 302 564-7428
  Selbyville (G-8459)
C KS Hairport Ltd Salon & Spa .... G 302 645-2246
  Lewes (G-3398)
Carme LLC .... F 302 832-8418
  Newark (G-6157)
Carol Inc .... E 302 386-4362
  Newark (G-6159)
Cartessa Aesthetics .... G 302 332-1991
  Hockessin (G-2978)
Cecilia Williams .... G 302 250-6269
  Wilmington (G-9607)
Center For Black Culture .... G 302 831-2991
  Newark (G-6176)
Charlotte Wilson .... G 302 500-1440
  Seaford (G-8191)
Cheveux Inc .... E 302 731-9202
  Newark (G-6195)
Chez Nichole Hair & Nail Salon ...... E 302 654-8888
  Wilmington (G-9659)
Christophers Hair Design .... G 302 378-1988
  Middletown (G-3990)
Cielo Salon & Spa Inc .... F 302 575-0400
  Wilmington (G-9702)
Clippers & Curls Hair Design .... G 302 684-1522
  Milton (G-4881)
CMC Corporation of Hockessin .... G 302 239-1960
  Hockessin (G-2990)

Coiffure Ltd .... G 302 652-3443
  Wilmington (G-9763)
Coiffure Ltd .... G 302 652-3463
  Wilmington (G-9764)
Complexions Tanning Salon .... G 302 430-0150
  Milford (G-4363)
Currie Hair Skin Nailss .... G 302 777-7755
  Wilmington (G-9920)
Cut Above Hair Gallery .... G 302 539-0622
  Bethany Beach (G-394)
Cuts & Styles Barley Mill Inc .... G 302 999-8059
  Wilmington (G-9929)
Cuts R US Inc .... G 302 674-2223
  Dover (G-1333)
Delaware Learning Institue of .... F 302 732-6704
  Dagsboro (G-895)
Designer Braids and Trade .... G 718 783-9078
  Middletown (G-4037)
Donnas Family Cut & Curl Inc .... G 302 436-8999
  Selbyville (G-8482)
Elayne James Salon & Spa LLC ...... G 302 376-5290
  Middletown (G-4053)
Elegant Images LLP .... G 302 698-5250
  Camden (G-568)
Expecting Miracles LLC .... G 302 893-3220
  Wilmington (G-10460)
Fabrizio Salon .... G 302 254-3432
  Wilmington (G-10473)
Family Comb & Scissors .... G 302 398-8570
  Harrington (G-2840)
Fantasy Beauty Salon .... G 302 629-6762
  Seaford (G-8242)
Ferrari Hair Studio Ltd .... E 302 731-7505
  Wilmington (G-10525)
Fusion .... E 302 479-9444
  Wilmington (G-10650)
Gc New Castle Inc .... G 302 544-6128
  New Castle (G-5347)
Gemini Hair Designs .... G 302 654-9371
  Wilmington (G-10689)
George Marcus Salon Inc .... F 302 475-7530
  Wilmington (G-10702)
Girls Auto Clinic LLC .... G 484 679-6394
  New Castle (G-5354)
Glossgirl Inc .... G 302 888-4520
  Wilmington (G-10733)
Great Clips .... G 302 478-2022
  Wilmington (G-10768)
Hair 2 Please .... G 302 378-3349
  Middletown (G-4101)
Hair Academy Llc .... G 302 738-6251
  Newark (G-6701)
Hair Artistry .... G 302 645-7167
  Lewes (G-3529)
Hair Designs By Linda Inc .... G 302 478-7080
  Wilmington (G-10818)
Hair Designs By Regina .... G 302 652-8089
  Wilmington (G-10819)
Hair Levels .... G 302 212-0842
  Wilmington (G-10821)
Hair Sensations Inc .... G 302 731-0920
  New Castle (G-5372)
Hair Studio II .... G 302 945-5110
  Millsboro (G-4703)
Hairs To You .... G 302 436-1728
  Selbyville (G-8498)
Hairworks Inc .... F 302 656-0566
  Wilmington (G-10822)
Head Quarters .... G 302 798-1639
  Wilmington (G-10864)
Head Quarters Barbershop .... G 646 423-6767
  Middletown (G-4106)
Headquarters 2 Inc .... F 302 731-9600
  Newark (G-6715)
Hockessin Day Spa .... G 302 234-7573
  Hockessin (G-3050)
Island of Misfits LLC .... G 302 732-6704
  Dagsboro (G-895)
J and J Hair Fashions .... G 302 422-5117
  Milford (G-4454)
James & Jesses Barbr & Buty Sp ... G 302 658-9617
  Wilmington (G-11119)
Jersey Clippers LLC .... E 302 956-0138
  Bridgeville (G-486)
Jk Tangles Hair Salon .... F 302 698-1006
  Dover (G-1697)
JM Virgin Hair Company .... G 856 383-8588
  New Castle (G-5440)
Joanne Reuther .... G 302 945-8707
  Lewes (G-3571)

Key To Beauty .... G 302 398-9460
  Harrington (G-2861)
Kustom Kutz .... G 302 424-7556
  Milford (G-4468)
Lady PS Hair Designs Inc .... G 302 832-2668
  Bear (G-228)
Lavish Strands 1 .... G 302 333-5742
  New Castle (G-5474)
Lee Nails .... G 302 674-5001
  Dover (G-1777)
Les Nails .... G 302 449-5290
  Middletown (G-4129)
Lon Spa Inc .... G 302 368-4595
  Newark (G-6947)
Lux Spa & Nails .... G 302 834-4899
  Bear (G-241)
Main Event Inc .... G 302 737-2225
  Newark (G-6973)
Make Wave .... G 302 422-1247
  Milford (G-4484)
Mark IV Beauty Salon Inc .... G 302 737-4994
  Newark (G-6990)
Mary Zieken .... F 302 475-6714
  Wilmington (G-11559)
Mastercuts .... G 302 674-0300
  Dover (G-1826)
Maureen Freebery .... E 302 234-7800
  Wilmington (G-11575)
Maureens For Men & Women .... F 302 234-7800
  Wilmington (G-11576)
Maxim Hair & Nails LLC .... G 410 920-8656
  Selbyville (G-8517)
Maxines Hair Happenings Inc .... G 302 875-4055
  Laurel (G-3263)
Mdm Hair Studio .... G 302 312-6052
  Middletown (G-4151)
Michaelangelos Hair Designs .... G 302 734-8343
  Dover (G-1846)
Mr Chris Hair Design .... G 302 658-2121
  Wilmington (G-11766)
N&D Nail Salon .... G 302 834-4899
  Bear (G-261)
Nail Pros .... G 302 674-2988
  Dover (G-1882)
New Image Laser and Skin Care ..... G 302 537-4336
  Ocean View (G-7804)
New Trend Hair Salon .... G 302 998-3331
  Wilmington (G-11871)
Nu Attitude Styling Salon Ltd .... G 302 734-8638
  Dover (G-1908)
Oerigo Consulting LLC .... G 302 353-4719
  Smyrna (G-8686)
One Step Ahead Childcare .... G 302 292-1162
  Newark (G-7152)
Penache Beauty Salon .... G 302 731-5912
  Newark (G-7192)
Perfect Nails .... G 302 731-1964
  Newark (G-7201)
Petite Hair Designs .... G 302 945-2595
  Millsboro (G-4781)
Pizazz Beauty Studio .... G 302 761-9820
  Wilmington (G-12146)
Posh Salon .... F 302 655-7000
  Wilmington (G-12189)
Precious Nails .... G 302 292-1690
  Wilmington (G-12200)
Premier Salons Intl Inc .... G 302 477-3459
  Wilmington (G-12217)
Premier Solutions Intl .... G 302 477-1334
  Wilmington (G-12218)
Premiere Hair Design .... G 302 368-7711
  Newark (G-7245)
Pretty Nails .... G 302 628-3937
  Seaford (G-8363)
Ralphs Scissors Sensations .... G 302 764-2744
  Wilmington (G-12311)
Rape of The Locke Inc .... G 302 368-5370
  Newark (G-7297)
Ratner Companies LC .... F 302 226-9822
  Rehoboth Beach (G-8040)
Ratner Companies LC .... F 302 678-8081
  Dover (G-2010)
Ratner Companies LC .... G 302 999-7724
  Wilmington (G-12321)
Ratner Companies LC .... F 302 836-3749
  Bear (G-297)
Ratner Companies LC .... E 302 366-9032
  Newark (G-7299)
Ratner Companies LC .... F 302 376-3568
  Middletown (G-4212)

SIC SECTION 72 PERSONAL SERVICES

Ratner Companies LC F 302 537-4624
Millville *(G-4854)*
Ratner Companies LC F 302 478-9978
Wilmington *(G-12322)*
Regis Corporation G 302 376-6165
Middletown *(G-4214)*
Regis Corporation G 302 654-4477
Wilmington *(G-12361)*
Regis Corporation G 302 430-0881
Milford *(G-4535)*
Regis Corporation G 302 697-6220
Camden *(G-598)*
Regis Corporation G 302 834-1272
Bear *(G-299)*
Regis Corporation G 302 856-2575
Georgetown *(G-2634)*
Regis Corporation F 302 454-2800
Newark *(G-7311)*
Regis Corporation G 302 227-9730
Rehoboth Beach *(G-8046)*
Regis Corporation F 302 834-9916
Bear *(G-300)*
Regis Corporation G 302 629-2916
Seaford *(G-8375)*
Regis Corporation G 302 628-0484
Seaford *(G-8376)*
Regis Corporation G 302 478-5065
Wilmington *(G-12362)*
Rene Delyn Designs Inc F 302 736-6070
Dover *(G-2028)*
Resh LLC F 302 543-5469
New Castle *(G-5674)*
Robins Hair & Tanning G 302 529-9000
Wilmington *(G-12443)*
Royal Hair Design LLC G 302 312-4569
Smyrna *(G-8704)*
Salon By Dominic F 302 239-8282
Hockessin *(G-3141)*
Salon Rispoli Inc G 302 731-9202
Newark *(G-7380)*
Scissor Wizards Inc G 302 475-9575
Wilmington *(G-12562)*
Shear Magic Hair Design F 302 836-4001
Bear *(G-318)*
Shop Talk Inc G 302 322-5860
New Castle *(G-5705)*
Sky Nails G 302 322-5949
New Castle *(G-5715)*
Something Unique Inc G 302 678-0555
Dover *(G-2094)*
Sophisticuts Inc G 302 834-7427
Bear *(G-328)*
Star Nail Salon G 302 498-0702
Wilmington *(G-12741)*
Star Nails & Spa G 302 798-6245
Wilmington *(G-12742)*
Styles By US G 302 629-3244
Seaford *(G-8410)*
Sunco Salon G 302 456-0240
Newark *(G-7506)*
Sunlight Salon LLC G 302 456-1799
Newark *(G-7507)*
Supercuts Inc G 302 475-5001
Wilmington *(G-12805)*
Supreme Hair Design G 302 672-7255
Dover *(G-2118)*
Sylvia Saienna E 302 683-9082
Wilmington *(G-12829)*
Today Nails G 302 286-7937
Newark *(G-7572)*
Todds F 302 658-0387
Wilmington *(G-12924)*
Top Nails G 302 644-2261
Lewes *(G-3788)*
Town and Country Salon Inc E 302 737-1855
Newark *(G-7579)*
Trilogy Salon and Day Spa Inc E 302 292-3511
Newark *(G-7591)*
Ultimate Images Inc F 302 479-0292
Wilmington *(G-13008)*
Unisex Palace E 302 674-0950
Dover *(G-2179)*
Uppercut Inc F 302 736-1661
Dover *(G-2181)*
Vision Salon & Barbershop G 302 934-9301
Millsboro *(G-4821)*
Visions Hair Design G 302 477-0820
Wilmington *(G-13093)*
Vivians Style G 302 645-9444
Lewes *(G-3809)*
White Mink Beauty Salon F 302 737-2081
Newark *(G-7692)*
Womens Wellness Ctr & Med Spa G 302 643-2500
Newark *(G-7716)*
Wyatt Ridley Corp G 302 998-8860
Wilmington *(G-13311)*
Xanadu Concepts LLC G 302 449-2677
Middletown *(G-4292)*
Yankee Clippers Hair Designer G 302 422-2748
Milford *(G-4615)*

7241 Barber Shops

A Gentlemans Touch Inc F 302 655-7015
Wilmington *(G-8878)*
Altered Images Hair Studio G 302 234-2151
Newark *(G-5947)*
Amstel Barbershop LLC G 302 635-7686
Hockessin *(G-2957)*
Bethany Bch Hair Snippery Inc G 302 539-8344
Millville *(G-4837)*
CMC Corporation of Hockessin G 302 239-1960
Hockessin *(G-2990)*
Cuts & Styles Barley Mill Inc G 302 999-8059
Wilmington *(G-9929)*
Cutting Edge of Delaware Inc F 302 834-8723
Wilmington *(G-9930)*
Georve V Sawyer G 302 736-1474
Dover *(G-1591)*
Hair Studio II G 302 945-5110
Millsboro *(G-4703)*
Haircut & Company Inc F 302 239-3236
Newark *(G-6702)*
His Image Barbershop G 302 256-2792
Wilmington *(G-10916)*
House of Hair G 302 697-6088
Dover *(G-1657)*
Joes Barber Shop G 302 478-2837
Wilmington *(G-11166)*
Jstanley Salon G 302 778-1885
Wilmington *(G-11205)*
Millcreek Barber Shop F 302 998-2174
Wilmington *(G-11689)*
Rape of The Locke Inc G 302 368-5370
Newark *(G-7297)*
Ratner Companies LC G 302 378-8565
Middletown *(G-4211)*
Styles Millenium G 302 472-3427
Wilmington *(G-12783)*
The Professionals G 302 764-5501
Wilmington *(G-12892)*
Toms Barber Shop G 302 992-9635
Wilmington *(G-12925)*
United States Mle MNS Hair Cre G 302 368-1273
Newark *(G-7615)*
Vision Salon & Barbershop G 302 934-9301
Millsboro *(G-4821)*
Visions Hair Design G 302 477-0820
Wilmington *(G-13093)*

7251 Shoe Repair & Shoeshine Parlors

Curzon Corp E 302 655-5551
Wilmington *(G-9922)*
Fast Feet Inc G 302 478-5300
Wilmington *(G-10503)*
Parkway Dry Cleaners Inc G 302 737-2406
Newark *(G-7178)*

7261 Funeral Svcs & Crematories

A Douglas Melson G 302 732-6606
Frankford *(G-2344)*
Austin Cox Home Services G 410 334-6406
Georgetown *(G-2441)*
Beeson Funeral Home G 302 764-2900
Wilmington *(G-9281)*
Bennie Smith Funeral Home Inc G 302 678-8747
Dover *(G-1193)*
Bennie Smith Funeral Home Inc G 302 934-9019
Millsboro *(G-4643)*
Berry Short Funeral Home Inc G 302 422-8091
Milford *(G-4324)*
Charles P Arcaro Funeral Home G 302 658-9095
Wilmington *(G-9635)*
Congo Funeral Home F 302 652-6640
Wilmington *(G-9822)*
Delaware Prof Fnrl Svcs Inc E 302 731-5459
Newark *(G-6404)*
Direct Cremation Services Del F 302 656-6873
Wilmington *(G-10160)*
Dohery Funeral Homes Inc F 302 999-8277
Wilmington *(G-10184)*
Edward R Bell G 302 658-1555
Wilmington *(G-10358)*
Ews Funeral Home G 302 494-1847
Bear *(G-146)*
Faries Funeral Directors Inc G 302 653-8816
Smyrna *(G-8633)*
Gebhart Funeral Home Inc E 302 798-7726
Claymont *(G-750)*
Gore Funeral Services G 610 364-9900
New Castle *(G-5357)*
Hannigan Short Disharoonk G 302 875-3637
Laurel *(G-3237)*
House of Wright Mortuary F 302 762-8448
Wilmington *(G-10960)*
James T Chandler & Son Inc F 302 478-7100
Wilmington *(G-11124)*
John F Yasik Funeral Services G 302 428-9986
Wilmington *(G-11169)*
John F Yasik Inc G 302 652-5114
Wilmington *(G-11170)*
Krienen-Griffith Inc G 302 994-9614
Wilmington *(G-11295)*
Lofland Funeral Home Inc G 302 422-5416
Milford *(G-4476)*
McCrery Funeral Homes Inc G 302 478-2204
Wilmington *(G-11592)*
Melson Funeral Services G 302 945-9000
Millsboro *(G-4741)*
Melson Funeral Services Ltd G 302 732-9000
Frankford *(G-2373)*
Melsons Cape Hnlopen Crematory G 302 537-2441
Frankford *(G-2374)*
Michael A Mealey & Sons Inc F 302 652-5913
Wilmington *(G-11654)*
Michael A Mealey & Sons Inc F 302 654-3005
Wilmington *(G-11655)*
Parsell Funeral Entps Inc G 302 645-9520
Lewes *(G-3679)*
Robert T Jones & Foard Inc G 302 731-4627
Newark *(G-7352)*
Ryland Funeral Home Inc G 302 764-7711
Wilmington *(G-12503)*
Short Funeral Home Inc G 302 846-9814
Delmar *(G-1028)*
Short Funeral Home Inc G 302 875-3637
Laurel *(G-3288)*
Spicer Mullikin Funeral Homes E 302 368-9500
New Castle *(G-5729)*
Spicer Mullikin Funeral Homes F 302 368-9500
Newark *(G-7471)*
Thomas E Melvin Son Inc G 302 398-3884
Harrington *(G-2899)*
Torbert Funeral Chapel Inc F 302 734-3341
Dover *(G-2153)*
Trader Funeral Home Inc G 302 734-4620
Dover *(G-2158)*
Warwick Funeral Home G 302 368-9500
Newark *(G-7677)*
Watson Funeral Home Inc F 302 934-7842
Millsboro *(G-4824)*
Watson-Yates Funeral Home Inc G 302 629-8561
Seaford *(G-8435)*
Zwaanendael LLC G 302 645-6466
Lewes *(G-3837)*

7291 Tax Return Preparation Svcs

Adkins & Assoc CPA G 302 737-2390
Wilmington *(G-8938)*
Advantage Delaware LLC G 302 479-7764
Wilmington *(G-8959)*
Affordable Tax Services LLC G 302 399-3867
Bear *(G-23)*
Basic Block Corp F 302 645-2000
Rehoboth Beach *(G-7855)*
David Wentworth G 302 856-3272
Georgetown *(G-2493)*
Dbw Tax Services G 302 276-0428
Bear *(G-100)*
Ekww Inc G 302 234-2877
Hockessin *(G-3018)*
Elite Tax Services LLC G 302 256-0401
Wilmington *(G-10377)*
H&R Block Inc G 302 934-6178
Millsboro *(G-4702)*
H&R Block Inc F 302 378-8931
Middletown *(G-4100)*
H&R Block Inc F 302 999-7488
Wilmington *(G-10812)*

S I C

Employee Codes: A=Over 500 employees, B=251-500
C=101-250, D=51-100, E=20-50, F=10-19, G=1-9
2020 Harris Directory of
Delaware Businesses
521

H&R Block Inc .... F 302 328-7320
New Castle *(G-5370)*
H&R Block Inc .... F 302 652-3286
New Castle *(G-5371)*
H&R Block Inc .... F 302 836-2700
Bear *(G-174)*
H&R Block Inc .... F 302 478-9140
Wilmington *(G-10813)*
H&R Block Inc .... F 302 479-5717
Newark *(G-6699)*
H&R Block Inc .... F 302 478-6300
Wilmington *(G-10814)*
Horty & Horty PA .... E 302 730-4560
Dover *(G-1656)*
Jackson Hewitt Inc .... G 302 934-7430
Millsboro *(G-4712)*
Jackson Hewitt Tax Service .... G 302 629-4548
Seaford *(G-8276)*
Kelly Robert & Assoc LLC .... F 302 737-7785
Newark *(G-6873)*
Michael Eller Income Tax Svc .... G 302 652-5916
Wilmington *(G-11659)*
Miller & Associates PA .... G 302 234-0678
Wilmington *(G-11693)*
Oates Consultants LLC .... G 302 477-0109
Wilmington *(G-11929)*
Papaleo Rosen Chelf & Pinder .... F 302 644-8600
Lewes *(G-3678)*
Prefered Tax Service Inc .... G 302 654-4388
Wilmington *(G-12210)*
R E Wllams Prof Acctg Frm Tax .... G 302 598-7171
Wilmington *(G-12294)*
Ronald Midaugh .... F 410 860-1040
Dover *(G-2041)*
Sandra S Gulledge CPA .... G 302 674-1585
Dover *(G-2058)*
Slacum & Doyle Tax Service LLC .... E 302 734-1850
Dover *(G-2088)*
Tax Management Service Inc .... G 703 845-5900
Milford *(G-4575)*
Tax Masters of Delaware .... G 302 832-1313
Bear *(G-348)*
Thomson Reuters (grc) Inc .... A 212 227-7357
Wilmington *(G-12904)*
Wahid Consultants LLC .... E 315 400-0955
New Castle *(G-5821)*
Walls & Davenport Inc .... G 302 653-4779
Smyrna *(G-8739)*
Wentworth Inc .... F 302 629-6284
Seaford *(G-8436)*

7299 Miscellaneous Personal Svcs, NEC

A Fields Unlimited LLC .... G 800 484-2331
Newark *(G-5866)*
Adpese LLC .... G 302 223-5411
Wilmington *(G-8943)*
Alternative Therapy LLC .... G 302 368-0800
Newark *(G-5949)*
Beach Tans and Hair Design .... G 302 645-8267
Rehoboth Beach *(G-7858)*
Bennett & Bennett Inc .... F 302 990-8939
New Castle *(G-5081)*
Boutique The Bridal Ltd .... G 302 335-5948
Milford *(G-4329)*
Bridal & Tuxedo Outlet Inc .... G 302 731-8802
Newark *(G-6118)*
Candlelight Bridal Formal Tlrg .... G 302 934-8009
Millsboro *(G-4654)*
Celebrations Design Group Ltd .... G 302 793-3893
Claymont *(G-711)*
Cnu Fit LLC .... G 302 744-9037
Dover *(G-1298)*
Community Services Corporation .... F 302 368-4400
Newark *(G-6272)*
Covenant Asset Mgmt & Financl .... G 302 324-5655
New Castle *(G-5205)*
Deep Muscle Therapy Center Del .... F 302 397-8073
Wilmington *(G-9992)*
Delaware AG Museum & Vlg .... G 302 734-1618
Dover *(G-1357)*
Delcastle Golf Club Management .... E 302 998-9505
Wilmington *(G-10098)*
Domian International Svc LLC .... G 804 837-3616
Smyrna *(G-8624)*
Dream Clean Team LP .... F 302 981-5154
Newark *(G-6473)*
Electric Beach Tanning Company .... G 302 730-8266
Dover *(G-1513)*
Endless Summer Tanning Salon .... G 302 369-0455
Newark *(G-6526)*
Essencia Salon and Day Spa .... G 302 234-9144
Hockessin *(G-3023)*
Eventc2 LLC .... G 301 467-5780
Newark *(G-6545)*
Events A La Carte .... G 302 753-7462
Middletown *(G-4065)*
Everybody Needs Ink .... G 302 633-0866
Wilmington *(G-10450)*
Formal Affairs Inc .... F 302 737-1519
Newark *(G-6606)*
Fremont Hall .... G 302 731-2431
Newark *(G-6620)*
Fresh Start Marketplace LLC .... F 302 240-3002
Dover *(G-1569)*
Fresh Start Transformations .... G 302 219-0221
Newark *(G-6623)*
Gb Home Improvement .... G 302 654-5411
Wilmington *(G-10681)*
Grofos International LLC .... G 302 635-4805
Newark *(G-6693)*
Hand & Spa .... G 302 478-1700
Wilmington *(G-10830)*
Hollywood Tan .... G 302 995-2692
Wilmington *(G-10932)*
Hollywood Tans .... G 302 478-8267
Wilmington *(G-10933)*
Independent Studio Inc .... G 302 436-5581
Selbyville *(G-8506)*
Jenny Craig Wght Loss Ctrs Inc .... G 302 477-9202
Wilmington *(G-11149)*
Jenny Craig Wght Loss Ctrs Inc .... G 302 454-0991
Newark *(G-6834)*
Km Klacko & Associate .... G 302 652-1482
Wilmington *(G-11278)*
Knowland Group LLC .... F 302 645-9777
Lewes *(G-3584)*
Luxiasuites LLC .... G 302 778-3000
Wilmington *(G-11460)*
M & P Adventures Inc .... E 302 645-6271
Lewes *(G-3614)*
Matthew Smith .... G 302 654-4853
Wilmington *(G-11572)*
Nixon Unf Rntl Svc of Lncaster .... G 302 656-2774
New Castle *(G-5570)*
Oink Oink LLC .... G 302 924-5034
Dover *(G-1914)*
Paxful Inc .... F 865 272-9385
Wilmington *(G-12047)*
Poppycock Tattoo .... G 302 543-7973
Wilmington *(G-12187)*
Quail Associates Inc .... E 302 697-4660
Camden Wyoming *(G-651)*
Rendezvous Inc .... G 302 645-7400
Lewes *(G-3715)*
Robins Hair & Tanning .... G 302 529-9000
Wilmington *(G-12443)*
Sanctuary Spa and Saloon .... F 302 475-1469
Wilmington *(G-12537)*
Selwor Enterprises Inc .... F 302 454-9454
Newark *(G-7404)*
Shechinah Empower Center Inc .... G 302 858-4467
Georgetown *(G-2653)*
Snap Fitness .... G 302 741-2444
Dover *(G-2090)*
Stephanie Galbraith .... G 302 290-2235
Wilmington *(G-12753)*
Storyworth Inc .... G 415 967-1531
Claymont *(G-808)*
Tantini LLC .... G 302 444-4024
Newark *(G-7538)*
Therapy At Beach .... G 302 313-5555
Lewes *(G-3781)*
U Tan Inc .... G 302 674-8040
Dover *(G-2170)*
University of Delaware .... F 302 831-2792
Newark *(G-7619)*
Weather or Not Dog Walkers .... G 302 304-8399
Wilmington *(G-13131)*
White Eagle Integrations .... G 302 464-0550
Middletown *(G-4285)*
Worcester Golf Club Inc .... F 610 222-0200
Milton *(G-4981)*

73 BUSINESS SERVICES

7311 Advertising Agencies

Advertising Healthy Inc .... G 302 366-7502
Newark *(G-5912)*
Almm Ventures LLC .... G 302 778-1300
Wilmington *(G-9026)*
Aloysius Butlr Clark Assoc Inc .... D 302 655-1552
Wilmington *(G-9029)*
Bayshore Communications Inc .... F 302 737-2164
Newark *(G-6057)*
Beanstock Media Inc .... E 415 912-1530
Wilmington *(G-9273)*
Chilay Inc .... G 302 559-6014
Newark *(G-6196)*
Cohesive Strategies Inc .... E 302 429-9120
Wilmington *(G-9762)*
Convention Coach .... G 302 335-5459
Magnolia *(G-3887)*
Delaware Design Company .... G 302 737-9700
Newark *(G-6375)*
Diamond State Promotions .... G 302 999-1900
Wilmington *(G-10145)*
Digital Generation Inc .... F 302 368-0002
Newark *(G-6445)*
Effective Advertising Seaford .... G 302 628-1946
Seaford *(G-8233)*
Epic Marketing Cons Corp .... E 302 285-9790
Middletown *(G-4061)*
Essential Health Brands LLC .... G 302 322-1249
Wilmington *(G-10438)*
Extreme Reach Inc .... F 302 366-7538
Newark *(G-6557)*
Ezangacom Inc .... E 888 439-2642
Middletown *(G-4067)*
Grind or Starve LLC .... G 302 322-1679
Wilmington *(G-10786)*
Industrial Training Cons Inc .... F 302 266-6100
Newark *(G-6774)*
Janet Hughes and Associates .... F 302 656-5252
Wilmington *(G-11128)*
Jay Gundel and Associates Inc .... G 302 658-1674
Wilmington *(G-11132)*
K F Dunn & Associates .... F 302 328-3347
Wilmington *(G-11215)*
Kiosked Corporation .... G 803 993-8463
Wilmington *(G-11270)*
Koncordia Group LLC .... F 302 427-1350
Wilmington *(G-11288)*
New ERA Media LLC .... G 302 731-2003
Newark *(G-7105)*
Paragon Design Inc .... G 302 292-1523
Newark *(G-7175)*
Remline Corp .... E 302 737-7228
Newark *(G-7316)*
Shiny Agency LLC .... G 302 384-6494
Wilmington *(G-12603)*
Shor Associates Inc .... G 302 764-1701
Wilmington *(G-12608)*
Simplymiddle LLC .... F 302 217-3460
Wilmington *(G-12629)*
Top Rated Media Inc .... E 888 550-9273
Wilmington *(G-12930)*
Unified Companies Inc .... G 866 936-0515
Wilmington *(G-13011)*
Wh2p Inc .... G 302 530-6555
Wilmington *(G-13180)*

7312 Outdoor Advertising Svcs

Carvertise Inc .... G 302 273-1889
Wilmington *(G-9583)*
Clear Channel Outdoor Inc .... E 302 658-5520
Wilmington *(G-9739)*
United Outdoor Advertising .... G 302 652-3177
Wilmington *(G-13025)*

7313 Radio, TV & Publishers Adv Reps

Burris & Baxter Communications .... G 302 454-8511
Newark *(G-6138)*
Melody Entertainment USA Inc .... G 305 505-7659
Wilmington *(G-11627)*
Social Work Helper Pbc .... G 302 233-7422
Dover *(G-2093)*
Yield Nexus LLC .... F 308 380-3788
Dover *(G-2245)*

7319 Advertising, NEC

Get Cents LLC .... E 203 856-0841
Lewes *(G-3512)*
Gkua Inc .... F 415 971-5341
Wilmington *(G-10718)*
Gotshadeonline Inc .... G 302 832-8468
Bear *(G-168)*
Innospec Inc .... G 302 454-8100
Newark *(G-6783)*

U Transit Inc .... G 302 227-1197
Rehoboth Beach *(G-8102)*

7322 Adjustment & Collection Svcs

Advanced Rcvable Solutions Inc .... E 302 225-6001
Wilmington *(G-8955)*
Andrews & Wells LLC .... G 302 359-5417
Camden *(G-538)*
Baines Shapiro & Associates .... G 302 384-2322
New Castle *(G-5064)*
Beach Associates Inc .... F 866 744-9911
Dover *(G-1183)*
Byron & Davis Cccc .... G 302 792-2334
Wilmington *(G-9517)*
Capitol Credit Services Inc .... F 302 678-1735
Dover *(G-1253)*
Commercial Recovery Group Inc .... F 302 730-4040
Dover *(G-1305)*
Commtrak Corporation .... G 302 644-1600
Lewes *(G-3443)*
Firstcollect Inc .... G 302 644-6804
Lewes *(G-3500)*
G & D Collection Group Inc .... F 302 482-2512
Wilmington *(G-10656)*
Jsd Management Inc .... E 302 735-4628
Dover *(G-1713)*
Kearns Brinen & Monaghan Inc .... F 302 736-6481
Dover *(G-1727)*
Matthews Pierce & Lloyd Inc .... E 302 678-5500
Dover *(G-1829)*
Phillips & Cohen Assoc Ltd .... D 609 518-9000
Wilmington *(G-12117)*
Phillips & Cohen Assoc Ltd .... D 302 355-3500
Newark *(G-7214)*
Simm Associates Inc .... C 302 283-2800
Newark *(G-7430)*
SLM Corporation .... D 302 451-0200
Newark *(G-7441)*
Stevenson Ventures LLC .... G 302 752-4449
Milford *(G-4571)*
Wyatt & Brown Inc .... G 302 786-2793
Harrington *(G-2910)*

7323 Credit Reporting Svcs

D & H Credit Services Inc .... F 302 832-6980
Newark *(G-6340)*
Groupe Victoire LLC .... G 302 384-5355
Wilmington *(G-10790)*
Lexisnexis Risk Assets Inc .... A 800 458-9410
Wilmington *(G-11378)*
S Wallace Holdings LLC .... G 917 304-1164
Wilmington *(G-12509)*

7331 Direct Mail Advertising Svcs

Bcd Systems .... G 302 328-2070
New Castle *(G-5076)*
Copy Craft Inc .... E 302 633-1313
Wilmington *(G-9856)*
D & B Printing and Mailing Inc .... G 302 838-7111
Newark *(G-6339)*
Hibbert Company .... E 609 394-7500
New Castle *(G-5394)*
Mail Center .... G 302 422-2200
Milford *(G-4483)*
Million Group .... G 302 543-8354
Wilmington *(G-11696)*
Valassis Direct Mail Inc .... C 302 861-3567
Newark *(G-7639)*

7334 Photocopying & Duplicating Svcs

◆ **Amer Inc** .... G 302 654-2498
Wilmington *(G-9039)*
ARC Document Solutions Inc .... E 302 654-2365
Wilmington *(G-9114)*
Braun Engineering & Surveying .... F 302 698-0701
Camden Wyoming *(G-621)*
Copy Craft Inc .... E 302 633-1313
Wilmington *(G-9856)*
Fedex Office & Print Svcs Inc .... E 302 475-9501
Wilmington *(G-10517)*
Fedex Office & Print Svcs Inc .... G 302 652-2151
Wilmington *(G-10518)*
Fedex Office & Print Svcs Inc .... F 302 368-5080
Newark *(G-6576)*
Fedex Office & Print Svcs Inc .... G 302 996-0264
Wilmington *(G-10519)*
Garile Inc .... E 302 366-0848
Newark *(G-6639)*
Medical Copy Services .... G 302 654-4741
Wilmington *(G-11616)*
Mr Copy Inc .... G 302 227-4666
Rehoboth Beach *(G-8015)*
Reliable Copy Service Inc .... F 302 654-8080
Wilmington *(G-12373)*
Reprographics Center Inc .... G 302 328-5019
New Castle *(G-5672)*
Windswept Enterprises .... G 302 678-0805
Dover *(G-2233)*

7335 Commercial Photography

Colourworks Photographic Svcs .... G 302 428-0222
Wilmington *(G-9778)*
Cut Out Image Inc .... G 844 866-5577
Newark *(G-6333)*
Dean Digital Imaging Inc .... G 302 655-6992
Wilmington *(G-9989)*
Firefly Drone Operations Llc .... G 305 206-6955
Wilmington *(G-10543)*
Floyd Dean Inc .... G 302 655-7193
Wilmington *(G-10581)*
Herbert Studios .... G 302 836-3122
Newark *(G-6724)*
Horizon Helicopters Inc .... G 302 368-5135
Newark *(G-6745)*

7336 Commercial Art & Graphic Design

9193 4323 Quebec Inc .... G 855 824-0795
Newark *(G-5862)*
Advangelists LLC .... G 734 546-4989
Wilmington *(G-8958)*
Aztec Copies LLC .... F 302 575-1993
Wilmington *(G-9204)*
Bear Associates LLC .... G 302 735-5558
Dover *(G-1184)*
Brand Design Co Inc .... G 302 234-2356
Yorklyn *(G-13364)*
De Nest Studio .... G 302 836-1316
Bear *(G-101)*
De Novo Corporation .... E 302 234-7407
Wilmington *(G-9987)*
Dean Dsign/Marketing Group Inc .... G 717 898-9800
Lincoln *(G-3844)*
Envision It Publications LLC .... G 800 329-9411
Bear *(G-144)*
Eye35design LLC .... G 470 236-3933
Dover *(G-1535)*
Graphics Unlimited Inc .... G 302 398-3898
Harrington *(G-2842)*
Green Crescent LLC .... G 800 735-9620
Dover *(G-1611)*
Growth Inc .... F 302 366-8586
Newark *(G-6694)*
Gulch Group LLC .... G 202 697-1756
Rehoboth Beach *(G-7956)*
Hamilton Associates .... G 302 629-4949
Seaford *(G-8257)*
Harting Graphics Ltd .... G 302 762-6397
Wilmington *(G-10845)*
Hplusmedia LLC .... G 347 480-8996
Lewes *(G-3548)*
Initially Yours Inc .... G 302 999-0562
Wilmington *(G-11035)*
Integrated Solutions Planning .... G 302 297-9215
Georgetown *(G-2567)*
Little Nests Portraits .... F 610 459-8622
Wilmington *(G-11405)*
Miller Mauro Group Inc .... G 302 426-6565
Wilmington *(G-11694)*
Mitchell Associates Inc .... E 302 594-9400
Wilmington *(G-11714)*
Pixxy Solutions LLC .... E 631 609-6686
Claymont *(G-795)*
Plugdin Inc .... G 347 726-1831
Dover *(G-1972)*
Pond Publishing & Productions .... G 302 284-0200
Felton *(G-2313)*
Precision Color Graphics LLC .... G 302 661-2595
Wilmington *(G-12202)*
Promotion Zone LLC .... G 302 832-8565
Newark *(G-7269)*
Promotions Plus Inc .... G 302 836-2820
Newark *(G-7270)*
Seaside Graphics Corp .... F 302 436-9460
Selbyville *(G-8543)*
Sunshine Graphics and Printing .... G 302 724-5127
Dover *(G-2115)*
Visual Arts Studio Inc .... G 302 652-0925
Wilmington *(G-13094)*
Xcs Corporation .... G 302 514-0600
Wilmington *(G-13316)*

7338 Secretarial & Court Reporting Svcs

Chancery Court Reporters .... G 302 255-0515
Wilmington *(G-9628)*
Dale Hawkins .... G 302 658-6697
Wilmington *(G-9948)*
Federal Court Reporters .... G 302 573-6195
Wilmington *(G-10512)*
Garile Inc .... E 302 366-0848
Newark *(G-6639)*
Linkedin Profile Services LLC .... F 703 679-7719
Wilmington *(G-11397)*
Maples Fiduciary Svcs Del Inc .... G 302 338-9130
Wilmington *(G-11517)*
Wilcox & Fetzer Ltd .... E 302 655-0477
Wilmington *(G-13200)*

7342 Disinfecting & Pest Control Svcs

Accurate Pest Control Company .... E 302 875-2725
Laurel *(G-3189)*
Activ Pest & Lawn Inc .... F 302 645-1502
Lewes *(G-3324)*
Air Quality Remediation LLC .... F 302 464-1050
Townsend *(G-8755)*
Brasures Pest Control Inc .... E 302 436-8140
Selbyville *(G-8462)*
Bug Rite Extreminator Comp .... G 302 738-4373
Wilmington *(G-9502)*
Corteva Inc .... E 302 485-3000
Wilmington *(G-9869)*
Crystal Graham .... F 302 669-9318
Middletown *(G-4016)*
Delaware Mosquito Control LLC .... G 302 504-6757
Newark *(G-6398)*
Delmar Termite & Pest Control .... G 302 658-5010
Wilmington *(G-10101)*
Diamond Pest Control .... G 302 654-2300
Wilmington *(G-10141)*
Diamond State Commercial Clg .... G 215 888-2575
Bear *(G-116)*
Elkton Exterminating Co Inc .... F 302 368-9116
Newark *(G-6516)*
Guy Bug .... G 302 242-5254
Dover *(G-1619)*
Home Paramount Pest Control .... G 302 894-9201
New Castle *(G-5401)*
Ladybug Pest Management Inc .... G 302 846-2295
Delmar *(G-1014)*
Maguire & Sons Inc .... G 302 798-1200
Wilmington *(G-11488)*
Orkin LLC .... F 302 322-9569
New Castle *(G-5591)*
R W Home Services Inc .... F 302 539-4683
Ocean View *(G-7810)*
Rentokil North America Inc .... F 302 325-2687
Newark *(G-7319)*
Rentokil North America Inc .... F 302 337-8100
Bridgeville *(G-519)*
Rentokil North America Inc .... E 302 733-0851
Newark *(G-7318)*
Royal Pest Management .... G 302 322-3600
New Castle *(G-5687)*
Royal Pest Solutions Inc .... E 302 322-6665
New Castle *(G-5688)*
Royal Termite & Pest Ctrl Inc .... E 302 322-3600
New Castle *(G-5689)*
Terminix Intl Co Ltd Partnr .... E 302 653-4866
New Castle *(G-5761)*
Think Clean & Grounds Up LLC .... F 904 250-1614
New Castle *(G-5767)*
Total Pest Solutions .... G 302 275-7159
Camden Wyoming *(G-660)*
Tri State Termite & Pest Ctrl .... G 302 239-0512
Newark *(G-7585)*
True Pest Control Services .... G 302 834-0867
Middletown *(G-4270)*

7349 Building Cleaning & Maintenance Svcs, NEC

A1 Striping Inc .... G 302 738-5016
Newark *(G-5872)*
Able Whelling and Machiene .... G 302 436-1929
Selbyville *(G-8446)*
ABM Industries Incorporated .... E 302 999-1898
Wilmington *(G-8905)*
ABM Janitorial Services Inc .... A 302 571-9900
Wilmington *(G-8906)*

S I C

Employee Codes: A=Over 500 employees, B=251-500
C=101-250, D=51-100, E=20-50, F=10-19, G=1-9
2020 Harris Directory of
Delaware Businesses
523

73 BUSINESS SERVICES

Name	Code	Phone
Abrahams Seed LLC	G	302 588-1913
Clayton (G-831)		
Advanced Bizz Innovations LLC	G	302 397-1162
Townsend (G-8753)		
All Clean Services	G	302 378-7376
Townsend (G-8756)		
All Pro Maids Inc	E	302 645-9247
Lewes (G-3334)		
Als Power Washing Service	G	302 399-3406
Dover (G-1112)		
Alvins Professional Services	F	302 544-6634
New Castle (G-5028)		
Aqua Pro Inc	G	302 659-6593
Smyrna (G-8575)		
Aqua Wash Inc	G	302 994-1720
Newark (G-5992)		
Arrowsmith Cleaning Solutions	G	302 377-5614
Townsend (G-8759)		
Blue Chip Services Ltd	G	302 798-5010
Wilmington (G-9374)		
Bravo Building Services Inc	A	302 322-5959
New Castle (G-5108)		
Briggs Services LLC	G	302 569-5230
Ellendale (G-2258)		
Carr Paris	F	302 401-1203
Wilmington (G-9578)		
Catch-A-Web Cleaning Inc	E	302 836-1970
Bear (G-67)		
Chaffin Cleaning Service Inc	E	302 369-2704
Newark (G-6183)		
Christopher Handy	G	302 934-1018
Millsboro (G-4661)		
City Window Cleaning of Del	E	302 633-0633
Wilmington (G-9726)		
Clean Force Building Services	F	302 494-9330
Newark (G-6247)		
Clean Hands LLC	F	215 681-1435
Smyrna (G-8598)		
Clean Sweep	G	302 422-6085
Milford (G-4355)		
Cleaners Sunny	G	302 827-2095
Lewes (G-3428)		
Clearview Windows LLC	G	302 491-6768
Milford (G-4356)		
Coastal Maintenance LLC	G	302 536-1290
Seaford (G-8200)		
Colonial Cleaning Services Inc	G	302 660-2067
Wilmington (G-9773)		
Commercial Cleaning Services	G	302 764-3424
Wilmington (G-9785)		
Community Services Corporation	F	302 368-4400
Newark (G-6272)		
▲ Corporation Service Company	B	302 636-5400
Wilmington (G-9866)		
County Building Services Inc	D	302 377-4213
Middletown (G-4012)		
Crystal Graham	F	302 669-9318
Middletown (G-4016)		
D A Jones Inc	G	302 836-9238
Selbyville (G-8476)		
D C S Company	G	302 328-5138
New Castle (G-5212)		
David Jenkins	G	302 304-5568
Bear (G-96)		
Delmarva Cleaning & Maint Inc	C	302 734-1856
Dover (G-1409)		
Delores Welch	G	302 856-7989
Georgetown (G-2510)		
Diamond State Commercial Clg	G	215 888-2575
Bear (G-116)		
Dm Home Maintenance	G	302 945-5050
Millsboro (G-4679)		
Don-Lee Margin Corporation	E	302 629-7567
Seaford (G-8225)		
Dover Nunan LLC	G	302 697-9776
Dover (G-1461)		
Dream Clean Team LP	F	302 981-5154
Newark (G-6473)		
Dryzone LLC	G	302 684-5034
Milton (G-4899)		
Dss - Integrity LLC	E	302 677-0111
Dover (G-1482)		
Dss Services Inc	F	302 677-0111
Dover (G-1483)		
Dss Urban Joint Venture LLC	F	302 677-0111
Dover (G-1484)		
Ducts R US LLC	G	302 284-4006
Felton (G-2288)		
Dust Away Cleaning Svcs Inc	E	302 658-8803
Wilmington (G-10269)		
Eckels Family LLC	E	302 465-5224
Felton (G-2290)		
Efficient Services Inc	G	302 629-2124
Seaford (G-8234)		
Elite Commercial Cleaning Inc	D	302 366-8900
Newark (G-6514)		
Focus Solutions Services Inc	F	302 318-1345
Newark (G-6597)		
Fortress Home Maintenance Serv	G	302 539-3446
Ocean View (G-7785)		
Gemini Building Systems LLC	D	302 654-5310
Wilmington (G-10688)		
Gutter Connection LLC	G	302 736-0105
Dover (G-1617)		
H&S Cleaning Service Inc	E	302 449-2928
Townsend (G-8791)		
Harmon Investments LLC	G	302 383-2176
Wilmington (G-10837)		
Hood Man LLC	G	302 422-4564
Lincoln (G-3855)		
J & W Mc Cormick Ltd	E	302 798-0336
Wilmington (G-11099)		
JBA Enterprises	G	302 834-6685
Bear (G-198)		
Jrw Cleaning Solutions LLC	G	484 942-9995
Wilmington (G-11203)		
JV s Cleaning Services	G	302 345-7679
Bear (G-208)		
Kleen-Comp LLC	G	302 981-0791
Newark (G-6897)		
L & M Services Inc	F	302 658-3735
Wilmington (G-11306)		
M T O Clean of Sussex County	G	302 854-0204
Milton (G-4929)		
Maid For Shore	G	302 344-1857
Lewes (G-3617)		
Maids For You Inc	F	302 328-9050
New Castle (G-5500)		
Maintenance Tech	G	302 322-6410
New Castle (G-5502)		
Maintenance Troubleshooti	G	302 477-1045
Wilmington (G-11493)		
Markatos Services Inc	E	302 792-0606
Wilmington (G-11532)		
Marlings Inc	F	302 325-1759
New Castle (G-5509)		
Master Klean Company	G	302 539-4290
Ocean View (G-7802)		
Maude Burton	G	302 674-4210
Dover (G-1830)		
McClain Custodial Service	G	302 645-6597
Lewes (G-3629)		
Mebro Inc	E	302 992-0104
Wilmington (G-11613)		
Merry Maids Inc	F	302 698-9038
Dover (G-1841)		
Mid-Atlantic Services A-Team	D	302 984-9559
Wilmington (G-11681)		
Mid-Atlantic Services A-Team	E	302 628-3403
Seaford (G-8310)		
Nu World Building Service	F	302 678-2578
Dover (G-1909)		
Oceanside Elite Clg Bldg Svcs	E	302 339-7777
Lewes (G-3665)		
Optima Cleaning Systems Inc	D	302 652-3979
Wilmington (G-11963)		
Otis Kamara		443 207-2643
Dover (G-1925)		
Penwood Property Preservation	G	302 469-5318
Felton (G-2308)		
Pride Klean Inc	E	302 994-8500
Wilmington (G-12225)		
Priority Services LLC	E	302 918-3070
Newark (G-7258)		
Proclean	G	302 654-1074
New Castle (G-5649)		
Quality Assured Inc	E	302 652-4151
Wilmington (G-12277)		
R W Home Services Inc	F	302 539-4683
Ocean View (G-7810)		
Ras Addis & Associates Inc	G	302 571-1683
Wilmington (G-12318)		
Schoon Inc	G	302 894-7574
Newark (G-7394)		
Schweizer Cleaning Service	G	302 995-2816
Wilmington (G-12557)		
Serpro of Bear New Castle	G	302 392-6000
Bear (G-317)		
ServiceMaster of Newark	F	302 834-8006
Newark (G-7410)		
Simply Clean Jantr Svcs Inc	E	302 744-9100
Dover (G-2084)		
Slater Fireplaces Inc	G	302 999-1200
Wilmington (G-12645)		
St Andrews Maintenance	G	302 832-2675
Bear (G-335)		
Stl & Associates LLC	G	302 359-2801
Smyrna (G-8725)		
Superior Commercial Cleaning	G	302 897-2544
Newark (G-7513)		
Sussex Floor	G	302 629-5620
Seaford (G-8415)		
Swift Services Inc	G	302 328-1145
New Castle (G-5747)		
Teagle and Sons	G	302 682-8639
Seaford (G-8419)		
Teff Inc	F	302 856-9768
Georgetown (G-2689)		
Tlaloc Building Services Inc	F	302 559-6459
Bear (G-354)		
TMI Company Store Holding Corp	E	302 992-0220
Wilmington (G-12920)		
TNT Window Cleaning	G	302 326-2411
Newark (G-7570)		
Todds Janitorial Service Inc	G	302 378-8212
Middletown (G-4262)		
Top of The Line Jantr Svcs	G	302 645-2668
Lewes (G-3790)		
Tornado II Janitorial Service	F	302 898-1370
New Castle (G-5774)		
Totally Clean	F	302 376-3626
Middletown (G-4263)		
University of Delaware	C	302 831-1141
Newark (G-7625)		
Valet Cleaning Service	G	302 653-0233
Clayton (G-872)		
Vicks Commercial Clg & Maint	G	302 697-9591
Dover (G-2191)		
Whaleys Seed Store Inc	G	302 875-7833
Laurel (G-3308)		
Wilkins Enterprises Inc	G	302 945-4142
Lewes (G-3824)		

7352 Medical Eqpt Rental & Leasing

Name	Code	Phone
American Homepatient Inc	D	302 454-4941
Newark (G-5953)		
Apria Healthcare LLC	E	302 737-7979
Newark (G-5990)		
Broad Creek Medical Service	F	302 629-0202
Seaford (G-8174)		
Lincare Inc	G	302 424-8302
Felton (G-2305)		
Quinn-Miller Group Inc	G	302 738-9742
Wilmington (G-12290)		
Univita of Florida Inc	E	239 936-4449
Wilmington (G-13032)		

7353 Heavy Construction Eqpt Rental & Leasing

Name	Code	Phone
Active Crane Rentals Inc	E	302 998-1000
Wilmington (G-8927)		
▲ Blade Platforms LLC	G	646 431-1666
Wilmington (G-9366)		
Chesapeake Supply & Eqp Co	G	302 284-1000
Felton (G-2283)		
Don D Corp	E	302 994-5793
Wilmington (G-10192)		
Dozr Ltd	E	844 218-3697
Wilmington (G-10216)		
Eagle Power and Equipment Corp	F	302 652-3028
New Castle (G-5274)		
First State Crane Service	F	302 398-8885
Felton (G-2292)		
Heavy Equipment Rental Inc	F	302 654-5716
New Castle (G-5388)		
Interstate Aerials LLC	G	302 838-1117
Bear (G-190)		
▼ Iron Source LLC	G	302 856-7545
Georgetown (G-2568)		
Judd Brook 5 LLC	G	302 846-3355
Delmar (G-1011)		
Knight Hauling Inc	G	610 494-6800
Wilmington (G-11281)		
Raven Crane & Equipment Co LLC	G	302 998-1000
New Castle (G-5667)		
Sunbelt Rentals Inc	F	302 907-1921
Delmar (G-1032)		
Sunbelt Rentals Inc	G	302 669-0595
New Castle (G-5743)		

7359 Equipment Rental & Leasing, NEC

A V Resources Inc ....G.... 302 994-1488
Wilmington *(G-8886)*
A-1 Sanitation Service Inc ....F.... 302 322-1074
New Castle *(G-4995)*
AAA Portable Restroom Co Inc ....G.... 909 981-0090
Camden Wyoming *(G-610)*
Aardvark Party Rentals LLC ....G.... 302 331-1929
Bear *(G-8)*
Aarons Inc ....G.... 302 221-1200
New Castle *(G-4996)*
Aarons Sales & Leasing ....G.... 302 628-8870
Seaford *(G-8136)*
Action Rental Inc ....G.... 302 366-0749
Newark *(G-5894)*
Action Unlimited Resources Inc ....E.... 302 323-1455
New Castle *(G-5001)*
Actors Attic ....G.... 302 734-8214
Dover *(G-1084)*
American Furniture Rentals Inc ....E.... 302 323-1682
New Castle *(G-5032)*
Arrow Leasing Corp ....F.... 302 834-4546
Bear *(G-36)*
B Williams Holding Corp ....F.... 302 656-8596
Wilmington *(G-9214)*
Brandywine Electronics Corp ....F.... 302 324-9992
Bear *(G-56)*
Brewster Products Inc ....G.... 302 798-1988
Wilmington *(G-9468)*
Burke Equipment Company ....D.... 302 697-3200
Felton *(G-2278)*
Carrier Rental Systems Inc ....E.... 302 836-3000
Bear *(G-65)*
Celera Services Inc ....G.... 302 378-7778
Middletown *(G-3982)*
Chesapeake Supply & Eqp Co ....G.... 302 284-1000
Felton *(G-2283)*
Coastal Rentals Hydraulics LLC ....G.... 302 251-3103
Millville *(G-4840)*
Darby Leasing LLC ....G.... 302 477-0500
Wilmington *(G-9960)*
Diamond Chemical & Supply Co ....E.... 302 656-7786
Wilmington *(G-10139)*
Diamond State Pty Rentl & Sls ....E.... 302 777-6677
Wilmington *(G-10146)*
Dover Rent-All Inc ....F.... 302 739-0860
Dover *(G-1469)*
Enterprise Flasher Co Inc ....F.... 302 999-0856
Wilmington *(G-10407)*
Excape Entertainment US Ltd ....G.... 949 943-9219
Wilmington *(G-10457)*
Gge Amusements ....G.... 302 227-0661
Rehoboth Beach *(G-7947)*
Gian-Co ....E.... 302 798-7100
Claymont *(G-753)*
Grand Rental Station ....G.... 302 227-7368
Rehoboth Beach *(G-7954)*
Groff Tractor & Equipment LLC ....F.... 302 349-5760
Greenwood *(G-2742)*
Home Depot USA Inc ....C.... 302 838-6818
Newark *(G-6739)*
Home Depot USA Inc ....C.... 302 395-1260
New Castle *(G-5400)*
Home Depot USA Inc ....C.... 302 735-8864
Dover *(G-1652)*
J R Rents Inc ....F.... 302 266-8090
Newark *(G-6820)*
J&S Leasing Co Inc ....G.... 302 328-1066
New Castle *(G-5432)*
Junttan USA Inc ....G.... 302 500-1274
Laurel *(G-3246)*
Material Handling Supply Inc ....F.... 302 571-0176
New Castle *(G-5511)*
Mid South Audio LLC ....G.... 302 856-6993
Georgetown *(G-2603)*
Milford Rent All Inc ....G.... 302 422-0100
Milford *(G-4503)*
Milford Rental Center Inc ....G.... 302 422-0315
Dover *(G-1857)*
Morton Electric Co ....G.... 302 645-9414
Lewes *(G-3650)*
National Rig Rental LLC ....G.... 302 539-1963
Frankford *(G-2378)*
Penske Truck Leasing Co LP ....E.... 302 325-9290
New Castle *(G-5617)*
Professional Leasing Inc ....G.... 302 629-4350
Seaford *(G-8365)*
Queen B Tbl Chair Rentals LLC ....G.... 215 960-6303
Dover *(G-2002)*
Quillens Rent All Inc ....G.... 302 227-3151
Rehoboth Beach *(G-8039)*
Rent Co Inc ....F.... 302 674-1177
Dover *(G-2029)*
Rent-A-Center Inc ....G.... 302 653-3701
Smyrna *(G-8700)*
Rent-A-Center Inc ....E.... 302 322-4335
New Castle *(G-5671)*
Rent-A-Center Inc ....G.... 302 731-7900
Newark *(G-7317)*
Rent-A-Center Inc ....G.... 302 654-7700
Wilmington *(G-12380)*
Rent-A-Center Inc ....G.... 302 678-4676
Dover *(G-2030)*
Rent-A-Center Inc ....G.... 302 838-7333
Bear *(G-302)*
Rent-A-Center Inc ....G.... 302 674-5060
Dover *(G-2031)*
Rent-A-Center Inc ....G.... 302 934-6700
Millsboro *(G-4788)*
Rent-A-Center Inc ....G.... 302 629-8925
Seaford *(G-8377)*
Rent-A-Center Inc ....G.... 302 734-3505
Dover *(G-2032)*
Rent-A-Center Inc ....G.... 302 856-9200
Georgetown *(G-2636)*
Rent-A-Center Inc ....G.... 302 422-1230
Milford *(G-4537)*
Right Way Flagging and Sign Co ....E.... 302 698-5229
Camden Wyoming *(G-653)*
Ryder Truck Rental Inc ....E.... 302 798-1472
Wilmington *(G-12501)*
Shell We Bounce ....G.... 302 727-5411
Rehoboth Beach *(G-8073)*
Sussex Protection Service LLC ....F.... 302 337-0209
Bridgeville *(G-522)*
Temp-Air Inc ....F.... 302 369-3880
Newark *(G-7555)*
◆ **Ten Talents Enterprises Inc** ....G.... 302 409-0718
Middletown *(G-4255)*
Total Construction Rentals Inc ....F.... 302 575-1132
New Castle *(G-5775)*
United Rentals North Amer Inc ....E.... 302 328-2900
New Castle *(G-5807)*
United Rentals North Amer Inc ....F.... 302 846-0955
Delmar *(G-1045)*
Video Den ....G.... 302 628-9835
Seaford *(G-8431)*

7361 Employment Agencies

924 Inc ....E.... 302 656-6100
Wilmington *(G-8870)*
A&F Group LLC ....G.... 302 504-9937
Wilmington *(G-8887)*
Access Labor Service Inc ....F.... 302 326-2575
New Castle *(G-5000)*
Accu Personnel Inc ....F.... 302 384-8777
Wilmington *(G-8917)*
Adecco Usa Inc ....G.... 302 669-4005
New Castle *(G-5003)*
Alpha Technologies Consulting ....F.... 302 898-2862
Townsend *(G-8757)*
Altea Resources LLC ....D.... 713 242-1460
Dover *(G-1113)*
Barbizon of Delaware Inc ....E.... 302 658-6666
Wilmington *(G-9249)*
Barrett Business Services Inc ....G.... 302 674-2206
Dover *(G-1173)*
Bernard and Bernard Inc ....G.... 302 999-7213
Wilmington *(G-9306)*
Careers Usa Inc ....G.... 302 737-3600
New Castle *(G-5132)*
Caring N Action Nursing ....G.... 302 368-2273
Newark *(G-6155)*
CBI Group LLc ....E.... 302 266-0860
Newark *(G-6174)*
Centrix Hr ....G.... 302 777-7818
Wilmington *(G-9616)*
Christiana Care Home Health ....F.... 302 698-4300
Camden *(G-549)*
Christiana Consulting Inc ....G.... 302 454-7000
Newark *(G-6221)*
Coastal Hospitality LLC ....G.... 302 304-3156
Wilmington *(G-9752)*
Community Integrated Services ....E.... 215 238-7411
Milford *(G-4362)*
Computer Staffing Services LLC ....E.... 302 737-4920
Newark *(G-6278)*
Conducerent Incorporated ....G.... 302 543-8525
Wilmington *(G-9816)*
Congruence Consulting Group ....G.... 320 290-6155
Newark *(G-6286)*
Contemprary Stffing Sltons Inc ....G.... 302 328-1300
New Castle *(G-5192)*
D-Staffing Consulting Svcs LLC ....D.... 302 402-5678
Dover *(G-1336)*
Delaware Registry Ltd ....G.... 302 477-9800
Wilmington *(G-10078)*
Delaware Valley Group LLC ....G.... 302 777-7007
Wilmington *(G-10095)*
Dkmrbh Inc ....F.... 302 250-4428
Wilmington *(G-10173)*
Elite Office Staff Inc ....D.... 302 387-4158
Dover *(G-1514)*
Exclusively Legal Inc ....F.... 302 239-5990
Hockessin *(G-3025)*
Global Network Executive Inc ....F.... 302 251-8940
Wilmington *(G-10728)*
Global Recruiters Network Inc ....G.... 302 455-9500
Newark *(G-6667)*
Hastin-Karin Inc ....G.... 347 377-8415
Wilmington *(G-10851)*
Hornberger Management Company ....G.... 302 573-2541
Wilmington *(G-10956)*
Howroyd-Wright Emplymnt Agcy ....G.... 302 738-4022
Newark *(G-6752)*
Hyper Jobs LLC ....E.... 786 667-0905
Newark *(G-6757)*
Insignia Global Corporation ....G.... 302 310-4107
Wilmington *(G-11039)*
Integrity Staffing Solutions ....A.... 302 661-8770
Newark *(G-6792)*
Jobs For Delaware Graduates ....E.... 302 734-9341
Dover *(G-1699)*
Joseph Moore ....G.... 302 478-5659
Wilmington *(G-11194)*
Kna Solutions LLC ....G.... 302 709-1215
Dover *(G-1753)*
Majestique Ventures & Hlth Cre ....E.... 302 633-4010
Wilmington *(G-11495)*
Marine Corps United States ....G.... 302 376-3590
Middletown *(G-4145)*
Mwidm Inc ....E.... 302 298-0101
Wilmington *(G-11785)*
Nurses Connection ....G.... 302 421-3687
Wilmington *(G-11923)*
Opportunity Center Inc ....D.... 302 762-0300
New Castle *(G-5589)*
Opus Financial Svcs USA Inc ....G.... 646 435-5616
Wilmington *(G-11966)*
Premier Staffing Solutions Inc ....G.... 302 344-5996
Georgetown *(G-2625)*
Premier Staffing Solutions Inc ....D.... 302 628-7700
Seaford *(G-8362)*
Professional Recruiting Cons ....G.... 302 479-9550
Wilmington *(G-12239)*
Ramona Clay ....G.... 866 448-0834
Wilmington *(G-12314)*
Randstad Professionals Us LLC ....F.... 302 658-6181
Wilmington *(G-12316)*
Redleo Software Inc ....F.... 302 691-9072
Wilmington *(G-12348)*
Relig Staffing Inc ....E.... 312 219-6786
Dover *(G-2022)*
Robert Half International Inc ....E.... 302 252-3162
Wilmington *(G-12439)*
Service General Corp ....C.... 302 856-3500
Georgetown *(G-2651)*
Servicexpress Corporation ....A.... 302 854-9118
Seaford *(G-8399)*
Servicexpress Corporation ....C.... 302 424-3500
Milford *(G-4556)*
Servicexpress Corporation ....G.... 302 856-3500
Georgetown *(G-2652)*
Silicon Valley Ht Partners LP ....G.... 213 272-0088
Camden *(G-600)*
Staffmark Investment LLC ....G.... 302 422-0606
Milford *(G-4569)*
Staffmark Investment LLC ....G.... 302 854-0650
Georgetown *(G-2665)*
Trinity Cloud Company ....E.... 973 494-8190
Wilmington *(G-12974)*
Whitecrow Research Inc ....F.... 908 752-4200
Wilmington *(G-13193)*
Whitehook Solutions LLC ....G.... 302 222-5177
Smyrna *(G-8744)*
Wilmington Senior Center Inc ....F.... 302 651-3440
Wilmington *(G-13256)*

S I C

Employee Codes: A=Over 500 employees, B=251-500
C=101-250, D=51-100, E=20-50, F=10-19, G=1-9
2020 Harris Directory of Delaware Businesses
525

73 BUSINESS SERVICES

7363 Help Supply Svcs

Access Labor Service Inc .... E 302 741-2575
  Dover *(G-1081)*
Adecco Usa Inc .... G 302 457-4059
  Newark *(G-5899)*
Aero Ways Inc .... F 302 324-9970
  New Castle *(G-5014)*
Aerotek Inc .... E 302 561-6300
  New Castle *(G-5015)*
Barrett Business Services Inc .... G 302 674-2206
  Dover *(G-1173)*
Benitime Solutions Inc .... G 302 476-8097
  Wilmington *(G-9302)*
Bestemps .... G 302 674-4357
  Dover *(G-1198)*
BP Staffing Inc .... G 302 999-7213
  Wilmington *(G-9407)*
Career Associates Inc .... G 302 674-4357
  Dover *(G-1255)*
County of Kent .... D 302 735-2180
  Dover *(G-1317)*
County of Sussex .... D 302 854-5050
  Georgetown *(G-2489)*
Eden Hill Express Care LLC .... E 302 674-1999
  Dover *(G-1504)*
Employers Bench Inc .... F 973 757-1912
  Christiana *(G-667)*
Fladger & Associates Inc .... E 302 836-3100
  Bear *(G-155)*
GSM Systems Inc .... F 302 284-8304
  Viola *(G-8836)*
Haymy Resources LLC .... G 402 218-6787
  Lewes *(G-3537)*
Integrity Staffing Solutions .... A 520 276-7775
  Newark *(G-6791)*
Interim Health Care .... G 302 322-2743
  New Castle *(G-5422)*
Interim Healthcare Del LLC .... C 302 322-2743
  Smyrna *(G-8658)*
J&J Staffing Resources Inc .... G 302 738-7800
  Newark *(G-6821)*
Kelly Services Inc .... F 302 323-4748
  New Castle *(G-5459)*
Kelly Services Inc .... G 302 674-8087
  Dover *(G-1731)*
Manpowergroup Inc .... G 302 674-8600
  Dover *(G-1813)*
Partsquarry-Aviation Div .... G 302 703-7195
  Wilmington *(G-12029)*
Placers Inc of Delaware .... F 302 709-0973
  Newark *(G-7221)*
Staffmark Investment LLC .... E 302 834-2303
  Bear *(G-336)*
Timber Ridge Inc .... E 302 239-9239
  Hockessin *(G-3161)*
Transworld Diversfd Svcs Inc .... F 302 777-5902
  Wilmington *(G-12959)*
Triglia Trans Co .... E 302 846-3795
  Delmar *(G-1041)*
Walker & Sons Inc .... F 302 653-5635
  Smyrna *(G-8738)*
Webro Holdings LLC .... G 302 314-3334
  Rehoboth Beach *(G-8109)*

7371 Custom Computer Programming Svcs

1 Software Place .... G 302 533-0344
  Newark *(G-5851)*
360tovisit Inc .... F 302 526-0575
  Newark *(G-5858)*
3rdgp LLC .... F 905 330-3335
  Dover *(G-1069)*
A2ps Consulting and Sftwr LLC .... F 331 201-6101
  Wilmington *(G-8891)*
Accelertrain Company Limited ...... G 413 599-0450
  Dover *(G-1079)*
Adferns Media LLC .... G 315 444-7720
  Dover *(G-1086)*
Afrikelist Corporation .... F 800 767-1744
  Wilmington *(G-8974)*
Agora Net Inc .... F 302 224-2475
  Newark *(G-5920)*
Aila Pty Inc .... E 626 693-0598
  Newark *(G-5922)*
Alias Technology LLC .... G 302 856-9488
  Georgetown *(G-2428)*
Ampx2 Inc .... G 650 521-5750
  Dover *(G-1121)*
Angee Inc .... E 650 320-1775
  Wilmington *(G-9083)*
Animatra Inc .... G 303 350-9264
  Lewes *(G-3342)*
Annexus Health LLC .... F 302 547-4154
  Wilmington *(G-9087)*
Anotherai Inc .... G 408 987-1927
  Lewes *(G-3343)*
Antitoxin Technologies Inc .... E 650 304-0608
  Dover *(G-1129)*
Apphive Inc .... G 240 898-4661
  Newark *(G-5984)*
Appic Stars LLC .... G 903 224-6469
  Dover *(G-1131)*
Applied Control Engrg Inc .... D 302 738-8800
  Newark *(G-5987)*
Apploye Inc .... G 925 452-6102
  Newark *(G-5989)*
ARA Technologies Inc .... G 215 605-5707
  Wilmington *(G-9109)*
Ardexo Inc .... G 855 617-7500
  Dover *(G-1134)*
Aries Security LLC .... G 302 365-0026
  Wilmington *(G-9128)*
Arnab Mobility Inc .... F 774 316-6767
  Newark *(G-5997)*
Ask Connoisseur LLC .... G 302 482-8026
  Claymont *(G-695)*
Atoze Inc .... G 415 992-7936
  Newark *(G-6025)*
Aum LLC .... F 302 385-6767
  Wilmington *(G-9182)*
Autoweb Technologies Inc .... G 443 485-4200
  Wilmington *(G-9192)*
B&H Insurance LLC .... E 302 995-2247
  Newark *(G-6036)*
Babilonia Inc .... G 415 237-3339
  Newark *(G-6039)*
Bantam Technologies LLC .... G 302 256-5823
  Wilmington *(G-9245)*
Bar Code Software Inc .... G 410 360-7455
  Frankford *(G-2346)*
Barclays PLC .... E 302 622-8990
  Wilmington *(G-9252)*
Bathwa Limited .... D 213 550-3812
  New Castle *(G-5068)*
Bbest LLC .... F 302 581-9963
  Wilmington *(G-9269)*
Biomedic Data Systems Inc .... A 302 628-4100
  Seaford *(G-8171)*
Birdie Ssot LLC .... G 857 361-6883
  Dover *(G-1205)*
Bits & Bytes Inc .... G 302 674-2999
  Dover *(G-1207)*
Black Math Labs Inc .... G 858 349-9446
  Dover *(G-1208)*
Blair Computing Systems Inc .... F 302 453-8947
  Newark *(G-6091)*
Blaze Systems Corporation .... G 302 733-7235
  Newark *(G-6092)*
Blix Inc .... E 347 753-8035
  Newark *(G-6094)*
Blu Dragon Studio Inc .... G 302 722-6227
  Newark *(G-6097)*
Bml App Development .... G 302 528-7281
  Wilmington *(G-9386)*
Bolt Innovation LLC .... G 800 293-5249
  Dover *(G-1220)*
Booking Bullet Inc .... G 416 988-2354
  Newark *(G-6106)*
Boxhero Inc .... G 827 867-4320
  Middletown *(G-3971)*
Breckenridge Software Tech .... G 302 656-8460
  Wilmington *(G-9464)*
Brittons Wise Computers Inc .... G 302 659-0343
  Smyrna *(G-8587)*
Brown Eagle Inc .... E 302 295-3816
  Wilmington *(G-9489)*
Bryant Technologies Inc .... G 302 289-2044
  Felton *(G-2276)*
Bsbv Inc .... G 631 201-2044
  Lewes *(G-3392)*
Buzlin Inc .... G 800 829-0115
  Camden *(G-542)*
Bysness Inc .... F 937 687-8701
  Wilmington *(G-9518)*
Capture Technologies Inc .... G 650 772-8006
  Wilmington *(G-9559)*
Carzaty Inc .... F 650 396-0144
  Dover *(G-1258)*
Cell Point LLC .... D 302 658-9200
  Wilmington *(G-9610)*
Change Shop LLC .... G 301 363-7188
  Newark *(G-6187)*
Channelpro Mobile LLC .... F 757 620-4635
  Newark *(G-6188)*
Chemaxon LLC .... G 281 528-0485
  Wilmington *(G-9645)*
Cim Concepts Incorporated .... F 302 613-5400
  New Castle *(G-5161)*
Classroomapp Inc .... G 833 257-7761
  Lewes *(G-3426)*
Client Monster LLC .... G 866 799-5433
  Newark *(G-6250)*
Clinpharma Clinical RES LLC ...... G 646 961-3437
  Wilmington *(G-9744)*
Cloud Software Development LLC ... G 703 957-9847
  Wilmington *(G-9747)*
Cloudbees Inc .... F 804 767-5481
  Lewes *(G-3430)*
Cloudbees Inc .... F 323 842-7783
  Lewes *(G-3431)*
Clymene LLC .... G 888 679-3310
  Lewes *(G-3433)*
Codeship Inc .... F 617 515-3664
  Lewes *(G-3440)*
Collections Marketing Center .... E 302 830-9262
  Wilmington *(G-9769)*
Commtrak Corporation .... G 302 644-1600
  Lewes *(G-3443)*
Compassred Inc .... G 302 383-2856
  Wilmington *(G-9803)*
Computer Aid Inc .... C 302 831-5500
  Newark *(G-6276)*
Conci LLC .... D 847 665-9285
  Wilmington *(G-9808)*
Congruence Consulting Group ..... G 320 290-6155
  Newark *(G-6286)*
Conrep Inc .... G 302 528-8383
  Middletown *(G-4007)*
Construct App Inc .... F 415 702-0634
  Wilmington *(G-9834)*
Contact Info Inc .... G 917 817-7939
  Dover *(G-1312)*
Continuum Media LLC .... F 310 295-9997
  Camden *(G-552)*
Conventra LLC .... G 302 378-4461
  Middletown *(G-4008)*
Corvant LLC .... F 302 299-1570
  Newark *(G-6302)*
Covant Solutions Inc .... G 302 607-2678
  Newark *(G-6307)*
Cratis Solutions Inc .... G 515 423-7259
  Dover *(G-1320)*
Cubics Inc .... G 302 261-5751
  Newark *(G-6324)*
Cyber Seven Technologies LLC ... G 302 635-7122
  Newark *(G-6335)*
Data Age International LLC .... E 302 760-9222
  Wilmington *(G-9961)*
Data-Bi LLC .... G 302 290-3138
  Wilmington *(G-9962)*
Datatech Enterprises Inc .... F 540 370-0010
  Selbyville *(G-8478)*
Dax-Wave Consulting LLC .... G 424 543-6662
  Wilmington *(G-9974)*
DC Consulting Service LLC .... F 617 594-9780
  Wilmington *(G-9976)*
Decisivedge Inc .... G 302 299-1570
  Newark *(G-6357)*
Dekadu Inc .... G 763 390-3266
  Wilmington *(G-9996)*
Delaware Beacon Network LLC ... G 302 218-2755
  Wilmington *(G-10006)*
Digital Penguin Inc .... G 484 387-7803
  Newark *(G-6448)*
Dining Software Group Inc .... G 720 236-9572
  Camden *(G-562)*
Discidium Technology Inc .... G 347 220-5979
  Newark *(G-6455)*
DOE Technologies Inc .... E 302 792-1285
  Wilmington *(G-10181)*
Done Again Software LLC .... G 301 466-7858
  Lewes *(G-3469)*
Dream Weaver LLC .... G 302 352-9473
  Wilmington *(G-10232)*
Drop Table LLC .... G 650 669-8753
  Wilmington *(G-10237)*
E2e LLC .... G 703 906-5353
  Hockessin *(G-3014)*
Eagle Eye America Inc .... G 302 392-3600
  Bear *(G-134)*

2020 Harris Directory of Delaware Businesses

SIC SECTION
73 BUSINESS SERVICES

Company	Code	Phone
Ekalt LLC	G	302 300-4853
Wilmington (G-10365)		
Encross LLC	F	302 351-2593
Wilmington (G-10396)		
Endevor LLC	G	302 543-5055
Wilmington (G-10397)		
English Tech LLC	G	844 707-9904
Dover (G-1524)		
Epic Kings LLC	G	302 669-9018
Claymont (G-739)		
Epiq Systems Inc	E	302 574-2600
Wilmington (G-10426)		
Epotec Inc	C	302 654-3090
Wilmington (G-10427)		
Et International Inc	F	302 266-6426
Newark (G-6541)		
Eventzilla Corporation	G	888 817-2837
Wilmington (G-10444)		
Evolution Rx LLC	G	614 344-4600
Townsend (G-8786)		
Exa Solutions Inc	G	302 273-9320
Newark (G-6548)		
Extreme Scale Solutions LLC	G	302 540-7149
Newark (G-6558)		
Fabby Inc	F	408 891-7991
Wilmington (G-10470)		
Fabit Corp	G	832 217-0864
Wilmington (G-10471)		
Falcons Media Group Inc	G	201 247-6489
Wilmington (G-10483)		
Famoid Technology LLC	G	530 601-7284
New Castle (G-5303)		
Fever Labs Inc	G	646 781-7359
Camden (G-571)		
Figgo Inc	F	734 560-1300
Newark (G-6578)		
File Right LLC	G	302 757-7107
Middletown (G-4070)		
Fitwise Inc	G	812 929-2696
Middletown (G-4073)		
Fleek Inc	G	888 870-1291
Wilmington (G-10572)		
Flowpay Corporation	G	720 425-3244
Wilmington (G-10580)		
Four Point Solutions Ltd	E	613 907-6400
Wilmington (G-10605)		
Foxfire Industries LLC	G	817 602-4900
Newark (G-6609)		
Franchise Command Inc	E	714 832-7767
Newark (G-6611)		
Ftl Technologies Corporation	F	703 873-7801
Lewes (G-3505)		
Fx-Edge LLC	E	718 404-9362
Lewes (G-3507)		
Gamers4gamers LLC	G	302 722-6289
Newark (G-6636)		
Gatesair Inc	G	513 459-3400
Wilmington (G-10676)		
Genex Technologies Inc	D	302 266-6161
Newark (G-6647)		
Geo-Fence Inc	G	763 516-8934
Dover (G-1589)		
Getresponse Inc	G	302 573-3895
Wilmington (G-10705)		
Ghg Enterprises LLC	G	817 705-0313
Wilmington (G-10709)		
Giesela Inc	G	855 556-4338
Newark (G-6653)		
Gigkloud Inc	F	301 375-5008
Lewes (G-3514)		
Global Exterior LLC	G	302 722-1969
Middletown (G-4089)		
Golden Shell Corp	G	917 951-6118
Dover (G-1599)		
Gossamer Games LLC	G	302 645-7400
Lewes (G-3520)		
Got Health-E LLC	G	203 583-5447
Wilmington (G-10755)		
Gotit Inc	F	408 382-1300
Dover (G-1602)		
Gulch Group LLC	G	202 697-1756
Rehoboth Beach (G-7956)		
Gw Solutions LLC	G	240 578-5981
Bethany Beach (G-402)		
Gyst Inc	G	631 680-4307
Dover (G-1620)		
Har-Lex LLC	G	302 476-2322
Wilmington (G-10835)		
Hashr8 Software LLC	G	702 473-0426
Newark (G-6713)		
Healex Systems Ltd	E	302 235-5750
Wilmington (G-10866)		
Hexact Inc	G	850 716-1616
Newark (G-6726)		
Himalaya Trading Inc	G	702 833-0485
Dover (G-1647)		
Homself Limited	D	213 269-5469
Middletown (G-4108)		
Hoover Computer Services Inc	G	302 529-7050
Wilmington (G-10950)		
Horizon Systems Inc	G	302 983-3203
New Castle (G-5404)		
Hubgets Inc	G	239 206-2995
Wilmington (G-10970)		
Hypergames Inc	G	424 343-6370
Wilmington (G-10982)		
Imagine Technologies	G	240 428-8406
Newark (G-6767)		
Implify Inc	G	302 533-2345
Newark (G-6769)		
Inbit Inc	G	302 603-7437
Dover (G-1669)		
Inclind Inc	G	302 856-2802
Lewes (G-3556)		
Infevo Technologies Co Ltd	G	626 703-8197
Newark (G-6777)		
Informal Inc	G	415 504-2106
Newark (G-6780)		
Innclude LLC	G	310 430-6552
Wilmington (G-11037)		
Insight Engineering Solutions	G	302 378-4842
Townsend (G-8797)		
Intelligent Systems Inc	G	302 388-0566
Newark (G-6795)		
Intouch Inc	G	302 313-2594
Dover (G-1683)		
Intoyou Inc	G	818 309-5115
Milford (G-4451)		
Inumsoft Inc	G	302 533-5403
Bear (G-191)		
Iroi Management LLC	F	516 373-5269
Lewes (G-3562)		
Itango Inc	G	302 648-2646
Wilmington (G-11091)		
Itennisyou LLC	G	305 890-3234
Newark (G-6810)		
Iveeapp Corp	G	610 999-6290
Wilmington (G-11094)		
Ivychat Inc	F	201 567-5694
Newark (G-6811)		
Joincube Inc	F	214 532-9997
Dover (G-1706)		
Jsi Group LLC	G	267 582-5850
Hockessin (G-3070)		
Juni Holdings Inc	F	415 949-4860
Wilmington (G-11209)		
Kaleido Health Solutions Inc	G	908 721-7020
Wilmington (G-11221)		
Keyboarders LLC	G	302 438-8055
Wilmington (G-11250)		
Keylent Inc	E	401 864-6498
Wilmington (G-11251)		
Kissflow Inc	C	650 396-7692
Wilmington (G-11276)		
Knowt Inc	F	848 391-0575
Lewes (G-3585)		
Kortech Consulting Inc	F	302 559-4612
Bear (G-220)		
Kwikbuck Inc	G	774 517-8959
Wilmington (G-11305)		
Labware Inc	E	302 658-8444
Wilmington (G-11319)		
Labware Global Services Inc	F	302 658-8444
Wilmington (G-11321)		
Labware Holdings Inc	E	302 658-8444
Wilmington (G-11322)		
Lamed LLC	G	302 597-9018
Newark (G-6914)		
LAp Studios Inc	F	213 357-0825
Newark (G-6917)		
Live Typing Inc	G	415 670-9601
Wilmington (G-11412)		
Lnbe LLC	E	302 393-2201
Wilmington (G-11417)		
Loom Network Inc	F	404 939-1294
Wilmington (G-11434)		
Lumulabs Inc	G	302 261-5284
Newark (G-6957)		
Maan Softwares Inc	E	531 203-9141
Lewes (G-3615)		
Made By Tilde Inc	G	302 766-7215
Newark (G-6970)		
Madrona Labs Inc	G	216 375-1978
Wilmington (G-11483)		
Maestrik Inc	E	312 925-3116
Newark (G-6971)		
Makave International Trdg LLC	E	302 288-0670
Dover (G-1812)		
Mara Labs Inc	G	650 564-4971
Wilmington (G-11518)		
Mayjuun LLC	G	865 300-7738
Lewes (G-3628)		
Medici Ventures Inc	E	801 319-7029
Wilmington (G-11617)		
Mentor Consultants Inc	G	610 566-4004
Wilmington (G-11633)		
Metaquotes Software Corp	E	657 859-6918
Wilmington (G-11648)		
Mican Technologies Inc	F	302 703-0708
Bear (G-252)		
Microcom Tech LLC	G	858 775-5559
Rehoboth Beach (G-8005)		
Microlog Corporation Maryland	G	301 540-5501
Rehoboth Beach (G-8006)		
Microsoft Corporation	E	302 669-0200
Newark (G-7025)		
Middleware Inc	G	415 213-2625
Wilmington (G-11683)		
Mightyinvoice LLC	G	302 415-3000
Dover (G-1854)		
Minoti Inc	F	720 725-0720
Lewes (G-3644)		
Miss Mafia LLC	F	800 246-2677
Wilmington (G-11713)		
Mithril Cable Network Inc	F	213 373-4381
Claymont (G-783)		
Mobile Alerts LLC	E	202 596-8709
Dover (G-1867)		
Modern Masters Inc	G	240 800-6622
Dover (G-1868)		
Morrow Limited	D	213 631-3534
Montchanin (G-4987)		
Moscase Inc	G	786 520-8062
Dover (G-1874)		
Moving Sciences LLC	E	617 871-9892
Wilmington (G-11764)		
Mssgme Inc	G	786 233-7592
Dover (G-1877)		
Must App Corp	F	905 537-5522
Wilmington (G-11779)		
Mymedchoices Inc	G	302 932-1920
Hockessin (G-3100)		
Myschedule Inc	G	877 235-6825
Wilmington (G-11790)		
Naiva Solutions Inc	F	612 987-6350
Newark (G-7082)		
Nationwide Hlth Info Tech Inc	G	302 295-5033
Wilmington (G-11815)		
Neutec Corp	G	302 697-6752
Dover (G-1896)		
New Concept Technologies LLC	E	518 533-5367
Wilmington (G-11860)		
Next Music Inc	G	650 300-4881
Wilmington (G-11881)		
Next Trucking Inc	E	213 568-0388
Wilmington (G-11882)		
Ninety One Holding Inc	E	212 203-7900
Bethany Beach (G-418)		
Noble Master	G	302 261-2018
Lewes (G-3660)		
Novo Financial Corp	F	844 260-6800
Dover (G-1906)		
Nvcomputers Inc	G	860 878-0525
Wilmington (G-11924)		
Objects Worldwide Inc	G	703 623-7861
Wilmington (G-11931)		
Omni Games Inc	G	302 652-4800
Wilmington (G-11949)		
Omninet International Inc	E	208 246-5022
Wilmington (G-11950)		
One System Incorporated	G	888 311-1110
Wilmington (G-11956)		
Operata LLC	G	302 525-0190
Newark (G-7156)		
Orbeex Trading Inc	F	786 403-9124
Wilmington (G-11970)		
Otw Technologies Inc	G	813 230-4212
Dover (G-1926)		
Ovo Digital Services LLC	G	415 741-1615
Wilmington (G-11986)		

Employee Codes: A=Over 500 employees, B=251-500
C=101-250, D=51-100, E=20-50, F=10-19, G=1-9

2020 Harris Directory of Delaware Businesses

Pathao Inc....G.... 845 242-3834
Dover *(G-1939)*
Pathscale Inc....E.... 408 520-0811
Wilmington *(G-12031)*
PDr Vc Ltd Liability Company....G.... 424 281-4669
Wilmington *(G-12056)*
Peeper Vehicle Technology Corp....G.... 800 971-4134
Dover *(G-1943)*
People Over Profit LLC....G.... 718 612-0328
Dover *(G-1947)*
Perkwiz Inc....G.... 702 866-9122
Hockessin *(G-3116)*
Petcube Inc....E.... 786 375-9065
Wilmington *(G-12093)*
Phly LLC....G.... 778 882-2391
Wilmington *(G-12122)*
Pike Creek Computer Company....F.... 302 239-5113
Wilmington *(G-12137)*
Pks & Company PA....G.... 302 645-5757
Lewes *(G-3693)*
Play US Media LLC....G.... 302 924-5034
Dover *(G-1965)*
Playphone Inc....G.... 415 307-0246
Dover *(G-1967)*
Playsight Interactive USA Inc....F.... 800 246-2677
Wilmington *(G-12156)*
PLM Consulting Inc....F.... 302 984-2698
Wilmington *(G-12160)*
Pointlook Corporation....G.... 415 448-6002
Wilmington *(G-12179)*
Polar Strategy Inc....G.... 703 628-0001
Lewes *(G-3695)*
Polymorphic Software Inc....G.... 786 612-0257
Wilmington *(G-12185)*
Precisioncure LLC....G.... 302 622-9119
Wilmington *(G-12208)*
Professionals LLC....G.... 302 295-2330
Wilmington *(G-12240)*
Progressive Software Cmpt Inc....C.... 302 479-9700
Wilmington *(G-12244)*
Project Assistants Inc....E.... 302 477-9711
Wilmington *(G-12246)*
Protech Solutions Group LLC....G.... 844 744-2418
Wilmington *(G-12254)*
Protocol Labs Inc....F.... 302 703-7194
Wilmington *(G-12256)*
Purpose Ministries Inc....G.... 302 753-0435
Newark *(G-7273)*
Pxe Group LLC....G.... 561 295-1451
Dover *(G-2000)*
Qmobi Inc....E.... 800 246-2677
Wilmington *(G-12275)*
Qsr Group LLC....G.... 302 268-6909
Wilmington *(G-12276)*
Quavo Inc....E.... 484 802-4693
Wilmington *(G-12284)*
Raas Infotek LLC....E.... 302 894-3184
Newark *(G-7294)*
Radiocut Inc....G.... 302 613-1280
Wilmington *(G-12301)*
Rainmaker Software Group LLC....G.... 800 616-6701
Wilmington *(G-12307)*
Ram Tech Systems Inc....E.... 302 832-6600
Middletown *(G-4210)*
Rct Studio Inc....G.... 669 255-1562
Wilmington *(G-12336)*
Reporting Solutions LLC....G.... 857 284-3583
Newark *(G-7321)*
Ritchie Sawyer Corporation....F.... 302 475-1971
Wilmington *(G-12426)*
Rockey & Associates Inc....G.... 610 640-4880
Lewes *(G-3723)*
Rovier LLC....G.... 302 832-6726
Newark *(G-7368)*
Royal Era LLC....G.... 484 574-0260
Newark *(G-7369)*
Safer Technologies LLC....G.... 302 497-0333
Wilmington *(G-12521)*
Saferwatch LLC....E.... 844 449-2824
Lewes *(G-3728)*
Sailnovo Limited....D.... 213 550-3897
Dover *(G-2054)*
Sain Cosmos LLC....F.... 936 244-7017
Wilmington *(G-12523)*
Scanpoint Inc....G.... 603 429-0777
Wilmington *(G-12552)*
Scanta Inc....E.... 302 645-7400
Lewes *(G-3732)*
Scope One Inc....G.... 415 429-9347
Dover *(G-2061)*
Scorelogix LLC....E.... 302 294-6532
Newark *(G-7396)*
Sensofusion Inc....F.... 570 239-4912
Milton *(G-4967)*
Server Management LLC....G.... 302 300-1745
Wilmington *(G-12584)*
Seven Tech LLC....G.... 302 464-6488
Middletown *(G-4238)*
◆ Severn Trent Inc....E.... 302 427-5990
Wilmington *(G-12588)*
Sherweb Inc....G.... 888 567-6610
Newark *(G-7416)*
Shipshap LLC....G.... 425 298-5215
Middletown *(G-4240)*
Shore Consultants Ltd....F.... 302 737-3375
Newark *(G-7417)*
Shouldr LLC....G.... 917 331-1384
Lewes *(G-3741)*
Singular Key Inc....F.... 408 753-5848
Wilmington *(G-12631)*
Sitengle Technology LLC....F.... 719 822-0710
Dover *(G-2086)*
Sketches and Pixels LLC....G.... 312 834-4402
Newark *(G-7435)*
Skinary App Inc....G.... 773 744-5407
Middletown *(G-4242)*
SM Technomine Inc....F.... 312 492-4386
Wilmington *(G-12647)*
Smartstudents LLC....G.... 302 597-6586
Wilmington *(G-12655)*
Softmogul Inc....G.... 414 426-1650
Wilmington *(G-12671)*
Software Services of De Inc....E.... 302 654-3172
Wilmington *(G-12672)*
Spearhead Inc....G.... 347 670-2699
Bear *(G-331)*
Speedrid LLC....D.... 213 550-5462
Dover *(G-2097)*
Sqrin Technologies LLC....G.... 540 330-1379
Lewes *(G-3761)*
Stylelabs Inc....E.... 347 674-7993
Wilmington *(G-12782)*
Subcodevs Inc....G.... 704 234-6780
Wilmington *(G-12784)*
Sumuri LLC....G.... 302 570-0015
Camden *(G-601)*
Supply Chain Consultants Inc....E.... 302 738-9215
Wilmington *(G-12812)*
Surge Networks Inc....G.... 206 432-5047
Newark *(G-7515)*
Swit Inc....C.... 302 792-0175
Wilmington *(G-12826)*
Sygul Inc....E.... 315 384-1848
Newark *(G-7524)*
Syncretic Software Inc....F.... 302 762-2600
Wilmington *(G-12835)*
Tabella Inc....G.... 415 799-2389
Newark *(G-7528)*
Tandem Hosted Resources Inc....F.... 302 740-7099
Newark *(G-7537)*
Tech Central LLC....F.... 717 273-3301
Wilmington *(G-12866)*
Technosecure Corporation....E.... 732 302-9005
Bear *(G-350)*
Thinkruptive Media Inc....F.... 310 779-4748
Dover *(G-2142)*
Tiki Interactive Inc....G.... 408 306-4393
Lewes *(G-3785)*
Toolook Inc....F.... 240 330-3307
Wilmington *(G-12926)*
Toptracker LLC....B.... 415 230-0131
Wilmington *(G-12934)*
Touchstone Systems Inc....F.... 302 324-5322
New Castle *(G-5779)*
Town of Middletown....G.... 302 378-2711
Middletown *(G-4265)*
Town of Middletown....E.... 302 376-9950
Middletown *(G-4264)*
Transactional Web Inc....G.... 908 216-5054
Wilmington *(G-12954)*
Trialogics LLC....F.... 302 313-9000
Wilmington *(G-12969)*
Trifecta Health Solutions Inc....G.... 614 582-4184
Middletown *(G-4268)*
Truck Lagbe Inc....E.... 860 810-8677
Lewes *(G-3795)*
True Intelligence Tech Inc....G.... 979 209-0335
Wilmington *(G-12987)*
True Life Church Newark Inc....G.... 302 283-9003
Bear *(G-361)*
Turnkey Lender Inc....G.... 888 299-4892
Lewes *(G-3799)*
Twyne Inc....G.... 213 675-9518
Camden *(G-603)*
U Scope Solutions LLC....F.... 844 872-6732
Wilmington *(G-13003)*
Unikie Inc....F.... 408 839-1920
Dover *(G-2177)*
Unite USA Inc....E.... 609 915-9130
Wilmington *(G-13020)*
Uno Messenger LLC....G.... 513 703-8091
Wilmington *(G-13033)*
US Telex Corporation....E.... 302 652-2707
Wilmington *(G-13040)*
Vam Apps Co....G.... 786 220-4826
Wilmington *(G-13046)*
Vedaham Inc....F.... 302 250-4594
Wilmington *(G-13055)*
Vensoft LLC....E.... 302 392-9000
Wilmington *(G-13057)*
Veristuffcom Inc....G.... 972 545-2434
Wilmington *(G-13060)*
Vertigo Group Inc....F.... 302 298-0825
Wilmington *(G-13068)*
Vertrius Corp....F.... 800 770-1913
Lewes *(G-3808)*
Veteran It Pro LLC....F.... 302 824-3111
Hockessin *(G-3167)*
Vew Technologies Inc....G.... 310 560-3814
Wilmington *(G-13073)*
Volvant Inc....G.... 805 456-6464
Wilmington *(G-13103)*
Vortex Labs LLC....G.... 302 231-1294
Wilmington *(G-13104)*
Vpn Vpn Vpn Proxy....G.... 415 758-8354
Lewes *(G-3810)*
W23 S12 Holdings LLC....G.... 610 348-3825
Wilmington *(G-13110)*
Wabisabi Design Inc....G.... 650 451-8501
Newark *(G-7673)*
Wallor Wearables LLC....G.... 505 310-6099
Lewes *(G-3814)*
We Cobble LLC....F.... 302 504-4294
Wilmington *(G-13130)*
Web Applications Inc....G.... 302 834-0282
Newark *(G-7680)*
Webbrowser Media Inc....G.... 302 830-3664
Wilmington *(G-13134)*
Webstudy Inc....G.... 888 326-4058
Harbeson *(G-2802)*
Wgames Incorporated....G.... 206 618-3699
Wilmington *(G-13178)*
Whitaker LLC....G.... 302 633-2740
Wilmington *(G-13187)*
Windy Weather World Inc....G.... 650 204-7941
Claymont *(G-823)*
Wna Infotech LLC....E.... 302 668-5977
Bear *(G-379)*
Workplace Rebels LLC....G.... 917 771-8286
Dover *(G-2237)*
Workweek Inc....G.... 423 708-4565
Dover *(G-2238)*
Writingwizards Inc....G.... 650 382-1357
Lewes *(G-3830)*
Wutap LLC....G.... 610 457-3559
Newark *(G-7725)*
Wutopia Group US Ltd....F.... 302 488-0248
Dover *(G-2241)*
Xcs Corporation....G.... 302 514-0600
Wilmington *(G-13316)*
Xerafy Inc....G.... 817 938-4197
Wilmington *(G-13317)*
Xxl Cloud Inc....G.... 302 298-0050
Wilmington *(G-13324)*
Yello Technologies Inc....G.... 954 802-6089
Lewes *(G-3833)*
Youshop Inc....E.... 302 526-0521
Dover *(G-2249)*
Youyu Home Technology LLC....F.... 347 796-4305
Wilmington *(G-13336)*
Z Data Inc....G.... 302 566-5351
Newark *(G-7734)*
Z Data Inc....G.... 302 566-5351
Newark *(G-7735)*
Zax Mobile LLC....G.... 302 261-3232
Newark *(G-7738)*
Zenbanx Holding Ltd....G.... 310 749-3101
Claymont *(G-829)*
Zilpa Ltd....G.... 800 504-5368
Wilmington *(G-13351)*

- **Zir LLC** G 203 524-1215 — Lewes *(G-3835)*
- **Zumra Solutions LLC** G 302 504-4423 — Lewes *(G-3836)*

7372 Prepackaged Software

- **7c Infotech Inc** G 717 288-8686 — Wilmington *(G-8866)*
- **Abcware LLC** G 888 755-1485 — Wilmington *(G-8900)*
- **Accessquint LLC** F 302 351-4064 — Wilmington *(G-8915)*
- **Acorn Energy Inc** G 302 656-1708 — Wilmington *(G-8923)*
- **Acumen Health Technologies LLC** F 800 941-0356 — Wilmington *(G-8930)*
- **Advangelists LLC** G 734 546-4989 — Wilmington *(G-8958)*
- **Advice Wallet Inc** F 510 280-2475 — Wilmington *(G-8961)*
- **AEG International LLC** G 302 750-6411 — Laurel *(G-3190)*
- **Aeres Corporation** G 858 926-8626 — New Castle *(G-5013)*
- **Aivo America Corp** G 415 849-2288 — Dover *(G-1099)*
- **Alfa-Order LLC** G 302 319-2663 — Wilmington *(G-9006)*
- **All Lives Matter LLC** G 252 767-9291 — Dover *(G-1106)*
- **Allosentry LLC** G 617 838-7608 — Newark *(G-5941)*
- **Almond Toc Inc** G 347 756-2318 — Wilmington *(G-9027)*
- **Altr Solutions LLC** F 888 757-2587 — Dover *(G-1114)*
- **Amdisvet LLC** G 302 514-9130 — Smyrna *(G-8568)*
- **Anamo Inc** G 702 852-2992 — Dover *(G-1122)*
- **Anchor App Inc** G 302 421-6890 — Wilmington *(G-9076)*
- **Anvil Enterprises LLC** G 323 230-9376 — Wilmington *(G-9091)*
- **App Pros LLC** G 646 441-0788 — Wilmington *(G-9098)*
- **Apploye Inc** G 925 452-6102 — Newark *(G-5989)*
- **Appmotion Inc** G 347 513-6333 — Wilmington *(G-9103)*
- **Ardexo Inc** G 855 617-7500 — Dover *(G-1134)*
- **Atapy Software LLC** G 657 221-9370 — Lewes *(G-3351)*
- **Audtra Benefit Corp** G 800 991-5156 — Dover *(G-1159)*
- **Baabao Inc** G 415 990-6767 — Wilmington *(G-9216)*
- **Babel Inc** G 866 327-3465 — Wilmington *(G-9218)*
- **Basemark Inc** G 832 483-7093 — Dover *(G-1177)*
- **Batescainelli LLC** G 202 618-2040 — Rehoboth Beach *(G-7856)*
- **Bayesian Health Inc** G 408 205-8035 — Wilmington *(G-9265)*
- **Bbhotel Corp** G 939 272-3953 — Wilmington *(G-9270)*
- **Beatdapp Inc** G 310 903-0244 — Dover *(G-1185)*
- **Bijoti Inc** F 908 916-7764 — Wilmington *(G-9336)*
- **Biomechsys Incorporated** G 818 305-4436 — Dover *(G-1204)*
- **Biritek LLC** G 949 556-3943 — Dover *(G-1206)*
- **Bk 2 Si LLC** G 800 246-2677 — Wilmington *(G-9344)*
- **Blaze Systems Corporation** G 302 733-7235 — Newark *(G-6092)*
- **Bluevault LLC** F 302 425-4367 — Wilmington *(G-9385)*
- **Business Services Corp** G 302 645-0400 — Lewes *(G-3395)*
- **Calmeet Inc** G 469 223-0863 — Newark *(G-6145)*
- **Cansurround Pbc** G 302 540-2270 — Wilmington *(G-9552)*
- **Chameleon City Inc** G 415 964-0054 — Newark *(G-6184)*
- **Chart Exchange** G 850 376-6435 — Claymont *(G-714)*
- **Charter Dynamics LLC** G 888 260-4579 — Wilmington *(G-9640)*
- **Chatngo Corporation** G 302 504-4291 — Wilmington *(G-9642)*
- **Clairvyant Technosolutions Inc** E 302 999-7172 — Wilmington *(G-9728)*
- **Coditas Inc** G 888 220-6200 — Lewes *(G-3441)*
- **Colorimetrix Inc** G 347 560-0037 — New Castle *(G-5184)*
- **Communicate U Media LLC** G 610 453-6501 — Middletown *(G-4001)*
- **Conformit** G 302 451-9167 — Newark *(G-6285)*
- **Conventra LLC** G 302 378-4461 — Middletown *(G-4008)*
- **Coqonut Inc** G 347 419-7709 — Wilmington *(G-9857)*
- **Core Purchase LLC** G 616 328-5715 — Wilmington *(G-9859)*
- **Cosmodog Software Inc** G 302 762-2437 — Wilmington *(G-9872)*
- **Crossknowledge** D 646 699-5983 — Dover *(G-1324)*
- **Cryptomarket Inc** G 860 222-0318 — Wilmington *(G-9908)*
- **CT Corporation System** E 302 658-4968 — Wilmington *(G-9914)*
- **Cybele Software Inc** G 302 892-9625 — Wilmington *(G-9931)*
- **Cyber 20/20 Inc** F 203 802-8742 — Newark *(G-6334)*
- **Cyber Seven Technologies LLC** G 302 635-7122 — Newark *(G-6335)*
- **Cyberwolf Software Inc** G 302 324-8442 — Bear *(G-91)*
- **Damon Baca** G 858 837-0800 — Dover *(G-1338)*
- **Datatech Enterprises Inc** F 540 370-0010 — Selbyville *(G-8478)*
- **Derby Software LLC** G 502 435-1371 — Dover *(G-1415)*
- **Digital Penguin Inc** G 484 387-7803 — Newark *(G-6448)*
- **Dimensional Insight Inc** G 302 791-0687 — Wilmington *(G-10156)*
- **Directrestore LLC** F 650 276-0384 — Dover *(G-1428)*
- **Discidium Technology Inc** G 347 220-5979 — Newark *(G-6455)*
- **Dodd Health Innovation LLC** G 410 598-7266 — Ocean View *(G-7784)*
- **Done Again Software LLC** G 301 466-7858 — Lewes *(G-3469)*
- **Donr LLC** G 857 400-8679 — Wilmington *(G-10200)*
- **Dream Weaver LLC** G 302 352-9473 — Wilmington *(G-10232)*
- **Dresslikeme LLC** G 302 450-1046 — Dover *(G-1480)*
- **Dxc Technology Company** G 302 391-2762 — Newark *(G-6482)*
- **Eagle Eye America Inc** G 302 392-3600 — Bear *(G-134)*
- **Easy Analytic Software Inc** G 302 762-4271 — Wilmington *(G-10330)*
- **Eclipse Software Inc** G 212 727-1136 — Wilmington *(G-10338)*
- **Edaura Inc** G 707 330-9836 — Wilmington *(G-10343)*
- **Eitv USA Inc** G 305 517-7715 — Wilmington *(G-10364)*
- **Eksab Corporation** G 319 371-1669 — Camden *(G-567)*
- **Enclave Digital Development Co** G 203 807-0400 — Lewes *(G-3482)*
- **Enth Inc** G 630 986-8700 — Wilmington *(G-10416)*
- **Fabmanianet** G 302 994-5801 — Wilmington *(G-10472)*
- **Famealy Inc** G 650 492-5009 — Newark *(G-6565)*
- **Famoid Technology LLC** G 530 601-7284 — New Castle *(G-5303)*
- **Farnam Hall Ventures LLC** G 347 687-2152 — Wilmington *(G-10500)*
- **Feastfox Inc** G 650 250-6887 — Dover *(G-1546)*
- **Fever Labs Inc** G 646 781-7359 — Camden *(G-571)*
- **Fitovate LLC** G 302 463-9790 — Wilmington *(G-10565)*
- **Floristware Inc** G 888 531-3012 — Wilmington *(G-10577)*
- **Flowpay Corporation** G 720 425-3244 — Wilmington *(G-10580)*
- **Fluent Forever Inc** F 262 725-1707 — Lewes *(G-3501)*
- **Four Point Solutions Ltd** E 613 907-6400 — Wilmington *(G-10605)*
- **Foxfire Industries LLC** G 817 602-4900 — Newark *(G-6609)*
- **Free Psychic Reading LLC** G 305 439-1455 — Dover *(G-1566)*
- **Freshbooks Usa Inc** G 416 525-5384 — Wilmington *(G-10637)*
- **Full Game Ahead USA LLC** G 302 281-0102 — Wilmington *(G-10646)*
- **Fun Bakery LLC** G 858 220-0946 — Dover *(G-1572)*
- **Genex Technologies Inc** D 302 266-6161 — Newark *(G-6647)*
- **Get Takeout LLC** G 800 785-6218 — Lewes *(G-3513)*
- **Giesela Inc** G 855 556-4338 — Newark *(G-6653)*
- **Givfolio LLC** G 213 949-1964 — Newark *(G-6657)*
- **Global Computers Networks LLC** G 484 686-8374 — Middletown *(G-4088)*
- **Global Gaming Business** G 302 994-3898 — Wilmington *(G-10725)*
- **Go Go Go Inc** G 302 645-7400 — Lewes *(G-3517)*
- **Gulch Group LLC** G 202 697-1756 — Rehoboth Beach *(G-7956)*
- **Halligan Inc** G 314 488-9400 — Lewes *(G-3530)*
- **Harbin LLC** G 302 219-3320 — Lewes *(G-3532)*
- **Heavy Key Studios LLC** G 302 356-6832 — New Castle *(G-5389)*
- **Hells Kitchen Software Ltd** G 302 983-5644 — Newark *(G-6722)*
- **Henderson Software** G 302 239-7573 — Wilmington *(G-10884)*
- **Hoard Inc** F 980 333-1703 — Wilmington *(G-10922)*
- **Hullo Inc** G 415 939-6534 — Dover *(G-1662)*
- **Hungrosity LLC** G 401 527-1133 — Wilmington *(G-10972)*
- **Hyper Jobs LLC** E 786 667-0905 — Newark *(G-6757)*
- **Idf Connect Inc** G 888 765-1611 — Wilmington *(G-10992)*
- **Iexperienceilearn LLC** G 718 704-4870 — New Castle *(G-5409)*
- **Ifi Inc** G 718 791-7669 — Newark *(G-6764)*
- **Innclude LLC** G 310 430-6552 — Wilmington *(G-11037)*
- **Inspectware** G 302 999-9601 — Wilmington *(G-11041)*
- **Isaac Fair Corporation** E 302 324-8015 — New Castle *(G-5426)*
- **Island Boy Enterprise LLC** G 904 347-4563 — Bethany Beach *(G-405)*
- **Itango Inc** G 302 648-2646 — Wilmington *(G-11091)*
- **Ithaca Holdco 2 LLC** G 650 385-5000 — Wilmington *(G-11092)*
- **Johnny Walker Enterprises LLC** G 408 500-6439 — Lewes *(G-3575)*
- **Joto Inc** G 260 337-3362 — Wilmington *(G-11197)*
- **Kankana LLC** G 302 597-6998 — Wilmington *(G-11224)*
- **Kera Cable Products LLC** G 917 383-4013 — Dover *(G-1743)*
- **Keystack Inc** G 510 629-5099 — Newark *(G-6879)*
- **Knowt Inc** F 848 391-0575 — Lewes *(G-3585)*
- **KOA Technologies LLC** G 760 471-5726 — Wilmington *(G-11285)*
- **Labware Inc** G 302 658-8444 — Wilmington *(G-11320)*

73 BUSINESS SERVICES

Labware Global Services Inc .... F 302 658-8444
　Wilmington *(G-11321)*
Labware Holdings Inc .... E 302 658-8444
　Wilmington *(G-11322)*
Laurel Bridge Software Inc .... G 302 453-0222
　Newark *(G-6919)*
Life Before Us LLC .... G 917 690-3380
　Wilmington *(G-11384)*
Lifesquared Inc .... G 415 475-9090
　Dover *(G-1785)*
Lityx LLC .... G 888 548-9947
　Wilmington *(G-11411)*
Loadbalancerorginc .... G 888 867-9504
　Wilmington *(G-11418)*
Localspin LLC .... G 917 232-7203
　Wilmington *(G-11421)*
Locksign LLC .... G 917 573-6582
　Lewes *(G-3610)*
Lognex Inc .... G 786 650-7755
　Wilmington *(G-11426)*
Lookinn Inc .... G 302 839-2088
　Dover *(G-1796)*
Lyra Software Inc .... G 347 506-5287
　Newark *(G-6962)*
Machine Learning Systems LLC ..... G 302 299-2621
　Wilmington *(G-11479)*
Magneco LLC .... G 302 613-0080
　Wilmington *(G-11487)*
Marble City Software Inc .... G 302 658-2583
　Wilmington *(G-11519)*
Matter Music Inc .... F 650 793-7749
　Wilmington *(G-11568)*
Medibid .... G 888 855-6334
　Wilmington *(G-11615)*
Merix LLC .... G 425 659-1425
　Lewes *(G-3638)*
Mimix Company .... G 305 916-8602
　Dover *(G-1859)*
Mindcentral Inc .... G 302 273-1011
　Newark *(G-7042)*
Mm Mobile LLC .... G 917 297-9534
　Dover *(G-1864)*
Money Galaxy Inc .... F 302 319-2008
　Wilmington *(G-11731)*
Moving Sciences LLC .... G 617 871-9892
　Wilmington *(G-11764)*
Mresource LLC .... G 312 608-4789
　Wilmington *(G-11768)*
Mwidm Inc .... E 302 298-0101
　Wilmington *(G-11785)*
My Easy Team LLC .... G 302 722-6821
　Newark *(G-7075)*
Neon Dojo LLC .... G 650 275-2395
　Dover *(G-1892)*
Neon Fun LLC .... G 858 220-0946
　Dover *(G-1893)*
Nerd Boy LLC .... G 302 857-0243
　Dover *(G-1894)*
Nevron Software LLC .... F 302 792-0175
　Wilmington *(G-11847)*
Next Generation Plant Svcs Inc .... G 302 654-7584
　Wilmington *(G-11880)*
Noble Master .... G 302 261-2018
　Lewes *(G-3660)*
Nortonlifelock Inc .... G 650 527-8000
　Wilmington *(G-11909)*
Odyssey Technologies LLC .... D 302 525-8184
　Newark *(G-7143)*
Office Bpo LLC .... G 248 716-5136
　Wilmington *(G-11938)*
Open Barn Inc .... G 669 254-7747
　Lewes *(G-3670)*
Oppa Inc .... G 732 540-0308
　Lewes *(G-3671)*
Oppameet LLC .... G 732 540-0308
　Lewes *(G-3672)*
Ordering Inc .... F 888 443-6203
　Wilmington *(G-11972)*
Oto Global Inc .... G 966 597-9694
　Newark *(G-7163)*
Outcome Associates LLC .... G 302 368-3637
　Newark *(G-7164)*
Pangeamart Inc .... G 914 374-0913
　Lewes *(G-3677)*
Paperbasket LLC .... G 516 360-3500
　Dover *(G-1933)*
Paypergigs Inc .... A 917 336-2162
　Newark *(G-7187)*
Pbtv Global Inc .... G 302 292-1400
　Wilmington *(G-12050)*

Peas and Love Corporation .... G 301 537-3593
　Wilmington *(G-12058)*
Peeper Vehicle Technology Corp .... G 800 971-4134
　Dover *(G-1943)*
Percebe Music Inc .... G 850 341-9594
　Dover *(G-1949)*
Perceri LLC .... G 217 721-8731
　Dover *(G-1950)*
Pfpc Worldwide Inc .... F 302 791-1700
　Wilmington *(G-12105)*
Pharmacy Technologies Inc .... G 877 655-3846
　Lewes *(G-3686)*
Platenger LLC .... G 302 298-0896
　Wilmington *(G-12152)*
Play US Media LLC .... G 302 924-5034
　Dover *(G-1965)*
Point of Sale Technologies .... G 302 659-5119
　Clayton *(G-867)*
Pointless Technology LLC .... G 917 403-2264
　Dover *(G-1975)*
Process Academy LLC .... G 302 415-3104
　Wilmington *(G-12238)*
Promenta LLC .... G 302 552-2922
　Wilmington *(G-12250)*
Prosift LLC .... G 302 678-2386
　Dover *(G-1991)*
Qrepublik Inc .... G 559 475-8262
　Claymont *(G-798)*
Quantus Innovations LLC .... G 302 356-1661
　Wilmington *(G-12282)*
Queryloop Inc .... G 412 253-6265
　Newark *(G-7286)*
Raad360 LLC .... F 855 722-3360
　Newark *(G-7293)*
Ram Tech Systems Inc .... E 302 832-6600
　Middletown *(G-4210)*
Re-Up App Inc .... G 267 972-1183
　Wilmington *(G-12339)*
Readyb Inc .... G 323 813-8710
　Dover *(G-2015)*
Red Rhino Labs LLC .... G 650 275-2464
　Newark *(G-7307)*
Refrating LLC .... G 617 358-2789
　New Castle *(G-5670)*
Relytv LLC .... G 213 373-5988
　Dover *(G-2023)*
Remote Inc .... G 302 636-5440
　Wilmington *(G-12379)*
Renderapps LLC .... G 919 274-0582
　Dover *(G-2027)*
Rendezvous Inc .... G 302 645-7400
　Lewes *(G-3715)*
Retrocode Inc .... G 302 570-0002
　Newark *(G-7328)*
Rfx Analyst Inc .... G 302 244-5650
　Dover *(G-2034)*
Rogue Elephants LLC .... G 979 264-2845
　Lewes *(G-3724)*
Romie LLC .... G 866 698-0052
　Wilmington *(G-12468)*
Ru Inc .... C 917 346-0285
　Wilmington *(G-12488)*
Scholarjet PBc .... G 617 407-9851
　Lewes *(G-3733)*
SEI Robotics Corporation .... C 858 752-8675
　Newark *(G-7402)*
Shore Consultants Ltd .... F 302 737-3375
　Newark *(G-7417)*
Sinc Business Corporation .... G 480 210-1798
　Wilmington *(G-12630)*
Singular Key Inc .... F 408 753-5848
　Wilmington *(G-12631)*
Siriusiq Mobile LLC .... F 888 414-2047
　Newark *(G-7433)*
Sitwa Group LLC .... G 786 802-4155
　Wilmington *(G-12636)*
Software Bananas LLC .... G 302 348-8488
　Newark *(G-7453)*
Solufy Corp .... E 877 476-5839
　Wilmington *(G-12679)*
Statwhiz Ventures LLC .... G 310 819-5427
　Wilmington *(G-12746)*
Stay Prime Inc .... G 612 770-6753
　Wilmington *(G-12747)*
Stealthorg LLC .... G 302 724-6461
　Dover *(G-2107)*
Stream App LLC .... G 610 420-5864
　Wilmington *(G-12775)*
Sumuri LLC .... G 302 570-0015
　Camden *(G-601)*

Sweat Social LLC .... G 504 510-1973
　Dover *(G-2123)*
Switchedon Inc .... E 415 271-1172
　Lewes *(G-3775)*
Symmetry Dimensions Inc .... F 302 918-5536
　Wilmington *(G-12831)*
Sysod Inc .... G 973 333-4848
　Wilmington *(G-12838)*
Tableart LLC .... G 650 587-8769
　Wilmington *(G-12847)*
Talk Aware LLC .... G 302 645-7400
　Lewes *(G-3776)*
Tap 99 LLC .... G 301 541-7395
　Wilmington *(G-12853)*
Taply LLC .... G 650 275-2395
　Dover *(G-2129)*
Thoroughbred Software Intl .... G 302 339-8383
　Georgetown *(G-2692)*
Tom Miller Remodeling .... G 302 674-1637
　Dover *(G-2150)*
Topiary Tech LLC .... G 302 636-5440
　Wilmington *(G-12931)*
Tricky Minute Games Inc .... G 302 319-5137
　Wilmington *(G-12971)*
Trumove Inc .... G 917 379-7427
　Lewes *(G-3797)*
Ufo Development Group Inc .... G 408 995-3217
　Lewes *(G-3802)*
Unadori LLC .... G 917 539-2128
　Dover *(G-2174)*
Unfold Creative LLC .... G 509 850-1337
　Dover *(G-2176)*
Verde Advantage Group LLC .... G 302 333-5701
　Wilmington *(G-13059)*
Version 40 Software LLC .... G 302 270-0245
　Magnolia *(G-3911)*
Vitellus LLC .... G 718 782-3539
　Wilmington *(G-13096)*
Voice 4 Impact Inc .... G 484 410-0111
　Wilmington *(G-13099)*
Vshield Software Corp .... G 302 531-0855
　Dover *(G-2200)*
Walltag Inc .... G 917 725-1715
　Lewes *(G-3815)*
Wavertech LLC .... G 877 735-0897
　Wilmington *(G-13124)*
Wbi Capital Advisors LLC .... G 856 361-6362
　Wilmington *(G-13127)*
Webstudy Inc .... G 888 326-4058
　Harbeson *(G-2802)*
Wepro LLC .... G 310 650-8622
　Wilmington *(G-13157)*
Winker Labs LLC .... G 630 449-8130
　Wilmington *(G-13271)*
Wutap LLC .... G 610 457-3559
　Newark *(G-7725)*
Xapix Inc .... G 408 508-4324
　Wilmington *(G-13313)*
Yorokobi Inc .... G 323 591-3466
　Newark *(G-7731)*
Zimple Inc .... G 877 494-6753
　Dover *(G-2252)*
Zumidian .... G 302 219-3500
　Wilmington *(G-13354)*

7373 Computer Integrated Systems Design

924 Inc .... E 302 656-6100
　Wilmington *(G-8870)*
Access Versalign Inc .... G 302 225-7800
　Wilmington *(G-8914)*
Aigc Games Inc .... G 214 499-8654
　Lewes *(G-3331)*
Applied Control Engrg Inc .... D 302 738-8800
　Newark *(G-5987)*
Ardexo Inc .... G 855 617-7500
　Dover *(G-1134)*
Averest Inc .... G 302 281-2062
　Wilmington *(G-9198)*
Batescainelli LLC .... G 202 618-2040
　Rehoboth Beach *(G-7856)*
Blu Dragon Studio Inc .... G 302 722-6227
　Newark *(G-6097)*
Blue Ocean Systems LLC .... G 866 355-5989
　Wilmington *(G-9379)*
◆ Bluent LLC .... D 832 476-8459
　Lewes *(G-3388)*
Bothub Ai Limited .... F 669 278-7485
　Newark *(G-6108)*
Brittons Wise Computers Inc .... G 302 659-0343
　Smyrna *(G-8587)*

Central Firm LLC ... G ... 610 470-9836
Wilmington *(G-9615)*
Cim Concepts Incorporated ... F ... 302 613-5400
New Castle *(G-5161)*
Cloudcoffer LLC ... E ... 412 620-3203
Wilmington *(G-9748)*
Cloudxperts LLC ... G ... 302 257-5686
Dover *(G-1295)*
Congruence Consulting Group ... G ... 320 290-6155
Newark *(G-6286)*
Consult Dynamics Inc ... E ... 302 654-1019
Wilmington *(G-9837)*
Cyber Seven Technologies LLC ... G ... 302 635-7122
Newark *(G-6335)*
Data-Bi LLC ... G ... 302 290-3138
Wilmington *(G-9962)*
Datatech Enterprises Inc ... F ... 540 370-0010
Selbyville *(G-8478)*
Delaware Business Systems Inc ... E ... 302 395-0900
New Castle *(G-5226)*
Dennek LLC ... G ... 302 703-0790
Wilmington *(G-10109)*
Discidium Technology Inc ... G ... 347 220-5979
Newark *(G-6455)*
Dodd Health Innovation LLC ... G ... 410 598-7266
Ocean View *(G-7784)*
E-Dmz Security LLC ... E ... 302 791-9370
Wilmington *(G-10312)*
Ebc Systems LLC ... G ... 302 472-1896
Wilmington *(G-10334)*
Encross LLC ... F ... 302 351-2593
Wilmington *(G-10396)*
Enterprise Services LLC ... C ... 302 454-7622
Newark *(G-6533)*
Genex Technologies Inc ... D ... 302 266-6161
Newark *(G-6647)*
Gyst Inc ... G ... 631 680-4307
Dover *(G-1620)*
Horizon Systems Inc ... G ... 302 983-3203
New Castle *(G-5404)*
Inclind Inc ... G ... 302 856-2802
Lewes *(G-3556)*
Indelible Blue Inc ... F ... 302 231-5200
Lewes *(G-3557)*
Info Systems LLC ... C ... 302 633-9800
Wilmington *(G-11026)*
Insight Engineering Solutions ... G ... 302 378-4842
Townsend *(G-8797)*
Internet Business Pubg Corp ... F ... 302 875-7700
Laurel *(G-3241)*
Itiyam LLC ... F ... 703 291-1600
Wilmington *(G-11093)*
Knowpro LLC ... G ... 772 538-6477
Wilmington *(G-11284)*
Kortech Consulting Inc ... F ... 302 559-4612
Bear *(G-220)*
Linkedin Profile Services LLC ... F ... 703 679-7719
Wilmington *(G-11397)*
M C Tek LLC ... G ... 302 644-9695
Rehoboth Beach *(G-7992)*
Majalco LLC ... G ... 703 507-5298
Wilmington *(G-11494)*
Medictek Inc ... F ... 302 351-4924
Wilmington *(G-11618)*
Omnimaven Inc ... G ... 302 378-8918
Middletown *(G-4178)*
Panzeea ... F ... 770 573-3672
Seaford *(G-8340)*
Pentius Inc ... E ... 855 825-3778
Wilmington *(G-12078)*
PHD Technology Solutions LLC ... E ... 410 961-7895
Newark *(G-7211)*
Play US Media LLC ... G ... 302 924-5034
Dover *(G-1965)*
Polar Strategy Inc ... G ... 703 628-0001
Lewes *(G-3695)*
Progressive Software Cmpt Inc ... C ... 302 479-9700
Wilmington *(G-12244)*
Public Systems Inc ... E ... 302 326-4500
New Castle *(G-5652)*
Ram Tech Systems Inc ... E ... 302 832-6600
Middletown *(G-4210)*
Rave Business Systems LLC ... F ... 302 407-2270
Lewes *(G-3708)*
Recoveryip Innovations LLC ... G ... 617 901-3414
Newark *(G-7305)*
Riders App Inc ... G ... 347 484-4344
Wilmington *(G-12416)*
Sahave Inc ... F ... 630 401-5211
Wilmington *(G-12522)*
Scientific Games Corporation ... F ... 302 737-4300
Newark *(G-7395)*
Sensofusion Inc ... F ... 570 239-4912
Milton *(G-4967)*
Sevone Inc ... E ... 302 319-5400
Newark *(G-7412)*
Sharlay Computer Systems ... G ... 302 588-3170
Smyrna *(G-8714)*
Smartis ... G ... 302 653-8355
Dover *(G-2089)*
Sync It LLC ... G ... 904 697-1132
Wilmington *(G-12832)*
Systmade Technologies LLC ... F ... 888 944-3546
Dover *(G-2124)*
Tandem Hosted Resources Inc ... F ... 302 740-7099
Newark *(G-7537)*
United3 Services Inc ... G ... 302 233-5985
Millsboro *(G-4817)*
Vel Micro Works Incorporated ... G ... 302 239-4661
Hockessin *(G-3166)*
Verizon Delaware LLC ... C ... 302 571-1571
Wilmington *(G-13062)*
Versatus Corp ... G ... 203 293-3597
Wilmington *(G-13064)*
Webstudy Inc ... G ... 888 326-4058
Harbeson *(G-2802)*
Xcs Corporation ... G ... 302 514-0600
Wilmington *(G-13316)*

7374 Data & Computer Processing & Preparation

Ample Business Solutions Inc ... E ... 302 752-4270
Wilmington *(G-9071)*
Analyttica Datalab Inc ... E ... 917 300-3325
Wilmington *(G-9074)*
Brandywine Cad Design Inc ... E ... 302 478-8334
Wilmington *(G-9420)*
Cadrender LLC ... G ... 302 657-0700
Wilmington *(G-9532)*
Cgs Infotech Inc ... E ... 302 351-2434
Wilmington *(G-9623)*
Computer Aid Inc ... C ... 302 831-5500
Newark *(G-6276)*
Computer Services of Delaware ... G ... 302 697-8644
Dover *(G-1309)*
Conch Island ... G ... 302 226-9378
Rehoboth Beach *(G-7899)*
Court Record & Data MGT Svcs ... G ... 732 955-6567
Wilmington *(G-9877)*
Creaform USA Inc ... G ... 407 732-4103
Newark *(G-6312)*
Cyberdaptive Inc ... G ... 302 388-3506
Newark *(G-6336)*
Data Drum Inc ... G ... 347 502-8485
Newark *(G-6347)*
Data-Bi LLC ... G ... 302 290-3138
Wilmington *(G-9962)*
Datatech Enterprises Inc ... F ... 540 370-0010
Selbyville *(G-8478)*
Fine Line It Consulting LLP ... G ... 302 645-4549
Lewes *(G-3496)*
GOBLIN Technologies LLC ... G ... 844 733-5724
Newark *(G-6669)*
Hangster Inc ... G ... 619 871-8086
Wilmington *(G-10833)*
Hap LLC ... G ... 302 645-7400
Lewes *(G-3531)*
Herox Pbc ... F ... 604 681-3651
Wilmington *(G-10894)*
Infinity Intellectuals Inc ... C ... 302 565-4830
Newark *(G-6778)*
Invensis Inc ... C ... 302 351-3509
Wilmington *(G-11072)*
Ipr International LLC ... E ... 302 304-8774
Wilmington *(G-11080)*
J P Morgan Services Inc ... A ... 302 634-1000
Newark *(G-6818)*
John Snow Labs Inc ... E ... 302 786-5227
Lewes *(G-3574)*
Mobius New Media Inc ... G ... 302 475-9880
Wilmington *(G-11719)*
My Qme Inc ... E ... 302 218-8730
Wilmington *(G-11789)*
National Dcument MGT Solutions ... G ... 302 535-9263
Marydel *(G-3921)*
Native Communications LLC ... G ... 302 439-0640
Wilmington *(G-11817)*
Planet Payment Solutions Inc ... E ... 516 670-3200
New Castle *(G-5625)*
Pointlook Corporation ... G ... 415 448-6002
Wilmington *(G-12179)*
Professionale Inc ... G ... 646 262-9101
Bear *(G-293)*
SM Technomine Inc ... F ... 312 492-4386
Wilmington *(G-12647)*
Techno Goober ... F ... 302 645-7177
Lewes *(G-3780)*
Valiu Inc ... G ... 317 853-5081
Lewes *(G-3807)*
Vpn Express Incorporated ... E ... 302 351-8029
Wilmington *(G-13106)*
Web N App LLC ... G ... 810 309-8242
Smyrna *(G-8741)*
Webstudy Inc ... G ... 888 326-4058
Harbeson *(G-2802)*
Wilkinson Technology Svcs LLC ... G ... 302 384-7770
Wilmington *(G-13204)*

7375 Information Retrieval Svcs

Aidbits Inc ... G ... 647 692-3494
Lewes *(G-3330)*
American Domain Names LLC ... F ... 253 785-0332
Wilmington *(G-9044)*
Braincore Inc ... F ... 302 999-9221
New Castle *(G-5103)*
Digital Whale LLC ... G ... 302 526-0115
Camden *(G-561)*
Eagle Eye America Inc ... G ... 302 392-3600
Bear *(G-134)*
Homeland SEC Verification LLC ... G ... 888 791-4614
Wilmington *(G-10941)*
Hughes Network Systems LLC ... G ... 302 335-4138
Frederica *(G-2406)*
Instanode Inc ... G ... 352 327-8872
Wilmington *(G-11042)*
Lexisnexis Risk Assets Inc ... A ... 800 458-9410
Wilmington *(G-11378)*
Merix LLC ... G ... 425 659-1425
Lewes *(G-3638)*
Plai Apps Inc ... G ... 661 678-3740
Dover *(G-1962)*
Quantumfly LLC ... F ... 312 618-5739
Dover *(G-2001)*
Veteran It Pro LLC ... F ... 302 824-3111
Hockessin *(G-3167)*
Webstudy Inc ... G ... 888 326-4058
Harbeson *(G-2802)*
Xcs Corporation ... G ... 302 514-0600
Wilmington *(G-13316)*

7376 Computer Facilities Management Svcs

Absolute Computer Support LLC ... E ... 717 917-8900
Newark *(G-5887)*
Datatech Enterprises Inc ... F ... 540 370-0010
Selbyville *(G-8478)*
Herbert R Martin Associates ... G ... 302 239-1700
Hockessin *(G-3046)*
Information Safeguard Inc ... G ... 410 604-2660
Wilmington *(G-11027)*
Insight Engineering Solutions ... G ... 302 378-4842
Townsend *(G-8797)*
Veteran It Pro LLC ... F ... 302 824-3111
Hockessin *(G-3167)*

7377 Computer Rental & Leasing

34m LLC ... E ... 302 444-8290
Newark *(G-5857)*

7378 Computer Maintenance & Repair

Access Versalign Inc ... G ... 302 225-7800
Wilmington *(G-8914)*
Biz TEC Inc ... G ... 302 227-1967
Rehoboth Beach *(G-7870)*
Coastal It Consulting ... G ... 302 226-9395
Rehoboth Beach *(G-7893)*
Computer Jocks ... G ... 302 544-6448
Bear *(G-81)*
Confluent Corporation ... G ... 301 440-4100
Georgetown *(G-2481)*
Curvature Inc ... G ... 302 525-9525
Newark *(G-6328)*
Diamond Computer Inc ... G ... 302 674-4064
Dover *(G-1420)*
Eagle Eye America Inc ... G ... 302 392-3600
Bear *(G-134)*
First Tech ... E ... 302 421-3650
Wilmington *(G-10557)*

SIC

Laser Images of Delaware Inc ...G ... 302 836-8610
Bear *(G-229)*
Motto Computer Inc ...G ... 302 633-6783
Wilmington *(G-11763)*
PC Supplies Inc ...G ... 302 368-4800
Newark *(G-7189)*
Response Computer Group Inc ...F ... 302 335-3400
Milford *(G-4540)*
Secure Data Cmpt Solutions Inc ...G ... 302 346-7327
Dover *(G-2065)*
Software Services of De Inc ...E ... 302 654-3172
Wilmington *(G-12672)*
Steven Abdill ...G ... 443 243-6864
Wilmington *(G-12758)*
Tech Impact ...E ... 302 256-5015
Wilmington *(G-12867)*
Technicare Inc ...G ... 302 322-7766
Newark *(G-7545)*
Teleplan Vdeocom Solutions Inc ...C ... 302 323-8503
New Castle *(G-5760)*
Tower Business Machines Inc ...G ... 302 395-1445
New Castle *(G-5780)*
Zerowait Corporation ...F ... 302 996-9408
Wilmington *(G-13349)*

7379 Computer Related Svcs, NEC

2ndquadrant Inc ...G ... 650 378-1218
Wilmington *(G-8856)*
34m LLC ...E ... 302 444-8290
Newark *(G-5857)*
3d Tech LLC ...G ... 610 268-2350
Hockessin *(G-2947)*
4sight Group LLC ...G ... 800 490-2131
Wilmington *(G-8864)*
Aegisnet Inc ...E ... 302 325-2122
New Castle *(G-5011)*
Ait Advanced Infotech Inc ...G ... 302 454-8620
Bear *(G-24)*
Aleric International Inc ...F ... 302 547-4846
Middletown *(G-3934)*
Almm Ventures LLC ...G ... 302 778-1300
Wilmington *(G-9026)*
Antenna House Inc ...G ... 302 427-2456
Newark *(G-5973)*
Applied Control Engrg Inc ...D ... 302 738-8800
Newark *(G-5987)*
Applied Technologies Inc ...G ... 302 670-4601
Camden Wyoming *(G-614)*
Apps Complex LLC ...F ... 705 600-0729
Lewes *(G-3344)*
Axiom Resources LLC ...F ... 410 756-0440
Dover *(G-1163)*
Bamboozle Web Services Inc ...G ... 833 380-4600
Newark *(G-6041)*
Biritek LLC ...G ... 949 556-3943
Dover *(G-1206)*
Blackthorn Advisory Group LLC ...G ... 302 442-6484
Wilmington *(G-9365)*
◆ **Bluent LLC** ...D ... 832 476-8459
Lewes *(G-3388)*
Burgeon It Services LLC ...F ... 302 613-0999
Wilmington *(G-9506)*
Capgemini America Inc ...G ... 302 656-7491
Wilmington *(G-9555)*
Compd Holdings Inc ...G ... 929 436-5252
Middletown *(G-4005)*
Computer Sciences Corporation ...B ... 302 391-8347
Newark *(G-6277)*
Conectiv Communications Inc ...E ... 302 224-1177
Newark *(G-6282)*
Congruence Consulting Group ...G ... 320 290-6155
Newark *(G-6286)*
Conventra LLC ...G ... 302 378-4461
Middletown *(G-4008)*
Counterpoint Software Inc ...G ... 302 426-6500
Wilmington *(G-9875)*
Csols Inc ...E ... 302 731-5290
Newark *(G-6322)*
Data-Bi LLC ...G ... 302 290-3138
Wilmington *(G-9962)*
Datatech Enterprises Inc ...F ... 540 370-0010
Selbyville *(G-8478)*
Dax-Wave Consulting LLC ...G ... 424 543-6662
Wilmington *(G-9974)*
Delasoft Inc ...C ... 302 533-7912
New Castle *(G-5222)*
Delmarvavoip LLC ...G ... 855 645-8647
Lewes *(G-3460)*
Delt LLC ...G ... 215 869-7409
Newark *(G-6431)*
Dew Softech Inc ...E ... 302 834-2555
Newark *(G-6441)*
Diamond Technologies Inc ...E ... 302 421-8252
Wilmington *(G-10149)*
Digital Technology ...F ... 416 829-8400
Wilmington *(G-10153)*
Diligent Bus Solutions LLC ...G ... 302 897-5993
Newark *(G-6449)*
Discidium Technology Inc ...G ... 347 220-5979
Newark *(G-6455)*
E-Dmz Security LLC ...E ... 302 791-9370
Wilmington *(G-10312)*
E2e LLC ...G ... 703 906-5353
Hockessin *(G-3014)*
Eagle Eye America Inc ...G ... 302 392-3600
Bear *(G-134)*
Edward Land Consulting Inc ...G ... 302 838-7003
Bear *(G-140)*
Efotolabcom Inc ...G ... 302 984-0807
Wilmington *(G-10361)*
Encross LLC ...F ... 302 351-2593
Wilmington *(G-10396)*
Ets & Ycp LLC ...G ... 302 525-4111
Newark *(G-6543)*
Even & Odd Minds LLC ...F ... 619 663-7284
Wilmington *(G-10443)*
Evocati Group Corporation ...F ... 206 551-9087
Dover *(G-1533)*
Evonsys LLC ...G ... 302 544-2156
Wilmington *(G-10451)*
Feast Kitchen Inc ...G ... 415 758-8779
Dover *(G-1545)*
Forward Discovery Inc ...G ... 703 647-6364
Camden Wyoming *(G-641)*
Frontier Technologies Inc ...G ... 302 225-2530
Wilmington *(G-10644)*
G B Tech Inc ...E ... 302 378-5600
Middletown *(G-4081)*
GBA Enterprises Inc ...G ... 302 323-1080
New Castle *(G-5346)*
Genesec Inc ...G ... 917 656-5742
Claymont *(G-751)*
Genovesius Solutia LLC ...G ... 302 252-7506
Hockessin *(G-3036)*
Gmg Solutions LLC ...E ... 302 781-3008
Wilmington *(G-10734)*
Goodworld Inc ...G ... 845 325-2232
Wilmington *(G-10750)*
Headstream Inc ...D ... 302 356-0156
Wilmington *(G-10865)*
Hoover Computer Services Inc ...G ... 302 529-7050
Wilmington *(G-10950)*
Horizon Systems Inc ...G ... 302 983-3203
New Castle *(G-5404)*
Icuelab LLC ...G ... 302 983-8924
Newark *(G-6761)*
Iji Inc ...E ... 732 485-9427
Wilmington *(G-10997)*
Ik Solutions Inc ...G ... 302 861-6775
Newark *(G-6766)*
Implify Inc ...E ... 302 533-2345
Newark *(G-6769)*
Inetworkz LLC ...F ... 407 401-9384
Lewes *(G-3558)*
Inov8 Inc ...G ... 302 465-5124
Camden Wyoming *(G-646)*
Instadapp Labs LLC ...G ... 469 605-1661
Lewes *(G-3560)*
Intercontinental Tech LLC ...G ... 302 984-2111
Wilmington *(G-11057)*
Internet Working Technologies ...G ... 302 424-1855
Milford *(G-4450)*
Intrinsic Partners LLC ...D ... 610 388-0853
Wilmington *(G-11071)*
Inumsoft Inc ...G ... 302 533-5403
Bear *(G-191)*
It Resources Inc ...E ... 203 521-6945
Newark *(G-6809)*
It Tigers LLC ...G ... 732 898-2793
Lewes *(G-3565)*
Jhonston and Associates ...G ... 302 368-9790
Newark *(G-6838)*
Keyboarders LLC ...G ... 302 438-8055
Wilmington *(G-11250)*
Kogut Tech Consulting Inc ...G ... 302 455-0388
Newark *(G-6901)*
Kortech Consulting Inc ...F ... 302 559-4612
Bear *(G-220)*
Lambro Technologies LLC ...G ... 302 351-2559
Wilmington *(G-11325)*
Layercake LLC ...G ... 571 449-7538
Newark *(G-6924)*
Licensing Assurance LLC ...F ... 305 851-3545
Lewes *(G-3607)*
Lifesquared Inc ...G ... 415 475-9090
Dover *(G-1785)*
Liveware Inc ...F ... 302 791-9446
Claymont *(G-775)*
Luxcore LLC ...F ... 302 777-0538
Wilmington *(G-11457)*
Maan Softwares Inc ...E ... 531 203-9141
Lewes *(G-3615)*
Maven Security Consulting Inc ...G ... 302 365-6862
Bear *(G-248)*
McSglobal Inc ...G ... 302 427-6970
Wilmington *(G-11607)*
Mozeweb LLC ...G ... 302 355-0692
Newark *(G-7065)*
My Digital Shield ...G ... 423 310-8977
Wilmington *(G-11787)*
Naiva Solutions Inc ...G ... 612 987-6350
Newark *(G-7082)*
Net Monarch ...G ... 302 994-9407
Wilmington *(G-11837)*
Network Design Technologies ...G ... 610 991-2929
Wilmington *(G-11839)*
Network Security Services Inc ...F ... 703 319-0411
Dover *(G-1895)*
Nspire Automation LLC ...G ... 404 545-0821
Wilmington *(G-11917)*
Orpheus Companies Ltd ...G ... 302 328-3451
New Castle *(G-5592)*
Partners Plus Inc ...G ... 302 529-3700
New Castle *(G-5605)*
Pathscale Inc ...E ... 408 520-0811
Wilmington *(G-12031)*
Paymenex Inc ...D ... 302 504-6044
Wilmington *(G-12048)*
Petcube Inc ...E ... 786 375-9065
Wilmington *(G-12093)*
Play US Media LLC ...G ... 302 924-5034
Dover *(G-1965)*
PLM Consulting Inc ...F ... 302 984-2698
Wilmington *(G-12160)*
Precisionists Inc ...G ... 610 241-5354
Wilmington *(G-12209)*
Private Family Network LLC ...F ... 302 760-9684
Dover *(G-1988)*
Proactive Prfmce Solutions Inc ...F ... 302 375-0451
Newark *(G-7264)*
Quickborn Consulting LLC ...G ... 302 407-0922
Wilmington *(G-12288)*
Raas Infotek LLC ...E ... 302 894-3184
Newark *(G-7294)*
Ram Tech Systems Inc ...E ... 302 832-6600
Middletown *(G-4210)*
Rave Business Systems LLC ...F ... 302 407-2270
Lewes *(G-3708)*
Ru Inc ...C ... 917 346-0285
Wilmington *(G-12488)*
Sanjaban Corp ...G ... 612 805-5971
Wilmington *(G-12540)*
SC Foster LLC ...F ... 302 383-0201
Wilmington *(G-12548)*
Scicom Scntific Communications ...G ... 302 475-2694
Wilmington *(G-12558)*
Scinorx Technologies Inc ...G ... 302 268-5447
Wilmington *(G-12560)*
Securenetmd LLC ...E ... 302 645-7770
Lewes *(G-3736)*
Sendsafely LLC ...F ... 917 375-5891
Newark *(G-7407)*
Sherweb Inc ...G ... 888 567-6610
Newark *(G-7416)*
Sigma Data Systems Inc ...G ... 302 453-8812
Newark *(G-7426)*
Skiplist Inc ...G ... 440 855-0319
Newark *(G-7436)*
SM Technomine Inc ...F ... 312 492-4386
Wilmington *(G-12647)*
Smart Armor Protected LLC ...G ... 480 823-8122
Newark *(G-7444)*
Solid Idea Solutions LLC ...G ... 646 982-2890
Lewes *(G-3755)*
Swit Inc ...C ... 302 792-0175
Wilmington *(G-12826)*
Symbiosys Consulting LLC ...F ... 302 507-7649
Wilmington *(G-12830)*
Syncretic Software Inc ...F ... 302 762-2600
Wilmington *(G-12835)*

SIC SECTION

73 BUSINESS SERVICES

Tapp Networks LLC	G	302 222-3384
Newark (G-7539)		
Tech International Corp	G	302 478-2301
Wilmington (G-12868)		
Techno Soft Inc	F	302 392-5200
Wilmington (G-12871)		
Tecs Plus	G	302 437-6890
Newark (G-7550)		
Tekstrom Inc	E	302 709-5900
Wilmington (G-12876)		
Threatstop Inc	F	760 542-1550
Dover (G-2146)		
Toptal LLC	D	650 843-9206
Wilmington (G-12933)		
Total Risc Technology USA LLC	D	972 422-9135
Wilmington (G-12940)		
Ublerb	G	773 569-9686
Dover (G-2171)		
University of Delaware	C	302 831-6041
Newark (G-7621)		
Vensoft LLC	E	302 392-9000
Wilmington (G-13057)		
Verito Technologies LLC	F	855 583-7486
Wilmington (G-13061)		
Vitalus Technologies Inc	G	302 383-9100
Clayton (G-873)		
Vls It Consulting Inc	F	302 368-5656
Newark (G-7662)		
Vsg Business Solutions LLC	E	302 261-3209
Bear (G-367)		
Wahed Inc	E	646 961-7063
Lewes (G-3813)		
Wahid Consultants LLC	E	315 400-0955
New Castle (G-5821)		
Warain Corp	G	762 670-3452
Wilmington (G-13118)		
Webbit	G	302 725-6024
Milford (G-4600)		
Wenova Inc	G	847 477-0489
New Castle (G-5829)		
Wyndham Group Inc	G	704 905-9750
Wilmington (G-13312)		
Xtium LLC	E	302 351-6177
Wilmington (G-13323)		
Yes Hardsoft Solutions Inc	G	609 632-0397
Claymont (G-828)		
Yesamerica Corporation	F	800 872-1548
Middletown (G-4294)		
Z Data Inc	G	302 566-5351
Newark (G-7735)		
Ziras Technologies Inc	F	302 286-7303
Newark (G-7741)		

7381 Detective & Armored Car Svcs

ADT LLC	F	302 918-1016
Newark (G-5902)		
Advantage Security Inc	F	302 652-3060
Wilmington (G-8960)		
Alliedbarton Security Svcs LLC	G	302 498-0450
Wilmington (G-9024)		
Alpha Omega Invstgtons Wrkmans	G	302 323-8111
New Castle (G-5025)		
Base Enterprise Inc	G	302 337-0548
Bridgeville (G-452)		
Bennett Det Prtective Agcy Inc	G	302 734-2480
Dover (G-1192)		
Black Dragon Corporation	D	617 470-9230
Newark (G-6089)		
Command Security Corporation	C	302 478-7003
Wilmington (G-9782)		
Conmac Security Systems Inc	E	302 529-9286
Wilmington (G-9824)		
Delaware Acdemy Pub Safety SEC	F	302 377-1465
New Castle (G-5223)		
Delaware Detective Group LLC	G	302 373-3678
Middletown (G-4027)		
Dunbar Armored Inc	E	302 892-4950
Wilmington (G-10247)		
Dunbar Armored Inc	E	302 628-5401
Seaford (G-8228)		
Dupont Esl Security	E	302 695-1657
Wilmington (G-10254)		
G4s Secure Solutions (usa)	G	302 395-9930
New Castle (G-5340)		
Garda CL Atlantic Inc	E	302 762-5444
Wilmington (G-10670)		
Global Protection MGT LLC	D	302 425-4190
Wilmington (G-10729)		
Int Investigation Security Inc	G	609 727-8317
Lewes (G-3561)		
Ironhouse Security Group Inc	G	443 312-9932
Dover (G-1684)		
JR Gettier & Associates Inc	B	302 478-0911
Wilmington (G-11202)		
Lenar Detective Agency Inc	C	302 994-3011
Wilmington (G-11369)		
Multi-Cble Adv SEC Sltns Inc	G	703 909-6239
Wilmington (G-11774)		
Resort Investigation & Patrol	E	302 539-5808
Millville (G-4855)		
S & H Enterprises Inc	F	302 999-9911
Wilmington (G-12505)		
Securitas SEC Svcs USA Inc	C	302 573-6802
Wilmington (G-12569)		
Security Watch Corp	F	302 286-6728
Newark (G-7401)		
Social Security Administration	G	302 736-3688
Dover (G-2092)		
SOS Security Incorporated	G	302 425-4755
Wilmington (G-12683)		
T & B Invstgtions SEC Agcy LLC	G	302 476-4087
Middletown (G-4252)		
Zicherheit LLC	F	302 510-3718
Selbyville (G-8557)		

7382 Security Systems Svcs

A Plus Electric & Security	G	302 455-1725
Newark (G-5869)		
Action Security	G	302 838-2852
Newark (G-5895)		
ADT LLC	F	302 325-3125
New Castle (G-5006)		
Advanced Protection LLC	G	302 539-6041
Ocean View (G-7754)		
Advanced Security Systems Inc	G	302 998-7222
Wilmington (G-8956)		
Advantech Incorporated	E	302 674-8405
Dover (G-1090)		
Anaconda Prtctive Concepts Inc	F	302 834-1125
Newark (G-5965)		
B Safe Inc	E	302 633-1833
Wilmington (G-9213)		
B Safe Inc	E	302 422-3916
Dover (G-1167)		
Bantam Technologies LLC	G	302 256-5823
Wilmington (G-9245)		
Berley Security Systems Inc	F	302 791-9056
Wilmington (G-9305)		
Besecure LLC	E	855 897-0650
Lewes (G-3377)		
BTS Enterprises Inc	G	302 428-6080
Wilmington (G-9496)		
Chesapeake SEC Investigations	E	302 429-7505
New Castle (G-5146)		
Delta Risk LLC	F	312 203-8307
Wilmington (G-10107)		
Emergncy Response Protocol LLC	G	302 994-2600
Wilmington (G-10391)		
IMNa Solutions Inc	F	347 821-8238
Wilmington (G-11006)		
Int Investigation Security Inc	G	609 727-8317
Lewes (G-3561)		
Integrated Tech Systems LLC	G	302 613-2111
New Castle (G-5420)		
Ip Camera Warehouse LLC	G	302 358-2690
Wilmington (G-11079)		
Johnson Cntrls SEC Sltions LLC	D	302 328-2800
New Castle (G-5442)		
Prevent Alarm Company LLC	G	302 478-6647
New Castle (G-5639)		
Protect America Inc	G	302 999-9045
Wilmington (G-12255)		
S & B Pro Security LLC	G	800 841-9907
Dover (G-2047)		
Safe Home Control Inc	G	302 504-6300
Wilmington (G-12515)		
Securitas Electronic SEC Inc	E	302 992-7950
Wilmington (G-12568)		
Security Inc	F	302 652-5276
Claymont (G-802)		
Security Instrument Corp Del	F	302 674-2891
Milton (G-4966)		
Security Instrument Corp Del	D	302 998-2261
Wilmington (G-12571)		
Security Quality	G	302 286-1200
Newark (G-7400)		
Sobieski Life Safety	G	800 321-1332
Newark (G-7451)		
Sound-N-Secure Inc	G	302 424-3670
Milford (G-4563)		
Vector Security Inc	E	302 422-7031
Milford (G-4589)		

7383 News Syndicates

Associated Press	G	302 737-1628
Newark (G-6012)		
Dover Post Co Inc	D	302 678-3616
Dover (G-1467)		
Nk Consulting Inc	F	330 269-5775
Wilmington (G-11891)		

7384 Photofinishing Labs

▲ Avalanche Strategies LLC	C	302 436-7060
Selbyville (G-8452)		
Cameras Etc Inc	G	302 453-9400
Newark (G-6146)		
Colourworks Photographic Svcs	G	302 428-0222
Wilmington (G-9778)		
Delaware Color Lab	G	302 529-1339
Wilmington (G-10021)		
Fujifilm Imaging Colorants Inc	D	302 472-1245
New Castle (G-5335)		

7389 Business Svcs, NEC

1 Fair Chiropractic & Med Inc	G	302 528-1068
Wilmington (G-8840)		
1313 Innovation	G	302 407-0420
Wilmington (G-8846)		
1st State Accessibility LLC	G	844 663-4396
Wilmington (G-8850)		
313design Lab Inc	G	929 399-6426
Lewes (G-3316)		
3ti Coatings LLC	G	302 379-1265
Hockessin (G-2948)		
6 Star Fundraising LLC	E	302 250-5085
Newark (G-5861)		
7c Infotech Inc	G	717 288-8686
Wilmington (G-8866)		
A and D Plumbing LLC	G	302 387-9232
Magnolia (G-3877)		
A1 Nationwide LLC	G	302 327-9302
Wilmington (G-8889)		
A2a Intgrted Phrmceuticals LLC	G	270 202-2461
Lewes (G-3320)		
A2ps Consulting and Sftwr LLC	F	331 201-6101
Wilmington (G-8891)		
Abba Monument Co Inc	G	302 738-0272
Newark (G-5880)		
Abcware LLC	G	888 755-1485
Wilmington (G-8900)		
Abha Architects Inc	E	302 658-6426
Wilmington (G-8902)		
ABS Engineering LLC	G	302 595-9081
Newark (G-5886)		
Acentium Inc	F	617 938-3938
Wilmington (G-8920)		
Acorn Site Furnishings	G	302 249-4979
Bridgeville (G-443)		
Adferns Media LLC	G	315 444-7720
Dover (G-1086)		
Aecom Technology Corporation	E	302 468-5878
Wilmington (G-8962)		
Aeres Corporation	G	858 926-8626
New Castle (G-5013)		
African Markets Fund LLC	G	703 944-1514
Dover (G-1092)		
Agricltral Asssmnts Intl Corp	G	240 463-6677
Laurel (G-3191)		
Aids Delaware Inc	E	302 652-6776
Wilmington (G-8986)		
Aldas Refinishing Company	G	302 528-5028
Hockessin (G-2955)		
Alias Inc	G	302 481-5556
Wilmington (G-9010)		
All Lives Matter LLC	G	252 767-9291
Dover (G-1106)		
Allegiant Fire Protection LLC	G	302 276-1300
Newark (G-5938)		
Alliance Bus Dev Concepts LLC	F	803 814-4004
Clayton (G-832)		
Amdisvet LLC	G	302 514-9130
Smyrna (G-8568)		
American-Eurasian Exch Co LLC	G	202 701-4009
Wilmington (G-9060)		
Ampx2 Inc	G	650 521-5750
Dover (G-1121)		
Andrews Construction LLC	G	302 604-8166
Seaford (G-8153)		

Employee Codes: A=Over 500 employees, B=251-500
C=101-250, D=51-100, E=20-50, F=10-19, G=1-9

2020 Harris Directory of
Delaware Businesses

73 BUSINESS SERVICES

Angle Planning Concepts ....F...... 302 735-7526
  Dover *(G-1126)*
Apphive Inc ....G...... 240 898-4661
  Newark *(G-5984)*
Applied Card Holdings Inc ....G...... 302 326-4200
  Wilmington *(G-9101)*
Applied Virtual Solutions LLC .....G...... 302 312-8548
  Newark *(G-5988)*
Aptustech LLC ....G...... 347 254-5619
  Wilmington *(G-9105)*
Arangodb Inc ....G...... 415 659-5938
  Wilmington *(G-9111)*
Arqitecture LLC ....G...... 302 777-5666
  Winterthur *(G-13356)*
Arrim LLC ....G...... 617 697-7914
  Wilmington *(G-9134)*
Ascension Industries LLC ....G...... 302 659-1778
  Smyrna *(G-8576)*
◆ Aspenologies LLC ....G...... 302 234-4346
  Wilmington *(G-9153)*
Asphalt Striping Svcs Del LLC ....G...... 302 456-9820
  Wilmington *(G-9154)*
At Systems Atlantic Inc ....F...... 302 762-5444
  Wilmington *(G-9170)*
Atlantic Sun Screen Prtg Inc ......F...... 302 731-5100
  Newark *(G-6021)*
Atlantic Water Products ....E...... 302 326-1166
  New Castle *(G-5052)*
Atr Electrical Services Inc ....G...... 302 373-7769
  Middletown *(G-3954)*
Aviman Management LLC ....E...... 302 377-5788
  Wilmington *(G-9199)*
B&W Tek LLC ....G...... 302 368-7824
  Newark *(G-6037)*
Bangus Business Services ....G...... 302 266-7285
  Newark *(G-6044)*
Bar & Associates Ltd ....G...... 302 999-9233
  Wilmington *(G-9246)*
Barutopia Inc ....G...... 858 284-8830
  Camden *(G-540)*
Batescainelli LLC ....G...... 202 618-2040
  Rehoboth Beach *(G-7856)*
Bayshore Communications Inc ....F...... 302 737-2164
  Newark *(G-6057)*
Bayville Postal Svc ....G...... 302 436-2715
  Selbyville *(G-8455)*
Be Blessed Design Group LLC ....G...... 302 561-3793
  Bear *(G-45)*
Beauty Purse Inc ....G...... 424 210-7474
  Dover *(G-1187)*
Beebe Medical Foundation ....G...... 302 644-2900
  Lewes *(G-3373)*
Beeline Services LLC ....G...... 302 376-7399
  Middletown *(G-3965)*
Bernardon PC ....F...... 302 622-9550
  Wilmington *(G-9309)*
Bethany Beach Vlntr Fire Co ......E...... 302 539-7700
  Bethany Beach *(G-388)*
BETz&betz Enterprises LLC ....G...... 302 602-0613
  Wilmington *(G-9318)*
Bever Mobility Products Inc ....G...... 312 375-0300
  Wilmington *(G-9319)*
Big Tomorrow LLC ....F...... 650 714-3912
  Wilmington *(G-9333)*
Bill Torbert ....F...... 302 734-9804
  Dover *(G-1202)*
Bitta Monk Entertainment Inc .....G...... 916 969-4430
  Newark *(G-6085)*
Bk 2 Si LLC ....G...... 800 246-2677
  Wilmington *(G-9344)*
Bki Enterprises LLC ....G...... 302 541-5317
  Ocean View *(G-7768)*
Blaze Coin LLC ....G...... 509 768-2249
  Dover *(G-1209)*
BLJ&d Flagging Llc ....F...... 302 272-0574
  Dover *(G-1210)*
Blue Hen Auction Co LLC ....G...... 302 697-6096
  Dover *(G-1213)*
Blue Pie Productions USA LLC ...F...... 917 817-7174
  Wilmington *(G-9380)*
Bml App Development ....G...... 302 528-7281
  Wilmington *(G-9386)*
Bolt Innovation LLC ....G...... 800 293-5249
  Dover *(G-1220)*
Bookaway ....E...... 888 250-3414
  Newark *(G-6105)*
Bovell Lowinger Bail Bonds ....G...... 302 427-9000
  Wilmington *(G-9401)*
Brandywine Hundred Fire Co 1 ...D...... 302 764-4901
  Wilmington *(G-9438)*

Brandywine Process Servers ....G...... 302 475-2600
  Wilmington *(G-9451)*
Brooks Courier Service Inc ....C...... 302 762-4661
  Wilmington *(G-9485)*
Buck Simpers Archt + Assoc Inc ..F...... 302 658-9300
  Wilmington *(G-9498)*
Building Inspection Undrwrtr ......G...... 302 266-9057
  Newark *(G-6133)*
Business At International LLC ....E...... 605 610-4885
  Lewes *(G-3394)*
Business Move Solutions Inc ......E...... 302 324-0080
  New Castle *(G-5124)*
Byte Technology Systems Inc ....G...... 347 687-7240
  Lewes *(G-3396)*
C&G Dental Studio LLC ....G...... 302 345-4995
  Bear *(G-60)*
C4-Nvis USA LLC ....G...... 213 465-5089
  Dover *(G-1246)*
▲ Cad Import Inc ....E...... 302 628-4178
  New Castle *(G-5128)*
Cadtech Inc ....F...... 302 832-2255
  Bear *(G-61)*
Captains Grant Solar 1 Inc ....G...... 410 375-2092
  Millsboro *(G-4655)*
Cargo Cube Licensing LLC ....G...... 844 200-2823
  Wilmington *(G-9568)*
Carolina Street Garden & Home ..G...... 302 539-2405
  Fenwick Island *(G-2332)*
Carr Paris ....F...... 302 401-1203
  Wilmington *(G-9578)*
Carter Pool Management LLC .....F...... 302 236-6952
  Lewes *(G-3409)*
Catholic Docese Wilmington Inc ..G...... 302 764-2717
  Wilmington *(G-9595)*
Center For A Pstive Hmnity LLC ..G...... 302 703-1036
  Felton *(G-2281)*
Center For Community Justice ....G...... 302 424-0890
  Milford *(G-4343)*
Chesapeake Design Center LLC ..G...... 302 875-8570
  Laurel *(G-3212)*
Chime Inc ....E...... 978 844-1162
  Wilmington *(G-9666)*
Christmas Corporation ....G...... 424 645-5001
  Lewes *(G-3420)*
Citifinancial Inc ....G...... 302 834-6677
  Bear *(G-73)*
Citigroup Inc ....E...... 302 631-3530
  Newark *(G-6237)*
City of Dover ....E...... 302 736-7035
  Dover *(G-1289)*
City of Dover - McKee Run ....G...... 302 672-6306
  Dover *(G-1291)*
Classerium Corporation ....G...... 773 306-3297
  Dover *(G-1292)*
Clinton Craddock ....F...... 267 505-2671
  Middletown *(G-3999)*
Cmp Fire LLC ....G...... 410 620-2062
  Newark *(G-6255)*
Coastal Marine AVI Svc LLC ......G...... 904 200-2749
  Wilmington *(G-9753)*
Cointigo LLC ....F...... 817 681-7131
  Middletown *(G-4000)*
Comprehensive Bus Svcs LLC ....F...... 302 994-2000
  Wilmington *(G-6274)*
Conducerent Incorporated ....G...... 302 543-8525
  Wilmington *(G-9816)*
Conference Group LLC ....E...... 302 224-8255
  Newark *(G-6284)*
Continental Finance Co LLC ....E...... 302 456-1930
  Wilmington *(G-9840)*
Contract Environments Inc ....G...... 302 658-0668
  Wilmington *(G-9843)*
Conzurge Inc ....F...... 267 507-6039
  Newark *(G-6294)*
Coolpop Nation ....G...... 302 584-8833
  Wilmington *(G-9852)*
Coqonut Inc ....G...... 347 419-7709
  Wilmington *(G-9857)*
Cordjia LLC ....E...... 302 743-1297
  Newark *(G-6296)*
Core Functions LLC ....G...... 443 956-9626
  Selbyville *(G-8471)*
Couture Denim LLC ....G...... 302 220-8339
  New Castle *(G-5204)*
▲ Cpmg Inc ....G...... 302 429-8688
  Wilmington *(G-9888)*
Crystal Graham ....F...... 302 669-9318
  Middletown *(G-4016)*
Custom Creations By Design ......G...... 302 482-2267
  Wilmington *(G-9925)*

Customs Benefits ....G...... 302 798-2884
  Wilmington *(G-9927)*
Cyber 20/20 Inc ....F...... 203 802-8742
  Newark *(G-6334)*
Cyber Seven Technologies LLC ...G...... 302 635-7122
  Newark *(G-6335)*
Cybersecurity Trust LLC ....G...... 844 240-2287
  Middletown *(G-4017)*
Cycology 202 LLC ....F...... 610 202-0518
  Lewes *(G-3447)*
D A B Productions ....G...... 302 670-9407
  Harrington *(G-2829)*
D&F Joint Ventures De LLC ....G...... 302 652-5151
  Wilmington *(G-9944)*
Dabvasan Inc ....G...... 302 529-1100
  Wilmington *(G-9946)*
Damon Baca ....G...... 858 837-0800
  Dover *(G-1338)*
▲ Data MGT Internationale Inc ..E...... 302 656-1151
  New Castle *(G-5215)*
David G Horsey & Sons Inc ....D...... 302 875-3033
  Laurel *(G-3221)*
David Popovich LLC ....G...... 855 464-9653
  Wilmington *(G-9971)*
Davin Management Group LLC ...F...... 302 367-6563
  Bear *(G-99)*
Dbd Wholesale LLC ....G...... 215 301-6277
  Wilmington *(G-9975)*
DC Consulting Service LLC ....F...... 617 594-9780
  Wilmington *(G-9976)*
Dcc Design Group LLC ....G...... 302 777-2100
  Wilmington *(G-9978)*
De Cheaper Trash LLC ....G...... 302 325-0670
  New Castle *(G-5219)*
Deafinitions & Interpreting ....F...... 302 563-7714
  Bear *(G-102)*
Deangelis & Son Inc ....G...... 302 337-8699
  Bridgeville *(G-464)*
Dekadu Inc ....G...... 763 390-3266
  Wilmington *(G-9996)*
Delaware 87ers LLC ....E...... 302 351-5385
  Wilmington *(G-10000)*
Delaware Bail Bonds ....G...... 302 734-9881
  Dover *(G-1358)*
Delaware Barter Corp ....G...... 800 343-1322
  Newark *(G-6365)*
Delaware Botanic Gardens Inc ....G...... 202 262-9501
  Bethany Beach *(G-397)*
Delaware Ecumenical Council .....G...... 302 225-1040
  Wilmington *(G-10043)*
Delaware Fncl Edcatn Alnce Inc ..G...... 302 674-0288
  Dover *(G-1371)*
Delaware Innovation Space Inc ..G...... 302 695-2201
  Wilmington *(G-10058)*
Delaware Merchant Services ......G...... 302 838-9100
  Wilmington *(G-10066)*
Delaware Mosquito Control LLC ..G...... 302 504-6757
  Newark *(G-6398)*
Delaware Retired Schl Prsnl ....E...... 302 674-8252
  Wilmington *(G-10079)*
Delaware Valley Field Svcs LLC ..G...... 302 384-8617
  Wilmington *(G-10094)*
Dell Oem Inc ....G...... 302 294-0060
  Newark *(G-6425)*
Delmarva Space Scnces Fndation .G...... 302 236-2761
  Millsboro *(G-4676)*
Delmarva Water Solutions ....G...... 302 674-0509
  Dover *(G-1412)*
Dempsey Farms LLC ....F...... 302 734-4937
  Dover *(G-1413)*
Dennek LLC ....G...... 302 703-0790
  Wilmington *(G-10109)*
Derby Software LLC ....G...... 502 435-1371
  Dover *(G-1415)*
Design Services Ltd ....J...... 302 475-5663
  Wilmington *(G-10122)*
Designer Consigner Inc ....G...... 302 239-4034
  Hockessin *(G-3008)*
Dewitt Heating and AC Inc ....G...... 267 228-7355
  Bear *(G-115)*
Dfs Corporate Services LLC ....B...... 302 735-3902
  Dover *(G-1419)*
Diamond State Door ....G...... 302 743-4667
  Wilmington *(G-10142)*
Dibiasos Clg Rstration Svc Inc ....G...... 302 376-7111
  Townsend *(G-8784)*
Digital Broadcast Corporation .....F...... 215 285-0912
  Wilmington *(G-10151)*
▲ DLS Discovery LLC ....D...... 302 888-2060
  Wilmington *(G-10176)*

2020 Harris Directory of Delaware Businesses

SIC SECTION 73 BUSINESS SERVICES

Dmg Clearances Inc..............G....... 302 239-6337
Hockessin *(G-3010)*
DOE Technologies Inc..............E....... 302 792-1285
Wilmington *(G-10181)*
Domian International Svc LLC..............G....... 804 837-3616
Smyrna *(G-8624)*
Donald Walker..............G....... 240 507-9805
Harrington *(G-2834)*
DOT Matrix Inc..............G....... 917 657-4918
Dover *(G-1439)*
Drafting By Design Inc..............G....... 302 292-8304
Newark *(G-6472)*
Dream Weaver Interiors Inc..............G....... 302 644-0800
Rehoboth Beach *(G-7921)*
Drfish LLC..............G....... 978 393-1212
Lewes *(G-3473)*
Du Pont Foreign Sales Corp..............A....... 302 774-1000
Wilmington *(G-10244)*
Dustntime..............F....... 302 858-7876
Rehoboth Beach *(G-7922)*
Dynamic Support Services Inc..............G....... 202 820-3113
Wilmington *(G-10272)*
E I Du Pont De Nemours & Co..............B....... 302 892-8832
Wilmington *(G-10284)*
E I Du Pont De Nemours & Co..............A....... 302 999-5072
Wilmington *(G-10303)*
E-Carauctions LLC..............G....... 302 677-1552
New Castle *(G-5272)*
Eastern Bison Association..............F....... 434 660-6036
Greenwood *(G-2735)*
▲ **Eastern Shore Metals LLC**..............F....... 302 629-6629
Seaford *(G-8231)*
Ebube Group & Co LLC..............G....... 215 821-7490
Newark *(G-6501)*
Echelon Interiors LLC..............G....... 302 519-9151
Rehoboth Beach *(G-7924)*
Ecomo Inc..............G....... 412 567-3867
Dover *(G-1502)*
Edokk LLC..............G....... 305 434-7227
Lewes *(G-3479)*
Eduqc LLC..............F....... 800 346-4646
Dover *(G-1508)*
Ekalt LLC..............G....... 302 300-4853
Wilmington *(G-10365)*
Electric Motor Wholesale Inc..............F....... 302 222-2090
Camden Wyoming *(G-634)*
Elsmere Fire Co 1 Inc..............G....... 302 999-0183
Wilmington *(G-10383)*
Emendo Bio Inc..............G....... 516 595-1849
Wilmington *(G-10389)*
Emmert Auction Associates..............F....... 302 227-1433
Rehoboth Beach *(G-7926)*
Empire Flippers LLC..............F....... 323 638-0438
Wilmington *(G-10394)*
Enclave Digital Development Co..............G....... 203 807-0400
Lewes *(G-3482)*
Envirtech Enviromental Consltg..............G....... 302 645-6491
Lewes *(G-3484)*
Envision It Publications LLC..............G....... 800 329-9411
Bear *(G-144)*
Ergos Consultores LLC..............F....... 549 404-6360
Wilmington *(G-10433)*
European Coach Werkes Inc..............G....... 302 436-2277
Frankford *(G-2362)*
Evans Farms LLC..............G....... 302 337-8130
Bridgeville *(G-469)*
Exo Works Inc..............G....... 302 531-1139
Dover *(G-1534)*
Eye35design LLC..............G....... 470 236-3933
Dover *(G-1535)*
Factory Technologies Inc..............G....... 302 266-1290
Newark *(G-6563)*
Fareed Services..............G....... 302 559-8594
Wilmington *(G-10499)*
Fast Bailbonds LLC..............G....... 302 778-4400
Wilmington *(G-10502)*
Federal Technical Associates..............G....... 302 697-7951
Dover *(G-1547)*
Ferrara Asset Management Inc..............G....... 401 286-8464
Wilmington *(G-10523)*
Fia Card Services Nat Assn..............D....... 800 362-6255
Wilmington *(G-10529)*
Fidelity National Fincl Inc..............D....... 302 658-2102
Wilmington *(G-10534)*
Firefly Drone Operations Llc..............G....... 305 206-6955
Wilmington *(G-10543)*
First State Inspection Agency..............G....... 302 422-3859
Milford *(G-4413)*
First State Inspection Agency..............G....... 302 449-5383
Middletown *(G-4072)*

Fitzgerald Auto Salvage Inc..............D....... 302 422-7584
Lincoln *(G-3849)*
Flute Pro Shop Inc..............G....... 302 479-5000
Wilmington *(G-10583)*
Food Equipment Service Inc..............F....... 302 996-9363
Wilmington *(G-10586)*
Forum To Advnce Mnrties In Eng..............E....... 302 777-3254
Wilmington *(G-10595)*
Fourth Floor..............G....... 302 472-8416
Wilmington *(G-10606)*
Fresh Start Transformations..............G....... 302 219-0221
Newark *(G-6623)*
Freshbooks Usa Inc..............G....... 416 525-5384
Wilmington *(G-10637)*
Frizbee Medical Inc..............G....... 424 901-1534
Wilmington *(G-10643)*
Fur Baby Tracker LLC..............G....... 610 563-3294
Wilmington *(G-10649)*
Fyrbeacon Inc..............E....... 562 569-0547
Wilmington *(G-10655)*
Gamers4gamers LLC..............G....... 302 722-6289
Newark *(G-6636)*
Garth Troescher Jr LLC..............G....... 302 927-0106
Frankford *(G-2364)*
Gaudlitz Inc..............G....... 202 468-3876
Dover *(G-1585)*
GE Capital Intl Holdings Corp..............F....... 302 658-7581
Wilmington *(G-10684)*
Gensource Fincl Asrn Co LLC..............F....... 302 415-3030
Wilmington *(G-10695)*
Get Takeout LLC..............G....... 800 785-6218
Lewes *(G-3513)*
Giesela Inc..............G....... 855 556-4338
Newark *(G-6653)*
Giumarra International Mktg..............G....... 302 652-4009
Wilmington *(G-10717)*
Gjv Inc..............G....... 302 455-1600
Newark *(G-6659)*
Global Merchant Partners LLC..............G....... 302 425-3567
Rehoboth Beach *(G-7950)*
Global Shipping Center LLC..............G....... 302 798-4321
Claymont *(G-754)*
Global Shopaholics LLC..............F....... 703 608-7108
Wilmington *(G-10731)*
Golden Globe Intl Svcs Ltd..............C....... 302 487-0022
Wilmington *(G-10737)*
Goldfinch Group Inc..............G....... 646 300-0716
Dover *(G-1600)*
Golt Adj Service Inc..............E....... 302 798-5500
Wilmington *(G-10744)*
Goodworld Inc..............G....... 845 325-2232
Wilmington *(G-10750)*
Grahams Wireless Solutions Inc..............F....... 717 943-0717
Millsboro *(G-4698)*
Great I AM Prod Studios Inc..............G....... 302 463-2483
New Castle *(G-5361)*
Greater Wilmington Convention..............G....... 302 652-4088
Wilmington *(G-10769)*
Green Crescent LLC..............G....... 800 735-9620
Dover *(G-1611)*
Greenlea LLC..............G....... 302 227-7868
Rehoboth Beach *(G-7955)*
GSM Systems Inc..............F....... 302 284-8304
Viola *(G-8836)*
Gt Designs Inc..............G....... 302 275-8100
Middletown *(G-4096)*
Gt USA Wilmington LLC..............G....... 302 472-7679
Wilmington *(G-10794)*
Gulch Group LLC..............G....... 202 697-1756
Rehoboth Beach *(G-7956)*
Guy & Lady Barrel LLC..............G....... 302 399-3069
Dover *(G-1618)*
◆ **H&H Trading International LLC**..............G....... 480 580-3911
Wilmington *(G-10811)*
Haloali Teeth Whitening LLC..............G....... 302 300-4042
Claymont *(G-760)*
Har-Lex LLC..............G....... 302 476-2322
Wilmington *(G-10835)*
Harbin LLC..............G....... 302 219-3320
Lewes *(G-3532)*
Harrel Stefoni..............G....... 302 344-3269
Dover *(G-1628)*
Harriet Tubman Safe House Inc..............G....... 302 351-4434
Wilmington *(G-10841)*
Harry H Mc Robie..............G....... 302 846-9784
Delmar *(G-1001)*
HARt Group LLC..............G....... 302 782-9742
Dover *(G-1636)*
Hatfield Gas Connections Inc..............G....... 302 945-2354
Lewes *(G-3536)*

Haymy Resources LLC..............G....... 402 218-6787
Lewes *(G-3537)*
Hcac..............G....... 302 266-8100
Newark *(G-6714)*
Henderson Services Inc..............F....... 302 424-1999
Milford *(G-4438)*
Hera Sports Surfaces LLC..............E....... 781 392-4094
Newark *(G-6723)*
Hifu Services Inc..............G....... 650 867-4972
Wilmington *(G-10902)*
Highway Traffic Controllers..............E....... 302 697-7117
Camden Wyoming *(G-645)*
Hindin Media LLC..............G....... 302 463-4612
Wilmington *(G-10915)*
Holland Corp..............G....... 302 245-5645
Selbyville *(G-8503)*
Hoops For Hope Delaware..............F....... 302 229-7600
Wilmington *(G-10949)*
Hq Global Workplaces Inc..............G....... 302 295-4800
Wilmington *(G-10963)*
Hts 20 LLP..............G....... 800 690-2029
Milton *(G-4916)*
Hx Innovations Inc..............G....... 302 983-9705
Middletown *(G-4110)*
Hypergames Inc..............G....... 424 343-6370
Wilmington *(G-10982)*
Icase LLC..............F....... 302 703-7854
Lewes *(G-3550)*
ICS America Inc..............G....... 215 979-1620
Wilmington *(G-10990)*
Inc Plan (usa)..............G....... 302 428-1200
Wilmington *(G-11011)*
Incolor Inc..............G....... 302 984-2695
Wilmington *(G-11014)*
Industrial Training Cons Inc..............F....... 302 266-6100
Newark *(G-6774)*
Inetworkz LLC..............F....... 407 401-9384
Lewes *(G-3558)*
Initial Trading Co..............G....... 302 428-1132
Wilmington *(G-11034)*
Inov8 Inc..............G....... 302 465-5124
Camden Wyoming *(G-646)*
Instantuptime Inc..............F....... 302 608-0890
Dover *(G-1680)*
Interactive Marketing Services..............E....... 302 456-9810
Newark *(G-6796)*
Iron HI Aprsal Prperty MGT LLC..............G....... 302 454-1404
Newark *(G-6808)*
Itconnectus Inc..............G....... 302 531-1139
Dover *(G-1685)*
J L Carpenter Farms LLC..............G....... 302 684-8601
Milton *(G-4919)*
James Stewart Rostocki..............G....... 302 250-5541
Wilmington *(G-11123)*
James T Vaughn..............G....... 302 653-9261
Smyrna *(G-8663)*
Jarel Industries LLC..............G....... 336 782-0697
Camden *(G-585)*
Jayu LLC..............F....... 888 534-3018
Wilmington *(G-11134)*
JBA Enterprises..............F....... 302 834-6685
Bear *(G-198)*
Jbm Petroleum Service LLC..............G....... 302 752-6105
Lincoln *(G-3857)*
Jbr Contractors Inc..............E....... 856 296-9594
Millsboro *(G-4714)*
Jed T James..............G....... 302 875-0101
Georgetown *(G-2572)*
Jeffrey Hatch..............G....... 443 496-0449
Marydel *(G-3919)*
Ji DCI Jv-II..............F....... 302 652-4221
Wilmington *(G-11156)*
Jl Mechanical Inc..............G....... 302 337-7855
Bridgeville *(G-487)*
Jni CCC Jv1..............G....... 302 654-6611
Wilmington *(G-11162)*
▲ **Johnny Janosik Inc**..............C....... 302 875-5955
Laurel *(G-3243)*
Jon Irby III..............G....... 302 652-0564
Wilmington *(G-11180)*
Jthan LLC..............G....... 302 994-2534
Wilmington *(G-11206)*
Kamara LLC..............G....... 302 220-9570
New Castle *(G-5450)*
Keefer Mountain Enterprise..............G....... 814 657-3998
Rehoboth Beach *(G-7977)*
Kent County Tourism Corp..............G....... 302 734-1736
Dover *(G-1733)*
Kenya Gather Foundation..............F....... 302 382-8227
Millsboro *(G-4716)*

S
I
C

Employee Codes: A=Over 500 employees, B=251-500
C=101-250, D=51-100, E=20-50, F=10-19, G=1-9

73 BUSINESS SERVICES

▲ Kid Agains Inc .... G 631 830-5228
Dover *(G-1746)*
Kintyre Solutions LLC .... G 888 636-0010
Wilmington *(G-11269)*
Kirks Flowers Inc .... E 302 737-3931
Newark *(G-6890)*
Kleen-Comp LLC .... G 302 981-0791
Newark *(G-6897)*
Knight Hauling Inc .... G 610 494-6800
Wilmington *(G-11281)*
Knowt Inc .... F 848 391-0575
Lewes *(G-3585)*
Kortech Consulting Inc .... F 302 559-4612
Bear *(G-220)*
Kriss Contracting Inc .... E 302 492-3502
Hartly *(G-2932)*
Kwikbuck Inc .... G 774 517-8959
Wilmington *(G-11305)*
Lamar Bags .... G 302 492-8566
Hartly *(G-2933)*
Lawrence JP & Associates .... F 313 293-2692
Wilmington *(G-11345)*
Leadership Forum LLC .... G 919 309-4025
Dover *(G-1773)*
Lifesquared Inc .... G 415 475-9090
Dover *(G-1785)*
Litcharts LLC .... G 646 481-4807
Wilmington *(G-11400)*
Live Typing Inc .... E 415 670-9601
Wilmington *(G-11412)*
Living Well Magazine .... G 302 355-0929
Newark *(G-6943)*
Local TV Finance LLC .... E 302 636-5401
Wilmington *(G-11420)*
Loftcom Inc .... G 800 563-6900
Wilmington *(G-11425)*
Lookinn Inc .... G 302 839-2088
Dover *(G-1796)*
Looksiebin LLC .... G 410 869-2192
Wilmington *(G-11433)*
Lumber Industries Inc .... G 302 655-9651
Wilmington *(G-11448)*
Lynn and Rachel Walsh .... G 302 422-2893
Milford *(G-4482)*
M R Designs Inc .... G 302 684-8082
Milton *(G-4928)*
Maan Softwares Inc .... E 531 203-9141
Lewes *(G-3615)*
Mail Rooms Ltd .... G 302 629-4838
Seaford *(G-8300)*
Mail Stop .... G 302 947-4704
Millsboro *(G-4731)*
Mainline Masonry Inc .... E 302 998-2499
Middletown *(G-4142)*
Majalco LLC .... G 703 507-5298
Wilmington *(G-11494)*
Mark Showell Interiors Ltd .... F 302 227-2272
Rehoboth Beach *(G-7999)*
Martys Contracting .... G 302 234-8690
Hockessin *(G-3091)*
Maryann Metrinko LLC .... G 410 643-1472
Lewes *(G-3623)*
Matter Music Inc .... F 650 793-7749
Wilmington *(G-11568)*
Mayjuun LLC .... G 865 300-7738
Lewes *(G-3628)*
Mazzpac LLC .... G 973 641-9159
Newark *(G-7009)*
MBNA Marketing Systems Inc .... A 302 456-8588
Wilmington *(G-11583)*
McConnell Bros Inc .... G 302 218-4240
Wilmington *(G-11588)*
McCormick Contracting & Suppor .... G 443 987-2099
Wilmington *(G-11591)*
Mdnewsline Inc .... G 773 759-4363
Dover *(G-1834)*
Mellon Private Wealth MGT .... G 302 421-2306
Wilmington *(G-11626)*
Mercantile Processing Inc .... G 302 524-8000
Millville *(G-4849)*
Mergers Acqstons Strtegies LLC ..... G 302 992-0400
Wilmington *(G-11640)*
Merix LLC .... G 425 659-1425
Lewes *(G-3638)*
Metal Shop .... F 302 846-2988
Delmar *(G-1020)*
Metaquotes Software Corp .... E 657 859-6918
Wilmington *(G-11648)*
Michael Pdmnczky Cnsrvator LLC ... G 302 388-0656
Wilmington *(G-11664)*

Michaels Home Repair Services ...... G 302 333-2235
New Castle *(G-5521)*
Microcom Tech LLC .... G 858 775-5559
Rehoboth Beach *(G-8005)*
Mid South Audio LLC .... G 302 856-6993
Georgetown *(G-2603)*
Middle Dept Insptn Agcy Inc .... G 302 875-4514
Laurel *(G-3265)*
Middle Dept Insptn Agcy Inc .... G 302 999-0243
Wilmington *(G-11682)*
Midnight Blue Inc .... F 302 436-9665
Selbyville *(G-8522)*
Miss Mafia LLC .... F 800 246-2677
Wilmington *(G-11713)*
Mission Movement Transport LLC ... G 302 480-9401
Lincoln *(G-3863)*
Mitchell Associates Inc .... E 302 594-9400
Wilmington *(G-11714)*
Mitek Holdings Inc .... G 302 429-1816
Wilmington *(G-11715)*
ML Whiteman and Sons Inc .... G 302 659-1001
Townsend *(G-8811)*
Modern Masters Inc .... G 240 800-6622
Dover *(G-1868)*
Moghul Life Inc .... G 347 560-9124
Wilmington *(G-11724)*
Montesino Technologies Inc .... G 302 888-2355
Wilmington *(G-11737)*
Morgan Stnley Smith Barney LLC ... G 302 636-5500
Wilmington *(G-11754)*
Morning After Inc .... G 302 562-5190
Hartly *(G-2936)*
Morningstar Maids LLC .... G 302 829-3030
Hockessin *(G-3099)*
Moscase Inc .... G 786 520-8062
Dover *(G-1874)*
Movetec Fitness Equipment LLC ..... G 302 563-4487
Newark *(G-7064)*
Moving Sciences LLC .... G 617 871-9892
Wilmington *(G-11764)*
Mr Gregory Michael Hausmann .... G 302 635-7675
Newark *(G-7066)*
Msb Enterprise Partners LLC .... G 302 947-0736
Millsboro *(G-4757)*
Mumford-Bjorkman Associates .... F 302 655-8234
Wilmington *(G-11775)*
Murry Trucking Llc .... F 302 653-4811
Smyrna *(G-8683)*
Nancy Conklin Interiors .... G 302 655-0877
Wilmington *(G-11796)*
Nancy Dufresne .... G 302 378-7236
Townsend *(G-8812)*
Nanticoke Consulting Inc .... G 302 424-0750
Greenwood *(G-2755)*
National Opprtnities Unlimited .... F 913 905-2261
New Castle *(G-5547)*
National Signing Source LLC .... E 773 885-3285
Wilmington *(G-11810)*
Nettel Partners LLC .... F 215 290-7383
Rehoboth Beach *(G-8016)*
New ERA Media LLC .... G 302 731-2003
Newark *(G-7105)*
New Vision Services Inc .... F 484 350-6495
Newark *(G-7108)*
Newrez LLC .... G 302 455-6600
Middletown *(G-4174)*
Nk Consulting Inc .... F 330 269-5775
Wilmington *(G-11891)*
No Joke I LLC .... G 302 395-0882
New Castle *(G-5573)*
Nouvir Lightning Corporation .... G 302 628-9888
Seaford *(G-8331)*
Novo Financial Corp .... G 844 260-6800
Dover *(G-1906)*
Nrai Services LLC .... F 302 674-4089
Dover *(G-1907)*
Nvcomputers Inc .... G 860 878-0525
Wilmington *(G-11924)*
Objects Worldwide Inc .... G 703 623-7861
Wilmington *(G-11931)*
Oerigo Consulting LLC .... G 302 353-4719
Smyrna *(G-8686)*
Oink Oink LLC .... G 302 924-5034
Dover *(G-1914)*
Olivar & Greb Capital MGT LLC ...... F 508 598-7590
Lewes *(G-3667)*
One Hour Translation Inc .... G 800 720-3722
Lewes *(G-3668)*
ONeal J C & Sons Auctioneers .... G 302 875-5261
Laurel *(G-3268)*

Orbeex Trading Inc .... F 786 403-9124
Wilmington *(G-11970)*
Ovo Digital Services LLC .... G 415 741-1615
Wilmington *(G-11986)*
P A Cnmri .... D 302 678-8100
Dover *(G-1928)*
Pacer International One LLC .... F 302 588-9500
Wilmington *(G-12003)*
Patriot Systems Inc .... G 302 472-9727
Wilmington *(G-12036)*
Pcu Systems LLC .... G 888 780-9728
Wilmington *(G-12053)*
Peeper Vehicle Technology Corp ... G 800 971-4134
Dover *(G-1943)*
Perastic LLC .... G 917 592-4219
Wilmington *(G-12083)*
Percebe Music Inc .... G 850 341-9594
Dover *(G-1949)*
Perceri LLC .... G 217 721-8731
Dover *(G-1950)*
Perkwiz Inc .... G 702 866-9122
Hockessin *(G-3116)*
Perpetual Invstments Group LLC ... E 718 795-3394
Wilmington *(G-12087)*
Phalco Inc .... G 302 654-2620
Wilmington *(G-12107)*
Phazebreak Coatings LLC .... G 844 467-4293
Wilmington *(G-12111)*
Phillip T Bradley Inc .... G 302 947-2741
Lewes *(G-3687)*
Pierce Design & Tool .... G 302 222-3339
Dover *(G-1958)*
Pixstorm LLC .... G 617 365-4949
Dover *(G-1961)*
Plai Apps Inc .... G 661 678-3740
Dover *(G-1962)*
Plain & Fancy Inc .... G 302 656-9901
Wilmington *(G-12148)*
Positioneering LLC .... G 302 415-3200
Wilmington *(G-12191)*
Power Financial Group Inc .... G 302 992-7971
Wilmington *(G-12196)*
Pradhan Energy Projects .... G 305 428-2123
Hockessin *(G-3124)*
Premier Nat Ln & Lsg Group LLC ... E 302 295-2194
Wilmington *(G-12216)*
Prism Events Inc .... G 424 252-1070
Newark *(G-7259)*
Private Family Network LLC .... F 302 760-9684
Dover *(G-1988)*
Process Academy LLC .... G 302 415-3104
Wilmington *(G-12238)*
Proclean .... G 302 654-1074
New Castle *(G-5649)*
Protech Delivery & Assembly .... F 302 449-5003
New Castle *(G-5650)*
Quality Distributors Inc .... G 917 335-6662
Wilmington *(G-12279)*
Quality III Fire Protection .... G 302 762-8262
Wilmington *(G-12281)*
Ralph Paul Inc .... G 302 764-9162
Wilmington *(G-12309)*
Rays and Sons Mechanical LLC ..... G 302 697-2100
Seaford *(G-8372)*
Rbc Capital Markets LLC .... G 302 252-9444
Wilmington *(G-12334)*
Reagan-Watson Auctions LLC .... G 302 422-2392
Milford *(G-4534)*
Red Sun Custom Apparel Inc .... E 302 988-8230
Selbyville *(G-8538)*
Redzun LLC .... G 512 657-4100
Wilmington *(G-12349)*
Regal Painting & Decorating .... F 302 994-8943
Wilmington *(G-12354)*
Registered Agents Ltd .... E 302 421-5750
Wilmington *(G-12363)*
Regus Corporation .... G 302 318-1300
Newark *(G-7312)*
Regus Corporation .... G 302 295-4800
Wilmington *(G-12366)*
Reliable Home Inspection .... F 302 455-1200
Wilmington *(G-12374)*
Renderapps LLC .... G 919 274-0582
Dover *(G-2027)*
Rendezvous Inc .... G 302 645-7400
Lewes *(G-3715)*
Retail Services Wis Corp .... D 302 477-0667
Wilmington *(G-12392)*
Reyes Rebeca .... G 302 276-9132
New Castle *(G-5677)*

SIC SECTION — 75 AUTOMOTIVE REPAIR, SERVICES, AND PARKING

Company	Code	Phone
Richard L Sapp Farms LLC — Milton *(G-4957)*	F	302 684-4727
Right Way Flagging and Sign Co — Camden Wyoming *(G-653)*	E	302 698-5229
Rmv Workforce Corp — Milton *(G-4963)*	F	302 408-1061
Rockwood Financial Group Inc — Wilmington *(G-12457)*	G	302 791-0237
Rogers Sign Company Inc — Milton *(G-4965)*	F	302 684-8338
Rogue Elephants LLC — Lewes *(G-3724)*	G	979 264-2845
Rohma Inc — Newark *(G-7360)*	G	909 234-5381
Rooah LLC — Dover *(G-2042)*	G	305 233-7557
RPR Environmental Solutions — Lincoln *(G-3866)*	G	302 362-0687
S Brown Appraisals LLC — Harrington *(G-2882)*	G	302 672-0694
Safeplace Corporation — Wilmington *(G-12520)*	G	302 479-9000
Sayhi LLC — Wilmington *(G-12547)*	G	860 631-7725
Scientific USA Inc — Wilmington *(G-12559)*	G	425 681-9462
Scottish Ventures LLC — New Castle *(G-5695)*	G	302 382-6057
Sean E Chipman — New Castle *(G-5697)*	F	302 300-4307
Sensofusion Inc — Milton *(G-4967)*	F	570 239-4912
Server Management LLC — Wilmington *(G-12584)*	G	302 300-1745
Shopify Payments (usa) Inc — Wilmington *(G-12607)*	G	613 241-2828
Shore Answer LLC — Georgetown *(G-2654)*	F	302 253-8381
Simple Space LLC — Wilmington *(G-12625)*	G	801 520-3680
Sitengle Technology LLC — Dover *(G-2086)*	F	719 822-0710
Six Angels Development Inc — Wilmington *(G-12637)*	G	302 218-1548
Sky World Traveler — Wilmington *(G-12643)*	F	844 591-9060
Sleeper Creeper Inc — Georgetown *(G-2656)*	G	302 519-4553
SM Technomine Inc — Wilmington *(G-12648)*	F	312 492-4386
SM Technomine Inc — Wilmington *(G-12647)*	F	312 492-4386
Smart Hospitality & MGT LLC — Wilmington *(G-12654)*	E	212 444-1989
Smartstudents LLC — Wilmington *(G-12655)*	G	302 597-6586
Society For Acpuncture RES Inc — Lewes *(G-3752)*	F	302 222-1832
Solar Foundations Usa Inc — Newark *(G-7454)*	G	518 935-3360
Solar Unlimited North Amer LLC — Lewes *(G-3754)*	G	302 542-4580
Southern Del Trck Growers Assn — Laurel *(G-3292)*	E	302 875-3147
Sovereign Capitl MGT Group Inc — Wilmington *(G-12689)*	A	619 294-8989
Specialized Carier Systems Inc — Milford *(G-4567)*	G	302 424-4548
Spences Bazaar & Auction LLC — Dover *(G-2098)*	F	302 734-3441
Springleaf Fincl Holdings LLC — Wilmington *(G-12715)*	B	302 543-6767
Staikos Associates Architects — Wilmington *(G-12730)*	G	302 764-1678
Statwhiz Ventures LLC — Wilmington *(G-12746)*	G	310 819-5427
Stauffer Family LLC — Rehoboth Beach *(G-8087)*	G	302 227-5820
Stealthorg LLC — Dover *(G-2107)*	G	302 724-6461
Stephen Cropper — Frankford *(G-2390)*	G	302 732-3730
Stericycle Comm Solutions Inc — Wilmington *(G-12757)*	F	302 656-0630
Stl & Associates LLC — Smyrna *(G-8725)*	G	302 359-2801
Strands Prprty Prservation LLC — Millsboro *(G-4805)*	G	302 381-9792
Strategic Fund Raising Inc — Wilmington *(G-12774)*	E	651 649-0404
Stream App LLC — Wilmington *(G-12775)*	G	610 420-5864
Strike Exchange Inc — Lewes *(G-3766)*	F	310 995-5653
Stuart Kingston Galleries Inc — Wilmington *(G-12780)*	F	302 652-7978
Sun Exchange Inc — Lewes *(G-3769)*	G	917 747-9527
Super C Inc — Newark *(G-7510)*	G	302 533-6024
Susan Straughen — Georgetown *(G-2673)*	G	302 856-7703
Swami Enterprises Inc — Wilmington *(G-12822)*	G	302 999-8077
Swift Financial LLC — Wilmington *(G-12825)*	E	302 374-7019
Systems Approach Ltd — Newark *(G-7526)*	G	302 743-6331
T & B Invstgtions SEC Agcy LLC — Middletown *(G-4252)*	G	302 476-4087
T & H Bail Bond Inc — Wilmington *(G-12841)*	G	302 777-7982
T & H Bail Bonds Agency LLC — Wilmington *(G-12842)*	G	302 777-7982
Tableart LLC — Wilmington *(G-12847)*	G	650 587-8769
Tag Sale By Changeover — Wilmington *(G-12849)*	F	302 478-2450
Tarpon Strategies LLC — Newark *(G-7540)*	G	215 806-2723
Techgas Inc — Georgetown *(G-2688)*	G	302 856-4111
Techxponent Inc — Newark *(G-7548)*	F	410 701-0089
Tecnatom USA Corporation — Wilmington *(G-12873)*	G	412 265-7226
Thinkruptive Media Inc — Dover *(G-2142)*	F	310 779-4748
Transworld Diversfd Svcs Inc — Wilmington *(G-12959)*	F	302 777-5902
Travel Agency — Lewes *(G-3794)*	G	302 381-0205
Tristate Courier & Carriage — Wilmington *(G-12980)*	E	302 654-3345
Turning Point Collection LLC — Wilmington *(G-12993)*	G	302 416-0092
Twin Creek Farms LLC — Milford *(G-4581)*	G	302 249-2294
Two Roses United LLC — Wilmington *(G-12999)*	G	302 593-2453
UBS Financial Services Inc — Wilmington *(G-13007)*	F	302 657-5331
Unikie Inc — Dover *(G-2177)*	F	408 839-1920
Unique Image LLC — Wilmington *(G-13017)*	E	302 658-2266
University of De Printing — Newark *(G-7618)*	E	302 831-2153
▲ Vanguard Manufacturing Inc — Wilmington *(G-13049)*	G	302 994-9302
Vera Bradley Designs Inc — Newark *(G-7650)*	G	302 733-0880
Vetdiet Usa Inc — Wilmington *(G-13069)*	G	514 622-7313
Veteran It Pro LLC — Hockessin *(G-3167)*	F	302 824-3111
Village Green Inc — Wilmington *(G-13082)*	E	302 764-2234
Vinsys Corporation — Newark *(G-2194)*	D	732 983-4150
Violet Aura Inc — Wilmington *(G-13086)*	F	302 654-4008
Virion Therapeutics LLC — Newark *(G-7660)*	G	800 841-9303
Vitellus LLC — Wilmington *(G-13096)*	G	718 782-3539
Voice 4 Impact Inc — Wilmington *(G-13099)*	G	484 410-0111
Voitlex Corp — Dover *(G-2198)*	F	302 288-0670
Vtms LLC — Dover *(G-2201)*	G	302 264-9094
Wahid Consultants LLC — New Castle *(G-5821)*	E	315 400-0955
Watercraft LLC — Wilmington *(G-13122)*	G	302 757-0786
Webstudy Inc — Harbeson *(G-2802)*	G	888 326-4058
Wetzel & Associates PA — Wilmington *(G-13175)*	G	302 652-1200
When Poets Dream Inc — Dover *(G-2222)*	G	818 738-6954
Whipper Snapper Transport LLC — Milford *(G-4604)*	G	302 265-2437
Williamson Building Corp — Lewes *(G-3825)*	G	302 644-0605
Wilmington Resources — Wilmington *(G-13244)*	F	302 746-7162
Wilmington Trust Corporation — Wilmington *(G-13263)*	E	302 651-8378
Wilsons Auction Sales Inc — Lincoln *(G-3874)*	G	302 422-3454
Win From Wthin Xc Camp/Tatnall — Wilmington *(G-13269)*	E	302 494-5312
Windy Inc — Dover *(G-2234)*	F	224 707-0442
Winker Labs LLC — Wilmington *(G-13271)*	G	630 449-8130
Wmk Financing Inc — Wilmington *(G-13283)*	G	302 576-2697
World Wide Com Corporation — Newark *(G-7721)*	F	646 810-8624
Wowdesk Inc — Newark *(G-7724)*	G	310 871-5251
Wuji Inc — Dover *(G-2240)*	G	815 274-6777
Wutap LLC — Newark *(G-7725)*	G	610 457-3559
◆ Xenopia LLC — Lewes *(G-3832)*	G	302 703-7050
Yello Technologies Inc — Lewes *(G-3833)*	G	954 802-6089
Zahn Incorporated — Wilmington *(G-13339)*	G	302 425-3700
Zen Health Technology Inc — Newark *(G-7739)*	G	551 194-2345
Zest-Index Investments LLC — Middletown *(G-4295)*	G	503 908-2110
Zicherheit LLC — Selbyville *(G-8557)*	F	302 510-3718
Zogo Inc — Newark *(G-7743)*	G	978 810-8895

75 AUTOMOTIVE REPAIR, SERVICES, AND PARKING

7513 Truck Rental & Leasing, Without Drivers

Company	Code	Phone
Action Rental Inc — Newark *(G-5894)*	G	302 366-0749
▼ Bayshore Ford Truck Sales Inc — New Castle *(G-5075)*	D	302 656-3160
Budget Truck Rental LLC — Rehoboth Beach *(G-7880)*	F	302 644-0132
Clifton Leasing Co Inc — Dover *(G-1293)*	E	302 674-2300
D E Leager Construction — Wilmington *(G-9939)*	G	302 994-1060
Dependable Trucking Inc — New Castle *(G-5248)*	F	302 655-6271
Dover Leasing Co Inc — Dover *(G-1456)*	F	302 674-2300
Esl Inc — Seaford *(G-8239)*	G	302 629-4553
Lee Mc Neill Associates — Wilmington *(G-11356)*	G	302 593-6172
Livingston Healthcare Svcs Inc — Newark *(G-6944)*	B	302 631-5000
Martin Newark Dealership Inc — Newark *(G-6996)*	C	302 454-9300
Morton Electric Co — Lewes *(G-3650)*	G	302 645-9414
Penske Truck Leasing Co LP — Wilmington *(G-12076)*	F	302 994-7899
Penske Truck Leasing Co LP — New Castle *(G-5617)*	E	302 325-9290
Penske Truck Leasing Corp — Seaford *(G-8352)*	F	302 629-5373
Penske Truck Leasing Corp — Wilmington *(G-12077)*	F	302 658-3255
Penske Truck Leasing Corp — Rehoboth Beach *(G-8030)*	F	302 260-7039
Penske Truck Leasing Corp — Middletown *(G-4188)*	F	302 449-9294
▲ Rollins Leasing LLC — Wilmington *(G-12466)*	C	302 426-2700
Ryder Truck Rental Inc — Wilmington *(G-12500)*	F	302 571-4210
Ryder Truck Rental Inc — Wilmington *(G-12501)*	E	302 798-1472

Employee Codes: A=Over 500 employees, B=251-500, C=101-250, D=51-100, E=20-50, F=10-19, G=1-9

75 AUTOMOTIVE REPAIR, SERVICES, AND PARKING

Ryder Truck Rental Inc .... F 302 995-9607
  Newark (G-7371)
Spallco Enterprises Inc .... G 302 762-3825
  Wilmington (G-12692)
Tat Trucking Inc .... F 302 261-5444
  Bear (G-347)
U Haul Co Independent Dealers ...... G 302 424-3189
  Milford (G-4582)
U Haul Company Independent Dlr ... G 302 369-8230
  Newark (G-7605)
U Haul Neighborhood Dealer .... G 302 613-0207
  Bear (G-362)
U-Haul International Inc .... G 302 762-6445
  Wilmington (G-13004)
U-Haul Neighborhood Dealer .... G 302 644-4316
  Lewes (G-3800)
U-Haul Neighborhood Dealer .... G 302 703-0376
  Lewes (G-3801)
U-Haul Neighborhood Dealer .... G 302 326-1875
  New Castle (G-5800)
U-Haul Neighborhood Dealer .... G 302 449-7379
  Middletown (G-4272)
Watkins System Inc .... E 302 658-8561
  New Castle (G-5827)
▼ Winner Ford of Newark Inc .... C 302 731-2415
  Newark (G-7710)

7514 Passenger Car Rental

Ace Rent-A-Car Inc .... E 302 368-5950
  Newark (G-5892)
Avis Rent A Car System Inc .... F 302 322-2092
  New Castle (G-5058)
Budget Rent A Car System Inc .... G 302 652-0629
  Wilmington (G-9500)
Burke Equipment Company .... F 302 629-7500
  Delmar (G-977)
Dela Belle Inv Group Corp .... G 901 279-2742
  Middletown (G-4026)
Ean Holdings LLC .... G 302 422-1167
  Milford (G-4398)
Ean Holdings LLC .... G 302 674-5553
  Dover (G-1494)
Ean Holdings LLC .... G 302 376-5606
  Middletown (G-4047)
Enterprise Lsg Phladelphia LLC .... G 302 425-4404
  Wilmington (G-10409)
Enterprise Lsg Phladelphia LLC .... G 302 266-7777
  Newark (G-6531)
Enterprise Lsg Phladelphia LLC .... G 302 479-7829
  Wilmington (G-10410)
Enterprise Lsg Phladelphia LLC .... G 302 656-5464
  Wilmington (G-10411)
Enterprise Lsg Phladelphia LLC .... G 302 761-4545
  Wilmington (G-10412)
Enterprise Lsg Phladelphia LLC .... G 302 732-3534
  Dagsboro (G-900)
Enterprise Lsg Phladelphia LLC .... G 302 292-0524
  Newark (G-6532)
Enterprise Rent-A-Car .... G 302 323-0850
  New Castle (G-5291)
Enterprise Rent-A-Car .... G 302 934-1216
  Millsboro (G-4685)
Enterprise Rent-A-Car .... G 302 575-1021
  Wilmington (G-10414)
Enterprise Rent-A-Car .... G 302 653-4330
  Smyrna (G-8629)
Go4spin .... G 310 400-2588
  (G-10735)
Golden Chariot Transportaion .... G 302 730-3882
  Dover (G-1598)
Hertz Corporation .... E 302 654-8312
  Wilmington (G-10895)
Hertz Corporation .... E 302 428-0637
  New Castle (G-5390)
Hertz Corporation .... E 302 428-0637
  New Castle (G-5391)
Hertz Corporation .... E 302 428-0637
  Wilmington (G-10896)
Hertz Corporation .... E 302 428-0637
  New Castle (G-5392)
Hertz Local Edition Corp .... G 302 678-0700
  Dover (G-1642)
Kent Leasing Company Inc .... E 302 697-3000
  Dover (G-1736)
Spallco Enterprises Inc .... G 302 368-5950
  Newark (G-7463)
Spallco Enterprises Inc .... G 302 762-3825
  Wilmington (G-12692)
Winner Group Inc .... B 302 764-5900
  Wilmington (G-13272)

Wreck Masters Demo Derby .... F 302 368-5544
  Bear (G-381)

7515 Passenger Car Leasing

Delaware Motor Sales Inc .... C 302 656-3100
  Wilmington (G-10067)
Esl Inc .... G 302 629-4553
  Seaford (G-8239)
Future Ford Sales Inc .... D 302 999-0261
  Wilmington (G-10654)
Martin Newark Dealership Inc .... C 302 454-9300
  Newark (G-6996)
New Car Connection .... F 302 328-7000
  New Castle (G-5553)
Professional Leasing Inc .... G 302 629-4350
  Seaford (G-8365)
Star States Leasing Corp .... E 302 283-4500
  Newark (G-7484)
▼ Winner Ford of Newark Inc .... C 302 731-2415
  Newark (G-7710)
Winner Group Inc .... E 302 292-8200
  Newark (G-7711)

7519 Utility Trailers & Recreational Vehicle Rental

Complete Rsrvtion Slutions LLC .... F 800 672-8522
  Dover (G-1307)
Morton Electric Co .... G 302 645-9414
  Lewes (G-3650)
Penske Truck Leasing Co LP .... E 302 325-9290
  New Castle (G-5617)
Sussex Suites LLC .... G 302 856-3351
  Georgetown (G-2684)

7521 Automobile Parking Lots & Garages

City of Newark .... F 302 366-0457
  Newark (G-6242)
Colonial Parking Inc .... E 302 651-3600
  Wilmington (G-9775)
Colonial Parking Inc .... G 302 651-3618
  Wilmington (G-9776)
Go Go Go Inc .... G 302 645-7400
  Lewes (G-3517)
Landmark Parking Inc .... F 302 651-3610
  Wilmington (G-11328)
Sp Plus Corporation .... G 302 652-1410
  Wilmington (G-12690)
Wilmington Parking Authority .... E 302 655-4442
  Wilmington (G-13241)

7532 Top, Body & Upholstery Repair & Paint Shops

A R Myers Corporation .... E 302 652-3164
  Wilmington (G-8882)
ABRA Auto Body & Glass LP .... F 302 279-1007
  Middletown (G-3927)
Allen Body Works Inc .... G 302 875-3208
  Laurel (G-3192)
Armigers Auto Center Inc .... G 302 875-7642
  Laurel (G-3193)
Auto Collision Service .... G 302 328-5611
  New Castle (G-5055)
Auto Works Collision Ctr LLC .... F 302 732-3902
  Dagsboro (G-879)
Automotive Services Inc .... F 302 762-0100
  Wilmington (G-9190)
▼ Autoport Inc .... E 302 658-5100
  New Castle (G-5057)
Betts Texaco and B & G GL Inc .... G 302 834-2284
  Newark (G-6076)
Brandywine Body Shop Inc .... G 302 998-0424
  Wilmington (G-9418)
Brasures Body Shop Inc .... G 302 732-6157
  Frankford (G-2349)
Car Tech Auto Center .... G 302 368-4104
  Newark (G-6151)
Chets Auto Body Inc .... G 302 875-3376
  Laurel (G-3213)
Christiana Body Shop Inc .... G 302 655-1085
  Wilmington (G-9674)
Classic Auto Body Inc .... G 302 655-4044
  Wilmington (G-9733)
Colliers Trim Shop Inc .... G 302 227-8398
  Rehoboth Beach (G-7897)
Complete Auto Body Inc .... E 302 629-3955
  Seaford (G-8203)
Dent Pro Inc .... G 302 628-0978
  Seaford (G-8222)

Dominos Body Shop .... G 302 697-3801
  Camden Wyoming (G-630)
Doug Richmonds Body Shop .... F 302 453-1173
  Newark (G-6463)
Dunnings Body Shop .... G 302 653-9615
  Clayton (G-843)
East Coast Auto Body Inc .... G 302 265-6830
  Dover (G-1498)
Eastern Auto Body Inc .... G 302 731-1200
  Bear (G-138)
Edward J Henry & Sons Inc .... G 302 658-4324
  Wilmington (G-10357)
Ellmore Auto Collision .... G 302 762-2301
  Wilmington (G-10381)
Executive Auto Repairs Inc .... G 302 995-6220
  Wilmington (G-10459)
Future Ford Sales Inc .... D 302 999-0261
  Wilmington (G-10654)
Gas & Go Inc .... G 302 734-8234
  Dover (G-1582)
Henry Bros Autobody & Pnt Sp .... F 302 994-4438
  Wilmington (G-10885)
Hertrich Collision Ctr of .... G 302 839-0550
  Milford (G-4440)
Housers Auto Trim Inc .... G 302 422-1290
  Milford (G-4445)
Jewell Enterprises Inc .... G 302 737-8460
  Newark (G-6837)
Joes Paint & Body Shop Inc .... G 302 855-0281
  Georgetown (G-2576)
Johns Body Shop Inc .... G 302 658-5133
  Wilmington (G-11177)
Kns09 Inc .... F 302 697-3499
  Dover (G-1756)
Kpkm Inc .... G 302 678-0271
  Dover (G-1757)
Lewes Body Works Inc .... G 302 645-5595
  Lewes (G-3596)
Maaco Collision Repr Auto Pntg ...... G 610 628-3867
  Wilmington (G-11475)
Mackmetts Auto Body .... G 302 366-8107
  Townsend (G-8807)
Martin Dealership .... G 302 738-5200
  Newark (G-6995)
Master Tech Inc .... E 302 832-1660
  Bear (G-247)
New Car Connection .... F 302 328-7000
  New Castle (G-5553)
Omniway Corporation .... F 302 738-5076
  Newark (G-7147)
Penuel Sign Co .... G 302 856-7265
  Georgetown (G-2616)
Performance Auto Body & Paint .... G 302 655-6170
  Wilmington (G-12084)
Pine Valley Corvettes .... G 302 834-1268
  Middletown (G-4193)
Puzs Body Shop Inc .... G 302 368-8265
  Newark (G-7274)
Quillen Signs LLC .... G 302 684-3661
  Milton (G-4954)
Rayco Auto & Marine Uphl Inc .... G 302 323-8844
  Hockessin (G-3129)
Red Barn Inc .... F 302 678-0271
  Dover (G-2017)
Rex Auto Body Inc .... G 302 731-4707
  Newark (G-7331)
Rhodes Custom Auto Works Inc ...... G 302 378-1701
  Townsend (G-8819)
Rickards Auto Body .... G 302 934-9600
  Millsboro (G-4790)
Rossi Auto Body Inc .... G 302 999-7707
  Wilmington (G-12480)
Rudlyn Inc .... F 302 764-5677
  Wilmington (G-12490)
Stokes Garage Inc .... G 302 994-0613
  Wilmington (G-12768)
Techniques Inc .... G 302 422-7760
  Newark (G-7546)
Whites Body Shop .... G 302 655-4369
  Wilmington (G-13194)
Willis Ford Inc .... E 302 653-5900
  Smyrna (G-8746)
Wilmington Collision Ctr LLC .... G 302 764-3520
  Wilmington (G-13227)
Winner Premier Collision Ctr .... E 302 571-5200
  Wilmington (G-13275)

7533 Automotive Exhaust System Repair Shops

Bernard Limpert ......G 302 674-8280
Dover *(G-1195)*
C-Met Inc ......G 302 652-1884
New Castle *(G-5127)*
Daves Disc Mfflers of Dver De ......G 302 678-8803
Dover *(G-1342)*
Leeds West Inv Group LLC ......E 302 998-0533
Wilmington *(G-11358)*
Meineke Car Care Center ......G 302 995-2020
Wilmington *(G-11625)*
Monro Inc ......G 302 999-0237
Wilmington *(G-11733)*
Monro Inc ......G 302 328-2945
New Castle *(G-5535)*
Roy Covey ......G 302 995-2900
Wilmington *(G-12482)*
Scott Muffler LLC ......G 302 674-8280
Dover *(G-2063)*
Tomall Inc ......G 302 424-4004
Milford *(G-4579)*
Walls Service Center Inc ......G 302 422-8110
Milford *(G-4596)*
Wilcon North Inc ......G 302 798-1699
Claymont *(G-820)*

7534 Tire Retreading & Repair Shops

Ajacks Tire Service Inc ......G 302 834-5200
New Castle *(G-5020)*
Bridgestone Ret Operations LLC ......F 302 995-2487
Wilmington *(G-9472)*
Bridgestone Ret Operations LLC ......F 302 734-4522
Dover *(G-1232)*
Bridgestone Ret Operations LLC ......G 302 656-2529
New Castle *(G-5112)*
Clarksville Auto Service Ctr ......E 302 539-1700
Ocean View *(G-7777)*
Diamond State Tire Inc ......F 302 836-1919
Bear *(G-118)*
Service Tire Truck Center Inc ......F 302 629-5533
Seaford *(G-8398)*

7536 Automotive Glass Replacement Shops

A R Myers Corporation ......E 302 652-3164
Wilmington *(G-8882)*
Delmarva Auto Glass Inc ......G 302 934-8600
Dagsboro *(G-896)*
Go-Glass Corporation ......F 302 674-3390
Dover *(G-1596)*
Mikes Glass Service Inc ......F 302 658-7936
Wilmington *(G-11686)*
Parags Glass Company ......G 302 737-0101
Newark *(G-7176)*
Pro-Bond Auto Glass ......G 302 324-8500
New Castle *(G-5648)*
Safelite Fulfillment Inc ......G 302 678-9600
Dover *(G-2052)*
Safelite Fulfillment Inc ......F 302 999-9908
Wilmington *(G-12518)*
Safelite Fulfillment Inc ......G 302 856-7175
Georgetown *(G-2646)*
Safelite Glass Corp ......G 877 800-2727
Dover *(G-2053)*
Safelite Glass Corp ......F 302 656-4640
Wilmington *(G-12519)*
U A G Inc ......F 302 731-2747
Newark *(G-7604)*

7537 Automotive Transmission Repair Shops

AAMCO Transmissions ......G 302 322-3454
Bear *(G-7)*
All Trans Transmission Inc ......G 302 366-0104
Newark *(G-5937)*
Benchmark Transmission Inc ......G 302 792-2300
Claymont *(G-701)*
Benchmark Transmissions Inc ......G 302 999-9400
Wilmington *(G-9296)*
Challenge Automotive Svcs Inc ......G 302 629-3058
Seaford *(G-8186)*
Cottman Transmission ......G 302 322-4600
New Castle *(G-5199)*
Dynamic Converters LLC ......G 302 454-9203
Newark *(G-6483)*
Js Automotive AAMCO ......G 302 678-5660
Dover *(G-1711)*
K & J Automotive Inc ......G 302 798-3635
Claymont *(G-771)*
Lst Insvestment LLC ......G 302 322-3454
Bear *(G-239)*
Powertrain Technology Inc ......G 302 368-4900
Newark *(G-7237)*
Scott Muffler LLC ......G 302 378-9247
Middletown *(G-4233)*
Trans Plus Inc ......G 302 323-3051
New Castle *(G-5784)*
Walls Service Center Inc ......G 302 422-8110
Milford *(G-4596)*
World Transmissions Inc ......G 302 735-5535
Dover *(G-2239)*

7538 General Automotive Repair Shop

4n Car Inc ......G 302 856-7434
Georgetown *(G-2417)*
A2b Auto Group ......G 302 786-2331
Wilmington *(G-8890)*
Admiral Tire ......G 302 734-5911
Dover *(G-1087)*
Alderman Automotive Enterprise ......G 302 652-3733
New Castle *(G-5021)*
All American Truck Brokers ......G 302 654-6101
Wilmington *(G-9011)*
ASAP Automotive ......G 302 444-8659
Bear *(G-39)*
AV Auto Worx LLC ......F 302 384-7646
Wilmington *(G-9194)*
B & F Towing & Salvage Co Inc ......E 302 328-4146
New Castle *(G-5062)*
▼ **Bayshore Ford Truck Sales Inc** ......D 302 656-3160
New Castle *(G-5075)*
Bernard Limpert ......G 302 674-8280
Dover *(G-1195)*
Bill Cannons Garage Inc ......F 302 436-4200
Selbyville *(G-8457)*
Blue Hen Spring Works Inc ......F 302 422-6600
Milford *(G-4328)*
Bradleys Auto Center Inc ......G 302 762-2247
Wilmington *(G-9413)*
Bullfeathers Auto Sound Inc ......G 302 846-0434
Laurel *(G-3205)*
Cammocks Auto Works LLC ......G 302 597-0204
New Castle *(G-5129)*
Car Clinic Inc ......G 302 421-9100
Wilmington *(G-9560)*
◆ **Careys Diesel Inc** ......F 302 678-3797
Leipsic *(G-3313)*
Careys Foreign & Domestic Repr ......G 302 856-2779
Georgetown *(G-2462)*
Careys Inc ......E 302 875-5674
Laurel *(G-3207)*
Caribb Transport Inc ......G 302 274-2112
Wilmington *(G-9570)*
Chriss Auto Repair ......G 302 791-0699
Claymont *(G-716)*
Classic Auto Sales & Service ......G 302 684-8126
Harbeson *(G-2775)*
Coastal Towing Inc ......G 302 645-6300
Lewes *(G-3439)*
Coveys Car Care Inc ......G 302 629-2746
Seaford *(G-8210)*
Deals On Wheels Inc ......E 302 999-9955
Wilmington *(G-9988)*
Delaware Fleet Service Inc ......G 302 778-5000
New Castle *(G-5229)*
Delmarva Pump Center Inc ......E 302 492-1245
Marydel *(G-3915)*
Delmarva Rv Center Inc ......E 302 424-4505
Milford *(G-4385)*
Dempseys Service Center Inc ......G 302 239-4996
Newark *(G-6435)*
Donald Briggs ......G 267 476-2712
Middletown *(G-4042)*
Donaway Corporation ......G 302 934-6226
Millsboro *(G-4680)*
Dover Volkswagen Inc ......E 302 734-4761
Dover *(G-1472)*
Durkee Automotive Inc ......G 302 798-5656
Claymont *(G-737)*
E & M Enterprises Inc ......G 302 736-6391
Dover *(G-1490)*
Elite Auto LLC ......G 302 690-2948
Middletown *(G-4054)*
European Performance Inc ......G 302 633-1122
Wilmington *(G-10442)*
Everest Autoworks Auto Spa LLC ......G 302 737-8424
Newark *(G-6546)*
First Choice Auto & Truck Repr ......G 302 656-1433
New Castle *(G-5311)*
Four Brothers Auto Service ......G 302 482-2932
Wilmington *(G-10604)*
Four States LLC ......F 302 655-3400
New Castle *(G-5325)*
Fox Run Automotive Inc ......F 302 834-1200
Bear *(G-159)*
Freedom Rides Auto ......G 302 422-4559
Seaford *(G-8247)*
Furrs Tire Service Inc ......G 302 678-0800
Dover *(G-1573)*
Girls Auto Clinic LLC ......G 484 679-6394
New Castle *(G-5354)*
Golden Car Care ......G 302 856-2219
Georgetown *(G-2550)*
Goodyear Tire & Rubber Company ......G 302 737-2461
Newark *(G-6677)*
Griff Son Hometown Auto Rep ......G 302 786-2143
Harrington *(G-2843)*
Gumboro Service Center Inc ......G 302 238-7040
Frankford *(G-2366)*
H & H Truck and Trailer Repair ......G 302 653-1446
Smyrna *(G-8648)*
Harris Towing and Auto Service ......G 302 736-9901
Dover *(G-1632)*
Harvey Road Automotive Inc ......G 302 654-7500
Wilmington *(G-10849)*
Henrys Car Care Inc ......G 302 994-5766
Wilmington *(G-10886)*
High Horse Performance Inc ......G 302 894-1115
Smyrna *(G-8652)*
Hoban Auto & Machineshop Inc ......G 302 436-8013
Selbyville *(G-8502)*
Horton and Bros Inc ......G 302 738-7221
Newark *(G-6747)*
IG Burton & Company Inc ......D 302 422-3041
Milford *(G-4447)*
IG Burton & Company Inc ......E 302 424-3041
Milford *(G-4448)*
Isaacs Automotive Inc ......G 302 995-2519
Wilmington *(G-11087)*
J & K Auto Repair Inc ......G 302 834-8025
Bear *(G-194)*
J V Auto Service Inc ......F 302 999-0786
Wilmington *(G-11112)*
K & S Garage Inc ......G 302 731-7997
Newark *(G-6863)*
Kent Sussex Auto Care Inc ......G 302 422-3337
Milford *(G-4465)*
Kirkwood Auto Center LLC ......F 302 995-6179
Wilmington *(G-11273)*
Kirkwood Tires Inc ......G 302 737-2460
Newark *(G-6894)*
Lee Lynn Inc ......F 302 678-9978
Dover *(G-1775)*
Lube Depot ......G 302 659-3329
Smyrna *(G-8677)*
M Tech European Autohouse Inc ......G 302 472-6813
Wilmington *(G-11473)*
Maliks Auto Repair ......G 302 325-2555
New Castle *(G-5504)*
Manor Exxon Inc ......G 302 834-6691
Bear *(G-243)*
Martel & Son Foreign Car Ctr ......G 302 674-5556
Dover *(G-1820)*
Martin Newark Dealership Inc ......C 302 454-9300
Newark *(G-6996)*
Middletown Car Care ......G 302 449-1550
Middletown *(G-4154)*
Millcreek Texaco Station ......G 302 571-8489
Wilmington *(G-11691)*
Monro Inc ......F 302 378-3801
Middletown *(G-4168)*
Monro Inc ......G 302 846-2732
Delmar *(G-1022)*
Nallys Auto Plaza Inc ......G 302 543-8126
Wilmington *(G-11795)*
New Car Connection ......F 302 328-7000
New Castle *(G-5553)*
Ocean Pines Auto Service Ctr ......E 410 641-7800
Ocean View *(G-7806)*
Oil Spot Express Lube Center ......G 302 628-9866
Seaford *(G-8335)*
Patriot Auto & Truck Care LLC ......G 302 257-5715
Dover *(G-1940)*
Paul F Campanella Inc ......F 302 777-7170
Wilmington *(G-12041)*
Petes Garage Inc ......G 302 286-6069
Newark *(G-7206)*
Pettyjohns Custom Engine ......G 302 684-8888
Milton *(G-4950)*

S I C

Employee Codes: A=Over 500 employees, B=251-500
C=101-250, D=51-100, E=20-50, F=10-19, G=1-9
2020 Harris Directory of Delaware Businesses
539

75 AUTOMOTIVE REPAIR, SERVICES, AND PARKING

Phillip E Weir ....G....... 302 652-1312
  Wilmington (G-12115)
Powertrain Technology Inc ....G....... 302 368-4900
  Newark (G-7237)
Preferred Auto and Cycle LLC ....G....... 302 855-0169
  Dagsboro (G-931)
Pro Trans Inc ....G....... 302 328-1550
  Bear (G-292)
Pughs Service Inc ....F....... 302 678-2408
  Dover (G-1999)
R & K Motors & Machine Shop ....G....... 302 737-4596
  Newark (G-7290)
Rbs Auto Repair Inc ....G....... 302 678-8803
  Dover (G-2012)
Redmill Auto Repair ....G....... 302 292-2155
  Newark (G-7310)
Rinehimer Body Shop Inc ....F....... 302 737-7350
  Newark (G-7342)
Rittenhouse Motor Co Inc ....E....... 302 731-5059
  Newark (G-7345)
Roccos Automotive Service ....F....... 302 998-2234
  Wilmington (G-12445)
Ronnies Auto Repairs Inc ....G....... 302 994-4703
  Wilmington (G-12472)
Route 9 Auto Center ....G....... 302 856-3941
  Georgetown (G-2643)
Sals Garage Inc ....G....... 302 655-4981
  Wilmington (G-12527)
Scott Muffler LLC ....G....... 302 378-9247
  Middletown (G-4233)
Service King Holdings LLC ....E....... 302 797-8783
  Claymont (G-804)
Sevys Auto Service Inc ....G....... 302 328-0839
  New Castle (G-5701)
Shark Service Center LLC ....G....... 302 337-8233
  Bridgeville (G-520)
Silview Auto Care ....G....... 302 994-1617
  Wilmington (G-12622)
Smiths Jack Towing & Svc Ctr ....G....... 302 798-6667
  Wilmington (G-12663)
Smittys Auto Repair Inc ....G....... 302 398-8419
  Harrington (G-2890)
Sports Car Service Inc ....F....... 302 764-7439
  Wilmington (G-12709)
Stokes Garage Inc ....G....... 302 994-0613
  Wilmington (G-12768)
Tbc Retail Group Inc ....E....... 302 478-8013
  Wilmington (G-12855)
Three Js Disc Tire & Auto Svc ....E....... 302 995-6141
  Wilmington (G-12906)
Truck Tech Inc ....F....... 302 832-8000
  New Castle (G-5796)
TSC Enterprises LLC ....G....... 302 934-6158
  Millsboro (G-4815)
Tune-Up III of MD Inc ....G....... 410 655-9500
  Frankford (G-2395)
United Auto Sales Inc ....G....... 302 325-3000
  New Castle (G-5803)
Universalfleet ....G....... 302 428-0661
  New Castle (G-5810)
Wallis Repair Inc ....G....... 302 378-4301
  Middletown (G-4279)
Wiedman Enterprises Inc ....G....... 302 226-2407
  Rehoboth Beach (G-8115)
William Chambers and Son ....G....... 302 284-9655
  Viola (G-8838)
William T Wadkins Garage Inc ....G....... 302 422-0265
  Milford (G-4608)
Willis Ford Inc ....E....... 302 653-5900
  Smyrna (G-8746)
Winner Group Inc ....E....... 302 292-8200
  Newark (G-7711)
Winner Infiniti Inc ....E....... 302 764-5900
  Wilmington (G-13274)
Wolfs Elite Autos ....G....... 302 999-9199
  Wilmington (G-13287)

7539 Automotive Repair Shops, NEC

Accurate Machine Inc ....G....... 302 992-9606
  Wilmington (G-8918)
B & E Tire Alignment Inc ....G....... 302 732-6091
  Frankford (G-2345)
Bargain Tire & Service Inc ....F....... 302 764-8900
  Wilmington (G-9254)
Bear Alignment Center ....G....... 302 655-9219
  Wilmington (G-9274)
Benchmark Transmission Inc ....G....... 302 792-2300
  Claymont (G-701)
Bernard Limpert ....G....... 302 674-8280
  Dover (G-1195)

Blue Hen Spring Works Inc ....F....... 302 422-6600
  Milford (G-4328)
Brandywine Chrysler Jeep Dodge ....D....... 302 998-0458
  Wilmington (G-9424)
Buckleys Inc ....G....... 302 999-8285
  Wilmington (G-9499)
Buntings Garage Inc ....F....... 302 732-9021
  Dagsboro (G-886)
Coastal Towing Inc ....G....... 302 645-6300
  Lewes (G-3439)
Cod Lift Truck Inc ....G....... 302 656-7731
  Wilmington (G-9757)
D & H Automotive & Towing Inc ....G....... 302 655-7611
  Wilmington (G-9936)
Dave Smagala ....G....... 302 383-2761
  Claymont (G-729)
Els Tire Service Inc ....F....... 302 834-1997
  Newark (G-6518)
Ewings Towing Service Inc ....G....... 302 366-8806
  Newark (G-6547)
Farmers Radiator & AC ....G....... 302 235-5922
  Newark (G-6572)
Garage ....G....... 302 645-7288
  Rehoboth Beach (G-7943)
Goodchild Inc ....G....... 302 368-1681
  Newark (G-6675)
Gould Motor Technologies Inc ....G....... 618 932-8446
  Wilmington (G-10756)
H & H Truck and Trailer Repair ....G....... 302 653-1446
  Smyrna (G-8648)
H&H Services Electrical Contrs ....G....... 302 373-4950
  New Castle (G-5369)
Harvey Road Automotive Inc ....G....... 302 475-0369
  Newark (G-6547)
Hidden Hitch & Trailer Parts ....G....... 410 398-5949
  Bear (G-183)
J & K Auto Repair Inc ....G....... 302 834-8025
  Bear (G-194)
Just Right Tires Inc ....F....... 302 268-2825
  Bear (G-207)
Kent Sign Company Inc ....F....... 302 697-2181
  Dover (G-1739)
McHugh Electric Inc ....G....... 302 995-9091
  Wilmington (G-11597)
Meadowood Mobil Station ....G....... 302 731-5602
  Newark (G-7013)
Monro Inc ....G....... 302 328-2945
  New Castle (G-5535)
Pike Creek Automotive Inc ....G....... 302 998-2234
  Wilmington (G-12135)
Quality Auto Care Centers ....G....... 302 992-7978
  Wilmington (G-12278)
Reliable Trailer Inc ....F....... 856 962-7900
  Felton (G-2316)
◆ Robert Bayly ....G....... 302 846-9752
  Laurel (G-3283)
Roy Covey ....G....... 302 995-2900
  Wilmington (G-12482)
Schrider Enterprises Inc ....G....... 302 934-1900
  Millsboro (G-4799)
Semper Program LLC ....G....... 302 535-6769
  Middletown (G-4236)
Sevys Auto Service Inc ....G....... 302 328-0839
  New Castle (G-5701)
Staplefords Sales and Service ....E....... 302 834-4568
  Saint Georges (G-8130)
Tomall Inc ....G....... 302 424-4004
  Milford (G-4579)
US Telex Corporation ....E....... 302 652-2707
  Wilmington (G-13040)

7542 Car Washes

Attention To Detail In Smyrna ....G....... 302 388-1267
  Smyrna (G-8578)
Big Toy Custom Car Care Inc ....G....... 302 668-6729
  Wilmington (G-9334)
Briscoes Onsite Detailing ....G....... 302 420-1629
  Wilmington (G-9478)
Car Wash of Prices Corner ....E....... 302 994-9274
  Wilmington (G-9561)
Cleanpro Detail Center ....G....... 302 834-6878
  Bear (G-77)
Delaware Detailing Services ....G....... 302 414-0755
  New Castle (G-5227)
Diamond Car Wash Inc ....G....... 302 449-5696
  Middletown (G-4038)
Dover Soft Touch Car Wash ....E....... 302 736-6011
  Dover (G-1470)
Duck In Car Wash ....G....... 302 536-7056
  Seaford (G-8227)

Gas & Go Inc ....G....... 302 734-8234
  Dover (G-1582)
Greenhill Express Car Wash ....G....... 302 464-1031
  Middletown (G-4092)
HI Line Auto Detailing ....G....... 302 420-5368
  Wilmington (G-10901)
Logue Brothers Inc ....F....... 302 762-1896
  Wilmington (G-11427)
Maaco Collision Repr Auto Pntg ....G....... 610 628-3867
  Wilmington (G-11475)
Magic Car Wash Inc ....E....... 302 479-5911
  Wilmington (G-11486)
Magic Touch ....F....... 302 655-6430
  New Castle (G-5495)
Mr Royal Touch MBL Detailing ....G....... 302 229-0161
  Wilmington (G-11767)
Newport Ventures Inc ....F....... 302 998-1693
  Wilmington (G-11879)
Ocean Waves LLC ....G....... 302 344-1282
  Fenwick Island (G-2338)
Rehoboth Car Wash Inc ....E....... 302 227-6177
  Rehoboth Beach (G-8053)
Richard Addington Co ....G....... 302 422-2668
  Milford (G-4543)
Wilkins Enterprises Inc ....G....... 302 945-4142
  Milton (G-4980)
Willies Auto Detail Service ....G....... 302 734-1010
  Dover (G-2228)

7549 Automotive Svcs, Except Repair & Car Washes

All Hked Up Twing Recovery LLC ....G....... 302 545-1205
  Newark (G-5934)
Auto Sun Roof Inc ....F....... 302 325-3001
  New Castle (G-5056)
▼ Autoport Inc ....G....... 302 658-5100
  New Castle (G-5057)
B & F Towing & Salvage Co Inc ....E....... 302 328-4146
  New Castle (G-5062)
Basher & Son Enterprises Inc ....G....... 302 239-6584
  Hockessin (G-2962)
Bauls Towing & Services LLC ....G....... 302 999-9919
  Newark (G-6054)
Big Time Towing LLC ....G....... 302 510-1160
  Wilmington (G-9332)
Car Clinic Inc ....G....... 302 421-9100
  Wilmington (G-9560)
Careys Inc ....E....... 302 875-5674
  Laurel (G-3207)
Chambers Motors Inc ....E....... 302 629-3553
  Seaford (G-8187)
Coastal Towing Inc ....G....... 302 645-6300
  Lewes (G-3439)
Continental Warranty Corp ....E....... 302 375-0401
  Claymont (G-723)
D & H Automotive & Towing Inc ....G....... 302 655-7611
  Wilmington (G-9936)
D&G Inc ....G....... 302 378-4877
  Townsend (G-8778)
Daves Towing Inc ....G....... 302 697-9073
  Dover (G-1343)
Donald Briggs ....G....... 267 476-2712
  Middletown (G-4042)
Dover Lubricants Inc ....F....... 302 674-8282
  Dover (G-1458)
Ellmore Auto Collision ....G....... 302 762-2301
  Wilmington (G-10381)
Ewings Towing Service Inc ....G....... 302 366-8806
  Newark (G-6547)
Fast4wrd Towing & Repair LLC ....G....... 302 331-5157
  Wilmington (G-10504)
Fred Drake Automotive Inc ....G....... 302 378-4877
  Townsend (G-8788)
Goodchild Inc ....G....... 302 368-1681
  Newark (G-6675)
Harris Towing and Auto Service ....G....... 302 736-9901
  Dover (G-1632)
Holly Oak Towing and Service ....G....... 302 792-1500
  Wilmington (G-10928)
Horton Brothers Recovery Inc ....G....... 302 266-7339
  Newark (G-6748)
Hound Dog Recovery LLC ....G....... 302 836-3806
  Smyrna (G-8655)
Jiffy Lube International Inc ....F....... 302 738-5494
  Newark (G-6839)
Jim Sellers ....G....... 302 738-4149
  Newark (G-6840)
Kraemer & Sons LLC ....G....... 302 832-1534
  Bear (G-222)

Loyalty Is Earned Inc....G.... 347 606-6383
Wilmington (G-11445)
Mag Towing....G.... 302 462-5686
Frankford (G-2371)
Martel & Son Foreign Car Ctr....G.... 302 674-5556
Dover (G-1820)
Matthews Towing & Recovery....G.... 302 463-1108
Smyrna (G-8680)
Midway Towing Inc....G.... 302 323-4850
New Castle (G-5528)
Monro Inc....G.... 302 846-2732
Delmar (G-1022)
Pennzoil-Quaker State Company....E.... 302 999-7323
Wilmington (G-12074)
Pughs Service Inc....F.... 302 678-2408
Dover (G-1999)
Quality Auto Care Centers....G.... 302 992-7978
Wilmington (G-12278)
◆ Robert Bayly....G.... 302 846-9752
Laurel (G-3283)
Rossi Auto Body Inc....G.... 302 999-7707
Wilmington (G-12480)
Sals Auto Services Inc....G.... 302 654-1168
Wilmington (G-12526)
Schrider Enterprises Inc....F.... 302 934-1900
Millsboro (G-4799)
Sears Roebuck and Co....D.... 302 995-9295
Wilmington (G-12566)
Shore Tint & More Inc....G.... 302 947-4624
Harbeson (G-2800)
Smiths Jack Towing & Svc Ctr....G.... 302 798-6667
Wilmington (G-12663)
Swift Towing & Recovery....G.... 302 650-4579
New Castle (G-5748)
Uris LLC....G.... 302 469-7000
Millsboro (G-4818)
V B Towing Inc....G.... 302 238-7705
Frankford (G-2396)
Wilson Fleet & Equipment....G.... 302 422-7159
Milford (G-4610)
Winners Circle Inc....E.... 302 661-2100
Wilmington (G-13276)
Worthys Towing LLC....G.... 302 259-5265
Greenwood (G-2769)

76 MISCELLANEOUS REPAIR SERVICES

7622 Radio & TV Repair Shops

Als TV Service....G.... 302 653-3711
Smyrna (G-8567)
C B Joe TV & Appliances Inc....F.... 302 322-7600
New Castle (G-5125)
Computers Fixed Today....G.... 302 724-6411
Wilmington (G-9807)
Corporate Arcft Technical Svcs....G.... 302 383-9400
Wilmington (G-9864)
ET Communications LLC....F.... 302 322-2222
New Castle (G-5296)
Far Rezolutions Inc....G.... 302 547-6850
Newark (G-6570)
G & S TV & Antenna....G.... 302 422-5733
Milford (G-4419)
Overture LLC....G.... 302 226-1940
Rehoboth Beach (G-8025)
Summit Aviation Inc....D.... 302 834-5400
Middletown (G-4250)
Video Tech Center Inc....E.... 302 691-7213
Wilmington (G-13080)
Wireless Electronics Inc....G.... 302 652-1301
Wilmington (G-13278)

7623 Refrigeration & Air Conditioning Svc & Repair Shop

Berry Refrigeration Co....E.... 302 733-0933
Newark (G-6073)
Burns & McBride Inc....D.... 302 656-5110
New Castle (G-5121)
Commercial Equipment Service....G.... 302 475-6682
Wilmington (G-9786)
Delmarva Refrigeration Inc....G.... 302 846-2727
Delmar (G-992)
Morans Refrigeration Service....F.... 703 642-1200
Rehoboth Beach (G-8011)
Roto-Rooter Services Company....E.... 302 659-7637
Newark (G-7367)
United Technologies Corp....F.... 800 227-7437
New Castle (G-5808)

7629 Electrical & Elex Repair Shop, NEC

ABC Sales & Service Inc....E.... 302 652-3683
Wilmington (G-8899)
B Williams Holding Corp....F.... 302 656-8596
Wilmington (G-9214)
Blue Skies Solar & Wind Power....E.... 302 326-0856
New Castle (G-5097)
CMI Electric Inc....E.... 302 731-5556
Newark (G-6253)
Del-Mar Appliance of Delaware....G.... 302 674-2414
Dover (G-1352)
Delaware Hearing Aids....G.... 302 652-3558
Wilmington (G-10051)
Excel Business Systems Inc....E.... 302 453-1500
Newark (G-6550)
Food Equipment Service Inc....F.... 302 996-9363
Wilmington (G-10586)
Johns Washer Repair....G.... 302 792-2333
Claymont (G-769)
Kral Electronics Inc....F.... 302 737-1300
Newark (G-6902)
Mark D Garrett....G.... 302 674-2825
Dover (G-1818)
Martel Inc....F.... 302 744-9566
Dover (G-1821)
Master Klean Company....G.... 302 539-4290
Ocean View (G-7802)
Micro Ovens of Delaware....G.... 302 998-8444
Wilmington (G-11674)
Modern Controls Inc....E.... 302 325-6800
New Castle (G-5532)
Morton Electric Co....G.... 302 645-9414
Lewes (G-3650)
Naes Corporation....F.... 856 299-0020
New Castle (G-5542)
Qoe Inc....G.... 302 455-1234
Newark (G-7279)
Quality Appliance Services....G.... 302 766-4808
Newark (G-7282)
Ram Tech Systems Inc....E.... 302 832-6600
Middletown (G-4210)
Roys Electrical Service Inc....G.... 302 674-3199
Cheswold (G-663)
Smith Brothers Communication....G.... 302 293-5224
Newark (G-7450)
Tower Business Machines Inc....G.... 302 395-1445
New Castle (G-5780)
Video Tech Center Inc....E.... 302 691-7213
Wilmington (G-13080)
Visual Communications Inc....G.... 302 792-9500
Claymont (G-816)

7631 Watch, Clock & Jewelry Repair

Bellingers Jewelers....G.... 302 227-6410
Rehoboth Beach (G-7866)
Bridgewater Jewelers....G.... 302 328-2101
New Castle (G-5113)
Continental Jewelers Inc....F.... 302 475-2000
Wilmington (G-9841)
Del Haven of Wilmington Inc....G.... 302 999-9040
Newark (G-6361)
Michael Gallagher Jewelers....G.... 302 836-2925
Bear (G-254)
Precision Jewelry Inc....G.... 302 422-7138
Milford (G-4528)
Turquoise Shop Inc....F.... 302 366-7448
Newark (G-7601)
Whittens Fine Jewelry....G.... 302 995-7464
Wilmington (G-13196)

7641 Reupholstery & Furniture Repair

Advance Office Instlltions Inc....E.... 302 777-5599
New Castle (G-5008)
Barlows Upholstery Inc....G.... 302 655-3955
Wilmington (G-9255)
Calloways Custom Interiors Co....G.... 302 994-7931
Wilmington (G-9538)
Charles Andrews....G.... 302 378-7116
Townsend (G-8769)
Colliers Trim Shop Inc....G.... 302 227-8398
Rehoboth Beach (G-7897)
Color Dye Systems and Co....G.... 302 454-1754
Newark (G-6265)
Melroys Furniture Refinishing....G.... 302 645-1856
Lewes (G-3636)
New Life Furniture Systems....G.... 302 994-9054
Wilmington (G-11864)
Timothy Blawn....G.... 302 697-3843
Camden Wyoming (G-659)

7692 Welding Repair

3rd State Welding Supply LLC....G.... 302 777-1088
Wilmington (G-8858)
Allied Precision Inc....G.... 302 376-6844
Middletown (G-3936)
Basher & Son Enterprises Inc....G.... 302 239-6584
Hockessin (G-2962)
Bear Forge and Machine Co Inc....G.... 302 322-5199
Bear (G-47)
Bg Welding LLC....G.... 302 228-7260
Bridgeville (G-453)
Blm Industries Inc....G.... 302 238-7745
Millsboro (G-4645)
Boyds Trailor Hitches....G.... 302 697-9000
Camden Wyoming (G-619)
Boyds Welding Inc....G.... 302 697-9000
Camden Wyoming (G-620)
Bruces Welding Inc....G.... 302 629-3891
Seaford (G-8176)
C&C Welding....G.... 402 414-2485
New Castle (G-5126)
Cat Welding LLC....G.... 302 846-3509
Delmar (G-981)
Chets Welding Service....G.... 302 492-1003
Hartly (G-2915)
Chuck George Inc....E.... 302 994-7444
Wilmington (G-9697)
Dana S Wright....G.... 610 563-6070
Newark (G-6345)
Davis Welding Service Llc....G.... 302 465-3004
Seaford (G-8217)
Dempseys Specialized Services....G.... 302 530-7856
Newark (G-6436)
Diamond State Welding LLC....G.... 302 644-8489
Milton (G-4894)
Donaway Corporation....G.... 302 934-6226
Millsboro (G-4680)
East Coast Machine Works....G.... 302 349-5180
Greenwood (G-2734)
George Swire Sr....G.... 302 690-6995
Clayton (G-853)
▲ George W Plummer & Son Inc....G.... 302 645-9531
Lewes (G-3511)
Gj Chalfant Welding....G.... 302 545-6404
Newark (G-6658)
GJ Chalfant Welding LLC....G.... 302 983-0822
Port Penn (G-7834)
Graydie Welding LLC....G.... 302 753-0695
Wilmington (G-10764)
Haines Fabrication & Mch LLC....F.... 302 436-1929
Selbyville (G-8497)
Hot Rod Welding....G.... 302 725-5485
Harrington (G-2851)
Indian River Golf Cars Dr Wldg....G.... 302 947-2044
Millsboro (G-4708)
Joe Falco Portable Welding....G.... 302 998-1115
Wilmington (G-11164)
Js Knotts Inc....G.... 302 284-4888
Felton (G-2299)
Jumpers Welding Inc....G.... 302 519-7941
Middletown (G-4118)
Jvl Automotive....G.... 302 335-3942
Frederica (G-2408)
K L Vincent Welding Svc Inc....F.... 302 398-9357
Harrington (G-2860)
L & J Sheet Metal....F.... 302 875-2822
Laurel (G-3249)
Leland Oakley Welding....G.... 302 469-5746
Felton (G-2302)
Leroy H Smith....G.... 302 875-5976
Laurel (G-3258)
Lloyds Wldg & Fabrication LLC....G.... 302 384-7662
Wilmington (G-11416)
Marvel Portable Welding Inc....G.... 302 732-9480
Dagsboro (G-917)
Mastercraft Welding....G.... 302 697-3932
Dover (G-1824)
Metal-Tech Inc....E.... 302 322-7770
New Castle (G-5518)
Miller JW Wldg Boiler Repr Co....G.... 302 449-1575
Middletown (G-4166)
Mitchell S Welding LLC....G.... 302 632-1089
Camden Wyoming (G-650)
Moore Qlty Wldg Fbrication LLC....G.... 302 731-4818
Newark (G-7056)
Moore Quality Welding Fab....G.... 302 250-7136
Middletown (G-4169)
Newarc Welding Inc....G.... 302 376-1801
Middletown (G-4173)

S I C

Nicks Welding Repair LLC ....G.... 302 545-1494
Wilmington *(G-11889)*
Peninsula Technical Services I ....G.... 302 907-0554
Delmar *(G-1025)*
Pts Professional Welding ....G.... 302 632-2079
Houston *(G-3180)*
R & J Welding & Fabrication ....G.... 302 236-5618
Laurel *(G-3276)*
R C Fabricators Inc ....D.... 302 573-8989
Wilmington *(G-12293)*
Richard M White Welding ....G.... 302 684-4461
Milton *(G-4959)*
Ronald P Wilson ....G.... 302 539-4139
Frankford *(G-2384)*
Sapps Welding Service ....G.... 302 491-6319
Lincoln *(G-3868)*
Seaford Machine Works Inc ....F.... 302 629-6034
Seaford *(G-8392)*
Terrys Welding LLC ....G.... 302 349-5260
Greenwood *(G-2766)*
Truck Tech Inc ....F.... 302 832-8000
New Castle *(G-5796)*
Welding By Jackson ....G.... 302 846-3090
Delmar *(G-1047)*
William Stele Wldg Fabrication ....G.... 302 422-7444
Milford *(G-4607)*

7694 Armature Rewinding Shops

Dills Electric ....G.... 302 674-3444
Dover *(G-1426)*
Electric Motor Repair Svc ....G.... 302 322-1179
New Castle *(G-5281)*
F and D Equipment & Repair LLC ....G.... 302 378-1999
Middletown *(G-4068)*
HP Motors Inc ....G.... 302 368-4543
Newark *(G-6753)*
Roys Electrical Service Inc ....G.... 302 674-3199
Cheswold *(G-663)*
Warren Electric Co Inc ....G.... 302 629-9134
Seaford *(G-8433)*

7699 Repair Shop & Related Svcs, NEC

1st State Power Clean LLC ....G.... 302 735-7974
Dover *(G-1067)*
5 JS Sanitation ....G.... 302 945-7086
Georgetown *(G-2418)*
A & R Fence Co Inc ....G.... 302 366-8550
Newark *(G-5864)*
A-1 Sanitation Service Inc ....F.... 302 322-1074
New Castle *(G-4995)*
A1 Sanitation Service Inc ....F.... 302 653-9591
Smyrna *(G-8559)*
Acanthus & Reed Ltd ....G.... 212 628-9290
New Castle *(G-4999)*
Allied Lock & Safe Company ....G.... 302 658-3172
Wilmington *(G-9023)*
Almars Outboard Service & Sls ....G.... 302 328-8541
New Castle *(G-5023)*
Alvins Professional Services ....F.... 302 544-6634
New Castle *(G-5028)*
◆ **Anderson Group Inc** ....G.... 302 478-6160
Wilmington *(G-9078)*
Arrow Leasing Corp ....F.... 302 834-4546
Bear *(G-36)*
Arteaga Properties LLC ....G.... 808 339-6906
Wilmington *(G-9136)*
Bg Truck & Trailor Repair ....G.... 302 455-9171
Middletown *(G-3967)*
Blades H V A C Services ....G.... 302 539-4436
Dagsboro *(G-884)*
Blue Sky Clean ....G.... 302 584-5800
Wilmington *(G-9381)*
Board of Public Works Inc ....G.... 302 645-6450
Lewes *(G-3390)*
Bobs Marine Service Inc ....F.... 302 539-3711
Ocean View *(G-7769)*
Brooks Machine Inc ....G.... 302 674-5900
Dover *(G-1235)*
▲ **Bruce Industrial Co Inc** ....D.... 302 655-9616
New Castle *(G-5118)*
Budget Rooter Inc ....F.... 302 322-3011
New Castle *(G-5120)*
Burns & McBride Inc ....D.... 302 656-5110
New Castle *(G-5121)*
C H P T Manufacturing Inc ....G.... 302 856-7660
Georgetown *(G-2461)*
C&B Complete Cleaning & Cnstr ....G.... 302 436-9622
Frankford *(G-2352)*
Candlelight Cleaning ....G.... 302 270-1218
Smyrna *(G-8590)*
Carspecken-Scott Inc ....G.... 302 655-7173
Wilmington *(G-9580)*
Certified Lock & Access LLC ....G.... 302 383-7507
Wilmington *(G-9618)*
Charles Offroad ....G.... 443 365-0630
Laurel *(G-3211)*
Clean Delaware Inc ....F.... 302 684-4221
Milton *(G-4879)*
Clean Delaware LLC ....E.... 302 684-4221
Lewes *(G-3427)*
Cleaning Frenzy LLC ....G.... 302 453-8800
Newark *(G-6248)*
Clifton Leasing Co Inc ....E.... 302 674-2300
Dover *(G-1293)*
Columbia Vending Service Inc ....F.... 302 856-7000
Delmar *(G-985)*
Community Auto Repair ....G.... 302 856-3333
Georgetown *(G-2478)*
▲ **Cooper Bearings Inc** ....F.... 302 858-5056
Georgetown *(G-2484)*
Costline Cleaning Service ....G.... 302 420-3000
Harbeson *(G-2778)*
Croosroads Auto Repair Inc ....G.... 302 436-9100
Selbyville *(G-8473)*
Deangelis & Son Inc ....G.... 302 337-8699
Bridgeville *(G-464)*
◆ **Delaware Capital Holdings Inc** ....G.... 302 793-4921
Wilmington *(G-10011)*
Delaware Rural Water Assn ....G.... 302 398-9633
Harrington *(G-2830)*
Delaware Septic Service LLC ....G.... 302 376-6412
Townsend *(G-8780)*
Drain Kings LLC ....G.... 302 399-8980
Smyrna *(G-8626)*
Dustntime ....F.... 302 858-7876
Rehoboth Beach *(G-7922)*
Earls Place LLC ....G.... 302 538-8909
Felton *(G-2289)*
Econerd ....G.... 302 669-9279
Middletown *(G-4049)*
Elite Chemical and Supply Inc ....G.... 302 366-8900
Newark *(G-6513)*
F and M Equipment Ltd ....G.... 302 715-5382
Laurel *(G-3229)*
Fiduks Industrial Services Inc ....F.... 302 994-2534
Wilmington *(G-10536)*
Flute Pro Shop Inc ....G.... 302 479-5000
Wilmington *(G-10583)*
Foulk Lawn & Equipment Co Inc ....G.... 302 475-3233
Wilmington *(G-10599)*
Freedom Cycle LLC ....G.... 302 286-6900
Newark *(G-6615)*
Gale Force Cleaning & Restore ....F.... 302 539-4683
Ocean View *(G-7789)*
General Separation Tech Inc ....G.... 302 533-5646
Newark *(G-6645)*
George Hardcastle & Sons Inc ....G.... 302 655-5230
Wilmington *(G-10700)*
Groff Tractor & Equipment LLC ....F.... 302 349-5760
Greenwood *(G-2742)*
Gtech Cleaning Services LLC ....E.... 302 494-2102
Claymont *(G-759)*
Halls We Clean Service LLC ....G.... 302 422-7787
Milford *(G-4431)*
Hayes Sewing Machine Company ....F.... 302 764-9033
Wilmington *(G-10856)*
HCC Corporation LLC ....G.... 302 421-9306
Wilmington *(G-10860)*
Heavy Equipment Rental Inc ....F.... 302 654-5716
New Castle *(G-5388)*
Hickman Overhead Door Company ....F.... 302 422-4249
Milford *(G-4441)*
Hockessin Tractor Inc ....G.... 302 239-4201
Hockessin *(G-3055)*
Homeimprovement E B&S ....G.... 302 465-1828
Dover *(G-1655)*
Igal Biochemical LLC ....G.... 302 525-2090
Newark *(G-6765)*
Industrial Resource Netwrk Inc ....F.... 302 888-2905
Wilmington *(G-11022)*
Integrity Cleaning Svcs LLC ....G.... 302 353-9315
Clayton *(G-856)*
International Electrical Svcs ....G.... 302 438-6096
Wilmington *(G-11065)*
J & A Grinding Inc ....F.... 302 368-8760
Newark *(G-6812)*
Jbm Petroleum Service LLC ....G.... 302 752-6105
Lincoln *(G-3857)*
Keene Enterprises Inc ....G.... 302 422-2856
Ellendale *(G-2261)*
Kelly Appliance Service ....G.... 302 628-5396
Seaford *(G-8286)*
Kompressed Air Delaware Inc ....G.... 302 275-1985
New Castle *(G-5469)*
Kream Puff Clean ....F.... 251 509-1639
Smyrna *(G-8668)*
Laser Tone Bus Systems LLC ....G.... 302 335-2510
Milford *(G-4471)*
Lee Lynn Inc ....F.... 302 678-9978
Dover *(G-1775)*
Linda & Richard Partnership ....G.... 302 697-9758
Dover *(G-1790)*
Links Outboard LLC ....G.... 302 368-2860
Newark *(G-6937)*
Lion Totalcare Inc ....E.... 610 444-1700
Wilmington *(G-11398)*
M&J Services LLC ....G.... 302 227-8725
Rehoboth Beach *(G-7993)*
Man Maid Cleaning Inc ....G.... 302 226-5050
Rehoboth Beach *(G-7995)*
Matties Cleaning Service ....F.... 302 229-3585
Wilmington *(G-11574)*
Mc Mullen Septic Service Inc ....G.... 302 629-6221
Seaford *(G-8305)*
Messick & Gray Cnstr Inc ....E.... 302 337-8777
Bridgeville *(G-497)*
Messick & Gray Cnstr Inc ....F.... 302 337-8445
Bridgeville *(G-498)*
Metal Shop ....F.... 302 846-2988
Delmar *(G-1020)*
Michael Matthew Sponaugle ....G.... 302 566-1010
Harrington *(G-2868)*
Mid Atlntic Scientific Svc Inc ....G.... 302 328-4440
New Castle *(G-5524)*
Midlantic Marine Center Inc ....F.... 302 436-2628
Selbyville *(G-8521)*
Modern Controls Inc ....E.... 302 325-6800
New Castle *(G-5532)*
Multi Koastal Services ....G.... 302 436-8822
Frankford *(G-2377)*
Pat T Clean Inc ....G.... 302 239-5354
Hockessin *(G-3111)*
Pike Creek Bike Line Inc ....G.... 610 747-1200
Wilmington *(G-12136)*
Pinnacle Garage Door Company ....G.... 302 505-4531
Felton *(G-2310)*
Poof Power Wash & Ldscpg LLC ....G.... 302 595-1576
Dover *(G-1976)*
Precision Door Service ....G.... 302 343-6394
Wilmington *(G-12204)*
Progressive Systems Inc ....G.... 302 732-3321
Frankford *(G-2381)*
Pughs Service Inc ....F.... 302 678-2408
Dover *(G-1999)*
Reliable Trailer Inc ....F.... 856 962-7900
Felton *(G-2316)*
▼ **Revod Corporation** ....G.... 302 477-1795
Wilmington *(G-12396)*
Richards Investment Group Corp ....G.... 302 399-0450
Smyrna *(G-8701)*
Rommel Cycles LLC ....D.... 302 658-8800
Smyrna *(G-8703)*
Roto-Rooter Services Company ....E.... 302 659-7637
Newark *(G-7367)*
Rudy Marine Inc ....F.... 302 999-8735
Wilmington *(G-12491)*
Sawyers Sanitation Service ....G.... 302 678-8240
Leipsic *(G-3314)*
Seagreen Bicycle LLP ....G.... 302 226-2323
Rehoboth Beach *(G-8070)*
Shark Service Center LLC ....G.... 302 337-8233
Bridgeville *(G-520)*
Square One Electric Service Co ....F.... 302 678-0400
Dover *(G-2099)*
State Line Machine Inc ....F.... 302 478-0285
Wilmington *(G-12745)*
Suburban Lawn & Equipment Inc ....G.... 302 475-4300
Wilmington *(G-12785)*
Summit Aviation Inc ....D.... 302 834-5400
Middletown *(G-4250)*
Super Perfection Clg Svcs LLC ....G.... 267 619-4441
Wilmington *(G-12803)*
Superior Maids ....F.... 302 284-2012
Felton *(G-2323)*
Sussex Hydraulics Sales & Svcs ....G.... 302 846-9702
Delmar *(G-1033)*
T & T Small Engines Inc ....G.... 302 492-8677
Hartly *(G-2943)*
T&T Cleaning LLC ....F.... 609 575-0458
Dover *(G-2127)*

SIC SECTION

79 AMUSEMENT AND RECREATION SERVICES

Talleys Garage Inc .... G 302 652-0463
   Wilmington *(G-12850)*
True Mobility Inc .... G 302 836-4110
   New Castle *(G-5797)*
Tucker Mechanical Service Inc .... G 302 536-7730
   Seaford *(G-8426)*
Vertical Blind Factory Inc .... F 302 998-9616
   Wilmington *(G-13067)*
Vesta Wash LLC .... G 302 559-7533
   Newark *(G-7654)*
Weaver Sanitation .... G 302 653-8777
   Smyrna *(G-8740)*
Widgeon Enterprises Inc .... G 302 846-9763
   Delmar *(G-1049)*
Willey Knives Inc .... G 302 349-4070
   Greenwood *(G-2768)*
Woodward Enterprises Inc .... F 302 378-2849
   Middletown *(G-4291)*
Xerox Corporation .... E 302 792-5100
   Wilmington *(G-13319)*
Yoder Overhead Door Company .... G 302 875-0663
   Delmar *(G-1050)*
Youve Been Framed .... G 302 366-8029
   Newark *(G-7732)*

78 MOTION PICTURES

7812 Motion Picture & Video Tape Production

Avian Productions Inc .... G 302 526-0542
   Dover *(G-1161)*
Brandywine Electronics Corp .... F 302 324-9992
   Bear *(G-56)*
Continuum Media LLC .... F 310 295-9997
   Camden *(G-552)*
Cornerstone Media Production .... G 302 855-9380
   Georgetown *(G-2486)*
Electro Sound Systems Inc .... F 302 543-2292
   Newport *(G-7748)*
Everett Robinson .... F 302 530-6574
   Wilmington *(G-10446)*
▲ Imcg Global Inc .... G 800 559-6140
   Lewes *(G-3553)*
Ken-Del Productions Inc .... F 302 999-1111
   Wilmington *(G-11239)*
Maxwell World .... G 937 463-3579
   Dagsboro *(G-918)*
Melody Entertainment USA Inc .... G 305 505-7659
   Wilmington *(G-11627)*
OK Video .... F 302 762-2333
   Wilmington *(G-11942)*
▲ Petes Big Tvs Inc .... G 302 328-3551
   New Castle *(G-5619)*
Point Eght Third Prdctions LLC .... G 302 317-9419
   Wilmington *(G-12177)*
Pond Publishing & Productions .... G 302 284-0200
   Felton *(G-2313)*
Productions For Purpose Inc .... G 302 388-9883
   Middletown *(G-4199)*
Teleduction Associates Inc .... G 302 429-0303
   Wilmington *(G-12877)*
Waco Lid Films Inc .... G 302 378-7053
   Townsend *(G-8831)*

7819 Services Allied To Motion Picture Prdtn

Risingplatformproductions LLC .... G 660 283-0183
   Newark *(G-7344)*

7822 Motion Picture & Video Tape Distribution

Bernieface Productions LLC .... G 302 561-0273
   Bear *(G-51)*
Bew Productions .... G 302 547-8661
   Wilmington *(G-9322)*
Brewster Products Inc .... G 302 798-1988
   New Castle *(G-5111)*
CB Productions .... G 302 715-1015
   Laurel *(G-3209)*
Digital Heart Productions .... G 302 737-6158
   Newark *(G-6446)*
Echelon Studios Inc .... F 800 208-9052
   Wilmington *(G-10335)*
Far Flung Bungy LLC .... F 302 421-8226
   Wilmington *(G-10497)*
Fish & Monkey Productions LLC .... F 302 897-4318
   Wilmington *(G-10559)*
J Alexander Productions LLC .... F 302 559-6667
   Wilmington *(G-11103)*
J Chance Productions .... G 302 322-2251
   New Castle *(G-5428)*

Jam Productions .... G 302 369-3629
   Newark *(G-6824)*
Kamproductions .... G 302 228-1852
   Lincoln *(G-3858)*
Michael Woody Productions .... F 302 584-2082
   Bear *(G-255)*
Moghul Life Inc .... G 347 560-9124
   Wilmington *(G-11724)*
New Cndlelight Productions Inc .... E 302 475-2313
   Wilmington *(G-11856)*
Nkognito Productions LLC .... G 302 943-0399
   Magnolia *(G-3901)*
Peristalsis Productions Inc .... G 302 366-1106
   Newark *(G-7204)*
Short Wars Productions LLC .... F 302 932-0707
   Wilmington *(G-12609)*
Trauma Film Production PR LLC .... G 623 582-2287
   Dover *(G-2162)*

7832 Motion Picture Theaters, Except Drive-In

Assoc Community Talents Inc .... G 302 378-7038
   Middletown *(G-3944)*
Associated Cmnty Talents Inc .... G 302 378-1200
   Middletown *(G-3945)*
Carmike Cinemas Inc .... E 302 734-5249
   Dover *(G-1256)*
Cinemark Usa Inc .... G 302 994-7280
   Wilmington *(G-9707)*
Foot Light Production Inc .... F 302 645-7220
   Lewes *(G-3502)*
Regal Cinemas Inc .... E 302 479-0753
   Wilmington *(G-12353)*
Regal Cinemas Inc .... D 302 834-8515
   Christiana *(G-679)*
Rich Hebert & Associates .... F 202 255-3474
   Selbyville *(G-8541)*
Westown Movies LLC .... G 330 244-1633
   Middletown *(G-4283)*
Wilkins Enterprises .... G 302 732-3744
   Dagsboro *(G-944)*

7841 Video Tape Rental

California Video 2 .... G 302 477-6944
   Wilmington *(G-9537)*
Extreme Audio & Video .... G 302 533-7404
   Newark *(G-6555)*
Pat Cirelli .... G 302 322-6751
   New Castle *(G-5607)*
Video Den .... G 302 628-9835
   Seaford *(G-8431)*

79 AMUSEMENT AND RECREATION SERVICES

7911 Dance Studios, Schools & Halls

A Dance Class .... G 302 422-2633
   Milford *(G-4301)*
Barbaras Dance Academy .... G 302 883-4355
   Dover *(G-1172)*
Brandywine Center For Dance & .... G 302 798-0124
   Wilmington *(G-9423)*
Dance Conservatory .... G 302 734-9717
   Dover *(G-1339)*
Dancedelaware .... G 302 998-1222
   Wilmington *(G-9954)*
Delaware Arts Conservatory .... F 302 595-4160
   Bear *(G-103)*
Delaware Dance Center Inc .... G 302 454-1440
   Wilmington *(G-10035)*
Delaware Dance Company Inc .... E 302 738-2023
   Newark *(G-6374)*
Hockessin Dance Center Inc .... G 302 738-3838
   Newark *(G-6733)*
Il Extreme Entertainment .... G 302 389-8525
   New Castle *(G-5412)*
Mid-Atlantic Ballet Inc .... G 302 266-6362
   Newark *(G-7028)*
New Castle Dance Academy .... F 302 836-2060
   Bear *(G-263)*
Take Lead Dance Studio .... G 302 234-0909
   Hockessin *(G-3156)*
Tri-State Cheernastics Inc .... G 302 322-4020
   New Castle *(G-5787)*

7922 Theatrical Producers & Misc Theatrical Svcs

B & B Tickettown Inc .... G 302 656-9797
   Wilmington *(G-9208)*
Clear Space Theatre Company .... G 302 227-2270
   Rehoboth Beach *(G-7892)*
Delaware Theatre Company .... E 302 594-1100
   Wilmington *(G-10090)*
Dickens Parlour Theatre .... G 302 829-1071
   Millville *(G-4842)*
Earle Teate Music .... G 302 736-1937
   Dover *(G-1495)*
Everett Robinson .... F 302 530-6574
   Wilmington *(G-10446)*
Friends of Capitol Theater Inc .... G 302 678-3583
   Dover *(G-1570)*
Gobos Togo Inc .... G 302 426-1898
   New Castle *(G-5355)*
Grand Opera House Inc .... E 302 652-5577
   Wilmington *(G-10759)*
Heidis Academy of Prfrmg Arts .... F 302 293-7868
   Bear *(G-181)*
▲ Imcg Global Inc .... G 800 559-6140
   Lewes *(G-3553)*
Joshua M Freeman Foundation .... F 302 436-3003
   Selbyville *(G-8510)*
Light Action Inc .... F 302 328-7800
   New Castle *(G-5481)*
Main Light Industries Inc .... C 302 998-8017
   Wilmington *(G-11491)*
Michael Schwartz .... F 302 791-9999
   Wilmington *(G-11666)*
Mirworth Enterprise Inc .... G 302 846-0218
   Delmar *(G-1021)*
Operadelaware Inc .... G 302 658-8063
   Wilmington *(G-11962)*
Pieces of A Dream Inc .... G 302 593-6172
   Wilmington *(G-12132)*
Rehoboth Summer Chld Theatre .... F 302 227-6766
   Rehoboth Beach *(G-8056)*
Rhodeside Inc .... G 505 261-4568
   Wilmington *(G-12402)*
Wilmington String Ensemble .... E 302 764-1201
   Wilmington *(G-13258)*
Worldwind Inc .... G 302 762-0556
   Wilmington *(G-13305)*

7929 Bands, Orchestras, Actors & Entertainers

Alex Vaughan Mobile Entrtnmnt .... G 302 674-2464
   Dover *(G-1102)*
Aqua Flow Sprinklers .... G 302 369-3629
   Newark *(G-5991)*
Bihbrand Inc .... F 302 223-4330
   Lewes *(G-3384)*
Bobby Wilson Entertainment LLC .... G 302 233-6463
   Dover *(G-1217)*
Coastal Concerts Inc .... G 302 645-1539
   Lewes *(G-3437)*
Comfort Zone Jazz LLC .... G 302 745-2019
   Milton *(G-4882)*
Continuum Media LLC .... F 310 295-9997
   Camden *(G-552)*
Cube Media L L C .... G 716 239-2789
   Wilmington *(G-9915)*
Delaware Symphony Association .... D 302 656-7442
   Wilmington *(G-10089)*
Dj First Class .... F 302 345-0602
   New Castle *(G-5256)*
Dover Motorsports Inc .... G 302 328-6820
   New Castle *(G-5259)*
Dover Symphony Orchestra Inc .... G 302 734-1701
   Dover *(G-1471)*
E I Du Pont De Nemours & Co .... F 302 888-0200
   Wilmington *(G-10296)*
Everett Robinson .... F 302 530-6574
   Wilmington *(G-10446)*
First State Strings Inc .... G 302 331-7362
   Camden Wyoming *(G-640)*
Gge Amusements .... G 302 227-0661
   Rehoboth Beach *(G-7947)*
Jammin Productions .... G 302 670-7302
   Dover *(G-1693)*
K&B Investors LLC .... G 302 357-9723
   Wilmington *(G-11216)*
Levi Calling .... G 302 449-0017
   Townsend *(G-8806)*
Lune Rouge Entrmt USA Inc .... E 514 556-2101
   Wilmington *(G-11451)*

Employee Codes: A=Over 500 employees, B=251-500
C=101-250, D=51-100, E=20-50, F=10-19, G=1-9

79 AMUSEMENT AND RECREATION SERVICES

Mid Atlantic Grand Prix LLC ....E...... 302 656-5278 New Castle *(G-5522)*	Afterglo Beauty Spa ....G...... 302 537-7546 Millville *(G-4832)*	Pike Creek Court Club Inc ....D...... 302 239-6688 Wilmington *(G-12138)*
Milford Community Band Inc ....D...... 302 422-6304 Milford *(G-4497)*	Alternative Therapy LLC ....G...... 302 368-0800 Newark *(G-5949)*	Plexus Fitness ....F...... 302 654-9642 Wilmington *(G-12159)*
Mobile Muzic Inc ....G...... 302 998-5951 Wilmington *(G-11718)*	American Karate Studios ....E...... 302 737-9500 Newark *(G-5954)*	Powerhouse Gym ....G...... 302 262-0262 Seaford *(G-8360)*
PDr Vc Ltd Liability Company ....G...... 424 281-4669 Wilmington *(G-12056)*	▼ American Martial Arts Inst ....F...... 302 834-4060 Bear *(G-27)*	Retro Fitness ....E...... 302 276-0828 Bear *(G-303)*
Premier Entertainment III LLC ....E...... 302 674-4600 Dover *(G-1982)*	Anytime Fitness ....G...... 302 475-2404 Wilmington *(G-9092)*	Ricks Fitness & Health Inc ....G...... 302 684-0316 Milton *(G-4962)*
Raymond Entrmt Group LLC ....G...... 302 731-2000 Newark *(G-7300)*	Anytime Fitness ....G...... 302 738-3040 Newark *(G-5978)*	Sanctuary Spa and Saloon ....F...... 302 475-1469 Wilmington *(G-12537)*
Real Life Entertainment ....G...... 516 413-2782 Newark *(G-7304)*	Anytime Fitness ....G...... 302 653-4496 Smyrna *(G-8572)*	Semp Wellness LLC ....G...... 302 525-9612 Newark *(G-7406)*
Smooth Sound Dance Band ....E...... 302 398-8467 Harrington *(G-2891)*	Avenue Day Spa ....F...... 302 227-5649 Rehoboth Beach *(G-7852)*	Silverback Gyms LLC ....G...... 302 539-8282 Ocean View *(G-7813)*
Soucialize Inc ....G...... 916 803-1057 Lewes *(G-3756)*	B Fit Enterprises ....F...... 302 292-1785 Newark *(G-6035)*	Smakkfitness LLC ....G...... 213 280-7569 Wilmington *(G-12649)*
Studio J Entrmt & AP & Cof Bar ......G...... 410 422-3155 Laurel *(G-3296)*	Bear-Glasgow YMCA ....G...... 302 836-9622 Newark *(G-6066)*	Snap Fitness ....G...... 302 741-2444 Dover *(G-2090)*
Wilmington String Ensemble ....E...... 302 764-1201 Wilmington *(G-13258)*	Body and Soul Fitness LLC ....G...... 302 536-1278 Seaford *(G-8172)*	Spa At Corolla Inc ....F...... 302 292-2858 Newark *(G-7462)*
Zone Laser Tag Inc ....F...... 302 730-8888 Dover *(G-2254)*	Christophers Hair Design ....G...... 302 378-1988 Middletown *(G-3990)*	Taekwondo Fitness Ctr of Del ....G...... 302 836-8264 Bear *(G-346)*
	Cnu Fit LLC ....G...... 302 744-9037 Dover *(G-1298)*	Tri-State Cheernastics Inc ....G...... 302 322-4020 New Castle *(G-5787)*
## 7933 Bowling Centers	Crossfit Bear ....G...... 302 540-4394 Bear *(G-89)*	Via Mdical Day Spa Pasca Salon ......G...... 302 757-2830 Wilmington *(G-13074)*
AMF Bowling Centers Inc ....E...... 302 998-5316 Wilmington *(G-9068)*	Crossfit Diamond State LLC ....G...... 201 803-1159 Wilmington *(G-9904)*	W23 S12 Holdings LLC ....G...... 610 348-3825 Wilmington *(G-13110)*
Bowlerama Inc ....E...... 302 654-0704 New Castle *(G-5100)*	Crossfit Dover LLC ....G...... 302 242-5400 Magnolia *(G-3888)*	Womens Fitness ....G...... 302 239-5088 Wilmington *(G-13291)*
Brunswick Doverama ....G...... 302 734-7501 Dover *(G-1238)*	Curves ....G...... 302 731-2617 Newark *(G-6329)*	Young Mens Christian Associat ......D...... 302 571-6935 Wilmington *(G-13331)*
Delaware Womens Bowling Assn ......F...... 302 834-7002 Bear *(G-114)*	Curves For Women ....F...... 302 477-9400 Wilmington *(G-9921)*	Young Mens Christian Associat ......D...... 302 296-9622 Rehoboth Beach *(G-8121)*
Inspection Lanes ....G...... 302 853-1003 Georgetown *(G-2566)*	Curves International Inc ....G...... 302 698-1481 Camden *(G-554)*	Young Mens Christian Associat ......F...... 302 472-9622 Wilmington *(G-13333)*
Inspection Lanes ....G...... 302 744-2514 Dover *(G-1678)*	Cycology 202 LLC ....F...... 610 202-0518 Lewes *(G-3447)*	Young Mens Christian Associat ......C...... 302 571-6900 Wilmington *(G-13332)*
Keglers Korner Pro Shop ....G...... 302 526-2249 Dover *(G-1729)*	David L Townsend Co Inc ....G...... 302 378-7967 Smyrna *(G-8611)*	YWCA Delaware ....D...... 302 655-0039 Wilmington *(G-13337)*
Leftys Alley & Eats ....F...... 302 864-6000 Lewes *(G-3593)*	Delaware Rock Gym Inc ....G...... 302 838-5850 Bear *(G-111)*	YWCA Delaware ....F...... 302 224-4060 Newark *(G-7733)*
Midcoast Gymnstics Dnce Studio ....G...... 302 436-6007 Selbyville *(G-8520)*	Energy Gym ....F...... 302 436-9001 Selbyville *(G-8488)*	
Milford Bowling Lanes Inc ....E...... 302 422-9456 Milford *(G-4496)*	Fitness Mtivation Inst of Amer ....G...... 302 628-3488 Seaford *(G-8245)*	## 7992 Public Golf Courses
Millsboro Lanes Inc ....F...... 302 934-0400 Millsboro *(G-4750)*	Forever Fit Foundation ....G...... 302 698-5201 Dover *(G-1561)*	American Classic Golf Club LLC ......G...... 302 703-6662 Lewes *(G-3336)*
Pleasant Hill Lanes Inc ....E...... 302 998-8811 Wilmington *(G-12158)*	Frontline Crossfit ....G...... 302 229-6467 New Castle *(G-5332)*	Arpago Corp ....G...... 302 645-7955 Lewes *(G-3347)*
	Gold Medal Gymnastics Inc ....G...... 302 659-5569 Smyrna *(G-8643)*	Back Creek Golf Shop ....E...... 302 378-6499 Middletown *(G-3958)*
## 7941 Professional Sports Clubs & Promoters	Golds Gym ....G...... 302 226-4653 Rehoboth Beach *(G-7951)*	Bayside Golf LLC DBA Bear Trap ......F...... 302 537-5600 Ocean View *(G-7760)*
Five Star Franchising LLC ....G...... 646 838-3992 Wilmington *(G-10567)*	Harts Two ....G...... 302 741-2119 Camden Wyoming *(G-644)*	Bayside Resort Golf Club ....E...... 302 436-3400 Selbyville *(G-8453)*
Wilmington Blue Rocks Baseball ......F...... 302 888-2015 Wilmington *(G-13224)*	Haus of Lacquer LLC ....E...... 302 690-0309 Wilmington *(G-10855)*	Baywood Greens Golf Club ....E...... 302 947-9225 Millsboro *(G-4638)*
	HB Fitness Delaware Inc ....F...... 302 384-7245 Wilmington *(G-10859)*	Baywood Greens Golf Club ....E...... 302 947-9800 Millsboro *(G-4639)*
## 7948 Racing & Track Operations	Higher Power Yoga and Fitness ......G...... 302 526-2077 Dover *(G-1644)*	Bear Trap Partners ....F...... 302 537-5600 Ocean View *(G-7761)*
Advanced Motorsports ....G...... 302 629-3301 Seaford *(G-8139)*	Hockessin Day Spa ....G...... 302 234-7573 Hockessin *(G-3050)*	City of Seaford Inc ....F...... 302 629-2890 Seaford *(G-8197)*
Delaware Racing Association ....B...... 302 355-1000 Newark *(G-6405)*	Jennifers Spa ....G...... 302 740-6363 Newark *(G-6833)*	Delaware Park Racing LLC ....G...... 302 994-6700 Wilmington *(G-10073)*
▲ Delaware Racing Association ......A...... 302 994-2521 Wilmington *(G-10076)*	Kirkwood Ftnes Racquetball CLB ....F...... 302 529-1865 Wilmington *(G-11275)*	Delcastle Golf Club ....G...... 302 995-1990 Wilmington *(G-10097)*
Dover Downs Inc ....A...... 302 674-4600 Dover *(G-1445)*	La Bella Vita Salon & Day Spa ....G...... 302 883-2597 Dover *(G-1762)*	Delcastle Golf Club Management ....E...... 302 998-9505 Wilmington *(G-10098)*
Dover Intl Speedway Inc ....G...... 302 857-2114 Dover *(G-1455)*	Last Tangle Salon and Spa ....G...... 302 653-6638 Smyrna *(G-8670)*	Dover Golf Center ....G...... 302 674-8275 Dover *(G-1451)*
Dover Motorsports Inc ....G...... 302 328-6820 New Castle *(G-5259)*	Legion Transformation Ctr LLC ......G...... 302 543-4922 Wilmington *(G-11363)*	Frog Hollow Golf Course ....E...... 302 376-6500 Middletown *(G-4079)*
Dover Motorsports Inc ....D...... 302 883-6500 Dover *(G-1460)*	Lillys Personal Training ....G...... 302 538-6723 Dover *(G-1789)*	Garrisons Lake Golf Club ....G...... 302 659-1206 Smyrna *(G-8639)*
▲ Harrington Raceway Inc ....F...... 302 398-4920 Harrington *(G-2845)*	Midway Fitness Center ....G...... 302 645-0407 Rehoboth Beach *(G-8007)*	Golf Course At Garrisons Lake ....G...... 302 659-1206 Smyrna *(G-8644)*
Penske Performance Inc ....D...... 302 656-2082 Wilmington *(G-12075)*	Missy Muller ....F...... 302 376-0760 Middletown *(G-4167)*	Greens At Broadview LLC ....E...... 302 684-3000 Milton *(G-4910)*
Premier Entertainment III LLC ....E...... 302 674-4600 Dover *(G-1982)*	More Than Fitness Inc ....G...... 302 690-5655 Wilmington *(G-11748)*	Jonathans Landing ....E...... 302 697-8204 Magnolia *(G-3896)*
Sharp Farm ....G...... 302 652-7729 Wilmington *(G-12594)*	National Fitness LLC ....G...... 301 841-8066 Bethany Beach *(G-417)*	Lynx Golf Ltd ....G...... 778 755-4107 Dover *(G-1809)*
Sharp Farm ....F...... 302 378-9606 Middletown *(G-4239)*	Neuro Fitness Therapy ....G...... 302 753-2700 Wilmington *(G-11844)*	Meadowbrook Golf Group Inc ....E...... 302 571-9041 Wilmington *(G-11611)*
U S 13 Dragway Inc ....D...... 302 875-1911 Delmar *(G-1044)*	Paladin Sports Club Inc ....F...... 302 764-5335 Wilmington *(G-12008)*	Odessa National Golf Crse LLC ......F...... 302 464-1007 Townsend *(G-8814)*
## 7991 Physical Fitness Facilities		Par 3 Inc ....G...... 302 674-8275 Dover *(G-1934)*
1110 On Parkway Nedi Spa ....F...... 302 576-1110 Wilmington *(G-8843)*		

79 AMUSEMENT AND RECREATION SERVICES

Peninsula At Long Neck LLC ....G....... 302 947-4717
  Millsboro (G-4775)
Rock Manor Golf Course ....G....... 302 295-1400
  Wilmington (G-12447)
Rookery Golf Courses South ....G....... 302 422-7010
  Milford (G-4548)
Vinces Sports Center Inc ....G....... 302 738-4859
  Newark (G-7659)
Worcester Golf Club Inc ....F....... 610 222-0200
  Milton (G-4981)

7993 Coin-Operated Amusement Devices & Arcades

Delaware Racing Association ....B....... 302 355-1000
  Newark (G-6405)
▲ Delaware Racing Association ....A....... 302 994-2521
  Wilmington (G-10076)
Harrington Raceway Inc ....B....... 302 398-5346
  Harrington (G-2846)
Orbit Research LLC ....G....... 302 683-1063
  Wilmington (G-11971)
Seaside Amusements Inc ....G....... 302 227-1921
  Rehoboth Beach (G-8071)

7996 Amusement Parks

Fun Sport Inc ....G....... 302 644-2042
  Rehoboth Beach (G-7939)

7997 Membership Sports & Recreation Clubs

20dollar Club Association ....G....... 978 908-6047
  Wilmington (G-8853)
Adkins Management Company ....F....... 302 684-3000
  Milford (G-4303)
AMC Museum Foundation ....G....... 302 677-5938
  Dover (G-1116)
American Sports Licensing ....D....... 302 288-0122
  Wilmington (G-9057)
Army & Air Force Exchange Svc ....G....... 302 677-6365
  Dover (G-1139)
Bayside At Bthany Lkes Clbhuse ....F....... 302 539-4378
  Ocean View (G-7759)
Bayside Resort Golf Club ....E....... 302 436-3400
  Selbyville (G-8453)
Bayside Sports Club LLC ....F....... 302 436-3550
  Selbyville (G-8454)
Bear Trap Sales ....G....... 302 541-5454
  Ocean View (G-7762)
Beast of East Baseball LLC ....G....... 302 545-9094
  New Castle (G-5079)
Bethany Club Tennis LLC ....G....... 302 539-5111
  Ocean View (G-7766)
Big Stone Hunting Club ....G....... 302 424-7592
  Milford (G-4326)
Bob Lafazia ....G....... 302 633-1456
  Wilmington (G-9389)
Bowlamisha LLC ....G....... 302 727-4969
  Newark (G-6109)
Brandywine Country Club ....D....... 302 478-4604
  Wilmington (G-9428)
Brandywine Lacrosse Club ....G....... 302 249-1840
  Wilmington (G-9441)
Brandywine Volleyball Club ....G....... 302 898-6452
  Wilmington (G-9461)
Bridgeville Lions Club Inc ....E....... 302 629-9543
  Bridgeville (G-455)
Cambridge Club Assoc Partn ....G....... 302 674-3500
  Hockessin (G-2975)
Camden-Wyoming Rotary Club ....G....... 302 697-2724
  Camden Wyoming (G-622)
Can Collecting Club ....G....... 302 420-5768
  Wilmington (G-9547)
Cavaliers of Delaware Inc ....D....... 302 731-5600
  Newark (G-6173)
Champions Club ....G....... 215 380-1273
  Magnolia (G-3884)
Clementes Clubhouse ....G....... 302 455-0936
  Newark (G-6249)
Club Brennan ....G....... 302 838-9530
  Bear (G-79)
Club Mantis Boxing LLC ....G....... 302 943-2580
  Lincoln (G-3842)
Coastal Club Schell Brothers ....G....... 302 966-0063
  Lewes (G-3435)
Country Swim Club Inc ....G....... 302 420-5043
  Wilmington (G-9876)
Credit Share Club LLC ....G....... 302 401-6450
  Dover (G-1321)
Cripple Creek Golf & Cntry CLB ....E....... 302 539-1446
  Dagsboro (G-894)

Dale Maple Country Club Inc ....E....... 302 674-2505
  Dover (G-1337)
Del Bay Retriever Club ....G....... 302 678-8583
  Dover (G-1350)
Delaware Boat Registration ....G....... 302 739-9916
  Dover (G-1359)
Delaware Cobras Inc ....G....... 302 983-3500
  Bear (G-106)
Delaware Lacrosse Foundation ....F....... 302 831-8661
  Wilmington (G-10061)
Delaware Riders Basbal CLB Inc ....G....... 302 475-1915
  Wilmington (G-10080)
Delaware Trail Spinners ....G....... 302 738-0177
  Newark (G-6420)
Diamond State Curling Club ....G....... 856 577-3747
  Hockessin (G-3009)
Down Under Boxing Club ....G....... 302 745-4392
  Bridgeville (G-467)
Drummond Hill Swim Club ....G....... 302 366-9882
  Newark (G-6474)
Eastern Athletic Clubs LLC ....D....... 302 239-6688
  Hockessin (G-3016)
Emblem At Christiana Clubhouse ....G....... 302 525-6692
  Newark (G-6523)
Factory Sports ....G....... 302 313-4186
  Lewes (G-3489)
▲ Fieldstone Golf Club LP ....D....... 302 254-4569
  Wilmington (G-10538)
Five 1 Five Ice Sports Group L ....G....... 302 266-0777
  Newark (G-6590)
Forewinds Hospitality LLC ....G....... 302 368-6640
  Newark (G-6605)
Graylyn Crest III Swim Club ....G....... 302 547-5809
  Wilmington (G-10766)
Greater Newark Baseball L ....G....... 302 635-0562
  Newark (G-6685)
Greenville Country Club Inc ....E....... 302 652-3255
  Wilmington (G-10779)
Hagerty Drivers Club LLC ....G....... 302 504-6086
  Wilmington (G-10817)
Hartly Ruritan Club ....G....... 302 492-8337
  Hartly (G-2924)
Hellenic Univ CLB Wilmington ....G....... 302 479-8811
  Wilmington (G-10883)
Henlopen Acres Beach Club Inc ....G....... 302 227-9919
  Rehoboth Beach (G-7960)
Hockessin Soccer Club ....F....... 302 234-1444
  Hockessin (G-3054)
Hunt Vicmead Club ....G....... 302 655-3336
  Wilmington (G-10973)
Hunt Vicmead Club ....G....... 302 655-9601
  Wilmington (G-10974)
Hunt Wandendale Club ....G....... 302 945-3369
  Millsboro (G-4707)
Indian River Soccer Club ....G....... 302 542-6397
  Ocean View (G-7793)
Itennisyou LLC ....G....... 305 890-3234
  Newark (G-6810)
Kent Swimming Club Inc ....F....... 302 674-3283
  Dover (G-1741)
Kings Creek Country Club Inc ....F....... 302 227-8951
  Rehoboth Beach (G-7982)
Kirkwood Ftnes Racquetball CLB ....F....... 302 529-1865
  Wilmington (G-11275)
Little Gym ....G....... 302 856-2310
  Georgetown (G-2592)
Little League Baseball Inc ....G....... 302 227-0888
  Rehoboth Beach (G-7987)
Little League Baseball Inc ....G....... 302 276-0375
  New Castle (G-5486)
Lumber Jacks Axe Club LLC ....F....... 215 900-0318
  New Castle (G-5490)
Mako Swim Club LLC ....G....... 631 682-2131
  Harbeson (G-2790)
Mears Baseball Instruction ....G....... 302 448-9713
  Millsboro (G-4739)
Michael Lo Sapio ....G....... 201 919-2643
  Townsend (G-8810)
Middletown Sports Complex LLC ....G....... 302 299-8630
  Middletown (G-4160)
Midway Little League ....F....... 302 737-3104
  Newark (G-7037)
Millsboro Little League ....F....... 302 934-1806
  Millsboro (G-4751)
Milton Garden Club ....D....... 302 684-8315
  Milton (G-4940)
New Castle Sailing Club ....G....... 302 307-3060
  New Castle (G-5487)
Newark Country Club ....G....... 302 368-7008
  Newark (G-7114)

Newark National Little League ....E....... 302 738-0881
  Newark (G-7125)
Northeast Rally Club ....G....... 302 934-1246
  Millsboro (G-4762)
Ocean CLB Rsort Rservation Ctr ....G....... 302 369-1420
  Newark (G-7141)
Paladin Sports Club Inc ....F....... 302 764-5335
  Wilmington (G-12008)
Peninsula ....G....... 302 945-4768
  Millsboro (G-4774)
Penn Acres Swim Club ....E....... 302 322-6501
  New Castle (G-5613)
Pike Creek Court Club Inc ....D....... 302 239-6688
  Wilmington (G-12138)
Police & Fire Rod & Gun Club ....G....... 302 655-0304
  New Castle (G-5630)
Polish American Civic Assn ....G....... 302 652-9324
  Wilmington (G-12182)
Quail Associates Inc ....E....... 302 697-4660
  Camden Wyoming (G-651)
Rehoboth Bay Sailing Assn ....G....... 302 227-9008
  Rehoboth Beach (G-8048)
Rehoboth Beach Country Club ....D....... 302 227-3811
  Rehoboth Beach (G-8049)
Resort Poker League ....G....... 302 604-8706
  Selbyville (G-8539)
Rockland Sports LLC ....D....... 302 654-4435
  Wilmington (G-12454)
Ronald L Barrows ....F....... 302 227-3616
  Rehoboth Beach (G-8062)
Sache Social Club ....G....... 302 287-4813
  Wilmington (G-12512)
Saint Anthonys Club ....G....... 302 328-9440
  New Castle (G-5693)
Salem County Amateur Radio CLB .....G....... 302 689-8127
  Wilmington (G-12524)
Salt Pond Associates ....G....... 302 539-2750
  Bethany Beach (G-430)
Shellcrest Swim Club ....G....... 302 529-1464
  Wilmington (G-12598)
Silverside Club Inc ....F....... 302 478-4568
  Talleyville (G-8751)
Skating Club of Wilmington Inc ....F....... 302 656-5005
  Wilmington (G-12642)
Skim USA ....F....... 302 227-4011
  Rehoboth Beach (G-8078)
Softball World LLC ....G....... 302 856-7922
  Georgetown (G-2658)
Spring Lake Bath & Tennis Club ....G....... 302 227-6136
  Rehoboth Beach (G-8085)
Studio 11 ....G....... 302 622-9959
  Wilmington (G-12781)
Sussex Pines Country Club ....E....... 302 856-6283
  Georgetown (G-2682)
Terrace Athletic Club Inc ....G....... 302 652-9059
  New Castle (G-5762)
Vacation Club ....G....... 302 628-1144
  Seaford (G-8429)
Velo Amis ....G....... 302 757-2783
  Newark (G-7649)
Wilmington Aquatic Club Inc ....G....... 302 322-2487
  New Castle (G-5835)
Wilmington Country Club ....C....... 302 655-6171
  Wilmington (G-13228)
Wilmington Turners Club ....F....... 302 658-9011
  Wilmington (G-13266)
Womens Civic Club Bethany Bch ....G....... 302 539-7515
  Bethany Beach (G-439)
Womens Tennis C N C C ....G....... 302 762-2078
  Wilmington (G-13293)
Woodland Ferry Beagle Club ....G....... 302 856-2186
  Georgetown (G-2707)
YMCA Central Branch LLC ....F....... 302 571-6950
  Wilmington (G-13328)
Young Mens Christian Associat ....D....... 302 571-6935
  Wilmington (G-13331)
Young Mens Christian Associat ....D....... 302 296-9622
  Rehoboth Beach (G-8121)
Young Mens Christian Associat ....C....... 302 571-6900
  Wilmington (G-13332)
Young MNS Chrstn Assn Wlmngton ...E....... 302 221-9622
  Wilmington (G-13334)

7999 Amusement & Recreation Svcs, NEC

Aikikai Foundation of Delaware ....G....... 302 369-2454
  Newark (G-5921)
American Karate Studio ....F....... 302 529-7800
  Wilmington (G-9052)
American Karate Studios ....E....... 302 737-9500
  Newark (G-5954)

79 AMUSEMENT AND RECREATION SERVICES

▼American Martial Arts Inst ....F 302 834-4060
  Bear *(G-27)*
Anglers Marina ....G 302 644-4533
  Lewes *(G-3340)*
B & B Tickettown Inc ....G 302 656-9797
  Wilmington *(G-9208)*
Books & Tobaccos Inc ....F 302 994-3156
  Wilmington *(G-9393)*
▲Bridge Studio of Delaware ....G 302 479-5431
  Wilmington *(G-9471)*
Capitol Billiards Inc ....G 302 629-0298
  Seaford *(G-8182)*
Childrens Beach House Inc ....F 302 645-9184
  Lewes *(G-3413)*
City of Newark ....E 302 366-7060
  Newark *(G-6243)*
David Marshall & Associates ....E 302 539-4488
  Bethany Beach *(G-396)*
Days of Knights ....G 302 366-0963
  Newark *(G-6351)*
Del Bay Charter Fishing LLC ....G 302 542-1930
  Milton *(G-4886)*
Delaware Learning Institue of ....F 302 732-6704
  Dagsboro *(G-895)*
Delaware Skating Center Ltd ....E 302 697-3218
  Dover *(G-1391)*
Delaware Skating Center Ltd ....E 302 366-0473
  Newark *(G-6412)*
Delaware State Fair Inc ....E 302 398-3269
  Harrington *(G-2831)*
Doubleudiamond LLC ....G 206 502-0144
  Wilmington *(G-10209)*
Dover Downs Inc ....A 302 674-4600
  Dover *(G-1445)*
Elcoach Inc ....G 302 261-3794
  Wilmington *(G-10366)*
Elevated Studios Hq ....G 302 407-3229
  Wilmington *(G-10372)*
Frightland LLC ....G 302 838-0256
  Middletown *(G-4078)*
G Rehoboth ....G 302 278-7677
  Rehoboth Beach *(G-7941)*
Harrington Raceway Inc ....B 302 398-5346
  Harrington *(G-2846)*
Historic Red Clay Valley Inc ....G 302 998-1930
  Wilmington *(G-10917)*
Hook Em & Cook Em LLC ....G 302 226-8220
  Milford *(G-4444)*
Judy V ....G 302 226-2214
  Rehoboth Beach *(G-7975)*
Kensington Tours Ltd ....D 888 903-2001
  Wilmington *(G-11243)*
Kent County ....G 302 330-8873
  Frederica *(G-2409)*
Korean Martial Arts Institute ....F 302 992-7999
  Wilmington *(G-11289)*
Little Gym of Ncc ....G 302 543-5524
  Wilmington *(G-11404)*
Lon Spa Inc ....G 302 368-4595
  Newark *(G-6947)*
Megan Hegenbarth ....G 302 477-9872
  Wilmington *(G-11623)*
Michael Schwartz ....F 302 791-9999
  Wilmington *(G-11666)*
Mid Atlantic Grand Prix LLC ....E 302 656-5278
  New Castle *(G-5522)*
Noble Eagle Sales LLC ....F 302 736-5166
  Dover *(G-1898)*
Nothing But Net Inc ....G 302 476-0453
  New Castle *(G-5580)*
Olympiad Schools Inc ....F 302 636-0606
  Wilmington *(G-11946)*
Paintball Action of Delware ....F 302 234-1735
  Hockessin *(G-3110)*
Parks & Recreation Del Div ....F 302 571-7788
  Wilmington *(G-12024)*
Playfit Education Inc ....G 302 438-3257
  Wilmington *(G-12155)*
Pond Inc ....E 302 266-0777
  Newark *(G-7232)*
Posidon Adventure Inc ....F 302 543-5024
  Wilmington *(G-12190)*
Premier Entertainment III LLC ....E 302 674-4600
  Dover *(G-1982)*
Rigbys Karate Academy ....G 302 735-9637
  Dover *(G-2036)*
S F F Art Inc ....G 302 226-9410
  Rehoboth Beach *(G-8064)*
Scientific Games Corporation ....F 302 737-4300
  Newark *(G-7395)*

Sea Colony Tennis Center ....G 302 539-4488
  Bethany Beach *(G-431)*
Shooters Choice Inc ....G 302 736-5166
  Dover *(G-2079)*
Skateworld Inc ....E 302 875-2121
  Seaford *(G-8402)*
Somerville Manning Gallery ....G 302 652-0271
  Wilmington *(G-12681)*
Torc Yoga LLC ....G 856 408-9118
  Wilmington *(G-12935)*
Tri-State Cheernastics Inc ....G 302 322-4020
  New Castle *(G-5787)*
Vinces Sports Center Inc ....G 302 738-4859
  Newark *(G-7659)*
Wellspring Farm Inc ....G 302 798-2407
  Wilmington *(G-13154)*
Wta Inc ....E 302 397-8142
  Wilmington *(G-13309)*
Xbos ....G 302 653-1800
  Smyrna *(G-8748)*
Yogo Factory ....G 302 266-4506
  Newark *(G-7728)*
Young Mens Christian Associat ....F 302 472-9622
  Wilmington *(G-13333)*

80 HEALTH SERVICES

8011 Offices & Clinics Of Doctors Of Medicine

A Center For Mntal Wllness Inc ....F 302 674-1397
  Dover *(G-1074)*
A I Dupont Hospital For Child ....G 302 651-4186
  Wilmington *(G-8879)*
Aaron S Chidekel M D ....G 302 651-6400
  Wilmington *(G-8894)*
Abad & Salameda PA ....G 302 652-4705
  Wilmington *(G-8897)*
Abby L Allen Fnp ....G 302 856-1773
  Georgetown *(G-2421)*
Abby Medical Center ....G 302 999-0003
  Newark *(G-5882)*
Abel Center For Oculofacial ....G 302 998-3220
  Wilmington *(G-8901)*
Abigail E Martin M D ....G 302 651-4000
  Wilmington *(G-8903)*
Abigail Family Medicine LLC ....G 302 738-3770
  Newark *(G-5884)*
Adriane Hohmann ....G 302 253-2020
  Georgetown *(G-2424)*
Advanced Anesthesiology & Pain .....G 302 283-3300
  Wilmington *(G-8949)*
Advanced Endoscopy Center LLC ....G 302 678-0725
  Dover *(G-1089)*
Advanced Plastic Surgery Cente ......F 302 623-4004
  Newark *(G-5906)*
Advanced Surgical Specialists ....G 302 475-4900
  Wilmington *(G-8957)*
Aesthtic Plstic Surgery Del PA ....F 302 656-0214
  Wilmington *(G-8966)*
Affinity Womens Health LLC ....G 302 468-4320
  Bear *(G-20)*
Alfieri Anthony D Do Facc ....G 302 397-8199
  Wilmington *(G-9007)*
Alfred Idpont Hosp For Chldren ....A 302 651-4000
  Wilmington *(G-9008)*
All About Women LLC ....E 302 224-8400
  Newark *(G-5932)*
Allergy Associates PA ....G 302 834-3401
  Newark *(G-5939)*
Allergy Associates PA Inc ....F 302 798-8070
  Wilmington *(G-9020)*
Allied Anesthesia Assoc LLC ....G 302 547-3620
  Dover *(G-1110)*
Alpha Care Medical LLC ....G 302 398-0888
  Harrington *(G-2807)*
Alpha Care Medical LLC ....G 800 818-8680
  Millsboro *(G-4628)*
Alyvant Therapeutics Inc ....G 646 767-5878
  Wilmington *(G-9037)*
Amick Mart J MD ....F 302 633-1700
  Wilmington *(G-9069)*
Amy Wachter MD ....G 302 661-3070
  Wilmington *(G-9072)*
Andre M D Hoffman ....G 302 892-2710
  Newark *(G-5967)*
Andreas Rauer MD PA ....G 302 734-1760
  Dover *(G-1124)*
Andrew J Glick MD ....E 302 652-8990
  Wilmington *(G-9079)*

Andrew Nowakowski MD PA ....G 410 838-8900
  Bear *(G-29)*
Andrew Weinstein MD Inc ....G 302 428-1675
  Wilmington *(G-9082)*
Andrey Georgieff MD ....G 302 998-1866
  Newark *(G-5968)*
Angela Saldarriaga ....G 302 633-1182
  Wilmington *(G-9084)*
Anthony Lee Cucuzzella MD ....F 302 623-4370
  Newark *(G-5974)*
Antonio C Narvaez MD ....G 302 453-1002
  Newark *(G-5975)*
Armand De MD Sanctic ....F 302 475-2535
  Wilmington *(G-9131)*
Arminio Joseph A MD & Assoc PA ...F 302 654-6245
  Wilmington *(G-9132)*
Arthritis and Osteoporosis LLC ....G 302 628-8300
  Seaford *(G-8155)*
Asher B Carey III ....G 302 678-3443
  Dover *(G-1144)*
Ashish B Parikh ....F 302 338-9444
  Newark *(G-6010)*
Associates In Medicine PA ....G 302 645-6644
  Lewes *(G-3350)*
Assoction Pathology Chairs Inc ....G 301 634-7880
  Wilmington *(G-9161)*
Asthma and Allergy Care Del ....G 302 995-2952
  Wilmington *(G-9164)*
Athena T Jolly M D ....G 302 454-3020
  Newark *(G-6014)*
Atlantic Adult & Pediatric ....F 302 644-1300
  Lewes *(G-3352)*
Atlantic Family Physician LLC ....G 302 856-4092
  Georgetown *(G-2437)*
Atlantic Family Physicians ....G 302 856-4092
  Milton *(G-4864)*
Attitude LLC None ....G 302 422-3356
  Milford *(G-4313)*
Aviado Domingo G MD ....G 302 430-7600
  Milford *(G-4316)*
Bay Area Womens Care ....G 302 424-2200
  Milford *(G-4318)*
Bayada Home Health Care Inc ....D 302 424-8200
  Milford *(G-4319)*
Bayhealth Medical Group Ent ....G 302 339-8040
  Georgetown *(G-2448)*
Bayside Health Assn Chartered ....E 302 645-4700
  Lewes *(G-3364)*
Beacon Medical Group PA ....G 302 947-9767
  Rehoboth Beach *(G-7859)*
Beacon Pediatrics LLC ....F 302 645-8212
  Rehoboth Beach *(G-7860)*
Beebe Medical Center Inc ....D 302 393-2056
  Milford *(G-4321)*
Beebe Medical Center Inc ....D 302 541-4175
  Millville *(G-4836)*
Beebe Medical Center Inc ....D 302 645-3289
  Rehoboth Beach *(G-7863)*
Beebe Medical Center Inc ....C 302 645-3010
  Rehoboth Beach *(G-7864)*
Beebe Medical Center Inc ....G 302 856-9729
  Georgetown *(G-2453)*
Beebe Physician Network Inc ....E 302 645-1805
  Lewes *(G-3374)*
Bellevue Heart Group LLC ....G 302 468-4500
  Wilmington *(G-9290)*
Beth A Renzulli M D ....G 302 449-0420
  Middletown *(G-3966)*
Bethany Primary Care ....G 302 537-1100
  Bethany Beach *(G-390)*
Bhaskar Palekar MD PA ....G 302 645-1805
  Lewes *(G-3381)*
Bhaskar S Palekar MD PA ....G 302 645-1806
  Lewes *(G-3382)*
Bijan K Sorouri MD PA ....G 302 453-9171
  Newark *(G-6080)*
Birth Center Holistic Women ....F 302 658-2229
  Newark *(G-6083)*
Blanca O Lim MD ....E 302 653-1669
  Smyrna *(G-8581)*
BMA of Smyrna ....G 302 659-5220
  Smyrna *(G-8583)*
Boulos Magdy I MD PA ....G 302 571-9750
  Wilmington *(G-9399)*
Boyd Jeffrey MD ....G 302 454-8800
  Newark *(G-6111)*
Bradford Family Physicians LLC ......G 302 730-3750
  Dover *(G-1227)*
Brandi Wine Pediatric Inc ....E 302 478-7805
  Wilmington *(G-9416)*

SIC SECTION
80 HEALTH SERVICES

Business	Code	Phone
Brandywine Care L L C	F	302 658-5822
Wilmington (G-9421)		
Brandywine Cosmetic Surgery	G	302 652-3331
Wilmington (G-9425)		
Brandywine Cosmetic Surgery	G	302 652-3331
Newark (G-6115)		
Brandywine Family Medicine	G	302 475-5000
Wilmington (G-9432)		
Brandywine Ob Gyn	G	302 477-1375
Wilmington (G-9445)		
Brandywine Urology Cons PA	E	302 652-8990
Wilmington (G-9457)		
Brdly M Winston Pdrtcs Prctc	F	302 424-1650
Milford (G-4333)		
Bruce C Turner MD	G	302 366-0938
Newark (G-6128)		
Bruce E Katz M D	G	302 478-5500
Wilmington (G-9492)		
Burke Dermatology	F	302 703-6585
Rehoboth Beach (G-7881)		
Burke Dermatology	G	302 734-3376
Dover (G-1242)		
Burke Dermatology	G	302 230-3376
Newark (G-6136)		
Camp Chiropractic Inc	G	302 378-2899
Middletown (G-3980)		
Cape Medical Associates PA	F	302 645-2805
Lewes (G-3402)		
Cape Surgical Associates PA	G	302 645-7050
Lewes (G-3403)		
Cardio-Kinetics Inc	G	302 738-6635
Newark (G-6152)		
Cardiology Consultants	F	302 645-1233
Lewes (G-3405)		
Cardiology Consultants	G	302 541-8138
Millville (G-4838)		
Cardiology Physicans PA Inc	E	302 366-8600
Newark (G-6153)		
Cardiology Specialists	G	302 453-0624
Wilmington (G-9565)		
Caridad Rosal MA MD	E	302 653-6174
Smyrna (G-8591)		
Carol A Tavani MD	G	302 454-9900
Newark (G-6160)		
Caruso Richard F MD PA	G	302 645-6698
Lewes (G-3410)		
Casscells Orthopaedics Sp	G	302 832-6220
Newark (G-6166)		
Cataract and Laser Center LLC	F	302 454-8802
Newark (G-6168)		
Ccmc Inc	G	302 477-9660
Wilmington (G-9602)		
Center For Human Reproduction	F	302 738-4600
Newark (G-6178)		
Center For Intrvntnal Pain SPI	G	302 792-1370
Wilmington (G-9612)		
Center For Neurology	D	302 422-0800
Milford (G-4344)		
Central Del Endoscopy Unit	F	302 422-3393
Milford (G-4346)		
Central Del Gstrntrology Assoc	G	302 422-3393
Milford (G-4347)		
Central Delaware Fmly Medicine	F	302 735-1616
Dover (G-1266)		
Charles Wang MD PA	G	302 655-1500
Wilmington (G-9639)		
Chesapeake Neurology Service	G	302 563-7253
Wilmington (G-9655)		
Children Youth & Their Fam	E	302 633-2600
Wilmington (G-9663)		
Chistine E Woods	G	302 709-4497
Newark (G-6201)		
Choudhary Arabinda K MD	G	302 651-4000
Wilmington (G-9671)		
Christana Ctr For Wns Wellness	G	302 454-9800
Newark (G-6204)		
Christiana Care	F	302 633-3750
Wilmington (G-9676)		
Christiana Care Health Sys Inc	G	302 428-4110
Claymont (G-717)		
Christiana Care Health Sys Inc	F	302 733-2410
Newark (G-6210)		
Christiana Care Health Sys Inc	G	302 529-1975
Wilmington (G-9678)		
Christiana Care Health Sys Inc	F	302 659-4401
Smyrna (G-8594)		
Christiana Care Health Sys Inc	G	302 477-6500
Wilmington (G-9680)		
Christiana Care Hlth Svcs Inc	F	302 623-0100
Newark (G-6214)		
Christiana Care Hlth Svcs Inc	G	302 477-3960
Wilmington (G-9683)		
Christiana Counseling	G	302 995-1680
Wilmington (G-9686)		
Christiana Csmtc Srgry Cnsltnt	F	302 368-9611
Newark (G-6222)		
Christiana Medical Group PA	G	302 366-1800
Newark (G-6225)		
Christiana Neonatal Practice	F	302 733-2410
Newark (G-6226)		
Christine W Maynard M D	G	302 225-6110
Newark (G-6230)		
Christopher A Bowens MD	G	302 834-3700
Newark (G-6231)		
Christopher Casscells MD	G	302 832-6220
Newark (G-6232)		
Christopher H Wendel Md PA	G	302 540-2979
Hockessin (G-2988)		
Claravall Odilon	G	302 875-7753
Laurel (G-3215)		
Clinic By Sea	G	302 644-0999
Lewes (G-3429)		
Clinical Crdlgy Spcialists LLC	G	302 834-3700
Newark (G-6251)		
Cnmri	G	302 422-0800
Milford (G-4360)		
Cntrl De Gstroenterolgyassoc I	G	302 678-9002
Dover (G-1297)		
Coastal Kid Watch	F	302 537-0793
Millville (G-4839)		
Coastal Kids Pediatric Dntstry	G	302 644-4460
Rehoboth Beach (G-7894)		
Coastal Pain Care Physcians PA	G	302 644-8330
Lewes (G-3438)		
Colon Rectal Surgery Assoc Del	G	302 737-5444
Newark (G-6262)		
Columbia Care New York LLC	G	302 297-8614
Smyrna (G-8602)		
Comprhensive Neurology Ctr LLC	F	302 996-9010
Newark (G-6275)		
Concentra Inc	F	302 738-0103
Newark (G-6279)		
Concord Med Spine & Pain Ctr	G	302 652-1107
Wilmington (G-9813)		
Connections Development Corp	F	302 984-3380
Wilmington (G-9829)		
Corizon Health Inc	D	302 266-8230
Wilmington (G-6298)		
Critical Care Systems Intl Inc	G	302 765-4132
Wilmington (G-9900)		
Curtis A Smith	G	302 875-6800
Laurel (G-3218)		
Cynthia P Mangubat MD	G	302 674-1356
Dover (G-1334)		
D C Medical Services LLC	G	302 855-0915
Georgetown (G-2492)		
David B Ettinger DMD MD	G	302 369-1000
Newark (G-6348)		
David C Larned MD	G	302 655-7600
Wilmington (G-9968)		
David G Reyes MD	G	302 735-7780
Dover (G-1344)		
Dcmfm At Christiana Care	G	302 543-7543
Newark (G-6352)		
Debay Surgical Service	F	302 644-4954
Lewes (G-3449)		
Deborah A Wingel Do	G	302 239-6200
Hockessin (G-3003)		
Deborah Kirk	G	302 653-6022
Smyrna (G-8613)		
Dedicated To Women Ob Gyn	E	302 674-0223
Dover (G-1348)		
Dedicated To Women Obgyn	F	302 285-5545
Middletown (G-4024)		
Del Marva Hand Specialists LLC	G	302 644-0940
Lewes (G-3452)		
Delaware Clncal Lab Physcans P	E	302 737-7700
Newark (G-6370)		
Delaware County Pain MGT	G	302 575-1145
Wilmington (G-10029)		
Delaware Crdovascular Assoc PA	F	302 644-7676
Lewes (G-3456)		
Delaware Crdovascular Assoc PA	G	302 993-7676
Wilmington (G-6371)		
Delaware Crdovascular Assoc PA	G	302 734-7676
Dover (G-1362)		
Delaware Crdovascular Assoc PA	G	302 543-4800
Wilmington (G-10030)		
Delaware Dermatolgy PA	G	302 736-1800
Dover (G-1366)		
Delaware Diagnostic Group LLC	G	302 472-5555
Wilmington (G-10040)		
Delaware Ear Nose & Throat Hea	G	302 738-6014
Newark (G-6377)		
Delaware Eye Institute PA	E	302 645-2300
Rehoboth Beach (G-7912)		
Delaware Eye Surgeons	G	302 956-0285
Wilmington (G-10045)		
Delaware Eye Surgery Center	G	302 645-2300
Rehoboth Beach (G-7913)		
Delaware Heart & Vascular PA	G	302 734-1414
Dover (G-1377)		
Delaware Imaging Network	G	302 836-4200
Newark (G-6386)		
Delaware Imaging Network	G	302 652-3016
Newark (G-6387)		
Delaware Imaging Network	G	302 449-5400
Middletown (G-4028)		
Delaware Imaging Network	G	302 644-2590
Newark (G-6388)		
Delaware Imaging Network	F	302 478-1100
Wilmington (G-10056)		
Delaware Institue Pain MGT	G	302 698-3994
Camden (G-558)		
Delaware Interventional Spine	G	302 674-8444
Dover (G-1379)		
Delaware Medical Care Inc	E	302 225-6868
Wilmington (G-10065)		
Delaware Modern Pediatrics	F	302 392-2077
Newark (G-6397)		
Delaware Nurosurgical Group PA	F	302 731-3017
Newark (G-6399)		
Delaware Obgyn & Womens Health	G	302 730-0633
Dover (G-1383)		
Delaware Open M R I	G	302 479-5400
Wilmington (G-10069)		
Delaware Open M R I & C T	G	302 734-5800
Dover (G-1384)		
Delaware Open M R I LLC	G	302 449-2300
Middletown (G-4030)		
Delaware Ophthalmology Cons PA	E	302 479-3937
Wilmington (G-10070)		
Delaware Orthopaedic Specialis	E	302 633-3555
Wilmington (G-10071)		
Delaware Orthopedic	G	302 730-0840
Dover (G-1385)		
Delaware Pain & Spine Center	G	302 737-0800
Wilmington (G-10072)		
Delaware Plastic & Recon	F	302 994-8492
Newark (G-6402)		
Delaware Plstic/Recons Srgy PA	G	302 994-8492
Newark (G-6403)		
Delaware Primary Care LLC	G	302 730-0554
Dover (G-1388)		
Delaware Sleep Dsrder Ctrs LLC	E	302 669-6141
Wilmington (G-10084)		
Delaware Soc Orthpd Surgeons	G	302 366-1400
Newark (G-6413)		
▲ Delaware Surgery Center LLC	E	302 730-0217
Dover (G-1401)		
Delaware Surgical Arts	G	302 225-0177
Newark (G-6416)		
Delaware Surgical Group PA	G	302 892-2100
Wilmington (G-10088)		
Delawre Ctr For Mtrnal & Fetal	E	302 319-5680
Newark (G-6424)		
Delmarva Bariatric Fitnes Ctr		410 341-6180
Lewes (G-3459)		
Delmarva Surgery Center	G	302 369-1700
Newark (G-6428)		
Doctors Pathology Services PA	E	302 677-0000
Dover (G-1436)		
Donald A Girard MD	G	302 633-5755
Wilmington (G-10194)		
Douglas J Lavenburg MD PA	F	302 993-0722
Newark (G-6465)		
Douglas R Johnston M D	G	302 651-4000
Wilmington (G-10214)		
Dover Family Physicians PA	E	302 734-2500
Dover (G-1448)		
Dover Ophthalmology Asc LLC	F	302 724-4720
Dover (G-1462)		
Dover Oral and Maxillofacial S	G	302 674-1140
Dover (G-1463)		
Dover Pulmonary PA	G	302 734-0400
Dover (G-1468)		
Dover Surgicenter LLC	E	302 346-3171
Middletown (G-4045)		
Dr Azarcon & Assoc	G	302 478-2969
Wilmington (G-10218)		

Employee Codes: A=Over 500 employees, B=251-500
C=101-250, D=51-100, E=20-50, F=10-19, G=1-9

2020 Harris Directory of Delaware Businesses

547

80 HEALTH SERVICES

Name	Loc	Phone
Dr Fanny Berg P C Wilmington (G-10221)	G	302 475-8000
Dr Mehdi Balakhani Wilmington (G-10227)	G	302 368-8900
Dr Monika Gupta PA Newark (G-6471)	G	302 737-5074
Du Pont Lynne M MD Wilmington (G-10240)	G	302 777-7966
Duncan Elisabeth D MD Dover (G-1486)	G	302 677-2730
Duque Nieva MD PA Bear (G-130)	G	302 838-9712
Duque Nieva MD PA Wilmington (G-10266)	G	302 655-2048
Duque Nieva MD PA Wilmington (G-10267)	G	302 655-5661
Dushuttle Richard P MD PA Dover (G-1488)	F	302 678-8447
Dynamic Therapy Services LLC Dover (G-1489)	F	302 526-2148
E N T Associates Dover (G-1491)	F	302 674-3752
Eden Hill Medical Center LLC Dover (G-1505)	G	302 883-0097
Edward S Jaoude Milton (G-4901)	E	302 684-2020
Edwin C Katzman MD Newark (G-6504)	G	302 368-2501
Edwina C Granada MD Seaford (G-8232)	G	302 629-7555
Elias Mamberg MD Wilmington (G-10375)	G	302 428-0337
Elizabeth Jackovic MD Newark (G-6515)	G	302 623-0240
Elva G Pearson MD Newark (G-6521)	G	302 623-4144
Ent Allergy Center Seaford (G-8237)	G	302 629-3400
Ent and Allergy Delaware LLC Wilmington (G-10405)	E	302 478-8467
Ent and Allergy Delaware LLC Wilmington (G-10406)	F	302 998-0300
Ent and Allergy Delaware LLC Newark (G-6530)	G	302 832-8700
Epstein Kplan OpthImlogist LLP New Castle (G-5293)	G	302 322-4444
Eranga Cardiology Dover (G-1529)	G	302 747-7486
Erik M D Stancofski Lewes (G-3487)	G	302 645-7050
Eugene E Godfrey Do Dover (G-1532)	G	302 674-1356
Eugene M DAmico III DDS PA Newark (G-6544)	G	302 292-1600
Eye Care of Delaware Newark (G-6559)	E	302 454-8800
Eye Consultants LLC Wilmington (G-10464)	G	302 998-2333
Eye Physicians and Surgeons PA Wilmington (G-10465)	E	302 225-1018
F H Everett & Associates Inc Dover (G-1536)	G	302 674-2380
Family Ear Nose & Throad Wilmington (G-10490)	E	302 998-0300
Family Ent Physicians Inc Wilmington (G-10491)	E	302 998-0300
Family Health Delaware Inc Dover (G-1538)	G	302 734-2444
Family Medical Centre PA Dover (G-1539)	F	302 678-0510
Family Medicine At Greenville Wilmington (G-10492)	F	302 429-5870
Family Medicine Ctr Naticchia Wilmington (G-10493)	G	302 477-3300
Family Practice Center Lewes (G-3491)	F	302 645-2833
Family Practice Cntr of New CA Newark (G-6569)	G	302 999-0933
Family Practice Hockessin PA Hockessin (G-3027)	G	302 239-4500
Fataneh M Ziari MD Newark (G-6575)	G	302 836-8533
Fenwick Medical Center Fenwick Island (G-2335)	G	302 539-2399
First State Anesthesia Svcs Newark (G-6581)	G	302 225-2990
First State Gastroenterology A Dover (G-1557)	G	302 677-1617
First State Medical Assoc LLC Wilmington (G-10552)	G	302 999-8169
First State Pediatrics LLC Newark (G-6584)	F	302 292-1559
First State Surgery Center LLC Newark (G-6586)	F	302 683-0700
First State Vein and Laser Ctr Wilmington (G-10556)	G	302 294-0700
Foundtion For A Btter Tomorrow Dover (G-1563)	G	302 674-1397
Francis Mase Pediatrics Wilmington (G-10611)	F	302 762-5656
Frank Falco MD Bear (G-160)	F	302 392-6501
Frensenius Medical Ctr Wilmington (G-10634)	G	302 762-2903
Fresenius Medical Care Souther Dover (G-1568)	E	302 678-2181
Future Bright Pediatrics Dover (G-1574)	G	302 883-3266
Future Bright Pediatrics LLC Camden (G-573)	F	302 538-6258
Gabriel Jr Timoteo R MD Wilmington (G-10661)	G	302 998-0300
Gary I Markowitz MD Milford (G-4420)	G	302 422-5155
Gary Quiroga Dover (G-1580)	G	302 697-3352
Gastroenterology Associates PA Newark (G-6641)	E	302 738-5300
George Mtstsos MD Crdiolgy LLC Wilmington (G-10703)	G	302 482-2035
Georgetown Family Medicine Georgetown (G-2545)	G	302 856-4092
Georgetown Medical Assoc LLC Georgetown (G-2546)	F	302 856-3737
GI Associates of Delaware Dover (G-1592)	G	302 678-5008
GI Specialists of De Newark (G-6651)	G	302 832-1545
Gilani Malik Javed MD Wilmington (G-10710)	G	302 737-8116
Glasgow Medical Associates PA Newark (G-6661)	C	302 836-3539
Glasgow Medical Associates PA Newark (G-6663)	F	302 836-8350
Glasgow Medical Center LLC Newark (G-6664)	C	302 836-8350
Habib Bolourchi MD Facc Rehoboth Beach (G-7957)	G	302 645-7672
Halpern Opthalmology Assoc Dover (G-1624)	G	302 678-2210
Harmonious Mind LLC Wilmington (G-10838)	G	302 668-1059
Harry A Lehman III Md PA Bridgeville (G-479)	F	302 629-5050
Harsha Tankala MD Dover (G-1635)	G	302 674-1818
Hcsg Regal Hghts Regal41 Hockessin (G-3044)	G	302 998-0181
Health & Social Svcs Del Dept Wilmington (G-10867)	G	302 577-3420
Health Care Assoc PA Milton (G-4912)	G	302 684-2033
Healthy Outcomes LLC Georgetown (G-2557)	G	302 856-4022
Hearsay Services of Delaware Milford (G-4437)	G	302 422-3312
Helena Schroyer MD Wilmington (G-10882)	G	302 429-5870
Henlopen Cardiology PA Rehoboth Beach (G-7961)	G	302 645-7671
Heritage Medical Associates PA Wilmington (G-10893)	G	302 998-3334
Horizons Family Practice PA Wilmington (G-10898)	F	302 918-6300
Ian Myers MD LLC Newark (G-6759)	G	302 832-7600
Ierardi Vascular Clinic LLC Newark (G-6763)	G	302 655-8272
III John F Glenn MD Dover (G-1667)	G	302 735-8850
Imaging Group Delaware PA Wilmington (G-11005)	G	302 421-4300
Indian River Golf Cars Dr Wldg Millsboro (G-4708)	G	302 947-2044
Infectious Disease Association Newark (G-6775)	G	302 368-2883
Infusion Solutions of De Dover (G-1723)	F	302 674-4627
Institute of Christiana Newark (G-6785)	F	302 892-9900
Internal Medicine Associates Wilmington (G-11064)	F	302 633-1700
Internal Medicine Bridgeville Bridgeville (G-484)	G	302 337-3300
Internal Medicine Delaware LLC Middletown (G-4111)	G	302 261-2269
Internal Medicine Dover PA Dover (G-1681)	G	302 678-4488
International Spine Pain Wilmington (G-11067)	G	302 478-7001
IPC Healthcare Newark (G-6803)	G	302 984-2577
IPC Healthcare Inc Newark (G-6804)	E	302 368-2630
Irene C Szeto MD Bear (G-192)	G	302 832-1560
Irwin L Lifrak MD PC Wilmington (G-11085)	G	302 654-7317
James Fierro Do PA Wilmington (G-11120)	G	302 529-2255
James H Hays MD Wilmington (G-11121)	G	302 633-1212
Janice Tildon-Burton MD Newark (G-6828)	G	302 832-1124
Jarrell Benson Giles & Sweeney Dover (G-1694)	F	302 678-4488
Jay D Lufty MD Wilmington (G-11131)	F	302 658-0404
Jeanes Radiology Associates PC Newark (G-6830)	G	302 738-1700
Jeff Ezell Dr Wilmington (G-11142)	G	302 654-5955
Jennifer M D Hung Rehoboth Beach (G-7971)	G	302 644-0690
Jiao Junfang MD Smyrna (G-8664)	G	302 453-1342
Joaquin Cabrera MD Seaford (G-8280)	G	302 629-8977
▲ Joel R Temple MD Dover (G-1700)	G	302 678-1343
John D Mannion M D Dover (G-1704)	G	302 744-7980
John F Reinhardt MD PA Newark (G-6842)	G	302 731-0800
John Hocutt Jr MD Wilmington (G-11171)	G	302 475-7800
John Johnson Dr Wilmington (G-11174)	G	302 999-7104
John R Stump MD Milford (G-4459)	G	302 422-3937
John T Malcynski MD Milford (G-4460)	G	302 424-7522
Jonathan L Kates M D Dover (G-1707)	G	302 730-4366
Jose A Pando MD Lewes (G-3576)	F	302 644-2302
Jose D Manalo MD PA Inc Wilmington (G-11183)	G	302 655-0355
Jose H Austria MD Lewes (G-3577)	G	302 645-8954
Jose Picazo M D P A Newark (G-6850)	G	302 738-6535
Joseph A Kuhn MD LLC Wilmington (G-11185)	G	302 656-3801
Joseph Bryer MD Wilmington (G-11187)	G	302 426-9440
Joseph G Goldberg Od Wilmington (G-11191)	G	302 999-1286
Joseph J Danyo MD Wilmington (G-11192)	G	302 888-0508
Joseph Schwartz Psyd Rehoboth Beach (G-7974)	G	302 213-3287
Joseph Schwartz Psyd Lewes (G-3579)	G	302 213-3287
Joshua Kalin MD Newark (G-6852)	G	302 737-6900
Just For Women Ob/Gyn PA Newark (G-6860)	F	302 224-9400
K F W Medical Inst De LLC Newark (G-6865)	G	302 533-6406
K V Associates Inc New Castle (G-5448)	G	302 322-1353
Kalin Eye Assoc Newark (G-6866)	G	302 292-2020
Kathleen M Cronan MD Wilmington (G-11229)	E	302 651-5860
Kathryn L Ford Fmly Practice Dover (G-1723)	G	302 674-8088
Kaza Medical Group Inc Dover (G-1725)	F	302 674-2616

Kent General Hospital Inc ....G.... 302 430-5705
Milford (G-4464)
Kent Pediatrics LLC ....G.... 302 264-9691
Dover (G-1737)
Kent Pulmonary Associates LLC ....G.... 302 674-7155
Dover (G-1738)
Kentmere Healthcare Cnsltng ....G.... 302 478-7600
Wilmington (G-11245)
Kerry S Kirifides MD PA ....G.... 302 918-6400
Newark (G-6876)
Khaja Yezdani MD ....F.... 302 322-1794
New Castle (G-5463)
Khan Ob Gyn Associates ....F.... 302 735-8720
Dover (G-1745)
Khan Pediatrics Inc ....G.... 302 449-5791
Newark (G-6884)
Kiddocs ....G.... 302 892-3300
Wilmington (G-11258)
Kids Teens Pediatrics of Dover ....G.... 302 538-5624
Dover (G-1749)
Kirk Family Practice ....G.... 302 423-2049
Wilmington (G-11272)
Klaus Dr Robert MD ....G.... 302 422-3500
Wilmington (G-11277)
Kristen Smith ....F.... 302 623-6320
Wilmington (G-11296)
Lakeside Physical Therapy LLC ....F.... 302 280-6920
Laurel (G-3251)
Laser & Plastic Surgery Center ....G.... 302 674-4865
Dover (G-1766)
Laurel Medical Group ....G.... 302 875-7753
Laurel (G-3255)
Lawall Prosthetics - Orthotics ....G.... 302 677-0693
Dover (G-1769)
Lawall Prosthetics - Orthotics ....F.... 302 427-3668
Wilmington (G-11341)
Lawall Prosthetics - Orthotics ....E.... 302 429-7625
Wilmington (G-11342)
Lawrence M Lewandoski MD ....G.... 302 698-1100
Dover (G-1771)
▲ Lee M Dennis MD ....G.... 302 735-1888
Dover (G-1776)
Lewes Orthopedic Ctr ....G.... 302 645-4939
Lewes (G-3603)
Lewes Surgery Center ....G.... 302 644-3466
Lewes (G-3605)
Lewes Surgical and Med Assoc ....F.... 302 945-9730
Millsboro (G-4719)
Limestone Medical Center Inc ....D.... 302 992-0500
Wilmington (G-11389)
Limestone Open Mri LLC ....F.... 302 246-2001
Wilmington (G-11390)
Limestone Open Mri LLC ....G.... 302 834-4500
Bear (G-235)
Long Neck Med Entreprises LLC ....G.... 302 945-9730
Millsboro (G-4723)
Longneck Family Practice ....G.... 302 947-9767
Millsboro (G-4726)
Loughran Medical Group PA ....G.... 302 479-8464
Wilmington (G-11439)
Lowell Scott MD PA ....G.... 302 684-1119
Milton (G-4926)
Lowell Scott MD PA ....G.... 302 684-1119
Milford (G-4478)
Luis L David MD PA ....G.... 302 422-9768
Milford (G-4480)
Lynnanne Kasarda MD ....G.... 302 655-5822
Wilmington (G-11463)
M Diana Metzger MD ....F.... 302 731-0942
Newark (G-6965)
M Imran MD ....G.... 302 453-7399
Newark (G-6966)
Macfarlane A Radford MD PA ....F.... 302 633-6338
Wilmington (G-11478)
Malek Abdollah Dr ....G.... 302 994-8492
Newark (G-6978)
Manveen Duggal MD ....G.... 302 734-5438
Dover (G-1817)
Marita F Fallorina MD ....G.... 302 322-0660
New Castle (G-5507)
Mark Glassner MD ....F.... 302 369-9002
Newark (G-6989)
Mark Menendez ....G.... 302 644-8500
Lewes (G-3619)
Mark W Wingel ....G.... 302 239-6200
Hockessin (G-3090)
Marshall T Williams MD PHD ....F.... 302 994-9692
Newark (G-6992)
Mary Kobak MD ....G.... 302 623-0260
Newark (G-6997)

Maternity Associates PA ....G.... 302 478-7973
Wilmington (G-11567)
Maternity Gynecology Assoc PA ....E.... 302 368-9000
Newark (G-7002)
Matthew Gotthold Dr ....G.... 302 762-6222
Wilmington (G-11569)
Matthew Gotthold Dr ....G.... 302 762-6222
Wilmington (G-11570)
Matthew W Lawrence Do ....F.... 302 652-6050
Wilmington (G-11573)
Medical Associates Bear Inc ....G.... 302 832-6768
Bear (G-250)
Medical Center of Harrington ....G.... 302 398-8704
Harrington (G-2866)
Medical Oncology Hematology ....E.... 302 999-8095
Newark (G-7017)
Melissa A Mackel Do ....G.... 302 674-4070
Dover (G-1837)
Michael A Mc Culloch MD ....G.... 302 651-6600
Wilmington (G-11653)
Michael Butterworth Dr ....G.... 302 732-9850
Dagsboro (G-922)
Michael K Rosenthal ....G.... 302 652-3469
Wilmington (G-11661)
Michael L Mattern MD PA ....F.... 302 734-3416
Dover (G-1845)
Michael Matthias ....G.... 302 575-0100
Wilmington (G-11662)
Michael T Teixido MD ....G.... 302 998-0300
Wilmington (G-11668)
Michael W Lankiewicz MD ....G.... 302 737-7700
Newark (G-7023)
Michelle E Papa Do ....G.... 302 656-5424
Wilmington (G-11672)
Mid Atlantic Spine ....F.... 302 369-1700
Newark (G-7027)
Mid Atlantic Surgical Practice ....F.... 302 652-6050
Wilmington (G-11679)
Mid Delaware Imaging Inc ....F.... 302 734-9888
Dover (G-1849)
Mid-Atlantic Fmly Practice LLC ....E.... 302 934-0944
Millsboro (G-4746)
Mid-Atlantic Fmly Practice LLC ....F.... 302 644-6860
Lewes (G-3641)
Middltown Familycare Assoc LLC ....F.... 302 378-4779
Middletown (G-4162)
Mike Walsh Physical Therapy ....G.... 302 724-5593
Dover (G-1855)
Milford Anesthesia Assoc LLC ....A.... 203 783-1831
Newark (G-7041)
Milford Medical Associates PA ....F.... 302 424-0600
Milford (G-4501)
Milford Medical Associates PA ....G.... 302 329-9517
Milton (G-4937)
Milford Pulmonary Assoc LLC ....G.... 302 424-3100
Milford (G-4502)
Millsboro Eye Care LLC ....E.... 302 684-2020
Milton (G-4938)
Millsboro Family Practice PA ....G.... 302 934-5626
Millsboro (G-4749)
Milton Enterprises Inc ....G.... 302 684-2000
Milton (G-4939)
Milton Family Practice ....F.... 302 684-2000
Lewes (G-3642)
Minimally Invasive Surgcl & Ne ....E.... 302 738-0300
Newark (G-7043)
Mitchell C Stickler MD Inc ....F.... 302 644-6400
Lewes (G-3645)
Morgan Kalman Clinic PA ....F.... 302 529-5500
Wilmington (G-11749)
Morgan Kalman Clinic ....F.... 610 869-5757
Wilmington (G-11750)
Mri Consultants LLC ....G.... 302 295-3367
Newark (G-7067)
Mymedchoices Inc ....G.... 302 932-1920
Hockessin (G-3100)
Nancy A Union MD ....G.... 302 645-6644
Lewes (G-3654)
Nanticoke Cardiology ....E.... 302 629-9099
Seaford (G-8316)
Nanticoke Ear Nose and Throat ....G.... 302 629-9067
Seaford (G-8317)
Nanticoke Gastroenterology ....G.... 302 629-2229
Seaford (G-8319)
Nanticoke Health Services Inc ....E.... 302 629-4240
Seaford (G-8320)
Nanticoke Health Services Inc ....E.... 302 628-6344
Seaford (G-8321)
Nanticoke Health Services Inc ....E.... 302 856-7099
Georgetown (G-2608)

Nanticoke Health Services Inc ....D.... 302 629-3923
Seaford (G-8322)
Nanticoke Obgyn Associates P A ....F.... 302 629-2434
Seaford (G-8326)
Narinder Singh MD ....G.... 302 737-2600
Newark (G-7083)
Nemours Foundation ....G.... 302 422-4559
Milford (G-4512)
Nemours Foundation ....E.... 302 651-6811
Wilmington (G-11834)
Nemours Foundation ....C.... 302 629-5030
Seaford (G-8328)
Nemours Foundation ....E.... 302 651-4400
Wilmington (G-11835)
Nemours Fundation Pension Plan ....E.... 302 629-5030
Seaford (G-8329)
Nemours Fundation Pension Plan ....C.... 302 836-7820
Newark (G-7091)
Nephrology Associates PA ....E.... 302 225-0451
Newark (G-7093)
Neuro Ophthalmologic Asso ....G.... 302 792-1616
Claymont (G-789)
Neurology Associates PA ....E.... 302 731-3017
Newark (G-7095)
Neurosurgery Consultants PA ....G.... 302 738-9145
Newark (G-7096)
Neurosurgical Associates PA ....G.... 302 738-9543
Newark (G-7097)
New Ark Pediatrics Inc ....F.... 302 738-4800
Newark (G-7098)
New Castle Family Care PA ....G.... 302 275-3428
Newark (G-7102)
New Image Laser and Skin Care ....G.... 302 537-4336
Ocean View (G-7804)
Newark Emergency Center Inc ....E.... 302 738-4300
Newark (G-7118)
Newark Pediatrician Inc ....F.... 302 738-4800
Newark (G-7126)
North Bay Medical Associates ....F.... 302 731-4620
Newark (G-7137)
Novacare Rehabilitation ....G.... 302 674-4192
Dover (G-1904)
Ob-Gyn Associates of Dover P A ....E.... 302 674-0223
Dover (G-1912)
Ocean Medical Imaging Del LLC ....G.... 302 684-5151
Milton (G-4943)
Omega Imaging Associates LLC ....E.... 302 738-9300
Newark (G-7146)
Omega Imaging Associates LLC ....G.... 302 654-5245
Wilmington (G-11947)
Onpoint Oncology Inc ....G.... 610 274-0188
Newark (G-7154)
Open Mri At Trolley Square LLC ....F.... 302 472-5555
Wilmington (G-11961)
Orthopaedic Specialists PA ....E.... 302 655-9494
Wilmington (G-11978)
Orthopdic Assoc Suthern Del PA ....E.... 302 644-3311
Lewes (G-3673)
Orthopedic Properties LLC ....G.... 302 998-2310
Newark (G-7159)
Orthopedic Specialists ....E.... 302 351-4848
Newark (G-7160)
Orthopedic Spine Center P A ....G.... 302 734-9700
Dover (G-1923)
Otolaryngology Consultants ....F.... 302 328-1331
Hockessin (G-3108)
Outpatent Ansthsia Spclists PA ....F.... 302 995-1860
Wilmington (G-11984)
Ovation Health Intl LLC ....G.... 302 765-7595
Wilmington (G-11985)
P A Alfieri Cardiology ....E.... 302 731-0001
Wilmington (G-11990)
P A Anesthesia Services ....G.... 302 709-4709
New Castle (G-5596)
P A Brandywine Pediatrics ....F.... 302 479-9610
Wilmington (G-11992)
P A Cnmri ....D.... 302 678-8100
Dover (G-1928)
P A Ortho-Surg ....G.... 302 658-4800
Wilmington (G-11993)
Pain MGT & Rehabilitation Ctr ....F.... 302 734-7246
Dover (G-1929)
Palermo Francis A MD Facc PA ....G.... 302 994-1100
Newark (G-7171)
Pamela M D Leclaire ....G.... 302 677-2600
Dover (G-1930)
Panzer Dermatology Assoc PA ....G.... 302 633-7550
Newark (G-7174)
Parviz Sorouri Md PA ....G.... 302 453-9171
Newark (G-7179)

S I C

80 HEALTH SERVICES

Name	Type	Phone
Pasquale Fucci MD	G	302 652-4705
Wilmington (G-12030)		
Patricia H Purcell MD	G	302 428-1142
Wilmington (G-12033)		
Patrick Swier Mdpa Kar	G	302 645-7737
Lewes (G-3681)		
Paul C Anisman M D	G	302 651-6600
Wilmington (G-12040)		
Paul H Aguillon MD	G	302 629-6664
Seaford (G-8342)		
Paul Imber Do	G	302 478-5647
Wilmington (G-12042)		
Paul Sica MD	G	302 652-3469
Wilmington (G-12044)		
Pediatric & Adolescent Center	G	302 684-0561
Milton (G-4946)		
Pediatric Associates PA	E	302 368-8612
Newark (G-7190)		
Peninsula Allergy and Asthma	G	302 734-4434
Dover (G-1944)		
Peninsula Plastic Surgery PC	G	302 663-0119
Millsboro (G-4778)		
Peninsula Regional Medical Ctr	G	302 436-8004
Selbyville (G-8529)		
Peninsula Regional Medical Ctr	F	302 732-8400
Dagsboro (G-929)		
Persante Sleep Center	G	302 508-2130
Smyrna (G-8688)		
Persephone Jones MD	G	302 651-4000
Wilmington (G-12090)		
Perspective Counseling Center	G	302 677-1758
Felton (G-2309)		
Peter F Townsend MD	E	302 633-3555
Wilmington (G-12096)		
Peter R Coggins MD	G	302 655-1115
Wilmington (G-12097)		
Philips B Eric DMD PA	F	302 738-7303
Newark (G-7213)		
Physician Dspnsng Solutions	G	302 734-7246
Wilmington (G-12129)		
Pike Creek Assoc In Wns Care	F	302 995-7062
Wilmington (G-12134)		
Pike Creek Imaging Center	F	302 995-2037
Wilmington (G-12139)		
Pike Creek Pediatric Assoc	F	302 239-7755
Wilmington (G-12140)		
Pregnacy Health Center	G	302 698-9311
Dover (G-1980)		
Premier Othpdic Bone Jint Care	G	302 422-6506
Milford (G-4529)		
Premiere Oral and Facial Surg	G	302 273-8300
Wilmington (G-12219)		
Premiere Physicians PA	G	302 762-6675
Newark (G-7246)		
Prospect Crozer LLC	G	302 798-8785
Claymont (G-797)		
Pulmonary & Sleep Cons LLC	G	302 994-4060
Wilmington (G-12267)		
Pulmonary Associates PA	G	302 656-2213
Wilmington (G-12268)		
Quality Family Physicians PA	G	302 235-2351
Hockessin (G-3127)		
Quinn Pediatric Dentistry	G	302 674-8000
Dover (G-2004)		
R G Altschuler MD	G	302 652-3771
Wilmington (G-12295)		
R M Villasenor MD	G	302 629-4078
Seaford (G-8368)		
Raafat Z Abdel-Misih MD	G	302 658-7533
Wilmington (G-12300)		
Radiation Oncology	E	302 733-1830
Newark (G-7295)		
Radiology Associates Inc	E	302 832-5590
Wilmington (G-12302)		
Rafi Soofi MD	G	302 999-1644
Wilmington (G-12305)		
Ramachandra U Hosmane MD	G	302 645-2274
Lewes (G-3707)		
Rebecca Jaffee MD	F	302 992-0200
Wilmington (G-12344)		
Regional Hmatology Oncology PA	E	302 731-7782
Wilmington (G-12358)		
Regional Orthopaedic Assoc	E	302 633-3555
Wilmington (G-12360)		
Rehabilitation Associates	G	302 529-8783
Newark (G-7313)		
Rehabilitation Associates PA	G	302 832-8894
Newark (G-7314)		
Reproductive Associates Del PA	G	302 478-8000
Wilmington (G-12382)		
Reproductive Associates Del PA	E	302 623-4242
Newark (G-7322)		
Rescue Surgical Solutions LLC	G	302 722-5877
Newark (G-7324)		
Retinovitreous Associates Ltd	F	302 351-1087
Wilmington (G-12393)		
Retinovitreous Associates Ltd	G	302 351-1085
Wilmington (G-12394)		
Richard L Sherry MD	F	302 475-1880
Wilmington (G-12410)		
Richard L Sherry MD	F	302 836-3937
Wilmington (G-7338)		
Ricks Fitness & Health Inc	G	302 684-0316
Milton (G-4962)		
Robert A Heinle M D	G	302 651-6400
Wilmington (G-12434)		
Robert Donlick MD	G	302 653-8916
Smyrna (G-8702)		
Robert J Varipapa MD	G	302 678-8100
Wilmington (G-12037)		
Robert S Callahan MD PA	G	302 731-0942
Newark (G-7351)		
Robinson & Cook Eyes Surgical	E	302 645-2300
Rehoboth Beach (G-8060)		
Rochelle E Haas M D	G	302 651-5600
Wilmington (G-12446)		
Rockland Surgery Center LP	E	302 999-0200
Wilmington (G-12455)		
Rodney Baltazar	G	302 283-3300
Middletown (G-4222)		
Roger Alexander MD	G	302 422-5223
Milford (G-4547)		
Rosalina Dejesus-Jiloca MD	F	302 629-4238
Seaford (G-8382)		
Ryan C Gough MD	G	302 677-6527
Dover (G-2046)		
Samaha Michel R MD	G	302 422-3100
Milford (G-4552)		
Schwartz Eric Wm MD	E	302 234-5770
Hockessin (G-3142)		
Seaford Endoscopy Center	G	302 629-7177
Seaford (G-8388)		
Serene Minds	G	302 478-6199
Wilmington (G-12583)		
Seth Ivins Dr MD	G	302 824-7280
Newark (G-7411)		
Shashikala Patel MD	G	302 737-5074
Newark (G-7413)		
Shore Community Medical	G	302 827-4365
Rehoboth Beach (G-8074)		
Silverside Open Mri Imaging	G	302 246-2000
Wilmington (G-12621)		
Sleep Disorder Center Del Inc	G	302 224-6000
Newark (G-7439)		
Smyrna Medical Associates PA	E	302 653-6174
Smyrna (G-8719)		
Southbrdge Med Advsory Council	E	302 655-6187
Wilmington (G-12686)		
Southern Delaware Imaging LLP	F	302 645-7919
Lewes (G-3758)		
Southern Delaware Med Group	G	302 424-3900
Dover (G-2095)		
Southern Delaware Med Group PA	E	302 424-3900
Milford (G-4566)		
Southside Family Practice	G	302 735-1880
Dover (G-2096)		
Spine Care of Delaware	G	302 894-1900
Newark (G-7473)		
Spine Group LLC	G	302 595-3030
Wilmington (G-12706)		
St Francis Bariatric Center	G	302 421-4121
Newark (G-7476)		
▼ Stephen F Penny MD	G	302 678-8100
Dover (G-2108)		
Stephen F Wetherill MD	G	302 478-3700
Wilmington (G-12755)		
Stewart Septimus MD	G	302 992-9940
Wilmington (G-12764)		
Stone Harbor Square LLC	G	302 227-5227
Rehoboth Beach (G-8088)		
Stoney Batter Family Medicine	G	302 234-9109
Wilmington (G-12770)		
Summit Orthopaedic HM Care LLC	G	302 703-0800
Lewes (G-3768)		
Sunwise Drmatology Surgery LLC	G	302 378-7981
Middletown (G-4251)		
Surgical Associates PA	F	302 346-4502
Dover (G-2119)		
Surgical Critical Assoc	G	302 623-4370
Newark (G-7516)		
Surgical Nanticoke Assoc PA	G	302 629-8662
Seaford (G-8411)		
Sussex Pain Relief Center LLC	E	302 519-0100
Georgetown (G-2681)		
Teresa H Keller MD	G	302 422-2022
Milford (G-4578)		
Terry L Horton	G	302 320-4900
Wilmington (G-12884)		
Textronics Inc	F	302 351-2109
Wilmington (G-12889)		
Theresa Little MD	G	302 735-1616
Dover (G-2141)		
Timothy Liveright MD	G	302 655-7293
Wilmington (G-12914)		
Tooze & Easter MD PA	E	302 735-8700
Dover (G-2152)		
Total Care Physicians	E	302 998-2977
Wilmington (G-12937)		
Total Care Physicians	G	302 798-0666
Wilmington (G-12938)		
Total Care Physicians	G	302 836-4200
Newark (G-7577)		
Total Health & Rehabilitation	G	302 999-9202
Wilmington (G-12939)		
Tri-State Health	G	302 368-2563
Newark (G-7588)		
Trinity Medical Assoc	G	302 762-6675
Wilmington (G-12977)		
Trinity Medical Center PA	G	302 846-0618
Delmar (G-1043)		
Trolley Sq Opn Mri & Imgng Ctr	F	302 472-5555
Wilmington (G-12983)		
Tru Beauti LLC	E	302 353-9249
Middletown (G-4269)		
Ty Jennifer MD	G	302 651-4459
Wilmington (G-13000)		
Uma Chatterjee MD	G	302 995-7500
Newark (G-7608)		
Urology Assoc Southern Del PA	G	302 422-5569
Milford (G-4588)		
Urology Associates Dover PA	E	302 674-1728
Dover (G-2182)		
VA Medical Center	F	302 994-2511
Wilmington (G-13043)		
Van Buren Medical Associates	E	302 998-1151
Wilmington (G-13047)		
Vascular Specialists Del PA	G	302 733-5700
Newark (G-7645)		
Veterans Health Administration	B	302 994-2511
Wilmington (G-13070)		
Veterans Health Administration	G	302 994-1660
Wilmington (G-13071)		
Vision Center of Delaware Inc	F	302 656-8867
Wilmington (G-13092)		
Visionquest Eye Care Center	E	302 678-3545
Dover (G-2196)		
W Lee Mackewiz Od PA	G	302 834-2020
Bear (G-368)		
Wayne I Tucker	G	302 838-1100
Bear (G-372)		
Westover Cardiology	G	302 482-2035
Middletown (G-4282)		
Westside Family Healthcare Inc	F	302 575-1414
Wilmington (G-13171)		
Westside Family Healthcare Inc	F	302 836-2864
Bear (G-376)		
Westside Family Healthcare Inc	C	302 652-2455
New Castle (G-5831)		
Westside Family Healthcare Inc	F	302 455-0900
Newark (G-7689)		
Westside Family Healthcare Inc	F	302 656-8292
Wilmington (G-13172)		
Westside Family Healthcare Inc	F	302 656-8292
Wilmington (G-13173)		
William A Ellert MD	G	302 369-9370
Newark (G-7696)		
William B Funk MD	G	302 731-0900
Newark (G-7697)		
William M Kaplan MD	G	302 422-3393
Milford (G-4606)		
Wilm Otolarngology	F	302 658-0404
Wilmington (G-13220)		
Wilmington Medical Associates	F	302 478-0400
Wilmington (G-13237)		
Wilmington Otolrynglgy Assc	G	302 658-0404
Wilmington (G-13239)		
Wilson Family Practice	G	302 422-6677
Milford (G-4609)		
Wolf Creek Surgeons PA	F	302 678-3627
Dover (G-2235)		

SIC SECTION 80 HEALTH SERVICES

Women First LLC .... G 302 368-3257
Newark *(G-7714)*

Women To Women Ob/Gyn Assoc PA .... G 302 778-2229
Wilmington *(G-13290)*

Womens Medical Center Inc .... G 302 629-5409
Seaford *(G-8442)*

Womens Wellness Ctr & Med Spa .... G 302 643-2500
Newark *(G-7716)*

Zabel PLStc&recnstrctve Surgy .... G 302 996-6400
Newark *(G-7736)*

Zarek Donohue LLC .... E 302 543-5454
Wilmington *(G-13340)*

Zarraga & Zarraga Internl Medc .... G 302 422-9140
Milford *(G-4616)*

Zeina Jeha Md MPH .... G 302 503-4200
Lewes *(G-3834)*

8021 Offices & Clinics Of Dentists

A D Alpine DMD .... F 302 239-4600
Wilmington *(G-8875)*

Aaron B Poleck D M D LLC .... G 302 623-4190
Newark *(G-5877)*

Aaron B Poleck DDS .... G 302 533-7649
Newark *(G-5878)*

Access Dental LLC .... G 302 674-3303
Dover *(G-1080)*

Adam C Sydell DDS .... G 302 684-1100
Milton *(G-4860)*

Ahl Orthodontics .... G 302 678-3000
Dover *(G-1096)*

Alan R Levine DDS .... F 302 475-3743
Wilmington *(G-8999)*

Alexis A Senholzi DMD .... G 302 234-2728
Hockessin *(G-2956)*

Alfred B Lauder DDS .... G 302 697-7188
Camden Wyoming *(G-612)*

Alfred Lauder DDS .... G 302 678-9742
Dover *(G-1103)*

Ali S Husain Orthodontist .... F 302 838-1400
Newark *(G-5931)*

All Smiles Family & Cosme .... G 302 734-5303
Dover *(G-1107)*

Allan C Goldfeder DMD .... G 302 994-1782
Wilmington *(G-9017)*

Aloe & Carr PA .... G 302 736-6631
Dover *(G-1111)*

Alpine Rafetto Orthodontics .... G 302 239-2304
Wilmington *(G-9033)*

Alvis D Burris .... G 302 697-3125
Camden *(G-537)*

Anna Marie Mazoch DDS PA .... G 302 998-9594
Wilmington *(G-9086)*

Anzilotti Orthodontics .... G 302 750-0117
Wilmington *(G-9093)*

Apex Dental Center LLC .... G 302 633-7550
Newark *(G-5980)*

Areas USA Dd LLC .... G 302 674-1946
Dover *(G-1135)*

Arthur L Young Dentist Jr .... G 302 737-9065
Newark *(G-6006)*

Arthur W Henry DDS Inc .... G 302 734-8101
Dover *(G-1141)*

Avalon Dental .... G 302 999-8822
Wilmington *(G-9195)*

Avalon Dental LLC Bldg G4 .... G 302 292-8899
Newark *(G-6030)*

B James Rogge DDS .... G 302 736-1423
Dover *(G-1164)*

Baker James Ccjr DDS .... G 302 658-9511
Wilmington *(G-9222)*

Barry Kayne DDS .... G 302 456-0400
Newark *(G-6048)*

Barry Klassman DDS RES .... G 302 478-0475
Wilmington *(G-9256)*

Bear Glasgow Dental .... F 302 836-3750
Newark *(G-6064)*

Bear-Glasgow Dental LLC .... G 302 836-9330
Bear *(G-49)*

Beautiful Smiles of Delaware .... G 302 656-0558
Wilmington *(G-9279)*

Bernard A Lewis DDS .... G 302 943-0456
Dover *(G-1194)*

Bernardo Anthony J Jr Dr DDS .... G 302 998-9244
Wilmington *(G-9308)*

Blair A Jones DDS .... G 302 226-1115
Lewes *(G-3386)*

Blog - Care First Dental Team .... G 302 741-2044
Dover *(G-1212)*

Blue Diamond Dental PA .... G 302 655-8387
Wilmington *(G-9375)*

Blue Hen Dental LLC .... G 302 538-0448
Smyrna *(G-8582)*

Brafman Family Dentistry PC .... F 302 732-3852
Dagsboro *(G-885)*

Brandywine Dental Care .... G 302 421-9960
Wilmington *(G-9429)*

Brian A Wisk .... G 302 653-5011
Smyrna *(G-8585)*

Brian McAllister DDS .... G 302 376-0617
Middletown *(G-3972)*

Brice Darla M DDS Ms .... G 302 478-4700
Wilmington *(G-9470)*

Bright Dental .... E 302 376-7882
Middletown *(G-3973)*

Bruce E Matthews DDS PA .... G 302 234-2440
Hockessin *(G-2971)*

Bruce E Matthews DDS PA .... F 302 475-9220
Wilmington *(G-9493)*

Bruce G Fay DMD PA .... G 302 778-3822
Wilmington *(G-9494)*

Caimar Corporation .... G 302 653-5011
Smyrna *(G-8589)*

Carter Karen DMD .... G 302 832-2200
Bear *(G-66)*

Cathy L Harris DDS .... G 302 453-1400
Newark *(G-6171)*

Cha Moon DDS .... G 302 297-3750
Newark *(G-6182)*

Charles D Calhoon DDS P .... G 302 731-0202
Wilmington *(G-9631)*

Charles J Veith DMD .... G 302 658-7354
Wilmington *(G-9632)*

Christiana Family Dental Care .... G 302 623-4190
Newark *(G-6224)*

Christianna Dental Center .... G 302 369-3200
Newark *(G-6227)*

Christina Ctr For Oral Surgery .... G 302 328-3053
New Castle *(G-5160)*

Christine E Fox DDS .... G 302 732-9850
Dagsboro *(G-892)*

Christine Fox DDS .... G 302 703-2838
Lewes *(G-3419)*

Christopher Baran DDS .... G 903 968-7467
Wilmington *(G-9692)*

Christopher Fortin DDS .... G 302 422-9791
Milford *(G-4352)*

Clay White Dental Associates .... F 302 731-4225
Newark *(G-6245)*

Clifford L Anzilotti DDS PC .... F 302 475-2050
Wilmington *(G-9741)*

Clifford L Anzilotti DDS PC .... F 302 378-2778
Middletown *(G-3997)*

Coastal Kids Pediatric Dntstry .... G 302 644-4460
Rehoboth Beach *(G-7894)*

Collins Associates .... F 302 834-4000
Newark *(G-6261)*

Concord Dental .... G 302 836-3750
Wilmington *(G-9811)*

Conley & Wright DDS .... G 302 645-6671
Rehoboth Beach *(G-7900)*

Connie F Cicorelli DDS PA .... G 302 798-5797
Wilmington *(G-9830)*

Cook & Cook Ltd Partnership .... E 302 428-0109
Wilmington *(G-9849)*

▲ Cook G Legih DDS& Cook Jefry .... G 302 378-4416
Middletown *(G-4009)*

Crescent Dental Associates .... G 302 230-0000
Wilmington *(G-9897)*

Crescent Dental Associates .... G 302 836-6968
Bear *(G-88)*

Curtis J Leciejewski DDS PA .... G 302 226-7960
Rehoboth Beach *(G-7905)*

Cynthia A Mumma DDS .... G 302 652-2451
Wilmington *(G-9932)*

D B Nibouar DDS .... F 302 239-0502
Wilmington *(G-9937)*

D R Deakyne DDS .... G 302 653-6661
Smyrna *(G-8610)*

D S Williams DMD PA .... F 302 239-5272
Wilmington *(G-9942)*

Dann J Gladnick Dmd PA .... G 302 654-7243
Wilmington *(G-9959)*

David A King DDS .... G 302 998-0331
Wilmington *(G-9965)*

David E Mastrota DMD PA .... G 302 654-0100
Wilmington *(G-9969)*

David L Isaacs DDS .... F 302 654-2904
Wilmington *(G-9970)*

Dd Snacks LLC .... G 302 652-3850
Wilmington *(G-9983)*

Deakyne Dental Associates PA .... G 302 653-6661
Smyrna *(G-8612)*

Deborah J Halligan DDS .... G 302 738-5766
Newark *(G-6356)*

Delaware Dental Care Centers .... G 410 474-5520
Dover *(G-1363)*

Delaware Dentistry .... G 302 475-6900
Wilmington *(G-10036)*

Delaware Gentle Dental Group .... G 302 514-6200
Smyrna *(G-8615)*

Delaware Mobile Dentistry .... G 302 698-9901
Dover *(G-1381)*

Delaware Modern Dental LLC .... G 302 366-8668
Newark *(G-6396)*

Delaware Periodontics .... G 302 658-7871
Wilmington *(G-10074)*

Delaware Star Dental .... G 302 994-3093
Wilmington *(G-10085)*

Delaware Valley Orthodontics .... G 302 239-3531
Wilmington *(G-10096)*

Delmarva Prosthodontics .... G 302 674-8331
Dover *(G-1411)*

Dental Associates PA .... G 302 571-0878
Wilmington *(G-10111)*

Dental Associates Delaware PA .... E 302 477-4900
Wilmington *(G-10112)*

Dental Associates Delaware PA .... E 302 378-8600
Middletown *(G-4035)*

Dental Associates Delaware PA .... F 302 477-4900
Wilmington *(G-10113)*

Dental Associates Hockessin .... G 302 239-5917
Wilmington *(G-10114)*

Dental Diagnostics & Services .... G 302 655-2626
Wilmington *(G-10115)*

Dental Group .... G 302 645-8993
Lewes *(G-3461)*

Dental Sleep Solution .... G 302 235-8249
Wilmington *(G-10116)*

Dentistry For Children .... F 302 475-7640
Wilmington *(G-10117)*

Devon Sadlowski DMD .... F 302 735-8940
Dover *(G-1418)*

Dominic Gioffre DDS PA .... F 302 239-0410
Wilmington *(G-10191)*

Dougherty Dental Solutions LLC .... G 302 475-3270
Wilmington *(G-10212)*

Douglas Ditty DMD MD .... G 302 644-2977
Lewes *(G-3471)*

Dover Dental Associates .... F 302 734-7634
Dover *(G-1444)*

Dover Fmly Csmtc Dentistry LLC .... G 302 672-7766
Dover *(G-1450)*

Dover Junior A DDS .... G 302 836-3750
Newark *(G-6466)*

Dr Amit Dua .... G 302 239-5917
Hockessin *(G-3011)*

Dr Bruce Matthews DDS .... G 302 234-2440
Hockessin *(G-3012)*

Dr Christopher Burns .... G 302 674-8331
Dover *(G-1475)*

Dr Clyde A Maxwell Jr .... G 302 765-3373
Wilmington *(G-10219)*

Dr Dawn Grandison DDS .... G 302 678-3384
Dover *(G-1476)*

Dr Fay Mintz-Guttin DMD .... G 302 356-0392
Wilmington *(G-10222)*

Dr Howard Giles - Wilmington .... G 302 477-4900
Wilmington *(G-10223)*

Dr James Kramer .... G 302 436-5133
Selbyville *(G-8483)*

Dr Jeffrey E Felzer DMD PC .... G 302 995-6979
Wilmington *(G-10225)*

Dr John Fontana III .... G 302 734-1950
Dover *(G-1477)*

Dr Robert M Collins .... G 302 239-3655
Wilmington *(G-10228)*

Dr Robert Webster .... G 302 674-1080
Dover *(G-1479)*

Dr Shefali Pandya .... G 302 421-9960
Wilmington *(G-10229)*

Dr Weidong Yang Dental Office .... G 302 409-3050
Bear *(G-127)*

Edward B Bayley DMD .... G 302 766-4633
Wilmington *(G-10355)*

Edward S Yalisove DDS PA .... G 302 658-4124
Wilmington *(G-10359)*

Edwin S Kuipers DDS .... G 302 455-0333
Newark *(G-6505)*

Edwin S Kuipers DDS .... G 302 652-3775
Wilmington *(G-10360)*

SIC

Employee Codes: A=Over 500 employees, B=251-500
C=101-250, D=51-100, E=20-50, F=10-19, G=1-9
2020 Harris Directory of
Delaware Businesses
551

80 HEALTH SERVICES

Elkington I Kent DDS .... G 302 629-3008
  Seaford *(G-8235)*
Emil W Tetzner D M D .... G 302 744-9900
  Dover *(G-1518)*
Emory & Marier PA .... F 302 422-2020
  Milford *(G-4405)*
Enhanced Dental Care .... G 302 645-7200
  Rehoboth Beach *(G-7927)*
Equidental .... G 302 423-0851
  Dover *(G-1526)*
Eric S Balliet .... F 302 856-7423
  Georgetown *(G-2524)*
Erik S Bradley DDS .... G 302 239-5917
  Wilmington *(G-10435)*
Erin N Macko DDS LLC .... G 302 368-7463
  Newark *(G-6538)*
Eugene M DAmico III DDS PA ..... G 302 292-1600
  Newark *(G-6544)*
Eugene M DAmico III DDS PA ..... G 302 376-3700
  Middletown *(G-4063)*
Family Denistry .... G 302 368-0054
  Newark *(G-6567)*
Family Dental Associates Inc ...... F 302 674-8810
  Dover *(G-1537)*
Family Dental Care .... G 302 999-7600
  Wilmington *(G-10487)*
Family Dental Center .... F 302 656-8266
  Wilmington *(G-10488)*
Family Dentistry Milford PA .... G 302 422-6924
  Milford *(G-4409)*
Family Dentistry Wilmington .... G 302 656-2434
  Wilmington *(G-10489)*
First State Oral & M .... G 302 674-4450
  Dover *(G-1558)*
Foulk Road Dental & Associates ... F 302 652-3775
  Wilmington *(G-10602)*
Franklin Pancko DDS .... G 302 674-1140
  Dover *(G-1565)*
Fred L Wright DDS .... G 302 239-1641
  Wilmington *(G-10624)*
Fred S Fink Orthodontist .... G 302 478-6930
  Wilmington *(G-10625)*
Frederick N Hartman .... G 302 479-5068
  Wilmington *(G-10628)*
Freedom Dental Management Inc ... G 302 836-3750
  Newark *(G-6616)*
G B Lyons DDS .... F 302 654-1765
  Wilmington *(G-10657)*
G Leigh Cook DMD .... F 302 453-8700
  Newark *(G-6631)*
G W Keller DDS .... F 302 652-3586
  Wilmington *(G-10659)*
Gary L Waite DMD .... G 302 239-8586
  Wilmington *(G-10673)*
Gary R Collins DDS .... G 302 239-3531
  Wilmington *(G-10674)*
Gentle Touch Dentistry .... G 302 765-3373
  Wilmington *(G-10696)*
George E Frattali DDS .... G 302 651-4408
  Wilmington *(G-10697)*
Glenwood Dental Associates LLP ... G 302 653-5011
  Smyrna *(G-8642)*
Gonce William E Dr DDS PA .... G 302 235-2400
  Hockessin *(G-3039)*
Gordon C Honig DMD PA .... G 302 737-6333
  Newark *(G-6678)*
Gordon C Honig DMD PA .... G 302 696-4020
  Middletown *(G-4091)*
Graylyn Dental .... G 302 475-5555
  Wilmington *(G-10767)*
Greeley & Nista Orthodontics ..... F 302 475-4102
  Wilmington *(G-10770)*
H Dean McSpadden DDS .... G 302 239-5917
  Hockessin *(G-3042)*
H Dean McSpadden DDS .... G 302 571-0680
  Wilmington *(G-10808)*
Hammond M Knox DDS .... G 302 383-6696
  Newark *(G-6704)*
Harry He DDS .... G 302 836-3711
  Newark *(G-6711)*
Herbert T Casalena DDS .... F 302 984-1712
  Wilmington *(G-10888)*
Hockessin Dental .... G 302 239-7277
  Hockessin *(G-3051)*
Hounsell Dental LLC .... G 302 691-8132
  Wilmington *(G-10959)*
Ignacio S Gispert DDS .... G 302 322-2303
  New Castle *(G-5410)*
Isaacs Isacs Fmly Dentistry PA ... F 302 654-1328
  Wilmington *(G-11088)*

J A Pyne Jr DDS PA .... G 302 994-7730
  Wilmington *(G-11102)*
J Michael Fay DDS PA .... F 302 998-2244
  Wilmington *(G-11108)*
J R Forshey DMD PA .... F 302 322-0245
  New Castle *(G-5430)*
J R Williamson DDS .... G 302 734-8887
  Dover *(G-1688)*
J S McKelvey DDS .... G 302 239-0303
  Wilmington *(G-11110)*
James S Pillsbury DDS .... G 302 734-0330
  Dover *(G-1692)*
James Tigani III DDS .... G 302 571-8740
  Wilmington *(G-11125)*
Jay J Harris PC .... G 302 453-1400
  Newark *(G-6829)*
Jeanette Y Son Dentist .... G 302 998-8283
  Wilmington *(G-11138)*
Jeena M Jolly DDS .... G 302 655-2626
  Wilmington *(G-11141)*
Jeffrey A Bright DMD .... E 302 832-1371
  Middletown *(G-4113)*
Jeffrey L Cook D M D .... G 302 453-8700
  Newark *(G-6831)*
Jennifer L Joseph DDS .... G 302 239-6677
  Wilmington *(G-11147)*
Jerome C Kayatta DDS .... G 302 737-6761
  Newark *(G-6835)*
Jessica S Dicerbo DDS .... G 302 644-4460
  Rehoboth Beach *(G-7972)*
Jill Garrido DDS .... G 302 475-3110
  Wilmington *(G-11158)*
Jillann I Hounsell DDS .... G 302 239-5917
  Hockessin *(G-3066)*
Jillann I Hounsell DDS .... G 302 691-3000
  Wilmington *(G-11159)*
Jiten Patel DDS .... G 302 690-8629
  Milford *(G-4458)*
John A Capodanno DDS PA .... G 302 697-7859
  Dover *(G-1701)*
John B Fontana Jr DDS .... G 302 656-2434
  Wilmington *(G-11167)*
John C Lynch DDS PA .... G 302 629-7115
  Seaford *(G-8282)*
John H Hatfield DDS .... G 302 698-0567
  Dover *(G-1705)*
John J Thaler II DDS .... G 302 478-9000
  Wilmington *(G-11173)*
John N Russo DDS .... F 302 652-3775
  Wilmington *(G-11175)*
John Nista DDS .... G 302 292-1552
  Newark *(G-6845)*
John Wasniewski DMD .... G 302 266-0200
  Newark *(G-6846)*
John Wasniewski III DMD .... G 302 832-1371
  Bear *(G-203)*
Johnson Orthodontics .... G 302 645-5554
  Rehoboth Beach *(G-7973)*
Joseph C Kelly DDS .... G 302 475-5555
  Wilmington *(G-11188)*
Joseph Cornatzer DDS .... G 302 239-5917
  Hockessin *(G-3069)*
Joseph F Spera DMD PA .... G 302 475-1122
  Wilmington *(G-11190)*
Jr Walter J Kaminski DDS .... F 302 738-3666
  Christiana *(G-670)*
Judith E McCann DMD .... G 302 368-7463
  Newark *(G-6857)*
Julie Q Nies DDS .... G 302 242-9085
  Dover *(G-1715)*
Junior Anderson Dover .... G 302 376-7979
  Townsend *(G-8803)*
Karl J Zeren DDS .... G 302 644-2773
  Rehoboth Beach *(G-7976)*
Kelly Ann Hatton .... G 484 571-5369
  Wilmington *(G-11237)*
Kelly Walker DDS .... G 302 832-2200
  Bear *(G-214)*
Kidd Robert W III DDS .... F 302 678-1440
  Dover *(G-1747)*
King & Minsk PA Inc .... G 302 475-3270
  Wilmington *(G-11268)*
Kirkwood Dental Associates PA ... F 302 994-2582
  Wilmington *(G-11274)*
Kirkwood Dental Associates PA ... G 302 834-7700
  Newark *(G-6892)*
L F Conlin DDS .... G 302 764-0930
  Wilmington *(G-11310)*
Laima V Anthaney DMD .... G 302 645-4726
  Lewes *(G-3588)*

Laurel Dental .... G 302 875-4271
  Laurel *(G-3252)*
Laurie Jacobs .... G 302 239-6257
  Hockessin *(G-3078)*
Lawrence A Louie DMD .... G 302 674-5437
  Dover *(G-1770)*
Leo J Kituskie DDS .... G 302 479-3937
  Wilmington *(G-11370)*
Lisa A Fagioletti DMD LLC .... G 302 514-9064
  Smyrna *(G-8673)*
Lois James DDS .... G 302 537-4500
  Ocean View *(G-7800)*
Louis K Rafetto DMD .... G 302 477-1800
  Wilmington *(G-11440)*
Louis P Martin DDS .... G 302 994-4900
  Wilmington *(G-11441)*
Lrk Dental .... G 302 629-7115
  Seaford *(G-8297)*
Margaret M Munley DDS .... G 302 475-2626
  Wilmington *(G-11523)*
Mark A Fortunato .... E 302 477-4900
  Wilmington *(G-11530)*
Mark B Brown DDS .... G 302 537-1200
  Bethany Beach *(G-413)*
Mark C Gladnick DDS .... G 302 994-2660
  Wilmington *(G-11531)*
Mark Wieczorek Dmd PC .... F 302 838-3384
  Bear *(G-246)*
Marsico & Weinstien DDS .... G 302 998-8474
  Wilmington *(G-11546)*
Marta Biskup DDS .... G 302 478-0000
  Wilmington *(G-11547)*
Marta Blackhurst DMD .... G 302 478-1504
  Wilmington *(G-11548)*
Mary Sweeney-Lehr .... G 302 764-0589
  Wilmington *(G-11558)*
Mary Ziomek DDS .... G 301 984-9646
  Milton *(G-4931)*
Maryann K Bailey DDS .... G 302 655-5822
  Wilmington *(G-11560)*
Mattern & Piccioni Md PA .... F 302 730-8060
  Dover *(G-1827)*
Maxillofacial Southern De Oral ... G 302 644-2977
  Lewes *(G-3627)*
Mercer Dental Associates .... G 302 664-1385
  Milton *(G-4934)*
Michael A Poleck DDS .... G 302 644-4100
  Lewes *(G-3639)*
Michael A Poleck DDS PA .... G 302 994-7730
  Wilmington *(G-11657)*
Michael Butterworth Dr .... G 302 732-9850
  Dagsboro *(G-922)*
Michael J Ryan DDS .... G 302 378-8600
  Middletown *(G-4153)*
Michael L Cahoon Dr .... G 302 644-4171
  Lewes *(G-3640)*
Michael Matthias .... G 302 575-0100
  Wilmington *(G-11662)*
Michael S Wirosloff DMD .... G 302 998-8588
  Wilmington *(G-11665)*
Michael T Rosen DDS PA .... G 866 561-5067
  Wilmington *(G-11667)*
Michele Broder .... G 302 652-1533
  Wilmington *(G-11670)*
Middletown Family Dentist .... G 302 376-1959
  Middletown *(G-4156)*
Mill Creek Select .... G 302 995-2090
  Wilmington *(G-11688)*
Milltown Dental LLC .... G 302 998-3332
  Wilmington *(G-11697)*
Milunsky Family Dentistry .... G 610 566-5322
  Wilmington *(G-11701)*
Milunsky Family Dentistry PC .... G 610 872-8042
  Wilmington *(G-11702)*
Modern Dental .... G 302 478-1748
  Wilmington *(G-11720)*
Monica Mehring DDS .... F 302 368-0054
  Newark *(G-7051)*
Ms Governors Square Shopping C ... G 302 838-3384
  Bear *(G-258)*
Mullen Thomas R DMD PA .... G 302 629-3588
  Seaford *(G-8312)*
Nathaniel Jon Bent DDS PA .... G 302 731-4907
  Newark *(G-7084)*
Neena Mukkamala DDS .... G 302 734-5305
  Dover *(G-1890)*
Neil G McAneny DDS .... G 302 368-0329
  Newark *(G-7089)*
Neil G McAneny DDS PC .... F 302 731-4907
  Newark *(G-7090)*

New Castle Dental Assoc PA ....F 302 328-1513
New Castle *(G-5556)*
New Concept Dental ....G....... 302 778-3822
Wilmington *(G-11859)*
Newark Dental Assoc Inc ....E....... 302 737-5170
Newark *(G-7117)*
Nicholas J Punturieri ....G....... 302 834-7700
Newark *(G-7131)*
Norman M Lippman DDS..........................G....... 302 674-1140
Dover *(G-1900)*
Norman S Steward DDS PA......................G....... 302 422-9791
Milford *(G-4514)*
OConnor Orthodontics.............................G....... 302 678-1441
Dover *(G-1913)*
Ofc Partners Xiv Bellevue ....G....... 302 439-3345
Wilmington *(G-11937)*
Oral & Maxillofacial Surgery ....G....... 302 998-0331
Wilmington *(G-11967)*
Oral Mxllfcial Srgery Assoc PA...............F 302 655-6183
Wilmington *(G-11968)*
Orthodontics On Silver Lake ....G....... 302 672-7776
Dover *(G-1921)*
Orthodontics On Silver Lake PA.............G....... 302 672-7776
Dover *(G-1922)*
Pace Enterprises LLC.............................G....... 302 529-2500
Wilmington *(G-12001)*
Park Place Dental...................................G....... 302 455-0333
Newark *(G-7177)*
Park Place Dental...................................G....... 302 652-3775
Wilmington *(G-12020)*
Paul G Collins DDS ....G....... 302 934-8005
Millsboro *(G-4771)*
Paul R Christian DMD..............................G....... 302 376-9600
Middletown *(G-4184)*
Peninsula Dental LLC..............................G....... 302 297-3750
Millsboro *(G-4776)*
Penna Orthodontics.................................G....... 302 998-8783
Wilmington *(G-12068)*
Peter F Subach...G....... 302 995-1870
Wilmington *(G-12095)*
Peter Patellis ....G....... 302 537-1200
Bethany Beach *(G-421)*
Premier Comprehensive Dental..............G....... 302 378-3131
Middletown *(G-4197)*
Premier Dentistry Christiana ....G....... 302 366-7636
Newark *(G-7243)*
Progresive Dental Arts ....F 302 455-9569
Newark *(G-7268)*
Progressive Dental Arts ....G....... 302 234-2222
Wilmington *(G-12241)*
Prudent Endodontics...............................G....... 302 475-3803
Wilmington *(G-12258)*
Qlean Implants Inc...................................G....... 302 613-0804
Rehoboth Beach *(G-8038)*
R M Quinn DDS ....F 302 674-8000
Dover *(G-2007)*
Ralph Tomases DDS PA ....G....... 302 652-8656
Wilmington *(G-12310)*
Ramon Galvan..G....... 201 797-7172
Wilmington *(G-12313)*
Rawlins Orthodontics..............................G....... 302 239-3533
Wilmington *(G-12324)*
Raymond L Para DDS ....F 302 234-2728
Hockessin *(G-3130)*
Raymond W Petrunich.............................G....... 302 836-3565
Newark *(G-7303)*
Rebekah Fedele DMD PA........................G....... 302 994-9555
Wilmington *(G-12345)*
Rehoboth Beach Dent ....G....... 302 226-7960
Rehoboth Beach *(G-8050)*
Richard E Chodroff DMD.........................G....... 302 995-6979
Wilmington *(G-12406)*
Richard J Tananis DDS LLC....................G....... 302 875-4271
Laurel *(G-3281)*
Richard S Jacobs DDS ....G....... 302 792-2648
Claymont *(G-800)*
Robert A Penna DMD...............................G....... 302 623-4060
Newark *(G-7349)*
Robert C Director DDS ....G....... 302 658-7358
Wilmington *(G-12436)*
Robert P Hart DDS ....G....... 302 328-1513
New Castle *(G-5681)*
Rodriguez Marieve O Dmd PA ....G....... 302 655-5862
Wilmington *(G-12462)*
Russell J Tibbetts DDS PA......................G....... 302 479-5959
Wilmington *(G-12496)*
Russo Mary Claire Real Estate ....G....... 302 529-2653
Wilmington *(G-12498)*
Rutledge Dental Assoc Inc......................G....... 302 378-8705
Middletown *(G-4228)*
S D Nemcic DDS......................................G....... 302 734-1950
Dover *(G-2049)*
Sarah K Smith DDS..................................G....... 302 442-3233
Newark *(G-7386)*
Sattar A Syed DMD PA ....G....... 302 994-3093
Wilmington *(G-12544)*
Sedation Center PA.................................G....... 302 678-3384
Dover *(G-2066)*
Silly Smiles LLC ....G....... 302 838-1865
Newark *(G-7429)*
Silverside Dental Associates ....G....... 302 478-4700
Wilmington *(G-12620)*
Small Wonder Dental ....G....... 302 525-6463
Newark *(G-7443)*
Smile Brite Dental Care LLC ....G....... 302 384-8448
Wilmington *(G-12657)*
Smile Brite Dental Care LLC ....F 302 838-8306
Newark *(G-7449)*
Smile Place..G....... 302 514-6200
Smyrna *(G-8717)*
Smile Solutions By Emmi Dental............G....... 302 999-8113
Wilmington *(G-12658)*
Smiles Jolly PA ....G....... 302 378-3384
Middletown *(G-4244)*
Smyrna Dental Center PA.......................G....... 302 223-6194
Smyrna *(G-8718)*
Southern Del Assoc Dntl Spc ....G....... 302 226-1606
Rehoboth Beach *(G-8082)*
Southern Delaware Dental Spec............G....... 302 855-9499
Georgetown *(G-2661)*
Southern Dental LLC ....G....... 302 536-7589
Seaford *(G-8406)*
Sparkle Mobile Dental Services.............G....... 302 762-4322
Wilmington *(G-12694)*
Stanley Goleburn DDS............................G....... 302 297-3750
Newark *(G-7482)*
Stanley H Goloskov DDS PA...................G....... 302 475-0600
Wilmington *(G-12737)*
Stephen A Niemoeller DMD PA ....G....... 302 737-3320
Newark *(G-7489)*
Steven Alban DDS PA ....G....... 302 422-9637
Milford *(G-4570)*
Suk-Young Carr DDS ....G....... 302 736-6631
Dover *(G-2112)*
Sussex Orthodontics...............................G....... 302 644-4100
Dover *(G-2121)*
Swiatowicz Dental Associates...............G....... 302 476-8185
Wilmington *(G-12824)*
Terry Bryan..G....... 302 698-9901
Dover *(G-2139)*
Thomas Baldwin DDS..............................G....... 302 829-1243
Ocean View *(G-7820)*
Thomas Dougherty DDS..........................G....... 302 239-2500
Wilmington *(G-12899)*
Thomas Jenkins DMD..............................F 302 426-0526
Wilmington *(G-12902)*
Thomas Postlethwait DDS ....G....... 302 674-8283
Dover *(G-2143)*
Thomas W Mercer DMD...........................G....... 302 678-2942
Dover *(G-2144)*
Tigani Family Dentistry PA.....................G....... 302 571-8740
Wilmington *(G-12908)*
Timothy and Rosemary Clay DMD ....F 302 998-0500
Wilmington *(G-12912)*
Todd Rowen DMD ....G....... 302 994-5887
Wilmington *(G-12922)*
Townsend Fmly Cosmtc Dentistry ....G....... 302 376-7979
Townsend *(G-8827)*
Two Dds LLC ....G....... 302 300-1259
Middletown *(G-4271)*
Victor J Venturena DDS ....G....... 302 656-0558
Wilmington *(G-13076)*
Victor L Gregory Jr DMD.........................G....... 302 239-1827
Wilmington *(G-13077)*
W H Thomas DDS.....................................G....... 302 697-1152
Dover *(G-2202)*
Wahl Family Dentistry ....E 302 655-1228
Wilmington *(G-13113)*
Weatherhill Dental...................................G....... 302 239-6677
Wilmington *(G-13132)*
Westside Family Healthcare Inc ....E 302 678-4622
Dover *(G-2217)*
Westside Family Healthcare Inc ....F 302 575-1414
Wilmington *(G-13171)*
Westside Family Healthcare Inc ....F 302 836-2864
Bear *(G-376)*
Westside Family Healthcare Inc ....F 302 455-0900
Newark *(G-7689)*
Westside Family Healthcare Inc ....F 302 656-8292
Wilmington *(G-13172)*
Westside Family Healthcare Inc ....F 302 656-8292
Wilmington *(G-13173)*
William Gonce ....G....... 302 235-2400
Newark *(G-7698)*
William P Smith DDS ....G....... 302 737-7274
Newark *(G-7699)*
Wilmington Dental Assoc PA..................F 302 654-6915
Wilmington *(G-13229)*
Woodmill Dental......................................G....... 302 998-8588
Wilmington *(G-13298)*
Woodmill Dental......................................G....... 302 998-8588
Wilmington *(G-13299)*
Wright Bruce B DDS Office RES.............G....... 302 227-8707
Rehoboth Beach *(G-8119)*
Xgate Dental Inc......................................G....... 302 613-2142
Wilmington *(G-13320)*
Your Dentistry Today Inc.........................G....... 302 575-0100
Wilmington *(G-13335)*
Zachary Chipman DMD PA......................G....... 302 994-8696
Wilmington *(G-13338)*

8031 Offices & Clinics Of Doctors Of Osteopathy

Abby Medical Center ....G....... 302 999-0003
Newark *(G-5882)*
Alan Warrington Do ....G....... 302 239-9599
Wilmington *(G-9000)*
Alfieri Anthony D Do Facc.......................G....... 302 397-8199
Wilmington *(G-9007)*
Andrew W Donohue D O ....G....... 302 999-7386
Wilmington *(G-9081)*
Anthony A Vasile Do................................G....... 302 764-2072
Wilmington *(G-9090)*
Battaglia Joseph A & Diamond...............G....... 302 655-8868
Wilmington *(G-9261)*
Brandywine Family Medicine..................G....... 302 475-5000
Wilmington *(G-9432)*
Christiana Care ....G....... 302 654-4925
Wilmington *(G-9675)*
Christiana Care Health Sys Inc...............F 302 659-4401
Smyrna *(G-8594)*
Cynthia P Mangubat MD..........................G....... 302 674-1356
Dover *(G-1334)*
Dr Jason Parker Do..................................G....... 302 651-5874
Wilmington *(G-10224)*
Dr Jillian G Stevens Do ....G....... 302 762-7332
Wilmington *(G-10226)*
Dr Marisa E Conti Do ....G....... 302 678-4488
Dover *(G-1478)*
Dr Ronald R Blanck Do............................G....... 302 541-4137
Fenwick Island *(G-2334)*
Family Doctors ....G....... 302 368-3600
Newark *(G-6568)*
Family Medicine Smyrna Clayton...........G....... 302 653-1050
Smyrna *(G-8631)*
Family Practice Hockessin PA................G....... 302 239-4500
Hockessin *(G-3027)*
International Spine Pain..........................G....... 302 478-7001
Wilmington *(G-11067)*
John B Coll Do ....G....... 302 678-8100
Dover *(G-1702)*
Joseph Parise Do.....................................G....... 302 735-8855
Dover *(G-1709)*
Milford Medical Associates PA...............G....... 302 329-9517
Milton *(G-4937)*
N O Biasotto Do ....G....... 302 998-1211
Newark *(G-7079)*
Nicholas O Biasotto Co............................G....... 302 998-1235
Newark *(G-7132)*
P A Womencare..G....... 302 731-2900
Newark *(G-7166)*
Paul Imber Do...G....... 302 478-5647
Wilmington *(G-12042)*
Pulmonary & Sleep Cons LLC ....G....... 302 994-4060
Wilmington *(G-12267)*
Ralph Burdick Do......................................G....... 302 834-3600
Delaware City *(G-966)*
Robert S Callahan MD PA.......................G....... 302 731-0942
Newark *(G-7351)*
Southern Delaware Med Group ....G....... 302 424-3900
Dover *(G-2095)*
Sullivan Anna Marie Do ....G....... 302 454-1680
Newark *(G-7501)*
To Do Yard Guys ....G....... 302 947-9475
Millsboro *(G-4813)*
Total Care Physicians...............................G....... 302 836-4200
Newark *(G-7577)*
Trinity Medical Center PA........................G....... 302 846-0618
Delmar *(G-1043)*

S I C

80 HEALTH SERVICES

Urology Assoc Southern Del PA .... G 302 422-5569
 Milford (G-4588)
Vincent Lobo Dr PA .... G 302 398-8163
 Harrington (G-2905)

8041 Offices & Clinics Of Chiropractors

1 Fair Chiropractic & Med Inc .... G 302 528-1068
 Wilmington (G-8840)
American Chiropractic Center .... G 302 450-3153
 Dover (G-1118)
Atlantic Chiropractic Associat .... G 302 854-9300
 Georgetown (G-2436)
Atlantic Chiropractic Associat .... F 302 703-6108
 Lewes (G-3353)
Atlantic Chiropractic Associat .... F 302 422-3100
 Milford (G-4311)
Beachview Chiropractic Center .... G 302 539-7063
 Millville (G-4834)
Bear Chiropractic Center DC .... G 302 836-8361
 Bear (G-46)
Brandywine Total Health Care .... G 302 478-3028
 Wilmington (G-9455)
Camp Chiropractic Inc .... G 302 378-2899
 Middletown (G-3980)
Carrick Chiropractic Centre PA .... G 302 478-1443
 Wilmington (G-9579)
Chiropractic Services PA .... G 302 654-0404
 Wilmington (G-9669)
Christiana Chiropractic LLC .... G 302 633-6335
 Newark (G-6220)
Coastal Chiropractic LLC .... G 302 933-0700
 Millsboro (G-4663)
Concord Med Spine & Pain Ctr .... G 302 652-1107
 Wilmington (G-9813)
Davis Chiropractic Inc .... G 302 856-2225
 Georgetown (G-2494)
Delaware Backpan Rhblttn Assoc .... E 302 529-8783
 Wilmington (G-10004)
Delaware Chiropractic At Louvi .... G 302 738-7300
 Newark (G-6368)
Delaware County Pain MGT .... G 302 575-1145
 Wilmington (G-10029)
Delaware Spine & Rehab LLC .... G 813 965-0903
 Seaford (G-8219)
Diamond Chiropractic Inc .... F 302 892-9355
 Newark (G-6443)
Dover Family Chiropractic .... G 302 531-1900
 Camden (G-565)
Elizabeth C Parberry Dr .... G 302 436-1803
 Selbyville (G-8487)
Family Chiropractic Office PA .... G 302 993-9113
 Wilmington (G-10485)
Feeney Chropractic Care Ctr PA .... F 302 328-0200
 Bear (G-150)
First Choice Health Care Inc .... G 302 836-6150
 Bear (G-151)
First State Health & Wellness .... F 302 645-6681
 Rehoboth Beach (G-7933)
First State Health & Wellness .... G 302 239-1600
 Hockessin (G-3029)
First State Physicia NS .... G 302 836-6150
 Bear (G-154)
Glasgow Chiropractic .... G 302 453-4043
 Newark (G-6660)
Hockessin Chrpractic Centre PA .... G 302 239-8550
 Hockessin (G-3048)
Howmedica Osteonics Corp .... G 302 655-3239
 Wilmington (G-10962)
Kenneth De Grout DC .... G 302 475-5600
 Wilmington (G-11240)
Lewes Chiropractic Center .... G 302 645-9171
 Lewes (G-3597)
Lodes Chiropractic Center PA .... G 302 477-1565
 Wilmington (G-11423)
Main Street Fmly Chiropractic .... G 302 737-8667
 Newark (G-6974)
Matthew J McIlrath DC .... G 302 798-7033
 Wilmington (G-11571)
Newark Chropractic Hlth Ctr PA .... G 302 239-1600
 Hockessin (G-3103)
Nowcare LLC .... G 302 777-5551
 Wilmington (G-11916)
P A Chadley .... G 302 234-1115
 Hockessin (G-3109)
Peninsula Chiropractic Center .... G 302 629-4344
 Seaford (G-8346)
Pro Rehab Chiropractic .... G 302 200-9102
 Lewes (G-3698)
Pro Rehab Chiropractors .... G 302 652-2225
 Wilmington (G-12235)

Pure Wellness LLC .... G 302 449-0149
 Middletown (G-4204)
Pure Wellness LLC .... F 302 365-5470
 Newark (G-7272)
Pure Wellness LLC .... G 302 543-5679
 Wilmington (G-12271)
Pyne Chiropractic PA .... G 302 644-1792
 Rehoboth Beach (G-8037)
Renu Chiropractic Wellness .... G 302 368-0124
 Newark (G-7320)
Richard C McKay DC PA .... G 302 368-1300
 Newark (G-7337)
Roger C Allen DC .... G 302 734-9824
 Dover (G-2040)
Rosenthal Chiropractic Offs PA .... G 302 999-0633
 Wilmington (G-12476)
Schreppler Chiropractic Offs PA .... G 302 653-5525
 Smyrna (G-8712)
Stephen G Puzio DC .... G 302 234-4045
 Hockessin (G-3149)
Stephen Jankovic Chiropractor .... G 302 384-8540
 Wilmington (G-12756)
Sussex Pain Relief Center LLC .... E 302 519-0100
 Georgetown (G-2681)
T Shane Palmer DC .... G 302 328-2656
 New Castle (G-5750)
Todd A Richardson Dcpa .... G 302 449-0149
 Middletown (G-4261)
Travis Chiropractic .... G 610 485-9800
 Wilmington (G-12962)
Trevor Ennis DC .... G 302 730-8848
 Dover (G-2163)
Trevor Ennis DC .... G 302 389-2225
 Smyrna (G-8732)
Walsh Chiropractic Center .... G 302 422-0622
 Milford (G-4597)
Wellness Health Inc .... G 302 424-4100
 Milford (G-4601)

8042 Offices & Clinics Of Optometrists

Allan S Tocker Od .... G 302 995-9060
 Wilmington (G-9018)
Amy M Farrall OD LLC .... G 302 737-5777
 Newark (G-5964)
Bryan K Sterling LLC .... G 302 734-3511
 Dover (G-1239)
Chambers Optometrist .... G 302 543-6492
 Wilmington (G-9626)
Delaware Eye Care Center .... E 302 674-1121
 Dover (G-1368)
Dr Andrew Berman .... G 302 678-1000
 Dover (G-1474)
Halpern Eye Associates Inc .... G 302 734-5861
 Middletown (G-4102)
Halpern Eye Associates Inc .... G 302 537-0234
 Millville (G-4846)
Halpern Eye Associates Inc .... E 302 734-5861
 Dover (G-1623)
Halpern Eye Associates Inc .... G 302 422-2020
 Milford (G-4432)
Halpern Eye Associates Inc .... F 302 629-6816
 Seaford (G-8256)
Halpern Eye Associates Inc .... G 302 838-0800
 Bear (G-176)
Halpern Eye Associates Inc .... G 302 653-3400
 Smyrna (G-8649)
Howard B Stromwasser .... G 302 368-4424
 Newark (G-6751)
In Vision Eye Care .... F 302 655-1952
 Wilmington (G-11010)
In Vision Eye Care Inc .... G 302 235-7031
 Hockessin (G-3057)
John M Otto Od .... G 302 623-0170
 Newark (G-6844)
Joseph G Goldberg Od .... G 302 999-1286
 Wilmington (G-11191)
Kneisley Eye Care PA .... G 302 224-3000
 Newark (G-6899)
Larry Wallis 856 456-3925
 Wilmington (G-11331)
Ronald S Pogach Od RES .... G 302 994-3300
 Newark (G-7364)
Simon Eye Associates PA .... E 302 834-4305
 Bear (G-322)
Simon Eye Associates PA .... G 302 655-8180
 Wilmington (G-12623)
Simon Eye Associates PA .... F 302 239-1389
 Wilmington (G-12624)
Steve O Quillin Od .... G 302 398-8404
 Harrington (G-2894)

Susan J Betts Od .... G 302 629-6691
 Seaford (G-8412)
Sussex Eye Center PA .... G 302 856-2020
 Georgetown (G-2679)
Sussex Eye Center PA .... G 302 436-2020
 Selbyville (G-8551)
Timothy Westgate 302 629-9197
 Seaford (G-8423)

8043 Offices & Clinics Of Podiatrists

Advanced Foot & Ankle Center .... G 302 355-0056
 Newark (G-5905)
Brandywine Podiatry PA .... G 302 658-1129
 Wilmington (G-9450)
Delaware Foot & Ankle Assoc .... G 302 834-3575
 Newark (G-6380)
Delaware Podiatrist Medicine .... G 302 674-9255
 Dover (G-1387)
Delaware Valley Ent Inc .... G 302 427-2444
 Wilmington (G-10093)
Edwin M Mow DPM Facfas .... G 302 424-1760
 Milford (G-4403)
Foot & Ankle Associates .... F 302 652-5767
 Wilmington (G-10587)
Foot & Ankle Ctr of Delaware .... G 302 945-1221
 Millsboro (G-4692)
▲ Foot Care Group Inc .... E 302 998-0178
 Wilmington (G-10588)
Foot Care Group Inc .... F 302 285-0292
 Middletown (G-4075)
Garcia Podiatry Group .... G 302 994-5956
 Wilmington (G-10669)
James F Palmer .... G 302 629-6162
 Seaford (G-8277)
James F Palmer .... G 302 644-3980
 Lewes (G-3570)
John Hocutt Jr MD .... G 302 475-7800
 Wilmington (G-11171)
Lisa Ryan Hobbs DPM .... G 302 629-3000
 Seaford (G-8295)
Raymond V Feehery Jr DPM .... G 302 999-8511
 Newark (G-7302)
Southern Delaware Foot .... G 302 404-5915
 Seaford (G-8405)
Sussex Podiatry Group .... G 302 645-8555
 Lewes (G-3773)
Tri State Foot & Ankle Ctr LLC .... G 302 475-1299
 Wilmington (G-12966)

8049 Offices & Clinics Of Health Practitioners, NEC

Akhtar Javed .... G 606 515-3698
 Magnolia (G-3879)
All Therapy LLC .... G 302 376-5578
 Middletown (G-3935)
Amy Donovan .... G 302 245-8957
 Lewes (G-3337)
Annette Rickolt .... G 302 285-4200
 Middletown (G-3940)
Associates In Hlth Psychology .... F 302 428-0205
 Wilmington (G-9156)
Aston Home Health .... F 302 421-3686
 Wilmington (G-9165)
ATI Holdings LLC .... E 302 422-6670
 Milford (G-4310)
ATI Holdings LLC .... E 302 993-1450
 Wilmington (G-9173)
ATI Holdings LLC .... E 302 836-5670
 Bear (G-40)
ATI Holdings LLC .... E 302 226-2230
 Rehoboth Beach (G-7849)
ATI Holdings LLC .... E 302 894-1600
 Newark (G-6016)
ATI Holdings LLC .... E 302 285-0700
 Middletown (G-3947)
ATI Holdings LLC .... E 302 659-3102
 Smyrna (G-8577)
ATI Holdings LLC .... E 302 994-1200
 Wilmington (G-9174)
ATI Holdings LLC .... E 302 786-3008
 Harrington (G-2814)
ATI Holdings LLC .... E 302 536-5562
 Seaford (G-8157)
ATI Holdings LLC .... E 302 838-2165
 Newark (G-6017)
ATI Holdings LLC .... E 302 677-0100
 Dover (G-1155)
ATI Holdings LLC .... E 302 392-3400
 Bear (G-41)

SIC SECTION

80 HEALTH SERVICES

Company	Code	Phone
ATI Holdings LLC — Wilmington (G-9175)	E	302 475-7500
ATI Holdings LLC — Wilmington (G-9176)	E	302 351-0302
ATI Holdings LLC — Dover (G-1156)	E	302 741-0200
ATI Holdings LLC — New Castle (G-5050)	E	302 654-1700
ATI Holdings LLC — Wilmington (G-9177)	E	302 656-2521
ATI Holdings LLC — Millsboro (G-4631)	E	302 297-0700
ATI Holdings LLC — Wilmington (G-9178)	F	302 658-7800
Austrlian Phystherapy Ctrs Ltd — Wilmington (G-9185)	G	631 298-5367
Back Clinic Inc — Wilmington (G-9220)	F	302 995-2100
Basco Physical Therapy — Dover (G-1176)	G	302 730-1294
Bayada Home Health Care Inc — Wilmington (G-9264)	G	302 655-1333
Bayada Home Health Care Inc — Milford (G-4319)	D	302 424-8200
Blue Hen Physical Therapy Inc — Newark (G-6100)	E	302 453-1588
Brandywine Pain Center — Wilmington (G-9447)	F	302 998-2585
Brdly M Winston Pdrtcs Prctc — Milford (G-4333)	G	302 424-1650
Catherine Kotalis — Dover (G-1259)	G	302 526-1470
Christiana Care Hlth Svcs Inc — Wilmington (G-9681)	F	302 428-6662
Christiana Care Hlth Svcs Inc — Wilmington (G-9682)	F	302 477-3300
Christiana Care Hlth Svcs Inc — New Castle (G-5156)	E	302 327-5555
Christiana Chiropractic LLC — Newark (G-6220)	G	302 633-6335
Christina Newton — Bear (G-72)	G	302 454-2400
Christine W Maynard MD — Wilmington (G-9691)	G	302 995-7073
Christopher A Bowens MD — Newark (G-6231)	G	302 834-3700
Chuck B Barker Pt Dpt Ocs Atc — Dover (G-1281)	G	302 730-4800
Coastal Care Physical Therapy — Selbyville (G-8469)	G	480 236-3863
Connections Community Support — Wilmington (G-9826)	D	302 984-2302
Cristy Anna Care Physcl Thrapy — Middletown (G-4015)	G	302 378-6111
Delaware Curative — Bear (G-107)	G	302 836-5670
Delaware Curative Workshop — Wilmington (G-10033)	D	302 656-2521
Delaware Orthopedic and Sports — Smyrna (G-8618)	E	302 653-8389
Delaware Vein Center — Georgetown (G-2505)	G	302 258-8853
Dorilyn English PHD — Wilmington (G-10202)	G	302 655-6506
Dorinda F Dove — Wilmington (G-10203)	G	302 658-2229
Dynamic Therapy Services LLC — Newark (G-6485)	F	302 691-5603
Dynamic Therapy Services LLC — Dover (G-1489)	F	302 526-2148
Dynamic Therapy Services LLC — Middletown (G-4046)	F	302 376-4315
Dynamic Therapy Services LLC — Wilmington (G-10273)	F	302 778-0810
Dynamic Therapy Services LLC — New Castle (G-5270)	F	302 544-4388
Dynamic Therapy Services LLC — Lewes (G-3476)	F	302 703-2355
Dynamic Therapy Services LLC — Newark (G-6486)	G	302 292-3454
Dynamic Therapy Services LLC — Wilmington (G-10274)	F	302 998-9880
Dynamic Therapy Services LLC — Bear (G-131)	E	302 834-1550
Ellingson & Associates — Newark (G-6517)	F	302 650-6437
Eric Barsky — Newark (G-6536)	G	856 495-6988
Family Care Associates — Newark (G-6566)	G	302 454-8880
Hcr Manor Care Svc Fla III Inc — Wilmington (G-10862)	G	302 764-0181
Healing Adults & Adolescents — Bear (G-180)	G	302 836-4000
Hillside Center — Wilmington (G-10909)	F	302 652-1181
Hockessin Chrpractic Centre PA — Hockessin (G-3048)	G	302 239-8550
Jackson Massage and Cft — Newark (G-6822)	G	302 525-6808
James Friesa Acupuncture — Dover (G-1691)	G	302 674-4204
Javed Gilani MD — Wilmington (G-11130)	G	302 478-7160
Jill Dusak — Wilmington (G-11157)	G	302 652-4705
John Johnson Dr — Wilmington (G-11174)	G	302 999-7104
Kalin Eye Assoc — Newark (G-6866)	G	302 292-2020
Kathryn M Gehret — Lewes (G-3581)	G	610 420-7233
Lakeside Physical Therapy LLC — Laurel (G-3251)	F	302 280-6920
Laurie Ann Fishinger — Millsboro (G-4718)	G	570 460-4370
Lucila Carmichael Rn — New Castle (G-5489)	G	302 324-8901
Lynn Holiday Shynea — Dover (G-1808)	G	302 674-4700
Marsha S Eddorlov — Wilmington (G-11544)	G	302 994-4014
Mary Dodson — Wilmington (G-11556)	G	302 479-0100
Maryruth L Nich — Newark (G-6998)	G	302 623-1929
Massage By Alicia — Wilmington (G-11563)	G	352 401-4328
Medical Massage Delaware LLC — Newark (G-7016)	G	888 757-1951
Melissa A Wolf — Lewes (G-3635)	G	716 465-7093
Michelle S Jones — Wilmington (G-11673)	G	302 651-4801
Mike Walsh Physical Therapy — Dover (G-1855)	G	302 724-5593
Nanticoke Memorial Hosp Inc — Seaford (G-8325)	G	302 629-6875
Naomi Ruth Howard — Smyrna (G-8684)	G	828 284-8721
New Perspectives Inc — Wilmington (G-11869)	G	302 489-0220
Norman S Broudy M D — Wilmington (G-11896)	G	302 655-7110
Nurse Next Door Home Care Svcs — Camden (G-594)	G	302 264-1021
Orthopaedic & Sports Phys — Wilmington (G-11977)	G	302 683-0782
Peak Cryotherapy — Wilmington (G-12057)	G	302 502-3160
Performance Physcl Therapy Inc — Hockessin (G-3115)	F	302 234-2288
Phoenix Rehabilitation and Hea — Milford (G-4526)	G	302 725-5720
Phoenix Rhbilitation Hlth Svcs — Wilmington (G-12125)	G	302 764-2008
Physical Therapist — Middletown (G-4190)	G	302 983-4151
Physical Therapy Services Inc — Wilmington (G-1955)	E	302 678-3100
Physiotherapy Associates Inc — Wilmington (G-12130)	G	302 655-8989
Physiotherapy Associates Inc — Dover (G-1957)	F	302 674-1269
Physiotherapy Associates Inc — Wilmington (G-12131)	G	610 444-1270
Physiotherapy Corporation — Seaford (G-8357)	G	302 628-8568
Pike Creek Psychological Ctr PA — Middletown (G-4192)	G	302 449-2223
Pike Creek Psychological Ctr PA — Newark (G-7217)	F	302 738-6859
Prelude Therapeutics Inc — Wilmington (G-12214)	E	302 644-5427
Premier Physical Therapy & — Smyrna (G-8691)	G	302 389-7855
Primary Care Delaware L L C — Dover (G-1986)	G	302 744-9645
Pro Physical Therapy PA — New Castle (G-5647)	F	302 654-1700
Pro Physl Therapy Ftns Acct — Wilmington (G-12234)	F	302 658-7800
Psychological Services — Wilmington (G-12262)	G	302 489-0213
Psychotherapeutic Services — Dover (G-1995)	G	302 678-9962
Reddish Walton — Seaford (G-8373)	G	302 629-4787
Rehabilitation Consultants Inc — Wilmington (G-12367)	E	302 478-5240
Roberto A Uribe PHD — Newark (G-7353)	G	302 524-0814
Samuel Blumberg PHD — Wilmington (G-12535)	G	302 652-7733
Select Physical Therapy — Dover (G-2067)	G	302 760-9966
Southern Del Physcl Therapy — Millsboro (G-4802)	G	302 947-4460
Southern Del Physcl Therapy — Georgetown (G-2660)	G	302 854-9600
Southern Del Physcl Therapy — Smyrna (G-8723)	G	302 659-0173
Southern Del Physcl Therapy — Rehoboth Beach (G-8083)	G	302 227-2008
Southern Del Physcl Therapy — Lewes (G-3757)	F	302 644-2530
Specialty Rehabilitation Inc — Newark (G-7468)	F	302 709-0440
Speech Clinic — Wilmington (G-12701)	E	302 999-0702
Speech Therapeutics Inc — Hockessin (G-3147)	G	302 234-9226
Spine & Orthopedic Specialist — Newark (G-7472)	G	302 633-1280
Tammy S Bennett — Laurel (G-3298)	G	302 875-6550
Thrive Physical Therapy — Middletown (G-4258)	G	302 834-8400
Tidewater Physcl Thrpy and REB — Milton (G-4976)	G	302 684-2829
Tidewater Physcl Thrpy and REB — Georgetown (G-2693)	G	302 856-2446
Tidewater Physcl Thrpy and REB — Harrington (G-2900)	G	302 398-7982
Tidewater Physcl Thrpy and REB — Ocean View (G-7821)	G	302 537-7260
Tidewater Physcl Thrpy and REB — Seaford (G-8422)	G	302 629-4024
Tidewater Physcl Thrpy and REB — Lewes (G-3784)	G	302 945-5111
Timothy W McHugh — Bear (G-353)	G	302 633-1280
Total Health & Rehabilitation — Wilmington (G-12939)	G	302 999-9202
Wellness Health Inc — Milford (G-4601)	G	302 424-4100
Wilderman Physical Therapy LLC — Wilmington (G-13201)	G	717 873-6836
Wilmington Psychiatric Svcs — Newark (G-7704)	G	302 999-8602
Woodlyn Physical Therapy Inc — Newark (G-7718)	G	610 583-1133
Yanez & De Yanez MD PC — Wilmington (G-13325)	G	302 655-2991
Zuber & Associates Inc — Wilmington (G-13353)	G	302 478-1618

8051 Skilled Nursing Facilities

Company	Code	Phone
100 St Clire Drv Oprations LLC — Hockessin (G-2945)	C	610 444-6350
100 St Clire Drv Oprations LLC — Hockessin (G-2946)	C	302 234-5420
1080 Slver Lk Blvd Oprtons LLC — Dover (G-1063)	C	610 444-6350
1203 Walker Rd Operations LLC — Dover (G-1064)	C	302 735-8800
1203 Walker Rd Operations LLC — Dover (G-1065)	A	610 444-6350
500 South Dupont Boule — Milford (G-4297)	E	302 422-8700
700 Marvel Road Operations LLC — Milford (G-4298)	A	302 422-3303
715 East King St Oprations LLC — Seaford (G-8134)	C	302 628-3000
810 Suth Broom St Oprtions LLC — Wilmington (G-8868)	C	302 655-1375
Beebe School of Nursing — Lewes (G-3375)	F	302 645-3251
Birth Center Holistic Women — Newark (G-6083)	F	302 658-2229

80 HEALTH SERVICES

Brandywine Nursing & Rehab .... C 302 683-0444
  Wilmington (G-9444)
Brandywine Snior Lving MGT LLC .... D 302 226-8750
  Rehoboth Beach (G-7874)
Cadbury At Lewes Inc .... D 302 644-6382
  Lewes (G-3399)
Cadia Rhabilitation Pike Creek .... E 302 455-0808
  Wilmington (G-9529)
Cadia Rhabilitation Silverside .... E 302 478-8889
  Wilmington (G-9530)
Cadia Rverside Healthcare Svcs .... G 302 455-0808
  Wilmington (G-9531)
Capitol Nursg & Rhb Cntr LLC .... C 302 734-1199
  Dover (G-1254)
Chancellor Care Ctr of Delmar .... C 302 846-3077
  Delmar (G-982)
Christiana Care Hlth Svcs Inc .... F 302 733-6510
  Newark (G-6218)
Churchman Village Center LLC .... G 302 998-6900
  Newark (G-6234)
Commonspirit Health .... D 302 234-5420
  Hockessin (G-2994)
Compassionate Care Hospice of .... D 302 994-1704
  Wilmington (G-9801)
Country Meadow Propco LLC .... G 330 633-0555
  Dover (G-1315)
Courtland Manor Inc .... D 302 674-0566
  Dover (G-1318)
Emeritus Corporation .... E 302 674-4407
  Dover (G-1517)
Exceptional Care For Children .... D 302 894-1001
  Newark (G-6551)
Five Star Quality Care Inc .... G 302 266-9255
  Newark (G-6592)
Five Star Quality Care Inc .... G 302 366-0160
  Newark (G-6593)
Five Star Quality Care Inc .... D 302 655-6249
  Wilmington (G-10568)
Five Star Quality Care Inc .... G 302 792-5115
  Wilmington (G-10569)
Five Star Senior Living Inc .... D 302 283-0540
  Newark (G-6594)
Five Star Senior Living Inc .... D 302 478-4296
  Wilmington (G-10570)
Genesis Eldercare Nat Ctrs Inc .... C 302 734-5990
  Dover (G-1588)
Genesis Halthcare - Main Voice .... G 302 536-6390
  Seaford (G-8251)
Genesis Healthcare Corporation .... G 302 422-3754
  Milford (G-4422)
Genesis Healthcare Seafood Ctr .... C 302 629-3575
  Seaford (G-8252)
Green Acres Health Systems .... C 302 934-7300
  Millsboro (G-4699)
Green Valley Pavilion .... E 302 653-5085
  Smyrna (G-8646)
Green Valley Terrace Snf LLC .... C 302 934-7300
  Millsboro (G-4700)
Greenvlle Retirement Cmnty LLC .... C 302 658-6200
  Wilmington (G-10781)
Harrison Snior Lving Gorgetown .... G 302 856-4574
  Georgetown (G-2555)
Hcr Manorcare Med Svcs Fla LLC .... C 302 239-8583
  Wilmington (G-10863)
Health & Social Svcs Del Dept .... A 302 223-1000
  Smyrna (G-8650)
Hillside Center .... F 302 652-1181
  Wilmington (G-10909)
Home For Aged Wmn-Mnquadale HM .... C 302 654-1810
  Wilmington (G-10935)
Home of Merciful Rest Society .... C 302 652-3311
  Wilmington (G-10939)
Ingleside Homes Inc .... E 302 984-0950
  Wilmington (G-11032)
Ivy Gables LLC .... F 302 475-9400
  Wilmington (G-11095)
Just Like Home .... G 302 653-0605
  Smyrna (G-8665)
Manor House .... F 302 629-4368
  Seaford (G-8301)
Milton & Hattie Kutz Home Inc .... C 302 764-7000
  Wilmington (G-11700)
New Castle HEAlth&rehab Cntr .... C 302 328-2580
  New Castle (G-5559)
Nursing Board .... G 302 744-4500
  Dover (G-1911)
Oak Hrc New Castle LLC .... D 302 328-2580
  New Castle (G-5584)
Odyssey Healthcare Inc .... E 302 478-1297
  Wilmington (G-11936)

Onix Silverside LLC .... D 484 731-2500
  Wilmington (G-11960)
Parkview Covalescent Center .... G 302 655-0955
  Wilmington (G-12025)
Peninsula Untd Mthdst Hmes Inc .... B 302 235-6810
  Hockessin (G-3113)
Peninsula Untd Mthdst Hmes Inc .... C 302 654-5101
  Wilmington (G-12064)
Presbyterian Senior Living .... C 302 744-3600
  Dover (G-1984)
Public Health Nursing .... F 302 856-5136
  Georgetown (G-2630)
Regal Hgts Hlthcare Ctr LLC .... D 302 998-0181
  Hockessin (G-3133)
Regency Hlthcare Rehab Ctr LLC .... C 302 654-8400
  Wilmington (G-12355)
Riverside Healthcare Center .... D 302 764-2615
  Wilmington (G-12429)
Rockland Place .... E 302 777-3099
  Wilmington (G-12453)
Steven E Diamond M D .... G 302 655-8868
  Wilmington (G-12760)
Summit Retirement Community .... F 888 933-2300
  Hockessin (G-3154)
Sunrise Senior Living LLC .... D 302 475-9163
  Wilmington (G-12801)
Weston Senior Living Center .... F 302 994-4434
  Wilmington (G-13170)

8052 Intermediate Care Facilities

Brookdale Senior Living Inc .... E 302 239-3200
  Hockessin (G-2970)
Chancellor Care Ctr of Delmar .... C 302 846-3077
  Delmar (G-982)
Community Alternatives Ind Inc .... F 302 323-1436
  New Castle (G-5187)
Community Systems and Svcs Inc ...... C 302 325-1500
  New Castle (G-5189)
Compassionate Care .... G 302 654-5401
  Wilmington (G-9799)
Compassionate Care Hospi of Ce ...... G 302 993-9090
  Wilmington (G-9800)
Delaware Hospice .... G 302 934-9018
  Millsboro (G-4675)
Delaware Hospice Inc .... D 302 478-5707
  Newark (G-6384)
Elderly Comfort Corporation .... F 302 530-6680
  Wilmington (G-10367)
Home of Merciful Rest Society .... C 302 652-3311
  Wilmington (G-10939)
Ingleside Homes Inc .... E 302 984-0950
  Wilmington (G-11032)
Little Sisters of The Poor .... D 302 368-5886
  Newark (G-6941)
Lutheran Senior Services Inc .... E 302 654-4490
  Wilmington (G-11454)
Martin Luther Homes East Inc .... G 302 475-4920
  Wilmington (G-11550)
Mary Campbell Center Inc .... G 302 762-6025
  Wilmington (G-11555)
Milton & Hattie Kutz Home Inc .... C 302 764-7000
  Wilmington (G-11700)
Mosaic .... C 302 456-5995
  Newark (G-7060)
Mosaic .... C 302 456-5995
  Newark (G-7062)
Mossaic .... G 302 428-1680
  Wilmington (G-11762)
Premier Healthcare Inc .... E 302 731-5576
  Wilmington (G-7244)
RES-Care Inc .... E 302 323-1436
  New Castle (G-5673)
Seaside Pointe .... G 302 226-8750
  Rehoboth Beach (G-8072)
Seasons Hspice Plltive Care De ...... E 847 692-1000
  Newark (G-7399)
Summit At Hockessin .... G 302 235-8388
  Hockessin (G-3153)

8059 Nursing & Personal Care Facilities, NEC

A and H Nursing Administra .... G 302 544-4474
  Bear (G-3)
Akzo Nobel Inc .... G 312 544-7000
  Millsboro (G-4625)
Bk Temp Home Care .... G 302 575-1400
  Wilmington (G-9345)
Bove Psychological Svcs LLC .... G 302 299-5193
  Wilmington (G-9400)
Broadmeadow Investment LLC .... C 302 449-3400
  Middletown (G-3977)

Brookdale Senior Living Inc .... E 302 239-3200
  Hockessin (G-2970)
Capitol Nursg & Rhb Cntr LLC .... C 302 734-1199
  Dover (G-1254)
Courtland Manor Inc .... D 302 674-0566
  Dover (G-1318)
E I Du Pont De Nemours & Co .... E 302 774-1000
  Newark (G-6489)
Edlyncare LLC .... G 267 474-0486
  Middletown (G-4050)
Green Valley Pavilion .... E 302 653-5085
  Smyrna (G-8646)
Hillside Center .... F 302 652-1181
  Wilmington (G-10909)
Infusion Care Delaware Home .... G 302 423-2511
  Wilmington (G-11028)
Kreske Kares LLC .... G 302 893-5600
  Bear (G-223)
Lauren Farms Group Home .... G 302 836-1379
  Bear (G-230)
Little Sisters of The Poor .... D 302 368-5886
  Newark (G-6941)
Lodge Lane Assisted Living .... E 302 757-8100
  Wilmington (G-11424)
Macklyn Home Care .... G 302 253-8208
  Georgetown (G-2594)
Miss Kittys Kiddies .... G 302 571-1547
  Wilmington (G-11712)
Nicole L Scott Np-C Adult .... G 302 690-1692
  Hockessin (G-3104)
North Eastern Waffles LLC .... G 302 697-2226
  Dover (G-1901)
Oncology Care Home .... G 610 274-2437
  Newark (G-7149)
Peninsula Home Care LLC .... G 302 629-4914
  Seaford (G-8347)
Presbyterian Senior Living .... C 302 744-3600
  Dover (G-1984)
PSC Technology Incorporated .... G 866 866-1466
  Lewes (G-3701)
Quality Care Homes LLC .... G 302 858-3999
  Lewes (G-3702)
Quality Lawn Care Home RE .... G 302 331-5892
  Camden Wyoming (G-652)
Serenity Gardens Assisted Livi .... F 302 442-5330
  Middletown (G-4237)
Solution On-Call Services LLC .... E 302 353-4328
  New Castle (G-5722)
Ten Blade Enterprises LLC .... G 484 843-4811
  Wilmington (G-12882)
Turning Pt Counseling Ctr LLC .... G 214 883-5148
  Camden (G-602)
United Adult Care Ltd .... G 302 725-0708
  Harrington (G-2902)

8062 General Medical & Surgical Hospitals

Ai Dupont Hosp For Children .... A 302 651-4620
  Wilmington (G-8984)
Atlantic General Hospital Corp .... F 302 524-5007
  Selbyville (G-8451)
Bayhealth Med Ctr Inc-OCC Hlth .... E 302 678-1303
  Dover (G-1180)
Bayhealth Medical Center Inc .... A 302 422-3311
  Milford (G-4320)
Bayhealth Medical Center Inc .... E 302 422-3311
  Dover (G-1182)
Bayview Endoscopy Center .... F 302 644-0455
  Lewes (G-3365)
Beebe Healthcare .... G 302 934-5052
  Millsboro (G-4641)
Beebe Hospital Hs .... G 302 645-3565
  Lewes (G-3369)
Beebe Medical Center Inc .... C 302 645-3100
  Rehoboth Beach (G-7862)
Beebe Medical Center Inc .... A 302 645-3300
  Lewes (G-3370)
Beebe Medical Center Inc .... C 302 645-3300
  Lewes (G-3371)
Beebe Medical Center Inc .... E 302 645-3629
  Lewes (G-3372)
Beebe Medical Center Inc .... G 302 947-9767
  Millsboro (G-4642)
Beebe Medical Center Inc .... G 302 856-9729
  Georgetown (G-2453)
Brandywine Veterinary Hospital .... G 302 476-8779
  Wilmington (G-9460)
Brian Costleigh LLC .... G 302 645-3775
  Rehoboth Beach (G-7876)
Cancer Care Ctrs At Bay Hlth .... F 302 674-4401
  Dover (G-1249)

80 HEALTH SERVICES

Company	Code	Phone
Catholic Health East New Castle *(G-5137)*	G	302 325-4900
Cedar Tree Surgical Center Millsboro *(G-4658)*	F	302 945-9766
Central Del Endoscopy Unit Dover *(G-1264)*	G	302 677-1617
Central Delaware Surgery Ctr Dover *(G-1268)*	F	302 744-6801
Christana Care Vsclar Spcalist Newark *(G-6203)*	F	302 733-5700
Christiana Care Wilmington *(G-9675)*	G	302 654-4925
Christiana Care Wilmington *(G-9676)*	F	302 633-3750
Christiana Care Health Sys Inc Wilmington *(G-9677)*	F	302 623-7500
Christiana Care Health Sys Inc Newark *(G-6212)*	G	302 733-1000
Christiana Care Health Sys Inc Middletown *(G-3988)*	G	302 449-3000
Christiana Care Health Sys Inc Newark *(G-6213)*	G	302 733-5700
Christiana Care Health Sys Inc Wilmington *(G-9679)*	C	302 733-1000
Christiana Care Hlth Svcs Inc New Castle *(G-5154)*	F	302 327-5820
Christiana Care Hlth Svcs Inc Newark *(G-6215)*	B	302 733-1900
Christiana Care Hlth Svcs Inc New Castle *(G-5155)*	C	302 327-3959
Christiana Care Hlth Svcs Inc Newark *(G-6216)*	E	302 733-5437
Christiana Care Hlth Svcs Inc Newark *(G-6217)*	C	302 623-7201
Christiana Care Hlth Svcs Inc Wilmington *(G-9684)*	G	302 733-1805
Cuhiana Care Health System Newark *(G-6325)*	G	302 733-1780
Cynthia Crosser DC Fiama Wilmington *(G-9933)*	G	302 239-5014
David E Driban New Castle *(G-5216)*	G	302 322-0860
Delaware Bay Surgical Svc PA Lewes *(G-3454)*	F	302 645-5650
Delaware Center For Oral Srgry Newark *(G-6367)*	F	302 369-1000
Delaware Outpatient Center Newark *(G-6401)*	D	302 738-0300
Endoscopy Center of Deleware Newark *(G-6527)*	F	302 892-2710
Envision Healthcare Corp Lewes *(G-3485)*	F	302 644-3852
Frenius Medical Care Wilmington *(G-10633)*	G	302 421-9177
Healthpartners Delmarva LLC Dover *(G-1641)*	G	302 744-6008
Hospitalists of Delaware Wilmington *(G-10958)*	G	302 984-2577
Iqarus Americas Inc Wilmington *(G-11081)*	E	407 222-5726
Jr Board of Kent Gen Hospital Dover *(G-1710)*	G	302 744-7128
Kent General Hospital Dover *(G-1734)*	G	302 744-7688
Kent General Hospital Middletown *(G-4120)*	G	302 378-1199
Kent General Hospital Dover *(G-1735)*	D	302 674-4700
Kent General Hospital Milford *(G-4463)*	E	302 430-5731
Kent General Hospital Smyrna *(G-8667)*	G	302 653-2010
Nemours Foundation Wilmington *(G-11833)*	A	302 651-4000
North Wilmington Womens Center Wilmington *(G-11902)*	G	302 529-7900
Peninsula Regional Medical Ctr Selbyville *(G-8529)*	G	302 436-8004
Peninsula Regional Medical Ctr Dagsboro *(G-929)*	F	302 732-8400
Rockford Center Newark *(G-7354)*	D	302 996-5480
Route 24 Animal Hospital Millsboro *(G-4796)*	G	302 945-2330
Select Medical Corporation Wilmington *(G-12574)*	D	302 421-4545
Southern Delaware Surgery Ctr Rehoboth Beach *(G-8084)*	F	302 644-6992
St Francis Family Care New Castle *(G-5734)*	G	302 554-5127
St Francis Hospital Newark *(G-7477)*	G	302 369-9370
St Francis Hospital Inc Wilmington *(G-12722)*	A	616 685-3538
Trinity Health Corporation Wilmington *(G-12976)*	F	302 421-4100
Womens Health Ctr Christn Care Wilmington *(G-13292)*	F	302 428-5810
World Hospital Inc Bear *(G-380)*	G	609 254-3391

8063 Psychiatric Hospitals

Company	Code	Phone
Alternative Solutions Georgetown *(G-2429)*	G	302 542-9081
Children Youth & Their Fam New Castle *(G-5147)*	D	302 577-4270
Health & Social Svcs Del Dept New Castle *(G-5384)*	F	302 255-2700
Health & Social Svcs Del Dept New Castle *(G-5386)*	A	302 255-2700
Phc Inc New Castle *(G-5621)*	F	313 831-3500
Psychotherapeutic Services Dover *(G-1994)*	E	302 672-7159
Rockford Center Newark *(G-7354)*	D	302 996-5480
Social Health Innovations Inc Dover *(G-2091)*	G	917 476-9355

8069 Specialty Hospitals, Except Psychiatric

Company	Code	Phone
1212 Corporation Wilmington *(G-8844)*	G	302 764-4048
Advanced Treatment Systems Claymont *(G-687)*	F	302 792-0700
Aquila of Delaware Inc Georgetown *(G-2432)*	G	302 856-9746
B M A Central Delaware Dover *(G-1165)*	G	302 678-5718
Brandywine Counseling Newark *(G-6116)*	F	302 454-3020
Central Delaware Committee Georgetown *(G-2466)*	G	302 854-0172
Children Fmilies First Del Inc Georgetown *(G-2468)*	E	302 856-2388
Compassionate Care Hospice Georgetown *(G-2480)*	G	302 856-1486
Crest Central Dover *(G-1322)*	F	302 736-0576
Encompass Health Corporation Middletown *(G-4058)*	C	302 464-3400
Gina Madaline MS CCC/Slp Wilmington *(G-10713)*	G	302 220-0931
Health & Social Svcs Del Dept Smyrna *(G-8650)*	A	302 223-1000
Home of Divine Providence Inc Wilmington *(G-10938)*	G	302 654-1184
Horizon House Inc Claymont *(G-764)*	G	302 798-1960
Jamie H Keskeny Wilmington *(G-11126)*	G	302 651-6060
Lawall Prosthetics - Orthotics Dover *(G-1769)*	G	302 677-0693
Otolaryngology Consultants New Castle *(G-5593)*	G	302 328-1331
Presbyterian Senior Living Dover *(G-1984)*	C	302 744-3600
Select Specialty Hospital Wilmington *(G-12575)*	D	302 421-4590
Thresholds Inc Lewes *(G-3783)*	G	302 827-4478
Westside N Begnings Yth Imprvm Rehoboth Beach *(G-8113)*	G	302 227-5442

8071 Medical Laboratories

Company	Code	Phone
Agro Lab Harrington *(G-2805)*	G	302 265-2734
Allied Diagnstc Pathology Cons Wilmington *(G-9021)*	G	302 575-8103
Arcpoint Labs Wilmington *(G-9125)*	G	302 268-6560
Armed Forces Med Examiner Sys Dover *(G-1137)*	D	302 346-8653
Beebe Medical Foundation Milton *(G-4868)*	G	302 684-8579
Brandywine Imaging LLC Wilmington *(G-9440)*	E	302 654-5300
Breast Imaging Center Newark *(G-6117)*	E	302 623-9729
CD Diagnostics Inc Claymont *(G-709)*	F	302 367-7770
Christiana Care Health Sys Inc Newark *(G-6207)*	B	302 733-1601
Clinical Breast Imaging Wilmington *(G-9743)*	G	302 658-4800
Clinpharma Clinical RES LLC Wilmington *(G-9744)*	G	646 961-3437
Cogtest Inc Newark *(G-6259)*	F	302 454-1265
Delaware Clinical & Labortry Wilmington *(G-10019)*	G	302 999-8095
Delaware Diagnostic Labs LLC Newark *(G-6376)*	G	302 996-9585
Delaware Imaging Network Middletown *(G-4028)*	G	302 449-5400
Delaware Imaging Network Newark *(G-6388)*	F	302 644-2590
Delaware Public Health Lab Smyrna *(G-8620)*	G	302 223-1520
Delaware Womens Imaging LLC Newark *(G-6422)*	E	302 738-9100
Exalenz Bioscience Inc Wilmington *(G-10456)*	G	888 392-5369
F P T & W Medical Associates Wilmington *(G-10469)*	F	800 421-2368
◆ Glaxosmithkline Holdings Wilmington *(G-10720)*	C	302 984-6932
Laboratory Corporation America Smyrna *(G-8669)*	G	302 653-5119
Laboratory Corporation America Wilmington *(G-11315)*	G	302 651-9502
Laboratory Corporation America Dover *(G-1763)*	G	302 735-4694
Laboratory Corporation America Middletown *(G-4126)*	G	302 376-6146
Laboratory Corporation America Middletown *(G-4127)*	G	302 449-0246
Laboratory Corporation America Seaford *(G-8289)*	G	302 629-3182
Laboratory Corporation America New Castle *(G-5472)*	G	302 655-5673
Laboratory Corporation America Bear *(G-227)*	G	302 834-6845
Laboratory Corporation America Newark *(G-6908)*	G	302 834-1359
Laboratory Corporation America Newark *(G-6909)*	E	302 737-3525
Laboratory Corporation America Wilmington *(G-11316)*	E	302 798-2520
Laboratory Corporation America Wilmington *(G-11317)*	E	302 998-7340
Laboratory Corporation America Wilmington *(G-11318)*	G	302 994-8575
Laboratory Corporation America Hockessin *(G-3076)*	E	302 234-0493
Laboratory Corporation America Newark *(G-6910)*	G	302 731-0244
Maria Lazar MD Newark *(G-6986)*	G	302 838-2210
Medlab Environmental Testing New Castle *(G-5514)*	G	302 655-5227
Molecular Imaging Services Inc Bear *(G-257)*	G	302 450-4505
Omega Imaging Associates LLC Wilmington *(G-11947)*	G	302 654-5245
Omega Imaging Associates LLC Wilmington *(G-11948)*	F	302 995-2037
Paul Renzi Wilmington *(G-12043)*	G	302 478-3166
Professional Imaging Smyrna *(G-8694)*	G	302 653-3522
Quest Diagnostics Incorporated New Castle *(G-5659)*	F	302 322-4651
Quest Diagnostics Incorporated Millville *(G-4853)*	F	302 537-3862
Quest Diagnostics Incorporated Milford *(G-4532)*	G	302 424-4504
Quest Diagnostics Incorporated Wilmington *(G-12286)*	G	302 478-1100
Quest Diagnostics Incorporated Seaford *(G-8366)*	G	302 628-3078
Quest Diagnostics Incorporated Wilmington *(G-12287)*	F	302 239-5273
Quest Diagnostics Incorporated Dover *(G-2003)*	G	302 735-4555
Quest Diagnostics Incorporated Newark *(G-7287)*	G	302 455-0720
Quest Diagnostics Incorporated Middletown *(G-4205)*	G	302 376-8675

Employee Codes: A=Over 500 employees, B=251-500, C=101-250, D=51-100, E=20-50, F=10-19, G=1-9

8072 Dental Laboratories

All Denture Center ....F 302 656-8202
Wilmington *(G-9013)*
Chromium Dental LLC ....F 302 731-5582
Newark *(G-6233)*
Mittelman Dental Lab ....F 302 798-7440
Claymont *(G-784)*
National Dentex LLC ....D 302 661-6000
New Castle *(G-5544)*
Precision Dental Laboratory ....G 302 478-5608
Wilmington *(G-12203)*
Sonshine Dental Labs Inc ....F 302 731-5582
Newark *(G-7459)*
Welsh Family Dentistry ....G 302 836-3711
Hockessin *(G-3172)*
Wilmington & Newark Dental ....G 302 571-0526
Wilmington *(G-13222)*

8082 Home Health Care Svcs

Acts Rtrmnt-Life Cmmnities Inc ....A 302 654-5101
Wilmington *(G-8928)*
Addus Healthcare Inc ....G 302 995-9010
Wilmington *(G-8936)*
Addus Healthcare Inc ....E 302 424-4842
Milford *(G-4302)*
Aegle Health ....G 302 468-0235
New Castle *(G-5012)*
Affinity Homecare Services ....G 302 264-9363
Dover *(G-1091)*
Almost Home Day Care ....G 302 220-6731
Newark *(G-5946)*
Always Best Care ....G 302 409-3710
Milton *(G-4862)*
Amedisys Inc ....E 302 678-4764
Dover *(G-1117)*
Anderson Lawn & Home Care ....G 302 376-7115
Middletown *(G-3938)*
Angels Visiting ....G 302 691-8700
Wilmington *(G-9085)*
At Home Care Agency ....G 302 883-2059
Dover *(G-1151)*
At Home Infucare LLC ....G 302 883-2059
Dover *(G-1152)*
Atkins Home Health Aid Agency ....G 302 832-0315
Bear *(G-42)*
Bayada Home Health Care Inc ....D 302 424-8200
Milford *(G-4319)*
Bayada Home Health Care Inc ....D 302 655-1333
Wilmington *(G-9263)*
Bayada Home Health Care Inc ....F 856 231-1000
New Castle *(G-5073)*
Bayada Home Health Care Inc ....G 302 322-2300
New Castle *(G-5074)*
Bayada Home Health Care Inc ....F 302 836-1000
Newark *(G-6055)*
Bayada Home Health Care Inc ....G 302 655-1333
Wilmington *(G-9264)*
Bc Home Health Care Services ....G 302 746-7844
Claymont *(G-700)*
Bills Home Care Service LLC ....G 302 526-2071
Dover *(G-1203)*
Biotek Remedys Inc ....E 877 246-9104
New Castle *(G-5092)*
Blue Ridge Home Care Inc ....G 302 397-8211
Dover *(G-1215)*
By The Shore ....G 302 462-0496
Milton *(G-4871)*
Cain Home Health Services ....F 302 268-6919
Wilmington *(G-9535)*
Careportmd LLC ....F 302 202-3020
Wilmington *(G-9567)*
Caring For Life Inc ....E 302 892-2214
New Castle *(G-5133)*
Caring Hearts Home Care LLC ....G 302 734-9000
Hartly *(G-2914)*
Caring Matters Home Care ....G 302 993-1121
Camden *(G-545)*
Caroline M Wiesner ....G 877 220-9755
Wilmington *(G-9575)*
Carpe Vita Home Care ....G 302 482-4305
Wilmington *(G-9576)*
Chesapeakecaregivers LLC ....G 302 841-9686
Seaford *(G-8192)*
Christana Care HM Hlth Cmnty S ....B 302 327-5583
New Castle *(G-5152)*
Christiana Care Home Health ....F 302 995-8448
Wilmington *(G-9685)*
Christiana Care Home Health ....F 302 698-4300
Camden *(G-549)*
Christiana Care Infusion ....G 302 623-0345
Newark *(G-6219)*
Cindys Home Away From Hme Fam ....G 302 378-0487
Middletown *(G-3991)*
Comfort Care At Home Inc ....E 302 737-8078
Newark *(G-6266)*
Comfort Keepers ....G 302 378-0994
Townsend *(G-8771)*
Dedicated To Home Care LLC ....G 484 470-5013
New Castle *(G-5220)*
Delaware Home Health Care ....F 302 856-3600
Georgetown *(G-2500)*
Delaware Hospice Inc ....E 302 678-4444
Dover *(G-1378)*
Delaware Hospice Inc ....E 302 856-7717
Milford *(G-4379)*
Dover Health Care Center LLC ....G 302 270-5238
Dover *(G-1452)*
Envolve Inc ....B 314 349-3571
Wilmington *(G-10423)*
Epic Health Services Inc ....G 302 504-4092
Christiana *(G-668)*
Excellent Home Care ....G 302 327-0147
New Castle *(G-5299)*
Expert Home Care ....G 856 870-6691
Middletown *(G-4066)*
Fogarty LLC ....G 610 731-4804
Seaford *(G-8246)*
General Hlthcare Resources LLC ....C 302 998-0469
Wilmington *(G-10691)*
Generations Home Care Inc ....E 302 322-3100
Wilmington *(G-10692)*
Grace Visitation Services ....D 302 329-9475
Milton *(G-4909)*
Griswold Home Care ....G 302 750-4564
Wilmington *(G-10787)*
Hallies Helping Hands Home ....G 844 277-8911
Townsend *(G-8792)*
Health Care Consultants Inc ....C 302 892-9210
Wilmington *(G-10869)*
Healthy At Home Care LLC ....G 571 228-5935
Rehoboth Beach *(G-7958)*
Heartland Hospice Services LLC ....D 302 737-7080
Newark *(G-6718)*
Heartland Hospice Services LLC ....D 419 252-5743
Newark *(G-6719)*
Home Care Assistance De ....G 856 625-9934
Bear *(G-186)*
Home Health Corp America Inc ....F 302 678-4764
Dover *(G-1653)*
Home Health Heartfel ....G 302 660-2686
Wilmington *(G-10936)*
Home Health Services By TLC ....E 302 322-5510
Wilmington *(G-10937)*
Home Instead Senior Care ....G 302 697-6435
Dover *(G-1654)*
Homewatch Caregivers ....G 302 644-1888
Lewes *(G-3545)*
Homewatch Caregivers LLC ....F 302 691-5358
Wilmington *(G-10944)*
Ind Swift Laboratories Inc ....G 302 233-1564
Dover *(G-1670)*
Ingleside Homes Inc ....D 302 575-0250
Wilmington *(G-11031)*
Interim Healthcare Del LLC ....C 302 322-2743
Smyrna *(G-8658)*
Kindheart Homecare ....G 484 479-6582
Middletown *(G-4124)*
La Red Health Care ....G 757 709-5072
Georgetown *(G-2586)*
Lieske E2e Home Hlth Care Inc ....E 302 898-1563
Middletown *(G-4131)*
Lifetime Skills Services LLC ....E 302 378-2911
Middletown *(G-4132)*
Lynne Betts ....G 302 265-5602
Seaford *(G-8298)*
Macklyn Home Care ....G 302 690-9397
Wilmington *(G-11481)*
Macklyn Home Care ....G 302 253-8208
Georgetown *(G-2594)*
Maxim Healthcare Services Inc ....F 302 478-3434
Wilmington *(G-11579)*
Mayjuun LLC ....G 865 300-7738
Lewes *(G-3628)*
National Mentor Holdings Inc ....E 732 627-9890
Millsboro *(G-4760)*
National Mentor Holdings Inc ....F 302 934-0512
Millsboro *(G-4761)*
Near and Dear Home Care ....G 302 530-6498
Newark *(G-7088)*
Neighborly Home Care ....G 610 420-1868
Wilmington *(G-11831)*
No Place Like Home LLC ....G 302 528-8682
Bear *(G-266)*
Nurse Next Door Home Care Svcs ....G 302 264-1021
Camden *(G-594)*
Nurses N Kids Inc ....E 302 424-1770
Milford *(G-4515)*
Option Care Enterprises Inc ....E 302 355-6100
Newark *(G-7158)*
Pennsula Home Care LLC ....G 302 629-4914
Seaford *(G-8351)*
Perry & Assoc ....G 302 472-8701
Wilmington *(G-12088)*
Philadelph Ft Ankl Asscts ....G 215 465-5342
Wilmington *(G-12112)*
Phyllis M Green ....G 302 354-6986
Bear *(G-283)*
Premier Immediate Med Care LLC ....G 610 226-6200
Hockessin *(G-3125)*
Private Duty Home Care ....G 302 482-3502
Wilmington *(G-12232)*
Pro 2 Respiratory Services ....G 302 514-9843
Smyrna *(G-8693)*
R&R Homecare ....G 302 478-3448
Wilmington *(G-12299)*
Ridgaway Philips of Delaware ....G 302 323-1436
New Castle *(G-5679)*
Right At Home ....G 302 652-1550
Wilmington *(G-12422)*
Robert Bird ....F 302 654-4003
Wilmington *(G-12435)*
Saint Home Health Care ....G 302 514-9597
Milford *(G-4551)*
Senior Home Help LLC ....G 302 335-4243
Felton *(G-2320)*
Seniortech Inc ....G 302 234-1274
Hockessin *(G-3143)*
Shorecare of Delaware ....G 302 724-5235
Dover *(G-2080)*
Shorecare of Delaware ....G 302 724-5235
Dover *(G-2081)*
Special Care Inc ....F 302 644-6990
Lewes *(G-3760)*
Special Care Inc ....G 302 456-9904
Wilmington *(G-12695)*
T & L Consulting Services LLC ....G 302 573-1585
Wilmington *(G-12843)*
TLC Home Care ....G 302 983-5720
Wilmington *(G-12917)*
Trinity Home Health Care Corp ....E 302 838-2710
Newark *(G-7594)*
Trinity Home Health Care LLC ....G 410 620-9366
Newark *(G-7595)*
Vitas Healthcare Corporation ....D 302 451-4000
Newark *(G-7661)*
Vna of Delaware ....G 302 454-5422
Newark *(G-7663)*
▲ **Wow Tech USA Ltd** ....G 613 828-6678
Wilmington *(G-13306)*

8092 Kidney Dialysis Centers

Bio-Mdcal Applications Del Inc ....G 302 366-0129
Newark *(G-6081)*
Bio-Mdical Applications of Del ....E 302 998-7568
Newark *(G-6082)*
DSI Laurel LLC ....D 302 715-3060
Laurel *(G-3224)*
Fresenius Med Care S Delaware ....F 302 934-6342
Millsboro *(G-4694)*
Fresenius Med Cre N Delaware ....E 302 239-4704
Hockessin *(G-3032)*
Fresenius Medical Care ....E 302 736-1340
Dover *(G-1567)*
Fresenius Medical Care ....E 302 337-8789
Bridgeville *(G-473)*
Fresenius Medical Care N Amer ....F 302 328-9044
New Castle *(G-5330)*
Fresenius Medical Care N Amer ....G 302 633-6228
Wilmington *(G-10635)*
Fresenius Medical Care Nephr ....G 302 836-6093
Bear *(G-161)*
Fresenius Medical Care Vero Be ....E 302 453-8834
Newark *(G-6621)*
Fresenius Usa Inc ....F 302 422-9739
Milford *(G-4417)*
Fresenius Usa Inc ....E 302 455-0454
Newark *(G-6622)*
Fresenius Usa Inc ....E 302 658-7469
Wilmington *(G-10636)*

Liberty Dalysis Wilmington LLC ....F 302 429-0142
Wilmington *(G-11379)*
National Medical Care Inc ....F 302 658-7469
Wilmington *(G-11808)*
Renal Care Center Dover ....E 302 678-5718
Dover *(G-2025)*
Renal Care Group Inc ....E 302 678-8744
Dover *(G-2026)*

8093 Specialty Outpatient Facilities, NEC

Acupoint Therapeutics ....G 302 734-7716
Dover *(G-1085)*
Advanced Behavioral Care Inc ....G 410 599-7400
Lewes *(G-3326)*
Advancexing Pain & Rehabltatn ....F 302 384-7439
Newark *(G-5910)*
Ah Therapy Services LLC ....G 302 379-0528
Wilmington *(G-8982)*
All The Difference Inc ....F 302 738-6353
Newark *(G-5936)*
Angelic Therapy ....G 717 870-4618
Lewes *(G-3339)*
Aod Smyma 43 ....G 302 659-5060
Smyrna *(G-8573)*
Applied Biofeedback Solutions ....G 302 674-3225
Dover *(G-1132)*
ARS New Castle LLC ....G 302 323-9400
New Castle *(G-5046)*
Barker Benchark Therpy & Rehab ....G 302 659-7552
Smyrna *(G-8580)*
Behavioral Health Assoc ....G 302 429-6200
Wilmington *(G-9282)*
Body Ease Therapy ....G 610 314-0780
Newark *(G-6103)*
Body/Mind & Spirit Massage Thr ....G 302 453-8151
Newark *(G-6104)*
Brandywine Counseling ....D 302 655-9880
Wilmington *(G-9427)*
Brandywine Occpational Therapy ....G 302 740-4798
Wilmington *(G-9446)*
Brownstarr Therapy ....G 302 838-2645
Newark *(G-6127)*
Capitol Nursg & Rhb Cntr LLC ....C 302 734-1199
Dover *(G-1254)*
Cardio-Kinetics Inc ....E 302 738-6635
Newark *(G-6152)*
Central Delaware Committee ....E 302 735-7790
Dover *(G-1265)*
Chelsea McHugh Music Therapy ....G 302 827-2335
Milton *(G-4878)*
Christiana Care Health Sys Inc ....F 302 623-0390
Newark *(G-6208)*
Christina Care Vna ....E 302 327-5212
New Castle *(G-5159)*
Chuck B Barker Pt Dpt Ocs Atc ....G 302 730-4800
Dover *(G-1281)*
Connections ....G 302 221-6605
New Castle *(G-5190)*
Connections Community Support ....D 302 653-1505
Smyrna *(G-8604)*
Connections Community Support ....D 302 536-1952
Seaford *(G-8204)*
Connections CSP Inc Dover ....G 302 672-9276
Dover *(G-1311)*
Corinthian House ....G 302 858-1493
Georgetown *(G-2485)*
Corizon LLC ....F 302 998-3958
Wilmington *(G-9862)*
Defy Therapy Services LLC ....G 302 290-9562
Wilmington *(G-9995)*
Delaware Back PAln&sprts Rehab ....D 302 529-8783
Newark *(G-6364)*
Delaware Councl On Gmblng Prbl ....G 302 655-3261
Wilmington *(G-10027)*
Delaware Curative Workshop ....D 302 656-2521
Wilmington *(G-10033)*
Delaware Rehabilitation Inst ....G 302 831-0315
Newark *(G-6407)*
Delaware Spine Rehabilitation ....G 302 883-2292
Dover *(G-1394)*
Delmarva Surgery Ctr ....G 443 245-3470
Newark *(G-6430)*
Dima II Inc ....G 302 427-0787
Wilmington *(G-10155)*
Doris V Obenshain ....G 302 448-1450
Middletown *(G-4043)*
Dynamic Therapy Services LLC ....G 302 280-6953
Laurel *(G-3225)*
Dynamic Therapy Services LLC ....G 302 566-6624
Harrington *(G-2836)*
Easter Seal Delaware ....E 302 678-3353
Dover *(G-1499)*
Elwyn ....D 302 658-8860
Wilmington *(G-10385)*
Emory Massage Therapy ....G 302 290-0003
Dover *(G-1520)*
Empowered Therapy Services ....G 302 234-4820
Hockessin *(G-3021)*
Family Planning ....G 302 856-5225
Georgetown *(G-2525)*
Fellowship Hlth Resources Inc ....G 302 422-6699
Milford *(G-4412)*
First State Rehab Home LLC ....G 443 252-7367
Wilmington *(G-10553)*
Focus Behavioral Health ....F 302 762-2285
Wilmington *(G-10584)*
Focus Health Care Delaware LLC ....D 302 395-1111
New Castle *(G-5322)*
Foundtion For A Btter Tomorrow ....G 302 674-1397
Dover *(G-1563)*
Golo LLC ....G 302 635-7245
Newark *(G-6673)*
Health & Social Svcs Del Dept ....F 302 368-6700
Newark *(G-6716)*
Health & Social Svcs Del Dept ....G 302 283-7500
Newark *(G-6717)*
Health & Social Svcs Del Dept ....D 302 857-5000
Dover *(G-1639)*
Henlopen Music Therapy SE ....G 302 593-7784
Lewes *(G-3542)*
Hogar Crea Int of Delaware ....G 302 762-2875
Wilmington *(G-10925)*
Hope Rising Therapy ....G 302 273-3194
Newark *(G-6744)*
Hudson House Services ....G 302 856-4363
Georgetown *(G-2563)*
Hysiotherapy Associates Inc ....E 610 444-1270
Wilmington *(G-10983)*
Informed Touch Massage Therapy ....G 302 229-8239
Townsend *(G-8796)*
Intouch Body Therapy LLC ....G 302 537-0510
Bethany Beach *(G-404)*
Iveeapp Corp ....G 610 999-6290
Wilmington *(G-11094)*
Jan Stern Eqine Asssted Thrapy ....G 302 234-9835
Wilmington *(G-11127)*
Jennifer Lopez Moya Rpt ....G 302 836-1495
Newark *(G-6832)*
Joselow Beth Lpcmh ....G 302 644-0130
Lewes *(G-3578)*
Kenneth Butler ....G 302 561-8114
Newark *(G-6874)*
Kent Sussex Community Services ....F 302 384-6926
Dover *(G-1740)*
Lake Therapy Creations ....G 410 920-7130
Newark *(G-6913)*
Lewes Expressive Therapy ....G 302 727-3275
Lewes *(G-3599)*
Management Pain LLC ....G 302 543-5180
Wilmington *(G-11499)*
Marc Wsburg Lpcmh Mntal Hlth C ....G 302 798-4400
Wilmington *(G-11520)*
Matrix Rehabilitation Delaware ....G 302 424-1714
Milford *(G-4490)*
McCormick Assoc Middletown LLC ....G 302 449-0710
Middletown *(G-4149)*
Medi-Weightloss Clinics ....G 302 763-3455
Hockessin *(G-3093)*
Mend ME Massage Therapy Inc ....G 302 229-1250
Wilmington *(G-11630)*
Mental Health Assn In Del ....G 302 654-6833
Wilmington *(G-11632)*
Midatlantic Pain Institute ....D 302 369-1700
Newark *(G-7034)*
Moore Physcial Therapy ....G 302 654-8142
Wilmington *(G-11746)*
National Stress Clinic LLC ....G 646 571-8627
Wilmington *(G-11812)*
Necessary Luxury ....G 302 764-4032
Wilmington *(G-11827)*
Nemours Foundation ....A 302 651-4000
Wilmington *(G-11836)*
Northeast Treatment Ctrs Inc ....E 302 691-0140
Wilmington *(G-11904)*
Novacare Rehabilitation ....G 302 537-7762
Ocean View *(G-7805)*
Novacare Rehabilitation ....G 302 597-9256
Bear *(G-268)*
Novacare Rehabilitation Dover ....G 302 760-9966
Dover *(G-1905)*
Novacare Rehabilitation Seafor ....G 302 990-2951
Seaford *(G-8332)*
Occupational Therapy Sour ....G 302 234-2273
Hockessin *(G-3107)*
On National Alliance ....E 302 427-0787
Wilmington *(G-11951)*
On The Spot Massage ....G 302 545-5200
Bear *(G-272)*
Oneness Massage Therapy ....G 302 893-0348
Newark *(G-7153)*
Pace Inc ....E 302 999-9812
Wilmington *(G-12002)*
Pain & Sleep Therapy Center ....G 302 314-1409
Wilmington *(G-12005)*
Planned Parenthood of Delaware ....E 302 655-7293
Wilmington *(G-12150)*
Planned Parenthood of Delaware ....G 302 678-5200
Dover *(G-1963)*
Planned Parenthood of Delaware ....G 302 731-7801
Newark *(G-7222)*
Point Hope Brain Injury Spport ....G 302 731-7676
New Castle *(G-5629)*
Premier Spine & Rehab ....G 302 730-4878
Dover *(G-1983)*
Premier Spine and Rehab ....G 302 404-5293
Seaford *(G-8361)*
Presicson Pain Rhbltation Svcs ....G 302 827-2321
Rehoboth Beach *(G-8036)*
Pro Rehab Chiropractic ....G 302 200-9102
Lewes *(G-3698)*
Pro Weight Loss ....G 302 220-9555
Newark *(G-7263)*
Psychotherapeutic Svc Assn Inc ....G 302 284-8370
Dover *(G-1996)*
R H D Brandywine Hills ....E 302 764-3660
Wilmington *(G-12296)*
Rehabilitation Consultants ....E 302 478-2131
Wilmington *(G-12368)*
Relaxing Tours LLC ....G 610 905-3852
Greenwood *(G-2759)*
Richard L Todd PHD ....G 302 853-0559
Milton *(G-4958)*
S T Progressive Strides ....G 410 775-8103
Bear *(G-313)*
Safe Space Delaware Inc ....F 302 691-7946
Wilmington *(G-12516)*
Shauna Sullivan Lcsw ....G 302 383-6826
Wilmington *(G-12595)*
Sleep Disorders Ctr-Christiana ....G 302 623-0650
Newark *(G-7440)*
Sodat of Delaware Inc ....F 302 656-2810
Wilmington *(G-12670)*
Sussex Pregnancy Care Center ....G 302 856-4344
Georgetown *(G-2683)*
Swedish Massage Therapy ....G 302 841-3166
Ocean View *(G-7819)*
Talk With Twila Ministries ....G 302 525-6472
Newark *(G-7535)*
Therapy Concierge ....G 302 319-3040
Bear *(G-351)*
Therapy Services of Delaw ....G 302 239-2285
Hockessin *(G-3158)*
Tidewater Physcl Thrpy and REB ....G 302 629-4024
Seaford *(G-8422)*
Tidewater Physcl Thrpy and REB ....G 302 945-5111
Lewes *(G-3784)*
Total Health & Rehabilitation ....G 302 999-9202
Wilmington *(G-12939)*
Unique Massage Therapy ....G 302 359-5982
Dover *(G-2178)*
US Dept of the Air Force ....B 302 677-2525
Dover *(G-2183)*
Wilmington Pain/Rehab Cntr PA ....G 302 575-1776
Wilmington *(G-13240)*
Worlds Best Massage Therapy ....G 302 366-8777
Newark *(G-7723)*
Zen Therapy & Body Work ....G 302 252-1733
Wilmington *(G-13343)*

8099 Health & Allied Svcs, NEC

166th Medical Squadron ....D 302 323-3385
New Castle *(G-4989)*
Access Quality Healthcare ....G 302 947-4437
Millsboro *(G-4621)*
Acuhealth & Wellness ....G 302 438-4493
Middletown *(G-3930)*
Ambient Medical Care ....G 302 629-3099
Seaford *(G-8145)*
American Sleep Medicine LLC ....E 302 366-0111
Newark *(G-5957)*

80 HEALTH SERVICES

Business	Location/ID	Rating	Phone
Animatra Inc	Lewes (G-3342)	G	303 350-9264
Bancroft Behavioral Health Inc	Newark (G-6043)	G	302 502-3255
Bancroft Neurohealth	Wilmington (G-9236)	E	302 691-8531
Bayhealth Medical Center Inc	Dover (G-1181)	D	302 744-7033
Beachview Family Health	Millville (G-4835)	G	302 537-8318
Blood Bank of Delmarva Inc	Newark (G-6095)	F	302 737-1151
Blood Bank of Delmarva Inc	Wilmington (G-9371)	G	302 737-8400
Brandx Heirloom Tomatoes	Townsend (G-8765)	G	302 287-1782
Christiana Care Health Sys Inc	Newark (G-6209)	F	302 838-4750
Claymont Methadone Clinic	Claymont (G-722)	G	855 244-7803
Compassonate Certification Ctr	Middletown (G-4004)	G	888 316-9085
Cpr Solutions Inc	Wilmington (G-9889)	G	302 477-1114
Csl Plasma Inc	Newark (G-6321)	G	302 565-0003
Das Financial Health LLC	Dover (G-1341)	G	570 947-7931
Delaware Eye Clinics	Milton (G-4887)	G	302 645-2338
Delaware Health and Fitnes LLC	Hockessin (G-3004)	G	302 584-7531
Delaware Health Net Inc	Wilmington (G-10050)	G	410 788-9715
Delaware Imaging Network	Newark (G-6385)	G	302 737-5990
Delaware Integrative Medical C	Georgetown (G-2501)	G	302 559-5959
Delaware Med Care Assoc LLC	Newark (G-6393)	G	302 633-9033
Delaware Medical Associates PA	Wilmington (G-10064)	F	302 475-2535
Delaware Occupational Health S	Newark (G-6400)	E	302 368-5100
Diagnostic Medical Services	Newark (G-6442)	G	302 292-2700
Diocese of Wilmington	Wilmington (G-10158)	E	302 368-0146
Douglas Morrow	Wilmington (G-10213)	G	302 750-9161
Dover Behavorl Hlth 249	Dover (G-1442)	G	302 741-0140
Dr Debra Wolf Encore Health	Newark (G-6470)	G	302 737-1918
Dupont De Nemours Inc	Wilmington (G-10251)	B	302 774-1000
▲ Eagle Mhc Company	Clayton (G-847)	B	302 653-3000
Epic Health Services Inc	Georgetown (G-2523)	G	302 422-3176
Eternal Health LLC	Wilmington (G-10441)	G	302 635-7421
Exam Master Corporation	Newark (G-6549)	E	302 378-3842
Fidelity Mntal Hlth Sltons LLC	Dover (G-1550)	G	302 304-2974
First State Health & Wellness	Milton (G-4906)	G	302 684-1995
Fusion Health Works	Wilmington (G-10651)	G	302 543-4714
Green Clinics Laboratory LLC	Dover (G-1610)	G	302 734-5050
Halo Medical Technologies LLC	Wilmington (G-10826)	G	302 475-2300
Health Support Services	Wilmington (G-10870)	G	302 287-4952
Heckessin Health Partners	Hockessin (G-3045)	G	302 234-2597
Ierardi Vascular Clinic LLC	Newark (G-6763)	G	302 655-8272
Javed Gilani MD	Wilmington (G-11130)	G	302 478-7160
Johnny Walker Enterprises LLC	Lewes (G-3575)	G	408 500-6439
Kent General Hospital Inc	Milford (G-4464)	G	302 430-5705
La Red Health Center Inc	Georgetown (G-2587)	D	302 855-1233
Laurel Highschool Wellness Ctr	Laurel (G-3254)	G	302 875-6164
Life At St Frncis Hlthcare Inc	(G-11383)	G	302 660-3297
Lily Intrnl Medicine Asscs LLC	Milford (G-4474)	G	302 424-1000
Medical Reimbursement Sol	Millsboro (G-4740)	G	516 809-6812
Medicine Woman	Milton (G-4933)	G	302 684-8048
Middelaware Family Medicine	Dover (G-1853)	G	302 724-5125
Mind Mechanix	Milford (G-4505)	G	302 503-5142
Nanticoke Health Services Inc	Seaford (G-8323)	E	302 629-6611
New U Nutrition Inc	(G-11872)	G	302 543-4555
One Stop Medical Inc	Milford (G-4518)	G	302 450-4479
Panzeea	Seaford (G-8340)	F	770 573-3672
Paradigm Health LLC	Bear (G-277)	G	301 233-7221
Patient First Medical LLC	Seaford (G-8341)	G	302 536-7740
Pearl Clinic LLC	Millsboro (G-4772)	G	302 648-2099
Peninsula Health LLC	Millsboro (G-4777)	G	302 945-0440
Peninsula Regional Medical Ctr	Millville (G-4852)	C	302 537-1457
Pinnacle Rhbilitation Hlth Ctr	Smyrna (G-8689)	F	302 653-5085
Pivotal Medical	Bethany Beach (G-422)	G	302 299-5795
Precision Care & Wellness LLC	Wilmington (G-12201)	G	302 407-5222
Produce For Btter Hlth Fndtion	Hockessin (G-3126)	E	302 235-2329
Pure Wellness LLC	Smyrna (G-8695)	G	302 389-8915
Regional Medical Group LLC	Wilmington (G-12359)	G	302 993-7890
Rekindle Family Medicine	Wilmington (G-12372)	G	302 565-4799
Repotmecom Inc	Georgetown (G-2637)	G	301 315-2344
Rose Health Center Inc	Lewes (G-3725)	G	302 441-5987
Select Health Services LLC	Newark (G-7403)	G	504 737-4300
Sleep Disorders Center	Lewes (G-3747)	G	302 645-3186
Spirits Path To Wellness LLC	Wilmington (G-12707)	G	302 998-0074
Sunrise Medical Center	Georgetown (G-2671)	G	302 854-9006
▲ Sussex Eye Care & Medical Asso	Lewes (G-3772)	G	302 644-8007
Telemed Health Group	Dover (G-2137)	G	561 922-3953
Transforming Wellness LLC	Millville (G-4856)	G	302 249-2526
United Medical Clinics of De	Bear (G-365)	F	302 451-5607
Vision & Hearing Inc	(G-13091)	G	302 475-8897
Wellness and Rejuvenation	Millsboro (G-4825)	G	732 977-6958
Wellness From Within	Lewes (G-3818)	G	717 884-3908
Womens Imaging Center Delaware	Newark (G-7715)	E	302 738-9494

81 LEGAL SERVICES

8111 Legal Svcs

Business	Location/ID	Rating	Phone
Abrams & Bayliss LLP	Wilmington (G-8908)	F	302 778-1000
Allmond & Eastburn	Wilmington (G-9025)	G	302 764-2193
American Incorporators Ltd	Wilmington (G-9049)	F	302 421-5752
Archer & Greiner PC	Wilmington (G-9122)	G	302 777-4350
Archer & Greiner PC	Georgetown (G-2433)	G	302 858-5151
Ashby & Geddes	Wilmington (G-9148)	E	302 654-1888
Atlantic Law Group LLC	Georgetown (G-2439)	E	302 854-0380
Baird Mandalas Brockstedt LLC	Dover (G-1168)	F	302 677-0061
Balick & Balick Pllc	Wilmington (G-9226)	G	302 658-4265
Ballard Spahr LLP	Wilmington (G-9227)	G	302 252-4465
Barnett Tom D Law Firm	Georgetown (G-2446)	G	302 855-9252
Barros Mc Namara Malkwcz & Tay	Dover (G-1174)	E	302 734-8400
Benesch Friedlander Coplan &	Wilmington (G-9301)	F	216 363-4500
Betts & Abram PA LLC	Georgetown (G-2454)	G	302 856-7755
Beverly L Bove PA	Wilmington (G-9320)	G	302 777-3500
Bifferato Gentilotti LLC	Wilmington (G-9329)	G	302 429-1900
Bifferato Gentilotti LLC	Wilmington (G-9330)	G	302 429-1900
Biggs & Battaglia	Wilmington (G-9335)	F	302 655-9677
Blank Rome LLP	Wilmington (G-9368)	E	302 425-6400
Bodell Bove LLC	Wilmington (G-9390)	F	302 655-6749
Bonnie M Benson PA	Camden (G-541)	G	302 697-4900
Boudart & Mensinger LLP	Wilmington (G-9397)	G	302 428-0100
Brown Shiels & OBrien	Dover (G-1236)	F	302 734-4766
Brown Shels Bauregard LLC	Dover (G-1237)	G	302 226-2270
Brown Stone Nimeroff LLC	Wilmington (G-9490)	E	302 428-8142
Bruce A Rogers PA	Georgetown (G-2460)	G	302 856-7161
Business Centric Svcs Group	Wilmington (G-9509)	G	302 984-3800
Capitol Credit Services Inc	Dover (G-1253)	F	302 678-1735
Carmine Potter & Associates	Newark (G-6158)	G	302 832-6000
Carmine Potter & Associates	Wilmington (G-9573)	G	302 658-8940
Casarino Christman Shalk	Wilmington (G-9586)	E	302 594-4500
Central Firm LLC	Wilmington (G-9615)	G	610 470-9836
Charles S Knothe Inc	Wilmington (G-9636)	G	302 478-8800
Charles Slanina	Hockessin (G-2983)	G	302 234-1605
Ciconte Roseman & Wasserman	Wilmington (G-9701)	F	302 658-7101
Cindy L Szabo	Georgetown (G-2472)	G	302 855-9505
Cogency Global Inc	Dover (G-1301)	G	800 483-1140
Cohen Seglias Pallas	Wilmington (G-9761)	E	302 425-5089
Cole Schotz PC	Wilmington (G-9767)	E	302 984-9541
Community Legal Aid Society	Wilmington (G-9795)	D	302 757-7001
Community Legal Aid Society	Dover (G-1306)	G	302 674-8500
Community Legal Aid Society	Georgetown (G-2479)	F	302 856-0038
Cooch & Taylor Attys	Wilmington (G-9847)	F	302 652-3641
Cooch and Taylor A Prof Assn	Wilmington (G-9848)	E	302 984-3800
Cooper Levenson PA	Bear (G-84)	G	302 838-2600
Corp1 Inc	Dover (G-1313)	F	720 644-6144
Countermeasures Assessment	New Castle (G-5200)	G	302 322-9600
Cozen OConnor	Wilmington (G-9886)	G	302 295-2000
Cross & Simon LLC	Wilmington (G-9903)	E	302 777-4200
Crossland and Associates	Hockessin (G-2996)	G	302 658-2100
CSC Corporate Domains Inc	Wilmington (G-9910)	F	902 746-5201
Curley & Benton LLC	Dover (G-1329)	G	302 674-3333

2020 Harris Directory of Delaware Businesses

81 LEGAL SERVICES

Curran James P Law Offices .... G 302 894-1111
Newark *(G-6327)*

Cynthia L Carroll .... G 302 733-0411
Newark *(G-6338)*

Dalton & Associates PA .... G 302 652-2050
Wilmington *(G-9950)*

David A Dorey Esq .... F 302 425-6400
Wilmington *(G-9964)*

David I Walsh Esquire PA .... G 302 498-0760
Lewes *(G-3448)*

De Workers Cmpnstion Legal Ctr .... G 302 888-1111
Hockessin *(G-3002)*

Deirde A McCartney .... G 302 644-8330
Lewes *(G-3451)*

Delaware Bus Incorporators Inc .... G 302 996-5819
Wilmington *(G-10009)*

Delaware Claims Agency LLC .... G 212 957-2180
Wilmington *(G-10017)*

Delaware Counsel Group LLP .... G 302 543-4870
Rockland *(G-8123)*

Delaware Counsel Group LLP .... G 302 576-9600
Wilmington *(G-10028)*

Delaware Department Finance .... E 302 739-5291
Dover *(G-1364)*

Delaware Law Office of Larry .... G 302 286-6336
Newark *(G-6392)*

Delaware Tchncal Cmnty College .... C 302 259-6160
Georgetown *(G-2504)*

Dla Piper LLP (us) .... B 302 654-3025
Wilmington *(G-10174)*

Doroshow Pasquale Karwitz Sieg .... E 302 998-2397
Wilmington *(G-10204)*

Doroshow Pasquale Karwitz Sieg .... F 302 674-7100
Dover *(G-1438)*

Doroshow Pasquale Karwitz Sieg .... F 302 934-9400
Millsboro *(G-4681)*

Doroshow Pasquale Karwitz Sieg .... F 302 424-7744
Milford *(G-4391)*

Doroshow Pasquale Karwitz Sieg .... F 302 832-3200
Bear *(G-124)*

Doroshow Pasquale Karwitz Sieg .... F 302 998-0100
Wilmington *(G-10205)*

Dorsey and Whitney Del LLP .... G 302 425-7171
Wilmington *(G-10206)*

Draper & Goldberg Pllc .... G 302 448-4040
Georgetown *(G-2514)*

Drinker Biddle & Reath LLP .... F 302 467-4200
Wilmington *(G-10236)*

Eckert Smans Chrin Mellott LLC .... D 302 574-7400
Wilmington *(G-10336)*

Elzufon Austin Reardon Tarlov .... G 302 644-0144
Lewes *(G-3481)*

Elzufon Austin Reardon Tarlov .... E 302 428-3181
Wilmington *(G-10386)*

Eric M Doroshow .... G 302 934-9400
Millsboro *(G-4687)*

Express Legal Documents LLC .... E 212 710-1374
Wilmington *(G-10463)*

Ferrara Haley & Bevis .... F 302 656-7247
Wilmington *(G-10524)*

Ferry Joseph & Pearce PA .... G 302 856-3706
Georgetown *(G-2530)*

Ferry Joseph & Pearce PA .... G 302 575-1555
Wilmington *(G-10526)*

Fish & Richardson PC .... E 302 652-5070
Wilmington *(G-10560)*

Fish & Richardson PC .... E 302 652-5070
Wilmington *(G-10561)*

Flowers Counsel Group LLC .... G 302 656-7370
Wilmington *(G-10578)*

Fox Rothschild LLP .... F 302 654-7444
Wilmington *(G-10608)*

Franta Rchard E Attrney At Law .... G 302 428-1800
Wilmington *(G-10620)*

Frederick K Funk .... G 302 368-6233
Newark *(G-6614)*

Freibott Law Firm .... F 302 633-9000
Wilmington *(G-10631)*

Friedlander and Gorris .... G 302 573-3500
Wilmington *(G-10638)*

Fuqua & Yori P A .... G 302 856-7777
Georgetown *(G-2536)*

Gary A Bryde PA .... G 302 239-3700
Hockessin *(G-3035)*

Gill Edward Law Offices of .... F 302 854-5400
Georgetown *(G-2548)*

Giordano Delcollo & Werb LLC .... G 302 234-6855
Wilmington *(G-10714)*

Goldfein & Hosmer PC .... G 302 656-3301
Wilmington *(G-10739)*

Goldfinch Group Inc .... G 646 300-0716
Dover *(G-1600)*

Gonser and Gonser P A .... G 302 478-4445
Wilmington *(G-10745)*

Gordon Fournaris Mammarella PA ..... E 302 652-2900
Wilmington *(G-10754)*

Grady & Hampton LLC .... G 302 678-1265
Dover *(G-1606)*

Grant & Eisenhofer PA .... E 302 622-7000
Wilmington *(G-10760)*

Greenberg Praurig LLC .... E 302 661-7000
Wilmington *(G-10776)*

GSB&b LLC .... G 302 425-5800
Wilmington *(G-10793)*

Haller & Hudson .... G 302 856-4525
Georgetown *(G-2554)*

Hamilton Pepper LLP .... E 302 777-6500
Wilmington *(G-10828)*

Harris Berger LLC .... G 302 665-1140
Wilmington *(G-10842)*

Hartnett & Hartnett .... G 302 239-4220
Hockessin *(G-3043)*

Harvard Business Services Inc .... E 302 645-7400
Lewes *(G-3534)*

Harvey Macelree Ltd .... F 302 654-4454
Wilmington *(G-10848)*

Heckler & Frabizzio PA .... G 302 573-4800
Wilmington *(G-10879)*

Heiman Gouge & Kaufman LLP .... G 302 658-1800
Wilmington *(G-10880)*

Heiman Aber Goldlust & Baker .... G 302 658-1800
Wilmington *(G-10881)*

Herdeg Dupont Dalle Pazze LLP .... G 302 655-6500
Wilmington *(G-10891)*

Hogan & Veith PA .... G 302 656-7540
Wilmington *(G-10924)*

Hudson Jnes Jaywork Fisher LLC ...... E 302 734-7401
Dover *(G-1661)*

Hudson Jnes Jaywork Fisher LLC ...... G 302 227-9441
Rehoboth Beach *(G-7966)*

Jackson Thmas C Attrney At Law ...... G 302 736-1723
Dover *(G-1690)*

Jacobs & Crumplar PA .... E 302 656-5445
Wilmington *(G-11117)*

James L Holzman .... E 302 888-6500
Wilmington *(G-11122)*

Jeffrey K Martin PC .... G 302 777-4681
Wilmington *(G-11144)*

John E Sullivan .... G 302 234-6855
Wilmington *(G-11168)*

John Williams PA .... G 302 571-4780
Wilmington *(G-11176)*

Jonmor Investments Inc .... G 302 477-1380
Wilmington *(G-11182)*

Joseph A Hurley PA .... G 302 658-8980
Wilmington *(G-11184)*

Joseph Longobardi Atty .... G 302 575-1502
Wilmington *(G-11193)*

Joseph W Benson PA .... G 302 656-8811
Wilmington *(G-11195)*

K and L Gates .... G 302 416-7000
Wilmington *(G-11213)*

Karen Y Vcks Law Offces of LLC .... G 302 674-1100
Dover *(G-1722)*

Katharine L Mayer Atty .... F 302 984-6312
Wilmington *(G-11227)*

Katherine Laffey .... G 302 651-7999
Wilmington *(G-11228)*

Kenneth R Schuster .... G 302 984-1000
Wilmington *(G-11241)*

Kimberly A Leaman PA .... G 301 261-4115
Selbyville *(G-8512)*

Kimmel Carter Roman & Peltz .... F 302 565-6100
Christiana *(G-671)*

Knepper & Stratton .... G 302 658-1717
Wilmington *(G-11279)*

Knepper & Stratton .... G 302 658-1717
Dover *(G-1754)*

La Esperanza Inc .... G 302 854-9262
Georgetown *(G-2585)*

Labaton Sucharow LLP .... G 302 573-6938
Wilmington *(G-11313)*

Laffey Kathryn J The Law Off .... G 302 651-7999
Wilmington *(G-11324)*

Landis Rath & Cobb LLP .... G 302 467-4400
Wilmington *(G-11327)*

Law Firm .... F 302 472-4900
Wilmington *(G-11340)*

Law Office Laura A Yiengst LLC .... G 302 264-9780
Dover *(G-1767)*

Law Office of James Curra .... G 302 894-1111
Newark *(G-6920)*

Law Office of R I Masten Jr .... G 302 358-2044
Newark *(G-6921)*

Law Offices Gary R Dodge PA .... G 302 674-5400
Dover *(G-1768)*

Lawrence Levinson Attorney .... G 302 656-3393
Wilmington *(G-11346)*

Leech Tshman Fscaldo Lampl LLC .... G 302 421-9379
Wilmington *(G-11357)*

Legal Services Corp Delaware .... G 302 575-0408
Wilmington *(G-11361)*

Legal Services of Delaware .... F 302 575-0408
Wilmington *(G-11362)*

Legalnature LLC .... G 888 881-1139
Dover *(G-1779)*

Leonard L Williams .... G 302 652-3141
Wilmington *(G-11373)*

Liguori Morris & Reddin .... G 302 678-9900
Dover *(G-1788)*

Linarducci & Butler PA .... G 302 325-2400
New Castle *(G-5483)*

Loizides & Associates PC .... G 302 654-0248
Wilmington *(G-11428)*

Losco and Marconi PA .... G 302 656-7776
Wilmington *(G-11437)*

Lyons David J Law Office .... G 302 777-5698
Wilmington *(G-11464)*

Lyons Doughty & Veldhuis .... D 302 428-1670
Wilmington *(G-11465)*

Macelree & Harvey Ltd .... G 302 654-4454
Wilmington *(G-11477)*

Malik John S Atty At Law .... G 302 427-2247
Wilmington *(G-11496)*

Manning Gross + Massenburg LLP .... F 302 657-2100
Wilmington *(G-11504)*

Margolis Edelstein .... E 302 888-1112
Wilmington *(G-11524)*

Marin Bayard .... G 302 658-4200
Wilmington *(G-11525)*

Marks ONeill OBrien Doher .... E 302 658-6538
Wilmington *(G-11540)*

Maron Mrvel Brdley Anderson PA ..... D 302 425-5177
Wilmington *(G-11542)*

Marshall Dennehey .... E 302 552-4300
Wilmington *(G-11545)*

Martin Daniel D & Assoc LLC .... G 302 658-2884
Wilmington *(G-11549)*

Mattleman Weinroth & Miller PC .... G 302 731-8349
Newark *(G-7003)*

McCarter & English LLP .... D 302 984-6300
Wilmington *(G-11586)*

McGivney Kluger & Cook PC .... F 302 656-1200
Wilmington *(G-11596)*

McLaughlin Gordon L Law Office .... G 302 651-7979
Wilmington *(G-11602)*

McLaughlin Morton Holdg Co LLC ..... G 302 426-1313
Wilmington *(G-11603)*

Michael B Joseph .... F 302 656-0123
Wilmington *(G-11658)*

Michael P Morton PA .... G 302 426-1313
Wilmington *(G-11663)*

Montgomery McCracken .... E 302 504-7800
Wilmington *(G-11739)*

Monzack Mersky McLaughlin .... E 302 656-8162
Wilmington *(G-11741)*

Mooney & Andrew PA .... G 302 856-3070
Georgetown *(G-2605)*

Morgan Lewis International LLC .... G 302 574-3000
Wilmington *(G-11751)*

Morris and Morris .... G 302 426-0400
Wilmington *(G-11755)*

Morris James LLP .... F 302 655-2599
Wilmington *(G-11756)*

Morris James LLP .... F 302 888-6800
Wilmington *(G-11757)*

Morris James LLP .... G 302 260-7290
Rehoboth Beach *(G-8014)*

Morris James LLP .... G 302 678-8815
Dover *(G-1873)*

Morris James LLP .... D 302 888-6863
Wilmington *(G-11758)*

Morris Jmes Htchens Wllams LLP ..... G 302 368-4200
Newark *(G-7059)*

Morris Nchols Arsht Tnnell LLP .... C 302 658-9200
Wilmington *(G-11759)*

Murphy & Landon PC .... F 302 472-8100
Wilmington *(G-11776)*

Nolan Williams & Plumhoff .... E 410 823-7800
Newark *(G-7135)*

Employee Codes: A=Over 500 employees, B=251-500
C=101-250, D=51-100, E=20-50, F=10-19, G=1-9

Nolte & Brodoway PA G 302 777-1700
Wilmington (G-11893)
Novak Druce Cnnlly Bv+qigg LLP C 302 252-9922
Wilmington (G-11911)
O Kelly Ernst Belli Wallen LLC G 302 778-4001
Wilmington (G-11925)
Office John M Law G 302 427-2369
Wilmington (G-11939)
P A Bayard D 302 429-4212
Wilmington (G-11991)
Parkowski Guerke & Swayze PA E 302 678-3262
Dover (G-1936)
Parkway Law LLC G 302 449-0400
Townsend (G-8815)
Patricia P McGonigle F 302 888-7605
Wilmington (G-12034)
Patrick Scanlon PA G 302 424-1996
Milford (G-4523)
Philip M Finestrauss PA G 302 984-1600
Wilmington (G-12114)
Phillips Gldmn McLghln & Hll E 302 655-4200
Wilmington (G-12116)
Pinckney Wdnger Urban Jyce LLC G 302 504-1497
Wilmington (G-12141)
Poolside Cnstr & Renovation G 302 436-9711
Selbyville (G-8533)
Potter Anderson & Corroon LLP C 302 984-6000
Wilmington (G-12195)
Pratcher Krayer LLC G 302 803-5291
Wilmington (G-12197)
Prentice-Hall Corp System Inc F 302 636-5440
Wilmington (G-12220)
R Stokes Nolte Esquire & G 302 777-1700
Wilmington (G-12298)
Rahaim & Saints Attys At Law F 302 892-9200
Wilmington (G-12306)
Ramunno & Ramunno & Scerba PA F 302 656-9400
Wilmington (G-12315)
Raskaukas Joseph C Aty Law G 302 537-2000
Bethany Beach (G-425)
Ratner & Prestia PC F 302 778-2500
Wilmington (G-12320)
Raymond E Tomassetti Esq G 302 539-3041
Fenwick Island (G-2339)
Raymond E Tomassetti Esq G 302 995-2840
Wilmington (G-12326)
Reger Rizzo & Darnall LLP F 302 652-3611
Wilmington (G-12356)
Reilly Janiczek & McDevitt PC F 302 777-1700
Wilmington (G-12370)
Rhoades & Morrow LLC F 302 427-9500
Wilmington (G-12401)
Richard S Cobb Esquire F 302 467-4430
Wilmington (G-12411)
Richards Layton & Finger P A E 302 651-7700
Wilmington (G-12412)
Richards Layton & Finger P A B 302 651-7700
Wilmington (G-12413)
Ridrodsky & Long PA F 302 691-8822
Wilmington (G-12419)
Robinson Grayson and Ward PA G 302 655-6262
Wilmington (G-12444)
Roeberg Moore & Associates PA F 302 658-4757
Wilmington (G-12463)
Roger D Anderson E 302 652-8400
Wilmington (G-12464)
Ronald D Jr Attorney At Law G 302 856-9860
Georgetown (G-2642)
Rosen Moss Snyder Bleefeld G 302 475-8060
Wilmington (G-12475)
Rosenthal Monhait Goddess PA F 302 656-4433
Wilmington (G-12477)
Rosner Law Group LLC G 302 295-4877
Wilmington (G-12478)
Ross Aronstam & Moritz LLP F 302 576-1600
Wilmington (G-12479)
Saul Ewing Arnstein & Lehr LLP E 302 654-1413
Wilmington (G-12546)
Schab & Barnett PA F 302 856-9024
Georgetown (G-2648)
Schmittinger & Rodriguez PA D 302 674-0140
Dover (G-2059)
Schnader Hrrson Sgal Lewis LLP D 302 888-4554
Wilmington (G-12554)
Schoenbeck & Schoenbeck PA G 302 239-9316
Wilmington (G-12555)
Schwartz & Schwartz Atty At La G 302 678-8700
Dover (G-2060)
Seitz Vanogtrop & Green F 302 888-0600
Wilmington (G-12573)
Sergovic & Carmean P A G 302 855-1260
Georgetown (G-2649)
Sergovic Carmean Weidman F 302 855-0551
Georgetown (G-2650)
Skadden Arps Slate Meagher C 302 651-3000
Wilmington (G-12639)
Skadden Arps Slate Meagher & F B 302 651-3000
Wilmington (G-12640)
Smith Firm LLC G 302 875-5595
Seaford (G-8403)
Smith Fnberg McCrtney Berl LLP E 302 644-8330
Lewes (G-3750)
Smith Fnberg McCrtney Berl LLP E 302 856-7082
Georgetown (G-2657)
Smith Katzenstein & Furlow LLP E 302 652-8400
Wilmington (G-12660)
Snyder Associates PA G 302 657-8300
Wilmington (G-12667)
Steen Waehler Schrider Fox LLC G 302 539-7900
Ocean View (G-7814)
Steven J Stirparo G 302 479-9555
Wilmington (G-12761)
Stevens & Lee PC E 302 654-5180
Wilmington (G-12762)
Stewart Law Firm E 302 652-5200
Wilmington (G-12763)
Street & Ellis P A G 302 735-8408
Dover (G-2110)
Stumpf Vickers and Sandy F 302 856-3561
Georgetown (G-2669)
Supreme Court of The State Del G 302 255-0544
Wilmington (G-12815)
Tarabicos Grosso G 302 757-7800
New Castle (G-5753)
Thomas J Allingham II E 302 651-3000
Wilmington (G-12901)
Thomson Reuters (grc) Inc A 212 227-7357
Wilmington (G-12904)
Tighe and Cottrell PA F 302 658-6400
Wilmington (G-12909)
Tunnell & Raysor PA E 302 856-7313
Georgetown (G-2696)
Tunnell & Raysor PA G 302 226-4420
Rehoboth Beach (G-8100)
Tunnell & Raysor PA G 302 644-4442
Lewes (G-3798)
Tybout Redfearn & Pell PA D 302 658-6901
Wilmington (G-13001)
UAW-GM Legal Services Plan F 302 562-8212
Newark (G-7606)
Vance A Funk III G 302 368-2561
Newark (G-7643)
Vivian A Houghton Esquire G 302 658-0518
Wilmington (G-13097)
Vps Services LLC G 302 376-6710
Middletown (G-4278)
Ward & Taylor LLC G 302 227-1403
Rehoboth Beach (G-8108)
Ward & Taylor LLC E 302 225-3350
Wilmington (G-13119)
Weber Gallagher Simpson G 302 346-6377
Dover (G-2209)
Weik Nitsche & Dougherty E 302 655-4040
Wilmington (G-13138)
Weiss & Saville PA G 302 656-0400
Wilmington (G-13140)
Werb & Sullivan F 302 652-1100
Wilmington (G-13160)
Wharton Levin Ehrmantraut G 302 252-0090
Wilmington (G-13181)
Whitaker Corporation F 302 633-2740
Wilmington (G-13186)
White and Williams LLP F 302 654-0424
Wilmington (G-13189)
Whittington & Aulgur G 302 235-5800
Yorklyn (G-13368)
Whittington & Aulgur F 302 378-1661
Odessa (G-7833)
Whittington & Aulgur F 302 378-1661
Middletown (G-4286)
Wilbraham Lawler & Buba PC G 302 421-9922
Wilmington (G-13199)
Wilks Lukoff & Bracegirdle LLC G 302 225-0850
Wilmington (G-13205)
William E Ward PA F 302 225-3350
Wilmington (G-13208)
William W Erhart PA G 302 651-0113
Wilmington (G-13216)
Williams Law Firm PA G 302 575-0873
Wilmington (G-13218)
Wilson Halbrook & Bayard PA F 302 856-0015
Georgetown (G-2705)
Woloshin and Lynch Associates F 302 449-2606
Middletown (G-4289)
Woloshin and Lynch Associates F 302 477-3200
Wilmington (G-13288)
Womble Bond Dickinson (us) LLP D 302 252-4320
Wilmington (G-13289)
Young & McNelis G 302 674-8822
Dover (G-2246)
Young and Malmberg PA F 302 672-5600
Dover (G-2247)
▲ Young Cnway Strgatt Taylor LLP C 302 571-6600
Wilmington (G-13330)

83 SOCIAL SERVICES

8322 Individual & Family Social Svcs

A Bail Bond By Resto & Co Inc G 302 312-7714
New Castle (G-4992)
A Door of Hope Inc G 302 998-9000
Wilmington (G-8876)
A Seed Hope Counseling Ctr LLC G 302 605-6702
Wilmington (G-8883)
Absalom Jones Senior Center G 302 998-0363
Wilmington (G-8909)
Achieve Solutions G 302 598-1457
Hockessin (G-2950)
Active Day Inc F 302 831-6774
Newark (G-5896)
Adirondack Bhvral Hlthcare LLC G 302 832-1282
Christiana (G-665)
Adoptions From Heart Inc G 302 658-8883
Wilmington (G-8940)
Aids Delaware Inc E 302 652-6776
Wilmington (G-8986)
Allow ME Errand Service LLC F 302 480-0954
Newark (G-5942)
Alzheimers Assn Del Chapter C 302 633-4420
Wilmington (G-9038)
American Institute For Pub Svc G 302 622-9101
Wilmington (G-9051)
AMS of Delaware G 302 227-1320
Rehoboth Beach (G-7840)
Angels Messiahs Foundation F 302 465-1647
Bear (G-30)
ARC A Resource Ctr For Youth G 302 658-6134
Wilmington (G-9113)
ARC of Delaware E 302 996-9400
Wilmington (G-9118)
Autism Delaware Inc F 302 224-6020
Newark (G-6027)
Balanced Mind Cnseling Ctr LLC G 302 377-6911
Middletown (G-3962)
Bear-Glasgow YMCA G 302 836-9622
Newark (G-6066)
Beautiful Gate Outreach Center F 302 472-3002
Wilmington (G-9277)
Bellevue Community Center G 302 429-5859
Wilmington (G-9288)
Bellwether Behavioral Health F 856 769-2042
Bear (G-50)
Bernard ND Ruth Siegel Jcc D 302 478-5660
Wilmington (G-9307)
Bfpe International Inc F 302 346-4800
Dover (G-1200)
Big Brthers Big Sisters of Del F 302 998-3577
Wilmington (G-9331)
Blossom Philadelphia F 215 242-4200
Wilmington (G-9373)
Brandy Wine Senior Center G 302 798-5562
Claymont (G-704)
Brandywine Assisted Living B 302 436-0808
Selbyville (G-8460)
Brandywine Center For Autism G 302 762-2636
Wilmington (G-9422)
Brandywine Counseling E 302 762-7120
Wilmington (G-9426)
Brandywine Hundred Fire Co 1 D 302 764-4901
Wilmington (G-9438)
Bridge Counseling Center LLC G 302 856-9190
Georgetown (G-2459)
Bridgeville Senior Center G 302 337-8771
Bridgeville (G-456)
Brownstein Meryl Med Lpcmh G 302 479-5060
Wilmington (G-9491)
Cancer Support Cmnty Del Inc G 302 995-2850
Wilmington (G-9549)
Cape Henlopen Senior Center G 302 227-2055
Rehoboth Beach (G-7883)

83 SOCIAL SERVICES

Carpe Dia Organization .... G 302 333-7546
  Newark *(G-6161)*
Catholic Charities Inc .... G 302 856-9578
  Georgetown *(G-2463)*
Catholic Charities Inc .... E 302 573-3122
  Wilmington *(G-9592)*
Catholic Charities Inc .... F 302 654-1184
  Wilmington *(G-9593)*
Catholic Charities Inc .... G 302 674-1600
  Dover *(G-1260)*
Catholic Charities Inc .... E 302 655-9624
  Wilmington *(G-9594)*
Catholic Charities Inc .... G 302 684-8694
  Milton *(G-4876)*
Catholic Charities Inc .... G 302 674-1600
  Dover *(G-1261)*
Center For A Pstive Hmnity LLC .... G 302 703-1036
  Felton *(G-2281)*
Chase Center On River .... G 302 655-2187
  Wilmington *(G-9641)*
Cheer Inc .... F 302 856-5641
  Georgetown *(G-2467)*
Cheer Inc .... G 302 645-9239
  Lewes *(G-3412)*
Child Inc .... C 302 832-5451
  Newark *(G-6197)*
Child Inc .... E 302 762-8989
  Wilmington *(G-9661)*
Children Youth & Their Fam .... G 302 577-6011
  Wilmington *(G-9662)*
Children Youth & Their Fam .... F 302 628-2024
  Seaford *(G-8193)*
Children Fmilies First Del Inc .... E 302 629-6996
  Seaford *(G-8194)*
Children Fmilies First Del Inc .... D 302 658-5177
  Wilmington *(G-9664)*
Children Fmilies First Del Inc .... G 302 674-8384
  Dover *(G-1276)*
Children Fmilies First Del Inc .... E 302 856-2388
  Georgetown *(G-2468)*
Childrens Advocacy Ctr of Del .... F 302 854-0323
  Georgetown *(G-2469)*
Childrens Beach House Inc .... E 302 655-4288
  Wilmington *(G-9665)*
Childrens Choice Inc .... G 302 731-9512
  Newark *(G-6198)*
Christiana Care Home Health .... F 302 995-8448
  Wilmington *(G-9685)*
Christiana Community Ctr Inc .... G 302 353-6796
  Christiana *(G-666)*
Claymont Community Center Inc ...... E 302 792-2757
  Claymont *(G-721)*
Claymore Senior Center Inc .... G 302 428-3170
  Wilmington *(G-9735)*
Connections Community Support ..... E 302 659-0512
  Townsend *(G-8773)*
Connections Community Support ..... D 302 536-1952
  Seaford *(G-8204)*
Connections Community Support ..... D 302 984-2302
  Wilmington *(G-9826)*
Connections Community Support ..... F 302 654-9289
  Wilmington *(G-9828)*
Contactlifeline Inc .... F 302 761-9800
  Wilmington *(G-9838)*
Cornerstone Senior Center .... G 302 836-6463
  Bear *(G-85)*
Cosey Gabre .... G 302 233-0658
  Felton *(G-2284)*
Counseling Services Inc .... G 302 894-1477
  Wilmington *(G-9874)*
Crossroads of Delaware .... G 302 744-9999
  Dover *(G-1325)*
Delaware Adlescent Program Inc ...... E 302 531-0257
  Camden *(G-557)*
Delaware Breast Cancer Coalit .... G 302 644-6844
  Lewes *(G-3455)*
Delaware Breast Cancer Coalit .... F 302 778-1102
  Wilmington *(G-10007)*
Delaware Breast Cancer Coalit .... G 302 672-6435
  Dover *(G-1360)*
Delaware Clitn Agnst Dmstc Vln ...... G 302 658-2958
  Wilmington *(G-10020)*
Delaware Councl On Gmblng Prbl ..... G 302 226-5041
  Rehoboth Beach *(G-7911)*
Delaware Ctr For Hmless Vtrans ...... F 302 898-2647
  Wilmington *(G-10031)*
Delaware Dagnstc Rehabilitatio .... G 302 777-3955
  Wilmington *(G-10034)*
Delaware Diagnostic & Rehab .... G 302 777-3955
  Wilmington *(G-10039)*

Delaware Drnking Drver Program ..... G 302 736-4326
  Dover *(G-1367)*
Delaware Drnking Drver Program ..... F 302 856-1835
  Georgetown *(G-2499)*
Delaware Guidance Ser .... E 302 678-3020
  Dover *(G-1373)*
Delaware Guidance Services For ...... F 302 455-9333
  Newark *(G-6382)*
Delaware Guidance Services For ...... F 302 652-3948
  Wilmington *(G-10048)*
Delaware Hiv Services Inc .... F 302 654-5471
  Wilmington *(G-10053)*
Delaware Juniors Volleyball .... G 302 463-4218
  Newark *(G-6391)*
Delaware S P C A .... E 302 998-2281
  Newark *(G-6409)*
Delaware Senior Olympics Inc .... G 302 736-5698
  Dover *(G-1390)*
Delaware Teen Challenge Inc .... F 302 629-8824
  Seaford *(G-8220)*
Delaware Wic Program .... G 302 741-2900
  Dover *(G-1405)*
Delaware Wic Program .... G 302 857-5000
  Dover *(G-1406)*
Dimarquez Intl Ministries Inc .... F 302 256-4847
  New Castle *(G-5253)*
Division Svcs For Agng Adlts .... G 302 255-9390
  New Castle *(G-5255)*
Door of Second Chances Inc .... E 302 898-3959
  Wilmington *(G-10201)*
Dover Educational & Cmnty Ctr .... G 302 883-3092
  Dover *(G-1446)*
Dover Interfaith Mission Fr Ho .... F 302 736-3600
  Dover *(G-1454)*
Dunamis-Homes of Divine .... G 302 393-5778
  Camden Wyoming *(G-631)*
Easter Seal Delaware .... C 302 324-4444
  New Castle *(G-5276)*
Elohim Community Dev Corp .... G 302 856-4551
  Georgetown *(G-2521)*
Epilepsy Foundation of Del .... G 302 999-9313
  Newark *(G-6535)*
F H Everett & Associates Inc .... G 302 674-2380
  Dover *(G-1536)*
Family Cnsling Ctr St Puls Inc .... F 302 576-4136
  Wilmington *(G-10486)*
Family Promise of Northern New ..... G 302 998-2222
  Wilmington *(G-10495)*
Family Wrkplace Connection Inc ..... D 302 479-1660
  Wilmington *(G-10496)*
Fellowship Hlth Resources Inc .... F 302 854-0626
  Georgetown *(G-2528)*
First State Cmnty Action Agcy .... D 302 674-1355
  Dover *(G-1553)*
First State Cmnty Action Agcy .... F 302 856-7761
  Georgetown *(G-2532)*
Forgotten Few Foundation Inc .... G 302 494-6212
  Wilmington *(G-10594)*
Frederica Senior Center Inc .... G 302 335-4555
  Frederica *(G-2402)*
Freedom Ctr For Ind Living Inc .... G 302 376-4399
  Middletown *(G-4077)*
Friends & Family Practice .... G 302 537-3740
  Millville *(G-4845)*
Friendship House Incorporated .... F 302 652-8033
  Wilmington *(G-10640)*
Friendship House Incorporated .... G 302 652-8133
  Wilmington *(G-10641)*
Gem-Gradually Expanding Minds ..... G 302 322-3701
  Wilmington *(G-6643)*
Girl Scouts of The Cheasapea .... E 302 456-7150
  Newark *(G-6656)*
Good Samaritan Aid .... G 302 875-2425
  Laurel *(G-3233)*
Gull House Adult Activity .... G 302 226-2160
  Lewes *(G-3526)*
Habitat For Humanity .... F 302 652-0365
  Wilmington *(G-10815)*
Habitat For Humanity Intl Inc .... G 302 855-1156
  Georgetown *(G-2553)*
Harrington Senior Center Inc .... G 302 398-4224
  Harrington *(G-2847)*
Harrison Hse Cmnty Prgrams Inc ..... G 302 427-8438
  New Castle *(G-5375)*
Health & Social Svcs Del Dept .... G 302 337-8261
  Bridgeville *(G-480)*
Health & Social Svcs Del Dept .... D 302 857-5000
  Dover *(G-1639)*
Health & Social Svcs Del Dept .... F 302 856-5586
  Georgetown *(G-2556)*

Health & Social Svcs Del Dept .... D 302 391-3505
  New Castle *(G-5387)*
Health & Social Svcs Del Dept .... F 302 255-9500
  Dover *(G-1640)*
Health & Social Svcs Del Dept .... E 302 552-3530
  Wilmington *(G-10868)*
Hillside Center .... F 302 652-1181
  Wilmington *(G-10909)*
Home For Aged Wmn-Mnquadale HM ...C 302 654-1810
  Wilmington *(G-10935)*
Horizon House of Delaware Inc .... E 302 658-2392
  Wilmington *(G-10953)*
Housing Alliance Delaware Inc .... F 302 654-0126
  Wilmington *(G-10961)*
Howard Weston Senior Center .... G 302 328-6425
  New Castle *(G-5406)*
Hrnx LLC .... F 844 700-0090
  Dover *(G-1658)*
Idrch3 Ministries .... G 302 344-6957
  Camden *(G-581)*
Independent Resources Inc .... F 302 735-4599
  Dover *(G-1674)*
Ingleside Homes Inc .... D 302 575-0250
  Wilmington *(G-11031)*
Jewish Community Center Inc .... E 302 478-5660
  Wilmington *(G-11152)*
Jewish Family Service of Del .... G 302 798-0600
  Claymont *(G-768)*
Jungle Gym LLC .... F 302 734-1515
  Dover *(G-1716)*
Karen Kim Zogheib Lcsw .... G 786 897-3022
  Wilmington *(G-11226)*
Kent Cnty Cmnty Actn Agncy Inc ..... F 302 678-1949
  Dover *(G-1732)*
Keystone Service Systems Inc .... G 302 273-3952
  Newark *(G-6882)*
Khanyi Media Corporation .... G 302 482-8142
  Wilmington *(G-11257)*
Kristina Brandis 516 457-2717
  Middletown *(G-4125)*
La Esperanza Inc .... F 302 854-9262
  Georgetown *(G-2585)*
Latin American Cmnty Ctr Corp ...... D 302 655-7338
  Wilmington *(G-11336)*
Laurel Senior Center Inc .... G 302 875-2536
  Laurel *(G-3256)*
Lewes Senior Citizens Center .... G 302 645-9293
  Lewes *(G-3604)*
Lisa R Savage .... G 302 353-7052
  Newark *(G-6940)*
Lost and Found Dog Rescue Adop ... G 302 613-0394
  New Castle *(G-5487)*
Lutheran Community Services .... G 302 654-8886
  Wilmington *(G-11453)*
Luz D Reynoso .... G 302 358-6237
  Newark *(G-6959)*
M O T Senior Citizen Center .... F 302 378-3041
  Middletown *(G-4138)*
Madison Adoption Associates .... F 302 475-8977
  Claymont *(G-778)*
Martin Luther Homes East Inc .... G 302 475-4920
  Wilmington *(G-11550)*
MB Veterans Center LLC .... G 302 384-2350
  Wilmington *(G-11582)*
Meals On Wheels Delaware Inc .... G 302 656-6451
  Wilmington *(G-11612)*
Meals On Whels of Lwes Rhoboth ... G 302 645-7449
  Lewes *(G-3631)*
Merakey USA .... D 302 325-3540
  New Castle *(G-5516)*
Methodist Mission and Church E ..... G 302 225-5862
  Wilmington *(G-11649)*
Metropltan Wlmngton Urban Leag ... G 302 778-8300
  Wilmington *(G-11650)*
Middletown Counseling .... G 302 376-0621
  Middletown *(G-4155)*
Middltown Odssa Twnsend Snior .... F 302 378-4758
  Middletown *(G-4163)*
Milford Senior Center Inc .... F 302 422-3385
  Milford *(G-4504)*
Millenium Counseling .... G 302 995-9188
  Wilmington *(G-11692)*
Mind and Body Consortium LLC ..... E 302 674-2380
  Dover *(G-1860)*
Ministry of Caring Inc .... G 302 652-0904
  Wilmington *(G-11706)*
Ministry of Caring Inc .... G 302 658-6123
  Wilmington *(G-11707)*
Ministry of Caring Inc .... G 302 652-5522
  Wilmington *(G-11708)*

Ministry of Caring Inc ....G.... 302 652-0970
Wilmington (G-11709)
Ministry of Caring Inc ....G.... 302 652-0969
Wilmington (G-11710)
Modern Maturity Center Inc ....C.... 302 734-1200
Dover (G-1869)
Mosaic ....C.... 302 456-5995
Newark (G-7062)
My Sisters Place Inc ....G.... 302 737-5303
Newark (G-7076)
N U Friendship Outreach Inc ....G.... 302 836-0404
Bear (G-260)
Nehemiah Gtwy Cmnty Dev Corp ....G.... 302 655-0803
Wilmington (G-11829)
Neighborhood House Inc ....F.... 302 658-5404
Wilmington (G-11830)
New Castle Senior Center ....G.... 302 326-4209
New Castle (G-5565)
Newark Family Counceling Ctr ....G.... 302 368-6895
Newark (G-7119)
Newark Senior Center Inc ....E.... 302 737-2336
Newark (G-7128)
Oak Grove Senior Center Inc ....G.... 302 998-3319
Wilmington (G-11927)
One Village Alliance Inc ....G.... 302 275-1715
Wilmington (G-11957)
Open Door Inc ....F.... 302 731-1504
Newark (G-7155)
Open Door Inc ....G.... 302 629-7900
Seaford (G-8338)
Outreach Team LLC ....G.... 302 744-9550
Dover (G-1927)
Patricia Ayers ....G.... 609 335-8923
Newark (G-7181)
Pauls House Inc ....F.... 302 384-2350
Wilmington (G-12046)
PDr Vc Ltd Liability Company ....G.... 424 281-4669
Wilmington (G-12056)
People Builders Inc ....G.... 302 250-0716
Newark (G-7198)
Peoples Place II Inc ....G.... 302 422-8033
Milford (G-4524)
Peoples Settlement Assc of WI ....E.... 302 658-4133
Wilmington (G-12079)
Phc Inc ....F.... 313 831-3500
New Castle (G-5621)
Pike Creek Psychlogical Ctr PA ....F.... 302 738-6859
Newark (G-7217)
Pioneer House ....E.... 302 286-0892
Newark (G-7219)
Point of Hope Inc ....G.... 302 731-7676
Christiana (G-677)
Precious Moments Edu ....F.... 302 697-9374
Dover (G-1979)
Pressley Ridge Foundation ....G.... 302 677-1590
Dover (G-1985)
Prison Ministries Delaware Inc ....F.... 302 737-2792
Newark (G-7260)
Puzzles of Life ....G.... 302 339-0327
Wilmington (G-12272)
Rain of Light Inc ....G.... 302 312-7642
Newark (G-7296)
Rauma Survivors Foundation ....G.... 302 275-9705
Wilmington (G-12323)
Reach Riverside Dev Corp ....G.... 302 540-1698
Wilmington (G-12340)
Reeds Refuge Center Inc ....D.... 302 428-1830
Wilmington (G-12351)
Reliable Home Services LLC ....G.... 302 246-6000
Wilmington (G-12375)
Resources For Human Dev Inc ....D.... 215 951-0300
Newark (G-7327)
Retired Senior Volunteer ....G.... 610 565-5563
Wilmington (G-12395)
Ronald McDonald House Delaware ....F.... 302 428-5299
Wilmington (G-12469)
Rose Hill Community Center ....F.... 302 656-8513
New Castle (G-5684)
Ryerson Geralyn ....G.... 302 547-3060
Wilmington (G-12502)
Salvation Army ....F.... 302 628-2020
Seaford (G-8384)
Salvation Army ....C.... 302 934-3730
Millsboro (G-4797)
Salvation Army ....E.... 302 996-9400
Wilmington (G-12528)
Salvation Army ....D.... 302 656-1696
Wilmington (G-12529)
Samaritan Outreach ....G.... 302 594-9476
Wilmington (G-12532)
Sellers Senior Center Inc ....G.... 302 762-2050
Wilmington (G-12576)
Senior Nanticoke Center Inc ....F.... 302 629-4939
Seaford (G-8396)
Shechinah Empower Center Inc ....G.... 302 858-4467
Georgetown (G-2653)
Shelatia J Dennis ....G.... 302 465-0630
Dover (G-2075)
Shepherd Place Inc ....F.... 302 678-1909
Dover (G-2076)
Sojourners Place Inc ....E.... 302 764-4592
Wilmington (G-12673)
South Coastal ....G.... 302 542-5668
Frankford (G-2389)
Special Olympics Inc ....F.... 302 831-4653
Newark (G-7466)
Special Olympics Delaware Inc ....F.... 302 831-4653
Newark (G-7467)
St Anthonys Community Center ....E.... 302 421-3721
Wilmington (G-12720)
St Patrick Center Inc ....G.... 302 652-6219
Wilmington (G-12728)
Suburban Psychiatric Svcs LLC ....F.... 302 999-9834
Wilmington (G-12787)
Supreme Court United States ....E.... 302 252-2950
Wilmington (G-12814)
Survivors Abuse In Rcovery Inc ....G.... 302 651-0181
Wilmington (G-12818)
Sussex Community Crisis ....F.... 302 856-2246
Georgetown (G-2675)
Sussex County Senior Ctr Svcs ....G.... 302 539-2671
Ocean View (G-7817)
Sussex County Senior Svcs Inc ....G.... 302 854-2882
Georgetown (G-2678)
Sussex Family Counseling LLC ....G.... 302 864-7970
Georgetown (G-2680)
Sussex Pregnancy Care Center ....G.... 302 856-4344
Georgetown (G-2683)
Tatsapod-Aame ....F.... 302 897-8963
Wilmington (G-12854)
Techno Relief Limited ....G.... 416 453-9393
Wilmington (G-12870)
Tidewater Physcl Thrpy and REB ....G.... 302 684-2829
Milton (G-4976)
Tranquility Counseling Inc ....G.... 302 636-0700
Newark (G-7581)
Transitional Youth ....F.... 302 423-7543
Greenwood (G-2767)
Tri-State Cheernastics Inc ....G.... 302 322-4020
New Castle (G-5787)
Troy Farmer ....G.... 888 711-0094
Bear (G-360)
Turning Point At Peoples Place ....G.... 302 424-2420
Milford (G-4580)
United Cerebral Palsy of De ....F.... 302 764-6216
Wilmington (G-13022)
United Cerebral Palsy of De ....E.... 302 764-2400
Wilmington (G-13023)
United Cerebral Palsy of De ....G.... 302 335-3739
Felton (G-2324)
United Way of Delaware Inc ....E.... 302 573-3700
Wilmington (G-13028)
Unity Perspectives Inc ....G.... 302 265-2854
Milford (G-4587)
University of Delaware ....E.... 302 831-2501
Newark (G-7622)
Urbanpromise Wilmington Inc ....F.... 302 425-5502
Wilmington (G-13036)
Veterans Re-Entry Resources ....F.... 302 384-2350
Wilmington (G-13072)
Way Home Inc ....G.... 302 856-9870
Georgetown (G-2702)
We Deserve It Shs For Kids Inc ....G.... 302 521-7255
Dover (G-2208)
Wellspring Counseling Services ....G.... 302 373-8904
Smyrna (G-8742)
West End Neighborhood Hse Inc ....G.... 302 654-2131
Wilmington (G-13165)
West End Neighborhood Hse Inc ....D.... 302 658-4171
Wilmington (G-13166)
Whatcoat Social Service Agency ....F.... 302 734-0319
Dover (G-2220)
William Hcks Andrson Cmnty Ctr ....E.... 302 571-4266
Wilmington (G-13213)
Wilmington Senior Center Inc ....E.... 302 651-3400
Wilmington (G-13257)
Young Mens Christian Associat ....C.... 302 571-6900
Wilmington (G-13332)
Young Mens Christian Associat ....D.... 302 296-9622
Rehoboth Beach (G-8121)
YWCA Delaware ....F.... 302 224-4060
Newark (G-7733)

8331 Job Training & Vocational Rehabilitation Svcs

Academy Massage & Bdy Work Ltd ....G.... 302 392-6768
Bear (G-10)
Advanced Training Acadmey ....F.... 302 369-8800
Newark (G-5909)
Chimes Inc ....G.... 302 382-4500
New Castle (G-5148)
Corelink Ministries ....G.... 610 505-6043
Wilmington (G-9861)
Delmarva Clergy United Inc ....F.... 302 422-2350
Ellendale (G-2259)
Easter Seal Delaware ....E.... 302 856-7364
Georgetown (G-2519)
Easter Seal Delaware ....E.... 302 678-3353
Dover (G-1499)
Easter Seal Delaware ....C.... 302 324-4444
New Castle (G-5276)
Elwyn ....D.... 302 658-8860
Wilmington (G-10385)
Fursan Consulting Services ....F.... 240 654-5784
New Castle (G-5336)
Goodwill Inds Del Del Cnty Inc ....E.... 302 761-4640
Wilmington (G-10749)
Health & Social Svcs Del Dept ....E.... 302 255-9800
New Castle (G-5383)
Health & Social Svcs Del Dept ....E.... 302 255-9855
New Castle (G-5385)
Industrial Training Cons Inc ....F.... 302 266-6100
Newark (G-6774)
Jobs For Delaware Graduates ....G.... 302 995-7175
Wilmington (G-11163)
Leadership Caddie ....F.... 302 743-6456
Bear (G-232)
Leadership Institute Inc ....F.... 302 368-7292
Newark (G-6925)
Opportunity Center Inc ....D.... 302 762-0300
New Castle (G-5589)
Service Quest ....G.... 302 235-0173
Hockessin (G-3144)
Telamon Corp/Early Chldhd Pgrm ....G.... 302 934-1642
Georgetown (G-2690)
Telamon Corporation ....F.... 302 398-9196
Harrington (G-2898)
Telamon Corporation ....G.... 302 684-3234
Milton (G-4975)
Telamon Corporation ....G.... 302 629-5557
Seaford (G-8420)
Telamon Corporation ....G.... 302 424-2335
Milford (G-4577)

8351 Child Day Care Svcs

A Better Chnce For Our Chldren ....G.... 302 725-5008
Milford (G-4300)
A Childs Potential ....G.... 302 249-6929
Lewes (G-3319)
A Childs World LLC ....F.... 302 322-9386
Bear (G-4)
A Leap of Faith Inc ....F.... 302 543-6256
Wilmington (G-8881)
A Place To Grow Fmly Chld Care ....G.... 302 897-8944
Claymont (G-684)
Academy of Early Learning ....G.... 302 659-0750
Smyrna (G-8560)
Acclaim Academy LLC ....E.... 215 848-7827
Wilmington (G-8916)
Advanced Care Centers Delaware ....G.... 302 472-4878
Wilmington (G-8950)
All About ME Day Care ....F.... 302 424-8322
Milford (G-4304)
All My Children Inc ....F.... 302 995-9191
Wilmington (G-9015)
Amemg Inc ....F.... 302 220-7132
New Castle (G-5029)
American Universal LLC ....G.... 302 836-9790
Newark (G-5960)
Angels In Heaven ....G.... 302 398-7820
Harrington (G-2811)
Angels Lindas ....E.... 302 328-3700
New Castle (G-5039)
Anns Family Daycare ....G.... 302 836-8910
Newark (G-5972)
Army & Air Force Exchange Svc ....D.... 302 677-3716
Dover (G-1138)
Atlantic Dawn Ltd ....F.... 302 737-8854
Newark (G-6019)

SIC SECTION
83 SOCIAL SERVICES

Attic Away From Home ....G.... 302 378-2600
Townsend *(G-8761)*
Ave Preschool ....F.... 302 422-8775
Milford *(G-4315)*
Babes On Square ....G.... 302 477-9190
Wilmington *(G-9219)*
Barbara L McKinney ....G.... 302 266-9594
Newark *(G-6046)*
Beach Babies Child Care ....E.... 302 644-1585
Lewes *(G-3366)*
Beach Babies Child Care ....F.... 302 378-4778
Townsend *(G-8763)*
Bear Early Education Center ....G.... 302 836-5000
Newark *(G-6063)*
Bear-Glasgow YMCA ....G.... 302 836-9622
Newark *(G-6066)*
Beetles Playhouse Day Care ....G.... 302 593-7321
Newark *(G-6068)*
Beginning Blssngs Chldcare LLC ....G.... 302 893-1726
New Castle *(G-5080)*
Beginning Bridges Child Care ....G.... 302 875-7428
Laurel *(G-3197)*
Beginnings and Beyond Inc ....F.... 302 734-2464
Dover *(G-1190)*
Bernices Edtl Scl AG Ctr Inc ....G.... 302 651-0286
Wilmington *(G-9310)*
Bethel United Methodist Church ....E.... 302 645-9426
Lewes *(G-3379)*
Beverlys Help In Hand ....G.... 302 651-9304
Wilmington *(G-9321)*
Bizzy Bees Home Daycare LLC ....G.... 302 376-9245
Middletown *(G-3969)*
Blessed Beginnings Lrng Ctr ....G.... 302 838-9112
Bear *(G-52)*
Boost Learning LLC ....G.... 302 691-5821
Wilmington *(G-9394)*
Bowman Linda Group Day Care ....G.... 302 737-5479
Newark *(G-6110)*
Brees Home Day Care ....G.... 302 762-0876
Wilmington *(G-9467)*
Bright Beginnings Child Care C ....G.... 302 934-1249
Millsboro *(G-4649)*
Bright Bgnnngs Lrng Acdemy LLC ....G.... 302 655-1346
Wilmington *(G-9473)*
Bright Futures Inc ....E.... 610 905-0506
Middletown *(G-3974)*
Bright Horizons Chld Ctrs LLC ....D.... 302 456-8913
Newark *(G-6119)*
Bright Horizons Chld Ctrs LLC ....G.... 302 282-6378
Wilmington *(G-9474)*
Bright Horizons Chld Ctrs LLC ....E.... 302 477-1023
Wilmington *(G-9475)*
Bright Horizons Chld Ctrs LLC ....E.... 302 453-2050
Newark *(G-6120)*
Bright Kidz Inc ....F.... 302 369-6929
Newark *(G-6121)*
Bright New Beginnings ....G.... 610 637-9809
Wilmington *(G-9476)*
Bright Stars Home Daycare ....G.... 302 378-8142
Middletown *(G-3975)*
Brilliant Little Minds ....G.... 302 376-9889
Middletown *(G-3976)*
Brown Lisha ....G.... 302 832-9529
Newark *(G-6126)*
Building Blocks Academy Ltd ....F.... 302 284-8797
Felton *(G-2277)*
Building Blocks For Learni ....G.... 302 677-0248
Dover *(G-1241)*
Cacc Montessori School ....E.... 302 239-2917
Hockessin *(G-2974)*
Caesar Rodney School District ....D.... 302 697-3207
Dover *(G-1248)*
Capital School District ....G.... 302 678-8394
Dover *(G-1250)*
Carmen R Benitez ....G.... 302 793-2061
Claymont *(G-707)*
Catholic Charities Inc ....G.... 302 674-1600
Dover *(G-1261)*
Catholic Docese Wilmington Inc ....E.... 302 731-2210
Newark *(G-6169)*
Cdb Ventures Inc ....E.... 302 235-0414
Hockessin *(G-2981)*
Celebree Holding Inc ....G.... 302 834-0436
Bear *(G-69)*
Center For Child Developement ....G.... 302 292-1334
Newark *(G-6177)*
Chester Bethel United Methodis ....F.... 302 475-3549
Wilmington *(G-9656)*
Child Inc ....F.... 302 335-8652
Magnolia *(G-3886)*

Children First Lrng Ctr Inc ....G.... 302 674-5227
Dover *(G-1275)*
Children First Preschool ....G.... 302 239-3544
Hockessin *(G-2985)*
Children S Secret Garden ....F.... 302 730-1717
Dover *(G-1277)*
Childrens Beach House Inc ....F.... 302 645-9184
Lewes *(G-3413)*
Childrens Place ....G.... 302 698-0969
Camden *(G-548)*
Childrens Place Child Dev Ce ....G.... 302 947-4808
Millsboro *(G-4659)*
Childs Play At Home LLC ....G.... 302 644-3445
Lewes *(G-3414)*
Childs Play By Bay ....G.... 302 703-6234
Lewes *(G-3415)*
Christ Care Cardiac Surgery ....G.... 302 644-4282
Lewes *(G-3418)*
Christ Ch Episcpal Preschool ....E.... 302 472-0021
Wilmington *(G-9673)*
Church of God In Christ ....F.... 302 678-1949
Dover *(G-1282)*
Circle Time Learning Center ....G.... 302 384-7193
Wilmington *(G-9711)*
Claremont School LLC ....G.... 302 478-4531
Wilmington *(G-9729)*
Connections Development Corp ....G.... 302 436-3292
Frankford *(G-2356)*
Corporate Kids Lrng Ctr Inc ....E.... 302 678-0688
Dover *(G-1314)*
Country Kids Child ....G.... 302 349-5888
Greenwood *(G-2724)*
Country Kids Home Day Care ....G.... 302 653-4134
Townsend *(G-8774)*
Covenant Preschool ....F.... 302 764-8503
Wilmington *(G-9879)*
Cozy Critters Child Care Corp ....E.... 302 541-8210
Frankford *(G-2357)*
Creative Learning Academy Inc ....G.... 302 834-5259
Bear *(G-87)*
Creative Learning Child Care ....G.... 302 691-3167
Wilmington *(G-9895)*
Creative Minds Daycare ....G.... 302 378-0741
Townsend *(G-8775)*
Dawn L Conly ....G.... 302 378-1890
Middletown *(G-4020)*
Day School For Children ....G.... 302 652-4651
New Castle *(G-5218)*
Dcc Inc ....G.... 302 750-1207
Wilmington *(G-9979)*
De Colores Family Child Care ....G.... 302 883-3298
Dover *(G-1347)*
Deanne Naples Family Daycare ....G.... 302 376-1408
Middletown *(G-4022)*
Dees Learning Care ....G.... 908 623-7685
Newark *(G-6359)*
Developing Minds Preschool ....G.... 302 995-9611
Wilmington *(G-10129)*
Diane Spence Day Care ....G.... 302 335-4460
Frederica *(G-2401)*
Diocesan Council Inc ....E.... 302 475-4688
Wilmington *(G-10157)*
Dis Daycare ....F.... 302 888-0350
Wilmington *(G-10162)*
Discovery Island Preschool ....F.... 302 732-7529
Dagsboro *(G-898)*
Ditrocchio Maria Antonetta ....G.... 302 450-6790
Dover *(G-1432)*
Dog Dayz Dog Day Care Center ....G.... 302 655-5506
Wilmington *(G-10182)*
Dover Educational & Cmnty Ctr ....F.... 302 883-3092
Dover *(G-1446)*
Dovers Childrens Villag ....F.... 302 672-6476
Dover *(G-1473)*
Durrell Sandblasting & Pntg Co ....G.... 302 836-1113
Newark *(G-6481)*
Early Childhood Lab ....G.... 302 857-6731
Dover *(G-1496)*
Early Learning Center ....G.... 302 831-0584
Wilmington *(G-10317)*
Early Learning Center ....E.... 302 239-3033
Hockessin *(G-3015)*
Ebenezer United Methdst Chruch ....F.... 302 731-9495
Newark *(G-6500)*
Eden Land Care ....G.... 302 379-2405
Wilmington *(G-10345)*
Edgemoor Community Center Inc ....E.... 302 762-1391
Wilmington *(G-10348)*
Education Svcs Unlimited LLC ....F.... 302 650-4210
Wilmington *(G-10352)*

Educational Enrichment Center ....E.... 302 478-8697
Wilmington *(G-10354)*
Eisele Celine ....G.... 302 684-3201
Milton *(G-4902)*
Elaine Leonard ....F.... 302 376-5553
Middletown *(G-4052)*
Elementary Workshop Inc ....F.... 302 656-1498
Wilmington *(G-10369)*
Elsmere Presbyterian Church ....F.... 302 998-6365
Wilmington *(G-10384)*
Emma Jefferies Day Care ....G.... 302 762-3235
Wilmington *(G-10392)*
Enterprise Learning Solutions ....G.... 302 762-6595
Wilmington *(G-10408)*
Estelles Child Dev Ctr Inc ....F.... 302 792-9065
New Castle *(G-5294)*
Esther V Graham ....G.... 302 422-6667
Milford *(G-4406)*
Expanding Our Kids World ....E.... 302 659-0293
Smyrna *(G-8630)*
Ezion Fair Community Academy ....F.... 302 652-9114
Wilmington *(G-10466)*
Fairchild Day School ....G.... 302 478-4646
Wilmington *(G-10476)*
Faith Presbyterian Church ....F.... 302 764-8615
Wilmington *(G-10478)*
Faith Victory Christn Academy ....F.... 302 333-0855
Claymont *(G-744)*
Family Wrkplace Connection Inc ....D.... 302 479-1660
Wilmington *(G-10496)*
Favored Childcare Academy Inc ....G.... 302 698-1266
Dover *(G-1543)*
First Steps Preschool-Milford ....G.... 302 424-4470
Milford *(G-4415)*
Foot Steps Two Heaven Daycare ....G.... 302 738-5519
Newark *(G-6601)*
Foulk Pre-Schl & Day Cre Cntr ....G.... 302 529-1580
Wilmington *(G-10600)*
Foulk Pre-Schl & Day Cre Cntr ....G.... 302 478-3047
Wilmington *(G-10601)*
Fun 2 Learn Day Care ....G.... 302 875-3393
Laurel *(G-3231)*
Funstep Inc ....F.... 302 731-9618
Newark *(G-6629)*
Future Development Learning ....G.... 302 652-7500
Wilmington *(G-10653)*
Future Leaders ....G.... 862 262-7312
Smyrna *(G-8638)*
Gaudenzia Inc ....G.... 302 421-9945
Wilmington *(G-10679)*
Gb Jacobs LLC ....E.... 302 378-9100
Middletown *(G-4084)*
Gift Love Early Learning Ctr ....G.... 302 659-1984
Smyrna *(G-8641)*
Good Beginnings Preschool ....G.... 302 875-5507
Laurel *(G-3232)*
Graceland Daycare ....G.... 302 698-0414
Magnolia *(G-3892)*
Great New Beginnings ....G.... 302 218-8332
Bear *(G-170)*
Green Acres Pre School ....F.... 302 378-9250
Odessa *(G-7827)*
Greenbank Child Dev Ctr ....G.... 302 994-8574
Wilmington *(G-10775)*
Growing Palace ....F.... 302 376-5553
Middletown *(G-4094)*
Growing Palace III ....F.... 302 376-5553
Middletown *(G-4095)*
Guardian Angel Child Care ....G.... 302 428-3620
Wilmington *(G-10796)*
Guardian Angel Day Care ....G.... 302 934-0130
Georgetown *(G-2552)*
Hand -N- Hand Early Lrng Ctr ....F.... 302 422-0702
Ellendale *(G-2260)*
Happy Kids Academy Inc ....E.... 302 369-6929
Newark *(G-6706)*
Happy Place Day Care LLC ....G.... 302 737-7603
Newark *(G-6707)*
Happyland Childcare ....G.... 302 424-3868
Lincoln *(G-3854)*
Harrison House Cmnty Program ....E.... 302 595-3370
Newark *(G-6710)*
Hartly Family Learning Ctr LLC ....F.... 302 492-1152
Hartly *(G-2923)*
Harvest Community Dev Corp ....E.... 302 654-2613
Wilmington *(G-10847)*
Head Start Harrington ....G.... 302 398-9196
Harrington *(G-2848)*
Heart Start Er Training Inc ....G.... 302 420-1917
Wilmington *(G-10876)*

SIC

Employee Codes: A=Over 500 employees, B=251-500
C=101-250, D=51-100, E=20-50, F=10-19, G=1-9
2020 Harris Directory of
Delaware Businesses
565

Heart To Hand Daycare LLC G 302 256-4524
Lewes *(G-3539)*
Hill Luth Day Care Center E 302 656-3224
Wilmington *(G-10908)*
Hilltop Lutheran Neighborhd E 302 656-3224
Wilmington *(G-10910)*
Hockessin Montessori School E 302 234-1240
Hockessin *(G-3053)*
Hope House Daycare F 302 407-3404
Wilmington *(G-10951)*
Independence School Inc D 302 239-0330
Newark *(G-6771)*
J N Hooker Inc E 302 838-5650
Bear *(G-195)*
Jacqueline Allens Daycare G 302 368-3633
Newark *(G-6823)*
Janis Dicristofaro Day Care G 302 998-6630
Wilmington *(G-11129)*
Jjs Learning Experience LLC F 302 398-9000
Harrington *(G-2856)*
Jumpin Jacks G 302 762-7604
Wilmington *(G-11207)*
Junebugs Little Rubies LLC G 302 494-7552
Wilmington *(G-11208)*
Karen Schreiber G 302 628-3007
Seaford *(G-8284)*
Karen Schreiber G 302 875-7733
Laurel *(G-3248)*
Karries Daycare G 302 328-7369
New Castle *(G-5451)*
Kenton Child Care G 302 674-8142
Dover *(G-1742)*
Kerry & G Inc G 302 999-0022
Wilmington *(G-11247)*
Kiddie Academy of Middletown E 302 376-5112
Middletown *(G-4122)*
Kids Cottage LLC E 302 644-7690
Rehoboth Beach *(G-7981)*
Kids Inc G 302 422-9099
Milford *(G-4467)*
Kids Korner Day Care G 302 998-4606
Wilmington *(G-11259)*
Kids Nest Day Care G 302 731-7017
Newark *(G-6886)*
Kids R US Learning Center Inc G 302 678-1234
Dover *(G-1748)*
Kidscom Daycare G 302 544-5655
New Castle *(G-5464)*
Kidz Akademy Corp G 302 732-6077
Dagsboro *(G-913)*
Kidz Ink E 302 838-1500
Bear *(G-218)*
Kidz Ink G 302 376-1700
Middletown *(G-4123)*
Kidz Klub G 302 652-5439
Wilmington *(G-11260)*
Kidz Kottage Club Inc F 302 398-4067
Harrington *(G-2862)*
Kimberly Sue Kester G 302 732-1093
Dagsboro *(G-914)*
Kind Mind Kids G 302 545-0380
Wilmington *(G-11263)*
Kindercare Learning Ctrs LLC E 302 234-8680
Hockessin *(G-3071)*
Kindercare Learning Ctrs LLC F 302 834-6931
Newark *(G-6888)*
Kindercare Learning Ctrs LLC F 302 322-3102
New Castle *(G-5465)*
Kindercare Learning Ctrs LLC E 302 475-2212
Wilmington *(G-11265)*
Kindercare Learning Ctrs LLC F 302 731-7138
Wilmington *(G-11266)*
Kingdom Kids Day Care F 302 492-0207
Hartly *(G-2931)*
La Petite Academy Inc E 302 234-2574
Hockessin *(G-3075)*
Lake Forest School District F 302 398-8945
Harrington *(G-2864)*
Learning Care Group Inc E 302 235-5702
Wilmington *(G-11350)*
Learning Circle Child Care G 302 834-1473
Bear *(G-233)*
Learning Ctr At Madison St LLC F 302 543-7588
Wilmington *(G-11351)*
Learning Express Academy E 302 737-8260
Newark *(G-6926)*
Learning Express Preschool F 302 737-8990
Newark *(G-6927)*
Learning Patch Kids G 302 368-7208
Newark *(G-6928)*
Learning Train LLC F 302 731-0944
Newark *(G-6929)*
Learning Tree Network G 302 645-7199
Milton *(G-4923)*
Learning Years Preschool G 302 241-4781
Dover *(G-1774)*
Learning4 Lrng Professionals G 302 994-0451
Wilmington *(G-11352)*
Lessons Learnd Dy Care /Presch E 302 777-2200
Wilmington *(G-11375)*
Lewes Montessori School G 302 644-7482
Lewes *(G-3602)*
Lighted Pathway Day Care Ctr F 302 629-8583
Seaford *(G-8294)*
Lil Red Hen Nursery Schl Inc E 302 846-2777
Delmar *(G-1017)*
Limestone Country Day School F 302 239-9041
Wilmington *(G-11388)*
Linda Putnam Day Care G 302 836-1033
Bear *(G-236)*
Lindas Angels Chldcare Dev Ctr F 302 328-3700
New Castle *(G-5484)*
Lisa Trabaudo Day Care G 302 653-3529
Smyrna *(G-8674)*
Little Blessings Daycare F 302 655-8962
Wilmington *(G-11401)*
Little Einsteins Preschool G 302 933-0600
Millsboro *(G-4721)*
Little Folks Too Day Care G 302 652-3420
Wilmington *(G-11402)*
Little Folks Too Day Care E 302 652-1238
Wilmington *(G-11403)*
Little Kids Swagg Lrng Ctr LLC G 302 480-4404
Smyrna *(G-8675)*
Little Learner Inc F 302 798-5570
Claymont *(G-774)*
Little People Child Dev G 302 328-1481
Christiana *(G-673)*
Little People Day Care G 302 528-4336
Middletown *(G-4134)*
Little Peoples College G 302 998-4929
Wilmington *(G-11406)*
Little Pople Child Dev Ctr Inc F 302 836-5900
Bear *(G-237)*
Little Scholars Learning Ctr F 302 656-8785
Wilmington *(G-11407)*
Little School Inc F 302 734-3040
Dover *(G-1792)*
Little Star Inc F 302 995-2920
Wilmington *(G-11408)*
Little Stars Inc F 302 737-9759
Newark *(G-6942)*
Little Steps Daycare G 302 654-4867
Wilmington *(G-11409)*
Little Trooper Day Care G 302 378-7355
Middletown *(G-4135)*
Love N Learn Nursery Too G 302 678-0445
Dover *(G-1797)*
Loving Care Nursery School G 302 653-6990
Smyrna *(G-8676)*
Lullaby Learning Center Inc F 302 703-2871
Harbeson *(G-2789)*
Lynns Home Daycare G 302 337-0186
Bridgeville *(G-490)*
Magic Yrs Child Care Lrng Cntr F 302 322-3102
New Castle *(G-5496)*
Mahavir LLC E 302 651-7995
Wilmington *(G-11489)*
Malgiero Helen A Day Care G 302 834-9060
Delaware City *(G-960)*
Mamie Sturgis Handy Day Care G 302 875-4703
Laurel *(G-3260)*
Marlette R Lofland G 302 628-1521
Bridgeville *(G-494)*
Mary E Herring Daycare Center G 302 652-5978
Wilmington *(G-11557)*
Marys Little Lambs Daycare G 302 436-5796
Selbyville *(G-8516)*
Maxines Daycare G 302 652-7242
Wilmington *(G-11580)*
Mercy Land Academy Inc G 302 378-2013
Middletown *(G-4152)*
MI-Dee Inc E 302 453-7326
Newark *(G-7022)*
Milford Early Learning Center G 302 331-6612
Camden Wyoming *(G-649)*
Mom Home Daycare G 302 265-2668
Milford *(G-4511)*
Moms House Inc G 302 658-3433
Wilmington *(G-11730)*
Moms House Inc G 302 678-8688
Dover *(G-1870)*
Montessori Learning Centre G 302 478-2575
Wilmington *(G-11738)*
Mother Goose Childrens Center G 302 934-8454
Millsboro *(G-4754)*
Mother Hubbard Child Care Ctr F 302 368-7584
Newark *(G-7063)*
Ms Hathers Lrng Ctr Childcare G 302 994-2448
Wilmington *(G-11770)*
Nagengast Janet Day Care G 302 656-6898
Wilmington *(G-11794)*
Neenee Wees Daycare G 302 730-3630
Dover *(G-1891)*
Neighborhood House Inc F 302 658-5404
Wilmington *(G-11830)*
New Castle County Head Start F 302 452-1500
Newark *(G-7101)*
New Castle County Head Start E 302 999-8480
Wilmington *(G-11852)*
New Castle County Head Start F 302 832-2212
Bear *(G-262)*
New Day Montessori G 302 235-2554
Wilmington *(G-11862)*
New Direction Early Headstart E 302 831-0584
Newark *(G-7104)*
Newark Christian Childcare G 302 369-3000
Newark *(G-7113)*
Newark Ctr For Creative Lrng F 302 368-7772
Newark *(G-7115)*
Newark Day-Nursery Association E 302 731-4925
Newark *(G-7116)*
Newark Montessori Preschool G 302 366-1481
Newark *(G-7124)*
Newark United Methodist E 302 368-8774
Newark *(G-7129)*
Northeast Early Learning Ctr F 302 762-5803
Wilmington *(G-11903)*
Nurses N Kids Inc E 302 323-1118
New Castle *(G-5583)*
Odessa Early Education Center G 302 376-5254
Townsend *(G-8813)*
Ogletown Baptist Church E 302 737-2511
Newark *(G-7144)*
Our Childrens Learning Ctr G 302 565-1272
Bear *(G-274)*
Our Future Child Care Ctr LLC G 302 762-8645
Wilmington *(G-11983)*
Over Rainbow Daycare G 302 328-6574
New Castle *(G-5594)*
Panda Early Education Ctr Inc E 302 832-1891
Christiana *(G-674)*
Panda Early Education Ctr Inc F 302 832-1891
Bear *(G-276)*
Passion Care Services Inc F 302 832-2622
Bear *(G-278)*
Patricia Degirolano Day Care G 302 947-2874
Millsboro *(G-4770)*
Patricia Disario Day Care G 302 737-8889
Newark *(G-7182)*
Patricia McKay G 302 563-5334
Bear *(G-280)*
Peoples Place II Inc D 302 934-0300
Millsboro *(G-4780)*
Peoples Place II Inc D 302 730-1321
Dover *(G-1948)*
Peoples Settlement Assc of WI E 302 658-4133
Wilmington *(G-12079)*
Pirulos Child Care Center LLC G 302 836-3520
Newark *(G-7220)*
Playhouse Nursery School G 302 747-7007
Dover *(G-1966)*
Precious Knwldg Erly Lrng Ctr G 302 293-2588
Newark *(G-7238)*
Precious Little Angels Daycare G 302 378-2912
Townsend *(G-8817)*
Precious Little Hands Childcar G 302 298-5027
Wilmington *(G-12199)*
Precious Moments Day Care G 302 856-2346
Georgetown *(G-2623)*
Precious Years Child Care LLC G 302 322-1701
New Castle *(G-5635)*
Primeros Pasos Inc G 302 856-7406
Georgetown *(G-2627)*
Pyle Child Development Center F 302 732-1443
Frankford *(G-2382)*
Rainbow Day Care & Pre-Sch G 302 628-1020
Seaford *(G-8370)*
Regina Coleman G 215 476-4682
Wilmington *(G-12357)*

Company	Code	Phone
Renzi Rust Inc	F	302 424-4470
Milford (G-4538)		
Rising Stars Child Care Inc	F	302 998-7682
Wilmington (G-12424)		
Robin S Wright	G	302 249-2105
Lewes (G-3721)		
Rosa M Custis	G	302 934-0541
Millsboro (G-4795)		
Rose Hill Community Center	F	302 656-8513
New Castle (G-5684)		
Saint Johns Lutheran Church	E	302 734-7078
Dover (G-2055)		
Salvation Army	D	302 656-1696
Wilmington (G-12529)		
Sandy Rose Inc	F	302 454-1649
Newark (G-7383)		
Scalias Day Care Center Inc	G	302 366-1430
Newark (G-7392)		
Seeds of Jesus Day Care LLC	F	302 494-6568
Wilmington (G-12572)		
Selwor Enterprises Inc	F	302 454-9454
Newark (G-7404)		
Shavone Loves Kids Day Care	G	302 544-6170
New Castle (G-5704)		
Shelias Childcare Center	G	302 472-9648
Wilmington (G-12597)		
Shells Child Care Center III	F	302 398-9778
Harrington (G-2888)		
Shining Time Day Care Center	G	302 335-2770
Felton (G-2321)		
Slaughter Neck Educational and	G	302 684-1834
Lincoln (G-3870)		
Small Wonder Day Care Inc	E	302 654-2269
Wilmington (G-12651)		
Smalls Stepping Stone	E	302 652-3011
Wilmington (G-12653)		
Smarty Pants Early Education	G	302 985-3770
Bear (G-325)		
Smyrna School District	E	302 653-3135
Smyrna (G-8721)		
St Marks United Methodist Ch	E	302 994-0400
Wilmington (G-12726)		
St Michaels School Inc	E	302 656-3389
Wilmington (G-12727)		
Step Up Daycare	G	302 762-3183
Wilmington (G-12752)		
Sunshine Home Daycare	G	302 674-2009
Dover (G-2116)		
Sunshine Kids Academy	F	302 444-4270
Newark (G-7508)		
Susan R Austin	G	302 322-4685
New Castle (G-5744)		
Susan T Fischer	G	302 832-2570
Newark (G-7517)		
Sussex Prschool Erly Care Ctrs	G	302 732-7529
Seaford (G-8417)		
Tadpole Academy LLC	G	302 658-2141
Wilmington (G-12848)		
Telamon Corp Head Start Prgram	D	302 653-3766
Smyrna (G-8729)		
Telamon Corporation	E	302 736-5933
Dover (G-2136)		
Telamon Corporation Headstart	F	302 875-7718
Laurel (G-3299)		
Tender Hearts	F	302 674-2565
Dover (G-2138)		
Tender Loving Kare	E	302 464-1014
Middletown (G-4256)		
Tender Loving Kare Child Care	E	302 653-5677
Smyrna (G-8730)		
Thirst 2 Learn	G	302 293-2304
Bear (G-352)		
Thirst 2 Learn LLC	G	302 475-7080
Wilmington (G-12898)		
Thomas Jffrson Lrng Foundation	F	302 856-3300
Georgetown (G-2691)		
Timber Heart Learning Center	F	302 674-2565
Dover (G-2148)		
Tinas Tiny Tots Daycare	G	302 536-7077
Seaford (G-8424)		
Tiny Tots Childcare and Learni	G	302 651-9060
Wilmington (G-12915)		
Todays Kid Inc (not Inc)	G	302 834-5620
Newark (G-7573)		
Toddlers Tech Inc	F	302 655-4487
Wilmington (G-12923)		
Toy Box Child Care Center	G	302 427-8438
New Castle (G-5781)		
Tutor Time Learning Ctrs LLC	E	302 235-5701
Wilmington (G-12995)		
Tutor Time Lrng Systems Inc	E	302 478-7366
Wilmington (G-12996)		
United Cerebral Palsy of De	F	302 856-3490
Georgetown (G-2698)		
Universal Design Company	G	302 328-8391
New Castle (G-5809)		
V Quinton Inc	F	302 449-1711
Middletown (G-4274)		
Village Sq Acdemy Lrng Ctr LLC	G	302 539-5000
Ocean View (G-7823)		
Wagstaff Day Care Center Inc	F	302 998-7818
Wilmington (G-13112)		
Wee Care Day Care Salv Army	G	302 472-0712
Wilmington (G-13136)		
Wesley Play Care Center	F	302 678-8987
Dover (G-2213)		
West Center Cy Early Lrng Ctr	E	302 656-0485
Wilmington (G-13163)		
West Wilmington Svnth Day Adv	G	302 998-3961
Wilmington (G-13168)		
Whatcoat Christian Preschool	G	302 698-2108
Dover (G-2219)		
White Oak Head Start	G	302 736-5933
Dover (G-2224)		
Wilmington Head Start	G	302 762-8038
Wilmington (G-13231)		
Wilmington Headstart Inc	G	302 421-3620
Wilmington (G-13232)		
Wilmington Headstart Inc	G	302 762-8038
Wilmington (G-13233)		
Wilmington Montessori School	D	302 475-0555
Wilmington (G-13238)		
Wilson Care Wilson Co	G	302 897-5059
Newark (G-7709)		
Wonder Years Kids Club	F	302 398-0563
Harrington (G-2909)		
Wright Choice Child Care	G	302 798-0758
Claymont (G-827)		
Xavier Inc	G	302 655-1962
Wilmington (G-13314)		
Young Mens Christian Associat	D	302 296-9622
Rehoboth Beach (G-8121)		
Young Mens Christian Associat	C	302 571-6900
Wilmington (G-13332)		
YWCA Delaware	F	302 224-4060
Newark (G-7733)		

8361 Residential Care

Company	Code	Phone
Active Day Inc	F	302 831-6774
Newark (G-5896)		
Advo Opco LLC	A	302 365-8051
Bear (G-16)		
Advoserv Inc	E	302 365-8050
Bear (G-17)		
Advoserv Nj Inc	F	302 365-8050
Bear (G-18)		
Advoserv Nj Inc	D	302 365-8050
Bear (G-19)		
Assisted Living Concepts LLC	G	302 735-8800
Dover (G-1148)		
Associated Svc Specialist Inc	F	302 672-7159
Dover (G-1149)		
Catholic Mnstry To Elderly Inc	F	302 368-2784
Newark (G-6170)		
Changing Faces Inc	F	302 397-4164
Lincoln (G-3841)		
Children Fmilies First Del Inc	E	302 629-6996
Seaford (G-8194)		
Chimes Inc	G	302 678-3270
Dover (G-1279)		
Chimes Inc	D	302 452-3400
Newark (G-6199)		
Choice For Cmnty Lvng-Byview 1	G	302 328-4176
New Castle (G-5151)		
Choice For Community	G	302 734-9020
Dover (G-1280)		
Choices For Community Living	G	302 398-0446
Harrington (G-2825)		
Churchman Village Center LLC	G	302 998-6900
Newark (G-6234)		
Connections Community Support	D	302 389-1118
Smyrna (G-8603)		
Connections Community Support	D	302 984-2302
Wilmington (G-9826)		
Correction Delaware Department	B	302 856-5280
Georgetown (G-2487)		
Dunamis-Homes of Divine	G	302 393-5778
Camden Wyoming (G-631)		
Elderwood Village Dover LLC	D	516 496-1505
Dover (G-1511)		
Elizabeth W Murphey School Inc	D	302 734-7478
Dover (G-1515)		
Fellowship Hlth Resources Inc	F	302 854-0626
Georgetown (G-2528)		
Fellowship Hlth Resources Inc	F	302 856-7642
Georgetown (G-2529)		
Gateway House Inc	F	302 571-8885
Wilmington (G-10677)		
Green Valley Pavilion	E	302 653-5085
Smyrna (G-8646)		
Heritage At Milford	F	302 422-8700
Milford (G-4439)		
Home For Aged Wmn-Mnquadale HM	C	302 654-1810
Wilmington (G-10935)		
Ingleside Homes Inc	D	302 575-0250
Wilmington (G-11031)		
Kencrest Services	G	302 834-3365
Saint Georges (G-8127)		
Keystone Autism Services	G	302 731-3115
Newark (G-6880)		
Keystone Service Systems Inc	C	302 286-7234
Newark (G-6881)		
Keystone Service Systems Inc	C	302 273-3952
Newark (G-6882)		
Little Sisters of The Poor	D	302 368-5886
Newark (G-6941)		
Living Harvest Interntl Minst	G	302 757-4273
Wilmington (G-11413)		
Majalco LLC	G	703 507-5298
Wilmington (G-11494)		
Mary Campbell Center Inc	C	302 762-6025
Wilmington (G-11555)		
Mosaic	G	302 366-0257
Newark (G-7061)		
National Mentor Holdings Inc	E	732 627-9890
Millsboro (G-4760)		
National Mentor Holdings Inc	F	302 934-0512
Millsboro (G-4761)		
New Vision Services Inc	F	484 350-6495
Newark (G-7108)		
Peninsula Untd Mthdst Hmes Inc	F	302 235-6800
Hockessin (G-3114)		
Peninsula Untd Mthdst Hmes Inc	C	302 654-5101
Wilmington (G-12064)		
People In Transition Inc	G	302 784-5214
New Castle (G-5618)		
Pressley Ridge Foundation	G	302 366-0490
Christiana (G-678)		
Sacred Heart Village I Inc	E	302 428-0801
Wilmington (G-12513)		
Sacred Heart Village II Inc	E	302 428-3702
Wilmington (G-12514)		
Sunday Breakfast Mission	F	302 656-8542
Wilmington (G-12799)		
Sunrise Senior Living LLC	D	302 475-9163
Wilmington (G-12801)		
Visionquest Nonprofit Corp	E	302 735-1666
Dover (G-2197)		
Westminster Village Dover	G	302 744-3527
Dover (G-2216)		
Windsor Place	G	302 239-3200
Hockessin (G-3174)		
Young Mens Christian Associat	C	302 571-6900
Wilmington (G-13332)		

8399 Social Services, NEC

Company	Code	Phone
AARP	F	202 434-2277
Wilmington (G-8895)		
Agh Parent LLC	A	919 298-2267
Wilmington (G-8976)		
Aids Delaware Inc	G	302 226-3519
Rehoboth Beach (G-7838)		
ARC Finance Ltd	G	914 478-3851
Wilmington (G-9115)		
Article 19 Inc	G	302 295-4959
Wilmington (G-9138)		
Beth Sholom Congregation	D	302 734-5578
Dover (G-1199)		
Central Delaware Habitat For	G	302 526-2366
Dover (G-1267)		
Champions For Childrens Mh	G	302 249-6788
Newark (G-6185)		
Children Fmilies First Del Inc	G	302 674-8384
Dover (G-1276)		
Childrens Advocacy Ctr of Del	F	302 741-2123
Dover (G-1278)		
Click For Savings LLC	G	302 300-0202
Bear (G-78)		
Colonial Chapter of	G	302 861-6671
Newark (G-6263)		

Employee Codes: A=Over 500 employees, B=251-500 C=101-250, D=51-100, E=20-50, F=10-19, G=1-9

Community Interactions Inc..................G....... 302 993-7846
Wilmington *(G-9794)*
Connections Community Support.........E....... 302 654-7120
Wilmington *(G-9827)*
Cornerstone West Cmnty Dev Co.........G....... 302 658-4171
Wilmington *(G-9863)*
Coverdale Community Council..............G....... 302 337-7179
Bridgeville *(G-461)*
Delaware Center For Digestive.............F....... 302 565-6596
Newark *(G-6366)*
Delaware Center For Justice..................F....... 302 658-7174
Wilmington *(G-10013)*
Delaware Hmanities Council Inc...........G....... 302 657-0650
Wilmington *(G-10054)*
Easter Seal Delaware............................E....... 302 856-7364
Georgetown *(G-2519)*
Eastside Bluprt Cmnty Dev Corp..........F....... 302 384-2350
Wilmington *(G-10329)*
Family Outrch Multi-Purpose Com..........G....... 302 422-2158
Lincoln *(G-3847)*
Fathers Day Gala Inc............................G....... 302 981-4117
Wilmington *(G-10507)*
First State Cmnty Action Agcy.............D....... 302 856-7761
Georgetown *(G-2532)*
Food Bank of Delaware Inc..................E....... 302 424-3301
Milford *(G-4416)*
Food Bank of Delaware Inc..................E....... 302 292-1305
Newark *(G-6598)*
Fort Miles Historical Assn Inc...............G....... 302 645-0753
Lewes *(G-3503)*
Georgetown Playground & Pk Inc.........G....... 302 856-7111
Georgetown *(G-2547)*
Ggc Inc...G....... 267 893-8052
Lincoln *(G-3850)*
Global Childrens Advocacy LLC...........G....... 484 383-3900
Dover *(G-1594)*
Greene Business Support S.................G....... 302 480-3725
Dover *(G-1613)*
Health & Social Svcs Del Dept..............E....... 302 552-3530
Wilmington *(G-10868)*
Hete Tech Support................................G....... 302 226-1892
Rehoboth Beach *(G-7963)*
Hidden Acres Rest Home Inc................F....... 302 492-1962
Marydel *(G-3918)*
Hispanic Personal Dev LLC.................G....... 302 738-4782
Newark *(G-6731)*
Homes For Life Foundation..................F....... 302 571-1217
Wilmington *(G-10942)*
Homeward Bound Inc...........................F....... 302 737-2241
Newark *(G-6741)*
Independence Support Svcs LLC..........G....... 484 450-6662
New Castle *(G-5413)*
Jewish Federation of Delaware............F....... 302 478-5660
Wilmington *(G-11153)*
Knights York Cross of Honour.............G....... 302 731-4817
Newark *(G-6900)*
Leukemia & Lymphoma Soc Inc...........G....... 302 661-7300
Wilmington *(G-11377)*
Long Term Care Residents Div.............F....... 302 424-8600
Milford *(G-4477)*
Loris Hands Inc....................................G....... 302 440-5454
Newark *(G-6950)*
Mad Delaware Chapter..........................G....... 910 284-6286
Lewes *(G-3616)*
March of Dimes Inc..............................G....... 302 225-1020
Wilmington *(G-11521)*
Meghan House Inc...............................G....... 302 253-8261
Georgetown *(G-2601)*
Ministry of Caring Inc...........................C....... 302 652-8947
Wilmington *(G-11704)*
Navy Operational Support Ctr W..........G....... 312 998-3328
Wilmington *(G-11825)*
Ncf Supporting Organization................G....... 850 776-2789
Wilmington *(G-11826)*
Northern Del Youth For Chrst..............G....... 302 995-6937
Wilmington *(G-11906)*
Pathways of Delaware Inc....................D....... 302 573-5073
Wilmington *(G-12032)*
Pcmh Support Team - Privacy..............G....... 267 254-2111
Wilmington *(G-12051)*
Powell Life Skills Inc...........................C....... 302 378-2706
Townsend *(G-8816)*
Quinn-Miller Group Inc.........................G....... 302 738-9742
Wilmington *(G-12290)*
Richard Allen Coalition.........................G....... 302 258-7182
Georgetown *(G-2638)*
Royal Mission & Ministries...................G....... 302 249-8863
Laurel *(G-3286)*
Saint Georges Cultr & Arts Rev............G....... 302 836-8202
Saint Georges *(G-8129)*
Salvation Army.....................................E....... 302 654-8808
Wilmington *(G-12530)*
Simplymiddle..F....... 302 200-0102
Newark *(G-7432)*
Simplymiddle LLC.................................F....... 302 217-3460
Wilmington *(G-12629)*
St Matthew Grand Chapter...................G....... 302 834-9552
Dover *(G-2101)*
Supportive Care Solutions LLC............G....... 302 598-4797
Wilmington *(G-12813)*
Thedigitalsupport.................................G....... 347 305-4006
Wilmington *(G-12893)*
Uzuakoli Dev & Cultural Assn..............G....... 302 465-3266
Dover *(G-2185)*
Veterans Re-Entry Resources...............F....... 302 384-2350
Wilmington *(G-13072)*
Volunteers For Adolescent...................G....... 302 658-3331
Wilmington *(G-13102)*
West Rhoboth Cmnty Land Tr Inc.........G....... 302 260-9519
Rehoboth Beach *(G-8112)*
Wilmington Renaissance Corp.............G....... 302 425-5500
Wilmington *(G-13243)*

84 MUSEUMS, ART GALLERIES, AND BOTANICAL AND ZOOLOGICAL GARDENS

8412 Museums & Art Galleries

AMC Museum Foundation.....................G....... 302 677-5938
Dover *(G-1116)*
Biggs Swell C Mseum Amercn Art........G....... 302 674-2111
Dover *(G-1201)*
Commission On Archvs In Hstory.........G....... 302 335-5544
Frederica *(G-2400)*
Delaware AG Museum & Vlg.................G....... 302 734-1618
Dover *(G-1357)*
Delaware Art Museum Inc....................E....... 302 571-9590
Wilmington *(G-10001)*
Delaware Children S Museum...............G....... 302 654-2340
Wilmington *(G-10015)*
Delaware Childrens Museum Inc..........G....... 302 654-2340
Wilmington *(G-10016)*
Delaware Museum of Natural...............E....... 302 658-9111
Wilmington *(G-10068)*
Eleuthrian Mlls-Hgley Fndtion..............C....... 302 658-2400
Wilmington *(G-10370)*
Filipino Heritg & Arts Museum.............G....... 302 731-5899
Newark *(G-6579)*
For Delaware Center............................F....... 302 656-6466
Wilmington *(G-10589)*
Friends of Bellaca Airfield....................G....... 302 322-3816
New Castle *(G-5331)*
Gallery One...G....... 302 537-5055
Ocean View *(G-7790)*
Hale Byrnes House..............................F....... 302 998-3792
Newark *(G-6703)*
Historical & Cultural Afairs...................F....... 302 792-0285
Claymont *(G-761)*
Historical & Cultural Afairs...................F....... 302 323-4453
New Castle *(G-5396)*
Historical & Cultural Afairs...................F....... 302 739-3277
Dover *(G-1650)*
Historical Society of Del Inc.................E....... 302 295-2400
Wilmington *(G-10918)*
Historical Society of Del Inc.................E....... 302 322-8411
New Castle *(G-5397)*
◆ **Historical Society of Delware**...........E....... 302 655-7161
Wilmington *(G-10919)*
Kalmar Nyckel Foundation....................G....... 302 429-7447
Wilmington *(G-11223)*
Lewes Historical Society.......................G....... 302 645-7670
Lewes *(G-3601)*
Maxwell World.......................................G....... 937 463-3579
Dagsboro *(G-918)*
Milton Historical Society.......................F....... 302 684-1010
Milton *(G-4941)*
Mispillion Art League Inc......................G....... 302 430-7646
Milford *(G-4506)*
Nanticoke Indian Museum....................G....... 302 945-7022
Millsboro *(G-4758)*
New Castle Historical Society...............F....... 302 322-2794
New Castle *(G-5560)*
Odessa Historic Foundation..................E....... 302 378-4119
Odessa *(G-7832)*
Overfalls Maritime Museum..................D....... 302 644-8050
Lewes *(G-3674)*
Rehoboth Art League Inc......................G....... 302 227-8408
Rehoboth Beach *(G-8047)*
Rehoboth Beach Historical Soc............G....... 302 227-7310
Rehoboth Beach *(G-8052)*
Rh Gallery and Studios.........................G....... 302 218-5182
Hockessin *(G-3135)*
Rockwood Museum...............................G....... 302 761-4340
Wilmington *(G-12458)*
Sewell C Biggs Trust.............................F....... 302 674-2111
Dover *(G-2073)*
Somerville Manning Gallery..................G....... 302 652-0271
Wilmington *(G-12681)*
Winterthur Museum..............................G....... 302 740-9771
Wilmington *(G-13277)*
▲ **Winterthur Museum Garden & Lib**....E....... 302 888-4600
Winterthur *(G-13357)*

86 MEMBERSHIP ORGANIZATIONS

8611 Business Associations

Alias Inc..G....... 302 481-5556
Wilmington *(G-9010)*
Assocted Bldrs Cntrs Del Chpte...........G....... 302 328-1111
New Castle *(G-5048)*
Bethany-Fenwick Chamber...................G....... 302 539-2100
Fenwick Island *(G-2331)*
Better Business Bureau of De...............G....... 302 221-5255
New Castle *(G-5089)*
C S C Corporation Texas Inc................D....... 302 636-5440
Wilmington *(G-9524)*
Central Del Chmber of Commerce........G....... 302 734-7513
Dover *(G-1263)*
Clark Associates Inc.............................E....... 302 421-9950
New Castle *(G-5172)*
Corporate Relocation Assn...................G....... 302 239-9314
Newark *(G-6300)*
Delaware Comm Reinvstmnt Actn........G....... 302 298-3250
Wilmington *(G-10022)*
Delaware Credit Union Leag Inc...........G....... 302 322-9341
Newark *(G-6372)*
Delaware Dept Transportation..............C....... 302 577-3278
Dover *(G-1365)*
Delaware Healthcare Assn...................G....... 302 674-2853
Dover *(G-1376)*
Delaware Racing Association...............D....... 302 994-6700
Wilmington *(G-10075)*
Delaware Restaurant Assn....................G....... 302 738-2545
Newark *(G-6408)*
Delaware State Chamber......................F....... 302 655-7221
Wilmington *(G-10087)*
Delaware State Farm Bureau................G....... 302 697-3183
Camden *(G-560)*
Delaware Stndrdbre Ownrs Assc..........G....... 302 678-3058
Dover *(G-1398)*
Delmarva Poultry Industry Inc...............G....... 302 856-9037
Georgetown *(G-2507)*
Dtg General Contractor.........................G....... 321 439-0893
Wilmington *(G-10239)*
Establishing Black Men LLC..................G....... 215 432-7469
Claymont *(G-740)*
Georgetown Chamber Commerce.........F....... 302 856-1544
Georgetown *(G-2543)*
Insurance Networks Aliance LLC..........G....... 302 268-1010
Wilmington *(G-11045)*
Nemours Hlth & Prevention Svcs..........G....... 302 366-1929
Newark *(G-7092)*
New Cstle Cnty Chmber Commerce......F....... 302 737-4343
Wilmington *(G-11861)*
Parks & Recreation Del Div...................F....... 302 761-6963
Wilmington *(G-12023)*
Pride of Delaware Lodge.......................G....... 215 453-9236
Newark *(G-7251)*
Rehoboth Beach Dewey Beach Cha.....F....... 302 227-2233
Rehoboth Beach *(G-8051)*
Service Corps Retired Execs................E....... 302 573-6552
Wilmington *(G-12585)*
Seth Ral & Associates Inc.....................G....... 302 478-9020
Wilmington *(G-12587)*
Small Business Development Ctr..........F....... 302 571-1555
Wilmington *(G-12650)*
Stapler Athletic Association.................G....... 302 652-9769
Wilmington *(G-12740)*
Sussex County Assn Realtors..............G....... 302 855-2300
Georgetown *(G-2677)*
Uacj Trading America Co Ltd...............F....... 312 636-5941
Wilmington *(G-13005)*

8621 Professional Membership Organizations

American Birding Assn Inc...................G....... 302 838-3660
Delaware City *(G-948)*

86 MEMBERSHIP ORGANIZATIONS

American Heart Association Inc .... F 302 454-0613
Newark *(G-5952)*
American Lung Assn of Del .... G 302 737-6414
Newark *(G-5955)*
American Lung Association .... G 302 674-9701
Dover *(G-1120)*
American Philosophical Assn .... F 302 831-1112
Newark *(G-5956)*
Association For The Rights .... F 302 996-9400
Wilmington *(G-9159)*
Assoction Pathology Chairs Inc .... G 301 634-7880
Wilmington *(G-9161)*
Bethany Dental Association .... F 302 537-1200
Bethany Beach *(G-389)*
Central and Southern Delaware .... G 302 545-8067
Milford *(G-4345)*
Cramer & Dimichele PA .... G 302 293-1230
Wilmington *(G-9893)*
Dcor .... G 302 227-9341
Rehoboth Beach *(G-7908)*
Delaware Association .... G 302 622-9177
Wilmington *(G-10002)*
Delaware Association For Blind .... F 302 998-5913
Wilmington *(G-10003)*
Delaware Health Care Comm .... F 302 739-2730
Dover *(G-1374)*
Delaware Health Info Netwrk .... F 302 678-0220
Dover *(G-1375)*
Delaware Helpline Inc .... F 302 255-1810
Wilmington *(G-10052)*
Delaware Rural Water Assn .... G 302 424-3792
Milford *(G-4380)*
Delaware State Bar Association .... G 302 658-5279
Wilmington *(G-10086)*
Delaware State Dental Society .... F 302 368-7634
Newark *(G-6414)*
Family Practice Association PA .... E 302 656-5416
Wilmington *(G-10494)*
International Literacy Assn .... D 302 731-1600
Newark *(G-6797)*
Jones Francina .... G 302 245-4139
Delmar *(G-1010)*
LLC Levy Wilson .... F 302 888-1088
Wilmington *(G-11415)*
Medical Society of Delaware .... E 302 366-1400
Newark *(G-7018)*
National Society Inc .... G 302 656-9572
Wilmington *(G-11811)*
Navy League of United States .... G 302 456-4410
Wilmington *(G-11824)*
Nonprofit Bus Solutions LLC .... F 302 353-4606
Wilmington *(G-11894)*
Seamens Center Wilmington Inc .... F 302 575-1300
Wilmington *(G-12565)*
Society For Whole-Body Autorad .... G 302 369-5240
Newark *(G-7452)*
State Education Agency Di .... F 302 739-4111
Dover *(G-2103)*
Volume Mob Inc .... G 302 433-6629
Wilmington *(G-13101)*

8631 Labor Unions & Similar Organizations

American Federation .... G 302 283-1330
Newark *(G-5951)*
American Federation of State .... F 302 323-2121
New Castle *(G-5031)*
American Postal Workers Union .... E 302 322-8994
New Castle *(G-5035)*
Christina Education Assn .... F 302 454-7700
Newark *(G-6228)*
Contemprary Stffing Sltons Inc .... G 302 328-1300
New Castle *(G-5192)*
Delaware Nature Society .... D 302 239-1283
Hockessin *(G-3006)*
Delaware State Education Assn .... E 302 734-5834
Dover *(G-1396)*
Delaware State Education Assn .... G 302 366-8440
Newark *(G-6415)*
Diamond State Tele Coml Un .... F 302 999-1100
Wilmington *(G-10148)*
General Teamsters Local Un 326 .... G 302 328-2387
New Castle *(G-5349)*
Iron Workers Local 451 .... G 302 994-0946
Wilmington *(G-11082)*
Laborers Intl Un N Amer .... G 302 654-2880
Newark *(G-6911)*
Laborers Intl Un N Amer .... F 302 934-7376
Georgetown *(G-2588)*
Millwrights Local Union 1548 .... F 410 355-0011
Wilmington *(G-11698)*

National Assn Ltr Carriers .... G 302 652-2933
Newport *(G-7751)*
Pace Local 2 898 .... G 302 737-8898
Newark *(G-7169)*
Plumbers Pipefitters Local 74 .... G 302 636-7400
Newark *(G-7223)*
Smart .... F 302 655-6084
New Castle *(G-5717)*
Transport Wkrs Un Amer Intl Un .... G 302 652-1503
Wilmington *(G-12957)*
United Auto Workers Local 435 .... F 302 995-6001
Newark *(G-7611)*
United Steelworkers .... E 302 999-0412
Wilmington *(G-13026)*
United Tele Wkrs Local 13101 .... G 302 737-0400
Newark *(G-7616)*

8641 Civic, Social & Fraternal Associations

1122 Condominium .... G 302 234-4860
New Castle *(G-4988)*
1401 Condominium Association .... E 302 656-8171
Wilmington *(G-8847)*
Alpha PHI Delta Fraternity .... E 302 531-7854
Camden *(G-536)*
American Legion .... G 302 398-3566
Harrington *(G-2809)*
American Legion .... G 302 628-5221
Seaford *(G-8147)*
American Legion Log Cabin .... G 302 629-9915
Seaford *(G-8148)*
American Lgion Amblance Stn 64 .... G 302 653-6465
Smyrna *(G-8569)*
Angola By Bay Prprty Ownr Assn .... F 302 945-2700
Lewes *(G-3341)*
Arise Africa Foundation Inc .... G 877 829-5500
New Castle *(G-5043)*
Battle Proven Foundation .... G 703 216-1986
Dover *(G-1178)*
Bay Forest Homeowners Assn .... G 302 537-6580
Ocean View *(G-7757)*
Baynard House Condominiums .... G 302 319-3740
Wilmington *(G-9266)*
Baywood Greens .... G 302 947-9800
Millsboro *(G-4637)*
Bear-Glasgow YMCA .... G 302 836-9622
Newark *(G-6066)*
Benevolent & Protective Order .... G 302 424-2401
Milford *(G-4322)*
Benevolent Protectve Ordr Elks .... F 302 629-2458
Seaford *(G-8165)*
Best Buddies International Inc .... G 302 691-3187
Wilmington *(G-9313)*
Boys & Girls Club of De .... G 302 677-6376
Dover *(G-1224)*
Boys & Girls Club of Milford .... G 302 422-4453
Milford *(G-4330)*
Boys & Girls Clubs Del Inc .... F 302 422-3757
Milford *(G-4331)*
Boys & Girls Clubs Del Inc .... B 302 658-1870
Wilmington *(G-9404)*
Boys & Girls Clubs Del Inc .... E 302 836-6464
Newark *(G-6112)*
Boys & Girls Clubs Del Inc .... F 302 655-8569
New Castle *(G-5102)*
Boys & Girls Clubs Del Inc .... G 302 678-5182
Dover *(G-1225)*
Boys & Girls Clubs Del Inc .... G 302 678-5182
Dover *(G-1226)*
Boys & Girls Clubs Del Inc .... G 302 656-1386
Wilmington *(G-9405)*
Boys & Girls Clubs Del Inc .... G 302 655-4591
Wilmington *(G-9406)*
Boys & Girls Clubs Del Inc .... F 302 856-4903
Georgetown *(G-2457)*
Boys & Girls Clubs Del Inc .... G 302 628-3789
Seaford *(G-8173)*
Boys & Girls Clubs of America .... F 302 659-5610
Smyrna *(G-8584)*
Boys & Girls Clubs of America .... G 302 875-1200
Laurel *(G-3204)*
Boys Girls Clubs .... G 302 260-9864
Rehoboth Beach *(G-7873)*
Brandywine Club Inc .... G 302 798-9891
Claymont *(G-705)*
Brandywine Park Condos .... G 302 655-2262
Wilmington *(G-9448)*
Brenden Bailey & Chandler VFW .... G 302 239-0797
Hockessin *(G-3096)*
Center For Inland Bays Inc .... G 302 226-8105
Rehoboth Beach *(G-7885)*

Coffee Run Condo Council Inc .... G 302 239-4134
Hockessin *(G-2991)*
Community Business Dev Corp .... G 302 544-1709
Newark *(G-6271)*
Council of Devon .... F 302 658-5366
Wilmington *(G-9873)*
Del Ray Foundatins LLC .... G 302 272-6153
Milford *(G-4372)*
Del-Mr-Va Cncil Inc Boy Scuts .... E 302 622-3300
Wilmington *(G-9998)*
Delaware City Recreation Club .... G 302 834-9900
Delaware City *(G-953)*
Delaware Ffa Foundation Inc .... G 302 857-6493
Dover *(G-1369)*
Delaware Nature Society .... D 302 239-1283
Hockessin *(G-3006)*
Delaware Parents Association .... F 302 678-9288
Dover *(G-1386)*
Delaware Retired Schl Prsnl .... E 302 674-8252
Wilmington *(G-10079)*
Delaware Saengerbund Lib Assn .... G 302 366-9454
Newark *(G-6410)*
Delaware Veterans Home Inc .... D 302 424-6000
Milford *(G-4382)*
Delaware Wild Lands Inc .... G 302 378-2736
Odessa *(G-7825)*
Diamond State Home Auxiliary .... G 302 652-9331
Newport *(G-7747)*
Disabled American Veterans .... E 302 697-9061
Camden *(G-563)*
Early Foundations Therapeutic .... G 302 384-6905
Wilmington *(G-10316)*
East Millsboro Elem School Pto .... G 302 238-0176
Millsboro *(G-4684)*
East Sussex Moose Lodge .... G 302 436-2088
Frankford *(G-2361)*
Eastern Bison Association .... F 434 660-6036
Greenwood *(G-2735)*
Farpath Foundation .... G 302 645-8328
Lewes *(G-3492)*
Forest Oak Elementary Pta .... G 302 540-2873
Newark *(G-6603)*
Fraternal Order Eagles Inc .... G 302 764-6100
Wilmington *(G-10621)*
Fraternal Order of Eagles BR .... G 302 616-2935
Ocean View *(G-7786)*
Freelee Foundation .... G 302 607-8053
Newark *(G-6619)*
Georgetown Boys and Girls Club .... F 302 856-4903
Georgetown *(G-2542)*
Girl Scouts of The Cheasapea .... E 302 456-7150
Newark *(G-6656)*
Girls Incorporate of Delaware .... E 302 575-1041
Wilmington *(G-10716)*
Greater Dover Foundation .... G 302 734-2513
Dover *(G-1609)*
Hall Burke VFW Post 5447 Inc .... F 302 798-2052
Wilmington *(G-10824)*
Hamilton House Condominium .... G 302 658-7787
Wilmington *(G-10827)*
Helopen Condominium Council .... G 302 227-6409
Rehoboth Beach *(G-7959)*
Indo-American Association Del .... F 302 234-0214
Newark *(G-6772)*
Intercollegiate Studies Inst .... D 302 656-3292
Wilmington *(G-11054)*
Knights of Columbus .... F 302 559-9959
Wilmington *(G-11282)*
Kristol Ctr For Jewish Lf Inc .... G 302 453-0479
Newark *(G-6903)*
League of Wmen Vters New Cstle .... F 302 571-8948
Wilmington *(G-11349)*
Lincoln Community Hall Inc .... G 302 242-1747
Lincoln *(G-3859)*
Linden Hill Elementary Pta .... E 302 454-3406
Wilmington *(G-11395)*
Longview Farms Civic Assn .... G 302 475-6684
Wilmington *(G-11432)*
Loyal Order Mose Lwes Rehoboth .... G 302 684-4004
Lewes *(G-3613)*
Mallerd Lakes .... F 443 783-2993
Selbyville *(G-8514)*
Maplewood Home Owners Clubhous .... G 302 645-9925
Rehoboth Beach *(G-7997)*
Mariners Court Condo Assn .... E 443 742-7812
Rehoboth Beach *(G-7998)*
Millcreek Foundation .... G 302 239-3811
Hockessin *(G-3096)*
Moose International Inc .... G 302 684-4004
Lewes *(G-3649)*

Employee Codes: A=Over 500 employees, B=251-500
C=101-250, D=51-100, E=20-50, F=10-19, G=1-9

2020 Harris Directory of
Delaware Businesses

Natio Assoc For The Advan of..............F....... 302 655-0998
Wilmington *(G-11804)*
New Temple Corp..............G....... 302 998-6475
Wilmington *(G-11870)*
Noor Foundation International..............G....... 302 234-8860
Hockessin *(G-3105)*
North Star Pta..............G....... 302 234-7200
Hockessin *(G-3106)*
Oak Orchard-Riverdale American..............F....... 302 945-1673
Millsboro *(G-4766)*
Objective Zero Foundation..............F....... 202 573-9660
Wilmington *(G-11930)*
Omega PSI PHI Fraternity..............G....... 908 463-2197
Dover *(G-1917)*
One Commerce Ctr Condo Council..............G....... 302 573-2513
Wilmington *(G-11953)*
One Virginia..............G....... 302 227-9533
Rehoboth Beach *(G-8023)*
Park Plaza Condo Association..............G....... 302 658-3526
Wilmington *(G-12021)*
PHI Service Co..............F....... 302 451-5224
Newark *(G-7212)*
Police Athc Leag Wlmington Inc..............G....... 302 764-6170
Wilmington *(G-12181)*
Police Athletic League Del..............G....... 302 656-9501
New Castle *(G-5631)*
Polish Library Association..............G....... 302 652-9555
Wilmington *(G-12183)*
Pride of Delaw..............G....... 302 861-6857
Newark *(G-7250)*
Pta Delaware Military Academy..............E....... 302 998-0745
Wilmington *(G-12263)*
Pta Lombardy Elementary..............G....... 302 478-6054
Wilmington *(G-12264)*
Public Allies Deleware Inc..............G....... 302 573-4438
Wilmington *(G-12265)*
Raskob Foundation For Catholic..............F....... 302 655-4440
Wilmington *(G-12319)*
Richardson Park Community..............E....... 302 428-1247
Wilmington *(G-12414)*
Rockford Park Condominium Home..............G....... 302 658-7842
Wilmington *(G-12451)*
Rotary International..............F....... 302 378-2488
Middletown *(G-4224)*
Rotary International..............F....... 302 227-5862
Rehoboth Beach *(G-8063)*
Salvation Army..............E....... 302 654-8808
Wilmington *(G-12530)*
Seaford Police Dept..............E....... 302 629-6644
Seaford *(G-8394)*
Silver Lake Elem Sch Pta..............D....... 302 378-5023
Middletown *(G-4241)*
Solar Foundations Usa Inc..............F....... 855 738-7200
New Castle *(G-5721)*
Solutions Property Management..............G....... 302 581-9060
Rehoboth Beach *(G-8081)*
South Bowers Ladies Auxiliary..............E....... 302 335-4135
Milford *(G-4564)*
St Stephens Evang Lutheran Ch..............G....... 302 652-7623
Wilmington *(G-12729)*
Star of The Sea Assoc of Ownrs..............G....... 302 227-6006
Rehoboth Beach *(G-8086)*
Supreme Grand Lodge of U S A..............G....... 302 998-3549
Wilmington *(G-12816)*
Sussex Cnty Manufactrd Housing..............G....... 302 945-2122
Millsboro *(G-4806)*
The Nature Conservancy..............F....... 302 654-4707
Wilmington *(G-12891)*
Tiffany Pines I Condo Assn..............G....... 302 227-0913
Rehoboth Beach *(G-8098)*
United Tele Wkrs Local 13101..............G....... 302 737-0400
Newark *(G-7616)*
Universty & Whist Club Wlmgton..............F....... 302 658-5125
Wilmington *(G-13031)*
V F W Post Home..............G....... 302 366-8438
Newark *(G-7637)*
V F W Sussex Mem Post 7422..............G....... 302 934-9967
Millsboro *(G-4819)*
V F W Virgil Wilson Post..............G....... 302 629-3092
Seaford *(G-8428)*
Veterans of Foreign Wars Newmn..............G....... 302 653-8801
Smyrna *(G-8736)*
VFW Post 6483..............G....... 302 422-4412
Milford *(G-4591)*
Voiture Nationale La Society..............G....... 302 478-7591
Wilmington *(G-13100)*
Walter L Fox Post 2 Inc..............E....... 302 674-1741
Dover *(G-2205)*
Wdbid Management Company..............D....... 302 425-5374
Wilmington *(G-13129)*
Willow Run Civic Association..............G....... 302 994-2250
Wilmington *(G-13219)*
Wilmington Club Inc..............E....... 302 658-4287
Wilmington *(G-13226)*
Wilmington Elks Home Inc..............G....... 302 652-0313
Wilmington *(G-13230)*
Wilmington Trap Association..............E....... 302 834-9320
Newark *(G-7708)*
Wilmington Youth Organization..............G....... 302 761-9030
Wilmington *(G-13267)*
Young Mens Christian Associat..............D....... 302 296-9622
Rehoboth Beach *(G-8121)*
YWCA Delaware..............F....... 302 224-4060
Newark *(G-7733)*
YWCA Delaware..............D....... 302 655-0039
Wilmington *(G-13337)*

8651 Political Organizations

Republican State Committee Del..............G....... 302 668-1954
Wilmington *(G-12384)*

8699 Membership Organizations, NEC

A Fresh Start Clg Svcs Corp..............G....... 302 257-1099
Newark *(G-5867)*
AAA Club Alliance Inc..............B....... 302 368-8175
Newark *(G-5873)*
AAA Club Alliance Inc..............F....... 302 674-8020
Dover *(G-1075)*
Afgceaa Corporation..............G....... 617 314-0814
Wilmington *(G-8972)*
American Frnds of The Ryal Soc..............G....... 302 295-4959
Wilmington *(G-9045)*
American Soc Cytopathology Inc..............G....... 302 543-6583
Wilmington *(G-9056)*
Association Eductional Publr..............F....... 302 295-8350
Wilmington *(G-9158)*
Astrazeneca Foundation..............G....... 302 886-3000
Wilmington *(G-9167)*
Athari Inc..............F....... 312 358-4933
Dover *(G-1154)*
Attention Dficit Disorder Assn..............G....... 302 478-0255
Talleyville *(G-8749)*
Because Love Allows Compassion..............E....... 302 674-2496
Dover *(G-1188)*
Benevlent Prtective Order Elks..............E....... 302 736-1903
Dover *(G-1191)*
Bethany Beach Vlntr Fire Co..............E....... 302 539-7700
Bethany Beach *(G-388)*
Blackwater Village Association..............G....... 302 541-4700
Dagsboro *(G-883)*
Blessed Giving..............G....... 302 856-4551
Georgetown *(G-2456)*
Blindsight Delaware LLC..............E....... 302 998-5913
Wilmington *(G-9370)*
Brain Injury Association Del..............F....... 302 346-2083
Dover *(G-1228)*
Cape Henlopen Senior Center..............G....... 302 227-2055
Rehoboth Beach *(G-7883)*
Catholic Docese Wilmington Inc..............G....... 302 764-2717
Wilmington *(G-9595)*
Challenge Program..............G....... 302 655-0945
Wilmington *(G-9624)*
Child Inc..............E....... 302 762-8989
Wilmington *(G-9661)*
Christian Science Reading Room..............G....... 302 456-1428
Newark *(G-6206)*
Christian Science Reading Room..............F....... 302 227-7650
Rehoboth Beach *(G-7888)*
Christina Cultural Arts Center..............E....... 302 652-0101
Wilmington *(G-9690)*
Collegiate Network Inc..............G....... 302 652-4600
Wilmington *(G-9771)*
Curiosity Service Foundation..............G....... 302 628-4140
Seaford *(G-8215)*
Dcrac..............G....... 302 298-3289
Wilmington *(G-9981)*
Delaware Chpr Amer Acdmy Pedtc..............G....... 302 218-1075
Newark *(G-6369)*
Delaware Comm Reinvstmnt Actn..............G....... 302 298-3250
Wilmington *(G-10022)*
Delaware Ctr For Hrtclture Inc..............F....... 302 658-6262
Wilmington *(G-10032)*
Delaware Friends of Folk..............G....... 302 678-1423
Dover *(G-1372)*
Delaware Humane Association..............E....... 302 571-0111
Wilmington *(G-10055)*
Delaware Lacrosse Foundation..............F....... 302 831-8661
Wilmington *(G-10061)*
Delaware S P C A..............E....... 302 998-2281
Newark *(G-6409)*
Delaware S P C A..............G....... 302 856-6361
Georgetown *(G-2502)*
Delaware Spca..............G....... 302 698-3006
Camden *(G-559)*
Dewey Artist Collaboration Inc..............G....... 302 212-9798
Rehoboth Beach *(G-7915)*
East Sussex Moose Lodge..............G....... 302 436-2088
Frankford *(G-2361)*
Fairwinds Baptist Church Inc..............G....... 302 322-1029
Bear *(G-149)*
Faithful Friends Inc..............D....... 302 427-8514
Wilmington *(G-10479)*
Family & Friends Caring Perola..............F....... 302 683-0611
Wilmington *(G-10484)*
Foundation Source Philanthropi..............E....... 800 839-1754
Wilmington *(G-10603)*
Frets4vetsorg..............G....... 302 382-1426
Georgetown *(G-2534)*
Friends of University Sussex..............F....... 302 295-4959
Wilmington *(G-10639)*
Gene and Taffin A Ray Family..............F....... 800 839-1754
Wilmington *(G-10690)*
Gods Way To Recovery Inc..............G....... 302 856-7375
Georgetown *(G-2549)*
Harrison House Cmnty Program..............E....... 302 595-3370
Newark *(G-6710)*
Harvest Ministries Inc..............E....... 302 846-3001
Delmar *(G-1002)*
Hispanic American Assn of Del..............G....... 302 562-2705
Newark *(G-6730)*
Iaad..............F....... 302 234-0214
Newark *(G-6758)*
▲ Independent Resources Inc..............F....... 302 765-0191
Wilmington *(G-11017)*
Keith D Stoltz Foundation..............F....... 302 654-3600
Wilmington *(G-11234)*
Kent County Scty For The Prvnt..............E....... 302 698-3006
Camden *(G-587)*
Khan Family Foundation Inc..............G....... 800 839-1754
Wilmington *(G-11256)*
Kind To Kids Foundation..............G....... 302 654-5440
Wilmington *(G-11264)*
Knights York Cross of Honour..............G....... 302 731-4817
Newark *(G-6900)*
Leukemia & Lymphoma Soc Inc..............G....... 302 661-7300
Wilmington *(G-11377)*
Lewes Senior Citizens Center..............G....... 302 645-9293
Lewes *(G-3604)*
Little League Baseball Inc..............G....... 302 276-0375
New Castle *(G-5486)*
Lituation Creative Designs Inc..............F....... 302 494-4399
Wilmington *(G-11410)*
Lodge Lane Assisted Living..............E....... 302 757-8100
Wilmington *(G-11424)*
Mass For The Homeless Inc..............G....... 302 368-1030
Wilmington *(G-11562)*
Millsboro Art League Inc..............G....... 302 934-6440
Millsboro *(G-4748)*
Ministry of Caring Inc..............G....... 302 428-3702
Wilmington *(G-11705)*
Moms Club..............G....... 302 738-8822
Wilmington *(G-11729)*
Morning After Inc..............G....... 302 562-5190
Hartly *(G-2936)*
National Guard Association Del..............F....... 302 326-7125
New Castle *(G-5545)*
Nehemiah Gtwy Cmnty Dev Corp..............G....... 302 655-0803
Wilmington *(G-11829)*
Norbertine Fathers..............G....... 302 449-1840
Middletown *(G-4175)*
Piedmont Baseball League Inc..............G....... 302 234-9437
Hockessin *(G-3120)*
Plantation Lakes Homeowners..............G....... 302 934-5200
Millsboro *(G-4782)*
Pressley Ridge Foundation..............G....... 302 854-9782
Georgetown *(G-2626)*
Read-Alouddelaware Inc..............G....... 302 656-5256
Wilmington *(G-12341)*
Retrosheet Inc..............G....... 302 731-1570
Newark *(G-7329)*
Rising Sunset Publishing LLC..............G....... 877 231-5425
Newark *(G-7343)*
Rotary International..............F....... 302 738-0827
Newark *(G-7366)*
Skim USA..............F....... 302 227-4011
Rehoboth Beach *(G-8078)*
Society of St Vincent De Paul..............G....... 302 328-5166
Wilmington *(G-12668)*
Spca..............G....... 302 698-3006
Newark *(G-7465)*

Summer Lrng Collaborative Inc.............G....... 860 751-9887
Wilmington *(G-12791)*
Unidel Foundation Inc.............G....... 302 658-9200
Wilmington *(G-13010)*
Water Is Life Kenya Inc.............G....... 302 894-7335
Newark *(G-7678)*
Welfare Foundation Inc.............G....... 302 683-8200
Wilmington *(G-13141)*
What Is Your Voice Inc.............F....... 443 653-2067
Lewes *(G-3820)*
Wilmington Youth Rowing Assn.............F....... 302 777-4533
Wilmington *(G-13268)*
Windview Inc.............G....... 610 345-9001
Middletown *(G-4288)*

87 ENGINEERING, ACCOUNTING, RESEARCH, MANAGEMENT, AND RELATED SERVICES

8711 Engineering Services

AC Group Inc.............G....... 201 840-5566
Wilmington *(G-8910)*
Acorn Energy Inc.............G....... 302 656-1708
Wilmington *(G-8923)*
Aecom Global II LLC.............D....... 302 933-0200
Millsboro *(G-4623)*
Aecom Usa Inc.............E....... 302 781-5963
Wilmington *(G-8963)*
Ai Construction Services LLC.............G....... 619 732-0250
Middletown *(G-3933)*
Altea Resources LLC.............D....... 713 242-1460
Dover *(G-1113)*
American Hardscapes LLC.............F....... 302 253-8237
Georgetown *(G-2431)*
Ames Engineering Corp.............E....... 302 658-6945
Wilmington *(G-9067)*
Apex Engineering Inc.............F....... 302 994-1900
Wilmington *(G-9095)*
ARA Technologies Inc.............G....... 215 605-5707
Wilmington *(G-9109)*
Arcadis US Inc.............E....... 302 658-1718
Wilmington *(G-9120)*
Arenarts Inc.............F....... 302 408-0887
Claymont *(G-694)*
Aries Security LLC.............G....... 302 365-0026
Wilmington *(G-9128)*
B E & K Inc.............B....... 302 452-9000
Newark *(G-6033)*
B E & K Engineering Company.............G....... 302 452-9000
Newark *(G-6034)*
Batta Ramesh C Associates PA.............E....... 302 998-9463
Wilmington *(G-9260)*
Beacon Engineering LLC.............G....... 302 864-8825
Georgetown *(G-2451)*
Becker Morgan Group Inc.............F....... 302 734-7950
Dover *(G-1189)*
Beckley Associates LLC.............G....... 301 943-7343
Ocean View *(G-7763)*
Biehl & Co LP.............G....... 302 594-9700
Wilmington *(G-9327)*
Black & Veatch Corporation.............E....... 302 798-0200
Wilmington *(G-9346)*
Blake and Vaughan Engrg Inc.............F....... 302 888-1780
Wilmington *(G-9367)*
Brandywine Cad Design Inc.............E....... 302 478-8334
Wilmington *(G-9420)*
Brightfields Inc.............E....... 302 656-9600
Wilmington *(G-9477)*
Cabe Associates Inc.............F....... 302 674-9280
Dover *(G-1247)*
Calvin R Clendaniel Associates.............G....... 302 422-5347
Lincoln *(G-3840)*
Carzo & Associates Inc.............G....... 302 575-0336
Wilmington *(G-9584)*
Cda Engineering Inc.............G....... 302 998-9202
Wilmington *(G-9604)*
Cecon Group LLC.............G....... 302 994-8000
Wilmington *(G-9608)*
Century Engineering Inc.............D....... 302 734-9188
Dover *(G-1270)*
Cgc Consulting LLC.............G....... 302 489-2280
Wilmington *(G-9622)*
Civil Engineering Assoc LLC.............G....... 302 376-8833
Middletown *(G-3993)*
Cmy Solutions LLC.............G....... 321 732-1866
Newark *(G-6256)*
Cohawk.............G....... 302 422-5176
Milford *(G-4361)*
Commerce Global Inc.............G....... 302 478-0853
Wilmington *(G-9784)*
Corporate Arcft Technical Svcs.............G....... 302 383-9400
Wilmington *(G-9864)*
Corrosion Testing Laboratories.............F....... 302 454-8200
Newark *(G-6301)*
Cotten Engineering LLC.............G....... 302 628-9164
Seaford *(G-8209)*
Criterium Jagiasi Engineers.............G....... 302 498-5600
Wilmington *(G-9899)*
De Technologies Inc.............G....... 302 285-0353
Middletown *(G-4021)*
Dedc LLC.............D....... 302 738-7172
Newark *(G-6358)*
Delaware Engineering & Design.............D....... 302 738-7172
Newark *(G-6378)*
Delaware Secretary of State.............E....... 302 472-7678
Wilmington *(G-10083)*
Delmarva Energy Solutions LLC.............G....... 302 684-3418
Milton *(G-4890)*
Delmarva Power & Light Company.............G....... 302 454-4040
Newark *(G-6427)*
Delta Engineering Corporation.............F....... 302 325-9320
New Castle *(G-5247)*
Delux Engineering LLC.............G....... 610 304-0606
Newark *(G-6434)*
Diamond Mechanical Inc.............E....... 302 697-7694
Dover *(G-1422)*
Drafting By Design Inc.............G....... 302 292-8304
Newark *(G-6472)*
Duffield Associates Inc.............D....... 302 239-6634
Wilmington *(G-10245)*
Dupont Aviation Corp.............E....... 302 996-8000
New Castle *(G-5266)*
Dupont Prfmce Coatings Inc.............A....... 302 892-1064
Wilmington *(G-10258)*
E I Du Pont De Nemours & Co.............E....... 302 999-4356
Wilmington *(G-10291)*
E-Merge Systems Inc.............G....... 302 894-3860
Newark *(G-6493)*
East West Engineering Inc.............G....... 302 528-0652
Bear *(G-137)*
Edc LLC.............F....... 302 645-0777
Lewes *(G-3478)*
Em Photonics Inc.............F....... 302 456-9003
Newark *(G-6522)*
Evocati Group Corporation.............F....... 206 551-9087
Dover *(G-1533)*
Flowline Technologies Inc.............G....... 302 256-5825
Wilmington *(G-10579)*
Foresite Assoc Inc.............G....... 302 351-3421
New Castle *(G-5323)*
Gahagan & Bryant Assoc Inc.............F....... 302 652-4948
Wilmington *(G-10662)*
Game Changing Industries LLC.............G....... 302 498-8321
Wilmington *(G-10667)*
Gannett Fleming Inc.............E....... 302 378-2256
Middletown *(G-4083)*
Gcora Corp.............G....... 302 310-1000
Milford *(G-4421)*
George Miles & Buhr LLC.............G....... 302 628-1421
Seaford *(G-8253)*
Gif North America LLC.............B....... 703 969-9243
Rehoboth Beach *(G-7948)*
Hardcore Cmpstes Oprations Llc.............D....... 302 442-5900
New Castle *(G-5374)*
Hillis-Carnes Engrg Assoc Inc.............E....... 302 744-9855
Dover *(G-1646)*
Hough Associates Inc.............F....... 302 322-7800
Newark *(G-6750)*
I 3 A LLC.............G....... 302 659-0909
Smyrna *(G-8656)*
Ibi Group (us) Inc.............C....... 949 833-5588
Wilmington *(G-10987)*
Integrated Solutions Planning.............G....... 302 297-9215
Georgetown *(G-2567)*
Jaed Corporation.............F....... 302 832-1652
Bear *(G-196)*
Ji DCI Jv-II.............F....... 302 652-4221
Wilmington *(G-11156)*
Johnson Mirmiran Thompson Inc.............E....... 302 266-9600
Newark *(G-6847)*
Karins Engineering Inc.............E....... 302 369-2900
Newark *(G-6867)*
Kci Protection Tech LLC.............G....... 302 543-8340
Newark *(G-6870)*
Kci Technologies Inc.............E....... 302 731-9176
Newark *(G-6871)*
Kercher Group Inc.............F....... 302 894-1098
Newark *(G-6875)*
Koch Accounting Services LLC.............E....... 877 446-8478
Wilmington *(G-11286)*
Kubota Research Associates.............G....... 302 683-0199
Hockessin *(G-3072)*
Landmark Engineering Inc.............D....... 302 323-9377
Newark *(G-6915)*
Landmark Engineering Inc.............G....... 302 734-9597
Newark *(G-6916)*
Larson Engineering Inc.............G....... 302 731-7434
Newark *(G-6918)*
Lindsay and Associates Limited.............G....... 703 631-5840
Milton *(G-4924)*
Long & Tann & D Onofrio Inc.............G....... 302 477-1970
Wilmington *(G-11430)*
Luriware Consulting Agricultur.............G....... 302 244-1947
Dover *(G-1799)*
Lutz Engineering Inc.............G....... 302 479-9017
Wilmington *(G-11456)*
Macintosh Engineering Inc.............F....... 302 252-9200
Wilmington *(G-11480)*
Magowi Consulting Group LLC.............F....... 832 301-9230
Newark *(G-6972)*
Mahaffy & Associates Inc.............E....... 302 656-8381
Middletown *(G-4141)*
Merestone Consultants Inc.............F....... 302 992-7900
Wilmington *(G-11639)*
Merestone Consultants Inc.............F....... 302 226-5880
Lewes *(G-3637)*
Merge Industrial Solutions LLC.............E....... 302 400-2157
Dover *(G-1838)*
Meridian Architects Engineers.............E....... 302 643-9928
Milton *(G-4935)*
Merit Construction Engineers.............F....... 302 992-9810
Wilmington *(G-11643)*
Michael-Bruno LLC.............G....... 315 941-8514
Wilmington *(G-11669)*
Mig Consulting LLC.............G....... 302 999-1888
Wilmington *(G-11684)*
Morris & Ritchie Assoc Inc.............E....... 302 855-5734
Georgetown *(G-2607)*
Morris & Ritchie Assoc Inc.............F....... 302 326-2200
New Castle *(G-5536)*
Mountain Consulting Inc.............G....... 302 744-9875
Dover *(G-1876)*
Mvl Structures Group LLC.............E....... 302 652-7580
Wilmington *(G-11782)*
Network Mapping Inc.............G....... 310 560-4142
Wilmington *(G-11840)*
On Board Engineering Corp.............D....... 302 613-5030
New Castle *(G-5587)*
P C Bohler Engineering.............E....... 302 644-1155
Rehoboth Beach *(G-8026)*
Panelmatic Inc.............G....... 302 324-9193
New Castle *(G-5600)*
▼ Panelmatic East Inc.............F....... 302 324-9193
New Castle *(G-5601)*
Paragon Engineering Corp.............E....... 302 762-6010
Wilmington *(G-12016)*
Pelsa Company Inc.............G....... 302 834-3771
Newark *(G-7191)*
Pennoni.............E....... 302 234-4600
Newark *(G-7196)*
Pennoni Associates Inc.............E....... 302 684-8030
Milton *(G-4947)*
Pennoni Associates Inc.............E....... 302 655-4451
Newark *(G-7197)*
Phase Snsitive Innovations Inc.............F....... 302 456-9003
Newark *(G-7210)*
Philadelphia Control Systems.............G....... 302 368-4333
Christiana *(G-675)*
Pilottown Engineering LLC.............G....... 302 703-1770
Lewes *(G-3691)*
Polar Mechanical Inc.............E....... 302 994-9566
Wilmington *(G-12180)*
Power Delivery Solutions LLC.............E....... 302 260-3114
Newark *(G-7236)*
Precise Alignment Mch Tl Co.............G....... 302 832-2922
Newark *(G-7239)*
Premier Restoration Inc.............F....... 302 645-1611
Lewes *(G-3696)*
Pro-Tech Engineering Inc.............E....... 302 998-1717
Wilmington *(G-12236)*
Qbeck Inspection Group.............E....... 302 452-9257
Newark *(G-7277)*
Quinteccent Inc.............G....... 443 838-5447
Selbyville *(G-8536)*
RDS Engineering LLC.............G....... 417 763-3727
Lewes *(G-3710)*
Retained Logic Group Inc.............G....... 302 530-3692
Middletown *(G-4219)*

S I C

Employee Codes: A=Over 500 employees, B=251-500 C=101-250, D=51-100, E=20-50, F=10-19, G=1-9
2020 Harris Directory of Delaware Businesses
571

Robert A Chagnon ....G.... 302 489-1932
Hockessin (G-3138)
Rummel Klepper & Kahl LLP ....E.... 302 468-4880
Wilmington (G-12493)
Sargent & Lundy LLC ....C.... 302 622-7200
Wilmington (G-12542)
Sauer Holdings Inc ....E.... 302 656-8989
Wilmington (G-12545)
Scott Engineering Inc ....G.... 302 736-3058
Dover (G-2062)
Sinnott Exc Consulting LLC ....G.... 302 656-2898
Wilmington (G-12632)
South Bowers Volunteer Fire Co ....E.... 302 335-4666
Milford (G-4565)
Spaceport Support Services ....G.... 302 524-4020
Selbyville (G-8547)
Summer Consultants Inc ....F.... 484 493-4150
Newark (G-7502)
Suretronix Solutions LLC ....G.... 302 407-3146
Wilmington (G-12817)
Taylor McCormick Inc ....E.... 302 738-0203
Christiana (G-682)
Tech International Corp ....G.... 302 478-2301
Wilmington (G-12868)
Techmer Engineered Solutions ....G.... 800 401-8181
New Castle (G-5758)
Techncal Stffing Resources LLC ....G.... 302 452-9933
Newark (G-7544)
Technology Transfers Inc ....G.... 302 234-4718
Newark (G-7547)
Telgian Corporation ....E.... 480 753-5444
Wilmington (G-12880)
Telgian Engrg & Consulting LLC ....F.... 480 282-5392
Wilmington (G-12881)
Ten Bears Environmental LLC ....G.... 302 731-8633
Newark (G-7556)
Tetra Tech Inc ....F.... 302 738-7551
Newark (G-7559)
Tetra Tech Inc ....E.... 302 738-7551
Newark (G-7560)
Trim Waste Management LLC ....G.... 302 738-2500
Newark (G-7592)
TY Lin International Group ....G.... 302 883-3662
Dover (G-2168)
Unitrack Industries Inc ....E.... 302 424-5050
Milford (G-4586)
Urban Engineers Inc ....G.... 302 689-0260
New Castle (G-5811)
URS Group Inc ....D.... 302 731-7824
Newark (G-7634)
Vandemark & Lynch Inc ....E.... 302 764-7635
Wilmington (G-13048)
VD&I Holdings Inc ....D.... 302 764-7635
Wilmington (G-13052)
Wallace Montgomery & Assoc LLP ....E.... 302 510-1080
Newark (G-7674)
Whitman Requardt and Assoc LLP ....F.... 302 571-9001
Wilmington (G-13195)
Woodin + Associates LLC ....F.... 302 378-7300
Middletown (G-4290)
Xcs Corporation ....G.... 302 514-0600
Wilmington (G-13316)
Yellow Pine Associates Inc ....G.... 302 994-9500
Wilmington (G-13326)

8712 Architectural Services

Abha Architects Inc ....E.... 302 658-6426
Wilmington (G-8902)
Aecom Technology Corporation ....E.... 302 468-5878
Wilmington (G-8962)
Andersen Ford Architects LLC ....G.... 302 388-7862
Wilmington (G-9077)
Architecture Plus Pa ....G.... 302 999-1614
Wilmington (G-9124)
Arqitecture LLC ....G.... 302 777-5666
Winterthur (G-13356)
◆ Balfour Beatty LLC ....G.... 302 573-3873
Wilmington (G-9225)
Becker Morgan Group Inc ....F.... 302 734-7950
Dover (G-1189)
Bernardon PC ....F.... 302 622-9550
Wilmington (G-9309)
Brandywine Cad Design Inc ....E.... 302 478-8334
Wilmington (G-9420)
Breckstone Group Inc ....G.... 302 654-3646
Wilmington (G-9465)
Buck Simpers Archt + Assoc Inc ....F.... 302 658-9300
Wilmington (G-9498)
Cadrender LLC ....G.... 302 657-0700
Wilmington (G-9532)
Cooperson Associates LLC ....G.... 302 655-1105
Wilmington (G-9853)
Cooperson Associates Inc ....G.... 302 655-1105
Wilmington (G-9854)
Davis Bowen & Friedel Inc ....E.... 302 424-1441
Milford (G-4371)
Delaware Architects LLC ....G.... 302 491-6047
Milford (G-4375)
Design Collaborative Inc ....F.... 302 652-4221
Wilmington (G-10120)
Design Delmarva ....G.... 302 644-8884
Lewes (G-3462)
Edc LLC ....F.... 302 645-0777
Lewes (G-3478)
Fearn-Clndaniel Architects Inc ....G.... 302 998-7615
Wilmington (G-10510)
G A Hastings & Associates ....G.... 302 537-5760
Ocean View (G-7788)
Homsey Architects Inc ....F.... 302 656-4491
Wilmington (G-10946)
Jaed Corporation ....F.... 302 832-1652
Bear (G-196)
Ji DCI Joint Venture 1 ....G.... 302 652-4221
Wilmington (G-11155)
Ji DCI Jv-II ....F.... 302 652-4221
Wilmington (G-11156)
Kci Technologies Inc ....E.... 302 731-9176
Newark (G-6871)
Montchanin Design Group Inc ....F.... 302 652-3008
Wilmington (G-11735)
Moonlight Architechture Inc ....G.... 302 645-9361
Lewes (G-3648)
R G Architects LLC ....G.... 302 376-8100
Middletown (G-4208)
Staikos Associates Architects ....G.... 302 764-1678
Wilmington (G-12730)
Tevebaugh Associates Inc ....F.... 302 984-1400
Wilmington (G-12887)
William Byler Jr Architect Inc ....G.... 302 653-3550
Clayton (G-874)
Zahn Incorporated ....G.... 302 425-3700
Wilmington (G-13339)

8713 Surveying Services

Adams Kemp Associates Inc ....G.... 302 856-6699
Georgetown (G-2423)
Amplified Gchmical Imaging LLC ....G.... 302 266-2428
Newark (G-5963)
Batta Ramesh C Associates PA ....E.... 302 998-9463
Wilmington (G-9260)
Braun Engineering & Surveying ....F.... 302 698-0701
Camden Wyoming (G-621)
Charles D Murphy Associates ....F.... 302 422-7327
Milford (G-4348)
Christian Raymond F & Assoc ....G.... 302 738-3016
Newark (G-6205)
Clifton L Bakhsh Jr Inc ....F.... 302 378-8009
Middletown (G-3998)
Coast Survey ....G.... 302 645-7184
Lewes (G-3434)
Compass Point Associates LLC ....G.... 302 684-2980
Harbeson (G-2777)
Davis Bowen & Friedel Inc ....E.... 302 424-1441
Milford (G-4371)
Design Consultants Group LLC ....E.... 302 684-8030
Milton (G-4892)
Firefly Drone Operations Llc ....G.... 305 206-6955
Wilmington (G-10543)
Landmark Engineering Inc ....D.... 302 323-9377
Newark (G-6915)
Landmark Engineering Inc ....G.... 302 734-9597
Newark (G-6916)
Landtech LLC ....G.... 302 539-2366
Ocean View (G-7798)
Lewis Miller Inc ....G.... 302 629-9895
Seaford (G-8293)
McBride and Ziegler Inc ....E.... 302 737-9138
Newark (G-7011)
Merestone Consultants Inc ....F.... 302 992-7900
Wilmington (G-11639)
Merestone Consultants Inc ....F.... 302 226-5880
Lewes (G-3637)
Morris & Ritchie Assoc Inc ....E.... 302 855-5734
Georgetown (G-2607)
Morris & Ritchie Assoc Inc ....F.... 302 326-2200
New Castle (G-5536)
Professional Roof Services Inc ....G.... 302 731-5770
Newark (G-7266)
Retained Logic Group Inc ....G.... 302 530-3692
Middletown (G-4219)
Robert Larimore ....G.... 302 730-8682
Camden Wyoming (G-654)
Rod-AES Surveryors Co ....G.... 302 993-1059
Wilmington (G-12459)
Scott Engineering Inc ....G.... 302 736-3058
Dover (G-2062)
Simpler Surveying & Associates ....G.... 302 539-7873
Frankford (G-2387)
Woodin + Associates LLC ....F.... 302 378-7300
Middletown (G-4290)

8721 Accounting, Auditing & Bookkeeping Svcs

Accounting & Bookkeeping Svc ....G.... 302 376-7857
Middletown (G-3929)
Accutax ....G.... 302 735-9747
Dover (G-1082)
Advantdge Hlthcare Sltions Inc ....G.... 302 224-5678
Newark (G-5911)
Alma Company ....G.... 302 731-4427
Newark (G-5945)
Automotive Accounting Service ....F.... 302 378-9551
Middletown (G-3955)
Baffone & Associates LLC ....G.... 302 655-1544
Wilmington (G-9221)
Baker Tilly Virchow Krause LLP ....G.... 302 442-4600
Wilmington (G-9223)
Bank of New York Mellon Corp ....G.... 302 791-1700
Wilmington (G-9244)
Barbacane Thornton & Company ....E.... 302 478-8940
Wilmington (G-9247)
Bastianelli Group Inc ....G.... 302 658-1500
Newark (G-6050)
Bdo Usa LLP ....D.... 302 656-5500
Wilmington (G-9272)
Belfint Lyons & Shuman P A ....D.... 302 225-0600
Wilmington (G-9287)
Bireley & Kortvelesy PA ....G.... 302 539-0311
Ocean View (G-7767)
Boyer & Boyer ....G.... 302 998-3700
Wilmington (G-9403)
Breakwater Accounting Advisory ....G.... 302 543-4564
Rockland (G-8122)
Brousseau & Brousseau C P A ....G.... 302 234-1976
Wilmington (G-9486)
Bumpers & Company ....F.... 302 798-3300
Wilmington (G-9505)
Chandler and Lynch CPA ....F.... 302 478-9800
Wilmington (G-9629)
Christiana Care Hlth Svcs Inc ....C.... 302 623-7201
Newark (G-6217)
Christiana Incorporators Inc ....G.... 302 998-2008
Wilmington (G-9687)
City of Dover ....G.... 302 736-7018
Dover (G-1288)
Consult Dynamics Inc ....E.... 302 295-4700
Wilmington (G-9836)
Corcoran & Associates PA CPA ....G.... 302 478-9515
Wilmington (G-9858)
Cover & Rossiter PA ....E.... 302 656-6632
Wilmington (G-9882)
Danny G Perez Ea MST ....G.... 302 422-2600
Milford (G-4370)
Delaware Clean Service ....G.... 302 838-1650
Bear (G-105)
Delaware Medical MGT Svcs LLC ....E.... 302 283-3300
Newark (G-6394)
Delaware Occupational Health S ....E.... 302 368-5100
Newark (G-6400)
Diehl & Co CPA ....G.... 302 644-4441
Lewes (G-3465)
Dingle & Kane PA ....G.... 302 731-5200
Newark (G-6450)
Diversified Financial Cons ....G.... 302 765-3500
Wilmington (G-10170)
Doherty & Associates Inc ....F.... 302 239-3500
Wilmington (G-10183)
DSouza and Associates Inc ....F.... 302 239-2300
Hockessin (G-3013)
Dss International LLC ....G.... 302 836-0270
Newark (G-6476)
Ekww Inc ....G.... 302 234-2877
Hockessin (G-3018)
Elite Tax Services LLC ....G.... 302 256-0401
Wilmington (G-10377)
Estep Douglas E Pub Accountant ....G.... 302 322-4621
New Castle (G-5295)
Faw Casson & Co LLP ....E.... 302 674-4305
Dover (G-1544)

Faw Casson ....G.... 302 226-1919
Rehoboth Beach *(G-7932)*
Fields & Company Inc ....G.... 302 234-2775
Hockessin *(G-3028)*
First State Cpas LLC ....G.... 302 736-6657
Dover *(G-1555)*
Gallagher & Associates PA ....G.... 302 239-5501
Wilmington *(G-10665)*
Gary Sj CPA ....G.... 302 730-3737
Dover *(G-1581)*
Genoese Miller & Associates ....F.... 302 655-9505
Wilmington *(G-10694)*
Global Merchant Partners LLC ....G.... 302 425-3567
Rehoboth Beach *(G-7950)*
Grabowski Sprano Vnclette Cpas ....G.... 302 999-7300
Wilmington *(G-10757)*
Gunnip & Company ....D.... 302 225-5000
Wilmington *(G-10802)*
H&R Block Inc ....F.... 302 999-7488
Wilmington *(G-10812)*
Hartnett Accounting & Tax Serv ....G.... 302 477-0660
Wilmington *(G-10846)*
Horty & Horty PA ....E.... 302 652-4194
Wilmington *(G-10957)*
Horty & Horty PA ....E.... 302 730-4560
Dover *(G-1656)*
Hospital Blling Cllctn Svc Ltd ....B.... 302 552-8000
New Castle *(G-5405)*
Howard Wimbrow CPA ....G.... 302 539-0829
Frankford *(G-2368)*
Jane L Stayton CPA ....F.... 302 856-4141
Georgetown *(G-2571)*
Jefferson Urian Dane Strner PA ....E.... 302 856-3900
Georgetown *(G-2573)*
Jefferson Urian Dane Strner PA ....F.... 302 539-5543
Ocean View *(G-7795)*
Jefferson Urian Dane Strner PA ....F.... 302 678-1425
Dover *(G-1695)*
Kupferman & Associates LLC ....G.... 302 656-7566
Wilmington *(G-11300)*
Lachall Lee LLP ....G.... 302 644-9952
Lewes *(G-3587)*
Lank Johnson and Tull ....G.... 302 422-3308
Milford *(G-4470)*
Lank Johnson and Tull ....G.... 302 629-9543
Seaford *(G-8291)*
Lester & Co PC ....G.... 302 684-5980
Lewes *(G-3595)*
Lexisnexis Risk Assets Inc ....A.... 800 458-9410
Wilmington *(G-11378)*
Luff & Associates CPA PA ....G.... 302 422-9699
Milford *(G-4479)*
M3r & Assoc Inc ....G.... 302 324-1040
New Castle *(G-5494)*
Maillie LLP ....F.... 302 324-0780
New Castle *(G-5501)*
Marshall Wagner & Associates ....G.... 302 227-2537
Rehoboth Beach *(G-8001)*
Master Sidlow & Associates PA ....E.... 302 384-9780
Newark *(G-7001)*
Medical Billing & MGT Svcs Inc ....G.... 610 564-5314
Newark *(G-7015)*
Miller & Associates PA ....G.... 302 234-0678
Wilmington *(G-11693)*
Mitten & Winters CPA ....F.... 302 736-6100
Dover *(G-1861)*
Multi-Pro Business Svcs LLC ....G.... 800 571-7017
Newark *(G-7072)*
Nannas Haines & Schiavo PA ....E.... 302 479-8800
Wilmington *(G-11797)*
Orth & Kowalick PA ....G.... 302 697-2159
Dover *(G-1920)*
Papaleo Rosen Chelf & Pinder ....F.... 302 644-8600
Lewes *(G-3678)*
Paths LLC ....E.... 302 294-1494
Newark *(G-7180)*
Patterson & Kelly PA ....G.... 302 736-6657
Dover *(G-1941)*
Payroll Management Assistants ....G.... 302 456-6816
Newark *(G-7188)*
Perioperative Services LLC ....D.... 302 733-0806
Newark *(G-7203)*
Pfpc Worldwide Inc ....F.... 302 791-1700
Wilmington *(G-12105)*
Progar & Co ....G.... 302 645-6216
Lewes *(G-3699)*
R T Accountants Co ....G.... 302 670-5117
Dover *(G-2008)*
Raymond F Book III ....E.... 302 734-5826
Dover *(G-2011)*
Ritchie Sawyer Corporation ....F.... 302 475-1971
Wilmington *(G-12426)*
Robert B Gregg ....G.... 302 994-9300
Newport *(G-7752)*
Robert G Starkey CPA ....G.... 302 422-0108
Milford *(G-4545)*
Robert Hoyt & Co ....G.... 302 934-6688
Millsboro *(G-4793)*
Ross W Burnam CPA PA ....G.... 302 453-8161
Newark *(G-7365)*
Santora CPA Group Pa ....E.... 302 737-6200
Newark *(G-7385)*
Scassociates Inc ....F.... 302 454-1100
Middletown *(G-4231)*
Sean E Chipman ....F.... 302 300-4307
New Castle *(G-5697)*
Siegfried Group LLP ....C.... 302 984-1800
Wilmington *(G-12610)*
Simon Mstr & Sidlow Assoc Inc ....E.... 302 652-3480
Newark *(G-7431)*
Snyder & Company PA ....F.... 302 475-1600
Wilmington *(G-12666)*
Sombar & Co CPA PA ....G.... 302 856-6712
Georgetown *(G-2659)*
Stephano Slack LLC ....G.... 302 777-7400
Wilmington *(G-12754)*
Szewczyk Company P A ....G.... 302 998-1117
Wilmington *(G-12840)*
Tax Management Service Inc ....G.... 703 845-5900
Milford *(G-4575)*
Thomson Reuters (grc) Inc ....A.... 212 227-7357
Wilmington *(G-12904)*
Timothy D Humphreys ....F.... 302 225-3000
Wilmington *(G-12913)*
TLC Personal Assistants ....G.... 302 290-9902
Wilmington *(G-12918)*
University of Delaware ....E.... 302 831-2961
Newark *(G-7623)*
Wahid Consultants LLC ....E.... 315 400-0955
New Castle *(G-5821)*
Wendy Cpa LLC ....G.... 302 377-7165
Bear *(G-375)*
Wheeler Wolfenden & Dwares CPA ....F.... 302 254-8240
Wilmington *(G-13183)*
William Humphreys & Co LLC ....G.... 302 225-3904
Wilmington *(G-13214)*
Zenker and Styer PA ....G.... 302 475-9006
Wilmington *(G-13346)*
Zimny & Associates PA ....G.... 302 325-6900
New Castle *(G-5847)*

8731 Commercial Physical & Biological Research

Advanced Materials Technology ....G.... 302 477-2510
Wilmington *(G-8953)*
Algorithm Sciences LLC ....G.... 734 904-9491
Wilmington *(G-9009)*
Alpha Omega Scientific LLC ....G.... 302 415-4499
New Castle *(G-5026)*
Applied Research Assoc Inc ....D.... 302 677-4147
Dover *(G-1133)*
Aries Security LLC ....G.... 302 365-0026
Wilmington *(G-9128)*
▲ **Arkion Life Sciences LLC** ....E.... 302 504-7400
New Castle *(G-5044)*
Batescainelli LLC ....G.... 202 618-2040
Rehoboth Beach *(G-7856)*
Beatdapp Inc ....G.... 310 903-0244
Dover *(G-1185)*
Biomatik Usa LLC ....F.... 416 273-4858
Wilmington *(G-9340)*
C M-Tec Inc ....G.... 302 369-6166
Newark *(G-6141)*
Charles River Labs Intl Inc ....G.... 302 292-8888
Newark *(G-6190)*
Chuck George Inc ....E.... 302 994-7444
Wilmington *(G-9697)*
Cowie Technology Corp ....G.... 302 998-7037
Wilmington *(G-9885)*
Delaware Innovation Space Inc ....G.... 302 695-2201
Wilmington *(G-10058)*
Delaware Sstnble Enrgy Utility ....G.... 302 883-3038
Dover *(G-1395)*
Diversified Chemical Pdts Inc ....G.... 302 656-5293
Wilmington *(G-10169)*
Dupont Displays Inc ....E.... 805 562-9293
Wilmington *(G-10253)*
Dupont Specialty Pdts USA LLC ....E.... 302 695-3295
Wilmington *(G-10262)*
E I Du Pont De Nemours & Co ....G.... 302 774-1000
Wilmington *(G-10288)*
E I Du Pont De Nemours & Co ....D.... 302 774-1000
Wilmington *(G-10308)*
E I Du Pont De Nemours & Co ....E.... 805 562-5307
Wilmington *(G-10304)*
Ener-G Group Inc ....F.... 917 281-0020
Wilmington *(G-10400)*
Environmental Consulting Svcs ....F.... 302 378-9881
Middletown *(G-4059)*
Environmental Protection Agcy ....A.... 302 739-9917
Dover *(G-1525)*
Environmental Testing Inc ....G.... 302 378-5341
Middletown *(G-4060)*
Ezy Biotech LLC ....G.... 212 247-4261
Wilmington *(G-10467)*
Fbk Medical Tubing Inc ....E.... 302 855-0585
Georgetown *(G-2527)*
Fraunhofer Usa Inc ....D.... 302 369-1708
Newark *(G-6613)*
Frontier Scientific Inc ....G.... 302 266-6891
Newark *(G-6626)*
Frontier Scientific Svcs Inc ....G.... 302 266-6891
Newark *(G-6627)*
IEC ....E.... 302 831-6231
Newark *(G-6762)*
Jenrin Discovery LLC ....G.... 302 379-1679
Wilmington *(G-11150)*
M-Cap Technologies Intl ....G.... 302 695-5329
Wilmington *(G-11474)*
Merck Holdings LLC ....G.... 302 234-1401
Wilmington *(G-11637)*
MMR Group Inc ....E.... 302 328-0500
New Castle *(G-5531)*
Modern Water Inc ....E.... 302 669-6900
New Castle *(G-5533)*
Moscase Inc ....G.... 786 520-8062
Dover *(G-1874)*
Napigen Inc ....G.... 302 419-8117
Wilmington *(G-11801)*
Neurorx Inc ....F.... 202 340-1352
Wilmington *(G-11846)*
▲ **Nichino America Inc** ....E.... 302 636-9001
Wilmington *(G-11887)*
Omnimaven Inc ....G.... 302 378-8918
Middletown *(G-4178)*
Partnership For De Estuary ....G.... 302 655-4990
Wilmington *(G-12027)*
Penn Labs Inc ....F.... 215 751-4000
Wilmington *(G-12065)*
Red Clay Inc ....G.... 302 239-2018
Hockessin *(G-3132)*
Research & Innovation Co ....G.... 302 281-3600
Wilmington *(G-12385)*
Romie LLC ....G.... 866 698-0052
Wilmington *(G-12468)*
Sdix LLC ....D.... 302 456-6789
Newark *(G-7398)*
Separation Methods Tech Inc ....F.... 302 368-0610
Newark *(G-7408)*
Stereochemical Inc ....G.... 302 266-0700
Newark *(G-7490)*
Stride Services Inc ....F.... 302 540-4713
Wilmington *(G-12776)*
Sun Coal & Coke LLC ....A.... 630 824-1000
Wilmington *(G-12792)*
Synchrgnix Info Strategies LLC ....E.... 302 892-4800
Wilmington *(G-12833)*
Timtec LLC ....F.... 302 292-8500
Newark *(G-7567)*
Ultrafine Technologies Inc ....G.... 302 384-6513
Wilmington *(G-13009)*
University of Delaware ....B.... 302 831-8149
Newark *(G-7627)*
University of Delaware ....D.... 302 831-6300
Newark *(G-7628)*
W7energy LLC ....G.... 302 897-1653
Wilmington *(G-13111)*
Warehouse Technology Inc ....G.... 302 516-7791
New Castle *(G-5823)*
White Dog Labs Inc ....F.... 302 220-4760
New Castle *(G-5832)*
Wilmington Pharmatech Co LLC ....E.... 302 737-9916
Newark *(G-7703)*

8732 Commercial Economic, Sociological & Educational Research

431 Corporation ....G.... 352 385-1427
Bear *(G-1)*

S I C

87 ENGINEERING, ACCOUNTING, RESEARCH, MANAGEMENT, AND RELATED SERVICES

Ayala Pharmaceuticals Inc ..... F 857 444-0553
  Wilmington (G-9202)
China Monitor Inc ..... F 302 351-2324
  Wilmington (G-9667)
Circus Associates Intelligence ..... E 757 663-7864
  Lewes (G-3422)
Digital Wish Inc ..... G 802 375-6721
  Milton (G-4895)
Environics Analytics Inc ..... E 302 600-0304
  Wilmington (G-10418)
Envision It Publications LLC ..... G 800 329-9411
  Bear (G-144)
Fast Intrcnnect Tchologies Inc ..... G 302 465-5344
  Dover (G-1542)
Gbc International Corp ..... G 404 860-2533
  Wilmington (G-10682)
Ibope Media LLC ..... G 305 529-0062
  Lewes (G-3549)
Incenco International ..... F 302 478-8400
  Wilmington (G-11012)
Ivychat Inc ..... F 201 567-5694
  Newark (G-6811)
Ka Analytics & Tech LLC ..... G 800 520-8178
  Dover (G-1720)
Kc & Associates Inc ..... G 302 633-3300
  Wilmington (G-11231)
Pelsa Company Inc ..... G 302 834-3771
  Newark (G-7191)
Readhowyouwant LLC ..... G 302 730-4560
  Dover (G-2014)
Remline Corp ..... E 302 737-7228
  Newark (G-7316)
Sanosil International LLC ..... F 302 454-8102
  New Castle (G-5694)
SM Technomine Inc ..... G 312 492-4386
  Wilmington (G-12647)
Sparkia Inc ..... G 302 636-5440
  Wilmington (G-12693)
Taq Incorporated ..... G 302 734-8300
  Dover (G-2130)
University of Delaware ..... E 302 831-2136
  Newark (G-7626)
Wboc Inc ..... F 302 734-9262
  Dover (G-2207)
Wherebyus Enterprises Inc ..... G 305 988-0808
  Claymont (G-819)
Willowflare LLC ..... G 312 428-0159
  Lewes (G-3827)

8733 Noncommercial Research Organizations

A66 Inc ..... G 800 444-0446
  Wilmington (G-8892)
Analytical Biological Svcs Inc ..... E 302 654-4492
  Wilmington (G-9073)
Atria Medical Inc ..... G 407 334-5190
  Dover (G-1158)
Avantix Labratories Inc ..... F 302 832-1008
  Newark (G-6031)
Delaware Acdemy of Mdicine Inc ..... F 302 733-3900
  Newark (G-6363)
Delaware Community Foundation ..... F 302 571-8004
  Wilmington (G-10023)
Delaware Native Plants Society ..... G 302 735-8918
  Dover (G-1382)
Delaware Nature Society ..... D 302 239-1283
  Hockessin (G-3006)
Delaware Vly Outcomes RES LLC ..... G 302 444-9363
  Newark (G-6421)
Disaster Research Center ..... E 302 831-6618
  Newark (G-6454)
Epic Research LLC ..... G 703 297-8121
  Wilmington (G-10425)
Galvin Industries LLC ..... G 703 505-7860
  Georgetown (G-2537)
Global Institute ..... G 732 776-7360
  Newark (G-6666)
Indonesian Cultural Institute ..... G 302 981-7780
  Newark (G-6773)
Invistas Applied RES Centre ..... F 302 731-6800
  Newark (G-6802)
Mid Atlantic Pain Institute ..... G 302 369-1700
  Milford (G-4494)
Minder Foundation ..... F 917 477-7661
  Lewes (G-3643)
Signal Garden Research Corp ..... G 708 715-3646
  Lewes (G-3743)
Smid Aerospace Corporation ..... G 443 205-0881
  Bear (G-326)

Society For Acpuncture RES Inc ..... F 302 222-1832
  Lewes (G-3752)
Tdm Pharmaceutical RES LLC ..... G 302 832-1008
  Newark (G-7543)
Thomson Reuters (grc) Inc ..... A 212 227-7357
  Wilmington (G-12904)
Towle Institute ..... G 302 993-1408
  Wilmington (G-12943)
Ubinet Inc ..... G 302 722-6015
  Wilmington (G-13006)
University of Delaware ..... E 302 831-4811
  Newark (G-7620)
University of Delaware ..... G 302 831-2833
  Newark (G-7624)
University of Delaware ..... F 302 831-2802
  Newark (G-7629)
Zinger Enterprizes Inc ..... G 302 381-6761
  Laurel (G-3312)

8734 Testing Laboratories

3sigma Labs Inc ..... G 925 236-2618
  Wilmington (G-8859)
Accugenix Inc ..... E 302 292-8888
  Newark (G-5890)
Agera Laboratories ..... G 302 888-1500
  Wilmington (G-8975)
Alias Technology LLC ..... G 302 856-9488
  Georgetown (G-2428)
Christiana Care Health Sys Inc ..... G 302 477-6500
  Wilmington (G-9680)
Compact Membrane Systems Inc ..... E 302 999-7996
  Wilmington (G-9797)
Corrosion Testing Laboratories ..... F 302 454-8200
  Newark (G-6301)
E I Du Pont De Nemours & Co ..... D 302 695-5300
  Wilmington (G-10306)
Ecg Industries Inc ..... G 302 453-0535
  Newark (G-6502)
Element Mtls Tech Wlmngton Inc ..... F 302 636-0202
  Wilmington (G-10368)
Envirocorp Inc ..... F 302 398-3869
  Harrington (G-2837)
Eurofins Qc Inc ..... E 302 276-0432
  New Castle (G-5297)
Evans ..... G 302 629-0545
  Seaford (G-8240)
Geo-Technology Associates Inc ..... E 302 326-2100
  New Castle (G-5351)
Integrity Testlabs LLC ..... D 302 325-2365
  New Castle (G-5421)
K & S Technical Services Inc ..... G 302 737-9133
  Newark (G-6864)
Lehigh Testing Laboratories ..... E 302 328-0500
  New Castle (G-5476)
Lewis Research Inc ..... G 302 644-0881
  Lewes (G-3606)
Micron Incorporated ..... G 302 998-1184
  Wilmington (G-11676)
Mid-Atlantic Envmtl Labs Inc ..... F 302 654-1340
  New Castle (G-5525)
Midi Labs Inc ..... E 302 737-4297
  Newark (G-7035)
MMR Group Inc ..... E 302 328-0500
  New Castle (G-5531)
Quinteccent Inc ..... G 443 838-5447
  Selbyville (G-8536)
R L Laboratories Inc ..... F 302 328-1686
  New Castle (G-5663)
Red Lion Medical Safety Inc ..... G 302 731-8600
  Newark (G-7306)
Stereochemical Inc ..... G 302 266-0700
  Newark (G-7490)
Tell Lab ..... G 302 831-7121
  Newark (G-7554)
Wm Systems Inc ..... G 302 450-4482
  Wilmington (G-13282)

8741 Management Services

1995 Property Management Inc ..... G 302 745-1187
  Seaford (G-8133)
Aark Network Inc ..... D 302 399-3945
  Newark (G-5876)
Advance Central Services Inc ..... E 302 830-9732
  Wilmington (G-8945)
Affinity Wealth Management ..... F 302 652-6767
  Wilmington (G-8971)
Agile 1 ..... F 302 791-6900
  Wilmington (G-8977)
AMC - Commercial Inc ..... G 302 229-0051
  Claymont (G-689)

Ameken Network Group Inc ..... F 302 545-3472
  Claymont (G-691)
Antebellum Hospitality Inc ..... G 302 436-4375
  Selbyville (G-8449)
Apartment Communities Corp ..... D 302 656-7781
  Wilmington (G-9094)
Aquatic Management ..... G 302 235-1818
  Wilmington (G-9106)
Ardexo Inc ..... G 855 617-7500
  Dover (G-1134)
Ashby Management Corporation ..... G 302 894-1200
  Newark (G-6009)
Atlantic Management ..... G 302 222-3919
  Rehoboth Beach (G-7850)
Atlantic Management Ltd ..... F 302 645-9511
  Rehoboth Beach (G-7851)
Avantys Health LLC ..... G 302 521-2848
  Wilmington (G-9196)
Axia Management ..... B 302 674-2200
  Dover (G-1162)
◆ Balfour Beatty LLC ..... G 302 573-3873
  Wilmington (G-9225)
Bayshore Records MGT LLC ..... G 302 731-4477
  Newark (G-6058)
Beachview Mgmt Inc ..... G 302 227-3280
  Georgetown (G-2450)
Bellevue Holding Company ..... E 302 655-1561
  Wilmington (G-9291)
Bpgs Construction LLC ..... D 302 691-2111
  Wilmington (G-9412)
Brandywine Contractors Inc ..... G 302 325-2700
  New Castle (G-5107)
Brownstone LLC ..... G 302 300-4370
  New Castle (G-5117)
Buck Simpers Archt + Assoc Inc ..... F 302 658-9300
  Wilmington (G-9498)
Business Integration Solution ..... G 302 355-3512
  Newark (G-6139)
Bz Construction Services Inc ..... G 302 999-7505
  Wilmington (G-9519)
C & S Consultants Inc ..... G 302 236-5211
  Milford (G-4339)
C and L Bradford and Assoc ..... G 302 529-8566
  Wilmington (G-9522)
Cactus Annies Restaurant & Bar ..... G 302 655-9004
  Wilmington (G-9528)
Cafe Management Associates ..... G 302 655-4959
  Wilmington (G-9534)
Cap Managmnt Services LLC ..... G 302 846-0120
  Delmar (G-978)
Capano Management Company ..... D 302 429-8700
  Wilmington (G-9554)
Case Management Services ..... G 302 354-3711
  Wilmington (G-9587)
Ceo-Hqcom LLC ..... G 302 883-8555
  Hockessin (G-2982)
Cetaris Inc ..... G 416 679-9555
  Dover (G-1271)
Christiana Care Health Sys Inc ..... B 302 733-1601
  Newark (G-6207)
Christiana Care Health Sys Inc ..... F 302 623-0390
  Newark (G-6208)
Christiana Care Health Sys Inc ..... G 302 366-1929
  Newark (G-6211)
Christiana Care Health Sys Inc ..... C 302 733-1000
  Wilmington (G-9679)
Cht Holdings LLC ..... F 954 864-2008
  Lewes (G-3421)
Chubb INA Ovrseas Holdings Inc ..... F 302 476-6000
  Wilmington (G-9694)
Clearwater Enrgy Resources LLC ..... G 510 267-8921
  Wilmington (G-9740)
Cloud Services Solutions Inc ..... G 888 335-3132
  Wilmington (G-9746)
Columbus Inn Management I ..... G 302 429-8700
  Wilmington (G-9779)
Construction MGT Svcs Inc ..... A 302 478-4200
  Wilmington (G-9835)
Corrado Management Svcs LLC ..... E 302 225-0700
  New Castle (G-5198)
Coventry Health Care Inc ..... G 800 833-7423
  Newark (G-6309)
Craftsman Cbntry Woodworks Inc ..... G 302 841-5274
  Selbyville (G-8472)
Crestline Hotels & Resorts LLC ..... C 302 655-0400
  Wilmington (G-9898)
Crystal Holdings Inc ..... D 302 421-5700
  Wilmington (G-9909)
CSC Entity Services LLC ..... G 302 654-7584
  Wilmington (G-9911)

SIC SECTION — 87 ENGINEERING, ACCOUNTING, RESEARCH, MANAGEMENT, AND RELATED SERVICES

Davin Management Group LLC ....F 302 367-6563
  Bear (G-99)
Dax-Wave Consulting LLC ....G...... 424 543-6662
  Wilmington (G-9974)
Delaware Innovation Space Inc ....G...... 302 695-2201
  Wilmington (G-10058)
Dis Management ....G...... 302 543-4481
  Wilmington (G-10163)
Dnrec Air Waste Management ....G...... 302 739-9406
  Dover (G-1435)
Eagle Hospitality Group LLC ....F 302 678-8388
  Dover (G-1493)
Easy Corp Ltd ....F 302 824-0109
  Wilmington (G-10331)
Ekww Inc ....G...... 302 234-2877
  Hockessin (G-3018)
Eprintit Usa Inc ....F 613 299-7105
  Wilmington (G-10428)
Erickson Management ....G...... 302 235-0855
  Newark (G-6537)
Everest Hotel Group LLC ....F 213 272-0088
  Camden (G-569)
Everett Robinson ....F 302 530-6574
  Wilmington (G-10446)
Faith Family Management Co ....G...... 302 832-5936
  Newark (G-6564)
First State Management LLC ....G...... 302 268-8176
  Lincoln (G-3848)
Glen Playa Inc ....G...... 302 703-7512
  Lewes (G-3515)
Harvey Development Co ....C 302 323-9300
  New Castle (G-5381)
Hfm Investment Advisors Inc ....G...... 302 234-9777
  Newark (G-6727)
Highmarks Inc ....G...... 302 421-3000
  Wilmington (G-10906)
Hlh Construction MGT Svcs Inc ....F 302 654-7508
  Wilmington (G-10920)
Hyas US Inc ....G...... 250 327-9743
  Wilmington (G-10981)
Inov8 Inc ....G...... 302 465-5124
  Camden Wyoming (G-646)
Integrated Solutions Planning ....G...... 302 297-9215
  Georgetown (G-2567)
J P Morgan Services Inc ....A 302 634-1000
  Newark (G-6818)
J T Mican & Associates Inc ....G...... 302 323-8152
  New Castle (G-5431)
J&D Management ....G...... 302 239-2489
  Hockessin (G-3062)
K W Lands LLC ....E 302 674-2200
  Dover (G-1718)
Keep Selling Property LLC ....G...... 302 235-3066
  New Castle (G-5458)
Keystate Corporate MGT LLC ....G...... 302 425-5158
  Wilmington (G-11253)
Kubera Global Solutions LLC ....F 480 241-5124
  Wilmington (G-11299)
Lau & Assoc Ltd ....F 302 792-5955
  Wilmington (G-11337)
Lawrence Kennedy ....F 302 533-5880
  Newark (G-6923)
Lighthouse Construction Inc ....F 302 677-1965
  Magnolia (G-3898)
Locker Construction Inc ....G...... 302 239-2859
  Newark (G-6946)
Lutheran Community Services ....G...... 302 654-8886
  Wilmington (G-11453)
M C Tek LLC ....G...... 302 644-9695
  Rehoboth Beach (G-7992)
Magetti Gorup LLC ....D 302 355-5540
  Wilmington (G-11485)
Majalco LLC ....G...... 703 507-5298
  Wilmington (G-11494)
Marta Group ....G...... 302 737-2008
  Newark (G-6993)
McDonalds ....G...... 302 674-2095
  Dover (G-1832)
McNeil and Fmly MGT Group LLC ....F 302 830-3267
  Wilmington (G-11605)
Mera Rd 2 LLC ....G...... 305 577-3443
  Wilmington (G-11634)
Merman Management Inc ....G...... 302 456-9904
  Wilmington (G-11645)
Mid Atlantic Grand Prix LLC ....E 302 656-5278
  New Castle (G-5522)
Minatee Business Group ....G...... 302 543-5092
  Wilmington (G-11703)
Montchanin Design Group Inc ....F 302 652-3008
  Wilmington (G-11735)

Moorway Painting Management ....G...... 302 764-5002
  Wilmington (G-11747)
Mosaic ....C 302 456-5995
  Newark (G-7062)
Natural House Inc ....G...... 302 218-0338
  Newark (G-7087)
New Balance Retail Management ....G...... 302 230-3062
  Wilmington (G-11850)
Omniway Corporation ....F 302 738-5076
  Newark (G-7147)
Orion Group LLC ....G...... 302 357-9137
  Wilmington (G-11973)
Palmetto MGT & Engrg LLC ....C 302 993-2766
  Wilmington (G-12009)
Peek Performance Group LLC ....E 480 242-6087
  Wilmington (G-12059)
Pro Pest Management of De Inc ....F 302 994-2847
  Wilmington (G-12233)
Procaccianti Group LLC ....G...... 401 946-4600
  Wilmington (G-12237)
Prorank Business Solutions LLC ....G...... 302 256-0642
  Wilmington (G-12253)
Prosperity Unlimited Ente ....G...... 302 379-2494
  Middletown (G-4200)
Providence At Heritage Sh ....G...... 302 337-1040
  Bridgeville (G-513)
Registered Agnts Legal Svcs LLC ....G...... 302 427-6970
  Wilmington (G-12364)
Richman Wealth Management ....G...... 443 536-6936
  Rehoboth Beach (G-8058)
Right Property MGT Co LLC ....F 302 227-1155
  Rehoboth Beach (G-8059)
Roberts Property MGT LLC ....G...... 302 537-5371
  Bethany Beach (G-429)
Safe Harbor Property MGT LLC ....G...... 302 436-9882
  Selbyville (G-8542)
Saggio Management Group Inc ....G...... 302 659-6560
  Smyrna (G-8710)
Secure Management ....G...... 302 999-8342
  Middletown (G-4234)
Service General Corp ....C 302 856-3500
  Georgetown (G-2651)
◆ Severn Trent Inc ....E 302 427-5990
  Wilmington (G-12588)
Signature Group Management Co ....G...... 302 691-1010
  New Castle (G-5713)
Signature Property Management ....G...... 302 212-2381
  Lewes (G-3745)
Six Plus Inc ....G...... 302 652-3296
  Wilmington (G-12638)
Smart Printing MGT LLC ....G...... 855 549-4900
  Newark (G-7447)
Sodel Concepts II LLC ....G...... 302 228-3786
  Rehoboth Beach (G-8080)
St Anthonys Housing Mgt Corp ....G...... 302 421-3756
  Wilmington (G-12721)
Strands Prprty Prservation LLC ....G...... 302 381-9792
  Millsboro (G-4805)
▼ Syngenta Corporation ....E 302 425-2000
  Wilmington (G-12836)
Tdc Partners Ltd ....G...... 302 827-2137
  Lewes (G-3779)
Teksolv Usd Inc ....D 302 738-1050
  Newark (G-7553)
Telamon Corp Head Start Prgram ....D 302 653-3766
  Smyrna (G-8729)
Tgx Holdings LLC ....C 212 260-6300
  Wilmington (G-12890)
Thomson Reuters (grc) Inc ....A 212 227-7357
  Wilmington (G-12904)
Tm Management LLC ....G...... 302 654-4940
  Wilmington (G-12919)
Totaltranslogistics LLC ....G...... 302 325-4245
  New Castle (G-5777)
Tpw Management LLC ....G...... 302 227-7878
  Lewes (G-3793)
Twin Hearts Management LLC ....G...... 302 777-5700
  Dover (G-2167)
Unity Construction Inc ....E 302 998-0531
  Wilmington (G-13030)
Vest Management Inc ....G...... 302 856-3100
  Georgetown (G-2700)
Walnut Green Asset MGT LL ....G...... 302 689-3798
  Wilmington (G-13116)
Waste Management Inc ....F 302 854-5304
  Laurel (G-3305)
Wellington Management Group ....G...... 215 569-8900
  Wilmington (G-13143)
Whispering Meadows LLC ....G...... 302 698-1073
  Dover (G-2223)

Wilmington Trust Corporation ....E 302 651-8378
  Wilmington (G-13263)
Winifred Ellen Erbe ....G...... 302 541-0889
  Frankford (G-2399)
Wohlsen Construction Company ....E 302 324-9900
  Wilmington (G-13284)
Xenith Solutions LLC ....G...... 703 963-3523
  Selbyville (G-8556)

8742 Management Consulting Services

924 Inc ....E 302 656-6100
  Wilmington (G-8870)
AA Smith & Associates LLC ....F 973 477-3052
  Middletown (G-3926)
Above and Beyond Coverage LLC .....E 201 417-5189
  Wilmington (G-8907)
Abridge Partners LLC ....G...... 302 378-1882
  Middletown (G-3928)
ABS Engineering LLC ....G...... 302 595-9081
  Newark (G-5886)
Adamlouis Ltd Liability Co ....G...... 973 937-7524
  Wilmington (G-8932)
Adjuvant Research Services Inc ....F 302 737-5513
  Newark (G-5900)
ADP Pacific Inc ....G...... 302 657-4060
  Wilmington (G-8942)
Advanced Internet Solutions ....G...... 302 584-4641
  Wilmington (G-8952)
Advanced Systems Inc ....G...... 302 368-1211
  Newark (G-5908)
Aesthtic Special Care Assoc PA ....F 302 482-4444
  Wilmington (G-8967)
Alder Associates LLC ....G...... 360 833-0988
  Wilmington (G-9004)
All In One Brands LLC ....G...... 301 323-8144
  Dover (G-1105)
Alliance Bus Dev Concepts LLC ....F 803 814-4004
  Clayton (G-832)
America Group ....G...... 302 529-1320
  Wilmington (G-9041)
American Institute For Pub Svc ....G...... 302 622-9101
  Wilmington (G-9051)
Anq LLC ....G...... 408 837-3678
  Wilmington (G-9089)
Arm Chair Scouts LLC ....F 315 360-8692
  Wilmington (G-9130)
Ascension Industries LLC ....G...... 302 659-1778
  Smyrna (G-8576)
Austin Alliance Electric Inc ....E 843 297-8078
  Wilmington (G-9184)
▲ Avalanche Strategies LLC ....C 302 436-7060
  Selbyville (G-8452)
Batescainelli LLC ....G...... 202 618-0340
  Rehoboth Beach (G-7856)
Bennett & Bennett Inc ....F 302 990-8939
  New Castle (G-5081)
Big Tomorrow LLC ....F 650 714-3912
  Wilmington (G-9333)
Blackgrid Consulting LLC ....G...... 302 319-2013
  Wilmington (G-9348)
Bloom Consulting ....G...... 302 584-1592
  Wilmington (G-9372)
Blue Ridge Air Inc ....G...... 302 323-4800
  New Castle (G-5096)
Boothe Investment Group ....G...... 302 734-7526
  Dover (G-1221)
BP Staffing Inc ....G...... 302 999-7213
  Wilmington (G-9407)
Breckenridge Software Tech ....G...... 302 656-8460
  Wilmington (G-9464)
Brs Consulting Inc ....G...... 302 786-2326
  Harrington (G-2819)
Byron & Davis Cccc ....G...... 302 792-2334
  Wilmington (G-9517)
Carr Paris ....F 302 401-1203
  Wilmington (G-9578)
Central Firm LLC ....G...... 610 470-9836
  Wilmington (G-9615)
Circus Associates Intelligence ....E 757 663-7864
  Lewes (G-3422)
Cloud Services Solutions Inc ....G...... 888 335-3132
  Wilmington (G-9746)
Cmy Solutions LLC ....G...... 321 732-1866
  Newark (G-6256)
Cognition Group Inc ....G...... 302 454-1265
  Wilmington (G-9760)
▲ Company Corporation ....D 302 636-5440
  Wilmington (G-9798)
Comprehensive Bus Cons Inc ....G...... 302 635-7711
  Hockessin (G-2995)

Employee Codes: A=Over 500 employees, B=251-500
C=101-250, D=51-100, E=20-50, F=10-19, G=1-9

Conducerent Incorporated...G... 302 543-8525
Wilmington *(G-9816)*
Congruence Consulting Group...G... 320 290-6155
Newark *(G-6286)*
Connecting Generations Inc...F... 302 656-2122
Wilmington *(G-9825)*
Convergence Group Inc...F... 302 234-7400
Wilmington *(G-9845)*
Cool Nerds Marketing Inc...F... 302 304-3440
Wilmington *(G-9851)*
Core Functions LLC...G... 443 956-9626
Selbyville *(G-8471)*
Core Value Global LLC...G... 908 312-4070
Wilmington *(G-9860)*
Corporate Holding Services...G... 302 428-0515
Wilmington *(G-9865)*
Countermeasures Assessment...G... 302 322-9600
New Castle *(G-5200)*
County of Sussex...E... 302 855-7878
Georgetown *(G-2490)*
Cr24 LLC...F... 888 427-9357
Wilmington *(G-9890)*
Crimson Strategy Group LLP...G... 302 503-5698
Dover *(G-1323)*
Csi Solutions LLC...F... 202 506-7573
Newark *(G-6320)*
Cypress Capital Management LLC...F... 302 429-8436
Wilmington *(G-9934)*
Da Vinci Ebusiness Ltd...G... 610 399-3988
Wilmington *(G-9945)*
Daimlerchrysler N Amrca Financ...F... 302 292-6840
Newark *(G-6344)*
Daniel M McDermott Chfc Cfp...G... 302 778-5677
Wilmington *(G-9956)*
David G Major Associates Inc...E... 703 642-7450
Millsboro *(G-4673)*
DCH Auto Group (usa) Inc...G... 302 478-4600
Wilmington *(G-9980)*
De Catering Inc...E... 302 607-7200
Wilmington *(G-9985)*
Decisivedge LLC...G... 302 299-1570
Newark *(G-6357)*
Delaware Enterprises Inc...E... 302 324-5660
New Castle *(G-5228)*
Delaware Healthcare Assn...G... 302 674-2853
Dover *(G-1376)*
Delaware Incorporation Svcs...F... 302 658-1733
Wilmington *(G-10057)*
Delaware Intercorp Inc...G... 302 266-9367
Wilmington *(G-10059)*
Delaware Marketing Partners...G... 302 575-1610
Wilmington *(G-10062)*
Delaware Mfg EXT Partnr Inc...G... 302 283-3131
Newark *(G-6395)*
Delaware Registered Agents...G... 320 733-0600
Newark *(G-6406)*
Delaware State Education Assn...E... 302 734-5834
Dover *(G-1396)*
Design Tribe Republic LLC...G... 302 918-5279
Wilmington *(G-10124)*
Dfs Corporate Services LLC...A... 302 323-7191
New Castle *(G-5250)*
Diamond State Fincl Group Inc...E... 302 366-0366
Newark *(G-6444)*
Dojupa LLC...G... 302 300-2009
Wilmington *(G-10185)*
Dominring Blgcal RES Group LLC...F... 951 327-8062
Rehoboth Beach *(G-7919)*
Dorey Financial Services Inc...G... 302 856-0970
Georgetown *(G-2513)*
Douglas C Loew & Associates...G... 302 453-0550
Newark *(G-6464)*
Dreamville LLC...G... 662 524-0917
Lewes *(G-3472)*
Drw Funding LLC...G... 404 631-7127
Dover *(G-1481)*
Dss International LLC...G... 302 836-0270
Newark *(G-6476)*
Dumont Group LLC...G... 302 777-1003
New Castle *(G-5265)*
Dynamic Devices LLC...F... 302 994-2401
Wilmington *(G-10271)*
Eco SBC 2015-1 REO 167061 LLC...E... 302 652-8013
Wilmington *(G-10340)*
Ecsquared Inc...G... 302 750-8554
Wilmington *(G-10341)*
Emory Hill & Company...D... 302 322-4400
New Castle *(G-5287)*
Encima Group Inc...D... 302 352-1714
Newark *(G-6525)*
Enhanced Corporate Prfmce LLC...E... 302 545-8541
Newark *(G-6529)*
Enterprise Rsurce Planners Inc...G... 800 716-3660
Wilmington *(G-10415)*
Epic Marketing Cons Corp...E... 302 285-9790
Middletown *(G-4061)*
Esis Inc...G... 215 640-1000
Wilmington *(G-10436)*
Even & Odd Minds LLC...F... 619 663-7284
Wilmington *(G-10443)*
Exo Works Inc...G... 302 531-1139
Dover *(G-1534)*
Express Legal Documents LLC...E... 212 710-1374
Wilmington *(G-10463)*
Ezprohub LLC...G... 302 327-4222
Newark *(G-6560)*
F D Hammond Enterprises Inc...F... 302 424-8455
Milford *(G-4407)*
Fair Square Financial LLC...G... 571 205-0305
Wilmington *(G-10475)*
Femmepal Corporation...E... 888 406-0804
Lewes *(G-3494)*
Financial House Inc...F... 302 654-5451
Wilmington *(G-10540)*
Financial Services...E... 302 478-4707
Wilmington *(G-10541)*
Fiscal Associates...F... 302 894-0500
Newark *(G-6588)*
Five Sixty Enterprise LLC...E... 302 268-6530
Wilmington *(G-10566)*
Franklin Kennet LLC...F... 302 655-6536
Wilmington *(G-10617)*
Functionalit Inc...G... 703 566-6624
Selbyville *(G-8495)*
Fursan Consulting Services...F... 240 654-5784
New Castle *(G-5336)*
Gale and Associates LLC...G... 302 698-4253
Dover *(G-1578)*
Gateway International 360 LLC...G... 302 250-4990
New Castle *(G-5345)*
Gavinsolmonese...F... 302 655-8997
Wilmington *(G-10680)*
Genovesius Solutia LLC...G... 302 252-7506
Hockessin *(G-3036)*
Gkua Inc...F... 415 971-5341
Wilmington *(G-10718)*
Global Data Mining LLC...G... 551 208-1316
Lewes *(G-3516)*
Global Vision Xtreme Corp...F... 302 287-4822
Claymont *(G-755)*
Golden Thorns Inc...G... 861 598-6748
Lewes *(G-3519)*
Government Mrktplace Ltd Lblty...E... 302 297-9694
Newark *(G-6679)*
Green Interest Enterprises LLC...G... 228 355-0708
Dover *(G-1612)*
Grind or Starve LLC...G... 302 322-1679
Wilmington *(G-10786)*
Grofos International LLC...G... 302 635-4805
Newark *(G-6693)*
Gulf Development Partners LLC...G... 646 334-1245
Wilmington *(G-10800)*
Haccp Navigator LLC...G... 302 531-7922
Lincoln *(G-3853)*
Hardin & Associates Inc...G... 302 654-9923
Wilmington *(G-10836)*
Harvey Hanna & Associates Inc...G... 302 323-9300
Newport *(G-7750)*
Hat Blue Group LLC...F... 225 288-2962
Lewes *(G-3535)*
Honey Bee Seasonal Kit & Mkt...G... 302 407-5579
Wilmington *(G-10947)*
Host Nation Perspectives LLC...G... 443 292-6702
Selbyville *(G-8504)*
Ibr Group Inc...F... 610 986-8545
Newark *(G-6760)*
Iceteccom Inc...G... 302 477-1792
Wilmington *(G-10988)*
Iconic Skus LLC...G... 302 722-4547
Wilmington *(G-10989)*
Ignis Group LLC...E... 302 645-7400
Lewes *(G-3552)*
Incenco International...F... 302 478-8400
Wilmington *(G-11012)*
Independent School MGT Inc...E... 302 656-4944
Wilmington *(G-11018)*
Inflection Point Ventures LP...G... 302 452-1120
Newark *(G-6779)*
Insurance & Fincl Svcs Ltd Del...G... 302 234-1200
Wilmington *(G-11044)*
Integrated AVI Solutions LLC...G... 302 351-3427
Wilmington *(G-11047)*
Intercontinental Marketing...G... 302 429-7555
Wilmington *(G-11056)*
Intercontinental Tech LLC...G... 302 984-2111
Wilmington *(G-11057)*
Intrinsic Partners LLC...D... 610 388-0853
Wilmington *(G-11071)*
Isis North America Inc...G... 508 653-7318
Lewes *(G-3563)*
It Tigers LLC...G... 732 898-2793
Lewes *(G-3565)*
Jack Donovan...G... 410 715-0504
Millsboro *(G-4711)*
Johnston Associates...G... 302 521-2984
Newark *(G-6848)*
K and L Gates...G... 302 416-7000
Wilmington *(G-11213)*
Kc & Associates Inc...G... 302 633-3300
Wilmington *(G-11231)*
Kch Ventures LLC...G... 302 737-6260
Newark *(G-6869)*
Keen Consulting Inc...G... 302 684-5270
Georgetown *(G-2580)*
Kelmar Associates LLC...D... 781 213-6926
Wilmington *(G-11238)*
Key Advisors Group LLC...G... 302 735-9909
Dover *(G-1744)*
Kfs Strategic MGT Svcs LLC...F... 302 545-7640
Bear *(G-217)*
Kintyre Solutions LLC...G... 888 636-0010
Wilmington *(G-11269)*
Kirk & Associates LLC...F... 302 444-4733
Christiana *(G-672)*
Kmh Contracting...G... 302 331-4894
Magnolia *(G-3897)*
Kortech Consulting Inc...F... 302 559-4612
Bear *(G-220)*
KS Kitchen LLC...G... 302 743-4349
Newark *(G-6904)*
Lawter Planning Group Inc...G... 302 736-6065
Dover *(G-1772)*
Lifesource Consulting Svcs LLC...F... 302 257-6247
Dover *(G-1784)*
Linda McCormick...G... 443 987-2099
Wilmington *(G-11392)*
Lockheed Martin Overseas LLC...G... 301 897-6923
Wilmington *(G-11422)*
Longo and Associates LLP...G... 302 477-7500
Wilmington *(G-11431)*
Maintenance Troubleshooting...G... 302 692-0871
Newark *(G-6976)*
Mallard Advisors LLC...F... 302 239-1654
Hockessin *(G-3086)*
Management Options Inc...F... 302 234-0836
Newark *(G-6980)*
Market Edge LLC...E... 302 442-6800
Wilmington *(G-11534)*
Marketing Creators Inc...D... 302 409-0344
Wilmington *(G-11536)*
Marketing Enterprise Capyuring...G... 302 293-9250
Wilmington *(G-11537)*
McNichol Enterprises Inc...F... 302 633-9348
Wilmington *(G-11606)*
Mediguide America LLC...E... 302 425-5900
Wilmington *(G-11619)*
Mentor Consultants Inc...G... 610 566-4004
Wilmington *(G-11633)*
Merion Realty Services LLC...G... 302 656-8543
Wilmington *(G-11642)*
Metropolitan Revenue Assoc LLC...G... 302 449-7490
New Castle *(G-5520)*
Mid States Sales & Marketing...E... 302 888-2475
Wilmington *(G-11680)*
Modernthink LLC...F... 302 764-4477
Wilmington *(G-11721)*
Moghul Life Inc...G... 347 560-9124
Wilmington *(G-11724)*
Momentum Management Group Inc...G... 302 477-9730
Wilmington *(G-11728)*
Money Bax LLC...G... 302 360-8577
Lewes *(G-3646)*
Money Galaxy Inc...F... 302 319-2008
Wilmington *(G-11731)*
Montesino Associates...G... 302 888-2355
Wilmington *(G-11736)*
Moore International LLC...G... 302 603-7262
Wilmington *(G-11745)*
Morning Report Research Inc...G... 302 730-3793
Dover *(G-1872)*

Mountain Consulting Inc ....G.... 302 744-9875
Dover *(G-1876)*
Mozeweb LLC ....G.... 302 355-0692
Newark *(G-7065)*
Mtc Usa LLC ....F.... 980 999-8888
Newark *(G-7069)*
MV Farinola Inc ....G.... 302 545-8492
Wilmington *(G-11781)*
Mwidm Inc ....E.... 302 298-0101
Wilmington *(G-11785)*
My Market Quest Inc ....F.... 213 265-9767
Wilmington *(G-11788)*
My Qme Inc ....E.... 302 218-8730
Wilmington *(G-11789)*
Nemours Hlth & Prevention Svcs ....G.... 302 366-1929
Newark *(G-7092)*
Newrez LLC ....G.... 302 455-6600
Middletown *(G-4174)*
Newton One Advisors ....F.... 302 731-1326
Newark *(G-7130)*
Nhb Advisors Inc ....G.... 610 660-0060
Wilmington *(G-11886)*
Nova RE & Bus Consulting LLC ....F.... 302 258-2193
Lewes *(G-3661)*
Oceanstar Technologies Inc ....G.... 302 542-1900
Bear *(G-270)*
Ohana Companies Inc ....F.... 302 225-5505
Wilmington *(G-11941)*
Omninet International Inc ....E.... 208 246-5022
Wilmington *(G-11950)*
Omniway Corporation ....F.... 302 738-5076
Newark *(G-7147)*
On Point Partners LLC ....G.... 302 655-5606
Wilmington *(G-11952)*
Openexo Inc ....F.... 617 965-5057
Dover *(G-1919)*
P A Aba Intl Inc ....F.... 800 979-5106
Lewes *(G-3675)*
Pabian Ventures LLC ....G.... 302 762-1992
Wilmington *(G-11999)*
Parent Information Ctr Del Inc ....G.... 302 999-7394
Wilmington *(G-12019)*
Paul Associates ....G.... 302 584-0064
Wilmington *(G-12039)*
Performance Based Results ....G.... 302 478-4443
Talleyville *(G-8750)*
Perinatal Assocation Delaware ....E.... 302 654-1088
Wilmington *(G-12086)*
Perry and Associates Inc ....F.... 302 898-2327
Hockessin *(G-3117)*
Phs Corporate Services Inc ....G.... 302 571-1128
Wilmington *(G-12128)*
Pierce Professional Services ....G.... 302 331-1154
Magnolia *(G-3903)*
Pineal Consulting Group LLC ....F.... 302 219-4822
Newark *(G-7218)*
Positioneering LLC ....G.... 302 415-3200
Wilmington *(G-12191)*
Postal Associates Inc ....G.... 302 584-1244
Wilmington *(G-12193)*
Precisionists Inc ....G.... 610 241-5354
Wilmington *(G-12209)*
Printify LLC ....G.... 415 968-6351
Wilmington *(G-12230)*
Pro Automated Inc ....D.... 302 294-6121
Newark *(G-7262)*
Project of Providence LLC ....G.... 302 438-8970
Wilmington *(G-12247)*
Project Otr LLC ....G.... 404 964-2244
Wilmington *(G-12248)*
Pyramid Group MGT Svcs Corp ....G.... 302 737-1770
Newark *(G-7275)*
Quintecent Inc ....G.... 443 838-5447
Selbyville *(G-8536)*
Red Clay Consolidated Schl Dst ....G.... 302 992-5580
Wilmington *(G-12347)*
Red Clay Inc ....G.... 302 239-2018
Hockessin *(G-3132)*
Redleo Software Inc ....F.... 302 691-9072
Wilmington *(G-12348)*
Resources For Human Dev Inc ....E.... 302 691-7574
Wilmington *(G-12387)*
Resources For Human Dev Inc ....E.... 302 731-5283
Newark *(G-7326)*
Sam Walts & Associates ....G.... 302 777-2211
Wilmington *(G-12531)*
Scottish Ventures LLC ....G.... 302 382-6057
New Castle *(G-5695)*
Second Chance Solutions LLC ....G.... 302 204-0551
Wilmington *(G-12567)*
Sfin 3 Inc ....G.... 302 472-9276
Wilmington *(G-12591)*
Simpler Logistics LLC ....G.... 800 619-8321
Wilmington *(G-12626)*
Siriusiq Mobile LLC ....F.... 888 414-2047
Newark *(G-7433)*
Solace Lifesciences Inc ....G.... 302 275-4195
Wilmington *(G-12674)*
Sopo-360 LLC ....G.... 703 585-3706
Newark *(G-7460)*
Strategic Solutions Intl Inc ....G.... 302 525-6313
Newark *(G-7493)*
Supply Chain Consultants Inc ....E.... 302 738-9215
Wilmington *(G-12812)*
Sweat Social LLC ....G.... 504 510-1973
Dover *(G-2123)*
Sweeny and Associates ....G.... 302 453-1645
Newark *(G-7519)*
Tecnologika Usa Inc ....G.... 302 597-7611
Wilmington *(G-12874)*
Timtec LLC ....F.... 302 292-8500
Newark *(G-7567)*
Tipton Communications Group ....G.... 302 454-7901
Newark *(G-7568)*
TLC Personal Assistants ....G.... 302 290-9902
Wilmington *(G-12918)*
Trellist Inc ....E.... 302 778-1300
Wilmington *(G-12964)*
Ubivis Management LLC ....E.... 833 824-8476
Rehoboth Beach *(G-8103)*
Unique Creations By Chloe LLC ....E.... 855 942-0477
Wilmington *(G-13016)*
United Worldwide Express LLC ....G.... 347 651-5111
Wilmington *(G-13029)*
V2s Corporation ....D.... 302 384-9947
Wilmington *(G-13042)*
Vcg LLC ....G.... 302 336-8151
Dover *(G-2188)*
Vector Marketing Corp ....G.... 716 373-6141
Wilmington *(G-13053)*
Velocity Pointe LLC ....G.... 302 351-8305
Wilmington *(G-13056)*
Veteran It Pro LLC ....F.... 302 824-3111
Hockessin *(G-3167)*
Vironex Envmtl Field Svcs Inc ....E.... 302 661-1400
Wilmington *(G-13088)*
Vtms LLC ....G.... 302 264-9094
Dover *(G-2201)*
Wang Consultants Inc ....G.... 626 483-0265
Wilmington *(G-13117)*
Wartrude Services Inc ....F.... 302 213-3944
Wilmington *(G-13120)*
Weelwork Inc ....G.... 800 546-8607
Claymont *(G-818)*
Well Done Cleaning Services ....G.... 443 407-3064
Wilmington *(G-13142)*
White & Associates ....G.... 302 765-3736
Wilmington *(G-13188)*
Winner Group Management Inc ....E.... 302 571-5200
Wilmington *(G-13273)*
Wyndham Group Inc ....G.... 704 905-9750
Wilmington *(G-13312)*
Xcutivescom Inc ....G.... 888 245-9996
Dover *(G-2242)*
Xonex Relocation LLC ....D.... 302 323-9000
New Castle *(G-5843)*
Zir LLC ....G.... 203 524-1215
Lewes *(G-3835)*
Zumra Solutions LLC ....G.... 302 504-4423
Lewes *(G-3836)*
Zutz Risk Management ....D.... 302 658-8000
Wilmington *(G-13355)*

8743 Public Relations Svcs

Alexander Rv Service Center ....G.... 302 653-3250
Smyrna *(G-8563)*
Aloysius Butlr Clark Assoc Inc ....D.... 302 655-1552
Wilmington *(G-9029)*
Bgp Publicity Inc ....G.... 302 234-9500
Hockessin *(G-2964)*
Kimos Hawaiian Shave Ice ....G.... 302 998-1763
Wilmington *(G-11261)*
Middletown Main Street Inc ....G.... 302 378-2977
Middletown *(G-4159)*
One System Incorporated ....F.... 888 311-1110
Wilmington *(G-11956)*
Remline Corp ....E.... 302 737-7228
Newark *(G-7316)*
SC Marketing US Inc ....G.... 714 352-4992
Wilmington *(G-12549)*
Spark Productions LLC ....G.... 302 436-0183
Selbyville *(G-8548)*
The Ascendant Group Inc ....F.... 302 450-4494
Newark *(G-7561)*
Tipton Communications Group ....G.... 302 454-7901
Newark *(G-7568)*
Willis Groupllc ....G.... 302 632-9898
Dover *(G-2229)*

8744 Facilities Support Mgmt Svcs

Brandywine Zoo ....E.... 302 571-7747
Wilmington *(G-9462)*
Brightfields Inc ....E.... 302 656-9600
Wilmington *(G-9477)*
Cognitive Group LLC ....F.... 301 585-1444
Dover *(G-1302)*
Day and Zimmermann Inc ....C.... 302 368-1609
Newark *(G-6350)*
Dibiasos Clg Rstration Svc Inc ....G.... 302 376-7111
Townsend *(G-8784)*
Ecg Industries Inc ....G.... 302 453-0535
Newark *(G-6502)*
Environmental Versacorp ....G.... 302 798-1839
Wilmington *(G-10420)*
Focus Solutions Services Inc ....F.... 302 318-1345
Newark *(G-6597)*
H2o Pro LLC ....G.... 302 321-7077
Frankford *(G-2367)*
Professional Roof Services Inc ....G.... 302 731-5770
Newark *(G-7266)*
Seaford Mission Inc ....F.... 302 629-2559
Seaford *(G-8393)*

8748 Business Consulting Svcs, NEC

ABC Systems Inc ....G.... 302 528-8875
Newark *(G-5883)*
AC Group Inc ....G.... 201 840-5566
Wilmington *(G-8910)*
Action Environmental Service ....G.... 302 798-3100
Wilmington *(G-8926)*
Acuitive Inc ....G.... 214 738-1099
Wilmington *(G-8929)*
Acumen Strategies Inc ....G.... 302 218-3949
Hockessin *(G-2951)*
Aecom Usa Inc ....E.... 302 781-5963
Wilmington *(G-8963)*
African Wood Inc ....G.... 302 884-6738
Wilmington *(G-8973)*
Agricltral Assssmnts Intl Corp ....G.... 240 463-6677
Laurel *(G-3191)*
Alliance Bus Dev Concepts LLC ....F.... 803 814-4004
Clayton *(G-832)*
Ameresco Inc ....G.... 302 284-1480
Felton *(G-2271)*
Ameresco Inc ....G.... 302 875-0696
Georgetown *(G-2430)*
American Gen Trdg Contg US Inc ....G.... 804 739-1480
Dover *(G-1119)*
Applied Research Assoc Inc ....D.... 302 677-4147
Dover *(G-1133)*
Aquila of Delaware Inc ....F.... 302 999-1106
Wilmington *(G-9107)*
ARC HUD I Inc ....G.... 302 996-9400
Wilmington *(G-9116)*
ARC HUD VII Inc ....G.... 302 996-9400
Wilmington *(G-9117)*
Aspira of Delaware Inc ....G.... 302 292-1463
Newark *(G-6011)*
Assoction Brds Thlgcal Educatn ....G.... 302 654-7770
Wilmington *(G-9160)*
Atlantic Duncan Inc ....F.... 302 383-0740
Newark *(G-6020)*
Atlantic Resource Management ....F.... 302 539-2029
Ocean View *(G-7756)*
Atlantic Training LLC ....F.... 302 464-0341
Middletown *(G-3951)*
B Rich Enterprises ....G.... 302 530-6865
Middletown *(G-3957)*
Bastianelli Group Inc ....G.... 302 658-1500
Newark *(G-6050)*
Batescainelli LLC ....G.... 202 618-2040
Rehoboth Beach *(G-7856)*
Batta Inc ....E.... 302 737-3376
Newark *(G-6051)*
Batta Environmental Assoc Inc ....E.... 302 737-3376
Newark *(G-6052)*
Bishop Enterprises Corporation ....E.... 302 379-2884
Wilmington *(G-9342)*
Bluestone AM LLC ....F.... 302 477-0370
Wilmington *(G-9383)*

S I C

Employee Codes: A=Over 500 employees, B=251-500
C=101-250, D=51-100, E=20-50, F=10-19, G=1-9
2020 Harris Directory of
Delaware Businesses
577

87 ENGINEERING, ACCOUNTING, RESEARCH, MANAGEMENT, AND RELATED SERVICES

Company	Code	Phone
Brightfields Inc — Wilmington (G-9477)	E	302 656-9600
Burton Enterprises Inc — Bear (G-57)	G	302 838-0115
C and L Bradford and Assoc — (G-9522)	G	302 529-8566
C4-Nvis USA LLC — Dover (G-1246)	G	213 465-5089
Cannon Cold Storage LLC — Bridgeville (G-457)	E	302 337-5500
Capitol Environmental Svcs Inc — Newark (G-6150)	G	302 652-8999
Capstone Homes LLC — Lewes (G-3404)	G	302 644-0300
Cardiovascular Consultants of — Ocean View (G-7774)	G	302 541-8138
Cardno Inc — Newark (G-6154)	F	302 395-1919
Carter Firm LLC — Wilmington (G-9582)	G	267 420-0717
Cda Group Inc — Claymont (G-710)	G	302 793-0693
Cecon Group LLC — Wilmington (G-9608)	G	302 994-8000
Cleantech Energy Solutions LLC — Wilmington (G-9738)	G	301 704-2831
Cleaver — Smyrna (G-8599)	G	302 659-1707
Cloudcoffer LLC — Wilmington (G-9748)	E	412 620-3203
Cognitive Group LLC — Dover (G-1302)	F	301 585-1444
Commonwealth Group — Wilmington (G-9790)	G	302 995-6400
Compliance Environmental Inc — Dover (G-1308)	G	302 674-4427
Congruence Consulting Group — Newark (G-6286)	G	320 290-6155
Consulttive Rview Rhbilitation — Newark (G-6290)	G	302 366-0356
Convergone Gvrnment Sltons LLC — Wilmington (G-9846)	G	302 999-7020
Core Construction LLC — Smyrna (G-8605)	G	302 449-4186
Corporations & Companies Inc — Wilmington (G-9867)	G	302 652-4800
Countermeasures Assessment — New Castle (G-5200)	G	302 322-9600
Creative Micro Designs Inc — Newark (G-6314)	G	302 456-5800
Cyclesolv LLC — Newark (G-6337)	G	302 894-9400
D & H Credit Services Inc — Newark (G-6340)	F	302 832-6980
D E Enterprises LLC — Clayton (G-841)	G	302 653-5493
De Novo Corporation — Wilmington (G-9987)	E	302 234-7407
Decoy Magazine — Lewes (G-3450)	G	302 644-9001
Delaware Family Voices Inc — Wilmington (G-10046)	F	302 588-4908
Delaware Innovation Space Inc — Wilmington (G-10058)	G	302 695-2201
Delaware Safety Council Inc — New Castle (G-5239)	G	302 276-0660
Design Tribe Republic LLC — Wilmington (G-10124)	G	302 918-5279
Diamond State CLT Inc — Dover (G-1424)	F	800 282-0477
Dolan Manufacturing Solutions — Middletown (G-4040)	G	302 378-4981
Drh Enterprises LLC — Seaford (G-8226)	G	302 864-0060
Dvhd Inc — Wilmington (G-10270)	G	302 584-3547
E I Du Pont De Nemours & Co — Newark (G-6490)	D	302 774-1000
Eagle Us Inc — Wilmington (G-10315)	A	484 913-0300
East Coast Seed LLC — Georgetown (G-2518)	G	302 856-7018
Eden Green LLC — Wilmington (G-10344)	F	817 999-1570
Elevationtv — Wilmington (G-10373)	G	978 317-9285
Ellis Fall Sfety Solutions LLC — Wilmington (G-10379)	G	302 571-8470
Ementum Inc — Milton (G-4903)	E	866 984-1999
▲ Emerald Bioagriculture Corp — Hockessin (G-3019)	F	517 882-7370
Encross LLC — Wilmington (G-10396)	F	302 351-2593
Endocrinology Consultant — Dover (G-1521)	G	302 734-2782
Endovascular Consultants LLC — Wilmington (G-10398)	G	302 482-1333
Environmental Alliance Inc — Wilmington (G-10419)	E	302 995-7544
Environmental Consulting Svcs — Middletown (G-4059)	F	302 378-9881
Environmental Resources Inc — Selbyville (G-8489)	G	302 436-9637
Environmental Services Inc — New Castle (G-5292)	G	302 669-6812
Environmental Testing Inc — Middletown (G-4060)	F	302 378-5341
Envirotech Envmtl Consulting — Lewes (G-3483)	G	302 684-5201
Envision Consulting LLC — Wilmington (G-10421)	G	302 658-9027
Envision Solution LLC — Wilmington (G-10422)	F	302 442-7329
Etechpublish Inc — Newark (G-6542)	G	302 294-1678
Fareed Services — Wilmington (G-10499)	G	302 559-8594
Fireside Partners Inc — Dover (G-1551)	G	302 613-2165
First State Sealcoating — Camden Wyoming (G-639)	G	302 632-1234
Flex Ip Solutions Inc — Wilmington (G-10573)	G	610 359-5812
Flexera Inc — Harbeson (G-2783)	E	302 945-6870
Fshery Mid-Atlntic MGT Council — Dover (G-1571)	F	302 674-2331
Gamut Color Inc — Wilmington (G-10668)	G	302 652-7171
Geo-Technology Associates Inc — New Castle (G-5351)	E	302 326-2100
Geo-Technology Associates Inc — Georgetown (G-2538)	G	302 855-5775
Georgetown Construction Co — Georgetown (G-2544)	D	302 856-7601
Gift Solutions LLC — Newark (G-6654)	G	585 317-4465
GL Gray Consulting Services LL — Magnolia (G-3891)	G	302 698-3339
Global Dev Partners Inc — Wilmington (G-10723)	G	480 330-7931
Good Home Solutions LLC — Wilmington (G-10746)	G	302 540-3190
Graceland Group Inc — Dewey Beach (G-1058)	G	302 226-1373
Grape Solutions — Wilmington (G-10761)	G	201 784-9797
Greenwing Solutions Inc — Wilmington (G-10782)	G	302 295-5690
Gwantel Intl Corp Engrg & Tech — Newark (G-6696)	G	302 377-6235
H Clemons Consulting Inc — Wilmington (G-10805)	E	302 295-5097
Har-Lex LLC — Wilmington (G-10835)	G	302 476-2322
Harvard Environmental Inc — Bear (G-178)	F	302 326-2333
Hedgeforce LLC — Bear (G-6720)	G	305 600-0085
Highdef Transportation LLC — Bear (G-184)	G	610 212-8596
I AM Consulting Group Inc — Bear (G-187)	F	302 521-4999
Incorporators USA LLC — Wilmington (G-11015)	F	800 441-5940
Industry ARC — Wilmington (G-11023)	G	614 588-8538
Inrg of Delaware Inc — Lewes (G-3559)	G	302 369-1412
Insight Engineering Solutions — Townsend (G-8797)	G	302 378-4842
Intelligent Signage Inc — Wilmington (G-11052)	G	302 762-4100
International Spine Pain — Wilmington (G-11067)	G	302 478-7001
J C Wells & Sons LP — Milford (G-4455)	G	302 422-4732
Jackson Contracting Inc — Dover (G-1689)	F	302 678-2011
JD Rellek Company Inc — Felton (G-2298)	G	302 284-7042
Jeris LLC — Selbyville (G-8508)	F	443 745-9023
Joseph T Hardy & Son Inc — New Castle (G-5446)	E	302 328-9457
JR Gettier & Associates Inc — Wilmington (G-11202)	B	302 478-0911
Kfs Strategic MGT Svcs LLC — Bear (G-217)	G	302 545-7640
Koala Enterprises Inc — Frankford (G-2370)	G	302 436-9950
Kramer Group LLC — Wilmington (G-11291)	G	717 368-2117
La Jolla Fincl Partners LLC — Wilmington (G-11312)	G	858 864-0146
Landmark Engineering Inc — Newark (G-6915)	D	302 323-9377
Leadership Caddie — Bear (G-232)	F	302 743-6456
Lens Tolic LLC — Hockessin (G-3081)	G	800 343-5697
Lindco — Wilmington (G-11393)	G	302 652-0708
Lityx LLC — Wilmington (G-11411)	G	888 548-9947
Maryann Metrinko LLC — Lewes (G-3623)	G	410 643-1472
McNichol Enterprises Inc — Wilmington (G-11606)	F	302 633-9348
Medevice Services LLC — Dover (G-1835)	G	877 202-1588
Mefta LLC — Wilmington (G-11622)	F	804 433-3566
Mehar Investment Group LLC — Wilmington (G-11624)	G	302 999-1888
Mentor Consultants Inc — Wilmington (G-11633)	G	610 566-4004
Moghul Life Inc — Wilmington (G-11724)	G	347 560-9124
Monterey Enterprises LLC — Newark (G-7053)	G	302 504-4901
Mtk Enterprises LLC — Newark (G-7070)	G	302 266-9611
Multicultural A Delaware — Dover (G-1878)	F	302 399-6118
My Benefit Advisor LLC — Wilmington (G-11786)	G	302 588-7242
Nabstar Hospitality — Newark (G-7080)	G	302 453-1700
Nations Equity Investments Inc — Wilmington (G-11814)	G	302 257-9287
Ncall Research Inc — Dover (G-1888)	E	302 678-9400
Netinstincts Inc — Wilmington (G-11838)	F	302 521-9478
Netragy LLC — Newark (G-7094)	G	973 846-7018
New Castle Cnty Shoppers Guide — New Castle (G-5554)	E	302 325-6600
New Covenant Elec Svcs Inc — Middletown (G-4172)	G	302 454-1165
Newark Heritage Partners I LLC — Newark (G-7121)	G	302 283-0540
Nova Consultants Ltd — New Castle (G-5581)	F	302 328-1686
Nr Hudson Consulting Inc — Laurel (G-3267)	G	302 875-5276
Nucar Consulting Inc — Odessa (G-7831)	E	302 696-6000
Ocean First Enterprises LLC — Wilmington (G-11933)	F	302 232-8547
Office Partners Xiv Bellevue — Wilmington (G-11940)	G	302 691-2100
Orchard Park Group Inc — New Castle (G-5590)	E	302 356-1139
Paragon Group — Claymont (G-792)	F	302 798-5777
Performance Materials Na Inc — Wilmington (G-12085)	A	302 892-7009
Perrone Enterprises Inc — Selbyville (G-8530)	G	302 436-8031
Pmcaa Inc — Wilmington (G-12163)	G	302 439-6028
Princeton Coml Holdings LLC — Newark (G-7253)	G	302 449-4836
Professional Roof Services Inc — Newark (G-7266)	G	302 731-5770
Project Widgets Inc — Wilmington (G-12249)	G	302 439-3414

Pyramid Educational Cons .... E 302 368-2515
New Castle *(G-5655)*
Qsr Group LLC .... G 302 268-6909
Wilmington *(G-12276)*
Quinteccent Inc .... G 443 838-5447
Selbyville *(G-8536)*
Rallypoint Solutions LLC .... F 302 543-8087
Wilmington *(G-12308)*
Reading Assist Institute .... F 302 425-4080
Wilmington *(G-12342)*
Renaissance Square LLC .... G 302 943-5118
Dover *(G-2024)*
RFS Enterprises Inc .... G 302 888-0143
Wilmington *(G-12398)*
Ricore Inc .... G 302 656-8158
New Castle *(G-5678)*
Rockledge Global Partners Ltd ..... F 800 659-1102
Wilmington *(G-12456)*
Sandler Occptnal Mdicine Assoc .. E 302 369-0171
Newark *(G-7381)*
Sandy Knoll Enterprises LLC .... G 302 875-3916
Laurel *(G-3287)*
Santora CPA Group Pa .... E 302 737-6200
Newark *(G-7385)*
Schatz Messick Enterprises LLC ... G 302 398-8646
Harrington *(G-2883)*
Scio Risk Group Llc .... F 302 897-1534
Wilmington *(G-12561)*
Sentinel-Sg LLC .... G 580 458-9184
Wilmington *(G-12580)*
Sereduke Design Cons LLC .... G 302 478-3468
Wilmington *(G-12582)*
Siemanowski Consulting Inc .... G 302 368-1081
Newark *(G-7423)*
Sinnott Exc Consulting LLC .... G 302 656-2898
Wilmington *(G-12632)*
Six Angels Development Inc .... G 302 218-1548
Wilmington *(G-12637)*
Southern States Coop Inc .... G 302 875-3635
Laurel *(G-3293)*
Spectrum Tax Consultants USA ... G 866 544-1408
Wilmington *(G-12700)*
Spine Group LLC .... G 302 595-3030
Wilmington *(G-12706)*
Sqs Global Solutions LLC .... F 302 691-9682
Wilmington *(G-12718)*
Strategy House Inc .... G 302 658-1500
Newark *(G-7494)*
Suffex Conservation .... G 302 856-2105
Georgetown *(G-2670)*
Sustainable-Generation LLC .... G 917 678-6947
Wilmington *(G-12820)*
Systems Tech & Science LLC ...... G 703 757-2010
Dagsboro *(G-937)*
Tade Info Tech Solutions .... G 302 832-1449
Newark *(G-7529)*
Tarpon Strategies LLC .... G 215 806-2723
Newark *(G-7540)*
Tech Management Services Inc ... G 302 539-4837
Bethany Beach *(G-435)*
Tek Electronics LLC .... G 302 449-6947
Middletown *(G-4254)*
Tek Tree LLC .... F 302 368-2730
Newark *(G-7551)*
Telgian Corporation .... E 480 753-5444
Wilmington *(G-12880)*
Ten Bears Environmental LLC ..... G 302 731-8633
Newark *(G-7556)*

Terra Systems Inc .... F 302 798-9553
Claymont *(G-810)*
Trainor Consulting LLC .... G 302 428-1677
Wilmington *(G-12950)*
Treehouse Wellness Center LLC .. F 302 893-1001
Wilmington *(G-12963)*
Trellist Inc .... G 302 593-1432
Wilmington *(G-12965)*
Trinet Consultants Inc .... F 302 633-9348
Wilmington *(G-12973)*
Trinity Gold Consulting LLC .... G 302 476-9774
Wilmington *(G-12975)*
Umbrella Corporation .... E 302 603-7100
Rehoboth Beach *(G-8104)*
▼ Verscom LLC .... E 866 238-9189
Wilmington *(G-13065)*
Virtual Business Entps LLC .... G 302 472-9100
Wilmington *(G-13089)*
Vtms LLC .... G 302 264-9094
Dover *(G-2201)*
Wagamon Technology Group LLC ...G 302 424-1855
Milford *(G-4593)*
Wheeler Wolfenden & Dwares PA ..... E 302 254-8240
Wilmington *(G-13184)*
Wiedmann Enterprises Inc .... G 302 645-2028
Lewes *(G-3822)*
Wik Associates Inc .... G 302 322-2558
Newark *(G-7694)*
Wilmington Metropolitan Area P ... F 302 737-6205
Newark *(G-7702)*
Wise Power Systems Inc .... F 302 351-4613
Wilmington *(G-13279)*
Woods Hole Group Inc .... G 302 222-6720
Dover *(G-2236)*
Yellow Pine Associates Inc .... G 302 994-9500
Wilmington *(G-13326)*
Yph Consultants LLC .... F 302 674-4766
Dover *(G-2250)*
Zahn Incorporated .... G 302 425-3700
Wilmington *(G-13339)*
Zieta Technologies LLC .... F 302 252-5249
Wilmington *(G-13350)*

89 SERVICES, NOT ELSEWHERE CLASSIFIED

8999 Services Not Elsewhere Classified

Agriculture United States Dept ..... G 302 741-2600
Dover *(G-1095)*
American Diagnostic Svcs Inc ...... G 302 628-4209
Seaford *(G-8146)*
B P Services .... G 302 399-4132
Dover *(G-1166)*
Beach Butler Services LLC .... F 302 227-0114
Rehoboth Beach *(G-7857)*
Biblion .... G 302 644-2210
Lewes *(G-3383)*
Brightfields Inc .... E 302 656-9600
Wilmington *(G-9477)*
Carr Paris .... F 302 401-1203
Wilmington *(G-9578)*
Congo Capital Management LLC ... F 732 337-6643
Wilmington *(G-9820)*
Delaware Arts Conservatory .... F 302 595-4160
Bear *(G-103)*
Delaware Secretary of State .... F 302 736-7400
Dover *(G-1389)*

Delmarva Communications Inc .... F 302 324-1230
New Castle *(G-5244)*
Destiny Rescue Intl Inc .... G 574 529-2238
Lewes *(G-3463)*
Dialog News Paper Inc .... G 302 573-3109
Wilmington *(G-10138)*
Dj First Class .... F 302 345-0602
New Castle *(G-5256)*
Du Pont Delaware Inc .... G 302 774-1000
Wilmington *(G-10242)*
Dynamic Packet Corp .... F 302 448-2222
Newark *(G-6484)*
Elevationtv .... G 978 317-9285
Wilmington *(G-10373)*
Envision It Publications LLC .... G 800 329-9411
Bear *(G-144)*
Evergreen Resources Group LLC ... G 302 477-0189
Wilmington *(G-10449)*
Fort Delaware Society .... G 302 834-1630
Delaware City *(G-959)*
Government Information Center ... G 302 857-3020
Dover *(G-1604)*
Ibg Enterprise Inc .... G 302 494-5017
New Castle *(G-5408)*
Info Solutions North Amer LLC .... F 302 793-9200
New Castle *(G-5418)*
J & J Services .... G 302 422-2684
Milford *(G-4452)*
Joshua A Beck .... G 302 529-9426
Wilmington *(G-11196)*
Landmark Engineering Inc .... D 302 323-9377
Newark *(G-6915)*
M & D Poultry Service .... G 302 934-7050
Millsboro *(G-4729)*
Michael Pdmnczky Cnsrvator LLC ... G 302 388-0656
Wilmington *(G-11664)*
Mid Sussex Rescue Squad Inc .... E 302 945-2680
Millsboro *(G-4744)*
Moran Envmtl Recovery LLC .... F 302 322-6008
Newark *(G-7057)*
New Castle Conservation Dst ...... E 302 832-3100
Newark *(G-7099)*
New Perspectives Inc .... G 302 489-0220
Wilmington *(G-11869)*
Performance Cons Group Inc ...... E 302 738-7532
Newark *(G-7202)*
Prestege LLC .... G 302 312-8548
Newark *(G-7247)*
PSI-TEC Corporation .... G 425 943-9493
Wilmington *(G-12259)*
Psychotherapeutic Svcs Assoc .... E 302 672-7159
Dover *(G-1997)*
Qbr Telecom Inc .... F 302 510-1155
Wilmington *(G-12274)*
Rama LLC .... G 202 596-9547
Wilmington *(G-12312)*
Ribodynamics LLC .... G 518 339-6605
Wilmington *(G-12405)*
Stride Services Inc .... F 302 540-4713
Wilmington *(G-12776)*
Sussex Conservation District .... E 302 856-2105
Georgetown *(G-2676)*
Technical Writers Inc .... E 302 477-1972
Wilmington *(G-12869)*
Wdbid DBA Downtown Visions .... E 302 425-5374
Wilmington *(G-13128)*
Whole Child App Inc .... F 302 570-2002
Lewes *(G-3821)*

ALPHABETIC SECTION

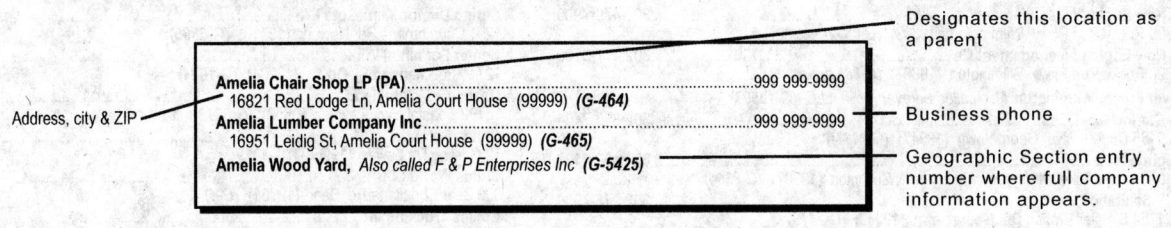

- Designates this location as a parent
- Address, city & ZIP
- Business phone
- Geographic Section entry number where full company information appears.

See footnotes for symbols and codes identification.
* Companies listed alphabetically.
* Complete physical or mailing address.

1 A Lifesafer Inc 800 634-3077
   101 Clark St Harrington (19952) *(G-2803)*
1 A Lifesafer Inc 800 634-3077
   1300 Rd 535 Seaford (19973) *(G-8132)*
1 A Lifesafer Inc 800 634-3077
   23095 Lwes Georgetown Hwy Georgetown (19947) *(G-2416)*
1 A Lifesafer Inc 800 634-3077
   26905 Lwes Georgetown Hwy Harbeson (19951) *(G-2771)*
1 A Lifesafer Inc 800 634-3077
   27380 William Street Rd Millsboro (19966) *(G-4617)*
1 A Lifesafer Inc 800 634-3077
   280 E Main St Newark (19711) *(G-5850)*
1 A Lifesafer Inc 800 634-3077
   280 N Dupont Hwy Dover (19901) *(G-1062)*
1 A Lifesafer Inc 800 634-3077
   317 S Rehoboth Blvd Milford (19963) *(G-4296)*
1 A Lifesafer Inc 800 634-3077
   32393 Lwes Georgetown Hwy Lewes (19958) *(G-3315)*
1 A Lifesafer Inc 800 634-3077
   333 Naamans Rd Ste 41 Claymont (19703) *(G-683)*
1 Fair Chiropractic & Med Inc 302 528-1068
   811 Windsor St Wilmington (19801) *(G-8840)*
1 Hour Martinizing, Wilmington *Also called McKelvey Hires Dry Cleaning (G-11601)*
1 Smart Home, Dagsboro *Also called Communications & Wiring Co (G-893)*
1 Software Place 302 533-0344
   18 Ethan Allen Ct Newark (19711) *(G-5851)*
1-800 Got Junk, Greenwood *Also called Draw Incorporated (G-2732)*
100 St Clire Drv Oprations LLC 610 444-6350
   100 Saint Claire Dr Hockessin (19707) *(G-2945)*
100 St Clire Drv Oprations LLC 302 234-5420
   100 Saint Claire Dr Hockessin (19707) *(G-2946)*
1000 Degrees Pizzeria 609 382-3022
   4500 New Linden Rd Wilmington (19808) *(G-8841)*
1080 Slver Lk Blvd Oprtons LLC 610 444-6350
   1080 Silver Lake Blvd Dover (19904) *(G-1063)*
1102 West Street Ltd Partnr 302 429-7600
   1102 N West St Wilmington (19801) *(G-8842)*
1110 On Parkway Nedi Spa 302 576-1110
   1110 N Bancroft Pkwy # 2 Wilmington (19805) *(G-8843)*
1122 Condominium (PA) 302 234-4860
   610 W 11th St New Castle (19720) *(G-4988)*
1203 Walker Rd Operations LLC 302 735-8800
   1203 Walker Rd Dover (19904) *(G-1064)*
1203 Walker Rd Operations LLC 610 444-6350
   1203 Walker Rd Dover (19904) *(G-1065)*
1212 Corporation 302 764-4048
   2700 N Washington St Wilmington (19802) *(G-8844)*
1300 Publishing Company LLC 302 268-2684
   1306 W 6th St Wilmington (19805) *(G-8845)*
1313 Innovation 302 407-0420
   1313 N Market St 1150nw Wilmington (19801) *(G-8846)*
1401 Condominium Association 302 656-8171
   1401 Pennsylvania Ave # 108 Wilmington (19806) *(G-8847)*
1401 Hair Designs Ltd 302 655-1401
   1401 Penns Ave Ste 102 Wilmington (19806) *(G-8848)*
166th Medical Squadron 302 323-3385
   2600 Spruance Dr New Castle (19720) *(G-4989)*
190 Stadium LLC 302 659-3635
   190 Stadium St Smyrna (19977) *(G-8558)*
1995 Property Management Inc 302 745-1187
   25309 Church Rd Seaford (19973) *(G-8133)*
1st Capitol Mortgage Inc 302 674-5540
   9 E Loockerman St Ste 207 Dover (19901) *(G-1066)*
1st Class Glass LLC 302 229-9203
   108 A St Wilmington (19801) *(G-8849)*
1st Impression Inc 302 738-4918
   933 Branch Rd Newark (19711) *(G-5852)*
1st State Accessibility LLC 844 663-4396
   105 Brookside Dr Wilmington (19804) *(G-8850)*

1st State Home Services 302 339-5573
   25935 Starboard Dr Millsboro (19966) *(G-4618)*
1st State PC Training 302 697-0347
   500 E Cherry Dr Magnolia (19962) *(G-3876)*
1st State Power Clean LLC 302 735-7974
   1609 Forrest Ave Dover (19904) *(G-1067)*
2 Days Bath LLC 302 798-0103
   6603 Governor Printz Blvd Wilmington (19809) *(G-8851)*
20 20 Fincl Advisors of Del 302 777-2020
   100 S Dupont Rd Wilmington (19804) *(G-8852)*
20dollar Club Association 978 908-6047
   2716 Jacqueline Dr K23 Wilmington (19810) *(G-8853)*
21st Century Insurance Company 302 252-2000
   3 Beaver Valley Rd # 100 Wilmington (19803) *(G-8854)*
21st Century N Amer Insur Co (HQ) 877 310-5687
   3 Beaver Valley Rd Wilmington (19803) *(G-8855)*
2300 PA Ave Condo Assoc, Wilmington *Also called Paul Sica MD (G-12044)*
24 Hr Truck Services LLC 609 516-7307
   1 Innovation Way Ste 400 Newark (19711) *(G-5853)*
2ndquadrant Inc 650 378-1218
   1000 N West St Ste 1200 Wilmington (19801) *(G-8856)*
2nu Photonics LLC 302 388-2261
   113 E Main St Unit 404 Newark (19711) *(G-5854)*
3-D Fabrications Inc 302 292-3501
   100 Gabor Dr Newark (19711) *(G-5855)*
302 Aquatics LLC 302 222-4807
   79 Aintree Ln Dover (19904) *(G-1068)*
302 Properties LLC 302 753-8383
   250 Corporate Blvd Ste L Newark (19702) *(G-5856)*
302 Sports 302 650-8479
   116 Winston Ave Wilmington (19804) *(G-8857)*
313design Lab Inc 929 399-6426
   16192 Coastal Hwy Lewes (19958) *(G-3316)*
321 Down Street Press Inc 302 376-3965
   62 Chancellorsville Cir Middletown (19709) *(G-3924)*
326 Associates LP 302 328-4101
   110 N Dupont Hwy New Castle (19720) *(G-4990)*
34m LLC 302 444-8290
   40 E Main St 1196 Newark (19711) *(G-5857)*
36 Builders Inc 302 349-9480
   16255 Sussex Hwy Bridgeville (19933) *(G-441)*
360tovisit Inc 302 526-0575
   2035 Sunset Lake Rd Newark (19702) *(G-5858)*
3d Internet Group Inc 302 376-7900
   609 Colchester Ct Middletown (19709) *(G-3925)*
3d Microwave LLC 302 497-0223
   7795 Bethel Rd Laurel (19956) *(G-3188)*
3d Tech LLC 610 268-2350
   7454 Lancaster Pike 308 Hockessin (19707) *(G-2947)*
3M Company 302 286-2480
   650 Dawson Dr Newark (19713) *(G-5859)*
3rd State Welding Supply LLC 302 777-1088
   32 Germay Dr Ste C Wilmington (19804) *(G-8858)*
3rdgp LLC 905 330-3335
   8 The Grn Ste A Dover (19901) *(G-1069)*
3sigma Labs Inc 925 236-2618
   300 Delaware Ave Ste 210 Wilmington (19801) *(G-8859)*
3ti Coatings LLC 302 379-1265
   780 Brookwood Ln Hockessin (19707) *(G-2948)*
4 Corners LLC 302 723-2264
   511 W 37th St Wilmington (19802) *(G-8860)*
4 Seasons Nails & Spa 302 663-9474
   28662 Dupont Blvd Millsboro (19966) *(G-4619)*
4-N Car, Georgetown *Also called 4n Car Inc (G-2417)*
422 Hotel LLC 401 946-4600
   422 Delaware Ave Wilmington (19801) *(G-8861)*
431 Corporation 352 385-1427
   4185 Krkwood St Georges Bear (19701) *(G-1)*
436th Medical Group, Dover *Also called US Dept of the Air Force (G-2183)*

(PA)=Parent Co (HQ)=Headquarters (DH)=Div Headquarters   2020 Harris Directory of Delaware Businesses

44 Aasha Hospitality Assoc LLC 302 674-3784
1706 N Dupont Hwy Dover (19901) ***(G-1070)***
44 New England Management Co 302 479-7900
300 Rocky Run Pkwy Wilmington (19803) ***(G-8862)***
44 New England Management Co 302 477-9500
320 Rocky Run Pkwy Wilmington (19803) ***(G-8863)***
4ever Fresh, Wilmington *Also called Forever Fresh LLC* ***(G-10593)***
4n Car Inc 302 856-7434
20185 Dupont Blvd Georgetown (19947) ***(G-2417)***
4sight Group LLC 800 490-2131
4023 Knnett Pike Wlmngton Wilmington Wilmington (19807) ***(G-8864)***
5 JS Sanitation 302 945-7086
21754 Simpler Branch Rd Georgetown (19947) ***(G-2418)***
5 Roads, Newark *Also called Grofos International LLC* ***(G-6693)***
500 South Dupont Boule 302 422-8700
500 S Dupont Blvd Milford (19963) ***(G-4297)***
51 and Prospect 443 944-1934
227 S Dillwyn Rd Newark (19711) ***(G-5860)***
6 Star Fundraising LLC 302 250-5085
16 Revelstone Ct Newark (19711) ***(G-5861)***
700 Marvel Road Operations LLC 302 422-3303
700 Marvel Rd Milford (19963) ***(G-4298)***
700 Nrth King St Wlmington LLC 302 655-0400
700 N King St Wilmington (19801) ***(G-8865)***
715 East King St Oprations LLC 302 628-3000
715 E King St Seaford (19973) ***(G-8134)***
764 Dover Leipsic LLC 302 736-1204
1654 N Dupont Hwy Dover (19901) ***(G-1071)***
7c Infotech Inc (PA) 717 288-8686
108 W 13th St Wilmington (19801) ***(G-8866)***
7day Farmers Market LLC 302 476-8924
3901 Lancaster Pike Wilmington (19805) ***(G-8867)***
7p Networks LLC 938 777-7662
16192 Coastal Hwy Lewes (19958) ***(G-3317)***
810 Suth Broom St Oprtions LLC 302 655-1375
810 S Broom St Wilmington (19805) ***(G-8868)***
887 The Bridge 302 422-6909
1977 Bay Rd Milford (19963) ***(G-4299)***
8th Baptist Church, Wilmington *Also called Resurrection Center* ***(G-12391)***
900 F Street Owner LLC 212 355-1500
251 Little Falls Dr Wilmington (19808) ***(G-8869)***
911 Emergency, Dover *Also called County of Kent* ***(G-1317)***
9193 4323 Quebec Inc 855 824-0795
2915 Ogletown Rd # 2385 Newark (19713) ***(G-5862)***
924 Inc 302 656-6100
4550 Linden Hill Rd # 100 Wilmington (19808) ***(G-8870)***
A & A Air Services Inc (PA) 302 436-4800
35130 Bennett Rd Frankford (19945) ***(G-2342)***
A & A Electrical Inc 302 436-4800
35130 Bennett Rd Frankford (19945) ***(G-2343)***
A & A Mechanical Service Inc 302 234-9949
517 Erickson Ave Hockessin (19707) ***(G-2949)***
A & B Electric 302 349-4050
25 Adamsville Rd Greenwood (19950) ***(G-2710)***
A & D Enterprises, Ocean View *Also called Clover Farms Meats* ***(G-7778)***
A & G Kramedas Associates LLC 302 674-3300
222 S Dupont Hwy Dover (19901) ***(G-1072)***
A & G Lawn Care LLC 302 584-8719
13 Hackney Dr Bear (19701) ***(G-2)***
A & G Realty LLC 302 674-3300
222 S Dupont Hwy Dover (19901) ***(G-1073)***
A & H Metals Inc 302 366-7540
249 E Chestnut Hill Rd Newark (19713) ***(G-5863)***
A & H Plumbing & Heating Inc 302 223-8027
811 Clayton Delaney Rd Clayton (19938) ***(G-830)***
A & J Custom Woodworking, Middletown *Also called Peirce James Townsend III* ***(G-4187)***
A & R Fence Co Inc 302 366-8550
1126 Ralph Rd Newark (19713) ***(G-5864)***
A + Floor Store Inc 302 698-2166
166 Roundabout Trl Camden Wyoming (19934) ***(G-609)***
A and D Plumbing LLC 302 387-9232
128 Glenn Forest Rd Magnolia (19962) ***(G-3877)***
A and H Nursing Administra 302 544-4474
94 Dasher Ave Bear (19701) ***(G-3)***
A B C Lending Corp 302 655-5313
1944 Maryland Ave Wilmington (19805) ***(G-8871)***
A B C Ticket Co, Wilmington *Also called Michael Schwartz* ***(G-11666)***
A B Fab & Machining LLC 302 293-4945
170 Earland Dr New Castle (19720) ***(G-4991)***
A Bail Bond By Resto & Co Inc 302 312-7714
7 Corkwood Ln New Castle (19720) ***(G-4992)***
A Better Chnce For Our Chldren 302 725-5008
805 S Dupont Blvd Milford (19963) ***(G-4300)***
A C Electric Company 302 764-7429
3406 Broom Pl Wilmington (19802) ***(G-8872)***
A C Emsley & Associates 302 429-9191
12 S Union St Wilmington (19805) ***(G-8873)***
A C Schultes of Delaware Inc (HQ) 302 337-0700
16289 Sussex Hwy Bridgeville (19933) ***(G-442)***
A Caring Doctor Minnesota PA 302 478-3910
3010 Brandywine Pkwy Wilmington (19803) ***(G-8874)***
A Caring Doctor Minnesota PA 302 266-0122
1291 Churchmans Rd Newark (19713) ***(G-5865)***
A Center For Mntal Wllness Inc 302 674-1397
121 W Loockerman St Dover (19904) ***(G-1074)***
A Chance To Write It LLC 202 256-4524
16192 Coastal Hwy Lewes (19958) ***(G-3318)***
A Childs Potential 302 249-6929
12 Gosling Dr Lewes (19958) ***(G-3319)***
A Childs World LLC 302 322-9386
300 Bear Christiana Rd Bear (19701) ***(G-4)***
A Collins Trucking Inc 302 438-8334
314 Turnberry Ct Bear (19701) ***(G-5)***
A Cut Above, Wilmington *Also called Hair Designs By Regina* ***(G-10819)***
A D Alpine DMD 302 239-4600
4901 Limestone Rd Wilmington (19808) ***(G-8875)***
A Dance Class 302 422-2633
107 S Maple Ave Milford (19963) ***(G-4301)***
A Door of Hope Inc (PA) 302 998-9000
3407 Lancaster Pike Ste B Wilmington (19805) ***(G-8876)***
A Douglas Melson 302 732-6606
40 Thatcher St Frankford (19945) ***(G-2344)***
A Duie Pyle Inc 302 326-9440
204 Quigley Blvd New Castle (19720) ***(G-4993)***
A E Moore Incorporated 302 934-7055
25872 W State St Millsboro (19966) ***(G-4620)***
A F R, New Castle *Also called American Furniture Rentals Inc* ***(G-5032)***
A Felix Dupont Jr Co 302 658-5244
3120 Kennett Pike Wilmington (19807) ***(G-8877)***
A Fields Unlimited LLC 800 484-2331
200 Continental Dr Newark (19713) ***(G-5866)***
A Fresh Start Clg Svcs Corp 302 257-1099
3 Linette Ct Newark (19702) ***(G-5867)***
A G Concrete Works LLC 302 841-2227
31883 New St Dagsboro (19939) ***(G-876)***
A Gentlemans Touch Inc 302 655-7015
1321 Lancaster Ave Ste A Wilmington (19805) ***(G-8878)***
A I Dupont Hosp For Children, Wilmington *Also called Alfred Idpont Hosp For Chldren* ***(G-9008)***
A I Dupont Hospital For Child 302 651-4186
24 Hurst Rd Wilmington (19803) ***(G-8879)***
A I O, Georgetown *Also called Atlantic Industrial Optics* ***(G-2438)***
A I T, Wilmington *Also called Amer Industrial Tech Inc* ***(G-9040)***
A J Dauphin & Son Inc 302 994-1454
3313 Elizabeth Ave Wilmington (19808) ***(G-8880)***
A L N Construction Inc 302 292-1580
104 Sandy Dr Newark (19713) ***(G-5868)***
A Leap Faith Child Dev Ctr, Wilmington *Also called A Leap of Faith Inc* ***(G-8881)***
A Leap of Faith Inc 302 543-6256
1715 W 4th St Wilmington (19805) ***(G-8881)***
A Little Veterinary Clinic PA 302 398-3367
6902 Mlford Hrrington Hwy Harrington (19952) ***(G-2804)***
A M T General Contracting, Dover *Also called Troutman Machine Company Inc* ***(G-2164)***
A Nod To Stella Embroidery 302 697-6308
120 Pine St Wyoming (19934) ***(G-13358)***
A P Croll & Son Inc 302 856-6177
22997 Lwes Georgetown Hwy Georgetown (19947) ***(G-2419)***
A P Linen Service, Milford *Also called AP Linens Inc* ***(G-4308)***
A Place To Grow Fmly Chld Care 302 897-8944
3067 W Court Ave Claymont (19703) ***(G-684)***
A Plus Electric & Security 302 455-1725
94 Stardust Dr Newark (19702) ***(G-5869)***
A Plus Floor Store, Camden Wyoming *Also called A + Floor Store Inc* ***(G-609)***
A R Myers Auto Body, Wilmington *Also called A R Myers Corporation* ***(G-8882)***
A R Myers Corporation 302 652-3164
1300 E 18th St Wilmington (19801) ***(G-8882)***
A R Nails 302 858-4592
401 College Park Ln Georgetown (19947) ***(G-2420)***
A S A P Insulation Inc 302 836-9040
3019 Mcdaniel Ln Newark (19702) ***(G-5870)***
A S C, Wilmington *Also called American Soc Cytopathology Inc* ***(G-9056)***
A S I, Milton *Also called Atlantic Screen & Mfg Inc* ***(G-4865)***
A S I Controls 302 629-7730
221 High St Seaford (19973) ***(G-8135)***
A Seed Hope Counseling Ctr LLC 302 605-6702
1601 Milltown Rd Ste 1 Wilmington (19808) ***(G-8883)***
A Stitch In Time 302 395-1306
101 Harrison Ave New Castle (19720) ***(G-4994)***
A T I Funding Corporation (HQ) 302 656-8937
801 N West St Fl 2 Wilmington (19801) ***(G-8884)***
A To Z Landscaping Services 302 994-1552
11 Lewis Cir Wilmington (19804) ***(G-8885)***
A Toll Building Systems, Newark *Also called Case Construction Inc* ***(G-6164)***
A V C Inc 302 227-2549
20807 Coastal Hwy Ste 4 Rehoboth Beach (19971) ***(G-7835)***
A V Resources Inc 302 994-1488
240 N James St Ste B2 Wilmington (19804) ***(G-8886)***

ALPHABETIC SECTION Accelcomm, Wilmington

A Womans Touch Moving & Pkg 302 265-4729
109 Shady Ridge Dr Rehoboth Beach (19971) ***(G-7836)***
A&F Group LLC 302 504-9937
750 Shipyard Dr Ste 300 Wilmington (19801) ***(G-8887)***
A&V Landscaping 302 684-8609
704 Chestnut St Milton (19968) ***(G-4859)***
A+ Printing 302 273-3147
501 Birmingham Ave Wilmington (19804) ***(G-8888)***
A-1 Air Cndtning Htg Refrigera, Newport *Also called A-1 Air Conditioning Heating* ***(G-7744)***
A-1 Air Conditioning Heating 302 998-5634
3 Gregg Ave Newport (19804) ***(G-7744)***
A-1 Sanitation Service Inc 302 322-1074
1009 River Rd New Castle (19720) ***(G-4995)***
A-Del Construction Company Inc 302 453-8286
10 Adel Dr Newark (19702) ***(G-5871)***
A-Stover Management Group LLC 866 299-0709
238 Turnberry Ct Ste A Bear (19701) ***(G-6)***
A1 Nationwide LLC 302 327-9302
1201 N Orange St Ste 7037 Wilmington (19801) ***(G-8889)***
A1 Sanitation Service Inc 302 653-9591
27 E Chestnut St Smyrna (19977) ***(G-8559)***
A1 Striping Inc 302 738-5016
902 Irish Bank Rd Newark (19702) ***(G-5872)***
A2a Intgrted Phrmceuticals LLC 270 202-2461
16192 Coastal Hwy Lewes (19958) ***(G-3320)***
A2b Auto Group 302 786-2331
1211 E 15th St Wilmington (19802) ***(G-8890)***
A2ps Consulting and Sftwr LLC 331 201-6101
2711 Centerville Rd # 120 Wilmington (19808) ***(G-8891)***
A66 Inc 800 444-0446
2711 Centerville Rd # 400 Wilmington (19808) ***(G-8892)***
AA Smith & Associates LLC 973 477-3052
364 E Main St Ste 403 Middletown (19709) ***(G-3926)***
AAA Club Alliance Inc (PA) 302 299-4700
1 River Pl Wilmington (19801) ***(G-8893)***
AAA Club Alliance Inc 302 368-8175
200 Commerce Dr Newark (19713) ***(G-5873)***
AAA Club Alliance Inc 302 283-4300
200 Continental Dr # 402 Newark (19713) ***(G-5874)***
AAA Club Alliance Inc 302 674-8020
124 Greentree Dr Dover (19904) ***(G-1075)***
AAA Dover, Dover *Also called AAA Club Alliance Inc* ***(G-1075)***
AAA Keystone, Wilmington *Also called AAA Club Alliance Inc* ***(G-8893)***
AAA Portable Restroom Co Inc 909 981-0090
108 Gardengate Rd Camden Wyoming (19934) ***(G-610)***
Aafton Research & Media Inc 617 407-6619
73 Greentree Dr 47 Dover (19904) ***(G-1076)***
Aag La LLC 305 801-7900
160 Greentree Dr Ste 101 Dover (19904) ***(G-1077)***
AAL Drtc 302 229-5891
200 Gbc Dr Newark (19702) ***(G-5875)***
AAMCO Transmissions, Seaford *Also called Challenge Automotive Svcs Inc* ***(G-8186)***
AAMCO Transmissions, Dover *Also called Js Automotive AAMCO* ***(G-1711)***
AAMCO Transmissions, Claymont *Also called K & J Automotive Inc* ***(G-771)***
AAMCO Transmissions, Bear *Also called Lst Insvestment LLC* ***(G-239)***
AAMCO Transmissions 302 322-3454
819 Pulaski Hwy Bear (19701) ***(G-7)***
Aardvark Party Rentals LLC 302 331-1929
37 Deer Cir Bear (19701) ***(G-8)***
Aark Network Inc 302 399-3945
1142 Elkton Rd Newark (19711) ***(G-5876)***
Aaron B Poleck D M D LLC 302 623-4190
4735 Ogletown Stanton Rd # 1101 Newark (19713) ***(G-5877)***
Aaron B Poleck DDS 302 533-7649
50 Omega Dr Newark (19713) ***(G-5878)***
Aaron S Chidekel M D 302 651-6400
1600 Rockland Rd Wilmington (19803) ***(G-8894)***
Aaron's F244, Seaford *Also called Aarons Sales & Leasing* ***(G-8136)***
Aaron's Rental Purchase, Newark *Also called J R Rents Inc* ***(G-6820)***
Aarons Inc 302 221-1200
511 E Basin Rd New Castle (19720) ***(G-4996)***
Aarons Sales & Leasing 302 628-8870
850 Norman Eskridge Hwy Seaford (19973) ***(G-8136)***
AARP 202 434-2277
222 Delaware Ave Ste 1610 Wilmington (19801) ***(G-8895)***
AARP Delaware, Wilmington *Also called AARP* ***(G-8895)***
AB Creative Publishing LLC 202 802-6909
1104 Philadelphia Pike Wilmington (19809) ***(G-8896)***
AB Group Packaging Inc 302 607-3281
1800 Ogletown Rd Newark (19711) ***(G-5879)***
AB&c, Wilmington *Also called Aloysius Butlr Clark Assoc Inc* ***(G-9029)***
Aba PA, Lewes *Also called P A Aba Intl Inc* ***(G-3675)***
Aba Travl & Ent Inc 305 374-0838
16192 Coastal Hwy Lewes (19958) ***(G-3321)***
Abad & Salameda PA 302 652-4705
1508 Penns Ave Ste 1c Wilmington (19806) ***(G-8897)***
Abba Monument Co Inc 302 738-0272
94 Albe Dr Ste 1 Newark (19702) ***(G-5880)***
Abbey Lein Inc 302 239-2712
28 Meteor Ct Newark (19711) ***(G-5881)***
Abbey Walk Apts, Newark *Also called Mid-Atlantic Realty Co Inc* ***(G-7031)***
Abby Family Practice, Newark *Also called Family Practice Cntr of New CA* ***(G-6569)***
Abby L Allen Fnp 302 856-1773
20797 Professional Prk Bl Georgetown (19947) ***(G-2421)***
Abby Medical Center 302 999-0003
1 Centurian Dr Ste 301 Newark (19713) ***(G-5882)***
Abbycare, Newark *Also called Abigail Family Medicine LLC* ***(G-5884)***
Abc Inc 302 429-0189
500 W 2nd St Wilmington (19801) ***(G-8898)***
ABC Payday & Title Lending 302 322-0233
624 E Basin Rd New Castle (19720) ***(G-4997)***
ABC Sales & Service Inc 302 652-3683
2520 W 6th St Wilmington (19805) ***(G-8899)***
ABC Supply 31, Wilmington *Also called American Bldrs Contrs Sup Inc* ***(G-9042)***
ABC Systems Inc 302 528-8875
92 White Clay Cres Newark (19711) ***(G-5883)***
Abcware LLC 888 755-1485
2207 Concord Pike 816 Wilmington (19803) ***(G-8900)***
Abel Center For Oculofacial 302 998-3220
1941 Limestone Rd Ste 201 Wilmington (19808) ***(G-8901)***
ABG Designs, Middletown *Also called Ten Talents Enterprises Inc* ***(G-4255)***
Abha Architects Inc 302 658-6426
1621 N Lincoln St Wilmington (19806) ***(G-8902)***
Abigail E Martin M D 302 651-4000
1600 Rockland Rd Wilmington (19803) ***(G-8903)***
Abigail Family Medicine LLC 302 738-3770
412 Suburban Dr Newark (19711) ***(G-5884)***
Able Recycling Inc 302 324-1760
3711 Valley Brook Dr Wilmington (19808) ***(G-8904)***
Able Welding & Machine, Selbyville *Also called Able Whelling and Machiene* ***(G-8446)***
Able Whelling and Machiene 302 436-1929
45 Railroad Ave Selbyville (19975) ***(G-8446)***
ABM Industries Incorporated 302 999-1898
2110 Duncan Rd Wilmington (19808) ***(G-8905)***
ABM Janitorial Services Inc 302 571-9900
2110 Duncan Rd Wilmington (19808) ***(G-8906)***
Above All Gtter Gardening Svcs 302 478-0762
44 Fairway Rd Apt 2a Newark (19711) ***(G-5885)***
Above and Beyond Coverage LLC 201 417-5189
3616 Kirkwood Hwy Wilmington (19808) ***(G-8907)***
Above Beyond Unisex Hair Salon 302 276-0187
1111 Wilmington Rd New Castle (19720) ***(G-4998)***
ABRA Auto Body & Glass LP 302 279-1007
5077 Summit Bridge Rd Middletown (19709) ***(G-3927)***
Abrahams Seed LLC 302 588-1913
246 Coldwater Dr Clayton (19938) ***(G-831)***
Abrams & Bayliss LLP 302 778-1000
20 Montchanin Rd Ste 200 Wilmington (19807) ***(G-8908)***
Abridge Partners LLC (PA) 302 378-1882
6 Crawford St Middletown (19709) ***(G-3928)***
ABS, Wilmington *Also called Analytical Biological Svcs Inc* ***(G-9073)***
ABS Engineering LLC 302 595-9081
417 Jaymar Blvd Newark (19702) ***(G-5886)***
Absalom Jones Senior Center 302 998-0363
310 Kiamensi Rd Ste B Wilmington (19804) ***(G-8909)***
Absolute Computer Support LLC 717 917-8900
249 E Main St Ste 1 Newark (19711) ***(G-5887)***
Absolute Cyber Defense 850 532-0233
8 The Grn Ste A Dover (19901) ***(G-1078)***
Absolute Equity 302 983-2591
501 Clinton St Delaware City (19706) ***(G-945)***
Absolutely Green Inc 302 731-1616
995 S Chapel St Ste 3 Newark (19713) ***(G-5888)***
AC Electric, Wilmington *Also called A C Electric Company* ***(G-8872)***
AC Engineering 215 873-6482
135 Emerald Ridge Dr Bear (19701) ***(G-9)***
AC Group Inc 201 840-5566
3422 Old Capitol Trl # 163 Wilmington (19808) ***(G-8910)***
Aca Mortgage Co Inc 302 225-1390
3202 Kirkwood Hwy Ste 205 Wilmington (19808) ***(G-8911)***
Academy Bind Body Arts, Newark *Also called American Karate Studios* ***(G-5954)***
Academy Business Mch & Prtg Co 302 654-3200
12 S Maryland Ave Wilmington (19804) ***(G-8912)***
Academy Express 302 537-4805
52 Atlantic Ave Ocean View (19970) ***(G-7753)***
Academy Massage & Bdy Work Ltd 302 392-6768
1218 Pulaski Hwy Ste 324 Bear (19701) ***(G-10)***
Academy of Early Learning 302 659-0750
310 N Main St Bldg A Smyrna (19977) ***(G-8560)***
Academy Printing, Wilmington *Also called Academy Business Mch & Prtg Co* ***(G-8912)***
Acadia Realty Trust 302 479-5510
3001 Brandywine Pkwy Wilmington (19803) ***(G-8913)***
Acanthus & Reed Ltd 212 628-9290
106 E 3rd St New Castle (19720) ***(G-4999)***
Acanthus and Reed, New Castle *Also called Acanthus & Reed Ltd* ***(G-4999)***
Accelcomm, Wilmington *Also called AC Group Inc* ***(G-8910)***

ALPHABETIC

Accelertrain Company Limited........413 599-0450
8 The Grn Ste A Dover (19901) ***(G-1079)***
Accent Coatings, Newark *Also called Raymond Harner* ***(G-7301)***
Accent On Travel, Rehoboth Beach *Also called Ans Corporation* ***(G-7844)***
Access Dental LLC........302 674-3303
446a S New St Dover (19904) ***(G-1080)***
Access Labor Service Inc (PA)........302 326-2575
2203 N Dupont Hwy New Castle (19720) ***(G-5000)***
Access Labor Service Inc........302 741-2575
1102 S State St Ste 1 Dover (19901) ***(G-1081)***
Access Quality Healthcare........302 947-4437
32026 Long Neck Rd Millsboro (19966) ***(G-4621)***
Access Versalign Inc (PA)........302 225-7800
701 Cornell Dr Ste 13 Wilmington (19801) ***(G-8914)***
Access4u Inc........800 355-7025
510 Railroad Ave Lewes (19958) ***(G-3322)***
Accessible Home Builders Inc........302 628-9571
28412 Dupont Blvd Ste 103 Millsboro (19966) ***(G-4622)***
Accessquint LLC........302 351-4064
300 Delaware Ave Ste 200 Wilmington (19801) ***(G-8915)***
Acclaim Academy LLC........215 848-7827
1521 Concord Pike Ste 301 Wilmington (19803) ***(G-8916)***
Accountemps, Wilmington *Also called Robert Half International Inc* ***(G-12439)***
Accounting & Bookkeeping Svc........302 376-7857
18 Manassas Dr Middletown (19709) ***(G-3929)***
Accounting Dept, Newark *Also called University of Delaware* ***(G-7623)***
Accu Personnel Inc........302 384-8777
1707 Concord Pike Wilmington (19803) ***(G-8917)***
Accudyne Systems Inc (PA)........302 369-5390
210 Executive Dr Ste 5 Newark (19702) ***(G-5889)***
Accugenix, Newark *Also called Charles River Labs Intl Inc* ***(G-6190)***
Accugenix Inc........302 292-8888
223 Lake Dr Newark (19702) ***(G-5890)***
Accurate Machine Inc........302 992-9606
304 Falco Dr Wilmington (19804) ***(G-8918)***
Accurate Pest Control Company........302 875-2725
30139 Sussex Hwy Laurel (19956) ***(G-3189)***
Accurate Power, Wilmington *Also called Accurate Machine Inc* ***(G-8918)***
Accurate Termite & Pest Ctrl, Laurel *Also called Accurate Pest Control Company* ***(G-3189)***
Accurate-Energy LLC........302 947-9560
35180 South Dr Lewes (19958) ***(G-3323)***
Accutax........302 735-9747
408 Martin St Dover (19901) ***(G-1082)***
Ace American Insurance Company........302 476-6000
1 Beaver Valley Rd Wilmington (19803) ***(G-8919)***
Ace Cash Express Inc........302 737-3785
14 Marrows Rd Ste B Newark (19713) ***(G-5891)***
Ace Cash Express Inc........302 628-0422
22978 Sussex Hwy Seaford (19973) ***(G-8137)***
Ace Global Solution, Wilmington *Also called Chubb US Holding Inc* ***(G-9696)***
Ace Monitoring, Claymont *Also called Security Inc* ***(G-802)***
Ace Rent-A-Car Inc........302 368-5950
915 S Chapel St Newark (19713) ***(G-5892)***
Acentium Inc........617 938-3938
251 Little Falls Dr Wilmington (19808) ***(G-8920)***
Achieve Logistic Systems........302 654-4701
510 A St Wilmington (19801) ***(G-8921)***
Achieve Solutions........302 598-1457
1 Foxview Cir Hockessin (19707) ***(G-2950)***
Aci Energy Inc........302 588-3024
1105 N Market St Ste 650 Wilmington (19801) ***(G-8922)***
Acm Corp........302 736-3864
218 Canal St Dover (19904) ***(G-1083)***
Acolyst, Selbyville *Also called Datatech Enterprises Inc* ***(G-8478)***
Acopia LLC........302 286-5172
220 Continental Dr # 203 Newark (19713) ***(G-5893)***
Acorn Books Inc........302 508-2219
727 Lexington Ave Smyrna (19977) ***(G-8561)***
Acorn Energy Inc (PA)........302 656-1708
1000 N West St Ste 1200 Wilmington (19801) ***(G-8923)***
Acorn Site Furnishings........302 249-4979
5218 Federalsburg Rd Bridgeville (19933) ***(G-443)***
Acoustic Audio Tek LLC........302 685-2113
1000 N West St Ste 1200 Wilmington (19801) ***(G-8924)***
Acre Mortgage & Financial........302 737-5853
56 W Main St Ste 107 Christiana (19702) ***(G-664)***
Act One, Wilmington *Also called Agile 1* ***(G-8977)***
Act Program, Dover *Also called Delaware Guidance Ser* ***(G-1373)***
Action Automotive Inc........302 429-0643
2200 Rodman Rd Wilmington (19805) ***(G-8925)***
Action Enterprise Inc........302 537-7223
27 W Bayard St Fenwick Island (19944) ***(G-2328)***
Action Environmental Service........302 798-3100
501 Silverside Rd Ste 114 Wilmington (19809) ***(G-8926)***
Action Rental Inc........302 366-0749
8 Mill Park Ct Newark (19713) ***(G-5894)***
Action Security, Bear *Also called M D Electric LLC* ***(G-242)***
Action Security........302 838-2852
100 Peoples Dr Newark (19702) ***(G-5895)***
Action Unlimited Resources Inc........302 323-1455
230 Quigley Blvd New Castle (19720) ***(G-5001)***
Activ Pest & Lawn Inc........302 645-1502
16861 New Rd Lewes (19958) ***(G-3324)***
Active Crane Rentals Inc........302 998-1000
103 Water St Wilmington (19804) ***(G-8927)***
Active Day Inc........302 831-6774
200 Whitechapel Dr Newark (19713) ***(G-5896)***
Active Supply LLC........888 843-0243
465 Carson Dr Bear (19701) ***(G-11)***
Actors Attic........302 734-8214
540 Otis Dr Dover (19901) ***(G-1084)***
Acts Rtrmnt-Life Cmmnities Inc........302 654-5101
4830 Kennett Pike Wilmington (19807) ***(G-8928)***
Acuhealth & Wellness........302 438-4493
134 Tywyn Dr Middletown (19709) ***(G-3930)***
Acuitive Inc........214 738-1099
4001 Kennett Pike Ste 134 Wilmington (19807) ***(G-8929)***
Acuity Brands Lighting Inc........302 476-2055
19 Blevins Dr New Castle (19720) ***(G-5002)***
Acumen Health Technologies LLC........800 941-0356
2207 Concord Pike 224 Wilmington (19803) ***(G-8930)***
Acumen Strategies Inc........302 218-3949
7454 Lancaster Pike # 334 Hockessin (19707) ***(G-2951)***
Acupoint Therapeutics........302 734-7716
165 Chucker Xing Dover (19904) ***(G-1085)***
Acuren Inspection Inc........302 836-0165
6 Verdun Ct Newark (19702) ***(G-5897)***
Acurio LLC........201 932-8160
108 W 13th St Wilmington (19801) ***(G-8931)***
Ad-Art Signs Georgetown Inc........302 856-7446
24383 Mariner Cir Georgetown (19947) ***(G-2422)***
Adam Basement (PA)........302 983-8446
563 Walther Rd Newark (19702) ***(G-5898)***
Adam C Sydell DDS........302 684-1100
524 Union St Milton (19968) ***(G-4860)***
Adam Hobbs & Son Inc........302 697-2090
344 Fitzbrian Dr Felton (19943) ***(G-2269)***
Adamlouis Ltd Liability Co........973 937-7524
427 N Tatnall St Wilmington (19801) ***(G-8932)***
Adams Auto Parts Inc (PA)........302 655-9693
1601 Northeast Blvd Wilmington (19802) ***(G-8933)***
Adams Bakery Corporation........802 863-2696
2711 Centerville Rd # 400 Wilmington (19808) ***(G-8934)***
Adams Kemp Associates Inc........302 856-6699
217 S Race St Georgetown (19947) ***(G-2423)***
Adams Oceanfront Resort........302 227-3030
4 Read Ave Dewey Beach (19971) ***(G-1051)***
Adams Oceanfront Villas, Dewey Beach *Also called Adams Oceanfront Resort* ***(G-1051)***
Adams Oil Co Inc........302 629-4531
Pine St Extd Seaford (19973) ***(G-8138)***
Adandy Farm........302 349-5116
13450 Adandy Farm Ln Greenwood (19950) ***(G-2711)***
Addalli Landscaping........302 836-2002
2546 Red Lion Rd Bear (19701) ***(G-12)***
Additive Mfg Tech Inc........540 577-9260
919 N Market St Ste 950 Wilmington (19801) ***(G-8935)***
Addus Healthcare Inc........302 995-9010
3521 Silverside Rd Wilmington (19810) ***(G-8936)***
Addus Healthcare Inc........302 424-4842
1675 S State St Milford (19963) ***(G-4302)***
Addy Sea........302 539-3707
99 Ocean View Pkwy Bethany Beach (19930) ***(G-382)***
Addy Sea, The, Bethany Beach *Also called Addy Sea* ***(G-382)***
Adecco Staffing, Newark *Also called Adecco Usa Inc* ***(G-5899)***
Adecco Usa Inc........302 669-4005
40 Reads Way New Castle (19720) ***(G-5003)***
Adecco Usa Inc........302 457-4059
1000 Samoset Dr Newark (19713) ***(G-5899)***
Aderyn Woodworks........219 229-5070
11 Villas Dr Apt 9 New Castle (19720) ***(G-5004)***
Adesis Inc........302 323-4880
27 Mccullough Dr New Castle (19720) ***(G-5005)***
Adferns Media LLC........315 444-7720
8 The Grn Dover (19901) ***(G-1086)***
Adh Holdings LLC........302 482-4138
908 E 17th St Wilmington (19802) ***(G-8937)***
Adirondack Bhvral Hlthcare LLC........302 832-1282
1400 Peoples Plz Ste 204 Christiana (19702) ***(G-665)***
Adjuvant Research Services Inc........302 737-5513
1 Innovation Way Ste 400 Newark (19711) ***(G-5900)***
Adkess Transport Services LLC........978 235-3924
14 Winchester Ct Bear (19701) ***(G-13)***
Adkins & Assoc CPA........302 737-2390
2615 E Riding Dr Wilmington (19808) ***(G-8938)***
Adkins & Associates CPA, Wilmington *Also called Adkins & Assoc CPA* ***(G-8938)***
Adkins Management Company........302 684-3000
421 Kings Hwy Milford (19963) ***(G-4303)***

Administrative Office, Dover *Also called Delaware Wic Program* ***(G-1405)***
Admiral Hotel.....302 227-2103
2 Baltimore Ave Rehoboth Beach (19971) ***(G-7837)***
Admiral Motel, Wilmington *Also called Admiral West Inc* ***(G-8939)***
Admiral Tire.....302 734-5911
280 Cowgill St Dover (19901) ***(G-1087)***
Admiral West Inc.....609 729-0031
726 Greenwood Rd Wilmington (19807) ***(G-8939)***
Admirals Club Apartments, Newark *Also called Admirals Club Apts2c* ***(G-5901)***
Admirals Club Apts2c.....302 737-8496
41 Fairway Rd Ofc 2c Newark (19711) ***(G-5901)***
Adoptions From Heart Inc.....302 658-8883
18a Trolley Sq Wilmington (19806) ***(G-8940)***
ADP Capital Management Inc.....302 657-4060
800 Delaware Ave Ste 601 Wilmington (19801) ***(G-8941)***
ADP Pacific Inc.....302 657-4060
800 Delaware Ave Ste 601 Wilmington (19801) ***(G-8942)***
Adpese LLC.....302 223-5411
3616 Kirkwood Hwy Wilmington (19808) ***(G-8943)***
Adriane Hohmann.....302 253-2020
501 College Park Ln Georgetown (19947) ***(G-2424)***
ADS, New Castle *Also called Affordable Delivery Svcs LLC* ***(G-5016)***
ADT LLC.....302 918-1016
130 Executive Dr Ste 2 Newark (19702) ***(G-5902)***
ADT LLC.....302 325-3125
140 Quigley Blvd New Castle (19720) ***(G-5006)***
Adv Fuel Polishing Service.....302 477-1040
950 Ridge Rd Ste A6 Claymont (19703) ***(G-685)***
Advacare LLC.....302 448-5045
3601 Old Capitol Trl A5a6 Wilmington (19808) ***(G-8944)***
Advance America Cash Advance.....302 999-0145
527 E Basin Rd New Castle (19720) ***(G-5007)***
Advance Auto Parts Inc.....302 644-0141
17884 Coastal Hwy Unit 1 Lewes (19958) ***(G-3325)***
Advance Central Services Inc (PA).....302 830-9732
1313 N Market St Fl 10 Wilmington (19801) ***(G-8945)***
Advance Construction Co Del.....302 697-9444
280 Banning Rd Camden Wyoming (19934) ***(G-611)***
Advance Magazine Group, Wilmington *Also called Advance Magazine Publs Inc* ***(G-8946)***
Advance Magazine Publs Inc.....302 830-4630
1201 N Market St Ste 600 Wilmington (19801) ***(G-8946)***
Advance Marine LLC.....302 656-2111
900 Smiths Bridge Rd Wilmington (19807) ***(G-8947)***
Advance Nanotech Inc.....212 583-0080
1000 N West St Fl 10 Wilmington (19801) ***(G-8948)***
Advance Office Instlltions Inc.....302 777-5599
37 Lukens Dr Ste B New Castle (19720) ***(G-5008)***
Advance Paving Services, Wilmington *Also called Stripe-A-Lot Inc* ***(G-12777)***
Advance Wndw/Sprior Siding Inc.....302 324-8890
11 Mcmillan Way Ste A Newark (19713) ***(G-5903)***
Advanced Anesthesiology & Pain.....302 283-3300
5307 Limestone Rd Ste 103 Wilmington (19808) ***(G-8949)***
Advanced Automotive Tech, Wilmington *Also called Htk Automotive USA Corporation* ***(G-10969)***
Advanced Back & Neck Pain Ctr, Newark *Also called Richard C McKay DC PA* ***(G-7337)***
Advanced Behavioral Care Inc.....410 599-7400
19 Cedarwood Dr Lewes (19958) ***(G-3326)***
Advanced Bio-Energy Tech Inc.....347 363-9927
3500 S Dupont Hwy Dover (19901) ***(G-1088)***
Advanced Bizz Innovations LLC.....302 397-1162
405 South St Townsend (19734) ***(G-8753)***
Advanced Care Centers Delaware.....302 472-4878
3910 Concord Pike Wilmington (19803) ***(G-8950)***
Advanced Cnstr Techniques, Wilmington *Also called Advanced Cnstr Techniques Inc* ***(G-8951)***
Advanced Cnstr Techniques Inc (HQ).....302 295-4868
1000 N West St Ste 1200 Wilmington (19801) ***(G-8951)***
Advanced Coatings Engrg LLC.....888 607-0000
2915 Ogletown Rd Newark (19713) ***(G-5904)***
Advanced Endoscopy Center LLC.....302 678-0725
742 S Governors Ave Ste 2 Dover (19904) ***(G-1089)***
Advanced Foot & Ankle Center.....302 355-0056
774 Christiana Rd Ste 105 Newark (19713) ***(G-5905)***
Advanced Internet Solutions.....302 584-4641
14 Ashley Pl Wilmington (19804) ***(G-8952)***
Advanced Machinery Sales Inc.....302 322-2226
2 Mccullough Dr Ste 2 # 2 New Castle (19720) ***(G-5009)***
Advanced Materials Technology.....302 477-2510
3521 Silvr Rd Ste 1k Qui Wilmington (19810) ***(G-8953)***
Advanced Metal Concepts Inc.....302 421-9905
1823 Choptank Rd Middletown (19709) ***(G-3931)***
Advanced Motorsports.....302 629-3301
8734 Concord Rd Seaford (19973) ***(G-8139)***
Advanced Networking Inc.....302 442-6199
1316 Philadelphia Pike Wilmington (19809) ***(G-8954)***
Advanced Office Systems & Sups.....302 629-7505
9683 Tharp Rd Seaford (19973) ***(G-8140)***
Advanced Plastic Surgery Cente.....302 623-4004
4735 Ogletown Stanton Rd Newark (19713) ***(G-5906)***
Advanced Power Control Inc (HQ).....302 368-0443
126 Sandy Dr Newark (19713) ***(G-5907)***
Advanced Power Generation.....302 375-6145
950 Ridge Rd Ste A6 Claymont (19703) ***(G-686)***
Advanced Protection LLC.....302 539-6041
9 Briarcliffe Ct Ocean View (19970) ***(G-7754)***
Advanced Rcvable Solutions Inc.....302 225-6001
1300 First State Blvd Wilmington (19804) ***(G-8955)***
Advanced Security Systems Inc.....302 998-7222
1800 Milltown Rd Wilmington (19808) ***(G-8956)***
Advanced Surgical Specialists.....302 475-4900
1401 Foulk Rd Ste 207 Wilmington (19803) ***(G-8957)***
Advanced Systems Inc.....302 368-1211
202 Cheltenham Rd Newark (19711) ***(G-5908)***
Advanced Thermal Packaging.....302 326-2222
420 Churchmans Rd New Castle (19720) ***(G-5010)***
Advanced Training Acadmey.....302 369-8800
9 Prospect Ave Newark (19711) ***(G-5909)***
Advanced Treatment Systems.....302 792-0700
2999 Philadelphia Pike Claymont (19703) ***(G-687)***
Advancexing Pain & Rehabltatn.....302 384-7439
620 Stanton Christiana Rd # 202 Newark (19713) ***(G-5910)***
Advangelists LLC.....734 546-4989
919 N Market St Ste 425 Wilmington (19801) ***(G-8958)***
Advantage Delaware.....302 365-5398
134 Antlers Ln Bear (19701) ***(G-14)***
Advantage Delaware LLC.....302 479-7764
3524 Silverside Rd Wilmington (19810) ***(G-8959)***
Advantage Security Inc.....302 652-3060
802 First State Blvd Wilmington (19804) ***(G-8960)***
Advantage Travel Inc.....302 674-8747
1218 Pulaski Hwy Ste 336 Bear (19701) ***(G-15)***
Advantdge Hlthcare Sltions Inc.....302 224-5678
307 Ruthar Dr Newark (19711) ***(G-5911)***
Advantech Incorporated.....302 674-8405
151 Garrison Oak Dr Dover (19901) ***(G-1090)***
Adventures Lrning Erly Chood, New Castle *Also called Amemg Inc* ***(G-5029)***
Advertising Healthy Inc.....302 366-7502
210 Sweetgrass Run Newark (19702) ***(G-5912)***
Advice Wallet Inc.....510 280-2475
1811 Silverside Rd Wilmington (19810) ***(G-8961)***
Advo Opco LLC (PA).....302 365-8051
2520 Wrangle Hill Rd # 210 Bear (19701) ***(G-16)***
Advoserv, Bear *Also called Advo Opco LLC* ***(G-16)***
Advoserv Inc.....302 365-8050
2520 Wrangle Hill Rd # 200 Bear (19701) ***(G-17)***
Advoserv Nj Inc (HQ).....302 365-8050
2520 Wrangle Hill Rd # 200 Bear (19701) ***(G-18)***
Advoserv Nj Inc.....302 365-8050
2520 Wrangle Hill Rd # 200 Bear (19701) ***(G-19)***
Aearo Technologies LLC.....302 283-5497
650 Dawson Dr Newark (19713) ***(G-5913)***
Aecom Energy & Cnstr Inc.....302 234-1445
2 York Way Hockessin (19707) ***(G-2952)***
Aecom Global II LLC.....302 933-0200
28485 Dupont Blvd Millsboro (19966) ***(G-4623)***
Aecom Technology Corporation.....302 468-5878
1013 Centre Rd Ste 222 Wilmington (19805) ***(G-8962)***
Aecom Usa Inc.....302 781-5963
1013 Centre Rd Ste 222 Wilmington (19805) ***(G-8963)***
Aeec, Wilmington *Also called American-Eurasian Exch Co LLC* ***(G-9060)***
AEG International LLC.....302 750-6411
30931 Sussex Hwy Laurel (19956) ***(G-3190)***
Aegisnet Inc (PA).....302 325-2122
42 Reads Way New Castle (19720) ***(G-5011)***
Aegle Health.....302 468-0235
27 Chelwynne Rd New Castle (19720) ***(G-5012)***
Aeolus Pharmaceuticals Inc (PA).....949 481-9825
824 N Market St Ste 1000 Wilmington (19801) ***(G-8964)***
Aeres Corporation.....858 926-8626
2035 Sunset Lk Rd Ste B-2 New Castle (19720) ***(G-5013)***
Aero Enterprises Inc.....302 378-1396
1270 Caldwell Corner Rd Townsend (19734) ***(G-8754)***
Aero Marine Laminates, Seaford *Also called Aero-Marine Laminates Inc* ***(G-8141)***
Aero Taxi Inc.....302 328-3430
1315 Chadwick Rd Wilmington (19803) ***(G-8965)***
Aero Ways Inc.....302 324-9970
131 N Dupont Hwy New Castle (19720) ***(G-5014)***
Aero-Marine Laminates Inc.....302 628-3944
22762 Sussex Hwy Seaford (19973) ***(G-8141)***
Aerotek Inc.....302 561-6300
100 W Cmmons Blvd Ste 425 New Castle (19720) ***(G-5015)***
AES Foods, Newark *Also called American Express Shuttle Inc* ***(G-5950)***
AES Foods.....302 420-8377
83 Albe Dr Ste F Newark (19702) ***(G-5914)***
AES Surveyors, Wilmington *Also called Rod-AES Surveyors Co* ***(G-12459)***
Aesops Gables Inc.....302 737-2683
9 Whitfield Rd Newark (19711) ***(G-5915)***
Aesthetic Surgical Associates, Wilmington *Also called Peter R Coggins MD* ***(G-12097)***

ALPHABETIC

(PA)=Parent Co (HQ)=Headquarters (DH)=Div Headquarters
2020 Harris Directory of Delaware Businesses
585

Aesthetis Special Care Assoc, Wilmington *Also called Thomas Jenkins DMD* ***(G-12902)***
Aesthtic Plstic Surgery Del PA...302 656-0214
1600 Penns Ave Ste A Wilmington (19806) ***(G-8966)***
Aesthtic Special Care Assoc PA...302 482-4444
2323 Penns Ave Ste Ll Wilmington (19806) ***(G-8967)***
Aet Films, Newark *Also called Taghleef Industries Inc* ***(G-7532)***
Aetna Banquet Hall, Newark *Also called Aetna Hose Hook & Ladder Co 9* ***(G-5916)***
Aetna Hose Hook & Ladder Co 9...302 454-3305
400 Ogletown Rd Newark (19711) ***(G-5916)***
Aetna Hose Hook and Ladder Co...302 454-3300
31 Academy St Newark (19711) ***(G-5917)***
Aetna Inc...860 808-3458
750 Prides Xing Ste 200 Newark (19713) ***(G-5918)***
Aezi Electrical Services LLC...302 547-5734
131 Azbury Loop Middletown (19709) ***(G-3932)***
Affilate Marks Investments Inc...302 478-7451
3411 Silverside Rd Wilmington (19810) ***(G-8968)***
Affiliate Venture Group...302 379-6961
2419 Kirkwood Hwy Wilmington (19805) ***(G-8969)***
Affinity Homecare Services...302 264-9363
1040 S State St Dover (19901) ***(G-1091)***
Affinity Research Chemicals...302 525-4060
406 Meco Dr Wilmington (19804) ***(G-8970)***
Affinity Wealth Management...302 652-6767
2961 Centerville Rd # 310 Wilmington (19808) ***(G-8971)***
Affinity Womens Health LLC...302 468-4320
121 Becks Woods Dr # 100 Bear (19701) ***(G-20)***
Affordable Delivery Svcs LLC...302 276-0246
217 Lisa Dr Ste D New Castle (19720) ***(G-5016)***
Affordable Heating & AC...302 328-9220
1700 Wilmington Rd New Castle (19720) ***(G-5017)***
Affordable Insur Netwrk Del...302 392-4500
1218 Pulaski Hwy Ste 490 Bear (19701) ***(G-21)***
Affordable Insurance...302 834-9641
1218 Pulaski Hwy Ste 490 Bear (19701) ***(G-22)***
Affordable Recreation LLC...603 635-2101
16192 Coastal Hwy Lewes (19958) ***(G-3327)***
Affordable Sod Inc...302 545-0275
1 S Wynwyd Dr Newark (19711) ***(G-5919)***
Affordable Tax Services LLC...302 399-3867
241 Shai Cir Bear (19701) ***(G-23)***
Afgceaa Corporation...617 314-0814
1521 Concord Pike Ste 303 Wilmington (19803) ***(G-8972)***
African Markets Fund LLC...703 944-1514
8 The Grn Ste A Dover (19901) ***(G-1092)***
African Wood Inc...302 884-6738
1201 N Orange St Ste 902 Wilmington (19801) ***(G-8973)***
Afrikelist Corporation...800 767-1744
1201 N Orange St Ste 700 Wilmington (19801) ***(G-8974)***
Afrwood, Wilmington *Also called African Wood Inc* ***(G-8973)***
Afscme-Council 81, New Castle *Also called American Federation of State* ***(G-5031)***
After Hours Heating & Air...302 945-3310
24436 Hollyville Rd Millsboro (19966) ***(G-4624)***
Afterglo Beauty Spa...302 537-7546
22 Cedar Dr Millville (19967) ***(G-4832)***
Aftermath Services LLC...302 357-3780
160 Greentree Dr Ste 101 Dover (19904) ***(G-1093)***
Afternoon Little, Dover *Also called Little School Inc* ***(G-1792)***
AG & G Sheet Metal Inc...302 653-4111
129 N Union St Smyrna (19977) ***(G-8562)***
AG Concrete Works, Dagsboro *Also called A G Concrete Works LLC* ***(G-876)***
Agera Laboratories...302 888-1500
2 Mill Rd Wilmington (19806) ***(G-8975)***
Agfirst Farm Credit Bank...302 734-7534
1410 S State St Dover (19901) ***(G-1094)***
Agfirst Farm Credit Bank...302 856-9081
20816 Dupont Blvd Georgetown (19947) ***(G-2425)***
Agh Parent LLC...919 298-2267
1209 N Orange St Wilmington (19801) ***(G-8976)***
Agile 1...302 791-6900
1013 Centre Rd Ste 200 Wilmington (19805) ***(G-8977)***
Agilent Technologies Inc...408 345-8886
300 Century Blvd Wilmington (19808) ***(G-8978)***
Agilent Technologies Inc...877 424-4536
2850 Centerville Rd Wilmington (19808) ***(G-8979)***
Agora Net Inc...302 224-2475
314 E Main St Ste 1 Newark (19711) ***(G-5920)***
Agree Arlington TX LLC...302 683-3008
2801 Centerville Rd # 300 Wilmington (19808) ***(G-8980)***
Agricltral Asssmnts Intl Corp...240 463-6677
101 Lake Dr Laurel (19956) ***(G-3191)***
Agriculture United States Dept...302 741-2600
800 S Bay Rd Ste 2 Dover (19901) ***(G-1095)***
Agrima Postal Solutions LLC...302 394-6939
16192 Coastal Hwy Lewes (19958) ***(G-3328)***
Agro Lab...302 265-2734
101 Clukey Dr Harrington (19952) ***(G-2805)***
Agrolab Inc...302 535-6591
101 Clukey Dr Harrington (19952) ***(G-2806)***

Agtus, Dover *Also called American Gen Trdg Contg US Inc* ***(G-1119)***
Agvisory LLC...302 270-5165
125 Lakeside Dr Lewes (19958) ***(G-3329)***
Ah (uk) Inc (HQ)...302 288-0115
1011 Centre Rd Ste 322 Wilmington (19805) ***(G-8981)***
Ah Therapy Services LLC...302 379-0528
725 Halstead Rd Wilmington (19803) ***(G-8982)***
Ahl Orthodontics...302 678-3000
1004 S State St Dover (19901) ***(G-1096)***
AHP, Wilmington *Also called Associates In Hlth Psychology* ***(G-9156)***
Ai Construction Services LLC...619 732-0250
651 N Broad St Ste 206 Middletown (19709) ***(G-3933)***
Ai Dupont...302 528-6520
2200 Concord Pike Wilmington (19803) ***(G-8983)***
Ai Dupont Hosp For Children...302 651-4620
1600 Rockland Rd Wilmington (19803) ***(G-8984)***
Ai Enterprises...302 764-2342
234 Philadelphia Pike # 10 Wilmington (19809) ***(G-8985)***
AIA...302 407-2252
4058 New Castle Ave New Castle (19720) ***(G-5018)***
Aidbits Inc...647 692-3494
16192 Coastal Hwy Lewes (19958) ***(G-3330)***
Aids Delaware Inc...302 226-3519
37201 Rehoboth Avenue Ext # 1 Rehoboth Beach (19971) ***(G-7838)***
Aids Delaware Inc (PA)...302 652-6776
100 W 10th St Ste 315 Wilmington (19801) ***(G-8986)***
AIG AIG...302 252-4683
3 Beaver Valley Rd Wilmington (19803) ***(G-8987)***
AIG Federal Savings Bank...302 661-8992
503 Carr Rd 130 Wilmington (19809) ***(G-8988)***
Aigc Games Inc...214 499-8654
16192 Coastal Hwy Lewes (19958) ***(G-3331)***
Aikikai Foundation of Delaware...302 369-2454
103 Jupiter Rd Ste A Newark (19711) ***(G-5921)***
Aila Pty Inc...626 693-0598
2035 Sunset Lake Rd B2 Newark (19702) ***(G-5922)***
Aim Metals & Alloys USA Inc (PA)...212 450-4519
1209 N Orange St Wilmington (19801) ***(G-8989)***
Aim Research Co...302 235-5940
5936 Limestone Rd Ste 302 Hockessin (19707) ***(G-2953)***
Aimco/Bethesda GP LLC...303 757-8101
2711 Centerville Rd Wilmington (19808) ***(G-8990)***
Aion Prides Court LLC...302 737-2085
6 Sussex Rd Ofc F Newark (19713) ***(G-5923)***
Aion University Village LLC...302 366-8000
2017 Mederia Cir Newark (19702) ***(G-5924)***
Air Doctorx Inc...302 492-1333
4639 Halltown Rd Ste B Hartly (19953) ***(G-2912)***
Air Enterprises Inc...302 335-5141
4403 Irish Hill Rd Magnolia (19962) ***(G-3878)***
Air Intrnational US Sbusid Inc (PA)...248 819-1602
2711 Centerville Rd # 300 Wilmington (19808) ***(G-8991)***
Air Liquide America LP...302 225-2132
305 Water St Wilmington (19804) ***(G-8992)***
Air Liquide Medal Div, Wilmington *Also called Air Liquide America LP* ***(G-8992)***
Air Lqide Advanced Separations...302 225-1100
305 Water St Newport (19804) ***(G-7745)***
Air Lqide Advanced Tech US LLC...302 225-1100
200 Gbc Dr Newark (19702) ***(G-5925)***
Air Lqide Advanced Tech US LLC...302 225-1100
305 Water St Wilmington (19804) ***(G-8993)***
Air Methods Corporation...302 363-3168
21479 Rudder Ln Georgetown (19947) ***(G-2426)***
Air Natures Way Inc...302 738-3063
5 Myers Rd Newark (19713) ***(G-5926)***
Air Quality Remediation LLC...302 464-1050
1274 Caldwell Corner Rd Townsend (19734) ***(G-8755)***
Airbase Carpet Mart Abct Dist...302 323-8800
76 Southgate Blvd New Castle (19720) ***(G-5019)***
Airbnb Inc...415 800-5959
2711 Centerville Rd Wilmington (19808) ***(G-8994)***
Aircraft Specialties...302 762-0816
106 Baynard Blvd Wilmington (19803) ***(G-8995)***
Airespa Worldwide Whl LLC...908 227-4441
8 The Grn Dover (19901) ***(G-1097)***
Airgas Inc...302 575-1822
1521 Concord Pike Ste 101 Wilmington (19803) ***(G-8996)***
Airgas Usa LLC...302 834-7404
4442 Wrangle Rd Delaware City (19706) ***(G-946)***
Airgas Usa LLC...302 286-5400
200 Gbc Dr Newark (19702) ***(G-5927)***
Airport Plaza Branch, New Castle *Also called Wilmington Savings Fund Soc* ***(G-5837)***
Airsled Inc...302 292-8911
70 Aleph Dr Ste A Newark (19702) ***(G-5928)***
Airsoft Shortyusa.com, Hockessin *Also called Shorty USA Inc* ***(G-3146)***
Airwave Technology...302 734-7838
1238 Forrest Ave Dover (19904) ***(G-1098)***
Airwick/Delaware, Wilmington *Also called Diamond Chemical & Supply Co* ***(G-10139)***
Ait Advanced Infotech Inc...302 454-8620
467 Carson Dr Bear (19701) ***(G-24)***

Aiu North America, Wilmington *Also called American Gen Lf Insur Co Del (G-9046)*
Aivo America Corp 415 849-2288
160 Greentree Dr Dover (19904) *(G-1099)*
Ajacks Tire Service Inc 302 834-5200
819 S Dupont Hwy New Castle (19720) *(G-5020)*
Ajedium Film Group LLC 302 452-6609
100 Interchange Blvd Newark (19711) *(G-5929)*
Ajs Crochets 302 257-0381
1679 S State St Trlr A32 Dover (19901) *(G-1100)*
Akhtar Javed 606 515-3698
658 W Birdie Ln Magnolia (19962) *(G-3879)*
Aku Transport Inc (PA) 302 500-8127
24559 Dupont Blvd Georgetown (19947) *(G-2427)*
Akzo Nobel Inc 312 544-7000
29160 Intervet Ln Millsboro (19966) *(G-4625)*
Al Jusant Travel 302 427-2594
1801 W 4th St Frnt Ste Wilmington (19805) *(G-8997)*
Al's Vinyl Cleaning Service, Dover *Also called Als Power Washing Service (G-1112)*
Alamad Investments LLC 833 311-8899
16192 Coastal Hwy Lewes (19958) *(G-3332)*
Alamo, Wilmington *Also called Enterprise Lsg Phladelphia LLC (G-10409)*
Alan B Evantash, Wilmington *Also called Christiana Care Hlth Svcs Inc (G-9684)*
Alan M Billingsley Jr 302 998-7907
2502 Tigani Dr Wilmington (19808) *(G-8998)*
Alan R Levine DDS 302 475-3743
2018 Naamans Rd Ste A2 Wilmington (19810) *(G-8999)*
Alan Warrington Do 302 239-9599
5307 Limestone Rd Ste 202 Wilmington (19808) *(G-9000)*
Alarm Cmmncations Sytems Group, Rehoboth Beach *Also called Yacht Anything Ltd (G-8120)*
Alarm Systems Co of Delaware 302 239-7754
735 Montgomery Woods Dr Hockessin (19707) *(G-2954)*
Alaskawild Seafoods 302 337-0710
8589 Cannon Rd Seaford (19973) *(G-8142)*
Alban Associates 302 656-1827
1600 Bonwood Rd Wilmington (19805) *(G-9001)*
Alban Tractor Co Inc 302 284-4100
13074 S Dupont Hwy Felton (19943) *(G-2270)*
Albatross Industries LLC 850 447-2150
16192 Coastal Hwy Lewes (19958) *(G-3333)*
Albert S Lambertson Inc 302 734-9649
2433 Central Church Rd Dover (19904) *(G-1101)*
Albireo Energy, Newark *Also called Advanced Power Control Inc (G-5907)*
ALC Funding Corporation 302 656-8923
1403 Foulk Rd Ste 200 Wilmington (19803) *(G-9002)*
Alcatel-Lucent USA Inc 302 529-3900
1415 Foulk Rd Ste 104 Wilmington (19803) *(G-9003)*
Alcoa, Newark *Also called Reynolds Metals Company LLC (G-7333)*
Aldas Refinishing Company 302 528-5028
606 Chanin Ct Hockessin (19707) *(G-2955)*
Alder Associates LLC 360 833-0988
1209 N Orange St Wilmington (19801) *(G-9004)*
Alderman Automotive Enterprise 302 652-3733
2317 N Dupont Hwy New Castle (19720) *(G-5021)*
Alderman Automotive Machine Sp, New Castle *Also called Alderman Automotive Enterprise (G-5021)*
Aleric International Inc 302 547-4846
116 Saint Andrews Ct Middletown (19709) *(G-3934)*
Alex and Ani LLC 302 731-1420
132 Christiana Mall Newark (19702) *(G-5930)*
Alex and Ani LLC 302 227-7360
36494 Seaside Outlet Dr # 1420 Rehoboth Beach (19971) *(G-7839)*
Alex Vaughan Mobile Entrtnmnt 302 674-2464
509 Dyke Branch Rd Dover (19901) *(G-1102)*
Alexander Rv Service Center (PA) 302 653-3250
5710 Dupont Pkwy Smyrna (19977) *(G-8563)*
Alexis A Senholzi DMD 302 234-2728
720 Yorklyn Rd Ste 120 Hockessin (19707) *(G-2956)*
Alexis Wirt 302 654-4236
610 Harrington St Wilmington (19805) *(G-9005)*
Alfa-Order LLC 302 319-2663
3422 Old Capitol Trl # 1824 Wilmington (19808) *(G-9006)*
Alfieri Anthony D Do Facc 302 397-8199
701 Foulk Rd Ste 2b Wilmington (19803) *(G-9007)*
Alfred B Lauder DDS 302 697-7188
508 Eagle Nest Dr Camden Wyoming (19934) *(G-612)*
Alfred I Dupont Hospital, Wilmington *Also called Nemours Foundation (G-11836)*
Alfred Idpont Hosp For Chldren (HQ) 302 651-4000
1600 Rockland Rd Wilmington (19803) *(G-9008)*
Alfred Lauder DDS 302 678-9742
33 Gooden Ave Dover (19904) *(G-1103)*
Alfred Moore 302 653-7600
1057 Wheatleys Pond Rd Smyrna (19977) *(G-8564)*
Alfreda Hicks LLC 302 312-8721
701 E Hazeldell Ave Ste 2 New Castle (19720) *(G-5022)*
Algorithm Sciences LLC 734 904-9491
702 N West St Ste 101 Wilmington (19801) *(G-9009)*
Ali S Husain Orthodontist (PA) 302 838-1400
1400 Peoples Plz Ste 312 Newark (19702) *(G-5931)*
Alias Inc 302 481-5556
913 N Market St Wilmington (19801) *(G-9010)*
Alias Technology LLC 302 856-9488
25100 Trinity Dr Georgetown (19947) *(G-2428)*
Alibel, Smyrna *Also called Tender Loving Kare Child Care (G-8730)*
Alice M Mehaffey 302 697-1893
1896 Upper King Rd Dover (19904) *(G-1104)*
Alive, Wilmington *Also called Almm Ventures LLC (G-9026)*
All About Kidz, Bear *Also called J N Hooker Inc (G-195)*
All About ME Day Care 302 424-8322
104 Mccoy St Milford (19963) *(G-4304)*
All About U Evada Concept (PA) 302 539-1925
35825 Atlantic Ave Millville (19967) *(G-4833)*
All About Women LLC 302 224-8400
4735 Ogletown Stanton Rd # 2300 Newark (19713) *(G-5932)*
All American Electric Svcs LLC 410 479-0277
680 Hickman Rd Greenwood (19950) *(G-2712)*
All American Truck Brokers 302 654-6101
2205 E Huntington Dr Wilmington (19808) *(G-9011)*
All Appliance Repair, Wilmington *Also called Micro Ovens of Delaware (G-11674)*
All Around Moverz 302 494-9925
314 W 35th St Wilmington (19802) *(G-9012)*
All Classics Ltd 302 738-2190
66 Albe Dr Newark (19702) *(G-5933)*
All Clean Services 302 378-7376
859 Union Church Rd Townsend (19734) *(G-8756)*
All Denture Center 302 656-8202
1 Winston Ave Wilmington (19804) *(G-9013)*
All Hked Up Twing Recovery LLC 302 545-1205
102 Pattie Dr Newark (19702) *(G-5934)*
All In One Brands LLC 301 323-8144
8 The Grn Ste 6817 Dover (19901) *(G-1105)*
All In One Transportation LLC 302 482-3222
32 Brookside Dr Wilmington (19894) *(G-9014)*
All Lives Matter LLC 252 767-9291
8 The Grn Ste A Dover (19901) *(G-1106)*
All My Children Elsmere, Wilmington *Also called All My Children Inc (G-9015)*
All My Children Inc 302 995-9191
8 Walnut Ave Wilmington (19805) *(G-9015)*
All Peoples Food LLC 302 690-4881
62 Albe Dr Ste B Newark (19702) *(G-5935)*
All Pets Medical Center 302 653-2300
10 Artisan Dr Smyrna (19977) *(G-8565)*
All Pro Maids Inc 302 645-9247
1546 Savannah Rd Lewes (19958) *(G-3334)*
All Restored Inc 302 222-3537
1638 Thicket Rd Camden Wyoming (19934) *(G-613)*
All Rock & Mulch LLC 302 838-7625
1570 Red Lion Rd Bear (19701) *(G-25)*
All Smiles Family & Cosme 302 734-5303
95 Wolf Creek Blvd Ste 3 Dover (19901) *(G-1107)*
All Star Linen and Uniform Co 302 897-9003
3217 Heathwood Rd Wilmington (19810) *(G-9016)*
All The Difference Inc 302 738-6353
119 Saint Regis Dr Newark (19711) *(G-5936)*
All Therapy LLC 302 376-5578
212 Carter Dr Ste C Middletown (19709) *(G-3935)*
All Trans Transmission Inc 302 366-0104
18 Albe Dr Ste F Newark (19702) *(G-5937)*
All United Prpts Solutions LLC 310 853-2223
4034 Willow Grove Rd Camden (19934) *(G-535)*
All-Med Services of Florida,, Wilmington *Also called Univita of Florida Inc (G-13032)*
All-Span Inc (PA) 302 349-9460
9347 Allspan Dr Bridgeville (19933) *(G-444)*
Allan C Goldfeder DMD 302 994-1782
2415 Milltown Rd Wilmington (19808) *(G-9017)*
Allan Myers Materials Inc 302 734-8632
3700 S Bay Rd Dover (19901) *(G-1108)*
Allan Myers Md Inc 302 883-3501
440 Twin Oak Dr Dover (19904) *(G-1109)*
Allan S Tocker Od 302 995-9060
5151 W Woodmill Dr Wilmington (19808) *(G-9018)*
Allandale Village Apartments, Newark *Also called Westover Management Company LP (G-7687)*
Allegiant Fire Protection LLC 302 276-1300
118 Sandy Dr Ste 6 Newark (19713) *(G-5938)*
Allen Biotech LLC 302 629-9136
29984 Pinnacle Way Millsboro (19966) *(G-4626)*
Allen Body Works Inc 302 875-3208
421 N Central Ave Laurel (19956) *(G-3192)*
Allen Chiropractic, Dover *Also called Roger C Allen DC (G-2040)*
Allen Chorman & Son, Milton *Also called Allen Chorman Inc (G-4861)*
Allen Chorman Inc 302 684-2770
30475 E Mill Run Milton (19968) *(G-4861)*
Allen Harim, Millsboro *Also called Allen Biotech LLC (G-4626)*
Allen Harim Farms LLC 302 629-9136
29984 Pinnacle Way Millsboro (19966) *(G-4627)*
Allen Harim Foods LLC (HQ) 302 629-9136
126 N Shipley St Seaford (19973) *(G-8143)*

ALPHABETIC

Allen Harim Foods LLC 302 732-9511
26867 Nine Foot Rd Dagsboro (19939) *(G-877)*
Allen Harim Foods LLC 302 629-9460
20799 Allen Rd Seaford (19973) *(G-8144)*
Allen Insurance Group (PA) 302 654-8823
410 Delaware Ave Wilmington (19801) *(G-9019)*
Allergy Associates PA 302 834-3401
2600 Glasgow Ave Ste 201 Newark (19702) *(G-5939)*
Allergy Associates PA Inc 302 798-8070
1400 Philadelphia Pike A6 Wilmington (19809) *(G-9020)*
Alliance Bus Dev Concepts LLC 803 814-4004
1480 Alley Corner Rd Clayton (19938) *(G-832)*
Alliance Electric Inc 302 366-0295
1003 S Chapel St Ste D Newark (19702) *(G-5940)*
Alliance International Elec 302 838-3880
608 Carson Dr Bear (19701) *(G-26)*
Allied Anesthesia Assoc LLC 302 547-3620
75 Old Mill Rd Dover (19901) *(G-1110)*
Allied Barton Security Svcs, Wilmington *Also called Alliedbarton Security Svcs LLC (G-9024)*
Allied Behavioral Health, Christiana *Also called Adirondack Bhvral Hlthcare LLC (G-665)*
Allied Diagnstc Pathology Cons 302 575-8103
701 N Clayton St Wilmington (19805) *(G-9021)*
Allied Elec Solutions Ltd 302 893-0257
4661 Malden Dr Wilmington (19803) *(G-9022)*
Allied Lock & Safe Company 302 658-3172
709 N Shipley St Wilmington (19801) *(G-9023)*
Allied Precision Inc 302 376-6844
106 Sleepy Hollow Dr C Middletown (19709) *(G-3936)*
Alliedbarton Security Svcs LLC 302 498-0450
824 N Market St Ste 102 Wilmington (19801) *(G-9024)*
Allmond & Eastburn 302 764-2193
409 Glenside Ave Wilmington (19803) *(G-9025)*
Allmond, Charles M III, Wilmington *Also called Allmond & Eastburn (G-9025)*
Allosentry LLC 617 838-7608
2035 Sunset Lake Rd B2 Newark (19702) *(G-5941)*
Allow ME Errand Service LLC 302 480-0954
5 Peddlers Row Newark (19702) *(G-5942)*
Allpower Generator Sales & Svc 302 793-1690
100 Naamans Rd Ste 1h Claymont (19703) *(G-688)*
Allstate, Milford *Also called Marvel Agency Inc (G-4488)*
Allstate, New Castle *Also called Joseph Devane Enterprises Inc (G-5444)*
Allstate, Newark *Also called Tom Wiseley Insurance Agency (G-7574)*
Allstate Accounting Services, New Castle *Also called M3r & Assoc Inc (G-5494)*
Allstate Van & Storage Corp 302 369-0230
910 Interchange Blvd Newark (19711) *(G-5943)*
Allstates Technical Services, Newark *Also called Techncal Stffing Resources LLC (G-7544)*
Allura Bath & Kitchen Inc 302 731-2851
704 Interchange Blvd Newark (19711) *(G-5944)*
Allure Salon 302 653-6125
599 Jimmy Dr Ste 15 Smyrna (19977) *(G-8566)*
Alma Company 302 731-4427
625 Barksdale Rd Newark (19711) *(G-5945)*
Almars Outboard Service & Sls 302 328-8541
701 Washington St New Castle (19720) *(G-5023)*
Almm Ventures LLC 302 778-1300
117 N Market St Ste 300 Wilmington (19801) *(G-9026)*
Almond Toc Inc 347 756-2318
1209 N Orange St Wilmington (19801) *(G-9027)*
Almost Home Child Care Center, Milford *Also called Renzi Rust Inc (G-4538)*
Almost Home Day Care 302 220-6731
1129 Capitol Trl Newark (19711) *(G-5946)*
Aloe & Carr PA 302 736-6631
850 S State St Ste 2 Dover (19901) *(G-1111)*
Aloft Aeroarchitects, Georgetown *Also called Pats Aircraft LLC (G-2613)*
Aloft Canvas LLC 302 893-0144
511 Delaware St New Castle (19720) *(G-5024)*
Aloha Movers 302 559-4310
4306 Miller Rd Wilmington (19802) *(G-9028)*
Aloysius Butlr Clark Assoc Inc 302 655-1552
819 N Washington St Wilmington (19801) *(G-9029)*
Alpha Care Medical LLC (PA) 302 398-0888
1000 Midway Dr Ste 3 Harrington (19952) *(G-2807)*
Alpha Care Medical LLC 800 818-8680
29787 John J Williams Hwy # 8 Millsboro (19966) *(G-4628)*
Alpha Chemicals, Hockessin *Also called Economic Laundry Solutions (G-3017)*
Alpha Omega Invstgtons Wrkmans 302 323-8111
42 Reads Way New Castle (19720) *(G-5025)*
Alpha Omega Scientific LLC 302 415-4499
129 Freedom Trl New Castle (19720) *(G-5026)*
Alpha PHI Delta Fraternity 302 531-7854
257 E Camden Wyoming Ave A Camden (19934) *(G-536)*
Alpha Technologies Consulting 302 898-2862
1405 Gibraltar Ct Townsend (19734) *(G-8757)*
Alpha To Omega Signs 302 846-3865
14413 Pepperbox Rd Delmar (19940) *(G-969)*
AlphaGraphics, Wilmington *Also called Ancar Enterprises LLC (G-9075)*
AlphaGraphics, Newark *Also called Ancar Enterprises LLC (G-5966)*
AlphaGraphics Franchising Inc 302 559-8369
248 Weldin Ridge Rd Wilmington (19803) *(G-9030)*
Alphasense Inc 302 998-1116
470 Century Blvd Wilmington (19808) *(G-9031)*
Alphasure Technologies 302 992-0900
5909 Old Capitol Trl Wilmington (19808) *(G-9032)*
Alpine Rafetto Orthodontics 302 239-2304
4901 Limestone Rd Ste 4 Wilmington (19808) *(G-9033)*
Als Power Washing Service 302 399-3406
213 Rose Bowl Rd Dover (19904) *(G-1112)*
Als TV Service 302 653-3711
1200 Wheatleys Pond Rd Smyrna (19977) *(G-8567)*
Alsco Inc 302 322-2136
30 Mccullough Dr New Castle (19720) *(G-5027)*
Altea Resources LLC 713 242-1460
3500 S Dupont Hwy Dover (19901) *(G-1113)*
Altered Images Hair Studio 302 234-2151
45 Abelia Ln Newark (19711) *(G-5947)*
Alternative Eco Energy LLC 404 434-0660
6 S Dillwyn Rd Newark (19711) *(G-5948)*
Alternative Solutions 302 542-9081
532 S Bedford St Georgetown (19947) *(G-2429)*
Alternative Therapy LLC 302 368-0800
4629 Ogletown Stanton Rd Newark (19713) *(G-5949)*
Altitude Trampoline Park, Wilmington *Also called Wta Inc (G-13309)*
Altr Solutions LLC 888 757-2587
8 The Grn Ste A Dover (19901) *(G-1114)*
Altra Cargo Inc 302 256-0748
4004 N Market St Wilmington (19802) *(G-9034)*
Altschuler Micki Designs 302 655-6867
4001 Montchanin Rd Wilmington (19807) *(G-9035)*
Alutech Awnings, Selbyville *Also called Alutech United Inc (G-8447)*
Alutech United Inc (PA) 302 436-6005
117 Dixon St Selbyville (19975) *(G-8447)*
Alvatek Electronics LLC 302 655-5870
1200 Penns Ave Ste 101 Wilmington (19806) *(G-9036)*
Alvins Professional Services 302 544-6634
241 Old Churchmans Rd New Castle (19720) *(G-5028)*
Alvis D Burris 302 697-3125
199 South St Camden (19934) *(G-537)*
Always Best Care 302 409-3710
624 Mulberry St Milton (19968) *(G-4862)*
Alycia, Wilmington *Also called Holly Oak Towing and Service (G-10928)*
Alyvant Therapeutics Inc 646 767-5878
251 Little Falls Dr Wilmington (19808) *(G-9037)*
Alzheimers Assn Del Chapter 302 633-4420
2306 Kirkwood Hwy Wilmington (19805) *(G-9038)*
AM Custom Tackle Inc 302 945-7921
25889 Kings Ln Millsboro (19966) *(G-4629)*
Amaa Management Corporation 302 677-0505
764 Dover Leipsic Rd Dover (19901) *(G-1115)*
Amakor Inc 302 834-8664
72 Clinton St Delaware City (19706) *(G-947)*
Amato & Associates Insurance, Bear *Also called Affordable Insurance (G-22)*
Amazon Steel Construction Inc 302 751-1146
2537 Bay Rd Milford (19963) *(G-4305)*
Ambient Medical Care 302 629-3099
24459 Sussex Hwy Ste 2 Seaford (19973) *(G-8145)*
AMC - Commercial Inc 302 229-0051
316 Governor Printz Blvd Claymont (19703) *(G-689)*
AMC Museum Foundation 302 677-5938
1301 Heritage Rd Dover (19902) *(G-1116)*
Amdisvet LLC 302 514-9130
230 Ashton Ct Ste 100 Smyrna (19977) *(G-8568)*
Amears Contractors Inc 302 791-7767
905 Cedartree Ln Apt 6 Claymont (19703) *(G-690)*
Amedisys Inc 302 678-4764
1221 College Park Dr # 203 Dover (19904) *(G-1117)*
Ameken Network Group Inc 302 545-3472
405 Maple Ln Claymont (19703) *(G-691)*
Amemg Inc 302 220-7132
32 Phoebe Farms Ln New Castle (19720) *(G-5029)*
Amer Inc 302 654-2498
1010 N Union St Ste D Wilmington (19805) *(G-9039)*
Amer Industrial Tech Inc 302 765-3318
100 Amer Rd Ste 200 Wilmington (19809) *(G-9040)*
Amer Masonry T A Marino 302 834-1511
811 Reybold Dr New Castle (19720) *(G-5030)*
Ameresco Inc 302 284-1480
1119 Willow Grove Rd Felton (19943) *(G-2271)*
Ameresco Inc 302 875-0696
29086 Landfill Ln Georgetown (19947) *(G-2430)*
America Group 302 529-1320
2036 Foulk Rd Ste 104 Wilmington (19810) *(G-9041)*
American Birding Assn Inc (PA) 302 838-3660
93 Clinton St Ste Aba Delaware City (19706) *(G-948)*
American Bldrs Contrs Sup Inc 302 994-1166
1550 First State Blvd Wilmington (19804) *(G-9042)*
American Cabinetry LLC 302 655-4064
307 Commercial Dr Wilmington (19805) *(G-9043)*

ALPHABETIC SECTION

American Cedar & Millwork Inc (PA)..................................302 645-9580
  17993 American Way Lewes (19958) *(G-3335)*
American Chiropractic Center..302 450-3153
  230 Beiser Blvd Ste 101 Dover (19904) *(G-1118)*
American Classic Golf Club LLC......................................302 703-6662
  18485 Bethpage Dr Ste 1 Lewes (19958) *(G-3336)*
American Consumer Marketing, Dover Also called Acm Corp *(G-1083)*
American Diagnostic Svcs Inc..302 628-4209
  1109 Middleford Rd Seaford (19973) *(G-8146)*
American Domain Names LLC...253 785-0332
  3422 Old Capitol Trl Wilmington (19808) *(G-9044)*
American Express Shuttle Inc...302 420-8377
  83 Albe Dr Ste F Newark (19702) *(G-5950)*
American Federation...302 283-1330
  698 Old Baltimore Pike Newark (19702) *(G-5951)*
American Federation of State...302 323-2121
  91 Christiana Rd New Castle (19720) *(G-5031)*
American Finance LLC..302 674-0365
  17507 S Dupont Hwy Harrington (19952) *(G-2808)*
American Frnds of The Ryal Soc.......................................302 295-4959
  1000 N West St Ste 1200 Wilmington (19801) *(G-9045)*
American Furniture Rentals Inc..302 323-1682
  490 W Basin Rd New Castle (19720) *(G-5032)*
American Gen Lf Insur Co Del...302 575-5200
  503 Carr Rd Wilmington (19809) *(G-9046)*
American Gen Trdg Contg US Inc......................................804 739-1480
  73 Greentree Dr 519 Dover (19904) *(G-1119)*
American General..302 575-5200
  405 N King St Wilmington (19801) *(G-9047)*
American Hardscapes LLC...302 253-8237
  20099 Gravel Hill Rd Georgetown (19947) *(G-2431)*
American Heart Association Inc.......................................302 454-0613
  200 Continental Dr # 101 Newark (19713) *(G-5952)*
American Heritage, Lewes Also called Thomas R Wyshock *(G-3782)*
American Homepatient Inc..302 454-4941
  701 Interchange Blvd Newark (19711) *(G-5953)*
American Ice, Milford Also called United States Cold Storage Inc *(G-4584)*
American Income Life Insurance......................................610 277-9499
  1521 Concord Pike Ste 301 Wilmington (19803) *(G-9048)*
American Incorporators, Wilmington Also called Incorporators USA LLC *(G-11015)*
American Incorporators Ltd..302 421-5752
  1013 Centre Rd Ste 403a Wilmington (19805) *(G-9049)*
American Industries LLC...302 585-0129
  124 Broadkill Rd Ste 436 Milton (19968) *(G-4863)*
American Insert Flange Co Inc..302 777-7464
  1603 Jessup St Ste 6 Wilmington (19802) *(G-9050)*
American Institute For Pub Svc..302 622-9101
  100 W 10th St Ste 1005 Wilmington (19801) *(G-9051)*
American K9 Doggie Daycare & T......................................302 376-9663
  128 Patriot Dr Unit 12 Middletown (19709) *(G-3937)*
American Karate Studio...302 529-7800
  1812 Marsh Rd Ste 421 Wilmington (19810) *(G-9052)*
American Karate Studios..302 737-9500
  1150 Capitol Trl Newark (19711) *(G-5954)*
American Kidney Care, Newark Also called American Universal LLC *(G-5960)*
American Legion...302 398-3566
  17448 S Dupont Hwy Harrington (19952) *(G-2809)*
American Legion (PA)...302 628-5221
  601 Bridgeville Hwy # 213 Seaford (19973) *(G-8147)*
American Legion Ckrt Post 7, Harrington Also called American Legion *(G-2809)*
American Legion Log Cabin..302 629-9915
  230 N Front St Unit 6 Seaford (19973) *(G-8148)*
American Lgion Amblance Stn 64.....................................302 653-6465
  900 Smyrna Clayton Blvd Smyrna (19977) *(G-8569)*
American Life Insurance Co (HQ).....................................302 594-2000
  1 Alico Plz Wilmington (19801) *(G-9053)*
American Lung Assn In Del, Dover Also called American Lung Association *(G-1120)*
American Lung Assn of Del..302 737-6414
  630 Churchmans Rd Ste 202 Newark (19702) *(G-5955)*
American Lung Association...302 674-9701
  422 S Governors Ave Dover (19904) *(G-1120)*
American Male Hair Care, Newark Also called United States Mle MNS Hair Cre *(G-7615)*
American Martial Arts Inst...302 834-4060
  414 Eden Cir Bear (19701) *(G-27)*
American Meter Holdings Corp (HQ).................................302 477-0208
  1105 N Market St Ste 1300 Wilmington (19801) *(G-9054)*
American Minerals Inc..302 652-3301
  301 Pigeon Point Rd New Castle (19720) *(G-5033)*
American Minerals Partnership..302 652-3301
  301 Pigeon Point Rd New Castle (19720) *(G-5034)*
American Neon Products Company..................................302 856-3400
  715c S Washington St Milford (19963) *(G-4306)*
American Philosophical Assn...302 831-1112
  31 Amstel Ave Newark (19716) *(G-5956)*
American Postal Workers Union.......................................302 322-8994
  271 Christiana Rd New Castle (19720) *(G-5035)*
American Precast Inc..302 629-6688
  301 Nanticoke Ave Seaford (19973) *(G-8149)*
American Prtable Mini Stor Inc..302 934-9898
  24139 Fishers Pt Millsboro (19966) *(G-4630)*
American Records Management, Newark Also called American Van Storage Corp *(G-5961)*
American Seaboard Exteriors...302 571-9896
  14 Ashley Pl Wilmington (19804) *(G-9055)*
American Sleep Medicine LLC..302 366-0111
  200 Continental Dr # 112 Newark (19713) *(G-5957)*
American Soc Cytopathology Inc......................................302 543-6583
  100 W 10th St Ste 605 Wilmington (19801) *(G-9056)*
American Speedy Printing, Wilmington Also called OConnell Speedy Printing Inc *(G-11935)*
American Spirit Federal Cr Un..302 738-4515
  1110 Elkton Rd Newark (19711) *(G-5958)*
American Spirit Federal Cr Un..302 738-4515
  1110 Elkton Rd Newark (19711) *(G-5959)*
American Sports, Newark Also called Versatile Impex Inc *(G-7652)*
American Sports Licensing (PA).......................................302 288-0122
  1011 Centre Rd Ste 310 Wilmington (19805) *(G-9057)*
American Timber Brokerage...302 655-8471
  1305 N Dupont St B Wilmington (19806) *(G-9058)*
American Universal LLC..302 836-9790
  1415 Pulaski Hwy Ste 2 Newark (19702) *(G-5960)*
American Van Storage Corp..302 369-0900
  900 Interchange Blvd Newark (19711) *(G-5961)*
American Water Well System..302 629-3796
  1129 A Brickyard Rd Seaford (19973) *(G-8150)*
American-Amicable Holding Inc (HQ)..............................302 427-0355
  1105 N Market St Ste 1300 Wilmington (19801) *(G-9059)*
American-Eurasian Exch Co LLC.....................................202 701-4009
  4023 Kennett Pike 267 Wilmington (19807) *(G-9060)*
AmericInn, Rehoboth Beach Also called Sunny Hospitality LLC *(G-8092)*
AmericInn International LLC..302 398-3900
  1259 Corn Crib Rd Harrington (19952) *(G-2810)*
AmericInn Ldge Stes Harrington, Harrington Also called Sunny Hospitality LLC *(G-2895)*
AmericInn Lodge & Suites, Bear Also called Innpros Inc *(G-188)*
AmericInn Lodging & Suites, Milford Also called Milford Lodging LLC *(G-4500)*
Ameriprise Financial Services..302 476-8000
  2 Righter Pkwy Wilmington (19803) *(G-9061)*
Ameriprise Financial Svcs Inc..302 543-5784
  5195 W Woodmill Dr 27 Wilmington (19808) *(G-9062)*
Ameriprise Financial Svcs Inc..302 475-5105
  1805 Foulk Rd Ste A Wilmington (19810) *(G-9063)*
Ameriprise Financial Svcs Inc..302 468-8200
  1011 Centre Rd Ste 100 Wilmington (19805) *(G-9064)*
Ameriprise Financial Svcs Inc..302 475-2357
  2106 Silverside Rd # 201 Wilmington (19810) *(G-9065)*
Amerirpise...302 656-7773
  1 Righter Pkwy Ste 250 Wilmington (19803) *(G-9066)*
Ames Engineering Corp..302 658-6945
  805 E 13th St Wilmington (19802) *(G-9067)*
Ametek Inc..302 456-4400
  455 Corporate Blvd Newark (19702) *(G-5962)*
AMF Bowling Centers Inc..302 998-5316
  3215 Kirkwood Hwy Wilmington (19808) *(G-9068)*
Amh Enterprises LLC..302 337-0300
  8805 Newton Rd Bridgeville (19933) *(G-445)*
Amick Farms LLC..302 846-9511
  10392 Allens Mill Rd Delmar (19940) *(G-970)*
Amick Mart J MD...302 633-1700
  3105 Limestone Rd Ste 301 Wilmington (19808) *(G-9069)*
AMP Electric LLC...302 337-8050
  302 Earlee Ave Bridgeville (19933) *(G-446)*
AMP-In, Wilmington Also called Whitaker LLC *(G-13187)*
Ampco Ues Sub Inc..302 691-6420
  103 Foulk Rd Ste 202 Wilmington (19803) *(G-9070)*
Ample Business Solutions Inc...302 752-4270
  501 Silverside Rd Wilmington (19809) *(G-9071)*
Amplified Gchmical Imaging LLC.....................................302 266-2428
  210 Executive Dr Ste 1 Newark (19702) *(G-5963)*
Ampx2 Inc..650 521-5750
  615 S Dupont Hwy Dover (19901) *(G-1121)*
AMS of Delaware..302 227-1320
  20576 Coastal Hwy Rehoboth Beach (19971) *(G-7840)*
Amspec Chemical Corporation..302 392-1702
  703 Carson Dr Bear (19701) *(G-28)*
Amstel Barbershop LLC..302 635-7686
  7313 Lancaster Pike Ste 4 Hockessin (19707) *(G-2957)*
Amstel Mechanical Contractors......................................302 836-6469
  1183 S Dupont Hwy New Castle (19720) *(G-5036)*
Amy Donovan..302 245-8957
  32855 Ocean Reach Dr Lewes (19958) *(G-3337)*
Amy M Farrall OD LLC...302 737-5777
  317 E Main St Newark (19711) *(G-5964)*
Amy Wachter MD...302 661-3070
  3506 Kennett Pike Wilmington (19807) *(G-9072)*
An Inn By Bay...302 644-8878
  205 E Savannah Rd Lewes (19958) *(G-3338)*
Anaconda Prtctive Concepts Inc......................................302 834-1125
  210 Executive Dr Ste 6 Newark (19702) *(G-5965)*
Analtech, Newark Also called Miles Scientific Corporation *(G-7039)*

Analytical Biological Svcs Inc 302 654-4492
701 Cornell Dr Ste 4 Wilmington (19801) *(G-9073)*
Analyttica Datalab Inc 917 300-3325
1007 N Orange St Fl 4 Wilmington (19801) *(G-9074)*
Anamo Inc 702 852-2992
28 Old Rudnick Ln Dover (19901) *(G-1122)*
Anatrope Inc 202 507-9441
3500 S Dupont Hwy Dover (19901) *(G-1123)*
Ancar Enterprises LLC (PA) 302 477-1884
3411 Silverside Rd 103 Wilmington (19810) *(G-9075)*
Ancar Enterprises LLC 302 453-2600
703 Interchange Blvd Newark (19711) *(G-5966)*
Anchor App Inc 302 421-6890
222 Delaware Ave Ste 1200 Wilmington (19801) *(G-9076)*
Anchor Electric Inc 302 221-6111
185 Old Churchmans Rd New Castle (19720) *(G-5037)*
Anchor Enterprises 302 629-7969
22 W High St Seaford (19973) *(G-8151)*
Anchorage Motel Inc 302 645-8320
18809 Coastal Hwy Rehoboth Beach (19971) *(G-7841)*
Andersen Ford Architects LLC 302 388-7862
611 Haverhill Rd Wilmington (19803) *(G-9077)*
Anderson Floor Coverings Inc 302 227-3244
4286 Highway One Rehoboth Beach (19971) *(G-7842)*
Anderson Group Inc 302 478-6160
3411 Silverside Rd # 103 Wilmington (19810) *(G-9078)*
Anderson Landscaping 302 423-3904
95 Jump Dr Smyrna (19977) *(G-8570)*
Anderson Lawn & Home Care 302 376-7115
813 W Creek Ln Middletown (19709) *(G-3938)*
Andover Companies Inc 410 705-1503
207 S Paula Lynne Dr Seaford (19973) *(G-8152)*
Andre M D Hoffman 302 892-2710
1090 Old Churchmans Rd Newark (19713) *(G-5967)*
Andre Noel Thalia 302 747-0813
550 S Dupont Hwy Apt 11b New Castle (19720) *(G-5038)*
Andreas Rauer MD PA 302 734-1760
16 Old Rudnick Ln Dover (19901) *(G-1124)*
Andrei S Remo 302 569-4555
35948 Haven Dr Unit 305 Rehoboth Beach (19971) *(G-7843)*
Andrew J Glick MD 302 652-8990
2000 Foulk Rd Ste F Wilmington (19810) *(G-9079)*
Andrew Nowakowski MD PA 410 838-8900
22 Riva Ridge Ln Bear (19701) *(G-29)*
Andrew Pipon 949 337-2249
8231 Woods Edge Cir Milford (19963) *(G-4307)*
Andrew Simoff Horse Trnsp 302 994-1433
3719 Old Capitol Trl Wilmington (19808) *(G-9080)*
Andrew W Donohue D O 302 999-7386
34 Harlech Dr Wilmington (19807) *(G-9081)*
Andrew Weinstein MD Inc 302 428-1675
111 Walnut Ridge Rd Wilmington (19807) *(G-9082)*
Andrews & Wells LLC 302 359-5417
195 Captain Davis Dr Camden (19934) *(G-538)*
Andrews Construction LLC 302 604-8166
25489 Janice Dr Seaford (19973) *(G-8153)*
Andrews, Joseph F MD, Dover *Also called Delaware Dermatolgy PA* *(G-1366)*
Andrey Georgieff MD 302 998-1866
83 E Main St 3 Newark (19716) *(G-5968)*
Andy Mast 302 653-5014
1269 Seeneytown Rd Dover (19904) *(G-1125)*
Angee Inc (PA) 650 320-1775
1201 N Orange St Ste 7419 Wilmington (19801) *(G-9083)*
Angel Nails 302 449-5067
480 Middletown Warwick Rd Middletown (19709) *(G-3939)*
Angel's In Heaven Daycare, Harrington *Also called Angels In Heaven* *(G-2811)*
Angela Saldarriaga 302 633-1182
5578 Kirkwood Hwy Wilmington (19808) *(G-9084)*
Angelic Therapy 717 870-4618
17436 Slipper Shell Way # 11 Lewes (19958) *(G-3339)*
Angels In Heaven 302 398-7820
333 Weiner Ave Harrington (19952) *(G-2811)*
Angels Lindas 302 328-3700
6 Parkway Ct New Castle (19720) *(G-5039)*
Angels Messiahs Foundation 302 465-1647
360 Fox Hunt Dr Bear (19701) *(G-30)*
Angels Visiting 302 691-8700
3101 Limestone Rd Ste E Wilmington (19808) *(G-9085)*
Angita Pharmard LLC 302 234-6794
24 Tall Oaks Dr Hockessin (19707) *(G-2958)*
Angle Planning Concepts 302 735-7526
31 Saulsbury Rd B Dover (19904) *(G-1126)*
Angle Wireless Wholesale LLC 302 883-7788
11 Avignon Dr Newark (19702) *(G-5969)*
Angler Plumbing LLC 302 293-5691
37 Dempsey Dr Newark (19713) *(G-5970)*
Anglers Fishing Center, Lewes *Also called Anglers Marina* *(G-3340)*
Anglers Marina 302 644-4533
213 Anglers Rd Lewes (19958) *(G-3340)*
Anglin Aircraft Recovery Svc, Clayton *Also called Anglin Associates LLC* *(G-833)*
Anglin Associates LLC 302 653-3500
4901 Holletts Corner Rd Clayton (19938) *(G-833)*
Angola By Bay Prprty Ownr Assn 302 945-2700
33457 Woodland Cir Lewes (19958) *(G-3341)*
Angry 8 LLC (PA) 203 304-9256
200 Continental Dr # 401 Newark (19713) *(G-5971)*
Animal Haven Veterinary Center 302 326-1400
757 Pulaski Hwy Ste 6 Bear (19701) *(G-31)*
Animal Health Sales Inc 302 436-8286
44 Rte 113 Selbyville (19975) *(G-8448)*
Animal Inn Inc 302 653-5560
2308 Seeneytown Rd Dover (19904) *(G-1127)*
Animal Veterinary Center LLC 302 322-6488
160 Bear Christiana Rd Bear (19701) *(G-32)*
Animatra Inc (PA) 303 350-9264
16192 Coastal Hwy Lewes (19958) *(G-3342)*
Ann Jackson Vmd 302 659-3624
310 N Main St Bldg N Smyrna (19977) *(G-8571)*
Anna Marie Mazoch DDS PA 302 998-9594
2601 Annand Dr Ste 18 Wilmington (19808) *(G-9086)*
Annette Rickolt 302 285-4200
350 Noxontown Rd Middletown (19709) *(G-3940)*
Annexus Health LLC 302 547-4154
1105 N Market St Fl 11 Wilmington (19801) *(G-9087)*
Anniemac Home Mortgage LLC 302 234-2956
4839 Limestone Rd Wilmington (19808) *(G-9088)*
Anns Family Daycare 302 836-8910
30 Reubens Cir Newark (19702) *(G-5972)*
Annual Conf of United Meth Ch, Frederica *Also called Commission On Archvs In Hstory* *(G-2400)*
Anotherai Inc (PA) 408 987-1927
16192 Coastal Hwy Lewes (19958) *(G-3343)*
Anq LLC 408 837-3678
3422 Old Capitol Trl # 510 Wilmington (19808) *(G-9089)*
Ans Corporation (PA) 410 296-8330
37156 Rehoboth Avenue Ext Rehoboth Beach (19971) *(G-7844)*
Anta Import/Export LLC 302 653-4542
428 Christiana River Dr Clayton (19938) *(G-834)*
Antebellum Hospitality Inc 302 436-4375
118 W Church St Selbyville (19975) *(G-8449)*
Antenna House Inc 302 427-2456
500 Creek View Rd Ste 107 Newark (19711) *(G-5973)*
Anthony A Vasile Do 302 764-2072
700 W Lea Blvd Ste 301 Wilmington (19802) *(G-9090)*
Anthony J Nappa 716 888-0553
56 Cedarfield Rd Magnolia (19962) *(G-3880)*
Anthony J Poppiti Signs, Wilmington *Also called Poppiti Signs Inc* *(G-12186)*
Anthony Lee Cucuzzella MD 302 623-4370
4735 Ogletown Stanton Rd # 3302 Newark (19713) *(G-5974)*
Anthony Street 302 528-2861
24 Verona Ct Dover (19904) *(G-1128)*
Anthony, Harry C MD, Georgetown *Also called Nanticoke Health Services Inc* *(G-2608)*
Antitoxin Technologies Inc 650 304-0608
8 The Grn Ste A Dover (19901) *(G-1129)*
Antonio C Narvaez MD 302 453-1002
2602 Eastburn Ctr Newark (19711) *(G-5975)*
Antonios Lawn Service LLC 302 293-1200
8 W 9th St New Castle (19720) *(G-5040)*
Anvil Enterprises LLC 323 230-9376
300 Delaware Ave Ste 210a Wilmington (19801) *(G-9091)*
Anya International LLC 847 850-0920
113 Barksdale Pro Ctr Newark (19711) *(G-5976)*
Anything Under Sun LLC 302 292-1023
3027 Rosetree Ln Newark (19702) *(G-5977)*
Anytime Fitness 302 475-2404
1851 Marsh Rd Wilmington (19810) *(G-9092)*
Anytime Fitness 302 738-3040
201 Louviers Dr Newark (19711) *(G-5978)*
Anytime Fitness 302 653-4496
599 Jimmy Dr Ste 18 Smyrna (19977) *(G-8572)*
Anzilotti Orthodontics 302 750-0117
203 Montchanin Rd Wilmington (19807) *(G-9093)*
Aod Smyrna 43 302 659-5060
222 N Dupont Blvd Smyrna (19977) *(G-8573)*
Aoz Food and Gas LLC 302 981-2966
9 Wenark Dr Apt 8 Newark (19713) *(G-5979)*
AP Linens Inc 302 430-0851
713 S Washington St Milford (19963) *(G-4308)*
Apartment Communities, Wilmington *Also called Woods Edge Apartments* *(G-13300)*
Apartment Communities Corp 302 656-7781
402 Foulk Rd Apt 1a9 Wilmington (19803) *(G-9094)*
Apartment Communities Inc 302 798-9100
31 Harbor Dr Apt 2 Claymont (19703) *(G-692)*
Aperture Photography 302 377-6590
106 Redden Ln Middletown (19709) *(G-3941)*
Apex Arabians Inc 302 242-6272
671 Williamsville Rd Houston (19954) *(G-3176)*
Apex Dental Center LLC 302 633-7550
537 Stanton Christn Rd # 211 Newark (19713) *(G-5980)*

Apex Engineering Inc 302 994-1900
27 W Market St Wilmington (19804) *(G-9095)*
Apex Manufacturing Group Inc 484 888-6252
825 Dawson Dr Ste 1&2 Newark (19712) *(G-5981)*
Apex Manufacturing Group Inc (PA) 484 888-6252
825 Dawson Dr Ste 1 Newark (19713) *(G-5982)*
Apex Piping Systems Inc 302 998-5272
3629 Old Capitol Trl Wilmington (19808) *(G-9096)*
Apex Piping Systems Inc (PA) 302 995-6136
302 Falco Dr Wilmington (19804) *(G-9097)*
Apex Stable, Houston *Also called Apex Arabians Inc (G-3176)*
Apgar Turf Farm Inc 302 653-9389
1381 Smyrna Leipsic Rd Smyrna (19977) *(G-8574)*
API, Smyrna *Also called Aqua Pro Inc (G-8575)*
Apollo Scitech LLC 302 861-6557
18 Shea Way Ste 108 Newark (19713) *(G-5983)*
Aponte, Lourdes MD, Lewes *Also called Nancy A Union MD (G-3654)*
App Pros LLC 646 441-0788
2404 Jacqueline Dr Apt A9 Wilmington (19810) *(G-9098)*
Appa Inc 302 440-1448
8 The Grn Ste 7868 Dover (19901) *(G-1130)*
Apparel & Advanced Textiles, Wilmington *Also called Lycra Company LLC (G-11462)*
Apphive Inc 240 898-4661
2035 Sunset Lake Rd Newark (19702) *(G-5984)*
Appic Stars LLC 903 224-6469
8 The Grn Ste 4524 Dover (19901) *(G-1131)*
Apple Electric Inc 302 645-5105
18854 John J Williams Hwy Rehoboth Beach (19971) *(G-7845)*
Apple One, Newark *Also called Howroyd-Wright Emplymnt Agcy (G-6752)*
Appleby Apartments Assoc LP 302 219-5014
401 Bedford Ln New Castle (19720) *(G-5041)*
Appliances Zone 302 280-6073
34936 Sussex Hwy Delmar (19940) *(G-971)*
Applied Analytics Inc 781 791-5005
113 Barksdale Pro Ctr Newark (19711) *(G-5985)*
Applied Bank 302 326-4200
2200 Concord Pike Wilmington (19803) *(G-9099)*
Applied Bank 302 227-3044
37012 Country Club Rd Rehoboth Beach (19971) *(G-7846)*
Applied Bank 302 326-4200
660 Plaza De Rte 89 Newark (19713) *(G-5986)*
Applied Bank (PA) 302 326-4200
2200 Concord Pike Ste 102 Wilmington (19803) *(G-9100)*
Applied Biofeedback Solutions 302 674-3225
1485 S Governors Ave Dover (19904) *(G-1132)*
Applied Card Holdings Inc 302 326-4200
601 Delaware Ave Ste 100 Wilmington (19801) *(G-9101)*
Applied Constructal Inc 203 606-1656
7730 Main St Bethel (19931) *(G-440)*
Applied Control Engrg Inc (PA) 302 738-8800
700 Creek View Rd Newark (19711) *(G-5987)*
Applied Diamond Inc 302 999-1132
3825 Lancaster Pike # 200 Wilmington (19805) *(G-9102)*
Applied Research Assoc Inc 302 677-4147
909 Arnold Drive Ext Dover (19902) *(G-1133)*
Applied Technologies Inc 302 670-4601
169 Roundabout Trl Camden Wyoming (19934) *(G-614)*
Applied Virtual Solutions LLC 302 312-8548
16 N Bellwoode Dr Newark (19702) *(G-5988)*
Apploye Inc 925 452-6102
2035 Sunset Lake Rd B2 Newark (19702) *(G-5989)*
Appmotion Inc 347 513-6333
1000 N West St Ste 1200 Wilmington (19801) *(G-9103)*
Appoquinimink Development Inc 302 378-0878
103 E Park Pl Middletown (19709) *(G-3942)*
Appraisal Associates Inc 302 652-0710
2101 N Tatnall St Wilmington (19802) *(G-9104)*
Apps Complex LLC 705 600-0729
16192 Coastal Hwy Lewes (19958) *(G-3344)*
Apria Healthcare LLC 302 737-7979
225 Lake Dr Newark (19702) *(G-5990)*
APS Cleaning Services, New Castle *Also called Alvins Professional Services (G-5028)*
Aptustech LLC 347 254-5619
1209 Ornge St Corp Tr Ctr Wilmington (19801) *(G-9105)*
Aqua Flow Sprinklers 302 369-3629
52 W Stephen Dr Newark (19713) *(G-5991)*
Aqua Pro Inc 302 659-6593
104 Big Woods Rd Smyrna (19977) *(G-8575)*
Aqua Wash Inc 302 994-1720
4142 Ogletown Stanton Rd Newark (19713) *(G-5992)*
Aquacast Liner LLC 302 535-3728
100 Lake Dr Ste 200 Newark (19702) *(G-5993)*
Aquaflow Pump & Supply Company (PA) 302 834-1311
1561 Pulaski Hwy Bear (19701) *(G-33)*
Aquatic Management 302 235-1818
4905 Mermaid Blvd Wilmington (19808) *(G-9106)*
Aquatic Rehabilitation, Bear *Also called Dynamic Therapy Services LLC (G-131)*
Aquila of Delaware Inc (PA) 302 999-1106
1812 Newport Gap Pike Wilmington (19808) *(G-9107)*
Aquila of Delaware Inc 302 856-9746
6 N Railroad Ave Georgetown (19947) *(G-2432)*
Aquila Trading LLC 302 290-5566
17 Amberfield Ln Hockessin (19707) *(G-2959)*
Aquion Inc 847 725-3000
2711 Centerville Rd Ste 4 Wilmington (19808) *(G-9108)*
AR Solutions Inc 609 751-9611
650 Naamans Rd Ste 207 Claymont (19703) *(G-693)*
ARA Technologies Inc 215 605-5707
7703 Pleasant Ct Wilmington (19802) *(G-9109)*
Aracent Healthcare LLC 302 478-8865
3411 Silve Road Bayna Bui Wilmington (19810) *(G-9110)*
Arangodb Inc 415 659-5938
251 Little Falls Dr Wilmington (19808) *(G-9111)*
Arbor Management LLC 302 764-6450
4 Denny Rd Ste 1 Wilmington (19809) *(G-9112)*
Arbor Pointe, Wilmington *Also called Vintage Properties LLC (G-13084)*
ARC A Resource Ctr For Youth 302 658-6134
2005 Baynard Blvd Wilmington (19802) *(G-9113)*
ARC Document Solutions Inc 302 654-2365
110 S Poplar St Wilmington (19801) *(G-9114)*
ARC Finance Ltd 914 478-3851
251 Little Falls Dr Wilmington (19808) *(G-9115)*
ARC HUD I Inc 302 996-9400
2 S Augustine St Wilmington (19804) *(G-9116)*
ARC HUD VII Inc 302 996-9400
2 S Augustine St Wilmington (19804) *(G-9117)*
ARC of Delaware, Wilmington *Also called Association For The Rights (G-9159)*
ARC of Delaware 302 996-9400
2 S Augustine St Ste B Wilmington (19804) *(G-9118)*
ARC Offshore Investments Inc 561 670-9938
3511 Silverside Rd # 105 Wilmington (19810) *(G-9119)*
Arcadia Fencing Inc 302 398-7700
166 Hopkins Cemetery Rd Harrington (19952) *(G-2812)*
Arcadis US Inc 302 658-1718
824 N Market St Ste 820 Wilmington (19801) *(G-9120)*
Arcangel Inc 347 771-0789
1013 Centre Rd Ste 403 Wilmington (19805) *(G-9121)*
Archer & Greiner PC 302 777-4350
300 Delaware Ave Ste 1100 Wilmington (19801) *(G-9122)*
Archer & Greiner PC 302 858-5151
406 S Bedford St Ste 1 Georgetown (19947) *(G-2433)*
Archer Exteriors Inc 302 877-0650
22295 Lwes Georgetown Hwy Georgetown (19947) *(G-2434)*
Archer Group, The, Wilmington *Also called Cohesive Strategies Inc (G-9762)*
Architect Engineer Ins Co Risk 302 658-2342
4001 Kennett Pike Ste 318 Wilmington (19807) *(G-9123)*
Architects Engineers Loss Ctrl, Wilmington *Also called Architect Engineer Ins Co Risk (G-9123)*
Architecture Plus Pa 302 999-1614
234 N James St Wilmington (19804) *(G-9124)*
Arcpoint Labs 302 268-6560
222 Philadelphia Pike # 5 Wilmington (19809) *(G-9125)*
Arctec Air Heating & Cooling 302 629-7129
21965 Palomino Way Bridgeville (19933) *(G-447)*
Ardexo Inc 855 617-7500
8 The Grn Ste 4810 Dover (19901) *(G-1134)*
Ardexo Housing Solutions, Dover *Also called Ardexo Inc (G-1134)*
Areas USA Dd LLC 302 674-1946
1131 N Dupont Hwy Dover (19901) *(G-1135)*
Arena Signs 302 644-8300
34696 Jiffy Way Lewes (19958) *(G-3345)*
Arenarts Inc 302 408-0887
619 New York Ave Claymont (19703) *(G-694)*
Arex Holding Inc 646 216-2091
501 Silverside Rd Ste 105 Wilmington (19809) *(G-9126)*
Arg Communications, Wilmington *Also called Arugie Enterprises Corp (G-9145)*
Argilla Brewing Company 302 731-8200
2667 Kirkwood Hwy Newark (19711) *(G-5994)*
Argo Financial Services Inc 302 322-7788
104 Penn Mart Shopg Ctr New Castle (19720) *(G-5042)*
Arhc McNwdny01 LLC 518 213-1000
2711 Centerville Rd # 400 Wilmington (19808) *(G-9127)*
Aries Security LLC 302 365-0026
1226 N King St Wilmington (19801) *(G-9128)*
Ariio Inc 562 481-8717
8 The Grn Ste 8074 Dover (19901) *(G-1136)*
ARINC Ctrl & Info Systems LLC (PA) 302 658-7581
1209 N Orange St Wilmington (19801) *(G-9129)*
Arise Africa Foundation Inc 877 829-5500
10 Elks Trl New Castle (19720) *(G-5043)*
Aritisans Wilmington Bank, Wilmington *Also called Artisans Bank Inc (G-9143)*
Arkieva, Wilmington *Also called Supply Chain Consultants Inc (G-12812)*
Arkion Life Sciences LLC (PA) 302 504-7400
551 Mews Dr Ste J New Castle (19720) *(G-5044)*
Arlon LLC (HQ) 302 834-2100
1100 Governor Lea Rd Bear (19701) *(G-34)*
Arlon Mtl Tech Microwave Mtls, Bear *Also called Arlon LLC (G-34)*

ALPHABETIC

ALPHABETIC SECTION

Arlon Partners Inc...302 595-1234
　1100 Governor Lea Rd Bear (19701) *(G-35)*
Arm Chair Scouts LLC...315 360-8692
　427 N Tatnall St 24852 Wilmington (19801) *(G-9130)*
Armand De MD Sanctic.......................................302 475-2535
　2101 Foulk Rd Wilmington (19810) *(G-9131)*
Armed Forces Driving School.............................302 981-6903
　14 Waltham St Newark (19713) *(G-5995)*
Armed Forces Med Examiner Sys........................302 346-8653
　115 Purple Heart Ave Dover (19902) *(G-1137)*
Armigers Auto Center Inc (PA)............................302 875-7642
　28866 Sussex Hwy Laurel (19956) *(G-3193)*
Arminio Joseph A MD & Assoc PA......................302 654-6245
　1701 Augustine Cut Off Wilmington (19803) *(G-9132)*
Armor Graphics Inc..302 737-8790
　1102 Ogletown Rd Newark (19711) *(G-5996)*
Armored Fire Protection LLC.............................302 563-3516
　33 Mailly Dr Townsend (19734) *(G-8758)*
Armstrong Cork Finance LLC (HQ)......................302 652-1520
　818 N Washington St Wilmington (19801) *(G-9133)*
Armstrong Relocation Co LLC.............................302 323-9000
　20 E Commons Blvd New Castle (19720) *(G-5045)*
Army & Air Force Exchange Svc.........................302 677-3716
　260 Chad St Dover (19902) *(G-1138)*
Army & Air Force Exchange Svc.........................302 677-6365
　447 Tuskegee Blvd Dover (19902) *(G-1139)*
Army & Air Force Exchange Svc.........................302 734-8262
　266 Galaxy St Dover (19902) *(G-1140)*
Arnab Mobility Inc..774 316-6767
　2035 Sunset Lake Rd B2 Newark (19702) *(G-5997)*
Arnold International Inc...................................302 266-4441
　573 Bellevue Rd Ste B Newark (19713) *(G-5998)*
Arnold Powerwash LLC......................................302 542-9783
　18197 Robinsonville Rd Lewes (19958) *(G-3346)*
Around Clock Htg AC Inc....................................302 856-9306
　22343 Bunting Rd Georgetown (19947) *(G-2435)*
Arpago Corp..302 645-7955
　34578 Pinnacle Rd Lewes (19958) *(G-3347)*
Arqitecture LLC..302 777-5666
　5105 Kennett Pike Winterthur (19735) *(G-13356)*
Array of Monograms...302 998-2381
　300 Megan Ave Seaford (19973) *(G-8154)*
Arrc, Hockessin Also called Atlantic Remediation *(G-2960)*
Arrim LLC (PA)..617 697-7914
　919 N Market St Ste 950 Wilmington (19801) *(G-9134)*
Arrow Leasing Corp..302 834-4546
　1772 Pulaski Hwy Bear (19701) *(G-36)*
Arrow Safety Device Co.....................................302 856-2516
　123 Dixon St Selbyville (19975) *(G-8450)*
Arrow Sanitary Service, Bear Also called Arrow Leasing Corp *(G-36)*
Arrow Shuttle Service.......................................302 836-5658
　105 Ascot Ct Bear (19701) *(G-37)*
Arrowsmith Cleaning Solutions.........................302 377-5614
　34 Dornoch Way Townsend (19734) *(G-8759)*
ARS New Castle LLC...302 323-9400
　263 Quigley Blvd Ste 1b New Castle (19720) *(G-5046)*
Art Beat...302 834-5700
　2431 Sunset Lake Rd Newark (19702) *(G-5999)*
Art Floor Inc...302 636-9201
　9 Jefferson Ave Wilmington (19805) *(G-9135)*
Art Guild Inc...302 420-8056
　200 Anchor Mill Rd New Castle (19720) *(G-5047)*
Arteaga Properties LLC....................................808 339-6906
　2711 Centerville Rd # 200 Wilmington (19808) *(G-9136)*
Artesian Resources Corporation (PA)................302 453-6900
　664 Churchmans Rd Newark (19702) *(G-6000)*
Artesian Utility Dev Inc....................................800 332-5114
　664 Churchmans Rd Newark (19702) *(G-6001)*
Artesian Wastewater MD Inc............................302 453-6900
　664 Churchmans Rd Newark (19702) *(G-6002)*
Artesian Wastewater MGT Inc..........................302 453-6900
　664 Churchmans Rd Newark (19702) *(G-6003)*
Artesian Water Company Inc...........................302 453-6900
　664 Churchmans Rd Newark (19702) *(G-6004)*
Artesian Water Maryland Inc...........................302 453-6900
　664 Churchmans Rd Newark (19702) *(G-6005)*
Artevet LLC...443 255-0016
　1000 N West St Ste 1200 Wilmington (19801) *(G-9137)*
Artguild, New Castle Also called Art Guild Inc *(G-5047)*
Arthritis and Osteoporosis LLC (PA).................302 628-8300
　1350 Middleford Rd # 502 Seaford (19973) *(G-8155)*
Arthur Bradley & Son, Milford Also called Bradley Arthur & Son Cnstr *(G-4332)*
Arthur L Young Dentist Jr.................................302 737-9065
　6 Millbourne Dr Newark (19711) *(G-6006)*
Arthur W Henry DDS Inc...................................302 734-8101
　748 S New St Dover (19904) *(G-1141)*
Article 19 Inc..302 295-4959
　1000 N West St Ste 1200 Wilmington (19801) *(G-9138)*
Artisan Electrical Inc..302 645-5844
　119 S Washington Ave Lewes (19958) *(G-3348)*

Artisan Woodworks LLC..................................302 841-5182
　28205 Johnson Ln Harbeson (19951) *(G-2772)*
Artisans Bank Clefco Branch, Newark Also called Artisans Bank Inc *(G-6007)*
Artisans Bank Inc..302 656-8188
　223 W 9th St Wilmington (19801) *(G-9139)*
Artisans Bank Inc (PA).....................................302 658-6881
　2961 Centerville Rd # 101 Wilmington (19808) *(G-9140)*
Artisans Bank Inc..302 838-6700
　2424 Pulaski Hwy Newark (19702) *(G-6007)*
Artisans Bank Inc..302 479-2553
　3631 Silverside Rd Wilmington (19810) *(G-9141)*
Artisans Bank Inc..302 479-2550
　1706 Marsh Rd Wilmington (19810) *(G-9142)*
Artisans Bank Inc..302 674-3214
　1555 S Governors Ave Dover (19904) *(G-1142)*
Artisans Bank Inc..302 993-8220
　4901 Kirkwood Hwy Wilmington (19808) *(G-9143)*
Artisans Bank Inc..302 738-3744
　4551 New Linden Hill Rd Wilmington (19808) *(G-9144)*
Artisans Bank Inc..302 834-8800
　1124 Pulaski Hwy Bear (19701) *(G-38)*
Artisans Bank Inc..302 430-7681
　100 Aerenson Dr Milford (19963) *(G-4309)*
Artisans Bank Inc..302 296-0155
　19358 Miller Rd Rehoboth Beach (19971) *(G-7847)*
Artistic Designs Salon......................................302 644-2009
　20361 John J Williams Hwy Lewes (19958) *(G-3349)*
Artists At Work Inc..302 424-4427
　20879 Hummingbird Rd Ellendale (19941) *(G-2257)*
Arttista Accessories..302 455-0195
　105 Woodring Ln Newark (19702) *(G-6008)*
Aruanno Enterprises Inc..................................302 530-1217
　524 E Creek Ln Middletown (19709) *(G-3943)*
Arugie Enterprises Corp..................................302 225-2000
　612 S Colonial Ave Ste A Wilmington (19805) *(G-9145)*
Arundel Trailer Sales.......................................302 398-6288
　344 Jefferson Woods Dr Harrington (19952) *(G-2813)*
Aryvve Technologies LLC.................................678 977-1252
　1675 S State St Ste B Dover (19901) *(G-1143)*
Asa V Peugh Inc...302 629-7969
　22 W High St Seaford (19973) *(G-8156)*
ASAP Automotive..302 444-8659
　807 Pulaski Hwy Bear (19701) *(G-39)*
ASAP Mass Spectrometry, Newark Also called M&M Mass Spec Consulting LLC *(G-6967)*
ASAP Tickets, Wilmington Also called International Travel Network *(G-11069)*
Asari, Julie Y MD, Wilmington Also called Christiana Care Health Sys Inc *(G-9677)*
Asbury Carbons Inc..302 652-0266
　103 Foulk Rd Ste 202 Wilmington (19803) *(G-9146)*
Ascension Industries LLC................................302 659-1778
　104 Needham Dr Smyrna (19977) *(G-8576)*
Asdi, Newark Also called Frontier Scientific Svcs Inc *(G-6627)*
Asferik LLC..302 981-6519
　717 W Oakmeade Dr Wilmington (19810) *(G-9147)*
Ashby & Geddes...302 654-1888
　500 Delaware Ave Ste 8 Wilmington (19801) *(G-9148)*
Ashby Management Corporation......................302 894-1200
　108 W Main St Newark (19711) *(G-6009)*
Ashcraft Masonry Inc......................................302 537-4298
　30171 Jump Ln Ocean View (19970) *(G-7755)*
Asher B Carey III (PA)......................................302 678-3443
　200 Banning St Ste 370 Dover (19904) *(G-1144)*
Ashford Capital Management..........................302 655-1750
　1 Walkers Mill Rd Wilmington (19807) *(G-9149)*
Ashish B Parikh...302 338-9444
　620 Stanton Christiana Rd # 203 Newark (19713) *(G-6010)*
Ashland Credit Union, Wilmington Also called Ashland LLC *(G-9150)*
Ashland LLC..302 995-4180
　500 Hercules Rd Wilmington (19808) *(G-9150)*
Ashland LLC..302 594-5000
　1313 N Market St Fl 8 Wilmington (19801) *(G-9151)*
Ashland Spcalty Ingredients GP......................302 995-3000
　8145 Blazer Dr Wilmington (19808) *(G-9152)*
Ashland Water Technologies, Wilmington Also called Solenis LLC *(G-12678)*
Asi Transport LLC..302 349-9460
　9347 Allspan Dr Bridgeville (19933) *(G-448)*
Ask Connoisseur LLC.......................................302 482-8026
　2093 Philadelphia Pike # 3353 Claymont (19703) *(G-695)*
Aslin Inc..302 674-1900
　2143 Lockwood Chapel Rd Dover (19904) *(G-1145)*
Aspenologies..302 234-4346
　106 Belmont Dr Wilmington (19808) *(G-9153)*
Asphalt Paving Eqp & Sups.............................302 683-0105
　26822 Lwes Georgetown Hwy Harbeson (19951) *(G-2773)*
Asphalt Striping Svcs Del LLC..........................302 456-9820
　12 Hosta Ct Wilmington (19808) *(G-9154)*
Aspira of Delaware Inc...................................302 292-1463
　326 Ruthar Dr Newark (19711) *(G-6011)*
Aspire Energy LLC..330 682-7726
　909 Silver Lake Blvd Dover (19904) *(G-1146)*

Asplundh Tree Expert Co 302 678-4702
100 Carlsons Way Ste 14 Dover (19901) *(G-1147)*
Asset Management Alliance 302 656-5238
222 Delaware Ave Ste 109 Wilmington (19801) *(G-9155)*
Assisted Living Concepts LLC 302 735-8800
1203 Walker Rd Dover (19904) *(G-1148)*
Assoc Community Talents Inc 302 378-7038
41 W Main St Middletown (19709) *(G-3944)*
ASSOCIATED BUILDERS & CONTRACT, New Castle *Also called Assocted Bldrs Cntrs Del Chpte (G-5048)*
Associated Cmnty Talents Inc 302 378-1200
45 W Main St Middletown (19709) *(G-3945)*
Associated Press 302 737-1628
100 Addison Dr Newark (19702) *(G-6012)*
Associated Svc Specialist Inc 302 672-7159
630 W Division St Ste E Dover (19904) *(G-1149)*
Associates Contracting Inc 302 734-4311
1661 S Dupont Hwy Dover (19901) *(G-1150)*
Associates In Hlth Psychology (PA) 302 428-0205
1521 Concord Pike Ste 103 Wilmington (19803) *(G-9156)*
Associates In Medicine PA 302 645-6644
1302 Savannah Rd Lewes (19958) *(G-3350)*
Associates International Inc 302 656-4500
100 Rogers Rd Wilmington (19801) *(G-9157)*
Association Eductional Publr 302 295-8350
300 Mrtin Lther King Blvd Wilmington (19801) *(G-9158)*
Association For The Rights (PA) 302 996-9400
1016 Centre Rd Ste 1 Wilmington (19805) *(G-9159)*
Assocted Bldrs Cntrs Del Chpte (PA) 302 328-1111
31 Blevins Dr Ste B New Castle (19720) *(G-5048)*
Assoction Brds Thlgcal Educatn 302 654-7770
100 W 10th St Ste 703 Wilmington (19801) *(G-9160)*
Assoction Pathology Chairs Inc 301 634-7880
100 W 10th St Ste 603 Wilmington (19801) *(G-9161)*
Assurance Media LLC 302 892-3540
590 Century Blvd Ste B Wilmington (19808) *(G-9162)*
Assurance Partners Intl 302 478-0173
1201 N Market St Ste 1600 Wilmington (19801) *(G-9163)*
Astec Inc 302 378-2717
1554 Lorewood Grove Rd Middletown (19709) *(G-3946)*
Asthma Allergy Care Delaware, Wilmington *Also called Andrew Weinstein MD Inc (G-9082)*
Asthma and Allergy Care Del (PA) 302 995-2952
1941 Limestone Rd Ste 209 Wilmington (19808) *(G-9164)*
Aston Home Health 302 421-3686
1021 Gilpin Ave Ste 100 Wilmington (19806) *(G-9165)*
Astra Zeneca Pharmaceuticals, Wilmington *Also called Zeneca Holdings Inc (G-13344)*
Astral Plane Woodworks Inc 302 654-8666
28 Germay Dr Ste 28b Wilmington (19804) *(G-9166)*
Astrazeneca Foundation 302 886-3000
1800 Concord Pike Wilmington (19850) *(G-9167)*
Astrazeneca LP (HQ) 302 886-3000
1800 Concord Pike Wilmington (19803) *(G-9168)*
Astrazeneca Pharmaceuticals LP 302 286-3500
587 Old Baltimore Pike Newark (19702) *(G-6013)*
Astute General Contracting LLC 302 383-4942
306 Stanton Rd Wilmington (19804) *(G-9169)*
Asw Machinery Inc (HQ) 899 792-5288
2 Lukens Dr Ste 300 New Castle (19720) *(G-5049)*
At Home Care Agency 302 883-2059
57 Saulsbury Rd Dover (19904) *(G-1151)*
At Home Infucare LLC 302 883-2059
373 W North St Ste A Dover (19904) *(G-1152)*
At Systems Atlantic Inc 302 762-5444
4200 Governor Printz Blvd Wilmington (19802) *(G-9170)*
At The Bch Repr & Maintainance, Harbeson *Also called Custom Framers Inc (G-2781)*
AT&T, Wilmington *Also called New Cingular Wireless Svcs Inc (G-11855)*
AT&T Authorized Retailer, Millsboro *Also called Spring Communications Inc (G-4803)*
AT&T Authorized Retailer, Wilmington *Also called Spring Communications Inc (G-12713)*
AT&T Corp 302 644-4529
19354 Miller Rd Ste A Rehoboth Beach (19971) *(G-7848)*
AT&T Mobility LLC 302 674-4888
275 N Dupont Hwy Dover (19901) *(G-1153)*
AT&T Wireless, Wilmington *Also called New Cingular Wireless Svcs Inc (G-11854)*
Atapy Software LLC 657 221-9370
16192 Coastal Hwy Lewes (19958) *(G-3351)*
Atechnologie LLC 781 325-5230
1521 Concord Pike Ste 301 Wilmington (19803) *(G-9171)*
Atg Trading LLC 909 348-0620
1013 Centre Rd Ste 403b Wilmington (19805) *(G-9172)*
Athari Inc 312 358-4933
278 Jordan Dr Dover (19904) *(G-1154)*
Athena T Jolly M D 302 454-3020
24 Brookhill Dr Newark (19702) *(G-6014)*
ATI, New Castle *Also called Pro Physical Therapy PA (G-5647)*
ATI Flat Rlled Pdts Hldngs LLC 302 368-7350
48 Prestbury Sq 18 Newark (19713) *(G-6015)*
ATI Funding, Wilmington *Also called A T I Funding Corporation (G-8884)*
ATI Holdings LLC 302 422-6670
941 N Dupont Blvd Ste C Milford (19963) *(G-4310)*
ATI Holdings LLC 302 993-1450
1208 Kirkwood Hwy Wilmington (19805) *(G-9173)*
ATI Holdings LLC 302 836-5670
1015 E Songsmith Dr Bear (19701) *(G-40)*
ATI Holdings LLC 302 226-2230
19266 Coastal Hwy Unit 9 Rehoboth Beach (19971) *(G-7849)*
ATI Holdings LLC 302 894-1600
4051 Ogletown Rd Ste 104 Newark (19713) *(G-6016)*
ATI Holdings LLC 302 285-0700
114 Sandhill Dr Ste 103 Middletown (19709) *(G-3947)*
ATI Holdings LLC 302 659-3102
1000 Smyrna Clayton Blvd # 4 Smyrna (19977) *(G-8577)*
ATI Holdings LLC 302 994-1200
100 Valley Center Rd Wilmington (19808) *(G-9174)*
ATI Holdings LLC 302 786-3008
16819 S Dupont Hwy # 500 Harrington (19952) *(G-2814)*
ATI Holdings LLC 302 536-5562
22832 Sussex Hwy Seaford (19973) *(G-8157)*
ATI Holdings LLC 302 838-2165
2600 Glasgow Ave Ste 105 Newark (19702) *(G-6017)*
ATI Holdings LLC 302 677-0100
1288 S Governors Ave Dover (19904) *(G-1155)*
ATI Holdings LLC 302 392-3400
100 Becks Woods Dr Bear (19701) *(G-41)*
ATI Holdings LLC 302 475-7500
1812 Marsh Rd Ste 505 Wilmington (19810) *(G-9175)*
ATI Holdings LLC 302 351-0302
914 Justison St Wilmington (19801) *(G-9176)*
ATI Holdings LLC 302 741-0200
260 Beiser Blvd Ste 102 Dover (19904) *(G-1156)*
ATI Holdings LLC 302 654-1700
2032 New Castle Ave New Castle (19720) *(G-5050)*
ATI Holdings LLC 302 656-2521
1600 N Washington St Wilmington (19802) *(G-9177)*
ATI Holdings LLC 302 297-0700
28535 Dupont Blvd Unit 1 Millsboro (19966) *(G-4631)*
ATI Holdings LLC 302 658-7800
213 Greenhill Ave Ste C Wilmington (19805) *(G-9178)*
ATI Physical Therapy, Milford *Also called ATI Holdings LLC (G-4310)*
ATI Physical Therapy, Wilmington *Also called ATI Holdings LLC (G-9173)*
ATI Physical Therapy, Bear *Also called ATI Holdings LLC (G-40)*
ATI Physical Therapy, Rehoboth Beach *Also called ATI Holdings LLC (G-7849)*
ATI Physical Therapy, Newark *Also called ATI Holdings LLC (G-6016)*
ATI Physical Therapy, Middletown *Also called ATI Holdings LLC (G-3947)*
ATI Physical Therapy, Smyrna *Also called ATI Holdings LLC (G-8577)*
ATI Physical Therapy, Wilmington *Also called ATI Holdings LLC (G-9174)*
ATI Physical Therapy, Harrington *Also called ATI Holdings LLC (G-2814)*
ATI Physical Therapy, Seaford *Also called ATI Holdings LLC (G-8157)*
ATI Physical Therapy, Newark *Also called ATI Holdings LLC (G-6017)*
ATI Physical Therapy, Dover *Also called ATI Holdings LLC (G-1155)*
ATI Physical Therapy, Bear *Also called ATI Holdings LLC (G-41)*
ATI Physical Therapy, Wilmington *Also called ATI Holdings LLC (G-9176)*
ATI Physical Therapy, Dover *Also called ATI Holdings LLC (G-1156)*
ATI Physical Therapy, New Castle *Also called ATI Holdings LLC (G-5050)*
ATI Physical Therapy, Wilmington *Also called ATI Holdings LLC (G-9177)*
ATI Physical Therapy, Millsboro *Also called ATI Holdings LLC (G-4631)*
ATI Physical Therapy, Wilmington *Also called ATI Holdings LLC (G-9178)*
Atkins Home Health Aid Agency 302 832-0315
18 Calvarese Dr Bear (19701) *(G-42)*
Atlantic Adult & Pediatric 302 644-1300
34453 King Street Row # 1 Lewes (19958) *(G-3352)*
Atlantic Aluminum Products Inc 302 349-9091
12136 Sussex Hwy Greenwood (19950) *(G-2713)*
Atlantic Aviation Corporation 302 613-4747
120 Old Churchmans Rd New Castle (19720) *(G-5051)*
Atlantic Barter, Newark *Also called Delaware Barter Corp (G-6365)*
Atlantic Broadband 302 378-0780
5350 Summit Bridge Rd # 101 Middletown (19709) *(G-3948)*
Atlantic Budget Inn Millsboro 302 934-6711
28534 Dupont Blvd Millsboro (19966) *(G-4632)*
Atlantic Bulk Carriers 302 378-6300
364 E Main St Middletown (19709) *(G-3949)*
Atlantic Bulk Ltd 302 378-6300
421 Boyds Corner Rd Middletown (19709) *(G-3950)*
Atlantic Business Contracting 302 337-7490
18089 Sussex Hwy Bridgeville (19933) *(G-449)*
Atlantic Chiropractic Associat 302 854-9300
2 Lee Ave Unit 103 Georgetown (19947) *(G-2436)*
Atlantic Chiropractic Associat 302 703-6108
12001 Old Vine Blvd Lewes (19958) *(G-3353)*
Atlantic Chiropractic Associat (PA) 302 422-3100
375 Mullet Run Milford (19963) *(G-4311)*
Atlantic City Electric Company (HQ) 202 872-2000
500 N Wakefield Dr Fl 2 Newark (19702) *(G-6018)*
Atlantic Concrete Company Inc (PA) 302 422-8017
New Wharf Rd Milford (19963) *(G-4312)*

Atlantic Concrete Company Inc 302 398-8920
Newworf Rd Harrington (19952) ***(G-2815)***
Atlantic Concrete Company Inc 302 856-7847
1 Country Ln Lewes (19958) ***(G-3354)***
Atlantic Control Systems Inc 302 284-9700
7873 S Dupont Hwy Ste 2 Felton (19943) ***(G-2272)***
Atlantic Dawn Ltd 302 737-8854
430 Old Baltimore Pike Newark (19702) ***(G-6019)***
Atlantic Duncan Inc 302 383-0740
5 Magil Ct Newark (19702) ***(G-6020)***
Atlantic Elevators 302 537-8304
31023 Country Gdns Sf3 Dagsboro (19939) ***(G-878)***
Atlantic Enterprises LLC 302 542-5427
20684 John J Williams Hwy # 1 Lewes (19958) ***(G-3355)***
Atlantic Family Physician LLC 302 856-4092
2 Lee Ave Unit 103 Georgetown (19947) ***(G-2437)***
Atlantic Family Physicians 302 856-4092
100 Eaton Ln Milton (19968) ***(G-4864)***
Atlantic General Hospital Corp 302 524-5007
38394 Dupont Blvd Unit 6 Selbyville (19975) ***(G-8451)***
Atlantic Heat Treat, Wilmington *Also called Industrial Metal Treating Corp* ***(G-11021)***
Atlantic Homes LLC 302 947-0223
20684 John J Williams Hwy # 1 Lewes (19958) ***(G-3356)***
Atlantic Industrial Optics 302 856-7905
21348 Cedar Creek Ave Georgetown (19947) ***(G-2438)***
Atlantic Irrigation Spc Inc 302 846-3527
14413 Pepperbox Rd Delmar (19940) ***(G-972)***
Atlantic Kitchen & Bath LLC 302 947-9001
18355 Coastal Hwy Lewes (19958) ***(G-3357)***
Atlantic Landscape Co 302 661-1950
800 A St Wilmington (19801) ***(G-9179)***
Atlantic Law Group LLC 302 854-0380
512 E Market St Georgetown (19947) ***(G-2439)***
Atlantic Management 302 222-3919
34821 Derrickson Dr Rehoboth Beach (19971) ***(G-7850)***
Atlantic Management Ltd 302 645-9511
29 Midway Shopping Ctr Rehoboth Beach (19971) ***(G-7851)***
Atlantic Marketing Inc 302 674-7036
5 Maggies Way Ste 6 Dover (19901) ***(G-1157)***
Atlantic Oil & Gas LLC 302 898-2862
1405 Gibraltar Ct Townsend (19734) ***(G-8760)***
Atlantic Realty Management 302 629-0770
100 Hitch Pond Cir Seaford (19973) ***(G-8158)***
Atlantic Refrigeration & AC, Lewes *Also called Atlantic Refrigeration Inc* ***(G-3358)***
Atlantic Refrigeration Inc 302 645-9321
17553 Nassau Commons Blvd Lewes (19958) ***(G-3358)***
Atlantic Remediation 610 444-5513
1074 Yorklyn Rd E Hockessin (19707) ***(G-2960)***
Atlantic Resource Management 302 539-2029
37448 Club House Rd Ocean View (19970) ***(G-7756)***
Atlantic Sands Hotel, Rehoboth Beach *Also called Sands Inc* ***(G-8067)***
Atlantic Screen & Mfg Inc 302 684-3197
142 Broadkill Rd Milton (19968) ***(G-4865)***
ATLANTIC SHORES REHABILITATION, Millsboro *Also called Green Valley Terrace Snf LLC* ***(G-4700)***
Atlantic Source Contg Inc 302 645-5207
35 Bridge Ridge Cir Lewes (19958) ***(G-3359)***
Atlantic Sun Screen Prtg Inc 302 731-5100
700 Peoples Plz Newark (19702) ***(G-6021)***
Atlantic Surgical, Milford *Also called John T Malcynski MD* ***(G-4460)***
Atlantic Tractor LLC 302 834-0114
2688 Pulaski Hwy Newark (19702) ***(G-6022)***
Atlantic Tractor LLC 302 653-8536
315 Main St Clayton (19938) ***(G-835)***
Atlantic Training LLC 302 464-0341
101 N Broad St Middletown (19709) ***(G-3951)***
Atlantic Veterinary Center, Middletown *Also called Atlantic Veterinary Svcs Inc* ***(G-3952)***
Atlantic Veterinary Svcs Inc 302 376-7506
741 N Broad St Middletown (19709) ***(G-3952)***
Atlantic View Motel 302 227-3878
2 Clayton St Dewey Beach (19971) ***(G-1052)***
Atlantic Water Products 302 326-1166
74 Southgate Blvd New Castle (19720) ***(G-5052)***
Atlantis Industries Corp 302 684-8542
21490 Baltimore Ave Georgetown (19947) ***(G-2440)***
Atlas Glass & Metal LLC 302 456-5958
110 Coopers Dr Newark (19702) ***(G-6023)***
Atlas Management Inc (HQ) 302 576-2749
103 Foulk Rd Wilmington (19803) ***(G-9180)***
Atlas Van Lines Agents 302 369-0900
900 Interchange Blvd Newark (19711) ***(G-6024)***
Atlas Wldg & Fabrication Inc 302 326-1900
728 Grantham Ln New Castle (19720) ***(G-5053)***
Atlas World Express LLC 202 536-5238
119 Plymouth Pl Middletown (19709) ***(G-3953)***
Atom Alloys LLC 786 975-3771
3411 Silverside Rd Ste Wilmington (19810) ***(G-9181)***
Atom Solutions United States, Wilmington *Also called Atom Alloys LLC* ***(G-9181)***
Atoze Inc 415 992-7936
2035 Sunset Lake Rd B2 Newark (19702) ***(G-6025)***
Atr Electrical Services Inc 302 373-7769
14 Manassas Dr Middletown (19709) ***(G-3954)***
Atria Medical Inc (PA) 407 334-5190
160 Greentree Dr Ste 101 Dover (19904) ***(G-1158)***
Attention Dficit Disorder Assn 302 478-0255
101 Brandywine Blvd A Talleyville (19803) ***(G-8749)***
Attention To Detail In Smyrna 302 388-1267
5702 Dupont Pkwy Smyrna (19977) ***(G-8578)***
Attic Away From Home 302 378-2600
893 Noxontown Rd Townsend (19734) ***(G-8761)***
Attitude LLC None 302 422-3356
808 Seabury Ave Milford (19963) ***(G-4313)***
Attorney Rymond H Lemischs Off, Wilmington *Also called Benesch Friedlander Coplan &* ***(G-9301)***
Audi Wilmington, Wilmington *Also called Winners Circle Inc* ***(G-13276)***
Audio Visual Communications, Rehoboth Beach *Also called A V C Inc* ***(G-7835)***
Audioscience Inc (PA) 302 324-5333
42 Reads Way New Castle (19720) ***(G-5054)***
Audtra Benefit Corp 800 991-5156
8 The Grn Ste A Dover (19901) ***(G-1159)***
Aum LLC 302 385-6767
20c Trolley Sq Wilmington (19806) ***(G-9182)***
Auragin LLC 800 383-5109
427 N Tatnall St Wilmington (19801) ***(G-9183)***
Aurista Technologies Inc 302 792-4900
100 Naamans Rd Ste 3c Claymont (19703) ***(G-696)***
Aurum Capital Ventures Inc 877 467-7780
3500 S Dupont Hwy Dover (19901) ***(G-1160)***
Austenitex, Wilmington *Also called Vertex Industries Inc* ***(G-13066)***
Austin & Bednash Construction 302 376-5590
32 Brookhill Dr Newark (19702) ***(G-6026)***
Austin Alliance Electric Inc 843 297-8078
300 Delaware Ave Ste 210a Wilmington (19801) ***(G-9184)***
Austin Cox Home Services 410 334-6406
22945 E Piney Grove Rd Georgetown (19947) ***(G-2441)***
Austin Signs 302 697-7321
351 Captain Davis Dr Camden Wyoming (19934) ***(G-615)***
Austrlian Phystherapy Ctrs Ltd 631 298-5367
300 Delaware Ave Ste 1014 Wilmington (19801) ***(G-9185)***
Autism Delaware Inc 302 224-6020
924 Old Harmony Rd # 201 Newark (19713) ***(G-6027)***
Auto Collision Service (PA) 302 328-5611
501 Churchmans Rd New Castle (19720) ***(G-5055)***
Auto Equity Loans 302 834-2500
1146 Pulaski Hwy Bear (19701) ***(G-43)***
Auto Equity Loans 302 731-0073
1241 Churchmans Rd Newark (19713) ***(G-6028)***
Auto Equity Loans 302 998-3009
4701 Kirkwood Hwy Wilmington (19808) ***(G-9186)***
Auto Parts of Greenwood 302 349-9601
8316 Greenwood Rd Farmington (19950) ***(G-2265)***
Auto Sun Roof Inc 302 325-3001
26 Parkway Cir Ste 5 New Castle (19720) ***(G-5056)***
Auto Works Collision Ctr LLC 302 732-3902
27420 Auto Works Ave Dagsboro (19939) ***(G-879)***
Automation & Controls Tech LLC 913 908-4344
16610 Bluestone Ter Milton (19968) ***(G-4866)***
Automation Air Inc 973 875-6676
16782 Oak Rd Bridgeville (19933) ***(G-450)***
Automation Inc 302 999-0971
408 Harvey Dr Wilmington (19804) ***(G-9187)***
Automation Partnership 302 478-9060
502 First State Blvd Wilmington (19804) ***(G-9188)***
Automation Solutions Inc 302 478-9060
20 Montchanin Rd Ste 200 Wilmington (19807) ***(G-9189)***
Automotive Accounting Service 302 378-9551
680 N Broad St Middletown (19709) ***(G-3955)***
Automotive Services Inc 302 762-0100
2510 Northeast Blvd Wilmington (19802) ***(G-9190)***
Autopart International Inc 302 998-2920
401 Marsh Ln Ste 5 Wilmington (19804) ***(G-9191)***
Autoport Inc 302 658-5100
203 Pigeon Point Rd New Castle (19720) ***(G-5057)***
Autoteam Delaware, Wilmington *Also called Delaware Motor Sales Inc* ***(G-10067)***
Autotote Canada Inc 302 737-4300
100 Bellevue Rd Newark (19713) ***(G-6029)***
Autotype Holdings (usa) Inc 302 378-3100
701 Industrial Rd Middletown (19709) ***(G-3956)***
Autoweb Technologies Inc 443 485-4200
2801 Cntrvlle Rd Fl 1 Flr 1 Wilmington (19808) ***(G-9192)***
Autumn Hill Patio & Landscape 302 293-1183
242 Barberry Dr Wilmington (19808) ***(G-9193)***
AV Auto Worx LLC 302 384-7646
124 Middleboro Rd Wilmington (19804) ***(G-9194)***
AV Logistics LLC 302 725-5407
14 Patriots Pass Milford (19963) ***(G-4314)***
Avalanche Strategies LLC 302 436-7060
144 Dixon St Selbyville (19975) ***(G-8452)***

Avalon Dental 302 999-8822
34 Kiamensi Rd Wilmington (19804) *(G-9195)*
Avalon Dental LLC Bldg G4 302 292-8899
420 Christiana Med Ctr Newark (19702) *(G-6030)*
Avantix Labratories Inc 302 832-1008
100 Biddle Ave Ste 202 Newark (19702) *(G-6031)*
Avantys Health LLC 302 521-2848
1000 N West St Ste 1200 Wilmington (19801) *(G-9196)*
Avatar Instruments Inc 302 703-6865
16587 Coastal Hwy Lewes (19958) *(G-3360)*
Ave Preschool 302 422-8775
20 N Church Ave Milford (19963) *(G-4315)*
Avenue Apothecary and Spa, Rehoboth Beach *Also called Avenue Day Spa (G-7852)*
Avenue Condominium, Rehoboth Beach *Also called One Virginia (G-8023)*
Avenue Cuts Inc 302 655-1718
1700 N Scott St Lowr Lowr Wilmington (19806) *(G-9197)*
Avenue Day Spa 302 227-5649
110 Rehoboth Ave Ste A Rehoboth Beach (19971) *(G-7852)*
Avenue Imparts, Wyoming *Also called Imparts Inc (G-13363)*
Avenue Inn, Rehoboth Beach *Also called Kenny Simpler (G-7978)*
Avenue Medical, New Castle *Also called Marosa Surgical Industries (G-5510)*
Averest Inc 302 281-2062
2201 Valley Ave Wilmington (19810) *(G-9198)*
Aviado Domingo G MD 302 430-7600
18 S Dupont Blvd Milford (19963) *(G-4316)*
Avian Productions Inc 302 526-0542
8 The Grn Ste 4876 Dover (19901) *(G-1161)*
Aviman Management LLC 302 377-5788
910 Gilpin Ave Wilmington (19806) *(G-9199)*
Avis Rent A Car System Inc 302 322-2092
151 N Dupont Hwy New Castle (19720) *(G-5058)*
Avis Rent A Car Systems, New Castle *Also called Avis Rent A Car System Inc (G-5058)*
Avkin Inc 302 562-7468
113 J And M Dr Fl 2 New Castle (19720) *(G-5059)*
Avs Industries LLC 302 221-1705
21 Bellecor Dr Ste C New Castle (19720) *(G-5060)*
Aw Layman Machine, Wilmington *Also called Awl Machine (G-9200)*
Awl Machine 302 888-0440
327 7th Ave Wilmington (19805) *(G-9200)*
Axa Equitable Life Insur Co 302 655-7231
200 Bellevue Pkwy Ste 200 # 200 Wilmington (19809) *(G-9201)*
Axe Bail Bonds, Harrington *Also called D A B Productions (G-2829)*
Axess Corporation (PA) 302 292-8500
91 Lukens Dr Ste E New Castle (19720) *(G-5061)*
Axia Management 302 674-2200
222 S Dupont Hwy Frnt Dover (19901) *(G-1162)*
Axial Medical Printing Inc 518 620-4479
2803 Philadelphia Pike B Claymont (19703) *(G-697)*
Axiom Resources LLC 410 756-0440
160 Greentree Dr Ste 101 Dover (19904) *(G-1163)*
Axxess Marine LLC 954 225-1744
16192 Coastal Hwy Lewes (19958) *(G-3361)*
Ayala Pharmaceuticals Inc 857 444-0553
1313 N Market St Ste 51 Wilmington (19801) *(G-9202)*
Ayon Landscaping 302 275-0205
313 Orinda Dr Wilmington (19804) *(G-9203)*
Aztec Copies LLC 302 575-1993
3636 Silverside Rd Wilmington (19810) *(G-9204)*
Aztec Printing and Design, Wilmington *Also called Aztec Copies LLC (G-9204)*
Aztech Contracting Inc 302 526-2145
68 Elijah Ln Felton (19943) *(G-2273)*
Azur Gcs Inc 302 884-6713
1201 N Orange St Ste 7293 Wilmington (19801) *(G-9205)*
Azurite03 Inc 866 667-5119
1104 Philadelphia Pike Wilmington (19809) *(G-9206)*
Azzota Corporation 877 649-2746
100 Naamans Rd Ste 5i Claymont (19703) *(G-698)*
B & B Contracting, Wilmington *Also called Alan M Billingsley Jr (G-8998)*
B & B Industries Inc 302 655-6156
1507 A St Wilmington (19801) *(G-9207)*
B & B Tickettown Inc 302 656-9797
1601 Concord Pike Ste 61 Wilmington (19803) *(G-9208)*
B & E Tire Alignment Inc 302 732-6091
Rr 113 Frankford (19945) *(G-2345)*
B & F Ceramics 302 475-4721
2644 Boxwood Dr Wilmington (19810) *(G-9209)*
B & F Towing & Salvage Co Inc 302 328-4146
449 Old Airport Rd New Castle (19720) *(G-5062)*
B & M Electric Inc 302 745-3807
19460 Savannah Rd Georgetown (19947) *(G-2442)*
B & M Meats Inc 302 655-5521
21 Commerce St Wilmington (19801) *(G-9210)*
B & R Boyer Pressure Washing 302 875-3603
16835 Arvey Rd Laurel (19956) *(G-3194)*
B & T Contracting 302 492-8415
4158 Westville Rd Camden Wyoming (19934) *(G-616)*
B & W Tek Inc 302 368-7788
18 Shea Way Ste 103 Newark (19713) *(G-6032)*
B A C, Milford *Also called Baltimore Aircoil Company Inc (G-4317)*
B and C Awning 302 629-4465
709 Washington Ave Seaford (19973) *(G-8159)*
B B Construction, Clayton *Also called Bartlett & Bartlett LLC (G-838)*
B D Welding, Newark *Also called Dana S Wright (G-6345)*
B Diamond Feed Company 302 697-7576
2140 Jebb Rd Camden Wyoming (19934) *(G-617)*
B Doherty Inc 302 239-3500
5301 Limestone Rd Ste 100 Wilmington (19808) *(G-9211)*
B E & K Inc 302 452-9000
Ashford Bldg 242 Chpmn Rd 242 Chapman Newark (19702) *(G-6033)*
B E & K Engineering Company 302 452-9000
242 Chapman Rd Newark (19702) *(G-6034)*
B F Shin of Salisbury Inc 302 652-3521
1715 Lovering Ave Wilmington (19806) *(G-9212)*
B Fit Enterprises (PA) 302 292-1785
35 Salem Church Rd Ste 23 Newark (19713) *(G-6035)*
B G Halko & Sons Inc 302 322-2020
204 Old Churchmans Rd New Castle (19720) *(G-5063)*
B James Rogge DDS 302 736-1423
838 Walker Rd Ste 21-1 Dover (19904) *(G-1164)*
B M A Central Delaware 302 678-5718
655 S Bay Rd Ste 4m Dover (19901) *(G-1165)*
B P Services 302 399-4132
547 N Bradford St Dover (19904) *(G-1166)*
B Rich Enterprises 302 530-6865
808 Sweet Hollow Ct Middletown (19709) *(G-3957)*
B Ritter LLC 302 945-7294
20478 Beaver Dam Rd Harbeson (19951) *(G-2774)*
B Safe Inc 302 422-3916
1490 E Lebanon Rd Dover (19901) *(G-1167)*
B Safe Inc (PA) 302 633-1833
109 Baltimore Ave Wilmington (19805) *(G-9213)*
B Walls Son Htg & A Conditions 302 856-4045
22424 Peterkins Rd Georgetown (19947) *(G-2443)*
B Williams Holding Corp (HQ) 302 656-8596
1403 Foulk Rd Ste 200 Wilmington (19803) *(G-9214)*
B&H Insurance LLC 302 995-2247
111 Ruthar Dr Newark (19711) *(G-6036)*
B&P Transit 302 653-8466
979 Mount Friendship Rd Smyrna (19977) *(G-8579)*
B&W Tek LLC 302 368-7824
19 Shea Way Ste 301 Newark (19713) *(G-6037)*
B&W Tek LLC 302 368-7824
19 Shea Way Ste 301 Newark (19713) *(G-6038)*
B'Nai B'Rith House, Claymont *Also called BNai Brith Snior Ctzens Hsing (G-703)*
B-Line Printing 302 628-1311
22876 Sussex Hwy Unit 7 Seaford (19973) *(G-8160)*
Ba Credit Card Trust 704 386-5681
1100 N King St Wilmington (19884) *(G-9215)*
Baabao Inc 415 990-6767
300 Delaware Ave Ste 210a Wilmington (19801) *(G-9216)*
Babe Styling Studio Inc 302 543-7738
213 N Market St Wilmington (19801) *(G-9217)*
Babel Inc 866 327-3465
1 Commerce St Wilmington (19801) *(G-9218)*
Babes On Square 302 477-9190
1411 Foulk Rd Ste A Wilmington (19803) *(G-9219)*
Babilonia Inc 415 237-3339
2035 Sunset Lake Rd B2 Newark (19702) *(G-6039)*
Baby Tel Communications Inc 302 368-3969
727 Art Ln Newark (19713) *(G-6040)*
Back Bay Plumbing 302 945-1210
34140 Meadow Ln Millsboro (19966) *(G-4633)*
Back Clinic Inc 302 995-2100
5550 Kirkwood Hwy Wilmington (19808) *(G-9220)*
Back Creek Golf Course, Middletown *Also called Back Creek Golf Shop (G-3958)*
Back Creek Golf Shop 302 378-6499
101 Back Creek Dr Middletown (19709) *(G-3958)*
Bacon, Alfred, Newark *Also called Infectious Disease Association (G-6775)*
Bad Hair Day Inc 302 226-4247
20 Lake Ave Rehoboth Beach (19971) *(G-7853)*
Badger Electric, Wilmington *Also called M Auger Enterprise Inc (G-11470)*
Baffone & Associates LLC 302 655-1544
1211 N King St Fl 1 Wilmington (19801) *(G-9221)*
Bafundo & Associates, Wilmington *Also called Let US Lift It Inc (G-11376)*
Bahars Company 302 856-2966
110 N Race St Ste 101 Georgetown (19947) *(G-2444)*
Bahtiarian, Gregory Do, Lewes *Also called Bayside Health Assn Chartered (G-3364)*
Baileys Lawn and Landscape LLC 302 376-9113
5101 Summit Bridge Rd Middletown (19709) *(G-3959)*
Baines Shapiro & Associates 302 384-2322
30 Queen Ave New Castle (19720) *(G-5064)*
Baird Mandalas Brockstedt LLC (PA) 302 677-0061
6 S State St Dover (19901) *(G-1168)*
Baked LLC 302 212-5202
2000 Coastal Hwy Dewey Beach (19971) *(G-1053)*
Baker James Ccjr DDS 302 658-9511
1304 N Broom St Uppr Wilmington (19806) *(G-9222)*

(PA)=Parent Co (HQ)=Headquarters (DH)=Div Headquarters
2020 Harris Directory of Delaware Businesses
595

Baker & Sons Paving ... 302 945-6333
116 Bakerfield Dr Middletown (19709) ***(G-3960)***
Baker Farms Inc ... 302 378-3750
665 Shallcross Lake Rd Middletown (19709) ***(G-3961)***
Baker Safety Equipment Inc ... 302 376-9302
107 Delilah Dr Bear (19701) ***(G-44)***
Baker Tilly Virchow Krause LLP ... 302 442-4600
1105 N Market St Ste 700 Wilmington (19801) ***(G-9223)***
Bakhsh Surveyors, Middletown *Also called Clifton L Bakhsh Jr Inc* ***(G-3998)***
Balanceco2 Inc ... 302 494-9476
103 Ascension Dr Wilmington (19808) ***(G-9224)***
Balanced Audio Technology, Wilmington *Also called Bat Electronics Inc* ***(G-9259)***
Balanced Mind Cnseling Ctr LLC ... 302 377-6911
115 N Broad St Ste 4a Middletown (19709) ***(G-3962)***
Baldwin Sayre Inc ... 302 337-0309
17882 Potato Ln Bridgeville (19933) ***(G-451)***
Baldwin, Thomas E, Ocean View *Also called Thomas Baldwin DDS* ***(G-7820)***
Balfour Beatty LLC (HQ) ... 302 573-3873
1011 Centre Rd Ste 322 Wilmington (19805) ***(G-9225)***
Balick & Balick Pllc ... 302 658-4265
711 N King St Wilmington (19801) ***(G-9226)***
Ball Room By Bill ... 302 328-4014
166 S Du Pont Pkwy New Castle (19720) ***(G-5065)***
Ballard Builders LLC ... 302 363-1677
101 S Bassett St Clayton (19938) ***(G-836)***
Ballard Spahr LLP ... 302 252-4465
919 N Market St Ste 1201 Wilmington (19801) ***(G-9227)***
Ballet Theatre of Dover, Dover *Also called Dance Conservatory* ***(G-1339)***
Ballistics Technology Intl Ltd (PA) ... 877 291-1111
2207 Concord Pike 657 Wilmington (19803) ***(G-9228)***
Bally Holding Company Delaware (HQ) ... 610 845-7511
3411 Silverside Rd 108wb Wilmington (19810) ***(G-9229)***
Baltazar Women's Care, Middletown *Also called Rodney Baltazar* ***(G-4222)***
Baltimore Aircoil Company Inc ... 302 424-2583
1162 Holly Hill Rd Milford (19963) ***(G-4317)***
Bamboozle Web Services Inc ... 833 380-4600
2035 Sunset Lake Rd Newark (19702) ***(G-6041)***
Bambu Candles LLC ... 917 903-2563
210 Cullen Way Newark (19711) ***(G-6042)***
Banacom Signs Inc ... 302 429-6243
3201 Miller Rd Ste A Wilmington (19802) ***(G-9230)***
Banana Boat Products, Dover *Also called Sun Pharmaceuticals Corp* ***(G-2113)***
Bancorp Inc (PA) ... 302 385-5000
409 Silverside Rd Ste 105 Wilmington (19809) ***(G-9231)***
Bancorp Bank (HQ) ... 302 385-5000
409 Silverside Rd Ste 105 Wilmington (19809) ***(G-9232)***
BANCORP.COM, Wilmington *Also called Bancorp Bank* ***(G-9232)***
Bancroft Behavioral Health Inc ... 302 502-3255
1107 Drummond Plz Newark (19711) ***(G-6043)***
Bancroft Carpentry Company (HQ) ... 302 655-3434
44 Bancroft Mills Rd Wilmington (19806) ***(G-9233)***
Bancroft Construction Company (PA) ... 302 655-3434
1300 N Grant Ave Ste 101 Wilmington (19806) ***(G-9234)***
Bancroft Family Care, Wilmington *Also called Helena Schroyer MD* ***(G-10882)***
Bancroft Homes Inc ... 302 655-5461
1300 N Grant Ave Ste 204 Wilmington (19806) ***(G-9235)***
Bancroft Internal Medicine, Wilmington *Also called R G Altschuler MD* ***(G-12295)***
Bancroft Neurohealth ... 302 691-8531
321 E 11th St Wilmington (19801) ***(G-9236)***
Bancroft Pkwy Open Mri & Imgng, Wilmington *Also called Trolley Sq Opn Mri & Imgng Ctr* ***(G-12983)***
Bane Clene Way ... 610 485-1234
950 Ridge Rd Ste B25 Claymont (19703) ***(G-699)***
Banfield & Temperley Inc ... 347 878-6057
8 The Grn Ste A Dover (19901) ***(G-1169)***
Banfield Pet Hospital 1103, Wilmington *Also called A Caring Doctor Minnesota PA* ***(G-8874)***
Bangus Business Services ... 302 266-7285
18 Marvin Dr Apt B4 Newark (19713) ***(G-6044)***
Bank America National Assn ... 302 478-1005
5215 Concord Pike Wilmington (19803) ***(G-9237)***
Bank America National Assn ... 302 674-5379
1404 Forrest Ave Ste 5 Dover (19904) ***(G-1170)***
Bank America National Assn ... 302 656-5399
3816 Kennett Pike Wilmington (19807) ***(G-9238)***
Bank America National Assn ... 302 765-2108
1100 N King St Wilmington (19884) ***(G-9239)***
Bank America National Assn ... 302 464-1745
655 Paper Mill Rd Newark (19711) ***(G-6045)***
Bank of America Child Dev Ctr, Newark *Also called Bright Horizons Chld Ctrs LLC* ***(G-6119)***
Bank of America Corporation ... 302 432-0407
1100 N Market St Wilmington (19890) ***(G-9240)***
Bank of Delmar ... 302 732-3610
601 Main St Dagsboro (19939) ***(G-880)***
Bank of Delmar ... 302 875-5901
200 E Market St Laurel (19956) ***(G-3195)***
Bank of Delmarva ... 302 226-8900
4575 Highway One Rehoboth Beach (19971) ***(G-7854)***
Bank of Delmarva ... 302 629-2700
910 Norman Eskridge Hwy Seaford (19973) ***(G-8161)***
Bank of New Castle ... 800 347-3301
12 Reads Way New Castle (19720) ***(G-5066)***
Bank of New York Mellon ... 302 421-2207
4005 Kennett Pike Wilmington (19807) ***(G-9241)***
Bank of New York Mellon Corp ... 302 416-6283
4005 Kennett Pike Fl 1 Wilmington (19807) ***(G-9242)***
Bank of New York Mellon Corp ... 302 421-2335
3801 Kennett Pike E155 Wilmington (19807) ***(G-9243)***
Bank of New York Mellon Corp ... 302 791-1700
301 Bellevue Pkwy Wilmington (19809) ***(G-9244)***
Bank of Ocean City ... 410 723-4944
904 Coastal Hwy Fenwick Island (19944) ***(G-2329)***
Banknorth Massachusetts, Wilmington *Also called Td Bank NA* ***(G-12862)***
Banks Farm LLC ... 302 542-4100
30190 Whites Neck Rd Dagsboro (19939) ***(G-881)***
Bantam Technologies LLC ... 302 256-5823
1201 N Orange St 700-7019 Wilmington (19801) ***(G-9245)***
Baq Logistics LLC ... 302 401-6466
8 The Grn Ste 8118 Dover (19901) ***(G-1171)***
Bar & Associates Intr Design, Wilmington *Also called Bar & Associates Ltd* ***(G-9246)***
Bar & Associates Ltd ... 302 999-9233
3410 Old Capitol Trl # 2 Wilmington (19808) ***(G-9246)***
Bar Code Software Inc ... 410 360-7455
34295 Wilgus Cemetery Rd Frankford (19945) ***(G-2346)***
Barbacane Thornton & Company ... 302 478-8940
3411 Silverside Rd 200s Wilmington (19810) ***(G-9247)***
Barbara Graphics Inc ... 302 636-9040
506 First State Blvd Wilmington (19804) ***(G-9248)***
Barbara L McKinney ... 302 266-9594
5 Knickerbocker Dr Newark (19713) ***(G-6046)***
Barbaras Dance Academy ... 302 883-4355
1151 E Lebanon Rd Ste F Dover (19901) ***(G-1172)***
Barbizon of Delaware Inc ... 302 658-6666
17 Trolley Sq Ste B Wilmington (19806) ***(G-9249)***
Barbizon School of Modeling, Wilmington *Also called Barbizon of Delaware Inc* ***(G-9249)***
Barbosa Manufacturing ... 302 856-6343
24965 Kruger Rd Georgetown (19947) ***(G-2445)***
Barclay Farms ... 302 697-6939
1 Paynters Way Camden (19934) ***(G-539)***
BARCLAYCARD US, Wilmington *Also called Barclays Bank Delaware* ***(G-9250)***
Barclays Bank Delaware (HQ) ... 302 255-8000
100 S West St Wilmington (19801) ***(G-9250)***
Barclays Financial Corporation ... 302 652-6201
100 S West St Wilmington (19801) ***(G-9251)***
Barclays PLC ... 302 622-8990
125 S West St Wilmington (19801) ***(G-9252)***
Bardon U S Corporation (HQ) ... 302 552-3136
300 Delaware Ave Fl 9 Wilmington (19801) ***(G-9253)***
Bargain Tire & Service Inc ... 302 764-8900
3415 N Market St Ste 17 Wilmington (19802) ***(G-9254)***
Baritc Lawn Care LLC ... 302 420-6072
621 Delaware St New Castle (19720) ***(G-5067)***
Barker Benchark Therpy & Rehab ... 302 659-7552
208 N Dupont Blvd Smyrna (19977) ***(G-8580)***
Barker Therapy Rehabilitation, Milford *Also called Matrix Rehabilitation Delaware* ***(G-4490)***
Barker-Mtrix Thrapy Rhbltation, Dover *Also called Physiotherapy Associates Inc* ***(G-1957)***
Barlow Upholstery, Wilmington *Also called Barlows Upholstery Inc* ***(G-9255)***
Barlows Upholstery Inc ... 302 655-3955
1002 W 28th St Wilmington (19802) ***(G-9255)***
Barnett Tom D Law Firm ... 302 855-9252
512 E Market St Georgetown (19947) ***(G-2446)***
Barnett, Norman C, Georgetown *Also called Market Street Center Inc* ***(G-2598)***
Barnhart, Ryan DDS, Lewes *Also called Dental Group* ***(G-3461)***
Barrett Business Services Inc ... 302 674-2206
116 E Water St Dover (19901) ***(G-1173)***
Barrettes Run Apartments ... 302 368-3400
100 N Barrett Ln Newark (19702) ***(G-6047)***
Barros Mc Namara Malkwcz & Tay ... 302 734-8400
2 W Loockerman St Dover (19904) ***(G-1174)***
Barry Kayne DDS ... 302 456-0400
58 Omega Dr Ste F58 Newark (19713) ***(G-6048)***
Barry Klassman DDS RES ... 302 478-0475
706 Bristol Rd Wilmington (19803) ***(G-9256)***
Barry USA Inc (PA) ... 800 305-2673
104 Alan Dr Newark (19711) ***(G-6049)***
Barry USA Inc ... 800 305-2673
874 Walker Rd Ste C Dover (19904) ***(G-1175)***
Barrys Cleaning Service ... 302 653-0110
2472 Chance Rd Clayton (19938) ***(G-837)***
Barsgr LLC (PA) ... 302 645-6665
32193 Winery Way Lewes (19958) ***(G-3362)***
Barsgr LLC ... 302 945-3410
32087 Holly Lake Rd Millsboro (19966) ***(G-4634)***
Bartlett & Bartlett LLC ... 302 653-7200
392 Hopewell Dr Clayton (19938) ***(G-838)***
Bartol Research Institute, Newark *Also called University of Delaware* ***(G-7620)***

Bartons Landscaping/Lawn Inc ...302 629-2213
20689 Sussex Hwy Seaford (19973) ***(G-8162)***
Bartsch John C, Dover *Also called Sunnyfield Contractors Inc* ***(G-2114)***
Barutopia Inc ...858 284-8830
2140 S Dupont Hwy Camden (19934) ***(G-540)***
Bas Home and Landscape Svcs ...302 354-0178
416 Hockessin Hills Rd Hockessin (19707) ***(G-2961)***
Basco Physical Therapy ...302 730-1294
1410 Joshua Clayton Rd Dover (19904) ***(G-1176)***
Base Enterprise Inc ...302 337-0548
14021 Quiddity Way Bridgeville (19933) ***(G-452)***
Base Line Transports L ...302 438-3092
452 Goodwick Dr Middletown (19709) ***(G-3963)***
Basell Capital Corporation ...302 683-8000
2 Righter Pkwy Ste 300 Wilmington (19803) ***(G-9257)***
Basemark Inc (PA) ...832 483-7093
3500 S Dupont Hwy Dover (19901) ***(G-1177)***
BASF Corporation ...302 992-5600
205 S James St Wilmington (19804) ***(G-9258)***
Basher & Son Enterprises Inc ...302 239-6584
1072 Yorklyn Rd Hockessin (19707) ***(G-2962)***
Basher & Son Welding, Hockessin *Also called Basher & Son Enterprises Inc* ***(G-2962)***
Basic Block Corp ...302 645-2000
4590 Highway One Ste 118 Rehoboth Beach (19971) ***(G-7855)***
Bastianelli Group Inc ...302 658-1500
231 Executive Dr Ste 15 Newark (19702) ***(G-6050)***
Bat Electronics Inc ...302 999-8855
1300 First State Blvd Wilmington (19804) ***(G-9259)***
Batescainelli LLC ...202 618-2040
319 Byview Ave Rhboth Bch Rehoboth Beach Rehoboth Beach (19971) ***(G-7856)***
Bathwa Limited ...213 550-3812
702 Delaware St New Castle (19720) ***(G-5068)***
Batta Inc ...302 737-3376
6 Garfield Way Newark (19713) ***(G-6051)***
Batta Environmental Assoc Inc (PA) ...302 737-3376
6 Garfield Way Newark (19713) ***(G-6052)***
Batta Laboratory, Newark *Also called Batta Environmental Assoc Inc* ***(G-6052)***
Batta Ramesh C Associates PA (PA) ...302 998-9463
4600 New Linden Hill Rd Wilmington (19808) ***(G-9260)***
Battaglia Associates Inc ...302 325-6100
11 Industrial Blvd New Castle (19720) ***(G-5069)***
Battaglia Electric Inc ...302 325-6100
11 Industrial Blvd New Castle (19720) ***(G-5070)***
Battaglia Joseph A & Diamond ...302 655-8868
900 Foulk Rd Ste 200 Wilmington (19803) ***(G-9261)***
Battaglia Mechanical Inc ...302 325-6100
11 Industrial Blvd New Castle (19720) ***(G-5071)***
Battle Proven Foundation ...703 216-1986
368 Artis Dr Dover (19904) ***(G-1178)***
Bauer Farms ...302 284-9722
396 Hayfield Rd Harrington (19952) ***(G-2816)***
Bauguess Electrical Svcs Inc ...302 737-5614
1400 Interchange Blvd Newark (19711) ***(G-6053)***
Bauls Towing & Services LLC ...302 999-9919
543 Old Baltimore Pike Newark (19702) ***(G-6054)***
Baumann Industries Inc ...302 593-1049
2412 W Heather Rd Ste 200 Wilmington (19803) ***(G-9262)***
Bausum & Duckett Elc Co Inc ...302 846-0536
38190 Old Stage Rd Delmar (19940) ***(G-973)***
Baxter Farms Inc ...302 856-1818
23073 Zoar Rd Georgetown (19947) ***(G-2447)***
Bay Animal Hospital LLC ...302 279-1082
3891 Dupont Pkwy Townsend (19734) ***(G-8762)***
Bay Area Market Place, Wilmington *Also called Hs Capital LLC* ***(G-10964)***
Bay Area Womens Care ...302 424-2200
306 Polk Ave Milford (19963) ***(G-4318)***
Bay Developers Inc ...302 736-0924
200 Weston Dr Dover (19904) ***(G-1179)***
Bay Forest Homeowners Assn ...302 537-6580
36115 Bay Forest Dr Ocean View (19970) ***(G-7757)***
Bay Resort Motel, Dewey Beach *Also called Moore Partnership* ***(G-1059)***
Bay Shippers LLC ...302 652-5005
1535 Matassino Rd New Castle (19720) ***(G-5072)***
Bay To Beach Builders Inc ...302 349-5099
11582 Sussex Hwy Farmington (19950) ***(G-2266)***
Bayada Home Health Care Inc ...302 424-8200
1016 N Walnut St Milford (19963) ***(G-4319)***
Bayada Home Health Care Inc ...302 655-1333
750 S Madison St Wilmington (19801) ***(G-9263)***
Bayada Home Health Care Inc ...856 231-1000
32 Reads Way New Castle (19720) ***(G-5073)***
Bayada Home Health Care Inc ...302 322-2300
15 Reads Way Ste 205 New Castle (19720) ***(G-5074)***
Bayada Home Health Care Inc ...302 655-1333
750 Shipyard Dr Ste 101 Wilmington (19801) ***(G-9264)***
Bayada Home Health Care Inc ...302 836-1000
200 Biddle Ave Ste 101 Newark (19702) ***(G-6055)***
Bayada Nurses, Newark *Also called Bayada Home Health Care Inc* ***(G-6055)***
Bayard House, Wilmington *Also called Home of Divine Providence Inc* ***(G-10938)***
Bayard, Eugene H, Georgetown *Also called Wilson Halbrook & Bayard PA* ***(G-2705)***
Bayesian Health Inc ...408 205-8035
251 Little Falls Dr Wilmington (19808) ***(G-9265)***
Bayhealth Med Ctr Inc-OCC Hlth ...302 678-1303
1275 S State St Dover (19901) ***(G-1180)***
Bayhealth Medical Center, Middletown *Also called Kent General Hospital* ***(G-4120)***
Bayhealth Medical Center Inc ...302 422-3311
21 W Clarke Ave Milford (19963) ***(G-4320)***
Bayhealth Medical Center Inc ...302 744-7033
35 Commerce Way Ste 100 Dover (19904) ***(G-1181)***
Bayhealth Medical Center Inc (PA) ...302 422-3311
640 S State St Dover (19901) ***(G-1182)***
Bayhealth Medical Group Ent ...302 339-8040
20930 Dupont Blvd # 202 Georgetown (19947) ***(G-2448)***
Bayly's Garage, Laurel *Also called Robert Bayly* ***(G-3283)***
Baymont Inn & Suites Newark ...302 453-1700
630 S College Ave Newark (19713) ***(G-6056)***
Baynard House Condominiums ...302 319-3740
2400 Baynard Blvd Wilmington (19802) ***(G-9266)***
Baynum Enterprises Inc (PA) ...302 629-6104
300 W Stein Hwy Seaford (19973) ***(G-8163)***
Baynum Enterprises Inc ...302 875-4477
307 N Central Ave Unit A Laurel (19956) ***(G-3196)***
Baynum Enterprises Inc ...302 934-8699
28632 Dupont Blvd Unit 20 Millsboro (19966) ***(G-4635)***
Bayshore Communications Inc ...302 737-2164
2839 Ogletown Rd Newark (19713) ***(G-6057)***
Bayshore Ford Truck Sales Inc (PA) ...302 656-3160
4003 N Dupont Hwy New Castle (19720) ***(G-5075)***
Bayshore Inc ...302 539-7200
Rr 1 Box 252 Ocean View (19970) ***(G-7758)***
Bayshore Records MGT LLC ...302 731-4477
300 Pencader Dr Newark (19702) ***(G-6058)***
Bayshore Trnsp Sys Inc (PA) ...302 366-0220
901 Dawson Dr Newark (19713) ***(G-6059)***
Bayshore Trnsp Sys Inc ...302 366-0220
300 Pencader Dr Newark (19702) ***(G-6060)***
Bayside At Bthany Lkes Clbhuse ...302 539-4378
38335 Old Mill Way Ocean View (19970) ***(G-7759)***
Bayside Exteriors LLC ...302 727-5288
32295 Nassau Rd Lewes (19958) ***(G-3363)***
Bayside Golf LLC DBA Bear Trap ...302 537-5600
7 Clubhouse Dr Ocean View (19970) ***(G-7760)***
Bayside Health Assn Chartered (PA) ...302 645-4700
1535 Savannah Rd Lewes (19958) ***(G-3364)***
Bayside Limousine ...302 644-6999
34026 Annas Way Unit 1 Millsboro (19966) ***(G-4636)***
Bayside Resort Golf Club ...302 436-3400
31806 Lakeview Dr Selbyville (19975) ***(G-8453)***
Bayside Sealcoating Supply ...302 697-6441
6453 Mud Mill Rd Camden Wyoming (19934) ***(G-618)***
Bayside Sports Club LLC ...302 436-3550
31381 Sorsyphia Selbyville (19975) ***(G-8454)***
Baytown Packhouse Inc ...936 340-2122
112 Capitol Trl Newark (19711) ***(G-6061)***
Baytown Systems Inc ...302 689-3421
2711 Centerville Rd # 400 Wilmington (19808) ***(G-9267)***
Bayview Endoscopy Center ...302 644-0455
33663 Bayview Med Dr 3 Lewes (19958) ***(G-3365)***
Bayville Postal Svc ...302 436-2715
37232 Lighthouse Rd Selbyville (19975) ***(G-8455)***
Baywood Greens ...302 947-9800
34026 Annas Way Unit 5 Millsboro (19966) ***(G-4637)***
Baywood Greens Golf Club ...302 947-9225
24 Ofc Rte Millsboro (19966) ***(G-4638)***
Baywood Greens Golf Club (PA) ...302 947-9800
32267 Clubhouse Way Millsboro (19966) ***(G-4639)***
Bb Custom Instruments ...302 339-3826
300a Nancy St Georgetown (19947) ***(G-2449)***
Bb Technologies Inc ...302 652-2300
801 N West St Fl 2 Wilmington (19801) ***(G-9268)***
Bbdg, Bear *Also called Be Blessed Design Group LLC* ***(G-45)***
Bbest LLC ...302 581-9963
1232 N King St Wilmington (19801) ***(G-9269)***
Bbg2x Transportation, Magnolia *Also called Hodges L Wooten* ***(G-3895)***
Bbhotel Corp (PA) ...939 272-3953
108 W 13th St Wilmington (19801) ***(G-9270)***
Bbsi, Dover *Also called Barrett Business Services Inc* ***(G-1173)***
Bc Consulting Inc ...302 234-7710
4905 Mermaid Blvd Wilmington (19808) ***(G-9271)***
Bc Home Health Care Services ...302 746-7844
3301 Green St Claymont (19703) ***(G-700)***
Bcbg, Wilmington *Also called Runway Liquidation LLC* ***(G-12494)***
Bcd Systems ...302 328-2070
34 Blevins Dr Ste 1 New Castle (19720) ***(G-5076)***
BCI, New Castle *Also called Brandywine Contractors Inc* ***(G-5106)***
Bdc-Healthit, Ocean View *Also called Dodd Health Innovation LLC* ***(G-7784)***
Bdo Usa LLP ...302 656-5500
4250 Lancaster Pike # 120 Wilmington (19805) ***(G-9272)***

ALPHABETIC

Be Better Hotels, Wilmington *Also called Bbhotel Corp* ***(G-9270)***
Be Blessed Design Group LLC 302 561-3793
808 Lowell Dr Bear (19701) ***(G-45)***
BE&k, Newark *Also called B E & K Engineering Company* ***(G-6034)***
Beach Associates Inc 866 744-9911
9 E Loockerman St Ste 2a Dover (19901) ***(G-1183)***
Beach Babies Child Care (PA) 302 644-1585
31169 Learning Ln Lewes (19958) ***(G-3366)***
Beach Babies Child Care 302 378-4778
6020 Summit Bridge Rd Townsend (19734) ***(G-8763)***
Beach Break & Bakrie 302 537-3800
123 Garfield Pkwy Bethany Beach (19930) ***(G-383)***
Beach Butler Services LLC 302 227-0114
28 Manor Dr Rehoboth Beach (19971) ***(G-7857)***
Beach House Dewey Hotel, Dewey Beach *Also called Dewey Beach House* ***(G-1055)***
Beach House Resources 703 980-3336
29l Atlantic Ave 199 Bethany Beach (19930) ***(G-384)***
Beach House Services 302 645-2554
26 Cripple Creek Run Milton (19968) ***(G-4867)***
Beach Mobile Home Supply 302 945-5611
32695 Long Neck Rd Unit 1 Millsboro (19966) ***(G-4640)***
Beach Tans & Hair Designs, Rehoboth Beach *Also called Beach Tans and Hair Design* ***(G-7858)***
Beach Tans and Hair Design 302 645-8267
23 Midway Shopping Ctr Rehoboth Beach (19971) ***(G-7858)***
Beach Time 302 644-2850
32191 Nassau Rd Lewes (19958) ***(G-3367)***
Beach View Motel, Rehoboth Beach *Also called Cooper Simpler Associates Inc* ***(G-7901)***
Beach-Net.com, Fenwick Island *Also called Coastal Images Inc* ***(G-2333)***
Beachballs Com LLC 302 628-8888
112 S Bradford St Seaford (19973) ***(G-8164)***
Beachview Chiropractic Center 302 539-7063
35202 Atlantic Ave Millville (19967) ***(G-4834)***
Beachview Family Health 302 537-8318
35202 Atlantic Ave Millville (19967) ***(G-4835)***
Beachview Mgmt Inc 302 227-3280
24049 Lews Georgtwn Hwy # 22 Georgetown (19947) ***(G-2450)***
Beacon Air Inc 302 323-1688
23 Parkway Cir Ste 9 New Castle (19720) ***(G-5077)***
Beacon Engineering LLC 302 864-8825
23318 Cedar Ln Georgetown (19947) ***(G-2451)***
Beacon Hospitality 302 249-0502
22297 Dupont Blvd Georgetown (19947) ***(G-2452)***
Beacon Medical Group PA 302 947-9767
18947 John J Williams Hwy # 303 Rehoboth Beach (19971) ***(G-7859)***
Beacon Motel 302 645-4888
514 E Savannah Rd Lewes (19958) ***(G-3368)***
Beacon Pediatrics LLC 302 645-8212
18947 J J Williams Hwy311 Rehoboth Beach (19971) ***(G-7860)***
Beam Construction Inc 302 537-2787
1 E Atlantic St Fenwick Island (19944) ***(G-2330)***
Beanstock Media Inc (PA) 415 912-1530
300 Delaware Ave Ste 1100 Wilmington (19801) ***(G-9273)***
Bear Alignment Center 302 655-9219
1317 N Scott St Wilmington (19806) ***(G-9274)***
Bear Associates LLC 302 735-5558
209 Massey Dr Dover (19904) ***(G-1184)***
Bear Chiropractic Center DC 302 836-8361
811 Governors Pl Bear (19701) ***(G-46)***
Bear Concrete, Bear *Also called Greggo & Ferrara Inc* ***(G-173)***
Bear Concrete Construction 302 834-3333
595 Walther Rd Newark (19702) ***(G-6062)***
Bear Early Education Center 302 836-5000
2884 Glasgow Ave Newark (19702) ***(G-6063)***
Bear Eye Assoc, Bear *Also called W Lee Mackewiz Od PA* ***(G-368)***
Bear Forge and Machine Co Inc 302 322-5199
147 School Bell Rd Bear (19701) ***(G-47)***
Bear Glasgow Dental 302 836-3750
1290 Peoples Plz Newark (19702) ***(G-6064)***
Bear Hospitality Inc 302 326-2500
875 Pulaski Hwy Bear (19701) ***(G-48)***
Bear Industries Inc 302 368-1311
15 Albe Dr Newark (19702) ***(G-6065)***
Bear Materials LLC (PA) 302 658-5241
4048 New Castle Ave New Castle (19720) ***(G-5078)***
Bear Trap Dunes, Ocean View *Also called Bear Trap Partners* ***(G-7761)***
Bear Trap Partners 302 537-5600
County Rte 84 Ocean View (19970) ***(G-7761)***
Bear Trap Sales 302 541-5454
21 Vil Grn Dr 101 Ocean View (19970) ***(G-7762)***
Bear-Glasgow Dental LLC 302 836-9330
1106 Pulaski Hwy Bear (19701) ***(G-49)***
Bear-Glasgow YMCA 302 836-9622
351 George Williams Way Newark (19702) ***(G-6066)***
Beasley Broadcast Group Inc 302 765-1160
812 Philadelphia Pike # 2 Wilmington (19809) ***(G-9275)***
Beasley FM Acquisition Corp 302 765-1160
812 Philadelphia Pike Wilmington (19809) ***(G-9276)***
Beast of East Baseball LLC 302 545-9094
916 Gray St New Castle (19720) ***(G-5079)***
Beatdapp Inc 310 903-0244
9 E Loockerman St Ste 311 Dover (19901) ***(G-1185)***
Beautiful Gate Outreach Center 302 472-3002
604 N Walnut St Wilmington (19801) ***(G-9277)***
Beautiful Lashes 302 983-9521
2513 N Tatnall St Wilmington (19802) ***(G-9278)***
Beautiful Smiles of Delaware 302 656-0558
4901 Limestone Rd Ste 1 Wilmington (19808) ***(G-9279)***
Beauty Max Inc 302 735-1705
1634 S Governors Ave Dover (19904) ***(G-1186)***
Beauty Purse Inc 424 210-7474
3500 S Dupont Hwy Dover (19901) ***(G-1187)***
Beaver Tree Service Inc 302 226-3564
108 2nd St Rehoboth Beach (19971) ***(G-7861)***
Beaverdam Pet Food 302 349-5299
12933 Sussex Hwy Greenwood (19950) ***(G-2714)***
Beazer Homes Corp 302 378-4161
202 Ann Dr Middletown (19709) ***(G-3964)***
Because Love Allows Compassion 302 674-2496
270 Beechwood Ave Dover (19901) ***(G-1188)***
Becker Morgan Group Inc 302 734-7950
309 S Governors Ave Dover (19904) ***(G-1189)***
Beckers Chimney and Roofg LLC 302 463-8294
209 Main St Wilmington (19804) ***(G-9280)***
Beckley Associates LLC 301 943-7343
32615 Widgeon Rd Ocean View (19970) ***(G-7763)***
Beebe Healthcare, Lewes *Also called Beebe Medical Center Inc* ***(G-3372)***
Beebe Healthcare 302 934-5052
28538 Dupont Blvd Unit 2 Millsboro (19966) ***(G-4641)***
Beebe Hospital Hs 302 645-3565
424 E Savannah Rd Lewes (19958) ***(G-3369)***
Beebe Imaging, Georgetown *Also called Beebe Medical Center Inc* ***(G-2453)***
Beebe Medical Center Inc 302 393-2056
810 Seabury Ave Milford (19963) ***(G-4321)***
Beebe Medical Center Inc 302 645-3100
18947 John J Williams Hwy # 201 Rehoboth Beach (19971) ***(G-7862)***
Beebe Medical Center Inc (PA) 302 645-3300
424 Savannah Rd Lewes (19958) ***(G-3370)***
Beebe Medical Center Inc 302 645-3300
440 Market St Lewes (19958) ***(G-3371)***
Beebe Medical Center Inc 302 645-3629
431 Savannah Rd Bldg C Lewes (19958) ***(G-3372)***
Beebe Medical Center Inc 302 541-4175
32550 Docs Pl Millville (19967) ***(G-4836)***
Beebe Medical Center Inc 302 947-9767
Long Neck Rd Millsboro (19966) ***(G-4642)***
Beebe Medical Center Inc 302 856-9729
21635 Biden Ave Georgetown (19947) ***(G-2453)***
Beebe Medical Center Inc 302 645-3289
38149 Terrace Rd Rehoboth Beach (19971) ***(G-7863)***
Beebe Medical Center Inc 302 645-3010
18941 John J Williams Hwy Rehoboth Beach (19971) ***(G-7864)***
BEEBE MEDICAL CENTER HOME HEAL, Lewes *Also called Beebe Medical Center Inc* ***(G-3370)***
BEEBE MEDICAL CENTER HOME HEAL, Lewes *Also called Beebe Physician Network Inc* ***(G-3374)***
BEEBE MEDICAL CENTER HOME HEAL, Lewes *Also called Beebe Medical Foundation* ***(G-3373)***
Beebe Medical Foundation 302 684-8579
611 Federal St Ste 2 Milton (19968) ***(G-4868)***
Beebe Medical Foundation (HQ) 302 644-2900
902 Savannah Rd Lewes (19958) ***(G-3373)***
Beebe Physician Network Inc 302 645-1805
1515 Savannah Rd Ste 103 Lewes (19958) ***(G-3374)***
Beebe School of Nursing 302 645-3251
424 Savannah Rd Lewes (19958) ***(G-3375)***
Beech Hill Press 302 588-0315
85 Beech Hill Dr Newark (19711) ***(G-6067)***
Beeline Services LLC 302 376-7399
865 Vance Neck Rd Middletown (19709) ***(G-3965)***
Beeson Funeral Home (PA) 302 764-2900
412 Philadelphia Pike Wilmington (19809) ***(G-9281)***
Beetles Playhouse Day Care 302 593-7321
1 Coronet Ct Newark (19713) ***(G-6068)***
Beginning Blessings Daycare, New Castle *Also called Beginning Blssngs Chldcare LLC* ***(G-5080)***
Beginning Blssngs Chldcare LLC 302 893-1726
23 Karen Ct New Castle (19720) ***(G-5080)***
Beginning Bridges Child Care 302 875-7428
6721 Sharptown Rd Laurel (19956) ***(G-3197)***
Beginnings and Beyond Inc 302 734-2464
402 Cowgill St Dover (19901) ***(G-1190)***
Behavioral Health Assoc 302 429-6200
1303 Del Ave Apt 1216 Wilmington (19806) ***(G-9282)***
Beimac LLC 302 677-1965
859 Golf Links Ln Magnolia (19962) ***(G-3881)***

Bekart Holding LLC 302 600-7000
1201 N Orange St Ste 7524 Wilmington (19801) ***(G-9283)***
Belchim Crop Prtection US Corp (HQ) 302 407-3590
2751 Centerville Rd # 100 Wilmington (19808) ***(G-9284)***
Belchim Crop Prtection USA LLC 302 407-3590
2751 Centerville Rd # 100 Wilmington (19808) ***(G-9285)***
Belco Inc 302 655-1561
909 Delaware Ave Wilmington (19806) ***(G-9286)***
Belfint Lyons & Shuman P A 302 225-0600
1011 Centre Rd Ste 310 Wilmington (19805) ***(G-9287)***
Bell Buoy Motel 302 227-6000
21 Vandyke St Dewey Beach (19971) ***(G-1054)***
Bell Manufacturing Company Inc 302 703-2684
31971 Carneros Ave Lewes (19958) ***(G-3376)***
Bell Painting & Wall Covering 302 738-8854
667 Dawson Dr Ste F Newark (19713) ***(G-6069)***
Bell Rock Capital LLC (PA) 302 227-7607
35568 Airport Rd Rehoboth Beach (19971) ***(G-7865)***
Bella Terra Landscapes LLC 302 422-9000
21429 Bella Terra Dr Lincoln (19960) ***(G-3838)***
Bellbuoy Inn, Dewey Beach *Also called Bell Buoy Motel* ***(G-1054)***
Belles and Beaus Photography 302 368-2468
238 E Seneca Dr Newark (19702) ***(G-6070)***
Bellevue Community Center 302 429-5859
500 Duncan Rd Ofc A Wilmington (19809) ***(G-9288)***
Bellevue Contractors LLC 302 655-1522
909 Delaware Ave Wilmington (19806) ***(G-9289)***
Bellevue Heart Group LLC 302 468-4500
1016 Delaware Ave Wilmington (19806) ***(G-9290)***
Bellevue Holding Company (PA) 302 655-1561
909 Delaware Ave Wilmington (19806) ***(G-9291)***
Bellevue Realty Co 302 655-1818
909 Delaware Ave Wilmington (19806) ***(G-9292)***
Bellevue Remodel & Design LLC 302 482-7200
222 Philadelphia Pike # 9 Wilmington (19809) ***(G-9293)***
Bellevue State Park, Wilmington *Also called Parks & Recreation Del Div* ***(G-12023)***
Bellex International Corp (PA) 302 791-5180
200 Bellevue Pkwy Ste 180 Wilmington (19809) ***(G-9294)***
Bellingers Jewelers 302 227-6410
20747 Coastal Hwy Rehoboth Beach (19971) ***(G-7866)***
Bellmoor, The, Rehoboth Beach *Also called Coastal Properties I LLC* ***(G-7895)***
Bells of Hope, New Castle *Also called Dimarquez Intl Ministries Inc* ***(G-5253)***
Bellwether Behavioral Health 856 769-2042
2520 Wrangle Hill Rd # 200 Bear (19701) ***(G-50)***
Belmont Villa Condominiums 302 368-1633
60 Welsh Tract Rd Ste 2b Newark (19713) ***(G-6071)***
Belotti R Landscaping & Nurs, Georgetown *Also called Richard Belotti* ***(G-2639)***
Ben-Dom Printing Company 302 737-9144
35 Salem Church Rd 43e Newark (19713) ***(G-6072)***
Benchmark Builders Inc (PA) 302 995-6945
818 First State Blvd Wilmington (19804) ***(G-9295)***
Benchmark Transmission Inc 302 792-2300
2610 Philadelphia Pike 1a Claymont (19703) ***(G-701)***
Benchmark Transmissions, Newark *Also called Powertrain Technology Inc* ***(G-7237)***
Benchmark Transmissions Inc 302 999-9400
1301 Centerville Rd Wilmington (19808) ***(G-9296)***
Bender Farms Llc 302 349-5574
13060 Bender Farm Rd Greenwood (19950) ***(G-2715)***
Bendom Printing, Newark *Also called Ben-Dom Printing Company* ***(G-6072)***
Beneficial Consumer Disc Co (HQ) 302 425-2500
301 N Walnut St Wilmington (19801) ***(G-9297)***
Beneficial Oklahoma Inc (HQ) 302 529-8701
301 N Walnut St Wilmington (19801) ***(G-9298)***
Benefit Administrators Del 302 234-1978
5708 Limestone Rd Wilmington (19808) ***(G-9299)***
Benefit Services Unlimited 302 479-5696
2500 Grubb Rd Ste 140 Wilmington (19810) ***(G-9300)***
Benesch Friedlander Coplan & 216 363-4500
222 Delaware Ave Ste 801 Wilmington (19801) ***(G-9301)***
Benevlent Prtective Order Elks 302 736-1903
200 Saulsbury Rd Dover (19904) ***(G-1191)***
Benevolent & Protective Order 302 424-2401
18951 Elks Lodge Rd Milford (19963) ***(G-4322)***
Benevolent Protectve Ordr Elks 302 629-2458
8846 Elks Rd Seaford (19973) ***(G-8165)***
Benitime Solutions Inc 302 476-8097
701 Foulk Rd Ste 2f Wilmington (19803) ***(G-9302)***
Benjamin Tanei 302 521-2033
404 Sitka Spruce Ln Townsend (19734) ***(G-8764)***
Benjamin B Smith Builders Inc 302 537-1916
54 Central Ave Ocean View (19970) ***(G-7764)***
Bennett & Bennett Inc 302 990-8939
122 Delaware St New Castle (19720) ***(G-5081)***
Bennett Det Prtective Agcy Inc (PA) 302 734-2480
335 Martin St Dover (19901) ***(G-1192)***
Bennett Electric, Frankford *Also called Wayne Bennett* ***(G-2397)***
Bennett Farms Inc 302 684-1627
24139 Sugar Hill Rd Milford (19963) ***(G-4323)***
Bennett Realty, Bethany Beach *Also called D M F Associates Inc* ***(G-395)***
Bennett Security Service, Dover *Also called Bennett Det Prtective Agcy Inc* ***(G-1192)***
Bennie Smith Funeral Home Inc (PA) 302 678-8747
717 W Division St Dover (19904) ***(G-1193)***
Bennie Smith Funeral Home Inc 302 934-9019
216 S Washington St Millsboro (19966) ***(G-4643)***
Benson Enterprise Inc 302 344-9183
11676 Park Dr Seaford (19973) ***(G-8166)***
Bentley Mills Inc 800 423-4709
2711 Centerville Rd # 400 Wilmington (19808) ***(G-9303)***
Benz Hydraulic Service, New Castle *Also called Benz Hydraulics Inc* ***(G-5082)***
Benz Hydraulics Inc (PA) 302 328-6648
153 S Dupont Hwy New Castle (19720) ***(G-5082)***
Beracah Homes Inc 302 349-4561
9590 Nantcke Bus Pk Dr Greenwood (19950) ***(G-2716)***
Berg, Fanny J MD, Wilmington *Also called Dr Fanny Berg P C* ***(G-10221)***
Berkshire At Limestone 302 635-7495
1526 Braken Ave Wilmington (19808) ***(G-9304)***
Berkshire Hataway Home Svcs 302 235-6431
88 Lantana Dr Hockessin (19707) ***(G-2963)***
Berley Security Systems Inc 302 791-9056
6701 Governor Printz Blvd Wilmington (19809) ***(G-9305)***
Berman Development Corp 302 323-1197
30 Highland Blvd New Castle (19720) ***(G-5083)***
Berman Development Corp 302 323-9522
2801 Stonebridge Blvd New Castle (19720) ***(G-5084)***
Bernard A Lewis DDS 302 943-0456
149 Great Geneva Dr Dover (19901) ***(G-1194)***
Bernard and Bernard Inc 302 999-7213
5187 W Woodmill Dr Ste 1 Wilmington (19808) ***(G-9306)***
Bernard Limpert 302 674-8280
1465 S Governors Ave Dover (19904) ***(G-1195)***
Bernard ND Ruth Siegel Jcc 302 478-5660
101 Garden Of Eden Rd Wilmington (19803) ***(G-9307)***
Bernard Personnel, Wilmington *Also called BP Staffing Inc* ***(G-9407)***
Bernardo Anthony J Jr Dr DDS 302 998-9244
301 S Dupont Rd Wilmington (19805) ***(G-9308)***
Bernardon PC 302 622-9550
123 S Justison St Ste 101 Wilmington (19801) ***(G-9309)***
Bernices Edtl Scl AG Ctr Inc 302 651-0286
2516 W 4th St Wilmington (19805) ***(G-9310)***
Bernieface Productions LLC 302 561-0273
11 Wildfields Ct Bear (19701) ***(G-51)***
Berrodin South Inc 302 575-0500
20 Mccullough Dr New Castle (19720) ***(G-5085)***
Berry International Inc 302 674-1300
606 Pear St Unit 1 Dover (19904) ***(G-1196)***
Berry Refrigeration Co 302 733-0933
2 Garfield Way Newark (19713) ***(G-6073)***
Berry Short Funeral Home Inc 302 422-8091
119 Nw Front St Milford (19963) ***(G-4324)***
Berry Van Lines, Dover *Also called Diamond State Corporation* ***(G-1425)***
Besecure LLC 855 897-0650
16192 Coastal Hwy Lewes (19958) ***(G-3377)***
Bessemer Trust Company 302 230-2675
1007 N Orange St Ste 1450 Wilmington (19801) ***(G-9311)***
Bessemer Trust Company Del NA 212 708-9182
1007 N Orange St Ste 1450 Wilmington (19801) ***(G-9312)***
Best Buddies International Inc 302 691-3187
1401 Penns Ave Ste 104 Wilmington (19806) ***(G-9313)***
Best Granite LLC 302 644-8302
95 Tulip Dr Lewes (19958) ***(G-3378)***
Best Office Pros 302 629-4561
26082 Butler Branch Rd Seaford (19973) ***(G-8167)***
Best Roofing and Siding Co 302 678-5700
5091 N Dupont Hwy Dover (19901) ***(G-1197)***
Best Stoneworks of Delaware 302 765-3497
3015 Bellevue Ave Wilmington (19802) ***(G-9314)***
Best Stucco LLC 302 650-3620
304 Jefferson Ave New Castle (19720) ***(G-5086)***
Best Western, Dover *Also called Mark One LLC* ***(G-1819)***
Best Western Goldleaf Ht LLC 302 226-1100
1400 Hwy 1 Rehoboth Beach (19971) ***(G-7867)***
Best Western Newark 302 738-3400
260 Chapman Rd Newark (19702) ***(G-6074)***
Best Western Plus, Bear *Also called Bear Hospitality Inc* ***(G-48)***
Best Western Smyrna Inn, Smyrna *Also called 190 Stadium LLC* ***(G-8558)***
Bestemps 302 674-4357
385 W North St Dover (19904) ***(G-1198)***
Bestemps Career Asso Resume Sv, Dover *Also called Career Associates Inc* ***(G-1255)***
Bestemps of Dover, Dover *Also called Bestemps* ***(G-1198)***
Bestfield Associates Inc 302 633-6361
200 Mary Ella Dr Wilmington (19805) ***(G-9315)***
Bestfield Homes, Wilmington *Also called Bestfield Associates Inc* ***(G-9315)***
Bestrans Inc 302 824-0909
19 Davidson Ln Frnt Frnt New Castle (19720) ***(G-5087)***
Beth A Renzulli M D 302 449-0420
102 Sleepy Hollow Dr # 200 Middletown (19709) ***(G-3966)***
Beth Sholom Congregation 302 734-5578
340 N Queen St Dover (19904) ***(G-1199)***

ALPHABETIC

Beth Trucking Inc — 918 814-2970
129 Crikmoe Blvd Newark (19702) *(G-6075)*
Bethany Auto Parts Inc (PA) — 302 539-0555
13 Atlantic Ave Ocean View (19970) *(G-7765)*
Bethany Bch Hair Snippery Inc — 302 539-8344
32566 Docs Pl Unit 6 Millville (19967) *(G-4837)*
Bethany Beach Bed & Breakfast — 301 651-2278
33391 Ocean Pines Ln Bethany Beach (19930) *(G-385)*
Bethany Beach Books — 302 539-2522
99 Garfield Pkwy Bethany Beach (19930) *(G-386)*
Bethany Beach Ocean — 302 539-3201
99 Hollywood St Bethany Beach (19930) *(G-387)*
Bethany Beach Vlntr Fire Co (PA) — 302 539-7700
215 Hollywood St Bethany Beach (19930) *(G-388)*
Bethany Club Tennis LLC — 302 539-5111
30078 Cedar Neck Rd Ocean View (19970) *(G-7766)*
Bethany Dental Association — 302 537-1200
32895 Coastal Hwy # 102 Bethany Beach (19930) *(G-389)*
Bethany Primary Care — 302 537-1100
33188 Coastal Hwy Unit 4 Bethany Beach (19930) *(G-390)*
Bethany Resort Furn Whse — 302 251-4101
145 Dixon St Selbyville (19975) *(G-8456)*
Bethany Tennis Ctr,, Ocean View Also called Bethany Club Tennis LLC *(G-7766)*
Bethany Travel Inc — 302 933-0955
28412 Dupont Blvd Ste 103 Millsboro (19966) *(G-4644)*
Bethany-Fenwick Chamber — 302 539-2100
36913 Coastal Hwy Fenwick Island (19944) *(G-2331)*
Bethel United Methodist Church — 302 645-9426
129 W 4th St Lewes (19958) *(G-3379)*
Bethel Villa Apartments, Wilmington Also called Roizman & Associates Inc *(G-12465)*
Bethel Villa Associates LP — 302 426-9688
506 E 5th St Fl 2 Wilmington (19801) *(G-9316)*
Bethel Villas 2009 Assoc LP — 610 278-1733
506 E 5th St Wilmington (19801) *(G-9317)*
Bethrant Industries LLC — 484 343-5435
7 Midfield Rd New Castle (19720) *(G-5088)*
Bettan Trucking LLC — 302 841-3834
19347 Beaver Dam Rd Lewes (19958) *(G-3380)*
Better Business Bureau of De — 302 221-5255
60 Reads Way New Castle (19720) *(G-5089)*
Better Homes Laurel II Inc — 302 875-4282
2600 Daniel St 3000 Laurel (19956) *(G-3198)*
Better Homes of Laurel Inc — 302 875-4281
3000 Daniel St Laurel (19956) *(G-3199)*
Betterlving Ptio Snroms Dlmrva — 302 251-0000
32442 Royal Blvd Unit 1 Dagsboro (19939) *(G-882)*
Betts & Abram PA LLC — 302 856-7755
15 S Race St Georgetown (19947) *(G-2454)*
Betts Garage, Newark Also called Betts Texaco and B & G GL Inc *(G-6076)*
Betts Texaco and B & G GL Inc — 302 834-2284
2806 Pulaski Hwy Newark (19702) *(G-6076)*
Bettys — 302 233-2675
140 N Landing Dr Milford (19963) *(G-4325)*
BETz&betz Enterprises LLC — 302 602-0613
528 W 3rd St Wilmington (19801) *(G-9318)*
Bever Mobility Products Inc — 312 375-0300
2711 Centerville Rd Wilmington (19808) *(G-9319)*
Beverly Bove Attorney At Law, Wilmington Also called Beverly L Bove PA *(G-9320)*
Beverly L Bove PA — 302 777-3500
1020 W 18th St Ste 2 Wilmington (19802) *(G-9320)*
Beverlys Help In Hand — 302 651-9304
2520 W 4th St Wilmington (19805) *(G-9321)*
Bew Productions — 302 547-8661
1004 Berkeley Rd Wilmington (19807) *(G-9322)*
Bewitched, Dover Also called Actors Attic *(G-1084)*
Beyond The Studs, Wilmington Also called BTS Enterprises Inc *(G-9496)*
BF Disc Inc — 302 691-6351
103 Foulk Rd Wilmington (19803) *(G-9323)*
BFI Waste Services LLC — 302 284-4440
907 Willow Grove Rd Felton (19943) *(G-2274)*
BFI Waste Services LLC — 302 658-4097
1420 New York Ave Wilmington (19801) *(G-9324)*
Bfpe International Inc — 302 346-4800
155 Commerce Way Dover (19904) *(G-1200)*
Bg Farms Inc — 302 875-2167
Watson Rd Laurel (19956) *(G-3200)*
Bg Truck & Trailor Repair — 302 455-9171
4917 Summit Bridge Rd Middletown (19709) *(G-3967)*
Bg Welding LLC — 302 228-7260
14047 Redden Rd Bridgeville (19933) *(G-453)*
Bgdedge — 302 477-1734
3652 Silverside Rd Wilmington (19810) *(G-9325)*
Bgi Print Solutions — 302 234-2825
4142 Ogletown Stanton Rd Newark (19713) *(G-6077)*
Bgi Print Solutions — 302 234-2825
1109 Oakland Ct Newark (19711) *(G-6078)*
Bgp Publicity Inc — 302 234-9500
1214 Old Lancaster Pike # 1 Hockessin (19707) *(G-2964)*
Bhaskar Palekar MD PA — 302 645-1805
1526 Savannah Rd Ste 1 Lewes (19958) *(G-3381)*

Bhaskar S Palekar MD PA — 302 645-1806
1526 Savannah Rd Ste 2 Lewes (19958) *(G-3382)*
Bi-State Feeders LLC — 302 398-3408
16054 S Dupont Hwy Harrington (19952) *(G-2817)*
Bia Separations Inc — 510 740-4045
1000 N West St Ste 1200 Wilmington (19801) *(G-9326)*
BIAD, Dover Also called Brain Injury Association Del *(G-1228)*
Biblion — 302 644-2210
205 2nd St Lewes (19958) *(G-3383)*
Biddle Capital Management Inc — 302 369-6789
220 Continental Dr # 202 Newark (19713) *(G-6079)*
Biderman Golf Club, Wilmington Also called Hunt Vicmead Club *(G-10974)*
Bidermann Golf Course, Wilmington Also called Hunt Vicmead Club *(G-10973)*
Biehl & Co LP — 302 594-9700
1 Hausel Rd Wilmington (19801) *(G-9327)*
Bif III Holtwood LLC — 819 561-2722
2711 Centerville Rd # 400 Wilmington (19808) *(G-9328)*
Bifferato Gentilotti LLC (PA) — 302 429-1900
4250 Lancaster Pike Ste 1 Wilmington (19805) *(G-9329)*
Bifferato Gentilotti LLC — 302 429-1900
4250 Lancaster Pike Wilmington (19805) *(G-9330)*
Big Brthers Big Sisters of Del — 302 998-3577
413 Larch Cir Wilmington (19804) *(G-9331)*
Big Centric, Wilmington Also called Dongjin Usa Inc *(G-10198)*
Big Chill Inc — 302 727-5568
19406 Coastal Hwy Rehoboth Beach (19971) *(G-7868)*
Big Dog Farm LLC — 302 841-7721
12 Crossgate Dr Seaford (19973) *(G-8168)*
Big Stone Hunting Club — 302 424-7592
687 New Wharf Rd Milford (19963) *(G-4326)*
Big Time Towing LLC — 302 510-1160
913 N Market St Ste 200 Wilmington (19801) *(G-9332)*
Big Tomorrow LLC — 650 714-3912
800 Delaware Ave Wilmington (19801) *(G-9333)*
Big Toy Custom Car Care Inc — 302 668-6729
1806 Tulip St Wilmington (19805) *(G-9334)*
Biggs & Battaglia — 302 655-9677
921 N Orange St Wilmington (19801) *(G-9335)*
Biggs Museum of American Art, Dover Also called Biggs Swell C Mseum Amercn Art *(G-1201)*
Biggs Swell C Mseum Amercn Art — 302 674-2111
406 Federal St Dover (19901) *(G-1201)*
Bihbrand Inc — 302 223-4330
16192 Coastal Hwy Lewes (19958) *(G-3384)*
Bijan K Sorouri MD PA — 302 453-9171
10 Darwin Dr Ste C Newark (19711) *(G-6080)*
Bijan Sorouri, Newark Also called Parviz Sorouri Md PA *(G-7179)*
Bijoti Inc — 908 916-7764
1808 N Washington St Wilmington (19802) *(G-9336)*
Bilcare Research Inc — 302 838-3200
1389 School House Rd Delaware City (19706) *(G-949)*
Bill Cannons Garage Inc — 302 436-4200
Rr 2 Box 125 Selbyville (19975) *(G-8457)*
Bill Luke Team, Wilmington Also called Real Estate Partners LLC *(G-12343)*
Bill M Douthat Jr — 407 977-2273
17468 Slipper Shell Way # 16 Lewes (19958) *(G-3385)*
Bill Rust Plumbing — 302 422-6061
64 Deer Valley Rd Harrington (19952) *(G-2818)*
Bill Torbert — 302 734-9804
335 Grey Fox Ln Dover (19904) *(G-1202)*
Bill Ward Inc — 302 762-6600
1010 Philadelphia Pike Wilmington (19809) *(G-9337)*
Billows Electric Supply Co Inc — 302 996-9133
480 First State Blvd Wilmington (19804) *(G-9338)*
Bills Home Care Service LLC — 302 526-2071
160 Beech Dr Dover (19904) *(G-1203)*
Bills Printers Service — 302 798-0482
718 Elmtree Ln Claymont (19703) *(G-702)*
Billy Warren Son — 302 349-5767
286 Burrsville Rd Greenwood (19950) *(G-2717)*
Bilski, William F Do, Newark Also called Family Doctors *(G-6568)*
Bimbo Bakeries Usa Inc — 302 328-7970
78 Southgate Blvd New Castle (19720) *(G-5090)*
Bimbo Bakeries Usa Inc — 302 328-0837
32 Parkway Cir New Castle (19720) *(G-5091)*
Bin 66 Fine Wine & Spirit — 302 227-6966
20729 Coastal Hwy Rehoboth Beach (19971) *(G-7869)*
Binkley Horticulture Services — 484 459-2391
1524 Clinton St Wilmington (19806) *(G-9339)*
Binkley Hurst LP — 302 628-3135
22375 Sussex Hwy Seaford (19973) *(G-8169)*
Bio Medic Corporation (PA) — 302 628-4300
742 Sussex Ave Seaford (19973) *(G-8170)*
Bio-Mdcal Applications Del Inc — 302 366-0129
230 E Main St Ste 325 Newark (19711) *(G-6081)*
Bio-Mdical Applications of Del — 302 998-7568
4923 Ogletown Stanton Rd Newark (19713) *(G-6082)*
Biomatik Usa LLC — 416 273-4858
105 Silverside Rd 501 Wilmington (19809) *(G-9340)*

ALPHABETIC SECTION

Biomechsys Incorporated 818 305-4436
  160 Greentree Dr Ste 101 Dover (19904) *(G-1204)*
Biomedic Data Systems Inc 302 628-4100
  1 Silas Rd Seaford (19973) *(G-8171)*
Biotek Remedys Inc (PA) 877 246-9104
  2 Penns Way Ste 404 New Castle (19720) *(G-5092)*
Birdie Ssot LLC 857 361-6883
  3500 S Dupont Hwy Dover (19901) *(G-1205)*
Birdsong Books 302 378-7274
  1322 Bayview Rd Middletown (19709) *(G-3968)*
Bireley & Kortvelesy PA 302 539-0311
  53 Atlantic Ave Ste 2 Ocean View (19970) *(G-7767)*
Biritek LLC 949 556-3943
  8 The Grn Ste A Dover (19901) *(G-1206)*
Birth Center Holistic Women 302 658-2229
  620 Churchmans Rd Ste 101 Newark (19702) *(G-6083)*
Birthdayboxio Inc 302 990-2616
  251 Little Falls Dr Wilmington (19808) *(G-9341)*
Bishop Associates 302 838-1270
  1235 Peoples Plz Newark (19702) *(G-6084)*
Bishop Enterprises Corporation 302 379-2884
  2207 Concord Pike Ste 412 Wilmington (19803) *(G-9342)*
Bits & Bytes Inc 302 674-2999
  3895 N Dupont Hwy Dover (19901) *(G-1207)*
Bitta Monk Entertainment Inc 916 969-4430
  25 Winchester Rd Apt G Newark (19713) *(G-6085)*
Bittenpixel, Rehoboth Beach *Also called Gulch Group LLC* *(G-7956)*
Biz TEC Inc 302 227-1967
  18806 John J Williams Hwy Rehoboth Beach (19971) *(G-7870)*
Bizboost Inc 732 865-8050
  4023 Kennett Pike 50297 Wilmington (19807) *(G-9343)*
Bizzy Bees Home Daycare LLC 302 376-9245
  815 S Cass St Middletown (19709) *(G-3969)*
Bjk Plumbing & Heating LLC 215 828-2556
  49 Macintosh Cir Magnolia (19962) *(G-3882)*
Bk 2 Si LLC 800 246-2677
  1201 N Orange St Ste 600 Wilmington (19801) *(G-9344)*
Bk Lord Trucking 302 284-7890
  1428 Turkey Point Rd Felton (19943) *(G-2275)*
Bk Temp Home Care 302 575-1400
  2101 N Tatnall St Wilmington (19802) *(G-9345)*
Bki Enterprises LLC 302 541-5317
  23 Willow Oak Ave Ocean View (19970) *(G-7768)*
Black & Decker Corporation 302 738-0250
  1207 Drummond Plz Newark (19711) *(G-6086)*
Black & Decker Inc (HQ) 860 827-3861
  1207 Drummond Plz Newark (19711) *(G-6087)*
Black & Veatch Corporation 302 798-0200
  200 Bellevue Pkwy Ste 430 Wilmington (19809) *(G-9346)*
Black Dog Construction LLC 302 530-4967
  1104 Oakland Ct Newark (19711) *(G-6088)*
Black Dragon Corporation 617 470-9230
  40 E Main St 1010 Newark (19711) *(G-6089)*
Black Math Labs Inc 858 349-9446
  8 The Grn Ste A Dover (19901) *(G-1208)*
Black Rock Inc 302 797-2009
  400 Bellevue Pkwy Wilmington (19809) *(G-9347)*
Blackgrid Consulting LLC 302 319-2013
  2711 Centerville Rd Wilmington (19808) *(G-9348)*
Blackrock Enhnced Globl Dvdend 800 441-7762
  100 Bellevue Pkwy Wilmington (19809) *(G-9349)*
Blackrock Financial Management 302 797-2000
  400 Bellevue Pkwy Wilmington (19809) *(G-9350)*
Blackrock Funds II 302 797-2000
  100 Bellevue Pkwy Wilmington (19809) *(G-9351)*
Blackrock Global Long 302 797-2000
  100 Bellevue Pkwy Wilmington (19809) *(G-9352)*
Blackrock Income Trust Inc 800 441-7762
  100 Bellevue Pkwy Wilmington (19809) *(G-9353)*
Blackrock Instnl Mgt Corp 302 797-2000
  100 Bellevue Pkwy Wilmington (19809) *(G-9354)*
Blackrock Intermediate 302 797-2000
  100 Bellevue Pkwy Wilmington (19809) *(G-9355)*
Blackrock LNG-Hrzon Eqity Fund 800 441-7762
  100 Bellevue Pkwy Wilmington (19809) *(G-9356)*
Blackrock Mncpl 2030 Trget Ter 800 882-0052
  100 Bellevue Pkwy Wilmington (19809) *(G-9357)*
Blackrock Mncpl Income Inv Qlt 800 441-7762
  100 Bellevue Pkwy Wilmington (19809) *(G-9358)*
Blackrock Mnhldngs Cal Qlty Fu 800 441-7762
  100 Bellevue Pkwy Wilmington (19809) *(G-9359)*
Blackrock Mnhldngs NJ Qlty Fun 800 441-7762
  100 Bellevue Pkwy Wilmington (19809) *(G-9360)*
Blackrock NY Mncpl Income Qlty 800 441-7762
  100 Bellevue Pkwy Wilmington (19809) *(G-9361)*
Blackrock NY Mncpl Income Tr I 800 441-7762
  100 Bellevue Pkwy Wilmington (19809) *(G-9362)*
Blackrock NY Municpl Income Tr 800 441-7762
  100 Bellevue Pkwy Wilmington (19809) *(G-9363)*
Blackrock Total, Wilmington *Also called Blackrock Funds II* *(G-9351)*

Blackstone Building Group LLC 302 824-4632
  3310 Coachman Rd Wilmington (19803) *(G-9364)*
Blackthorn Advisory Group LLC 302 442-6484
  750 Shipyard Dr Ste 200 Wilmington (19801) *(G-9365)*
Blacktop Sealcoating Inc 302 234-2243
  511 Paisley Pl Newark (19711) *(G-6090)*
Blackwater Village Association 302 541-4700
  31275 Mohican Dr Dagsboro (19939) *(G-883)*
Blade Platforms LLC 646 431-1666
  1000 N West St Wilmington (19801) *(G-9366)*
Blades H V A C Services 302 539-4436
  32798 Swamp Rd Dagsboro (19939) *(G-884)*
Blair Carmean Masonry 302 934-6103
  24373 Gravel Hill Rd Georgetown (19947) *(G-2455)*
Blair A Jones DDS 302 226-1115
  34359 Carpenters Way Lewes (19958) *(G-3386)*
Blair Computing Systems Inc 302 453-8947
  500 Creek View Rd Ste 200 Newark (19711) *(G-6091)*
Blake and Vaughan Engrg Inc 302 888-1780
  800 Woodlawn Ave Wilmington (19805) *(G-9367)*
Blake Computers 540 843-0656
  438 S Lake Dr Milton (19968) *(G-4869)*
Blanca O Lim MD 302 653-1669
  38 Deak Dr Smyrna (19977) *(G-8581)*
Blank Rome LLP 302 425-6400
  1201 N Market St Ste 800 Wilmington (19801) *(G-9368)*
Blaze Coin LLC 509 768-2249
  8 The Grn Ste B Dover (19901) *(G-1209)*
Blaze Systems Corporation 302 733-7235
  300 Creek View Rd Ste 204 Newark (19711) *(G-6092)*
Blenheim Homes, Newark *Also called Blenheim Management Company* *(G-6093)*
Blenheim Management Company 302 254-0100
  220 Continental Dr # 410 Newark (19713) *(G-6093)*
Blessed Beginnings Lrng Ctr 302 838-9112
  117 Portside Ct Bear (19701) *(G-52)*
Blessed Giving 302 856-4551
  40 Ingramtown Rd Georgetown (19947) *(G-2456)*
Blind Factory 302 838-1211
  3316 Kirkwood Hwy Wilmington (19808) *(G-9369)*
Blindsight Delaware LLC 302 998-5913
  2915 Newport Gap Pike Wilmington (19808) *(G-9370)*
Blix Inc 347 753-8035
  40 E Main St Ste 556 Newark (19711) *(G-6094)*
BLJ&d Flagging Llc 302 272-0574
  820 Carvel Dr Dover (19901) *(G-1210)*
Blm Industries Inc 302 238-7745
  19930 Lowes Crossing Rd Millsboro (19966) *(G-4645)*
Blockfreight Inc 614 350-2252
  16192 Coastal Hwy Lewes (19958) *(G-3387)*
Blockweather Holdings LLC 844 644-6837
  8 The Grn Ste 6338 Dover (19901) *(G-1211)*
Blog - Care First Dental Team 302 741-2044
  1250 S Governors Ave Dover (19904) *(G-1212)*
Blood Bank of Delmarva Inc (PA) 302 737-1151
  100 Hygeia Dr Newark (19713) *(G-6095)*
Blood Bank of Delmarva Inc 302 737-8400
  913 N Market St Ste 905 Wilmington (19801) *(G-9371)*
Bloom Consulting 302 584-1592
  2812 Landon Dr Wilmington (19810) *(G-9372)*
Bloom Energy Corporation 302 733-7524
  611 Interchange Blvd Newark (19711) *(G-6096)*
Bloomfield Trucking Inc 302 834-6922
  P.O. Box 1284 Middletown (19709) *(G-3970)*
Blossic, Tamara DC, Hockessin *Also called Hockessin Chrpractic Centre PA* *(G-3048)*
Blossom Philadelphia 215 242-4200
  3518 Silverside Rd Ste 22 Wilmington (19810) *(G-9373)*
Blu Dragon Studio Inc 302 722-6227
  2035 Sunset Lake Rd B2 Newark (19702) *(G-6097)*
Blu H20 Ltd 302 875-4810
  120 Horsey Ave Laurel (19956) *(G-3201)*
Bluchill Inc 302 658-2638
  19 Davidson Ln Bldg 7 New Castle (19720) *(G-5093)*
Blue Arrow Contract Manufactur 302 738-2583
  115 Pencader Dr Newark (19702) *(G-6098)*
Blue Chip Services Ltd 302 798-5010
  501 Silverside Rd Ste 90 Wilmington (19809) *(G-9374)*
Blue Cross, Wilmington *Also called Highmarks Inc* *(G-10906)*
Blue Diamond Dental PA 302 655-8387
  2300 Penns Ave Ste 2c Wilmington (19806) *(G-9375)*
Blue Energy International LLC 480 941-5100
  1209 N Orange St Wilmington (19801) *(G-9376)*
Blue Energy Partners LLC 480 941-5100
  1209 N Orange St Wilmington (19801) *(G-9377)*
Blue Hen Auction Co LLC 302 697-6096
  1528 E Lebanon Rd Dover (19901) *(G-1213)*
Blue Hen Bzzrds Dspose-All LLC 302 856-0913
  34026 Annas Way Unit 3 Millsboro (19966) *(G-4646)*
Blue Hen Courier, Camden Wyoming *Also called Charles E Carlson* *(G-623)*
Blue Hen Dental LLC 302 538-0448
  231 S Dupont Blvd Smyrna (19977) *(G-8582)*

ALPHABETIC SECTION

Blue Hen Hotel LLC 302 266-0354
400 David Hollowell Dr Newark (19716) *(G-6099)*

Blue Hen Insulation Inc 302 424-4482
2844 Deer Valley Rd Milford (19963) *(G-4327)*

Blue Hen Masonry Inc 302 398-8737
3296 Andrewville Rd Greenwood (19950) *(G-2718)*

Blue Hen Photography 302 690-3259
111 Clear Creek Dr Bear (19701) *(G-53)*

Blue Hen Physical Therapy Inc 302 453-1588
1501 Casho Mill Rd Ste 6 Newark (19711) *(G-6100)*

Blue Hen Spring Works Inc 302 422-6600
112 N Rehoboth Blvd Milford (19963) *(G-4328)*

Blue Hen Surgery Center The, Dover Also called Dover Ophthalmology Asc LLC *(G-1462)*

Blue Hen Utility Services Inc 302 273-3167
473 Old Airport Rd Bldg 4 New Castle (19720) *(G-5094)*

Blue Heron Discount Cards, Bear Also called Blue Heron Ent Inc *(G-54)*

Blue Heron Ent Inc 302 834-1521
600 Garron Point Pass Bear (19701) *(G-54)*

Blue Marble Logistics LLC (PA) 302 661-4390
800 N King St Ste 102 Wilmington (19801) *(G-9378)*

Blue Marlin Ice LLC 302 697-7800
273 Walnut Shade Rd Dover (19904) *(G-1214)*

Blue Mountain Apparel La LLC 646 787-5679
40 E Main St Ste 899 Newark (19711) *(G-6101)*

Blue Ocean Systems LLC 866 355-5989
3511 Silverside Rd # 204 Wilmington (19810) *(G-9379)*

Blue Pie Productions USA LLC 917 817-7174
3 Germay Dr Ste 44002 Wilmington (19804) *(G-9380)*

Blue Ribbon Oil Company Inc 302 832-7601
819 S Dupont Hwy New Castle (19720) *(G-5095)*

Blue Ribbon Petroleum, New Castle Also called Blue Ribbon Oil Company Inc *(G-5095)*

Blue Ridge Air Inc 302 323-4800
137 N Dupont Hwy New Castle (19720) *(G-5096)*

Blue Ridge Home Care Inc 302 397-8211
9 E Loockerman St Ste 210 Dover (19901) *(G-1215)*

Blue Skies Solar & Wind Power 302 326-0856
261 Airport Rd New Castle (19720) *(G-5097)*

Blue Sky Clean 302 584-5800
293 Carlow Dr Wilmington (19808) *(G-9381)*

Blue Sky Management, Frankford Also called Winifred Ellen Erbe *(G-2399)*

Blue Swan Cleaners Inc (PA) 302 652-7607
2001 Delaware Ave Wilmington (19806) *(G-9382)*

Blueberry Lne Brry Frm & Orchd 302 238-7067
24133 Blueberry Ln Frankford (19945) *(G-2347)*

Bluedot Technologies Inc 415 800-1890
2035 Sunset Lake Rd B2 Newark (19702) *(G-6102)*

Bluent LLC 832 476-8459
16192 Coastal Hwy Lewes (19958) *(G-3388)*

Bluestone AI LLC 302 477-0370
728 Westcliff Rd Wilmington (19803) *(G-9383)*

Bluestone Communication 302 478-4200
3600 Silverside Rd Wilmington (19810) *(G-9384)*

Bluevault LLC 302 425-4367
1300 N Broom St Wilmington (19806) *(G-9385)*

Bluewater Wind LLC 302 731-7020
700 Pilottown Rd Lewes (19958) *(G-3389)*

Bluffs, The, Newark Also called Sheldon Limited Partnership *(G-7414)*

BMA of Smyrna 302 659-5220
Gateway Shopping Ctr N Smyrna (19977) *(G-8583)*

Bml App Development 302 528-7281
123 Berry Dr Wilmington (19808) *(G-9386)*

Bmo Delaware Trust Company 302 652-1660
20 Montchanin Rd Ste 240 Wilmington (19807) *(G-9387)*

Bmp Sunstone Corporation 610 940-1675
3711 Kennett Pike Ste 200 Wilmington (19807) *(G-9388)*

BNai Brith Snor Ctzens Hsing 302 798-6846
8000 Society Dr Claymont (19703) *(G-703)*

Bny Mellon, Wilmington Also called Bank of New York Mellon Corp *(G-9243)*

Board of Public Works Inc 302 645-6450
116 American Legion Rd Lewes (19958) *(G-3390)*

Boardwalk Builders Inc 302 227-5754
37395 Main St Rehoboth Beach (19971) *(G-7871)*

Boardwalk Plaza Incorporated (PA) 302 227-0441
2 Olive Ave Rehoboth Beach (19971) *(G-7872)*

Bob Lafazia 302 633-1456
2635 Grenton Dr Wilmington (19808) *(G-9389)*

Bob Reynolds Backhoe Services 302 239-4711
1124 Old Wilmington Rd Hockessin (19707) *(G-2965)*

Bob Simmons Agency 302 698-1970
1460 E Lebanon Rd Dover (19901) *(G-1216)*

Bob's Custom Clubs, Wilmington Also called Bob Lafazia *(G-9389)*

Bobby Wilson Entertainment LLC 302 233-6463
1561 Nthan Mitchell Rd Dover (19904) *(G-1217)*

Bobcat of New Castle LLC (PA) 732 780-6880
325 Quigley Blvd New Castle (19720) *(G-5098)*

Bobcat of Sussex County, Delmar Also called Judd Brook 5 LLC *(G-1011)*

Bobola Farm Florist 302 492-3367
5268 Forrest Ave Dover (19904) *(G-1218)*

Bobola Farm, Dover Also called Bobola Farm & Florist *(G-1218)*

Bobs Marine Service Inc 302 539-3711
Routes 17 & 26 Ocean View (19970) *(G-7769)*

Bodell Bove LLC 302 655-6749
1225 N King St Ste 1000 Wilmington (19801) *(G-9390)*

Bodied By Tru, Middletown Also called Tru Beauti LLC *(G-4269)*

Bodies Dar Mkts Coin Laundries, Georgetown Also called Om Shiv Groceries Inc *(G-2611)*

Body and Soul Fitness LLC 302 536-1278
1035 W Stein Hwy Seaford (19973) *(G-8172)*

Body Double Swimwear 302 537-1444
1007 Coastal Hwy Selbyville (19944) *(G-8458)*

Body Ease Therapy 610 314-0780
105 Louviers Dr Newark (19711) *(G-6103)*

Body/Mind & Spirit Massage Thr 302 453-8151
1215 Janice Dr Newark (19713) *(G-6104)*

Boeing Company 302 735-2922
639 Evreux St Dover (19902) *(G-1219)*

Bold Industries LLC 302 858-7237
37424 Dale Earnhardt Blvd Frankford (19945) *(G-2348)*

Bolt Innovation LLC 800 293-5249
8 The Grn 4594 Dover (19901) *(G-1220)*

Bombay Hook Ltd 302 571-8644
1105 N Market St Wilmington (19801) *(G-9391)*

Bombonais Cable Tech LLC 302 444-1199
218 Mccallmont Rd New Castle (19720) *(G-5099)*

Bombshell Beauty Inc 302 559-3011
331 Rockmeade Dr Wilmington (19810) *(G-9392)*

Bond Network, The, New Castle Also called A Bail Bond By Resto & Co Inc *(G-4992)*

Bond, Donald T DDS, Newark Also called Clay White Dental Associates *(G-6245)*

Bonna-Agela Technologies Inc 302 438-8798
217 Cherry Blossom Pl Hockessin (19707) *(G-2966)*

Bonnie M Benson PA (PA) 302 697-4900
306 E Camden Wyoming Ave Camden (19934) *(G-541)*

Bookaway 888 250-3414
2035 Sunset Lake Rd Newark (19702) *(G-6105)*

Booking Bullet Inc (PA) 416 988-2354
2035 Sunset Lake Rd B2 Newark (19702) *(G-6106)*

Books & Tobaccos Inc 302 994-3156
4555 Kirkwood Hwy Wilmington (19808) *(G-9393)*

Boomers Staffing USA, Wilmington Also called Ramona Clay *(G-12314)*

Boost Learning LLC 302 691-5821
721 Ambleside Dr Wilmington (19808) *(G-9394)*

Boothe Investment Group 302 734-7526
450 Kings Hwy Dover (19901) *(G-1221)*

Booths Services Plbg Htg & AC 302 454-7385
1088 1/2 S Chapel St Newark (19702) *(G-6107)*

Boozer Excavation Co Inc 302 542-0290
18208 Beech Tree Path Milton (19968) *(G-4870)*

BOPyer & Boyer CPA, Wilmington Also called Boyer & Boyer *(G-9403)*

Borsello Inc 302 472-2600
720 Yorklyn Rd Ste 5 Hockessin (19707) *(G-2967)*

Borsello Landscaping, Hockessin Also called Cheap-Scape Inc *(G-2984)*

Bos Construction Company 302 875-9120
7045 Sharptown Rd Laurel (19956) *(G-3202)*

Bosco Insurance Agency 302 678-0647
625 S Dupont Hwy Ste 101 Dover (19901) *(G-1222)*

Boston Land Co Mgt Svcs Inc 302 571-0100
200 N Washington St Ofc 1 Wilmington (19801) *(G-9395)*

Bothub Ai Limited 669 278-7485
113 Darksdale Prof Ctr Newark (19711) *(G-6108)*

Botica Cbd Inc 619 800-5857
300 Delaware Ave Ste 210 Wilmington (19801) *(G-9396)*

Bottle of Smoke Press 302 399-1856
902 Wilson Dr Dover (19904) *(G-1223)*

Botts Industries 302 934-1628
29535 Whitstone Ln Millsboro (19966) *(G-4647)*

Boudart & Mensinger LLP 302 428-0100
2710 Centerville Rd # 101 Wilmington (19808) *(G-9397)*

Boulden Buses Inc 302 998-5463
32 Honeysuckle Ln Wilmington (19804) *(G-9398)*

Boulos Magdy I MD PA 302 571-9750
1306 N Broom St Ofc 1 Wilmington (19806) *(G-9399)*

Boutique The Bridal Ltd 302 335-5948
2454 Bay Rd Milford (19963) *(G-4329)*

Bove Psychological Svcs LLC 302 299-5193
108 Peirce Rd Wilmington (19803) *(G-9400)*

Bovell Lowinger Bail Bonds 302 427-9000
1900 W 4th St Wilmington (19805) *(G-9401)*

Bowlamisha LLC 302 727-4969
105 Holiday Pl Newark (19702) *(G-6109)*

Bowlerama Inc 302 654-0704
3031 New Castle Ave Ste 2 New Castle (19720) *(G-5100)*

Bowman Linda Group Day Care 302 737-5479
21 Oklahoma State Dr Newark (19713) *(G-6110)*

Boxhero Inc 827 867-4320
651 N Broad St Ste 205 Middletown (19709) *(G-3971)*

Boxwood Electric Inc 302 368-3257
10 King Ave New Castle (19720) *(G-5101)*

Boxwood Planing Mill Inc 302 999-0249
2 Meco Cir Wilmington (19804) *(G-9402)*

Boyces Electrical Service 302 875-5877
229 E Market St Laurel (19956) *(G-3203)*
Boyd Jeffrey MD 302 454-8800
4102 Ogletown Stanton Rd Newark (19713) *(G-6111)*
Boyds Crane, Camden Wyoming *Also called Boyds Trailor Hitches (G-619)*
Boyds Trailor Hitches 302 697-9000
3178 S State St Camden Wyoming (19934) *(G-619)*
Boyds Welding Inc 302 697-9000
3178 S State St Camden Wyoming (19934) *(G-620)*
Boyer & Boyer (PA) 302 998-3700
2392 Limestone Rd Wilmington (19808) *(G-9403)*
Boys & Girls Club of De 302 677-6376
864 Center Rd Dover (19901) *(G-1224)*
Boys & Girls Club of Dover, Dover *Also called Boys & Girls Clubs Del Inc (G-1225)*
Boys & Girls Club of Milford 302 422-4453
105 Ne Front St Milford (19963) *(G-4330)*
Boys & Girls Clubs Del Inc 302 422-3757
101 Dlaware Veterans Blvd Milford (19963) *(G-4331)*
Boys & Girls Clubs Del Inc (PA) 302 658-1870
669 S Union St Wilmington (19805) *(G-9404)*
Boys & Girls Clubs Del Inc 302 836-6464
109 Glasgow Dr Newark (19702) *(G-6112)*
Boys & Girls Clubs Del Inc 302 655-8569
19 Lambson Ln New Castle (19720) *(G-5102)*
Boys & Girls Clubs Del Inc 302 678-5182
375 Simon Cir Dover (19904) *(G-1225)*
Boys & Girls Clubs Del Inc 302 678-5182
9 E Loockerman St Ste 2c Dover (19901) *(G-1226)*
Boys & Girls Clubs Del Inc 302 656-1386
1601 N Spruce St Wilmington (19802) *(G-9405)*
Boys & Girls Clubs Del Inc 302 655-4591
669 S Union St Wilmington (19805) *(G-9406)*
Boys & Girls Clubs Del Inc 302 856-4903
115 N Race St Georgetown (19947) *(G-2457)*
Boys & Girls Clubs Del Inc 302 628-3789
310 Virginia Ave Seaford (19973) *(G-8173)*
Boys & Girls Clubs of America 302 659-5610
240 E Commerce St Smyrna (19977) *(G-8584)*
Boys & Girls Clubs of America 302 875-1200
454 N Central Ave Laurel (19956) *(G-3204)*
Boys & Girls Clubs Wstn Sussex, Seaford *Also called Boys & Girls Clubs Del Inc (G-8173)*
Boys Girls CLB Greater Newark, Newark *Also called Boys & Girls Clubs Del Inc (G-6112)*
Boys Girls Clubs 302 260-9864
19285 Holland Glade Rd Rehoboth Beach (19971) *(G-7873)*
BP, Dover *Also called B P Services (G-1166)*
BP Staffing Inc 302 999-7213
5187 W Woodmill Dr Ste 1 Wilmington (19808) *(G-9407)*
Bpg, Wilmington *Also called Buccini/Pollin Group Inc (G-9497)*
Bpg Hotel Partners X LLC 302 453-9700
640 S College Ave Newark (19713) *(G-6113)*
Bpg International, Wilmington *Also called Brandywine PDT Group Intl Inc (G-9449)*
Bpg Office Invstors III/IV LLC 302 691-2100
1000 N West St Ste 900 Wilmington (19801) *(G-9408)*
Bpg Office Partners Viii LLC 302 250-3065
1000 N West St Ste 900 Wilmington (19801) *(G-9409)*
Bpg Real Estate Services LLC 302 478-1190
3505 Silverside Rd # 105 Wilmington (19810) *(G-9410)*
Bpg Real Estate Services LLC (PA) 302 777-2000
1000 N West St Ste 1000 # 1000 Wilmington (19801) *(G-9411)*
Bpgs Construction LLC 302 691-2111
1000 N West St Wilmington (19801) *(G-9412)*
Brackenville Center, Hockessin *Also called 100 St Clire Drv Oprations LLC (G-2945)*
Bradford Family Physicians LLC 302 730-3750
1055 S Bradford St Dover (19904) *(G-1227)*
Bradley & Sons Designer Con 302 836-8031
1 Tammie Dr Bear (19701) *(G-55)*
Bradley Arthur & Son Cnstr 302 422-9391
720 Meadow Brook Ln Milford (19963) *(G-4332)*
Bradley, Michael J Do, Dover *Also called Dover Family Physicians PA (G-1448)*
Bradleys Auto Center Inc 302 762-2247
5 E 41st St Wilmington (19802) *(G-9413)*
Brafman Family Dentistry PC 302 732-3852
31381 Dogwood Acres Dr # 2 Dagsboro (19939) *(G-885)*
Brain Injury Association Del 302 346-2083
840 Walker Rd Ste A Dover (19904) *(G-1228)*
Brainbase Inc (PA) 412 515-9000
1000 N West St Ste 1200 Wilmington (19801) *(G-9414)*
Braincore Inc 302 999-9221
35 Industrial Blvd New Castle (19720) *(G-5103)*
Brakes Engine & Tracks LLC 302 476-9450
501 Silverside Rd Pmb 29 Wilmington (19809) *(G-9415)*
Bramble Construction Co Inc 302 856-6723
812 E Market St Georgetown (19947) *(G-2458)*
Brand Design Co Inc 302 234-2356
1145 York Lane Rd Yorklyn (19736) *(G-13364)*
Brandi Wine Pediatric Inc 302 478-7805
3521 Silverside Rd Ste 1f Wilmington (19810) *(G-9416)*
Brandon Tatum 302 564-7428
36666 Bluewater Run W # 7 Selbyville (19975) *(G-8459)*

Brandx Heirloom Tomatoes 302 287-1782
103 Ashley Ann Ct Townsend (19734) *(G-8765)*
Brandy Bine Medical Associates, Wilmington *Also called Abad & Salameda PA (G-8897)*
Brandy Wine, Newark *Also called Richard L Sherry MD (G-7338)*
Brandy Wine Senior Center 302 798-5562
3301 Green St Claymont (19703) *(G-704)*
Brandywine Apartment Assoc LP 302 475-8600
2702 Jacqueline Dr H19 Wilmington (19810) *(G-9417)*
Brandywine Assisted Living 302 436-0808
21111 Arrington Dr # 101 Selbyville (19975) *(G-8460)*
Brandywine Auto Parts, Wilmington *Also called Action Automotive Inc (G-8925)*
Brandywine Balustrades 302 893-1837
1225 Old Coochs Bridge Rd Newark (19713) *(G-6114)*
Brandywine Body Shop Inc 302 998-0424
1325 Newport Gap Pike Wilmington (19804) *(G-9418)*
Brandywine Botanicals LLC 302 354-4650
318 Tindall Rd Wilmington (19805) *(G-9419)*
Brandywine Cad Design Inc 302 478-8334
3204 Concord Pike Wilmington (19803) *(G-9420)*
Brandywine Care L L C 302 658-5822
1300 Delaware Ave Ste 1 Wilmington (19806) *(G-9421)*
Brandywine Center For Autism 302 762-2636
210 Bellefonte Ave Wilmington (19809) *(G-9422)*
Brandywine Center For Dance & 302 798-0124
2700 Ebright Rd Wilmington (19810) *(G-9423)*
Brandywine Chemical Company 302 656-5428
600 Terminal Ave Ste 1 New Castle (19720) *(G-5104)*
Brandywine Chrysler Jeep Dodge (PA) 302 998-0458
3807 Kirkwood Hwy Wilmington (19808) *(G-9424)*
Brandywine Club Inc 302 798-9891
135 Princeton Ave Claymont (19703) *(G-705)*
Brandywine Com Rsrc Cncl, Claymont *Also called Claymont Community Center Inc (G-721)*
Brandywine Construction Co 302 571-9773
101 Pigeon Point Rd New Castle (19720) *(G-5105)*
Brandywine Contractors Inc 302 325-2700
34 Industrial Blvd New Castle (19720) *(G-5106)*
Brandywine Contractors Inc 302 325-2700
34 Industrial Blvd New Castle (19720) *(G-5107)*
Brandywine Cosmetic Surgery (PA) 302 652-3331
410 Foulk Rd Ste 201 Wilmington (19803) *(G-9425)*
Brandywine Cosmetic Surgery 302 652-3331
Medical Arts Pvilion 13 Newark (19713) *(G-6115)*
Brandywine Counseling 302 454-3020
24 Brookhill Dr Newark (19702) *(G-6116)*
Brandywine Counseling 302 762-7120
500 Duncan Rd Ofc 1 Wilmington (19809) *(G-9426)*
Brandywine Counseling (PA) 302 655-9880
2713 Lancaster Ave Wilmington (19805) *(G-9427)*
Brandywine Country Club 302 478-4604
302 River Rd Apt D2 Wilmington (19809) *(G-9428)*
Brandywine Dental Care 302 421-9960
707 Foulk Rd Ste 201 Wilmington (19803) *(G-9429)*
Brandywine Elec Ltd Belcom, Bear *Also called Brandywine Electronics Corp (G-56)*
Brandywine Electronics Corp 302 324-9992
611 Carson Dr Bear (19701) *(G-56)*
Brandywine Elevator Co Inc (PA) 866 636-0102
300 B And O Ln Wilmington (19804) *(G-9430)*
Brandywine Exteriors Corp 302 746-7134
221 Valley Rd Wilmington (19804) *(G-9431)*
Brandywine Eye Center, Wilmington *Also called Richard L Sherry MD (G-12410)*
Brandywine Family Medicine 302 475-5000
2500 Grubb Rd Ste 212 Wilmington (19810) *(G-9432)*
Brandywine Fine Properties 302 691-3052
5701 Kennett Pike Wilmington (19807) *(G-9433)*
Brandywine Fund Inc 302 656-3017
3711 Kennett Pike Ste 100 Wilmington (19807) *(G-9434)*
Brandywine Graphics Inc 302 655-7571
500 S Colonial Ave Wilmington (19805) *(G-9435)*
Brandywine Hills Apartments 302 764-3242
4310 Miller Rd Apt 106 Wilmington (19802) *(G-9436)*
Brandywine Hndred Vtrnary Hosp 302 792-2777
806 Silverside Rd Wilmington (19809) *(G-9437)*
Brandywine Hundred Fire Co 1 302 764-4901
1006 Brandywine Blvd Wilmington (19809) *(G-9438)*
BRANDYWINE HUNDRED FIRE CO NO, Wilmington *Also called Brandywine Hundred Fire Co 1 (G-9438)*
Brandywine I & 2 Apts 302 475-8600
2702 Jacqueline Dr H19 Wilmington (19810) *(G-9439)*
Brandywine Imaging LLC 302 654-5300
3206 Concord Pike Wilmington (19803) *(G-9440)*
Brandywine Ingredient Tech, Wilmington *Also called McShares Inc (G-11608)*
Brandywine Lacrosse Club 302 249-1840
2403 W Heather Rd Wilmington (19803) *(G-9441)*
Brandywine Management, Wilmington *Also called Brandywine Realty Management (G-9452)*
Brandywine Mill Work 302 652-3008
1907 N Market St Wilmington (19802) *(G-9442)*
Brandywine Nurseries Inc 302 429-0865
4 James Ct Wilmington (19801) *(G-9443)*

ALPHABETIC

Brandywine Nursing & Rehab........302 683-0444
505 Greenbank Rd Wilmington (19808) ***(G-9444)***
Brandywine Ob Gyn........302 477-1375
3520 Silverside Rd 2l1 Wilmington (19810) ***(G-9445)***
Brandywine Occpational Therapy........302 740-4798
800 Carr Rd Wilmington (19809) ***(G-9446)***
Brandywine Pain Center........302 998-2585
4512 Kirkwood Hwy Ste 200 Wilmington (19808) ***(G-9447)***
Brandywine Park Condominiums, Wilmington *Also called Brandywine Park Condos* ***(G-9448)***
Brandywine Park Condos........302 655-2262
1704 N Park Dr Apt 115 Wilmington (19806) ***(G-9448)***
Brandywine PDT Group Intl Inc........302 472-1463
3 Mill Rd Ste 202 Wilmington (19806) ***(G-9449)***
Brandywine Podiatry PA (PA)........302 658-1129
1010 N Bancroft Pkwy # 12 Wilmington (19805) ***(G-9450)***
Brandywine Process Servers........302 475-2600
2500 Delaware Ave Wilmington (19806) ***(G-9451)***
Brandywine Realty Management........302 656-1058
3200 Lancaster Ave Wilmington (19805) ***(G-9452)***
Brandywine Realty Trust........302 655-5900
300 Delaware Ave Ste 1630 Wilmington (19801) ***(G-9453)***
Brandywine Rubber Mills LLC........267 499-3993
1704 N Park Dr Apt 508 Wilmington (19806) ***(G-9454)***
Brandywine Snior Lving MGT LLC........302 226-8750
36101 Seaside Blvd Rehoboth Beach (19971) ***(G-7874)***
Brandywine Sr Care, Selbyville *Also called Brandywine Assisted Living* ***(G-8460)***
Brandywine Technology, Wilmington *Also called 924 Inc* ***(G-8870)***
Brandywine Total Health Care........302 478-3028
3214 Naamans Rd Wilmington (19810) ***(G-9455)***
Brandywine Town Center 16, Wilmington *Also called Regal Cinemas Inc* ***(G-12353)***
Brandywine Tree and Shrub LLC........302 475-7594
214 Alders Dr Wilmington (19803) ***(G-9456)***
Brandywine Trust Co........302 234-5750
7234 Lancaster Pike 300a Hockessin (19707) ***(G-2968)***
Brandywine Urology Cons PA (PA)........302 652-8990
2000 Foulk Rd Ste F Wilmington (19810) ***(G-9457)***
Brandywine Valley Properties........302 475-7660
1806 Breen Ln Wilmington (19810) ***(G-9458)***
Brandywine Valley Woodworking........302 743-5640
1212 Bruce Rd Wilmington (19803) ***(G-9459)***
Brandywine Vending, Claymont *Also called Gian-Co* ***(G-753)***
Brandywine Veterinary Hospital........302 476-8779
3848 Kennett Pike Wilmington (19807) ***(G-9460)***
Brandywine Vly Fire Safety Div, Wilmington *Also called McDonald Safety Equipment Inc* ***(G-11594)***
Brandywine Volleyball Club........302 898-6452
3023 Maple Shade Ln Wilmington (19810) ***(G-9461)***
Brandywine Wods Aprtmnts Sites, Bear *Also called Town and Country Trust* ***(G-356)***
Brandywine Zoo, Wilmington *Also called Parks & Recreation Del Div* ***(G-12024)***
Brandywine Zoo........302 571-7747
1001 N Park Dr Wilmington (19802) ***(G-9462)***
Brandywood Plaza Assoc LLC........302 633-9134
2126 W Newport Pike Wilmington (19804) ***(G-9463)***
Brasures Body Shop Inc........302 732-6157
Rr 113 Frankford (19945) ***(G-2349)***
Brasures Carpet Care Inc (PA)........302 436-5652
35131 Lighthouse Rd Selbyville (19975) ***(G-8461)***
Brasures Pest Control Inc........302 436-8140
38187 Dickerson Rd Selbyville (19975) ***(G-8462)***
Braun Engineering & Surveying........302 698-0701
863 Allabands Mill Rd Camden Wyoming (19934) ***(G-621)***
Bravo Building Services Inc........302 322-5959
34 Blevins Dr Ste 7 New Castle (19720) ***(G-5108)***
Brdly M Winston Pdrtcs Prctc........302 424-1650
375 Mullet Run Milford (19963) ***(G-4333)***
Breakers Associates........302 227-6688
105 2nd St Rehoboth Beach (19971) ***(G-7875)***
Breakers Hotel, The, Rehoboth Beach *Also called Breakers Associates* ***(G-7875)***
Breakthru Beverage Delaware, New Castle *Also called Breakthru Beverage Group LLC* ***(G-5109)***
Breakthru Beverage Group LLC........302 356-3500
411 Churchmans Rd New Castle (19720) ***(G-5109)***
Breakthrugh Cpitl Partners LLC........212 381-4420
16192 Coastal Hwy Lewes (19958) ***(G-3391)***
Breakwater Accounting Advisory........302 543-4564
100 S Rockland Falls Rd Rockland (19732) ***(G-8122)***
Breakwater Construction Envmtl........302 945-5800
4 Chief Joseph Trl Millsboro (19966) ***(G-4648)***
Breast Imaging Center........302 623-9729
4735 Ogletown Stanton Rd # 2112 Newark (19713) ***(G-6117)***
Breckenridge Software Tech (PA)........302 656-8460
2514 Eaton Rd Wilmington (19810) ***(G-9464)***
Breckstone Architecture, Wilmington *Also called Breckstone Group Inc* ***(G-9465)***
Breckstone Group Inc........302 654-3646
2417 Lancaster Ave Wilmington (19805) ***(G-9465)***
Breeding & Day Inc (PA)........302 478-4585
3316 Silverside Rd Wilmington (19810) ***(G-9466)***
Brees Home Day Care........302 762-0876
915 E 26th St Wilmington (19802) ***(G-9467)***
Breeze Construction LLC........302 522-9201
39 Basalt St Townsend (19734) ***(G-8766)***
Brenden Bailey & Chandler VFW........302 239-0797
7620 Lancaster Pike Hockessin (19707) ***(G-2969)***
Brendon T Warfel Construction........302 422-7814
940 Ne Front Street Ext Milford (19963) ***(G-4334)***
Brenford Animal Hospital P A (PA)........302 678-9418
4118 N Dupont Hwy Dover (19901) ***(G-1229)***
Brennan Title Company........302 541-0400
31634 Hickory Manor Rd Frankford (19945) ***(G-2350)***
Breslin Contracting Inc........302 322-0320
18 King Ct New Castle (19720) ***(G-5110)***
Brewster Products Inc........302 798-1988
2305 Swynford Rd Wilmington (19810) ***(G-9468)***
Brewster Products Inc........302 798-1988
3020 Bowlarama Dr New Castle (19720) ***(G-5111)***
Brewster Products Inc........302 764-4463
3607 Downing Dr Ste E Wilmington (19802) ***(G-9469)***
Brian A Wisk........302 653-5011
17 W Glenwood Ave Smyrna (19977) ***(G-8585)***
Brian Costleigh LLC........302 645-3775
1 Beach Ave Rehoboth Beach (19971) ***(G-7876)***
Brian Garnsey........302 463-1985
34 Debs Way Dover (19901) ***(G-1230)***
Brian McAllister DDS........302 376-0617
200 Cleaver Farms Rd # 101 Middletown (19709) ***(G-3972)***
Brice Darla M DDS Ms........302 478-4700
3512 Silverside Rd Ste 3 Wilmington (19810) ***(G-9470)***
Brick Doctor Inc (PA)........302 678-3380
130 Kruser Blvd Dover (19901) ***(G-1231)***
Bridal & Tuxedo Outlet Inc (PA)........302 731-8802
124 Astro Shopping Ctr Newark (19711) ***(G-6118)***
Bridal & Tuxedo Shoppe, Newark *Also called Bridal & Tuxedo Outlet Inc* ***(G-6118)***
Bridge Counseling Center LLC........302 856-9190
21635 Biden Ave Georgetown (19947) ***(G-2459)***
Bridge Studio of Delaware........302 479-5431
1409 Foulk Rd Ste 101 Wilmington (19803) ***(G-9471)***
Bridgestone Ret Operations LLC........302 422-4508
103 Causey Ave Bldg 103 # 103 Milford (19963) ***(G-4335)***
Bridgestone Ret Operations LLC........302 995-2487
3301 Old Capitol Trl Wilmington (19808) ***(G-9472)***
Bridgestone Ret Operations LLC........302 734-4522
625 S Bay Rd Dover (19901) ***(G-1232)***
Bridgestone Ret Operations LLC........302 656-2529
2098 New Castle Ave New Castle (19720) ***(G-5112)***
Bridgeville Auto Center Inc........302 337-3100
Rr 13 Box S Bridgeville (19933) ***(G-454)***
Bridgeville Lions Club Inc........302 629-9543
P.O. Box 414 Bridgeville (19933) ***(G-455)***
Bridgeville Machining, Bridgeville *Also called Messick & Gray Cnstr Inc* ***(G-497)***
Bridgeville Senior Center........302 337-8771
414 Market St Bridgeville (19933) ***(G-456)***
Bridgeville State Services, Bridgeville *Also called Health & Social Svcs Del Dept* ***(G-480)***
Bridgewater Jewelers........302 328-2101
318 Delaware St New Castle (19720) ***(G-5113)***
Briggs Company, Georgetown *Also called John L Briggs & Co* ***(G-2577)***
Briggs Company (PA)........302 328-9471
3 Bellecor Dr New Castle (19720) ***(G-5114)***
Briggs Services LLC........302 569-5230
14546 S Old State Rd Ellendale (19941) ***(G-2258)***
Bright Beginnings Child Care C........302 934-1249
29753 John J Williams Hwy Millsboro (19966) ***(G-4649)***
Bright Bgnnngs Lrng Acdemy LLC........302 655-1346
111 N Cleveland Ave Wilmington (19805) ***(G-9473)***
Bright Dental........302 376-7882
600 N Broad St Ste 7 Middletown (19709) ***(G-3973)***
Bright Finish LLC........888 974-4747
56 Arrowood Dr Smyrna (19977) ***(G-8586)***
Bright Future Pediatrics, Camden *Also called Future Bright Pediatrics LLC* ***(G-573)***
BRIGHT FUTURE PEDIATRICS, Dover *Also called Future Bright Pediatrics* ***(G-1574)***
Bright Futures Inc........610 905-0506
125 Sleepy Hollow Dr Middletown (19709) ***(G-3974)***
Bright Horizons Child Care Ctr, Wilmington *Also called Bright Horizons Chld Ctrs LLC* ***(G-9475)***
Bright Horizons Chld Ctrs LLC........302 456-8913
950 Samoset Dr Newark (19713) ***(G-6119)***
Bright Horizons Chld Ctrs LLC........302 282-6378
201 N Walnut St Wilmington (19801) ***(G-9474)***
Bright Horizons Chld Ctrs LLC........302 477-1023
3515 Silverside Rd # 102 Wilmington (19810) ***(G-9475)***
Bright Horizons Chld Ctrs LLC........302 453-2050
1089 Prides Xing Newark (19713) ***(G-6120)***
Bright Kidz Inc........302 369-6929
273 Old Baltimore Pike Newark (19702) ***(G-6121)***
Bright New Beginnings........610 637-9809
8 W Holly Oak Rd Wilmington (19809) ***(G-9476)***

Bright Stars Home Daycare....302 378-8142
302 Northhampton Way Middletown (19709) ***(G-3975)***
Brightfields Inc (PA)....302 656-9600
801 Industrial St Wilmington (19801) ***(G-9477)***
Brighton Hotels LLC....302 227-5780
34 Wilmington Ave Rehoboth Beach (19971) ***(G-7877)***
Brighton Suites, Rehoboth Beach *Also called Packem Associates Partnership* ***(G-8027)***
Brighton Suites Hotel, Rehoboth Beach *Also called Brighton Hotels LLC* ***(G-7877)***
Brightview Landscapes LLC....302 731-4162
22 Brookhill Dr Newark (19702) ***(G-6122)***
Brilliant Little Minds....302 376-9889
102 Sandhill Dr Middletown (19709) ***(G-3976)***
Briscoe Trucking Inc....302 836-1327
28 Chambord Dr Newark (19702) ***(G-6123)***
Briscoes Onsite Detailing....302 420-1629
100 Greenhill Ave Ste C Wilmington (19805) ***(G-9478)***
Bristol Industrial Corporation....302 322-1100
1010 River Rd New Castle (19720) ***(G-5115)***
Bristol-Myers Squibb Company....800 321-1335
1209 N Orange St Wilmington (19801) ***(G-9479)***
Brite Lite Supply, New Castle *Also called Colonial Electric Supply Co* ***(G-5181)***
Brittingham Inc....302 656-8173
5809 Kennett Pike Wilmington (19807) ***(G-9480)***
Brittons Wise Computers Inc....302 659-0343
777 Paddock Rd Smyrna (19977) ***(G-8587)***
Broad Acres Inc....302 734-2910
8853 Bayside Dr Dover (19901) ***(G-1233)***
Broad Creek Medical Service....302 629-0202
1601 Middleford Rd Seaford (19973) ***(G-8174)***
Broadberry Data Systems LLC....302 295-1086
1308 Delaware Ave Wilmington (19806) ***(G-9481)***
Broadberry Data Systems LLC (PA)....800 496-9918
501 Silverside Rd Ste 119 Wilmington (19809) ***(G-9482)***
Broadcreek Medical Service, Seaford *Also called Broad Creek Medical Service* ***(G-8174)***
BROADMEADOW HEALTHCARE, Middletown *Also called Broadmeadow Investment LLC* ***(G-3977)***
Broadmeadow Investment LLC....302 449-3400
500 S Broad St Middletown (19709) ***(G-3977)***
Broadpoint Construction LLC....302 567-2100
37251 Rehoboth Avenue Ext Rehoboth Beach (19971) ***(G-7878)***
Broadpoint Custom Homes, Rehoboth Beach *Also called Broadpoint Construction LLC* ***(G-7878)***
Broadwater Oyster Company LLC....610 220-7776
4 S Lake Ter Rehoboth Beach (19971) ***(G-7879)***
Brocks Soy Candles....609 841-5121
105 Hobbyhorse Ct Dover (19904) ***(G-1234)***
Brodie Invitations....302 999-7889
229 Linden Ave Wilmington (19805) ***(G-9483)***
Broker Post....302 628-8467
1310 Bridgeville Hwy Seaford (19973) ***(G-8175)***
Bronco Manufacturing Inc....302 475-1210
1605 Forrest Rd Wilmington (19810) ***(G-9484)***
Brookdale Senior Living Inc....302 239-3200
6677 Lancaster Pike Hockessin (19707) ***(G-2970)***
Brooks Courier Service Inc....302 762-4661
831 E 28th St Wilmington (19802) ***(G-9485)***
Brooks Machine Inc (PA)....302 674-5900
716 S West St Dover (19904) ***(G-1235)***
BROOKS METAL SAWS REPAIR, Dover *Also called Brooks Machine Inc* ***(G-1235)***
Brookside Laundromat....302 369-3366
69 Marrows Rd Newark (19713) ***(G-6124)***
Brookside Plaza Apartments LLC....302 737-2008
885 Marrows Rd Apt D6 Newark (19713) ***(G-6125)***
Brousseau & Brousseau C P A....302 234-1976
5708 Limestone Rd Wilmington (19808) ***(G-9486)***
Brown Shiels & OBrien....302 734-4766
108 E Water St Dover (19901) ***(G-1236)***
Brown Advisory Incorporated....302 351-7600
5701 Kennett Pike 100 Wilmington (19807) ***(G-9487)***
Brown Brothers Harriman & Co....302 552-4040
919 N Market St Ste 710 Wilmington (19801) ***(G-9488)***
Brown Eagle Inc....302 295-3816
1000 N West St Ste 1200 Wilmington (19801) ***(G-9489)***
Brown Lisha....302 832-9529
33 Wellington Dr Newark (19702) ***(G-6126)***
Brown Shels Bauregard LLC....302 226-2270
148 S Bradford St Dover (19904) ***(G-1237)***
Brown Stone Nimeroff LLC....302 428-8142
901 N Market St Wilmington (19801) ***(G-9490)***
Browne USA Inc....302 326-4802
802 Centerpoint Blvd New Castle (19720) ***(G-5116)***
Brownstarr Therapy....302 838-2645
6 Bristol Ct Newark (19702) ***(G-6127)***
Brownstein Meryl Med Lpcmh....302 479-5060
3526 Silverside Rd Ste 36 Wilmington (19810) ***(G-9491)***
Brownstone LLC....302 300-4370
200 Centerpoint Blvd A New Castle (19720) ***(G-5117)***
Brs Consulting Inc....302 786-2326
293 Jackson Ditch Rd Harrington (19952) ***(G-2819)***

Bruce A Rogers PA....302 856-7161
12 S Front St Georgetown (19947) ***(G-2460)***
Bruce C Turner MD....302 366-0938
8 Sunrise Cir Newark (19713) ***(G-6128)***
Bruce E Katz M D....302 478-5500
1401 Foulk Rd Ste 101 Wilmington (19803) ***(G-9492)***
Bruce E Matthews DDS PA....302 234-2440
451 Hockessin Cors Hockessin (19707) ***(G-2971)***
Bruce E Matthews DDS PA (PA)....302 475-9220
1403 Silverside Rd Ste A Wilmington (19810) ***(G-9493)***
Bruce G Fay DMD PA....302 778-3822
900 Foulk Rd Ste 203 Wilmington (19803) ***(G-9494)***
Bruce Industrial Co Inc....302 655-9616
4049 New Castle Ave New Castle (19720) ***(G-5118)***
Bruce Mears Designer-Builder....302 539-2355
31370 Railway Rd 2 Ocean View (19970) ***(G-7770)***
Bruces Welding Inc....302 629-3891
21263 Nattell Ln Seaford (19973) ***(G-8176)***
Brunswick Doverama....302 734-7501
1600 S Governors Ave Dover (19904) ***(G-1238)***
Bryan & Brittingham Inc....302 846-9500
38148 Bi State Blvd Delmar (19940) ***(G-974)***
Bryan K Sterling LLC....302 734-3511
773 S Queen St Ste A Dover (19904) ***(G-1239)***
Bryant Technologies Inc....302 289-2044
2368 Paradise Alley Rd Felton (19943) ***(G-2276)***
Bryn Mawr Trust Company....302 529-5984
5301 Limestone Rd Ste 106 Wilmington (19808) ***(G-9495)***
Bsbv Inc....631 201-2044
16192 Coastal Hwy Lewes (19958) ***(G-3392)***
Bsr Trade LLC....646 250-4409
8 The Grn Ste 6258 Dover (19901) ***(G-1240)***
BTS Enterprises Inc....302 428-6080
2702 Lancaster Ave Wilmington (19805) ***(G-9496)***
Bubba Game Calls....302 332-2004
158 Blackbird Station Rd Townsend (19734) ***(G-8767)***
Buccini/Pollin Group Inc (PA)....302 691-2100
1000 N West St Ste 1000 # 1000 Wilmington (19801) ***(G-9497)***
Buchi Corporation (HQ)....302 652-3000
19 Lukens Dr Ste 400 New Castle (19720) ***(G-5119)***
Buchspot LLC....302 715-1253
16192 Coastal Hwy Lewes (19958) ***(G-3393)***
Buck Simpers Archt + Assoc Inc....302 658-9300
954 Justison St Wilmington (19801) ***(G-9498)***
Buck's Barber Shop, Dover *Also called Georve V Sawyer* ***(G-1591)***
Buckingham Pl Twnhuse Aprtmnts, Newark *Also called Galman Group Inc* ***(G-6635)***
Buckley's Autocare, Wilmington *Also called Buckleys Inc* ***(G-9499)***
Buckleys Inc....302 999-8285
1604 E Newport Pike Wilmington (19804) ***(G-9499)***
Buddycable, Dover *Also called Bolt Innovation LLC* ***(G-1220)***
Budget Blinds, Milton *Also called Rementer Brothers Inc* ***(G-4956)***
Budget Rent A Car System Inc....302 652-0629
100 S Front St Wilmington (19801) ***(G-9500)***
Budget Rooter Inc....302 322-3011
1015 River Rd New Castle (19720) ***(G-5120)***
Budget Truck Rental LLC....302 644-0132
18744 John J Williams Hwy Rehoboth Beach (19971) ***(G-7880)***
Buffalo Concrete Co Inc....302 378-4421
307 A St Ste A Wilmington (19801) ***(G-9501)***
Buffalo Consulting Group, New Castle *Also called Delaware Enterprises Inc* ***(G-5228)***
Buford Manlove Grdns Assoc LP....302 652-3991
722 Yorklyn Rd Ste 350 Hockessin (19707) ***(G-2972)***
Bug Rite Extreminator Comp....302 738-4373
303 Portland Ave Wilmington (19804) ***(G-9502)***
Builders Firstsource Inc....302 731-0678
54 Albe Dr Newark (19702) ***(G-6129)***
Builders LLC General....302 533-6528
99 Albe Dr Ste A Newark (19702) ***(G-6130)***
Building Blocks Academy Ltd....302 284-8797
333 Ludlow Ln Felton (19943) ***(G-2277)***
Building Blocks For Learni....302 677-0248
88 Beech Dr Dover (19904) ***(G-1241)***
Building Concepts America Inc....302 292-0200
101 Peoples Dr Newark (19702) ***(G-6131)***
Building Fasteners Inc....302 738-0671
955 Dawson Dr Ste 1 Newark (19713) ***(G-6132)***
Building Inspection Undrwrtr....302 266-9057
1 Liberty Plz Ste C Newark (19711) ***(G-6133)***
Building Insptn Underwriters, Newark *Also called Building Inspection Undrwrtr* ***(G-6133)***
Building Systems and Svcs Inc....302 996-0900
1504 Kirkwood Hwy Wilmington (19805) ***(G-9503)***
Built-Rite Fence Co Inc....302 366-8329
34 Hidden Valley Dr Newark (19711) ***(G-6134)***
Buker Limousine & Trnsp Svc....302 234-7600
517 Paisley Pl Newark (19711) ***(G-6135)***
Bullens Bucktails Inc....302 998-6288
3906 Chestnut St Wilmington (19808) ***(G-9504)***
Bullfeathers Auto Sound Inc....302 846-0434
28368 Beaver Dam Br Rd Laurel (19956) ***(G-3205)***

Bumpers & Company...302 798-3300
1104 Philadelphia Pike Wilmington (19809) ***(G-9505)***
Bunting & Bertrand Inc...302 732-6836
15 Hickory St Frankford (19945) ***(G-2351)***
Bunting & Murray Cnstr Corp...302 436-5144
32996 Lighthouse Rd Selbyville (19975) ***(G-8463)***
Bunting Construction Corp...302 436-5124
32996 Lighthouse Rd Selbyville (19975) ***(G-8464)***
Buntings Garage Inc...302 732-9021
28506 Carebear Ln Dagsboro (19939) ***(G-886)***
Burgeon It Services LLC...302 613-0999
1601 Concord Pike Ste 36e Wilmington (19803) ***(G-9506)***
Burke Dermatology...302 703-6585
18947 John J Williams Hwy Rehoboth Beach (19971) ***(G-7881)***
Burke Dermatology (PA)...302 734-3376
95 Wolf Creek Blvd Ste 1 Dover (19901) ***(G-1242)***
Burke Dermatology (PA)...302 230-3376
774 Christiana Rd Ste 107 Newark (19713) ***(G-6136)***
Burke Equipment Company (PA)...302 697-3200
54 Andrews Lake Rd Felton (19943) ***(G-2278)***
Burke Equipment Company...302 248-7070
11196 E Snake Rd Delmar (19940) ***(G-975)***
Burke Equipment Company...302 248-7070
11196 E Snake Rd Delmar (19940) ***(G-976)***
Burke Equipment Company...302 629-7500
11196 E Snake Rd Delmar (19940) ***(G-977)***
Burke Painting Co Inc...302 998-8500
25 Brookside Dr Wilmington (19804) ***(G-9507)***
Burke Roofing, Dover *Also called Martin J Burke Inc* ***(G-1823)***
Burlington Manor Apartments, Wilmington *Also called Burlington Manor Associates* ***(G-9508)***
Burlington Manor Associates...609 387-3184
4 Denny Rd Wilmington (19809) ***(G-9508)***
Burns & Ellis Realty Co...302 674-4220
490 N Dupont Hwy Dover (19901) ***(G-1243)***
Burns & Fiorina Demolition...732 888-1076
46 Vansant Rd Newark (19711) ***(G-6137)***
Burns & McBride Inc (PA)...302 656-5110
18 Boulden Cir Ste 30 New Castle (19720) ***(G-5121)***
Burris & Baxter Communications...302 454-8511
256 Chapman Rd Ste 201 Newark (19702) ***(G-6138)***
Burris Freight Management LLC...800 805-8135
501 Se 5th St Milford (19963) ***(G-4336)***
Burris Logistics (PA)...302 839-4531
501 Se 5th St Milford (19963) ***(G-4337)***
Burris Logistics...302 221-4100
1000 Centerpoint Blvd New Castle (19720) ***(G-5122)***
Burris Logistics...302 398-5050
111 Reese Ave Harrington (19952) ***(G-2820)***
Burris Refrigerated Logistics, New Castle *Also called Burris Logistics* ***(G-5122)***
Burris Retail Logistics, Milford *Also called Burris Logistics* ***(G-4337)***
Burton Enterprises Inc...302 838-0115
241 Rice Dr Bear (19701) ***(G-57)***
Burton Hg & Company Inc...302 245-3384
32973 Main St Dagsboro (19939) ***(G-887)***
Burton Realty Inc...302 945-5100
24808 John J Williams Hwy Millsboro (19966) ***(G-4650)***
Bushwick Metals LLC...302 328-0590
100 Steel Dr New Castle (19720) ***(G-5123)***
Business At International LLC...605 610-4885
16192 Coastal Hwy Lewes (19958) ***(G-3394)***
Business Centric Svcs Group...302 984-3800
1000 N West St Ste 1000 # 1000 Wilmington (19801) ***(G-9509)***
Business History Conference...302 658-2400
298 Buck Rd Wilmington (19807) ***(G-9510)***
Business Insurance Services...302 655-5300
109 N Dupont Rd Wilmington (19807) ***(G-9511)***
Business Integration Solution...302 355-3512
220 Continental Dr # 213 Newark (19713) ***(G-6139)***
Business Move Solutions Inc...302 324-0080
11 Boulden Cir New Castle (19720) ***(G-5124)***
Business Services Corp...302 645-0400
11 New Hampshire Ave Lewes (19958) ***(G-3395)***
Business Slip LLC...302 563-3660
201 E 39th St Ste 201 # 201 Wilmington (19802) ***(G-9512)***
Busy Bees Home Learning Center, Dover *Also called Ditrocchio Maria Antonetta* ***(G-1432)***
Busymama Cupcakes...302 259-9988
328 E Poplar St Seaford (19973) ***(G-8177)***
Butamax Advanced Biofuels LLC...302 695-3617
200 Powder Mill Rd Wilmington (19803) ***(G-9513)***
Butamax Advanced Biofuels LLC (PA)...302 695-6787
Henry Clay Rr 141 Wilmington (19880) ***(G-9514)***
Butler Financial Ltd...302 778-2170
900 Foulk Rd Ste 201 Wilmington (19803) ***(G-9515)***
Butler Woodcrafters...302 764-0744
1204 Brook Dr Wilmington (19803) ***(G-9516)***
Butlers Sewing Center Inc...302 629-9155
1023 W Stein Hwy Seaford (19973) ***(G-8178)***
Buy and Sell Rags, Newark *Also called Commodities Plus Inc* ***(G-6269)***
Buzlin Inc...800 829-0115
2140 S Dupont Hwy Camden (19934) ***(G-542)***
Buzzards Inc...302 945-3500
Longneck Rd Millsboro (19966) ***(G-4651)***
BW Electric Inc...302 566-6248
15342 S Dupont Hwy Harrington (19952) ***(G-2821)***
Bwci Animal Hospital MGT Sys, Smyrna *Also called Brittons Wise Computers Inc* ***(G-8587)***
Bwe Electric, Harrington *Also called BW Electric Inc* ***(G-2821)***
By Feel Farms, Felton *Also called Francis Bergold* ***(G-2293)***
By The Shore...302 462-0496
5005 Beverly Ln Milton (19968) ***(G-4871)***
Byers Industrial Services LLC...302 836-4790
1501 Porter Rd Bear (19701) ***(G-58)***
Byler Sawmill...302 730-4208
2846 Yoder Dr Dover (19904) ***(G-1244)***
Bylers Woodworking Shop...302 492-1375
2021 Pearsons Corner Rd Hartly (19953) ***(G-2913)***
Byron & Davis Cccc...302 792-2334
601 Philadelphia Pike Wilmington (19809) ***(G-9517)***
Byron H Jefferson Engineering...302 422-9568
10045 Clendaniel Pond Rd Lincoln (19960) ***(G-3839)***
Bysness Inc...937 687-8701
1521 Concord Pike Ste 303 Wilmington (19803) ***(G-9518)***
Byte Technology Systems Inc...347 687-7240
16192 Coastal Hwy Lewes (19958) ***(G-3396)***
Byzantium Sky Press...302 258-6116
27567 Bristol Ct Milton (19968) ***(G-4872)***
Bz Construction Services Inc...302 999-7505
120 E Ayre St Wilmington (19804) ***(G-9519)***
C & A Ink...302 565-9866
42 Stallion Dr Newark (19713) ***(G-6140)***
C & B Construct...302 378-9862
150 Vickers Rd Milford (19963) ***(G-4338)***
C & B Internet Services LLC...302 384-9804
704 N King St Ste 500 Wilmington (19801) ***(G-9520)***
C & C Technologies Inc...302 653-7623
P.O. Box 1081 Clayton (19938) ***(G-8588)***
C & D Contractors Inc...302 764-2020
14 E 40th St Lowr Wilmington (19802) ***(G-9521)***
C & J Paving, Milton *Also called C&J Paving Inc* ***(G-4873)***
C & K Builders LLC...302 324-9811
334 Bear Christiana Rd Bear (19701) ***(G-59)***
C & M Roofing & Siding, Millsboro *Also called C&M Construction Company LLC* ***(G-4652)***
C & S Consultants Inc...302 236-5211
6 E Clarke Ave Milford (19963) ***(G-4339)***
C & W Auto Parts Co Inc...302 697-2684
851 Sorghum Mill Rd Magnolia (19962) ***(G-3883)***
C and C Alpaca Factory...609 752-7894
17219 Sweetbriar Rd Lewes (19958) ***(G-3397)***
C and L Bradford and Assoc...302 529-8566
1604 Trevalley Rd Wilmington (19810) ***(G-9522)***
C B Joe TV & Appliances Inc...302 322-7600
348 Churchmans Rd New Castle (19720) ***(G-5125)***
C Edgar Wood Inc (PA)...302 674-3500
1154 S Governors Ave Dover (19904) ***(G-1245)***
C H P T Manufacturing Inc...302 856-7660
21388 Cedar Creek Ave Georgetown (19947) ***(G-2461)***
C K F, Seaford *Also called Creative Kitchens and Floors* ***(G-8214)***
C K'S Hair Port, Lewes *Also called C KS Hairport Ltd Salon & Spa* ***(G-3398)***
C KS Hairport Ltd Salon & Spa...302 645-2246
34410 Tenley Ct Unit 5 Lewes (19958) ***(G-3398)***
C L Burchenal Oil Co Inc...302 697-1517
109 S Main St Camden (19934) ***(G-543)***
C M C, Wilmington *Also called Collections Marketing Center* ***(G-9769)***
C M L Management...302 537-5599
35837 Atlantic Ave Ocean View (19967) ***(G-7771)***
C M-Tec Inc...302 369-6166
1 Innovation Way Ste 100 Newark (19711) ***(G-6141)***
C P M Industries Inc...302 478-8200
3511 Silverside Rd # 210 Wilmington (19810) ***(G-9523)***
C S C, Wilmington *Also called Corporation Service Company* ***(G-9866)***
C S C Corporation Texas Inc...302 636-5440
2711 Centerville Rd # 400 Wilmington (19808) ***(G-9524)***
C V International Inc...302 427-0440
603 Christiana Ave Wilmington (19801) ***(G-9525)***
C Wallace & Associates...302 528-2182
805 Grande Ln Hockessin (19707) ***(G-2973)***
C White & Sons LLC...302 629-4848
5635 Neals School Rd Seaford (19973) ***(G-8179)***
C&B Complete Cleaning & Cnstr...302 436-9622
36007 Zion Church Rd Frankford (19945) ***(G-2352)***
C&C Welding...402 414-2485
50 N Purdue Ave New Castle (19720) ***(G-5126)***
C&G Dental Studio LLC...302 345-4995
3 Lotus Cir N Bear (19701) ***(G-60)***
C&H Environmental Services...302 376-0178
112 Gillespie Ave Middletown (19709) ***(G-3978)***
C&J Paving Inc...302 684-0211
12518 Union Street Ext Milton (19968) ***(G-4873)***

C&M Construction Company LLC...302 663-0936
27324 Johan Williams Hwy Millsboro (19966) ***(G-4652)***
C&S Farms Inc...302 249-0458
8947 Woodland Ferry Rd Laurel (19956) ***(G-3206)***
C-Met Inc...302 652-1884
1604 N Dupont Hwy New Castle (19720) ***(G-5127)***
C-Perl, Newark *Also called Chesapeake Perl Inc* ***(G-6193)***
C-West Entertainment, Wilmington *Also called Everett Robinson* ***(G-10446)***
C21 Gold Key Realty...302 250-6801
260 E Main St Frnt Newark (19711) ***(G-6142)***
C4-Nvis USA LLC...213 465-5089
8 The Grn Ste 6794 Dover (19901) ***(G-1246)***
CA Cassidy Vmd...302 998-2995
3705 Lancaster Pike Wilmington (19805) ***(G-9526)***
Cabe Associates Inc...302 674-9280
144 S Governors Ave Dover (19904) ***(G-1247)***
Cabell Corp...302 398-8125
131 W Center St Apt 33 Harrington (19952) ***(G-2822)***
Cabinetry Unlimited LLC...302 436-5030
7 Hosier St Selbyville (19975) ***(G-8465)***
Cablicons LLC...843 458-7702
1201 N Orange St Ste 600 Wilmington (19801) ***(G-9527)***
Cacc Montessori School...302 239-2917
1313 Little Baltimore Rd Hockessin (19707) ***(G-2974)***
Cactus Annies Restaurant & Bar...302 655-9004
211 W 9th St Wilmington (19801) ***(G-9528)***
Cad Import Inc...302 628-4178
650 Centerpoint Blvd New Castle (19720) ***(G-5128)***
Cadapult Ltd...302 733-0477
2644 Kirkwood Hwy Ste 140 Newark (19711) ***(G-6143)***
Cadbury At Lewes Inc...302 644-6382
17028 Cadbury Cir Lewes (19958) ***(G-3399)***
Cadia Rhabilitation Pike Creek, Wilmington *Also called Cadia Rhabilitation Pike Creek* ***(G-9529)***
Cadia Rhabilitation Pike Creek...302 455-0808
3540 Three Little Bkrs Bl Wilmington (19808) ***(G-9529)***
Cadia Rhabilitation Silverside...302 478-8889
3322 Silverside Rd Wilmington (19810) ***(G-9530)***
Cadia Rverside Healthcare Svcs...302 455-0808
3540 Three Little Bakers Wilmington (19808) ***(G-9531)***
Cadrender LLC...302 657-0700
716 N Tatnall St Wilmington (19801) ***(G-9532)***
Cadtech Inc...302 832-2255
2500 Wrangle Hill Rd # 105 Bear (19701) ***(G-61)***
Cae(us) Inc (HQ)...813 885-7481
1011 Ct Rd Ste 322 Wilmington (19805) ***(G-9533)***
Caesar Rodney School District...302 697-3207
950 Center Rd Dover (19901) ***(G-1248)***
Cafe Management Associates...302 655-4959
1428 N Clayton St Wilmington (19806) ***(G-9534)***
Cahill Contracting...302 378-9650
104 Sleepy Hollow Dr # 201 Middletown (19709) ***(G-3979)***
Cahill Electrical Contractors, Middletown *Also called Cahill Contracting* ***(G-3979)***
Cahill Plumbing & Heating Inc...302 894-1802
325 Markus Ct Newark (19713) ***(G-6144)***
Caimar Corporation...302 653-5011
17 W Glenwood Ave Smyrna (19977) ***(G-8589)***
Cain Home Health Services...302 268-6919
913 N Market St Ste 200 Wilmington (19801) ***(G-9535)***
Cakes By Dee...302 934-7483
30790 Hickory Hill Rd Millsboro (19966) ***(G-4653)***
Calatlantic Group Inc...302 834-5472
8 Meridian Blvd Bear (19701) ***(G-62)***
Calfo & Haight Inc...302 998-3852
21 Glover Cir Wilmington (19804) ***(G-9536)***
California Video 2...302 477-6944
1716 Marsh Rd Wilmington (19810) ***(G-9537)***
Callaway Farnell and Moore...302 629-4514
500 W Stein Hwy Seaford (19973) ***(G-8180)***
Callaway Furniture Inc...302 398-8858
15152 S Dupont Hwy Harrington (19952) ***(G-2823)***
Calloway's Interiors, Wilmington *Also called Calloways Custom Interiors Co* ***(G-9538)***
Calloways Custom Interiors Co...302 994-7931
211 Brookland Ave Wilmington (19805) ***(G-9538)***
Calmeet Inc...469 223-0863
113 Barksdale Pro Ctr Newark (19711) ***(G-6145)***
Calmet Corporation...714 505-6765
717 N Union St Ste 100 Wilmington (19805) ***(G-9539)***
Calpine Corporation...302 764-4478
198 Hay Rd Wilmington (19809) ***(G-9540)***
Calpine Corporation...302 824-4779
200 Hay Rd Wilmington (19809) ***(G-9541)***
Calpine Operating Svcs Co Inc...302 468-5400
500 Delaware Ave Ste 600 Wilmington (19801) ***(G-9542)***
Calvert Comfort Cooling & Htg, Wilmington *Also called Calvert Mechanical Systems Inc* ***(G-9543)***
Calvert Mechanical Systems Inc...302 998-0460
410 Meco Dr Wilmington (19804) ***(G-9543)***
Calvin B Taylor Bnkg Berlin MD...302 541-0500
50 Atlantic Ave Ocean View (19970) ***(G-7772)***
Calvin R Clendaniel Associates...302 422-5347
1 Buttler Ave Lincoln (19960) ***(G-3840)***
Calvin Sheets...302 832-0600
254 Foxhunt Dr Bear (19701) ***(G-63)***
Cambridge Club Assoc Partn...302 674-3500
726 Yorklyn Rd Ste 200 Hockessin (19707) ***(G-2975)***
Camdel Metals, Camden *Also called Handytube Corporation* ***(G-575)***
Camden Drywall Inc...302 697-9653
203 Harrison Ave Wyoming (19934) ***(G-13359)***
Camden Metals, Camden *Also called Handytube Corporation* ***(G-576)***
Camden-Wyoming Rotary Club...302 697-2724
6 Bob White Pl Camden Wyoming (19934) ***(G-622)***
Camdenwyoming Sewer & Wtr Auth...302 697-6372
16 S West St Camden (19934) ***(G-544)***
Cameck Publishing...302 598-4799
3306 Coachman Rd Wilmington (19803) ***(G-9544)***
Camels Hump Inc...302 227-5719
63 Fields End Rehoboth Beach (19971) ***(G-7882)***
Cameras Etc Inc (PA)...302 764-9400
2303 Baynard Blvd Wilmington (19802) ***(G-9545)***
Cameras Etc Inc...302 453-9400
165 E Main St Newark (19711) ***(G-6146)***
Cameras Etc T V & Video, Wilmington *Also called Cameras Etc Inc* ***(G-9545)***
Cameras Etc TV & Video, Newark *Also called Cameras Etc Inc* ***(G-6146)***
Cammarato & Aloe PA, Dover *Also called Aloe & Carr PA* ***(G-1111)***
Cammock Boy Auto, New Castle *Also called Cammocks Auto Works LLC* ***(G-5129)***
Cammocks Auto Works LLC...302 597-0204
314 Bay West Blvd Ste 5a New Castle (19720) ***(G-5129)***
Camp Arrowhead Busine...302 448-6919
913 Wilson Rd Wilmington (19803) ***(G-9546)***
Camp Chiropractic Inc...302 378-2899
272 Carter Dr Ste 120 Middletown (19709) ***(G-3980)***
Campbell's Custom Cabinet Shop, Greenwood *Also called Custom Cabinet Shop Inc* ***(G-2725)***
Campbells Landscape Svc Inc...302 266-0117
22 Deer Run Newark (19711) ***(G-6147)***
Can Collecting Club...302 420-5768
1524 Seton Dr Wilmington (19809) ***(G-9547)***
Canada Dry Distrg Wilmington, New Castle *Also called Canada Dry Dstrg Wilmington De* ***(G-5130)***
Canada Dry Dstrg Wilmington De (PA)...302 322-1856
650 Ships Landing Way New Castle (19720) ***(G-5130)***
Canal New Orleans Hotel LLC (PA)...504 962-0500
1209 N Orange St Wilmington (19801) ***(G-9548)***
Canby Park Apartments, Wilmington *Also called Alban Associates* ***(G-9001)***
Cancer Care Ctrs At Bay Hlth...302 674-4401
793 S Queen St Dover (19904) ***(G-1249)***
Cancer Support Cmnty Del Inc...302 995-2850
4810 Lancaster Pike Wilmington (19807) ***(G-9549)***
Candle Parlour...302 408-0890
12 Commonwealth Ave Claymont (19703) ***(G-706)***
Candlelight Bridal Formal Tlrg...302 934-8009
314 Main St Millsboro (19966) ***(G-4654)***
Candlelight Cleaning...302 270-1218
379 Lake Dr Smyrna (19977) ***(G-8590)***
Candyland Farm, Middletown *Also called Pck Associates Inc* ***(G-4186)***
Cann Printing, Wilmington *Also called William N Cann Inc* ***(G-13215)***
Cann-Erikson Bindery Inc...302 995-6636
1 Meco Cir Wilmington (19804) ***(G-9550)***
Cannon Cold Storage LLC...302 337-5500
500 Market St Bridgeville (19933) ***(G-457)***
Cannon Enterprises...302 629-6746
22719 Bridgeville Hwy Seaford (19973) ***(G-8181)***
Cannon Sline LLC...302 658-1420
103 Carroll Dr New Castle (19720) ***(G-5131)***
Cannons Cake and Candy Sups...302 738-3321
2638 Kirkwood Hwy Newark (19711) ***(G-6148)***
Canon Solutions America Inc...302 792-8700
300 Bellevue Pkwy Ste 135 Wilmington (19809) ***(G-9551)***
Cansurround Pbc...302 540-2270
1815 W 13th St Ste 5 Wilmington (19806) ***(G-9552)***
Canterbury Homes Inc (PA)...302 284-0351
120 Crestwood Dr Ste A Felton (19943) ***(G-2279)***
CAP, Wilmington *Also called Richardson Park Community* ***(G-12414)***
Cap Managment Services LLC...302 846-0120
10977 State St Unit 6 Delmar (19940) ***(G-978)***
Cap Title of Delaware LLC...302 537-3788
29 Atlantic Ave Ste E Ocean View (19970) ***(G-7773)***
Capano Homes Inc...302 384-7980
4120 Concord Pike Ste D Wilmington (19803) ***(G-9553)***
Capano Management, Wilmington *Also called Capano Homes Inc* ***(G-9553)***
Capano Management Company...302 429-8700
105 Foulk Rd Wilmington (19803) ***(G-9554)***
Capano Management Company...302 737-8056
33 Marrows Rd Newark (19713) ***(G-6149)***

ALPHABETIC C

Cape Canvas 302 684-8201
12 Meadowridge Ln Milton (19968) *(G-4874)*
Cape Financial Services Inc 302 645-6274
16117 Willow Creek Rd Lewes (19958) *(G-3400)*
Cape Gazette Ltd 302 645-7700
17585 Nassau Commons Blvd # 6 Lewes (19958) *(G-3401)*
Cape Henlopen Senior Center 302 227-2055
11 Christian St Rehoboth Beach (19971) *(G-7883)*
Cape Hnlpen Nntcoke Drmatology, Lewes Also called Mitchell C Stickler MD Inc *(G-3645)*
Cape May-Lewes Ferry, Lewes Also called Delaware River & Bay Authority *(G-3457)*
Cape Medical Associates PA 302 645-2805
701 Savannah Rd Ste B Lewes (19958) *(G-3402)*
Cape Surgical Associates PA 302 645-7050
750 Kings Hwy Ste 103 Lewes (19958) *(G-3403)*
Capes & Open Glass, Georgetown Also called Joes Paint & Body Shop Inc *(G-2576)*
Capgemini America Inc 302 656-7491
405 N King St Wilmington (19801) *(G-9555)*
Capital Commercial Realty LLC 302 734-4400
5307 Limestone Rd Ste 102 Wilmington (19808) *(G-9556)*
Capital Crematorium, Dover Also called Torbert Funeral Chapel Inc *(G-2153)*
Capital Gaines LLC 302 433-6777
4023 Kennett Pike 2082 Wilmington (19807) *(G-9557)*
CAPITAL HEALTHCARE SERVICES, N, Dover Also called Capitol Nursg & Rhb Cntr LLC *(G-1254)*
Capital One National Assn 302 658-3302
1 S Orange St Wilmington (19801) *(G-9558)*
Capital One National Assn 302 645-1360
19268 Old Landing Rd Rehoboth Beach (19971) *(G-7884)*
Capital School District 302 678-8394
88 Carpenter St Dover (19901) *(G-1250)*
Capitaql Environmental, Newark Also called Capitol Environmental Svcs Inc *(G-6150)*
Capitol Billiards Inc 302 629-0298
735 Nylon Blvd Seaford (19973) *(G-8182)*
Capitol Cleaners & Launderers 302 378-4744
600 N Broad St Ste 14 Middletown (19709) *(G-3981)*
Capitol Cleaners & Launderers (PA) 302 674-1511
195 Commerce Way Dover (19904) *(G-1251)*
Capitol Cleaners & Launderers 302 674-0500
217 S New St Dover (19904) *(G-1252)*
Capitol Credit Services Inc (PA) 302 678-1735
872 Walker Rd Ste B Dover (19904) *(G-1253)*
Capitol Environmental Svcs Inc 302 652-8999
200 Biddle Ave Ste 205 Newark (19702) *(G-6150)*
Capitol Nursg & Rhb Cntr LLC 302 734-1199
1225 Walker Rd Dover (19904) *(G-1254)*
Capitol Uniform & Linen Svc, Dover Also called Capitol Cleaners & Launderers *(G-1251)*
Capriottis of Milford 302 424-3309
684 N Dupont Blvd Milford (19963) *(G-4340)*
Capstone Homes 302 684-4480
27423 Walking Run Milton (19968) *(G-4875)*
Capstone Homes LLC 302 644-0300
33712 Wescoats Rd Unit 5 Lewes (19958) *(G-3404)*
Captain's Catch, Wilmington Also called Meltrone Inc *(G-11628)*
Captains Grant Hoa, Millsboro Also called Captains Grant Solar 1 Inc *(G-4655)*
Captains Grant Solar 1 Inc 410 375-2092
32499 Captains Way Millsboro (19966) *(G-4655)*
Capture Technologies Inc 650 772-8006
1013 Centre Rd Ste 403b Wilmington (19805) *(G-9559)*
Car Clinic Inc 302 421-9100
59 Germay Dr Wilmington (19804) *(G-9560)*
Car Tech Auto Center 302 368-4104
102 Albe Dr Ste A Newark (19702) *(G-6151)*
Car Wash of Prices Corner 302 994-9274
3213 Kirkwood Hwy Wilmington (19808) *(G-9561)*
Cara Guitars Manufacturing 302 521-0119
112 Water St Wilmington (19804) *(G-9562)*
Cara Plastics Inc 302 622-7070
1201 N Market St Ste 2100 Wilmington (19801) *(G-9563)*
Carbocycle Co 212 214-4068
919 N Market St Ste 425 Wilmington (19801) *(G-9564)*
Cardenti Electric 302 834-1278
109 E Scotland Dr Bear (19701) *(G-64)*
Cardiac Diagnostic Center, Wilmington Also called Christiana Care Health Sys Inc *(G-9680)*
Cardio-Kinetics Inc 302 738-6635
52 N Chapel St Ste 101 Newark (19711) *(G-6152)*
Cardiology Consultants 302 645-1233
16704 Kings Hwy Lewes (19958) *(G-3405)*
Cardiology Consultants (PA) 302 541-8138
35141 Atlantic Ave Unit 3 Millville (19967) *(G-4838)*
Cardiology Physicans PA Inc 302 366-8600
1 Centurian Dr Ste 200 Newark (19713) *(G-6153)*
Cardiology Specialists 302 453-0624
106 Saint Moritz Dr Wilmington (19807) *(G-9565)*
Cardiomo Care Inc 929 360-5107
919 N Market St Ste 425 Wilmington (19801) *(G-9566)*
Cardiovascular Consultants of 302 541-8138
609 Atlantic Ave Ocean View (19967) *(G-7774)*
Cardno Inc 302 395-1919
121 Continental Dr # 308 Newark (19713) *(G-6154)*

Career Associates Inc 302 674-4357
385 W North St Ste A Dover (19904) *(G-1255)*
Careers Usa Inc 302 737-3600
2 Reads Way Ste 224 New Castle (19720) *(G-5132)*
Careportmd LLC 302 202-3020
4365 Kirkwood Hwy Wilmington (19808) *(G-9567)*
Carey Ins & Fin Services Inc 302 934-8383
30618 Dupont Blvd Unit 1 Dagsboro (19939) *(G-888)*
Carey Jr James E Inc (PA) 302 934-8383
30618 Dupont Blvd Unit 1 Dagsboro (19939) *(G-889)*
Careys Diesel Inc 302 678-3797
168 Denny St Leipsic (19901) *(G-3313)*
Careys Foreign & Domestic Repr 302 856-2779
7 Bridgeville Rd Georgetown (19947) *(G-2462)*
Careys Inc 302 875-5674
30986 Sussex Hwy Laurel (19956) *(G-3207)*
Careys Towing, Laurel Also called Careys Inc *(G-3207)*
Cargo Cube Licensing LLC 844 200-2823
2711 Centerville Rd # 400 Wilmington (19808) *(G-9568)*
Cargoex Inc 800 850-9493
1208 First State Blvd Wilmington (19804) *(G-9569)*
Caribb Moto Cars, Wilmington Also called Caribb Transport Inc *(G-9570)*
Caribb Transport Inc 302 274-2112
2800 Governor Printz Blvd # 3 Wilmington (19802) *(G-9570)*
Caridad Rosal MA MD 302 653-6174
38 Deak Dr Smyrna (19977) *(G-8591)*
Caring For Life Inc 302 892-2214
92 Reads Way Ste 207 New Castle (19720) *(G-5133)*
Caring Hearts Home Care LLC 302 734-9000
971 Burris Rd Hartly (19953) *(G-2914)*
Caring Matters Home Care 302 993-1121
283 Orchard Grove Dr Camden (19934) *(G-545)*
Caring N Action Nursing 302 368-2273
15 Prestbury Sq Newark (19713) *(G-6155)*
Carl Deputy & Son Builders LLC 302 284-3041
5564 Lttle Mstens Crnr Rd Felton (19943) *(G-2280)*
Carl King Tire Co Inc (PA) 302 697-9506
109 S Main St Camden (19934) *(G-546)*
Carl King Tire Co Inc 302 644-4070
96 Tulip Dr Lewes (19958) *(G-3406)*
Carl M Freeman Associates Inc 302 436-3000
21 Village Green Dr # 101 Ocean View (19970) *(G-7775)*
Carl M Freeman Associates Inc 302 539-6961
Pennsylvania Ave Rr 1 Bethany Beach (19930) *(G-391)*
Carleton Court Apartments, Wilmington Also called Carleton Court Associates LP *(G-9571)*
Carleton Court Associates LP 302 454-1800
4 Denny Rd Wilmington (19809) *(G-9571)*
Carlisle Farms Inc 302 349-5692
12733 Shawnee Rd Greenwood (19950) *(G-2719)*
Carlisle Group 302 475-3010
2801 Ebright Rd Wilmington (19810) *(G-9572)*
Carlisle Machine Shop Inc 302 653-2584
970 Blackbird Landing Rd Townsend (19734) *(G-8768)*
Carlo Porter Michael 267 709-6370
2015 Cervantes Ct Newark (19702) *(G-6156)*
Carlson , John C MD, Wilmington Also called Maternity Associates PA *(G-11567)*
Carlyle Cocoa Co LLC 302 428-3800
23 Harbor View Dr New Castle (19720) *(G-5134)*
Carme LLC 302 832-8418
1420 Pulaski Hwy Newark (19702) *(G-6157)*
Carmen R Benitez 302 793-2061
3047 Greenshire Ave Claymont (19703) *(G-707)*
Carmike Cinemas Inc 302 734-5249
1365 N Dupont Hwy # 3020 Dover (19901) *(G-1256)*
Carmine Potter & Associates 302 832-6000
1400 Peoples Plz Ste 104 Newark (19702) *(G-6158)*
Carmine Potter & Associates (PA) 302 658-8940
840 N Union St Wilmington (19805) *(G-9573)*
Carney Machinery Co (PA) 302 571-8382
500 E Front St Wilmington (19801) *(G-9574)*
Carol Inc 302 386-4362
106 Peoples Plz Newark (19702) *(G-6159)*
Carol A Tavani MD 302 454-9900
4745 Ogltn Stntn Rd # 124 Newark (19713) *(G-6160)*
Carol Boyd Heron 302 645-0551
520 E Savannah Rd Lewes (19958) *(G-3407)*
Carolina Street Garden & Home 302 539-2405
40118 E Sc St Fenwick Island (19944) *(G-2332)*
Caroline M Wiesner 877 220-9755
3322 Englewood Rd Wilmington (19810) *(G-9575)*
Carolyn A Drkowski Ht Ascp LLC 443 831-4854
20845 Crest Ct Lewes (19958) *(G-3408)*
Carolyn Palmatary 302 239-5744
519 Pershing Rd Hockessin (19707) *(G-2976)*
Carpe Dia Organization 302 333-7546
241 Goldfinch Turn Newark (19711) *(G-6161)*
Carpe Vita Home Care 302 482-4305
240 N James St Wilmington (19804) *(G-9576)*
Carpediem Health LLC 347 467-4444
8 The Grn Ste 240 Dover (19901) *(G-1257)*

Carpenter Investments Inc 302 656-5664
1105 N Market St Fl 1 Wilmington (19801) ***(G-9577)***
Carpentry Unlimited, Bear *Also called Kevin Garber* ***(G-216)***
Carquest Auto Parts, Ocean View *Also called Bethany Auto Parts Inc* ***(G-7765)***
Carr Paris 302 401-1203
511 N Union St Apt 2f Wilmington (19805) ***(G-9578)***
Carr Courier Service Inc 302 846-9826
12294 Coachmen Ln Delmar (19940) ***(G-979)***
Carrick Chiropractic Centre PA 302 478-1443
1309 Veale Rd Ste 12 Wilmington (19810) ***(G-9579)***
Carrie Construction Inc 302 239-5386
403 Hockessin Hills Rd Hockessin (19707) ***(G-2977)***
Carrier Rental Systems Inc 302 836-3000
500 Carson Dr Bear (19701) ***(G-65)***
Carrington Way Apartments, Newark *Also called Kimberton Apartments Assoc LP* ***(G-6887)***
Carroll Brothers Electric LLC 302 947-4754
24853 Rivers Edge Rd Millsboro (19966) ***(G-4656)***
Carspecken-Scott Inc (PA) 302 655-7173
1707 N Lincoln St Wilmington (19806) ***(G-9580)***
Carspecken-Scott Inc 302 762-7955
3007 Rosemont Ave Wilmington (19802) ***(G-9581)***
Carter Firm LLC 267 420-0717
2600 N Van Buren St Wilmington (19802) ***(G-9582)***
Carter Karen DMD 302 832-2200
1991 Pulaski Hwy Bear (19701) ***(G-66)***
Carter Pool Management LLC 302 236-6952
35740 Cutter Ct Lewes (19958) ***(G-3409)***
Carter Printing and Design 302 655-2343
427 Martin Dr New Castle (19720) ***(G-5135)***
Carters Inc 302 731-1432
3132 Fashion Center Blvd Newark (19702) ***(G-6162)***
Cartessa Aesthetics 302 332-1991
210 Peoples Way Hockessin (19707) ***(G-2978)***
Carthage Group Inc 610 931-8493
407 Stanley Plaza Blvd Newark (19713) ***(G-6163)***
Caruso Richard F MD PA 302 645-6698
130 Savannah Rd Ste B Lewes (19958) ***(G-3410)***
CARVEL GARDEN, Laurel *Also called Better Homes of Laurel Inc* ***(G-3199)***
Carvel Gardens Annex, Laurel *Also called Better Homes Laurel II Inc* ***(G-3198)***
Carvel Gardens Associates LP 302 875-4281
801 Daniel St Laurel (19956) ***(G-3208)***
Carvertise Inc 302 273-1889
319 6th Ave Wilmington (19805) ***(G-9583)***
Carzaty Inc 650 396-0144
874 Walker Rd Ste C Dover (19904) ***(G-1258)***
Carzo & Associates Inc 302 575-0336
3401 Montchanin Rd Wilmington (19807) ***(G-9584)***
Casa San Francisco, Milton *Also called Catholic Charities Inc* ***(G-4876)***
Casale Marble Imports Inc 561 404-4213
3518 Silverside Rd Ste 22 Wilmington (19810) ***(G-9585)***
Casarino Christman Shalk 302 594-4500
1007 N Orange St Wilmington (19801) ***(G-9586)***
Case, New Castle *Also called Countermeasures Assessment* ***(G-5200)***
Case Construction Inc 302 737-3800
17 Mcmillan Way Newark (19713) ***(G-6164)***
Case Hndyman Svcs W Chster LLC 302 234-6558
510 Thorndale Dr Hockessin (19707) ***(G-2979)***
Case Management Services 302 354-3711
234 Philadelphia Pike # 6 Wilmington (19809) ***(G-9587)***
Cash Advance Plus 302 846-3900
38650 Sussex Hwy Unit 8 Delmar (19940) ***(G-980)***
Cash Advance Plus (PA) 302 629-6266
N607 N 607 N Dual Hwy Rr Seaford (19973) ***(G-8183)***
Cash Connect Inc 302 283-4100
500 Creek View Rd Ste 100 Newark (19711) ***(G-6165)***
Cashtoday Financial Centers, Claymont *Also called Frascella Enterprises Inc* ***(G-748)***
Casscells Orthopaedics Sp 302 832-6220
2600 Glasgow Ave Ste 104 Newark (19702) ***(G-6166)***
Cassidy Painting Inc 302 683-0710
20 Germay Dr Wilmington (19804) ***(G-9588)***
Castle Bag Company 302 656-1001
115 Valley Rd Wilmington (19804) ***(G-9589)***
Castle Construction Del Inc 302 326-3600
185 Old Churchmans Rd New Castle (19720) ***(G-5136)***
Castle Consultants, Wilmington *Also called Ciancon Global LLC* ***(G-9699)***
Castle Mortage Services Inc 302 366-0912
4 Vantage Ct Newark (19711) ***(G-6167)***
Castrol Industrial N Amer Inc 302 934-9100
28569 Dupont Blvd Millsboro (19966) ***(G-4657)***
Castrol Premium Lube Express, Millsboro *Also called Castrol Industrial N Amer Inc* ***(G-4657)***
Cat Welding LLC 302 846-3509
37544 Horsey Church Rd Delmar (19940) ***(G-981)***
Catalyst Handling Resources 302 798-2200
950 Ridge Rd Ste E3 Claymont (19703) ***(G-708)***
Cataract and Laser Center LLC 302 454-8802
4102 Ogltn Stntn Rd # 1 Newark (19713) ***(G-6168)***
Catch-A-Web Cleaning Inc 302 836-1970
2099 Red Lion Rd Bear (19701) ***(G-67)***
Caterpillar, New Castle *Also called Giles & Ransome Inc* ***(G-5353)***
Caterpillar Authorized Dealer, Bear *Also called Foley Incorporated* ***(G-157)***
Caterpillar Authorized Dealer, Felton *Also called Alban Tractor Co Inc* ***(G-2270)***
Cathedral Cemetary, Wilmington *Also called Catholic Cemetaries Inc* ***(G-9590)***
Catherine Deane, Wilmington *Also called Arcangel Inc* ***(G-9121)***
Catherine Kotalis 302 526-1470
540 S Governors Ave Dover (19904) ***(G-1259)***
Catholic Cemetaries Inc (PA) 302 254-4701
2400 Lancaster Ave Wilmington (19805) ***(G-9590)***
Catholic Cemetaries Inc 302 737-2524
6001 Kirkwood Hwy Wilmington (19808) ***(G-9591)***
Catholic Charities Inc 302 856-9578
406 S Bedford St Georgetown (19947) ***(G-2463)***
Catholic Charities Inc 302 573-3122
2307 Kentmere Pkwy Wilmington (19806) ***(G-9592)***
Catholic Charities Inc 302 654-1184
300 Bayard Ave Wilmington (19805) ***(G-9593)***
Catholic Charities Inc 302 674-1600
2099 S Dupont Hwy Dover (19901) ***(G-1260)***
Catholic Charities Inc (PA) 302 655-9624
2601 W 4th St Wilmington (19805) ***(G-9594)***
Catholic Charities Inc 302 684-8694
127 Broad St Milton (19968) ***(G-4876)***
Catholic Charities Inc 302 674-1600
1155 Walker Rd Dover (19904) ***(G-1261)***
Catholic Charities Thrift Ctr, Wilmington *Also called Catholic Docese Wilmington Inc* ***(G-9595)***
Catholic Docese Wilmington Inc 302 764-2717
1320 E 23rd St Wilmington (19802) ***(G-9595)***
Catholic Docese Wilmington Inc 302 731-2210
82 Possum Park Rd Newark (19711) ***(G-6169)***
Catholic Health East 302 325-4900
612 Ferry Cut Off St New Castle (19720) ***(G-5137)***
Catholic Mnstry To Elderly Inc 302 368-2784
135 Jeandell Dr Newark (19713) ***(G-6170)***
Cathy L Harris DDS 302 453-1400
220 Christiana Med Ctr Newark (19702) ***(G-6171)***
Cato Corporation 302 854-9548
509 N Dupont Hwy Georgetown (19947) ***(G-2464)***
Cavalier Apartments, Wilmington *Also called Cavalier Group* ***(G-9596)***
Cavalier Apts, Newark *Also called Cavalier Group* ***(G-6172)***
Cavalier Group (PA) 302 429-8700
105 Foulk Rd Wilmington (19803) ***(G-9596)***
Cavalier Group 302 368-7437
25 Golf View Dr Ofc A4 Newark (19702) ***(G-6172)***
Cavaliers Country Club, Newark *Also called Cavaliers of Delaware Inc* ***(G-6173)***
Cavaliers of Delaware Inc 302 731-5600
100 Addison Dr Newark (19702) ***(G-6173)***
Caveman Design Inc 302 234-9969
359 Lower Snuff Mill Rd Hockessin (19707) ***(G-2980)***
Cawsl Enterprises Inc (HQ) 302 478-6160
3411 Silverside Rd Wilmington (19810) ***(G-9597)***
CB Productions 302 715-1015
33434 Ellis Grove Rd Laurel (19956) ***(G-3209)***
CB Richard Ellis RE Svcs LLC 302 661-6700
1007 N Orange St Ste 100 Wilmington (19801) ***(G-9598)***
Cbbc Opco LLC (PA) 863 967-0636
200 Bellevue Pkwy Ste 210 Wilmington (19809) ***(G-9599)***
Cbc Holding Inc 302 254-2000
1201 N Market St Fl 9 Wilmington (19801) ***(G-9600)***
Cbd Pro LLC 443 736-9002
6625 Millcreek Rd Laurel (19956) ***(G-3210)***
CBI Group LLc (PA) 302 266-0860
1501 Casho Mill Rd Ste 9 Newark (19711) ***(G-6174)***
CBI Services LLC 302 325-8400
24 Reads Way New Castle (19720) ***(G-5138)***
Cbre Inc 302 661-6700
1007 N Orange St Ste 100 Wilmington (19801) ***(G-9601)***
CBS, Delmar *Also called Concrete Bldg Systems Del Inc* ***(G-986)***
CC Enterprises LLC 302 265-3677
105 Anita Dr Newark (19713) ***(G-6175)***
Cchs Logistics Center, New Castle *Also called Christiana Care Health Sys Inc* ***(G-5153)***
Ccmc Inc 302 477-9660
2106 Silverside Rd # 202 Wilmington (19810) ***(G-9602)***
CD Clean Energy and Infrastruc (PA) 480 653-8450
251 Little Falls Dr Wilmington (19808) ***(G-9603)***
CD Cream 302 832-5425
32 Clinton St Delaware City (19706) ***(G-950)***
CD Diagnostics Inc (HQ) 302 367-7770
650 Naamans Rd Ste 100 Claymont (19703) ***(G-709)***
Cda Engineering Inc 302 998-9202
6 Larch Ave Ste 401 Wilmington (19804) ***(G-9604)***
Cda Group Inc 302 793-0693
15 Delaware Ave Claymont (19703) ***(G-710)***
Cdb Ventures Inc 302 235-0414
157 Lantana Dr Hockessin (19707) ***(G-2981)***
CDI Inc Sofr System LLC 302 536-7325
1330 Middleford Rd Seaford (19973) ***(G-8184)***
Cdo USA Inc 347 429-5110
1013 Centre Rd Ste 403a Wilmington (19805) ***(G-9605)***

ALPHABETIC

Cecil Vault & Memorial Co Inc 302 994-3806
5701 Kirkwood Hwy Wilmington (19808) ***(G-9606)***
Cecilia Williams 302 250-6269
3710 N Market St Wilmington (19802) ***(G-9607)***
Ceco Inc 302 732-3919
27515 Hodges Ln Unit N1 Dagsboro (19939) ***(G-890)***
Cecon Group LLC 302 994-8000
242 N James St Ste 202 Wilmington (19804) ***(G-9608)***
Cedar Chase Apartments, Dover *Also called Udr Inc* ***(G-2172)***
Cedar Creek Custom Cabinets 302 542-7794
7816 Cedar Creek Ct Milford (19963) ***(G-4341)***
Cedar Creek Marina 302 422-2040
100 Marina Ln Milford (19963) ***(G-4342)***
Cedar Hardscaping L L C 877 569-9859
1782 Red Lion Rd Bear (19701) ***(G-68)***
Cedar Lane Inc 302 328-7232
310 Delaware St New Castle (19720) ***(G-5139)***
Cedar Neck Decor LLC 918 497-7179
30980 Country Gdns Q1 Dagsboro (19939) ***(G-891)***
Cedar Tree Apartments, Wilmington *Also called Panco Management Corporation* ***(G-12012)***
Cedar Tree Medical Center, Millsboro *Also called Lewes Surgical and Med Assoc* ***(G-4719)***
Cedar Tree Surgical Center 302 945-9766
32711 Long Neck Rd Millsboro (19966) ***(G-4658)***
Celanese International Corp 972 443-4000
Silverside Rd Rodney 34 Wilmington (19810) ***(G-9609)***
Celebrations Design Group Ltd 302 793-3893
950 Ridge Rd Ste D8 Claymont (19703) ***(G-711)***
Celebree Holding Inc 302 834-0436
1205 Quintilio Dr Bear (19701) ***(G-69)***
Celebree Learning Centers, Bear *Also called Celebree Holding Inc* ***(G-69)***
Celera Services Inc 302 378-7778
364 E Main St Middletown (19709) ***(G-3982)***
Cell Point LLC 302 658-9200
1201 N Market St Wilmington (19801) ***(G-9610)***
Cellco Partnership 302 376-6049
580 W Main St Middletown (19709) ***(G-3983)***
Cellco Partnership 302 530-4620
4407 Concord Pike Wilmington (19803) ***(G-9611)***
Cellco Partnership 302 653-8183
239 N Dupont Blvd Smyrna (19977) ***(G-8592)***
Cellco Partnership 302 697-8340
386 Walmart Dr Camden (19934) ***(G-547)***
Cellco Partnership 302 730-5200
1045 N Dupont Hwy Dover (19901) ***(G-1262)***
Cemex Materials LLC 302 378-8920
800 Industrial Rd Middletown (19709) ***(G-3984)***
Center 213, Newark *Also called Csl Plasma Inc* ***(G-6321)***
Center For A Pstive Hmnity LLC 302 703-1036
86 Ludlow Ln Felton (19943) ***(G-2281)***
Center For Advnced Srgcal Arts, Wilmington *Also called Rockland Surgery Center LP* ***(G-12455)***
Center For Black Culture 302 831-2991
192 S College Ave Newark (19716) ***(G-6176)***
Center For Child Developement 302 292-1334
256 Chapman Rd Ste 201 Newark (19702) ***(G-6177)***
Center For Community Justice 302 424-0890
1129 Airport Rd Milford (19963) ***(G-4343)***
Center For Composite Material, Newark *Also called University of Delaware* ***(G-7628)***
Center For Human Reproduction (PA) 302 738-4600
4745 Ogletown Stanton Rd Newark (19713) ***(G-6178)***
Center For Inland Bays Inc 302 226-8105
39375 Inlet Rd Rehoboth Beach (19971) ***(G-7885)***
Center For Intrvntnal Pain SPI 302 792-1370
405 Silverside Rd Ste 100 Wilmington (19809) ***(G-9612)***
Center For Neurology 302 422-0800
111 Neurology Way Milford (19963) ***(G-4344)***
Center For Plastic/Rconstructv, Dover *Also called Asher B Carey III* ***(G-1144)***
Center For Rehabilitation, Wilmington *Also called Christiana Care Health Sys Inc* ***(G-9679)***
Center For Women's Health, Wilmington *Also called Ccmc Inc* ***(G-9602)***
Center of Hope, Newark *Also called William A Ellert MD* ***(G-7696)***
Center Stage Auto Auction 302 325-2277
741 Hamburg Rd New Castle (19720) ***(G-5140)***
Centerville Company Contrs 302 656-8666
5714 Kennett Pike Wilmington (19807) ***(G-9613)***
Centerville Veterinary Hosp 302 655-3315
5804 Kennett Pike Wilmington (19807) ***(G-9614)***
Central Amer Hlth Buty Distrs, Georgetown *Also called Central America Distrs LLC* ***(G-2465)***
Central America Distrs LLC 302 628-4178
11 E Market St Ste 2 Georgetown (19947) ***(G-2465)***
Central and Southern Delaware 302 545-8067
221 S Rehoboth Blvd Milford (19963) ***(G-4345)***
Central Backhoe Service 302 398-6420
28247 Rund Pole Bridge Rd Milton (19968) ***(G-4877)***
Central Del Chmber of Commerce 302 734-7513
435 N Dupont Hwy Dover (19901) ***(G-1263)***
Central Del Endoscopy Unit 302 422-3393
302 Polk Ave Milford (19963) ***(G-4346)***
Central Del Endoscopy Unit (PA) 302 677-1617
644 S Queen St Ste 105 Dover (19904) ***(G-1264)***
Central Del Gstrntrology Assoc 302 422-3393
302 Polk Ave Milford (19963) ***(G-4347)***
Central Delaware Committee 302 854-0172
20728 Dupont Blvd # 315 Georgetown (19947) ***(G-2466)***
Central Delaware Committee (PA) 302 735-7790
1241 College Park Dr Dover (19904) ***(G-1265)***
Central Delaware Fmly Medicine 302 735-1616
95 Wolf Creek Blvd Ste 2 Dover (19901) ***(G-1266)***
Central Delaware Habitat For 302 526-2366
2311 S Dupont Hwy Dover (19901) ***(G-1267)***
Central Delaware Surgery Ctr, Dover *Also called Central Delaware Surgery Ctr* ***(G-1268)***
Central Delaware Surgery Ctr 302 744-6801
640 S State St Dover (19901) ***(G-1268)***
Central Firm LLC 610 470-9836
1201 N Orange St Ste 7016 Wilmington (19801) ***(G-9615)***
Central Pacific Helicopters 760 786-4163
16192 Coastal Hwy Lewes (19958) ***(G-3411)***
Central Storage 302 678-1919
650 W Division St Dover (19904) ***(G-1269)***
Centrix Hr 302 777-7818
213 W 4th St Wilmington (19801) ***(G-9616)***
Century 21 Fantini Realty 302 798-6688
3724 Philadelphia Pike Claymont (19703) ***(G-712)***
Century 21 Mann & Sons 302 227-9477
19606 Coastal Hwy # 205 Rehoboth Beach (19971) ***(G-7886)***
Century 21 Tom Livizos Inc 302 737-9000
701 Capitol Trl Newark (19711) ***(G-6179)***
Century Engineering Inc 302 734-9188
550 S Bay Rd Dover (19901) ***(G-1270)***
Century Seals Inc 302 629-0324
503 Harrington St Seaford (19973) ***(G-8185)***
Ceo-Hqcom LLC 302 883-8555
7209 Lancaster Pike # 41023 Hockessin (19707) ***(G-2982)***
Ceramic Tile Supply Co 302 737-4968
375 Bellevue Rd Newark (19713) ***(G-6180)***
Certapro Painters of Delaware, Wilmington *Also called Jgarvey Enterprises Inc* ***(G-11154)***
Certified Assets MGT Intl LLC 302 765-3352
100 Todds Ln Wilmington (19802) ***(G-9617)***
Certified Lock & Access LLC 302 383-7507
3 Germay Dr Ste 7 Wilmington (19804) ***(G-9618)***
Certified Mechanical Contrs 302 559-3727
117 David Rd Wilmington (19804) ***(G-9619)***
Cesn Partners Inc 302 537-1814
34541 Atlantic Ave Ocean View (19970) ***(G-7776)***
Cetaris Inc (PA) 416 679-9555
73 Greentree Dr 540 Dover (19904) ***(G-1271)***
Ceventry Health Care Delaware, Newark *Also called Coventry Health Care Inc* ***(G-6309)***
Cfd Group Inc 242 698-1039
919 N Market St Ste 950 Wilmington (19801) ***(G-9620)***
Cfg Lab Inc 302 261-3403
1521 Concord Pike Ste 301 Wilmington (19803) ***(G-9621)***
CFS Construction, Lewes *Also called Cape Financial Services Inc* ***(G-3400)***
Cft Ambulance Service Inc 302 984-2255
33 Pear Dr Bear (19701) ***(G-70)***
Cgc Consulting LLC 302 489-2280
5400 Limestone Rd Ste 200 Wilmington (19808) ***(G-9622)***
Cge Landscape Design 302 983-4847
15 Fox Den Rd Newark (19711) ***(G-6181)***
Cgs Infotech Inc 302 351-2434
501 Silverside Rd Ste 105 Wilmington (19809) ***(G-9623)***
Cha Moon DDS 302 297-3750
1290 Peoples Plz Newark (19702) ***(G-6182)***
Chabbott Ptrosky Coml Realtors 302 678-3276
2 N State St Dover (19901) ***(G-1272)***
Chaffin Cleaning Service Inc 302 369-2704
3 Whitfield Rd Newark (19711) ***(G-6183)***
Challenge Automotive Svcs Inc 302 629-3058
22598 Sussex Hwy Seaford (19973) ***(G-8186)***
Challenge Program 302 655-0945
1124 E 7th St Wilmington (19801) ***(G-9624)***
CHAMBER OF COMMERCE OF CENTRAL, Dover *Also called Central Del Chmber of Commerce* ***(G-1263)***
Chambers Bus Service Inc 302 284-9655
8964 S Dupont Hwy Viola (19979) ***(G-8834)***
Chambers Insurance Agency Inc 302 655-5300
109 N Dupont Rd Wilmington (19807) ***(G-9625)***
Chambers Ldscpg & Lawncare Inc 302 328-1312
41 Don Ave New Castle (19720) ***(G-5141)***
Chambers Motors Inc 302 629-3553
20610 Sussex Hwy Seaford (19973) ***(G-8187)***
Chambers Optometrist 302 543-6492
2323 Pennsylvania Ave Wilmington (19806) ***(G-9626)***
Chameleon City Inc (PA) 415 964-0054
2035 Sunset Lake Rd Newark (19702) ***(G-6184)***
Chamish, Steven E, New Castle *Also called New Castle Dental Assoc PA* ***(G-5556)***
Champion Builders, New Castle *Also called No Joke I LLC* ***(G-5573)***
Champion Exterminators, Millsboro *Also called Mark Wilson Diguardi* ***(G-4735)***

ALPHABETIC SECTION

Champion Window Cleaners, Selbyville Also called D A Jones Inc *(G-8476)*
Champions + Legends Corp 702 605-2522
  251 Little Falls Dr Wilmington (19808) *(G-9627)*
Champions Club 215 380-1273
  488 Augusta National Dr Magnolia (19962) *(G-3884)*
Champions For Childrens Mh 302 249-6788
  119 Timberline Dr Newark (19711) *(G-6185)*
Championship Apparel Corp 302 731-5917
  60 N College Ave Newark (19711) *(G-6186)*
Chancellor Care Center Delmar, Delmar Also called Chancellor Care Ctr of Delmar *(G-982)*
Chancellor Care Ctr of Delmar 302 846-3077
  101 Delaware Ave Delmar (19940) *(G-982)*
Chancery Court Reporters 302 255-0515
  500 N King St Ste 11400 Wilmington (19801) *(G-9628)*
Chandler and Lynch CPA 302 478-9800
  3510 Silverside Rd Ste 4 Wilmington (19810) *(G-9629)*
Chandler Funeral Homes, Wilmington Also called James T Chandler & Son Inc *(G-11124)*
Chandler Heights II LP 302 629-8048
  802 Clementine Ct Seaford (19973) *(G-8188)*
Chaney Enterprises 302 990-5039
  22223 Eskridge Rd Seaford (19973) *(G-8189)*
Change Shop LLC 301 363-7188
  2035 Sunset Lake Rd B2 Newark (19702) *(G-6187)*
Changing Faces Inc 302 397-4164
  19500 Pine Rd Lincoln (19960) *(G-3841)*
Channelpro Mobile LLC 757 620-4635
  19 Kris Ct Newark (19702) *(G-6188)*
Chapis Drafting & Blue Print 302 629-6373
  8057 Hearns Pond Rd Seaford (19973) *(G-8190)*
Chapman Hospitality Inc 302 738-3400
  260 Chapman Rd Newark (19702) *(G-6189)*
Charlan Neighborhood Home, Newark Also called Mosaic *(G-7060)*
Charles A Klein & Sons Inc 410 549-6960
  3 Mason Dr Selbyville (19975) *(G-8466)*
Charles A Zonko Builders Inc 302 436-0222
  37116 Lighthouse Rd Selbyville (19975) *(G-8467)*
Charles Allen Ltd 302 475-5048
  9 W Greenbriar Rd Wilmington (19810) *(G-9630)*
Charles Andrews 302 378-7116
  3305 Harris Rd Townsend (19734) *(G-8769)*
Charles Andrews Upholstery, Townsend Also called Charles Andrews *(G-8769)*
Charles D Calhoon DDS P 302 731-0202
  4600 New Linden Hl 102 Wilmington (19808) *(G-9631)*
Charles D Murphy Associates 302 422-7327
  14 S Maple Ave Milford (19963) *(G-4348)*
Charles Dempsey Farms 302 734-4937
  1708 Fast Landing Rd Dover (19901) *(G-1273)*
Charles E Carlson 302 284-3184
  3670 Willow Grove Rd Camden Wyoming (19934) *(G-623)*
Charles E Hill MD, Wilmington Also called Brandywine Care L L C *(G-9421)*
Charles H West Farms Inc 302 335-3936
  2953 Tub Mill Pond Rd Milford (19963) *(G-4349)*
Charles J Veith DMD 302 658-7354
  2300 Penns Ave Ste 5c Wilmington (19806) *(G-9632)*
Charles M Wallace 302 998-1412
  1906 Newport Gap Pike Wilmington (19808) *(G-9633)*
Charles Moon Plumbing & Htg, Ocean View Also called Cesn Partners Inc *(G-7776)*
Charles Moon Plumbing & Htg (PA) 302 798-6666
  2505 Philadelphia Pike C Claymont (19703) *(G-713)*
Charles Offroad 443 365-0630
  33418 Horsey Church Rd Laurel (19956) *(G-3211)*
Charles Ogden 305 606-4512
  2205 Jones Ln Wilmington (19810) *(G-9634)*
Charles P Arcaro Funeral Home 302 658-9095
  2309 Lancaster Ave Wilmington (19805) *(G-9635)*
Charles R Reed 302 284-3353
  93 Paradise Cove Way Felton (19943) *(G-2282)*
Charles River Labs Intl Inc 302 292-8888
  614 Interchange Blvd Newark (19711) *(G-6190)*
Charles S Knothe Inc 302 478-8800
  3516 Silverside Rd Ste 14 Wilmington (19810) *(G-9636)*
Charles S Reskovitz Inc 302 999-9455
  1018 Liberty Rd Wilmington (19804) *(G-9637)*
Charles Schwab & Co Inc 302 622-3600
  602 Delaware Ave Wilmington (19801) *(G-9638)*
Charles Slanina 302 234-1605
  724 Yorklyn Rd Ste 210 Hockessin (19707) *(G-2983)*
Charles Wang MD PA 302 655-1500
  1700 Wawaset St Ste 200 Wilmington (19806) *(G-9639)*
Charlotte Wilson 302 500-1440
  629 Rosemary Dr Seaford (19973) *(G-8191)*
Chart Exchange 850 376-6435
  3001 Philadelphia Pike Claymont (19703) *(G-714)*
Charter Dynamics LLC 888 260-4579
  427 N Ttnall St Ste 70775 Wilmington (19802) *(G-9640)*
Chas Pools Inc 302 737-9224
  600 N Broad St Ste 11 Middletown (19709) *(G-3985)*
Chase Center On River 302 655-2187
  815 Justison St Ste B Wilmington (19801) *(G-9641)*

Chase Manhattan, Newark Also called Jpmorgan Chase Bank Nat Assn *(G-6856)*
Chasemont Apartments 302 731-0784
  54 Cheswold Blvd Newark (19713) *(G-6191)*
Chatngo Corporation 302 504-4291
  901 N Market St Wilmington (19801) *(G-9642)*
Cheap-Scape Inc 302 472-2600
  720 Yorklyn Rd Ste 5 Hockessin (19707) *(G-2984)*
Cheer Inc (PA) 302 856-5641
  546 S Bedford St Georgetown (19947) *(G-2467)*
Cheer Inc 302 645-9239
  34211 Woods Edge Dr Lewes (19958) *(G-3412)*
Chelsea McHugh Music Therapy 302 827-2335
  28784 Fisher Rd Milton (19968) *(G-4878)*
Chelten Apartments, New Castle Also called Chelten Preservation Assoc LLC *(G-5142)*
Chelten Apartments, New Castle Also called Leon N Weiner & Associates Inc *(G-5479)*
Chelten Apartments Assoc LP 302 322-6323
  4 Denny Rd Wilmington (19809) *(G-9643)*
Chelten Preservation Assoc LLC 302 322-6323
  431 Old Forge Rd New Castle (19720) *(G-5142)*
Chem Tech Inc 302 798-9675
  6725 Governor Printz Blvd Wilmington (19809) *(G-9644)*
Chemax Manufacturing Corp 302 328-2440
  1025 River Rd New Castle (19720) *(G-5143)*
Chemaxon LLC 281 528-0485
  3511 Silverside Rd # 105 Wilmington (19810) *(G-9645)*
Chemfirst Inc (HQ) 302 774-1000
  1007 Market St Wilmington (19898) *(G-9646)*
Chemlime NJ Inc 302 697-2115
  198 Records Dr Magnolia (19962) *(G-3885)*
Chemours Co Fc LLC 302 353-5003
  200 Powder Mill Rd Wilmington (19803) *(G-9647)*
Chemours Company (PA) 302 773-1000
  1007 Market St Wilmington (19898) *(G-9648)*
Chemours Company Fc LLC (HQ) 302 773-1000
  1007 Market St Wilmington (19898) *(G-9649)*
Chemours Company Fc LLC 302 773-1267
  1007 Market St Wilmington (19898) *(G-9650)*
Chemours Company Fc LLC 678 427-1530
  4301 Lncaster Pike Barley Wilmington (19805) *(G-9651)*
Chemours Company Fc LLC 302 540-5423
  Chestnut Run Wilmington (19880) *(G-9652)*
Chemours Company Fc LLC 302 545-0072
  1007 Market St Wilmington (19898) *(G-9653)*
Chemring North Amer Group Inc (HQ) 302 658-5687
  1105 N Market St Wilmington (19801) *(G-9654)*
Chemstar Corp 302 465-3175
  686 N Dupont Blvd Milford (19963) *(G-4350)*
Cherry Island Landfill, Dover Also called Delaware Solid Waste Authority *(G-1393)*
Cherry Island LLC 302 658-5241
  4048 New Castle Ave New Castle (19720) *(G-5144)*
Cherryrich Publishing 302 533-6354
  4 Four Seasons Pkwy Newark (19702) *(G-6192)*
CHESAPEAKE, Dover Also called Eastern Shore Natural Gas Co *(G-1500)*
Chesapeake Climate Control LLC 302 732-6006
  34913 Delaware Ave Frankford (19945) *(G-2353)*
Chesapeake Design Center LLC 302 875-8570
  32852 Sussex Hwy Laurel (19956) *(G-3212)*
Chesapeake Insurance Advisors 302 544-6900
  10 Corporate Cir Ste 215 New Castle (19720) *(G-5145)*
Chesapeake Neurology Service 302 563-7253
  12 Stable Ln Wilmington (19803) *(G-9655)*
Chesapeake Perl Inc (PA) 302 533-3540
  7 Mcmillan Way Ste 7 # 7 Newark (19713) *(G-6193)*
Chesapeake Plumbing & Htg Inc 302 732-6006
  34913 Delaware Ave Frankford (19945) *(G-2354)*
Chesapeake Rehab Equipment Inc 302 266-6234
  810 Interchange Blvd Newark (19711) *(G-6194)*
Chesapeake Seaglass Jewelry 410 778-4999
  11505 W Sand Cove Rd Selbyville (19975) *(G-8468)*
Chesapeake SEC Investigations 302 429-7505
  122 Delaware St 5 New Castle (19720) *(G-5146)*
Chesapeake Supply & Eqp Co 302 284-1000
  12915 S Dupont Hwy Felton (19943) *(G-2283)*
Chesapeake Utilities Corp (PA) 302 734-6799
  909 Silver Lake Blvd Dover (19904) *(G-1274)*
Chesapeakecaregivers LLC 302 841-9686
  10105 Concord Rd Seaford (19973) *(G-8192)*
Chesapeakemaine Trey 302 226-3600
  316 Rehoboth Ave Rehoboth Beach (19971) *(G-7887)*
Cheslantic Overhead Door 443 880-0378
  23 Shannon St Delmar (19940) *(G-983)*
Chester Bethel Preschool, Wilmington Also called Chester Bethel United Methodis *(G-9656)*
Chester Bethel United Methodis 302 475-3549
  2619 Foulk Rd Wilmington (19810) *(G-9656)*
Chester Cnty Ortho Sprts Physc, Wilmington Also called Hysiotherapy Associates Inc *(G-10983)*
Chestnut Investors II Inc 302 478-5142
  590 Madison Ave Fl 30 Wilmington (19899) *(G-9657)*

Chestnut Run Federal Cr Un (PA).....302 999-2967
974 Centre Rd Wilmington (19805) ***(G-9658)***
Chets Auto Body Inc.....302 875-3376
425 N Central Ave Laurel (19956) ***(G-3213)***
Chets Welding Service.....302 492-1003
1308 Taraila Rd Hartly (19953) ***(G-2915)***
Cheveux Inc.....302 731-9202
1115 Churchmans Rd Newark (19713) ***(G-6195)***
Chez Nichole Beauty Salon, Wilmington *Also called Chez Nichole Hair & Nail Salon* ***(G-9659)***
Chez Nichole Hair & Nail Salon.....302 654-8888
1901 W 11th St Ste B Wilmington (19805) ***(G-9659)***
Chichester Business Park LLC.....302 379-3140
1940 Rising Sun Ln Wilmington (19807) ***(G-9660)***
Chick Harness & Supply Inc (PA).....302 398-4630
18011 S Dupont Hwy Harrington (19952) ***(G-2824)***
Chick/Brook LLC.....302 337-7141
20015 Wilson Farm Rd Bridgeville (19933) ***(G-458)***
Chicken Little Child Care, Dagsboro *Also called Kimberly Sue Kester* ***(G-914)***
Chicks Graphics Unlimited, Harrington *Also called Graphics Unlimited Inc* ***(G-2842)***
Chieffo Electric Inc.....302 292-6813
108 W Cedarwood Dr Middletown (19709) ***(G-3986)***
Chilay Inc.....302 559-6014
40 E Main St 111 Newark (19711) ***(G-6196)***
Child Inc.....302 832-5451
148 Flamingo Dr Newark (19702) ***(G-6197)***
Child Inc (PA).....302 762-8989
507 Philadelphia Pike Wilmington (19809) ***(G-9661)***
Child Inc.....302 335-8652
776 Tullamore Ct Magnolia (19962) ***(G-3886)***
Children Youth & Their Fam.....302 577-6011
321 E 11th St Fl 1 Wilmington (19801) ***(G-9662)***
Children Youth & Their Fam.....302 628-2024
350 Virginia Ave Seaford (19973) ***(G-8193)***
Children Youth & Their Fam.....302 577-4270
10 Central Ave New Castle (19720) ***(G-5147)***
Children Youth & Their Fam.....302 633-2600
1825 Faulkland Rd Wilmington (19805) ***(G-9663)***
Children First Lrng Ctr Inc.....302 674-5227
760 Townsend Blvd Dover (19901) ***(G-1275)***
Children First Preschool.....302 239-3544
728 Yorklyn Rd Hockessin (19707) ***(G-2985)***
Children Fmilies First Del Inc.....302 629-6996
400 N Market Street Ext Seaford (19973) ***(G-8194)***
Children Fmilies First Del Inc (PA).....302 658-5177
809 N Washington St Wilmington (19801) ***(G-9664)***
Children Fmilies First Del Inc.....302 674-8384
91 Wolf Creek Blvd Dover (19901) ***(G-1276)***
Children Fmilies First Del Inc.....302 856-2388
410 S Bedford St Georgetown (19947) ***(G-2468)***
Children S Secret Garden.....302 730-1717
717 Hatchery Rd Dover (19901) ***(G-1277)***
Children's Place, The, Magnolia *Also called Child Inc* ***(G-3886)***
Children's Theater of Delmarva, Delmar *Also called Mirworth Enterprise Inc* ***(G-1021)***
Childrens Advocacy Ctr of Del.....302 854-0323
410 S Bedford St Georgetown (19947) ***(G-2469)***
Childrens Advocacy Ctr of Del (PA).....302 741-2123
611 S Dupont Hwy Ste 201 Dover (19901) ***(G-1278)***
Childrens Beach House Inc (PA).....302 655-4288
100 W 10th St Ste 411 Wilmington (19801) ***(G-9665)***
Childrens Beach House Inc.....302 645-9184
1800 Bay Ave Lewes (19958) ***(G-3413)***
Childrens Choice Inc.....302 731-9512
25 S Old Baltmre Pike # 101 Newark (19702) ***(G-6198)***
Childrens Place.....302 698-0969
3377 S Dupont Hwy Camden (19934) ***(G-548)***
Childrens Place Child Dev Ce.....302 947-4808
32362 Long Neck Rd Unit 1 Millsboro (19966) ***(G-4659)***
Childs Play At Home LLC.....302 644-3445
11 Hartford Way Lewes (19958) ***(G-3414)***
Childs Play By Bay.....302 703-6234
1510 Savannah Rd Lewes (19958) ***(G-3415)***
Chilimidos LLC.....302 388-1880
7209 Lancaster Pike Ste 4 Hockessin (19707) ***(G-2986)***
Chime Inc.....978 844-1162
1013 Centre Rd Ste 403 Wilmington (19805) ***(G-9666)***
Chimes Inc.....302 678-3270
3499 Cypress St Dover (19901) ***(G-1279)***
Chimes Inc.....302 382-4500
130 Quigley Blvd New Castle (19720) ***(G-5148)***
Chimes Inc.....302 452-3400
514 Interchange Blvd Newark (19711) ***(G-6199)***
Chimes Metro Inc.....302 452-3400
323 E 14th St New Castle (19720) ***(G-5149)***
Chimpark LLC.....226 219-7771
257 Old Churchmans Rd New Castle (19720) ***(G-5150)***
China Monitor Inc.....302 351-2324
134 Chatenay Ln Wilmington (19807) ***(G-9667)***
Chiorino Inc (PA).....302 292-1906
125 Ruthar Dr Harm K Y Business Par Newark (19711) ***(G-6200)***
Chip Vickio.....302 448-0211
30845 Phillips Branch Rd Millsboro (19966) ***(G-4660)***
Chiquita Brands LLC.....302 571-9781
101 River Rd Wilmington (19801) ***(G-9668)***
Chiropractic Services PA.....302 654-0404
536 Greenhill Ave Wilmington (19805) ***(G-9669)***
Chistine E Woods.....302 709-4497
111 Continental Dr # 412 Newark (19713) ***(G-6201)***
Chocolate Editions Inc.....302 479-8400
2614 Philadelphia Pike Claymont (19703) ***(G-715)***
Chocolate Swirl LLC.....718 407-0034
401 Justison St Apt 312 Wilmington (19801) ***(G-9670)***
Chocolette Distribution LLC.....917 547-8905
16192 Coastal Hwy Lewes (19958) ***(G-3416)***
Choctaw- Kaul Distribution Co, New Castle *Also called Kaul Glove and Mfg Co* ***(G-5454)***
Choice Builders LLC.....302 856-7234
23105 Parker Rd Georgetown (19947) ***(G-2470)***
Choice For Cmnty Lvng-Byview 1.....302 328-4176
713 Dora Moors Ln New Castle (19720) ***(G-5151)***
Choice For Community.....302 734-9020
210 Hiawatha Ln Dover (19904) ***(G-1280)***
Choice Medwaste LLC.....302 366-1187
16 Tyre Ave Newark (19711) ***(G-6202)***
Choice Rmdlg & Restoration Inc.....717 917-0601
110 Ramunno Cir Hockessin (19707) ***(G-2987)***
Choicepoint, Wilmington *Also called Lexisnexis Risk Assets Inc* ***(G-11378)***
Choices For Community Living (PA).....302 398-0446
100 Kings Ct Harrington (19952) ***(G-2825)***
Choptank Excavation.....302 378-8114
410 Joshua Ln Middletown (19709) ***(G-3987)***
Choudhary Arabinda K MD.....302 651-4000
1600 Rockland Rd Wilmington (19803) ***(G-9671)***
Choy Wilson Cdgn.....302 424-4141
329 Mullet Run Milford (19963) ***(G-4351)***
Chpt Manufacturing, Georgetown *Also called C H P T Manufacturing Inc* ***(G-2461)***
Chpt Mfg Inc.....302 645-4314
100 Dock Dr Lewes (19958) ***(G-3417)***
Chrias, Newark *Also called Institute of Christiana* ***(G-6785)***
Chris Kissell.....302 547-4800
1474 Big Woods Rd Smyrna (19977) ***(G-8593)***
Chriss Auto Repair.....302 791-0699
950 Ridge Rd Ste A3 Claymont (19703) ***(G-716)***
Chrissinger and Baumberger.....302 777-0100
3 Mill Rd Ste 301 Wilmington (19806) ***(G-9672)***
Christ Care Cardiac Surgery.....302 644-4282
400 Savannah Rd Ste C Lewes (19958) ***(G-3418)***
Christ Ch Episcpal Preschool.....302 472-0021
505 E Buck Rd Wilmington (19807) ***(G-9673)***
Christana Care Crdiolgy Conslt, Newark *Also called Christiana Care Health Sys Inc* ***(G-6211)***
Christana Care HM Hlth Cmnty S (HQ).....302 327-5583
1 Reads Way Ste 100 New Castle (19720) ***(G-5152)***
Christana Care Vsclar Spcalist.....302 733-5700
4765 Ogletown Stanton Rd 1e20 Newark (19713) ***(G-6203)***
Christana Care Vsting Nrse Ass, New Castle *Also called Christana Care HM Hlth Cmnty S* ***(G-5152)***
Christana Ctr For Wns Wellness.....302 454-9800
4745 Ogletown Stanton Rd Newark (19713) ***(G-6204)***
Christany Care Healthcare, Newark *Also called Christiana Care Health Sys Inc* ***(G-6210)***
Christian Raymond F & Assoc.....302 738-3016
226 W Park Pl Newark (19711) ***(G-6205)***
Christian Recovery Spa, Seaford *Also called Charlotte Wilson* ***(G-8191)***
Christian Science Reading Room.....302 456-1428
92 E Main St Ste 7 Newark (19711) ***(G-6206)***
Christian Science Reading Room.....302 227-7650
801 Bayard Ave Rehoboth Beach (19971) ***(G-7888)***
Christiana Body Shop Inc.....302 655-1085
96 Germay Dr Wilmington (19804) ***(G-9674)***
Christiana Care.....302 654-4925
601 Delaware Ave Ste 300 Wilmington (19801) ***(G-9675)***
Christiana Care.....302 633-3750
1941 Limestone Rd Ste 204 Wilmington (19808) ***(G-9676)***
Christiana Care Dover, Camden *Also called Christiana Care Home Health* ***(G-549)***
Christiana Care Health Sys Inc.....302 733-1601
4755 Stanton Ogletown Newark (19718) ***(G-6207)***
Christiana Care Health Sys Inc.....302 623-0390
200 Hygeia Dr Newark (19713) ***(G-6208)***
Christiana Care Health Sys Inc.....302 838-4750
300 Biddle Ave Ste 200 Newark (19702) ***(G-6209)***
Christiana Care Health Sys Inc.....302 428-4110
2401 Philadelphia Pike Claymont (19703) ***(G-717)***
Christiana Care Health Sys Inc.....302 733-2410
4745 Ogltwn Stn Mp 1 217 Newark (19718) ***(G-6210)***
Christiana Care Health Sys Inc.....302 623-3970
11 Boulden Cir New Castle (19720) ***(G-5153)***
Christiana Care Health Sys Inc.....302 623-7500
4512 Kirkwood Hwy Ste 300 Wilmington (19808) ***(G-9677)***
Christiana Care Health Sys Inc.....302 366-1929
252 Chapman Rd Ste 150 Newark (19702) ***(G-6211)***

Christiana Care Health Sys Inc 302 529-1975
2002 Foulk Rd Ste C Wilmington (19810) ***(G-9678)***
Christiana Care Health Sys Inc 302 733-1000
501 W 14th St Wilmington (19801) ***(G-9679)***
Christiana Care Health Sys Inc (HQ) 302 733-1000
200 Hygeia Dr Newark (19713) ***(G-6212)***
Christiana Care Health Sys Inc 302 449-3000
124 Sleepy Hollow Dr # 203 Middletown (19709) ***(G-3988)***
Christiana Care Health Sys Inc 302 659-4401
100 S Main St Ste 105 Smyrna (19977) ***(G-8594)***
Christiana Care Health Sys Inc 302 733-5700
4755 Ogletown Stanton Rd Newark (19718) ***(G-6213)***
Christiana Care Health Sys Inc 302 477-6500
3521 Silverside Rd Ste 1a Wilmington (19810) ***(G-9680)***
Christiana Care Hlth Svcs Inc 302 327-5820
11 Reads Way New Castle (19720) ***(G-5154)***
Christiana Care Hlth Svcs Inc 302 428-6662
501 W 14th St Ste 8 Wilmington (19801) ***(G-9681)***
Christiana Care Hlth Svcs Inc 302 477-3300
1401 Foulk Rd Ste 100 Wilmington (19803) ***(G-9682)***
Christiana Care Hlth Svcs Inc 302 623-0100
200 Hygeia Dr Unit B Newark (19713) ***(G-6214)***
Christiana Care Hlth Svcs Inc 302 733-1900
4755 Ogle Town Newark (19718) ***(G-6215)***
Christiana Care Hlth Svcs Inc 302 477-3960
2501 Ebright Rd Wilmington (19810) ***(G-9683)***
Christiana Care Hlth Svcs Inc 302 327-3959
1 Reads Way Ste 200 New Castle (19720) ***(G-5155)***
Christiana Care Hlth Svcs Inc 302 327-5555
100 W Cmmons Blvd Ste 100 New Castle (19720) ***(G-5156)***
Christiana Care Hlth Svcs Inc 302 733-5437
4755 Ogletown Stanton Rd Newark (19718) ***(G-6216)***
Christiana Care Hlth Svcs Inc 302 623-7201
200 Hygeia Dr Newark (19713) ***(G-6217)***
Christiana Care Hlth Svcs Inc 302 733-1805
2302 W 16th St Wilmington (19806) ***(G-9684)***
Christiana Care Hlth Svcs Inc 302 733-6510
4755 Ogletown Stanton Rd # 1249 Newark (19718) ***(G-6218)***
Christiana Care Home Health 302 995-8448
3000 Newport Gap Pike Wilmington (19808) ***(G-9685)***
Christiana Care Home Health 302 698-4300
2116 S Dupont Hwy Ste 2 Camden (19934) ***(G-549)***
Christiana Care Infusion 302 623-0345
600 White Clay Center Dr Newark (19711) ***(G-6219)***
Christiana Care Wound Care Ctr, Wilmington *Also called Critical Care Systems Intl Inc* ***(G-9900)***
Christiana Chiropractic LLC 302 633-6335
1 Centurian Dr Ste 303 Newark (19713) ***(G-6220)***
Christiana Community Ctr Inc 302 353-6796
50 N Old Baltimore Pike Christiana (19702) ***(G-666)***
Christiana Consulting Inc 302 454-7000
2608 Eastburn Ctr Newark (19711) ***(G-6221)***
Christiana Cosmetics Surgery, Newark *Also called Christiana Csmtc Srgry Cnsltnt* ***(G-6222)***
Christiana Counseling 302 995-1680
5235 W Woodmill Dr Ste 47 Wilmington (19808) ***(G-9686)***
Christiana Csmtc Srgry Cnsltnt 302 368-9611
62e Omega Dr Newark (19713) ***(G-6222)***
Christiana Excavating Company 302 738-8660
2016 Sunset Lake Rd Newark (19702) ***(G-6223)***
Christiana Family Dental Care 302 623-4190
50 Omega Dr Newark (19713) ***(G-6224)***
Christiana Fire Company 302 834-2433
1714 Porter Rd Bear (19701) ***(G-71)***
Christiana High Sch Wellness, Newark *Also called Vna of Delaware* ***(G-7663)***
Christiana Hosp Satellite Off, Newark *Also called John M Otto Od* ***(G-6844)***
Christiana Hospital, Newark *Also called Christiana Care Health Sys Inc* ***(G-6212)***
Christiana Incorporators Inc 302 998-2008
508 Main St Wilmington (19804) ***(G-9687)***
Christiana Mall, Newark *Also called Preit-Rubin Inc* ***(G-7242)***
Christiana Materials Inc 302 633-5600
305 W Newport Pike Wilmington (19804) ***(G-9688)***
Christiana Meadows Apartments, Bear *Also called Schoolhouse Trust Inc* ***(G-315)***
Christiana Mechanical Inc 302 378-7308
109 Sleepy Hollow Dr A Middletown (19709) ***(G-3989)***
Christiana Medical Group PA 302 366-1800
131 Continental Dr # 410 Newark (19713) ***(G-6225)***
Christiana Motor Freight Inc (PA) 302 655-6271
520 Terminal Ave Ste C New Castle (19720) ***(G-5157)***
Christiana Neonatal Practice 302 733-2410
4745 Ogltn Stntn Rd # 217 Newark (19713) ***(G-6226)***
Christiana Physcl Therapy Plus, Wilmington *Also called Christiana Care Hlth Svcs Inc* ***(G-9682)***
Christiana Psychiatric Svcs, Newark *Also called Carol A Tavani MD* ***(G-6160)***
Christiana Skating Center, Newark *Also called Delaware Skating Center Ltd* ***(G-6412)***
Christiana Village Apts 302 427-0403
225 W 4th St Apt 3a Wilmington (19801) ***(G-9689)***
Christiana Wood LLC 302 322-1172
218 Villas Dr New Castle (19720) ***(G-5158)***
Christianity Care Pathology, Newark *Also called Christiana Care Health Sys Inc* ***(G-6207)***
Christianna Dental Center 302 369-3200
330 Christiana Med Ctr Newark (19702) ***(G-6227)***
Christina Care Vna 302 327-5212
1 Reads Way Ste 100 New Castle (19720) ***(G-5159)***
Christina Ctr For Oral Surgery 302 328-3053
112 2nd Ave New Castle (19720) ***(G-5160)***
Christina Cultural Arts Center 302 652-0101
705 N Market St Wilmington (19801) ***(G-9690)***
Christina Education Assn 302 454-7700
4135 Ogletown Stanton Rd Newark (19713) ***(G-6228)***
Christina Landing, Wilmington *Also called Luxiasuites LLC* ***(G-11461)***
Christina Mill Apartments, Newark *Also called ML Newark LLC* ***(G-7048)***
Christina Newton 302 454-2400
925 Bear Corbitt Rd Bear (19701) ***(G-72)***
Christina School District 302 454-2281
400 Wyoming Rd Newark (19711) ***(G-6229)***
Christine E Fox DDS 302 732-9850
31059 Dupont Blvd Dagsboro (19939) ***(G-892)***
Christine Fox DDS 302 703-2838
32792 Ocean Reach Dr Lewes (19958) ***(G-3419)***
Christine W Maynard M D 302 225-6110
4735 Ogletown Stanton Rd Newark (19713) ***(G-6230)***
Christine W Maynard MD 302 995-7073
4600 New Lndn Hll Rd 20 Wilmington (19808) ***(G-9691)***
Christmas Corporation 424 645-5001
16192 Coastal Hwy Lewes (19958) ***(G-3420)***
Christopher A Bowens MD 302 834-3700
2600 Glasgow Ave Ste 108 Newark (19702) ***(G-6231)***
Christopher Baran DDS 903 968-7467
1601 Milltown Rd Ste 19 Wilmington (19808) ***(G-9692)***
Christopher Casscells MD 302 832-6220
Glasgow Med Ctr Ste 104 Newark (19702) ***(G-6232)***
Christopher Fortin DDS 302 422-9791
214 S Walnut St Milford (19963) ***(G-4352)***
Christopher H Wendel Md PA 302 540-2979
P.O. Box 250 Hockessin (19707) ***(G-2988)***
Christopher Handy 302 934-1018
24872 Doe Bridge Ln Millsboro (19966) ***(G-4661)***
Christopher T Parsons 302 947-2380
162 White Pine Dr Millsboro (19966) ***(G-4662)***
Christopher's Salon & Spa, Middletown *Also called Christophers Hair Design* ***(G-3990)***
Christophers Hair Design 302 378-1988
423 N Broad St Ste 5 Middletown (19709) ***(G-3990)***
Chromium Dental LLC 302 731-5582
300 Creek View Rd Ste 105 Newark (19711) ***(G-6233)***
Chruch Creek, Dover *Also called Liberto Development Ltd* ***(G-1782)***
Chrystal Holdings 302 655-2398
222 Delaware Ave Wilmington (19801) ***(G-9693)***
Cht Holdings LLC 954 864-2008
16192 Coastal Hwy Lewes (19958) ***(G-3421)***
Chubb INA Ovrseas Holdings Inc (HQ) 302 476-6000
1 Beaver Valley Rd Wilmington (19803) ***(G-9694)***
Chubb Insurance Company 302 477-1892
1 Beaver Valley Rd Wilmington (19803) ***(G-9695)***
Chubb US Holding Inc 215 640-1000
1 Beaver Valley Rd 4e Wilmington (19803) ***(G-9696)***
Chuck B Barker Pt Dpt Ocs Atc 302 730-4800
1015 S Governors Ave Dover (19904) ***(G-1281)***
Chuck George Inc 302 994-7444
400 Water St Wilmington (19804) ***(G-9697)***
Chudasama Enterprises LLC 302 856-7532
313 N Dupont Hwy Georgetown (19947) ***(G-2471)***
Church of God In Christ 302 678-1949
120a S Governors Ave Dover (19904) ***(G-1282)***
Church Street Associates 302 227-1599
33 Baltimore Ave Ste H Rehoboth Beach (19971) ***(G-7889)***
Churchman Village Center LLC 302 998-6900
4949 Ogletown Stanton Rd Newark (19713) ***(G-6234)***
Churchmens Machine Company 302 994-8660
401 Brookside Ave Wilmington (19805) ***(G-9698)***
Churman Village Center, Newark *Also called Churchman Village Center LLC* ***(G-6234)***
Ci Centre, Millsboro *Also called David G Major Associates Inc* ***(G-4673)***
Ciancon Global LLC 302 365-0956
501 Silverside Rd Ste 105 Wilmington (19809) ***(G-9699)***
Ciba Specialty Chem N Amer 302 992-5600
205 S James St Wilmington (19804) ***(G-9700)***
Ciconte Roseman & Wasserman 302 658-7101
1300 N King St Wilmington (19801) ***(G-9701)***
Cielo Salon & Spa Inc 302 575-0400
600 Delaware Ave Wilmington (19801) ***(G-9702)***
Cigarette City Inc (PA) 302 836-4889
460 Peoples Plz Newark (19702) ***(G-6235)***
Cigna Corporate Services LLC 302 792-4906
300 Bellevue Pkwy Ste 101 Wilmington (19809) ***(G-9703)***
Cigna Corporation 302 792-4906
300 Bellevue Pkwy Wilmington (19809) ***(G-9704)***
Cigna Corporation 302 792-4906
300 Bellevue Pkwy Wilmington (19809) ***(G-9705)***

ALPHABETIC

Cigna Global Holdings Inc (HQ) 302 797-3469
590 Naamans Rd Claymont (19703) ***(G-718)***
Cigna Holdings Inc (HQ) 215 761-1000
590 Naamans Rd Claymont (19703) ***(G-719)***
Cigna Real Estate Inc (HQ) 302 476-3337
1 Beaver Valley Rd Wilmington (19803) ***(G-9706)***
Cim Concepts Incorporated 302 613-5400
100 W Cmmons Blvd Ste 101 New Castle (19720) ***(G-5161)***
Cimentum 302 635-7262
17 Springbrook Ln Newark (19711) ***(G-6236)***
Cindy L Szabo 302 855-9505
9 N Front St Georgetown (19947) ***(G-2472)***
Cindys Home Away From Hme Fam 302 378-0487
22 Canary Ct Middletown (19709) ***(G-3991)***
Cinemark Movies 10, Wilmington *Also called Cinemark Usa Inc* ***(G-9707)***
Cinemark Usa Inc 302 994-7280
1796 W Newport Pike Wilmington (19804) ***(G-9707)***
Cinemavericks Media LLC 302 438-1144
2433 Hammond Pl Wilmington (19808) ***(G-9708)***
Cingular Wireless, Dover *Also called AT&T Mobility LLC* ***(G-1153)***
Cintas Corporation No 2 ....302 765-6460
2925 Northeast Blvd Wilmington (19802) ***(G-9709)***
Cintas J98, Wilmington *Also called Cintas Corporation No 2* ***(G-9709)***
CIO Story LLC 408 915-5559
19c Trolley Sq Wilmington (19806) ***(G-9710)***
Cipolloni Brothers LLC 302 449-0960
879 Black Diamond Rd Smyrna (19977) ***(G-8595)***
Circle C Outfit LLC 302 337-8828
9801 Orchards End Bridgeville (19933) ***(G-459)***
Circle Time Learning Center 302 384-7193
1002 S Grant Ave Wilmington (19805) ***(G-9711)***
Circle Veterinary Clinic 302 652-6587
1212 E Newport Pike Wilmington (19804) ***(G-9712)***
Circus Associates Intelligence 757 663-7864
16192 Coastal Hwy Lewes (19958) ***(G-3422)***
Circus Associates, The, Lewes *Also called Circus Associates Intelligence* ***(G-3422)***
Cirillo Bros Inc 302 326-1540
761 Grantham Ln New Castle (19720) ***(G-5162)***
Cisco Systems Inc 302 492-1735
850 Arthursville Rd Hartly (19953) ***(G-2916)***
Ciseaux Hair Design Studio, Dover *Also called Jk Tangles Hair Salon* ***(G-1697)***
Citibank, New Castle *Also called Citigroup Asia PCF Holdg Corp* ***(G-5169)***
Citibank National Association 302 477-5418
1 Penns Way New Castle (19721) ***(G-5163)***
Citibank Overseas Inv Corp (HQ) 302 323-3600
1 Penns Way New Castle (19720) ***(G-5164)***
Citicorp Banking Corporation (HQ) 302 323-3140
1 Penns Way New Castle (19721) ***(G-5165)***
Citicorp Del-Lease Inc (HQ) 302 323-3801
1 Penns Way New Castle (19721) ***(G-5166)***
Citicorp Delaware Services Inc 302 323-3124
1 Penns Way New Castle (19721) ***(G-5167)***
Citicorp Trust Bank (HQ) 302 737-7803
1 Penns Way New Castle (19721) ***(G-5168)***
Citifinancial, Newark *Also called One Main Financial* ***(G-7151)***
Citifinancial Inc 302 834-6677
619 Governors Pl Bear (19701) ***(G-73)***
Citifinancial Credit Company 302 628-9253
22974 Sussex Hwy Seaford (19973) ***(G-8195)***
Citifinancial Credit Company 302 834-6677
619 Governors Pl Bear (19701) ***(G-74)***
Citifinancial Credit Company 302 678-8226
1057 N Dupont Hwy Dover (19901) ***(G-1283)***
Citifinancial Services Inc 302 875-2813
11212 Trussum Pond Rd Laurel (19956) ***(G-3214)***
Citigroup, New Castle *Also called Citicorp Banking Corporation* ***(G-5165)***
Citigroup Inc 302 631-3530
500 White Clay Center Dr Newark (19711) ***(G-6237)***
Citigroup Asia PCF Holdg Corp (HQ) 302 323-3100
1 Penns Way Fl 1 # 1 New Castle (19721) ***(G-5169)***
Citigroup Global Markets Inc 302 888-4100
222 Delaware Ave Fl 7 Wilmington (19801) ***(G-9713)***
Citizens Bank National Assn 302 360-6101
34161 Citizen Dr Lewes (19958) ***(G-3423)***
Citizens Bank National Assn 302 734-0200
8 W Loockerman St Dover (19904) ***(G-1284)***
Citizens Bank National Assn 302 292-6401
100 Suburban Dr Newark (19711) ***(G-6238)***
Citizens Bank National Assn 302 456-7100
117 E Main St Newark (19711) ***(G-6239)***
Citizens Bank National Assn 302 856-4231
13 The Cir Georgetown (19947) ***(G-2473)***
Citizens Bank National Assn 302 645-2024
131 2nd St Lewes (19958) ***(G-3424)***
Citizens Bank National Assn 302 283-5600
1 University Plz Newark (19702) ***(G-6240)***
Citizens Bank National Assn 302 628-6150
22870 Sussex Hwy Seaford (19973) ***(G-8196)***
Citizens Bank National Assn 302 456-7111
40 Chestnut Hill Plz Newark (19713) ***(G-6241)***
Citizens Bank National Assn 302 235-4321
128 Lantana Dr Hockessin (19707) ***(G-2989)***
Citizens Bank National Assn 302 633-4503
4435 Kirkwood Hwy Wilmington (19808) ***(G-9714)***
Citizens Bank National Assn 302 734-0231
1399 Forrest Ave Dover (19904) ***(G-1285)***
Citizens Bank National Assn 302 422-5010
610 N Dupont Blvd Milford (19963) ***(G-4353)***
Citizens Bank National Assn 302 653-9245
7 W Glenwood Ave Smyrna (19977) ***(G-8596)***
Citizens Bank National Assn 302 477-1205
1620 Marsh Rd Wilmington (19803) ***(G-9715)***
Citizens Bank National Assn 302 633-3080
4720 Limestone Rd Wilmington (19808) ***(G-9716)***
Citizens Bank National Assn 302 376-3641
460 E Main St Middletown (19709) ***(G-3992)***
Citizens Bank National Assn 302 529-6100
2084 Naamans Rd Wilmington (19810) ***(G-9717)***
Citizens Bank National Assn 302 322-0525
130 N Dupont Hwy New Castle (19720) ***(G-5170)***
Citizens Bank National Assn 302 421-2229
919 N Market St Ste 200 Wilmington (19801) ***(G-9718)***
Citizens Bank National Assn 302 834-2611
146 Foxhunt Dr Bear (19701) ***(G-75)***
Citizens Bank National Assn 302 421-2240
1422 N Dupont St Wilmington (19806) ***(G-9719)***
Citrosuco North America Inc 302 652-8763
1000 Ferry Rd Wilmington (19801) ***(G-9720)***
City Cab of Delware Inc 302 734-5968
716 S Governors Ave Dover (19904) ***(G-1286)***
City Cab of Delware Inc 302 227-8294
164 Henlopen Ave Rehoboth Beach (19971) ***(G-7890)***
City Cab of Delware Inc (PA) 302 734-5968
1203 State College Rd Dover (19904) ***(G-1287)***
City Electric Contracting Co 302 764-0775
204 Channel Rd Wilmington (19809) ***(G-9721)***
City Electric Supply Company 302 777-5300
6 Medori Blvd Wilmington (19801) ***(G-9722)***
City Mist LLC 302 342-1377
1005 Willings Way New Castle (19720) ***(G-5171)***
City Mist Logistics, New Castle *Also called City Mist LLC* ***(G-5171)***
City of Dover 302 736-7018
5 E Reed St Dover (19901) ***(G-1288)***
City of Dover 302 736-7035
5 E Reed St Ste 100 Dover (19901) ***(G-1289)***
City of Dover 302 736-7070
860 Buttner Pl Dover (19904) ***(G-1290)***
City of Dover - McKee Run 302 672-6306
880 Buttner Pl Dover (19904) ***(G-1291)***
City of Milford 302 422-1110
180 Vickers Rd Milford (19963) ***(G-4354)***
City of Newark 302 366-0457
45 E Main St Ste 205 Newark (19711) ***(G-6242)***
City of Newark 302 366-7060
220 S Main St Newark (19711) ***(G-6243)***
City of Seaford Inc 302 629-2890
1019 W Locust St Seaford (19973) ***(G-8197)***
City of Wilmington 302 576-2584
800 N French St Fl 1 Wilmington (19801) ***(G-9723)***
City One Hour Cleaners 302 658-0001
615 N King St Wilmington (19801) ***(G-9724)***
City Systems Inc 302 655-9914
13 Gale Ln Wilmington (19807) ***(G-9725)***
City Theater Co Inc 302 831-2206
110 Tanglewood Ln Newark (19711) ***(G-6244)***
City Wide Transportation Inc 302 792-1225
6705 Governor Printz Blvd Claymont (19703) ***(G-720)***
City Window Cleaning of Del 302 633-0633
130b Middleboro Rd Wilmington (19804) ***(G-9726)***
Citywide Transportation Inc 302 792-0159
6705 Governor Printz Blvd Wilmington (19809) ***(G-9727)***
Civil Engineering Assoc LLC 302 376-8833
55 W Main St Middletown (19709) ***(G-3993)***
CK Construction Inc 302 698-3207
4181 Berrytown Rd Camden (19934) ***(G-550)***
Clairvyant Technosolutions Inc 302 999-7172
5700 Kirkwood Hwy Ste 107 Wilmington (19808) ***(G-9728)***
Claravall Odilon 302 875-7753
1124 S Central Ave Laurel (19956) ***(G-3215)***
Claremont School LLC 302 478-4531
1501 Marsh Rd Wilmington (19803) ***(G-9729)***
Clarence Fraim, Wilmington *Also called Boys & Girls Clubs Del Inc* ***(G-9406)***
Clarion Hotel - The Belle, New Castle *Also called Sabre Amb LLC* ***(G-5692)***
Clarios 302 996-0309
812 First State Blvd Wilmington (19804) ***(G-9730)***
Clarios LLC 302 378-9885
700 N Broad St Middletown (19709) ***(G-3994)***

ALPHABETIC SECTION — Clymene LLC

Clarios LLC 302 696-3221
50 Patriot Dr Middletown (19709) *(G-3995)*

Clarius Mobile Health Corp 778 800-9975
16192 Coastal Hwy Lewes (19958) *(G-3425)*

Clark & Sons Inc (PA) 302 998-7552
314 E Ayre St Wilmington (19804) *(G-9731)*

Clark & Sons Inc 302 856-3372
500 W Market St Georgetown (19947) *(G-2474)*

Clark & Sons Overhead Doors 302 998-7552
314 E Ayre St Wilmington (19804) *(G-9732)*

Clark Associates Inc 302 421-9950
3065 New Castle Ave New Castle (19720) *(G-5172)*

Clark Bffone Mtthews Insur AGC 302 322-2261
100 W Cmmons Blvd Ste 302 New Castle (19720) *(G-5173)*

Clark Seed Company Inc 302 653-9249
1467 Seven Hickories Rd Clayton (19938) *(G-839)*

Clark Services Inc Delaware 302 834-0556
900 Julian Ln Bear (19701) *(G-76)*

Clark Services Inc of Del 302 322-1118
107 J And M Dr New Castle (19720) *(G-5174)*

Clark Video Productions, Newark Also called Kral Electronics Inc *(G-6902)*

Clarke Association, New Castle Also called Clark Associates Inc *(G-5172)*

Clarke Service Groupdotcom LLC 302 875-0300
109 E Front St Laurel (19956) *(G-3216)*

Clarks Glasgow Pools Inc (PA) 302 834-0200
109 J And M Dr New Castle (19720) *(G-5175)*

Clarks Pool and Spa, New Castle Also called Clarks Glasgow Pools Inc *(G-5175)*

Clarks Swimming Pools Inc 302 629-8835
22855 Sussex Hwy Seaford (19973) *(G-8198)*

Clarksville Auto Service Ctr (PA) 302 539-1700
34461 Atlantic Ave Ocean View (19970) *(G-7777)*

Clarksville Parts Plus, Ocean View Also called Clarksville Auto Service Ctr *(G-7777)*

Class Limousine Service 302 653-1166
1271 S Dupont Blvd Smyrna (19977) *(G-8597)*

Classerium Corporation 773 306-3297
8 The Grn Ste 4534 Dover (19901) *(G-1292)*

Classic Auto Body Inc 302 655-4044
103 Brookside Dr Wilmington (19804) *(G-9733)*

Classic Auto Body Wilmington, Wilmington Also called Classic Auto Body Inc *(G-9733)*

Classic Auto Sales & Service 302 684-8126
26905 Lwes Georgetown Hwy Harbeson (19951) *(G-2775)*

Classic Canvas LLC 443 359-0150
3505 May Twilley Rd Delmar (19940) *(G-984)*

Classic Cookies of Dowingtown 302 494-9662
2628 Longwood Dr Wilmington (19810) *(G-9734)*

Classic Image Clrs Laundromat, New Castle Also called Classic Image Inc *(G-5176)*

Classic Image Inc 302 658-7281
21 Stamm Blvd New Castle (19720) *(G-5176)*

Classroomapp Inc 833 257-7761
16192 Coastal Hwy Lewes (19958) *(G-3426)*

Clay White Dental Associates 302 731-4225
12 Polly Drummond Hill Rd Newark (19711) *(G-6245)*

Claymont Branch, Claymont Also called Wilmington Savings Fund Soc *(G-821)*

Claymont Community Center Inc 302 792-2757
3301 Green St Claymont (19703) *(G-721)*

Claymont Foods, Claymont Also called Estia Hospitality Group Inc *(G-741)*

Claymont Methadone Clinic 855 244-7803
2999 Philadelphia Pike Claymont (19703) *(G-722)*

Claymore Senior Center Inc 302 428-3170
504 S Clayton St Wilmington (19805) *(G-9735)*

Clayton Court Apartments, Wilmington Also called Pennrose Management Company *(G-12070)*

Clayton Theatre, Dagsboro Also called Wilkins Enterprises *(G-944)*

Cleamol LLC 513 885-3462
330 Water St Ste 105 Wilmington (19804) *(G-9736)*

Clean As A Whistle 302 757-5024
46 Cheswold Blvd Newark (19713) *(G-6246)*

Clean As A Whistle Inc 302 376-1388
107 Lynn Cir Middletown (19709) *(G-3996)*

Clean Cut Interlocking Pavers, Lewes Also called Road Site Construction Inc *(G-3720)*

Clean Delaware Inc 302 684-4221
Rr 404 Milton (19968) *(G-4879)*

Clean Delaware LLC 302 684-4221
33852 Clay Rd Lewes (19958) *(G-3427)*

Clean Earth New Castle Inc 302 427-6633
94 Pyles Ln New Castle (19720) *(G-5177)*

Clean Energy Usa LLC (PA) 302 227-1337
20184 Phillips St Rehoboth Beach (19971) *(G-7891)*

Clean Force Building Services 302 494-9330
36 Ashkirk Pl Newark (19702) *(G-6247)*

Clean Hands LLC 215 681-1435
60 Markham Ct Smyrna (19977) *(G-8598)*

Clean Sweep 302 422-6085
5862 Old Shawnee Rd Milford (19963) *(G-4355)*

Clean-A-Tank Inc 302 250-4229
207 S Ogle Ave Wilmington (19805) *(G-9737)*

Cleaners Sunny 302 827-2095
17601 Coastal Hwy Lewes (19958) *(G-3428)*

Cleaning Frenzy LLC 302 453-8800
2860 Ogletown Rd Bldg 6-1 Newark (19713) *(G-6248)*

Cleanpro Detail Center 302 834-6878
200 Connor Blvd Bear (19701) *(G-77)*

Cleantech Energy Solutions LLC 301 704-2831
300 Delaware Ave Ste 210a Wilmington (19801) *(G-9738)*

Clear Brook Farms Inc 302 337-7678
18800 Wesley Church Rd Bridgeville (19933) *(G-460)*

Clear Channel Outdoor Inc 302 658-5520
24 Germay Dr Wilmington (19804) *(G-9739)*

Clear Space Theatre Company 302 227-2270
20 Baltimore Ave Rehoboth Beach (19971) *(G-7892)*

Clearview Windows LLC 302 491-6768
600 Ne Front Street Ext H Milford (19963) *(G-4356)*

Clearwater Enrgy Resources LLC 510 267-8921
2711 Centerville Rd Wilmington (19808) *(G-9740)*

Cleaver 302 659-1707
246 Nursery Ln Smyrna (19977) *(G-8599)*

Clementes Clubhouse 302 455-0936
321 Shisler Ct Newark (19702) *(G-6249)*

Clendaniel Plbg Htg & Coolg, Milton Also called Clendaniel Plbg Htg & Coolg *(G-4880)*

Clendaniel Plbg Htg & Coolg 302 684-3152
18052 Gravel Hill Rd Milton (19968) *(G-4880)*

Click For Savings LLC 302 300-0202
5104 Christiana Mdws Bear (19701) *(G-78)*

Clickloot, Wilmington Also called Drop Table LLC *(G-10237)*

Client Monster LLC 866 799-5433
1300 Helen Dr Unit 112 Newark (19702) *(G-6250)*

Clifford L Anzilotti DDS PC (PA) 302 475-2050
2101 Foulk Rd Wilmington (19810) *(G-9741)*

Clifford L Anzilotti DDS PC 302 378-2778
112 Saint Annes Church Rd Middletown (19709) *(G-3997)*

Clifton Farms Inc 302 424-8340
306 Warner Rd Milford (19963) *(G-4357)*

Clifton L Bakhsh Jr Inc 302 378-8009
4450 Summit Bridge Rd Middletown (19709) *(G-3998)*

Clifton Leasing Co Inc (PA) 302 674-2300
613 Clara St Dover (19904) *(G-1293)*

Climate Control Heating Inc 302 349-5778
9703 Woodyard Rd Greenwood (19950) *(G-2720)*

Climate Solutions Services 302 275-9919
2426 Calf Run Dr Wilmington (19808) *(G-9742)*

Clinic By Sea 302 644-0999
16295 Willow Creek Rd Lewes (19958) *(G-3429)*

Clinical Breast Imaging 302 658-4800
2401 Penns Ave Ste 115 Wilmington (19806) *(G-9743)*

Clinical Crdlgy Spcialists LLC 302 834-3700
1400 Peoples Plz Ste 111 Newark (19702) *(G-6251)*

Clinpharma Clinical RES LLC 646 961-3437
1000 N West St Ste 1200 Wilmington (19801) *(G-9744)*

Clinton Craddock 267 505-2671
511 Cilantro Ct Middletown (19709) *(G-3999)*

Clipper Advisor LLC 203 428-5251
2711 Centerville Rd # 400 Wilmington (19808) *(G-9745)*

Clippers & Curls Hair Design 302 684-1522
620 Clipper Sq 620 Mulbry Milton (19968) *(G-4881)*

Clique Digital Media Mktg LLC 305 704-2128
8 The Grn Ste A Dover (19901) *(G-1294)*

Close Cuts Lawn Svc & Ldscpg 302 422-2248
24 Ne 10th St Milford (19963) *(G-4358)*

Cloud Services Solutions Inc 888 335-3132
1521 Concord Pike Ste 301 Wilmington (19803) *(G-9746)*

Cloud Software Development LLC 703 957-9847
3411 Silverside Rd # 104 Wilmington (19810) *(G-9747)*

Cloudbees Inc 804 767-5481
16192 Coastal Hwy Lewes (19958) *(G-3430)*

Cloudbees Inc (PA) 323 842-7783
16192 Coastal Hwy Lewes (19958) *(G-3431)*

Cloudburst Lawn Sprink, Wilmington Also called D F Distribution Inc *(G-9940)*

Cloudburst Sprinkler Systems, Wilmington Also called Lightscapes Inc *(G-11387)*

Cloudcoffer LLC 412 620-3203
1201 N Orange St Ste 600 Wilmington (19801) *(G-9748)*

Cloudxperts LLC 302 257-5686
8 The Grn Ste 5210 Dover (19901) *(G-1295)*

Clouto Inc 302 966-9282
40 E Main St 1202 Newark (19711) *(G-6252)*

Clover Farms Meats 610 428-8066
15 William Ave Ocean View (19970) *(G-7778)*

Clover Yarns Inc (PA) 302 422-4518
715 S Washington St Milford (19963) *(G-4359)*

Club Brennan 302 838-9530
1 Primrose Dr Bear (19701) *(G-79)*

Club Mantis Boxing LLC 302 943-2580
16424 Fitzgeralds Rd Lincoln (19960) *(G-3842)*

Clyde Bergemann Pwr Group LLC 770 557-3600
16192 Coastal Hwy Lewes (19958) *(G-3432)*

Clyde Spinelli 302 328-7679
500 S Dupont Hwy Apt 225 New Castle (19720) *(G-5178)*

Clymene LLC 888 679-3310
16192 Coastal Hwy Lewes (19958) *(G-3433)*

(PA)=Parent Co (HQ)=Headquarters (DH)=Div Headquarters

Cmas, Wilmington *Also called Coastal Marine AVI Svc LLC* ***(G-9753)***
CMC Corporation of Hockessin 302 239-1960
721 Yorklyn Rd Hockessin (19707) ***(G-2990)***
CMH Capital Inc (HQ) 302 651-7947
1105 N Market St Ste 1300 Wilmington (19801) ***(G-9749)***
CMI, Middletown *Also called Christiana Mechanical Inc* ***(G-3989)***
CMI Electric Inc 302 731-5556
83 Albe Dr Ste E Newark (19702) ***(G-6253)***
CMI Electric Inc (PA) 302 731-5556
83 Albe Dr Ste A Newark (19702) ***(G-6254)***
CMI Solar Electric, Newark *Also called CMI Electric Inc* ***(G-6254)***
Cmp Fire LLC 410 620-2062
1820 Otts Chapel Rd Newark (19702) ***(G-6255)***
CMS, Wilmington *Also called Bluevault LLC* ***(G-9385)***
Cmy Solutions LLC 321 732-1866
2035 Sunset Lake Rd B2 Newark (19702) ***(G-6256)***
Cnc Insurance Associates Inc 302 678-3860
20 E Division St Ste A Dover (19901) ***(G-1296)***
Cnh Cptal Oprting Lase Eqp Rcv 262 636-6011
1209 N Orange St Wilmington (19801) ***(G-9750)***
CNJ Contracting LLC 302 659-3750
1189 Alabam Rd Smyrna (19977) ***(G-8600)***
Cnmri 302 422-0800
111 Neurology Way Milford (19963) ***(G-4360)***
Cns Construction Corp 302 224-0450
116 Sandy Dr Ste B Newark (19713) ***(G-6257)***
Cntrl De Gstroenterolgyassoc I 302 678-9002
644 S Queen St Ste 106 Dover (19904) ***(G-1297)***
Cnu Fit LLC 302 744-9037
1404 Forrest Ave Ste 9 Dover (19904) ***(G-1298)***
CNW Enterprise, Wilmington *Also called Brandywine Graphics Inc* ***(G-9435)***
Cnwynn Publications 484 753-1568
1102 Dwight Ct Dover (19904) ***(G-1299)***
Co Fs Holding Company LLC 302 894-1244
502 S College Ave Newark (19713) ***(G-6258)***
Coast Survey 302 645-7184
32261 Nassau Rd Lewes (19958) ***(G-3434)***
Coastal 302 319-4061
1201 N Orange St Ste 700 Wilmington (19801) ***(G-9751)***
Coastal Cabinetry LLC 302 542-4155
400 Megan Ave Seaford (19973) ***(G-8199)***
Coastal Care Physical Therapy 480 236-3863
37197 E Stoney Run Selbyville (19975) ***(G-8469)***
Coastal Chiropractic LLC 302 933-0700
28467 Dupont Blvd Unit 1 Millsboro (19966) ***(G-4663)***
Coastal Club Schell Brothers 302 966-0063
31605 Exeter Way Lewes (19958) ***(G-3435)***
Coastal Coatings Inc 302 645-1399
17993 American Way Lewes (19958) ***(G-3436)***
Coastal Concerts Inc 302 645-1539
Bethel United Methodist Lewes (19958) ***(G-3437)***
Coastal Concrete Works LLC 302 381-5261
27220 Buckskin Trl Harbeson (19951) ***(G-2776)***
Coastal Credit LLC 302 734-1312
1406 Forrest Ave Ste 2 Dover (19904) ***(G-1300)***
Coastal Hospitality LLC 302 304-3156
1000 N West St Ste 1200 Wilmington (19801) ***(G-9752)***
Coastal Images Inc 302 539-6001
711 Coastal Hwy Fenwick Island (19944) ***(G-2333)***
Coastal It Consulting 302 226-9395
4 Tall Oaks Ct Rehoboth Beach (19971) ***(G-7893)***
Coastal Kid Watch 302 537-0793
32566 Docs Pl Millville (19967) ***(G-4839)***
Coastal Kids Pediatric Dntstry 302 644-4460
18947 John J Williams Hwy Rehoboth Beach (19971) ***(G-7894)***
Coastal Maintenance LLC 302 536-1290
26253 Sussex Hwy Seaford (19973) ***(G-8200)***
Coastal Marine AVI Svc LLC 904 200-2749
3422 Old Capitol Trl # 1388 Wilmington (19808) ***(G-9753)***
Coastal Mechanical 302 994-9100
1 Carsdale Ct Wilmington (19808) ***(G-9754)***
Coastal Pain Care Physcians PA 302 644-8330
1606 Savannah Rd Ste 8 Lewes (19958) ***(G-3438)***
Coastal Point 302 539-1788
111 Atlantic Ave Ste 2 Ocean View (19970) ***(G-7779)***
Coastal Printing Company 302 537-1700
Shops Of Millville Rr 26 Ocean View (19970) ***(G-7780)***
Coastal Properties I LLC 302 227-5800
6 Christian St Rehoboth Beach (19971) ***(G-7895)***
Coastal Pump & Tank Inc 302 398-3061
17401 S Dupont Hwy Harrington (19952) ***(G-2826)***
Coastal Rentals Hydraulics LLC 302 251-3103
35283 Atlantic Ave Millville (19967) ***(G-4840)***
Coastal Sun Roms Prch Enclsres 302 537-3679
36017 Pine Bark Ln Frankford (19945) ***(G-2355)***
Coastal Towing Inc 302 645-6300
33012 Cedar Grove Rd Lewes (19958) ***(G-3439)***
Coastal Veterinary 302 524-8550
33053 Lighthouse Rd Selbyville (19975) ***(G-8470)***
Coastal Wood Industries 302 398-9601
6621 Mlford Hrrington Hwy Harrington (19952) ***(G-2827)***
Coastal Woodcraft 302 856-7947
404 Robinson St Georgetown (19947) ***(G-2475)***
Coating Effects Div, Wilmington *Also called BASF Corporation* ***(G-9258)***
Coatings Inc 302 661-1962
30 Commerce St Wilmington (19801) ***(G-9755)***
Coatings With A Purpose Inc 302 462-1465
21166 Greenway Pl Georgetown (19947) ***(G-2476)***
Coblentz Woodworking, Hartly *Also called Leroy A Coblentz* ***(G-2934)***
Cobra Razors 302 540-0464
4007 Montchanin Rd Wilmington (19807) ***(G-9756)***
Cochran Oil, New Castle *Also called Federal Mechanical Contractors* ***(G-5305)***
Cochran-Trivits Inc 302 328-2945
401 S Dupont Hwy New Castle (19720) ***(G-5179)***
Cod Lift Truck Inc 302 656-7731
1240 E 16th St Wilmington (19802) ***(G-9757)***
Codemessaging, Newark *Also called Generation Consultants LLC* ***(G-6646)***
Codeship Inc 617 515-3664
16192 Coastal Hwy Lewes (19958) ***(G-3440)***
Coditas Inc 888 220-6200
16192 Coastal Hwy Lewes (19958) ***(G-3441)***
Coffee Artisan LLC 302 297-8800
718 Phillips Hill Dr Millsboro (19966) ***(G-4664)***
Coffee Run Condo Council Inc 302 239-4134
614 Loveville Rd Ofc Hockessin (19707) ***(G-2991)***
Coffin Hardwood Flooring Inc 302 934-6414
28539 Dupont Blvd Millsboro (19966) ***(G-4665)***
Cogency Global Inc 800 483-1140
850 New Burton Rd Dover (19904) ***(G-1301)***
Cogentrix Delaware Holdings (HQ) 847 908-2800
1105 N Market St Ste 1108 Wilmington (19801) ***(G-9758)***
Coghan-Haes LLC 302 325-4210
101 S Mary St Wilmington (19804) ***(G-9759)***
Cognition Group Inc 302 454-1265
2055 Limestone Rd Ste 200 Wilmington (19808) ***(G-9760)***
Cognitive Group LLC 301 585-1444
160 Greentree Dr Ste 101 Dover (19904) ***(G-1302)***
Cogtest Inc 302 454-1265
Topkis Bldg Ste 100254c Newark (19702) ***(G-6259)***
Cohawk 302 422-5176
611 Abbott Dr Milford (19963) ***(G-4361)***
Cohen Seglias Pallas 302 425-5089
1007 N Orange St Ste 1130 Wilmington (19801) ***(G-9761)***
Cohesive Strategies Inc 302 429-9120
600 N King St Ste 2 Wilmington (19801) ***(G-9762)***
Coiffure Ltd (PA) 302 652-3443
2401 Penns Ave Ste 104 Wilmington (19806) ***(G-9763)***
Coiffure Ltd 302 652-3463
4031 Kennett Pike Wilmington (19807) ***(G-9764)***
Cointigo LLC 817 681-7131
651 N Broad St Ste 205 Middletown (19709) ***(G-4000)***
Cokesbury Village, Hockessin *Also called Peninsula Untd Mthdst Hmes Inc* ***(G-3113)***
Coko Prints 302 507-1683
3 Doe Run Ct Apt 1b Wilmington (19808) ***(G-9765)***
Coldwell Banker, Rehoboth Beach *Also called Rehoboth Realty Inc* ***(G-8055)***
Coldwell Banker 302 539-4086
39682 Sunrise Ct Bethany Beach (19930) ***(G-392)***
Coldwell Banker Rehoboth Resrt 302 227-5000
20184 Coastal Hwy Rehoboth Beach (19971) ***(G-7896)***
Coldwell Bnkr Coml Amato Assoc 302 224-7700
100 Christiana Med Ctr Newark (19702) ***(G-6260)***
Cole and Latz Inc 702 234-2784
38 Phoebe Farms Ln New Castle (19720) ***(G-5180)***
Cole Realty Inc 302 764-4700
705 Philadelphia Pike Wilmington (19809) ***(G-9766)***
Cole Schotz PC 302 984-9541
500 Delaware Ave Ste 1410 Wilmington (19801) ***(G-9767)***
Colgate-Palmolive Company 302 428-1554
1105 N Market St Ste 1300 Wilmington (19801) ***(G-9768)***
Collateral Department, Wilmington *Also called Td Bank NA* ***(G-12861)***
Collections Marketing Center (PA) 302 830-9262
112 S French St Ste 500 Wilmington (19801) ***(G-9769)***
College Ave Student Loans, Wilmington *Also called College Avenue Student Ln LLC* ***(G-9770)***
College Avenue Student Ln LLC 302 684-6070
233 N King St Ste 400 Wilmington (19801) ***(G-9770)***
Collegiate Network Inc 302 652-4600
3901 Centerville Rd Wilmington (19807) ***(G-9771)***
Collender Griffith Chang Inc 302 992-0600
1601 Milltown Rd Ste 9 Wilmington (19808) ***(G-9772)***
Collett & Son Welding Inc 302 376-1830
550 Green Giant Rd Townsend (19734) ***(G-8770)***
Collett and Sons Welding 302 223-6525
370 N Main St Smyrna (19977) ***(G-8601)***
Colliers Trim Shop Inc 302 227-8398
2206 Hwy One Rehoboth Beach (19971) ***(G-7897)***
Collins Associates 302 834-4000
38 Peoples Plz Newark (19702) ***(G-6261)***

Collins Brothers Farms...302 238-7822
37161 Millsboro Hwy Millsboro (19966) ***(G-4666)***
Collins Mechanical Inc...302 398-8877
15294 S Dupont Hwy Harrington (19952) ***(G-2828)***
Colon Rectal Surgery Assoc Del...302 737-5444
4745 Ogletown Stanton Rd # 216 Newark (19713) ***(G-6262)***
Colonial Chapter of...302 861-6671
700 Barksdale Rd Ste 6 Newark (19711) ***(G-6263)***
Colonial Cleaning, Wilmington *Also called Colonial Construction Company* ***(G-9774)***
Colonial Cleaning Services Inc...302 660-2067
126b Middleboro Rd Wilmington (19804) ***(G-9773)***
Colonial Construction Company...302 994-5705
126 Middleboro Rd Wilmington (19804) ***(G-9774)***
Colonial East LP...302 644-4758
16 Manor House Ln Lewes (19958) ***(G-3442)***
Colonial Electric Supply Co...302 998-9993
88 Quigley Blvd New Castle (19720) ***(G-5181)***
Colonial Garden Apartments, Newark *Also called Colonial Rlty Assoc Ltd Partnr* ***(G-6264)***
Colonial Inv Managment Co...302 736-0674
9 E Loockerman St Ste C Dover (19901) ***(G-1303)***
Colonial Masonry Ltd...302 349-4945
219 Wheatfield Rd Greenwood (19950) ***(G-2721)***
Colonial Oaks Hotel LLC...302 645-7766
19113 Coastal Hwy Rehoboth Beach (19971) ***(G-7898)***
Colonial Parking Inc (HQ)...302 651-3600
715 N Orange St Fl 1 Wilmington (19801) ***(G-9775)***
Colonial Parking Inc...302 651-3618
800 N French St Wilmington (19801) ***(G-9776)***
Colonial Rlty Assoc Ltd Partnr...302 737-1254
334 E Main St Bldg B Newark (19711) ***(G-6264)***
Colonial School District...302 323-2700
1617 Matassino Rd New Castle (19720) ***(G-5182)***
Colonial Secrity Service, Wilmington *Also called Lenar Detective Agency Inc* ***(G-11369)***
Colony North Apartments...302 762-0405
319 E Lea Blvd Wilmington (19802) ***(G-9777)***
Color Dye Systems and Co...302 454-1754
663 Dawson Dr Ste B Newark (19713) ***(G-6265)***
Color Works Painting Inc...302 324-8411
251 Edwards Ave New Castle (19720) ***(G-5183)***
Colorful World Daycare, Bridgeville *Also called Marlette R Lofland* ***(G-494)***
Colorimetrix Inc...347 560-0037
122 Delaware St Ste M New Castle (19720) ***(G-5184)***
Colourworks Photographic Svcs...302 428-0222
1902 Superfine Ln Wilmington (19802) ***(G-9778)***
Colton Cleaners...302 234-9422
146 Lantana Dr Hockessin (19707) ***(G-2992)***
Columbia Care New York LLC...302 297-8614
200 S Dupont Blvd Smyrna (19977) ***(G-8602)***
Columbia Vending Service Inc...302 856-7000
10000 Old Racetrack Rd Delmar (19940) ***(G-985)***
Columbus Inn Management I...302 429-8700
105 Foulk Rd Wilmington (19803) ***(G-9779)***
Comcast Cablevision of Del...302 661-4465
5 Bellecor Dr New Castle (19720) ***(G-5185)***
Comcast Cablevision of Del (HQ)...302 856-4591
426a N Dupont Hwy Georgetown (19947) ***(G-2477)***
Comcast Cble Cmmunications LLC...302 323-9200
22 Reads Way New Castle (19720) ***(G-5186)***
Comcast Corporation...302 262-8996
500 High St Seaford (19973) ***(G-8201)***
Comcast Corporation...302 495-5612
2 Schulze Rd Greenwood (19950) ***(G-2722)***
Comcast MO Investments LLC...302 594-8705
1201 N Market St Ste 1000 Wilmington (19801) ***(G-9780)***
Comcast of Delmarva LLC...215 286-3345
5729 W Denneys Rd Dover (19904) ***(G-1304)***
Comenity Bank (HQ)...614 729-4000
1 Righter Pkwy Ste 100 Wilmington (19803) ***(G-9781)***
Comfort Care At Home Inc...302 737-8078
260 Chapman Rd Ste 201 Newark (19702) ***(G-6266)***
Comfort Inn, Newark *Also called Keval Corp* ***(G-6877)***
Comfort Inn, Dover *Also called Amaa Management Corporation* ***(G-1115)***
Comfort Inn, Dover *Also called A & G Realty LLC* ***(G-1073)***
Comfort Inn, Georgetown *Also called J & P Management Inc* ***(G-2569)***
Comfort Inn, Dover *Also called A & G Kramedas Associates LLC* ***(G-1072)***
Comfort Inn, Rehoboth Beach *Also called Resort Hotel LLC* ***(G-8057)***
Comfort Inn & Suites...302 737-3900
3 Concord Ln Newark (19713) ***(G-6267)***
Comfort Keepers, New Castle *Also called Caring For Life Inc* ***(G-5133)***
Comfort Keepers...302 378-0994
6303 Summit Bridge Rd Townsend (19734) ***(G-8771)***
Comfort Service Company, Seaford *Also called National HVAC Service* ***(G-8327)***
Comfort Suites, Dover *Also called 764 Dover Leipsic LLC* ***(G-1071)***
Comfort Suites...302 628-5400
23420 Sussex Hwy Seaford (19973) ***(G-8202)***
Comfort Suites Motel...302 266-6600
181 Thompson Dr Hockessin (19707) ***(G-2993)***
Comfort Zone Jazz LLC...302 745-2019
14620 Oyster Rocks Rd Milton (19968) ***(G-4882)***
Command Security Corporation...302 478-7003
3511 Silverside Rd Wilmington (19810) ***(G-9782)***
Commerce Associates LP...302 573-2500
1201 N Orange St Ste 700 Wilmington (19801) ***(G-9783)***
Commerce Global Inc...302 478-0853
2419 Dorval Rd Wilmington (19810) ***(G-9784)***
Commercial & Trauma Clg Entp, Middletown *Also called Crystal Graham* ***(G-4016)***
Commercial Cleaning Services...302 764-3424
814 Philadelphia Pike A Wilmington (19809) ***(G-9785)***
Commercial Credit, Dover *Also called Citifinancial Credit Company* ***(G-1283)***
Commercial Equipment Service...302 475-6682
1411 Windybush Rd Wilmington (19810) ***(G-9786)***
Commercial Food Equipment Repr, Wilmington *Also called Elmer Schultz Services Inc* ***(G-10382)***
Commercial Ground Care Inc...302 762-5410
852 Cranbrook Dr Wilmington (19803) ***(G-9787)***
Commercial Insurance Assoc...610 436-4608
256 Chapman Rd Ste 203 Newark (19702) ***(G-6268)***
Commercial Recovery Group Inc...302 730-4040
1012 College Rd Ste 203 Dover (19904) ***(G-1305)***
Commercial Residential Contrs, Dover *Also called Scuba World Inc* ***(G-2064)***
Commercial Waterman...302 659-3031
518 Flemings Landing Rd Townsend (19734) ***(G-8772)***
Commission On Archvs In Hstory (PA)...302 335-5544
6362 Bay Rd Frederica (19946) ***(G-2400)***
Commodities Plus Inc...302 376-5219
132 Sandy Dr Newark (19713) ***(G-6269)***
Common Sense Solutions LLC...302 875-4510
14127 Rottwaller Rd Laurel (19956) ***(G-3217)***
Commonspirit Health...302 234-5420
100 Saint Claire Dr Hockessin (19707) ***(G-2994)***
Commonwealth Construction...302 654-6611
2317 Pennsylvania Ave Wilmington (19806) ***(G-9788)***
Commonwealth Contruction Co...302 654-6611
2317 Pennsylvania Ave Wilmington (19806) ***(G-9789)***
Commonwealth Group...302 995-6400
4550 New Linden Hill Rd Wilmington (19808) ***(G-9790)***
Commonwealth Group LLC (PA)...302 472-7200
300 Water St Ste 300 # 300 Wilmington (19801) ***(G-9791)***
Commonwealth Trust Co...302 658-7214
29 Bancroft Mills Rd Wilmington (19806) ***(G-9792)***
Commtrak Corporation...302 644-1600
17493 Nassau Commons Blvd Lewes (19958) ***(G-3443)***
Communicate U Media LLC...610 453-6501
1010 Camelot Dr Middletown (19709) ***(G-4001)***
Communications & Wiring Co...302 539-0809
34423 Sylvan Vue Dr Dagsboro (19939) ***(G-893)***
Communications Printing Inc...302 229-9369
2850 Ogletown Rd Newark (19713) ***(G-6270)***
Community Alternatives Ind Inc...302 323-1436
908 Churchmans Road Ext B New Castle (19720) ***(G-5187)***
Community Auto Repair...302 856-3333
514 W Market St Georgetown (19947) ***(G-2478)***
Community Bank Delaware (PA)...302 348-8600
16982 Kings Hwy Lewes (19958) ***(G-3444)***
Community Business Dev Corp...302 544-1709
25 Hempstead Dr Newark (19702) ***(G-6271)***
Community Heating & AC...302 422-6839
10511 N Union Church Rd Lincoln (19960) ***(G-3843)***
Community Housing Inc (PA)...302 652-3991
613 N Washington St Wilmington (19801) ***(G-9793)***
Community Integrated Services...215 238-7411
24 Nw Front St Ste 300 Milford (19963) ***(G-4362)***
Community Interactions Inc...302 993-7846
625 W Newport Pike Wilmington (19804) ***(G-9794)***
Community Legal Aid Society (PA)...302 757-7001
100 W 10th St Ste 801 Wilmington (19801) ***(G-9795)***
Community Legal Aid Society...302 674-8500
840 Walker Rd Dover (19904) ***(G-1306)***
Community Legal Aid Society...302 856-0038
20151 Office Cir Georgetown (19947) ***(G-2479)***
Community Publications Inc...302 239-4644
24 W Main St Middletown (19709) ***(G-4002)***
Community Pwered Federal Cr Un (PA)...302 392-2930
1758 Pulaski Hwy Bear (19701) ***(G-80)***
Community Pwered Federal Cr Un...302 324-1441
4 Quigley Blvd New Castle (19720) ***(G-5188)***
Community Services Corporation...302 368-4400
116 Haines St Newark (19711) ***(G-6272)***
Community Systems and Svcs Inc...302 325-1500
2 Penns Way Ste 301 New Castle (19720) ***(G-5189)***
Community Twered Federal Cr Un...302 994-3617
3670 Kirkwood Hwy Wilmington (19808) ***(G-9796)***
Community Twered Federal Cr Un (PA)...302 368-2396
401 Eagle Run Rd Newark (19702) ***(G-6273)***
Compact Membrane Systems Inc...302 999-7996
335 Water St Wilmington (19804) ***(G-9797)***
Companion Therapy Lasers, New Castle *Also called Litecure LLC* ***(G-5485)***

ALPHABETIC

(PA)=Parent Co (HQ)=Headquarters (DH)=Div Headquarters
2020 Harris Directory of Delaware Businesses
617

Company Corporation (HQ)...302 636-5440
2711 Centerville Rd # 400 Wilmington (19808) ***(G-9798)***
Compass Graphics...302 378-1977
137 Back Creek Dr Middletown (19709) ***(G-4003)***
Compass Point Associates LLC...302 684-2980
26373 Lwes Georgetown Hwy Harbeson (19951) ***(G-2777)***
Compassionate Care...302 654-5401
405 Marsh Ln Ste 4 Wilmington (19804) ***(G-9799)***
Compassionate Care Hospi of Ce...302 993-9090
702 Wilmington Ave B Wilmington (19805) ***(G-9800)***
Compassionate Care Hospice...302 856-1486
20165 Office Cir Georgetown (19947) ***(G-2480)***
Compassionate Care Hospice of...302 994-1704
405 Marsh Ln Ste 4 Wilmington (19804) ***(G-9801)***
Compassionate Care Trnspt LLC...215 847-9836
510 Howard St Wilmington (19804) ***(G-9802)***
Compassonate Certification Ctr...888 316-9085
364 E Main St Ste 2001 Middletown (19709) ***(G-4004)***
Compassred Inc...302 383-2856
605 N Market St Fl 2 Wilmington (19801) ***(G-9803)***
Compd Holdings Inc...929 436-5252
651 N Broad St Ste 205 Middletown (19709) ***(G-4005)***
Competition Game Calls...302 345-7463
208 Brookland Ave Wilmington (19805) ***(G-9804)***
Complete Auto Body Inc...302 629-3955
26907 Sussex Hwy Seaford (19973) ***(G-8203)***
Complete Lawn Care, Millsboro *Also called Complete Tree Care Inc* ***(G-4667)***
Complete Properties Services...302 242-8666
116 Sarah Cir Ste D Camden Wyoming (19934) ***(G-624)***
Complete Rsrvtion Slutions LLC...800 672-8522
8 The Grn Ste 5863 Dover (19901) ***(G-1307)***
Complete Tree Care Inc...302 945-8289
30598 Cordrey Rd Millsboro (19966) ***(G-4667)***
Complex Systems Inc...302 651-8300
1105 N Market St Ste 1300 Wilmington (19801) ***(G-9805)***
Complexions Tanning Salon...302 430-0150
280 N Rehoboth Blvd Milford (19963) ***(G-4363)***
Compliance Environmental Inc...302 674-4427
150 S Bradford St Dover (19904) ***(G-1308)***
Comprehensive Bus Cons Inc...302 635-7711
3 Larchmont Ct Hockessin (19707) ***(G-2995)***
Comprehensive Bus Svcs LLC (PA)...302 994-2000
112 Capitol Trl Newark (19711) ***(G-6274)***
Comprhensive Neurology Ctr LLC...302 996-9010
537 Stanton Christiana Rd # 106 Newark (19713) ***(G-6275)***
Comprhnsive Spine Spt Medicine, Bear *Also called Frank Falco MD* ***(G-160)***
Compton Apartments, Wilmington *Also called Compton Pk Prsrvtion Assoc LLC* ***(G-9806)***
Compton Pk Prsrvtion Assoc LLC...302 654-4369
4 Denny Rd Wilmington (19809) ***(G-9806)***
Compton Towne House Apartments, Wilmington *Also called New Compton Towne Assoc LP* ***(G-11858)***
Computer Aid Inc...302 831-5500
500 Creek View Rd Ste 300 Newark (19711) ***(G-6276)***
Computer Jocks...302 544-6448
726 Pulaski Hwy Bear (19701) ***(G-81)***
Computer Sciences Corporation...302 391-8347
500 Creek View Rd Newark (19711) ***(G-6277)***
Computer Services of Delaware...302 697-8644
1991 S State St Ste B Dover (19901) ***(G-1309)***
Computer Staffing Services LLC (PA)...302 737-4920
263 E Main St Ste A Newark (19711) ***(G-6278)***
Computer User, Newark *Also called Burris & Baxter Communications* ***(G-6138)***
Computers Fixed Today...302 724-6411
301 E Lea Blvd Wilmington (19802) ***(G-9807)***
Computing & Network Service, Newark *Also called University of Delaware* ***(G-7621)***
Comstock Custom Cabinets Inc...302 422-2928
6706 Shawnee Rd Milford (19963) ***(G-4364)***
Concentra Inc...302 738-0103
4110 Stanton Ogletown Rd Newark (19713) ***(G-6279)***
Conch Island...302 226-9378
211 Rehoboth Ave Rehoboth Beach (19971) ***(G-7899)***
Conci LLC...847 665-9285
1013 Centre Rd Wilmington (19805) ***(G-9808)***
Concord Agency Inc...302 478-4000
3520 Silverside Rd Ste 28 Wilmington (19810) ***(G-9809)***
Concord Corporate Services Inc (HQ)...302 791-8200
1100 Carr Rd Wilmington (19809) ***(G-9810)***
Concord Dental...302 836-3750
2304 Concord Pike Wilmington (19803) ***(G-9811)***
Concord Mall LLC...302 478-9271
4737 Concord Pike Fl 3 Wilmington (19803) ***(G-9812)***
Concord Med Spine & Pain Ctr...302 652-1107
6 Sharpley Rd Wilmington (19803) ***(G-9813)***
Concord Towers Inc...302 737-2700
1201 Christiana Rd Newark (19713) ***(G-6280)***
Concrete Bldg Systems Del Inc...302 846-3645
9283 Old Racetrack Rd Delmar (19940) ***(G-986)***
Concrete Co Inc...302 652-1101
101 Brookside Dr Wilmington (19804) ***(G-9814)***
Concrete Services Inc...302 883-2883
794 Rose Valley School Rd Dover (19904) ***(G-1310)***
Concrete Walls Inc...302 293-7061
3415 Wrangle Hill Rd # 2 Bear (19701) ***(G-82)***
Cond Nast's, Wilmington *Also called Conde Nast International Inc* ***(G-9815)***
Conde Nast International Inc (HQ)...515 243-3273
1313 N Market St Fl 11 Wilmington (19801) ***(G-9815)***
Condor Technologies Inc...302 698-4444
110 N Main St Ste H Camden (19934) ***(G-551)***
Conducerent Incorporated...302 543-8525
1011 Centre Rd Ste 104 Wilmington (19805) ***(G-9816)***
Conectiv LLC (HQ)...202 872-2680
800 N King St Ste 400 Wilmington (19801) ***(G-9817)***
Conectiv LLC...800 375-7117
630 Mrtin Lther King Blvd Wilmington (19801) ***(G-9818)***
Conectiv LLC...302 429-3018
375 N Wakefield Dr Newark (19702) ***(G-6281)***
Conectiv Communications Inc (HQ)...302 224-1177
252 Chapman Rd Newark (19702) ***(G-6282)***
Conectiv Energy Supply Inc (HQ)...302 454-0300
500 N Wakefield Dr Newark (19702) ***(G-6283)***
Confab Inc...302 429-0140
1216 D St Wilmington (19801) ***(G-9819)***
Conference Group LLC...302 224-8255
254 Chapman Rd Ste 200 Newark (19702) ***(G-6284)***
Confluent Corporation...301 440-4100
19640 Buck Run Georgetown (19947) ***(G-2481)***
Conformit...302 451-9167
2915 Ogletown Rd Ste 2636 Newark (19713) ***(G-6285)***
Congo Capital Management LLC (HQ)...732 337-6643
3911 Concord Pike Wilmington (19803) ***(G-9820)***
Congo Capital Management LLC...732 337-6643
3911 Concord Pike Wilmington (19803) ***(G-9821)***
Congo Funeral Home (PA)...302 652-6640
2317 N Market St Wilmington (19802) ***(G-9822)***
Congruence Consulting Group...320 290-6155
87 Madison Dr Ste A Newark (19711) ***(G-6286)***
Conley & Wright DDS...302 645-6671
18913 John J Williams Hwy Rehoboth Beach (19971) ***(G-7900)***
Conlin Corporation...302 633-9174
737 Ambleside Dr Wilmington (19808) ***(G-9823)***
Conmac Security Systems Inc...302 529-9286
205 Beau Tree Dr Wilmington (19810) ***(G-9824)***
Connecticut Metallurgical, New Castle *Also called MMR Group Inc* ***(G-5531)***
Connecting Generations Inc...302 656-2122
100 W 10th St Ste 1115 Wilmington (19801) ***(G-9825)***
Connections...302 221-6605
204 Gordy Pl New Castle (19720) ***(G-5190)***
Connections Community Support...302 659-0512
994 Blackbird Landing Rd Townsend (19734) ***(G-8773)***
Connections Community Support...302 536-1952
105 N Front St Seaford (19973) ***(G-8204)***
Connections Community Support (PA)...302 984-2302
3821 Lancaster Pike Wilmington (19805) ***(G-9826)***
Connections Community Support...302 389-1118
676 Black Diamond Rd Smyrna (19977) ***(G-8603)***
Connections Community Support...302 654-7120
604 N West St Wilmington (19801) ***(G-9827)***
Connections Community Support...302 653-1505
222 N Dupont Blvd Smyrna (19977) ***(G-8604)***
Connections Community Support...302 654-9289
500 W 10th St Wilmington (19801) ***(G-9828)***
Connections CSP Inc Dover...302 672-9276
698 S Bay Rd Dover (19901) ***(G-1311)***
Connections Development Corp...302 436-3292
35906 Zion Church Rd Frankford (19945) ***(G-2356)***
Connections Development Corp (PA)...302 984-3380
3821 Lancaster Pike Wilmington (19805) ***(G-9829)***
Connell Construction Co...302 738-9428
808 N Country Club Dr Newark (19711) ***(G-6287)***
Connie F Cicorelli DDS PA...302 798-5797
1401 Silverside Rd Ste 2a Wilmington (19810) ***(G-9830)***
Connie's Market, Bear *Also called Jcholley LLC* ***(G-199)***
Connolly Flooring Inc...302 996-9470
315 Water St Wilmington (19804) ***(G-9831)***
Connolly Options LLC...302 998-2016
83 Christiana Rd New Castle (19720) ***(G-5191)***
Connor Charles & Sons Painting...302 945-1746
14219 Road 526 Georgetown (19947) ***(G-2482)***
Connor Marketing Inc...302 376-6037
434 Boxwood Ln Middletown (19709) ***(G-4006)***
Connor Sweeping Inc...302 368-2210
2016 Sunset Lake Rd Newark (19702) ***(G-6288)***
Conrep Inc...302 528-8383
292 Carter Dr Ste C Middletown (19709) ***(G-4007)***
Consoldted Fabrication Constrs...302 654-9001
1216 D St Wilmington (19801) ***(G-9832)***
Consolidated LLC...302 654-9001
1216 D St Wilmington (19801) ***(G-9833)***

Consolidated Construction Svcs 302 629-6070
7450 Rivershore Dr Seaford (19973) *(G-8205)*
Construct App Inc 415 702-0634
2711 Centerville Rd # 400 Wilmington (19808) *(G-9834)*
Construction Layout Services 302 998-1800
304 Mason Dr Newark (19711) *(G-6289)*
Construction MGT Svcs Inc (PA) 302 478-4200
3600 Silverside Rd Wilmington (19810) *(G-9835)*
Construction Unlimited Inc 302 836-3140
705 Elizabeth Ln Bear (19701) *(G-83)*
Consult Dynamics Inc 302 295-4700
1204 N West St Wilmington (19801) *(G-9836)*
Consult Dynamics Inc (PA) 302 654-1019
1016 Delaware Ave Wilmington (19806) *(G-9837)*
Consulting Experts Online, Hockessin *Also called Ceo-Hqcom LLC (G-2982)*
Consulttive Rview Rhbilitation 302 366-0356
630 Churchmans Rd Ste 105 Newark (19702) *(G-6290)*
Consumer Injury Alert, Newark *Also called Chilay Inc (G-6196)*
Contact Info Inc 917 817-7939
8 The Grn Ste A Dover (19901) *(G-1312)*
Contactlifeline Inc (PA) 302 761-9800
314 Brandywine Blvd Wilmington (19809) *(G-9838)*
Contemprary Stffing Sltons Inc 302 328-1300
10 Corporate Cir Ste 210 New Castle (19720) *(G-5192)*
Conti Electric of N J Inc 302 996-3905
2633 Skylark Rd Wilmington (19808) *(G-9839)*
Continental Case 302 322-1765
64 Shields Ln Newark (19702) *(G-6291)*
Continental Finance Co LLC (PA) 302 456-1930
4550 Linden Hill Rd # 400 Wilmington (19808) *(G-9840)*
Continental Jewelers Inc 302 475-2000
2209 Silverside Rd Wilmington (19810) *(G-9841)*
Continental Mortgage Corp 302 996-5807
3422 Old Capitol Trl Wilmington (19808) *(G-9842)*
Continental Warranty Corp 302 375-0401
99 Wiltshire Rd Claymont (19703) *(G-723)*
Continuum Media LLC 310 295-9997
2140 S Dupont Hwy Camden (19934) *(G-552)*
Contract Environments Inc 302 658-0668
1020 W 18th St Ste 1 Wilmington (19802) *(G-9843)*
Contractor Materials LLC 302 658-5241
4048 New Castle Ave New Castle (19720) *(G-5193)*
Contractors Materials, New Castle *Also called Contractor Materials LLC (G-5193)*
Contractors Materials LLC 302 656-6066
925 S Heald St Wilmington (19801) *(G-9844)*
Contractual Carriers Inc 302 453-1420
104 Alan Dr Newark (19711) *(G-6292)*
Contruction Jones and Ldscpg 302 423-6456
5169 Mud Mill Rd Camden Wyoming (19934) *(G-625)*
Convention Coach 302 335-5459
554 Lexington Mill Rd Magnolia (19962) *(G-3887)*
Conventional Builders Inc 302 422-2429
846 School St Houston (19954) *(G-3177)*
Conventioneer Pubg Co Inc 301 487-3907
24948 Green Fern Dr Georgetown (19947) *(G-2483)*
Conventra LLC 302 378-4461
25 S Cummings Dr Middletown (19709) *(G-4008)*
Convergence Group Inc 302 234-7400
1011 Centre Rd Ste 104 Wilmington (19805) *(G-9845)*
Convergone Gvrnment Sltons LLC 302 999-7020
242 N James St Ste 201 Wilmington (19804) *(G-9846)*
Conway Construction LLC 302 453-9260
521 Dougfield Rd Newark (19713) *(G-6293)*
Conzurge Inc 267 507-6039
2035 Sunset Lake Rd B2 Newark (19702) *(G-6294)*
Cooch & Taylor Attys 302 652-3641
1000 N West St Fl 10 Wilmington (19801) *(G-9847)*
Cooch and Taylor A Prof Assn (PA) 302 984-3800
1007 N Orange St Ste 1120 Wilmington (19801) *(G-9848)*
Cooch and Taylor Attys At Law, Wilmington *Also called Cooch and Taylor A Prof Assn (G-9848)*
Coogan, Kevin P Vmd, Wilmington *Also called Kentmere Veterinary Hospital (G-11246)*
Cook & Cook Ltd Partnership 302 428-0109
304 Centennial Cir Wilmington (19807) *(G-9849)*
Cook Awesome Food LLC 302 990-2665
1308 W 13th St Apt 2 Wilmington (19806) *(G-9850)*
Cook G Legih DDS& Cook Jefry 302 378-4416
12 Pennington St Ste 300 Middletown (19709) *(G-4009)*
Cook Hauling LLC 302 378-6451
350 Misty Vale Dr Middletown (19709) *(G-4010)*
Cook Plastering Inc 302 737-0778
1026 Summit View Dr Newark (19713) *(G-6295)*
Cool Branch Associates LLC 302 629-5363
100 Hitch Pond Cir Seaford (19973) *(G-8206)*
Cool Nerds Marketing Inc 302 304-3440
300 N Market St Ste 208 Wilmington (19801) *(G-9851)*
Coolpop Nation 302 584-8833
2418 Rambler Rd Wilmington (19810) *(G-9852)*
Coon, Chris E Dvm, Dover *Also called Dover Animal Hospital (G-1441)*
Cooper Bearings Inc 302 858-5056
21629 Baltimore Ave Georgetown (19947) *(G-2484)*
Cooper Bros Inc 302 323-0717
62 Southgate Blvd Frnt New Castle (19720) *(G-5194)*
Cooper Levenson PA 302 838-2600
30 Foxhunt Dr U30 Bear (19701) *(G-84)*
Cooper Simpler Associates Inc 302 227-2999
6 Wilmington Ave Rehoboth Beach (19971) *(G-7901)*
Cooper, Stephen MD, Dover *Also called E N T Associates (G-1491)*
Cooper-Wilbert Vault Co Inc 302 376-1331
4971 Summit Bridge Rd Middletown (19709) *(G-4011)*
Cooperealty Associates Inc (PA) 302 629-6693
615 W Stein Hwy Seaford (19973) *(G-8207)*
Cooperson Associates LLC 302 655-1105
1504 N French St Wilmington (19801) *(G-9853)*
Cooperson Associates Inc 302 655-1105
2417 Lancaster Ave 2 Wilmington (19805) *(G-9854)*
Copart Inc 302 628-5412
26029 Bethel Concord Rd Seaford (19973) *(G-8208)*
Copp Seafood, Lewes *Also called Steven P Copp (G-3765)*
Copra Inc 917 224-1727
1000 N West St Ste 1501 Wilmington (19801) *(G-9855)*
Copy Craft Inc 302 633-1313
707 Kirkwood Hwy Wilmington (19805) *(G-9856)*
Copy Print, Georgetown *Also called Rogers Graphics Inc (G-2641)*
Copy Systems, Newark *Also called Digital Office Solutions Inc (G-6447)*
Coqonut Inc (PA) 347 419-7709
251 Little Falls Dr Wilmington (19808) *(G-9857)*
Corcoran & Associates PA CPA 302 478-9515
3801 Kennett Pike C100 Wilmington (19807) *(G-9858)*
Corcoran & Company PA CPA, Wilmington *Also called Corcoran & Associates PA CPA (G-9858)*
Cordjia LLC (PA) 302 743-1297
131 Continental Dr # 409 Newark (19713) *(G-6296)*
Core & Main LP 302 684-3452
25414 Primehook Rd # 100 Milton (19968) *(G-4883)*
Core & Main LP 302 737-1500
22 Garfield Way Newark (19713) *(G-6297)*
Core Construction LLC 302 449-4186
115 E Glenwood Ave Smyrna (19977) *(G-8605)*
Core Functions LLC 443 956-9626
21142 Arrington Dr Selbyville (19975) *(G-8471)*
Core Purchase LLC 616 328-5715
910 Foulk Rd Ste 201 Wilmington (19803) *(G-9859)*
Core Value Global LLC 908 312-4070
1209 N Orange St Wilmington (19801) *(G-9860)*
Corelink Ministries 610 505-6043
2207 Concord Pike Wilmington (19803) *(G-9861)*
Corelink Solution, The, Wilmington *Also called Corelink Ministries (G-9861)*
Corexcel, Wilmington *Also called Momentum Management Group Inc (G-11728)*
Corinthian House 302 858-1493
219 S Race St Georgetown (19947) *(G-2485)*
Corizon LLC 302 998-3958
200 Greenbank Rd Wilmington (19808) *(G-9862)*
Corizon Health Inc 302 266-8230
111 Continental Dr # 211 Newark (19713) *(G-6298)*
Corlo Services Inc 302 737-3207
100 Peoples Dr Newark (19702) *(G-6299)*
Cornerstone CPA, Bear *Also called Wendy Cpa LLC (G-375)*
Cornerstone Media Production 302 855-9380
41 Bramhall St Georgetown (19947) *(G-2486)*
Cornerstone Senior Center 302 836-6463
3135 Summit Bridge Rd Bear (19701) *(G-85)*
Cornerstone West Cmnty Dev Co 302 658-4171
710 N Lincoln St Wilmington (19805) *(G-9863)*
Corp1 Inc 720 644-6144
614 N Dupont Hwy Ste 210 Dover (19901) *(G-1313)*
Corporate Arcft Technical Svcs 302 383-9400
415 Riblett Ln Wilmington (19808) *(G-9864)*
Corporate Holding Services (PA) 302 428-0515
818 N Washington St Wilmington (19801) *(G-9865)*
Corporate Interiors Inc (PA) 302 322-1008
223 Lisa Dr New Castle (19720) *(G-5195)*
Corporate Interiors Delaware, New Castle *Also called Corporate Interiors Inc (G-5195)*
Corporate Kids Lrng Ctr Inc 302 678-0688
605 S Bay Rd Dover (19901) *(G-1314)*
Corporate Relocation Assn 302 239-9314
663 Arbour Dr Newark (19713) *(G-6300)*
Corporation, Wilmington *Also called Swit Inc (G-12826)*
Corporation Service Company (PA) 302 636-5400
251 Little Falls Dr Wilmington (19808) *(G-9866)*
Corporations & Companies Inc 302 652-4800
910 Foulk Rd Ste 201 Wilmington (19803) *(G-9867)*
Corrado American LLC 302 655-6501
200 Marsh Ln New Castle (19720) *(G-5196)*
Corrado Construction Co LLC 302 652-3339
210 Marsh Ln New Castle (19720) *(G-5197)*
Corrado Fleet Services, New Castle *Also called Heavy Equipment Rental Inc (G-5388)*

ALPHABETIC

Corrado Management Svcs LLC ... 302 225-0700
204 Marsh Ln New Castle (19720) ***(G-5198)***
Correction Delaware Department ... 302 856-5280
23203 Dupont Blvd Georgetown (19947) ***(G-2487)***
Corrective Chiropractic, Hockessin *Also called P A Chadley* ***(G-3109)***
Corrin Expert Tree Care, Bear *Also called Corrin Tree & Landscape Co* ***(G-86)***
Corrin Tree & Landscape Co ... 302 753-8733
1276 Porter Rd Bear (19701) ***(G-86)***
Corrin Tree Landscape ... 302 521-8333
1307 N Rodney St Wilmington (19806) ***(G-9868)***
Corrosion Testing Laboratories ... 302 454-8200
60 Blue Hen Dr Newark (19713) ***(G-6301)***
Corteva Inc (PA) ... 302 485-3000
974 Centre Rd Bldg 735 Wilmington (19805) ***(G-9869)***
Corteva Agriscience, Wilmington *Also called Corteva Inc* ***(G-9869)***
Corvant LLC ... 302 299-1570
131 Continental Dr # 409 Newark (19713) ***(G-6302)***
Cosey Gabre ... 302 233-0658
23 Lake Cove Ln Felton (19943) ***(G-2284)***
Cosmetic Innovators LLC ... 310 310-9784
1201 N Orange St Ste 7198 Wilmington (19801) ***(G-9870)***
Cosmic Custom Screen Printing ... 302 933-0920
28116 John J Williams Hwy Millsboro (19966) ***(G-4668)***
Cosmic Strands LLC ... 302 660-3268
913 N Market St Ste 200 Wilmington (19801) ***(G-9871)***
Cosmodog Software Inc ... 302 762-2437
309 Grandview Ave Wilmington (19809) ***(G-9872)***
Cosmoprof, Newark *Also called Sally Beauty Supply LLC* ***(G-7378)***
Costa and Rihl Mech Contrs, Wilmington *Also called J Rihl Inc* ***(G-11109)***
Costleigh, Brian J MD, Dover *Also called Cancer Care Ctrs At Bay Hlth* ***(G-1249)***
Costline Cleaning Service ... 302 420-3000
22791 Dozer Ln Unit 5 Harbeson (19951) ***(G-2778)***
Cotten Engineering LLC ... 302 628-9164
10087 Concord Rd Seaford (19973) ***(G-8209)***
Cottman Transmission ... 302 322-4600
1600 N Dupont Hwy New Castle (19720) ***(G-5199)***
Council of Devon ... 302 658-5366
2401 Penns Ave Apt 606 Wilmington (19806) ***(G-9873)***
Counseling Services Inc ... 302 894-1477
18c Trolley Sq Wilmington (19806) ***(G-9874)***
Countermeasures Assessment ... 302 322-9600
110 Quigley Blvd New Castle (19720) ***(G-5200)***
Counterparts LLC ... 302 349-0400
12952 Sussex Hwy Greenwood (19950) ***(G-2723)***
Counterpoint Software Inc ... 302 426-6500
1901 N Lincoln St Wilmington (19806) ***(G-9875)***
Country Comforts ... 302 242-8527
6309 Mud Mill Rd Camden Wyoming (19934) ***(G-626)***
Country Green Landscaping ... 302 653-1600
949 S Dupont Blvd Smyrna (19977) ***(G-8606)***
Country House, Wilmington *Also called Acts Rtrmnt-Life Cmmnities Inc* ***(G-8928)***
Country House, The, Wilmington *Also called Peninsula Untd Mthdst Hmes Inc* ***(G-12064)***
Country Inns Suites ... 302 266-6400
1024 Old Churchmans Rd Newark (19713) ***(G-6303)***
Country Kids Child ... 302 349-5888
12400 Sussex Hwy Greenwood (19950) ***(G-2724)***
Country Kids Home Day Care ... 302 653-4134
1069 Vndyke Grenspring Rd Townsend (19734) ***(G-8774)***
Country Lawn Care & Maint ... 302 593-3393
30435 Hollymount Rd Harbeson (19951) ***(G-2779)***
Country Life Homes Milford De ... 302 265-2257
610 Marshall St Milford (19963) ***(G-4365)***
Country Maid Launderette, Claymont *Also called Wolfe Resources Ltd* ***(G-825)***
Country Meadow Propco LLC ... 330 633-0555
850 New Burton Rd Dover (19904) ***(G-1315)***
Country Roads Veterinary Svc ... 302 514-9087
2681 Shaws Corner Rd Clayton (19938) ***(G-840)***
Country Store ... 302 653-5111
11 S Main St Kenton (19955) ***(G-3184)***
Country Suites By Carlson, Newark *Also called Khanna Entps Ltd A Ltd Partnr* ***(G-6885)***
Country Suites By Carlson, Newark *Also called Country Inns Suites* ***(G-6303)***
Country Swim Club Inc ... 302 420-5043
2700 Centerville Rd Wilmington (19808) ***(G-9876)***
Country Villa Motel ... 814 938-8330
1036 N Walnut St Milford (19963) ***(G-4366)***
Country Village Apartments ... 302 674-0991
480 Country Dr Dover (19901) ***(G-1316)***
Countryside Lawn & Landscape ... 302 832-1320
1604 Pulaski Hwy Newark (19702) ***(G-6304)***
Countryside Nursery & Grdn Ctr, Newark *Also called Countryside Lawn & Landscape* ***(G-6304)***
County Bank ... 302 684-2300
140 Broadkill Rd Milton (19968) ***(G-4884)***
County Bank ... 302 947-7300
25933 School Ln Millsboro (19966) ***(G-4669)***
County Bank ... 302 537-0900
36754 Old Mill Rd Millville (19967) ***(G-4841)***
County Bank ... 302 855-2000
13 N Bedford St Georgetown (19947) ***(G-2488)***
County Bank ... 302 645-8880
1609 Savannah Rd Lewes (19958) ***(G-3445)***
County Bank ... 302 424-2500
100 E Masten Cir Milford (19963) ***(G-4367)***
County Bank (PA) ... 302 226-9800
19927 Shuttle Rd Rehoboth Beach (19971) ***(G-7902)***
County Building Services Inc ... 302 377-4213
8 Knightsbridge Rd Middletown (19709) ***(G-4012)***
County Environmental Inc ... 302 322-8946
461 Churchmans Rd New Castle (19720) ***(G-5201)***
County Group Companies, New Castle *Also called County Environmental Inc* ***(G-5201)***
County Insulation Co ... 302 322-8946
461 Churchmans Rd New Castle (19720) ***(G-5202)***
County of Kent ... 302 735-2180
911 Public Safety Blvd Dover (19901) ***(G-1317)***
County of Sussex ... 302 854-5050
22215 Dupont Blvd Georgetown (19947) ***(G-2489)***
County of Sussex ... 302 947-0864
29445 Inland Bay Rd Millsboro (19966) ***(G-4670)***
County of Sussex ... 302 855-7878
2 The Cir Georgetown (19947) ***(G-2490)***
County Women S Journal ... 302 236-1435
17252 N Village Main Blvd # 9 Lewes (19958) ***(G-3446)***
Court Record & Data MGT Svcs ... 732 955-6567
1300 First State Blvd H Wilmington (19804) ***(G-9877)***
Courtesy Trnsp Svcs Inc ... 302 322-9722
4 Parkway Cir New Castle (19720) ***(G-5203)***
Courtland Manor Inc ... 302 674-0566
889 S Little Creek Rd Dover (19901) ***(G-1318)***
Courtyard By Marriott, Wilmington *Also called 1102 West Street Ltd Partnr* ***(G-8842)***
Courtyard By Marriott, Wilmington *Also called 44 New England Management Co* ***(G-8863)***
Courtyard By Marriott, Newark *Also called Courtyard Management Corp* ***(G-6305)***
Courtyard Management Corp ... 302 429-7600
1102 N West St Wilmington (19801) ***(G-9878)***
Courtyard Management Corp ... 302 456-3800
48 Geoffrey Dr Newark (19713) ***(G-6305)***
Courtyard Newark At Ud ... 302 737-0900
400 David Hollowell Dr Newark (19716) ***(G-6306)***
Couture Denim LLC ... 302 220-8339
3 Silsbee Rd New Castle (19720) ***(G-5204)***
Covant Solutions Inc ... 302 607-2678
220 Continental Dr # 314 Newark (19713) ***(G-6307)***
Covenant Asset Mgmt & Financl ... 302 324-5655
42 Reads Way New Castle (19720) ***(G-5205)***
Covenant Preschool ... 302 764-8503
503 Duncan Rd Wilmington (19809) ***(G-9879)***
Covenant Properties I ... 302 234-5655
15 Middleton Dr Wilmington (19808) ***(G-9880)***
Coventry Health Care Inc ... 302 995-6100
750 Prides Xing Ste 200 Newark (19713) ***(G-6308)***
Coventry Health Care Inc ... 800 833-7423
750 Prdes Crssing Ste 200 Newark (19713) ***(G-6309)***
Coventry Health Care Del Inc ... 302 995-6100
2751 Centerville Rd # 400 Wilmington (19808) ***(G-9881)***
Cover & Rossiter PA ... 302 656-6632
2711 Centerville Rd # 100 Wilmington (19808) ***(G-9882)***
Coverdale Community Council ... 302 337-7179
11575 Fisher Cir Bridgeville (19933) ***(G-461)***
Coverdeck Systems Inc ... 302 427-7578
408 Meco Dr A Wilmington (19804) ***(G-9883)***
Coveys Car Care Inc ... 302 629-2746
1300 Middleford Rd Seaford (19973) ***(G-8210)***
Cowchok Tf Inc ... 302 475-4510
2615 Kimbrough Dr Wilmington (19810) ***(G-9884)***
Cowie Technology Corp ... 856 692-2828
18 Boulden Cir Ste 28 New Castle (19720) ***(G-5206)***
Cowie Technology Corp ... 302 998-7037
510 1st Blvd State Wilmington (19804) ***(G-9885)***
Cox Electric Inc ... 302 629-5448
10851 Airport Rd Unit 1 Seaford (19973) ***(G-8211)***
Cox Industries Inc ... 302 332-8470
111 Lake Dr Ste C Newark (19702) ***(G-6310)***
Cozen OConnor ... 302 295-2000
1201 N Market St Ste 1001 Wilmington (19801) ***(G-9886)***
Cozy Critters Child Care Corp ... 302 541-8210
35371 Beaver Dam Rd Frankford (19945) ***(G-2357)***
Cpex Pharmaceuticals Inc ... 302 651-8300
1105 N Market St Ste 1300 Wilmington (19801) ***(G-9887)***
Cpmg Inc ... 302 429-8688
2207 Concord Pike Wilmington (19803) ***(G-9888)***
Cpr Construction Inc ... 302 322-5770
106 E 14th St New Castle (19720) ***(G-5207)***
Cpr Solutions Inc ... 302 477-1114
2502 Silverside Rd Ste 6 Wilmington (19810) ***(G-9889)***
Cr Newlin Trucking Inc ... 302 678-9124
2199 Fast Landing Rd Dover (19901) ***(G-1319)***
Cr24 LLC ... 888 427-9357
221 W 9th St Ste 224 Wilmington (19801) ***(G-9890)***

Crabby Dick's Creamery, Delaware City *Also called CD Cream* ***(G-950)***
Craft Bookbinding Co, Wilmington *Also called L E Stansell Inc* ***(G-11308)***
Crafts Report Publishing Co 302 656-2209
100 Rogers Rd Wilmington (19801) ***(G-9891)***
Craftsman Cbntry Woodworks Inc 302 841-5274
37357 Tree Top Ln Selbyville (19975) ***(G-8472)***
Craig Ball Sales Inc 302 628-9900
103 Davis Dr Seaford (19973) ***(G-8212)***
Craig Joyner Entertainment, Wilmington *Also called Worldwind Inc* ***(G-13305)***
Craig Technologies Inc (PA) 302 628-9900
103 Davis Dr Seaford (19973) ***(G-8213)***
Craigs Woodworks LLC 302 998-4201
2017 S Woodmill Dr Wilmington (19808) ***(G-9892)***
Cramaro Tarpaulin Systems Inc 302 292-2170
131 Sandy Dr Newark (19713) ***(G-6311)***
Cramer & Dimichele PA 302 293-1230
1801 W Newport Pike Wilmington (19804) ***(G-9893)***
Cranston Hall Apartments 302 999-7001
3314 Old Capitol Trl # 2 Wilmington (19808) ***(G-9894)***
Cratis Solutions Inc 515 423-7259
8 The Grn Ste 5910 Dover (19901) ***(G-1320)***
Crazy Coatings 302 378-0888
4783 Summit Bridge Rd Middletown (19709) ***(G-4013)***
Crazy Ladyz LLC 302 541-4040
9 Atlantic Ave Ocean View (19970) ***(G-7781)***
Crds, Wilmington *Also called Court Record & Data MGT Svcs* ***(G-9877)***
Creaform USA Inc 407 732-4103
220 E Delaware Ave Newark (19711) ***(G-6312)***
Creative Assemblies Inc 302 956-6194
17053 Tatman Farm Rd Bridgeville (19933) ***(G-462)***
Creative Builders Inc 302 228-8153
20593 Rust Rd Harbeson (19951) ***(G-2780)***
Creative Children, Wilmington *Also called Regina Coleman* ***(G-12357)***
Creative Courtyards 302 226-1994
20184 Phillips St Rehoboth Beach (19971) ***(G-7903)***
Creative Devices Inc 302 378-5433
361 Misty Vale Dr Middletown (19709) ***(G-4014)***
Creative Flooring Contrs Inc 302 653-7521
100c E Glenwood Ave Smyrna (19977) ***(G-8607)***
Creative Floors Inc 302 455-9045
105 Sandy Dr Newark (19713) ***(G-6313)***
Creative Hairdressers, Rehoboth Beach *Also called Ratner Companies LC* ***(G-8040)***
Creative Hairdressers, Wilmington *Also called Ratner Companies LC* ***(G-12321)***
Creative Hairdressers, Bear *Also called Ratner Companies LC* ***(G-297)***
Creative Hairdressers, Newark *Also called Ratner Companies LC* ***(G-7299)***
Creative Hairdressers, Wilmington *Also called Ratner Companies LC* ***(G-12322)***
Creative Impressions, Rehoboth Beach *Also called S F F Art Inc* ***(G-8064)***
Creative Kitchens and Floors 302 629-3166
507 Hickory Ln Seaford (19973) ***(G-8214)***
Creative Learning Academy Inc 302 834-5259
1458 Bear Corbitt Rd Bear (19701) ***(G-87)***
Creative Learning Child Care 302 691-3167
1220 Apple St Wilmington (19801) ***(G-9895)***
Creative Learning Preschool, Bear *Also called Creative Learning Academy Inc* ***(G-87)***
Creative Micro Designs Inc 302 456-5800
645 Dawson Dr Ste B Newark (19713) ***(G-6314)***
Creative Minds Daycare 302 378-0741
2 Mica St Townsend (19734) ***(G-8775)***
Creative Promotions 302 697-7896
38 South St Camden (19934) ***(G-553)***
Creative Solutions Intl, Wilmington *Also called De Novo Corporation* ***(G-9987)***
Creative Spaces, Claymont *Also called Wire Works* ***(G-824)***
Creative Travel Inc 302 658-2900
908 Old Harmony Rd Newark (19713) ***(G-6315)***
Credit Share Club LLC 302 401-6450
8 The Grn Ste 8360 Dover (19901) ***(G-1321)***
Creditshop LLC 302 588-0107
123 S Justison St Ste 602 Wilmington (19801) ***(G-9896)***
Crescent Dental Associates 302 230-0000
129 S West St Wilmington (19801) ***(G-9897)***
Crescent Dental Associates 302 836-6968
100 Becks Woods Dr Bear (19701) ***(G-88)***
Cressona Associates LLC 302 792-2737
1308 Society Dr Claymont (19703) ***(G-724)***
Crest Central 302 736-0576
300 W Water St Dover (19904) ***(G-1322)***
Crestline Hotels & Resorts LLC 302 655-0400
700 N King St Wilmington (19801) ***(G-9898)***
Crestwood Garden Apts, Georgetown *Also called Service General Corp* ***(G-2651)***
Crimson Group LLC 301 252-3779
17 Dubb Dr Newark (19702) ***(G-6316)***
Crimson Strategy Group LLP 302 503-5698
8 The Grn Ste 10235 Dover (19901) ***(G-1323)***
Cripple Creek Golf & Cntry CLB 302 539-1446
29494 Cripple Creek Dr Dagsboro (19939) ***(G-894)***
Cristy Anna Care Physcl Thrapy 302 378-6111
200 Cleaver Farms Rd Middletown (19709) ***(G-4015)***
Criterium Jagiasi Engineers 302 498-5600
1500 Shallcross Ave Wilmington (19806) ***(G-9899)***
Critical Care Systems Intl Inc 302 765-4132
700 W Lea Blvd Ste 300 Wilmington (19802) ***(G-9900)***
Crochet Creations By Debbie 302 287-2462
1219 Mckennans Church Rd Wilmington (19808) ***(G-9901)***
Croda Inc 302 429-5249
321 Cherry Ln New Castle (19720) ***(G-5208)***
Croda Inc 302 429-5200
315 Cherry Ln New Castle (19720) ***(G-5209)***
Croda Atlas Point, New Castle *Also called Croda Uniqema Inc* ***(G-5210)***
Croda Uniqema Inc 302 429-5599
315 Cherry Ln New Castle (19720) ***(G-5210)***
Croesus Inc 302 472-9260
1007 N Orange St Wilmington (19801) ***(G-9902)***
Croker Oars Usa Inc 302 897-6705
212 Karins Blvd Townsend (19734) ***(G-8776)***
Croosroads Auto Repair Inc 302 436-9100
32469 Lighthouse Rd Selbyville (19975) ***(G-8473)***
Cross & Simon LLC 302 777-4200
913 N Market St Ste 1100 Wilmington (19801) ***(G-9903)***
Cross Border It, Dover *Also called Damon Baca* ***(G-1338)***
Cross Over Camo LLC 302 798-1898
7205 Governor Printz Blvd Claymont (19703) ***(G-725)***
Crossfit Bear 302 540-4394
2611 Del Laws Rd Bear (19701) ***(G-89)***
Crossfit Diamond State LLC 201 803-1159
1801 Lincoln Ave Wilmington (19809) ***(G-9904)***
Crossfit Dover LLC 302 242-5400
177 Windrow Way Magnolia (19962) ***(G-3888)***
Crossings At Oak Orchard 302 231-8243
27825 Sandy Dr Millsboro (19966) ***(G-4671)***
Crossknowledge 646 699-5983
874 Walker Rd Ste C Dover (19904) ***(G-1324)***
Crossland and Associates 302 658-2100
724 Yorklyn Rd Ste 100 Hockessin (19707) ***(G-2996)***
Crossroads of Delaware 302 744-9999
2 Forest St Dover (19904) ***(G-1325)***
Crossroads Veterinary Clinic 302 436-5984
36774 Dupont Blvd Selbyville (19975) ***(G-8474)***
Crossroads Wireless Holdg LLC 405 946-1200
919 N Market St Ste 600 Wilmington (19801) ***(G-9905)***
Crosswinds Motel, Rehoboth Beach *Also called Lomas Properties LLC* ***(G-7990)***
Crothers Doors and More I 302 678-3667
11361 Willow Grove Rd Camden Wyoming (19934) ***(G-627)***
Crowley and Assoc Rlty Inc 302 227-6131
20250 Coastal Hwy Rehoboth Beach (19971) ***(G-7904)***
Crown Cork & Seal Receivables (HQ) 215 698-5100
5301 Limestone Rd Ste 221 Wilmington (19808) ***(G-9906)***
Crown Cork Seal Receivables De, Wilmington *Also called Crown Cork & Seal Receivables* ***(G-9906)***
Crown Equine LLC 302 629-2782
14274 Cokesbury Rd Georgetown (19947) ***(G-2491)***
Crown Molding Man 302 455-1204
187 Scottfield Dr Newark (19713) ***(G-6317)***
Crown Shipping 617 909-3357
15 Brittingham Dr Dover (19904) ***(G-1326)***
Crowne Plaza Wilmington North, Claymont *Also called Delaware Hotel Associates LP* ***(G-732)***
Crude Gold Research LLC 646 681-7317
8 The Grn Ste A Dover (19901) ***(G-1327)***
Cruise Holidays Brandywine Vly 302 239-6400
7460 Lancaster Pike Ste 6 Hockessin (19707) ***(G-2997)***
Cruise One 302 698-6468
159 Orchard Grove Ct Camden Wyoming (19934) ***(G-628)***
Cruise Ship Centers 302 999-0202
760 Peoples Plz Newark (19702) ***(G-6318)***
Cruise Shoppe Inc 302 737-7220
26 Valerie Dr Bear (19701) ***(G-90)***
Cruiseone 302 945-4620
32317 Mulligan Way Millsboro (19966) ***(G-4672)***
Cruz Publishing Group 302 287-2938
64 Representative Ln Dover (19904) ***(G-1328)***
Crw Parts Inc 302 651-9300
3 James Ct Wilmington (19801) ***(G-9907)***
Cryptomarket Inc (PA) 860 222-0318
1209 N Orange St Wilmington (19801) ***(G-9908)***
Cryptomkt, Wilmington *Also called Cryptomarket Inc* ***(G-9908)***
Crystal Diamond Publishing 302 737-2130
1 Mabry Ct Newark (19702) ***(G-6319)***
Crystal Graham 302 669-9318
415 E Main St Middletown (19709) ***(G-4016)***
Crystal Holdings Inc (PA) 302 421-5700
110 S Poplar St Ste 400 Wilmington (19801) ***(G-9909)***
Crystal Penn Avenue LP 302 846-0613
9317 Old Racetrack Rd Delmar (19940) ***(G-987)***
Crystal Steel Fabricators Inc 302 846-0277
N 2nd Delmar (19940) ***(G-988)***

ALPHABETIC

(PA)=Parent Co (HQ)=Headquarters (DH)=Div Headquarters
2020 Harris Directory of Delaware Businesses
621

Crystal Steel Fabricators Inc (PA) 302 846-0613
 9317 Old Racetrack Rd Delmar (19940) *(G-989)*
Cs Webb Daughters & Son Inc 302 239-2801
 1028 Yorklyn Rd Hockessin (19707) *(G-2998)*
CSC, Wilmington *Also called Company Corporation* *(G-9798)*
CSC Corporate Domains Inc 902 746-5201
 251 Little Falls Dr Wilmington (19808) *(G-9910)*
CSC Entity Services LLC 302 654-7584
 103 Foulk Rd Ste 200 Wilmington (19803) *(G-9911)*
CSC Tem Ingersoll Rand 302 765-3208
 4899 Limestone Rd Wilmington (19808) *(G-9912)*
Csi Solutions LLC 202 506-7573
 200 Continental Dr # 401 Newark (19713) *(G-6320)*
Csi Plasma Inc 302 565-0003
 77 Marrows Rd Newark (19713) *(G-6321)*
Csols Inc 302 731-5290
 750 Prdes Crssing Ste 305 Newark (19713) *(G-6322)*
CSP Supervised Apartments, Wilmington *Also called Connections Community Support* *(G-9828)*
CSS Technical Staffing, Newark *Also called Computer Staffing Services LLC* *(G-6278)*
CSX Transportation Inc 302 998-8613
 1155 Centerville Rd Wilmington (19804) *(G-9913)*
CT Corporation System (PA) 302 658-4968
 1209 N Orange St Wilmington (19801) *(G-9914)*
CTA Roofing & Waterproofing 302 454-8551
 91 Blue Hen Dr Newark (19713) *(G-6323)*
Cube Media L L C 716 239-2789
 501 Silverside Rd 345 Wilmington (19809) *(G-9915)*
Cubic Products LLC 781 990-3886
 2711 Centerville Rd # 300 Wilmington (19808) *(G-9916)*
Cubics Inc 302 261-5751
 2035 Sunset Lake Rd B2 Newark (19702) *(G-6324)*
Cuhiana Care Health System 302 733-1780
 4755 Ogletown Stanton Rd Newark (19718) *(G-6325)*
Culiquip LLC 302 654-4974
 20 Germay Dr Wilmington (19804) *(G-9917)*
Cummins Power Generation Inc 302 762-2027
 1706 E 12th St Wilmington (19809) *(G-9918)*
Cunningham Homes LLC 267 473-0895
 5 Rudloff Ct Newark (19702) *(G-6326)*
Curbs Etc Inc 302 653-3511
 3528 S Dupont Blvd Smyrna (19977) *(G-8608)*
Curiosity Service Foundation 302 628-4140
 2001 Bridgeville Hwy Seaford (19973) *(G-8215)*
Curley & Benton LLC 302 674-3333
 250 Beiser Blvd Ste 202 Dover (19904) *(G-1329)*
Curley and Funk, Dover *Also called Curley & Benton LLC* *(G-1329)*
Curran James P Law Offices 302 894-1111
 256 Chapman Rd Ste 107 Newark (19702) *(G-6327)*
Currency Technics Metrics Inc 302 482-4846
 4200 Governor Printz Blvd Wilmington (19802) *(G-9919)*
Current Services, Georgetown *Also called Jed T James* *(G-2572)*
Current Solutions 302 724-5243
 1160 Rose Valley Schl Rd Dover (19904) *(G-1330)*
Current Solutions Inc 302 736-5210
 1100 Apple Grove Schl Rd Camden Wyoming (19934) *(G-629)*
Currie Hair Skin Nailss 302 777-7755
 317 Justison St Wilmington (19801) *(G-9920)*
Curry Industries LLC 732 858-1794
 380 David Hall Rd Dover (19904) *(G-1331)*
Curtis A Smith 302 875-6800
 314 S Central Ave Laurel (19956) *(G-3218)*
Curtis J Leciejewski DDS PA 302 226-7960
 19643 Blue Bird Ln Unit 1 Rehoboth Beach (19971) *(G-7905)*
Curvature Inc 302 525-9525
 645 Paper Mill Rd Newark (19711) *(G-6328)*
Curves 302 731-2617
 7 Chestnut Hill Plz Newark (19713) *(G-6329)*
Curves For Women 302 477-9400
 2001 Concord Pike 202 Wilmington (19803) *(G-9921)*
Curves Franchise, Camden Wyoming *Also called Harts Two* *(G-644)*
Curves International Inc 302 698-1481
 103 South St 2 Camden (19934) *(G-554)*
Curzon Corp 302 655-5551
 900 N Union St Wilmington (19805) *(G-9922)*
Cushman & Wakefield Del Inc 302 655-9621
 1 Commerce St Ste 782 Wilmington (19801) *(G-9923)*
Custom America 856 516-1103
 173 Edgemoor Rd Wilmington (19809) *(G-9924)*
Custom Cabinet Shop Inc 302 337-8241
 Rr 13 Greenwood (19950) *(G-2725)*
Custom Ceramics, Middletown *Also called Joel Gonzalez* *(G-4115)*
Custom Creations By Design 302 482-2267
 1 Murphy Rd Wilmington (19803) *(G-9925)*
Custom Decor Inc 302 735-7600
 1585 Mckee Rd 1 Dover (19904) *(G-1332)*
Custom Drywall Inc 302 369-3266
 573 Bellevue Rd Ste C Newark (19713) *(G-6330)*

Custom Framers Inc 302 684-5377
 26526 Lwes Georgetown Hwy Harbeson (19951) *(G-2781)*
Custom House Ulc 302 737-4085
 132 Christiana Mall Newark (19702) *(G-6331)*
Custom Improvers Inc 302 731-9246
 89 Albe Dr Newark (19702) *(G-6332)*
Custom Mechanical Inc 302 537-5611
 State Routes 370 Bethany Beach (19930) *(G-393)*
Custom Mechanical Inc (PA) 302 537-1150
 34799 Daisey Rd Frankford (19945) *(G-2358)*
Custom Porcelain Inc 302 659-6590
 54 Cart Rd Townsend (19734) *(G-8777)*
Custom Satellite and Sound, Wilmington *Also called Weyl Enterprises Inc* *(G-13176)*
Custom Sheet Metal of Delaware 302 998-6865
 464 E Ayre St Wilmington (19804) *(G-9926)*
Customer Services Department, Dover *Also called City of Dover* *(G-1289)*
Customs Benefits 302 798-2884
 501 Silverside Rd Ste 120 Wilmington (19809) *(G-9927)*
Cut Above Hair Gallery 302 539-0622
 1 N Pennsylvania Ave Bethany Beach (19930) *(G-394)*
Cut Out Image Inc 844 866-5577
 2035 Sunset Lake Rd B2 Newark (19702) *(G-6333)*
Cutem Up Tree Care Del Inc 302 629-4655
 10404 Old Furnace Rd Seaford (19973) *(G-8216)*
Cutler Industries Inc 302 689-3779
 2711 Centerville Rd # 400 Wilmington (19808) *(G-9928)*
Cuts & Styles Barley Mill Inc 302 999-8059
 4300 Lancaster Pike Wilmington (19805) *(G-9929)*
Cuts R US Inc 302 674-2223
 51 Roosevelt Ave Dover (19901) *(G-1333)*
Cutting Edge 302 834-8723
 511 5th St Delaware City (19706) *(G-951)*
Cutting Edge of Delaware Inc 302 834-8723
 511 E 5th St Wilmington (19801) *(G-9930)*
Cutting of Precision Concrete 302 543-5833
 213 Maryland Ave Newport (19804) *(G-7746)*
Cybele Software Inc 302 892-9625
 3422 Old Capitol Trl Wilmington (19808) *(G-9931)*
Cyber 20/20 Inc 203 802-8742
 1 Innovation Way Unit 2 Newark (19711) *(G-6334)*
Cyber Seven Technologies LLC 302 635-7122
 465 Upper Pike Creek Rd Newark (19711) *(G-6335)*
Cyberdaptive Inc 302 388-3506
 P.O. Box 7989 Newark (19714) *(G-6336)*
Cybersecurity Trust LLC 844 240-2287
 45 Millwood Dr Middletown (19709) *(G-4017)*
Cyberwolf Software Inc 302 324-8442
 8 Willhelen Ct Bear (19701) *(G-91)*
Cyclesolv LLC 302 894-9400
 301 Ruthar Dr Ste C Newark (19711) *(G-6337)*
Cycology 202 LLC (PA) 610 202-0518
 23924 Sunny Cove Ct Lewes (19958) *(G-3447)*
Cygnet Construction Corp 302 436-5212
 50 Saw Mill Ln Selbyville (19975) *(G-8475)*
Cynthia A Mumma DDS 302 652-2451
 1304 N Broom St Ste 1 Wilmington (19806) *(G-9932)*
Cynthia Crosser DC Fiama 302 239-5014
 3101 Limestone Rd Ste B Wilmington (19808) *(G-9933)*
Cynthia L Carroll 302 733-0411
 262 Chapman Rd Ste 108 Newark (19702) *(G-6338)*
Cynthia P Mangubat MD 302 674-1356
 22 Old Rudnick Ln Dover (19901) *(G-1334)*
Cynwood Apartments, Wilmington *Also called Panco Management Corporation* *(G-12011)*
Cynwyd Club Apartments, Wilmington *Also called Delaware Equity Fund IV* *(G-10044)*
Cypress Capital Management LLC 302 429-8436
 3801 Kennett Pike C304 Wilmington (19807) *(G-9934)*
Cytec Industries Inc 302 530-7665
 3 Weldin Park Dr Wilmington (19803) *(G-9935)*
D & B Printing and Mailing Inc 302 838-7111
 3 Brookmont Dr Newark (19702) *(G-6339)*
D & C Mechanical LLC 302 604-9025
 13500 Wolf Rd Greenwood (19950) *(G-2726)*
D & D Contractors Inc 302 378-9724
 206 Blckbird Grnspring Rd Smyrna (19977) *(G-8609)*
D & D Screen Printing 302 349-4231
 12794 Shawnee Rd Greenwood (19950) *(G-2727)*
D & H Automotive & Towing Inc 302 655-7611
 4016th Ave Ste B Wilmington (19805) *(G-9936)*
D & H Credit Services Inc 302 832-6980
 171 Haut Brion Ave Newark (19702) *(G-6340)*
D & J Recycling Inc 302 422-0163
 5688 Betty St Milford (19963) *(G-4368)*
D & S Warehousing Inc 302 731-7440
 104 Alan Dr Newark (19711) *(G-6341)*
D A B Productions 302 670-9407
 604 Fernwood Dr Harrington (19952) *(G-2829)*
D A Jones Inc 302 836-9238
 37479 Leisure Dr Selbyville (19975) *(G-8476)*
D B Nibouar DDS 302 239-0502
 5317 Limestone Rd Wilmington (19808) *(G-9937)*

D B S, New Castle *Also called Delaware Business Systems Inc* ***(G-5226)***
D By D Printing LLC 302 659-3373
5083 N Dupont Hwy Dover (19901) ***(G-1335)***
D C A Net, Wilmington *Also called Consult Dynamics Inc* ***(G-9836)***
D C A Net, Wilmington *Also called Consult Dynamics Inc* ***(G-9837)***
D C I, Wilmington *Also called Design Collaborative Inc* ***(G-10120)***
D C J L Partnership (PA) 302 328-8040
A-1 Paisely Ln New Castle (19720) ***(G-5211)***
D C Medical Services LLC 302 855-0915
10 W Laurel St Georgetown (19947) ***(G-2492)***
D C Mitchell LLC 302 998-1181
8 Hadco Rd Ste B Wilmington (19804) ***(G-9938)***
D C Painting Corp 302 218-1211
410 Uxbridge Way Hockessin (19707) ***(G-2999)***
D C S Company 302 328-5138
233 Gordy Pl New Castle (19720) ***(G-5212)***
D E Enterprises LLC 302 653-5493
1826 Clayton Delaney Rd Clayton (19938) ***(G-841)***
D E I Farms Inc 302 684-3415
114 S White Cedar Dr Milton (19968) ***(G-4885)***
D E Leager Construction 302 994-1060
3725 Washington Ave Wilmington (19808) ***(G-9939)***
D F Distribution Inc 302 798-5999
6603 Gov Prince Blvd Stea Wilmington (19809) ***(G-9940)***
D F Quillen & Sons Inc (PA) 302 227-2531
803 Rehoboth Ave Ste F Rehoboth Beach (19971) ***(G-7906)***
D Gingerich Concrete & Masnry 302 492-8662
952 Myers Dr Hartly (19953) ***(G-2917)***
D L Printing, Claymont *Also called Dragons Lair Printing LLC* ***(G-735)***
D M F Associates Inc 302 539-0606
Evergreen St Rr 1 Bethany Beach (19930) ***(G-395)***
D M I, New Castle *Also called Data MGT Internationale Inc* ***(G-5215)***
D M Peoples Investment Corp 302 836-1500
2750 Wrangle Hill Rd Bear (19701) ***(G-92)***
D M S Stucco Construction Co 302 368-2618
47 Wedgewood Rd Newark (19711) ***(G-6342)***
D P Investment L L C 302 998-7031
400 B And O Ln Ste A Wilmington (19804) ***(G-9941)***
D R Deakyne DDS 302 653-6661
231 N New St Smyrna (19977) ***(G-8610)***
D S Williams DMD PA 302 239-5272
5317 Limestone Rd Wilmington (19808) ***(G-9942)***
D Shinn Inc 302 792-2033
1409 Haines Ave Wilmington (19809) ***(G-9943)***
D&C Logging 302 846-3982
16075 Russell Rd Delmar (19940) ***(G-990)***
D&F Joint Ventures De LLC 302 652-5151
2002 N Bancroft Pkwy Wilmington (19806) ***(G-9944)***
D&G Inc 302 378-4877
4195 Dupont Pkwy Townsend (19734) ***(G-8778)***
D&N Bus Service Inc 302 422-3869
140 Vickers Rd Milford (19963) ***(G-4369)***
D&S Construction Company 302 650-3209
58 Millwood Dr Middletown (19709) ***(G-4018)***
D-Staffing Consulting Svcs LLC 302 402-5678
8 The Grn Ste 6060 Dover (19901) ***(G-1336)***
Da Vinci Ebusiness Ltd 610 399-3988
2207 Concord Pike Ste 181 Wilmington (19803) ***(G-9945)***
Da Vinci Painting 302 229-0644
5 Wenark Dr Apt 11 Newark (19713) ***(G-6343)***
Dabvasan Inc 302 529-1100
1812 Marsh Rd Ste 6 Wilmington (19810) ***(G-9946)***
Dack Realty Corp (PA) 302 792-2737
1308 Society Dr Claymont (19703) ***(G-726)***
Dack Trading LLC 917 576-4432
18585 Cstl Hwy Unt10 Ofc Rehoboth Beach (19971) ***(G-7907)***
Dad's Workwear, Laurel *Also called Dads Workwear Inc* ***(G-3219)***
Dads Workwear Inc (PA) 302 663-0068
11480 Commercial Ln Laurel (19956) ***(G-3219)***
Dagsboro Family Practice, Dagsboro *Also called Peninsula Regional Medical Ctr* ***(G-929)***
Dagsboro Serv-Dagsboro BR, Dagsboro *Also called Southern States Coop Inc* ***(G-934)***
Daimlerchrysler N Amrca Financ 302 292-6840
131 Continental Dr Newark (19713) ***(G-6344)***
Daisy Construction Company 302 658-4417
102 Larch Cir Ste 301 Wilmington (19804) ***(G-9947)***
Dal Construction 302 538-5310
8331 Willow Grove Rd Camden (19934) ***(G-555)***
Dale Hawkins 302 658-6697
715 N King St Ste 200 Wilmington (19801) ***(G-9948)***
Dale Insulation Co of Delaware 302 324-9332
13 King Ct Ste 5 New Castle (19720) ***(G-5213)***
Dale Maple Country Club Inc 302 674-2505
180 Mapledale Cir Dover (19904) ***(G-1337)***
Dalstrong America Inc 716 380-4998
3411 Silverside Rd Wilmington (19810) ***(G-9949)***
Dalton & Associates PA 302 652-2050
1106 W 10th St Wilmington (19806) ***(G-9950)***
Damon Baca 858 837-0800
8 The Grn Ste 8 # 8 Dover (19901) ***(G-1338)***
Dan H Beachy & Sons Inc 302 492-1493
1298 Lockwood Chapel Rd Hartly (19953) ***(G-2918)***
Dan Licale 302 888-2133
Corner Kirk Rd And 100 Montchanin (19710) ***(G-4984)***
Dana Container Inc 302 652-8550
1280 Railcar Ave Wilmington (19802) ***(G-9951)***
Dana E Herbert 302 721-5798
22 Peterson Pl Bear (19701) ***(G-93)***
Dana Railcare, Wilmington *Also called Dana Container Inc* ***(G-9951)***
Dana Railcare Inc 302 652-8550
1280 Railcar Ave Wilmington (19802) ***(G-9952)***
Dana S Wright 610 563-6070
94 Albe Dr Newark (19702) ***(G-6345)***
Danaher Corporation 302 798-5741
501 Silverside Rd Ste 105 Wilmington (19809) ***(G-9953)***
Dance Conservatory 302 734-9717
522 Otis Dr Dover (19901) ***(G-1339)***
Dance Hdc, Newark *Also called Hockessin Dance Center Inc* ***(G-6733)***
Dancedelaware 302 998-1222
2005 Concord Pike Ste 204 Wilmington (19803) ***(G-9954)***
Dandy Signs 301 399-8746
37384 Club House Rd Ocean View (19970) ***(G-7782)***
Dane Waters 302 377-9999
1 Hillside Rd Claymont (19703) ***(G-727)***
Daniel A Yoder 302 730-4076
2956 Yoder Dr Dover (19904) ***(G-1340)***
Daniel D Rappa Inc 302 994-1199
1624 E Ayre St Wilmington (19804) ***(G-9955)***
Daniel George Bebee Inc 443 359-1542
32353 Cobbs Creek Rd Laurel (19956) ***(G-3220)***
Daniel M McDermott Chfc Cfp 302 778-5677
3520 Silverside Rd Ste 25 Wilmington (19810) ***(G-9956)***
Daniels + Tansey LLP 302 594-1070
1013 Centre Rd Ste 220 Wilmington (19805) ***(G-9957)***
Daniels Lawn Care 302 218-0173
1211 Gary Ave Wilmington (19808) ***(G-9958)***
Dann J Gladnick Dmd PA 302 654-7243
1104 N Broom St Wilmington (19806) ***(G-9959)***
Danny G Perez Ea MST 302 422-2600
233 Ne Front St Milford (19963) ***(G-4370)***
Dannys Custom Upholstery 302 436-8200
34799 Lighthouse Rd Selbyville (19975) ***(G-8477)***
Dans Pallets & Services 302 836-4848
8 Andrew Ln Bear (19701) ***(G-94)***
Dans Taxi & Shuttle 302 383-8826
152 Bayard Dr Claymont (19703) ***(G-728)***
Dap, Milford *Also called Delaware Animal Products LLC* ***(G-4374)***
Darby Leasing LLC 302 477-0500
3411 Silverside Rd # 104 Wilmington (19810) ***(G-9960)***
Darlington Postal Company LLC 410 917-4147
1217 Cooches Bridge Rd Newark (19713) ***(G-6346)***
Dart First State, Dover *Also called Delaware Dept Transportation* ***(G-1365)***
Das Financial Health LLC 570 947-7931
53 Chatham Ct Dover (19901) ***(G-1341)***
Dassault Aircraft Svcs Corp 302 322-7000
191 N Dupont Hwy New Castle (19720) ***(G-5214)***
Data Age International LLC 302 760-9222
2701 Centerville Rd Wilmington (19808) ***(G-9961)***
Data Drum Inc 347 502-8485
2035 Sunset Lake Rd Newark (19702) ***(G-6347)***
Data Guard Recycling Inc 302 337-8870
9174 Redden Rd Bridgeville (19933) ***(G-463)***
Data MGT Internationale Inc (PA) 302 656-1151
55 Lukens Dr Ste A New Castle (19720) ***(G-5215)***
Data-Bi LLC 302 290-3138
601 Entwisle Ct Wilmington (19808) ***(G-9962)***
Datatech Enterprises Inc (PA) 540 370-0010
36322 Sunflower Blvd Selbyville (19975) ***(G-8478)***
Datwyler Pharma Packg USA Inc 302 603-8020
571 Merrimac Ave Middletown (19709) ***(G-4019)***
Dave Arletta 302 475-8013
2621 Epping Rd Wilmington (19810) ***(G-9963)***
Dave Smagala 302 383-2761
26 Rolling Rd Claymont (19703) ***(G-729)***
Daves Contracting Inc 302 436-5129
37172 Brickman Ln Selbyville (19975) ***(G-8479)***
Daves Disc Mfflers of Dver De 302 678-8803
1312 S Dupont Hwy Dover (19901) ***(G-1342)***
Daves Lawn Care & Landscaping, Bear *Also called David M Wagner* ***(G-98)***
Daves Towing Inc 302 697-9073
1927 Peachtree Run Rd Dover (19901) ***(G-1343)***
David A Dorey Esq 302 425-6400
1201 N Market St Ste 800 Wilmington (19801) ***(G-9964)***
David A King DDS 302 998-0331
2601 Annand Dr Ste 10 Wilmington (19808) ***(G-9965)***
David B Ettinger DMD MD 302 369-1000
131 E Chestnut Hill Rd Newark (19713) ***(G-6348)***
David Bridge 302 429-3317
245 Benjamin Blvd Bear (19701) ***(G-95)***

ALPHABETIC

(PA)=Parent Co (HQ)=Headquarters (DH)=Div Headquarters
2020 Harris Directory of Delaware Businesses
623

David Brown Gear Systems USA (PA) 540 416-2062
300 Delaware Ave Ste 1370 Wilmington (19801) ***(G-9966)***
David Brown Gear Systems USA 540 943-8375
300 Delaware Ave Ste 1370 Wilmington (19801) ***(G-9967)***
David C Larned MD 302 655-7600
2300 Penns Ave Ste 3a Wilmington (19806) ***(G-9968)***
David E Driban 302 322-0860
239 Christiana Rd New Castle (19720) ***(G-5216)***
David E Mastrota DMD PA 302 654-0100
2215 Pennsylvania Ave Wilmington (19806) ***(G-9969)***
David G Horsey & Sons Inc 302 875-3033
28107 Beaver Dam Br Rd Laurel (19956) ***(G-3221)***
David G Major Associates Inc 703 642-7450
30165 Ethan Allen Ct Millsboro (19966) ***(G-4673)***
David G Reyes MD 302 735-7780
29 Gooden Ave Dover (19904) ***(G-1344)***
David I Walsh Esquire PA 302 498-0760
20640 Hopkins Rd Lewes (19958) ***(G-3448)***
David Jenkins 302 304-5568
522 Liam Pl Bear (19701) ***(G-96)***
David L Isaacs DDS 302 654-2904
707 Foulk Rd Ste 103 Wilmington (19803) ***(G-9970)***
David L Townsend Co Inc 302 378-7967
1041 Clyton Grenspring Rd Smyrna (19977) ***(G-8611)***
David M Sartin Sr 302 838-1074
1984 Porter Rd Bear (19701) ***(G-97)***
David M Wagner 302 832-8336
812 Archer Pl Bear (19701) ***(G-98)***
David Marshall & Associates 302 539-4488
Kent Avenue Westley Dr Bethany Beach (19930) ***(G-396)***
David Oppenheimer and Co I LLC 302 533-0779
200 Continental Dr # 301 Newark (19713) ***(G-6349)***
David P Roser Inc (PA) 302 239-7605
19 Roser Ln Hockessin (19707) ***(G-3000)***
David Popovich LLC 855 464-9653
19c Trolley Sq Ste 20c Wilmington (19806) ***(G-9971)***
David Rockwell & Associates 302 478-9900
208 W Pembrey Dr Wilmington (19803) ***(G-9972)***
David Saunders General Contrs 302 998-0056
1204 E Willow Run Dr Wilmington (19805) ***(G-9973)***
David Waters & Son 302 235-8653
1862 Graves Rd Hockessin (19707) ***(G-3001)***
David Wentworth 302 856-3272
418 N Dupont Hwy Georgetown (19947) ***(G-2493)***
Davidson Associates, Wilmington *Also called Yellow Pine Associates Inc* ***(G-13326)***
Davin Management Group LLC 302 367-6563
808 Jeffrey Pine Dr Bear (19701) ***(G-99)***
Davis Bowen & Friedel Inc 302 424-1441
1 Park Ave Milford (19963) ***(G-4371)***
Davis Chiropractic Inc 302 856-2225
20461 Dupont Blvd Ste 1 Georgetown (19947) ***(G-2494)***
Davis Insurance Group Inc 302 652-4700
And Rockland Rd Rr 100 Montchanin (19710) ***(G-4985)***
Davis Trucking & Family LLC 302 381-6358
38254 Millsboro Hwy Millsboro (19966) ***(G-4674)***
Davis Welding Service Llc 302 465-3004
26075 River Rd Seaford (19973) ***(G-8217)***
Davis Young Associates Inc (PA) 610 388-0932
2896 Creek Rd Yorklyn (19736) ***(G-13365)***
Dawn Arrow Inc 302 328-9695
602 Brant Ave New Castle (19720) ***(G-5217)***
Dawn L Conly 302 378-1890
266 Bucktail Dr Middletown (19709) ***(G-4020)***
Dawson Bus Service Inc (PA) 302 697-9501
405 E Camden Wyoming Ave Camden (19934) ***(G-556)***
Dawson Bus Service Inc 302 678-2594
1 Weston Dr Ste A Dover (19904) ***(G-1345)***
Dax-Wave Consulting LLC 424 543-6662
1000 N West St Ste 1200 Wilmington (19801) ***(G-9974)***
Day and Zimmermann Inc 302 368-1609
504 Interchange Blvd Newark (19711) ***(G-6350)***
Day School For Children 302 652-4651
3071 New Castle Ave New Castle (19720) ***(G-5218)***
Day Town Pack House, Newark *Also called Baytown Packhouse Inc* ***(G-6061)***
Days Inn, New Castle *Also called Jay Ambe Inc* ***(G-5436)***
Days Inn and Suites Seaford 302 629-4300
23450 Sussex Hwy Seaford (19973) ***(G-8218)***
Days Inn Dover Downtown 302 674-8002
272 N Dupont Hwy Dover (19901) ***(G-1346)***
Days Inn Wilmington, Wilmington *Also called Dipna Inc* ***(G-10159)***
Days of Knights 302 366-0963
173 E Main St Lowr Newark (19711) ***(G-6351)***
Dbd Maangment, Wilmington *Also called Edward B De Seta & Associates* ***(G-10356)***
Dbd Wholesale LLC 215 301-6277
213 Sunset Dr Wilmington (19809) ***(G-9975)***
Dbot, Wilmington *Also called Delaware Bd Trade Holdings Inc* ***(G-10005)***
Dbw Tax Services 302 276-0428
222 Guilford St Bear (19701) ***(G-100)***
DC Consulting Service LLC 617 594-9780
3422 Old Capitol Trl Wilmington (19808) ***(G-9976)***
DC Printing Inc 302 545-6666
2305 Pennsylvania Ave Wilmington (19806) ***(G-9977)***
Dcat Transit LLC 302 855-1231
18800 Whaleys Corner Rd Georgetown (19947) ***(G-2495)***
Dcc Design Group LLC 302 777-2100
2 Mill Rd Ste 103 Wilmington (19806) ***(G-9978)***
Dcc Inc 302 750-1207
2639 Grendon Dr Wilmington (19808) ***(G-9979)***
Dcca, Wilmington *Also called For Delaware Center* ***(G-10589)***
DCH, Wilmington *Also called Delaware Ctr For Hrtclture Inc* ***(G-10032)***
DCH Auto Group (usa) Inc 302 478-4600
3411 Silverside Rd 108 Wilmington (19810) ***(G-9980)***
Dcmfm At Christiana Care 302 543-7543
1 Centurian Dr Ste 312 Newark (19713) ***(G-6352)***
Dcor 302 227-9341
37545 Atlantic Ave Rehoboth Beach (19971) ***(G-7908)***
Dcrac 302 298-3289
600 S Harrison St Wilmington (19805) ***(G-9981)***
Dct, Newark *Also called Dream Clean Team LP* ***(G-6473)***
Dd & E Investment Group Inc 302 319-2780
1000 N St Wilmington (19801) ***(G-9982)***
Dd Inc De LLC 302 669-9269
907 Providence Ave Claymont (19703) ***(G-730)***
Dd Snacks LLC 302 652-3850
230 Alban Dr Wilmington (19805) ***(G-9983)***
Ddh Advanced Mtls Systems Inc 515 441-1313
625 Dawson Dr Ste B Newark (19713) ***(G-6353)***
Ddk 302 999-1132
3825 Lancaster Pike Wilmington (19805) ***(G-9984)***
De Atlantic Elevator, Dagsboro *Also called Atlantic Elevators* ***(G-878)***
De Catering Inc 302 607-7200
913 Brandywine Blvd Wilmington (19809) ***(G-9985)***
De Cheaper Trash LLC 302 325-0670
29 Prosperity Rd New Castle (19720) ***(G-5219)***
De Colores Family Child Care 302 883-3298
917 Monroe Ter Dover (19904) ***(G-1347)***
De Homecare, Wilmington *Also called Maxim Healthcare Services Inc* ***(G-11579)***
De Nest Studio 302 836-1316
216 Lake Arrowhead Cir Bear (19701) ***(G-101)***
De Nisio General Construction 302 656-9460
1306 N Bancroft Pkwy Wilmington (19806) ***(G-9986)***
De Novo Corporation (PA) 302 234-7407
1011 Centre Rd Ste 104 Wilmington (19805) ***(G-9987)***
De Sales and Service 302 456-1660
1210 Janice Dr Newark (19713) ***(G-6354)***
De Technologies Inc 302 285-0353
118 Sleepy Hollow Dr # 1 Middletown (19709) ***(G-4021)***
De Turf Sports Complex, Frederica *Also called Kent County* ***(G-2409)***
De Workers Cmpnstion Legal Ctr (PA) 302 888-1111
32 Barley Glen Ct Hockessin (19707) ***(G-3002)***
Dead On Construction 302 462-5023
P.O. Box 1092 Selbyville (19975) ***(G-8480)***
Deadcow Computers 302 239-5974
14 Deer Track Ln Newark (19711) ***(G-6355)***
Deafinitions & Interpreting 302 563-7714
1148 Pulaski Hwy Ste 236 Bear (19701) ***(G-102)***
Deakyne Dental Associates PA 302 653-6661
27 Deak Dr Smyrna (19977) ***(G-8612)***
Deals On Wheels Inc (PA) 302 999-9955
1220 Centerville Rd Wilmington (19808) ***(G-9988)***
Deals On Wheels Used Cars, Wilmington *Also called Deals On Wheels Inc* ***(G-9988)***
Dean Digital Imaging Inc 302 655-6992
2 S Poplar St Ste B Wilmington (19801) ***(G-9989)***
Dean Dsign/Marketing Group Inc 717 898-9800
13 Water St Lincoln (19960) ***(G-3844)***
Deangelis & Son Inc (PA) 302 337-8699
19489 Handy Rd Bridgeville (19933) ***(G-464)***
Deanne Naples Family Daycare 302 376-1408
225 Manchester Way Middletown (19709) ***(G-4022)***
Deaton McCue & Co Inc 302 658-7789
62 Rockford Rd Ste 10a Wilmington (19806) ***(G-9990)***
Deaven Development Corp 302 994-5793
1615 E Ayre St Wilmington (19804) ***(G-9991)***
Debay Surgical Service 302 644-4954
33664 Bayview Medical Dr Lewes (19958) ***(G-3449)***
Debbie Gill 302 547-5182
108 Fox Hunt Ln Middletown (19709) ***(G-4023)***
Debbie Reed 302 227-3818
319 Rehoboth Ave Rehoboth Beach (19971) ***(G-7909)***
Deborah A Wingel Do 302 239-6200
724 Yorklyn Rd Ste 125 Hockessin (19707) ***(G-3003)***
Deborah J Halligan DDS 302 738-5766
414 Capitol Trl Newark (19711) ***(G-6356)***
Deborah Kirk 302 653-6022
100 S Main St Ste 205 Smyrna (19977) ***(G-8613)***
Decalgirl.com, Rehoboth Beach *Also called Skinify LLC* ***(G-8079)***
Decg, Wilmington *Also called Delaware Counsel Group LLP* ***(G-10028)***
Decisivedge LLC (PA) 302 299-1570
131 Continental Dr # 409 Newark (19713) ***(G-6357)***

Decoded USA, Wilmington *Also called Htk Automotive USA Corp* ***(G-10968)***
Decoy Magazine....302 644-9001
102 2nd St Lewes (19958) ***(G-3450)***
Decrane Aircraft Systems....302 253-0390
21583 Baltimore Ave Georgetown (19947) ***(G-2496)***
Dedc LLC....302 738-7172
315 S Chapel St Newark (19711) ***(G-6358)***
Dedicated To Home Care LLC....484 470-5013
2 Yorktown Rd New Castle (19720) ***(G-5220)***
Dedicated To Women Ob Gyn....302 674-0223
200 Banning St Ste 320 Dover (19904) ***(G-1348)***
Dedicated To Women Obgyn....302 285-5545
209 E Main St Middletown (19709) ***(G-4024)***
Dee & Doreens Team....302 677-0030
1671 S State St Dover (19901) ***(G-1349)***
Dee's Cleaning Service, Georgetown *Also called Delores Welch* ***(G-2510)***
Deep Muscle Therapy Center Del....302 397-8073
5700 Kirkwood Hwy Ste 206 Wilmington (19808) ***(G-9992)***
Deeps On Massage, Wilmington *Also called Deep Muscle Therapy Center Del* ***(G-9992)***
Deerborne Woods Sales Center, Wilmington *Also called Handler Builders Inc* ***(G-10831)***
Dees Learning Care....908 623-7685
128 Auckland Dr Newark (19702) ***(G-6359)***
Def Com, Wilmington *Also called Defense Communication LLC* ***(G-9993)***
Defense Communication LLC....850 348-0708
3422 Old Capitol Trl # 700 Wilmington (19808) ***(G-9993)***
Defense Shield Trust....540 815-8248
504 N Broom St Wilmington (19805) ***(G-9994)***
Defy Therapy Services LLC....302 290-9562
2213 Beaumont Rd Wilmington (19803) ***(G-9995)***
Degussa International Inc....302 731-9250
220 Continental Dr # 204 Newark (19713) ***(G-6360)***
Deirde A McCartney....302 644-8330
34382 Carpenters Way # 1 Lewes (19958) ***(G-3451)***
Deiter Inc....302 875-9167
27840 Woodcrest Dr Georgetown (19947) ***(G-2497)***
Deja Vu Record Album Cover Art....302 227-8909
35982 Bay Dr Rehoboth Beach (19971) ***(G-7910)***
Dekadu Inc....763 390-3266
2711 Centerville Rd # 400 Wilmington (19808) ***(G-9996)***
Del Bay Charter Fishing LLC....302 542-1930
23602 Harvest Run Reach Milton (19968) ***(G-4886)***
Del Bay Retriever Club....302 678-8583
68 Mcbry Dr Dover (19901) ***(G-1350)***
Del Campo Plumbing & Heating....302 998-3648
2429 Hartley Pl Wilmington (19808) ***(G-9997)***
Del Haven of Wilmington Inc (PA)....302 999-9040
152 Kane Dr Newark (19702) ***(G-6361)***
Del Homes Inc (PA)....302 697-8204
1309 Ponderosa Dr Magnolia (19962) ***(G-3889)***
Del Homes Inc....302 730-1479
1567 Mckee Rd Dover (19904) ***(G-1351)***
Del Lawn Service....302 525-4148
5 Matthews Rd Newark (19713) ***(G-6362)***
Del Marva Hand Specialists LLC....302 644-0940
701 Savannah Rd Ste B Lewes (19958) ***(G-3452)***
Del Ray Foundatins LLC....302 272-6153
48 Goosebriar Ln Milford (19963) ***(G-4372)***
Del-Mar Appliance of Delaware (PA)....302 674-2414
230 S Governors Ave Dover (19904) ***(G-1352)***
Del-Mar Door Services Inc....800 492-2392
515 Janvier Dr Middletown (19709) ***(G-4025)***
Del-Mr-Va Cncil Inc Boy Scuts (PA)....302 622-3300
100 W 10th St Ste 915 Wilmington (19801) ***(G-9998)***
Del-One Federal Credit Union....302 739-2390
150 E Water St Ste 1 Dover (19901) ***(G-1353)***
Del-One Federal Credit Union....302 739-4496
270 Beiser Blvd Dover (19904) ***(G-1354)***
Del-One Federal Credit Union....302 739-4496
201 Pharmacy Dr Smyrna (19977) ***(G-8614)***
Del-One Federal Credit Union....302 424-2969
100 Credit Union Way Milford (19963) ***(G-4373)***
Del-One Federal Credit Union (PA)....302 739-4496
270 Beiser Blvd Dover (19904) ***(G-1355)***
Del-One Federal Credit Union....302 577-2667
824 N Market St Ste 104 Wilmington (19801) ***(G-9999)***
Del-One Federal Credit Union....302 323-4578
80 Christiana Rd New Castle (19720) ***(G-5221)***
Del-One Federal Credit Union....302 739-6389
635 S Bay Rd Dover (19901) ***(G-1356)***
Del-One Federal Credit Union....302 856-5100
30 Georgetown Plz Georgetown (19947) ***(G-2498)***
Dela Belle Inv Group Corp....901 279-2742
651 N Broad St Ste 205 Middletown (19709) ***(G-4026)***
Delamed Supplies Inc....917 517-4492
950 Ridge Rd Ste C29 Claymont (19703) ***(G-731)***
Delasoft Inc....302 533-7912
92 Reads Way Ste 204 New Castle (19720) ***(G-5222)***
Delaware 87ers LLC....302 351-5385
300 Martin L King Blvd # 200 Wilmington (19801) ***(G-10000)***
Delaware Acdemy of Mdicine Inc....302 733-3900
4765 Ogletown Stanton Rd Newark (19713) ***(G-6363)***
Delaware Acdemy Pub Safety SEC....302 377-1465
179 Stanton Christiana Rd New Castle (19720) ***(G-5223)***
Delaware Adlescent Program Inc....302 531-0257
185 South St Camden (19934) ***(G-557)***
Delaware AG Museum & Vlg....302 734-1618
866 N Dupont Hwy Dover (19901) ***(G-1357)***
Delaware Aliance Federal Cr Un....302 429-0404
2320 N Dupont Hwy New Castle (19720) ***(G-5224)***
Delaware Animal Products LLC....302 423-7754
662 Log Cabin Rd Milford (19963) ***(G-4374)***
Delaware Architects LLC....302 491-6047
16558 Retreat Cir Milford (19963) ***(G-4375)***
Delaware Art Museum Inc....302 571-9590
2301 Kentmere Pkwy Wilmington (19806) ***(G-10001)***
Delaware Arts Conservatory....302 595-4160
723 Rue Madora Ste 4 Bear (19701) ***(G-103)***
Delaware Association....302 622-9177
100 W 10th St Ste 103 Wilmington (19801) ***(G-10002)***
Delaware Association For Blind (PA)....302 998-5913
2915 Newport Gap Pike Wilmington (19808) ***(G-10003)***
Delaware Auto Salvage Inc....302 322-2328
445 Old Airport Rd New Castle (19720) ***(G-5225)***
Delaware Back PAln&sprts Rehab....302 529-8783
2006 Foulk Rd Ste B Newark (19702) ***(G-6364)***
Delaware Backpan Rhblttn Assoc....302 529-8783
2006 Foulk Rd Ste B Wilmington (19810) ***(G-10004)***
Delaware Bail Bonds....302 734-9881
414 Denison St Dover (19901) ***(G-1358)***
Delaware Barter Corp....800 343-1322
4 Mill Park Ct F Newark (19713) ***(G-6365)***
Delaware Bay & River....302 645-7861
700 Pilottown Rd Lewes (19958) ***(G-3453)***
Delaware Bay Launch Service....302 422-7604
100 Passwaters Dr Milford (19963) ***(G-4376)***
Delaware Bay Surgical Svc PA....302 645-5650
33664 Bayvw Med Dr Ste 2 Lewes (19958) ***(G-3454)***
Delaware Bd Trade Holdings Inc....302 298-0600
1313 N Market St Fl 8 Wilmington (19801) ***(G-10005)***
Delaware Beacon Network LLC....302 218-2755
1201 N Market St Fl 1 Wilmington (19801) ***(G-10006)***
Delaware Beer Works Inc....302 836-2739
219 Governors Pl Bear (19701) ***(G-104)***
Delaware Boat Registration....302 739-9916
89 Kings Hwy Dover (19901) ***(G-1359)***
Delaware Botanic Gardens Inc....202 262-9501
201 Ashwood St Bethany Beach (19930) ***(G-397)***
Delaware Brast Cncer Coalition, Dover *Also called Delaware Breast Cancer Coalit* ***(G-1360)***
Delaware Breast Cancer Coalit....302 644-6844
16529 Coastal Hwy Lewes (19958) ***(G-3455)***
Delaware Breast Cancer Coalit (PA)....302 778-1102
100 W 10th St Ste 209 Wilmington (19801) ***(G-10007)***
Delaware Breast Cancer Coalit....302 672-6435
165 Commerce Way Ste 2 Dover (19904) ***(G-1360)***
Delaware Brick Company (PA)....302 994-0948
1114 Centerville Rd Wilmington (19804) ***(G-10008)***
Delaware Brick Company....302 883-2807
492 Webbs Ln Dover (19904) ***(G-1361)***
Delaware Building Supply Corp....302 424-3505
141 Mullet Run Milford (19963) ***(G-4377)***
Delaware Bus Incorporators Inc....302 996-5819
3422 Old Capitol Trl Wilmington (19808) ***(G-10009)***
Delaware Business Systems Inc....302 395-0900
191 Airport Rd New Castle (19720) ***(G-5226)***
Delaware Capital Formation Inc (HQ)....302 793-4921
501 Silverside Rd Ste 5 Wilmington (19809) ***(G-10010)***
Delaware Capital Holdings Inc (HQ)....302 793-4921
501 Silverside Rd Ste 5 Wilmington (19809) ***(G-10011)***
Delaware Car Company....302 655-6665
Second & Lombard St Wilmington (19801) ***(G-10012)***
Delaware Center For Digestive....302 565-6596
71 Omega Dr Bldg D Newark (19713) ***(G-6366)***
Delaware Center For Justice....302 658-7174
100 W 10th St Ste 905 Wilmington (19801) ***(G-10013)***
Delaware Center For Oral Srgry....302 369-1000
131 E Chestnut Hill Rd Newark (19713) ***(G-6367)***
Delaware Chapter, Wilmington *Also called March of Dimes Inc* ***(G-11521)***
Delaware Chemical Corporation....302 234-1463
1105 N Market St Ste 1300 Wilmington (19801) ***(G-10014)***
Delaware Children S Museum....302 654-2340
550 Justison St Wilmington (19801) ***(G-10015)***
Delaware Childrens Museum Inc....302 654-2340
550 Justison St Wilmington (19801) ***(G-10016)***
Delaware Chiropractic At Louvi....302 738-7300
105 Louviers Dr Newark (19711) ***(G-6368)***
Delaware Chpr Amer Acdmy Pedtc....302 218-1075
4765 Ogletown Stanton Rd Newark (19713) ***(G-6369)***
Delaware City Fire Co No 1....302 834-9336
815 5th St Delaware City (19706) ***(G-952)***

ALPHABETIC

Delaware City Recreation Club 302 834-9900
  5th And Wahington Delaware City (19706) *(G-953)*
Delaware City Refining Co LLC 302 834-6000
  4550 Wrangle Hill Rd Delaware City (19706) *(G-954)*
Delaware Claims Agency LLC 212 957-2180
  230 N Market St Wilmington (19801) *(G-10017)*
Delaware Claims Proc Fcilty 302 427-8913
  1007 N Orange St Wilmington (19801) *(G-10018)*
Delaware Clean Service 302 838-1650
  4 Winchester Ct Bear (19701) *(G-105)*
Delaware Clinical & Lab Physcn, Newark Also called Michael W Lankiewicz MD *(G-7023)*
Delaware Clinical & Labortry 302 999-8095
  4512 Kirkwood Hwy Ste 200 Wilmington (19808) *(G-10019)*
Delaware Clitn Agnst Dmstc Vln 302 658-2958
  100 W 10th St Ste 903 Wilmington (19801) *(G-10020)*
Delaware Clncal Lab Physcans P (PA) 302 737-7700
  4701 Ogletown Stanton Rd Newark (19713) *(G-6370)*
Delaware Coast Line RR Co (PA) 302 422-9200
  8266 N Union Church Rd Milford (19963) *(G-4378)*
Delaware Cobras Inc 302 983-3500
  122 Honora Dr Bear (19701) *(G-106)*
Delaware Color Lab 302 529-1339
  2107 Naamans Rd Wilmington (19810) *(G-10021)*
Delaware Comm Reinvstmnt Actn 302 298-3250
  600 S Harrison St Wilmington (19805) *(G-10022)*
Delaware Community Foundation (PA) 302 571-8004
  100 W 10th St Ste 115 Wilmington (19801) *(G-10023)*
Delaware Community Inv Corp 302 655-1420
  100 W 10th St Ste 303 Wilmington (19801) *(G-10024)*
Delaware Consistory, The, Wilmington Also called New Temple Corp *(G-11870)*
Delaware Contract Testing LLC 302 650-4030
  4517 Verona Dr Wilmington (19808) *(G-10025)*
Delaware Corporate Agents Inc 302 762-8637
  4406 Tennyson Rd Wilmington (19802) *(G-10026)*
Delaware Councl On Gmblng Prbl 302 226-5041
  37201 Rehoboth Avenue Ext Rehoboth Beach (19971) *(G-7911)*
Delaware Councl On Gmblng Prbl (PA) 302 655-3261
  100 W 10th St Ste 303 Wilmington (19801) *(G-10027)*
Delaware Counsel Group LLP 302 543-4870
  100 S Rockland Falls Rd Rockland (19732) *(G-8123)*
Delaware Counsel Group LLP (PA) 302 576-9600
  2 Mill Rd Ste 108 Wilmington (19806) *(G-10028)*
Delaware County Pain MGT 302 575-1145
  208 N Union St Wilmington (19805) *(G-10029)*
Delaware Crdovascular Assoc PA 302 644-7676
  34453 King Street Row Lewes (19958) *(G-3456)*
Delaware Crdovascular Assoc PA 302 993-7676
  537 Stanton Christiana Rd Newark (19713) *(G-6371)*
Delaware Crdovascular Assoc PA 302 734-7676
  1113 S State St Ste 100 Dover (19901) *(G-1362)*
Delaware Crdovascular Assoc PA 302 543-4800
  1403 Foulk Rd Ste 101 Wilmington (19803) *(G-10030)*
Delaware Credit Union Leag Inc 302 322-9341
  262 Chapman Rd Ste 101 Newark (19702) *(G-6372)*
Delaware Ctr For Hmless Vtrans 302 898-2647
  1405 Veale Rd Wilmington (19810) *(G-10031)*
Delaware Ctr For Hrtclture Inc 302 658-6262
  1810 N Dupont St Wilmington (19806) *(G-10032)*
Delaware Curative 302 836-5670
  609 Governors Pl Bear (19701) *(G-107)*
Delaware Curative Workshop (PA) 302 656-2521
  1600 N Washington St Wilmington (19802) *(G-10033)*
Delaware Cy Vlntr Fire Co No 1 .... 302 834-9336
  815 5th St Delaware City (19706) *(G-955)*
Delaware D G Co LLC 302 731-0500
  1007 S Chapel St Newark (19702) *(G-6373)*
Delaware Dagnstc Rehabilitatio 302 777-3955
  P.O. Box 4056 Wilmington (19807) *(G-10034)*
Delaware Dance Center Inc 302 454-1440
  4751 Shopp Of Lndnhill Rd Wilmington (19808) *(G-10035)*
Delaware Dance Company Inc 302 738-2023
  168 S Main St Ste 101 Newark (19711) *(G-6374)*
Delaware Day Treatment, Dover Also called Catholic Charities Inc *(G-1261)*
Delaware Dental Care Centers 410 474-5520
  73 Greentree Dr 407 Dover (19904) *(G-1363)*
Delaware Dentistry 302 475-6900
  2505 Silverside Rd Wilmington (19810) *(G-10036)*
Delaware Department Finance 302 739-5291
  1575 Mckee Rd Ste 102 Dover (19904) *(G-1364)*
Delaware Depository Svc Co LLC 302 762-2635
  3601 N Market St Wilmington (19802) *(G-10037)*
Delaware Dept Transportation 302 577-3278
  655 S Bay Rd Ste 4g Dover (19901) *(G-1365)*
Delaware Dermatolgy PA 302 736-1800
  737 S Queen St Ste 1 Dover (19904) *(G-1366)*
Delaware Dermatologic 302 593-8625
  14 Alders Ln Wilmington (19807) *(G-10038)*
Delaware Design Company 302 737-9700
  29 S Old Baltimore Pike Newark (19702) *(G-6375)*

Delaware Detailing Services 302 414-0755
  800 Washington St New Castle (19720) *(G-5227)*
Delaware Detective Group LLC 302 373-3678
  364 E Main St Middletown (19709) *(G-4027)*
Delaware Dgnstc Rhbltation Cen, Wilmington Also called Delaware Diagnostic & Rehab *(G-10039)*
Delaware Diagnostic & Rehab 302 777-3955
  131 S West St Wilmington (19801) *(G-10039)*
Delaware Diagnostic Group LLC 302 472-5555
  2060 Limestone Rd Wilmington (19808) *(G-10040)*
Delaware Diagnostic Labs LLC 302 996-9585
  1 Centurian Dr Ste 103 Newark (19713) *(G-6376)*
Delaware Diamond Knives Inc 302 999-7476
  3825 Lancaster Pike # 200 Wilmington (19805) *(G-10041)*
Delaware Direct Inc 302 658-8223
  220 Valley Rd Wilmington (19804) *(G-10042)*
Delaware Document Retrieval, Wilmington Also called Parcels Inc *(G-12018)*
Delaware Document Retrieval, Dover Also called Parcels Inc *(G-1935)*
Delaware Drnking Drver Program (PA) 302 736-4326
  1661 S Dupont Hwy Dover (19901) *(G-1367)*
Delaware Drnking Drver Program 302 856-1835
  20505 Dupont Blvd Unit 1 Georgetown (19947) *(G-2499)*
Delaware Dry Goods, Newark Also called Delaware D G Co LLC *(G-6373)*
Delaware Ear Nose & Throat Hea 302 738-6014
  4745 Ogletown Stanton Rd # 112 Newark (19713) *(G-6377)*
Delaware Early Childhood Ctr, Harrington Also called Lake Forest School District *(G-2864)*
Delaware Ecumenical Council 302 225-1040
  240 N James St Ste 111 Wilmington (19804) *(G-10043)*
Delaware Electric Signal, Dover Also called B Safe Inc *(G-1167)*
Delaware Elwyn, Wilmington Also called Elwyn *(G-10385)*
Delaware Engineering & Design 302 738-7172
  315 S Chapel St Newark (19711) *(G-6378)*
Delaware Enterprises Inc 302 324-5660
  42 Reads Way New Castle (19720) *(G-5228)*
Delaware Equity Fund IV 302 655-1420
  100 W 10th St Ste 303 Wilmington (19801) *(G-10044)*
Delaware Eye Care Center (PA) 302 674-1121
  833 S Governors Ave Dover (19904) *(G-1368)*
Delaware Eye Clinic, Milton Also called Millsboro Eye Care LLC *(G-4938)*
Delaware Eye Clinics 302 645-2338
  16924 Lilly Pad Dr Milton (19968) *(G-4887)*
Delaware Eye Institute PA 302 645-2300
  18791 J J Williams Hwy Rehoboth Beach (19971) *(G-7912)*
Delaware Eye Optical, Rehoboth Beach Also called Delaware Eye Institute PA *(G-7912)*
Delaware Eye Surgeons 302 956-0285
  2710 Centerville Rd # 102 Wilmington (19808) *(G-10045)*
Delaware Eye Surgery Center 302 645-2300
  18791 John J Williams Hwy Rehoboth Beach (19971) *(G-7913)*
Delaware Family Care Assoc, Wilmington Also called Delaware Medical Care Inc *(G-10065)*
Delaware Family Voices Inc 302 588-4908
  3301 Englewood Rd Wilmington (19810) *(G-10046)*
DELAWARE FARM BUREAU, Camden Also called Delaware State Farm Bureau *(G-560)*
Delaware Fedral Credit Union, Wilmington Also called Del-One Federal Credit Union *(G-9999)*
Delaware Ffa Foundation Inc 302 857-6493
  35 Commerce Way Ste 1 Dover (19904) *(G-1369)*
Delaware Field Office, Wilmington Also called The Nature Conservancy *(G-12891)*
Delaware Film & Tape Vault Co, Wilmington Also called Ken-Del Productions Inc *(G-11239)*
Delaware Financial Capital (PA) 302 266-9500
  22 Polly Drummond Hill Rd Newark (19711) *(G-6379)*
Delaware First Federal Cr Un (PA) 302 998-0665
  1815 Newport Gap Pike # 1 Wilmington (19808) *(G-10047)*
Delaware First Media Corp 302 857-7096
  1200 N Dupont Hwy Dover (19901) *(G-1370)*
Delaware Fleet Service Inc 302 778-5000
  550 Pigeon Point Rd New Castle (19720) *(G-5229)*
Delaware Flooring Supply Inc 302 276-0031
  520 South St New Castle (19720) *(G-5230)*
Delaware Fncl Edcatn Alnce Inc 302 674-0288
  8 W Loockerman St Ste 200 Dover (19904) *(G-1371)*
Delaware Foot & Ankle Assoc 302 834-3575
  2600 Glasgow Ave Ste 101 Newark (19702) *(G-6380)*
Delaware Friends of Folk 302 678-1423
  275 Simms Woods Rd Dover (19901) *(G-1372)*
Delaware Gentle Dental Group 302 514-6200
  17 N Main St Smyrna (19977) *(G-8615)*
Delaware Geological Survey, Newark Also called University of Delaware *(G-7624)*
Delaware Grapevine LLC 302 731-8400
  16 Martine Ct Newark (19711) *(G-6381)*
Delaware Guidance Ser 302 678-3020
  103 Mont Blanc Blvd Dover (19904) *(G-1373)*
Delaware Guidance Services For 302 455-9333
  Polly Drummond Ofc Newark (19711) *(G-6382)*
Delaware Guidance Services For (PA) 302 652-3948
  1213 Delaware Ave Wilmington (19806) *(G-10048)*
Delaware Guitar School 302 697-2341
  200 Southern Blvd Wyoming (19934) *(G-13360)*

ALPHABETIC SECTION — Delaware Plastic & Recon

Delaware Hardscape Supply LLC 302 996-6464
4701 B And O Ln Wilmington (19804) *(G-10049)*

Delaware Health and Fitnes LLC 302 584-7531
204 Lantana Dr Hockessin (19707) *(G-3004)*

Delaware Health Care Comm 302 739-2730
Oneill Bldg 410 Federal Dover (19901) *(G-1374)*

Delaware Health Info Netwrk 302 678-0220
107 Wolf Creek Blvd Ste 2 Dover (19901) *(G-1375)*

Delaware Health Net Inc 410 788-9715
601 New Castle Ave Wilmington (19801) *(G-10050)*

Delaware Healthcare Assn 302 674-2853
1280 S Governors Ave Dover (19904) *(G-1376)*

Delaware Hearing Aids 302 652-3558
1601 Concord Pike Ste 65 Wilmington (19803) *(G-10051)*

Delaware Heart & Vascular PA 302 734-1414
200 Banning St Ste 340 Dover (19904) *(G-1377)*

Delaware Heating & AC 302 738-4669
713 Millcreek Ln Bear (19701) *(G-108)*

Delaware Heating & AC Svcs Inc 302 738-4669
11 Mcmillan Way Newark (19713) *(G-6383)*

Delaware Helpline Inc 302 255-1810
625 N Orange St Fl 3 Wilmington (19801) *(G-10052)*

Delaware Hiv Services Inc 302 654-5471
100 W 10th St Ste 415 Wilmington (19801) *(G-10053)*

Delaware Hmanities Council Inc 302 657-0650
100 W 10th St Ste 509 Wilmington (19801) *(G-10054)*

Delaware Home Health Care 302 856-3600
22251 Lews Georgtwn Hwy Georgetown (19947) *(G-2500)*

Delaware Homes Inc (PA) 302 378-9510
401 Main St Townsend (19734) *(G-8779)*

Delaware Homes Inc 302 223-6258
200 S Dupont Blvd Ste 105 Smyrna (19977) *(G-8616)*

Delaware Hosp For Chrnclly Ill, Smyrna Also called Health & Social Svcs Del Dept *(G-8650)*

Delaware Hospice 302 934-9018
315 Old Landing Rd Unit 1 Millsboro (19966) *(G-4675)*

Delaware Hospice Inc (PA) 302 478-5707
16 Polly Drmmd Shpg Ctr 2 Newark (19711) *(G-6384)*

Delaware Hospice Inc. 302 678-4444
911 S Dupont Hwy Dover (19901) *(G-1378)*

Delaware Hospice Inc. 302 856-7717
100 Patriots Way Milford (19963) *(G-4379)*

Delaware Hotel Associates LP 302 792-2700
630 Naamans Rd Claymont (19703) *(G-732)*

Delaware Humane Association 302 571-0111
701 A St Wilmington (19801) *(G-10055)*

Delaware Imaging Network 302 737-5990
40 Polly Drummond Hill Rd Newark (19711) *(G-6385)*

Delaware Imaging Network 302 836-4200
2600 Glasgow Ave Ste 122 Newark (19702) *(G-6386)*

Delaware Imaging Network (HQ) 302 652-3016
40 Polly Drmmnd Hl Rd 4 Newark (19711) *(G-6387)*

Delaware Imaging Network 302 449-5400
114 Sandhill Dr Ste 201 Middletown (19709) *(G-4028)*

Delaware Imaging Network 302 644-2590
40 Polly Drmmnd Hl Rd 4 Newark (19711) *(G-6388)*

Delaware Imaging Network 302 478-1100
2700 Silverside Rd Ste 1b Wilmington (19810) *(G-10056)*

Delaware Importers Inc 302 656-4487
615 Lambson Ln New Castle (19720) *(G-5231)*

Delaware Incorporation Svcs 302 658-1733
704 N King St Ste 500 Wilmington (19801) *(G-10057)*

Delaware Industries For Blind, New Castle Also called Health & Social Svcs Del Dept *(G-5385)*

Delaware Innovation Space Inc 302 695-2201
200 Powder Mill Rd E500 Wilmington (19803) *(G-10058)*

Delaware Inst For Rep, Newark Also called Center For Human Reproduction *(G-6178)*

Delaware Institue Pain MGT 302 698-3994
6 E Camden Wyoming Ave Camden (19934) *(G-558)*

Delaware Instrument Lab LLC 302 737-6250
2106 Chelmsford Cir Newark (19713) *(G-6389)*

Delaware Insur Guarantee Assn 302 456-3656
220 Continental Dr # 309 Newark (19713) *(G-6390)*

Delaware Integrative Medical C 302 559-5959
20930 Dupont Blvd # 203 Georgetown (19947) *(G-2501)*

Delaware Intercorp Inc 302 266-9367
3511 Silverside Rd # 105 Wilmington (19810) *(G-10059)*

Delaware Interventional Spine 302 674-8444
1673 S State St Ste B Dover (19901) *(G-1379)*

Delaware Intl Speedway, Delmar Also called U S 13 Dragway Inc *(G-1044)*

Delaware Italian-American 302 545-6406
2208 Highland Pl Wilmington (19805) *(G-10060)*

Delaware Juniors Volleyball 302 463-4218
4142 Ogletree Stanton Rd # 229 Newark (19713) *(G-6391)*

Delaware Lacrosse Foundation 302 831-8661
P.O. Box 5066 Wilmington (19808) *(G-10061)*

Delaware Landscaping Inc 302 698-3001
106 Semans Dr Dover (19904) *(G-1380)*

Delaware Law Office of Larry 302 286-6336
111 Barksdale Pro Ctr Newark (19711) *(G-6392)*

Delaware Lawn & Tree Service 302 834-7406
1756 Bear Corbitt Rd Bear (19701) *(G-109)*

Delaware Learning Institue of 302 732-6704
32448 Royal Blvd Unit 1 Dagsboro (19939) *(G-895)*

Delaware Marketing Group, Wilmington Also called Delaware Marketing Partners *(G-10062)*

Delaware Marketing Partners 302 575-1610
3801 Kennett Pike D301 Wilmington (19807) *(G-10062)*

Delaware Meat Company LLC 302 438-0252
28 Brookside Dr Wilmington (19804) *(G-10063)*

Delaware Med Care Assoc LLC 302 633-9033
550 Stanton Christiana Rd # 103 Newark (19713) *(G-6393)*

Delaware Medical Associates PA 302 475-2535
2101 Foulk Rd Ste 2 Wilmington (19810) *(G-10064)*

Delaware Medical Care Inc 302 225-6868
2700 Silverside Rd Ste 2 Wilmington (19810) *(G-10065)*

Delaware Medical Courier 302 670-1247
17048 W Holly Dr Milton (19968) *(G-4888)*

Delaware Medical MGT Svcs LLC 302 283-3300
71 Omega Dr Newark (19713) *(G-6394)*

Delaware Mentor, Millsboro Also called National Mentor Holdings Inc *(G-4760)*

Delaware Mentor, Millsboro Also called National Mentor Holdings Inc *(G-4761)*

Delaware Merchant Services 302 838-9100
510 Century Blvd Wilmington (19808) *(G-10066)*

Delaware Metals, Wilmington Also called Chuck George Inc *(G-9697)*

Delaware Mfg EXT Partnr Inc 302 283-3131
400 Stanton Christiana Rd Newark (19713) *(G-6395)*

Delaware Millwork 302 376-8324
110 W Green St Middletown (19709) *(G-4029)*

Delaware Mobile Dentistry 302 698-9901
189 S Fairfield Dr Dover (19901) *(G-1381)*

Delaware Modern Dental LLC 302 366-8668
850 Library Ave Ste 102 Newark (19711) *(G-6396)*

Delaware Modern Pediatrics 302 392-2077
300 Biddle Ave Ste 206 Newark (19702) *(G-6397)*

Delaware Monument and Vault 302 540-2387
203 Wyndtree Ct S Hockessin (19707) *(G-3005)*

Delaware Mosquito Control LLC 302 504-6757
4 Cobblestone Xing Newark (19702) *(G-6398)*

Delaware Motel and Rv Park 302 328-3114
235 S Dupont Hwy New Castle (19720) *(G-5232)*

Delaware Motor Sales Inc (PA) 302 656-3100
1606 Pennsylvania Ave Wilmington (19806) *(G-10067)*

Delaware Moving & Storage Inc 302 322-0311
214 Bear Christiana Rd Bear (19701) *(G-110)*

Delaware Municipal Elc Corp 302 653-2733
22 Artisan Dr Smyrna (19977) *(G-8617)*

Delaware Museum of Natural 302 658-9111
4840 Kennett Pike Wilmington (19807) *(G-10068)*

Delaware Native Plants Society 302 735-8918
163 Mitscher Rd Dover (19901) *(G-1382)*

Delaware Nature Society (PA) 302 239-1283
3511 Barley Mill Rd Hockessin (19707) *(G-3006)*

Delaware Nurosurgical Group PA 302 731-3017
774 Christiana Rd Ste 202 Newark (19713) *(G-6399)*

Delaware Obgyn & Womens Health 302 730-0633
1057 S Bradford St Dover (19904) *(G-1383)*

Delaware Occupational Health S 302 368-5100
15 Omega Dr Bldg K15 Newark (19713) *(G-6400)*

Delaware Open M R I, Newark Also called Jeanes Radiology Associates PC *(G-6830)*

Delaware Open M R I 302 479-5400
3211a Concord Pike Wilmington (19803) *(G-10069)*

Delaware Open M R I & C T 302 734-5800
1030 Forrest Ave Ste 105 Dover (19904) *(G-1384)*

Delaware Open M R I LLC 302 449-2300
374 E Main St Middletown (19709) *(G-4030)*

Delaware Ophthalmology Cons PA (PA) 302 479-3937
3501 Silverside Rd Wilmington (19810) *(G-10070)*

Delaware Orthopaedic Specialis 302 633-3555
1941 Limestone Rd Ste 101 Wilmington (19808) *(G-10071)*

Delaware Orthopedic 302 730-0840
230 Beiser Blvd Ste 100 Dover (19904) *(G-1385)*

Delaware Orthopedic and Sports 302 653-8389
208 N Dupont Blvd Smyrna (19977) *(G-8618)*

Delaware Outpatient Center 302 738-0300
774 Christiana Rd Ste 2 Newark (19713) *(G-6401)*

Delaware Pain & Spine Center 302 737-0800
2055 Limestone Rd Ste 201 Wilmington (19808) *(G-10072)*

Delaware Parents Association 302 678-9288
101 W Loockerman St 3a Dover (19904) *(G-1386)*

Delaware Park, Wilmington Also called Delaware Racing Association *(G-10076)*

Delaware Park Racing LLC 302 994-6700
777 Delaware Park Blvd Wilmington (19804) *(G-10073)*

Delaware Periodontics 302 658-7871
1110 N Bancroft Pkwy # 1 Wilmington (19805) *(G-10074)*

Delaware Pharmacist Society 302 659-3088
27 N Main St Smyrna (19977) *(G-8619)*

Delaware Plastic & Recon, Newark Also called Delaware Plastic & Recon *(G-6402)*

Delaware Plastic & Recon 302 994-8492
1 Centurian Dr Ste 301 Newark (19713) *(G-6402)*

Delaware Plstic/Recons Srgy PA 302 994-8492
1 Centurian Dr Ste 301 Newark (19713) ***(G-6403)***
Delaware Plumbing Supply Co 302 656-5437
2309 N Dupont Hwy New Castle (19720) ***(G-5233)***
Delaware Podiatrist Medicine (PA) 302 674-9255
22 Old Rudnick Ln Dover (19901) ***(G-1387)***
Delaware Primary Care LLC 302 730-0554
810 New Burton Rd Ste 3 Dover (19904) ***(G-1388)***
Delaware Prof Fnrl Svcs Inc 302 731-5459
635 Churchmans Rd Newark (19702) ***(G-6404)***
Delaware Protection Agency, Middletown *Also called Clinton Craddock* ***(G-3999)***
Delaware Psychiatric Center, New Castle *Also called Health & Social Svcs Del Dept* ***(G-5384)***
Delaware Public Auto Auction 302 656-0500
2323 N Dupont Hwy New Castle (19720) ***(G-5234)***
Delaware Public Health Lab 302 223-1520
30 Sunnyside Rd Smyrna (19977) ***(G-8620)***
Delaware Racing Association 302 994-6700
777 Delaware Park Blvd Wilmington (19804) ***(G-10075)***
Delaware Racing Association 302 355-1000
2701 Kirkwood Hwy Newark (19711) ***(G-6405)***
Delaware Racing Association (PA) 302 994-2521
777 Delaware Park Blvd Wilmington (19804) ***(G-10076)***
Delaware RE Advisors LLC 302 998-4030
1013 Centre Rd Ste 201 Wilmington (19805) ***(G-10077)***
Delaware Realty Group Inc 302 227-4800
317 Rehoboth Ave Rehoboth Beach (19971) ***(G-7914)***
Delaware Recyclable Products 302 655-1360
246 Marsh Ln New Castle (19720) ***(G-5235)***
Delaware Registered Agents 302 733-0600
19 Kris Ct Newark (19702) ***(G-6406)***
Delaware Registry Ltd 302 477-9800
3511 Silverside Rd # 105 Wilmington (19810) ***(G-10078)***
Delaware Rehabilitation Inst 302 831-0315
540 S College Ave Rm 201k Newark (19713) ***(G-6407)***
Delaware Restaurant Assn 302 738-2545
500 Creek View Rd Ste 103 Newark (19711) ***(G-6408)***
Delaware Retired Schl Prsnl 302 674-8252
100 Galewood Ct Wilmington (19803) ***(G-10079)***
Delaware Riders Basbal CLB Inc 302 475-1915
2214 Nassau Dr Wilmington (19810) ***(G-10080)***
Delaware River & Bay Authority 302 571-6474
I 295 N Rte 9 New Castle (19720) ***(G-5236)***
Delaware River & Bay Authority (PA) 302 571-6303
Interstate 295 New Castle New Castle (19720) ***(G-5237)***
Delaware River & Bay Authority 800 643-3779
43 Cape Henlopen Dr Lewes (19958) ***(G-3457)***
Delaware River Stevedores Inc 302 657-0472
1 Hausel Rd Ste 115 Wilmington (19801) ***(G-10081)***
Delaware Rock Gym Inc 302 838-5850
520 Carson Dr Bear (19701) ***(G-111)***
Delaware Rug Co Inc 302 998-8881
5 Forrest Ave Wilmington (19805) ***(G-10082)***
Delaware Rural Water Assn 302 424-3792
210 Vickers Rd Milford (19963) ***(G-4380)***
Delaware Rural Water Assn 302 398-9633
27 Commerce St Ste 27c Harrington (19952) ***(G-2830)***
Delaware Rver Bay Auth Emplyee 302 571-6320
P.O. Box 71 New Castle (19720) ***(G-5238)***
Delaware S P C A (PA) 302 998-2281
455 Stanton Christiana Rd Newark (19713) ***(G-6409)***
Delaware S P C A 302 856-6361
22918 Dupont Blvd Georgetown (19947) ***(G-2502)***
Delaware Saengerbund Lib Assn 302 366-9454
49 Salem Church Rd Newark (19713) ***(G-6410)***
Delaware Safety Council Inc 302 276-0660
2 Penns Way Ste 201 New Castle (19720) ***(G-5239)***
Delaware Screen Printing Inc 302 378-4231
350 Strawberry Ln Middletown (19709) ***(G-4031)***
Delaware Secretary of State 302 736-7400
21 The Grn A Dover (19901) ***(G-1389)***
Delaware Secretary of State 302 472-7678
1 Hausel Rd Lbby Wilmington (19801) ***(G-10083)***
Delaware Secretary of State 302 834-8046
2465 Chesapeake City Rd Bear (19701) ***(G-112)***
Delaware Senior Olympics Inc 302 736-5698
1121 Forrest Ave Dover (19904) ***(G-1390)***
Delaware Septic Service LLC 302 376-6412
893 Noxontown Rd Townsend (19734) ***(G-8780)***
Delaware Settlement Services 302 731-2500
930 Old Harmony Rd Ste F1 Newark (19713) ***(G-6411)***
Delaware Siding Company Inc 302 836-6971
723 Rue Madora Ste 8 Bear (19701) ***(G-113)***
Delaware Sign Co 302 469-5656
411 E Railroad Ave Felton (19943) ***(G-2285)***
Delaware Skating Center Ltd 302 697-3218
2201 S Dupont Hwy Dover (19901) ***(G-1391)***
Delaware Skating Center Ltd (PA) 302 366-0473
801 Christiana Rd Newark (19713) ***(G-6412)***
Delaware Sleep Dsrder Ctrs LLC (PA) 302 669-6141
701 Foulk Rd Ste 1g Wilmington (19803) ***(G-10084)***
Delaware Smile Center 302 285-7645
201 Carter Dr Ste A Middletown (19709) ***(G-4032)***
Delaware Soc Orthpd Surgeons 302 366-1400
900 Prides Xing Newark (19713) ***(G-6413)***
Delaware Soc Rdlgy Profession, Wilmington *Also called National Society Inc* ***(G-11811)***
Delaware Solid Waste Authority 302 378-1407
276 Pine Tree Rd Townsend (19734) ***(G-8781)***
Delaware Solid Waste Authority (PA) 302 739-5361
1128 S Bradford St Dover (19904) ***(G-1392)***
Delaware Solid Waste Authority 302 764-2732
1128 S Bradford St Dover (19904) ***(G-1393)***
Delaware Spca 302 698-3006
32 Shelter Cir Camden (19934) ***(G-559)***
Delaware Specialty Dist, Wilmington *Also called Fluorogistx LLC* ***(G-10582)***
Delaware Spine & Rehab LLC 813 965-0903
105 New St Ste 1 Seaford (19973) ***(G-8219)***
Delaware Spine Institute, Dover *Also called Delaware Interventional Spine* ***(G-1379)***
Delaware Spine Rehabilitation 302 883-2292
642 S Queen St Dover (19904) ***(G-1394)***
Delaware Sstnble Enrgy Utility 302 883-3038
500 W Loockerman St # 400 Dover (19904) ***(G-1395)***
Delaware St Historic Pres, Dover *Also called Delaware Secretary of State* ***(G-1389)***
Delaware Star Dental 302 994-3093
5507 Kirkwood Hwy Wilmington (19808) ***(G-10085)***
Delaware State Bar Association 302 658-5279
405 N King St Ste 100 Wilmington (19801) ***(G-10086)***
Delaware State Chamber 302 655-7221
1201 N Orange St Ste 200 Wilmington (19801) ***(G-10087)***
Delaware State Dental Society 302 368-7634
200 Continental Dr # 111 Newark (19713) ***(G-6414)***
Delaware State Education Assn (PA) 302 734-5834
136 E Water St Dover (19901) ***(G-1396)***
Delaware State Education Assn 302 366-8440
4135 Ogltn Stntn Rd # 101 Newark (19713) ***(G-6415)***
Delaware State Fair Inc (PA) 302 398-3269
18500 S Dupont Hwy Harrington (19952) ***(G-2831)***
Delaware State Farm Bureau 302 697-3183
233 S Dupont Hwy Camden (19934) ***(G-560)***
Delaware State Hospital, New Castle *Also called Health & Social Svcs Del Dept* ***(G-5386)***
Delaware State Lottery, Dover *Also called Delaware Department Finance* ***(G-1364)***
Delaware State News, Dover *Also called Independent Newsmedia USA Inc* ***(G-1673)***
Delaware State Police Federal 302 324-8141
235 Christiana Rd New Castle (19720) ***(G-5240)***
Delaware State Police Federal (PA) 302 856-3501
700 N Bedford St Georgetown (19947) ***(G-2503)***
Delaware State Printing 302 228-9431
110 Galaxy Dr Dover (19901) ***(G-1397)***
Delaware Stndrdbre Ownrs Assc 302 678-3058
830 Walker Rd Dover (19904) ***(G-1398)***
Delaware Storage & Pipeline Co 302 736-1774
987 Port Mahon Rd Dover (19901) ***(G-1399)***
Delaware Storefronts LLC 302 697-1850
720 S Governors Ave Dover (19904) ***(G-1400)***
Delaware Surgery Center LLC 302 730-0217
200 Banning St Ste 110 Dover (19904) ***(G-1401)***
Delaware Surgical Arts 302 225-0177
537 Stanton Christn Rd # 109 Newark (19713) ***(G-6416)***
Delaware Surgical Group PA (PA) 302 892-2100
1941 Limestone Rd Ste 213 Wilmington (19808) ***(G-10088)***
Delaware Surgical Service, Lewes *Also called Debay Surgical Service* ***(G-3449)***
Delaware Symphony Association 302 656-7442
100 W 10th St Ste 1003 Wilmington (19801) ***(G-10089)***
DELAWARE SYMPHONY ORCHESTRA, Wilmington *Also called Delaware Symphony Association* ***(G-10089)***
Delaware Tchncal Cmnty College 302 259-6160
21179 College Dr Georgetown (19947) ***(G-2504)***
Delaware Technology Park Inc 302 452-1100
1 Innovation Way Ste 300 Newark (19711) ***(G-6417)***
Delaware Teen Challenge Inc (PA) 302 629-8824
611 3rd St Seaford (19973) ***(G-8220)***
Delaware Temp System, Wilmington *Also called Bernard and Bernard Inc* ***(G-9306)***
Delaware Theatre Company 302 594-1100
200 Water St Wilmington (19801) ***(G-10090)***
Delaware Thrmplastic Specialty 302 424-4722
720 Mccolley St Ste D Milford (19963) ***(G-4381)***
Delaware Tire Center Inc 302 674-0234
207 S Governors Ave Dover (19904) ***(G-1402)***
Delaware Tire Center Inc (PA) 302 368-2531
616 S College Ave Newark (19713) ***(G-6418)***
Delaware Title Loans Inc 302 368-2131
2431 Pulaski Hwy Ste 1 Newark (19702) ***(G-6419)***
Delaware Title Loans Inc 302 629-8843
22994 Sussex Hwy Seaford (19973) ***(G-8221)***
Delaware Title Loans Inc 302 328-7482
505 N Dupont Hwy New Castle (19720) ***(G-5241)***
Delaware Title Loans Inc 302 478-8505
3300 Concord Pike Ste 2 Wilmington (19803) ***(G-10091)***
Delaware Title Loans Inc 302 653-8315
202 N Dupont Blvd Smyrna (19977) ***(G-8621)***

Delaware Title Loans Inc 302 644-3640
17672 Coastal Hwy Lewes (19958) *(G-3458)*
Delaware Tool Cleaning, Wilmington *Also called Conlin Corporation (G-9823)*
Delaware Trail Spinners 302 738-0177
1013 Tulip Tree Ln Newark (19713) *(G-6420)*
Delaware Transit, Wilmington *Also called Transportation Delaware Dept (G-12958)*
Delaware Transportation Auth 302 760-2000
800 S Bay Rd Dover (19901) *(G-1403)*
Delaware Trnsp Svcs Inc 302 981-6562
130 Falmouth Way Dover (19904) *(G-1404)*
Delaware Trust 208, Dover *Also called Wells Fargo Bank National Assn (G-2212)*
Delaware Trust 221, Hockessin *Also called Wells Fargo Bank National Assn (G-3169)*
Delaware Valley Brokerage Inc 302 477-9700
1415 Foulk Rd Ste 103 Wilmington (19803) *(G-10092)*
Delaware Valley Dev LLC 302 235-2500
726 Yorklyn Rd Ste 150 Hockessin (19707) *(G-3007)*
Delaware Valley Ent Inc 302 427-2444
1508 Penns Ave Ste 1a Wilmington (19806) *(G-10093)*
Delaware Valley Fence & Iron 302 322-8193
47 University Ave New Castle (19720) *(G-5242)*
Delaware Valley Field Svcs LLC 302 384-8617
321 Robinson Ln Wilmington (19805) *(G-10094)*
Delaware Valley Group LLC 302 777-7007
1720 Gilpin Ave Wilmington (19806) *(G-10095)*
Delaware Valley Housing Dev, Wilmington *Also called Dvhd Inc (G-10270)*
Delaware Valley Orthodontics 302 239-3531
5500 Skyline Dr Ste 1 Wilmington (19808) *(G-10096)*
Delaware Vein Center 302 258-8853
20930 Dupont Blvd # 202 Georgetown (19947) *(G-2505)*
Delaware Veterans Home Inc 302 424-6000
100 Dlaware Veterans Blvd Milford (19963) *(G-4382)*
Delaware Vly Outcomes RES LLC 302 444-9363
17 Henderson Hill Rd Newark (19711) *(G-6421)*
Delaware Wic Program (PA) 302 741-2900
635 S Bay Rd 1c Dover (19901) *(G-1405)*
Delaware Wic Program 302 857-5000
805 River Rd Dover (19901) *(G-1406)*
Delaware Wild Lands Inc 302 378-2736
315 Main St Odessa (19730) *(G-7825)*
Delaware Womens Bowling Assn 302 834-7002
9 Winchester Ct Bear (19701) *(G-114)*
Delaware Womens Imaging LLC 302 738-9100
J24 26 Omega Dr Newark (19713) *(G-6422)*
Delawareblack Com LLC 302 388-1444
560 Peoples Plz Ste 288 Newark (19702) *(G-6423)*
Delawre Ctr For Mtrnal & Fetal 302 319-5680
1 Centurian Dr Ste 312 Newark (19713) *(G-6424)*
Delawres Fnest Hardwood Floors 302 376-0742
1461 Cedar Lane Rd Middletown (19709) *(G-4033)*
Delcarm LLC (PA) 610 345-9001
1482 Levels Rd Townsend (19734) *(G-8782)*
Delcastle Golf Club 302 995-1990
801 Mckennans Church Rd Wilmington (19808) *(G-10097)*
Delcastle Golf Club Management 302 998-9505
3800 Valley Brook Dr Wilmington (19808) *(G-10098)*
Delchem Inc 302 426-1800
1318 E 12th St Ste 1 Wilmington (19802) *(G-10099)*
Delcollo Security Technologies 302 994-5400
226 Brookside Dr Wilmington (19804) *(G-10100)*
Delcon Builders Inc (PA) 609 499-7747
124 Delaware St Fl 3 New Castle (19720) *(G-5243)*
Deldeo Builders Inc 302 791-0243
100 Naamans Rd Ste 3f Claymont (19703) *(G-733)*
Delduca, Vincent Jr MD, Newark *Also called Medical Oncology Hematology (G-7017)*
Deleware Heart Group, Newark *Also called Christopher A Bowens MD (G-6231)*
Delight Housing Complex, Lincoln *Also called Ggc Inc (G-3850)*
Dell Oem Inc 302 294-0060
705 Dawson Dr Newark (19713) *(G-6425)*
Delmaco Manufacturing Inc 302 856-6345
21424 Cedar Creek Ave Georgetown (19947) *(G-2506)*
Delmar Termite & Pest Control 302 658-5010
700 Cornell Dr Wilmington (19801) *(G-10101)*
Delmar Vapor Lounge 302 907-0125
38660 Sussex Hwy Unit 2 Delmar (19940) *(G-991)*
Delmarv Orthtcs & Prosthtcs 302 678-8311
30 E Division St Dover (19901) *(G-1407)*
Delmarva 2000 Ltd 302 645-2226
21 Shay Ln Milton (19968) *(G-4889)*
Delmarva Anmal Emrgncy Ctr LLC 302 697-0850
1482 E Lebanon Rd Dover (19901) *(G-1408)*
Delmarva Auto Glass Inc 302 934-8600
30667 Dupont Blvd Dagsboro (19939) *(G-896)*
Delmarva Bariatric Fitnes Ctr 410 341-6180
17487 Taramino Pl Lewes (19958) *(G-3459)*
Delmarva Broadcasting, Milford *Also called Lnp Media Group Inc (G-4475)*
Delmarva Broadcasting Co Inc (PA) 302 478-2700
2727 Shipley Rd Wilmington (19810) *(G-10102)*
Delmarva Broadcasting Co Inc 302 422-7575
1666 Blairs Pond Rd Milford (19963) *(G-4383)*
Delmarva Builders Inc 302 629-9123
20846 Camp Rd Bridgeville (19933) *(G-465)*
Delmarva Cleaning & Maint Inc 302 734-1856
1131 N Dupont Hwy Fl 2 Dover (19901) *(G-1409)*
Delmarva Clergy United Inc 302 422-2350
13726 S Old State Rd Ellendale (19941) *(G-2259)*
Delmarva Communications Inc 302 324-1230
113 J And M Dr New Castle (19720) *(G-5244)*
Delmarva Concrete Pumping Inc 302 537-4118
34090 Central Ave Frankford (19945) *(G-2359)*
Delmarva Digital Media Group, Laurel *Also called Internet Business Pubg Corp (G-3241)*
Delmarva Energy Solutions LLC 302 684-3418
115 Atlantic Ave Milton (19968) *(G-4890)*
Delmarva Equine Clinic 302 735-4735
1008 S Governors Ave Dover (19904) *(G-1410)*
Delmarva Hardwood Products 302 349-4101
28950 Seaford Rd Laurel (19956) *(G-3222)*
Delmarva Insulation, Georgetown *Also called Southland Insulators Del LLC (G-2662)*
Delmarva Kenworth Trucks, Dover *Also called Clifton Leasing Co Inc (G-1293)*
Delmarva Laboratories Inc 302 645-2226
21 Shay Ln Milton (19968) *(G-4891)*
Delmarva Plastics Co 302 398-1000
800 Pine Pitch Rd Harrington (19952) *(G-2832)*
Delmarva Pole Building Sup Inc 302 698-3636
317 N Layton Ave Wyoming (19934) *(G-13361)*
Delmarva Poultry Industry Inc 302 856-9037
16686 County Seat Hwy Georgetown (19947) *(G-2507)*
Delmarva Power & Light Company (HQ) 302 454-0300
500 N Wakefield Dr Fl 2 Newark (19702) *(G-6426)*
Delmarva Power & Light Company 302 454-4040
401 Eagle Run Rd Newark (19702) *(G-6427)*
Delmarva Power & Light Company 302 454-4450
I 95 Rr 273 Newark (19714) *(G-6428)*
Delmarva Power & Light Company 302 429-3376
630 Mrtin Lther King Blvd Wilmington (19801) *(G-10103)*
Delmarva Power & Light Company 302 454-0300
200 Hay Rd Wilmington (19809) *(G-10104)*
Delmarva Precision Grinding 302 393-3008
906 Se 2nd St Milford (19963) *(G-4384)*
Delmarva Prosthodontics 302 674-8331
871 S Governors Ave Ste 1 Dover (19904) *(G-1411)*
Delmarva Pump Center Inc (PA) 302 492-1245
335 Strauss Ave Marydel (19964) *(G-3915)*
Delmarva Refrigeration Inc 302 846-2727
504 N Pennsylvania Ave Delmar (19940) *(G-992)*
Delmarva Roofing & Coating Inc 302 349-5174
12982 Mennonite School Rd Greenwood (19950) *(G-2728)*
Delmarva Rubber & Gasket Co 302 424-8300
16356 Sussex Hwy Bridgeville (19933) *(G-466)*
Delmarva Rv Center Inc 302 424-4505
702 Milford Harrington Hw Milford (19963) *(G-4385)*
Delmarva Sign Co 302 934-6188
24835 Lawson Rd Georgetown (19947) *(G-2508)*
Delmarva Space Scnces Fndation 302 236-2761
10046 Iron Pointe Drv Ext Millsboro (19966) *(G-4676)*
Delmarva Sports Action Mag, Fenwick Island *Also called Action Enterprise Inc (G-2328)*
Delmarva Spray Foam LLC 302 752-1080
22976 Sussex Ave Georgetown (19947) *(G-2509)*
Delmarva Surgery Center 302 369-1700
139 E Chestnut Hill Rd Newark (19713) *(G-6429)*
Delmarva Surgery Ctr 443 245-3470
100 Biddle Ave Ste 101 Newark (19702) *(G-6430)*
Delmarva Transportation Inc 302 349-0840
101 Maryland Ave Greenwood (19950) *(G-2729)*
Delmarva Truss and Panel LLC 302 270-8888
317 N Layton Ave Wyoming (19934) *(G-13362)*
Delmarva Water Solutions 302 674-0509
1039 Fowler Ct Dover (19901) *(G-1412)*
Delmarvalous 302 200-2001
30748 Long Leaf Rd Dagsboro (19939) *(G-897)*
Delmarvavoip LLC 855 645-8647
16557 Coastal Hwy Lewes (19958) *(G-3460)*
Delnet, Middletown *Also called Delstar Technologies Inc (G-4034)*
Delores Welch 302 856-7989
22812 Cedar Ln Georgetown (19947) *(G-2510)*
Delp Trucking 302 275-6541
71 Lenora Dr Smyrna (19977) *(G-8622)*
Delpa Builders LLC 302 731-7304
10 King Ave New Castle (19720) *(G-5245)*
Delphi Capital, Wilmington *Also called Chestnut Investors II Inc (G-9657)*
Delphi Financial Group Inc (HQ) 302 478-5142
1105 N Market St Ste 1230 Wilmington (19801) *(G-10105)*
Delport Holding Company 302 655-7300
529 Terminal Ave New Castle (19720) *(G-5246)*
Delstar Technologies Inc (HQ) 302 378-8888
601 Industrial Rd Middletown (19709) *(G-4034)*
Delt LLC 215 869-7409
201 Ruthar Dr Ste 4 Newark (19711) *(G-6431)*
Delta Engineering Corporation 302 325-9320
13 Drba Way New Castle (19720) *(G-5247)*

ALPHABETIC

Delta Forms Inc 302 652-3266
  5 Germay Dr Wilmington (19804) *(G-10106)*
Delta Machine & Tool Company 302 738-1788
  201 Ruthar Dr Ste 3 Newark (19711) *(G-6432)*
Delta Risk LLC 312 203-8307
  108 W 13th St Wilmington (19801) *(G-10107)*
Delta Sales Corp 302 436-6063
  5 W Church St Selbyville (19975) *(G-8481)*
Deltrans Inc 302 453-8213
  759 Old Baltimore Pike Newark (19702) *(G-6433)*
Delux Engineering LLC 610 304-0606
  550 S College Ave Newark (19716) *(G-6434)*
Delvina I Willson 302 659-3672
  300 Garrisons Cir Smyrna (19977) *(G-8623)*
DEMEP, Newark Also called Delaware Mfg EXT Partnr Inc *(G-6395)*
Dempsey Farms LLC 302 734-4937
  1708 Fast Landing Rd Dover (19901) *(G-1413)*
Dempseys Service Center Inc 302 239-4996
  604 Corner Ketch Rd Newark (19711) *(G-6435)*
Dempseys Specialized Services 302 530-7856
  304b Markus Ct Newark (19713) *(G-6436)*
Denco Inc 302 798-4200
  501 Silverside Rd Ste 132 Wilmington (19809) *(G-10108)*
Denices Ragged Wreath 302 220-7377
  691 Churchmans Rd Newark (19702) *(G-6437)*
Denim Duo-Vers 302 632-6943
  113 Lovers Ln Milford (19963) *(G-4386)*
Denise Beam 302 539-1900
  112 Atlantic Ave Ocean View (19970) *(G-7783)*
Dennek LLC 302 703-0790
  7 Rockford Rd Apt C5 Wilmington (19806) *(G-10109)*
Denney Electric Supply Del Inc 302 934-8855
  28635 Dupont Blvd Millsboro (19966) *(G-4677)*
Dennis H Snyder Assoc, Wilmington Also called Snyder & Company PA *(G-12666)*
Dennis Woltemate Lawn Corp 302 738-5266
  117 N Dillwyn Rd Newark (19711) *(G-6438)*
Denovix Inc 302 442-6911
  3411 Silverside Rd Wilmington (19810) *(G-10110)*
Denovix Inc., Wilmington Also called Denovix Inc *(G-10110)*
Dent Pro Inc 302 628-0978
  14470 Baker Mill Rd Seaford (19973) *(G-8222)*
Dental Assoc Del Mddletown Off, Middletown Also called Dental Associates Delaware PA *(G-4035)*
Dental Associates PA 302 571-0878
  2300 Penns Ave Ste 6cd Wilmington (19806) *(G-10111)*
Dental Associates Delaware PA (PA) 302 477-4900
  1415 Foulk Rd Ste 200 Wilmington (19803) *(G-10112)*
Dental Associates Delaware PA 302 378-8600
  106 Saint Annes Church Rd Middletown (19709) *(G-4035)*
Dental Associates Delaware PA 302 477-4900
  1415 Foulk Rd Ste 200 Wilmington (19803) *(G-10113)*
Dental Associates Hockessin 302 239-5917
  1415 Foulk Rd Ste 201 Wilmington (19803) *(G-10114)*
Dental Diagnostics & Services 302 655-2626
  217 W 9th St Wilmington (19801) *(G-10115)*
Dental Group 302 645-8993
  34359 Carpenters Way Lewes (19958) *(G-3461)*
Dental Health Assoc Pike Creek, Wilmington Also called J S McKelvey DDS *(G-11110)*
Dental Management Strategies, Wilmington Also called Dental Associates Delaware PA *(G-10113)*
Dental Sleep Solution 302 235-8249
  4901 Limestone Rd Wilmington (19808) *(G-10116)*
Dentistry For Children 302 475-7640
  2036 Foulk Rd Ste 200 Wilmington (19810) *(G-10117)*
Dentsply Sirona Inc 302 422-4511
  38 W Clarke Ave Milford (19963) *(G-4387)*
Dentsply Sirona Inc 302 422-4511
  38 W Clarke Ave Milford (19963) *(G-4388)*
Dentsply Sirona Inc 302 422-1043
  779 E Masten Cir Milford (19963) *(G-4389)*
Dentsply Sirona Inc 302 430-7474
  412 Mccolley St Milford (19963) *(G-4390)*
Deo Trucking 302 744-9832
  2505 White Oak Rd Dover (19901) *(G-1414)*
Dependable Lawn Care Inc 302 834-0159
  1421 Pole Bridge Rd Middletown (19709) *(G-4036)*
Dependable Trucking Inc 302 655-6271
  520 Terminal Ave New Castle (19720) *(G-5248)*
Depository Trust Co Del LLC 302 762-2635
  3601 N Market St Wilmington (19802) *(G-10118)*
Depro Serical, Townsend Also called Depro-Serical USA Inc *(G-8783)*
Depro-Serical USA Inc 302 368-8040
  4676 Dupont Pkwy Townsend (19734) *(G-8783)*
Dept of Anthropology, Newark Also called University of Delaware *(G-7629)*
Derby Software LLC (PA) 502 435-1371
  8 The Grn Ste A Dover (19901) *(G-1415)*
Derco USA, Newark Also called OConnor Belting Intl Inc *(G-7142)*
Deride Igo 302 234-4121
  28 Findail Dr Newark (19711) *(G-6439)*

Desai, Parul MD, Wilmington Also called Rebecca Jaffee MD *(G-12344)*
Desangosse US Inc 302 691-6137
  103 Foulk Rd Wilmington (19803) *(G-10119)*
Deshong & Sons Contractors 302 453-8500
  2606 Ogletown Rd Newark (19713) *(G-6440)*
Design Collaborative Inc 302 652-4221
  1211 Delaware Ave Ste Dc1 Wilmington (19806) *(G-10120)*
Design Consultants Group LLC 302 684-8030
  10872d Davidson Dr Milton (19968) *(G-4892)*
Design Contracting Inc 302 429-6900
  1000 N Heald St Wilmington (19802) *(G-10121)*
Design Craft 302 834-3720
  104 Clark Cir Delaware City (19706) *(G-956)*
Design Delmarva 302 644-8884
  1304 Savannah Rd Lewes (19958) *(G-3462)*
Design Services Ltd 302 475-5663
  1403 Silverside Rd Ste C Wilmington (19810) *(G-10122)*
Design Specific US Inc 650 318-6473
  501 Silverside Rd Ste 105 Wilmington (19809) *(G-10123)*
Design Technology, Seaford Also called Nouvir Lightning Corporation *(G-8331)*
Design Tribe Republic LLC 302 918-5279
  300 Delaware Ave Ste 210a Wilmington (19801) *(G-10124)*
Designer Braids and Trade 718 783-9078
  148 Vincent Cir Middletown (19709) *(G-4037)*
Designer Consigner Inc (PA) 302 239-4034
  7185 Lancaster Pike Hockessin (19707) *(G-3008)*
Despatch Section, Magnolia Also called Chemlime NJ Inc *(G-3885)*
Dess Machine & Manufacturing 302 736-7457
  5049 N Dupont Hwy Dover (19901) *(G-1416)*
Desserts By Dana, Bear Also called Dana E Herbert *(G-93)*
Destiny Rescue Intl Inc 574 529-2238
  16192 Coastal Hwy Lewes (19958) *(G-3463)*
Detroit Desl Rmnfacturing Corp 302 427-3564
  1105 N Market St Ste 1300 Wilmington (19801) *(G-10125)*
Detweilers Lighting 302 678-5804
  285 Pearsons Corner Rd R Hartly (19953) *(G-2919)*
Deutsche Bank Tr Co Americas 302 636-3301
  1011 Centre Rd Ste 200 Wilmington (19805) *(G-10126)*
Deutsche Bank Trust Co Del 302 636-3300
  1011 Centre Rd Ste 200 Wilmington (19805) *(G-10127)*
Deutsche Bnk US Fncl Mkts Hldg 302 636-3301
  1011 Centre Rd Ste 200 Wilmington (19805) *(G-10128)*
Devanlay, Rehoboth Beach Also called Lacoste Usa Inc *(G-7984)*
Devary Electric Inc 302 674-4560
  3 Forrest Hills Ct Dover (19904) *(G-1417)*
Devastator Game Calls LLC 302 875-5328
  12009 Lahoba Ln Laurel (19956) *(G-3223)*
Developing Minds Preschool 302 995-9611
  2106 Saint James Ch Rd Wilmington (19808) *(G-10129)*
Devils Party Press 310 904-3660
  204 Sundance Ln Milton (19968) *(G-4893)*
Devon Sadlowski DMD 302 735-8940
  882 Walker Rd Ste A Dover (19904) *(G-1418)*
Dew Softech Inc 302 834-2555
  200 Biddle Ave Ste 212 Newark (19702) *(G-6441)*
Dewberry Insurance Agency Inc 302 995-9550
  5700 Kirkwood Hwy Ste 103 Wilmington (19808) *(G-10130)*
Dewey Artist Collaboration Inc 302 212-9798
  19817 Hebron Rd Rehoboth Beach (19971) *(G-7915)*
Dewey Beach House 302 227-4000
  1710 Coastal Hwy Dewey Beach (19971) *(G-1055)*
Dewey Beer & Food Company LLC 302 227-1182
  2100 Coastal Hwy Dewey Beach (19971) *(G-1056)*
Dewey Beer Company, Dewey Beach Also called Dewey Beer & Food Company LLC *(G-1056)*
Dewitt Heating and AC Inc 267 228-7355
  1 Joanne Ct Bear (19701) *(G-115)*
Dewson Construction Company 302 427-2250
  7 S Lincoln St Wilmington (19805) *(G-10131)*
Dexsta Federal Credit Union 302 996-4893
  300 Foulk Rd Ste 100 Wilmington (19803) *(G-10132)*
Dexsta Federal Credit Union (PA) 302 996-4893
  1310 Centerville Rd Wilmington (19808) *(G-10133)*
Dexsta Federal Credit Union 302 695-3888
  E444-108 Wilmington (19880) *(G-10134)*
Dezins Unlimited Inc 302 652-4545
  323 Clubhouse Ln Wilmington (19810) *(G-10135)*
Dfc Industries Inc 215 292-1572
  4 Bellecor Dr Unit B New Castle (19720) *(G-5249)*
Dfs Corporate Services LLC 302 323-7191
  12 Reads Way New Castle (19720) *(G-5250)*
Dfs Corporate Services LLC 302 349-4512
  502 E Market St Greenwood (19950) *(G-2730)*
Dfs Corporate Services LLC 302 735-3902
  34 Starlifter Ave Dover (19901) *(G-1419)*
Dgs, Newark Also called Delaware Guidance Services For *(G-6382)*
DH Tech Wilmington De 215 680-9194
  1 Limousine Dr Wilmington (19803) *(G-10136)*

Dhm Wilmington LLC 302 656-8952
700 N King St Wilmington (19801) ***(G-10137)***
Di Sabatino, M P DDS, Smyrna *Also called Caimar Corporation* ***(G-8589)***
Diagnostic Imaging Assoc, Wilmington *Also called Pike Creek Imaging Center* ***(G-12139)***
Diagnostic Imaging Associates, Newark *Also called Omega Imaging Associates LLC* ***(G-7146)***
Diagnostic Imaging Associates, Wilmington *Also called Brandywine Imaging LLC* ***(G-9440)***
Diagnostic Medical Services 302 292-2700
25 S Old Baltimore Pike # 104 Newark (19702) ***(G-6442)***
Dialog News Paper Inc 302 573-3109
1925 Delaware Ave Fl 3 Wilmington (19806) ***(G-10138)***
Diamond Car Wash Inc 302 449-5896
104 Sandhill Dr Middletown (19709) ***(G-4038)***
Diamond Chemical & Supply Co 302 656-7786
524 S Walnut St Ste B Wilmington (19801) ***(G-10139)***
Diamond Chiropractic Inc 302 892-9355
1101 Twin Ceiling Ln 20 Newark (19713) ***(G-6443)***
Diamond Computer Inc 302 674-4064
4608 S Dupont Hwy Ste 4 Dover (19901) ***(G-1420)***
Diamond Dance Co, Milford *Also called A Dance Class* ***(G-4301)***
Diamond Electric Inc 302 697-3296
3566 Peachtree Run Rd # 1 Dover (19901) ***(G-1421)***
Diamond Glo Cleaning Solutions, Bear *Also called David Jenkins* ***(G-96)***
Diamond Hill Inc 302 999-0302
34 Industrial Blvd 104 New Castle (19720) ***(G-5251)***
Diamond Materials LLC 302 658-6524
242 N James St Ste 102 Wilmington (19804) ***(G-10140)***
Diamond Mechanical Inc 302 697-7694
3588 Peachtree Run Rd Dover (19901) ***(G-1422)***
Diamond Motor Sports Inc 302 697-3222
4595 S Dupont Hwy Dover (19901) ***(G-1423)***
Diamond Pest Control 302 654-2300
6 Weldin Park Dr Wilmington (19803) ***(G-10141)***
Diamond State Cabinetry 302 250-3531
32627 Millsboro Hwy Millsboro (19966) ***(G-4678)***
Diamond State Chiropractic, Newark *Also called Diamond Chiropractic Inc* ***(G-6443)***
Diamond State CLT Inc 800 282-0477
9 E Loockerman St Ste 205 Dover (19901) ***(G-1424)***
Diamond State Commercial Clg 215 888-2575
9 S Sherman Dr Bear (19701) ***(G-116)***
DIAMOND STATE COMMUNITY LAND T, Dover *Also called Diamond State CLT Inc* ***(G-1424)***
Diamond State Corporation (PA) 302 674-1300
602 Pear St Dover (19904) ***(G-1425)***
Diamond State Curling Club 856 577-3747
8 E Aldine Dr Hockessin (19707) ***(G-3009)***
Diamond State Door 302 743-4667
2107 Othoson Ave Wilmington (19808) ***(G-10142)***
Diamond State Express LLC 302 563-3514
1610 E Newport Pike Spc 5 Wilmington (19804) ***(G-10143)***
Diamond State Fincl Group Inc 302 366-0366
121 Continental Dr # 110 Newark (19713) ***(G-6444)***
Diamond State Graphics Inc 302 325-1100
200 Century Park New Castle (19720) ***(G-5252)***
Diamond State Home Auxiliary 302 652-9331
8 S Dupont Rd Newport (19804) ***(G-7747)***
Diamond State Machining Inc (PA) 302 398-8437
207 Main St Farmington (19950) ***(G-2267)***
Diamond State Pole Bldings LLC (PA) 302 387-1710
7288 S Dupont Hwy Felton (19943) ***(G-2286)***
Diamond State Port Corporation 302 472-7678
1 Hausel Rd Lbby Wilmington (19801) ***(G-10144)***
Diamond State Promotions 302 999-1900
5231 W Woodmill Dr Wilmington (19808) ***(G-10145)***
Diamond State Props 302 528-7146
463 Granger Dr Bear (19701) ***(G-117)***
Diamond State Pty Rentl & Sls 302 777-6677
53 Germay Dr Wilmington (19804) ***(G-10146)***
Diamond State Recycling Corp 302 655-1501
1600 Bowers St Wilmington (19802) ***(G-10147)***
Diamond State Tele Coml Un 302 999-1100
1819 Newport Rd Ste A Wilmington (19808) ***(G-10148)***
Diamond State Tire Inc 302 836-1919
3482 Wrangle Hill Rd Bear (19701) ***(G-118)***
Diamond State Welding LLC 302 644-8489
13307 Jefferson Rd Milton (19968) ***(G-4894)***
Diamond State Whsng & Dist, New Castle *Also called First State Warehousing* ***(G-5319)***
Diamond Technologies Inc 302 421-8252
221 W 9th St 200 Wilmington (19801) ***(G-10149)***
Diane Spence Day Care 302 335-4460
19 Ruyter Dr Frederica (19946) ***(G-2401)***
Dianes Bus Service 302 629-4336
Rr 2 Box 79 Seaford (19973) ***(G-8223)***
Dibiasos Clg Rstration Svc Inc 302 376-7111
690 Blackbird Station Rd Townsend (19734) ***(G-8784)***
Dick Broadbent Insurance 302 998-0137
715 Greenbank Rd Wilmington (19808) ***(G-10150)***
Dick Ennis Inc 302 945-2627
22357 John J Williams Hwy Lewes (19958) ***(G-3464)***
Dick Palmer Woodworking 302 227-8419
Near Midway Rd 1 Rehoboth Beach (19971) ***(G-7916)***
Dickens Parlour Theatre 302 829-1071
35715 Atlantic Ave Millville (19967) ***(G-4842)***
Dickerson Fence Co Inc 302 846-2227
36947 Saint George Rd Delmar (19940) ***(G-993)***
Diehl & Co CPA 302 644-4441
18306 Coastal Hwy Lewes (19958) ***(G-3465)***
Dienay Distribution Corp 732 766-0814
101 Trupenny Turn Ste 1b Middletown (19709) ***(G-4039)***
Dieste Mark Design Build LLC 301 921-9050
32895 Coastal Hwy # 201 Bethany Beach (19930) ***(G-398)***
Digen Auto Group, Middletown *Also called Lifetime Skills Services LLC* ***(G-4132)***
Digital Broadcast Corporation 215 285-0912
2207 Concord Pike 619 Wilmington (19803) ***(G-10151)***
Digital Generation Inc 302 368-0002
450 Corporate Blvd Newark (19702) ***(G-6445)***
Digital Heart Productions 302 737-6158
112 Entre Ln Newark (19702) ***(G-6446)***
Digital Ink Sciences LLC 951 757-0027
3 Germay Dr Ste 4 Wilmington (19804) ***(G-10152)***
Digital Legal, Wilmington *Also called DLS Discovery LLC* ***(G-10176)***
Digital Office Solutions Inc 302 286-6706
101 Sandy Dr Newark (19713) ***(G-6447)***
Digital Penguin Inc 484 387-7803
625 Dawson Dr Ste A Newark (19713) ***(G-6448)***
Digital Technology 416 829-8400
1201 N Orange St Ste 71 Wilmington (19801) ***(G-10153)***
Digital Whale LLC 302 526-0115
110 N Main St Ste F Camden (19934) ***(G-561)***
Digital Wish Inc 802 375-6721
15187 Hudson Rd Milton (19968) ***(G-4895)***
Diligent Bus Solutions LLC 302 897-5993
1 Marra Pl Newark (19702) ***(G-6449)***
Diligent Detail 302 482-2836
2203 Mitch Rd Wilmington (19804) ***(G-10154)***
Dillon Distributors LLC 302 226-9700
35584 Airport Rd Rehoboth Beach (19971) ***(G-7917)***
Dills Electric 302 674-3444
4508 N Dupont Hwy Dover (19901) ***(G-1426)***
Dima II Inc 302 427-0787
2400 W 4th St Wilmington (19805) ***(G-10155)***
Dimarquez Intl Ministries Inc 302 256-4847
417 Moores Ln New Castle (19720) ***(G-5253)***
Dimensional Insight Inc 302 791-0687
501 Silverside Rd Ste 2 Wilmington (19809) ***(G-10156)***
Dimo Corp 302 324-8100
46 Industrial Blvd New Castle (19720) ***(G-5254)***
Dimple Construction Inc 302 559-7535
3310 Wrangle Hill Rd # 112 Bear (19701) ***(G-119)***
Dingle & Kane PA 302 731-5200
356 E Main St Ste A Newark (19711) ***(G-6450)***
Dining Software Group Inc 720 236-9572
2140 S Dupont Hwy Camden (19934) ***(G-562)***
Diocesan Council Inc 302 475-4688
2320 Grubb Rd Wilmington (19810) ***(G-10157)***
Diocese of Wilmington 302 368-0146
3000 Videre Dr Wilmington (19808) ***(G-10158)***
Dipna Inc 302 478-0300
5209 Concord Pike Wilmington (19803) ***(G-10159)***
Dippold Marble Granite 302 734-8505
101 Hatchery Rd Dover (19901) ***(G-1427)***
Direct Cremation Services Del 302 656-6873
1900 Delaware Ave Wilmington (19806) ***(G-10160)***
Direct Importer LLC 302 838-2183
843 Salem Church Rd Newark (19702) ***(G-6451)***
Direct Mobile Transit Inc 302 218-5106
2110 Duncan Rd 3 Wilmington (19808) ***(G-10161)***
Direct Radiography Corp 302 631-2700
600 Technology Dr Newark (19702) ***(G-6452)***
Directfit, Wilmington *Also called Robert Fickling* ***(G-12437)***
Directrestore LLC 650 276-0384
3500 S Dupont Hwy Dover (19901) ***(G-1428)***
Dirt Works Inc 302 947-2429
22547 Waterview Rd Lewes (19958) ***(G-3466)***
Dis Daycare 302 888-0350
1725 W 7th St Wilmington (19805) ***(G-10162)***
Dis Inc (PA) 302 834-1633
268 Cornell Dr Newark (19702) ***(G-6453)***
Dis Management 302 543-4481
713 Greenbank Rd Wilmington (19808) ***(G-10163)***
Disabatino Construction Co 302 652-3838
1 S Cleveland Ave Wilmington (19805) ***(G-10164)***
Disabatino Enterprises LLC 302 652-3838
1 S Cleveland Ave Wilmington (19805) ***(G-10165)***
Disabatino Landscaping Inc 302 764-0408
471 B And O Ln Wilmington (19804) ***(G-10166)***
Disabatino Ldscpg Tree Svc Inc 302 764-0408
471 B And O Ln Wilmington (19804) ***(G-10167)***
Disabilities Law Program, Dover *Also called Community Legal Aid Society* ***(G-1306)***

ALPHABETIC

(PA)=Parent Co (HQ)=Headquarters (DH)=Div Headquarters
2020 Harris Directory of Delaware Businesses
631

Disabilities Law Program, Georgetown *Also called Community Legal Aid Society (G-2479)*
Disabled American Veterans 302 697-9061
183 South St Camden (19934) *(G-563)*
Disanto, Joseph MD, Wilmington *Also called Brandi Wine Pediatric Inc (G-9416)*
Disaster Research Center 302 831-6618
111 Academy St Rm 166 Newark (19716) *(G-6454)*
Discidium Technologies, Newark *Also called Discidium Technology Inc (G-6455)*
Discidium Technology Inc 347 220-5979
100 Cullen Way Newark (19711) *(G-6455)*
Discount Cigarette Depot 302 398-4447
1 Liberty Plz Harrington (19952) *(G-2833)*
Discount Oil LLC 302 737-6560
2126 Old Kirkwood Rd Bear (19701) *(G-120)*
DISCOVER, New Castle *Also called Bank of New Castle (G-5066)*
Discover Bank (HQ) 302 349-4512
502 E Market St Greenwood (19950) *(G-2731)*
Discover Financial Services, New Castle *Also called Dfs Corporate Services LLC (G-5250)*
Discovery Cove Learning Center, Laurel *Also called Karen Schreiber (G-3248)*
Discovery Island Preschool, Seaford *Also called Sussex Prschool Erly Care Ctrs (G-8417)*
Discovery Island Preschool 302 732-7529
32532 Smith Dr Dagsboro (19939) *(G-898)*
Discovery Solutions Inc 410 929-0025
16192 Coastal Hwy Lewes (19958) *(G-3467)*
Dish Network LLC 302 387-0341
2 S Main St Camden (19934) *(G-564)*
Disrupt Industries Deleware 424 229-9300
8 The Grn Dover (19901) *(G-1429)*
Disrupt Pharma Tech Africa Inc 312 945-8002
8 The Grn Ste A Dover (19901) *(G-1430)*
Distillate Media LLC 302 270-7945
141 Shinnecock Rd Dover (19904) *(G-1431)*
Distribution Headquarters, Wilmington *Also called Casale Marble Imports Inc (G-9585)*
Distribution Marketing of Del 302 658-6397
818 S Heald St Ste A Wilmington (19801) *(G-10168)*
District Council 21, Wilmington *Also called Painters Local Union 277 (G-12006)*
Ditrocchio Maria Antonetta 302 450-6790
814 S Governors Ave Dover (19904) *(G-1432)*
Diversified Chemical Pdts Inc 302 656-5293
60 Germay Dr Wilmington (19804) *(G-10169)*
Diversified Financial Cons 302 765-3500
2200 Concord Pike 104 Wilmington (19803) *(G-10170)*
Diversified Lighting Assoc Inc 302 286-6370
5466 Fairmont Dr Wilmington (19808) *(G-10171)*
Divine Element Hbb 302 538-5209
405 W Lebanon Rd Dover (19901) *(G-1433)*
Division For Visually Impaired, New Castle *Also called Health & Social Svcs Del Dept (G-5383)*
Division of Child Spprt &, Georgetown *Also called Health & Social Svcs Del Dept (G-2556)*
Division of Family Services, Seaford *Also called Children Youth & Their Fam (G-8193)*
Division of Social Services, Wilmington *Also called Health & Social Svcs Del Dept (G-10868)*
Division Svcs For Agng Adlts 302 255-9390
1901 N Dupont Hwy Fl 1 New Castle (19720) *(G-5255)*
Division-Developmental Dsblts 302 836-2110
2540 Wrangle Hill Rd Bear (19701) *(G-121)*
Dixie Construction Company Inc 302 858-5007
22237 Lwes Georgetown Hwy Georgetown (19947) *(G-2511)*
Dixie Line Farm Inc 302 236-7402
9455 Airport Rd Seaford (19973) *(G-8224)*
Dixon Brothers LLC 302 377-8289
3 Francis Cir Newark (19711) *(G-6456)*
Dixon Contracting Inc 302 653-4623
1614 Seeneytown Rd Dover (19904) *(G-1434)*
Diy Tool Supply LLC 302 253-8461
23135 Lewes Georgetown Georgetown (19947) *(G-2512)*
Dj First Class 302 345-0602
20 Robins Nest Ln New Castle (19720) *(G-5256)*
Djont/Jpm Wilmington Lsg LLC 302 478-6000
4727 Concord Pike Wilmington (19803) *(G-10172)*
Dkmrbh Inc 302 250-4428
704 N King St Ste 500 Wilmington (19801) *(G-10173)*
Dla Piper LLP (us) 302 654-3025
919 N Market St Wilmington (19801) *(G-10174)*
DLS Discovery 302 654-3345
824 N Market St Wilmington (19801) *(G-10175)*
DLS Discovery LLC 302 888-2060
1007 N Orange St Ste 510 Wilmington (19801) *(G-10176)*
Dm Home Maintenance 302 945-5050
34079 Taylor Dr S Millsboro (19966) *(G-4679)*
DMC Power Inc 302 276-0303
98 Quigley Blvd New Castle (19720) *(G-5257)*
DMD Business Forms & Prtg Co 302 998-8200
204 S Maryland Ave Wilmington (19804) *(G-10177)*
Dmg Clearances Inc 302 239-6337
13 Robin Dr Hockessin (19707) *(G-3010)*
Dmi, Wilmington *Also called Sign Express (G-12613)*
DMI Commodities Inc 877 364-3644
2915 Ogletown Rd Newark (19713) *(G-6457)*
Dml Creation, Newark *Also called 9193 4323 Quebec Inc (G-5862)*
Dmms, Newark *Also called Delaware Medical MGT Svcs LLC (G-6394)*
Dnd Limousine Service 302 998-5856
104c S John St Wilmington (19804) *(G-10178)*
Dnrec Air Waste Management 302 739-9406
30 S American Ave Dover (19901) *(G-1435)*
Do It Wiser LLC (PA) 800 816-0944
3422 Old Capitol Trl Wilmington (19808) *(G-10179)*
Docs Medical LLC 301 401-1489
25 Dynasty Dr Bear (19701) *(G-122)*
Doctor Laubers Karate Plus, Bear *Also called Taekwondo Fitness Ctr of Del (G-346)*
Doctors Pathology Services PA 302 677-0000
1253 College Park Dr Dover (19904) *(G-1436)*
Dodd Dental Laboratory, New Castle *Also called National Dentex LLC (G-5544)*
Dodd Health Innovation LLC 410 598-7266
31027 Scissorbill Rd Ocean View (19970) *(G-7784)*
DOE Legal, Wilmington *Also called DOE Technologies Inc (G-10181)*
DOE Legal LLC 302 798-7500
1200 Philadelphia Pike # 1 Wilmington (19809) *(G-10180)*
DOE Technologies Inc 302 792-1285
1200 Philadelphia Pike # 1 Wilmington (19809) *(G-10181)*
Dog Anya 302 456-0108
918 Kenilworth Ave Newark (19711) *(G-6458)*
Dog Dayz Dog Day Care Center 302 655-5506
3000 W 2nd St Wilmington (19805) *(G-10182)*
Dog Works South 302 366-8161
2201 Ogletown Rd Newark (19711) *(G-6459)*
Dogfish Head Brewings & Eats, Rehoboth Beach *Also called Dogfish Head Inc (G-7918)*
Dogfish Head Companies LLC 302 684-1000
6 Cannery Vlg Milton (19968) *(G-4896)*
Dogfish Head Craft Brewery LLC 302 684-1000
Cannery Vlg Ctr Ste 6 Milton (19968) *(G-4897)*
Dogfish Head Inc 302 226-2739
320 Rehoboth Ave Rehoboth Beach (19971) *(G-7918)*
Dogfish Inn 302 644-8292
105 Savannah Rd Lewes (19958) *(G-3468)*
Doherty & Associates Inc 302 239-3500
5301 Limestone Rd Ste 100 Wilmington (19808) *(G-10183)*
Dohery Funeral Homes Inc 302 999-8277
3200 Limestone Rd Wilmington (19808) *(G-10184)*
Dojupa LLC 302 300-2009
5586 Kirkwood Hwy Wilmington (19808) *(G-10185)*
Dolan Manufacturing Solutions 302 378-4981
424 Spring Hollow Dr Middletown (19709) *(G-4040)*
Dole Food Company Inc 302 652-6060
Port Of Wilmington Lbr Rd Wilmington (19899) *(G-10186)*
Dole Fresh Fruit Company 302 652-6484
70 Gist Rd Wilmington (19801) *(G-10187)*
Dole Fresh Fruit Company 302 652-2215
1 Hausel Rd Wilmington (19801) *(G-10188)*
Dolphin Design & Communic, Newark *Also called Delaware Design Company (G-6375)*
Dolphin Ship Services Ltd (PA) 302 832-0410
235 Hope Ct W Bear (19701) *(G-123)*
Domain Hr Solutions 302 357-9401
364 E Main St Ste 1012 Middletown (19709) *(G-4041)*
Domenic Di Donato Plbg Htg Inc 856 207-4919
128 Shrewsbury Dr Wilmington (19810) *(G-10189)*
Domian International Svc LLC 804 837-3616
22 Zion Dr Smyrna (19977) *(G-8624)*
Dominic A Di Febo & Sons 302 425-5054
812 Rose St Wilmington (19805) *(G-10190)*
Dominic Gioffre DDS PA 302 239-0410
4901 Limestone Rd Ste 1 Wilmington (19808) *(G-10191)*
Dominick P Ferrari, President, Wilmington *Also called Wholesale Janitor Supply Co (G-13197)*
Dominos Body Shop 302 697-3801
467 Moose Lodge Rd Camden Wyoming (19934) *(G-630)*
Dominring Blgcal RES Group LLC 951 327-8062
19266 Coastal Hwy Rehoboth Beach (19971) *(G-7919)*
Don D Corp 302 994-5793
1615 E Ayre St Wilmington (19804) *(G-10192)*
Don Noel Professional Services, Middletown *Also called Donald Briggs (G-4042)*
Don Rogers Inc (PA) 302 658-6524
242 N James St Ste 102 Wilmington (19804) *(G-10193)*
Don-Lee Margin Corporation 302 629-7567
25271 Figgs Rd Seaford (19973) *(G-8225)*
Donald A Girard MD 302 633-5755
2601 Annand Dr Ste 19 Wilmington (19808) *(G-10194)*
Donald Briggs 267 476-2712
400 W Harvest Ln Middletown (19709) *(G-4042)*
Donald C Savoy Inc 888 992-6755
200 Continental Dr # 209 Newark (19713) *(G-6460)*
Donald C Savoy Inc 302 697-4100
5158 S Dupont Hwy Dover (19901) *(G-1437)*
Donald Eichholz 302 792-1236
210 Cordon Rd Wilmington (19803) *(G-10195)*
Donald F Deaven Inc 302 994-5793
1615 E Ayre St Wilmington (19804) *(G-10196)*
Donald G Varnes & Sons Inc 302 737-5953
27 Albe Dr Ste A Newark (19702) *(G-6461)*

ALPHABETIC SECTION — Dover Place, Dover

Donald Jaffey Enterprises, Claymont *Also called Dack Realty Corp* *(G-726)*
Donald Walker 240 507-9805
142 W Milby St Harrington (19952) *(G-2834)*
Donaldson Electric 302 660-7534
124 Middleboro Rd Wilmington (19804) *(G-10197)*
Donaway Corporation (PA) 302 934-6226
Rr 24 Millsboro (19966) *(G-4680)*
Donaway Service Station, Millsboro *Also called Donaway Corporation* *(G-4680)*
Done Again Software LLC 301 466-7858
31736 Marsh Island Ave Lewes (19958) *(G-3469)*
Done Done Fitness, Middletown *Also called Missy Muller* *(G-4167)*
Dongjin Usa Inc 302 691-8510
175 Edgemoor Rd Wilmington (19809) *(G-10198)*
Donnas Family Cut & Curl Inc 302 436-8999
106 Bayville Shopping Ctr Selbyville (19975) *(G-8482)*
Donne Delle & Associates Inc (PA) 302 325-1111
200 Continental Dr # 200 Newark (19713) *(G-6462)*
Donner Corporation 302 778-0844
919 N Market St Ste 601 Wilmington (19801) *(G-10199)*
Donovan Transport, Newark *Also called John A Donovan* *(G-6841)*
Donovan, Jack, Seminars, Millsboro *Also called Jack Donovan* *(G-4711)*
Donr LLC 857 400-8679
251 Little Falls Dr Wilmington (19808) *(G-10200)*
Door & Gate Co LLC 888 505-6962
130 Hickman Rd Ste 26 Claymont (19703) *(G-734)*
Door of Second Chances Inc 302 898-3959
604 W 32nd St Wilmington (19802) *(G-10201)*
Dorey Financial Services Inc 302 856-0970
13 Bridgeville Rd Georgetown (19947) *(G-2513)*
Dorilyn English PHD 302 655-6506
18c Trolley Sq Wilmington (19806) *(G-10202)*
Dorinda F Dove 302 658-2229
1508 W 7th St Wilmington (19805) *(G-10203)*
Doris Obenshain Counseling, Middletown *Also called Doris V Obenshain* *(G-4043)*
Doris V Obenshain 302 448-1450
100 W Green St Middletown (19709) *(G-4043)*
Doroshow Pasquale Karwitz Sieg (PA) 302 998-2397
1202 Kirkwood Hwy Wilmington (19805) *(G-10204)*
Doroshow Pasquale Karwitz Sieg 302 674-7100
500 W Loockerman St # 120 Dover (19904) *(G-1438)*
Doroshow Pasquale Karwitz Sieg 302 934-9400
28535 Dupont Blvd Unit 2 Millsboro (19966) *(G-4681)*
Doroshow Pasquale Karwitz Sieg 302 424-7744
903 Lakeview Ave Milford (19963) *(G-4391)*
Doroshow Pasquale Karwitz Sieg 302 832-3200
1701 Pulaski Hwy Bear (19701) *(G-124)*
Doroshow Pasquale Karwitz Sieg 302 998-0100
1208 Kirkwood Hwy Wilmington (19805) *(G-10205)*
Doroshow Pasquale Law Offices, Wilmington *Also called Doroshow Pasquale Karwitz Sieg* *(G-10204)*
Doroshow Pasquale Law Offices, Millsboro *Also called Doroshow Pasquale Karwitz Sieg* *(G-4681)*
Dorsey and Whitney Del LLP 302 425-7171
300 Delaware Ave Ste 1010 Wilmington (19801) *(G-10206)*
Dorsia Alliance Ltd 302 492-5052
717 N Union St Ste 125 Wilmington (19805) *(G-10207)*
DOT Foods Inc 302 300-4239
301 American Blvd Bear (19701) *(G-125)*
DOT Matrix Inc (PA) 917 657-4918
3500 S Dupont Hwy Dover (19901) *(G-1439)*
DOT Pop Inc 302 691-3160
1010 N Union St Ste D Wilmington (19805) *(G-10208)*
Dotty Sweicicki Dvm 302 674-1380
748 Hazlettville Rd Hartly (19953) *(G-2920)*
Double Diamone Builders Inc 302 945-2512
25187 Banks Rd Millsboro (19966) *(G-4682)*
Double R Holdings Inc 302 645-5555
1009 Kings Hwy Lewes (19958) *(G-3470)*
Double S Co, Bear *Also called Double S Developers Inc* *(G-126)*
Double S Developers Inc 302 838-8880
1919 Red Lion Rd Bear (19701) *(G-126)*
Double Tree By Hilton, Wilmington *Also called Driftwood Hospitality MGT LLC* *(G-10235)*
Doubletree Downtown Wilmington, Wilmington *Also called 700 Nrth King St Wlmington LLC* *(G-8865)*
Doubletree Hotel, Wilmington *Also called Wilmington Hotel Venture* *(G-13234)*
Doubletree Hotel Wilmington, Wilmington *Also called Dhm Wilmington LLC* *(G-10137)*
Doubleudiamond LLC 206 502-0144
1209 N Orange St Wilmington (19801) *(G-10209)*
Doubltree By Hilton Wilmington, Wilmington *Also called Djont/Jpm Wilmington Lsg LLC* *(G-10172)*
Doubltree Htels Suites Resorts 302 478-6000
4727 Concord Pike Wilmington (19803) *(G-10210)*
Doug Green Woodworking 302 652-6522
330 N Maryland Ave Wilmington (19804) *(G-10211)*
Doug Richmonds Body Shop 302 453-1173
854 Dawson Dr Newark (19713) *(G-6463)*

Dougherty Dental Solutions LLC 302 475-3270
1805 Foulk Rd Wilmington (19810) *(G-10212)*
Douglas Bennetti Insur Agcy (PA) 302 724-4490
43 Voshell Mill Rd Dover (19904) *(G-1440)*
Douglas C Loew & Associates 302 453-0550
248 E Chestnut Hill Rd # 4 Newark (19713) *(G-6464)*
Douglas Ditty DMD MD 302 644-2977
37718 Wescoats Rd Lewes (19958) *(G-3471)*
Douglas J Lavenburg MD PA (PA) 302 993-0722
1 Centurian Dr Ste 114 Newark (19713) *(G-6465)*
Douglas Morrow 302 750-9161
211 Beau Tree Dr Ste 100 Wilmington (19810) *(G-10213)*
Douglas R Johnston M D 302 651-4000
1600 Rockland Rd Wilmington (19803) *(G-10214)*
Dover, Dover *Also called Midatlantic Farm Credit* *(G-1852)*
Dover Afb Aero Club, Dover *Also called Army & Air Force Exchange Svc* *(G-1139)*
Dover Afb Beauty Salon, Dover *Also called Army & Air Force Exchange Svc* *(G-1140)*
Dover Afb Child Care Center, Dover *Also called Army & Air Force Exchange Svc* *(G-1138)*
Dover Animal Hospital, Smyrna *Also called All Pets Medical Center* *(G-8565)*
Dover Animal Hospital 302 746-2688
1151 S Governors Ave Dover (19904) *(G-1441)*
Dover Auto Repair, Dover *Also called E & M Enterprises Inc* *(G-1490)*
Dover Automotive Inc 302 653-9234
5 E Glenwood Ave Smyrna (19977) *(G-8625)*
Dover Behavorl Hlth 249 .... 302 741-0140
725 Horsepond Rd Dover (19901) *(G-1442)*
Dover Budget Inn, Dover *Also called Gulab Management Inc* *(G-1615)*
Dover Consulting Services Inc 302 736-1365
555 E Loockerman St # 102 Dover (19901) *(G-1443)*
Dover Dental Associates 302 734-7634
65 N Dupont Hwy Dover (19901) *(G-1444)*
Dover Downs Inc 302 674-4600
1131 N Dupont Hwy Dover (19901) *(G-1445)*
Dover Downs Gaming & Entrmt, Dover *Also called Premier Entertainment III LLC* *(G-1982)*
Dover Downs Hotel & Casino, Dover *Also called Dover Downs Inc* *(G-1445)*
Dover Educational & Cmnty Ctr 302 883-3092
744 River Rd Dover (19901) *(G-1446)*
Dover Electric Supply Co Inc (PA) 302 674-0115
1631 S Dupont Hwy Dover (19901) *(G-1447)*
Dover Electric Supply Co Inc 302 645-0555
18585 Curstol Hwy Ste 15 Rehoboth Beach (19971) *(G-7920)*
Dover Family Chiropractic 302 531-1900
120 Old Camden Rd Ste C Camden (19934) *(G-565)*
Dover Family Physicians PA 302 734-2500
1342 S Governors Ave Dover (19904) *(G-1448)*
Dover Federal Credit Union (PA) 302 678-8000
1075 Silver Lake Blvd Dover (19904) *(G-1449)*
Dover Federal Credit Union 302 322-4230
499 Pulaski Hwy New Castle (19720) *(G-5258)*
Dover Fmly Csmtc Dentistry LLC 302 672-7766
1113 S State St Ste 201 Dover (19901) *(G-1450)*
Dover Garden Court Apartments, Dover *Also called Colonial Inv Managment Co* *(G-1303)*
Dover Golf Center 302 674-8275
924 Artis Dr Dover (19904) *(G-1451)*
Dover Health Care Center LLC 302 270-5238
212 S Queen St Dover (19904) *(G-1452)*
Dover Home Dialysis Center, Dover *Also called Fresenius Medical Care* *(G-1567)*
Dover Hospitality Group LLC 302 677-0900
655 N Dupont Hwy Dover (19901) *(G-1453)*
Dover Inn, Dover *Also called Umiya Inc* *(G-2173)*
Dover Interfaith Mission Fr Ho 302 736-3600
684 Forest St Dover (19904) *(G-1454)*
Dover Intl Speedway Inc 302 857-2114
1131 N Dupont Hwy Dover (19901) *(G-1455)*
Dover Junior A DDS 302 836-3750
1290 Peoples Plz Newark (19702) *(G-6466)*
Dover Leasing Co Inc 302 674-2300
613 Clara St Dover (19904) *(G-1456)*
Dover Litho Printing Co 302 698-5292
21 Chadwick Dr Dover (19901) *(G-1457)*
Dover Lubricants Inc 302 674-8282
236 S Dupont Hwy Dover (19901) *(G-1458)*
Dover Mall LLC 302 678-4000
1365 N Dupont Hwy # 5061 Dover (19901) *(G-1459)*
Dover Millwork Inc 302 349-5070
10862 Shawnee Rd Harrington (19952) *(G-2835)*
Dover Mntessori Cntry Day Schl, Dover *Also called Capital School District* *(G-1250)*
Dover Motorsports Inc 302 328-6820
162 Old Churchmans Rd New Castle (19720) *(G-5259)*
Dover Motorsports Inc (PA) 302 883-6500
1131 N Dupont Hwy Dover (19901) *(G-1460)*
Dover Nunan LLC 302 697-9776
607 Otis Dr Dover (19901) *(G-1461)*
Dover Ophthalmology Asc LLC 302 724-4720
655 S Bay Rd Ste 5b Dover (19901) *(G-1462)*
Dover Oral and Maxillofacial S 302 674-1140
1004 S State St Ste 1 Dover (19901) *(G-1463)*
Dover Place, Dover *Also called Assisted Living Concepts LLC* *(G-1148)*

(PA)=Parent Co (HQ)=Headquarters (DH)=Div Headquarters

Dover Plumbing Supply Co 302 674-0333
3626 N Dupont Hwy Dover (19901) *(G-1464)*
Dover Pool & Patio Center Inc (PA) 302 346-7665
1255 S State St Ste 1 Dover (19901) *(G-1465)*
Dover Pool & Patio Center Inc. 302 839-3300
1055 N Walnut St Milford (19963) *(G-4392)*
Dover Post Co Inc (PA) 302 653-2083
609 E Division St Dover (19901) *(G-1466)*
Dover Post Co Inc. 302 378-9531
24 W Main St Middletown (19709) *(G-4044)*
Dover Post Co Inc. 302 678-3616
1196 S Little Creek Rd Dover (19901) *(G-1467)*
Dover Post Inc 304 222-6025
12 S Walnut St Milford (19963) *(G-4393)*
Dover Post News Paper, Dover *Also called Gatehouse Media Inc (G-1583)*
Dover Post Web Printing, Dover *Also called Dover Post Co Inc (G-1467)*
Dover Pulmonary PA 302 734-0400
31 Gooden Ave Dover (19904) *(G-1468)*
Dover Rent-All Inc 302 739-0860
35 Commerce Way Ste 180 Dover (19904) *(G-1469)*
Dover Rental, Dover *Also called Dover Rent-All Inc (G-1469)*
Dover Security, Dover *Also called Dover Mall LLC (G-1459)*
Dover Skating Center, Dover *Also called Delaware Skating Center Ltd (G-1391)*
Dover Soft Touch Car Wash 302 736-6011
226 N Dupont Hwy Dover (19901) *(G-1470)*
Dover Surgicenter LLC 302 346-3171
108 Patriot Dr Ste A Middletown (19709) *(G-4045)*
Dover Symphony Orchestra Inc 302 734-1701
P.O. Box 163 Dover (19903) *(G-1471)*
Dover Volkswagen Inc. 302 734-4761
1387 N Dupont Hwy Dover (19901) *(G-1472)*
Dover Windows and Doors, Harrington *Also called Dover Millwork Inc (G-2835)*
Dovers Childrens Villag 302 672-6476
726 Woodcrest Dr Dover (19904) *(G-1473)*
Dovington Training Center LLC 302 284-2114
595 Black Swamp Rd Felton (19943) *(G-2287)*
Dow Chemical Company 302 368-4169
451 Bellevue Rd Bldg 9 Newark (19713) *(G-6467)*
Dow Chemical Company 302 366-0500
231 Lake Dr Newark (19702) *(G-6468)*
Dow Electronic Materials, Newark *Also called Rohm Haas Electronic Mtls LLC (G-7358)*
Down Under Boxing Club 302 745-4392
19124 Wesley Church Rd Bridgeville (19933) *(G-467)*
Downs Insurance Associates 302 422-8863
1047 N Walnut St Milford (19963) *(G-4394)*
Downtown Parking, Newark *Also called City of Newark (G-6242)*
DOWNTOWN VISIONS, Wilmington *Also called Wdbid Management Company (G-13129)*
Doyjul Apartments 302 998-0088
3403 Lancaster Pike Wilmington (19805) *(G-10215)*
Doyjul Center, Wilmington *Also called Doyjul Apartments (G-10215)*
Dozr Ltd 844 218-3697
3411 Silverside Rd Wilmington (19810) *(G-10216)*
Dp Fire & Safety Inc. 302 998-5430
411 Orinda Dr Wilmington (19804) *(G-10217)*
Dpc Emergency Equipment, Marydel *Also called Delmarva Pump Center Inc (G-3915)*
DPI, Georgetown *Also called Delmarva Poultry Industry Inc (G-2507)*
Dpnl LLC 302 366-8097
270 Chapman Rd Newark (19702) *(G-6469)*
DPs Custom Painting LLC 302 732-3232
33099 Thunder Rd Frankford (19945) *(G-2360)*
Dr Amit Dua 302 239-5917
500 Lantana Dr Hockessin (19707) *(G-3011)*
Dr Andrew Berman 302 678-1000
446 S New St Dover (19904) *(G-1474)*
Dr Azarcon & Assoc 302 478-2969
3411 Silverside Rd 107r Wilmington (19810) *(G-10218)*
Dr Bruce Matthews DDS 302 234-2440
451 Hockessin Cors Hockessin (19707) *(G-3012)*
Dr Christopher Burns 302 674-8331
871 S Governors Ave Ste 1 Dover (19904) *(G-1475)*
Dr Clyde A Maxwell Jr 302 765-3373
4201 Miller Rd Wilmington (19802) *(G-10219)*
Dr Dawn Grandison DDS 302 678-3384
429 S Governors Ave Dover (19904) *(G-1476)*
Dr Debra Wolf Encore Health 302 737-1918
19 Green Meadow Ct Newark (19711) *(G-6470)*
Dr Dunner Usa Inc 302 656-1950
103 Foulk Rd Wilmington (19803) *(G-10220)*
Dr Fanny Berg P C 302 475-8000
2000 Foulk Rd Ste A Wilmington (19810) *(G-10221)*
Dr Fay Mintz-Guttin DMD 302 356-0392
623 Kilburn Rd Wilmington (19803) *(G-10222)*
Dr Howard Giles - Wilmington 302 477-4900
1415 Foulk Rd Ste 200 Wilmington (19803) *(G-10223)*
Dr James Kramer 302 436-5133
13 S Main St 348 Selbyville (19975) *(G-8483)*
Dr Jason Parker Do 302 651-5874
1600 Rockland Rd Wilmington (19803) *(G-10224)*
Dr Jeffrey E Felzer DMD PC 302 995-6979
3105 Limestone Rd Ste 203 Wilmington (19808) *(G-10225)*
Dr Jillian G Stevens Do 302 762-7332
812 Bezel Rd Wilmington (19803) *(G-10226)*
Dr John Fontana III 302 734-1950
910 Walker Rd Ste A Dover (19904) *(G-1477)*
Dr Mackler, Seaford *Also called Nanticoke Gastroenterology (G-8319)*
Dr Marisa E Conti Do 302 678-4488
725 S Queen St Dover (19904) *(G-1478)*
Dr Mehdi Balakhani 302 368-8900
2319 Pennsylvania Ave Wilmington (19806) *(G-10227)*
Dr Monika Gupta PA 302 737-5074
314 E Main St Ste 404 Newark (19711) *(G-6471)*
Dr Robert M Collins 302 239-3655
5500 Skyline Dr Ste 3 Wilmington (19808) *(G-10228)*
Dr Robert Webster 302 674-1080
1522 S State St Dover (19901) *(G-1479)*
Dr Ronald R Blanck Do 302 541-4137
1613 Bay St Fenwick Island (19944) *(G-2334)*
Dr Shefali Pandya 302 421-9960
707 Foulk Rd Wilmington (19803) *(G-10229)*
Dr Stanley Strauss, Wilmington *Also called Vision & Hearing Inc (G-13091)*
Dr Weidong Yang Dental Office 302 409-3050
131 Becks Woods Dr Bear (19701) *(G-127)*
Dr. Armand Neal Dsanctis Jr MD, Wilmington *Also called Delaware Medical Associates PA (G-10064)*
Drafting By Design Inc (PA) 302 292-8304
170 E Main St Ste 1 Newark (19711) *(G-6472)*
Dragon Cloud Inc. 702 508-2676
1 Commerce St Wilmington (19801) *(G-10230)*
Dragons Lair Printing LLC 302 798-4465
130 Hickman Rd Ste 24 Claymont (19703) *(G-735)*
Drain Kings LLC 302 399-8980
3867 Wheatleys Pond Rd Smyrna (19977) *(G-8626)*
Draper & Goldberg Pllc 302 448-4040
512 E Market St Georgetown (19947) *(G-2514)*
Draper Communications Inc. 302 684-8962
1 Square Milton (19968) *(G-4898)*
Draperies Etc Inc 302 422-7323
723 Mccolley St Milford (19963) *(G-4395)*
Drass Insurance Agency Inc. 302 998-1331
205 N James St Wilmington (19804) *(G-10231)*
Draw Incorporated 410 208-9513
12528 Utica Rd Greenwood (19950) *(G-2732)*
Drba Police Fund 302 571-6326
And I 295 Rr 9 New Castle (19720) *(G-5260)*
Dream Clean Team LP 302 981-5154
217 Sleepy Hollow Ct Newark (19711) *(G-6473)*
Dream Graphics 302 328-6264
9 King Ave New Castle (19720) *(G-5261)*
Dream Vacations, Millsboro *Also called Bethany Travel Inc (G-4644)*
Dream View Exteriors Group LLC 302 358-9530
201 Primary Ave Georgetown (19947) *(G-2515)*
Dream Weaver Interiors Inc 302 644-0800
34 Midway Shopping Ctr Rehoboth Beach (19971) *(G-7921)*
Dream Weaver LLC. 302 352-9473
1521 Concord Pike Ste 301 Wilmington (19803) *(G-10232)*
Dream Weavers Embroidery 302 998-4264
8 Whitehall Cir Wilmington (19808) *(G-10233)*
Dreamscape Landscaping 302 354-5247
60 Colby Ave Claymont (19703) *(G-736)*
Dreamville LLC 662 524-0917
16192 Coastal Hwy Lewes (19958) *(G-3472)*
Dresslikeme LLC 302 450-1046
8 The Grn Ste 1 Dover (19901) *(G-1480)*
Drfish LLC 978 393-1212
16192 Coastal Hwy Lewes (19958) *(G-3473)*
DRG Holdco Inc 610 974-9760
2711 Centerville Rd Wilmington (19808) *(G-10234)*
Drh Enterprises LLC 302 864-0060
6796 Hearns Pond Rd Seaford (19973) *(G-8226)*
Drhealing, Milford *Also called Drnaturalhealing Inc (G-4396)*
Driftwood Cabinetry LLC 302 645-4876
1009 Kings Hwy Lewes (19958) *(G-3474)*
Driftwood Candles LLC 302 858-1600
23 Thornberry Rd Millville (19967) *(G-4843)*
Driftwood Club Apartments, Wilmington *Also called Evergreen Realty Inc (G-10448)*
Driftwood Hospitality MGT LLC 302 655-0400
700 N King St Wilmington (19801) *(G-10235)*
Drinker Biddle & Reath LLP 302 467-4200
222 Delaware Ave Ste 1400 Wilmington (19801) *(G-10236)*
Driveway Mint Pvng/Slcting LLC. 302 228-2644
7031 Cannon Rd Bridgeville (19933) *(G-468)*
Drnaturalhealing Inc 302 265-2213
111 Mccoy St Milford (19963) *(G-4396)*
Drone Delivery Systems Corp 757 903-5006
33572 Westgate Cir Unit 1 Lewes (19958) *(G-3475)*
Drop A Tot Pre-School Day Care, Dover *Also called Church of God In Christ (G-1282)*

ALPHABETIC SECTION — Duque Nieva MD PA

Drop Table LLC 650 669-8753
Trolley Sq Ste 20c Wilmington (19806) *(G-10237)*
Drummond Hill Swim Club 302 366-9882
Alton Dr Newark (19711) *(G-6474)*
Drw Funding LLC 404 631-7127
8 The Grn Ste B Dover (19901) *(G-1481)*
Dry Wall Associates Ltd 302 737-3220
58 Albe Dr Newark (19702) *(G-6475)*
Dry Wall Inc 302 838-6500
13 King Ct Ste 3 New Castle (19720) *(G-5262)*
Dryzone LLC 302 684-5034
115 Atlantic Ave Milton (19968) *(G-4899)*
Ds Paving 302 832-3748
426 Woods Rd Bear (19701) *(G-128)*
DSI Laurel LLC 302 715-3060
30214 Sussex Hwy Laurel (19956) *(G-3224)*
DSI Wilmington Dialysis, Wilmington Also called Liberty Dalysis Wilmington LLC *(G-11379)*
DSM Desotech Inc 302 328-5435
52 Reads Way New Castle (19720) *(G-5263)*
DSM Somos Technology Center, New Castle Also called DSM Desotech Inc *(G-5263)*
DSouza and Associates Inc 302 239-2300
530 Schoolhouse Rd Ste A Hockessin (19707) *(G-3013)*
Dss - Integrity LLC 302 677-0111
1679 S Dupont Hwy Ste 5 Dover (19901) *(G-1482)*
Dss International LLC 302 836-0270
203 Peoples Plz Newark (19702) *(G-6476)*
Dss Services Inc 302 677-0111
373 W North St Ste B Dover (19904) *(G-1483)*
Dss Urban Joint Venture LLC 302 677-0111
373 W North St Ste B Dover (19904) *(G-1484)*
Dssf, Millsboro Also called Delmarva Space Scnces Fndation *(G-4676)*
DSU Student Housing LLC 302 857-7966
430 College Rd Dover (19904) *(G-1485)*
Dt Investment Partners LLC 302 442-6203
1013 Centre Rd Wilmington (19805) *(G-10238)*
Dtg General Contractor 321 439-0893
220 East Ct Wilmington (19810) *(G-10239)*
Du Pont Lynne M MD 302 777-7966
910 Foulk Rd Wilmington (19803) *(G-10240)*
Du Pont Chem Enrgy Oprtons Inc (HQ) 302 774-1000
974 Centre Rd Wilmington (19805) *(G-10241)*
Du Pont Delaware Inc (HQ) 302 774-1000
974 Centre Rd Chestnut Wilmington (19805) *(G-10242)*
Du Pont Elastomers LP 302 774-1000
974 Centre Rd Wilmington (19805) *(G-10243)*
Du Pont Foreign Sales Corp 302 774-1000
974 Centre Rd Wilmington (19805) *(G-10244)*
Duane Edward Ruark 302 846-2332
6988 Beagle Dr Delmar (19940) *(G-994)*
Duck Creek Printing LLC 302 653-5121
228 E Glenwood Ave Smyrna (19977) *(G-8627)*
Duck In Car Wash 302 536-7056
9817 Spotless St Seaford (19973) *(G-8227)*
Ducts R US LLC 302 284-4006
6084 Hopkins Cemetery Rd Felton (19943) *(G-2288)*
Ducts Unlimited Inc 302 378-4125
339 W Mount Vernon St Smyrna (19977) *(G-8628)*
Duffield Associates Inc (PA) 302 239-6634
5400 Limestone Rd Wilmington (19808) *(G-10245)*
Dugan Dt Roofing Inc 302 636-9300
20 S Woodward Ave Wilmington (19805) *(G-10246)*
Dugan, Dt Roofing Co, Wilmington Also called Dugan Dt Roofing Inc *(G-10246)*
Duhadaway Tool and Die Sp Inc 302 366-0113
801 Dawson Dr Newark (19713) *(G-6477)*
Dulin Brothers 302 653-5365
938 Blackiston Church Rd Clayton (19938) *(G-842)*
Dumont Aviation, New Castle Also called Dumont Group LLC *(G-5265)*
Dumont Aviation LLC (PA) 302 777-1003
2000 Brett Rd New Castle (19720) *(G-5264)*
Dumont Group LLC 302 777-1003
2000 Brett Rd New Castle (19720) *(G-5265)*
Dunamis-Homes of Divine 302 393-5778
1328 Rising Sun Rd Ste 1 Camden Wyoming (19934) *(G-631)*
Dunbar Armored Inc 302 892-4950
320 Water St Ste A Wilmington (19804) *(G-10247)*
Dunbar Armored Inc 302 628-5401
186 Kent Dr Seaford (19973) *(G-8228)*
Dunbarton Oaks Associates 302 856-7719
301 Dunbarton Georgetown (19947) *(G-2516)*
Duncan Elisabeth D MD 302 677-2730
300 Tuskegee Blvd Dover (19902) *(G-1486)*
Duncan S Concrete 302 395-1552
324 N Red Lion Ter Bear (19701) *(G-129)*
Dunkin' Donuts, Wilmington Also called Swami Enterprises Inc *(G-12822)*
Dunkle, Mark F, Dover Also called Parkowski Guerke & Swayze PA *(G-1936)*
Dunkley Enterprises LLC 302 275-0100
139 Wallace Rd Odessa (19730) *(G-7826)*
Dunnings Body Shop 302 653-9615
2399 Sudlersville Rd Clayton (19938) *(G-843)*

Dupont, Wilmington Also called E I Du Pont De Nemours & Co *(G-10278)*
Dupont, Wilmington Also called E I Du Pont De Nemours & Co *(G-10279)*
Dupont, Wilmington Also called E I Du Pont De Nemours & Co *(G-10280)*
Dupont, Wilmington Also called E I Du Pont De Nemours & Co *(G-10281)*
Dupont, Newark Also called E I Du Pont De Nemours & Co *(G-6488)*
Dupont, Wilmington Also called E I Du Pont De Nemours & Co *(G-10282)*
Dupont, Wilmington Also called E I Du Pont De Nemours & Co *(G-10283)*
Dupont, Wilmington Also called E I Du Pont De Nemours & Co *(G-10291)*
Dupont, Wilmington Also called E I Du Pont De Nemours & Co *(G-10292)*
Dupont, Wilmington Also called E I Du Pont De Nemours & Co *(G-10293)*
Dupont, Wilmington Also called E I Du Pont De Nemours & Co *(G-10294)*
Dupont, Newark Also called E I Du Pont De Nemours & Co *(G-6490)*
Dupont, Wilmington Also called E I Du Pont De Nemours & Co *(G-10295)*
Dupont, Wilmington Also called E I Du Pont De Nemours & Co *(G-10297)*
Dupont, Wilmington Also called E I Du Pont De Nemours & Co *(G-10298)*
Dupont, Wilmington Also called E I Du Pont De Nemours & Co *(G-10299)*
Dupont, Wilmington Also called E I Du Pont De Nemours & Co *(G-10300)*
Dupont, Wilmington Also called Du Pont Delaware Inc *(G-10242)*
Dupont, Wilmington Also called Du Pont Chem Enrgy Oprtons Inc *(G-10241)*
Dupont, Newark Also called E I Du Pont De Nemours & Co *(G-6492)*
Dupont, New Castle Also called E I Du Pont De Nemours & Co *(G-5271)*
Dupont Accounts Payable, Wilmington Also called E I Du Pont De Nemours & Co *(G-10285)*
Dupont Asia Pacific Limited (HQ) 302 774-1000
974 Centre Rd Wilmington (19805) *(G-10248)*
Dupont Athntcation Systems LLC 800 345-9999
4417 Lancaster Pike Wilmington (19805) *(G-10249)*
Dupont Aviation Corp 302 996-8000
199 N Dupont Hwy New Castle (19720) *(G-5266)*
Dupont Building Innovations, Wilmington Also called E I Du Pont De Nemours & Co *(G-10284)*
Dupont Capital Management Corp 302 477-6000
1 Righter Pkwy Ste 3200 Wilmington (19803) *(G-10250)*
Dupont Country Club, Wilmington Also called Rockland Sports LLC *(G-12454)*
Dupont De Nemours Inc (PA) 302 774-1000
974 Centre Rd Wilmington (19805) *(G-10251)*
Dupont De Nemours Inc 302 999-7932
4250 Lancaster Pike Wilmington (19805) *(G-10252)*
Dupont De Nemours Ei & Co 302 659-1079
1238 Lynnbury Woods Rd Dover (19904) *(G-1487)*
Dupont Displays Inc (HQ) 805 562-9293
974 Centre Rd Wilmington (19805) *(G-10253)*
Dupont Esl Security 302 695-1657
200 Powder Mill Rd Wilmington (19803) *(G-10254)*
Dupont Experimental Station, Wilmington Also called E I Du Pont De Nemours & Co *(G-10302)*
Dupont Flaments - Americas LLC 302 774-1000
974 Centre Rd Wilmington (19805) *(G-10255)*
Dupont Industrial Biosciences, Wilmington Also called E I Du Pont De Nemours & Co *(G-10286)*
Dupont North America Inc 302 774-1000
1007 N Market St Wilmington (19801) *(G-10256)*
Dupont Nutrition and Health 302 451-0112
1301 Ogletown Rd Newark (19711) *(G-6478)*
Dupont Nutrition Usa Inc 302 774-1000
974 Centre Rd Wilmington (19805) *(G-10257)*
Dupont Personal Protection, Wilmington Also called Dupont Specialty Pdts USA LLC *(G-10263)*
Dupont Prfmce Coatings Inc 302 892-1064
4417 Lncaster Pike Barley Wilmington (19805) *(G-10258)*
Dupont Prfmce Elastomers LLC (HQ) 302 774-1000
4417 Lancaster Pike # 72 Wilmington (19805) *(G-10259)*
Dupont Specialty Pdts USA LLC 302 774-1000
350 Bellevue Rd Newark (19713) *(G-6479)*
Dupont Specialty Pdts USA LLC 302 451-0717
5 Tralee Industrial Park Newark (19711) *(G-6480)*
Dupont Specialty Pdts USA LLC (HQ) 302 774-1000
974 Centre Rd Wilmington (19805) *(G-10260)*
Dupont Specialty Pdts USA LLC 302 774-1000
974 Centre Rd Chestnu Chestnut Run Wilmington (19805) *(G-10261)*
Dupont Specialty Pdts USA LLC 302 695-3295
Rising Sun Ln Rr 141 Wilmington (19803) *(G-10262)*
Dupont Specialty Pdts USA LLC 302 774-1000
974 Centre Rd Ches Chestnut Run Wilmington (19805) *(G-10263)*
Dupont Stine Haskell RES Ctr, Newark Also called E I Du Pont De Nemours & Co *(G-6489)*
Dupont Tate Lyle Bio Pdts LLC 865 408-1962
1007 Market St Fl 2 Wilmington (19898) *(G-10264)*
Dupont Txtles Intriors Del Inc (HQ) 302 774-1000
974 Centre Rd Wilmington (19805) *(G-10265)*
Duque Nieva MD PA 302 838-9712
121 Becks Woods Dr Bear (19701) *(G-130)*
Duque Nieva MD PA (PA) 302 655-2048
1010 N Bancroft Pkwy L3 Wilmington (19805) *(G-10266)*
Duque Nieva MD PA 302 655-5661
12 Trolley Sq Ste B Wilmington (19806) *(G-10267)*

(PA)=Parent Co (HQ)=Headquarters (DH)=Div Headquarters   2020 Harris Directory of Delaware Businesses

Durafiber Tech DFT Entps Inc (HQ) — 704 912-3770
  300 Delaware Ave Ste 1100 Wilmington (19801) *(G-10268)*
Duralex Usa Inc — 302 326-4804
  802 Centerpoint Blvd New Castle (19720) *(G-5267)*
Durkee Automotive Inc — 302 798-5656
  8400 Governor Printz Blvd Claymont (19703) *(G-737)*
Durrell Sandblasting & Pntg Co — 302 836-1113
  829 Salem Church Rd Newark (19702) *(G-6481)*
Dushuttle Richard P MD PA — 302 678-8447
  240 Beiser Blvd Ste 101 Dover (19904) *(G-1488)*
Dust Away Cleaning Svcs Inc — 302 658-8803
  700 Cornell Dr Ste E1 Wilmington (19801) *(G-10269)*
Dust Your Stuff Cleaning Svc, Dover Also called Maude Burton *(G-1830)*
Dustntime — 302 858-7876
  36181 Field Ln Rehoboth Beach (19971) *(G-7922)*
Dutch Village Motel Inc — 302 328-6246
  111 S Dupont Hwy New Castle (19720) *(G-5268)*
Dvhd Inc — 302 584-3547
  1716 Shallcross Ave Ste 2 Wilmington (19806) *(G-10270)*
Dxc Technology Company — 302 391-2762
  645 Paper Mill Rd Newark (19711) *(G-6482)*
Dxl, Wilmington Also called Dojupa LLC *(G-10185)*
Dycom Industries Inc — 302 613-0958
  34 Blevins Dr Ste 5 New Castle (19720) *(G-5269)*
Dynamic Converters LLC — 302 454-9203
  122 Sandy Dr Ste F Newark (19713) *(G-6483)*
Dynamic Devices LLC — 302 994-2401
  8 Lewis Cir Wilmington (19804) *(G-10271)*
Dynamic Packet Corp — 302 448-2222
  40 E Main St Ste 4000 Newark (19711) *(G-6484)*
Dynamic Physical Therapy, Newark Also called Dynamic Therapy Services LLC *(G-6486)*
Dynamic Recycling Enterprise, Wilmington Also called Delaware Valley Group LLC *(G-10095)*
Dynamic Support Services Inc — 202 820-3113
  1209 N Orange St Wilmington (19801) *(G-10272)*
Dynamic Therapy Services LLC — 302 280-6953
  400 S Central Ave Laurel (19956) *(G-3225)*
Dynamic Therapy Services LLC — 302 691-5603
  550 Stanton Christn Rd # 203 Newark (19713) *(G-6485)*
Dynamic Therapy Services LLC — 302 526-2148
  487 S Queen St Dover (19904) *(G-1489)*
Dynamic Therapy Services LLC — 302 376-4315
  432 E Main St Middletown (19709) *(G-4046)*
Dynamic Therapy Services LLC — 302 778-0810
  305 N Union St 101 Wilmington (19805) *(G-10273)*
Dynamic Therapy Services LLC — 302 544-4388
  1218 Beaver Brook Plz A New Castle (19720) *(G-5270)*
Dynamic Therapy Services LLC — 302 566-6624
  2000 Midway Dr Harrington (19952) *(G-2836)*
Dynamic Therapy Services LLC — 302 703-2355
  1415 Savannah Rd Unit 1 Lewes (19958) *(G-3476)*
Dynamic Therapy Services LLC — 302 292-3454
  2717 Pulaski Hwy Newark (19702) *(G-6486)*
Dynamic Therapy Services LLC — 302 998-9880
  4709 Kirkwood Hwy Wilmington (19808) *(G-10274)*
Dynamic Therapy Services LLC — 302 834-1550
  1651-53 Pulaski Hwy Bear (19701) *(G-131)*
E & J Trucking Inc — 302 349-4284
  14907 Nichols Run Rd Greenwood (19950) *(G-2733)*
E & M Enterprises Inc — 302 736-6391
  5102 N Dupont Hwy Dover (19901) *(G-1490)*
E A Slack Bus Service Inc — 302 697-2012
  751 Oak Point School Rd Camden Wyoming (19934) *(G-632)*
E A Zando Custom Designs Inc — 302 684-4601
  210 Chandler St Milton (19968) *(G-4900)*
E B D Management Inc — 302 428-1313
  4001 Kennett Pike Ste 10 Wilmington (19807) *(G-10275)*
E C I Motorsports Inc — 302 239-6376
  9 Polaris Dr Newark (19711) *(G-6487)*
E D Custom Contracting Inc — 302 653-2646
  94 Green Heather Ln Clayton (19938) *(G-844)*
E D I S Interiors, Wilmington Also called Chrystal Holdings *(G-9693)*
E E Rosser Inc — 302 762-9643
  5109 Governor Printz Blvd Wilmington (19809) *(G-10276)*
E Earle Downing Inc — 302 656-9908
  1221 Bowers St Ste 5 Wilmington (19802) *(G-10277)*
E F AG Products & Service — 302 945-2415
  26805 Anderson Corner Rd Harbeson (19951) *(G-2782)*
E I Du Pont De Nemours & Co (HQ) — 302 485-3000
  974 Centre Rd Bldg 735 Wilmington (19805) *(G-10278)*
E I Du Pont De Nemours & Co. — 302 999-3301
  702 Canter Rd Wilmington (19810) *(G-10279)*
E I Du Pont De Nemours & Co. — 302 695-7141
  407 Cheer Ct Bear (19701) *(G-132)*
E I Du Pont De Nemours & Co. — 302 774-1000
  970 Centre Rd 709 Wilmington (19805) *(G-10280)*
E I Du Pont De Nemours & Co. — 302 892-8832
  4417 Lancaster Pike Wilmington (19805) *(G-10281)*
E I Du Pont De Nemours & Co. — 302 239-9424
  6 Meteor Ln Newark (19711) *(G-6488)*
E I Du Pont De Nemours & Co — 302 774-1000
  4117 Lancaster Pike Wilmington (19805) *(G-10282)*
E I Du Pont De Nemours & Co — 302 999-2826
  974 Centre Rd Bldg 730 Wilmington (19805) *(G-10283)*
E I Du Pont De Nemours & Co — 302 892-8832
  4417 Lancaster Pike 735 Wilmington (19805) *(G-10284)*
E I Du Pont De Nemours & Co — 302 774-1000
  1090 Elkton Rd Newark (19711) *(G-6489)*
E I Du Pont De Nemours & Co — 615 847-6920
  P.O. Box 80040 Wilmington (19880) *(G-10285)*
E I Du Pont De Nemours & Co — 302 695-7228
  200 Power Mill Rd Wilmington (19803) *(G-10286)*
E I Du Pont De Nemours & Co — 843 335-5934
  1 Righter Pkwy Wilmington (19803) *(G-10287)*
E I Du Pont De Nemours & Co — 302 774-1000
  Chestnut Run Plz Bldg 7 Wilmington (19805) *(G-10288)*
E I Du Pont De Nemours & Co — 844 773-2436
  1007 Market St Wilmington (19898) *(G-10289)*
E I Du Pont De Nemours & Co — 800 441-7515
  974 Chestnut Run Plz B Wilmington (19805) *(G-10290)*
E I Du Pont De Nemours & Co — 302 999-4356
  Chestnt Run Plz 708 141 Wilmington (19805) *(G-10291)*
E I Du Pont De Nemours & Co — 302 792-4371
  300 Delaware Ave Wilmington (19801) *(G-10292)*
E I Du Pont De Nemours & Co — 302 996-4000
  Barley Mill Plaza Wilmington (19898) *(G-10293)*
E I Du Pont De Nemours & Co — 302 774-1000
  974 Centre Rd Wilmington (19805) *(G-10294)*
E I Du Pont De Nemours & Co — 302 774-1000
  1007 Mkt St De Nmurs Bldg Newark (19702) *(G-6490)*
E I Du Pont De Nemours & Co — 302 774-1000
  Rt 141 Lancaster Pike Wilmington (19898) *(G-10295)*
E I Du Pont De Nemours & Co — 302 888-0200
  901 N Market St Wilmington (19801) *(G-10296)*
E I Du Pont De Nemours & Co — 302 654-8198
  1011 Centre Rd Ste 200 Wilmington (19805) *(G-10297)*
E I Du Pont De Nemours & Co — 302 774-1000
  22 Barley Mill Dr Wilmington (19807) *(G-10298)*
E I Du Pont De Nemours & Co — 302 774-1000
  Corporate Data Ctr Wilmington (19899) *(G-10299)*
E I Du Pont De Nemours & Co — 302 999-4329
  Faulkland Rd & Centre Rd Wilmington (19808) *(G-10300)*
E I Du Pont De Nemours & Co — 302 366-5763
  1090 Elkton Rd Newark (19711) *(G-6491)*
E I Du Pont De Nemours & Co — 302 892-5655
  4417 Lancaster Pike Wilmington (19805) *(G-10301)*
E I Du Pont De Nemours & Co — 302 695-3742
  200 Powder Mill Rd Wilmington (19803) *(G-10302)*
E I Du Pont De Nemours & Co — 302 999-5072
  4417 Lancaster Pike Wilmington (19805) *(G-10303)*
E I Du Pont De Nemours & Co — 805 562-5307
  4417 Lancaster Pike Wilmington (19805) *(G-10304)*
E I Du Pont De Nemours & Co — 302 774-1000
  4417 Lancaster Pike Ste 2 Wilmington (19805) *(G-10305)*
E I Du Pont De Nemours & Co — 302 452-9000
  242 Chapman Rd Newark (19702) *(G-6492)*
E I Du Pont De Nemours & Co — 302 695-5300
  Experimentl Statn Bdg 400 Wilmington (19880) *(G-10306)*
E I Du Pont De Nemours & Co — 302 658-7796
  4417 Lancaster Pike Wilmington (19805) *(G-10307)*
E I Du Pont De Nemours & Co — 302 774-1000
  Chestnut Run Plz Bldg 722 Wilmington (19805) *(G-10308)*
E I Du Pont De Nemours & Co — 302 772-0016
  1001 Lambson Ln New Castle (19720) *(G-5271)*
E M C Process Company Inc — 302 999-9204
  1663 E Ayre St Wilmington (19804) *(G-10309)*
E N T Associates — 302 674-3752
  826 S Governors Ave Dover (19904) *(G-1491)*
E W Brown Inc — 302 652-6612
  1202 E 16th St Wilmington (19802) *(G-10310)*
E Z Cash of Delaware Inc (PA) — 302 846-2920
  300 N Bi State Blvd Ste 1 Delmar (19940) *(G-995)*
E Z Cash of Delaware Inc — 302 424-4013
  658 N Dupont Blvd Milford (19963) *(G-4397)*
E&N Surgical LLC — 860 471-0786
  251 Little Falls Dr Wilmington (19808) *(G-10311)*
E-Carauctions LLC (PA) — 302 677-1552
  1602 N Dupont Hwy New Castle (19720) *(G-5272)*
E-Commerce, Wilmington Also called Bbest LLC *(G-9269)*
E-Commerce, Wilmington Also called Lnbe LLC *(G-11417)*
E-Dmz Security LLC — 302 791-9370
  501 Silverside Rd Ste 143 Wilmington (19809) *(G-10312)*
E-Industrial Suppliers LLC — 302 251-6210
  2207 Concord Pike Ste 648 Wilmington (19803) *(G-10313)*
E-Lyte Transportation — 808 269-0283
  8 The Grn Dover (19901) *(G-1492)*
E-Merge Systems Inc — 302 894-3860
  254 Cadmin Rd Newark (19702) *(G-6493)*
E2e LLC — 703 906-5353
  177 Thompson Dr Ste 888 Hockessin (19707) *(G-3014)*

ALPHABETIC SECTION Easy Analytic Software Inc

Eager Gear 302 727-5831
19413 Jingle Shell Way # 6 Lewes (19958) ***(G-3477)***
Eagle 97.7 FM, Milford *Also called Wafl Wyus Broadcasting Inc* ***(G-4592)***
Eagle Bldg & Grounds Maint LLC 302 264-7058
3507 Sudlersville Rd Clayton (19938) ***(G-845)***
Eagle Building and Grounds 302 508-5403
2817 Shaws Corner Rd Clayton (19938) ***(G-846)***
Eagle Erectors Inc 302 832-9586
3500 Wrangle Hill Rd Bear (19701) ***(G-133)***
Eagle Eye America Inc 302 392-3600
405 Bergenia Loop Bear (19701) ***(G-134)***
Eagle Foodservice, Clayton *Also called Metal Msters Fdservice Eqp Inc* ***(G-863)***
Eagle Group, Clayton *Also called Eagle Mhc Company* ***(G-847)***
Eagle Hospitality Group LLC 302 678-8388
201 Stover Blvd Dover (19901) ***(G-1493)***
Eagle Limousine Inc (PA) 302 325-4200
77 Mccullough Dr Ste 5 New Castle (19720) ***(G-5273)***
Eagle Mhc Company 302 653-3000
100 Industrial Blvd Clayton (19938) ***(G-847)***
Eagle One Federal Credit Union 302 798-7749
3301 Philadelphia Pike Claymont (19703) ***(G-738)***
Eagle Plaza Associates Inc 302 999-0708
234 N James St Wilmington (19804) ***(G-10314)***
Eagle Power and Equipment Corp 302 652-3028
2211 N Du Pont Pkwy New Castle (19720) ***(G-5274)***
Eagle Transportation, New Castle *Also called Eagle Limousine Inc* ***(G-5273)***
Eagle Us Inc 484 913-0300
1105 N Market St Ste 1300 Wilmington (19801) ***(G-10315)***
Eagle's Nest, Wilmington *Also called Bright Horizons Chld Ctrs LLC* ***(G-9474)***
Ean Holdings LLC 302 422-1167
411 N Rehoboth Blvd Milford (19963) ***(G-4398)***
Ean Holdings LLC 302 674-5553
580 S Bay Rd Dover (19901) ***(G-1494)***
Ean Holdings LLC 302 376-5606
5207 Summit Bridge Rd Middletown (19709) ***(G-4047)***
Ear Enterprise LLC 302 836-8334
123 Pinion Pl Bear (19701) ***(G-135)***
Earle Teate Music (PA) 302 736-1937
3098 N Dupont Hwy Dover (19901) ***(G-1495)***
Earls Place LLC 302 538-8909
9989 S Dupont Hwy Ste 4 Felton (19943) ***(G-2289)***
EARLY CHILDHOOD ASSISTANCE PRO, Wilmington *Also called Hilltop Lutheran Neighborhd* ***(G-10910)***
EARLY CHILDHOOD EDUCATION ARTS, Wilmington *Also called Christina Cultural Arts Center* ***(G-9690)***
Early Childhood Lab 302 857-6731
1200 N Dupont Hwy Dover (19901) ***(G-1496)***
Early Essentials, Middletown *Also called Elaine Leonard* ***(G-4052)***
Early Foundation Preschool, Wilmington *Also called Early Foundations Therapeutic* ***(G-10316)***
Early Foundations Therapeutic 302 384-6905
2814 W 2nd St Wilmington (19805) ***(G-10316)***
Early Learning Center 302 831-0584
1218 B St Wilmington (19801) ***(G-10317)***
Early Learning Center 302 239-3033
7250 Lancaster Pike Hockessin (19707) ***(G-3015)***
Earth Wind and Expedition, Wilmington *Also called Megan Hegenbarth* ***(G-11623)***
Earthscapes LLC 302 678-0478
6336 Pearsons Corner Rd Dover (19904) ***(G-1497)***
East Coast Auto Body Inc 302 265-6830
216 South St Dover (19904) ***(G-1498)***
East Coast Builders Inc 302 629-3551
Rr 1 Box 350 Seaford (19973) ***(G-8229)***
East Coast Cleaning Co LLC 302 762-6820
528 Ruxton Dr Wilmington (19809) ***(G-10318)***
East Coast Cstm Cabinetry LLC 302 245-3040
23636 Saulsbury Ln Georgetown (19947) ***(G-2517)***
East Coast Elastomerics Inc 302 524-8004
38298 London Ave Unit 4 Selbyville (19975) ***(G-8484)***
East Coast Electric Inc 302 998-1577
824 Kiamensi Rd Wilmington (19804) ***(G-10319)***
East Coast Erectors Inc 302 323-1800
1144 River Rd New Castle (19720) ***(G-5275)***
East Coast Games Inc 302 838-0669
24 Eaton Pl Bear (19701) ***(G-136)***
East Coast Kite Sports 302 359-0749
10 N Main St Magnolia (19962) ***(G-3890)***
East Coast Lawn Services Inc 302 453-8400
2860 Ogletown Rd Apt 2 Newark (19713) ***(G-6494)***
East Coast Machine Works 302 349-5180
12773 Tuckers Rd Greenwood (19950) ***(G-2734)***
East Coast Minority Supplier 302 656-3337
610 W 8th St Wilmington (19801) ***(G-10320)***
East Coast Perennials Inc 302 945-5853
30366 Cordrey Rd Millsboro (19966) ***(G-4683)***
East Coast Poured Walls Inc 302 430-0630
331 S Rehoboth Blvd Milford (19963) ***(G-4399)***
East Coast Property MGT Inc (HQ) 302 629-8612
977 E Masten Cir Milford (19963) ***(G-4400)***
East Coast Seed LLC 302 856-7018
17741 Davis Rd Georgetown (19947) ***(G-2518)***
East Coast Signs & Graph 302 335-5824
853 S Bowers Rd Milford (19963) ***(G-4401)***
East Coast Stainless Inc 302 366-0675
30 Albe Dr Ste E Newark (19702) ***(G-6495)***
East Coast Stainless & Alloys 302 366-0675
30 Albe Dr Ste E Newark (19702) ***(G-6496)***
East Millsboro Elem School Pto 302 238-0176
29343 Iron Branch Rd Millsboro (19966) ***(G-4684)***
East Pointe Apartments, Claymont *Also called Rp Management Inc* ***(G-801)***
East Side Cmmty Lrng Cntr Fndt 302 762-5834
3000 N Claymont St Wilmington (19802) ***(G-10321)***
East Sussex Moose Lodge 302 436-2088
35993 Zion Church Rd Frankford (19945) ***(G-2361)***
East Sussex Public Brdcstg 302 644-7385
13 Breakwater Dr Rehoboth Beach (19971) ***(G-7923)***
East West Engineering Inc 302 528-0652
130 Wynnefield Rd Bear (19701) ***(G-137)***
Easter Seal Delaware (PA) 302 324-4444
61 Corporate Cir New Castle (19720) ***(G-5276)***
Easter Seal Delaware 302 856-7364
22317 Dupont Blvd Georgetown (19947) ***(G-2519)***
Easter Seal Delaware 302 678-3353
100 Enterprise Pl Ste 1 Dover (19904) ***(G-1499)***
Eastern Athletic Clubs LLC 302 239-6688
100 Fitness Way Hockessin (19707) ***(G-3016)***
Eastern Auto Body Inc 302 731-1200
700 Elizabeth Ln Bear (19701) ***(G-138)***
Eastern Bison Association 434 660-6036
10685 Buffalo Rd Greenwood (19950) ***(G-2735)***
Eastern Group Inc 302 737-6603
931 S Chapel St Newark (19713) ***(G-6497)***
Eastern Home Improvements Inc (PA) 302 655-9920
3112 Lancaster Ave Wilmington (19805) ***(G-10322)***
Eastern Hospitality Management 302 322-9480
215 S Dupont Hwy New Castle (19720) ***(G-5277)***
Eastern Hwy Specialists Inc 302 777-7673
920 N Church St Wilmington (19801) ***(G-10323)***
Eastern Industrial Svcs Inc 302 455-1400
196 Quigley Blvd Ste A New Castle (19720) ***(G-5278)***
Eastern Lift Truck Co Inc 302 286-6660
137 Sandy Dr Newark (19713) ***(G-6498)***
Eastern Lift Truck Co Inc 302 875-4031
11512 Commercial Ln Laurel (19956) ***(G-3226)***
Eastern Mail Transport Inc 302 838-0500
900 Julian Ln Bear (19701) ***(G-139)***
Eastern Marine, Newark *Also called Eastern Group Inc* ***(G-6497)***
Eastern Metals Inc 302 454-7886
679 Dawson Dr Newark (19713) ***(G-6499)***
Eastern Ornamentals LLC 302 684-8733
24675 Bakerfield Rd Milford (19963) ***(G-4402)***
Eastern Percision, Newark *Also called Trimble Navigation Limited* ***(G-7593)***
Eastern Property Group Inc 302 764-7112
3408 Miller Rd C7 Wilmington (19802) ***(G-10324)***
Eastern Prosperity Group 302 764-7112
3408 Miller Rd Wilmington (19802) ***(G-10325)***
Eastern Shore Energy Inc 302 697-9230
11550 Willow Grove Rd Camden (19934) ***(G-566)***
Eastern Shore Equipment Co 302 697-3300
Vepco Indus Park Bldg 7 Camden Wyoming (19934) ***(G-633)***
Eastern Shore Gastroenterology, Lewes *Also called Bayview Endoscopy Center* ***(G-3365)***
Eastern Shore Leasing, Seaford *Also called Esl Inc* ***(G-8239)***
Eastern Shore Lite Industries 302 653-8687
5908 Judith Rd Clayton (19938) ***(G-848)***
Eastern Shore Metal Detectors 302 628-1985
20380 Wesley Church Rd Seaford (19973) ***(G-8230)***
Eastern Shore Metals LLC 302 629-6629
102 Park Ave Seaford (19973) ***(G-8231)***
Eastern Shore Natural Gas Co 302 734-6716
909 Silver Lake Blvd Dover (19904) ***(G-1500)***
Eastern Shore Porch Patio Inc 302 436-9520
17 Mason Dr Selbyville (19975) ***(G-8485)***
Eastern Shore Poultry Company 302 855-1350
21724 Broad Creek Ave Georgetown (19947) ***(G-2520)***
Eastern Shore Veterinary Hosp 302 875-5941
32384 Sussex Hwy Laurel (19956) ***(G-3227)***
Eastern States Cnstr Svc Inc 302 995-2259
702 First State Blvd Wilmington (19804) ***(G-10326)***
Eastern States Develpment Inc 302 998-0683
702 First State Blvd Wilmington (19804) ***(G-10327)***
Eastlake Apartments LLC 302 764-0215
2412 Thatcher St Wilmington (19802) ***(G-10328)***
Eastlake Village, Wilmington *Also called Eastlake Apartments LLC* ***(G-10328)***
Eastside Bluprt Cmnty Dev Corp 302 384-2350
121 N Poplar St Wilmington (19801) ***(G-10329)***
Easy Analytic Software Inc 302 762-4271
21 Paladin Dr Wilmington (19802) ***(G-10330)***

ALPHABETIC

Easy Corp Ltd....302 824-0109
3422 Old Capitol Trl Wilmington (19808) ***(G-10331)***
Easy Diagnostics....302 674-4089
160 Greentree Dr Ste 101 Dover (19904) ***(G-1501)***
Easy Lawn Inc....302 815-6500
9599 Nantcke Bus Pk Dr # 1 Greenwood (19950) ***(G-2736)***
Ebanks Construction LLC....302 420-7584
507 Florence Fields Ln New Castle (19720) ***(G-5279)***
EBc Carpet Services Corp....302 995-7461
1300 First State Blvd 1 Wilmington (19804) ***(G-10332)***
Ebc National Inc....302 995-7461
1300 First State Blvd Wilmington (19804) ***(G-10333)***
Ebc Systems LLC....302 472-1896
1 Ave Of The Arts Wilmington (19801) ***(G-10334)***
Ebenezer Preschool, Newark *Also called Ebenezer United Methdst Chruch* ***(G-6500)***
Ebenezer United Methdst Chruch....302 731-9495
525 Polly Drummond Hl Rd Newark (19711) ***(G-6500)***
Ebube Group & Co LLC....215 821-7490
40 E Main St Newark (19711) ***(G-6501)***
Ece Weatherguard, Selbyville *Also called East Coast Elastomerics Inc* ***(G-8484)***
Ecg Industries Inc (PA)....302 453-0535
254 Chapman Rd Ste 203 Newark (19702) ***(G-6502)***
Echelon Interiors LLC....302 519-9151
55 Cascade Ln Ste A Rehoboth Beach (19971) ***(G-7924)***
Echelon Studios Inc (PA)....800 208-9052
19c Trolley Sq Wilmington (19806) ***(G-10335)***
Eckels Family LLC....302 465-5224
141 Hunters Run Blvd Felton (19943) ***(G-2290)***
Eckert Smans Chrin Mellott LLC....302 574-7400
222 Delaware Ave Fl 7 Wilmington (19801) ***(G-10336)***
Eclipes Erection Inc....302 633-1421
330 Water St Wilmington (19804) ***(G-10337)***
Eclipse Software Inc....212 727-1136
908 Greenhill Ave Wilmington (19805) ***(G-10338)***
Eco Plastic Products Del Inc....302 575-9227
18 Germay Dr Wilmington (19804) ***(G-10339)***
Eco SBC 2015-1 REO 167061 LLC....302 652-8013
824 N Market St Wilmington (19801) ***(G-10340)***
Ecomo Inc....412 567-3867
160 Greentree Dr Ste 101 Dover (19904) ***(G-1502)***
Econat Inc....201 925-5239
651 N Broad St Ste 206 Middletown (19709) ***(G-4048)***
Econerd....302 669-9279
117 Zachary Ln Middletown (19709) ***(G-4049)***
Econo Lodge, New Castle *Also called Sun Hotel Inc* ***(G-5742)***
Econo Lodge Inn Suites Resort....302 227-0500
19540 Coastal Hwy Rehoboth Beach (19971) ***(G-7925)***
Economic Laundry Solutions....302 234-7627
14 Cinnamon Dr Hockessin (19707) ***(G-3017)***
Ecsquared Inc....302 750-8554
1801 Forrest Rd Wilmington (19810) ***(G-10341)***
Ed Hileman Drywall Inc....302 436-6277
36722 Roxana Rd Selbyville (19975) ***(G-8486)***
Ed Hunt Inc (PA)....302 339-8443
8 The Grn Ste 9487 Dover (19901) ***(G-1503)***
Ed Oliver Golf Club, Wilmington *Also called Meadowbrook Golf Group Inc* ***(G-11611)***
Ed Turulski Custom Woodworking....302 658-2221
1020 Liberty Rd Wilmington (19804) ***(G-10342)***
Edaura Inc....707 330-9836
1209 N Orange St Wilmington (19801) ***(G-10343)***
Edc LLC....302 645-0777
115 W Market St Fl 2 Lewes (19958) ***(G-3478)***
Edelsohn, Lanny MD, Newark *Also called Neurology Associates PA* ***(G-7095)***
Eden Green LLC....817 999-1570
300 Delaware Ave Ste 210a Wilmington (19801) ***(G-10344)***
Eden Hill Express Care LLC....302 674-1999
200 Banning St Ste 170 Dover (19904) ***(G-1504)***
Eden Hill Medical Center, Dover *Also called Surgical Associates PA* ***(G-2119)***
Eden Hill Medical Center LLC....302 883-0097
200 Banning St Ste 330 Dover (19904) ***(G-1505)***
Eden Land Care....302 379-2405
202 New Rd Unit 7 Wilmington (19805) ***(G-10345)***
Edge Construction Corp....302 778-5200
300 M L King Blvd 300 Wilmington (19801) ***(G-10346)***
Edge Moor Dupont Employees....302 761-2282
104 Hay Rd Wilmington (19809) ***(G-10347)***
Edge Water Tire, Dover *Also called Admiral Tire* ***(G-1087)***
Edgemoor Community Center Inc....302 762-1391
500 Duncan Rd Ofc A Wilmington (19809) ***(G-10348)***
Edgewell Personal Care LLC....302 678-6000
50 N Dupont Hwy Dover (19901) ***(G-1506)***
Edgewell Personal Care Company....302 678-6191
185 Saulsbury Rd Dover (19904) ***(G-1507)***
Edis Building Systems Inc....302 421-5700
110 S Poplar St Ste 400 Wilmington (19801) ***(G-10349)***
Edis Company....302 421-5700
110 S Poplar St Ste 400 Wilmington (19801) ***(G-10350)***
Edit Inc....302 478-7069
1026 Sedwick Dr Wilmington (19803) ***(G-10351)***
Edlyncare LLC....267 474-0486
261 Ann Dr Middletown (19709) ***(G-4050)***
Edokk LLC....305 434-7227
16192 Coastal Hwy Lewes (19958) ***(G-3479)***
Edu-Care Preschool & Daycare, Newark *Also called MI-Dee Inc* ***(G-7022)***
Education Svcs Unlimited LLC....302 650-4210
500 Mckennans Church Rd Wilmington (19808) ***(G-10352)***
Educational Assets Corp....302 288-0149
1011 Centre Rd Ste 320 Wilmington (19805) ***(G-10353)***
Educational Enrichment Center....302 478-8697
730 Halstead Rd Wilmington (19803) ***(G-10354)***
Edufar, Newark *Also called Sygul Inc* ***(G-7524)***
Eduqc LLC....800 346-4646
3500 S Dupont Hwy Dover (19901) ***(G-1508)***
Edward B Bayley DMD....302 766-4633
1610 Sunset Ln Wilmington (19810) ***(G-10355)***
Edward B De Seta & Associates, Wilmington *Also called E B D Management Inc* ***(G-10275)***
Edward B De Seta & Associates....302 428-1313
4001 Kennett Pike Ste 10 Wilmington (19807) ***(G-10356)***
Edward J Henry & Sons Inc....302 658-4324
2300 W 4th St Wilmington (19805) ***(G-10357)***
Edward Land Consulting Inc....302 838-7003
27 Rose Hill Dr Bear (19701) ***(G-140)***
Edward R Bell....302 658-1555
909 Clifford Brown Walk Wilmington (19801) ***(G-10358)***
Edward S Jaoude....302 684-2020
28322 Lwes Georgetown Hwy Milton (19968) ***(G-4901)***
Edward S Yalisove DDS PA....302 658-4124
1111 N Franklin St Wilmington (19806) ***(G-10359)***
Edward Varnes Hardwood Floors....302 292-0919
634 Old Baltimore Pike Newark (19702) ***(G-6503)***
Edwards Paul Crpt Installation....302 672-7847
547 Otis Dr Dover (19901) ***(G-1509)***
Edwin C Katzman MD....302 368-2501
210 Christiana Med Ctr Newark (19702) ***(G-6504)***
Edwin M Mow DPM Facfas....302 424-1760
505 Lakeview Ave Milford (19963) ***(G-4403)***
Edwin S Kuipers DDS....302 455-0333
210 W Park Pl Newark (19711) ***(G-6505)***
Edwin S Kuipers DDS....302 652-3775
300 Foulk Rd Ste 101 Wilmington (19803) ***(G-10360)***
Edwina C Granada MD....302 629-7555
9109 Middleford Rd Seaford (19973) ***(G-8232)***
Edythe L Pridgen....302 652-8887
450 S Hyde Pl Bear (19701) ***(G-141)***
Eec, Wilmington *Also called Educational Enrichment Center* ***(G-10354)***
Eeco Inc (HQ)....302 456-1448
850 Library Ave Ste 204c Newark (19711) ***(G-6506)***
Eecoo LLC....315 503-1477
19 Kris Ct Newark (19702) ***(G-6507)***
Ef Technologies Inc....302 451-1088
119b Sandy Dr Newark (19713) ***(G-6508)***
Effective Advertising Seaford....302 628-1946
511 N Phillips St Seaford (19973) ***(G-8233)***
Efficient Services Inc....302 629-2124
24660 German Rd Seaford (19973) ***(G-8234)***
Efotolabcom Inc....302 984-0807
1900 Superfine Ln Wilmington (19802) ***(G-10361)***
Egg Harbor City Apartments LLC....302 543-6514
9 Courtyard Ln Wilmington (19802) ***(G-10362)***
Eggplant Inc....302 737-1073
1918 Kirkwood Hwy Newark (19711) ***(G-6509)***
Egli, Michelle D Dvm, Dover *Also called Delmarva Equine Clinic* ***(G-1410)***
Egolf Forest Harvesting Inc....302 846-0634
36642 Horsey Church Rd Delmar (19940) ***(G-996)***
Egs Financial Care Inc....800 227-4000
P.O. Box 15110 Wilmington (19850) ***(G-10363)***
Ehlrlich, J C Pest Control, Bridgeville *Also called Rentokil North America Inc* ***(G-519)***
Eichholz Services, Wilmington *Also called Donald Eichholz* ***(G-10195)***
Eisele Celine....302 684-3201
225 Bayport Business Park Milton (19968) ***(G-4902)***
Eisi, New Castle *Also called Eastern Industrial Svcs Inc* ***(G-5278)***
Eitv USA Inc....305 517-7715
501 Silverside Rd Ste 105 Wilmington (19809) ***(G-10364)***
Ej Usa Inc....302 378-1100
401 Industrial Rd Middletown (19709) ***(G-4051)***
EKA Jewelers, Milford *Also called Precision Jewelry Inc* ***(G-4528)***
Ekalt LLC....302 300-4853
20c Trolley Sq Wilmington (19806) ***(G-10365)***
Eksab Corporation....319 371-1669
2140 S Dupont Hwy Camden (19934) ***(G-567)***
Ekww Inc....302 234-2877
720 Yorklyn Rd Ste 100 Hockessin (19707) ***(G-3018)***
El Tiempo Hispano, Newark *Also called Hola Delaware LLC* ***(G-6735)***
Elaine Leonard....302 376-5553
111 Patriot Dr Ste A&B Middletown (19709) ***(G-4052)***
Elanco Inc....302 731-8500
723 Rue Madora Ste 6 Bear (19701) ***(G-142)***

Elayne James Salon & Spa LLC........302 376-5290
462 W Main St Middletown (19709) ***(G-4053)***
Elcoach Inc........302 261-3794
251 Little Falls Dr Wilmington (19808) ***(G-10366)***
Elcriton Inc........864 921-5146
15 Reads Way New Castle (19720) ***(G-5280)***
Eld, Wilmington *Also called Express Legal Documents LLC* ***(G-10463)***
Eldas Kitchen LLC (PA)........925 260-6156
8 The Grn 6947 Dover (19901) ***(G-1510)***
ELDAS KITCHEN COOKING & GRILLI, Dover *Also called Eldas Kitchen LLC* ***(G-1510)***
Elderly Comfort Corporation........302 530-6680
800 N West St Fl 3 Wilmington (19801) ***(G-10367)***
Elderwood Village Dover LLC........516 496-1505
21 N State St Dover (19901) ***(G-1511)***
Elec Integrity........302 388-3430
6253 N Dupont Hwy Dover (19901) ***(G-1512)***
Electric, Kenton *Also called Shure-Line Construction Inc* ***(G-3185)***
Electric Beach Tanning Company........302 730-8266
650 S Bay Rd Dover (19901) ***(G-1513)***
Electric Department, Milford *Also called City of Milford* ***(G-4354)***
Electric Department, Dover *Also called City of Dover* ***(G-1290)***
Electric Motor Repair Svc........302 322-1179
263 Quigley Blvd Ste 12 New Castle (19720) ***(G-5281)***
Electric Motor Wholesale Inc........302 222-2090
2629 Morgans Choice Rd Camden Wyoming (19934) ***(G-634)***
Electric Motor Wholesale Inc........302 653-1844
2575 Morgans Choice Rd Camden Wyoming (19934) ***(G-635)***
Electrical Associates Inc........302 678-1068
959 Hazlettville Rd Hartly (19953) ***(G-2921)***
Electrical Integrity LLC........302 388-3430
117 J And M Dr New Castle (19720) ***(G-5282)***
Electrical Power Systems Inc (PA)........302 325-3502
240a Churchmans Rd New Castle (19720) ***(G-5283)***
Electro Sound Systems Inc........302 543-2292
330 Water St Ste 108 Newport (19804) ***(G-7748)***
Electro Temp Technology, Wilmington *Also called Reil Machines USA Inc* ***(G-12369)***
Electro-Art Sign Company........302 322-1108
107 J And M Dr New Castle (19720) ***(G-5284)***
Electronic Security, Dover *Also called S & B Pro Security LLC* ***(G-2047)***
Electronic Systems Specialist........302 738-4165
Polly Drummond Shr Bldg 1 Newark (19711) ***(G-6510)***
Electronics Exchange Inc........302 322-5401
282 Quigley Blvd New Castle (19720) ***(G-5285)***
Elegance, Newark *Also called Leeber Limited USA* ***(G-6930)***
Elegant Images LLP........302 698-5250
10 S West St Camden (19934) ***(G-568)***
Elegant Stone Veneer LLC........302 547-4780
4 Carriage Ln Newark (19711) ***(G-6511)***
Element........302 645-0777
115 W Market St Lewes (19958) ***(G-3480)***
Element Design Group, Lewes *Also called Edc LLC* ***(G-3478)***
Element Mtls Tech Wlmngton Inc........302 636-0202
1300 First State Blvd Wilmington (19804) ***(G-10368)***
Elementary Workshop Inc........302 656-1498
502 N Pine St Wilmington (19801) ***(G-10369)***
Elements Beauty Supply North........302 738-7732
1309 Churchmans Rd Newark (19713) ***(G-6512)***
Eleuthrian Mlls-Hgley Fndtion........302 658-2400
200 Hagley Rd Wilmington (19807) ***(G-10370)***
Elevate Dvm Inc........302 761-9650
3 Penny Lane Ct Wilmington (19803) ***(G-10371)***
Elevated Studios Hq........302 407-3229
34a Trolley Sq Wilmington (19806) ***(G-10372)***
Elevationtv........978 317-9285
108 W 13th St Wilmington (19801) ***(G-10373)***
Eleven Twenty Two Condominium, New Castle *Also called 1122 Condominium* ***(G-4988)***
Elf Homes Inc........650 918-7829
3616 Kirkwood Hwy Ste A Wilmington (19808) ***(G-10374)***
Elias Mamberg MD........302 428-0337
1301 N Harrison St # 104 Wilmington (19806) ***(G-10375)***
Elison Db 2015-1, Wilmington *Also called Eco SBC 2015-1 REO 167061 LLC* ***(G-10340)***
Elite Auto LLC........302 690-2948
364 E Main St Ste 204 Middletown (19709) ***(G-4054)***
Elite Chemical and Supply Inc........302 366-8900
630 Churchmans Rd Ste 106 Newark (19702) ***(G-6513)***
Elite Cleaning Company, Newark *Also called Elite Commercial Cleaning Inc* ***(G-6514)***
Elite Commercial Cleaning Inc........302 366-8900
630 Churchmans Rd Ste 106 Newark (19702) ***(G-6514)***
Elite Feet LLC........302 464-1028
5238 Summit Bridge Rd Middletown (19709) ***(G-4055)***
Elite Landscape........302 543-7305
414 Meco Dr Wilmington (19804) ***(G-10376)***
Elite Mechanical........302 321-9215
29810 Beach A Landing Rd Dagsboro (19939) ***(G-899)***
Elite Office Staff Inc........302 387-4158
8 The Grn Ste 5421 Dover (19901) ***(G-1514)***
Elite Tax Services LLC........302 256-0401
30b Trolley Sq Wilmington (19806) ***(G-10377)***
Elite Trnspt & Logistics Inc........302 348-8480
300 Delaware Ave Ste 210 Wilmington (19801) ***(G-10378)***
Elizabeth Beverage Company LLC........302 322-9895
650 Ships Landing Way New Castle (19720) ***(G-5286)***
Elizabeth Bottling Company, New Castle *Also called Elizabeth Beverage Company LLC* ***(G-5286)***
Elizabeth C Parberry Dr........302 436-1803
37600 Bearhole Rd Selbyville (19975) ***(G-8487)***
Elizabeth Jackovic MD........302 623-0240
200 Hygeia Dr Newark (19713) ***(G-6515)***
Elizabeth Malbert........302 422-9015
242 Cedar Dr Lincoln (19960) ***(G-3845)***
Elizabeth W Murphey School Inc........302 734-7478
42 Kings Hwy Dover (19901) ***(G-1515)***
Elkington I Kent DDS........302 629-3008
218 Pennsylvania Ave Seaford (19973) ***(G-8235)***
ELKS LODGE, Seaford *Also called Benevolent Protectve Ordr Elks* ***(G-8165)***
ELKS LODGE 1903, Dover *Also called Benevlent Prtective Order Elks* ***(G-1191)***
Elks Lodge 307, Wilmington *Also called Wilmington Elks Home Inc* ***(G-13230)***
Elkton Exterminating Co Inc........302 368-9116
1040 S Chapel St Newark (19702) ***(G-6516)***
Ellingsen & Associates........302 650-6437
113 Barksdale Pro Ctr Newark (19711) ***(G-6517)***
Elliott Holdings Corporation........650 241-8646
651 N Broad St Ste 20512 Middletown (19709) ***(G-4056)***
Elliott John........302 846-2487
36411 August Rd Delmar (19940) ***(G-997)***
Ellis Fall Sfety Solutions LLC........302 571-8470
306 Country Club Dr Wilmington (19803) ***(G-10379)***
Ellis Ladder Improvements........302 571-8470
306 Country Club Dr Wilmington (19803) ***(G-10380)***
Ellmore Auto Collision........302 762-2301
4921 Governor Printz Blvd Wilmington (19809) ***(G-10381)***
Elmer Schultz Services Inc........302 655-8900
36 Belmont Ave Wilmington (19804) ***(G-10382)***
Elohim Community Dev Corp........302 856-4551
40 Ingramtown Rd Georgetown (19947) ***(G-2521)***
Elrod, Michael E DC, Lewes *Also called Lewes Chiropractic Center* ***(G-3597)***
Els........302 312-3645
13 Dunleary Dr Bear (19701) ***(G-143)***
Els Tire Service Inc........302 834-1997
2724 Pulaski Hwy Newark (19702) ***(G-6518)***
Elsicon Inc........302 266-7030
5 Innovation Way Ste 100 Newark (19711) ***(G-6519)***
Elsmere Fire Co 1 Inc........302 999-0183
1107 Kirkwood Hwy Wilmington (19805) ***(G-10383)***
Elsmere Presbyterian Church........302 998-6365
606 New Rd Wilmington (19805) ***(G-10384)***
Eluktronics Inc........302 380-3242
9 Albe Dr Ste E Newark (19702) ***(G-6520)***
Elva G Pearson MD........302 623-4144
4735 Ogletown Stanton Rd Newark (19713) ***(G-6521)***
Elvin Schrock and Sons Inc........302 349-4384
10725 Beach Hwy Greenwood (19950) ***(G-2737)***
Elwyn........302 658-8860
321 E 11th St Fl 1 Wilmington (19801) ***(G-10385)***
Elzufon Austin Reardon Tarlov........302 644-0144
1413 Savannah Rd Unit 1 Lewes (19958) ***(G-3481)***
Elzufon Austin Reardon Tarlov (PA)........302 428-3181
300 Delaware Ave Ste 1700 Wilmington (19801) ***(G-10386)***
Em Photonics Inc........302 456-9003
51 E Main St Ste 203 Newark (19711) ***(G-6522)***
Emblem At Christiana Clubhouse........302 525-6692
1150 Helen Dr Newark (19702) ***(G-6523)***
Embrace Home Loans Inc........302 635-7998
5341 Limestone Rd Ste 101 Wilmington (19808) ***(G-10387)***
Embroid Me LLC........302 993-0204
4385 Kirkwood Hwy Wilmington (19808) ***(G-10388)***
Embroidery Enterprises, Milford *Also called Andrew Pipon* ***(G-4307)***
Emeca/Spe Usa LLC........302 875-0760
200 W 10th St Laurel (19956) ***(G-3228)***
Emendo Bio Inc........516 595-1849
1811 Silverside Rd Wilmington (19810) ***(G-10389)***
Ementum Inc (PA)........866 984-1999
2841 S Bay Shore Dr Mlton Milton Milton (19968) ***(G-4903)***
Emerald Bioagriculture Corp (PA)........517 882-7370
726 Yorklyn Rd Ste 420 Hockessin (19707) ***(G-3019)***
Emerald City Wash World........302 734-1230
730 W Division St Dover (19904) ***(G-1516)***
Emerald Green........302 836-6909
992 Port Penn Rd Middletown (19709) ***(G-4057)***
Emerald Industries LLC........302 450-1416
4157 Concord Pike Wilmington (19803) ***(G-10390)***
Emerald Lawn and Ldscpg LLC........302 228-1468
701 Lindsay Ln Milford (19963) ***(G-4404)***
Emergency Medical Mgmnt, Wilmington *Also called Douglas Morrow* ***(G-10213)***
Emergency Room, Wilmington *Also called Kathleen M Cronan MD* ***(G-11229)***
Emergncy Response Protocol LLC........302 994-2600
101 W Ayre St Wilmington (19804) ***(G-10391)***

A L P H A B E T I C

(PA)=Parent Co (HQ)=Headquarters (DH)=Div Headquarters
2020 Harris Directory of Delaware Businesses
639

Emeritus Corporation....302 674-4407
150 Saulsbury Rd Dover (19904) *(G-1517)*
Emerson & Klair....302 239-6362
853 Old Wilmington Rd Hockessin (19707) *(G-3020)*
Emil W Tetzner D M D....302 744-9900
804 S State St Ste 1 Dover (19901) *(G-1518)*
Emlyn Construction Co....302 697-8247
1341 Walnut Shade Rd Dover (19901) *(G-1519)*
Emma Jefferies Day Care....302 762-3235
603 W 39th St Wilmington (19802) *(G-10392)*
Emmanuel Diningroom, Wilmington *Also called Ministry of Caring Inc (G-11707)*
Emment A Oat Contractor Inc....302 999-1567
501 W Newport Pike Wilmington (19804) *(G-10393)*
Emmert Auction Associates....302 227-1433
4270d Rehoboth Svc Ctr Rehoboth Beach (19971) *(G-7926)*
Emory & Marier PA....302 422-2020
771 E Masten Cir Ste 107 Milford (19963) *(G-4405)*
Emory Agency Inc....302 855-2100
20650 Dupont Blvd Georgetown (19947) *(G-2522)*
Emory Hill, New Castle *Also called Mid-Atlantic Realty Co Inc (G-5526)*
Emory Hill & Company (PA)....302 322-4400
10 Corporate Cir Ste 100 New Castle (19720) *(G-5287)*
Emory Hill RE Svcs Inc (PA)....302 322-9500
10 Corporate Cir New Castle (19720) *(G-5288)*
Emory Massage Therapy....302 290-0003
155 Willis Rd Apt G Dover (19901) *(G-1520)*
Empire Building and Dev, Newark *Also called Empire Construction Company (G-6524)*
Empire Construction Company....302 235-2093
1 Tenby Chase Dr Newark (19711) *(G-6524)*
Empire Flippers LLC....323 638-0438
427 N Tatnall St 34425 Wilmington (19801) *(G-10394)*
Empire Investments Inc....302 838-0631
201 Jestan Blvd New Castle (19720) *(G-5289)*
Employers Bench Inc....973 757-1912
40 W Main St Ste 855 Christiana (19702) *(G-667)*
Empower Materials Inc....302 225-0100
91 Lukens Dr Ste E New Castle (19720) *(G-5290)*
Empowered Therapy Services....302 234-4820
118 Dandelion Dr Hockessin (19707) *(G-3021)*
Emulsion Products Company....302 629-3505
25938 Nanticoke Ave Seaford (19973) *(G-8236)*
Emw Publications....302 438-9879
351 Mockingbird Hill Rd Hockessin (19707) *(G-3022)*
Encima Group Inc....302 352-1714
1 Innovation Way Ste 400 Newark (19711) *(G-6525)*
Enclave Digital Development Co (PA)....203 807-0400
16192 Coastal Hwy Lewes (19958) *(G-3482)*
Encompass Elements, New Castle *Also called Fox Specialties Inc (G-5326)*
Encompass Health Corporation....302 464-3400
250 E Hampden Rd Middletown (19709) *(G-4058)*
Encore Designs Inc....302 798-5678
1607 Walton Rd Wilmington (19803) *(G-10395)*
Encross LLC....302 351-2593
1521 Concord Pike Ste 301 Wilmington (19803) *(G-10396)*
Endevor LLC....302 543-5055
3844 Kennett Pike Ste 210 Wilmington (19807) *(G-10397)*
Endless Summer Tanning Salon (PA)....302 369-0455
60 N College Ave Ste A Newark (19711) *(G-6526)*
Endocrinology Consultant....302 734-2782
111 Wolf Creek Blvd Dover (19901) *(G-1521)*
Endoscopy Center of Delaware, Newark *Also called Endoscopy Center of Deleware (G-6527)*
Endoscopy Center of Deleware....302 892-2710
1090 Old Churchmans Rd Newark (19713) *(G-6527)*
Endovascular Consultants LLC....302 482-1333
701 N Clayton St 601 Wilmington (19805) *(G-10398)*
Endurnce Reinsurance Corp Amer....973 898-9575
1209 N Orange St Wilmington (19801) *(G-10399)*
Ener-G Group Inc....917 281-0020
3422 Old Capitol Trl Wilmington (19808) *(G-10400)*
Energizer Holdings Inc....302 678-6767
50 N Dupont Hwy Dover (19901) *(G-1522)*
Energy Assistance Program, Dover *Also called Catholic Charities Inc (G-1260)*
Energy Center Dover LLC....302 678-4666
1280 W North St Dover (19904) *(G-1523)*
Energy Gym....302 436-9001
36666 Bluewater Run W # 1 Selbyville (19975) *(G-8488)*
Energy Systems Tech Inc....302 368-0443
126a Sandy Dr Newark (19713) *(G-6528)*
Enerkem Miss Biofuels LLC....514 875-0284
222 Delaware Ave Fl 9 Wilmington (19801) *(G-10401)*
Engineered Systems & Designs....302 456-0446
3 S Tatnall St Wilmington (19801) *(G-10402)*
Engineering Incorporated....302 995-6862
6 Lewis Cir Wilmington (19804) *(G-10403)*
English Tech LLC....844 707-9904
3500 S Dupont Hwy Dover (19901) *(G-1524)*
English Village, Newark *Also called Panco Management Corporation (G-7173)*
Enhanced Corporate Prfmce LLC....302 545-8541
1 Morning Glen Ln Newark (19711) *(G-6529)*
Enhanced Dental Care....302 645-7200
18947 John J Williams Hwy Rehoboth Beach (19971) *(G-7927)*
Ensinger Penn Fibre Inc....302 349-4505
220 S Church & Snider St Greenwood (19950) *(G-2738)*
Ensyn GA Biorefinery I LLC....303 425-3740
1521 Concord Pike Ste 205 Wilmington (19803) *(G-10404)*
Ent Allergy Center....302 629-3400
8468 Herring Run Rd Seaford (19973) *(G-8237)*
Ent and Allergy Delaware LLC (PA)....302 478-8467
1401 Foulk Rd Ste 205 Wilmington (19803) *(G-10405)*
Ent and Allergy Delaware LLC....302 998-0300
1941 Limestone Rd Wilmington (19808) *(G-10406)*
Ent and Allergy Delaware LLC....302 832-8700
2600 Glasgow Ave Ste 221 Newark (19702) *(G-6530)*
Enteraxion, Wilmington *Also called Charter Dynamics LLC (G-9640)*
Enterprise Flasher Co Inc....302 999-0856
4 Hadco Rd Wilmington (19804) *(G-10407)*
Enterprise Learning Solutions....302 762-6595
236 Weldin Ridge Rd Wilmington (19803) *(G-10408)*
Enterprise Lsg Phladelphia LLC....302 425-4404
100 S French St Unit 115a Wilmington (19801) *(G-10409)*
Enterprise Lsg Phladelphia LLC....302 266-7777
409 E Cleveland Ave Newark (19711) *(G-6531)*
Enterprise Lsg Phladelphia LLC....302 479-7829
4727 Concord Pike Wilmington (19803) *(G-10410)*
Enterprise Lsg Phladelphia LLC....302 656-5464
520 S Walnut St Wilmington (19801) *(G-10411)*
Enterprise Lsg Phladelphia LLC....302 761-4545
100 Philadelphia Pike Wilmington (19809) *(G-10412)*
Enterprise Lsg Phladelphia LLC....302 732-3534
27424 Auto Works Ave Dagsboro (19939) *(G-900)*
Enterprise Lsg Phladelphia LLC....302 292-0524
430 Newark Shopping Ctr Newark (19711) *(G-6532)*
Enterprise Masonry Corporation....302 764-6858
3010 Bellevue Ave Wilmington (19802) *(G-10413)*
Enterprise Rent-A-Car, Newark *Also called Enterprise Lsg Phladelphia LLC (G-6531)*
Enterprise Rent-A-Car, Wilmington *Also called Enterprise Lsg Phladelphia LLC (G-10410)*
Enterprise Rent-A-Car, Wilmington *Also called Enterprise Lsg Phladelphia LLC (G-10411)*
Enterprise Rent-A-Car, Wilmington *Also called Enterprise Lsg Phladelphia LLC (G-10412)*
Enterprise Rent-A-Car, Dagsboro *Also called Enterprise Lsg Phladelphia LLC (G-900)*
Enterprise Rent-A-Car, Newark *Also called Enterprise Lsg Phladelphia LLC (G-6532)*
Enterprise Rent-A-Car....302 323-0850
190 S Dupont Hwy New Castle (19720) *(G-5291)*
Enterprise Rent-A-Car....302 934-1216
28656 Dupont Blvd Millsboro (19966) *(G-4685)*
Enterprise Rent-A-Car....302 575-1021
2415 Lancaster Ave Wilmington (19805) *(G-10414)*
Enterprise Rent-A-Car....302 653-4330
119 N Dupont Blvd Ste F Smyrna (19977) *(G-8629)*
Enterprise Rsurce Planners Inc (PA)....800 716-3660
4023 Kennett Pike 312 Wilmington (19807) *(G-10415)*
Enterprise Services LLC....302 454-7622
248 Chapman Rd Ste 100 Newark (19702) *(G-6533)*
Entertainment Production Svcs, Wilmington *Also called Bew Productions (G-9322)*
Enth Inc....630 986-8700
3422 Old Capitol Trl # 2096 Wilmington (19808) *(G-10416)*
Entourage Financial Group LLC....302 352-9473
1703 N Pine St Wilmington (19802) *(G-10417)*
Envirocorp Inc....302 398-3869
51 Clark St Harrington (19952) *(G-2837)*
Environics Analytics Inc....302 600-0304
1000 N West St Ste 1200 Wilmington (19801) *(G-10418)*
Environmental Alliance Inc (PA)....302 995-7544
5341 Limestone Rd Wilmington (19808) *(G-10419)*
Environmental Consulting Svcs (PA)....302 378-9881
100 S Cass St Middletown (19709) *(G-4059)*
Environmental Protection Agcy....302 739-9917
89 Kings Hwy Dover (19901) *(G-1525)*
Environmental Resources Inc....302 436-9637
38173 Dupont Blvd Selbyville (19975) *(G-8489)*
Environmental Services Inc....302 669-6812
461 Churchmans Rd New Castle (19720) *(G-5292)*
Environmental Testing Inc....302 378-5341
100 S Cass St Middletown (19709) *(G-4060)*
Environmental Versacorp (PA)....302 798-1839
501 Silverside Rd Ste 98 Wilmington (19809) *(G-10420)*
Envirotech Envmtl Consulting....302 684-5201
17605 Nassau Commons Blvd Lewes (19958) *(G-3483)*
Envirtech Enviromental Consltg....302 645-6491
34634 Bay Crossing Blvd Lewes (19958) *(G-3484)*
Envision Consulting LLC....302 658-9027
2008 Woodlawn Ave Wilmington (19806) *(G-10421)*
Envision Healthcare Corp....302 644-3852
1451 Kings Hwy Ste 4a Lewes (19958) *(G-3485)*
Envision It Publications LLC....800 329-9411
1148 Pulaski Hwy Bear (19701) *(G-144)*
Envision Solution LLC....302 442-7329
3422 Old Capitol Trl # 714 Wilmington (19808) *(G-10422)*

ALPHABETIC SECTION

Envolve Inc (PA) ... 314 349-3571
  1209 N Orange St Wilmington (19801) *(G-10423)*
Envoy Flight Systems Inc ... 302 738-1788
  201 Ruthar Dr Ste 3 Newark (19711) *(G-6534)*
EPA, Dover Also called Environmental Protection Agcy *(G-1525)*
Epb Associates Inc ... 302 475-7301
  107 W Sutton Pl Wilmington (19810) *(G-10424)*
Epic Health Services Inc ... 302 504-4092
  56 W Main St Ste 211 Christiana (19702) *(G-668)*
Epic Health Services Inc ... 302 422-3176
  20093 Office Cir 205 Georgetown (19947) *(G-2523)*
Epic Kings LLC ... 302 669-9018
  2093 Philadelphia Pike Claymont (19703) *(G-739)*
Epic Manufacturing, Greenwood Also called Hydroseeding Company LLC *(G-2745)*
Epic Marketing Cons Corp ... 302 285-9790
  10 Jackie Cir Middletown (19709) *(G-4061)*
Epic Research LLC ... 703 297-8121
  1105 N Market St Ste 1600 Wilmington (19801) *(G-10425)*
Epilepsy Foundation of Del (PA) ... 302 999-9313
  527 Stanton Christiana Rd Newark (19713) *(G-6535)*
Epiq Systems Inc ... 302 574-2600
  824 N Market St Wilmington (19801) *(G-10426)*
Epotec Inc ... 302 654-3090
  62 Rockford Rd Wilmington (19806) *(G-10427)*
Eprintit Usa Inc ... 613 299-7105
  1000 N West St Wilmington (19801) *(G-10428)*
Epstein Kplan OpthImlogist LLP ... 302 322-4444
  169 Christiana Rd New Castle (19720) *(G-5293)*
Epthi Inc ... 917 821-1935
  300 Delaware Ave Wilmington (19801) *(G-10429)*
Equidental ... 302 423-0851
  21 Wilder Rd Dover (19904) *(G-1526)*
Equine Wholesalers, Harrington Also called Chick Harness & Supply Inc *(G-2824)*
Equitable Life Assurance, Wilmington Also called Axa Equitable Life Insur Co *(G-9201)*
Equity Contracting LLC ... 302 504-1468
  102 Robino Ct Ste 203 Wilmington (19804) *(G-10430)*
Equity Lifestyle Prpts Inc ... 302 645-5770
  32045 Janice Rd Lewes (19958) *(G-3486)*
Equity Lifestyle Prpts Inc ... 302 945-1544
  126 Pine St Millsboro (19966) *(G-4686)*
ERA, Dover Also called Harrington Realty Inc *(G-1630)*
ERA, Wilmington Also called Cole Realty Inc *(G-9766)*
ERA, Dover Also called Harrington Realty Inc *(G-1631)*
ERA Harrington Realty (PA) ... 302 674-4663
  1404 Forrest Ave Ste A Dover (19904) *(G-1527)*
ERA Harrington Realty ... 302 363-1796
  516 Jefferic Blvd Ste C Dover (19901) *(G-1528)*
Eranga Cardiology ... 302 747-7486
  200 Banning St Ste 310 Dover (19904) *(G-1529)*
Erco Ceilings Inc ... 302 994-6200
  2 S Dupont Rd Wilmington (19805) *(G-10431)*
Erco Ceilings & Blinds, Harrington Also called Erco Ceilings & Interiors Inc *(G-2838)*
Erco Ceilings & Interiors Inc (HQ) ... 302 994-6200
  2 S Dupont Rd Wilmington (19805) *(G-10432)*
Erco Ceilings & Interiors Inc ... 302 398-3200
  512 Shaw Ave Harrington (19952) *(G-2838)*
Ergos Consultores LLC ... 549 404-6360
  3411 Silverside Rd # 104 Wilmington (19810) *(G-10433)*
Ergosix Corporation ... 844 603-1181
  615 S Dupont Hwy Dover (19901) *(G-1530)*
Eri Investments Inc ... 302 656-8089
  801 N West St Fl 2 Wilmington (19801) *(G-10434)*
Eric Barsky ... 856 495-6988
  19 Autumnwood Dr Newark (19711) *(G-6536)*
Eric Cline ... 302 629-3984
  22366 Sussex Hwy Seaford (19973) *(G-8238)*
Eric Hobbs Trucking Inc ... 302 697-2090
  3292 Turkey Point Rd Viola (19979) *(G-8835)*
Eric M Doroshow ... 302 934-9400
  213 E Dupont Hwy Millsboro (19966) *(G-4687)*
Eric S Balliet ... 302 856-7423
  212 W Market St Georgetown (19947) *(G-2524)*
Erickson Management ... 302 235-0855
  447 Coldspring Run Newark (19711) *(G-6537)*
Erik M D Stancofski ... 302 645-7050
  431 Savannah Rd Lewes (19958) *(G-3487)*
Erik S Bradley DDS ... 302 239-5917
  1415 Foulk Rd Ste 200 Wilmington (19803) *(G-10435)*
Erin N Macko DDS LLC ... 302 368-7463
  625 Barksdale Rd Ste 101 Newark (19711) *(G-6538)*
Ernie Deangelis (PA) ... 302 226-9533
  19791 Coastal Hwy Rehoboth Beach (19971) *(G-7928)*
Erosion Control Products Corp ... 302 815-6500
  9599 Nantcke Bus Pk Dr Greenwood (19950) *(G-2739)*
Erosion Control Services De ... 302 218-8913
  1432 Elk Way Bear (19701) *(G-145)*
ESA P Portfolio LLC ... 302 283-0800
  333 Continental Dr Newark (19713) *(G-6539)*
Esd, Wilmington Also called Engineered Systems & Designs *(G-10402)*
Eseco, Camden Wyoming Also called Eastern Shore Equipment Co *(G-633)*
Esis Inc ... 215 640-1000
  P.O. Box 15054 Wilmington (19850) *(G-10436)*
Esl Inc ... 302 629-4553
  Rr 13 Box South Seaford (19973) *(G-8239)*
Esposito Mansory LLC ... 302 996-4961
  471 B And O Ln Wilmington (19804) *(G-10437)*
Espositos Woodworking & Cnstr ... 302 245-5474
  99 Falls Rd Milton (19968) *(G-4904)*
Esquire Plumbing & Heating Co ... 302 378-7001
  7 Wood St Middletown (19709) *(G-4062)*
Essencia Salon and Day Spa ... 302 234-9144
  1240 Old Lancaster Pike Hockessin (19707) *(G-3023)*
Essential Health Brands LLC ... 302 322-1249
  1000 N West St Ste 1200 Wilmington (19801) *(G-10438)*
Essentially Hair, Newark Also called Regis Corporation *(G-7311)*
Essies Kitchen LLC ... 302 465-2856
  218 Samuel Paynter Dr Dover (19904) *(G-1531)*
Essilor America Holding Co Inc (HQ) ... 214 496-4000
  1209 N Orange St Wilmington (19801) *(G-10439)*
Est, Wilmington Also called Exploration Systems & Tech *(G-10461)*
Establishing Black Men LLC ... 215 432-7469
  P.O. Box 182 Claymont (19703) *(G-740)*
Estacionamiento Inteligente, Lewes Also called Go Go Go Inc *(G-3517)*
Estate Planning Delaware Vly, Wilmington Also called Occidental L Transamerica *(G-11932)*
Estate Servicing LLC ... 302 731-1119
  901 Barksdale Rd Newark (19711) *(G-6540)*
Estelles Child Dev Ctr Inc ... 302 792-9065
  132 Colesbery Dr New Castle (19720) *(G-5294)*
Estep Douglas E Pub Accountant ... 302 322-4621
  193 Christiana Rd New Castle (19720) *(G-5295)*
Esther V Graham ... 302 422-6667
  901 N Dupont Blvd Milford (19963) *(G-4406)*
Estia Hospitality Group Inc (PA) ... 302 798-5319
  3526 Philadelphia Pike Claymont (19703) *(G-741)*
ET Communications LLC ... 302 322-2222
  270 Quigley Blvd New Castle (19720) *(G-5296)*
Et International Inc ... 302 266-6426
  10 Fountainview Dr Newark (19713) *(G-6541)*
Etechboys Inc ... 800 549-4208
  3616 Kirkwood Hwy Ste A Wilmington (19808) *(G-10440)*
Etechpublish Inc ... 302 294-1678
  35 Stature Dr Newark (19713) *(G-6542)*
Eternal Health LLC ... 302 635-7421
  4837 Limestone Rd Wilmington (19808) *(G-10441)*
Ets & Ycp LLC ... 302 525-4111
  113 Barksdale Pro Ctr Newark (19711) *(G-6543)*
Eugene E Godfrey Do ... 302 674-1356
  22 Old Rudnick Ln 2 Dover (19901) *(G-1532)*
Eugene M DAmico III DDS PA (PA) ... 302 292-1600
  4735 Ogletown Stanton Rd # 1115 Newark (19713) *(G-6544)*
Eugene M DAmico III DDS PA ... 302 376-3700
  114 Saint Annes Church Rd Middletown (19709) *(G-4063)*
Eurofins Qc Inc ... 302 276-0432
  272 Quigley Blvd New Castle (19720) *(G-5297)*
European Coach Werkes Inc ... 302 436-2277
  Rr 20 Frankford (19945) *(G-2362)*
European Performance Inc ... 302 633-1122
  806 Wilmington Ave Wilmington (19805) *(G-10442)*
Evan Hurst Lawn & Landscaping, Claymont Also called Evan Hurst Property Management *(G-742)*
Evan Hurst Property Management ... 302 375-0398
  100 Naamans Rd Claymont (19703) *(G-742)*
Evanix Enterprises LLC ... 302 384-1806
  49 W Sarazen Dr Middletown (19709) *(G-4064)*
Evans ... 302 629-0545
  604 S Market St Seaford (19973) *(G-8240)*
Evans Farms LLC ... 302 337-8130
  9843 Seashore Hwy Bridgeville (19933) *(G-469)*
Even & Odd Minds LLC (PA) ... 619 663-7284
  1521 Concord Pike Ste 301 Wilmington (19803) *(G-10443)*
Eventc2 LLC ... 301 467-5780
  23 Oklahoma State Dr Newark (19713) *(G-6545)*
Events A La Carte ... 302 753-7462
  3 N Cummings Dr Middletown (19709) *(G-4065)*
Eventzilla Corporation (PA) ... 888 817-2837
  19c Trolley Sq Wilmington (19806) *(G-10444)*
Ever Green Lawns, Millsboro Also called Jason M Bradford *(G-4713)*
Everest Autoworks Auto Spa LLC ... 302 737-8424
  690 Kirkwood Hwy Newark (19711) *(G-6546)*
Everest Granite LLC ... 302 229-4733
  3410 Old Capitol Trl Wilmington (19808) *(G-10445)*
Everest Grocery, New Castle Also called GBA Enterprises Inc *(G-5346)*
Everest Hotel Group LLC (PA) ... 213 272-0088
  2140 S Dupont Hwy Camden (19934) *(G-569)*
Everest Sonoma Management LLC ... 213 272-0088
  2140 S Dupont Hwy Camden (19934) *(G-570)*
Everett Robinson ... 302 530-6574
  1 Margit Ln Wilmington (19810) *(G-10446)*

EVERETT THEATRE, Middletown Also called Associated Cmnty Talents Inc *(G-3945)*
Evergreen Center Alzheimer, Wilmington Also called Christiana Care Home Health *(G-9685)*
Evergreen Led..302 218-7819
 29 Dornoch Way Townsend (19734) *(G-8785)*
Evergreen Reallty, Wilmington Also called Brandywine Hills Apartments *(G-9436)*
Evergreen Realty...302 999-8805
 100 Ethan Ct Apt H Wilmington (19804) *(G-10447)*
Evergreen Realty Inc..302 998-0354
 125 Greenbank Rd Apt A4 Wilmington (19808) *(G-10448)*
Evergreen Resources Group LLC..302 477-0189
 2 Righter Pkwy Ste 120 Wilmington (19803) *(G-10449)*
Evergreen Waste Services LLC..302 635-7055
 839 Valley Rd Hockessin (19707) *(G-3024)*
Everlift Wind Technology...240 683-9787
 31798 Carneros Ave Lewes (19958) *(G-3488)*
Everybody Needs Ink..302 633-0866
 209 Lister Dr Wilmington (19808) *(G-10450)*
Evocati Group Corporation..206 551-9087
 9 E Loockerman St Ste 3a Dover (19901) *(G-1533)*
Evolution Rx LLC..614 344-4600
 512 Aviemore Dr Townsend (19734) *(G-8786)*
Evonsys LLC...302 544-2156
 4550 New Lnden Hl Rd Ste Wilmington (19808) *(G-10451)*
Evoqua Water Technologies LLC..302 322-6247
 259 Quigley Blvd New Castle (19720) *(G-5298)*
Evoqua Water Technologies LLC..302 654-3712
 1020 Christiana Ave Ste 1 Wilmington (19801) *(G-10452)*
Evraz Clymont Stl Holdings Inc..302 792-5400
 4001 Philadelphia Pike Claymont (19703) *(G-743)*
Evs Lawn Service Inc..302 475-9222
 2609 Ebright Rd Wilmington (19810) *(G-10453)*
Ewaste Express...302 691-8052
 6 Rosetree Ct Wilmington (19810) *(G-10454)*
Ewebvalet Co Inc..302 893-0903
 22 Center Meeting Rd Wilmington (19807) *(G-10455)*
Ewings Towing Service Inc..302 366-8806
 1111 Elkton Rd Newark (19711) *(G-6547)*
Ews Funeral Home...302 494-1847
 219 Niobrara Ln Bear (19701) *(G-146)*
Exa Solutions Inc...302 273-9320
 2035 Sunset Lake Rd B2 Newark (19702) *(G-6548)*
Exalenz Bioscience Inc...888 392-5369
 1313 N Market St Wilmington (19801) *(G-10456)*
Exam Master Corporation...302 378-3842
 100 Lake Dr Ste 6 Newark (19702) *(G-6549)*
Excape Entertainment US Ltd..949 943-9219
 704 N King St Ste 500 Wilmington (19801) *(G-10457)*
Excel Business Systems Inc (PA)..302 453-1500
 201 Ruthar Dr Ste 10 Newark (19711) *(G-6550)*
Excel Property Management LLC.......................................302 541-5312
 35370 Atlantic Ave Millville (19967) *(G-4844)*
Excellent Home Care...302 327-0147
 122 Delaware St New Castle (19720) *(G-5299)*
Exceptional Care For Children...302 894-1001
 11 Independence Way Newark (19713) *(G-6551)*
Exclusively Legal Inc...302 239-5990
 7301 Lancaster Pike Ste 2 Hockessin (19707) *(G-3025)*
Exco Inc (HQ)..905 477-3065
 1007 N Orange St Wilmington (19801) *(G-10458)*
Executive Auto Repairs Inc..302 995-6220
 480 B And O Ln Wilmington (19804) *(G-10459)*
Executive Brdband Cmmnications, Newark Also called Executive Broadband *(G-6552)*
Executive Broadband...302 463-4335
 6 Jaymar Blvd Newark (19702) *(G-6552)*
Executive Offices Inc...302 323-8100
 42 Reads Way New Castle (19720) *(G-5300)*
Executive Touch, Dover Also called Anthony Streett *(G-1128)*
Executive Transportation Inc...302 337-3455
 12643 Rock Rd Greenwood (19950) *(G-2740)*
Exo Works Inc...302 531-1139
 3500 S Dupont Hwy Yy101 Dover (19901) *(G-1534)*
Expanding Our Kids World..302 659-0293
 3460 S Dupont Blvd Smyrna (19977) *(G-8630)*
Expecting Miracles LLC..302 893-3220
 2506 Teal Rd Wilmington (19805) *(G-10460)*
Experienced Auto Parts Inc...302 322-3344
 461 Old Airport Rd New Castle (19720) *(G-5301)*
Expert Home Care...856 870-6691
 504 Silverhill Xing Middletown (19709) *(G-4066)*
Exploration Systems & Tech...302 335-3911
 1209 N Orange St Wilmington (19801) *(G-10461)*
Explorer New Build LLC...305 436-4000
 2711 Centerville Rd # 120 Wilmington (19808) *(G-10462)*
Express Electric Inc...302 456-1919
 P.O. Box 9560 Newark (19714) *(G-6553)*
Express Hotel Inc..302 227-4030
 19953 Shuttle Rd Rehoboth Beach (19971) *(G-7929)*
Express Legal Documents LLC (HQ)...................................212 710-1374
 1201 N Orange St Wilmington (19801) *(G-10463)*
Express Vpn LLC...310 601-8492
 113 Barksdale Pro Ctr Newark (19711) *(G-6554)*
Expressions Hair Salon, Selbyville Also called Hairs To You *(G-8498)*
Extended Stay America, Inc., Newark Also called ESA P Portfolio LLC *(G-6539)*
Extreme Audio & Video...302 533-7404
 19a Albe Dr Newark (19702) *(G-6555)*
Extreme Machining LLC..302 368-7595
 111 Lake Dr Ste A Newark (19702) *(G-6556)*
Extreme Reach Inc..302 366-7538
 450 Corporate Blvd Newark (19702) *(G-6557)*
Extreme Scale Solutions LLC..302 540-7149
 256 Chapman Rd Ste 107 Newark (19702) *(G-6558)*
Exxon, Wilmington Also called Newport Ventures Inc *(G-11879)*
Eye Care of Delaware...302 454-8800
 4102 Ogletown Rd Ste 1 Newark (19713) *(G-6559)*
Eye Center of Delaware, Wilmington Also called Vision Center of Delaware *(G-13092)*
Eye Consultants LLC..302 998-2333
 1941 Limestone Rd Ste 200 Wilmington (19808) *(G-10464)*
Eye Physicians and Surgeons PA.......................................302 225-1018
 1207 N Scott St Ste 1 Wilmington (19806) *(G-10465)*
Eye35design LLC...470 236-3933
 28 Old Rudnick Ln Dover (19901) *(G-1535)*
EZ Cash of New Hampshire Inc..302 846-0464
 300 N Bi State Blvd Ste 2 Delmar (19940) *(G-998)*
EZ Loans Inc (PA)..302 934-5563
 28273 Dupont Blvd Millsboro (19966) *(G-4688)*
EZ Manufacturing Company LLC..302 653-6567
 500 N Bassett St Clayton (19938) *(G-849)*
Ezangacom Inc..888 439-2642
 222 Carter Dr Ste 201 Middletown (19709) *(G-4067)*
Ezion Fair Community Academy..302 652-9114
 1400 B St Wilmington (19801) *(G-10466)*
Ezprohub LLC..302 327-4222
 100 Biddle Ave Ste 112 Newark (19702) *(G-6560)*
Eztread, New Castle Also called Delaware Flooring Supply Inc *(G-5230)*
Ezy Biotech LLC..212 247-4261
 3513 Concord Pike # 3100 Wilmington (19803) *(G-10467)*
F & G Construction Co Inc..302 994-1406
 25 Maple Ave Wilmington (19804) *(G-10468)*
F & N Vazquez Concrete LLC...302 725-5305
 18577 Sherman Ave Lincoln (19960) *(G-3846)*
F & S Boat Works..302 838-5500
 353 Summit Pointe Cir Bear (19701) *(G-147)*
F & S Property Management Co, Seaford Also called Integra ADM Group Inc *(G-8271)*
F and D Equipment & Repair LLC......................................302 378-1999
 213 W Lake St Unit F Middletown (19709) *(G-4068)*
F and M Equipment Ltd..302 715-5382
 28587 Sussex Hwy Laurel (19956) *(G-3229)*
F D Hammond Enterprises Inc..302 424-8455
 1111 N Dupont Blvd Milford (19963) *(G-4407)*
F H Everett & Associates Inc..302 674-2380
 1151 Walker Rd Ste 100 Dover (19904) *(G-1536)*
F M C Biopolymore, Newark Also called FMC Corporation *(G-6596)*
F P T & W Medical Associates...800 421-2368
 1508 Penns Ave Ste 2b Wilmington (19806) *(G-10469)*
F S C Wallcoverings, Newark Also called F Schumacher & Co *(G-6561)*
F Sartin Tyson Inc..302 834-4571
 4376 Krkwood St Gorges Rd Saint Georges (19733) *(G-8125)*
F Schumacher & Co...302 454-3200
 131 Continental Dr # 300 Newark (19713) *(G-6561)*
Fa webb & Sons..302 335-4548
 3277 Milford Neck Rd Milford (19963) *(G-4408)*
Fabby Inc..408 891-7991
 1013 Centre Rd Ste 403b Wilmington (19805) *(G-10470)*
Fabit Corp..832 217-0864
 1201 N Orange St Ste 775 Wilmington (19801) *(G-10471)*
Fabmanianet..302 994-5801
 2834 W Oakland Dr Wilmington (19808) *(G-10472)*
Fabreeka Intl Holdings Inc...302 452-2500
 315 Ruthar Dr Newark (19711) *(G-6562)*
Fabri-Zone Cleaning Systems, Ocean View Also called Schrider Enterprises Inc *(G-7812)*
Fabrizio Salon...302 254-3432
 1604 W 16th St Wilmington (19806) *(G-10473)*
Fabrizio Salon & Spa, Wilmington Also called Fabrizio Salon *(G-10473)*
Facepainting...302 344-3145
 260 Christiana Rd Apt F10 New Castle (19720) *(G-5302)*
Facility Services Group Inc...302 317-3029
 300 Cornell Dr Ste A1 Wilmington (19801) *(G-10474)*
Factors Etc Inc..302 834-1625
 1218 Pulaski Hwy Ste 484 Bear (19701) *(G-148)*
Factory Sports..302 313-4186
 17543 Nassau Commons Blvd Lewes (19958) *(G-3489)*
Factory Technologies Inc..302 266-1290
 2035 Sunset Lake Rd B2 Newark (19702) *(G-6563)*
Fae McKenzie..302 227-6700
 54 Baltimore Ave Rehoboth Beach (19971) *(G-7930)*
Fair Square Financial LLC..571 205-0305
 1000 N West St Ste 1100 Wilmington (19801) *(G-10475)*

Fairchild Day School.......302 478-4646
103 Lyndhurst Ave Wilmington (19803) ***(G-10476)***
Fairfax Eye Works, Wilmington *Also called In Vision Eye Care* ***(G-11010)***
Fairfax Neighborhood Home, Wilmington *Also called Mossaic* ***(G-11762)***
Fairfax Vision Center, Hockessin *Also called In Vision Eye Care Inc* ***(G-3057)***
Fairfield Inn, New Castle *Also called Jay Devi Inc* ***(G-5437)***
Fairfield Inn, Dover *Also called Dover Hospitality Group LLC* ***(G-1453)***
Fairfield Inn, Newark *Also called Sage Hospitality Resources LLC* ***(G-7376)***
Fairfield Inn Suites Rehoboth, Rehoboth Beach *Also called Colonial Oaks Hotel LLC* ***(G-7898)***
Fairview Inn, Wilmington *Also called Nab Motel Inc* ***(G-11793)***
Fairville Management Co LLC (PA).......302 489-2000
726 Yorklyn Rd Ste 200 Hockessin (19707) ***(G-3026)***
Fairville Products Inc.......302 425-4400
41 Germay Dr Ste 1 Wilmington (19804) ***(G-10477)***
Fairway Manufacturing Company (HQ).......302 398-4630
51 Clark St Harrington (19952) ***(G-2839)***
Fairwinds Baptist Church Inc.......302 322-1029
801 Seymour Rd Bear (19701) ***(G-149)***
Fairwinds Christian School, Bear *Also called Fairwinds Baptist Church Inc* ***(G-149)***
Faith Day Care and Preschool, Wilmington *Also called Faith Presbyterian Church* ***(G-10478)***
Faith Family Management Co.......302 832-5936
63 Marrows Rd Newark (19713) ***(G-6564)***
Faith Fmly Friends Holdg LLC.......202 256-4524
16192 Coastal Hwy Lewes (19958) ***(G-3490)***
Faith Presbyterian Church.......302 764-8615
720 Marsh Rd Wilmington (19803) ***(G-10478)***
Faith Victory Christn Academy.......302 333-0855
301 Commonwealth Ave Claymont (19703) ***(G-744)***
Faithful Friends Animal Soc, Wilmington *Also called Faithful Friends Inc* ***(G-10479)***
Faithful Friends Inc.......302 427-8514
12 Germay Dr Wilmington (19804) ***(G-10479)***
Falasco Masonry Inc.......302 697-8971
3152 S State St Camden Wyoming (19934) ***(G-636)***
Falcidian LLC.......302 656-5500
270 Presidential Dr Wilmington (19807) ***(G-10480)***
Falco Industries Inc.......302 628-1170
200 Bedford Falls Dr # 1 Seaford (19973) ***(G-8241)***
Falcon Crest Inv Intl Inc.......240 701-1746
1201 N Orange St Ste 600 Wilmington (19801) ***(G-10481)***
Falcon Steel Co.......302 571-0890
811 S Market St Wilmington (19801) ***(G-10482)***
Falcons Media Group Inc.......201 247-6489
251 Little Falls Dr Wilmington (19808) ***(G-10483)***
Fame, Wilmington *Also called Forum To Advnce Mnrties In Eng* ***(G-10595)***
Famealy Inc (PA).......650 492-5009
2035 Sunset Lake Rd B2 Newark (19702) ***(G-6565)***
Family & Friends Caring Perola.......302 683-0611
14 Oxford Way Wilmington (19807) ***(G-10484)***
Family Benefit Home Care, Wilmington *Also called Caroline M Wiesner* ***(G-9575)***
Family Care Associates, New Castle *Also called K V Associates Inc* ***(G-5448)***
Family Care Associates.......302 454-8880
510 Christiana Med Ctr Newark (19702) ***(G-6566)***
Family Chiropractic Office PA.......302 993-9113
3105 Limestone Rd Ste 303 Wilmington (19808) ***(G-10485)***
Family Cnsling Ctr St Puls Inc.......302 576-4136
301 N Van Buren St Wilmington (19805) ***(G-10486)***
Family Comb & Scissors.......302 398-8570
100 W Milby St Harrington (19952) ***(G-2840)***
Family Denistry.......302 368-0054
179 W Chestnut Hill Rd # 4 Newark (19713) ***(G-6567)***
Family Dental Associates Inc.......302 674-8810
385 Saulsbury Rd Dover (19904) ***(G-1537)***
Family Dental Care.......302 999-7600
1601 Milltown Rd Ste 19 Wilmington (19808) ***(G-10487)***
Family Dental Center.......302 656-8266
1 Winston Ave Wilmington (19804) ***(G-10488)***
Family Dentistry Milford PA.......302 422-6924
100 Sussex Ave Milford (19963) ***(G-4409)***
Family Dentistry Wilmington.......302 656-2434
1708 Lovering Ave Ste 101 Wilmington (19806) ***(G-10489)***
Family Doctors.......302 368-3600
4 Polly Drummond Hill Rd Newark (19711) ***(G-6568)***
Family Ear Nose & Throad.......302 998-0300
1941 Limestone Rd Ste 210 Wilmington (19808) ***(G-10490)***
Family Ear Nose/Throat Physcn, Wilmington *Also called Gabriel Jr Timoteo R MD* ***(G-10661)***
Family Ent Physicians Inc (PA).......302 998-0300
1941 Limestone Rd Ste 210 Wilmington (19808) ***(G-10491)***
Family Health Delaware Inc.......302 734-2444
640 S Queen St Dover (19904) ***(G-1538)***
Family Mediation Services, Wilmington *Also called Katherine Laffey* ***(G-11228)***
Family Medical Associates, Wilmington *Also called Jose D Manalo MD PA Inc* ***(G-11183)***
Family Medical Centre PA.......302 678-0510
111 Wolf Creek Blvd Ste 2 Dover (19901) ***(G-1539)***
Family Medicine At Greenville.......302 429-5870
213 Greenhill Ave Ste B Wilmington (19805) ***(G-10492)***
Family Medicine Ctr Naticchia.......302 477-3300
1400 N Washington St Wilmington (19801) ***(G-10493)***
Family Medicine Smyrna Clayton.......302 653-1050
319 N Carter Rd Smyrna (19977) ***(G-8631)***
Family Outrch Multi-Purpse Com.......302 422-2158
19227 Young Ln Lincoln (19960) ***(G-3847)***
Family Planning.......302 856-5225
544 S Bedford St Georgetown (19947) ***(G-2525)***
Family Practice Association PA.......302 656-5416
2701 Kirkwood Hwy Wilmington (19805) ***(G-10494)***
Family Practice Center.......302 645-2833
7 Dunes Ter Lewes (19958) ***(G-3491)***
Family Practice Cntr of New CA.......302 999-0933
1 Centurian Dr Ste 105 Newark (19713) ***(G-6569)***
Family Practice Hockessin PA.......302 239-4500
5936 Limestone Rd Ste 202 Hockessin (19707) ***(G-3027)***
Family Promise of Northern New.......302 998-2222
2104 St James Church Rd Wilmington (19808) ***(G-10495)***
Family Respiratory & Med Supl.......302 653-3602
5609 Dupont Pkwy Ste 15 Smyrna (19977) ***(G-8632)***
FAMILY TO FAMILY, Wilmington *Also called Delaware Family Voices Inc* ***(G-10046)***
Family Wrkplace Connection Inc (PA).......302 479-1660
2005 Baynard Blvd Wilmington (19802) ***(G-10496)***
Famoid Technology LLC.......530 601-7284
607 Deemer Pl New Castle (19720) ***(G-5303)***
Fannon Color Printing LLC.......302 227-2164
20 Harbor Rd Rehoboth Beach (19971) ***(G-7931)***
Fantast Costumes Inc.......302 455-2006
8 The Grn Ste A Dover (19901) ***(G-1540)***
Fantasy Beauty Salon.......302 629-6762
224 High St Seaford (19973) ***(G-8242)***
Far Flung Bungy LLC.......302 421-8226
4405 Whittier Rd Wilmington (19802) ***(G-10497)***
Far Rezolutions Inc.......302 547-6850
218 Margaux Cir Newark (19702) ***(G-6570)***
Far Trucking LLC.......302 266-8034
23 O Rourke Ct Newark (19702) ***(G-6571)***
Fare4air LLC.......844 663-4040
500 Delaware Ave Wilmington (19899) ***(G-10498)***
Fareed Services.......302 559-8594
9202 Westview Rd Wilmington (19802) ***(G-10499)***
Faries Funeral Directors Inc (PA).......302 653-8816
29 S Main St Smyrna (19977) ***(G-8633)***
Farlow-Taylor Construction.......302 436-9660
7 Discovery Ln Selbyville (19975) ***(G-8490)***
Farlow-Taylor Woodworks, Selbyville *Also called Farlow-Taylor Construction* ***(G-8490)***
Farm Financial Services Inc.......302 854-9760
P.O. Box 769 Georgetown (19947) ***(G-2526)***
Farmers First Services Inc (PA).......302 424-8340
306 Warner Rd Milford (19963) ***(G-4410)***
Farmers Harvest Inc.......302 734-7708
2826 Seven Hickories Rd Dover (19904) ***(G-1541)***
Farmers Radiator & AC.......302 235-5922
15 Deer Track Ln Newark (19711) ***(G-6572)***
Farmers Radiator & AC Sho, Newark *Also called Farmers Radiator & AC* ***(G-6572)***
Farnam Hall Ventures LLC.......347 687-2152
3422 Old Capitol Trl Wilmington (19808) ***(G-10500)***
Farnell & Gast Insurance, Seaford *Also called Callaway Farnell and Moore* ***(G-8180)***
Farpath Foundation.......302 645-8328
800 Bay Ave Lewes (19958) ***(G-3492)***
Farrand Village Apartments.......302 998-5796
16 Deville Cir Wilmington (19808) ***(G-10501)***
Farrell Roofing Inc.......302 378-7663
201 W Lake St Middletown (19709) ***(G-4069)***
Fas Mart / Shore Stop 286 LLC.......302 366-9694
1400 Capitol Trl Newark (19711) ***(G-6573)***
Fast Bailbonds LLC.......302 778-4400
1224 N King St Wilmington (19801) ***(G-10502)***
Fast Feet Inc.......302 478-5300
4737 Concord Pike Ste 415 Wilmington (19803) ***(G-10503)***
Fast Feet Shoe Repair, Wilmington *Also called Fast Feet Inc* ***(G-10503)***
Fast Intrcnnect Tchologies Inc.......302 465-5344
73 Greentree Dr Ste 30 Dover (19904) ***(G-1542)***
Fast Pipe Lining East Inc.......302 368-7414
563 Walther Rd Newark (19702) ***(G-6574)***
Fast4wrd Towing & Repair LLC.......302 331-5157
10 Meco Cir Wilmington (19804) ***(G-10504)***
Fastenal Company.......302 424-4149
205 Mullet Run Milford (19963) ***(G-4411)***
Fastsigns, Wilmington *Also called Jenner Enterprises Inc* ***(G-11146)***
Fastsigns.......302 998-6755
1300 Frst State Blvd Ste Wilmington (19804) ***(G-10505)***
Fasttrak.......302 761-5454
1500 Eastlawn Ave Wilmington (19802) ***(G-10506)***
Fataneh M Ziari MD.......302 836-8533
2600 Glasgow Ave Ste 212 Newark (19702) ***(G-6575)***
Fathers Day Gala Inc.......302 981-4117
436 S Buttonwood St Wilmington (19801) ***(G-10507)***
Faust Sheet Metal Works Inc.......302 645-9509
1636 Savannah Rd Ste A Lewes (19958) ***(G-3493)***

A L P H A B E T I C

Faustin Enterprises LLC ... 302 543-2687
1224 N King St Wilmington (19801) *(G-10508)*
Favored Childcare Academy Inc ... 302 698-1266
2319 S Dupont Hwy Dover (19901) *(G-1543)*
Faw Casson & Co LLP ... 302 674-4305
160 Greentree Dr Ste 203 Dover (19904) *(G-1544)*
Faw Casson ... 302 226-1919
20376 Coastal Hwy Ste 204 Rehoboth Beach (19971) *(G-7932)*
Faw Casson & Co, Dover Also called Faw Casson & Co LLP *(G-1544)*
FB Door-Delaware LLC ... 302 995-1000
330 Water St Newport (19804) *(G-7749)*
Fbk Graphico Inc ... 302 743-4784
2207 Concord Pike Wilmington (19803) *(G-10509)*
Fbk Medical Tubing Inc ... 302 855-0585
21649 Cedar Creek Ave Georgetown (19947) *(G-2527)*
Fcw, Wilmington Also called Carspecken-Scott Inc *(G-9581)*
Fearn-CIndaniel Architects Inc ... 302 998-7615
6 Larch Ave Ste 398 Wilmington (19804) *(G-10510)*
Feast Kitchen Inc ... 415 758-8779
1679 S Dupont Hwy Ste 100 Dover (19901) *(G-1545)*
Feastfox Inc ... 650 250-6887
8 The Grn Dover (19901) *(G-1546)*
Febys Fishery Inc ... 302 998-9501
3701 Lancaster Pike Wilmington (19805) *(G-10511)*
Federal Court Reporters ... 302 573-6195
844 N King St Unit 24 Wilmington (19801) *(G-10512)*
Federal Energy Inf ... 858 521-3300
251 Little Falls Dr Wilmington (19808) *(G-10513)*
Federal Express Corporation ... 800 463-3339
1209 N Orange St Wilmington (19801) *(G-10514)*
Federal Express Corporation ... 302 577-2667
827 N King St Wilmington (19801) *(G-10515)*
Federal Express Corporation ... 800 463-3339
2 W Commons Blvd New Castle (19720) *(G-5304)*
Federal Home Loan ADM Inc ... 855 345-2669
1201 N Orange St Ste 600 Wilmington (19801) *(G-10516)*
Federal Mechanical Contractors ... 302 656-2998
229 Hillview Ave New Castle (19720) *(G-5305)*
Federal Technical Associates ... 302 697-7951
50 Westview Ave Dover (19901) *(G-1547)*
Fedex, Wilmington Also called Federal Express Corporation *(G-10514)*
Fedex, Wilmington Also called Federal Express Corporation *(G-10515)*
Fedex, New Castle Also called Federal Express Corporation *(G-5304)*
Fedex Freight Corporation ... 800 218-6570
617 Lambson Ln New Castle (19720) *(G-5306)*
Fedex Ground Package Sys Inc ... 800 463-3339
6 Dock View Dr New Castle (19720) *(G-5307)*
Fedex Ground Package Sys Inc ... 800 463-3339
161 Venture Dr Seaford (19973) *(G-8243)*
Fedex Office & Print Svcs Inc ... 302 475-9501
4120 Concord Pike Wilmington (19803) *(G-10517)*
Fedex Office & Print Svcs Inc ... 302 652-2151
1201 N Market St Ste 1200 Wilmington (19801) *(G-10518)*
Fedex Office & Print Svcs Inc ... 302 368-5080
132 S Main St Newark (19711) *(G-6576)*
Fedex Office & Print Svcs Inc ... 302 996-0264
4721a Kirkwood Hwy Wilmington (19808) *(G-10519)*
Feeney Chropractic Care Ctr PA ... 302 328-0200
835 Pulaski Hwy Bear (19701) *(G-150)*
Feeney Chrprctic Care Cntre PA, Bear Also called Feeney Chiropractic Care Ctr PA *(G-150)*
Feick, Judith MD, Wilmington Also called Pike Creek Pediatric Assoc *(G-12140)*
Felder USA, New Castle Also called Asw Machinery Inc *(G-5049)*
Felixcem Corporation Inc ... 302 324-9101
314 Bay West Blvd New Castle (19720) *(G-5308)*
Fellowship Hlth Resources Inc ... 302 422-6699
7549 Wilkins Rd Milford (19963) *(G-4412)*
Fellowship Hlth Resources Inc ... 302 854-0626
505 W Market St Ste 110 Georgetown (19947) *(G-2528)*
Fellowship Hlth Resources Inc ... 302 856-7642
23769 Shortly Rd Georgetown (19947) *(G-2529)*
Fells Point Surf Co LLC ... 302 212-2005
23 Bellevue St Dewey Beach (19971) *(G-1057)*
Felton Community Fire Co Inc ... 302 284-9552
9 E Main St Felton (19943) *(G-2291)*
Felton Residential Trtmnt Ctr, Dover Also called Psychotherapeutic Svc Assn Inc *(G-1996)*
Femmepal Corporation ... 888 406-0804
16192 Coastal Hwy Lewes (19958) *(G-3494)*
Fencemaxcom Inc ... 302 343-9063
2210 Bryants Corner Rd Hartly (19953) *(G-2922)*
Fenwick Island Marine LLC ... 302 436-4702
Rr 1 Selbyville (19975) *(G-8491)*
Fenwick Medical Center ... 302 539-2399
1209 Coastal Hwy Fenwick Island (19944) *(G-2335)*
Ferguson 1991, New Castle Also called Ferguson Enterprises LLC *(G-5309)*
Ferguson Enterprises LLC ... 302 656-4421
2000 Maryland Ave Wilmington (19805) *(G-10520)*
Ferguson Enterprises LLC ... 302 747-2032
10 Maggies Way Dover (19901) *(G-1548)*

Ferguson Enterprises LLC ... 302 934-6040
118 E Dupont Hwy Millsboro (19966) *(G-4689)*
Ferguson Enterprises LLC ... 302 322-2836
77 Mccullough Dr Ste 12 New Castle (19720) *(G-5309)*
Ferm Development LLC ... 302 792-1102
501 Silverside Rd Wilmington (19809) *(G-10521)*
Ferrante & Associates Inc ... 781 891-4328
175 Fairhill Dr Wilmington (19808) *(G-10522)*
Ferrara Asset Management Inc ... 401 286-8464
2711 Centerville Rd # 120 Wilmington (19808) *(G-10523)*
Ferrara Haley & Bevis ... 302 656-7247
1716 Wawaset St Wilmington (19806) *(G-10524)*
Ferrari Hair Studio Ltd ... 302 731-7505
4559 New Linden Hill Rd Wilmington (19808) *(G-10525)*
Ferrell Cooling & Heating Inc ... 302 436-2922
32971 Lighthouse Rd Selbyville (19975) *(G-8492)*
Ferry Joseph & Pearce PA ... 302 856-3706
6 W Market St Georgetown (19947) *(G-2530)*
Ferry Joseph & Pearce PA (PA) ... 302 575-1555
824 N Market St Ste 1000 Wilmington (19801) *(G-10526)*
Fessenden Hall Incorporated ... 302 674-4505
1037 Fowler Ct Dover (19901) *(G-1549)*
Fessenden Hall of Delaware, Dover Also called Fessenden Hall Incorporated *(G-1549)*
Fever Labs Inc (PA) ... 646 781-7359
2140 S Dupont Hwy Camden (19934) *(G-571)*
Ffi General Contractor In ... 302 420-1242
13 Perth Dr Wilmington (19803) *(G-10527)*
Fia Card Services Nat Assn ... 302 457-0517
11 King St Wilmington (19884) *(G-10528)*
Fia Card Services Nat Assn (HQ) ... 800 362-6255
1100 N King St Wilmington (19884) *(G-10529)*
Fia Card Services Nat Assn ... 302 432-1573
1200 N French St Wilmington (19884) *(G-10530)*
Fiber One Inc ... 302 834-0890
2812 Old County Rd Newark (19702) *(G-6577)*
Fibre Processing Corporation ... 302 654-3659
701 Garasches Ln Wilmington (19801) *(G-10531)*
Fidelitrade Incorporated (PA) ... 302 762-6200
3601 N Market St Wilmington (19802) *(G-10532)*
Fidelity Income Advisors Co ... 302 223-9444
3911 Concord Pike # 8030 Wilmington (19803) *(G-10533)*
Fidelity Mntal Hlth Sltons LLC ... 302 304-2974
365 United Way Dover (19901) *(G-1550)*
Fidelity National Fincl Inc ... 302 658-2102
1220 N Market St Ste 201 Wilmington (19801) *(G-10534)*
Fidelity National Info Svcs (PA) ... 302 658-2102
600 N King St Fl 10 Wilmington (19801) *(G-10535)*
Fiduks Industrial Services Inc (PA) ... 302 994-2534
7 Meco Cir Wilmington (19804) *(G-10536)*
Fiduks Industrial Services Inc ... 302 994-2534
7 Meco Cir Wilmington (19804) *(G-10537)*
Fields & Company Inc ... 302 234-2775
7460 Lancaster Pike Ste 3 Hockessin (19707) *(G-3028)*
Fieldstone Golf Club LP ... 302 254-4569
1000 Dean Rd Wilmington (19807) *(G-10538)*
Fifer Orchards Inc ... 302 697-2141
1919 Allabands Mill Rd Camden Wyoming (19934) *(G-637)*
Fifty Plus Monthly ... 302 645-2938
16587 John Rowland Trl Milton (19968) *(G-4905)*
Figgo Inc ... 734 560-1300
2035 Sunset Lake Rd B2 Newark (19702) *(G-6578)*
File Right LLC ... 302 757-7107
364 E Main St Middletown (19709) *(G-4070)*
Filipino Heritg & Arts Museum ... 302 731-5899
58 S Skyward Dr Newark (19713) *(G-6579)*
Final Finishes Inc ... 302 995-1850
708 Woodtop Rd Wilmington (19804) *(G-10539)*
Finance Department, Dover Also called City of Dover *(G-1288)*
Financial House Inc ... 302 654-5451
5818 Kennett Pike Wilmington (19807) *(G-10540)*
Financial Services ... 302 478-4707
1000 N West St Ste 1200 Wilmington (19801) *(G-10541)*
Finding A Voice Inc ... 315 333-7567
16193 Coastal Hwy Lewes (19958) *(G-3495)*
Fine Line It Consulting LLP ... 302 645-4549
16678 Kings Hwy Ste 1 Lewes (19958) *(G-3496)*
Finocchiaro Landscape Inc ... 302 792-2201
41 N Cliffe Dr Wilmington (19809) *(G-10542)*
Firefly Drone Operations Llc ... 305 206-6955
2643 Bittersweet Dr Wilmington (19810) *(G-10543)*
Firefly Drone Ops, Wilmington Also called Firefly Drone Operations Llc *(G-10543)*
Fireplace Shoppe, Wilmington Also called Slater Fireplaces Inc *(G-12645)*
Fireplace Specialities LLC ... 302 436-9250
44 Rte 113 Selbyville (19975) *(G-8493)*
Fireside Heart & Home ... 302 337-3025
18109 Sussex Hwy Bridgeville (19933) *(G-470)*
Fireside Partners Inc ... 302 613-2165
60 Starlifter Ave Dover (19901) *(G-1551)*
Firestone, New Castle Also called Cochran-Trivits Inc *(G-5179)*
Firestone, Milford Also called Bridgestone Ret Operations LLC *(G-4335)*

ALPHABETIC SECTION Fisher Auto Parts Inc

Firestone, Wilmington *Also called Bridgestone Ret Operations LLC* ***(G-9472)***
Firestone, Dover *Also called Bridgestone Ret Operations LLC* ***(G-1232)***
Firestone, New Castle *Also called Bridgestone Ret Operations LLC* ***(G-5112)***
Firing Distance...302 337-9094
6515 Ray Rd Bridgeville (19933) ***(G-471)***
Firsd Tea North America LLC (HQ)...302 322-1255
34 Blevins Dr Ste 1&2 New Castle (19720) ***(G-5310)***
First Access Inc...949 455-4027
427 N Tatnall St Wilmington (19801) ***(G-10544)***
First American Title Insur Co...302 855-2120
106 N Bedford St Georgetown (19947) ***(G-2531)***
First American Title Insur Co...302 421-9440
704 N King St Wilmington (19801) ***(G-10545)***
First Atlantic Mortgage Svcs, Lewes *Also called First Atlantic Mrtg Svcs LLC* ***(G-3497)***
First Atlantic Mrtg Svcs LLC...302 841-8435
16678 Kings Hwy Ste 2 Lewes (19958) ***(G-3497)***
First Chice Auto Trck Mddltown...302 376-6333
128 Patriot Dr Middletown (19709) ***(G-4071)***
First Choice Auto & Truck Repr...302 656-1433
533 Rogers Rd New Castle (19720) ***(G-5311)***
First Choice Health Care Inc...302 836-6150
12 Fox Hunt Dr Bear (19701) ***(G-151)***
First Choice Home Med Equipt (PA)...302 323-8700
259 Quigley Blvd Ste 1 New Castle (19720) ***(G-5312)***
First Choice Services Inc...302 648-7877
33334 Main St Dagsboro (19939) ***(G-901)***
First Church of Christ, Rehoboth Beach *Also called Christian Science Reading Room* ***(G-7888)***
First Class Cards LLC...302 653-0111
131 Stirrup Rd Clayton (19938) ***(G-850)***
First Class Heating & AC Inc...302 934-8900
28418 Dupont Blvd Millsboro (19966) ***(G-4690)***
First Class Heating AC...302 834-1036
6 Shea Way Newark (19713) ***(G-6580)***
First Class Limousine (PA)...302 836-9500
734 Staghorn Dr New Castle (19720) ***(G-5313)***
First Class Properties Del LLC (PA)...302 677-0770
1641 E Lebanon Rd Dover (19901) ***(G-1552)***
First Command Fincl Plg Inc...302 535-8132
1378 Rising Sun Rd Camden Wyoming (19934) ***(G-638)***
First Lincoln Holdings Inc...302 429-4900
1219 N West St Wilmington (19801) ***(G-10546)***
First Line Defense LLC...302 287-2764
885 Mount Friendship Rd Smyrna (19977) ***(G-8634)***
First Montgomery Properties...302 834-8272
900 Woodchuck Pl Bear (19701) ***(G-152)***
First National Bank, Harrington *Also called Wilmington Savings Fund Soc* ***(G-2907)***
First National Bank, Viola *Also called Wilmington Savings Fund Soc* ***(G-8839)***
First National Bnk of Wyoming...302 697-2666
4566 S Dupont Hwy Camden (19934) ***(G-572)***
First Power LLC...610 247-5750
22 Peirce Rd Wilmington (19803) ***(G-10547)***
First Republic Bank...302 777-2699
1201 N Market St Ste 1002 Wilmington (19801) ***(G-10548)***
First Sight Laser Center, Wilmington *Also called Laser Management Group LLC* ***(G-11332)***
First State, New Castle *Also called Fresenius Medical Care N Amer* ***(G-5330)***
First State Anesthesia Svcs...302 225-2990
537 Stanton Christiana Rd # 201 Newark (19713) ***(G-6581)***
First State Automation LLC...302 743-4798
34 Blevins Dr Ste 3 New Castle (19720) ***(G-5314)***
First State Building LLC...302 803-5082
720 Stanton Christiana Rd Wilmington (19804) ***(G-10549)***
First State Carpentry LLC...302 738-8849
14 Thomas Ln N Newark (19711) ***(G-6582)***
First State Cmnty Action Agcy...302 674-1355
655 S Bay Rd Ste 4j Dover (19901) ***(G-1553)***
First State Cmnty Action Agcy (PA)...302 856-7761
308 N Railroad Ave Georgetown (19947) ***(G-2532)***
First State Coin Co...302 734-7776
53 Greentree Dr Dover (19904) ***(G-1554)***
First State Container LLC...603 888-1315
100 Lake Dr Ste 106 Newark (19702) ***(G-6583)***
First State Controls Inc...302 559-7822
2207 Concord Pike 220 Wilmington (19803) ***(G-10550)***
First State Cpas LLC...302 736-6657
970 N State St Dover (19901) ***(G-1555)***
First State Crane Service...302 398-8885
13326 S Dupont Hwy Felton (19943) ***(G-2292)***
First State Disposal...302 644-3885
15 Bridle Reach Ct Lewes (19958) ***(G-3498)***
First State Distributors Inc...302 655-8266
222a 7th Ave Wilmington (19805) ***(G-10551)***
First State Electric Company...302 322-0140
25 King Ct New Castle (19720) ***(G-5315)***
First State Fabrication LLC...302 875-2417
26546 Seaford Rd Seaford (19973) ***(G-8244)***
First State Federal Credit Un...302 674-5281
58 Carver Rd Dover (19904) ***(G-1556)***
First State Firearms & ACC LLC...302 322-1126
178 S Dupont Hwy New Castle (19720) ***(G-5316)***
First State Gastroenterology A...302 677-1617
644 S Queen St Ste 106 Dover (19904) ***(G-1557)***
First State Health & Wellness, Newark *Also called Christiana Chiropractic LLC* ***(G-6220)***
First State Health & Wellness (PA)...302 645-6681
18585 Coastal Hwy Unit 26 Rehoboth Beach (19971) ***(G-7933)***
First State Health & Wellness...302 239-1600
310 Lantana Dr Hockessin (19707) ***(G-3029)***
First State Health & Wellness...302 684-1995
113 Union St Unit A Milton (19968) ***(G-4906)***
First State Inspection Agency (PA)...302 422-3859
1001 Mattlind Way Milford (19963) ***(G-4413)***
First State Inspection Agency...302 449-5383
811 N Broad St Ste 201 Middletown (19709) ***(G-4072)***
First State Landscaping...302 420-8604
214 Springwood Dr Bear (19701) ***(G-153)***
First State Management LLC...302 268-8176
37 Major St Lincoln (19960) ***(G-3848)***
First State Manufacturing Inc...302 424-4520
301 Se 4th St Milford (19963) ***(G-4414)***
First State Medical Assoc LLC...302 999-8169
2055 Limestone Rd Ste 111 Wilmington (19808) ***(G-10552)***
First State Motor Sports...302 798-7000
950 Ridge Rd Ste B18 Claymont (19703) ***(G-745)***
First State Oral & M...302 674-4450
1004 S State St Ste 1 Dover (19901) ***(G-1558)***
First State Orthopaedics, Newark *Also called First State Surgery Center LLC* ***(G-6586)***
First State Pediatrics LLC (PA)...302 292-1559
210 Christiana Med Ctr Newark (19702) ***(G-6584)***
First State Petroleum Services...302 398-9704
714 Gallo Rd Harrington (19952) ***(G-2841)***
First State Physicia NS (PA)...302 836-6150
12 Fox Hunt Dr Bear (19701) ***(G-154)***
First State Plaza, Wilmington *Also called Wilmington Savings Fund Soc* ***(G-13246)***
First State Press LLC...302 731-9058
14 Eileen Dr Newark (19711) ***(G-6585)***
First State Printing, Newark *Also called Luke Destefano Inc* ***(G-6955)***
First State Refinery...302 838-8303
118 Jestan Blvd New Castle (19720) ***(G-5317)***
First State Rehab Home LLC...443 252-7367
111 Oxford Pl Wilmington (19803) ***(G-10553)***
First State Sealcoating...302 632-1234
787 Darling Farm Rd Camden Wyoming (19934) ***(G-639)***
First State Services...302 985-1560
205 Admiral Dr Wilmington (19804) ***(G-10554)***
First State Signs Inc...302 744-9990
122 Rosemary Rd Dover (19901) ***(G-1559)***
First State Steel Drum Co...302 655-2422
4030 New Castle Ave New Castle (19720) ***(G-5318)***
First State Strings Inc...302 331-7362
140 Metz Dr Camden Wyoming (19934) ***(G-640)***
First State Surgery Center LLC...302 683-0700
1000 Twin C Ln Ste 200 Newark (19713) ***(G-6586)***
First State Trust Company...302 573-5967
1 Righter Pkwy Ste 120 Wilmington (19803) ***(G-10555)***
First State Twr & Antenna Svc, Smyrna *Also called Chris Kissell* ***(G-8593)***
First State Vein and Laser Ctr...302 294-0700
1300 N Franklin St Wilmington (19806) ***(G-10556)***
First State Warehousing...302 426-0802
300 Pigeon Blvd New Castle (19720) ***(G-5319)***
First Steps Preschool-Milford...302 424-4470
104 Mccoy St Milford (19963) ***(G-4415)***
FIRST STEPS PRIMEROS PASOS, Georgetown *Also called Primeros Pasos Inc* ***(G-2627)***
First Student Inc...302 995-9607
750 Stanton Christiana Rd Newark (19713) ***(G-6587)***
First Tech...302 421-3650
700 Cornell Dr Ste E5 Wilmington (19801) ***(G-10557)***
First Un Fincl Investments Inc...646 652-6580
2711 Centerville Rd # 400 Wilmington (19808) ***(G-10558)***
Firstchoice Group America LLC...425 242-8626
16192 Coastal Hwy Lewes (19958) ***(G-3499)***
Firstcollect Inc...302 644-6804
12000 Old Vine Blvd Lewes (19958) ***(G-3500)***
Fiscal Associates...302 894-0500
16 Fairfield Dr Newark (19711) ***(G-6588)***
Fish & Monkey Productions LLC...302 897-4318
1612 W 16th St Wilmington (19806) ***(G-10559)***
Fish & Richardson PC...302 652-5070
222 Delaware Ave Wilmington (19801) ***(G-10560)***
Fish & Richardson PC...302 652-5070
222 Delaware Ave Ste 1700 Wilmington (19801) ***(G-10561)***
Fish Window Cleaning Services, Milford *Also called Clearview Windows LLC* ***(G-4356)***
Fisher Auto Parts Inc...302 653-9241
5736 Dupont Pkwy Smyrna (19977) ***(G-8635)***
Fisher Auto Parts Inc...302 856-2507
117 E Market St Georgetown (19947) ***(G-2533)***
Fisher Auto Parts Inc...302 998-3111
1600 E Newport Pike Ste C Wilmington (19804) ***(G-10562)***

ALPHABETIC

(PA)=Parent Co (HQ)=Headquarters (DH)=Div Headquarters
2020 Harris Directory of Delaware Businesses
645

Fishers Auto Parts Inc.......302 934-8088
422 Union St Millsboro (19966) ***(G-4691)***
Fishers Popcorn Fenwick LLC.......302 539-8833
37081 Coastal Hwy Fenwick Island (19944) ***(G-2336)***
Fishing Inc.......302 999-9961
503 Windsor Ave Wilmington (19804) ***(G-10563)***
Fishtail Print Company.......302 408-4800
18585 Coastal Hwy Rehoboth Beach (19971) ***(G-7934)***
Fishtail Print Company.......302 682-3053
125 Cornwall Rd Rehoboth Beach (19971) ***(G-7935)***
Fisons US Investment Holdings (HQ).......302 777-7222
3711 Kennett Pike Ste 334 Wilmington (19807) ***(G-10564)***
Fit ME By Crystal.......302 573-1235
1600 Helen Dr Unit 205 Newark (19702) ***(G-6589)***
Fitness Mtivation Inst of Amer.......302 628-3488
26685 Sussex Hwy Seaford (19973) ***(G-8245)***
Fitovate LLC.......302 463-9790
2702 E Landsdowne Dr Wilmington (19810) ***(G-10565)***
Fitwise Inc.......812 929-2696
651 N Broad St Middletown (19709) ***(G-4073)***
Fitzgerald Auto Salvage Inc.......302 422-7584
17115 Fitzgeralds Rd Lincoln (19960) ***(G-3849)***
Five 1 Five Ice Sports Group L.......302 266-0777
101 John F Campbell Rd Newark (19711) ***(G-6590)***
Five In One Oven Inc.......888 401-3911
200 Continental Dr # 401 Newark (19713) ***(G-6591)***
Five Points, Lewes *Also called County Bank* ***(G-3445)***
Five Sixty Enterprise LLC.......302 268-6530
501 Silverside Rd Ste 505 Wilmington (19809) ***(G-10566)***
Five Star Franchising LLC (HQ).......646 838-3992
1209 N Orange St Wilmington (19801) ***(G-10567)***
Five Star Quality Care Inc.......302 266-9255
501 S Harmony Rd Newark (19713) ***(G-6592)***
Five Star Quality Care Inc.......302 366-0160
255 Possum Park Rd Newark (19711) ***(G-6593)***
Five Star Quality Care Inc.......302 655-6249
407 Foulk Rd Wilmington (19803) ***(G-10568)***
Five Star Quality Care Inc.......302 792-5115
1912 Marsh Rd Wilmington (19810) ***(G-10569)***
Five Star Senior Living Inc.......302 283-0540
4175 Ogletown Rd Newark (19713) ***(G-6594)***
Five Star Senior Living Inc.......302 478-4296
1212 Foulk Rd Ste 1 Wilmington (19803) ***(G-10570)***
Five Stars Embroidery.......443 466-9692
224 Milford Dr Middletown (19709) ***(G-4074)***
Five-Star Basketball, Wilmington *Also called Five Star Franchising LLC* ***(G-10567)***
Fladger & Associates Inc.......302 836-3100
204 Stewards Ct Bear (19701) ***(G-155)***
Flapdoodles Inc (PA).......302 731-9793
725 Dawson Dr Newark (19713) ***(G-6595)***
Flavors & More Inc.......917 887-9241
2711 Centerville Rd # 400 Wilmington (19808) ***(G-10571)***
Fleek Fleet, Wilmington *Also called Fleek Inc* ***(G-10572)***
Fleek Inc.......888 870-1291
3616 Kirkwood Hwy A1470 Wilmington (19808) ***(G-10572)***
Flemings Electrical Service.......302 258-9386
15199 Trap Pond Rd Laurel (19956) ***(G-3230)***
Fletcher Plumbing Htg & AC Inc (PA).......302 653-6277
18 Myrtle St Smyrna (19977) ***(G-8636)***
Flex Ip Solutions Inc.......610 359-5812
2313 Shipley Rd Wilmington (19803) ***(G-10573)***
Flexera Inc.......302 945-6870
22791 Dozer Ln Unit 8 Harbeson (19951) ***(G-2783)***
Flexible Packaging Group, New Castle *Also called Printpack Inc* ***(G-5645)***
Flight Centre Travel Group USA.......302 633-1996
3616 Kirkwood Hwy Ste B Wilmington (19808) ***(G-10574)***
Flight Centre Travel Group USA.......302 479-7581
4737 Concord Pike Ste 835 Wilmington (19803) ***(G-10575)***
Flo Mechanical LLC.......302 239-7299
507 Baxter Ct Hockessin (19707) ***(G-3030)***
Floor Coatings Etc Inc.......302 322-4177
110 J And M Dr New Castle (19720) ***(G-5320)***
Flooring Solutions Inc.......302 655-8001
500 A St Wilmington (19801) ***(G-10576)***
Floristware Inc.......888 531-3012
19c Trolley Sq Wilmington (19806) ***(G-10577)***
Flowers Counsel Group LLC (PA).......302 656-7370
1105 N Market St Ste 800 Wilmington (19801) ***(G-10578)***
Flowline Technologies Inc.......302 256-5825
1201 N Orange St Ste 600 Wilmington (19801) ***(G-10579)***
Flowpay Corporation.......720 425-3244
221 W 9th St Ste 300 Wilmington (19801) ***(G-10580)***
Flowrite Inc.......302 547-5657
102 Country Woods Dr Bear (19701) ***(G-156)***
Flowrite Plumbing, Bear *Also called Flowrite Inc* ***(G-156)***
Floyd Dean Inc.......302 655-7193
2 S Poplar St Ste B Wilmington (19801) ***(G-10581)***
Fluent Forever Inc.......262 725-1707
16192 Coastal Hwy Lewes (19958) ***(G-3501)***
Fluorogistx LLC.......302 479-7614
3704 Kennett Pike Ste 100 Wilmington (19807) ***(G-10582)***
Fluoroproducts, Wilmington *Also called Chemours Company Fc LLC* ***(G-9652)***
Flute Pro Shop Inc.......302 479-5000
4023 Kennett Pike Ste 30 Wilmington (19807) ***(G-10583)***
Flutterby Stitches & EMB.......302 531-7784
203 Doveview Dr Unit 403 Dover (19904) ***(G-1560)***
Flw Wood Products Inc.......410 259-4674
33290 Bayberry Ct Dagsboro (19939) ***(G-902)***
Flyadvanced LLC.......302 324-9970
131 N Dupont Hwy New Castle (19720) ***(G-5321)***
FM Electric Inc.......302 492-3900
436 Strauss Ave Marydel (19964) ***(G-3916)***
FMC Corporation.......302 451-0100
1301 Ogletown Rd Newark (19711) ***(G-6596)***
Fme Lighting LLC.......877 234-8460
21019 Rogers Ave Rehoboth Beach (19971) ***(G-7936)***
Fmj Electrical Contracting.......215 669-2085
912 Parkside Blvd Claymont (19703) ***(G-746)***
Foard R T & Jones Funeral Home, Newark *Also called Robert T Jones & Foard Inc* ***(G-7352)***
Focus Behavioral Health.......302 762-2285
410 Foulk Rd Ste 105 Wilmington (19803) ***(G-10584)***
Focus Health Care Delaware LLC.......302 395-1111
575 S Dupont Hwy New Castle (19720) ***(G-5322)***
Focus Solutions Services Inc.......302 318-1345
262 Chapman Rd Ste 200 Newark (19702) ***(G-6597)***
Foe 74, Wilmington *Also called Fraternal Order Eagles Inc* ***(G-10621)***
Fogarty LLC.......610 731-4804
5 Coty Ln Seaford (19973) ***(G-8246)***
Foldfast Goals LLC.......302 478-7881
1211 Stony Run Dr Wilmington (19803) ***(G-10585)***
Foley Incorporated.......302 328-4131
720 Pulaski Hwy Bear (19701) ***(G-157)***
Food Bank of Delaware Inc.......302 424-3301
1040 Mattlind Way Milford (19963) ***(G-4416)***
Food Bank of Delaware Inc (PA).......302 292-1305
222 Lake Dr Newark (19702) ***(G-6598)***
Food Equipment Service Inc.......302 996-9363
3316a Old Capitol Trl Wilmington (19808) ***(G-10586)***
Food For Pets USA Inc.......514 831-4876
2915 Ogletown Rd Ste 2846 Newark (19713) ***(G-6599)***
Foodliner Inc.......302 368-4204
206 Hansen Ct Newark (19713) ***(G-6600)***
Foot & Ankle Associates.......302 652-5767
3801 Kennett Pike A102 Wilmington (19807) ***(G-10587)***
Foot & Ankle Ctr of Delaware.......302 945-1221
26744 John J Williams Hwy Millsboro (19966) ***(G-4692)***
Foot Care Group Inc (PA).......302 998-0178
1601 Milltown Rd Ste 24 Wilmington (19808) ***(G-10588)***
Foot Care Group Inc.......302 285-0292
272 Carter Dr Ste 220 Middletown (19709) ***(G-4075)***
Foot Light Production Inc.......302 645-7220
516 Kings Hwy Lewes (19958) ***(G-3502)***
Foot Steps Two Heaven Daycare.......302 738-5519
606 Lisbeth Rd Newark (19713) ***(G-6601)***
Footcare Technologies Inc.......704 301-6966
124 Broadkill Rd Ste 472 Milton (19968) ***(G-4907)***
For Delaware Center.......302 656-6466
200 S Madison St Wilmington (19801) ***(G-10589)***
Foraker Oil Inc.......302 834-7595
5th & Clinton St Delaware City (19706) ***(G-957)***
Forcebeyond Inc.......302 995-6588
1521 Concord Pike Ste 301 Wilmington (19803) ***(G-10590)***
Foresee Pharmaceuticals Inc.......302 396-5243
3 Innovation Way Ste 240 Newark (19711) ***(G-6602)***
Foresite Assoc Inc.......302 351-3421
208 Delaware St New Castle (19720) ***(G-5323)***
Forest Oak Elementary Pta.......302 540-2873
55 S Meadowood Dr Newark (19711) ***(G-6603)***
Forest Park Apartments.......302 737-6151
5501 Limeric Cir Ofc 33 Wilmington (19808) ***(G-10591)***
Forest View Nursery.......302 653-7757
1313 Blackbird Forest Rd Clayton (19938) ***(G-851)***
Forever Inc (PA).......302 594-0400
1006 W 27th St Wilmington (19802) ***(G-10592)***
Forever Inc.......302 449-2100
328 E Main St Middletown (19709) ***(G-4076)***
Forever Inc.......302 368-1440
334 Suburban Dr Newark (19711) ***(G-6604)***
Forever Fit Foundation.......302 698-5201
1510 E Lebanon Rd Dover (19901) ***(G-1561)***
Forever Fresh LLC.......302 510-8538
6 Denny Rd Ste 303 Wilmington (19809) ***(G-10593)***
Forever Green Landscaping Inc.......302 322-9535
340 Churchmans Rd New Castle (19720) ***(G-5324)***
Forewinds Hospitality LLC (HQ).......302 368-6640
507 Thompson Station Rd Newark (19711) ***(G-6605)***
Forgotten Few Foundation Inc.......302 494-6212
1927 W 4th St Wilmington (19805) ***(G-10594)***

Formal Affairs Inc ... 302 737-1519
257 E Main St 100 Newark (19711) ***(G-6606)***
Formosa Plastics Corp Delaware ... 302 836-2200
Schoolhouse Rd Delaware City (19706) ***(G-958)***
Formula One Tinting Graphics, Bear *Also called Gotshadeonline Inc* ***(G-168)***
Forrest Avenue Animal Hospital ... 302 736-3000
3156 Forrest Ave Dover (19904) ***(G-1562)***
Forrest Fencing, Felton *Also called J & M Fencing Inc* ***(G-2295)***
Fort Delaware Society ... 302 834-1630
33 Staff Ln Delaware City (19706) ***(G-959)***
Fort Miles Historical Assn Inc ... 302 645-0753
120 E Wild Rabbit Run Lewes (19958) ***(G-3503)***
Forte Sports Incorporated ... 302 731-0776
314 E Main St Ste 1 Newark (19711) ***(G-6607)***
Forthright Consulting, Wilmington *Also called Trellist Inc* ***(G-12965)***
Fortress Home Maintenance Serv ... 302 539-3446
111 Atlantic Ave Ste 7 Ocean View (19970) ***(G-7785)***
Forum To Advnce Mnrties In Eng ... 302 777-3254
2005 Baynard Blvd Wilmington (19802) ***(G-10595)***
Forward Discovery Inc ... 703 647-6364
27 Milbourn Manor Dr Camden Wyoming (19934) ***(G-641)***
Forward Motion Inc ... 302 658-2829
735 S Market St Ste D Wilmington (19801) ***(G-10596)***
Forwood Manor, Wilmington *Also called Five Star Quality Care Inc* ***(G-10569)***
Foschi Fine Photography, Wilmington *Also called Delaware Color Lab* ***(G-10021)***
Foschi Studio ... 302 439-4457
2107 Naamans Rd Wilmington (19810) ***(G-10597)***
Foss-Brown Inc (PA) ... 610 940-6040
3411 Silverside Rd 100wb Wilmington (19810) ***(G-10598)***
Foulk Lawn & Equipment Co Inc ... 302 475-3233
2018 Foulk Rd Wilmington (19810) ***(G-10599)***
Foulk Manor North, Wilmington *Also called Five Star Senior Living Inc* ***(G-10570)***
Foulk Manor South, Wilmington *Also called Five Star Quality Care Inc* ***(G-10568)***
Foulk Pre-Schl & Day Cre Cntr ... 302 529-1580
2711 Carpenter Station Rd Wilmington (19810) ***(G-10600)***
Foulk Pre-Schl & Day Cre Cntr (PA) ... 302 478-3047
2 Tenby Dr Wilmington (19803) ***(G-10601)***
Foulk Road Dental & Associates ... 302 652-3775
300 Foulk Rd Ste 101 Wilmington (19803) ***(G-10602)***
Foundation Source Philanthropi ... 800 839-1754
501 Silverside Rd Wilmington (19809) ***(G-10603)***
Foundtion For A Btter Tomorrow ... 302 674-1397
121 W Loockerman St Dover (19904) ***(G-1563)***
Four Brothers Auto Service ... 302 482-2932
101 N Union St Wilmington (19805) ***(G-10604)***
Four Paws Animal Hospital PA ... 302 629-7297
21804 Eskridge Rd Bridgeville (19933) ***(G-472)***
Four Point Solutions Ltd ... 613 907-6400
3422 Old Capitol Trl Wilmington (19808) ***(G-10605)***
Four Points By Sheraton ... 302 266-6600
56 S Old Baltimore Pike Newark (19702) ***(G-6608)***
Four Seasons Sunrooms, Wilmington *Also called Eastern Home Improvements Inc* ***(G-10322)***
Four States LLC ... 302 655-3400
520 Terminal Ave Ste D New Castle (19720) ***(G-5325)***
Fourth Floor ... 302 472-8416
1205 N Orange St Wilmington (19801) ***(G-10606)***
Fox & Roach LLC ... 302 239-2343
88 Lantana Dr Hockessin (19707) ***(G-3031)***
Fox & Roach LP ... 302 836-2888
1126 Pulaski Hwy Bear (19701) ***(G-158)***
Fox & Roach LP ... 302 477-5500
2200 Concord Pike 1 Wilmington (19803) ***(G-10607)***
Fox Landscaping Corp ... 302 945-5656
24659 Banks Rd Millsboro (19966) ***(G-4693)***
Fox Point Programs Inc ... 800 499-7242
3001 Philadelphia Pike # 1 Claymont (19703) ***(G-747)***
Fox Pointe ... 302 744-9442
352 Fox Pointe Dr Dover (19904) ***(G-1564)***
Fox Rothschild LLP ... 302 654-7444
919 N Market St Ste 1300 Wilmington (19801) ***(G-10608)***
Fox Run Apartments, Bear *Also called First Montgomery Properties* ***(G-152)***
Fox Run Automotive Inc ... 302 834-1200
610 Connor Blvd Bear (19701) ***(G-159)***
Fox Specialties Inc ... 302 322-5200
1500 Johnson Way New Castle (19720) ***(G-5326)***
Foxfire Industries LLC ... 817 602-4900
2035 Sunset Lake Rd B2 Newark (19702) ***(G-6609)***
Foxwood Apts Rehab ... 302 366-8790
15 Fox Hall Ofc Newark (19711) ***(G-6610)***
FPL Energy American Wind LLC ... 302 655-0632
3801 Kennett Pike C200 Wilmington (19807) ***(G-10609)***
Franchise Command Inc ... 714 832-7767
40 E Main St Ste 70 Newark (19711) ***(G-6611)***
Francis Bergold ... 302 284-8101
918 Midstate Rd Felton (19943) ***(G-2293)***
Francis Enterprises LLC ... 302 276-1316
261 Quigley Blvd Ste 10 New Castle (19720) ***(G-5327)***
Francis Kelly Sons Inc ... 302 999-7400
8 Meco Cir Wilmington (19804) ***(G-10610)***
Francis Mase Pediatrics ... 302 762-5656
700 W Lea Blvd Ste 209 Wilmington (19802) ***(G-10611)***
Francis Pollinger & Son Inc ... 302 655-8097
57 Germay Dr Wilmington (19804) ***(G-10612)***
Frank Bartsch Saw Mill ... 302 653-9721
186 Mckays Corner Rd Townsend (19734) ***(G-8787)***
Frank Deramo & Son Inc ... 302 328-0102
10 King Ct New Castle (19720) ***(G-5328)***
Frank Falco MD ... 302 392-6501
100 Becks Woods Dr # 102 Bear (19701) ***(G-160)***
Frank R Yocum Sons Wlpr Blind (PA) ... 302 888-2000
5716 Kennett Pike Wilmington (19807) ***(G-10613)***
Frank Smths Twing Atobody Repr, Wilmington *Also called Ellmore Auto Collision* ***(G-10381)***
Franke USA Holding Inc (HQ) ... 615 462-4000
1105 N Market St Ste 1300 Wilmington (19801) ***(G-10614)***
Frankel Enterprises Inc ... 302 652-6364
1300 N Harrison St A100 Wilmington (19806) ***(G-10615)***
Frankford Custom Woodworks Inc ... 302 732-9570
34139 Dupont Blvd Frankford (19945) ***(G-2363)***
Franklin Fibre-Lamitex Corp ... 302 652-3621
903 E 13th St Wilmington (19802) ***(G-10616)***
Franklin Jester PA ... 302 368-3080
603 Lisbeth Rd Newark (19713) ***(G-6612)***
Franklin Kennet LLC ... 302 655-6536
1113 N Franklin St Wilmington (19806) ***(G-10617)***
Franklin Pancko DDS ... 302 674-1140
712 S Governors Ave Dover (19904) ***(G-1565)***
Franklin Rubber Stamp Co Inc ... 302 654-8841
301 W 8th St Frnt Ste Wilmington (19801) ***(G-10618)***
Franklin T Varone Inc ... 302 475-6200
1403 Silverside Rd Ste A Wilmington (19810) ***(G-10619)***
Franta Rchard E Attrney At Law ... 302 428-1800
1301 N Harrison St # 102 Wilmington (19806) ***(G-10620)***
Frascella Enterprises Inc ... 267 467-4496
650 Naamans Rd Ste 300 Claymont (19703) ***(G-748)***
Fraternal Order Eagles Inc ... 302 764-6100
415 Philadelphia Pike Wilmington (19809) ***(G-10621)***
Fraternal Order of Eagles BR ... 302 616-2935
35083 Atlantic Ave Ocean View (19970) ***(G-7786)***
Fraunhofer Center For Molecula, Newark *Also called Fraunhofer Usa Inc* ***(G-6613)***
Fraunhofer Usa Inc ... 302 369-1708
9 Innovation Way Newark (19711) ***(G-6613)***
Frazzberry ... 302 543-7791
4734 Limestone Rd Wilmington (19808) ***(G-10622)***
Freakin Fresh Salsa Inc ... 302 750-9789
2 Biltmore Ct Wilmington (19808) ***(G-10623)***
Fred Drake Automotive Inc ... 302 378-4877
4195 Dupont Pkwy Townsend (19734) ***(G-8788)***
Fred Drake Salvage, Townsend *Also called Fred Drake Automotive Inc* ***(G-8788)***
Fred L Wright DDS ... 302 239-1641
5309 Limestone Rd A Wilmington (19808) ***(G-10624)***
Fred S Fink Orthodontist ... 302 478-6930
23 The Commons Wilmington (19810) ***(G-10625)***
Fred S Smalls Insurance (PA) ... 302 633-1980
5227 W Woodmill Dr Ste 43 Wilmington (19808) ***(G-10626)***
Frederica Senior Center Inc ... 302 335-4555
216 Market St Frederica (19946) ***(G-2402)***
Frederick Enterprises Inc ... 302 994-5786
810 Stanton Rd Wilmington (19804) ***(G-10627)***
Frederick K Funk ... 302 368-6233
24 Polly Drummond Hill Rd Newark (19711) ***(G-6614)***
Frederick N Hartman ... 302 479-5068
1410 Jan Dr Wilmington (19803) ***(G-10628)***
Free Psychic Reading LLC ... 305 439-1455
8 The Grn Ste 7048 Dover (19901) ***(G-1566)***
Freedom Ctr For Ind Living Inc ... 302 376-4399
400 N Broad St Ste A Middletown (19709) ***(G-4077)***
Freedom Cycle LLC ... 302 286-6900
1110 Ogletown Rd Newark (19711) ***(G-6615)***
Freedom Dental Management Inc ... 302 836-3750
1290 Peoples Plz Newark (19702) ***(G-6616)***
Freedom Landscape & Irrigation ... 302 436-7100
38488 Dupont Blvd Selbyville (19975) ***(G-8494)***
Freedom Materials ... 302 281-0085
721 Dawson Dr Newark (19713) ***(G-6617)***
Freedom Mortgage Corporation ... 302 368-7100
220 Continental Dr # 315 Newark (19713) ***(G-6618)***
Freedom Paper Company LLC ... 443 542-5845
1201 N Orange St Ste 700 Wilmington (19801) ***(G-10629)***
Freedom Rides Auto ... 302 422-4559
26831 Sussex Hwy Seaford (19973) ***(G-8247)***
Freehold Cartage Inc ... 302 658-2005
350 Pigeon Point Rd New Castle (19720) ***(G-5329)***
Freelee Foundation ... 302 607-8053
1400 Helen Dr Unit 104 Newark (19702) ***(G-6619)***
Freemarkets Investment Co Inc ... 302 427-2089
1105 N Market St Ste 1300 Wilmington (19801) ***(G-10630)***

Freibott Law Firm 302 633-9000
  1711 E Newport Pike Wilmington (19804) *(G-10631)*
Fremont Hall 302 731-2431
  82 Possum Park Rd Newark (19711) *(G-6620)*
French Street Management 302 571-8597
  1105 N Market St Ste 1300 Wilmington (19801) *(G-10632)*
Frenius Medical Care 302 421-9177
  7 S Clayton St Wilmington (19805) *(G-10633)*
Frensenius Medical Ctr 302 762-2903
  4000 N Washington St Wilmington (19802) *(G-10634)*
Fresenius Kdney Care Brdgville, Bridgeville Also called Fresenius Medical Care *(G-473)*
Fresenius Kidney Care Lantana, Hockessin Also called Fresenius Med Cre N Delaware *(G-3032)*
Fresenius Kidney Care Main St, Newark Also called Bio-Mdcal Applications Del Inc *(G-6081)*
Fresenius Kidney Care N Dover, Dover Also called Fresenius Medical Care Souther *(G-1568)*
Fresenius Med Care Brandywine, Wilmington Also called National Medical Care Inc *(G-11808)*
Fresenius Med Care Millsboro, Millsboro Also called Fresenius Med Care S Delaware *(G-4694)*
Fresenius Med Care S Delaware 302 934-6342
  30164 Commerce Dr Millsboro (19966) *(G-4694)*
Fresenius Med Cre N Delaware 302 239-4704
  704 Lantana Dr Hockessin (19707) *(G-3032)*
Fresenius Medcl Care Brndywine, Newark Also called Bio-Mdical Applications of Del *(G-6082)*
Fresenius Medical Care, Dover Also called Renal Care Center Dover *(G-2025)*
Fresenius Medical Care 302 736-1340
  1198 S Governors Ave Dover (19904) *(G-1567)*
Fresenius Medical Care 302 337-8789
  9115 Antique Aly Unit 1 Bridgeville (19933) *(G-473)*
Fresenius Medical Care Fox Run, Bear Also called Fresenius Medical Care Nephr *(G-161)*
Fresenius Medical Care N Amer 302 328-9044
  608 Ferry Cut Off St New Castle (19720) *(G-5330)*
Fresenius Medical Care N Amer 302 633-6228
  605 W Newport Pike Wilmington (19804) *(G-10635)*
Fresenius Medical Care Nephr 302 836-6093
  2520 Wrangle Hill Rd Bear (19701) *(G-161)*
Fresenius Medical Care Souther 302 678-2181
  80 Salt Creek Dr Dover (19901) *(G-1568)*
Fresenius Medical Care Vero Be 302 453-8834
  63 University Plz Newark (19702) *(G-6621)*
Fresenius Medical Services, Smyrna Also called BMA of Smyrna *(G-8583)*
Fresenius Usa Inc 302 422-9739
  656 N Dupont Blvd Milford (19963) *(G-4417)*
Fresenius Usa Inc 302 455-0454
  61 University Plz Newark (19702) *(G-6622)*
Fresenius Usa Inc 302 658-7469
  303 A St Wilmington (19801) *(G-10636)*
Fresh Accents LLC 301 717-3757
  134 New Castle Dr Bethany Beach (19930) *(G-399)*
Fresh Industries Ltd 205 737-3747
  37385 Henlopen Jct Rehoboth Beach (19971) *(G-7937)*
Fresh Start Marketplace LLC 302 240-3002
  8 The Grn Dover (19901) *(G-1569)*
Fresh Start Transformations 302 219-0221
  4604 Tracy Dr Newark (19702) *(G-6623)*
Freshbooks Usa Inc 416 525-5384
  2711 Centerville Rd # 300 Wilmington (19808) *(G-10637)*
Frets4vetsorg 302 382-1426
  300a Nancy St Georgetown (19947) *(G-2534)*
Friedlander and Gorris 302 573-3500
  1201 N Market St Ste 2200 Wilmington (19801) *(G-10638)*
Friendly Oil Co, Newark Also called Durrell Sandblasting & Pntg Co *(G-6481)*
Friends & Family Practice 302 537-3740
  35141 Atlantic Ave Unit 1 Millville (19967) *(G-4845)*
Friends and Sign 302 368-4794
  61 Matthews Rd Newark (19713) *(G-6624)*
Friends of Bellaca Airfield 302 322-3816
  Ctr Pt Blvd Rr 273 New Castle (19720) *(G-5331)*
Friends of Capitol Theater Inc 302 678-3583
  226 S State St Dover (19901) *(G-1570)*
Friends of University Sussex 302 295-4959
  1000 N West St Ste 1200 Wilmington (19801) *(G-10639)*
Friendship House Incorporated 302 652-8033
  720 N Orange St Wilmington (19801) *(G-10640)*
Friendship House Incorporated (PA) 302 652-8133
  226 N Walnut St Wilmington (19801) *(G-10641)*
Friess Associates LLC 302 656-3017
  3711 Kennett Pike Ste 100 Wilmington (19807) *(G-10642)*
Frightland LLC 302 838-0256
  309 Port Penn Rd Middletown (19709) *(G-4078)*
Frizbee Medical Inc 424 901-1534
  1013 Centre Rd Wilmington (19805) *(G-10643)*
Frog Hollow Golf Course 302 376-6500
  1 Wittington Way Middletown (19709) *(G-4079)*
Froggys Industrial Supply Inc 302 508-2340
  370 N Main St Smyrna (19977) *(G-8637)*

From Ground Up Construction 302 747-0996
  26 Evergreen Dr Newark (19702) *(G-6625)*
Frontgate LLC 302 245-6654
  33258 Kent Ave Bethany Beach (19930) *(G-400)*
Frontier Agricultural Sciences, Newark Also called Frontier Scientific Inc *(G-6626)*
Frontier Scientific Inc 302 266-6891
  601 Interchange Blvd Newark (19711) *(G-6626)*
Frontier Scientific Svcs Inc 302 266-6891
  601 Interchange Blvd Newark (19711) *(G-6627)*
Frontier Technologies Inc (PA) 302 225-2530
  1521 Concord Pike Ste 302 Wilmington (19803) *(G-10644)*
Frontline LLC 302 526-0877
  16192 Coastal Hwy Lewes (19958) *(G-3504)*
Frontline Crossfit 302 229-6467
  4060 N Dupont Hwy 1 New Castle (19720) *(G-5332)*
Frst State Ceramics & Marble, Milton Also called Robert McMann *(G-4964)*
Fruitbearer Publishing LLC 302 856-6649
  107 Elizabeth St Georgetown (19947) *(G-2535)*
Fry Farms Inc 302 422-9112
  5846 Williamsville Rd Milford (19963) *(G-4418)*
Fshery Mid-Atlntic MGT Council 302 674-2331
  800 N State St Ste 201 Dover (19901) *(G-1571)*
Ftl Technologies Corporation 703 873-7801
  16192 Coastal Hwy Lewes (19958) *(G-3505)*
Fuji Film 302 477-8000
  233 Cherry Ln New Castle (19720) *(G-5333)*
Fujifilm Imaging Colorants Inc (HQ) 302 477-8022
  233 Cherry Ln New Castle (19720) *(G-5334)*
Fujifilm Imaging Colorants Inc 302 472-1245
  233 Cherry Ln New Castle (19720) *(G-5335)*
Fulcrum Pharmacy MGT Inc 302 658-8020
  501 N Shipley St Wilmington (19801) *(G-10645)*
Full Game Ahead USA LLC 302 281-0102
  Trolley Sq Ste 20c Wilmington (19806) *(G-10646)*
Fulton Bank National Assn 302 407-3291
  800 Foulk Rd Wilmington (19803) *(G-10647)*
Fulton Bank National Assn 302 737-7766
  281 E Main St Newark (19711) *(G-6628)*
Fulton Bank National Assn 302 378-4575
  468 W Main St Middletown (19709) *(G-4080)*
Fulton Bank National Assn 302 227-0330
  20281 Coastal Hwy Rehoboth Beach (19971) *(G-7938)*
Fulton Bank National Assn 302 539-8031
  60 Atlantic Ave Ocean View (19970) *(G-7787)*
Fulton Bank National Assn 302 934-5911
  28412 Dupont Blvd Ste 106 Millsboro (19966) *(G-4695)*
Fulton Bank National Assn 302 644-4900
  34346 Carpenters Way Lewes (19958) *(G-3506)*
Fulton Financial Advisors, Wilmington Also called Fulton Bank National Assn *(G-10647)*
Fulton Financial Advisors, Newark Also called Fulton Bank National Assn *(G-6628)*
Fulton Financial Advisors, Middletown Also called Fulton Bank National Assn *(G-4080)*
Fulton Financial Advisors, Rehoboth Beach Also called Fulton Bank National Assn *(G-7938)*
Fulton Financial Advisors, Ocean View Also called Fulton Bank National Assn *(G-7787)*
Fulton Financial Advisors, Lewes Also called Fulton Bank National Assn *(G-3506)*
Fulton Paper, Middletown Also called Forever Inc *(G-4076)*
Fulton Paper & Party Supply, Wilmington Also called Forever Inc *(G-10592)*
Fulton Paper Co, Newark Also called Forever Inc *(G-6604)*
Fulton Paper Company 302 594-0400
  1006 W 27th St Wilmington (19802) *(G-10648)*
Fun 2 Learn Day Care 302 875-3393
  7119 Airport Rd Laurel (19956) *(G-3231)*
Fun Bakery LLC 858 220-0946
  3500 S Dupont Hwy Dover (19901) *(G-1572)*
Fun Sport Inc 302 644-2042
  Rr 1 Rehoboth Beach (19971) *(G-7939)*
Functionalit Inc 703 566-6624
  31454 Forsythia Dr Selbyville (19975) *(G-8495)*
Funland, Rehoboth Beach Also called Seaside Amusements Inc *(G-8071)*
Funstep Inc 302 731-9618
  1805 Capitol Trl Newark (19711) *(G-6629)*
Fuqua & Yori P A 302 856-7777
  26 The Cir Georgetown (19947) *(G-2536)*
Fuqua, James A Jr, Georgetown Also called Fuqua & Yori P A *(G-2536)*
Fur Baby Tracker LLC 610 563-3294
  302 Taft Ave Wilmington (19805) *(G-10649)*
Furniture Solution, Bear Also called Furniture Whl Connection Inc *(G-162)*
Furniture Whl Connection Inc 302 836-6000
  1890 Pulaski Hwy Bear (19701) *(G-162)*
Furrs Tire Service Inc 302 678-0800
  1251 S Bay Rd Dover (19901) *(G-1573)*
Fursan Consulting Services 240 654-5784
  42 Reads Way New Castle (19720) *(G-5336)*
Fusco Enterprises, New Castle Also called Fusco Management Inc *(G-5338)*
Fusco Enterprises (PA) 302 328-6251
  200 Airport Rd New Castle (19720) *(G-5337)*
Fusco Management Inc 302 328-6251
  200 Airport Rd New Castle (19720) *(G-5338)*

Fusion...302 479-9444
3444 Naamans Rd Fl 1 Wilmington (19810) ***(G-10650)***
Fusion Health Works...302 543-4714
829 N Harrison St Wilmington (19806) ***(G-10651)***
Fusura LLC...302 397-2200
800 Delaware Ave Ste 500 Wilmington (19801) ***(G-10652)***
Future Bright Pediatrics...302 883-3266
938 S Bradford St Dover (19904) ***(G-1574)***
Future Bright Pediatrics LLC (PA)...302 538-6258
120 Old Camden Rd Ste B Camden (19934) ***(G-573)***
Future Development Learning...302 652-7500
500 Maryland Ave Wilmington (19805) ***(G-10653)***
Future Ford Sales Inc (PA)...302 999-0261
4001 Kirkwood Hwy Wilmington (19808) ***(G-10654)***
Future Leaders...862 262-7312
906 Boxwood Dr Smyrna (19977) ***(G-8638)***
Future Option Trading Company, Newark *Also called Futuretech Inv Group Inc* ***(G-6630)***
Futuretech Inv Group Inc...302 476-9529
12 Timber Creek Ln Newark (19711) ***(G-6630)***
Fx-Edge LLC...718 404-9362
16192 Coastal Hwy Lewes (19958) ***(G-3507)***
Fyrbeacon Inc...562 569-0547
2711 Centerville Rd # 400 Wilmington (19808) ***(G-10655)***
G & D Collection Group Inc...302 482-2512
234 Philadelphia Pike # 9 Wilmington (19809) ***(G-10656)***
G & E Welding Supply Co...302 322-9353
281 Airport Rd New Castle (19720) ***(G-5339)***
G & G Flight Service Inc...302 674-3264
144 Cherry St Dover (19904) ***(G-1575)***
G & S TV & Antenna...302 422-5733
20450 Sapp Rd Milford (19963) ***(G-4419)***
G A Hastings & Associates...302 537-5760
102 Central Ave Ste 1 Ocean View (19970) ***(G-7788)***
G B Lyons DDS...302 654-1765
100 W Rockwind Rd Wilmington (19801) ***(G-10657)***
G B Tech Inc...302 378-5600
651 N Broad St Ste 301 Middletown (19709) ***(G-4081)***
G E N, Wilmington *Also called Global Network Executive Inc* ***(G-10728)***
G Fedale General Contrs LLC...302 225-7663
160 Thompson Dr Hockessin (19707) ***(G-3033)***
G Fedale Roofing & Siding, Hockessin *Also called G Fedale General Contrs LLC* ***(G-3033)***
G Fedale Roofing and Siding...302 225-7663
101 S Mary St Wilmington (19804) ***(G-10658)***
G G + A LLC...302 376-6122
1050 Industrial Rd # 110 Middletown (19709) ***(G-4082)***
G I Associates of Delaware, Dover *Also called GI Associates of Delaware* ***(G-1592)***
G K Associates Inc...302 381-2824
19 Eagles Lndg Unit 2 Rehoboth Beach (19971) ***(G-7940)***
G L K Inc (PA)...302 697-3838
55 Beloit Ave Dover (19901) ***(G-1576)***
G Leigh Cook DMD...302 453-8700
16 Peddlers Row Newark (19702) ***(G-6631)***
G N G Insurance, Wilmington *Also called Williams Insurance Agency Inc* ***(G-13217)***
G Rehoboth...302 278-7677
234 Rehoboth Ave Rehoboth Beach (19971) ***(G-7941)***
G T Painting Inc...302 734-7771
1206 White Oak Rd Dover (19901) ***(G-1577)***
G W Keller DDS...302 652-3586
1110 N Bancroft Pkwy # 2 Wilmington (19805) ***(G-10659)***
G.C.E., Newark *Also called Dis Inc* ***(G-6453)***
G2 Group Inc...302 836-4202
88 Loblolly Ln Bear (19701) ***(G-163)***
G2 Lab Group, Bear *Also called G2 Group Inc* ***(G-163)***
G2 Performance Band ACC...800 554-8523
2207 Concord Pike Ste 220 Wilmington (19803) ***(G-10660)***
G4s Secure Solutions (usa)...302 395-9930
38 Reads Way New Castle (19720) ***(G-5340)***
Gabriel Jr Timoteo R MD...302 998-0300
1941 Limestone Rd Ste 210 Wilmington (19808) ***(G-10661)***
Gahagan & Bryant Assoc Inc...302 652-4948
3801 Kennett Pike C302 Wilmington (19807) ***(G-10662)***
Gai Communications Inc...609 254-1470
560 Peoples Plz 136 Newark (19702) ***(G-6632)***
Gainor Awnings Inc...302 998-8611
1 Elm Ave Wilmington (19805) ***(G-10663)***
Galaxy Sign & Lighting...302 757-5349
2117 Armour Dr Wilmington (19808) ***(G-10664)***
Gale and Associates LLC...302 698-4253
113 Jillian Dr Dover (19901) ***(G-1578)***
Gale Force Cleaning & Restore...302 539-4683
14 Atlantic Ave Ocean View (19970) ***(G-7789)***
Gale Force Clg & Restoration, Ocean View *Also called R W Home Services Inc* ***(G-7810)***
Gallagher & Associates PA...302 239-5501
5500 Skyline Dr Ste 6 Wilmington (19808) ***(G-10665)***
Gallery One...302 537-5055
125 Atlantic Ave Ocean View (19967) ***(G-7790)***
Galleyware Company Inc...302 996-9480
330 Water St Ste 107 Wilmington (19804) ***(G-10666)***
Gallo Realty Inc...888 624-6794
33292 Coastal Hwy Bethany Beach (19930) ***(G-401)***
Gallo Realty Inc (PA)...302 945-7368
37230 Rehoboth Avenue Ext Rehoboth Beach (19971) ***(G-7942)***
Galloway Court Apts...302 328-0488
400 S Dupont Hwy Ofc 125 New Castle (19720) ***(G-5341)***
Galloway Electric Co Inc...302 453-8385
19 Albe Dr Newark (19702) ***(G-6633)***
Galloway Leasing Inc...302 453-8385
19 Albe Dr Newark (19702) ***(G-6634)***
Gallucios Lawn Care...302 324-8182
24 Farragut Ln New Castle (19720) ***(G-5342)***
Galman Group Inc...302 737-5550
25b Windsor Cir Newark (19702) ***(G-6635)***
Galvin Industries LLC...703 505-7860
202 W Laurel St Georgetown (19947) ***(G-2537)***
Game Changing Industries LLC (PA)...302 498-8321
3422 Old Capitol Trl Wilmington (19808) ***(G-10667)***
Gamers4gamers LLC...302 722-6289
40 E Main St Ste 649 Newark (19711) ***(G-6636)***
Gamestop Inc...302 266-7362
326 Suburban Dr Newark (19711) ***(G-6637)***
Gaming Morning Report, Dover *Also called Morning Report Research Inc* ***(G-1872)***
Gamma Theta Lambda Ed...302 983-9429
2 N Sherman Dr Bear (19701) ***(G-164)***
Gamut Color Inc...302 652-7171
1600 N Scott St Wilmington (19806) ***(G-10668)***
Gannett Co Inc...302 325-6600
950 W Basin Rd New Castle (19720) ***(G-5343)***
Gannett Fleming Inc...302 378-2256
651 N Broad St Middletown (19709) ***(G-4083)***
Garage...302 645-7288
18791 Coastal Hwy Rehoboth Beach (19971) ***(G-7943)***
Garage...302 453-1930
132 Christiana Mall Newark (19702) ***(G-6638)***
Garcia Landscaping Services...302 324-8789
14 Mark Dr New Castle (19720) ***(G-5344)***
Garcia Podiatry Group...302 994-5956
1941 Limestone Rd Ste 208 Wilmington (19808) ***(G-10669)***
Garcia, Luis M Jr DPM, Wilmington *Also called Garcia Podiatry Group* ***(G-10669)***
Garda CL Atlantic Inc (HQ)...302 762-5444
4200 Governor Printz Blvd Wilmington (19802) ***(G-10670)***
Garden Design Group Inc...302 234-3000
787 Valley Rd Hockessin (19707) ***(G-3034)***
Gardner Asphalt, Seaford *Also called Emulsion Products Company* ***(G-8236)***
Gardner Asphalt Corporation...302 629-3505
25938 Nanticoke Ave Seaford (19973) ***(G-8248)***
Gardner Industries Inc...302 448-9195
25938 Nanticoke Ave Seaford (19973) ***(G-8249)***
Gardner-Gibson Inc...302 628-4290
25938 Nanticoke Ave Seaford (19973) ***(G-8250)***
Garile Inc...302 366-0848
311 Ruthar Dr Newark (19711) ***(G-6639)***
Garrett Motion Inc...973 867-7017
251 Little Falls Dr Wilmington (19808) ***(G-10671)***
Garrett Transportation I Inc (HQ)...973 455-2000
251 Little Falls Dr Wilmington (19808) ***(G-10672)***
Garrison Calpine...302 562-5661
450 Garrison Oak Dr Dover (19901) ***(G-1579)***
Garrison Custom Homes...302 644-4008
19413 Jingle Shell Way # 5 Lewes (19958) ***(G-3508)***
Garrisons Lake Golf Club...302 659-1206
101 W Fairways Cir Smyrna (19977) ***(G-8639)***
Garth Troescher Jr LLC...302 927-0106
34105 Shockley Town Rd Frankford (19945) ***(G-2364)***
Gary A Bryde PA...302 239-3700
724 Yorklyn Rd Ste 100 Hockessin (19707) ***(G-3035)***
Gary I Markowitz MD...302 422-5155
110 Ne Front St Milford (19963) ***(G-4420)***
Gary L Waite DMD...302 239-8586
5500 Skyline Dr Ste 2 Wilmington (19808) ***(G-10673)***
Gary M Munch Inc...302 525-8301
995 S Chapel St Ste 1 Newark (19713) ***(G-6640)***
Gary Quiroga...302 697-3352
34 S Fairfield Dr Dover (19901) ***(G-1580)***
Gary R Collins DDS...302 239-3531
5500 Skyline Dr Ste 1 Wilmington (19808) ***(G-10674)***
Gary Sj CPA...302 730-3737
809 Monroe Ter Dover (19904) ***(G-1581)***
Gas & Go Inc...302 734-8234
805 Forest St Dover (19904) ***(G-1582)***
Gas Div, Wilmington *Also called Delmarva Power & Light Company* ***(G-10103)***
Gastroenterology Associates PA (PA)...302 738-5300
4745 Ogletown Stanton Rd # 134 Newark (19713) ***(G-6641)***
Gatehouse Media Inc...302 678-3616
1196 S Little Creek Rd Dover (19901) ***(G-1583)***
Gatehuse Mdia Del Holdings Inc...302 678-3616
1196 S Little Creek Rd Dover (19901) ***(G-1584)***
Gates and Company LLC...302 428-1338
4001 Kennett Pike Ste 206 Wilmington (19807) ***(G-10675)***

ALPHABETIC

(PA)=Parent Co (HQ)=Headquarters (DH)=Div Headquarters
2020 Harris Directory of Delaware Businesses
649

Gatesair Inc ALPHABETIC SECTION

Gatesair Inc ... 513 459-3400
2711 Centerville Rd Wilmington (19808) ***(G-10676)***
Gateway Construction Inc ... 302 653-4400
498 Sudlersville Rd Clayton (19938) ***(G-852)***
Gateway House Inc ... 302 571-8885
121 N Poplar St Apt A11 Wilmington (19801) ***(G-10677)***
Gateway International 360 LLC ... 302 250-4990
260 Quigley Blvd Ste 135 New Castle (19720) ***(G-5345)***
Gatto Graphix LLC ... 302 598-5377
2412 Greenleaf Dr Wilmington (19810) ***(G-10678)***
Gaudenzia Fresh Start, Wilmington *Also called Gaudenzia Inc* ***(G-10679)***
Gaudenzia Inc ... 302 421-9945
604 W 10th St Wilmington (19801) ***(G-10679)***
Gaudlitz Inc ... 202 468-3876
160 Greentree Dr Ste 101 Dover (19904) ***(G-1585)***
Gaudlitz Plastic Technologies, Dover *Also called Gaudlitz Inc* ***(G-1585)***
Gauri Inc ... 302 731-5300
306 Suburban Dr Newark (19711) ***(G-6642)***
Gavinsolmonese ... 302 655-8997
919 N Market St Wilmington (19801) ***(G-10680)***
Gb Home Improvement ... 302 654-5411
100 Greenhill Ave Ste F Wilmington (19805) ***(G-10681)***
Gb Jacobs LLC ... 302 378-9100
2486 N Dupont Pkwy Middletown (19709) ***(G-4084)***
Gb Shades LLC (PA) ... 302 798-3028
100 Naamans Rd Ste 5f Claymont (19703) ***(G-749)***
GBA, Wilmington *Also called Newmarkkfsm* ***(G-11876)***
GBA, Wilmington *Also called Gahagan & Bryant Assoc Inc* ***(G-10662)***
GBA Enterprises Inc ... 302 323-1080
208 Churchmans Rd New Castle (19720) ***(G-5346)***
Gbc International Corp (PA) ... 404 860-2533
2711 Centerville Rd # 400 Wilmington (19808) ***(G-10682)***
Gbg USA Inc ... 888 342-7243
1209 N Orange St Wilmington (19801) ***(G-10683)***
Gc New Castle Inc ... 302 544-6128
1508 Beaver Creek Xing New Castle (19720) ***(G-5347)***
Gcg Capital LLC ... 302 703-7610
16192 Coastal Hwy Lewes (19958) ***(G-3509)***
Gcl A, Wilmington *Also called Garda CL Atlantic Inc* ***(G-10670)***
Gcora Corp ... 302 310-1000
30 Rosebush Ct Milford (19963) ***(G-4421)***
GE Capital Intl Holdings Corp (HQ) ... 302 658-7581
1209 N Orange St Wilmington (19801) ***(G-10684)***
GE Tf Trust ... 302 636-6196
Rodney Sq N 1100 N Mkt St Wilmington (19890) ***(G-10685)***
Gearhalo Us Inc ... 780 239-2120
8 The Grn Dover (19901) ***(G-1586)***
Gearhart Construction Inc ... 302 674-5466
5075 N Dupont Hwy Dover (19901) ***(G-1587)***
Gears Mechanical Company, Frankford *Also called Robert Gears* ***(G-2383)***
Gebhart Funeral Home Inc ... 302 798-7726
3401 Philadelphia Pike Claymont (19703) ***(G-750)***
Geekytek, Rehoboth Beach *Also called M C Tek LLC* ***(G-7992)***
Geico Corporation ... 302 998-9192
4541 Kirkwood Hwy Wilmington (19808) ***(G-10686)***
Gelfand Group Inc ... 310 666-2362
341 Raven Cir Camden Wyoming (19934) ***(G-642)***
Gellert Scali Busenkell Brown, Wilmington *Also called GSB&b LLC* ***(G-10793)***
Gem Group LP ... 302 762-2008
501 Carr Rd Wilmington (19809) ***(G-10687)***
Gem Merchant LLC ... 734 274-1280
16192 Coastal Hwy Lewes (19958) ***(G-3510)***
Gem-Gradually Expanding Minds ... 302 322-3701
523 Concord Bridge Pl Newark (19702) ***(G-6643)***
Gemini Building Systems LLC ... 302 654-5310
1607 E Newport Pike Wilmington (19804) ***(G-10688)***
Gemini Hair Designs ... 302 654-9371
22a Trolley Sq Wilmington (19806) ***(G-10689)***
Genalyze LLC ... 732 917-4893
410 N Ramunno Dr Ut1806 Middletown (19709) ***(G-4085)***
Gene and Taffin A Ray Family ... 800 839-1754
501 Silverside Rd Ste 123 Wilmington (19809) ***(G-10690)***
General Automotive Repair, Dover *Also called Patriot Auto & Truck Care LLC* ***(G-1940)***
General Coatings LLC ... 302 841-7958
26492 Shasta Way Millsboro (19966) ***(G-4696)***
General Contractor, Dover *Also called Kings Contracting Inc* ***(G-1751)***
General Crpt-Mech Sply ... 302 322-1847
4 Nonesuch Pl New Castle (19720) ***(G-5348)***
General Electric Company ... 302 631-1300
400 Bellevue Rd Newark (19713) ***(G-6644)***
General Hlthcare Resources LLC ... 302 998-0469
5700 Kirkwood Hwy Ste 203 Wilmington (19808) ***(G-10691)***
General Refrigeration Company (PA) ... 302 846-3073
36615 Old Stage Rd Delmar (19940) ***(G-999)***
General Separation Tech Inc ... 302 533-5646
625 Dawson Dr Ste A Newark (19713) ***(G-6645)***
General Teamsters Local Un 326 ... 302 328-2387
451 Churchmans Rd New Castle (19720) ***(G-5349)***
Generation Consultants LLC ... 302 722-4884
362 Wedgewood Rd Ste 2a Newark (19711) ***(G-6646)***
Generations Home Care Inc ... 302 322-3100
5211 W Woodmill Dr Wilmington (19808) ***(G-10692)***
Genes Limousine Service Inc ... 410 479-8470
501 Market St Bridgeville (19933) ***(G-474)***
Genesec Inc ... 917 656-5742
62 Lake Forest Blvd Claymont (19703) ***(G-751)***
Genesis Eldercare Nat Ctrs Inc ... 302 734-5990
1080 Silver Lake Blvd Dover (19904) ***(G-1588)***
Genesis Halthcare - Main Voice ... 302 536-6390
1100 Norman Eskridge Hwy Seaford (19973) ***(G-8251)***
GENESIS HEALTH CARE, Wilmington *Also called Hillside Center* ***(G-10909)***
Genesis Health Care, Wilmington *Also called 810 Suth Broom St Oprtions LLC* ***(G-8868)***
Genesis Healthcare Corporation ... 302 422-3754
700 Marvel Rd Milford (19963) ***(G-4422)***
Genesis Healthcare Seafood Ctr ... 302 629-3575
1100 Norman Eskridge Hwy Seaford (19973) ***(G-8252)***
Genesis Laboratories Inc (PA) ... 832 217-8585
11 Middleton Dr Wilmington (19808) ***(G-10693)***
Genex Technologies Inc ... 302 266-6161
100 Lake Dr Ste 6 Newark (19702) ***(G-6647)***
Genoese Miller & Associates ... 302 655-9505
615 W 18th St Wilmington (19802) ***(G-10694)***
Genovesius Solutia LLC ... 302 252-7506
521 Cabot Dr Hockessin (19707) ***(G-3036)***
Gens Trucking Inc ... 302 421-3522
512 Golding Ave New Castle (19720) ***(G-5350)***
Gensource Fincl Asrn Co LLC ... 302 415-3030
3422 Old Capitol Trl Wilmington (19808) ***(G-10695)***
Gentle Care Family Dentistry, Wilmington *Also called Rodriguez Marieve O Dmd PA* ***(G-12462)***
Gentle Touch Dentistry ... 302 765-3373
303 E Lea Blvd Wilmington (19802) ***(G-10696)***
Gentleman Door Company Inc ... 302 239-4045
506 Dawson Tract Rd Yorklyn (19736) ***(G-13366)***
Genuine Parts Company ... 610 494-6355
319 Ridge Rd Claymont (19703) ***(G-752)***
Geo-Fence Inc ... 763 516-8934
8 The Grn Ste A Dover (19901) ***(G-1589)***
Geo-Technology Associates Inc ... 302 326-2100
18 Boulden Cir Ste 36 New Castle (19720) ***(G-5351)***
Geo-Technology Associates Inc ... 302 855-5775
21133 Sterling Ave Unit 7 Georgetown (19947) ***(G-2538)***
George Miles & Buhr LLC ... 302 628-1421
400 High St Seaford (19973) ***(G-8253)***
George & Lynch Inc (PA) ... 302 736-3031
150 Lafferty Ln Dover (19901) ***(G-1590)***
George & Lynch Inc ... 302 238-7289
20631 Betts Rd Millsboro (19966) ***(G-4697)***
George and Son Seafood Market ... 302 239-7204
1216 Old Lancaster Pike Hockessin (19707) ***(G-3037)***
George E Frattali DDS ... 302 651-4408
1801 Rockland Rd Ste 100 Wilmington (19803) ***(G-10697)***
George F Kempf Supply Co Inc ... 302 658-3760
1101 E 7th St Wilmington (19801) ***(G-10698)***
George H Bunting Jr ... 302 227-3891
19716 Sea Air Ave 1 Rehoboth Beach (19971) ***(G-7944)***
George H Burns Inc ... 302 658-0752
200 N Ford Ave Wilmington (19805) ***(G-10699)***
George Hardcastle & Sons Inc (PA) ... 302 655-5230
5714 Kennett Pike Wilmington (19807) ***(G-10700)***
George J Weiner Associates ... 302 658-0218
2961 Centerville Rd # 300 Wilmington (19808) ***(G-10701)***
George K Rickards Inc ... 302 539-7550
26 Central Ave Ocean View (19970) ***(G-7791)***
George M Howard & Sons Inc ... 302 645-9655
18682 Munchy Branch Rd Rehoboth Beach (19971) ***(G-7945)***
George Marcus Salon Inc ... 302 475-7530
3629 Silverside Rd Ste 1 Wilmington (19810) ***(G-10702)***
George Metz ... 302 227-4343
37385 Rehoboth Avenue Ext Rehoboth Beach (19971) ***(G-7946)***
George Mtstsos MD Crdiolgy LLC ... 302 482-2035
3521 Silverside Rd Ste 2k Wilmington (19810) ***(G-10703)***
George P Stewart ... 302 737-4927
488 Walther Rd Newark (19702) ***(G-6648)***
George Products Company Inc ... 302 449-0199
110 Sleepy Hollow Dr Middletown (19709) ***(G-4086)***
George Read II House, New Castle *Also called Historical Society of Del Inc* ***(G-5397)***
George Staats ... 302 653-9729
1570 Vndyke Grenspring Rd Smyrna (19977) ***(G-8640)***
George Swire Sr ... 302 690-6995
790 Daisey Rd Clayton (19938) ***(G-853)***
George W Oppel ... 302 398-4433
3202 Gun And Rod Club Rd Houston (19954) ***(G-3178)***
George W Plummer & Son Inc ... 302 645-9531
18370 Coastal Hwy Lewes (19958) ***(G-3511)***
Georges Custom Woodworking ... 302 541-4599
34885 Wingate Ct Dagsboro (19939) ***(G-903)***
Georgetown, Georgetown *Also called Boys & Girls Clubs Del Inc* ***(G-2457)***

Georgetown Air Services.....302 855-2355
21553 Rudder Ln Unit 1 Georgetown (19947) ***(G-2539)***
Georgetown Air Services LLC.....302 855-2355
21553 Rudder Ln Unit 1 Georgetown (19947) ***(G-2540)***
Georgetown Animal Hospital PA.....302 856-2623
20784 Dupont Blvd Georgetown (19947) ***(G-2541)***
Georgetown Apartments, Wilmington *Also called Georgtown Prsrvation Assoc LLC* ***(G-10704)***
Georgetown Apts, Georgetown *Also called Leon N Weiner & Associates Inc* ***(G-2590)***
Georgetown Boys and Girls Club.....302 856-4903
115 N Race St Georgetown (19947) ***(G-2542)***
Georgetown Chamber Commerce.....302 856-1544
87 E Market St Georgetown (19947) ***(G-2543)***
Georgetown Construction Co.....302 856-7601
25136 Dupont Blvd Georgetown (19947) ***(G-2544)***
Georgetown Family Medicine.....302 856-4092
201 W Market St Georgetown (19947) ***(G-2545)***
Georgetown Manor Apartments.....302 328-6231
260 Christiana Rd Ofc B4 New Castle (19720) ***(G-5352)***
Georgetown Medical Assoc LLC.....302 856-3737
20930 Dupont Blvd # 101 Georgetown (19947) ***(G-2546)***
Georgetown Playground & Pk Inc.....302 856-7111
212 Wilson St Georgetown (19947) ***(G-2547)***
Georgtown Prsrvation Assoc LLC.....302 856-1557
4 Denny Rd Wilmington (19809) ***(G-10704)***
Georve V Sawyer.....302 736-1474
2296 Forrest Ave Dover (19904) ***(G-1591)***
Geotech LLC.....302 353-9769
13 Shull Dr Newark (19711) ***(G-6649)***
Gerace Signs, Wilmington *Also called Joe Gerace* ***(G-11165)***
Gerald Brown.....302 335-5211
3232 Thompsonville Rd Milford (19963) ***(G-4423)***
Geris Auto Financial Services.....302 660-9719
23 Geneva Ct Apt B4 Newark (19702) ***(G-6650)***
Gerone C Hudson Elec Contr.....302 539-3332
35944 Bayard Rd Frankford (19945) ***(G-2365)***
Get Cents LLC.....203 856-0841
16192 Coastal Hwy Lewes (19958) ***(G-3512)***
Get Real On Line Classifieds.....302 234-6522
30 Robin Dr Hockessin (19707) ***(G-3038)***
Get Takeout LLC.....800 785-6218
16192 Coastal Hwy Lewes (19958) ***(G-3513)***
Getresponse Inc.....302 573-3895
1011 Centre Rd Ste 322 Wilmington (19805) ***(G-10705)***
Gettakeout.com, Lewes *Also called Get Takeout LLC* ***(G-3513)***
Gettier Security, Wilmington *Also called JR Gettier & Associates Inc* ***(G-11202)***
Gettier Staffing Services Inc.....302 478-0911
2 Centerville Rd Wilmington (19808) ***(G-10706)***
GF McLaughlin LLC.....302 279-6018
800 W 20th St Wilmington (19802) ***(G-10707)***
Gfp Cement Contractors LLC.....302 998-7687
14 Hadco Rd Wilmington (19804) ***(G-10708)***
Gg Shuttle Service.....302 684-8818
28379 Martins Farm Rd Milton (19968) ***(G-4908)***
Gga, Georgetown *Also called Geo-Technology Associates Inc* ***(G-2538)***
Ggc Inc.....267 893-8052
19544 Pine Rd Lincoln (19960) ***(G-3850)***
Gge Amusements.....302 227-0661
34974 Oyster House Rd Rehoboth Beach (19971) ***(G-7947)***
Ghg Enterprises LLC.....817 705-0313
1209 N Orange St Wilmington (19801) ***(G-10709)***
Gl Associates of Delaware.....302 678-5008
742 S Governors Ave Ste 3 Dover (19904) ***(G-1592)***
Gl Specialists of De.....302 832-1545
2600 Glasgow Ave Ste 106 Newark (19702) ***(G-6651)***
Gian-Co.....302 798-7100
2 Stockdale Ave Claymont (19703) ***(G-753)***
Gibbons Innovations Inc.....302 265-4220
P.O. Box 99 Lincoln (19960) ***(G-3851)***
Gibellino Construction Co.....302 455-0500
1213 Old Coochs Bridge Rd Newark (19713) ***(G-6652)***
Gibson Industries.....302 653-7874
2712 Shaws Corner Rd Clayton (19938) ***(G-854)***
Giesela Inc.....855 556-4338
2035 Sunset Lake Rd B2 Newark (19702) ***(G-6653)***
Gif North America LLC.....703 969-9243
18227 Shockley Dr Rehoboth Beach (19971) ***(G-7948)***
Gift Love Early Learning Ctr.....302 659-1984
115 E North St Smyrna (19977) ***(G-8641)***
Gift Solutions LLC.....585 317-4465
16 Townsend Rd Newark (19711) ***(G-6654)***
Gigkloud Inc.....301 375-5008
16192 Coastal Hwy Lewes (19958) ***(G-3514)***
Gilani Malik Javed MD.....302 737-8116
1309 Veale Rd Ste 11 Wilmington (19810) ***(G-10710)***
Gildea Enterprises Inc.....302 475-1184
2100 Willow Way Wilmington (19810) ***(G-10711)***
Giles & Ransome Inc.....302 777-5800
2225 N Dupont Hwy New Castle (19720) ***(G-5353)***
Giles, Christopher MD, Dover *Also called Jarrell Benson Giles & Sweeney* ***(G-1694)***
Gill Edward Law Offices of.....302 854-5400
16 N Bedford St Georgetown (19947) ***(G-2548)***
GILPIN HALL, Wilmington *Also called Home For Aged Wmn-Mnquadale HM* ***(G-10935)***
Gilpin Mortgage.....302 656-5400
1400 N Dupont St Wilmington (19806) ***(G-10712)***
Gina Madaline MS CCC/Slp.....302 220-0931
2504 Pennington Dr Wilmington (19810) ***(G-10713)***
Ginch Gonch Corp.....713 240-9900
2915 Ogletown Rd Newark (19713) ***(G-6655)***
Giordano Delcollo & Werb LLC.....302 234-6855
5315 Limestone Rd Wilmington (19808) ***(G-10714)***
Giordano, Delcollo Werb Gdw, Wilmington *Also called Giordano Delcollo & Werb LLC* ***(G-10714)***
Giordano, Lawrence S, Wilmington *Also called Peter F Subach* ***(G-12095)***
Giorgi Kitchens Inc.....302 762-1121
4 Meco Cir Wilmington (19804) ***(G-10715)***
Girl Scouts of The Cheasapea (PA).....302 456-7150
225 Old Baltimore Pike Newark (19702) ***(G-6656)***
Girls Auto Clinic LLC.....484 679-6394
35 Antioch Ct New Castle (19720) ***(G-5354)***
Girls Incorporate of Delaware (PA).....302 575-1041
1019 Brown St Wilmington (19805) ***(G-10716)***
Giumarra International Mktg.....302 652-4009
11 Gist Rd Ste 101 Wilmington (19801) ***(G-10717)***
Givfolio LLC (PA).....213 949-1964
2035 Sunset Lake Rd B2 Newark (19702) ***(G-6657)***
Gj Chalfant Welding.....302 545-6404
1123 Mayflower Dr Newark (19711) ***(G-6658)***
GJ Chalfant Welding LLC.....302 983-0822
119 S Congress St Port Penn (19731) ***(G-7834)***
Gjv Inc (PA).....302 455-1600
4142 Ogletown Stanton Rd Newark (19713) ***(G-6659)***
Gkua Inc.....415 971-5341
1000 N West St Ste 1200 Wilmington (19801) ***(G-10718)***
GL Gray Consulting Services LL.....302 698-3339
1563 Autumn Moon Ln Magnolia (19962) ***(G-3891)***
Glasgo Plaza Shopping Center, Newark *Also called Wilmington Savings Fund Soc* ***(G-7705)***
Glasgow Chiropractic.....302 453-4043
650 Plaza Dr Newark (19702) ***(G-6660)***
Glasgow Medical Associates PA.....302 836-3539
2600 Glasgow Ave Ste 106 Newark (19702) ***(G-6661)***
Glasgow Medical Associates PA.....302 836-8350
2600 Glasgow Ave Ste 100 Newark (19702) ***(G-6662)***
Glasgow Medical Associates PA (PA).....302 836-8350
2600 Glasgow Ave Ste 126 Newark (19702) ***(G-6663)***
Glasgow Medical Center, Newark *Also called Total Care Physicians* ***(G-7577)***
Glasgow Medical Center, Newark *Also called Glasgow Medical Associates PA* ***(G-6663)***
Glasgow Medical Center LLC.....302 836-8350
2600 Glasgow Ave Ste 226 Newark (19702) ***(G-6664)***
Glasgow Shopping Center Corp.....302 836-1503
2750 Wrangle Hill Rd Bear (19701) ***(G-165)***
Glass Doctor of Delaware, New Castle *Also called West Ventures Inc* ***(G-5830)***
Glass Technologists Inc.....240 682-0966
32 S Main St Middletown (19709) ***(G-4087)***
Glass Works Company, The, Newark *Also called Gregory D Thacker* ***(G-6689)***
Glaxosmithkline Capital Inc.....302 656-5280
1105 N Market St Ste 622 Wilmington (19801) ***(G-10719)***
Glaxosmithkline Company, Wilmington *Also called Penn Labs Inc* ***(G-12065)***
Glaxosmithkline Holdings (HQ).....302 984-6932
1105 N Market St Wilmington (19801) ***(G-10720)***
Glaxosmithkline Svcs Unlimited, Wilmington *Also called Glaxosmithkline Holdings* ***(G-10720)***
Glen Eagle Villiage, Newark *Also called Westover Management Company LP* ***(G-7688)***
Glen Playa Inc.....302 703-7512
16192 Coastal Hwy Lewes (19958) ***(G-3515)***
Glenmede Trust Co Nat Assn.....302 661-2900
1201 N Market St Ste 1501 Wilmington (19801) ***(G-10721)***
Glenwood Dental Associates LLP.....302 653-5011
17 W Glenwood Ave Smyrna (19977) ***(G-8642)***
Glimpse Global Inc.....305 216-7667
8 The Grn Ste A Dover (19901) ***(G-1593)***
Global Air Strategy Inc.....302 229-5889
40 E Main St Ste 275 Newark (19711) ***(G-6665)***
Global Childrens Advocacy LLC.....484 383-3900
8 The Grn Ste B Dover (19901) ***(G-1594)***
Global Computers Networks LLC.....484 686-8374
718 Pinewood Dr Ste 2 Middletown (19709) ***(G-4088)***
Global Currents Inv MGT LLC.....302 476-3800
2 Righter Pkwy Wilmington (19803) ***(G-10722)***
Global Data Mining LLC.....551 208-1316
16192 Coastal Hwy Lewes (19958) ***(G-3516)***
Global Dev Partners Inc.....480 330-7931
2711 Centerville Rd # 400 Wilmington (19808) ***(G-10723)***
Global Entp Worldwide LLC (PA).....713 260-9687
1201 N Orange St Ste 700 Wilmington (19801) ***(G-10724)***
Global Exterior LLC.....302 722-1969
1057 Boyds Corner Rd Middletown (19709) ***(G-4089)***

ALPHABETIC

Global Financial Advisors Netw 302 697-3565
38291 Blackstone Ave Rehoboth Beach (19971) ***(G-7949)***
Global Gaming Business 302 994-3898
2413 Horace Dr Wilmington (19808) ***(G-10725)***
Global Garments (usa) LLC 617 340-3329
1 Commerce St Wilmington (19801) ***(G-10726)***
Global Innovation Holding LLC 877 276-7701
191 N Market St 425 Wilmington (19801) ***(G-10727)***
Global Innovation Institute, Wilmington *Also called Global Innovation Holding LLC* ***(G-10727)***
Global Institute 732 776-7360
10 Eileen Dr Newark (19711) ***(G-6666)***
Global Institute, The, Wilmington *Also called Intercontinental Marketing* ***(G-11056)***
Global Logistics and Trnsp, New Castle *Also called Courtesy Trnsp Svcs Inc* ***(G-5203)***
Global Merchant Partners LLC 302 425-3567
38131 West Dr Unit 730 Rehoboth Beach (19971) ***(G-7950)***
Global Network Executive Inc 302 251-8940
702 N West St Ste 101 Wilmington (19801) ***(G-10728)***
Global Protection MGT LLC 302 425-4190
1105 N Market St Ste 400 Wilmington (19801) ***(G-10729)***
Global Recruiters Network Inc 302 455-9500
3202 Drummond Plz Newark (19711) ***(G-6667)***
Global Scientific Glass Inc 302 429-9330
3 S Tatnall St Wilmington (19801) ***(G-10730)***
Global Shipping Center LLC 302 798-4321
2803 Philadelphia Pike B Claymont (19703) ***(G-754)***
Global Shopaholics LLC 703 608-7108
601 Cornell Dr Unit G11 Wilmington (19801) ***(G-10731)***
Global Vision Xtreme Corp 302 287-4822
21 Benning Rd Claymont (19703) ***(G-755)***
Globaltec Networks Inc 646 321-8627
1013 Centre Rd Wilmington (19805) ***(G-10732)***
Glory Contracting 302 275-5430
231 Ratledge Rd Townsend (19734) ***(G-8789)***
Glossgirl Inc 302 888-4520
1320 N Union St Wilmington (19806) ***(G-10733)***
Glushakow, Robert S, Newark *Also called Nolan Williams & Plumhoff* ***(G-7135)***
Glycomira LLC 704 651-9789
160 Greentree Dr Ste 101 Dover (19904) ***(G-1595)***
Gmb - Seaford, Seaford *Also called George Miles & Buhr LLC* ***(G-8253)***
Gmg Solutions LLC 302 781-3008
4550 Linden Hill Rd # 301 Wilmington (19808) ***(G-10734)***
Go Ahead Make My Ring 302 235-8172
1 Great Circle Rd Newark (19711) ***(G-6668)***
Go Go Go Inc 302 645-7400
16192 Coastal Hwy Lewes (19958) ***(G-3517)***
Go Mozaic LLC 302 438-4141
3042 Greenshire Ave Claymont (19703) ***(G-756)***
Go Tees LLC 708 703-1788
101 Arcadia Pkwy Middletown (19709) ***(G-4090)***
Go-Glass Corporation 302 674-3390
3895 N Dupont Hwy Dover (19901) ***(G-1596)***
Go4spin 310 400-2588
251 Little Falls Dr Wilmington (19808) ***(G-10735)***
GOBLIN Technologies LLC 844 733-5724
63 Bay Blvd Newark (19702) ***(G-6669)***
Gobos Togo Inc 302 426-1898
136 Quigley Blvd New Castle (19720) ***(G-5355)***
Goddard Early Learning Center, Newark *Also called Selwor Enterprises Inc* ***(G-7404)***
Goddard School, The, Wilmington *Also called Mahavir LLC* ***(G-11489)***
Gods Way To Recovery Inc 302 856-7375
20785 Dupont Blvd Georgetown (19947) ***(G-2549)***
Golage Inc 302 526-1181
8 The Grn Ste 5568 Dover (19901) ***(G-1597)***
Gold Care Center, Newark *Also called Abby Medical Center* ***(G-5882)***
Gold Label Transportation LLC 302 668-2383
36 Cardenti Ct Newark (19702) ***(G-6670)***
Gold Leaf Services LLC 302 373-3333
1591 Letitia Ln Wilmington (19809) ***(G-10736)***
Gold Medal Gymnastics Inc 302 659-5569
56 Artisan Dr Ste 1 Smyrna (19977) ***(G-8643)***
Gold Star Services 302 376-7677
665 Dawson Dr Ste A Newark (19713) ***(G-6671)***
Golden Car Care 302 856-2219
19395 Substation Rd Georgetown (19947) ***(G-2550)***
Golden Chariot Transportaion 302 730-3882
622 W Division St Dover (19904) ***(G-1598)***
Golden Coastal Realty 302 360-0226
33815 Clay Rd Ste 5 Lewes (19958) ***(G-3518)***
Golden Globe Intl Svcs Ltd 302 487-0022
913 N Market St Ste 200 Wilmington (19801) ***(G-10737)***
Golden Horse Shoe Gaming, Wilmington *Also called Ghg Enterprises LLC* ***(G-10709)***
Golden Merger Corp 302 737-8100
245 E Cleveland Ave Newark (19711) ***(G-6672)***
Golden Rubber Stamp Co 302 658-7343
841 N Tatnall St Wilmington (19801) ***(G-10738)***
Golden Shell Corp 917 951-6118
8 The Grn Dover (19901) ***(G-1599)***
Golden Thorns Inc 861 598-6748
16192 Coastal Hwy Lewes (19958) ***(G-3519)***
Goldenopp RE Solutions 908 565-0510
936 King James Ct Bear (19701) ***(G-166)***
Goldfein & Hosmer PC 302 656-3301
3513 Concord Pike # 2000 Wilmington (19803) ***(G-10739)***
Goldfinch Group Inc 646 300-0716
9 E Loockerman St Ste 3a Dover (19901) ***(G-1600)***
Goldis Enterprises Inc (PA) 302 764-3100
120 Hay Rd Wilmington (19809) ***(G-10740)***
Goldis Holdings Inc (PA) 302 764-3100
120 Hay Rd Wilmington (19809) ***(G-10741)***
Goldmine Enterprises Inc 302 834-4314
930 Woods Rd Bear (19701) ***(G-167)***
Golds Gym 302 226-4653
3712 Highway One Rehoboth Beach (19971) ***(G-7951)***
Goldsboro Sand and Gravel 410 310-0402
2904 Willow Grove Rd Camden Wyoming (19934) ***(G-643)***
Goldstar Cash, Wilmington *Also called Goldstar- Cash LLC* ***(G-10742)***
Goldstar- Cash LLC (PA) 302 427-2535
711 N Market St Wilmington (19801) ***(G-10742)***
Golegik Technologies, Wilmington *Also called Steven Abdill* ***(G-12758)***
Golf Bayside, Selbyville *Also called Bayside Resort Golf Club* ***(G-8453)***
Golf Course At Garrisons Lake 302 659-1206
101 W Fairways Cir Smyrna (19977) ***(G-8644)***
Golfclub LLC 908 770-7892
1209 Orange St Wilmington Wilmington (19801) ***(G-10743)***
Golo LLC 302 635-7245
630 Churchmans Rd Ste 200 Newark (19702) ***(G-6673)***
Golt Adj Service Inc 302 798-5500
3516 Silverside Rd Ste 16 Wilmington (19810) ***(G-10744)***
Gonce William E Dr DDS PA 302 235-2400
1127 Valley Rd Ste 4 Hockessin (19707) ***(G-3039)***
Gonser and Gonser P A 302 478-4445
3411 Silverside Rd 203hg Wilmington (19810) ***(G-10745)***
Good Beginnings Preschool 302 875-5507
10024 Woodland Ferry Rd Laurel (19956) ***(G-3232)***
Good Home Solutions LLC 302 540-3190
20 North Ave Wilmington (19804) ***(G-10746)***
Good Manufacturing Practices 302 222-6808
80 Coventry Ct Dover (19901) ***(G-1601)***
Good Samaritan Aid 302 875-2425
115 W Market St Laurel (19956) ***(G-3233)***
GOOD SAMARITAN THRIFT SHOP, TH, Laurel *Also called Good Samaritan Aid* ***(G-3233)***
Good To Go Delivery LLC 302 893-2734
831 N Union St Wilmington (19805) ***(G-10747)***
Goodales Naturals 302 743-6455
84 Warren Dr Newark (19702) ***(G-6674)***
Goodchild Inc 302 368-1681
6 Brookhill Dr Newark (19702) ***(G-6675)***
Goodeals Inc 302 999-1737
537 Main St Wilmington (19804) ***(G-10748)***
Goodman Manufacturing Co LP 302 894-1010
230 Executive Dr Ste 5 Newark (19702) ***(G-6676)***
Goodwill Center, Wilmington *Also called Goodwill Inds Del Del Cnty Inc* ***(G-10749)***
Goodwill Inds Del Del Cnty Inc (PA) 302 761-4640
300 E Lea Blvd Wilmington (19802) ***(G-10749)***
Goodwill Industries Delaware 302 337-8561
18178 Sussex Hwy Bridgeville (19933) ***(G-475)***
Goodwin Brothers Shading & Spc, Claymont *Also called Gb Shades LLC* ***(G-749)***
Goodworld Inc 845 325-2232
2711 Centerville Rd # 400 Wilmington (19808) ***(G-10750)***
Goodyear Tire & Rubber Company 302 737-2461
1929 Kirkwood Hwy Newark (19711) ***(G-6677)***
Goodyear Tire & Rubber Company 302 998-0428
3217 Kirkwood Hwy Wilmington (19808) ***(G-10751)***
Goorland and Mann Inc 302 655-1514
825 N Union St Wilmington (19805) ***(G-10752)***
Goorland Enterprises LLC 302 229-4573
800b Plant St Wilmington (19801) ***(G-10753)***
Gordon C Honig DMD PA (PA) 302 737-6333
2707 Kirkwood Hwy Newark (19711) ***(G-6678)***
Gordon C Honig DMD PA 302 696-4020
104 Sleepy Hollow Dr Middletown (19709) ***(G-4091)***
Gordon Fournaris Mammarella PA 302 652-2900
1925 Lovering Ave Wilmington (19806) ***(G-10754)***
Gordy Enterprises, New Castle *Also called Gordy Management Inc* ***(G-5356)***
Gordy Management Inc 302 322-3723
265 N Dupont Hwy Fl 2 New Castle (19720) ***(G-5356)***
Gordys Lumber Inc 302 875-3502
28950 Seaford Rd Laurel (19956) ***(G-3234)***
Gore Funeral Services 610 364-9900
812 Arthur Springs Ln New Castle (19720) ***(G-5357)***
Gossamer Games LLC 302 645-7400
16192 Coastal Hwy Lewes (19958) ***(G-3520)***
Got Health-E LLC 203 583-5447
3616 Kirkwood Hwy Ste A Wilmington (19808) ***(G-10755)***
Gotit Inc 408 382-1300
3500 S Dupont Hwy Dover (19901) ***(G-1602)***
Gotshadeonline Inc 302 832-8468
1700 Firedancer Ln Bear (19701) ***(G-168)***

Gould Motor Technologies Inc 618 932-8446
100 S West St Wilmington (19801) *(G-10756)*
Govbizconnect Inc 860 341-1925
850 New Burton Rd Dover (19904) *(G-1603)*
Government Information Center 302 857-3020
121 Martin Luther King Dover (19901) *(G-1604)*
Government Mrktplace Ltd Lblty 302 297-9694
200 Continental Dr 401o Newark (19713) *(G-6679)*
Government Portfolio LLC 301 718-9742
35546 Hatteras Ct Rehoboth Beach (19971) *(G-7952)*
Governors Ave Animal Hospital 302 734-5588
1008 S Governors Ave Dover (19904) *(G-1605)*
Governors Place Townhomes 302 653-6655
17 Providence Dr Smyrna (19977) *(G-8645)*
Gpe Construction LLC 267 595-8942
129 Mendel Ct Bear (19701) *(G-169)*
GPM Investments LLC 302 436-6330
36345 Lighthouse Rd # 301 Selbyville (19975) *(G-8496)*
Grabowski Sprano Vnclette Cpas 302 999-7300
1814 Newport Gap Pike Wilmington (19808) *(G-10757)*
Grace Visitation Services 302 329-9475
28350 Lwes Georgetown Hwy Milton (19968) *(G-4909)*
Graceland Daycare 302 698-0414
342 Ponderosa Dr Magnolia (19962) *(G-3892)*
Graceland Group Inc 302 226-1373
113 Dickinson St Dewey Beach (19971) *(G-1058)*
Gracelawn Memorial Park Inc (PA) 302 654-6158
2220 N Dupont Hwy New Castle (19720) *(G-5358)*
Grady & Hampton LLC 302 678-1265
6 N Bradford St Dover (19904) *(G-1606)*
Graham Packaging Co Europe LLC 302 453-9464
1601 Ogletown Rd Newark (19711) *(G-6680)*
Grahams Wireless Solutions Inc 717 943-0717
24817 Rivers Edge Rd Millsboro (19966) *(G-4698)*
Grainger 595, New Castle *Also called WW Grainger Inc* *(G-5842)*
Gramonoli Enterprises Inc 302 227-1288
21 Rehoboth Ave Rehoboth Beach (19971) *(G-7953)*
Grand National USA Inc 416 746-3511
2711 Centerville Rd # 400 Wilmington (19808) *(G-10758)*
Grand Opera House Inc 302 652-5577
818 N Market St Fl 2 Wilmington (19801) *(G-10759)*
Grand Rental Station, Rehoboth Beach *Also called Quillens Rent All Inc* *(G-8039)*
Grand Rental Station 302 227-7368
19897 Hebron Rd Unit G Rehoboth Beach (19971) *(G-7954)*
Grandma ZS Maple Haus 412 297-3324
171 Harbor Dr Apt 1 Claymont (19703) *(G-757)*
Grant & Eisenhofer PA (PA) 302 622-7000
123 S Justison St Ste 700 Wilmington (19801) *(G-10760)*
Grant & Sons Roofing & Siding, Milford *Also called Robert Grant Inc* *(G-4546)*
Grant Pharmaceuticals Inc 855 364-7268
200 Continental Dr # 401 Newark (19713) *(G-6681)*
Grape Solutions 201 784-9797
3210 Wilson Ave Wilmington (19808) *(G-10761)*
Grapetree Inc 302 655-1950
901 Mount Lebanon Rd Wilmington (19803) *(G-10762)*
Graphics Unlimited Inc 302 398-3898
51 Clark St Harrington (19952) *(G-2842)*
Grass Busters Landscaping Co 302 292-1166
935 Rahway Dr Newark (19711) *(G-6682)*
Grass Works Lawn Care Service, Wilmington *Also called Grassworks Lawn Care Service* *(G-10763)*
Grassworks Lawn Care Service 302 683-0833
809a Kiamensi Rd Wilmington (19804) *(G-10763)*
Grassy Creek Quilting 302 528-1653
4 W Rivers End Dr Claymont (19703) *(G-758)*
Gravely Hockessin, Hockessin *Also called Hockessin Tractor Inc* *(G-3055)*
Graver Separations Inc 302 731-1700
200 Lake Dr Newark (19702) *(G-6683)*
Graver Technologies LLC (HQ) 302 731-1700
200 Lake Dr Newark (19702) *(G-6684)*
Gray Audograph Agency Inc 302 658-1700
2340 N Dupont Hwy New Castle (19720) *(G-5359)*
Graybar Electric Company Inc 302 322-2200
43 Boulden Blvd New Castle (19720) *(G-5360)*
Graydie Welding LLC 302 753-0695
42 W Reamer Ave Wilmington (19804) *(G-10764)*
Graydon Hurst & Son Inc 302 762-2444
2901 Baynard Blvd Ste 4 Wilmington (19802) *(G-10765)*
Grayling Industries Inc 770 751-9095
1 Moonwalker Rd Frederica (19946) *(G-2403)*
Grayling Industries Inc 302 629-6860
2 Moonwalker Rd Frederica (19946) *(G-2404)*
Graylyn Crest III Swim Club 302 547-5809
2015 Kynwyd Rd Wilmington (19810) *(G-10766)*
Graylyn Dental 302 475-5555
2205 Silverside Rd Ste 2 Wilmington (19810) *(G-10767)*
Grays Fine Printing, Wilmington *Also called Stanley Golden* *(G-12736)*
Grays Peak LLC (PA) 302 288-0670
8 The Grn Ste A Dover (19901) *(G-1607)*

Great Clips, Bridgeville *Also called Jersey Clippers LLC* *(G-486)*
Great Clips 302 478-2022
4235 Concord Pike Wilmington (19803) *(G-10768)*
Great Clips Hair Cut Salon, New Castle *Also called Gc New Castle Inc* *(G-5347)*
Great Graphic Originals Ltd 302 734-7600
5374 Pearsons Corner Rd Dover (19904) *(G-1608)*
Great I AM Prod Studios Inc 302 463-2483
25 Rose Ln New Castle (19720) *(G-5361)*
Great New Beginnings 302 218-8332
14 Saint Andrews Dr Bear (19701) *(G-170)*
Great Whites Dental, Wilmington *Also called David E Mastrota DMD PA* *(G-9969)*
Greater Dover Foundation 302 734-2513
101 W Loockerman St 1b Dover (19904) *(G-1609)*
Greater Newark Baseball L 302 635-0562
P.O. Box 7212 Newark (19714) *(G-6685)*
Greater Wilmington Convention (PA) 302 652-4088
100 W 10th St Ste 20 Wilmington (19801) *(G-10769)*
Greeley & Nista Orthodontics 302 475-4102
1405 Silverside Rd Ste A Wilmington (19810) *(G-10770)*
Green Acres Farm Inc 302 645-8652
18186 Dairy Farm Rd Lewes (19958) *(G-3521)*
Green Acres Health Systems 302 934-7300
231 S Washington St Millsboro (19966) *(G-4699)*
Green Acres Pre School 302 378-9250
411 N 6th St Odessa (19730) *(G-7827)*
Green Blade Irrigation & Turf 302 736-8873
2203 Ponderosa Dr Magnolia (19962) *(G-3893)*
Green Clinics Laboratory LLC 302 734-5050
740 S New St Ste B Dover (19904) *(G-1610)*
Green Crescent LLC 800 735-9620
8 The Grn Ste 4710 Dover (19901) *(G-1611)*
Green Crescent Translations, Dover *Also called Green Crescent LLC* *(G-1611)*
Green DOT Capital LLC 302 395-0500
203 Cornwell Dr Bear (19701) *(G-171)*
Green Earth Tech Group LLC 302 257-5617
1000 N West St Wilmington (19801) *(G-10771)*
Green Interest Enterprises LLC 228 355-0708
81 Rye Oak Ct Dover (19904) *(G-1612)*
Green Meadows At Latrobe, Dover *Also called Emeritus Corporation* *(G-1517)*
Green Oak Real Estate LP 212 359-7800
1209 N Orange St Wilmington (19801) *(G-10772)*
Green Outfitters, Bethany Beach *Also called Fresh Accents LLC* *(G-399)*
Green Pages Technologies Inc 626 497-6363
2035 Sunset Lake Rd B2 Newark (19702) *(G-6686)*
Green Recovery Tech LLC 302 317-0062
42 Lukens Dr Ste 100 New Castle (19720) *(G-5362)*
Green Room Restaurant 302 594-3100
100 W 11th St Wilmington (19801) *(G-10773)*
Green Roots LLC 516 643-2621
16192 Coastal Hwy Lewes (19958) *(G-3522)*
Green Stay CA, Wilmington *Also called Elf Homes Inc* *(G-10374)*
Green Valley Pavilion 302 653-5085
3034 S Dupont Blvd Smyrna (19977) *(G-8646)*
Green Valley Terrace Snf LLC 302 934-7300
231 S Washington St Millsboro (19966) *(G-4700)*
Green Valley Terrance, Millsboro *Also called Green Acres Health Systems* *(G-4699)*
Greenamoyer Construction 302 999-8235
212 S Woodward Ave Wilmington (19805) *(G-10774)*
Greenbank Child Dev Ctr 302 994-8574
708 Greenbank Rd Wilmington (19808) *(G-10775)*
Greenberg Praurig LLC 302 661-7000
1007 N Orange St Ste 1200 Wilmington (19801) *(G-10776)*
Greenberg Supply Co Inc 302 656-4496
809 E 5th St Wilmington (19801) *(G-10777)*
Greenbrook Tms Neurohealth Ctr 302 994-4010
121 Becks Woods Dr # 204 Bear (19701) *(G-172)*
Greene Business Support S 302 480-3725
3 Heritage Dr Dover (19904) *(G-1613)*
Greene Tweed of Delaware Inc 302 888-2560
1105 N Market St Ste 1300 Wilmington (19801) *(G-10778)*
Greenhill Auto Service, Wilmington *Also called Phillip E Weir* *(G-12115)*
Greenhill Express Car Wash 302 464-1031
299 E Main St Middletown (19709) *(G-4092)*
Greenlea LLC 302 227-7868
31 Rolling Rd Rehoboth Beach (19971) *(G-7955)*
Greenleaf Services Inc 302 836-9050
20393 John J Williams Hwy Lewes (19958) *(G-3523)*
Greenleaf Turf Solutions Inc 302 731-1075
9 Albe Dr Ste C Newark (19702) *(G-6687)*
Greens At Broadview LLC 302 684-3000
27052 Broadkill Rd Milton (19968) *(G-4910)*
Greensorb.com, Wilmington *Also called Sorbent Green LLC* *(G-12682)*
Greenview Gardens Inc 302 422-8109
Sherman Ave Lincoln (19960) *(G-3852)*
Greenville Community Newspaper, Middletown *Also called Community Publications Inc* *(G-4002)*
Greenville Country Club Inc 302 652-3255
201 Owls Nest Rd Wilmington (19807) *(G-10779)*

ALPHABETIC

(PA)=Parent Co (HQ)=Headquarters (DH)=Div Headquarters
2020 Harris Directory of Delaware Businesses
653

Greenville Travel Agency Inc ... 302 658-3585
3926 Kennett Pike Wilmington (19807) *(G-10780)*

Greenvlle Retirement Cmnty LLC ... 302 658-6200
4031 Kennett Pike Wilmington (19807) *(G-10781)*

Greenwich Aerogroup Inc ... 302 834-5400
4200 Summit Bridge Rd Middletown (19709) *(G-4093)*

Greenwing Solutions Inc ... 302 295-5690
1201 N Orange St Ste 700 Wilmington (19801) *(G-10782)*

Greenwood Liquor Inc ... 302 349-4767
12599 Sussex Hwy Greenwood (19950) *(G-2741)*

Greenwood Pallet Co ... 302 337-8181
16849 Road Runner Dr Bridgeville (19933) *(G-476)*

Greg Elect ... 215 651-1477
547 Ashland Ridge Rd Hockessin (19707) *(G-3040)*

Greg Smith Equipment Sales ... 302 894-9333
250 Executive Dr Ste 1 Newark (19702) *(G-6688)*

Gregg & Sons Mechanical LLC ... 302 223-8145
256 Gum Bush Rd Townsend (19734) *(G-8790)*

Gregg Bus Service, Wilmington Also called Krapfs Coaches Inc *(G-11292)*

Greggo & Ferrara Inc ... 302 834-3333
595 Walther Rd Bear (19701) *(G-173)*

Gregory D Thacker ... 302 239-0879
20 Lamatan Rd Newark (19711) *(G-6689)*

Greyhound 5511, Wilmington Also called Wilmington Transportation Ctr *(G-13259)*

Grier Signs ... 302 737-4823
4 Bridgeview Ct Newark (19711) *(G-6690)*

Griff Son Hometown Auto Rep ... 302 786-2143
201 Delaware Ave Harrington (19952) *(G-2843)*

Griffen Corporate Services ... 302 576-2890
300 Delaware Ave Fl 9 Wilmington (19801) *(G-10783)*

Griffin Home Builders Inc ... 302 629-5615
118 N Pine St Seaford (19973) *(G-8254)*

Griffith Industrial Supply ... 302 731-0574
153 Scottfield Dr Newark (19713) *(G-6691)*

Griffs Signs LLC ... 302 784-5596
101 Westmoreland Ave Wilmington (19804) *(G-10784)*

Grillo Holdings Inc ... 302 261-9668
2711 Centerville Rd # 400 Wilmington (19808) *(G-10785)*

Grime Busters USA Inc ... 302 834-7006
3 Misty Ct Newark (19702) *(G-6692)*

Grind or Starve LLC ... 302 322-1679
608 W Lea Blvd Apt C4 Wilmington (19802) *(G-10786)*

Grindstone Aviation LLC ... 302 324-1993
13 1/2 Penns Way New Castle (19720) *(G-5363)*

Griswold Home Care ... 302 750-4564
115 Christina Landing Dr # 708 Wilmington (19801) *(G-10787)*

Griswold Special Care, Wilmington Also called Special Care Inc *(G-12695)*

Grizzlys Landscape Sup & Svcs ... 302 644-0654
20144 John J Williams Hwy Lewes (19958) *(G-3524)*

Grm Pro Imaging LLC ... 302 999-8162
401 Marsh Ln Ste 3 Wilmington (19804) *(G-10788)*

Grn Wilmington, Newark Also called Global Recruiters Network Inc *(G-6667)*

Grobman, Marc Do, Claymont Also called Prospect Crozer LLC *(G-797)*

Groff Tractor & Equipment LLC ... 302 349-5760
12420 Sussex Hwy Greenwood (19950) *(G-2742)*

Grofos International LLC (PA) ... 302 635-4805
1 Innovation Way Ste 426 Newark (19711) *(G-6693)*

Gross Lighting Center, New Castle Also called Grossman Electric Supply Inc *(G-5364)*

Grossman Electric Supply Inc ... 302 655-5561
30 W 5th St New Castle (19720) *(G-5364)*

Group Investments Associates, Wilmington Also called Dental Associates Delaware PA *(G-10112)*

Group Three Inc (PA) ... 302 658-4158
1100 Duncan St Ste A Wilmington (19805) *(G-10789)*

Groupe Victoire LLC ... 302 384-5355
800 Delaware Ave Wilmington (19801) *(G-10790)*

Grow & Learn Childcare Center, Middletown Also called Gb Jacobs LLC *(G-4084)*

Grow USA Press ... 302 725-5195
503 Gilcrest St Milford (19963) *(G-4424)*

Growing Palace ... 302 376-5553
111 Patriot Dr Ste A Middletown (19709) *(G-4094)*

Growing Palace 3, The, Middletown Also called Growing Palace III *(G-4095)*

Growing Palace III ... 302 376-5553
111 Patriot Dr Ste A Middletown (19709) *(G-4095)*

Growmark Fs LLC (HQ) ... 302 422-3002
308 Ne Front St Milford (19963) *(G-4425)*

Growmark Fs LLC ... 302 875-7511
31052 N Poplar St Laurel (19956) *(G-3235)*

Growmark Fs LLC ... 302 422-3001
339 Mlford Harrington Hwy Milford (19963) *(G-4426)*

Growth Inc ... 302 366-8586
311 Ruthar Dr Newark (19711) *(G-6694)*

Grubb Lumber Company Inc ... 302 652-2800
200 A St Wilmington (19801) *(G-10791)*

Grubb Road Neighborhood Home, Wilmington Also called Martin Luther Homes East Inc *(G-11550)*

Grupo Acosta Ecuador Limited ... 302 231-2981
501 Silverside Rd Wilmington (19809) *(G-10792)*

Gs - Tek, Newark Also called General Separation Tech Inc *(G-6645)*

Gs Racing Photos ... 302 855-1165
18063 Deer Forest Rd Georgetown (19947) *(G-2551)*

GSB&b LLC ... 302 425-5800
1201 N Orange St Ste 300 Wilmington (19801) *(G-10793)*

GSM Systems Inc ... 302 284-8304
215 E Evens Rd Viola (19979) *(G-8836)*

Gt Designs Inc ... 302 275-8100
109 Wellington Way Middletown (19709) *(G-4096)*

Gt USA Wilmington LLC ... 302 472-7679
1 Hausel Rd Wilmington (19801) *(G-10794)*

Gt World Machineries Usa Inc ... 800 242-4935
40 W Main St Christiana (19702) *(G-669)*

Gtech Cleaning Services LLC ... 302 494-2102
950 Ridge Rd Ste B5 Claymont (19703) *(G-759)*

Gti Millwork, Wilmington Also called Group Three Inc *(G-10789)*

GTS Technical Sales LLC ... 302 778-1362
122 Middleboro Rd Wilmington (19804) *(G-10795)*

Gtv Live Shopping LLC ... 844 694-8688
724 Yorklyn Rd Ste 248 Hockessin (19707) *(G-3041)*

Guap International Enterprise, Townsend Also called Nancy Dufresne *(G-8812)*

Guardian Angel Child Care ... 302 428-3620
1000 Wilson St Wilmington (19801) *(G-10796)*

Guardian Angel Day Care ... 302 934-0130
25193 Zoar Rd Georgetown (19947) *(G-2552)*

Guardian Construction Co Inc (HQ) ... 302 834-1000
1617 Matassino Rd New Castle (19720) *(G-5365)*

Guardian Envmtl Svcs Co Inc ... 302 918-3070
70 Albe Dr Newark (19702) *(G-6695)*

Guardian Fence Co ... 302 834-3044
4783 Summit Bridge Rd Middletown (19709) *(G-4097)*

Guardian Property MGT LLC ... 302 227-7878
17298 Coastal Hwy Unit 1 Lewes (19958) *(G-3525)*

Guco, Wilmington Also called Guedon Co *(G-10797)*

Guedon Co ... 302 375-6151
1106 Cypress Rd Wilmington (19810) *(G-10797)*

Guidance Gaming ... 724 708-2321
1033 High St Dover (19901) *(G-1614)*

Guide Idler and Conveyor Belt ... 302 762-7564
8 S Stuyvesant Dr Wilmington (19809) *(G-10798)*

Guiding Hearts Family Daycare, New Castle Also called Susan R Austin *(G-5744)*

Guinevere Associates Inc ... 302 635-7798
2 Nob Hill Rd Wilmington (19808) *(G-10799)*

Gulab Management Inc ... 302 422-8089
1036 N Walnut St Milford (19963) *(G-4427)*

Gulab Management Inc ... 302 398-4206
17101 Dupont Hwy Harrington (19952) *(G-2844)*

Gulab Management Inc ... 302 934-6126
729 Bay Rd Milford (19963) *(G-4428)*

Gulab Management Inc (PA) ... 302 734-4433
1426 N Dupont Hwy Dover (19901) *(G-1615)*

Gulch Group LLC ... 202 697-1756
38 Olive Ave 1 Rehoboth Beach (19971) *(G-7956)*

Gulf Development Partners LLC ... 646 334-1245
910 Foulk Rd Ste 201 Wilmington (19803) *(G-10800)*

Gulfstream Development Corp ... 302 539-6178
27 Atlantic Ave Ste 101 Ocean View (19970) *(G-7792)*

Gull House Adult Activity ... 302 226-2160
34382 Carpenters Way # 1 Lewes (19958) *(G-3526)*

Gull's Way Campground, Dagsboro Also called Gulls Way Inc *(G-905)*

Gulls Way Campground ... 302 732-6383
Rr 26 Dagsboro (19939) *(G-904)*

Gulls Way Inc ... 302 732-9629
Rural Route 2 Box 45 Dagsboro (19939) *(G-905)*

Gumboro Service Center Inc ... 302 238-7040
22181 Charles West Rd Frankford (19945) *(G-2366)*

Gund Securities Corporation ... 302 479-9210
1105 N Market St Ste 1300 Wilmington (19801) *(G-10801)*

Gunn Shot Photography ... 302 399-3094
154 Cathleen Dr Smyrna (19977) *(G-8647)*

Gunnip & Company ... 302 225-5000
2751 Centerville Rd # 300 Wilmington (19808) *(G-10802)*

Gunnip Employment Services, Wilmington Also called Gunnip & Company *(G-10802)*

Gunton Corporation ... 302 999-0535
3617 Kirkwood Hwy Wilmington (19808) *(G-10803)*

Gurukrupa Inc ... 302 328-6691
133 S Dupont Hwy New Castle (19720) *(G-5366)*

Gushen America Inc ... 630 853-3135
1679 S Dupont Hwy Ste 100 Dover (19901) *(G-1616)*

Gutter Connection LLC ... 302 736-0105
2559 Mckee Rd Dover (19904) *(G-1617)*

Guy & Lady Barrel Cigars, Dover Also called Guy & Lady Barrel LLC *(G-1618)*

Guy & Lady Barrel LLC ... 302 399-3069
198 Hatteras Dr Dover (19904) *(G-1618)*

Guy Bug ... 302 242-5254
1017 Westview Ter Dover (19904) *(G-1619)*

Gvx, Claymont Also called Global Vision Xtreme Corp *(G-755)*

Gw Solutions LLC ... 240 578-5981
237 Oyster Shell Cv Bethany Beach (19930) *(G-402)*

Gwantel Intl Corp Engrg & Tech.......302 377-6235
21 Hidden Valley Dr Fl B Newark (19711) ***(G-6696)***
Gwantel-Usa, Newark *Also called Gwantel Intl Corp Engrg & Tech* ***(G-6696)***
Gym Source.......302 478-4069
3901 Concord Pike Wilmington (19803) ***(G-10804)***
Gyst Inc.......631 680-4307
8 The Grn Ste A Dover (19901) ***(G-1620)***
H & A Electric Co.......302 678-8252
59 Roosevelt Ave Dover (19901) ***(G-1621)***
H & C Insulation LLC.......302 448-0777
14329 Saint Johnstown Rd Greenwood (19950) ***(G-2743)***
H & H Truck and Trailer Repair.......302 653-1446
738 Paddock Rd Smyrna (19977) ***(G-8648)***
H & J Wright Family Farms LLC.......302 841-9002
4814 Blackwater Branch Rd Delmar (19940) ***(G-1000)***
H & M Construction.......302 645-6639
4 Bradford Ln Lewes (19958) ***(G-3527)***
H & R Block, Millsboro *Also called H&R Block Inc* ***(G-4702)***
H & R Block, Rehoboth Beach *Also called Basic Block Corp* ***(G-7855)***
H & R Block, Middletown *Also called H&R Block Inc* ***(G-4100)***
H & R Block, Wilmington *Also called H&R Block Inc* ***(G-10812)***
H & R Block, Seaford *Also called Wentworth Inc* ***(G-8436)***
H & R Block, New Castle *Also called H&R Block Inc* ***(G-5370)***
H & R Block, New Castle *Also called H&R Block Inc* ***(G-5371)***
H & R Block, Smyrna *Also called Walls & Davenport Inc* ***(G-8739)***
H & R Block, Bear *Also called H&R Block Inc* ***(G-174)***
H & R Block, Wilmington *Also called H&R Block Inc* ***(G-10813)***
H & R Block, Georgetown *Also called David Wentworth* ***(G-2493)***
H & R Block, Newark *Also called H&R Block Inc* ***(G-6699)***
H & R Block, Wilmington *Also called H&R Block Inc* ***(G-10814)***
H & R Heating & AC.......302 323-9919
7 King Ct New Castle (19720) ***(G-5367)***
H & T Builders Inc.......302 422-0745
6650 Shawnee Rd Milford (19963) ***(G-4429)***
H & V Farms Inc.......302 934-1320
341 Grace St Millsboro (19966) ***(G-4701)***
H B P Inc (PA).......302 378-9693
110 W Green St Middletown (19709) ***(G-4098)***
H C Davis Inc.......302 337-7001
Pine Aly Bridgeville (19933) ***(G-477)***
H Clemons Consulting Inc.......302 295-5097
1000 N West St Ste 1200 Wilmington (19801) ***(G-10805)***
H D C Inc.......302 323-9300
405 Marsh Ln Ste 1 Wilmington (19804) ***(G-10806)***
H D Lee Company Inc (HQ).......302 477-3930
3411 Silverside Rd 200hb Wilmington (19810) ***(G-10807)***
H Dean McSpadden DDS.......302 239-5917
500 Lantana Dr Hockessin (19707) ***(G-3042)***
H Dean McSpadden DDS.......302 571-0680
11 Old Barley Mill Rd Wilmington (19807) ***(G-10808)***
H G Investments LLC.......302 734-5017
27 E Walnut St Magnolia (19962) ***(G-3894)***
H H Builders Inc.......302 735-9900
3947 Forrest Ave Dover (19904) ***(G-1622)***
H I E Contractors Inc.......302 224-3032
324 Markus Ct Newark (19713) ***(G-6697)***
H Juarez Transport Inc.......302 407-5102
3314 Old Capitol Trl L5 Wilmington (19808) ***(G-10809)***
H K Griffith Inc.......302 368-4635
115 Happy Ln Newark (19711) ***(G-6698)***
H P Electric Motors, Newark *Also called HP Motors Inc* ***(G-6753)***
H R Phillips Inc (PA).......302 422-4518
715 S Washington St Milford (19963) ***(G-4430)***
H S B C Overseas Corp De.......302 657-8400
300 Delaware Ave Ste 1400 Wilmington (19801) ***(G-10810)***
H T G Consulting LLC.......302 322-4100
2 Penns Way Ste 300 New Castle (19720) ***(G-5368)***
H&H Customs Inc.......302 378-0810
708 Lorewood Grove Rd Middletown (19709) ***(G-4099)***
H&H Services Electrical Contrs.......302 373-4950
507 Sterling Ave New Castle (19720) ***(G-5369)***
H&H Trading International LLC.......480 580-3911
1201 N Orange St Ste 600 Wilmington (19801) ***(G-10811)***
H&K Group Inc.......302 934-7635
30548 Thoroughgood Rd Dagsboro (19939) ***(G-906)***
H&L Construction Corp.......302 875-5634
5673 Woodland Ferry Rd Seaford (19973) ***(G-8255)***
H&R Block Inc.......302 934-6178
28417 Dupont Blvd Unit 4 Millsboro (19966) ***(G-4702)***
H&R Block Inc.......302 378-8931
Middletown Shopping Ctr Middletown (19709) ***(G-4100)***
H&R Block Inc.......302 999-7488
4711 Kirkwood Hwy Wilmington (19808) ***(G-10812)***
H&R Block Inc.......302 328-7320
196 Penn Mart Ctr Unit 11 New Castle (19720) ***(G-5370)***
H&R Block Inc.......302 652-3286
232 New Castle Ave New Castle (19720) ***(G-5371)***
H&R Block Inc.......302 836-2700
54 Foxhunt Dr Bear (19701) ***(G-174)***
H&R Block Inc.......302 478-9140
1720 Marsh Rd Wilmington (19810) ***(G-10813)***
H&R Block Inc.......302 479-5717
860 Peoples Plz Newark (19702) ***(G-6699)***
H&R Block Inc.......302 478-6300
3629b Silverside Rd Wilmington (19810) ***(G-10814)***
H&S Cleaning Service Inc.......302 449-2928
684 Southerness Dr Townsend (19734) ***(G-8791)***
H. Fletcher Brown, Wilmington *Also called Boys & Girls Clubs Del Inc* ***(G-9405)***
H2o Pro LLC.......302 321-7077
31765 Hickory Manor Rd Frankford (19945) ***(G-2367)***
Haart Program, Bear *Also called Healing Adults & Adolescents* ***(G-180)***
Hab Nab Trucking Inc.......302 245-6900
8805 Newton Rd Bridgeville (19933) ***(G-478)***
Habib Bolourchi MD Facc.......302 645-7672
4503 Hwy 1 Rehoboth Beach (19971) ***(G-7957)***
Habitat America LLC.......302 875-3525
101 Laurel Commons Ln Laurel (19956) ***(G-3236)***
Habitat Design Group.......302 335-4452
192 Bowers Beach Rd Frederica (19946) ***(G-2405)***
Habitat For Humanity (PA).......302 652-0365
1920 Hutton St Wilmington (19802) ***(G-10815)***
Habitat For Humanity Intl Inc.......302 855-1156
107 Depot St Georgetown (19947) ***(G-2553)***
Haccp Navigator LLC.......302 531-7922
10256 Webb Farm Rd Lincoln (19960) ***(G-3853)***
Hackett Industries LLC.......302 357-2539
701 S Franklin St Wilmington (19805) ***(G-10816)***
Hackney Business Solutions LLC.......843 496-7236
930 Alexandria Dr Newark (19711) ***(G-6700)***
Hage Tool and Machine Inc.......302 836-4850
3415 Wrangle Hill Rd # 7 Bear (19701) ***(G-175)***
Hagemeyer - Site X4, Delaware City *Also called Vallen Distribution Inc* ***(G-968)***
Hagerty Drivers Club LLC.......302 504-6086
2711 Centerville Rd # 400 Wilmington (19808) ***(G-10817)***
HAGLEY MUSEUM AND LIBRARY, Wilmington *Also called Eleuthrian Mlls-Hgley Fndtion* ***(G-10370)***
Hague Surfboards.......302 745-9336
102 Gosling Creek Rd Lewes (19958) ***(G-3528)***
Haines Fabrication & Mch LLC.......302 436-1929
45 Railroad Ave Selbyville (19975) ***(G-8497)***
Hair 2 Please.......302 378-3349
2484 Rte 13 Middletown (19709) ***(G-4101)***
Hair Academy Llc.......302 738-6251
160 Pencader Plz Newark (19713) ***(G-6701)***
Hair Acdemy Schl Brbering Buty, Newark *Also called Hair Academy Llc* ***(G-6701)***
Hair Artistry.......302 645-7167
33995 Clay Rd Lewes (19958) ***(G-3529)***
Hair Cuttery, Dover *Also called Ratner Companies LC* ***(G-2010)***
Hair Cuttery, Middletown *Also called Ratner Companies LC* ***(G-4212)***
Hair Cuttery, Millville *Also called Ratner Companies LC* ***(G-4854)***
Hair Designs By Linda Inc.......302 478-7080
704 W Matson Run Pkwy Wilmington (19802) ***(G-10818)***
Hair Designs By Regina.......302 652-8089
1920 Lancaster Ave Wilmington (19805) ***(G-10819)***
Hair Dimensions, Lewes *Also called Joanne Reuther* ***(G-3571)***
Hair Gallery.......302 475-6714
2080 Naamans Rd Wilmington (19810) ***(G-10820)***
Hair Levels.......302 212-0842
4737 Concord Pike Wilmington (19803) ***(G-10821)***
Hair Sensations Inc.......302 731-0920
55 Herbert Dr New Castle (19720) ***(G-5372)***
Hair Studio II.......302 945-5110
Long Neck Rd Millsboro (19966) ***(G-4703)***
Haircut & Company Inc.......302 239-3236
47 Tenby Chase Dr Newark (19711) ***(G-6702)***
Hairs To You.......302 436-1728
61 S Dupont Hwy Selbyville (19975) ***(G-8498)***
Hairworks Inc.......302 656-0566
1601 Concord Pike Ste 21 Wilmington (19803) ***(G-10822)***
Hajoca Corporation.......302 764-6000
303 E 30th St Wilmington (19802) ***(G-10823)***
Haldas Brothers, Wilmington *Also called Jabez Corp* ***(G-11113)***
Hale Byrnes House.......302 998-3792
606 Stanton Christiana Rd Newark (19713) ***(G-6703)***
Haley, David, Wilmington *Also called Foot Care Group Inc* ***(G-10588)***
Hall Burke VFW Post 5447 Inc.......302 798-2052
1605 Philadelphia Pike Wilmington (19809) ***(G-10824)***
Hall International Ind Corp.......302 777-2290
1000 N West St Ste 1200 Wilmington (19801) ***(G-10825)***
Haller & Hudson.......302 856-4525
101 S Bedford St Georgetown (19947) ***(G-2554)***
Hallies Helping Hands Home.......844 277-8911
616 Brittany Cir Townsend (19734) ***(G-8792)***
Halligan Inc.......314 488-9400
16192 Coastal Hwy Lewes (19958) ***(G-3530)***

ALPHABETIC

Halls We Clean Service LLC 302 422-7787
16332 Sarah St Milford (19963) ***(G-4431)***
Halo Medical Technologies LLC 302 475-2300
1805 Foulk Rd Ste G Wilmington (19810) ***(G-10826)***
Haloali Teeth Whitening LLC 302 300-4042
409 Fillmore Ct Claymont (19703) ***(G-760)***
Halosil International Inc 302 543-8095
91 Lukens Dr Ste A New Castle (19720) ***(G-5373)***
Halpern Eye Associates Inc 302 734-5861
223 E Main St Middletown (19709) ***(G-4102)***
Halpern Eye Associates Inc 302 537-0234
35786 Atlantic Ave Unit 1 Millville (19967) ***(G-4846)***
Halpern Eye Associates Inc (PA) 302 734-5861
885 S Governors Ave Dover (19904) ***(G-1623)***
Halpern Eye Associates Inc 302 422-2020
771 E Masten Cir Ste 109 Milford (19963) ***(G-4432)***
Halpern Eye Associates Inc 302 629-6816
1301 Bridgeville Hwy Seaford (19973) ***(G-8256)***
Halpern Eye Associates Inc 302 838-0800
1237 Quintilio Dr Bear (19701) ***(G-176)***
Halpern Eye Associates Inc 302 653-3400
201 Stadium St Smyrna (19977) ***(G-8649)***
Halpern Eye Care, Dover *Also called Halpern Eye Associates Inc* ***(G-1623)***
Halpern Opthalmology Assoc 302 678-2210
200 Banning St Dover (19904) ***(G-1624)***
Halpern Opthamology, Seaford *Also called Halpern Eye Associates Inc* ***(G-8256)***
Hamilton Associates 302 629-4949
413 High St Seaford (19973) ***(G-8257)***
Hamilton House Condominium 302 658-7787
1403 Shallcross Ave # 304 Wilmington (19806) ***(G-10827)***
Hamilton Pepper LLP 302 777-6500
1313 N Market St Ste 5100 Wilmington (19801) ***(G-10828)***
Hammer, Greg S, Dover *Also called Brenford Animal Hospital P A* ***(G-1229)***
Hammond Enterprises Inc 302 934-1700
1111 N Dupont Blvd Milford (19963) ***(G-4433)***
Hammond M Knox DDS 302 383-6696
13 Thomas Ln N Newark (19711) ***(G-6704)***
Hampshire Group Limited 212 840-5666
919 N Market St Ste 600 Wilmington (19801) ***(G-10829)***
Hampton Enterprises Delaware 302 378-7365
413 Prestwick Pl Townsend (19734) ***(G-8793)***
Hampton Inn, Wilmington *Also called Hollywood Grill Restaurant* ***(G-10930)***
Hampton Inn, Seaford *Also called Hollywood Grill Restaurant* ***(G-8265)***
Hampton Inn, Rehoboth Beach *Also called Midway Ventures LLC* ***(G-8009)***
Hampton Inn, Dover *Also called K W Lands LLC* ***(G-1718)***
Hampton Inn, Newark *Also called Hollywood Grill Restaurant* ***(G-6736)***
Hampton Inn 302 629-4500
22871 Sussex Hwy Seaford (19973) ***(G-8258)***
Hampton Inn 302 422-4320
800 Karken Pit Rd Milford (19963) ***(G-4434)***
Hampton Inn Dover, Dover *Also called Hampton Inn-Dover* ***(G-1625)***
Hampton Inn Middletown 302 378-5656
117 Sandhill Dr Middletown (19709) ***(G-4103)***
Hampton Inn Seaford 302 629-4500
799 N Dual Hwy Seaford (19973) ***(G-8259)***
Hampton Inn-Dover 302 736-3500
1568 N Dupont Hwy Dover (19901) ***(G-1625)***
Hanbang Group 626 506-7585
201 Ruthar Dr Newark (19711) ***(G-6705)***
Hanco Inc 302 734-9782
3975 Leipsic Rd Dover (19901) ***(G-1626)***
Hand & Spa 302 478-1700
3654 Concord Pike Wilmington (19803) ***(G-10830)***
Hand -N- Hand Early Lrng Ctr 302 422-0702
13724 S Old State Rd Ellendale (19941) ***(G-2260)***
Handler Builders Inc 302 999-9200
5169 W Woodmill Dr Wilmington (19808) ***(G-10831)***
Handler Corporation 302 999-9200
5169 W Woodmill Dr Ste 10 Wilmington (19808) ***(G-10832)***
Handy & Harman, Camden *Also called Handytube Corporation* ***(G-577)***
Handy & Harman 302 697-9521
12244 Willow Grove Rd Camden (19934) ***(G-574)***
Handy Man Maintenance, Millsboro *Also called Christopher Handy* ***(G-4661)***
Handytube Corporation 302 697-9521
12244 Willow Grove Rd Camden (19934) ***(G-575)***
Handytube Corporation 302 697-9521
124 Vepco Blvd Camden (19934) ***(G-576)***
Handytube Corporation (HQ) 302 697-9521
12244 Willow Grove Rd Camden (19934) ***(G-577)***
Hangster Inc 619 871-8086
1201 N Orange St Ste 600 Wilmington (19801) ***(G-10833)***
Hannahs Christian HM Day Care, Bear *Also called Phyllis M Green* ***(G-283)***
Hannas Phrm Sup Co Inc 302 571-8761
2505 W 6th St Wilmington (19805) ***(G-10834)***
Hannigan Short Disharoonk 302 875-3637
700 West St Laurel (19956) ***(G-3237)***
Hanover Foods Corporation 302 653-9281
Duck Creek Rd Rr 6 Clayton (19938) ***(G-855)***
Hap LLC 302 645-7400
16192 Coastal Hwy Lewes (19958) ***(G-3531)***
Happy Hoofer, Harrington *Also called Michael Matthew Sponaugle* ***(G-2868)***
Happy Hours 302 422-9766
2908 Mlford Hrrington Hwy Milford (19963) ***(G-4435)***
Happy Kids Academy Inc 302 369-6929
273 Old Baltimore Pike Newark (19702) ***(G-6706)***
Happy Place Day Care LLC 302 737-7603
4638 Ogletown Stanton Rd Newark (19713) ***(G-6707)***
Happyland Childcare 302 424-3868
18073 Johnson Rd Lincoln (19960) ***(G-3854)***
Happynest, Wilmington *Also called Vitellus LLC* ***(G-13096)***
Har-Lex LLC (PA) 302 476-2322
105 Chandler Ave Wilmington (19807) ***(G-10835)***
Harbin LLC 302 219-3320
16192 Coastal Hwy Lewes (19958) ***(G-3532)***
Harbor Club Apartments 302 738-3561
26 Cheswold Blvd Apt 2a Newark (19713) ***(G-6708)***
Harbor House Apts, Claymont *Also called Apartment Communities Inc* ***(G-692)***
Harbor House Seafood Inc (PA) 302 629-0444
504 Bridgeville Hwy Seaford (19973) ***(G-8260)***
Harbour Towne Associates LP 302 645-1003
34232 Woods Edge Dr # 313 Lewes (19958) ***(G-3533)***
Hardcastle Gallery, Wilmington *Also called George Hardcastle & Sons Inc* ***(G-10700)***
Hardcore Cmpstes Oprations Llc 302 442-5900
618 Lambson Ln New Castle (19720) ***(G-5374)***
Hardin & Associates Inc 302 654-9923
1300 N Grant Ave Ste 204 Wilmington (19806) ***(G-10836)***
Harding Limo Bus Cnnection LLC 302 376-1818
21 W Green St Middletown (19709) ***(G-4104)***
Hardwood Direct LLC 302 378-3692
4390 Smmit Brdge Rd Ste 5 Middletown (19709) ***(G-4105)***
Hardwood Mills Inc 302 697-7195
5237 S Dupont Hwy Dover (19901) ***(G-1627)***
Hardy Development 302 436-4496
32984 Lighthouse Rd Selbyville (19975) ***(G-8499)***
Hardy Environmental Services, New Castle *Also called Joseph T Hardy & Son Inc* ***(G-5446)***
Hardy's Development, Selbyville *Also called Hardy Development* ***(G-8499)***
Harim Usa Ltd (HQ) 302 629-9136
126 N Shipley St Seaford (19973) ***(G-8261)***
Harley-Davidson, Smyrna *Also called Rommel Cycles LLC* ***(G-8703)***
Harman Hay Publications Inc 302 669-9144
221 Cornwell Dr Bear (19701) ***(G-177)***
Harmon Investments LLC 302 383-2176
2626 Drayton Dr Wilmington (19808) ***(G-10837)***
Harmonious Mind LLC 302 668-1059
5189 W Woodmill Dr 30a Wilmington (19808) ***(G-10838)***
Harmoniously Pbc 302 291-1106
3 Germay Dr Ste 4-1696 Wilmington (19804) ***(G-10839)***
Harmony Construction Inc 302 737-8700
350 Salem Church Rd Newark (19702) ***(G-6709)***
Harmony Trucking Inc 302 633-5600
305 W Newport Pike Wilmington (19804) ***(G-10840)***
Harold W.T. Purnell II, Georgetown *Also called Archer & Greiner PC* ***(G-2433)***
Harrel Stefoni 302 344-3269
1040 Harvest Grove Trl Dover (19901) ***(G-1628)***
Harriet Tubman Safe House Inc 302 351-4434
914 E 7th St Wilmington (19801) ***(G-10841)***
Harrington Insurance 302 883-5000
736 N Dupont Hwy Dover (19901) ***(G-1629)***
Harrington Medical & Optical, Harrington *Also called Medical Center of Harrington* ***(G-2866)***
Harrington Raceway and Casino, Harrington *Also called Harrington Raceway Inc* ***(G-2846)***
Harrington Raceway Inc 302 398-4920
15 W Rider Rd Harrington (19952) ***(G-2845)***
Harrington Raceway Inc 302 398-5346
Rr 13 Harrington (19952) ***(G-2846)***
Harrington Realty Inc (PA) 302 736-0800
516 Jefferic Blvd Ste C Dover (19901) ***(G-1630)***
Harrington Realty Inc 302 422-2424
736 N Dupont Hwy B Dover (19901) ***(G-1631)***
Harrington Senior Center Inc 302 398-4224
102 Fleming St Harrington (19952) ***(G-2847)***
Harris Berger LLC (PA) 302 665-1140
1105 N Market St Ste 1100 Wilmington (19801) ***(G-10842)***
Harris Towing and Auto Service 302 736-9901
5360 N Dupont Hwy Dover (19901) ***(G-1632)***
Harrison House Cmnty Program 302 595-3370
1415 Pulaski Hwy Newark (19702) ***(G-6710)***
Harrison Hse Cmnty Prgrams Inc 302 427-8438
6 Halcyon Dr New Castle (19720) ***(G-5375)***
Harrison Properties Ltd Inc 302 888-2650
1311 N Rodney St Ste A Wilmington (19806) ***(G-10843)***
Harrison Snior Lving Gorgetown 302 856-4574
110 W North St Georgetown (19947) ***(G-2555)***
HARRISON, DAVID C POST #14 AME, Smyrna *Also called American Lgion Amblance Stn 64* ***(G-8569)***
Harrisons Asphalt Paving 302 674-1255
51 Union St Dover (19904) ***(G-1633)***

ALPHABETIC SECTION — Health Care Center of Dover, Dover

Harrold & Son Inc 302 629-9504
27129 Woodland Rd Seaford (19973) *(G-8262)*
Harry A Lehman III Md PA 302 629-5050
38 Snowy Egret Ct Bridgeville (19933) *(G-479)*
Harry Caswell Inc 302 945-5322
32645 Long Neck Rd Millsboro (19966) *(G-4704)*
Harry H Mc Robie 302 846-9784
6872 Delmar Rd Delmar (19940) *(G-1001)*
Harry He DDS 302 836-3711
1400 Peoples Plz Ste 207 Newark (19702) *(G-6711)*
Harry J Lawall & Son Inc 302 429-7630
1822 Augustine Cut Off Wilmington (19803) *(G-10844)*
Harry Joseph 302 684-3243
18749 Josephs Rd Milton (19968) *(G-4911)*
Harry Kenyon Incorporated 302 762-7776
259 Quigley Blvd Ste 1 New Castle (19720) *(G-5376)*
Harry L Adams Inc 302 328-5268
23 Parkway Cir Ste 14 New Castle (19720) *(G-5377)*
Harry Louies Laundry & Dry Clg 302 734-8195
129 S Governors Ave Dover (19904) *(G-1634)*
Harry McRobie Farm, Delmar Also called Harry H Mc Robie *(G-1001)*
Harrymirimax Logisitics 302 784-5578
26 Bellecor Dr Ste B New Castle (19720) *(G-5378)*
Harsha Tankala MD 302 674-1818
1055 S Bradford St Dover (19904) *(G-1635)*
Hart Construction Co Inc 302 737-7886
109 Dallas Ave Newark (19711) *(G-6712)*
HARt Group LLC 302 782-9742
8 The Grn Ste A Dover (19901) *(G-1636)*
Hart Management Group, Newark Also called Hart Construction Co Inc *(G-6712)*
Harting Graphics Ltd 302 762-6397
305 Brandywine Blvd Wilmington (19809) *(G-10845)*
Hartle Brian State Farm Agency 302 322-1741
239 Christiana Rd Ste C New Castle (19720) *(G-5379)*
Hartly Family Learning Ctr LLC 302 492-1152
21 North St Hartly (19953) *(G-2923)*
Hartly Ruritan Club 302 492-8337
683 Hartly Rd Hartly (19953) *(G-2924)*
Hartnett & Hartnett 302 239-4220
7301 Lancaster Pike Ste 2 Hockessin (19707) *(G-3043)*
Hartnett Accounting & Tax Serv 302 477-0660
1202 Foulk Rd Ste 5 Wilmington (19803) *(G-10846)*
Harts Two 302 741-2119
204 Grouse Trl Camden Wyoming (19934) *(G-644)*
Hartzell Industries Inc 302 322-4900
115 Quigley Blvd New Castle (19720) *(G-5380)*
Harvard Business Services Inc 302 645-7400
16192 Coastal Hwy Lewes (19958) *(G-3534)*
Harvard Environmental Inc 302 326-2333
760 Pulaski Hwy Bear (19701) *(G-178)*
Harvest Community Dev Corp 302 654-2613
2205 Lancaster Ave Wilmington (19805) *(G-10847)*
Harvest Consumer Products LLC 302 732-6624
350 Clayton St Dagsboro (19939) *(G-907)*
Harvest Ministries Inc 302 846-3001
305 N Bi State Blvd Delmar (19940) *(G-1002)*
Harvest Ridge Winery LLC 302 250-6583
447 Westville Rd Marydel (19964) *(G-3917)*
Harvey Development Co 302 323-9300
29 E Commons Blvd Ste 100 New Castle (19720) *(G-5381)*
Harvey Development Company, Wilmington Also called H D C Inc *(G-10806)*
Harvey Hanna & Associates Inc 302 323-9300
405 Marsh Ln Ste 1 Newport (19804) *(G-7750)*
Harvey Macelree Ltd 302 654-4454
5721 Kennett Pike Wilmington (19807) *(G-10848)*
Harvey Mack Sales & Svc Inc (PA) 302 324-8340
29 E Commons Blvd Ste 300 New Castle (19720) *(G-5382)*
Harvey Miller Construction 302 674-4128
371 Blue Heron Rd Dover (19904) *(G-1637)*
Harvey Road Automotive Inc 302 654-7500
1004 W 25th St Wilmington (19802) *(G-10849)*
Harvey Road Automotive Inc 302 475-0369
1503 Harvey Rd Wilmington (19810) *(G-10850)*
Harvey Truck Center, New Castle Also called Harvey Mack Sales & Svc Inc *(G-5382)*
Hashr8 Software LLC 702 473-0426
2035 Sunset Lake Rd B2 Newark (19702) *(G-6713)*
Haskell Laboratory, Newark Also called E I Du Pont De Nemours & Co *(G-6491)*
Hastin-Karin Inc 347 377-8415
704 N King St Wilmington (19801) *(G-10851)*
Hat Blue Group LLC 225 288-2962
16192 Coastal Hwy Lewes (19958) *(G-3535)*
Hat World, Dover Also called Lids Corporation *(G-1783)*
Hatch's Home Improvement, Marydel Also called Jeffrey Hatch *(G-3919)*
Hatfield Gas Connections Inc 302 945-2354
59 Aintree Dr Lewes (19958) *(G-3536)*
Hathworth Inc (PA) 302 884-7616
913 N Market St Ste 200 Wilmington (19801) *(G-10852)*
Hatzel & Buehler Inc (HQ) 302 478-4200
3600 Silverside Rd Ste A Wilmington (19810) *(G-10853)*

Hatzel & Buehler Inc 302 798-5422
1 Righter Pkwy Ste 110 Wilmington (19803) *(G-10854)*
Haunted Industries 302 836-5823
457 Buck Jersey Rd Bear (19701) *(G-179)*
Haus of Lacquer LLC (PA) 302 690-0309
300 N Market St Wilmington (19801) *(G-10855)*
Haven Lake Animal Hospital 302 422-8100
300 Milford Harrington Hw Milford (19963) *(G-4436)*
Hawkins Reporting Service, Wilmington Also called Dale Hawkins *(G-9948)*
Hay Road Power Complex, Wilmington Also called Calpine Corporation *(G-9540)*
Hayes Sewing Machine Company 302 764-9033
4425 Concord Pike Wilmington (19803) *(G-10856)*
Hayloft Enterprises Inc 302 656-7600
3 Mill Rd Wilmington (19806) *(G-10857)*
Haymy Resources LLC 402 218-6787
16192 Coastal Hwy Lewes (19958) *(G-3537)*
Hazardous Waste 302 739-9403
89 Kings Hwy Dover (19901) *(G-1638)*
Hazzard Electrical Contractors 302 645-8457
1 American Legion Rd Lewes (19958) *(G-3538)*
HB Dupont Plaza 302 998-7271
422 Delaware Ave Wilmington (19801) *(G-10858)*
HB Fitness Delaware Inc 302 384-7245
5810 Kirkwood Hwy Ste B Wilmington (19808) *(G-10859)*
Hbcs, New Castle Also called Hospital Blling Cllctn Svc Ltd *(G-5405)*
Hbnyc, Dover Also called Hypebeast Inc *(G-1663)*
Hbs, Lewes Also called Harvard Business Services Inc *(G-3534)*
Hcac 302 266-8100
301 Ruthar Dr Ste C Newark (19711) *(G-6714)*
HCC Corporation LLC 302 421-9306
505 S Market St Dept 2610 Wilmington (19801) *(G-10860)*
Hce, Wilmington Also called Hunte Corporate Enterprise LLC *(G-10975)*
Hchc Uk Holdings Inc 302 225-5007
2751 Centerville Rd # 342 Wilmington (19808) *(G-10861)*
Hcnrg Solutions, Wilmington Also called H Clemons Consulting Inc *(G-10805)*
Hcr Manor Care Svc Fla III Inc 302 764-0181
700 Foulk Rd Wilmington (19803) *(G-10862)*
Hcr Manorcare Med Svcs Fla LLC 302 239-8583
5651 Limestone Rd Wilmington (19808) *(G-10863)*
Hcsg Regal Hghts Regal41 .... 302 998-0181
6525 Lancaster Pike Hockessin (19707) *(G-3044)*
Head Masters Salon, Wilmington Also called Hair Gallery *(G-10820)*
Head Quarters 302 798-1639
1400 Philadelphia Pike A5 Wilmington (19809) *(G-10864)*
Head Quarters Barbershop 646 423-6767
217 E Main St Middletown (19709) *(G-4106)*
Head Start Harrington 302 398-9196
112 East St Harrington (19952) *(G-2848)*
Headmasters Beauty Salon, Wilmington Also called Mary Zieken *(G-11559)*
Headquarters 2 Inc 302 731-9600
6 Polly Drummond Shpg Ctr Newark (19711) *(G-6715)*
Headstream Inc 302 356-0156
5301 Limestone Rd Ste 204 Wilmington (19808) *(G-10865)*
Healex Systems Ltd 302 235-5750
11 Middleton Dr Wilmington (19808) *(G-10866)*
Healing Adults & Adolescents 302 836-4000
3560 Wrangle Hill Rd Bear (19701) *(G-180)*
Health & Social Svcs Del Dept 302 255-9800
1901 N Dupont Hwy New Castle (19720) *(G-5383)*
Health & Social Svcs Del Dept 302 368-6700
501 Ogletown Rd Newark (19711) *(G-6716)*
Health & Social Svcs Del Dept 302 255-2700
1901 N Dupont Hwy New Castle (19720) *(G-5384)*
Health & Social Svcs Del Dept 302 223-1000
100 Sunnyside Rd Smyrna (19977) *(G-8650)*
Health & Social Svcs Del Dept 302 577-3420
200 S Adams St Wilmington (19801) *(G-10867)*
Health & Social Svcs Del Dept 302 552-3530
1624 Jessup St Wilmington (19802) *(G-10868)*
Health & Social Svcs Del Dept 302 255-9855
1901 N Dupont Hwy New Castle (19720) *(G-5385)*
Health & Social Svcs Del Dept 302 255-2700
1901 N Dupont Hwy Fl 1 New Castle (19720) *(G-5386)*
Health & Social Svcs Del Dept 302 283-7500
501 Ogletown Rd Fl 3 Newark (19711) *(G-6717)*
Health & Social Svcs Del Dept 302 337-8261
400 Mill St Bridgeville (19933) *(G-480)*
Health & Social Svcs Del Dept 302 857-5000
805 River Rd Dover (19901) *(G-1639)*
Health & Social Svcs Del Dept 302 856-5586
20105 Office Cir Georgetown (19947) *(G-2556)*
Health & Social Svcs Del Dept 302 391-3505
1901 N Dupont Hwy New Castle (19720) *(G-5387)*
Health & Social Svcs Del Dept 302 255-9500
410 Federal St Ste 7 Dover (19901) *(G-1640)*
Health Care Assoc PA 302 684-2033
616 Mulberry St Milton (19968) *(G-4912)*
Health Care Center of Dover, Dover Also called Highmarks Inc *(G-1645)*

(PA)=Parent Co (HQ)=Headquarters (DH)=Div Headquarters   2020 Harris Directory of Delaware Businesses

Health Care Consultants Inc ALPHABETIC SECTION

Health Care Consultants Inc...302 892-9210
240 N James St Ste 111 Wilmington (19804) *(G-10869)*
Health Insurance Associates, Dover *Also called Donald C Savoy Inc (G-1437)*
Health Support Services...302 287-4952
512 W 22nd St Apt 2 Wilmington (19802) *(G-10870)*
Healthpartners Delmarva LLC...302 744-6008
640 S State St Dover (19901) *(G-1641)*
HealthSouth, Middletown *Also called Encompass Health Corporation (G-4058)*
Healthworks, Dover *Also called Bayhealth Med Ctr Inc-OCC Hlth (G-1180)*
Healthy At Home Care LLC...571 228-5935
7 Kendal Ln Rehoboth Beach (19971) *(G-7958)*
Healthy Homes De Inc...302 998-1001
2421 Kirkwood Hwy Wilmington (19805) *(G-10871)*
Healthy Kneads, Wilmington *Also called Stephanie Galbraith (G-12753)*
Healthy Outcomes LLC...302 856-4022
2 Lee Ave Unit 103 Georgetown (19947) *(G-2557)*
Healthy Smiles of Delaware PA...302 658-7200
1700 Shallcross Ave Ste 2 Wilmington (19806) *(G-10872)*
Healy & Long Inc...302 654-8039
2000 Rodman Rd Wilmington (19805) *(G-10873)*
Healy Long & Jevin Inc...302 654-8039
2000 Rodman Rd Wilmington (19805) *(G-10874)*
Hearsay Services of Delaware...302 422-3312
104 Ne Front St Milford (19963) *(G-4437)*
Hearst Media Services Conn LLC...203 330-6231
1209 N Orange St Wilmington (19801) *(G-10875)*
Heart and Vascular Clinic, Newark *Also called Ashish B Parikh (G-6010)*
Heart Start Er Training Inc...302 420-1917
2724 Jacqueline Dr M33 Wilmington (19810) *(G-10876)*
Heart To Hand Daycare LLC...202 256-4524
16192 Coastal Hwy Lewes (19958) *(G-3539)*
Heartfelt Books Publishing...866 557-6522
1000 N West St Ste 1200 Wilmington (19801) *(G-10877)*
Heartland, Wilmington *Also called Hcr Manor Care Svc Fla III Inc (G-10862)*
Heartland Hospice Services LLC...302 737-7080
256 Chapman Rd Ste 102 Newark (19702) *(G-6718)*
Heartland Hospice Services LLC...419 252-5743
750 Prides Xing Ste 110 Newark (19713) *(G-6719)*
Heartland Hospice Svcs 4668, Newark *Also called Heartland Hospice Services LLC (G-6718)*
Heated Wear LLC...347 510-7965
427 N Ttnall St Ste 16278 Wilmington (19801) *(G-10878)*
Heather Kraft...302 927-0072
33094 Main St Dagsboro (19939) *(G-908)*
Heavenly Hound Hotel...302 436-2926
33049 Lighthouse Rd Selbyville (19975) *(G-8500)*
Heavy Equipment Rental Inc...302 654-5716
218 Marsh Ln New Castle (19720) *(G-5388)*
Heavy Key Studios LLC...302 356-6832
320 N Dupont Hwy New Castle (19720) *(G-5389)*
Heckessin Health Partners...302 234-2597
5850 Limestone Rd Hockessin (19707) *(G-3045)*
Heckler & Frabizzio PA...302 573-4800
800 Delaware Ave Ste 200 Wilmington (19801) *(G-10879)*
Hedgeforce LLC...305 600-0085
9 Majestic Dr Newark (19713) *(G-6720)*
Heidis Academy of Prfrmg Arts...302 293-7868
1218 Pulaski Hwy Bear (19701) *(G-181)*
Heiman Gouge & Kaufman LLP...302 658-1800
800 N King St Ste 303 Wilmington (19801) *(G-10880)*
Heiman Aber Goldlust & Baker...302 658-1800
800 N King St Ste 303 Wilmington (19801) *(G-10881)*
Heiman, Henry A, Wilmington *Also called Heiman Aber Goldlust & Baker (G-10881)*
Heirloom Creations...302 659-1817
5899 Underwoods Corner Rd Smyrna (19977) *(G-8651)*
Helena Agri-Enterprises LLC...302 337-3881
16635 Adams Rd Bridgeville (19933) *(G-481)*
Helena Schroyer MD...302 429-5870
1010 N Bancroft Pkwy Wilmington (19805) *(G-10882)*
Helium3 Tech and Services LLC...302 766-2856
197 Harriet Ct Newark (19711) *(G-6721)*
Helix Inc Ta Audioworks...302 285-0555
478 Middletown Warwick Rd Middletown (19709) *(G-4107)*
Hellenic Univ CLB Wilmington...302 479-8811
1407 Foulk Rd Ste 100 Wilmington (19803) *(G-10883)*
Hellens Heating & Air I...302 945-1875
20949 Harbeson Rd Harbeson (19951) *(G-2784)*
Hellings Builders, Claymont *Also called RC Hellings Inc (G-799)*
Hells Kitchen Software Ltd...302 983-5644
12 Furman Ct Newark (19713) *(G-6722)*
Helopen Condominium Council...302 227-6409
527 N Boardwalk Rehoboth Beach (19971) *(G-7959)*
Helpern Eye Associates, Milford *Also called Halpern Eye Associates Inc (G-4432)*
Hematology/Oncology Office, Wilmington *Also called Delaware Clinical & Labortry (G-10019)*
Henderson Mechanical Inc...302 629-3753
105 New St Ste 2seaford Seaford (19973) *(G-8263)*
Henderson Services Inc...302 424-1999
219 N Rehoboth Blvd Milford (19963) *(G-4438)*
Henderson Software...302 239-7573
5 Citation Ct Wilmington (19808) *(G-10884)*
Henlopen Acres Beach Club Inc...302 227-9919
28 Dune Way Rehoboth Beach (19971) *(G-7960)*
Henlopen Cardiology, Rehoboth Beach *Also called Habib Bolourchi MD Facc (G-7957)*
Henlopen Cardiology PA (PA)...302 645-7671
18959 Coastal Hwy Ste A Rehoboth Beach (19971) *(G-7961)*
Henlopen Condominiums, Rehoboth Beach *Also called Helopen Condominium Council (G-7959)*
Henlopen Design LLC...302 265-4330
16192 Coastal Hwy Lewes (19958) *(G-3540)*
Henlopen Homes Inc...302 684-0860
17644 Coastal Hwy Lewes (19958) *(G-3541)*
Henlopen Homes LLC...302 684-0860
18427 Josephs Rd Milton (19968) *(G-4913)*
Henlopen Hotel Inc...302 227-2551
511 N Boardwalk Rehoboth Beach (19971) *(G-7962)*
Henlopen Music Therapy SE...302 593-7784
31618 Holly Ct Lewes (19958) *(G-3542)*
Henninger Printing Co Inc...302 934-8119
208 Main St Millsboro (19966) *(G-4705)*
HENRIETTA JOHNSON MEDICAL CENT, Wilmington *Also called Southbrdge Med Advsory Council (G-12686)*
Henry Auto Body Shop, Wilmington *Also called Edward J Henry & Sons Inc (G-10357)*
Henry Bros, Wilmington *Also called Henry Bros Autobody & Pnt Sp (G-10885)*
Henry Bros Autobody & Pnt Sp...302 994-4438
2013 W Newport Pike Wilmington (19804) *(G-10885)*
Henry Eashum & Son Inc...302 697-6164
20 S Dupont Hwy Camden (19934) *(G-578)*
Henrys Car Care Inc...302 994-5766
2207 Saint James Dr Wilmington (19808) *(G-10886)*
Hensco Glass Company, Harrington *Also called Hensco LLC (G-2849)*
Hensco LLC...302 423-1638
155 Argos Choice Harrington (19952) *(G-2849)*
Hentkowski Inc...302 998-2257
3420 Old Capitol Trl Wilmington (19808) *(G-10887)*
Hera Sports Surfaces LLC...781 392-4094
2915 Ogletown Rd Newark (19713) *(G-6723)*
Herbert R Martin Associates...302 239-1700
489 Valley Brook Dr Hockessin (19707) *(G-3046)*
Herbert Studios...302 836-3122
131 Canal Way Newark (19702) *(G-6724)*
Herbert T Casalena DDS...302 984-1712
2300 Penns Ave Ste 6a Wilmington (19806) *(G-10888)*
Hercules International Ltd LLC...302 594-5000
1313 N Market St Ste A Wilmington (19801) *(G-10889)*
Hercules LLC (HQ)...302 594-5000
500 Hercules Rd Wilmington (19808) *(G-10890)*
Herdeg Dupont Dalle Pazze LLP...302 655-6500
15 Center Meeting Rd Wilmington (19807) *(G-10891)*
Heritage At Dover, Dover *Also called 1203 Walker Rd Operations LLC (G-1064)*
Heritage At Dover, Dover *Also called 1203 Walker Rd Operations LLC (G-1065)*
Heritage At Milford...302 422-8700
500 S Dupont Blvd Milford (19963) *(G-4439)*
Heritage Concrete, Wilmington *Also called HMA Concrete LLC (G-10921)*
Heritage Interiors Inc...302 369-3199
113 Sandy Dr Newark (19713) *(G-6725)*
Heritage Machine Shop LLC...302 656-3313
2 James Ct Wilmington (19801) *(G-10892)*
Heritage Manor, Harrington *Also called Cabell Corp (G-2822)*
Heritage Medical Associates PA...302 998-3334
2601 Annand Dr Ste 4 Wilmington (19808) *(G-10893)*
Heritage Sports Rdo Netwrk LLC...302 492-1132
1841 Bryants Corner Rd Hartly (19953) *(G-2925)*
Herox Pbc...604 681-3651
3 Germay Dr Unit 4-402 Wilmington (19804) *(G-10894)*
Herr Foods Incorporated...302 628-9161
22706 Sussex Hwy Seaford (19973) *(G-8264)*
Herring Creek Builders Inc...302 684-3015
26085 Williams Farm Rd Milton (19968) *(G-4914)*
Hertiage Builders & Improvemen...302 275-8675
9 Linn Ct Bear (19701) *(G-182)*
Hertrich Collision Ctr of...302 839-0550
1449 Bay Rd Milford (19963) *(G-4440)*
Hertrich's Collision Center, Seaford *Also called Complete Auto Body Inc (G-8203)*
Hertz Corporation...302 654-8312
100 S French St Ste D Wilmington (19801) *(G-10895)*
Hertz Corporation...302 428-0637
100 Mrtin Lther King Blvd New Castle (19720) *(G-5390)*
Hertz Corporation...302 428-0637
191 N Dupont Hwy New Castle (19720) *(G-5391)*
Hertz Corporation...302 428-0637
500 Hercules Rd Wilmington (19808) *(G-10896)*
Hertz Corporation...302 428-0637
162 Old Churchmans Rd New Castle (19720) *(G-5392)*
Hertz Local Edition Corp...302 678-0700
1679 S Dupont Hwy Ste 17 Dover (19901) *(G-1642)*

Hes Sign Services LLC 302 232-2100
459 Old Airport Rd New Castle (19720) *(G-5393)*
Hete Tech Support 302 226-1892
45 Kings Creek Cir Rehoboth Beach (19971) *(G-7963)*
Hetrick, C H Associates, Wilmington *Also called Hetrick-Drake Associates Inc* *(G-10897)*
Hetrick-Drake Associates Inc 302 998-7500
2018 Duncan Rd Wilmington (19808) *(G-10897)*
Hewlett-Packard World Trade (PA) 877 424-4536
2850 Centerville Rd Wilmington (19808) *(G-10898)*
Hexact Inc 850 716-1616
2035 Sunset Lake Rd B2 Newark (19702) *(G-6726)*
Hexagon Metrology Inc 302 351-3580
800 First State Blvd Wilmington (19804) *(G-10899)*
Heyden, Edward B, Newark *Also called Newark Family Counceling Ctr* *(G-7119)*
Hfm Investment Advisors Inc 302 234-9777
5 Hunting Ct Newark (19711) *(G-6727)*
Hh Property Management 302 999-1414
6 Larch Ave Wilmington (19804) *(G-10900)*
HI Grade Dairy, Harrington *Also called Tuscan/Lehigh Dairies Inc* *(G-2901)*
HI Line Auto Detailing 302 420-5368
1618 Newport Gap Pike Wilmington (19808) *(G-10901)*
Hibbert Company 609 394-7500
890 Ships Landing Way New Castle (19720) *(G-5394)*
Hibbert Group, The, New Castle *Also called Hibbert Company* *(G-5394)*
Hickman Overhead Door Company 302 422-4249
1625 Bay Rd Milford (19963) *(G-4441)*
Hickory Hill Builders Inc 302 934-6109
25714 Timmons Ln Dagsboro (19939) *(G-909)*
Hickory Hill Metal Fabrication 302 382-6727
2134 Seven Hickories Rd Dover (19904) *(G-1643)*
Hidden Acres Rest Home Inc 302 492-1962
265 Mowely Ln Marydel (19964) *(G-3918)*
Hidden Hitch & Trailer Parts 410 398-5949
304 Connor Blvd Bear (19701) *(G-183)*
Hie, Bridgeville *Also called Horney Industrial Electronics* *(G-483)*
Hifu Services Inc 650 867-4972
3411 Silverside Rd Wilmington (19810) *(G-10902)*
Higgins House Victorian B & B 407 324-9238
140 River Bend Dr Dagsboro (19939) *(G-910)*
High Horse Performance Inc 302 894-1115
93 Artisan Dr Ste 6 Smyrna (19977) *(G-8652)*
High Point Mobil Park, Frederica *Also called Sun Communities Inc* *(G-2413)*
High Seas Motel 302 227-2022
12 Christian St Rehoboth Beach (19971) *(G-7964)*
High Tide News 302 727-0390
11243 Signature Blvd Selbyville (19975) *(G-8501)*
High Tide Trucking Inc 302 846-3537
10256 Beauchamp Ln Delmar (19940) *(G-1003)*
High Vue Logging Inc 302 697-3606
12090 Willow Grove Rd Camden (19934) *(G-579)*
High-Tech Machine Company Inc 302 636-0267
10 Lewis Cir Wilmington (19804) *(G-10903)*
Highdef Transportation LLC 610 212-8596
8 Dover Ct Bear (19701) *(G-184)*
Higher Power Yoga and Fitness 302 526-2077
96 Salt Creek Dr Unit 3 Dover (19901) *(G-1644)*
Highland Construction LLC 302 286-6990
3415 Wrangle Hill Rd # 10 Bear (19701) *(G-185)*
Highland Orchards (PA) 302 478-1392
4 Clyth Dr Wilmington (19803) *(G-10904)*
Highmark Blue Cross, Wilmington *Also called Highmarks Inc* *(G-10905)*
Highmarks Inc (PA) 302 421-3000
800 Delaware Ave Ste 900 Wilmington (19801) *(G-10905)*
Highmarks Inc 302 421-3000
800 W Delaware Ave Wilmington (19809) *(G-10906)*
Highmarks Inc 302 674-8492
870 S Governors Ave Dover (19904) *(G-1645)*
Highway Operations, Middletown *Also called Transportation Delaware Dept* *(G-4267)*
Highway Traffic Controllers 302 697-7117
6236 Mud Mill Rd Camden Wyoming (19934) *(G-645)*
Hill & Smith Inc 302 328-3220
18 Blevins Dr New Castle (19720) *(G-5395)*
Hill Bancshares Delaware Inc (PA) 302 651-8389
1105 N Market St Ste 1300 Wilmington (19801) *(G-10907)*
Hill Farms Inc 302 422-0219
2007 School St Houston (19954) *(G-3179)*
Hill Luth Day Care Center 302 656-3224
1018 W 6th St Wilmington (19805) *(G-10908)*
Hill Publishing Inc 917 826-3722
2035 Sunset Lake Rd Newark (19702) *(G-6728)*
Hill-Billy Towing Services, Newark *Also called Jim Sellers* *(G-6840)*
Hillandale Farms Delaware Inc 302 492-3644
149 Sydell Dr Hartly (19953) *(G-2926)*
Hillandale Farms of Delaware, Hartly *Also called Hillandale Farms of Pa Inc* *(G-2927)*
Hillandale Farms of Pa Inc 302 492-1537
149 Sydell Dr Hartly (19953) *(G-2927)*
Hillis-Carnes Engrg Assoc Inc 302 744-9855
1277 Mcd Dr Dover (19901) *(G-1646)*

Hillside Center 302 652-1181
810 S Broom St Wilmington (19805) *(G-10909)*
Hillside Oil Company Inc 302 738-4144
40 Brookhill Dr Newark (19702) *(G-6729)*
Hilltop Lutheran Neighborhd 302 656-3224
1018 W 6th St Wilmington (19805) *(G-10910)*
Hilo House, Wilmington *Also called W23 S12 Holdings LLC* *(G-13110)*
Hilton, Dover *Also called 44 Aasha Hospitality Assoc LLC* *(G-1070)*
Hilton, Dover *Also called Quintasian LLC* *(G-2005)*
Hilton Bus Service 302 697-7676
168 Vepco Blvd Camden (19934) *(G-580)*
Hilton Christiana, Newark *Also called Mj Wilmington Hotel Assoc LP* *(G-7046)*
Hilton Christiana, Newark *Also called Mj Wilmington Hotel Assoc LP* *(G-7047)*
Hilton Corp (PA) 302 994-3365
1900 Kirkwood Hwy Wilmington (19805) *(G-10911)*
Hilton Marine, Wilmington *Also called Hilton Corp* *(G-10911)*
Hilton Marine Supply Company 302 994-3365
1900 Kirkwood Hwy Wilmington (19805) *(G-10912)*
Hilyard's Business Solutions, Wilmington *Also called Hilyards Inc* *(G-10913)*
Hilyards Inc (PA) 302 995-2201
1616 Newport Gap Pike Wilmington (19808) *(G-10913)*
Himalaya Trading Inc 702 833-0485
8 The Grn Dover (19901) *(G-1647)*
Himont Inc 302 996-6000
2801 Centerville Rd Wilmington (19808) *(G-10914)*
Hindin Media LLC (PA) 302 463-4612
1116 Webster Dr Wilmington (19803) *(G-10915)*
Hippo Trailer 302 854-6661
14 Evergreen Dr Georgetown (19947) *(G-2558)*
Hirsh Industries Inc 302 678-4990
631 Ridgely St Dover (19904) *(G-1648)*
Hirsh Industries Inc 302 678-3456
1525 Mckee Rd Dover (19904) *(G-1649)*
His Image Barbershop 302 256-2792
505 N Lincoln St Wilmington (19805) *(G-10916)*
Hispanic American Assn of Del (PA) 302 562-2705
92 S Gerald Dr Ste A Newark (19713) *(G-6730)*
Hispanic Personal Dev LLC 302 738-4782
2 Rolling Dr Newark (19713) *(G-6731)*
Historic Red Clay Valley Inc (PA) 302 998-1930
1601 Railroad Ave Wilmington (19808) *(G-10917)*
Historical & Cultural Afairs 302 792-0285
1 Naamans Rd Claymont (19703) *(G-761)*
Historical & Cultural Afairs 302 323-4453
211 Delaware St New Castle (19720) *(G-5396)*
Historical & Cultural Afairs 302 739-3277
340 Kitts Hummock Rd Dover (19901) *(G-1650)*
Historical Society of Del Inc 302 295-2400
505 N Market St Wilmington (19801) *(G-10918)*
Historical Society of Del Inc 302 322-8411
42 The Strand New Castle (19720) *(G-5397)*
Historical Society of Delware (PA) 302 655-7161
505 N Market St Wilmington (19801) *(G-10919)*
Hither Creek Press 603 387-3444
197 Meadow Brook Ln Milford (19963) *(G-4442)*
Hlh Construction MGT Svcs Inc 302 654-7508
2000 Rodman Rd Wilmington (19805) *(G-10920)*
HM Defense Resources, Lewes *Also called Haymy Resources LLC* *(G-3537)*
HMA Concrete LLC 302 777-1235
307 A St Wilmington (19801) *(G-10921)*
Hoard Inc 980 333-1703
251 Little Falls Dr Wilmington (19808) *(G-10922)*
Hoban Auto & Machineshop Inc 302 436-8013
19 N Main St Selbyville (19975) *(G-8502)*
Hoban Service Center, Selbyville *Also called Hoban Auto & Machineshop Inc* *(G-8502)*
Hobbs Enterprises Inc 302 697-2090
4398 Turkey Point Rd Viola (19979) *(G-8837)*
Hobo News Press Inc 302 235-1066
8 Willow Creek Ln Newark (19711) *(G-6732)*
Hockessin Animal Hospital 302 239-9464
643 Yorklyn Rd Hockessin (19707) *(G-3047)*
Hockessin Athletic Club, Hockessin *Also called Eastern Athletic Clubs LLC* *(G-3016)*
Hockessin Chrpractic Centre PA 302 239-8550
724 Yorklyn Rd Ste 150 Hockessin (19707) *(G-3048)*
Hockessin Cleaners 302 239-6071
7313 Lancaster Pike Ste 1 Hockessin (19707) *(G-3049)*
Hockessin Dance Center Inc 302 738-3838
216 Louviers Dr Newark (19711) *(G-6733)*
Hockessin Day Spa 302 234-7573
1304 Old Lancaster Pike C Hockessin (19707) *(G-3050)*
Hockessin Dental 302 239-7277
6300 Limestone Rd Hockessin (19707) *(G-3051)*
Hockessin Electric Inc 302 239-9332
6 Fritze Ct Hockessin (19707) *(G-3052)*
Hockessin Family Medicine, Hockessin *Also called Mark W Wingel* *(G-3090)*
Hockessin Kinder Care 1633, Hockessin *Also called Kindercare Learning Ctrs LLC* *(G-3071)*
Hockessin Montessori School 302 234-1240
1000 Old Lancaster Pike Hockessin (19707) *(G-3053)*

Hockessin Sanitation, Hockessin *Also called Carolyn Palmatary* ***(G-2976)***
Hockessin Soccer Club....302 234-1444
740 Evanson Rd Hockessin (19707) ***(G-3054)***
Hockessin Tractor Inc....302 239-4201
654 Yorklyn Rd Hockessin (19707) ***(G-3055)***
Hodges International Inc....310 874-8516
8 The Grn Dover (19901) ***(G-1651)***
Hodges L Wooten....302 335-5162
120 Limerick Ln Magnolia (19962) ***(G-3895)***
Hoenen & Mitchell Inc....302 645-6193
18548 Arabian Acres Rd Lewes (19958) ***(G-3543)***
Hoerner Inc....302 762-4406
602 Elizabeth Ave Wilmington (19809) ***(G-10923)***
Hoeschel Inv & Insur Group....302 738-3535
106 Haines St Ste A Newark (19711) ***(G-6734)***
Hogan & Veith PA....302 656-7540
1311 Delaware Ave Ste 1 Wilmington (19806) ***(G-10924)***
Hogan McDaniel, Wilmington *Also called Hogan & Veith PA* ***(G-10924)***
Hogar Crea Int of Delaware....302 762-2875
1126 Brandywine St Wilmington (19802) ***(G-10925)***
Hola Delaware LLC....302 832-3620
100 Hickory Pl Newark (19702) ***(G-6735)***
Holiday Hair, Seaford *Also called Regis Corporation* ***(G-8375)***
Holiday Hair 141, Rehoboth Beach *Also called Regis Corporation* ***(G-8046)***
Holiday Hair 238, Bear *Also called Regis Corporation* ***(G-300)***
Holiday Inn, Newark *Also called Concord Towers Inc* ***(G-6280)***
Holiday Inn, Bethany Beach *Also called Paul Amos* ***(G-420)***
Holiday Inn, Dover *Also called Nazar Dover LLC* ***(G-1886)***
Holiday Inn, Claymont *Also called Interstate Hotels Resorts Inc* ***(G-766)***
Holiday Inn, Dover *Also called Shri SAI Dover LLC* ***(G-2083)***
Holiday Inn, Dover *Also called K W Lands North LLC* ***(G-1719)***
Holiday Inn Express....302 227-4030
19953 Shuttle Rd Rehoboth Beach (19971) ***(G-7965)***
Holiday Inn Express....302 398-8800
17271 S Dupont Hwy Harrington (19952) ***(G-2850)***
Holiday Inn Express & Suites, Middletown *Also called Lila Keshav Hospitality LLC* ***(G-4133)***
Holiday Inn Select....302 792-2700
630 Naamans Rd Claymont (19703) ***(G-762)***
Holland Corp....302 245-5645
33357 Deer Run Rd Selbyville (19975) ***(G-8503)***
Holland Mulch Inc....302 765-3100
135 Hay Rd Wilmington (19809) ***(G-10926)***
Hollie Enterprises LLC....903 721-1904
1201 N Orange St Ste 600 Wilmington (19801) ***(G-10927)***
Hollingsead International LLC....302 855-5888
21583 Baltimore Ave Georgetown (19947) ***(G-2559)***
Hollingsworth Heating & AC....302 422-7525
719 S Dupont Blvd Milford (19963) ***(G-4443)***
Holloway Bros Tools, New Castle *Also called Sid Tool Co Inc* ***(G-5707)***
Holly Hill Estates....302 653-7503
271 Berry Dr Smyrna (19977) ***(G-8653)***
Holly Lake Campsite, Millsboro *Also called Barsgr LLC* ***(G-4634)***
Holly Lake Campsites, Lewes *Also called Barsgr LLC* ***(G-3362)***
Holly Oak Towing and Service....302 792-1500
6521 Governor Printz Blvd Wilmington (19809) ***(G-10928)***
Hollywell Logistics LLC....267 901-4272
802 N West St Ste 105 Wilmington (19801) ***(G-10929)***
Hollywood Grill Restaurant (PA)....302 655-1348
1811 Concord Pike Wilmington (19803) ***(G-10930)***
Hollywood Grill Restaurant....302 629-4500
22871 Sussex Hwy Seaford (19973) ***(G-8265)***
Hollywood Grill Restaurant....302 479-2000
350 Rocky Run Pkwy Wilmington (19803) ***(G-10931)***
Hollywood Grill Restaurant....302 737-3900
3 Concord Ln Newark (19713) ***(G-6736)***
Hollywood Tan (PA)....302 995-2692
4575 Kirkwood Hwy Wilmington (19808) ***(G-10932)***
Hollywood Tans....302 478-8267
3100 Naamans Rd Ste 34 Wilmington (19810) ***(G-10933)***
Holman Moving Systems LLC (PA)....302 323-9000
20 E Commons Blvd New Castle (19720) ***(G-5398)***
Holman Moving Systems LLC....302 323-9000
20 E Commons Blvd New Castle (19720) ***(G-5399)***
Hologic Inc....302 631-2846
18 Bay Blvd Newark (19702) ***(G-6737)***
Hologic Inc....302 631-2700
600 Technology Dr Newark (19702) ***(G-6738)***
Holts Metal Works Inc....302 628-1609
3325 Horseshoe Rd Seaford (19973) ***(G-8266)***
Holy Angels School, Newark *Also called Catholic Docese Wilmington Inc* ***(G-6169)***
Home Care Assistance De....856 625-9934
11 Mcmahon Dr Bear (19701) ***(G-186)***
Home Depot USA Inc....302 838-6818
2000 Peoples Plz Newark (19702) ***(G-6739)***
Home Depot USA Inc....302 395-1260
138 Sunset Blvd New Castle (19720) ***(G-5400)***
Home Depot USA Inc....302 735-8864
801 N Dupont Hwy Dover (19901) ***(G-1652)***
Home Depot, The, Newark *Also called Home Depot USA Inc* ***(G-6739)***
Home Depot, The, New Castle *Also called Home Depot USA Inc* ***(G-5400)***
Home Depot, The, Dover *Also called Home Depot USA Inc* ***(G-1652)***
Home Finders Real Estate Co....302 655-8091
31 Trolley Sq Ste C Wilmington (19806) ***(G-10934)***
Home For Aged Wmn-Mnquadale HM....302 654-1810
1101 Gilpin Ave Wilmington (19806) ***(G-10935)***
Home Health Corp America Inc....302 678-4764
1221 College Park Dr # 203 Dover (19904) ***(G-1653)***
Home Health Heartfel....302 660-2686
5179 W Woodmill Dr Wilmington (19808) ***(G-10936)***
Home Health Services By TLC....302 322-5510
287 Christiana Ave Ste 24 Wilmington (19801) ***(G-10937)***
Home Helpers, Claymont *Also called Bc Home Health Care Services* ***(G-700)***
Home Hlth Care Amer An Amdisys, Dover *Also called Amedisys Inc* ***(G-1117)***
Home Instead Senior Care, Wilmington *Also called Robert Bird* ***(G-12435)***
Home Instead Senior Care....302 697-6435
755 Walker Rd Ste A Dover (19904) ***(G-1654)***
Home Media One LLC....302 644-0307
22344 Lwes Georgetown Hwy Georgetown (19947) ***(G-2560)***
Home of Divine Providence Inc....302 654-1184
300 Bayard Ave Wilmington (19805) ***(G-10938)***
Home of Merciful Rest Society....302 652-3311
1900 Lovering Ave Wilmington (19806) ***(G-10939)***
Home Paramount Pest Control....302 894-9201
769 S Dupont Hwy New Castle (19720) ***(G-5401)***
Home Services LLC....302 510-4580
3410 Old Capitol Trl # 2 Wilmington (19808) ***(G-10940)***
Home Services Unlimited....302 293-8726
22 Sailboat Cir Newark (19702) ***(G-6740)***
Home Team Realty....302 629-7711
959 Norman Eskridge Hwy Seaford (19973) ***(G-8267)***
Home Theater, Dover *Also called Smartis* ***(G-2089)***
Homeimprovement E B&S....302 465-1828
19 Carpenter St Dover (19901) ***(G-1655)***
Homeland SEC Verification LLC....888 791-4614
4001 Kennett Pike Wilmington (19807) ***(G-10941)***
Homeless Cat Helpers Inc....302 344-3015
550 N Pine St Seaford (19973) ***(G-8268)***
Homes For Life Foundation....302 571-1217
1106 Berkeley Rd Wilmington (19807) ***(G-10942)***
Homestar Remodeling LLC....302 528-5898
405 Silverside Rd Ste 250 Wilmington (19809) ***(G-10943)***
Homestead Camping Inc....302 684-4278
25165 Prettyman Rd Georgetown (19947) ***(G-2561)***
Hometown America LLC....302 945-5186
22971 Suburban Blvd Lewes (19958) ***(G-3544)***
Homeward Bound Inc....302 737-2241
34 Continental Ave Newark (19711) ***(G-6741)***
Homewatch Caregivers....302 644-1888
17527 Nassau Commons Blvd Lewes (19958) ***(G-3545)***
Homewatch Caregivers LLC....302 691-5358
5560 Kirkwood Hwy Wilmington (19808) ***(G-10944)***
Homewood Suites, Wilmington *Also called Hollywood Grill Restaurant* ***(G-10931)***
Homewood Suites, Newark *Also called Bpg Hotel Partners X LLC* ***(G-6113)***
Homewood Suites....302 565-2100
820 Justison St Wilmington (19801) ***(G-10945)***
Homewood Suites Newark....302 453-9700
640 S College Ave Newark (19713) ***(G-6742)***
Homself Limited....213 269-5469
200 Cleaver Farms Rd Middletown (19709) ***(G-4108)***
Homsey Architects Inc....302 656-4491
2003 N Scott St Wilmington (19806) ***(G-10946)***
Honey Alteration....302 519-2031
17370 Coastal Hwy Lewes (19958) ***(G-3546)***
Honey Bee Seasonal Kit & Mkt....302 407-5579
11a Trolley Sq Wilmington (19806) ***(G-10947)***
Honeywell Authorized Dealer, Newark *Also called Berry Refrigeration Co* ***(G-6073)***
Honeywell Authorized Dealer, Georgetown *Also called Megee Plumbing & Heating Co* ***(G-2600)***
Honeywell Authorized Dealer, Frankford *Also called Chesapeake Climate Control LLC* ***(G-2353)***
Honeywell Authorized Dealer, Wilmington *Also called George H Burns Inc* ***(G-10699)***
Honeywell Authorized Dealer, Frankford *Also called Koala Enterprises Inc* ***(G-2370)***
Honeywell Authorized Dealer, Dagsboro *Also called Blades H V A C Services* ***(G-884)***
Honeywell Authorized Dealer, Middletown *Also called Pierce Total Comfort LLC* ***(G-4191)***
Honeywell Authorized Dealer, Bear *Also called Delaware Heating & AC* ***(G-108)***
Honeywell Authorized Dealer, Delmar *Also called K and B Hvac Svcs LLC* ***(G-1012)***
Honeywell Authorized Dealer, Wilmington *Also called Hentkowski Inc* ***(G-10887)***
Honeywell Authorized Dealer, Newark *Also called Gold Star Services* ***(G-6671)***
Honeywell Authorized Dealer, New Castle *Also called National HVAC Service* ***(G-5546)***
Honeywell Authorized Dealer, Dover *Also called Traps Plumbing Heating A/C* ***(G-2161)***
Honeywell Authorized Dealer, Harbeson *Also called Hyett Refrigeration Inc* ***(G-2786)***
Honeywell Authorized Dealer, Frankford *Also called Custom Mechanical Inc* ***(G-2358)***
Honeywell Authorized Dealer, Millsboro *Also called After Hours Heating & Air* ***(G-4624)***

ALPHABETIC SECTION

Honeywell Authorized Dealer, Wilmington Also called Building Systems and Svcs Inc (G-9503)
Honeywell Authorized Dealer, Dagsboro Also called North Star Heating & Air Inc (G-925)
Honeywell Authorized Dealer, Dover Also called Associates Contracting Inc (G-1150)
Honeywell Authorized Dealer, Newark Also called Total Climate Control Inc (G-7578)
Honeywell Authorized Dealer, Wilmington Also called B Safe Inc (G-9213)
Honeywell Authorized Dealer, Frankford Also called A & A Air Services Inc (G-2342)
Honeywell Authorized Dealer, New Castle Also called Amstel Mechanical Contractors (G-5036)
Honeywell Authorized Dealer, Bridgeville Also called JI Mechanical Inc (G-487)
Honeywell Authorized Dealer, Hartly Also called Air Doctorx Inc (G-2912)
Honeywell International Inc 302 322-4071
  3 Boulden Cir New Castle (19720) (G-5402)
Honeywell International Inc 302 791-6700
  6100 Philadelphia Pike Claymont (19703) (G-763)
Honeywell Safety Pdts USA Inc (HQ) 302 636-5401
  2711 Centerville Rd Wilmington (19808) (G-10948)
Honig, Gordon C DMD, Newark Also called Gordon C Honig DMD PA (G-6678)
Hoober Inc 717 768-8231
  1130 Mddletown Warwick Rd Middletown (19709) (G-4109)
Hoober Equipment, Middletown Also called Hoober Inc (G-4109)
Hood Man LLC 302 422-4564
  10421 Jasmine Dr Lincoln (19960) (G-3855)
Hook Em & Cook Em LLC 302 226-8220
  24603 Bay Ave Milford (19963) (G-4444)
Hooper's Landing, Seaford Also called City of Seaford Inc (G-8197)
Hoopes Fire Prevention Inc 302 323-0220
  124 Sandy Dr Newark (19713) (G-6743)
Hoopin It Up Embroidery 302 945-5511
  34491 Sunset Dr Millsboro (19966) (G-4706)
Hoops For Hope Delaware 302 229-7600
  1204 B St Wilmington (19801) (G-10949)
Hoopty Do 302 324-1742
  5 Palmer Pl New Castle (19720) (G-5403)
Hoover Computer Services Inc 302 529-7050
  4611 Bedford Blvd Wilmington (19803) (G-10950)
Hope House Daycare 302 407-3404
  2814 W 2nd St Wilmington (19805) (G-10951)
Hope Rising Therapy 302 273-3194
  262 Chapman Rd Newark (19702) (G-6744)
Hopkins Construction Inc 302 337-3366
  18904 Maranatha Way # 1 Bridgeville (19933) (G-482)
Hopkins Granary Inc 302 684-8525
  611 Federal St Milton (19968) (G-4915)
Horizon Aeronautics Inc 409 504-2645
  300 Delaware Ave Ste 300 # 300 Wilmington (19801) (G-10952)
Horizon and Co, Wilmington Also called Kensington Tours Ltd (G-11243)
Horizon Helicopters Inc 302 368-5135
  2035 Sunset Lake Rd Ste A Newark (19702) (G-6745)
Horizon House Inc 302 798-1960
  134 Unit A Princeton Ave Claymont (19703) (G-764)
Horizon House of Delaware Inc 302 658-2392
  1902 Maryland Ave Wilmington (19805) (G-10953)
Horizon Intl Holdings LLC (HQ) 302 636-5401
  251 Little Falls Dr Wilmington (19808) (G-10954)
Horizon Services Inc (PA) 302 762-1200
  320 Century Blvd Wilmington (19808) (G-10955)
Horizon Systems Inc 302 983-3203
  42 Reads Way New Castle (19720) (G-5404)
Horizons Family Practice PA 302 918-6300
  2600 Glasgow Ave Ste 102 Newark (19702) (G-6746)
Hornberger Management Company (PA) 302 573-2541
  1 Commerce St Fl 7 Wilmington (19801) (G-10956)
Horney Industrial Electronics (PA) 302 337-3600
  114 N Main St Bridgeville (19933) (G-483)
Horns Machine Shop Inc 302 653-6663
  3652 Big Woods Rd Smyrna (19977) (G-8654)
Horsey Family, The, Laurel Also called David G Horsey & Sons Inc (G-3221)
Horsey Turf Farm LLC 302 875-7299
  28107 Beaver Dam Br Rd Laurel (19956) (G-3238)
Horton and Bros Inc 302 738-7221
  80 Aleph Dr Newark (19702) (G-6747)
Horton Brothers Recovery Inc 302 266-7339
  1001 S Chapel St Ste A Newark (19702) (G-6748)
Horton Brothers Towing, Newark Also called Horton and Bros Inc (G-6747)
Horty & Horty PA (PA) 302 652-4194
  503 Carr Rd Ste 120 Wilmington (19809) (G-10957)
Horty & Horty PA 302 730-4560
  3702 N Dupont Hwy Dover (19901) (G-1656)
Hospital Blling Cllctn Svc Ltd (PA) 302 552-8000
  118 Lukens Dr New Castle (19720) (G-5405)
Hospitalists of Delaware 302 984-2577
  701 Foulk Rd Ste 2f Wilmington (19803) (G-10958)
Host Integrado Inc 277 326-6719
  16192 Coastal Hwy Lewes (19958) (G-3547)
Host Nation Perspectives LLC 443 292-6702
  36970 Old Mill Bridge Rd Selbyville (19975) (G-8504)

Hosting.com, Newark Also called Lnh Inc (G-6945)
Hot Rod Welding 302 725-5485
  258 Sika Dr Harrington (19952) (G-2851)
Hot Shot Concepts 302 947-1808
  4 Sassafras Ln Harbeson (19951) (G-2785)
Hotel Dupont Company, Wilmington Also called Green Room Restaurant (G-10773)
Hotel Environments Inc 302 234-9294
  359 Mockingbird Hill Rd Hockessin (19707) (G-3056)
Hotelrunner Inc 302 956-9616
  2035 Sunset Lake Rd Newark (19702) (G-6749)
Hough Associates Inc 302 322-7800
  2605 Eastburn Ctr Newark (19711) (G-6750)
Hound Dog Recovery LLC 302 836-3806
  2151 S Dupont Blvd Smyrna (19977) (G-8655)
Hounsell Dental LLC 302 691-8132
  2300 Pennsylvania Ave Wilmington (19806) (G-10959)
House Industries, Yorklyn Also called Brand Design Co Inc (G-13364)
House of Deborah, Wilmington Also called Living Harvest Interntl Minst (G-11413)
House of Hair 302 697-6088
  1462 E Lebanon Rd Dover (19901) (G-1657)
House of Joseph, Wilmington Also called Ministry of Caring Inc (G-11706)
House of Wright Mortuary (PA) 302 762-8448
  208 E 35th St Wilmington (19802) (G-10960)
Housers Auto Trim Inc 302 422-1290
  112 Park Ave Milford (19963) (G-4445)
Housing Alliance Delaware Inc 302 654-0126
  100 W 10th St Ste 611 Wilmington (19801) (G-10961)
Howard B Stromwasser 302 368-4424
  210 Suburban Dr Newark (19711) (G-6751)
Howard Johnson, Newark Also called Shri Swami Narayan LLC (G-7418)
Howard M Joseph Inc (PA) 302 335-1300
  3235 Bay Rd Milford (19963) (G-4446)
Howard Weston Senior Center 302 328-6425
  1 Bassett Ave Ste 1 # 1 New Castle (19720) (G-5406)
Howard Wilkins & Sons Inc 302 270-4183
  7630 Wilkins Rd Lincoln (19960) (G-3856)
Howard Wimbrow CPA 302 539-0829
  35288 Honeysuckle Rd Frankford (19945) (G-2368)
Howmedica Osteonics Corp 302 655-3239
  2118 Kirkwood Hwy Ste A Wilmington (19805) (G-10962)
Howroyd-Wright Emplymnt Agcy 302 738-4022
  131 Continental Dr # 207 Newark (19713) (G-6752)
Hoy En Delaware LLC 302 854-0240
  105 Depot St Georgetown (19947) (G-2562)
Hoyt, Robert M & Co LLC CPA, Millsboro Also called Robert Hoyt & Co (G-4793)
HP, Wilmington Also called Hewlett-Packard World Trade (G-10898)
HP Motors Inc 302 368-4543
  38 Albe Dr Ste 14 Newark (19702) (G-6753)
Hplusmedia LLC 347 480-8996
  16192 Coastal Hwy Lewes (19958) (G-3548)
Hq Global Workplaces Inc 302 295-4800
  1000 N West St Ste 1200 Wilmington (19801) (G-10963)
Hrd Products Inc 302 757-3587
  68d Omega Dr Newark (19713) (G-6754)
Hrnx LLC 844 700-0090
  874 Walker Rd Ste C Dover (19904) (G-1658)
Hrupsa Farms Ltd Partnership 302 270-1817
  3418 Hopkins Cemetery Rd Harrington (19952) (G-2852)
Hs Capital LLC 302 598-2961
  847 Cranbrook Dr Wilmington (19803) (G-10964)
Hs Capital LLC 302 317-3614
  300 Delaware Ave Ste 1370 Wilmington (19801) (G-10965)
Hsbc Bank USA (HQ) 302 778-0169
  300 Delaware Ave Ste 1400 Wilmington (19801) (G-10966)
Hsbc North America Inc 302 652-4673
  1105 N Market St Fl 1 Wilmington (19801) (G-10967)
Hsi Service Corp 302 369-3709
  220 Continental Dr # 115 Newark (19713) (G-6755)
Htk Automotive USA Corp 888 998-9366
  3422 Old Capitol Trl Wilmington (19808) (G-10968)
Htk Automotive USA Corporation 310 504-2283
  3422 Old Capitol Trl # 1851 Wilmington (19808) (G-10969)
Htm Management, Wilmington Also called High-Tech Machine Company Inc (G-10903)
Hts 20 LLP 800 690-2029
  16394 Samuel Paynter Blvd # 103 Milton (19968) (G-4916)
Huawei Technologies Svc LLC 888 548-2934
  8 The Grn Ste A Dover (19901) (G-1659)
Hub Associates 302 674-2200
  222 S Dupont Hwy Dover (19901) (G-1660)
Hubgets Inc 239 206-2995
  4250 Lancaster Pike # 120 Wilmington (19805) (G-10970)
Hudson Farm Supply Co Inc 302 398-3654
  213 Harrington Ave Harrington (19952) (G-2853)
Hudson House Services 302 856-4363
  11 W Pine St Georgetown (19947) (G-2563)
Hudson Jnes Jaywork Fisher LLC (PA) 302 734-7401
  225 S State St Dover (19901) (G-1661)
Hudson Jnes Jaywork Fisher LLC 302 227-9441
  309 Rehoboth Ave Rehoboth Beach (19971) (G-7966)

Hudson Management & Entps LLC....302 645-9464
30045 Eagles Crest Rd Milton (19968) *(G-4917)*
Hudson State Service Center, Newark *Also called Health & Social Svcs Del Dept (G-6716)*
Hudson Valley Investment Corp....302 656-1825
3301 Lancaster Pike 5c Wilmington (19805) *(G-10971)*
Hudson Valley Magazine, Wilmington *Also called Hudson Valley Investment Corp (G-10971)*
Hugh H Hickman & Sons Inc....302 539-9741
300 Ocean View Pkwy Bethany Beach (19930) *(G-403)*
Hughes & Associates, Wilmington *Also called Janet Hughes and Associates (G-11128)*
Hughes Delaware Maid Scrapple....302 284-4370
8873 Burnite Mill Rd Felton (19943) *(G-2294)*
Hughes Network Systems LLC....302 335-4138
1 E David St Frederica (19946) *(G-2406)*
Hullo Inc....415 939-6534
3500 S Dupont Hwy Dover (19901) *(G-1662)*
Humphries Construction Company....302 349-9277
11533 Holly Tree Ln Greenwood (19950) *(G-2744)*
Hungrosity LLC....401 527-1133
1201 N Orange St Ste 600 Wilmington (19801) *(G-10972)*
Hungry Student Athletes, Odessa *Also called Dunkley Enterprises LLC (G-7826)*
Hunt Vicmead Club....302 655-3336
601 Adams Dam Rd Wilmington (19807) *(G-10973)*
Hunt Vicmead Club (PA)....302 655-9601
903 Owls Nest Rd Wilmington (19807) *(G-10974)*
Hunt Wandendale Club....302 945-3369
34068 Village Way Millsboro (19966) *(G-4707)*
Hunte Corporate Enterprise LLC (PA)....212 710-1341
1201 N Orange St Ste 7377 Wilmington (19801) *(G-10975)*
Hunters Crossing, Newark *Also called Palladian Management LLC (G-7172)*
Hunters Run Associates, Bear *Also called Reybold Group of Companies Inc (G-306)*
Huntington Auto Trust 2012-1....302 636-5401
Rodney Sq N 1100 N Mkt St Wilmington (19890) *(G-10976)*
Huntington Auto Trust 2012-2....302 636-5401
Rodney Sq N 1100 N Mkt St Wilmington (19890) *(G-10977)*
Huntington Towers, Wilmington *Also called Leon N Weiner & Associates Inc (G-11372)*
Hurlock Roofing Company....302 654-2783
26 Brookside Dr Wilmington (19804) *(G-10978)*
Husain, Ali S DMD Msd, Newark *Also called Ali S Husain Orthodontist (G-5931)*
Husband 4 Hire, Dover *Also called Brian Garnsey (G-1230)*
Huzala Inc (PA)....313 404-6941
4c Aleph Dr New Castle Co Newark (19702) *(G-6756)*
Hx Innovations Inc....302 983-9705
372 Northhampton Way Middletown (19709) *(G-4110)*
Hy-Point Dairy Farms Inc....302 478-1414
425 Beaver Valley Rd Wilmington (19803) *(G-10979)*
Hy-Point Equipment Co....302 478-0388
425 Beaver Valley Rd Wilmington (19803) *(G-10980)*
Hyas US Inc....250 327-9743
251 Little Falls Dr Wilmington (19808) *(G-10981)*
Hydroseeding Company LLC....302 815-6500
9599 Nantcke Bus Pk Dr # 3 Greenwood (19950) *(G-2745)*
Hyett Refrigeration Inc....302 684-4600
26451 Lwes Georgetown Hwy Harbeson (19951) *(G-2786)*
Hypebeast Inc....714 791-0755
3500 S Dupont Hwy Dover (19901) *(G-1663)*
Hyper Jobs LLC....786 667-0905
40 E Main St Ste 1212 Newark (19711) *(G-6757)*
Hypergames Inc....424 343-6370
919 N Market St Ste 950 Wilmington (19801) *(G-10982)*
Hypertec Usa Inc....480 626-9000
73 Greentree Dr Dover (19904) *(G-1664)*
Hysiotherapy Associates Inc....610 444-1270
3411 Silverside Rd # 105 Wilmington (19810) *(G-10983)*
I 3 A LLC....302 659-0909
5819 Underwoods Corner Rd Smyrna (19977) *(G-8656)*
I AM Consulting Group Inc....302 521-4999
12 Dunleary Dr Bear (19701) *(G-187)*
I C S, Wilmington *Also called Intercontinental Chem Svcs Inc (G-11055)*
I G Burton Chrysler, Milford *Also called IG Burton & Company Inc (G-4448)*
I G Burton Imports, Milford *Also called IG Burton & Company Inc (G-4447)*
I K O, Wilmington *Also called Goldis Enterprises Inc (G-10740)*
I K O Productions, Wilmington *Also called Goldis Holdings Inc (G-10741)*
I N I Holdings Inc (PA)....302 674-3600
110 Galaxy Dr Dover (19901) *(G-1665)*
I T M S, Newark *Also called Integrated Turf Management Sys (G-6789)*
I V F, New Castle *Also called Industrial Valves & Fittings (G-5417)*
I-Pulse Inc....604 689-8765
2711 Centerville Rd # 400 Wilmington (19808) *(G-10984)*
I9 Directcom, Wilmington *Also called Homeland SEC Verification LLC (G-10941)*
Iaa Inc....302 322-1808
417 Old Airport Rd New Castle (19720) *(G-5407)*
Iaad....302 234-0214
113 Jupiter Rd Newark (19711) *(G-6758)*
Iacchetta Builders Inc....302 436-4525
Rr 1 Box 79 Selbyville (19975) *(G-8505)*
Iacono - Summer Chase....302 994-2505
102 Robino Ct Ste 101 Wilmington (19804) *(G-10985)*
Ian Myers MD LLC....302 832-7600
2600 Glasgow Ave Ste 218 Newark (19702) *(G-6759)*
Ibg Enterprise Inc....302 494-5017
9 Nieole Ave New Castle (19720) *(G-5408)*
Ibi Group (delaware) Inc....614 818-4900
501 Silverside Rd # 307 Wilmington (19809) *(G-10986)*
Ibi Group (us) Inc (HQ)....949 833-5588
501 Silverside Rd # 307 Wilmington (19809) *(G-10987)*
Ibope Media LLC....305 529-0062
16192 Coastal Hwy Lewes (19958) *(G-3549)*
Ibr Group Inc....610 986-8545
1098 Elkton Rd Newark (19711) *(G-6760)*
Icase LLC....302 703-7854
16192 Coastal Hwy Lewes (19958) *(G-3550)*
Iceteccom Inc (PA)....302 477-1792
3411 Silverside Rd # 201 Wilmington (19810) *(G-10988)*
ICHDE, Wilmington *Also called Interfaith Cmnty Hsing of Del (G-11062)*
Iconic Skus LLC....302 722-4547
4023 Kennett Pike Ste 226 Wilmington (19807) *(G-10989)*
Iconic Tsunami LLC....302 223-3411
57 Pier Head Blvd Ste 2 Smyrna (19977) *(G-8657)*
ICS America Inc....215 979-1620
1209 N Orange St Wilmington (19801) *(G-10990)*
Ict, Wilmington *Also called Intercontinental Tech LLC (G-11057)*
Icuelab LLC....302 983-8924
51 W Kyla Marie Dr Newark (19702) *(G-6761)*
Icy Pup....302 777-1776
35432 Coastal Hwy Fenwick Island (19944) *(G-2337)*
ID Griffith Inc....302 656-8253
735 S Market St Frnt Wilmington (19801) *(G-10991)*
Identisource LLC....888 716-7498
16192 Coastal Hwy Lewes (19958) *(G-3551)*
Idf Connect Inc....888 765-1611
2207 Concord Pike 359 Wilmington (19803) *(G-10992)*
Idpa Holdings Inc....302 281-3600
200 Bellevue Pkwy Ste 300 Wilmington (19809) *(G-10993)*
Idrch3 Ministries....302 344-6957
49 Brenda Ln Camden (19934) *(G-581)*
Idtp Holdings Inc....302 281-3600
200 Bellevue Pkwy Ste 300 Wilmington (19809) *(G-10994)*
Idylc Homes LLC....302 295-3719
103 Cambridge Dr Wilmington (19803) *(G-10995)*
IEC....302 831-6231
451 Wyoming Rd Newark (19716) *(G-6762)*
Ieh Auto Parts LLC....302 994-7171
3315 Old Capitol Trl Wilmington (19808) *(G-10996)*
Ierardi Vascular Clinic LLC....302 655-8272
1 Centurian Dr Ste 307 Newark (19713) *(G-6763)*
Ies, Townsend *Also called Insight Engineering Solutions (G-8797)*
Iexperienceilearn LLC....718 704-4870
66 Buttonwood Ave New Castle (19720) *(G-5409)*
Ifi Inc....718 791-7669
2035 Sunset Lake Rd B2 Newark (19702) *(G-6764)*
Ifs, Wilmington *Also called Insurance & Fincl Svcs Ltd Del (G-11044)*
IG Burton & Company Inc (PA)....302 422-3041
793 Bay Rd Milford (19963) *(G-4447)*
IG Burton & Company Inc....302 629-2800
24799 Sussex Hwy Seaford (19973) *(G-8269)*
IG Burton & Company Inc....302 424-3041
605 Bay Rd Milford (19963) *(G-4448)*
Igal Biochemical LLC....302 525-2090
4142 Ogletown Stanton Rd Newark (19713) *(G-6765)*
Ignacio S Gispert DDS....302 322-2303
189 Christiana Rd New Castle (19720) *(G-5410)*
Ignis Group LLC....302 645-7400
16192 Coastal Hwy Lewes (19958) *(G-3552)*
Iheartcommunications Inc....302 674-1410
1575 Mckee Rd Ste 206 Dover (19904) *(G-1666)*
Iheartmedia Inc....302 395-9800
920 W Basin Rd Ste 400 New Castle (19720) *(G-5411)*
Il Extreme Entertainment....302 389-8525
100 Schafer Blvd New Castle (19720) *(G-5412)*
Ill John F Glenn MD....302 735-8850
737 S Queen St Ste 2 Dover (19904) *(G-1667)*
Iji Inc....732 485-9427
2711 Centerville Rd # 400 Wilmington (19808) *(G-10997)*
Ik Solutions Inc (PA)....302 861-6775
100 Commerce Dr Ste 201 Newark (19713) *(G-6766)*
Ikeno Tech Business Solutions, Newark *Also called Lawrence Kennedy (G-6923)*
Iko Industries Inc....302 764-3100
6 Denny Rd Ste 200 Wilmington (19809) *(G-10998)*
Iko Manufacturing, Wilmington *Also called Iko Production Inc (G-11000)*
Iko Manufacturing Inc....302 764-3100
120 Hay Rd Wilmington (19809) *(G-10999)*
Iko Production Inc (HQ)....302 764-3100
120 Hay Rd Wilmington (19809) *(G-11000)*
Iko Productions, Wilmington *Also called Iko Sales Inc (G-11001)*
Iko Sales Inc....302 764-3100
120 Hay Rd Wilmington (19809) *(G-11001)*

ALPHABETIC SECTION — Infusion Care Delaware Home

Iko Sales Ltd 302 764-3100
120 Hay Rd Wilmington (19809) *(G-11002)*
Iko Southeast Inc (HQ) 815 936-9600
6 Denny Rd Ste 200 Wilmington (19809) *(G-11003)*
Ila, Newark Also called International Literacy Assn *(G-6797)*
Ilc Dover LP (HQ) 302 335-3911
1 Moonwalker Rd Frederica (19946) *(G-2407)*
Ilgen Inc 518 369-0069
3422 Old Capitol Trl Wilmington (19808) *(G-11004)*
Illumination Technology Inc 410 430-5349
38024 N Spring Hill Rd Delmar (19940) *(G-1004)*
Illuminations Training, Coachi, Delmar Also called Jones Francina *(G-1010)*
Imaginations, Newark Also called Christiana Care Hlth Svcs Inc *(G-6216)*
Imagine Technologies 240 428-8406
110 Coopers Dr Newark (19702) *(G-6767)*
Imaging Group Delaware PA 302 421-4300
St Francis Hospital Depa Wilmington (19805) *(G-11005)*
Imaging Neuroscience Real Est 302 731-9656
774 Christiana Rd Newark (19713) *(G-6768)*
Imcg Global Asia, Lewes Also called Imcg Global Inc *(G-3553)*
Imcg Global Inc (PA) 800 559-6140
16192 Coastal Hwy Lewes (19958) *(G-3553)*
IMNa Solutions Inc 347 821-8238
704 N King St Ste 500 Wilmington (19801) *(G-11006)*
Impact Graphix 302 337-7076
415 Harrington St Seaford (19973) *(G-8270)*
Impact Irrgation Solutions Inc 484 723-3600
3213 Heathwood Rd Wilmington (19810) *(G-11007)*
Imparts Inc 302 697-0990
100 N Railroad Ave Wyoming (19934) *(G-13363)*
Imperial Dynasty Arts Program 302 521-8551
1008 S Broom St Wilmington (19805) *(G-11008)*
Imperial Farm, Smyrna Also called George Staats *(G-8640)*
Implify Inc 302 533-2345
260 Chapman Rd Ste 201c Newark (19702) *(G-6769)*
Impress 302 645-8411
616 Kings Hwy Lewes (19958) *(G-3554)*
Impulse Construction 302 644-0464
31622 Madison Dr Lewes (19958) *(G-3555)*
IMS, Bear Also called Interntional Mkt Suppliers Inc *(G-189)*
In A Stitch 302 678-2260
526 Rose Dale Ln Dover (19904) *(G-1668)*
In Home Veterinary Care, Newark Also called Karli Flanagan Dvm *(G-6868)*
In The Drivers Seat 302 475-3361
1811 Gravers Ln Wilmington (19810) *(G-11009)*
IN TRUST, Wilmington Also called Assoction Brds Thlgcal Educatn *(G-9160)*
In Vision Eye Care 302 655-1952
2205 Concord Pike Wilmington (19803) *(G-11010)*
In Vision Eye Care Inc 302 235-7031
210 Lantana Dr Hockessin (19707) *(G-3057)*
Inbit Inc 302 603-7437
8 The Grn Ste 10159 Dover (19901) *(G-1669)*
Inc Chimes 302 449-1926
409 Zamora Ct Townsend (19734) *(G-8794)*
Inc Plan (usa) 302 428-1200
26c Trolley Sq Wilmington (19806) *(G-11011)*
Incenco International 302 478-8400
1806 Jaybee Rd Wilmington (19803) *(G-11012)*
Incite Solutions Inc 302 655-8952
5714 Kennett Pike Ofc 3 Wilmington (19807) *(G-11013)*
Inclind Inc 302 856-2802
119 W 3rd St Ste 6 Lewes (19958) *(G-3556)*
Incolor Inc 302 984-2695
1401 Todds Ln Wilmington (19802) *(G-11014)*
Incorporators USA LLC 800 441-5940
1013 Centre Rd Ste 403a Wilmington (19805) *(G-11015)*
Incyte Corporation (PA) 302 498-6700
1801 Augustine Cut Off Wilmington (19803) *(G-11016)*
Ind Swift Laboratories Inc 302 233-1564
3500 S Dupont Hwy Dover (19901) *(G-1670)*
Indelible Blue Inc 302 231-5200
16192 Coastal Hwy Lewes (19958) *(G-3557)*
Independence Prosthtcs-Ortho (PA) 302 369-9476
31 Meadowood Dr Newark (19711) *(G-6770)*
Independence School Inc 302 239-0330
1300 Paper Mill Rd Newark (19711) *(G-6771)*
Independence Support Svcs LLC 484 450-6662
637 Dane Ct New Castle (19720) *(G-5413)*
Independence Wealth Advisors 302 763-1180
726 Yorklyn Rd Ste 300 Hockessin (19707) *(G-3058)*
Independent Disposal Services 302 378-5400
604 Cannery Ln Townsend (19734) *(G-8795)*
Independent Electrical Svcs, Claymont Also called Dave Smagala *(G-729)*
Independent Metal Strap Co Inc 516 621-0030
883 Horsepond Rd Dover (19901) *(G-1671)*
Independent Newsmedia Inc USA 302 422-1200
37a Walnut St Milford (19963) *(G-4449)*
Independent Newsmedia USA Inc (HQ) 302 674-3600
110 Galaxy Dr Dover (19901) *(G-1672)*

Independent Newsmedia USA Inc 302 674-3600
110 Galaxy Dr Dover (19901) *(G-1673)*
Independent Resources Inc (PA) 302 765-0191
6 Denny Rd Ste 101 Wilmington (19809) *(G-11017)*
Independent Resources Inc 302 735-4599
154 S Governors Ave Dover (19904) *(G-1674)*
Independent School MGT Inc (PA) 302 656-4944
1316 N Union St Wilmington (19806) *(G-11018)*
Independent Studio Inc 302 436-5581
36666 Bluewater Run W # 3 Selbyville (19975) *(G-8506)*
Independent Transfer Operators 302 420-4289
P.O. Box 1443 Hockessin (19707) *(G-3059)*
India Ink, New Castle Also called Zwd Products Corporation *(G-5848)*
Indian River Captains Assoc 302 227-3071
39415 Inlet Rd Rehoboth Beach (19971) *(G-7967)*
Indian River Golf Cars Dr Wldg 302 947-2044
26246 Kathys Way Millsboro (19966) *(G-4708)*
Indian River Land Company, Millsboro Also called Moore & Lind Inc *(G-4753)*
Indian River Power LLC 302 934-3527
29416 Power Plant Rd Dagsboro (19939) *(G-911)*
Indian River Soccer Club 302 542-6397
32221 Gum Rd Ocean View (19970) *(G-7793)*
Indian River Trust (PA) 302 661-2320
22855 Dupont Blvd Georgetown (19947) *(G-2564)*
Indo Amines Americas LLC 301 466-9902
5301 Limestone Rd Ste 100 Wilmington (19808) *(G-11019)*
Indo-American Association Del 302 234-0214
113 Jupiter Rd Newark (19711) *(G-6772)*
Indonesian Cultural Institute 302 981-7780
15 Anthony Dr Newark (19702) *(G-6773)*
Indoor American Assn Del, Newark Also called Iaad *(G-6758)*
Industraplate Corp 302 654-5210
5 James Ct Wilmington (19801) *(G-11020)*
Industrial Metal Treating Corp 302 656-1677
402 E Front St Wilmington (19801) *(G-11021)*
Industrial Physics Inc (PA) 302 613-5600
40 Mccullough Dr New Castle (19720) *(G-5414)*
Industrial Products of Del 302 328-6648
153 S Dupont Hwy New Castle (19720) *(G-5415)*
Industrial Resource Netwrk Inc 302 888-2905
707 S Church St Wilmington (19801) *(G-11022)*
Industrial Stl Structures Inc 302 275-8892
4049 New Castle Ave New Castle (19720) *(G-5416)*
Industrial Training Cons Inc 302 266-6100
13 Garfield Way Newark (19713) *(G-6774)*
Industrial Valves & Fittings 302 326-2494
55 Mccullough Dr New Castle (19720) *(G-5417)*
Industry ARC 614 588-8538
251 Little Falls Dr Wilmington (19808) *(G-11023)*
Ineos Chlor Americas Inc 302 529-9601
2036 Foulk Rd Ste 204 Wilmington (19810) *(G-11024)*
Inetworkz LLC 407 401-9384
16192 Coastal Hwy Lewes (19958) *(G-3558)*
Inf Head Start Center, Wilmington Also called Wilmington Headstart Inc *(G-13232)*
Infant Acid Reflux Solutions, Lewes Also called Phoenix Intl Resources LLC *(G-3689)*
Infarm - Indoor Urban Farming 561 809-5183
8 The Grn Ste 7929 Dover (19901) *(G-1675)*
Infectious Disease Association 302 368-2883
78 Omega Dr C Newark (19713) *(G-6775)*
Infectious Diseases Cons PA 302 994-9692
537 Stanton Christiana Rd # 201 Newark (19713) *(G-6776)*
Infevo Technologies Co Ltd 626 703-8197
200 Continental Dr # 401 Newark (19713) *(G-6777)*
Infinity Choppers 302 249-7282
24655 Dupont Blvd Georgetown (19947) *(G-2565)*
Infinity Intellectuals Inc 302 565-4830
113 Barksdale Pro Ctr Newark (19711) *(G-6778)*
Inflection Point Ventures LP 302 452-1120
1 Innovation Way Ste 500 Newark (19711) *(G-6779)*
Influencers Lab Media LLC 302 444-6990
300 Martin Luther King Wilmington (19801) *(G-11025)*
Info Solutions North Amer LLC 302 793-9200
12 Penns Way New Castle (19720) *(G-5418)*
Info Systems LLC (HQ) 302 633-9800
590 Century Blvd Wilmington (19808) *(G-11026)*
Info Titan LLC 510 495-4117
32 Loockerman Plz Ste 109 Dover (19901) *(G-1676)*
Informal Inc 415 504-2106
2035 Sunset Lake Rd B2 Newark (19702) *(G-6780)*
Information Retrieval Services, Bridgeville Also called Base Enterprise Inc *(G-452)*
Information Safeguard Inc (PA) 410 604-2660
1201 N Orange St Ste 700 Wilmington (19801) *(G-11027)*
Information Services, New Castle Also called Christiana Care Hlth Svcs Inc *(G-5155)*
Information Technology, Dover Also called Blaze Coin LLC *(G-1209)*
Informed Touch Massage Therapy 302 229-8239
905 Ibiza Ct Townsend (19734) *(G-8796)*
Infusion Care Delaware Home 302 423-2511
9 N Hampshire Ct Wilmington (19807) *(G-11028)*

Infusion Solutions of De 302 674-4627
1100 Forrest Ave Dover (19904) ***(G-1677)***
Ing Bank Fsb 302 255-3750
802 Delaware Ave Fl 1 Wilmington (19801) ***(G-11029)***
Ing Bank Fsb (HQ) 302 658-2200
802 Delaware Ave Wilmington (19801) ***(G-11030)***
Ing Direct, Wilmington *Also called Ing Bank Fsb* ***(G-11030)***
Ing Direct Wilmington Cafe, Wilmington *Also called Ing Bank Fsb* ***(G-11029)***
Ingleside Assisted Living, Wilmington *Also called Ingleside Homes Inc* ***(G-11032)***
Ingleside Homes Inc (PA) 302 575-0250
1005 N Franklin St Wilmington (19806) ***(G-11031)***
Ingleside Homes Inc 302 984-0950
1605 N Broom St Wilmington (19806) ***(G-11032)***
Ingleside Rtirement Apartments, Wilmington *Also called Ingleside Homes Inc* ***(G-11031)***
Ingleside Rtrment Aprtmnts LLC 302 575-0250
1005 N Franklin St Wilmington (19806) ***(G-11033)***
Initial Trading Co 302 428-1132
5716 Kennett Pike Ste D Wilmington (19807) ***(G-11034)***
Initially Yours Inc 302 999-0562
1412 Kirkwood Hwy Wilmington (19805) ***(G-11035)***
Inn At Montchanin Village, The, Montchanin *Also called Dan Licale* ***(G-4984)***
Inn At Wilmington, Wilmington *Also called 44 New England Management Co* ***(G-8862)***
Inn At Wilmington 302 479-7900
300 Rocky Run Pkwy Wilmington (19803) ***(G-11036)***
Inn LLC A-1 Dash 302 368-7964
380 E Chestnut Hill Rd Newark (19713) ***(G-6781)***
Innclude LLC 310 430-6552
3511 Silverside Rd # 105 Wilmington (19810) ***(G-11037)***
Innospec Inc 302 454-8100
200 Executive Dr Newark (19702) ***(G-6782)***
Innospec Inc 302 454-8100
220 Continental Dr # 115 Newark (19713) ***(G-6783)***
Innovation Ventures LP 302 777-1616
1601 Concord Pike Ste 82 Wilmington (19803) ***(G-11038)***
Innovative Music Group, Harrington *Also called Donald Walker* ***(G-2834)***
Innpros Inc 302 326-2500
875 Pulaski Hwy Bear (19701) ***(G-188)***
Inns of Rehoboth Beach LLC 302 645-8003
18826 Coastal Hwy Rehoboth Beach (19971) ***(G-7968)***
Inov8 Inc 302 465-5124
45 Milbourn Manor Dr Camden Wyoming (19934) ***(G-646)***
Inrg of Delaware Inc 302 369-1412
16949 Hudsons Turn Lewes (19958) ***(G-3559)***
Insight Engineering Solutions 302 378-4842
640 Ravenglass Dr Townsend (19734) ***(G-8797)***
Insignia Global Corporation 302 310-4107
913 N Market St Ste 200 Wilmington (19801) ***(G-11039)***
Insite Constructors Inc 302 479-5555
3201 Tanya Dr Wilmington (19803) ***(G-11040)***
Insley Insurance & Fincl Svc 302 286-0777
110 Christiana Med Ctr Newark (19702) ***(G-6784)***
Inspection Lanes 302 853-1003
23737 Dupont Blvd Georgetown (19947) ***(G-2566)***
Inspection Lanes 302 744-2514
415 Transportation Cir Dover (19901) ***(G-1678)***
Inspection of Gas/Chemical, Felton *Also called JD Rellek Company Inc* ***(G-2298)***
Inspectware 302 999-9601
123 E Ayre St Wilmington (19804) ***(G-11041)***
Insta Signs Plus Inc 302 324-8800
107 J And M Dr New Castle (19720) ***(G-5419)***
Instadapp Labs LLC 469 605-1661
16192 Coastal Hwy Lewes (19958) ***(G-3560)***
Instanode Inc 352 327-8872
501 Silverside Rd Ste 105 Wilmington (19809) ***(G-11042)***
Instant Global Services Corp 302 514-1047
8 The Grn Ste 8301 Dover (19901) ***(G-1679)***
Instant Imprints of Delaware, Wilmington *Also called Bgdedge Inc* ***(G-9325)***
Instantuptime Inc 302 608-0890
8 The Grn Ste A Dover (19901) ***(G-1680)***
Institute of Christiana 302 892-9900
537 Stanton Christiana Rd # 102 Newark (19713) ***(G-6785)***
Instruments & Thermal Products 302 378-6290
8 Millburn Ct Townsend (19734) ***(G-8798)***
Insurance & Financial Svcs Inc 302 239-5895
1523 Concord Pike Ste 400 Wilmington (19803) ***(G-11043)***
Insurance & Fincl Svcs Ltd Del 302 234-1200
1523 Concord Pike Ste 400 Wilmington (19803) ***(G-11044)***
Insurance Associates Inc 302 368-0888
720 New London Rd Newark (19711) ***(G-6786)***
Insurance Market Inc (PA) 302 875-7591
310 N Central Ave Laurel (19956) ***(G-3239)***
Insurance Market Inc 302 934-9006
17 Main St Millsboro (19966) ***(G-4709)***
Insurance Networks Aliance LLC 302 268-1010
3411 Silverside Rd Bynardb Wilmington (19810) ***(G-11045)***
Insurance Office America Inc 302 764-1000
900 Philadelphia Pike Wilmington (19809) ***(G-11046)***
Int Investigation Security Inc 609 727-8317
16192 Coastal Hwy Lewes (19958) ***(G-3561)***

Intech Services 302 366-1442
136 Pawnee Ct Newark (19702) ***(G-6787)***
Intech Services Inc 302 366-8530
211 Lake Dr Ste J Newark (19702) ***(G-6788)***
Integra ADM Group Inc (PA) 800 959-3518
110 S Shipley St Seaford (19973) ***(G-8271)***
Integra Realty Resources, Wilmington *Also called Delaware RE Advisors LLC* ***(G-10077)***
Integra Services Tech Inc 302 792-0346
100 Naamans Rd Ste 1f Claymont (19703) ***(G-765)***
Integraded Care of Dover, Dover *Also called David G Reyes MD* ***(G-1344)***
Integrated AVI Solutions LLC 302 351-3427
3700 Centerville Rd Wilmington (19807) ***(G-11047)***
Integrated Data Corp (PA) 302 295-5057
1000 N West St Ste 1200 Wilmington (19801) ***(G-11048)***
Integrated Dynmc Solutions LLC 818 406-8500
2140 S Dupont Hwy Camden (19934) ***(G-582)***
Integrated Green Partners LLC 402 871-8347
1209 N Orange St Wilmington (19801) ***(G-11049)***
Integrated Solutions Planning 302 297-9215
303 N Bedford St Georgetown (19947) ***(G-2567)***
Integrated Tech Systems LLC 302 613-2111
42 Reads Way New Castle (19720) ***(G-5420)***
Integrated Technology Systems 302 429-0560
1401 Penns Ave Apt 310 Wilmington (19806) ***(G-11050)***
Integrated Turf Management Sys 302 266-8000
200 Ruthar Dr Ste 7 Newark (19711) ***(G-6789)***
Integrated Wealth MGT LLC (PA) 302 442-4233
5511 Kirkwood Hwy Wilmington (19808) ***(G-11051)***
Integrated Wirg Solutions LLC 302 999-8448
1695 S Dupont Hwy Saint Georges (19733) ***(G-8126)***
Integrity Cleaning Svcs LLC 302 353-9315
331 Coldwater Dr Clayton (19938) ***(G-856)***
Integrity Corporation Inc (PA) 410 392-8665
1 Innovation Way Newark (19711) ***(G-6790)***
Integrity MGT Solution Inc 302 270-8976
312 Seeneytown Rd Clayton (19938) ***(G-857)***
Integrity Staffing Solutions 520 276-7775
700 Prides Xing Ste 300 Newark (19713) ***(G-6791)***
Integrity Staffing Solutions (PA) 302 661-8770
700 Prides Xing Ste 300 Newark (19713) ***(G-6792)***
Integrity Supply & Service, Newark *Also called Integrity Corporation Inc* ***(G-6790)***
Integrity Tech Solutions Inc 302 369-9093
200 Continental Dr # 401 Newark (19713) ***(G-6793)***
Integrity Testlabs LLC (PA) 302 325-2365
258 Quigley Blvd New Castle (19720) ***(G-5421)***
Intelexmicro Inc 302 907-9545
10253 Stone Creek Dr 1 Laurel (19956) ***(G-3240)***
Intelligent Building Mtls LLC 302 261-9922
40 E Main St Ste 611 Newark (19711) ***(G-6794)***
Intelligent Signage Inc (PA) 302 762-4100
4006 Coleridge Rd Wilmington (19802) ***(G-11052)***
Intelligent Systems Inc 302 388-0566
601 Interchange Blvd Newark (19711) ***(G-6795)***
Intellution, Rehoboth Beach *Also called Umbrella Corporation* ***(G-8104)***
Interactive Marketing Services 302 456-9810
200 University Plz Newark (19702) ***(G-6796)***
Intercoastal Title Agency Inc 302 478-7752
10 Cohee Cir Wilmington (19803) ***(G-11053)***
Intercollegiate Studies Inst 302 656-3292
3901 Centerville Rd Wilmington (19807) ***(G-11054)***
Intercontinental Chem Svcs Inc 302 654-6800
1020 Christiana Ave Ste B Wilmington (19801) ***(G-11055)***
Intercontinental Marketing 302 429-7555
807 Essex Rd Wilmington (19807) ***(G-11056)***
Intercontinental Tech LLC 302 984-2111
3106 Centerville Rd Wilmington (19807) ***(G-11057)***
Interdgital Communications Inc (HQ) 610 878-7800
200 Bellevue Pkwy Ste 300 Wilmington (19809) ***(G-11058)***
Interdgital Communications LLC, Wilmington *Also called Interdgital Communications Inc* ***(G-11058)***
Interdigital Inc (PA) 302 281-3600
200 Bellevue Pkwy Ste 300 Wilmington (19809) ***(G-11059)***
Interdigital Belgium LLC 302 281-3600
200 Bellevue Pkwy Wilmington (19809) ***(G-11060)***
Interdigital Wireless Inc (HQ) 302 281-3600
200 Bellevue Pkwy Ste 300 Wilmington (19809) ***(G-11061)***
Interfaith Cmnty Hsing of Del 302 652-3991
613 N Washington St Wilmington (19801) ***(G-11062)***
Interfaith Community Housing, Wilmington *Also called Management Associates Inc* ***(G-11498)***
Interim Health Care 302 322-2743
2 Reads Way Ste 209 New Castle (19720) ***(G-5422)***
Interim Healthcare Del LLC 302 322-2743
100 S Main St Ste 203 Smyrna (19977) ***(G-8658)***
Interim Services, New Castle *Also called Interim Health Care* ***(G-5422)***
Interior Alternative, The, Newark *Also called Loomcraft Textile & Supply Co* ***(G-6948)***
Interiors By Kim Inc 302 537-2480
33 Central Ave Ocean View (19970) ***(G-7794)***

ALPHABETIC SECTION

Interjet West Inc...209 848-0290
1013 Centre Rd Ste 403a Wilmington (19805) *(G-11063)*
Internal Medicine Associates...........................302 633-1700
3105 Limestone Rd Ste 301 Wilmington (19808) *(G-11064)*
Internal Medicine Bridgeville...........................302 337-3300
8991 Redden Rd Bridgeville (19933) *(G-484)*
Internal Medicine Delaware LLC......................302 261-2269
411 Hawks Nest Ct Middletown (19709) *(G-4111)*
Internal Medicine Dover PA..............................302 678-4488
725 S Queen St Dover (19904) *(G-1681)*
International Electrical Svcs............................302 438-6096
15 Atkins Ave Wilmington (19805) *(G-11065)*
International Game Technology........................302 674-3177
1281 Mcd Dr Dover (19901) *(G-1682)*
International Literacy Assn (PA)......................302 731-1600
800 Barksdale Rd Newark (19711) *(G-6797)*
International Petro Corp Del, Wilmington Also called International Petro Corp Del *(G-11066)*
International Petro Corp Del............................302 421-9306
505 S Market St Wilmington (19801) *(G-11066)*
International Spine Pain..................................302 478-7001
3411 Silverside Rd 103r Wilmington (19810) *(G-11067)*
International Std Elc Corp (HQ)......................302 427-3769
1105 N Market St Ste 1217 Wilmington (19801) *(G-11068)*
International Travel Network...........................415 840-0207
1000 N West St Ste 1200 Wilmington (19801) *(G-11069)*
Internet Business Pubg Corp..........................302 875-7700
220 Laureltowne Laurel (19956) *(G-3241)*
Internet Working Technologies........................302 424-1855
12 S Walnut St A Milford (19963) *(G-4450)*
Interntional Mkt Suppliers Inc.........................302 392-1840
400 Carson Dr Bear (19701) *(G-189)*
Interntnal Agrclture Prod Grou........................302 450-2008
22 Zion Dr Smyrna (19977) *(G-8659)*
Interrupcion Fair Trade, New Castle Also called Social Enterprise LLC *(G-5720)*
Interstate Aerials LLC.....................................302 838-1117
900 Julian Ln Bear (19701) *(G-190)*
Interstate Battery First State, Newark Also called S & K Enterprises Inc *(G-7373)*
Interstate Construction Inc.............................302 369-3590
1000 Dawson Dr Ste A Newark (19713) *(G-6798)*
Interstate Hotels Resorts Inc..........................302 792-2700
630 Naamans Rd Claymont (19703) *(G-766)*
Interstate Mortgage Corp Inc..........................302 733-7620
1933 Kirkwood Hwy Newark (19711) *(G-6799)*
Interstate Steel Co Inc....................................302 598-5159
11 Taylors Farm Dr Newark (19711) *(G-6800)*
Intervet Inc (HQ)...302 934-4341
29160 Intervet Ln Millsboro (19966) *(G-4710)*
Intervet USA, Millsboro Also called Akzo Nobel Inc *(G-4625)*
Intohost Inc..888 567-2607
501 Silverside Rd Ste 105 Wilmington (19809) *(G-11070)*
Intouch Body Therapy LLC..............................302 537-0510
33012 Coastal Hwy Unit 4 Bethany Beach (19930) *(G-404)*
Intouch Inc (PA)..302 313-2594
160 Greentree Dr Ste 101 Dover (19904) *(G-1683)*
Intoyou Inc...818 309-5115
203 Ne Front St Ste 101 Milford (19963) *(G-4451)*
Intrinsic Partners LLC....................................610 388-0853
4001 Kennett Pike Ste 134 Wilmington (19807) *(G-11071)*
Inumsoft Inc...302 533-5403
2500 Wrangle Hill Rd # 222 Bear (19701) *(G-191)*
Invensis Inc..302 351-3509
1000 N West St Ste 1200 Wilmington (19801) *(G-11072)*
Investment Property Services L.....................302 994-3907
102 Robino Ct Ste 101 Wilmington (19804) *(G-11073)*
Invisible Hand Labs LLC................................434 989-9642
2711 Centerville Rd # 400 Wilmington (19808) *(G-11074)*
Invista Capital Management LLC...................302 629-1100
25876 Dupont Rd Seaford (19973) *(G-8272)*
Invista Capital Management LLC (HQ)..........302 683-3000
2801 Centerville Rd Wilmington (19808) *(G-11075)*
Invista Capital Management LLC...................877 446-8478
4417 Lancaster Pike Wilmington (19805) *(G-11076)*
Invista Capital Management LLC...................302 731-6882
150 Red Mill Rd Newark (19711) *(G-6801)*
Invista SARL..302 683-3001
3 Little Leaf Ct Wilmington (19810) *(G-11077)*
Invistas Applied RES Centre..........................302 731-6800
150 Red Mill Rd Newark (19711) *(G-6802)*
Invoicegenius, Dover Also called Mightyinvoice LLC *(G-1854)*
Ion Power Inc...302 832-9550
720 Governor Lea Rd New Castle (19720) *(G-5423)*
Iovate Health Sciences USA Inc (HQ)...........888 334-4448
1105 N Market St Ste 1330 Wilmington (19801) *(G-11078)*
Ip Camera Warehouse LLC............................302 358-2690
3422 Old Capitol Trl Wilmington (19808) *(G-11079)*
Ipay, New Castle Also called Planet Payment Solutions Inc *(G-5625)*
IPC Healthcare...302 984-2577
111 Continental Dr # 406 Newark (19713) *(G-6803)*
IPC Healthcare Inc...302 368-2630
111 Continental Dr Newark (19713) *(G-6804)*

Ipd Technologies LLC....................................302 533-8850
240 Goldfinch Turn Newark (19711) *(G-6805)*
Ipm Inc...302 328-4030
247 Old Churchmans Rd New Castle (19720) *(G-5424)*
Ipr International LLC (PA)..............................302 304-8774
1201 N Market St Ste 201 Wilmington (19801) *(G-11080)*
Iqarus Americas Inc.......................................407 222-5726
1209 N Orange St Wilmington (19801) *(G-11081)*
Irene C Szeto MD...302 832-1560
121 Becks Woods Dr # 100 Bear (19701) *(G-192)*
Irg, Wilmington Also called Mgj Enterprises Inc *(G-11652)*
Irn, Wilmington Also called Industrial Resource Netwrk Inc *(G-11022)*
Iroi Management LLC.....................................516 373-5269
16192 Coastal Hwy Lewes (19958) *(G-3562)*
Iron Hill Apartments Assoc............................302 366-8228
2 Burleigh Ct Ofc A4 Newark (19702) *(G-6806)*
Iron Hill Fence...302 453-9060
1565 Old Baltimore Pike Newark (19702) *(G-6807)*
Iron HI Aprsal Prperty MGT LLC.....................302 454-1404
1 Penn State Dr Newark (19713) *(G-6808)*
Iron Lion Enterprises Inc...............................302 628-8320
22319 Dixie Ln Seaford (19973) *(G-8273)*
Iron Mountain Incorporated............................610 636-1424
6 Dock View Dr Ste 200 New Castle (19720) *(G-5425)*
Iron Source LLC..302 856-7545
25113 Dupont Blvd Georgetown (19947) *(G-2568)*
Iron Workers Local 451.................................302 994-0946
203 Old Dupont Rd Wilmington (19804) *(G-11082)*
Iron Works Inc..302 684-1887
14726 Gravel Hill Rd 1 Milton (19968) *(G-4918)*
Irondt Corp...347 539-6471
3411 Silverside Rd Wilmington (19810) *(G-11083)*
Ironhouse Security Group Inc........................443 312-9932
8 The Grn Ste A Dover (19901) *(G-1684)*
Irving IA Extract Diet Pills..............................302 218-0472
3717 Valley Brook Dr Wilmington (19808) *(G-11084)*
Irwin L Lifrak MD PC.....................................302 654-7317
1010 N Union St Ste 5 Wilmington (19805) *(G-11085)*
Irwin Landscaping Inc....................................302 239-9229
1080 Old Lancaster Pike Hockessin (19707) *(G-3060)*
ISA Professional Ltd......................................647 869-1552
919 N Market St Ste 425 Wilmington (19801) *(G-11086)*
Isaac Fair Corporation...................................302 324-8015
100 W Cmmons Blvd Ste 400 New Castle (19720) *(G-5426)*
Isaacs Automotive Inc....................................302 995-2519
15 W Ayre St Wilmington (19804) *(G-11087)*
Isaacs Isacs Fmly Dentistry PA.....................302 654-1328
707 Foulk Rd Ste 103 Wilmington (19803) *(G-11088)*
ISI Connect, Wilmington Also called Info Systems LLC *(G-11026)*
Isis North America Inc..................................508 653-7318
16192 Coastal Hwy Lewes (19958) *(G-3563)*
Island Boy Enterprise LLC.............................904 347-4563
35 Inlet View Ct Bethany Beach (19930) *(G-405)*
Island Genius LLC...888 529-5506
1201 N Market St Ste 2300 Wilmington (19801) *(G-11089)*
Island of Misfits LLC.....................................302 732-6704
32448 Royal Blvd Ste A Dagsboro (19939) *(G-912)*
Ism...302 656-2376
15 Sharpley Rd Wilmington (19803) *(G-11090)*
It Dept, Middletown Also called Town of Middletown *(G-4265)*
It Resources Inc...203 521-6945
220 Continental Dr # 104 Newark (19713) *(G-6809)*
It S Apples Oranges In..................................301 333-3696
121 Jefferson Ave Lewes (19958) *(G-3564)*
It Tigers LLC..732 898-2793
16192 Coastal Hwy Lewes (19958) *(G-3565)*
Itango Inc...302 648-2646
1201 N Orange St Ste 600 Wilmington (19801) *(G-11091)*
Itc Specialty, Newark Also called Industrial Training Cons Inc *(G-6774)*
Itconnectus Inc..302 531-1139
3500 S Dupont Hwy Dover (19901) *(G-1685)*
Itea Inc...302 328-3716
370 School Bell Rd Bear (19701) *(G-193)*
Itennisyou LLC...305 890-3234
2035 Sunset Lake Rd B2 Newark (19702) *(G-6810)*
Ithaca Holdco 2 LLC......................................650 385-5000
1209 N Orange St Wilmington (19801) *(G-11092)*
Itiyam LLC..703 291-1600
1000 N West St Ste 1200 Wilmington (19801) *(G-11093)*
Ivc, Newark Also called Ierardi Vascular Clinic LLC *(G-6763)*
Iveeapp Corp (PA)...610 999-6290
251 Little Falls Dr Wilmington (19808) *(G-11094)*
Ivy Gables LLC..302 475-9400
2210 Swiss Ln Wilmington (19810) *(G-11095)*
Ivychat Inc..201 567-5694
2035 Sunset Lake Rd B2 Newark (19702) *(G-6811)*
Izzys Lawn Service Inc..................................302 293-9221
1936 Seneca Rd Wilmington (19805) *(G-11096)*
J & A Grinding Inc...302 368-8760
307 Markus Ct Newark (19713) *(G-6812)*

(PA)=Parent Co (HQ)=Headquarters (DH)=Div Headquarters

J & A Overhead Door Inc 302 846-9915
16937 Whitesville Rd Delmar (19940) ***(G-1005)***
J & B Caulkers Co 302 653-7325
1414 Dexter Corner Rd Townsend (19734) ***(G-8799)***
J & G Acoustical Co 302 285-3630
118 Sleepy Hollow Dr Middletown (19709) ***(G-4112)***
J & J Bulkheading 302 436-2800
Snow Goose Ln Unit 3c Selbyville (19975) ***(G-8507)***
J & J Bus Service 302 744-9002
315 Billy Mitchell Ln E209 Dover (19901) ***(G-1686)***
J & J Services 302 422-2684
2908 Milford Hrrington Hwy Milford (19963) ***(G-4452)***
J & K Auto Repair Inc 302 834-8025
3310 Wrangle Hill Rd # 103 Bear (19701) ***(G-194)***
J & L Building Materials Inc 302 504-0350
59 Lukens Dr New Castle (19720) ***(G-5427)***
J & L Construction Co, Dover *Also called Gearhart Construction Inc* ***(G-1587)***
J & L Services Inc 410 943-3355
5670 Glestown Reliance Rd Seaford (19973) ***(G-8274)***
J & M Fencing Inc 302 284-9674
9867 S Dupont Hwy Felton (19943) ***(G-2295)***
J & M Industries Inc 302 575-0200
1014 S Market St Wilmington (19801) ***(G-11097)***
J & P Management Inc 302 854-9400
20530 Dupont Blvd Georgetown (19947) ***(G-2569)***
J & S General Contractors 302 658-4499
1815 Williamson St Wilmington (19806) ***(G-11098)***
J & S Moving & Dlvry Svc LLC 302 357-5675
603 Franklin Bldg Newark (19702) ***(G-6813)***
J & T Concrete Inc 302 368-4949
84 Salem Church Rd Newark (19713) ***(G-6814)***
J & V Shooters Supply 302 422-5417
7369 Shawnee Rd Milford (19963) ***(G-4453)***
J & W Mc Cormick Ltd 302 798-0336
508 First State Blvd Wilmington (19804) ***(G-11099)***
J A Banks & Associates LLC 914 260-2003
486 Joseph Wick Dr Smyrna (19977) ***(G-8660)***
J A E Seafood 302 765-2546
403 Philadelphia Pike # 1 Wilmington (19809) ***(G-11100)***
J A Moore & Sons Inc 302 765-0110
3201 Miller Rd Wilmington (19802) ***(G-11101)***
J A Pyne Jr DDS PA 302 994-7730
4925 Old Capitol Trl Wilmington (19808) ***(G-11102)***
J Alexander Productions LLC 302 559-6667
2208 Van Buren Pl Wilmington (19802) ***(G-11103)***
J and J Display 302 628-4190
101 Park Ave Unit 2 Seaford (19973) ***(G-8275)***
J and J Hair Fashions 302 422-5117
971 N Dupont Blvd Milford (19963) ***(G-4454)***
J B Landscaping 302 645-7202
15468 New Rd Lewes (19958) ***(G-3566)***
J B S Construction LLC 302 349-5705
8801 Greenwood Rd Greenwood (19950) ***(G-2746)***
J C C Fitness Center, Wilmington *Also called Jewish Community Center Inc* ***(G-11152)***
J C Wells & Sons LP 302 422-4732
7481 Wells Rd Milford (19963) ***(G-4455)***
J Chance Productions 302 322-2251
5 Stevens Ave New Castle (19720) ***(G-5428)***
J Culver Construction Inc 302 337-8136
18731 Progress School Rd Bridgeville (19933) ***(G-485)***
J D Construction 302 292-8789
5 Radnor Rd Newark (19713) ***(G-6815)***
J D Masonry Inc 302 684-1009
Rr 5 Harbeson (19951) ***(G-2787)***
J E Bailey & Sons Inc 302 349-4376
2135 Seashore Hwy Greenwood (19950) ***(G-2747)***
J E Pellegrino & Associates 302 655-2565
301 Robinson Ln Bldg 1 Wilmington (19805) ***(G-11104)***
J E Rispoli Contractor Inc 302 999-1310
402 Hillside Ave Wilmington (19805) ***(G-11105)***
J F Sobieski Mech Contrs Inc (PA) 302 993-0103
14 Hadco Rd Wilmington (19804) ***(G-11106)***
J Fredericks & Son Elec C 302 733-0307
16 Flint Hill Dr Newark (19702) ***(G-6816)***
J G M Associates 302 645-2159
17569 Nassau Commons Blvd Lewes (19958) ***(G-3567)***
J H Wilkerson & Son Inc 302 422-4306
Ne Front St Milford (19963) ***(G-4456)***
J I Beiler Homes LLC 302 697-1553
106 Orchard Grove Way Camden (19934) ***(G-583)***
J J White Inc 215 722-1000
101 Cirillo Cir New Castle (19720) ***(G-5429)***
J Kenneth Moore & Son Inc 302 736-0563
1876 E Denneys Rd Dover (19901) ***(G-1687)***
J L Carpenter Farms LLC 302 684-8601
27113 Carpenter Rd Milton (19968) ***(G-4919)***
J M Aja Transportation LLC 302 562-6028
524 W Holly Oak Rd Wilmington (19809) ***(G-11107)***
J M Industries 302 893-0363
845 Old Public Rd Hockessin (19707) ***(G-3061)***
J Melchiore & Sons, Lewes *Also called Melchiorre and Melchiorre* ***(G-3634)***
J Michael Fay DDS PA 302 998-2244
3105 Limestone Rd Ste 304 Wilmington (19808) ***(G-11108)***
J Michaels Painting Inc 302 738-8465
108 Unami Trl Newark (19711) ***(G-6817)***
J N Hooker Inc 302 838-5650
1799 Pulaski Hwy Bear (19701) ***(G-195)***
J P Morgan Services Inc 302 634-1000
500 Stanton Christiana Rd Newark (19713) ***(G-6818)***
J R Brooks Custom Framing LLC 302 538-3637
1791 Peach Basket Rd Felton (19943) ***(G-2296)***
J R Forshey DMD PA 302 322-0245
702 E Basin Rd Ste 1 New Castle (19720) ***(G-5430)***
J R Pini Electrical Contrs 302 368-2311
104 Sandy Dr Newark (19713) ***(G-6819)***
J R Rents Inc (PA) 302 266-8090
59 Marrows Rd Newark (19713) ***(G-6820)***
J R Williamson DDS 302 734-8887
900 Forest St Dover (19904) ***(G-1688)***
J Rihl Inc 856 778-5899
3518 Silverside Rd Ste 22 Wilmington (19810) ***(G-11109)***
J Rocco Construction LLC 302 856-4100
22476 Deep Branch Rd Georgetown (19947) ***(G-2570)***
J S McKelvey DDS 302 239-0303
4901 Limestone Rd Wilmington (19808) ***(G-11110)***
J Stachon Plumbing LLC 302 998-0938
1311 Hillside Blvd Wilmington (19803) ***(G-11111)***
J Star, Wilmington *Also called Three Js Disc Tire & Auto Svc* ***(G-12906)***
J T Mican & Associates Inc 302 323-8152
42 Reads Way New Castle (19720) ***(G-5431)***
J V Auto Service Inc 302 999-0786
1500 W Newport Pike Wilmington (19804) ***(G-11112)***
J V L Automotive & Custom Wldg, Frederica *Also called Jvl Automotive* ***(G-2408)***
J W Humphries Masonary 302 284-0510
1185 Berrytown Rd Felton (19943) ***(G-2297)***
J W Miller Wldg Boiler Repr Co, Middletown *Also called Miller JW Wldg Boiler Repr Co* ***(G-4166)***
J William Gordy Fuel Co (PA) 302 846-3425
106 N Pennsylvania Ave Delmar (19940) ***(G-1006)***
J&D Management 302 239-2489
1174 Old Wilmington Rd Hockessin (19707) ***(G-3062)***
J&G Building Group, Middletown *Also called J & G Acoustical Co* ***(G-4112)***
J&J Contracting Co Inc 302 227-0800
19287 Miller Rd Unit 4 Rehoboth Beach (19971) ***(G-7969)***
J&J Quality Wood, Wilmington *Also called American Timber Brokerage* ***(G-9058)***
J&J Staffing Resources Inc 302 738-7800
200 Continental Dr # 107 Newark (19713) ***(G-6821)***
J&J Systems 302 239-2969
10 Ridgewood Dr Hockessin (19707) ***(G-3063)***
J&K Fleet Service, Bear *Also called J & K Auto Repair Inc* ***(G-194)***
J&S Leasing Co Inc 302 328-1066
729 Grantham Ln Ste 12 New Castle (19720) ***(G-5432)***
Jaa Industries LLC 302 332-0388
16 W Point Ave New Castle (19720) ***(G-5433)***
Jaa's Crane Service and Eqp, New Castle *Also called Jaa Industries LLC* ***(G-5433)***
Jabez Corp 302 475-7600
2201 Silverside Rd Wilmington (19810) ***(G-11113)***
Jack Donovan 410 715-0504
23868 Samuel Adams Cir Millsboro (19966) ***(G-4711)***
Jack F Owens Campus, Georgetown *Also called Delaware Tchncal Cmnty College* ***(G-2504)***
Jack Hickman Real Estate 302 539-8000
33188 Coastal Hwy Unit 2 Bethany Beach (19930) ***(G-406)***
Jack Kelly's Landscaping, Hockessin *Also called Jack Kellys Ldscpg & Tree Svc* ***(G-3064)***
Jack Kellys Ldscpg & Tree Svc 302 239-7185
6 Crest Dr Hockessin (19707) ***(G-3064)***
Jack Lewis 302 475-2010
2018 Naamans Rd Ste A4 Wilmington (19810) ***(G-11114)***
Jack Lingo Inc Realtor (PA) 302 227-3883
246 Rehoboth Ave Rehoboth Beach (19971) ***(G-7970)***
Jack Lingo Inc Realtor 302 947-9030
1240 Kings Hwy Lewes (19958) ***(G-3568)***
Jack Lingo Realtor 302 645-2207
1240 Kings Hwy Lewes (19958) ***(G-3569)***
Jack Parisi Tile Co Inc 302 892-2455
2319 Frederick Ave Wilmington (19805) ***(G-11115)***
Jack Saxton Construction Co 302 764-5683
1228 Evergreen Rd Wilmington (19803) ***(G-11116)***
Jack Smith Towing, Wilmington *Also called Smiths Jack Towing & Svc Ctr* ***(G-12663)***
Jacks Bstro At Dvid Fnney Inn 302 544-5172
222 Delaware St New Castle (19720) ***(G-5434)***
Jackson Contracting Inc 302 678-2011
7242 Pearsons Corner Rd Dover (19904) ***(G-1689)***
Jackson Hewitt Inc 302 934-7430
28412 Dupont Blvd Ste 102 Millsboro (19966) ***(G-4712)***
Jackson Hewitt Tax Service, Millsboro *Also called Jackson Hewitt Inc* ***(G-4712)***
Jackson Hewitt Tax Service, Dover *Also called Ronald Midaugh* ***(G-2041)***
Jackson Hewitt Tax Service (PA) 302 629-4548
1004 W Stein Hwy Seaford (19973) ***(G-8276)***

Jackson Massage and Cft......302 525-6808
124 Wren Way Newark (19711) ***(G-6822)***
Jackson Thmas C Attrney At Law......302 736-1723
438 S State St Dover (19901) ***(G-1690)***
Jaco LLC......302 645-8068
21 Shay Ln Milton (19968) ***(G-4920)***
Jacobs & Crumplar PA......302 656-5445
750 Shipyard Dr Ste 200 Wilmington (19801) ***(G-11117)***
Jacqueline Allens Daycare......302 368-3633
17 Timberline Dr Newark (19711) ***(G-6823)***
Jade Enterprises Inc......302 378-3435
103 S Dupont Hwy Odessa (19730) ***(G-7828)***
Jaed Corporation (PA)......302 832-1652
2500 Wrangle Hill Rd # 110 Bear (19701) ***(G-196)***
Jaiden Jewels Shoes and ACC......302 659-2473
533 Brenford Station Rd Smyrna (19977) ***(G-8661)***
Jairus Enterprises Inc......302 834-1625
1218 Pulaski Hwy Ste 484 Bear (19701) ***(G-197)***
Jam Productions......302 369-3629
8 Hillcroft Rd Newark (19711) ***(G-6824)***
Jamark Enterprises Inc......302 652-2000
40 Germay Dr Wilmington (19804) ***(G-11118)***
James & Jesses Barbr & Buty Sp......302 658-9617
931 Bennett St Ste 933 Wilmington (19801) ***(G-11119)***
James A Peel & Sons Inc......302 738-1468
118 Sandy Dr Ste 1 Newark (19713) ***(G-6825)***
James Atkinson......302 236-7499
1911 Prospect Church Rd Harrington (19952) ***(G-2854)***
James F Givens Inc......302 875-5436
11213 County Seat Hwy Laurel (19956) ***(G-3242)***
James F Palmer (PA)......302 629-6162
8857 Riverside Dr Seaford (19973) ***(G-8277)***
James F Palmer......302 644-3980
33664 Bayview Medical Dr Lewes (19958) ***(G-3570)***
James Fierro Do PA......302 529-2255
1805 Foulk Rd Ste F Wilmington (19810) ***(G-11120)***
James Friesa Acupuncture......302 674-4204
1326 S Governors Ave Dover (19904) ***(G-1691)***
James H Hays MD......302 633-1212
4512 Kirkwood Hwy Ste 302 Wilmington (19808) ***(G-11121)***
James Hughes Company Inc......302 239-4529
508 Pershing Ct Hockessin (19707) ***(G-3065)***
James Jesses Barbr Maudes Buty, Wilmington *Also called James & Jesses Barbr & Buty Sp* ***(G-11119)***
James L Carpenter & Son Inc......302 684-8601
27113 Carpenter Rd Milton (19968) ***(G-4921)***
James L Holzman......302 888-6500
1310 N King St Wilmington (19801) ***(G-11122)***
James L Webb Paving Co Inc......302 697-2000
11804 Willow Grove Rd Camden (19934) ***(G-584)***
James Machine Shop Inc......302 798-5679
3102 W Brandywine Ave Claymont (19703) ***(G-767)***
James Marvel Jr MD, Lewes *Also called Cape Medical Associates PA* ***(G-3402)***
James P Curran, Newark *Also called Curran James P Law Offices* ***(G-6327)***
James Poole......215 407-4046
215 Hawkey Branch Rd Smyrna (19977) ***(G-8662)***
James Powell......302 539-2351
34309 Burton Farm Rd Frankford (19945) ***(G-2369)***
James Rice Jr Construction Co......302 731-9323
122 Upper Pike Creek Rd Newark (19711) ***(G-6826)***
James S Pillsbury DDS......302 734-0330
125 Greentree Dr B Dover (19904) ***(G-1692)***
James Stewart Rostocki......302 250-5541
14 Westover Cir Wilmington (19807) ***(G-11123)***
James Sutton......302 328-5438
807 Churchmans Road Ext New Castle (19720) ***(G-5435)***
James T Chandler & Son Inc (PA)......302 478-7100
2506 Concord Pike Wilmington (19803) ***(G-11124)***
James T Vaughn......302 653-9261
1181 Paddock Rd Smyrna (19977) ***(G-8663)***
James Thompson & Company Inc......302 349-4501
301 S Church St Greenwood (19950) ***(G-2748)***
James Tigani III DDS......302 571-8740
1021 Gilpin Ave Ste 205 Wilmington (19806) ***(G-11125)***
James Williams State Svc Ctr, Dover *Also called Health & Social Svcs Del Dept* ***(G-1639)***
JAMES, STEVENS & DANIELS, Dover *Also called Jsd Management Inc* ***(G-1713)***
Jamestown Painting & Dctg Inc......302 454-7344
830 Dawson Dr Newark (19713) ***(G-6827)***
Jamie H Keskeny......302 651-6060
1600 Rockland Rd Wilmington (19803) ***(G-11126)***
Jammin Productions......302 670-7302
2178 S State St Dover (19901) ***(G-1693)***
Jan Stern Eqine Asssted Thrapy......302 234-9835
112 Shinn Cir Wilmington (19808) ***(G-11127)***
Jane L Stayton CPA......302 856-4141
117 S Bedford St Georgetown (19947) ***(G-2571)***
Janet Hughes and Associates......302 656-5252
203 Plymouth Rd Wilmington (19803) ***(G-11128)***
Janette Redrow Ltd......302 659-3534
635 Cannery Ln Townsend (19734) ***(G-8800)***
Janice Tildon-Burton MD (PA)......302 832-1124
2600 Glasgow Ave Ste 207 Newark (19702) ***(G-6828)***
Janis Dicristofaro Day Care......302 998-6630
1104 Arundel Dr Wilmington (19808) ***(G-11129)***
Janitorial Services and Sups, Wilmington *Also called Gemini Building Systems LLC* ***(G-10688)***
Janvier Jewelers, Newark *Also called Turquoise Shop Inc* ***(G-7601)***
Jarel Industries LLC......336 782-0697
3411 S Dupont Hwy Camden (19934) ***(G-585)***
Jarrell Benson Giles & Sweeney......302 678-4488
725 S Queen St Dover (19904) ***(G-1694)***
Jason M Bradford......302 236-8236
24681 Wesley Dr Millsboro (19966) ***(G-4713)***
Javed Gilani MD......302 478-7160
1309 Veale Rd Ste 11 Wilmington (19810) ***(G-11130)***
Jay Ambe Inc......302 654-5400
3 Memorial Dr New Castle (19720) ***(G-5436)***
Jay D Lufty MD......302 658-0404
2300 Penns Ave Ste 2a Wilmington (19806) ***(G-11131)***
Jay Devi Inc......302 777-4700
2117 N Dupont Hwy New Castle (19720) ***(G-5437)***
Jay Ganesh LLC......302 322-1800
140 S Dupont Hwy New Castle (19720) ***(G-5438)***
Jay Gundel and Associates Inc......302 658-1674
2502 Silverside Rd Ste 8 Wilmington (19810) ***(G-11132)***
Jay J Harris PC......302 453-1400
220 Christiana Med Ctr Newark (19702) ***(G-6829)***
Jaykal Led Solutions Inc......302 295-0015
26832 Lewes Georgetown Hw Harbeson (19951) ***(G-2788)***
Jaysons LLC......302 656-9436
1807 Concord Pike Wilmington (19803) ***(G-11133)***
Jayu LLC......888 534-3018
501 Silverside Rd 345 Wilmington (19809) ***(G-11134)***
JB Landscaping, Lewes *Also called J B Landscaping* ***(G-3566)***
JBA Enterprises......302 834-6685
109 Peace Ct W Bear (19701) ***(G-198)***
Jbm Petroleum Service LLC......302 752-6105
8913 Clendaniel Pond Rd Lincoln (19960) ***(G-3857)***
Jbr Contractors Inc......856 296-9594
30853 Short Cove Ct Millsboro (19966) ***(G-4714)***
Jbs Contracting......302 543-7264
2211 Bradmoor Rd Wilmington (19803) ***(G-11135)***
Jbs Souderton Inc......302 629-0725
4957 Stein Hwy Seaford (19973) ***(G-8278)***
JC Zimny Rod Co......302 998-9187
106 Whitekirk Dr Wilmington (19808) ***(G-11136)***
Jcholley LLC......302 653-6659
3661 Wrangle Hill Rd Bear (19701) ***(G-199)***
Jcr Enterprises Inc......302 629-9163
126 N Shipley St Seaford (19973) ***(G-8279)***
Jcr Systems LLC......302 420-6072
621 Delaware St New Castle (19720) ***(G-5439)***
JD Rellek Company Inc......302 284-7042
693 Irish Hill Rd Felton (19943) ***(G-2298)***
JD Sign Company LLC......302 786-2761
515 Smith Ave Harrington (19952) ***(G-2855)***
Jeandar Masonry Construction......302 994-2616
5905 Old Capitol Trl Wilmington (19808) ***(G-11137)***
Jeanes Radiology Associates PC......302 738-1700
42 Omega Dr Ste H Newark (19713) ***(G-6830)***
Jeanette Y Son Dentist......302 998-8283
2601 Annand Dr Ste 8 Wilmington (19808) ***(G-11138)***
Jeanne Jugan Residence, Newark *Also called Little Sisters of The Poor* ***(G-6941)***
Jeb Plastics Inc......302 479-9223
3521 Silverside Rd 2i-1 Wilmington (19810) ***(G-11139)***
Jed T James......302 875-0101
18066 Asketum Branch Rd Georgetown (19947) ***(G-2572)***
Jedi Inc (PA)......610 459-4477
409 Nichols Ave Wilmington (19803) ***(G-11140)***
Jeena M Jolly DDS......302 655-2626
217 W 9th St Wilmington (19801) ***(G-11141)***
Jeff Bartsch Trckg Excvtg Inc......302 653-9329
299 Saw Mill Rd Townsend (19734) ***(G-8801)***
Jeff Ezell Dr......302 654-5955
20 Westover Cir Wilmington (19807) ***(G-11142)***
Jeff Thomas......302 762-9154
4201 N Market St Wilmington (19802) ***(G-11143)***
Jefferson Awards, Wilmington *Also called American Institute For Pub Svc* ***(G-9051)***
JEFFERSON SCHOOL, THE, Georgetown *Also called Thomas Jffrson Lrng Foundation* ***(G-2691)***
Jefferson Urian Dane Strner PA (PA)......302 856-3900
651 N Bedford St Georgetown (19947) ***(G-2573)***
Jefferson Urian Dane Strner PA......302 539-5543
92 Atlantic Ave Ste D Ocean View (19970) ***(G-7795)***
Jefferson Urian Dane Strner PA......302 678-1425
107 Wolf Creek Blvd Ste 1 Dover (19901) ***(G-1695)***
Jeffrey A Bright DMD......302 832-1371
600 N Broad St Ste 7 Middletown (19709) ***(G-4113)***

ALPHABETIC

Jeffrey Hatch — ALPHABETIC SECTION

Jeffrey Hatch..................443 496-0449
233 Westville Rd Marydel (19964) *(G-3919)*
Jeffrey K Martin PC..................302 777-4681
1508 Penns Ave Ste 1c Wilmington (19806) *(G-11144)*
Jeffrey L Cook D M D..................302 453-8700
16 Peddlers Row Ste 16 # 16 Newark (19702) *(G-6831)*
Jeffs Mobile Power Washing..................302 753-4726
62 Old Creek Dr Clayton (19938) *(G-858)*
Jenner Enterprises Inc (PA)..................302 998-6755
1300 First State Blvd Wilmington (19804) *(G-11145)*
Jenner Enterprises Inc..................302 479-5686
3203 Concord Pike Wilmington (19803) *(G-11146)*
JENNER ENTERPRISES/DBA FASTSIGNS, Wilmington Also called Jenner Enterprises Inc *(G-11145)*
Jennifer L Joseph DDS..................302 239-6677
5317 Limestone Rd Ste 2 Wilmington (19808) *(G-11147)*
Jennifer Lopez Moya Rpt..................302 836-1495
8 Three Rivers Ct Newark (19702) *(G-6832)*
Jennifer M D Hung..................302 644-0690
18947 John J Williams Hwy Rehoboth Beach (19971) *(G-7971)*
Jennifers Spa..................302 740-6363
4 S Merriment Dr Newark (19702) *(G-6833)*
Jenns Tail Waggers..................302 475-9621
8 Carpenter Plz Wilmington (19810) *(G-11148)*
Jenny Craig Wght Loss Ctrs Inc..................302 477-9202
4447 Concord Pike Wilmington (19803) *(G-11149)*
Jenny Craig Wght Loss Ctrs Inc..................302 454-0991
108 Astro Shopping Ctr Newark (19711) *(G-6834)*
Jenrin Discovery LLC..................302 379-1679
2515 Lori Ln N Wilmington (19810) *(G-11150)*
Jeris LLC..................443 745-9023
37427 Kingfisher Dr Selbyville (19975) *(G-8508)*
Jerome C Kayatta DDS..................302 737-6761
192 Kenneth Ct Newark (19711) *(G-6835)*
Jerry A Fletcher..................302 875-9057
34301 Rider Rd Delmar (19940) *(G-1007)*
Jerry A Fletcher Catering, Delmar Also called Jerry A Fletcher *(G-1007)*
Jerry O Thompson Prntng..................302 832-1309
4 Ogden Ct Bear (19701) *(G-200)*
Jerrys Inc..................302 422-7676
17776 Oak Hill Dr Milford (19963) *(G-4457)*
Jersey Clippers LLC..................302 956-0138
134 Widgeon Way Bridgeville (19933) *(G-486)*
Jes-Made Bakery (PA)..................610 558-2131
314 N Dillwyn Rd Newark (19711) *(G-6836)*
Jesco Inc..................302 376-6946
1001 Industrial Rd Middletown (19709) *(G-4114)*
Jessica S Dicerbo DDS..................302 644-4460
18947 John J Williams Hwy Rehoboth Beach (19971) *(G-7972)*
Jet Products LLC (PA)..................877 453-8868
2207 Concord Pike 640 Wilmington (19803) *(G-11151)*
Jetset Travel Inc..................302 678-5050
222 S Dupont Hwy Ste 102 Dover (19901) *(G-1696)*
Jewelers of Wilmington, Newark Also called Del Haven of Wilmington Inc *(G-6361)*
Jewell Enterprises Inc..................302 737-8460
729 Dawson Dr Newark (19713) *(G-6837)*
Jewish Community Center Inc..................302 478-5660
101 Grde Of Eden Rd 102 Wilmington (19803) *(G-11152)*
Jewish Family Service of Del..................302 798-0600
8000 Society Dr Claymont (19703) *(G-768)*
Jewish Federation of Delaware..................302 478-5660
101 Garden Of Eden Rd Wilmington (19803) *(G-11153)*
JG Townsend Jr & Co Inc (PA)..................302 856-2525
316 N Race St Georgetown (19947) *(G-2574)*
JG Townsend Jr Frz Foods Inc..................302 856-2525
316 N Race St Georgetown (19947) *(G-2575)*
JG Wentworth HM Lending Inc..................302 725-0723
37901 Island Dr Ocean View (19970) *(G-7796)*
Jgarvey Enterprises Inc..................302 562-7282
405 Old Dupont Rd Wilmington (19804) *(G-11154)*
Jhonston and Associates..................302 368-9790
16 Farmhouse Rd Newark (19711) *(G-6838)*
Ji DCI Joint Venture 1..................302 652-4221
1211 Delaware Ave Wilmington (19806) *(G-11155)*
Ji DCI Jv-II..................302 652-4221
1211 Delaware Ave Wilmington (19806) *(G-11156)*
Jiao Junfang MD..................302 453-1342
315 N Carter Rd Smyrna (19977) *(G-8664)*
Jiffy Lube, Dover Also called Dover Lubricants Inc *(G-1458)*
Jiffy Lube 312, Wilmington Also called Pennzoil-Quaker State Company *(G-12074)*
Jiffy Lube International Inc..................302 738-5494
29 Liberty Plz Newark (19711) *(G-6839)*
Jill Dusak..................302 652-4705
1815 W 13th St Ste 1 Wilmington (19806) *(G-11157)*
Jill Garrido DDS..................302 475-3110
2000 Foulk Rd Ste C Wilmington (19810) *(G-11158)*
Jillann I Hounsell DDS..................302 239-5917
7197 Lancaster Pike Hockessin (19707) *(G-3066)*
Jillann I Hounsell DDS..................302 691-3000
2300 Penns Ave Ste 6a Wilmington (19806) *(G-11159)*
Jim Kounnas Optometrists (PA)..................302 722-6197
501 Silverside Rd Wilmington (19809) *(G-11160)*
Jim Sellers..................302 738-4149
40 Brookhill Dr Newark (19702) *(G-6840)*
Jireh Trucking, Lincoln Also called Elizabeth Malbert *(G-3845)*
Jiten Patel DDS..................302 690-8629
100 Sussex Ave Milford (19963) *(G-4458)*
Jjid Inc..................302 836-0414
100 Julian Ln Bear (19701) *(G-201)*
Jjs Industries LP..................302 690-2957
2424 E Parris Dr Wilmington (19808) *(G-11161)*
Jjs Learning Experience LLC..................302 398-9000
17001 S Dupont Hwy Harrington (19952) *(G-2856)*
Jk Tangles Hair Salon..................302 698-1006
1151 E Lebanon Rd Ste E Dover (19901) *(G-1697)*
Jkb Corp..................302 734-5017
1169 S Dupont Hwy Dover (19901) *(G-1698)*
Jl Mechanical Inc..................302 337-7855
5460 Hartzell Rd Bridgeville (19933) *(G-487)*
JLJ Enterprises Inc..................302 398-0229
6465 Milford Hrrington Hwy Harrington (19952) *(G-2857)*
JM Virgin Hair Company..................856 383-8588
12 Briarcliff Dr New Castle (19720) *(G-5440)*
Jmsp USA LLC..................337 254-1451
341 Rven Cir Cnty Of Kent County Of Kent Camden Wyoming (19934) *(G-647)*
Jmt, Newark Also called Johnson Mirmiran Thompson Inc *(G-6847)*
Jmt Inter LLC..................302 312-5177
415 Aldwych Dr Bear (19701) *(G-202)*
Jni CCC Jv1..................302 654-6611
2317 Pennsylvania Ave Wilmington (19806) *(G-11162)*
Joanne Reuther..................302 945-8707
20750 John J Williams Hwy # 17 Lewes (19958) *(G-3571)*
Joaquin Cabrera MD..................302 629-8977
8472 Herring Run Rd Seaford (19973) *(G-8280)*
Job Placement Center, Wilmington Also called Ministry of Caring Inc *(G-11708)*
Job Printing..................302 907-0416
36729 Bi State Blvd Delmar (19940) *(G-1008)*
Jobes Landscape Inc..................302 945-0195
20934 Robinsonville Rd Lewes (19958) *(G-3572)*
Jobs By Joe, Wilmington Also called Joseph Moore *(G-11194)*
Jobs For Delaware Graduates (PA)..................302 995-7175
5157 W Woodmill Dr Ste 16 Wilmington (19808) *(G-11163)*
Jobs For Delaware Graduates..................302 734-9341
381 W North St Dover (19904) *(G-1699)*
Joe Falco Portable Welding..................302 998-1115
4517 Roslyn Dr Wilmington (19804) *(G-11164)*
Joe Gerace..................302 994-3114
3315 Elizabeth Ave Wilmington (19808) *(G-11165)*
Joe Maggio Realty..................302 539-9300
8 N Pennsylvania Ave Bethany Beach (19930) *(G-407)*
Joel Gonzalez..................302 562-6878
21 Silver Lake Dr Middletown (19709) *(G-4115)*
Joel R Temple MD..................302 678-1343
9 E Loockerman St Ste 303 Dover (19901) *(G-1700)*
Joes Barber Shop..................302 478-2837
2505 Concord Pike Ste 1 Wilmington (19803) *(G-11166)*
Joes Paint & Body Shop Inc..................302 855-0281
501 N Bedford St Georgetown (19947) *(G-2576)*
John A Capodanno DDS PA..................302 697-7859
75 W Fairfield Dr Dover (19901) *(G-1701)*
John A Donovan..................302 540-7512
131 E Rutherford Dr Newark (19713) *(G-6841)*
John B Coll Do..................302 678-8100
1074 S State St Dover (19901) *(G-1702)*
John B Fontana Jr DDS..................302 656-2434
1708 Lovering Ave Ste 101 Wilmington (19806) *(G-11167)*
John Borden..................302 674-2992
450 S Dupont Hwy Ofc B Dover (19901) *(G-1703)*
John C Leverage..................302 629-3525
26876 Sussex Hwy Seaford (19973) *(G-8281)*
John C Lynch DDS PA..................302 629-7115
543 N Shipley St Ste E Seaford (19973) *(G-8282)*
John Campanelli & Sons Inc..................302 239-8573
7460 Lancaster Pike Hockessin (19707) *(G-3067)*
John D Mannion M D..................302 744-7980
540 S Governors Ave 101a Dover (19904) *(G-1704)*
John Deere Authorized Dealer, Harrington Also called Taylor and Messick Inc *(G-2897)*
John Deere Authorized Dealer, Wilmington Also called Foulk Lawn & Equipment Co Inc *(G-10599)*
John Deere Authorized Dealer, Middletown Also called Jesco Inc *(G-4114)*
John Deere Authorized Dealer, Newark Also called Atlantic Tractor LLC *(G-6022)*
John Deere Authorized Dealer, Clayton Also called Atlantic Tractor LLC *(G-835)*
John Dickinson Plantation, Dover Also called Historical & Cultural Affairs *(G-1650)*
John E Sullivan..................302 234-6855
5305 Limestone Rd Ste 200 Wilmington (19808) *(G-11168)*
John F Reinhardt MD PA..................302 731-0800
4745 Ogletown Stanton Rd # 138 Newark (19713) *(G-6842)*
John F Yasik Funeral Services..................302 428-9986
1900 Delaware Ave Wilmington (19806) *(G-11169)*

ALPHABETIC SECTION — Joseph T Richardson Inc

John F Yasik Inc 302 652-5114
607 S Harrison St Wilmington (19805) *(G-11170)*

John H Hatfield DDS 302 698-0567
1390 Lochmeath Way Dover (19901) *(G-1705)*

John H Miller Sons Plbg Htg AC, Camden Also called Miller John H Plumbing & Htg *(G-591)*

John Hiott Refrigeration & AC 302 697-3050
9166 Willow Grove Rd Camden Wyoming (19934) *(G-648)*

John Hocutt Jr MD 302 475-7800
3521 Silverside Rd Ste 2b Wilmington (19810) *(G-11171)*

John I Beiler Developers, Camden Also called J I Beiler Homes LLC *(G-583)*

John J Buckley Associates Inc 302 475-5443
105 Farm Ave Wilmington (19810) *(G-11172)*

John J Thaler II DDS 302 478-9000
3512 Silverside Rd Ste 13 Wilmington (19810) *(G-11173)*

John Johnson Dr 302 999-7104
325 S Dupont St Wilmington (19805) *(G-11174)*

John Koziol Inc 302 234-5430
724 Yorklyn Rd Ste 370 Hockessin (19707) *(G-3068)*

John L Briggs & Co 302 856-7033
106 E Laurel St Georgetown (19947) *(G-2577)*

John Lovett Inc 302 455-9460
520 Christiana Med Ctr Newark (19702) *(G-6843)*

John M Cooper Reverand 302 684-8639
Tall Pnes Lewes (19958) *(G-3573)*

John M Otto Od 302 623-0170
200 Hygeia Dr Ste 1420 Newark (19713) *(G-6844)*

John Mancuso and Associates, Lewes Also called J G M Associates *(G-3567)*

John Mobile Sndblst & Pain 302 270-5627
683 Hartly Rd Hartly (19953) *(G-2928)*

John N Russo DDS 302 652-3775
300 Foulk Rd Ste 101 Wilmington (19803) *(G-11175)*

John Nista DDS 302 292-1552
74 Omega Dr Newark (19713) *(G-6845)*

John Q Hammons Hotels, Wilmington Also called Tucson Hotels LP *(G-12991)*

John R Seiberlich Inc 302 356-2400
66 Southgate Blvd New Castle (19720) *(G-5441)*

John R Stump MD 302 422-3937
200 Kona Cir Milford (19963) *(G-4459)*

John Snow Labs Inc 302 786-5227
16192 Coastal Hwy Lewes (19958) *(G-3574)*

John T Brown Inc 302 398-8518
4795 Mlford Hrrington Hwy Harrington (19952) *(G-2858)*

John T Malcynski MD 302 424-7522
100 Wellness Way Milford (19963) *(G-4460)*

John T Rogers Jr 302 945-3016
Rr 6 Box 87a Millsboro (19966) *(G-4715)*

John Wasniewski DMD 302 266-0200
103 Louviers Dr Newark (19711) *(G-6846)*

John Wasniewski III DMD 302 832-1371
262 Foxhunt Dr Bear (19701) *(G-203)*

John Williams PA 302 571-4780
1225 N King St Ste 700 Wilmington (19801) *(G-11176)*

Johnny Janosik Inc (PA) 302 875-5955
11151 Trussum Pond Rd Laurel (19956) *(G-3243)*

Johnny Janosik World Furniture, Laurel Also called Johnny Janosik Inc *(G-3243)*

Johnny Walker Enterprises LLC 408 500-6439
16192 Coastal Hwy Ste 346 Lewes (19958) *(G-3575)*

Johns Auto Parts Inc 302 322-3273
10 Nick Ct Bear (19701) *(G-204)*

Johns Body Shop Inc 302 658-5133
2302 W 3rd St Wilmington (19805) *(G-11177)*

Johns Landscaping 302 507-4773
2306 W Newport Pike C Wilmington (19804) *(G-11178)*

Johns Maytag, Claymont Also called Johns Washer Repair *(G-769)*

Johns Washer Repair 302 792-2333
3309 Philadelphia Pike Claymont (19703) *(G-769)*

Johns Woodworking LLC 302 492-3527
84 Tack Shop Ln Hartly (19953) *(G-2929)*

Johnson & Johnson 302 652-3840
500 Swedes Landing Rd Wilmington (19801) *(G-11179)*

Johnson Cntrls SEC Sltions LLC 302 328-2800
18 Boulden Cir Ste 24 New Castle (19720) *(G-5442)*

Johnson Contrls Authorized Dlr, New Castle Also called United Refrigeration Inc *(G-5806)*

Johnson Controls, Middletown Also called Clarios LLC *(G-3994)*

Johnson Controls, Middletown Also called Clarios LLC *(G-3995)*

Johnson Controls, Wilmington Also called Clarios *(G-9730)*

Johnson Controls Inc 302 715-5208
34898 Sussex Hwy Delmar (19940) *(G-1009)*

Johnson Jr Henry & Son Farm 302 436-8501
37047 Johnson Rd Selbyville (19975) *(G-8509)*

Johnson Mirmiran Thompson Inc 302 266-9600
121 Continental Dr # 300 Newark (19713) *(G-6847)*

Johnson Orthodontics 302 645-5554
18947 John J Williams Hwy # 310 Rehoboth Beach (19971) *(G-7973)*

Johnston Associates 302 521-2984
5 Winsome Way Newark (19702) *(G-6848)*

Johnstone Supply, New Castle Also called WJC of Delaware LLC *(G-5839)*

Joincube Inc 214 532-9997
3500 S Dupont Hwy Dover (19901) *(G-1706)*

Joint Anlytcl Systms (amrcs) 302 607-0088
134a Sandy Dr Newark (19713) *(G-6849)*

Jolly Trolley, Rehoboth Beach Also called U Transit Inc *(G-8102)*

Jon Irby III 302 652-0564
204 W 21st St Wilmington (19802) *(G-11180)*

Jona D Gorra MD, Georgetown Also called D C Medical Services LLC *(G-2492)*

Jonathan L Kates M D 302 730-4366
540 S Governors Ave # 201 Dover (19904) *(G-1707)*

Jonathans Landing 302 697-8204
1309 Ponderosa Dr Magnolia (19962) *(G-3896)*

Jonathans Landing Pub Golf CLB, Magnolia Also called Jonathans Landing *(G-3896)*

Jones Francina 302 245-4139
36114 Horsey Church Rd Delmar (19940) *(G-1010)*

Jones Enterprises Incorporated 888 639-1194
1521 Concord Pike Ste 301 Wilmington (19803) *(G-11181)*

Jonmor Investments Inc 302 477-1380
3411 Silverside Rd 103 Wilmington (19810) *(G-11182)*

Jonny Nichols Ldscp Maint Inc 302 697-2200
273 Walnut Shade Rd Dover (19904) *(G-1708)*

Jor-Lin Charter Bus Service, Milford Also called Jor-Lin Inc *(G-4461)*

Jor-Lin Inc 302 424-4445
309 S Rehoboth Blvd Milford (19963) *(G-4461)*

Jorc Industrial LLC 302 395-0310
1146 River Rd Ste 100 New Castle (19720) *(G-5443)*

Jordan Cabinetry & WD Turning 302 792-1009
84 S Avon Dr Claymont (19703) *(G-770)*

Jordan Marketing 302 428-0147
678 Southerness Dr Townsend (19734) *(G-8802)*

Jose A Pando MD 302 644-2302
20268 Plantations Rd Lewes (19958) *(G-3576)*

Jose D Manalo MD PA Inc 302 655-0355
2300 Penns Ave Ste 1a Wilmington (19806) *(G-11183)*

Jose H Austria MD (PA) 302 645-8954
10 Pilot Pt Lewes (19958) *(G-3577)*

Jose Picazo M D P A 302 738-6535
600 Christiana Med Ctr Newark (19702) *(G-6850)*

Joselow Beth Lpcmh 302 644-0130
1307 Savannah Rd Lewes (19958) *(G-3578)*

Joseph & Cummings Builder 302 875-4279
34629 Hudson Rd Laurel (19956) *(G-3244)*

Joseph A Dudeck 302 559-5552
739 Idlewyld Dr Middletown (19709) *(G-4116)*

Joseph A Hurley PA 302 658-8980
1215 N King St Wilmington (19801) *(G-11184)*

Joseph A Kuhn MD LLC 302 656-3801
102 Haywood Rd Wilmington (19807) *(G-11185)*

Joseph A Santillo Inc 302 661-7313
2403 E Parris Dr Wilmington (19808) *(G-11186)*

Joseph Bryer MD 302 426-9440
2300 Penns Ave Ste 3b Wilmington (19806) *(G-11187)*

Joseph C Kelly DDS 302 475-5555
2205 Silverside Rd Ste 2 Wilmington (19810) *(G-11188)*

Joseph Cornatzer DDS 302 239-5917
500 Lantana Dr Hockessin (19707) *(G-3069)*

Joseph Devane Enterprises Inc 302 703-0493
240 S Dupont Hwy Ste 200 New Castle (19720) *(G-5444)*

Joseph E Stevens & Father 302 654-8556
715 Melrose Ave Wilmington (19809) *(G-11189)*

Joseph F Spera DMD PA 302 475-1122
2101 Foulk Rd Wilmington (19810) *(G-11190)*

Joseph Frederick & Sons, Wilmington Also called Frederick Enterprises Inc *(G-10627)*

Joseph G Goldberg Od 302 999-1286
801 E Newport Pike Wilmington (19804) *(G-11191)*

Joseph J Danyo MD 302 888-0508
3701 Kennett Pike 400b Wilmington (19807) *(G-11192)*

Joseph L Hinks 302 875-2260
32053 Gordy Rd Laurel (19956) *(G-3245)*

Joseph Longobardi Atty 302 575-1502
1303 Delaware Ave Ste 115 Wilmington (19806) *(G-11193)*

Joseph M L Sand & Gravel Co 302 856-7396
25136 Dupont Blvd Georgetown (19947) *(G-2578)*

Joseph M Press Mr 302 378-2053
375 Misty Vale Dr Middletown (19709) *(G-4117)*

Joseph Moore 302 478-5659
1412 Athens Rd Wilmington (19803) *(G-11194)*

Joseph Parise Do 302 735-8855
793 S Queen St Dover (19904) *(G-1709)*

Joseph Rizzo & Sons Cnstr Co 302 656-8116
13 Rizzo Ave New Castle (19720) *(G-5445)*

Joseph Schwartz Psyd 302 213-3287
19606 Coastal Hwy # 102 Rehoboth Beach (19971) *(G-7974)*

Joseph Schwartz Psyd 302 213-3287
17021 Old Orchard Rd # 1 Lewes (19958) *(G-3579)*

Joseph Smith & Sons Inc 302 492-8091
3221 Hartly Rd Hartly (19953) *(G-2930)*

Joseph T Hardy & Son Inc (PA) 302 328-9457
425 Old Airport Rd New Castle (19720) *(G-5446)*

Joseph T Richardson Inc 302 398-8101
105 E Center St Harrington (19952) *(G-2859)*

(PA)=Parent Co (HQ)=Headquarters (DH)=Div Headquarters

ALPHABETIC SECTION

Joseph T Ryerson & Son Inc 302 366-0555
700 Pencader Dr Newark (19702) *(G-6851)*
Joseph W Benson PA 302 656-8811
1701 N Market St Wilmington (19802) *(G-11195)*
Josephine Keir Limited 302 422-0270
27 S Walnut St Milford (19963) *(G-4462)*
Joshua A Beck 302 529-9426
2205 Rvera Ln Hlliday Hls Holliday Hls Wilmington (19810) *(G-11196)*
Joshua Kalin MD 302 737-6900
314 E Main St Ste 302 Newark (19711) *(G-6852)*
Joshua M Freeman Foundation 302 436-3003
31556 Winterberry Pkwy Selbyville (19975) *(G-8510)*
Joto Inc 260 337-3362
1209 N Orange St Wilmington (19801) *(G-11197)*
Journeys LLC 302 384-7843
5201 W Wdmill Dr Ste 31ll Wilmington (19808) *(G-11198)*
Joy Cleaners Inc 302 656-3537
301 Greenhill Ave Wilmington (19805) *(G-11199)*
Joyce Co 302 353-4011
3 Mill Rd Wilmington (19806) *(G-11200)*
JP Morgan Trust Company Del 302 634-3800
500 Stanton Christiana Rd Newark (19713) *(G-6853)*
JP Signdesign Co 302 733-7547
205 Tamara Cir Newark (19711) *(G-6854)*
Jpmorgan Chase & Co 312 732-2801
500 Stanton Christiana Rd Newark (19713) *(G-6855)*
Jpmorgan Chase Bank Nat Assn 302 634-1000
200 White Clay Center Dr Newark (19711) *(G-6856)*
Jpmorgan Chase Bank Nat Assn 302 282-1624
300 N King St Wilmington (19801) *(G-11201)*
Jr, Townsend *Also called Janette Redrow Ltd* *(G-8800)*
Jr Board of Kent Gen Hospital 302 744-7128
640 S State St Dover (19901) *(G-1710)*
JR Gettier & Associates Inc 302 478-0911
2 Centerville Rd Wilmington (19808) *(G-11202)*
Jr Walter J Kaminski DDS 302 738-3666
100 Chrstana Vlg Prof Ctr Christiana (19702) *(G-670)*
Jrw Cleaning Solutions LLC 484 942-9995
2405 N Madison St Wilmington (19802) *(G-11203)*
Js Automotive AAMCO 302 678-5660
3729 N Dupont Hwy Dover (19901) *(G-1711)*
Js Knotts Inc 302 284-4888
918 Midstate Rd Felton (19943) *(G-2299)*
Jsc Ventures LLC 302 336-8151
9 E Loockerman St Ste 202 Dover (19901) *(G-1712)*
Jsd Management Inc 302 735-4628
1283 College Park Dr Dover (19904) *(G-1713)*
Jsf Construction Co Inc 302 999-9573
316 Main St Wilmington (19804) *(G-11204)*
Jsi Group LLC 267 582-5850
7217 Lancaster Pike Ste F Hockessin (19707) *(G-3070)*
Jstanley Salon 302 778-1885
204 N Union St Wilmington (19805) *(G-11205)*
JT Hoover Concrete Inc 302 832-7699
3415 Wrangle Hill Rd # 1 Bear (19701) *(G-205)*
Jthan LLC 302 994-2534
7 Meco Cir Wilmington (19804) *(G-11206)*
Juan Saucedo 302 233-4539
1133 S Little Creek Rd Dover (19901) *(G-1714)*
Judd Brook 5 LLC 302 846-3355
36322 Sussex Hwy Delmar (19940) *(G-1011)*
Judith E McCann DMD 302 368-7463
101 Barksdale Pro Ctr Newark (19711) *(G-6857)*
Judy Tim Fuel Inc 302 349-5895
12386 Beach Hwy Greenwood (19950) *(G-2749)*
Judy V 302 226-2214
39401 Inlet Rd Rehoboth Beach (19971) *(G-7975)*
Juicefresh, Rehoboth Beach *Also called Fresh Industries Ltd* *(G-7937)*
Juiceplus+ 302 322-2616
15 W 3rd St New Castle (19720) *(G-5447)*
Julesk, Bethany Beach *Also called Frontgate LLC* *(G-400)*
Julie Q Nies DDS 302 242-9085
1380 S State St Dover (19901) *(G-1715)*
Jumpers Welding Inc 302 519-7941
808 Lorewood Grove Rd Middletown (19709) *(G-4118)*
Jumpin Jacks 302 762-7604
508 E 35th St Wilmington (19802) *(G-11207)*
Junebugs Little Rubies LLC 302 494-7552
1104-1106 D St Wilmington (19801) *(G-11208)*
Jungle Gym LLC 302 734-1515
1418 S State St Dover (19901) *(G-1716)*
Juni Holdings Inc 415 949-4860
251 Little Falls Dr Wilmington (19808) *(G-11209)*
Junior Anderson Dover 302 376-7979
3920 Dupont Pkwy Ste B Townsend (19734) *(G-8803)*
Junior Bd of Christiana Care 302 733-1100
4755 Stanton Ogletown Rd Newark (19718) *(G-6858)*
Juniper Bank 302 255-8000
100 S West St Wilmington (19801) *(G-11210)*

Junttan USA Inc 302 500-1274
10253 Stone Creek Dr Laurel (19956) *(G-3246)*
Just Be Holdings LLC 833 454-5273
200 Continental Dr # 401 Newark (19713) *(G-6859)*
Just For Women Ob/Gyn PA 302 224-9400
875 Aaa Blvd Newark (19713) *(G-6860)*
Just Kids Pediatrics, Newark *Also called Kerry S Kirifides MD PA* *(G-6876)*
Just Like Home 302 653-0605
314 W Mount Vernon St Smyrna (19977) *(G-8665)*
Just One Embroiderer 302 832-9655
17 Decidedly Ln Bear (19701) *(G-206)*
Just Right Tires Inc 302 268-2825
1148 Pulaski Hwy Ste 331 Bear (19701) *(G-207)*
Justin Tanks LLC 302 856-3521
21413 Cedar Creek Ave Georgetown (19947) *(G-2579)*
Justison Landing, Wilmington *Also called Luxiasuites LLC* *(G-11458)*
Juwelo Usa Inc 888 471-7614
1000 N West St Ste 1200 Wilmington (19801) *(G-11211)*
JV s Cleaning Services 302 345-7679
1148 Pulaski Hwy Ste 151 Bear (19701) *(G-208)*
Jvl Automotive 302 335-3942
411 Buffalo Rd Frederica (19946) *(G-2408)*
JW Tull Contracting Svcs LLC 302 494-8179
1203 Philadelphia Pike Wilmington (19809) *(G-11212)*
Jwr 1 LLC 302 379-9951
11 Biltmore Ct Bear (19701) *(G-209)*
Jz Road & Air Cargo Lines Inc 302 468-5988
40 E Main St Ste 1437 Newark (19711) *(G-6861)*
K & H Provision Co, Harrington *Also called Kirby & Holloway Provisions Co* *(G-2863)*
K & J Automotive Inc (PA) 302 798-3635
3111 Philadelphia Pike Claymont (19703) *(G-771)*
K & L Renovations LLC 302 456-0373
5 Garfield Way Ste A Newark (19713) *(G-6862)*
K & R Seal Coating LLC 302 530-3649
135 Willamette Dr Bear (19701) *(G-210)*
K & S Garage Inc 302 731-7997
1060 S Chapel St Newark (19702) *(G-6863)*
K & S Ironworks 302 658-0040
406 Draper Ln Middletown (19709) *(G-4119)*
K & S Technical Services Inc 302 737-9133
941 New London Rd Newark (19711) *(G-6864)*
K and B Hvac Svcs LLC 302 846-3111
18228 Whitesville Rd Delmar (19940) *(G-1012)*
K and L Gates 302 416-7000
600 N King St Ste 901 Wilmington (19801) *(G-11213)*
K Bank 302 645-9700
17021 Old Orchard Rd A Lewes (19958) *(G-3580)*
K BS Plumbing Incorporated 302 678-2757
518 Lochmeath Way Dover (19904) *(G-1717)*
K C G, Dover *Also called Keen Compressed Gas Co* *(G-1728)*
K C Weaver and Sons Inc 302 994-8399
108 E Keystone Ave Wilmington (19804) *(G-11214)*
K E Smart & Sons Inc 302 875-7002
29110 Discount Land Rd Laurel (19956) *(G-3247)*
K F Dunn & Associates 302 328-3347
819 N Washington St Wilmington (19801) *(G-11215)*
K F W Medical Inst De LLC 302 533-6406
1423 Capitol Trl Ste 3105 Newark (19711) *(G-6865)*
K K American Corporation 302 738-8982
231 Shai Cir Bear (19701) *(G-211)*
K L Vincent Welding Svc Inc 302 398-9357
19456 S Dupont Hwy Harrington (19952) *(G-2860)*
K V Associates Inc 302 322-1353
191 Christiana Rd Ste 3 New Castle (19720) *(G-5448)*
K W Lands LLC 302 674-2200
222 S Dupont Hwy Dover (19901) *(G-1718)*
K W Lands North LLC 302 678-0600
1780 N Dupont Hwy Dover (19901) *(G-1719)*
K&B Investors LLC 302 357-9723
1908 Oak Lane Rd Wilmington (19803) *(G-11216)*
K-Tron Investment Co (HQ) 856 589-0500
300 Delaware Ave Ste 900 Wilmington (19801) *(G-11217)*
K2 Advanced Media LLC (PA) 408 305-7007
108 W 13th St Wilmington (19802) *(G-11218)*
K9 Natural Foods USA LLC 855 596-2887
108 W 13th St Wilmington (19801) *(G-11219)*
Ka Analytics & Tech LLC 800 520-8178
1024 Avocado Ave Dover (19901) *(G-1720)*
Kad Industrial Rubber Products, New Castle *Also called Hartzell Industries Inc* *(G-5380)*
Kaeser Compressors Inc 410 242-8793
77 Mccullough Dr Ste 3 New Castle (19720) *(G-5449)*
Kahl Company Inc 302 478-8450
3526 Silverside Rd Ste 38 Wilmington (19810) *(G-11220)*
Kairos Home Pros LLC 302 233-7044
8 The Grn Ste 8086 Dover (19901) *(G-1721)*
Kalbrosky Associates, Ocean View *Also called Bki Enterprises LLC* *(G-7768)*
Kaleido Health Solutions Inc 908 721-7020
2810 N Church St Wilmington (19802) *(G-11221)*
Kalin Eye Assoc 302 292-2020
314 E Main St Ste 302 Newark (19711) *(G-6866)*

Kalin, Neil S MD, Newark *Also called Kalin Eye Assoc* ***(G-6866)***
Kalmar Investments Inc 302 658-7575
3701 Kennett Pike Ste 100 Wilmington (19807) ***(G-11222)***
Kalmar Nyckel Foundation 302 429-7447
1124 E 7th St Wilmington (19801) ***(G-11223)***
Kaman Industrial Technology, Dover *Also called Ruby Industrial Tech LLC* ***(G-2045)***
Kamara LLC 302 220-9570
260 Christiana Rd New Castle (19720) ***(G-5450)***
Kamproductions 302 228-1852
7768 Dobbin Ct Lincoln (19960) ***(G-3858)***
Kankana LLC 302 597-6998
1201 N Orange St Ste 600 Wilmington (19801) ***(G-11224)***
Kapa Inc LLC (PA) 302 740-1235
815 Norman Eskridge Hwy Seaford (19973) ***(G-8283)***
Kardmaster Graphics 610 434-5262
24 Colony Blvd Wilmington (19802) ***(G-11225)***
Karen Kim Zogheib Lcsw 786 897-3022
2110 Dunhill Dr Wilmington (19810) ***(G-11226)***
Karen Schreiber 302 628-3007
425 E Stein Hwy Seaford (19973) ***(G-8284)***
Karen Schreiber 302 875-7733
12034 County Seat Hwy Laurel (19956) ***(G-3248)***
Karen Y Vcks Law Offces of LLC 302 674-1100
500 W Loockerman St # 102 Dover (19904) ***(G-1722)***
Kari Heverin Photography 302 943-0176
582 Union Church Rd Townsend (19734) ***(G-8804)***
Karins & Associates, Newark *Also called Karins Engineering Inc* ***(G-6867)***
Karins Engineering Inc 302 369-2900
17 Polly Drummond Shpg Ct Newark (19711) ***(G-6867)***
Karl J Zeren DDS 302 644-2773
18947 John J Williams Hwy Rehoboth Beach (19971) ***(G-7976)***
Karli Flanagan Dvm 302 893-7872
18 Silverwood Blvd Newark (19711) ***(G-6868)***
Karries Daycare 302 328-7369
44 Lesley Ln New Castle (19720) ***(G-5451)***
Kate Gehret Ms, Lewes *Also called Kathryn M Gehret* ***(G-3581)***
Katharine L Mayer Atty 302 984-6312
919 N Market St Wilmington (19801) ***(G-11227)***
Katherine Klyc Intl LLC 917 312-0789
108 W 3rd St New Castle (19720) ***(G-5452)***
Katherine Laffey 302 651-7999
1509 Gilpin Ave Wilmington (19806) ***(G-11228)***
Kathleen M Cronan MD 302 651-5860
1600 Rockland Rd Wilmington (19803) ***(G-11229)***
Kathryn L Ford Fmly Practice 302 674-8088
870 S Governors Ave Dover (19904) ***(G-1723)***
Kathryn M Gehret 610 420-7233
17124 Poplar Dr Lewes (19958) ***(G-3581)***
Kathy Safford 302 734-8268
1 S Independence Blvd Dover (19904) ***(G-1724)***
Kathy Stabley 302 322-7884
9 King Ave New Castle (19720) ***(G-5453)***
Katie Bennett 302 697-2650
2150 S Dupont Hwy Camden (19934) ***(G-586)***
Katlyn Co Ceramics 302 528-1322
9 Moores Dr Bear (19701) ***(G-212)***
Kauffman Woodworks 302 836-1976
1967 Pulaski Hwy Bear (19701) ***(G-213)***
Kaul Glove and Mfg Co 302 292-2660
599 Ships Landing Way New Castle (19720) ***(G-5454)***
Kaye Construction 302 628-6962
22223 Eskridge Rd Seaford (19973) ***(G-8285)***
Kaza Medical Group Inc 302 674-2616
18 Old Rudnick Ln Dover (19901) ***(G-1725)***
Kaza, Janaki B MD, Dover *Also called Kaza Medical Group Inc* ***(G-1725)***
KB Coldiron Inc 302 436-4224
36546 Dupont Blvd Selbyville (19975) ***(G-8511)***
KB Electrical Services 302 276-5733
1 S Clayton St Wilmington (19805) ***(G-11230)***
Kbf Associates LP 302 328-5400
595 Tulip Ln New Castle (19720) ***(G-5455)***
Kc & Associates Inc 302 633-3300
155 Oldbury Dr Wilmington (19808) ***(G-11231)***
Kc Sign Wilmington, Wilmington *Also called Kgc Enterprises Inc* ***(G-11255)***
Kch Ventures LLC 302 737-6260
12 Timber Creek Ln Newark (19711) ***(G-6869)***
Kci Protection Tech LLC 302 543-8340
1352 Marrows Rd Ste 100 Newark (19711) ***(G-6870)***
Kci Technologies Inc 302 731-9176
1352 Marrows Rd Newark (19711) ***(G-6871)***
Kcs Sensational Vacations 267 886-0991
1206 S Farmview Dr Dover (19904) ***(G-1726)***
Kearns Brinen & Monaghan Inc 302 736-6481
20 E Division St Ste B Dover (19901) ***(G-1727)***
Keefer Mountain Enterprise 814 657-3998
56 Delaware Ave Rehoboth Beach (19971) ***(G-7977)***
Keen Compressed Gas, New Castle *Also called TEC-Con Inc* ***(G-5757)***
Keen Compressed Gas Co (PA) 302 594-4545
101 Rogers Rd Ste 200 Wilmington (19801) ***(G-11232)***
Keen Compressed Gas Co 302 736-6814
226 S New St Dover (19904) ***(G-1728)***
Keen Compressed Gas Co 302 594-4545
4063 New Castle Ave New Castle (19720) ***(G-5456)***
Keen Compressed Gas Co Inc (PA) 610 583-8770
4063 New Castle Ave New Castle (19720) ***(G-5457)***
Keen Consulting Inc 302 684-5270
26229 Prettyman Rd Georgetown (19947) ***(G-2580)***
Keene Enterprises Inc 302 422-2856
14247 Oakley Rd Ellendale (19941) ***(G-2261)***
Keener-Sensenig Co 302 453-8584
491 Gender Rd Newark (19713) ***(G-6872)***
Keep In Touch Systems Inc 510 868-8088
19c Trolley Sq Wilmington (19806) ***(G-11233)***
Keep Selling Property LLC 302 235-3066
2 Penns Way Ste 301 New Castle (19720) ***(G-5458)***
Keglers Korner Pro Shop 302 526-2249
1600 S Governors Ave Dover (19904) ***(G-1729)***
Keith D Stoltz Foundation 302 654-3600
20 Montchanin Rd Ste 250 Wilmington (19807) ***(G-11234)***
Keiths Boat Canvas 302 841-8081
16408 Seashore Hwy Georgetown (19947) ***(G-2581)***
Keller Truck Parts Inc 302 658-5107
5 Medori Blvd Wilmington (19801) ***(G-11235)***
Keller Williams Realty Ce 302 653-3624
1671 S State St Dover (19901) ***(G-1730)***
Kelly Robert & Assoc LLC 302 737-7785
418 Suburban Dr Newark (19711) ***(G-6873)***
Kelly & Assoc Insur Group Inc 302 661-6324
1201 N Orange St Ste 1100 Wilmington (19801) ***(G-11236)***
Kelly Ann Hatton 484 571-5369
1601 Milltown Rd Ste 1 Wilmington (19808) ***(G-11237)***
Kelly Appliance Service 302 628-5396
22251 Conrail Rd Seaford (19973) ***(G-8286)***
Kelly Benefit Strategy, Wilmington *Also called Kelly & Assoc Insur Group Inc* ***(G-11236)***
Kelly Maintenance Ltd Inc 302 539-3956
4 New Castle Ct Ocean View (19970) ***(G-7797)***
Kelly Services Inc 302 323-4748
34 Reads Way New Castle (19720) ***(G-5459)***
Kelly Services Inc 302 674-8087
160 Greentree Dr Ste 103 Dover (19904) ***(G-1731)***
Kelly Walker DDS 302 832-2200
1991 Pulaski Hwy Bear (19701) ***(G-214)***
Kelmar Associates LLC 781 213-6926
2200 Concord Pike 12 Wilmington (19803) ***(G-11238)***
Ken-Del Productions Inc 302 999-1111
1500 First State Blvd Wilmington (19804) ***(G-11239)***
Kenco Cnstr Drywall Special, Felton *Also called Kenco Drywall* ***(G-2300)***
Kenco Drywall 302 697-6489
7093 S Dupont Hwy Felton (19943) ***(G-2300)***
Kenco Group Inc 302 629-4295
1700 Dulany St Seaford (19973) ***(G-8287)***
Kenco Trophy Sales 302 846-3339
301 Lincoln Ave Delmar (19940) ***(G-1013)***
Kencrest Services 302 834-3365
240 Clarks Corner Rd Saint Georges (19733) ***(G-8127)***
Kennedy, Debra DC, Newark *Also called Rehabilitation Associates* ***(G-7313)***
Kenneth Butler 302 561-8114
34 Cheswold Blvd Apt 1b Newark (19713) ***(G-6874)***
Kenneth De Grout DC 302 475-5600
1401 Silverside Rd Ste 1 Wilmington (19810) ***(G-11240)***
Kenneth Deitch 302 838-2808
95 Loblolly Ln Bear (19701) ***(G-215)***
Kenneth R Schuster 302 984-1000
712 N West St Wilmington (19801) ***(G-11241)***
Kenny Brothers Produce LLC 302 337-3007
16440 Adams Rd Bridgeville (19933) ***(G-488)***
Kenny Simpler 302 226-2900
33 Wilmington Ave Rehoboth Beach (19971) ***(G-7978)***
Kens Lawn Service Inc 302 478-2714
732 Westcliff Rd Wilmington (19803) ***(G-11242)***
Kensington Cross Ltd (PA) 888 999-9360
18585 Coastal Hwy Rehoboth Beach (19971) ***(G-7979)***
Kensington Tours Ltd 888 903-2001
2207 Concord Pike 645 Wilmington (19803) ***(G-11243)***
Kent Cnty Cmnty Actn Agncy Inc 302 678-1949
120a S Governors Ave Dover (19904) ***(G-1732)***
Kent Construction Co (PA) 302 653-6469
2 Big Oak Rd Smyrna (19977) ***(G-8666)***
Kent County 302 330-8873
4000 Bay Rd Frederica (19946) ***(G-2409)***
Kent County Counseling Svcs, Dover *Also called Central Delaware Committee* ***(G-1265)***
Kent County Painting Inc 302 994-9628
1700 First State Blvd Wilmington (19804) ***(G-11244)***
Kent County Scty For The Prvnt 302 698-3006
32 Shelter Cir Camden (19934) ***(G-587)***
KENT COUNTY SPCA, Camden *Also called Kent County Scty For The Prvnt* ***(G-587)***
Kent County Tourism Corp 302 734-1736
435 N Dupont Hwy Dover (19901) ***(G-1733)***

ALPHABETIC

Kent General Hospital 302 744-7688
725 Horsepond Rd Dover (19901) *(G-1734)*
Kent General Hospital 302 378-1199
209 E Main St Middletown (19709) *(G-4120)*
Kent General Hospital (HQ) 302 674-4700
640 S State St Dover (19901) *(G-1735)*
Kent General Hospital 302 430-5731
100 Wellness Way Milford (19963) *(G-4463)*
Kent General Hospital 302 653-2010
401 N Carter Rd Smyrna (19977) *(G-8667)*
Kent General Hospital Inc 302 430-5705
301 Jefferson Ave Milford (19963) *(G-4464)*
Kent Landscaping Co LLC 302 535-4296
109 S Main St Camden (19934) *(G-588)*
Kent Leasing Company Inc 302 697-3000
2181 S Dupont Hwy Dover (19901) *(G-1736)*
Kent Pediatrics LLC 302 264-9691
1102 S Dupont Hwy Ste 1 Dover (19901) *(G-1737)*
Kent Pulmonary Associates LLC 302 674-7155
807 S Bradford St Dover (19904) *(G-1738)*
Kent Sign Company Inc 302 697-2181
2 E Bradys Ln Dover (19901) *(G-1739)*
Kent Sussex Auto Care Inc 302 422-3337
914 N Walnut St Milford (19963) *(G-4465)*
Kent Sussex Community Services 302 384-6926
1241 College Park Dr Dover (19904) *(G-1740)*
Kent Swimming Club Inc 302 674-3283
295 Cardinal Hills Pkwy Dover (19904) *(G-1741)*
Kent-Sussex Industries Inc 302 422-4014
301 N Rehoboth Blvd Milford (19963) *(G-4466)*
Kentmere Healthcare Cnsltng 302 478-7600
3511 Silverside Rd # 202 Wilmington (19810) *(G-11245)*
KENTMERE NURSING CARE CENTER, Wilmington Also called Home of Merciful Rest Society *(G-10939)*
Kentmere Veterinary Hospital 302 655-6610
1710 Lovering Ave Wilmington (19806) *(G-11246)*
Kenton Chair Shop 302 653-2411
291 Blackiston Rd Clayton (19938) *(G-859)*
Kenton Child Care 302 674-8142
1298 Mckee Rd Dover (19904) *(G-1742)*
Kenya Gather Foundation 302 382-8227
23246 Country Living Rd Millsboro (19966) *(G-4716)*
Keogh & Son Contracting Co, New Castle Also called Keoghs Contracting Company *(G-5460)*
Keoghs Contracting Company 302 656-0058
9 Bellecor Dr New Castle (19720) *(G-5460)*
Kera Cable Products LLC 917 383-4013
8 The Grn Ste A Dover (19901) *(G-1743)*
Kercher Group Inc (PA) 302 894-1098
254 Chapman Rd Ste 202 Newark (19702) *(G-6875)*
Kerry & G Inc 302 999-0022
1621 Willow Ave Wilmington (19804) *(G-11247)*
Kerry S Kirifides MD PA 302 918-6400
875 Aaa Blvd Ste C Newark (19713) *(G-6876)*
Kersey Homes Inc 302 934-8434
23090 Lakewood Cir Millsboro (19966) *(G-4717)*
Kershaw Industries 302 464-1051
110 W Main St Middletown (19709) *(G-4121)*
Keval Corp 302 453-9100
100 Mcintosh Plz Newark (19713) *(G-6877)*
Kevin Fleming 302 227-4994
37021 Rehobth Ave Ext Rehoboth Beach (19971) *(G-7980)*
Kevin Fleming Photography, Rehoboth Beach Also called Kevin Fleming *(G-7980)*
Kevin Garber 302 834-0639
148 Carlotta Dr Bear (19701) *(G-216)*
Kevin Lammers Ins 302 283-1210
18 Carriage Ln Newark (19711) *(G-6878)*
Kevins Masonry Concrete Co 302 382-7259
526 Reeves Crossing Rd Felton (19943) *(G-2301)*
Key Advisors Group LLC (PA) 302 735-9909
31 Saulsbury Rd Dover (19904) *(G-1744)*
Key National Trust Company Del 302 574-4702
1105 N Market St Ste 500 Wilmington (19801) *(G-11248)*
Key To Beauty 302 398-9460
7184 Mlford Hrrington Hwy Harrington (19952) *(G-2861)*
Key West Program, Wilmington Also called Corizon LLC *(G-9862)*
Key-Tel Communications Inc 302 475-3066
2642 Foulk Rd Wilmington (19810) *(G-11249)*
Keyboarders LLC 302 438-8055
501 Silverside Rd Ste 54 Wilmington (19809) *(G-11250)*
Keylent Inc 401 864-6498
1000 N West St Ste 1200 Wilmington (19801) *(G-11251)*
Keyrock LLC 818 605-7772
3524 Silverside Rd 35b Wilmington (19810) *(G-11252)*
Keystack Inc 510 629-5099
2035 Sunset Lake Rd Newark (19702) *(G-6879)*
Keystate Corporate MGT LLC 302 425-5158
824 N Market St Ste 210 Wilmington (19801) *(G-11253)*
Keystone Autism Services 302 731-3115
7 Firethorn Ct Newark (19711) *(G-6880)*

Keystone Automotive Inds Inc 302 764-8010
62 Southgate Blvd Ste D New Castle (19720) *(G-5461)*
Keystone Finishing Inc 925 825-2498
1800 Lovering Ave Wilmington (19806) *(G-11254)*
Keystone Granite and Tile Inc 302 323-0200
217 Lisa Dr Ste C New Castle (19720) *(G-5462)*
Keystone Service Systems Inc 302 286-7234
300 Creek View Rd Newark (19711) *(G-6881)*
Keystone Service Systems Inc 302 273-3952
824 N Barrett Ln Newark (19702) *(G-6882)*
Keystone Swine Services 302 329-9731
14356 Clydes Dr Milton (19968) *(G-4922)*
Kfs Strategic MGT Svcs LLC 302 545-7640
125 Rickey Blvd Unit 1650 Bear (19701) *(G-217)*
Kgc Enterprises Inc 302 668-1835
3617 Kirkwood Hwy Wilmington (19808) *(G-11255)*
Kha-Neke Inc 302 440-4728
25 Hempstead Dr Newark (19702) *(G-6883)*
Khaja Yezdani MD 302 322-1794
191 Christiana Rd Ste 3 New Castle (19720) *(G-5463)*
Khan Family Foundation Inc 800 839-1754
501 Silverside Rd Wilmington (19809) *(G-11256)*
Khan Ob Gyn Associates 302 735-8720
1113 S State St Dover (19901) *(G-1745)*
Khan Pediatrics Inc (PA) 302 449-5791
266 S College Ave Newark (19711) *(G-6884)*
Khanna Entps Ltd A Ltd Partnr 302 266-6400
1024 Old Churchmans Rd Newark (19713) *(G-6885)*
Khanyi Media Corporation 302 482-8142
105 Silverside Rd Ste 501 Wilmington (19809) *(G-11257)*
Kid Agains Inc 631 830-5228
33 Lindley Dr Dover (19904) *(G-1746)*
Kidd Mc, New Castle Also called Reyes Rebeca *(G-5677)*
Kidd Robert W III DDS 302 678-1440
850 S State St Dover (19901) *(G-1747)*
Kiddie Academy of Middletown 302 376-5112
915 Boyds Corner Rd Middletown (19709) *(G-4122)*
Kiddie Express, Newark Also called Barbara L McKinney *(G-6046)*
Kiddocs 302 892-3300
4600 New Linden Hl 204 Wilmington (19808) *(G-11258)*
Kids Cottage LLC 302 644-7690
35448 Wolfe Neck Rd Rehoboth Beach (19971) *(G-7981)*
Kids First Newark, Newark Also called Edwin C Katzman MD *(G-6504)*
Kids Inc 302 422-9099
613 Lakeview Ave Milford (19963) *(G-4467)*
Kids Korner Day Care 302 998-4606
706 W Newport Pike Wilmington (19804) *(G-11259)*
Kids Nest Day Care 302 731-7017
24 Donaldson Dr Newark (19713) *(G-6886)*
Kids R US Learning Center Inc 302 678-1234
425 Webbs Ln Dover (19904) *(G-1748)*
Kids Teens Pediatrics of Dover 302 538-5624
125 Greentree Dr Ste 1 Dover (19904) *(G-1749)*
Kids-R-Us Learning Center, Dover Also called Kids R US Learning Center Inc *(G-1748)*
Kidscom Daycare 302 544-5655
25 Wardor Ave New Castle (19720) *(G-5464)*
Kidz Akademy Corp 302 732-6077
32442 Royal Blvd Dagsboro (19939) *(G-913)*
Kidz Ink (PA) 302 838-1500
1703 Porter Rd Bear (19701) *(G-218)*
Kidz Ink 302 376-1700
125 Sleepy Hollow Dr Middletown (19709) *(G-4123)*
Kidz Klub 302 652-5439
200 N Union St Wilmington (19805) *(G-11260)*
Kidz Korner Home Daycare, Millsboro Also called Rosa M Custis *(G-4795)*
Kidz Kottage Club Inc 302 398-4067
17001 S Dupont Hwy Harrington (19952) *(G-2862)*
Kimberly A Leaman PA 301 261-4115
38178 Dockside Dr # 1262 Selbyville (19975) *(G-8512)*
Kimberly Sue Kester 302 732-1093
32315 Spring Ct Dagsboro (19939) *(G-914)*
Kimberton Apartments Assoc LP 302 368-0116
100 Kimberton Dr Newark (19713) *(G-6887)*
Kimbles AVI Lgistical Svcs Inc 334 663-4954
21785 Aviation Ave Georgetown (19947) *(G-2582)*
Kimbles DLS, Georgetown Also called Kimbles AVI Lgistical Svcs Inc *(G-2582)*
Kimmel Carter Roman & Peltz (PA) 302 565-6100
56 W Main St Ste 400 Christiana (19702) *(G-671)*
Kimos Hawaiian Shave Ice 302 998-1763
2628 Newell Dr Wilmington (19808) *(G-11261)*
Kims Cleaners 302 656-2397
3 Murphy Rd Wilmington (19803) *(G-11262)*
Kind Mind Kids 302 545-0380
111 Lands End Rd Wilmington (19807) *(G-11263)*
Kind To Kids Foundation 302 654-5440
100 W 10th St Ste 606 Wilmington (19801) *(G-11264)*
Kindercare Center 1006, Wilmington Also called Kindercare Learning Ctrs LLC *(G-11265)*
Kindercare Center 45, Wilmington Also called Kindercare Learning Ctrs LLC *(G-11266)*

Kindercare Learning Ctrs LLC 302 234-8680
6696 Lancaster Pike Hockessin (19707) *(G-3071)*
Kindercare Learning Ctrs LLC 302 834-6931
100 Paxson Dr Newark (19702) *(G-6888)*
Kindercare Learning Ctrs LLC 302 322-3102
327 Old State Rd New Castle (19720) *(G-5465)*
Kindercare Learning Ctrs LLC 302 475-2212
2018 Naamans Rd C Wilmington (19810) *(G-11265)*
Kindercare Learning Ctrs LLC 302 731-7138
3449 Hillock Ln Wilmington (19808) *(G-11266)*
Kindheart Homecare 484 479-6582
207 Parker Dr Middletown (19709) *(G-4124)*
Kinetic Skateboarding 856 375-2236
5319 Concord Pike Wilmington (19803) *(G-11267)*
King & Minsk PA Inc 302 475-3270
1805 Foulk Rd Ste D Wilmington (19810) *(G-11268)*
King of Sweets Inc 302 730-8200
47 S West St Dover (19904) *(G-1750)*
Kingdom Kids Day Care 302 492-0207
2899 Arthursville Rd Hartly (19953) *(G-2931)*
Kingdom of God Fellowship, Hartly *Also called Kingdom Kids Day Care* *(G-2931)*
Kings Contracting Inc 302 677-0363
378 Kentland Ave Dover (19901) *(G-1751)*
Kings Creek Country Club Inc 302 227-8951
1 Kings Creek Cir Rehoboth Beach (19971) *(G-7982)*
Kings Sealcoating 302 674-1568
416 Dogwood Ave Dover (19904) *(G-1752)*
Kinoland Logistics LLC 302 565-4505
256 Chapman Rd Ste 105 Newark (19702) *(G-6889)*
Kintyre Solutions LLC 888 636-0010
2817 Kennedy Rd Wilmington (19810) *(G-11269)*
Kiosked Corporation 803 993-8463
2711 Centerville Rd # 400 Wilmington (19808) *(G-11270)*
Kirby & Holloway Provisions Co 302 398-3705
966 Jackson Ditch Rd Harrington (19952) *(G-2863)*
Kirk & Associates LLC 302 444-4733
56 W Main St Ste 305 Christiana (19702) *(G-672)*
Kirk Cabinetry LLC 302 220-3377
601 Cornell Dr Ste 11-G Wilmington (19801) *(G-11271)*
Kirk Custom Furniture, Wilmington *Also called Kirk Cabinetry LLC* *(G-11271)*
Kirk Family Practice 302 423-2049
5 Courtney Rd Wilmington (19807) *(G-11272)*
Kirk Flowers, Newark *Also called Kirks Flowers Inc* *(G-6890)*
Kirkin Roofing LLC 302 483-7135
1053 Lower Twin Lane Rd New Castle (19720) *(G-5466)*
Kirks Flowers Inc 302 737-3931
7 Ash Ave Newark (19711) *(G-6890)*
Kirkwood Anmal Brding Grooming 302 737-1098
1501 Capitol Trl Newark (19711) *(G-6891)*
Kirkwood Auto Center LLC 302 995-6179
4913 Kirkwood Hwy Wilmington (19808) *(G-11273)*
Kirkwood Dental Associates PA (PA) 302 994-2582
710 Greenbank Rd Ste A Wilmington (19808) *(G-11274)*
Kirkwood Dental Associates PA 302 834-7700
1200 Peoples Plz Ste 1260 Newark (19702) *(G-6892)*
Kirkwood Detox, Wilmington *Also called Northeast Treatment Ctrs Inc* *(G-11904)*
Kirkwood Ftnes Racquetball CLB (PA) 302 529-1865
1800 Naamans Rd Wilmington (19810) *(G-11275)*
Kirkwood Smoke Shop 302 525-6718
151 E Main St Newark (19711) *(G-6893)*
Kirkwood Tires Inc 302 737-2460
1929 Kirkwood Hwy Newark (19711) *(G-6894)*
Kissangen Inc 414 446-4182
113 Barksdale Pro Ctr Newark (19711) *(G-6895)*
Kissflow Inc 650 396-7692
1000 N West St Ste 1200 Wilmington (19801) *(G-11276)*
Kite 302 324-9569
446 School Bell Rd Bear (19701) *(G-219)*
Kitschy Stitch 302 200-9889
18419 Berkeley Rd Lewes (19958) *(G-3582)*
Kitten's Quilting & Embroidery, Dover *Also called Alice M Mehaffey* *(G-1104)*
Kitty Jazzy Publishing 302 897-8842
702 Cobble Creek Curv Newark (19702) *(G-6896)*
Klaus Dr Robert MD 302 422-3500
1100 Lovering Ave Apt 810 Wilmington (19806) *(G-11277)*
Kleen-Comp LLC 302 981-0791
32 Edgebrooke Way Newark (19702) *(G-6897)*
Klh Industries LLC 800 348-0758
16192 Coastal Hwy Lewes (19958) *(G-3583)*
Km Klacko & Associate 302 652-1482
509 Redfern Ave Wilmington (19807) *(G-11278)*
Kmh Contracting 302 331-4894
133 Moores Dr Magnolia (19962) *(G-3897)*
Kmp Mechanical LLC 410 392-6126
406 Suburban Dr 155 Newark (19711) *(G-6898)*
Kna Solutions LLC 302 709-1215
8 The Grn Ste 4372 Dover (19901) *(G-1753)*
Kneisley Eye Care PA 302 224-3000
45 E Main St Ste 201 Newark (19711) *(G-6899)*
Knepper & Stratton (PA) 302 658-1717
1228 N King St Wilmington (19801) *(G-11279)*
Knepper & Stratton 302 658-1717
309 S State St Ste C Dover (19901) *(G-1754)*
Knight Capital Funding LLC 888 523-4363
9 E Lockmerman St Ste Dover (19901) *(G-1755)*
Knight Construction 610 496-6879
2508 Dorval Rd Wilmington (19810) *(G-11280)*
Knight Hauling Inc 610 494-6800
2508 Dorval Rd Wilmington (19810) *(G-11281)*
Knights Inn, New Castle *Also called Gurukrupa Inc* *(G-5366)*
Knights Inn, Georgetown *Also called Chudasama Enterprises LLC* *(G-2471)*
Knights of Columbus 302 559-9959
1801 Lancaster Ave Wilmington (19805) *(G-11282)*
Knights York Cross of Honour 302 731-4817
208 Sypherd Dr Newark (19711) *(G-6900)*
Knotts Construction Inc 302 475-7074
1504 Upsan Downs Ln Wilmington (19810) *(G-11283)*
Knotts Incorporated 302 322-0554
700 Wilmington Rd New Castle (19720) *(G-5467)*
Knowland Group LLC 302 645-9777
115 W Market St Lewes (19958) *(G-3584)*
Knowpro LLC 772 538-6477
1013 Centre Rd Ste 403 Wilmington (19805) *(G-11284)*
Knowt Inc 848 391-0575
16192 Coastal Hwy Lewes (19958) *(G-3585)*
Kns09 Inc 302 697-3499
1062 Lafferty Ln Dover (19901) *(G-1756)*
KOA Technologies LLC 760 471-5726
108 W 13th St Wilmington (19801) *(G-11285)*
Koala Enterprises Inc 302 436-9950
36382 Bayard Rd Frankford (19945) *(G-2370)*
Koch Accounting Services LLC 877 446-8478
2801 Centerville Rd Wilmington (19808) *(G-11286)*
Koch Methanol Investments LLC (PA) 302 658-7581
1209 N Orange St Wilmington (19801) *(G-11287)*
Kogut Tech Consulting Inc 302 455-0388
24 Ohio State Dr Newark (19713) *(G-6901)*
Kohr Brothers Inc 302 227-9354
5 Rehoboth Ave Rehoboth Beach (19971) *(G-7983)*
Kokoszka & Sons Inc 302 328-4807
68 Skyline Dr New Castle (19720) *(G-5468)*
Kokoszka Ent, Bear *Also called C & K Builders LLC* *(G-59)*
Kompressed Air Delaware Inc 302 275-1985
144 Quigley Blvd Ste 100 New Castle (19720) *(G-5469)*
Koncordia Group LLC 302 427-1350
1201 N Market St Ste 401 Wilmington (19801) *(G-11288)*
Korean Martial Arts Institute (PA) 302 992-7999
2419 W Newport Pike Wilmington (19804) *(G-11289)*
Kortech Consulting Inc 302 559-4612
13 Primrose Dr Bear (19701) *(G-220)*
Koty Inc 302 654-2665
850 N Church St Wilmington (19801) *(G-11290)*
Kpkm Inc 302 678-0271
1062 Lafferty Ln Dover (19901) *(G-1757)*
Kpv Enterprises Llc 302 500-9669
125 Mendel Ct Bear (19701) *(G-221)*
Kraemer & Sons LLC 302 832-1534
4077 Wrangle Hill Rd Bear (19701) *(G-222)*
Kraft Heinz Company 302 734-6100
1250 W North St Dover (19904) *(G-1758)*
Kral Electronics Inc 302 737-1300
2403 Ogletown Rd Newark (19711) *(G-6902)*
Kramer Group LLC 717 368-2117
2116 Peachtree Dr Wilmington (19805) *(G-11291)*
Krapfs Coaches Inc 302 993-7855
1400 First State Blvd Wilmington (19804) *(G-11292)*
Kratom Foundation LLC 302 645-7400
16192 Coastal Hwy Lewes (19958) *(G-3586)*
Krave Like LLC 302 482-4550
7 Deer Run Dr Wilmington (19807) *(G-11293)*
KRC Waste Management Inc 302 999-9276
P.O. Box 3115 Wilmington (19804) *(G-11294)*
Kream Puff Clean 251 509-1639
49 Trala St Smyrna (19977) *(G-8668)*
Kreske Kares LLC 302 893-5600
4 Cottage Ct Bear (19701) *(G-223)*
Krienen-Griffith Inc (PA) 302 994-9614
1400 Kirkwood Hwy Wilmington (19805) *(G-11295)*
Krienen-Griffith Funeral Home, Wilmington *Also called Krienen-Griffith Inc* *(G-11295)*
Krisallis 610 522-7273
2419 Porter Rd Bear (19701) *(G-224)*
Kriss Contracting Inc 302 492-3502
1523 Gunter Rd Hartly (19953) *(G-2932)*
Kristen Smith 302 623-6320
3706 Kennett Pike Wilmington (19807) *(G-11296)*
Kristin Construction, Claymont *Also called Kristin Konstruction Company* *(G-772)*
Kristin Konstruction Company 302 791-9670
950 Ridge Rd Ste C14 Claymont (19703) *(G-772)*

ALPHABETIC

(PA)=Parent Co (HQ)=Headquarters (DH)=Div Headquarters
2020 Harris Directory of Delaware Businesses
673

Kristina Brandis 516 457-2717
  208 Wickerberry Dr Middletown (19709) *(G-4125)*
Kristol Ctr For Jewish Lf Inc 302 453-0479
  47 W Delaware Ave Newark (19711) *(G-6903)*
Krm Stables 302 653-3838
  1225 Clyton Grenspring Rd Clayton (19938) *(G-860)*
Kroegers Salvage Inc 302 381-7082
  15896 White Pine Ln Bridgeville (19933) *(G-489)*
Kruger Farms Inc 302 856-2577
  24306 Dupont Blvd Georgetown (19947) *(G-2583)*
Kruger Trailers Inc 302 856-2577
  24306 Dupont Blvd Georgetown (19947) *(G-2584)*
KS Kitchen LLC 302 743-4349
  6 Smalleys Ct Newark (19702) *(G-6904)*
KSI CARTRIDGE SERVICE, Milford Also called Kent-Sussex Industries Inc *(G-4466)*
Ksn, Newark Also called Kissangen Inc *(G-6895)*
Kst Land Design Inc 302 328-1879
  2627 Skylark Rd Wilmington (19808) *(G-11297)*
KT&d Inc 302 429-8500
  1013 Centre Rd Ste 200 Wilmington (19805) *(G-11298)*
Ktc, Newark Also called Kogut Tech Consulting Inc *(G-6901)*
Kubera Global Solutions LLC 480 241-5124
  1521 Concord Pike Ste 301 Wilmington (19803) *(G-11299)*
Kubota Authorized Dealer, Felton Also called Burke Equipment Company *(G-2278)*
Kubota Authorized Dealer, Delmar Also called Burke Equipment Company *(G-975)*
Kubota Authorized Dealer, Newark Also called Newark Kubota Inc *(G-7123)*
Kubota Research Associates 302 683-0199
  100 Hobson Dr Hockessin (19707) *(G-3072)*
Kuehne Chemical Company Inc 302 834-4557
  1645 River Rd New Castle (19720) *(G-5470)*
Kulina, Patrick F MD, Lewes Also called Sussex Podiatry Group *(G-3773)*
Kupferman & Associates LLC 302 656-7566
  1701 Shallcross Ave Ste D Wilmington (19806) *(G-11300)*
Kuraray America Inc 302 992-4204
  2200 Concord Pike # 1101 Wilmington (19803) *(G-11301)*
Kuraray Intrlyer Solutions Off, Wilmington Also called Kuraray America Inc *(G-11301)*
Kurtz Collection 302 654-0442
  1010 N Union St Wilmington (19805) *(G-11302)*
Kushner Companies, Newark Also called University Village Apartment *(G-7630)*
Kustom Kutz 302 424-7556
  1007 N Walnut St Milford (19963) *(G-4468)*
Kvm Depot Inc 302 472-9190
  1007 N Orange St Wilmington (19801) *(G-11303)*
Kw Commercial 302 299-1123
  1521 Concord Pike Wilmington (19803) *(G-11304)*
Kw Garden 302 735-7770
  1784 N Dupont Hwy Dover (19901) *(G-1759)*
Kw Solar Solutions Inc 302 838-8400
  2444 Denny Rd Bear (19701) *(G-225)*
Kw Solar Solutions Inc 302 838-8400
  2444 Denny Rd Bear (19701) *(G-226)*
Kwikbuck Inc 774 517-8959
  Trolley Sq Ste 20c Wilmington (19806) *(G-11305)*
L & B Publishing 302 743-4061
  44 Lakewood Cir Newark (19711) *(G-6905)*
L & D Insurance Services LLC 302 235-2288
  1 Isabella Ct Hockessin (19707) *(G-3073)*
L & J Sheet Metal 302 875-2822
  8095 Airport Rd Laurel (19956) *(G-3249)*
L & L Carpet Discount Ctrs Inc 302 292-3712
  900 Interchange Blvd # 901 Newark (19711) *(G-6906)*
L & M Services Inc 302 658-3735
  617 Lafayette Blvd Wilmington (19801) *(G-11306)*
L & W Insurance Inc 302 674-3500
  1154 S Governors Ave Dover (19904) *(G-1760)*
L A Masonary Inc 302 239-6833
  125 Sun Ct Newark (19711) *(G-6907)*
L A S Trucking LLC 302 439-4433
  5 W Holly Oak Rd Wilmington (19809) *(G-11307)*
L E I, Newark Also called Landmark Engineering Inc *(G-6916)*
L E Stansell Inc 302 475-1534
  2525 Ebright Rd Wilmington (19810) *(G-11308)*
L E York Law LLC 302 234-8338
  182 Belmont Dr Wilmington (19808) *(G-11309)*
L F Conlin DDS 302 764-0930
  1202 Foulk Rd Wilmington (19803) *(G-11310)*
L F Systems Corp 302 322-0460
  249 Old Churchmans Rd New Castle (19720) *(G-5471)*
L&J Transportation LLC 302 234-3366
  4 Fox Run Dr Hockessin (19707) *(G-3074)*
L&W Insurance Agency, Dover Also called C Edgar Wood Inc *(G-1245)*
L3d LLC 302 677-0031
  1671 S State St Dover (19901) *(G-1761)*
La Bella Vita Salon & Day Spa 302 883-2597
  525 S Red Haven Ln Dover (19901) *(G-1762)*
La Esperanza Inc 302 854-9262
  216 N Race St Georgetown (19947) *(G-2585)*

LA ESPERANZA COMMUNITY CENTER, Georgetown Also called La Esperanza Inc *(G-2585)*
La Floresta Perdida Inc (PA) 302 478-8900
  3411 Silverside Rd 101wd Wilmington (19810) *(G-11311)*
La Jolla Fincl Partners LLC 858 864-0146
  2711 Centerville Rd # 400 Wilmington (19808) *(G-11312)*
La Petite Academy Inc 302 234-2574
  5986 Limestone Rd Hockessin (19707) *(G-3075)*
La Red Health Care 757 709-5072
  23659 Saulsbury Ln Georgetown (19947) *(G-2586)*
La Red Health Center Inc 302 855-1233
  21444 Carmean Way Georgetown (19947) *(G-2587)*
La Vere Electric Inc 302 422-9185
  840 Church Hill Rd Milford (19963) *(G-4469)*
Lab, Wilmington Also called Delaware Meat Company LLC *(G-10063)*
Lab Products Inc 302 628-4300
  742 Sussex Ave Seaford (19973) *(G-8288)*
Labaton Sucharow LLP 302 573-6938
  300 Delaware Ave Ste 1340 Wilmington (19801) *(G-11313)*
Labcorp of America, Middletown Also called Laboratory Corporation America *(G-4126)*
Labcorp of America, Middletown Also called Laboratory Corporation America *(G-4127)*
Labcorp of America, Seaford Also called Laboratory Corporation America *(G-8289)*
Laboratoires Esthederm USA Inc 514 270-3763
  2711 Centerville Rd # 300 Wilmington (19808) *(G-11314)*
Laboratory Corporation America 302 653-5119
  100 S Main St Smyrna (19977) *(G-8669)*
Laboratory Corporation America 302 651-9502
  2123 Concord Pike Wilmington (19803) *(G-11315)*
Laboratory Corporation America 302 735-4694
  200 Banning St Ste 160 Dover (19904) *(G-1763)*
Laboratory Corporation America 302 376-6146
  120 Sandhill Dr Ste 1 Middletown (19709) *(G-4126)*
Laboratory Corporation America 302 449-0246
  366 E Main St Middletown (19709) *(G-4127)*
Laboratory Corporation America 302 629-3182
  701 Health Services Dr Seaford (19973) *(G-8289)*
Laboratory Corporation America 302 655-5673
  212 Cherry Ln New Castle (19720) *(G-5472)*
Laboratory Corporation America 302 834-6845
  101 Becks Woods Dr Bear (19701) *(G-227)*
Laboratory Corporation America 302 834-1359
  2600 Glasgow Ave Newark (19702) *(G-6908)*
Laboratory Corporation America 302 737-3525
  4623 Ogletown Stanton Rd Newark (19713) *(G-6909)*
Laboratory Corporation America 302 798-2520
  1400 Philadelphia Pike Wilmington (19809) *(G-11316)*
Laboratory Corporation America 302 998-7340
  3105 Limestone Rd Ste 105 Wilmington (19808) *(G-11317)*
Laboratory Corporation America 302 994-8575
  1941 Limestone Rd Ste 109 Wilmington (19808) *(G-11318)*
Laboratory Corporation America 302 234-0493
  722 Yorklyn Rd Ste 154 Hockessin (19707) *(G-3076)*
Laboratory Corporation America 302 731-0244
  314 E Main St Ste 105 Newark (19711) *(G-6910)*
Laborers Intl Un N Amer 302 654-2880
  308 Markus Ct Newark (19713) *(G-6911)*
Laborers Intl Un N Amer 302 934-7376
  26351 Patriots Way Georgetown (19947) *(G-2588)*
Labrador, The, Millsboro Also called Wooley Bully Inc *(G-4829)*
Labshops, Claymont Also called Azzota Corporation *(G-698)*
Labware Inc (HQ) 302 658-8444
  3 Mill Rd Ste 102 Wilmington (19806) *(G-11319)*
Labware Inc 302 658-8444
  400 Burnt Mill Rd Wilmington (19807) *(G-11320)*
Labware Global Services Inc 302 658-8444
  3 Mill Rd Ste 102 Wilmington (19806) *(G-11321)*
Labware Holdings Inc (PA) 302 658-8444
  3 Mill Rd Ste 102 Wilmington (19806) *(G-11322)*
Lachall Lee LLP 302 644-9952
  17563 Nassau Commons Blvd Lewes (19958) *(G-3587)*
Lacieah Inc 302 365-5585
  14 Creek Ln Newark (19702) *(G-6912)*
Lacoste Usa Inc 302 227-9575
  36470 Seaside Outlet Dr Rehoboth Beach (19971) *(G-7984)*
Lady PS Hair Designs Inc 302 832-2668
  117 Emerald Ridge Dr Bear (19701) *(G-228)*
Ladybug Pest Management Inc 302 846-2295
  15307 Britt Ln Delmar (19940) *(G-1014)*
Lafazia Construction 302 234-1300
  149 Belmont Dr Wilmington (19808) *(G-11323)*
Laffey Kathryn J The Law Off 302 651-7999
  1500 Shallcross Ave 2b Wilmington (19806) *(G-11324)*
Laima V Anthaney DMD 302 645-4726
  1200 Savannah Rd Lewes (19958) *(G-3588)*
Lake Forest School District 302 398-8945
  100 W Mispillion St Harrington (19952) *(G-2864)*
Lake Therapy Creations 410 920-7130
  2271 Sunset Lake Rd Newark (19702) *(G-6913)*

Lakeside Greenhouses Inc (PA)......302 875-2457
31494 Greenhouse Ln Laurel (19956) *(G-3250)*
Lakeside Physical Therapy LLC......302 280-6920
200 Laurel Ct Unit 202 Laurel (19956) *(G-3251)*
Lamar Bags......302 492-8566
2090 Hartly Rd Hartly (19953) *(G-2933)*
Lambden Bus Service......302 629-4358
10174 Airport Rd Seaford (19973) *(G-8290)*
Lambertson Signs......302 645-6700
30444 Lwes Georgetown Hwy Lewes (19958) *(G-3589)*
Lambro Technologies LLC......302 351-2559
206 Kirk Ave Wilmington (19803) *(G-11325)*
Lamed LLC......302 597-9018
2915 Ogletown Rd Newark (19713) *(G-6914)*
Lan Rack Inc (PA)......949 587-5168
8 The Grn Ste 8284 Dover (19901) *(G-1764)*
Landis Ltd......302 656-9024
420 B And O Ln Wilmington (19804) *(G-11326)*
Landis Rath & Cobb LLP......302 467-4400
919 N Market St Ste 1800 Wilmington (19801) *(G-11327)*
Landmark Associates of Del......302 645-7070
9 Bradford Ln Lewes (19958) *(G-3590)*
Landmark Engineering Inc (PA)......302 323-9377
200 Continental Dr # 400 Newark (19713) *(G-6915)*
Landmark Engineering Inc......302 734-9597
200 Continental Dr # 400 Newark (19713) *(G-6916)*
Landmark Homes......302 388-8557
68 Representative Ln Dover (19904) *(G-1765)*
Landmark Homes Inc......302 242-1394
2 Reads Way Ste 224 New Castle (19720) *(G-5473)*
Landmark Parking Inc (HQ)......302 651-3610
1205 N Orange St Wilmington (19801) *(G-11328)*
Landmark Science & Engineering, Newark *Also called Landmark Engineering Inc (G-6915)*
Landtech Land Survey, Ocean View *Also called Landtech LLC (G-7798)*
Landtech LLC......302 539-2366
118 Atlantic Ave Ocean View (19970) *(G-7798)*
Lane Builders LLC......302 645-5555
1009 Kings Hwy Lewes (19958) *(G-3591)*
Lane Carpet Company, Newark *Also called L & L Carpet Discount Ctrs Inc (G-6906)*
Lane Home Services Inc......302 652-7663
45 Germay Dr Ste A Wilmington (19804) *(G-11329)*
Lane Roofing, Wilmington *Also called Lane Home Services Inc (G-11329)*
Lank Johnson and Tull (PA)......302 422-3308
268 Milford Harrington Hw Milford (19963) *(G-4470)*
Lank Johnson and Tull......302 629-9543
521 N Market Street Ext Seaford (19973) *(G-8291)*
Lanning Woodworks......302 353-4726
2404 Overlook Dr Wilmington (19810) *(G-11330)*
Lantana Chiropratic, Hockessin *Also called Newark Chropractic Hlth Ctr PA (G-3103)*
Lantana Veterinary Center Inc......302 234-3275
306 Lantana Dr Hockessin (19707) *(G-3077)*
Lantransit Enterprises LLC......302 722-4800
16192 Coastal Hwy Lewes (19958) *(G-3592)*
LAp Studios Inc......213 357-0825
2035 Sunset Lake Rd Newark (19702) *(G-6917)*
Larkins Bus Service LLC......302 653-5855
512 S Bassett St Clayton (19938) *(G-861)*
Larry Hill Farms Inc......302 875-0886
Rr 1 Box 518 Delmar (19940) *(G-1015)*
Larry Hill Farms LLC......302 245-6657
36292 Old Stage Rd Delmar (19940) *(G-1016)*
Larry Wallis......856 456-3925
20 Kentshire Ct Wilmington (19807) *(G-11331)*
Larry's Custom Drywall, Newark *Also called Custom Drywall Inc (G-6330)*
Larson Engineering Inc......302 731-7434
910 S Chapel St Ste 200 Newark (19713) *(G-6918)*
Laser & Plastic Surgery Center......302 674-4865
200 Banning St Ste 230 Dover (19904) *(G-1766)*
Laser Images of Delaware Inc......302 836-8610
100 E Scotland Dr Bear (19701) *(G-229)*
Laser Management Group LLC......302 992-9030
5590 Kirkwood Hwy Wilmington (19808) *(G-11332)*
Laser Marking Works LLC......786 307-6203
3511 Silverside Rd # 105 Wilmington (19810) *(G-11333)*
Laser Online LLC......302 261-5225
801 N King St Wilmington (19801) *(G-11334)*
Laser Tone Bus Systems LLC......302 335-2510
1973 Bay Rd Milford (19963) *(G-4471)*
Last Tangle Salon and Spa......302 653-6638
76 E Glenwood Ave Smyrna (19977) *(G-8670)*
Lasting Impression Inc A......302 762-9200
504 Philadelphia Pike Wilmington (19809) *(G-11335)*
Latin American Cmnty Ctr Corp......302 655-7338
403 N Van Buren St Wilmington (19805) *(G-11336)*
Latin American Community Ctr, Wilmington *Also called Latin American Cmnty Ctr Corp (G-11336)*
Lau & Assoc Ltd......302 792-5955
20 Montchanin Rd Wilmington (19807) *(G-11337)*
Laurel Adult Day Care, Laurel *Also called Laurel Senior Center Inc (G-3256)*
Laurel Bridge Software Inc......302 453-0222
500 Creek View Rd Ste 200 Newark (19711) *(G-6919)*
Laurel Dental......302 875-4271
10250 Stone Creek Dr # 1 Laurel (19956) *(G-3252)*
Laurel DMV North Growout Off, Laurel *Also called Perdue Farms Inc (G-3271)*
Laurel Grain Company......302 875-4231
10717 Georgetown Rd Laurel (19956) *(G-3253)*
Laurel Highschool Wellness Ctr......302 875-6164
1133 S Central Ave Laurel (19956) *(G-3254)*
Laurel Medical Group......302 875-7753
1124 S Central Ave Laurel (19956) *(G-3255)*
Laurel Senior Center Inc......302 875-2536
113 N Central Ave Laurel (19956) *(G-3256)*
Laurel Storage Center, Lewes *Also called Love Creek Marina MBL Hm Site (G-3611)*
Lauren Farms Group Home......302 836-1379
116 Walls Way Bear (19701) *(G-230)*
Laurie Ann Fishinger......570 460-4370
29441 Glenwood Dr Millsboro (19966) *(G-4718)*
Laurie Jacobs......302 239-6257
730 Brookwood Ln Hockessin (19707) *(G-3078)*
Lavish Strands 1......302 333-5742
1408 Stonebridge Blvd New Castle (19720) *(G-5474)*
Lavond Mackey......484 466-8055
2808 N Jefferson St Apt 1 Wilmington (19802) *(G-11338)*
Law Debenture Trust Company......302 655-3505
901 N Market St Wilmington (19801) *(G-11339)*
Law Firm......302 472-4900
702 N King St Ste 600 Wilmington (19801) *(G-11340)*
Law Firm Michael P Freebery PA, Hockessin *Also called De Workers Cmpnstion Legal Ctr (G-3002)*
Law Office Laura A Yiengst LLC......302 264-9780
314 S State St Dover (19901) *(G-1767)*
Law Office of James Curra......302 894-1111
256 Chapman Rd Ste 107 Newark (19702) *(G-6920)*
Law Office of R I Masten Jr......302 358-2044
500 Creek View Rd Ste 304 Newark (19711) *(G-6921)*
Law Offices Doroshow Pasquele, Dover *Also called Doroshow Pasquale Karwitz Sieg (G-1438)*
Law Offices Gary R Dodge PA......302 674-5400
250 Beiser Blvd Ste 202 Dover (19904) *(G-1768)*
Lawall Prosthetics & Orthotics, Wilmington *Also called Harry J Lawall & Son Inc (G-10844)*
Lawall Prosthetics - Orthotics......302 677-0693
514 N Dupont Hwy Dover (19901) *(G-1769)*
Lawall Prosthetics - Orthotics (PA)......302 427-3668
1822 Augustine Cut Off Wilmington (19803) *(G-11341)*
Lawall Prosthetics - Orthotics......302 429-7625
1600 Rockland Rd Wilmington (19803) *(G-11342)*
Lawfully Yours, Wilmington *Also called K&B Investors LLC (G-11216)*
Lawn Doctor Aston-Middletown, Wilmington *Also called Jedi Inc (G-11140)*
Lawn Doctor Dover-Middletown, Odessa *Also called Jade Enterprises Inc (G-7828)*
Lawn Doctor of Newark, Newark *Also called Absolutely Green Inc (G-5888)*
Lawn Doctor of Wilmington Inc......302 656-4900
203 N Dupont Rd Wilmington (19804) *(G-11343)*
Lawn Quenchers Inc......302 218-1909
2633 Denny Rd Bear (19701) *(G-231)*
Lawnworks Inc......302 368-5699
667 Dawson Dr Ste D Newark (19713) *(G-6922)*
Lawrence A Louie DMD......302 674-5437
250 Beiser Blvd Ste 101 Dover (19904) *(G-1770)*
Lawrence Agencies Inc......302 995-6936
113 Kirkwood Sq Wilmington (19808) *(G-11344)*
Lawrence JP & Associates......313 293-2692
3012 N Heald St Wilmington (19802) *(G-11345)*
Lawrence Kennedy......302 533-5880
262 Chapman Rd Ste 107 Newark (19702) *(G-6923)*
Lawrence Legates Masnry Co Inc......302 422-8043
2891 Mlford Hrrington Hwy Milford (19963) *(G-4472)*
Lawrence Levinson Attorney......302 656-3393
1326 N King St Wilmington (19801) *(G-11346)*
Lawrence M Lewandoski MD......302 698-1100
4601 S Dupont Hwy Ste 2 Dover (19901) *(G-1771)*
Lawter Planning Group Inc......302 736-6065
1305 S Governors Ave Dover (19904) *(G-1772)*
Layercake LLC......571 449-7538
42 Hawthorne Ave Newark (19711) *(G-6924)*
Layton Associates, Ocean View *Also called C M L Management (G-7771)*
Laytons Umbrellas......302 249-1958
35527 Jamie Ave Laurel (19956) *(G-3257)*
Lc Associates LLC......302 235-2500
726 Yorklyn Rd Ste 150 Hockessin (19707) *(G-3079)*
Lc Homes Inc......302 429-8700
105 Foulk Rd Wilmington (19803) *(G-11347)*
Lcd Wealth Management LLC......302 294-0013
42 Piersons Rdg Hockessin (19707) *(G-3080)*
Le Herbe LLC (PA)......949 317-1100
1209 N Orange St Wilmington (19801) *(G-11348)*
Leadership Caddie......302 743-6456
15 Waterton Dr Bear (19701) *(G-232)*

ALPHABETIC

Leadership Forum LLC ... 919 309-4025
850 New Burton Rd Ste 201 Dover (19904) ***(G-1773)***
Leadership Institute Inc ... 302 368-7292
76 Omega Dr Newark (19713) ***(G-6925)***
Leading Communication Contrs, New Castle *Also called Prince Telecom LLC* ***(G-5643)***
Leadsrain, Wilmington *Also called Aum LLC* ***(G-9182)***
Leager Construction Inc ... 302 653-8021
732 Smyrna Landing Rd Smyrna (19977) ***(G-8671)***
League of Wmen Vters New Cstle ... 302 571-8948
2400 W 17th St R Wilmington (19806) ***(G-11349)***
Learning Care Group Inc ... 302 235-5702
5305 Limestone Rd Wilmington (19808) ***(G-11350)***
Learning Circle Child Care ... 302 834-1473
765 Old Porter Rd Bear (19701) ***(G-233)***
Learning Ctr At Madison St LLC ... 302 543-7588
600 N Madison St Wilmington (19801) ***(G-11351)***
Learning Express Academy ... 302 737-8260
302 Darling St Newark (19702) ***(G-6926)***
Learning Express Preschool ... 302 737-8990
300 Darling St Newark (19702) ***(G-6927)***
Learning Patch Kids ... 302 368-7208
25 Red Mill Rd Newark (19711) ***(G-6928)***
Learning Train LLC ... 302 731-0944
309 Possum Park Rd Newark (19711) ***(G-6929)***
Learning Tree Network ... 302 645-7199
16581 John Rowland Trl Milton (19968) ***(G-4923)***
Learning Years Preschool ... 302 241-4781
2 Riverside Rd Dover (19904) ***(G-1774)***
Learning4 Lrng Professionals ... 302 994-0451
317 E Christian St Wilmington (19804) ***(G-11352)***
Led Sign City ... 866 343-4011
3422 Old Capitol Trl Wilmington (19808) ***(G-11353)***
Ledtolight (PA) ... 941 323-6664
Trolley Sq Ste 20c Wilmington (19806) ***(G-11354)***
Lee Bell Inc (HQ) ... 302 477-3930
3411 Silverside Rd Wilmington (19810) ***(G-11355)***
Lee Lynn Inc ... 302 678-9978
1020 S State St Dover (19901) ***(G-1775)***
Lee M Dennis MD ... 302 735-1888
960 Forest St Dover (19904) ***(G-1776)***
Lee Mc Neill Associates ... 302 593-6172
1302 Grinnell Rd Wilmington (19803) ***(G-11356)***
Lee Nails ... 302 674-5001
63 Greentree Dr Dover (19904) ***(G-1777)***
Lee Townsend Electrical Contr ... 302 697-3432
2577 Upper King Rd Dover (19904) ***(G-1778)***
Leeber Limited USA ... 302 733-0991
115 Pencader Dr Newark (19702) ***(G-6930)***
Leech Tshman Fscaldo Lampl LLC ... 302 421-9379
1007 N Orange St Fl 4 Wilmington (19801) ***(G-11357)***
Leeds West Inv Group LLC ... 302 998-0533
3425 Kirkwood Hwy Wilmington (19808) ***(G-11358)***
Lees Lawn Care ... 302 658-2546
224 S Cleveland Ave Wilmington (19805) ***(G-11359)***
Leftys Alley & Eats ... 302 864-6000
36450 Plaza Blvd Lewes (19958) ***(G-3593)***
Legacy Distilling LLC ... 302 983-1269
106 W Commerce St Smyrna (19977) ***(G-8672)***
Legacy Foods LLC ... 302 656-5540
915 S Heald St Wilmington (19801) ***(G-11360)***
Legacy Vulcan LLC ... 302 875-5733
14208 County Seat Hwy Seaford (19973) ***(G-8292)***
Legacy Vulcan LLC ... 302 875-0748
28272 Landfill Ln Georgetown (19947) ***(G-2589)***
Legal Services Corp Delaware ... 302 575-0408
100 W 10th St Ste 203 Wilmington (19801) ***(G-11361)***
Legal Services of Delaware (PA) ... 302 575-0408
100 W 10th St Ste 203 Wilmington (19801) ***(G-11362)***
Legalnature LLC (PA) ... 888 881-1139
8 The Grn Ste 1 Dover (19901) ***(G-1779)***
Leggs Hanes Bali Playtex Otlt ... 302 227-8943
36454 Seaside Outlet Dr Rehoboth Beach (19971) ***(G-7985)***
Legion Transformation Ctr LLC ... 302 543-4922
97 Galewood Rd Wilmington (19803) ***(G-11363)***
Legist Media Ltd ... 302 655-2730
605 N Market St Fl 2 Wilmington (19801) ***(G-11364)***
Legum & Norman Mid-West LLC ... 302 537-9499
4 4 Edgewater House Rd Bethany Beach (19930) ***(G-408)***
Legum & Norman Mid-West LLC ... 302 227-8448
12000 Old Vine Blvd # 114 Lewes (19958) ***(G-3594)***
Legum & Norman Realty, Lewes *Also called Legum & Norman Mid-West LLC* ***(G-3594)***
Lehanes Bus Service Inc ... 302 328-7100
1705 Wilmington Rd New Castle (19720) ***(G-5475)***
Lehigh Testing Laboratories ... 302 328-0500
308 W Basin Rd New Castle (19720) ***(G-5476)***
Lehigh Vly Safety Sup Co Inc ... 302 323-9166
1f King Ave New Castle (19720) ***(G-5477)***
Lehman Brothers/Gp Inc ... 877 740-0108
919 N Market St Ste 506 Wilmington (19801) ***(G-11365)***
Lehvoss North Amer Holdg Inc (HQ) ... 302 734-1450
615 S Dupont Hwy Dover (19901) ***(G-1780)***
Leidig, Gilbert A MD, Newark *Also called Cardiology Physicans PA Inc* ***(G-6153)***
Leiluna LLC ... 888 201-6444
4023 Kennett Pike # 5830 Wilmington (19807) ***(G-11366)***
Leiny Snacks ... 302 494-2499
3 Germay Dr Ste 7 Wilmington (19804) ***(G-11367)***
Leisure Pt MBL HM Pk Cmpground, Lewes *Also called Pine Acres Inc* ***(G-3692)***
Lekue USA Inc ... 302 326-4805
802 Centerpoint Blvd New Castle (19720) ***(G-5478)***
Lela Capital LLC ... 917 428-0304
37259 Fox Dr Ocean View (19970) ***(G-7799)***
Leland Oakley Welding ... 302 469-5746
93 Paradise Cove Way Felton (19943) ***(G-2302)***
Lemay Enterprises Inc ... 302 659-3278
480 Oak Hill School Rd Townsend (19734) ***(G-8805)***
Lenape Builders Inc ... 302 376-3971
700 Ash Blvd Middletown (19709) ***(G-4128)***
Lenape Properties MGT Inc ... 302 426-0200
903 N French St Ste 106 Wilmington (19801) ***(G-11368)***
Lenar Detective Agency Inc ... 302 994-3011
411 S Dupont St Wilmington (19805) ***(G-11369)***
Lending Manager Holdings LLC ... 888 501-0335
152 E Main St Newark (19711) ***(G-6931)***
Lens Tolic LLC ... 800 343-5697
7209 Lancaster Pike Hockessin (19707) ***(G-3081)***
Leo J Kituskie DDS ... 302 479-3937
1941 Limestone Rd Ste 120 Wilmington (19808) ***(G-11370)***
Leo Ritter & Co ... 302 674-1375
892 Woodcrest Dr Dover (19904) ***(G-1781)***
Leon N Weiner & Associates Inc (PA) ... 302 656-1354
1 Fox Pt Ctr 4 Denny Rd Wilmington (19809) ***(G-11371)***
Leon N Weiner & Associates Inc ... 302 737-9574
330 E Main St Apt 214 Newark (19711) ***(G-6932)***
Leon N Weiner & Associates Inc ... 860 447-2282
4 Denny Rd Ste 1 Wilmington (19809) ***(G-11372)***
Leon N Weiner & Associates Inc ... 302 856-2251
200 Ingramtown Rd Georgetown (19947) ***(G-2590)***
Leon N Weiner & Associates Inc ... 302 322-6323
431 Old Forge Rd Ofc Ofc New Castle (19720) ***(G-5479)***
Leon N Weiner & Associates Inc ... 302 422-3343
806a Moyer Cir E Milford (19963) ***(G-4473)***
Leon N Weiner & Associates Inc ... 302 798-3446
1114 Andrea Ct Claymont (19703) ***(G-773)***
Leonard L Williams ... 302 652-3141
1214 N King St Wilmington (19801) ***(G-11373)***
Leons Garden World Ej Inc ... 410 392-8630
137 S Dupont Hwy New Castle (19720) ***(G-5480)***
Leounes Catered Affairs ... 302 547-3233
511 Saint George Dr Wilmington (19809) ***(G-11374)***
Leroy A Coblentz ... 302 343-7434
5024 Halltown Rd Hartly (19953) ***(G-2934)***
Leroy Betts Construction Inc ... 302 284-9193
4020 Hopkins Cemetery Rd Felton (19943) ***(G-2303)***
Leroy H Smith ... 302 875-5976
8095 Airport Rd Laurel (19956) ***(G-3258)***
Les Nails ... 302 449-5290
372 E Main St Middletown (19709) ***(G-4129)***
Leslie Johnson Center, Wilmington *Also called Wilmington Head Start* ***(G-13231)***
Leslie Kopp Inc ... 302 541-5207
33298 Coastal Hwy Bethany Beach (19930) ***(G-409)***
Lessons Learnd Dy Care /Presch ... 302 777-2200
207 N Union St Wilmington (19805) ***(G-11375)***
Lester & Co PC ... 302 684-5980
17021 Old Orchard Rd # 4 Lewes (19958) ***(G-3595)***
Let US Lift It Inc ... 302 654-2221
802 W 20th St Wilmington (19802) ***(G-11376)***
Let's Have Fun Daycare, Newark *Also called Susan T Fischer* ***(G-7517)***
Letica Corporation ... 302 378-9853
801 Industrial Rd Middletown (19709) ***(G-4130)***
Leukemia & Lymphoma Soc Inc ... 302 661-7300
100 W 10th St Ste 209 Wilmington (19801) ***(G-11377)***
Levi Calling ... 302 449-0017
858 Green Giant Rd Townsend (19734) ***(G-8806)***
Lewes Body Works Inc ... 302 645-5595
16205 New Rd Lewes (19958) ***(G-3596)***
Lewes Building Co, The, Lewes *Also called Tlbc LLC* ***(G-3787)***
Lewes Cheer Center, Lewes *Also called Cheer Inc* ***(G-3412)***
Lewes Chiropractic Center ... 302 645-9171
1527 Savannah Rd Lewes (19958) ***(G-3597)***
Lewes Dairy Inc ... 302 645-6281
660 Pilottown Rd Lewes (19958) ***(G-3598)***
Lewes Expressive Therapy ... 302 727-3275
105 Dove Dr Lewes (19958) ***(G-3599)***
Lewes Fishhouse & Produce Inc ... 302 827-4074
17696 Coastal Hwy Lewes (19958) ***(G-3600)***
Lewes Historical Society ... 302 645-7670
110 Shipcarpenter St Lewes (19958) ***(G-3601)***
Lewes Montessori School ... 302 644-7482
32234 Conleys Chapel Rd Lewes (19958) ***(G-3602)***

Lewes Orthopedic Ctr........302 645-4939
16704 Kings Hwy 2 Lewes (19958) ***(G-3603)***
Lewes Physical Therapy, Lewes *Also called Southern Del Physcl Therapy* ***(G-3757)***
LEWES SENIOR CENTER, Lewes *Also called Lewes Senior Citizens Center* ***(G-3604)***
Lewes Senior Citizens Center........302 645-9293
32083 Janice Rd Lewes (19958) ***(G-3604)***
Lewes Surgery Center........302 644-3466
17015 Old Orchard Rd # 4 Lewes (19958) ***(G-3605)***
Lewes Surgical and Med Assoc........302 945-9730
32711 Long Neck Rd Millsboro (19966) ***(G-4719)***
Lewes Waste Water Trtmnt Plant, Lewes *Also called Board of Public Works Inc* ***(G-3390)***
Lewis Educational Games, Wilmington *Also called Sandebbarnanricway Corp* ***(G-12538)***
Lewis Miller Inc........302 629-9895
8957 Middleford Rd Seaford (19973) ***(G-8293)***
Lewis Research Inc........302 644-0881
33712 Wescoats Rd Unit 1 Lewes (19958) ***(G-3606)***
Lewis Sand and Gravel LLC........302 238-0169
38227 Firemans Rd Millsboro (19966) ***(G-4720)***
Lexatys LLC........302 715-5029
10253 Stone Creek Dr 1 Laurel (19956) ***(G-3259)***
Lexatys,, Laurel *Also called Intelexmicro Inc* ***(G-3240)***
Lexington Green Apartments........302 322-8959
1201 Kingston Bldg Newark (19702) ***(G-6933)***
Lexisnexis Risk Assets Inc (HQ)........800 458-9410
1105 N Market St Ste 501 Wilmington (19801) ***(G-11378)***
Liberto Development Ltd........302 698-1104
1500 E Lebanon Rd Dover (19901) ***(G-1782)***
Liberty Dalysis Wilmington LLC........302 429-0142
913 Delaware Ave Wilmington (19806) ***(G-11379)***
Liberty Electric LLC........410 275-9200
1102 Varsity Ln Bear (19701) ***(G-234)***
Liberty Elevator Experts LLC........302 650-4688
625 Barksdale Rd Ste 113 Newark (19711) ***(G-6934)***
Liberty Mechanical LLC........302 397-8863
2032 Duncan Rd Wilmington (19808) ***(G-11380)***
Liberty Mutual, Wilmington *Also called Chrissinger and Baumberger* ***(G-9672)***
Liberty Mutual Fire Insur Co........302 993-0500
1011 Centre Rd Ste 400 Wilmington (19805) ***(G-11381)***
Liberty Mutual Insurance Co........302 993-0500
1011 Centre Rd Ste 400 Wilmington (19805) ***(G-11382)***
Liberty Parks and Playgrounds........302 659-5083
319 Wheatleys Pond Rd Clayton (19938) ***(G-862)***
Liberty Pointe, Newark *Also called Aion University Village LLC* ***(G-5924)***
Liberty Square, Newark *Also called Aion Prides Court LLC* ***(G-5923)***
Liberty Tax Service, Dover *Also called Slacum & Doyle Tax Service LLC* ***(G-2088)***
Liberty Tax Service, Newark *Also called Kelly Robert & Assoc LLC* ***(G-6873)***
Licensing Assurance LLC........305 851-3545
16192 Coastal Hwy Lewes (19958) ***(G-3607)***
Lids / Hatworld, Rehoboth Beach *Also called Lids Corporation* ***(G-7986)***
Lids Corporation........302 226-8580
35706 Byside Outl Dr S440 Rehoboth Beach (19971) ***(G-7986)***
Lids Corporation........302 736-8465
1365 N Dupont Hwy # 4018 Dover (19901) ***(G-1783)***
Lie, Wilmington *Also called Loyalty Is Earned Inc* ***(G-11445)***
Lielles Investments LLC........215 874-0770
16192 Coastal Hwy Lewes (19958) ***(G-3608)***
Lieske E2e Home Hlth Care Inc........302 898-1563
53 Meadow Dr Middletown (19709) ***(G-4131)***
Life At St Frncis Hlthcare Inc........302 660-3297
1072 Justison St Wilmington (19801) ***(G-11383)***
Life Before Us LLC........917 690-3380
2711 Centerville Rd Wilmington (19808) ***(G-11384)***
Life Reach / Eap Systems, Dover *Also called F H Everett & Associates Inc* ***(G-1536)***
Life Sciences Intl LLC........603 436-9444
1209 N Orange St Wilmington (19801) ***(G-11385)***
Lifesource Consulting Svcs LLC........302 257-6247
8 The Grn Ste 8155 Dover (19901) ***(G-1784)***
Lifespan Development Centers, Wilmington *Also called Education Svcs Unlimited LLC* ***(G-10352)***
Lifesquared Inc........415 475-9090
1679 S Dupont Hwy Dover (19901) ***(G-1785)***
Lifestyle Document MGT Inc........302 856-6387
22277 Lwes Georgetown Hwy Georgetown (19947) ***(G-2591)***
Lifetime Skills Services LLC........302 378-2911
300 Brady Ln Middletown (19709) ***(G-4132)***
Lifetouch Portrait Studios Inc........302 453-8080
Christina Mall Ste 606 Newark (19702) ***(G-6935)***
Lifetouch Portrait Studios Inc........302 734-9870
5000 Dover Mall Dover (19901) ***(G-1786)***
Light Action Inc........302 328-7800
31 Blevins Dr Ste C New Castle (19720) ***(G-5481)***
Light My Fire Inc........239 777-0878
48 Old Rudnick Ln Dover (19901) ***(G-1787)***
Lighted Pathway Day Care Ctr........302 629-8583
425 W Stein Hwy Seaford (19973) ***(G-8294)***
Lighthouse Construction Inc........302 677-1965
859 Golf Ln Ste 1 Magnolia (19962) ***(G-3898)***
Lighthouse Masonry Inc........302 945-1392
20090 Beaver Dam Rd Lewes (19958) ***(G-3609)***
Lighthse Rstrnt Fshrmans Wharf, Lewes *Also called M & P Adventures Inc* ***(G-3614)***
Lights Out Screen Printing Co........302 409-0560
1805 Beech St Wilmington (19805) ***(G-11386)***
Lightscapes Inc........302 798-5451
6603a Gvernor Printz Blvd Wilmington (19809) ***(G-11387)***
Liguori Morris & Reddin........302 678-9900
46 The Grn Dover (19901) ***(G-1788)***
Lil Red Hen Nursery Schl Inc........302 846-2777
400 N Bi State Blvd Delmar (19940) ***(G-1017)***
Lila Keshav Hospitality LLC........302 696-2272
315 Auto Park Dr Middletown (19709) ***(G-4133)***
Lillys Personal Training........302 538-6723
106 Mast Cir Dover (19901) ***(G-1789)***
Lily Intrnl Medicine Asscs LLC........302 424-1000
1019 Mattlind Way Milford (19963) ***(G-4474)***
Lily Wreaths........202 251-6004
133 W Lucky Estates Dr Harrington (19952) ***(G-2865)***
Limestone Country Day School........302 239-9041
5671 Ocheltree Ln Wilmington (19808) ***(G-11388)***
Limestone Hills Day School, Wilmington *Also called Limestone Country Day School* ***(G-11388)***
Limestone Medical Aid Unit, Wilmington *Also called Limestone Medical Center Inc* ***(G-11389)***
Limestone Medical Center Inc........302 992-0500
1941 Limestone Rd Ste 113 Wilmington (19808) ***(G-11389)***
Limestone Open Mri LLC (PA)........302 246-2001
2060 Limestone Rd Wilmington (19808) ***(G-11390)***
Limestone Open Mri LLC........302 834-4500
101 Becks Woods Dr # 103 Bear (19701) ***(G-235)***
Limestone Veterinary Hospital........302 239-5415
6102 Limestone Rd Hockessin (19707) ***(G-3082)***
Limewood Investments Del Inc........302 656-8915
801 N West St Fl 2 Wilmington (19801) ***(G-11391)***
Limitless Project, The, Dover *Also called Global Childrens Advocacy LLC* ***(G-1594)***
Limo Exchange........302 322-1200
800 Washington St New Castle (19720) ***(G-5482)***
Limousine Unlimited LLC........302 284-1100
12600 S Dupont Hwy Felton (19943) ***(G-2304)***
Linarducci & Butler PA........302 325-2400
910 W Basin Rd Ste 100 New Castle (19720) ***(G-5483)***
Lincare Inc........302 424-8302
7012 S Dupont Hwy Felton (19943) ***(G-2305)***
Lincoln Community Hall Inc........302 242-1747
18881 Washington St Lincoln (19960) ***(G-3859)***
Linda & Richard Partnership........302 697-9758
107 Lake Front Dr Dover (19904) ***(G-1790)***
Linda McCormick........443 987-2099
200 Tyrone Ave Wilmington (19804) ***(G-11392)***
Linda Putnam Day Care........302 836-1033
525 Deer Run Bear (19701) ***(G-236)***
Lindas Angels Chldcare Dev Ctr........302 328-3700
6 Parkway Ct New Castle (19720) ***(G-5484)***
Lindco........302 652-0708
122 Alapocas Dr Wilmington (19803) ***(G-11393)***
Lindco Packaging, Wilmington *Also called Lindco* ***(G-11393)***
Linden Hill Cleaners Inc........302 368-9795
4561 New Linden Hill Rd Wilmington (19808) ***(G-11394)***
Linden Hill Elementary Pta........302 454-3406
3415 Skyline Dr Wilmington (19808) ***(G-11395)***
Lindsay and Associates Limited........703 631-5840
1610 Beach Plum Dr Milton (19968) ***(G-4924)***
Line-X Delaware Inc........302 672-7005
1053 Barl Ct Dover (19901) ***(G-1791)***
Linens of The Week, New Castle *Also called Palace Laundry Inc* ***(G-5598)***
Linguatext Ltd........302 453-8695
103 Walker Way Newark (19711) ***(G-6936)***
Link Metals LLC (PA)........302 295-5066
3524 Silverside Rd 35b Wilmington (19810) ***(G-11396)***
Linkedin Profile Services LLC........703 679-7719
108 W 13th St Wilmington (19801) ***(G-11397)***
Links Outboard LLC........302 368-2860
20 Brookhill Dr Newark (19702) ***(G-6937)***
Linne Industries LLC........302 454-1439
11 Bridlebrook Ln Newark (19711) ***(G-6938)***
Lion Totalcare Inc........610 444-1700
9 Germay Dr Ste 200a Wilmington (19804) ***(G-11398)***
Lip Balm Land LLC........302 319-9919
19c Trolley Sq Wilmington (19806) ***(G-11399)***
Liquid Filter Division, Newark *Also called Graver Technologies LLC* ***(G-6684)***
Lisa A Fagioletti DMD LLC........302 514-9064
25 W Commerce St Smyrna (19977) ***(G-8673)***
Lisa Broadbent Insurance Inc........302 731-0044
20 Polly Drummond Hill Rd Newark (19711) ***(G-6939)***
Lisa M Horsey........302 725-5767
8868 Cedar Creek Rd Lincoln (19960) ***(G-3860)***
Lisa M Horsey Bus Service, Lincoln *Also called Lisa M Horsey* ***(G-3860)***

ALPHABETIC

Lisa R Savage 302 353-7052
  260 Chapman Rd Ste 100b Newark (19702) *(G-6940)*
Lisa Ryan Hobbs DPM 302 629-3000
  543 N Shipley St Ste C Seaford (19973) *(G-8295)*
Lisa Trabaudo Day Care 302 653-3529
  316 Lisa Ct Smyrna (19977) *(G-8674)*
Litcharts LLC 646 481-4807
  2711 Centerville Rd # 400 Wilmington (19808) *(G-11400)*
Litecure LLC 302 709-0408
  101 Lukens Dr Ste G New Castle (19720) *(G-5485)*
Little Blessings Daycare 302 655-8962
  2010 N Market St Wilmington (19802) *(G-11401)*
Little Caboose The, Newark Also called Atlantic Dawn Ltd *(G-6019)*
Little Einsteins Preschool 302 933-0600
  28253 Dupont Blvd Millsboro (19966) *(G-4721)*
Little Folks Too Day Care 302 652-3420
  1318 N Market St Wilmington (19801) *(G-11402)*
Little Folks Too Day Care (PA) 302 652-1238
  1320 N Market St Wilmington (19801) *(G-11403)*
Little Gym 302 856-2310
  21500 Carmean Way Unit 4 Georgetown (19947) *(G-2592)*
Little Gym of Ncc 302 543-5524
  4758 Limestone Rd Ste A Wilmington (19808) *(G-11404)*
Little Gym, The, Wilmington Also called Little Gym of Ncc *(G-11404)*
Little Kids Swagg Lrng Ctr LLC 302 480-4404
  433 S Dupont Blvd Smyrna (19977) *(G-8675)*
Little League Baseball Inc 302 276-0375
  23 Blount Rd New Castle (19720) *(G-5486)*
Little League Baseball Inc 302 227-0888
  125 Beachfield Dr Rehoboth Beach (19971) *(G-7987)*
Little Learner Inc 302 798-5570
  41 N Avon Dr Claymont (19703) *(G-774)*
Little Nests Portraits (PA) 610 459-8622
  2100 N Bancroft Pkwy Wilmington (19806) *(G-11405)*
Little People Child Dev 302 328-1481
  122 E Main St Christiana (19702) *(G-673)*
Little People Day Care 302 528-4336
  17 Cole Blvd Middletown (19709) *(G-4134)*
Little Peoples College 302 998-4929
  3507 Old Capitol Trl Wilmington (19808) *(G-11406)*
Little Pople Child Dev Ctr Inc 302 836-5900
  3843 Wrangle Hill Rd Bear (19701) *(G-237)*
Little Scholars Learning Ctr 302 656-8785
  2511 W 4th St Ste A Wilmington (19805) *(G-11407)*
Little School Inc 302 734-3040
  105 Mont Blanc Blvd Dover (19904) *(G-1792)*
Little Sisters of The Poor 302 368-5886
  185 Salem Church Rd Newark (19713) *(G-6941)*
Little Sprouts Learning Academ, Seaford Also called Karen Schreiber *(G-8284)*
Little Star Inc 302 995-2920
  5702 Kirkwood Hwy Wilmington (19808) *(G-11408)*
Little Stars Inc 302 737-9759
  947 Old Harmony Rd Newark (19713) *(G-6942)*
Little Steps Daycare 302 654-4867
  212 W 21st St Wilmington (19802) *(G-11409)*
Little Sunshines, New Castle Also called Shavone Loves Kids Day Care *(G-5704)*
Little Thresa P MD Fmly Mdcine, Dover Also called Theresa Little MD *(G-2141)*
Little Trooper Day Care 302 378-7355
  329 Senator Dr Middletown (19709) *(G-4135)*
Lituation Creative Designs Inc 302 494-4399
  3201 N Jefferson St Wilmington (19802) *(G-11410)*
Lityx LLC 888 548-9947
  1000 N West St Ste 1200 Wilmington (19801) *(G-11411)*
Liuna, Georgetown Also called Laborers Intl Un N Amer *(G-2588)*
Live Typing Inc 415 670-9601
  1521 Concord Pike Ste 303 Wilmington (19803) *(G-11412)*
Liveware Inc 302 791-9446
  1506 Society Dr Claymont (19703) *(G-775)*
Living Harvest Interntl Minst 302 757-4273
  701 N Clnl Ave Apt 202 Wilmington (19805) *(G-11413)*
Living Well Magazine 302 355-0929
  1519 Old Coach Rd Newark (19711) *(G-6943)*
Livingston Healthcare Svcs Inc 302 631-5000
  220 Lake Dr Newark (19702) *(G-6944)*
Lkq Northeast Inc 800 223-0171
  1575 Mckee Rd Ste 5 Dover (19904) *(G-1793)*
Llb Acquisition LLC 212 750-8300
  1209 N Orange St Wilmington (19801) *(G-11414)*
LLC Levy Wilson 302 888-1088
  3801 Kennett Pike D204 Wilmington (19807) *(G-11415)*
LLC Schell Brothers 302 226-1994
  55 Cascade Ln B Rehoboth Beach (19971) *(G-7988)*
LLC Schell Brothers 302 376-0355
  758 Idlewyld Dr Middletown (19709) *(G-4136)*
Lloyds Wldg & Fabrication LLC 302 384-7662
  1101 E 8th St Wilmington (19801) *(G-11416)*
Lnbe LLC 302 393-2201
  1226 N King St Wilmington (19801) *(G-11417)*
Lnh Inc 302 731-4948
  650 Pencader Dr Newark (19702) *(G-6945)*

Lnp Media Group Inc 302 422-7575
  1666 Blairs Pond Rd Milford (19963) *(G-4475)*
Lns Delivery Inc 302 448-6848
  25905 Pear St Millsboro (19966) *(G-4722)*
Loadbalancerorginc 888 867-9504
  4550 Linden Hill Rd # 201 Wilmington (19808) *(G-11418)*
Loan Till Payday LLC 302 792-5001
  2604 Philadelphia Pike Claymont (19703) *(G-776)*
LOCAL 13100 CWA, Wilmington Also called Diamond State Tele Coml Un *(G-10148)*
LOCAL 199, Newark Also called Laborers Intl Un N Amer *(G-6911)*
Local Investments LLC 302 422-0731
  215 Sunset Dr Wilmington (19809) *(G-11419)*
Local TV Finance LLC 302 636-5401
  2711 Centerville Rd # 400 Wilmington (19808) *(G-11420)*
Local Vertical 302 242-2552
  69 Oakcrest Dr Dover (19901) *(G-1794)*
Localspin LLC 917 232-7203
  1521 Concord Pike Ste 301 Wilmington (19803) *(G-11421)*
Locker Construction Inc 302 239-2859
  314 Cox Rd Newark (19711) *(G-6946)*
Lockheed Martin Overseas LLC 301 897-6923
  251 Little Falls Dr Wilmington (19808) *(G-11422)*
Locksign LLC 917 573-6582
  16192 Coastal Hwy Lewes (19958) *(G-3610)*
Lockwood Design Construction 302 684-4844
  26412 Broadkill Rd Fl 1 Milton (19968) *(G-4925)*
Locust Cnstr & Contg Svcs, Wilmington Also called Linda McCormick *(G-11392)*
Lodes Chiropractic Center PA 302 477-1565
  3411 Silverside Rd 102hb Wilmington (19810) *(G-11423)*
Lodge Lane Assisted Living 302 757-8100
  1221 Lodge Ln Wilmington (19809) *(G-11424)*
Lofland Funeral Home Inc 302 422-5416
  102 Lakeview Ave Milford (19963) *(G-4476)*
Lofland Park Center, Seaford Also called 715 East King St Oprations LLC *(G-8134)*
Loftcom Inc 800 563-6900
  1000 N West St Fl 12 Wilmington (19801) *(G-11425)*
Lognex Inc 786 650-7755
  1000 N West St Ste 1200 Wilmington (19801) *(G-11426)*
Logo Motive Inc 302 645-2959
  35576 Airport Rd Rehoboth Beach (19971) *(G-7989)*
Logue Brothers Inc 302 762-1896
  3507 Miller Rd Wilmington (19802) *(G-11427)*
Lois James DDS 302 537-4500
  17 Atlantic Ave Ste 4 Ocean View (19970) *(G-7800)*
Loizides & Associates PC 302 654-0248
  1225 N King St Ste 800 Wilmington (19801) *(G-11428)*
Lolahsoul Jewelry Inc 888 771-7087
  P.O. Box 2576 Wilmington (19805) *(G-11429)*
Lomas Properties LLC 302 260-9245
  312 Rehoboth Ave Rehoboth Beach (19971) *(G-7990)*
Lon Spa Inc 302 368-4595
  330 Suburban Dr Newark (19711) *(G-6947)*
Lone Star Global Services Inc 302 744-9800
  9 E Loockerman St Ste 3a Dover (19901) *(G-1795)*
Long & Foster Companies Inc 302 539-9040
  1150 S Coastal Hwy Bethany Beach (19930) *(G-410)*
Long & Foster Companies Inc 302 539-9767
  33298 Coastal Hwy Unit 1 Bethany Beach (19930) *(G-411)*
Long & Foster Real Estate Inc 302 227-3821
  37156 Rehoboth Avenue Ext # 5 Rehoboth Beach (19971) *(G-7991)*
Long & Foster Realtors, Lewes Also called Richard Bryan *(G-3718)*
Long & Tann & D Onofrio Inc (PA) 302 477-1970
  3906 Concord Pike Ste F Wilmington (19803) *(G-11430)*
Long Neck Med Entreprises LLC 302 945-9730
  32711 Long Neck Rd Millsboro (19966) *(G-4723)*
Long Neck Water Co 302 947-9600
  32783 Long Neck Rd Unit 6 Millsboro (19966) *(G-4724)*
Long Term Care Residents Div 302 424-8600
  24 Nw Front St Milford (19963) *(G-4477)*
Longneck Backhoe 302 945-3429
  25509 Guinea Hollow Rd Millsboro (19966) *(G-4725)*
Longneck Family Practice 302 947-9767
  26744 J J Wllms Hwy 3 Millsboro (19966) *(G-4726)*
Longneck Housing Specialist, Millsboro Also called Manufctured Hsing Concepts LLC *(G-4734)*
Longo and Associates LLP 302 477-7500
  2010 Limestone Rd Wilmington (19808) *(G-11431)*
Longview Farms Civic Assn 302 475-6684
  1107 S Overhill Ct Wilmington (19810) *(G-11432)*
Lookinn Inc 302 839-2088
  8 The Grn Ste 5154 Dover (19901) *(G-1796)*
Looksiebin Inc 410 869-2192
  4708 Weatherhill Dr Wilmington (19808) *(G-11433)*
Loom Network Inc 404 939-1294
  427 N Tatnall St 38768 Wilmington (19801) *(G-11434)*
Loomcraft Textile & Supply Co 302 454-3232
  211 Executive Dr Ste 13 Newark (19702) *(G-6948)*
Lord & Wheeler, Georgetown Also called Eric S Balliet *(G-2524)*

Lord Printing LLC 302 439-3253
1812 Marsh Rd Ste 411 Wilmington (19810) ***(G-11435)***
Lords Landscaping Inc 302 539-6119
35577 Atlantic Ave Millville (19967) ***(G-4847)***
Lorelton 302 573-3580
2200 W 4th St Apt 229 Wilmington (19805) ***(G-11436)***
Lori Emory 302 737-7352
35 Winsome Way Newark (19702) ***(G-6949)***
Loris Hands Inc 302 440-5454
100 Discovery Blvd Fl 4 Newark (19713) ***(G-6950)***
Losco and Marconi PA 302 656-7776
1813 N Franklin St Wilmington (19802) ***(G-11437)***
Losemynumbercom LLC 302 778-9741
427 N Tatnall St # 10885 Wilmington (19801) ***(G-11438)***
Lost and Found Dog Rescue Adop 302 613-0394
70 Ivy Ln New Castle (19720) ***(G-5487)***
Lotus Blossom Learning Center, Lewes *Also called Robin S Wright* ***(G-3721)***
Loughran Medical Group PA 302 479-8464
3411 Silverside Rd 103wb Wilmington (19810) ***(G-11439)***
Louie Harry Laundry & Dry Clg, Dover *Also called Harry Louies Laundry & Dry Clg* ***(G-1634)***
Louis Capano and Associates 302 738-8000
6502 Winterhaven Dr Newark (19702) ***(G-6951)***
Louis K Rafetto DMD 302 477-1800
3512 Silverside Rd Ste 12 Wilmington (19810) ***(G-11440)***
Louis P Martin DDS 302 994-4900
1941 Limestone Rd Ste 105 Wilmington (19808) ***(G-11441)***
Louviers Federal Credit Union 302 571-9513
1007 N Market St Wilmington (19801) ***(G-11442)***
Louviers Federal Credit Union (PA) 302 733-0426
185 S Main St Newark (19711) ***(G-6952)***
Louviers Mortgage Corporation 302 234-4129
4839 Limestone Rd Wilmington (19808) ***(G-11443)***
Love Creek Marina MBL Hm Site (PA) 302 448-6492
31136 Conleys Chapel Rd Lewes (19958) ***(G-3611)***
Love N Learn Nursery Too 302 678-0445
1598 Forrest Ave Dover (19904) ***(G-1797)***
Loving Care Nursery School 302 653-6990
22 Dwight Ave Smyrna (19977) ***(G-8676)***
Lowe, Robert W Agency, Newark *Also called Interstate Mortgage Corp Inc* ***(G-6799)***
Lowell Scott MD PA 302 684-1119
611 Federal St Ste 3 Milton (19968) ***(G-4926)***
Lowell Scott MD PA 302 684-1119
807 Hickory Ln Milford (19963) ***(G-4478)***
Lowes Home Centers LLC 302 479-7799
3100 Brandywine Pkwy Fl 1 Wilmington (19803) ***(G-11444)***
Lowes Home Centers LLC 302 934-3740
26688 Centerview Dr Millsboro (19966) ***(G-4727)***
Lowes Home Centers LLC 302 376-3006
500 W Main St Middletown (19709) ***(G-4137)***
Lowes Home Centers LLC 302 735-7500
1450 N Dupont Hwy Dover (19901) ***(G-1798)***
Lowes Home Centers LLC 302 645-0900
20364 Plantations Rd Lewes (19958) ***(G-3612)***
Lowes Home Centers LLC 302 834-8508
800 Eden Cir Bear (19701) ***(G-238)***
Lowes Home Centers LLC 302 697-0700
516 Walmart Dr Camden (19934) ***(G-589)***
Lowes Home Centers LLC 302 781-1154
2000 Ogletown Rd Newark (19711) ***(G-6953)***
Lowes Home Centers LLC 302 536-4000
22880 Sussex Hwy Seaford (19973) ***(G-8296)***
Lowes Home Centers LLC 302 252-3228
2225 Hessler Blvd New Castle (19720) ***(G-5488)***
Loyal Orange Institution, Wilmington *Also called Supreme Grand Lodge of U S A* ***(G-12816)***
Loyal Order Mose Lwes Rehoboth 302 684-4004
28971 Lwes Georgetown Hwy Lewes (19958) ***(G-3613)***
Loyalty Is Earned Inc (PA) 347 606-6383
3616 Kirkwood Hwy Ste A Wilmington (19808) ***(G-11445)***
LRC North America Inc 302 427-2845
1105 N Market St Wilmington (19801) ***(G-11446)***
Lrk Dental 302 629-7115
543 N Shipley St Seaford (19973) ***(G-8297)***
Lsf Networks LLC 213 537-2402
300 Delaware Ave Ste 210a Wilmington (19801) ***(G-11447)***
Lsref4 Lighthouse Corp Acqstn 302 737-8500
146 Chestnut Crossing Dr Newark (19713) ***(G-6954)***
Lst Insvestment LLC 302 322-3454
819 Pulaski Hwy Bear (19701) ***(G-239)***
Ltc Pharmacy, Newark *Also called Pharmerica Long-Term Care LLC* ***(G-7209)***
Lube Depot 302 659-3329
205 W Glenwood Ave Smyrna (19977) ***(G-8677)***
Lucila Carmichael Rn 302 324-8901
1101 Delaware St New Castle (19720) ***(G-5489)***
Luff & Associates CPA PA 302 422-9699
223 S Rehoboth Blvd Milford (19963) ***(G-4479)***
Luff & Associates PA, Milford *Also called Luff & Associates CPA PA* ***(G-4479)***
Luis L David MD PA 302 422-9768
204 S Walnut St Milford (19963) ***(G-4480)***
Luke Destefano Inc 302 455-0710
107b Albe Dr Ste B Newark (19702) ***(G-6955)***
Lulla Woodworking 302 841-8800
1 New Castle Ct Ocean View (19970) ***(G-7801)***
Lullaby Learning Center Inc 302 703-2871
26324 Lwes Georgetown Hwy Harbeson (19951) ***(G-2789)***
Lumber Industries Inc 302 655-9651
5809 Kennett Pike Wilmington (19807) ***(G-11448)***
Lumber Jacks Axe Club LLC 215 900-0318
44 E 4th St New Castle (19720) ***(G-5490)***
Lumenty Technologies Inc 971 331-3113
3411 Silverside Rd # 104 Wilmington (19810) ***(G-11449)***
Lumhaa LLC 916 517-9972
108 W 13th St Wilmington (19801) ***(G-11450)***
Lumi Cases LLC 302 525-6971
501 Capitol Trl Apt 201 Newark (19711) ***(G-6956)***
Lums Pond Animal Hospital Inc 302 836-5585
3052 Wrangle Hill Rd Bear (19701) ***(G-240)***
Lumulabs Inc 302 261-5284
2035 Sunset Lake Rd B2 Newark (19702) ***(G-6957)***
Lundberg Tech Inc - America 302 738-2500
667 Dawson Dr Ste C Newark (19713) ***(G-6958)***
Lune Rouge Entrmt USA Inc 514 556-2101
251 Little Falls Dr Wilmington (19808) ***(G-11451)***
Luriware Consulting Agricultur 302 244-1947
155 S Bradford St 200a Dover (19904) ***(G-1799)***
Lusotrading Corp 302 288-0670
1521 Concord Pike Ste 303 Wilmington (19803) ***(G-11452)***
Luther Martin Foundation Dover 302 674-1408
430 Kings Hwy Ofc 727 Dover (19901) ***(G-1800)***
Luther Towers II, Wilmington *Also called Lutheran Senior Services Inc* ***(G-11455)***
Luther Towers III Dover Inc 302 674-1408
430 Kings Hwy Dover (19901) ***(G-1801)***
Luther Towers IV Dover Inc 302 674-1408
430 Kings Hwy Ofc 1021 Dover (19901) ***(G-1802)***
LUTHER TOWERS OF DOVER, Dover *Also called Lutheran Senior Svcs of Dover* ***(G-1807)***
Luther Towers of Dover Inc 302 674-1408
430 Kings Hwy Ofc 727 Dover (19901) ***(G-1803)***
LUTHER TOWERS OF MILTON,THE, Milton *Also called Lutheran Snr Srvcs Ssx Cnty* ***(G-4927)***
Luther Village I Dover Inc 302 674-1408
430 Kings Hwy Ofc 727 Dover (19901) ***(G-1804)***
Luther Village II Dover Inc 302 674-1408
430 Kings Hwy Dover (19901) ***(G-1805)***
Luther Village of Dover 302 674-3780
101 Babb Dr Unit 1000 Dover (19901) ***(G-1806)***
Lutheran Community Services 302 654-8886
2809 Baynard Blvd Wilmington (19802) ***(G-11453)***
Lutheran Senior Services Inc (PA) 302 654-4490
1201 N Harrison St # 1204 Wilmington (19806) ***(G-11454)***
Lutheran Senior Services Inc 302 654-4490
1420 N Franklin St Ste 1 Wilmington (19806) ***(G-11455)***
Lutheran Senior Svcs of Dover 302 674-1408
430 Kings Hwy Ofc 727 Dover (19901) ***(G-1807)***
Lutheran Snr Srvcs Ssx Cnty 302 684-1668
500 Palmer St Milton (19968) ***(G-4927)***
Lutz Engineering Inc 302 479-9017
3324 Hermitage Rd Wilmington (19810) ***(G-11456)***
Lux Spa & Nails 302 834-4899
122 Foxhunt Dr Bear (19701) ***(G-241)***
Luxcore LLC 302 777-0538
300 Delaware Ave Ste 210a Wilmington (19801) ***(G-11457)***
Luxiasuites LLC 302 654-8527
331 Justison St Wilmington (19801) ***(G-11458)***
Luxiasuites LLC (PA) 302 778-2900
322 A St Ste 300 Wilmington (19801) ***(G-11459)***
Luxiasuites LLC 302 778-3000
1007 N Orange St Wilmington (19801) ***(G-11460)***
Luxiasuites LLC 302 426-1200
115 Christina Landing Dr Wilmington (19801) ***(G-11461)***
Luxottica of America Inc 302 322-4131
124 Sunset Blvd New Castle (19720) ***(G-5491)***
Luz D Reynoso 302 358-6237
179 W Chestnut Hill Rd # 6 Newark (19713) ***(G-6959)***
Lweco Group LLC 302 296-8035
28428 Cedar Ridge Dr Millsboro (19966) ***(G-4728)***
Lycon Investment Company 302 732-0940
30983 Country Gdns Unit 1 Dagsboro (19939) ***(G-915)***
Lycra Company LLC (HQ) 316 226-9361
2711 Centerville Rd # 300 Wilmington (19808) ***(G-11462)***
Lycra Company LLC 302 731-6800
150 Red Mill Rd Newark (19711) ***(G-6960)***
Lynch Heights Fuel Corp 302 422-9195
840 Bay Rd Milford (19963) ***(G-4481)***
Lynn and Rachel Walsh 302 422-2893
6028 Old Shawnee Rd Milford (19963) ***(G-4482)***
Lynn Holiday Shynea 302 674-4700
540 S Governors Ave 101b Dover (19904) ***(G-1808)***
Lynnanne Kasarda MD 302 655-5822
1802 W 4th St Wilmington (19805) ***(G-11463)***
Lynne Betts 302 265-5602
28 N Pine Street Ext Seaford (19973) ***(G-8298)***

ALPHABETIC

Lynns Home Daycare.....302 337-0186
412 S Laws St Bridgeville (19933) ***(G-490)***
Lynx General Contracting.....302 368-9401
1267 Old Cooches Brdg Rd Newark (19713) ***(G-6961)***
Lynx Golf Ltd.....778 755-4107
160 Greentree Dr Ste 101 Dover (19904) ***(G-1809)***
Lyon 784, Dagsboro *Also called Lycon Investment Company* ***(G-915)***
Lyons David J Law Office.....302 777-5698
1526 Gilpin Ave Wilmington (19806) ***(G-11464)***
Lyons Doughty & Veldhuis.....302 428-1670
15 Ashley Pl Ste 2b Wilmington (19804) ***(G-11465)***
Lyons Insurance Agency Inc (PA).....302 227-7100
501 Carr Rd Ste 301 Wilmington (19809) ***(G-11466)***
Lyra Software Inc.....347 506-5287
2035 Sunset Lake Rd B2 Newark (19702) ***(G-6962)***
M & D Poultry Service.....302 934-7050
26518 Gravel Hill Rd Millsboro (19966) ***(G-4729)***
M & L Contractors Inc.....302 436-9303
13354 Blueberry Rd Selbyville (19975) ***(G-8513)***
M & M Construction Inc.....410 758-1071
101 Main St Odessa (19730) ***(G-7829)***
M & M Marketing Group LLC.....321 274-5352
1521 Concord Pike Wilmington (19803) ***(G-11467)***
M & P Adventures Inc.....302 645-6271
Corner Of Savannah Angler Lewes (19958) ***(G-3614)***
M & W Trucking Inc.....302 655-6994
44 Glen Ave New Castle (19720) ***(G-5492)***
M A K Roofing Inc.....302 737-5380
10 Deerborne Trl Newark (19702) ***(G-6963)***
M and J Industries.....302 559-5005
105 Hayman Pl Wilmington (19803) ***(G-11468)***
M and R.....302 421-9838
2909 Lancaster Ave Wilmington (19805) ***(G-11469)***
M Auger Enterprise Inc.....302 992-9922
101 Cassidy Dr Wilmington (19804) ***(G-11470)***
M B A, Wilmington *Also called Mumford-Bjorkman Associates* ***(G-11775)***
M C Tek LLC.....302 644-9695
19122 Coastal Hwy Unit B Rehoboth Beach (19971) ***(G-7992)***
M Cubed Technologies Inc.....302 454-8600
1300 Marrows Rd Newark (19711) ***(G-6964)***
M D Electric LLC.....302 838-2852
325 Meadow Glen Dr Bear (19701) ***(G-242)***
M D Plumbing Drain Cleaning.....302 492-8880
1500 Gunter Rd Marydel (19964) ***(G-3920)***
M Davis & Sons Inc (PA).....302 998-3385
19 Germay Dr Wilmington (19804) ***(G-11471)***
M Davis & Sons Inc.....302 998-3385
200 Hadco Rd Wilmington (19804) ***(G-11472)***
M Davis Farms LLC.....302 856-7018
17741 Davis Rd Georgetown (19947) ***(G-2593)***
M Diana Metzger MD.....302 731-0942
665 Churchmans Rd Newark (19702) ***(G-6965)***
M E C C Ad, Wilmington *Also called Marketing Enterprise Capyuring* ***(G-11537)***
M G Hamex Corporation.....302 832-9072
1063 Twin Lane Rd New Castle (19720) ***(G-5493)***
M Imran MD.....302 453-7399
2707 Kirkwood Hwy Ste 1 Newark (19711) ***(G-6966)***
M K Customer Elevator Pads.....302 698-3110
1644 Sorghum Mill Rd Dover (19901) ***(G-1810)***
M L Parker Construction Inc.....302 798-8530
950 Ridge Rd Ste C6 Claymont (19703) ***(G-777)***
M O T Senior Citizen Center.....302 378-3041
300 S Scott St Middletown (19709) ***(G-4138)***
M R Designs Inc.....302 684-8082
26342 Broadkill Rd Milton (19968) ***(G-4928)***
M T C, Newark *Also called Mtc Usa LLC* ***(G-7069)***
M T O Clean of Sussex County.....302 854-0204
2 N Aquarius Way Milton (19968) ***(G-4929)***
M Tech European Autohouse Inc.....302 472-6813
2517 W 6th St Wilmington (19805) ***(G-11473)***
M W Fogarty Inc.....302 658-5547
22 Bernard Blvd Hockessin (19707) ***(G-3083)***
M W U L, Wilmington *Also called Metropltan Wlmngton Urban Leag* ***(G-11650)***
M&J Services LLC.....302 227-8725
307 Bayview Ave Rehoboth Beach (19971) ***(G-7993)***
M&M Mass Spec Consulting LLC.....302 250-4488
28 Tenby Chase Dr Newark (19711) ***(G-6967)***
M&T, Wilmington *Also called Wilmington Trust Company* ***(G-13261)***
M&T, Lewes *Also called Manufacturers & Traders Tr Co* ***(G-3618)***
M&T, Georgetown *Also called Manufacturers & Traders Tr Co* ***(G-2595)***
M&T, Milton *Also called Manufacturers & Traders Tr Co* ***(G-4930)***
M&T, Newark *Also called Manufacturers & Traders Tr Co* ***(G-6981)***
M&T, Seaford *Also called Manufacturers & Traders Tr Co* ***(G-8302)***
M&T, Bethany Beach *Also called Manufacturers & Traders Tr Co* ***(G-412)***
M&T, Wilmington *Also called Manufacturers & Traders Tr Co* ***(G-11505)***
M&T, Middletown *Also called Manufacturers & Traders Tr Co* ***(G-4143)***
M&T, Wilmington *Also called Manufacturers & Traders Tr Co* ***(G-11506)***
M&T, Claymont *Also called Manufacturers & Traders Tr Co* ***(G-780)***
M&T, Dover *Also called Manufacturers & Traders Tr Co* ***(G-1814)***
M&T, Wilmington *Also called Manufacturers & Traders Tr Co* ***(G-11507)***
M&T, Milford *Also called Manufacturers & Traders Tr Co* ***(G-4485)***
M&T, Wilmington *Also called Manufacturers & Traders Tr Co* ***(G-11508)***
M&T, Wilmington *Also called Manufacturers & Traders Tr Co* ***(G-11509)***
M&T, Wilmington *Also called Manufacturers & Traders Tr Co* ***(G-11510)***
M&T, Wilmington *Also called Manufacturers & Traders Tr Co* ***(G-11511)***
M&T, Wilmington *Also called Manufacturers & Traders Tr Co* ***(G-11512)***
M&T, Wilmington *Also called Manufacturers & Traders Tr Co* ***(G-11513)***
M&T, Hockessin *Also called Manufacturers & Traders Tr Co* ***(G-3087)***
M&T, Bear *Also called Manufacturers & Traders Tr Co* ***(G-244)***
M&T, Rehoboth Beach *Also called Manufacturers & Traders Tr Co* ***(G-7996)***
M&T, Wilmington *Also called Manufacturers & Traders Tr Co* ***(G-11514)***
M&T, Laurel *Also called Manufacturers & Traders Tr Co* ***(G-3261)***
M&T, Millsboro *Also called Manufacturers & Traders Tr Co* ***(G-4732)***
M&T, Georgetown *Also called Manufacturers & Traders Tr Co* ***(G-2596)***
M&T, Middletown *Also called Manufacturers & Traders Tr Co* ***(G-4144)***
M&T, Millsboro *Also called Manufacturers & Traders Tr Co* ***(G-4733)***
M&T, Millville *Also called Manufacturers & Traders Tr Co* ***(G-4848)***
M&T, Newark *Also called Manufacturers & Traders Tr Co* ***(G-6982)***
M&T, Newark *Also called Manufacturers & Traders Tr Co* ***(G-6983)***
M&T, Seaford *Also called Manufacturers & Traders Tr Co* ***(G-8303)***
M&T, Dover *Also called Manufacturers & Traders Tr Co* ***(G-1815)***
M&T, New Castle *Also called Manufacturers & Traders Tr Co* ***(G-5505)***
M&T, Delmar *Also called Manufacturers & Traders Tr Co* ***(G-1018)***
M&T, Wilmington *Also called Manufacturers & Traders Tr Co* ***(G-11515)***
M&T, Wilmington *Also called Manufacturers & Traders Tr Co* ***(G-11516)***
M&T, Dover *Also called Manufacturers & Traders Tr Co* ***(G-1816)***
M-Cap Technologies Intl (PA).....302 695-5329
3521 Silverside Rd Wilmington (19810) ***(G-11474)***
M/S Hollow Metal Wholesale LLC.....302 349-9471
9644 Nantcke Bus Pk Dr Greenwood (19950) ***(G-2750)***
M3 Contracting LLC.....302 781-3143
13 Garfield Way Newark (19713) ***(G-6968)***
M3r & Assoc Inc.....302 324-1040
287 Christiana Rd Ste 24 New Castle (19720) ***(G-5494)***
MA Transportation LLC.....302 588-5435
34016 Sea Otter Way Millsboro (19966) ***(G-4730)***
Maaco Auto Painting, Newark *Also called Jewell Enterprises Inc* ***(G-6837)***
Maaco Auto Painting, Dover *Also called Red Barn Inc* ***(G-2017)***
Maaco Collision Repr Auto Pntg, Dover *Also called Kpkm Inc* ***(G-1757)***
Maaco Collision Repr Auto Pntg, Dover *Also called Kns09 Inc* ***(G-1756)***
Maaco Collision Repr Auto Pntg.....610 628-3867
2400 Northeast Blvd Wilmington (19802) ***(G-11475)***
Maalika K LLC.....844 622-5452
35 Stature Dr Newark (19713) ***(G-6969)***
Maan Softwares Inc.....531 203-9141
16192 Coastal Hwy Lewes (19958) ***(G-3615)***
Mabel R Cole.....302 378-2792
139 Wellington Way Middletown (19709) ***(G-4139)***
Mac Contractors Inc.....302 653-5765
131 Dodge Dr Smyrna (19977) ***(G-8678)***
Macan Manufacturing, Milton *Also called Jaco LLC* ***(G-4920)***
Maccari Companies Inc (PA).....302 994-9628
1700 First State Blvd Wilmington (19804) ***(G-11476)***
Macelree & Harvey Ltd.....302 654-4454
5721 Kennett Pike Wilmington (19807) ***(G-11477)***
Macfarlane A Radford MD PA.....302 633-6338
203 W Pembrey Dr Wilmington (19803) ***(G-11478)***
Machine Learning Systems LLC.....302 299-2621
123 Odyssey Dr Wilmington (19808) ***(G-11479)***
Macintosh Engineering Inc.....302 252-9200
2 Mill Rd Ste 100 Wilmington (19806) ***(G-11480)***
Mack Construction & Handy.....302 337-3448
3100 Craft Rd Bridgeville (19933) ***(G-491)***
Mackeys Complete Cnstr Co, Wilmington *Also called Lavond Mackey* ***(G-11338)***
Macklyn Home Care.....302 690-9397
5179 W Woodmill Dr Wilmington (19808) ***(G-11481)***
Macklyn Home Care.....302 253-8208
6 W Market St Georgetown (19947) ***(G-2594)***
Mackmetts Auto Body.....302 366-8107
300 Saw Mill Branch Rd Townsend (19734) ***(G-8807)***
Macknett's Body Shop, Townsend *Also called Mackmetts Auto Body* ***(G-8807)***
Macknife Specialties, Hockessin *Also called Macknyfe Specialties* ***(G-3084)***
Macknyfe Specialties.....302 239-4904
862 Auburn Mill Rd Hockessin (19707) ***(G-3084)***
Mad Delaware Chapter.....910 284-6286
34013 Woodland Cir Lewes (19958) ***(G-3616)***
Maddox Concrete Co Inc (PA).....302 656-2000
11 Millside Dr Wilmington (19801) ***(G-11482)***
Made By Tilde Inc.....302 766-7215
2035 Sunset Lake Rd B2 Newark (19702) ***(G-6970)***
Made Just For You, Middletown *Also called Debbie Gill* ***(G-4023)***

ALPHABETIC SECTION
Manufacturers & Traders Tr Co

Madison Adoption Associates (PA) 302 475-8977
1102 Society Dr Claymont (19703) ***(G-778)***
Madrona Labs Inc 216 375-1978
1209 N Orange St Wilmington (19801) ***(G-11483)***
Maestrik Inc 312 925-3116
2035 Sunset Lake Rd D2 Newark (19702) ***(G-6971)***
Maf Industries 302 249-1254
27797 Oneals Rd Seaford (19973) ***(G-8299)***
Mag Towing 302 462-5686
35001 Roxana Rd Frankford (19945) ***(G-2371)***
Magellan Midstream Partners LP 302 654-3717
1050 Christiana Ave Ste A Wilmington (19801) ***(G-11484)***
Magen Tactical Defense 484 589-0670
2083 Philadelphia Pike Claymont (19703) ***(G-779)***
Magetti Gorup LLC 302 355-5540
2711 Centerville Rd # 120 Wilmington (19808) ***(G-11485)***
Maggio/Shields Teams 302 226-3770
70 Rehoboth Ave Ste 101 Rehoboth Beach (19971) ***(G-7994)***
Magic Canvas 302 312-4122
900 S Cass St Middletown (19709) ***(G-4140)***
Magic Car Wash Inc 302 479-5911
3221 Naamans Rd Wilmington (19810) ***(G-11486)***
Magic Office Supply, Dover *Also called Mark D Garrett* ***(G-1818)***
Magic Touch 302 655-6430
1707 New Castle Ave New Castle (19720) ***(G-5495)***
Magic Yrs Child Care Lrng Cntr 302 322-3102
327 Old State Rd New Castle (19720) ***(G-5496)***
Magneco LLC 302 613-0080
19c Trolley Sq Wilmington (19806) ***(G-11487)***
Magnus Environmental Corp 302 655-4443
220 Marsh Ln New Castle (19720) ***(G-5497)***
Magowi Consulting Group LLC 832 301-9230
262 Chapman Rd Ste 107 Newark (19702) ***(G-6972)***
Magron Inc 302 324-8094
31 Palmetto Dr New Castle (19720) ***(G-5498)***
Maguire & Sons Inc 302 798-1200
1035 Philadelphia Pike C Wilmington (19809) ***(G-11488)***
Maguire Pest Control, Wilmington *Also called Maguire & Sons Inc* ***(G-11488)***
Mahaffy & Associates Inc 302 656-8381
4 Brightham Ln Middletown (19709) ***(G-4141)***
Mahavir LLC 302 651-7995
111 S West St Wilmington (19801) ***(G-11489)***
Maichle S Heating Air 302 328-4822
105 J And M Dr New Castle (19720) ***(G-5499)***
Maid For Shore 302 344-1857
22 Chesterfield Dr Lewes (19958) ***(G-3617)***
Maids, Wilmington *Also called TMI Company Store Holding Corp* ***(G-12920)***
Maids, Wilmington *Also called J & W Mc Cormick Ltd* ***(G-11099)***
Maids For You Inc 302 328-9050
3 Scottie Ln New Castle (19720) ***(G-5500)***
Mail Box Outlet, New Castle *Also called True-Pack Ltd* ***(G-5798)***
Mail Center 302 422-2200
686 N Dupont Blvd Milford (19963) ***(G-4483)***
Mail Rooms Ltd 302 629-4838
500 Arbutus Ave Seaford (19973) ***(G-8300)***
Mail Stop 302 947-4704
24832 John J Williams Hwy # 1 Millsboro (19966) ***(G-4731)***
Maillie LLP 302 324-0780
15 Reads Way Ste 200 New Castle (19720) ***(G-5501)***
Main Event Inc 302 737-2225
2601 Eastburn Ctr Newark (19711) ***(G-6973)***
Main Gate Laundry 302 998-9949
123 Kirkwood Sq Wilmington (19808) ***(G-11490)***
Main Light Industries Inc 302 998-8017
1614 Newport Gap Pike Wilmington (19808) ***(G-11491)***
Main Office Inc 302 732-3460
32096 Sussex St Dagsboro (19939) ***(G-916)***
Main Street Fmly Chiropractic 302 737-8667
280 E Main St Ste 111 Newark (19711) ***(G-6974)***
Main Towers, Newark *Also called Leon N Weiner & Associates Inc* ***(G-6932)***
Main Towers Apartments, Wilmington *Also called Main Towers Assoicates LP* ***(G-11492)***
Main Towers Assoicates LP 302 761-7327
4 Denny Rd Wilmington (19809) ***(G-11492)***
Main Twers Prsrvtion Assoc LLC 302 737-9574
330 E Main St Newark (19711) ***(G-6975)***
Mainline Masonry Inc 302 998-2499
415 Boxwood Ln Middletown (19709) ***(G-4142)***
Mainline Today, Wilmington *Also called Suburban Publishing Inc* ***(G-12788)***
MainStay Suites 302 678-8383
201 Stover Blvd Dover (19901) ***(G-1811)***
Maintenance Tech 302 322-6410
10 Strawbridge Ave New Castle (19720) ***(G-5502)***
Maintenance Troubleshooti 302 477-1045
2917 Cheshire Rd Wilmington (19810) ***(G-11493)***
Maintenance Troubleshooting 302 692-0871
2860 Ogletown Rd Newark (19713) ***(G-6976)***
Maitland Australian, Wilmington *Also called Austrlian Phystherapy Ctrs Ltd* ***(G-9185)***
Majalco LLC 703 507-5298
1013 Centre Rd Ste 403a Wilmington (19805) ***(G-11494)***
Majdell Group USA Inc 302 722-8223
40 E Main St 790 Newark (19711) ***(G-6977)***
Majestique Ventures & Hlth Cre 302 633-4010
4708 Kirkwood Hwy Ste D Wilmington (19808) ***(G-11495)***
Majo Hair Studio, Wilmington *Also called Sylvia Saienna* ***(G-12829)***
Makave International Trdg LLC 302 288-0670
8 The Grn Ste A Dover (19901) ***(G-1812)***
Make Wave 302 422-1247
628 Mlford Harrington Hwy Milford (19963) ***(G-4484)***
Makeshopncompany Inc 302 999-9961
312 Cherry Ln Ste 300 New Castle (19720) ***(G-5503)***
Makk-O Industries Inc 302 376-0160
4640 Dupont Pkwy Townsend (19734) ***(G-8808)***
Mako Swim Club LLC 631 682-2131
P.O. Box 231 Harbeson (19951) ***(G-2790)***
Malek Abdollah Dr 302 994-8492
1 Centurian Dr Ste 301 Newark (19713) ***(G-6978)***
Malgiero Helen A Day Care 302 834-9060
311 Monroe St Delaware City (19706) ***(G-960)***
Malik John S Atty At Law 302 427-2247
100 E 14th St Wilmington (19801) ***(G-11496)***
Maliks Auto Repair 302 325-2555
95 Christiana Rd New Castle (19720) ***(G-5504)***
Malins Jim E Plumbing & Htg 302 239-2755
538 Basher Ln Hockessin (19707) ***(G-3085)***
Mallard Advisors LLC 302 239-1654
7234 Lancaster Pike 220a Hockessin (19707) ***(G-3086)***
Mallard Advisors LLC (PA) 302 737-4546
750 Barksdale Rd Ste 3 Newark (19711) ***(G-6979)***
Mallerd Lakes 443 783-2993
37976 Pelican Ln Selbyville (19975) ***(G-8514)***
Malmberg Firm, The, Dover *Also called Young and Malmberg PA* ***(G-2247)***
Malvern Federal Savings Bank 302 477-7305
10 W Rockland Rd Montchanin (19710) ***(G-4986)***
Mamie Sturgis Handy Day Care 302 875-4703
31732 Old Stage Rd Laurel (19956) ***(G-3260)***
Mammele's Paint Stores, Wilmington *Also called Mammeles Inc* ***(G-11497)***
Mammeles Inc (PA) 302 998-0541
2300 Kirkwood Hwy Wilmington (19805) ***(G-11497)***
Man Maid Cleaning Inc 302 226-5050
29 Fox Creek Dr Rehoboth Beach (19971) ***(G-7995)***
Management Associates Inc 302 652-3991
613 N Washington St Wilmington (19801) ***(G-11498)***
Management Options Inc 302 234-0836
4142 Ogletown Stanton Rd Newark (19713) ***(G-6980)***
Management Pain LLC 302 543-5180
5231 W Woodmill Dr Ste 45 Wilmington (19808) ***(G-11499)***
Mancor US Inc 302 573-3858
1011 Centre Rd Ste 322 Wilmington (19805) ***(G-11500)***
Maneto Inc (HQ) 302 656-4285
103 Foulk Rd Wilmington (19803) ***(G-11501)***
Mangrove Holdings LLC 305 587-2950
1000 N West St Ste 1200 Wilmington (19801) ***(G-11502)***
Manley Hvac Inc 302 998-4654
3705 Wild Cherry Ln Wilmington (19808) ***(G-11503)***
Manlove Auto Parts, Smyrna *Also called Fisher Auto Parts Inc* ***(G-8635)***
Manlove Auto Parts, Georgetown *Also called Fisher Auto Parts Inc* ***(G-2533)***
Manlove Auto Parts, Wilmington *Also called Fisher Auto Parts Inc* ***(G-10562)***
Mann & Moore Associates, Rehoboth Beach *Also called Century 21 Mann & Sons* ***(G-7886)***
Manning Gross + Massenburg LLP 302 657-2100
1007 N Orange St Apt 1051 Wilmington (19801) ***(G-11504)***
Manor Exxon Inc 302 834-6691
131 W Savannah Dr Bear (19701) ***(G-243)***
Manor House 302 629-4368
1001 Middleford Rd Seaford (19973) ***(G-8301)***
Manorcare Hlth Svcs Pike Creek, Wilmington *Also called Hcr Manorcare Med Svcs Fla LLC* ***(G-10863)***
Manpowergroup Inc 302 674-8600
1012 College Rd Dover (19904) ***(G-1813)***
Mantech, Dover *Also called Applied Research Assoc Inc* ***(G-1133)***
Mantikote Podiaky, Seaford *Also called James F Palmer* ***(G-8277)***
Manufacturers & Traders Tr Co 302 644-9930
1515 Savannah Rd Ste 103 Lewes (19958) ***(G-3618)***
Manufacturers & Traders Tr Co 302 856-4410
22205 Dupont Blvd Georgetown (19947) ***(G-2595)***
Manufacturers & Traders Tr Co 302 855-2184
107 Front St Milton (19968) ***(G-4930)***
Manufacturers & Traders Tr Co 302 651-1618
82 E Main St Newark (19711) ***(G-6981)***
Manufacturers & Traders Tr Co 302 856-4470
509 W Stein Hwy Seaford (19973) ***(G-8302)***
Manufacturers & Traders Tr Co 302 539-3471
33364 S Pennsylvania Ave Bethany Beach (19930) ***(G-412)***
Manufacturers & Traders Tr Co 302 651-8738
3801 Kennett Pike Wilmington (19807) ***(G-11505)***
Manufacturers & Traders Tr Co 302 285-3277
399 E Main St Middletown (19709) ***(G-4143)***
Manufacturers & Traders Tr Co 302 472-3233
2301 Concord Pike Wilmington (19803) ***(G-11506)***

ALPHABETIC

Manufacturers & Traders Tr Co............302 472-3262
3503 Philadelphia Pike Claymont (19703) ***(G-780)***
Manufacturers & Traders Tr Co............302 735-2010
139 S State St Dover (19901) ***(G-1814)***
Manufacturers & Traders Tr Co............302 472-3141
1309 Kirkwood Hwy Wilmington (19805) ***(G-11507)***
Manufacturers & Traders Tr Co............302 855-2160
673 N Dupont Blvd Milford (19963) ***(G-4485)***
Manufacturers & Traders Tr Co............302 651-1757
2371 Limestone Rd Wilmington (19808) ***(G-11508)***
Manufacturers & Traders Tr Co............302 651-1803
1812 Marsh Rd Wilmington (19810) ***(G-11509)***
Manufacturers & Traders Tr Co............302 651-1544
100 N James St Wilmington (19804) ***(G-11510)***
Manufacturers & Traders Tr Co............302 656-1260
1207 N Union St Wilmington (19806) ***(G-11511)***
Manufacturers & Traders Tr Co............302 472-3161
15 W Lea Blvd Wilmington (19802) ***(G-11512)***
Manufacturers & Traders Tr Co............302 477-1761
5107 Concord Pike Wilmington (19803) ***(G-11513)***
Manufacturers & Traders Tr Co............302 472-3177
151 Lantana Dr Hockessin (19707) ***(G-3087)***
Manufacturers & Traders Tr Co............302 651-8828
10 Foxhunt Dr Bear (19701) ***(G-244)***
Manufacturers & Traders Tr Co............302 855-2227
302 Rehoboth Ave Rehoboth Beach (19971) ***(G-7996)***
Manufacturers & Traders Tr Co............302 651-1000
301 W 11th St Wilmington (19801) ***(G-11514)***
Manufacturers & Traders Tr Co............302 855-2873
101 W Market St Laurel (19956) ***(G-3261)***
Manufacturers & Traders Tr Co............302 934-2400
499 Mitchell St Millsboro (19966) ***(G-4732)***
Manufacturers & Traders Tr Co............302 856-4405
7 W Market St Georgetown (19947) ***(G-2596)***
Manufacturers & Traders Tr Co............302 449-2780
405 W Main St Middletown (19709) ***(G-4144)***
Manufacturers & Traders Tr Co............302 855-2891
28529 Dupont Blvd Millsboro (19966) ***(G-4733)***
Manufacturers & Traders Tr Co............302 541-8700
204 Atlantic Ave Millville (19967) ***(G-4848)***
Manufacturers & Traders Tr Co............302 472-3335
550 Suburban Dr Newark (19711) ***(G-6982)***
Manufacturers & Traders Tr Co............302 292-6060
102 Astro Shopping Ctr Newark (19711) ***(G-6983)***
Manufacturers & Traders Tr Co............302 855-2283
670 N Dual Hwy Seaford (19973) ***(G-8303)***
Manufacturers & Traders Tr Co............302 735-2075
1001 Walker Rd Dover (19904) ***(G-1815)***
Manufacturers & Traders Tr Co............302 472-3249
287 Christiana Rd Ste 16 New Castle (19720) ***(G-5505)***
Manufacturers & Traders Tr Co............302 855-2297
38716 Sussex Hwy Delmar (19940) ***(G-1018)***
Manufacturers & Traders Tr Co............302 636-6000
1100 N Market St Wilmington (19801) ***(G-11515)***
Manufacturers & Traders Tr Co............302 472-3309
4899 Limestone Rd Wilmington (19808) ***(G-11516)***
Manufacturers & Traders Tr Co............302 735-2020
1001 E Lebanon Rd Dover (19901) ***(G-1816)***
Manufctured Hsing Concepts LLC............302 934-8848
28862 Dupont Blvd Millsboro (19966) ***(G-4734)***
Manveen Duggal MD............302 734-5438
874 Walker Rd Ste B Dover (19904) ***(G-1817)***
Maples Fiduciary Svcs Del Inc............302 338-9130
4001 Kennett Pike Ste 302 Wilmington (19807) ***(G-11517)***
Mapleton Square Apartments, Dover *Also called West Minister Management* ***(G-2215)***
Maplewood Dental Associates, Rehoboth Beach *Also called Conley & Wright DDS* ***(G-7900)***
Maplewood Home Owners Clubhous............302 645-9925
12 Vassar Dr Rehoboth Beach (19971) ***(G-7997)***
Mara Labs Inc............650 564-4971
1013 Centre Rd Ste 403b Wilmington (19805) ***(G-11518)***
Marble City Software Inc............302 658-2583
1900 Gilpin Ave Wilmington (19806) ***(G-11519)***
Marble Source Unlimited Inc............302 337-7665
18089 Sussex Hwy Bridgeville (19933) ***(G-492)***
Marc Wsburg Lpcmh Mntal Hlth C............302 798-4400
1201 Philadelphia Pike Wilmington (19809) ***(G-11520)***
March of Dimes Inc............302 225-1020
236 N James St Ste C Wilmington (19804) ***(G-11521)***
Marcus Materials Co............302 731-7519
9 Renee Ct Newark (19711) ***(G-6984)***
Mardlantic Machinery, Laurel *Also called F and M Equipment Ltd* ***(G-3229)***
Margaret Harris-Nemtuda............302 477-5500
3513 Concord Pike # 1000 Wilmington (19803) ***(G-11522)***
Margaret Keith's Draperies, Wilmington *Also called Vertical Blind Factory Inc* ***(G-13067)***
Margaret M Munley DDS............302 475-2626
2004 Foulk Rd Ste 2 Wilmington (19810) ***(G-11523)***
Margherita Vincent & Anthony............302 834-9023
5 Misty Ct Newark (19702) ***(G-6985)***
Margolis Edelstein............302 888-1112
300 Delaware Ave Ste 800 Wilmington (19801) ***(G-11524)***
Maria Lazar MD............302 838-2210
1400 Peoples Plz Ste 305 Newark (19702) ***(G-6986)***
Mariachi House............302 635-7361
7313 Lancaster Pike Ste 3 Hockessin (19707) ***(G-3088)***
Marier, Robert P DDS, Milford *Also called Emory & Marier PA* ***(G-4405)***
Marin Bayard............302 658-4200
521 N West St Wilmington (19801) ***(G-11525)***
Marina Suites, Rehoboth Beach *Also called Marshall Hotels & Resorts Inc* ***(G-8000)***
Marine Corps United States............302 376-3590
705 N Broad St Middletown (19709) ***(G-4145)***
Marine Lubricants Inc............302 429-7570
1130 E 7th St Wilmington (19801) ***(G-11526)***
Mariner Finance LLC............302 628-3970
22826 Sussex Hwy Seaford (19973) ***(G-8304)***
Mariner Finance LLC............302 384-6047
3616 Kirkwood Hwy Wilmington (19808) ***(G-11527)***
Mariner's Cove, Millsboro *Also called Equity Lifestyle Prpts Inc* ***(G-4686)***
Mariners Court Condo Assn............443 742-7812
4 Laurel St Rehoboth Beach (19971) ***(G-7998)***
Marinhrdwremfg/Forcebeyond Inc............302 691-4787
201 Ruthar Dr Ste 2 Newark (19711) ***(G-6987)***
Marinis Bros Inc............302 322-9663
755 Grantham Ln New Castle (19720) ***(G-5506)***
Marino & Sons, New Castle *Also called Amer Masonry T A Marino* ***(G-5030)***
Mario F Medori Inc............302 239-4550
20 Millside Dr Wilmington (19801) ***(G-11528)***
Mario Medori Inc............302 656-8432
20 Millside Dr Wilmington (19801) ***(G-11529)***
Marita F Fallorina MD............302 322-0660
1 Catherine St Ste 1 # 1 New Castle (19720) ***(G-5507)***
Marjam Supply Co Inc............302 283-1020
200 Bellevue Rd Newark (19713) ***(G-6988)***
Marjano LLC............302 454-7446
14 Orchid Dr Bear (19701) ***(G-245)***
Mark A Fortunato............302 477-4900
1415 Foulk Rd Wilmington (19803) ***(G-11530)***
Mark B Brown DDS............302 537-1200
32895 Coastal Hwy # 102 Bethany Beach (19930) ***(G-413)***
Mark C Gladnick DDS............302 994-2660
5513 Kirkwood Hwy Wilmington (19808) ***(G-11531)***
Mark D Garrett............302 674-2825
4 Michael Ct Dover (19904) ***(G-1818)***
Mark Glassner MD............302 369-9002
324 E Main St Ste 202 Newark (19711) ***(G-6989)***
Mark IV Beauty Salon Inc............302 737-4994
240 College Sq Newark (19711) ***(G-6990)***
Mark IV Hair Design, Newark *Also called Mark IV Beauty Salon Inc* ***(G-6990)***
Mark IV Transportation Co Inc............302 337-9898
617 Market St Bridgeville (19933) ***(G-493)***
Mark Menendez............302 644-8500
33759 Clay Rd Unit 2 Lewes (19958) ***(G-3619)***
Mark One LLC............302 735-4700
1700 E Lebanon Rd Dover (19901) ***(G-1819)***
Mark Penuel............302 856-7724
522 E Market St Georgetown (19947) ***(G-2597)***
Mark Showell Interiors Ltd............302 227-2272
59 Baltimore Ave Rehoboth Beach (19971) ***(G-7999)***
Mark Ventresca Associates Inc............302 239-3925
19 Bernard Blvd Hockessin (19707) ***(G-3089)***
Mark W Wingel............302 239-6200
724 Yorklyn Rd Ste 125 Hockessin (19707) ***(G-3090)***
Mark Wieczorek Dmd PC............302 838-3384
494 Bear Christiana Rd Bear (19701) ***(G-246)***
Mark Wilson Diguardi............302 897-6625
27046 Merchantman Dr Millsboro (19966) ***(G-4735)***
Markatos Cleaning Services, Wilmington *Also called Markatos Services Inc* ***(G-11532)***
Markatos Services Inc............302 792-0606
1411 Philadelphia Pike B Wilmington (19809) ***(G-11532)***
Markes International Inc............302 656-5500
270 Presidential Dr Wilmington (19807) ***(G-11533)***
Market Edge LLC (PA)............302 442-6800
1003 Park Pl Wilmington (19806) ***(G-11534)***
Market Keys LLC............205 800-0285
108 W 13th St Wilmington (19801) ***(G-11535)***
Market Street Center Inc............302 856-9024
9 Chestnut St Georgetown (19947) ***(G-2598)***
Market Street Preservation Inc............302 422-8255
977 E Masten Cir Milford (19963) ***(G-4486)***
Market Street Preservation LP............302 422-8255
977 E Masten Cir Milford (19963) ***(G-4487)***
Marketing Creators Inc............302 409-0344
802 N West St Wilmington (19801) ***(G-11536)***
Marketing Enterprise Capyuring............302 293-9250
1600 Desmond Rd Wilmington (19805) ***(G-11537)***
Marking Services Inc............302 478-0381
3505 Silverside Rd # 101 Wilmington (19810) ***(G-11538)***
Markizon Printing............610 715-7989
111 Nevada Ave Wilmington (19803) ***(G-11539)***
Marks ONeill OBrien Doher............302 658-6538
300 Delaware Ave Ste 900 Wilmington (19801) ***(G-11540)***

Marksman Embroidery.....302 223-6740
1312 Twin Willows Rd Smyrna (19977) ***(G-8679)***
Marlenka America LLC (PA).....502 530-0720
16192 Coastal Hwy Lewes (19958) ***(G-3620)***
Marlette Funding LLC.....302 358-2730
1523 Concord Pike Ste 201 Wilmington (19803) ***(G-11541)***
Marlette R Lofland.....302 628-1521
20255 Wilson Farm Rd Bridgeville (19933) ***(G-494)***
Marlex Pharmaceuticals Inc.....302 328-3355
65 Lukens Dr New Castle New Castle (19720) ***(G-5508)***
Marling's Emergency Water, New Castle *Also called Marlings Inc* ***(G-5509)***
Marlings Inc.....302 325-1759
710 Wilmington Rd New Castle (19720) ***(G-5509)***
Marlyn Meadow Arabians.....302 378-8642
1210 Sharp Ln Middletown (19709) ***(G-4146)***
Maron Mrvel Brdley Anderson PA (PA).....302 425-5177
1201 N Market St Ste 900 Wilmington (19801) ***(G-11542)***
Marosa Surgical Industries.....302 674-0907
243 Quigley Blvd Ste J New Castle (19720) ***(G-5510)***
Marriott, Wilmington *Also called Courtyard Management Corp* ***(G-9878)***
Marriott International Inc.....800 441-7048
400 David Hollowell Dr Newark (19716) ***(G-6991)***
Mars James Hitchens & Williams, Wilmington *Also called Morris James LLP* ***(G-11758)***
Marsh USA Inc.....302 888-4300
1201 N Market St Ste 500 Wilmington (19801) ***(G-11543)***
Marsha S Eddorlov.....302 994-4014
Heritage Prosessional Plz Wilmington (19808) ***(G-11544)***
Marshall Dennehey.....302 552-4300
1220 N Market St Ste 201 Wilmington (19801) ***(G-11545)***
Marshall Hotels & Resorts Inc.....302 227-1700
1115 Hwy One Rehoboth Beach (19971) ***(G-8000)***
Marshall T Williams MD PHD.....302 994-9692
537 Stanton Christiana Rd Newark (19713) ***(G-6992)***
Marshall Wagner & Associates.....302 227-2537
19643 Blue Bird Ln Unit 2 Rehoboth Beach (19971) ***(G-8001)***
Marsico & Weinstien DDS.....302 998-8474
2390 Limestone Rd Wilmington (19808) ***(G-11546)***
Marsico Weinstien, Wilmington *Also called Marsico & Weinstien DDS* ***(G-11546)***
Marta Biskup DDS.....302 478-0000
3522 Silverside Rd Wilmington (19810) ***(G-11547)***
Marta Blackhurst DMD.....302 478-1504
3522 Silverside Rd Wilmington (19810) ***(G-11548)***
Marta Group.....302 737-2008
885 Marrows Rd Apt D6 Newark (19713) ***(G-6993)***
Martel & Son Foreign Car Ctr.....302 674-5556
1161 Horsepond Rd Dover (19901) ***(G-1820)***
Martel Inc.....302 744-9566
4608 S Dupont Hwy Ste 1 Dover (19901) ***(G-1821)***
Marthann Print Center LLC.....267 884-8130
1130 Charles Dr Dover (19904) ***(G-1822)***
Marthin Luther Homes of Del, Newark *Also called Mosaic* ***(G-7062)***
Martial Industries LLC.....302 983-5742
526 Barrymore Pkwy Middletown (19709) ***(G-4147)***
Martin Construction Svcs LLC.....302 200-0885
340 W Chestnut Hill Rd Newark (19713) ***(G-6994)***
Martin Daniel D & Assoc LLC.....302 658-2884
1301 N Harrison St Wilmington (19806) ***(G-11549)***
Martin Dealership.....302 738-5200
298 E Cleveland Ave Newark (19711) ***(G-6995)***
Martin Grey LLC.....302 990-0675
16192 Coastal Hwy Lewes (19958) ***(G-3621)***
Martin Honda, Newark *Also called Martin Newark Dealership Inc* ***(G-6996)***
Martin J Burke Inc.....302 741-2638
22 N Sandpiper Dr Dover (19901) ***(G-1823)***
Martin Luther Homes, Bear *Also called Lauren Farms Group Home* ***(G-230)***
Martin Luther Homes East Inc.....302 475-4920
2412 Grubb Rd Wilmington (19810) ***(G-11550)***
Martin Newark Dealership Inc.....302 454-9300
298 E Cleveland Ave Newark (19711) ***(G-6996)***
Martinelli Holdings LLC (PA).....302 656-1809
3301 Lancaster Pike 5c Wilmington (19805) ***(G-11551)***
Martins Landscaping LLC.....302 984-2887
703 Wilson Rd Wilmington (19803) ***(G-11552)***
Martom Landscaping Co Inc.....302 322-1920
1699 St Georges Bus Ctr Saint Georges (19733) ***(G-8128)***
Martys Contracting.....302 234-8690
1072 Yorklyn Rd Hockessin (19707) ***(G-3091)***
Maruko Holdings Usa LLC.....917 515-2776
16192 Coastal Hwy Lewes (19958) ***(G-3622)***
Marvel Agency Inc.....302 422-7844
15 N Walnut St Milford (19963) ***(G-4488)***
Marvel Portable Welding Inc.....302 732-9480
32887 Dupont Blvd Dagsboro (19939) ***(G-917)***
Marvi Cleaners Limited Inc.....302 764-3077
309 Philadelphia Pike Wilmington (19809) ***(G-11553)***
Marvin & Palmer Associates.....302 573-3570
200 Bellevue Pkwy Ste 220 Wilmington (19809) ***(G-11554)***
Mary Annes Landscaping Inc.....302 335-5433
96 Windward Dr Felton (19943) ***(G-2306)***
Mary Bryan Inc.....302 875-5099
4679 Old Sharptown Rd Laurel (19956) ***(G-3262)***
Mary Campbell Center Inc.....302 762-6025
4641 Weldin Rd Wilmington (19803) ***(G-11555)***
Mary Costas Woodworking.....302 227-6255
527 School Ln Rehoboth Beach (19971) ***(G-8002)***
Mary Dodson.....302 479-0100
1403 Foulk Rd Ste 105 Wilmington (19803) ***(G-11556)***
Mary E Herring Daycare Center.....302 652-5978
2450 N Market St Wilmington (19802) ***(G-11557)***
Mary Kobak MD.....302 623-0260
200 Hygeia Dr Newark (19713) ***(G-6997)***
Mary Mother of Hope House III, Wilmington *Also called Ministry of Caring Inc* ***(G-11709)***
Mary Sweeney-Lehr.....302 764-0589
3209 Coachman Rd Wilmington (19803) ***(G-11558)***
Mary Zieken.....302 475-6714
2080 Naamans Rd Wilmington (19810) ***(G-11559)***
Mary Ziomek DDS.....301 984-9646
317 Mariners Cir Milton (19968) ***(G-4931)***
Maryann K Bailey DDS.....302 655-5822
1802 W 4th St Wilmington (19805) ***(G-11560)***
Maryann Metrinko LLC.....410 643-1472
401 Samantha Dr Lewes (19958) ***(G-3623)***
MARYDALE RETIREMENT VILLAGE, Newark *Also called Catholic Mnstry To Elderly Inc* ***(G-6170)***
Maryland Agency Financial Grou.....410 420-8866
38781 Wilson Ave Selbyville (19975) ***(G-8515)***
Maryland Meadow Arabians, Middletown *Also called Marlyn Meadow Arabians* ***(G-4146)***
Maryland Park Apartments, Wilmington *Also called Westwood Properties Ltd* ***(G-13174)***
Maryruth L Nich.....302 623-1929
86 Omega Dr Newark (19713) ***(G-6998)***
Marys Little Lambs Daycare.....302 436-5796
31730 Phillips Rd Selbyville (19975) ***(G-8516)***
Masley Enterprises Inc.....302 427-9885
1601 Jessup St Wilmington (19802) ***(G-11561)***
Mason Building Group Inc.....302 292-0600
35 Albe Dr Newark (19702) ***(G-6999)***
Mass For The Homeless Inc.....302 368-1030
2817 Ambler Ct Wilmington (19808) ***(G-11562)***
Massage By Alicia.....352 401-4328
700 Garnet Rd Wilmington (19804) ***(G-11563)***
Masseys Landing Park Inc.....302 947-2600
20628 Long Beach Dr Millsboro (19966) ***(G-4736)***
Mast Harness Shop, Dover *Also called Andy Mast* ***(G-1125)***
Masten Insurance & Fincl Svcs, Georgetown *Also called Peninsula Health Alliance Inc* ***(G-2614)***
Master Industrical Catalog, Millsboro *Also called Lweco Group LLC* ***(G-4728)***
Master Interiors Inc (PA).....302 368-9361
113 Sandy Dr Newark (19713) ***(G-7000)***
Master Interiors Inc.....302 368-9361
160 Mullet Run Milford (19963) ***(G-4489)***
Master Klean Company.....302 539-4290
P.O. Box 1198 Bethany Beach (19930) ***(G-7802)***
Master Movers, Rehoboth Beach *Also called Walter Doring* ***(G-8107)***
Master Shower Doors, Newark *Also called R & J Taylor Inc* ***(G-7289)***
Master Sidlow & Associates PA.....302 384-9780
750 Prides Xing Ste 100 Newark (19713) ***(G-7001)***
Master Tech Inc.....302 832-1660
743 Rue Madora Bear (19701) ***(G-247)***
Master Tech Pnt Collision Ctr, Bear *Also called Master Tech Inc* ***(G-247)***
Master-Halco Inc.....302 475-6714
P.O. Box 1791 Wilmington (19899) ***(G-11564)***
Mastercraft Welding.....302 697-3932
4010 S Dupont Hwy Dover (19901) ***(G-1824)***
Mastercrafters Inc.....302 678-1470
1234 S Governors Ave A Dover (19904) ***(G-1825)***
Mastercuts.....302 674-0300
Dupont Hwy Dover Mall 8 Dover (19901) ***(G-1826)***
Mastermark Woodworking Inc.....302 945-9131
25205 Mastermark Ln Millsboro (19966) ***(G-4737)***
Mastriana Property Management.....302 234-4860
5500 Skyline Dr Ste 6 Wilmington (19808) ***(G-11565)***
Match Software, Wilmington *Also called Abcware LLC* ***(G-8900)***
Material Handling Supply Inc.....302 571-0176
243 Quigley Blvd Ste I New Castle (19720) ***(G-5511)***
Material Supply, New Castle *Also called Material Transit Inc* ***(G-5512)***
Material Supply Inc.....302 658-6524
924 S Heald St Wilmington (19801) ***(G-11566)***
Material Transit Inc.....302 395-0556
255 Airport Rd New Castle (19720) ***(G-5512)***
Maternity Associates PA.....302 478-7973
3524 Silverside Rd Ste 33 Wilmington (19810) ***(G-11567)***
Maternity Gynecology Assoc PA.....302 368-9000
4745 Ogletown Stanton Rd # 207 Newark (19713) ***(G-7002)***
Mathias, New Castle *Also called Staging Dimesions Inc* ***(G-5736)***
Matrix Rehabilitation Delaware.....302 424-1714
800 Airport Rd Ste 102 Milford (19963) ***(G-4490)***
Matt's Auto Care, Rehoboth Beach *Also called Wiedman Enterprises Inc* ***(G-8115)***

ALPHABETIC

Matt's Line Painting, Frankford *Also called Matts Management Family LLC* ***(G-2372)***
Matter Music Inc 650 793-7749
427 N Tatnall St 25426 Wilmington (19801) ***(G-11568)***
Mattern & Piccioni Md PA 302 730-8060
260 Beiser Blvd Ste 101 Dover (19904) ***(G-1827)***
Matthew Gotthold Dr 302 762-6222
1403 Foulk Rd Ste 103 Wilmington (19803) ***(G-11569)***
Matthew Gotthold Dr (PA) 302 762-6222
1409 Foulk Rd Ste 100 Wilmington (19803) ***(G-11570)***
Matthew J Mcllrath DC 302 798-7033
1201 Philadelphia Pike Wilmington (19809) ***(G-11571)***
Matthew Smith 302 654-4853
1810 W 4th St Wilmington (19805) ***(G-11572)***
Matthew Smith Bus Service 302 734-9311
206 N Queen St Dover (19904) ***(G-1828)***
Matthew W Lawrence Do 302 652-6050
1500 Shallcross Ave Wilmington (19806) ***(G-11573)***
Matthew's Formal Wear, Wilmington *Also called Matthew Smith* ***(G-11572)***
Matthews Pierce & Lloyd Inc (PA) 302 678-5500
830 Walker Rd Ste 12 Dover (19904) ***(G-1829)***
Matthews Towing & Recovery 302 463-1108
710 Black Diamond Rd Smyrna (19977) ***(G-8680)***
Matties Cleaning Service 302 229-3585
5 Sunset Ct Wilmington (19810) ***(G-11574)***
Mattleman Weinroth & Miller PC 302 731-8349
200 Continental Dr # 215 Newark (19713) ***(G-7003)***
Matts Fish Camp Lewes De LLC 302 539-4415
34401 Tenley Ct Lewes (19958) ***(G-3624)***
Matts Management Family LLC 302 732-3715
32397 Omar Rd Frankford (19945) ***(G-2372)***
Maude Burton 302 674-4210
657 Vista Ave Dover (19901) ***(G-1830)***
Maureen Freebery 302 234-7800
4801 Limestone Rd Wilmington (19808) ***(G-11575)***
Maureens Beauty Salon, Wilmington *Also called Maureen Freebery* ***(G-11575)***
Maureens For Men & Women 302 234-7800
4813 Limestone Rd Wilmington (19808) ***(G-11576)***
Maurten US Corporation 302 669-9085
1000 N West St Ste 1200 Wilmington (19801) ***(G-11577)***
Maven Security Consulting Inc 302 365-6862
512 Portrush Pass Bear (19701) ***(G-248)***
Maws Tails Mfg 302 740-7664
29621 Riverstone Dr Milton (19968) ***(G-4932)***
Mawuli Logistics LLC 302 544-5129
262 Chapman Rd 205-222 Newark (19702) ***(G-7004)***
Max One Printing 302 897-9050
310 Chattahoochee Dr Bear (19701) ***(G-249)***
Max RE Associates Inc 302 453-3200
228 Suburban Dr Newark (19711) ***(G-7005)***
Max RE Associates Inc (PA) 302 477-3900
3302 Concord Pike Wilmington (19803) ***(G-11578)***
Max RE Central 302 234-3800
1302 Old Lancaster Pike Hockessin (19707) ***(G-3092)***
Max Seal Inc 619 946-2650
16192 Coastal Hwy Lewes (19958) ***(G-3625)***
Max Virtual LLC 302 525-8112
40 E Main St 766 Newark (19711) ***(G-7006)***
Maxbright Inc 281 616-7999
16192 Coastal Hwy Lewes (19958) ***(G-3626)***
Maxillofacial Southern De Oral 302 644-2977
17605 Nassau Commons Blvd Lewes (19958) ***(G-3627)***
Maxim Hair & Nails LLC 410 920-8656
31225 Americana Pkwy # 7 Selbyville (19975) ***(G-8517)***
Maxim Healthcare Services Inc 302 478-3434
1523 Concord Pike Ste 100 Wilmington (19803) ***(G-11579)***
Maxines Daycare 302 652-7242
1027 Lancaster Ave Wilmington (19805) ***(G-11580)***
Maxines Hair Happenings Inc 302 875-4055
206 Laureltowne Laurel (19956) ***(G-3263)***
Maxwell Historic Preservation, Dagsboro *Also called Maxwell World* ***(G-918)***
Maxwell World (PA) 937 463-3579
29092a Piney Neck Rd Dagsboro (19939) ***(G-918)***
Mayfair Apartments, Wilmington *Also called Frankel Enterprises Inc* ***(G-10615)***
Mayjuun LLC (PA) 865 300-7738
16192 Coastal Hwy Lewes (19958) ***(G-3628)***
Mayse Painting & Contg LLC 443 553-6503
2250 Audubon Trl Middletown (19709) ***(G-4148)***
Mazindustries 302 292-3636
103 Greenfield Rd Newark (19713) ***(G-7007)***
Mazzola Construction, Newark *Also called Mazzola Systems Inc* ***(G-7008)***
Mazzola Systems Inc 302 738-6808
560 Peoples Plz Ste 112 Newark (19702) ***(G-7008)***
Mazzpac LLC 973 641-9159
94 Salem Church Rd Newark (19713) ***(G-7009)***
MB Aerospace Acp (PA) 586 772-2500
2711 Centerville Rd # 400 Wilmington (19808) ***(G-11581)***
MB Veterans Center LLC 302 384-2350
1405 Veale Rd Wilmington (19810) ***(G-11582)***
Mbanza Coffee Inc 813 403-8724
2035 Sunset Lake Rd Newark (19702) ***(G-7010)***
MBNA Bank Great Expectations, Newark *Also called Bright Horizons Chld Ctrs LLC* ***(G-6120)***
MBNA Marketing Systems Inc 302 456-8588
1100 N King St Wilmington (19884) ***(G-11583)***
Mc Cabe Enterprises Inc 302 436-5176
30175 Rabbit Naw Rd Selbyville (19975) ***(G-8518)***
Mc Ginnis Commercial RE 302 736-2700
555 E Loockerman St # 102 Dover (19901) ***(G-1831)***
Mc Mullen Septic Service Inc 302 629-6221
22593 Bridgeville Hwy Seaford (19973) ***(G-8305)***
MCB Landscaping LLC 215 421-1083
1020 Darley Rd Wilmington (19810) ***(G-11584)***
McBride and Ziegler Inc 302 737-9138
2607 Eastburn Ctr Newark (19711) ***(G-7011)***
McCabes Mechanical Service Inc 302 854-9001
16689 Seashore Hwy Georgetown (19947) ***(G-2599)***
McCall Brooks Insurance Agency 302 475-8200
1805 Foulk Rd Ste H Wilmington (19810) ***(G-11585)***
McCall Handling Co 302 846-2334
38431 Sussex Hwy Delmar (19940) ***(G-1019)***
McCarter & English LLP 302 984-6300
405 N King St Ste 800 Wilmington (19801) ***(G-11586)***
McCarter English, Wilmington *Also called Katharine L Mayer Atty* ***(G-11227)***
MCCARTNEY DEIRDE A, Lewes *Also called Deirde A McCartney* ***(G-3451)***
McClafferty Printing Company 302 652-8112
1600 N Scott St Wilmington (19806) ***(G-11587)***
McClain Custodial Service 302 645-6597
418 Burton Ave Lewes (19958) ***(G-3629)***
McClung-Logan Equipment Co Inc 302 337-3400
17941 Sussex Hwy Bridgeville (19933) ***(G-495)***
McComrick Insurance Services 302 732-6655
3394 N Main St Dagsboro (19939) ***(G-919)***
McConnell Bros Inc 302 218-4240
400 E Ayre St Wilmington (19804) ***(G-11588)***
McConnell Development Inc (PA) 302 428-0712
1201 N Market St Ste 400 Wilmington (19801) ***(G-11589)***
McConnell Johnson RE Co LLC 302 421-2000
1201 N Market St Ste 1605 Wilmington (19801) ***(G-11590)***
McCormick Assoc Middletown LLC 302 449-0710
5350 Summit Bridge Rd # 107 Middletown (19709) ***(G-4149)***
McCormick Contracting & Suppor 443 987-2099
200 Tyrone Ave Wilmington (19804) ***(G-11591)***
McCoy Enterprises, Newark *Also called Enhanced Corporate Prfmce LLC* ***(G-6529)***
McCracken M Jill, Wilmington *Also called Circle Veterinary Clinic* ***(G-9712)***
McCray Investments 302 836-8569
76 Three Rivers Dr Newark (19702) ***(G-7012)***
McCrea Equipment Company Inc 302 945-0821
22787 Dozer Ln Unit 2 Harbeson (19951) ***(G-2791)***
McCrery Funeral Homes Inc 302 478-2204
3924 Concord Pike Wilmington (19803) ***(G-11592)***
McDaniel Plumbing & Heating 302 322-3075
106 Rowland Park Blvd Wilmington (19803) ***(G-11593)***
McDonald Safety Equipment Inc 302 999-0151
581 Copper Dr Wilmington (19804) ***(G-11594)***
McDonalds 302 674-2095
1424 Forrest Ave Dover (19904) ***(G-1832)***
McElroy & Son Inc 302 995-2623
15 E Edmont Rd Wilmington (19804) ***(G-11595)***
McGinnis Commercial RE Co, Dover *Also called Mc Ginnis Commercial RE* ***(G-1831)***
McGinnis Farms LLC 302 841-8175
32738 Dupont Blvd Dagsboro (19939) ***(G-920)***
McGivney Kluger & Cook PC 302 656-1200
1201 N Orange St Ste 504 Wilmington (19801) ***(G-11596)***
McGraphix Advertising Products, Selbyville *Also called Midnight Blue Inc* ***(G-8522)***
McHugh Electric Inc 302 995-9091
100 Cassidy Dr Ste 105 Wilmington (19804) ***(G-11597)***
MCI Communications Corporation 302 791-4900
200 Bellevue Pkwy Ste 500 Wilmington (19809) ***(G-11598)***
MCI LLC 302 407-5034
452 E Ayre St Wilmington (19804) ***(G-11599)***
MCI LLC (PA) 302 293-0028
2102 Kirkwood Hwy Wilmington (19805) ***(G-11600)***
McKelvey Hires Dry Cleaning 302 998-9191
808 First State Blvd Wilmington (19804) ***(G-11601)***
McKenzie Paving Inc 302 376-8560
114 Bakerfield Dr Middletown (19709) ***(G-4150)***
McKie Foundation, The, Newark *Also called New Vision Services Inc* ***(G-7108)***
McLaughlin Gordon L Law Office 302 651-7979
1203 N Orange St Wilmington (19801) ***(G-11602)***
McLaughlin Morton Holdg Co LLC 302 426-1313
1203 N Orange St Fl 2 Wilmington (19801) ***(G-11603)***
McLeen Properties 302 482-1486
240 N James St Ste 100c Wilmington (19804) ***(G-11604)***
McMahon Heating & AC 302 945-4300
20378 John J Williams Hwy Lewes (19958) ***(G-3630)***
McNeil and Fmly MGT Group LLC 302 830-3267
2 White Oak Rd Wilmington (19809) ***(G-11605)***
McNeil Paving 302 945-7131
32758 Spring Water Dr Millsboro (19966) ***(G-4738)***

McNichol Enterprises Inc (PA) 302 633-9348
1106 Elderon Dr Wilmington (19808) *(G-11606)*
MCS, Wilmington *Also called Medical Copy Services (G-11616)*
McSglobal Inc 302 427-6970
1220 N Market St Wilmington (19801) *(G-11607)*
McShares Inc 302 656-3168
2207 Concord Pike 407 Wilmington (19803) *(G-11608)*
MD Freight & Logistics LLC 804 347-1196
8 The Grn Ste A Dover (19901) *(G-1833)*
Mda Lending Solutions Inc 302 433-8006
5300 Brandywine Pkwy # 100 Wilmington (19803) *(G-11609)*
Mdm Hair Studio 302 312-6052
187 Gloucester Blvd Middletown (19709) *(G-4151)*
Mdm McHncal Instlltion USA LLC 617 938-9634
1201 N Orange St Ste 700 Wilmington (19801) *(G-11610)*
Mdnewsline Inc 773 759-4363
28 Old Rudnick Ln Dover (19901) *(G-1834)*
Meade Inc 302 262-3394
22536 Sussex Hwy Seaford (19973) *(G-8306)*
Meadowbrook Golf Group Inc 302 571-9041
800 N Dupont Rd Wilmington (19807) *(G-11611)*
Meadowood Mobil Station 302 731-5602
2650 Kirkwood Hwy Newark (19711) *(G-7013)*
Meadowwood Behavioral Health, New Castle *Also called Focus Health Care Delaware LLC (G-5322)*
Mealey Fnrl Homes & Crematory, Wilmington *Also called Michael A Mealey & Sons Inc (G-11655)*
Mealey Funeral Homes, Wilmington *Also called Michael A Mealey & Sons Inc (G-11654)*
Meals On Wheels Delaware Inc 302 656-6451
100 W 10th St Ste 207 Wilmington (19801) *(G-11612)*
Meals On Whels of Lwes Rhoboth 302 645-7449
32409 Lwes Georgetown Hwy Lewes (19958) *(G-3631)*
Mears Baseball Instruction 302 448-9713
24975 Radish Rd Millsboro (19966) *(G-4739)*
Mebro Inc 302 992-0104
225 N James St Wilmington (19804) *(G-11613)*
Mechanical Systems Intl Corp 302 453-8315
9 Lewis St Newark (19711) *(G-7014)*
Mechanics Paradise Inc 302 652-8863
2335 N Dupont Hwy New Castle (19720) *(G-5513)*
MED Transport LLC 513 257-7626
3524 Silverside Rd 35b Wilmington (19810) *(G-11614)*
Medevice Services LLC 877 202-1588
3500 S Dupont Hwy Dover (19901) *(G-1835)*
Medford, William L Jr MD, Wilmington *Also called Wilmington Otolrynglgy Assc (G-13239)*
Medi-Weightloss Clinics 302 763-3455
502 Lantana Dr Hockessin (19707) *(G-3093)*
Mediacom LLC 302 732-9332
32441 Royal Blvd Dagsboro (19939) *(G-921)*
Medibid 888 855-6334
2711 Centerville Rd Wilmington (19808) *(G-11615)*
Medical Aid Unit At Christiana, Newark *Also called Glasgow Medical Center LLC (G-6664)*
Medical Associates Bear Inc 302 832-6768
121 Becks Woods Dr # 100 Bear (19701) *(G-250)*
Medical Billing & MGT Svcs Inc (PA) 610 564-5314
111 Continental Dr # 101 Newark (19713) *(G-7015)*
Medical Center of Harrington 302 398-8704
203 Shaw Ave 205 Harrington (19952) *(G-2866)*
Medical Copy Services 302 654-4741
901 N Market St Ste 460 Wilmington (19801) *(G-11616)*
Medical Massage Delaware LLC (PA) 888 757-1951
254 Chapman Rd Ste 112 Newark (19702) *(G-7016)*
Medical Oncology Hematology 302 999-8095
4701 Ogltn Stntn Rd # 2200 Newark (19713) *(G-7017)*
Medical Reimbursement Sol 516 809-6812
29517 Glenwood Dr Millsboro (19966) *(G-4740)*
Medical Society of Delaware (PA) 302 366-1400
900 Prides Xing Newark (19713) *(G-7018)*
Medical Technologies Intl 760 837-4778
8 The Grn Ste 1 Dover (19901) *(G-1836)*
Medici Ventures Inc 801 319-7029
1209 N Orange St Wilmington (19801) *(G-11617)*
Medicine Woman 302 684-8048
503 Canning House Row Milton (19968) *(G-4933)*
Medictek Inc 302 351-4924
902 N Market St Apt 805 Wilmington (19801) *(G-11618)*
Mediguide America LLC (PA) 302 425-5900
4001 Kennett Pike Ste 218 Wilmington (19807) *(G-11619)*
Medimmune LLC 301 398-1200
1800 Concord Pike Wilmington (19897) *(G-11620)*
Meding & Son Seafood 302 335-3944
3697 Bay Rd Milford (19963) *(G-4491)*
Medlab Environmental Testing 302 655-5227
212 Cherry Ln New Castle (19720) *(G-5514)*
Medrep Inc 302 571-0263
903 Berkeley Rd Wilmington (19807) *(G-11621)*
Medtix LLC (PA) 302 645-8070
221 S Rehoboth Blvd Milford (19963) *(G-4492)*
Medtix LLC 302 265-4550
16337 Coastal Hwy Lewes (19958) *(G-3632)*
Medtix Medical Supply, Milford *Also called Medtix LLC (G-4492)*
Mefta LLC 804 433-3566
1220 N Market St Wilmington (19801) *(G-11622)*
Megan Hegenbarth 302 477-9872
6 Onyx Ct Wilmington (19810) *(G-11623)*
Megee Plumbing & Heating Co 302 856-6311
22965 Lwes Georgetown Hwy Georgetown (19947) *(G-2600)*
Megellan Terminal, Wilmington *Also called Magellan Midstream Partners LP (G-11484)*
Meghan House Inc 302 253-8261
210 Rosa St Georgetown (19947) *(G-2601)*
Mehar Investment Group LLC (PA) 302 999-1888
1624 Newport Gap Pike Wilmington (19808) *(G-11624)*
Meherrin AG & Chem Co 302 337-0330
18441 Wesley Church Rd Bridgeville (19933) *(G-496)*
Meineke Car Care Center, Dover *Also called Rbs Auto Repair Inc (G-2012)*
Meineke Car Care Center 302 995-2020
1512 Kirkwood Hwy Wilmington (19805) *(G-11625)*
Meineke Discount Mufflers, Claymont *Also called Wilcon North Inc (G-820)*
Meineke Discount Mufflers, Dover *Also called Daves Disc Mfflers of Dver De (G-1342)*
Meineke Discount Mufflers, Wilmington *Also called Meineke Car Care Center (G-11625)*
Melcar Underground Ltd 484 653-8259
16192 Coastal Hwy Lewes (19958) *(G-3633)*
Melchiorre and Melchiorre 302 645-6311
17352 Coastal Hwy Lewes (19958) *(G-3634)*
Melissa A Mackel Do 302 674-4070
655 S Bay Rd Ste 1f Dover (19901) *(G-1837)*
Melissa A Wolf 716 465-7093
18512 Belle Grove Rd # 6 Lewes (19958) *(G-3635)*
Mellon Private Wealth MGT 302 421-2306
4005 Kennett Pike Wilmington (19807) *(G-11626)*
Melody Entertainment USA Inc 305 505-7659
717 N Union St Apt 68 Wilmington (19805) *(G-11627)*
Melroys Furniture Refinishing 302 645-1856
20597 Mulberry Knoll Rd Lewes (19958) *(G-3636)*
Melson Funeral Services, Frankford *Also called A Douglas Melson (G-2344)*
Melson Funeral Services 302 945-9000
Longneck Rd Millsboro (19966) *(G-4741)*
Melson Funeral Services Ltd 302 732-9000
43 Thatcher St Frankford (19945) *(G-2373)*
Melsons Cape Hnlopen Crematory 302 537-2441
41 Thatcher St Frankford (19945) *(G-2374)*
Melsons Henlipen Creammatury, Frankford *Also called Melson Funeral Services Ltd (G-2373)*
Meltrone Inc 302 998-3457
5828 Kirkwood Hwy Wilmington (19808) *(G-11628)*
Melvin Funeral Home, Harrington *Also called Thomas E Melvin Son Inc (G-2899)*
Melvin L Joseph Cnstr Co 302 856-7396
25136 Dupont Blvd Georgetown (19947) *(G-2602)*
Melvin's Sunoco, Dover *Also called Lee Lynn Inc (G-1775)*
Memorial Super Fuel 215 512-1012
3006 New Castle Ave New Castle (19720) *(G-5515)*
Menchaca Building Corp 302 475-4581
4 Lloyd Pl Wilmington (19810) *(G-11629)*
Mend ME Massage Therapy Inc 302 229-1250
6 W Salisbury Dr Wilmington (19809) *(G-11630)*
Menno Freight Logistics LLC 302 229-8137
504 E Boxborough Dr Wilmington (19810) *(G-11631)*
Mennos Woodworks 302 381-5525
10147 Shawnee Rd Greenwood (19950) *(G-2751)*
Mental Health Assn In Del 302 654-6833
100 W 10th St Ste 600 Wilmington (19801) *(G-11632)*
Mentor Consultants Inc 610 566-4004
3200 Concord Pike Wilmington (19803) *(G-11633)*
Mentoris, Wilmington *Also called Clairvyant Technosolutions Inc (G-9728)*
Mera Rd 2 LLC 305 577-3443
251 Little Falls Dr Wilmington (19808) *(G-11634)*
Mera Usa LLC 305 577-3443
251 Little Falls Dr Wilmington (19808) *(G-11635)*
Merakey USA 302 325-3540
2 Penns Way New Castle (19720) *(G-5516)*
Mercantile Press Inc 302 764-6884
3007 Bellevue Ave Wilmington (19802) *(G-11636)*
Mercantile Processing Inc 302 524-8000
32695 Roxana Rd Millville (19967) *(G-4849)*
Mercer and Sydell Dental, Milton *Also called Mercer Dental Associates (G-4934)*
Mercer Dental Associates, Dover *Also called Thomas W Mercer DMD (G-2144)*
Mercer Dental Associates 302 664-1385
524 Union St Milton (19968) *(G-4934)*
Merck & Co Inc 410 860-2227
28387 Dupont Blvd Millsboro (19966) *(G-4742)*
Merck and Company Inc 302 934-8051
29160 Intervet Ln Millsboro (19966) *(G-4743)*
Merck Animal Health, Millsboro *Also called Merck and Company Inc (G-4743)*
Merck Holdings Inc., Wilmington *Also called Merck Holdings LLC (G-11637)*
Merck Holdings LLC 302 234-1401
5307 Limestone Rd Ste 200 Wilmington (19808) *(G-11637)*

A L P H A B E T I C

Mercy Inc 302 764-7781
218 W 35th St Wilmington (19802) *(G-11638)*

Mercy Land Academy Inc 302 378-2013
211 E Main St Middletown (19709) *(G-4152)*

Meredith Salvage 302 349-4776
12206 Woodbridge Rd Greenwood (19950) *(G-2752)*

Merestone Consultants Inc (PA) 302 992-7900
5215 W Woodmill Dr Ste 38 Wilmington (19808) *(G-11639)*

Merestone Consultants Inc 302 226-5880
33516 Crossing Ave Unit 1 Lewes (19958) *(G-3637)*

Merge Industrial Solutions LLC 302 400-2157
3500 S Dupont Hwy Dover (19901) *(G-1838)*

Mergers Acqstons Strtegies LLC (PA) 302 992-0400
5183 W Woodmill Dr Ste 3 Wilmington (19808) *(G-11640)*

Meridian Architects Engineers 302 643-9928
26412 Broadkill Rd Milton (19968) *(G-4935)*

Meridian Bank 302 477-9449
1601 Concord Pike Ste 45 Wilmington (19803) *(G-11641)*

Meridian Limo LLC 800 462-1550
8 The Grn Dover (19901) *(G-1839)*

Merion Realty Services LLC 302 656-8543
1303 Delaware Ave Wilmington (19806) *(G-11642)*

Meris Gardens Bed & Breakfast 302 752-4962
33309 Kent Ave Bethany Beach (19930) *(G-414)*

Merit Construction Engineers 302 992-9810
5700 Kirkwood Hwy Ste 201 Wilmington (19808) *(G-11643)*

Merit Construction Engineers 302 992-9810
1605 E Ayre St Wilmington (19804) *(G-11644)*

Merit Mechanical Co Inc 302 366-8601
39 Albe Dr Newark (19702) *(G-7019)*

Merit Services Inc 302 366-8601
39 Albe Dr Newark (19702) *(G-7020)*

Merix LLC (PA) 425 659-1425
16192 Coastal Hwy Lewes (19958) *(G-3638)*

Merman Management Inc 302 456-9904
5145 W Woodmill Dr 22 Wilmington (19808) *(G-11645)*

Mernies Market 302 629-9877
4610 Woodland Church Rd Seaford (19973) *(G-8307)*

Merrill Lynch Pierce Fenner 302 736-7700
55 Kings Hwy Dover (19901) *(G-1840)*

Merrill Lynch Pierce Fenner 302 571-5100
1201 N Market St Ste 2000 Wilmington (19801) *(G-11646)*

Merrill Lynch Pierce Fenner 302 227-5159
19535 Carmelot Dr Rehoboth Beach (19971) *(G-8003)*

Merritt Marine Cnstr Inc 302 436-2881
32992 Lighthouse Rd Selbyville (19975) *(G-8519)*

Merry Maids Inc 302 698-9038
753 Walker Rd Ste A Dover (19904) *(G-1841)*

Messer LLC 302 798-9342
6000 Philadelphia Pike Claymont (19703) *(G-781)*

Messick & Gray Cnstr Inc (PA) 302 337-8777
9003 Fawn Rd Bridgeville (19933) *(G-497)*

Messick & Gray Cnstr Inc 302 337-8445
17016 N Main St Bridgeville (19933) *(G-498)*

Messick and Johnson LLc 302 628-3111
955 Norman Eskridge Hwy Seaford (19973) *(G-8308)*

Messick Signs & Service 302 629-6999
7684 Gum Branch Rd Seaford (19973) *(G-8309)*

Messicks Mobile Homes Inc 302 398-9166
17959 S Dupont Hwy Harrington (19952) *(G-2867)*

Messina Charles Plbg & Elc Co 302 674-5696
3681 S Little Creek Rd Dover (19901) *(G-1842)*

Meta Galaxic Publishing Inc 302 245-7939
2711 Centerville Rd # 1205323 Wilmington (19808) *(G-11647)*

Metal Msters Fdservice Eqp Inc (PA) 302 653-3000
100 Industrial Blvd Clayton (19938) *(G-863)*

Metal Partners International, New Castle Also called *Metal Partners Rebar LLC (G-5517)*

Metal Partners Rebar LLC 215 791-3491
20 Davidson Ln New Castle (19720) *(G-5517)*

Metal Shop 302 846-2988
10690 Allens Mill Rd Delmar (19940) *(G-1020)*

Metal Systems Div, Seaford Also called *Lab Products Inc (G-8288)*

Metal-Tech Inc 302 322-7770
265 Airport Rd New Castle (19720) *(G-5518)*

Metaquotes Software Corp 657 859-6918
602 Rockwood Rd Wilmington (19802) *(G-11648)*

Metatron Inc (PA) 619 550-4668
160 Greentree Dr Ste 101 Dover (19904) *(G-1843)*

Meter Service, Newark Also called *Hillside Oil Company Inc (G-6729)*

Meterpro Services Inc 302 227-8596
112 Stockley St Rehoboth Beach (19971) *(G-8004)*

Methodist Action Program, Wilmington Also called *Methodist Mission and Church E (G-11649)*

Methodist Mission and Church E 302 225-5862
1218 B St Wilmington (19801) *(G-11649)*

Meticulous Maids, The, Wilmington Also called *Harmon Investments LLC (G-10837)*

MetLife, Wilmington Also called *American Life Insurance Co (G-9053)*

MetLife, Newark Also called *Metropolitan Life Insur Co (G-7021)*

MetLife, Dover Also called *Metropolitan Life Insur Co (G-1844)*

Metrie Inc 302 337-0269
617 Market St Unit 4 Bridgeville (19933) *(G-499)*

Metrinko Office Interiors, Lewes Also called *Maryann Metrinko LLC (G-3623)*

Metro Merchant Services, Wilmington Also called *Delaware Merchant Services (G-10066)*

Metro Steel Incorporated 302 778-2288
4049 New Castle Ave New Castle (19720) *(G-5519)*

Metropltan Wlmngton Urban Leag 302 778-8300
100 W 10th St Ste 710 Wilmington (19801) *(G-11650)*

Metropolitan Life Insur Co 302 738-0888
111 Continental Dr # 305 Newark (19713) *(G-7021)*

Metropolitan Life Insur Co 302 734-5803
160 Greentree Dr Ste 105 Dover (19904) *(G-1844)*

Metropolitan Revenue Assoc LLC 302 449-7490
29 E Commons Blvd Ste 100 New Castle (19720) *(G-5520)*

Meyer & Meyer Inc 302 994-9600
2706 Kirkwood Hwy Wilmington (19805) *(G-11651)*

Meyer & Meyer Reatly, Wilmington Also called *Meyer & Meyer Inc (G-11651)*

Mf Stoneworks LLC 302 265-7732
23844 Dakotas Reach Milton (19968) *(G-4936)*

Mgj Enterprises Inc 866 525-8529
4023 Kennett Pike 624 Wilmington (19807) *(G-11652)*

Mgl Screen Printing 302 450-6250
47 S Longwood Ln Clayton (19938) *(G-864)*

Mgza, Wilmington Also called *Zahn Incorporated (G-13339)*

Mh Custom Cabinets 302 422-7082
624 Marshall St Milford (19963) *(G-4493)*

MHS Lift of Delaware, New Castle Also called *Material Handling Supply Inc (G-5511)*

MI-Dee Inc 302 453-7326
345 Polly Drummond Hl Newark (19711) *(G-7022)*

Mia Bellas Candles 302 331-7038
697 Judith Rd Hartly (19953) *(G-2935)*

Micahs General Contracting 302 437-4068
37 Primrose Dr Bear (19701) *(G-251)*

Mican Technologies Inc (PA) 302 703-0708
2500 Wrangle Hill Rd Bear (19701) *(G-252)*

Michael A Beecher 302 285-3357
1122 Dexter Corner Rd Townsend (19734) *(G-8809)*

Michael A Mc Culloch MD 302 651-6600
1600 Rockland Rd Wilmington (19803) *(G-11653)*

Michael A Mealey & Sons Inc (PA) 302 652-5913
703 N Broom St Wilmington (19805) *(G-11654)*

Michael A Mealey & Sons Inc 302 654-3005
2509 Limestone Rd Wilmington (19808) *(G-11655)*

Michael A OBrien & Sons 302 994-2894
405 E Ayre St Wilmington (19804) *(G-11656)*

Michael A Poleck DDS 302 644-4100
1632 Savannah Rd Lewes (19958) *(G-3639)*

Michael A Poleck DDS PA 302 994-7730
5501 Kirkwood Hwy Wilmington (19808) *(G-11657)*

Michael A Sinclair Inc 302 834-8144
705 Connell Dr Bear (19701) *(G-253)*

Michael B Joseph 302 656-0123
824 N Market St Fl 10 Wilmington (19801) *(G-11658)*

Michael Butterworth Dr 302 732-9850
31059 Dupont Blvd Dagsboro (19939) *(G-922)*

Michael C Rapa 302 236-4423
10596 Georgetown Rd Laurel (19956) *(G-3264)*

Michael Eller Income Tax Svc 302 652-5916
724 N Union St Wilmington (19805) *(G-11659)*

Michael Gallagher Jewelers 302 836-2925
102 Fox Hunt Dr Bear (19701) *(G-254)*

Michael Gioia 302 479-7780
3520 Silverside Rd Ste 27 Wilmington (19810) *(G-11660)*

Michael J Munroe 804 240-7188
811 Augusta National Dr Magnolia (19962) *(G-3899)*

Michael J Ryan DDS 302 378-8600
106 Saint Annes Church Rd Middletown (19709) *(G-4153)*

Michael K Rosenthal 302 652-3469
2300 Penns Ave Ste 3c Wilmington (19806) *(G-11661)*

Michael L Cahoon Dr 302 644-4171
750 Kings Hwy Ste 107 Lewes (19958) *(G-3640)*

Michael L Mattern MD PA 302 734-3416
724 S New St Dover (19904) *(G-1845)*

Michael Lo Sapio 201 919-2643
900 Grears Corner Rd Townsend (19734) *(G-8810)*

Michael Matthew Sponaugle 302 566-1010
2427 Flatiron Rd Harrington (19952) *(G-2868)*

Michael Matthias 302 575-0100
3801 Kennett Pike E207 Wilmington (19807) *(G-11662)*

Michael McCarthy Stones 302 539-8056
35283 Atlantic Ave Millville (19967) *(G-4850)*

Michael P Morton PA 302 426-1313
3704 Kennett Pike Ste 200 Wilmington (19807) *(G-11663)*

Michael Pdmnczky Cnsrvator LLC 302 388-0656
1715 N Rodney St Wilmington (19806) *(G-11664)*

Michael S Wirosloff DMD 302 998-8588
5185 W Woodmill Dr Ste 2 Wilmington (19808) *(G-11665)*

Michael Schwartz 302 791-9999
1400 Philadelphia Pike Wilmington (19809) *(G-11666)*

Michael T Rosen DDS PA...866 561-5067
2601 Annand Dr Ste 2 Wilmington (19808) ***(G-11667)***
Michael T Teixido MD...302 998-0300
1941 Limestone Rd Ste 210 Wilmington (19808) ***(G-11668)***
Michael W Fogarty Gen Contr...302 658-5547
22 Bernard Blvd Hockessin (19707) ***(G-3094)***
Michael W Lankiewicz MD...302 737-7700
4701 Ogletown Stanton Rd # 4200 Newark (19713) ***(G-7023)***
Michael Woody Productions...302 584-2082
210 Skeet Cir W Bear (19701) ***(G-255)***
Michael-Bruno LLC (PA)...315 941-8514
2711 Centerville Rd # 120 Wilmington (19808) ***(G-11669)***
Michaelangelos Hair Designs...302 734-8343
696 N Dupont Hwy Dover (19901) ***(G-1846)***
Michaels Home Repair Services...302 333-2235
550 S Dupont Hwy Apt 22k New Castle (19720) ***(G-5521)***
Michaelynne, Seaford *Also called Lynne Betts* ***(G-8298)***
Michele Broder...302 652-1533
2300 Penns Ave Ste 5c Wilmington (19806) ***(G-11670)***
Michelet Finance Inc...302 427-8751
1105 N Market St Ste 1300 Wilmington (19801) ***(G-11671)***
Michelin Corporation...864 458-4698
2724 Pulaski Hwy Newark (19702) ***(G-7024)***
Michelle E Papa Do...302 656-5424
1100 S Broom St Ste 1 Wilmington (19805) ***(G-11672)***
Michelle S Jones...302 651-4801
1600 Rockland Rd Wilmington (19803) ***(G-11673)***
Micro Ovens of Delaware...302 998-8444
309 Main St Wilmington (19804) ***(G-11674)***
Microcom Tech LLC...858 775-5559
18971 Goldfinch Cv Rehoboth Beach (19971) ***(G-8005)***
Microdry Inc...302 416-3021
913 N Market St Ste 200 Wilmington (19801) ***(G-11675)***
Microlog Corporation Maryland...301 540-5501
17027 Taramac Dr Rehoboth Beach (19971) ***(G-8006)***
Micron Incorporated...302 998-1184
3815 Lancaster Pike Wilmington (19805) ***(G-11676)***
Microsoft Corporation...302 669-0200
137 Christiana Mall Newark (19702) ***(G-7025)***
Microtel, Dover *Also called Shiv Sagar Inc* ***(G-2078)***
Microtel, Georgetown *Also called Beacon Hospitality* ***(G-2452)***
Microtune LP LLC...302 691-6037
103 Foulk Rd Ste 202 Wilmington (19803) ***(G-11677)***
Mid Atlantic Care LLC (PA)...302 266-8306
520 Robinson Ln Wilmington (19805) ***(G-11678)***
Mid Atlantic Farm Credit Aca...302 734-7534
1410 S State St Dover (19901) ***(G-1847)***
Mid Atlantic Grand Prix LLC...302 656-5278
4060 N Dupont Hwy Ste 11 New Castle (19720) ***(G-5522)***
Mid Atlantic Indus Belting...302 453-7353
15 Garfield Way Newark (19713) ***(G-7026)***
Mid Atlantic Industrial Sales...302 698-6356
26 Kathleen Ct Camden (19934) ***(G-590)***
Mid Atlantic Pain Institute...302 369-1700
550 S Dupont Blvd Ste C Milford (19963) ***(G-4494)***
Mid Atlantic Renewable Energy...302 672-0741
29 N State St Ste 300 Dover (19901) ***(G-1848)***
Mid Atlantic Retina, Wilmington *Also called Retinovitreous Associates Ltd* ***(G-12394)***
Mid Atlantic Spine...302 369-1700
100 Biddle Ave Ste 101 Newark (19702) ***(G-7027)***
Mid Atlantic Surgical Practice...302 652-6050
701 N Clayton St Wilmington (19805) ***(G-11679)***
Mid Atlantic Waste System...610 497-2405
314 Bay West Blvd Ste 3 New Castle (19720) ***(G-5523)***
Mid Atlntic Scientific Svc Inc...302 328-4440
62 Southgate Blvd Ste Ab New Castle (19720) ***(G-5524)***
Mid Delaware Imaging Inc...302 734-9888
710 S Queen St Dover (19904) ***(G-1849)***
Mid South Audio LLC...302 856-6993
52 Bramhall St Georgetown (19947) ***(G-2603)***
Mid States Sales & Marketing...302 888-2475
3411 Silverside Rd # 104 Wilmington (19810) ***(G-11680)***
Mid Sussex Rescue Squad Inc...302 945-2680
31738 Indian Mission Rd Millsboro (19966) ***(G-4744)***
Mid-Atlantic Ballet Inc...302 266-6362
506 Interchange Blvd Newark (19711) ***(G-7028)***
Mid-Atlantic Elec Svcs Inc...302 945-2555
24556 Betts Pond Rd Millsboro (19966) ***(G-4745)***
Mid-Atlantic Envmtl Labs Inc...302 654-1340
30 Lukens Dr Ste A New Castle (19720) ***(G-5525)***
Mid-Atlantic Fmly Practice LLC...302 934-0944
28538 Dupont Blvd Unit 1 Millsboro (19966) ***(G-4746)***
Mid-Atlantic Fmly Practice LLC (PA)...302 644-6860
20251 John J Williams Hwy Lewes (19958) ***(G-3641)***
Mid-Atlantic Packaging Company...800 284-1332
14 Starlifter Ave Dover (19901) ***(G-1850)***
Mid-Atlantic Realty Co Inc (PA)...302 658-7642
39 Abbey Ln Newark (19711) ***(G-7029)***
Mid-Atlantic Realty Co Inc...302 738-5325
911 Village Cir Ofc D Newark (19713) ***(G-7030)***
Mid-Atlantic Realty Co Inc...302 737-3110
39 Abbey Ln Newark (19711) ***(G-7031)***
Mid-Atlantic Realty Co Inc...302 322-9500
10 Corporate Cir Ste 100 New Castle (19720) ***(G-5526)***
Mid-Atlantic Region, Wilmington *Also called Securitas SEC Svcs USA Inc* ***(G-12569)***
Mid-Atlantic Services A-Team...302 984-9559
700 Cornell Dr Wilmington (19801) ***(G-11681)***
Mid-Atlantic Services A-Team (PA)...302 628-3403
8558 Elks Rd Seaford (19973) ***(G-8310)***
Mid-Atlantic Steel LLC...302 323-1800
1144 River Rd New Castle (19720) ***(G-5527)***
Mid-Atlantic Systems Dpn Inc (PA)...301 206-9510
802 Interchange Blvd Newark (19711) ***(G-7032)***
Mid-Atlantic Systems of D P N, Newark *Also called Mid-Atlntic Wtrproofing MD Inc* ***(G-7033)***
Mid-Atlntic Dismantlement Corp...302 678-9300
913 Horsepond Rd Dover (19901) ***(G-1851)***
Mid-Atlntic Wtrproofing MD Inc...855 692-4668
802 Interchange Blvd Newark (19711) ***(G-7033)***
Mid-Coast Gymnastic Studio, Selbyville *Also called Midcoast Gymnstics Dnce Studio* ***(G-8520)***
Mid-County Electric Inc...302 934-8304
24556 Betts Pond Rd Millsboro (19966) ***(G-4747)***
Mid-Shore Envmtl Svcs Inc...302 736-5504
7481 Federalsburg Rd Bridgeville (19933) ***(G-500)***
Midas Muffler, Wilmington *Also called Leeds West Inv Group LLC* ***(G-11358)***
Midas Muffler, New Castle *Also called C-Met Inc* ***(G-5127)***
Midatlantic Farm Credit...302 734-7534
1410 S State St Dover (19901) ***(G-1852)***
Midatlantic Farm Credit Aca...302 856-9081
20816 Dupont Blvd Georgetown (19947) ***(G-2604)***
Midatlantic Pain Institute...302 369-1700
100 Biddle Ave Ste 101 Newark (19702) ***(G-7034)***
Midatlantic Spine, Newark *Also called Midatlantic Pain Institute* ***(G-7034)***
Midatlntic Auto Rstration Sups...302 422-3812
6930 Shawnee Rd Milford (19963) ***(G-4495)***
Midcoast Gymnstics Dnce Studio...302 436-6007
15 Duke Street Ext Selbyville (19975) ***(G-8520)***
Middelaware Family Medicine...302 724-5125
1813 Windswept Cir Dover (19901) ***(G-1853)***
Middle Dept Insptn Agcy Inc...302 875-4514
11508 Commercial Ln Laurel (19956) ***(G-3265)***
Middle Dept Insptn Agcy Inc...302 999-0243
2024 Duncan Rd Fl 2 Wilmington (19808) ***(G-11682)***
Middle East Free Trade Assoc, Wilmington *Also called Mefta LLC* ***(G-11622)***
Middletown Car Care...302 449-1550
50 E Main St Middletown (19709) ***(G-4154)***
Middletown Counseling...302 376-0621
401 N Broad St Middletown (19709) ***(G-4155)***
Middletown Family Dentist...302 376-1959
122 Sandhill Dr Ste 101 Middletown (19709) ***(G-4156)***
Middletown Ink LLC...302 725-0705
126 Patriot Dr Middletown (19709) ***(G-4157)***
Middletown Kitchen and Bath...302 376-5766
987 Marl Pit Rd Middletown (19709) ***(G-4158)***
Middletown Liquors, Middletown *Also called Patel Sanjay* ***(G-4180)***
Middletown Main Street Inc...302 378-2977
216 N Broad St Middletown (19709) ***(G-4159)***
Middletown Police Department, Middletown *Also called Town of Middletown* ***(G-4264)***
Middletown Shopping Center, Middletown *Also called Capitol Cleaners & Launderers* ***(G-3981)***
Middletown Sports Complex LLC...302 299-8630
407 Draper Ln Middletown (19709) ***(G-4160)***
Middletown Transcript, Middletown *Also called Dover Post Co Inc* ***(G-4044)***
Middletown Veterinary Hospital...302 378-2342
366 Warwick Rd Middletown (19709) ***(G-4161)***
Middletown Well Drilling Co (PA)...302 378-9396
115 S 6th St Odessa (19730) ***(G-7830)***
Middleware Inc...415 213-2625
1000 N West St Ste 1200 Wilmington (19801) ***(G-11683)***
Middltown Familycare Assoc LLC...302 378-4779
114 Sandhill Dr Ste 101 Middletown (19709) ***(G-4162)***
Middltown Odssa Twnsend Snior...302 378-4758
300 S Scott St Middletown (19709) ***(G-4163)***
Midi Labs Inc...302 737-4297
125 Sandy Dr Newark (19713) ***(G-7035)***
Midlantic Marine Center Inc...302 436-2628
36624 Dupont Blvd Selbyville (19975) ***(G-8521)***
Midnight Blue Inc...302 436-9665
37091 E White Tail Dr Selbyville (19975) ***(G-8522)***
Midnite Air Corp...614 296-1678
35 Salem Church Rd Newark (19713) ***(G-7036)***
Midshore Electrical Services...302 945-2555
22787 Dozer Ln Unit A1 Harbeson (19951) ***(G-2792)***
Midway Chiropractic, Rehoboth Beach *Also called First State Health & Wellness* ***(G-7933)***
Midway Chiropractic, Hockessin *Also called First State Health & Wellness* ***(G-3029)***
Midway Fitnes Racquetball CLB, Rehoboth Beach *Also called Midway Fitness Center* ***(G-8007)***

ALPHABETIC

(PA)=Parent Co (HQ)=Headquarters (DH)=Div Headquarters
2020 Harris Directory of Delaware Businesses
687

Midway Fitness Center.......302 645-0407
28b Midway Shopping Ctr Rehoboth Beach (19971) ***(G-8007)***
Midway Little League.......302 737-3104
55 S Meadowood Dr Newark (19711) ***(G-7037)***
Midway LLC.......302 378-9156
102 Dungarvan Dr Middletown (19709) ***(G-4164)***
Midway Muffler Shop, Wilmington *Also called Roy Covey* ***(G-12482)***
Midway Par 3 Golf Course & Dri, Lewes *Also called Arpago Corp* ***(G-3347)***
Midway Realty Inc.......302 645-9511
29 Midway Shopping Ctr Rehoboth Beach (19971) ***(G-8008)***
Midway Services Inc.......302 422-8603
9446 Willow Pond Ln Lincoln (19960) ***(G-3861)***
Midway Speedway, Rehoboth Beach *Also called Fun Sport Inc* ***(G-7939)***
Midway Towing Inc.......302 323-4850
443 Old Airport Rd New Castle (19720) ***(G-5528)***
Midway Ventures LLC.......302 645-8003
18826 Coastal Hwy Rehoboth Beach (19971) ***(G-8009)***
Mifflin Run Apts, Dover *Also called Robino Management Group Inc* ***(G-2038)***
Mig Consulting LLC (PA).......302 999-1888
1624 Newport Gap Pike Wilmington (19808) ***(G-11684)***
Mig Environmental, Wilmington *Also called Mehar Investment Group LLC* ***(G-11624)***
Mightyinvoice LLC.......302 415-3000
8 The Grn Ste B Dover (19901) ***(G-1854)***
Mih International LLC.......301 908-4233
112 Capitol Trl Newark (19711) ***(G-7038)***
Mike Faella Inc.......302 475-2116
2208 Sconset Rd Wilmington (19810) ***(G-11685)***
Mike Molitor Contractor LLC.......302 528-6300
754 Morris Rd Hockessin (19707) ***(G-3095)***
Mike Walsh Physical Therapy.......302 724-5593
810 New Burton Rd Ste 2 Dover (19904) ***(G-1855)***
Miken Builders Inc.......302 537-4444
32782 Cedar Dr Unit 1 Millville (19967) ***(G-4851)***
Mikes Ceramic Tile Inc.......302 376-5743
624 Nesting Ln Middletown (19709) ***(G-4165)***
Mikes Glass Service Inc.......302 658-7936
108 A St Wilmington (19801) ***(G-11686)***
Mil International Incorporated.......302 234-7501
203 Alisons Way Wilmington (19807) ***(G-11687)***
Milcreek Barber Shop, Wilmington *Also called Millcreek Barber Shop* ***(G-11689)***
Miles Scientific Corporation.......302 737-6960
75 Blue Hen Dr Newark (19713) ***(G-7039)***
Milestone Construction Co Inc.......302 442-4252
4 Mill Park Ct Ste A Newark (19713) ***(G-7040)***
Milford Anesthesia Assoc LLC.......203 783-1831
111 Continental Dr # 412 Newark (19713) ***(G-7041)***
Milford Bowling Lanes Inc.......302 422-9456
809 N Dupont Blvd Milford (19963) ***(G-4496)***
Milford Boys & Girls Club, Milford *Also called Boys & Girls Clubs Del Inc* ***(G-4331)***
Milford Center, Milford *Also called 700 Marvel Road Operations LLC* ***(G-4298)***
Milford Community Band Inc.......302 422-6304
616 Cedarwood Ave Milford (19963) ***(G-4497)***
Milford Crossing Apartments, Milford *Also called Leon N Weiner & Associates Inc* ***(G-4473)***
Milford Early Learning Center, Milford *Also called Esther V Graham* ***(G-4406)***
Milford Early Learning Center.......302 331-6612
592 Ashland Ave Camden Wyoming (19934) ***(G-649)***
Milford Fertilizer, Milford *Also called Growmark Fs LLC* ***(G-4425)***
Milford Grain Co Inc.......302 422-6752
6789 Shawnee Rd Milford (19963) ***(G-4498)***
Milford Gutter Guys LLC.......302 424-1931
7074 Marshall St Lincoln (19960) ***(G-3862)***
Milford Housing Development.......302 678-0300
200 Harmony Ln Dover (19904) ***(G-1856)***
Milford Housing Development (PA).......302 422-8255
977 E Masten Cir Milford (19963) ***(G-4499)***
Milford Lodge 2401, Milford *Also called Benevolent & Protective Order* ***(G-4322)***
Milford Lodging LLC.......302 839-5000
699 N Dupont Blvd Milford (19963) ***(G-4500)***
Milford Medical Associates PA.......302 329-9517
611 Federal St Milton (19968) ***(G-4937)***
Milford Medical Associates PA (PA).......302 424-0600
310 Mullet Run Milford (19963) ***(G-4501)***
Milford Memorial Hospital, Dover *Also called Kent General Hospital* ***(G-1735)***
Milford Memorial Hospital, Milford *Also called Kent General Hospital* ***(G-4463)***
Milford Place, Milford *Also called 500 South Dupont Boule* ***(G-4297)***
Milford Pulmonary Assoc LLC.......302 424-3100
39 W Clarke Ave Milford (19963) ***(G-4502)***
Milford Rent All Inc.......302 422-0100
601 Marshall St Milford (19963) ***(G-4503)***
Milford Rental Center Inc.......302 422-0315
1679 S Dupont Hwy Dover (19901) ***(G-1857)***
Milford Senior Center Inc.......302 422-3385
111 Park Ave Milford (19963) ***(G-4504)***
Milford Stitching Co, Dover *Also called G L K Inc* ***(G-1576)***
Mill Creek Metals Inc.......302 529-7020
3 1/2 Yale Ave Claymont (19703) ***(G-782)***
Mill Creek Select.......302 995-2090
2006 Limestone Rd Wilmington (19808) ***(G-11688)***

Millcreek Barber Shop.......302 998-2174
4573 Kirkwood Hwy Wilmington (19808) ***(G-11689)***
Millcreek Foundation.......302 239-3811
3713 Mill Creek Rd Hockessin (19707) ***(G-3096)***
Millcreek Mobile Hm Pk Land Co.......302 998-3045
5600 Old Capitol Trl Wilmington (19808) ***(G-11690)***
Millcreek Pediatrics, Wilmington *Also called Macfarlane A Radford MD PA* ***(G-11478)***
Millcreek Texaco Station.......302 571-8489
109 Bellant Cir Wilmington (19807) ***(G-11691)***
Millcroft, Newark *Also called Five Star Quality Care Inc* ***(G-6593)***
Millenium Counseling.......302 995-9188
1601 Milltown Rd Ste 14 Wilmington (19808) ***(G-11692)***
Millennia Contracting Inc.......302 654-6200
3075 New Castle Ave New Castle (19720) ***(G-5529)***
Millennium Prcess Contrls Svcs.......302 455-1717
105 Carson Dr Bear (19701) ***(G-256)***
Miller & Associates Cpas, Wilmington *Also called Miller & Associates PA* ***(G-11693)***
Miller & Associates PA.......302 234-0678
5500 Skyline Dr Ste 5 Wilmington (19808) ***(G-11693)***
Miller John H Plumbing & Htg.......302 697-1012
220 Old North Rd Camden (19934) ***(G-591)***
Miller JW Wldg Boiler Repr Co.......302 449-1575
4917 Summit Bridge Rd Middletown (19709) ***(G-4166)***
Miller Lewis Surveyors, Seaford *Also called Lewis Miller Inc* ***(G-8293)***
Miller Mauro Group Inc.......302 426-6565
3512 Silverside Rd Ste 9 Wilmington (19810) ***(G-11694)***
Miller Metal Fabrication Inc.......302 337-2291
16356 Sussex Hwy Unit 4 Bridgeville (19933) ***(G-501)***
Miller Publishing Inc.......302 576-6579
5 Servan Ct Wilmington (19805) ***(G-11695)***
Miller's Beverage Center, Wilmington *Also called Wwd Inc* ***(G-13310)***
Millers Gun Center Inc.......302 328-9747
97 Jackson Ave New Castle (19720) ***(G-5530)***
Millies Scented Rocks LLC.......302 331-9232
83 Pitch Kettle Ct Magnolia (19962) ***(G-3900)***
Million Group.......302 543-8354
100 South Rd Wilmington (19809) ***(G-11696)***
Millsboro Art League Inc.......302 934-6440
103 Main St Millsboro (19966) ***(G-4748)***
Millsboro Bowling Center, Millsboro *Also called Millsboro Lanes Inc* ***(G-4750)***
Millsboro Eye Care LLC.......302 684-2020
28322 L Georgetown Hwy Milton (19968) ***(G-4938)***
Millsboro Family Practice PA.......302 934-5626
201 Laurel Rd Millsboro (19966) ***(G-4749)***
Millsboro Lanes Inc.......302 934-0400
213 Mitchell St Millsboro (19966) ***(G-4750)***
Millsboro Little League.......302 934-1806
262 W State St Millsboro (19966) ***(G-4751)***
Millsboro Village I LLC.......302 678-9400
701 Stanford Bratton Dr Millsboro (19966) ***(G-4752)***
Milltown Dental LLC.......302 998-3332
2601 Annand Dr Ste 18 Wilmington (19808) ***(G-11697)***
Millwrights Local Union 1548.......410 355-0011
1013 Centre Rd Ste 201 Wilmington (19805) ***(G-11698)***
Milton & Hattie Kutz Foundaton.......302 427-2100
101 Garden Of Eden Rd Wilmington (19803) ***(G-11699)***
Milton & Hattie Kutz Home Inc.......302 764-7000
704 River Rd Wilmington (19809) ***(G-11700)***
Milton Enterprises Inc.......302 684-2000
424 Mulberry St Ste 2 Milton (19968) ***(G-4939)***
Milton Family Practice, Milton *Also called Milton Enterprises Inc* ***(G-4939)***
Milton Family Practice.......302 684-2000
16529 Coastal Hwy Lewes (19958) ***(G-3642)***
Milton Garden Club.......302 684-8315
14354 Sand Hill Rd Milton (19968) ***(G-4940)***
Milton Historical Society.......302 684-1010
210 Union St Milton (19968) ***(G-4941)***
Milunsky Family Dentistry.......610 566-5322
103 Danforth Pl Wilmington (19810) ***(G-11701)***
Milunsky Family Dentistry PC.......610 872-8042
103 Danforth Pl Wilmington (19810) ***(G-11702)***
Mimesis Signs.......302 674-5566
1035 Fowler Ct Dover (19901) ***(G-1858)***
Mimix Company.......305 916-8602
8 The Grn Ste 6236 Dover (19901) ***(G-1859)***
Minatee Business Group.......302 543-5092
114 Lloyd St Wilmington (19804) ***(G-11703)***
Mind and Body Consortium LLC.......302 674-2380
156 S State St Dover (19901) ***(G-1860)***
Mind Body & Sole.......302 537-3668
32892 Coastal Hwy Unit 3 Bethany Beach (19930) ***(G-415)***
Mind Mechanix.......302 503-5142
556 S Dupont Blvd Ste I Milford (19963) ***(G-4505)***
Mindcentral Inc.......302 273-1011
2035 Sunset Lake Rd B2 Newark (19702) ***(G-7042)***
Minder Foundation.......917 477-7661
16192 Coastal Hwy Lewes (19958) ***(G-3643)***
Mindqube, Wilmington *Also called Polymorphic Software Inc* ***(G-12185)***

ALPHABETIC SECTION — Montchanin Design Group Inc

Minimally Invasive Surgcl & Ne 302 738-0300
774 Christiana Rd Ste 2 Newark (19713) *(G-7043)*

Ministry Caring Distribution, Wilmington Also called Ministry of Caring Inc *(G-11710)*

Ministry of Caring Inc 302 652-8947
830 N Spruce St Lowr Wilmington (19801) *(G-11704)*

Ministry of Caring Inc (PA) 302 428-3702
115 E 14th St Wilmington (19801) *(G-11705)*

Ministry of Caring Inc 302 652-0904
1328 W 3rd St Wilmington (19805) *(G-11706)*

Ministry of Caring Inc 302 658-6123
121 N Jackson St Wilmington (19805) *(G-11707)*

Ministry of Caring Inc 302 652-5522
1100 Lancaster Ave Wilmington (19805) *(G-11708)*

Ministry of Caring Inc 302 652-0970
515 N Broom St Wilmington (19805) *(G-11709)*

Ministry of Caring Inc 302 652-0969
1410 N Claymont St Wilmington (19802) *(G-11710)*

Minkers Construction Inc 302 239-9239
830 Dawson Dr Newark (19713) *(G-7044)*

Minor Figures Inc 714 875-3449
2140 S Dupont Hwy Camden (19934) *(G-592)*

Minoti Inc 720 725-0720
16192 Coastal Hwy Lewes (19958) *(G-3644)*

Minquadale Plant, Wilmington Also called New Castle Hot Mix Inc *(G-11853)*

Minute Loan Center 302 994-6588
3210 Kirkwood Hwy Wilmington (19808) *(G-11711)*

Minuteman Press, Wilmington Also called Lord Printing LLC *(G-11435)*

Mirworth Enterprise Inc 302 846-0218
404 Lincoln Ave Delmar (19940) *(G-1021)*

Mispillion Art League Inc 302 430-7646
5 N Walnut St Milford (19963) *(G-4506)*

Mispillion III 302 422-4429
504 Mispillion Apts Milford (19963) *(G-4507)*

Mispillion River Brewing LLC 302 491-6623
233 Mullet Run Milford (19963) *(G-4508)*

Miss Kittys Kiddies 302 571-1547
441 Anderson Dr Wilmington (19801) *(G-11712)*

Miss Mafia LLC 800 246-2677
919 N Market St Ste 950 Wilmington (19801) *(G-11713)*

Mission Bracelets 302 528-5065
1201 Woodland Beach Rd Smyrna (19977) *(G-8681)*

Mission Movement Transport LLC 302 480-9401
8604 First Born Church Rd Lincoln (19960) *(G-3863)*

Missy Muller 302 376-0760
5350 Summit Bridge Rd Middletown (19709) *(G-4167)*

Mistress of Spice, New Castle Also called Andre Noel Thalia *(G-5038)*

Mitchell Associates Inc (PA) 302 594-9400
1 Ave Of The Arts Ste B Wilmington (19801) *(G-11714)*

Mitchell C Stickler MD Inc (PA) 302 644-6400
750 Kings Hwy Ste 110 Lewes (19958) *(G-3645)*

Mitchell S Welding LLC 302 632-1089
1106 Steeles Ridge Rd Camden Wyoming (19934) *(G-650)*

Mitek Holdings Inc (HQ) 302 429-1816
802 N West St Wilmington (19801) *(G-11715)*

Mithril Cable Network Inc 213 373-4381
2093 Philadelphia Pike Claymont (19703) *(G-783)*

Mitsdarfer Bros Lawn Ldscpg I, Newark Also called Mitsdrfer Bros Lawn Ldscpg Inc *(G-7045)*

Mitsdrfer Bros Lawn Ldscpg Inc 302 633-1150
715 Stanton Christiana Rd Newark (19713) *(G-7045)*

Mittelman Dental Lab 302 798-7440
108 Delaware Ave Claymont (19703) *(G-784)*

Mitten & Winters CPA 302 736-6100
119 W Loockerman St Dover (19904) *(G-1861)*

Mitten Construction Co 302 697-2124
1420 E Lebanon Rd Dover (19901) *(G-1862)*

Mitusha International Corp 302 674-2977
626 Roberta Ave Dover (19901) *(G-1863)*

MJ Webb Farms Inc 302 349-4453
12608 Webb Farm Rd Greenwood (19950) *(G-2753)*

Mj Wilmington Hotel Assoc LP 302 454-1500
100 Continental Dr Newark (19713) *(G-7046)*

Mj Wilmington Hotel Assoc LP 302 454-1500
100 Continental Dr Newark (19713) *(G-7047)*

MJL Industrial Inc 302 234-0898
405 Uxbridge Way Hockessin (19707) *(G-3097)*

MJM Fabrications Inc 302 764-0163
506 Crest Rd Wilmington (19803) *(G-11716)*

MJM Publishing 302 943-3590
719 Tomahawk Ln Felton (19943) *(G-2307)*

Mk Krawlers, Laurel Also called Michael C Rapa *(G-3264)*

ML Newark LLC 302 737-2868
100 Christina Mill Dr Newark (19711) *(G-7048)*

ML Whiteman and Sons Inc 302 659-1001
261 Gum Bush Rd Townsend (19734) *(G-8811)*

Mm Mobile LLC 917 297-9534
874 Walker Rd Ste C Dover (19904) *(G-1864)*

Mmi Holdings Inc 302 455-2021
1360 Marrows Rd Newark (19711) *(G-7049)*

MMR Associates Inc 302 883-2984
679 Horsepond Rd Dover (19901) *(G-1865)*

MMR Group Inc (PA) 302 328-0500
308 W Basin Rd New Castle (19720) *(G-5531)*

MMR Industries Inc 302 999-9561
7 Dartmouth Rd Wilmington (19808) *(G-11717)*

Mnr Industries LLC 443 485-6213
200 Banning St Ste 170 Dover (19904) *(G-1866)*

Mobil, Wilmington Also called Sals Auto Services Inc *(G-12526)*

Mobile Alerts LLC 202 596-8709
160 Greentree Dr Ste 101 Dover (19904) *(G-1867)*

Mobile Muzic Inc 302 998-5951
2517 Nicholby Dr Wilmington (19808) *(G-11718)*

Mobius New Media Inc 302 475-9880
818 N Market St Fl 2r Wilmington (19801) *(G-11719)*

Modern Controls Inc 302 325-6800
7 Bellecor Dr New Castle (19720) *(G-5532)*

Modern Dental 302 478-1748
2 Righter Pkwy Ste 110 Wilmington (19803) *(G-11720)*

Modern Masters Inc 240 800-6622
8 The Grn Ste A Dover (19901) *(G-1868)*

Modern Maturity Center Inc 302 734-1200
1121 Forrest Ave Dover (19904) *(G-1869)*

Modern Water Inc 302 669-6900
15 Reads Way Ste 100 New Castle (19720) *(G-5533)*

Modernthink LLC 302 764-4477
2 Mill Rd Ste 102 Wilmington (19806) *(G-11721)*

Modified Thermoset Resins Inc 302 235-3710
2 Pixie Rd Wilmington (19810) *(G-11722)*

Modular Carpet Recycling Inc 484 885-5890
239 Lisa Dr New Castle (19720) *(G-5534)*

Modulation Therapeutics Inc 813 784-0033
2711 Centerville Rd # 400 Wilmington (19808) *(G-11723)*

Moghul Life Inc 347 560-9124
1201 N Orange St Ste 600 Wilmington (19801) *(G-11724)*

Mohammad Kamali, MD, Newark Also called Orthopedic Specialists *(G-7160)*

Mohawk Electrical Systems Inc 302 422-2500
251 S Rehoboth Blvd Milford (19963) *(G-4509)*

Mohawk Plastic Products Inc 302 424-4324
251 S Rehoboth Blvd Milford (19963) *(G-4510)*

Mohawk Tile MBL Distrs of Del 302 655-7164
2700 W 3rd St Wilmington (19805) *(G-11725)*

Mold Busters LLC 302 339-2204
27221 Buckskin Trl Harbeson (19951) *(G-2793)*

Mold Medics Global LLC 301 943-9428
300 Water St Ste 300 # 300 Wilmington (19801) *(G-11726)*

Molded Components Inc 302 588-2240
3817 Katherine Ave Wilmington (19808) *(G-11727)*

Molecular Imaging Services Inc 302 450-4505
10 Whitaker Ct Bear (19701) *(G-257)*

Mom Home Daycare 302 265-2668
8351 Collett Ln Milford (19963) *(G-4511)*

MOM'S HOUSE OF WILMINGTON, Wilmington Also called Moms House Inc *(G-11730)*

Momentum Management Group Inc 302 477-9730
3411 Silverside Rd 201w Wilmington (19810) *(G-11728)*

Moms Club 302 738-8822
5447 Crestline Rd Wilmington (19808) *(G-11729)*

Moms House Inc 302 658-3433
1718 Howland St Wilmington (19805) *(G-11730)*

Moms House Inc 302 678-8688
864 S State St Dover (19901) *(G-1870)*

Money Bax LLC 302 360-8577
33692 Reservoir Dr Lewes (19958) *(G-3646)*

Money Galaxy Inc 302 319-2008
1000 N West St Ste 1200 Wilmington (19801) *(G-11731)*

Moneykey - TX Inc 866 255-1668
3422 Old Capitol Trl Wilmington (19808) *(G-11732)*

Monge Woodworking 302 455-0175
4 Barnard St Newark (19711) *(G-7050)*

Monica Mehring DDS 302 368-0054
179 W Chestnut Hill Rd # 4 Newark (19713) *(G-7051)*

Monitor For Hire. Com, Hockessin Also called Pharma E Market LLC *(G-3119)*

Monogram Specialties 302 292-2424
701 Valley Rd Newark (19711) *(G-7052)*

Monro Inc 302 999-0237
600 Kirkwood Hwy Wilmington (19805) *(G-11733)*

Monro Inc 302 846-2732
5 Gerald Ct Delmar (19940) *(G-1022)*

Monro Inc 302 328-2945
401 S Dupont Hwy New Castle (19720) *(G-5535)*

Monro Inc 302 378-3801
430 Haveg Rd Middletown (19709) *(G-4168)*

Monro Muffler Brake, New Castle Also called Monro Inc *(G-5535)*

Monro Mufflers, Wilmington Also called Monro Inc *(G-11733)*

Monroe Iko Inc 302 764-3100
120 Hay Rd Wilmington (19809) *(G-11734)*

Monroe Mechanical Contracting 302 223-6020
370 Christiana River Dr Clayton (19938) *(G-865)*

Monseco Leather LLC 302 235-1777
724 Yorklyn Rd Ste 260 Hockessin (19707) *(G-3098)*

Montchanin Design Group Inc 302 652-3008
1907 N Market St Wilmington (19802) *(G-11735)*

Monterey Enterprises LLC.....302 504-4901
111 Continental Dr # 114 Newark (19713) ***(G-7053)***
Monterey SW LLC.....302 504-4901
111 Continental Dr # 114 Newark (19713) ***(G-7054)***
Monterey Swf LLC.....302 504-4901
111 Continental Dr # 114 Newark (19713) ***(G-7055)***
Montesino Associates.....302 888-2355
1719 Delaware Ave 3 Wilmington (19806) ***(G-11736)***
Montesino Technologies Inc.....302 888-2355
1719 Delaware Ave 3 Wilmington (19806) ***(G-11737)***
Montessor Teachers Association, Wilmington *Also called Elementary Workshop Inc* ***(G-10369)***
Montessori Learning Centre.....302 478-2575
2313 Concord Pike Wilmington (19803) ***(G-11738)***
Montgomery McCracken.....302 504-7800
300 Delaware Ave Ste 750 Wilmington (19801) ***(G-11739)***
Montgomery Kenneth John.....302 992-0484
610 Ohio Ave Wilmington (19805) ***(G-11740)***
Monzack Mersky McLaughlin.....302 656-8162
1201 N Orange St Ste 400 Wilmington (19801) ***(G-11741)***
Moon Shot Energy LLC.....512 297-2626
16192 Coastal Hwy Lewes (19958) ***(G-3647)***
Mooney & Andrew PA.....302 856-3070
11 S Race St Georgetown (19947) ***(G-2605)***
Moonlight Architechture Inc.....302 645-9361
29003 Lwes Georgetown Hwy Lewes (19958) ***(G-3648)***
Moony and Zeager Inc.....302 593-8166
2518 Pennington Way Wilmington (19810) ***(G-11742)***
Moor Instruments Inc.....302 798-7470
501 Silverside Rd Ste 66 Wilmington (19809) ***(G-11743)***
Moore & Lind Inc.....302 934-8818
28448 Dupont Blvd Millsboro (19966) ***(G-4753)***
Moore Farms.....302 629-4999
14619 Cokesbury Rd Georgetown (19947) ***(G-2606)***
Moore Insurance & Financial.....302 999-9101
1702 Kirkwood Hwy Ste 101 Wilmington (19805) ***(G-11744)***
Moore International LLC.....302 603-7262
913 N Market St Ste 200 Wilmington (19801) ***(G-11745)***
Moore Partnership.....302 227-5253
126 Bellevue St Dewey Beach (19971) ***(G-1059)***
Moore Physcial Therapy.....302 654-8142
1806 N Van Buren St # 110 Wilmington (19802) ***(G-11746)***
Moore Qlty Wldg Fbrication LLC.....302 731-4818
522 Stafford Ave Newark (19711) ***(G-7056)***
Moore Quality Welding Fab.....302 250-7136
328 W Dickerson Ln Middletown (19709) ***(G-4169)***
Moore, J A Construction Co, Wilmington *Also called J A Moore & Sons Inc* ***(G-11101)***
Moore, William X Jr, Wilmington *Also called Roeberg Moore & Associates PA* ***(G-12463)***
Moores Cabinet Refinishing Inc.....302 378-3055
939 Bethel Church Rd Middletown (19709) ***(G-4170)***
Moores Enterprises Inc.....302 227-8200
6 2nd St Rehoboth Beach (19971) ***(G-8010)***
Moorway Painting Management.....302 764-5002
1 Hayden Ave Wilmington (19804) ***(G-11747)***
Moose Family Center 646, Lewes *Also called Moose International Inc* ***(G-3649)***
Moose International Inc.....302 684-4004
28971 Lwes Georgetown Hwy Lewes (19958) ***(G-3649)***
Mopak, Seaford *Also called Jbs Souderton Inc* ***(G-8278)***
Morales Screen Printing.....302 465-8179
201 Cassidy Dr Ste C Dover (19901) ***(G-1871)***
Moran Envmtl Recovery LLC.....302 322-6008
9 Garfield Way Newark (19713) ***(G-7057)***
Moran Foods LLC.....302 798-5042
401 Naamans Dr Ste 3 Claymont (19703) ***(G-785)***
Morans Refrigeration Service.....703 642-1200
146 Glade Cir W Rehoboth Beach (19971) ***(G-8011)***
More Than Fitness Inc.....302 690-5655
718 Grandview Ave Wilmington (19809) ***(G-11748)***
Morgan Kalman Clinic PA.....302 529-5500
2501 Silverside Rd Ste 1 Wilmington (19810) ***(G-11749)***
Morgan Garanty Intl Fincl Corp.....302 634-1000
500 Stanton Christiana Rd Newark (19713) ***(G-7058)***
Morgan Kalman Clinic.....610 869-5757
2701 Kirkwood Hwy Wilmington (19805) ***(G-11750)***
Morgan Lewis International LLC (PA).....302 574-3000
1007 N Orange St Ste 500 Wilmington (19801) ***(G-11751)***
Morgan Stanley, Wilmington *Also called Ms Financing LLC* ***(G-11769)***
Morgan Stanley.....302 644-6600
55 Cascade Ln Rehoboth Beach (19971) ***(G-8012)***
Morgan Stanley & Co LLC.....302 573-4000
2751 Centerville Rd # 104 Wilmington (19808) ***(G-11752)***
Morgan Stnley Intl Hldings Inc.....302 657-2000
2751 Centerville Rd # 104 Wilmington (19808) ***(G-11753)***
Morgan Stnley Smith Barney LLC.....302 636-5500
2751 Centerville Rd # 104 Wilmington (19808) ***(G-11754)***
Morgan Stnley Smith Barney LLC.....302 644-6600
55 Cascade Ln Rehoboth Beach (19971) ***(G-8013)***
Morning After Inc.....302 562-5190
5006 Halltown Rd Hartly (19953) ***(G-2936)***
Morning Report Research Inc.....302 730-3793
32 W Loockerman St 101a Dover (19904) ***(G-1872)***
Morning Star Construction LLC.....302 539-0791
103 Wood Duck Ct Dagsboro (19939) ***(G-923)***
Morning Star Publications Inc.....302 629-9788
951 Norman Eskridge Hwy D Seaford (19973) ***(G-8311)***
Morningstar Maids LLC.....302 829-3030
987 Old Lancaster Pike Hockessin (19707) ***(G-3099)***
Morris & Ritchie Assoc Inc.....302 855-5734
8 W Market St Georgetown (19947) ***(G-2607)***
Morris & Ritchie Assoc Inc.....302 326-2200
18 Boulden Cir Ste 36 New Castle (19720) ***(G-5536)***
Morris and Morris.....302 426-0400
4001 Kennett Pike Ste 300 Wilmington (19807) ***(G-11755)***
Morris CT Trucking Inc.....302 653-2396
803 Masseys Church Rd Smyrna (19977) ***(G-8682)***
Morris E Justice Inc.....302 539-7731
33897 Em Calhoun Ln Dagsboro (19939) ***(G-924)***
Morris James LLP.....302 655-2599
803 N Broom St Wilmington (19806) ***(G-11756)***
Morris James LLP.....302 888-6800
500 Delaware Ave Ste 500 # 500 Wilmington (19801) ***(G-11757)***
Morris James LLP.....302 260-7290
19339 Coastal Hwy # 300 Rehoboth Beach (19971) ***(G-8014)***
Morris James LLP.....302 678-8815
850 New Burton Rd Ste 101 Dover (19904) ***(G-1873)***
Morris James LLP (PA).....302 888-6863
500 Delaware Ave Ste 1500 Wilmington (19801) ***(G-11758)***
Morris Jmes Htchens Wllams LLP.....302 368-4200
16 Polly Drummond Hill Rd Newark (19711) ***(G-7059)***
Morris Nchols Arsht Tnnell LLP.....302 658-9200
1201 N Market St Fl 16 Wilmington (19801) ***(G-11759)***
Morris, James, Dover *Also called Morris James LLP* ***(G-1873)***
Morrow Limited.....213 631-3534
4 W Rockland Rd Montchanin (19710) ***(G-4987)***
Mortgage America Inc.....302 239-0600
5315 Limestone Rd Wilmington (19808) ***(G-11760)***
Mortgage Capitol, Rehoboth Beach *Also called Union Mortgage Group Inc* ***(G-8105)***
Mortgage Network Solutions LLC.....302 252-0100
223 Pine Cliff Dr Wilmington (19810) ***(G-11761)***
Morton Electric Co.....302 645-9414
16867 Kings Hwy Lewes (19958) ***(G-3650)***
Mosaic.....302 456-5995
8 Stoddard Dr Newark (19702) ***(G-7060)***
Mosaic.....302 366-0257
223 E Seneca Dr Newark (19702) ***(G-7061)***
Mosaic.....302 456-5995
261 Chapman Rd Ste 201 Newark (19702) ***(G-7062)***
Moscase Inc.....786 520-8062
3500 S Dupont Hwy Dover (19901) ***(G-1874)***
Mosquito Joe of Delaware, Newark *Also called Delaware Mosquito Control LLC* ***(G-6398)***
Mossaic.....302 428-1680
219 Potomac Rd Wilmington (19803) ***(G-11762)***
MOT SENIOR CENTER, Middletown *Also called Middltown Odssa Twnsend Snior* ***(G-4163)***
Mother Goose Childrens Center.....302 934-8454
27275 Dagsboro Rd Millsboro (19966) ***(G-4754)***
Mother Hubbard Child Care Ctr.....302 368-7584
2050 S College Ave Newark (19702) ***(G-7063)***
Motion Industries Inc.....302 462-3130
38541 Sussex Hwy Delmar (19940) ***(G-1023)***
Motopods LLC.....818 641-4299
8 The Grn Ste 8095 Dover (19901) ***(G-1875)***
Motorsport Series, Wilmington *Also called Whisman John* ***(G-13185)***
Motto Computer Inc.....302 633-6783
3317 Old Capitol Trl C Wilmington (19808) ***(G-11763)***
Mount Aire Farms of Delawa.....302 934-4048
29005 John J Williams Hwy Millsboro (19966) ***(G-4755)***
Mountain Consulting Inc.....302 744-9875
103 S Bradford St Dover (19904) ***(G-1876)***
Mountaire Farms Delaware Inc (HQ).....302 934-1100
29005 John J Williams Hwy Millsboro (19966) ***(G-4756)***
Mountaire Farms Delaware Inc.....302 398-3296
615 Fairground Rd Harrington (19952) ***(G-2869)***
Mountaire Farms Inc.....302 988-6200
35 Railroad Ave Selbyville (19975) ***(G-8523)***
Mountaire Farms Inc.....302 732-6611
11 Daisey St Frankford (19945) ***(G-2375)***
Mountaire Farms Inc.....302 988-6289
37 Railroad Ave Selbyville (19975) ***(G-8524)***
Mountaire Farms Inc.....302 436-8241
Hoosier St Selbyville (19975) ***(G-8525)***
Mountaire Farms of Delmarva, Frankford *Also called Mountaire Farms Inc* ***(G-2375)***
Mountaire of Delmarva Inc.....302 988-6207
55 Hosier St Selbyville (19975) ***(G-8526)***
Move Crew.....302 290-4684
14 Fresconi Ct New Castle (19720) ***(G-5537)***
Movement Mortgage LLC.....302 344-6758
19413 Jingle Shell Way Lewes (19958) ***(G-3651)***
Movetec Fitness Equipment LLC (PA).....302 563-4487
790 Salem Church Rd Newark (19702) ***(G-7064)***

Moving Sciences LLC 617 871-9892
1201 N Orange St Ste 600 Wilmington (19801) ***(G-11764)***
Mow Foot & Ankle Center, Milford *Also called Edwin M Mow DPM Facfas* ***(G-4403)***
Moyer, Robert A MD, Dover *Also called Tooze & Easter MD PA* ***(G-2152)***
Mozeweb LLC 302 355-0692
40 E Main St Newark (19711) ***(G-7065)***
Mp Axle Inc 302 478-6442
1329 Tulane Rd Wilmington (19803) ***(G-11765)***
Mr Chris Beauty Salon, Wilmington *Also called Mr Chris Hair Design* ***(G-11766)***
Mr Chris Hair Design 302 658-2121
209 W 9th St Wilmington (19801) ***(G-11766)***
Mr Copy Inc 302 227-4666
20200 Coastal Hwy Ste A Rehoboth Beach (19971) ***(G-8015)***
Mr Go-Glass, Dover *Also called Go-Glass Corporation* ***(G-1596)***
Mr Gregory Michael Hausmann 302 635-7675
39 Tremont Ct Newark (19711) ***(G-7066)***
Mr Natural Bottled Water 302 436-7700
32482 Mccary Rd Frankford (19945) ***(G-2376)***
Mr Natural Bottled Water Inc 302 436-7700
31919 Christine Ln Ocean View (19970) ***(G-7803)***
Mr Royal Touch MBL Detailing 302 229-0161
230 Paynter Dr Wilmington (19804) ***(G-11767)***
Mr Tire 1210, Delmar *Also called Monro Inc* ***(G-1022)***
Mr Window Washer 302 588-3624
126 Glenrock Dr Claymont (19703) ***(G-786)***
Mr. Tire, Middletown *Also called Monro Inc* ***(G-4168)***
Mresource LLC (PA) 312 608-4789
1220 N Market St Ste 808 Wilmington (19801) ***(G-11768)***
Mri Consultants LLC 302 295-3367
1 Centurian Dr Ste 107 Newark (19713) ***(G-7067)***
Ms Financing LLC 212 276-1206
1209 N Orange St Wilmington (19801) ***(G-11769)***
Ms Governors Square Shopping C 302 838-3384
1229 Quintilio Dr Bear (19701) ***(G-258)***
Ms Hathers Lrng Ctr Childcare 302 994-2448
205 Brookland Ave Wilmington (19805) ***(G-11770)***
Ms Linda's, Newark *Also called Bowman Linda Group Day Care* ***(G-6110)***
MSA, New Castle *Also called Couture Denim LLC* ***(G-5204)***
MSA Recording, Georgetown *Also called Mid South Audio LLC* ***(G-2603)***
Msb Enterprise Partners LLC 302 947-0736
24912 Pot Bunker Way Millsboro (19966) ***(G-4757)***
MSC Industrial Direct Co Inc 302 998-1214
401 Marsh Ln Ste 2 Wilmington (19804) ***(G-11771)***
Mssgme Inc 786 233-7592
3500 S Dupont Hwy Dover (19901) ***(G-1877)***
Mstm LLC 302 239-4447
28 Tenby Chase Dr Newark (19711) ***(G-7068)***
Mtb Artisans LLC 303 475-9024
2205 Kentmere Pkwy Wilmington (19806) ***(G-11772)***
Mtc Delaware LLC 302 654-3400
2 Dock View Dr New Castle (19720) ***(G-5538)***
Mtc Usa LLC 980 999-8888
411 Woodlawn Ave Newark (19711) ***(G-7069)***
Mtk Enterprises LLC 302 266-9611
210 Nathan Ct Newark (19711) ***(G-7070)***
Mto Hose Solutions Inc (PA) 302 266-6555
214 Interchange Blvd Newark (19711) ***(G-7071)***
Muffler Mart, Milford *Also called Tomall Inc* ***(G-4579)***
Mullen Thomas R DMD PA 302 629-3588
8466 Herring Run Rd D Seaford (19973) ***(G-8312)***
Mullico General Construction 302 475-4400
510 Foulkstone Rd Wilmington (19803) ***(G-11773)***
Multi Koastal Services 302 436-8822
34756 Roxana Rd Frankford (19945) ***(G-2377)***
Multi-Cble Adv SEC Sltns Inc 703 909-6239
19c Trolley Sq Wilmington (19806) ***(G-11774)***
Multi-Pro Business Svcs LLC 800 571-7017
200 Continental Dr Newark (19713) ***(G-7072)***
Multicultural A Delaware 302 399-6118
365 United Way Dover (19901) ***(G-1878)***
Mumford and Miller Con Inc 302 378-7736
1005 Industrial Rd Middletown (19709) ***(G-4171)***
Mumford Sheet Metal Works Inc 302 436-8251
101 Cemetery Rd Selbyville (19975) ***(G-8527)***
Mumford-Bjorkman Associates 302 655-8234
222a 7th Ave Wilmington (19805) ***(G-11775)***
Muncie Insurance Services 302 678-2800
1889 S Dupont Hwy Dover (19901) ***(G-1879)***
Muncie Insurance Services (PA) 302 629-9414
1011 Norman Eskridge Hwy Seaford (19973) ***(G-8313)***
Mundy Industrial Contrs Inc 302 629-1100
25876 Dupont Rd Seaford (19973) ***(G-8314)***
Municipal Services Commission (PA) 302 323-2330
216 Chestnut St New Castle (19720) ***(G-5539)***
Munters Corporation 302 798-2455
100 Naamans Rd Ste 5l Claymont (19703) ***(G-787)***
Murphy & Landon PC 302 472-8100
1011 Centre Rd Ste 210 Wilmington (19805) ***(G-11776)***
Murphy Electric Inc 302 644-0404
30731 Sassafras Dr Lewes (19958) ***(G-3652)***
Murphy Marine Services Inc 302 571-4700
701 Christiana Ave Wilmington (19801) ***(G-11777)***
Murphy Spadaro & Landon, Wilmington *Also called Murphy & Landon PC* ***(G-11776)***
Murphy Steel Inc 302 366-8676
727 Dawson Dr Newark (19713) ***(G-7073)***
Murray Manor, Wilmington *Also called Millcreek Mobile Hm Pk Land Co* ***(G-11690)***
Murray Motors, Seaford *Also called Murrays Motors* ***(G-8315)***
Murrayphillipspa, Georgetown *Also called Ronald D Jr Attorney At Law* ***(G-2642)***
Murrays Motors 302 628-0500
26029 Bethel Concord Rd Seaford (19973) ***(G-8315)***
Murry Trucking Llc 302 653-4811
568 Blckbird Grnspring Rd Smyrna (19977) ***(G-8683)***
Murry's Steaks 8262, New Castle *Also called Murrys of Maryland Inc* ***(G-5540)***
Murrys of Maryland Inc 302 328-3361
1400 S Dupont Hwy New Castle (19720) ***(G-5540)***
Mushroom Supply & Services Inc 302 998-2008
227 Cullen Way Newark (19711) ***(G-7074)***
Musi Commercial Properties Inc 302 594-1000
5700 Kennett Pike Wilmington (19807) ***(G-11778)***
Must App Corp 905 537-5522
1013 Centre Rd Ste 403b Wilmington (19805) ***(G-11779)***
Muvers Inc 888 508-4849
427 N Tatnall St Wilmington (19801) ***(G-11780)***
MV Farinola Inc 302 545-8492
4023 Kennett Pike Ste 219 Wilmington (19807) ***(G-11781)***
Mvl Structures Group LLC 302 652-7580
1000 N West St Ste 1501 Wilmington (19801) ***(G-11782)***
Mvl-Al Othman Al Zamel JV LLC 832 302-2757
1000 N West St Ste 1501 Wilmington (19801) ***(G-11783)***
Mvl-Saqa JV LLC 832 302-2757
1000 N West St Ste 1501 Wilmington (19801) ***(G-11784)***
Mwidm Inc (PA) 302 298-0101
913 N Market St Ste 200 Wilmington (19801) ***(G-11785)***
My Baby's Heartbeat Bear, Bear *Also called Purushas Picks Inc* ***(G-295)***
My Benefit Advisor LLC 302 588-7242
2207 Concord Pike Ste 152 Wilmington (19803) ***(G-11786)***
My Digital Shield 423 310-8977
300 Delaware Ave Ste 210 Wilmington (19801) ***(G-11787)***
My Easy Team LLC 302 722-6821
200 Continental Dr Newark (19713) ***(G-7075)***
My Lip Stuff 302 945-5922
21002 Robinsonville Rd Lewes (19958) ***(G-3653)***
My Mailbox Store, Wilmington *Also called Cpmg Inc* ***(G-9888)***
My Market Quest Inc 213 265-9767
501 Silverside Rd Ste 105 Wilmington (19809) ***(G-11788)***
My Qme Inc 302 218-8730
1000 Kirk Ave Ste 1000 # 1000 Wilmington (19806) ***(G-11789)***
My Sisters Place Inc 302 737-5303
50 Currant Dr Newark (19702) ***(G-7076)***
Mymedchoices Inc 302 932-1920
407 Valley Brook Dr Hockessin (19707) ***(G-3100)***
Mymoroccanbazar Inc 323 238-5747
2035 Sunset Lake Rd Newark (19702) ***(G-7077)***
Mymortgageready.com, Dover *Also called Vtms LLC* ***(G-2201)***
Myrle Manufacturing LLC 302 249-9408
14866 Adamsville Rd Greenwood (19950) ***(G-2754)***
Myschedule Inc 877 235-6825
2711 Centerville Rd # 400 Wilmington (19808) ***(G-11790)***
Myserve Inc 302 528-4822
129 Jade Dr Wilmington (19810) ***(G-11791)***
Mysherpa, Wilmington *Also called Gmg Solutions LLC* ***(G-10734)***
N A A C P, Wilmington *Also called Natio Assoc For The Advan of* ***(G-11804)***
N A L C, Newport *Also called National Assn Ltr Carriers* ***(G-7751)***
N and J Delivery Service LLC 302 562-3220
125 Rickey Blvd Unit 246 Bear (19701) ***(G-259)***
N Daisy Jax Inc 302 387-3543
1585 Mckee Rd Ste 3 Dover (19904) ***(G-1880)***
N Mallari Gc Corp 302 516-7738
44 Bastille Loop Newark (19702) ***(G-7078)***
N O Biasotto Do 302 998-1211
620 Stanton Christn Rd # 2 Newark (19713) ***(G-7079)***
N U Friendship Outreach Inc 302 836-0404
20 Waterton Dr Bear (19701) ***(G-260)***
N&D Nail Salon 302 834-4899
14 Foxhunt Dr Bear (19701) ***(G-261)***
N. Barton Sheet Metal & Hvac, Wilmington *Also called Apex Piping Systems Inc* ***(G-9096)***
Naamans Creek Watershed 302 475-3037
2204 Hillside Rd Wilmington (19810) ***(G-11792)***
Nab Hospitality, Newark *Also called Towne Place Suites By Marriott* ***(G-7580)***
Nab Motel Inc 302 656-9431
1051 S Market St Wilmington (19801) ***(G-11793)***
Nabertherm Inc 302 322-3665
64 Reads Way New Castle (19720) ***(G-5541)***
Nabstar Hospitality 302 453-1700
630 S College Ave Newark (19713) ***(G-7080)***

A
L
P
H
A
B
E
T
I
C

Nacstar 302 453-1700
630 S College Ave Newark (19713) ***(G-7081)***
Naes Corporation 856 299-0020
13 Reads Way Ste 100 New Castle (19720) ***(G-5542)***
Nagengast Janet Day Care 302 656-6898
602 Ashford Rd Wilmington (19803) ***(G-11794)***
Nagorka 302 537-2392
303 Wellington Pkwy Bethany Beach (19930) ***(G-416)***
Nail It Down General Contrs, Dover *Also called Nail It Down General Contrs* ***(G-1881)***
Nail It Down General Contrs 302 698-3073
1474 E Lebanon Rd Dover (19901) ***(G-1881)***
Nail Pros 302 674-2988
1365 N Dupont Hwy # 5008 Dover (19901) ***(G-1882)***
Naiva Solutions Inc 612 987-6350
100 Biddle Ave Ste 124 Newark (19702) ***(G-7082)***
Nakuuruq Solutions 302 526-2223
206 Atlantic St Dover (19902) ***(G-1883)***
Nalco Company LLC 856 423-6417
204 Quigley Blvd New Castle (19720) ***(G-5543)***
Nallys Auto Plaza Inc (PA) 302 543-8126
2412 W Newport Pike Wilmington (19804) ***(G-11795)***
Nancy A Union MD 302 645-6644
1302 Savannah Rd Lewes (19958) ***(G-3654)***
Nancy Conklin Interiors 302 655-0877
3220 Swarthmore Rd Wilmington (19807) ***(G-11796)***
Nancy Dufresne 302 378-7236
4 Denny Lynn Dr Townsend (19734) ***(G-8812)***
Nannas & Schiavo, Wilmington *Also called Nannas Haines & Schiavo PA* ***(G-11797)***
Nannas Haines & Schiavo PA 302 479-8800
1407 Foulk Rd Ste 100 Wilmington (19803) ***(G-11797)***
Nanodrop Technologies LLC 302 479-7707
3411 Silverside Rd 100bc Wilmington (19810) ***(G-11798)***
Nanoshel LLC 302 268-6163
3422 Old Capitol Trl Wilmington (19808) ***(G-11799)***
Nanticoke Cardiology 302 629-9099
200 Federal St Seaford (19973) ***(G-8316)***
Nanticoke Consulting Inc 302 424-0750
7707 Lindale Rd Greenwood (19950) ***(G-2755)***
Nanticoke Consulting and McHy, Greenwood *Also called Nanticoke Consulting Inc* ***(G-2755)***
Nanticoke Ear Nose and Throat 302 629-9067
900 Middleford Rd Seaford (19973) ***(G-8317)***
Nanticoke Fence LLC 302 628-7808
23464 Sussex Hwy Seaford (19973) ***(G-8318)***
Nanticoke Gastroenterology 302 629-2229
924 Middleford Rd Seaford (19973) ***(G-8319)***
Nanticoke Health Services Inc 302 629-4240
1320 Middleford Rd Seaford (19973) ***(G-8320)***
Nanticoke Health Services Inc 302 628-6344
701 Middleford Rd Seaford (19973) ***(G-8321)***
Nanticoke Health Services Inc 302 856-7099
503 W Market St Ste 110b Georgetown (19947) ***(G-2608)***
Nanticoke Health Services Inc 302 629-3923
1309 Bridgeville Hwy Seaford (19973) ***(G-8322)***
Nanticoke Health Services Inc (PA) 302 629-6611
801 Middleford Rd Seaford (19973) ***(G-8323)***
Nanticoke Indian Museum 302 945-7022
27073 John J Williams Hwy Millsboro (19966) ***(G-4758)***
Nanticoke Industries LLC 302 245-8825
28986 Cannon Dr Seaford (19973) ***(G-8324)***
Nanticoke Memorial Hosp Inc 302 629-6875
543 N Shipley St Ste F Seaford (19973) ***(G-8325)***
Nanticoke Obgyn Associates P A 302 629-2434
10 Tidewater Dr Seaford (19973) ***(G-8326)***
Nanticoke Occptional Hlth Svcs, Seaford *Also called Nanticoke Memorial Hosp Inc* ***(G-8325)***
Nanticoke Podiatry, Lewes *Also called James F Palmer* ***(G-3570)***
Nanticoke Shores Assoc LLC 302 945-1500
26335 Goosepond Rd Millsboro (19966) ***(G-4759)***
Naomi Ruth Howard 828 284-8721
654 Brenford Station Rd Smyrna (19977) ***(G-8684)***
NAPA, Millsboro *Also called Fishers Auto Parts Inc* ***(G-4691)***
NAPA Auto Parts, Claymont *Also called Genuine Parts Company* ***(G-752)***
NAPA Auto Parts, Smyrna *Also called Dover Automotive Inc* ***(G-8625)***
NAPA M3 Inc 719 660-6263
1521 Concord Pike Ste 301 Wilmington (19803) ***(G-11800)***
Napigen Inc 302 419-8117
200 Powder Mill Rd E4003431 Wilmington (19803) ***(G-11801)***
Nappa Trading Company, Magnolia *Also called Anthony J Nappa* ***(G-3880)***
Narinder Singh MD 302 737-2600
295 E Main St Ste 100 Newark (19711) ***(G-7083)***
Nash Omniscaping LLC 302 654-4000
118 Valley Rd Wilmington (19804) ***(G-11802)***
Nason Construction Inc (PA) 302 529-2510
3411 Silverside Rd # 200 Wilmington (19810) ***(G-11803)***
Nassau Vly Vineyards & Winery 302 645-9463
32165 Winery Way Lewes (19958) ***(G-3655)***
Nathaniel Jon Bent DDS PA 302 731-4907
625 Barksdale Rd Ste 117 Newark (19711) ***(G-7084)***
Natio Assoc For The Advan of 302 655-0998
408 E 8th St Wilmington (19801) ***(G-11804)***
National Appliance Whse Inc 302 543-7636
2101 Concord Pike Wilmington (19803) ***(G-11805)***
National Assn Ltr Carriers 302 652-2933
8 S Dupont Rd Fl 2 Newport (19804) ***(G-7751)***
National Auto Movers LLC 302 229-9256
46 Bluegrass Blvd Smyrna (19977) ***(G-8685)***
National City Bank, Wilmington *Also called PNC Bank National Association* ***(G-12166)***
National Concrete Products LLC 302 349-5528
9466 Beach Hwy Greenwood (19950) ***(G-2756)***
National Cricket Associates 302 454-7294
12 Rocky Rd Newark (19702) ***(G-7085)***
National Dcument MGT Solutions 302 535-9263
301 Westville Rd Marydel (19964) ***(G-3921)***
National Dentex LLC 302 661-6000
24 Lukens Dr New Castle (19720) ***(G-5544)***
National Educatn Finical Svcs, Wilmington *Also called Nefsc Inc* ***(G-11828)***
National Fitness LLC 301 841-8066
726 Fox Tail Dr Bethany Beach (19930) ***(G-417)***
National Guard Association Del 302 326-7125
1 Vavala Way New Castle (19720) ***(G-5545)***
National Holding Investment Co (HQ) 302 573-3887
1011 Centre Rd Wilmington (19805) ***(G-11806)***
National HVAC Service 302 323-1776
42a Southgate Blvd New Castle (19720) ***(G-5546)***
National HVAC Service 570 825-2894
N Usa Rt 13 Seaford (19973) ***(G-8327)***
National Income Tax Service, Dover *Also called Sandra S Gulledge CPA* ***(G-2058)***
National Industries For The Bl 302 477-0860
3314 Tunison Dr Wilmington (19810) ***(G-11807)***
National Medical Care Inc 302 658-7469
303 A St Wilmington (19801) ***(G-11808)***
National Mentor Holdings Inc 732 627-9890
28417 Dupont Blvd Millsboro (19966) ***(G-4760)***
National Mentor Holdings Inc 302 934-0512
230 Mitchell St Millsboro (19966) ***(G-4761)***
National Opprtnities Unlimited 913 905-2261
42 Reads Way Ste 5 New Castle (19720) ***(G-5547)***
National Restortn & Faclty Svc 856 401-0100
1800 Walnut St Wilmington (19809) ***(G-11809)***
National Rig Rental LLC 302 539-1963
35322 Bayard Rd Frankford (19945) ***(G-2378)***
National Signing Source LLC 773 885-3285
1521 Concord Pike Ste 300 Wilmington (19803) ***(G-11810)***
National Society Inc 302 656-9572
1538 Cleland Crse Wilmington (19805) ***(G-11811)***
National Stress Clinic LLC 646 571-8627
1201 N Orange St Ste 600 Wilmington (19801) ***(G-11812)***
National Supply Contractors, Wilmington *Also called Ip Camera Warehouse LLC* ***(G-11079)***
National Tape Duplicators 302 999-1110
1500 First State Blvd Wilmington (19804) ***(G-11813)***
National Waterworks Inc 302 653-9096
25414 Primehook Rd # 100 Milton (19968) ***(G-4942)***
Nations Equity Investments Inc 302 257-9287
1201 N Orange St Ste 700 Wilmington (19801) ***(G-11814)***
Nationwide, Newark *Also called S T Good Insurance Inc* ***(G-7374)***
Nationwide, New Castle *Also called Clark Bffone Mtthews Insur AGC* ***(G-5173)***
Nationwide, Newark *Also called Insley Insurance & Fincl Svc* ***(G-6784)***
Nationwide, Wilmington *Also called Weymouth Swyze Crroon Insur In* ***(G-13177)***
Nationwide, Hockessin *Also called L & D Insurance Services LLC* ***(G-3073)***
Nationwide, Wilmington *Also called Insurance & Financial Svcs Inc* ***(G-11043)***
Nationwide, Wilmington *Also called Usi Inc* ***(G-13041)***
Nationwide, Wilmington *Also called Insurance Office America Inc* ***(G-11046)***
Nationwide, Delaware City *Also called Nickle Insurance Agency Inc* ***(G-961)***
Nationwide, Hockessin *Also called John Koziol Inc* ***(G-3068)***
Nationwide, Lewes *Also called Truitt Insurance Agency Inc* ***(G-3796)***
Nationwide, Wilmington *Also called Nickle Insurance* ***(G-11888)***
Nationwide, Dover *Also called Muncie Insurance Services* ***(G-1879)***
Nationwide, Wilmington *Also called Lyons Insurance Agency Inc* ***(G-11466)***
Nationwide, Wilmington *Also called McCall Brooks Insurance Agency* ***(G-11585)***
Nationwide, Seaford *Also called Muncie Insurance Services* ***(G-8313)***
Nationwide, Christiana *Also called Steinebach Robert and Assoc* ***(G-680)***
Nationwide, Newark *Also called Lisa Broadbent Insurance Inc* ***(G-6939)***
Nationwide, Bear *Also called Calvin Sheets* ***(G-63)***
Nationwide Corporation 302 761-9611
100 Penn Mart Shopg Ctr New Castle (19720) ***(G-5548)***
Nationwide Hlth Info Tech Inc 302 295-5033
1000 N West St Ste 1200 Wilmington (19801) ***(G-11815)***
Nationwide Insurance, Newark *Also called B&H Insurance LLC* ***(G-6036)***
Nationwide Insurance, Newark *Also called Poland & Sullivan Insurance* ***(G-7229)***
Nationwide Insurance, Wilmington *Also called Business Insurance Services* ***(G-9511)***
Nationwide Insurance Co 302 678-2223
1252 Forrest Ave Dover (19904) ***(G-1884)***
Nationwide Mutual Insurance Co 302 479-5560
501 Silverside Rd Ste 28 Wilmington (19809) ***(G-11816)***
Nationwide Mutual Insurance Co 302 234-5430
724 Yorklyn Rd Ste 200 Hockessin (19707) ***(G-3101)***

Native Communications LLC 302 439-0640
4023 Kennett Pike 176 Wilmington (19807) ***(G-11817)***
Natural By Nature, Newark *Also called Natural Dairy Products Corp* ***(G-7086)***
Natural Dairy Products Corp 302 455-1261
316 Markus Ct Newark (19713) ***(G-7086)***
Natural House Inc 302 218-0338
2515 Kirkwood Hwy Newark (19711) ***(G-7087)***
Natural Lawn Care of America, Dagsboro *Also called West Third Enterprises LLC* ***(G-943)***
Natural Lawn of America, Wilmington *Also called Jamark Enterprises Inc* ***(G-11118)***
Natural Stacks Inc 855 678-2257
16192 Coastal Hwy Lewes (19958) ***(G-3656)***
Naturalawn of America Inc 302 652-2000
40 Germay Dr Wilmington (19804) ***(G-11818)***
Natures Call LLC 302 777-7767
601 Philadelphia Pike Wilmington (19809) ***(G-11819)***
Natures Gourmet Candles 302 697-2785
2189 S State St Dover (19901) ***(G-1885)***
Naudain Enterprises LLC 302 239-6840
5840 Limestone Rd Hockessin (19707) ***(G-3102)***
Naughty Apple 954 300-7158
4209 Birch Cir Wilmington (19808) ***(G-11820)***
Navient Corporation (PA) 302 283-8000
123 S Justison St Ste 300 Wilmington (19801) ***(G-11821)***
Navient Corporation 302 283-8000
123 S Justison St Ste 300 Wilmington (19801) ***(G-11822)***
Navient Corporation 302 283-8000
123 S Justison St Ste 300 Wilmington (19801) ***(G-11823)***
Navient Dept Edcatn Ln Srvcing, Wilmington *Also called Navient Corporation* ***(G-11823)***
Navy League of United States 302 456-4410
2205 Glen Avon Rd Wilmington (19808) ***(G-11824)***
Navy Operational Support Ctr W 312 998-3328
3920 Kirkwood Hwy Wilmington (19808) ***(G-11825)***
Nazar Dover LLC 302 747-5050
561 N Dupont Hwy Dover (19901) ***(G-1886)***
Nazhat Enterprises Holdings 415 670-9262
8 The Grn Ste 7361 Dover (19901) ***(G-1887)***
Ncall Research Inc (PA) 302 678-9400
363 Saulsbury Rd Dover (19904) ***(G-1888)***
NCCSEFCU, New Castle *Also called New Castle County School Emplo* ***(G-5555)***
Nces, Middletown *Also called New Covenant Elec Svcs Inc* ***(G-4172)***
Ncf Supporting Organization 850 776-2789
15 Center Meeting Rd Wilmington (19807) ***(G-11826)***
Ncs Pearson Inc 302 736-8006
1012 College Rd Dover (19904) ***(G-1889)***
NDT, Wilmington *Also called Network Design Technologies* ***(G-11839)***
Near and Dear Home Care 302 530-6498
1002 Birchwood Dr Newark (19713) ***(G-7088)***
Necessary Luxury 302 764-4032
806 Woodsdale Rd Wilmington (19809) ***(G-11827)***
Necessary Lxury Mssage Therapy, Wilmington *Also called Necessary Luxury* ***(G-11827)***
Neena Mukkamala DDS 302 734-5305
95 Wolf Creek Blvd Ste 3 Dover (19901) ***(G-1890)***
Neenee Wees Daycare 302 730-3630
208 Mifflin Rd Dover (19904) ***(G-1891)***
Nefsc Inc 302 746-1771
405 Silverside Rd Ste 200 Wilmington (19809) ***(G-11828)***
Negri Bossi North America Inc 302 328-8020
311 Carroll Dr New Castle (19720) ***(G-5549)***
Negri Bossi Usa Inc 302 328-8020
311 Carroll Dr 100 New Castle (19720) ***(G-5550)***
Nehemiah Gtwy Cmnty Dev Corp 302 655-0803
201 W 23rd St Wilmington (19802) ***(G-11829)***
Neighborhood House Inc (PA) 302 658-5404
1218 B St Wilmington (19801) ***(G-11830)***
Neighborly Home Care 610 420-1868
2101 W 2nd St Wilmington (19805) ***(G-11831)***
Neil, Wilmington *Also called Nuclear Electric Insurance Ltd* ***(G-11921)***
Neil G McAneny DDS 302 368-0329
400 New London Rd Newark (19711) ***(G-7089)***
Neil G McAneny DDS PC 302 731-4907
117 Barksdale Pro Ctr Newark (19711) ***(G-7090)***
Nemours Dpont Pdatrics Milford, Milford *Also called Nemours Foundation* ***(G-4512)***
Nemours Dpont Pdatrics Seaford, Seaford *Also called Nemours Foundation* ***(G-8328)***
Nemours Energy (PA) 302 655-4838
400 W 9th St Ste 200 Wilmington (19801) ***(G-11832)***
Nemours Foundation 302 651-4000
1600 Rockland Rd Wilmington (19803) ***(G-11833)***
Nemours Foundation 302 422-4559
703 N Dupont Blvd Milford (19963) ***(G-4512)***
Nemours Foundation 302 651-6811
1600 Rockland Rd Wilmington (19803) ***(G-11834)***
Nemours Foundation 302 629-5030
49 Fallon Ave Seaford (19973) ***(G-8328)***
Nemours Foundation 302 651-4400
1801 Rockland Rd Wilmington (19803) ***(G-11835)***
Nemours Foundation 302 651-4000
1600 Rockland Rd Wilmington (19803) ***(G-11836)***
Nemours Fundation Pension Plan 302 629-5030
49 Fallon Ave Seaford (19973) ***(G-8329)***
Nemours Fundation Pension Plan 302 836-7820
1400 Peoples Plz Ste 300 Newark (19702) ***(G-7091)***
Nemours Hlth & Prevention Svcs (PA) 302 366-1929
252 Chapman Rd Ste 200 Newark (19702) ***(G-7092)***
Nemours Research Institute, Wilmington *Also called Nemours Foundation* ***(G-11834)***
Nemours Senior Care Wilmington, Wilmington *Also called Nemours Foundation* ***(G-11835)***
Neon Dojo LLC 650 275-2395
3500 S Dupont Hwy Dover (19901) ***(G-1892)***
Neon Fun LLC 858 220-0946
3500 S Dupont Hwy Dover (19901) ***(G-1893)***
Nephrology Associates PA 302 225-0451
4923 Ogletown Stanton Rd # 200 Newark (19713) ***(G-7093)***
Nerd Boy LLC 302 857-0243
800 N State St Ste 402 Dover (19901) ***(G-1894)***
Nesmith & Company Inc 215 755-4570
100 Naamans Rd Ste 2d Claymont (19703) ***(G-788)***
Nessus Investment Corporation 302 323-3104
1 Penns Way New Castle (19721) ***(G-5551)***
Nestle Usa Inc 302 325-0300
200 Lisa Dr New Castle (19720) ***(G-5552)***
Net Monarch 302 994-9407
5161 W Woodmill Dr Wilmington (19808) ***(G-11837)***
Netinstincts Inc 302 521-9478
501 Silverside Rd Ste 105 Wilmington (19809) ***(G-11838)***
Netproteus 206 203-2525
33107 Perrydale Grn Lewes (19958) ***(G-3657)***
Netproteus.com, Lewes *Also called Netproteus* ***(G-3657)***
Netragy LLC 973 846-7018
10 Cheswold Blvd Apt 1d Newark (19713) ***(G-7094)***
Nettel Partners LLC 215 290-7383
8 Venetian Dr Rehoboth Beach (19971) ***(G-8016)***
Network Design Technologies 610 991-2929
1000 N West St Ste 1200 Wilmington (19801) ***(G-11839)***
Network Mapping Inc 310 560-4142
1013 Centre Rd Ste 403a Wilmington (19805) ***(G-11840)***
Network Scrap Metal Corp (PA) 910 202-0655
1000 N West St Ste 1501 Wilmington (19801) ***(G-11841)***
Network Security Services Inc 703 319-0411
32 W Loockerman St # 108 Dover (19904) ***(G-1895)***
Neuberger & Berman Trust Co 302 658-8522
919 N Market St Ste 506 Wilmington (19801) ***(G-11842)***
Neuracon Biotech Inc 813 966-3129
1313 N Market St Ste 5100 Wilmington (19801) ***(G-11843)***
Neuro Fitness Therapy 302 753-2700
3300 Concord Pike Ste 4 Wilmington (19803) ***(G-11844)***
Neuro Ophthalmologic Asso 302 792-1616
1201 Society Dr Claymont (19703) ***(G-789)***
Neurolixis Inc (PA) 215 910-2261
251 Little Falls Dr Wilmington (19808) ***(G-11845)***
Neurology Associates PA 302 731-3017
774 Christiana Rd Ste 201 Newark (19713) ***(G-7095)***
Neurorx Inc 202 340-1352
913 N Market St Ste 200 Wilmington (19801) ***(G-11846)***
Neurosurgery Consultants PA 302 738-9145
79 Omega Dr Bldg C Newark (19713) ***(G-7096)***
Neurosurgical Associates PA 302 738-9543
249 E Main St Apt K Newark (19711) ***(G-7097)***
Neutec Corp 302 697-6752
29 Emerson Dr Dover (19901) ***(G-1896)***
Never Never Lnd Kennel Cattery 302 645-6140
34377 Neverland Rd Lewes (19958) ***(G-3658)***
Nevron Software LLC 302 792-0175
501 Silverside Rd Ste 105 Wilmington (19809) ***(G-11847)***
New Alden-Berkley Apartments, Wilmington *Also called New Alden-Berkley Assoc LLC* ***(G-11848)***
New Alden-Berkley Assoc LLC 207 774-5341
4 Denny Rd Wilmington (19809) ***(G-11848)***
New Ark Pediatrics Inc 302 738-4800
314 E Main St Ste 101 Newark (19711) ***(G-7098)***
New B & M Meats Inc 302 655-5331
21 Commerce St Wilmington (19801) ***(G-11849)***
New Balance Retail Management 302 230-3062
5300 Brandywine Pkwy Wilmington (19803) ***(G-11850)***
New Beginnings, New Castle *Also called Chimes Inc* ***(G-5148)***
New Behavorial Network, Wilmington *Also called Health Care Consultants Inc* ***(G-10869)***
New Car Connection 302 328-7000
174 N Dupont Hwy New Castle (19720) ***(G-5553)***
New Castel, West Coast Video, New Castle *Also called Pat Cirelli* ***(G-5607)***
New Castle Airport, New Castle *Also called Delaware River & Bay Authority* ***(G-5236)***
New Castle Assoc & Podiatry, Newark *Also called Raymond V Feehery Jr DPM* ***(G-7302)***
New Castle Boys & Girls Clubs, New Castle *Also called Boys & Girls Clubs Del Inc* ***(G-5102)***
New Castle Chiropractic Ctr PA, Newark *Also called Main Street Fmly Chiropractic* ***(G-6974)***
New Castle Cnty Bd of Realtors 302 762-4800
3615 Miller Rd Wilmington (19802) ***(G-11851)***
New Castle Cnty Shoppers Guide 302 325-6600
950 W Basin Rd New Castle (19720) ***(G-5554)***
New Castle Conservation Dst 302 832-3100
2430 Old County Rd Newark (19702) ***(G-7099)***

ALPHABETIC

(PA)=Parent Co (HQ)=Headquarters (DH)=Div Headquarters
2020 Harris Directory of Delaware Businesses
693

NEW CASTLE COUNTY CRISIS PREGN, Wilmington *Also called A Door of Hope Inc* ***(G-8876)***
New Castle County Flooring....302 218-0507
2923 Ogletown Rd Newark (19713) ***(G-7100)***
New Castle County Head Start (PA)....302 452-1500
256 Chapman Rd Ste 103 Newark (19702) ***(G-7101)***
New Castle County Head Start....302 999-8480
310 Kiamensi Rd Ste A Wilmington (19804) ***(G-11852)***
New Castle County Head Start....302 832-2212
931 Bear Corbitt Rd Bear (19701) ***(G-262)***
New Castle County School Emplo....302 613-5330
113 W 6th St New Castle (19720) ***(G-5555)***
New Castle Court House Museum, New Castle *Also called Historical & Cultural Afairs* ***(G-5396)***
New Castle Dance & Mus Academy, Bear *Also called New Castle Dance Academy* ***(G-263)***
New Castle Dance Academy....302 836-2060
460 Eden Cir Bear (19701) ***(G-263)***
New Castle Dental Assoc PA....302 328-1513
92 Reads Way Ste 200 New Castle (19720) ***(G-5556)***
New Castle Engraving Co....302 652-7551
133 Festone Ave New Castle (19720) ***(G-5557)***
New Castle Family Care PA....302 275-3428
14 Magil Ct Newark (19702) ***(G-7102)***
New Castle Farmers Market, New Castle *Also called 326 Associates LP* ***(G-4990)***
New Castle Glass Inc....302 322-6164
38 Lesley Ln New Castle (19720) ***(G-5558)***
New Castle Health&Rehab Cntr, New Castle *Also called New Castle HEAlth&rehab Cntr* ***(G-5559)***
New Castle HEAlth&rehab Cntr....302 328-2580
32 Buena Vista Dr New Castle (19720) ***(G-5559)***
New Castle Hearing Speech Ctr, Hockessin *Also called Otolaryngology Consultants* ***(G-3108)***
New Castle Hearing/Spch/Vstblr, New Castle *Also called Otolaryngology Consultants* ***(G-5593)***
New Castle Historical Society....302 322-2794
30 Market St New Castle (19720) ***(G-5560)***
New Castle Hot Mix Inc....302 655-2119
925 S Heald St Wilmington (19801) ***(G-11853)***
New Castle Insurance Ltd....302 328-6111
621 Delaware St Ste 100 New Castle (19720) ***(G-5561)***
New Castle Lodging Corporation....302 654-5544
1213 West Ave New Castle (19720) ***(G-5562)***
New Castle Precision Mch LLC....302 650-7849
729 Grantham Ln Ste 2 New Castle (19720) ***(G-5563)***
New Castle Sailing Club....302 307-3060
614 South St New Castle (19720) ***(G-5564)***
New Castle Senior Center....302 326-4209
400 South St New Castle (19720) ***(G-5565)***
New Castle Shuttle and Taxi SE....302 326-1855
38 Stevens Ave New Castle (19720) ***(G-5566)***
New Castle Travelodge, New Castle *Also called Shriji Hospitality (not Llc)* ***(G-5706)***
New Castle Travelodge, New Castle *Also called New Castle Lodging Corporation* ***(G-5562)***
New Castle Weekly Inc....302 328-6005
203 Delaware St New Castle (19720) ***(G-5567)***
New Cingular Wireless Svcs Inc....302 999-0055
3401 Kirkwood Hwy Wilmington (19808) ***(G-11854)***
New Cingular Wireless Svcs Inc....302 762-1366
4120 Concord Pike Ste 2 Wilmington (19803) ***(G-11855)***
New Cndlelight Productions Inc....302 475-2313
2208 Millers Rd Wilmington (19810) ***(G-11856)***
New Colony North Enterprises....302 762-0405
319 E Lea Blvd Wilmington (19802) ***(G-11857)***
New Compton Towne Assoc LP....302 571-0217
4 Denny Rd Wilmington (19809) ***(G-11858)***
New Concept Dental....302 778-3822
2004 Foulk Rd Ste 1 Wilmington (19810) ***(G-11859)***
New Concept Technologies LLC....518 533-5367
3422 Old Capitol Trl Wilmington (19808) ***(G-11860)***
New Covenant Elec Svcs Inc....302 454-1165
806 Old School House Rd Middletown (19709) ***(G-4172)***
New Creation Logistics Inc....302 438-3154
6 Sussex Rd Apt J Newark (19713) ***(G-7103)***
New Cstle Cmnty Mntal Hlth Ctr, Newark *Also called Health & Social Svcs Del Dept* ***(G-6717)***
New Cstle Cnty Chmber Commerce....302 737-4343
920 Justison St Wilmington (19801) ***(G-11861)***
New Cstle Cnty Del Em Fdral Cr....302 395-5350
100 Churchmans Rd New Castle (19720) ***(G-5568)***
New Cstle Hlth Rhblitation Ctr, New Castle *Also called Oak Hrc New Castle LLC* ***(G-5584)***
New Day Montessori....302 235-2554
1 Middleton Dr Wilmington (19808) ***(G-11862)***
New Direction Early Headstart....302 831-0584
321 S College Ave Newark (19716) ***(G-7104)***
New England Fellowship, Georgetown *Also called Fellowship Hlth Resources Inc* ***(G-2528)***
New ERA Media LLC....302 731-2003
31 Cordele Rd Newark (19711) ***(G-7105)***
New Hope Vehicle Exports LLC....302 275-6482
1000 S Market St Wilmington (19801) ***(G-11863)***
New Ilc Dover Inc (PA)....302 335-3911
1 Moonwalker Rd Frederica (19946) ***(G-2410)***
New Image Inc....302 738-6824
2401 Ogletown Rd Ste A Newark (19711) ***(G-7106)***
New Image Laser and Skin Care....302 537-4336
118 Atlantic Ave Ocean View (19970) ***(G-7804)***
New Life Furniture Systems....302 994-9054
1675 E Ayre St Wilmington (19804) ***(G-11864)***
New Life Medicals LLC....302 478-7973
3524 Silverside Rd 35b Wilmington (19810) ***(G-11865)***
New London Veterinary Center....302 738-5000
437 New London Rd Newark (19711) ***(G-7107)***
New Look Home Inc....302 994-4397
100 Bestfield Rd Wilmington (19804) ***(G-11866)***
New Nordic US Inc....514 390-2316
1000 N West St Wilmington (19801) ***(G-11867)***
New Nordic USA, Wilmington *Also called New Nordic US Inc* ***(G-11867)***
New Orleans Hotel Equity LLC....302 757-7300
1000 N West St Ste 1400 Wilmington (19801) ***(G-11868)***
New Perspectives Inc....302 489-0220
2055 Limestone Rd Ste 109 Wilmington (19808) ***(G-11869)***
New Process Fibre Company Inc....302 349-4535
12655 N 1st St Greenwood (19950) ***(G-2757)***
New R V Associates L P....302 798-6878
2610 Philadelphia Pike B6 Claymont (19703) ***(G-790)***
New Temple Corp....302 998-6475
818 N Market St Fl 3 Wilmington (19801) ***(G-11870)***
New Trend Hair Salon....302 998-3331
4569 Kirkwood Hwy Wilmington (19808) ***(G-11871)***
New U Nutrition Inc....302 543-4555
2801 Lancaster Ave Wilmington (19805) ***(G-11872)***
New Vision Services Inc....484 350-6495
812 Village Cir Apt B Newark (19713) ***(G-7108)***
New Visions Inv Group LLC....302 299-6234
31 Phoenix Ave Newark (19702) ***(G-7109)***
New Windsor Associates LLC....207 774-5341
4 Denny Rd Wilmington (19809) ***(G-11873)***
New Wndsor Apartments Assoc LP....302 656-1354
4 Denny Rd Wilmington (19809) ***(G-11874)***
New York Life, Wilmington *Also called Zavier J Decaire* ***(G-13341)***
New York Life Insurance Co....302 369-8500
200 Continental Dr # 306 Newark (19713) ***(G-7110)***
Newarc Welding & Fabricating....302 658-5214
30 Commerce St Wilmington (19801) ***(G-11875)***
Newarc Welding Inc....302 376-1801
222 Chestnut Way Middletown (19709) ***(G-4173)***
Newark Building Services LLC....302 377-7687
9 Cartier Ct Newark (19711) ***(G-7111)***
Newark Chinese Ldry & Dry Clrs....302 368-3305
810 Hilltop Rd Newark (19711) ***(G-7112)***
Newark Christian Childcare....302 369-3000
680 S Chapel St Newark (19713) ***(G-7113)***
Newark Chropractic Hlth Ctr PA....302 239-1600
310 Lantana Dr Hockessin (19707) ***(G-3103)***
Newark Country Club....302 368-7008
300 W Main St Newark (19711) ***(G-7114)***
Newark Ctr For Creative Lrng....302 368-7772
401 Phillips Ave Newark (19711) ***(G-7115)***
NEWARK DAY NURSERY AND CHILDRE, Newark *Also called Newark Day-Nursery Association* ***(G-7116)***
Newark Day-Nursery Association....302 731-4925
921 Barksdale Rd Newark (19711) ***(G-7116)***
Newark Dental Assoc Inc....302 737-5170
344 E Main St Newark (19711) ***(G-7117)***
Newark Emergency Center Inc....302 738-4300
324 E Main St Ste 100 Newark (19711) ***(G-7118)***
Newark Family Counceling Ctr....302 368-6895
501 Ogletown Rd Newark (19711) ***(G-7119)***
Newark Fence Co....302 368-5329
24 Briarcliffe Ct Newark (19702) ***(G-7120)***
Newark Glass & Mirror Inc....302 834-1158
151 Rickey Blvd Bear (19701) ***(G-264)***
Newark Heritage Partners I LLC....302 283-0540
501 S Harmony Rd Newark (19713) ***(G-7121)***
Newark Insulation Co Inc....302 731-8970
68 Albe Dr A Newark (19702) ***(G-7122)***
Newark Kubota Inc....302 365-6000
2063 Pulaski Hwy Newark (19702) ***(G-7123)***
Newark Manor, Newark *Also called Premier Healthcare Inc* ***(G-7244)***
Newark Montessori Preschool....302 366-1481
1031 S Chapel St Newark (19702) ***(G-7124)***
Newark National Little League....302 738-0881
P.O. Box 15031 Newark (19711) ***(G-7125)***
Newark Pediatrician Inc....302 738-4800
314 E Main St Ste 101 Newark (19711) ***(G-7126)***
Newark Recycling Center Inc....302 737-7300
6 Albe Dr Newark (19702) ***(G-7127)***
Newark Senior Center Inc....302 737-2336
200 Whitechapel Dr Newark (19713) ***(G-7128)***
Newark United Methodist....302 368-8774
69 E Main St Newark (19711) ***(G-7129)***

Newcosmos LLC....302 838-1935
52 Blue Spruce Dr Bear (19701) ***(G-265)***
Newmarkkfsm....302 655-0600
1105 N Market St Ste 1610 Wilmington (19801) ***(G-11876)***
Newphoenix Screen Printing....302 747-8991
305 Lotus St Dover (19901) ***(G-1897)***
Newport....302 995-2840
22 W Market St Wilmington (19804) ***(G-11877)***
Newport Builders & Windowland....302 994-3537
2 E Ayre St Wilmington (19804) ***(G-11878)***
Newport Ventures Inc....302 998-1693
20 N James St Wilmington (19804) ***(G-11879)***
Newrez LLC....302 455-6600
651 N Broad St Middletown (19709) ***(G-4174)***
News Journal, New Castle *Also called Gannett Co Inc* ***(G-5343)***
News Print Shop....302 337-8283
16694 Emma Jane Ln Bridgeville (19933) ***(G-502)***
News Radio 1450 Wilm, New Castle *Also called Iheartmedia Inc* ***(G-5411)***
News-Journal Company....302 324-2500
950 W Basin Rd New Castle (19720) ***(G-5569)***
Newton One Advisors....302 731-1326
131 Continental Dr # 206 Newark (19713) ***(G-7130)***
Newtown Family Dentistry, Bear *Also called Mark Wieczorek Dmd PC* ***(G-246)***
Nexsigns LLC....302 508-2615
711 Coldwater Dr Clayton (19938) ***(G-866)***
Next Generation Plant Svcs Inc....302 654-7584
103 Foulk Rd Ste 202 Wilmington (19803) ***(G-11880)***
Next Music Inc....650 300-4881
1811 Silverside Rd Wilmington (19810) ***(G-11881)***
Next Trucking Inc....213 568-0388
1209 N Orange St Wilmington (19801) ***(G-11882)***
Nexus Services America LLC (PA)....800 946-4626
2711 Centerville Rd # 400 Wilmington (19808) ***(G-11883)***
NGK North America Inc (HQ)....302 654-1344
1105 N Market St Ste 1300 Wilmington (19801) ***(G-11884)***
NGK Spark Plugs USA Holdg Inc (HQ)....302 288-0131
1011 Centre Rd Wilmington (19805) ***(G-11885)***
Nguyen, Keith C/O Aesthetic, Wilmington *Also called Aesthtic Special Care Assoc PA* ***(G-8967)***
Nhb Advisors Inc....610 660-0060
919 N Market St Ste 600 Wilmington (19801) ***(G-11886)***
Nic-O-Boli, Rehoboth Beach *Also called Nicola Pizza Inc* ***(G-8017)***
Nichino America Inc....302 636-9001
4550 Linden Hill Rd # 501 Wilmington (19808) ***(G-11887)***
Nicholas J Punturieri....302 834-7700
1200 Peoples Plz Newark (19702) ***(G-7131)***
Nicholas O Biasotto Co....302 998-1235
620 Stanton Christiana Rd # 205 Newark (19713) ***(G-7132)***
Nichols Excavation and Ldscp, Newark *Also called Nichols Nursery Inc* ***(G-7133)***
Nichols Nursery Inc....302 834-2426
324 Markus Ct Newark (19713) ***(G-7133)***
Nickle Elec Companies Inc....302 856-1006
540 S Bedford St Georgetown (19947) ***(G-2609)***
Nickle Elec Companies Inc (PA)....302 453-4000
14 Mill Park Ct Ste E Newark (19713) ***(G-7134)***
Nickle Insurance....302 654-0347
3920 Kennett Pike Wilmington (19807) ***(G-11888)***
Nickle Insurance Agency Inc....302 834-9700
119 Washington St Delaware City (19706) ***(G-961)***
Nicks Welding Repair LLC....302 545-1494
3705 Oak Ridge Rd Wilmington (19808) ***(G-11889)***
Nicola Pizza Inc....302 227-6211
8 N 1st St Rehoboth Beach (19971) ***(G-8017)***
Nicole L Scott Np-C Adult....302 690-1692
45 Forest Creek Dr Hockessin (19707) ***(G-3104)***
Nikko Capital Investments Ltd....832 324-5335
16192 Coastal Hwy Lewes (19958) ***(G-3659)***
Ninety One Holding Inc....212 203-7900
56140 Pine Cone Ln Bethany Beach (19930) ***(G-418)***
Nitro Impact Inc....347 694-7000
3422 Old Capitol Trl 68 Wilmington (19808) ***(G-11890)***
Nixon Unf Rntl Svc of Lncaster (PA)....302 656-2774
42 Lukens Dr Ste 100 New Castle (19720) ***(G-5570)***
Nixon Uniform Service Inc (PA)....302 325-2875
500 Centerpoint Blvd New Castle (19720) ***(G-5571)***
Nixon Uniform Service & Med Wr, New Castle *Also called Nixon Uniform Service Inc* ***(G-5571)***
Nk Consulting Inc....330 269-5775
427 N Ttnall St Ste 83747 Wilmington (19801) ***(G-11891)***
Nk News, Wilmington *Also called Nk Consulting Inc* ***(G-11891)***
Nkognito Productions LLC....302 943-0399
80 Braeburn Ter Magnolia (19962) ***(G-3901)***
NKS Distributors Inc (PA)....302 322-1811
399 Churchmans Rd New Castle (19720) ***(G-5572)***
NKS Distributors Inc....302 422-1220
759 E Masten Cir Milford (19963) ***(G-4513)***
Nnn 824 North Market St LLC....302 652-8013
824 N Market St Ste 111 Wilmington (19801) ***(G-11892)***

No Joke I LLC....302 395-0882
16 Stockton Dr New Castle (19720) ***(G-5573)***
No Nonsense Office Mchs LLC....302 856-7381
22416 Lwes Georgetown Hwy Georgetown (19947) ***(G-2610)***
No Place Like Home LLC....302 528-8682
1017 Bear Corbitt Rd Bear (19701) ***(G-266)***
Noble Eagle Sales LLC....302 736-5166
5105 N Dupont Hwy Dover (19901) ***(G-1898)***
Noble Finance Corp....302 995-2760
1708 E Lebanon Rd Ste 4 Dover (19901) ***(G-1899)***
Noble Master....302 261-2018
16192 Coastal Hwy Lewes (19958) ***(G-3660)***
Noble Master Games, Lewes *Also called Noble Master* ***(G-3660)***
Nolan Williams & Plumhoff....410 823-7800
4132 Ogletown Stanton Rd Newark (19713) ***(G-7135)***
Nolte & Associates, Wilmington *Also called R Stokes Nolte Esquire &* ***(G-12298)***
Nolte & Brodoway PA....302 777-1700
1013 Centre Rd Wilmington (19805) ***(G-11893)***
Nonprofit Bus Solutions LLC....302 353-4606
2701 Centerville Rd Wilmington (19808) ***(G-11894)***
Nonwovens Indus & Active Packg, Wilmington *Also called E I Du Pont De Nemours & Co* ***(G-10303)***
Noor Foundation International....302 234-8860
249 Peoples Way Hockessin (19707) ***(G-3105)***
Nora Lees Frnch Quarter Bistro....302 322-7675
124 Delaware St New Castle (19720) ***(G-5574)***
Noramco Inc....302 761-2923
500 Swedes Landing Rd Wilmington (19801) ***(G-11895)***
Norbertine Fathers....302 449-1840
1269 Bayview Rd Middletown (19709) ***(G-4175)***
Norkol Converting Corporation....302 283-1080
1800 Ogletown Rd Newark (19711) ***(G-7136)***
Norman Broudy MD and Assoc, Wilmington *Also called Norman S Broudy M D* ***(G-11896)***
Norman M Lippman DDS....302 674-1140
712 S Governors Ave Dover (19904) ***(G-1900)***
Norman S Broudy M D....302 655-7110
825 N Washington St Wilmington (19801) ***(G-11896)***
Norman S Steward DDS PA....302 422-9791
214 S Walnut St Milford (19963) ***(G-4514)***
Norris Village, Middletown *Also called Appoquinimink Development Inc* ***(G-3942)***
North American Brands Inc....519 680-0385
501 Silverside Rd Wilmington (19809) ***(G-11897)***
North American Hardwoods Ltd....516 848-7729
2711 Centerville Rd Wilmington (19808) ***(G-11898)***
North American Trnspt Co Inc....856 696-5483
92 Reads Way Ste 202 New Castle (19720) ***(G-5575)***
North ATL Intl Ocean Carier....786 275-5352
35 Davidson Ln New Castle (19720) ***(G-5576)***
North Atlantic Ocean Ship....302 652-3782
19 Davidson Ln New Castle (19720) ***(G-5577)***
North Bay Marina Incorporated....302 436-4211
36543 Lighthouse Rd Selbyville (19975) ***(G-8528)***
North Bay Medical Associates....302 731-4620
313 W Main St Ste A Newark (19711) ***(G-7137)***
North District Engrg Cnstr, Bear *Also called Transportation Delaware Dept* ***(G-357)***
North Dupont Shell....301 375-6000
102 N Dupont Hwy New Castle (19720) ***(G-5578)***
North East Contractors Inc....302 286-6324
87 Blue Hen Dr Newark (19713) ***(G-7138)***
North Eastern Waffles LLC....302 697-2226
4003 S Dupont Hwy # 1753 Dover (19901) ***(G-1901)***
North Face Apparel Corp....336 424-7755
3411 Silverside Rd Wilmington (19810) ***(G-11899)***
North Hills Cleaners Inc....302 764-1234
211 Philadelphia Pike Wilmington (19809) ***(G-11900)***
North Orthopedic and Hand Ctr, Wilmington *Also called ATI Holdings LLC* ***(G-9175)***
North Quarter Creole....302 691-7890
837 N Union St Wilmington (19805) ***(G-11901)***
North Star Heating & Air Inc....302 732-3967
30968 Vines Creek Rd Dagsboro (19939) ***(G-925)***
North Star Pta....302 234-7200
1340 Little Baltimore Rd Hockessin (19707) ***(G-3106)***
North Wilmington Womens Center....302 529-7900
2002 Foulk Rd Ste A Wilmington (19810) ***(G-11902)***
Northeast Agri Systems Inc....302 875-1886
28527 Boyce Rd Laurel (19956) ***(G-3266)***
Northeast Body Shop, Wilmington *Also called Automotive Services Inc* ***(G-9190)***
Northeast Coast Service Center, New Castle *Also called Tdw Services Inc* ***(G-5756)***
Northeast Early Learning Ctr....302 762-5803
3014 Governor Printz Blvd Wilmington (19802) ***(G-11903)***
Northeast Rally Club....302 934-1246
213 Dodd St Millsboro (19966) ***(G-4762)***
Northeast Treatment Ctrs Inc....302 691-0140
3315 Kirkwood Hwy Wilmington (19808) ***(G-11904)***
Northeastern Coating Systems....302 328-6545
140 Belmont Dr Wilmington (19808) ***(G-11905)***
Northeastern Supply Inc....302 698-1414
100 S Dupont Hwy Camden (19934) ***(G-593)***

ALPHABETIC

Northeastern Supply Inc...302 378-7880
104 Patriot Dr Middletown (19709) ***(G-4176)***
Northeastern Title Loans...302 672-7895
105 N Dupont Hwy Dover (19901) ***(G-1902)***
Northeastern Title Loans...302 326-2210
1560 N Dupont Hwy New Castle (19720) ***(G-5579)***
Northern Del Youth For Chrst...302 995-6937
310 Kiamensi Rd Ste A Wilmington (19804) ***(G-11906)***
Northern Steel International, Lewes *Also called Steel Buildings Inc* ***(G-3764)***
Northern Trust Company...302 428-8700
1313 N Market St Ste 5100 Wilmington (19801) ***(G-11907)***
Northernsigs Mfg LLC...302 383-9270
809 Taylor St Wilmington (19801) ***(G-11908)***
Nortonlifelock Inc...650 527-8000
1209 N Orange St Wilmington (19801) ***(G-11909)***
Nothing But Net Inc...302 476-0453
83 Charles Dr New Castle (19720) ***(G-5580)***
Notify Technology Inc...505 818-5888
2035 Sunset Lake Rd Newark (19702) ***(G-7139)***
Nouvir Lighting Corporation...302 628-9933
20915 Sussex Hwy Seaford (19973) ***(G-8330)***
Nouvir Lightning Corporation...302 628-9888
20915 Sussex Hwy Seaford (19973) ***(G-8331)***
Nouvir Research, Seaford *Also called Nouvir Lighting Corporation* ***(G-8330)***
Nova Consultants Ltd...302 328-1686
245 Quigley Blvd Ste B New Castle (19720) ***(G-5581)***
Nova Industries LLC...302 218-4837
47 Courtland Cir Bear (19701) ***(G-267)***
Nova Pangaea Technologies Inc...612 743-6266
160 Greentree Dr Ste 101 Dover (19904) ***(G-1903)***
Nova RE & Bus Consulting LLC...302 258-2193
16192 Coastal Hwy Lewes (19958) ***(G-3661)***
Novacare Rehabilitation, Wilmington *Also called Rehabilitation Consultants Inc* ***(G-12367)***
Novacare Rehabilitation, Newark *Also called Blue Hen Physical Therapy Inc* ***(G-6100)***
Novacare Rehabilitation...302 537-7762
118 Atlantic Ave Ste 302 Ocean View (19970) ***(G-7805)***
Novacare Rehabilitation...302 674-4192
128 Greentree Dr Dover (19904) ***(G-1904)***
Novacare Rehabilitation...302 597-9256
256 Foxhunt Dr Bear (19701) ***(G-268)***
Novacare Rehabilitation Dover...302 760-9966
230 Beiser Blvd Ste 103 Dover (19904) ***(G-1905)***
Novacare Rehabilitation Seafor...302 990-2951
300 Hlth Svcs Dr Ste 301 Seaford (19973) ***(G-8332)***
Novaeo LLC...832 643-2153
4023 Kennett Pike # 5823 Wilmington (19807) ***(G-11910)***
Novak Druce Cnnlly Bv+qigg LLP (PA)...302 252-9922
1007 N Orange St Wilmington (19801) ***(G-11911)***
Novartis Corporation...302 992-5610
205 S James St Wilmington (19804) ***(G-11912)***
Novin LLC...315 670-7979
919 N Market St Ste 425 Wilmington (19801) ***(G-11913)***
Novo Financial Corp...844 260-6800
850 New Burton Rd Ste 201 Dover (19904) ***(G-1906)***
Novo Nordisk Pharma Inc...302 691-6181
103 Foulk Rd Ste 282 Wilmington (19803) ***(G-11914)***
Novo Nrdisk US Coml Hldngs Inc (HQ)...302 691-6181
103 Foulk Rd Ste 282 Wilmington (19803) ***(G-11915)***
Nowcare LLC (PA)...302 777-5551
1010 Concord Ave Wilmington (19802) ***(G-11916)***
Nr Hudson Consulting Inc...302 875-5276
14617 Arvey Rd Laurel (19956) ***(G-3267)***
Nrai Services LLC...302 674-4089
160 Greentree Dr Ste 101 Dover (19904) ***(G-1907)***
NRG Energy Inc...302 934-3537
Burton Island Rd Millsboro (19966) ***(G-4763)***
Nsmc, Wilmington *Also called Network Scrap Metal Corp* ***(G-11841)***
Nspire Automation LLC...404 545-0821
251 Little Falls Dr Wilmington (19808) ***(G-11917)***
Nt Ezlinq Holdings LLC...302 351-3051
251 Little Falls Dr Wilmington (19808) ***(G-11918)***
Nt Philadelphia LLC...302 384-8967
3705 Concord Pike Ste 2 Wilmington (19803) ***(G-11919)***
NTL (triangle) LLC (HQ)...302 525-0027
2711 Centerville Rd Wilmington (19808) ***(G-11920)***
Nu Attitude Styling Salon Ltd...302 734-8638
49 S Dupont Hwy Dover (19901) ***(G-1908)***
Nu World Building Service...302 678-2578
148 Willis Rd Apt F Dover (19901) ***(G-1909)***
Nu-Look Painting Contractors...302 734-9203
149 Beech Dr Dover (19904) ***(G-1910)***
Nu-Tech Masonry Inc...302 934-5660
Rr 2 Box 332f Millsboro (19966) ***(G-4764)***
Nucar Consulting Inc...302 696-6000
313 N Dupont Hwy Ste 100 Odessa (19730) ***(G-7831)***
Nucelectric Insurance Limited, Wilmington *Also called Nuclear Service Organization* ***(G-11922)***
Nuclear Electric Insurance Ltd (PA)...302 888-3000
1201 N Market St Ste 1100 Wilmington (19801) ***(G-11921)***
Nuclear Service Organization (PA)...302 888-3000
1201 N Market St Ste 1100 Wilmington (19801) ***(G-11922)***
Numake-1 LLC...302 220-4760
239 Lisa Dr New Castle (19720) ***(G-5582)***
Nurse Next Door Home Care Svcs...302 264-1021
110 N Main St Ste A Camden (19934) ***(G-594)***
Nurses Connection...302 421-3687
1021 Gilpin Ave Wilmington (19806) ***(G-11923)***
Nurses N Kids Inc (PA)...302 323-1118
904 Churchmans Road Ext New Castle (19720) ***(G-5583)***
Nurses N Kids Inc...302 424-1770
705 North St Milford (19963) ***(G-4515)***
Nurses N Kids Southern Del, Milford *Also called Nurses N Kids Inc* ***(G-4515)***
Nursing Board...302 744-4500
861 Silver Lake Blvd Dover (19904) ***(G-1911)***
Nursing Resources, Newark *Also called Christiana Care Hlth Svcs Inc* ***(G-6218)***
Nutrien AG Solutions Inc...302 629-2780
8518 Potts Ln Seaford (19973) ***(G-8333)***
Nutrien AG Solutions Inc...302 422-3570
200 N Rehoboth Blvd Milford (19963) ***(G-4516)***
Nutrien AG Solutions Inc...302 629-3047
8562 Elks Rd Seaford (19973) ***(G-8334)***
Nutrition Dept Supervisor, Wilmington *Also called Red Clay Consolidated Schl Dst* ***(G-12347)***
Nuvim Inc...302 827-4052
18327 Port Cir Lewes (19958) ***(G-3662)***
Nvcomputers Inc...860 878-0525
300 Delaware Ave Ste 210 Wilmington (19801) ***(G-11924)***
Nvr Inc...302 732-9900
32448 Royal Blvd Ste B Dagsboro (19939) ***(G-926)***
Nvr Inc...302 731-5770
1302 Drummond Plz 1032 Newark (19711) ***(G-7140)***
O A Newton & Son Co...302 337-8211
16356 Sussex Hwy Bridgeville (19933) ***(G-503)***
O A Newton & Son Company...302 337-3782
16356 Sussex Hwy Unit 1 Bridgeville (19933) ***(G-504)***
O B Pntg & Powerwashing Inc...302 238-7384
23031 Dennis Ln Millsboro (19966) ***(G-4765)***
O Kelly Ernst Belli Wallen LLC...302 778-4001
901 N Market St Ste 1000 Wilmington (19801) ***(G-11925)***
O Morales Stucco Plaster Inc...302 834-8891
7 Hawkins Ct Bear (19701) ***(G-269)***
O&G Knwldge Sharing Consortium, Wilmington *Also called O&G Knwldge Shring Pltform LLC* ***(G-11926)***
O&G Knwldge Shring Pltform LLC...303 872-0533
808 W Boxborough Dr Wilmington (19810) ***(G-11926)***
Oak Construction...302 703-2013
788 Kings Hwy Lewes (19958) ***(G-3663)***
Oak Grove Senior Center Inc...302 998-3319
11 Poplar Ave Wilmington (19805) ***(G-11927)***
Oak Hrc New Castle LLC...302 328-2580
32 Buena Vista Dr New Castle (19720) ***(G-5584)***
Oak Knoll Books, New Castle *Also called Cedar Lane Inc* ***(G-5139)***
Oak Orchard AM Legion 28, Millsboro *Also called Oak Orchard-Riverdale American* ***(G-4766)***
Oak Orchard-Riverdale American...302 945-1673
31768 Legion Rd Millsboro (19966) ***(G-4766)***
Oakwood Funding Corporation...336 855-2400
913 N Market St Ste 410 Wilmington (19801) ***(G-11928)***
Oates Consultants LLC...302 477-0109
234 Philadelphia Pike # 9 Wilmington (19809) ***(G-11929)***
Ob-Gyn Associates of Dover P A...302 674-0223
200 Banning St Ste 320 Dover (19904) ***(G-1912)***
Objective Zero Foundation...202 573-9660
919 N Market St Ste 425 Wilmington (19801) ***(G-11930)***
Objects Worldwide Inc...703 623-7861
910 Foulk Rd Ste 201 Wilmington (19803) ***(G-11931)***
OBryan Woodworks...302 398-8202
5400 Vernon Rd Harrington (19952) ***(G-2870)***
Obsidian Investors LLC...954 560-1499
2336 E Palladio Pl Middletown (19709) ***(G-4177)***
Oc Car Shows, Selbyville *Also called Spark Productions LLC* ***(G-8548)***
Occidental Chemical Corp...302 834-3800
1657 River Rd New Castle (19720) ***(G-5585)***
Occidental L Transamerica...302 477-9700
1415 Foulk Rd Ste 103 Wilmington (19803) ***(G-11932)***
Occupational Therapy Sour...302 234-2273
14 Winding Hill Dr Hockessin (19707) ***(G-3107)***
Ocean Atlantic Agency Inc...302 227-6767
330 Rehoboth Ave Rehoboth Beach (19971) ***(G-8018)***
Ocean Atlantic Associates LLC...302 227-3573
18949 Coastal Hwy # 301 Rehoboth Beach (19971) ***(G-8019)***
Ocean Atlantic Companies, Rehoboth Beach *Also called Ocean Atlantic Management LLC* ***(G-8020)***
Ocean Atlantic Companies, Rehoboth Beach *Also called Ocean Atlantic Associates LLC* ***(G-8019)***
Ocean Atlantic Management LLC...302 227-3573
18949 Coastal Hwy # 301 Rehoboth Beach (19971) ***(G-8020)***

ALPHABETIC SECTION

Ocean CLB Rsort Rservation Ctr 302 369-1420
153 E Chestnut Hill Rd # 200 Newark (19713) *(G-7141)*
Ocean First Enterprises LLC 302 232-8547
501 Silverside Rd Ste 507 Wilmington (19809) *(G-11933)*
Ocean Medical Imaging Del LLC 302 684-5151
611 Federal St Ste 4 Milton (19968) *(G-4943)*
Ocean Pines Auto Service Ctr 410 641-7800
34461 Atlantic Ave Ocean View (19970) *(G-7806)*
Ocean Pines Parts, Ocean View Also called Ocean Pines Auto Service Ctr *(G-7806)*
Ocean Travel 302 227-1607
19478 Coastal Hwy Unit 7 Rehoboth Beach (19971) *(G-8021)*
Ocean View Animal Hospital 302 539-2273
118 Atlantic Ave Ste 101 Ocean View (19970) *(G-7807)*
Ocean View Farms Inc (PA) 302 537-4042
76 West Ave Ocean View (19970) *(G-7808)*
Ocean View Plumbing & Heating, Dagsboro Also called Ocean View Plumbing Inc *(G-927)*
Ocean View Plumbing Inc 302 732-9117
Rr 4 Box 21a Dagsboro (19939) *(G-927)*
Ocean Waves LLC 302 344-1282
Rr 3 Box 286d Fenwick Island (19944) *(G-2338)*
Oceanic Ventures Inc 302 645-5872
32292 Nassau Rd Unit 1 Lewes (19958) *(G-3664)*
Oceanport LLC 302 792-2212
6200 Philadelphia Pike Claymont (19703) *(G-791)*
Oceanside Elite Clg Bldg Svcs 302 339-7777
33033 Nassau Loop Lewes (19958) *(G-3665)*
Oceanside Seafood Mkt Deli LLC 302 313-5158
109 Savannah Rd Lewes (19958) *(G-3666)*
Oceanstar Technologies Inc 302 542-1900
203 Mariners Way Bear (19701) *(G-270)*
Oceanus Motel, Rehoboth Beach Also called Moores Enterprises Inc *(G-8010)*
Oci, New Castle Also called Opportunity Center Inc *(G-5589)*
Oci Melamine Americas Inc (HQ) 800 615-8284
1209 N Orange St Wilmington (19801) *(G-11934)*
Ockels Acres LLC 302 684-0456
17120 Ockles Ln Milton (19968) *(G-4944)*
Ockels Farms Inc 302 684-0456
17120 E Redden Rd Milton (19968) *(G-4945)*
OConnell Speedy Printing Inc 302 656-1475
715 N King St Wilmington (19801) *(G-11935)*
OConnor Belting Intl Inc 302 452-2500
728 Dawson Dr Newark (19713) *(G-7142)*
OConnor Orthodontics 302 678-1441
1004 S State St Dover (19901) *(G-1913)*
Odd Fellows Cmtry of Milford 302 422-4619
300 S Rehoboth Blvd Milford (19963) *(G-4517)*
Odessa Early Education Center 302 376-5254
27 Mailly Dr Townsend (19734) *(G-8813)*
Odessa Historic Foundation 302 378-4119
201 Main St Odessa (19730) *(G-7832)*
Odessa National Golf Crse LLC 302 464-1007
1131 Fieldsboro Rd Townsend (19734) *(G-8814)*
Odyssey Healthcare Inc 302 478-1297
1407 Foulk Rd Ste 200 Wilmington (19803) *(G-11936)*
Odyssey Technologies LLC 302 525-8184
2915 Ogletown Rd 1072 Newark (19713) *(G-7143)*
Oerigo Consulting LLC 302 353-4719
82 E Cayhill Ln Smyrna (19977) *(G-8686)*
Ofc Partners Xiv Bellevue 302 439-3345
300 Bellevue Pkwy Wilmington (19809) *(G-11937)*
Office Bpo LLC 248 716-5136
1201 N Orange St Ste 600 Wilmington (19801) *(G-11938)*
Office Furnish & Sup Bus Ctr, Bear Also called Kenneth Deitch *(G-215)*
Office John M Law 302 427-2369
100 E 14th St Wilmington (19801) *(G-11939)*
Office Movers, New Castle Also called Business Move Solutions Inc *(G-5124)*
Office of Chief Med Examiner, Wilmington Also called Health & Social Svcs Del Dept *(G-10867)*
Office of Ruben Tejeira MD The, Georgetown Also called Sunrise Medical Center *(G-2671)*
Office Partners Xiv Bellevue 302 691-2100
322 A St Ste 300 Wilmington (19801) *(G-11940)*
Office Pride, Felton Also called Eckels Family LLC *(G-2290)*
Ogletown Baptist Church 302 737-2511
316 Red Mill Rd Newark (19713) *(G-7144)*
Ohana Companies Inc 302 225-5505
1405 Foulk Rd Ste 200 Wilmington (19803) *(G-11941)*
Ohmyzip 302 322-8792
599 Ships Landing Way New Castle (19720) *(G-5586)*
Oil Spot Express Lube Center 302 628-9866
915 Norman Eskridge Hwy Seaford (19973) *(G-8335)*
Oilminers Cbd LLC 484 885-9417
22 Gershwin Cir Newark (19702) *(G-7145)*
Oink Oink LLC 302 924-5034
8 The Grn Ste A Dover (19901) *(G-1914)*
OK Video 302 762-2333
406 Philadelphia Pike Wilmington (19809) *(G-11942)*
Old Country Garden Center Inc 302 652-3317
414 Wilson Rd Wilmington (19803) *(G-11943)*

Old Dominion Freight Line Inc 302 337-8793
1664 Emma Jane Ln Bridgeville (19933) *(G-505)*
Old Inlet Bait and Tackle Inc (PA) 302 227-7974
25012 Coastal Hwy Rehoboth Beach (19971) *(G-8022)*
Old Landing II LP 302 934-1871
29320 White St Unit 400 Millsboro (19966) *(G-4767)*
Old Mill Crab House, Milford Also called Prouse Enterprises LLC *(G-4531)*
Old Republic Nat Title Insur 302 734-3570
32 The Grn Dover (19901) *(G-1915)*
Old Republic Nat Title Insur 302 661-1997
600 N King St 100 Wilmington (19801) *(G-11944)*
Old School Plating 302 345-0350
757 Rue Madora Bear (19701) *(G-271)*
Old Wood & Co LLC 302 684-3600
26804 Lwes Georgetown Hwy Harbeson (19951) *(G-2794)*
Olga N Ganoudis Jewelry 302 421-9820
1313 N Scott St Wilmington (19806) *(G-11945)*
Olivar & Greb Capital MGT LLC 508 598-7590
16192 Coastal Hwy Lewes (19958) *(G-3667)*
Olympiad Gymnastic, Wilmington Also called Olympiad Schools Inc *(G-11946)*
Olympiad Schools Inc 302 636-0606
380 Water St Wilmington (19804) *(G-11946)*
Om Shiv Groceries Inc (PA) 302 856-7014
208 N Bedford St Georgetown (19947) *(G-2611)*
Omega Endodontics, Newark Also called Philips B Eric DMD PA *(G-7213)*
Omega Imaging Associates LLC (PA) 302 738-9300
6 Omega Dr Newark (19713) *(G-7146)*
Omega Imaging Associates LLC 302 654-5245
1020 N Union St Ste C Wilmington (19805) *(G-11947)*
Omega Imaging Associates LLC 302 995-2037
3105 Limestone Rd Ste 106 Wilmington (19808) *(G-11948)*
Omega Industries Inc 302 734-3835
7 Messina Hill Rd Dover (19904) *(G-1916)*
Omega Medical Center, Newark Also called Delaware Occupational Health S *(G-6400)*
Omega Physical Therapy, Wilmington Also called Zuber & Associates Inc *(G-13353)*
Omega PSI PHI Fraternity 908 463-2197
1300 S Farmview Dr Dover (19904) *(G-1917)*
Omni Games Inc 302 652-4800
910 Foulk Rd Ste 201 Wilmington (19803) *(G-11949)*
Omnimaven Inc 302 378-8918
103 Cazier Dr Middletown (19709) *(G-4178)*
Omninet International Inc (PA) 208 246-5022
427 N Tatnall St Wilmington (19801) *(G-11950)*
Omniway Corporation (PA) 302 738-5076
2300 Waters Edge Dr Newark (19702) *(G-7147)*
On Board Engineering Corp 302 613-5030
2 Penns Way Ste 400 New Castle (19720) *(G-5587)*
On Demand Moving Services, Newark Also called On Demand Services LLC *(G-7148)*
On Demand Services LLC 302 388-1215
46 Chambord Dr Newark (19702) *(G-7148)*
On National Alliance 302 427-0787
2400 W 4th St Wilmington (19805) *(G-11951)*
On Point Partners LLC 302 655-5606
18 Germay Dr 2a Wilmington (19804) *(G-11952)*
On The Spot Massage 302 545-5200
2871 Red Lion Rd Bear (19701) *(G-272)*
On Time Construction, Wilmington Also called Thomas F Cavanaugh *(G-12900)*
On-Demand Services LLC 302 388-1215
412 Park Ave New Castle (19720) *(G-5588)*
Oncology Care Home 610 274-2437
267 E Main St Newark (19711) *(G-7149)*
One Commerce Ctr Condo Council 302 573-2513
1 Commerce St Ste 700 Wilmington (19801) *(G-11953)*
One EDM LLC 908 399-0536
3524 Silverside Rd Wilmington (19810) *(G-11954)*
One Hour Printing 302 220-1684
122 Balmoral Way Newark (19702) *(G-7150)*
One Hour Translation Inc 800 720-3722
16192 Coastal Hwy Lewes (19958) *(G-3668)*
One Hundred West Tenth St 302 651-1469
1100 N Market St Wilmington (19899) *(G-11955)*
One Main Financial 302 737-9456
420 Suburban Dr Newark (19711) *(G-7151)*
One Off Rod & Custom Inc 302 449-1489
118 Sleepy Hollow Dr Middletown (19709) *(G-4179)*
One Step Ahead Childcare 302 292-1162
432 Salem Church Rd Newark (19702) *(G-7152)*
One Stop Medical Inc 302 450-4479
515 S Dupont Blvd Bldg C Milford (19963) *(G-4518)*
One System Incorporated 888 311-1110
4023 Kennett Pike Ste 645 Wilmington (19807) *(G-11956)*
One Village Alliance Inc 302 275-1715
1401 A St Wilmington (19801) *(G-11957)*
One Virginia 302 227-9533
1 Virginia Ave Ste 1 # 1 Rehoboth Beach (19971) *(G-8023)*
ONeal J C & Sons Auctioneers 302 875-5261
1112 Laurel Rd Laurel (19956) *(G-3268)*
ONeill Woodworking LLC 443 669-3458
23292 Bridgeway Dr W Lewes (19958) *(G-3669)*

Onemain Financial Group LLC ... 302 834-6677
619 Governors Pl Bear (19701) ***(G-273)***
Onemain Financial Group LLC ... 302 628-9253
22974 Sussex Hwy Seaford (19973) ***(G-8336)***
Onemain Financial Group LLC ... 302 674-3900
1057 N Dupont Hwy Dover (19901) ***(G-1918)***
Onemain Financial Group LLC ... 302 422-9657
660 N Dupont Blvd Milford (19963) ***(G-4519)***
Onemain Financial Group LLC ... 302 478-8070
4325 Concord Pike Wilmington (19803) ***(G-11958)***
Oneness Massage Therapy ... 302 893-0348
10 Blue Jay Dr Newark (19713) ***(G-7153)***
Oni Acquisition Corp ... 212 271-3800
2711 Centerville Rd Wilmington (19808) ***(G-11959)***
Onix Silverside LLC ... 484 731-2500
3322 Silverside Rd Wilmington (19810) ***(G-11960)***
Online, Newark *Also called Cubics Inc* ***(G-6324)***
Onpoint Oncology Inc ... 610 274-0188
1184 Corner Ketch Rd Newark (19711) ***(G-7154)***
Onsite Construction Inc ... 302 628-4244
9654 Brickyard Rd Unit 2 Seaford (19973) ***(G-8337)***
Open Barn Inc ... 669 254-7747
16192 Coastal Hwy Lewes (19958) ***(G-3670)***
Open Door Inc (PA) ... 302 731-1504
254 E Main St Newark (19711) ***(G-7155)***
Open Door Inc ... 302 629-7900
107 Pennsylvania Ave Seaford (19973) ***(G-8338)***
Open Mri At Trolley Square LLC ... 302 472-5555
1010 N Bancroft Pkwy Wilmington (19805) ***(G-11961)***
Openexo Inc ... 617 965-5057
3500 S Dupont Hwy Dover (19901) ***(G-1919)***
Opera Studios, Wilmington *Also called Operadelaware Inc* ***(G-11962)***
Operadelaware Inc ... 302 658-8063
4 S Poplar St Wilmington (19801) ***(G-11962)***
Operata LLC ... 302 525-0190
2035 Sunset Lake Rd B2 Newark (19702) ***(G-7156)***
Oppa Inc ... 732 540-0308
16192 Coastal Hwy Lewes (19958) ***(G-3671)***
Oppameet LLC ... 732 540-0308
16192 Coastal Hwy Lewes (19958) ***(G-3672)***
Oppenheimer Group Inc ... 302 533-0779
200 Continental Dr # 301 Newark (19713) ***(G-7157)***
Oppenheimer Group, The, Newark *Also called David Oppenheimer and Co I LLC* ***(G-6349)***
Opportunity Center Inc (PA) ... 302 762-0300
13 Reads Way Ste 101 New Castle (19720) ***(G-5589)***
Optima Cleaning Systems Inc ... 302 652-3979
110 Valley Rd Wilmington (19804) ***(G-11963)***
Option Care Enterprises Inc ... 302 355-6100
604 White Clay Center Dr Newark (19711) ***(G-7158)***
Optometry Associates PC ... 302 654-6490
419 S Market St Wilmington (19801) ***(G-11964)***
Opus Design Build LLC ... 952 656-4444
1000 N West St Fl 10 Wilmington (19801) ***(G-11965)***
Opus Financial Svcs USA Inc ... 646 435-5616
19c Trolley Sq Wilmington (19806) ***(G-11966)***
Oral & Maxillofacial Surgery ... 302 998-0331
2601 Annand Dr Ste 10 Wilmington (19808) ***(G-11967)***
Oral Mxllfcial Srgery Assoc PA ... 302 655-6183
1304 N Broom St Wilmington (19806) ***(G-11968)***
Orange Power Electric Inc ... 205 886-5815
300 Delaware Ave Wilmington (19801) ***(G-11969)***
Orbeex Trading Inc ... 786 403-9124
3411 Silverside Rd Wilmington (19810) ***(G-11970)***
Orbit Research LLC (PA) ... 302 683-1063
3422 Old Capitol Trl # 25 Wilmington (19808) ***(G-11971)***
Orchard Park Group Inc ... 302 356-1139
42 Reads Way New Castle (19720) ***(G-5590)***
Ordering Inc ... 888 443-6203
2711 Centerville Rd # 400 Wilmington (19808) ***(G-11972)***
Orient Corp of America, Seaford *Also called Orient Corporation of America* ***(G-8339)***
Orient Corporation of America ... 302 628-1300
111 Park Ave Seaford (19973) ***(G-8339)***
Orion Group LLC ... 302 357-9137
2801 Centerville Rd Wilmington (19808) ***(G-11973)***
Orjam Ltd ... 302 482-5016
3602 Squirrel Hill Ct Wilmington (19808) ***(G-11974)***
Orkin LLC ... 302 322-9569
101 Johnson Way New Castle (19720) ***(G-5591)***
Orkin Pest Control 314, New Castle *Also called Orkin LLC* ***(G-5591)***
Orlando J Camp & Associates ... 302 478-3720
1808 Pan Rd Wilmington (19803) ***(G-11975)***
Orlov Counseling, Wilmington *Also called Marsha S Eddorlov* ***(G-11544)***
Oros Communications LLC ... 954 228-7399
2711 Centerville Rd # 400 Wilmington (19808) ***(G-11976)***
Orpheus Companies Ltd ... 302 328-3451
255 Old Churchmans Rd New Castle (19720) ***(G-5592)***
Orth & Kowalick PA ... 302 697-2159
1991 S State St Dover (19901) ***(G-1920)***
Ortho-Surg P.A. Pension Plan, Wilmington *Also called P A Ortho-Surg* ***(G-11993)***
Orthodontics On Silver Lake ... 302 672-7776
42 Hiawatha Ln Dover (19904) ***(G-1921)***
Orthodontics On Silver Lake PA ... 302 672-7776
42 Hiawatha Ln Dover (19904) ***(G-1922)***
Orthopaedic & Sports Phys ... 302 683-0782
617 W Newport Pike Wilmington (19804) ***(G-11977)***
Orthopaedic Specialists PA ... 302 655-9494
7 S Clayton St Ste 600 Wilmington (19805) ***(G-11978)***
Orthopdic Assoc Suthern Del PA ... 302 644-3311
17005 Old Orchard Rd Lewes (19958) ***(G-3673)***
Orthopedic Properties LLC ... 302 998-2310
1096 Old Churchmans Rd Newark (19713) ***(G-7159)***
Orthopedic Specialists ... 302 351-4848
1096 Old Churchmans Rd Newark (19713) ***(G-7160)***
Orthopedic Spine Center P A ... 302 734-9700
260 Beiser Blvd Dover (19904) ***(G-1923)***
Orville Sammons Ardens ... 302 492-8620
4272 Judith Rd Dover (19904) ***(G-1924)***
Osaka Gas Freedom Energy Corp, Wilmington *Also called Osaka Gas USA Corporation* ***(G-11979)***
Osaka Gas USA Corporation ... 302 658-7581
1209 N Orange St Wilmington (19801) ***(G-11979)***
Osfs Wlmngton Phldlphia Prvnce ... 302 656-8529
2200 Kentmere Pkwy Wilmington (19806) ***(G-11980)***
OSG America LP ... 212 578-1922
111 Continental Dr # 402 Newark (19713) ***(G-7161)***
Oso Grande Hv LLC ... 858 521-3300
251 Little Falls Dr Wilmington (19808) ***(G-11981)***
Osskin USA Inc ... 302 266-8200
2915 Ogletown Rd Newark (19713) ***(G-7162)***
Othg Inc ... 302 421-9187
1708 Tulip St Wilmington (19805) ***(G-11982)***
Otis Kamara ... 443 207-2643
P.O. Box 960 Dover (19903) ***(G-1925)***
Oto Global Inc ... 966 597-9694
2035 Sunset Lake Rd B2 Newark (19702) ***(G-7163)***
Otolaryngology Consultants (PA) ... 302 328-1331
10 Foxview Cir Hockessin (19707) ***(G-3108)***
Otolaryngology Consultants ... 302 328-1331
100 Christiana Rd New Castle (19720) ***(G-5593)***
Otw Technologies Inc ... 813 230-4212
8 The Grn Ste A Dover (19901) ***(G-1926)***
Our Childrens Learning Ctr ... 302 565-1272
313 Sun Blvd Bear (19701) ***(G-274)***
Our Future Child Care Ctr LLC ... 302 762-8645
3400 N Market St Wilmington (19802) ***(G-11983)***
Out & About, Wilmington *Also called T S N Publishing Co Inc* ***(G-12845)***
Outcome Associates LLC ... 302 368-3637
8 Linette Ct Newark (19702) ***(G-7164)***
Outdoor Design Group LLC ... 302 743-2363
935 Rahway Dr Newark (19711) ***(G-7165)***
Outlet Liquors ... 302 227-7700
19724 Coastal Hwy Unit 1 Rehoboth Beach (19971) ***(G-8024)***
Outpatent Ansthsia Spclists PA ... 302 995-1860
2006 Limestone Rd Ste 5 Wilmington (19808) ***(G-11984)***
Outreach Team LLC ... 302 744-9550
8 The Grn Ste R Dover (19901) ***(G-1927)***
Outside In, Newark *Also called CBI Group LLc* ***(G-6174)***
Ovation Health Intl LLC ... 302 765-7595
515 Giada Dr Wilmington (19808) ***(G-11985)***
Over Rainbow Daycare ... 302 328-6574
713 W 12th St New Castle (19720) ***(G-5594)***
Overfalls Maritime Museum ... 302 644-8050
219 Pilottown Rd Lewes (19958) ***(G-3674)***
Overhead Door Co Delmar Inc ... 302 424-4400
603 Marshall St Milford (19963) ***(G-4520)***
Overture LLC ... 302 226-1940
20660 Coastal Hwy Unit 1 Rehoboth Beach (19971) ***(G-8025)***
Ovo Digital Services LLC ... 415 741-1615
3616 Kirkwood Hwy 1547 Wilmington (19808) ***(G-11986)***
Ovocrm, Wilmington *Also called Ovo Digital Services LLC* ***(G-11986)***
Owens Corningfibreboard ... 302 654-4250
1105 N Market St Ste 1300 Wilmington (19801) ***(G-11987)***
Owi, Wilmington *Also called Objects Worldwide Inc* ***(G-11931)***
Owl's Nest Horticultural, Wilmington *Also called Owls Nest Horticultural Svcs* ***(G-11988)***
Owls Nest Horticultural Svcs ... 302 654-6989
805 Owls Nest Rd Wilmington (19807) ***(G-11988)***
Owners Management Company ... 302 422-0740
5 Linstone Ln Ofc 100 Milford (19963) ***(G-4521)***
Ox Pond Industries ... 703 608-7769
29489 Colony Dr Dagsboro (19939) ***(G-928)***
Oxford Plastic Systems LLC ... 800 567-9182
1011 Centre Rd Ste 312 Wilmington (19805) ***(G-11989)***
P & C Roofing Inc ... 302 322-6767
35 Southgate Blvd New Castle (19720) ***(G-5595)***
P & R Printing, Georgetown *Also called Conventioneer Pubg Co Inc* ***(G-2483)***
P A Aba Intl Inc ... 800 979-5106
16192 Coastal Hwy Lewes (19958) ***(G-3675)***

P A Alfieri Cardiology (PA) 302 731-0001
701 Foulk Rd Ste 2b Wilmington (19803) *(G-11990)*
P A Anesthesia Services 302 709-4709
2 Reads Way Ste 201 New Castle (19720) *(G-5596)*
P A Bayard 302 429-4212
600 N King St Ste 400 Wilmington (19801) *(G-11991)*
P A Brandywine Pediatrics 302 479-9610
3521 Silverside Rd Ste 1f Wilmington (19810) *(G-11992)*
P A C T T Child Care Center, Georgetown *Also called United Cerebral Palsy of De (G-2698)*
P A Chadley 302 234-1115
7503 Lancaster Pike Ste A Hockessin (19707) *(G-3109)*
P A Cnmri 302 678-8100
1074 S State St Dover (19901) *(G-1928)*
P A Ortho-Surg 302 658-4800
2401 Penns Ave Ste 115 Wilmington (19806) *(G-11993)*
P A Womencare 302 731-2900
4745 Ogletown Stanton Rd # 231 Newark (19713) *(G-7166)*
P B Investment Corp 302 266-7920
256 Chapman Rd Ste 100 Newark (19702) *(G-7167)*
P B R, Talleyville *Also called Performance Based Results (G-8750)*
P C Bohler Engineering 302 644-1155
18958 Coastal Hwy Rehoboth Beach (19971) *(G-8026)*
P D Supply Inc 302 655-3358
307 Commercial Dr Wilmington (19805) *(G-11994)*
P M O Advisors L L C 302 545-1159
700 Hopeton Rd Wilmington (19807) *(G-11995)*
P R C Management Co Inc 302 475-7643
2601 Carpenter Station Rd Wilmington (19810) *(G-11996)*
P S C Contracting Inc 302 838-2998
704 5th St Delaware City (19706) *(G-962)*
P S C Electric Contractor Inc 302 838-2998
704 5th St Delaware City (19706) *(G-963)*
P S I Maximus, New Castle *Also called Public Systems Inc (G-5652)*
P&L Transportation Inc (PA) 800 444-2580
301 N Market St Ste 1414 Wilmington (19801) *(G-11997)*
P&P Horse Transportation 302 388-7687
1101 Millstone Dr Newark (19711) *(G-7168)*
P-Ks Wholesale Grocer Inc 302 656-5540
915 S Heald St Wilmington (19801) *(G-11998)*
Pabian Ventures LLC 302 762-1992
101 N Maryland Ave Wilmington (19804) *(G-11999)*
Pace Electric 302 328-2600
3603 Old Capitol Trl B4 Wilmington (19808) *(G-12000)*
Pace Enterprises LLC 302 529-2500
1405 Silverside Rd Ste B Wilmington (19810) *(G-12001)*
Pace Inc 302 999-9812
5171 W Woodmill Dr Ste 9 Wilmington (19808) *(G-12002)*
Pace Local 2 898 .... 302 737-8898
25 S Old Baltimore Pike # 202 Newark (19702) *(G-7169)*
Pacer International One LLC 302 588-9500
16 Taylors Mill Ln Wilmington (19808) *(G-12003)*
Pacific Cargo LLC 302 521-6317
11 Gist Rd Ste 201 Wilmington (19801) *(G-12004)*
Pacifico Industrial Ltd 213 435-1181
113 Barksdale Pro Ctr Newark (19711) *(G-7170)*
Packem Associates Partnership 302 227-5780
34 Wilmington Ave Rehoboth Beach (19971) *(G-8027)*
Paducah & Louisville Railway, Wilmington *Also called P&L Transportation Inc (G-11997)*
Pagetech 845 624-4911
20418 Oakney St Lewes (19958) *(G-3676)*
Pagoda Hotel & Floating Rest, New Castle *Also called Pagoda Hotel Inc (G-5597)*
Pagoda Hotel Inc 808 922-1233
599 Ships Landing Way New Castle (19720) *(G-5597)*
Pain & Sleep Therapy Center 302 314-1409
4901 Limestone Rd Wilmington (19808) *(G-12005)*
Pain MGT & Rehabilitation Ctr 302 734-7246
240 Beiser Blvd Ste 201a Dover (19904) *(G-1929)*
Paintball Action of Delware 302 234-1735
102 Lucia Ln Hockessin (19707) *(G-3110)*
Painters Local Union 277 .... 302 994-7835
922 New Rd Ste 1 Wilmington (19805) *(G-12006)*
Pak Mail, Wilmington *Also called Dabvasan Inc (G-9946)*
Pala Tile & Carpet Contrs Inc 302 652-4500
600 S Colonial Ave Wilmington (19805) *(G-12007)*
Palace Laundry Inc 302 322-2136
30 Mccullough Dr New Castle (19720) *(G-5598)*
Paladin Sports & Social Club, Wilmington *Also called Paladin Sports Club Inc (G-12008)*
Paladin Sports Club Inc 302 764-5335
500 Paladin Dr Wilmington (19802) *(G-12008)*
Palermo Francis A MD Facc PA 302 994-1100
620 Stanton Christiana Rd Newark (19713) *(G-7171)*
Palermo, Francis A MD PA, Newark *Also called Palermo Francis A MD Facc PA (G-7171)*
Pall Aerospace, Newark *Also called Russell Associates Inc (G-7370)*
Palladian Management LLC 302 737-1971
41 Fairway Rd Ofc 2c Newark (19711) *(G-7172)*
Palmer & Associates Inc 302 834-9329
14 Lauren Dr Bear (19701) *(G-275)*
Palmer Chiropractic, New Castle *Also called T Shane Palmer DC (G-5750)*
Palmetto MGT & Engrg LLC 302 993-2766
4550 Linden Hill Rd # 400 Wilmington (19808) *(G-12009)*
Pam Pipes & Puppets 302 999-0078
18 Wordsworth Dr Wilmington (19808) *(G-12010)*
Pamela M D Leclaire 302 677-2600
300 Tuskegee Blvd Dover (19902) *(G-1930)*
Panco Management Corporation 302 366-1875
15 Fox Hall 15 # 15 Newark (19711) *(G-7173)*
Panco Management Corporation 302 995-6152
1302 Cynwyd Club Dr Wilmington (19808) *(G-12011)*
Panco Management Corporation 302 475-9337
2512 Cedar Tree Dr Ofc 2d Wilmington (19810) *(G-12012)*
Panda Early Education Ctr Inc 302 832-1891
122 E Main St Christiana (19702) *(G-674)*
Panda Early Education Ctr Inc (PA) 302 832-1891
105 Emerald Ridge Dr Bear (19701) *(G-276)*
Panda Sleep Inc 302 760-9754
8 The Grn Ste A Dover (19901) *(G-1931)*
Pandaciti LLC 226 219-7771
257 Old Churchmans Rd New Castle (19720) *(G-5599)*
Pandol Bros Inc 302 571-8923
Christiana Ctr Wilmington (19884) *(G-12013)*
Panelmatic Inc 302 324-9193
11 Southgate Blvd New Castle (19720) *(G-5600)*
Panelmatic East Inc 302 324-9193
11 Southgate Blvd New Castle (19720) *(G-5601)*
Pangeamart Inc 914 374-0913
16192 Coastal Hwy Lewes (19958) *(G-3677)*
Pano Development Inc 302 428-1062
1701 Augustine Cut Off # 15 Wilmington (19803) *(G-12014)*
Panzeea 770 573-3672
225 High St Seaford (19973) *(G-8340)*
Panzer Dermatology Assoc PA 302 633-7550
537 Stanton Christiana Rd # 207 Newark (19713) *(G-7174)*
Paoli Services Inc 302 998-7031
400 B And O Ln Wilmington (19804) *(G-12015)*
Papaleo Rosen Chelf & Pinder 302 644-8600
135 2nd St Lewes (19958) *(G-3678)*
Papastavros Assoc Med Imaging, Newark *Also called Delaware Imaging Network (G-6385)*
Papastavros Assoc Med Imaging, Middletown *Also called Delaware Imaging Network (G-4028)*
Papen Farms Inc 302 697-3291
847 Papen Ln Dover (19904) *(G-1932)*
Paperbasket LLC 516 360-3500
8 The Grn Ste A Dover (19901) *(G-1933)*
Par 3 Inc 302 674-8275
924 Artis Dr Dover (19904) *(G-1934)*
Par 4 Golf Inc 302 227-5663
38 Glade Cir E Rehoboth Beach (19971) *(G-8028)*
Paradigm Health LLC 301 233-7221
709 Observatory Dr Bear (19701) *(G-277)*
Paradise Grill 302 945-4500
27344 Bay Walk Millsboro (19966) *(G-4768)*
Paragon Contracting Inc 302 697-6565
220 Weeks Dr Camden (19934) *(G-595)*
Paragon Design Inc 302 292-1523
77 E Main St Ste 2 Newark (19711) *(G-7175)*
Paragon Engineering Corp 302 762-6010
708 Philadelphia Pike # 1 Wilmington (19809) *(G-12016)*
Paragon Group 302 798-5777
1304 Society Dr Claymont (19703) *(G-792)*
Paragon Masonry Corporation 302 798-7314
501 Silverside Rd Ste 1 Wilmington (19809) *(G-12017)*
Parags Glass Company 302 737-0101
107 Albe Dr Ste D Newark (19702) *(G-7176)*
Parcels Inc (PA) 302 888-1718
230 N Market St Wilmington (19801) *(G-12018)*
Parcels Inc 302 736-1777
1111 B S Govenanvce Ave Dover (19904) *(G-1935)*
Parent Information Ctr Del Inc (PA) 302 999-7394
6 Larch Ave Ste 404 Wilmington (19804) *(G-12019)*
Paris Carr US, Wilmington *Also called Carr Paris (G-9578)*
Park Place Dental 302 455-0333
210 W Park Pl Newark (19711) *(G-7177)*
Park Place Dental 302 652-3775
300 Foulk Rd Wilmington (19803) *(G-12020)*
Park Plaza Condo Association 302 658-3526
1100 Lovering Ave Ste 15 Wilmington (19806) *(G-12021)*
Park Plaza Condominiums, Wilmington *Also called Park Plaza Condo Association (G-12021)*
Park View 302 429-7288
1800 N Broom St Wilmington (19802) *(G-12022)*
Parker Block Co Inc (HQ) 302 934-9237
30234 Millsboro Hwy Millsboro (19966) *(G-4769)*
Parker Construction Inc 302 798-8530
950 Ridge Rd Ste C6 Claymont (19703) *(G-793)*
Parker Express Inc 302 221-5777
152 S Dupont Hwy New Castle (19720) *(G-5602)*
Parkowski Guerke & Swayze PA (PA) 302 678-3262
116 W Water St Dover (19904) *(G-1936)*

ALPHABETIC

Parks & Recreation Del Div 302 761-6963
800 Carr Rd Wilmington (19809) ***(G-12023)***
Parks & Recreation Del Div 302 571-7788
1001 N Park Dr Wilmington (19802) ***(G-12024)***
Parks Rcreation Dept Cy Newark, Newark *Also called City of Newark* ***(G-6243)***
Parkview Covalescent Center 302 655-0955
2801 W 6th St Wilmington (19805) ***(G-12025)***
Parkway Cleaners, Newark *Also called Parkway Dry Cleaners Inc* ***(G-7178)***
Parkway Dry Cleaners Inc (PA) 302 737-2406
13 Chestnut Hill Plz Newark (19713) ***(G-7178)***
Parkway Gravel Inc 302 658-5241
4048 New Castle Ave New Castle (19720) ***(G-5603)***
Parkway Gravel Inc 302 326-0554
13 Parkway Cir New Castle (19720) ***(G-5604)***
Parkway Law LLC 302 449-0400
3171 Dupont Pkwy Townsend (19734) ***(G-8815)***
Parkwood Trust Company 302 426-1220
919 N Market St Ste 429 Wilmington (19801) ***(G-12026)***
Parsell Fnrl Homes Crematorium, Lewes *Also called Parsell Funeral Entps Inc* ***(G-3679)***
Parsell Funeral Entps Inc 302 645-9520
16961 Kings Hwy Lewes (19958) ***(G-3679)***
Parson Thorne Apartments, Milford *Also called Parson Thorne Realty Assoc LP* ***(G-4522)***
Parson Thorne Realty Assoc LP 302 422-9367
505 Nw Front St Apt A24 Milford (19963) ***(G-4522)***
Partners Plus Inc 302 529-3700
2 Tenns Way Ste 403 New Castle (19720) ***(G-5605)***
Partnership For De Estuary 302 655-4990
110 S Poplar St Ste 202 Wilmington (19801) ***(G-12027)***
Partnrre Cpitl Invstments Corp 608 347-5824
1209 N Orange St Wilmington (19801) ***(G-12028)***
Parts Plus More LLC 302 300-4913
8 The Grn Ste 4469 Dover (19901) ***(G-1937)***
Partsquarry-Aviation Div 302 703-7195
110 W 9th St Wilmington (19801) ***(G-12029)***
Party Gas 302 730-3880
5200 N Dupont Hwy Dover (19901) ***(G-1938)***
Party Restaurant Outlet, Newark *Also called South Forks Inc* ***(G-7461)***
Parviz Sorouri Md PA 302 453-9171
10 Darwin Dr Ste C Newark (19711) ***(G-7179)***
Pascale Industries Inc 302 421-9400
55 Harbor View Dr New Castle (19720) ***(G-5606)***
Pasquale Fucci MD 302 652-4705
1508 Penns Ave Ste 1c Wilmington (19806) ***(G-12030)***
Passion Care Services Inc 302 832-2622
3727 Wrangle Hill Rd Bear (19701) ***(G-278)***
Passwaters Landscaping 302 542-8077
18956 Sussex Hwy Bridgeville (19933) ***(G-506)***
Pat Cirelli 302 322-6751
622 E Basin Rd New Castle (19720) ***(G-5607)***
Pat Press 302 836-2955
8 Eaton Pl Bear (19701) ***(G-279)***
Pat T Clean Inc 302 239-5354
519 Cabot Dr Hockessin (19707) ***(G-3111)***
Patel Sanjay 302 376-0136
745 N Broad St Middletown (19709) ***(G-4180)***
Patel, Ashok MD, Dover *Also called Harsha Tankala MD* ***(G-1635)***
Pathao Inc (PA) 845 242-3834
8 The Grn Ste A Dover (19901) ***(G-1939)***
Pathology Dept, Wilmington *Also called Allied Diagnstc Pathology Cons* ***(G-9021)***
Paths LLC 302 294-1494
1352 Marrows Rd Ste 110 Newark (19711) ***(G-7180)***
Pathscale Inc 408 520-0811
427 N Tatnall St 16370 Wilmington (19801) ***(G-12031)***
Pathways of Delaware Inc 302 573-5073
101 Rogers Rd Ste 102 Wilmington (19801) ***(G-12032)***
Patient First Medical LLC 302 536-7740
1330 Middleford Rd # 301 Seaford (19973) ***(G-8341)***
Patio Printing Co Inc 302 328-6881
197 Airport Rd New Castle (19720) ***(G-5608)***
Patio Systems Inc 302 644-6540
16083 New Rd Lewes (19958) ***(G-3680)***
Patricia Ayers 609 335-8923
20 Capano Dr Apt C3 Newark (19702) ***(G-7181)***
Patricia Degirolano Day Care 302 947-2874
32909 Long Neck Rd Millsboro (19966) ***(G-4770)***
Patricia Disario Day Care 302 737-8889
4 Cottonwood Ct Newark (19702) ***(G-7182)***
Patricia H Purcell MD 302 428-1142
601 Cheltenham Rd Wilmington (19808) ***(G-12033)***
Patricia Hoffmann 203 247-2635
98 Garfield Pkwy Bethany Beach (19930) ***(G-419)***
Patricia McKay 302 563-5334
337 Starboard Dr Bear (19701) ***(G-280)***
Patricia P McGonigle 302 888-7605
222 Delaware Ave Ste 1500 Wilmington (19801) ***(G-12034)***
Patrick Aircraft Group LLC 302 854-9300
21583 Baltimore Ave Georgetown (19947) ***(G-2612)***
Patrick J McCabe 302 368-3711
262 Chapman Rd Ste 109 Newark (19702) ***(G-7183)***
Patrick Scanlon PA 302 424-1996
203 Ne Front St Ste 101 Milford (19963) ***(G-4523)***
Patrick Swier Mdpa Kar 302 645-7737
1400 Savannah Rd Lewes (19958) ***(G-3681)***
Patriot Auto & Truck Care LLC 302 257-5715
497 S Dupont Hwy Dover (19901) ***(G-1940)***
Patriot Government Svcs Inc 302 655-3434
44 Bancroft Mills Rd Wilmington (19806) ***(G-12035)***
Patriot Systems Inc 302 472-9727
1204 First State Blvd Wilmington (19804) ***(G-12036)***
Pats Aircraft LLC (HQ) 855 236-1638
21652 Nanticoke Ave Georgetown (19947) ***(G-2613)***
Patterns 302 654-9075
2 Rockland Meadows Rd Rockland (19732) ***(G-8124)***
Patterson Price 302 378-9852
5 E Green St Wilmington (19801) ***(G-12037)***
Patterson & Kelly PA 302 736-6657
18 S State St Dover (19901) ***(G-1941)***
Patterson Price RE LLC 302 366-0200
1101 Millstone Dr Newark (19711) ***(G-7184)***
Patterson Price RE LLC (PA) 302 378-9550
5 E Green St Middletown (19709) ***(G-4181)***
Patterson Schwartz Real Estate, Middletown *Also called Patterson-Schwartz & Assoc Inc* ***(G-4182)***
Patterson Schwartz Real Estate, Wilmington *Also called Patterson-Schwartz & Assoc Inc* ***(G-12038)***
Patterson Schwartz Real Estate, Dover *Also called Patterson-Schwartz & Assoc Inc* ***(G-1942)***
Patterson-Schwartz & Assoc Inc (PA) 302 234-5250
7234 Lancaster Pike Hockessin (19707) ***(G-3112)***
Patterson-Schwartz & Assoc Inc 302 733-7000
680 S College Ave Newark (19713) ***(G-7185)***
Patterson-Schwartz & Assoc Inc 302 285-5100
4485 Summit Bridge Rd Middletown (19709) ***(G-4182)***
Patterson-Schwartz & Assoc Inc 302 429-4500
3705 Kennett Pike Wilmington (19807) ***(G-12038)***
Patterson-Schwartz & Assoc Inc 302 672-9400
140 Greentree Dr Dover (19904) ***(G-1942)***
Patterson-Schwartz Real Estate, Hockessin *Also called Patterson-Schwartz & Assoc Inc* ***(G-3112)***
Patty Cakes Childcare, Bear *Also called Patricia McKay* ***(G-280)***
Paul A Lange 302 378-1706
7 Claddagh Ct Middletown (19709) ***(G-4183)***
Paul Amos 302 541-9200
39642 Jefferson Bridge Rd Bethany Beach (19930) ***(G-420)***
Paul Associates 302 584-0064
304 Country Club Dr Wilmington (19803) ***(G-12039)***
Paul C Anisman M D 302 651-6600
1600 Rockland Rd Wilmington (19803) ***(G-12040)***
Paul Edwards Carpet Cleaning, Dover *Also called Edwards Paul Crpt Installation* ***(G-1509)***
Paul F Campanella Inc 302 777-7170
1703 Augustine Cut Off Wilmington (19803) ***(G-12041)***
Paul F Campanella Auto Service, Wilmington *Also called Paul F Campanella Inc* ***(G-12041)***
Paul G Collins DDS 302 934-8005
560 W Dupont Hwy Millsboro (19966) ***(G-4771)***
Paul H Aguillon MD 302 629-6664
401 Concord Rd Seaford (19973) ***(G-8342)***
Paul Imber Do 302 478-5647
2700 Silverside Rd Ste 3a Wilmington (19810) ***(G-12042)***
Paul J Renzi Masonary, Wilmington *Also called Paul Renzi* ***(G-12043)***
Paul R Christian DMD 302 376-9600
423 E Main St Middletown (19709) ***(G-4184)***
Paul Renzi 302 478-3166
6 Brookside Dr Wilmington (19804) ***(G-12043)***
Paul Sica MD 302 652-3469
2300 Penns Ave Ste 5b Wilmington (19806) ***(G-12044)***
Paul Sorvino Foods Inc 302 547-1977
4001 Kennett Pike Ste 134 Wilmington (19807) ***(G-12045)***
Paul Woerner 302 266-6282
610 Banyan Rd Newark (19713) ***(G-7186)***
Pauls House Inc 302 384-2350
1405 Veale Rd Wilmington (19810) ***(G-12046)***
Pauls Paving Inc 302 539-9123
37425 Dale Earnhardt Blvd Frankford (19945) ***(G-2379)***
Pauls Plastering Inc 302 654-5583
19 Davidson Ln Bldg 1 New Castle (19720) ***(G-5609)***
Paws & People Too 302 376-8234
4390 Summit Bridge Rd # 4 Middletown (19709) ***(G-4185)***
Paxful Inc 865 272-9385
3422 Old Capitol Trl Wilmington (19808) ***(G-12047)***
Paybysky Inc 519 641-1771
16192 Coastal Hwy Lewes (19958) ***(G-3682)***
Paymenex Inc 302 504-6044
501 Silverside Rd Ste 105 Wilmington (19809) ***(G-12048)***
Paypergigs Inc 917 336-2162
2035 Sunset Lake Rd B2 Newark (19702) ***(G-7187)***
Payroll Management Assistants 302 456-6816
409 White Clay Center Dr Newark (19711) ***(G-7188)***
Payroll Services of Delaware, Dover *Also called Computer Services of Delaware* ***(G-1309)***

Pb Reit, Newark *Also called P B Investment Corp* ***(G-7167)***
PB Trucking Inc 302 841-3209
8940 Greenwood Rd Greenwood (19950) ***(G-2758)***
Pbe Companies LLC 617 346-7459
2711 Centerville Rd Wilmington (19808) ***(G-12049)***
Pbtv Global Inc 302 292-1400
2105a W Newport Pike Wilmington (19804) ***(G-12050)***
PC Supplies Inc 302 368-4800
1003 S Chapel St Ste A Newark (19702) ***(G-7189)***
PCI of Virginia LLC (HQ) 302 655-7300
529 Terminal Ave New Castle (19720) ***(G-5610)***
Pck Associates Inc 302 378-7192
1343 Bohemia Mill Rd Middletown (19709) ***(G-4186)***
Pcmh Support Team - Privacy 267 254-2111
2607 N Harrison St Wilmington (19802) ***(G-12051)***
Pcms Holdings Inc 302 281-3600
200 Bellevue Pkwy Ste 300 Wilmington (19809) ***(G-12052)***
Pcu Systems LLC 888 780-9728
3524 Silverside Rd 35b Wilmington (19810) ***(G-12053)***
Pde I LLC 302 654-8300
422 Delaware Ave Wilmington (19801) ***(G-12054)***
PDM Incorporated 302 478-0768
3411 Silverside Rd 104wb Wilmington (19810) ***(G-12055)***
PDr Vc Ltd Liability Company 424 281-4669
427 N Tatnall St 92059 Wilmington (19801) ***(G-12056)***
Peak Cryotherapy 302 502-3160
3105 Limestone Rd Wilmington (19808) ***(G-12057)***
Pearce & Moretto Inc 302 326-0707
314 Bay West Blvd Ste 4 New Castle (19720) ***(G-5611)***
Pearl Clinic LLC 302 648-2099
230 Mitchell St Ste B Millsboro (19966) ***(G-4772)***
Peas and Love Corporation 301 537-3593
1209 N Orange St Wilmington (19801) ***(G-12058)***
Pebble Hill Apartments, Wilmington *Also called Eastern Property Group Inc* ***(G-10324)***
Pebble Hill Assoc A Partnr, Wilmington *Also called Eastern Prosperity Group* ***(G-10325)***
Pediatric & Adolescent Center 302 684-0561
424 Mulberry St Milton (19968) ***(G-4946)***
Pediatric Associates PA 302 368-8612
4735 Ogltn Stntn Rd # 1116 Newark (19713) ***(G-7190)***
Peek Performance Group LLC 480 242-6087
300 Delaware Ave Wilmington (19801) ***(G-12059)***
Peeper Vehicle Technology Corp 800 971-4134
8 The Grn Ste A Dover (19901) ***(G-1943)***
Pegasus Air Inc 302 875-3540
32524 Aero Dr Laurel (19956) ***(G-3269)***
Peirce James Townsend III 302 449-2279
19 Canary Ct Middletown (19709) ***(G-4187)***
Peirce-Phelps Inc 302 633-9352
360 Water St Wilmington (19804) ***(G-12060)***
Pelican Bay Group Inc 302 945-5900
100 Rudder Rd Millsboro (19966) ***(G-4773)***
Pella Window and Door, Wilmington *Also called Gunton Corporation* ***(G-10803)***
Pelsa Company Inc 302 834-3771
610 Peoples Plz Newark (19702) ***(G-7191)***
Pemco Lighting Products Inc 302 892-9000
150 Pemco Way Wilmington (19804) ***(G-12061)***
Pemco Lighting Products LLC 302 892-9000
150 Pemco Way Wilmington (19804) ***(G-12062)***
Penache Beauty Salon 302 731-5912
16 Polly Drmmond Shpg Ctr Newark (19711) ***(G-7192)***
Pencader Associates 302 838-7838
560 Peoples Plz Newark (19702) ***(G-7193)***
Pencader Mechanical Contrs 302 368-9144
2038 Sunset Lake Rd # 2040 Newark (19702) ***(G-7194)***
Penco Corporation (PA) 302 629-7911
1503 W Stein Hwy Seaford (19973) ***(G-8343)***
Penco Corporation 302 629-3061
1800 Dulany St 6 Seaford (19973) ***(G-8344)***
Penco Corporation 302 629-7911
1503 W Stein Hwy Seaford (19973) ***(G-8345)***
Penco Corporation 302 698-3108
2000 S Dupont Hwy Camden (19934) ***(G-596)***
Penco Corporation 302 227-9188
Rr 1 Rehoboth Beach (19971) ***(G-8029)***
Penco Corporation 302 738-3212
121 Sandy Dr Newark (19713) ***(G-7195)***
Penflex III LLC 302 998-0683
702 First State Blvd Wilmington (19804) ***(G-12063)***
Peninsula 302 945-4768
32981 Peninsula Esplanade Millsboro (19966) ***(G-4774)***
Peninsula Acoustical Co Inc 302 653-3551
441 Pier Head Blvd Smyrna (19977) ***(G-8687)***
Peninsula Allergy and Asthma 302 734-4434
200 Banning St Ste 280 Dover (19904) ***(G-1944)***
Peninsula Anmal Hosp Orthpdics 302 846-9011
38375 Old Stage Rd Delmar (19940) ***(G-1024)***
Peninsula At Long Neck LLC 302 947-4717
468 Bay Farm Rd Millsboro (19966) ***(G-4775)***
Peninsula Chiropractic Center 302 629-4344
26685 Sussex Hwy Seaford (19973) ***(G-8346)***
Peninsula Compost Company LLC 215 595-4218
529 Terminal Ave New Castle (19720) ***(G-5612)***
Peninsula Dental LLC 302 297-3750
26670 Centerview Dr # 19 Millsboro (19966) ***(G-4776)***
Peninsula Dry Cleaners, Seaford *Also called Kapa Inc LLC* ***(G-8283)***
Peninsula Energy Svcs Co Inc (HQ) 302 734-6799
909 Silver Lake Blvd Dover (19904) ***(G-1945)***
Peninsula Gallery, Lewes *Also called Carol Boyd Heron* ***(G-3407)***
Peninsula Health Alliance Inc 302 856-9778
13 Bridgeville Rd Georgetown (19947) ***(G-2614)***
Peninsula Health LLC 302 945-0440
26744 J J Williams 7 Millsboro (19966) ***(G-4777)***
Peninsula Home Care LLC 302 629-4914
8466 Herring Run Rd Seaford (19973) ***(G-8347)***
Peninsula Home Health Care 302 629-5672
514 W Stein Hwy Seaford (19973) ***(G-8348)***
Peninsula Masonry Inc 302 684-3410
26822 Lwes Georgetown Hwy Harbeson (19951) ***(G-2795)***
Peninsula Oil & Propane, Seaford *Also called Peninsula Oil Co Inc* ***(G-8349)***
Peninsula Oil Co Inc (PA) 302 422-6691
40 S Market St Seaford (19973) ***(G-8349)***
Peninsula Pave & Seal LLC 302 226-7283
20288 Asphalt Aly Georgetown (19947) ***(G-2615)***
Peninsula Paving, Georgetown *Also called Peninsula Pave & Seal LLC* ***(G-2615)***
Peninsula Plastic Surgery PC 302 663-0119
30265 Commerce Dr # 208 Millsboro (19966) ***(G-4778)***
Peninsula Poultry Eqp Co Inc 302 875-0889
30709 Sussex Hwy Laurel (19956) ***(G-3270)***
Peninsula Regional Medical Ctr 302 436-8004
15 N Williams St Selbyville (19975) ***(G-8529)***
Peninsula Regional Medical Ctr 302 537-1457
35786 Atlantic Ave Unit 3 Millville (19967) ***(G-4852)***
Peninsula Regional Medical Ctr 302 732-8400
Rts 113 & 26th Dagsboro (19939) ***(G-929)***
Peninsula Regional Prmry Care, Selbyville *Also called Peninsula Regional Medical Ctr* ***(G-8529)***
Peninsula Technical Services I 302 907-0554
38224 Old Stage Rd Delmar (19940) ***(G-1025)***
Peninsula Untd Mthdst Hmes Inc 302 235-6810
726 Loveville Rd Ste 3000 Hockessin (19707) ***(G-3113)***
Peninsula Untd Mthdst Hmes Inc (PA) 302 235-6800
726 Loveville Rd Ste 3000 Hockessin (19707) ***(G-3114)***
Peninsula Untd Mthdst Hmes Inc 302 654-5101
4830 Kennett Pike Wilmington (19807) ***(G-12064)***
Peninsula Veterinary Svcs LLC 302 947-0719
32038 Long Neck Rd Millsboro (19966) ***(G-4779)***
Penn Acres Swim Club 302 322-6501
30 Fithian Dr New Castle (19720) ***(G-5613)***
Penn Del Adjustment Service 302 999-0196
7 Lake Dr Bear (19701) ***(G-281)***
Penn Del Carriers LLC 484 424-3768
110 W Edinburgh Dr New Castle (19720) ***(G-5614)***
Penn Labs Inc 215 751-4000
2711 Centerville Rd # 400 Wilmington (19808) ***(G-12065)***
Penn Mutual Life Insurance Co 302 655-7151
1521 Concord Pike Ste 305 Wilmington (19803) ***(G-12066)***
Penn Virginia Holding Corp 302 288-0158
1011 Centre Rd Ste 310 Wilmington (19805) ***(G-12067)***
Penna Orthodontics 302 998-8783
2710 Centerville Rd Wilmington (19808) ***(G-12068)***
Pennengineering Holdings LLC (HQ) 302 576-2746
103 Foulk Rd Ste 108 Wilmington (19803) ***(G-12069)***
Pennengineering Holdings, Inc., Wilmington *Also called Pennengineering Holdings LLC* ***(G-12069)***
Penney Enterprises Inc 302 629-4430
9203 Brickyard Rd Seaford (19973) ***(G-8350)***
Pennisula Glass, Dover *Also called MMR Associates Inc* ***(G-1865)***
Pennoni 302 234-4600
121 Continental Dr # 207 Newark (19713) ***(G-7196)***
Pennoni Associates Inc 302 684-8030
18072 Davidson Dr Milton (19968) ***(G-4947)***
Pennoni Associates Inc 302 655-4451
121 Continental Dr # 207 Newark (19713) ***(G-7197)***
Pennrose Management Company 302 571-8295
502 N Dupont St Wilmington (19805) ***(G-12070)***
Pennsula Home Care LLC 302 629-4914
501 Health Services Dr Seaford (19973) ***(G-8351)***
Pennsylvania Brand Co 302 674-5774
550 S New St Dover (19904) ***(G-1946)***
Pennsylvania Inc 302 498-0904
1420 Lancaster Ave Wilmington (19805) ***(G-12071)***
Penny Cooper Sportswear & EMB 302 325-3710
204 Christiana Rd New Castle (19720) ***(G-5615)***
Penny Express Inc 302 571-0544
1202 E 13th St Wilmington (19802) ***(G-12072)***
Penny Hill Lawn & Landscaping 302 762-4406
602 Elizabeth Ave Wilmington (19809) ***(G-12073)***
Pennzoil-Quaker State Company 302 999-7323
3725 Kirkwood Hwy Wilmington (19808) ***(G-12074)***

ALPHABETIC

(PA)=Parent Co (HQ)=Headquarters (DH)=Div Headquarters
2020 Harris Directory of Delaware Businesses
701

Penobscot Properties LLC (PA) 302 322-4477
135 N Dupont Hwy Hngr B New Castle (19720) ***(G-5616)***
Penske Performance Inc (HQ) 302 656-2082
1105 N Market St Wilmington (19801) ***(G-12075)***
Penske Truck Leasing Co LP 302 994-7899
3625 Kirkwood Hwy Wilmington (19808) ***(G-12076)***
Penske Truck Leasing Co LP 302 325-9290
51 Boulden Blvd New Castle (19720) ***(G-5617)***
Penske Truck Leasing Corp 302 629-5373
24799 Sussex Hwy Seaford (19973) ***(G-8352)***
Penske Truck Leasing Corp 302 658-3255
4709 Ferris Dr Wilmington (19808) ***(G-12077)***
Penske Truck Leasing Corp 302 260-7039
19659 Blue Bird Ln Rehoboth Beach (19971) ***(G-8030)***
Penske Truck Leasing Corp 302 449-9294
921 Middletown Warwick Rd Middletown (19709) ***(G-4188)***
Pentius Inc 855 825-3778
1201 N Orange St Ste 7382 Wilmington (19801) ***(G-12078)***
Penuel Sign Co 302 856-7265
22832 E Trap Pond Rd Georgetown (19947) ***(G-2616)***
Penwood Property Preservation 302 469-5318
125 Dickens Ln Felton (19943) ***(G-2308)***
People Builders Inc 302 250-0716
38 Hempstead Dr Newark (19702) ***(G-7198)***
People In Transition Inc 302 784-5214
39 Thorn Ln New Castle (19720) ***(G-5618)***
People Over Profit LLC 718 612-0328
8 The Grn Ste A Dover (19901) ***(G-1947)***
People's Settlement Day Care, Wilmington *Also called Peoples Settlement Assc of WI* ***(G-12079)***
Peoples Place II Inc 302 934-0300
30265 Commerce Dr # 201 Millsboro (19966) ***(G-4780)***
Peoples Place II Inc 302 730-1321
165 Commerce Way Dover (19904) ***(G-1948)***
Peoples Place II Inc (PA) 302 422-8033
1129 Airport Rd Milford (19963) ***(G-4524)***
Peoples Plaza Cinema 17, Christiana *Also called Regal Cinemas Inc* ***(G-679)***
Peoples Settlement Assc of WI 302 658-4133
408 E 8th St Wilmington (19801) ***(G-12079)***
Peoples, R C, Bear *Also called Robert C Peoples Inc* ***(G-308)***
Pep-Up Inc (PA) 302 856-2555
24987 Dupont Blvd Georgetown (19947) ***(G-2617)***
Pep-Up Inc 302 645-2600
18979 Coastal Hwy Rehoboth Beach (19971) ***(G-8031)***
Pep-Up 11, Rehoboth Beach *Also called Pep-Up Inc* ***(G-8031)***
Pepco Holdings LLC 202 872-2000
401 Eagle Run Rd Newark (19702) ***(G-7199)***
Pepco Holdings LLC 202 872-2000
630 Mrtin Lthar King Blvd Wilmington (19801) ***(G-12080)***
Pepper Greenhouses 302 684-8092
13034 Mulberry Street Ext Milton (19968) ***(G-4948)***
Peppers Inc (PA) 302 645-0812
17601 Coastal Hwy Unit 1 Lewes (19958) ***(G-3683)***
Peppers Inc 302 644-6900
15608 Coastal Hwy Lewes (19958) ***(G-3684)***
Pepsi Bottling Ventures LLC 302 398-3415
58 Clukey Dr Harrington (19952) ***(G-2871)***
Pepsi-Cola Btlg of Wilmington 302 761-4848
3501 Governor Printz Blvd Wilmington (19802) ***(G-12081)***
Pepsi-Cola Metro Btlg Co Inc 302 764-6770
3501 Governor Printz Blvd Wilmington (19802) ***(G-12082)***
Pepsico, Harrington *Also called Pepsi Bottling Ventures LLC* ***(G-2871)***
Pera Trading Inc 302 292-1750
711 Interchange Blvd Newark (19711) ***(G-7200)***
Perastic LLC 917 592-4219
1704 N Park Dr Apt 508 Wilmington (19806) ***(G-12083)***
Percebe Music Inc 850 341-9594
8 The Grn Ste A Dover (19901) ***(G-1949)***
Perceri LLC 217 721-8731
160 Greentree Dr Ste 101 Dover (19904) ***(G-1950)***
Perdue Farms Inc 302 629-3216
1000 Nanticoke Ave Seaford (19973) ***(G-8353)***
Perdue Farms Inc 302 337-2210
16447 Adams Rd Bridgeville (19933) ***(G-507)***
Perdue Farms Inc 410 543-3424
300 New St Seaford (19973) ***(G-8354)***
Perdue Farms Inc 302 855-5681
10262 Stone Creek Dr Laurel (19956) ***(G-3271)***
Perdue Farms Inc 302 424-2600
225 S Rehoboth Blvd Milford (19963) ***(G-4525)***
Perdue Farms Incorporated 302 855-5635
20621 Savannah Rd Georgetown (19947) ***(G-2618)***
Perdue-Agrirecycle LLC 302 628-2360
28338 Enviro Way Seaford (19973) ***(G-8355)***
Perfect Finish Powder Coating 302 566-6189
3845 Whiteleysburg Rd Harrington (19952) ***(G-2872)***
Perfect Nails 302 731-1964
210 University Plz Newark (19702) ***(G-7201)***
Perfection Lawncare Ltd 215 624-7410
129 Gazebo Ln Middletown (19709) ***(G-4189)***
Performance Auto Body & Paint 302 655-6170
200 Bradford St Wilmington (19801) ***(G-12084)***
Performance Based Results 302 478-4443
400 Delaware Ave Talleyville (19803) ***(G-8750)***
Performance Cons Group Inc 302 738-7532
1 Innovation Way Ste 304c Newark (19711) ***(G-7202)***
Performance Lubricants, Wilmington *Also called Chemours Company Fc LLC* ***(G-9650)***
Performance Materials Na Inc 302 892-7009
974 Chestnut Run Plz Wilmington (19805) ***(G-12085)***
Performance Physcl Therapy Inc (PA) 302 234-2288
720 Yorklyn Rd Ste 150 Hockessin (19707) ***(G-3115)***
Perinatal Assocation Delaware 302 654-1088
715 N Tatnall St Wilmington (19801) ***(G-12086)***
Perioperative Services LLC (PA) 302 733-0806
111 Continental Dr # 412 Newark (19713) ***(G-7203)***
Peristalsis Productions Inc 302 366-1106
6 Newside Ct Newark (19711) ***(G-7204)***
Perkwiz Inc 702 866-9122
7209 Lancaster Pike Hockessin (19707) ***(G-3116)***
Perpetual Invstments Group LLC 718 795-3394
251 Little Falls Dr Wilmington (19808) ***(G-12087)***
Perrone Enterprises Inc 302 436-8031
36829 W Pond Cir Selbyville (19975) ***(G-8530)***
Perry & Assoc 302 472-8701
6 Larch Ave Ste 397 Wilmington (19804) ***(G-12088)***
Perry and Associates Inc 302 898-2327
540 Waterford Rd Hockessin (19707) ***(G-3117)***
Perry and Associates Services 302 581-3092
300 Delaware Ave Ste 210 Wilmington (19801) ***(G-12089)***
Persante Sleep Center 302 508-2130
100 S Main St Ste 201 Smyrna (19977) ***(G-8688)***
Persephone Jones MD 302 651-4000
1600 Rockland Rd Wilmington (19803) ***(G-12090)***
Persona Group LLC 302 335-5221
74 Wildflower Cir W Magnolia (19962) ***(G-3902)***
Persona Ink, Magnolia *Also called Persona Group LLC* ***(G-3902)***
Personal Health PDT Dev LLC 888 901-6150
4023 Kennett Pike Ste 622 Wilmington (19807) ***(G-12091)***
Perspective Counseling Center 302 677-1758
393 Fork Landing Rd Felton (19943) ***(G-2309)***
Perteh 302 200-0912
1800 Naamans Rd Wilmington (19810) ***(G-12092)***
Pessagno Equipment Inc 302 738-7001
109 Sandy Dr Newark (19713) ***(G-7205)***
Pet Medical Center 302 846-2869
Rr 13 Delmar (19940) ***(G-1026)***
Pet Poultry Products LLC 302 337-8223
7494 Federalsburg Rd Bridgeville (19933) ***(G-508)***
Petal Pushers Flowers, Wilmington *Also called Alexis Wirt* ***(G-9005)***
Petal Pushers LLC 302 945-0350
31341 Kendale Rd Lewes (19958) ***(G-3685)***
Petcube Inc 786 375-9065
2711 Centerville Rd # 400 Wilmington (19808) ***(G-12093)***
Peter D Furness Elc Co Inc 302 764-6030
1604 Todds Ln Wilmington (19802) ***(G-12094)***
Peter Domanski & Sons 302 475-3214
1562 Brackenville Rd Hockessin (19707) ***(G-3118)***
Peter F Subach 302 995-1870
1601 Milltown Rd Ste 17 Wilmington (19808) ***(G-12095)***
Peter F Townsend MD 302 633-3555
3519 Silverside Rd # 101 Wilmington (19810) ***(G-12096)***
Peter Patellis 302 537-1200
32895 Coastal Hwy # 102 Bethany Beach (19930) ***(G-421)***
Peter R Coggins MD 302 655-1115
5811 Kennett Pike Wilmington (19807) ***(G-12097)***
Peter Shin (PA) 302 498-0977
805 W 21st St Wilmington (19802) ***(G-12098)***
Peters Alan E Peters & Assoc 302 656-1007
1200 Penns Ave Ste 202 Wilmington (19806) ***(G-12099)***
Peters John Dvm 302 478-5981
136 Hitching Post Dr Wilmington (19803) ***(G-12100)***
Petes Big Tvs Inc (PA) 302 328-3551
22 Lukens Dr New Castle (19720) ***(G-5619)***
Petes Garage Inc 302 286-6069
78 Albe Dr Ste 8 Newark (19702) ***(G-7206)***
Petite Hair Designs 302 945-2595
Long Neck Rd Palmer Shpng Millsboro (19966) ***(G-4781)***
Petroleum Equipment Inc (PA) 302 734-7433
3799 N Dupont Hwy Dover (19901) ***(G-1951)***
Petroleum Equipment Inc 302 422-4281
3799 N Dupont Hwy Dover (19901) ***(G-1952)***
Petroserv Inc 302 398-3260
17436 S Dupont Hwy Harrington (19952) ***(G-2873)***
Petrucon Construction Inc 302 571-5781
100 N Cleveland Ave Wilmington (19805) ***(G-12101)***
Pettinaro Construction Co Inc (PA) 302 999-0708
234 N James St Wilmington (19804) ***(G-12102)***
Pettinaro Construction Co Inc 302 832-8823
100 Cindy Dr Newark (19702) ***(G-7207)***

Pettinaro Enterprises LLC 302 999-0708
234 N James St Wilmington (19804) *(G-12103)*
Pettitt Construction LLC 302 690-0831
12 Carlisle Rd Newark (19713) *(G-7208)*
Pettyjohn Farms Inc 302 684-4383
16771 Gravel Hill Rd Milton (19968) *(G-4949)*
Pettyjohn's Parts & Repair, Milton *Also called Pettyjohns Custom Engine (G-4950)*
Pettyjohns Custom Engine 302 684-8888
601 Federal St Milton (19968) *(G-4950)*
Pfister Insurance Inc 302 674-3100
625 S Dupont Hwy Ste 101 Dover (19901) *(G-1953)*
Pfpc Trust Company 302 791-2000
301 Bellevue Pkwy Fl 4 Wilmington (19809) *(G-12104)*
Pfpc Worldwide Inc (HQ) 302 791-1700
301 Bellevue Pkwy Wilmington (19809) *(G-12105)*
Pga Acquisitions V LLC 302 355-3500
1002 Justison St Wilmington (19801) *(G-12106)*
Pgw Auto Glass LLC 302 793-1486
130 Hickman Rd Ste 19 Claymont (19703) *(G-794)*
Pgw Autoglass, Claymont *Also called Pgw Auto Glass LLC (G-794)*
Phalco Inc 302 654-2620
10 Germay Dr Wilmington (19804) *(G-12107)*
Pharma E Market LLC 302 737-3711
726 Loveville Rd Apt 99 Hockessin (19707) *(G-3119)*
Pharmacy Technologies Inc 877 655-3846
16192 Coastal Hwy Lewes (19958) *(G-3686)*
Pharmadel LLC 302 322-1329
600 Ships Landing Way New Castle (19720) *(G-5620)*
Pharmerica Long-Term Care LLC 302 454-8234
111 Ruthar Dr Newark (19711) *(G-7209)*
Pharmunion LLC 415 307-5128
3524 Silverside Rd 35b Wilmington (19810) *(G-12108)*
Phase Flats II L P 717 291-1911
601 N Union St Wilmington (19805) *(G-12109)*
Phase I Flats L P 717 291-1911
401-535 N Union St Wilmington (19805) *(G-12110)*
Phase Snsitive Innovations Inc 302 456-9003
116 Sandy Dr Newark (19713) *(G-7210)*
Phazebreak Coatings LLC 844 467-4293
1105 N Market St Ste 1300 Wilmington (19801) *(G-12111)*
Phc Inc (HQ) 313 831-3500
575 S Dupont Hwy New Castle (19720) *(G-5621)*
PHD Technology Solutions LLC 410 961-7895
111 Continental Dr # 309 Newark (19713) *(G-7211)*
PHI Service Co 302 451-5224
P.O. Box 6066 Newark (19714) *(G-7212)*
Phil Hill 302 678-0499
3728 N Dupont Hwy Dover (19901) *(G-1954)*
Philadelph Ft Ankl Asscts 215 465-5342
503 E 35th St Wilmington (19802) *(G-12112)*
Philadelphia Control Systems 302 368-4333
56 W Main St Ste 103 Christiana (19702) *(G-675)*
Philadelphia Gear, New Castle *Also called Timken Gears & Services Inc (G-5770)*
Philadlphia Arms Town Hmes Inc 302 503-7216
18527 Pentecostal St Ellendale (19941) *(G-2262)*
Philadlphia Ball Rller Bearing 215 727-0982
701 Cornell Dr Ste 12 Wilmington (19801) *(G-12113)*
Philip M Finestrauss PA 302 984-1600
1404 N King St Wilmington (19801) *(G-12114)*
Philips B Eric DMD PA 302 738-7303
Omega Prof Ctr Ste J31 Newark (19713) *(G-7213)*
Phillip E Weir 302 652-1312
600 Greenhill Ave Wilmington (19805) *(G-12115)*
Phillip L Hrrs Fd/Cnsltnt 302 270-2905
40 Meadowood Ln Harrington (19952) *(G-2874)*
Phillip T Bradley Inc 302 947-2741
33057 Angola Rd Lewes (19958) *(G-3687)*
Phillips Gldmn McLghln & Hll 302 655-4200
1200 N Broom St Wilmington (19806) *(G-12116)*
Phillips & Cohen Assoc Ltd (PA) 609 518-9000
1002 Justison St Wilmington (19801) *(G-12117)*
Phillips & Cohen Assoc Ltd 302 355-3500
258 Chapman Rd Ste 205 Newark (19702) *(G-7214)*
Phillips Fabrication 302 875-4424
32846 Shockley Rd Laurel (19956) *(G-3272)*
Phillips Insulation Inc 302 655-6523
8 Brookside Dr Wilmington (19804) *(G-12118)*
Phillips Signs Inc 302 629-3550
20874 Sussex Hwy Seaford (19973) *(G-8356)*
Philly Plastics Corp 718 435-4808
1201 N Orange St Wilmington (19801) *(G-12119)*
Philly Pretzel 302 478-5658
4737 Concord Pike Wilmington (19803) *(G-12120)*
Philymack Games LLC 302 658-7581
1209 N Orange St Wilmington (19801) *(G-12121)*
Phippins Cabinetry 302 212-2189
20807 Coastal Hwy Apt 1 Rehoboth Beach (19971) *(G-8032)*
Phly LLC 778 882-2391
500 Delaware Ave Unit 1 Wilmington (19899) *(G-12122)*
Phocal Therapy Inc 917 803-7168
16192 Coastal Hwy Lewes (19958) *(G-3688)*
Phoenix Filtration Inc 302 998-8805
403 Marsh Ln Ste 2-4 Wilmington (19804) *(G-12123)*
Phoenix Home Theater Inc 302 295-1390
403 Marsh Ln 3 Wilmington (19804) *(G-12124)*
Phoenix Intl Resources LLC 954 309-0120
16192 Coastal Hwy Lewes (19958) *(G-3689)*
Phoenix Rehabilitation and Hea 302 725-5720
401 S Dupont Blvd Milford (19963) *(G-4526)*
Phoenix Restoration, Wilmington *Also called Phoenix Home Theater Inc (G-12124)*
Phoenix Rhbilitation Hlth Svcs 302 764-2008
4001 Miller Rd Ste 2 Wilmington (19802) *(G-12125)*
Phoenix Trnsp & Logistics Inc (HQ) 302 348-8814
1000 N West St Ste 1200 Wilmington (19801) *(G-12126)*
Phoenix Vitae Holdings LLC 302 351-3047
251 Little Falls Dr Wilmington (19808) *(G-12127)*
Phonecandiescom 215 385-1818
507 Grinnell Ct Bear (19701) *(G-282)*
Photodemy.com, Dover *Also called Classerium Corporation (G-1292)*
Photography By Dennis McD 610 678-0318
5 W Greenwing Dr Milton (19968) *(G-4951)*
Photon Programming 302 328-2925
58 Stockton Dr New Castle (19720) *(G-5622)*
Phresh Products, Wilmington *Also called Personal Health PDT Dev LLC (G-12091)*
Phs Corporate Services Inc 302 571-1128
1313 N Market St Wilmington (19801) *(G-12128)*
Phyllis M Green 302 354-6986
329 N Red Lion Ter Bear (19701) *(G-283)*
Physiatrist Assoc, Newark *Also called Anthony Lee Cucuzzella MD (G-5974)*
Physical Medical Rehab Assoc, Milford *Also called Center For Neurology (G-4344)*
Physical Therapist 302 983-4151
503 Pierce Ct Middletown (19709) *(G-4190)*
Physical Therapy Services Inc (PA) 302 678-3100
725 Walker Rd Dover (19904) *(G-1955)*
Physicchmcal Scences Inst Tech, Wilmington *Also called PSI-TEC Corporation (G-12259)*
Physician Dspnsng Solutions 302 734-7246
390 Mitch Rd Wilmington (19804) *(G-12129)*
Physicians Beauty Group LLC 866 270-9290
9 E Loockerman St Ste 202 Dover (19901) *(G-1956)*
Physio Therapy Association, Wilmington *Also called Physiotherapy Associates Inc (G-12131)*
Physiotherapy Associates Inc 302 655-8989
2401 Penns Ave Ste 112 Wilmington (19806) *(G-12130)*
Physiotherapy Associates Inc 302 674-1269
642 Suth Queen St Ste 101 Dover (19904) *(G-1957)*
Physiotherapy Associates Inc 610 444-1270
3411 Silverside Rd # 105 Wilmington (19810) *(G-12131)*
Physiotherapy Corporation 302 628-8568
300 Hlth Svcs Dr Unit 301 Seaford (19973) *(G-8357)*
Pictsweet Company 302 337-8206
18215 Wesley Church Rd Bridgeville (19933) *(G-509)*
Pieces of A Dream Inc 302 593-6172
2404 W 7th St Wilmington (19805) *(G-12132)*
Piedmont Baseball League Inc 302 234-9437
102 Wyeth Way Hockessin (19707) *(G-3120)*
Pierce Design & Tool 302 222-3339
20 Bailey Cir Dover (19901) *(G-1958)*
Pierce Fence Company Inc 302 674-1996
5751 N Dupont Hwy Dover (19901) *(G-1959)*
Pierce Professional Services 302 331-1154
501 Cypress Dr Magnolia (19962) *(G-3903)*
Pierce Total Comfort LLC 302 378-7714
24 Chancellorsville Cir Middletown (19709) *(G-4191)*
Pierpont Industries 302 998-9220
11 Harlech Dr Wilmington (19807) *(G-12133)*
Pierson Culver LLC 302 732-1145
27517 Hodges Ln Dagsboro (19939) *(G-930)*
Pike Creek Animal Hospital 302 454-7780
297 Polly Drummond Hl Rd Newark (19711) *(G-7215)*
Pike Creek Assoc In Wmncare PA, Wilmington *Also called Pike Creek Assoc In Wns Care (G-12134)*
Pike Creek Assoc In Wns Care (PA) 302 995-7062
4600 New Lndn Hill Rd 1 Wilmington (19808) *(G-12134)*
Pike Creek Automotive Inc 302 998-2234
2379 Limestone Rd Wilmington (19808) *(G-12135)*
Pike Creek Bike Line Inc 610 747-1200
4768 Limestone Rd Wilmington (19808) *(G-12136)*
Pike Creek Branch, Wilmington *Also called Wilmington Savings Fund Soc (G-13249)*
Pike Creek Computer Company 302 239-5113
2206 Milltown Rd Wilmington (19808) *(G-12137)*
Pike Creek Court Club Inc 302 239-6688
4905 Mermaid Blvd Ste B Wilmington (19808) *(G-12138)*
Pike Creek Fitness Club, Wilmington *Also called Pike Creek Court Club Inc (G-12138)*
Pike Creek Imaging Center 302 995-2037
3105 Limestone Rd Ste 106 Wilmington (19808) *(G-12139)*
Pike Creek Mortgage Group, Newark *Also called Pike Creek Mortgage Services (G-7216)*

ALPHABETIC

Pike Creek Mortgage Services (PA) 302 892-2811
2100 Drummond Plz Bldg 2 Newark (19711) ***(G-7216)***
Pike Creek Pediatric Assoc 302 239-7755
100 S Riding Blvd Wilmington (19808) ***(G-12140)***
Pike Creek Psychological Ctr PA 302 449-2223
252 Carter Dr Ste 100 Middletown (19709) ***(G-4192)***
Pike Creek Psychological Ctr PA (PA) 302 738-6859
8 Polly Drummond Hill Rd Newark (19711) ***(G-7217)***
Pike Creek Software, Wilmington *Also called Pike Creek Computer Company* ***(G-12137)***
Pilots Assn For Bay River Del 302 645-2229
41 Cape Henlopen Dr Lewes (19958) ***(G-3690)***
Pilottown Engineering LLC 302 703-1770
17585 Nssau Cmmons Blvd S Lewes (19958) ***(G-3691)***
Pimc, Wilmington *Also called Blackrock Instnl Mgt Corp* ***(G-9354)***
Pinckney Wdnger Urban Jyce LLC 302 504-1497
3711 Kennett Pike Ste 210 Wilmington (19807) ***(G-12141)***
Pine Acres Inc 302 945-2000
34385 Carpenters Way B Lewes (19958) ***(G-3692)***
Pine Breeze Farms Inc 302 337-7717
3583 Buck Fever Rd Bridgeville (19933) ***(G-510)***
Pine Derivatives Marketing, Wilmington *Also called PDM Incorporated* ***(G-12055)***
Pine Valley Corvettes 302 834-1268
108 Pine Valley Dr Middletown (19709) ***(G-4193)***
Pineal Consulting Group LLC 302 219-4822
40 E Main St 181 Newark (19711) ***(G-7218)***
Pineapple Stitchery 302 500-8050
26005 Gvernor Stockley Rd Georgetown (19947) ***(G-2619)***
Pinevalley Apartments, New Castle *Also called Clyde Spinelli* ***(G-5178)***
Pinewood Acres MBL Hm Pk L L C 302 678-1004
1 Pinewood Acres Ave Dover (19901) ***(G-1960)***
Pinewood Acres Mobile Home Pk, Dover *Also called Pinewood Acres MBL Hm Pk L L C* ***(G-1960)***
Pinnacle Funding Inc 302 657-0160
2002 Baynard Blvd Wilmington (19802) ***(G-12142)***
Pinnacle Garage Door Company 302 505-4531
764 Midstate Rd Felton (19943) ***(G-2310)***
Pinnacle Rhbilitation Hlth Ctr 302 653-5085
3034 S Dupont Blvd Smyrna (19977) ***(G-8689)***
Pioneer Behavioral Health, New Castle *Also called Phc Inc* ***(G-5621)***
Pioneer Distributors Inc 302 644-0791
16612 Howard Millman Ln Milton (19968) ***(G-4952)***
Pioneer Fence Co Inc 302 998-2892
109 S John St Wilmington (19804) ***(G-12143)***
Pioneer House 302 286-0892
413 Salem Church Rd Newark (19702) ***(G-7219)***
Pioneer Materials 302 284-3580
401 Lombard St Felton (19943) ***(G-2311)***
Piper, Glenn T, Lewes *Also called Landmark Associates of Del* ***(G-3590)***
Pirulos Child Care Center LLC 302 836-3520
799 Salem Church Rd Newark (19702) ***(G-7220)***
Pitney Bowes Intl Holdings (HQ) 302 656-8595
801 N West St Fl 2 Wilmington (19801) ***(G-12144)***
Pivotal Medical 302 299-5795
413 Salt Pond Rd Bethany Beach (19930) ***(G-422)***
Pixorize Inc 737 529-4404
251 Little Falls Dr Wilmington (19808) ***(G-12145)***
Pixstorm LLC 617 365-4949
160 Greentree Dr Ste 101 Dover (19904) ***(G-1961)***
Pixxy Solutions LLC 631 609-6686
2093 Philadelphia Pike # 4 Claymont (19703) ***(G-795)***
Pizazz Beauty Studio 302 761-9820
4001 N Market St Wilmington (19802) ***(G-12146)***
Pizza King, Seaford *Also called Baynum Enterprises Inc* ***(G-8163)***
Pizza King, Laurel *Also called Baynum Enterprises Inc* ***(G-3196)***
Pizzadili Partners LLC 302 284-9463
1683 Peach Basket Rd Felton (19943) ***(G-2312)***
PJ Fitzpatrick Inc (PA) 302 325-2360
21 Industrial Blvd New Castle (19720) ***(G-5623)***
Pkg LLC 269 651-8640
251 Little Falls Dr Wilmington (19808) ***(G-12147)***
Pks & Company PA 302 645-5757
1143 Savannah Rd Lewes (19958) ***(G-3693)***
Pks Food, Wilmington *Also called P-Ks Wholesale Grocer Inc* ***(G-11998)***
Pkwy Gravel 302 328-5182
820 Federal School Ln New Castle (19720) ***(G-5624)***
Placers Inc of Delaware 302 709-0973
1501 Casho Mill Rd Ste 9 Newark (19711) ***(G-7221)***
Plai Apps Inc 661 678-3740
850 New Burton Rd Ste 201 Dover (19904) ***(G-1962)***
Plain & Fancy Inc 302 656-9901
5716 Kennett Pike Ste E Wilmington (19807) ***(G-12148)***
Plain & Fancy Interiors, Wilmington *Also called Plain & Fancy Inc* ***(G-12148)***
Plan USA, Wilmington *Also called Inc Plan (usa)* ***(G-11011)***
Planet Payment Solutions Inc (HQ) 516 670-3200
100 W Cmmons Blvd Ste 200 New Castle (19720) ***(G-5625)***
Planet X Skateboards 484 886-9287
2400 Shellpot Dr Wilmington (19803) ***(G-12149)***
Planned Parenthood of Delaware (PA) 302 655-7293
625 N Shipley St Wilmington (19801) ***(G-12150)***
Planned Parenthood of Delaware 302 678-5200
805 S Governors Ave Dover (19904) ***(G-1963)***
Planned Parenthood of Delaware 302 731-7801
140 E Delaware Ave Newark (19711) ***(G-7222)***
Planned Poultry Renovation 302 875-4196
16244 Sycamore Rd Laurel (19956) ***(G-3273)***
Planned Residential Communites 302 475-4621
2601 Carpenter Station Rd Wilmington (19810) ***(G-12151)***
Plant Retrievers Whl Nurs 302 337-9833
13418 Seashore Hwy Georgetown (19947) ***(G-2620)***
Plantation Lakes Homeowners 302 934-5200
29787 Plntn Lakes Blvd Millsboro (19966) ***(G-4782)***
Plasti Pallets Corp 302 737-1977
6 Albe Dr Christiana (19702) ***(G-676)***
Platenger LLC 302 298-0896
1201 N Orange St Ste 7126 Wilmington (19801) ***(G-12152)***
Platinum US Distribution Inc 905 364-8713
1201 N Orange St Ste 741 Wilmington (19801) ***(G-12153)***
Play For Good Inc 312 520-9788
3411 Silverside Rd 104r Wilmington (19810) ***(G-12154)***
Play Game Sports 302 736-0606
222 Kentwood Dr Dover (19901) ***(G-1964)***
Play US Media LLC 302 924-5034
8 The Gree Ste 8136 Dover Dover (19901) ***(G-1965)***
Playfit Education Inc 302 438-3257
3575 Silverside Rd # 404 Wilmington (19810) ***(G-12155)***
Playhouse Nursery School 302 747-7007
1925 S Dupont Hwy Dover (19901) ***(G-1966)***
Playhouse On Rodney Square, Wilmington *Also called E I Du Pont De Nemours & Co* ***(G-10296)***
Playphone Inc 415 307-0246
3500 S Dupont Hwy Dover (19901) ***(G-1967)***
Playsight Interactive USA Inc 800 246-2677
1201 N Orange St Ste 600 Wilmington (19801) ***(G-12156)***
Playtex Investment Corporation 302 678-6000
50 N Dupont Hwy Dover (19901) ***(G-1968)***
Playtex Manufacturing Inc (HQ) 302 678-6000
50 N Dupont Hwy Dover (19901) ***(G-1969)***
Playtex Marketing Corp 302 678-6000
800 Silver Lake Blvd # 103 Dover (19904) ***(G-1970)***
Playtex Products LLC 302 678-6000
50 N Dupont Hwy Dover (19901) ***(G-1971)***
Plaza Apartments, Wilmington *Also called Stoltz Realty Co* ***(G-12769)***
Plaza Fuel 302 275-6242
2213 Concord Pike Wilmington (19803) ***(G-12157)***
Pleasant Distributors, Wilmington *Also called P D Supply Inc* ***(G-11994)***
Pleasant Hill Bowling Alley, Wilmington *Also called Pleasant Hill Lanes Inc* ***(G-12158)***
Pleasant Hill Lanes Inc 302 998-8811
1001 W Newport Pike Wilmington (19804) ***(G-12158)***
Plexus Fitness 302 654-9642
20 Montchanin Rd Ste 60 Wilmington (19807) ***(G-12159)***
PLM Consulting Inc 302 984-2698
828 N Jefferson St Wilmington (19801) ***(G-12160)***
Ploeners Automotive Pdts Co 302 655-4418
510 S Market St Wilmington (19801) ***(G-12161)***
Plp Financial, Seaford *Also called Professional Leasing Inc* ***(G-8365)***
Plugdin Inc 347 726-1831
8 The Grn Ste A Dover (19901) ***(G-1972)***
Plumbers Pipefitters Local 74 ....302 636-7400
201 Executive Dr Newark (19702) ***(G-7223)***
Plume Serum LLC 302 697-9044
1059 Ponderosa Dr Magnolia (19962) ***(G-3904)***
Plushbeds Inc (PA) 888 758-7423
1201 N Orange St Ste 7058 Wilmington (19801) ***(G-12162)***
Pma, Newark *Also called Produce Marketing Assn Inc* ***(G-7265)***
Pmb Associates LLC 302 436-0111
37816 Eagle Ln Unit 325 Selbyville (19975) ***(G-8531)***
PMC Publications LLC 302 268-4480
201 Michelle Ct Newark (19711) ***(G-7224)***
Pmcaa Inc 302 439-6028
913 N Market St Ste 200 Wilmington (19801) ***(G-12163)***
Pmh Financial, Wilmington *Also called Stewart Title Company* ***(G-12765)***
PNC Bancorp Inc (HQ) 302 427-5896
300 Delaware Ave Wilmington (19801) ***(G-12164)***
PNC Bank National Association 302 994-6337
2751 Centerville Rd # 101 Wilmington (19808) ***(G-12165)***
PNC Bank National Association (HQ) 877 762-2000
222 Delaware Ave Wilmington (19801) ***(G-12166)***
PNC Bank National Association 302 337-3500
100 S Laws St Bridgeville (19933) ***(G-511)***
PNC Bank National Association 302 735-3117
3 Loockerman Plz Frnt Dover (19901) ***(G-1973)***
PNC Bank National Association 302 934-3106
104 Main St Millsboro (19966) ***(G-4783)***
PNC Bank National Association 302 733-7150
201 Newark Shopping Ctr Newark (19711) ***(G-7225)***

PNC Bank National Association............302 653-2475
7 S Main St Smyrna (19977) ***(G-8690)***
PNC Bank National Association............302 326-4710
1 Penn Mart Ctr New Castle (19720) ***(G-5626)***
PNC Bank National Association............302 733-7170
25 Castle Mall Newark (19713) ***(G-7226)***
PNC Bank National Association............302 326-4701
1 E Basin Rd New Castle (19720) ***(G-5627)***
PNC Bank National Association............302 537-2600
2 S Pennsylvania Ave Bethany Beach (19930) ***(G-423)***
PNC Bank National Association............302 436-5400
31231 Americana Pkwy Selbyville (19975) ***(G-8532)***
PNC Bank National Association............302 378-4441
460 W Main St Middletown (19709) ***(G-4194)***
PNC Bank National Association............302 733-7160
84 University Plz Newark (19702) ***(G-7227)***
PNC Bank National Association............302 733-7190
4643 Stanton Ogletown Rd Newark (19713) ***(G-7228)***
PNC Bank National Association............302 629-5000
1200 W Stein Hwy Seaford (19973) ***(G-8358)***
PNC Bank National Association............302 429-1761
1009 N Union St Wilmington (19805) ***(G-12167)***
PNC Bank National Association............302 479-4529
1704 Marsh Rd Wilmington (19810) ***(G-12168)***
PNC Bank National Association............302 479-4520
4111 Concord Pike Wilmington (19803) ***(G-12169)***
PNC Bank National Association............302 993-3013
4725 Kirkwood Hwy Wilmington (19808) ***(G-12170)***
PNC Bank National Association............302 832-8750
100 Eden Cir Bear (19701) ***(G-284)***
PNC Bank National Association............302 478-7822
4301 Concord Pike Wilmington (19803) ***(G-12171)***
PNC Bank National Association............302 235-4010
5325 Limestone Rd Wilmington (19808) ***(G-12172)***
PNC Bank National Association............302 838-6782
100 Eden Cir Bear (19701) ***(G-285)***
PNC Bank National Association............302 422-1015
655 N Dupont Blvd Milford (19963) ***(G-4527)***
PNC Bank National Association............302 993-3000
2203 Kirkwood Hwy Wilmington (19805) ***(G-12173)***
PNC Bank National Association............302 429-1167
3840 Kennett Pike Wilmington (19807) ***(G-12174)***
PNC Bank National Association............302 735-2160
87 Greentree Dr Dover (19904) ***(G-1974)***
PNC Bank National Association............302 832-6180
250 Foxhunt Dr Bear (19701) ***(G-286)***
PNC Bank National Association............302 235-4000
7421 Lancaster Pike Hockessin (19707) ***(G-3121)***
PNC Bank National Association............302 645-4500
17725 Coastal Hwy Lewes (19958) ***(G-3694)***
PNC Bank National Association............302 855-0400
Alfred St Rr 113 Georgetown (19947) ***(G-2621)***
PNC Bank National Association............302 733-7192
4643 Stanton Ogletwown Rd New Castle (19720) ***(G-5628)***
PNC Financial Svcs Group Inc............302 429-1364
300 Delaware Ave Wilmington (19801) ***(G-12175)***
PNC National Bank of Delaware (HQ)............302 479-4529
300 Bellevue Pkwy Ste 200 Wilmington (19809) ***(G-12176)***
Point Coffee Shop and Bakery............302 260-9734
37140 Rehoboth Avenue Ext Rehoboth Beach (19971) ***(G-8033)***
Point Eght Third Prdctions LLC (PA)............302 317-9419
913 N Market St Ste 200 Wilmington (19801) ***(G-12177)***
Point Hope Brain Injury Spport............302 731-7676
34 Blevins Dr Ste 5 New Castle (19720) ***(G-5629)***
Point of Hope Inc............302 731-7676
19 Peddlers Row Christiana (19702) ***(G-677)***
Point of Sale Technologies............302 659-5119
412 Bryn Zion Rd Clayton (19938) ***(G-867)***
Pointe Snaps............260 602-0898
1000 Marsh Rd Wilmington (19803) ***(G-12178)***
Pointless Technology LLC............917 403-2264
9 E Loockerman St Ste 215 Dover (19901) ***(G-1975)***
Pointlook Corporation............415 448-6002
717 N Union St Wilmington (19805) ***(G-12179)***
Pointstrekker, Dover *Also called Instantuptime Inc* ***(G-1680)***
Poland & Sullivan Insurance............302 738-3535
106 Haines St Ste A Newark (19711) ***(G-7229)***
Polar Mechanical Inc............302 994-9566
330 Water St Wilmington (19804) ***(G-12180)***
Polar Strategy Inc............703 628-0001
16192 Coastal Hwy Lewes (19958) ***(G-3695)***
Polarstar Engineering & Mch............302 368-4639
5 Garfield Way Ste B Newark (19713) ***(G-7230)***
Police & Fire Rod & Gun Club............302 655-0304
1 Glen Ave New Castle (19720) ***(G-5630)***
Police Athc Leag Wlmington Inc............302 764-6170
3707 N Market St Wilmington (19802) ***(G-12181)***
Police Athletic Leag Del Inc-P, New Castle *Also called Police Athletic League Del* ***(G-5631)***
Police Athletic League Del (PA)............302 656-9501
26 Karlyn Dr New Castle (19720) ***(G-5631)***
Polish American Civic Assn............302 652-9324
618 S Franklin St Wilmington (19805) ***(G-12182)***
Polish Library Association............302 652-9555
433 S Van Buren St Wilmington (19805) ***(G-12183)***
Polydel Corporation............302 655-8200
820 N Buttonwood St Wilmington (19801) ***(G-12184)***
Polymart Inc............302 656-1470
710 Yorklyn Rd Ste 200 Hockessin (19707) ***(G-3122)***
Polymer Technologies Inc (PA)............302 738-9001
420 Corporate Blvd Newark (19702) ***(G-7231)***
Polymorphic Software Inc (PA)............786 612-0257
1521 Concord Pike Ste 301 Wilmington (19803) ***(G-12185)***
Polytechnic Resources Inc............302 629-4221
185 Kent Dr Seaford (19973) ***(G-8359)***
Pond Inc............302 266-0777
101 John F Campbell Rd Newark (19711) ***(G-7232)***
Pond Publishing & Productions............302 284-0200
5012 Killens Pond Rd Felton (19943) ***(G-2313)***
Pond The Ice Arena, Newark *Also called Pond Inc* ***(G-7232)***
Pony Run Kitchens LLC............302 492-3006
5066 Westville Rd Hartly (19953) ***(G-2937)***
Poof Power Wash & Ldscpg LLC............302 595-1576
182 Hatteras Dr Dover (19904) ***(G-1976)***
Pools & Spas Unlimited Milford, Milford *Also called Henderson Services Inc* ***(G-4438)***
Poolside Cnstr & Renovation............302 436-9711
Rr 54 Selbyville (19975) ***(G-8533)***
Poore's Propane Gas Service, Dover *Also called Petroleum Equipment Inc* ***(G-1952)***
Poores Propane, Dover *Also called Service Oil Company* ***(G-2072)***
Poores Propane Gas Service, Dover *Also called Petroleum Equipment Inc* ***(G-1951)***
Poppiti Signs Inc............302 999-8003
2513 Dean Dr Wilmington (19808) ***(G-12186)***
Poppycock Tattoo............302 543-7973
800 N Orange St Wilmington (19801) ***(G-12187)***
Port Contractors Inc (PA)............302 655-7300
529 Terminal Ave New Castle (19720) ***(G-5632)***
Port Del-Mar-Va Inc............302 227-7409
260 Port Delmarva Rehoboth Beach (19971) ***(G-8034)***
Port of Wilmington, Wilmington *Also called Delaware Secretary of State* ***(G-10083)***
Port of Wilmington, Wilmington *Also called Diamond State Port Corporation* ***(G-10144)***
Port To Port Intl Corp............302 654-2444
32 Pyles Ln New Castle (19720) ***(G-5633)***
Porter Broadcasting............302 535-8809
1991 S State St Dover (19901) ***(G-1977)***
Porter Nissan Buick Newark............302 368-6300
600 Ogletown Rd Newark (19711) ***(G-7233)***
Porter Sand & Gravel Inc............302 335-5132
640 Sandbox Rd Harrington (19952) ***(G-2875)***
Porter Trucking, Newark *Also called Carlo Porter Michael* ***(G-6156)***
Portrait Innovations Inc............302 477-1696
5601 Concord Pike Ste D Wilmington (19803) ***(G-12188)***
Pos Technologies, Clayton *Also called Point of Sale Technologies* ***(G-867)***
Posh Cupcake............302 234-4451
50 Westwoods Blvd Hockessin (19707) ***(G-3123)***
Posh Salon............302 655-7000
1017 N Lincoln St Wilmington (19805) ***(G-12189)***
Posidon Adventure Inc............302 543-5024
3301 Lancaster Pike 5a Wilmington (19805) ***(G-12190)***
Positioneering LLC............302 415-3200
19c Trolley Sq Wilmington (19806) ***(G-12191)***
Positive Results Cleaning Inc............302 575-1146
338 B And O Ln Wilmington (19804) ***(G-12192)***
Positive Signs............302 378-9559
14 Spring Arbor Dr Middletown (19709) ***(G-4195)***
Post Shipper LLC............302 444-8144
601 Carson Dr Bear (19701) ***(G-287)***
Postal Associates Inc............302 584-1244
110 Hoiland Dr Wilmington (19803) ***(G-12193)***
Postimpressions Incorporated............302 656-2271
1400 Maryland Ave Wilmington (19805) ***(G-12194)***
Potter Anderson & Corroon LLP............302 984-6000
1313 N Market St Fl 6 Wilmington (19801) ***(G-12195)***
Potts Wldg Boiler Repr Co Inc (HQ)............302 453-2550
1901 Ogletown Rd Newark (19711) ***(G-7234)***
Poultry Litter Solutions LLC............302 245-5577
28194 Fox Run Rd Millsboro (19966) ***(G-4784)***
Poured Foundations of De Inc............302 234-2050
409 Capitol Trl Newark (19711) ***(G-7235)***
Powell Construction L L C............302 745-1146
100 Murrays Ln Georgetown (19947) ***(G-2622)***
Powell Life Skills Inc............302 378-2706
209 Glenshee Dr Townsend (19734) ***(G-8816)***
Power Delivery Solutions LLC............302 260-3114
100 Commerce Dr Ste 201 Newark (19713) ***(G-7236)***
Power Electronics Inc............302 653-4822
310 S Bassett St Clayton (19938) ***(G-868)***
Power Financial Group Inc............302 992-7971
494 First State Blvd Wilmington (19804) ***(G-12196)***
Power Options, Wilmington *Also called Power Financial Group Inc* ***(G-12196)***

ALPHABETIC

Power Plus Electrical Contg..302 736-5070
  10 Janis Dr Dover (19901) (G-1978)
Power Trans Inc 302 337-3016
  9029 Fawn Rd Bridgeville (19933) (G-512)
Power Trans Inc 302 322-7110
  12 Mccullough Dr Ste 2 New Castle (19720) (G-5634)
Powerback Service LLC 302 934-1901
  30148 Mitchell St Millsboro (19966) (G-4785)
Powerhouse Gym 302 262-0262
  620 W Stein Hwy Seaford (19973) (G-8360)
Powers Publishing Group 302 519-8575
  29549 Whitstone Ln Millsboro (19966) (G-4786)
Powerscape LLC 302 945-4626
  34438 Dog Wood Rd Millsboro (19966) (G-4787)
Powertrain Technology Inc 302 368-4900
  2101 Ogletown Rd Newark (19711) (G-7237)
Ppc Coatings, Wilmington Also called Modified Thermoset Resins Inc (G-11722)
Pradhan Energy Projects 305 428-2123
  104 Hawthorne Ct W Hockessin (19707) (G-3124)
Pratcher Krayer LLC 302 803-5291
  1000 N West St Fl 10 Wilmington (19801) (G-12197)
Praxair Distribution Inc 302 654-8755
  2 Medori Blvd Wilmington (19801) (G-12198)
Prayon Inc 302 449-0875
  231 Casper Way Middletown (19709) (G-4196)
PRC, Wilmington Also called Professional Recruiting Cons (G-12239)
Precious Knwldg Erly Lrng Ctr 302 293-2588
  1000 Village Cir Newark (19713) (G-7238)
Precious Little Angels Daycare 302 378-2912
  123 Edgar Rd Townsend (19734) (G-8817)
Precious Little Hands Childcar 302 298-5027
  702b Kirkwood Hwy Wilmington (19805) (G-12199)
Precious Moments Day Care 302 856-2346
  18943 Shingle Point Rd Georgetown (19947) (G-2623)
Precious Moments Edu 302 697-9374
  4607 S Dupont Hwy Dover (19901) (G-1979)
Precious Nails 302 292-1690
  2607 Kirkwood Hwy Wilmington (19805) (G-12200)
Precious Paws Animal Hospital 302 539-2273
  118 Atlantic Ave Ste 101 Ocean View (19970) (G-7809)
Precious Years Child Care LLC 302 322-1701
  200 Robinson Dr New Castle (19720) (G-5635)
Precise Alignment Mch Tl Co 302 832-2922
  59 Avignon Dr Newark (19702) (G-7239)
Precise Technology Inc 302 737-4638
  220 Lake Dr Ste 4 Newark (19702) (G-7240)
Precision Airconvey Corp (PA) 302 999-8000
  465 Corporate Blvd Newark (19702) (G-7241)
Precision Care & Wellness LLC 302 407-5222
  4001 Miller Rd Ste 1 Wilmington (19802) (G-12201)
Precision Color Graphics LLC 302 661-2595
  1401 Todds Ln Wilmington (19802) (G-12202)
Precision Dental Laboratory 302 478-5608
  1403 Foulk Rd Ste 107 Wilmington (19803) (G-12203)
Precision Door Service 302 343-6394
  330 Water St Ste 109 Wilmington (19804) (G-12204)
Precision Drywall Inc 415 550-8880
  2711 Centerville Rd # 400 Wilmington (19808) (G-12205)
Precision Drywall Construction, Wilmington Also called Precision Drywall Inc (G-12205)
Precision Flow LLC 302 544-4417
  62 Southgate Blvd Ste L New Castle (19720) (G-5636)
Precision Jewelry Inc 302 422-7138
  607 N Dupont Blvd Milford (19963) (G-4528)
Precision Ldscpg & Lawn Care 302 492-1583
  286 Judith Rd Hartly (19953) (G-2938)
Precision Marine Construction 302 227-2711
  125 Blackpool Rd Rehoboth Beach (19971) (G-8035)
Precision Polyolefins LLC 301 588-3709
  2711 Centerville Rd # 400 Wilmington (19808) (G-12206)
Precision Systems Inds LLC 224 388-9837
  2711 Centerville Rd # 400 Wilmington (19808) (G-12207)
Precision Tune Auto Care, Frankford Also called Tune-Up III of MD Inc (G-2395)
Precisioncure LLC 302 622-9119
  2207 Concord Pike 301 Wilmington (19803) (G-12208)
Precisionists Inc 610 241-5354
  1 Righter Pkwy Ste 150 Wilmington (19803) (G-12209)
Prefered Tax Service Inc 302 654-4388
  2201 N Market St Ste A Wilmington (19802) (G-12210)
Preferred Auto and Cycle LLC 302 855-0169
  100 Deer Run Dagsboro (19939) (G-931)
Preferred Business Services, Wilmington Also called Prefered Tax Service Inc (G-12210)
Preferred Construction Inc 302 322-9568
  505 Churchmans Rd New Castle (19720) (G-5637)
Preferred Contractors Inc 302 798-5457
  204 S Park Dr Wilmington (19809) (G-12211)
Preferred Electric Inc 302 322-1217
  505 Churchmans Rd New Castle (19720) (G-5638)
Preferred Enviromental 610 364-1106
  2300 W Fourth St Ste E104 Clayton (19938) (G-869)

Preferred Fire Protection 302 256-0607
  4321 Miller Rd Wilmington (19802) (G-12212)
Preferred Security Inc 302 834-7800
  1570 Red Lion Rd Bear (19701) (G-288)
Preferred Travel 302 838-8966
  11 Mystic Dr Bear (19701) (G-289)
Preferred Trnsp Systems LLC 302 323-0828
  101 E Beaver Ct Bear (19701) (G-290)
Preffered Mechanical Services 302 993-1122
  330 Water St Ste 107 Wilmington (19804) (G-12213)
Pregnancy Health Center 302 698-9311
  811 S Governors Ave Dover (19904) (G-1980)
PREGNANCY HELP CENTER OF KENT, Dover Also called Pregnancy Health Center (G-1980)
Preit-Rubin Inc 302 731-9815
  715 Christiana Mall Newark (19702) (G-7242)
Prela S Lynch 302 856-2130
  409 N Front St Georgetown (19947) (G-2624)
Prelude Therapeutics Inc 302 644-5427
  200 Powder Mill Rd Wilmington (19803) (G-12214)
Premier Builders Inc 302 999-8500
  2601 Annand Dr Ste 21 Wilmington (19808) (G-12215)
Premier Capital Holding (PA) 302 730-1010
  1675 S State St Dover (19901) (G-1981)
Premier Comprehensive Dental 302 378-3131
  212 Celebration Ct Middletown (19709) (G-4197)
Premier Dentistry Christiana 302 366-7636
  4745 Ogltn Stntn Rd # 110 Newark (19713) (G-7243)
Premier Entertainment III LLC (HQ) 302 674-4600
  1131 N Dupont Hwy Dover (19901) (G-1982)
Premier Glass & Screen Inc 302 732-3101
  33937 Premire Dr Frankford (19945) (G-2380)
Premier Healthcare Inc 302 731-5576
  254 W Main St Newark (19711) (G-7244)
Premier Heating & AC 302 684-1888
  25111 Williams Farm Rd Milton (19968) (G-4953)
Premier Immediate Med Care LLC 610 226-6200
  316 Lantana Dr Hockessin (19707) (G-3125)
Premier Nat Ln & Lsg Group LLC 302 295-2194
  504 N Broom St Wilmington (19805) (G-12216)
Premier Othpdic Bone Jint Care 302 422-6506
  329 Mullet Run Milford (19963) (G-4529)
Premier Physical Therapy & 302 389-7855
  100 S Main St Ste 300 Smyrna (19977) (G-8691)
Premier Porch & Patio, Frankford Also called Premier Glass & Screen Inc (G-2380)
Premier Restoration Inc 302 645-1611
  145 Heather Dr Lewes (19958) (G-3696)
Premier Restoration Cnstr Inc (PA) 302 832-1288
  703 Industrial Rd Middletown (19709) (G-4198)
Premier Restorations, Middletown Also called Premier Restoration Cnstr Inc (G-4198)
Premier Salon, Wilmington Also called Premier Solutions Intl (G-12218)
Premier Salon 22920, Wilmington Also called Premier Salons Intl Inc (G-12217)
Premier Salons Intl Inc 302 477-3459
  4737 Concord Pike Wilmington (19803) (G-12217)
Premier Solutions Intl 302 477-1334
  4737 Concord Pike Ste 100 Wilmington (19803) (G-12218)
Premier Spine & Rehab 302 730-4878
  111 S West St Ste 5 Dover (19904) (G-1983)
Premier Spine and Rehab 302 404-5293
  8470 Herring Run Rd Seaford (19973) (G-8361)
Premier Staffing Solutions Inc (PA) 302 344-5996
  123 W Market St Georgetown (19947) (G-2625)
Premier Staffing Solutions Inc 302 628-7700
  809 Norman Eskridge Hwy Seaford (19973) (G-8362)
Premiere Hair Design 302 368-7711
  1450 Capitol Trl Ste 109 Newark (19711) (G-7245)
Premiere Oral and Facial Surg 302 273-8300
  1202 Foulk Rd Wilmington (19803) (G-12219)
Premiere Physicians PA 302 762-6675
  314 E Main St Ste 103 Newark (19711) (G-7246)
Prentice Hall Legal Fincl Svcs, Wilmington Also called Prentice-Hall Corp System Inc (G-12220)
Prentice-Hall Corp System Inc (PA) 302 636-5440
  2711 Centerville Rd # 120 Wilmington (19808) (G-12220)
Prepaid Legal Service Inc 302 836-1985
  214 Palermo Dr Bear (19701) (G-291)
Prepaid Legal Svc USA & Canada, Bear Also called Prepaid Legal Service Inc (G-291)
Presbyterian Senior Living 302 744-3600
  1175 Mckee Rd Dover (19904) (G-1984)
Prescription Center Inc 302 764-8564
  4616 Sylvanus Dr Wilmington (19803) (G-12221)
Presicson Pain Rhbltation Svcs 302 827-2321
  18958 Coastal Hwy Rehoboth Beach (19971) (G-8036)
Press, Christine M. Mrs., Middletown Also called Joseph M Press Mr (G-4117)
Pressair International 302 636-5440
  3501 Silverside Rd Wilmington (19810) (G-12222)
Pressley Ridge Foundation 302 366-0490
  56 W Main St Ste 203 Christiana (19702) (G-678)
Pressley Ridge Foundation 302 677-1590
  942 Walker Rd Ste A Dover (19904) (G-1985)

Pressley Ridge Foundation 302 854-9782
20461 Dupont Blvd Ste 2 Georgetown (19947) ***(G-2626)***
Pressley Ridge of Delaware, Dover *Also called Pressley Ridge Foundation* ***(G-1985)***
Prestege LLC 302 312-8548
16 N Bellwoode Dr Newark (19702) ***(G-7247)***
Prestige Contractors Inc 302 722-1032
2615 N Tatnall St Wilmington (19802) ***(G-12223)***
Prestige Powder Inc 302 737-7086
13 Tyler Way Newark (19713) ***(G-7248)***
Prestige Powder Finishing Inc 302 737-7500
13 Tyler Way Newark (19713) ***(G-7249)***
Prestwick House Inc 302 659-2070
58 Artisan Dr Smyrna (19977) ***(G-8692)***
Pretty Nails 302 628-3937
22986 Sussex Hwy Seaford (19973) ***(G-8363)***
Prevent Alarm Company LLC 302 478-6647
91 Lukens Dr Ste B New Castle (19720) ***(G-5639)***
Prevent Security and Tech, New Castle *Also called Prevent Alarm Company LLC* ***(G-5639)***
Prezoom LLC 302 414-8204
262 Quigley Blvd New Castle (19720) ***(G-5640)***
Price Honda, Dover *Also called Diamond Motor Sports Inc* ***(G-1423)***
Price Is Right Contracting LLC 215 760-1416
919 N Market St Ste 950 Wilmington (19801) ***(G-12224)***
Prices Corner Branch, Wilmington *Also called Wilmington Savings Fund Soc* ***(G-13251)***
Prices Corner Car Wash, Wilmington *Also called Car Wash of Prices Corner* ***(G-9561)***
Prickett Jones & Elliott, Wilmington *Also called James L Holzman* ***(G-11122)***
Pride of Delaw 302 861-6857
57 W Cleveland Ave Newark (19711) ***(G-7250)***
Pride Klean Inc 302 994-8500
301 S Maryland Ave Apt 2 Wilmington (19804) ***(G-12225)***
Pride Klean Service, Wilmington *Also called Pride Klean Inc* ***(G-12225)***
Pride of Delaware Lodge 215 453-9236
57 W Cleveland Ave Newark (19711) ***(G-7251)***
Prides Court Apartments 302 737-2085
6 Sussex Rd Ofc F Newark (19713) ***(G-7252)***
Pridestaff, Wilmington *Also called Benitime Solutions Inc* ***(G-9302)***
Primary Care Delaware L L C 302 744-9645
200 Banning St Ste 210 Dover (19904) ***(G-1986)***
Prime America, Newark *Also called John Lovett Inc* ***(G-6843)***
Prime Products Usa Inc 302 528-3866
15 Germay Dr Ste 100 Wilmington (19804) ***(G-12226)***
Primecare Medical Trnspt LLC 302 422-0900
568 Milford Harrington Hw Milford (19963) ***(G-4530)***
Primeros Pasos Inc 302 856-7406
20648 Savannah Rd Georgetown (19947) ***(G-2627)***
Primetime Limousine 302 425-5599
1812 Marsh Rd Ste 6 Wilmington (19810) ***(G-12227)***
Prince Manufacturing Co 646 747-4208
301 Pigeon Point Rd New Castle (19720) ***(G-5641)***
Prince Minerals LLC 646 747-4200
301 Pigeon Point Rd New Castle (19720) ***(G-5642)***
Prince Telecom LLC (HQ) 302 324-1800
551 Mews Dr Ste A New Castle (19720) ***(G-5643)***
Princeton Coml Holdings LLC 302 449-4836
113 Barksdale Pro Ctr Newark (19711) ***(G-7253)***
Principal Financial Group Inc 302 993-8045
1013 Centre Rd Ste 100 Wilmington (19805) ***(G-12228)***
Print Coast 2 Coast 302 381-4610
33073 E Light Dr Lewes (19958) ***(G-3697)***
Print On This 302 235-9475
3 Green Ct Newark (19702) ***(G-7254)***
Print Shack, Seaford *Also called Penney Enterprises Inc* ***(G-8350)***
Print Shack Inc 302 629-4430
9203 Brickyard Rd Seaford (19973) ***(G-8364)***
Print-N-Press Inc 302 994-6665
300 Cassidy Dr Ste 301 Wilmington (19804) ***(G-12229)***
Printcurement 302 249-6100
122 Delaware St Ste 300 New Castle (19720) ***(G-5644)***
Printed Solid Inc 302 439-0098
2860 Ogletown Rd Bldg 6-8 Newark (19713) ***(G-7255)***
Printify LLC (PA) 415 968-6351
108 W 13th St Wilmington (19801) ***(G-12230)***
Printit Solutions 302 380-3838
1155 E Lebanon Rd Dover (19901) ***(G-1987)***
Printpack Inc 302 323-4000
600 Grantham Ln New Castle (19720) ***(G-5645)***
Printpack Enterprises Inc (HQ) 302 323-0900
River Rd & Grantham Ln New Castle (19720) ***(G-5646)***
Prints and Princesses 703 881-1057
202 Hanover Pl Newark (19711) ***(G-7256)***
Printz Picks, Claymont *Also called Victor Kornbluth* ***(G-815)***
Priority Plus Federal Cr Un 302 633-6480
6 Lynam St Wilmington (19804) ***(G-12231)***
Priority Radio Inc 302 540-5690
179 Stanton Christiana Rd Newark (19702) ***(G-7257)***
Priority Services LLC 302 918-3070
70 Albe Dr Newark (19702) ***(G-7258)***
Priscilla Lancaster 302 792-8305
302 Harvey Rd Claymont (19703) ***(G-796)***
Prism Events Inc 424 252-1070
2035 Sunset Lake Rd B2 Newark (19702) ***(G-7259)***
Prison Ministries Delaware Inc 302 737-2792
1 Hartford Pl Newark (19711) ***(G-7260)***
Private Duty Home Care 302 482-3502
109 Clyde St Wilmington (19804) ***(G-12232)***
Private Family Network LLC 302 760-9684
8 The Grn Ste A Dover (19901) ***(G-1988)***
Priya Realty Corp 302 737-5050
268 E Main St Newark (19711) ***(G-7261)***
Pro 2 Respiratory Services 302 514-9843
56 Artisan Dr Ste 5 Smyrna (19977) ***(G-8693)***
Pro Automated Inc 302 294-6121
100 Lake Dr Ste 205 Newark (19702) ***(G-7262)***
Pro Clean Company, Delaware City *Also called Pro Clean Wilmington Inc* ***(G-964)***
Pro Clean Wilmington Inc 302 836-8080
210 Clinton St Delaware City (19706) ***(G-964)***
Pro Pest Management of De Inc 302 994-2847
200 Cassidy Dr Ste 201 Wilmington (19804) ***(G-12233)***
Pro Physical Therapy, Wilmington *Also called Pro Physl Therapy Ftns Acct* ***(G-12234)***
Pro Physical Therapy PA 302 654-1700
2032 New Castle Ave New Castle (19720) ***(G-5647)***
Pro Physl Therapy Ftns Acct 302 658-7800
1812 Marsh Rd Ste 505 Wilmington (19810) ***(G-12234)***
Pro Rehab Chiropractic 302 200-9102
105 W 4th St Lewes (19958) ***(G-3698)***
Pro Rehab Chiropractors 302 652-2225
215 Peirce Rd Wilmington (19803) ***(G-12235)***
Pro Trans Inc 302 328-1550
807 Pulaski Hwy Bear (19701) ***(G-292)***
Pro Weight Loss 302 220-9555
550 Stanton Christiana Rd Newark (19713) ***(G-7263)***
Pro-Bond Auto Glass 302 324-8500
23 Parkway Cir Ste 7 New Castle (19720) ***(G-5648)***
Pro-Grade Electric LLC 302 258-7745
20151 Sand Hill Rd Georgetown (19947) ***(G-2628)***
Pro-Tech Engineering Inc 302 998-1717
1200 First State Blvd Wilmington (19804) ***(G-12236)***
Proactive Prfmce Solutions Inc (PA) 302 375-0451
560 Peoples Plz Ste 139 Newark (19702) ***(G-7264)***
Procaccianti Group LLC 401 946-4600
422 Delaware Ave Wilmington (19801) ***(G-12237)***
Process Academy LLC 302 415-3104
4023 Kennett Pike Wilmington (19807) ***(G-12238)***
Proclean 302 654-1074
28 Mifflin Ave New Castle (19720) ***(G-5649)***
Proclean Inc 302 656-8080
P.O. Box 638 Delaware City (19706) ***(G-965)***
Procter & Gamble Paper Pdts Co 302 678-2600
1340 W North St Dover (19904) ***(G-1989)***
Produce For Btter Hlth Fndtion (PA) 302 235-2329
7465 Lancaster Pike Hockessin (19707) ***(G-3126)***
Produce Marketing Assn Inc 302 738-7100
1500 Casho Mill Rd Newark (19711) ***(G-7265)***
Productions For Purpose Inc 302 388-9883
10 Little Cir Middletown (19709) ***(G-4199)***
Professional Home Health Care, Dover *Also called Home Health Corp America Inc* ***(G-1653)***
Professional Imaging 302 653-3522
97 Nita Dr Smyrna (19977) ***(G-8694)***
Professional Leasing Inc 302 629-4350
740 Sussex Ave Seaford (19973) ***(G-8365)***
Professional Recruiting Cons 302 479-9550
3617a Silverside Rd Wilmington (19810) ***(G-12239)***
Professional Roof Services Inc (HQ) 302 731-5770
229 Lake Dr Newark (19702) ***(G-7266)***
Professional Window Tinting 302 456-3456
9 Albe Dr Ste A Newark (19702) ***(G-7267)***
Professionals LLC 302 295-2330
1000 N West St Ste 1283 Wilmington (19801) ***(G-12240)***
Professionsale Inc 646 262-9101
1148 Pulaski Hwy Ste 134 Bear (19701) ***(G-293)***
Professnal Arfication Svcs Inc 302 752-7003
4 Hollyberry Dr Georgetown (19947) ***(G-2629)***
Progar & Co 302 645-6216
33815 Clay Rd Ste 1 Lewes (19958) ***(G-3699)***
Progar & Company PA, Lewes *Also called Progar & Co* ***(G-3699)***
Progresive Dental Arts 302 455-9569
685 E Chestnut Hill Rd Newark (19713) ***(G-7268)***
Progressive Casualty Insur Co 302 734-7360
1241 N Dupont Hwy Dover (19901) ***(G-1990)***
Progressive Dental Arts 302 234-2222
5301 Limestone Rd Ste 212 Wilmington (19808) ***(G-12241)***
Progressive Health of Delaware, Wilmington *Also called Zarek Donohue LLC* ***(G-13340)***
Progressive Insurance, Dover *Also called Progressive Casualty Insur Co* ***(G-1990)***
Progressive Investment Co Inc 302 656-8597
801 N West St Fl 2 Wilmington (19801) ***(G-12242)***
Progressive Services Inc 302 658-7260
300 Commercial Dr Wilmington (19805) ***(G-12243)***
Progressive Software Cmpt Inc 302 479-9700
1 Righter Pkwy Ste 280 Wilmington (19803) ***(G-12244)***

ALPHABETIC

Progressive Systems Inc...302 732-3321
25 Hickory St Frankford (19945) ***(G-2381)***
Progressive Telecom LLC...302 883-8883
3422 Old Capitol Trl # 1483 Wilmington (19808) ***(G-12245)***
Project Assistants Inc...302 477-9711
1521 Concord Pike Ste 301 Wilmington (19803) ***(G-12246)***
Project of Providence LLC...302 438-8970
1007 Park Pl Apt A Wilmington (19806) ***(G-12247)***
Project Otr LLC...404 964-2244
1209 N Orange St Wilmington (19801) ***(G-12248)***
Project Widgets Inc...302 439-3414
501 Silverside Rd Ste 29 Wilmington (19809) ***(G-12249)***
Promenta LLC...302 552-2922
3422 Old Capitol Trl Wilmington (19808) ***(G-12250)***
Prominent Insurance Svcs Inc...302 351-3368
1201 N Orange St Ste 700 Wilmington (19801) ***(G-12251)***
Promotion Zone LLC...302 832-8565
50 Albe Dr Ste A Newark (19702) ***(G-7269)***
Promotions Plus Inc...302 836-2820
700 Peoples Plz Newark (19702) ***(G-7270)***
Promotora Systems Inc...302 304-3147
1224 N King St Wilmington (19801) ***(G-12252)***
Proper Pitch LLC...302 436-5442
131 Dixon St Selbyville (19975) ***(G-8534)***
Property Doctors LLC...302 249-7731
309 Millchop Ln Magnolia (19962) ***(G-3905)***
Property Improvements LLC...610 692-5343
144 Elizabeth Way Bethany Beach (19930) ***(G-424)***
Property Management Dept., of, Millsboro *Also called Fulton Bank National Assn* ***(G-4695)***
Prorank Business Solutions LLC...302 256-0642
1515 W 6th St Wilmington (19805) ***(G-12253)***
Prosift LLC...302 678-2386
1239 N Farmview Dr Dover (19904) ***(G-1991)***
Prospect Crozer LLC...302 798-8785
2999 Philadelphia Pike Claymont (19703) ***(G-797)***
Prosperity Unlimited Ente...302 379-2494
32 E Sarazen Dr Middletown (19709) ***(G-4200)***
Protech Delivery & Assembly...302 449-5003
106 Somers Ave New Castle (19720) ***(G-5650)***
Protech Solutions Group LLC...844 744-2418
1000 N West St Ste 1200 Wilmington (19801) ***(G-12254)***
Protect America Inc...302 999-9045
234 N James St Wilmington (19804) ***(G-12255)***
Protection One, Newark *Also called ADT LLC* ***(G-5902)***
Protermant Services, Newark *Also called University of Delaware* ***(G-7619)***
Protocol Labs Inc...302 703-7194
427 N Tatnall St 51207 Wilmington (19801) ***(G-12256)***
Prototek Machining & Dev...302 368-1226
307 Markus Ct Newark (19713) ***(G-7271)***
Prouse Enterprises LLC...302 846-9000
120 Mullet Run Milford (19963) ***(G-4531)***
Providence At Heritage Sh...302 337-1040
21 White Pelican Ct Bridgeville (19933) ***(G-513)***
Providence Hall Apartments, Wilmington *Also called Providence Hall Associates LP* ***(G-12257)***
Providence Hall Associates LP...518 828-4700
4 Denny Rd Wilmington (19809) ***(G-12257)***
Providence Media LLC...302 715-1757
119 Lake Dr Laurel (19956) ***(G-3274)***
Provident Federal Credit Union...302 734-1133
401 S New St Dover (19904) ***(G-1992)***
Proximity Malt LLC...414 755-8388
33222 Bi State Blvd Laurel (19956) ***(G-3275)***
Prudent Endodontics...302 475-3803
2036 Foulk Rd Wilmington (19810) ***(G-12258)***
Prudential Emerson and Company, Dover *Also called ERA Harrington Realty* ***(G-1527)***
Prudential Fox and Roach Realt...302 378-9500
1126 Pulaski Hwy Bear (19701) ***(G-294)***
Prudential Fox Roach Realtors, Hockessin *Also called Fox & Roach LLC* ***(G-3031)***
Prudential Fox Roach Realtors, Bear *Also called Fox & Roach LP* ***(G-158)***
Prudential Fox Roach Realtors, Wilmington *Also called Fox & Roach LP* ***(G-10607)***
Prudential Gallo Realtor, Rehoboth Beach *Also called Gallo Realty Inc* ***(G-7942)***
Prudential Gallo Realty...302 645-6661
16712 Kings Hwy Lewes (19958) ***(G-3700)***
Prudential Insur Co of Amer...302 734-7877
9 E Loockerman St Dover (19901) ***(G-1993)***
Prudential Insur Co of Amer...302 378-8811
208 N Broad St Middletown (19709) ***(G-4201)***
PSC Technology Incorporated (PA)...866 866-1466
16192 Coastal Hwy Lewes (19958) ***(G-3701)***
PSI, Frankford *Also called Progressive Systems Inc* ***(G-2381)***
PSI-TEC Corporation (PA)...425 943-9493
2320 Lighthouse Ln Wilmington (19810) ***(G-12259)***
Psp Corp...302 764-7730
203 Churchill Dr Wilmington (19803) ***(G-12260)***
Psycho Therapeutic Services, Dover *Also called Associated Svc Specialist Inc* ***(G-1149)***
Psychoanalytic Electronic...949 495-3332
1013 Centre Rd Wilmington (19805) ***(G-12261)***
Psychological Services...302 489-0213
422 Woodstock Ln Wilmington (19808) ***(G-12262)***
Psychotherapeutic Services...302 672-7159
630 W Division St Ste D Dover (19904) ***(G-1994)***
Psychotherapeutic Services...302 678-9962
942 Walker Rd Ste B Dover (19904) ***(G-1995)***
Psychotherapeutic Svc Assn Inc...302 284-8370
2015 Peachtree Run Rd Dover (19901) ***(G-1996)***
Psychotherapeutic Svcs Assoc...302 672-7159
630 W Division St Ste D Dover (19904) ***(G-1997)***
Pta Delaware Military Academy...302 998-0745
12 Middleboro Rd Wilmington (19804) ***(G-12263)***
Pta Lombardy Elementary...302 478-6054
442 Foulk Rd Wilmington (19803) ***(G-12264)***
Pteris Global (usa) Inc...516 593-5633
615 S Dupont Hwy Dover (19901) ***(G-1998)***
Ptm Manufacturing LLC...302 455-9733
196 Quigley Blvd Ste A New Castle (19720) ***(G-5651)***
Pts Professional Welding...302 632-2079
609 Broad St Houston (19954) ***(G-3180)***
Public Allies Deleware Inc...302 573-4438
100 W 10th St Ste 812 Wilmington (19801) ***(G-12265)***
Public Health Nursing...302 856-5136
544 S Bedford St Georgetown (19947) ***(G-2630)***
Public Systems Inc...302 326-4500
2 Penns Way Ste 406 New Castle (19720) ***(G-5652)***
Publica.la, Newark *Also called Queryloop Inc* ***(G-7286)***
Publication Print...302 992-2040
3846 Kennett Pike Wilmington (19807) ***(G-12266)***
Pughs Service Inc...302 678-2408
728 Dover Leipsic Rd Dover (19901) ***(G-1999)***
Puglisi Egg Farms Delaware LLC...302 376-1200
1881 Middle Neck Rd Middletown (19709) ***(G-4202)***
Pulmonary & Sleep Cons LLC...302 994-4060
4512 Kirkwood Hwy Wilmington (19808) ***(G-12267)***
Pulmonary Associates PA (PA)...302 656-2213
7 S Clayton St 500 Wilmington (19805) ***(G-12268)***
Pulsar Print LLC...302 394-9202
243 Quigley Blvd Ste K New Castle (19720) ***(G-5653)***
Pulte Home Corporation...302 378-9091
3 Garcia Dr Middletown (19709) ***(G-4203)***
Pulte Home Corporation...302 999-9525
206 Jestan Blvd New Castle (19720) ***(G-5654)***
Pumh, Hockessin *Also called Peninsula Untd Mthdst Hmes Inc* ***(G-3114)***
Pump and Corrosion Tech Inc...302 655-3490
310 Cornell Dr Ste B5 Wilmington (19801) ***(G-12269)***
Pure Air Holdings Corp (HQ)...302 655-7130
1105 N Market St Ste 1300 Wilmington (19801) ***(G-12270)***
Pure Wellness LLC...302 389-8915
699 S Carter Rd Unit 5 Smyrna (19977) ***(G-8695)***
Pure Wellness LLC...302 449-0149
708 Ash Blvd Middletown (19709) ***(G-4204)***
Pure Wellness LLC (PA)...302 365-5470
550 Stanton Christiana Rd # 302 Newark (19713) ***(G-7272)***
Pure Wellness LLC...302 543-5679
1010 N Bancroft Pkwy Wilmington (19805) ***(G-12271)***
Pure Wellness Chiropractic, Newark *Also called Pure Wellness LLC* ***(G-7272)***
Purpose Ministries Inc (PA)...302 753-0435
225 Old Baltimore Pike Newark (19702) ***(G-7273)***
Purushas Picks Inc...302 918-7663
3310 Wrangle Hill Rd # 107 Bear (19701) ***(G-295)***
Puzs Body Shop Inc...302 368-8265
97 Peoples Dr Newark (19702) ***(G-7274)***
Puzzles of Life...302 339-0327
831 N Market St Wilmington (19801) ***(G-12272)***
Pxe Group LLC...561 295-1451
8 The Grn Ste A Dover (19901) ***(G-2000)***
Pyle Child Development Center...302 732-1443
34314 Pyle Center Rd Frankford (19945) ***(G-2382)***
Pyne Chiropractic PA...302 644-1792
18977 Munchy Branch Rd # 3 Rehoboth Beach (19971) ***(G-8037)***
Pyramid Educational Cons...302 368-2515
350 Churchmans Rd Ste B New Castle (19720) ***(G-5655)***
Pyramid Group MGT Svcs Corp...302 737-1770
227 E Delaware Ave Newark (19711) ***(G-7275)***
Pyramid Transport Inc...302 337-9340
18119 Sussex Hwy Unit 2 Bridgeville (19933) ***(G-514)***
Q and R Electric LLC...302 670-1817
701 Brook Dr Newark (19713) ***(G-7276)***
Q Vandenberg & Sons Inc...800 242-2852
3422 Old Capitol Trl Wilmington (19808) ***(G-12273)***
Qbeck Inspection Group...302 452-9257
242 Chapman Rd Newark (19702) ***(G-7277)***
Qbr Telecom Inc...302 510-1155
913 N Market St Ste 200 Wilmington (19801) ***(G-12274)***
Qc Laboratories, New Castle *Also called Eurofins Qc Inc* ***(G-5297)***
QH&a, Wilmington *Also called Quality Htg Ar-Cnditioning Inc* ***(G-12280)***
Qienna Wealth Management Inc...610 765-6008
112 Capitol Trl Newark (19711) ***(G-7278)***

ALPHABETIC SECTION

Qlean Implants Inc 302 613-0804
   19266 Coastal Hwy Unit 4 Rehoboth Beach (19971) *(G-8038)*
Qmobi Inc 800 246-2677
   919 N Market St Ste 425 Wilmington (19801) *(G-12275)*
Qnectus, Newark Also called Tandem Hosted Resources Inc *(G-7537)*
Qoe Inc 302 455-1234
   955 Dawson Dr Ste 3 Newark (19713) *(G-7279)*
Qoro LLC 302 322-5900
   166 S Dupont Hwy Ste B New Castle (19720) *(G-5656)*
Qps LLC 302 369-3753
   110 Executive Dr Ste 7 Newark (19702) *(G-7280)*
Qps Holdings LLC (PA) 302 369-5601
   3 Innovation Way Ste 240 Newark (19711) *(G-7281)*
Qrepublik Inc 559 475-8262
   2093 Philadelphia Pike # 2012 Claymont (19703) *(G-798)*
Qsr Group LLC 302 268-6909
   913 N Market St Ste 200 Wilmington (19801) *(G-12276)*
Quail Associates Inc 302 697-4660
   1 Clubhouse Dr Camden Wyoming (19934) *(G-651)*
Quaker City Auto Parts Inc 302 436-5114
   12 N Main St Selbyville (19975) *(G-8535)*
Quaker Hill Place Co, Wilmington Also called Boston Land Co Mgt Svcs Inc *(G-9395)*
Quality Appliance Services 302 766-4808
   202 Nathaniel Rd Newark (19713) *(G-7282)*
Quality Assured Inc 302 652-4151
   223 Valley Rd Wilmington (19804) *(G-12277)*
Quality Auto Care Centers 302 992-7978
   4325 Kirkwood Hwy Wilmington (19808) *(G-12278)*
Quality Automotive, Wilmington Also called Quality Auto Care Centers *(G-12278)*
Quality Builders Inc 302 697-0664
   213 Willow Ave Camden (19934) *(G-597)*
Quality Care Homes LLC 302 858-3999
   20366 Hopkins Rd Lewes (19958) *(G-3702)*
Quality Clene, Claymont Also called Bane Clene Way *(G-699)*
Quality Construction Cleaning 302 956-0752
   8902 Cannon Rd Bridgeville (19933) *(G-515)*
Quality Distributors Inc 917 335-6662
   244 Steeplechase Cir Wilmington (19808) *(G-12279)*
Quality Exteriors Inc 302 398-9283
   60 Hopkins Cemetery Rd Harrington (19952) *(G-2876)*
Quality Family Construction, Wilmington Also called Moony and Zeager Inc *(G-11742)*
Quality Family Physicians PA 302 235-2351
   722 Yorklyn Rd Ste 400 Hockessin (19707) *(G-3127)*
Quality Finishers Inc 302 325-1963
   1 Merit Dr New Castle (19720) *(G-5657)*
Quality Htg Ar-Cnditioning Inc 302 654-5247
   31 Brookside Dr Wilmington (19804) *(G-12280)*
Quality III Fire Protection 302 762-8262
   1607 Todds Ln Wilmington (19802) *(G-12281)*
Quality Inn, New Castle Also called Skyways Motor Lodge Corp *(G-5716)*
Quality Inn, Harrington Also called Veer Hotels Inc *(G-2904)*
Quality Inn 302 292-1500
   48 Geoffrey Dr Newark (19713) *(G-7283)*
Quality Lawn Care Home RE 302 331-5892
   4 Turtle Dr Camden Wyoming (19934) *(G-652)*
Quality Masonry, Laurel Also called Joseph L Hinks *(G-3245)*
Quality Rofg Sup Lancaster Inc 302 644-4115
   1312 Hwy 1 Lewes (19958) *(G-3703)*
Quality Rofg Sup Lancaster Inc 302 322-8322
   9 Parkway Cir New Castle (19720) *(G-5658)*
Quantum Corporation 302 737-7012
   211 Executive Dr Ste 1 Newark (19702) *(G-7284)*
Quantum Polymers Corporation 302 737-7012
   211 Executive Dr Ste 1 Newark (19702) *(G-7285)*
Quantumfly LLC 312 618-5739
   9 E Loockerman St Ste 215 Dover (19901) *(G-2001)*
Quantus Innovations LLC 302 356-1661
   136 Fairhill Dr Wilmington (19808) *(G-12282)*
Quarta-Rad Inc 201 877-2002
   1201 N Orange St Ste 7234 Wilmington (19801) *(G-12283)*
Quavo Inc 484 802-4693
   1201 N Orange St Ste 7115 Wilmington (19801) *(G-12284)*
Quboai Corporation 484 889-5789
   3524 Silverside Rd Wilmington (19810) *(G-12285)*
Queen B Tbl Chair Rentals LLC 215 960-6303
   8 The Grn 8105 Dover (19901) *(G-2002)*
Queryloop Inc 412 253-6265
   2035 Sunset Lake Rd B2 Newark (19702) *(G-7286)*
Quest Diagnostics Incorporated 302 322-4651
   525 E Basin Rd New Castle (19720) *(G-5659)*
Quest Diagnostics Incorporated 302 537-3862
   38025 Town Center Dr Millville (19967) *(G-4853)*
Quest Diagnostics Incorporated 302 424-4504
   975 N Dupont Blvd Milford (19963) *(G-4532)*
Quest Diagnostics Incorporated 302 478-1100
   2700 Slverstone Rd Ste 1b Wilmington (19810) *(G-12286)*
Quest Diagnostics Incorporated 302 628-3078
   808 Middleford Rd Ste 4 Seaford (19973) *(G-8366)*
Quest Diagnostics Incorporated 302 239-5273
   1941 Limestone Rd Ste 108 Wilmington (19808) *(G-12287)*
Quest Diagnostics Incorporated 302 735-4555
   190 John Hunn Brown Rd Dover (19901) *(G-2003)*
Quest Diagnostics Incorporated 302 455-0720
   A98 100 Omega Dr Newark (19713) *(G-7287)*
Quest Diagnostics Incorporated 302 376-8675
   114 Sandhill Dr Ste 202 Middletown (19709) *(G-4205)*
Quest Pharmaceutical Services, Newark Also called Qps LLC *(G-7280)*
Questar Capital Corporation 302 856-9778
   13 Bridgeville Rd Georgetown (19947) *(G-2631)*
Quick Browser, Wilmington Also called Webbrowser Media Inc *(G-13134)*
Quickborn Consulting LLC (PA) 302 407-0922
   501 Silverside Rd Ste 105 Wilmington (19809) *(G-12288)*
Quillen Signs LLC 302 684-3661
   523 Federal St Milton (19968) *(G-4954)*
Quillens Rent All Inc 302 227-3151
   803 Rehoboth Ave Ste G Rehoboth Beach (19971) *(G-8039)*
Quilted Heirlooms 302 354-6061
   123 Back Creek Dr Middletown (19709) *(G-4206)*
Quinn Data Corporation 302 429-7450
   922 New Rd Ste 1 Wilmington (19805) *(G-12289)*
Quinn Pediatric Dentistry 302 674-8000
   1380 S State St Dover (19901) *(G-2004)*
Quinn-Miller Group Inc 302 738-9742
   34 Germay Dr Wilmington (19804) *(G-12290)*
Quintasian LLC 302 674-3784
   1706 N Dupont Hwy Dover (19901) *(G-2005)*
Quinteccent Inc 443 838-5447
   37808 Salty Way W Selbyville (19975) *(G-8536)*
Quip Laboratories Incorporated 302 761-2600
   1500 Eastlawn Ave Wilmington (19802) *(G-12291)*
Qwintry LLC 858 633-6353
   825 Dawson Dr Newark (19713) *(G-7288)*
R & E Excavation LLC 302 750-5226
   226 Harlequin Dr New Castle (19720) *(G-5660)*
R & J Taylor Inc 302 368-7888
   1712 Ogletown Rd Newark (19711) *(G-7289)*
R & J Welding & Fabrication 302 236-5618
   32812 Bi State Blvd Laurel (19956) *(G-3276)*
R & K Motors & Machine Shop 302 737-4596
   60 Aleph Dr Newark (19702) *(G-7290)*
R & S Fabrication Inc 302 629-0377
   7159 Seashore Hwy Bridgeville (19933) *(G-516)*
R & W Transportation Corp 703 670-5483
   201 N Walnut St Wilmington (19801) *(G-12292)*
R A Chance Plumbing Inc 302 292-1315
   11 Fern Ct Newark (19702) *(G-7291)*
R A Chance Plumbing Inc 302 324-8200
   23 Parkway Cir Ste 5 New Castle (19720) *(G-5661)*
R and H Filter Co Inc 302 856-2129
   21646 Baltimore Ave Georgetown (19947) *(G-2632)*
R C Fabricators Inc 302 573-8989
   824 N Locust St Wilmington (19801) *(G-12293)*
R D Arnold Construction Inc 610 255-4739
   33 E Stonewall Dr Middletown (19709) *(G-4207)*
R D Collins & Sons 302 834-3409
   19 Shellbark Dr Bear (19701) *(G-296)*
R E Michel Company LLC 302 678-0250
   550 S Queen St Dover (19904) *(G-2006)*
R E Michel Company LLC 302 322-7480
   184 Quigley Blvd New Castle (19720) *(G-5662)*
R E Michel Company LLC 302 645-0585
   32437 Lwes Georgetown Hwy Lewes (19958) *(G-3704)*
R E Michel Company LLC 302 368-9410
   904 Interchange Blvd Newark (19711) *(G-7292)*
R E WIllams Prof Acctg Frm Tax 302 598-7171
   3628 Silverside Rd Wilmington (19810) *(G-12294)*
R F Gentner & Son 302 947-2733
   22797 Dozer Ln Unit 15 Harbeson (19951) *(G-2796)*
R G Altschuler MD 302 652-3771
   1806 N Van Buren St # 200 Wilmington (19802) *(G-12295)*
R G Architects LLC 302 376-8100
   200 W Main St Middletown (19709) *(G-4208)*
R H D Brandywine Hills 302 764-3660
   710 W Matson Run Pkwy Wilmington (19802) *(G-12296)*
R J Baker Distillery 302 745-0967
   34171 Rider Rd Laurel (19956) *(G-3277)*
R J Farms Inc 302 629-2520
   2864 Long Acre Ln Seaford (19973) *(G-8367)*
R J K Transportation Inc 302 422-3188
   1118 School St Houston (19954) *(G-3181)*
R L Laboratories Inc 302 328-1686
   245 Quigley Blvd Ste B New Castle (19720) *(G-5663)*
R M Bell Industries Inc 302 542-3747
   1504 Savannah Rd Lewes (19958) *(G-3705)*
R M Quinn DDS 302 674-8000
   1380 S State St Ste 2 Dover (19901) *(G-2007)*
R M Villasenor MD 302 629-4078
   9726 N Shore Dr Seaford (19973) *(G-8368)*

R R Roofing Inc 2............302 218-7474
4807 Lancaster Pike Wilmington (19807) ***(G-12297)***
R S Bauer LLC............302 398-4668
17584 S Dupont Hwy Harrington (19952) ***(G-2877)***
R S C, Newark *Also called Roller Service Corporation* ***(G-7361)***
R Stanley Collier & Son Inc............302 398-7855
1832 Brownsville Rd Harrington (19952) ***(G-2878)***
R Stokes Nolte Esquire &............302 777-1700
1010 N Bancroft Pkwy # 21 Wilmington (19805) ***(G-12298)***
R T Accountants Co............302 670-5117
39 S Turnberry Dr Dover (19904) ***(G-2008)***
R W Home Services Inc............302 539-4683
14 Atlantic Ave Ocean View (19970) ***(G-7810)***
R W Morgan Farms Inc............302 542-7740
18126 Haflinger Rd Lincoln (19960) ***(G-3864)***
R&R Contractors, Middletown *Also called Roberts Wilbert* ***(G-4221)***
R&R Homecare............302 478-3448
100 Beauregard Ct Wilmington (19810) ***(G-12299)***
R&R Logistics Inc............302 629-4255
29299 Hearns Ln Seaford (19973) ***(G-8369)***
R.R. Beach Associates, Dover *Also called Beach Associates Inc* ***(G-1183)***
Raad360 LLC............855 722-3360
550 S College Ave 107ofc Newark (19716) ***(G-7293)***
Raafat Z Abdel-Misih MD............302 658-7533
1021 Gilpin Ave Ste 203 Wilmington (19806) ***(G-12300)***
Raas Infotek LLC............302 894-3184
262 Chapman Rd Ste 105a Newark (19702) ***(G-7294)***
Rabspan Inc............302 324-8104
13 King Ct Ste 1 New Castle (19720) ***(G-5664)***
Racqueteer............302 378-1596
125 Crystal Run Dr Middletown (19709) ***(G-4209)***
RAD Pets Inc............302 335-5718
685 Roesville Rd Felton (19943) ***(G-2314)***
Radiance Vr Inc............937 818-3988
16192 Coastal Hwy Lewes (19958) ***(G-3706)***
Radiation Oncology............302 733-1830
4755 Stanton Ogeltown Rd Newark (19718) ***(G-7295)***
Radio Station Wdel-AM, Wilmington *Also called Delmarva Broadcasting Co Inc* ***(G-10102)***
Radio Sussex, Rehoboth Beach *Also called East Sussex Public Brdcstg* ***(G-7923)***
Radiocut Inc............302 613-1280
251 Little Falls Dr Wilmington (19808) ***(G-12301)***
Radiology Associates, Newark *Also called Delaware Imaging Network* ***(G-6388)***
Radiology Associates Inc (PA)............302 832-5590
1701 Augustine Cut Off # 100 Wilmington (19803) ***(G-12302)***
Radius Rx Direct Inc............302 658-9196
501 N Shipley St Unit 2 Wilmington (19801) ***(G-12303)***
Radius Services LLC (PA)............302 993-0600
16 Hadco Rd Wilmington (19804) ***(G-12304)***
Rafetto, Ray S DMD, Wilmington *Also called A D Alpine DMD* ***(G-8875)***
Rafi Soofi MD............302 999-1644
1941 Limestone Rd Ste 216 Wilmington (19808) ***(G-12305)***
Rahaim & Saints Attys At Law (PA)............302 892-9200
2055 Limestone Rd Ste 211 Wilmington (19808) ***(G-12306)***
Railway Logistics, Wilmington *Also called Hollywell Logistics LLC* ***(G-10929)***
Rain of Light Inc............302 312-7642
28 Tyre Ave Newark (19711) ***(G-7296)***
Rainbow Charter Service, Newark *Also called Creative Travel Inc* ***(G-6315)***
Rainbow Day Care & Pre-Sch............302 628-1020
26630 Sussex Hwy Seaford (19973) ***(G-8370)***
Rainmaker Software Group LLC............800 616-6701
1925 Lovering Ave Wilmington (19806) ***(G-12307)***
Rallypoint Solutions LLC............302 543-8087
3411 Silverside Rd Wilmington (19810) ***(G-12308)***
Ralph and Paul Adams Inc............800 338-4727
103 Railroad Ave Bridgeville (19933) ***(G-517)***
Ralph Burdick Do............302 834-3600
900 5th St Delaware City (19706) ***(G-966)***
Ralph Cahall & Son Paving............302 653-4220
2284 Bryn Zion Rd Smyrna (19977) ***(G-8696)***
Ralph H Givens............302 629-4319
27545 Johnson Rd Seaford (19973) ***(G-8371)***
Ralph Paul Inc............302 764-9162
319 E Lea Blvd Wilmington (19802) ***(G-12309)***
Ralph Tomases DDS PA............302 652-8656
707 Foulk Rd Ste 203 Wilmington (19803) ***(G-12310)***
Ralphs Scissors Sensations............302 764-2744
511 Philadelphia Pike A Wilmington (19809) ***(G-12311)***
Ram Electric Inc............302 875-2356
34779 Whaleys Rd Laurel (19956) ***(G-3278)***
Ram Tech Systems Inc (PA)............302 832-6600
1050 Industrial Rd # 110 Middletown (19709) ***(G-4210)***
Rama Corporation............302 266-6600
181 Thompson Dr Hockessin (19707) ***(G-3128)***
Rama LLC............202 596-9547
300 Delaware Ave Ste 210a Wilmington (19801) ***(G-12312)***
Ramachandra U Hosmane MD............302 645-2274
1408 Savannah Rd Lewes (19958) ***(G-3707)***
Ramada Inn, Newark *Also called Chapman Hospitality Inc* ***(G-6189)***
Ramon Galvan............201 797-7172
814 W Boxborough Dr Wilmington (19810) ***(G-12313)***
Ramona Clay............866 448-0834
1313 Innovation 1313 N Wilmington (19801) ***(G-12314)***
Ramunno & Ramunno & Scerba PA............302 656-9400
903 N French St Ste 106 Wilmington (19801) ***(G-12315)***
Randolphs Refuse Service Inc............302 658-5674
28 Dover Ave New Castle (19720) ***(G-5665)***
Randstad Finance & Accounting, Wilmington *Also called Randstad Professionals Us LLC* ***(G-12316)***
Randstad Professionals Us LLC............302 658-6181
2 Mill Rd Ste 200 Wilmington (19806) ***(G-12316)***
Rangeland Nm LLC............800 316-6660
1675 S State St Ste B Dover (19901) ***(G-2009)***
Rapa Scrapple, Bridgeville *Also called Ralph and Paul Adams Inc* ***(G-517)***
Rape of The Locke Inc............302 368-5370
700 Barksdale Rd Ste 5 Newark (19711) ***(G-7297)***
Rapid Recycling Inc............302 324-5360
42 Reads Way New Castle (19720) ***(G-5666)***
Rapid Renovation and Repr LLC............302 475-5400
79 Pleasant Pine Ct Harrington (19952) ***(G-2879)***
Rapuano Iron Works Inc............302 571-1809
14 Whitekirk Dr Wilmington (19808) ***(G-12317)***
Ras Addis & Associates Inc............302 571-1683
460 Robinson Dr Wilmington (19801) ***(G-12318)***
Raskaukas Joseph C Aty Law............302 537-2000
33176 Coastal Hwy Bethany Beach (19930) ***(G-425)***
Raskob Foundation For Catholic............302 655-4440
10 Montchanin Rd Wilmington (19807) ***(G-12319)***
Rath Incorporated (HQ)............302 294-4446
300 Ruthar Dr Ste 1 Newark (19711) ***(G-7298)***
Rath Performance Fibers, Newark *Also called Rath Incorporated* ***(G-7298)***
Ratner & Prestia PC............302 778-2500
1007 N Orange St Ste 205 Wilmington (19801) ***(G-12320)***
Ratner Companies LC............302 226-9822
19323 Lighthouse Plaza Bl Rehoboth Beach (19971) ***(G-8040)***
Ratner Companies LC............302 378-8565
659 Middletown Warwick Rd Middletown (19709) ***(G-4211)***
Ratner Companies LC............302 678-8081
1005 N Dupont Hwy Dover (19901) ***(G-2010)***
Ratner Companies LC............302 999-7724
3218 Kirkwood Hwy Wilmington (19808) ***(G-12321)***
Ratner Companies LC............302 836-3749
1009 Governors Pl Bear (19701) ***(G-297)***
Ratner Companies LC............302 366-9032
591 College Sq Newark (19711) ***(G-7299)***
Ratner Companies LC............302 376-3568
282 Dove Run Dr Middletown (19709) ***(G-4212)***
Ratner Companies LC............302 537-4624
38069 Town Center Dr # 4 Millville (19967) ***(G-4854)***
Ratner Companies LC............302 478-9978
5607 Concord Pike Wilmington (19803) ***(G-12322)***
Rauma Survivors Foundation............302 275-9705
2055 Limestone Rd Ste 109 Wilmington (19808) ***(G-12323)***
Rave Business Systems LLC............302 407-2270
16192 Coastal Hwy Lewes (19958) ***(G-3708)***
Raven Crane & Equipment Co LLC............302 998-1000
196 Quigley Blvd Ste B New Castle (19720) ***(G-5667)***
Rawlins Ferguson Jones & Lewis............302 337-8231
119 Market St Bridgeville (19933) ***(G-518)***
Rawlins Orthodontics............302 239-3533
5500 Skyline Dr Ste 1 Wilmington (19808) ***(G-12324)***
Ray Book & Co, Dover *Also called Raymond F Book III* ***(G-2011)***
Ray's & Sons, Felton *Also called Rays Plumbing & Heating Svcs* ***(G-2315)***
Rayco Auto & Marine Uphl Inc............302 323-8844
113 Carriage Dr Hockessin (19707) ***(G-3129)***
Raymon James Financial Service, Wilmington *Also called Raymond James Financial Svc* ***(G-12329)***
Raymond A Stachecki............302 653-6004
3157 Big Oak Rd Smyrna (19977) ***(G-8697)***
Raymond Chung Industries Corp............302 384-9796
12 Sharons Way Wilmington (19808) ***(G-12325)***
Raymond E Tomassetti Esq (PA)............302 539-3041
1209 Coastal Hwy Fl 2 Fenwick Island (19944) ***(G-2339)***
Raymond E Tomassetti Esq............302 995-2840
14 W Market St Wilmington (19804) ***(G-12326)***
Raymond Entrmt Group LLC............302 731-2000
62 N Chapel St Ste 4 Newark (19711) ***(G-7300)***
Raymond F Book III (PA)............302 734-5826
220 Beiser Blvd Dover (19904) ***(G-2011)***
Raymond Harner............302 737-0755
317 Jaymar Blvd Newark (19702) ***(G-7301)***
Raymond James, Wilmington *Also called Raymond James & Associates Inc* ***(G-12328)***
Raymond James & Associates Inc............302 656-1534
20 Montchanin Rd Ste 280 Wilmington (19807) ***(G-12327)***
Raymond James & Associates Inc............302 798-9113
200 Bellevue Pkwy Ste 425 Wilmington (19809) ***(G-12328)***
Raymond James Financial Svc............302 778-2170
900 Foulk Rd Ste 201 Wilmington (19803) ***(G-12329)***

Raymond James Fincl Svcs Inc 302 227-0330
20281 Coastal Hwy Rehoboth Beach (19971) ***(G-8041)***
Raymond James Fincl Svcs Inc 302 645-8592
34346 Carpenters Way Lewes (19958) ***(G-3709)***
Raymond James Fincl Svcs Inc 302 539-3323
701 Bethany Loop Bethany Beach (19930) ***(G-426)***
Raymond James Fincl Svcs Inc 302 778-2170
900 Foulk Rd Ste 201 Wilmington (19803) ***(G-12330)***
Raymond James Fincl Svcs Inc 302 656-1534
20 Montchanin Rd Ste 280 Wilmington (19807) ***(G-12331)***
Raymond L Para DDS 302 234-2728
720 Yorklyn Rd Ste 120 Hockessin (19707) ***(G-3130)***
Raymond V Feehery Jr DPM 302 999-8511
620 Stanton Christiana Rd # 303 Newark (19713) ***(G-7302)***
Raymond W Petrunich 302 836-3565
1400 Peoples Plz Ste 124 Newark (19702) ***(G-7303)***
Rays and Sons Mechanical LLC 302 697-2100
307 S Winding Brooke Dr Seaford (19973) ***(G-8372)***
Rays Plumbing & Heating Svcs 302 697-3936
7244 S Dupont Hwy Felton (19943) ***(G-2315)***
Raytheon Company 302 656-1339
100 W 10th St Wilmington (19801) ***(G-12332)***
Rbah Inc 302 227-2009
20259 Coastal Hwy Rehoboth Beach (19971) ***(G-8042)***
Rbc 302 892-5901
2751 Centerville Rd # 212 Wilmington (19808) ***(G-12333)***
Rbc Capital Markets LLC 302 252-9444
1000 N West St Ste 110 Wilmington (19801) ***(G-12334)***
Rbc Trust Company Delaware Ltd 302 892-6900
4550 New Linden Hill Rd Wilmington (19808) ***(G-12335)***
Rbc Wealth Management, Wilmington *Also called Rbc Capital Markets LLC* ***(G-12334)***
Rbs Auto Repair Inc 302 678-8803
1312 S Dupont Hwy Dover (19901) ***(G-2012)***
RC Hellings Inc 302 798-6850
950 Ridge Rd Ste D3 Claymont (19703) ***(G-799)***
RC Turner Collection, Newark *Also called Kha-Neke Inc* ***(G-6883)***
Rcc Christiana, Newark *Also called Fresenius Medical Care Vero Be* ***(G-6621)***
Rcd Printing 302 424-8467
623 Abbott Dr Milford (19963) ***(G-4533)***
Rcd Timber Products Inc (PA) 302 778-5700
1699 Matassino Rd New Castle (19720) ***(G-5668)***
Rci, New Castle *Also called Reprographics Center Inc* ***(G-5672)***
Rck Soliatire LLC 551 358-8400
19266 Cstl Hwy Unit 4108 Rehoboth Beach (19971) ***(G-8043)***
Rct Studio Inc 669 255-1562
251 Little Falls Dr Wilmington (19808) ***(G-12336)***
Rcw Renovations Inc 302 239-3714
828 Westridge Dr Hockessin (19707) ***(G-3131)***
RDS Engineering LLC 417 763-3727
16192 Coastal Hwy Lewes (19958) ***(G-3710)***
RE Calloway Trnsp Inc 302 422-2471
897 School St Houston (19954) ***(G-3182)***
RE Community Holdings II Inc 302 778-9793
1101 Lambson Ln New Castle (19720) ***(G-5669)***
RE Max of Wilmington (PA) 302 234-2500
5307 Limestone Rd Ste 100 Wilmington (19808) ***(G-12337)***
RE Max of Wilmington 302 657-8000
2323 Pennsylvania Ave Wilmington (19806) ***(G-12338)***
Re-Up App Inc 267 972-1183
8603 Park Ct Wilmington (19802) ***(G-12339)***
Re/Max, Newark *Also called Max RE Associates Inc* ***(G-7005)***
Re/Max, Middletown *Also called Remax 1st Choice LLC* ***(G-4217)***
Re/Max, Lewes *Also called Remax Coast & Country* ***(G-3714)***
Re/Max, Rehoboth Beach *Also called Debbie Reed* ***(G-7909)***
Re/Max, Wilmington *Also called Remax Sunvest Realty Corp* ***(G-12378)***
Re/Max, Rehoboth Beach *Also called Delaware Realty Group Inc* ***(G-7914)***
Re/Max, Wilmington *Also called RE Max of Wilmington* ***(G-12337)***
Re/Max, Wilmington *Also called Max RE Associates Inc* ***(G-11578)***
Re/Max, Wilmington *Also called RE Max of Wilmington* ***(G-12338)***
RE/Max Horizons Inc 302 678-4300
1198 S Governors Ave Dover (19904) ***(G-2013)***
Re/Max Realty Group-Rentals 302 227-4800
323 Rehoboth Ave Ste A Rehoboth Beach (19971) ***(G-8044)***
Re/Max Twin Counties, Milford *Also called Watsons Auction & Realty Svc* ***(G-4599)***
Reach Riverside Dev Corp 302 540-1698
2300 Bowers St Wilmington (19802) ***(G-12340)***
READ ALOUD DELAWARE, Wilmington *Also called Read-Alouddelaware Inc* ***(G-12341)***
Read-Alouddelaware Inc (PA) 302 656-5256
100 W 10th St Ste 309 Wilmington (19801) ***(G-12341)***
Readhowyouwant LLC 302 730-4560
3702 N Dupont Hwy Dover (19901) ***(G-2014)***
Reading Assist Institute (PA) 302 425-4080
100 W 10th St Ste 910 Wilmington (19801) ***(G-12342)***
Ready Set Textiles Inc 302 518-6583
19266 Coastal Hwy Rehoboth Beach (19971) ***(G-8045)***
Readyb Inc 323 813-8710
8 The Grn Ste A Dover (19901) ***(G-2015)***

Reagan-Watson Auctions LLC 302 422-2392
115 N Washington St Milford (19963) ***(G-4534)***
Real Estate Partners LLC 302 656-0251
2800 Lancaster Ave Ste 8 Wilmington (19805) ***(G-12343)***
Real Life Entertainment 516 413-2782
Northway Dr Newark (19713) ***(G-7304)***
Rebecca Jaffee MD 302 992-0200
3105 Limestone Rd Ste 300 Wilmington (19808) ***(G-12344)***
Rebekah Fedele DMD PA 302 994-9555
3101 Limestone Rd Ste C Wilmington (19808) ***(G-12345)***
Recommunity, New Castle *Also called RE Community Holdings II Inc* ***(G-5669)***
Record Storage Center Inc 302 674-8571
602 Pear St Dover (19904) ***(G-2016)***
Records Gebhart Agency Inc 302 653-9211
2 N Market St Smyrna (19977) ***(G-8698)***
Records-Gebhart Insurance, Smyrna *Also called Records Gebhart Agency Inc* ***(G-8698)***
Recoveryip Innovations LLC 617 901-3414
200 Continental Dr # 401 Newark (19713) ***(G-7305)***
Red Barn Inc 302 678-0271
1062 Lafferty Ln Dover (19901) ***(G-2017)***
Red Bird Egg Farm Inc (PA) 302 834-2571
1701 Red Lion Rd Bear (19701) ***(G-298)***
Red Carpet Inn, Dover *Also called Seper 8 Motel* ***(G-2070)***
Red Carpet Travel Agency Inc (PA) 302 475-1220
1812 Marsh Rd Ste 413 Wilmington (19810) ***(G-12346)***
Red Clay Consolidated Schl Dst 302 992-5580
1798 Limestone Rd Wilmington (19804) ***(G-12347)***
Red Clay Inc 302 239-2018
2388 Brackenville Rd Hockessin (19707) ***(G-3132)***
Red Dog Plumbing and Heating 302 436-5024
37058 Roxana Rd Selbyville (19975) ***(G-8537)***
Red Ghost Interactive LLC 385 485-9100
651 N Broad St Ste 205 Middletown (19709) ***(G-4213)***
Red Lion Medical Safety Inc 302 731-8600
123a Sandy Dr Newark (19713) ***(G-7306)***
Red Mill Inn 302 645-9736
16218 Coastal Hwy Lewes (19958) ***(G-3711)***
Red Rhino Labs LLC 650 275-2464
2035 Sunset Lake Rd B2 Newark (19702) ***(G-7307)***
Red Roof 302 368-8521
1119 S College Ave Newark (19713) ***(G-7308)***
Red Roof Inn, Dover *Also called Shree Lalji LLC* ***(G-2082)***
Red Roof Inns Inc 302 292-2870
415 Stanton Christiana Rd Newark (19713) ***(G-7309)***
Red Sun Custom Apparel Inc 302 988-8230
1 Mason Dr Selbyville (19975) ***(G-8538)***
Reddish Walton 302 629-4787
11 Fallon Ave Seaford (19973) ***(G-8373)***
Reddix Transportation Inc 302 249-9331
31014 Oak Leaf Dr Lewes (19958) ***(G-3712)***
Reddix Trucking Inc 302 745-1277
31342 Kendale Rd Lewes (19958) ***(G-3713)***
Redhead Farms LLC 443 235-3990
34841 Columbia Rd Delmar (19940) ***(G-1027)***
Redi Call Corp 302 856-9000
543 S Bedford St Georgetown (19947) ***(G-2633)***
Redi-Call Communications, Georgetown *Also called Redi Call Corp* ***(G-2633)***
Redleo Software Inc 302 691-9072
1201 N Orange St Ste 7495 Wilmington (19801) ***(G-12348)***
Redmill Auto Repair 302 292-2155
1209 Capitol Trl Newark (19711) ***(G-7310)***
Redzun LLC 512 657-4100
108 W 13th St Wilmington (19801) ***(G-12349)***
Reed Elsevier Capital Inc 302 427-9299
1105 N Market St Ste 501 Wilmington (19801) ***(G-12350)***
Reed Trucking Company 302 684-8585
522 Chestnut St Milton (19968) ***(G-4955)***
Reeds Refuge Center Inc 302 428-1830
1601 N Pine St Wilmington (19802) ***(G-12351)***
Reese Agency Inc 302 678-5656
575 N Dupont Hwy Dover (19901) ***(G-2018)***
Reflection Biotechnologies Inc 212 765-2200
1013 Centre Rd Ste 403b Wilmington (19805) ***(G-12352)***
Refrating LLC 617 358-2789
92 Reads Way Ste 104 New Castle (19720) ***(G-5670)***
Regal Cinemas Inc 302 479-0753
3300 Brandywine Pkwy Wilmington (19803) ***(G-12353)***
Regal Cinemas Inc 302 834-8515
1100 Peoples Plz Christiana (19702) ***(G-679)***
Regal Contractors LLC 302 736-5000
13 Nobles Pond Xing Dover (19904) ***(G-2019)***
Regal Hgts Hlthcre Ctr LLC 302 998-0181
6525 Lancaster Pike Hockessin (19707) ***(G-3133)***
Regal Painting & Decorating 302 994-8943
209 S Woodward Ave Wilmington (19805) ***(G-12354)***
Regen Solutions LLC 323 362-4336
32 W Loockerman St # 201 Dover (19904) ***(G-2020)***
Regency Hlthcare Rehab Ctr LLC 302 654-8400
801 N Broom St Wilmington (19806) ***(G-12355)***

ALPHABETIC

Reger Rizzo & Darnall LLP....302 652-3611
1001 N Jefferson St # 202 Wilmington (19801) ***(G-12356)***
Regina Coleman....215 476-4682
2720 Chinchilla Dr Wilmington (19810) ***(G-12357)***
Regional Builders Inc....302 628-8660
100 Park Ave Seaford (19973) ***(G-8374)***
Regional Hmatology Oncology PA (PA)....302 731-7782
1010 N Bancroft Pkwy # 21 Wilmington (19805) ***(G-12358)***
Regional Medical Group LLC....302 993-7890
4512 Kirkwood Hwy Ste 202 Wilmington (19808) ***(G-12359)***
Regional Orthopaedic Assoc (PA)....302 633-3555
1941 Limestone Rd Ste 101 Wilmington (19808) ***(G-12360)***
Regis Corporation....302 376-6165
705 Middletown Warwick Rd Middletown (19709) ***(G-4214)***
Regis Corporation....302 654-4477
1406 N Du Pont St Wilmington (19806) ***(G-12361)***
Regis Corporation....302 430-0881
939 N Dupont Blvd Milford (19963) ***(G-4535)***
Regis Corporation....302 697-6220
263 Walmart Dr Camden (19934) ***(G-598)***
Regis Corporation....302 834-1272
1233 Quintilio Dr Bear (19701) ***(G-299)***
Regis Corporation....302 856-2575
6 College Park Ln Ste 1 Georgetown (19947) ***(G-2634)***
Regis Corporation....302 454-2800
105 Christiana Mall Newark (19702) ***(G-7311)***
Regis Corporation....302 227-9730
19330 Coastal Hwy Rehoboth Beach (19971) ***(G-8046)***
Regis Corporation....302 834-9916
420 Eden Cir Bear (19701) ***(G-300)***
Regis Corporation....302 629-2916
632 N Dual Hwy Seaford (19973) ***(G-8375)***
Regis Corporation....302 628-0484
22899 Sussex Hwy Seaford (19973) ***(G-8376)***
Regis Corporation....302 478-5065
1732 Marsh Rd Wilmington (19810) ***(G-12362)***
Register In Chancery, Wilmington *Also called Supreme Court of The State Del* ***(G-12815)***
Registered Agents, Wilmington *Also called American Incorporators Ltd* ***(G-9049)***
Registered Agents Ltd....302 421-5750
1013 Centre Rd Ste 403a Wilmington (19805) ***(G-12363)***
Registered Agents Limited, Wilmington *Also called Registered Agents Ltd* ***(G-12363)***
Registred Agnts Legal Svcs LLC....302 427-6970
1013 Centre Rd Ste 403s Wilmington (19805) ***(G-12364)***
Registry Furniture Inc....626 297-9508
1000 N West St Ste 1200 Wilmington (19801) ***(G-12365)***
Regulatory Insurance Services....302 678-2444
841 Silver Lake Blvd # 201 Dover (19904) ***(G-2021)***
Regus Corporation....302 318-1300
200 Continental Dr # 401 Newark (19713) ***(G-7312)***
Regus Corporation....302 295-4800
1000 N West St Ste 1200 Wilmington (19801) ***(G-12366)***
Rehabilitation Associates....302 529-8783
87 Omega Dr Bldg B Newark (19713) ***(G-7313)***
Rehabilitation Associates PA (PA)....302 832-8894
2600 Glasgow Ave Ste 210 Newark (19702) ***(G-7314)***
Rehabilitation Consultants Inc....302 478-5240
3411 Silverside Rd 105s Wilmington (19810) ***(G-12367)***
Rehabitation Consultants....302 478-2131
3411 Silverside Rd # 105 Wilmington (19810) ***(G-12368)***
Rehoboth Art League Inc....302 227-8408
12 Dodds Ln Rehoboth Beach (19971) ***(G-8047)***
Rehoboth Bay Mobile Home Cmnty, Rehoboth Beach *Also called Theta Vest Inc* ***(G-8096)***
Rehoboth Bay Sailing Assn....302 227-9008
Highway One Rehoboth Beach (19971) ***(G-8048)***
Rehoboth Beach Country Club....302 227-3811
221 W Side Dr Rehoboth Beach (19971) ***(G-8049)***
Rehoboth Beach Dent....302 226-7960
19643 Blue Bird Ln Rehoboth Beach (19971) ***(G-8050)***
Rehoboth Beach Dewey Beach Cha....302 227-2233
501 Rehoboth Ave Rehoboth Beach (19971) ***(G-8051)***
Rehoboth Beach Historical Soc (PA)....302 227-7310
17 Christian St Rehoboth Beach (19971) ***(G-8052)***
Rehoboth Beach Museum, Rehoboth Beach *Also called Rehoboth Beach Historical Soc* ***(G-8052)***
Rehoboth Beach, De Branch, Rehoboth Beach *Also called Td Bank NA* ***(G-8095)***
Rehoboth Car Wash Inc....302 227-6177
37053 Rehoboth Avenue Ext Rehoboth Beach (19971) ***(G-8053)***
Rehoboth Country Club, Rehoboth Beach *Also called Ronald L Barrows* ***(G-8062)***
Rehoboth Inn LLC....302 226-2410
20494 Coastal Hwy Rehoboth Beach (19971) ***(G-8054)***
Rehoboth Realty Inc....302 227-5000
4157 Highway One Rehoboth Beach (19971) ***(G-8055)***
Rehoboth Shores, Millsboro *Also called Nanticoke Shores Assoc LLC* ***(G-4759)***
Rehoboth Summer Chld Theatre....302 227-6766
20 Baltimore Ave Rehoboth Beach (19971) ***(G-8056)***
Rehrig Penn Logistics Inc....302 659-3337
171 Hemlock Way Smyrna (19977) ***(G-8699)***
Reico Kitchen & Bath, Millsboro *Also called Robinson Export & Import Corp* ***(G-4794)***
Reil Machines USA Inc....905 488-9263
3511 Silverside Rd # 105 Wilmington (19810) ***(G-12369)***
Reilly Janiczek & McDevitt PC....302 777-1700
1013 Centre Rd Ste 210 Wilmington (19805) ***(G-12370)***
Reilly Sweeping Inc....302 738-8961
10 Albe Dr Newark (19702) ***(G-7315)***
Reima Sportswear, Hockessin *Also called Sui Trading Co* ***(G-3151)***
Reis Enterprises LLC....302 740-8382
504 Connor Blvd Bear (19701) ***(G-301)***
Reiver Hyman & Co Inc....302 764-2040
4104 N Market St Wilmington (19802) ***(G-12371)***
Rekindle Family Medicine....302 565-4799
5590 Kirkwood Hwy Wilmington (19808) ***(G-12372)***
Relax Inn....302 875-1554
30702 Sussex Hwy Laurel (19956) ***(G-3279)***
Relaxing Tours LLC....610 905-3852
11546 Adamsville Rd Greenwood (19950) ***(G-2759)***
Reliable Copy Service Inc....302 654-8080
1007 N Orange St Ste 110 Wilmington (19801) ***(G-12373)***
Reliable Home Inspection (PA)....302 455-1200
100 Old Kennett Rd Wilmington (19807) ***(G-12374)***
Reliable Home Services LLC....302 246-6000
1821 Marsh Rd Wilmington (19810) ***(G-12375)***
Reliable Trailer Inc....856 962-7900
1603 Andrews Lake Rd Felton (19943) ***(G-2316)***
Reliance Egleford Upstream LLC....302 472-7437
1007 N Orange St Wilmington (19801) ***(G-12376)***
Reliance Mortgage Company Inc....302 376-7234
101 S Broad St Middletown (19709) ***(G-4215)***
Reliance Trust Company LLC....302 246-5400
200 Bellevue Pkwy Ste 220 Wilmington (19809) ***(G-12377)***
Relig Staffing Inc....312 219-6786
8 The Grn Ste 7460 Dover (19901) ***(G-2022)***
Relytv LLC....213 373-5988
8 The Grn Ste 8422 Dover (19901) ***(G-2023)***
Remarle....215 245-6448
427 Smee Rd Middletown (19709) ***(G-4216)***
Remax 1st Choice LLC....302 378-8700
100 S Broad St Middletown (19709) ***(G-4217)***
Remax By Sea....302 541-5000
R 1 5th D St Bethany Beach (19930) ***(G-427)***
Remax Coast & Country....302 645-0800
16392 Coastal Hwy Lewes (19958) ***(G-3714)***
Remax Sunvest Realty Corp (PA)....302 995-1589
2103a W Newport Pike Wilmington (19804) ***(G-12378)***
Remco Electric....302 422-6833
125 Causey Ave Milford (19963) ***(G-4536)***
Rementer Brothers Inc....302 249-4250
28348 Lwes Georgetown Hwy Milton (19968) ***(G-4956)***
Remline Corp....302 737-7228
456 Corporate Blvd Newark (19702) ***(G-7316)***
Remote Apps, Wilmington *Also called Remote Inc* ***(G-12379)***
Remote Inc....302 636-5440
2711 Centerville Rd # 400 Wilmington (19808) ***(G-12379)***
Renaissance Square LLC....302 943-5118
1534 S Governors Ave B Dover (19904) ***(G-2024)***
Renal Care Center Dover....302 678-5718
655 S Bay Rd Ste 4m Dover (19901) ***(G-2025)***
Renal Care Group Inc....302 678-8744
748 S New St Dover (19904) ***(G-2026)***
Renderapps LLC....919 274-0582
8 The Grn Ste A Dover (19901) ***(G-2027)***
Rendezvous Inc....302 645-7400
16192 Coastal Hwy Lewes (19958) ***(G-3715)***
Rene Delyn Designs Inc....302 736-6070
1744 N Dupont Hwy Dover (19901) ***(G-2028)***
Rene Delyn Hair Design Studio, Dover *Also called Rene Delyn Designs Inc* ***(G-2028)***
Renewable Energy Resources Inc....302 544-0054
105 S Race St Ste A Georgetown (19947) ***(G-2635)***
Renovate LLC....302 378-1768
786 Old School House Rd Middletown (19709) ***(G-4218)***
Rent Big Screens, New Castle *Also called Video Walltronics Inc* ***(G-5817)***
Rent Co Inc....302 674-1177
35 Commerce Way Ste 180 Dover (19904) ***(G-2029)***
Rent-A-Center Inc....302 653-3701
120 E Glenwood Ave Smyrna (19977) ***(G-8700)***
Rent-A-Center Inc....302 322-4335
185 Penn Mart Shopping Ct New Castle (19720) ***(G-5671)***
Rent-A-Center Inc....302 731-7900
19 Chestnut Hill Plz Newark (19713) ***(G-7317)***
Rent-A-Center Inc....302 654-7700
1932 Maryland Ave Wilmington (19805) ***(G-12380)***
Rent-A-Center Inc....302 678-4676
1013 N Dupont Hwy Dover (19901) ***(G-2030)***
Rent-A-Center Inc....302 838-7333
38 Foxhunt Dr 40 Bear (19701) ***(G-302)***
Rent-A-Center Inc....302 674-5060
288 S Dupont Hwy Dover (19901) ***(G-2031)***
Rent-A-Center Inc....302 934-6700
28544 Dupont Blvd Unit 9 Millsboro (19966) ***(G-4788)***

ALPHABETIC SECTION

Rent-A-Center Inc 302 629-8925
  23002 Sussex Hwy Seaford (19973) *(G-8377)*
Rent-A-Center Inc 302 734-3505
  1688 S Governors Ave Dover (19904) *(G-2032)*
Rent-A-Center Inc 302 856-9200
  12 Georgetown Plz Georgetown (19947) *(G-2636)*
Rent-A-Center Inc 302 422-1230
  678 N Dupont Blvd Milford (19963) *(G-4537)*
Rentokil North America Inc 302 733-0851
  1712 Ogletown Rd Newark (19711) *(G-7318)*
Rentokil North America Inc 302 325-2687
  701 Dawson Dr Newark (19713) *(G-7319)*
Rentokil North America Inc 302 337-8100
  18904 Maranatha Way Bridgeville (19933) *(G-519)*
Rentzs Sign Service 302 378-9607
  4676 Dupont Pkwy Townsend (19734) *(G-8818)*
Renu Chiropractic Wellness 302 368-0124
  907 S College Ave Newark (19713) *(G-7320)*
Renzi Group Inc 302 588-2603
  109 Mcdaniel Ave Wilmington (19803) *(G-12381)*
Renzi Rust Inc 302 424-4470
  6722 Griffith Lake Dr Milford (19963) *(G-4538)*
Reporting Solutions LLC 857 284-3583
  102 Cannonball Ln Newark (19702) *(G-7321)*
Repotmecom Inc 301 315-2344
  21657 Paradise Rd Georgetown (19947) *(G-2637)*
Reproductive Associates Del, Newark *Also called Reproductive Associates Del PA (G-7322)*
Reproductive Associates Del PA 302 478-8000
  2700 Silverside Rd Ste 2a Wilmington (19810) *(G-12382)*
Reproductive Associates Del PA (PA) 302 623-4242
  4735 Ogletown Stanton Rd Newark (19713) *(G-7322)*
Reprographics Center Inc 302 328-5019
  298 Churchmans Rd New Castle (19720) *(G-5672)*
Republic Services Inc 302 658-4097
  1420 New York Ave Wilmington (19801) *(G-12383)*
Republican State Committee Del 302 668-1954
  3301 Lancaster Pike 4b Wilmington (19805) *(G-12384)*
RES-Care Inc 302 323-1436
  908 Churchmans Road Ext New Castle (19720) *(G-5673)*
Rescue Printig 302 286-7266
  17 Lynch Farm Dr Newark (19713) *(G-7323)*
Rescue Surgical Solutions LLC 302 722-5877
  1305 Whittaker Rd Newark (19702) *(G-7324)*
Research & Innovation Co 302 281-3600
  200 Bellevue Pkwy Ste 300 Wilmington (19809) *(G-12385)*
Research Office Vice Provost, Newark *Also called University of Delaware (G-7626)*
Reserves At Sawmill 302 424-1910
  100a Valley Dr Milford (19963) *(G-4539)*
Resh LLC 302 543-5469
  206 Jestan Blvd New Castle (19720) *(G-5674)*
Residence Inn By Marriott LLC 302 453-9200
  240 Chapman Rd Newark (19702) *(G-7325)*
Residence Inn Dover 302 677-0777
  600 Jefferic Blvd Dover (19901) *(G-2033)*
Residences At City Center, Wilmington *Also called Luxiasuites LLC (G-11460)*
Resonate Forward LLC 302 893-9504
  503 Ridgeview Dr Hockessin (19707) *(G-3134)*
Resort At Massey's Landing, Millsboro *Also called Masseys Landing Park Inc (G-4736)*
Resort Broadcasting Co LP 302 945-2050
  31549 Dutton Ln Lewes (19958) *(G-3716)*
Resort Custom Homes 302 645-8222
  18355 Coastal Hwy Lewes (19958) *(G-3717)*
Resort Hotel LLC 302 226-1515
  19210 Coastal Hwy Rehoboth Beach (19971) *(G-8057)*
Resort Investigation & Patrol 302 539-5808
  19 Pine St Millville (19970) *(G-4855)*
Resort Poker League 302 604-8706
  38291 Osprey Ct Apt 1168 Selbyville (19975) *(G-8539)*
Resort Quest, Bethany Beach *Also called Sea Colony Tennis Center (G-431)*
Resort Quest Delaware Beaches, Bethany Beach *Also called Resortquest Delaware RE LLC (G-428)*
Resortquest Delaware RE LLC 302 436-1100
  37458 Lion Dr Unit 7 Selbyville (19975) *(G-8540)*
Resortquest Delaware RE LLC (HQ) 302 541-8999
  33546 Market Pl Bethany Beach (19930) *(G-428)*
Resource Center YMCA, Wilmington *Also called Young Mens Christian Associat (G-13333)*
Resource Intl Inc 302 762-4501
  18 Boulden Cir Ste 10 New Castle (19720) *(G-5675)*
Resource Mortgage Corp 302 657-0181
  3301 Lancaster Pike Ste 9 Wilmington (19805) *(G-12386)*
Resources For Human Dev Inc 302 691-7574
  2804 Grubb Rd Wilmington (19810) *(G-12387)*
Resources For Human Dev Inc 302 731-5283
  12 Montrose Dr Newark (19713) *(G-7326)*
Resources For Human Dev Inc 215 951-0300
  262 Chatman Rd Ste 102 Newark (19702) *(G-7327)*
Response Computer Group Inc 302 335-3400
  213 W Liberty Way Milford (19963) *(G-4540)*

Responsible Publishing 609 412-9621
  301 Snuff Mill Rd Wilmington (19807) *(G-12388)*
Restoration Dynamics LLC (PA) 302 378-3729
  215 Rodman St Wilmington (19805) *(G-12389)*
Restoration Guys LLC 302 542-4045
  10971 Pit Rd Seaford (19973) *(G-8378)*
Restore Incorporated 302 655-6257
  3411 Silverside Rd # 104 Wilmington (19810) *(G-12390)*
Resurrection Center (PA) 302 762-8311
  3301 N Market St Ste 1 Wilmington (19802) *(G-12391)*
Resurrection Parish, Wilmington *Also called Diocese of Wilmington (G-10158)*
Retail Services Wis Corp 302 477-0667
  3411 Silverside Rd # 205 Wilmington (19810) *(G-12392)*
Retained Logic Group Inc 302 530-3692
  1070a Shallcross Lake Rd Middletown (19709) *(G-4219)*
Retinovitreous Associates Ltd 302 351-1087
  1523 Concord Pike Ste 100 Wilmington (19803) *(G-12393)*
Retinovitreous Associates Ltd 302 351-1085
  1523 Concord Pike Ste 101 Wilmington (19803) *(G-12394)*
Retired Senior Volunteer 610 565-5563
  12 Yellow Pine Ct Wilmington (19808) *(G-12395)*
Retro Fitness, Wilmington *Also called HB Fitness Delaware Inc (G-10859)*
Retro Fitness 302 276-0828
  835 Pulaski Hwy Bear (19701) *(G-303)*
Retrocode Inc 302 570-0002
  2035 Sunset Lake Rd B2 Newark (19702) *(G-7328)*
Retrosheet Inc 302 731-1570
  20 Sunset Rd Newark (19711) *(G-7329)*
Review 302 831-2771
  325 Academy St Rm 201 Newark (19716) *(G-7330)*
Revnation Ltd Liability Co 202 672-4120
  64 Olde Field Dr Magnolia (19962) *(G-3906)*
Revod Corporation (HQ) 302 477-1795
  1403 Foulk Rd Wilmington (19803) *(G-12396)*
Revolution Recovery Del LLC 302 356-3000
  1101 Lambson Ln New Castle (19720) *(G-5676)*
Rew Material 302 424-2125
  150 Vickers Rd Milford (19963) *(G-4541)*
Rex Auto Body Inc 302 731-4707
  27 North St Newark (19711) *(G-7331)*
Rexmex Drywall LLC 302 343-9140
  449 Gibbs Chapel Rd Hartly (19953) *(G-2939)*
Reybold Construction Corp 302 832-7100
  116 E Scotland Dr Bear (19701) *(G-304)*
Reybold Group of Companies Inc (PA) 302 832-7100
  116 E Scotland Dr Bear (19701) *(G-305)*
Reybold Group of Companies Inc 302 834-2544
  114 E Scotland Dr Bear (19701) *(G-306)*
Reybold Homes Inc 302 834-3000
  2350 Pulaski Hwy Newark (19702) *(G-7332)*
Reyes Rebeca 302 276-9132
  1303 Goldeneye Dr New Castle (19720) *(G-5677)*
Reynolds Metals Company LLC 302 366-0555
  700 Pencader Dr Newark (19702) *(G-7333)*
Rfpc & Wabtec 302 573-3977
  1011 Centre Rd Ste 310 Wilmington (19805) *(G-12397)*
RFS Enterprises Inc 302 888-0143
  202 New Rd Unit 2 Wilmington (19805) *(G-12398)*
Rfx Analyst Inc 302 244-5650
  8 The Grn 5875 Dover (19901) *(G-2034)*
Rgp Holding Inc (PA) 302 661-0117
  1105 N Market St Wilmington (19801) *(G-12399)*
Rh Gallery and Studios 302 218-5182
  1304 Old Lancaster Pike D Hockessin (19707) *(G-3135)*
Rheumatology Consultant Del, Lewes *Also called Jose A Pando MD (G-3576)*
Rhi Refractories Holding Co (HQ) 302 655-6497
  1105 N Market St Ste 1300 Wilmington (19801) *(G-12400)*
Rhino Cabling Group Inc 302 312-1033
  528 Sepia Ct Newark (19702) *(G-7334)*
Rhino Lnngs Del Auto Style Inc 302 368-4660
  841 Old Baltimore Pike Newark (19702) *(G-7335)*
Rhino Smart Publications 302 737-3422
  55 Shull Dr Newark (19711) *(G-7336)*
Rhoades & Morrow LLC 302 427-9500
  1225 N King St Ste 1200 Wilmington (19801) *(G-12401)*
Rhodes Custom Auto Works & Col, Townsend *Also called Rhodes Custom Auto Works Inc (G-8819)*
Rhodes Custom Auto Works Inc 302 378-1701
  3445 Harris Rd Townsend (19734) *(G-8819)*
Rhodeside Inc 505 261-4568
  322 Compton Ct Wilmington (19801) *(G-12402)*
Rhondium Corporation 800 771-4364
  35a The Commons Wilmington (19810) *(G-12403)*
Rhue & Associates Inc 302 422-3058
  628 Mlford Harrington Hwy Milford (19963) *(G-4542)*
Rhue Insurance, Milford *Also called Rhue & Associates Inc (G-4542)*
RI Heritage Inn Topeka Inc 785 271-8903
  1209 N Orange St Wilmington (19801) *(G-12404)*
Ribodynamics LLC 518 339-6605
  2711 Centerville Rd # 400 Wilmington (19808) *(G-12405)*

Rich Hebert & Associates 202 255-3474
38027 Fenwick Shoals Blvd Selbyville (19975) ***(G-8541)***
Richard A Parsons Agency Inc 302 674-2810
57 Saulsbury Rd Ste C Dover (19904) ***(G-2035)***
Richard Addington Co 302 422-2668
316 N Rehoboth Blvd Milford (19963) ***(G-4543)***
Richard Allen Coalition 302 258-7182
16950 Deer Forest Rd Georgetown (19947) ***(G-2638)***
Richard Belotti 302 934-7585
22988 Lawson Rd Georgetown (19947) ***(G-2639)***
Richard Bryan 302 645-6100
117 Savannah Rd Lewes (19958) ***(G-3718)***
Richard C McKay DC PA 302 368-1300
54 Omega Dr Bldg F54 Newark (19713) ***(G-7337)***
Richard D Whaley Cnstr LLC 302 934-9525
29952 Lewis Rd Millsboro (19966) ***(G-4789)***
Richard E Chodroff DMD 302 995-6979
3105 Limestone Rd Ste 203 Wilmington (19808) ***(G-12406)***
Richard E Small Inc 302 875-7199
1130 S Central Ave Laurel (19956) ***(G-3280)***
Richard Earl Fisher 302 598-1957
820 Kiamensi Rd Wilmington (19804) ***(G-12407)***
Richard Hrrmann Strbilders Inc 302 654-4329
500 Robinson Ln Wilmington (19805) ***(G-12408)***
Richard J Leach Upholstery 302 764-2067
506 Grove Rd Wilmington (19807) ***(G-12409)***
Richard J Tananis DDS LLC 302 875-4271
10250 Stone Creek Dr # 1 Laurel (19956) ***(G-3281)***
Richard J Wadsley 302 545-7162
108 Sleepy Hollow Dr Middletown (19709) ***(G-4220)***
Richard L Sapp Farms LLC 302 684-4727
12698 Union Street Ext Milton (19968) ***(G-4957)***
Richard L Sherry MD (PA) 302 475-1880
2500 Grubb Rd Ste 234 Wilmington (19810) ***(G-12410)***
Richard L Sherry MD 302 836-3937
2600 Glasgow Ave Ste 206 Newark (19702) ***(G-7338)***
Richard L Todd PHD 302 853-0559
28312 Lwes Georgetown Hwy Milton (19968) ***(G-4958)***
Richard M White Welding 302 684-4461
14443 Collins St Milton (19968) ***(G-4959)***
Richard Margolin Apothecary, Wilmington *Also called Prescription Center Inc* ***(G-12221)***
Richard S Cobb Esquire 302 467-4430
919 N Market St Ste 600 Wilmington (19801) ***(G-12411)***
Richard S Jacobs DDS 302 792-2648
3716 Philadelphia Pike Claymont (19703) ***(G-800)***
Richard Sapp Farms 302 684-4727
12698 Union Street Ext Milton (19968) ***(G-4960)***
Richard Williamson, Dover *Also called J R Williamson DDS* ***(G-1688)***
Richard Woinski Trucking 302 644-1579
17157 Minos Conaway Rd Lewes (19958) ***(G-3719)***
Richard Y Johnson & Son Inc 302 422-3732
18404 Johnson Rd Lincoln (19960) ***(G-3865)***
Richards Investment Group Corp 302 399-0450
381 Grayton Dr Smyrna (19977) ***(G-8701)***
Richards Layton & Finger P A 302 651-7700
Uknown Wilmington (19801) ***(G-12412)***
Richards Layton & Finger P A 302 651-7700
1 Rodney Sq 920 N King St Wilmington (19801) ***(G-12413)***
Richardson Park Community 302 428-1247
701 S Maryland Ave Wilmington (19804) ***(G-12414)***
Richert Inc (PA) 302 684-0696
2836 S Bay Shore Dr Milton (19968) ***(G-4961)***
Richman Wealth Management 443 536-6936
19468 Manchester Dr Rehoboth Beach (19971) ***(G-8058)***
Richmonds Automotive, Newark *Also called Doug Richmonds Body Shop* ***(G-6463)***
Rickards Auto Body 302 934-9600
28656 Dupont Blvd Millsboro (19966) ***(G-4790)***
Ricks Fitness & Health Inc 302 684-0316
22893 Neptune Rd Milton (19968) ***(G-4962)***
Ricoh Usa Inc 302 737-8000
131 Continental Dr # 109 Newark (19713) ***(G-7339)***
Ricoh Usa Inc 302 573-3562
1 Commerce St Ste 850 Wilmington (19801) ***(G-12415)***
Ricore Inc 302 656-8158
13 Rizzo Ave New Castle (19720) ***(G-5678)***
Riddles Masonry 302 238-7225
22689 Riddle Rd Millsboro (19966) ***(G-4791)***
Riders App Inc 347 484-4344
1 Commerce St 1 # 1 Wilmington (19801) ***(G-12416)***
Ridgaway Philips of Delaware 302 323-1436
908 Churchmans Road Ext B New Castle (19720) ***(G-5679)***
Ridgewood Electric Power Tr V 302 888-7444
1314 N King St Wilmington (19801) ***(G-12417)***
Ridgewood Electric Pwr Tr III 302 888-7444
1314 N King St Wilmington (19801) ***(G-12418)***
Ridrodsky & Long PA (PA) 302 691-8822
300 Delaware Ave Ste LI Wilmington (19801) ***(G-12419)***
Riemel of Delaware LLC 302 998-5806
460 B And O Ln Wilmington (19804) ***(G-12420)***
Rigbys Karate Academy 302 735-9637
560 Otis Dr Dover (19901) ***(G-2036)***
Rigel Energy Group LLC 888 624-9844
300 Delaware Ave Wilmington (19801) ***(G-12421)***
Riggin Group 302 235-2903
530 Schoolhouse Rd Ste E Hockessin (19707) ***(G-3136)***
Right At Home 302 652-1550
1500 N French St Wilmington (19801) ***(G-12422)***
Right Property MGT Co LLC (PA) 302 227-1155
20245 Bay Vista Rd # 205 Rehoboth Beach (19971) ***(G-8059)***
Right Way Flagging and Sign Co 302 698-5229
173 Brenda Ln Ste C Camden Wyoming (19934) ***(G-653)***
Rigid Builders LLC 732 425-3443
24491 Blackberry Dr Georgetown (19947) ***(G-2640)***
Riley Electric 302 533-5918
1235 Old Coochs Bridge Rd Newark (19713) ***(G-7340)***
Riley Electric Inc 302 276-3581
1235 Old Coochs Bridge Rd Newark (19713) ***(G-7341)***
Rinehimer Auto Works, Newark *Also called Rinehimer Body Shop Inc* ***(G-7342)***
Rinehimer Body Shop Inc 302 737-7350
6 Mill Park Ct Newark (19713) ***(G-7342)***
Rippl Labs Inc (PA) 551 427-1997
2711 Centerville Rd # 400 Wilmington (19808) ***(G-12423)***
Rising Star Communication 302 462-5474
14830 Josephs Rd Seaford (19973) ***(G-8379)***
Rising Star Preschool, Wilmington *Also called Rising Stars Child Care Inc* ***(G-12424)***
Rising Stars Child Care Inc 302 998-7682
415 Milmar Rd Wilmington (19804) ***(G-12424)***
Rising Sunset Publishing LLC 877 231-5425
200 Continental Dr # 401 Newark (19713) ***(G-7343)***
Risingplatformproductions LLC 660 283-0183
2035 Sunset Lake Rd B2 Newark (19702) ***(G-7344)***
Risk Consultan 302 655-3350
720 Nottingham Rd Wilmington (19805) ***(G-12425)***
Rita Lynn Inc 302 422-3904
501 Point Dr Milford (19963) ***(G-4544)***
Ritchie Sawyer Corporation (PA) 302 475-1971
2502 Pin Oak Dr Wilmington (19810) ***(G-12426)***
Rite Way Distributors (PA) 302 535-8507
7385 S Dupont Hwy Felton (19943) ***(G-2317)***
Rittenhouse Motor Co Inc 302 731-5059
217 Hullihen Dr Newark (19711) ***(G-7345)***
Rivas Ulises 302 454-8595
31 Albe Dr Ste 3 Newark (19702) ***(G-7346)***
Rivas Ironworks, Newark *Also called Rivas Ulises* ***(G-7346)***
River Asphalt LLC 302 934-0881
30548 Thorogoods Rd Dagsboro (19939) ***(G-932)***
Rivera Transportation Inc 302 258-9023
205 W 7th St Laurel (19956) ***(G-3282)***
Riverdale Park LLC 302 945-2475
28301 Chief Rd Millsboro (19966) ***(G-4792)***
Riverfront Dev Corp Del 302 425-4890
815 Justison St Ste D Wilmington (19801) ***(G-12427)***
Riverfront Development Corp 302 425-4890
815 Justison St Ste D Wilmington (19801) ***(G-12428)***
Riverside Healthcare Center 302 764-2615
700 W Lea Blvd Ste 102 Wilmington (19802) ***(G-12429)***
Riverside Specialty Chem Inc 212 769-3440
400 Carson Dr Bear (19701) ***(G-307)***
Riverstone Financial II LLC 302 295-5310
901 N Market St Ste 463 Wilmington (19801) ***(G-12430)***
Rk Advisors LLC 302 561-5258
104 Country Center Ln Hockessin (19707) ***(G-3137)***
RK&k, Wilmington *Also called Rummel Klepper & Kahl LLP* ***(G-12493)***
Rkb Funeral Inc Trading, Millsboro *Also called Watson Funeral Home Inc* ***(G-4824)***
Rkj Construction Inc 302 690-0959
2252 Saint James Dr Wilmington (19808) ***(G-12431)***
Rlk Press Inc 267 565-5138
3511 Silverside Rd Wilmington (19810) ***(G-12432)***
Rls Associates, Wilmington *Also called Mergers Acqstons Strtegies LLC* ***(G-11640)***
Rmch, Wilmington *Also called Financial Services* ***(G-10541)***
Rmv Workforce Corp 302 408-1061
124 Broadkill Rd Ste 380 Milton (19968) ***(G-4963)***
Rnh Installation 302 731-8900
42 Albe Dr Ste E Newark (19702) ***(G-7347)***
Road & Rail Services Inc 302 731-2552
502 S College Ave Ste C Newark (19713) ***(G-7348)***
Road Site Construction Inc 302 645-1922
16192 Coastal Hwy Lewes (19958) ***(G-3720)***
Roadrunner Express Inc 302 426-9551
21 Millside Dr Wilmington (19801) ***(G-12433)***
Robbins Nest Farm Inc 302 422-4722
16900 Robbins Nest Rd Ellendale (19941) ***(G-2263)***
Robert A Chagnon 302 489-1932
726 Loveville Rd Apt 126 Hockessin (19707) ***(G-3138)***
Robert A Heinle M D 302 651-6400
1600 Rockland Rd Wilmington (19803) ***(G-12434)***
Robert A Penna DMD 302 623-4060
4735 Ogletown Stanton Rd # 1104 Newark (19713) ***(G-7349)***

Robert B Gregg 302 994-9300
301 S Dupont Rd Newport (19804) *(G-7752)*
Robert Bayly 302 846-9752
Dual Hwy Rr 13 Laurel (19956) *(G-3283)*
Robert Bird 302 654-4003
1701 Shallcross Ave Ste A Wilmington (19806) *(G-12435)*
Robert Bryan 302 875-5099
4679 Old Sharptown Rd Laurel (19956) *(G-3284)*
Robert C Director DDS 302 658-7358
1110 N Bancroft Pkwy # 2 Wilmington (19805) *(G-12436)*
Robert C Peoples Inc 302 834-5268
2750 Wrangle Hill Rd Bear (19701) *(G-308)*
Robert C Thompson 302 492-1053
671 Bryants Corner Rd Hartly (19953) *(G-2940)*
Robert Donlick MD 302 653-8916
16 Garrisons Cir Smyrna (19977) *(G-8702)*
Robert Elgart Automotive 800 220-7777
698 Pencader Dr Newark (19702) *(G-7350)*
Robert F Mullen Insurance Agcy 302 322-5331
887 Pulaski Hwy Bear (19701) *(G-309)*
Robert Fickling 980 422-4754
2307 Paulwynn Rd Wilmington (19810) *(G-12437)*
Robert G Burke Painting Co 302 998-2200
1614 E Ayre St Wilmington (19804) *(G-12438)*
Robert G Starkey CPA 302 422-0108
1043 N Walnut St Milford (19963) *(G-4545)*
Robert Gears 302 834-7487
34696 Daisey Rd Frankford (19945) *(G-2383)*
Robert Grant Inc 302 422-6090
606 Mlford Harrington Hwy Milford (19963) *(G-4546)*
Robert Half International Inc 302 252-3162
500 Delaware Ave Ste 700 Wilmington (19801) *(G-12439)*
Robert Hoyt & Co 302 934-6688
218 N Dupont Millsboro (19966) *(G-4793)*
Robert J Peoples Inc 302 984-2017
3020 Bowlarama Dr New Castle (19720) *(G-5680)*
Robert J Peoples Inc 302 322-0595
1 Westmoreland Ave Apt A Wilmington (19804) *(G-12440)*
Robert J Seward and Son 302 378-9414
134 Ebenezer Church Rd Townsend (19734) *(G-8820)*
Robert J Varipapa MD 302 678-8100
1074 S State St Dover (19901) *(G-2037)*
Robert Keating Excavating 302 239-4670
1610 Old Wilmington Rd Hockessin (19707) *(G-3139)*
Robert Larimore 302 730-8682
328 Moose Lodge Rd Camden Wyoming (19934) *(G-654)*
Robert McMann 302 329-9413
13259 Sunland Dr Milton (19968) *(G-4964)*
Robert Mullin 302 322-9002
208 N Spring Valley Rd Wilmington (19807) *(G-12441)*
Robert Oxygen Company 33, Seaford *Also called Roberts Oxygen Company Inc (G-8380)*
Robert P Hart DDS 302 328-1513
92 Reads Way Ste 101 New Castle (19720) *(G-5681)*
Robert S Callahan MD PA 302 731-0942
32 Omega Dr J Newark (19713) *(G-7351)*
Robert T Jones & Foard Inc 302 731-4627
122 W Main St Newark (19711) *(G-7352)*
Robert T Minner Jr 302 422-9206
2181 Deep Grass Ln Greenwood (19950) *(G-2760)*
Roberto A Uribe PHD 302 524-0814
300 Creek View Rd Ste 101 Newark (19711) *(G-7353)*
Roberts Wilbert 215 867-5655
303 E Harvest Ln Middletown (19709) *(G-4221)*
Roberts Const Co 302 335-4141
Frnt Main Sts Frederica (19946) *(G-2411)*
Roberts Electric Inc 302 233-3017
165 Barkers Landing Rd Magnolia (19962) *(G-3907)*
Roberts Oxygen Company Inc 302 337-9666
22785 Sussex Hwy 102 Seaford (19973) *(G-8380)*
Roberts Property MGT LLC 302 537-5371
107 Canal Rd Bethany Beach (19930) *(G-429)*
Robin S Wright 302 249-2105
19305 Beaver Dam Rd Lewes (19958) *(G-3721)*
Robino Management Group Inc 302 734-2944
1300 S Farmview Dr Bldg O Dover (19904) *(G-2038)*
Robino Management Group Inc 302 633-6001
5189 W Woodmill Dr 30a Wilmington (19808) *(G-12442)*
Robins Hair & Tanning 302 529-9000
2716 Naamans Rd Wilmington (19810) *(G-12443)*
Robinson Grayson and Ward PA 302 655-6262
910 Foulk Rd Ste 200 Wilmington (19803) *(G-12444)*
Robinson & Cook Eyes Surgical 302 645-2300
18791 John J Williams Hwy Rehoboth Beach (19971) *(G-8060)*
Robinson and Grayson, Wilmington *Also called Robinson Grayson and Ward PA (G-12444)*
Robinson Export & Import Corp 410 219-7200
28412 Dupont Blvd Ste 106 Millsboro (19966) *(G-4794)*
Robinson House, The, Claymont *Also called Historical & Cultural Afairs (G-761)*
Robinson Insurance Agency, Seaford *Also called Robinson Realestate (G-8381)*
Robinson Realestate 302 629-4574
605 N Hall St Seaford (19973) *(G-8381)*
Robinsons Sewage Disposial, Frankford *Also called James Powell (G-2369)*
Robotick Media, Dover *Also called Robotick New Media Network LLC (G-2039)*
Robotick New Media Network LLC 213 219-3083
8 The Grn Ste A Dover (19901) *(G-2039)*
Rocco Automotive, Wilmington *Also called Roccos Automotive Service (G-12445)*
Roccos Automotive Service 302 998-2234
2379 Limestone Rd Wilmington (19808) *(G-12445)*
Rochelle E Haas M D 302 651-5600
1600 Rockland Rd Wilmington (19803) *(G-12446)*
Rock Bottom Paving Inc 800 728-3160
8191 S Dupont Hwy Felton (19943) *(G-2318)*
Rock Manor Golf Course 302 295-1400
1319 Carruthers Ln Wilmington (19803) *(G-12447)*
Rock Solid Contracting and Dev 302 655-8250
1213 B St Wilmington (19801) *(G-12448)*
Rock Solid Servicing LLC 302 233-2569
89 Mandrake Dr Magnolia (19962) *(G-3908)*
Rocket Signs 302 645-1425
18388 Coastal Hwy Unit 4 Lewes (19958) *(G-3722)*
Rockey & Associates Inc 610 640-4880
18306 Coastal Hwy Lewes (19958) *(G-3723)*
Rockford Center 302 996-5480
100 Rockford Dr Newark (19713) *(G-7354)*
Rockford Ice 302 478-7280
1218 Glenside Ave Wilmington (19803) *(G-12449)*
Rockford Map Gallery LLC 302 740-1851
1800 Lovering Ave Wilmington (19806) *(G-12450)*
Rockford Park Condominium Home 302 658-7842
2302 Riddle Ave Ofc Wilmington (19806) *(G-12451)*
Rockland Builders Inc 302 995-6800
1605 E Ayre St Wilmington (19804) *(G-12452)*
Rockland Dental Associates, Wilmington *Also called H Dean McSpadden DDS (G-10808)*
Rockland Place 302 777-3099
1519 Rockland Rd Wilmington (19803) *(G-12453)*
Rockland Sports LLC 302 654-4435
1001 Rockland Rd Wilmington (19803) *(G-12454)*
Rockland Surgery Center LP 302 999-0200
2710 Centerville Rd # 100 Wilmington (19808) *(G-12455)*
Rockledge Global Partners Ltd 800 659-1102
1000 N West St Ste 1200 Wilmington (19801) *(G-12456)*
Rockteam, Lewes *Also called Rockey & Associates Inc (G-3723)*
Rockwood Apartments 302 832-8823
100 Cindy Dr Newark (19702) *(G-7355)*
Rockwood Financial Group Inc 302 791-0237
228 Philadelphia Pike A Wilmington (19809) *(G-12457)*
Rockwood Museum 302 761-4340
610 Shipley Rd Wilmington (19809) *(G-12458)*
Rocky Lac LLC 302 440-5561
1012 San Remo Ct Ste A Bear (19701) *(G-310)*
Rocky Mtn Elk Foundation Inc 302 697-3621
34 Milbourn Manor Dr Camden Wyoming (19934) *(G-655)*
Rocla Concrete Tie Inc 302 836-5304
268 E Scotland Dr Bear (19701) *(G-311)*
Rod-AES Surveryors Co 302 993-1059
3913 Old Capitol Trl Wilmington (19808) *(G-12459)*
Rodeway Inn, New Castle *Also called Dutch Village Motel Inc (G-5268)*
Rodeway Inn 302 227-0401
19604 Blue Bird Ln Rehoboth Beach (19971) *(G-8061)*
Rodney Baltazar 302 283-3300
120 Sandhill Dr Middletown (19709) *(G-4222)*
Rodney Rbnsn Ldscp Archts Inc 302 888-1544
30 Hill Rd Wilmington (19806) *(G-12460)*
Rodney Square Associates 302 652-1536
1 Rodney Sq Wilmington (19801) *(G-12461)*
Rodney Trust Co 302 737-1205
121 Continental Dr # 107 Newark (19713) *(G-7356)*
Rodney's Animal Crackers, Rehoboth Beach *Also called Stauffer Family LLC (G-8087)*
Rodriguez Marieve O Dmd PA 302 655-5862
1407 Foulk Rd Wilmington (19803) *(G-12462)*
Roeberg Moore & Associates PA 302 658-4757
910 Gilpin Ave Wilmington (19806) *(G-12463)*
Roger Alexander MD 302 422-5223
306 Lakeview Ave Milford (19963) *(G-4547)*
Roger C Allen DC 302 734-9824
884 Walker Rd Ste A Dover (19904) *(G-2040)*
Roger D Anderson 302 652-8400
800 Delaware Ave Ste 1000 Wilmington (19801) *(G-12464)*
Roger Rullo Brick Pointing 302 378-8100
915 Waterlilly Ln Middletown (19709) *(G-4223)*
Rogers Corporation 302 834-2100
1100 Governor Lea Rd Bear (19701) *(G-312)*
Rogers Graphics Inc (PA) 302 856-0028
32 Bridgeville Rd Georgetown (19947) *(G-2641)*
Rogers Graphics Inc 302 422-6694
26836 Lwes Georgetown Hwy Harbeson (19951) *(G-2797)*
Rogers Sign Company Inc 302 684-8338
110 Lavinia St Milton (19968) *(G-4965)*
Rogue Elephants LLC 979 264-2845
16192 Coastal Hwy Lewes (19958) *(G-3724)*

ALPHABETIC

(PA)=Parent Co (HQ)=Headquarters (DH)=Div Headquarters
2020 Harris Directory of Delaware Businesses
715

Rohm and Haas Co, Newark *Also called Rohm Haas Electronic Mtls LLC* ***(G-7359)***
Rohm and Haas Electronic (HQ)....302 366-0500
451 Bellevue Rd Newark (19713) ***(G-7357)***
Rohm Haas Electronic Mtls LLC....302 366-0500
451 Bellevue Rd Newark (19713) ***(G-7358)***
Rohm Haas Electronic Mtls LLC....302 366-0500
231 Lake Dr Newark (19702) ***(G-7359)***
Rohma Inc....909 234-5381
2035 Sunset Lake Rd B2 Newark (19702) ***(G-7360)***
Roizman & Associates Inc....302 426-9688
506 E 5th St Wilmington (19801) ***(G-12465)***
Roll-A-Bout Corporation....302 736-6151
3240 Barratts Chapel Rd Frederica (19946) ***(G-2412)***
Roller Service Corporation (PA)....302 737-5000
23 Mcmillan Way Newark (19713) ***(G-7361)***
Rollins Leasing LLC (HQ)....302 426-2700
2200 Concord Pike Wilmington (19803) ***(G-12466)***
Roman Industries Inc....302 420-9420
2421 E Heather Rd Wilmington (19803) ***(G-12467)***
Romano Masonry Inc....302 368-4155
322 Markus Ct Ste A Newark (19713) ***(G-7362)***
Romantic Gardens, Wilmington *Also called Renzi Group Inc* ***(G-12381)***
Romer Labs Technology Inc....855 337-6637
130 Sandy Dr Newark (19713) ***(G-7363)***
Romie LLC....866 698-0052
300 Delaware Ave Ste 210a Wilmington (19801) ***(G-12468)***
Rommel Cycles LLC (PA)....302 658-8800
450 Stadium St Smyrna (19977) ***(G-8703)***
Ron Ell Hardware Inc....302 328-8997
16 Darlington Rd New Castle (19720) ***(G-5682)***
Ronald D Jr Attorney At Law....302 856-9860
215 E Market St Georgetown (19947) ***(G-2642)***
Ronald L Barrows....302 227-3616
184 E Side Dr Rehoboth Beach (19971) ***(G-8062)***
Ronald McDonald House Delaware....302 428-5299
1901 Rockland Rd Wilmington (19803) ***(G-12469)***
Ronald Midaugh....410 860-1040
1030 Forrest Ave Ste 104 Dover (19904) ***(G-2041)***
Ronald P Wilson....302 539-4139
Rr 2 Box 182 Frankford (19945) ***(G-2384)***
Ronald S Pogach Od RES....302 994-3300
6 Ironwood Dr Newark (19711) ***(G-7364)***
Ronald W Peacock Inc....302 571-9313
110 Matthes Ave Wilmington (19804) ***(G-12470)***
Ronan Gill LLC....877 549-7712
717 N Union St Pmb 6 Wilmington (19805) ***(G-12471)***
Rondo Specialty Foods Ltd....800 724-6636
118 Quigley Blvd New Castle (19720) ***(G-5683)***
Ronnies Auto Repairs Inc (PA)....302 994-4703
4 S Mary St Wilmington (19804) ***(G-12472)***
Rons Mobile Home Sales Inc....302 398-9166
17959 S Dupont Hwy Harrington (19952) ***(G-2880)***
Rooah LLC....305 233-7557
768 Townsend Blvd Ste 3 Dover (19901) ***(G-2042)***
Roofers Inc....302 995-7027
404 Meco Dr Wilmington (19804) ***(G-12473)***
Rookery Golf Courses South....302 422-7010
6152 S Rehoboth Blvd Milford (19963) ***(G-4548)***
Rookery, The, Milton *Also called Greens At Broadview LLC* ***(G-4910)***
Roots Landscaping, Selbyville *Also called William J Winkler* ***(G-8554)***
Rope-It Golf LLC....305 767-3481
3 River Rd Wilmington (19809) ***(G-12474)***
Rosa M Custis....302 934-0541
436 Old Landing Rd Millsboro (19966) ***(G-4795)***
Rosalina Dejesus-Jiloca MD....302 629-4238
9835 Warrens Way Seaford (19973) ***(G-8382)***
Rosas Greek Btq....302 678-2147
338 Blue Heron Rd Dover (19904) ***(G-2043)***
Rosauri Builders & Remodelers....302 234-8464
1797 Yeatmans Mill Rd Hockessin (19707) ***(G-3140)***
Rose Health Center Inc....302 441-5987
31347 Point Cir Lewes (19958) ***(G-3725)***
Rose Hill Community Center....302 656-8513
19 Lambson Ln New Castle (19720) ***(G-5684)***
Rosen Moss Snyder Bleefeld....302 475-8060
501 Silverside Rd Ste 33 Wilmington (19809) ***(G-12475)***
Rosenthal Chiropractic Offs PA (PA)....302 999-0633
507 S Maryland Ave Wilmington (19804) ***(G-12476)***
Rosenthal Monhait Goddess PA....302 656-4433
919 N Market St Ste 1401 Wilmington (19801) ***(G-12477)***
Rosle U S A Corp....302 326-4801
802 Centerpoint Blvd New Castle (19720) ***(G-5685)***
Rosner Law Group LLC....302 295-4877
824 N Market St Ste 810 Wilmington (19801) ***(G-12478)***
Ross Aronstam & Moritz LLP....302 576-1600
100 S West St Wilmington (19801) ***(G-12479)***
Ross Bicycles LLC (PA)....888 392-5628
16192 Coastal Hwy Lewes (19958) ***(G-3726)***
Ross W Burnam CPA PA....302 453-8161
625 Barksdale Rd Ste 107 Newark (19711) ***(G-7365)***
Rossi Auto Body Inc....302 999-7707
512 Belmont Ave Wilmington (19804) ***(G-12480)***
Rotary International....302 378-2488
109 Stephen Ct Middletown (19709) ***(G-4224)***
Rotary International....302 738-0827
307 Stamford Dr Newark (19711) ***(G-7366)***
Rotary International....302 227-5862
58 Rolling Rd Rehoboth Beach (19971) ***(G-8063)***
Roto-Rooter Services Company....302 659-7637
1001 Dawson Dr Ste 3 Newark (19713) ***(G-7367)***
Rouse Insurance and Fincl LL....302 678-2223
1252 Forrest Ave Dover (19904) ***(G-2044)***
Route 13 Outlet Market....302 875-4800
11290 Trussum Pond Rd Laurel (19956) ***(G-3285)***
Route 24 Animal Hospital....302 945-2330
26984 John J Williams Hwy Millsboro (19966) ***(G-4796)***
Route 9 Auto Center....302 856-3941
23422 Park Ave Georgetown (19947) ***(G-2643)***
Routzhan Jessman....302 398-4206
17010 S Dupont Hwy Harrington (19952) ***(G-2881)***
Rovier LLC....302 832-6726
3 Dublin Dr Newark (19702) ***(G-7368)***
Rowe Industries Inc....443 458-5569
21649 Cedar Creek Ave Georgetown (19947) ***(G-2644)***
Roxlor LLC....302 778-4166
1013 Centre Rd Ste 106 Wilmington (19805) ***(G-12481)***
Roy Covey....302 995-2900
701 Kirkwood Hwy Wilmington (19805) ***(G-12482)***
Royal Bank America Leasing LLC....302 529-5984
1000 Rocky Run Pkwy Wilmington (19803) ***(G-12483)***
Royal Bank America Leasing LLC....302 798-1790
20 Montchanin Rd Ste 100 Wilmington (19807) ***(G-12484)***
Royal Cleaners....302 478-0955
3914 Concord Pike Wilmington (19803) ***(G-12485)***
Royal Era LLC....484 574-0260
406 Suburban Dr 188 Newark (19711) ***(G-7369)***
Royal Hair Design LLC....302 312-4569
129 E Glenwood Ave Smyrna (19977) ***(G-8704)***
Royal Instruments Inc....302 328-5900
266 Quigley Blvd New Castle (19720) ***(G-5686)***
Royal Mission & Ministries....302 249-8863
9751 Randall St Laurel (19956) ***(G-3286)***
Royal Pest Management....302 322-3600
53 Mccullough Dr New Castle (19720) ***(G-5687)***
Royal Pest Solutions Inc....302 322-6665
53 Mccullough Dr New Castle (19720) ***(G-5688)***
Royal Termite & Pest Ctrl Inc....302 322-3600
53 Mccullough Dr New Castle (19720) ***(G-5689)***
Royal Termite and Pest Control, New Castle *Also called Royal Termite & Pest Ctrl Inc* ***(G-5689)***
Royal Treatments....302 722-6733
14 S Main St Smyrna (19977) ***(G-8705)***
Roys Electrical Service Inc....302 674-3199
543 Main St Cheswold (19936) ***(G-663)***
Rp Management Inc....302 798-6878
2610 Philadelphia Pike B6 Claymont (19703) ***(G-801)***
Rp New Churchmans, New Castle *Also called Community Alternatives Ind Inc* ***(G-5187)***
Rp Ventures and Holdings Inc (PA)....410 398-3000
9 Bellecor Dr New Castle (19720) ***(G-5690)***
Rpj Waste Services Inc....302 653-9999
453 Pier Head Blvd Smyrna (19977) ***(G-8706)***
RPR Environmental Solutions....302 362-0687
20758 Jefferson Rd Lincoln (19960) ***(G-3866)***
RS Widdoes and Son Inc....302 764-7455
204 Channel Rd Wilmington (19809) ***(G-12486)***
Rsl Investors Inc....302 478-5142
1105 Market Ste Ste 1230 Wilmington (19899) ***(G-12487)***
Rt Minner & Sons, Greenwood *Also called Robert T Minner Jr* ***(G-2760)***
Rt Stover, New Castle *Also called PJ Fitzpatrick Inc* ***(G-5623)***
Rtcp Farm Partnership....302 584-3584
1095 Hollering Hill Rd Camden Wyoming (19934) ***(G-656)***
Ru Inc....917 346-0285
2711 Centerville Rd Wilmington (19808) ***(G-12488)***
Ruan T119....302 376-9300
819 Middletown Warwick Rd Middletown (19709) ***(G-4225)***
Ruan Transport Corporation....302 696-3270
50 Patriot Dr Middletown (19709) ***(G-4226)***
Rubio Construction LLC....302 377-0353
6 E 40th St Wilmington (19802) ***(G-12489)***
Ruby Industrial Tech LLC....302 674-2943
521 Otis Dr Dover (19901) ***(G-2045)***
Rudlyn Inc....302 764-5677
3900 Governor Printz Blvd Wilmington (19802) ***(G-12490)***
Rudy Auto Body, Wilmington *Also called Rudlyn Inc* ***(G-12490)***
Rudy Marine Inc (PA)....302 999-8735
411 S Maryland Ave Wilmington (19804) ***(G-12491)***
Rudy's Outboard Service, Wilmington *Also called Rudy Marine Inc* ***(G-12491)***
Rukket LLC....855 478-5538
5006 Kennett Pike Wilmington (19807) ***(G-12492)***

Rukket Sports, Wilmington *Also called Rukket LLC (G-12492)*
Rummel Klepper & Kahl LLP......302 468-4880
1 Riverwal Ctr 110 S Po Wilmington (19801) *(G-12493)*
Rumpstich Machine Works Inc......302 422-4816
305 S Rehoboth Blvd Milford (19963) *(G-4549)*
Runway Liquidation LLC......305 451-1481
2500 Grubb Rd Ste 234 Wilmington (19810) *(G-12494)*
Rush Realty LLC......302 219-6707
395 Southern View Dr Smyrna (19977) *(G-8707)*
Russell A Paulus & Son Inc......302 998-4494
193 Christina Landing Dr Wilmington (19801) *(G-12495)*
Russell Associates Inc......443 992-5777
560 Peoples Plz 125 Newark (19702) *(G-7370)*
Russell D Earnest & Assoc......302 659-0730
P.O. Box 1132 Clayton (19938) *(G-870)*
Russell D Earnest Assoc......302 659-0730
1278 Fords Corner Rd Hartly (19953) *(G-2941)*
Russell J Tibbetts DDS PA......302 479-5959
3516 Silverside Rd Ste 17 Wilmington (19810) *(G-12496)*
Russell Plywood Inc......302 689-0137
3 Mccullough Dr New Castle (19720) *(G-5691)*
Russo Brothers Inc......302 764-5562
16 White Oak Rd Wilmington (19809) *(G-12497)*
Russo Mary Claire Real Estate......302 529-2653
3211 Cardiff Dr Wilmington (19810) *(G-12498)*
Ruth N Dorsey Relief Shelter, Dover *Also called Whatcoat Social Service Agency (G-2220)*
Ruthie Franczek......302 659-1000
6827 Underwoods Corner Rd Smyrna (19977) *(G-8708)*
Rutkoske Bros Inc......302 378-8181
819 Middletown Warwick Rd Middletown (19709) *(G-4227)*
Rutledge Dental Assoc Inc......302 378-8705
410 N Cass St Middletown (19709) *(G-4228)*
Rw Greer Inc......302 764-0376
203 Philadelphia Pike Wilmington (19809) *(G-12499)*
Rw Heating & Air Inc......302 856-4330
20801 Doddtown Rd Harbeson (19951) *(G-2798)*
Rwm Embroidery & More LLC......302 653-8384
19 Village Sq Smyrna (19977) *(G-8709)*
Ryan C Gough MD......302 677-6527
300 Tuskegee Blvd Dover (19902) *(G-2046)*
Ryan Homes, Newark *Also called Nvr Inc (G-7140)*
Ryan Media Lab Inc......302 360-8847
31794 Carneros Ave Lewes (19958) *(G-3727)*
Ryder, Rehoboth Beach *Also called Budget Truck Rental LLC (G-7880)*
Ryder Truck Rental Inc......302 571-4210
300 S Madison St Wilmington (19801) *(G-12500)*
Ryder Truck Rental Inc......302 798-1472
6605 Governor Printz Blvd Wilmington (19809) *(G-12501)*
Ryder Truck Rental Inc......302 995-9607
750 Christiana Stanton Rd Newark (19713) *(G-7371)*
Ryerson Geralyn......302 547-3060
1601 Milltown Rd Ste 8 Wilmington (19808) *(G-12502)*
Ryland Funeral Home Inc......302 764-7711
9 W 30th St Lowr Ste Wilmington (19802) *(G-12503)*
S & A Holding Associates Inc......302 479-8314
4737 Concord Pike Ste 261 Wilmington (19803) *(G-12504)*
S & B Pro Security LLC......800 841-9907
1300 E Lebanon Rd Dover (19901) *(G-2047)*
S & F Monuments......302 722-8045
635 Churchmans Rd Newark (19702) *(G-7372)*
S & H Enterprises Inc......302 999-9911
112 Water St Wilmington (19804) *(G-12505)*
S & K Enterprises Inc......302 292-1250
205 Gabor Dr Newark (19711) *(G-7373)*
S & S Trucking, Dover *Also called Warren W Seaver (G-2206)*
S & S Wines and Spirits......302 678-9987
1007 Walker Rd Dover (19904) *(G-2048)*
S Brown Appraisals LLC......302 672-0694
16819 S Dupont Hwy # 300 Harrington (19952) *(G-2882)*
S C O R E 42, Wilmington *Also called Service Corps Retired Execs (G-12585)*
S D Nemcic DDS......302 734-1950
910 Walker Rd Ste A Dover (19904) *(G-2049)*
S Dorman Lawn Care Inc......302 947-2858
24676 Mallard Pond Ln Georgetown (19947) *(G-2645)*
S F F Art Inc (PA)......302 226-9410
200 Rehoboth Ave Ste A Rehoboth Beach (19971) *(G-8064)*
S G Williams & Bros Co (PA)......302 656-8167
301 N Tatnall St Wilmington (19801) *(G-12506)*
S G Williams of Dover Inc......302 678-1080
580 Lafferty Ln Dover (19901) *(G-2050)*
S J Desmond Inc......302 475-6520
22 Lloyd Pl Wilmington (19810) *(G-12507)*
S J Passwater General Cnstr......302 422-1061
715a S Washington St Milford (19963) *(G-4550)*
S L Pharma Labs, Inc., Wilmington *Also called Element Mtls Tech Wlmngton Inc (G-10368)*
S P A C E-Makers, Bear *Also called Space Makers Inc (G-330)*
S P S International Inv Co (HQ)......302 478-9055
1105 N Market St Ste 1300 Wilmington (19801) *(G-12508)*
S S C 7714-1, Laurel *Also called Southern States Coop Inc (G-3293)*
S S C 7777-1, Middletown *Also called Southern States Coop Inc (G-4246)*
S T Good Insurance Inc (HQ)......215 969-8385
875 Aaa Blvd Ste A Newark (19713) *(G-7374)*
S T Progressive Strides......410 775-8103
718 Thyme Dr Bear (19701) *(G-313)*
S U I, New Castle *Also called Service Unlimited Inc (G-5700)*
S Wallace Holdings LLC......917 304-1164
251 Little Falls Dr Wilmington (19808) *(G-12509)*
S&D Industries LLC......703 801-3643
2711 Centerville Rd # 400 Wilmington (19808) *(G-12510)*
S&H Investigative Services, Wilmington *Also called S & H Enterprises Inc (G-12505)*
S&H Logistics LLC......708 548-8982
8 The Grn 6451 Dover (19901) *(G-2051)*
S.O.A.R, Wilmington *Also called Survivors Abuse In Rcovery Inc (G-12818)*
Sabion Sound Reinforcement Co......302 427-0551
15 W Reamer Ave Wilmington (19804) *(G-12511)*
Sabre Amb LLC......302 299-1400
1612 N Dupont Hwy New Castle (19720) *(G-5692)*
Sache Social Club......302 287-4813
317 Townsend St Wilmington (19801) *(G-12512)*
Sachetta Machine & Development......302 378-5468
1823 Choptank Rd Middletown (19709) *(G-4229)*
Sacred Heart Village I Inc......302 428-0801
920 N Monroe St Wilmington (19801) *(G-12513)*
Sacred Heart Village II Inc......302 428-3702
625 E 10th St Wilmington (19801) *(G-12514)*
Saenger Porcelain......302 738-5349
18 Mimosa Dr Newark (19711) *(G-7375)*
Safe Harbor Property MGT LLC......302 436-9882
11 Polly Branch Rd Selbyville (19975) *(G-8542)*
Safe Home Control Inc......302 504-6300
1000 N West St Wilmington (19801) *(G-12515)*
Safe Space Delaware Inc......302 691-7946
500 W 2nd St Wilmington (19801) *(G-12516)*
Safeguard......301 299-8806
20 Cavendish Ct Rehoboth Beach (19971) *(G-8065)*
Safeguard Dx Laboratory......888 919-8275
110 S Poplar St Ste 200 Wilmington (19801) *(G-12517)*
Safelite Autoglass, Dover *Also called Safelite Glass Corp (G-2053)*
Safelite Autoglass, Dover *Also called Safelite Fulfillment Inc (G-2052)*
Safelite Autoglass, Georgetown *Also called Safelite Fulfillment Inc (G-2646)*
Safelite Autoglass, Wilmington *Also called Safelite Glass Corp (G-12519)*
Safelite Autoglass 363, Wilmington *Also called Safelite Fulfillment Inc (G-12518)*
Safelite Fulfillment Inc......302 678-9600
746 N Du Pont Hwy Dover (19901) *(G-2052)*
Safelite Fulfillment Inc......302 999-9908
4722 Kirkwood Hwy Wilmington (19808) *(G-12518)*
Safelite Fulfillment Inc......302 856-7175
22834 Dupont Blvd Georgetown (19947) *(G-2646)*
Safelite Glass Corp......877 800-2727
4200 N Dupont Hwy Ste 6 Dover (19901) *(G-2053)*
Safelite Glass Corp......302 656-4640
109 Rogers Rd Ste 4 Wilmington (19801) *(G-12519)*
Safeplace Corporation......302 479-9000
4 Chaville Way Wilmington (19807) *(G-12520)*
Safer Technologies LLC......302 497-0333
427 N Tatnall St Wilmington (19801) *(G-12521)*
Saferwatch LLC......844 449-2824
16192 Coastal Hwy Lewes (19958) *(G-3728)*
Safian, Gary D DDS, Wilmington *Also called Ralph Tomases DDS PA (G-12310)*
Sage Hospitality Resources LLC......302 292-1500
65 Geoffrey Dr Newark (19713) *(G-7376)*
Saggio Management Group Inc......302 659-6560
350 N High St Ext Smyrna (19977) *(G-8710)*
Saggio Management Group Inc......302 659-6560
665 S Carter Rd Unit 2 Smyrna (19977) *(G-8711)*
Sahave Inc......630 401-5211
919 N Market St Ste 950 Wilmington (19801) *(G-12522)*
Saheed Rufai, Wilmington *Also called Majestique Ventures & Hlth Cre (G-11495)*
Saienni Stairs LLC......302 292-2699
120 Sandy Dr Ste E Newark (19713) *(G-7377)*
Sailnovo Limited......213 550-3897
108 S Governors Ave Dover (19904) *(G-2054)*
Sain Cosmos LLC......936 244-7017
3524 Silverside Rd 35b Wilmington (19810) *(G-12523)*
Saint Anthonys Club......302 328-9440
1017 Gray St New Castle (19720) *(G-5693)*
Saint Georges Cultr & Arts Rev......302 836-8202
1 Delaware St Saint Georges (19733) *(G-8129)*
Saint Home Health Care......302 514-9597
1017 Mattlind Way Milford (19963) *(G-4551)*
Saint Jnes Ctr For Bhvral Hlth, Dover *Also called Kent General Hospital (G-1734)*
Saint Johns Lutheran Church......302 734-7078
113 Lotus St Dover (19901) *(G-2055)*
SAINT PATRICK'S CENTER, Wilmington *Also called St Patrick Center Inc (G-12728)*
Saints Cemetary, Wilmington *Also called Catholic Cemetaries Inc (G-9591)*
Sakura Inc......302 349-4628
600 Cattail Branch Rd Greenwood (19950) *(G-2761)*

ALPHABETIC

Salem County Amateur Radio CLB.......302 689-8127
2015 Bentwood Ct Wilmington (19804) **(G-12524)**
Salem Village, Newark *Also called Mid-Atlantic Realty Co Inc* **(G-7030)**
Salem Village Child Care, Newark *Also called Sandy Rose Inc* **(G-7383)**
Sallie Mae, Newark *Also called SLM Corporation* **(G-7441)**
Sallie Mae Financial, Newark *Also called SLM Financial Corporation* **(G-7442)**
Sally Beauty Supply 1497, Wilmington *Also called Sally Beauty Supply LLC* **(G-12525)**
Sally Beauty Supply 712, Dover *Also called Sally Beauty Supply LLC* **(G-2056)**
Sally Beauty Supply LLC.......302 731-0285
2665 Capitol Trl Newark (19711) **(G-7378)**
Sally Beauty Supply LLC.......302 629-5160
22883 Sussex Hwy Seaford (19973) **(G-8383)**
Sally Beauty Supply LLC.......302 995-6197
4395 Kirkwood Hwy Wilmington (19808) **(G-12525)**
Sally Beauty Supply LLC.......302 674-2201
283 N Dupont Hwy Ste D Dover (19901) **(G-2056)**
Sally Beauty Supply LLC.......302 737-8837
220 College Sq Newark (19711) **(G-7379)**
Salon By Dominic.......302 239-8282
130 Lantana Dr Hockessin (19707) **(G-3141)**
Salon Rispoli Inc.......302 731-9202
1115 Churchmans Rd Newark (19713) **(G-7380)**
Sals Auto Services Inc.......302 654-1168
3000 Lancaster Ave Wilmington (19805) **(G-12526)**
Sals Garage Inc.......302 655-4981
705 N Lincoln St Ste 1 Wilmington (19805) **(G-12527)**
Salt Pond Associates.......302 539-2750
400 Bethany Loop Bethany Beach (19930) **(G-430)**
Salt Pond Golf Club, Bethany Beach *Also called Salt Pond Associates* **(G-430)**
Salted Vines Vineyard Winery.......302 829-8990
32512 Blackwater Rd Frankford (19945) **(G-2385)**
Salvation Army.......302 628-2020
22943 Sussex Hwy Seaford (19973) **(G-8384)**
Salvation Army.......302 934-3730
559 E Dupont Hwy Millsboro (19966) **(G-4797)**
Salvation Army.......302 996-9400
2 S Augustine St Wilmington (19804) **(G-12528)**
Salvation Army.......302 656-1696
400 N Orange St Wilmington (19801) **(G-12529)**
Salvation Army.......302 654-8808
107 S Market St Wilmington (19801) **(G-12530)**
Sam Walts & Associates.......302 777-2211
11 Downs Dr Wilmington (19807) **(G-12531)**
Sam Waltz & Associates Counsel, Wilmington *Also called Sam Walts & Associates* **(G-12531)**
Sam Yoder and Son LLC.......302 398-4711
9387 Memory Rd Greenwood (19950) **(G-2762)**
Samaha Michel R MD.......302 422-3100
39 W Clarke Ave Milford (19963) **(G-4552)**
Samaritan Outreach.......302 594-9476
1410 N Claymont St Wilmington (19802) **(G-12532)**
Sams Construction LLC.......302 654-6542
1405 Haines Ave Wilmington (19809) **(G-12533)**
Sams Construction LLC.......302 654-6542
1227 E 15th St Wilmington (19802) **(G-12534)**
Sams Sign.......302 947-8152
25768 Salt Grass Rd Millsboro (19966) **(G-4798)**
Samson Communications Inc.......302 424-1013
9078 Attles Rd Lincoln (19960) **(G-3867)**
Samuel Blumberg PHD.......302 652-7733
2300 Pennsylvania Ave Wilmington (19806) **(G-12535)**
Sanco Construction Co Inc.......302 633-4156
24 Brookside Dr Wilmington (19804) **(G-12536)**
Sanctuary Spa and Saloon.......302 475-1469
1847 Marsh Rd Wilmington (19810) **(G-12537)**
Sand Hill Adult Program, Georgetown *Also called Sussex County Senior Svcs Inc* **(G-2678)**
Sandcastle Motel.......302 227-0400
123 2nd St Rehoboth Beach (19971) **(G-8066)**
Sandebbarnanricway Corp.......302 475-2705
2221 Inwood Rd Wilmington (19810) **(G-12538)**
Sanderson Albidress Agency.......302 368-3010
1211b Milltown Rd Wilmington (19808) **(G-12539)**
Sandler Occptnal Mdicine Assoc.......302 369-0171
168 S Main St Ste 206 Newark (19711) **(G-7381)**
Sandpiper Energy Inc.......302 736-7656
909 Silver Lake Blvd Dover (19904) **(G-2057)**
Sandra S Gulledge CPA.......302 674-1585
1037 S Dupont Hwy Dover (19901) **(G-2058)**
Sands Inc.......302 227-2511
101 N Boardwalk Rehoboth Beach (19971) **(G-8067)**
Sands Motel, Fenwick Island *Also called Sussex Sands Inc* **(G-2341)**
Sandwich Inc.......647 360-8300
16192 Coastal Hwy Lewes (19958) **(G-3729)**
Sandy Brae Laboratories Inc.......302 456-0446
119a Sandy Dr Newark (19713) **(G-7382)**
Sandy Hill Greenhouses Inc.......302 856-2412
18303 Sand Hill Rd Georgetown (19947) **(G-2647)**
Sandy Knoll Enterprises LLC.......302 875-3916
12254 Laurel Rd Laurel (19956) **(G-3287)**
Sandy Rose Inc.......302 454-1649
1000 Village Cir Newark (19713) **(G-7383)**
Sanford Day Camp, Wilmington *Also called Dave Arletta* **(G-9963)**
Sanjaban Corp.......612 805-5971
4023 Kennett Pike # 701 Wilmington (19807) **(G-12540)**
Sanosil International LLC.......302 454-8102
91 Lukens Dr Ste A New Castle (19720) **(G-5694)**
Santander Bank NA.......302 654-5182
824 N Market St Ste 100 Wilmington (19801) **(G-12541)**
Santo Stucco.......302 453-0901
13 Metten Rd Newark (19713) **(G-7384)**
Santora CPA Group Pa.......302 737-6200
220 Continental Dr # 112 Newark (19713) **(G-7385)**
Sapps Welding Service.......302 491-6319
8547 Sophies Way Lincoln (19960) **(G-3868)**
Sarah K Smith DDS.......302 442-3233
83 Beech Hill Dr Newark (19711) **(G-7386)**
Sardo & Sons Warehousing Inc (PA).......302 369-2100
111 Lake Dr Ste E Newark (19702) **(G-7387)**
Sardo & Sons Warehousing Inc.......302 737-3000
401 Pencader Dr Ste A Newark (19702) **(G-7388)**
Sardo & Sons Warehousing Inc.......302 369-0852
300 White Clay Center Dr Newark (19711) **(G-7389)**
Saregama India Limited.......859 490-0156
200 Continental Dr # 401 Newark (19713) **(G-7390)**
Sargent & Lundy LLC.......302 622-7200
500 Delaware Ave Ste 400 Wilmington (19801) **(G-12542)**
Sas Contracting, Middletown *Also called Steven Schmith* **(G-4248)**
Sas Nanotechnologies LLC.......214 235-1008
550 S College Ave Ste 110 Newark (19713) **(G-7391)**
Sassafras Veterinary Hospital, Smyrna *Also called Ann Jackson Vmd* **(G-8571)**
Satellite Connection Inc.......302 328-2462
4001 Kennett Pike Ste 134 Wilmington (19807) **(G-12543)**
Sattar A Syed DMD PA.......302 994-3093
5507 Kirkwood Hwy Wilmington (19808) **(G-12544)**
Satterfield & Ryan Inc.......302 422-4919
8266 N Union Church Rd Milford (19963) **(G-4553)**
Saturn, Newark *Also called Winner Group Inc* **(G-7711)**
Saucedos Landscaping, Dover *Also called Juan Saucedo* **(G-1714)**
Sauer Holdings Inc.......302 656-8989
1403 Foulk Rd Ste 200 Wilmington (19803) **(G-12545)**
Saul Ewing Arnstein & Lehr LLP.......302 654-1413
1201 N Market St Ste 2300 Wilmington (19801) **(G-12546)**
Savannah Inn.......302 645-0330
55 N Atlantic Dr Lewes (19958) **(G-3730)**
Savannah Logistics LLC.......302 893-7251
278 Liborio Dr Middletown (19709) **(G-4230)**
Sawyers Sanitation Service.......302 678-8240
184 Front St Leipsic (19901) **(G-3314)**
Saxton Maritime Services LLC.......415 870-3881
16192 Coastal Hwy Lewes (19958) **(G-3731)**
Sayhi LLC.......860 631-7725
1521 Concord Pike Ste 301 Wilmington (19803) **(G-12547)**
SC Foster LLC.......302 383-0201
43 Stonewold Way Wilmington (19807) **(G-12548)**
SC Marketing US Inc.......714 352-4992
2711 Centerville Rd # 120 Wilmington (19808) **(G-12549)**
SC&a Construction Inc.......302 478-6030
3411 Silverside Rd 202hg Wilmington (19810) **(G-12550)**
Scalia S Landscaping.......302 651-9822
504 N Dupont Rd Wilmington (19804) **(G-12551)**
Scalias Day Care Center Inc.......302 366-1430
701 Old Harmony Rd Newark (19711) **(G-7392)**
Scanpoint Inc.......603 429-0777
5700 Kirkwood Hwy Ste 202 Wilmington (19808) **(G-12552)**
Scanta Inc.......302 645-7400
16192 Coastal Hwy Lewes (19958) **(G-3732)**
Scassociates Inc.......302 454-1100
651 N Broad St Ste 103 Middletown (19709) **(G-4231)**
Schab & Barnett PA.......302 856-9024
9 Chestnut St Georgetown (19947) **(G-2648)**
Schagrin Gas Co (PA).......302 378-2000
1000 N Broad St Middletown (19709) **(G-4232)**
Schagringas Company, Middletown *Also called Schagrin Gas Co* **(G-4232)**
Schanne Mark State Farm Insur.......302 422-7231
915 S Dupont Blvd Milford (19963) **(G-4554)**
Schatz Messick Enterprises LLC.......302 398-8646
705 Andrewville Rd Harrington (19952) **(G-2883)**
Schell Brothers LLC (PA).......302 226-1994
20184 Phillips St Rehoboth Beach (19971) **(G-8068)**
Schiff Farms Inc (PA).......302 398-8014
16054 S Dupont Hwy Harrington (19952) **(G-2884)**
Schiff Transport LLC.......302 398-8014
16054 S Dupont Hwy Harrington (19952) **(G-2885)**
Schlegel Associates Inc.......302 477-1810
6 Palomino Ct Ste 101 Wilmington (19803) **(G-12553)**
Schlosser Assoc Mech Cntrs Inc.......302 738-7333
2047 Sunset Lake Rd Newark (19702) **(G-7393)**
Schmidt & Assoc.......610 255-3540
30213 Jump Ln Ocean View (19970) **(G-7811)**

ALPHABETIC SECTION

Security Quality

Schmittinger & Rodriguez PA (PA) 302 674-0140
   414 S State St Dover (19901) *(G-2059)*
Schnader Hrrson Sgal Lewis LLP 302 888-4554
   824 N Market St Ste 800 Wilmington (19801) *(G-12554)*
Schoenbeck & Schoenbeck PA 302 239-9316
   1211 Milltown Rd A Wilmington (19808) *(G-12555)*
Scholarjet PBc 617 407-9851
   16192 Coastal Hwy Lewes (19958) *(G-3733)*
School - Del Paul Mitchell, Newark Also called Carme LLC *(G-6157)*
School Bell Apartments LP 302 328-9500
   2000 Varsity Ln Bear (19701) *(G-314)*
School For Young Children, Wilmington Also called Xavier Inc *(G-13314)*
School Transportation Dept, Newark Also called Christina School District *(G-6229)*
Schoolhouse Trust Inc 302 322-6161
   265 Bear Christiana Rd Bear (19701) *(G-315)*
Schoon Inc 302 894-7574
   200 Continental Dr # 401 Newark (19713) *(G-7394)*
Schreppler Chropractic Offs PA 302 653-5525
   892 S Dupont Blvd Smyrna (19977) *(G-8712)*
Schrider Enterprises Inc 302 934-1900
   398 W State St Millsboro (19966) *(G-4799)*
Schrider Enterprises Inc 302 539-1036
   327 Atlantic Ave Ocean View (19967) *(G-7812)*
Schroedl Cleaning Svcs Sup Co, Wilmington Also called Schroedl Company *(G-12556)*
Schroedl Company 410 358-5500
   422 B And O Ln Wilmington (19804) *(G-12556)*
Schulze, S J, Newark Also called Siegfried J Schulze Inc *(G-7422)*
Schwartz & Schwartz Atty At La 302 678-8700
   1140 S State St Dover (19901) *(G-2060)*
Schwartz Center For The Arts, Dover Also called Friends of Capitol Theater Inc *(G-1570)*
Schwartz Eric Wm MD 302 234-5770
   726 Yorklyn Rd Ste 100 Hockessin (19707) *(G-3142)*
Schweizer Cleaning Service 302 995-2816
   317 Brookside Dr Wilmington (19804) *(G-12557)*
Schwerman Trucking Co 302 832-3103
   3340 Wrangle Hill Rd Bear. (19701) *(G-316)*
Schwezers Thrapy Rhabilitation, Middletown Also called Cristy Anna Care Physcl Thrapy *(G-4015)*
Schwezers Thrapy Rhabilitation, New Castle Also called Christiana Care Hlth Svcs Inc *(G-5156)*
Scicom Scntific Communications 302 475-2694
   101 Beauregard Ct Wilmington (19810) *(G-12558)*
Scicom Systems, Wilmington Also called Scicom Scntific Communications *(G-12558)*
Scientific Games Corporation 302 737-4300
   220 Continental Dr # 407 Newark (19713) *(G-7395)*
Scientific USA Inc 425 681-9462
   2711 Centerville Rd # 120 Wilmington (19808) *(G-12559)*
Scinorx Technologies Inc 302 268-5447
   1521 Concord Pike Wilmington (19803) *(G-12560)*
Scio Risk Group Llc 302 897-1534
   808 N Lincoln St Ste 1 Wilmington (19805) *(G-12561)*
Scissor Wizards Inc 302 475-9575
   1402 Harrison Ave Wilmington (19809) *(G-12562)*
Scituate Solar I LLC 212 419-4843
   2711 Centerville Rd # 400 Wilmington (19808) *(G-12563)*
Scj, Milford Also called Stevenson Ventures LLC *(G-4571)*
Scope One Inc 415 429-9347
   8 The Grn Ste D Dover (19901) *(G-2061)*
Scorelogix LLC 302 294-6532
   1 Innovation Way Ste 300 Newark (19711) *(G-7396)*
Scotch Hills Apartments, New Castle Also called Berman Development Corp *(G-5083)*
Scott & Sons Landscaping, Delmar Also called Shubert Enterprises Inc *(G-1029)*
Scott Engineering Inc 302 736-3058
   22 Old Rudnick Ln Ste 2 Dover (19901) *(G-2062)*
Scott Muffler LLC (PA) 302 674-8280
   1465 S Governors Ave Dover (19904) *(G-2063)*
Scott Muffler LLC 302 378-9247
   308 W Main St Middletown (19709) *(G-4233)*
Scott Pediatrics, Milford Also called Lowell Scott MD PA *(G-4478)*
Scott, Patricia A L MD, Wilmington Also called Matthew Gotthold Dr *(G-11570)*
Scottish Ventures LLC 302 382-6057
   5 Wildfire Ln New Castle (19720) *(G-5695)*
Scottrade Inc 302 658-6511
   1257 Churchmans Rd Newark (19713) *(G-7397)*
Scotts Co 302 777-4779
   100 W 10th St Lbby Wilmington (19801) *(G-12564)*
Scotts Refrigeration & AC 302 732-3736
   32327 Wingate Rd Frankford (19945) *(G-2386)*
Scottys Trucking Inc 302 629-5156
   11667 Park Dr Seaford (19973) *(G-8385)*
Scuba World Inc 302 698-1117
   4004 S Dupont Hwy Ste B Dover (19901) *(G-2064)*
Sdads, Rehoboth Beach Also called Southern Del Assoc Dntl Spc *(G-8082)*
Sdg Defense Industry LLC 302 526-4800
   42 N Independence Blvd New Castle (19720) *(G-5696)*
Sdix LLC 302 456-6789
   111 Pencader Dr Newark (19702) *(G-7398)*

Sea Air Village, Rehoboth Beach Also called Sun Communities Inc *(G-8091)*
Sea Colony, Bethany Beach Also called Carl M Freeman Associates Inc *(G-391)*
Sea Colony Tennis Center 302 539-4488
   Westway & Kent Ave Bethany Beach (19930) *(G-431)*
Sea Esta Motel 2, Millsboro Also called Pelican Bay Group Inc *(G-4773)*
Sea Esta Motel III, Rehoboth Beach Also called George Metz *(G-7946)*
Sea Witch Inc 302 226-3900
   65 Lake Ave Rehoboth Beach (19971) *(G-8069)*
Sea Witch Inn & Spa, Rehoboth Beach Also called Sea Witch Inc *(G-8069)*
Seafood City Inc 302 284-8486
   9996 S Dupont Hwy Felton (19943) *(G-2319)*
Seafood House, The, Seaford Also called Children Fmilies First Del Inc *(G-8194)*
Seaford Animal Hospital Inc 302 629-7325
   22661 Atlanta Rd Seaford (19973) *(G-8386)*
Seaford Center, Seaford Also called Genesis Healthcare Seafood Ctr *(G-8252)*
Seaford Concrete Products LLC 302 628-6964
   22288 Coverdale Rd Seaford (19973) *(G-8387)*
Seaford Dental Associates, Seaford Also called Elkington I Kent DDS *(G-8235)*
Seaford Endoscopy Center 302 629-7177
   13 Fallon Ave Seaford (19973) *(G-8388)*
Seaford Federal Credit Union (PA) 302 629-7852
   24488 Sussex Hwy Ste 1 Seaford (19973) *(G-8389)*
Seaford Feed Mill, Seaford Also called Allen Harim Foods LLC *(G-8144)*
Seaford Grain North, Seaford Also called Perdue Farms Inc *(G-8354)*
Seaford Ice 302 629-2562
   504 Bridgeville Hwy Seaford (19973) *(G-8390)*
Seaford Ice & Cold Storage, Seaford Also called Seaford Ice Inc *(G-8391)*
Seaford Ice Inc 302 629-2562
   111 S Dual Hwy Seaford (19973) *(G-8391)*
Seaford Machine Works Inc 302 629-6034
   1451 Middleford Rd Seaford (19973) *(G-8392)*
Seaford Meadows Apartments, Seaford Also called Seaford Preservation Assoc LLC *(G-8395)*
Seaford Mission Inc 302 629-2559
   611 3rd St Seaford (19973) *(G-8393)*
Seaford Police Dept 302 629-6644
   300 Virginia Ave Seaford (19973) *(G-8394)*
Seaford Preservation Assoc LLC 302 629-6416
   122 Seaford Meadows Dr Seaford (19973) *(G-8395)*
Seaford Star, Seaford Also called Morning Star Publications Inc *(G-8311)*
Seagreen Bicycle LLP 302 226-2323
   54 Baltimore Ave Rehoboth Beach (19971) *(G-8070)*
Seamens Center Wilmington Inc 302 575-1300
   Port Of Wilmington Wilmington (19899) *(G-12565)*
Sean E Chipman 302 300-4307
   200 Centerpoint Blvd A New Castle (19720) *(G-5697)*
Search LLC 858 348-4584
   16192 Coastal Hwy Lewes (19958) *(G-3734)*
Sears Roebuck and Co 302 995-9295
   4737 Concord Pike Ste 410 Wilmington (19803) *(G-12566)*
Seaside Amusements Inc 302 227-1921
   6 Delaware Ave Rehoboth Beach (19971) *(G-8071)*
Seaside Endoscopy Pavillion, Lewes Also called Envision Healthcare Corp *(G-3485)*
Seaside Graphics Corp 302 436-9460
   1 Mason Dr Selbyville (19975) *(G-8543)*
Seaside Gstrointerology Consit, Lewes Also called Caruso Richard F MD PA *(G-3410)*
Seaside Inn 302 251-5000
   1401 Coastal Hwy Fenwick Island (19944) *(G-2340)*
Seaside Pointe 302 226-8750
   36101 Seaside Blvd Rehoboth Beach (19971) *(G-8072)*
Seaside Service LLC 302 827-3775
   36360 Tarpon Dr Lewes (19958) *(G-3735)*
Seasons Hspice Plltive Care De 847 692-1000
   220 Continental Dr # 407 Newark (19713) *(G-7399)*
Second Chance Solutions LLC 302 204-0551
   913 N Market St Ste 200 Wilmington (19801) *(G-12567)*
Secure Data Cmpt Solutions Inc 302 346-7327
   910 Walker Rd Ste B Dover (19904) *(G-2065)*
Secure Management 302 999-8342
   1050 Industrial Rd # 100 Middletown (19709) *(G-4234)*
Secure Self Storage (PA) 302 832-0400
   1020 Bear Rd New Castle (19720) *(G-5698)*
Securenetmd LLC 302 645-7770
   16557 Coastal Hwy Lewes (19958) *(G-3736)*
Securitas Electronic SEC Inc 302 992-7950
   1100 First State Blvd Wilmington (19804) *(G-12568)*
Securitas SEC Svcs USA Inc 302 573-6802
   1220 N Market St Ste 800 Wilmington (19801) *(G-12569)*
Securitech Inc 302 996-9230
   205 N Marshall St Wilmington (19804) *(G-12570)*
Security Inc 302 652-5276
   8000 Society Dr Claymont (19703) *(G-802)*
Security Instrument Corp Del (PA) 302 998-2261
   309 W Newport Pike Wilmington (19804) *(G-12571)*
Security Instrument Corp Del 302 674-2891
   28226 Lwes Georgetown Hwy Milton (19968) *(G-4966)*
Security Quality 302 286-1200
   930 Old Harmony Rd Ste H Newark (19713) *(G-7400)*

Security Satellite....302 376-0241
5101 Summit Bridge Rd Middletown (19709) ***(G-4235)***
Security Satellite Systems, Middletown *Also called Security Satellite* ***(G-4235)***
Security Watch Corp....302 286-6728
260 Chapman Rd Ste 100c Newark (19702) ***(G-7401)***
Sedation Center PA....302 678-3384
429 S Governors Ave Dover (19904) ***(G-2066)***
Seeds of Jesus Day Care LLC....302 494-6568
12 Mary Ella Dr Wilmington (19805) ***(G-12572)***
SEI Robotics Corporation....858 752-8675
12 Timber Creek Ln Newark (19711) ***(G-7402)***
Seiberlich Trane, New Castle *Also called John R Seiberlich Inc* ***(G-5441)***
Seitz Vanogtrop & Green....302 888-0600
222 Delaware Ave Ste 1500 Wilmington (19801) ***(G-12573)***
Selbyville Auto Parts, Selbyville *Also called Quaker City Auto Parts Inc* ***(G-8535)***
Selbyville Cleaners Inc (PA)....302 249-3444
68 Hosier St Selbyville (19975) ***(G-8544)***
Selbyville Pet and Garden Ctr, Selbyville *Also called Animal Health Sales Inc* ***(G-8448)***
Select Amenities,, Hockessin *Also called Hotel Environments Inc* ***(G-3056)***
Select Financial Group....302 424-7777
556 S Dupont Blvd Ste G Milford (19963) ***(G-4555)***
Select Health Services LLC....504 737-4300
560 Peoples Plz Newark (19702) ***(G-7403)***
Select Management Resources, New Castle *Also called Northeastern Title Loans* ***(G-5579)***
Select Medical Corporation....302 421-4545
701 N Clayton St Fl 5 Wilmington (19805) ***(G-12574)***
Select Physical Therapy....302 760-9966
230 Beiser Blvd Ste 100 Dover (19904) ***(G-2067)***
Select Spclty Hsptal- Wlmngton, Wilmington *Also called Select Medical Corporation* ***(G-12574)***
Select Specialty Hospital....302 421-4590
701 N Clayton St Fl 5 Wilmington (19805) ***(G-12575)***
Select Stainless Products LLC....302 653-3062
100 Industrial Blvd Clayton (19938) ***(G-871)***
Select Suppliers Ltd....303 523-1813
30 Old Rudnick Ln Dover (19901) ***(G-2068)***
Sellers Senior Center Inc....302 762-2050
2800 Silverside Rd Wilmington (19810) ***(G-12576)***
Selling Dreams LLC....302 746-7999
2901 Philadelphia Pike Claymont (19703) ***(G-803)***
Selwor Enterprises Inc....302 454-9454
50 Polly Drummond Hill Rd Newark (19711) ***(G-7404)***
Semiconductor Technologies....302 420-1432
231 Lake Dr Newark (19702) ***(G-7405)***
Semiconductorplus Inc....302 330-7533
913 N Market St Ste 200 Wilmington (19801) ***(G-12577)***
Semp Wellness LLC....302 525-9612
173 Rhythm Ct Newark (19713) ***(G-7406)***
Semper Program LLC....302 535-6769
304 Bohemia Mill Pond Dr Middletown (19709) ***(G-4236)***
Sendsafely LLC....917 375-5891
40 E Main St Ste 897 Newark (19711) ***(G-7407)***
Senior Helpers, Hockessin *Also called Seniortech Inc* ***(G-3143)***
Senior Home Help LLC....302 335-4243
266 Lake Cove Ln Felton (19943) ***(G-2320)***
Senior Nanticoke Center Inc....302 629-4939
310 Virginia Ave Ste B Seaford (19973) ***(G-8396)***
Seniortech Inc....302 234-1274
726 Yorklyn Rd Ste 410 Hockessin (19707) ***(G-3143)***
Sensofusion Inc....570 239-4912
30061 Clam Shell Ln Milton (19968) ***(G-4967)***
Sentinel Self Storage (PA)....302 999-0704
200 First State Blvd Wilmington (19804) ***(G-12578)***
Sentinel Transportation LLC (HQ)....302 477-1640
3521 Silverside Rd Ste 2a Wilmington (19810) ***(G-12579)***
Sentinel-Sg LLC....580 458-9184
919 N Market St Ste 425 Wilmington (19801) ***(G-12580)***
Separation Methods Tech Inc....302 368-0610
31 Blue Hen Dr Newark (19713) ***(G-7408)***
Separe Inc....302 736-5000
529 Weaver Dr Dover (19901) ***(G-2069)***
Sepax Technologies Inc (PA)....302 366-1101
5 Innovation Way Ste 100 Newark (19711) ***(G-7409)***
Seper 8 Motel....302 734-5701
348 N Dupont Hwy Dover (19901) ***(G-2070)***
Sepia Cleaners....302 656-0700
336 S Heald St Wilmington (19801) ***(G-12581)***
Sereduke Design Cons LLC....302 478-3468
408 Concord Ave Wilmington (19803) ***(G-12582)***
Serene Minds....302 478-6199
410 Foulk Rd Ste 102 Wilmington (19803) ***(G-12583)***
Serenity Gardens Assisted Livi....302 442-5330
207 Ruth Dr Middletown (19709) ***(G-4237)***
Serenity Grdns Assisted Living, Middletown *Also called Serenity Gardens Assisted Livi* ***(G-4237)***
Sergovic & Carmean P A....302 855-1260
231 S Race St Georgetown (19947) ***(G-2649)***
Sergovic Carmean Weidman (PA)....302 855-0551
406 S Bedford St Ste 1 Georgetown (19947) ***(G-2650)***
Serpro of Bear New Castle....302 392-6000
301 Carson Dr Bear (19701) ***(G-317)***
Server Management LLC....302 300-1745
1201 N Orange St Wilmington (19801) ***(G-12584)***
Service Corps Retired Execs....302 573-6552
1105 N Market St Lbby 2 Wilmington (19801) ***(G-12585)***
Service Energy LLC....302 734-7433
29 Harbor View Dr New Castle (19720) ***(G-5699)***
Service Energy LLC (PA)....302 734-7433
3799 N Dupont Hwy Dover (19901) ***(G-2071)***
Service Energy LLC....302 645-9050
47 Clay Rd Lewes (19958) ***(G-3737)***
Service General, Georgetown *Also called Bahars Company* ***(G-2444)***
Service General Corp....302 856-3500
120 N Race St Georgetown (19947) ***(G-2651)***
Service Glass Inc....302 629-9139
Rr 20 Box W Seaford (19973) ***(G-8397)***
Service King Cllision Repr Ctr, Claymont *Also called Service King Holdings LLC* ***(G-804)***
Service King Holdings LLC....302 797-8783
130 Hickman Rd Claymont (19703) ***(G-804)***
Service Oil Company....302 734-7433
3799 N Dupont Hwy Dover (19901) ***(G-2072)***
Service Quest....302 235-0173
217 Louis Ln Hockessin (19707) ***(G-3144)***
Service Tire Truck Center Inc....302 629-5533
24873 Sussex Hwy Seaford (19973) ***(G-8398)***
Service Unlimited Inc....302 326-2665
19 Southgate Blvd Unit A New Castle (19720) ***(G-5700)***
ServiceMaster, Wilmington *Also called Quality Assured Inc* ***(G-12277)***
ServiceMaster of Newark....302 834-8006
116 Cann Rd Newark (19702) ***(G-7410)***
Servicexpress Corporation....302 854-9118
809 Norman Eskridge Hwy Seaford (19973) ***(G-8399)***
Servicexpress Corporation....302 424-3500
340 Ne Front St Milford (19963) ***(G-4556)***
Servicexpress Corporation (PA)....302 856-3500
120 N Ray St Georgetown (19947) ***(G-2652)***
Servo2gocom Ltd....877 378-0240
4023 Kennett Pike Ste 583 Wilmington (19807) ***(G-12586)***
SERVPRO, Georgetown *Also called Teff Inc* ***(G-2689)***
SERVPRO, Wilmington *Also called Mebro Inc* ***(G-11613)***
SERVPRO of Dover/Middletown, Dover *Also called Dover Nunan LLC* ***(G-1461)***
Seth Ivins Dr MD....302 824-7280
620 Stanton Christn Rd # 305 Newark (19713) ***(G-7411)***
Seth Ral & Associates Inc....302 478-9020
2308 Ruthwynn Dr Wilmington (19803) ***(G-12587)***
Sev One Technology Center, Newark *Also called Sevone Inc* ***(G-7412)***
Seven Tech LLC....302 464-6488
600 N Broad St Middletown (19709) ***(G-4238)***
Severn Trent Inc (HQ)....302 427-5990
1011 Centre Rd Ste 320 Wilmington (19805) ***(G-12588)***
Sevone Inc....302 319-5400
550 S College Ave Newark (19716) ***(G-7412)***
Sevys Auto Service Inc....302 328-0839
245 Christiana Rd New Castle (19720) ***(G-5701)***
Sew Right 4 You Embroidery, Smyrna *Also called Delvina I Willson* ***(G-8623)***
Sew There Embroidery....302 545-0127
188 Green Giant Rd Townsend (19734) ***(G-8821)***
Seward, R J & Son, Townsend *Also called Robert J Seward and Son* ***(G-8820)***
Sewell C Biggs Trust....302 674-2111
406 Federal St Dover (19901) ***(G-2073)***
Sewickley Capital Inc (PA)....302 793-4964
501 Silverside Rd Ste 67 Wilmington (19809) ***(G-12589)***
Seymour's Cleaners, Wilmington *Also called Curzon Corp* ***(G-9922)***
SF Express Corporation....302 407-6155
1140 River Rd New Castle (19720) ***(G-5702)***
SF Logistics Limited....302 317-3954
1140 River Rd New Castle (19720) ***(G-5703)***
SFE Solar Energy Inc....905 366-7037
2711 Centerville Rd # 400 Wilmington (19808) ***(G-12590)***
Sfin 3 Inc (PA)....302 472-9276
1007 N Orange St Wilmington (19801) ***(G-12591)***
Sft, Newark *Also called Supercritical Fluid Tech* ***(G-7511)***
Shacraft....302 995-6385
1904 Lincoln Ave Marshallton (19808) ***(G-3914)***
Shady Park Inc....302 436-8441
36773 Lighthouse Rd Selbyville (19975) ***(G-8545)***
Shadybrook Farms LLC....302 734-9966
6401 Bayside Dr Dover (19901) ***(G-2074)***
Shallcross Mortgage Co Inc (PA)....302 999-9800
410 Century Blvd Wilmington (19808) ***(G-12592)***
Shamrock Construction Inc....302 376-0320
380 Lake Dr Smyrna (19977) ***(G-8713)***
Shamrock Glass Co Inc....302 629-5500
200 N Delaware Ave Seaford (19973) ***(G-8400)***
Shamrock Services LLC....302 519-7609
22576 Waterview Rd Lewes (19958) ***(G-3738)***
Shamrock Taxi, Lewes *Also called Shamrock Services LLC* ***(G-3738)***

Sharda USA LLC 610 350-6930
7217 Lancaster Pike Ste A Hockessin (19707) ***(G-3145)***
Shark Service Center LLC 302 337-8233
616a Market St Bridgeville (19933) ***(G-520)***
Sharlay Computer Systems 302 588-3170
15 Delhi Ct Smyrna (19977) ***(G-8714)***
Sharon A Welsh DDS, Hockessin *Also called Welsh Family Dentistry* ***(G-3172)***
Sharon Alger-Little Dr 302 398-3367
6902 Mlford Hrrington Hwy Harrington (19952) ***(G-2886)***
Sharon Construction Inc 302 999-1345
4932 Old Capitol Trl Wilmington (19808) ***(G-12593)***
Sharp Farm (PA) 302 652-7729
5727 Kennett Pike Wilmington (19807) ***(G-12594)***
Sharp Farm 302 378-9606
1214 Sharp Ln Middletown (19709) ***(G-4239)***
Sharp Raingutters 302 398-4873
Rr 36 Harrington (19952) ***(G-2887)***
Shashikala Patel MD 302 737-5074
314 E Main St Ste 404 Newark (19711) ***(G-7413)***
Shauna Sullivan Lcsw 302 383-6826
3100 Naamans Rd Wilmington (19810) ***(G-12595)***
Shavone Loves Kids Day Care 302 544-6170
6 Darien Ct New Castle (19720) ***(G-5704)***
Shawnee Wood Farms Inc 302 422-3534
7237 Calhoun Rd Milford (19963) ***(G-4557)***
Shea Concrete Ltd 302 422-7221
4th & Montgomery St Milford (19963) ***(G-4558)***
Shear Magic Hair Design 302 836-4001
106 Foxhunt Dr Bear (19701) ***(G-318)***
Shechinah Empower Center Inc 302 858-4467
231 S Race St Georgetown (19947) ***(G-2653)***
Sheep Skin Gifts, New Castle *Also called Francis Enterprises LLC* ***(G-5327)***
Sheer Expressions, Wilmington *Also called Wyatt Ridley Corp* ***(G-13311)***
Sheet Metal Contracting Co 302 834-3727
3445 Wrangle Hill Rd Bear (19701) ***(G-319)***
Sheets Insurance Agency, Bear *Also called Sheets Insurance Inc* ***(G-320)***
Sheets Insurance Inc 302 832-0441
254 Foxhunt Dr Bear (19701) ***(G-320)***
Shekinah Glory Sign Company 302 256-0426
2608 Kirkwood Hwy Wilmington (19805) ***(G-12596)***
Shelatia J Dennis 302 465-0630
9 E Loockerman St Ste 302 Dover (19901) ***(G-2075)***
Sheldon Limited Partnership 302 738-3048
810 Sheldon Dr Newark (19711) ***(G-7414)***
Shelias Childcare Center 302 472-9648
1621 N Heald St Wilmington (19802) ***(G-12597)***
Shell Recreation Center, Milton *Also called Eisele Celine* ***(G-4902)***
Shell We Bounce 302 727-5411
20699 Coastal Hwy Rehoboth Beach (19971) ***(G-8073)***
Shellcrest Swim Club 302 529-1464
916 Wilson Rd Wilmington (19803) ***(G-12598)***
Shellhorn & Hill Inc (PA) 302 654-4200
501 S Market St Wilmington (19801) ***(G-12599)***
Shells Child Care Center III 302 398-9778
5332 Mlford Hrrington Hwy Harrington (19952) ***(G-2888)***
Shelly's We Do Everything, Wilmington *Also called Shellys of Delaware Inc* ***(G-12600)***
Shellys of Delaware Inc 302 656-3337
610 W 8th St Wilmington (19801) ***(G-12600)***
Shelter Development LLC 302 737-4999
200 Vinings Way Newark (19702) ***(G-7415)***
Shepherd Place Inc 302 678-1909
1362 S Governors Ave Dover (19904) ***(G-2076)***
Sheraton Suites Wilmington, Wilmington *Also called Pde I LLC* ***(G-12054)***
Sheraton Suites Wilmington, Wilmington *Also called Procaccianti Group LLC* ***(G-12237)***
Sheraton Suites Wilmington, Wilmington *Also called 422 Hotel LLC* ***(G-8861)***
Sheridan Ford Sales, Wilmington *Also called Future Ford Sales Inc* ***(G-10654)***
Sherm's Catering, Wilmington *Also called De Catering Inc* ***(G-9985)***
Sherman Heating Oils Inc 302 684-4008
223 Bay Front Rd G Milton (19968) ***(G-4968)***
Sherman Heating Oils Inc (PA) 302 684-4008
223g Bay Ave Milton (19968) ***(G-4969)***
Sherweb Inc 888 567-6610
2915 Ogletown Rd 1073 Newark (19713) ***(G-7416)***
Shields Brothers 302 999-1094
315 1st Ave Wilmington (19804) ***(G-12601)***
Shiloh Industries Inc 302 656-1950
103 Foulk Rd Ste 202 Wilmington (19803) ***(G-12602)***
Shining Time Day Care Center 302 335-2770
220 Fox Chase Rd Felton (19943) ***(G-2321)***
Shiny Agency LLC 302 384-6494
1800 Wawaset St Wilmington (19806) ***(G-12603)***
Shipley Associates Inc 302 652-1766
135 S West St Wilmington (19801) ***(G-12604)***
Shipshap LLC 425 298-5215
651 N Road St Ste 205478 Middletown (19709) ***(G-4240)***
Shipyard Center LLC 302 999-0708
234 N James St Wilmington (19804) ***(G-12605)***
Shire North American Group Inc (HQ) 484 595-8800
103 Foulk Rd Ste 202 Wilmington (19803) ***(G-12606)***
Shirkey Trucking Corp 302 349-2791
734 Cattail Branch Rd Greenwood (19950) ***(G-2763)***
Shiv Baba LLC 703 314-1203
100 Carlsons Way Ste 15 Dover (19901) ***(G-2077)***
Shiv Sagar Inc 302 674-3800
1703 E Lebanon Rd Dover (19901) ***(G-2078)***
Shockley Brothers Construction 302 424-3255
8772 Herring Branch Rd Lincoln (19960) ***(G-3869)***
Shoemobile Services, New Castle *Also called Lehigh Vly Safety Sup Co Inc* ***(G-5477)***
Shoolex LLC (PA) 866 697-3330
16192 Coastal Hwy Lewes (19958) ***(G-3739)***
Shooter's Choice, Dover *Also called Noble Eagle Sales LLC* ***(G-1898)***
Shooters Choice Inc 302 736-5166
5105 N Dupont Hwy Dover (19901) ***(G-2079)***
Shop Talk Inc 302 322-5860
101 E Franklin Ave New Castle (19720) ***(G-5705)***
Shopify Payments (usa) Inc 613 241-2828
1209 N Orange St Wilmington (19801) ***(G-12607)***
Shopworks, Milford *Also called Growmark Fs LLC* ***(G-4426)***
Shor Associates Inc 302 764-1701
240 Philadelphia Pike Wilmington (19809) ***(G-12608)***
Shore Answer LLC 302 253-8381
543 S Bedford St Georgetown (19947) ***(G-2654)***
Shore Community Medical 302 827-4365
18947 John J Williams Hwy # 215 Rehoboth Beach (19971) ***(G-8074)***
Shore Consultants Ltd 302 737-3375
179 W Chestnut Hill Rd # 7 Newark (19713) ***(G-7417)***
Shore Electric Inc 302 645-4503
34697 Jiffy Way Unit 4 Lewes (19958) ***(G-3740)***
Shore Masonry Inc 302 945-5933
32405 Mermaid Run Millsboro (19966) ***(G-4800)***
Shore Pride Foods, Bridgeville *Also called H C Davis Inc* ***(G-477)***
Shore Property Maintenance 302 947-4440
28828 Four Of Us Rd Harbeson (19951) ***(G-2799)***
Shore Property Maintenance LLC 302 227-7786
4 S Lake Ter Rehoboth Beach (19971) ***(G-8075)***
Shore Shutters and Shade 302 569-1738
26760 Meadowlark Loop Millsboro (19966) ***(G-4801)***
Shore Stop 294, Selbyville *Also called GPM Investments LLC* ***(G-8496)***
Shore Stop Store 286, Newark *Also called Fas Mart / Shore Stop 286 LLC* ***(G-6573)***
Shore Tint & More Inc 302 947-4624
22797 Dozer Ln Unit 13 Harbeson (19951) ***(G-2800)***
Shore United Bank 302 284-4600
120 W Main St Felton (19943) ***(G-2322)***
Shore United Bank 302 424-4600
698a N Dupont Blvd Milford (19963) ***(G-4559)***
Shore United Bank 302 698-1432
4580 S Dupont Hwy Camden (19934) ***(G-599)***
Shorecare of Delaware, Middletown *Also called Lieske E2e Home Hlth Care Inc* ***(G-4131)***
Shorecare of Delaware 302 724-5235
874 Walker Rd Ste D Dover (19904) ***(G-2080)***
Shorecare of Delaware 302 724-5235
874 Walker Rd Dover (19904) ***(G-2081)***
Short Funeral Home Inc (PA) 302 846-9814
13 E Grove St Delmar (19940) ***(G-1028)***
Short Funeral Home Inc 302 875-3637
700 West St Laurel (19956) ***(G-3288)***
Short Funeral Services, Milford *Also called Berry Short Funeral Home Inc* ***(G-4324)***
Short Insurance Associates 302 629-0999
106 N Pine St Seaford (19973) ***(G-8401)***
Short Wars Productions LLC 302 932-0707
1907 N Franklin St Wilmington (19802) ***(G-12609)***
Shorty USA Inc 302 234-7750
141 Ramunno Cir Hockessin (19707) ***(G-3146)***
Shouldr LLC 917 331-1384
16192 Coastal Hwy Lewes (19958) ***(G-3741)***
Shree Kishna Inc 302 839-5000
699 N Dupont Blvd Milford (19963) ***(G-4560)***
Shree Lalji LLC 302 730-8009
652 N Dupont Hwy Dover (19901) ***(G-2082)***
Shri SAI Dover LLC 302 747-5050
561 N Dupont Hwy Dover (19901) ***(G-2083)***
Shri Swami Narayan LLC 302 738-3198
1119 S College Ave Newark (19713) ***(G-7418)***
Shriji Hospitality (not Llc) 302 654-5544
1213 West Ave New Castle (19720) ***(G-5706)***
Shubert Enterprises Inc 302 846-3122
11077 Iron Hill Rd Delmar (19940) ***(G-1029)***
Shubert Enterprises Inc 714 595-5762
28091 Nine Foot Rd Dagsboro (19939) ***(G-933)***
Shure Line Electrical Inc 302 856-3110
24207 Dupont Blvd Georgetown (19947) ***(G-2655)***
Shure-Line Construction Inc 302 653-4610
281 W Commerce St Kenton (19955) ***(G-3185)***
Shure-Line Electrical Inc 302 389-1114
100 Artisan Dr Smyrna (19977) ***(G-8715)***
Shuttercase Inc 347 480-1614
2035 Sunset Lake Rd B2 Newark (19702) ***(G-7419)***

ALPHABETIC

(PA)=Parent Co (HQ)=Headquarters (DH)=Div Headquarters
2020 Harris Directory of Delaware Businesses
721

Si360 Inc 800 849-6058
2035 Sunset Lake Rd B2 Newark (19702) *(G-7420)*
SIC Biometrics Inc 866 499-8377
2915 Ogletown Rd Ste 1737 Newark (19713) *(G-7421)*
Sid Harvey Industries Inc 302 746-7760
130 Hickman Rd Ste 32 Claymont (19703) *(G-805)*
Sid Tool Co Inc 302 322-5441
19 E Commons Blvd New Castle (19720) *(G-5707)*
Sids Liquor, Wilmington Also called Vishva Inc *(G-13090)*
Sieck Wholesale Florist Inc 302 356-2000
11 Southgate Blvd New Castle (19720) *(G-5708)*
Siegfried Group LLP (PA) 302 984-1800
1201 N Market St Ste 700 Wilmington (19801) *(G-12610)*
Siegfried J Schulze Inc 302 737-0403
12 Mill Park Ct Newark (19713) *(G-7422)*
Siegfried Resources, Wilmington Also called Siegfried Group LLP *(G-12610)*
Siemanowski Consulting Inc 302 368-1081
13 Covered Bridge Ln Newark (19711) *(G-7423)*
Siemens 302 220-1544
4001 Vandever Ave Wilmington (19802) *(G-12611)*
Siemens AG 302 836-2933
217 Benjamin Blvd Bear (19701) *(G-321)*
Siemens Corporation 302 690-2046
100 Gbc Dr Newark (19702) *(G-7424)*
Siemens Corporation 302 220-1544
800 Centerpoint Blvd A New Castle (19720) *(G-5709)*
Siemens Healthcare Diagnostics 302 631-8006
200 Centerpoint Blvd New Castle (19720) *(G-5710)*
Siemens Hlthcare Dgnostics Inc 302 631-7357
500 Gbc Dr Newark (19702) *(G-7425)*
Siena Hall, Wilmington Also called Catholic Charities Inc *(G-9592)*
Sigma Data Systems Inc 302 453-8812
197 Possum Park Rd Newark (19711) *(G-7426)*
Sigma Telecom LLC 347 741-8397
501 Silverside Rd Ste 105 Wilmington (19809) *(G-12612)*
Sign and Graphics, Wilmington Also called DOT Pop Inc *(G-10208)*
Sign Express 302 999-0893
103 S Augustine St Wilmington (19804) *(G-12613)*
Sign Guys The, Newark Also called Paul Woerner *(G-7186)*
Sign Lnguage Blitz Pblc Benft 928 925-3842
16192 Coastal Hwy Lewes (19958) *(G-3742)*
Sign Shop 302 998-2443
146 Bungalow Ave Wilmington (19805) *(G-12614)*
Sign-A-Rama, Georgetown Also called Beachview Mgmt Inc *(G-2450)*
Sign-A-Rama, Newark Also called Gary M Munch Inc *(G-6640)*
Sign-A-Rama, Bear Also called Marjano LLC *(G-245)*
Signal Garden Research Corp 708 715-3646
16192 Coastal Hwy Lewes (19958) *(G-3743)*
Signature Alert, Ocean View Also called Advanced Protection LLC *(G-7754)*
Signature Cnstr & Design, New Castle Also called Signature Cnstr Svcs LLC *(G-5711)*
Signature Cnstr Svcs LLC 302 691-1010
3029 Bowlarama Dr New Castle (19720) *(G-5711)*
Signature Construction Svcs, New Castle Also called Signature Furniture Svcs LLC *(G-5712)*
Signature Fitness Eqp LLC 888 657-5357
16192 Coastal Hwy Lewes (19958) *(G-3744)*
Signature Furniture Svcs LLC 302 691-1010
3029 Bowlarama Dr New Castle (19720) *(G-5712)*
Signature Group Management Co 302 691-1010
3029 Bowlarama Dr New Castle (19720) *(G-5713)*
Signature Property Management 302 212-2381
20375 John J Williams Hwy Lewes (19958) *(G-3745)*
Signature Selections LLC (PA) 631 256-6900
110 Executive Dr Ste 5 Newark (19702) *(G-7427)*
Signs By Tomorrow, Newark Also called Tylaur Inc *(G-7603)*
Signs Now, Wilmington Also called Barbara Graphics Inc *(G-9248)*
Signs Rite 302 836-6144
11 Kings Bridge Ct Newark (19702) *(G-7428)*
Signs-Rite Lettering Graphics, Newark Also called Signs Rite *(G-7428)*
Signscape Designs & Signs 302 798-2926
1709 Philadelphia Pike # 1 Wilmington (19809) *(G-12615)*
Silicon Valley Ht Partners LP 213 272-0088
2140 S Dupont Hwy Camden (19934) *(G-600)*
Silis Security Group, Lewes Also called Ftl Technologies Corporation *(G-3505)*
Silly Smiles LLC 302 838-1865
200 Biddle Ave Ste 201 Newark (19702) *(G-7429)*
Silver Lake Center, Dover Also called 1080 Slver Lk Blvd Oprtons LLC *(G-1063)*
Silver Lake Elem Sch Pta 302 378-5023
200 E Cochran St Middletown (19709) *(G-4241)*
Silver Lakes Estates, Milford Also called Owners Management Company *(G-4521)*
Silver Lining Solutions LLC 302 691-7100
49 Bancroft Mills Rd P8 Wilmington (19806) *(G-12616)*
Silver Springs Apartments 302 992-0800
12 Mary Ella Dr Ste E Wilmington (19805) *(G-12617)*
Silver Works Inc 302 227-1707
149 Rehoboth Ave Rehoboth Beach (19971) *(G-8076)*
Silverback Gyms LLC 302 539-8282
2 Town Rd Ocean View (19970) *(G-7813)*

Silverbrook Cemetery Co 302 658-0953
3300 Lancaster Pike Wilmington (19805) *(G-12618)*
Silverside Club Inc 302 478-4568
418 Brandywine Blvd Talleyville (19803) *(G-8751)*
Silverside Contracting Inc 302 798-1907
2801 N Broom St Wilmington (19802) *(G-12619)*
Silverside Dental Associates 302 478-4700
3512 Silverside Rd Ste 6 Wilmington (19810) *(G-12620)*
Silverside Mall, Wilmington Also called Delaware Imaging Network *(G-10056)*
Silverside Medical Center, Wilmington Also called Ent and Allergy Delaware LLC *(G-10405)*
Silverside Open Mri Imaging 302 246-2000
2501 Silverside Rd Ste A Wilmington (19810) *(G-12621)*
Silview Auto Care 302 994-1617
806 W Newport Pike Wilmington (19804) *(G-12622)*
Simar Fuel Inc 302 304-1969
126 S Dupont Blvd Smyrna (19977) *(G-8716)*
Simm Associates Inc 302 283-2800
800 Pencader Dr Newark (19702) *(G-7430)*
Simmons Electrical Service LLC 410 543-1480
4663 White Deer Rd B Delmar (19940) *(G-1030)*
Simon Eye Associates PA 302 834-4305
116 Foxhunt Dr Ste 116 # 116 Bear (19701) *(G-322)*
Simon Eye Associates PA 302 655-8180
912 N Union St Wilmington (19805) *(G-12623)*
Simon Eye Associates PA (PA) 302 239-1389
5301 Limestone Rd Ste 128 Wilmington (19808) *(G-12624)*
Simon Mstr & Sidlow Assoc Inc 302 652-3480
750 Prides Xing Ste 100 Newark (19713) *(G-7431)*
Simple Space LLC 801 520-3680
300 Delaware Ave Ste 210a Wilmington (19801) *(G-12625)*
Simpler and Sons LLC 302 296-4400
37139 Rehoboth Avenue Ext Rehoboth Beach (19971) *(G-8077)*
Simpler Logistics LLC 800 619-8321
300 Delaware Ave Ste 210 Wilmington (19801) *(G-12626)*
Simpler Surveying & Associates 302 539-7873
32486 Powell Farm Rd Frankford (19945) *(G-2387)*
Simplex Time Recorder 557, New Castle Also called Simplex Time Recorder LLC *(G-5714)*
Simplex Time Recorder LLC 302 325-6300
18 Boulden Cir Ste 36 New Castle (19720) *(G-5714)*
Simply Clean Jantr Svcs Inc 302 744-9100
100 Carlsons Way Ste 6 Dover (19901) *(G-2084)*
Simply Green 302 256-0822
216 S Maryland Ave Wilmington (19804) *(G-12627)*
Simply Styling-Schl of Csmtlgy 302 778-1885
204 N Union St Wilmington (19805) *(G-12628)*
Simplymiddle 302 200-0102
26 Auckland Dr Newark (19702) *(G-7432)*
Simplymiddle LLC 302 217-3460
901 N Market St Ste 719 Wilmington (19801) *(G-12629)*
Simpson Gary Contracting LLC 302 398-7733
1994 Fox Hunters Rd Harrington (19952) *(G-2889)*
Simpson Log Homes, Dover Also called Aslin Inc *(G-1145)*
Sinc Business Corporation (PA) 480 210-1798
251 Little Falls Dr Wilmington (19808) *(G-12630)*
Sinc Time Clock, Wilmington Also called Sinc Business Corporation *(G-12630)*
Singular Key Inc 408 753-5848
251 Little Falls Dr Wilmington (19808) *(G-12631)*
Sinnott Exc Consulting LLC 302 656-2898
319 Hampton Rd Wilmington (19803) *(G-12632)*
Sinuswars LLC 212 901-0805
501 Silverside Rd Ste 105 Wilmington (19809) *(G-12633)*
SIP Inc of Delaware (HQ) 302 654-4533
1101 E 8th St Wilmington (19801) *(G-12634)*
Sir Speedy, Wilmington Also called Amer Inc *(G-9039)*
Sir Speedy, Newark Also called Garile Inc *(G-6639)*
Siriusiq Mobile LLC 888 414-2047
200 Continental Dr Newark (19713) *(G-7433)*
Sirkin Levine Dental Assoc, Wilmington Also called Alan R Levine DDS *(G-8999)*
Sisterhood of Congregation, Dover Also called Beth Sholom Congregation *(G-1199)*
Sisuaq Scientific 302 739-3073
1 Commerce St Wilmington (19801) *(G-12635)*
Site 321, Wilmington Also called BFI Waste Services LLC *(G-9324)*
Site 426, Felton Also called BFI Waste Services LLC *(G-2274)*
Site Source Contractor Supply 302 322-0444
613 Pulaski Hwy Bear (19701) *(G-323)*
Site Work Safety Supplies Inc 302 672-7011
4020 Hickories Rd Dover (19904) *(G-2085)*
Siteage LLC 302 380-3709
16192 Coastal Hwy Lewes (19958) *(G-3746)*
Sitengle Technology LLC 719 822-0710
8 The Grn Ste A Dover (19901) *(G-2086)*
Siteone Landscape Supply LLC 302 836-3903
711 Carson Dr Bear (19701) *(G-324)*
Sitwa Group LLC (PA) 786 802-4155
1925 Lovering Ave Wilmington (19806) *(G-12636)*
Six Angels Development Inc 302 218-1548
7 Medori Blvd Wilmington (19801) *(G-12637)*
Six Plus Inc 302 652-3296
5714 Kennett Pike Wilmington (19807) *(G-12638)*

Sjm Sales Inc 302 697-6748
500 Eagle Nest Dr Camden Wyoming (19934) *(G-657)*
Skab International Corporation 412 475-2221
15 Loockerman Plz Dover (19901) *(G-2087)*
Skadden Arps Slate Meagher 302 651-3000
920 N King St Ste 700 Wilmington (19801) *(G-12639)*
Skadden Arps Slate Meagher & F 302 651-3000
1 Rodney Sq Wilmington (19801) *(G-12640)*
Skajaquoda Capital LLC 302 504-4448
717 N Union St Ste 5 Wilmington (19805) *(G-12641)*
Skanska USA Building Inc 215 495-8790
313 Wyoming Rd Newark (19711) *(G-7434)*
Skateworld Inc (PA) 302 875-2121
23601 Dove Rd Seaford (19973) *(G-8402)*
Skating Club of Wilmington Inc 302 656-5005
1301 Carruthers Ln Wilmington (19803) *(G-12642)*
Sketches and Pixels LLC 312 834-4402
2035 Sunset Lake Rd B2 Newark (19702) *(G-7435)*
Skim USA 302 227-4011
1904 Highway One Rehoboth Beach (19971) *(G-8078)*
Skinary App Inc 773 744-5407
651 N Broad St Ste 205 Middletown (19709) *(G-4242)*
Skinify LLC 302 212-5689
35770 Airport Rd Rehoboth Beach (19971) *(G-8079)*
Skiplist Inc 440 855-0319
2035 Sunset Lake Rd B2 Newark (19702) *(G-7436)*
Sks Enterprise 302 310-2511
200 Continental Dr Newark (19713) *(G-7437)*
Sky Nails 302 322-5949
287 Christiana Rd Ste 15 New Castle (19720) *(G-5715)*
Sky Trax, Wilmington *Also called Xcs Corporation (G-13316)*
Sky World Traveler 844 591-9060
1013 Centre Rd Ste 403s Wilmington (19805) *(G-12643)*
Skyline Supply Inc 302 894-9190
62 Albe Dr Ste C Newark (19702) *(G-7438)*
Skynethostingnet Inc 302 384-1784
501 Silverside Rd Wilmington (19809) *(G-12644)*
Skyways Motor Lodge Corp 302 328-6666
147 N Dupont Hwy New Castle (19720) *(G-5716)*
Slacum & Doyle Tax Service LLC 302 734-1850
838 Walker Rd Ste 22-2 Dover (19904) *(G-2088)*
Slater Fireplaces Inc 302 999-1200
1726 Newport Gap Pike Wilmington (19808) *(G-12645)*
Slaughter Neck Educational and 302 684-1834
22942 Slaughter Neck Rd Lincoln (19960) *(G-3870)*
Sleep Disorder Center Del Inc 302 224-6000
4735 Ogltn Stntn Rd # 1225 Newark (19713) *(G-7439)*
Sleep Disorders Center 302 645-3186
424 Savannah Rd Lewes (19958) *(G-3747)*
Sleep Disorders Ctr-Christiana 302 623-0650
774 Christiana Rd Ste 103 Newark (19713) *(G-7440)*
Sleep Inn, Dover *Also called Kw Garden (G-1759)*
Sleep Inn, Newark *Also called Nacstar (G-7081)*
Sleep Inn & Suites 302 645-6464
18451 Coastal Hwy Lewes (19958) *(G-3748)*
Sleeper Creeper Inc 302 519-4553
17015 Sand Hill Rd Georgetown (19947) *(G-2656)*
Sleigh Financial Inc 302 684-2929
28266 Lwes Georgetown Hwy Milton (19968) *(G-4970)*
Slice of Wood LLC 315 335-0917
70 Clinton St Delaware City (19706) *(G-967)*
Slimstim Inc 310 560-4950
1209 N Orange St Wilmington (19801) *(G-12646)*
Sling With ME 302 424-0111
809 Ne 10th St Milford (19963) *(G-4561)*
SLM Corporation (PA) 302 451-0200
300 Continental Dr Newark (19713) *(G-7441)*
SLM Financial Corporation (HQ) 856 642-8300
300 Continental Dr Fl 1 Newark (19713) *(G-7442)*
SM Technomine Inc (PA) 312 492-4386
802 N West St Wilmington (19801) *(G-12647)*
SM Technomine Inc 312 492-4386
19c Trolley Sq Wilmington (19806) *(G-12648)*
SMA Pediatrics, Smyrna *Also called Caridad Rosal MA MD (G-8591)*
Smackerals By Michelle LLC 302 376-8272
109 Fox Hunt Ln Middletown (19709) *(G-4243)*
Smakkfitness LLC 213 280-7569
401 N Market St Wilmington (19801) *(G-12649)*
Small Bus Resource Info Cebter, Wilmington *Also called Small Business Development Ctr (G-12650)*
Small Business Development Ctr 302 571-1555
1318 N Market St Wilmington (19801) *(G-12650)*
Small Wonder Day Care Inc 302 654-2269
100 Greenhill Ave Ste A Wilmington (19805) *(G-12651)*
Small Wonder Dental 302 525-6463
715 Nottingham Rd Newark (19711) *(G-7443)*
Smalls Real Estate Company 302 633-1985
5227 W Woodmill Dr Ste 42 Wilmington (19808) *(G-12652)*
Smalls Stepping Stone 302 652-3011
1408 Clifford Brown Walk Wilmington (19801) *(G-12653)*
Smart 302 655-6084
12 Varmar Dr New Castle (19720) *(G-5717)*
Smart Armor Protected LLC 480 823-8122
19 Kris Ct Newark (19702) *(G-7444)*
Smart Hospitality & MGT LLC 212 444-1989
3411 Silverside Rd Wilmington (19810) *(G-12654)*
Smart International Inc 302 451-9517
2035 Sunset Lake Rd B2 Newark (19702) *(G-7445)*
Smart Plus Transport LLC 347 963-0980
624 N Barrett Ln Newark (19702) *(G-7446)*
Smart Printing MGT LLC 855 549-4900
560 Peoples Plz Ste 301 Newark (19702) *(G-7447)*
Smart Shoppers, Wilmington *Also called Gbc International Corp (G-10682)*
Smarter Home & Office LLC 302 723-9313
18 Monticello Blvd New Castle (19720) *(G-5718)*
Smartis 302 653-8355
73 Greentree Dr Dover (19904) *(G-2089)*
Smartstudents LLC 302 597-6586
4701 Limestone Rd Ste 182 Wilmington (19808) *(G-12655)*
Smartwheel Inc 617 542-7400
1521 Concord Pike Ste 303 Wilmington (19803) *(G-12656)*
Smarty Pants Early Education 302 985-3770
146 Willamette Dr Bear (19701) *(G-325)*
Smb Lighting 302 733-0664
36 Anthony Dr Newark (19702) *(G-7448)*
Smf Deliveries LLC 302 945-6693
17 Amberwood Way Lewes (19958) *(G-3749)*
Smid Aerospace Corporation 443 205-0881
104 Dorothy Dr Bear (19701) *(G-326)*
Smile Brite Dental Care LLC 302 384-8448
1401 Pennsylvania Ave # 106 Wilmington (19806) *(G-12657)*
Smile Brite Dental Care LLC (PA) 302 838-8306
300 Biddle Ave Ste 204 Newark (19702) *(G-7449)*
Smile Place 302 514-6200
17 N Main St Smyrna (19977) *(G-8717)*
Smile Solutions By Emmi Dental 302 999-8113
1601 Milltown Rd Ste 25 Wilmington (19808) *(G-12658)*
Smiles Jolly PA 302 378-3384
102 Sleepy Hollow Dr # 100 Middletown (19709) *(G-4244)*
Smith & Allen Insurance, Wilmington *Also called Allen Insurance Group (G-9019)*
Smith & Nephew Holdings Inc (HQ) 302 884-6720
1201 N Orange St Ste 788 Wilmington (19801) *(G-12659)*
Smith Barney Consulting Group, Wilmington *Also called Citigroup Global Markets Inc (G-9713)*
Smith Brothers Communication 302 293-5224
27 Harkfort Rd Newark (19702) *(G-7450)*
Smith Concrete Inc 302 270-9251
8473 N Union Church Rd Milford (19963) *(G-4562)*
Smith Firm LLC 302 875-5595
8866 Riverside Dr Seaford (19973) *(G-8403)*
Smith Fnberg McCrtney Berl LLP 302 644-8330
34382 Carpenters Way # 1 Lewes (19958) *(G-3750)*
Smith Fnberg McCrtney Berl LLP (PA) 302 856-7082
406 S Bedford St Georgetown (19947) *(G-2657)*
Smith Katzenstein & Furlow LLP 302 652-8400
1000 N West St Ste 1500 Wilmington (19801) *(G-12660)*
Smith Superior Home Services, Wilmington *Also called Smith Superior Pntg Repr Svcs (G-12661)*
Smith Superior Pntg Repr Svcs 302 384-6575
2911 N Franklin St Wilmington (19802) *(G-12661)*
Smith, Katzenscein and Jenkins, Wilmington *Also called Roger D Anderson (G-12464)*
Smith, Kenneth MD, Bridgeville *Also called Internal Medicine Bridgeville (G-484)*
Smithfeld Intl Investments Inc 302 477-1358
3411 Silverside Rd Wilmington (19810) *(G-12662)*
Smiths Jack Towing & Svc Ctr 302 798-6667
1806 Philadelphia Pike Wilmington (19809) *(G-12663)*
Smittys Auto Repair Inc 302 398-8419
17378 S Dupont Hwy Harrington (19952) *(G-2890)*
Smokeys Gulf Service Inc 302 378-2451
48 E Main St Middletown (19709) *(G-4245)*
Smooth Sound Dance Band 302 398-8467
201 Dorman St Harrington (19952) *(G-2891)*
Smoothies Soup and Sandwiches 302 280-6183
11290 Trussum Pond Rd Laurel (19956) *(G-3289)*
Smrc Smart Automotive 317 941-7257
1209 Ornge St Corp Tr Ctr R Ation Trust Ct Wilmington (19801) *(G-12664)*
SMS Systems Maintenance, Newark *Also called Curvature Inc (G-6328)*
Smw Sales LLC 302 875-7958
11432 Trussum Pond Rd Laurel (19956) *(G-3290)*
Smyrna Dental Center PA 302 223-6194
679 S Carter Rd Unit 5 Smyrna (19977) *(G-8718)*
Smyrna Medical Associates PA 302 653-6174
38 Deak Dr Smyrna (19977) *(G-8719)*
Smyrna News & Tobacco 302 653-9620
456 W Glenwood Ave Ste B2 Smyrna (19977) *(G-8720)*
Smyrna School District 302 653-3135
80 Monrovia Ave Smyrna (19977) *(G-8721)*
Smyrna-Clayton Sun Times, Dover *Also called Dover Post Co Inc (G-1466)*

ALPHABETIC

Snap Fitness........302 741-2444
1030 Forrest Ave Ste 100 Dover (19904) ***(G-2090)***
Snickers Ditch Trunk Company........302 325-1762
182 E 4th St New Castle (19720) ***(G-5719)***
Snow Farms Inc........302 653-7534
249 Raymond Neck Rd Smyrna (19977) ***(G-8722)***
Snow Pharmaceuticals LLC........302 436-8855
35998 Zion Church Rd Frankford (19945) ***(G-2388)***
Snowden Candles........302 398-4373
7184 Mlford Hrrington Hwy Harrington (19952) ***(G-2892)***
Sntc Holding Inc (HQ)........302 777-5261
919 N Market St Ste 200 Wilmington (19801) ***(G-12665)***
Snyder & Associates, Wilmington *Also called Snyder Associates PA* ***(G-12667)***
Snyder & Company PA........302 475-1600
1405 Silverside Rd Wilmington (19810) ***(G-12666)***
Snyder Associates PA........302 657-8300
300 Delaware Ave Ste 1014 Wilmington (19801) ***(G-12667)***
Sobieski J F Mechanical Contrs, Wilmington *Also called J F Sobieski Mech Contrs Inc* ***(G-11106)***
Sobieski Life Safety........800 321-1332
1325 Old Coochs Bridge Rd Newark (19713) ***(G-7451)***
Socal Auto Supply Inc (PA)........818 717-9982
16192 Postal Hwy Lewes (19958) ***(G-3751)***
Social Enterprise LLC........718 417-4076
250 Centerpoint Blvd New Castle (19720) ***(G-5720)***
Social Health Innovations Inc........917 476-9355
8 The Grn Ste 5175 Dover (19901) ***(G-2091)***
Social Security Administration........302 736-3688
655 S Bay Rd Ste 3j Dover (19901) ***(G-2092)***
Social Work Helper Pbc........302 233-7422
8 The Grn Ste 8043 Dover (19901) ***(G-2093)***
Society For Acpuncture RES Inc........302 222-1832
108 Dewey Ave Lewes (19958) ***(G-3752)***
Society For Whole-Body Autorad........302 369-5240
110 Executive Dr Ste 7 Newark (19702) ***(G-7452)***
Society Hill Apts, Claymont *Also called Stoltz Realty Co* ***(G-807)***
Society of St Vincent De Paul........302 328-5166
1414 N King St Wilmington (19801) ***(G-12668)***
Sociomatry Press........302 313-5341
103 Hornbill Ct Lewes (19958) ***(G-3753)***
Socraticlaw Co Inc........302 654-9191
3900 Centerville Rd Wilmington (19807) ***(G-12669)***
Sodat of Delaware Inc (PA)........302 656-2810
625 N Orange St Fl 2 Wilmington (19801) ***(G-12670)***
Sodel Concepts II LLC........302 228-3786
220 Rehoboth Ave Unit A Rehoboth Beach (19971) ***(G-8080)***
Softball World LLC........302 856-7922
22518 Lwes Georgetown Hwy Georgetown (19947) ***(G-2658)***
Softmogul Inc........414 426-1650
2711 Centerville Rd # 400 Wilmington (19808) ***(G-12671)***
Software Bananas LLC........302 348-8488
2915 Ogletown Rd Ste 2304 Newark (19713) ***(G-7453)***
Software Plus, Newark *Also called Shore Consultants Ltd* ***(G-7417)***
Software Services of De Inc (PA)........302 654-3172
1024 Justison St Wilmington (19801) ***(G-12672)***
Soil Service Inc........302 629-7054
117 New St Seaford (19973) ***(G-8404)***
Sojourners Place Inc........302 764-4592
2901 Northeast Blvd Wilmington (19802) ***(G-12673)***
Sokoloff, Bruce H MD, Wilmington *Also called Wilmington Medical Associates* ***(G-13237)***
Solace Lifesciences Inc........302 275-4195
501 Silverside Rd Ste 7 Wilmington (19809) ***(G-12674)***
Solar Foundations Usa Inc........518 935-3360
206 Mcfarland Dr Newark (19702) ***(G-7454)***
Solar Foundations Usa Inc........855 738-7200
1142 River Rd New Castle (19720) ***(G-5721)***
Solar Heating Inc........302 836-3943
21 E Savannah Dr Bear (19701) ***(G-327)***
Solar Unlimited North Amer LLC........302 542-4580
11 Kentucky Ave Lewes (19958) ***(G-3754)***
Solavitek Engineering Inc........514 949-6981
2915 Ogletown Rd Ste 2823 Newark (19713) ***(G-7455)***
Solenis Holdings 3 LLC (HQ)........866 337-1533
3 Beaver Valley Rd # 500 Wilmington (19803) ***(G-12675)***
Solenis International LLC (PA)........302 994-1698
3 Beaver Valley Rd # 500 Wilmington (19803) ***(G-12676)***
Solenis LLC (HQ)........866 337-1533
2475 Pinnacle Dr Wilmington (19803) ***(G-12677)***
Solenis LLC........302 594-5000
500 Hercules Rd Wilmington (19808) ***(G-12678)***
Solid Idea Solutions LLC........646 982-2890
16192 Coastal Hwy Lewes (19958) ***(G-3755)***
Solid Image Inc........302 877-0901
11244 Whitesville Rd Laurel (19956) ***(G-3291)***
Solufy Corp........877 476-5839
1201 N Orange St Ste 7228 Wilmington (19801) ***(G-12679)***
Solution On-Call Services LLC........302 353-4328
19 Lambson Ln Ste 108-B New Castle (19720) ***(G-5722)***
Solutions of Advant-Edge........302 533-6858
1 Shea Way Newark (19713) ***(G-7456)***
Solutions Property Management........302 581-9060
38 Hannah Loop Rehoboth Beach (19971) ***(G-8081)***
Solutions, I.P.E.M., Georgetown *Also called Integrated Solutions Planning* ***(G-2567)***
Solvay Spclty Polymers USA LLC........302 452-6609
100 Interchange Blvd Newark (19711) ***(G-7457)***
Solvetech Inc........302 798-5400
1711 Philadelphia Pike Wilmington (19809) ***(G-12680)***
Sombar & Co CPA PA (PA)........302 856-6712
109 S Bedford St Georgetown (19947) ***(G-2659)***
Somerford House Newark, Newark *Also called Five Star Quality Care Inc* ***(G-6592)***
Somerford Place Newark, Newark *Also called Five Star Senior Living Inc* ***(G-6594)***
Somerville Manning Gallery........302 652-0271
101 Stone Block Row Wilmington (19807) ***(G-12681)***
Something Unique Inc........302 678-0555
1014 Lafferty Ln Dover (19901) ***(G-2094)***
Sonesta........302 453-9200
240 Chapman Rd Newark (19702) ***(G-7458)***
Sonshine Dental Labs Inc........302 731-5582
300 Creek View Rd Ste 105 Newark (19711) ***(G-7459)***
Sophisticuts Inc........302 834-7427
3 Rice Dr Bear (19701) ***(G-328)***
Sopo-360 LLC........703 585-3706
1 Innovation Way Ste 400 Newark (19711) ***(G-7460)***
Sorbent Green LLC (PA)........800 259-3577
1209 N Orange St Wilmington (19801) ***(G-12682)***
SOS Security Incorporated........302 425-4755
1000 N West St Ste 200 Wilmington (19801) ***(G-12683)***
Soucialize Inc........916 803-1057
16192 Coastal Hwy Lewes (19958) ***(G-3756)***
Sound-N-Secure Inc........302 424-3670
20444 Pingue Dr Milford (19963) ***(G-4563)***
Soundboks Inc (PA)........213 436-5888
2711 Centerville Rd # 400 Wilmington (19808) ***(G-12684)***
Source Supply Inc........302 328-5110
6 Bellecor Dr Ste 104 New Castle (19720) ***(G-5723)***
Sourcing Time LLC........302 409-0890
3422 Old Capitol Trl Wilmington (19808) ***(G-12685)***
South Bowers Ladies Auxiliary........302 335-4135
57 Scotts Corner Rd Milford (19963) ***(G-4564)***
South Bowers Volunteer Fire Co........302 335-4666
57 Scotts Corner Rd Milford (19963) ***(G-4565)***
South Coastal........302 542-5668
33711 S Coastal Ln Frankford (19945) ***(G-2389)***
South Delaware Masonry Inc........302 378-1998
319 Main St Townsend (19734) ***(G-8822)***
South Forks Inc........302 731-0344
136 Sandy Dr Newark (19713) ***(G-7461)***
South Gate Apartments, Claymont *Also called South Gate Realty Assoc LLP* ***(G-806)***
South Gate Realty Assoc LLP........302 368-4535
1308 Society Dr Claymont (19703) ***(G-806)***
South Jersey Paving........856 498-8647
518 Turnberry Ct Bear (19701) ***(G-329)***
South Shore Provisions LLC........443 614-2442
18 Ruth St Selbyville (19975) ***(G-8546)***
Southbrdge Med Advsory Council (PA)........302 655-6187
601 New Castle Ave Wilmington (19801) ***(G-12686)***
Souther States Co-Op, Harrington *Also called Hudson Farm Supply Co Inc* ***(G-2853)***
Southern Crab Company........302 478-0181
2831 Kennedy Rd Wilmington (19810) ***(G-12687)***
Southern Del Assoc Dntl Spc........302 226-1606
20398 Silver Lake Dr # 2 Rehoboth Beach (19971) ***(G-8082)***
Southern Del Imaging Assoc, Lewes *Also called Southern Delaware Imaging LLP* ***(G-3758)***
Southern Del Physcl Therapy........302 947-4460
26089 Shpps At Long Nck Millsboro (19966) ***(G-4802)***
Southern Del Physcl Therapy........302 854-9600
2 Lee Ave Unit 101 Georgetown (19947) ***(G-2660)***
Southern Del Physcl Therapy........302 659-0173
207 Stadium St Smyrna (19977) ***(G-8723)***
Southern Del Physcl Therapy........302 227-2008
70 Rehoboth Ave 37155 Rehoboth Beach (19971) ***(G-8083)***
Southern Del Physcl Therapy (PA)........302 644-2530
701 Savannah Rd Ste A Lewes (19958) ***(G-3757)***
Southern Del Trck Growers Assn........302 875-3147
Dual Hwy & Georgetown Rd Laurel (19956) ***(G-3292)***
Southern Delaware Dental Spec........302 855-9499
20785 Prof Pk Blvd Georgetown (19947) ***(G-2661)***
Southern Delaware Foot........302 404-5915
543 N Shipley St Ste C Seaford (19973) ***(G-8405)***
Southern Delaware Imaging LLP........302 645-7919
17503 Nassau Commons Blvd Lewes (19958) ***(G-3758)***
Southern Delaware Med Group........302 424-3900
200 Banning St Ste 380 Dover (19904) ***(G-2095)***
Southern Delaware Med Group PA........302 424-3900
119 Neurology Way Milford (19963) ***(G-4566)***
Southern Delaware Signs........302 645-1425
18388 Coastal Hwy Unit 4 Lewes (19958) ***(G-3759)***
Southern Delaware Surgery Ctr........302 644-6992
18941 John J Williams Hwy Rehoboth Beach (19971) ***(G-8084)***
Southern Dental LLC........302 536-7589
703 Health Services Dr Seaford (19973) ***(G-8406)***

Southern Glazers Wine 302 656-4487
615 Lambson Ln New Castle (19720) **(G-5724)**
Southern Glazers Wine Spirits, New Castle *Also called Southern Wine Spirits Del LLC* **(G-5726)**
Southern Printing 302 832-3475
1053 Lower Twin Lane Rd New Castle (19720) **(G-5725)**
Southern States Coop Inc 302 378-9841
900 N Broad St Middletown (19709) **(G-4246)**
Southern States Coop Inc 302 732-6651
302 Clayton St Dagsboro (19939) **(G-934)**
Southern States Coop Inc 302 875-3635
102 Deshields St Laurel (19956) **(G-3293)**
Southern Wine Spirits Del LLC 800 292-7890
615 Lambson Ln New Castle (19720) **(G-5726)**
Southgate Concrete Company 302 376-5280
600 Industrial Rd Middletown (19709) **(G-4247)**
Southland Insulators Del LLC 302 854-0344
22976 Sussex Ave Georgetown (19947) **(G-2662)**
Southside Family Practice 302 735-1880
230 Beiser Blvd Ste 200 Dover (19904) **(G-2096)**
Southwest American Corp 302 652-7003
2200 N Grant Ave Wilmington (19806) **(G-12688)**
Sovereign Capital MGT Group, Wilmington *Also called Sovereign Capitl MGT Group Inc* **(G-12689)**
Sovereign Capitl MGT Group Inc 619 294-8989
1000 N West St Ste 1200 Wilmington (19801) **(G-12689)**
Sp Auto Parts Inc 302 337-8897
7514 Federalsburg Rd Bridgeville (19933) **(G-521)**
Sp Plus Corporation 302 652-1410
111 W 11th St Lowr Wilmington (19801) **(G-12690)**
Spa At Corolla Inc 302 292-2858
271 W Main St Newark (19711) **(G-7462)**
Space Makers Inc 302 322-4325
600 Pulaski Hwy Bear (19701) **(G-330)**
Spacecon LLC (HQ) 302 322-9285
292 Churchmans Rd New Castle (19720) **(G-5727)**
Spaceport Support Services 302 524-4020
6 Dixon St Selbyville (19975) **(G-8547)**
Spacetime Engineering, Wilmington *Also called Dorsia Alliance Ltd* **(G-10207)**
Spain Magic Rose LLC (PA) 941 312-2051
3411 Silverside Rd Wilmington (19810) **(G-12691)**
Spallco Car & Truck Rental, Newark *Also called Spallco Enterprises Inc* **(G-7463)**
Spallco Car & Truck Rentals, Wilmington *Also called Spallco Enterprises Inc* **(G-12692)**
Spallco Enterprises Inc 302 368-5950
915 S Chapel St Newark (19713) **(G-7463)**
Spallco Enterprises Inc (PA) 302 762-3825
702 Philadelphia Pike Wilmington (19809) **(G-12692)**
Sparano, Joseph C CPA, Wilmington *Also called Grabowski Sprano Vnclette Cpas* **(G-10757)**
Spark 302 324-2203
950 W Basin Rd New Castle (19720) **(G-5728)**
Spark Productions LLC 302 436-0183
38025 Fenwick Shoals Blvd Selbyville (19975) **(G-8548)**
Sparkia Inc 302 636-5440
2711 Centerville Rd # 400 Wilmington (19808) **(G-12693)**
Sparkle Mobile Dental Services 302 762-4322
718 W 38th St Wilmington (19802) **(G-12694)**
Sparklean Laundromat 302 838-2226
750 Peoples Plz Newark (19702) **(G-7464)**
Spca 302 698-3006
455 Stanton Christiana Rd Newark (19713) **(G-7465)**
Spearhead Inc 347 670-2699
2306 Porter Rd Bear (19701) **(G-331)**
Spec Processing Group Inc 302 295-2197
2266 Porter Rd Bear (19701) **(G-332)**
Special Care Inc 302 644-6990
16698 Kings Hwy Ste D Lewes (19958) **(G-3760)**
Special Care Inc 302 456-9904
5145 W Woodmill Dr 22 Wilmington (19808) **(G-12695)**
Special Olympics Inc 302 831-4653
619 S College Ave Newark (19716) **(G-7466)**
Special Olympics Delaware Inc 302 831-4653
Univer Of De 619 S Collge St Univer Of Newark (19716) **(G-7467)**
Special Olympics of Deleware, Newark *Also called Special Olympics Inc* **(G-7466)**
Special Services Center, Smyrna *Also called Smyrna School District* **(G-8721)**
Specialized Carier Systems Inc 302 424-4548
256 N Rehoboth Blvd Milford (19963) **(G-4567)**
Specialty Machine Works 302 429-8970
319 Robinson Ln Wilmington (19805) **(G-12696)**
Specialty Products N&H Inc (HQ) 302 774-1000
200 Powder Mill Rd Wilmington (19803) **(G-12697)**
Specialty Products N&H, LLC, Wilmington *Also called Specialty Products N&H Inc* **(G-12697)**
Specialty Rehabilitation Inc 302 709-0440
4701 Ogltn Stntn Rd # 4100 Newark (19713) **(G-7468)**
Spectr-Physics Hldings USA Inc 302 478-4600
3411 Silverside Rd Ste 10 Wilmington (19810) **(G-12698)**
Spectrum Hone & Lace Llc 313 268-5455
310 Haines St Ste 116 Newark (19717) **(G-7469)**
Spectrum Magnetics LLC (PA) 302 993-1070
1210 First State Blvd Wilmington (19804) **(G-12699)**
Spectrum Tax Consultants USA 866 544-1408
800 Delaware Ave Fl 10 Wilmington (19801) **(G-12700)**
Speech Clinic 302 999-0702
5147 W Woodmill Dr Ste 21 Wilmington (19808) **(G-12701)**
Speech Therapeutics Inc 302 234-9226
15 Elderberry Ct Hockessin (19707) **(G-3147)**
Speed Pro Imiging, Wilmington *Also called Grm Pro Imaging LLC* **(G-10788)**
Speedrid Ltd 213 550-5462
625 S Dupont Hwy Dover (19901) **(G-2097)**
Speedy Publishing LLC 888 248-4521
40 E Main St 1156 Newark (19711) **(G-7470)**
Spekciton Biosciences LLC 302 353-2694
2509 Berwyn Rd Wilmington (19810) **(G-12702)**
Spencer, Richard N Jr Vmd, Newark *Also called White Clay Creek Vtrinary Hosp* **(G-7691)**
Spences Bazaar & Auction LLC 302 734-3441
550 S New St Dover (19904) **(G-2098)**
Spg, Bear *Also called Spec Processing Group Inc* **(G-332)**
Spg International LLC 404 823-3934
841 Mud Mill Rd Marydel (19964) **(G-3922)**
SPI Holding Company 800 789-9755
503 Carr Rd Ste 210 Wilmington (19809) **(G-12703)**
SPI Pharma, Wilmington *Also called SPI Holding Company* **(G-12703)**
SPI Pharma Inc 302 262-3223
1800 Dulany St Seaford (19973) **(G-8407)**
SPI Pharma Inc (HQ) 302 576-8500
503 Carr Rd Ste 210 Wilmington (19809) **(G-12704)**
Spicer Mullikin Funeral Homes (PA) 302 368-9500
1000 N Dupont Hwy New Castle (19720) **(G-5729)**
Spicer Mullikin Funeral Homes 302 368-9500
121 W Park Pl Newark (19711) **(G-7471)**
Spikes Coach Lines 302 438-3644
34 Vining Ln Wilmington (19807) **(G-12705)**
Spine & Orthopedic Specialist 302 633-1280
1101 Twin C Ln Ste 203 Newark (19713) **(G-7472)**
Spine Care of Delaware 302 894-1900
4102b Ogletown Stanton Rd Newark (19713) **(G-7473)**
Spine Group LLC 302 595-3030
1426 N Clayton St Wilmington (19806) **(G-12706)**
Spirit-Trans Inc 302 290-9830
832 N Gwynn Ct Bear (19701) **(G-333)**
Spirits Path To Wellness LLC 302 998-0074
1405 Greenhill Ave Wilmington (19806) **(G-12707)**
Splash Lndrmat LLC - Gorgetown 302 249-8231
201 E Laurel St Georgetown (19947) **(G-2663)**
Sporting Goods Properties 302 774-1000
974 Centre Rd Wilmington (19805) **(G-12708)**
Sports At The Beach, Georgetown *Also called Softball World LLC* **(G-2658)**
Sports Car Service Inc 302 764-7439
3901 N Market St Wilmington (19802) **(G-12709)**
Sports Car Tire Inc 302 571-8473
1203 E 13th St Wilmington (19802) **(G-12710)**
Sportz Tees 302 280-6076
16536 Adams Rd Laurel (19956) **(G-3294)**
Sposato Irrigation Company 302 645-4773
16181 Hudson Rd Milton (19968) **(G-4971)**
Sposato Landscape Company Inc 302 645-4773
16181 Hudson Rd Milton (19968) **(G-4972)**
Sposato Lawn Care 302 645-4773
Rr 4 Box 265-B Milton (19968) **(G-4973)**
Spotlight Publications LLC 302 504-1329
3301 Lancaster Pike 5c Wilmington (19805) **(G-12711)**
Spratley Publishing 267 779-7353
1203 Apple St Wilmington (19801) **(G-12712)**
Spratley Publishing Co, Wilmington *Also called Spratley Publishing* **(G-12712)**
Spring Communications Inc 302 297-2000
26670 Centerview Dr # 14 Millsboro (19966) **(G-4803)**
Spring Communications Inc 302 475-1052
2090 Naamans Rd Wilmington (19810) **(G-12713)**
Spring Floor Tech LLC 302 528-3474
1m King Ave New Castle (19720) **(G-5730)**
Spring Lake Bath & Tennis Club 302 227-6136
323 Rehoboth Ave Rehoboth Beach (19971) **(G-8085)**
Springhaus Landscape Company, Bear *Also called Itea Inc* **(G-193)**
Springhaus LLC 302 397-5261
251 Little Falls Dr Wilmington (19808) **(G-12714)**
Springhill Seamless Gutter, Milford *Also called Hickman Overhead Door Company* **(G-4441)**
Springleaf Fincl Holdings LLC 302 543-6767
1 Righter Pkwy Wilmington (19803) **(G-12715)**
Springside LLC 302 838-7223
200 Biddle Ave Ste 205 Newark (19702) **(G-7474)**
Sprinkles Christian Daycare, Newark *Also called Brown Lisha* **(G-6126)**
Sprint 302 261-8500
710 Peoples Plz Newark (19702) **(G-7475)**
Sprint Communications Inc 302 613-4004
1505 N Dupont Hwy New Castle (19720) **(G-5731)**
Sprint Communications Inc 302 604-6125
6 College Park Ln Georgetown (19947) **(G-2664)**

ALPHABETIC

(PA)=Parent Co (HQ)=Headquarters (DH)=Div Headquarters
2020 Harris Directory of Delaware Businesses
725

Sprint Quality Printing Inc 302 478-0720
3609 Silverside Rd Wilmington (19810) ***(G-12716)***
Sprint Spectrum LP 302 993-3700
4511 Kirkwood Hwy Wilmington (19808) ***(G-12717)***
Sprint Spectrum LP 302 393-2060
120 Aerenson Dr Milford (19963) ***(G-4568)***
Sprint Spectrum LP 302 322-1712
118 N Dupont Hwy New Castle (19720) ***(G-5732)***
Sprint Sprint, New Castle *Also called Sprint Communications Inc* ***(G-5731)***
Sprint Sprint, Georgetown *Also called Sprint Communications Inc* ***(G-2664)***
Sqrin Technologies LLC 540 330-1379
16192 Coastal Hwy Lewes (19958) ***(G-3761)***
Sqs Global Solutions LLC 302 691-9682
1201 N Orange St Ste 7383 Wilmington (19801) ***(G-12718)***
Square One Electric Service Co 302 678-0400
347 Fork Branch Rd Dover (19904) ***(G-2099)***
SRS Distribution Inc 240 965-8350
1204 E 12th St Ste 5 Wilmington (19802) ***(G-12719)***
Ssd Technology Partners, Wilmington *Also called Software Services of De Inc* ***(G-12672)***
SSS Clutch Company Inc 302 322-8080
610 W Basin Rd New Castle (19720) ***(G-5733)***
St Andrews Apartments 302 834-8600
50 Turnberry Ct Bear (19701) ***(G-334)***
St Andrews Maintenance 302 832-2675
104 E Scotland Dr Bear (19701) ***(G-335)***
St Anthonys Community Center 302 421-3721
1703 W 10th St Wilmington (19805) ***(G-12720)***
St Anthonys Housing Mgt Corp 302 421-3756
1701 W 10th St Ste 200 Wilmington (19805) ***(G-12721)***
St David's Episcopal Day Sch, Wilmington *Also called Diocesan Council Inc* ***(G-10157)***
St Delware Electrical 302 857-5316
245 Mckee Rd Dover (19904) ***(G-2100)***
St Francis Bariatric Center 302 421-4121
537 Stanton Christiana Rd Newark (19713) ***(G-7476)***
St Francis Family Care 302 554-5127
612 Ferry Cut Off St New Castle (19720) ***(G-5734)***
St Francis Hospital 302 369-9370
1220 Capitol Trl Newark (19711) ***(G-7477)***
St Francis Hospital Inc 616 685-3538
701 N Clayton St Wilmington (19805) ***(G-12722)***
St James Place Associates 302 764-6450
4 Denny Rd Wilmington (19809) ***(G-12723)***
St Johns Early Learning Center, Dover *Also called Saint Johns Lutheran Church* ***(G-2055)***
St Lawrence Grant Ave Trust 302 652-7978
2010 Pennsylvania Ave Wilmington (19806) ***(G-12724)***
St Logistics 302 407-5931
812 Philadelphia Pike Wilmington (19809) ***(G-12725)***
St Mark's Pre-School, Wilmington *Also called St Marks United Methodist Ch* ***(G-12726)***
St Marks United Methodist Ch 302 994-0400
1700 Limestone Rd Wilmington (19804) ***(G-12726)***
St Matthew Grand Chapter 302 834-9552
450 Topaz Cir Dover (19904) ***(G-2101)***
St Michaels School Inc 302 656-3389
305 E 7th St Wilmington (19801) ***(G-12727)***
St Patrick Center Inc 302 652-6219
107 E 14th St Wilmington (19801) ***(G-12728)***
St Stephens Evang Lutheran Ch 302 652-7623
1301 N Broom St Wilmington (19806) ***(G-12729)***
St Stephens Lutheran Church, Wilmington *Also called St Stephens Evang Lutheran Ch* ***(G-12729)***
ST. FRANCIS CARE CENTER AT WIL, Wilmington *Also called Regency Hlthcare Rehab Ctr LLC* ***(G-12355)***
St. Francis Life, Wilmington *Also called Life At St Frncis Hlthcare Inc* ***(G-11383)***
Stacy K Gates 302 368-1968
33 Possum Park Mall Newark (19711) ***(G-7478)***
Staffmark Investment LLC 302 834-2303
1867 Pulaski Hwy Bear (19701) ***(G-336)***
Staffmark Investment LLC 302 422-0606
242 S Rehoboth Blvd Milford (19963) ***(G-4569)***
Staffmark Investment LLC 302 854-0650
132 E Market St Georgetown (19947) ***(G-2665)***
Stafford Precision, Bear *Also called Bear Forge and Machine Co Inc* ***(G-47)***
Stage One, Dover *Also called Bernard Limpert* ***(G-1195)***
Staging Dimensions Inc 302 328-4100
31 Blevins Dr Ste A New Castle (19720) ***(G-5735)***
Staging Dimesions Inc 302 328-4100
31 Blevins Dr Ste A New Castle (19720) ***(G-5736)***
Staikos Associates Architects (PA) 302 764-1678
502 Dell Hill Rd Wilmington (19809) ***(G-12730)***
Stainless Alloys Inc 800 499-7833
103 Foulk Rd Ste 202 Wilmington (19803) ***(G-12731)***
Stainless Steel Invest Inc 800 499-7833
103 Foulk Rd Ste 202 Wilmington (19803) ***(G-12732)***
Stallard Chassis Co 302 292-1800
123 Sandy Dr Newark (19713) ***(G-7479)***
Stamford Screen Printing Inc 302 654-2442
3801 Kennett Pike C107 Wilmington (19807) ***(G-12733)***
Stamps By Impression 302 645-7191
102 Dove Dr Lewes (19958) ***(G-3762)***
Stan Perkoskis Plumbing & Htg 302 529-1220
1818 Marsh Rd Wilmington (19810) ***(G-12734)***
Standard Distributing Co Inc (PA) 302 655-5511
100 Mews Dr New Castle (19720) ***(G-5737)***
Standard Distributing Co Inc 302 674-4591
Horse Pond Rd Lafferty Ln Dover (19901) ***(G-2102)***
Standard Industrial Supply Co 302 656-1631
1625 N Heald St Wilmington (19802) ***(G-12735)***
Standard Insurance Company 302 322-9922
10 Corporate Cir New Castle (19720) ***(G-5738)***
Standard Pipe Services LLC 302 286-0701
567 Walther Rd Newark (19702) ***(G-7480)***
Standlee Hay Feed LLC 302 737-5117
1800 Ogletown Rd Ste B Newark (19711) ***(G-7481)***
Stanley Golden 302 652-5626
841 N Tatnall St Wilmington (19801) ***(G-12736)***
Stanley Goleburn DDS 302 297-3750
1290 Peoples Plz Newark (19702) ***(G-7482)***
Stanley H Goloskov DDS PA 302 475-0600
2500 Grubb Rd Ste 130 Wilmington (19810) ***(G-12737)***
Stanley Steamer Carpet, New Castle *Also called Sum Inc* ***(G-5740)***
Stanley Steemer Intl Inc 302 907-0062
1 Gerald Ct Delmar (19940) ***(G-1031)***
Stapen Construction Inc 302 218-2190
9 Harlech Dr Wilmington (19807) ***(G-12738)***
Stapleford's Oldsmobile, Saint Georges *Also called Staplefords Sales and Service* ***(G-8130)***
Staplefords At Wilmington Inc 302 762-0637
315 Springhill Ave Wilmington (19809) ***(G-12739)***
Staplefords Sales and Service 302 834-4568
1402 S Dupont Hwy Saint Georges (19733) ***(G-8130)***
Stapler Athletic Association 302 652-9769
1900 N Scott St Wilmington (19806) ***(G-12740)***
Star Art Inc 302 261-6732
1272 Porter Rd Bear (19701) ***(G-337)***
Star Campus II 302 514-7586
550 S College Ave Ste 107 Newark (19716) ***(G-7483)***
Star Nail Salon 302 498-0702
16a Trolley Sq Wilmington (19806) ***(G-12741)***
Star Nails & Spa 302 798-6245
1518 Philadelphia Pike Wilmington (19809) ***(G-12742)***
Star of Sea Condominium, Rehoboth Beach *Also called Star of The Sea Assoc of Ownrs* ***(G-8086)***
Star of The Sea Assoc of Ownrs 302 227-6006
307 S Boardwalk Ste L2 Rehoboth Beach (19971) ***(G-8086)***
Star States Leasing Corp 302 283-4500
30 Blue Hen Dr Ste 200 Newark (19713) ***(G-7484)***
Starr Wright Insur Agcy Inc 302 483-0190
405 Silverside Rd 102b Wilmington (19809) ***(G-12743)***
Starr Wright USA, Wilmington *Also called Starr Wright Insur Agcy Inc* ***(G-12743)***
Stars Transportation LLC 770 530-1843
311 Cams Fortune Way Harrington (19952) ***(G-2893)***
State Del Veterans Mem Cmtry, Bear *Also called Delaware Secretary of State* ***(G-112)***
State Drywall Co Inc 302 239-2843
12 Ridon Dr Hockessin (19707) ***(G-3148)***
State Education Agency Di 302 739-4111
401 Federal St Ste 2 Dover (19901) ***(G-2103)***
State Farm Insurance, New Castle *Also called Hartle Brian State Farm Agency* ***(G-5379)***
State Farm Insurance, Bear *Also called Robert F Mullen Insurance Agcy* ***(G-309)***
State Farm Insurance, Wilmington *Also called State Farm Mutl Auto Insur Co* ***(G-12744)***
State Farm Insurance, Rehoboth Beach *Also called George H Bunting Jr* ***(G-7944)***
State Farm Insurance, Wilmington *Also called Jack Lewis* ***(G-11114)***
State Farm Insurance, Seaford *Also called John C Leverage* ***(G-8281)***
State Farm Insurance, Camden *Also called Katie Bennett* ***(G-586)***
State Farm Insurance, Georgetown *Also called Mark Penuel* ***(G-2597)***
State Farm Insurance, Newark *Also called Terry White* ***(G-7557)***
State Farm Insurance, Seaford *Also called Eric Cline* ***(G-8238)***
State Farm Insurance, Newark *Also called Stacy K Gates* ***(G-7478)***
State Farm Insurance, Newark *Also called Patrick J McCabe* ***(G-7183)***
State Farm Insurance, Ocean View *Also called Denise Beam* ***(G-7783)***
State Farm Insurance, Dover *Also called John Borden* ***(G-1703)***
State Farm Insurance, Dover *Also called Phil Hill* ***(G-1954)***
State Farm Insurance, Dover *Also called Kathy Safford* ***(G-1724)***
State Farm Insurance, Dover *Also called Bob Simmons Agency* ***(G-1216)***
State Farm Insurance 302 832-0344
1250 Peoples Plz Newark (19702) ***(G-7485)***
State Farm Mutl Auto Insur Co 302 434-3333
1601 Concord Pike Ste 88 Wilmington (19803) ***(G-12744)***
State Janitorial Supply Co 302 734-4814
525 Otis Dr Dover (19901) ***(G-2104)***
State Line Building Supply 302 436-8624
Rr 113 Selbyville (19975) ***(G-8549)***
State Line Construction Inc 302 349-4244
650 Hickman Rd Greenwood (19950) ***(G-2764)***

State Line Farms LLC 302 628-4506
26394 Old Carriage Rd Seaford (19973) *(G-8408)*
State Line Machine Inc 302 478-0285
200 State Line Rd Wilmington (19803) *(G-12745)*
State Line Machine Inc 302 875-2248
1154 S Central Ave Laurel (19956) *(G-3295)*
State Street Inn 302 734-2294
228 N State St Dover (19901) *(G-2105)*
State Wide Plumbing Inc 302 292-0924
27 Albe Dr Ste J Newark (19702) *(G-7486)*
Statewide Mechanical Inc 302 376-6117
3295 Harris Rd Townsend (19734) *(G-8823)*
Statewide Plumbing, Newark *Also called State Wide Plumbing Inc (G-7486)*
Statwhiz Ventures LLC 310 819-5427
1201 N Orange St Ste 600 Wilmington (19801) *(G-12746)*
Stauffer Family LLC 302 227-5820
36 Glade Cir E Rehoboth Beach (19971) *(G-8087)*
Stay Prime Inc 612 770-6753
1201 N Orange St Ste 600 Wilmington (19801) *(G-12747)*
Stay True Plumbing 302 464-1198
693 Old Porter Rd Bear (19701) *(G-338)*
Staybrdge Stes - Nwrk/Wlmngton, Newark *Also called Dpnl LLC (G-6469)*
Stb Management 302 737-5105
2202 Drummond Plz Newark (19711) *(G-7487)*
Steadfast Insurance Company (HQ) 847 605-6000
2 Loockerman Plz Ste 202 Dover (19901) *(G-2106)*
Stealthorg LLC 302 724-6461
8 The Grn Ste 8295 Dover (19901) *(G-2107)*
Steamboat Landing 302 645-6500
Coastal Hwy 1 Lewes (19958) *(G-3763)*
Steel and Metal Service (PA) 302 322-9960
407 Old Airport Rd New Castle (19720) *(G-5739)*
Steel Buildings Inc 302 644-0444
17515 Nassau Commons Blvd Lewes (19958) *(G-3764)*
Steel Suppliers Inc 302 654-5243
701 E Front St Wilmington (19801) *(G-12748)*
Steel Suppliers Erectors, Wilmington *Also called Steel Suppliers Inc (G-12748)*
Steen Waehler Schrider Fox LLC 302 539-7900
92 Atlantic Ave Ste B Ocean View (19970) *(G-7814)*
Steering Sltions Ip Holdg Corp 313 556-5000
1209 N Orange St Wilmington (19801) *(G-12749)*
Stein Tree Service Inc 302 731-1718
17 Austin Rd Wilmington (19810) *(G-12750)*
Steinebach Robert and Assoc 302 328-1212
20 Peddlers Row Christiana (19702) *(G-680)*
Steiner Company, Milford *Also called Clover Yarns Inc (G-4359)*
Stella ABG Acquisition Inc 302 654-6682
1105 N Market St Ste 1300 Wilmington (19801) *(G-12751)*
Step By Step Furn Installation 302 834-8257
246 Ingram St Newark (19702) *(G-7488)*
Step Up Daycare 302 762-3183
2715 N Tatnall St Wilmington (19802) *(G-12752)*
Step-Up Daycare, Wilmington *Also called Step Up Daycare (G-12752)*
Stephanie E Steckel DDS, Ms, Dover *Also called Orthodontics On Silver Lake PA (G-1922)*
Stephanie Galbraith 302 290-2235
1429 Stapler Pl Wilmington (19806) *(G-12753)*
Stephano Slack LLC 302 777-7400
1700 W 14th St Wilmington (19806) *(G-12754)*
Stephen A Niemoeller DMD PA 302 737-3320
523 Capitol Trl Newark (19711) *(G-7489)*
Stephen Cropper 302 732-3730
35029 Dupont Blvd Frankford (19945) *(G-2390)*
Stephen F Penny MD 302 678-8100
1074 S State St Dover (19901) *(G-2108)*
Stephen F Wetherill MD 302 478-3700
133 Montchan Dr Wilmington (19807) *(G-12755)*
Stephen G Puzio DC 302 234-4045
7460 Lancaster Pike Ste 8 Hockessin (19707) *(G-3149)*
Stephen Jankovic Chiropractor 302 384-8540
1309 Beale Rd Ste 12 Wilmington (19810) *(G-12756)*
Stephens Management Corp 302 629-4393
321 E Stein Hwy Seaford (19973) *(G-8409)*
Stereochemical Inc 302 266-0700
667 Dawson Dr Ste E Newark (19713) *(G-7490)*
Stericycle Comm Solutions Inc 302 656-0630
1521 Concord Pike Ste 202 Wilmington (19803) *(G-12757)*
Sterling Nursery Inc 302 653-7060
1575 Vndyke Grenspring Rd Smyrna (19977) *(G-8724)*
Steve O Quillin Od 302 398-8404
203 Shaw Ave 205 Harrington (19952) *(G-2894)*
Steven Abdill 443 243-6864
24a Trolley Sq Ste 101 Wilmington (19806) *(G-12758)*
Steven Alban DDS PA 302 422-9637
3 Sussex Ave Milford (19963) *(G-4570)*
Steven Augusiewicz Inc 302 738-1919
25 Monticello Dr Bear (19701) *(G-339)*
Steven Brown & Associates Inc 302 652-4722
9 S Cleveland Ave Wilmington (19805) *(G-12759)*
Steven E Diamond M D 302 655-8868
900 Foulk Rd Ste 200 Wilmington (19803) *(G-12760)*
Steven J Stirparo 302 479-9555
3622 Silverside Rd Wilmington (19810) *(G-12761)*
Steven P Copp 302 645-9112
Rr 3 Box 254a Lewes (19958) *(G-3765)*
Steven Sachs Appraisal Access 302 477-9676
19 Brandywine Blvd Talleyville (19803) *(G-8752)*
Steven Schmith 302 584-8394
408 Maplewood Dr Middletown (19709) *(G-4248)*
Stevens & Lee PC 302 654-5180
919 N Market St Ste 1300 Wilmington (19801) *(G-12762)*
Stevenson Ventures LLC 302 752-4449
26 N Walnut St Milford (19963) *(G-4571)*
Steves Painting Plus 302 684-8938
22235 Jefferson Rd Lincoln (19960) *(G-3871)*
Stewart and Martin, Wilmington *Also called Stewart Law Firm (G-12763)*
Stewart Law Firm 302 652-5200
301 N Market St Wilmington (19801) *(G-12763)*
Stewart Management Company, Wilmington *Also called Virtual Business Entps LLC (G-13089)*
Stewart Septimus MD 302 992-9940
2055 Limestone Rd Ste 117 Wilmington (19808) *(G-12764)*
Stewart Title Company 302 433-8766
5300 Brandywine Pkwy Wilmington (19803) *(G-12765)*
Stewart Title Guaranty Company 302 651-9201
1 Righter Pkwy Ste 160 Wilmington (19803) *(G-12766)*
Stewart's Brewing Company, Bear *Also called Delaware Beer Works Inc (G-104)*
Stifel Bank and Trust 302 478-8880
1413 Foulk Rd Ste 204 Wilmington (19803) *(G-12767)*
Still Industries Inc 302 368-8832
287 S Main St Newark (19711) *(G-7491)*
Stitch-Stash, Bethany Beach *Also called Patricia Hoffmann (G-419)*
Stl & Associates LLC 302 359-2801
198 Greens Branch Ln Smyrna (19977) *(G-8725)*
Stockley Materials LLC 302 856-7601
25154 Dupont Blvd Georgetown (19947) *(G-2666)*
Stockmarket 302 697-8878
2573 Woodlytown Rd Magnolia (19962) *(G-3909)*
Stokes Garage Inc 302 994-0613
101 Old Dupont Rd Wilmington (19805) *(G-12768)*
Stoltz Realty Co 302 656-8543
1303 Delaware Ave Ste 101 Wilmington (19806) *(G-12769)*
Stoltz Realty Co 302 798-8500
7120 Society Dr Claymont (19703) *(G-807)*
Stone Express 302 376-8876
5093 Summit Bridge Rd Middletown (19709) *(G-4249)*
Stone Harbor Square LLC 302 227-5227
42 Rehoboth Ave Ste 23 Rehoboth Beach (19971) *(G-8088)*
Stone Medic 302 233-6039
73 Kristin Ct Smyrna (19977) *(G-8726)*
Stone Shop, The, Wilmington *Also called Tile Market of Delaware Inc (G-12910)*
Stonebridge Apartments, New Castle *Also called Berman Development Corp (G-5084)*
Stonegate Granite 302 500-8081
25029 Dupont Blvd Georgetown (19947) *(G-2667)*
STONEGATES, Wilmington *Also called Greenvlle Retirement Cmnty LLC (G-10781)*
Stoney Batter Family Medicine 302 234-9109
5311 Limestone Rd Ste 201 Wilmington (19808) *(G-12770)*
Stoneybrook Apartments, Wilmington *Also called Stoneybrook Presvtn Assoc LLC (G-12772)*
Stoneybrook Apartments, Wilmington *Also called Stoneybrook Associates LP (G-12771)*
Stoneybrook Apts, Claymont *Also called Leon N Weiner & Associates Inc (G-773)*
Stoneybrook Associates LP 302 764-6450
4 Denny Rd Wilmington (19809) *(G-12771)*
Stoneybrook Presvtn Assoc LLC 302 764-9430
4 Denny Rd Wilmington (19809) *(G-12772)*
Stop Traffic 302 604-1176
408 Circle Rd Millsboro (19966) *(G-4804)*
Stork Electric Inc 302 654-9427
9 Germay Dr Ste 100 Wilmington (19804) *(G-12773)*
Stormblade Inc 302 206-1631
73 Greentree Dr 311 Dover (19904) *(G-2109)*
Storyworth Inc 415 967-1531
2093 Philadelphia Pike Claymont (19703) *(G-808)*
Stracar Insurance Group, Georgetown *Also called Farm Financial Services Inc (G-2526)*
Stracke Enterprises Inc 302 743-6515
5 Beacon Ln Newark (19711) *(G-7492)*
Straight Line Striping LLC 302 228-3335
17865 Hudson Ln Georgetown (19947) *(G-2668)*
Strands Prprty Prservation LLC 302 381-9792
26035 Oak St Ste 101 Millsboro (19966) *(G-4805)*
Strano-Feely Funeral Home, Newark *Also called Delaware Prof Fnrl Svcs Inc (G-6404)*
Strategic Fund Raising Inc (PA) 651 649-0404
300 Delaware Ave Ste 1370 Wilmington (19801) *(G-12774)*
Strategic Solutions Intl Inc 302 525-6313
700 Barksdale Rd Ste 6 Newark (19711) *(G-7493)*
Strategy House Inc 302 658-1500
231 Executive Dr Ste 15 Newark (19702) *(G-7494)*
Stratis Visuals LLC 860 482-1208
20 Tyler Way Newark (19713) *(G-7495)*

ALPHABETIC

Stream App LLC	610 420-5864
1500 Lancaster Ave Wilmington (19805) *(G-12775)*	
Street & Ellis P A	302 735-8408
426 S State St Dover (19901) *(G-2110)*	
Street Core Utility Service	302 239-4110
501 Erickson Ave Hockessin (19707) *(G-3150)*	
Stride Rite Corporation	302 226-2288
36474 Seaside Outlet Dr # 1570 Rehoboth Beach (19971) *(G-8089)*	
Stride Services Inc	302 540-4713
200 Powder Mill Rd Wilmington (19803) *(G-12776)*	
Strike Exchange Inc	310 995-5653
16192 Coastal Hwy Lewes (19958) *(G-3766)*	
Strike Social, Lewes Also called Strike Exchange Inc *(G-3766)*	
Stripe-A-Lot Inc	302 654-9175
55 Germay Dr Wilmington (19804) *(G-12777)*	
Strobert Tree Services	302 633-3478
1506 A St Wilmington (19801) *(G-12778)*	
Strobert Tree Services Inc	302 475-7089
1806 Zebley Rd Wilmington (19810) *(G-12779)*	
Stroehmann Bakeries 62, New Castle Also called Bimbo Bakeries Usa Inc *(G-5091)*	
Stryker Chiropractic, Wilmington Also called Howmedica Osteonics Corp *(G-10962)*	
Stuart Kingston Galleries Inc	302 652-7978
3704 Kennett Pike Ste 100 Wilmington (19807) *(G-12780)*	
Stuart Kingston Inc (PA)	302 227-2524
1 Grenoble Pl Rehoboth Beach (19971) *(G-8090)*	
Stuart Kingston Jewelers, Wilmington Also called Stuart Kingston Galleries Inc *(G-12780)*	
Stucco Smith Systems	302 245-8179
31912 Phillips Rd Selbyville (19975) *(G-8550)*	
Student Media Group	302 607-2580
500 Creek View Rd Ste 3e Newark (19711) *(G-7496)*	
Studentup Inc	951 427-7563
2035 Sunset Lake Rd Newark (19702) *(G-7497)*	
Studio 11	302 622-9959
2301 Penns Ave Apt D Wilmington (19806) *(G-12781)*	
Studio J Entrmt & AP & Cof Bar	410 422-3155
11290 Trussum Pond Rd F32 Laurel (19956) *(G-3296)*	
Studio Jaed, Bear Also called Jaed Corporation *(G-196)*	
Studio On 24 Inc	302 644-4424
20231 John J Williams Hwy Lewes (19958) *(G-3767)*	
Stump B Gone Inc	302 737-7779
17 Red Mill Rd Newark (19711) *(G-7498)*	
Stumpf Vickers and Sandy	302 856-3561
8 W Market St Georgetown (19947) *(G-2669)*	
Stylelabs Inc	347 674-7993
108 W 13th St Wilmington (19801) *(G-12782)*	
Styles By US	302 629-3244
324 E Stein Hwy Seaford (19973) *(G-8410)*	
Styles Millenium	302 472-3427
1923 W 4th St Wilmington (19805) *(G-12783)*	
Stylish Stylus, The, Bear Also called Envision It Publications LLC *(G-144)*	
Subcodevs Inc	704 234-6780
919 N Market St Wilmington (19801) *(G-12784)*	
Suburban Farmhouse	302 250-6254
108 Federal St Milton (19968) *(G-4974)*	
Suburban Lawn & Equipment Inc (PA)	302 475-4300
1601 Naamans Rd Wilmington (19810) *(G-12785)*	
Suburban Marketing Associates (PA)	302 656-8440
3301 Lancaster Pike 5c Wilmington (19805) *(G-12786)*	
Suburban Psychiatric Svcs LLC	302 999-9834
5177 W Woodmill Dr Ste 6 Wilmington (19808) *(G-12787)*	
Suburban Publishing Inc (PA)	302 656-1809
3301 Lancaster Pike 5c Wilmington (19805) *(G-12788)*	
Succulents Soap Sand Scents	302 757-0697
103 Rockrose Dr Newark (19711) *(G-7499)*	
Suds and Company, Dover Also called Suds Bar Soap & Essentials LLC *(G-2111)*	
Suds Bar Soap & Essentials LLC	302 674-1303
31 W Loockerman St Dover (19904) *(G-2111)*	
Suez North America Inc (HQ)	302 633-5670
2000 First State Blvd Wilmington (19804) *(G-12789)*	
Suez Water Delaware Inc	302 633-5905
2000 First State Blvd Wilmington (19804) *(G-12790)*	
Suffex Conservation	302 856-2105
23818 Shortly Rd Georgetown (19947) *(G-2670)*	
Suffex County Ems, Georgetown Also called County of Sussex *(G-2489)*	
Suffix Cutlers Sales, Millsboro Also called Crossings At Oak Orchard *(G-4671)*	
Sui Trading Co	302 239-2012
406 Hawthorne Ct E Hockessin (19707) *(G-3151)*	
Sujo Music Publishing	302 731-8575
402 Longfield Rd Newark (19713) *(G-7500)*	
Suk-Young Carr DDS	302 736-6631
850 S State St Ste 2 Dover (19901) *(G-2112)*	
Sullivan Anna Marie Do	302 454-1680
2 Polly Drummond Hill Rd Newark (19711) *(G-7501)*	
Sum Inc	302 322-0831
31 Southgate Blvd New Castle (19720) *(G-5740)*	
Summer Consultants Inc	484 493-4150
131 Continental Dr # 302 Newark (19713) *(G-7502)*	
Summer Hill Custom Home Bldr	302 462-5853
68 Atlantic Ave Ocean View (19970) *(G-7815)*	
Summer Lrng Collaborative Inc	860 751-9887
1313 N Market St 1150nw Wilmington (19801) *(G-12791)*	
Summers Logging LLC	302 234-8725
364 Skyline Orchard Dr Hockessin (19707) *(G-3152)*	
Summit At Hockessin	302 235-8388
5850 Limestone Rd Hockessin (19707) *(G-3153)*	
Summit Aviation Inc (HQ)	302 834-5400
4200 Summit Bridge Rd Middletown (19709) *(G-4250)*	
Summit Bridge Inv Prpts LLC	410 499-1456
912 Westerly Ct Newark (19702) *(G-7503)*	
Summit Chase Apartments, The, Wilmington Also called Egg Harbor City Apartments LLC *(G-10362)*	
Summit Heating and AC LLC (PA)	302 378-1203
4361 Dupont Pkwy Townsend (19734) *(G-8824)*	
Summit Industrial Corporation	302 368-2718
1109 Elkton Rd Newark (19711) *(G-7504)*	
Summit Mechanical Inc	302 836-8814
304 Carson Dr Bear (19701) *(G-340)*	
Summit North Marina	302 836-1800
3000 Summit Harbour Pl Bear (19701) *(G-341)*	
Summit Orthopaedic HM Care LLC	302 703-0800
1632 Savannah Rd Ste 8 Lewes (19958) *(G-3768)*	
Summit Pike Creek, Newark Also called Summit Properties Inc *(G-7505)*	
Summit Properties Inc	302 737-3747
100 Red Fox Ln Bldg 100 # 100 Newark (19711) *(G-7505)*	
Summit Retirement Community	888 933-2300
5850 Limestone Rd Ofc 1 Hockessin (19707) *(G-3154)*	
Summit Steel Inc	302 325-3220
201 Edwards Ave New Castle (19720) *(G-5741)*	
Sumuri LLC	302 570-0015
49 Brenda Ln Ste A Camden (19934) *(G-601)*	
Sun Coal & Coke LLC	630 824-1000
2401 Penns Ave Ste 111 Wilmington (19806) *(G-12792)*	
Sun Communities Inc	302 335-5444
2 Willow Dr Frederica (19946) *(G-2413)*	
Sun Communities Inc	302 227-8118
19837 Sea Air Ave Rehoboth Beach (19971) *(G-8091)*	
Sun Exchange Inc (PA)	917 747-9527
16192 Coastal Hwy 1 Lewes (19958) *(G-3769)*	
Sun Gabon Oil Company	302 293-6000
201 N Walnut St Ste 1300t Wilmington (19801) *(G-12793)*	
Sun Hotel Inc	302 322-0711
232 S Dupont Hwy New Castle (19720) *(G-5742)*	
Sun Malaysia Petroleum Company	302 293-6000
201 N Walnut St Ste 1300t Wilmington (19801) *(G-12794)*	
Sun Marine Maintenance Inc	302 539-6756
35322 Bayard Rd Frankford (19945) *(G-2391)*	
Sun National Bank	302 334-4091
4401 Concord Pike Wilmington (19803) *(G-12795)*	
Sun Noordzee Oil Company	302 293-6000
201 N Walnut St Ste 1300 Wilmington (19801) *(G-12796)*	
Sun Orient Exploration Company	302 293-6000
201 N Walnut St Ste 1300 Wilmington (19801) *(G-12797)*	
Sun Pharmaceuticals Corp	302 678-6000
50 S Dupont Hwy Dover (19901) *(G-2113)*	
Sun Piledriving Equipment LLC	302 539-6756
35322 Bayard Rd Frankford (19945) *(G-2392)*	
Sun West Homes, Wilmington Also called Southwest American Corp *(G-12688)*	
Sun-In-One Inc	302 762-3100
500 Philadelphia Pike # 1 Wilmington (19809) *(G-12798)*	
Sunbelt Rentals Inc	302 907-1921
36412 Sussex Hwy Delmar (19940) *(G-1032)*	
Sunbelt Rentals Inc	302 669-0595
453 Pulaski Hwy New Castle (19720) *(G-5743)*	
Sunco Salon	302 456-0240
67 Marrows Rd Newark (19713) *(G-7506)*	
Sunday Breakfast Mission	302 656-8542
600 E 5th St Apt C1 Wilmington (19801) *(G-12799)*	
Sundew Painting Inc	302 994-7004
500 S Colonial Ave Wilmington (19805) *(G-12800)*	
Sundew Painting Inc	302 684-5858
26836 L Georgetown Hwyb1e Harbeson (19951) *(G-2801)*	
Sunglobal Technologies, Wilmington Also called Vensoft LLC *(G-13057)*	
Sunhaven Awning Co	302 239-7990
2870 Creek Rd Yorklyn (19736) *(G-13367)*	
Sunlight Salon LLC	302 456-1799
610 Plaza Dr Newark (19702) *(G-7507)*	
Sunny Hospitality LLC	302 226-0700
36012 Airport Rd Rehoboth Beach (19971) *(G-8092)*	
Sunny Hospitality LLC	302 398-3900
1259 Corn Crib Rd Harrington (19952) *(G-2895)*	
Sunnyfield Contractors Inc	302 674-8610
150 Sunnyfield Ln Dover (19904) *(G-2114)*	
Sunrise Medical Center	302 854-9006
22549 Little St Georgetown (19947) *(G-2671)*	
Sunrise of Wilmington, Wilmington Also called Sunrise Senior Living LLC *(G-12801)*	
Sunrise Senior Living LLC	302 475-9163
2215 Shipley Rd Wilmington (19803) *(G-12801)*	
Sunshine Crepes	302 537-1765
100 Garfield Pkwy Bethany Beach (19930) *(G-432)*	

Sunshine Graphics and Printing.....302 724-5127
511 N West St Dover (19904) **(G-2115)**
Sunshine Home Daycare.....302 674-2009
370 Mimosa Ave Dover (19904) **(G-2116)**
Sunshine Kids Academy.....302 444-4270
924 Old Harmony Rd # 104 Newark (19713) **(G-7508)**
Sunshine Nut Company LLC.....781 352-7766
16192 Coastal Hwy Lewes (19958) **(G-3770)**
SunTrust Mortgage Inc.....302 453-2350
200 Continental Dr # 207 Newark (19713) **(G-7509)**
Sunwise Drmatology Surgery LLC.....302 378-7981
102 Sleepy Hollow Dr Middletown (19709) **(G-4251)**
Sunworks Corporation.....302 655-5772
30 Evergreen Dr Wilmington (19850) **(G-12802)**
Super 8 Motel, Harrington *Also called Gulab Management Inc* **(G-2844)**
Super 8 Motel, Milford *Also called Gulab Management Inc* **(G-4428)**
Super 8 Motel, Harrington *Also called Routzhan Jessman* **(G-2881)**
Super 8 Motel, New Castle *Also called Eastern Hospitality Management* **(G-5277)**
Super 8 Motel, Newark *Also called Priya Realty Corp* **(G-7261)**
Super C Inc.....302 533-6024
1352 Marrows Rd Ste 104 Newark (19711) **(G-7510)**
Super Eight Dover.....302 734-5701
348 N Dupont Hwy Dover (19901) **(G-2117)**
Super Perfection Clg Svcs LLC.....267 619-4441
7 Colony Blvd Apt 302 Wilmington (19802) **(G-12803)**
Super Suppers.....302 478-5935
3619 Silverside Rd Wilmington (19810) **(G-12804)**
Supercritical Fluid Tech (PA).....302 738-3420
1 Innovation Way Newark (19711) **(G-7511)**
Supercritical Fluid Tech.....302 738-3420
120 Sandy Dr Ste 2b Newark (19713) **(G-7512)**
Supercuts, Wilmington *Also called Regis Corporation* **(G-12362)**
Supercuts Inc.....302 475-5001
2504 Foulk Rd Wilmington (19810) **(G-12805)**
Superior Cleaners Wilmington, Wilmington *Also called Superior Clr of Wilmington Inc* **(G-12806)**
Superior Clr of Wilmington Inc.....302 633-3323
808 First State Blvd Wilmington (19804) **(G-12806)**
Superior Commercial Cleaning.....302 897-2544
446 Douglas D Alley Dr Newark (19713) **(G-7513)**
Superior Drywall Inc.....302 732-9800
30996 Country Gdns Ste R1 Dagsboro (19939) **(G-935)**
Superior Electric Service Co (PA).....302 658-5949
36 Germay Dr Wilmington (19804) **(G-12807)**
Superior Foundations Inc.....302 293-7061
445 County Rd Bear (19701) **(G-342)**
Superior Graphic & Printing.....302 290-3475
1432 Governor House Cir Wilmington (19809) **(G-12808)**
Superior Maids.....302 284-2012
1391 Chandlers Rd Felton (19943) **(G-2323)**
Superior Screen & Glass.....302 541-5399
1 Town Rd Ocean View (19970) **(G-7816)**
Superior Sealing Services D.....610 717-6237
613 Pulaski Hwy Bear (19701) **(G-343)**
Superior Yardworks Inc.....610 274-2255
211 Cherry Blossom Pl Hockessin (19707) **(G-3155)**
Superlodge.....302 654-5544
1213 N West St Wilmington (19801) **(G-12809)**
Supermarket Associates Inc.....302 547-1977
4001 Kennett Pike Wilmington (19807) **(G-12810)**
Superstore LLC.....302 200-4933
1000 N West St Ste 1200 Wilmington (19801) **(G-12811)**
Supply Chain Consultants Inc.....302 738-9215
5460 Fairmont Dr Wilmington (19808) **(G-12812)**
Supportive Care Solutions LLC.....302 598-4797
1606 Newport Gap Pike Wilmington (19808) **(G-12813)**
Supreme Court United States.....302 252-2950
824 N Market St Wilmington (19801) **(G-12814)**
Supreme Court of The State Del.....302 255-0544
500 N King St Ste 11600 Wilmington (19801) **(G-12815)**
Supreme Grand Lodge of U S A.....302 998-3549
1315 Biggs Rd Wilmington (19805) **(G-12816)**
Supreme Hair Design.....302 672-7255
309 Northdown Dr Dover (19904) **(G-2118)**
Sure Good Foods USA LLC.....905 288-1136
40 E Main St Ste 1187 Newark (19711) **(G-7514)**
Sure Line Electrical Inc.....302 856-3110
281 W Commerce St Georgetown (19947) **(G-2672)**
Surestay, Wilmington *Also called Jaysons LLC* **(G-11133)**
Suretronix Solutions LLC.....302 407-3146
111 Brookside Dr Wilmington (19804) **(G-12817)**
Surf Club.....302 227-7059
1 Read Ave Dewey Beach (19971) **(G-1060)**
Surface Protection, Wilmington *Also called Chemours Company Fc LLC* **(G-9653)**
Surge Networks Inc.....206 432-5047
2035 Sunset Lake Rd B2 Newark (19702) **(G-7515)**
Surgical Associates PA.....302 346-4502
200 Banning St Ste 200 # 200 Dover (19904) **(G-2119)**
Surgical Critical Assoc.....302 623-4370
4735 Ogletown Stanton Rd # 3301 Newark (19713) **(G-7516)**
Surgical Nanticoke Assoc PA.....302 629-8662
543 N Shipley St Ste A Seaford (19973) **(G-8411)**
Surplus & Excess Line Ltd.....302 653-5016
4 Village Sq Ste 900 Smyrna (19977) **(G-8727)**
Survey Supply Inc.....302 422-3338
726 Mccolley St Milford (19963) **(G-4572)**
Survivors Abuse In Rcovery Inc.....302 651-0181
405 Foulk Rd Wilmington (19803) **(G-12818)**
Susan J Betts Od.....302 629-6691
8500 Herring Run Rd Seaford (19973) **(G-8412)**
Susan R Austin.....302 322-4685
103 Lesley Ln New Castle (19720) **(G-5744)**
Susan Straughen.....302 856-7703
205 N Front St Georgetown (19947) **(G-2673)**
Susan T Fischer.....302 832-2570
57 Avignon Dr Newark (19702) **(G-7517)**
Sussex Aero Maintenance, Georgetown *Also called Georgetown Air Services LLC* **(G-2540)**
Sussex Chapter, Georgetown *Also called Delaware S P C A* **(G-2502)**
Sussex Cnty Habitat For Humani.....302 855-1153
206 Academy St Georgetown (19947) **(G-2674)**
Sussex Cnty Manufactrd Housing.....302 945-2122
35124 Seahawk Ln Millsboro (19966) **(G-4806)**
Sussex Community Crisis.....302 856-2246
204 E North St Georgetown (19947) **(G-2675)**
Sussex Conservation District.....302 856-2105
23818 Shortly Rd Georgetown (19947) **(G-2676)**
Sussex Correctional Instn, Georgetown *Also called Correction Delaware Department* **(G-2487)**
Sussex Countian.....302 856-0026
1196 S Little Creek Rd Dover (19901) **(G-2120)**
Sussex County Animal Assn.....302 628-5198
4503 Briarhook Rd Seaford (19973) **(G-8413)**
Sussex County Assn Realtors.....302 855-2300
23407 Park Ave Georgetown (19947) **(G-2677)**
Sussex County Counseling Svcs, Georgetown *Also called Central Delaware Committee* **(G-2466)**
Sussex County Federal Cr Un (PA).....302 629-0100
1941 Bridgeville Hwy Seaford (19973) **(G-8414)**
Sussex County Federal Cr Un.....302 422-9110
140 Aerenson Dr Milford (19963) **(G-4573)**
Sussex County Federal Cr Un.....302 644-7111
34686 Oldm Postal Ln Lewes (19958) **(G-3771)**
Sussex County Federal Cr Un.....302 322-7777
121 Centerpoint Blvd New Castle (19720) **(G-5745)**
Sussex County Planning & Zng, Georgetown *Also called County of Sussex* **(G-2490)**
Sussex County Senior Ctr Svcs.....302 539-2671
Cedar Neck Rd Ocean View (19970) **(G-7817)**
Sussex County Senior Svcs Inc.....302 854-2882
20520 Sand Hill Rd Georgetown (19947) **(G-2678)**
Sussex County Woman.....302 539-2612
23 Daisey Ave Ocean View (19970) **(G-7818)**
Sussex Electric, Bear *Also called Solar Heating Inc* **(G-327)**
Sussex Eye Care & Medical Asso.....302 644-8007
1306 Savannah Rd Lewes (19958) **(G-3772)**
Sussex Eye Center PA (PA).....302 856-2020
502 W Market St Georgetown (19947) **(G-2679)**
Sussex Eye Center PA.....302 436-2020
17 Lighthouse Rd Selbyville (19975) **(G-8551)**
Sussex Family Counseling LLC.....302 864-7970
26114 Kits Burrow Ct Georgetown (19947) **(G-2680)**
Sussex Fencing.....302 945-7008
John J Williams Hwy Millsboro (19966) **(G-4807)**
Sussex Floor.....302 629-5620
10271 Old Furnace Rd Seaford (19973) **(G-8415)**
Sussex Guide, Seaford *Also called Sussex Printing Corp* **(G-8416)**
Sussex Hydraulics Sales & Svcs.....302 846-9702
12619 Line Rd Delmar (19940) **(G-1033)**
Sussex Landscaping & Lawn Care, Millsboro *Also called Christopher T Parsons* **(G-4662)**
Sussex Lumber Company Inc.....302 934-8128
655 Mitchell St Millsboro (19966) **(G-4808)**
Sussex Machine Works Inc.....302 875-7958
11432 Trussum Pond Rd Laurel (19956) **(G-3297)**
Sussex Medical Center, Seaford *Also called Paul H Aguillon MD* **(G-8342)**
Sussex Orthodontics.....302 644-4100
1004 S State St Ste 3 Dover (19901) **(G-2121)**
Sussex Pain Relief Center LLC.....302 519-0100
18229 Dupont Blvd Georgetown (19947) **(G-2681)**
Sussex Pines Country Club.....302 856-6283
22426 Sussex Pines Rd Georgetown (19947) **(G-2682)**
Sussex Podiatry Group.....302 645-8555
1532 Savannah Rd Lewes (19958) **(G-3773)**
Sussex Post.....302 629-5505
37 N Walnut St Milford (19963) **(G-4574)**
Sussex Pregnancy Care Center.....302 856-4344
5 Burger King Dr Georgetown (19947) **(G-2683)**
Sussex Printing Corp.....302 629-9303
24904 Sussex Hwy Seaford (19973) **(G-8416)**

ALPHABETIC

Sussex Protection Service LLC (PA) 302 337-0209
100 Market St Bridgeville (19933) ***(G-522)***
Sussex Prschool Erly Care Ctrs 302 732-7529
126 N Shipley St Seaford (19973) ***(G-8417)***
Sussex Sand & Gravel Inc 302 628-6962
22223 Eskridge Rd Seaford (19973) ***(G-8418)***
Sussex Sands Inc 302 539-8200
1501 Coastal Hwy Fenwick Island (19944) ***(G-2341)***
Sussex Shores Water Co Corp 302 539-7611
Rr 1 Bethany Beach (19930) ***(G-433)***
Sussex Suites LLC 302 856-3351
22339 Sussex Pines Rd Georgetown (19947) ***(G-2684)***
Sussex Tree Inc 302 629-9899
20350 Nelson Dr Bridgeville (19933) ***(G-523)***
Sussex Veterinary Hospital 302 732-9433
30053 Vine St Rd Dagsboro (19939) ***(G-936)***
Sustainable Energy Utility 302 504-3071
1011 Centre Rd Ste 210 Wilmington (19805) ***(G-12819)***
Sustainable Generation, Wilmington *Also called Sustainable-Generation LLC* ***(G-12820)***
Sustainable-Generation LLC 917 678-6947
110 S Poplar St Ste 400 Wilmington (19801) ***(G-12820)***
Suthar Holding Corporation 302 291-2490
16192 Coastal Hwy Lewes (19958) ***(G-3774)***
Sutton Bus & Truck Co Inc 302 995-7444
5609 Old Capitol Trl Frnt Wilmington (19808) ***(G-12821)***
Svea Real Estate Group LLC (PA) 855 262-9665
1675 S State St Ste B Dover (19901) ***(G-2122)***
Svn Commercial Real Estate 410 543-2440
286 E Main St Delmar (19940) ***(G-1034)***
Swain Excavation Inc 302 422-4349
18678 Sherman Ave Unit 1 Lincoln (19960) ***(G-3872)***
Swami Enterprises Inc 302 999-8077
1702 Faulkland Rd Wilmington (19805) ***(G-12822)***
Swamp Machine Shop, Townsend *Also called Michael A Beecher* ***(G-8809)***
Swan Cleaners, Wilmington *Also called Blue Swan Cleaners Inc* ***(G-9382)***
Swan Financial Group 302 689-6095
251 Saundra St Frederica (19946) ***(G-2414)***
Swarovski US Holding Limited 302 737-4811
715 Christiana Mall Newark (19702) ***(G-7518)***
Swarthmore Financial Services 302 325-0700
15 Reads Way Ste 210 New Castle (19720) ***(G-5746)***
Swartzentruber Sawmill Co 302 492-1665
1191 Pearsons Corner Rd Hartly (19953) ***(G-2942)***
Sweat Social LLC 504 510-1973
8 The Grn Ste 7379 Dover (19901) ***(G-2123)***
Swedish Massage Therapy 302 841-3166
38227 Muddy Neck Rd Ocean View (19970) ***(G-7819)***
Sweeny and Associates 302 453-1645
112 Possum Hollow Rd Newark (19711) ***(G-7519)***
Sweet Luci, Newark *Also called Sweets By Samantha LLC* ***(G-7521)***
Sweet Potato Equipments, Dover *Also called Farmers Harvest Inc* ***(G-1541)***
Sweet Venom Effect LLC 302 674-5831
1004 Kirkwood St Ste 1 Wilmington (19801) ***(G-12823)***
Sweeten Companies Inc 302 737-6161
149 Salem Church Rd Newark (19713) ***(G-7520)***
Sweeten Solar, Newark *Also called Sweeten Companies Inc* ***(G-7520)***
Sweets By Samantha LLC 302 740-2218
3 Linette Ct Newark (19702) ***(G-7521)***
Swiatowicz Dental Associates 302 476-8185
1211 Milltown Rd Wilmington (19808) ***(G-12824)***
Swift Capital, Wilmington *Also called Swift Financial LLC* ***(G-12825)***
Swift Construction Co Inc 302 855-1011
24892 Pebblestone Ln Georgetown (19947) ***(G-2685)***
Swift Financial LLC (HQ) 302 374-7019
3505 Silverside Rd Wilmington (19810) ***(G-12825)***
Swift Pools Inc 302 738-9800
1123 Capitol Trl Newark (19711) ***(G-7522)***
Swift Services Inc 302 328-1145
2 3rd Ave New Castle (19720) ***(G-5747)***
Swift Towing & Recovery 302 650-4579
469 Old Airport Rd New Castle (19720) ***(G-5748)***
Swit Inc 302 792-0175
501 Silverside Rd Ste 105 Wilmington (19809) ***(G-12826)***
Switch Inc 302 738-7499
54 E Main St Newark (19711) ***(G-7523)***
Switch Skates & Snowboards, Newark *Also called Switch Inc* ***(G-7523)***
Switchedon Inc 415 271-1172
16192 Coastal Hwy Lewes (19958) ***(G-3775)***
Sword Parts LLC 302 246-1346
19266 Coastal Hwy 4-37 Rehoboth Beach (19971) ***(G-8093)***
Sybounheuang Group Inc 302 999-9339
514 Centerville Rd Wilmington (19808) ***(G-12827)***
Sydell-Hillandale Farms, Hartly *Also called Hillandale Farms Delaware Inc* ***(G-2926)***
Syf Industries 302 384-6214
1410 Prospect Dr Wilmington (19809) ***(G-12828)***
Sygul Inc 315 384-1848
2035 Sunset Lake Rd B2 Newark (19702) ***(G-7524)***
Sylvester Custom Cabinetry 302 398-6050
16869 S Dupont Hwy Harrington (19952) ***(G-2896)***
Sylvia Saienna 302 683-9082
100 Westgate Dr Wilmington (19808) ***(G-12829)***
Symbiosys Consulting LLC 302 507-7649
920 Justison St Wilmington (19801) ***(G-12830)***
Symmetry Dimensions Inc 302 918-5536
108 W 13th St Wilmington (19801) ***(G-12831)***
Sync It LLC 904 697-1132
1314 Oberlin Rd Wilmington (19803) ***(G-12832)***
Synchrgnix Info Strategies LLC (HQ) 302 892-4800
2 Righter Pkwy Ste 205 Wilmington (19803) ***(G-12833)***
Syncretic Press 443 723-8355
1137 Webster Dr Wilmington (19803) ***(G-12834)***
Syncretic Software Inc 302 762-2600
228 Philadelphia Pike Wilmington (19809) ***(G-12835)***
Synergy Direct Mortgage 302 283-0833
9 Peddlers Village Ctr Christiana (19702) ***(G-681)***
Synergy Medical USA Inc 302 444-0163
2915 Ogletown Rd Ste 2565 Newark (19713) ***(G-7525)***
Syngenta Corporation (HQ) 302 425-2000
3411 Silverside Rd # 100 Wilmington (19810) ***(G-12836)***
Syntec Corporation (PA) 302 421-8393
109 Rogers Rd Ste 5 Wilmington (19801) ***(G-12837)***
Sysod Inc 973 333-4848
300 Delaware Ave Ste 210a Wilmington (19801) ***(G-12838)***
System4 of Delaware, Newark *Also called Schoon Inc* ***(G-7394)***
Systematic Achievement Inc 302 479-5829
2404 Dorval Rd Wilmington (19810) ***(G-12839)***
Systems Approach Ltd 302 743-6331
309 Palomino Dr Newark (19711) ***(G-7526)***
Systems Tech & Science LLC 703 757-2010
34394 Indian River Dr Dagsboro (19939) ***(G-937)***
Systmade Technologies LLC 888 944-3546
8 The Grn Ste 6233 Dover (19901) ***(G-2124)***
Szewczyk and Company, Wilmington *Also called Szewczyk Company P A* ***(G-12840)***
Szewczyk Company P A 302 998-1117
3403 Lancaster Pike Ste 4 Wilmington (19805) ***(G-12840)***
T & B Invstgtions SEC Agcy LLC 302 476-4087
68 Haggis Rd Middletown (19709) ***(G-4252)***
T & C Enterprise Incorporated 302 934-8080
26007 Pugs Xing Millsboro (19966) ***(G-4809)***
T & H Bail Bond Inc (PA) 302 777-7982
625 N King St Apt 1 Wilmington (19801) ***(G-12841)***
T & H Bail Bonds Agency LLC 302 777-7982
625 N King St Frnt Wilmington (19801) ***(G-12842)***
T & J Murray Worldwide Svcs 302 736-1790
283 Persimmon Tree Ln Dover (19901) ***(G-2125)***
T & L Consulting Services LLC 302 573-1585
222 Philadelphia Pike # 4 Wilmington (19809) ***(G-12843)***
T & T Small Engines Inc 302 492-8677
6503 Halltown Rd Hartly (19953) ***(G-2943)***
T A H First Inc 302 653-6114
571 Kates Way Smyrna (19977) ***(G-8728)***
T A Rietdorf & Sons Inc 302 429-0341
735 S Market St Ste D Wilmington (19801) ***(G-12844)***
T B Painting Restoration 610 283-4100
162 Madison Dr Newark (19711) ***(G-7527)***
T C R, New Castle *Also called Total Construction Rentals Inc* ***(G-5775)***
T E S, New Castle *Also called Techmer Engnered Solutions LLC* ***(G-5759)***
T J Lane Construction Inc 302 734-1099
267 Fork Branch Rd Dover (19904) ***(G-2126)***
T K O Designs Inc 302 539-6992
100 Garfield Pkwy Bethany Beach (19930) ***(G-434)***
T M I Div, New Castle *Also called Testing Machines Inc* ***(G-5764)***
T P Composites Inc 610 358-9001
1600 Johnson Way New Castle (19720) ***(G-5749)***
T S N Publishing Co Inc 302 655-6483
307 A St Ste C Wilmington (19801) ***(G-12845)***
T S Smith & Sons Inc 302 337-8271
8899 Redden Rd Bridgeville (19933) ***(G-524)***
T Shane Palmer DC 302 328-2656
191 Christiana Rd Ste 1 New Castle (19720) ***(G-5750)***
T&T Cleaning LLC 609 575-0458
2888 Fast Landing Rd Dover (19901) ***(G-2127)***
T&T Custom Embroidery Inc 302 420-9454
51 Rawlings Dr Bear (19701) ***(G-344)***
T-Mobile 302 652-7738
724 N Market St Wilmington (19801) ***(G-12846)***
T-Mobile Preferred Retailer, Wilmington *Also called T-Mobile* ***(G-12846)***
T-Mobile Store 9730, Dover *Also called T-Mobile Usa Inc* ***(G-2128)***
T-Mobile Usa Inc 302 644-7222
18585 Coastal Hwy Unit 12 Rehoboth Beach (19971) ***(G-8094)***
T-Mobile Usa Inc 302 736-1980
1141 N Dupont Hwy Ste 3 Dover (19901) ***(G-2128)***
T-Mobile Usa Inc 302 838-4500
1102 Quintilio Dr Bear (19701) ***(G-345)***
T/A Pizza King, Millsboro *Also called Baynum Enterprises Inc* ***(G-4635)***
TA Farms LLC 302 492-3030
4664 Mud Mill Rd Camden Wyoming (19934) ***(G-658)***

ALPHABETIC SECTION — Techno Relief Limited

Ta Instruments - Waters LLC (HQ) 302 427-4000
  159 Lukens Dr New Castle (19720) *(G-5751)*
Tabella Inc 415 799-2389
  2035 Sunset Lake Rd Newark (19702) *(G-7528)*
Tableart LLC 650 587-8769
  3616 Kirkwood Hwy Wilmington (19808) *(G-12847)*
Tade Info Tech Solutions 302 832-1449
  60 Avignon Dr Newark (19702) *(G-7529)*
Tadpole Academy LLC 302 658-2141
  1238 N Walnut St Wilmington (19801) *(G-12848)*
Taekwondo Fitness Ctr of Del 302 836-8264
  1230 Pulaski Hwy Bear (19701) *(G-346)*
Tag Sale By Changeover 302 478-2450
  2501 Bryn Mawr Ave Wilmington (19803) *(G-12849)*
Taghleef Industries LLC 302 326-5500
  500 Creek View Rd Ste 300 Newark (19711) *(G-7530)*
Taghleef Industries Inc 302 326-5500
  500 Creek View Rd Ste 300 Newark (19711) *(G-7531)*
Taghleef Industries Inc (HQ) 302 326-5500
  500 Creek View Rd Ste 301 Newark (19711) *(G-7532)*
Tai Jun International Inc 302 239-9336
  511 Penn Manor Dr Newark (19711) *(G-7533)*
Tail Bangers Inc 302 947-4900
  24546 Betts Pond Rd Millsboro (19966) *(G-4810)*
Tailbangers 302 934-1125
  24546 Betts Pond Rd Millsboro (19966) *(G-4811)*
Tajan Holdings & Investments 302 300-1183
  600 N Broad St Ste 5 Middletown (19709) *(G-4253)*
Take Lead Dance Studio 302 234-0909
  320 Lantana Dr Hockessin (19707) *(G-3156)*
Talents Publishing LLC 302 353-4574
  220 E Delaware Ave Newark (19711) *(G-7534)*
Talk Aware LLC 302 645-7400
  16192 Coastal Hwy Lewes (19958) *(G-3776)*
Talk With Twila Ministries 302 525-6472
  260 Chapman Rd Newark (19702) *(G-7535)*
Tall Pines Associates Llc 302 684-0300
  29551 Persimmon Rd Lewes (19958) *(G-3777)*
Tall Pines Campground, Lewes *Also called Tall Pines Associates Llc (G-3777)*
Talley Brothers Inc 302 224-5376
  116 Sandy Dr Ste C Newark (19713) *(G-7536)*
Talleys Garage Inc 302 652-0463
  416 Roseanna Ave Wilmington (19803) *(G-12850)*
Talostech LLC 302 332-9236
  274 Quigley Blvd New Castle (19720) *(G-5752)*
Tammy S Bennett 302 875-6550
  30668 Sussex Hwy Laurel (19956) *(G-3298)*
Tandem Hosted Resources Inc 302 740-7099
  300 Creek View Rd Ste 202 Newark (19711) *(G-7537)*
Tangent Cable Systems Inc 302 994-4104
  3700 Washington Ave Wilmington (19808) *(G-12851)*
Tanner Operations Inc 302 464-2194
  39 Anchor Inn Rd Townsend (19734) *(G-8825)*
Tansley Associates (usa) Inc 403 569-8566
  1209 N Orange St Wilmington (19801) *(G-12852)*
Tantini LLC 302 444-4024
  136 S Main St Newark (19711) *(G-7538)*
Tantrough Farm 302 422-5547
  234 Blairs Pond Rd. Houston (19954) *(G-3183)*
Tap, Wilmington *Also called Automation Partnership (G-9188)*
Tap 99 LLC 301 541-7395
  1521 Concord Pike Wilmington (19803) *(G-12853)*
Taply LLC 650 275-2395
  3500 S Dupont Hwy Dover (19901) *(G-2129)*
Tapp Networks LLC 302 222-3384
  136 Woodland Rd Newark (19702) *(G-7539)*
Taq Incorporated 302 734-8300
  874 Walker Rd Ste C Dover (19904) *(G-2130)*
Tarabicos Grosso 302 757-7800
  100 W Commons Blvd # 415 New Castle (19720) *(G-5753)*
Targus U S A 302 644-2311
  32884 Ocean Reach Dr Lewes (19958) *(G-3778)*
Tarpon Strategies LLC 215 806-2723
  64 Thompson Cir Newark (19711) *(G-7540)*
Tasteables (PA) 267 777-9143
  333 Naamans Rd Ste 17b Claymont (19703) *(G-809)*
Tat Trucking Inc 302 261-5444
  3482 Wrangle Hill Rd Bear (19701) *(G-347)*
Tatsapod-Aame 302 897-8963
  1112 Newport Gap Pike Wilmington (19804) *(G-12854)*
Tax Free Liquors 302 846-0410
  38627 Benro Dr Unit 7 Delmar (19940) *(G-1035)*
Tax Management Service Inc 703 845-5900
  233 Ne Front St Milford (19963) *(G-4575)*
Tax Masters of Delaware 302 832-1313
  37 Carrick Ln Bear (19701) *(G-348)*
Taylor & Sons Inc 302 856-6962
  26511 E Trap Pond Rd Georgetown (19947) *(G-2686)*
Taylor and Messick Inc 302 398-3729
  325 Walt Messick Rd Harrington (19952) *(G-2897)*

Taylor Electric Service Inc 302 422-3966
  8 Columbia St Milford (19963) *(G-4576)*
Taylor Kline Inc 302 328-8306
  298b Churchmans Rd New Castle (19720) *(G-5754)*
Taylor McCormick Inc 302 738-0203
  56 W Main St Ste 300 Christiana (19702) *(G-682)*
Taylor Woodworks 302 745-2049
  34 Clearview Dr Dover (19901) *(G-2131)*
Taylor Woodworks 302 697-0155
  5140 S State St Magnolia (19962) *(G-3910)*
Tazelaar Roofing Service Inc 302 697-2643
  4869 S Dupont Hwy Dover (19901) *(G-2132)*
Tbc Retail Group Inc 302 478-8013
  5508 Concord Pike Wilmington (19803) *(G-12855)*
Tc Dental Equipment Services 302 740-9049
  262 Dogtown Rd Townsend (19734) *(G-8826)*
Tc Electric Company Inc 302 791-0378
  6701 Governor Printz Blvd Wilmington (19809) *(G-12856)*
Tc Logistics Incorporated 302 470-8557
  934 Roger Chaffee Sq C Bear (19701) *(G-349)*
Tc Trans Inc 302 339-7952
  24557 Duport Blvd Georgetown (19947) *(G-2687)*
Tcar Holdings LLC 720 328-0944
  1209 N Orange St Wilmington (19801) *(G-12857)*
TCI Inspections USA LLC 302 261-5208
  2711 Centerville Rd # 120 Wilmington (19808) *(G-12858)*
Td Ameritrade Inc 302 368-1050
  1257 Churchmans Rd Newark (19713) *(G-7541)*
Td Bank NA 302 455-1781
  230 E Delaware Ave Newark (19711) *(G-7542)*
Td Bank NA 302 234-8570
  7330 Lancaster Pike Hockessin (19707) *(G-3157)*
Td Bank NA 302 644-0952
  34980 Midway Outlet Dr Rehoboth Beach (19971) *(G-8095)*
Td Bank NA 302 655-5031
  300 Delaware Ave Ste 110 Wilmington (19801) *(G-12859)*
Td Bank NA 302 529-8727
  1803 Marsh Rd Wilmington (19810) *(G-12860)*
Td Bank NA 302 351-4560
  2035 Limestone Rd Wilmington (19808) *(G-12861)*
Td Bank NA 508 793-4188
  2035 Limestone Rd Wilmington (19808) *(G-12862)*
Tdc Partners Ltd 302 827-2137
  31781 Marsh Island Ave Lewes (19958) *(G-3779)*
Tdm Pharmaceutical RES LLC 302 832-1008
  100 Biddle Ave Ste 202 Newark (19702) *(G-7543)*
Tdp Wireless Inc 302 424-1900
  34 Salt Creek Dr Dover (19901) *(G-2133)*
Tdw Delaware Inc (HQ) 302 594-9880
  43 Harbor View Dr New Castle (19720) *(G-5755)*
Tdw Services Inc 302 594-9880
  261 Quigley Blvd Ste 18 New Castle (19720) *(G-5756)*
Tdy Holdings LLC (HQ) 302 254-4172
  1403 Foulk Rd Ste 200 Wilmington (19803) *(G-12863)*
Te Connectivity 302 633-2740
  4550 New Linden Hill Rd Wilmington (19808) *(G-12864)*
Teagle and Sons 302 682-8639
  6 N Street Ext Seaford (19973) *(G-8419)*
Teal Construction Inc 302 276-6034
  612 Mary St Dover (19904) *(G-2134)*
Team Wilson 302 888-1088
  3838 Kennett Pike Wilmington (19807) *(G-12865)*
TEC-Con Inc 610 583-8770
  4063 New Castle Ave New Castle (19720) *(G-5757)*
Tech Central LLC 717 273-3301
  501 Silverside Rd Ste 110 Wilmington (19809) *(G-12866)*
Tech Impact 302 256-5015
  100 W 10th St Ste 1007 Wilmington (19801) *(G-12867)*
Tech International Corp (PA) 302 478-2301
  3411 Silverside Rd 102w Wilmington (19810) *(G-12868)*
Tech Management Services Inc 302 539-4837
  134 Henlopen Dr Bethany Beach (19930) *(G-435)*
Techgas Inc 302 856-4111
  22251 Lwes Georgetown Hwy Georgetown (19947) *(G-2688)*
Techmer Engineered Solutions 800 401-8181
  1600 Johnson Way New Castle (19720) *(G-5758)*
Techmer Engnered Solutions LLC 610 548-5032
  1600 Johnson Way New Castle (19720) *(G-5759)*
Techncal Stffing Resources LLC 302 452-9933
  262 Chapman Rd Newark (19702) *(G-7544)*
Technical Writers Inc 302 477-1972
  3511 Silverside Rd # 201 Wilmington (19810) *(G-12869)*
Technicare Inc 302 322-7766
  39 Lakewood Cir Newark (19711) *(G-7545)*
Techniques Inc 302 422-7760
  20 Lenape Ln Newark (19713) *(G-7546)*
Techniques Inc Borden E Smith, Newark *Also called Techniques Inc (G-7546)*
Techno Goober 302 645-7177
  17527 Nssau Cmmons Blvd S Lewes (19958) *(G-3780)*
Techno Relief Limited 416 453-9393
  3511 Silverside Rd # 105 Wilmington (19810) *(G-12870)*

(PA)=Parent Co (HQ)=Headquarters (DH)=Div Headquarters

Techno Soft Inc (PA)....302 392-5200
4001 Knneth Pike Ste 250b Wilmington (19807) ***(G-12871)***
Technology Transfers Inc....302 234-4718
16 Anderson Ln Newark (19711) ***(G-7547)***
Technosecure Corporation....732 302-9005
705 Thyme Dr Bear (19701) ***(G-350)***
Technosoft Inc, Wilmington *Also called Techno Soft Inc* ***(G-12871)***
Techsolutions Inc....302 656-8324
5630 Kirkwood Hwy Wilmington (19808) ***(G-12872)***
Techxponent Inc....410 701-0089
131 Arielle Dr Newark (19702) ***(G-7548)***
Tecnatom USA Corporation....412 265-7226
1209 N Orange St Wilmington (19801) ***(G-12873)***
Tecnologika Usa Inc....302 597-7611
501 Silverside Rd Wilmington (19809) ***(G-12874)***
Tecot Electric Supply Co....302 368-9161
501 Interchange Blvd Newark (19711) ***(G-7549)***
Tecot Electric Supply Co....302 735-3300
1251 College Park Dr Dover (19904) ***(G-2135)***
Tecs Plus....302 437-6890
260 Chapman Rd Ste 104a Newark (19702) ***(G-7550)***
Ted Johnson Enterprises....302 349-5925
14403 Adamsville Rd Greenwood (19950) ***(G-2765)***
Teddy Bear Enterprises, Georgetown *Also called Susan Straughen* ***(G-2673)***
Tee Pees From Rattlesnks....302 654-0709
2001 Rockford Rd Wilmington (19806) ***(G-12875)***
Tee's Kitchen, Townsend *Also called Benjamin Tanei* ***(G-8764)***
Teff Inc....302 856-9768
109 E Laurel St Georgetown (19947) ***(G-2689)***
Tek Electronics LLC....302 449-6947
865 Bullen Dr Middletown (19709) ***(G-4254)***
Tek Tree LLC (PA)....302 368-2730
1106 Drummond Plz Newark (19711) ***(G-7551)***
Teksolv Usd Inc....302 738-1050
100 Lake Dr Newark (19702) ***(G-7552)***
Teksolv Usd Inc (PA)....302 738-1050
130 Executive Dr Ste 5 Newark (19702) ***(G-7553)***
Tekstrom Inc....302 709-5900
1301 Milltown Rd Wilmington (19808) ***(G-12876)***
Telamon - Laurel Head Start, Laurel *Also called Telamon Corporation Headstart* ***(G-3299)***
Telamon Corp Head Start Prgram....302 653-3766
204 Georges Aly Fl 2 Smyrna (19977) ***(G-8729)***
Telamon Corp Lincoln Hs, Milford *Also called Telamon Corporation* ***(G-4577)***
Telamon Corp/Early Chldhd Pgrm....302 934-1642
26351 Patriots Way Georgetown (19947) ***(G-2690)***
Telamon Corporation....302 398-9196
112 East St Harrington (19952) ***(G-2898)***
Telamon Corporation....302 684-3234
28607 W Meadowview Dr Milton (19968) ***(G-4975)***
Telamon Corporation....302 629-5557
517 Bridgeville Hwy Seaford (19973) ***(G-8420)***
Telamon Corporation....302 424-2335
518 N Church Ave Milford (19963) ***(G-4577)***
Telamon Corporation....302 736-5933
195 Willis Rd Dover (19901) ***(G-2136)***
Telamon Corporation Headstart....302 875-7718
30125 Discount Land Rd Laurel (19956) ***(G-3299)***
Telaris Communication Group, Wilmington *Also called Mangrove Holdings LLC* ***(G-11502)***
Telco Envirotrols Inc....302 846-9103
105 E State St Delmar (19940) ***(G-1036)***
Teleborg Pipe Seals US, Lewes *Also called Max Seal Inc* ***(G-3625)***
Teleduction Associates Inc....302 429-0303
1 Weldin Park Dr Wilmington (19803) ***(G-12877)***
Telemed Health Group....561 922-3953
8 The Grn Ste D Dover (19901) ***(G-2137)***
Telephone Answering Service, Georgetown *Also called Shore Answer LLC* ***(G-2654)***
Teleplan Vdeocom Solutions Inc....302 323-8503
100 W Cmmons Blvd Ste 415 New Castle (19720) ***(G-5760)***
Telesonic PC Inc (PA)....302 658-6945
805 E 13th St Wilmington (19802) ***(G-12878)***
Telesonic PC Inc....302 658-6945
1330 E 12th St Wilmington (19802) ***(G-12879)***
Telgian Corporation....480 753-5444
4001 Kennett Pike Ste 308 Wilmington (19807) ***(G-12880)***
Telgian Engrg & Consulting LLC....480 282-5392
4001 Kennett Pike Ste 308 Wilmington (19807) ***(G-12881)***
Tell Lab....302 831-7121
540 S College Ave Newark (19713) ***(G-7554)***
Telsec Answering Service, Newark *Also called Bayshore Communications Inc* ***(G-6057)***
Temp-Air Inc....302 369-3880
200 Happy Ln Newark (19711) ***(G-7555)***
Tempair, Newark *Also called Temp-Air Inc* ***(G-7555)***
Ten Bears Environmental LLC....302 731-8633
1080 S Chapel St Ste 200 Newark (19702) ***(G-7556)***
Ten Blade Enterprises LLC....484 843-4811
800 Industrial St Wilmington (19801) ***(G-12882)***
Ten Talents Enterprises Inc (PA)....302 409-0718
316 Braemar St Middletown (19709) ***(G-4255)***
Tender Hearts....302 674-2565
1339 S Governors Ave Dover (19904) ***(G-2138)***
Tender Loving Kare....302 464-1014
400 N Ramunno Dr Middletown (19709) ***(G-4256)***
Tender Loving Kare Child Care....302 653-5677
649 S Carter Rd Smyrna (19977) ***(G-8730)***
Tenmat Inc....302 633-6600
23 Copper Dr Ste 5 Wilmington (19804) ***(G-12883)***
Teresa H Keller MD....302 422-2022
16 S Dupont Blvd Milford (19963) ***(G-4578)***
Terminix Intl Co Ltd Partnr....302 653-4866
284 Quigley Blvd New Castle (19720) ***(G-5761)***
Terra Firma of Delmarva Inc....302 846-3350
36393 Sussex Hwy Delmar (19940) ***(G-1037)***
Terra Systems Inc....302 798-9553
130 Hickman Rd Ste 1 Claymont (19703) ***(G-810)***
Terrace Athletic Club Inc....302 652-9059
208 New Castle Ave New Castle (19720) ***(G-5762)***
Terry Bryan....302 698-9901
189 S Fairfield Dr Dover (19901) ***(G-2139)***
Terry Chld Psychiatric Ctr, New Castle *Also called Children Youth & Their Fam* ***(G-5147)***
Terry L Horton....302 320-4900
501 W 14th St Wilmington (19801) ***(G-12884)***
Terry White....302 652-4969
200 Continental Dr # 109 Newark (19713) ***(G-7557)***
Terrys Welding LLC....302 349-5260
1477 Hickman Rd Greenwood (19950) ***(G-2766)***
Tesla Industries Inc (PA)....302 324-8910
101 109 Centerpoint Blvd New Castle (19720) ***(G-5763)***
Tesla Nootropics Inc....514 718-2270
8 The Grn Ste 5757 Dover (19901) ***(G-2140)***
Testek Aerospace Holdings LLC....302 658-7581
1209 N Orange St Wilmington (19801) ***(G-12885)***
Testex Inc....302 731-5693
8 Fox Ln Newark (19711) ***(G-7558)***
Testing Machines Inc (PA)....302 613-5600
40 Mccullough Dr Unit A New Castle (19720) ***(G-5764)***
Tetra Tech Inc....302 738-7551
240 Continental Dr # 200 Newark (19713) ***(G-7559)***
Tetra Tech Inc....302 738-7551
240 Continental Dr # 200 Newark (19713) ***(G-7560)***
Tetra Tech Engrg & Arch Svcs, Newark *Also called Tetra Tech Inc* ***(G-7560)***
Tetris Company LLC....302 656-1950
103 Foulk Rd Ste 202 Wilmington (19803) ***(G-12886)***
Tetrus Led Co, Milford *Also called American Neon Products Company* ***(G-4306)***
Tevebaugh Associates Inc (PA)....302 984-1400
2 Mill Rd Ste 210 Wilmington (19806) ***(G-12887)***
Texaco, Wilmington *Also called Logue Brothers Inc* ***(G-11427)***
Texaco, Wilmington *Also called Jeff Thomas* ***(G-11143)***
Texavino LLC....302 295-0829
3422 Old Capitol Trl # 1444 Wilmington (19808) ***(G-12888)***
Textronics Inc....302 351-2109
3825 Lancaster Pike # 201 Wilmington (19805) ***(G-12889)***
Tgx Holdings LLC....212 260-6300
1201 N Market St Wilmington (19801) ***(G-12890)***
Th White General Contract....302 945-1829
32783 Long Neck Rd Unit 2 Millsboro (19966) ***(G-4812)***
Thales Inc....302 326-0830
100 W Cmmons Blvd New Castle (19720) ***(G-5765)***
Thales Holding Corporation....302 326-0830
100 W Cmmons Blvd Ste 302 New Castle (19720) ***(G-5766)***
That Granite Place LLC....302 337-7490
18089 Sussex Hwy Bridgeville (19933) ***(G-525)***
The Ascendant Group Inc....302 450-4494
2035 Sunset Lake Rd B2 Newark (19702) ***(G-7561)***
The Dog House, Dover *Also called Governors Ave Animal Hospital* ***(G-1605)***
The Goddard School, Hockessin *Also called Cdb Ventures Inc* ***(G-2981)***
The Nature Conservancy....302 654-4707
100 W 10th St Ste 1107 Wilmington (19801) ***(G-12891)***
The Professionals....302 764-5501
3812 Governor Printz Blvd Wilmington (19802) ***(G-12892)***
Thedigitalsupport....347 305-4006
5301 Limestone Rd Ste 100 Wilmington (19808) ***(G-12893)***
Therapy Architects....610 246-5705
2700 Silverside Rd Ste 4a Wilmington (19810) ***(G-12894)***
Therapy At Beach....302 313-5555
34444 King Street Row Lewes (19958) ***(G-3781)***
Therapy Concierge....302 319-3040
516 Daniels Ct Bear (19701) ***(G-351)***
Therapy Services of Delaw....302 239-2285
24 Gates Cir Hockessin (19707) ***(G-3158)***
Theresa Little MD....302 735-1616
1001 S Bradford St Ste 5 Dover (19904) ***(G-2141)***
Thermal Pipe Systems Inc (PA)....302 999-1588
5205 W Woodmill Dr Ste 33 Wilmington (19808) ***(G-12895)***
Thermal Transf Composites LLC (PA)....302 635-7156
724 Yorklyn Rd Ste 200 Hockessin (19707) ***(G-3159)***
Thermo King Chesapeake, Delmar *Also called Thermo King Corporation* ***(G-1038)***

Thermo King Corporation....302 907-0345
36550 Sussex Hwy Delmar (19940) *(G-1038)*
Thermo King Corporation....302 907-0345
36550 Sussex Hwy Delmar (19940) *(G-1039)*
Thermo King of Delaware, Delmar *Also called Thermo King Corporation (G-1039)*
Thermo Stack LLC....401 885-7781
7460 Lancaster Pike Hockessin (19707) *(G-3160)*
Thermoelectrics Unlimited Inc....302 764-6618
5109 Governor Printz Blvd Wilmington (19809) *(G-12896)*
Thermoplastic Processes, Georgetown *Also called Tpi Partners Inc (G-2694)*
Thesmilezone.com, Wilmington *Also called Dr Clyde A Maxwell Jr (G-10219)*
Theta Vest Inc....302 227-3745
21707 B St Rehoboth Beach (19971) *(G-8096)*
Thi (us) Inc (HQ)....302 792-1444
650 Naamans Rd Ste 307 Claymont (19703) *(G-811)*
Think Clean & Grounds Up LLC....904 250-1614
11 W 9th St New Castle (19720) *(G-5767)*
Think Fast Toys.com, Selbyville *Also called Avalanche Strategies LLC (G-8452)*
Thinkrupter Magazine, Dover *Also called Thinkruptive Media Inc (G-2142)*
Thinkruptive Media Inc....310 779-4748
8 The Grn Ste R Dover (19901) *(G-2142)*
Third Fdral Sav Ln Assn Clvlan (PA)....302 661-2009
103 Foulk Rd Ste 101 Wilmington (19803) *(G-12897)*
Thirst 2 Learn....302 293-2304
891 Pulaski Hwy Bear (19701) *(G-352)*
Thirst 2 Learn LLC....302 475-7080
802 Naamans Rd Wilmington (19810) *(G-12898)*
Thomas A Cochran & Sons Inc (PA)....302 656-6054
807 Washington St New Castle (19720) *(G-5768)*
Thomas Baldwin DDS....302 829-1243
31028 Waterthrush Ln Ocean View (19970) *(G-7820)*
Thomas Brothers LLC....302 366-1316
12 Oak Ave Newark (19711) *(G-7562)*
Thomas Building Group Inc....302 283-0600
35 Albe Dr Newark (19702) *(G-7563)*
Thomas Dougherty DDS....302 239-2500
5317 Limestone Rd Ste 5 Wilmington (19808) *(G-12899)*
Thomas E Melvin Son Inc....302 398-3884
15522 S Dupont Hwy Harrington (19952) *(G-2899)*
Thomas E Moore Inc....302 653-2000
6 Marlyn Ln Kenton (19955) *(G-3186)*
Thomas E Moore Inc....302 674-1500
6 Maryland Ave Kenton (19955) *(G-3187)*
Thomas E OGrady Masonry....302 378-8245
305 N Scott St Middletown (19709) *(G-4257)*
Thomas F Cavanaugh....302 995-2859
123 Hawthorne Ave Wilmington (19805) *(G-12900)*
Thomas Family Farms LLC....302 492-3688
896 Sandy Bend Rd Marydel (19964) *(G-3923)*
Thomas J Allingham II....302 651-3000
1 Rodney Sq Wilmington (19801) *(G-12901)*
Thomas Jenkins DMD....302 426-0526
2323 Penns Ave Ste LI Wilmington (19806) *(G-12902)*
Thomas Jffrson Lrng Foundation....302 856-3300
22051 Wilson Rd Georgetown (19947) *(G-2691)*
Thomas Postlethwait DDS....302 674-8283
1592 Lochmeath Way Dover (19901) *(G-2143)*
Thomas R Wyshock....302 645-5070
32832 Pear Tree Ct Lewes (19958) *(G-3782)*
Thomas Roofing Supply Company....302 629-4521
1164 Airport Rd Ste 13 Seaford (19973) *(G-8421)*
Thomas W Mercer DMD....302 678-2942
77 Saulsbury Rd Dover (19904) *(G-2144)*
Thomas, Irving O DDS, Wilmington *Also called Russell J Tibbetts DDS PA (G-12496)*
Thomco Inc....302 454-0361
314 E Main St Ste 401 Newark (19711) *(G-7564)*
Thompson Cleaners....302 998-0935
4746 Limestone Rd Ste A Wilmington (19808) *(G-12903)*
Thompson's Farm, Hartly *Also called Robert C Thompson (G-2940)*
Thomson Reuters (grc) Inc....212 227-7357
2711 Centerville Rd # 400 Wilmington (19808) *(G-12904)*
Thorn Electric Inc....302 653-4300
405 W Commerce St Smyrna (19977) *(G-8731)*
Thornley Company Inc....302 224-8300
1 Innovation Way Ste 100 Newark (19711) *(G-7565)*
Thoro-Goods Concrete Co Inc (PA)....302 934-8102
30548 Thorogoods Rd Dagsboro (19939) *(G-938)*
Thoroughbred Software Intl....302 339-8383
22536 Lakeshore Dr Georgetown (19947) *(G-2692)*
Thoroughthreads....302 356-0502
3605 Old Capitol Trl C3 Wilmington (19808) *(G-12905)*
Threads N Denims....302 678-0642
8 Senator Ave Dover (19901) *(G-2145)*
Threatstop Inc (PA)....760 542-1550
615 S Dupont Hwy Dover (19901) *(G-2146)*
Three Bs Painting Contractors....302 227-1497
37021 Rehoboth Avenue Ext D Rehoboth Beach (19971) *(G-8097)*
Three Js Disc Tire & Auto Svc....302 995-6141
3724 Kirkwood Hwy Wilmington (19808) *(G-12906)*
Thresholds, Georgetown *Also called Delaware Drnking Drver Program (G-2499)*
Thresholds Inc....302 827-4478
17577 Nassau Commons Blvd # 202 Lewes (19958) *(G-3783)*
Thrive Physical Therapy....302 834-8400
834 Kohl Ave Middletown (19709) *(G-4258)*
Thrupore Technologies Inc (PA)....205 657-0714
15 Reads Way Ste 107 New Castle (19720) *(G-5769)*
Thumbs Only, Wilmington *Also called Charles Ogden (G-9634)*
Tickle Toes, Newark *Also called TT Luxury Group LLC (G-7599)*
Tidewater Electricmyology, Seaford *Also called Tidewater Physcl Thrpy and REB (G-8422)*
Tidewater Physcl Thrpy and REB....302 684-2829
611 Federal St Ste 1 Milton (19968) *(G-4976)*
Tidewater Physcl Thrpy and REB....302 856-2446
10 Georgetown Plz Georgetown (19947) *(G-2693)*
Tidewater Physcl Thrpy and REB....302 398-7982
610 Gordon St Harrington (19952) *(G-2900)*
Tidewater Physcl Thrpy and REB....302 537-7260
63 Atlantic Ave Ocean View (19970) *(G-7821)*
Tidewater Physcl Thrpy and REB....302 629-4024
808 Middleford Rd Ste 7 Seaford (19973) *(G-8422)*
Tidewater Physcl Thrpy and REB....302 945-5111
20750 John J Williams Hwy # 1 Lewes (19958) *(G-3784)*
Tidewater Utilities Inc....302 674-8056
1100 S Little Creek Rd Dover (19901) *(G-2147)*
Tiedemann Trust Company (PA)....302 656-5644
200 Bellevue Pkwy Ste 525 Wilmington (19809) *(G-12907)*
Tiffany Pines I Condo Assn....302 227-0913
20037 Old Landing Rd Rehoboth Beach (19971) *(G-8098)*
Tigani Family Dentistry PA....302 571-8740
1021 Gilpin Ave Ste 205 Wilmington (19806) *(G-12908)*
Tiger Mart, Delmar *Also called J William Gordy Fuel Co (G-1006)*
Tighe and Cottrell PA (PA)....302 658-6400
704 N King St Fl 5005 Wilmington (19801) *(G-12909)*
Tiki Interactive Inc....408 306-4393
16192 Coastal Hwy Lewes (19958) *(G-3785)*
Tile Market of Delaware Inc....302 644-7100
17701 Dartmouth Dr Unit 1 Lewes (19958) *(G-3786)*
Tile Market of Delaware Inc (PA)....302 777-4663
405 Marsh Ln Ste 3 Wilmington (19804) *(G-12910)*
Tile Shop LLC....302 250-4889
1200 Rocky Run Pkwy Wilmington (19803) *(G-12911)*
Tim's Upholstry, Camden Wyoming *Also called Timothy Blawn (G-659)*
Timber Heart Learning Center....302 674-2565
1339 S Governors Ave Dover (19904) *(G-2148)*
Timber Ridge Inc....302 239-9239
710 Yorklyn Rd Hockessin (19707) *(G-3161)*
Timken Gears & Services Inc....302 633-4600
100 Anchor Mill Rd New Castle (19720) *(G-5770)*
Timmons, Bake Jr, Ocean View *Also called Ocean View Farms Inc (G-7808)*
Timothy and Rosemary Clay DMD....302 998-0500
533 Main St Wilmington (19804) *(G-12912)*
Timothy B OHare Custom Bldr....302 537-9559
31494 Railway Rd Ocean View (19970) *(G-7822)*
Timothy Blawn....302 697-3843
11178 Willow Grove Rd Camden Wyoming (19934) *(G-659)*
Timothy D Humphreys....302 225-3000
1831 Delaware Ave Wilmington (19806) *(G-12913)*
Timothy Liveright MD....302 655-7293
625 N Shipley St Wilmington (19801) *(G-12914)*
Timothy W McHugh....302 633-1280
121 Becks Woods Dr # 100 Bear (19701) *(G-353)*
Timothy Westgate....302 629-9197
1415 W Stein Hwy Seaford (19973) *(G-8423)*
Timtec Inc....302 292-8500
301 Ruthar Dr Ste A Newark (19711) *(G-7566)*
Timtec LLC....302 292-8500
301 Ruthar Dr Ste A Newark (19711) *(G-7567)*
Tinas Tiny Tots Daycare....302 536-7077
8779 Concord Rd Seaford (19973) *(G-8424)*
Tiny Tots Childcare and Learni....302 651-9060
1014 W 24th St Wilmington (19802) *(G-12915)*
Tipton Communications Group....302 454-7901
323 E Main St Newark (19711) *(G-7568)*
Tire Kingdom, Wilmington *Also called Tbc Retail Group Inc (G-12855)*
Tire Rack Inc....302 325-8260
300 Anchor Mill Rd New Castle (19720) *(G-5771)*
Tire Sales LLC....302 994-2900
70 Mccullough Dr New Castle (19720) *(G-5772)*
Tire Sales & Service Inc....302 658-8955
600 First State Blvd Wilmington (19804) *(G-12916)*
Titanium Black Exec Sltons LLC....813 785-7842
850 New Burton Rd Dover (19904) *(G-2149)*
Tj Custom Woodworks Inc....302 563-8535
4 Mistweave Ct Newark (19711) *(G-7569)*
Tj S Plumbing Heating L....302 228-7129
26577 Blueberry Ln Frankford (19945) *(G-2393)*
Tlaloc Building Services Inc....302 559-6459
738 Pulaski Hwy Trlr 29b Bear (19701) *(G-354)*

ALPHABETIC

Tlbc LLC 302 797-8700
105 2nd St Lewes (19958) ***(G-3787)***
TLC Home Care 302 983-5720
2055 Melson Rd Wilmington (19808) ***(G-12917)***
TLC Personal Assistants 302 290-9902
1214 Linden St Wilmington (19805) ***(G-12918)***
Tm Management LLC 302 654-4940
30 Hill Rd Wilmington (19806) ***(G-12919)***
TMI Company Store Holding Corp 302 992-0220
508 First State Blvd Wilmington (19804) ***(G-12920)***
Tmk Trucking LLC 302 449-5131
53 Cantwell Dr Middletown (19709) ***(G-4259)***
TNT Window Cleaning 302 326-2411
35 Salem Church Rd Newark (19713) ***(G-7570)***
To A Tee Printing 302 525-6336
2860 Ogletown Rd Newark (19713) ***(G-7571)***
To Do Yard Guys 302 947-9475
28244 Chippewa Ave Millsboro (19966) ***(G-4813)***
Today Media, Wilmington *Also called Martinelli Holdings LLC* ***(G-11551)***
Today Nails 302 286-7937
1129 Churchmans Rd Newark (19713) ***(G-7572)***
Todays Energy Solutions LLC 302 438-0285
608 Beaver Falls Pl Wilmington (19808) ***(G-12921)***
Todays Kid Inc (not Inc) 302 834-5620
10 Songsmith Dr Newark (19702) ***(G-7573)***
Todays Latino Magazine 302 981-5131
217 N Broad St Middletown (19709) ***(G-4260)***
Todd A Richardson Dcpa 302 449-0149
708 Ash Blvd Middletown (19709) ***(G-4261)***
Todd Rowen DMD 302 994-5887
25 Milltown Rd Ste A Wilmington (19808) ***(G-12922)***
Toddlers Tech Inc 302 655-4487
2704 W 4th St Wilmington (19805) ***(G-12923)***
Todds 302 658-0387
1601 Concord Pike Ste 49 Wilmington (19803) ***(G-12924)***
Todds Janitorial Service Inc 302 378-8212
407 E Lake St Middletown (19709) ***(G-4262)***
Toll Brothers Inc 302 832-1700
1100 Casey Dr New Castle (19720) ***(G-5773)***
Tolton Builders Inc 302 239-5357
7301 Lancaster Pike Hockessin (19707) ***(G-3162)***
Tom Miller Remodeling 302 674-1637
416 N State St Dover (19901) ***(G-2150)***
Tom Wiseley Insurance Agency 302 832-7700
1400 Peoples Plz Ste 228 Newark (19702) ***(G-7574)***
Tom Wright Real Estate 302 234-6026
7234 Lancaster Pike # 101 Hockessin (19707) ***(G-3163)***
Tomall Inc 302 424-4004
1109 N Dupont Blvd Milford (19963) ***(G-4579)***
Tomato Sunshine, Rehoboth Beach *Also called Ernie Deangelis* ***(G-7928)***
Toms Barber Shop 302 992-9635
3317 Old Capitol Trl A Wilmington (19808) ***(G-12925)***
Tony Ashburn Inc 302 677-1940
872 Walker Rd Ste A Dover (19904) ***(G-2151)***
Toolook Inc 240 330-3307
500 Delaware Ave Unit 1 Wilmington (19899) ***(G-12926)***
Tools & More, New Castle *Also called Mechanics Paradise Inc* ***(G-5513)***
Tooze & Easter MD PA 302 735-8700
720 S Queen St Dover (19904) ***(G-2152)***
Top Dog Best Games LLC 949 859-8869
3422 Old Capitol Trl Wilmington (19808) ***(G-12927)***
Top Nails 302 644-2261
17601 Coastal Hwy Unit 2 Lewes (19958) ***(G-3788)***
Top Notch Htg & A C & Rfrgn 302 645-7171
33806 Dreamweaver Ln Lewes (19958) ***(G-3789)***
Top of Hllbrndywine Apartments 302 798-9971
2101 Prior Rd Wilmington (19809) ***(G-12928)***
Top of The Hill-Brandwine Apts, Wilmington *Also called Top of Hllbrndywine Apartments* ***(G-12928)***
Top of The Line Jantr Svcs 302 645-2668
19602 Mulberry Knoll Rd Lewes (19958) ***(G-3790)***
Top Qality Indus Finishers Inc 302 778-5005
1204 E 12th St Ste 1 Wilmington (19802) ***(G-12929)***
Top Rated Media Inc 888 550-9273
1000 N West St Ste 1200 Wilmington (19801) ***(G-12930)***
Topaz & Associates LLC 302 448-8914
3 Francis Cir Ste 1 Newark (19711) ***(G-7575)***
Topeka Residence Inn, Wilmington *Also called Rl Heritage Inn Topeka Inc* ***(G-12404)***
Topiary Tech LLC 302 636-5440
2711 Centerville Rd # 400 Wilmington (19808) ***(G-12931)***
Topkis Financial Advisors LLC 302 654-4444
910 Foulk Rd Ste 200 Wilmington (19803) ***(G-12932)***
Topkis, William M Chfc, Wilmington *Also called Daniel M McDermott Chfc Cfp* ***(G-9956)***
Tops International Corp 302 738-8889
707 Interchange Blvd Newark (19711) ***(G-7576)***
Toptal LLC (PA) 650 843-9206
2810 N Church St # 36879 Wilmington (19802) ***(G-12933)***
Toptracker LLC 415 230-0131
2810 N Church St # 36879 Wilmington (19802) ***(G-12934)***
Torbert Funeral Chapel Inc 302 734-3341
61 S Bradford St Dover (19904) ***(G-2153)***
Torc Yoga LLC 856 408-9118
4 Caleb Ter Wilmington (19805) ***(G-12935)***
Tornado II Janitorial Service 302 898-1370
336 Hackberry Dr New Castle (19720) ***(G-5774)***
Toroville, Newark *Also called Management Options Inc* ***(G-6980)***
Toss That Junk LLC 302 326-3867
300 S Dragon Dr Bear (19701) ***(G-355)***
Tot's Turf Child Care Center, Camden *Also called Delaware Adlescent Program Inc* ***(G-557)***
Total Beauty Supply Inc 302 798-4647
2320 Sconset Rd Wilmington (19810) ***(G-12936)***
Total Care Physicians 302 998-2977
2601 Annand Dr Ste 4 Wilmington (19808) ***(G-12937)***
Total Care Physicians 302 836-4200
2600 Glasgow Ave Ste 124 Newark (19702) ***(G-7577)***
Total Care Physicians (PA) 302 798-0666
405 Silverside Rd Ste 111 Wilmington (19809) ***(G-12938)***
Total Climate Control Inc 302 836-6240
2694 Frazer Rd Newark (19702) ***(G-7578)***
Total Construction Rentals Inc 302 575-1132
19 Davidson Ln Bldg 4 New Castle (19720) ***(G-5775)***
Total Health & Rehabilitation 302 999-9202
2060 Limestone Rd Ste 202 Wilmington (19808) ***(G-12939)***
Total Pest Solutions 302 275-7159
309 Quail Run Camden Wyoming (19934) ***(G-660)***
Total Risc Technology USA LLC 972 422-9135
3411 Silverside Rd Wilmington (19810) ***(G-12940)***
Total Services Inc 302 575-1132
19 Davidson Ln Bldg 4 New Castle (19720) ***(G-5776)***
Total Turf & Landscaping 302 762-5410
852 Cranbrook Dr Wilmington (19803) ***(G-12941)***
Totalgreen Holland, Wilmington *Also called Q Vandenberg & Sons Inc* ***(G-12273)***
Totally Clean 302 376-3626
13 Kingfisher Ct Middletown (19709) ***(G-4263)***
Totaltranslogistics LLC 302 325-4245
8 Mccullough Dr New Castle (19720) ***(G-5777)***
Totaltrax Inc 302 514-0600
920 W Basin Rd Ste 400 New Castle (19720) ***(G-5778)***
Toubasam Inc 302 299-2954
710 N Market St Ste 2b Wilmington (19801) ***(G-12942)***
Touch of Italy Bakery LLC 302 827-2132
33323 E Chesapeake St # 31 Lewes (19958) ***(G-3791)***
Touchstone Systems Inc 302 324-5322
42c Reads Way New Castle (19720) ***(G-5779)***
Tough Luck LLC 302 644-8001
1030 Hwy One Lewes (19958) ***(G-3792)***
Tower Business Machines Inc 302 395-1445
278 Quigley Blvd New Castle (19720) ***(G-5780)***
Tower Business Systems, New Castle *Also called Tower Business Machines Inc* ***(G-5780)***
Towle Institute 302 993-1408
4210 Limestone Rd Wilmington (19808) ***(G-12943)***
Towles Electric Inc 302 674-4985
621 W Div St Dover Dover Dover (19904) ***(G-2154)***
Town and Country Salon Inc 302 737-1855
1923 Kirkwood Hwy Newark (19711) ***(G-7579)***
Town and Country Trust 302 328-8700
270 Brandywine Dr Bear (19701) ***(G-356)***
Town Court Apartments, Wilmington *Also called Apartment Communities Corp* ***(G-9094)***
Town of Middletown 302 376-9950
130 Hampden Rd Middletown (19709) ***(G-4264)***
Town of Middletown 302 378-2711
19 W Green St Middletown (19709) ***(G-4265)***
Towne & Country Cleaners Inc 302 478-8911
3301 Concord Pike Ste B Wilmington (19803) ***(G-12944)***
Towne Place Suites By Marriott 302 369-6212
410 Eagle Run Rd Newark (19702) ***(G-7580)***
Townsend Bros Inc 302 674-0100
21 Emerson Dr Dover (19901) ***(G-2155)***
Townsend Fitness Equipment, Smyrna *Also called David L Townsend Co Inc* ***(G-8611)***
Townsend Fmly Cosmtc Dentistry 302 376-7979
3920 Dupont Pkwy Townsend (19734) ***(G-8827)***
Townsend Kitchens Cabinets & 302 659-1007
1028 Blackbird Landing Rd Townsend (19734) ***(G-8828)***
Toxtrap Inc 302 698-1400
12 S Springview Dr Dover (19901) ***(G-2156)***
Toy Box Child Care Center 302 427-8438
6 Halcyon Dr New Castle (19720) ***(G-5781)***
Toy Box Child Care Ctr, New Castle *Also called Toy Box Child Care Center* ***(G-5781)***
Toyo Fibre USA Inc 302 475-3699
2706 Alexander Dr Wilmington (19810) ***(G-12945)***
TP Computing, Rehoboth Beach *Also called Biz TEC Inc* ***(G-7870)***
TP Indira and Mdpa, Dover *Also called Manveen Duggal MD* ***(G-1817)***
Tpi, Wilmington *Also called Precisionists Inc* ***(G-12209)***
Tpi Partners Inc (PA) 302 855-0139
21649 Cedar Creek Ave Georgetown (19947) ***(G-2694)***
Tpp Acquisition Inc 302 674-4805
1365 N Dupont Hwy # 4012 Dover (19901) ***(G-2157)***

Tpw Management LLC 302 227-7878
17577 Nassau Commons Blvd # 103 Lewes (19958) *(G-3793)*
Traction Wholesale Center Inc 302 743-8473
600 S Heald St Wilmington (19801) *(G-12946)*
Tracy Peoples LLC 302 927-0280
31039 Country Gdns Dagsboro (19939) *(G-939)*
Trademark Productions Inc 416 787-0365
2711 Cntrvlle Rd Pmb 7051 7051 Pmb Wilmington (19808) *(G-12947)*
Trademark Signs 484 832-5770
2621 Boxwood Dr Wilmington (19810) *(G-12948)*
Trader Funeral Home Inc 302 734-4620
12 Lotus St Dover (19901) *(G-2158)*
Tradeway Corporation 302 834-1957
549 Mason Dr New Castle (19720) *(G-5782)*
Traffic Sign Solutions Inc 302 295-4836
1000 N West St Ste 1200 Wilmington (19801) *(G-12949)*
Training Center, The, New Castle *Also called James Sutton (G-5435)*
Trainor Consulting LLC 302 428-1677
9 Carillon Ct Wilmington (19803) *(G-12950)*
Traitel Telecom Corp 619 331-1913
3422 Old Capitol Trl Wilmington (19808) *(G-12951)*
Trane US Inc 302 395-0200
66 Southgate Blvd New Castle (19720) *(G-5783)*
Tranquility Counseling Inc 302 636-0700
314 E Main St Ste 402 Newark (19711) *(G-7581)*
Trans Logistics LLC 267 244-6550
4000 N Market St Wilmington (19802) *(G-12952)*
Trans Plus Inc 302 323-3051
423 W 7th St New Castle (19720) *(G-5784)*
Trans Products, Milford *Also called F D Hammond Enterprises Inc (G-4407)*
Trans Un Sttlment Slutions Inc (HQ) 800 916-8800
5300 Brandywine Pkwy # 100 Wilmington (19803) *(G-12953)*
Transactional Web Inc 908 216-5054
8 W 13th St Wilmington (19801) *(G-12954)*
Transaxle LLC 302 322-8300
4060 N Dupont Hwy Ste 6 New Castle (19720) *(G-5785)*
Transcontinental Airways Corp 202 817-2020
1000 N West St Ste 1200 Wilmington (19801) *(G-12955)*
Transcore LP 302 838-7429
2111 Dupont Pkwy Middletown (19709) *(G-4266)*
Transcore LP 302 677-7262
26 Old Rudnick Ln Dover (19901) *(G-2159)*
Transflo Terminal Services Inc 302 994-3853
1205 Centerville Rd Wilmington (19808) *(G-12956)*
Transforming Wellness LLC 302 249-2526
35802 Atlantic Ave Millville (19967) *(G-4856)*
Transitional Youth 302 423-7543
8748 Greenwood Rd Greenwood (19950) *(G-2767)*
Transport Wkrs Un Amer Intl Un 302 652-1503
1524 Bonwood Rd Wilmington (19805) *(G-12957)*
Transport Wkrs Un O Local 2015, Wilmington *Also called Transport Wkrs Un Amer Intl Un (G-12957)*
Transportation Delaware Dept 302 326-8950
250 Bear Christiana Rd Bear (19701) *(G-357)*
Transportation Delaware Dept 302 653-4128
5369 Summit Bridge Rd Middletown (19709) *(G-4267)*
Transportation Delaware Dept 302 658-8960
119 Lwer Beech St Ste 100 Wilmington (19805) *(G-12958)*
Transportation Department, New Castle *Also called Colonial School District (G-5182)*
Transstate Jet Service Inc 302 346-3102
139 Davis Cir Dover (19904) *(G-2160)*
Transworld Diversfd Svcs Inc 302 777-5902
100 Sico Rd Wilmington (19801) *(G-12959)*
Traps Plumbing Heating A/C 302 677-1775
1851 S Dupont Hwy Dover (19901) *(G-2161)*
Trash Tech LLC 302 832-8000
755 Governor Lea Rd New Castle (19720) *(G-5786)*
Trauma Film Production PR LLC 623 582-2287
8 The Grn Ste A Dover (19901) *(G-2162)*
Travel Agency 302 381-0205
101 Breakwater Reach Lewes (19958) *(G-3794)*
Travel Co Inc 302 652-6263
1700 Augustine Cut Off Wilmington (19803) *(G-12960)*
Travel Travel Newark Inc 302 737-5555
760 Peoples Plz Newark (19702) *(G-7582)*
Travelers Inn, Milford *Also called Gulab Management Inc (G-4427)*
Travelway Group USA Inc 514 331-3130
251 Little Falls Dr Wilmington (19808) *(G-12961)*
Travis Chropractic 610 485-9800
1911 Foulk Rd Wilmington (19810) *(G-12962)*
Travis, Dr Arthur W, Wilmington *Also called Travis Chropractic (G-12962)*
Treatment Foster Care - Newark, Christiana *Also called Pressley Ridge Foundation (G-678)*
Treatment Fster Care - Grgtown, Georgetown *Also called Pressley Ridge Foundation (G-2626)*
Treehouse Wellness Center LLC 302 893-1001
714 W 11th St Wilmington (19801) *(G-12963)*
Trellist Inc (PA) 302 778-1300
117 N Market St Ste 300 Wilmington (19801) *(G-12964)*
Trellist Inc 302 593-1432
2317 Macdonough Rd # 100 Wilmington (19805) *(G-12965)*
Trelltex Inc 302 738-4313
211 Executive Dr Ste 9 Newark (19702) *(G-7583)*
Trenton Block Delaware Inc 302 684-0112
701 Federal St Milton (19968) *(G-4977)*
Trevor Ennis DC 302 730-8848
200 Banning St Dover (19904) *(G-2163)*
Trevor Ennis DC 302 389-2225
29 N East St Smyrna (19977) *(G-8732)*
Tri County Electrical Services, Laurel *Also called Daniel George Bebee Inc (G-3220)*
Tri State Battery and Auto Elc (PA) 302 292-2330
107 Albe Dr Ste H Newark (19702) *(G-7584)*
Tri State Foot & Ankle Ctr LLC 302 475-1299
2018 Naamans Rd Bldg 1 Wilmington (19810) *(G-12966)*
Tri State Imaging Consultants, Middletown *Also called Delaware Open M R I LLC (G-4030)*
Tri State Roofers, Wilmington *Also called Roofers Inc (G-12473)*
Tri State Termite & Pest Ctrl 302 239-0512
1170 Corner Ketch Rd Newark (19711) *(G-7585)*
Tri State Tree Service 302 645-7412
30534 E Mill Run Milton (19968) *(G-4978)*
Tri-State Bird Rescue RES Inc 302 737-9543
170 Possum Hollow Rd Newark (19711) *(G-7586)*
Tri-State Cheernastics Inc 302 322-4020
1 King Ave New Castle (19720) *(G-5787)*
Tri-State Drywall LLC 302 798-2709
2803b Philadelphia Pike Claymont (19703) *(G-812)*
Tri-State Fbrction McHning LLC 302 232-3133
251 Airport Rd New Castle (19720) *(G-5788)*
Tri-State Grouting LLC 302 286-0701
567 Walther Rd Newark (19702) *(G-7587)*
Tri-State Health 302 368-2563
266 S College Ave Newark (19711) *(G-7588)*
Tri-State Mobile Home Supply, Millsboro *Also called T & C Enterprise Incorporated (G-4809)*
Tri-State SEC & Contrls LLC 302 299-2175
2860 Ogletown Rd 23 Newark (19713) *(G-7589)*
Tri-State Technologies Inc 302 658-5400
701 Cornell Dr Ste 13 Wilmington (19801) *(G-12967)*
Tri-State Truck & Eqp Sls LLC 302 276-1253
201 E 6th St New Castle (19720) *(G-5789)*
Tri-State Underground Inc 302 836-8030
4369 Dupont Pkwy Townsend (19734) *(G-8829)*
Tri-State Underground Inc 302 293-9352
2141 Old Kirkwood Rd Bear (19701) *(G-358)*
Tri-State Waste Solutions Inc 302 622-8600
1600 Matassino Rd New Castle (19720) *(G-5790)*
Triad Construction Company LLC 302 652-3339
210 Marsh Ln New Castle (19720) *(G-5791)*
Triad Enterprises, Wilmington *Also called Carzo & Associates Inc (G-9584)*
Trial Transport Logistics 302 383-5907
400 Wyoming Ave Wilmington (19809) *(G-12968)*
Trialogics LLC 302 313-9000
3 Mill Rd Ste 306a Wilmington (19806) *(G-12969)*
Triangle Fastener Corporation 302 322-0600
243 Quigley Blvd Ste C New Castle (19720) *(G-5792)*
Tricklestar Inc 888 700-1098
251 Little Falls Dr Wilmington (19808) *(G-12970)*
Tricky Minute Games Inc 302 319-5137
108 W 13th St Wilmington (19801) *(G-12971)*
Tricomm Services Corporation 302 454-2975
604 Interchange Blvd Newark (19711) *(G-7590)*
Tricon Construction MGT Inc 302 838-6500
13 King Ct Ste 3 New Castle (19720) *(G-5793)*
Trifecta Health Solutions Inc 614 582-4184
651 N Broad St Ste 20515 Middletown (19709) *(G-4268)*
Triglia Express Inc 302 846-2248
38001 Bi State Blvd Delmar (19940) *(G-1040)*
Triglia Trans Co 302 846-3795
Bystate Blvd Delmar (19940) *(G-1041)*
Triglias Transportation Co 302 846-2141
Rr 13 Box A Delmar (19940) *(G-1042)*
Trihold Inc 302 475-4517
110 Hackney Cir Wilmington (19803) *(G-12972)*
Trilogy Salon and Day Spa Inc 302 292-3511
1200 Capitol Trl Newark (19711) *(G-7591)*
Trim Shop, Newark *Also called Color Dye Systems and Co (G-6265)*
Trim Waste Management LLC (PA) 302 738-2500
667 Dawson Dr Ste C Newark (19713) *(G-7592)*
Trimble Navigation Limited 302 368-2434
107c Albe Dr Ste C Newark (19702) *(G-7593)*
Trinet Consultants Inc (HQ) 302 633-9348
1106 Elderon Dr Wilmington (19808) *(G-12973)*
Trinity 3 Enterprises Inc 267 973-2666
38 Ayrshire St Bear (19701) *(G-359)*
Trinity Cloud Company 973 494-8190
1013 Centre Rd Ste 403s Wilmington (19805) *(G-12974)*
Trinity Gold Consulting LLC 302 476-9774
807 Brown St Wilmington (19805) *(G-12975)*
Trinity Health Corporation 302 421-4100
701 N Clayton St Wilmington (19805) *(G-12976)*

ALPHABETIC

(PA)=Parent Co (HQ)=Headquarters (DH)=Div Headquarters
2020 Harris Directory of Delaware Businesses
735

Trinity Home Health Care Corp (PA) ... 302 838-2710
1400 Peoples Plz Ste 215 Newark (19702) *(G-7594)*

Trinity Home Health Care LLC ... 410 620-9366
1400 Peoples Plz Ste 215 Newark (19702) *(G-7595)*

Trinity Logistics Inc ... 302 595-2116
23 Fantail Ct New Castle (19720) *(G-5794)*

Trinity Logistics Inc (HQ) ... 302 253-3900
50 Fallon Ave Seaford (19973) *(G-8425)*

Trinity Medical Assoc ... 302 762-6675
410 Foulk Rd Ste 200b Wilmington (19803) *(G-12977)*

Trinity Medical Center PA ... 302 846-0618
8 E Grove St Delmar (19940) *(G-1043)*

Triodent, Wilmington Also called Rhondium Corporation *(G-12403)*

Triple D Charters LLC ... 302 934-6837
24386 Godwin School Rd Millsboro (19966) *(G-4814)*

Trisco Foods LLC ... 719 352-3218
2711 Centerville Rd # 400 Wilmington (19808) *(G-12978)*

Tristar Solar Farm LLC ... 626 457-1381
1521 Concord Pike Wilmington (19803) *(G-12979)*

Tristate Courier & Carriage ... 302 654-3345
1001 N Jefferson St # 100 Wilmington (19801) *(G-12980)*

Tristate Mechanical, Wilmington Also called Coastal Mechanical *(G-9754)*

Tritek Corporation ... 302 239-1638
103 E Bridle Path Hockessin (19707) *(G-3164)*

Tritek Technologies, Hockessin Also called Tritek Corporation *(G-3164)*

Tritek Technologies Inc (PA) ... 302 239-1638
103 E Bridle Path Hockessin (19707) *(G-3165)*

Tritek Technologies Inc ... 302 573-5096
1 Medori Blvd Ste B Wilmington (19801) *(G-12981)*

Triton Construction Co Inc ... 516 780-8100
101 Pigeon Point Rd New Castle (19720) *(G-5795)*

Troisi, Ernest DPM PA, Newark Also called Delaware Foot & Ankle Assoc *(G-6380)*

Trolley Laundry ... 302 654-3538
33a Trolley Sq Wilmington (19806) *(G-12982)*

Trolley Sq Opn Mri & Imgng Ctr ... 302 472-5555
1010 N Bancroft Pkwy # 101 Wilmington (19805) *(G-12983)*

Trolley Square Branch 307, Wilmington Also called Wilmington Savings Fund Soc *(G-13250)*

Trophy Shop ... 302 656-4438
303 W 8th St Wilmington (19801) *(G-12984)*

Tropic Wholesale, Wilmington Also called Village Green Inc *(G-13082)*

Tropical Harvest Inc ... 302 682-9463
10 Cardiff Rd Rehoboth Beach (19971) *(G-8099)*

Trottys Concrete Pumping Inc ... 302 732-3100
34107 Dupont Blvd Frankford (19945) *(G-2394)*

Troutman Machine Company Inc ... 302 674-3540
1175 S Governors Ave Dover (19904) *(G-2164)*

Troy Farmer ... 888 711-0094
16 Catherine Ct Bear (19701) *(G-360)*

Troy Granite Inc (PA) ... 302 292-1750
711 Interchange Blvd Newark (19711) *(G-7596)*

Tru Beauti LLC ... 302 353-9249
307 Bald Eagle Way Middletown (19709) *(G-4269)*

Tru By Hilton Georgetown LLC ... 302 515-2100
301 College Park Ln Georgetown (19947) *(G-2695)*

Tru General Contractor Inc ... 302 354-0553
3307 Faulkland Rd Wilmington (19808) *(G-12985)*

Tru Green-Chemlawn, Wilmington Also called Trugreen Limited Partnership *(G-12988)*

Truck Lagbe Inc ... 860 810-8677
16192 Coastal Hwy Lewes (19958) *(G-3795)*

Truck Tech Inc ... 302 832-8000
1600 Matassino Rd New Castle (19720) *(G-5796)*

True Access Capital Corp ... 302 652-6774
100 W 10th St Ste 300 Wilmington (19801) *(G-12986)*

True Intelligence Tech Inc ... 979 209-0335
2711 Centerville Rd # 400 Wilmington (19808) *(G-12987)*

True Life Church Newark Inc (PA) ... 302 283-9003
33 Lotus Cir N Bear (19701) *(G-361)*

True Mobility Inc ... 302 836-4110
773 S Dupont Hwy New Castle (19720) *(G-5797)*

True Pest Control Services (PA) ... 302 834-0867
48 Loblolly Ln Middletown (19709) *(G-4270)*

True Religion Apparel Inc ... 302 894-9425
132 Christiana Mall Newark (19702) *(G-7597)*

True Value, Rehoboth Beach Also called D F Quillen & Sons Inc *(G-7906)*

True-Pack Ltd (PA) ... 302 326-2222
420 Churchmans Rd New Castle (19720) *(G-5798)*

Trugreen Limited Partnership ... 302 724-6620
1350 First State Blvd Wilmington (19804) *(G-12988)*

Truitt Insurance Agency Inc ... 302 645-9344
365 Savannah Rd Lewes (19958) *(G-3796)*

Trumove Inc ... 917 379-7427
16192 Coastal Hwy Lewes (19958) *(G-3797)*

Trutrac LLC ... 833 878-8722
1201 N Orange St Ste 700 Wilmington (19801) *(G-12989)*

TS Air Enterprises LLC ... 302 533-7458
700 Barksdale Rd Ste 3 Newark (19711) *(G-7598)*

TSC Enterprises LLC ... 302 934-6158
27380 William Street Rd Millsboro (19966) *(G-4815)*

Tspkeycom, Wilmington Also called Market Keys LLC *(G-11535)*

TT Luxury Group LLC ... 732 242-9795
46 Vansant Rd Newark (19711) *(G-7599)*

Ttna Energy Systems LLC ... 302 384-9147
3422 Old Capitol Trl # 1468 Wilmington (19808) *(G-12990)*

Tuckahoe Acres Camping Resort ... 302 539-1841
36031 Tuckahoe Trl Dagsboro (19939) *(G-940)*

Tucker Mechanical Service Inc ... 302 536-7730
8185 Bethel Rd Seaford (19973) *(G-8426)*

Tucson Hotels LP (PA) ... 678 830-2438
2711 Centerville Rd # 400 Wilmington (19808) *(G-12991)*

Tudor Electric Inc ... 302 736-1444
801 Otis Dr Dover (19901) *(G-2165)*

Tudor Enterprises L L C ... 302 736-8255
1031 Fowler Ct Dover (19901) *(G-2166)*

Tull Brothers Inc ... 302 629-3071
24960 Dairy Ln Seaford (19973) *(G-8427)*

Tune-Up III of MD Inc (PA) ... 410 655-9500
112 Setting Sun Way Frankford (19945) *(G-2395)*

Tunnel Industries, Millsboro Also called Tunnell Companies LP *(G-4816)*

Tunnell & Raysor PA (PA) ... 302 856-7313
30 E Pine St Georgetown (19947) *(G-2696)*

Tunnell & Raysor PA ... 302 226-4420
323 Rehoboth Ave Ste E Rehoboth Beach (19971) *(G-8100)*

Tunnell & Raysor PA ... 302 644-4442
770 Kings Hwy Lewes (19958) *(G-3798)*

Tunnell Companies LP (PA) ... 302 945-9300
34026 Annas Way Unit 1 Millsboro (19966) *(G-4816)*

Turf Pro Inc ... 302 218-3530
103 Sandy Dr Ste 100 Newark (19713) *(G-7600)*

Turfhound Inc ... 215 783-8143
5500 Skyline Dr Ste 6 Wilmington (19808) *(G-12992)*

Turning Point At Peoples Place ... 302 424-2420
1131 Airport Rd Milford (19963) *(G-4580)*

Turning Point Collection LLC ... 302 416-0092
1020 W 18th St Wilmington (19802) *(G-12993)*

Turning Pt Counseling Ctr LLC ... 214 883-5148
1 N Main St Camden (19934) *(G-602)*

Turnkey Lender Inc ... 888 299-4892
16192 Coastal Hwy Lewes (19958) *(G-3799)*

Turnstone Builders LLC ... 302 227-8876
37395 Oyster House Rd Rehoboth Beach (19971) *(G-8101)*

Turquoise Shop Inc ... 302 366-7448
543 Christiana Mall Newark (19702) *(G-7601)*

Tuscan/Lehigh Dairies Inc ... 302 398-8321
17267 S Dupont Hwy Harrington (19952) *(G-2901)*

Tusi and Son Mechanical Inc ... 302 731-8228
675a Dawson Dr Newark (19713) *(G-7602)*

Tusi Brothers Inc ... 302 998-6383
1 Copper Dr Ste 1 # 1 Wilmington (19804) *(G-12994)*

Tutor Time Learning Ctrs LLC ... 302 235-5701
5305 Limestone Rd Wilmington (19808) *(G-12995)*

Tutor Time Lrng Systems Inc ... 302 478-7366
2001 Brandywine Pkwy Wilmington (19803) *(G-12996)*

Twaddell Plumbing and Heating ... 302 475-5577
1907 Zebley Rd Wilmington (19810) *(G-12997)*

Twin Creek Farms LLC ... 302 249-2294
638 Canterbury Rd Milford (19963) *(G-4581)*

Twin Hearts Management LLC ... 302 777-5700
200 Banning St Ste 340 Dover (19904) *(G-2167)*

Twinco Romax LLC ... 302 998-3019
1 Crowell St Wilmington (19804) *(G-12998)*

Twm, Newark Also called Trim Waste Management LLC *(G-7592)*

Two Dds LLC ... 302 300-1259
153 Jane Ct Middletown (19709) *(G-4271)*

Two Farms Inc ... 302 653-8345
304 N Dupont Blvd Smyrna (19977) *(G-8733)*

Two Men and A Truck, Dover Also called Jkb Corp *(G-1698)*

Two Men and A Truck, Magnolia Also called H G Investments LLC *(G-3894)*

Two Men and A Truck, New Castle Also called Connolly Options LLC *(G-5191)*

Two Roses United LLC ... 302 593-2453
543 E 35th St Wilmington (19802) *(G-12999)*

Twyne Inc ... 213 675-9518
2140 S Dupont Hwy Camden (19934) *(G-603)*

Ty Jennifer MD ... 302 651-4459
1600 Rockland Rd Wilmington (19803) *(G-13000)*

TY Lin International Group ... 302 883-3662
222 S Dupont Hwy Dover (19901) *(G-2168)*

Tybout Redfearn & Pell PA ... 302 658-6901
750 Shipyard Dr Ste 400 Wilmington (19801) *(G-13001)*

Tycos General Contractors Inc ... 302 478-9267
2112 Silverside Rd Wilmington (19810) *(G-13002)*

Tylaur Inc ... 302 894-9330
2659 Kirkwood Hwy Newark (19711) *(G-7603)*

U A G Inc ... 302 731-2747
841 Old Baltimore Pike Newark (19702) *(G-7604)*

U A W Legal Services, Newark Also called UAW-GM Legal Services Plan *(G-7606)*

U and I Builders Inc ... 302 697-1645
1633 Sorghum Mill Rd Dover (19901) *(G-2169)*

U Haul Co Independent Dealers ... 302 424-3189
601 Marshall St Milford (19963) *(G-4582)*

U Haul Company Independent Dlr 302 369-8230
8 Mill Park Ct Newark (19713) *(G-7605)*
U Haul Neighborhood Dealer 302 613-0207
214 Bear Christiana Rd Bear (19701) *(G-362)*
U S 13 Dragway Inc (PA) 302 875-1911
36952 Sussex Hwy Delmar (19940) *(G-1044)*
U S Express Taxi Company LLC 302 357-1908
260 Christiana Rd Apt N18 New Castle (19720) *(G-5799)*
U S Mail Transport, Lewes *Also called Lantransit Enterprises LLC (G-3592)*
U S Male Mens Hair Care Ctrs, Hockessin *Also called CMC Corporation of Hockessin (G-2990)*
U Scope Solutions LLC 844 872-6732
2711 Centerville Rd # 400 Wilmington (19808) *(G-13003)*
U Tan Inc 302 674-8040
650 S Bay Rd Ste 11 Dover (19901) *(G-2170)*
U Transit Inc 302 227-1197
12 Hazlett St Rehoboth Beach (19971) *(G-8102)*
U-Haul, Lewes *Also called Morton Electric Co (G-3650)*
U-Haul, Milford *Also called U Haul Co Independent Dealers (G-4582)*
U-Haul, Newark *Also called U Haul Company Independent Dlr (G-7605)*
U-Haul International Inc 302 762-6445
2920 Governor Printz Blvd Wilmington (19802) *(G-13004)*
U-Haul Neighborhood Dealer 302 644-4316
33012 Cedar Grove Rd Lewes (19958) *(G-3800)*
U-Haul Neighborhood Dealer 302 703-0376
17649 Coastal Hwy Lewes (19958) *(G-3801)*
U-Haul Neighborhood Dealer 302 326-1875
1713 Wilmington Rd New Castle (19720) *(G-5800)*
U-Haul Neighborhood Dealer 302 449-7379
5101 Summit Bridge Rd Middletown (19709) *(G-4272)*
U-Save Auto, Milford *Also called William T Wadkins Garage Inc (G-4608)*
Uacj Trading America Co Ltd (PA) 312 636-5941
1209 N Orange St Wilmington (19801) *(G-13005)*
UAW-GM Legal Services Plan 302 562-8212
4051 Ogletown Rd Ste 201 Newark (19713) *(G-7606)*
Ubinet Inc 302 722-6015
831 N Tatnall St Wilmington (19801) *(G-13006)*
Ubivis Management LLC 833 824-8476
19266 Coastal Hwy 4-1065 Rehoboth Beach (19971) *(G-8103)*
Ublerb 773 569-9686
9 E Loockerman St Ste 215 Dover (19901) *(G-2171)*
UBS Financial Services Inc 302 657-5331
500 Delaware Ave Ste 901 Wilmington (19801) *(G-13007)*
Ucp, Newark *Also called United Cocoa Processor Inc (G-7613)*
Udaan Inc 267 408-3001
5 Brittany Ln Bear (19701) *(G-363)*
Udel Holdings LLC 877 833-8737
91 Thorn Ln Ofc 2 Newark (19711) *(G-7607)*
Udr Inc 302 674-8887
1700 N Dupont Hwy Ste 1 Dover (19901) *(G-2172)*
Uet International Inc 302 834-0234
9 Riva Ridge Ln Bear (19701) *(G-364)*
Ufo Development Group Inc 408 995-3217
16192 Coastal Hwy Lewes (19958) *(G-3802)*
Ultimate Express Inc 443 523-0800
37976 Bayview Cir E Selbyville (19975) *(G-8552)*
Ultimate Images Inc 302 479-0292
3100 Naamans Rd Ste 8 Wilmington (19810) *(G-13008)*
Ultrachem Inc 302 325-9880
900 Centerpoint Blvd New Castle (19720) *(G-5801)*
Ultrafine Technologies Inc 302 384-6513
405 Derby Way Wilmington (19810) *(G-13009)*
Uma Chatterjee MD 302 995-7500
620 Stanton Christiana Rd Newark (19713) *(G-7608)*
Umbrella Corporation 302 603-7100
19266 Coastal Hwy 4-73r Rehoboth Beach (19971) *(G-8104)*
Umbrella Transport Group Inc 301 919-1623
39 Glennwood Dr Newark (19702) *(G-7609)*
Umiya Inc 302 674-4011
428 N Dupont Hwy Dover (19901) *(G-2173)*
Unadori LLC 917 539-2128
8 The Grn Ste A Dover (19901) *(G-2174)*
Uncorked Canvas Parties 302 724-7625
125 W Loockerman St Dover (19904) *(G-2175)*
Uncorked Canvas Parties LLC 302 659-1396
1477 Sunnyside Rd Smyrna (19977) *(G-8734)*
Under Whistle 302 250-8400
49 N Bellwoode Dr Newark (19702) *(G-7610)*
Under/Comm Inc 302 424-1554
198 Mullet Run Milford (19963) *(G-4583)*
Underground, Lewes *Also called Femmepal Corporation (G-3494)*
Underground Locating Services 302 856-9626
24497 Dupont Blvd Georgetown (19947) *(G-2697)*
Unfold Creative LLC (PA) 509 850-1337
9 E Loockerman St Ste 311 Dover (19901) *(G-2176)*
UNI Printing Solutionsllc 631 438-6045
42 Reads Way New Castle (19720) *(G-5802)*
Unicare Transport Service, Lewes *Also called Bill M Douthat Jr (G-3385)*
Unidel Foundation Inc 302 658-9200
3801 Kennett Pike C303 Wilmington (19807) *(G-13010)*
Unified Biz Club, Wilmington *Also called Unified Companies Inc (G-13011)*
Unified Companies Inc 866 936-0515
1201 N Orange St Ste 600 Wilmington (19801) *(G-13011)*
Uniforest Wood Products Inc 302 450-4541
501 Silverside Rd Ste 105 Wilmington (19809) *(G-13012)*
Uniglobe, Wilmington *Also called Red Carpet Travel Agency Inc (G-12346)*
Unikie Inc 408 839-1920
615 S Dupont Hwy Dover (19901) *(G-2177)*
Union Mortgage Group Inc 302 227-6687
323 Rehoboth Ave Ste D Rehoboth Beach (19971) *(G-8105)*
Union Press Printing Inc 302 652-0496
1723 W 8th St Wilmington (19805) *(G-13013)*
Union Whl Acoustical Sup Co, Wilmington *Also called Union Whl Acoustical Sup Co (G-13014)*
Union Whl Acoustical Sup Co 302 656-4462
500 E Front St Ste 1 Wilmington (19801) *(G-13014)*
Union Wholesale Co (HQ) 302 656-4462
500 E Front St Ste 1 Wilmington (19801) *(G-13015)*
Unique Creations By Chloe LLC 855 942-0477
501 Silverside Rd Wilmington (19809) *(G-13016)*
Unique Image LLC 302 658-2266
4577 Kirkwood Hwy Wilmington (19808) *(G-13017)*
Unique Image T-Shirts Company, Wilmington *Also called Unique Image LLC (G-13017)*
Unique Massage Therapy 302 359-5982
124 Lynnbroom Ln Dover (19904) *(G-2178)*
Unique Pro-Co LLC 302 723-2365
1301 Birch Ln Wilmington (19809) *(G-13018)*
Unique Tracking LLC 912 220-3522
1013 Centre Rd Ste 403a Wilmington (19805) *(G-13019)*
Unisex Palace 302 674-0950
1365 N Dupont Hwy # 2046 Dover (19901) *(G-2179)*
Unite USA Inc (PA) 609 915-9130
2207 Concord Pike Ste 301 Wilmington (19803) *(G-13020)*
United Adult Care Ltd 302 725-0708
3 Commerce St Harrington (19952) *(G-2902)*
United Air Lines Inc (HQ) 872 825-1911
2711 Centerville Rd # 120 Wilmington (19808) *(G-13021)*
United Airlines, Inc., Wilmington *Also called United Air Lines Inc (G-13021)*
United Auto Sales Inc 302 325-3000
300 Churchmans Rd New Castle (19720) *(G-5803)*
United Auto Workers Local 435 ....302 995-6001
698 Old Baltimore Pike Newark (19702) *(G-7611)*
United Brokerage Packaging 302 294-6782
110 Executive Dr Ste 5 Newark (19702) *(G-7612)*
United Cerebral Palsy of De 302 764-6216
700 River Rd Wilmington (19809) *(G-13022)*
United Cerebral Palsy of De (PA) 302 764-2400
700 River Rd Apt A Wilmington (19809) *(G-13023)*
United Cerebral Palsy of De 302 335-3739
3249 Midstate Rd Felton (19943) *(G-2324)*
United Cerebral Palsy of De 302 856-3490
17099 County Seat Hwy Georgetown (19947) *(G-2698)*
United Check Cashing, New Castle *Also called Argo Financial Services Inc (G-5042)*
United Check Cashing 302 792-2545
95 Naamans Rd Ste 37a Claymont (19703) *(G-813)*
United Cocoa Processor Inc 302 731-0825
701 Pencader Dr Ste F Newark (19702) *(G-7613)*
United Distribution Inc 302 429-0400
1000 N West St Ste 1200 Wilmington (19801) *(G-13024)*
United Electric Supply Co Inc (PA) 800 322-3374
10 Bellecor Dr New Castle (19720) *(G-5804)*
United Electric Supply Co Inc 302 674-8351
551 S Dupont Hwy Dover (19901) *(G-2180)*
United Electric Supply Co Inc 302 732-1291
27519 Hodges Ln Bldg P Dagsboro (19939) *(G-941)*
United Group Real Estate LLC 929 999-1277
607 Deemer Pl New Castle (19720) *(G-5805)*
United Medical Clinics of De 302 451-5607
121 Becks Woods Dr # 100 Bear (19701) *(G-365)*
United Outdoor Advertising 302 652-3177
2502 W 6th St Wilmington (19805) *(G-13025)*
United Parcel Service Inc 302 453-7462
211 Lake Dr Newark (19702) *(G-7614)*
United Refrigeration Inc 302 322-1836
818 W Basin Rd New Castle (19720) *(G-5806)*
United Rentals North Amer Inc 302 328-2900
248 S Dupont Hwy New Castle (19720) *(G-5807)*
United Rentals North Amer Inc 302 846-0955
38352 Sussex Hwy Delmar (19940) *(G-1045)*
United Rentals North Amer Inc 302 907-0292
38190 Old Stage Rd A Delmar (19940) *(G-1046)*
United States Cold Storage Inc 302 422-7536
419 Mlford Harrington Hwy Milford (19963) *(G-4584)*
United States Cold Storage Inc 302 422-7536
P.O. Box 242 Milford (19963) *(G-4585)*
United States Mle MNS Hair Cre (PA) 302 368-1273
169 E Main St Newark (19711) *(G-7615)*

ALPHABETIC

United Steelworkers 302 999-0412
3847 Evelyn Dr Wilmington (19808) ***(G-13026)***
United Technologies Corp 800 227-7437
276 Quigley Blvd New Castle (19720) ***(G-5808)***
United Tele Wkrs Delaware-C W, Newark *Also called United Tele Wkrs Local 13101* ***(G-7616)***
United Tele Wkrs Local 13101 302 737-0400
350 Gooding Dr Newark (19702) ***(G-7616)***
United Telecommunications 302 654-6108
103 Foulk Rd Ste 226 Wilmington (19803) ***(G-13027)***
United Transit Company L L C 302 838-3575
1 Main St Saint Georges (19733) ***(G-8131)***
United Water Delaware, Wilmington *Also called Suez North America Inc* ***(G-12789)***
United Water Delaware Inc., Wilmington *Also called Suez Water Delaware Inc* ***(G-12790)***
United Way of Delaware Inc (PA) 302 573-3700
625 N Orange St Fl 3 Wilmington (19801) ***(G-13028)***
United Worldwide Express LLC 347 651-5111
1202 E 16th St Wilmington (19802) ***(G-13029)***
United3 Services Inc 302 233-5985
24789 Rivers Edge Rd Millsboro (19966) ***(G-4817)***
Unitrack Industries Inc 302 424-5050
967 E Masten Cir Milford (19963) ***(G-4586)***
Unity Construction Inc 302 998-0531
3403 Lancaster Pike Ste 2 Wilmington (19805) ***(G-13030)***
Unity Development, Wilmington *Also called Unity Construction Inc* ***(G-13030)***
Unity Perspectives Inc 302 265-2854
702 North St Milford (19963) ***(G-4587)***
Univ of Del, Newark *Also called University of Delaware* ***(G-7622)***
Universal Bev Importers LLC 302 276-0619
505 E Glen Mare Dr Middletown (19709) ***(G-4273)***
Universal Design Company 302 328-8391
18 Baldt Ave New Castle (19720) ***(G-5809)***
Universal Forest Products 302 855-1250
22976 Sussex Ave Georgetown (19947) ***(G-2699)***
Universalfleet 302 428-0661
2019 Walmsley Dr New Castle (19720) ***(G-5810)***
University De Active Day Ctr, Newark *Also called Active Day Inc* ***(G-5896)***
University Garden Apts, Newark *Also called University Garden Associates* ***(G-7617)***
University Garden Associates 302 368-3823
281 Beverly Rd Apt H5 Newark (19711) ***(G-7617)***
University of De Printing 302 831-2153
222 Suth Chapel St Rm 124 Newark (19702) ***(G-7618)***
UNIVERSITY OF DELAWARE, Newark *Also called American Philosophical Assn* ***(G-5956)***
University of Delaware 302 831-2792
222 S Chapel St Rm 133 Newark (19716) ***(G-7619)***
University of Delaware 302 831-4811
104 The Grn Rm 217 Newark (19716) ***(G-7620)***
University of Delaware 302 831-6041
192 S Chapel St Newark (19716) ***(G-7621)***
University of Delaware 302 831-2501
363 New London Rd Newark (19711) ***(G-7622)***
University of Delaware 302 831-2961
42 Amstel Ave Rm 206 Newark (19716) ***(G-7623)***
University of Delaware 302 831-2833
257 Academy St Newark (19716) ***(G-7624)***
University of Delaware 302 831-1141
200 Academy St Newark (19716) ***(G-7625)***
University of Delaware 302 831-2136
162 The Grn Rm 210 Newark (19716) ***(G-7626)***
University of Delaware 302 831-8149
101 Academy St Ste 202 Newark (19716) ***(G-7627)***
University of Delaware 302 831-6300
7 Mcmillan Way Ste 3 Newark (19713) ***(G-7628)***
University of Delaware 302 831-2802
135 Monroe Hl Newark (19716) ***(G-7629)***
University Plaza Branch, Newark *Also called Wilmington Savings Fund Soc* ***(G-7707)***
University Village Apartment 302 731-5972
207 Mederia Cir Newark (19702) ***(G-7630)***
Universty & Whist Club Wlmgton 302 658-5125
805 N Broom St Wilmington (19806) ***(G-13031)***
Univita of Florida Inc 239 936-4449
1000 N King St Wilmington (19801) ***(G-13032)***
Uno Messenger LLC 513 703-8091
300 Delaware Ave Ste 210a Wilmington (19801) ***(G-13033)***
Upper Cut The, Dover *Also called Uppercut Inc* ***(G-2181)***
Uppercut Inc 302 736-1661
119 S Dupont Hwy Dover (19901) ***(G-2181)***
UPS, Newark *Also called Gjv Inc* ***(G-6659)***
UPS, Newark *Also called United Parcel Service Inc* ***(G-7614)***
UPS Supply Chain Solutions Inc 302 631-5259
220 Lake Dr Ste 1 Newark (19702) ***(G-7631)***
Urban Engineers Inc 302 689-0260
2 Penns Way Ste 400 New Castle (19720) ***(G-5811)***
Urban Retail Properties LLC 302 479-8314
4737 Concord Pike Wilmington (19803) ***(G-13034)***
Urban Retail Properties Co, Wilmington *Also called Urban Retail Properties LLC* ***(G-13034)***
Urban Svcs Fcilities Maint LLC 302 993-6363
2707 N Market St Wilmington (19802) ***(G-13035)***
Urbanpromise Wilmington Inc 302 425-5502
2401 Thatcher St Wilmington (19802) ***(G-13036)***
Urbn Steamlab LLC 267 738-3096
16192 Coastal Hwy Lewes (19958) ***(G-3803)***
Urgent Ambulance Service Inc (PA) 302 454-1821
8 Tyler Way Newark (19713) ***(G-7632)***
Urgent Ambulance Service Inc 302 454-1821
8 Tyler Way Newark (19713) ***(G-7633)***
Urgent Ambulance Svc Newark, Newark *Also called Urgent Ambulance Service Inc* ***(G-7633)***
Urie & Blanton Inc 302 658-8604
510 A St Wilmington (19801) ***(G-13037)***
Urigen Pharmaceuticals Inc (PA) 732 640-0160
501 Silverside Rd Pmb 95 Wilmington (19809) ***(G-13038)***
Uris LLC (PA) 302 469-7000
32783 Long Neck Rd Unit 3 Millsboro (19966) ***(G-4818)***
Uris Salvage Auto Inspections, Millsboro *Also called Uris LLC* ***(G-4818)***
Urology Assoc Southern Del PA 302 422-5569
810 Seabury Ave Milford (19963) ***(G-4588)***
Urology Associates Dover PA 302 674-1728
200 Banning St Ste 250 Dover (19904) ***(G-2182)***
URS Group Inc 302 731-7824
4051 Ogletown Rd Ste 300 Newark (19713) ***(G-7634)***
US Bortek LLC 888 203-7686
2140 S Dupont Hwy Camden (19934) ***(G-604)***
US Dept of the Air Force 302 677-2525
300 Tuskegee Blvd 1b22 Dover (19902) ***(G-2183)***
Us Engineering Corporation 302 645-7400
16192 Coastal Hwy Lewes (19958) ***(G-3804)***
US Green Battery Inc 347 723-5963
157 S Dupont Hwy Fl 2 New Castle (19720) ***(G-5812)***
US Installation Group Inc 302 994-1644
355 Water St Wilmington (19804) ***(G-13039)***
US Lawns Dover 302 703-2818
16856 Ketch Ct Lewes (19958) ***(G-3805)***
US Probation Pretrial, Wilmington *Also called Supreme Court United States* ***(G-12814)***
US Renal Care Laurel Dialysis, Laurel *Also called DSI Laurel LLC* ***(G-3224)***
US Telex Corporation 302 652-2707
4001 Kennett Pike Ste 300 Wilmington (19807) ***(G-13040)***
Usi Inc 302 658-8000
1007 N Orange St Ste 1115 Wilmington (19801) ***(G-13041)***
Uswa, Wilmington *Also called United Steelworkers* ***(G-13026)***
Utilicon Solutions Ltd 302 337-9980
18109 Sussex Hwy Bridgeville (19933) ***(G-526)***
Utilisite Inc 302 945-5022
20721 Robinsonville Rd Lewes (19958) ***(G-3806)***
Utility Audit Group Inc 302 398-8505
93 Clark St Harrington (19952) ***(G-2903)***
Utility Billing, Wilmington *Also called City of Wilmington* ***(G-9723)***
Utility Lines Cnstr Svcs LLC 302 337-9980
18109 Sussex Hwy Bridgeville (19933) ***(G-527)***
Utility/Eastern 302 337-7400
9126 Redden Rd Bridgeville (19933) ***(G-528)***
Uzin Utz Manufacturing N Amer 336 456-4624
200 Garrison Oak Dr Dover (19901) ***(G-2184)***
Uzuakoli Dev & Cultural Assn 302 465-3266
2319 S Dupont Hwy Dover (19901) ***(G-2185)***
V & A Trucking LLC 302 276-5548
10 Malvern Ave Newark (19713) ***(G-7635)***
V & P Custom Finishers Inc 302 376-6367
139 Ratledge Rd Townsend (19734) ***(G-8830)***
V and S Phldelphia Galvanizing, New Castle *Also called Voigt & Schweitzer LLC* ***(G-5820)***
V B Towing Inc 302 238-7705
22167 Cypress Rd Frankford (19945) ***(G-2396)***
V C A Kirkwood Animal Hospital, Newark *Also called Kirkwood Anmal Brding Grooming* ***(G-6891)***
V E Guerrazzi Inc 302 369-5557
122 Sandy Dr Ste D Newark (19713) ***(G-7636)***
V F W Post Home 302 366-8438
100 Veterans Dr Newark (19711) ***(G-7637)***
V F W Sussex Mem Post 7422 302 934-9967
28659 Dupont Blvd Millsboro (19966) ***(G-4819)***
V F W Virgil Wilson Post 302 629-3092
Middleford Rd Seaford (19973) ***(G-8428)***
V F W Virgil Wilson Post 4961, Seaford *Also called V F W Virgil Wilson Post* ***(G-8428)***
V P Produce Inc 302 249-0718
32228 Old Hickory Rd Laurel (19956) ***(G-3300)***
V Quinton Inc 302 449-1711
400 N Ramunno Dr Middletown (19709) ***(G-4274)***
V T I, Newark *Also called Val-Tech Inc* ***(G-7638)***
V2s Corporation 302 384-9947
1013 Centre Rd Ste 403a Wilmington (19805) ***(G-13042)***
VA Medical Center 302 994-2511
1601 Kirkwood Hwy Wilmington (19805) ***(G-13043)***
Vacation Club 302 628-1144
9290 River Vista Dr Seaford (19973) ***(G-8429)***
Vader LLC 302 565-9684
108 E Scotland Dr Bear (19701) ***(G-366)***
Vader.ro, Bear *Also called Vader LLC* ***(G-366)***

Val-Tech Inc........302 738-0500
24 Mcmillan Way Newark (19713) *(G-7638)*
Valassis Direct Mail Inc........302 861-3567
300 Mcintire Dr Newark (19711) *(G-7639)*
Valco Enterprises LLC........514 938-8474
4142 Ogletown Stanton Rd Newark (19713) *(G-7640)*
Valentina Liquors........302 368-3264
430 Old Baltimore Pike Newark (19702) *(G-7641)*
Valet Cleaning Service........302 653-0233
3234 Downs Chapel Rd Clayton (19938) *(G-872)*
Valiu Inc........317 853-5081
16192 Coastal Hwy Lewes (19958) *(G-3807)*
Vallen Distribution Inc........302 992-5604
205 S James St Wilmington (19804) *(G-13044)*
Vallen Distribution Inc........856 542-1453
4550 Wrangle Hill Rd Delaware City (19706) *(G-968)*
Valley Landscaping and Con Inc........302 922-5020
8 The Grn Dover (19901) *(G-2186)*
Valley Run Apartments, Wilmington *Also called Planned Residential Communites* *(G-12151)*
Valley Stream Village Apts........302 733-0844
500 Valley Stream Dr Newark (19702) *(G-7642)*
Valour Arabians........302 653-4066
1950 Vndyke Grenspring Rd Smyrna (19977) *(G-8735)*
Value Furniture, Felton *Also called Rite Way Distributors* *(G-2317)*
Value Rate Cleaners........302 477-9191
4405 Concord Pike Wilmington (19803) *(G-13045)*
Valuewrite........302 593-0694
204 Tralee Dr Middletown (19709) *(G-4275)*
Vam Apps Co........786 220-4826
1013 Centre Rd Ste 403b Wilmington (19805) *(G-13046)*
Van Buren Medical Associates........302 998-1151
1941 Limestone Rd Ste 211 Wilmington (19808) *(G-13047)*
Vance A Funk III........302 368-2561
273 E Main St Ste 100 Newark (19711) *(G-7643)*
Vance Phillips Inc........302 542-1501
7472 Portsville Rd Laurel (19956) *(G-3301)*
Vandemark & Lynch Inc........302 764-7635
4305 Miller Rd Wilmington (19802) *(G-13048)*
Vanguard Construction Inc........302 697-9187
2089 S Dupont Hwy Dover (19901) *(G-2187)*
Vanguard Manufacturing Inc........302 994-9302
11 Lewis Cir Wilmington (19804) *(G-13049)*
Vannies Hats........302 765-7094
4 Andover Ct New Castle (19720) *(G-5813)*
Vape Escape........302 737-8273
1834 Capitol Trl Newark (19711) *(G-7644)*
Vapp, Wilmington *Also called Volunteers For Adolescent* *(G-13102)*
Vari Builders, Wilmington *Also called Vari Development Corp* *(G-13050)*
Vari Development Corp........302 479-5571
1309 Veale Rd Ste 20 Wilmington (19810) *(G-13050)*
Varone Insurance Offices, Wilmington *Also called Franklin T Varone Inc* *(G-10619)*
Vascular Specialists Del PA........302 733-5700
1 Centurian Dr Ste 307 Newark (19713) *(G-7645)*
Vassallo Michael Elec Contr........302 455-9405
4 Mill Park Ct Newark (19713) *(G-7646)*
Vaughan Bckley Modular Sls Inc........215 259-7509
1521 Concord Pike Ste 301 Wilmington (19803) *(G-13051)*
VCA Animal Hospitals Inc........302 834-1118
650 Peoples Plz Newark (19702) *(G-7647)*
VCA Glasglow, Newark *Also called VCA Animal Hospitals Inc* *(G-7647)*
VCA Hockessin Animal Hospital, Newark *Also called Golden Merger Corp* *(G-6672)*
VCA Inc........302 737-1098
1501 Kirkwood Hwy Newark (19711) *(G-7648)*
Vcg LLC........302 336-8151
9 E Loockerman St 3a-522 Dover (19901) *(G-2188)*
Vci, Claymont *Also called Visual Communications Inc* *(G-816)*
VD&I Holdings Inc........302 764-7635
4305 Miller Rd Wilmington (19802) *(G-13052)*
Vector Marketing Corp........716 373-6141
5301 Limestone Rd Ste 105 Wilmington (19808) *(G-13053)*
Vector Security Inc........302 422-7031
409 S Dupont Blvd Milford (19963) *(G-4589)*
Vectorvance LLC (PA)........347 779-9932
1201 N Orange St Ste 600 Wilmington (19801) *(G-13054)*
Vedaham Inc........302 250-4594
2711 Centerville Rd # 400 Wilmington (19808) *(G-13055)*
Veer Hotels Inc........302 398-3900
1259 Corn Crib Rd Harrington (19952) *(G-2904)*
Vehattire LLC........302 221-2000
174 N Dupont Hwy New Castle (19720) *(G-5814)*
Vel Micro Works Incorporated........302 239-4661
726 Yorklyn Rd Ste 400 Hockessin (19707) *(G-3166)*
Velo Amis........302 757-2783
24 Nightingale Cir Newark (19711) *(G-7649)*
Velocity Pointe LLC........302 351-8305
20 Whitekirk Dr Wilmington (19808) *(G-13056)*
Vending Solutions LLC........302 674-2222
1624 N Little Creek Rd Dover (19901) *(G-2189)*
Vensoft LLC........302 392-9000
4001 Kennett Pike Ste 250 Wilmington (19807) *(G-13057)*
Venus On Halfshell........302 227-9292
136 Dagsworthy Ave Dewey Beach (19971) *(G-1061)*
Vera Bradley Designs Inc........302 733-0880
510 Christiana Mall Newark (19702) *(G-7650)*
Veramorph LLC........401 473-1318
200 Powder Mill Rd E50 Wilmington (19803) *(G-13058)*
Veramorph Materials, Wilmington *Also called Veramorph LLC* *(G-13058)*
Verde Advantage Group LLC........302 333-5701
1000 N West St Ste 1200 Wilmington (19801) *(G-13059)*
Verisoft Inc........602 908-7151
48 Kings Hwy Dover (19901) *(G-2190)*
Veristuffcom Inc........972 545-2434
1313 N Market St Ste 5100 Wilmington (19801) *(G-13060)*
Verito Technologies LLC........855 583-7486
251 Little Falls Dr Wilmington (19808) *(G-13061)*
Verizon, Wilmington *Also called Cellco Partnership* *(G-9611)*
Verizon, Dover *Also called Cellco Partnership* *(G-1262)*
Verizon Business, Wilmington *Also called MCI LLC* *(G-11599)*
Verizon Business, Wilmington *Also called MCI LLC* *(G-11600)*
Verizon Business, Wilmington *Also called MCI Communications Corporation* *(G-11598)*
Verizon Communications Inc........302 324-1385
124 Sunset Blvd New Castle (19720) *(G-5815)*
Verizon Delaware LLC (HQ)........302 571-1571
901 N Tatnall St Fl 2 Wilmington (19801) *(G-13062)*
Verizon Delaware LLC........302 761-6079
3900 N Washington St Fl 1 Wilmington (19802) *(G-13063)*
Verizon Delaware LLC........302 629-4502
8722 Concord Rd Seaford (19973) *(G-8430)*
Verizon Delaware LLC........302 422-1430
2 S Industrial Ln Milford (19963) *(G-4590)*
Verizon Wireless, Middletown *Also called Cellco Partnership* *(G-3983)*
Verizon Wireless, New Castle *Also called Verizon Communications Inc* *(G-5815)*
Verizon Wireless, Smyrna *Also called Cellco Partnership* *(G-8592)*
Verizon Wireless, Camden *Also called Cellco Partnership* *(G-547)*
Verizon Wireless Inc........302 737-5028
1209 Churchmans Rd Newark (19713) *(G-7651)*
Verizon Wreless Authorized Ret, Wilmington *Also called WER Wireless Inc* *(G-13158)*
Versatile Impex Inc........302 369-9480
74 Albe Dr Ste 3 Newark (19702) *(G-7652)*
Versatus Corp........203 293-3597
919 N Market St Ste 425 Wilmington (19801) *(G-13064)*
Verscom LLC (PA)........866 238-9189
501 Silverside Rd Ste 105 Wilmington (19809) *(G-13065)*
VERSCOM CARRIER, Wilmington *Also called Verscom LLC* *(G-13065)*
Version 40 Software LLC........302 270-0245
662 Tullamore Ct Magnolia (19962) *(G-3911)*
Versitron Inc........302 894-0699
83 Albe Dr Ste C Newark (19702) *(G-7653)*
Vertex Industries Inc........302 472-0601
818 S Heald St Ste C Wilmington (19801) *(G-13066)*
Vertical Blind Factory Inc (PA)........302 998-9616
3 Meco Cir Wilmington (19804) *(G-13067)*
Vertigo Group Inc........302 298-0825
200 N Market St Wilmington (19801) *(G-13068)*
Vertrius Corp........800 770-1913
16192 Coastal Hwy Lewes (19958) *(G-3808)*
Vest Management Inc........302 856-3100
18591 Sand Hill Rd Georgetown (19947) *(G-2700)*
Vesta Wash LLC........302 559-7533
146 Woodland Rd Newark (19702) *(G-7654)*
Vet Housecall Service........302 656-7291
2602 Jefferson Ave Claymont (19703) *(G-814)*
Vet Spa, The, Newark *Also called Kenneth Butler* *(G-6874)*
Vetcon Industries LLC........850 207-6723
2035 Sunset Lake Rd B2 Newark (19702) *(G-7655)*
Vetdiet International, Wilmington *Also called Vetdiet Usa Inc* *(G-13069)*
Vetdiet Usa Inc........514 622-7313
1209 N Orange St Wilmington (19801) *(G-13069)*
Veteran It Pro LLC........302 824-3111
37 Staten Dr Hockessin (19707) *(G-3167)*
Veteran Owned Cleaning Svcs, Dover *Also called Otis Kamara* *(G-1925)*
Veterans Fgn Wars Nwman L-Urba, Smyrna *Also called Veterans of Foreign Wars Newmn* *(G-8736)*
Veterans Health Administration........302 994-2511
1601 Kirkwood Hwy Wilmington (19805) *(G-13070)*
Veterans Health Administration........302 994-1660
2710 Centerville Rd Wilmington (19808) *(G-13071)*
Veterans of Foreign Wars Newmn........302 653-8801
4941 Wheatleys Pond Rd Smyrna (19977) *(G-8736)*
Veterans Re-Entry Resources........302 384-2350
1405 Veale Rd Wilmington (19810) *(G-13072)*
Veterinary Emergency Ctr Del, New Castle *Also called Veternary Specialty Ctr Del PA* *(G-5816)*
Veternary Specialty Ctr Del PA........302 322-6933
290 Churchmans Rd New Castle (19720) *(G-5816)*

ALPHABETIC

Vew Technologies Inc 310 560-3814
3422 Old Capitol Trl Wilmington (19808) *(G-13073)*
Veze Wireless of Concord Inc, Wilmington *Also called WER Wireless of Concord Inc (G-13159)*
VFW Post 2863, Newport *Also called Diamond State Home Auxiliary (G-7747)*
VFW Post 475, Newark *Also called V F W Post Home (G-7637)*
VFW Post 5892, Hockessin *Also called Brenden Bailey & Chandler VFW (G-2969)*
VFW Post 6483 .... 302 422-4412
77 Veterans Cir Milford (19963) *(G-4591)*
Via Mdical Day Spa Pasca Salon 302 757-2830
3212 Brookline Rd Wilmington (19808) *(G-13074)*
Via Networks Inc 314 727-2087
2711 Centerville Rd # 400 Wilmington (19808) *(G-13075)*
Viacard Concepts 302 537-4602
322 Baywinds Ct Dagsboro (19939) *(G-942)*
Vickers Heating & Air, Millsboro *Also called Blm Industries Inc (G-4645)*
Vickie York At Beach Realty (PA) 302 539-2145
518 Atlantic Ave Millville (19967) *(G-4857)*
Vicks Commercial Clg & Maint 302 697-9591
378 Mannering Dr Dover (19901) *(G-2191)*
Victor Colbert Construction 302 834-1174
1612 Pulaski Hwy Newark (19702) *(G-7656)*
Victor Colbert Construction 302 368-7270
723 Old Baltimore Pike Newark (19702) *(G-7657)*
Victor J Venturena DDS 302 656-0558
1117 N Franklin St Wilmington (19806) *(G-13076)*
Victor Kornbluth 302 791-9777
106 Governor Printz Blvd Claymont (19703) *(G-815)*
Victor L Gregory Jr DMD 302 239-1827
5301 Limestone Rd Ste 211 Wilmington (19808) *(G-13077)*
Victoria Mews LP Delnware Vall 302 489-2000
722 Yorklyn Rd Ste 350 Hockessin (19707) *(G-3168)*
Victorian Apartments LLC 302 678-0968
123 W Loockerman St Dover (19904) *(G-2192)*
Victorian Glassworks 302 798-4847
1800 Harrison Ave Wilmington (19809) *(G-13078)*
Victorias Scret Pink Main Line 302 644-1035
35000 Midway Outlet Dr Rehoboth Beach (19971) *(G-8106)*
Victory Racing Chassis Inc 302 593-2255
12 Hadco Rd Wilmington (19804) *(G-13079)*
Video Den 302 628-9835
27180 Williams Ave Seaford (19973) *(G-8431)*
Video Tech Center Inc (PA) 302 691-7213
2400 Kingman Dr Wilmington (19810) *(G-13080)*
Video Walltronics Inc 302 328-4511
22 Lukens Dr New Castle (19720) *(G-5817)*
Villa Belmont, Newark *Also called Belmont Villa Condominiums (G-6071)*
Village At Fox Point 302 762-7480
1436 Kynlyn Dr Wilmington (19809) *(G-13081)*
Village Graphics LLC 302 697-9288
69 Peyton St # 3 Dover (19901) *(G-2193)*
Village Green Inc 302 764-2234
4303 Miller Rd Wilmington (19802) *(G-13082)*
Village of Barrett's Run The, Newark *Also called Barrettes Run Apartments (G-6047)*
Village of Canterbury, Wilmington *Also called Iacono - Summer Chase (G-10985)*
Village of Cool Branch Homes, Seaford *Also called Atlantic Realty Management (G-8158)*
Village Sq Acdemy Lrng Ctr LLC 302 539-5000
30792 Whites Neck Rd Ocean View (19970) *(G-7823)*
Village Windhover Apartments 302 834-1168
104 Sandburg Pl Newark (19702) *(G-7658)*
Village Wines & Spirits 302 376-5583
718 Ash Blvd Middletown (19709) *(G-4276)*
Village Wndhver Rent Aprtments, Newark *Also called Village Windhover Apartments (G-7658)*
Villas Apartments, New Castle *Also called Christiana Wood LLC (G-5158)*
Vincent Farms Inc 302 875-5707
12487 Salt Barn Rd Laurel (19956) *(G-3302)*
Vincent J Daniels DMD, Wilmington *Also called Blue Diamond Dental PA (G-9375)*
Vincent Lobo Dr PA 302 398-8163
203 Shaw Ave 205 Harrington (19952) *(G-2905)*
Vincenza & Margherita Bistro 302 479-7999
1717 Marsh Rd Wilmington (19810) *(G-13083)*
Vinces Produce Inc 302 322-0386
380 Pulaski Hwy New Castle (19720) *(G-5818)*
Vinces Sports Center Inc 302 738-4859
14 Gender Rd Newark (19713) *(G-7659)*
Vine Creek Mobile Home Park, Ocean View *Also called Bayshore Inc (G-7758)*
Vinings At Christiana, Newark *Also called Shelter Development LLC (G-7415)*
Vinsys Corporation 732 983-4150
160 Greentree Dr Ste 101 Dover (19904) *(G-2194)*
Vintage Candle Company 302 643-9343
16734 Oak Rd Bridgeville (19933) *(G-529)*
Vintage Properties LLC 302 994-4442
4000 Dawnbrook Dr Wilmington (19804) *(G-13084)*
Vintage Properties LLC (PA) 302 994-2505
102 Robino Ct Ste 101 Wilmington (19804) *(G-13085)*
Violet Aura Inc 302 654-4008
5412 Delray Dr Wilmington (19808) *(G-13086)*
Virgil P Ellwanger 302 934-8083
Mllsboro Vlg Grn Rr 24 Millsboro (19966) *(G-4820)*
Virion Therapeutics LLC 800 841-9303
7 Creek Bend Ct Newark (19711) *(G-7660)*
Vironex Inc (PA) 302 661-1400
3 Owls Nest Rd Wilmington (19807) *(G-13087)*
Vironex Envmtl Field Svcs Inc 302 661-1400
3 Owls Nest Rd Wilmington (19807) *(G-13088)*
Virtual Business Entps LLC 302 472-9100
Farmers Bank Bldg 301ste Wilmington (19801) *(G-13089)*
Visamtion LLC 302 268-2177
607 Deemer Pl New Castle (19720) *(G-5819)*
Vishva Inc 302 425-3801
1104 Maryland Ave Wilmington (19805) *(G-13090)*
Vision & Hearing Inc 302 475-8897
1809 Marsh Rd Wilmington (19810) *(G-13091)*
Vision Center of Delaware Inc (PA) 302 656-8867
213 Greenhill Ave Ste A Wilmington (19805) *(G-13092)*
Vision Optik, Newark *Also called Howard B Stromwasser (G-6751)*
Vision Salon & Barbershop 302 934-9301
401 W Dupont Hwy Ste 103 Millsboro (19966) *(G-4821)*
Visionary Energy Systems Inc 410 739-4342
325 Alder Rd Dover (19904) *(G-2195)*
Visionquest Eye Care Center 302 678-3545
820 Walker Rd Dover (19904) *(G-2196)*
Visionquest Nonprofit Corp 302 735-1666
1001 S Bradford St Ste 1 Dover (19904) *(G-2197)*
Visions Hair Design 302 477-0820
2807 Concord Pike Wilmington (19803) *(G-13093)*
Visiting Angel of Sussex, De, Milton *Also called Grace Visitation Services (G-4909)*
Visual Arts Studio Inc 302 652-0925
4 Forest Creek Ln Wilmington (19809) *(G-13094)*
Visual Communications Inc 302 792-9500
3724 Philadelphia Pike Claymont (19703) *(G-816)*
Vital Renewable Energy Company (PA) 202 595-2944
2711 Centerville Rd Wilmington (19808) *(G-13095)*
Vitalus Technologies Inc 302 383-9100
5644 Millington Rd Clayton (19938) *(G-873)*
Vitas Healthcare Corporation 302 451-4000
100 Cmmrce Dr Chrstina Newark (19713) *(G-7661)*
Vitellus LLC (PA) 718 782-3539
1209 N Orange St Wilmington (19801) *(G-13096)*
Vivian A Houghton Esquire 302 658-0518
800 N West St Fl 2 Wilmington (19801) *(G-13097)*
Vivians Style 302 645-9444
33516 Crossing Ave Unit 2 Lewes (19958) *(G-3809)*
Vivid Colors Carpet LLC 302 335-3933
43 Bayview Ave Frederica (19946) *(G-2415)*
Vivig Shoes 302 427-2700
3801 Kennett Pike C103 Wilmington (19807) *(G-13098)*
Vls It Consulting Inc 302 368-5656
260 Chapman Rd Ste 104a Newark (19702) *(G-7662)*
Vna of Delaware 302 454-5422
190 Salem Church Rd Newark (19713) *(G-7663)*
Vogue On 54, Selbyville *Also called Brandon Tatum (G-8459)*
Voice 4 Impact Inc 484 410-0111
515 Lennox Rd Wilmington (19809) *(G-13099)*
Voice Radio LLC 302 858-5118
20254 Dupont Blvd Georgetown (19947) *(G-2701)*
Voigt & Schweitzer LLC 302 322-1420
511 Carroll Dr New Castle (19720) *(G-5820)*
Voitlex Corp 302 288-0670
8 The Grn Ste A Dover (19901) *(G-2198)*
Voiture Nationale La Society 302 478-7591
1017 Faun Rd Wilmington (19803) *(G-13100)*
Voltvault Inc 302 981-5339
134 Sandy Dr Newark (19713) *(G-7664)*
Volume Mob Inc 302 433-6629
3616 Kirkwood Hwy Ste A Wilmington (19808) *(G-13101)*
Volunteer Brewing Company LLC 610 721-2836
120 W Main St Middletown (19709) *(G-4277)*
Volunteers For Adolescent 302 658-3331
611 W 18th St Wilmington (19802) *(G-13102)*
Volvant Inc (PA) 805 456-6464
919 N Market St Ste 950 Wilmington (19801) *(G-13103)*
Vortex Labs LLC 302 231-1294
1209 N Orange St Wilmington (19801) *(G-13104)*
Voshell Bros Welding Inc 302 674-1414
1769 Kenton Rd Dover (19904) *(G-2199)*
Voshell Brothers, Dover *Also called Voshell Bros Welding Inc (G-2199)*
Voxx Electronics Corp 302 656-5303
2302 Concord Pike Wilmington (19803) *(G-13105)*
Voyyp Inc 833 342-5667
2035 Sunset Lake Rd B2 Newark (19702) *(G-7665)*
Vp Racing Fuels Inc 302 368-1500
16 Brookhill Dr Newark (19702) *(G-7666)*
Vpn Express Incorporated 302 351-8029
427 N Ttnail St Ste 99229 Wilmington (19801) *(G-13106)*
Vpn Vpn Vpn Proxy 415 758-8354
16192 Coastal Hwy Lewes (19958) *(G-3810)*

Vps International LLC 800 493-9356
16192 Coastal Hwy Lewes (19958) *(G-3811)*
Vps Services LLC 302 376-6710
651 N Broad St Ste 308 Middletown (19709) *(G-4278)*
Vsg Business Solutions LLC 302 261-3209
221 Cornwell Dr Bear (19701) *(G-367)*
Vshield Software Corp 302 531-0855
3500 S Dupont Hwy Dover (19901) *(G-2200)*
Vtms LLC 302 264-9094
3 Mineral Ct Dover (19904) *(G-2201)*
Vulcan International Corp (PA) 302 428-3181
300 Delaware Ave Ste 1704 Wilmington (19801) *(G-13107)*
Vulcraft Sales Corp (HQ) 302 427-5832
300 Delaware Ave Ste 210 Wilmington (19801) *(G-13108)*
Vvs Inc 302 827-2525
115 Rodney Ave Lewes (19958) *(G-3812)*
W B Mason Co Inc 888 926-2766
100 Interchange Blvd Newark (19711) *(G-7667)*
W B Simpson Elementary School, Dover *Also called Caesar Rodney School District (G-1248)*
W C Ungerer Insurance Agency 302 368-8505
124 Autumn Horseshoe Newark (19702) *(G-7668)*
W D Pressley Inc 302 653-4381
5779 Dupont Pkwy Smyrna (19977) *(G-8737)*
W Enterprises LLC 302 875-0430
12793 Laurel Rd Laurel (19956) *(G-3303)*
W F Construction Inc 302 420-6747
74 Albe Dr Ste 8 Newark (19702) *(G-7669)*
W Gifford Inc 302 420-6112
807 Chesapeake Ct Newark (19702) *(G-7670)*
W H Thomas DDS 302 697-1152
1981 S State St Dover (19901) *(G-2202)*
W L Gore & Associates Inc 410 506-7787
555 Paper Mill Rd Newark (19711) *(G-7671)*
W L Gore & Associates Inc 302 368-3700
1901 Barksdale Rd Newark (19711) *(G-7672)*
W Lee Mackewiz Od PA 302 834-2020
725 Pulaski Hwy Bear (19701) *(G-368)*
W R Grace & Co 410 531-4000
1521 Concord Pike Ste 341 Wilmington (19803) *(G-13109)*
W S M S Bank, Newark *Also called Cash Connect Inc (G-6165)*
W Sharp Paynter & Sons Inc 302 684-8508
28443 Paynter Rd Milton (19968) *(G-4979)*
W T Schrider & Sons Inc 302 934-1900
24572 Betts Pond Rd Millsboro (19966) *(G-4822)*
W W Snyder Excavating & Masnry, Middletown *Also called Walter W Snyder (G-4280)*
W23 S12 Holdings LLC 610 348-3825
2000 Pnsylvnia Ave Ste 10 Wilmington (19806) *(G-13110)*
W7energy LLC 302 897-1653
200 Powder Mill Rd E400-3 Wilmington (19803) *(G-13111)*
Wabisabi Design Inc 650 451-8501
2035 Sunset Lake Rd B2 Newark (19702) *(G-7673)*
Wac, New Castle *Also called Wilmington Aquatic Club Inc (G-5835)*
Waco Lid Films Inc 302 378-7053
467 Blackbird Station Rd Townsend (19734) *(G-8831)*
Wade Kimball Construction Inc 302 284-4732
1736 Henry Cowgill Rd Camden Wyoming (19934) *(G-661)*
Wafl Wyus Broadcasting Inc 302 422-7575
1666 Blairs Pond Rd Milford (19963) *(G-4592)*
Wagamon Technology Group LLC 302 424-1855
12 S Walnut St A Milford (19963) *(G-4593)*
Wagner N J & Sons Trucking 302 242-7731
5972 Hopkins Cemetery Rd Felton (19943) *(G-2325)*
Wagstaff Day Care Center Inc 302 998-7818
310 Kiamensi Rd Rm 301 Wilmington (19804) *(G-13112)*
Wahed Inc (PA) 646 961-7063
16192 Coastal Hwy Lewes (19958) *(G-3813)*
Wahid Consultants LLC 315 400-0955
51 Villas Dr Apt 8 New Castle (19720) *(G-5821)*
Wahl Family Dentistry 302 655-1228
2003 Concord Pike Wilmington (19803) *(G-13113)*
Wahl, John MD, Wilmington *Also called Eye Physicians and Surgeons PA (G-10465)*
Walan Specialty Cnstr Pdts LLC 724 545-2300
501 Christiana Ave Wilmington (19801) *(G-13114)*
Walden LLC 302 998-8112
1 Henry Ct Wilmington (19808) *(G-13115)*
Walden Townhomes, Wilmington *Also called Walden LLC (G-13115)*
Walker & Sons Inc 302 653-5635
838 Sunnyside Rd Smyrna (19977) *(G-8738)*
Walkers Marine Corporation 302 629-8666
26912 Walker Rd Seaford (19973) *(G-8432)*
Wallace Montgomery & Assoc LLP 302 510-1080
111 Continental Dr # 104 Newark (19713) *(G-7674)*
Wallce & Associates, Hockessin *Also called C Wallace & Associates (G-2973)*
Walleys Trucking Inc 302 893-8652
29 Emerald Ridge Dr Bear (19701) *(G-369)*
Wallflowers Press 302 454-1411
503 Windsor Dr Newark (19711) *(G-7675)*
Wallis Repair Inc 302 378-4301
106 Patriot Dr Middletown (19709) *(G-4279)*
Wallor Wearables LLC 505 310-6099
16192 Coastal Hwy Lewes (19958) *(G-3814)*
Walls & Davenport Inc 302 653-4779
94 E Glenwood Ave Smyrna (19977) *(G-8739)*
Walls Farm and Garden Ctr Inc 302 422-4565
833 S Dupont Blvd Milford (19963) *(G-4594)*
Walls Irrigation Inc (PA) 302 422-2262
833 S Dupont Blvd Milford (19963) *(G-4595)*
Walls Service Center Inc 302 422-8110
220 Ne Front St Milford (19963) *(G-4596)*
Walltag Inc 917 725-1715
16192 Coastal Hwy Lewes (19958) *(G-3815)*
Walnut Green Asset MGT LL 302 689-3798
1301 Walnut Green Rd Wilmington (19807) *(G-13116)*
Walnut Grove Cabinets LLC 302 678-2694
308 Rose Valley School Rd Dover (19904) *(G-2203)*
Walnut Street Y M C A, Wilmington *Also called Young Mens Christian Associat (G-13331)*
Walo US Holdings Inc 212 691-4537
1675 S State St Ste B Dover (19901) *(G-2204)*
Walsh Chiropractic Center 302 422-0622
800 Airport Rd Ste 103 Milford (19963) *(G-4597)*
Walter Doring 302 727-6773
35584 Airport Rd Rehoboth Beach (19971) *(G-8107)*
Walter L Fox Post 2 Inc 302 674-1741
835 S Bay Rd Dover (19901) *(G-2205)*
Walter W Snyder 302 378-1817
1844 Choptank Rd Middletown (19709) *(G-4280)*
Wanamakers Associates LLC 302 834-3491
203 Cornwell Dr Bear (19701) *(G-370)*
Wanex Electrical Service LLC 302 326-1700
261 Airport Rd New Castle (19720) *(G-5822)*
Wang Consultants Inc 626 483-0265
4023 Kennett Pike Ste 603 Wilmington (19807) *(G-13117)*
Warain Corp 762 670-3452
P.O. Box 13133 Wilmington (19850) *(G-13118)*
Ward & Taylor LLC 302 227-1403
37212 Rehoboth Avenue Ext Rehoboth Beach (19971) *(G-8108)*
Ward & Taylor LLC (PA) 302 225-3350
2710 Centerville Rd # 210 Wilmington (19808) *(G-13119)*
Warehouse Technology Inc 302 516-7791
2 Lukens Dr Ste 600 New Castle (19720) *(G-5823)*
Warfel Construction Co Inc 302 422-8927
246 S Rehoboth Blvd Milford (19963) *(G-4598)*
Warner Tansey Inc 302 539-3001
Pennsylvania Ave Bethany Beach (19930) *(G-436)*
Warren A Reid Custon Builders, Laurel *Also called Warren Reid (G-3304)*
Warren Electric Co Inc 302 629-9134
21621 Sussex Hwy Seaford (19973) *(G-8433)*
Warren Reid 302 877-0901
14234 Sycamore Rd Laurel (19956) *(G-3304)*
Warren Truss Co (PA) 302 368-8566
10 Aleph Dr Newark (19702) *(G-7676)*
Warren Truss Co 302 337-9470
16632 Nates Way Bridgeville (19933) *(G-530)*
Warren W Seaver 302 674-8969
3619 Bayside Dr Dover (19901) *(G-2206)*
Warsal, Nabil F MD, Wilmington *Also called Arminio Joseph A MD & Assoc PA (G-9132)*
Wartrude Services Inc 302 213-3944
1601 Milltown Rd Wilmington (19808) *(G-13120)*
Warwick Funeral Home 302 368-9500
121 W Park Pl Newark (19711) *(G-7677)*
Wash Depot, The, Wilmington *Also called Pennsylvania Inc (G-12071)*
Wash-N-Wag 302 644-2466
34680 Jiffy Way Lewes (19958) *(G-3816)*
Washington Group, Hockessin *Also called Aecom Energy & Cnstr Inc (G-2952)*
Waste Industries LLC 302 934-1364
28471 John J Williams Hwy Millsboro (19966) *(G-4823)*
Waste Management Inc 302 854-5304
11323 Trussum Pond Rd Laurel (19956) *(G-3305)*
Waste Management Delaware Inc 302 994-0944
300 Harvey Dr Wilmington (19804) *(G-13121)*
Waste Management Delaware Inc 302 854-5301
11323 Trussum Pond Rd Laurel (19956) *(G-3306)*
Waste Management Michigan Inc 302 655-1360
246 Marsh Ln New Castle (19720) *(G-5824)*
Waste Masters Solutions LLC 302 824-0909
19 Davidson Ln New Castle (19720) *(G-5825)*
Wasteflo LLC 410 202-0802
207 N Poplar St Laurel (19956) *(G-3307)*
Water Is Life Kenya Inc 302 894-7335
314 E Main St Ste 2 Newark (19711) *(G-7678)*
Water's Edge, Newark *Also called Omniway Corporation (G-7147)*
Watercraft LLC 302 757-0786
801 Owls Nest Rd Wilmington (19807) *(G-13122)*
Waterford Mhc Inc 302 834-9514
205 Joan Dr Bear (19701) *(G-371)*
Waterlogic Usa Inc 302 323-2100
77 Mccullough Dr Ste 9 New Castle (19720) *(G-5826)*
Watkins Dealership, New Castle *Also called Watkins System Inc (G-5827)*

ALPHABETIC

(PA)=Parent Co (HQ)=Headquarters (DH)=Div Headquarters
2020 Harris Directory of Delaware Businesses
741

Watkins System Inc...302 658-8561
4031 New Castle Ave New Castle (19720) ***(G-5827)***
Watson Funeral Home Inc...302 934-7842
211 S Washington St Millsboro (19966) ***(G-4824)***
Watson-Marlow Flow Smart Inc...302 536-6388
213 Nesbitt Dr Seaford (19973) ***(G-8434)***
Watson-Yates Funeral Home Inc...302 629-8561
609 E King St Seaford (19973) ***(G-8435)***
Watsons Auction & Realty Svc...302 422-2392
115 N Washington St Milford (19963) ***(G-4599)***
Watts Electric Company...302 529-1183
2027 Harwyn Rd Wilmington (19810) ***(G-13123)***
Wave, Wilmington *Also called Chime Inc* ***(G-9666)***
Wave Newspaper...302 537-1881
Coastal Hwy Bethany Beach (19930) ***(G-437)***
Waverly Orthopaedic, Milford *Also called Choy Wilson Cdgn* ***(G-4351)***
Wavertech LLC...877 735-0897
913 N Market St Ste 200 Wilmington (19801) ***(G-13124)***
Wavertise, Wilmington *Also called Wavertech LLC* ***(G-13124)***
Way Home Inc...302 856-9870
413 E Market St Georgetown (19947) ***(G-2702)***
Way To Go Led Lighting Company...844 312-4574
702 Interchange Blvd Newark (19711) ***(G-7679)***
Wayden Inc (PA)...302 798-1642
205 Ridge Rd Claymont (19703) ***(G-817)***
Wayden Paper, Claymont *Also called Wayden Inc* ***(G-817)***
Wayman Fire Protection Inc...302 994-5757
403 Meco Dr Wilmington (19804) ***(G-13125)***
Wayman Transportation Svc...302 363-5139
160 Carnation Dr Magnolia (19962) ***(G-3912)***
Wayne Bennett...302 436-2379
35484 Honeysuckle Rd Frankford (19945) ***(G-2397)***
Wayne I Tucker...302 838-1100
100 Becks Woods Dr # 202 Bear (19701) ***(G-372)***
Wayne Industries Inc (PA)...302 478-6160
1105 N Market St Ste 1300 Wilmington (19801) ***(G-13126)***
Wb Paving LLC...302 838-1886
1387 Red Lion Rd Bear (19701) ***(G-373)***
Wbi Capital Advisors LLC (PA)...856 361-6362
251 Little Falls Dr Wilmington (19808) ***(G-13127)***
Wboc Inc...302 734-9262
1839 S Dupont Hwy Dover (19901) ***(G-2207)***
Wboc-TV, Dover *Also called Wboc Inc* ***(G-2207)***
Wdbid DBA Downtown Visions...302 425-5374
409 N Orange St Wilmington (19801) ***(G-13128)***
Wdbid Management Company...302 425-5374
409 N Orange St Wilmington (19801) ***(G-13129)***
Wdov AM, Dover *Also called Iheartcommunications Inc* ***(G-1666)***
We Cobble LLC...302 504-4294
4023 Kennett Pike # 50098 Wilmington (19807) ***(G-13130)***
We Deserve It Shs For Kids Inc...302 521-7255
363 Frear Dr Dover (19901) ***(G-2208)***
WEANAS, Newark *Also called Huzala Inc* ***(G-6756)***
Weather or Not Dog Walkers...302 304-8399
1300 Tulane Rd Wilmington (19803) ***(G-13131)***
Weather or Not Inc...302 436-7533
38294 London Ave Unit 3 Selbyville (19975) ***(G-8553)***
Weatherhill Dental...302 239-6677
5317 Limestone Rd Ste 2 Wilmington (19808) ***(G-13132)***
Weaver Sanitation...302 653-8777
6 Manor Dr Smyrna (19977) ***(G-8740)***
Weavers Construction Inc...302 270-8876
6806 Canterbury Rd Felton (19943) ***(G-2326)***
Web Advantage Inc...302 479-7634
216 Paddock Ln Wilmington (19803) ***(G-13133)***
Web Applications Inc...302 834-0282
2604 Cindy Dr Ste 4 Newark (19702) ***(G-7680)***
Web N App LLC...810 309-8242
58 Burnside Dr Smyrna (19977) ***(G-8741)***
Webbit...302 725-6024
6200 Kirby Rd Milford (19963) ***(G-4600)***
Webbrowser Media Inc...302 830-3664
3422 Old Capitol Trl Wilmington (19808) ***(G-13134)***
Webbs Cleaners Corp (PA)...302 798-0655
1403 Philadelphia Pike A Wilmington (19809) ***(G-13135)***
Webcasting Media LLC...302 261-5178
16192 Coastal Hwy Lewes (19958) ***(G-3817)***
Weber Gallagher Simpson (PA)...302 346-6377
19 S State St Ste 102 Dover (19901) ***(G-2209)***
Weber Sign & Art Studio, Frankford *Also called Weber Sign Co* ***(G-2398)***
Weber Sign Co...302 732-1429
16 Hickory St Frankford (19945) ***(G-2398)***
Webro Holdings LLC (PA)...302 314-3334
19266 Coastal Hwy 4-1049 Rehoboth Beach (19971) ***(G-8109)***
Webstudy Inc (PA)...888 326-4058
30649 Hollymount Rd Harbeson (19951) ***(G-2802)***
Wee Care Day Care Salv Army...302 472-0712
400 N Orange St Wilmington (19801) ***(G-13136)***
Weelwork Inc...800 546-8607
619 New York Ave Claymont (19703) ***(G-818)***
Weepor Company Inc...302 575-9945
103 Foulk Rd Ste 202 Wilmington (19803) ***(G-13137)***
Wegman Bros Inc...302 738-4328
2612 Ogletown Rd Newark (19713) ***(G-7681)***
Weik Nitsche & Dougherty...302 655-4040
305 N Union St Unit 2 Wilmington (19805) ***(G-13138)***
Weiner Development LLC...302 764-9430
4 Denny Rd Ste 1 Wilmington (19809) ***(G-13139)***
Weinstein Supply Div, Wilmington *Also called Hajoca Corporation* ***(G-10823)***
Weiss & Saville PA...302 656-0400
1105 N Market St Ste 200 Wilmington (19801) ***(G-13140)***
Weitron Inc (PA)...800 398-3816
801 Pencader Dr Newark (19702) ***(G-7682)***
Welcome Aboard Travel Ltd...302 678-9480
57 Saulsbury Rd Ste C Dover (19904) ***(G-2210)***
Welding By Jackson...302 846-3090
10178 Jackson St Delmar (19940) ***(G-1047)***
Welfare Foundation Inc...302 683-8200
100 W 10th St Ste 1109 Wilmington (19801) ***(G-13141)***
Well Done Cleaning Services...443 407-3064
401 S Broom St Wilmington (19805) ***(G-13142)***
Weller's Utility Trailers, Bridgeville *Also called Wellers Tire Service Inc* ***(G-531)***
Wellers Tire Service Inc...302 337-8228
16889 N Main St Bridgeville (19933) ***(G-531)***
Wellington Management Group...215 569-8900
300 Delaware Ave Ste 1380 Wilmington (19801) ***(G-13143)***
Wellness and Rejuvenation...732 977-6958
30996 Puseys Rd Millsboro (19966) ***(G-4825)***
Wellness Centers, Wilmington *Also called Christiana Care Hlth Svcs Inc* ***(G-9683)***
Wellness From Within...717 884-3908
33253 Waterview Ct Lewes (19958) ***(G-3818)***
Wellness Health Center, Milford *Also called Wellness Health Inc* ***(G-4601)***
Wellness Health Inc...302 424-4100
106 Nw Front St Milford (19963) ***(G-4601)***
Wellnx Life Sciences USA, Wilmington *Also called Platinum US Distribution Inc* ***(G-12153)***
Wells Agency Inc...302 422-2121
995 N Dupont Blvd Milford (19963) ***(G-4602)***
Wells Fargo Advisors, Newark *Also called Wells Fargo Clearing Svcs LLC* ***(G-7685)***
Wells Fargo Advisors, Newark *Also called Wells Fargo Clearing Svcs LLC* ***(G-7686)***
Wells Fargo Advisors, Wilmington *Also called Wells Fargo Clearing Svcs LLC* ***(G-13152)***
Wells Fargo Bank National Assn...302 631-1500
2624 Capitol Trl Newark (19711) ***(G-7683)***
Wells Fargo Bank National Assn...302 736-2910
101 W Loockerman St Dover (19904) ***(G-2211)***
Wells Fargo Bank National Assn...302 449-5485
310 Dove Run Centre Dr Middletown (19709) ***(G-4281)***
Wells Fargo Bank National Assn...302 541-8660
38011 Town Center Dr Millville (19967) ***(G-4858)***
Wells Fargo Bank National Assn...302 765-5534
505 Carr Rd Ste 200 Wilmington (19809) ***(G-13144)***
Wells Fargo Bank National Assn...302 428-8600
3801 Kennett Pike Wilmington (19807) ***(G-13145)***
Wells Fargo Bank National Assn...302 529-2550
2024 Naamans Rd Wilmington (19810) ***(G-13146)***
Wells Fargo Bank National Assn...302 736-2920
100 N Du Pont Hwy Dover (19901) ***(G-2212)***
Wells Fargo Bank National Assn...302 235-4300
7270 Lancaster Pike Hockessin (19707) ***(G-3169)***
Wells Fargo Bank National Assn...302 832-6100
2450 Glasgow Ave Newark (19702) ***(G-7684)***
Wells Fargo Bank National Assn...302 644-6351
4600 Hwy 1 Rehoboth Beach (19971) ***(G-8110)***
Wells Fargo Bank National Assn...302 326-4304
1424 N Dupont Hwy New Castle (19720) ***(G-5828)***
Wells Fargo Bank National Assn...302 421-7508
2011 Concord Pike Wilmington (19803) ***(G-13147)***
Wells Fargo Bank National Assn...302 636-4306
3215 Old Capitol Trl Wilmington (19808) ***(G-13148)***
Wells Fargo Bank National Assn...302 761-1300
814 Philadelphia Pike Wilmington (19809) ***(G-13149)***
Wells Fargo Bank National Assn...302 622-3350
100 W 10th St Lbby 1 Wilmington (19801) ***(G-13150)***
Wells Fargo Bank National Assn...302 421-7820
4015 Kennett Pike Wilmington (19807) ***(G-13151)***
Wells Fargo Bank National Assn...302 832-6104
1601 Governors Pl Bear (19701) ***(G-374)***
Wells Fargo Bank National Assn...302 235-4304
5801 Limestone Rd Hockessin (19707) ***(G-3170)***
Wells Fargo Clearing Svcs LLC...302 428-5969
4 Creek Bend Ct Newark (19711) ***(G-7685)***
Wells Fargo Clearing Svcs LLC...302 731-2131
131 Continental Dr # 102 Newark (19713) ***(G-7686)***
Wells Fargo Clearing Svcs LLC...302 428-8600
3801 Kennett Pike Wilmington (19807) ***(G-13152)***
Wells Fargo Delaware Trust Co...302 575-2002
919 N Market St Ste 1600 Wilmington (19801) ***(G-13153)***

Wells Fargo Home Mortgage Inc 302 227-5700
18977 Munchy Branch Rd # 6 Rehoboth Beach (19971) ***(G-8111)***
Wells Fargo Home Mortgage Inc 302 239-6300
7465 Lancaster Pike Ste C Hockessin (19707) ***(G-3171)***
Wells Farms Inc 302 422-4732
7481 Wells Rd Milford (19963) ***(G-4603)***
Wellspring Counseling Services 302 373-8904
115 E Glenwood Ave Smyrna (19977) ***(G-8742)***
Wellspring Farm Inc 302 798-2407
800 Carr Rd Wilmington (19809) ***(G-13154)***
Wellspring Tack Shop, Wilmington *Also called Wellspring Farm Inc* ***(G-13154)***
Welsh Family Dentistry 302 836-3711
34 Withers Way Hockessin (19707) ***(G-3172)***
Wen International Inc 845 354-1773
101 Wayland Rd Wilmington (19807) ***(G-13155)***
Wendy Cpa LLC 302 377-7165
39 Maureen Way Bear (19701) ***(G-375)***
Wenova Inc (PA) 847 477-0489
42 Reads Way New Castle (19720) ***(G-5829)***
Wentworth Group 302 998-2115
4100 Dawnbrook Dr Wilmington (19804) ***(G-13156)***
Wentworth Inc 302 629-6284
22946 Sussex Hwy Seaford (19973) ***(G-8436)***
Wentzel Transportation 302 355-9465
33 Brenford Station Rd Smyrna (19977) ***(G-8743)***
Wepro LLC (PA) 310 650-8622
901 N Market St Ste 705 Wilmington (19801) ***(G-13157)***
WER Wireless Inc 302 478-7748
4737 Concord Pike Ste 416 Wilmington (19803) ***(G-13158)***
WER Wireless of Concord Inc 302 478-7748
4737 Concord Pike Ste 416 Wilmington (19803) ***(G-13159)***
Werb & Sullivan 302 652-1100
300 Delaware Ave Ste 1300 Wilmington (19801) ***(G-13160)***
Wertz & Co 302 658-5186
116 Valley Rd Wilmington (19804) ***(G-13161)***
Wesco Distribution Inc 302 655-9611
11 Brookside Dr Wilmington (19804) ***(G-13162)***
Wesley College, Dover *Also called Boys & Girls Clubs Del Inc* ***(G-1226)***
Wesley Play Care Center 302 678-8987
209 S State St Dover (19901) ***(G-2213)***
Wesley Preschool, Dover *Also called Wesley Play Care Center* ***(G-2213)***
West Center Cy Early Lrng Ctr 302 656-0485
600 N Madison St Wilmington (19801) ***(G-13163)***
West Dover Butcher Shop Inc 302 734-5447
3997 Hazlettville Rd Dover (19904) ***(G-2214)***
West End Machine Shop Inc 302 654-8436
1405 Brown St Wilmington (19805) ***(G-13164)***
West End Neighborhood Hse Inc 302 654-2131
1725 W 8th St Wilmington (19805) ***(G-13165)***
West End Neighborhood Hse Inc (PA) 302 658-4171
710 N Lincoln St Wilmington (19805) ***(G-13166)***
West End Nghbrhd Chld Care, Wilmington *Also called West End Neighborhood Hse Inc* ***(G-13165)***
West Minister Management, Newark *Also called Prides Court Apartments* ***(G-7252)***
West Minister Management 302 678-4515
177 Willis Rd Dover (19901) ***(G-2215)***
West Orange Office Exec Pk LLC 973 320-3227
2711 Centerville Rd # 400 Wilmington (19808) ***(G-13167)***
West Photography 302 858-6003
16848 Old Furnace Rd Georgetown (19947) ***(G-2703)***
West Rhoboth Cmnty Land Tr Inc 302 260-9519
19801 Norwood St Rehoboth Beach (19971) ***(G-8112)***
West Third Enterprises LLC 302 732-3133
30996 Country Gdns Dagsboro (19939) ***(G-943)***
West Ventures Inc 307 737-9900
13 King Ct Ste 1 New Castle (19720) ***(G-5830)***
West Wilmington Svnth Day Adv 302 998-3961
3003 Mill Creek Rd Wilmington (19808) ***(G-13168)***
Western Sussex Animal Hosp Inc 302 337-7387
16487 Sussex Hwy Bridgeville (19933) ***(G-532)***
Westlake Chemical Products 302 691-6028
103 Foulk Rd Wilmington (19803) ***(G-13169)***
Westminster Village Dover 302 744-3527
181 Westminster Dr Dover (19904) ***(G-2216)***
Westminster Village Health Ctr, Dover *Also called Presbyterian Senior Living* ***(G-1984)***
Westmor Industries 302 398-3253
17409 S Dupont Hwy Harrington (19952) ***(G-2906)***
Westmor Industries 302 956-0243
16941 Sussex Hwy Bridgeville (19933) ***(G-533)***
Weston Senior Living Center 302 994-4434
4800 Lancaster Pike Wilmington (19807) ***(G-13170)***
Weston Sr Living Ctr, Wilmington *Also called Weston Senior Living Center* ***(G-13170)***
Westover Cardiology 302 482-2035
222 Carter Dr Middletown (19709) ***(G-4282)***
Westover Management Company LP 302 738-5775
1 Allandale Dr Newark (19713) ***(G-7687)***
Westover Management Company LP 302 731-1638
24 Sandalwood Dr Ofc 5 Newark (19713) ***(G-7688)***
Westown Movies LLC 330 244-1633
150 Commerce Dr Middletown (19709) ***(G-4283)***
Westside Car Wash, Dover *Also called Gas & Go Inc* ***(G-1582)***
Westside Family Healthcare Inc 302 575-1414
908 E 16th St Ste B Wilmington (19802) ***(G-13171)***
Westside Family Healthcare Inc 302 836-2864
404 Foxhunt Dr Bear (19701) ***(G-376)***
Westside Family Healthcare Inc 302 652-2455
2 Penns Way Ste 412 New Castle (19720) ***(G-5831)***
Westside Family Healthcare Inc 302 678-4622
1020 Forrest Ave Dover (19904) ***(G-2217)***
Westside Family Healthcare Inc 302 455-0900
27 Marrows Rd Newark (19713) ***(G-7689)***
Westside Family Healthcare Inc (PA) 302 656-8292
300 Water St Ste 200 Wilmington (19801) ***(G-13172)***
Westside Family Healthcare Inc 302 656-8292
1802 W 4th St Wilmington (19805) ***(G-13173)***
Westside N Begnings Yth Imprvm 302 227-5442
19801 Norwood St Rehoboth Beach (19971) ***(G-8113)***
Westwood Farms Incorporated 302 238-7141
21906 Esham Ln Millsboro (19966) ***(G-4826)***
Westwood Properties Ltd 302 655-0274
699 Robinson Ln Wilmington (19805) ***(G-13174)***
Wetsu Tackle Distributors, Rehoboth Beach *Also called Old Inlet Bait and Tackle Inc* ***(G-8022)***
Wetzel & Associates PA 302 652-1200
2201 W 11th St Wilmington (19805) ***(G-13175)***
Weyl Enterprises Inc 302 993-1248
1206 Kirkwood Hwy Wilmington (19805) ***(G-13176)***
Weymouth Swyze Crroon Insur In 302 655-3705
5710 Kennett Pike Wilmington (19807) ***(G-13177)***
Wgames Incorporated 206 618-3699
1209 N Orange St Wilmington (19801) ***(G-13178)***
Wgmd, Lewes *Also called Resort Broadcasting Co LP* ***(G-3716)***
Wh Nutritionals LLC 302 357-3611
1000 N West St Fl 17 Wilmington (19801) ***(G-13179)***
Wh2p Inc 302 530-6555
3704 Kennett Pike Ste 400 Wilmington (19807) ***(G-13180)***
Whaleys Seed Store Inc 302 875-7833
106 W 8th St Laurel (19956) ***(G-3308)***
Wharton Levin Ehrmantraut 302 252-0090
300 Delaware Ave Ste 1704 Wilmington (19801) ***(G-13181)***
Whartons Landscaping LLC 302 947-0913
20503 Wil King Rd Lewes (19958) ***(G-3819)***
Whartons Landscaping Grdn Ctr 302 426-4854
19385 Old Landing Rd Rehoboth Beach (19971) ***(G-8114)***
What If Y Not Everything Inc 732 898-0241
8 The Grn Ste A Dover (19901) ***(G-2218)***
What Is Your Voice Inc 443 653-2067
30428 E Barrier Reef Blvd Lewes (19958) ***(G-3820)***
Whatcoat Christian Preschool 302 698-2108
16 Main St Dover (19901) ***(G-2219)***
Whatcoat Social Service Agency 302 734-0319
381 College Rd Dover (19904) ***(G-2220)***
Whatcoat Village Assoc LLC 856 596-0500
992 Whatcoat Dr Apt 12 Dover (19904) ***(G-2221)***
Whatever It Takes Services, Wilmington *Also called Wit Services LLC* ***(G-13280)***
Whayland Company Inc 302 875-5445
30613 Sussex Hwy Laurel (19956) ***(G-3309)***
Whayland Company LLC 302 875-5445
100 W 10th St Laurel (19956) ***(G-3310)***
Wheatley Farms Inc 302 337-7286
19115 Freeland Ln Bridgeville (19933) ***(G-534)***
Wheelchair Mechanix 302 478-0858
2110 Shipley Rd Wilmington (19803) ***(G-13182)***
Wheeler Wolfenden & Dwares CPA 302 254-8240
4550 New Linden Hl Rd # 201 Wilmington (19808) ***(G-13183)***
Wheeler Wolfenden & Dwares PA 302 254-8240
824 N Market St Ste 720 Wilmington (19801) ***(G-13184)***
When Poets Dream Inc 818 738-6954
1679 S Dupont Hwy Ste 100 Dover (19901) ***(G-2222)***
Wherebyus Enterprises Inc 305 988-0808
2093 Philadelphia Pike Claymont (19703) ***(G-819)***
Whet Industries Inc 302 236-2182
560 Peoples Plz Ste 144 Newark (19702) ***(G-7690)***
Whipper Snapper Transport LLC 302 265-2437
278 Canterbury Rd Milford (19963) ***(G-4604)***
Whisman John 302 530-1676
5201 W Woodmill Dr Ste 31 Wilmington (19808) ***(G-13185)***
Whispering Meadows LLC 302 698-1073
4110b Connecticut Ln Dover (19901) ***(G-2223)***
Whispering Pines Community Ctr, Lewes *Also called Equity Lifestyle Prpts Inc* ***(G-3486)***
Whitaker Corporation 302 633-2740
4550 New Lndn Hll Rd 14 Wilmington (19808) ***(G-13186)***
Whitaker LLC 302 633-2740
4550 New Linden Wilmington (19808) ***(G-13187)***
White & Associates 302 765-3736
114 W 40th St Ste A Wilmington (19802) ***(G-13188)***
White & Williams, Wilmington *Also called White and Williams LLP* ***(G-13189)***

ALPHABETIC

White and Williams LLP...302 654-0424
600 N King St Ste 800 Wilmington (19801) ***(G-13189)***
White Clay Creek Vtrinary Hosp...302 738-9611
107 Albe Dr Ste A Newark (19702) ***(G-7691)***
White Dog Labs Inc (PA)...302 220-4760
239 Lisa Dr New Castle (19720) ***(G-5832)***
White Drilling Corp...302 422-4057
Us 113 Lincoln (19960) ***(G-3873)***
White Eagle Electrical Contg...302 378-3366
709 Guido Dr Middletown (19709) ***(G-4284)***
White Eagle Integrations...302 464-0550
635 Lorewood Grove Rd Middletown (19709) ***(G-4285)***
White Horse Winery...302 388-4850
15 Guyencourt Rd Wilmington (19807) ***(G-13190)***
White House Beach Inc...302 945-3032
35266 Fishermans Rd # 2 Millsboro (19966) ***(G-4827)***
White Mink Beauty Salon...302 737-2081
330 College Sq Newark (19711) ***(G-7692)***
White Oak Head Start...302 736-5933
195 Willis Rd Dover (19901) ***(G-2224)***
White Oak Landscape MGT Inc...302 652-7533
17 Owls Nest Rd Wilmington (19807) ***(G-13191)***
White Robbins Company...302 478-5555
3513 Concord Pike # 2100 Wilmington (19803) ***(G-13192)***
White Robbins Condo & Assn, Wilmington *Also called White Robbins Company* ***(G-13192)***
White's Creek Manor, Bethany Beach *Also called Jack Hickman Real Estate* ***(G-406)***
Whitecrow Research Inc...908 752-4200
2711 Centerville Rd # 300 Wilmington (19808) ***(G-13193)***
Whitehook Solutions LLC...302 222-5177
219 Garrisons Cir Smyrna (19977) ***(G-8744)***
Whitemans Paving Inc...302 378-1828
501 Toledo Ct Townsend (19734) ***(G-8832)***
Whiteoptics, New Castle *Also called Acuity Brands Lighting Inc* ***(G-5002)***
Whites Auto Repair & Body Shop, Wilmington *Also called Whites Body Shop* ***(G-13194)***
Whites Body Shop...302 655-4369
436 S Buttonwood St Wilmington (19801) ***(G-13194)***
Whites Family Trucking LLC...302 393-1401
714 Main St Ellendale (19941) ***(G-2264)***
Whitetail Country Log & Hlg, Delmar *Also called Whitetail Country Log & Hlg* ***(G-1048)***
Whitetail Country Log & Hlg...302 846-3982
16075 Russell Rd Delmar (19940) ***(G-1048)***
Whiting-Turner Contracting Co...302 292-0676
131 Continental Dr # 404 Newark (19713) ***(G-7693)***
Whitman Requardt and Assoc, Wilmington *Also called Whitman Requardt and Assoc LLP* ***(G-13195)***
Whitman Requardt and Assoc LLP...302 571-9001
1013 Centre Rd Ste 302 Wilmington (19805) ***(G-13195)***
Whittens Fine Jewelry...302 995-7464
4719 Kirkwood Hwy Wilmington (19808) ***(G-13196)***
Whittington & Aulgur (PA)...302 235-5800
2979 Barley Mill Rd Yorklyn (19736) ***(G-13368)***
Whittington & Aulgur...302 378-1661
313 N Dupont Hwy Ste 110 Odessa (19730) ***(G-7833)***
Whittington & Aulgur...302 378-1661
651 N Broad St Ste 206 Middletown (19709) ***(G-4286)***
Whole Child App Inc...302 570-2002
16192 Coastal Hwy Lewes (19958) ***(G-3821)***
Wholesale, Wilmington *Also called Forcebeyond Inc* ***(G-10590)***
Wholesale Asgard, Wilmington *Also called Peter Shin* ***(G-12098)***
Wholesale Auto Inc...302 322-6190
53 Collingsdale Ave New Castle (19720) ***(G-5833)***
Wholesale Janitor Supply Co...302 655-5722
26 Germay Dr Wilmington (19804) ***(G-13197)***
Wholesale Jewelry Outlet Inc...302 994-5114
3616 Kirkwood Hwy Wilmington (19808) ***(G-13198)***
Wholesale Jewlery Outlet, Wilmington *Also called Whittens Fine Jewelry* ***(G-13196)***
Wholesale Millwork Inc (PA)...888 964-8746
107 Park Ave Seaford (19973) ***(G-8437)***
Wibsc, Wilmington *Also called A Gentlemans Touch Inc* ***(G-8878)***
Wic State Office of Delaware, Dover *Also called Delaware Wic Program* ***(G-1406)***
Widgeon Enterprises Inc...302 846-9763
38204 Old Stage Rd Delmar (19940) ***(G-1049)***
Wiedman Enterprises Inc...302 226-2407
38335 Martins Ln Rehoboth Beach (19971) ***(G-8115)***
Wiedmann Enterprises Inc...302 645-2028
18013 Robinsonville Rd Lewes (19958) ***(G-3822)***
Wik Associates Inc...302 322-2558
10 Donaldson Dr Newark (19713) ***(G-7694)***
Wilbraham Lawler & Buba PC...302 421-9922
901 N Market St Ste 800 Wilmington (19801) ***(G-13199)***
Wilcon North Inc...302 798-1699
3005 Philadelphia Pike Claymont (19703) ***(G-820)***
Wilcox & Fetzer Ltd...302 655-0477
1330 N King St Wilmington (19801) ***(G-13200)***
Wilcox Landscaping...302 322-3002
230 S Dupont Hwy New Castle (19720) ***(G-5834)***
Wild Bets, Dover *Also called Play US Media LLC* ***(G-1965)***
Wild Meadows Homes...302 730-4700
529 Weaver Dr Dover (19901) ***(G-2225)***
Wild Quail Golf & Country Club, Camden Wyoming *Also called Quail Associates Inc* ***(G-651)***
Wild Smiles, Newark *Also called Jay J Harris PC* ***(G-6829)***
Wilderman Physical Therapy LLC...717 873-6836
2626 Belaire Dr Wilmington (19808) ***(G-13201)***
Wiley-Liss Inc...302 429-8627
1105 N Market St Ste 1300 Wilmington (19801) ***(G-13202)***
Wilgus Associates Inc (PA)...302 539-7511
32904 Coastal Hwy Bethany Beach (19930) ***(G-438)***
Wilgus Associates Inc...302 644-2960
1520 Savannah Rd Lewes (19958) ***(G-3823)***
Wilgus Glamorama, Selbyville *Also called Selbyville Cleaners Inc* ***(G-8544)***
Wilkerson Water Co, Milford *Also called J H Wilkerson & Son Inc* ***(G-4456)***
Wilkins Enterprises...302 732-3744
E S Main St Dagsboro (19939) ***(G-944)***
Wilkins Enterprises Inc...302 945-4142
Pettyjohn Rd Milton (19968) ***(G-4980)***
Wilkins Enterprises Inc...302 945-4142
34994 Holly Dr Lewes (19958) ***(G-3824)***
Wilkins Fuel Co...302 422-5597
701 S Washington St Milford (19963) ***(G-4605)***
Wilkinson Roofing & Siding Inc...302 998-0176
1000 First State Blvd Wilmington (19804) ***(G-13203)***
Wilkinson Technology Svcs LLC...302 384-7770
4 Squirrel Run Wilmington (19807) ***(G-13204)***
Wilkisons Marking Service Inc...302 697-3669
22 Stevens St Dover (19901) ***(G-2226)***
Wilks Lukoff & Bracegirdle LLC...302 225-0850
1300 N Grant Ave Ste 100 Wilmington (19806) ***(G-13205)***
Will C & Will Fuels...302 366-1915
1218 Grayrock Rd Newark (19713) ***(G-7695)***
Willard Agri Service Greenw...302 349-4100
22272 S Dupont Hwy Farmington (19950) ***(G-2268)***
Willey and Co...302 629-3327
11588 Commercial Ln Laurel (19956) ***(G-3311)***
Willey Farms Inc...302 378-8441
4092 Dupont Pkwy Townsend (19734) ***(G-8833)***
Willey Knives Inc...302 349-4070
14210 Sugar Hill Rd Greenwood (19950) ***(G-2768)***
William A Ellert MD...302 369-9370
620 Stanton Christiana Rd Newark (19713) ***(G-7696)***
William A O'Day Ands Son, Seaford *Also called William A ODay* ***(G-8438)***
William A ODay...302 629-7854
4148 Woodland Ferry Rd Seaford (19973) ***(G-8438)***
William A ODay & Son LLC...302 629-7854
4148 Woodland Ferry Rd Seaford (19973) ***(G-8439)***
William B Funk MD...302 731-0900
665 Churchmans Rd Newark (19702) ***(G-7697)***
William Byler Jr Architect Inc...302 653-3550
2652 Chance Rd Clayton (19938) ***(G-874)***
William Chambers and Son...302 284-9655
8964 S Dupont Hwy Viola (19979) ***(G-8838)***
William D Shellady Inc...302 652-3106
112 A St Wilmington (19801) ***(G-13206)***
William Delcampo Mechanical SE...302 992-9748
2429 Hartley Pl Wilmington (19808) ***(G-13207)***
William E Ward PA...302 225-3350
2710 Centerville Rd # 200 Wilmington (19808) ***(G-13208)***
William G Day Company...302 427-3700
1603 Jessup St Ste 4 Wilmington (19802) ***(G-13209)***
William G Robelen Inc...302 656-8726
3110 Lancaster Ave Wilmington (19805) ***(G-13210)***
William Gonce...302 235-2400
410 Smith Mill Rd Newark (19711) ***(G-7698)***
William Grant & Sons USA Corp...302 573-3880
1011 Centre Rd Ste 310 Wilmington (19805) ***(G-13211)***
William H McDaniel Inc...302 764-2020
14 E 40th St Lowr Wilmington (19802) ***(G-13212)***
William H Radford Ldscp Contrs, Smyrna *Also called William H Rdford Nurseries Inc* ***(G-8745)***
William H Rdford Nurseries Inc...302 659-3130
853 Black Diamond Rd Smyrna (19977) ***(G-8745)***
William Hcks Andrson Cmnty Ctr...302 571-4266
501 N Madison St Wilmington (19801) ***(G-13213)***
William Humphreys & Co LLC...302 225-3904
1701 Shallcross Ave Wilmington (19806) ***(G-13214)***
William J Winkler...302 732-0866
36226 Dupont Blvd Selbyville (19975) ***(G-8554)***
William M Kaplan MD...302 422-3393
302 Polk Ave Milford (19963) ***(G-4606)***
William N Cann Inc...302 995-0820
1 Meco Cir Wilmington (19804) ***(G-13215)***
William P Smith DDS...302 737-7274
29 Meadowood Dr Newark (19711) ***(G-7699)***
William Penn Vlg Appartment, New Castle *Also called Kbf Associates LP* ***(G-5455)***
William R Knotts & Son Inc...302 674-3496
4786 Forrest Ave Dover (19904) ***(G-2227)***

ALPHABETIC SECTION — Wilmington Trust Corporation

William Stele Wldg Fabrication 302 422-7444
200 Mullet Run Milford (19963) *(G-4607)*

William T Wadkins Garage Inc 302 422-0265
402 Ne Front St Milford (19963) *(G-4608)*

William W Erhart PA 302 651-0113
2961 Centerville Rd Wilmington (19808) *(G-13216)*

Williams Insurance Agency Inc (PA) 302 227-2501
20220 Coastal Hwy Rehoboth Beach (19971) *(G-8116)*

Williams Insurance Agency Inc 302 239-5500
5301 Limestone Rd Ste 100 Wilmington (19808) *(G-13217)*

Williams Law Firm PA 302 575-0873
1201 N Orange St Ste 600 Wilmington (19801) *(G-13218)*

Williams-Garcia & Associates, Felton Also called Center For A Pstive Hmnity LLC *(G-2281)*

Williams-Sonoma Stores Inc 302 368-7707
178 Christiana Mall Newark (19702) *(G-7700)*

Williamson Building Corp 302 644-0605
130 New Rd Lewes (19958) *(G-3825)*

Willies Auto Detail Service 302 734-1010
17 Weston Dr Dover (19904) *(G-2228)*

Willin Farms LLC 302 629-2520
2864 Long Acre Ln Seaford (19973) *(G-8440)*

Willis Ford Inc 302 653-5900
15 N Dupont Blvd Smyrna (19977) *(G-8746)*

Willis Groupllc 302 632-9898
4 The Grn Dover (19901) *(G-2229)*

Willow Run Civic Association 302 994-2250
1504 Bondridge Rd Wilmington (19805) *(G-13219)*

Willow Tree Equity Holding LLC 213 479-4077
16192 Coastal Hwy Lewes (19958) *(G-3826)*

Willow Winters Publishing LLC 570 885-2513
164 N Bayberry Pkwy Middletown (19709) *(G-4287)*

Willowflare LLC 312 428-0159
16192 Coastal Hwy Lewes (19958) *(G-3827)*

Wilm Otolarngology 302 658-0404
2300 Penns Ave Ste 2a Wilmington (19806) *(G-13220)*

Wilmapco, Newark Also called Wilmington Metropolitan Area P *(G-7702)*

Wilmington 302 357-4509
1201 N Orange St Ste 7463 Wilmington (19801) *(G-13221)*

Wilmington & Newark Dental 302 571-0526
2300 Penns Ave Ste Ll Wilmington (19806) *(G-13222)*

WILMINGTON & WESTERN RAILROAD, Wilmington Also called Historic Red Clay Valley Inc *(G-10917)*

Wilmington 1st Walk-In, Wilmington Also called Precision Care & Wellness LLC *(G-12201)*

Wilmington Animal Hospital 302 762-2694
828 Philadelphia Pike Wilmington (19809) *(G-13223)*

Wilmington Aquatic Club Inc 302 322-2487
212 W Grant Ave New Castle (19720) *(G-5835)*

Wilmington Blue Rocks Baseball 302 888-2015
801 Shipyard Dr Wilmington (19801) *(G-13224)*

Wilmington Brew Works LLC 302 757-4971
3201 Miller Rd Wilmington (19802) *(G-13225)*

Wilmington Christiana Cou 302 456-3800
48 Geoffrey Dr Newark (19713) *(G-7701)*

Wilmington Club Inc 302 658-4287
1103 N Market St Wilmington (19801) *(G-13226)*

Wilmington Collision Ctr LLC 302 764-3520
214 E Lea Blvd Wilmington (19802) *(G-13227)*

Wilmington Country Club 302 655-6171
4825 Kennett Pike Wilmington (19807) *(G-13228)*

Wilmington Dental Assoc PA 302 654-6915
2309 Pennsylvania Ave Wilmington (19806) *(G-13229)*

Wilmington Elks Home Inc 302 652-0313
1310 Carruthers Ln Wilmington (19803) *(G-13230)*

Wilmington Fibre Specialty Co 302 328-7525
700 Washington St New Castle (19720) *(G-5836)*

Wilmington Head Start 302 762-8038
2401 Northeast Blvd Wilmington (19802) *(G-13231)*

Wilmington Headstart Inc 302 421-3620
1238 N Walnut St Wilmington (19801) *(G-13232)*

Wilmington Headstart Inc (PA) 302 762-8038
100 W 10th St Ste 1016 Wilmington (19801) *(G-13233)*

Wilmington Hotel Venture 302 655-0400
700 N King St Wilmington (19801) *(G-13234)*

Wilmington Housing Partnr Corp 302 576-3000
800 N French St Fl 7 Wilmington (19801) *(G-13235)*

Wilmington Infrared Tech 302 234-6761
108 Shinn Cir Wilmington (19808) *(G-13236)*

Wilmington Junior Academy, Wilmington Also called West Wilmington Svnth Day Adv *(G-13168)*

Wilmington Medical Associates 302 478-0400
2700 Silverside Rd Ste 3 Wilmington (19810) *(G-13237)*

Wilmington Metropolitan Area P 302 737-6205
100 Discovery Blvd # 800 Newark (19713) *(G-7702)*

Wilmington Montessori School 302 475-0555
1400 Harvey Rd Wilmington (19810) *(G-13238)*

Wilmington Mri Center, Wilmington Also called Omega Imaging Associates LLC *(G-11947)*

Wilmington Otolrynglgy Assc 302 658-0404
2300 Penns Ave Ste 2a Wilmington (19806) *(G-13239)*

Wilmington Pain/Rehab Cntr PA 302 575-1776
1021 Gilpin Ave Ste 101 Wilmington (19806) *(G-13240)*

Wilmington Parking Authority (PA) 302 655-4442
625 N Orange St Ste 2c Wilmington (19801) *(G-13241)*

Wilmington Pharmatech Co LLC (PA) 302 737-9916
229 Lake Dr Newark (19702) *(G-7703)*

Wilmington Police and Fire Fed 302 654-0818
1701 Shallcross Ave Ste B Wilmington (19806) *(G-13242)*

Wilmington Psychiatric Svcs 302 999-8602
71 Omega Dr D Newark (19713) *(G-7704)*

Wilmington Renaissance Corp 302 425-5500
100 W 10th St Ste 206 Wilmington (19801) *(G-13243)*

Wilmington Resources 302 746-7162
106 Clifton Park Cir Wilmington (19802) *(G-13244)*

Wilmington Savings Fund Soc (HQ) 302 792-6000
500 Delaware Ave Ste 500 # 500 Wilmington (19801) *(G-13245)*

Wilmington Savings Fund Soc 302 360-0020
25926 Plaza Dr Millsboro (19966) *(G-4828)*

Wilmington Savings Fund Soc 302 389-3151
400 Jimmy Dr Smyrna (19977) *(G-8747)*

Wilmington Savings Fund Soc 302 697-8891
4566 S Dupont Hwy Camden (19934) *(G-605)*

Wilmington Savings Fund Soc 302 436-4179
38394 Dupont Blvd Selbyville (19975) *(G-8555)*

Wilmington Savings Fund Soc 302 832-7842
2400 Peoples Plz Newark (19702) *(G-7705)*

Wilmington Savings Fund Soc 302 999-1227
1600 W Newport Pike Wilmington (19804) *(G-13246)*

Wilmington Savings Fund Soc 302 360-0440
22820 Sussex Hwy Seaford (19973) *(G-8441)*

Wilmington Savings Fund Soc 302 571-7242
500 Creek View Rd Ste 100 Newark (19711) *(G-7706)*

Wilmington Savings Fund Soc 888 665-9609
3801 Kennett Pike Wilmington (19807) *(G-13247)*

Wilmington Savings Fund Soc 302 838-6300
210 Foxhunt Dr Bear (19701) *(G-377)*

Wilmington Savings Fund Soc 302 571-6508
211 N Union St Wilmington (19805) *(G-13248)*

Wilmington Savings Fund Soc 302 360-0004
69 Atlantic Ave Ocean View (19970) *(G-7824)*

Wilmington Savings Fund Soc 302 677-1891
1486 Forrest Ave Dover (19904) *(G-2230)*

Wilmington Savings Fund Soc 302 792-6043
3512 Philadelphia Pike Claymont (19703) *(G-821)*

Wilmington Savings Fund Soc 302 456-6404
21 University Plz Newark (19702) *(G-7707)*

Wilmington Savings Fund Soc 302 633-5700
4730 Limestone Rd Wilmington (19808) *(G-13249)*

Wilmington Savings Fund Soc 302 571-6516
1711 Delaware Ave Wilmington (19806) *(G-13250)*

Wilmington Savings Fund Soc 302 633-5704
3202 Kirkwood Hwy Frnt Wilmington (19808) *(G-13251)*

Wilmington Savings Fund Soc 302 235-7600
7450 Lancaster Pike Hockessin (19707) *(G-3173)*

Wilmington Savings Fund Soc 302 398-3232
7 Commerce St Harrington (19952) *(G-2907)*

Wilmington Savings Fund Soc 302 571-6500
2005 Concord Pike Wilmington (19803) *(G-13252)*

Wilmington Savings Fund Soc 302 324-5800
144 N Dupont Hwy New Castle (19720) *(G-5837)*

Wilmington Savings Fund Soc 302 284-3201
105 Irish Hl Rd Viola (19979) *(G-8839)*

Wilmington Savings Fund Soc 302 226-5648
19335 Coastal Hwy Rehoboth Beach (19971) *(G-8117)*

Wilmington Savings Fund Soc 302 529-9300
2522 Foulk Rd Wilmington (19810) *(G-13253)*

Wilmington Savings Fund Soc 302 792-6435
2105 Philadelphia Pike Claymont (19703) *(G-822)*

Wilmington Savings Fund Soc 302 792-6000
Wsfs Bank Ctr 500 Del Ave Wsfs Bank Center Wilmington (19801) *(G-13254)*

Wilmington Savings Fund Soc 302 571-7090
500 Delaware Ave Ste 3 Wilmington (19801) *(G-13255)*

Wilmington Senior Center, Wilmington Also called Wilmington Senior Center Inc *(G-13256)*

Wilmington Senior Center Inc 302 651-3440
1909 N Market St Wilmington (19802) *(G-13256)*

Wilmington Senior Center Inc (PA) 302 651-3400
1901 N Market St Wilmington (19802) *(G-13257)*

Wilmington String Ensemble 302 764-1201
1310 Hillside Blvd Wilmington (19803) *(G-13258)*

Wilmington Transportation Ctr 302 655-6111
101 N French St Wilmington (19801) *(G-13259)*

Wilmington Trap Association 302 834-9320
2828 Pulaski Hwy Newark (19702) *(G-7708)*

Wilmington Trust 302 651-1000
Rodney Sq N 1100 N Mkt St Wilmington (19890) *(G-13260)*

Wilmington Trust Company (HQ) 302 651-1000
1100 N Market St Wilmington (19890) *(G-13261)*

Wilmington Trust Company TT 302 427-4812
1100 N Market St Wilmington (19890) *(G-13262)*

Wilmington Trust Corporation 302 651-8378
Rodney Sq N 1100 N Mkt St Wilmington (19890) *(G-13263)*

(PA)=Parent Co (HQ)=Headquarters (DH)=Div Headquarters

Wilmington Trust Sp Services (HQ) 302 427-7650
1105 N Market St Ste 1300 Wilmington (19801) ***(G-13264)***
Wilmington Tug Inc (PA) 302 652-1666
11 Gist Rd Ste 200 Wilmington (19801) ***(G-13265)***
Wilmington Turners Club 302 658-9011
701 S Clayton St Wilmington (19805) ***(G-13266)***
Wilmington VAM&roc, Wilmington *Also called Veterans Health Administration* ***(G-13070)***
Wilmington Vet Center, Wilmington *Also called Veterans Health Administration* ***(G-13071)***
Wilmington Youth Organization 302 761-9030
615 W 37th St Wilmington (19802) ***(G-13267)***
Wilmington Youth Rowing Assn 302 777-4533
500 E Front St Frnt Frnt Wilmington (19801) ***(G-13268)***
Wilson Care Wilson Co 302 897-5059
5 William Davis Ct Newark (19702) ***(G-7709)***
Wilson Construction Co Inc 302 856-3115
23054 Park Ave Georgetown (19947) ***(G-2704)***
Wilson Family Practice 302 422-6677
901 Lakeview Ave Milford (19963) ***(G-4609)***
Wilson Fleet & Equipment 302 422-7159
961 E Masten Cir Milford (19963) ***(G-4610)***
Wilson Halbrook & Bayard PA 302 856-0015
107 W Market St Georgetown (19947) ***(G-2705)***
Wilson Masonry Corp 302 398-8240
78 Pond View Ln Harrington (19952) ***(G-2908)***
Wilson Publications LLC 215 237-2344
331 N Red Lion Ter Bear (19701) ***(G-378)***
Wilson's Welding, Frankford *Also called Ronald P Wilson* ***(G-2384)***
Wilsons Auction Sales Inc 302 422-3454
10120 Dupont Blvd Lincoln (19960) ***(G-3874)***
Win From Wthin Xc Camp/Tatnall 302 494-5312
10 Courtney Rd Wilmington (19807) ***(G-13269)***
Windcrest Animal Hospital, Hockessin *Also called Hockessin Animal Hospital* ***(G-3047)***
Windcrest Animal Hospital 302 239-9464
3705 Lancaster Pike Wilmington (19805) ***(G-13270)***
Windham Enterprises Inc 302 678-5777
435 S Dupont Hwy Dover (19901) ***(G-2231)***
Windham Travel, Dover *Also called Windham Enterprises Inc* ***(G-2231)***
Windham Travel Inc 302 678-5777
435 S Dupont Hwy Dover (19901) ***(G-2232)***
Windsor Forest Town Homes 302 328-1260
101 Paisley Ln New Castle (19720) ***(G-5838)***
Windsor Place 302 239-3200
6677 Lancaster Pike Hockessin (19707) ***(G-3174)***
Windsors Flowers Plants Shrubs, Laurel *Also called Lakeside Greenhouses Inc* ***(G-3250)***
Windswept Enterprises 302 678-0805
251 N Dupont Hwy Dover (19901) ***(G-2233)***
Windswept Enterprising, Dover *Also called Windswept Enterprises* ***(G-2233)***
Windview Inc (PA) 610 345-9001
1482 Levels Rd Middletown (19709) ***(G-4288)***
Windy Inc 224 707-0442
8 The Grn Ste A Dover (19901) ***(G-2234)***
Windy Weather World Inc 650 204-7941
2093 Philadelphia Pike # 7 Claymont (19703) ***(G-823)***
Wing2wind Technology Inc 240 683-9787
31798 Carneros Ave Lewes (19958) ***(G-3828)***
Winifred Ellen Erbe 302 541-0889
38397 Hemlock Dr Frankford (19945) ***(G-2399)***
Winker Labs LLC 630 449-8130
2711 Centerville Rd # 400 Wilmington (19808) ***(G-13271)***
Winner Automotive Group, Wilmington *Also called Winner Group Management Inc* ***(G-13273)***
Winner Ford of Newark Inc 302 731-2415
303 E Cleveland Ave Newark (19711) ***(G-7710)***
Winner Group Inc 302 292-8200
1801 Ogletown Rd Newark (19711) ***(G-7711)***
Winner Group Inc (PA) 302 764-5900
911 N Tatnall St Wilmington (19801) ***(G-13272)***
Winner Group Management Inc (PA) 302 571-5200
520 S Walnut St Wilmington (19801) ***(G-13273)***
Winner Infiniti Inc 302 764-5900
1300 N Union St Wilmington (19806) ***(G-13274)***
Winner Porsche, Wilmington *Also called Winner Infiniti Inc* ***(G-13274)***
Winner Premier Collision Ctr 302 571-5200
520 S Walnut St Wilmington (19801) ***(G-13275)***
Winners Circle Inc 302 661-2100
1300 N Union St Wilmington (19806) ***(G-13276)***
Winterset Farms, Wilmington *Also called Carlisle Group* ***(G-9572)***
Winterthur Museum 302 740-9771
1520 N Rodney St Wilmington (19806) ***(G-13277)***
Winterthur Museum Garden & Lib 302 888-4600
5105 Kennett Pike Winterthur (19735) ***(G-13357)***
Wire Works 302 792-8305
302 Harvey Rd Claymont (19703) ***(G-824)***
Wiregateit LLC 302 538-1304
1 Latour Ln Newark (19702) ***(G-7712)***
Wireless Electronics Inc 302 652-1301
32 Germay Dr Ste C Wilmington (19804) ***(G-13278)***
Wireless Traders, Dover *Also called Shiv Baba LLC* ***(G-2077)***
Wirelisity Inc 213 816-1957
16192 Coastal Hwy Lewes (19958) ***(G-3829)***
Wise Power Systems Inc 302 351-4613
500 Philadelphia Pike # 100 Wilmington (19809) ***(G-13279)***
Wit Services LLC 302 995-2983
1174 Elderon Dr Wilmington (19808) ***(G-13280)***
Withyouwithme Inc 202 377-9743
1209 N Orange St Wilmington (19801) ***(G-13281)***
Witors America LLC 646 247-4836
2140 S Dupont Hwy Camden (19934) ***(G-606)***
WJC of Delaware LLC (PA) 302 323-9600
19 E Commons Blvd Ste 3 New Castle (19720) ***(G-5839)***
Wjwk 302 856-2567
20200 Dupont Blvd Georgetown (19947) ***(G-2706)***
Wm Systems Inc 302 450-4482
2711 Centerville Rd # 120 Wilmington (19808) ***(G-13282)***
Wm V Sipple & Son Inc 302 422-4214
300 S Rehoboth Blvd Milford (19963) ***(G-4611)***
Wmk Financing Inc 302 576-2697
300 Delaware Ave Wilmington (19801) ***(G-13283)***
Wna Infotech LLC 302 668-5977
2306 Porter Rd Bear (19701) ***(G-379)***
Wohlsen Construction Company 302 324-9900
501 Carr Rd Ste 100 Wilmington (19809) ***(G-13284)***
Wolanski & Sons Electric Inc 302 999-0838
22 Main Ave Wilmington (19804) ***(G-13285)***
Wolf Creek Surgeons PA 302 678-3627
103 Wolf Creek Blvd Ste 1 Dover (19901) ***(G-2235)***
Wolf Wood Works LLC 302 275-7227
4 Star Pine Cir Wilmington (19808) ***(G-13286)***
Wolfe Backhoe Service 302 737-2628
8 Springlake Dr Newark (19711) ***(G-7713)***
Wolfe Neck Treatment Plant 302 644-2761
36160 Wolfe Neck Rd Rehoboth Beach (19971) ***(G-8118)***
Wolfe Resources Ltd (PA) 302 798-6397
2087 Philadelphia Pike Claymont (19703) ***(G-825)***
Wolfs Elite Autos 302 999-9199
2130 W Newport Pike Wilmington (19804) ***(G-13287)***
Woloshin and Lynch Associates 302 449-2606
22 W Main St Middletown (19709) ***(G-4289)***
Woloshin and Lynch Associates (PA) 302 477-3200
3200 Concord Pike Wilmington (19803) ***(G-13288)***
Wolvesuff, Wilmington *Also called David Popovich LLC* ***(G-9971)***
Womble Bond Dickinson (us) LLP 302 252-4320
1313 N Market St Fl 12 Wilmington (19801) ***(G-13289)***
Women First LLC 302 368-3257
4745 Ogltn Stntn Rd # 106 Newark (19713) ***(G-7714)***
Women To Women Ob/Gyn Assoc PA 302 778-2229
1100 N Grant Ave Ste C Wilmington (19805) ***(G-13290)***
Women's Imaging Center, Rehoboth Beach *Also called Beebe Medical Center Inc* ***(G-7864)***
Women's Medical Center PA, Seaford *Also called Womens Medical Center Inc* ***(G-8442)***
Womens Civic Club Bethany Bch 302 539-7515
332 Sandpiper Dr Bethany Beach (19930) ***(G-439)***
Womens Fitness 302 239-5088
4811 Limestone Rd Wilmington (19808) ***(G-13291)***
Womens Health Ctr Christn Care 302 428-5810
501 W 14th St Wilmington (19801) ***(G-13292)***
Womens Imaging Center Delaware, Newark *Also called Delaware Womens Imaging LLC* ***(G-6422)***
Womens Imaging Center Delaware 302 738-9494
46 Omega Dr Ste J24 Newark (19713) ***(G-7715)***
Womens Medical Center Inc 302 629-5409
1301 Middleford Rd Seaford (19973) ***(G-8442)***
Womens Tennis C N C C 302 762-2078
507 Rockwood Rd Wilmington (19802) ***(G-13293)***
Womens Wellness Ctr & Med Spa 302 643-2500
1400 Peoples Plz Ste 301 Newark (19702) ***(G-7716)***
Wonder Years Kids Club 302 398-0563
17629 S Dupont Hwy Harrington (19952) ***(G-2909)***
Wood Creations By Bill 302 764-6497
26 Windsor Rd Wilmington (19809) ***(G-13294)***
Wood Expressions Incorporated 302 738-6189
2 Savoy Rd Newark (19702) ***(G-7717)***
Woodacres Apts, Claymont *Also called Woodacres Associates LP* ***(G-826)***
Woodacres Associates LP 302 792-0243
915 Cedartree Ln Claymont (19703) ***(G-826)***
Woodchuck Enterprises Inc 302 239-8336
1070 Sharpless Rd Hockessin (19707) ***(G-3175)***
Woodcrest Apartments, Dover *Also called Leo Ritter & Co* ***(G-1781)***
Woodin + Associates LLC 302 378-7300
111 Patriot Dr Ste D Middletown (19709) ***(G-4290)***
Woodland Apartments LP 302 994-9003
1201 Centre Rd Wilmington (19805) ***(G-13295)***
Woodland Ferry Beagle Club 302 856-2186
26858 Johnson Rd Georgetown (19947) ***(G-2707)***
Woodland Hill Preservation 302 764-6450
4 Denny Rd Wilmington (19809) ***(G-13296)***
Woodlawn Trustees Inc 302 655-6215
2201 W 11th St Wilmington (19805) ***(G-13297)***

Woodlyn Physical Therapy Inc 610 583-1133
1082 Old Churchmans Rd # 101 Newark (19713) *(G-7718)*
Woodmill Dental 302 998-8588
5185 W Woodmill Dr Ste 2 Wilmington (19808) *(G-13298)*
Woodmill Dental 302 998-8588
5185 W Woodmill Dr Ste 2 Wilmington (19808) *(G-13299)*
Woods Edge Apartments 302 762-8300
1204 Terra Hill Dr Apt 3b Wilmington (19809) *(G-13300)*
Woods General Contracting 302 856-4047
22403 Peterkins Rd Georgetown (19947) *(G-2708)*
Woods Hole Group Inc 302 222-6720
301 Cassidy Dr Ste D Dover (19901) *(G-2236)*
Woods Neighborhood Home, Newark *Also called Mosaic (G-7061)*
Woodward Enterprises Inc 302 378-2849
226 W Main St Middletown (19709) *(G-4291)*
Woodward Outdoor Equipment, Middletown *Also called Woodward Enterprises Inc (G-4291)*
Woodworks 302 995-0800
550 Copper Dr Wilmington (19804) *(G-13301)*
Woolard Properties 302 731-1944
42 Vansant Rd Newark (19711) *(G-7719)*
Wooley Bully Inc 302 542-3613
25605 Rogers Rd Millsboro (19966) *(G-4829)*
Worcester Golf Club Inc 610 222-0200
121 W Shore Dr Milton (19968) *(G-4981)*
Work First Casualty Company (PA) 302 477-1710
501 Silverside Rd Ste 39 Wilmington (19809) *(G-13302)*
Workaway Ventures Inc 843 608-9108
1521 Concord Pike Ste 303 Wilmington (19803) *(G-13303)*
Workmans Inc 302 934-9228
20135 Hardscrabble Rd Georgetown (19947) *(G-2709)*
Workplace Rebels LLC 917 771-8286
310 Alder Rd Dover (19904) *(G-2237)*
Workroom Enterprises LLC 417 621-5577
300 Delaware Ave Ste 210a Wilmington (19801) *(G-13304)*
Workweek Inc 423 708-4565
160 Greentree Dr Ste 101 Dover (19904) *(G-2238)*
World Class Products LLC 302 737-1441
375 Wedgewood Rd Newark (19711) *(G-7720)*
World Class Supply, Newark *Also called World Class Products LLC (G-7720)*
World Hospital Inc 609 254-3391
102 Sweethollow Dr Bear (19701) *(G-380)*
World Transmissions Inc 302 735-5535
2860 N Dupont Hwy Dover (19901) *(G-2239)*
World Wide Com Corporation 646 810-8624
40 E Main St Ste 614 Newark (19711) *(G-7721)*
World Wide Trading Brokers 302 368-7041
606 Benham Ct Newark (19711) *(G-7722)*
Worlds Best Massage Therapy 302 366-8777
412 Capitol Trl Newark (19711) *(G-7723)*
Worldwind Inc (PA) 302 762-0556
202 E 29th St Wilmington (19802) *(G-13305)*
Worms Quality Carpet Care 302 629-3114
21729 Maple Dr Seaford (19973) *(G-8443)*
Worthys Property MGT LLC 302 265-8301
8989 Herring Branch Rd Lincoln (19960) *(G-3875)*
Worthys Towing LLC 302 259-5265
9763 Blacksmith Shop Rd Greenwood (19950) *(G-2769)*
Wow Tech USA Ltd 613 828-6678
103 Foulk Rd Ste 200 Wilmington (19803) *(G-13306)*
Wowdesk Inc 310 871-5251
2035 Sunset Lake Rd Be Newark (19702) *(G-7724)*
Wrdx 302 395-9739
920 W Basin Rd Ste 400 New Castle (19720) *(G-5840)*
Wreck Masters Demo Derby 302 368-5544
221 Kline St Bear (19701) *(G-381)*
Wrenches 302 422-2690
1958 Bloomfield Dr Milford (19963) *(G-4612)*
Wright Bruce B DDS Office RES 302 227-8707
15 Venetian Dr Rehoboth Beach (19971) *(G-8119)*
Wright Choice Child Care 302 798-0758
3031 W Court Ave Claymont (19703) *(G-827)*
Wrights Lawn Care Inc 302 684-3058
14174 Union Street Ext Milton (19968) *(G-4982)*
Writingwizards Inc 650 382-1357
16192 Coastal Hwy Lewes (19958) *(G-3830)*
Ws One Investment Usa LLC 302 317-2610
298 Cherry Ln New Castle (19720) *(G-5841)*
Wsd Contracting Inc 302 492-8606
952 Myers Dr Hartly (19953) *(G-2944)*
WSFS, Wilmington *Also called Wilmington Savings Fund Soc (G-13245)*
Wsfs Bank, Claymont *Also called Wilmington Savings Fund Soc (G-822)*
Wsfs Credit, Newark *Also called Star States Leasing Corp (G-7484)*
Wsfs Financial Corporation (PA) 302 792-6000
500 Delaware Ave Wilmington (19801) *(G-13307)*
Wsfs Financial Corporation 302 346-2930
688 N Dupont Blvd Milford (19963) *(G-4613)*
Wsfs Investment Group Inc 302 573-3258
838 N Market St Wilmington (19801) *(G-13308)*
Wta, Newark *Also called Wilmington Trap Association (G-7708)*
Wta Inc 302 397-8142
510 Justison St Wilmington (19801) *(G-13309)*
Wuji Inc 815 274-6777
8 The Grn Ste A Dover (19901) *(G-2240)*
Wutap LLC 610 457-3559
6 Savoy Rd Newark (19702) *(G-7725)*
Wutopia Comics, Dover *Also called Wutopia Group US Ltd (G-2241)*
Wutopia Group US Ltd 302 488-0248
8 The Grn Ste 501 Dover (19901) *(G-2241)*
WW Grainger Inc 302 322-1840
117 Quigley Blvd New Castle (19720) *(G-5842)*
Wwc III 302 238-7778
34564 Pear Tree Rd Millsboro (19966) *(G-4830)*
Wwc III Trucking LLC 302 238-7778
34564 Pear Tree Rd Millsboro (19966) *(G-4831)*
Wwd Inc 302 994-4553
5998 Kirkwood Hwy Wilmington (19808) *(G-13310)*
Wxpz FM 101.3, Lincoln *Also called Samson Communications Inc (G-3867)*
Wyatt & Brown Inc 302 786-2793
15602 S Dupont Hwy Harrington (19952) *(G-2910)*
Wyatt Ridley Corp 302 998-8860
109 Kirkwood Sq Wilmington (19808) *(G-13311)*
Wyndham Group Inc 704 905-9750
2207 Concord Pike 696 Wilmington (19803) *(G-13312)*
Wyoming Millwork Co 302 684-3150
23000 Tracks End Ln Milton (19968) *(G-4983)*
Wyoming Millwork Co (PA) 302 697-8650
140 Vepco Blvd Camden (19934) *(G-607)*
X Leader LLC 800 345-2677
16192 Coastal Hwy Lewes (19958) *(G-3831)*
X Screen Graphix 302 422-4550
1514 Bay Rd Milford (19963) *(G-4614)*
X/L Mechanical Inc 203 233-3329
282 Apple Blossom Dr Camden (19934) *(G-608)*
Xanadu Concepts LLC 302 449-2677
104 W Main St Ste 4a Middletown (19709) *(G-4292)*
Xapix Inc (PA) 408 508-4324
1209 N Orange St Wilmington (19801) *(G-13313)*
Xavier Inc 302 655-1962
1315 N Union St Wilmington (19806) *(G-13314)*
Xbos 302 653-1800
456 W Glenwood Ave Ste D Smyrna (19977) *(G-8748)*
Xcmg Machinery Us LLC 786 796-1094
901 N Market St Ste 705 Wilmington (19801) *(G-13315)*
Xcs Corporation 302 514-0600
500 Water St Wilmington (19804) *(G-13316)*
Xcutivescom Inc 888 245-9996
3500 S Dupont Hwy Dover (19901) *(G-2242)*
Xenith Solutions LLC 703 963-3523
26211 Crosswinds Lndg Selbyville (19975) *(G-8556)*
Xenopia LLC 302 703-7050
16192 Coastal Hwy Lewes (19958) *(G-3832)*
Xerafy Inc 817 938-4197
3511 Silverside Rd Ste 10 Wilmington (19810) *(G-13317)*
Xergy Inc 302 629-5768
299 Cluckey Dr Ste A Harrington (19952) *(G-2911)*
Xerox Corporation 585 422-0272
2711 Centerville Rd # 400 Wilmington (19808) *(G-13318)*
Xerox Corporation 302 792-5100
200 Bellevue Pkwy Ste 300 Wilmington (19809) *(G-13319)*
Xgate Dental Inc 302 613-2142
913 N Market St Ste 200 Wilmington (19801) *(G-13320)*
Xinnix Ticketing Inc 302 778-1818
3 W 4th St Wilmington (19801) *(G-13321)*
Xonex Relocation LLC 302 323-9000
20 E Commons Blvd New Castle (19720) *(G-5843)*
Xpo Logistics Freight Inc 302 629-5228
104 Park Ave Seaford (19973) *(G-8444)*
Xrosswater USA LLC 917 310-1344
40 E Main St Ste 118 Newark (19711) *(G-7726)*
Xsc Ip LLC 305 384-6700
1201 N Market St Ste 2300 Wilmington (19801) *(G-13322)*
Xtium LLC 302 351-6177
2207 Concord Pike 242 Wilmington (19803) *(G-13323)*
Xxl Cloud Inc 302 298-0050
913 N Market St Ste 200 Wilmington (19801) *(G-13324)*
Xynomic Pharmaceuticals Inc 650 430-7561
3500 S Dupont Hwy Dover (19901) *(G-2243)*
Yacht Anything Ltd 302 226-3335
20913 Coastal Hwy Rehoboth Beach (19971) *(G-8120)*
Yanez & Associates, Wilmington *Also called Yanez & De Yanez MD PC (G-13325)*
Yanez & De Yanez MD PC 302 655-2991
2401 Penns Ave Ste 110 Wilmington (19806) *(G-13325)*
Yankee Clippers Hair Designer 302 422-2748
30 Nw 10th St Ste A Milford (19963) *(G-4615)*
Yardscape Inc 302 540-0311
303 Bald Eagle Way Middletown (19709) *(G-4293)*
Yasik, John F & Son, Wilmington *Also called John F Yasik Inc (G-11170)*
Yello Technologies Inc (PA) 954 802-6089
16192 Coastal Hwy Lewes (19958) *(G-3833)*

ALPHABETIC

(PA)=Parent Co (HQ)=Headquarters (DH)=Div Headquarters

2020 Harris Directory of Delaware Businesses

747

Yellow Light Publishing LLC ALPHABETIC SECTION

Yellow Light Publishing LLC 302 242-0990
25 Governors Ave Greenwood (19950) *(G-2770)*
Yellow Pine Associates Inc (PA) 302 994-9500
18 Yellow Pine Ct Wilmington (19808) *(G-13326)*
Yellow Trans 302 628-2805
26902 Bethel Concord Rd Seaford (19973) *(G-8445)*
Yellow Transportation, New Castle *Also called Yrc Inc (G-5844)*
Yencer Builders Inc 302 284-9989
925 Marshyhope Rd Felton (19943) *(G-2327)*
Yerkie Corp 302 653-1321
567 Seeneytown Rd Clayton (19938) *(G-875)*
Yerkie Enterprises, Clayton *Also called Yerkie Corp (G-875)*
Yes Hardsoft Solutions Inc 609 632-0397
351 Lenape Way Claymont (19703) *(G-828)*
Yesamerica Corporation 800 872-1548
651 N Broad St 205-908 Middletown (19709) *(G-4294)*
Yesco Sign Ltg Southeastern PA, New Castle *Also called Hes Sign Services LLC (G-5393)*
Yesliberia Inc 302 898-6338
10 W Christina Pl Newark (19702) *(G-7727)*
Yesllama LLC 714 270-8731
8 The Grn Ste A Dover (19901) *(G-2244)*
Yesteryars Phtgraphic Emporium, Rehoboth Beach *Also called Gramonoli Enterprises Inc (G-7953)*
Yhp Holdings LLC 302 636-5401
251 Little Falls Dr Wilmington (19808) *(G-13327)*
Yield Nexus LLC 308 380-3788
1679 S Dupont Hwy Ste 100 Dover (19901) *(G-2245)*
YMCA, Rehoboth Beach *Also called Young Mens Christian Associat (G-8121)*
YMCA, Wilmington *Also called Young Mens Christian Associat (G-13332)*
YMCA Central Branch LLC 302 571-6950
501 W 11th St Ste 100 Wilmington (19801) *(G-13328)*
YMCA of Delaware, Wilmington *Also called Young MNS Chrstn Assn Wlmngton (G-13334)*
Yoder Overhead Door Co., Delmar *Also called Yoder Overhead Door Company (G-1050)*
Yoder Overhead Door Company 302 875-0663
36318 Sussex Hwy Delmar (19940) *(G-1050)*
Yogo Factory 302 266-4506
2610 Kirkwood Hwy Newark (19711) *(G-7728)*
Yogurt City 302 292-8881
157 E Main St Newark (19711) *(G-7729)*
Yoko Trading 302 353-4506
4 Medill Ln Newark (19711) *(G-7730)*
Yokodanadotcom, Newark *Also called Yoko Trading (G-7730)*
Yorokobi Inc 323 591-3466
2035 Sunset Lake Rd B2 Newark (19702) *(G-7731)*
Yotta Games LLC 425 247-0756
1013 Centre Rd Ste 403s Wilmington (19805) *(G-13329)*
Young & McNelis 302 674-8822
300 S State St Dover (19901) *(G-2246)*
Young and Malmberg PA 302 672-5600
30 The Grn Dover (19901) *(G-2247)*
Young Cnway Strgatt Taylor LLP (PA) 302 571-6600
1000 N King St Wilmington (19801) *(G-13330)*
Young Mens Christian Associat 302 571-6935
1000 N Walnut St Wilmington (19801) *(G-13331)*
Young Mens Christian Associat 302 296-9622
20080 Church St Rehoboth Beach (19971) *(G-8121)*
Young Mens Christian Associat 302 571-6900
501 W 11th St Ste 100 Wilmington (19801) *(G-13332)*
Young Mens Christian Associat 302 472-9622
1000 N Walnut St Wilmington (19801) *(G-13333)*
Young MNS Chrstn Assn Wlmngton (PA) 302 221-9622
100 W 10th St Ste 1100 Wilmington (19801) *(G-13334)*
Young, Conaway & Associates, Wilmington *Also called Young Cnway Strgatt Taylor LLP (G-13330)*
Youngs Studio of Photography 302 736-2661
4 Carolee Dr Dover (19901) *(G-2248)*
Your Dentistry Today Inc 302 575-0100
3801 Kennett Pike E207 Wilmington (19807) *(G-13335)*
Your Personal Health Center, Dover *Also called Yph Consultants LLC (G-2250)*
Your Service, Wilmington *Also called Video Tech Center Inc (G-13080)*
Youshop Inc 302 526-0521
3500 S Dupont Hwy Dover (19901) *(G-2249)*
Youve Been Framed 302 366-8029
211 E Cobblefield Ct Newark (19713) *(G-7732)*
Youyu Home Technology LLC 347 796-4305
108 W 13th St Wilmington (19801) *(G-13336)*
Yph Consultants LLC 302 674-4766
700 Otis Dr Dover (19901) *(G-2250)*
Yrc Inc 302 322-5111
316 Churchmans Rd New Castle (19720) *(G-5844)*
Yvonne Hall Inc 302 677-1300
1671 S State St Dover (19901) *(G-2251)*
Yvonne Hall Realty, Dover *Also called Yvonne Hall Inc (G-2251)*
YWCA Delaware (PA) 302 655-0039
100 W 10th St Ste 515 Wilmington (19801) *(G-13337)*
YWCA Delaware 302 224-4060
153 E Chestnut Hill Rd # 102 Newark (19713) *(G-7733)*

Z Data Inc 302 566-5351
40 E Main St Ste 610 Newark (19711) *(G-7734)*
Z Data Inc 302 566-5351
40 E Main St 610 Newark (19711) *(G-7735)*
Zabel PLStc&recnstrctve Surgry 302 996-6400
550 Stanton Christiana Rd Newark (19713) *(G-7736)*
Zachary Chipman DMD PA 302 994-8696
5505 Kirkwood Hwy Wilmington (19808) *(G-13338)*
Zacros America Inc 302 368-7354
220 Lake Dr Ste 1 Newark (19702) *(G-7737)*
Zacros America Hedwin Division, Newark *Also called Zacros America Inc (G-7737)*
Zacs Inc 302 242-4653
31 Par Ct Magnolia (19962) *(G-3913)*
Zahn Incorporated 302 425-3700
110 S Poplar St Ste 200 Wilmington (19801) *(G-13339)*
Zarek Donohue LLC 302 543-5454
3521 Silverside Rd Ste 2j Wilmington (19810) *(G-13340)*
Zarraga & Zarraga Internl Medc 302 422-9140
219 S Walnut St Milford (19963) *(G-4616)*
Zavier J Decaire 302 658-0218
300 Delaware Ave Fl 8 Wilmington (19801) *(G-13341)*
Zax Mobile LLC 302 261-3232
152 W Main St Newark (19711) *(G-7738)*
Zdata Mt, Newark *Also called Z Data Inc (G-7734)*
Zeal Print Co LLC 302 407-5745
129 S Cleveland Ave Wilmington (19805) *(G-13342)*
Zeina Jeha Md MPH 302 503-4200
16295 Willow Creek Rd Lewes (19958) *(G-3834)*
Zen Health Technology Inc 551 194-2345
2035 Sunset Lake Rd B2 Newark (19702) *(G-7739)*
Zen Therapy & Body Work 302 252-1733
201 S Maryland Ave Wilmington (19804) *(G-13343)*
Zenbanx Holding Ltd 310 749-3101
650 Naamans Rd Ste 300 Claymont (19703) *(G-829)*
Zeneca Holdings Inc (HQ) 302 886-3000
1800 Concord Pike Wilmington (19897) *(G-13344)*
Zeneca Inc (HQ) 302 886-3000
1800 Concord Pike Wilmington (19897) *(G-13345)*
Zenith Home Corp 302 326-8200
400 Lukens Dr New Castle (19720) *(G-5845)*
Zenith Products 302 322-2190
499 Ships Landing Way New Castle (19720) *(G-5846)*
Zenker & Styer, Wilmington *Also called Zenker and Styer PA (G-13346)*
Zenker and Styer PA 302 475-9006
1202 Foulk Rd Ste 5 Wilmington (19803) *(G-13346)*
Zenpay Inc 650 336-6512
200 Belview Pkwy Ste 420 Wilmington (19808) *(G-13347)*
Zephyr Aluminum LLC 302 571-0585
50 Germay Dr Ste 2 Wilmington (19804) *(G-13348)*
Zerowait Corporation 302 996-9408
707 Kirkwood Hwy Wilmington (19805) *(G-13349)*
Zest-Index Investments LLC 503 908-2110
651 N Broad St Ste 205 Middletown (19709) *(G-4295)*
Zhc, New Castle *Also called Zenith Home Corp (G-5845)*
Zicherheit LLC 302 510-3718
38824 Wilson Ave Selbyville (19975) *(G-8557)*
Zieta Technologies LLC (PA) 302 252-5249
501 Silverside Rd Ste 39 Wilmington (19809) *(G-13350)*
Ziggy's Wood Floor Mechanics, Newark *Also called Ziggys Inc (G-7740)*
Ziggys Inc 302 453-1285
885 New London Rd Newark (19711) *(G-7740)*
Zilpa Ltd 800 504-5368
300 Delaware Ave Ste 210 Wilmington (19801) *(G-13351)*
Zimmer US Inc 617 272-0062
82 Brookwood Dr Camden Wyoming (19934) *(G-662)*
Zimny & Associates PA 302 325-6900
92 Reads Way Ste 104 New Castle (19720) *(G-5847)*
Zimple Inc 877 494-6753
1679 S Dupont Hwy Ste 10 Dover (19901) *(G-2252)*
Zinger Enterprizes Inc 302 381-6761
9224 Sharptown Rd Laurel (19956) *(G-3312)*
Zir LLC 203 524-1215
16192 Coastal Hwy Lewes (19958) *(G-3835)*
Ziras Technologies Inc 302 286-7303
260 Chapman Rd Ste 200 Newark (19702) *(G-7741)*
Ziv Investments Co 302 573-5080
4001 Kennett Pike Ste 316 Wilmington (19807) *(G-13352)*
Zizo Taxi Cab LLC 302 528-5663
69 Northfield Rd Newark (19713) *(G-7742)*
Zober Contracting Services Inc 302 270-3078
155 Old Mill Rd Dover (19901) *(G-2253)*
Zogo Inc 978 810-8895
2035 Sunset Lake Rd Newark (19702) *(G-7743)*
Zone Laser Tag Inc 302 730-8888
419 Webbs Ln Dover (19904) *(G-2254)*
Zone Systems Inc 302 730-8888
419 Webbs Ln Dover (19904) *(G-2255)*
Zuber & Associates Inc 302 478-1618
16 Burnett Dr Wilmington (19810) *(G-13353)*
Zucchini Brothers, Wilmington *Also called Trolley Laundry (G-12982)*

Zuhatrend LLC 302 883-2656
207 W Loockerman St Dover (19904) *(G-2256)*

Zumidian 302 219-3500
501 Silverside Rd Wilmington (19809) *(G-13354)*

Zumra Solutions LLC 302 504-4423
16192 Coastal Hwy Lewes (19958) *(G-3836)*

Zutz Risk Management 302 658-8000
300 Delaware Ave Ste 1600 Wilmington (19801) *(G-13355)*

Zwaanendael LLC 302 645-6466
142 2nd St Lewes (19958) *(G-3837)*

Zwd Products Corporation (HQ) 302 326-8200
400 Lukens Dr New Castle (19720) *(G-5848)*

Zzhouse Inc 302 354-3474
34 Blevins Dr Ste 1 New Castle (19720) *(G-5849)*

PRODUCT INDEX

• Product categories are listed in alphabetical order.

A

ABRASIVES
ACADEMIC TUTORING SVCS
ACADEMY
ACCELERATION INDICATORS & SYSTEM COMPONENTS: Aerospace
ACCIDENT INSURANCE CARRIERS
ACCOMMODATION LOCATING SVCS
ACCOUNTING SVCS, NEC
ACCOUNTING SVCS: Certified Public
ACUPUNCTURISTS' OFFICES
ADHESIVES
ADOPTION SVCS
ADULT DAYCARE CENTERS
ADVERTISING AGENCIES
ADVERTISING AGENCIES: Consultants
ADVERTISING DISPLAY PRDTS
ADVERTISING MATERIAL DISTRIBUTION
ADVERTISING REPRESENTATIVES: Electronic Media
ADVERTISING REPRESENTATIVES: Media
ADVERTISING SPECIALTIES, WHOLESALE
ADVERTISING SVCS, NEC
ADVERTISING SVCS: Billboards
ADVERTISING SVCS: Direct Mail
ADVERTISING SVCS: Display
ADVERTISING SVCS: Outdoor
ADVERTISING SVCS: Transit
ADVOCACY GROUP
AEROBIC DANCE & EXERCISE CLASSES
AGENTS, BROKERS & BUREAUS: Personal Service
AGENTS: Loan
AGRICULTURAL CREDIT INSTITUTIONS
AGRICULTURAL EQPT: Clippers, Animal, Hand Or Electric
AGRICULTURAL EQPT: Irrigation Eqpt, Self-Propelled
AGRICULTURAL EQPT: Tractors, Farm
AGRICULTURAL EQPT: Turf & Grounds Eqpt
AGRICULTURAL MACHINERY & EQPT REPAIR
AGRICULTURAL MACHINERY & EQPT: Wholesalers
AID TO FAMILIES WITH DEPENDENT CHILDREN OR AFDC
AIR CLEANING SYSTEMS
AIR CONDITIONERS: Motor Vehicle
AIR CONDITIONING & VENTILATION EQPT & SPLYS: Wholesales
AIR CONDITIONING EQPT
AIR CONDITIONING EQPT, WHOLE HOUSE: Wholesalers
AIR CONDITIONING REPAIR SVCS
AIR DUCT CLEANING SVCS
AIR PURIFICATION EQPT
AIRCRAFT & HEAVY EQPT REPAIR SVCS
AIRCRAFT ASSEMBLY PLANTS
AIRCRAFT CONTROL SYSTEMS:
AIRCRAFT ENGINES & ENGINE PARTS: Lubrication Systems
AIRCRAFT ENGINES & ENGINE PARTS: Research & Development, Mfr
AIRCRAFT ENGINES & ENGINE PARTS: Starting Vibrators
AIRCRAFT ENGINES & PARTS
AIRCRAFT EQPT & SPLYS WHOLESALERS
AIRCRAFT FLIGHT INSTRUMENT REPAIR SVCS
AIRCRAFT MAINTENANCE & REPAIR SVCS
AIRCRAFT PARTS & AUXILIARY EQPT: Aircraft Training Eqpt
AIRCRAFT PARTS & AUXILIARY EQPT: Assemblies, Fuselage
AIRCRAFT PARTS & AUXILIARY EQPT: Body Assemblies & Parts
AIRCRAFT PARTS & AUXILIARY EQPT: Refueling Eqpt, In Flight
AIRCRAFT PARTS & AUXILIARY EQPT: Research & Development, Mfr
AIRCRAFT PARTS & EQPT, NEC
AIRCRAFT PARTS WHOLESALERS
AIRCRAFT RADIO EQPT REPAIR SVCS
AIRCRAFT SEATS
AIRCRAFT SERVICING & REPAIRING
AIRCRAFT UPHOLSTERY REPAIR SVCS
AIRCRAFT: Airplanes, Fixed Or Rotary Wing
AIRLINE TRAINING
AIRPORT TERMINAL SVCS

AIRPORTS, FLYING FIELDS & SVCS
ALARMS: Fire
ALCOHOL TREATMENT CLINIC, OUTPATIENT
ALCOHOLISM COUNSELING, NONTREATMENT
ALL-TERRAIN VEHICLE DEALERS
ALUMINUM PRDTS
AMATEUR THEATRICAL COMPANY
AMBULANCE SVCS
AMBULANCE SVCS: Air
AMBULATORY SURGICAL CENTERS
AMMUNITION: Small Arms
AMUSEMENT & REC SVCS: Baseball Club, Exc Pro & Semi-Pro
AMUSEMENT & RECREATION SVCS, NEC
AMUSEMENT & RECREATION SVCS: Agricultural Fair
AMUSEMENT & RECREATION SVCS: Art Gallery, Commercial
AMUSEMENT & RECREATION SVCS: Aviation Club, Membership
AMUSEMENT & RECREATION SVCS: Boating Club, Membership
AMUSEMENT & RECREATION SVCS: Card & Game Svcs
AMUSEMENT & RECREATION SVCS: Diving Instruction, Underwater
AMUSEMENT & RECREATION SVCS: Fishing Boat Operations, Party
AMUSEMENT & RECREATION SVCS: Gambling & Lottery Svcs
AMUSEMENT & RECREATION SVCS: Gambling, Coin Machines
AMUSEMENT & RECREATION SVCS: Game Parlor
AMUSEMENT & RECREATION SVCS: Golf Club, Membership
AMUSEMENT & RECREATION SVCS: Gun Club, Membership
AMUSEMENT & RECREATION SVCS: Ice Skating Rink
AMUSEMENT & RECREATION SVCS: Ice Sports
AMUSEMENT & RECREATION SVCS: Indoor Court Clubs
AMUSEMENT & RECREATION SVCS: Indoor Or Outdoor Court Clubs
AMUSEMENT & RECREATION SVCS: Instruction Schools, Camps
AMUSEMENT & RECREATION SVCS: Karate Instruction
AMUSEMENT & RECREATION SVCS: Lawn Bowling Club, Membership
AMUSEMENT & RECREATION SVCS: Lottery Tickets, Sales
AMUSEMENT & RECREATION SVCS: Massage Instruction
AMUSEMENT & RECREATION SVCS: Outdoor Field Clubs
AMUSEMENT & RECREATION SVCS: Outfitters, Recreation
AMUSEMENT & RECREATION SVCS: Physical Fitness Instruction
AMUSEMENT & RECREATION SVCS: Racquetball Club, Membership
AMUSEMENT & RECREATION SVCS: Recreation Center
AMUSEMENT & RECREATION SVCS: Recreation SVCS
AMUSEMENT & RECREATION SVCS: Scenic Railroads, Amusement
AMUSEMENT & RECREATION SVCS: School, Basketball Instruction
AMUSEMENT & RECREATION SVCS: Shooting Range
AMUSEMENT & RECREATION SVCS: Soccer Club, Exc Pro/Semi-Pro
AMUSEMENT & RECREATION SVCS: Swimming Club, Membership
AMUSEMENT & RECREATION SVCS: Tennis & Professionals
AMUSEMENT & RECREATION SVCS: Tennis Club, Membership
AMUSEMENT & RECREATION SVCS: Tennis Courts, Non-Member
AMUSEMENT & RECREATION SVCS: Tour & Guide
AMUSEMENT & RECREATION SVCS: Trampoline Operation
AMUSEMENT & RECREATION SVCS: Yoga Instruction
AMUSEMENT & RECREATION SVCS: Zoological Garden, Commercial
AMUSEMENT ARCADES
AMUSEMENT PARKS

AMUSEMENT/REC SVCS: Ticket Sales, Sporting Events, Contract
ANALYZERS: Moisture
ANALYZERS: Network
ANIMAL FEED & SUPPLEMENTS: Livestock & Poultry
ANIMAL FEED: Wholesalers
ANIMAL FOOD & SUPPLEMENTS: Chicken Feeds, Prepared
ANIMAL FOOD & SUPPLEMENTS: Feed Concentrates
ANIMAL FOOD & SUPPLEMENTS: Feed Premixes
ANIMAL FOOD & SUPPLEMENTS: Feed Supplements
ANIMAL FOOD & SUPPLEMENTS: Livestock
ANTIBIOTICS
ANTIPOVERTY BOARD
ANTIQUE & CLASSIC AUTOMOBILE RESTORATION
ANTIQUE FURNITURE RESTORATION & REPAIR
APARTMENT LOCATING SVCS
APPAREL DESIGNERS: Commercial
APPAREL FILLING MATERIALS: Cotton Waste, Kapok/Related Matl
APPLICATIONS SOFTWARE PROGRAMMING
APPRAISAL SVCS, EXC REAL ESTATE
AQUATIC WEED MAINTENANCE SVCS
ARBITRATION & CONCILIATION SVCS
ARCHEOLOGICAL EXPEDITIONS
ARCHITECTURAL SVCS
ARCHITECTURAL SVCS: Engineering
ARCHITECTURAL SVCS: Engineering
ARCHITECTURAL SVCS: House Designer
ARMATURES: Ind
ARMORED CAR SVCS
ARRESTERS & COILS: Lightning
ART DEALERS & GALLERIES
ART DESIGN SVCS
ART GALLERIES
ART GALLERY, NONCOMMERCIAL
ART GOODS, WHOLESALE
ART RELATED SVCS
ARTISTS' AGENTS & BROKERS
ARTISTS' EQPT
ARTS & CRAFTS SCHOOL
ASPHALT & ASPHALT PRDTS
ASPHALT COATINGS & SEALERS
ASSEMBLING & PACKAGING SVCS: Cosmetic Kits
ASSOCIATION FOR THE HANDICAPPED
ASSOCIATIONS: Bar
ASSOCIATIONS: Business
ASSOCIATIONS: Dentists'
ASSOCIATIONS: Fraternal
ASSOCIATIONS: Homeowners
ASSOCIATIONS: Manufacturers'
ASSOCIATIONS: Parent Teacher
ASSOCIATIONS: Real Estate Management
ASSOCIATIONS: Scientists'
ASSOCIATIONS: Trade
ATHLETIC CLUB & GYMNASIUMS, MEMBERSHIP
ATHLETIC ORGANIZATION
ATOMIZERS
AUCTION SVCS: Motor Vehicle
AUCTIONEERS: Fee Basis
AUDIO & VIDEO EQPT, EXC COMMERCIAL
AUDIO ELECTRONIC SYSTEMS
AUDIO-VISUAL PROGRAM PRODUCTION SVCS
AUTHORS' AGENTS & BROKERS
AUTO & HOME SUPPLY STORES: Auto & Truck Eqpt & Parts
AUTO & HOME SUPPLY STORES: Auto Air Cond Eqpt, Sell/Install
AUTO & HOME SUPPLY STORES: Automotive Access
AUTO & HOME SUPPLY STORES: Automotive parts
AUTO & HOME SUPPLY STORES: Batteries, Automotive & Truck
AUTO & HOME SUPPLY STORES: Trailer Hitches, Automotive
AUTO & HOME SUPPLY STORES: Truck Eqpt & Parts
AUTOMATED TELLER MACHINE NETWORK
AUTOMATIC REGULATING CONTROL: Building Svcs Monitoring, Auto
AUTOMOBILE FINANCE LEASING
AUTOMOBILE RECOVERY SVCS

PRODUCT INDEX

AUTOMOBILES & OTHER MOTOR VEHICLES WHOLESALERS
AUTOMOBILES: Midget, Power Driven
AUTOMOBILES: Off-Road, Exc Recreational Vehicles
AUTOMOBILES: Wholesalers
AUTOMOTIVE & TRUCK GENERAL REPAIR SVC
AUTOMOTIVE BATTERIES WHOLESALERS
AUTOMOTIVE BODY SHOP
AUTOMOTIVE BODY, PAINT & INTERIOR REPAIR & MAINTENANCE SVC
AUTOMOTIVE BRAKE REPAIR SHOPS
AUTOMOTIVE COLLISION SHOPS
AUTOMOTIVE CUSTOMIZING SVCS, NONFACTORY BASIS
AUTOMOTIVE DEALERS, NEC
AUTOMOTIVE GLASS REPLACEMENT SHOPS
AUTOMOTIVE LETTERING & PAINTING SVCS
AUTOMOTIVE PAINT SHOP
AUTOMOTIVE PARTS, ACCESS & SPLYS
AUTOMOTIVE PARTS: Plastic
AUTOMOTIVE PRDTS: Rubber
AUTOMOTIVE RADIATOR REPAIR SHOPS
AUTOMOTIVE REPAIR SHOPS: Brake Repair
AUTOMOTIVE REPAIR SHOPS: Diesel Engine Repair
AUTOMOTIVE REPAIR SHOPS: Electrical Svcs
AUTOMOTIVE REPAIR SHOPS: Engine Rebuilding
AUTOMOTIVE REPAIR SHOPS: Engine Repair
AUTOMOTIVE REPAIR SHOPS: Fuel System Repair
AUTOMOTIVE REPAIR SHOPS: Machine Shop
AUTOMOTIVE REPAIR SHOPS: Muffler Shop, Sale/Rpr/Installation
AUTOMOTIVE REPAIR SHOPS: Rebuilding & Retreading Tires
AUTOMOTIVE REPAIR SHOPS: Shock Absorber Replacement
AUTOMOTIVE REPAIR SHOPS: Tire Recapping
AUTOMOTIVE REPAIR SHOPS: Tire Repair Shop
AUTOMOTIVE REPAIR SHOPS: Trailer Repair
AUTOMOTIVE REPAIR SHOPS: Truck Engine Repair, Exc Indl
AUTOMOTIVE REPAIR SHOPS: Wheel Alignment
AUTOMOTIVE REPAIR SVC
AUTOMOTIVE SPLYS & PARTS, NEW, WHOLESALE: Brakes
AUTOMOTIVE SPLYS & PARTS, NEW, WHOLESALE: Radiators
AUTOMOTIVE SPLYS & PARTS, NEW, WHOLESALE: Tools & Eqpt
AUTOMOTIVE SPLYS & PARTS, NEW, WHOLESALE: Trailer Parts
AUTOMOTIVE SPLYS & PARTS, NEW, WHOLESALE: Wheels
AUTOMOTIVE SPLYS & PARTS, USED, RETAIL ONLY: Tires, Used
AUTOMOTIVE SPLYS & PARTS, USED, WHOL: Testing Eqpt, Elec
AUTOMOTIVE SPLYS & PARTS, USED, WHOL: Trailer Parts/Access
AUTOMOTIVE SPLYS & PARTS, USED, WHOLESALE
AUTOMOTIVE SPLYS & PARTS, USED, WHOLESALE: Access, NEC
AUTOMOTIVE SPLYS & PARTS, USED, WHOLESALE: Garage Svc Eqpt
AUTOMOTIVE SPLYS & PARTS, WHOLESALE, NEC
AUTOMOTIVE SPLYS, USED, WHOLESALE & RETAIL
AUTOMOTIVE SVCS
AUTOMOTIVE SVCS, EXC REP & CARWASHES: Do-It-Yourself Garages
AUTOMOTIVE SVCS, EXC REPAIR & CARWASHES: Customizing
AUTOMOTIVE SVCS, EXC REPAIR & CARWASHES: Glass Tinting
AUTOMOTIVE SVCS, EXC REPAIR & CARWASHES: Insp & Diagnostic
AUTOMOTIVE SVCS, EXC REPAIR & CARWASHES: Lubrication
AUTOMOTIVE SVCS, EXC REPAIR & CARWASHES: Maintenance
AUTOMOTIVE SVCS, EXC REPAIR & CARWASHES: Trailer Maintenance
AUTOMOTIVE SVCS, EXC REPAIR: Carwash, Automatic
AUTOMOTIVE SVCS, EXC REPAIR: Carwash, Self-Service
AUTOMOTIVE SVCS, EXC REPAIR: Washing & Polishing
AUTOMOTIVE SVCS, EXC RPR/CARWASHES: High Perf Auto Rpr/Svc
AUTOMOTIVE TOWING & WRECKING SVC
AUTOMOTIVE TOWING SVCS
AUTOMOTIVE TRANSMISSION REPAIR SVC
AUTOMOTIVE UPHOLSTERY SHOPS
AUTOMOTIVE WELDING SVCS
AUTOMOTIVE: Seating
AWNINGS & CANOPIES
AWNINGS & CANOPIES: Awnings, Fabric, From Purchased Matls

B

BACKHOES
BAGS & CONTAINERS: Textile, Exc Sleeping
BAGS: Grocers', Made From Purchased Materials
BAGS: Paper, Made From Purchased Materials
BAGS: Plastic
BAGS: Plastic, Made From Purchased Materials
BAGS: Tea, Fabric, Made From Purchased Materials
BAGS: Textile
BAIL BONDING SVCS
BAKERIES, COMMERCIAL: On Premises Baking Only
BAKERY PRDTS: Cakes, Bakery, Exc Frozen
BAKERY PRDTS: Cookies
BAKERY PRDTS: Cookies & crackers
BAKERY PRDTS: Wholesalers
BAKERY: Wholesale Or Wholesale & Retail Combined
BALLASTS: Lighting
BALLOON SHOPS
BALLOONS: Hot Air
BANKRUPTCY REFEREE
BANKS: Commercial, NEC
BANKS: Mortgage & Loan
BANKS: National Commercial
BANKS: Other Activities, NEC
BANKS: State Commercial
BANQUET HALL FACILITIES
BAR
BARBER SHOPS
BARS: Concrete Reinforcing, Fabricated Steel
BARTERING SVCS
BASES, BEVERAGE
BATHING SUIT STORES
BATHROOM FIXTURE REGLAZING SVCS
BATTERIES: Storage
BATTERIES: Wet
BATTERY CHARGERS
BATTERY CHARGERS: Storage, Motor & Engine Generator Type
BAUXITE MINING
BEARINGS: Roller & Parts
BEAUTY & BARBER SHOP EQPT
BEAUTY & BARBER SHOP EQPT & SPLYS WHOLESALERS
BEAUTY CULTURE SCHOOL
BEAUTY SALONS
BED & BREAKFAST INNS
BEDS & ACCESS STORES
BEDSPREADS & BED SETS, FROM PURCHASED MATERIALS
BEEKEEPERS' SPLYS: Honeycomb Foundations
BEER & ALE WHOLESALERS
BEER & ALE, WHOLESALE: Beer & Other Fermented Malt Liquors
BEER & ALE, WHOLESALE: Porter
BEER, WINE & LIQUOR STORES: Wine
BELTS: Conveyor, Made From Purchased Wire
BELTS: Drive
BEVERAGE BASES & SYRUPS
BEVERAGE POWDERS
BEVERAGE PRDTS: Malt, Barley
BEVERAGE, NONALCOHOLIC: Iced Tea/Fruit Drink, Bottled/Canned
BEVERAGES, ALCOHOLIC: Ale
BEVERAGES, ALCOHOLIC: Beer
BEVERAGES, ALCOHOLIC: Beer & Ale
BEVERAGES, ALCOHOLIC: Distilled Liquors
BEVERAGES, ALCOHOLIC: Rum
BEVERAGES, ALCOHOLIC: Wine Coolers
BEVERAGES, ALCOHOLIC: Wines
BEVERAGES, NONALCOHOLIC: Bottled & canned soft drinks
BEVERAGES, NONALCOHOLIC: Carbonated
BEVERAGES, NONALCOHOLIC: Carbonated, Canned & Bottled, Etc
BEVERAGES, NONALCOHOLIC: Soft Drinks, Canned & Bottled, Etc
BEVERAGES, WINE & DISTILLED ALCOHOLIC, WHOLESALE: Liquor
BEVERAGES, WINE & DISTILLED ALCOHOLIC, WHOLESALE: Wine
BEVERAGES, WINE/DISTILLED ALCOHOLIC, WHOL: Bttlg Wine/Liquor
BICYCLE ASSEMBLY SVCS
BICYCLE REPAIR SHOP
BICYCLE SHOPS
BICYCLES WHOLESALERS
BICYCLES, PARTS & ACCESS
BILLIARD & POOL PARLORS
BILLIARD EQPT & SPLYS WHOLESALERS
BILLING & BOOKKEEPING SVCS
BINDING SVC: Books & Manuals
BIOLOGICAL PRDTS: Exc Diagnostic
BIOLOGICAL PRDTS: Extracts
BIOLOGICAL PRDTS: Serums
BIOLOGICAL PRDTS: Vaccines & Immunizing
BIOLOGICAL PRDTS: Veterinary
BIRD PROOFING SVCS
BLADES: Knife
BLANKBOOKS: Albums, Record
BLANKETS: Horse
BLASTING SVC: Sand, Metal Parts
BLINDS & SHADES: Vertical
BLINDS : Window
BLOCKS & BRICKS: Concrete
BLOCKS: Landscape Or Retaining Wall, Concrete
BLOOD BANK
BLOOD RELATED HEALTH SVCS
BLOWERS & FANS
BLUEPRINTING SVCS
BOAT BUILDING & REPAIR
BOAT BUILDING & REPAIRING: Fiberglass
BOAT BUILDING & REPAIRING: Yachts
BOAT BUILDING & RPRG: Fishing, Small, Lobster, Crab, Oyster
BOAT DEALERS
BOAT DEALERS: Marine Splys & Eqpt
BOAT DEALERS: Motor
BOAT REPAIR SVCS
BOAT YARD: Boat yards, storage & incidental repair
BOILER & HEATING REPAIR SVCS
BOLTS: Metal
BOND & MORTGAGE COMPANIES
BOOK STORES
BOOK STORES: Comic
BOOKS, WHOLESALE
BOTTLED GAS DEALERS: Liquefied Petro, Dlvrd To Customers
BOTTLED GAS DEALERS: Propane
BOTTLES: Plastic
BOWLING CENTERS
BOWLING EQPT & SPLY STORES
BOXES & CRATES: Rectangular, Wood
BOXES & SHOOK: Nailed Wood
BOXES: Corrugated
BRICK, STONE & RELATED PRDTS WHOLESALERS
BRIDAL SHOPS
BROADCASTING STATIONS, RADIO: Contemporary Music
BROADCASTING STATIONS, RADIO: Country Music
BROADCASTING STATIONS, RADIO: Educational
BROADCASTING STATIONS, RADIO: Music Format
BROADCASTING STATIONS, RADIO: Sports
BROKERS & DEALERS: Mortgages, Buying & Selling
BROKERS & DEALERS: Securities
BROKERS & DEALERS: Security
BROKERS & DEALERS: Stock
BROKERS' SVCS
BROKERS, MARINE TRANSPORTATION
BROKERS: Business
BROKERS: Commodity Contracts
BROKERS: Food
BROKERS: Loan
BROKERS: Mortgage, Arranging For Loans
BROKERS: Printing
BROKERS: Security
BROOMS & BRUSHES: Household Or Indl
BUILDING & OFFICE CLEANING SVCS
BUILDING & STRUCTURAL WOOD MEMBERS
BUILDING CLEANING & MAINTENANCE SVCS
BUILDING CLEANING SVCS
BUILDING COMPONENTS: Structural Steel
BUILDING EXTERIOR CLEANING SVCS

PRODUCT INDEX

BUILDING INSPECTION SVCS
BUILDING MAINTENANCE SVCS, EXC REPAIRS
BUILDING PRDTS & MATERIALS DEALERS
BUILDING STONE, ARTIFICIAL: Concrete
BUILDINGS, PREFABRICATED: Wholesalers
BUILDINGS: Farm & Utility
BUILDINGS: Portable
BUILDINGS: Prefabricated, Metal
BUILDINGS: Prefabricated, Wood
BUILDINGS: Prefabricated, Wood
BULLION, PRECIOUS METAL, WHOLESALE
BURGLAR ALARM MAINTENANCE & MONITORING SVCS
BURIAL VAULTS: Concrete Or Precast Terrazzo
BUS CHARTER SVC: Local
BUS CHARTER SVC: Long-Distance
BUSINESS & SECRETARIAL SCHOOLS
BUSINESS ACTIVITIES: Non-Commercial Site
BUSINESS COLLEGE OR SCHOOLS
BUSINESS FORMS WHOLESALERS
BUSINESS FORMS: Printed, Manifold
BUSINESS FORMS: Strip, Manifold
BUSINESS MACHINE REPAIR, ELECTRIC
BUSINESS SUPPORT SVCS
BUSINESS TRAINING SVCS

C

CABINETS & CASES: Show, Display & Storage, Exc Wood
CABINETS: Bathroom Vanities, Wood
CABINETS: Entertainment Units, Household, Wood
CABINETS: Factory
CABINETS: Kitchen, Metal
CABINETS: Kitchen, Wood
CABINETS: Show, Display, Etc, Wood, Exc Refrigerated
CABLE & OTHER PAY TELEVISION DISTRIBUTION
CABLE & PAY TELEVISION SVCS: Direct Broadcast Satellite
CABLE TELEVISION
CABLE TELEVISION PRDTS
CABLE: Fiber
CABLE: Fiber Optic
CAGES: Wire
CAMERA & PHOTOGRAPHIC SPLYS STORES: Cameras
CAMERAS & RELATED EQPT: Photographic
CAMPGROUNDS
CAMPSITES
CANDLES
CANDY MAKING GOODS & SPLYS, WHOLESALE
CANDY, NUT & CONFECTIONERY STORE: Popcorn, Incl Caramel Corn
CANNED SPECIALTIES
CANS: Aluminum
CANS: Metal
CAR LOADING SVCS
CAR WASH EQPT
CAR WASHES
CARAFES: Plastic
CARBON PAPER & INKED RIBBONS
CARDIOVASCULAR SYSTEM DRUGS, EXC DIAGNOSTIC
CARDS: Greeting
CARDS: Identification
CARPET & RUG CLEANING & REPAIRING PLANTS
CARPET & UPHOLSTERY CLEANING SVCS
CARPET & UPHOLSTERY CLEANING SVCS: Carpet/Furniture, On Loc
CARPET & UPHOLSTERY CLEANING SVCS: On Customer Premises
CARPET DYEING & FINISHING
CARPETS, RUGS & FLOOR COVERING
CARPETS: Textile Fiber
CARRIAGES: Horse Drawn
CARRYING CASES, WHOLESALE
CASES: Carrying
CASINGS: Sheet Metal
CASTINGS GRINDING: For The Trade
CASTINGS: Commercial Investment, Ferrous
CATALOG & MAIL-ORDER HOUSES
CATALOG SALES
CATALYSTS: Chemical
CATERERS
CEMENT: Hydraulic
CEMETERIES
CEMETERIES: Real Estate Operation
CERAMIC FLOOR & WALL TILE WHOLESALERS
CESSPOOL CLEANING SVCS
CHAMBERS OF COMMERCE
CHASSIS: Motor Vehicle

CHECK CASHING SVCS
CHECK CLEARING SVCS
CHEMICAL ELEMENTS
CHEMICAL SPLYS FOR FOUNDRIES
CHEMICALS & ALLIED PRDTS WHOLESALERS, NEC
CHEMICALS & ALLIED PRDTS, WHOL: Gases, Compressed/Liquefied
CHEMICALS & ALLIED PRDTS, WHOLESALE: Alkalines & Chlorine
CHEMICALS & ALLIED PRDTS, WHOLESALE: Carbon Dioxide
CHEMICALS & ALLIED PRDTS, WHOLESALE: Chemical Additives
CHEMICALS & ALLIED PRDTS, WHOLESALE: Chemicals, Indl
CHEMICALS & ALLIED PRDTS, WHOLESALE: Chemicals, Indl & Heavy
CHEMICALS & ALLIED PRDTS, WHOLESALE: Compressed Gas
CHEMICALS & ALLIED PRDTS, WHOLESALE: Detergents
CHEMICALS & ALLIED PRDTS, WHOLESALE: Manmade Fibers
CHEMICALS & ALLIED PRDTS, WHOLESALE: Plastics Materials, NEC
CHEMICALS & ALLIED PRDTS, WHOLESALE: Plastics Prdts, NEC
CHEMICALS & ALLIED PRDTS, WHOLESALE: Polyurethane Prdts
CHEMICALS & ALLIED PRDTS, WHOLESALE: Resins
CHEMICALS & ALLIED PRDTS, WHOLESALE: Spec Clean/Sanitation
CHEMICALS, AGRICULTURE: Wholesalers
CHEMICALS: Agricultural
CHEMICALS: Alcohols
CHEMICALS: Ammonium Compounds, Exc Fertilizers, NEC
CHEMICALS: Boron Compounds, Not From Mines, NEC
CHEMICALS: High Purity Grade, Organic
CHEMICALS: High Purity, Refined From Technical Grade
CHEMICALS: Inorganic, NEC
CHEMICALS: Medicinal, Organic, Uncompounded, Bulk
CHEMICALS: NEC
CHEMICALS: Organic, NEC
CHEMICALS: Reagent Grade, Refined From Technical Grade
CHEMICALS: Water Treatment
CHICKS WHOLESALERS
CHILD & YOUTH SVCS, NEC
CHILD DAY CARE SVCS
CHILDBIRTH PREPARATION CLINIC
CHILDREN'S & INFANTS' CLOTHING STORES
CHILDREN'S AID SOCIETY
CHILDREN'S HOME
CHILDREN'S WEAR STORES
CHIMES: Electric
CHIMNEY CLEANING SVCS
CHIROPRACTORS' OFFICES
CHLORINE
CHOCOLATE, EXC CANDY FROM BEANS: Chips, Powder, Block, Syrup
CHOCOLATE, EXC CANDY FROM PURCH CHOC: Chips, Powder, Block
CHROMATOGRAPHY EQPT
CHURCHES
CIGAR & CIGARETTE HOLDERS
CIGAR STORES
CIRCUIT BOARDS, PRINTED: Television & Radio
CIRCUITS: Electronic
CLAIMS ADJUSTING SVCS
CLAY: Ground Or Treated
CLEANING & DYEING PLANTS, EXC RUGS
CLEANING OR POLISHING PREPARATIONS, NEC
CLEANING PRDTS: Ammonia, Household
CLEANING PRDTS: Automobile Polish
CLEANING PRDTS: Disinfectants, Household Or Indl Plant
CLEANING PRDTS: Sanitation Preps, Disinfectants/Deodorants
CLEANING PRDTS: Specialty
CLEANING SVCS
CLEANING SVCS: Industrial Or Commercial
CLIPPERS: Fingernail & Toenail
CLOSET BOWLS: Vitreous China
CLOTHING & ACCESS, WOMEN, CHILD & INFANT, WHSLE: Sportswear
CLOTHING & ACCESS, WOMEN, CHILD/INFANT, WHOLESALE: Child

CLOTHING & ACCESS, WOMEN, CHILDREN & INFANT, WHOL: Access
CLOTHING & ACCESS, WOMEN, CHILDREN & INFANT, WHOL: Handbags
CLOTHING & ACCESS: Handicapped
CLOTHING & APPAREL STORES: Custom
CLOTHING & FURNISHINGS, MEN'S & BOYS', WHOLESALE: Gloves
CLOTHING & FURNISHINGS, MEN'S & BOYS', WHOLESALE: Hats
CLOTHING & FURNISHINGS, MEN'S & BOYS', WHOLESALE: Shirts
CLOTHING STORES, NEC
CLOTHING STORES: Caps & Gowns
CLOTHING STORES: Formal Wear
CLOTHING STORES: Leather
CLOTHING STORES: Lingerie & Corsets, Underwear
CLOTHING STORES: T-Shirts, Printed, Custom
CLOTHING: Access
CLOTHING: Athletic & Sportswear, Men's & Boys'
CLOTHING: Athletic & Sportswear, Women's & Girls'
CLOTHING: Band Uniforms
CLOTHING: Blouses, Women's & Girls'
CLOTHING: Children & Infants'
CLOTHING: Clergy Vestments
CLOTHING: Coats, Hunting & Vests, Men's
CLOTHING: Costumes
CLOTHING: Dresses
CLOTHING: Gowns & Dresses, Wedding
CLOTHING: Hospital, Men's
CLOTHING: Knit Underwear & Nightwear
CLOTHING: Mens & Boys Jackets, Sport, Suede, Leatherette
CLOTHING: Neckwear
CLOTHING: Outerwear, Knit
CLOTHING: Outerwear, Women's & Misses' NEC
CLOTHING: Shirts, Dress, Men's & Boys'
CLOTHING: Socks
CLOTHING: Suits & Skirts, Women's & Misses'
CLOTHING: Sweaters, Men's & Boys'
CLOTHING: Swimwear, Women's & Misses'
CLOTHING: T-Shirts & Tops, Knit
CLOTHING: Tuxedos, From Purchased Materials
CLOTHING: Underwear, Women's & Children's
CLOTHING: Uniforms, Ex Athletic, Women's, Misses' & Juniors'
CLOTHING: Uniforms, Men's & Boys'
CLOTHING: Uniforms, Military, Men/Youth, Purchased Materials
CLOTHING: Uniforms, Work
CLUTCHES, EXC VEHICULAR
COAL & OTHER MINERALS & ORES WHOLESALERS
COAL, MINERALS & ORES, WHOLESALE: Iron Ore
COATING SVC
COATING SVC: Hot Dip, Metals Or Formed Prdts
COATING SVC: Metals & Formed Prdts
COFFEE MAKERS: Electric
COIN OPERATED LAUNDRIES & DRYCLEANERS
COIN-OPERATED DRYCLEANING
COIN-OPERATED LAUNDRY
COINS, WHOLESALE
COLLECTION AGENCIES
COLLECTION AGENCY, EXC REAL ESTATE
COMBINED ELEMENTARY & SECONDARY SCHOOLS, PRIVATE
COMMERCIAL & LITERARY WRITINGS
COMMERCIAL & OFFICE BUILDINGS RENOVATION & REPAIR
COMMERCIAL ART & GRAPHIC DESIGN SVCS
COMMERCIAL ART & ILLUSTRATION SVCS
COMMERCIAL EQPT WHOLESALERS, NEC
COMMERCIAL EQPT, WHOLESALE: Restaurant, NEC
COMMERCIAL EQPT, WHOLESALE: Scales, Exc Laboratory
COMMERCIAL EQPT, WHOLESALE: Vending Machines, Coin-Operated
COMMERCIAL PHOTOGRAPHIC STUDIO
COMMERCIAL PRINTING & NEWSPAPER PUBLISHING COMBINED
COMMODITY CONTRACT TRADING COMPANIES
COMMODITY CONTRACTS BROKERS, DEALERS
COMMODITY INVESTORS
COMMON SAND MINING
COMMUNICATIONS CARRIER: Wired
COMMUNICATIONS EQPT & SYSTEMS, NEC
COMMUNICATIONS EQPT REPAIR & MAINTENANCE
COMMUNICATIONS EQPT WHOLESALERS

PRODUCT INDEX

COMMUNICATIONS SVCS
COMMUNICATIONS SVCS, NEC
COMMUNICATIONS SVCS: Cellular
COMMUNICATIONS SVCS: Data
COMMUNICATIONS SVCS: Internet Connectivity Svcs
COMMUNICATIONS SVCS: Internet Host Svcs
COMMUNICATIONS SVCS: Online Svc Providers
COMMUNICATIONS SVCS: Phone Cable, Svcs, Land Or Submarine
COMMUNICATIONS SVCS: Proprietary Online Svcs Networks
COMMUNICATIONS SVCS: Telephone, Broker
COMMUNICATIONS SVCS: Telephone, Data
COMMUNICATIONS SVCS: Telephone, Local
COMMUNICATIONS SVCS: Telephone, Local & Long Distance
COMMUNICATIONS SVCS: Telephone, Long Distance
COMMUNICATIONS SVCS: Telephone, Voice
COMMUNITY ACTION AGENCY
COMMUNITY CENTER
COMMUNITY CENTERS: Adult
COMMUNITY CENTERS: Youth
COMMUNITY DEVELOPMENT GROUPS
COMMUNITY SVCS EMPLOYMENT TRAINING PROGRAM
COMMUNITY THEATER PRODUCTION SVCS
COMPACT LASER DISCS: Prerecorded
COMPOST
COMPRESSORS, AIR CONDITIONING: Wholesalers
COMPRESSORS: Air & Gas
COMPRESSORS: Repairing
COMPRESSORS: Wholesalers
COMPUTER & COMPUTER SOFTWARE STORES
COMPUTER & COMPUTER SOFTWARE STORES: Peripheral Eqpt
COMPUTER & COMPUTER SOFTWARE STORES: Personal Computers
COMPUTER & COMPUTER SOFTWARE STORES: Software & Access
COMPUTER & COMPUTER SOFTWARE STORES: Software, Bus/Non-Game
COMPUTER & DATA PROCESSING EQPT REPAIR & MAINTENANCE
COMPUTER & OFFICE MACHINE MAINTENANCE & REPAIR
COMPUTER & SFTWR STORE: Modem, Monitor, Terminal/Disk Drive
COMPUTER FACILITIES MANAGEMENT SVCS
COMPUTER GRAPHICS SVCS
COMPUTER HARDWARE REQUIREMENTS ANALYSIS
COMPUTER PERIPHERAL EQPT REPAIR & MAINTENANCE
COMPUTER PERIPHERAL EQPT, NEC
COMPUTER PERIPHERAL EQPT, WHOLESALE
COMPUTER PLOTTERS
COMPUTER PROCESSING SVCS
COMPUTER PROGRAMMING SVCS
COMPUTER PROGRAMMING SVCS: Custom
COMPUTER RELATED MAINTENANCE SVCS
COMPUTER RELATED SVCS, NEC
COMPUTER SERVICE BUREAU
COMPUTER SOFTWARE DEVELOPMENT
COMPUTER SOFTWARE DEVELOPMENT & APPLICATIONS
COMPUTER SOFTWARE SYSTEMS ANALYSIS & DESIGN: Custom
COMPUTER SOFTWARE WRITERS
COMPUTER SOFTWARE WRITERS: Freelance
COMPUTER STORAGE DEVICES, NEC
COMPUTER SYSTEMS ANALYSIS & DESIGN
COMPUTER TERMINALS
COMPUTER-AIDED SYSTEM SVCS
COMPUTERS, NEC
COMPUTERS, NEC, WHOLESALE
COMPUTERS, PERIPH & SOFTWARE, WHLSE: Personal & Home Entrtn
COMPUTERS, PERIPHERALS & SOFTWARE, WHOLESALE: Printers
COMPUTERS, PERIPHERALS & SOFTWARE, WHOLESALE: Software
COMPUTERS: Personal
CONCERT MANAGEMENT SVCS
CONCRETE PLANTS
CONCRETE PRDTS
CONCRETE: Ready-Mixed
CONDENSERS: Heat Transfer Eqpt, Evaporative

CONFECTIONERY PRDTS WHOLESALERS
CONFECTIONS & CANDY
CONFINEMENT SURVEILLANCE SYS MAINTENANCE & MONITORING SVCS
CONNECTORS: Electrical
CONSERVATION PROGRAMS ADMINISTRATION SVCS
CONSTRUCTION & MINING MACHINERY WHOLESALERS
CONSTRUCTION EQPT REPAIR SVCS
CONSTRUCTION EQPT: Buckets, Excavating, Clamshell, Etc
CONSTRUCTION EQPT: Bulldozers
CONSTRUCTION EQPT: Line Markers, Self-Propelled
CONSTRUCTION EQPT: Rakes, Land Clearing, Mechanical
CONSTRUCTION EQPT: SCRAPERS, GRADERS, ROLLERS & SIMILAR EQPT
CONSTRUCTION EQPT: Tractors
CONSTRUCTION EQPT: Wrecker Hoists, Automobile
CONSTRUCTION MATERIALS, WHOLESALE: Air Ducts, Sheet Metal
CONSTRUCTION MATERIALS, WHOLESALE: Brick, Exc Refractory
CONSTRUCTION MATERIALS, WHOLESALE: Building Stone
CONSTRUCTION MATERIALS, WHOLESALE: Building Stone, Granite
CONSTRUCTION MATERIALS, WHOLESALE: Building Stone, Marble
CONSTRUCTION MATERIALS, WHOLESALE: Building, Exterior
CONSTRUCTION MATERIALS, WHOLESALE: Building, Interior
CONSTRUCTION MATERIALS, WHOLESALE: Ceiling Systems & Prdts
CONSTRUCTION MATERIALS, WHOLESALE: Cement
CONSTRUCTION MATERIALS, WHOLESALE: Ceramic, Exc Refractory
CONSTRUCTION MATERIALS, WHOLESALE: Concrete Mixtures
CONSTRUCTION MATERIALS, WHOLESALE: Door Frames
CONSTRUCTION MATERIALS, WHOLESALE: Doors, Garage
CONSTRUCTION MATERIALS, WHOLESALE: Gravel
CONSTRUCTION MATERIALS, WHOLESALE: Lime, Exc Agricultural
CONSTRUCTION MATERIALS, WHOLESALE: Limestone
CONSTRUCTION MATERIALS, WHOLESALE: Metal Buildings
CONSTRUCTION MATERIALS, WHOLESALE: Millwork
CONSTRUCTION MATERIALS, WHOLESALE: Pallets, Wood
CONSTRUCTION MATERIALS, WHOLESALE: Paving Materials
CONSTRUCTION MATERIALS, WHOLESALE: Plywood
CONSTRUCTION MATERIALS, WHOLESALE: Prefabricated Structures
CONSTRUCTION MATERIALS, WHOLESALE: Roof, Asphalt/Sheet Metal
CONSTRUCTION MATERIALS, WHOLESALE: Roofing & Siding Material
CONSTRUCTION MATERIALS, WHOLESALE: Tile & Clay Prdts
CONSTRUCTION MATERIALS, WHOLESALE: Wallboard
CONSTRUCTION MATERIALS, WHOLESALE: Windows
CONSTRUCTION MATLS, WHOL: Lumber, Rough, Dressed/Finished
CONSTRUCTION SITE PREPARATION SVCS
CONSTRUCTION: Agricultural Building
CONSTRUCTION: Apartment Building
CONSTRUCTION: Athletic & Recreation Facilities
CONSTRUCTION: Athletic & Recreation Facilities
CONSTRUCTION: Bridge
CONSTRUCTION: Chemical Facility
CONSTRUCTION: Commercial & Institutional Building
CONSTRUCTION: Commercial & Office Building, New
CONSTRUCTION: Commercial & Office Buildings, Prefabricated
CONSTRUCTION: Condominium
CONSTRUCTION: Dams, Waterways, Docks & Other Marine
CONSTRUCTION: Dock
CONSTRUCTION: Drainage System
CONSTRUCTION: Factory
CONSTRUCTION: Farm Building
CONSTRUCTION: Food Prdts Manufacturing or Packing Plant
CONSTRUCTION: Garage
CONSTRUCTION: Greenhouse
CONSTRUCTION: Harbor
CONSTRUCTION: Heavy

CONSTRUCTION: Heavy Highway & Street
CONSTRUCTION: Indl Building & Warehouse
CONSTRUCTION: Indl Building, Prefabricated
CONSTRUCTION: Indl Buildings, New, NEC
CONSTRUCTION: Indl Plant
CONSTRUCTION: Land Preparation
CONSTRUCTION: Marine
CONSTRUCTION: Multi-family Dwellings, New
CONSTRUCTION: Nonresidential Buildings, Custom
CONSTRUCTION: Oil & Gas Pipeline Construction
CONSTRUCTION: Parking Lot
CONSTRUCTION: Pipeline, NEC
CONSTRUCTION: Power & Communication Transmission Tower
CONSTRUCTION: Railroad & Subway
CONSTRUCTION: Refineries
CONSTRUCTION: Residential, Nec
CONSTRUCTION: School Building
CONSTRUCTION: Sewer Line
CONSTRUCTION: Sidewalk
CONSTRUCTION: Single-Family Housing
CONSTRUCTION: Single-family Housing, New
CONSTRUCTION: Single-family Housing, Prefabricated
CONSTRUCTION: Steel Buildings
CONSTRUCTION: Street Surfacing & Paving
CONSTRUCTION: Swimming Pools
CONSTRUCTION: Telephone & Communication Line
CONSTRUCTION: Utility Line
CONSTRUCTION: Warehouse
CONSTRUCTION: Waste Water & Sewage Treatment Plant
CONSTRUCTION: Water Main
CONSULTING SVC: Actuarial
CONSULTING SVC: Business, NEC
CONSULTING SVC: Computer
CONSULTING SVC: Data Processing
CONSULTING SVC: Educational
CONSULTING SVC: Engineering
CONSULTING SVC: Executive Placement & Search
CONSULTING SVC: Financial Management
CONSULTING SVC: Human Resource
CONSULTING SVC: Management
CONSULTING SVC: Marketing Management
CONSULTING SVC: Online Technology
CONSULTING SVC: Personnel Management
CONSULTING SVC: Sales Management
CONSULTING SVC: Telecommunications
CONSULTING SVCS, BUSINESS: Agricultural
CONSULTING SVCS, BUSINESS: City Planning
CONSULTING SVCS, BUSINESS: Communications
CONSULTING SVCS, BUSINESS: Energy Conservation
CONSULTING SVCS, BUSINESS: Environmental
CONSULTING SVCS, BUSINESS: Publishing
CONSULTING SVCS, BUSINESS: Safety Training Svcs
CONSULTING SVCS, BUSINESS: Sys Engnrg, Exc Computer/Prof
CONSULTING SVCS, BUSINESS: Systems Analysis & Engineering
CONSULTING SVCS, BUSINESS: Systems Analysis Or Design
CONSULTING SVCS, BUSINESS: Testing, Educational Or Personnel
CONSULTING SVCS, BUSINESS: Urban Planning & Consulting
CONSULTING SVCS: Oil
CONSULTING SVCS: Psychological
CONSULTING SVCS: Scientific
CONSUMER PURCHASING SVCS
CONTAINERS: Food & Beverage
CONTAINERS: Glass
CONTAINERS: Metal
CONTAINERS: Plastic
CONTRACT FOOD SVCS
CONTRACTOR: Framing
CONTRACTORS: Access Control System Eqpt
CONTRACTORS: Acoustical & Ceiling Work
CONTRACTORS: Antenna Installation
CONTRACTORS: Asbestos Removal & Encapsulation
CONTRACTORS: Asphalt
CONTRACTORS: Awning Installation
CONTRACTORS: Banking Machine Installation & Svc
CONTRACTORS: Bathtub Refinishing
CONTRACTORS: Boiler & Furnace
CONTRACTORS: Bricklaying
CONTRACTORS: Bridge Painting
CONTRACTORS: Building Board-up

PRODUCT INDEX

CONTRACTORS: Building Eqpt & Machinery Installation
CONTRACTORS: Building Front Installation, Metal
CONTRACTORS: Building Sign Installation & Mntnce
CONTRACTORS: Building Site Preparation
CONTRACTORS: Cable TV Installation
CONTRACTORS: Carpentry Work
CONTRACTORS: Carpentry, Cabinet & Finish Work
CONTRACTORS: Carpentry, Cabinet Building & Installation
CONTRACTORS: Carpentry, Finish & Trim Work
CONTRACTORS: Carpet Laying
CONTRACTORS: Central Vacuum Cleaning System Installation
CONTRACTORS: Ceramic Floor Tile Installation
CONTRACTORS: Chimney Construction & Maintenance
CONTRACTORS: Closed Circuit Television Installation
CONTRACTORS: Closet Organizers, Installation & Design
CONTRACTORS: Coating, Caulking & Weather, Water & Fire
CONTRACTORS: Commercial & Office Building
CONTRACTORS: Communications Svcs
CONTRACTORS: Computer Installation
CONTRACTORS: Concrete
CONTRACTORS: Concrete Block Masonry Laying
CONTRACTORS: Concrete Pumping
CONTRACTORS: Concrete Reinforcement Placing
CONTRACTORS: Construction Caulking
CONTRACTORS: Construction Site Cleanup
CONTRACTORS: Corrosion Control Installation
CONTRACTORS: Countertop Installation
CONTRACTORS: Curb & Sidewalk
CONTRACTORS: Decontamination Svcs
CONTRACTORS: Demolition, Building & Other Structures
CONTRACTORS: Demountable Partition Installation
CONTRACTORS: Driveway
CONTRACTORS: Drywall
CONTRACTORS: Earthmoving
CONTRACTORS: Electric Power Systems
CONTRACTORS: Electrical
CONTRACTORS: Electronic Controls Installation
CONTRACTORS: Energy Management Control
CONTRACTORS: Environmental Controls Installation
CONTRACTORS: Erection & Dismantling, Poured Concrete Forms
CONTRACTORS: Excavating
CONTRACTORS: Exterior Concrete Stucco
CONTRACTORS: Exterior Painting
CONTRACTORS: Fence Construction
CONTRACTORS: Fiber Optic Cable Installation
CONTRACTORS: Fire Detection & Burglar Alarm Systems
CONTRACTORS: Fire Sprinkler System Installation Svcs
CONTRACTORS: Floor Laying & Other Floor Work
CONTRACTORS: Flooring
CONTRACTORS: Food Svcs Eqpt Installation
CONTRACTORS: Foundation & Footing
CONTRACTORS: Foundation Building
CONTRACTORS: Garage Doors
CONTRACTORS: Gasoline Pump Installation
CONTRACTORS: General Electric
CONTRACTORS: Glass Tinting, Architectural & Automotive
CONTRACTORS: Glass, Glazing & Tinting
CONTRACTORS: Gutters & Downspouts
CONTRACTORS: Heating & Air Conditioning
CONTRACTORS: Heating Systems Repair & Maintenance Svc
CONTRACTORS: Highway & Street Construction, General
CONTRACTORS: Highway & Street Paving
CONTRACTORS: Home & Office Intrs Finish, Furnish/Remodel
CONTRACTORS: Hotel & Motel Renovation
CONTRACTORS: Hotel, Motel/Multi-Family Home Renovtn/Remodel
CONTRACTORS: Hydraulic Eqpt Installation & Svcs
CONTRACTORS: Hydronics Heating
CONTRACTORS: Indl Building Renovation, Remodeling & Repair
CONTRACTORS: Insulation Installation, Building
CONTRACTORS: Kitchen & Bathroom Remodeling
CONTRACTORS: Lighting Syst
CONTRACTORS: Machinery Installation
CONTRACTORS: Masonry & Stonework
CONTRACTORS: Mechanical
CONTRACTORS: Millwrights
CONTRACTORS: Mobile Home Site Set-Up
CONTRACTORS: Multi-Family Home Remodeling
CONTRACTORS: Office Furniture Installation
CONTRACTORS: Oil & Gas Wells Pumping Svcs

CONTRACTORS: Oil/Gas Well Construction, Rpr/Dismantling Svcs
CONTRACTORS: On-Site Mobile Home Repair Svcs
CONTRACTORS: On-Site Welding
CONTRACTORS: Ornamental Metal Work
CONTRACTORS: Paint & Wallpaper Stripping
CONTRACTORS: Painting & Wall Covering
CONTRACTORS: Painting, Commercial
CONTRACTORS: Painting, Commercial, Exterior
CONTRACTORS: Painting, Indl
CONTRACTORS: Painting, Residential
CONTRACTORS: Painting, Residential, Interior
CONTRACTORS: Patio & Deck Construction & Repair
CONTRACTORS: Pavement Marking
CONTRACTORS: Petroleum Storage Tanks, Pumping & Draining
CONTRACTORS: Pile Driving
CONTRACTORS: Pipe & Boiler Insulating
CONTRACTORS: Plaster & Drywall Work
CONTRACTORS: Plastering, Plain or Ornamental
CONTRACTORS: Plumbing
CONTRACTORS: Pollution Control Eqpt Installation
CONTRACTORS: Post Disaster Renovations
CONTRACTORS: Prefabricated Window & Door Installation
CONTRACTORS: Refractory or Acid Brick Masonry
CONTRACTORS: Refrigeration
CONTRACTORS: Roof Repair
CONTRACTORS: Roofing
CONTRACTORS: Roofing & Gutter Work
CONTRACTORS: Roustabout Svcs
CONTRACTORS: Safety & Security Eqpt
CONTRACTORS: Sandblasting Svc, Building Exteriors
CONTRACTORS: Screening, Window & Door
CONTRACTORS: Septic System
CONTRACTORS: Sheet Metal Work, NEC
CONTRACTORS: Sheet metal Work, Architectural
CONTRACTORS: Sidewalk
CONTRACTORS: Siding
CONTRACTORS: Single-Family Home Fire Damage Repair
CONTRACTORS: Single-family Home General Remodeling
CONTRACTORS: Skylight Installation
CONTRACTORS: Solar Energy Eqpt
CONTRACTORS: Sound Eqpt Installation
CONTRACTORS: Special Trades, NEC
CONTRACTORS: Specialized Public Building
CONTRACTORS: Spraying, Nonagricultural
CONTRACTORS: Sprinkler System
CONTRACTORS: Stone Masonry
CONTRACTORS: Store Fixture Installation
CONTRACTORS: Structural Iron Work, Structural
CONTRACTORS: Structural Steel Erection
CONTRACTORS: Stucco, Interior
CONTRACTORS: Svc Station Eqpt
CONTRACTORS: Svc Station Eqpt Installation, Maint & Repair
CONTRACTORS: Terrazzo Work
CONTRACTORS: Tile Installation, Ceramic
CONTRACTORS: Tuck Pointing & Restoration
CONTRACTORS: Underground Utilities
CONTRACTORS: Unit Paver Installation
CONTRACTORS: Wall Covering
CONTRACTORS: Warm Air Heating & Air Conditioning
CONTRACTORS: Water Intake Well Drilling Svc
CONTRACTORS: Water Well Drilling
CONTRACTORS: Water Well Servicing
CONTRACTORS: Waterproofing
CONTRACTORS: Well Bailing, Cleaning, Swabbing & Treating Svc
CONTRACTORS: Well Cleaning Svcs
CONTRACTORS: Window Treatment Installation
CONTRACTORS: Windows & Doors
CONTRACTORS: Wood Floor Installation & Refinishing
CONTRACTORS: Wrecking & Demolition
CONTROL EQPT: Buses Or Trucks, Electric
CONTROL EQPT: Electric
CONTROL PANELS: Electrical
CONTROLS & ACCESS: Indl, Electric
CONTROLS: Automatic Temperature
CONTROLS: Environmental
CONTROLS: Marine & Navy, Auxiliary
CONTROLS: Relay & Ind
CONVALESCENT HOME
CONVALESCENT HOMES
CONVENIENCE STORES
CONVENTION & TRADE SHOW SVCS

CONVERTERS: Data
CONVERTERS: Rotary, Electrical
CONVEYORS & CONVEYING EQPT
COOKING & FOOD WARMING EQPT: Commercial
COOKING & FOODWARMING EQPT: Coffee Brewing
COOLING TOWERS: Metal
COPPER ORES
COPY MACHINES WHOLESALERS
CORRECTIONAL INSTITUTIONS
COSMETIC PREPARATIONS
COSMETICS & TOILETRIES
COSMETICS WHOLESALERS
COSMETOLOGIST
COSMETOLOGY & BEAUTY SCHOOLS
COSMETOLOGY & PERSONAL HYGIENE SALONS
COSMETOLOGY SCHOOL
COSTUME JEWELRY & NOVELTIES: Apparel, Exc Precious Metals
COSTUME JEWELRY & NOVELTIES: Bracelets, Exc Precious Metals
COSTUME JEWELRY & NOVELTIES: Exc Semi & Precious
COUGH MEDICINES
COUNCIL FOR SOCIAL AGENCY
COUNTER & SINK TOPS
COUNTRY CLUBS
COURIER OR MESSENGER SVCS
COURIER SVCS, AIR: Letter Delivery, Private
COURIER SVCS, AIR: Package Delivery, Private
COURIER SVCS: Air
COURIER SVCS: Ground
COURIER SVCS: Package By Vehicle
COURIER SVCS: Parcel By Vehicle
COURT REPORTING SVCS
COURTS
COVERS: Canvas
COVERS: Slip Made Of Fabric, Plastic, Etc.
CRANE & AERIAL LIFT SVCS
CREATIVE SVCS: Advertisers, Exc Writers
CREDIT & OTHER FINANCIAL RESPONSIBILITY INSURANCE
CREDIT AGENCIES: Federal & Federally Sponsored
CREDIT AGENCIES: Federal Land Banks
CREDIT AGENCIES: Student Loan Marketing Association
CREDIT BUREAUS
CREDIT CARD SVCS
CREDIT INSTITUTIONS, SHORT-TERM BUS: Wrkg Capital Finance
CREDIT INSTITUTIONS, SHORT-TERM BUSINESS: Factoring Svcs
CREDIT INSTITUTIONS: Personal
CREDIT INSTITUTIONS: Short-Term Business
CREDIT INVESTIGATION SVCS
CREDIT UNIONS: Federally Chartered
CREDIT UNIONS: State Chartered
CREMATORIES
CRISIS CENTER
CRISIS INTERVENTION CENTERS
CRUCIBLES
CRUDE PETROLEUM & NATURAL GAS PRODUCTION
CRUDE PETROLEUM PRODUCTION
CULTURE MEDIA
CUTLERY, NEC
CUTOUTS: Distribution
CYCLIC CRUDES & INTERMEDIATES
CYLINDERS: Pressure
CYLINDERS: Pump

D

DAIRY PRDTS WHOLESALERS: Fresh
DAIRY PRDTS: Butter
DAIRY PRDTS: Dietary Supplements, Dairy & Non-Dairy Based
DAIRY PRDTS: Evaporated Milk
DAIRY PRDTS: Frozen Desserts & Novelties
DAIRY PRDTS: Ice Cream, Bulk
DAIRY PRDTS: Milk & Cream, Cultured & Flavored
DAIRY PRDTS: Milk, Fluid
DAIRY PRDTS: Milk, Processed, Pasteurized, Homogenized/Btld
DAIRY PRDTS: Processed Cheese
DAMAGED MERCHANDISE SALVAGING, SVCS ONLY
DANCE BAND
DANCE INSTRUCTOR & SCHOOL
DANCE INSTRUCTOR & SCHOOL SVCS
DATA PROCESSING & PREPARATION SVCS

PRODUCT INDEX

DATA PROCESSING SVCS
DATABASE INFORMATION RETRIEVAL SVCS
DATING SVCS
DEBT COUNSELING OR ADJUSTMENT SVCS: Individuals
DECORATIVE WOOD & WOODWORK
DEFENSE SYSTEMS & EQPT
DEHUMIDIFIERS: Electric
DELIVERY SVCS, BY VEHICLE
DENTAL EQPT
DENTAL EQPT & SPLYS
DENTAL EQPT & SPLYS WHOLESALERS
DENTAL EQPT & SPLYS: Enamels
DENTAL EQPT & SPLYS: Glue
DENTISTS' OFFICES & CLINICS
DEPARTMENT STORES
DEPARTMENT STORES: Army-Navy Goods
DEPARTMENT STORES: Country General
DEPILATORIES, COSMETIC
DEPOSIT INSURANCE
DERMATOLOGICALS
DESIGN SVCS, NEC
DESIGN SVCS: Commercial & Indl
DESIGN SVCS: Computer Integrated Systems
DETECTIVE & ARMORED CAR SERVICES
DETECTIVE AGENCY
DETOXIFICATION CENTERS, OUTPATIENT
DEVELOPING & LABORATORY SVCS: Motion Picture
DIAGNOSTIC SUBSTANCES
DIAGNOSTIC SUBSTANCES OR AGENTS: In Vitro
DIATOMACEOUS EARTH MINING SVCS
DIET & WEIGHT REDUCING CENTERS
DIODES: Light Emitting
DIRECT SELLING ESTABLISHMENTS: Telemarketing
DIRECT SELLING ESTABLSHS: Furnishings, Door-To-Door
DISC JOCKEYS
DISCS & TAPE: Optical, Blank
DISHES: Plastic, Exc Foam
DISINFECTING & DEODORIZING SVCS
DISINFECTING SVCS
DISKETTE DUPLICATING SVCS
DISPLAY LETTERING SVCS
DISTRIBUTORS: Motor Vehicle Engine
DIVING EQPT STORES
DOCUMENT EMBOSSING SVCS
DOCUMENT STORAGE SVCS
DOCUMENTATION CENTER
DOOR & WINDOW REPAIR SVCS
DOOR OPERATING SYSTEMS: Electric
DOORS & WINDOWS WHOLESALERS: All Materials
DOORS: Garage, Overhead, Metal
DOORS: Garage, Overhead, Wood
DRAFTING SPLYS WHOLESALERS
DRAFTING SVCS
DRAPERIES & CURTAINS
DRAPERIES & DRAPERY FABRICS, COTTON
DRAPERIES: Plastic & Textile, From Purchased Materials
DRAPERY & UPHOLSTERY STORES: Draperies
DRAWBACK SVCS: Customs
DRINKING PLACES: Alcoholic Beverages
DRINKING PLACES: Beer Garden
DRINKING WATER COOLERS WHOLESALERS: Mechanical
DRONES: Target, Used By Ships, Metal
DRUG CLINIC, OUTPATIENT
DRUG STORES
DRUGS & DRUG PROPRIETARIES, WHOLESALE
DRUGS & DRUG PROPRIETARIES, WHOLESALE: Animal Medicines
DRUGS & DRUG PROPRIETARIES, WHOLESALE: Patent Medicines
DRUGS & DRUG PROPRIETARIES, WHOLESALE: Pharmaceuticals
DRUGS & DRUG PROPRIETARIES, WHOLESALE: Vitamins & Minerals
DRUGS ACTING ON THE CENTRAL NERVOUS SYSTEM & SENSE ORGANS
DRYCLEANING & LAUNDRY SVCS: Commercial & Family
DRYCLEANING PLANTS
DRYCLEANING SVC: Collecting & Distributing Agency
DRYCLEANING SVC: Drapery & Curtain
DUCTS: Sheet Metal
DURABLE GOODS WHOLESALERS, NEC
DYES & PIGMENTS: Organic
DYES & TINTS: Household

E

EARTH SCIENCE SVCS
EATING PLACES
EDITORIAL SVCS
EDUCATIONAL SVCS
EDUCATIONAL SVCS, NONDEGREE GRANTING: Continuing Education
EGG WHOLESALERS
ELECTRIC & OTHER SERVICES COMBINED
ELECTRIC MOTOR REPAIR SVCS
ELECTRIC POWER DISTRIBUTION TO CONSUMERS
ELECTRIC POWER GENERATION: Fossil Fuel
ELECTRIC POWER, COGENERATED
ELECTRIC SERVICES
ELECTRIC SVCS, NEC: Power Generation
ELECTRICAL APPARATUS & EQPT WHOLESALERS
ELECTRICAL APPLIANCES, TELEVISIONS & RADIOS WHOLESALERS
ELECTRICAL CONSTRUCTION MATERIALS WHOLESALERS
ELECTRICAL CURRENT CARRYING WIRING DEVICES
ELECTRICAL DEVICE PARTS: Porcelain, Molded
ELECTRICAL EQPT & SPLYS
ELECTRICAL EQPT REPAIR & MAINTENANCE
ELECTRICAL EQPT REPAIR SVCS
ELECTRICAL EQPT: Automotive, NEC
ELECTRICAL GOODS, WHOL: Antennas, Receiving/Satellite Dishes
ELECTRICAL GOODS, WHOL: Vid Camera-Aud Recorders/Camcorders
ELECTRICAL GOODS, WHOLESALE: Air Conditioning Appliances
ELECTRICAL GOODS, WHOLESALE: Batteries, Storage, Indl
ELECTRICAL GOODS, WHOLESALE: Capacitors
ELECTRICAL GOODS, WHOLESALE: Closed Circuit Television Or TV
ELECTRICAL GOODS, WHOLESALE: Electrical Appliances, Major
ELECTRICAL GOODS, WHOLESALE: Electronic Parts
ELECTRICAL GOODS, WHOLESALE: Fans, Household
ELECTRICAL GOODS, WHOLESALE: Fire Alarm Systems
ELECTRICAL GOODS, WHOLESALE: Fittings & Construction Mat
ELECTRICAL GOODS, WHOLESALE: Generators
ELECTRICAL GOODS, WHOLESALE: Household Appliances, NEC
ELECTRICAL GOODS, WHOLESALE: Insulators
ELECTRICAL GOODS, WHOLESALE: Light Bulbs & Related Splys
ELECTRICAL GOODS, WHOLESALE: Lighting Fittings & Access
ELECTRICAL GOODS, WHOLESALE: Lighting Fixtures, Comm & Indl
ELECTRICAL GOODS, WHOLESALE: Mobile telephone Eqpt
ELECTRICAL GOODS, WHOLESALE: Motor Ctrls, Starters & Relays
ELECTRICAL GOODS, WHOLESALE: Motors
ELECTRICAL GOODS, WHOLESALE: Radio & TV Or TV Eqpt & Parts
ELECTRICAL GOODS, WHOLESALE: Security Control Eqpt & Systems
ELECTRICAL GOODS, WHOLESALE: Signaling, Eqpt
ELECTRICAL GOODS, WHOLESALE: Sound Eqpt
ELECTRICAL GOODS, WHOLESALE: Switches, Exc Electronic, NEC
ELECTRICAL GOODS, WHOLESALE: Telephone & Telegraphic Eqpt
ELECTRICAL GOODS, WHOLESALE: Video Eqpt
ELECTRICAL GOODS, WHOLESALE: Wire & Cable, Electronic
ELECTRICAL HOUSEHOLD APPLIANCE REPAIR
ELECTRICAL INDL APPARATUS, NEC
ELECTRICAL SPLYS
ELECTROMEDICAL EQPT
ELECTROMETALLURGICAL PRDTS
ELECTRONIC COMPONENTS
ELECTRONIC PARTS & EQPT WHOLESALERS
ELECTRONIC SHOPPING
ELEMENTARY & SECONDARY SCHOOLS, PRIVATE NEC
ELEMENTARY & SECONDARY SCHOOLS, PUBLIC
ELEMENTARY & SECONDARY SCHOOLS, SPECIAL EDUCATION
ELEMENTARY SCHOOLS, NEC
ELEMENTARY SCHOOLS, PRIVATE
ELEMENTARY SCHOOLS, PUBLIC
ELEVATOR: Grain, Storage Only
ELEVATORS & EQPT
ELEVATORS WHOLESALERS
ELEVATORS: Installation & Conversion
EMBLEMS: Embroidered
EMBROIDERING & ART NEEDLEWORK FOR THE TRADE
EMBROIDERING SVC
EMBROIDERY ADVERTISING SVCS
EMBROIDERY KITS
EMERGENCY & RELIEF SVCS
EMERGENCY ALARMS
EMERGENCY SHELTERS
EMPLOYEE LEASING SVCS
EMPLOYMENT AGENCY SVCS
EMPLOYMENT SVCS: Labor Contractors
EMPLOYMENT SVCS: Model Registry
EMPLOYMENT SVCS: Nurses' Registry
EMPLOYMENT SVCS: Registries
ENGINEERING HELP SVCS
ENGINEERING SVCS
ENGINEERING SVCS: Aviation Or Aeronautical
ENGINEERING SVCS: Building Construction
ENGINEERING SVCS: Chemical
ENGINEERING SVCS: Civil
ENGINEERING SVCS: Construction & Civil
ENGINEERING SVCS: Electrical Or Electronic
ENGINEERING SVCS: Energy conservation
ENGINEERING SVCS: Fire Protection
ENGINEERING SVCS: Heating & Ventilation
ENGINEERING SVCS: Industrial
ENGINEERING SVCS: Marine
ENGINEERING SVCS: Mechanical
ENGINEERING SVCS: Professional
ENGINEERING SVCS: Structural
ENGINES: Internal Combustion, NEC
ENGRAVING SVC, NEC
ENGRAVING SVCS: Tombstone
ENGRAVINGS: Plastic
ENTERTAINERS & ENTERTAINMENT GROUPS
ENTERTAINMENT PROMOTION SVCS
ENTERTAINMENT SVCS
ENVELOPES
ENVIRONMENTAL QUALITY PROGS ADMIN, GOVT: Recreational
EQUIPMENT: Rental & Leasing, NEC
ESTIMATING SVCS: Construction
ETHYLENE-PROPYLENE RUBBERS: EPDM Polymers
EXCAVATING MACHINERY & EQPT WHOLESALERS
EXECUTIVE OFFICES: Federal, State & Local
EXERCISE EQPT STORES
EXERCISE FACILITY
EXERCISE SALON
EXHAUST HOOD OR FAN CLEANING SVCS
EXHIBITORS, ITINERANT, MOTION PICTURE
EXPLOSIVES: Emulsions
EXTENDED CARE FACILITY
EXTERMINATING & FUMIGATING SVCS
EXTERMINATING PRDTS: Household Or Indl Use
EYEGLASSES

F

FABRIC STORES
FABRICATED METAL PRODUCTS, NEC
FABRICS: Alpacas, Cotton
FABRICS: Apparel & Outerwear, Broadwoven
FABRICS: Broadwoven, Synthetic Manmade Fiber & Silk
FABRICS: Canvas
FABRICS: Denims
FABRICS: Jean
FABRICS: Nonwoven
FABRICS: Nylon, Broadwoven
FABRICS: Shoe
FABRICS: Trimmings
FACILITIES SUPPORT SVCS
FACILITIES: Inspection & fixed
FACILITY RENTAL & PARTY PLANNING SVCS
FACSIMILE COMMUNICATION EQPT
FAMILY CLOTHING STORES
FAMILY COUNSELING SVCS
FAMILY OR MARRIAGE COUNSELING
FAMILY PLANNING CLINIC
FARM & GARDEN MACHINERY WHOLESALERS
FARM PRDTS, RAW MATERIAL, WHOLESALE: Tobacco & Tobacco Prdts

PRODUCT INDEX

FARM PRDTS, RAW MATERIALS, WHOLESALE: Cotton Merchants
FARM PRDTS, RAW MATERIALS, WHOLESALE: Farm Animals
FARM PRDTS, RAW MATERIALS, WHOLESALE: Oil Nuts, Kernel/Seed
FARM SPLY STORES
FARM SPLYS WHOLESALERS
FARM SPLYS, WHOLESALE: Equestrian Eqpt
FARM SPLYS, WHOLESALE: Feed
FARM SPLYS, WHOLESALE: Garden Splys
FARM SPLYS, WHOLESALE: Greenhouse Eqpt & Splys
FARM SPLYS, WHOLESALE: Hay
FASTENERS WHOLESALERS
FASTENERS: Metal
FASTENERS: Notions, Hooks & Eyes
FAUCETS & SPIGOTS: Metal & Plastic
FEDERAL SAVINGS & LOAN ASSOCIATIONS
FEDERAL SAVINGS BANKS
FELT: Polishing
FENCE POSTS: Iron & Steel
FENCING DEALERS
FENCING MATERIALS: Plastic
FERRIES: Operating Across Rivers Or Within Harbors
FERTILIZER, AGRICULTURAL: Wholesalers
FERTILIZERS: NEC
FERTILIZERS: Nitrogenous
FERTILIZERS: Phosphatic
FIBER & FIBER PRDTS: Protein
FIBER & FIBER PRDTS: Synthetic Cellulosic
FIBER OPTICS
FILLERS & SEALERS: Wood
FILM & SHEET: Unsuppported Plastic
FILM DEVELOPING & PRINTING SVCS
FILM PROCESSING & FINISHING LABORATORY
FILTERS
FILTERS & STRAINERS: Pipeline
FILTERS: Air Intake, Internal Combustion Engine, Exc Auto
FILTERS: Motor Vehicle
FILTRATION DEVICES: Electronic
FINANCIAL INVESTMENT ADVICE
FINANCIAL SVCS
FINISHING AGENTS: Textile
FINISHING SCHOOLS, CHARM & MODELING
FINISHING SVCS
FIRE ARMS, SMALL: Shotguns Or Shotgun Parts, 30 mm & Below
FIRE CONTROL OR BOMBING EQPT: Electronic
FIRE EXTINGUISHER SVC
FIRE EXTINGUISHERS, WHOLESALE
FIRE INSURANCE UNDERWRITERS' LABORATORIES
FIRE PROTECTION SVCS: Contracted
FIRE PROTECTION, GOVERNMENT: Local
FIREARMS & AMMUNITION, EXC SPORTING, WHOLESALE
FIREBRICK: Clay
FIREPLACE EQPT & ACCESS
FISH & SEAFOOD MARKETS
FISH & SEAFOOD WHOLESALERS
FITTINGS & ASSEMBLIES: Hose & Tube, Hydraulic Or Pneumatic
FITTINGS: Pipe
FLEA MARKET
FLIGHT TRAINING SCHOOLS
FLOOR COVERING STORES
FLOOR COVERING STORES: Carpets
FLOOR COVERING STORES: Floor Tile
FLOOR COVERING STORES: Rugs
FLOOR COVERING: Plastic
FLOOR COVERINGS WHOLESALERS
FLOOR WAXING SVCS
FLOORING: Hard Surface
FLOORING: Hardwood
FLORIST: Flowers, Fresh
FLORISTS
FLORISTS' ARTICLES: Pottery
FLOTATION COMPANIES
FLOTATION COMPANIES: Securities
FLOWERS & FLORISTS' SPLYS WHOLESALERS
FLOWERS, FRESH, WHOLESALE
FLUID POWER PUMPS & MOTORS
FOOD PRDTS, CANNED OR FRESH PACK: Vegetable Juices
FOOD PRDTS, CANNED: Barbecue Sauce
FOOD PRDTS, CANNED: Chili Sauce, Tomato
FOOD PRDTS, CANNED: Fruits
FOOD PRDTS, CANNED: Italian
FOOD PRDTS, CANNED: Mexican, NEC
FOOD PRDTS, CANNED: Mushrooms
FOOD PRDTS, CANNED: Vegetables
FOOD PRDTS, CONFECTIONERY, WHOLESALE: Snack Foods
FOOD PRDTS, FISH & SEAFOOD, WHOLESALE: Seafood
FOOD PRDTS, FISH & SEAFOOD: Codfish, Salted
FOOD PRDTS, FISH & SEAFOOD: Seafood, Frozen, Prepared
FOOD PRDTS, FROZEN: Dinners, Packaged
FOOD PRDTS, FROZEN: Ethnic Foods, NEC
FOOD PRDTS, FROZEN: Fruits & Vegetables
FOOD PRDTS, FROZEN: Fruits, Juices & Vegetables
FOOD PRDTS, FROZEN: NEC
FOOD PRDTS, FROZEN: Vegetables, Exc Potato Prdts
FOOD PRDTS, FRUITS & VEGETABLES, FRESH, WHOLESALE
FOOD PRDTS, FRUITS & VEGETABLES, FRESH, WHOLESALE: Fruits
FOOD PRDTS, FRUITS & VEGETABLES, FRESH, WHOLESALE: Vegetable
FOOD PRDTS, MEAT & MEAT PRDTS, WHOLESALE: Fresh
FOOD PRDTS, POULTRY, WHOLESALE: Poultry Prdts, NEC
FOOD PRDTS, WHOL: Canned Goods, Fruit, Veg, Seafood/Meats
FOOD PRDTS, WHOLESALE: Beverages, Exc Coffee & Tea
FOOD PRDTS, WHOLESALE: Chocolate
FOOD PRDTS, WHOLESALE: Coffee & Tea
FOOD PRDTS, WHOLESALE: Condiments
FOOD PRDTS, WHOLESALE: Cookies
FOOD PRDTS, WHOLESALE: Corn
FOOD PRDTS, WHOLESALE: Dog Food
FOOD PRDTS, WHOLESALE: Dried or Canned Foods
FOOD PRDTS, WHOLESALE: Flavorings & Fragrances
FOOD PRDTS, WHOLESALE: Grain Elevators
FOOD PRDTS, WHOLESALE: Grains
FOOD PRDTS, WHOLESALE: Health
FOOD PRDTS, WHOLESALE: Juices
FOOD PRDTS, WHOLESALE: Organic & Diet
FOOD PRDTS, WHOLESALE: Sandwiches
FOOD PRDTS, WHOLESALE: Sauces
FOOD PRDTS, WHOLESALE: Specialty
FOOD PRDTS, WHOLESALE: Spices & Seasonings
FOOD PRDTS, WHOLESALE: Sugar, Refined
FOOD PRDTS, WHOLESALE: Tea
FOOD PRDTS, WHOLESALE: Water, Mineral Or Spring, Bottled
FOOD PRDTS: Chicken, Processed, Frozen
FOOD PRDTS: Cocoa & Cocoa Prdts
FOOD PRDTS: Coffee
FOOD PRDTS: Dessert Mixes & Fillings
FOOD PRDTS: Flour
FOOD PRDTS: Flour & Other Grain Mill Products
FOOD PRDTS: Fruit Juices
FOOD PRDTS: Gelatin Dessert Preparations
FOOD PRDTS: Ice, Blocks
FOOD PRDTS: Nuts & Seeds
FOOD PRDTS: Olive Oil
FOOD PRDTS: Potato & Corn Chips & Similar Prdts
FOOD PRDTS: Poultry Sausage, Lunch Meats/Other Poultry Prdts
FOOD PRDTS: Poultry, Processed, NEC
FOOD PRDTS: Preparations
FOOD PRDTS: Seasonings & Spices
FOOD PRDTS: Syrup, Maple
FOOD PRDTS: Tea
FOOD PRDTS: Vegetables, Freeze-Dried
FOOD PRODUCTS MACHINERY
FOOD STORES: Convenience, Chain
FOOD STORES: Convenience, Independent
FOOD STORES: Cooperative
FOOTWEAR, WHOLESALE: Shoe Access
FOOTWEAR, WHOLESALE: Shoes
FORGINGS
FORGINGS: Bearing & Bearing Race, Nonferrous
FORGINGS: Gear & Chain
FOUNDRIES: Nonferrous
FOUNDRIES: Steel Investment
FRANCHISES, SELLING OR LICENSING
FREIGHT CAR LOADING & UNLOADING SVCS
FREIGHT FORWARDING ARRANGEMENTS
FREIGHT FORWARDING ARRANGEMENTS: Domestic
FREIGHT FORWARDING ARRANGEMENTS: Foreign
FREIGHT TRANSPORTATION ARRANGEMENTS
FRICTION MATERIAL, MADE FROM POWDERED METAL
FRUIT & VEGETABLE MARKETS
FRUITS & VEGETABLES WHOLESALERS: Fresh
FUEL ADDITIVES
FUEL DEALERS, NEC
FUEL OIL DEALERS
FUELS: Ethanol
FUELS: Jet
FUELS: Oil
FUND RAISING ORGANIZATION, NON-FEE BASIS
FUNDRAISING SVCS
FUNERAL DIRECTOR
FUNERAL HOME
FUNERAL HOMES & SVCS
FUNGICIDES OR HERBICIDES
FURNACES & OVENS: Indl
FURNITURE & CABINET STORES: Custom
FURNITURE REFINISHING SVCS
FURNITURE STORES
FURNITURE STORES: Office
FURNITURE STORES: Outdoor & Garden
FURNITURE UPHOLSTERY REPAIR SVCS
FURNITURE WHOLESALERS
FURNITURE, HOUSEHOLD: Wholesalers
FURNITURE, OFFICE: Wholesalers
FURNITURE, WHOLESALE: Racks
FURNITURE: Cabinets & Vanities, Medicine, Metal
FURNITURE: Chairs, Household Wood
FURNITURE: Foundations & Platforms
FURNITURE: Hospital
FURNITURE: Household, Metal
FURNITURE: Household, NEC
FURNITURE: Household, Wood
FURNITURE: Institutional, Exc Wood
FURNITURE: Juvenile, Wood
FURNITURE: Laboratory
FURNITURE: Mattresses, Box & Bedsprings
FURNITURE: Office, Exc Wood
FURNITURE: Office, Wood
FURNITURE: Picnic Tables Or Benches, Park
FURNITURE: Sleep
FURNITURE: Upholstered

G

GAMBLING MACHINE, OPERATIONS
GAMBLING: Lotteries
GAME MACHINES, COIN-OPERATED, WHOLESALE
GAMES & TOYS: Banks
GAMES & TOYS: Board Games, Children's & Adults'
GAMES & TOYS: Electronic
GAMES & TOYS: Game Machines, Exc Coin-Operated
GAMES & TOYS: Models, Boat & Ship, Toy & Hobby
GAMING: Slot Machines
GARAGE DOOR REPAIR SVCS
GARMENT: Pressing & cleaners' agents
GAS & OIL FIELD EXPLORATION SVCS
GAS & OIL FIELD SVCS, NEC
GAS & OTHER COMBINED SVCS
GAS APPLIANCE REPAIR SVCS
GAS FIELD MACHINERY & EQPT
GAS PRODUCTION & DISTRIBUTION
GAS STATIONS
GASES: Helium
GASES: Hydrogen
GASES: Indl
GASES: Nitrogen
GASES: Oxygen
GASKETS
GASKETS & SEALING DEVICES
GASOLINE FILLING STATIONS
GASOLINE WHOLESALERS
GEARS: Power Transmission, Exc Auto
GEMSTONE & INDL DIAMOND MINING SVCS
GENERAL & INDUSTRIAL LOAN INSTITUTIONS
GENERAL COUNSELING SVCS
GENERAL MERCHANDISE, NONDURABLE, WHOLESALE
GENERATOR REPAIR SVCS
GENERATORS: Automotive & Aircraft
GENERATORS: Electric
GENERATORS: Gas
GERIATRIC RESIDENTIAL CARE FACILITY
GERIATRIC SOCIAL SVCS
GIFT SHOP
GIFT, NOVELTY & SOUVENIR STORES: Party Favors
GIFTS & NOVELTIES: Wholesalers

PRODUCT INDEX

GLASS FABRICATORS
GLASS PRDTS, FROM PURCHASED GLASS: Insulating
GLASS PRDTS, FROM PURCHASED GLASS: Windshields
GLASS PRDTS, PRESSED OR BLOWN: Scientific Glassware
GLASS STORES
GLASS, AUTOMOTIVE: Wholesalers
GLASS: Fiber
GLASS: Leaded
GLASS: Pressed & Blown, NEC
GLASS: Stained
GLASSWARE WHOLESALERS
GLASSWARE: Laboratory
GLASSWARE: Laboratory & Medical
GLOBAL POSITIONING SYSTEMS & EQPT
GLOVES: Fabric
GLOVES: Leather, Work
GLOVES: Welders'
GOLF COURSES: Public
GOLF EQPT
GOLF GOODS & EQPT
GOVERNMENT, EXECUTIVE OFFICES: Mayors'
GOVERNMENT, GENERAL: Administration
GOVERNMENT, GENERAL: Administration, Local
GOVERNMENT, GENERAL: Administration, State
GRADING SVCS
GRANITE: Cut & Shaped
GRANITE: Dimension
GRANTMAKING FOUNDATIONS
GRAPHIC ARTS & RELATED DESIGN SVCS
GRASSES: Artificial & Preserved
GRAVEL MINING
GROCERIES WHOLESALERS, NEC
GROCERIES, GENERAL LINE WHOLESALERS
GROUP DAY CARE CENTER
GROUP FOSTER HOME
GROUP HOSPITALIZATION PLANS
GUARD PROTECTIVE SVCS
GUARD SVCS
GUIDED MISSILES & SPACE VEHICLES
GUTTERS: Sheet Metal
GYMNASTICS INSTRUCTION

H

HAIR DRESSING, FOR THE TRADE
HAIR STYLIST: Men
HAIRDRESSERS
HALFWAY GROUP HOME, PERSONS WITH SOCIAL OR PERSONAL PROBLEMS
HANDBAGS
HARDWARE
HARDWARE & EQPT: Stage, Exc Lighting
HARDWARE STORES
HARDWARE STORES: Chainsaws
HARDWARE STORES: Door Locks & Lock Sets
HARDWARE STORES: Tools
HARDWARE WHOLESALERS
HARDWARE, WHOLESALE: Bolts
HARDWARE, WHOLESALE: Builders', NEC
HARDWARE, WHOLESALE: Nozzles
HARDWARE, WHOLESALE: Nuts
HARDWARE, WHOLESALE: Power Tools & Access
HARDWARE, WHOLESALE: Security Devices, Locks
HARDWARE: Rubber
HARNESS HORSE RACING
HARNESSES, HALTERS, SADDLERY & STRAPS
HEAD START CENTER, EXC IN CONJUNCTION WITH SCHOOL
HEALTH & ALLIED SERVICES, NEC
HEALTH & WELFARE COUNCIL
HEALTH AIDS: Exercise Eqpt
HEALTH CLUBS
HEALTH INSURANCE CARRIERS
HEALTH MAINTENANCE ORGANIZATION: Insurance Only
HEALTH PRACTITIONERS' OFFICES, NEC
HEALTH SCREENING SVCS
HEALTH SYSTEMS AGENCY
HEARING AID REPAIR SVCS
HEARING TESTING SVCS
HEAT EXCHANGERS: After Or Inter Coolers Or Condensers, Etc
HEAT TREATING: Metal
HEATERS: Room & Wall, Including Radiators
HEATING & AIR CONDITIONING EQPT & SPLYS WHOLESALERS
HEAVY DISTILLATES

HEELS, BOOT OR SHOE: Rubber, Composition Or Fiber
HELICOPTERS
HELP SUPPLY SERVICES
HIGHWAY & STREET MAINTENANCE SVCS
HISTORICAL SOCIETY
HOBBY & COLLECTORS SVCS
HOBBY, TOY & GAME STORES: Chess, Backgammon/Other Drbl Games
HOLDING COMPANIES, NEC
HOLDING COMPANIES: Banks
HOLDING COMPANIES: Investment, Exc Banks
HOLDING COMPANIES: Personal, Exc Banks
HOLDING COMPANIES: Public Utility
HOME CENTER STORES
HOME ENTERTAINMENT EQPT: Electronic, NEC
HOME FOR THE DESTITUTE
HOME FOR THE MENTALLY HANDICAPPED
HOME FOR THE MENTALLY RETARDED, EXC SKILLED OR INTERMEDIATE
HOME FURNISHINGS WHOLESALERS
HOME HEALTH CARE SVCS
HOME IMPROVEMENT & RENOVATION CONTRACTOR AGENCY
HOMEBUILDERS & OTHER OPERATIVE BUILDERS
HOMEFURNISHING STORES: Cutlery
HOMEFURNISHING STORES: Fireplaces & Wood Burning Stoves
HOMEFURNISHING STORES: Lighting Fixtures
HOMEFURNISHING STORES: Window Furnishings
HOMEFURNISHINGS & SPLYS, WHOLESALE: Decorative
HOMEFURNISHINGS, WHOLESALE: Blankets
HOMEFURNISHINGS, WHOLESALE: Draperies
HOMEFURNISHINGS, WHOLESALE: Fireplace Eqpt & Access
HOMEFURNISHINGS, WHOLESALE: Kitchenware
HOMEFURNISHINGS, WHOLESALE: Sheets, Textile
HOMEMAKERS' SVCS
HOMES FOR THE ELDERLY
HOMES, MODULAR: Wooden
HONES
HOOKS: Gate
HORSES WHOLESALERS
HORSES, RACING
HORSESHOEING SVCS
HOSES & BELTING: Rubber & Plastic
HOSPITALS: AMA Approved Residency
HOSPITALS: Children's
HOSPITALS: Chronic Disease
HOSPITALS: Maternity
HOSPITALS: Medical & Surgical
HOSPITALS: Mental Retardation
HOSPITALS: Mental, Exc For The Mentally Retarded
HOSPITALS: Psychiatric
HOSPITALS: Rehabilitation, Alcoholism
HOSPITALS: Rehabilitation, Drug Addiction
HOSPITALS: Specialty, NEC
HOTEL & MOTEL RESERVATION SVCS
HOTEL: Franchised
HOTEL: YMCA/YMHA
HOTELS & MOTELS
HOUSE & BABYSITTING SVCS
HOUSEHOLD APPLIANCE REPAIR SVCS
HOUSEHOLD APPLIANCE STORES
HOUSEHOLD APPLIANCE STORES: Electric
HOUSEHOLD APPLIANCE STORES: Electric Household, Major
HOUSEHOLD APPLIANCE STORES: Garbage Disposals
HOUSEHOLD APPLIANCE STORES: Gas Appliances
HOUSEHOLD ARTICLES, EXC FURNITURE: Cut Stone
HOUSEHOLD FURNISHINGS, NEC
HOUSEKEEPING & MAID SVCS
HOUSES: Rooming & Boarding
HOUSEWARES, ELECTRIC: Heating Units, Electric Appliances
HOUSEWARES, ELECTRIC: Roasters
HOUSEWARES: Dishes, Plastic
HOUSING AUTHORITY OPERATOR
HUMAN RESOURCE, SOCIAL WORK & WELFARE ADMINISTRATION SVCS
HUMANE SOCIETIES
HYDRAULIC EQPT REPAIR SVC

I

ICE
ICE CREAM & ICES WHOLESALERS

INCINERATORS
INDL & PERSONAL SVC PAPER WHOLESALERS
INDL & PERSONAL SVC PAPER, WHOL: Bags, Paper/Disp Plastic
INDL & PERSONAL SVC PAPER, WHOL: Paper, Wrap/Coarse/Prdts
INDL & PERSONAL SVC PAPER, WHOLESALE: Boxes & Containers
INDL & PERSONAL SVC PAPER, WHOLESALE: Towels, Paper
INDL EQPT CLEANING SVCS
INDL EQPT SVCS
INDL MACHINERY & EQPT WHOLESALERS
INDL MACHINERY REPAIR & MAINTENANCE
INDL PROCESS INSTRUMENTS: Analyzers
INDL PROCESS INSTRUMENTS: Control
INDL PROCESS INSTRUMENTS: Digital Display, Process Variables
INDL PROCESS INSTRUMENTS: Indl Flow & Measuring
INDL PROCESS INSTRUMENTS: On-Stream Gas Or Liquid Analysis
INDL PROCESS INSTRUMENTS: Water Quality Monitoring/Cntrl Sys
INDL SPLYS WHOLESALERS
INDL SPLYS, WHOL: Fasteners, Incl Nuts, Bolts, Screws, Etc
INDL SPLYS, WHOLESALE: Abrasives
INDL SPLYS, WHOLESALE: Bearings
INDL SPLYS, WHOLESALE: Drums, New Or Reconditioned
INDL SPLYS, WHOLESALE: Electric Tools
INDL SPLYS, WHOLESALE: Filters, Indl
INDL SPLYS, WHOLESALE: Fittings
INDL SPLYS, WHOLESALE: Hydraulic & Pneumatic Pistons/Valves
INDL SPLYS, WHOLESALE: Power Transmission, Eqpt & Apparatus
INDL SPLYS, WHOLESALE: Rubber Goods, Mechanical
INDL SPLYS, WHOLESALE: Tools
INDL SPLYS, WHOLESALE: Tools, NEC
INDL SPLYS, WHOLESALE: Valves & Fittings
INDL TOOL GRINDING SVCS
INDUSTRIAL & COMMERCIAL EQPT INSPECTION SVCS
INFORMATION BUREAU SVCS
INFORMATION RETRIEVAL SERVICES
INFORMATION SVCS: Consumer
INGOTS: Steel
INK: Printing
INNS
INSECTICIDES
INSPECTION & TESTING SVCS
INSPECTION SVCS, TRANSPORTATION
INSTRUMENTS & METERS: Measuring, Electric
INSTRUMENTS, LAB: Spectroscopic/Optical Properties Measuring
INSTRUMENTS, LABORATORY: Differential Thermal Analysis
INSTRUMENTS, LABORATORY: Gas Analyzing
INSTRUMENTS, LABORATORY: Infrared Analytical
INSTRUMENTS, LABORATORY: Mass Spectrometers
INSTRUMENTS, MEASURING & CNTRL: Gauges, Auto, Computer
INSTRUMENTS, MEASURING & CNTRL: Testing, Abrasion, Etc
INSTRUMENTS, MEASURING & CNTRLG: Thermometers/Temp Sensors
INSTRUMENTS, MEASURING & CONTROLLING: Breathalyzers
INSTRUMENTS, MEASURING/CNTRL: Gauging, Ultrasonic Thickness
INSTRUMENTS, MEASURING/CNTRLG: Meters, Nuclear Rad Cnt Rate
INSTRUMENTS, SURGICAL & MEDICAL: Blood & Bone Work
INSTRUMENTS, SURGICAL & MEDICAL: Optometers
INSTRUMENTS, SURGICAL/MED: Microsurgical, Exc Electromedical
INSTRUMENTS: Analytical
INSTRUMENTS: Elec Lab Stds, Resist, Inductance/Capacitance
INSTRUMENTS: Flow, Indl Process
INSTRUMENTS: Indl Process Control
INSTRUMENTS: Laser, Scientific & Engineering
INSTRUMENTS: Measurement, Indl Process
INSTRUMENTS: Measuring & Controlling
INSTRUMENTS: Measuring Electricity
INSTRUMENTS: Medical & Surgical
INSTRUMENTS: Optical, Analytical

PRODUCT INDEX

INSTRUMENTS: Test, Digital, Electronic & Electrical Circuits
INSTRUMENTS: Test, Electrical, Engine
INSTRUMENTS: Thermal Property Measurement
INSULATION & ROOFING MATERIALS: Wood, Reconstituted
INSULATION MATERIALS WHOLESALERS
INSULATION: Fiberglass
INSULATORS, PORCELAIN: Electrical
INSURANCE AGENCIES & BROKERS
INSURANCE AGENTS, NEC
INSURANCE BROKERS, NEC
INSURANCE CARRIERS: Automobile
INSURANCE CARRIERS: Bank Deposit
INSURANCE CARRIERS: Dental
INSURANCE CARRIERS: Direct Accident & Health
INSURANCE CARRIERS: Disability
INSURANCE CARRIERS: Hospital & Medical
INSURANCE CARRIERS: Life
INSURANCE CARRIERS: Property & Casualty
INSURANCE CARRIERS: Title
INSURANCE CLAIM ADJUSTERS, NOT EMPLOYED BY INSURANCE COMPANY
INSURANCE CLAIM PROCESSING, EXC MEDICAL
INSURANCE EDUCATION SVCS
INSURANCE INFORMATION & CONSULTING SVCS
INSURANCE INFORMATION BUREAUS
INSURANCE: Agents, Brokers & Service
INTEGRATED CIRCUITS, SEMICONDUCTOR NETWORKS, ETC
INTERIOR DECORATING SVCS
INTERIOR DESIGN SVCS, NEC
INTERIOR DESIGNING SVCS
INTERIOR REPAIR SVCS
INTERMEDIATE CARE FACILITY
INVENTOR
INVENTORY COMPUTING SVCS
INVERTERS: Nonrotating Electrical
INVESTMENT ADVISORY SVCS
INVESTMENT BANKERS
INVESTMENT COUNSELORS
INVESTMENT FIRM: General Brokerage
INVESTMENT FUNDS, NEC
INVESTMENT FUNDS: Open-Ended
INVESTMENT OFFICES: Management, Closed-End
INVESTMENT OFFICES: Money Market Mutual
INVESTMENT OFFICES: Mutual Fund Sales, On Own Account
INVESTORS, NEC
INVESTORS: Real Estate, Exc Property Operators
IRON ORES
IRRIGATION EQPT WHOLESALERS
IRRIGATION SYSTEMS, NEC Water Distribution Or Sply Systems

J

JANITORIAL & CUSTODIAL SVCS
JANITORIAL EQPT & SPLYS WHOLESALERS
JEWELRY FINDINGS & LAPIDARY WORK
JEWELRY REPAIR SVCS
JEWELRY STORES
JEWELRY STORES: Precious Stones & Precious Metals
JEWELRY STORES: Watches
JEWELRY, WHOLESALE
JEWELRY: Decorative, Fashion & Costume
JEWELRY: Precious Metal
JIGS & FIXTURES
JOB COUNSELING
JOB PRINTING & NEWSPAPER PUBLISHING COMBINED
JOB TRAINING & VOCATIONAL REHABILITATION SVCS
JOB TRAINING SVCS
JOISTS: Long-Span Series, Open Web Steel
JUICE, FROZEN: Wholesalers
JUNIOR COLLEGE, NEC

K

KIDNEY DIALYSIS CENTERS
KINDERGARTEN
KITCHEN ARTICLES: Semivitreous Earthenware
KITCHEN CABINET STORES, EXC CUSTOM
KITCHEN CABINETS WHOLESALERS
KITCHEN TOOLS & UTENSILS WHOLESALERS
KITCHEN UTENSILS: Food Handling & Processing Prdts, Wood
KITCHEN UTENSILS: Wooden
KITCHENWARE: Plastic

L

LABOR RESOURCE SVCS
LABOR UNION
LABORATORIES, TESTING: Food
LABORATORIES, TESTING: Forensic
LABORATORIES, TESTING: Metallurgical
LABORATORIES, TESTING: Prdt Certification, Sfty/Performance
LABORATORIES, TESTING: Product Testing
LABORATORIES, TESTING: Soil Analysis
LABORATORIES, TESTING: Water
LABORATORIES: Biological
LABORATORIES: Biological Research
LABORATORIES: Biotechnology
LABORATORIES: Blood Analysis
LABORATORIES: Commercial Nonphysical Research
LABORATORIES: Dental
LABORATORIES: Dental & Medical X-Ray
LABORATORIES: Dental, Crown & Bridge Production
LABORATORIES: Electronic Research
LABORATORIES: Environmental Research
LABORATORIES: Medical
LABORATORIES: Medical Pathology
LABORATORIES: Noncommercial Research
LABORATORIES: Physical Research, Commercial
LABORATORIES: Testing
LABORATORIES: Testing
LABORATORY APPARATUS & FURNITURE
LABORATORY CHEMICALS: Organic
LABORATORY EQPT, EXC MEDICAL: Wholesalers
LABORATORY EQPT: Clinical Instruments Exc Medical
LABORATORY EQPT: Incubators
LABORATORY INSTRUMENT REPAIR SVCS
LAMINATED PLASTICS: Plate, Sheet, Rod & Tubes
LAMP & LIGHT BULBS & TUBES
LAND SUBDIVIDERS & DEVELOPERS: Commercial
LAND SUBDIVIDERS & DEVELOPERS: Residential
LAND SUBDIVISION & DEVELOPMENT
LASER SYSTEMS & EQPT
LAUNDRIES, EXC POWER & COIN-OPERATED
LAUNDRY & DRYCLEANER AGENTS
LAUNDRY & DRYCLEANING SVCS, EXC COIN-OPERATED: Garment Press
LAUNDRY & DRYCLEANING SVCS, EXC COIN-OPERATED: Pickup
LAUNDRY & DRYCLEANING SVCS, EXC COIN-OPERATED: Retail Agent
LAUNDRY & GARMENT SVCS, NEC
LAUNDRY & GARMENT SVCS, NEC: Fur Cleaning, Repairing/Storage
LAUNDRY & GARMENT SVCS, NEC: Garment Alteration & Repair
LAUNDRY & GARMENT SVCS, NEC: Garment Making, Alter & Repair
LAUNDRY & GARMENT SVCS: Tailor Shop, Exc Custom/Merchant
LAUNDRY SVC: Indl Eqpt
LAUNDRY SVCS: Indl
LAWN & GARDEN EQPT
LAWN & GARDEN EQPT STORES
LAWN MOWER REPAIR SHOP
LEASING & RENTAL SVCS: Computer Hardware, Exc Finance
LEASING & RENTAL SVCS: Cranes & Aerial Lift Eqpt
LEASING & RENTAL: Automobile With Driver
LEASING & RENTAL: Construction & Mining Eqpt
LEASING & RENTAL: Medical Machinery & Eqpt
LEASING & RENTAL: Mobile Home Sites
LEASING & RENTAL: Modular Office Trailers
LEASING & RENTAL: Other Real Estate Property
LEASING & RENTAL: Trucks, Without Drivers
LEASING & RENTAL: Utility Trailers & RV's
LEASING: Passenger Car
LEASING: Residential Buildings
LEATHER & CUT STOCK WHOLESALERS
LEATHER GOODS, EXC FOOTWEAR, GLOVES, LUGGAGE/BELTING, WHOL
LEATHER GOODS: Feed Bags, Horse
LEATHER GOODS: Garments
LEATHER GOODS: Harnesses Or Harness Parts
LEATHER GOODS: Wallets
LEATHER, LEATHER GOODS & FURS, WHOLESALE
LEATHER: Indl Prdts
LEATHER: Saddlery

LECTURE BUREAU
LEGAL AID SVCS
LEGAL OFFICES & SVCS
LEGAL PROCESS SERVERS
LEGAL SVCS: Administrative & Government Law
LEGAL SVCS: Bankruptcy Law
LEGAL SVCS: Criminal Law
LEGAL SVCS: Debt Collection Law
LEGAL SVCS: Divorce & Family Law
LEGAL SVCS: General Practice Attorney or Lawyer
LEGAL SVCS: General Practice Law Office
LEGAL SVCS: Immigration & Naturalization Law
LEGAL SVCS: Malpractice & Negligence Law
LEGAL SVCS: Real Estate Law
LEGAL SVCS: Securities Law
LEGAL SVCS: Specialized Law Offices, Attorney
LEGITIMATE LIVE THEATER PRODUCERS
LESSORS: Farm Land
LIABILITY INSURANCE
LIFE INSURANCE CARRIERS
LIFESAVING & SURVIVAL EQPT, EXC MEDICAL, WHOLESALE
LIGHTERS, CIGARETTE & CIGAR, WHOLESALE
LIGHTING EQPT: Outdoor
LIGHTING FIXTURES WHOLESALERS
LIGHTING FIXTURES, NEC
LIGHTING FIXTURES: Indl & Commercial
LIGHTING FIXTURES: Motor Vehicle
LIGHTING FIXTURES: Residential
LIGHTING FIXTURES: Residential, Electric
LIMOUSINE SVCS
LINEN SPLY SVC
LINEN SPLY SVC: Towel
LINEN SPLY SVC: Uniform
LINEN STORES
LININGS: Fabric, Apparel & Other, Exc Millinery
LIP BALMS
LIQUEFIED PETROLEUM GAS DEALERS
LIQUEFIED PETROLEUM GAS WHOLESALERS
LOAN CORRESPONDENTS
LOBBYING SVCS
LOCKS
LOCKSMITHS
LOGGING
LOGGING CAMPS & CONTRACTORS
LOOSELEAF BINDERS
LOTIONS OR CREAMS: Face
LOTIONS: SHAVING
LUBRICANTS: Corrosion Preventive
LUBRICATING OIL & GREASE WHOLESALERS
LUGGAGE & BRIEFCASES
LUGGAGE WHOLESALERS
LUMBER & BLDG MATLS DEALER, RET: Garage Doors, Sell/Install
LUMBER & BLDG MATRLS DEALERS, RET: Bath Fixtures, Eqpt/Sply
LUMBER & BLDG MTRLS DEALERS, RET: Greenhouse Kits, Prefab
LUMBER & BLDG MTRLS DEALERS, RET: Windows, Storm, Wood/Metal
LUMBER & BUILDING MATERIALS DEALER, RET: Door & Window Prdts
LUMBER & BUILDING MATERIALS DEALER, RET: Masonry Matls/Splys
LUMBER & BUILDING MATERIALS DEALERS, RET: Solar Heating Eqpt
LUMBER & BUILDING MATERIALS DEALERS, RETAIL: Brick
LUMBER & BUILDING MATERIALS DEALERS, RETAIL: Countertops
LUMBER & BUILDING MATERIALS DEALERS, RETAIL: Modular Homes
LUMBER & BUILDING MATERIALS DEALERS, RETAIL: Tile, Ceramic
LUMBER: Hardwood Dimension
LUMBER: Hardwood Dimension & Flooring Mills
LUMBER: Rails, Fence, Round Or Split
LUMBER: Treated
LUMBER: Veneer, Hardwood

M

MACHINE PARTS: Stamped Or Pressed Metal
MACHINE SHOPS
MACHINE TOOL ACCESS: Diamond Cutting, For Turning, Etc
MACHINE TOOL ACCESS: Pushers
MACHINE TOOL ACCESS: Tools & Access

PRODUCT INDEX

MACHINE TOOLS, METAL CUTTING: Tool Replacement & Rpr Parts
MACHINE TOOLS, METAL FORMING: Mechanical, Pneumatic Or Hyd
MACHINE TOOLS: Metal Cutting
MACHINE TOOLS: Metal Forming
MACHINERY & EQPT FINANCE LEASING
MACHINERY & EQPT, AGRICULTURAL, WHOL: Farm Eqpt Parts/Splys
MACHINERY & EQPT, AGRICULTURAL, WHOLESALE: Agricultural, NEC
MACHINERY & EQPT, AGRICULTURAL, WHOLESALE: Farm Implements
MACHINERY & EQPT, AGRICULTURAL, WHOLESALE: Garden, NEC
MACHINERY & EQPT, AGRICULTURAL, WHOLESALE: Landscaping Eqpt
MACHINERY & EQPT, AGRICULTURAL, WHOLESALE: Lawn & Garden
MACHINERY & EQPT, AGRICULTURAL, WHOLESALE: Poultry Eqpt
MACHINERY & EQPT, AGRICULTURAL, WHOLESALE: Tractors
MACHINERY & EQPT, INDL, WHOL: Brewery Prdts Mfrg, Commercial
MACHINERY & EQPT, INDL, WHOL: Controlling Instruments/Access
MACHINERY & EQPT, INDL, WHOLESALE: Chemical Process
MACHINERY & EQPT, INDL, WHOLESALE: Cranes
MACHINERY & EQPT, INDL, WHOLESALE: Drilling, Exc Bits
MACHINERY & EQPT, INDL, WHOLESALE: Engines & Parts, Diesel
MACHINERY & EQPT, INDL, WHOLESALE: Fans
MACHINERY & EQPT, INDL, WHOLESALE: Food Manufacturing
MACHINERY & EQPT, INDL, WHOLESALE: Food Product Manufacturng
MACHINERY & EQPT, INDL, WHOLESALE: Hydraulic Systems
MACHINERY & EQPT, INDL, WHOLESALE: Indl Machine Parts
MACHINERY & EQPT, INDL, WHOLESALE: Lift Trucks & Parts
MACHINERY & EQPT, INDL, WHOLESALE: Machine Tools & Access
MACHINERY & EQPT, INDL, WHOLESALE: Measure/Test, Electric
MACHINERY & EQPT, INDL, WHOLESALE: Metal Refining
MACHINERY & EQPT, INDL, WHOLESALE: Recycling
MACHINERY & EQPT, INDL, WHOLESALE: Robots
MACHINERY & EQPT, INDL, WHOLESALE: Safety Eqpt
MACHINERY & EQPT, INDL, WHOLESALE: Sawmill
MACHINERY & EQPT, INDL, WHOLESALE: Tractors, Indl
MACHINERY & EQPT, INDL, WHOLESALE: Water Pumps
MACHINERY & EQPT, INDL, WHOLESALE: Woodworking
MACHINERY & EQPT, WHOLESALE: Bailey Bridges
MACHINERY & EQPT, WHOLESALE: Construction, General
MACHINERY & EQPT, WHOLESALE: Contractors Materials
MACHINERY & EQPT, WHOLESALE: Masonry
MACHINERY & EQPT, WHOLESALE: Oil Field Eqpt
MACHINERY & EQPT: Farm
MACHINERY & EQPT: Gas Producers, Generators/Other Rltd Eqpt
MACHINERY & EQPT: Liquid Automation
MACHINERY BASES
MACHINERY, COMMERCIAL LAUNDRY: Washing, Incl Coin-Operated
MACHINERY, FOOD PRDTS: Food Processing, Smokers
MACHINERY, MAILING: Mailing
MACHINERY, METALWORKING: Rotary Slitters, Metalworking
MACHINERY, OFFICE: Stapling, Hand Or Power
MACHINERY, PRINTING TRADES: Printing Trade Parts & Attchts
MACHINERY/EQPT, AGRICULTURAL, WHOL: Wind Mach, Frost Protctn
MACHINERY/EQPT, INDL, WHOL: Cleaning, High Press, Sand/Steam
MACHINERY: Construction
MACHINERY: Cryogenic, Industrial
MACHINERY: Custom
MACHINERY: Engraving
MACHINERY: Industrial, NEC
MACHINERY: Metalworking
MACHINERY: Packaging
MACHINERY: Plastic Working
MACHINERY: Printing Presses
MACHINISTS' TOOLS: Precision
MAGAZINES, WHOLESALE
MAGNESITE MINING
MAIL-ORDER BOOK CLUBS
MAIL-ORDER HOUSE, NEC
MAIL-ORDER HOUSES: Computer Eqpt & Electronics
MAIL-ORDER HOUSES: Computer Software
MAIL-ORDER HOUSES: General Merchandise
MAILBOX RENTAL & RELATED SVCS
MAILING & MESSENGER SVCS
MAILING LIST: Compilers
MAILING SVCS, NEC
MANAGEMENT CONSULTING SVCS: Administrative
MANAGEMENT CONSULTING SVCS: Automation & Robotics
MANAGEMENT CONSULTING SVCS: Banking & Finance
MANAGEMENT CONSULTING SVCS: Business
MANAGEMENT CONSULTING SVCS: Business Planning & Organizing
MANAGEMENT CONSULTING SVCS: Compensation & Benefits Planning
MANAGEMENT CONSULTING SVCS: Construction Project
MANAGEMENT CONSULTING SVCS: Corporate Objectives & Policies
MANAGEMENT CONSULTING SVCS: Corporation Organizing
MANAGEMENT CONSULTING SVCS: Distribution Channels
MANAGEMENT CONSULTING SVCS: Food & Beverage
MANAGEMENT CONSULTING SVCS: Franchising
MANAGEMENT CONSULTING SVCS: General
MANAGEMENT CONSULTING SVCS: Hospital & Health
MANAGEMENT CONSULTING SVCS: Incentive Or Award Program
MANAGEMENT CONSULTING SVCS: Industrial & Labor
MANAGEMENT CONSULTING SVCS: Industry Specialist
MANAGEMENT CONSULTING SVCS: Information Systems
MANAGEMENT CONSULTING SVCS: Management Engineering
MANAGEMENT CONSULTING SVCS: Manufacturing
MANAGEMENT CONSULTING SVCS: Merchandising
MANAGEMENT CONSULTING SVCS: New Products & Svcs
MANAGEMENT CONSULTING SVCS: Programmed Instruction
MANAGEMENT CONSULTING SVCS: Public Utilities
MANAGEMENT CONSULTING SVCS: Quality Assurance
MANAGEMENT CONSULTING SVCS: Real Estate
MANAGEMENT CONSULTING SVCS: Restaurant & Food
MANAGEMENT CONSULTING SVCS: Retail Trade Consultant
MANAGEMENT CONSULTING SVCS: Training & Development
MANAGEMENT CONSULTING SVCS: Transportation
MANAGEMENT SERVICES
MANAGEMENT SVCS, FACILITIES SUPPORT: Environ Remediation
MANAGEMENT SVCS: Administrative
MANAGEMENT SVCS: Business
MANAGEMENT SVCS: Construction
MANAGEMENT SVCS: Financial, Business
MANAGEMENT SVCS: Hospital
MANAGEMENT SVCS: Hotel Or Motel
MANAGEMENT SVCS: Personnel
MANAGEMENT SVCS: Restaurant
MANGANESE ORES MINING
MANHOLES & COVERS: Metal
MANPOWER POOLS
MANUFACTURED & MOBILE HOME DEALERS
MANUFACTURING INDUSTRIES, NEC
MARBLE, BUILDING: Cut & Shaped
MARINAS
MARINE BASIN OPERATIONS
MARINE CARGO HANDLING SVCS
MARINE CARGO HANDLING SVCS: Waterfront Terminal Operations
MARINE ENGINE REPAIR SVCS
MARINE HARDWARE
MARINE SPLY DEALERS
MARINE SPLYS WHOLESALERS
MARKETS: Meat & fish
MARKING DEVICES
MARTIAL ARTS INSTRUCTION
MASSAGE PARLOR & STEAM BATH SVCS
MASSAGE PARLORS
MASSAGE THERAPIST
MATERIALS HANDLING EQPT WHOLESALERS
MATTRESS STORES
MEAL DELIVERY PROGRAMS
MEAT & FISH MARKETS: Freezer Provisioners, Meat
MEAT & FISH MARKETS: Seafood
MEAT & MEAT PRDTS WHOLESALERS
MEAT MARKETS
MEAT PRDTS: Boxed Beef, From Slaughtered Meat
MEAT PRDTS: Prepared Beef Prdts From Purchased Beef
MEAT PRDTS: Sausages, From Purchased Meat
MEAT PRDTS: Scrapple, From Purchased Meat
MEAT PROCESSED FROM PURCHASED CARCASSES
MEATS, PACKAGED FROZEN: Wholesalers
MEDICAL & HOSPITAL EQPT WHOLESALERS
MEDICAL & SURGICAL SPLYS: Abdominal Support, Braces/Trusses
MEDICAL & SURGICAL SPLYS: Crutches & Walkers
MEDICAL & SURGICAL SPLYS: Dressings, Surgical
MEDICAL & SURGICAL SPLYS: Limbs, Artificial
MEDICAL & SURGICAL SPLYS: Orthopedic Appliances
MEDICAL & SURGICAL SPLYS: Personal Safety Eqpt
MEDICAL & SURGICAL SPLYS: Prosthetic Appliances
MEDICAL & SURGICAL SPLYS: Supports, Abdominal, Ankle, Etc
MEDICAL & SURGICAL SPLYS: Welders' Hoods
MEDICAL CENTERS
MEDICAL EQPT: Laser Systems
MEDICAL EQPT: MRI/Magnetic Resonance Imaging Devs, Nuclear
MEDICAL FIELD ASSOCIATION
MEDICAL HELP SVCS
MEDICAL SUNDRIES: Rubber
MEDICAL SVCS ORGANIZATION
MEDICAL, DENTAL & HOSPITAL EQPT, WHOL: Dentists' Prof Splys
MEDICAL, DENTAL & HOSPITAL EQPT, WHOL: Hosptl Eqpt/Furniture
MEDICAL, DENTAL & HOSPITAL EQPT, WHOLESALE: Med Eqpt & Splys
MEDICAL, DENTAL & HOSPITAL EQPT, WHOLESALE: Medical Lab
MEDICAL, DENTAL & HOSPITAL EQPT, WHOLESALE: Safety
MEDICAL, DENTAL & HOSPITAL EQPT, WHOLESALE: Therapy
MEDITATION THERAPY
MELAMINE RESINS: Melamine-Formaldehyde
MEMBER ORGS, CIVIC, SOCIAL & FRATERNAL: Bars & Restaurants
MEMBERSHIP HOTELS
MEMBERSHIP ORGANIZATIONS, BUSINESS: Better Business Bureau
MEMBERSHIP ORGANIZATIONS, BUSINESS: Community Affairs & Svcs
MEMBERSHIP ORGANIZATIONS, BUSINESS: Contractors' Association
MEMBERSHIP ORGANIZATIONS, BUSINESS: Merchants' Association
MEMBERSHIP ORGANIZATIONS, CIVIC, SOCIAL & FRAT: Tenant Assoc
MEMBERSHIP ORGANIZATIONS, CIVIC, SOCIAL/FRAT: Boy Scout Org
MEMBERSHIP ORGANIZATIONS, CIVIC, SOCIAL/FRAT: Rec Assoc
MEMBERSHIP ORGANIZATIONS, CIVIC, SOCIAL/FRAT: Social Assoc
MEMBERSHIP ORGANIZATIONS, CIVIC, SOCIAL/FRAT: Youth Orgs
MEMBERSHIP ORGANIZATIONS, NEC: Amateur Sports Promotion
MEMBERSHIP ORGANIZATIONS, NEC: Art Council
MEMBERSHIP ORGANIZATIONS, NEC: Automobile Owner Association
MEMBERSHIP ORGANIZATIONS, NEC: Charitable
MEMBERSHIP ORGANIZATIONS, NEC: Christian Science Reading Rm
MEMBERSHIP ORGANIZATIONS, NEC: Food Co-Operative
MEMBERSHIP ORGANIZATIONS, NEC: Literary, Film Or Cultural
MEMBERSHIP ORGANIZATIONS, NEC: Personal Interest
MEMBERSHIP ORGANIZATIONS, NEC: Reading Room, Religious Mat
MEMBERSHIP ORGANIZATIONS, POLITICAL: Political Fundraising

PRODUCT INDEX

MEMBERSHIP ORGANIZATIONS, PROF: Education/Teacher Assoc
MEMBERSHIP ORGANIZATIONS, PROFESSIONAL: Health Association
MEMBERSHIP ORGANIZATIONS, REL: Churches, Temples & Shrines
MEMBERSHIP ORGANIZATIONS, RELIGIOUS: Baptist Church
MEMBERSHIP ORGANIZATIONS, RELIGIOUS: Catholic Church
MEMBERSHIP ORGANIZATIONS, RELIGIOUS: Episcopal Church
MEMBERSHIP ORGANIZATIONS, RELIGIOUS: Lutheran Church
MEMBERSHIP ORGANIZATIONS, RELIGIOUS: Methodist Church
MEMBERSHIP ORGANIZATIONS, RELIGIOUS: Nonchurch
MEMBERSHIP ORGANIZATIONS, RELIGIOUS: Presbyterian Church
MEMBERSHIP ORGANIZATIONS, RELIGIOUS: Religious Instruction
MEMBERSHIP ORGS, CIVIC, SOCIAL & FRAT: Dwelling-Related
MEMBERSHIP ORGS, CIVIC, SOCIAL & FRAT: Girl Scout
MEMBERSHIP ORGS, CIVIC, SOCIAL & FRATERNAL: Civic Assoc
MEMBERSHIP ORGS, CIVIC, SOCIAL & FRATERNAL: Condo Assoc
MEMBERSHIP ORGS, CIVIC, SOCIAL & FRATERNAL: Protection
MEMBERSHIP ORGS, CIVIC, SOCIAL & FRATERNAL: University Club
MEMBERSHIP ORGS, CIVIC, SOCIAL/FRAT: Educator's Assoc
MEMBERSHIP ORGS, LABOR UNIONS/SIMILAR: Employees' Assoc
MEMBERSHIP ORGS, LABOR UNIONS: Collective Bargaining
MEMBERSHIP SPORTS & RECREATION CLUBS
MEN'S & BOYS' CLOTHING STORES
MEN'S & BOYS' CLOTHING WHOLESALERS, NEC
MEN'S & BOYS' SPORTSWEAR WHOLESALERS
MEN'S & BOYS' UNDERWEAR WHOLESALERS
MEN'S & BOYS' WORK CLOTHING WHOLESALERS
MEN'S CLOTHING STORES: Everyday, Exc Suits & Sportswear
MENTAL HEALTH CLINIC, OUTPATIENT
MENTAL HEALTH PRACTITIONERS' OFFICES
MERCHANDISING MACHINE OPERATORS: Vending
METAL CUTTING SVCS
METAL DETECTORS
METAL FABRICATORS: Architechtural
METAL FABRICATORS: Plate
METAL FABRICATORS: Sheet
METAL FABRICATORS: Structural, Ship
METAL MINING SVCS
METAL SERVICE CENTERS & OFFICES
METAL SLITTING & SHEARING
METAL STAMPINGS: Ornamental
METALS SVC CENTERS & WHOLESALERS: Casting, Rough,Iron/Steel
METALS SVC CENTERS & WHOLESALERS: Piling, Iron & Steel
METALS SVC CENTERS & WHOLESALERS: Pipe & Tubing, Steel
METALS SVC CENTERS & WHOLESALERS: Sheets, Metal
METALS SVC CENTERS & WHOLESALERS: Steel
METALS SVC CTRS & WHOLESALERS: Aluminum Bars, Rods, Etc
METALWORK: Miscellaneous
METALWORK: Ornamental
METALWORKING MACHINERY WHOLESALERS
METERING DEVICES: Gas Meters, Domestic & Large Cap, Indl
METERING DEVICES: Water Quality Monitoring & Control Systems
MICROFILM SVCS
MICROWAVE COMPONENTS
MICROWAVE OVENS: Household
MILK, FLUID: Wholesalers
MILLWORK
MINE EXPLORATION SVCS: Nonmetallic Minerals
MINERAL WOOL
MINIATURE GOLF COURSES
MISC FIN INVEST ACT: Shares, RE, Entertain & Eqpt, Sales

MIXERS: Hot Metal
MIXTURES & BLOCKS: Asphalt Paving
MOBILE COMMUNICATIONS EQPT
MOBILE HOME DEALERS: Mobile Home Eqpt
MOBILE HOMES
MOBILE HOMES WHOLESALERS
MOBILE HOMES, EXC RECREATIONAL
MODELS: General, Exc Toy
MOLDED RUBBER PRDTS
MOLDINGS: Picture Frame
MOLDS: Indl
MONEY ORDER ISSUANCE SVCS
MONTESSORI CHILD DEVELOPMENT CENTER
MONUMENTS & GRAVE MARKERS, EXC TERRAZZO
MONUMENTS: Concrete
MONUMENTS: Cut Stone, Exc Finishing Or Lettering Only
MORTGAGE BANKERS
MOTEL
MOTEL: Franchised
MOTION PICTURE & VIDEO DISTRIBUTION
MOTION PICTURE & VIDEO PRODUCTION SVCS
MOTION PICTURE DISTRIBUTION
MOTION PICTURE DISTRIBUTION, EXCLUSIVE OF PRODUCTION
MOTOR REPAIR SVCS
MOTOR VEHICLE ASSEMBLY, COMPLETE: Autos, Incl Specialty
MOTOR VEHICLE ASSEMBLY, COMPLETE: Fire Department Vehicles
MOTOR VEHICLE DEALERS: Automobiles, New & Used
MOTOR VEHICLE DEALERS: Cars, Used Only
MOTOR VEHICLE DEALERS: Pickups, New & Used
MOTOR VEHICLE DEALERS: Trucks, Tractors/Trailers, New & Used
MOTOR VEHICLE PARTS & ACCESS: Acceleration Eqpt
MOTOR VEHICLE PARTS & ACCESS: Instrument Board Assemblies
MOTOR VEHICLE PARTS & ACCESS: Trailer Hitches
MOTOR VEHICLE PARTS & ACCESS: Transmissions
MOTOR VEHICLE RACING & DRIVER SVCS
MOTOR VEHICLE SPLYS & PARTS WHOLESALERS: New
MOTOR VEHICLE SPLYS & PARTS WHOLESALERS: Used
MOTOR VEHICLES & CAR BODIES
MOTOR VEHICLES, WHOLESALE: Fire Trucks
MOTOR VEHICLES, WHOLESALE: Recreational, All-Terrain
MOTOR VEHICLES, WHOLESALE: Trailers, Truck, New & Used
MOTOR VEHICLES, WHOLESALE: Truck bodies
MOTOR VEHICLES, WHOLESALE: Trucks, commercial
MOTORCYCLE DEALERS
MOTORCYCLE DEALERS: Bicycles, Motorized
MOTORCYCLE PARTS & ACCESS DEALERS
MOTORCYCLE REPAIR SHOPS
MOTORCYCLES & RELATED PARTS
MOTORS: Generators
MOVIE THEATERS, EXC DRIVE-IN
MOVING SVC & STORAGE: Local
MOVING SVC: Local
MOVING SVC: Long-Distance
MULTI-SVCS CENTER
MUSEUMS
MUSEUMS & ART GALLERIES
MUSIC ARRANGING & COMPOSING SVCS
MUSIC BROADCASTING SVCS
MUSIC DISTRIBUTION SYSTEM SVCS
MUSIC RECORDING PRODUCER
MUSIC VIDEO PRODUCTION SVCS
MUSICAL ENTERTAINERS
MUSICAL INSTRUMENT REPAIR
MUSICAL INSTRUMENTS & ACCESS: NEC
MUSICAL INSTRUMENTS & PARTS: Percussion
MUSICAL INSTRUMENTS & SPLYS STORES: Organs
MUSICAL INSTRUMENTS & SPLYS STORES: Pianos
MUSICAL INSTRUMENTS: Guitars & Parts, Electric & Acoustic

N

NAIL SALONS
NAILS WHOLESALERS
NATIONAL SECURITY, GOVERNMENT: Air Force
NATIONAL SECURITY, GOVERNMENT: Army
NATURAL GAS COMPRESSING SVC, On-Site
NATURAL GAS DISTRIBUTION TO CONSUMERS
NATURAL GAS TRANSMISSION & DISTRIBUTION
NATURAL PROPANE PRODUCTION

NATURAL RESOURCE PRESERVATION SVCS
NAUTICAL REPAIR SVCS
NAVIGATIONAL SYSTEMS & INSTRUMENTS
NEIGHBORHOOD DEVELOPMENT GROUP
NEW & USED,CAR DEALERS
NEWS SYNDICATES
NEWSPAPERS & PERIODICALS NEWS REPORTING SVCS
NEWSPAPERS, WHOLESALE
NONDURABLE GOODS WHOLESALERS, NEC
NOTARIES PUBLIC
NOVELTIES, DURABLE, WHOLESALE
NOZZLES & SPRINKLERS Lawn Hose
NUCLEAR DETECTORS: Solid State
NUCLEAR ELECTRIC POWER GENERATION
NURSERIES & LAWN & GARDEN SPLY STORES, RETAIL: Fertilizer
NURSERIES & LAWN/GARDEN SPLY STORE, RET: Lawnmowers/Tractors
NURSERIES & LAWN/GARDEN SPLY STORES, RET: Garden Splys/Tools
NURSERIES/LAWN/GRDN SPLY STORE, RET: Nursery Stck, Seed/Bulb
NURSERY & GARDEN CENTERS
NURSERY SCHOOLS
NURSERY STOCK, WHOLESALE
NURSING & PERSONAL CARE FACILITIES, NEC
NURSING CARE FACILITIES: Skilled
NURSING HOME, EXC SKILLED & INTERMEDIATE CARE FACILITY
NUTRITION SVCS
NYLON FIBERS

O

OFC/CLINIC OF MED DRS: Special, Phys Or Surgeon, Eye Or ENT
OFC/CLINIC OF MED DRS: Specl, Phys Or Surgeon, Occup & Indl
OFC/CLINIC, MED DRS: Specl, Phys Or Surgeon, Infect Disease
OFCS & CLINICS,MEDICAL DRS: Specl, Physician Or Surgn, ENT
OFFICE EQPT & ACCESSORY CUSTOMIZING SVCS
OFFICE EQPT WHOLESALERS
OFFICE EQPT, WHOLESALE: Duplicating Machines
OFFICE EQPT, WHOLESALE: Photocopy Machines
OFFICE FURNITURE REPAIR & MAINTENANCE SVCS
OFFICE MANAGEMENT SVCS
OFFICE SPLY & STATIONERY STORES
OFFICE SPLY & STATIONERY STORES: Office Forms & Splys
OFFICE SPLYS, NEC, WHOLESALE
OFFICES & CLINICS DOCTORS OF MED: Intrnl Med Practitioners
OFFICES & CLINICS DRS OF MED: Psychiatrists/Psychoanalysts
OFFICES & CLINICS HLTH PRACTITNRS: Psychiatric Social Wrkr
OFFICES & CLINICS OF DENTISTS: Dental Clinic
OFFICES & CLINICS OF DENTISTS: Dental Clinics & Offices
OFFICES & CLINICS OF DENTISTS: Dental Surgeon
OFFICES & CLINICS OF DENTISTS: Dentists' Office
OFFICES & CLINICS OF DENTISTS: Endodontist
OFFICES & CLINICS OF DENTISTS: Oral Pathologist
OFFICES & CLINICS OF DENTISTS: Pedodontist
OFFICES & CLINICS OF DENTISTS: Periodontist
OFFICES & CLINICS OF DENTISTS: Prosthodontist
OFFICES & CLINICS OF DENTISTS: Specialist, Maxillofacial
OFFICES & CLINICS OF DENTISTS: Specialist, Practitioners
OFFICES & CLINICS OF DOCTORS OF MEDICINE: Allergist
OFFICES & CLINICS OF DOCTORS OF MEDICINE: Anesthesiologist
OFFICES & CLINICS OF DOCTORS OF MEDICINE: Dermatologist
OFFICES & CLINICS OF DOCTORS OF MEDICINE: Dispensary
OFFICES & CLINICS OF DOCTORS OF MEDICINE: Endocrinologist
OFFICES & CLINICS OF DOCTORS OF MEDICINE: Gastronomist
OFFICES & CLINICS OF DOCTORS OF MEDICINE: Gynecologist
OFFICES & CLINICS OF DOCTORS OF MEDICINE: Hematologist
OFFICES & CLINICS OF DOCTORS OF MEDICINE: Nephrologist

PRODUCT INDEX

OFFICES & CLINICS OF DOCTORS OF MEDICINE: Neurologist
OFFICES & CLINICS OF DOCTORS OF MEDICINE: Neurosurgeon
OFFICES & CLINICS OF DOCTORS OF MEDICINE: Obstetrician
OFFICES & CLINICS OF DOCTORS OF MEDICINE: Oncologist
OFFICES & CLINICS OF DOCTORS OF MEDICINE: Ophthalmologist
OFFICES & CLINICS OF DOCTORS OF MEDICINE: Pathologist
OFFICES & CLINICS OF DOCTORS OF MEDICINE: Pediatrician
OFFICES & CLINICS OF DOCTORS OF MEDICINE: Psychiatrist
OFFICES & CLINICS OF DOCTORS OF MEDICINE: Radiologist
OFFICES & CLINICS OF DOCTORS OF MEDICINE: Surgeon
OFFICES & CLINICS OF DOCTORS OF MEDICINE: Surgeon, Plastic
OFFICES & CLINICS OF DOCTORS OF MEDICINE: Urologist
OFFICES & CLINICS OF DOCTORS, MEDICINE: Gen & Fam Practice
OFFICES & CLINICS OF DRS OF MED: Cardiologist & Vascular
OFFICES & CLINICS OF DRS OF MED: Clinic, Op by Physicians
OFFICES & CLINICS OF DRS OF MED: Em Med Ctr, Freestanding
OFFICES & CLINICS OF DRS OF MED: Health Maint Org Or HMO
OFFICES & CLINICS OF DRS OF MED: Physician/Surgeon, Int Med
OFFICES & CLINICS OF DRS OF MED: Physician/Surgeon, Phy Med
OFFICES & CLINICS OF DRS OF MEDICINE: Med Clinic, Pri Care
OFFICES & CLINICS OF DRS OF MEDICINE: Physician, Orthopedic
OFFICES & CLINICS OF DRS OF MEDICINE: Pulmonary
OFFICES & CLINICS OF DRS OF MEDICINE: Rheumatology
OFFICES & CLINICS OF DRS, MED: Specialized Practitioners
OFFICES & CLINICS OF HEALTH PRACTITIONERS: Nurse & Med Asst
OFFICES & CLINICS OF HEALTH PRACTITIONERS: Nutrition
OFFICES & CLINICS OF HEALTH PRACTITIONERS: Nutritionist
OFFICES & CLINICS OF HEALTH PRACTITIONERS: Occu Therapist
OFFICES & CLINICS OF HEALTH PRACTITIONERS: Physical Therapy
OFFICES & CLINICS OF HEALTH PRACTITIONERS: Physiotherapist
OFFICES & CLINICS OF HEALTH PRACTITIONERS: Speech Pathology
OFFICES & CLINICS OF HEALTH PRACTITIONERS: Speech Specialist
OFFICES & CLINICS OF HEALTH PRACTITIONERS: Speech Therapist
OFFICES & CLINICS OF HEALTH PRACTRS: Clinical Psychologist
OFFICES & CLINICS OF HLTH PRACTITIONERS: Reg/Practical Nurse
OFFICES & CLINICS OF OPTOMETRISTS: Specialist, Contact Lens
OFFICES & CLINICS OF OPTOMETRISTS: Specialist, Optometrists
OIL & GAS FIELD MACHINERY
OIL BURNER REPAIR SVCS
OIL FIELD MACHINERY & EQPT
OIL FIELD SVCS, NEC
OILS & ESSENTIAL OILS
OILS & GREASES: Lubricating
OILS: Lubricating
OLD AGE ASSISTANCE
OLEFINS
ON-LINE DATABASE INFORMATION RETRIEVAL SVCS
OPERA COMPANIES
OPERATIVE BUILDERS: Condominiums
OPERATIVE BUILDERS: Cooperative Apartment
OPERATOR TRAINING, COMPUTER
OPERATOR: Apartment Buildings
OPERATOR: Nonresidential Buildings
OPHTHALMIC GOODS
OPHTHALMIC GOODS WHOLESALERS
OPHTHALMIC GOODS, NEC, WHOLESALE: Frames
OPHTHALMIC GOODS: Frames, Lenses & Parts, Eyeglasses
OPTICAL GOODS STORES
OPTICAL GOODS STORES: Contact Lenses, Prescription
OPTICAL GOODS STORES: Eyeglasses, Prescription
OPTICAL INSTRUMENTS & LENSES
OPTICAL SCANNING SVCS
OPTOMETRISTS' OFFICES
ORCHESTRAS & BANDS
ORGANIZATIONS & UNIONS: Labor
ORGANIZATIONS, NEC
ORGANIZATIONS: Civic & Social
ORGANIZATIONS: Educational Research Agency
ORGANIZATIONS: Medical Research
ORGANIZATIONS: Noncommercial Biological Research
ORGANIZATIONS: Professional
ORGANIZATIONS: Religious
ORGANIZATIONS: Research Institute
ORGANIZATIONS: Scientific Research Agency
ORGANIZATIONS: Veterans' Membership
ORTHODONTIST
OUTBOARD MOTOR DEALERS
OUTLETS: Electric, Convenience
OUTREACH PROGRAM

P

PACKAGED FROZEN FOODS WHOLESALERS, NEC
PACKAGING & LABELING SVCS
PACKAGING MATERIALS, WHOLESALE
PACKAGING MATERIALS: Paper
PACKAGING MATERIALS: Plastic Film, Coated Or Laminated
PACKAGING MATERIALS: Polystyrene Foam
PACKAGING: Blister Or Bubble Formed, Plastic
PACKING & CRATING SVC
PACKING SVCS: Shipping
PAGERS: One-way
PAINT & PAINTING SPLYS STORE
PAINT STORE
PAINTING SVC: Metal Prdts
PAINTS & ALLIED PRODUCTS
PAINTS, VARNISHES & SPLYS WHOLESALERS
PAINTS, VARNISHES & SPLYS, WHOLESALE: Paints
PALLETS
PALLETS: Plastic
PALLETS: Wooden
PAPER & BOARD: Die-cut
PAPER MANUFACTURERS: Exc Newsprint
PAPER PRDTS: Panty Liners, Made From Purchased Materials
PAPER PRDTS: Sanitary
PAPER PRDTS: Tampons, Sanitary, Made From Purchased Material
PAPER PRDTS: Towels, Napkins/Tissue Paper, From Purchd Mtrls
PAPER: Coated & Laminated, NEC
PAPER: Gift Wrap
PARKING GARAGE
PARKING LOTS
PARKING LOTS & GARAGES
PARTITIONS & FIXTURES: Except Wood
PARTS: Metal
PARTY & SPECIAL EVENT PLANNING SVCS
PASSENGER AIRLINE SVCS
PASSENGER TRAIN SVCS
PATCHING PLASTER: Household
PATENT OWNERS & LESSORS
PATENT SOLICITOR
PATTERNS: Indl
PAVERS
PAVING MIXTURES
PAYROLL SVCS
PENSION & RETIREMENT PLAN CONSULTANTS
PENSION FUNDS
PENSIONS
PERFORMING ARTS CENTER PRODUCTION SVCS
PERSONAL & HOUSEHOLD GOODS REPAIR, NEC
PERSONAL APPEARANCE SVCS
PERSONAL CARE FACILITY
PERSONAL CREDIT INSTITUTION: Indl Loan Bank, Non Deposit
PERSONAL CREDIT INSTITUTIONS: Auto Loans, Incl Insurance
PERSONAL CREDIT INSTITUTIONS: Consumer Finance Companies
PERSONAL CREDIT INSTITUTIONS: Finance Licensed Loan Co's, Sm
PERSONAL CREDIT INSTITUTIONS: Financing, Autos, Furniture
PERSONAL CREDIT INSTITUTIONS: Install Sales Finance
PERSONAL CREDIT INSTITUTIONS: Licensed Loan Companies, Small
PERSONAL DOCUMENT & INFORMATION SVCS
PERSONAL FINANCIAL SVCS
PERSONAL INVESTIGATION SVCS
PERSONAL SVCS
PEST CONTROL IN STRUCTURES SVCS
PEST CONTROL SVCS
PESTICIDES WHOLESALERS
PET FOOD WHOLESALERS
PET SPLYS
PET SPLYS WHOLESALERS
PET-SITTING SVC: In-Home
PETROLEUM & PETROLEUM PRDTS, WHOL Svc Station Splys, Petro
PETROLEUM & PETROLEUM PRDTS, WHOLESALE Crude Oil
PETROLEUM & PETROLEUM PRDTS, WHOLESALE Fuel Oil
PETROLEUM & PETROLEUM PRDTS, WHOLESALE: Bulk Stations
PETROLEUM BULK STATIONS & TERMINALS
PETROLEUM PRDTS WHOLESALERS
PETROLEUM REFINERY INSPECTION SVCS
PHARMACEUTICAL PREPARATIONS: Druggists' Preparations
PHARMACEUTICAL PREPARATIONS: Medicines, Capsule Or Ampule
PHARMACEUTICAL PREPARATIONS: Pills
PHARMACEUTICAL PREPARATIONS: Powders
PHARMACEUTICAL PREPARATIONS: Proprietary Drug PRDTS
PHARMACEUTICAL PREPARATIONS: Tinctures
PHARMACEUTICALS
PHARMACEUTICALS: Medicinal & Botanical Prdts
PHOTOCOPY MACHINES
PHOTOCOPYING & DUPLICATING SVCS
PHOTOELECTRIC CELLS: Electronic Eye, Solid State
PHOTOFINISHING LABORATORIES
PHOTOGRAMMATIC MAPPING SVCS
PHOTOGRAPHIC CONTROL SYSTEMS: Electronic
PHOTOGRAPHIC EQPT & SPLYS
PHOTOGRAPHIC EQPT & SPLYS WHOLESALERS
PHOTOGRAPHIC EQPT & SPLYS, WHOLESALE: Printing Apparatus
PHOTOGRAPHIC EQPT & SPLYS: Reels, Film
PHOTOGRAPHIC EQPT & SPLYS: Tripods, Camera & Projector
PHOTOGRAPHIC EQPT/SPLYS, WHOL: Cameras/Projectors/Eqpt/Splys
PHOTOGRAPHIC SVCS
PHOTOGRAPHY SVCS: Commercial
PHOTOGRAPHY SVCS: Portrait Studios
PHOTOGRAPHY SVCS: Still Or Video
PHOTOGRAPHY: Aerial
PHYSICAL EXAMINATION & TESTING SVCS
PHYSICAL FITNESS CENTERS
PHYSICAL FITNESS CLUBS WITH TRAINING EQPT
PHYSICIANS' OFFICES & CLINICS: Medical
PHYSICIANS' OFFICES & CLINICS: Medical doctors
PHYSICIANS' OFFICES & CLINICS: Osteopathic
PICTURE FRAMES: Wood
PICTURE FRAMING SVCS, CUSTOM
PIECE GOODS, NOTIONS & DRY GOODS, WHOL: Textiles, Woven
PIECE GOODS, NOTIONS & DRY GOODS, WHOL: Yard Goods, Woven
PIECE GOODS, NOTIONS & OTHER DRY GOODS, WHOLESALE: Bridal
PIECE GOODS, NOTIONS & OTHER DRY GOODS, WHOLESALE: Fabrics
PIECE GOODS, NOTIONS/DRY GOODS, WHOL: Fabrics, Synthetic
PIECE GOODS, NOTIONS/DRY GOODS, WHOL: Sewing Splys/Notions
PILOT SVCS: Aviation

PRODUCT INDEX

PIPE & FITTING: Fabrication
PIPE SECTIONS, FABRICATED FROM PURCHASED PIPE
PIPE, IRRIGATION: Concrete
PIPE: Irrigation, Sheet Metal
PIPELINE & POWER LINE INSPECTION SVCS
PIPELINE TERMINAL FACILITIES: Independent
PIPELINES: Natural Gas
PIPES & TUBES
PIPES & TUBES: Steel
PIPES & TUBES: Welded
PLANING MILLS: Millwork
PLANT CARE SVCS
PLANTS, POTTED, WHOLESALE
PLANTS: Artificial & Preserved
PLASTIC COLORING & FINISHING
PLASTICS FILM & SHEET
PLASTICS FILM & SHEET: Photographic & X-Ray
PLASTICS FILM & SHEET: Polyethylene
PLASTICS FILM & SHEET: Polypropylene
PLASTICS FILM & SHEET: Polyvinyl
PLASTICS MATERIAL & RESINS
PLASTICS PROCESSING
PLASTICS: Finished Injection Molded
PLASTICS: Injection Molded
PLASTICS: Molded
PLASTICS: Polystyrene Foam
PLASTICS: Thermoformed
PLATEMAKING SVC: Letterpress
PLATES: Steel
PLATING & POLISHING SVC
PLATING SVC: NEC
PLAYGROUND EQPT
PLUMBING & HEATING EQPT & SPLY, WHOL: Htg Eqpt/Panels, Solar
PLUMBING & HEATING EQPT & SPLY, WHOLESALE: Hydronic Htg Eqpt
PLUMBING & HEATING EQPT & SPLYS WHOLESALERS
PLUMBING & HEATING EQPT & SPLYS, WHOL: Pipe/Fitting, Plastic
PLUMBING & HEATING EQPT & SPLYS, WHOL: Plumbing Fitting/Sply
PLUMBING & HEATING EQPT & SPLYS, WHOL: Plumbng/Heatng Valves
PLUMBING & HEATING EQPT & SPLYS, WHOL: Water Purif Eqpt
PLUMBING FIXTURES
PODIATRISTS' OFFICES
POINT OF SALE DEVICES
POLICE PROTECTION: Local Government
POLISHING SVC: Metals Or Formed Prdts
POLYETHYLENE RESINS
POLYHYDRIC ALCOHOL ESTERS, AMINOS, ETC
POLYTETRAFLUOROETHYLENE RESINS
POLYURETHANE RESINS
POLYVINYL CHLORIDE RESINS
PORCELAIN: Chemical
PORTRAITS, WHOLESALE
POSTAL STATION SVC, CONTRACTED
POTPOURRI
POTTERY
POULTRY & POULTRY PRDTS WHOLESALERS
POULTRY & SMALL GAME SLAUGHTERING & PROCESSING
POWDER: Metal
POWER TRANSMISSION EQPT: Mechanical
PRECIOUS METALS WHOLESALERS
PRECIOUS STONES & METALS, WHOLESALE
PRECIOUS STONES WHOLESALERS
PRERECORDED TAPE, CD/RECORD STORES: Video Tapes, Prerecorded
PRERECORDED TAPE, COMPACT DISC & RECORD STORES
PRESCHOOL CENTERS
PRESS SVCS
PRESSES
PRESTRESSED CONCRETE PRDTS
PRINT CARTRIDGES: Laser & Other Computer Printers
PRINTED CIRCUIT BOARDS
PRINTERS & PLOTTERS
PRINTING & BINDING: Books
PRINTING & ENGRAVING: Invitation & Stationery
PRINTING MACHINERY
PRINTING MACHINERY, EQPT & SPLYS: Wholesalers
PRINTING TRADES MACHINERY & EQPT REPAIR SVCS
PRINTING, COMMERCIAL: Bags, Plastic, NEC
PRINTING, COMMERCIAL: Business Forms, NEC
PRINTING, COMMERCIAL: Decals, NEC
PRINTING, COMMERCIAL: Promotional
PRINTING, COMMERCIAL: Screen
PRINTING, LITHOGRAPHIC: Color
PRINTING, LITHOGRAPHIC: Decals
PRINTING, LITHOGRAPHIC: Maps
PRINTING, LITHOGRAPHIC: Promotional
PRINTING, LITHOGRAPHIC: Schedules, Transportation
PRINTING, LITHOGRAPHIC: Transfers, Decalcomania Or Dry
PRINTING: Books
PRINTING: Commercial, NEC
PRINTING: Gravure, Business Form & Card
PRINTING: Gravure, Labels
PRINTING: Gravure, Rotogravure
PRINTING: Letterpress
PRINTING: Lithographic
PRINTING: Offset
PRINTING: Screen, Broadwoven Fabrics, Cotton
PRINTING: Screen, Fabric
PRIVATE INVESTIGATOR SVCS
PROBATION OFFICE
PRODUCT ENDORSEMENT SVCS
PRODUCTION CREDIT ASSOCIATION, AGRICULTURAL
PROFESSIONAL EQPT & SPLYS, WHOLESALE: Analytical Instruments
PROFESSIONAL EQPT & SPLYS, WHOLESALE: Law Enforcement
PROFESSIONAL EQPT & SPLYS, WHOLESALE: Optical Goods
PROFESSIONAL EQPT & SPLYS, WHOLESALE: Theatrical
PROGRAM ADMIN, GOVT: Energy Devpt & Conservation Agency
PROGRAM ADMINISTRATION, GOVERNMENT: Social & Human Resources
PROGRAM ADMINISTRATION, GOVERNMENT: Social & Manpower, State
PROMOTION SVCS
PROPELLERS: Boat & Ship, Machined
PROPERTY & CASUALTY INSURANCE AGENTS
PROPERTY DAMAGE INSURANCE
PUBLIC FINANCE, TAX & MONETARY POLICY, GOVT: Lottery Cntrl
PUBLIC HEALTH PROGRAM ADMINISTRATION, GOVERNMENT: State
PUBLIC HEALTH PROGRAMS ADMINISTRATION SVCS
PUBLIC LIBRARY
PUBLIC RELATIONS & PUBLICITY SVCS
PUBLIC RELATIONS SVCS
PUBLISHERS: Art Copy & Poster
PUBLISHERS: Book
PUBLISHERS: Books, No Printing
PUBLISHERS: Directories, Telephone
PUBLISHERS: Magazines, No Printing
PUBLISHERS: Miscellaneous
PUBLISHERS: Music Book & Sheet Music
PUBLISHERS: Newsletter
PUBLISHERS: Newspaper
PUBLISHERS: Newspapers, No Printing
PUBLISHERS: Pamphlets, No Printing
PUBLISHERS: Periodical, With Printing
PUBLISHERS: Periodicals, Magazines
PUBLISHING & BROADCASTING: Internet Only
PUBLISHING & PRINTING: Books
PUBLISHING & PRINTING: Comic Books
PUBLISHING & PRINTING: Guides
PUBLISHING & PRINTING: Magazines: publishing & printing
PUBLISHING & PRINTING: Newsletters, Business Svc
PUBLISHING & PRINTING: Newspapers
PUBLISHING & PRINTING: Textbooks
PULP MILLS
PUMPS
PUMPS & PUMPING EQPT REPAIR SVCS
PUMPS & PUMPING EQPT WHOLESALERS
PUPPETS & MARIONETTES
PURCHASING SVCS
PURIFICATION & DUST COLLECTION EQPT

Q

QUARTZ CRYSTALS: Electronic
QUILTING SVC & SPLYS, FOR THE TRADE

R

RACETRACKS
RACETRACKS: Auto
RACETRACKS: Horse
RADIO & TELEVISION COMMUNICATIONS EQUIPMENT
RADIO BROADCASTING & COMMUNICATIONS EQPT
RADIO BROADCASTING STATIONS
RADIO REPAIR SHOP, NEC
RADIO, TELEVISION & CONSUMER ELECTRONICS STORES: Eqpt, NEC
RADIO, TELEVISION & CONSUMER ELECTRONICS STORES: TV Sets
RADIO, TV & CONSUMER ELEC STORES: Tape Recorders/Players
RADIO, TV & CONSUMER ELECTRONICS: VCR & Access
RADIO, TV/CONSUMER ELEC STORES: Antennas, Satellite Dish
RAILROAD CAR RENTING & LEASING SVCS
RAILROAD CAR REPAIR SVCS
RAILROAD CARGO LOADING & UNLOADING SVCS
RAILROAD EQPT
RAILROAD EQPT & SPLYS WHOLESALERS
RAILROAD EQPT: Street Cars & Eqpt
RAILROAD MAINTENANCE & REPAIR SVCS
RAILROAD TIES: Concrete
RAILROADS: Long Haul
RAZORS, RAZOR BLADES
REAL ESTATE AGENCIES & BROKERS
REAL ESTATE AGENCIES: Buying
REAL ESTATE AGENCIES: Commercial
REAL ESTATE AGENCIES: Leasing & Rentals
REAL ESTATE AGENCIES: Multiple Listing Svc
REAL ESTATE AGENCIES: Rental
REAL ESTATE AGENCIES: Residential
REAL ESTATE AGENCIES: Selling
REAL ESTATE AGENTS & MANAGERS
REAL ESTATE APPRAISERS
REAL ESTATE AUCTION
REAL ESTATE BOARDS
REAL ESTATE BROKERS: Manufactured Homes, On-Site
REAL ESTATE ESCROW AGENCIES
REAL ESTATE FIDUCIARIES' OFFICES
REAL ESTATE INVESTMENT TRUSTS
REAL ESTATE LISTING SVCS
REAL ESTATE MANAGERS: Condominium
REAL ESTATE MANAGERS: Cooperative Apartment
REAL ESTATE OPERATORS, EXC DEVELOPERS: Apartment Hotel
REAL ESTATE OPERATORS, EXC DEVELOPERS: Commercial/Indl Bldg
REAL ESTATE OPERATORS, EXC DEVELOPERS: Residential Hotel
REAL ESTATE OPERATORS, EXC DEVELOPERS: Retirement Hotel
REAL ESTATE OPERATORS, EXC DEVELOPERS: Shopping Ctr
REAL ESTATE OPS, EXC DEVELOPER: Residential Bldg, 4 Or Less
RECREATIONAL & SPORTING CAMPS
RECREATIONAL DEALERS: Camper & Travel Trailers
RECREATIONAL VEHICLE REPAIR SVCS
RECREATIONAL VEHICLE REPAIRS
RECYCLABLE SCRAP & WASTE MATERIALS WHOLESALERS
RECYCLING: Paper
REELS: Cable, Metal
REFINERS & SMELTERS: Gold, Secondary
REFINERS & SMELTERS: Nonferrous Metal
REFINING: Petroleum
REFRACTORIES: Clay
REFRIGERATION & HEATING EQUIPMENT
REFRIGERATION EQPT & SPLYS WHOLESALERS
REFRIGERATION EQPT & SPLYS, WHOLESALE: Commercial Eqpt
REFRIGERATION EQPT: Complete
REFRIGERATION REPAIR SVCS
REFRIGERATION SVC & REPAIR
REFUSE SYSTEMS
REGULATION & ADMIN, GOVT: Port Authority/Dist, Nonoperating
REGULATION/ADMIN, GOVT: Water Vessel & Port Regulting Agency
REHABILITATION CENTER, OUTPATIENT TREATMENT
REHABILITATION SVCS
REINSURANCE CARRIERS: Accident & Health
RELIGIOUS SCHOOL
RELOCATION SVCS
REMOVERS & CLEANERS

PRODUCT INDEX

RENT-A-CAR SVCS
RENTAL CENTERS: Furniture
RENTAL CENTERS: General
RENTAL CENTERS: Party & Banquet Eqpt & Splys
RENTAL CENTERS: Tools
RENTAL SVCS: Appliance
RENTAL SVCS: Audio-Visual Eqpt & Sply
RENTAL SVCS: Business Machine & Electronic Eqpt
RENTAL SVCS: Clothing
RENTAL SVCS: Electronic Eqpt, Exc Computers
RENTAL SVCS: Eqpt, Theatrical
RENTAL SVCS: Home Cleaning & Maintenance Eqpt
RENTAL SVCS: Home Entertainment Eqpt
RENTAL SVCS: Office Facilities & Secretarial Svcs
RENTAL SVCS: Propane Eqpt
RENTAL SVCS: Stores & Yards Eqpt
RENTAL SVCS: Tuxedo
RENTAL SVCS: Vending Machine
RENTAL SVCS: Video Cassette Recorder & Access
RENTAL SVCS: Video Disk/Tape, To The General Public
RENTAL SVCS: Work Zone Traffic Eqpt, Flags, Cones, Etc
RENTAL: Passenger Car
RENTAL: Portable Toilet
RENTAL: Trucks, With Drivers
RENTAL: Video Tape & Disc
REPAIR SERVICES, NEC
REPAIR TRAINING, COMPUTER
REPOSSESSION SVCS
RESEARCH & DEVELOPMENT SVCS, COMMERCIAL: Engineering Lab
RESEARCH, DEV & TESTING SVCS, COMM: Chem Lab, Exc Testing
RESEARCH, DEVEL & TEST SVCS, COMM: Sociological & Education
RESEARCH, DEVELOPMENT & TEST SVCS, COMM: Business Analysis
RESEARCH, DEVELOPMENT & TEST SVCS, COMM: Cmptr Hardware Dev
RESEARCH, DEVELOPMENT & TEST SVCS, COMM: Research, Exc Lab
RESEARCH, DEVELOPMENT & TESTING SVCS, COMM: Agricultural
RESEARCH, DEVELOPMENT & TESTING SVCS, COMM: Bus Economic Sve
RESEARCH, DEVELOPMENT & TESTING SVCS, COMM: Natural Resource
RESEARCH, DEVELOPMENT & TESTING SVCS, COMM: Research Lab
RESEARCH, DEVELOPMENT & TESTING SVCS, COMMERCIAL: Business
RESEARCH, DEVELOPMENT & TESTING SVCS, COMMERCIAL: Education
RESEARCH, DEVELOPMENT & TESTING SVCS, COMMERCIAL: Energy
RESEARCH, DEVELOPMENT & TESTING SVCS, COMMERCIAL: Medical
RESEARCH, DEVELOPMENT & TESTING SVCS, COMMERCIAL: Physical
RESEARCH, DEVELOPMENT SVCS, COMMERCIAL: Indl Lab
RESEARCH, DVLPT & TEST SVCS, COMM: Mkt Analysis or Research
RESEARCH, DVLPT & TESTING SVCS, COMM: Mkt, Bus & Economic
RESEARCH, DVLPT & TESTING SVCS, COMM: Survey, Mktg
RESERVATION SVCS
RESIDENTIAL CARE FOR CHILDREN
RESIDENTIAL CARE FOR THE HANDICAPPED
RESIDENTIAL MENTAL HEALTH & SUBSTANCE ABUSE FACILITIES
RESIDENTIAL MENTALLY HANDICAPPED FACILITIES
RESIDENTIAL REMODELERS
RESORT HOTEL: Franchised
RESORT HOTELS
RESPIRATORY THERAPY CLINIC
RESTAURANTS: Delicatessen
RESTAURANTS:Full Svc, American
RESTAURANTS:Full Svc, Family, Independent
RESTAURANTS:Full Svc, Seafood
RESTAURANTS:Limited Svc, Coffee Shop
RESTAURANTS:Limited Svc, Fast-Food, Chain
RESTAURANTS:Limited Svc, Frozen Yogurt Stand
RESTAURANTS:Limited Svc, Pizza

RESTAURANTS:Limited Svc, Sandwiches & Submarines Shop
RESTROOM CLEANING SVCS
RESUME WRITING SVCS
RETAIL BAKERY: Bread
RETAIL BAKERY: Doughnuts
RETAIL FIREPLACE STORES
RETAIL STORES, NEC
RETAIL STORES: Alarm Signal Systems
RETAIL STORES: Alcoholic Beverage Making Eqpt & Splys
RETAIL STORES: Audio-Visual Eqpt & Splys
RETAIL STORES: Awnings
RETAIL STORES: Batteries, Non-Automotive
RETAIL STORES: Business Machines & Eqpt
RETAIL STORES: Cake Decorating Splys
RETAIL STORES: Cleaning Eqpt & Splys
RETAIL STORES: Coins
RETAIL STORES: Communication Eqpt
RETAIL STORES: Cosmetics
RETAIL STORES: Electronic Parts & Eqpt
RETAIL STORES: Farm Eqpt & Splys
RETAIL STORES: Farm Tractors
RETAIL STORES: Fire Extinguishers
RETAIL STORES: Flags
RETAIL STORES: Hair Care Prdts
RETAIL STORES: Hearing Aids
RETAIL STORES: Ice
RETAIL STORES: Medical Apparatus & Splys
RETAIL STORES: Mobile Telephones & Eqpt
RETAIL STORES: Monuments, Finished To Custom Order
RETAIL STORES: Motors, Electric
RETAIL STORES: Orthopedic & Prosthesis Applications
RETAIL STORES: Plumbing & Heating Splys
RETAIL STORES: Safety Splys & Eqpt
RETAIL STORES: Swimming Pools, Above Ground
RETAIL STORES: Telephone & Communication Eqpt
RETAIL STORES: Telephone Eqpt & Systems
RETAIL STORES: Tents
RETAIL STORES: Theatrical Eqpt & Splys
RETAIL STORES: Tombstones
RETAIL STORES: Vaults & Safes
RETAIL STORES: Water Purification Eqpt
RETIREMENT COMMUNITIES WITH NURSING
REUPHOLSTERY SVCS
RIDING STABLES
ROAD CONSTRUCTION EQUIPMENT WHOLESALERS
ROCK SALT MINING
ROLLS & ROLL COVERINGS: Rubber
ROOFING GRANULES
ROOFING MATERIALS: Asphalt
ROOMING & BOARDING HOUSES: Dormitory, Commercially Operated
ROOMING & BOARDING HOUSES: Lodging House, Exc Organization
RUBBER
RUBBER PRDTS
RUBBER PRDTS: Automotive, Mechanical
RUBBER PRDTS: Silicone
RUBBER STAMP, WHOLESALE
RUGS : Tufted

S

SADDLERY STORES
SAFETY EQPT & SPLYS WHOLESALERS
SALES PROMOTION SVCS
SAND & GRAVEL
SAND MINING
SAND: Hygrade
SAND: Silica
SANDBLASTING SVC: Building Exterior
SANITARY SVCS: Disease Control
SANITARY SVCS: Environmental Cleanup
SANITARY SVCS: Hazardous Waste, Collection & Disposal
SANITARY SVCS: Liquid Waste Collection & Disposal
SANITARY SVCS: Nonhazardous Waste Disposal Sites
SANITARY SVCS: Oil Spill Cleanup
SANITARY SVCS: Refuse Collection & Disposal Svcs
SANITARY SVCS: Rubbish Collection & Disposal
SANITARY SVCS: Sanitary Landfill, Operation Of
SANITARY SVCS: Sewage Treatment Facility
SANITARY SVCS: Waste Materials, Recycling
SANITATION CHEMICALS & CLEANING AGENTS
SATELLITE COMMUNICATIONS EQPT
SATELLITES: Communications
SAVINGS INSTITUTIONS: Federally Chartered

SAWING & PLANING MILLS
SAWING & PLANING MILLS: Custom
SCALE REPAIR SVCS
SCANNING DEVICES: Optical
SCHOOL BUS SVC
SCHOOL FOR PHYSICALLY HANDICAPPED, NEC
SCIENTIFIC EQPT REPAIR SVCS
SCIENTIFIC INSTRUMENTS WHOLESALERS
SCRAP & WASTE MATERIALS, WHOLESALE: Auto Wrecking For Scrap
SCRAP & WASTE MATERIALS, WHOLESALE: Ferrous Metal
SCRAP & WASTE MATERIALS, WHOLESALE: Junk & Scrap
SCRAP & WASTE MATERIALS, WHOLESALE: Metal
SCRUBBERS: CATV System
SEALANTS
SEALING COMPOUNDS: Sealing, synthetic rubber or plastic
SEALS: Hermetic
SEARCH & NAVIGATION SYSTEMS
SEARCH & RESCUE SVCS
SECRETARIAL & COURT REPORTING
SECRETARIAL SVCS
SECURE STORAGE SVC: Document
SECURE STORAGE SVC: Household & Furniture
SECURITIES DEALING
SECURITY & COMMODITY EXCHANGES
SECURITY CONTROL EQPT & SYSTEMS
SECURITY DEVICES
SECURITY EQPT STORES
SECURITY GUARD SVCS
SECURITY PROTECTIVE DEVICES MAINTENANCE & MONITORING SVCS
SECURITY SYSTEMS SERVICES
SELF-HELP GROUP HOME
SELF-HELP ORGANIZATION, NEC
SEMICONDUCTORS & RELATED DEVICES
SENSORS: Infrared, Solid State
SEPTIC TANK CLEANING SVCS
SERVICE STATION EQPT REPAIR SVCS
SERVICES, NEC
SETTLEMENT HOUSE
SEWAGE & WATER TREATMENT EQPT
SEWAGE FACILITIES
SEWER CLEANING & RODDING SVC
SEWER CLEANING EQPT: Power
SEWING CONTRACTORS
SEWING MACHINE STORES
SEWING, NEEDLEWORK & PIECE GOODS STORES: Sewing Splys
SHAPES & PILINGS, STRUCTURAL: Steel
SHEET METAL SPECIALTIES, EXC STAMPED
SHIPPING AGENTS
SHIPPING DOCUMENTS PREPARATION SVCS
SHOE & BOOT ACCESS
SHOE MATERIALS: Quarters
SHOE MATERIALS: Rands
SHOE REPAIR SHOP
SHOE STORES
SHOE STORES: Athletic
SHOE STORES: Boots, Men's
SHOES & BOOTS WHOLESALERS
SHOPPING CENTERS & MALLS
SHOWER STALLS: Plastic & Fiberglass
SHREDDERS: Indl & Commercial
SHUTTERS, DOOR & WINDOW: Metal
SIGN PAINTING & LETTERING SHOP
SIGNALING DEVICES: Sound, Electrical
SIGNALS: Transportation
SIGNS & ADVERTISING SPECIALTIES
SIGNS & ADVERTISING SPECIALTIES: Artwork, Advertising
SIGNS & ADVERTISING SPECIALTIES: Novelties
SIGNS & ADVERTISING SPECIALTIES: Signs
SIGNS, ELECTRICAL: Wholesalers
SIGNS, EXC ELECTRIC, WHOLESALE
SIGNS: Electrical
SILK SCREEN DESIGN SVCS
SILVERWARE
SILVERWARE & PLATED WARE
SIZES
SKATING RINKS: Roller
SKILL TRAINING CENTER
SKIN CARE PRDTS: Suntan Lotions & Oils
SLAG PRDTS
SMALL BUSINESS INVESTMENT COMPANIES
SOAPS & DETERGENTS
SOCIAL CLUBS

PRODUCT INDEX

SOCIAL SERVICES INFORMATION EXCHANGE
SOCIAL SERVICES, NEC
SOCIAL SVCS CENTER
SOCIAL SVCS, HANDICAPPED
SOCIAL SVCS: Individual & Family
SOCIAL WORKER
SOFT DRINKS WHOLESALERS
SOFTWARE PUBLISHERS: Application
SOFTWARE PUBLISHERS: Business & Professional
SOFTWARE PUBLISHERS: Computer Utilities
SOFTWARE PUBLISHERS: Education
SOFTWARE PUBLISHERS: Home Entertainment
SOFTWARE PUBLISHERS: NEC
SOFTWARE PUBLISHERS: Operating Systems
SOFTWARE PUBLISHERS: Publisher's
SOFTWARE TRAINING, COMPUTER
SOLAR CELLS
SOLAR HEATING EQPT
SOLID CONTAINING UNITS: Concrete
SOUND EQPT: Electric
SOUND RECORDING STUDIOS
SPACE FLIGHT OPERATIONS, EXC GOVERNMENT
SPAS
SPEAKER SYSTEMS
SPECIAL EDUCATION SCHOOLS, PUBLIC
SPECIALIZED LEGAL SVCS
SPECIALTY FOOD STORES: Health & Dietetic Food
SPECIALTY OUTPATIENT CLINICS, NEC
SPECULATIVE BUILDERS: Single-Family Housing
SPEED READING INSTRUCTION
SPICE & HERB STORES
SPORTING & ATHLETIC GOODS: Balls, Baseball, Football, Etc
SPORTING & ATHLETIC GOODS: Bowling Pins
SPORTING & ATHLETIC GOODS: Cricket Eqpt, NEC
SPORTING & ATHLETIC GOODS: Driving Ranges, Golf, Electronic
SPORTING & ATHLETIC GOODS: Fishing Eqpt
SPORTING & ATHLETIC GOODS: Game Calls
SPORTING & ATHLETIC GOODS: Gymnasium Eqpt
SPORTING & ATHLETIC GOODS: Lacrosse Eqpt & Splys, NEC
SPORTING & ATHLETIC GOODS: Mitts & Gloves, Baseball
SPORTING/ATHLETIC GOODS: Rods & Rod Parts, Fishing
SPORTING & ATHLETIC GOODS: Scoops, Crab & Fish
SPORTING & ATHLETIC GOODS: Shafts, Golf Club
SPORTING & ATHLETIC GOODS: Shooting Eqpt & Splys, General
SPORTING & ATHLETIC GOODS: Skateboards
SPORTING & ATHLETIC GOODS: Snowshoes
SPORTING & ATHLETIC GOODS: Strings, Tennis Racket
SPORTING & REC GOODS, WHOLESALE: Camping Eqpt & Splys
SPORTING & RECREATIONAL GOODS & SPLYS WHOLESALERS
SPORTING & RECREATIONAL GOODS, WHOLESALE: Diving
SPORTING & RECREATIONAL GOODS, WHOLESALE: Exercise
SPORTING & RECREATIONAL GOODS, WHOLESALE: Fishing
SPORTING & RECREATIONAL GOODS, WHOLESALE: Fitness
SPORTING & RECREATIONAL GOODS, WHOLESALE: Gymnasium
SPORTING & RECREATIONAL GOODS, WHOLESALE: Outboard Motors
SPORTING CAMPS
SPORTING FIREARMS WHOLESALERS
SPORTING GOODS
SPORTING GOODS STORES, NEC
SPORTING GOODS STORES: Bait & Tackle
SPORTING GOODS STORES: Firearms
SPORTING GOODS STORES: Fishing Eqpt
SPORTING GOODS STORES: Martial Arts Eqpt & Splys
SPORTING GOODS STORES: Team sports Eqpt
SPORTING GOODS: Surfboards
SPORTS APPAREL STORES
SPORTS CLUBS, MANAGERS & PROMOTERS
SPORTS TEAMS & CLUBS: Baseball
SPRINGS: Wire
STAFFING, EMPLOYMENT PLACEMENT
STAGE LIGHTING SYSTEMS
STAINLESS STEEL
STAIRCASES & STAIRS, WOOD

STAMPINGS: Automotive
STATE CREDIT UNIONS, NOT FEDERALLY CHARTERED
STATE SAVINGS BANKS, NOT FEDERALLY CHARTERED
STATIC ELIMINATORS: Ind
STATIONARY & OFFICE SPLYS, WHOLESALE: Looseleaf Binders
STATIONERY & OFFICE SPLYS WHOLESALERS
STATUARY GOODS, EXC RELIGIOUS: Wholesalers
STEEL & ALLOYS: Tool & Die
STEEL FABRICATORS
STEEL MILLS
STEEL, HOT-ROLLED: Sheet Or Strip
STEEL: Cold-Rolled
STENCILS
STEVEDORING SVCS
STOCK SHAPES: Plastic
STONE: Crushed & Broken, NEC
STONE: Quarrying & Processing, Own Stone Prdts
STORES: Auto & Home Supply
STRAPS: Bindings, Textile
STUCCO
STUDIOS: Artist's
STUDIOS: Artists & Artists' Studios
SUB-LESSORS: Real Estate
SUBSCRIPTION FULFILLMENT SVCS: Magazine, Newspaper, Etc
SUBSTANCE ABUSE CLINICS, OUTPATIENT
SUGAR SUBSTITUTES: Organic
SUMMER CAMPS, EXC DAY & SPORTS INSTRUCTIONAL
SUMMER THEATER
SUNDRIES & RELATED PRDTS: Medical & Laboratory, Rubber
SUNROOMS: Prefabricated Metal
SUPERMARKETS & OTHER GROCERY STORES
SURFACE ACTIVE AGENTS: Oils & Greases
SURGICAL & MEDICAL INSTRUMENTS WHOLESALERS
SURGICAL APPLIANCES & SPLYS
SURGICAL EQPT: See Also Instruments
SURGICAL IMPLANTS
SURVEYING & MAPPING: Land Parcels
SURVEYING INSTRUMENTS WHOLESALERS
SURVEYING SVCS: Aerial Digital Imaging
SURVEYING SVCS: Photogrammetric Engineering
SVC ESTABLISH EQPT, WHOLESALE: Carpet/Rug Clean Eqpt & Sply
SVC ESTABLISHMENT EQPT & SPLYS WHOLESALERS
SVC ESTABLISHMENT EQPT, WHOL: Cleaning & Maint Eqpt & Splys
SVC ESTABLISHMENT EQPT, WHOL: Concrete Burial Vaults & Boxes
SVC ESTABLISHMENT EQPT, WHOL: Stress Reducing Eqpt, Electric
SVC ESTABLISHMENT EQPT, WHOLESALE: Beauty Parlor Eqpt & Sply
SVC ESTABLISHMENT EQPT, WHOLESALE: Firefighting Eqpt
SVC ESTABLISHMENT EQPT, WHOLESALE: Laundry Eqpt & Splys
SVC ESTABLISHMENT EQPT, WHOLESALE: Sprinkler Systems
SVC ESTABLISHMENT EQPT, WHOLESALE: Vending Machines & Splys
SWIMMING POOL & HOT TUB CLEANING & MAINTENANCE SVCS
SWIMMING POOL SPLY STORES
SWITCHES: Electronic
SWITCHES: Electronic Applications
SYMPHONY ORCHESTRA
SYSTEMS ENGINEERING: Computer Related
SYSTEMS INTEGRATION SVCS
SYSTEMS INTEGRATION SVCS: Local Area Network
SYSTEMS INTEGRATION SVCS: Office Computer Automation
SYSTEMS SOFTWARE DEVELOPMENT SVCS

T

TABLE OR COUNTERTOPS, PLASTIC LAMINATED
TABLEWARE: Vitreous China
TAILORS: Custom
TANKS & OTHER TRACKED VEHICLE CMPNTS
TANKS: Fuel, Including Oil & Gas, Metal Plate
TANKS: Plastic & Fiberglass
TANNING SALON EQPT & SPLYS, WHOLESALE
TANNING SALONS
TANTALITE MINING

TARGET DRONES
TARPAULINS, WHOLESALE
TATTOO PARLORS
TAX RETURN PREPARATION SVCS
TAXI CABS
TECHNICAL WRITING SVCS
TELECOMMUNICATION EQPT REPAIR SVCS, EXC TELEPHONES
TELECOMMUNICATION SYSTEMS & EQPT
TELECOMMUNICATIONS CARRIERS & SVCS: Wired
TELECOMMUNICATIONS CARRIERS & SVCS: Wireless
TELECONFERENCING SVCS
TELEMARKETING BUREAUS
TELEPHONE ANSWERING SVCS
TELEPHONE CENTRAL OFFICE EQPT: Dial Or Manual
TELEPHONE EQPT INSTALLATION
TELEPHONE EQPT: NEC
TELEPHONE SET REPAIR SVCS
TELEPHONE SVCS
TELEPHONE: Automatic Dialers
TELEPHONE: Fiber Optic Systems
TELEVISION BROADCASTING STATIONS
TELEVISION FILM PRODUCTION SVCS
TELEVISION REPAIR SHOP
TEMPORARY HELP SVCS
TEMPORARY RELIEF SVCS
TEN PIN CENTERS
TENTS: All Materials
TESTERS: Physical Property
TEXTILE PRDTS: Hand Woven & Crocheted
TEXTILE: Finishing, Cotton Broadwoven
TEXTILE: Finishing, Raw Stock NEC
TEXTILE: Goods, NEC
TEXTILES: Jute & Flax Prdts
THEATER COMPANIES
THEATRICAL LIGHTING SVCS
THEATRICAL PRODUCERS & SVCS
THERMOELECTRIC DEVICES: Solid State
THERMOPLASTIC MATERIALS
THREAD & YARN, RUBBER: Fabric Covered
TICKET OFFICES & AGENCIES: Theatrical
TILE: Wall & Floor, Ceramic
TILE: Wall, Ceramic
TIMBER PRDTS WHOLESALERS
TIN ORE MINING
TIRE & TUBE REPAIR MATERIALS, WHOLESALE
TIRE DEALERS
TIRE RECAPPING & RETREADING
TIRES & INNER TUBES
TIRES & TUBES WHOLESALERS
TIRES & TUBES, WHOLESALE: Automotive
TIRES & TUBES, WHOLESALE: Truck
TITANIUM MILL PRDTS
TITLE & TRUST COMPANIES
TITLE ABSTRACT & SETTLEMENT OFFICES
TITLE INSURANCE: Real Estate
TOBACCO & PRDTS, WHOLESALE: Cigars
TOBACCO & PRDTS, WHOLESALE: Smokeless
TOBACCO & TOBACCO PRDTS WHOLESALERS
TOBACCO STORES & STANDS
TOBACCO: Cigarettes
TOILETRIES, COSMETICS & PERFUME STORES
TOILETRIES, WHOLESALE: Toiletries
TOILETS, PORTABLE, WHOLESALE
TOLL BRIDGE OPERATIONS
TOLL OPERATIONS
TOOLS & EQPT: Used With Sporting Arms
TOOLS: Hand
TOOLS: Hand, Power
TOURIST INFORMATION BUREAU
TOWELS: Paper
TOWING & TUGBOAT SVC
TOWING SVCS: Marine
TOYS
TOYS & HOBBY GOODS & SPLYS, WHOLESALE: Video Games
TOYS: Dolls, Stuffed Animals & Parts
TOYS: Kites
TOYS: Rubber
TRACTOR REPAIR SVCS
TRADERS: Commodity, Contracts
TRADERS: Security
TRAFFIC CONTROL FLAGGING SVCS
TRAILER PARKS
TRAILERS & PARTS: Truck & Semi's

PRODUCT INDEX

TRAILERS & TRAILER EQPT
TRAILERS: Bodies
TRANSLATION & INTERPRETATION SVCS
TRANSPORTATION AGENTS & BROKERS
TRANSPORTATION ARRANGEMENT SVCS, PASS: Sightseeing Tour Co's
TRANSPORTATION ARRANGEMENT SVCS, PASSENGER: Airline Ticket
TRANSPORTATION ARRANGEMENT SVCS, PASSENGER: Carpool/Vanpool
TRANSPORTATION ARRANGEMENT SVCS, PASSENGER: Tours, Conducted
TRANSPORTATION ARRANGEMNT SVCS, PASS: Travel Tour Pkgs, Whol
TRANSPORTATION BROKERS: Truck
TRANSPORTATION EPQT & SPLYS, WHOL: Aircraft Engs/Eng Parts
TRANSPORTATION EPQT & SPLYS, WHOLESALE: Marine Crafts/Splys
TRANSPORTATION EPQT/SPLYS, WHOL: Marine Propulsn Mach/Eqpt
TRANSPORTATION EQPT & SPLYS WHOLESALERS, NEC
TRANSPORTATION PROGRAMS REGULATION & ADMINISTRATION SVCS
TRANSPORTATION SVCS, AIR, NONSCHEDULED: Air Cargo Carriers
TRANSPORTATION SVCS, AIR, NONSCHEDULED: Helicopter Carriers
TRANSPORTATION SVCS, DEEP SEA: Intercoastal, Freight
TRANSPORTATION SVCS, NEC
TRANSPORTATION SVCS, WATER: River, Exc St Lawrence Seaway
TRANSPORTATION SVCS, WATER: Water Taxis
TRANSPORTATION SVCS: Airport
TRANSPORTATION SVCS: Airport Limousine, Scheduled Svcs
TRANSPORTATION SVCS: Bus Line Operations
TRANSPORTATION SVCS: Bus Line, Intercity
TRANSPORTATION SVCS: Highway, Intercity, Special Svcs
TRANSPORTATION SVCS: Railroad Terminals
TRANSPORTATION SVCS: Vanpool Operation
TRANSPORTATION: Air, Nonscheduled Passenger
TRANSPORTATION: Air, Nonscheduled, NEC
TRANSPORTATION: Air, Scheduled Freight
TRANSPORTATION: Air, Scheduled Passenger
TRANSPORTATION: Bus Transit Systems
TRANSPORTATION: Bus Transit Systems
TRANSPORTATION: Deep Sea Foreign Freight
TRANSPORTATION: Deep Sea Passenger
TRANSPORTATION: Local Passenger, NEC
TRANSPORTATION: Transit Systems, NEC
TRANSPORTATION: Trolley Systems
TRAVEL AGENCIES
TRAVEL ARRANGEMENT SVCS: Passenger
TRAVELER ACCOMMODATIONS, NEC
TRAVELERS' AID
TRUCK & BUS BODIES: Farm Truck
TRUCK & FREIGHT TERMINALS & SUPPORT ACTIVITIES
TRUCK BODIES: Body Parts
TRUCK BODY SHOP
TRUCK DRIVER SVCS
TRUCK GENERAL REPAIR SVC
TRUCK PAINTING & LETTERING SVCS
TRUCK PARTS & ACCESSORIES: Wholesalers
TRUCKING & HAULING SVCS: Contract Basis
TRUCKING & HAULING SVCS: Furniture Moving & Storage, Local
TRUCKING & HAULING SVCS: Garbage, Collect/Transport Only
TRUCKING & HAULING SVCS: Haulage & Cartage, Light, Local
TRUCKING & HAULING SVCS: Heavy, NEC
TRUCKING & HAULING SVCS: Liquid Petroleum, Exc Local
TRUCKING & HAULING SVCS: Mail Carriers, Contract
TRUCKING & HAULING SVCS: Mobile Homes
TRUCKING, ANIMAL
TRUCKING, AUTOMOBILE CARRIER
TRUCKING, DUMP

TRUCKING, REFRIGERATED: Long-Distance
TRUCKING: Except Local
TRUCKING: Local, With Storage
TRUCKING: Local, Without Storage
TRUCKING: Long-Distance, Less Than Truckload
TRUCKS & TRACTORS: Industrial
TRUCKS, INDL: Wholesalers
TRUCKS: Forklift
TRUNKS
TRUSSES & FRAMING: Prefabricated Metal
TRUSSES: Wood, Roof
TRUST COMPANIES: National With Deposits, Commercial
TRUST COMPANIES: State Accepting Deposits, Commercial
TRUST MANAGEMENT SVC, EXC EDUCATIONAL, RELIGIOUS & CHARITY
TRUST MANAGEMENT SVCS: Charitable
TRUST MANAGEMENT SVCS: Educational
TRUST MANAGEMENT SVCS: Personal Investment
TRUST MGMT SVCS: Priv Estate, Personal Invest/Vacation Fund
TUBING, COLD-DRAWN: Mech Or Hypodermic Sizes, Stainless
TUBING: Electrical Use, Quartz
TUBING: Plastic
TURBINE GENERATOR SET UNITS: Hydraulic, Complete
TURBINES & TURBINE GENERATOR SETS
TURKEY PROCESSING & SLAUGHTERING
TYPESETTING SVC

U

UNISEX HAIR SALONS
UNIVERSITY
UPHOLSTERY WORK SVCS
URBAN PLANNING & COMMUNITY & RURAL DEVELOPMENT SVCS
USED CAR DEALERS
USED MERCHANDISE STORES
USED MERCHANDISE STORES: Furniture
UTENSILS: Household, Cooking & Kitchen, Metal
UTILITY TRAILER DEALERS

V

VACATION LODGES
VACUUM CLEANER REPAIR SVCS
VACUUM CLEANER STORES
VACUUM CLEANERS: Household
VALUE-ADDED RESELLERS: Computer Systems
VALVES
VALVES & PIPE FITTINGS
VALVES: Indl
VALVES: Regulating & Control, Automatic
VARIETY STORE MERCHANDISE, WHOLESALE
VARIETY STORES
VEHICLES: All Terrain
VENDING MACHINE OPERATORS: Candy & Snack Food
VENDING MACHINE OPERATORS: Sandwich & Hot Food
VENDING MACHINE REPAIR SVCS
VENDING MACHINES & PARTS
VENTILATING EQPT: Metal
VENTURE CAPITAL COMPANIES
VESSELS: Process, Indl, Metal Plate
VETERANS AFFAIRS ADMINISTRATION SVCS
VETERANS' AFFAIRS ADMINISTRATION, GOVERNMENT: Federal
VIDEO PRODUCTION SVCS
VIDEO TAPE PRODUCTION SVCS
VINYL RESINS, NEC
VISA PROCUREMENT SVCS
VISITING NURSE
VISUAL COMMUNICATIONS SYSTEMS
VITAMINS: Natural Or Synthetic, Uncompounded, Bulk
VOCATIONAL TRAINING AGENCY

W

WALL COVERING STORE
WALLPAPER STORE
WAREHOUSING & STORAGE FACILITIES, NEC

WAREHOUSING & STORAGE, REFRIGERATED: Cold Storage Or Refrig
WAREHOUSING & STORAGE, REFRIGERATED: Frozen Or Refrig Goods
WAREHOUSING & STORAGE: General
WAREHOUSING & STORAGE: General
WAREHOUSING & STORAGE: Miniwarehouse
WAREHOUSING & STORAGE: Oil & Gasoline, Caverns For Hire
WAREHOUSING & STORAGE: Self Storage
WARM AIR HEATING & AC EQPT & SPLYS, WHOLESALE Air Filters
WARM AIR HEATING/AC EQPT/SPLYS, WHOL Warm Air Htg Eqpt/Splys
WASHERS
WASTE CLEANING SVCS
WATCH REPAIR SVCS
WATCHES
WATER SOFTENER SVCS
WATER SOFTENING WHOLESALERS
WATER SPLY: Irrigation
WATER SUPPLY
WATER TREATMENT EQPT: Indl
WATER: Pasteurized & Mineral, Bottled & Canned
WATERPROOFING COMPOUNDS
WEATHER RELATED SVCS
WEB SEARCH PORTALS: Internet
WEIGHING MACHINERY & APPARATUS
WELDING EQPT & SPLYS WHOLESALERS
WELDING EQPT REPAIR SVCS
WELDING EQPT: Electric
WELDING REPAIR SVC
WELDING SPLYS, EXC GASES: Wholesalers
WESTERN APPAREL STORES
WHEELCHAIR LIFTS
WHEELCHAIRS
WHISTLES
WIG & HAIRPIECE STORES
WINDOW BLIND REPAIR SVCS
WINDOW CLEANING SVCS
WINDOW FURNISHINGS WHOLESALERS
WINE & DISTILLED ALCOHOLIC BEVERAGES WHOLESALERS
WIRE
WIRE & CABLE: Aluminum
WIRE & WIRE PRDTS
WIRE FENCING & ACCESS WHOLESALERS
WIRE ROPE CENTERS
WIRE: Communication
WOMEN'S & CHILDREN'S CLOTHING WHOLESALERS, NEC
WOMEN'S & GIRLS' SPORTSWEAR WHOLESALERS
WOMEN'S CLOTHING STORES
WOMEN'S CLOTHING STORES: Ready-To-Wear
WOOD & WOOD BY-PRDTS, WHOLESALE
WOOD CHIPS, WHOLESALE
WOOD PRDTS
WOOD PRDTS: Applicators
WOOD PRDTS: Lasts, Boot & Shoe
WOOD PRDTS: Mulch Or Sawdust
WOOD PRDTS: Mulch, Wood & Bark
WOOD PRDTS: Novelties, Fiber
WOOD PRDTS: Trophy Bases
WOOD TREATING: Wood Prdts, Creosoted
WREATHS: Artificial

X

X-RAY EQPT & TUBES

Y

YARN MILLS: Rewinding
YOGURT WHOLESALERS
YOUTH CAMPS

PRODUCT & SERVICES SECTION

Indicates approximate employment figure
A = Over 500 employees, B = 251-500
C = 101-250, D = 51-100, E = 20-50
F = 10-19, G = 1-9

Product category — **BOXES: Folding**
Edgar & Son Paperboard .... G 999 999-9999
Yourtown *(G-11480)*
Ready Box Co .... E 999 999-9999
City — Anytown *(G-7097)*

Business phone

Geographic Section entry number where full company information appears.

See footnotes for symbols and codes identification.
- *Refer to the Industrial Product Index preceding this section to locate product headings.*

ABRASIVES
Dow Chemical Company .... B 302 368-4169
Newark *(G-6467)*

ACADEMIC TUTORING SVCS
Neighborhood House Inc .... F 302 658-5404
Wilmington *(G-11830)*

ACADEMY
West Wilmington Svnth Day Adv .... G 302 998-3961
Wilmington *(G-13168)*

ACCELERATION INDICATORS & SYSTEM COMPONENTS: Aerospace
Russell Associates Inc .... G 443 992-5777
Newark *(G-7370)*

ACCIDENT INSURANCE CARRIERS
Cigna Corporation .... C 302 792-4906
Wilmington *(G-9704)*

ACCOMMODATION LOCATING SVCS
GE Capital Intl Holdings Corp .... F 302 658-7581
Wilmington *(G-10684)*
Wetzel & Associates PA .... G 302 652-1200
Wilmington *(G-13175)*

ACCOUNTING SVCS, NEC
Alma Company .... G 302 731-4427
Newark *(G-5945)*
Automotive Accounting Service .... F 302 378-9551
Middletown *(G-3955)*
Bank of New York Mellon Corp .... G 302 791-1700
Wilmington *(G-9244)*
Belfint Lyons & Shuman P A .... D 302 225-0600
Wilmington *(G-9287)*
Bumpers & Company .... G 302 798-3300
Wilmington *(G-9505)*
Faw Casson & Co LLP .... E 302 674-4305
Dover *(G-1544)*
Hartnett Accounting & Tax Serv ...... G 302 477-0660
Wilmington *(G-10846)*
Lachall Lee LLP .... G 302 644-9952
Lewes *(G-3587)*
Lank Johnson and Tull .... G 302 422-3308
Milford *(G-4470)*
Mitten & Winters CPA .... F 302 736-6100
Dover *(G-1861)*
Nannas Haines & Schiavo PA .... E 302 479-8800
Wilmington *(G-11797)*
Pfpc Worldwide Inc .... F 302 791-1700
Wilmington *(G-12105)*
Thomson Reuters (grc) Inc .... A 212 227-7357
Wilmington *(G-12904)*
University of Delaware .... E 302 831-2961
Newark *(G-7623)*

ACCOUNTING SVCS: Certified Public
Baffone & Associates LLC .... G 302 655-1544
Wilmington *(G-9221)*
Baker Tilly Virchow Krause LLP ...... G 302 442-4600
Wilmington *(G-9223)*
Barbacane Thornton & Company ..... E 302 478-8940
Wilmington *(G-9247)*
Bdo Usa LLP .... D 302 656-5500
Wilmington *(G-9272)*

Bireley & Kortvelesy PA .... G 302 539-0311
Ocean View *(G-7767)*
Boyer & Boyer .... G 302 998-3700
Wilmington *(G-9403)*
Brousseau & Brousseau C P A .... G 302 234-1976
Wilmington *(G-9486)*
Christiana Incorporators Inc .... G 302 998-2008
Wilmington *(G-9687)*
Corcoran & Associates PA CPA ...... G 302 478-9515
Wilmington *(G-9858)*
Cover & Rossiter PA .... E 302 656-6632
Wilmington *(G-9882)*
Danny G Perez Ea MST .... G 302 422-2600
Milford *(G-4370)*
Diehl & Co CPA .... G 302 644-4441
Lewes *(G-3465)*
Dingle & Kane PA .... G 302 731-5200
Newark *(G-6450)*
Ekww Inc .... G 302 234-2877
Hockessin *(G-3018)*
Estep Douglas E Pub Accountant .... G 302 322-4621
New Castle *(G-5295)*
First State Cpas LLC .... G 302 736-6657
Dover *(G-1555)*
Gallagher & Associates PA .... G 302 239-5501
Wilmington *(G-10665)*
Gary Sj CPA .... G 302 730-3737
Dover *(G-1581)*
Grabowski Sprano Vnclette Cpas .... G 302 999-7300
Wilmington *(G-10757)*
Gunnip & Company .... D 302 225-5000
Wilmington *(G-10802)*
Horty & Horty PA .... E 302 652-4194
Wilmington *(G-10957)*
Horty & Horty PA .... E 302 730-4560
Dover *(G-1656)*
Howard Wimbrow CPA .... G 302 539-0829
Frankford *(G-2368)*
Jane L Stayton CPA .... F 302 856-4141
Georgetown *(G-2571)*
Jefferson Urian Dane Strner PA ...... E 302 856-3900
Georgetown *(G-2573)*
Jefferson Urian Dane Strner PA ...... F 302 539-5543
Ocean View *(G-7795)*
Jefferson Urian Dane Strner PA ...... F 302 678-1425
Dover *(G-1695)*
Kupferman & Associates LLC .... G 302 656-7566
Wilmington *(G-11300)*
Lank Johnson and Tull .... G 302 629-9543
Seaford *(G-8291)*
Lester & Co PC .... G 302 684-5980
Lewes *(G-3595)*
Luff & Associates CPA PA .... G 302 422-9699
Milford *(G-4479)*
Maillie LLP .... F 302 324-0780
New Castle *(G-5501)*
Marshall Wagner & Associates .... G 302 227-2537
Rehoboth Beach *(G-8001)*
Master Sidlow & Associates PA ...... E 302 384-9780
Newark *(G-7001)*
Miller & Associates PA .... G 302 234-0678
Wilmington *(G-11693)*
Orth & Kowalick PA .... G 302 697-2159
Dover *(G-1920)*
Patterson & Kelly PA .... G 302 736-6657
Dover *(G-1941)*
Progar & Co .... G 302 645-6216
Lewes *(G-3699)*
Raymond F Book III .... E 302 734-5826
Dover *(G-2011)*
Robert G Starkey CPA .... G 302 422-0108
Milford *(G-4545)*

Robert Hoyt & Co .... G 302 934-6688
Millsboro *(G-4793)*
Ross W Burnam CPA PA .... G 302 453-8161
Newark *(G-7365)*
Santora CPA Group Pa .... E 302 737-6200
Newark *(G-7385)*
Scassociates Inc .... F 302 454-1100
Middletown *(G-4231)*
Siegfried Group LLP .... C 302 984-1800
Wilmington *(G-12610)*
Simon Mstr & Sidlow Assoc Inc ...... E 302 652-3480
Newark *(G-7431)*
Snyder & Company PA .... F 302 475-1600
Wilmington *(G-12666)*
Sombar & Co CPA PA .... G 302 856-6712
Georgetown *(G-2659)*
Stephano Slack LLC .... G 302 777-7400
Wilmington *(G-12754)*
Szewczyk Company P A .... G 302 998-1117
Wilmington *(G-12840)*
Timothy D Humphreys .... F 302 225-3000
Wilmington *(G-12913)*
Wendy Cpa LLC .... G 302 377-7165
Bear *(G-375)*
Wheeler Wolfenden & Dwares CPA .. F 302 254-8240
Wilmington *(G-13183)*
William Humphreys & Co LLC .... G 302 225-3904
Wilmington *(G-13214)*
Zenker and Styer PA .... G 302 475-9006
Wilmington *(G-13346)*
Zimny & Associates PA .... G 302 325-6900
New Castle *(G-5847)*

ACUPUNCTURISTS' OFFICES
Christiana Chiropractic LLC .... G 302 633-6335
Newark *(G-6220)*
James Friesa Acupuncture .... G 302 674-4204
Dover *(G-1691)*
Psychotherapeutic Services .... G 302 678-9962
Dover *(G-1995)*

ADHESIVES
Hercules LLC .... C 302 594-5000
Wilmington *(G-10890)*

ADOPTION SVCS
Adoptions From Heart Inc .... G 302 658-8883
Wilmington *(G-8940)*
Delaware S P C A .... E 302 998-2281
Newark *(G-6409)*
Lost and Found Dog Rescue Adop ... G 302 613-0394
New Castle *(G-5487)*
Madison Adoption Associates .... F 302 475-8977
Claymont *(G-778)*

ADULT DAYCARE CENTERS
Active Day Inc .... F 302 831-6774
Newark *(G-5896)*
Angels Messiahs Foundation .... F 302 465-1647
Bear *(G-30)*
Christiana Care Home Health .... F 302 995-8448
Wilmington *(G-9685)*
Gull House Adult Activity .... G 302 226-2160
Lewes *(G-3526)*
Sussex County Senior Svcs Inc ...... G 302 854-2882
Georgetown *(G-2678)*

ADVERTISING AGENCIES

ADVERTISING AGENCIES

Advertising Healthy Inc .... G 302 366-7502
  Newark *(G-5912)*
Bayshore Communications Inc .... F 302 737-2164
  Newark *(G-6057)*
Chilay Inc .... G 302 559-6014
  Newark *(G-6196)*
Diamond State Promotions .... G 302 999-1900
  Wilmington *(G-10145)*
Effective Advertising Seaford .... G 302 628-1946
  Seaford *(G-8233)*
Epic Marketing Cons Corp .... E 302 285-9790
  Middletown *(G-4061)*
Essential Health Brands LLC .... G 302 322-1249
  Wilmington *(G-10438)*
Extreme Reach Inc .... F 302 366-7538
  Newark *(G-6557)*
Ezangacom Inc .... E 888 439-2642
  Middletown *(G-4067)*
Industrial Training Cons Inc .... F 302 266-6100
  Newark *(G-6774)*
K F Dunn & Associates .... F 302 328-3347
  Wilmington *(G-11215)*
Kiosked Corporation .... G 803 993-8463
  Wilmington *(G-11270)*
New ERA Media LLC .... G 302 731-2003
  Newark *(G-7105)*
Remline Corp .... E 302 737-7228
  Newark *(G-7316)*
Shiny Agency LLC .... G 302 384-6494
  Wilmington *(G-12603)*
Simplymiddle LLC .... F 302 217-3460
  Wilmington *(G-12629)*
Top Rated Media Inc .... E 888 550-9273
  Wilmington *(G-12930)*
Wh2p Inc .... G 302 530-6555
  Wilmington *(G-13180)*

ADVERTISING AGENCIES: Consultants

Almm Ventures LLC .... G 302 778-1300
  Wilmington *(G-9026)*
Aloysius Butlr Clark Assoc Inc .... D 302 655-1552
  Wilmington *(G-9029)*
Beanstock Media Inc .... E 415 912-1530
  Wilmington *(G-9273)*
Cohesive Strategies Inc .... E 302 429-9120
  Wilmington *(G-9762)*
Convention Coach .... G 302 335-5459
  Magnolia *(G-3887)*
Delaware Design Company .... G 302 737-9700
  Newark *(G-6375)*
Digital Generation Inc .... F 302 368-0002
  Newark *(G-6445)*
Grind or Starve LLC .... G 302 322-1679
  Wilmington *(G-10786)*
Janet Hughes and Associates .... F 302 656-5252
  Wilmington *(G-11128)*
Jay Gundel and Associates Inc .... G 302 658-1674
  Wilmington *(G-11132)*
Koncordia Group LLC .... F 302 427-1350
  Wilmington *(G-11288)*
Paragon Design Inc .... G 302 292-1523
  Newark *(G-7175)*
Shor Associates Inc .... G 302 764-1701
  Wilmington *(G-12608)*
Unified Companies Inc .... G 866 936-0515
  Wilmington *(G-13011)*

ADVERTISING DISPLAY PRDTS

Loyalty Is Earned Inc .... G 347 606-6383
  Wilmington *(G-11445)*

ADVERTISING MATERIAL DISTRIBUTION

Get Cents LLC .... E 203 856-0841
  Lewes *(G-3512)*

ADVERTISING REPRESENTATIVES: Electronic Media

Social Work Helper Pbc .... G 302 233-7422
  Dover *(G-2093)*
Yield Nexus LLC .... F 308 380-3788
  Dover *(G-2245)*

ADVERTISING REPRESENTATIVES: Media

Burris & Baxter Communications .... G 302 454-8511
  Newark *(G-6138)*

Melody Entertainment USA Inc .... G 305 505-7659
  Wilmington *(G-11627)*

ADVERTISING SPECIALTIES, WHOLESALE

Bill Ward Inc .... G 302 762-6600
  Wilmington *(G-9337)*
Convention Coach .... G 302 335-5459
  Magnolia *(G-3887)*
Creative Promotions .... G 302 697-7896
  Camden *(G-553)*
Goodman Manufacturing Co LP .... G 302 894-1010
  Newark *(G-6676)*
Jordan Marketing .... G 302 428-0147
  Townsend *(G-8802)*
New Image Inc .... G 302 738-6824
  Newark *(G-7106)*
Promotion Zone LLC .... G 302 832-8565
  Newark *(G-7269)*
Remline Corp .... E 302 737-7228
  Newark *(G-7316)*
Stamford Screen Printing Inc .... G 302 654-2442
  Wilmington *(G-12733)*

ADVERTISING SVCS, NEC

Gkua Inc .... F 415 971-5341
  Wilmington *(G-10718)*

ADVERTISING SVCS: Billboards

Clear Channel Outdoor Inc .... E 302 658-5520
  Wilmington *(G-9739)*
United Outdoor Advertising .... G 302 652-3177
  Wilmington *(G-13025)*

ADVERTISING SVCS: Direct Mail

Hibbert Company .... E 609 394-7500
  New Castle *(G-5394)*
Million Group .... G 302 543-8354
  Wilmington *(G-11696)*
Valassis Direct Mail Inc .... C 302 861-3567
  Newark *(G-7639)*

ADVERTISING SVCS: Display

Innospec Inc .... G 302 454-8100
  Newark *(G-6783)*
U Transit Inc .... G 302 227-1197
  Rehoboth Beach *(G-8102)*

ADVERTISING SVCS: Outdoor

Carvertise Inc .... G 302 273-1889
  Wilmington *(G-9583)*

ADVERTISING SVCS: Transit

Gotshadeonline Inc .... G 302 832-8468
  Bear *(G-168)*

ADVOCACY GROUP

Agh Parent LLC .... A 919 298-2267
  Wilmington *(G-8976)*
Aids Delaware Inc .... G 302 226-3519
  Rehoboth Beach *(G-7838)*
Champions For Childrens Mh .... G 302 249-6788
  Newark *(G-6185)*
Click For Savings LLC .... G 302 300-0202
  Bear *(G-78)*
Colonial Chapter of .... G 302 861-6671
  Newark *(G-6263)*
Community Interactions Inc .... G 302 993-7846
  Wilmington *(G-9794)*
Delaware Center For Digestive .... F 302 565-6596
  Newark *(G-6366)*
Global Childrens Advocacy LLC .... G 484 383-3900
  Dover *(G-1594)*
Greene Business Support S .... G 302 480-3725
  Dover *(G-1613)*
Hete Tech Support .... G 302 226-1892
  Rehoboth Beach *(G-7963)*
Hispanic Personal Dev LLC .... G 302 738-4782
  Newark *(G-6731)*
Independence Support Svcs LLC .... G 484 450-6662
  New Castle *(G-5413)*
Jewish Federation of Delaware .... F 302 478-5660
  Wilmington *(G-11153)*
Mad Delaware Chapter .... G 910 284-6286
  Lewes *(G-3616)*
Navy Operational Support Ctr W .... G 312 998-3328
  Wilmington *(G-11825)*

Ncf Supporting Organization .... G 850 776-2789
  Wilmington *(G-11826)*
Pcmh Support Team - Privacy .... G 267 254-2111
  Wilmington *(G-12051)*
Richard Allen Coalition .... G 302 258-7182
  Georgetown *(G-2638)*
Salvation Army .... E 302 654-8808
  Wilmington *(G-12530)*
St Matthew Grand Chapter .... G 302 834-9552
  Dover *(G-2101)*
Supportive Care Solutions LLC .... G 302 598-4797
  Wilmington *(G-12813)*
Thedigitalsupport .... G 347 305-4006
  Wilmington *(G-12893)*

AEROBIC DANCE & EXERCISE CLASSES

American Karate Studios .... E 302 737-9500
  Newark *(G-5954)*

AGENTS, BROKERS & BUREAUS: Personal Service

American-Eurasian Exch Co LLC .... G 202 701-4009
  Wilmington *(G-9060)*
At Systems Atlantic Inc .... F 302 762-5444
  Wilmington *(G-9170)*
Delaware Ecumenical Council .... G 302 225-1040
  Wilmington *(G-10043)*
Domian International Svc LLC .... G 804 837-3616
  Smyrna *(G-8624)*
Drfish LLC .... G 978 393-1212
  Lewes *(G-3473)*
Du Pont Foreign Sales Corp .... A 302 774-1000
  Wilmington *(G-10244)*
Forum To Advnce Mnrties In Eng .... E 302 777-3254
  Wilmington *(G-10595)*
ICS America Inc .... G 215 979-1620
  Wilmington *(G-10990)*
Incolor Inc .... G 302 984-2695
  Wilmington *(G-11014)*
James T Vaughn .... G 302 653-9261
  Smyrna *(G-8663)*
Susan Straughen .... G 302 856-7703
  Georgetown *(G-2673)*
Techgas Inc .... G 302 856-4111
  Georgetown *(G-2688)*

AGENTS: Loan

Creditshop LLC .... F 302 588-0107
  Wilmington *(G-9896)*
Delaware Title Loans Inc .... G 302 644-3640
  Lewes *(G-3458)*
Geris Auto Financial Services .... G 302 660-9719
  Newark *(G-6650)*
Innovation Ventures LP .... G 302 777-1616
  Wilmington *(G-11038)*
Loan Till Payday LLC .... E 302 792-5001
  Claymont *(G-776)*

AGRICULTURAL CREDIT INSTITUTIONS

American Finance LLC .... D 302 674-0365
  Harrington *(G-2808)*
Midatlantic Farm Credit .... F 302 734-7534
  Dover *(G-1852)*
Midatlantic Farm Credit Aca .... G 302 856-9081
  Georgetown *(G-2604)*

AGRICULTURAL EQPT: Clippers, Animal, Hand Or Electric

Macknyfe Specialties .... G 302 239-4904
  Hockessin *(G-3084)*

AGRICULTURAL EQPT: Irrigation Eqpt, Self-Propelled

Wilmington .... G 302 357-4509
  Wilmington *(G-13221)*

AGRICULTURAL EQPT: Tractors, Farm

Cnh Cptal Oprting Lase Eqp Rcv .... B 262 636-6011
  Wilmington *(G-9750)*

AGRICULTURAL EQPT: Turf & Grounds Eqpt

Turfhound Inc .... G 215 783-8143
  Wilmington *(G-12992)*

PRODUCT & SERVICES SECTION

AGRICULTURAL MACHINERY & EQPT REPAIR

Tucker Mechanical Service Inc .... G 302 536-7730
  Seaford (G-8426)

AGRICULTURAL MACHINERY & EQPT: Wholesalers

Baxter Farms Inc .... G 302 856-1818
  Georgetown (G-2447)
Northeast Agri Systems Inc .... G 302 875-1886
  Laurel (G-3266)
Richard Sapp Farms .... G 302 684-4727
  Milton (G-4960)
Taylor and Messick Inc .... F 302 398-3729
  Harrington (G-2897)
Willard Agri Service Greenw .... G 302 349-4100
  Farmington (G-2268)

AID TO FAMILIES WITH DEPENDENT CHILDREN OR AFDC

Aids Delaware Inc .... E 302 652-6776
  Wilmington (G-8986)

AIR CLEANING SYSTEMS

Ptm Manufacturing LLC .... G 302 455-9733
  New Castle (G-5651)

AIR CONDITIONERS: Motor Vehicle

Air Intrnational US Sbusid Inc .... D 248 819-1602
  Wilmington (G-8991)

AIR CONDITIONING & VENTILATION EQPT & SPLYS: Wholesales

Delmarva Refrigeration Inc .... G 302 846-2727
  Delmar (G-992)
Greenberg Supply Co Inc .... E 302 656-4496
  Wilmington (G-10777)
Peirce-Phelps Inc .... G 302 633-9352
  Wilmington (G-12060)

AIR CONDITIONING EQPT

Omega Industries Inc .... G 302 734-3835
  Dover (G-1916)

AIR CONDITIONING EQPT, WHOLE HOUSE: Wholesalers

R E Michel Company LLC .... G 302 322-7480
  New Castle (G-5662)

AIR CONDITIONING REPAIR SVCS

Berry Refrigeration Co .... E 302 733-0933
  Newark (G-6073)
Burns & McBride Inc .... D 302 656-5110
  New Castle (G-5121)
Commercial Equipment Service .... G 302 475-6682
  Wilmington (G-9786)

AIR DUCT CLEANING SVCS

Colonial Cleaning Services Inc .... G 302 660-2067
  Wilmington (G-9773)
Ducts R US LLC .... G 302 284-4006
  Felton (G-2288)

AIR PURIFICATION EQPT

TS Air Enterprises LLC .... G 302 533-7458
  Newark (G-7598)

AIRCRAFT & HEAVY EQPT REPAIR SVCS

Arteaga Properties LLC .... G 808 339-6906
  Wilmington (G-9136)

AIRCRAFT ASSEMBLY PLANTS

Aircraft Specialties .... G 302 762-0816
  Wilmington (G-8995)
Anthony Streett .... G 302 528-2861
  Dover (G-1128)
Grindstone Aviation LLC .... G 302 324-1993
  New Castle (G-5363)
Pats Aircraft LLC .... C 855 236-1638
  Georgetown (G-2613)
Pegasus Air Inc .... G 302 875-3540
  Laurel (G-3269)
Webro Holdings LLC .... G 302 314-3334
  Rehoboth Beach (G-8109)

AIRCRAFT CONTROL SYSTEMS:

Tesla Industries Inc .... E 302 324-8910
  New Castle (G-5763)

AIRCRAFT ENGINES & ENGINE PARTS: Lubrication Systems

Acurio LLC .... G 201 932-8160
  Wilmington (G-8931)

AIRCRAFT ENGINES & ENGINE PARTS: Research & Development, Mfr

Greenwich Aerogroup Inc .... G 302 834-5400
  Middletown (G-4093)

AIRCRAFT ENGINES & ENGINE PARTS: Starting Vibrators

Tesla Industries Inc .... E 302 324-8910
  New Castle (G-5763)

AIRCRAFT ENGINES & PARTS

Garrett Transportation I Inc .... G 973 455-2000
  Wilmington (G-10672)
General Electric Company .... C 302 631-1300
  Newark (G-6644)
Honeywell International Inc .... A 302 322-4071
  New Castle (G-5402)
MB Aerospace Acp .... G 586 772-2500
  Wilmington (G-11581)
S&H Logistics LLC .... G 708 548-8982
  Dover (G-2051)
Webro Holdings LLC .... G 302 314-3334
  Rehoboth Beach (G-8109)

AIRCRAFT EQPT & SPLYS WHOLESALERS

Delta Engineering Corporation .... F 302 325-9320
  New Castle (G-5247)

AIRCRAFT FLIGHT INSTRUMENT REPAIR SVCS

Summit Aviation Inc .... D 302 834-5400
  Middletown (G-4250)

AIRCRAFT MAINTENANCE & REPAIR SVCS

Aero Enterprises Inc .... G 302 378-1396
  Townsend (G-8754)
Dassault Aircraft Svcs Corp .... G 302 322-7000
  New Castle (G-5214)
Dumont Aviation LLC .... G 302 777-1003
  New Castle (G-5264)
Georgetown Air Services .... G 302 855-2355
  Georgetown (G-2539)
Georgetown Air Services LLC .... F 302 855-2355
  Georgetown (G-2540)

AIRCRAFT PARTS & AUXILIARY EQPT: Aircraft Training Eqpt

Nakuuruq Solutions .... G 302 526-2223
  Dover (G-1883)

AIRCRAFT PARTS & AUXILIARY EQPT: Assemblies, Fuselage

Pats Aircraft LLC .... C 855 236-1638
  Georgetown (G-2613)

AIRCRAFT PARTS & AUXILIARY EQPT: Body Assemblies & Parts

Decrane Aircraft Systems .... A 302 253-0390
  Georgetown (G-2496)

AIRCRAFT PARTS & AUXILIARY EQPT: Refueling Eqpt, In Flight

Patrick Aircraft Group LLC .... E 302 854-9300
  Georgetown (G-2612)

AIRCRAFT PARTS & AUXILIARY EQPT: Research & Development, Mfr

Envoy Flight Systems Inc .... G 302 738-1788
  Newark (G-6534)

AIRCRAFT PARTS & EQPT, NEC

Exploration Systems & Tech .... G 302 335-3911
  Wilmington (G-10461)
Global Air Strategy Inc .... G 302 229-5889
  Newark (G-6665)
Webro Holdings LLC .... G 302 314-3334
  Rehoboth Beach (G-8109)

AIRCRAFT PARTS WHOLESALERS

Dimo Corp .... E 302 324-8100
  New Castle (G-5254)

AIRCRAFT RADIO EQPT REPAIR SVCS

Corporate Arcft Technical Svcs .... G 302 383-9400
  Wilmington (G-9864)
Summit Aviation Inc .... D 302 834-5400
  Middletown (G-4250)

AIRCRAFT SEATS

First State Manufacturing Inc .... D 302 424-4520
  Milford (G-4414)

AIRCRAFT SERVICING & REPAIRING

Atlantic Aviation Corporation .... E 302 613-4747
  New Castle (G-5051)

AIRCRAFT UPHOLSTERY REPAIR SVCS

Pats Aircraft LLC .... C 855 236-1638
  Georgetown (G-2613)
Rayco Auto & Marine Uphl Inc .... G 302 323-8844
  Hockessin (G-3129)

AIRCRAFT: Airplanes, Fixed Or Rotary Wing

Boeing Company .... A 302 735-2922
  Dover (G-1219)

AIRLINE TRAINING

Favored Childcare Academy Inc .... G 302 698-1266
  Dover (G-1543)
Haymy Resources LLC .... G 402 218-6787
  Lewes (G-3537)

AIRPORT TERMINAL SVCS

Summit Aviation Inc .... D 302 834-5400
  Middletown (G-4250)

AIRPORTS, FLYING FIELDS & SVCS

Brian Garnsey .... G 302 463-1985
  Dover (G-1230)
Delaware River & Bay Authority .... E 302 571-6474
  New Castle (G-5236)
Flyadvanced LLC .... G 302 324-9970
  New Castle (G-5321)

ALARMS: Fire

Wayman Fire Protection Inc .... C 302 994-5757
  Wilmington (G-13125)

ALCOHOL TREATMENT CLINIC, OUTPATIENT

Brandywine Counseling .... D 302 655-9880
  Wilmington (G-9427)
Sodat of Delaware Inc .... F 302 656-2810
  Wilmington (G-12670)

ALCOHOLISM COUNSELING, NONTREATMENT

AMS of Delaware .... G 302 227-1320
  Rehoboth Beach (G-7840)
Delaware Drnking Drver Program ...... G 302 736-4326
  Dover (G-1367)
Delaware Drnking Drver Program ...... F 302 856-1835
  Georgetown (G-2499)

Employee Codes: A=Over 500 employees, B=251-500
C=101-250, D=51-100, E=20-50, F=10-19, G=1-9

2020 Harris Directory of Delaware Businesses

ALL-TERRAIN VEHICLE DEALERS

ALL-TERRAIN VEHICLE DEALERS

Walls Farm and Garden Ctr Inc ....G...... 302 422-4565
  Milford *(G-4594)*

ALUMINUM PRDTS

Uacj Trading America Co Ltd ....F...... 312 636-5941
  Wilmington *(G-13005)*

AMATEUR THEATRICAL COMPANY

Mirworth Enterprise Inc ....E...... 302 846-0218
  Delmar *(G-1021)*

AMBULANCE SVCS

Bill M Douthat Jr ....F...... 407 977-2273
  Lewes *(G-3385)*
Cft Ambulance Service Inc ....E...... 302 984-2255
  Bear *(G-70)*
Christiana Care Health Sys Inc ....F...... 302 623-3970
  New Castle *(G-5153)*
Christiana Fire Company ....G...... 302 834-2433
  Bear *(G-71)*
Delaware Cy Vlntr Fire Co No 1 ....C...... 302 834-9336
  Delaware City *(G-955)*
Felton Community Fire Co Inc ....C...... 302 284-9552
  Felton *(G-2291)*
Mid Atlantic Care LLC ....G...... 302 266-8306
  Wilmington *(G-11678)*
Primecare Medical Trnspt LLC ....E...... 302 422-0900
  Milford *(G-4530)*
Urgent Ambulance Service Inc ....E...... 302 454-1821
  Newark *(G-7632)*
Urgent Ambulance Service Inc ....E...... 302 454-1821
  Newark *(G-7633)*

AMBULANCE SVCS: Air

Air Methods Corporation ....G...... 302 363-3168
  Georgetown *(G-2426)*

AMBULATORY SURGICAL CENTERS

Dover Ophthalmology Asc LLC ....F...... 302 724-4720
  Dover *(G-1462)*
Dover Surgicenter LLC ....E...... 302 346-3171
  Middletown *(G-4045)*

AMMUNITION: Small Arms

Du Pont Chem Enrgy Oprtons Inc ....G...... 302 774-1000
  Wilmington *(G-10241)*

AMUSEMENT & REC SVCS: Baseball Club, Exc Pro & Semi-Pro

Beast of East Baseball LLC ....G...... 302 545-9094
  New Castle *(G-5079)*
Delaware Cobras Inc ....G...... 302 983-3500
  Bear *(G-106)*
Greater Newark Baseball L ....G...... 302 635-0562
  Newark *(G-6685)*
Little League Baseball Inc ....G...... 302 227-0888
  Rehoboth Beach *(G-7987)*
Mears Baseball Instruction ....G...... 302 448-9713
  Millsboro *(G-4739)*
Midway Little League ....F...... 302 737-3104
  Newark *(G-7037)*

AMUSEMENT & RECREATION SVCS, NEC

Frightland LLC ....G...... 302 838-0256
  Middletown *(G-4078)*
Paintball Action of Delware ....F...... 302 234-1735
  Hockessin *(G-3110)*

AMUSEMENT & RECREATION SVCS: Agricultural Fair

Delaware State Fair Inc ....E...... 302 398-3269
  Harrington *(G-2831)*

AMUSEMENT & RECREATION SVCS: Art Gallery, Commercial

S F F Art Inc ....G...... 302 226-9410
  Rehoboth Beach *(G-8064)*
Somerville Manning Gallery ....G...... 302 652-0271
  Wilmington *(G-12681)*

AMUSEMENT & RECREATION SVCS: Aviation Club, Membership

AMC Museum Foundation ....G...... 302 677-5938
  Dover *(G-1116)*
Army & Air Force Exchange Svc ....G...... 302 677-6365
  Dover *(G-1139)*

AMUSEMENT & RECREATION SVCS: Boating Club, Membership

Delaware Boat Registration ....G...... 302 739-9916
  Dover *(G-1359)*

AMUSEMENT & RECREATION SVCS: Card & Game Svcs

Doubleudiamond LLC ....G...... 206 502-0144
  Wilmington *(G-10209)*
Premier Entertainment III LLC ....E...... 302 674-4600
  Dover *(G-1982)*

AMUSEMENT & RECREATION SVCS: Diving Instruction, Underwater

Posidon Adventure Inc ....F...... 302 543-5024
  Wilmington *(G-12190)*

AMUSEMENT & RECREATION SVCS: Fishing Boat Operations, Party

Anglers Marina ....G...... 302 644-4533
  Lewes *(G-3340)*
Del Bay Charter Fishing LLC ....G...... 302 542-1930
  Milton *(G-4886)*
Hook Em & Cook Em LLC ....G...... 302 226-8220
  Milford *(G-4444)*
Judy V ....G...... 302 226-2214
  Rehoboth Beach *(G-7975)*

AMUSEMENT & RECREATION SVCS: Gambling & Lottery Svcs

Harrington Raceway Inc ....B...... 302 398-5346
  Harrington *(G-2846)*

AMUSEMENT & RECREATION SVCS: Gambling, Coin Machines

Harrington Raceway Inc ....B...... 302 398-5346
  Harrington *(G-2846)*

AMUSEMENT & RECREATION SVCS: Game Parlor

Days of Knights ....G...... 302 366-0963
  Newark *(G-6351)*

AMUSEMENT & RECREATION SVCS: Golf Club, Membership

Adkins Management Company ....F...... 302 684-3000
  Milford *(G-4303)*
Bayside Resort Golf Club ....E...... 302 436-3400
  Selbyville *(G-8453)*
Bear Trap Sales ....G...... 302 541-5454
  Ocean View *(G-7762)*
Brandywine Country Club ....D...... 302 478-4604
  Wilmington *(G-9428)*
Fieldstone Golf Club LP ....D...... 302 254-4569
  Wilmington *(G-10538)*
Forewinds Hospitality LLC ....G...... 302 368-6640
  Newark *(G-6605)*
Hunt Vicmead Club ....G...... 302 655-3336
  Wilmington *(G-10973)*
Hunt Vicmead Club ....E...... 302 655-9601
  Wilmington *(G-10974)*
Quail Associates Inc ....E...... 302 697-4660
  Camden Wyoming *(G-651)*
Salt Pond Associates ....F...... 302 539-2750
  Bethany Beach *(G-430)*
Silverside Club Inc ....F...... 302 478-4568
  Talleyville *(G-8751)*

AMUSEMENT & RECREATION SVCS: Gun Club, Membership

Police & Fire Rod & Gun Club ....G...... 302 655-0304
  New Castle *(G-5630)*

PRODUCT & SERVICES SECTION

AMUSEMENT & RECREATION SVCS: Ice Skating Rink

Pond Inc ....E...... 302 266-0777
  Newark *(G-7232)*

AMUSEMENT & RECREATION SVCS: Ice Sports

Five 1 Five Ice Sports Group L ....G...... 302 266-0777
  Newark *(G-6590)*
Skating Club of Wilmington Inc ....F...... 302 656-5005
  Wilmington *(G-12642)*

AMUSEMENT & RECREATION SVCS: Indoor Court Clubs

Mid Atlantic Grand Prix LLC ....E...... 302 656-5278
  New Castle *(G-5522)*

AMUSEMENT & RECREATION SVCS: Indoor Or Outdoor Court Clubs

Paladin Sports Club Inc ....F...... 302 764-5335
  Wilmington *(G-12008)*
Softball World LLC ....G...... 302 856-7922
  Georgetown *(G-2658)*

AMUSEMENT & RECREATION SVCS: Instruction Schools, Camps

Childrens Beach House Inc ....F...... 302 645-9184
  Lewes *(G-3413)*

AMUSEMENT & RECREATION SVCS: Karate Instruction

American Karate Studio ....F...... 302 529-7800
  Wilmington *(G-9052)*
Korean Martial Arts Institute ....F...... 302 992-7999
  Wilmington *(G-11289)*

AMUSEMENT & RECREATION SVCS: Lawn Bowling Club, Membership

Bowlamisha LLC ....G...... 302 727-4969
  Newark *(G-6109)*

AMUSEMENT & RECREATION SVCS: Lottery Tickets, Sales

Books & Tobaccos Inc ....F...... 302 994-3156
  Wilmington *(G-9393)*

AMUSEMENT & RECREATION SVCS: Massage Instruction

Delaware Learning Institute of ....F...... 302 732-6704
  Dagsboro *(G-895)*

AMUSEMENT & RECREATION SVCS: Outdoor Field Clubs

Lumber Jacks Axe Club LLC ....F...... 215 900-0318
  New Castle *(G-5490)*
Newark National Little League ....E...... 302 738-0881
  Newark *(G-7125)*

AMUSEMENT & RECREATION SVCS: Outfitters, Recreation

Kent County ....G...... 302 330-8873
  Frederica *(G-2409)*

AMUSEMENT & RECREATION SVCS: Physical Fitness Instruction

Elcoach Inc ....G...... 302 261-3794
  Wilmington *(G-10366)*
Playfit Education Inc ....G...... 302 438-3257
  Wilmington *(G-12155)*

AMUSEMENT & RECREATION SVCS: Racquetball Club, Membership

Kirkwood Ftnes Racquetball CLB ....F...... 302 529-1865
  Wilmington *(G-11275)*

PRODUCT & SERVICES SECTION

AMUSEMENT & RECREATION SVCS: Recreation Center

Business	Code	Phone
Bridge Studio of Delaware — Wilmington (G-9471)	G	302 479-5431
City of Newark — Newark (G-6243)	E	302 366-7060
Xbos — Smyrna (G-8748)	G	302 653-1800

AMUSEMENT & RECREATION SVCS: Recreation SVCS

Business	Code	Phone
G Rehoboth — Rehoboth Beach (G-7941)	G	302 278-7677
Young Mens Christian Associat — Wilmington (G-13333)	F	302 472-9622

AMUSEMENT & RECREATION SVCS: Scenic Railroads, Amusement

Business	Code	Phone
Historic Red Clay Valley Inc — Wilmington (G-10917)	G	302 998-1930

AMUSEMENT & RECREATION SVCS: School, Basketball Instruction

Business	Code	Phone
Nothing But Net Inc — New Castle (G-5580)	G	302 476-0453

AMUSEMENT & RECREATION SVCS: Shooting Range

Business	Code	Phone
Noble Eagle Sales LLC — Dover (G-1898)	F	302 736-5166
Shooters Choice Inc — Dover (G-2079)	G	302 736-5166

AMUSEMENT & RECREATION SVCS: Soccer Club, Exc Pro/Semi-Pro

Business	Code	Phone
Indian River Soccer Club — Ocean View (G-7793)	G	302 542-6397

AMUSEMENT & RECREATION SVCS: Swimming Club, Membership

Business	Code	Phone
Club Brennan — Bear (G-79)	G	302 838-9530
Country Swim Club Inc — Wilmington (G-9876)	G	302 420-5043
Drummond Hill Swim Club — Newark (G-6474)	G	302 366-9882
Graylyn Crest III Swim Club — Wilmington (G-10766)	G	302 547-5809
Kent Swimming Club Inc — Dover (G-1741)	F	302 674-3283
Ocean CLB Rsort Rservation Ctr — Newark (G-7141)	G	302 369-1420
Penn Acres Swim Club — New Castle (G-5613)	E	302 322-6501
Shellcrest Swim Club — Wilmington (G-12598)	G	302 529-1464

AMUSEMENT & RECREATION SVCS: Tennis & Professionals

Business	Code	Phone
David Marshall & Associates — Bethany Beach (G-396)	E	302 539-4488

AMUSEMENT & RECREATION SVCS: Tennis Club, Membership

Business	Code	Phone
Bethany Club Tennis LLC — Ocean View (G-7766)	G	302 539-5111
Eastern Athletic Clubs LLC — Hockessin (G-3016)	D	302 239-6688

AMUSEMENT & RECREATION SVCS: Tennis Courts, Non-Member

Business	Code	Phone
Lon Spa Inc — Newark (G-6947)	G	302 368-4595
Sea Colony Tennis Center — Bethany Beach (G-431)	G	302 539-4488

AMUSEMENT & RECREATION SVCS: Tour & Guide

Business	Code	Phone
Kensington Tours Ltd — Wilmington (G-11243)	D	888 903-2001
Megan Hegenbarth — Wilmington (G-11623)	G	302 477-9872

AMUSEMENT & RECREATION SVCS: Trampoline Operation

Business	Code	Phone
Wta Inc — Wilmington (G-13309)	E	302 397-8142

AMUSEMENT & RECREATION SVCS: Yoga Instruction

Business	Code	Phone
Torc Yoga LLC — Wilmington (G-12935)	G	856 408-9118
Yogo Factory — Newark (G-7728)	G	302 266-4506

AMUSEMENT & RECREATION SVCS: Zoological Garden, Commercial

Business	Code	Phone
Parks & Recreation Del Div — Wilmington (G-12024)	F	302 571-7788

AMUSEMENT ARCADES

Business	Code	Phone
Orbit Research LLC — Wilmington (G-11971)	G	302 683-1063
Seaside Amusements Inc — Rehoboth Beach (G-8071)	G	302 227-1921

AMUSEMENT PARKS

Business	Code	Phone
Fun Sport Inc — Rehoboth Beach (G-7939)	G	302 644-2042

AMUSEMENT/REC SVCS: Ticket Sales, Sporting Events, Contract

Business	Code	Phone
B & B Tickettown Inc — Wilmington (G-9208)	G	302 656-9797
Michael Schwartz — Wilmington (G-11666)	F	302 791-9999

ANALYZERS: Moisture

Business	Code	Phone
Ametek Inc — Newark (G-5962)	D	302 456-4400
Atlantic Remediation — Hockessin (G-2960)	F	610 444-5513

ANALYZERS: Network

Business	Code	Phone
Steven Abdill — Wilmington (G-12758)	G	443 243-6864

ANIMAL FEED & SUPPLEMENTS: Livestock & Poultry

Business	Code	Phone
Green Recovery Tech LLC — New Castle (G-5362)	G	302 317-0062
Nutrien AG Solutions Inc — Seaford (G-8333)	G	302 629-2780
Southern States Coop Inc — Middletown (G-4246)	F	302 378-9841
Southern States Coop Inc — Dagsboro (G-934)	F	302 732-6651

ANIMAL FEED: Wholesalers

Business	Code	Phone
B Diamond Feed Company — Camden Wyoming (G-617)	G	302 697-7576
E F AG Products & Service — Harbeson (G-2782)	G	302 945-2415

ANIMAL FOOD & SUPPLEMENTS: Chicken Feeds, Prepared

Business	Code	Phone
Mountaire Farms Inc — Frankford (G-2375)	E	302 732-6611

ANIMAL FOOD & SUPPLEMENTS: Feed Concentrates

Business	Code	Phone
Numake-1 LLC — New Castle (G-5582)	G	302 220-4760

ANIMAL FOOD & SUPPLEMENTS: Feed Premixes

Business	Code	Phone
Springhaus LLC — Wilmington (G-12714)	G	302 397-5261

ANIMAL FOOD & SUPPLEMENTS: Feed Supplements

Business	Code	Phone
Bi-State Feeders LLC — Harrington (G-2817)	G	302 398-3408

ANIMAL FOOD & SUPPLEMENTS: Livestock

Business	Code	Phone
B Diamond Feed Company — Camden Wyoming (G-617)	G	302 697-7576
Jbs Souderton Inc — Seaford (G-8278)	G	302 629-0725

ANTIBIOTICS

Business	Code	Phone
Glaxosmithkline Holdings — Wilmington (G-10720)	C	302 984-6932

ANTIPOVERTY BOARD

Business	Code	Phone
First State Cmnty Action Agcy — Georgetown (G-2532)	D	302 856-7761

ANTIQUE & CLASSIC AUTOMOBILE RESTORATION

Business	Code	Phone
Omniway Corporation — Newark (G-7147)	F	302 738-5076

ANTIQUE FURNITURE RESTORATION & REPAIR

Business	Code	Phone
New Life Furniture Systems — Wilmington (G-11864)	G	302 994-9054

APARTMENT LOCATING SVCS

Business	Code	Phone
Luxiasuites LLC — Wilmington (G-11460)	G	302 778-3000

APPAREL DESIGNERS: Commercial

Business	Code	Phone
Be Blessed Design Group LLC — Bear (G-45)	G	302 561-3793
Envision It Publications LLC — Bear (G-144)	G	800 329-9411

APPAREL FILLING MATERIALS: Cotton Waste, Kapok/Related Matl

Business	Code	Phone
Be Blessed Design Group LLC — Bear (G-45)	G	302 561-3793

APPLICATIONS SOFTWARE PROGRAMMING

Business	Code	Phone
Alias Technology LLC — Georgetown (G-2428)	G	302 856-9488
Arnab Mobility Inc — Newark (G-5997)	F	774 316-6767
Black Math Labs Inc — Dover (G-1208)	G	858 349-9446
Cloudbees Inc — Lewes (G-3430)	F	804 767-5481
Conventra LLC — Middletown (G-4008)	G	302 378-4461
Evolution Rx LLC — Townsend (G-8786)	G	614 344-4600
Falcons Media Group Inc — Wilmington (G-10483)	G	201 247-6489
Fever Labs Inc — Camden (G-571)	G	646 781-7359
Genex Technologies Inc — Newark (G-6647)	D	302 266-6161
One System Incorporated — Wilmington (G-11956)	F	888 311-1110
Operata LLC — Newark (G-7156)	G	302 525-0190
Scanpoint Inc — Wilmington (G-12552)	G	603 429-0777
Seven Tech LLC — Middletown (G-4238)	G	302 464-6488
SM Technomine Inc — Wilmington (G-12647)	F	312 492-4386
Syncretic Software Inc — Wilmington (G-12835)	G	302 762-2600

Employee Codes: A=Over 500 employees, B=251-500, C=101-250, D=51-100, E=20-50, F=10-19, G=1-9

2020 Harris Directory of Delaware Businesses

APPLICATIONS SOFTWARE PROGRAMMING

Unikie Inc ....F 408 839-1920
  Dover *(G-2177)*
Wna Infotech LLC ....E 302 668-5977
  Bear *(G-379)*
Xcs Corporation ....G 302 514-0600
  Wilmington *(G-13316)*
Zax Mobile LLC ....G 302 261-3232
  Newark *(G-7738)*

APPRAISAL SVCS, EXC REAL ESTATE

S Brown Appraisals LLC ....G 302 672-0694
  Harrington *(G-2882)*
Tag Sale By Changeover ....F 302 478-2450
  Wilmington *(G-12849)*

AQUATIC WEED MAINTENANCE SVCS

Envirtech Enviromental Consltg ....G 302 645-6491
  Lewes *(G-3484)*

ARBITRATION & CONCILIATION SVCS

Center For Community Justice ....G 302 424-0890
  Milford *(G-4343)*

ARCHEOLOGICAL EXPEDITIONS

University of Delaware ....F 302 831-2802
  Newark *(G-7629)*

ARCHITECTURAL SVCS

Architecture Plus Pa ....G 302 999-1614
  Wilmington *(G-9124)*
Arqitecture LLC ....G 302 777-5666
  Winterthur *(G-13356)*
Becker Morgan Group Inc ....F 302 734-7950
  Dover *(G-1189)*
Brandywine Cad Design Inc ....E 302 478-8334
  Wilmington *(G-9420)*
Breckstone Group Inc ....G 302 654-3646
  Wilmington *(G-9465)*
Cadrender LLC ....G 302 657-0700
  Wilmington *(G-9532)*
Delaware Architects LLC ....G 302 491-6047
  Milford *(G-4375)*
Edc LLC ....F 302 645-0777
  Lewes *(G-3478)*
Ji DCI Joint Venture 1 ....G 302 652-4221
  Wilmington *(G-11155)*
Ji DCI Jv-II ....F 302 652-4221
  Wilmington *(G-11156)*
Kci Technologies Inc ....E 302 731-9176
  Newark *(G-6871)*
Tevebaugh Associates Inc ....F 302 984-1400
  Wilmington *(G-12887)*
William Byler Jr Architect Inc ....G 302 653-3550
  Clayton *(G-874)*
Zahn Incorporated ....G 302 425-3700
  Wilmington *(G-13339)*

ARCHITECTURAL SVCS: Engineering

Cooperson Associates LLC ....G 302 655-1105
  Wilmington *(G-9853)*
Davis Bowen & Friedel Inc ....E 302 424-1441
  Milford *(G-4371)*

ARCHITECTURAL SVCS: Engineering

Abha Architects Inc ....E 302 658-6426
  Wilmington *(G-8902)*
Aecom Technology Corporation ....E 302 468-5878
  Wilmington *(G-8962)*
Andersen Ford Architects LLC ....G 302 388-7862
  Wilmington *(G-9077)*
Balfour Beatty LLC ....G 302 573-3873
  Wilmington *(G-9225)*
Bernardon PC ....F 302 622-9550
  Wilmington *(G-9309)*
Buck Simpers Archt + Assoc Inc ....F 302 658-9300
  Wilmington *(G-9498)*
Cooperson Associates Inc ....G 302 655-1105
  Wilmington *(G-9854)*
Design Collaborative Inc ....F 302 652-4221
  Wilmington *(G-10120)*
Fearn-CIndaniel Architects Inc ....G 302 998-7615
  Wilmington *(G-10510)*
Homsey Architects Inc ....F 302 656-4491
  Wilmington *(G-10946)*
Jaed Corporation ....F 302 832-1652
  Bear *(G-196)*

Montchanin Design Group Inc ....F 302 652-3008
  Wilmington *(G-11735)*
Moonlight Architechture Inc ....G 302 645-9361
  Lewes *(G-3648)*
R G Architects LLC ....F 302 376-8100
  Middletown *(G-4208)*
Staikos Associates Architects ....G 302 764-1678
  Wilmington *(G-12730)*

ARCHITECTURAL SVCS: House Designer

Design Delmarva ....G 302 644-8884
  Lewes *(G-3462)*
G A Hastings & Associates ....G 302 537-5760
  Ocean View *(G-7788)*

ARMATURES: Ind

AC Engineering ....G 215 873-6482
  Bear *(G-9)*

ARMORED CAR SVCS

Dunbar Armored Inc ....E 302 892-4950
  Wilmington *(G-10247)*
Dunbar Armored Inc ....E 302 628-5401
  Seaford *(G-8228)*
Garda CL Atlantic Inc ....E 302 762-5444
  Wilmington *(G-10670)*

ARRESTERS & COILS: Lightning

Nouvir Lightning Corporation ....G 302 628-9888
  Seaford *(G-8331)*

ART DEALERS & GALLERIES

George Hardcastle & Sons Inc ....G 302 655-5230
  Wilmington *(G-10700)*
Stuart Kingston Inc ....F 302 227-2524
  Rehoboth Beach *(G-8090)*
Youve Been Framed ....G 302 366-8029
  Newark *(G-7732)*

ART DESIGN SVCS

Bear Associates LLC ....G 302 735-5558
  Dover *(G-1184)*
Hplusmedia LLC ....G 347 480-8996
  Lewes *(G-3548)*
Little Nests Portraits ....F 610 459-8622
  Wilmington *(G-11405)*

ART GALLERIES

Gallery One ....G 302 537-5055
  Ocean View *(G-7790)*
Rh Gallery and Studios ....G 302 218-5182
  Hockessin *(G-3135)*

ART GALLERY, NONCOMMERCIAL

Mispillion Art League Inc ....G 302 430-7646
  Milford *(G-4506)*

ART GOODS, WHOLESALE

Netproteus ....G 206 203-2525
  Lewes *(G-3657)*

ART RELATED SVCS

Michael Pdmnczky Cnsrvator LLC ....G 302 388-0656
  Wilmington *(G-11664)*

ARTISTS' AGENTS & BROKERS

Transworld Diversfd Svcs Inc ....F 302 777-5902
  Wilmington *(G-12959)*

ARTISTS' EQPT

Artists At Work Inc ....G 302 424-4427
  Ellendale *(G-2257)*

ARTS & CRAFTS SCHOOL

Northeast Early Learning Ctr ....F 302 762-5803
  Wilmington *(G-11903)*

ASPHALT & ASPHALT PRDTS

Bardon U S Corporation ....G 302 552-3136
  Wilmington *(G-9253)*
Chemstar Corp ....G 302 465-3175
  Milford *(G-4350)*

Emulsion Products Company ....E 302 629-3505
  Seaford *(G-8236)*

ASPHALT COATINGS & SEALERS

Gardner Asphalt Corporation ....E 302 629-3505
  Seaford *(G-8248)*
Iko Manufacturing Inc ....D 302 764-3100
  Wilmington *(G-10999)*
Ipm Inc ....G 302 328-4030
  New Castle *(G-5424)*
Kings Sealcoating ....G 302 674-1568
  Dover *(G-1752)*

ASSEMBLING & PACKAGING SVCS: Cosmetic Kits

Scientific USA Inc ....G 425 681-9462
  Wilmington *(G-12559)*

ASSOCIATION FOR THE HANDICAPPED

Mosaic ....C 302 456-5995
  Newark *(G-7062)*
Special Olympics Delaware Inc ....F 302 831-4653
  Newark *(G-7467)*
United Cerebral Palsy of De ....E 302 764-2400
  Wilmington *(G-13023)*
United Cerebral Palsy of De ....G 302 335-3739
  Felton *(G-2324)*

ASSOCIATIONS: Bar

Delaware State Bar Association ....G 302 658-5279
  Wilmington *(G-10086)*

ASSOCIATIONS: Business

Alias Inc ....G 302 481-5556
  Wilmington *(G-9010)*
C S C Corporation Texas Inc ....D 302 636-5440
  Wilmington *(G-9524)*
Corporate Relocation Assn ....G 302 239-9314
  Newark *(G-6300)*
Delaware Comm Reinvstmnt Actn ....G 302 298-3250
  Wilmington *(G-10022)*
Delaware Dept Transportation ....C 302 577-3278
  Dover *(G-1365)*
Delaware State Farm Bureau ....G 302 697-3183
  Camden *(G-560)*
Delaware Stndrdbre Ownrs Assc ....G 302 678-3058
  Dover *(G-1398)*
Parks & Recreation Del Div ....F 302 761-6963
  Wilmington *(G-12023)*
Service Corps Retired Execs ....E 302 573-6552
  Wilmington *(G-12585)*
Small Business Development Ctr ....F 302 571-1555
  Wilmington *(G-12650)*
Uacj Trading America Co Ltd ....F 312 636-5941
  Wilmington *(G-13005)*

ASSOCIATIONS: Dentists'

Delaware State Dental Society ....F 302 368-7634
  Newark *(G-6414)*

ASSOCIATIONS: Fraternal

Benevolent & Protective Order ....G 302 424-2401
  Milford *(G-4322)*
Brandywine Club Inc ....G 302 798-9891
  Claymont *(G-705)*
Fraternal Order Eagles Inc ....G 302 764-6100
  Wilmington *(G-10621)*
Fraternal Order of Eagles BR ....G 302 616-2935
  Ocean View *(G-7786)*
Knights of Columbus ....F 302 559-9959
  Wilmington *(G-11282)*
New Temple Corp ....G 302 998-6475
  Wilmington *(G-11870)*
Voiture Nationale La Society ....G 302 478-7591
  Wilmington *(G-13100)*

ASSOCIATIONS: Homeowners

Angola By Bay Prprty Ownr Assn ....F 302 945-2700
  Lewes *(G-3341)*
Bay Forest Homeowners Assn ....G 302 537-6580
  Ocean View *(G-7757)*
Baywood Greens ....G 302 947-9800
  Millsboro *(G-4637)*

PRODUCT & SERVICES SECTION

AUTO & HOME SUPPLY STORES: Trailer Hitches, Automotive

ASSOCIATIONS: Manufacturers'

Seth Ral & Associates Inc .... G 302 478-9020
Wilmington *(G-12587)*

ASSOCIATIONS: Parent Teacher

Delaware Parents Association .... F 302 678-9288
Dover *(G-1386)*
East Millsboro Elem School Pto .... G 302 238-0176
Millsboro *(G-4684)*
Forest Oak Elementary Pta .... G 302 540-2873
Newark *(G-6603)*
Linden Hill Elementary Pta .... E 302 454-3406
Wilmington *(G-11395)*
North Star Pta .... G 302 234-7200
Hockessin *(G-3106)*
Pta Delaware Military Academy .... E 302 998-0745
Wilmington *(G-12263)*
Pta Lombardy Elementary .... G 302 478-6054
Wilmington *(G-12264)*
Silver Lake Elem Sch Pta .... D 302 378-5023
Middletown *(G-4241)*

ASSOCIATIONS: Real Estate Management

Arbor Management LLC .... C 302 764-6450
Wilmington *(G-9112)*
Asset Management Alliance .... F 302 656-5238
Wilmington *(G-9155)*
Bc Consulting Inc .... G 302 234-7710
Wilmington *(G-9271)*
Boston Land Co Mgt Svcs Inc .... G 302 571-0100
Wilmington *(G-9395)*
Brandywine Realty Management .... F 302 656-1058
Wilmington *(G-9452)*
Capano Management Company .... G 302 737-8056
Newark *(G-6149)*
Commonwealth Group LLC .... E 302 472-7200
Wilmington *(G-9791)*
Cressona Associates LLC .... F 302 792-2737
Claymont *(G-724)*
Crystal Holdings Inc .... D 302 421-5700
Wilmington *(G-9909)*
Dack Realty Corp .... G 302 792-2737
Claymont *(G-726)*
Deaton McCue & Co Inc .... G 302 658-7789
Wilmington *(G-9990)*
Delaware Valley Dev LLC .... F 302 235-2500
Hockessin *(G-3007)*
East Coast Property MGT Inc .... F 302 629-8612
Milford *(G-4400)*
Excel Property Management LLC .... G 302 541-5312
Millville *(G-4844)*
French Street Management .... F 302 571-8597
Wilmington *(G-10632)*
Guardian Property MGT LLC .... E 302 227-7878
Lewes *(G-3525)*
Harrison Properties Ltd Inc .... G 302 888-2650
Wilmington *(G-10843)*
Hh Property Management .... G 302 999-1414
Wilmington *(G-10900)*
Legum & Norman Mid-West LLC .... G 302 537-9499
Bethany Beach *(G-408)*
Lenape Properties MGT Inc .... G 302 426-0200
Wilmington *(G-11368)*
Mastriana Property Management .... G 302 234-4860
Wilmington *(G-11565)*
Mid-Atlantic Realty Co Inc .... G 302 738-5325
Newark *(G-7030)*
Mid-Atlantic Realty Co Inc .... G 302 737-3110
Newark *(G-7031)*
Milford Housing Development .... F 302 422-8255
Milford *(G-4499)*
One Hundred West Tenth St .... F 302 651-1469
Wilmington *(G-11955)*
P R C Management Co Inc .... F 302 475-7643
Wilmington *(G-11996)*
Panco Management Corporation .... F 302 366-1875
Newark *(G-7173)*
Panco Management Corporation .... G 302 995-6152
Wilmington *(G-12011)*
Panco Management Corporation .... F 302 475-9337
Wilmington *(G-12012)*
Patterson Price .... F 302 378-9852
Wilmington *(G-12037)*
Reybold Group of Companies Inc .... E 302 832-7100
Bear *(G-305)*
Robino Management Group Inc .... E 302 633-6001
Wilmington *(G-12442)*
Stephens Management Corp .... G 302 629-4393
Seaford *(G-8409)*
White Robbins Company .... G 302 478-5555
Wilmington *(G-13192)*
Woodlawn Trustees Inc .... E 302 655-6215
Wilmington *(G-13297)*

ASSOCIATIONS: Scientists'

American Birding Assn Inc .... G 302 838-3660
Delaware City *(G-948)*
Society For Whole-Body Autorad .... G 302 369-5240
Newark *(G-7452)*

ASSOCIATIONS: Trade

Delaware Credit Union Leag Inc .... G 302 322-9341
Newark *(G-6372)*
Delaware Healthcare Assn .... G 302 674-2853
Dover *(G-1376)*
Delaware Restaurant Assn .... G 302 738-2545
Newark *(G-6408)*
Delmarva Poultry Industry Inc .... G 302 856-9037
Georgetown *(G-2507)*
Insurance Networks Aliance LLC .... G 302 268-1010
Wilmington *(G-11045)*

ATHLETIC CLUB & GYMNASIUMS, MEMBERSHIP

Delaware Rock Gym Inc .... G 302 838-5850
Bear *(G-111)*
Gold Medal Gymnastics Inc .... G 302 659-5569
Smyrna *(G-8643)*
Midway Fitness Center .... G 302 645-0407
Rehoboth Beach *(G-8007)*
Paladin Sports Club Inc .... F 302 764-5335
Wilmington *(G-12008)*
Powerhouse Gym .... G 302 262-0262
Seaford *(G-8360)*

ATHLETIC ORGANIZATION

Little League Baseball Inc .... G 302 276-0375
New Castle *(G-5486)*
Piedmont Baseball League Inc .... G 302 234-9437
Hockessin *(G-3120)*
Wilmington Youth Rowing Assn .... F 302 777-4533
Wilmington *(G-13268)*
Windview Inc .... G 610 345-9001
Middletown *(G-4288)*

ATOMIZERS

Brandywine PDT Group Intl Inc .... E 302 472-1463
Wilmington *(G-9449)*
Falco Industries Inc .... G 302 628-1170
Seaford *(G-8241)*
Nova Industries LLC .... G 302 218-4837
Bear *(G-267)*
Pierpont Industries .... G 302 998-9220
Wilmington *(G-12133)*

AUCTION SVCS: Motor Vehicle

Center Stage Auto Auction .... G 302 325-2277
New Castle *(G-5140)*
Copart Inc .... F 302 628-5412
Seaford *(G-8208)*
Delaware Public Auto Auction .... E 302 656-0500
New Castle *(G-5234)*
Iaa Inc .... G 302 322-1808
New Castle *(G-5407)*

AUCTIONEERS: Fee Basis

Emmert Auction Associates .... F 302 227-1433
Rehoboth Beach *(G-7926)*
ONeal J C & Sons Auctioneers .... G 302 875-5261
Laurel *(G-3268)*
Reagan-Watson Auctions LLC .... G 302 422-2392
Milford *(G-4534)*
Southern Del Trck Growers Assn .... E 302 875-3147
Laurel *(G-3292)*
Spences Bazaar & Auction LLC .... F 302 734-3441
Dover *(G-2098)*
Wilsons Auction Sales Inc .... G 302 422-3454
Lincoln *(G-3874)*

AUDIO & VIDEO EQPT, EXC COMMERCIAL

Acoustic Audio Tek LLC .... G 302 685-2113
Wilmington *(G-8924)*
Brandywine Electronics Corp .... F 302 324-9992
Bear *(G-56)*

AUDIO ELECTRONIC SYSTEMS

Bat Electronics Inc .... G 302 999-8855
Wilmington *(G-9259)*
Helix Inc Ta Audioworks .... G 302 285-0555
Middletown *(G-4107)*
Sound-N-Secure Inc .... G 302 424-3670
Milford *(G-4563)*

AUDIO-VISUAL PROGRAM PRODUCTION SVCS

Petes Big Tvs Inc .... G 302 328-3551
New Castle *(G-5619)*

AUTHORS' AGENTS & BROKERS

Inc Plan (usa) .... G 302 428-1200
Wilmington *(G-11011)*

AUTO & HOME SUPPLY STORES: Auto & Truck Eqpt & Parts

Adams Auto Parts Inc .... F 302 655-9693
Wilmington *(G-8933)*
Dover Automotive Inc .... G 302 653-9234
Smyrna *(G-8625)*
Fishers Auto Parts Inc .... G 302 934-8088
Millsboro *(G-4691)*
Genuine Parts Company .... G 610 494-6355
Claymont *(G-752)*
T & J Murray Worldwide Svcs .... F 302 736-1790
Dover *(G-2125)*
True Mobility Inc .... G 302 836-4110
New Castle *(G-5797)*

AUTO & HOME SUPPLY STORES: Auto Air Cond Eqpt, Sell/Install

Cammocks Auto Works LLC .... G 302 597-0204
New Castle *(G-5129)*

AUTO & HOME SUPPLY STORES: Automotive Access

Geo-Fence Inc .... G 763 516-8934
Dover *(G-1589)*

AUTO & HOME SUPPLY STORES: Automotive parts

Action Automotive Inc .... G 302 429-0643
Wilmington *(G-8925)*
Bethany Auto Parts Inc .... G 302 539-0555
Ocean View *(G-7765)*
Bill Cannons Garage Inc .... F 302 436-4200
Selbyville *(G-8457)*
C & W Auto Parts Co Inc .... G 302 697-2684
Magnolia *(G-3883)*
Deltrans Inc .... F 302 453-8213
Newark *(G-6433)*
Fisher Auto Parts Inc .... G 302 998-3111
Wilmington *(G-10562)*
Fitzgerald Auto Salvage Inc .... D 302 422-7584
Lincoln *(G-3849)*
Forward Motion Inc .... G 302 658-2829
Wilmington *(G-10596)*
IG Burton & Company Inc .... E 302 424-3041
Milford *(G-4448)*
Just Right Tires Inc .... F 302 268-2825
Bear *(G-207)*
Ocean Pines Auto Service Ctr .... E 410 641-7800
Ocean View *(G-7806)*
Pettyjohns Custom Engine .... G 302 684-8888
Milton *(G-4950)*
Willis Ford Inc .... E 302 653-5900
Smyrna *(G-8746)*
Winner Infiniti Inc .... E 302 764-5900
Wilmington *(G-13274)*

AUTO & HOME SUPPLY STORES: Batteries, Automotive & Truck

Advance Auto Parts Inc .... G 302 644-0141
Lewes *(G-3325)*

AUTO & HOME SUPPLY STORES: Trailer Hitches, Automotive

Boyds Trailor Hitches .... G 302 697-9000
Camden Wyoming *(G-619)*

Employee Codes: A=Over 500 employees, B=251-500
C=101-250, D=51-100, E=20-50, F=10-19, G=1-9

2020 Harris Directory of Delaware Businesses

AUTO & HOME SUPPLY STORES: Truck Eqpt & Parts

Rhino Lnngs Del Auto Style Inc	F	302 368-4660
Newark (G-7335)		
Service Tire Truck Center Inc	F	302 629-5533
Seaford (G-8398)		
Transaxle LLC	G	302 322-8300
New Castle (G-5785)		

AUTOMATED TELLER MACHINE NETWORK

| Cash Connect Inc | E | 302 283-4100 |
| Newark (G-6165) | | |

AUTOMATIC REGULATING CONTROL: Building Svcs Monitoring, Auto

| Totaltrax Inc | D | 302 514-0600 |
| New Castle (G-5778) | | |

AUTOMOBILE FINANCE LEASING

| Star States Leasing Corp | E | 302 283-4500 |
| Newark (G-7484) | | |

AUTOMOBILE RECOVERY SVCS

Beeline Services LLC	G	302 376-7399
Middletown (G-3965)		
European Coach Werkes Inc	G	302 436-2277
Frankford (G-2362)		
Registered Agents Ltd	E	302 421-5750
Wilmington (G-12363)		

AUTOMOBILES & OTHER MOTOR VEHICLES WHOLESALERS

Dd Inc De LLC	G	302 669-9269
Claymont (G-730)		
Diamond Motor Sports Inc	D	302 697-3222
Dover (G-1423)		
Future Ford Sales Inc	D	302 999-0261
Wilmington (G-10654)		
Winner Ford of Newark Inc	C	302 731-2415
Newark (G-7710)		

AUTOMOBILES: Midget, Power Driven

| Stallard Chassis Co | F | 302 292-1800 |
| Newark (G-7479) | | |

AUTOMOBILES: Off-Road, Exc Recreational Vehicles

| Michael C Rapa | G | 302 236-4423 |
| Laurel (G-3264) | | |

AUTOMOBILES: Wholesalers

One Off Rod & Custom Inc	F	302 449-1489
Middletown (G-4179)		
Porter Nissan Buick Newark	D	302 368-6300
Newark (G-7233)		
Staplefords Sales and Service	E	302 834-4568
Saint Georges (G-8130)		
Winner Group Inc	E	302 292-8200
Newark (G-7711)		

AUTOMOTIVE & TRUCK GENERAL REPAIR SVC

4n Car Inc	G	302 856-7434
Georgetown (G-2417)		
A2b Auto Group	G	302 786-2331
Wilmington (G-8890)		
Admiral Tire	G	302 734-5911
Dover (G-1087)		
Alderman Automotive Enterprise	G	302 652-3733
New Castle (G-5021)		
ASAP Automotive	G	302 444-8659
Bear (G-39)		
AV Auto Worx LLC	F	302 384-7646
Wilmington (G-9194)		
Bayshore Ford Truck Sales Inc	D	302 656-3160
New Castle (G-5075)		
Bernard Limpert	G	302 674-8280
Dover (G-1195)		
Bill Cannons Garage Inc	F	302 436-4200
Selbyville (G-8457)		
Bullfeathers Auto Sound Inc	G	302 846-0434
Laurel (G-3205)		
Cammocks Auto Works LLC	G	302 597-0204
New Castle (G-5129)		
Car Clinic Inc	G	302 421-9100
Wilmington (G-9560)		
Careys Foreign & Domestic Repr	G	302 856-2779
Georgetown (G-2462)		
Caribb Transport Inc	G	302 274-2112
Wilmington (G-9570)		
Chriss Auto Repair	G	302 791-0699
Claymont (G-716)		
Classic Auto Sales & Service	G	302 684-8126
Harbeson (G-2775)		
Coveys Car Care Inc	G	302 629-2746
Seaford (G-8210)		
Deals On Wheels Inc	E	302 999-9955
Wilmington (G-9988)		
Donald Briggs		267 476-2712
Middletown (G-4042)		
Donaway Corporation	G	302 934-6226
Millsboro (G-4680)		
Dover Volkswagen Inc	E	302 734-4761
Dover (G-1472)		
E & M Enterprises Inc	G	302 736-6391
Dover (G-1490)		
Elite Auto LLC	G	302 690-2948
Middletown (G-4054)		
Everest Autoworks Auto Spa LLC	G	302 737-8424
Newark (G-6546)		
First Choice Auto & Truck Repr	G	302 656-1433
New Castle (G-5311)		
Four Brothers Auto Service	G	302 482-2932
Wilmington (G-10604)		
Fox Run Automotive Inc	F	302 834-1200
Bear (G-159)		
Freedom Rides Auto	G	302 422-4559
Seaford (G-8247)		
Furrs Tire Service Inc	G	302 678-0800
Dover (G-1573)		
Girls Auto Clinic LLC		484 679-6394
New Castle (G-5354)		
Golden Car Care	G	302 856-2219
Georgetown (G-2550)		
Goodyear Tire & Rubber Company	G	302 737-2461
Newark (G-6677)		
Griff Son Hometown Auto Rep	G	302 786-2143
Harrington (G-2843)		
Gumboro Service Center Inc	G	302 238-7040
Frankford (G-2366)		
Harris Towing and Auto Service	G	302 736-9901
Dover (G-1632)		
Harvey Road Automotive Inc	G	302 654-7500
Wilmington (G-10849)		
Henrys Car Care Inc	G	302 994-5766
Wilmington (G-10886)		
High Horse Performance Inc	G	302 894-1115
Smyrna (G-8652)		
Hoban Auto & Machineshop Inc	G	302 436-8013
Selbyville (G-8502)		
Horton and Bros Inc	G	302 738-7221
Newark (G-6747)		
IG Burton & Company Inc	D	302 422-3041
Milford (G-4447)		
IG Burton & Company Inc	D	302 424-3041
Milford (G-4448)		
J & K Auto Repair Inc	G	302 834-8025
Bear (G-194)		
J V Auto Service Inc	F	302 999-0786
Wilmington (G-11112)		
K & S Garage Inc	G	302 731-7997
Newark (G-6863)		
Kent Sussex Auto Care Inc	G	302 422-3337
Milford (G-4465)		
Kirkwood Auto Center LLC	F	302 995-6179
Wilmington (G-11273)		
Kirkwood Tires Inc	G	302 737-2460
Newark (G-6894)		
Lee Lynn Inc	F	302 678-9978
Dover (G-1775)		
Lube Depot	G	302 659-3329
Smyrna (G-8677)		
M Tech European Autohouse Inc	G	302 472-6813
Wilmington (G-11473)		
Maliks Auto Repair		302 325-2555
New Castle (G-5504)		
Manor Exxon Inc	G	302 834-6691
Bear (G-243)		
Martel & Son Foreign Car Ctr	G	302 674-5556
Dover (G-1820)		
Martin Newark Dealership Inc	C	302 454-9300
Newark (G-6996)		
Middletown Car Care	G	302 449-1550
Middletown (G-4154)		
Millcreek Texaco Station	G	302 571-8489
Wilmington (G-11691)		
Monro Inc	F	302 378-3801
Middletown (G-4168)		
Monro Inc	G	302 846-2732
Delmar (G-1022)		
Nallys Auto Plaza Inc	G	302 543-8126
Wilmington (G-11795)		
New Car Connection	F	302 328-7000
New Castle (G-5553)		
Ocean Pines Auto Service Ctr	E	410 641-7800
Ocean View (G-7806)		
Oil Spot Express Lube Center	G	302 628-9866
Seaford (G-8335)		
Patriot Auto & Truck Care LLC	G	302 257-5715
Dover (G-1940)		
Paul F Campanella Inc	F	302 777-7170
Wilmington (G-12041)		
Petes Garage Inc	G	302 286-6069
Newark (G-7206)		
Pettyjohns Custom Engine	G	302 684-8888
Milton (G-4950)		
Phillip E Weir	G	302 652-1312
Wilmington (G-12115)		
Powertrain Technology Inc	G	302 368-4900
Newark (G-7237)		
Preferred Auto and Cycle LLC	G	302 855-0169
Dagsboro (G-931)		
Pro Trans Inc	G	302 328-1550
Bear (G-292)		
Rbs Auto Repair Inc	G	302 678-8803
Dover (G-2012)		
Redmill Auto Repair	G	302 292-2155
Newark (G-7310)		
Rinehimer Body Shop Inc	F	302 737-7350
Newark (G-7342)		
Rittenhouse Motor Co Inc	E	302 731-5059
Newark (G-7345)		
Ronnies Auto Repairs Inc	G	302 994-4703
Wilmington (G-12472)		
Route 9 Auto Center	G	302 856-3941
Georgetown (G-2643)		
Sals Garage Inc	G	302 655-4981
Wilmington (G-12527)		
Scott Muffler LLC	G	302 378-9247
Middletown (G-4233)		
Service King Holdings LLC	E	302 797-8783
Claymont (G-804)		
Sevys Auto Service Inc	G	302 328-0839
New Castle (G-5701)		
Silview Auto Care	G	302 994-1617
Wilmington (G-12622)		
Smiths Jack Towing & Svc Ctr	G	302 798-6667
Wilmington (G-12663)		
Smittys Auto Repair Inc	G	302 398-8419
Harrington (G-2890)		
Sports Car Service Inc	F	302 764-7439
Wilmington (G-12709)		
Stokes Garage Inc	G	302 994-0613
Wilmington (G-12768)		
Tbc Retail Group Inc	E	302 478-8013
Wilmington (G-12855)		
Three Js Disc Tire & Auto Svc	E	302 995-6141
Wilmington (G-12906)		
TSC Enterprises LLC	G	302 934-6158
Millsboro (G-4815)		
Tune-Up III of MD Inc	G	410 655-9500
Frankford (G-2395)		
United Auto Sales Inc	G	302 325-3000
New Castle (G-5803)		
Wallis Repair Inc	G	302 378-4301
Middletown (G-4279)		
Wiedman Enterprises Inc	G	302 226-2407
Rehoboth Beach (G-8115)		
William T Wadkins Garage Inc	G	302 422-0265
Milford (G-4608)		
Willis Ford Inc	E	302 653-5900
Smyrna (G-8746)		
Winner Group Inc	E	302 292-8200
Newark (G-7711)		
Winner Infiniti Inc	E	302 764-5900
Wilmington (G-13274)		
Wolfs Elite Autos	G	302 999-9199
Wilmington (G-13287)		

AUTOMOTIVE BATTERIES WHOLESALERS

| Carl King Tire Co Inc | E | 302 697-9506 |
| Camden (G-546) | | |

PRODUCT & SERVICES SECTION

AUTOMOTIVE REPAIR SHOPS: Engine Repair

Delaware Tire Center Inc .... F 302 674-0234
  Dover *(G-1402)*
Tri State Battery and Auto Elc .... F 302 292-2330
  Newark *(G-7584)*

AUTOMOTIVE BODY SHOP

ABRA Auto Body & Glass LP .... F 302 279-1007
  Middletown *(G-3927)*
Allen Body Works Inc .... G 302 875-3208
  Laurel *(G-3192)*
Armigers Auto Center Inc .... G 302 875-7642
  Laurel *(G-3193)*
Auto Works Collision Ctr LLC .... F 302 732-3902
  Dagsboro *(G-879)*
Automotive Services Inc .... F 302 762-0100
  Wilmington *(G-9190)*
Brandywine Body Shop Inc .... G 302 998-0424
  Wilmington *(G-9418)*
Brasures Body Shop Inc .... G 302 732-6157
  Frankford *(G-2349)*
Chets Auto Body Inc .... G 302 875-3376
  Laurel *(G-3213)*
Christiana Body Shop Inc .... G 302 655-1085
  Wilmington *(G-9674)*
Classic Auto Body Inc .... G 302 655-4044
  Wilmington *(G-9733)*
Complete Auto Body Inc .... E 302 629-3955
  Seaford *(G-8203)*
Dent Pro Inc .... G 302 628-0978
  Seaford *(G-8222)*
Dominos Body Shop .... G 302 697-3801
  Camden Wyoming *(G-630)*
Doug Richmonds Body Shop .... F 302 453-1173
  Newark *(G-6463)*
Dunnings Body Shop .... G 302 653-9615
  Clayton *(G-843)*
East Coast Auto Body Inc .... G 302 265-6830
  Dover *(G-1498)*
Eastern Auto Body Inc .... G 302 731-1200
  Bear *(G-138)*
Edward J Henry & Sons Inc .... F 302 658-4324
  Wilmington *(G-10357)*
Ellmore Auto Collision .... G 302 762-2301
  Wilmington *(G-10381)*
Executive Auto Repairs Inc .... G 302 995-6220
  Wilmington *(G-10459)*
Henry Bros Autobody & Pnt Sp .... F 302 994-4438
  Wilmington *(G-10885)*
Joes Paint & Body Shop Inc .... G 302 855-0281
  Georgetown *(G-2576)*
Johns Body Shop Inc .... F 302 658-5133
  Wilmington *(G-11177)*
Maaco Collision Repr Auto Pntg .... G 610 628-3867
  Wilmington *(G-11475)*
Mackmetts Auto Body .... G 302 366-8107
  Townsend *(G-8807)*
Martin Dealership .... G 302 738-5200
  Newark *(G-6995)*
Master Tech Inc .... E 302 832-1660
  Bear *(G-247)*
Puzs Body Shop Inc .... G 302 368-8265
  Newark *(G-7274)*
Rex Auto Body Inc .... G 302 731-4707
  Newark *(G-7331)*
Rossi Auto Body Inc .... G 302 999-7707
  Wilmington *(G-12480)*
Rudlyn Inc .... F 302 764-5677
  Wilmington *(G-12490)*
Techniques Inc .... G 302 422-7760
  Newark *(G-7546)*
Whites Body Shop .... G 302 655-4369
  Wilmington *(G-13194)*

AUTOMOTIVE BODY, PAINT & INTERIOR REPAIR & MAINTENANCE SVC

Autoport Inc .... E 302 658-5100
  New Castle *(G-5057)*
Car Tech Auto Center .... G 302 368-4104
  Newark *(G-6151)*
Future Ford Sales Inc .... D 302 999-0261
  Wilmington *(G-10654)*
Gas & Go Inc .... G 302 734-8234
  Dover *(G-1582)*
Housers Auto Trim Inc .... G 302 422-1290
  Milford *(G-4445)*
New Car Connection .... F 302 328-7000
  New Castle *(G-5553)*
Pine Valley Corvettes .... G 302 834-1268
  Middletown *(G-4193)*

Willis Ford Inc .... E 302 653-5900
  Smyrna *(G-8746)*

AUTOMOTIVE BRAKE REPAIR SHOPS

Bernard Limpert .... G 302 674-8280
  Dover *(G-1195)*
J & K Auto Repair Inc .... G 302 834-8025
  Bear *(G-194)*
Sevys Auto Service Inc .... G 302 328-0839
  New Castle *(G-5701)*
Tomall Inc .... G 302 424-4004
  Milford *(G-4579)*

AUTOMOTIVE COLLISION SHOPS

Auto Collision Service .... G 302 328-5611
  New Castle *(G-5055)*
Betts Texaco and B & G GL Inc .... G 302 834-2284
  Newark *(G-6076)*
Hertrich Collision Ctr of .... G 302 839-0550
  Milford *(G-4440)*
Lewes Body Works Inc .... G 302 645-5595
  Lewes *(G-3596)*
Wilmington Collision Ctr LLC .... G 302 764-3520
  Wilmington *(G-13227)*
Winner Premier Collision Ctr .... E 302 571-5200
  Wilmington *(G-13275)*

AUTOMOTIVE CUSTOMIZING SVCS, NONFACTORY BASIS

Rhodes Custom Auto Works Inc .... G 302 378-1701
  Townsend *(G-8819)*

AUTOMOTIVE DEALERS, NEC

New Car Connection .... F 302 328-7000
  New Castle *(G-5553)*

AUTOMOTIVE GLASS REPLACEMENT SHOPS

A R Myers Corporation .... E 302 652-3164
  Wilmington *(G-8882)*
Delmarva Auto Glass Inc .... G 302 934-8600
  Dagsboro *(G-896)*
Go-Glass Corporation .... F 302 674-3390
  Dover *(G-1596)*
Mikes Glass Service Inc .... F 302 658-7936
  Wilmington *(G-11686)*
Parags Glass Company .... G 302 737-0101
  Newark *(G-7176)*
Pro-Bond Auto Glass .... G 302 324-8500
  New Castle *(G-5648)*
Safelite Fulfillment Inc .... G 302 678-9600
  Dover *(G-2052)*
Safelite Fulfillment Inc .... F 302 999-9908
  Wilmington *(G-12518)*
Safelite Fulfillment Inc .... G 302 856-7175
  Georgetown *(G-2646)*
Safelite Glass Corp 877 800-2727
  Dover *(G-2053)*
Safelite Glass Corp .... F 302 656-4640
  Wilmington *(G-12519)*
U A G Inc .... F 302 731-2747
  Newark *(G-7604)*

AUTOMOTIVE LETTERING & PAINTING SVCS

Quillen Signs LLC .... G 302 684-3661
  Milton *(G-4954)*

AUTOMOTIVE PAINT SHOP

A R Myers Corporation .... E 302 652-3164
  Wilmington *(G-8882)*
Jewell Enterprises Inc .... F 302 737-8460
  Newark *(G-6837)*
Kns09 Inc .... F 302 697-3499
  Dover *(G-1756)*
Kpkm Inc .... G 302 678-0271
  Dover *(G-1757)*
Performance Auto Body & Paint .... G 302 655-6170
  Wilmington *(G-12084)*
Red Barn Inc .... G 302 678-0271
  Dover *(G-2017)*
Rickards Auto Body .... G 302 934-9600
  Millsboro *(G-4790)*

AUTOMOTIVE PARTS, ACCESS & SPLYS

Alternative Eco Energy LLC .... G 404 434-0660
  Newark *(G-5948)*
Bever Mobility Products Inc .... G 312 375-0300
  Wilmington *(G-9319)*
Craig Ball Sales Inc .... G 302 628-9900
  Seaford *(G-8212)*
Forward Motion Inc .... G 302 658-2829
  Wilmington *(G-10596)*
Gif North America LLC .... B 703 969-9243
  Rehoboth Beach *(G-7948)*
Lkq Northeast Inc .... G 800 223-0171
  Dover *(G-1793)*
NAPA M3 Inc 719 660-6263
  Dover *(G-11800)*
NGK North America Inc .... G 302 654-1344
  Wilmington *(G-11884)*
Pressair International .... G 302 636-5440
  Wilmington *(G-12222)*
Steering Sltions Ip Holdg Corp .... G 313 556-5000
  Wilmington *(G-12749)*
Wilmington Fibre Specialty Co .... E 302 328-7525
  New Castle *(G-5836)*

AUTOMOTIVE PARTS: Plastic

Resource Intl Inc .... F 302 762-4501
  New Castle *(G-5675)*
Smrc Smart Automotive .... G 317 941-7257
  Wilmington *(G-12664)*

AUTOMOTIVE PRDTS: Rubber

Forcebeyond Inc .... E 302 995-6588
  Wilmington *(G-10590)*

AUTOMOTIVE RADIATOR REPAIR SHOPS

Farmers Radiator & AC .... G 302 235-5922
  Newark *(G-6572)*

AUTOMOTIVE REPAIR SHOPS: Brake Repair

Blue Hen Spring Works Inc .... F 302 422-6600
  Milford *(G-4328)*
Meadowood Mobil Station .... G 302 731-5602
  Newark *(G-7013)*
Quality Auto Care Centers .... G 302 992-7978
  Wilmington *(G-12278)*

AUTOMOTIVE REPAIR SHOPS: Diesel Engine Repair

Careys Diesel Inc .... F 302 678-3797
  Leipsic *(G-3313)*
Careys Inc .... E 302 875-5674
  Laurel *(G-3207)*
R & K Motors & Machine Shop .... G 302 737-4596
  Newark *(G-7290)*

AUTOMOTIVE REPAIR SHOPS: Electrical Svcs

Dave Smagala .... G 302 383-2761
  Claymont *(G-729)*
Gould Motor Technologies Inc .... G 618 932-8446
  Wilmington *(G-10756)*
H&H Services Electrical Contrs .... G 302 373-4950
  New Castle *(G-5369)*
Kent Sign Company Inc .... F 302 697-2181
  Dover *(G-1739)*
McHugh Electric Inc .... G 302 995-9091
  Wilmington *(G-11597)*
US Telex Corporation .... E 302 652-2707
  Wilmington *(G-13040)*

AUTOMOTIVE REPAIR SHOPS: Engine Rebuilding

Bradleys Auto Center Inc .... G 302 762-2247
  Wilmington *(G-9413)*
European Performance Inc .... G 302 633-1122
  Wilmington *(G-10442)*

AUTOMOTIVE REPAIR SHOPS: Engine Repair

Dempseys Service Center Inc .... G 302 239-4996
  Newark *(G-6435)*
Pughs Service Inc .... F 302 678-2408
  Dover *(G-1999)*

Employee Codes: A=Over 500 employees, B=251-500
C=101-250, D=51-100, E=20-50, F=10-19, G=1-9

AUTOMOTIVE REPAIR SHOPS: Engine Repair

Roccos Automotive Service ....F 302 998-2234
　Wilmington *(G-12445)*

AUTOMOTIVE REPAIR SHOPS: Fuel System Repair

Semper Program LLC ....G....... 302 535-6769
　Middletown *(G-4236)*

AUTOMOTIVE REPAIR SHOPS: Machine Shop

Accurate Machine Inc ....G....... 302 992-9606
　Wilmington *(G-8918)*

AUTOMOTIVE REPAIR SHOPS: Muffler Shop, Sale/Rpr/Installation

Bernard Limpert ....G....... 302 674-8280
　Dover *(G-1195)*
C-Met Inc ....G....... 302 652-1884
　New Castle *(G-5127)*
Daves Disc Mfflers of Dver De ....G....... 302 678-8803
　Dover *(G-1342)*
Leeds West Inv Group LLC ....E....... 302 998-0533
　Wilmington *(G-11358)*
Meineke Car Care Center ....G....... 302 995-2020
　Wilmington *(G-11625)*
Monro Inc ....G....... 302 999-0237
　Wilmington *(G-11733)*
Monro Inc ....G....... 302 328-2945
　New Castle *(G-5535)*
Roy Covey ....G....... 302 995-2900
　Wilmington *(G-12482)*
Scott Muffler LLC ....G....... 302 674-8280
　Dover *(G-2063)*
Tomall Inc ....G....... 302 424-4004
　Milford *(G-4579)*
Walls Service Center Inc ....G....... 302 422-8110
　Milford *(G-4596)*
Wilcon North Inc ....G....... 302 798-1699
　Claymont *(G-820)*

AUTOMOTIVE REPAIR SHOPS: Rebuilding & Retreading Tires

Bridgestone Ret Operations LLC ....F 302 995-2487
　Wilmington *(G-9472)*
Bridgestone Ret Operations LLC ....F 302 734-4522
　Dover *(G-1232)*
Bridgestone Ret Operations LLC ....G....... 302 656-2529
　New Castle *(G-5112)*

AUTOMOTIVE REPAIR SHOPS: Shock Absorber Replacement

Bargain Tire & Service Inc ....F 302 764-8900
　Wilmington *(G-9254)*
Roy Covey ....G....... 302 995-2900
　Wilmington *(G-12482)*

AUTOMOTIVE REPAIR SHOPS: Tire Recapping

Service Tire Truck Center Inc ....F 302 629-5533
　Seaford *(G-8398)*

AUTOMOTIVE REPAIR SHOPS: Tire Repair Shop

Ajacks Tire Service Inc ....G....... 302 834-5200
　New Castle *(G-5020)*

AUTOMOTIVE REPAIR SHOPS: Trailer Repair

H & H Truck and Trailer Repair ....G....... 302 653-1446
　Smyrna *(G-8648)*
Hidden Hitch & Trailer Parts ....G....... 410 398-5949
　Bear *(G-183)*
Reliable Trailer Inc ....F 856 962-7900
　Felton *(G-2316)*

AUTOMOTIVE REPAIR SHOPS: Truck Engine Repair, Exc Indl

Four States LLC ....F 302 655-3400
　New Castle *(G-5325)*
William Chambers and Son ....G....... 302 284-9655
　Viola *(G-8838)*

AUTOMOTIVE REPAIR SHOPS: Wheel Alignment

B & E Tire Alignment Inc ....G....... 302 732-6091
　Frankford *(G-2345)*
Bear Alignment Center ....G....... 302 655-9219
　Wilmington *(G-9274)*
Monro Inc ....G....... 302 328-2945
　New Castle *(G-5535)*

AUTOMOTIVE REPAIR SVC

Benchmark Transmission Inc ....G....... 302 792-2300
　Claymont *(G-701)*
Brandywine Chrysler Jeep Dodge ....D....... 302 998-0458
　Wilmington *(G-9424)*
Buckleys Inc ....G....... 302 999-8285
　Wilmington *(G-9499)*
Buntings Garage Inc ....F 302 732-9021
　Dagsboro *(G-886)*
Coastal Towing Inc ....G....... 302 645-6300
　Lewes *(G-3439)*
Cod Lift Truck Inc ....G....... 302 656-7731
　Wilmington *(G-9757)*
D & H Automotive & Towing Inc ....G....... 302 655-7611
　Wilmington *(G-9936)*
Els Tire Service Inc ....F 302 834-1997
　Newark *(G-6518)*
Ewings Towing Service Inc ....G....... 302 366-8806
　Newark *(G-6547)*
Garage ....G....... 302 645-7288
　Rehoboth Beach *(G-7943)*
Goodchild Inc ....G....... 302 368-1681
　Newark *(G-6675)*
Harvey Road Automotive Inc ....G....... 302 475-0369
　Wilmington *(G-10850)*
Just Right Tires Inc ....F 302 268-2825
　Bear *(G-207)*
Pike Creek Automotive Inc ....G....... 302 998-2234
　Wilmington *(G-12135)*
Robert Bayly ....G....... 302 846-9752
　Laurel *(G-3283)*
Schrider Enterprises Inc ....F 302 934-1900
　Millsboro *(G-4799)*
Staplefords Sales and Service ....E....... 302 834-4568
　Saint Georges *(G-8130)*

AUTOMOTIVE SPLYS & PARTS, NEW, WHOLESALE: Brakes

Wrenches ....G....... 302 422-2690
　Milford *(G-4612)*

AUTOMOTIVE SPLYS & PARTS, NEW, WHOLESALE: Radiators

Garage ....G....... 302 645-7288
　Rehoboth Beach *(G-7943)*

AUTOMOTIVE SPLYS & PARTS, NEW, WHOLESALE: Tools & Eqpt

Greg Smith Equipment Sales ....G....... 302 894-9333
　Newark *(G-6688)*

AUTOMOTIVE SPLYS & PARTS, NEW, WHOLESALE: Trailer Parts

Arundel Trailer Sales ....G....... 302 398-6288
　Harrington *(G-2813)*
Utility/Eastern ....E....... 302 337-7400
　Bridgeville *(G-528)*

AUTOMOTIVE SPLYS & PARTS, NEW, WHOLESALE: Wheels

Sports Car Tire Inc ....E....... 302 571-8473
　Wilmington *(G-12710)*

AUTOMOTIVE SPLYS & PARTS, USED, RETAIL ONLY: Tires, Used

Hammond Enterprises Inc ....G....... 302 934-1700
　Milford *(G-4433)*

AUTOMOTIVE SPLYS & PARTS, USED, WHOL: Testing Eqpt, Elec

Htk Automotive USA Corporation ....E....... 310 504-2283
　Wilmington *(G-10969)*

AUTOMOTIVE SPLYS & PARTS, USED, WHOL: Trailer Parts/Access

Arundel Trailer Sales ....G....... 302 398-6288
　Harrington *(G-2813)*

AUTOMOTIVE SPLYS & PARTS, USED, WHOLESALE

Auto Parts of Greenwood ....G....... 302 349-9601
　Farmington *(G-2265)*
Delaware Auto Salvage Inc ....G....... 302 322-2328
　New Castle *(G-5225)*
Deltrans Inc ....F 302 453-8213
　Newark *(G-6433)*
Murrays Motors ....G....... 302 628-0500
　Seaford *(G-8315)*

AUTOMOTIVE SPLYS & PARTS, USED, WHOLESALE: Access, NEC

Vehattire LLC ....F 302 221-2000
　New Castle *(G-5814)*

AUTOMOTIVE SPLYS & PARTS, USED, WHOLESALE: Garage Svc Eqpt

Pinnacle Garage Door Company ....G....... 302 505-4531
　Felton *(G-2310)*

AUTOMOTIVE SPLYS & PARTS, WHOLESALE, NEC

Action Automotive Inc ....G....... 302 429-0643
　Wilmington *(G-8925)*
Adams Auto Parts Inc ....F 302 655-9693
　Wilmington *(G-8933)*
Advance Auto Parts Inc ....G....... 302 644-0141
　Lewes *(G-3325)*
Andover Companies Inc ....G....... 410 705-1503
　Seaford *(G-8152)*
Autopart International Inc ....F 302 998-2920
　Wilmington *(G-9191)*
Berrodin South Inc ....E....... 302 575-0500
　New Castle *(G-5085)*
Bethany Auto Parts Inc ....G....... 302 539-0555
　Ocean View *(G-7765)*
Bridgestone Ret Operations LLC ....G....... 302 422-4508
　Milford *(G-4335)*
C & W Auto Parts Co Inc ....G....... 302 697-2684
　Magnolia *(G-3883)*
Clarksville Auto Service Ctr ....E....... 302 539-1700
　Ocean View *(G-7777)*
Cochran-Trivits Inc ....G....... 302 328-2945
　New Castle *(G-5179)*
Coveys Car Care Inc ....G....... 302 629-2746
　Seaford *(G-8210)*
Crw Parts Inc ....F 302 651-9300
　Wilmington *(G-9907)*
Fisher Auto Parts Inc ....G....... 302 653-9241
　Smyrna *(G-8635)*
Fisher Auto Parts Inc ....G....... 302 856-2507
　Georgetown *(G-2533)*
Fisher Auto Parts Inc ....G....... 302 998-3111
　Wilmington *(G-10562)*
Fishers Auto Parts Inc ....G....... 302 934-8088
　Millsboro *(G-4691)*
Fitzgerald Auto Salvage Inc ....D....... 302 422-7584
　Lincoln *(G-3849)*
Future Ford Sales Inc ....D....... 302 999-0261
　Wilmington *(G-10654)*
Genuine Parts Company ....G....... 610 494-6355
　Claymont *(G-752)*
Housers Auto Trim Inc ....G....... 302 422-1290
　Milford *(G-4445)*
Ieh Auto Parts LLC ....E....... 302 994-7171
　Wilmington *(G-10996)*
Imparts Inc ....G....... 302 697-0990
　Wyoming *(G-13363)*
Irondt Corp ....G....... 347 539-6471
　Wilmington *(G-11083)*
Johns Auto Parts Inc ....F 302 322-3273
　Bear *(G-204)*
Keystone Automotive Inds Inc ....F 302 764-8010
　New Castle *(G-5461)*
NGK North America Inc ....G....... 302 654-1344
　Wilmington *(G-11884)*
Quaker City Auto Parts Inc ....G....... 302 436-5114
　Selbyville *(G-8535)*

PRODUCT & SERVICES SECTION

AUTOMOTIVE: Seating

S & K Enterprises Inc ....G...... 302 292-1250
  Newark *(G-7373)*
Scott Muffler LLC ....G...... 302 378-9247
  Middletown *(G-4233)*
Sp Auto Parts Inc ....G...... 302 337-8897
  Bridgeville *(G-521)*
Townsend Bros Inc ....D...... 302 674-0100
  Dover *(G-2155)*
Wholesale Auto Inc ....G...... 302 322-6190
  New Castle *(G-5833)*

AUTOMOTIVE SPLYS, USED, WHOLESALE & RETAIL

Afrikelist Corporation ....F...... 800 767-1744
  Wilmington *(G-8974)*
Averest Inc. ....G...... 302 281-2062
  Wilmington *(G-9198)*
Goodchild Inc ....G...... 302 368-1681
  Newark *(G-6675)*
Hollie Enterprises LLC ....G...... 903 721-1904
  Wilmington *(G-10927)*
Parts Plus More LLC ....E...... 302 300-4913
  Dover *(G-1937)*
Uacj Trading America Co Ltd ....F...... 312 636-5941
  Wilmington *(G-13005)*
Wilmington Resources ....F...... 302 746-7162
  Wilmington *(G-13244)*

AUTOMOTIVE SVCS

Wilson Fleet & Equipment ....G...... 302 422-7159
  Milford *(G-4610)*

AUTOMOTIVE SVCS, EXC REP & CARWASHES: Do-It-Yourself Garages

Sals Auto Services Inc ....G...... 302 654-1168
  Wilmington *(G-12526)*

AUTOMOTIVE SVCS, EXC REPAIR & CARWASHES: Customizing

Auto Sun Roof Inc ....F...... 302 325-3001
  New Castle *(G-5056)*
Autoport Inc. ....E...... 302 658-5100
  New Castle *(G-5057)*
Continental Warranty Corp ....E...... 302 375-0401
  Claymont *(G-723)*

AUTOMOTIVE SVCS, EXC REPAIR & CARWASHES: Glass Tinting

Shore Tint & More Inc ....G...... 302 947-4624
  Harbeson *(G-2800)*

AUTOMOTIVE SVCS, EXC REPAIR & CARWASHES: Insp & Diagnostic

Uris LLC ....G...... 302 469-7000
  Millsboro *(G-4818)*

AUTOMOTIVE SVCS, EXC REPAIR & CARWASHES: Lubrication

Dover Lubricants Inc ....F...... 302 674-8282
  Dover *(G-1458)*
Jiffy Lube International Inc ....F...... 302 738-5494
  Newark *(G-6839)*
Pennzoil-Quaker State Company ....E...... 302 999-7323
  Wilmington *(G-12074)*
Quality Auto Care Centers ....G...... 302 992-7978
  Wilmington *(G-12278)*
Schrider Enterprises Inc ....F...... 302 934-1900
  Millsboro *(G-4799)*

AUTOMOTIVE SVCS, EXC REPAIR & CARWASHES: Maintenance

Monro Inc. ....G...... 302 846-2732
  Delmar *(G-1022)*
Sears Roebuck and Co ....D...... 302 995-9295
  Wilmington *(G-12566)*
Winners Circle Inc. ....E...... 302 661-2100
  Wilmington *(G-13276)*

AUTOMOTIVE SVCS, EXC REPAIR & CARWASHES: Trailer Maintenance

Basher & Son Enterprises Inc ....G...... 302 239-6584
  Hockessin *(G-2962)*

AUTOMOTIVE SVCS, EXC REPAIR: Carwash, Automatic

Gas & Go Inc ....G...... 302 734-8234
  Dover *(G-1582)*
Greenhill Express Car Wash ....G...... 302 464-1031
  Middletown *(G-4092)*
Logue Brothers Inc ....F...... 302 762-1896
  Wilmington *(G-11427)*
Maaco Collision Repr Auto Pntg ....G...... 610 628-3867
  Wilmington *(G-11475)*
Magic Touch ....F...... 302 655-6430
  New Castle *(G-5495)*
Rehoboth Car Wash Inc ....E...... 302 227-6177
  Rehoboth Beach *(G-8053)*

AUTOMOTIVE SVCS, EXC REPAIR: Carwash, Self-Service

Newport Ventures Inc ....F...... 302 998-1693
  Wilmington *(G-11879)*

AUTOMOTIVE SVCS, EXC REPAIR: Washing & Polishing

Attention To Detail In Smyrna ....G...... 302 388-1267
  Smyrna *(G-8578)*
Briscoes Onsite Detailing ....G...... 302 420-1629
  Wilmington *(G-9478)*
Cleanpro Detail Center ....G...... 302 834-6878
  Bear *(G-77)*
Delaware Detailing Services ....G...... 302 414-0755
  New Castle *(G-5227)*
Diamond Car Wash Inc ....G...... 302 449-5896
  Middletown *(G-4038)*
Duck In Car Wash ....G...... 302 536-7056
  Seaford *(G-8227)*
Hl Line Auto Detailing ....G...... 302 420-5368
  Wilmington *(G-10901)*
Magic Car Wash Inc ....E...... 302 479-5911
  Wilmington *(G-11486)*
Mr Royal Touch MBL Detailing ....G...... 302 229-0161
  Wilmington *(G-11767)*
Richard Addington Co ....G...... 302 422-2668
  Milford *(G-4543)*

AUTOMOTIVE SVCS, EXC RPR/CARWASHES: High Perf Auto Rpr/Svc

Donald Briggs ....G...... 267 476-2712
  Middletown *(G-4042)*

AUTOMOTIVE TOWING & WRECKING SVC

Bauls Towing & Services LLC ....G...... 302 999-9919
  Newark *(G-6054)*
Big Time Towing LLC ....G...... 302 510-1160
  Wilmington *(G-9332)*
D&G Inc ....G...... 302 378-4877
  Townsend *(G-8778)*
Daves Towing Inc ....G...... 302 697-9073
  Dover *(G-1343)*
Ewings Towing Service Inc ....G...... 302 366-8806
  Newark *(G-6547)*
Fast4wrd Towing & Repair LLC ....G...... 302 331-5157
  Wilmington *(G-10504)*
Goodchild Inc ....G...... 302 368-1681
  Newark *(G-6675)*
Hound Dog Recovery LLC ....G...... 302 836-3806
  Smyrna *(G-8655)*
Kraemer & Sons LLC ....G...... 302 832-1534
  Bear *(G-222)*
Loyalty Is Earned Inc ....G...... 347 606-6383
  Wilmington *(G-11445)*
Midway Towing Inc ....G...... 302 323-4850
  New Castle *(G-5528)*
Pughs Service Inc ....F...... 302 678-2408
  Dover *(G-1999)*
Robert Bayly ....G...... 302 846-9752
  Laurel *(G-3283)*
Smiths Jack Towing & Svc Ctr ....G...... 302 798-6667
  Wilmington *(G-12663)*
Swift Towing & Recovery ....G...... 302 650-4579
  New Castle *(G-5748)*
V B Towing Inc ....G...... 302 238-7705
  Frankford *(G-2396)*
Worthys Towing LLC ....G...... 302 259-5265
  Greenwood *(G-2769)*

AUTOMOTIVE TOWING SVCS

All Hked Up Twing Recovery LLC ....G...... 302 545-1205
  Newark *(G-5934)*
B & F Towing & Salvage Co Inc ....E...... 302 328-4146
  New Castle *(G-5062)*
Car Clinic Inc ....G...... 302 421-9100
  Wilmington *(G-9560)*
Careys Inc ....E...... 302 875-5674
  Laurel *(G-3207)*
Chambers Motors Inc ....E...... 302 629-3553
  Seaford *(G-8187)*
Coastal Towing Inc ....G...... 302 645-6300
  Lewes *(G-3439)*
D & H Automotive & Towing Inc ....G...... 302 655-7611
  Wilmington *(G-9936)*
Ellmore Auto Collision ....G...... 302 762-2301
  Wilmington *(G-10381)*
Fred Drake Automotive Inc ....G...... 302 378-4877
  Townsend *(G-8788)*
Harris Towing and Auto Service ....G...... 302 736-9901
  Dover *(G-1632)*
Holly Oak Towing and Service ....G...... 302 792-1500
  Wilmington *(G-10928)*
Horton Brothers Recovery Inc ....F...... 302 266-7339
  Newark *(G-6748)*
Jim Sellers ....G...... 302 738-4149
  Newark *(G-6840)*
Mag Towing ....G...... 302 462-5686
  Frankford *(G-2371)*
Martel & Son Foreign Car Ctr ....G...... 302 674-5556
  Dover *(G-1820)*
Matthews Towing & Recovery ....G...... 302 463-1108
  Smyrna *(G-8680)*
Rossi Auto Body Inc ....G...... 302 999-7707
  Wilmington *(G-12480)*

AUTOMOTIVE TRANSMISSION REPAIR SVC

AAMCO Transmissions ....G...... 302 322-3454
  Bear *(G-7)*
All Trans Transmission Inc ....G...... 302 366-0104
  Newark *(G-5937)*
Benchmark Transmission Inc ....G...... 302 792-2300
  Claymont *(G-701)*
Benchmark Transmissions Inc ....G...... 302 999-9400
  Wilmington *(G-9296)*
Challenge Automotive Svcs Inc ....G...... 302 629-3058
  Seaford *(G-8186)*
Cottman Transmission ....G...... 302 322-4600
  New Castle *(G-5199)*
Dynamic Converters LLC ....G...... 302 454-9203
  Newark *(G-6483)*
Js Automotive AAMCO ....G...... 302 678-5660
  Dover *(G-1711)*
K & J Automotive Inc ....G...... 302 798-3635
  Claymont *(G-771)*
Lst Insvestment LLC ....G...... 302 322-3454
  Bear *(G-239)*
Powertrain Technology Inc ....G...... 302 368-4900
  Newark *(G-7237)*
Scott Muffler LLC ....G...... 302 378-9247
  Middletown *(G-4233)*
Trans Plus Inc. ....G...... 302 323-3051
  New Castle *(G-5784)*
Walls Service Center Inc ....G...... 302 422-8110
  Milford *(G-4596)*
World Transmissions Inc ....G...... 302 735-5535
  Dover *(G-2239)*

AUTOMOTIVE UPHOLSTERY SHOPS

Rayco Auto & Marine Uphl Inc ....G...... 302 323-8844
  Hockessin *(G-3129)*

AUTOMOTIVE WELDING SVCS

Blm Industries Inc ....G...... 302 238-7745
  Millsboro *(G-4645)*
Donaway Corporation ....G...... 302 934-6226
  Millsboro *(G-4680)*
Jvl Automotive ....G...... 302 335-3942
  Frederica *(G-2408)*

AUTOMOTIVE: Seating

Clarios ....G...... 302 996-0309
  Wilmington *(G-9730)*
Johnson Controls Inc ....G...... 302 715-5208
  Delmar *(G-1009)*

AWNINGS & CANOPIES

Sunhaven Awning Co .... G 302 239-7990
Yorklyn *(G-13367)*

AWNINGS & CANOPIES: Awnings, Fabric, From Purchased Matls

B and C Awning .... G 302 629-4465
Seaford *(G-8159)*
Callaway Furniture Inc .... G 302 398-8858
Harrington *(G-2823)*
E W Brown Inc .... G 302 652-6612
Wilmington *(G-10310)*
Gainor Awnings Inc .... G 302 998-8611
Wilmington *(G-10663)*

BACKHOES

Bob Reynolds Backhoe Services .... G 302 239-4711
Hockessin *(G-2965)*
Central Backhoe Service .... G 302 398-6420
Milton *(G-4877)*
Longneck Backhoe .... G 302 945-3429
Millsboro *(G-4725)*
Wolfe Backhoe Service .... G 302 737-2628
Newark *(G-7713)*

BAGS & CONTAINERS: Textile, Exc Sleeping

Great Graphic Originals Ltd .... G 302 734-7600
Dover *(G-1608)*
Vanguard Manufacturing Inc .... G 302 994-9302
Wilmington *(G-13049)*

BAGS: Grocers', Made From Purchased Materials

Idylc Homes LLC .... G 302 295-3719
Wilmington *(G-10995)*

BAGS: Paper, Made From Purchased Materials

AB Group Packaging Inc .... G 302 607-3281
Newark *(G-5879)*

BAGS: Plastic

Jeb Plastics Inc .... G 302 479-9223
Wilmington *(G-11139)*
Printpack Inc .... C 302 323-4000
New Castle *(G-5645)*
Printpack Enterprises Inc .... G 302 323-0900
New Castle *(G-5646)*
Richard Earl Fisher .... G 302 598-1957
Wilmington *(G-12407)*
Toyo Fibre USA Inc .... G 302 475-3699
Wilmington *(G-12945)*

BAGS: Plastic, Made From Purchased Materials

Castle Bag Company .... G 302 656-1001
Wilmington *(G-9589)*
Grayling Industries Inc .... E 770 751-9095
Frederica *(G-2403)*

BAGS: Tea, Fabric, Made From Purchased Materials

Firsd Tea North America LLC .... G 302 322-1255
New Castle *(G-5310)*

BAGS: Textile

Lori Emory .... G 302 737-7352
Newark *(G-6949)*

BAIL BONDING SVCS

Bovell Lowinger Bail Bonds .... G 302 427-9000
Wilmington *(G-9401)*
D A B Productions .... G 302 670-9407
Harrington *(G-2829)*
Delaware Bail Bonds .... G 302 734-9881
Dover *(G-1358)*
Fast Bailbonds LLC .... G 302 778-4400
Wilmington *(G-10502)*
Harriet Tubman Safe House Inc .... G 302 351-4434
Wilmington *(G-10841)*

T & H Bail Bond Inc .... G 302 777-7982
Wilmington *(G-12841)*
T & H Bail Bonds Agency LLC .... G 302 777-7982
Wilmington *(G-12842)*

BAKERIES, COMMERCIAL: On Premises Baking Only

Busymama Cupcakes .... G 302 259-9988
Seaford *(G-8177)*
Kraft Heinz Company .... A 302 734-6100
Dover *(G-1758)*
Pennsylvania Brand Co .... G 302 674-5774
Dover *(G-1946)*
Posh Cupcake .... G 302 234-4451
Hockessin *(G-3123)*
Smackerals By Michelle LLC .... G 302 376-8272
Middletown *(G-4243)*

BAKERY PRDTS: Cakes, Bakery, Exc Frozen

Cakes By Dee .... G 302 934-7483
Millsboro *(G-4653)*
Sweets By Samantha LLC .... F 302 740-2218
Newark *(G-7521)*

BAKERY PRDTS: Cookies

Stauffer Family LLC .... G 302 227-5820
Rehoboth Beach *(G-8087)*

BAKERY PRDTS: Cookies & crackers

Philly Pretzel .... G 302 478-5658
Wilmington *(G-12120)*

BAKERY PRDTS: Wholesalers

Baked LLC .... G 302 212-5202
Dewey Beach *(G-1053)*
Beach Break & Bakrie .... G 302 537-3800
Bethany Beach *(G-383)*
Bimbo Bakeries Usa Inc .... E 302 328-0837
New Castle *(G-5091)*
Jes-Made Bakery .... G 610 558-2131
Newark *(G-6836)*
Pioneer Distributors Inc .... G 302 644-0791
Milton *(G-4952)*
Point Coffee Shop and Bakery .... G 302 260-9734
Rehoboth Beach *(G-8033)*
Touch of Italy Bakery LLC .... G 302 827-2132
Lewes *(G-3791)*

BAKERY: Wholesale Or Wholesale & Retail Combined

Adams Bakery Corporation .... A 802 863-2696
Wilmington *(G-8934)*
Bimbo Bakeries Usa Inc .... E 302 328-7970
New Castle *(G-5090)*
Sweet Venom Effect LLC .... E 302 674-5831
Wilmington *(G-12823)*

BALLASTS: Lighting

Rigel Energy Group LLC .... F 888 624-9844
Wilmington *(G-12421)*

BALLOON SHOPS

Forever Inc .... E 302 594-0400
Wilmington *(G-10592)*

BALLOONS: Hot Air

Ilc Dover LP .... B 302 335-3911
Frederica *(G-2407)*

BANKRUPTCY REFEREE

Woloshin and Lynch Associates .... F 302 477-3200
Wilmington *(G-13288)*

BANKS: Commercial, NEC

Artisans Bank Inc .... G 302 834-8800
Bear *(G-38)*
Artisans Bank Inc .... G 302 430-7681
Milford *(G-4309)*
Artisans Bank Inc .... G 302 738-3744
Wilmington *(G-9144)*
Bancorp Bank .... E 302 385-5000
Wilmington *(G-9232)*

Bank of Delmar .... G 302 875-5901
Laurel *(G-3195)*
Bank of Delmarva .... G 302 226-8900
Rehoboth Beach *(G-7854)*
Bank of Delmarva .... G 302 629-2700
Seaford *(G-8161)*
Bryn Mawr Trust Company .... F 302 529-5984
Wilmington *(G-9495)*
County Bank .... G 302 537-0900
Millville *(G-4841)*
K Bank .... G 302 645-9700
Lewes *(G-3580)*
Manufacturers & Traders Tr Co .... G 302 644-9930
Lewes *(G-3618)*
Maryland Agency Financial Grou .... G 410 420-8866
Selbyville *(G-8515)*
Royal Bank America Leasing LLC .... G 302 529-5984
Wilmington *(G-12483)*
Td Bank NA .... G 302 644-0952
Rehoboth Beach *(G-8095)*
Wilmington Savings Fund Soc .... G 888 665-9609
Wilmington *(G-13247)*
Wilmington Savings Fund Soc .... G 302 838-6300
Bear *(G-377)*
Wilmington Savings Fund Soc .... G 302 571-6508
Wilmington *(G-13248)*
Wilmington Savings Fund Soc .... G 302 677-1891
Dover *(G-2230)*
Wilmington Savings Fund Soc .... G 302 529-9300
Wilmington *(G-13253)*
Wilmington Savings Fund Soc .... F 302 792-6000
Wilmington *(G-13254)*

BANKS: Mortgage & Loan

1st Capitol Mortgage Inc .... G 302 674-5540
Dover *(G-1066)*
Acre Mortgage & Financial .... G 302 737-5853
Christiana *(G-664)*
Bank America National Assn .... G 302 674-5379
Dover *(G-1170)*
Bank of Ocean City .... G 410 723-4944
Fenwick Island *(G-2329)*
Delaware Community Inv Corp .... G 302 655-1420
Wilmington *(G-10024)*
Embrace Home Loans Inc .... G 302 635-7998
Wilmington *(G-10387)*
Movement Mortgage LLC .... G 302 344-6758
Lewes *(G-3651)*
Oakwood Funding Corporation .... G 336 855-2400
Wilmington *(G-11928)*
SLM Financial Corporation .... F 856 642-8300
Newark *(G-7442)*
Stifel Bank and Trust .... G 302 478-8880
Wilmington *(G-12767)*
SunTrust Mortgage Inc .... F 302 453-2350
Newark *(G-7509)*
Union Mortgage Group Inc .... G 302 227-6687
Rehoboth Beach *(G-8105)*

BANKS: National Commercial

Applied Bank .... F 302 326-4200
Wilmington *(G-9099)*
Applied Bank .... F 302 227-3044
Rehoboth Beach *(G-7846)*
Applied Bank .... F 302 326-4200
Newark *(G-5986)*
Applied Bank .... E 302 326-4200
Wilmington *(G-9100)*
Bancorp Inc .... E 302 385-5000
Wilmington *(G-9231)*
Bank America National Assn .... F 302 478-1005
Wilmington *(G-9237)*
Bank America National Assn .... F 302 656-5399
Wilmington *(G-9238)*
Bank America National Assn .... F 302 765-2108
Wilmington *(G-9239)*
Bank America National Assn .... F 302 464-1745
Newark *(G-6045)*
Bank of America Corporation .... F 302 432-0407
Wilmington *(G-9240)*
Bessemer Trust Company Del NA .... E 212 708-9182
Wilmington *(G-9312)*
Citibank National Association .... F 302 477-5418
New Castle *(G-5163)*
Citicorp Banking Corporation .... C 302 323-3140
New Castle *(G-5165)*
Citicorp Delaware Services Inc .... F 302 323-3124
New Castle *(G-5167)*
Citicorp Trust Bank .... G 302 737-7803
New Castle *(G-5168)*

Citigroup Asia PCF Holdg Corp............G....... 302 323-3100
New Castle *(G-5169)*
County Bank............G....... 302 947-7300
Millsboro *(G-4669)*
County Bank............G....... 302 537-0900
Millville *(G-4841)*
County Bank............G....... 302 855-2000
Georgetown *(G-2488)*
County Bank............G....... 302 645-8880
Lewes *(G-3445)*
County Bank............G....... 302 424-2500
Milford *(G-4367)*
County Bank............F....... 302 226-9800
Rehoboth Beach *(G-7902)*
Deutsche Bank Tr Co Americas............E....... 302 636-3301
Wilmington *(G-10126)*
Deutsche Bank Trust Co Del............C....... 302 636-3300
Wilmington *(G-10127)*
Fia Card Services Nat Assn............C....... 302 457-0517
Wilmington *(G-10528)*
Fia Card Services Nat Assn............B....... 302 432-1573
Wilmington *(G-10530)*
First National Bnk of Wyoming............D....... 302 697-2666
Camden *(G-572)*
Fulton Bank National Assn............G....... 302 378-4575
Middletown *(G-4080)*
Fulton Bank National Assn............G....... 302 227-0330
Rehoboth Beach *(G-7938)*
Fulton Bank National Assn............G....... 302 644-4900
Lewes *(G-3506)*
Hsbc Bank USA............A....... 302 778-0169
Wilmington *(G-10966)*
Hsbc North America Inc............F....... 302 652-4673
Wilmington *(G-10967)*
JP Morgan Trust Company Del............F....... 302 634-3800
Newark *(G-6853)*
Jpmorgan Chase & Co............E....... 312 732-2801
Newark *(G-6855)*
Jpmorgan Chase Bank Nat Assn............A....... 302 634-1000
Newark *(G-6856)*
Law Debenture Trust Company............G....... 302 655-3505
Wilmington *(G-11339)*
Manufacturers & Traders Tr Co............G....... 302 644-9930
Lewes *(G-3618)*
Meridian Bank............E....... 302 477-9449
Wilmington *(G-11641)*
Nessus Investment Corporation............G....... 302 323-3104
New Castle *(G-5551)*
Northern Trust Company............E....... 302 428-8700
Wilmington *(G-11907)*
PNC Bank National Association............C....... 877 762-2000
Wilmington *(G-12166)*
PNC Bank National Association............E....... 302 735-3117
Dover *(G-1973)*
PNC Bank National Association............F....... 302 653-2475
Smyrna *(G-8690)*
PNC Bank National Association............E....... 302 326-4701
New Castle *(G-5627)*
PNC Bank National Association............G....... 302 436-5400
Selbyville *(G-8532)*
PNC Bank National Association............F....... 302 733-7190
Newark *(G-7228)*
PNC Bank National Association............F....... 302 479-4529
Wilmington *(G-12168)*
PNC Bank National Association............F....... 302 479-4520
Wilmington *(G-12169)*
PNC Bank National Association............F....... 302 993-3013
Wilmington *(G-12170)*
PNC Bank National Association............F....... 302 422-1015
Milford *(G-4527)*
PNC Bank National Association............F....... 302 429-1167
Wilmington *(G-12174)*
PNC Bank National Association............F....... 302 832-6180
Bear *(G-286)*
PNC Financial Svcs Group Inc............F....... 302 429-1364
Wilmington *(G-12175)*
Reliance Trust Company LLC............G....... 302 246-5400
Wilmington *(G-12377)*
Sun National Bank............G....... 302 334-4091
Wilmington *(G-12795)*
Td Bank NA............G....... 302 655-5031
Wilmington *(G-12859)*
Td Bank NA............F....... 302 529-8727
Wilmington *(G-12860)*
Td Bank NA............G....... 302 351-4560
Wilmington *(G-12861)*
Td Bank NA............G....... 508 793-4188
Wilmington *(G-12862)*
Td Bank NA............G....... 302 644-0952
Rehoboth Beach *(G-8095)*
Tracy Peoples LLC............G....... 302 927-0280
Dagsboro *(G-939)*
Wells Fargo Bank National Assn............G....... 302 631-1500
Newark *(G-7683)*
Wells Fargo Bank National Assn............F....... 302 736-2910
Dover *(G-2211)*
Wells Fargo Bank National Assn............G....... 302 449-5485
Middletown *(G-4281)*
Wells Fargo Bank National Assn............F....... 302 541-8660
Millville *(G-4858)*
Wells Fargo Bank National Assn............F....... 302 765-5534
Wilmington *(G-13144)*
Wells Fargo Bank National Assn............F....... 302 428-8600
Wilmington *(G-13145)*
Wells Fargo Bank National Assn............F....... 302 529-2550
Wilmington *(G-13146)*
Wells Fargo Bank National Assn............G....... 302 736-2920
Dover *(G-2212)*
Wells Fargo Bank National Assn............F....... 302 235-4300
Hockessin *(G-3169)*
Wells Fargo Bank National Assn............F....... 302 832-6100
Newark *(G-7684)*
Wells Fargo Bank National Assn............F....... 302 644-6351
Rehoboth Beach *(G-8110)*
Wells Fargo Bank National Assn............F....... 302 326-4304
New Castle *(G-5828)*
Wells Fargo Bank National Assn............E....... 302 421-7508
Wilmington *(G-13147)*
Wells Fargo Bank National Assn............F....... 302 636-4306
Wilmington *(G-13148)*
Wells Fargo Bank National Assn............G....... 302 761-1300
Wilmington *(G-13149)*
Wells Fargo Bank National Assn............G....... 302 622-3350
Wilmington *(G-13150)*
Wells Fargo Bank National Assn............G....... 302 421-7820
Wilmington *(G-13151)*
Wells Fargo Bank National Assn............G....... 302 832-6104
Bear *(G-374)*
Wells Fargo Bank National Assn............G....... 302 235-4304
Hockessin *(G-3170)*
Wells Fargo Home Mortgage Inc............G....... 302 239-6300
Hockessin *(G-3171)*
Wilmington Savings Fund Soc............F....... 302 398-3232
Harrington *(G-2907)*
Wsfs Financial Corporation............D....... 302 792-6000
Wilmington *(G-13307)*

BANKS: Other Activities, NEC

Juniper Bank............F....... 302 255-8000
Wilmington *(G-11210)*

BANKS: State Commercial

1st State Home Services............G....... 302 339-5573
Millsboro *(G-4618)*
1st State PC Training............G....... 302 697-0347
Magnolia *(G-3876)*
Bank of Delmar............G....... 302 732-3610
Dagsboro *(G-880)*
Bank of Delmar............G....... 302 875-5901
Laurel *(G-3195)*
Bank of Delmarva............G....... 302 629-2700
Seaford *(G-8161)*
Bank of Ocean City............G....... 410 723-4944
Fenwick Island *(G-2329)*
Bmo Delaware Trust Company............G....... 302 652-1660
Wilmington *(G-9387)*
Cbc Holding Inc............C....... 302 254-2000
Wilmington *(G-9600)*
Citicorp Del-Lease Inc............D....... 302 323-3801
New Castle *(G-5166)*
Citizens Bank National Assn............F....... 302 360-6101
Lewes *(G-3423)*
Citizens Bank National Assn............F....... 302 734-0200
Dover *(G-1284)*
Citizens Bank National Assn............F....... 302 292-6401
Newark *(G-6238)*
Citizens Bank National Assn............F....... 302 456-7100
Newark *(G-6239)*
Citizens Bank National Assn............G....... 302 856-4231
Georgetown *(G-2473)*
Citizens Bank National Assn............G....... 302 645-2024
Lewes *(G-3424)*
Citizens Bank National Assn............F....... 302 283-5600
Newark *(G-6240)*
Citizens Bank National Assn............F....... 302 628-6150
Seaford *(G-8196)*
Citizens Bank National Assn............F....... 302 456-7111
Newark *(G-6241)*
Citizens Bank National Assn............F....... 302 235-4321
Hockessin *(G-2989)*
Citizens Bank National Assn............G....... 302 633-4503
Wilmington *(G-9714)*
Citizens Bank National Assn............G....... 302 422-5010
Milford *(G-4353)*
Citizens Bank National Assn............F....... 302 633-3080
Wilmington *(G-9716)*
Citizens Bank National Assn............G....... 302 376-3641
Middletown *(G-3992)*
Citizens Bank National Assn............G....... 302 529-6100
Wilmington *(G-9717)*
Citizens Bank National Assn............F....... 302 322-0525
New Castle *(G-5170)*
Citizens Bank National Assn............F....... 302 421-2229
Wilmington *(G-9718)*
Citizens Bank National Assn............F....... 302 834-2611
Bear *(G-75)*
Citizens Bank National Assn............G....... 302 421-2240
Wilmington *(G-9719)*
Comenity Bank............G....... 614 729-4000
Wilmington *(G-9781)*
County Bank............G....... 302 684-2300
Milton *(G-4884)*
First Republic Bank............C....... 302 777-2699
Wilmington *(G-10548)*
First State Motor Sports............G....... 302 798-7000
Claymont *(G-745)*
Fulton Bank National Assn............G....... 302 407-3291
Wilmington *(G-10647)*
Fulton Bank National Assn............G....... 302 737-7766
Newark *(G-6628)*
Fulton Bank National Assn............G....... 302 539-8031
Ocean View *(G-7787)*
Fulton Bank National Assn............G....... 302 934-5911
Millsboro *(G-4695)*
Hill Bancshares Delaware Inc............G....... 302 651-8389
Wilmington *(G-10907)*
Jpmorgan Chase Bank Nat Assn............E....... 302 282-1624
Wilmington *(G-11201)*
K Bank............G....... 302 645-9700
Lewes *(G-3580)*
Manufacturers & Traders Tr Co............G....... 302 644-9930
Lewes *(G-3618)*
Manufacturers & Traders Tr Co............D....... 302 856-4410
Georgetown *(G-2595)*
Manufacturers & Traders Tr Co............G....... 302 855-2184
Milton *(G-4930)*
Manufacturers & Traders Tr Co............E....... 302 651-1618
Newark *(G-6981)*
Manufacturers & Traders Tr Co............F....... 302 856-4470
Seaford *(G-8302)*
Manufacturers & Traders Tr Co............G....... 302 539-3471
Bethany Beach *(G-412)*
Manufacturers & Traders Tr Co............F....... 302 651-8738
Wilmington *(G-11505)*
Manufacturers & Traders Tr Co............G....... 302 472-3262
Claymont *(G-780)*
Manufacturers & Traders Tr Co............G....... 302 472-3141
Wilmington *(G-11507)*
Manufacturers & Traders Tr Co............G....... 302 472-3161
Wilmington *(G-11512)*
Manufacturers & Traders Tr Co............G....... 302 477-1761
Wilmington *(G-11513)*
Manufacturers & Traders Tr Co............F....... 302 472-3177
Hockessin *(G-3087)*
Manufacturers & Traders Tr Co............F....... 302 651-8828
Bear *(G-244)*
Manufacturers & Traders Tr Co............G....... 302 855-2227
Rehoboth Beach *(G-7996)*
Manufacturers & Traders Tr Co............G....... 302 651-1000
Wilmington *(G-11514)*
Manufacturers & Traders Tr Co............G....... 302 855-2873
Laurel *(G-3261)*
Manufacturers & Traders Tr Co............G....... 302 934-2400
Millsboro *(G-4732)*
Manufacturers & Traders Tr Co............G....... 302 449-2780
Middletown *(G-4144)*
Manufacturers & Traders Tr Co............G....... 302 855-2891
Millsboro *(G-4733)*
Manufacturers & Traders Tr Co............G....... 302 541-8700
Millville *(G-4848)*
Manufacturers & Traders Tr Co............G....... 302 472-3335
Newark *(G-6982)*
Manufacturers & Traders Tr Co............F....... 302 292-6060
Newark *(G-6983)*
Manufacturers & Traders Tr Co............G....... 302 855-2283
Seaford *(G-8303)*
Manufacturers & Traders Tr Co............F....... 302 735-2075
Dover *(G-1815)*
Manufacturers & Traders Tr Co............E....... 302 472-3249
New Castle *(G-5505)*

BANKS: State Commercial

Manufacturers & Traders Tr Co ....F....... 302 855-2297
  Delmar (G-1018)
Manufacturers & Traders Tr Co ....F....... 302 636-6000
  Wilmington (G-11515)
Manufacturers & Traders Tr Co ....F....... 302 472-3309
  Wilmington (G-11516)
Manufacturers & Traders Tr Co ....F....... 302 735-2020
  Dover (G-1816)
PNC Bank National Association ....F....... 302 235-4000
  Hockessin (G-3121)
PNC National Bank of Delaware ....D....... 302 479-4529
  Wilmington (G-12176)
Royal Bank America Leasing LLC ....F....... 302 798-1790
  Wilmington (G-12484)
Santander Bank NA ....F....... 302 654-5182
  Wilmington (G-12541)
Shore United Bank ....G....... 302 284-4600
  Felton (G-2322)
Shore United Bank ....F....... 302 424-4600
  Milford (G-4559)
Shore United Bank ....F....... 302 698-1432
  Camden (G-599)
Td Bank NA ....F....... 302 455-1781
  Newark (G-7542)
Td Bank NA ....F....... 302 234-8570
  Hockessin (G-3157)
Wilmington Savings Fund Soc ....C....... 302 792-6000
  Wilmington (G-13245)
Wilmington Savings Fund Soc ....G....... 302 360-0020
  Millsboro (G-4828)
Wilmington Savings Fund Soc ....G....... 302 389-3151
  Smyrna (G-8747)
Wilmington Savings Fund Soc ....E....... 302 697-8891
  Camden (G-605)
Wilmington Savings Fund Soc ....E....... 302 436-4179
  Selbyville (G-8555)
Wilmington Savings Fund Soc ....G....... 302 832-7842
  Newark (G-7705)
Wilmington Savings Fund Soc ....G....... 302 999-1227
  Wilmington (G-13246)
Wilmington Savings Fund Soc ....G....... 302 360-0440
  Seaford (G-8441)
Wilmington Savings Fund Soc ....G....... 302 571-7242
  Newark (G-7706)
Wilmington Savings Fund Soc ....G....... 302 360-0004
  Ocean View (G-7824)
Wilmington Savings Fund Soc ....F....... 302 456-6404
  Newark (G-7707)
Wilmington Savings Fund Soc ....G....... 302 633-5700
  Wilmington (G-13249)
Wilmington Savings Fund Soc ....F....... 302 633-5704
  Wilmington (G-13251)
Wilmington Savings Fund Soc ....G....... 302 235-7600
  Hockessin (G-3173)
Wilmington Savings Fund Soc ....F....... 302 324-5800
  New Castle (G-5837)
Wilmington Savings Fund Soc ....F....... 302 284-3201
  Viola (G-8839)
Wilmington Savings Fund Soc ....G....... 302 792-6435
  Claymont (G-822)
Wilmington Trust Company TT ....G....... 302 427-4812
  Wilmington (G-13262)
Wsfs Financial Corporation ....G....... 302 346-2930
  Milford (G-4613)

BANQUET HALL FACILITIES

Delcastle Golf Club Management ....E....... 302 998-9505
  Wilmington (G-10098)
Fremont Hall ....G....... 302 731-2431
  Newark (G-6620)
M & P Adventures Inc ....E....... 302 645-6271
  Lewes (G-3614)
Quail Associates Inc ....E....... 302 697-4660
  Camden Wyoming (G-651)
Worcester Golf Club Inc ....F....... 610 222-0200
  Milton (G-4981)

BAR

Camels Hump Inc ....F....... 302 227-5719
  Rehoboth Beach (G-7882)
Country Villa Motel ....F....... 814 938-8330
  Milford (G-4366)
Millsboro Lanes Inc ....F....... 302 934-0400
  Millsboro (G-4750)

BARBER SHOPS

A Gentlemans Touch Inc ....F....... 302 655-7015
  Wilmington (G-8878)

Altered Images Hair Studio ....G....... 302 234-2151
  Newark (G-5947)
Amstel Barbershop LLC ....G....... 302 635-7686
  Hockessin (G-2957)
Bethany Bch Hair Snippery Inc ....G....... 302 539-8344
  Millville (G-4837)
CMC Corporation of Hockessin ....G....... 302 239-1960
  Hockessin (G-2990)
Cuts & Styles Barley Mill Inc ....G....... 302 999-8059
  Wilmington (G-9929)
Cutting Edge of Delaware Inc ....F....... 302 834-8723
  Wilmington (G-9930)
Georve V Sawyer ....G....... 302 736-1474
  Dover (G-1591)
Hair Studio II ....G....... 302 945-5110
  Millsboro (G-4703)
His Image Barbershop ....G....... 302 256-2792
  Wilmington (G-10916)
Joes Barber Shop ....G....... 302 478-2837
  Wilmington (G-11166)
Jstanley Salon ....G....... 302 778-1885
  Wilmington (G-11205)
Millcreek Barber Shop ....F....... 302 998-2174
  Wilmington (G-11689)
Rape of The Locke Inc ....G....... 302 368-5370
  Newark (G-7297)
Ratner Companies LC ....G....... 302 378-8565
  Middletown (G-4211)
Styles Millenium ....G....... 302 472-3427
  Wilmington (G-12783)
The Professionals ....G....... 302 764-5501
  Wilmington (G-12892)
United States Mle MNS Hair Cre ....G....... 302 368-1273
  Newark (G-7615)
Vision Salon & Barbershop ....G....... 302 934-9301
  Millsboro (G-4821)
Visions Hair Design ....G....... 302 477-0820
  Wilmington (G-13093)

BARS: Concrete Reinforcing, Fabricated Steel

Confab Inc ....G....... 302 429-0140
  Wilmington (G-9819)

BARTERING SVCS

Delaware Barter Corp ....G....... 800 343-1322
  Newark (G-6365)

BASES, BEVERAGE

Bettys ....G....... 302 233-2675
  Milford (G-4325)

BATHING SUIT STORES

Body Double Swimwear ....G....... 302 537-1444
  Selbyville (G-8458)
Endless Summer Tanning Salon ....G....... 302 369-0455
  Newark (G-6526)

BATHROOM FIXTURE REGLAZING SVCS

1st State Accessibility LLC ....G....... 844 663-4396
  Wilmington (G-8850)

BATTERIES: Storage

Clarios LLC ....B....... 302 378-9885
  Middletown (G-3994)
Clarios LLC ....F....... 302 696-3221
  Middletown (G-3995)
Talostech LLC ....G....... 302 332-9236
  New Castle (G-5752)

BATTERIES: Wet

Energizer Holdings Inc ....G....... 302 678-6767
  Dover (G-1522)
Talostech LLC ....G....... 302 332-9236
  New Castle (G-5752)

BATTERY CHARGERS

Wirelisity Inc ....G....... 213 816-1957
  Lewes (G-3829)

BATTERY CHARGERS: Storage, Motor & Engine Generator Type

Kissangen Inc ....E....... 414 446-4182
  Newark (G-6895)

BAUXITE MINING

American Minerals Partnership ....C....... 302 652-3301
  New Castle (G-5034)

BEARINGS: Roller & Parts

Roller Service Corporation ....E....... 302 737-5000
  Newark (G-7361)

BEAUTY & BARBER SHOP EQPT

Baumann Industries Inc ....G....... 302 593-1049
  Wilmington (G-9262)
Chemax Manufacturing Corp ....G....... 302 328-2440
  New Castle (G-5143)
Cytec Industries Inc ....G....... 302 530-7665
  Wilmington (G-9935)
Hirsh Industries Inc ....G....... 302 678-4990
  Dover (G-1648)
ISA Professional Ltd ....G....... 647 869-1552
  Wilmington (G-11086)
Klh Industries LLC ....G....... 800 348-0758
  Lewes (G-3583)
Raymond Chung Industries Corp ....G....... 302 384-9796
  Wilmington (G-12325)
W L Gore & Associates Inc ....D....... 410 506-7787
  Newark (G-7671)

BEAUTY & BARBER SHOP EQPT & SPLYS WHOLESALERS

Hair Gallery ....F....... 302 475-6714
  Wilmington (G-10820)
Simply Styling-Schl of Csmtlgy ....G....... 302 778-1885
  Wilmington (G-12628)

BEAUTY CULTURE SCHOOL

Center For Black Culture ....G....... 302 831-2991
  Newark (G-6176)

BEAUTY SALONS

A Gentlemans Touch Inc ....F....... 302 655-7015
  Wilmington (G-8878)
Afterglo Beauty Spa ....G....... 302 537-7546
  Millville (G-4832)
Army & Air Force Exchange Svc ....G....... 302 734-8262
  Dover (G-1140)
Avenue Cuts Inc ....G....... 302 655-1718
  Wilmington (G-9197)
Beauty Max Inc ....G....... 302 735-1705
  Dover (G-1186)
Bethany Bch Hair Snippery Inc ....G....... 302 539-8344
  Millville (G-4837)
Cecilia Williams ....G....... 302 250-6269
  Wilmington (G-9607)
Cielo Salon & Spa Inc ....F....... 302 575-0400
  Wilmington (G-9702)
Clippers & Curls Hair Design ....G....... 302 684-1522
  Milton (G-4881)
CMC Corporation of Hockessin ....G....... 302 239-1960
  Hockessin (G-2990)
Coiffure Ltd ....G....... 302 652-3463
  Wilmington (G-9764)
Complexions Tanning Salon ....G....... 302 430-0150
  Milford (G-4363)
Cut Above Hair Gallery ....G....... 302 539-0622
  Bethany Beach (G-394)
Cuts R US Inc ....G....... 302 674-2223
  Dover (G-1333)
Designer Braids and Trade ....G....... 718 783-9078
  Middletown (G-4037)
Donnas Family Cut & Curl Inc ....G....... 302 436-8999
  Selbyville (G-8482)
Elayne James Salon & Spa LLC ....G....... 302 376-5290
  Middletown (G-4053)
Elegant Images LLP ....G....... 302 698-5250
  Camden (G-568)
Expecting Miracles LLC ....G....... 302 893-3220
  Wilmington (G-10460)
Fantasy Beauty Salon ....G....... 302 629-6762
  Seaford (G-8242)
Fusion ....E....... 302 479-9444
  Wilmington (G-10650)
Hair Designs By Linda Inc ....G....... 302 478-7080
  Wilmington (G-10818)
Hair Studio II ....G....... 302 945-5110
  Millsboro (G-4703)
Hairs To You ....G....... 302 436-1728
  Selbyville (G-8498)

Hockessin Day Spa	G	302 234-7573
Hockessin (G-3050)		
Key To Beauty	G	302 398-9460
Harrington (G-2861)		
Kustom Kutz	G	302 424-7556
Milford (G-4468)		
Lady PS Hair Designs Inc	G	302 832-2668
Bear (G-228)		
Lavish Strands 1	G	302 333-5742
New Castle (G-5474)		
Main Event Inc	G	302 737-2225
Newark (G-6973)		
Make Wave	G	302 422-1247
Milford (G-4484)		
Mary Zieken	F	302 475-6714
Wilmington (G-11559)		
Maureen Freebery	E	302 234-7800
Wilmington (G-11575)		
Maureens For Men & Women	F	302 234-7800
Wilmington (G-11576)		
New Image Laser and Skin Care	G	302 537-4336
Ocean View (G-7804)		
Oerigo Consulting LLC	G	302 353-4719
Smyrna (G-8686)		
One Step Ahead Childcare	G	302 292-1162
Newark (G-7152)		
Premier Salons Intl Inc	G	302 477-3459
Wilmington (G-12217)		
Shop Talk Inc	G	302 322-5860
New Castle (G-5705)		
Sunco Salon	G	302 456-0240
Newark (G-7506)		
Supreme Hair Design	G	302 672-7255
Dover (G-2118)		
Unisex Palace	E	302 674-0950
Dover (G-2179)		
Vision Salon & Barbershop	G	302 934-9301
Millsboro (G-4821)		
White Mink Beauty Salon	F	302 737-2081
Newark (G-7692)		
Wyatt Ridley Corp	G	302 998-8860
Wilmington (G-13311)		

BED & BREAKFAST INNS

Addy Sea	G	302 539-3707
Bethany Beach (G-382)		
An Inn By Bay	F	302 644-8878
Lewes (G-3338)		
Beach House Resources	G	703 980-3336
Bethany Beach (G-384)		
Dan Licale	D	302 888-2133
Montchanin (G-4984)		
Higgins House Victorian B & B	G	407 324-9238
Dagsboro (G-910)		
Meris Gardens Bed & Breakfast	G	302 752-4962
Bethany Beach (G-414)		
Savannah Inn	G	302 645-0330
Lewes (G-3730)		
Sea Witch Inc	G	302 226-3900
Rehoboth Beach (G-8069)		
State Street Inn	G	302 734-2494
Dover (G-2105)		

BEDS & ACCESS STORES

Johnny Janosik Inc	C	302 875-5955
Laurel (G-3243)		

BEDSPREADS & BED SETS, FROM PURCHASED MATERIALS

G L K Inc	G	302 697-3838
Dover (G-1576)		

BEEKEEPERS' SPLYS: Honeycomb Foundations

Warren W Seaver	G	302 674-8969
Dover (G-2206)		

BEER & ALE WHOLESALERS

Argilla Brewing Company	G	302 731-8200
Newark (G-5994)		
Southern Glazers Wine	E	302 656-4487
New Castle (G-5724)		

BEER & ALE, WHOLESALE: Beer & Other Fermented Malt Liquors

Delaware Importers Inc	D	302 656-4487
New Castle (G-5231)		
NKS Distributors Inc	C	302 322-1811
New Castle (G-5572)		
NKS Distributors Inc	E	302 422-1220
Milford (G-4513)		
Standard Distributing Co Inc	D	302 655-5511
New Castle (G-5737)		

BEER & ALE, WHOLESALE: Porter

Carlo Porter Michael	G	267 709-6370
Newark (G-6156)		

BEER, WINE & LIQUOR STORES: Wine

Pizzadili Partners LLC	G	302 284-9463
Felton (G-2312)		

BELTS: Conveyor, Made From Purchased Wire

Guide Idler and Conveyor Belt	G	302 762-7564
Wilmington (G-10798)		
Mid Atlantic Indus Belting	G	302 453-7353
Newark (G-7026)		
OConnor Belting Intl Inc	E	302 452-2500
Newark (G-7142)		

BELTS: Drive

Chiorino Inc	E	302 292-1906
Newark (G-6200)		

BEVERAGE BASES & SYRUPS

Trisco Foods LLC	D	719 352-3218
Wilmington (G-12978)		

BEVERAGE POWDERS

Le Herbe LLC	G	949 317-1100
Wilmington (G-11348)		

BEVERAGE PRDTS: Malt, Barley

Proximity Malt LLC	F	414 755-8388
Laurel (G-3275)		

BEVERAGE, NONALCOHOLIC: Iced Tea/Fruit Drink, Bottled/Canned

Cole and Latz Inc	G	702 234-2784
New Castle (G-5180)		

BEVERAGES, ALCOHOLIC: Ale

Dogfish Head Craft Brewery LLC	D	302 684-1000
Milton (G-4897)		
Mispillion River Brewing LLC	G	302 491-6623
Milford (G-4508)		

BEVERAGES, ALCOHOLIC: Beer

Delaware Beer Works Inc	E	302 836-2739
Bear (G-104)		
Dewey Beer & Food Company LLC	G	302 227-1182
Dewey Beach (G-1056)		
Wilmington Brew Works LLC	G	302 757-4971
Wilmington (G-13225)		

BEVERAGES, ALCOHOLIC: Beer & Ale

Chesapeakemaine Trey	G	302 226-3600
Rehoboth Beach (G-7887)		
Dogfish Head Inc	F	302 226-2739
Rehoboth Beach (G-7918)		
Volunteer Brewing Company LLC	G	610 721-2836
Middletown (G-4277)		

BEVERAGES, ALCOHOLIC: Distilled Liquors

Beach Time	G	302 644-2850
Lewes (G-3367)		
Dogfish Head Companies LLC	G	302 684-1000
Milton (G-4896)		
Legacy Distilling LLC	G	302 983-1269
Smyrna (G-8672)		
R J Baker Distillery	G	302 745-0967
Laurel (G-3277)		

William Grant & Sons USA Corp	G	302 573-3880
Wilmington (G-13211)		

BEVERAGES, ALCOHOLIC: Rum

Breakthru Beverage Group LLC	C	302 356-3500
New Castle (G-5109)		

BEVERAGES, ALCOHOLIC: Wine Coolers

Universal Bev Importers LLC	G	302 276-0619
Middletown (G-4273)		

BEVERAGES, ALCOHOLIC: Wines

Delaware Meat Company LLC	G	302 438-0252
Wilmington (G-10063)		
Harvest Ridge Winery LLC	G	302 250-6583
Marydel (G-3917)		
Nassau Vly Vineyards & Winery	G	302 645-9463
Lewes (G-3655)		
Pizzadili Partners LLC	G	302 284-9463
Felton (G-2312)		
Signature Selections LLC	G	631 256-6900
Newark (G-7427)		
Texavino LLC	G	302 295-0829
Wilmington (G-12888)		
White Horse Winery	G	302 388-4850
Wilmington (G-13190)		

BEVERAGES, NONALCOHOLIC: Bottled & canned soft drinks

Canada Dry Dstrg Wilmington De	E	302 322-1856
New Castle (G-5130)		
Moon Shot Energy LLC	G	512 297-2626
Lewes (G-3647)		

BEVERAGES, NONALCOHOLIC: Carbonated

Pepsi Bottling Ventures LLC	D	302 398-3415
Harrington (G-2871)		
Pepsi-Cola Btlg of Wilmington	C	302 761-4848
Wilmington (G-12081)		

BEVERAGES, NONALCOHOLIC: Carbonated, Canned & Bottled, Etc

Maurten US Corporation	G	302 669-9085
Wilmington (G-11577)		

BEVERAGES, NONALCOHOLIC: Soft Drinks, Canned & Bottled, Etc

Krave Like LLC	G	302 482-4550
Wilmington (G-11293)		
Minor Figures Inc	G	714 875-3449
Camden (G-592)		
Pepsi-Cola Metro Btlg Co Inc	C	302 764-6770
Wilmington (G-12082)		

BEVERAGES, WINE & DISTILLED ALCOHOLIC, WHOLESALE: Liquor

Delaware Importers Inc	D	302 656-4487
New Castle (G-5231)		
Greenwood Liquor Inc	G	302 349-4767
Greenwood (G-2741)		
Outlet Liquors	G	302 227-7700
Rehoboth Beach (G-8024)		
Patel Sanjay	G	302 376-0136
Middletown (G-4180)		
Tax Free Liquors	G	302 846-0410
Delmar (G-1035)		
Vishva Inc	G	302 425-3801
Wilmington (G-13090)		

BEVERAGES, WINE & DISTILLED ALCOHOLIC, WHOLESALE: Wine

Bin 66 Fine Wine & Spirit	G	302 227-6966
Rehoboth Beach (G-7869)		
NKS Distributors Inc	C	302 322-1811
New Castle (G-5572)		
S & S Wines and Spirits	G	302 678-9987
Dover (G-2048)		
Salted Vines Vineyard Winery	F	302 829-8990
Frankford (G-2385)		
Standard Distributing Co Inc	D	302 655-5511
New Castle (G-5737)		
Village Wines & Spirits	G	302 376-5583
Middletown (G-4276)		

BEVERAGES, WINE/DISTILLED ALCOHOLIC, WHOL: Bttlg Wine/Liquor

Southern Glazers Wine .... E 302 656-4487
New Castle *(G-5724)*

William Grant & Sons USA Corp .... G 302 573-3880
Wilmington *(G-13211)*

BICYCLE ASSEMBLY SVCS

Protech Delivery & Assembly .... F 302 449-5003
New Castle *(G-5650)*

BICYCLE REPAIR SHOP

Pike Creek Bike Line Inc 610 747-1200
Wilmington *(G-12136)*

Seagreen Bicycle LLP .... G 302 226-2323
Rehoboth Beach *(G-8070)*

BICYCLE SHOPS

Pike Creek Bike Line Inc .... G 610 747-1200
Wilmington *(G-12136)*

BICYCLES WHOLESALERS

Seagreen Bicycle LLP .... G 302 226-2323
Rehoboth Beach *(G-8070)*

BICYCLES, PARTS & ACCESS

Ross Bicycles LLC .... G 888 392-5628
Lewes *(G-3726)*

BILLIARD & POOL PARLORS

Capitol Billiards Inc .... G 302 629-0298
Seaford *(G-8182)*

BILLIARD EQPT & SPLYS WHOLESALERS

Capitol Billiards Inc .... G 302 629-0298
Seaford *(G-8182)*

BILLING & BOOKKEEPING SVCS

Accounting & Bookkeeping Svc .... G 302 376-7857
Middletown *(G-3929)*

Advantdge Hlthcare Sltions Inc .... G 302 224-5678
Newark *(G-5911)*

Consult Dynamics Inc .... E 302 295-4700
Wilmington *(G-9836)*

Delaware Clean Service .... G 302 838-1650
Bear *(G-105)*

Delaware Medical MGT Svcs LLC .... E 302 283-3300
Newark *(G-6394)*

Delaware Occupational Health S .... E 302 368-5100
Newark *(G-6400)*

Doherty & Associates Inc .... F 302 239-3500
Wilmington *(G-10183)*

DSouza and Associates Inc .... F 302 239-2300
Hockessin *(G-3013)*

Hospital Blling Cllctn Svc Ltd .... B 302 552-8000
New Castle *(G-5405)*

Medical Billing & MGT Svcs Inc .... G 610 564-5314
Newark *(G-7015)*

Paths LLC .... E 302 294-1494
Newark *(G-7180)*

Perioperative Services LLC .... D 302 733-0806
Newark *(G-7203)*

TLC Personal Assistants .... G 302 290-9902
Wilmington *(G-12918)*

BINDING SVC: Books & Manuals

Amer Inc .... G 302 654-2498
Wilmington *(G-9039)*

Ben-Dom Printing Company .... F 302 737-9144
Newark *(G-6072)*

Dover Post Co Inc .... D 302 678-3616
Dover *(G-1467)*

Dupont Txtles Intriors Del Inc .... G 302 774-1000
Wilmington *(G-10265)*

Garile Inc .... E 302 366-0848
Newark *(G-6639)*

L E Stansell Inc .... G 302 475-1534
Wilmington *(G-11308)*

William N Cann Inc .... E 302 995-0820
Wilmington *(G-13215)*

BIOLOGICAL PRDTS: Exc Diagnostic

Analytical Biological Svcs Inc .... E 302 654-4492
Wilmington *(G-9073)*

Cleamol LLC .... G 513 885-3462
Wilmington *(G-9736)*

Genalyze LLC .... G 732 917-4893
Middletown *(G-4085)*

Reflection Biotechnologies Inc .... G 212 765-2200
Wilmington *(G-12352)*

BIOLOGICAL PRDTS: Extracts

Irving IA Extract Diet Pills .... G 302 218-0472
Wilmington *(G-11084)*

BIOLOGICAL PRDTS: Serums

Plume Serum LLC .... G 302 697-9044
Magnolia *(G-3904)*

BIOLOGICAL PRDTS: Vaccines & Immunizing

Glaxosmithkline Holdings .... C 302 984-6932
Wilmington *(G-10720)*

BIOLOGICAL PRDTS: Veterinary

Artevet LLC .... E 443 255-0016
Wilmington *(G-9137)*

Intervet Inc .... B 302 934-4341
Millsboro *(G-4710)*

BIRD PROOFING SVCS

Rentokil North America Inc .... E 302 733-0851
Newark *(G-7318)*

BLADES: Knife

Dalstrong America Inc .... G 716 380-4998
Wilmington *(G-9949)*

Delaware Diamond Knives Inc .... E 302 999-7476
Wilmington *(G-10041)*

BLANKBOOKS: Albums, Record

Deja Vu Record Album Cover Art .... G 302 227-8909
Rehoboth Beach *(G-7910)*

BLANKETS: Horse

Fairway Manufacturing Company .... G 302 398-4630
Harrington *(G-2839)*

BLASTING SVC: Sand, Metal Parts

Industrial Metal Treating Corp .... F 302 656-1677
Wilmington *(G-11021)*

BLINDS & SHADES: Vertical

Blind Factory .... G 302 838-1211
Wilmington *(G-9369)*

Local Vertical 302 242-2552
Dover *(G-1794)*

BLINDS : Window

Vertical Blind Factory Inc .... F 302 998-9616
Wilmington *(G-13067)*

BLOCKS & BRICKS: Concrete

Elegant Stone Veneer LLC .... G 302 547-4780
Newark *(G-6511)*

BLOCKS: Landscape Or Retaining Wall, Concrete

All Rock & Mulch LLC .... G 302 838-7625
Bear *(G-25)*

Valley Landscaping and Con Inc .... G 302 922-5020
Dover *(G-2186)*

BLOOD BANK

Blood Bank of Delmarva Inc .... F 302 737-1151
Newark *(G-6095)*

Blood Bank of Delmarva Inc .... G 302 737-8400
Wilmington *(G-9371)*

Csl Plasma Inc .... G 302 565-0003
Newark *(G-6321)*

BLOOD RELATED HEALTH SVCS

Ambient Medical Care .... G 302 629-3099
Seaford *(G-8145)*

American Sleep Medicine LLC .... E 302 366-0111
Newark *(G-5957)*

Bancroft Neurohealth Inc .... E 302 691-8531
Wilmington *(G-9236)*

Delaware Imaging Network .... G 302 737-5990
Newark *(G-6385)*

Delaware Integrative Medical C .... G 302 559-5959
Georgetown *(G-2501)*

Eagle Mhc Company .... B 302 653-3000
Clayton *(G-847)*

Epic Health Services Inc .... G 302 422-3176
Georgetown *(G-2523)*

Kent General Hospital Inc .... G 302 430-5705
Milford *(G-4464)*

Pinnacle Rhbilitation Hlth Ctr .... F 302 653-5085
Smyrna *(G-8689)*

BLOWERS & FANS

Air Liquide America LP .... G 302 225-2132
Wilmington *(G-8992)*

Delaware Contract Testing LLC .... G 302 650-4030
Wilmington *(G-10025)*

BLUEPRINTING SVCS

Reliable Copy Service Inc .... F 302 654-8080
Wilmington *(G-12373)*

Reprographics Center Inc .... G 302 328-5019
New Castle *(G-5672)*

Windswept Enterprises .... G 302 678-0805
Dover *(G-2233)*

BOAT BUILDING & REPAIR

Croker Oars Usa Inc .... G 302 897-6705
Townsend *(G-8776)*

Saxton Maritime Services LLC .... G 415 870-3881
Lewes *(G-3731)*

BOAT BUILDING & REPAIRING: Fiberglass

F & S Boat Works .... E 302 838-5500
Bear *(G-147)*

BOAT BUILDING & REPAIRING: Yachts

Nanticoke Industries LLC .... G 302 245-8825
Seaford *(G-8324)*

BOAT BUILDING & RPRG: Fishing, Small, Lobster, Crab, Oyster

Broadwater Oyster Company LLC .... G 610 220-7776
Rehoboth Beach *(G-7879)*

BOAT DEALERS

Bobs Marine Service Inc .... F 302 539-3711
Ocean View *(G-7769)*

Cedar Creek Marina .... G 302 422-2040
Milford *(G-4342)*

Proper Pitch LLC .... G 302 436-5442
Selbyville *(G-8534)*

BOAT DEALERS: Marine Splys & Eqpt

Hilton Corp .... G 302 994-3365
Wilmington *(G-10911)*

BOAT DEALERS: Motor

North Bay Marina Incorporated .... F 302 436-4211
Selbyville *(G-8528)*

Rudy Marine Inc .... F 302 999-8735
Wilmington *(G-12491)*

Walkers Marine Corporation .... G 302 629-8666
Seaford *(G-8432)*

BOAT REPAIR SVCS

Bobs Marine Service Inc .... F 302 539-3711
Ocean View *(G-7769)*

Links Outboard LLC .... G 302 368-2860
Newark *(G-6937)*

PRODUCT & SERVICES SECTION

BOAT YARD: Boat yards, storage & incidental repair

Cedar Creek Marina .... G 302 422-2040
Milford (G-4342)
Midlantic Marine Center Inc .... F 302 436-2628
Selbyville (G-8521)
North Bay Marina Incorporated .... F 302 436-4211
Selbyville (G-8528)

BOILER & HEATING REPAIR SVCS

Blades H V A C Services .... G 302 539-4436
Dagsboro (G-884)

BOLTS: Metal

Anthony J Nappa .... G 716 888-0553
Magnolia (G-3880)

BOND & MORTGAGE COMPANIES

Federal Home Loan ADM Inc .... D 855 345-2669
Wilmington (G-10516)

BOOK STORES

Prestwick House Inc .... E 302 659-2070
Smyrna (G-8692)
Whole Child App Inc .... F 302 570-2002
Lewes (G-3821)

BOOK STORES: Comic

Biblion .... G 302 644-2210
Lewes (G-3383)

BOOKS, WHOLESALE

Bethany Beach Books .... G 302 539-2522
Bethany Beach (G-386)
Linguatext Ltd .... G 302 453-8695
Newark (G-6936)
Maintenance Troubleshooting .... G 302 692-0871
Newark (G-6976)

BOTTLED GAS DEALERS: Liquefied Petro, Dlvrd To Customers

Pep-Up Inc .... F 302 856-2555
Georgetown (G-2617)
Pep-Up Inc .... G 302 645-2600
Rehoboth Beach (G-8031)

BOTTLED GAS DEALERS: Propane

Keen Compressed Gas Co .... E 302 594-4545
New Castle (G-5456)
Schagrin Gas Co .... E 302 378-2000
Middletown (G-4232)

BOTTLES: Plastic

First State Container LLC .... E 603 888-1315
Newark (G-6583)

BOWLING CENTERS

Brunswick Doverama .... G 302 734-7501
Dover (G-1238)
Keglers Korner Pro Shop .... G 302 526-2249
Dover (G-1729)
Leftys Alley & Eats .... F 302 864-6000
Lewes (G-3593)
Midcoast Gymnstics Dnce Studio ...... G 302 436-6007
Selbyville (G-8520)

BOWLING EQPT & SPLY STORES

Pleasant Hill Lanes Inc .... E 302 998-8811
Wilmington (G-12158)

BOXES & CRATES: Rectangular, Wood

H&H Customs Inc .... G 302 378-0810
Middletown (G-4099)

BOXES & SHOOK: Nailed Wood

Elwyn .... D 302 658-8860
Wilmington (G-10385)

BOXES: Corrugated

True-Pack Ltd .... E 302 326-2222
New Castle (G-5798)

BRICK, STONE & RELATED PRDTS WHOLESALERS

Azurite03 Inc .... G 866 667-5119
Wilmington (G-9206)
Delaware Brick Company .... G 302 883-2807
Dover (G-1361)
Depro-Serical USA Inc .... G 302 368-8040
Townsend (G-8783)
Michael McCarthy Stones .... G 302 539-8056
Millville (G-4850)
Parker Block Co Inc .... E 302 934-9237
Millsboro (G-4769)

BRIDAL SHOPS

Boutique The Bridal Ltd .... G 302 335-5948
Milford (G-4329)
Bridal & Tuxedo Outlet Inc .... G 302 731-8802
Newark (G-6118)

BROADCASTING STATIONS, RADIO: Contemporary Music

Delmarva Broadcasting Co Inc .... D 302 478-2700
Wilmington (G-10102)

BROADCASTING STATIONS, RADIO: Country Music

Iheartcommunications Inc .... E 302 674-1410
Dover (G-1666)

BROADCASTING STATIONS, RADIO: Educational

East Sussex Public Brdcstg .... G 302 644-7385
Rehoboth Beach (G-7923)
Gamma Theta Lambda Ed .... G 302 983-9429
Bear (G-164)

BROADCASTING STATIONS, RADIO: Music Format

Resort Broadcasting Co LP .... E 302 945-2050
Lewes (G-3716)

BROADCASTING STATIONS, RADIO: Sports

302 Sports .... G 302 650-8479
Wilmington (G-8857)
Myserve Inc .... G 302 528-4822
Wilmington (G-11791)
Play Game Sports .... G 302 736-0606
Dover (G-1964)

BROKERS & DEALERS: Mortgages, Buying & Selling

John Lovett Inc .... D 302 455-9460
Newark (G-6843)
Meyer & Meyer Inc .... E 302 994-9600
Wilmington (G-11651)

BROKERS & DEALERS: Securities

Freemarkets Investment Co Inc .... G 302 427-2089
Wilmington (G-10630)
Gates and Company LLC .... F 302 428-1338
Wilmington (G-10675)
Gund Securities Corporation .... F 302 479-9210
Wilmington (G-10801)
Ing Bank Fsb .... E 302 658-2200
Wilmington (G-11030)
Lehman Brothers/Gp Inc .... F 877 740-0108
Wilmington (G-11365)
Navient Corporation .... D 302 283-8000
Wilmington (G-11821)
Navient Corporation .... D 302 283-8000
Wilmington (G-11822)
Navient Corporation .... D 302 283-8000
Wilmington (G-11823)
Rbc .... G 302 892-5901
Wilmington (G-12333)
Stb Management .... E 302 737-5105
Newark (G-7487)

BROKERS & DEALERS: Security

Boothe Investment Group .... G 302 734-7526
Dover (G-1221)
Citigroup Global Markets Inc .... D 302 888-4100
Wilmington (G-9713)
Deutsche Bank Tr Co Americas .... E 302 636-3301
Wilmington (G-10126)
Merrill Lynch Pierce Fenner .... D 302 571-5100
Wilmington (G-11646)
Merrill Lynch Pierce Fenner .... E 302 227-5159
Rehoboth Beach (G-8003)
Wells Fargo Clearing Svcs LLC .... E 302 428-5969
Newark (G-7685)

BROKERS & DEALERS: Stock

Brittingham Inc .... G 302 656-8173
Wilmington (G-9480)
Merrill Lynch Pierce Fenner .... E 302 736-7700
Dover (G-1840)
Scottrade Inc .... G 302 658-6511
Newark (G-7397)
Td Ameritrade Inc .... E 302 368-1050
Newark (G-7541)

BROKERS' SVCS

Giumarra International Mktg .... G 302 652-4009
Wilmington (G-10717)
Turning Point Collection LLC .... G 302 416-0092
Wilmington (G-12993)

BROKERS, MARINE TRANSPORTATION

C V International Inc .... G 302 427-0440
Wilmington (G-9525)
Explorer New Build LLC .... G 305 436-4000
Wilmington (G-10462)
Umbrella Transport Group Inc .... G 301 919-1623
Newark (G-7609)

BROKERS: Business

Empire Flippers LLC .... F 323 638-0438
Wilmington (G-10394)
Mergers Acqstons Strtegies LLC .... G 302 992-0400
Wilmington (G-11640)

BROKERS: Commodity Contracts

DMI Commodities Inc .... F 877 364-3644
Newark (G-6457)

BROKERS: Food

Acm Corp .... F 302 736-3864
Dover (G-1083)
Hughes Delaware Maid Scrapple .... G 302 284-4370
Felton (G-2294)
Oppenheimer Group Inc .... F 302 533-0779
Newark (G-7157)
Supermarket Associates Inc .... G 302 547-1977
Wilmington (G-12810)
Thomas E Moore Inc .... F 302 674-1500
Kenton (G-3187)
Valco Enterprises LLC .... G 514 938-8474
Newark (G-7640)

BROKERS: Loan

A B C Lending Corp .... G 302 655-5313
Wilmington (G-8871)
ABC Payday & Title Lending .... G 302 322-0233
New Castle (G-4997)
American Spirit Federal Cr Un .... F 302 738-4515
Newark (G-5958)
Del-One Federal Credit Union .... E 302 739-4496
Dover (G-1355)
Delaware First Federal Cr Un .... F 302 998-0665
Wilmington (G-10047)
Delaware Title Loans Inc .... F 302 478-8505
Wilmington (G-10091)
Goldstar- Cash LLC .... G 302 427-2535
Wilmington (G-10742)
Lending Manager Holdings LLC .... G 888 501-0335
Newark (G-6931)
Mda Lending Solutions Inc .... F 302 433-8006
Wilmington (G-11609)
Navient Corporation .... D 302 283-8000
Wilmington (G-11821)
Provident Federal Credit Union .... F 302 734-1133
Dover (G-1992)

Employee Codes: A=Over 500 employees, B=251-500
C=101-250, D=51-100, E=20-50, F=10-19, G=1-9

BROKERS: Loan

Stewart Title Company .... G 302 433-8766
  Wilmington (G-12765)
Union Mortgage Group Inc .... G 302 227-6687
  Rehoboth Beach (G-8105)

BROKERS: Mortgage, Arranging For Loans

Aca Mortgage Co Inc .... E 302 225-1390
  Wilmington (G-8911)
Delaware Financial Capital .... F 302 266-9500
  Newark (G-6379)
First Atlantic Mrtg Svcs LLC .... G 302 841-8435
  Lewes (G-3497)
Interstate Mortgage Corp Inc .... G 302 733-7620
  Newark (G-6799)
JG Wentworth HM Lending Inc .... E 302 725-0723
  Ocean View (G-7796)
John Lovett Inc .... D 302 455-9460
  Newark (G-6843)
Louviers Mortgage Corporation .... F 302 234-4129
  Wilmington (G-11443)
Nefsc Inc .... G 302 746-1771
  Wilmington (G-11828)
Pike Creek Mortgage Services .... F 302 892-2811
  Newark (G-7216)
Reliance Mortgage Company Inc .... G 302 376-7234
  Middletown (G-4215)
Resource Mortgage Corp .... F 302 657-0181
  Wilmington (G-12386)
Synergy Direct Mortgage .... F 302 283-0833
  Christiana (G-681)

BROKERS: Printing

University of De Printing .... E 302 831-2153
  Newark (G-7618)

BROKERS: Security

Charles Schwab & Co Inc .... F 302 622-3600
  Wilmington (G-9638)
Morgan Stanley & Co LLC .... E 302 573-4000
  Wilmington (G-11752)
Raymond James & Associates Inc ..... G 302 656-1534
  Wilmington (G-12327)
Raymond James & Associates Inc ..... G 302 798-9113
  Wilmington (G-12328)
Raymond James Financial Svc .... G 302 778-2170
  Wilmington (G-12329)
Raymond James Fincl Svcs Inc .... F 302 645-8592
  Lewes (G-3709)
Raymond James Fincl Svcs Inc .... G 302 539-3323
  Bethany Beach (G-426)
Raymond James Fincl Svcs Inc .... F 302 778-2170
  Wilmington (G-12330)
Raymond James Fincl Svcs Inc .... G 302 656-1534
  Wilmington (G-12331)
Wells Fargo Clearing Svcs LLC .... E 302 428-8600
  Wilmington (G-13152)

BROOMS & BRUSHES: Household Or Indl

Dupont Flaments - Americas LLC ...... G 302 774-1000
  Wilmington (G-10255)

BUILDING & OFFICE CLEANING SVCS

Aqua Wash Inc .... G 302 994-1720
  Newark (G-5992)
Carr Paris .... F 302 401-1203
  Wilmington (G-9578)
Clean Hands LLC .... F 215 681-1435
  Smyrna (G-8598)
Cleaners Sunny .... G 302 827-2095
  Lewes (G-3428)
Crystal Graham .... F 302 669-9318
  Middletown (G-4016)
Diamond State Commercial Clg .... G 215 888-2575
  Bear (G-116)
Gemini Building Systems LLC .... D 302 654-5310
  Wilmington (G-10688)
Jrw Cleaning Solutions LLC .... G 484 942-9995
  Wilmington (G-11203)
Kleen-Comp LLC .... G 302 981-0791
  Newark (G-6897)
M T O Clean of Sussex County .... G 302 854-0204
  Milton (G-4929)
Oceanside Elite Clg Bldg Svcs .... E 302 339-7777
  Lewes (G-3665)

BUILDING & STRUCTURAL WOOD MEMBERS

Delmarva Truss and Panel LLC .... G 302 270-8888
  Wyoming (G-13362)
Universal Forest Products .... G 302 855-1250
  Georgetown (G-2699)

BUILDING CLEANING & MAINTENANCE SVCS

A1 Striping Inc .... G 302 738-5016
  Newark (G-5872)
Able Whelling and Machiene .... G 302 436-1929
  Selbyville (G-8446)
Abrahams Seed LLC .... G 302 588-1913
  Clayton (G-831)
Christopher Handy .... G 302 934-1018
  Millsboro (G-4661)
Coastal Maintenance LLC .... G 302 536-1290
  Seaford (G-8200)
Commercial Cleaning Services .... G 302 764-3424
  Wilmington (G-9785)
Corporation Service Company .... B 302 636-5400
  Wilmington (G-9866)
Dm Home Maintenance .... G 302 945-5050
  Millsboro (G-4679)
Dover Nunan LLC .... G 302 697-9776
  Dover (G-1461)
Fortress Home Maintenance Serv ..... G 302 539-3446
  Ocean View (G-7785)
Gutter Connection LLC .... G 302 736-0105
  Dover (G-1617)
Maintenance Tech .... G 302 322-6410
  New Castle (G-5502)
Maintenance Troubleshooti .... G 302 477-1045
  Wilmington (G-11493)
Marlings Inc .... F 302 325-1759
  New Castle (G-5509)
McClain Custodial Service .... G 302 645-6597
  Lewes (G-3629)
Mebro Inc .... E 302 992-0104
  Wilmington (G-11613)
Penwood Property Preservation .... G 302 469-5318
  Felton (G-2308)
Priority Services LLC .... E 302 918-3070
  Newark (G-7258)
Quality Assured Inc .... E 302 652-4151
  Wilmington (G-12277)
Serpro of Bear New Castle .... G 302 392-6000
  Bear (G-317)
ServiceMaster of Newark .... F 302 834-8006
  Newark (G-7410)
St Andrews Maintenance .... G 302 832-2675
  Bear (G-335)
Teagle and Sons .... G 302 682-8639
  Seaford (G-8419)
Teff Inc .... F 302 856-9768
  Georgetown (G-2689)
Tornado II Janitorial Service .... F 302 898-1370
  New Castle (G-5774)
University of Delaware .... C 302 831-1141
  Newark (G-7625)
Vicks Commercial Clg & Maint .... G 302 697-9591
  Dover (G-2191)
Whaleys Seed Store Inc .... G 302 875-7833
  Laurel (G-3308)

BUILDING CLEANING SVCS

Community Services Corporation ..... F 302 368-4400
  Newark (G-6272)
County Building Services Inc .... D 302 377-4213
  Middletown (G-4012)
H&S Cleaning Service Inc .... E 302 449-2928
  Townsend (G-8791)
Maude Burton .... G 302 674-4210
  Dover (G-1830)
Nu World Building Service .... F 302 678-2578
  Dover (G-1909)
Tlaloc Building Services Inc .... F 302 559-6459
  Bear (G-354)
Valet Cleaning Service .... G 302 653-0233
  Clayton (G-872)

BUILDING COMPONENTS: Structural Steel

Crystal Steel Fabricators Inc .... C 302 846-0613
  Delmar (G-989)
Mancor US Inc .... G 302 573-3858
  Wilmington (G-11500)

Steel Suppliers Inc .... C 302 654-5243
  Wilmington (G-12748)
Summit Steel Inc .... D 302 325-3220
  New Castle (G-5741)

BUILDING EXTERIOR CLEANING SVCS

American Seaboard Exteriors .... E 302 571-9896
  Wilmington (G-9055)
Arnold Powerwash LLC .... G 302 542-9783
  Lewes (G-3346)
Proclean Inc .... E 302 656-8080
  Delaware City (G-965)
Wilkins Enterprises Inc .... G 302 945-4142
  Lewes (G-3824)

BUILDING INSPECTION SVCS

Aecom Technology Corporation ...... E 302 468-5878
  Wilmington (G-8962)
Building Inspection Undrwrtr .... G 302 266-9057
  Newark (G-6133)
First State Inspection Agency .... G 302 449-5383
  Middletown (G-4072)
Ji DCI Jv-Il .... F 302 652-4221
  Wilmington (G-11156)
McConnell Bros Inc .... G 302 218-4240
  Wilmington (G-11588)
Middle Dept Insptn Agcy Inc .... G 302 875-4514
  Laurel (G-3265)
Middle Dept Insptn Agcy Inc .... G 302 999-0243
  Wilmington (G-11682)
Reliable Home Inspection .... F 302 455-1200
  Wilmington (G-12374)
Safeplace Corporation .... G 302 479-9000
  Wilmington (G-12520)

BUILDING MAINTENANCE SVCS, EXC REPAIRS

Dryzone LLC .... G 302 684-5034
  Milton (G-4899)

BUILDING PRDTS & MATERIALS DEALERS

American Cedar & Millwork Inc .... D 302 645-9580
  Lewes (G-3335)
Case Construction Inc .... E 302 737-3800
  Newark (G-6164)
Custom Cabinet Shop Inc .... F 302 337-8241
  Greenwood (G-2725)
D F Quillen & Sons Inc .... E 302 227-2531
  Rehoboth Beach (G-7906)
East Coast Minority Supplier .... E 302 656-3337
  Wilmington (G-10320)
Erco Ceilings & Interiors Inc .... F 302 994-6200
  Wilmington (G-10432)
Erco Ceilings & Interiors Inc .... F 302 398-3200
  Harrington (G-2838)
Lowes Home Centers LLC .... C 302 479-7799
  Wilmington (G-11444)
Lowes Home Centers LLC .... C 302 934-3740
  Millsboro (G-4727)
Lowes Home Centers LLC .... C 302 735-7500
  Dover (G-1798)
Lowes Home Centers LLC .... C 302 697-0700
  Camden (G-589)
Lowes Home Centers LLC .... C 302 781-1154
  Newark (G-6953)
Marjam Supply Co Inc .... F 302 283-1020
  Newark (G-6988)
Mechanics Paradise Inc .... F 302 652-8863
  New Castle (G-5513)
P D Supply Inc .... G 302 655-3358
  Wilmington (G-11994)

BUILDING STONE, ARTIFICIAL: Concrete

Best Stoneworks of Delaware .... G 302 765-3497
  Wilmington (G-9314)

BUILDINGS, PREFABRICATED: Wholesalers

Edis Building Systems Inc .... G 302 421-5700
  Wilmington (G-10349)

BUILDINGS: Farm & Utility

Street Core Utility Service .... F 302 239-4110
  Hockessin (G-3150)

PRODUCT & SERVICES SECTION

BUILDINGS: Portable

Steel Buildings Inc..........................G....... 302 644-0444
  Lewes (G-3764)

BUILDINGS: Prefabricated, Metal

Regional Builders Inc.....................E....... 302 628-8660
  Seaford (G-8374)
Vaughan Bckley Modular Sls Inc....G....... 215 259-7509
  Wilmington (G-13051)

BUILDINGS: Prefabricated, Wood

Fox Pointe....................................G....... 302 744-9442
  Dover (G-1564)

BUILDINGS: Prefabricated, Wood

Beracah Homes Inc........................E....... 302 349-4561
  Greenwood (G-2716)
Howard M Joseph Inc.....................G....... 302 335-1300
  Milford (G-4446)

BULLION, PRECIOUS METAL, WHOLESALE

Fidelitrade Incorporated..................F....... 302 762-6200
  Wilmington (G-10532)

BURGLAR ALARM MAINTENANCE & MONITORING SVCS

ADT LLC..F....... 302 325-3125
  New Castle (G-5006)
Anaconda Prtctive Concepts Inc.....F....... 302 834-1125
  Newark (G-5965)
B Safe Inc.....................................E....... 302 633-1833
  Wilmington (G-9213)
B Safe Inc.....................................E....... 302 422-3916
  Dover (G-1167)
Berley Security Systems Inc...........F....... 302 791-9056
  Wilmington (G-9305)
Johnson Cntrls SEC Sltions LLC....D....... 302 328-2800
  New Castle (G-5442)
Prevent Alarm Company LLC.........G....... 302 478-6647
  New Castle (G-5639)
Protect America Inc.......................G....... 302 999-9045
  Wilmington (G-12255)
Security Inc..................................F....... 302 652-5276
  Claymont (G-802)
Security Instrument Corp Del.........D....... 302 998-2261
  Wilmington (G-12571)
Security Quality............................G....... 302 286-1200
  Newark (G-7400)
Sound-N-Secure Inc......................G....... 302 424-3670
  Milford (G-4563)
Vector Security Inc........................E....... 302 422-7031
  Milford (G-4589)

BURIAL VAULTS: Concrete Or Precast Terrazzo

Cecil Vault & Memorial Co Inc.......G....... 302 994-3806
  Wilmington (G-9606)
Cooper-Wilbert Vault Co Inc..........G....... 302 376-1331
  Middletown (G-4011)
Delaware Monument and Vault......G....... 302 540-2387
  Hockessin (G-3005)

BUS CHARTER SVC: Local

Krapfs Coaches Inc.......................E....... 302 993-7855
  Wilmington (G-11292)
R J K Transportation Inc................F....... 302 422-3188
  Houston (G-3181)
Staplefords Sales and Service........E....... 302 834-4568
  Saint Georges (G-8130)
Transportation Delaware Dept........G....... 302 658-8960
  Wilmington (G-12958)
Triple D Charters LLC....................G....... 302 934-6837
  Millsboro (G-4814)

BUS CHARTER SVC: Long-Distance

Dawson Bus Service Inc................D....... 302 697-9501
  Camden (G-556)
Dawson Bus Service Inc................F....... 302 678-2594
  Dover (G-1345)
First Student Inc...........................C....... 302 995-9607
  Newark (G-6587)
Harding Limo Bus Cnnection LLC..F....... 302 376-1818
  Middletown (G-4104)

Jor-Lin Inc....................................E....... 302 424-4445
  Milford (G-4461)
Krapfs Coaches Inc.......................E....... 302 993-7855
  Wilmington (G-11292)
Matthew Smith Bus Service...........E....... 302 734-9311
  Dover (G-1828)
Wilmington Transportation Ctr......G....... 302 655-6111
  Wilmington (G-13259)

BUSINESS & SECRETARIAL SCHOOLS

H&R Block Inc..............................F....... 302 652-3286
  New Castle (G-5371)

BUSINESS ACTIVITIES: Non-Commercial Site

1 Fair Chiropractic & Med Inc........G....... 302 528-1068
  Wilmington (G-8840)
3ti Coatings LLC...........................G....... 302 379-1265
  Hockessin (G-2948)
7c Infotech Inc..............................G....... 717 288-8686
  Wilmington (G-8866)
A2a Intgrted Phrmceuticals LLC....G....... 270 202-2461
  Lewes (G-3320)
A2ps Consulting and Sftwr LLC....F....... 331 201-6101
  Wilmington (G-8891)
Abcware LLC................................G....... 888 755-1485
  Wilmington (G-8900)
Acorn Site Furnishings..................G....... 302 249-4979
  Bridgeville (G-443)
Adferns Media LLC.......................G....... 315 444-7720
  Dover (G-1086)
Aeres Corporation.........................G....... 858 926-8626
  New Castle (G-5013)
Agricltral Asssmnts Intl Corp.........G....... 240 463-6677
  Laurel (G-3191)
Aldas Refinishing Company...........G....... 302 528-5028
  Hockessin (G-2955)
All Lives Matter LLC.....................G....... 252 767-9291
  Dover (G-1106)
Amdisvet LLC...............................G....... 302 514-9130
  Smyrna (G-8568)
Ampx2 Inc...................................G....... 650 521-5750
  Dover (G-1121)
Andrews Construction LLC............G....... 302 604-8166
  Seaford (G-8153)
Aptustech LLC..............................G....... 347 254-5619
  Wilmington (G-9105)
Arangodb Inc................................G....... 415 659-5938
  Wilmington (G-9111)
Arrim LLC....................................G....... 617 697-7914
  Wilmington (G-9134)
Ascension Industries LLC..............G....... 302 659-1778
  Smyrna (G-8576)
Aspenologies LLC.........................G....... 302 234-4346
  Wilmington (G-9153)
Asphalt Striping Svcs Del LLC.......G....... 302 456-9820
  Wilmington (G-9154)
Atr Electrical Services Inc..............G....... 302 373-7769
  Middletown (G-3954)
Aviman Management LLC.............E....... 302 377-5788
  Wilmington (G-9199)
B&W Tek LLC...............................G....... 302 368-7824
  Newark (G-6037)
Barutopia Inc................................G....... 858 284-8830
  Camden (G-540)
Batescainelli LLC..........................G....... 202 618-2040
  Rehoboth Beach (G-7856)
BETz&betz Enterprises LLC..........G....... 302 602-0613
  Wilmington (G-9318)
Bever Mobility Products Inc..........G....... 312 375-0300
  Wilmington (G-9319)
Big Tomorrow LLC........................F....... 650 714-3912
  Wilmington (G-9333)
Bill Torbert..................................F....... 302 734-9804
  Dover (G-1202)
Bk 2 Si LLC..................................G....... 800 246-2677
  Wilmington (G-9344)
Blaze Coin LLC.............................G....... 509 768-2249
  Dover (G-1209)
Bml App Development..................G....... 302 528-7281
  Wilmington (G-9386)
C&G Dental Studio LLC................G....... 302 345-4995
  Bear (G-60)
C4-Nvis USA LLC.........................G....... 213 465-5089
  Dover (G-1246)
Captains Grant Solar 1 Inc...........G....... 410 375-2092
  Millsboro (G-4655)
Carr Paris....................................F....... 302 401-1203
  Wilmington (G-9578)

Chime Inc....................................E....... 978 844-1162
  Wilmington (G-9666)
City of Dover - McKee Run............G....... 302 672-6306
  Dover (G-1291)
Classerium Corporation.................G....... 773 306-3297
  Dover (G-1292)
Clinton Craddock..........................F....... 267 505-2671
  Middletown (G-3999)
Cointigo LLC................................G....... 817 681-7131
  Middletown (G-4000)
Conducerent Incorporated.............G....... 302 543-8525
  Wilmington (G-9816)
Coolpop Nation.............................G....... 302 584-8833
  Wilmington (G-9852)
Core Functions LLC......................G....... 443 956-9626
  Selbyville (G-8471)
Couture Denim LLC......................G....... 302 220-8339
  New Castle (G-5204)
Crystal Graham............................F....... 302 669-9318
  Middletown (G-4016)
Cyber 20/20 Inc...........................F....... 203 802-8742
  Newark (G-6334)
Cyber Seven Technologies LLC.....G....... 302 635-7122
  Newark (G-6335)
Cycology 202 LLC........................F....... 610 202-0518
  Lewes (G-3447)
David Popovich LLC.....................G....... 855 464-9653
  Wilmington (G-9971)
Davin Management Group LLC.....F....... 302 367-6563
  Bear (G-99)
Dbd Wholesale LLC......................G....... 215 301-6277
  Wilmington (G-9975)
DC Consulting Service LLC...........F....... 617 594-9780
  Wilmington (G-9976)
De Cheaper Trash LLC..................G....... 302 325-0670
  New Castle (G-5219)
Deangelis & Son Inc.....................G....... 302 337-8699
  Bridgeville (G-464)
Dekadu Inc..................................G....... 763 390-3266
  Wilmington (G-9996)
Delaware Botanic Gardens Inc......G....... 202 262-9501
  Bethany Beach (G-397)
Delaware Fncl Edcatn Alnce Inc....G....... 302 674-0288
  Dover (G-1371)
Delaware Mosquito Control LLC...G....... 302 504-6757
  Newark (G-6398)
Delaware Retired Schl Prsnl.........E....... 302 674-8252
  Wilmington (G-10079)
Dell Oem Inc................................G....... 302 294-0060
  Newark (G-6425)
Delmarva Space Scnces Fndation.G....... 302 236-2761
  Millsboro (G-4676)
Dempsey Farms LLC....................F....... 302 734-4937
  Dover (G-1413)
Dennek LLC.................................G....... 302 703-0790
  Wilmington (G-10109)
Derby Software LLC....................G....... 502 435-1371
  Dover (G-1415)
Dewitt Heating and AC Inc............G....... 267 228-7355
  Bear (G-115)
Diamond State Door......................G....... 302 743-4667
  Wilmington (G-10142)
Dustntime....................................F....... 302 858-7876
  Rehoboth Beach (G-7922)
Dynamic Support Services Inc......G....... 202 820-3113
  Wilmington (G-10272)
Eastern Bison Association.............F....... 434 660-6036
  Greenwood (G-2735)
Ecomo Inc....................................G....... 412 567-3867
  Dover (G-1502)
Ekalt LLC.....................................G....... 302 300-4853
  Wilmington (G-10365)
Electric Motor Wholesale Inc........F....... 302 222-2090
  Camden Wyoming (G-634)
Emendo Bio Inc............................G....... 516 595-1849
  Wilmington (G-10389)
Enclave Digital Development Co...G....... 203 807-0400
  Lewes (G-3482)
Ergos Consultores LLC.................F....... 549 404-6360
  Wilmington (G-10433)
Evans Farms LLC.........................G....... 302 337-8130
  Bridgeville (G-469)
Exo Works Inc..............................C....... 302 531-1139
  Dover (G-1534)
Eye35design LLC.........................G....... 470 236-3933
  Dover (G-1535)
Fareed Services............................G....... 302 559-8594
  Wilmington (G-10499)
Ferrara Asset Management Inc....G....... 401 286-8464
  Wilmington (G-10523)

Employee Codes: A=Over 500 employees, B=251-500
C=101-250, D=51-100, E=20-50, F=10-19, G=1-9

BUSINESS ACTIVITIES: Non-Commercial Site PRODUCT & SERVICES SECTION

Firefly Drone Operations Llc.................G....... 305 206-6955
Wilmington *(G-10543)*

Fresh Start Transformations.................G....... 302 219-0221
Newark *(G-6623)*

Freshbooks Usa Inc.................G....... 416 525-5384
Wilmington *(G-10637)*

Frizbee Medical Inc.................G....... 424 901-1534
Wilmington *(G-10643)*

Fur Baby Tracker LLC.................G....... 610 563-3294
Wilmington *(G-10649)*

Gamers4gamers LLC.................G....... 302 722-6289
Newark *(G-6636)*

Garth Troescher Jr LLC.................G....... 302 927-0106
Frankford *(G-2364)*

Gaudlitz Inc.................G....... 202 468-3876
Dover *(G-1585)*

Get Takeout LLC.................G....... 800 785-6218
Lewes *(G-3513)*

Giesela Inc.................G....... 855 556-4338
Newark *(G-6653)*

Goldfinch Group Inc.................G....... 646 300-0716
Dover *(G-1600)*

Goodworld Inc.................G....... 845 325-2232
Wilmington *(G-10750)*

Grahams Wireless Solutions Inc.................F....... 717 943-0717
Millsboro *(G-4698)*

Greenlea LLC.................G....... 302 227-7868
Rehoboth Beach *(G-7955)*

GSM Systems Inc.................F....... 302 284-8304
Viola *(G-8836)*

Gt USA Wilmington LLC.................G....... 302 472-7679
Wilmington *(G-10794)*

Gulch Group LLC.................G....... 202 697-1756
Rehoboth Beach *(G-7956)*

Guy & Lady Barrel LLC.................G....... 302 399-3069
Dover *(G-1618)*

H&H Trading International LLC.................G....... 480 580-3911
Wilmington *(G-10811)*

Haloali Teeth Whitening LLC.................G....... 302 300-4042
Claymont *(G-760)*

Harbin LLC.................G....... 302 219-3320
Lewes *(G-3532)*

Harrel Stefoni.................G....... 302 344-3269
Dover *(G-1628)*

Harry H Mc Robie.................G....... 302 846-9784
Delmar *(G-1001)*

Hatfield Gas Connections Inc.................G....... 302 945-2354
Lewes *(G-3536)*

Hera Sports Surfaces LLC.................E....... 781 392-4094
Newark *(G-6723)*

Hifu Services Inc.................G....... 650 867-4972
Wilmington *(G-10902)*

Hindin Media LLC.................G....... 302 463-4612
Wilmington *(G-10915)*

Hoops For Hope Delaware.................F....... 302 229-7600
Wilmington *(G-10949)*

Hts 20 LLP.................G....... 800 690-2029
Milton *(G-4916)*

Hx Innovations Inc.................G....... 302 983-9705
Middletown *(G-4110)*

Hypergames Inc.................G....... 424 343-6370
Wilmington *(G-10982)*

Icase LLC.................F....... 302 703-7854
Lewes *(G-3550)*

Inetworkz LLC.................F....... 407 401-9384
Lewes *(G-3558)*

Inov8 Inc.................G....... 302 465-5124
Camden Wyoming *(G-646)*

Instantuptime Inc.................F....... 302 608-0890
Dover *(G-1680)*

J L Carpenter Farms LLC.................G....... 302 684-8601
Milton *(G-4919)*

James Stewart Rostocki.................G....... 302 250-5541
Wilmington *(G-11123)*

Jarel Industries LLC.................G....... 336 782-0697
Camden *(G-585)*

Jayu LLC.................F....... 888 534-3018
Wilmington *(G-11134)*

JBA Enterprises.................F....... 302 834-6685
Bear *(G-198)*

Jbr Contractors Inc.................E....... 856 296-9594
Millsboro *(G-4714)*

Jed T James.................G....... 302 875-0101
Georgetown *(G-2572)*

Jeffrey Hatch.................G....... 443 496-0449
Marydel *(G-3919)*

Jni CCC Jv1.................G....... 302 654-6611
Wilmington *(G-11162)*

Kamara LLC.................G....... 302 220-9570
New Castle *(G-5450)*

Kenya Gather Foundation.................F....... 302 382-8227
Millsboro *(G-4716)*

Kid Agains Inc.................G....... 631 830-5228
Dover *(G-1746)*

Kintyre Solutions LLC.................G....... 888 636-0010
Wilmington *(G-11269)*

Kleen-Comp LLC.................G....... 302 981-0791
Newark *(G-6897)*

Knight Hauling Inc.................G....... 610 494-6800
Wilmington *(G-11281)*

Kortech Consulting Inc.................F....... 302 559-4612
Bear *(G-220)*

Kriss Contracting Inc.................E....... 302 492-3502
Hartly *(G-2932)*

Kwikbuck Inc.................G....... 774 517-8959
Wilmington *(G-11305)*

Lamar Bags.................G....... 302 492-8566
Hartly *(G-2933)*

Leadership Forum LLC.................G....... 919 309-4025
Dover *(G-1773)*

Lifesquared Inc.................G....... 415 475-9090
Dover *(G-1785)*

Litcharts LLC.................G....... 646 481-4807
Wilmington *(G-11400)*

Live Typing Inc.................E....... 415 670-9601
Wilmington *(G-11412)*

Living Well Magazine.................G....... 302 355-0929
Newark *(G-6943)*

Looksiebin LLC.................G....... 410 869-2192
Wilmington *(G-11433)*

Maan Softwares Inc.................E....... 531 203-9141
Lewes *(G-3615)*

Majalco LLC.................G....... 703 507-5298
Wilmington *(G-11494)*

Martys Contracting.................G....... 302 234-8690
Hockessin *(G-3091)*

Matter Music Inc.................F....... 650 793-7749
Wilmington *(G-11568)*

Mayjuun LLC.................G....... 865 300-7738
Lewes *(G-3628)*

Mazzpac LLC.................G....... 973 641-9159
Newark *(G-7009)*

McCormick Contracting & Suppor.................G....... 443 987-2099
Wilmington *(G-11591)*

Merix LLC.................G....... 425 659-1425
Lewes *(G-3638)*

Metaquotes Software Corp.................E....... 657 859-6918
Wilmington *(G-11648)*

Michael Pdmnczky Cnsrvator LLC.................G....... 302 388-0656
Wilmington *(G-11664)*

Microcom Tech LLC.................G....... 858 775-5559
Rehoboth Beach *(G-8005)*

ML Whiteman and Sons Inc.................G....... 302 659-1001
Townsend *(G-8811)*

Modern Masters Inc.................G....... 240 800-6622
Dover *(G-1868)*

Moghul Life Inc.................G....... 347 560-9124
Wilmington *(G-11724)*

Morning After Inc.................G....... 302 562-5190
Hartly *(G-2936)*

Morningstar Maids LLC.................G....... 302 829-3030
Hockessin *(G-3099)*

Movetec Fitness Equipment LLC.................G....... 302 563-4487
Newark *(G-7064)*

Moving Sciences LLC.................G....... 617 871-9892
Wilmington *(G-11764)*

Mr Gregory Michael Hausmann.................G....... 302 635-7675
Newark *(G-7066)*

Murry Trucking Llc.................F....... 302 653-4811
Smyrna *(G-8683)*

Nancy Dufresne.................G....... 302 378-7236
Townsend *(G-8812)*

Nanticoke Consulting Inc.................G....... 302 424-0750
Greenwood *(G-2755)*

New ERA Media LLC.................G....... 302 731-2003
Newark *(G-7105)*

New Vision Services Inc.................F....... 484 350-6495
Newark *(G-7108)*

No Joke I LLC.................G....... 302 395-0882
New Castle *(G-5573)*

Nvcomputers Inc.................G....... 860 878-0525
Wilmington *(G-11924)*

Objects Worldwide Inc.................G....... 703 623-7861
Wilmington *(G-11931)*

Oerigo Consulting LLC.................G....... 302 353-4719
Smyrna *(G-8686)*

Olivar & Greb Capital MGT LLC.................F....... 508 598-7590
Lewes *(G-3667)*

Orbeex Trading Inc.................F....... 786 403-9124
Wilmington *(G-11970)*

Ovo Digital Services LLC.................G....... 415 741-1615
Wilmington *(G-11986)*

P A Cnmri.................D....... 302 678-8100
Dover *(G-1928)*

Pacer International One LLC.................F....... 302 588-9500
Wilmington *(G-12003)*

Pcu Systems LLC.................G....... 888 780-9728
Wilmington *(G-12053)*

Peeper Vehicle Technology Corp.................G....... 800 971-4134
Dover *(G-1943)*

Perastic LLC.................G....... 917 592-4219
Wilmington *(G-12083)*

Percebe Music Inc.................G....... 850 341-9594
Dover *(G-1949)*

Perceri LLC.................G....... 217 721-8731
Dover *(G-1950)*

Phazebreak Coatings LLC.................G....... 844 467-4293
Wilmington *(G-12111)*

Phillip T Bradley Inc.................G....... 302 947-2741
Lewes *(G-3687)*

Pixstorm LLC.................G....... 617 365-4949
Dover *(G-1961)*

Plai Apps Inc.................G....... 661 678-3740
Dover *(G-1962)*

Positioneering LLC.................G....... 302 415-3200
Wilmington *(G-12191)*

Pradhan Energy Projects.................G....... 305 428-2123
Hockessin *(G-3124)*

Prism Events Inc.................G....... 424 252-1070
Newark *(G-7259)*

Private Family Network LLC.................F....... 302 760-9684
Dover *(G-1988)*

Process Academy LLC.................G....... 302 415-3104
Wilmington *(G-12238)*

Proclean.................G....... 302 654-1074
New Castle *(G-5649)*

Quality Distributors Inc.................G....... 917 335-6662
Wilmington *(G-12279)*

Rays and Sons Mechanical LLC.................G....... 302 697-2100
Seaford *(G-8372)*

Redzun LLC.................G....... 512 657-4100
Wilmington *(G-12349)*

Renderapps LLC.................G....... 919 274-0582
Dover *(G-2027)*

Rendezvous Inc.................G....... 302 645-7400
Lewes *(G-3715)*

Reyes Rebeca.................G....... 302 276-9132
New Castle *(G-5677)*

Richard L Sapp Farms LLC.................F....... 302 684-4727
Milton *(G-4957)*

Rmv Workforce Corp.................F....... 302 408-1061
Milton *(G-4963)*

Rohma Inc.................G....... 909 234-5381
Newark *(G-7360)*

Rooah LLC.................G....... 305 233-7557
Dover *(G-2042)*

RPR Environmental Solutions.................G....... 302 362-0687
Lincoln *(G-3866)*

Scottish Ventures LLC.................G....... 302 382-6057
New Castle *(G-5695)*

Sensofusion Inc.................F....... 570 239-4912
Milton *(G-4967)*

Server Management LLC.................G....... 302 300-1745
Wilmington *(G-12584)*

Simple Space LLC.................G....... 801 520-3680
Wilmington *(G-12625)*

Sitengle Technology LLC.................F....... 719 822-0710
Dover *(G-2086)*

Six Angels Development Inc.................G....... 302 218-1548
Wilmington *(G-12637)*

Sleeper Creeper Inc.................G....... 302 519-4553
Georgetown *(G-2656)*

Smartstudents LLC.................G....... 302 597-6586
Wilmington *(G-12655)*

Society For Acpuncture RES Inc.................F....... 302 222-1832
Lewes *(G-3752)*

Solar Foundations Usa Inc.................G....... 518 935-3360
Newark *(G-7454)*

Solar Unlimited North Amer LLC.................G....... 302 542-4580
Lewes *(G-3754)*

Staikos Associates Architects.................G....... 302 764-1678
Wilmington *(G-12730)*

Statwhiz Ventures LLC.................G....... 310 819-5427
Wilmington *(G-12746)*

Stauffer Family LLC.................G....... 302 227-5820
Rehoboth Beach *(G-8087)*

Stealthorg LLC.................G....... 302 724-6461
Dover *(G-2107)*

Stl & Associates LLC.................G....... 302 359-2801
Smyrna *(G-8725)*

PRODUCT & SERVICES SECTION — CABLE TELEVISION

Company	Code	Phone
Strands Prprty Prservation LLC	G	302 381-9792
Millsboro (G-4805)		
Stream App LLC	G	610 420-5864
Wilmington (G-12775)		
Super C Inc	G	302 533-6024
Newark (G-7510)		
Tableart LLC	G	650 587-8769
Wilmington (G-12847)		
Tarpon Strategies LLC	G	215 806-2723
Newark (G-7540)		
Techxponent Inc	F	410 701-0089
Newark (G-7548)		
Tecnatom USA Corporation	G	412 265-7226
Wilmington (G-12873)		
Travel Agency	G	302 381-0205
Lewes (G-3794)		
Twin Creek Farms LLC	G	302 249-2294
Milford (G-4581)		
Two Roses United LLC	G	302 593-2453
Wilmington (G-12999)		
Unikie Inc	F	408 839-1920
Dover (G-2177)		
Vetdiet Usa Inc	G	514 622-7313
Wilmington (G-13069)		
Vinsys Corporation	D	732 983-4150
Dover (G-2194)		
Violet Aura Inc	F	302 654-4008
Wilmington (G-13086)		
Virion Therapeutics LLC	G	800 841-9303
Newark (G-7660)		
Voice 4 Impact Inc	G	484 410-0111
Wilmington (G-13099)		
Vtms LLC	G	302 264-9094
Dover (G-2201)		
Wahid Consultants LLC	E	315 400-0955
New Castle (G-5821)		
Webstudy Inc	G	888 326-4058
Harbeson (G-2802)		
When Poets Dream Inc	G	818 738-6954
Dover (G-2222)		
Whipper Snapper Transport LLC	G	302 265-2437
Milford (G-4604)		
Williamson Building Corp	G	302 644-0605
Lewes (G-3825)		
Wilmington Resources	F	302 746-7162
Wilmington (G-13244)		
Win From Wthin Xc Camp/Tatnall	E	302 494-5312
Wilmington (G-13269)		
Winker Labs LLC	G	630 449-8130
Wilmington (G-13271)		
Wuji Inc	G	815 274-6777
Dover (G-2240)		
Wutap LLC	G	610 457-3559
Newark (G-7725)		
Xenopia LLC	G	302 703-7050
Lewes (G-3832)		

BUSINESS COLLEGE OR SCHOOLS

Company	Code	Phone
Project of Providence LLC	G	302 438-8970
Wilmington (G-12247)		

BUSINESS FORMS WHOLESALERS

Company	Code	Phone
Brandywine Graphics Inc	G	302 655-7571
Wilmington (G-9435)		

BUSINESS FORMS: Printed, Manifold

Company	Code	Phone
Go Mozaic LLC	G	302 438-4141
Claymont (G-756)		
Safeguard	G	301 299-8806
Rehoboth Beach (G-8065)		

BUSINESS FORMS: Strip, Manifold

Company	Code	Phone
Brandywine Graphics Inc	G	302 655-7571
Wilmington (G-9435)		

BUSINESS MACHINE REPAIR, ELECTRIC

Company	Code	Phone
B Williams Holding Corp	F	302 656-8596
Wilmington (G-9214)		
Excel Business Systems Inc	E	302 453-1500
Newark (G-6550)		
Mark D Garrett	G	302 674-2825
Dover (G-1818)		
Ram Tech Systems Inc	E	302 832-6600
Middletown (G-4210)		
Tower Business Machines Inc	G	302 395-1445
New Castle (G-5780)		
Visual Communications Inc	G	302 792-9500
Claymont (G-816)		

BUSINESS SUPPORT SVCS

Company	Code	Phone
Acentium Inc	F	617 938-3938
Wilmington (G-8920)		
Apphive Inc	G	240 898-4661
Newark (G-5984)		
Bangus Business Services	G	302 266-7285
Newark (G-6044)		
Beauty Purse Inc	G	424 210-7474
Dover (G-1187)		
Byte Technology Systems Inc	G	347 687-7240
Lewes (G-3396)		
Cargo Cube Licensing LLC	G	844 200-2823
Wilmington (G-9568)		
Christmas Corporation	G	424 645-5001
Lewes (G-3420)		
Coastal Marine AVI Svc LLC	G	904 200-2749
Wilmington (G-9753)		
Conzurge Inc	F	267 507-6039
Newark (G-6294)		
Cybersecurity Trust LLC	G	844 240-2287
Middletown (G-4017)		
D&F Joint Ventures De LLC	G	302 652-5151
Wilmington (G-9944)		
David G Horsey & Sons Inc	D	302 875-3033
Laurel (G-3221)		
DOT Matrix Inc	G	917 657-4918
Dover (G-1439)		
Ebube Group & Co LLC	G	215 821-7490
Newark (G-6501)		
Edokk LLC	G	305 434-7227
Lewes (G-3479)		
Eduqc LLC	F	800 346-4646
Dover (G-1508)		
Factory Technologies Inc	G	302 266-1290
Newark (G-6563)		
Flute Pro Shop Inc	G	302 479-5000
Wilmington (G-10583)		
Fyrbeacon Inc	E	562 569-0547
Wilmington (G-10655)		
Global Shopaholics LLC	F	703 608-7108
Wilmington (G-10731)		
Har-Lex LLC	G	302 476-2322
Wilmington (G-10835)		
Jon Irby III	G	302 652-0564
Wilmington (G-11180)		
Jthan LLC	G	302 994-2534
Wilmington (G-11206)		
Keefer Mountain Enterprise	G	814 657-3998
Rehoboth Beach (G-7977)		
Knowt Inc	F	848 391-0575
Lewes (G-3585)		
Lawrence JP & Associates	F	313 293-2692
Wilmington (G-11345)		
Loftcom Inc	G	800 563-6900
Wilmington (G-11425)		
Michaels Home Repair Services	G	302 333-2235
New Castle (G-5521)		
Moscase Inc	G	786 520-8062
Dover (G-1874)		
Perpetual Invstments Group LLC	E	718 795-3394
Wilmington (G-12087)		
Ralph Paul Inc	G	302 764-9162
Wilmington (G-12309)		
Rogue Elephants LLC	G	979 264-2845
Lewes (G-3724)		
Sky World Traveler	F	844 591-9060
Wilmington (G-12643)		
Swami Enterprises Inc	G	302 999-8077
Wilmington (G-12822)		
Voitlex Corp	F	302 288-0670
Dover (G-2198)		
Wowdesk Inc	G	310 871-5251
Newark (G-7724)		
Zen Health Technology Inc	G	551 194-2345
Newark (G-7739)		
Zest-Index Investments LLC	G	503 908-2110
Middletown (G-4295)		
Zogo Inc	G	978 810-8895
Newark (G-7743)		

BUSINESS TRAINING SVCS

Company	Code	Phone
Fursan Consulting Services	F	240 654-5784
New Castle (G-5336)		
Tipton Communications Group	G	302 454-7901
Wilmington (G-7568)		
Treehouse Wellness Center LLC	F	302 893-1001
Wilmington (G-12963)		

CABINETS & CASES: Show, Display & Storage, Exc Wood

Company	Code	Phone
Stone Medic	G	302 233-6039
Smyrna (G-8726)		

CABINETS: Bathroom Vanities, Wood

Company	Code	Phone
Zenith Products	G	302 322-2190
New Castle (G-5846)		
Zwd Products Corporation	B	302 326-8200
New Castle (G-5848)		

CABINETS: Entertainment Units, Household, Wood

Company	Code	Phone
Jordan Cabinetry & WD Turning	G	302 792-1009
Claymont (G-770)		

CABINETS: Factory

Company	Code	Phone
Cubic Products LLC	E	781 990-3886
Wilmington (G-9916)		

CABINETS: Kitchen, Metal

Company	Code	Phone
Pony Run Kitchens LLC	G	302 492-3006
Hartly (G-2937)		

CABINETS: Kitchen, Wood

Company	Code	Phone
Bancroft Carpentry Company	G	302 655-3434
Wilmington (G-9233)		
Bylers Woodworking Shop	G	302 492-1375
Hartly (G-2913)		
Cedar Creek Custom Cabinets	G	302 542-7794
Milford (G-4341)		
Coastal Cabinetry LLC	G	302 542-4155
Seaford (G-8199)		
Culiquip LLC	D	302 654-4974
Wilmington (G-9917)		
Custom Cabinet Shop Inc	F	302 337-8261
Greenwood (G-2725)		
Diamond State Cabinetry	G	302 250-3531
Millsboro (G-4678)		
Driftwood Cabinetry LLC	G	302 645-4876
Lewes (G-3474)		
East Coast Cstm Cabinetry LLC	G	302 245-3040
Georgetown (G-2517)		
Mh Custom Cabinets	G	302 422-7082
Milford (G-4493)		
Michael A OBrien & Sons	G	302 994-2894
Wilmington (G-11656)		
Moores Cabinet Refinishing Inc	G	302 378-3055
Middletown (G-4170)		
Phippins Cabinetry	G	302 212-2189
Rehoboth Beach (G-8032)		
Sylvester Custom Cabinetry	G	302 398-6050
Harrington (G-2896)		
Taylor Woodworks	G	302 745-2049
Dover (G-2131)		
Townsend Kitchens Cabinets &	G	302 659-1007
Townsend (G-8828)		
Walnut Grove Cabinets LLC	G	302 678-2694
Dover (G-2203)		

CABINETS: Show, Display, Etc, Wood, Exc Refrigerated

Company	Code	Phone
3-D Fabrications Inc	E	302 292-3501
Newark (G-5855)		

CABLE & OTHER PAY TELEVISION DISTRIBUTION

Company	Code	Phone
Comcast MO Investments LLC	G	302 594-8705
Wilmington (G-9780)		

CABLE & PAY TELEVISION SVCS: Direct Broadcast Satellite

Company	Code	Phone
Central Firm LLC	G	610 470-9836
Wilmington (G-9615)		
Dish Network LLC	E	302 387-0341
Camden (G-564)		
Satellite Connection Inc	G	302 328-2462
Wilmington (G-12543)		

CABLE TELEVISION

Company	Code	Phone
Atlantic Broadband	G	302 378-0780
Middletown (G-3948)		

Employee Codes: A=Over 500 employees, B=251-500
C=101-250, D=51-100, E=20-50, F=10-19, G=1-9

CABLE TELEVISION

Bombonais Cable Tech LLC ....G....... 302 444-1199
  New Castle *(G-5099)*
Comcast Cablevision of Del ....E....... 302 661-4465
  New Castle *(G-5185)*
Comcast Cablevision of Del ....F....... 302 856-4591
  Georgetown *(G-2477)*
Comcast Cble Cmmunications LLC .....F....... 302 323-9200
  New Castle *(G-5186)*
Comcast Corporation ....D....... 302 262-8996
  Seaford *(G-8201)*
Comcast Corporation ....D....... 302 495-5612
  Greenwood *(G-2722)*
Comcast of Delmarva LLC ....D....... 215 286-3345
  Dover *(G-1304)*
Executive Broadband ....G....... 302 463-4335
  Newark *(G-6552)*
Mediacom LLC ....D....... 302 732-9332
  Dagsboro *(G-921)*
NTL (triangle) LLC ....F....... 302 525-0027
  Wilmington *(G-11920)*

CABLE TELEVISION PRDTS

Executive Broadband ....G....... 302 463-4335
  Newark *(G-6552)*

CABLE: Fiber

Cablicons LLC ....G....... 843 458-7702
  Wilmington *(G-9527)*

CABLE: Fiber Optic

Nouvir Lighting Corporation ....F....... 302 628-9933
  Seaford *(G-8330)*
Nouvir Lightning Corporation ....G....... 302 628-9888
  Seaford *(G-8331)*

CAGES: Wire

Bio Medic Corporation ....F....... 302 628-4300
  Seaford *(G-8170)*

CAMERA & PHOTOGRAPHIC SPLYS STORES: Cameras

Cameras Etc Inc ....F....... 302 764-9400
  Wilmington *(G-9545)*
Cameras Etc Inc ....G....... 302 453-9400
  Newark *(G-6146)*

CAMERAS & RELATED EQPT: Photographic

RDS Engineering LLC ....G....... 417 763-3727
  Lewes *(G-3710)*

CAMPGROUNDS

Gulls Way Campground ....G....... 302 732-6383
  Dagsboro *(G-904)*
Gulls Way Inc ....G....... 302 732-9629
  Dagsboro *(G-905)*
Masseys Landing Park Inc ....G....... 302 947-2600
  Millsboro *(G-4736)*
Port Del-Mar-Va Inc ....G....... 302 227-7409
  Rehoboth Beach *(G-8034)*
Steamboat Landing ....G....... 302 645-6500
  Lewes *(G-3763)*
Tall Pines Associates Llc ....F....... 302 684-0300
  Lewes *(G-3777)*

CAMPSITES

Barsgr LLC ....G....... 302 645-6665
  Lewes *(G-3362)*
Barsgr LLC ....E....... 302 945-3410
  Millsboro *(G-4634)*
Bayshore Inc ....G....... 302 539-7200
  Ocean View *(G-7758)*
Homestead Camping Inc ....G....... 302 684-4278
  Georgetown *(G-2561)*
Pine Acres Inc ....F....... 302 945-2000
  Lewes *(G-3692)*

CANDLES

Barbosa Manufacturing ....G....... 302 856-6343
  Georgetown *(G-2445)*
Brocks Soy Candles ....G....... 609 841-5121
  Dover *(G-1234)*
Candle Parlour ....G....... 302 408-0890
  Claymont *(G-706)*
Driftwood Candles LLC ....G....... 302 858-1600
  Millville *(G-4843)*

Mia Bellas Candles ....G....... 302 331-7038
  Hartly *(G-2935)*
Natures Gourmet Candles ....G....... 302 697-2785
  Dover *(G-1885)*
Snowden Candles ....G....... 302 398-4373
  Harrington *(G-2892)*
Vintage Candle Company ....G....... 302 643-9343
  Bridgeville *(G-529)*

CANDY MAKING GOODS & SPLYS, WHOLESALE

Cannons Cake and Candy Sups ....G....... 302 738-3321
  Newark *(G-6148)*

CANDY, NUT & CONFECTIONERY STORE: Popcorn, Incl Caramel Corn

Fishers Popcorn Fenwick LLC ....E....... 302 539-8833
  Fenwick Island *(G-2336)*

CANNED SPECIALTIES

Hanover Foods Corporation ....C....... 302 653-9281
  Clayton *(G-855)*

CANS: Aluminum

Reynolds Metals Company LLC ....E....... 302 366-0555
  Newark *(G-7333)*

CANS: Metal

Crown Cork & Seal Receivables ....G....... 215 698-5100
  Wilmington *(G-9906)*

CAR LOADING SVCS

Hodges L Wooten ....G....... 302 335-5162
  Magnolia *(G-3895)*

CAR WASH EQPT

B & R Boyer Pressure Washing ....G....... 302 875-3603
  Laurel *(G-3194)*
Jeff Thomas ....G....... 302 762-9154
  Wilmington *(G-11143)*

CAR WASHES

Big Toy Custom Car Care Inc ....G....... 302 668-6729
  Wilmington *(G-9334)*
Car Wash of Prices Corner ....E....... 302 994-9274
  Wilmington *(G-9561)*
Dover Soft Touch Car Wash ....E....... 302 736-6011
  Dover *(G-1470)*
Ocean Waves LLC ....G....... 302 344-1282
  Fenwick Island *(G-2338)*
Wilkins Enterprises Inc ....G....... 302 945-4142
  Milton *(G-4980)*
Willies Auto Detail Service ....G....... 302 734-1010
  Dover *(G-2228)*

CARAFES: Plastic

Cara Plastics Inc ....G....... 302 622-7070
  Wilmington *(G-9563)*

CARBON PAPER & INKED RIBBONS

Identisource LLC ....G....... 888 716-7498
  Lewes *(G-3551)*

CARDIOVASCULAR SYSTEM DRUGS, EXC DIAGNOSTIC

Cpex Pharmaceuticals Inc ....F....... 302 651-8300
  Wilmington *(G-9887)*
Fisons US Investment Holdings ....G....... 302 777-7222
  Wilmington *(G-10564)*

CARDS: Greeting

Sussex Printing Corp ....D....... 302 629-9303
  Seaford *(G-8416)*

CARDS: Identification

Viacard Concepts ....G....... 302 537-4602
  Dagsboro *(G-942)*

CARPET & RUG CLEANING & REPAIRING PLANTS

EBc Carpet Services Corp ....E....... 302 995-7461
  Wilmington *(G-10332)*

CARPET & UPHOLSTERY CLEANING SVCS

ABM Janitorial Services Inc ....A....... 302 571-9900
  Wilmington *(G-8906)*
Colonial Cleaning Services Inc ....G....... 302 660-2067
  Wilmington *(G-9773)*
Crystal Graham ....F....... 302 669-9318
  Middletown *(G-4016)*
Dibiasos Clg Rstration Svc Inc ....G....... 302 376-7111
  Townsend *(G-8784)*
Ebc National Inc ....G....... 302 995-7461
  Wilmington *(G-10333)*
Hampton Enterprises Delaware ....G....... 302 378-7365
  Townsend *(G-8793)*
Marlings Inc ....F....... 302 325-1759
  New Castle *(G-5509)*
Positive Results Cleaning Inc ....G....... 302 575-1146
  Wilmington *(G-12192)*
Vivid Colors Carpet LLC ....G....... 302 335-3933
  Frederica *(G-2415)*

CARPET & UPHOLSTERY CLEANING SVCS: Carpet/Furniture, On Loc

Brasures Carpet Care Inc ....G....... 302 436-5652
  Selbyville *(G-8461)*
Delaware Rug Co Inc ....G....... 302 998-8881
  Wilmington *(G-10082)*
Proclean Inc ....E....... 302 656-8080
  Delaware City *(G-965)*
Schrider Enterprises Inc ....G....... 302 539-1036
  Ocean View *(G-7812)*
Stanley Steemer Intl Inc ....E....... 302 907-0062
  Delmar *(G-1031)*
Sum Inc ....E....... 302 322-0831
  New Castle *(G-5740)*
Worms Quality Carpet Care ....G....... 302 629-3114
  Seaford *(G-8443)*
Worthys Property MGT LLC ....F....... 302 265-8301
  Lincoln *(G-3875)*

CARPET & UPHOLSTERY CLEANING SVCS: On Customer Premises

Bane Clene Way ....G....... 610 485-1234
  Claymont *(G-699)*
Edwards Paul Crpt Installation ....G....... 302 672-7847
  Dover *(G-1509)*
Grime Busters USA Inc ....G....... 302 834-7006
  Newark *(G-6692)*
L & M Services Inc ....F....... 302 658-3735
  Wilmington *(G-11306)*
Oceanside Elite Clg Bldg Svcs ....E....... 302 339-7777
  Lewes *(G-3665)*

CARPET DYEING & FINISHING

Vivid Colors Carpet LLC ....G....... 302 335-3933
  Frederica *(G-2415)*

CARPETS, RUGS & FLOOR COVERING

Hardwood Mills Inc ....G....... 302 697-7195
  Dover *(G-1627)*
Josephine Keir Limited ....G....... 302 422-0270
  Milford *(G-4462)*
Kurtz Collection ....G....... 302 654-0442
  Wilmington *(G-11302)*

CARPETS: Textile Fiber

Bentley Mills Inc ....G....... 800 423-4709
  Wilmington *(G-9303)*
Trademark Productions Inc ....F....... 416 787-0365
  Wilmington *(G-12947)*

CARRIAGES: Horse Drawn

Circle C Outfit LLC ....G....... 302 337-8828
  Bridgeville *(G-459)*

CARRYING CASES, WHOLESALE

Tai Jun International Inc ....G....... 302 239-9336
  Newark *(G-7533)*

PRODUCT & SERVICES SECTION

CHEMICALS, AGRICULTURE: Wholesalers

CASES: Carrying
Continental Case................................G...... 302 322-1765
  Newark (G-6291)

CASINGS: Sheet Metal
Seaside Service LLC..........................G...... 302 827-3775
  Lewes (G-3735)

CASTINGS GRINDING: For The Trade
Delmarva Precision Grinding..............G...... 302 393-3008
  Milford (G-4384)

CASTINGS: Commercial Investment, Ferrous
Forcebeyond Inc..................................E...... 302 995-6588
  Wilmington (G-10590)

CATALOG & MAIL-ORDER HOUSES
Brown Eagle Inc..................................E...... 302 295-3816
  Wilmington (G-9489)
Management Options Inc...................F...... 302 234-0836
  Newark (G-6980)
Two Roses United LLC.......................G...... 302 593-2453
  Wilmington (G-12999)

CATALOG SALES
Sitengle Technology LLC....................F...... 719 822-0710
  Dover (G-2086)

CATALYSTS: Chemical
Ddh Advanced Mtls Systems Inc........G...... 515 441-1313
  Newark (G-6353)
W R Grace & Co..................................C...... 410 531-4000
  Wilmington (G-13109)

CATERERS
Efficient Services Inc..........................G...... 302 629-2124
  Seaford (G-8234)
Leounes Catered Affairs....................G...... 302 547-3233
  Wilmington (G-11374)

CEMENT: Hydraulic
Cimentum..G...... 302 635-7262
  Newark (G-6236)

CEMETERIES
Odd Fellows Cmtry of Milford.............G...... 302 422-4619
  Milford (G-4517)

CEMETERIES: Real Estate Operation
Catholic Cemeteries Inc.....................F...... 302 254-4701
  Wilmington (G-9590)
Catholic Cemeteries Inc.....................E...... 302 737-2524
  Wilmington (G-9591)
Silverbrook Cemetery Co....................G...... 302 658-0953
  Wilmington (G-12618)

CERAMIC FLOOR & WALL TILE WHOLESALERS
Consolidated Construction Svcs........F...... 302 629-6070
  Seaford (G-8205)
Mohawk Tile MBL Distrs of Del..........G...... 302 655-7164
  Wilmington (G-11725)

CESSPOOL CLEANING SVCS
Sawyers Sanitation Service................G...... 302 678-8240
  Leipsic (G-3314)

CHAMBERS OF COMMERCE
Bethany-Fenwick Chamber.................G...... 302 539-2100
  Fenwick Island (G-2331)
Central Del Chmber of Commerce.....G...... 302 734-7513
  Dover (G-1263)
Delaware State Chamber....................F...... 302 655-7221
  Wilmington (G-10087)
Georgetown Chamber Commerce......F...... 302 856-1544
  Georgetown (G-2543)
New Cstle Cnty Chmber Commerce...F...... 302 737-4343
  Wilmington (G-11861)
Rehoboth Beach Dewey Beach Cha...F...... 302 227-2233
  Rehoboth Beach (G-8051)

CHASSIS: Motor Vehicle
Victory Racing Chassis Inc.................G...... 302 593-2255
  Wilmington (G-13079)

CHECK CASHING SVCS
Ace Cash Express Inc........................G...... 302 737-3785
  Newark (G-5891)
Bahars Company.................................F...... 302 856-2966
  Georgetown (G-2444)
E Z Cash of Delaware Inc...................G...... 302 846-2920
  Delmar (G-995)
EZ Cash of New Hampshire Inc.........G...... 302 846-0464
  Delmar (G-998)
Goldstar- Cash LLC.............................G...... 302 427-2535
  Wilmington (G-10742)
Service General Corp..........................C...... 302 856-3500
  Georgetown (G-2651)
United Check Cashing........................G...... 302 792-2545
  Claymont (G-813)

CHECK CLEARING SVCS
Ace Cash Express Inc........................G...... 302 628-0422
  Seaford (G-8137)
Argo Financial Services Inc................G...... 302 322-7788
  New Castle (G-5042)
Citigroup Inc.......................................E...... 302 631-3530
  Newark (G-6237)

CHEMICAL ELEMENTS
Divine Element Hbb............................G...... 302 538-5209
  Dover (G-1433)

CHEMICAL SPLYS FOR FOUNDRIES
Blue Sky Clean....................................G...... 302 584-5800
  Wilmington (G-9381)

CHEMICALS & ALLIED PRDTS WHOLESALERS, NEC
Action Unlimited Resources Inc.........E...... 302 323-1455
  New Castle (G-5001)
Ashland LLC..E...... 302 995-4180
  Wilmington (G-9150)
Bellex International Corp....................G...... 302 791-5180
  Wilmington (G-9294)
Blue Ribbon Oil Company Inc............F...... 302 832-7601
  New Castle (G-5095)
Cfg Lab Inc...G...... 302 261-3403
  Wilmington (G-9621)
Ciba Specialty Chem N Amer............F...... 302 992-5600
  Wilmington (G-9700)
Degussa International Inc..................G...... 302 731-9250
  Newark (G-6360)
DSM Desotech Inc..............................D...... 302 328-5435
  New Castle (G-5263)
Interntional Mkt Suppliers Inc............F...... 302 392-1840
  Bear (G-189)
PDM Incorporated...............................G...... 302 478-0768
  Wilmington (G-12055)
Progressive Systems Inc....................G...... 302 732-3321
  Frankford (G-2381)
Riverside Specialty Chem Inc............G...... 212 769-3440
  Bear (G-307)
Sepax Technologies Inc.....................F...... 302 366-1101
  Newark (G-7409)
Solenis LLC..G...... 302 594-5000
  Wilmington (G-12678)
Tenmat Inc..G...... 302 633-6600
  Wilmington (G-12883)
Thornley Company Inc.......................G...... 302 224-8300
  Newark (G-7565)
Ultrafine Technologies Inc..................G...... 302 384-6513
  Wilmington (G-13009)

CHEMICALS & ALLIED PRDTS, WHOL: Gases, Compressed/Liquefied
Keen Compressed Gas Co..................F...... 302 594-4545
  Wilmington (G-11232)
Keen Compressed Gas Co..................E...... 302 594-4545
  New Castle (G-5456)
Weitron Inc..E...... 800 398-3816
  Newark (G-7682)

CHEMICALS & ALLIED PRDTS, WHOLESALE: Alkalines & Chlorine
Ashland LLC..E...... 302 594-5000
  Wilmington (G-9151)

CHEMICALS & ALLIED PRDTS, WHOLESALE: Carbon Dioxide
Airgas Usa LLC...................................E...... 302 834-7404
  Delaware City (G-946)

CHEMICALS & ALLIED PRDTS, WHOLESALE: Chemical Additives
Mil International Incorporated............G...... 302 234-7501
  Wilmington (G-11687)

CHEMICALS & ALLIED PRDTS, WHOLESALE: Chemicals, Indl
C P M Industries Inc...........................G...... 302 478-8200
  Wilmington (G-9523)
Croda Inc..F...... 302 429-5200
  New Castle (G-5209)
Diamond Chemical & Supply Co........E...... 302 656-7786
  Wilmington (G-10139)
MJL Industrial Inc...............................G...... 302 234-0898
  Hockessin (G-3097)

CHEMICALS & ALLIED PRDTS, WHOLESALE: Chemicals, Indl & Heavy
Syntec Corporation..............................F...... 302 421-8393
  Wilmington (G-12837)

CHEMICALS & ALLIED PRDTS, WHOLESALE: Compressed Gas
E E Rosser Inc....................................G...... 302 762-9643
  Wilmington (G-10276)
Roberts Oxygen Company Inc...........G...... 302 337-9666
  Seaford (G-8380)

CHEMICALS & ALLIED PRDTS, WHOLESALE: Detergents
Brewster Products Inc........................G...... 302 798-1988
  Wilmington (G-9468)

CHEMICALS & ALLIED PRDTS, WHOLESALE: Manmade Fibers
Rath Incorporated...............................D...... 302 294-4446
  Newark (G-7298)

CHEMICALS & ALLIED PRDTS, WHOLESALE: Plastics Materials, NEC
Polymart Inc..G...... 302 656-1470
  Hockessin (G-3122)

CHEMICALS & ALLIED PRDTS, WHOLESALE: Plastics Prdts, NEC
Industrial Resource Netwrk Inc..........F...... 302 888-2905
  Wilmington (G-11022)

CHEMICALS & ALLIED PRDTS, WHOLESALE: Polyurethane Prdts
Grayling Industries Inc.......................E...... 770 751-9095
  Frederica (G-2403)

CHEMICALS & ALLIED PRDTS, WHOLESALE: Resins
Ion Power Inc......................................G...... 302 832-9550
  New Castle (G-5423)

CHEMICALS & ALLIED PRDTS, WHOLESALE: Spec Clean/Sanitation
A E Moore Incorporated.....................F...... 302 934-7055
  Millsboro (G-4620)

CHEMICALS, AGRICULTURE: Wholesalers
Emerald Bioagriculture Corp..............F...... 517 882-7370
  Hockessin (G-3019)

Employee Codes: A=Over 500 employees, B=251-500
C=101-250, D=51-100, E=20-50, F=10-19, G=1-9

CHEMICALS, AGRICULTURE: Wholesalers

Helena Agri-Enterprises LLC .... G 302 337-3881
Bridgeville *(G-481)*
Nutrien AG Solutions Inc .... F 302 629-3047
Seaford *(G-8334)*

CHEMICALS: Agricultural

A Felix Dupont Jr Co .... G 302 658-5244
Wilmington *(G-8877)*
Ai Dupont .... G 302 528-6520
Wilmington *(G-8983)*
Belchim Crop Prtection USA LLC ...... F 302 407-3590
Wilmington *(G-9285)*
Chemours Company .... B 302 773-1000
Wilmington *(G-9648)*
Chemours Company Fc LLC .... B 302 773-1000
Wilmington *(G-9649)*
Chemours Company Fc LLC .... C 678 427-1530
Wilmington *(G-9651)*
Dupont Asia Pacific Limited .... G 302 774-1000
Wilmington *(G-10248)*
Dupont De Nemours Inc .... G 302 999-7932
Wilmington *(G-10252)*
Dupont De Nemours Ei & Co .... G 302 659-1079
Dover *(G-1487)*
E C I Motorsports Inc .... G 302 239-6376
Newark *(G-6487)*
E I Du Pont De Nemours & Co .... A 302 485-3000
Wilmington *(G-10278)*
E I Du Pont De Nemours & Co .... B 302 695-7141
Bear *(G-132)*
E I Du Pont De Nemours & Co .... G 302 239-9424
Newark *(G-6488)*
E I Du Pont De Nemours & Co .... B 302 999-2826
Wilmington *(G-10283)*
E I Du Pont De Nemours & Co .... G 302 695-7228
Wilmington *(G-10286)*
E I Du Pont De Nemours & Co .... G 844 773-2436
Wilmington *(G-10289)*
E I Du Pont De Nemours & Co .... G 800 441-7515
Wilmington *(G-10290)*
E I Du Pont De Nemours & Co .... B 302 892-5655
Wilmington *(G-10301)*
E I Du Pont De Nemours & Co .... C 302 774-1000
Wilmington *(G-10305)*
E I Du Pont De Nemours & Co .... C 302 658-7796
Wilmington *(G-10307)*
Els .... G 302 312-3645
Bear *(G-143)*
HB Dupont Plaza .... G 302 998-7271
Wilmington *(G-10858)*
Meherrin AG & Chem Co .... G 302 337-0330
Bridgeville *(G-496)*
North Dupont Shell .... G 301 375-6000
New Castle *(G-5578)*
Specialty Products N&H Inc .... G 302 774-1000
Wilmington *(G-12697)*
Syngenta Corporation .... E 302 425-2000
Wilmington *(G-12836)*

CHEMICALS: Alcohols

Breakthru Beverage Group LLC .... C 302 356-3500
New Castle *(G-5109)*

CHEMICALS: Ammonium Compounds, Exc Fertilizers, NEC

Timtec Inc .... F 302 292-8500
Newark *(G-7566)*

CHEMICALS: Boron Compounds, Not From Mines, NEC

Honeywell International Inc .... D 302 791-6700
Claymont *(G-763)*

CHEMICALS: High Purity Grade, Organic

Veramorph LLC .... G 401 473-1318
Wilmington *(G-13058)*

CHEMICALS: High Purity, Refined From Technical Grade

Indo Amines Americas LLC .... G 301 466-9902
Wilmington *(G-11019)*

CHEMICALS: Inorganic, NEC

Affinity Research Chemicals .... G 302 525-4060
Wilmington *(G-8970)*

Amspec Chemical Corporation .... G 302 392-1702
Bear *(G-28)*
Brandywine Chemical Company .... G 302 656-5428
New Castle *(G-5104)*
Celanese International Corp .... G 972 443-4000
Wilmington *(G-9609)*
Chemours Company Fc LLC .... E 302 545-0072
Wilmington *(G-9653)*
Delaware Chemical Corporation .... G 302 234-1463
Wilmington *(G-10014)*
Dow Chemical Company .... C 302 366-0500
Newark *(G-6468)*
Du Pont Chem Enrgy Oprtons Inc ...... G 302 774-1000
Wilmington *(G-10241)*
Dupont Athntcation Systems LLC ...... G 800 345-9999
Wilmington *(G-10249)*
Dupont Specialty Pdts USA LLC .... E 302 774-1000
Wilmington *(G-10261)*
E I Du Pont De Nemours & Co .... E 302 999-3301
Wilmington *(G-10279)*
E I Du Pont De Nemours & Co .... G 302 774-1000
Wilmington *(G-10280)*
E I Du Pont De Nemours & Co .... B 302 892-8832
Wilmington *(G-10281)*
E I Du Pont De Nemours & Co .... D 615 847-6920
Wilmington *(G-10285)*
E I Du Pont De Nemours & Co .... D 302 792-4371
Wilmington *(G-10292)*
E I Du Pont De Nemours & Co .... D 302 774-1000
Wilmington *(G-10295)*
E I Du Pont De Nemours & Co .... E 302 774-1000
Wilmington *(G-10298)*
E I Du Pont De Nemours & Co .... G 302 774-1000
Wilmington *(G-10299)*
E I Du Pont De Nemours & Co .... F 302 999-4329
Wilmington *(G-10300)*
E I Du Pont De Nemours & Co .... D 302 695-3742
Wilmington *(G-10302)*
Element .... G 302 645-0777
Lewes *(G-3480)*
John J Buckley Associates Inc .... G 302 475-5443
Wilmington *(G-11172)*
Kuehne Chemical Company Inc .... E 302 834-4557
New Castle *(G-5470)*
Rohm Haas Electronic Mtls LLC .... G 302 366-0500
Newark *(G-7358)*
Rohm Haas Electronic Mtls LLC .... G 302 366-0500
Newark *(G-7359)*
Solvay Spclty Polymers USA LLC ..... G 302 452-6609
Newark *(G-7457)*
W L Gore & Associates Inc .... C 302 368-3700
Newark *(G-7672)*

CHEMICALS: Medicinal, Organic, Uncompounded, Bulk

Wilmington .... G 302 357-4509
Wilmington *(G-13221)*

CHEMICALS: NEC

Chemours Co Fc LLC .... G 302 353-5003
Wilmington *(G-9647)*
Chemours Company Fc LLC .... D 302 540-5423
Wilmington *(G-9652)*
Croda Inc .... F 302 429-5249
New Castle *(G-5208)*
Croda Inc .... F 302 429-5200
New Castle *(G-5209)*
Diversified Chemical Pdts Inc .... G 302 656-5293
Wilmington *(G-10169)*
E I Du Pont De Nemours & Co .... F 843 335-5934
Wilmington *(G-10287)*
Frontier Scientific Inc .... G 302 266-6891
Newark *(G-6626)*
Frontier Scientific Svcs Inc .... G 302 266-6891
Newark *(G-6627)*
Honeywell International Inc .... D 302 791-6700
Claymont *(G-763)*
Hrd Products Inc .... G 302 757-3587
Newark *(G-6754)*
Koch Methanol Investments LLC .... G 302 658-7581
Wilmington *(G-11287)*
Lehvoss North Amer Holdg Inc .... G 302 734-1450
Dover *(G-1780)*
Nova Consultants Ltd .... F 302 328-1686
New Castle *(G-5581)*
Orient Corporation of America .... E 302 628-1300
Seaford *(G-8339)*
Polydel Corporation .... F 302 655-8200
Wilmington *(G-12184)*

Thrupore Technologies Inc .... G 205 657-0714
New Castle *(G-5769)*
Twinco Romax LLC .... G 302 998-3019
Wilmington *(G-12998)*
Zeneca Holdings Inc .... E 302 886-3000
Wilmington *(G-13344)*

CHEMICALS: Organic, NEC

Ashland Spcalty Ingredients GP .... D 302 995-3000
Wilmington *(G-9152)*
Basell Capital Corporation .... G 302 683-8000
Wilmington *(G-9257)*
BASF Corporation .... C 302 992-5600
Wilmington *(G-9258)*
Butamax Advanced Biofuels LLC ...... F 302 695-6787
Wilmington *(G-9514)*
Dupont Nutrition Usa Inc .... G 302 774-1000
Wilmington *(G-10257)*
Elcriton Inc .... G 864 921-5146
New Castle *(G-5280)*
Enerkem Miss Biofuels LLC .... G 514 875-0284
Wilmington *(G-10401)*
Ensyn GA Biorefinery I LLC .... G 303 425-3740
Wilmington *(G-10404)*
Grayling Industries Inc .... E 770 751-9095
Frederica *(G-2403)*
Honeywell International Inc .... D 302 791-6700
Claymont *(G-763)*
Nova Pangaea Technologies Inc .... G 612 743-6266
Dover *(G-1903)*
Riverside Specialty Chem Inc .... G 212 769-3440
Bear *(G-307)*
Rohm Haas Electronic Mtls LLC .... G 302 366-0500
Newark *(G-7358)*
Sas Nanotechnologies LLC .... G 214 235-1008
Newark *(G-7391)*
Sorbent Green LLC .... G 800 259-3577
Wilmington *(G-12682)*
Stereochemical Inc .... G 302 266-0700
Newark *(G-7490)*
Syntec Corporation .... F 302 421-8393
Wilmington *(G-12837)*

CHEMICALS: Reagent Grade, Refined From Technical Grade

Debbie Gill .... G 302 547-5182
Middletown *(G-4023)*

CHEMICALS: Water Treatment

Solenis International LLC .... E 302 994-1698
Wilmington *(G-12676)*

CHICKS WHOLESALERS

Chick/Brook LLC .... G 302 337-7141
Bridgeville *(G-458)*

CHILD & YOUTH SVCS, NEC

Children Youth & Their Fam .... G 302 577-6011
Wilmington *(G-9662)*
Children Fmlies First Del Inc .... E 302 629-6996
Seaford *(G-8194)*
Children Fmlies First Del Inc .... D 302 658-5177
Wilmington *(G-9664)*
Childrens Advocacy Ctr of Del .... F 302 854-0323
Georgetown *(G-2469)*
Family Wrkplace Connection Inc .... D 302 479-1660
Wilmington *(G-10496)*
Health & Social Svcs Del Dept .... F 302 856-5586
Georgetown *(G-2556)*
Health & Social Svcs Del Dept .... F 302 255-9500
Dover *(G-1640)*
Pressley Ridge Foundation .... G 302 677-1590
Dover *(G-1985)*

CHILD DAY CARE SVCS

A Better Chnce For Our Chldren .... G 302 725-5008
Milford *(G-4300)*
A Place To Grow Fmly Chld Care ...... G 302 897-8944
Claymont *(G-684)*
Advanced Care Centers Delaware ..... G 302 472-4878
Wilmington *(G-8950)*
All About ME Day Care .... F 302 424-8322
Milford *(G-4304)*
Amemg Inc .... F 302 220-7132
New Castle *(G-5029)*
American Universal LLC .... G 302 836-9790
Newark *(G-5960)*

PRODUCT & SERVICES SECTION — CHILD DAY CARE SVCS

Business	Code	Phone
Anns Family Daycare — Newark (G-5972)	G	302 836-8910
Attic Away From Home — Townsend (G-8761)	G	302 378-2600
Barbara L McKinney — Newark (G-6046)	G	302 266-9594
Bear-Glasgow YMCA — Newark (G-6066)	G	302 836-9622
Beetles Playhouse Day Care — Newark (G-6068)	G	302 593-7321
Beginning Blssngs Chldcare LLC — New Castle (G-5080)	G	302 893-1726
Beginning Bridges Child Care — Laurel (G-3197)	G	302 875-7428
Bernices Edtl Scl AG Ctr Inc — Wilmington (G-9310)	G	302 651-0286
Bizzy Bees Home Daycare LLC — Middletown (G-3969)	G	302 376-9245
Blessed Beginnings Lrng Ctr — Bear (G-52)	G	302 838-9112
Bowman Linda Group Day Care — Newark (G-6110)	G	302 737-5479
Brees Home Day Care — Wilmington (G-9467)	G	302 762-0876
Bright Beginnings Child Care C — Millsboro (G-4649)	G	302 934-1249
Bright Bgnnngs Lrng Acdemy LLC — Wilmington (G-9473)	G	302 655-1346
Bright Futures Inc — Middletown (G-3974)	E	610 905-0506
Bright Kidz Inc — Newark (G-6121)	F	302 369-6929
Bright New Beginnings — Wilmington (G-9476)	G	610 637-9809
Building Blocks For Learni — Dover (G-1241)	G	302 677-0248
Cacc Montessori School — Hockessin (G-2974)	E	302 239-2917
Caesar Rodney School District — Dover (G-1248)	D	302 697-3207
Center For Child Developement — Newark (G-6177)	G	302 292-1334
Chester Bethel United Methodis — Wilmington (G-9656)	F	302 475-3549
Child Inc — Magnolia (G-3886)	F	302 335-8652
Childrens Place — Camden (G-548)	G	302 698-0969
Childrens Place Child Dev Ce — Millsboro (G-4659)	G	302 947-4808
Childs Play At Home LLC — Lewes (G-3414)	G	302 644-3445
Childs Play By Bay — Lewes (G-3415)	G	302 703-6234
Christ Care Cardiac Surgery — Lewes (G-3418)	G	302 644-4282
Church of God In Christ — Dover (G-1282)	F	302 678-1949
Circle Time Learning Center — Wilmington (G-9711)	G	302 384-7193
Country Kids Child — Greenwood (G-2724)	G	302 349-5888
Country Kids Home Day Care — Townsend (G-8774)	G	302 653-4134
Creative Learning Academy Inc — Bear (G-87)	G	302 834-5259
Creative Learning Child Care — Wilmington (G-9895)	G	302 691-3167
Dawn L Conly — Middletown (G-4020)	G	302 378-1890
Day School For Children — New Castle (G-5218)	G	302 652-4651
Dcc Inc — Wilmington (G-9979)	F	302 750-1207
De Colores Family Child Care — Dover (G-1347)	G	302 883-3298
Dees Learning Care — Newark (G-6359)	G	908 623-7685
Diane Spence Day Care — Frederica (G-2401)	G	302 335-4460
Diocesan Council Inc — Wilmington (G-10157)	E	302 475-4688
Ditrocchio Maria Antonetta — Dover (G-1432)	G	302 450-6790
Dog Dayz Dog Day Care Center — Wilmington (G-10182)	G	302 655-5506
Durrell Sandblasting & Pntg Co — Newark (G-6481)	G	302 836-1113
Early Learning Center — Wilmington (G-10317)	G	302 831-0584
Eden Land Care — Wilmington (G-10345)	G	302 379-2405
Edgemoor Community Center Inc — Wilmington (G-10348)	E	302 762-1391
Elementary Workshop Inc — Wilmington (G-10369)	F	302 656-1498
Elsmere Presbyterian Church — Wilmington (G-10384)	F	302 998-6365
Enterprise Learning Solutions — Wilmington (G-10408)	G	302 762-6595
Esther V Graham — Milford (G-4406)	G	302 422-6667
Ezion Fair Community Academy — Wilmington (G-10466)	F	302 652-9114
Faith Presbyterian Church — Wilmington (G-10478)	F	302 764-8615
Faith Victory Christn Academy — Claymont (G-744)	F	302 333-0855
Family Wrkplace Connection Inc — Wilmington (G-10496)	D	302 479-1660
Foot Steps Two Heaven Daycare — Newark (G-6601)	G	302 738-5519
Fun 2 Learn Day Care — Laurel (G-3231)	G	302 875-3393
Future Development Learning — Wilmington (G-10653)	G	302 652-7500
Future Leaders — Smyrna (G-8638)	G	862 262-7312
Gaudenzia Inc — Wilmington (G-10679)	G	302 421-9945
Great New Beginnings — Bear (G-170)	G	302 218-8332
Growing Palace — Middletown (G-4094)	G	302 376-5553
Growing Palace III — Middletown (G-4095)	F	302 376-5553
Guardian Angel Day Care — Georgetown (G-2552)	G	302 934-0130
Hand -N- Hand Early Lrng Ctr — Ellendale (G-2260)	F	302 422-0702
Happy Place Day Care LLC — Newark (G-6707)	G	302 737-7603
Happyland Childcare — Lincoln (G-3854)	G	302 424-3868
Harrison House Cmnty Program — Newark (G-6710)	E	302 595-3370
Harvest Community Dev Corp — Wilmington (G-10847)	E	302 654-2613
Heart To Hand Daycare LLC — Lewes (G-3539)	G	202 256-4524
Hill Luth Day Care Center — Wilmington (G-10908)	E	302 656-3224
Hope House Daycare — Wilmington (G-10951)	F	302 407-3404
Independence School Inc — Newark (G-6771)	D	302 239-0330
J N Hooker Inc — Bear (G-195)	E	302 838-5650
Jacqueline Allens Daycare — Newark (G-6823)	G	302 368-3633
Janis Dicristofaro Day Care — Wilmington (G-11129)	G	302 998-6630
Jjs Learning Experience LLC — Harrington (G-2856)	F	302 398-9000
Jumpin Jacks — Wilmington (G-11207)	G	302 762-7604
Junebugs Little Rubies LLC — Wilmington (G-11208)	G	302 494-7552
Kenton Child Care — Dover (G-1742)	G	302 674-8142
Kerry & G Inc — Wilmington (G-11247)	G	302 999-0022
Kiddie Academy of Middletown — Middletown (G-4122)	E	302 376-5112
Kids Korner Day Care — Wilmington (G-11259)	G	302 998-4606
Kids R US Learning Center Inc — Dover (G-1748)	G	302 678-1234
Kidz Klub — Wilmington (G-11260)	G	302 652-5439
Kidz Kottage Club Inc — Harrington (G-2862)	F	302 398-4067
Kimberly Sue Kester — Dagsboro (G-914)	G	302 732-1093
Kind Mind Kids — Wilmington (G-11263)	G	302 545-0380
Lake Forest School District — Harrington (G-2864)	F	302 398-8945
Learning Circle Child Care — Bear (G-233)	G	302 834-1473
Learning Ctr At Madison St LLC — Wilmington (G-11351)	F	302 543-7588
Learning Patch Kids — Newark (G-6928)	G	302 368-7208
Learning Train LLC — Newark (G-6929)	G	302 731-0944
Learning Tree Network — Milton (G-4923)	G	302 645-7199
Learning4 Lrng Professionals — Wilmington (G-11352)	G	302 994-0451
Lessons Learnd Dy Care /Presch	E	302 777-2200
Lessons Learnd Dy Care /Presch (G-11375)		
Lighted Pathway Day Care Ctr — Seaford (G-8294)	F	302 629-8583
Linda Putnam Day Care — Bear (G-236)	G	302 836-1033
Lindas Angels Chldcare Dev Ctr — New Castle (G-5484)	F	302 328-3700
Lisa Trabaudo Day Care — Smyrna (G-8674)	G	302 653-3529
Little Kids Swagg Lrng Ctr LLC — Smyrna (G-8675)	G	302 480-4404
Little People Child Dev — Christiana (G-673)	G	302 328-1481
Little People Day Care — Middletown (G-4134)	G	302 528-4336
Little Peoples College — Wilmington (G-11406)	G	302 998-4929
Little Trooper Day Care — Middletown (G-4135)	G	302 378-7355
Love N Learn Nursery Too — Dover (G-1797)	G	302 678-0445
Lullaby Learning Center Inc — Harbeson (G-2789)	F	302 703-2871
Magic Yrs Child Care Lrng Cntr — New Castle (G-5496)	F	302 322-3102
Malgiero Helen A Day Care — Delaware City (G-960)	G	302 834-9060
Mamie Sturgis Handy Day Care — Laurel (G-3260)	G	302 875-4703
Marys Little Lambs Daycare — Selbyville (G-8516)	G	302 436-5796
Mercy Land Academy Inc — Middletown (G-4152)	G	302 378-2013
Mom Home Daycare — Milford (G-4511)	G	302 265-2668
Moms House Inc — Wilmington (G-11730)	G	302 658-3433
Montessori Learning Centre — Wilmington (G-11738)	G	302 478-2575
Ms Hathers Lrng Ctr Childcare — Wilmington (G-11770)	G	302 994-2448
Nagengast Janet Day Care — Wilmington (G-11794)	G	302 656-6898
Neighborhood House Inc — Wilmington (G-11830)	G	302 658-5404
Newark Ctr For Creative Lrng — Newark (G-7115)	F	302 368-7772
Northeast Early Learning Ctr — Wilmington (G-11903)	F	302 762-5803
Nurses N Kids Inc — New Castle (G-5583)	E	302 323-1118
Ogletown Baptist Church — Newark (G-7144)	E	302 737-2511
Our Childrens Learning Ctr — Bear (G-274)	G	302 565-1272
Our Future Child Care Ctr LLC — Wilmington (G-11983)	G	302 762-8645
Peoples Place II Inc — Millsboro (G-4780)	G	302 934-0300
Peoples Place II Inc — Dover (G-1948)	D	302 730-1321
Peoples Settlement Assc of WI — Wilmington (G-12079)	E	302 658-4133
Precious Knwldg Erly Lrng Ctr — Newark (G-7238)	G	302 293-2588
Precious Little Hands Childcar — Wilmington (G-12199)	G	302 298-5027
Precious Years Child Care LLC — New Castle (G-5635)	G	302 322-1701
Pyle Child Development Center — Frankford (G-2382)	F	302 732-1443
Robin S Wright — Lewes (G-3721)	G	302 249-2105
Saint Johns Lutheran Church — Dover (G-2055)	E	302 734-7078
Salvation Army — Wilmington (G-12529)	D	302 656-1696
Seeds of Jesus Day Care LLC — Wilmington (G-12572)	G	302 494-6568

Employee Codes: A=Over 500 employees, B=251-500, C=101-250, D=51-100, E=20-50, F=10-19, G=1-9

2020 Harris Directory of Delaware Businesses

CHILD DAY CARE SVCS

Shavone Loves Kids Day Care ....G....... 302 544-6170
  New Castle (G-5704)
Shining Time Day Care Center ....G....... 302 335-2770
  Felton (G-2321)
Smarty Pants Early Education ....G....... 302 985-3770
  Bear (G-325)
Smyrna School District ....E....... 302 653-3135
  Smyrna (G-8721)
Sunshine Kids Academy ....F....... 302 444-4270
  Newark (G-7508)
Susan R Austin ....G....... 302 322-4685
  New Castle (G-5744)
Tender Hearts ....F....... 302 674-2565
  Dover (G-2138)
Tender Loving Kare Child Care ....E....... 302 653-5677
  Smyrna (G-8730)
Thirst 2 Learn ....G....... 302 293-2304
  Bear (G-352)
Thirst 2 Learn LLC ....G....... 302 475-7080
  Wilmington (G-12898)
Tiny Tots Childcare and Learni ....G....... 302 651-9060
  Wilmington (G-12915)
Todays Kid Inc (not Inc) ....G....... 302 834-5620
  Newark (G-7573)
Toy Box Child Care Center ....G....... 302 427-8438
  New Castle (G-5781)
Wee Care Day Care Salv Army ....F....... 302 472-0712
  Wilmington (G-13136)
Wesley Play Care Center ....F....... 302 678-8987
  Dover (G-2213)
West Center Cy Early Lrng Ctr ....E....... 302 656-0485
  Wilmington (G-13163)
Wilson Care Wilson Co ....G....... 302 897-5059
  Newark (G-7709)
Wonder Years Kids Club ....F....... 302 398-0563
  Harrington (G-2909)
Wright Choice Child Care ....G....... 302 798-0758
  Claymont (G-827)
Xavier Inc ....G....... 302 655-1962
  Wilmington (G-13314)
Young Mens Christian Associat ....D....... 302 296-9622
  Rehoboth Beach (G-8121)
Young Mens Christian Associat ....C....... 302 571-6900
  Wilmington (G-13332)
YWCA Delaware ....F....... 302 224-4060
  Newark (G-7733)

CHILDBIRTH PREPARATION CLINIC

Christiana Care Health Sys Inc ....F....... 302 838-4750
  Newark (G-6209)
Ierardi Vascular Clinic LLC ....G....... 302 655-8272
  Newark (G-6763)
Peninsula Regional Medical Ctr ....C....... 302 537-1457
  Millville (G-4852)
Pure Wellness LLC ....G....... 302 389-8915
  Smyrna (G-8695)
Sunrise Medical Center ....G....... 302 854-9006
  Georgetown (G-2671)

CHILDREN'S & INFANTS' CLOTHING STORES

Cato Corporation ....G....... 302 854-9548
  Georgetown (G-2464)

CHILDREN'S AID SOCIETY

Childrens Beach House Inc ....E....... 302 655-4288
  Wilmington (G-9665)
Kent Cnty Cmnty Actn Agncy Inc ....F....... 302 678-1949
  Dover (G-1732)
We Deserve It Shs For Kids Inc ....G....... 302 521-7255
  Dover (G-2208)

CHILDREN'S HOME

Associated Svc Specialist Inc ....F....... 302 672-7159
  Dover (G-1149)
Mary Campbell Center Inc ....C....... 302 762-6025
  Wilmington (G-11555)

CHILDREN'S WEAR STORES

Carters Inc ....G....... 302 731-1432
  Newark (G-6162)

CHIMES: Electric

Chimes Metro Inc ....G....... 302 452-3400
  New Castle (G-5149)
Inc Chimes ....G....... 302 449-1926
  Townsend (G-8794)

CHIMNEY CLEANING SVCS

Clean Sweep ....G....... 302 422-6085
  Milford (G-4355)
Swift Services Inc ....G....... 302 328-1145
  New Castle (G-5747)

CHIROPRACTORS' OFFICES

1 Fair Chiropractic & Med Inc ....G....... 302 528-1068
  Wilmington (G-8840)
American Chiropractic Center ....G....... 302 450-3153
  Dover (G-1118)
Atlantic Chiropractic Associat ....G....... 302 854-9300
  Georgetown (G-2436)
Atlantic Chiropractic Associat ....F....... 302 703-6108
  Lewes (G-3353)
Atlantic Chiropractic Associat ....F....... 302 422-3100
  Milford (G-4311)
Beachview Chiropractic Center ....G....... 302 539-7063
  Millville (G-4834)
Bear Chiropractic Center DC ....G....... 302 836-8361
  Bear (G-46)
Brandywine Total Health Care ....G....... 302 478-3028
  Wilmington (G-9455)
Camp Chiropractic Inc ....G....... 302 378-2899
  Middletown (G-3980)
Carrick Chiropractic Centre PA ....G....... 302 478-1443
  Wilmington (G-9579)
Chiropractic Services PA ....G....... 302 654-0404
  Wilmington (G-9669)
Christiana Chiropractic LLC ....G....... 302 633-6335
  Newark (G-6220)
Coastal Chiropractic LLC ....G....... 302 933-0700
  Millsboro (G-4663)
Concord Med Spine & Pain Ctr ....G....... 302 652-1107
  Wilmington (G-9813)
Davis Chiropractic Inc ....G....... 302 856-2225
  Georgetown (G-2494)
Delaware Backpan Rhbittn Assoc ....E....... 302 529-8783
  Wilmington (G-10004)
Delaware Chiropractic At Louvi ....G....... 302 738-7300
  Newark (G-6368)
Delaware County Pain MGT ....G....... 302 575-1145
  Wilmington (G-10029)
Delaware Spine & Rehab LLC ....G....... 813 965-0903
  Seaford (G-8219)
Diamond Chiropractic Inc ....F....... 302 892-9355
  Newark (G-6443)
Dover Family Chiropractic ....G....... 302 531-1900
  Camden (G-565)
Elizabeth C Parberry Dr ....G....... 302 436-1803
  Selbyville (G-8487)
Family Chiropractic Office PA ....G....... 302 993-9113
  Wilmington (G-10485)
Feeney Chropractic Care Ctr PA ....F....... 302 328-0200
  Bear (G-150)
First Choice Health Care Inc ....G....... 302 836-6150
  Bear (G-151)
First State Health & Wellness ....F....... 302 645-6681
  Rehoboth Beach (G-7933)
First State Health & Wellness ....G....... 302 239-1600
  Hockessin (G-3029)
First State Physicia NS ....G....... 302 836-6150
  Bear (G-154)
Glasgow Chiropractic ....G....... 302 453-4043
  Newark (G-6660)
Hockessin Chrpractic Centre PA ....G....... 302 239-8550
  Hockessin (G-3048)
Howmedica Osteonics Corp ....G....... 302 655-3239
  Wilmington (G-10962)
Kenneth De Grout DC ....G....... 302 475-5600
  Wilmington (G-11240)
Lewes Chiropractic Center ....G....... 302 645-9171
  Lewes (G-3597)
Lodes Chiropractic Center PA ....G....... 302 477-1565
  Wilmington (G-11423)
Main Street Fmly Chiropractic ....G....... 302 737-8667
  Newark (G-6974)
Matthew J McIlrath DC ....G....... 302 798-7033
  Wilmington (G-11571)
Newark Chropractic Hlth Ctr PA ....G....... 302 239-1600
  Hockessin (G-3103)
Nowcare LLC ....G....... 302 777-5551
  Wilmington (G-11916)
P A Chadley ....G....... 302 234-1115
  Hockessin (G-3109)
Peninsula Chiropractic Center ....G....... 302 629-4344
  Seaford (G-8346)
Pro Rehab Chiropractic ....G....... 302 200-9102
  Lewes (G-3698)
Pro Rehab Chiropractors ....G....... 302 652-2225
  Wilmington (G-12235)
Pure Wellness LLC ....G....... 302 449-0149
  Middletown (G-4204)
Pure Wellness LLC ....F....... 302 365-5470
  Newark (G-7272)
Pure Wellness LLC ....G....... 302 543-5679
  Wilmington (G-12271)
Pyne Chiropractic PA ....G....... 302 644-1792
  Rehoboth Beach (G-8037)
Renu Chiropractic Wellness ....G....... 302 368-0124
  Newark (G-7320)
Richard C McKay DC PA ....G....... 302 368-1300
  Newark (G-7337)
Roger C Allen DC ....G....... 302 734-9824
  Dover (G-2040)
Rosenthal Chiropractic Offs PA ....G....... 302 999-0633
  Wilmington (G-12476)
Schreppler Chropractic Offs PA ....G....... 302 653-5525
  Smyrna (G-8712)
Stephen G Puzio DC ....G....... 302 234-4045
  Hockessin (G-3149)
Stephen Jankovic Chiropractor ....G....... 302 384-8540
  Wilmington (G-12756)
Sussex Pain Relief Center LLC ....E....... 302 519-0100
  Georgetown (G-2681)
T Shane Palmer DC ....G....... 302 328-2656
  New Castle (G-5750)
Todd A Richardson Dcpa ....G....... 302 449-0149
  Middletown (G-4261)
Travis Chropractic ....G....... 610 485-9800
  Wilmington (G-12962)
Trevor Ennis DC ....G....... 302 730-8848
  Dover (G-2163)
Trevor Ennis DC ....G....... 302 389-2225
  Smyrna (G-8732)
Walsh Chiropractic Center ....G....... 302 422-0622
  Milford (G-4597)
Wellness Health Inc ....G....... 302 424-4100
  Milford (G-4601)

CHLORINE

Kuehne Chemical Company Inc ....E....... 302 834-4557
  New Castle (G-5470)

CHOCOLATE, EXC CANDY FROM BEANS: Chips, Powder, Block, Syrup

Kraft Heinz Company ....A....... 302 734-6100
  Dover (G-1758)
Witors America LLC ....G....... 646 247-4836
  Camden (G-606)

CHOCOLATE, EXC CANDY FROM PURCH CHOC: Chips, Powder, Block

Chocolate Editions Inc ....G....... 302 479-8400
  Claymont (G-715)
United Cocoa Processor Inc ....E....... 302 731-0825
  Newark (G-7613)

CHROMATOGRAPHY EQPT

Joint Anlytcl Systms (amrcs) ....G....... 302 607-0088
  Newark (G-6849)
Miles Scientific Corporation ....F....... 302 737-6960
  Newark (G-7039)

CHURCHES

True Life Church Newark Inc ....G....... 302 283-9003
  Bear (G-361)

CIGAR & CIGARETTE HOLDERS

Discount Cigarette Depot ....G....... 302 398-4447
  Harrington (G-2833)

CIGAR STORES

Guy & Lady Barrel LLC ....G....... 302 399-3069
  Dover (G-1618)

CIRCUIT BOARDS, PRINTED: Television & Radio

Via Networks Inc ....G....... 314 727-2087
  Wilmington (G-13075)

PRODUCT & SERVICES SECTION CLOTHING: Band Uniforms

CIRCUITS: Electronic

Eeco Inc .... G 302 456-1448
  Newark (G-6506)
Lexatys LLC .... F 302 715-5029
  Laurel (G-3259)
Suretronix Solutions LLC .... G 302 407-3146
  Wilmington (G-12817)

CLAIMS ADJUSTING SVCS

Hetrick-Drake Associates Inc .... G 302 998-7500
  Wilmington (G-10897)

CLAY: Ground Or Treated

Sorbent Green LLC .... G 800 259-3577
  Wilmington (G-12682)

CLEANING & DYEING PLANTS, EXC RUGS

Curzon Corp .... E 302 655-5551
  Wilmington (G-9922)
Hockessin Cleaners .... G 302 239-6071
  Hockessin (G-3049)
Kapa Inc LLC .... G 302 740-1235
  Seaford (G-8283)
Linden Hill Cleaners Inc .... G 302 368-9795
  Wilmington (G-11394)
Marvi Cleaners Limited Inc .... G 302 764-3077
  Wilmington (G-11553)
McKelvey Hires Dry Cleaning .... F 302 998-9191
  Wilmington (G-11601)
North Hills Cleaners Inc .... F 302 764-1234
  Wilmington (G-11900)
Royal Cleaners .... G 302 478-0955
  Wilmington (G-12485)
Sepia Cleaners .... G 302 656-0700
  Wilmington (G-12581)
Superior Clr of Wilmington Inc .... G 302 633-3323
  Wilmington (G-12806)
Webbs Cleaners Corp .... G 302 798-0655
  Wilmington (G-13135)

CLEANING OR POLISHING PREPARATIONS, NEC

Chem Tech Inc .... G 302 798-9675
  Wilmington (G-9644)
Quip Laboratories Incorporated .... E 302 761-2600
  Wilmington (G-12291)

CLEANING PRDTS: Ammonia, Household

Sanosil International LLC .... F 302 454-8102
  New Castle (G-5694)

CLEANING PRDTS: Automobile Polish

Diligent Detail .... G 302 482-2836
  Wilmington (G-10154)

CLEANING PRDTS: Disinfectants, Household Or Indl Plant

Halosil International Inc .... G 302 543-8095
  New Castle (G-5373)

CLEANING PRDTS: Sanitation Preps, Disinfectants/Deodorants

Gearhalo Us Inc .... G 780 239-2120
  Dover (G-1586)

CLEANING PRDTS: Specialty

Jeffs Mobile Power Washing .... G 302 753-4726
  Clayton (G-858)

CLEANING SVCS

1st State Power Clean LLC .... G 302 735-7974
  Dover (G-1067)
Alvins Professional Services .... F 302 544-6634
  New Castle (G-5028)
Blue Sky Clean .... G 302 584-5800
  Wilmington (G-9381)
C&B Complete Cleaning & Cnstr .... G 302 436-9622
  Frankford (G-2352)
Candlelight Cleaning .... G 302 270-1218
  Smyrna (G-8590)
Clean Delaware LLC .... E 302 684-4221
  Lewes (G-3427)
Cleaning Frenzy LLC .... G 302 453-8800
  Newark (G-6248)
Costline Cleaning Service .... G 302 420-3000
  Harbeson (G-2778)
Dustntime .... F 302 858-7876
  Rehoboth Beach (G-7922)
Elite Chemical and Supply Inc .... G 302 366-8900
  Newark (G-6513)
Gale Force Cleaning & Restore .... F 302 539-4683
  Ocean View (G-7789)
Gtech Cleaning Services LLC .... E 302 494-2102
  Claymont (G-759)
Halls We Clean Service LLC .... G 302 422-7787
  Milford (G-4431)
Integrity Cleaning Svcs LLC .... G 302 353-9315
  Clayton (G-856)
Kream Puff Clean .... F 251 509-1639
  Smyrna (G-8668)
M&J Services LLC .... G 302 227-8725
  Rehoboth Beach (G-7993)
Man Maid Cleaning Inc .... G 302 226-5050
  Rehoboth Beach (G-7995)
Matties Cleaning Service .... F 302 229-3585
  Wilmington (G-11574)
Pat T Clean Inc .... G 302 239-5354
  Hockessin (G-3111)
Poof Power Wash & Ldscpg LLC .... G 302 595-1576
  Dover (G-1976)
Super Perfection Clg Svcs LLC .... G 267 619-4441
  Wilmington (G-12803)
Superior Maids .... G 302 284-2012
  Felton (G-2323)
T&T Cleaning LLC .... F 609 575-0458
  Dover (G-2127)
Vesta Wash LLC .... G 302 559-7533
  Newark (G-7654)

CLEANING SVCS: Industrial Or Commercial

Aqua Pro Inc .... G 302 659-6593
  Smyrna (G-8575)
Blue Chip Services Ltd .... G 302 798-5010
  Wilmington (G-9374)
D C S Company .... G 302 328-5138
  New Castle (G-5212)
Focus Solutions Services Inc .... F 302 318-1345
  Newark (G-6597)
JV s Cleaning Services .... G 302 345-7679
  Bear (G-208)
Maid For Shore .... G 302 344-1857
  Lewes (G-3617)
Optima Cleaning Systems Inc .... D 302 652-3979
  Wilmington (G-11963)
R W Home Services Inc .... F 302 539-4683
  Ocean View (G-7810)
Schoon Inc .... G 302 894-7574
  Newark (G-7394)
Schweizer Cleaning Service .... G 302 995-2816
  Wilmington (G-12557)
Totally Clean .... F 302 376-3626
  Middletown (G-4263)
Wilkins Enterprises Inc .... G 302 945-4142
  Lewes (G-3824)

CLIPPERS: Fingernail & Toenail

LRC North America Inc .... E 302 427-2845
  Wilmington (G-11446)

CLOSET BOWLS: Vitreous China

Sylvester Custom Cabinetry .... G 302 398-6050
  Harrington (G-2896)

CLOTHING & ACCESS, WOMEN, CHILD & INFANT, WHSLE: Sportswear

Huzala Inc .... G 313 404-6941
  Newark (G-6756)

CLOTHING & ACCESS, WOMEN, CHILD/INFANT, WHOLESALE: Child

Flapdoodles Inc .... D 302 731-9793
  Newark (G-6595)

CLOTHING & ACCESS, WOMEN, CHILDREN & INFANT, WHOL: Access

Vivig Shoes .... F 302 427-2700
  Wilmington (G-13098)

CLOTHING & ACCESS, WOMEN, CHILDREN & INFANT, WHOL: Handbags

Tai Jun International Inc .... G 302 239-9336
  Newark (G-7533)

CLOTHING & ACCESS: Handicapped

Advacare LLC .... G 302 448-5045
  Wilmington (G-8944)

CLOTHING & APPAREL STORES: Custom

Be Blessed Design Group LLC .... G 302 561-3793
  Bear (G-45)

CLOTHING & FURNISHINGS, MEN'S & BOYS', WHOLESALE: Gloves

Sui Trading Co .... G 302 239-2012
  Hockessin (G-3151)

CLOTHING & FURNISHINGS, MEN'S & BOYS', WHOLESALE: Hats

Lids Corporation .... G 302 226-8580
  Rehoboth Beach (G-7986)

CLOTHING & FURNISHINGS, MEN'S & BOYS', WHOLESALE: Shirts

Great Graphic Originals Ltd .... G 302 734-7600
  Dover (G-1608)

CLOTHING STORES, NEC

Cato Corporation .... G 302 854-9548
  Georgetown (G-2464)

CLOTHING STORES: Caps & Gowns

Lids Corporation .... G 302 736-8465
  Dover (G-1783)

CLOTHING STORES: Formal Wear

Candlelight Bridal Formal Tlrg .... G 302 934-8009
  Millsboro (G-4654)
Formal Affairs Inc .... F 302 737-1519
  Newark (G-6606)

CLOTHING STORES: Leather

Francis Enterprises LLC .... F 302 276-1316
  New Castle (G-5327)

CLOTHING STORES: Lingerie & Corsets, Underwear

Victorias Scret Pink Main Line .... G 302 644-1035
  Rehoboth Beach (G-8106)

CLOTHING STORES: T-Shirts, Printed, Custom

Slater Fireplaces Inc .... G 302 999-1200
  Wilmington (G-12645)

CLOTHING: Access

Mymoroccanbazar Inc .... G 323 238-5747
  Newark (G-7077)

CLOTHING: Athletic & Sportswear, Men's & Boys'

Carpediem Health LLC .... G 347 467-4444
  Dover (G-1257)
Huzala Inc .... G 313 404-6941
  Newark (G-6756)
Majdell Group USA Inc .... G 302 722-8223
  Newark (G-6977)

CLOTHING: Athletic & Sportswear, Women's & Girls'

Carpediem Health LLC .... G 347 467-4444
  Dover (G-1257)

CLOTHING: Band Uniforms

G2 Performance Band ACC .... G 800 554-8523
  Wilmington (G-10660)

Employee Codes: A=Over 500 employees, B=251-500
C=101-250, D=51-100, E=20-50, F=10-19, G=1-9

2020 Harris Directory of Delaware Businesses

CLOTHING: Blouses, Women's & Girls'
Lee Bell Inc .... G 302 477-3930
  Wilmington *(G-11355)*

CLOTHING: Children & Infants'
Carters Inc .... G 302 731-1432
  Newark *(G-6162)*

CLOTHING: Clergy Vestments
John M Cooper Reverand .... G 302 684-8639
  Lewes *(G-3573)*
Nagorka .... G 302 537-2392
  Bethany Beach *(G-416)*

CLOTHING: Coats, Hunting & Vests, Men's
Heated Wear LLC .... G 347 510-7965
  Wilmington *(G-10878)*

CLOTHING: Costumes
Fantast Costumes Inc .... F 302 455-2006
  Dover *(G-1540)*

CLOTHING: Dresses
Runway Liquidation LLC .... G 305 451-1481
  Wilmington *(G-12494)*

CLOTHING: Gowns & Dresses, Wedding
Arcangel Inc .... G 347 771-0789
  Wilmington *(G-9121)*

CLOTHING: Hospital, Men's
Nixon Uniform Service Inc .... C 302 325-2875
  New Castle *(G-5571)*

CLOTHING: Knit Underwear & Nightwear
Ginch Gonch Corp .... G 713 240-9900
  Newark *(G-6655)*

CLOTHING: Mens & Boys Jackets, Sport, Suede, Leatherette
Lee Bell Inc .... G 302 477-3930
  Wilmington *(G-11355)*

CLOTHING: Neckwear
Aptustech LLC .... G 347 254-5619
  Wilmington *(G-9105)*
Mercy Inc .... G 302 764-7781
  Wilmington *(G-11638)*

CLOTHING: Outerwear, Knit
Flapdoodles Inc .... D 302 731-9793
  Newark *(G-6595)*

CLOTHING: Outerwear, Women's & Misses' NEC
City Theater Co Inc .... G 302 831-2206
  Newark *(G-6244)*

CLOTHING: Shirts, Dress, Men's & Boys'
Lee Bell Inc .... G 302 477-3930
  Wilmington *(G-11355)*

CLOTHING: Socks
Heated Wear LLC .... G 347 510-7965
  Wilmington *(G-10878)*

CLOTHING: Suits & Skirts, Women's & Misses'
Maalika K LLC .... G 844 622-5452
  Newark *(G-6969)*

CLOTHING: Sweaters, Men's & Boys'
Hampshire Group Limited .... D 212 840-5666
  Wilmington *(G-10829)*

CLOTHING: Swimwear, Women's & Misses'
Body Double Swimwear .... G 302 537-1444
  Selbyville *(G-8458)*

CLOTHING: T-Shirts & Tops, Knit
Great Graphic Originals Ltd .... G 302 734-7600
  Dover *(G-1608)*

CLOTHING: Tuxedos, From Purchased Materials
Zuhatrend LLC .... G 302 883-2656
  Dover *(G-2256)*

CLOTHING: Underwear, Women's & Children's
Perteh .... G 302 200-0912
  Wilmington *(G-12092)*
Victorias Srcret Pink Main Line .... G 302 644-1035
  Rehoboth Beach *(G-8106)*

CLOTHING: Uniforms, Ex Athletic, Women's, Misses' & Juniors'
Fresh Accents LLC .... G 301 717-3757
  Bethany Beach *(G-399)*

CLOTHING: Uniforms, Men's & Boys'
Fresh Accents LLC .... G 301 717-3757
  Bethany Beach *(G-399)*

CLOTHING: Uniforms, Military, Men/Youth, Purchased Materials
Cross Over Camo LLC .... G 302 798-1898
  Claymont *(G-725)*

CLOTHING: Uniforms, Work
Fresh Accents LLC .... G 301 717-3757
  Bethany Beach *(G-399)*

CLUTCHES, EXC VEHICULAR
SSS Clutch Company Inc .... G 302 322-8080
  New Castle *(G-5733)*

COAL & OTHER MINERALS & ORES WHOLESALERS
Banfield & Temperley Inc .... G 347 878-6057
  Dover *(G-1169)*

COAL, MINERALS & ORES, WHOLESALE: Iron Ore
Network Scrap Metal Corp .... G 910 202-0655
  Wilmington *(G-11841)*

COATING SVC
Coastal Coatings Inc .... G 302 645-1399
  Lewes *(G-3436)*
General Coatings LLC .... G 302 841-7958
  Millsboro *(G-4696)*
Raymond Harner .... G 302 737-0755
  Newark *(G-7301)*

COATING SVC: Hot Dip, Metals Or Formed Prdts
Top Qality Indus Finishers Inc .... G 302 778-5005
  Wilmington *(G-12929)*

COATING SVC: Metals & Formed Prdts
Chemring North Amer Group Inc .... G 302 658-5687
  Wilmington *(G-9654)*
Crazy Coatings .... G 302 378-0888
  Middletown *(G-4013)*
E M C Process Company Inc .... G 302 999-9204
  Wilmington *(G-10309)*
Perfect Finish Powder Coating .... G 302 566-6189
  Harrington *(G-2872)*

COFFEE MAKERS: Electric
Idylc Homes LLC .... G 302 295-3719
  Wilmington *(G-10995)*

COIN OPERATED LAUNDRIES & DRYCLEANERS
Sparklean Laundromat .... G 302 838-2226
  Newark *(G-7464)*
Splash Lndrmat LLC - Gorgetown .... G 302 249-8231
  Georgetown *(G-2663)*

COIN-OPERATED DRYCLEANING
Classic Image Inc .... G 302 658-7281
  New Castle *(G-5176)*

COIN-OPERATED LAUNDRY
Brookside Laundromat .... G 302 369-3366
  Newark *(G-6124)*
Emerald City Wash World .... G 302 734-1230
  Dover *(G-1516)*
Om Shiv Groceries Inc .... G 302 856-7014
  Georgetown *(G-2611)*
Pennsylvania Inc .... G 302 498-0904
  Wilmington *(G-12071)*
Trolley Laundry .... G 302 654-3538
  Wilmington *(G-12982)*
Wolfe Resources Ltd .... F 302 798-6397
  Claymont *(G-825)*

COINS, WHOLESALE
Certified Assets MGT Intl LLC .... G 302 765-3352
  Wilmington *(G-9617)*

COLLECTION AGENCIES
Andrews & Wells LLC .... G 302 359-5417
  Camden *(G-538)*
Baines Shapiro & Associates .... G 302 384-2322
  New Castle *(G-5064)*
Phillips & Cohen Assoc Ltd .... D 609 518-9000
  Wilmington *(G-12117)*
Phillips & Cohen Assoc Ltd .... D 302 355-3500
  Newark *(G-7214)*
SLM Corporation .... D 302 451-0200
  Newark *(G-7441)*

COLLECTION AGENCY, EXC REAL ESTATE
Advanced Rcvable Solutions Inc .... E 302 225-6001
  Wilmington *(G-8955)*
Beach Associates Inc .... F 866 744-9911
  Dover *(G-1183)*
Byron & Davis Cccc .... G 302 792-2334
  Wilmington *(G-9517)*
Capitol Credit Services Inc .... F 302 678-1735
  Dover *(G-1253)*
Commercial Recovery Group Inc .... F 302 730-4040
  Dover *(G-1305)*
Commtrak Corporation .... G 302 644-1600
  Lewes *(G-3443)*
Firstcollect Inc .... G 302 644-6804
  Lewes *(G-3500)*
G & D Collection Group Inc .... F 302 482-2512
  Wilmington *(G-10656)*
Jsd Management Inc .... E 302 735-4628
  Dover *(G-1713)*
Kearns Brinen & Monaghan Inc .... F 302 736-6481
  Dover *(G-1727)*
Matthews Pierce & Lloyd Inc .... E 302 678-5500
  Dover *(G-1829)*
Simm Associates Inc .... C 302 283-2800
  Newark *(G-7430)*
Stevenson Ventures LLC .... G 302 752-4449
  Milford *(G-4571)*
Wyatt & Brown Inc .... G 302 786-2793
  Harrington *(G-2910)*

COMBINED ELEMENTARY & SECONDARY SCHOOLS, PRIVATE
Independence School Inc .... D 302 239-0330
  Newark *(G-6771)*

COMMERCIAL & LITERARY WRITINGS
Carr Paris .... F 302 401-1203
  Wilmington *(G-9578)*
Envision It Publications LLC .... G 800 329-9411
  Bear *(G-144)*

PRODUCT & SERVICES SECTION

COMMERCIAL & OFFICE BUILDINGS RENOVATION & REPAIR

Benjamin B Smith Builders Inc............G...... 302 537-1916
  Ocean View *(G-7764)*
Breslin Contracting Inc.......................E...... 302 322-0320
  New Castle *(G-5110)*
Colonial Construction Company.........F...... 302 994-5705
  Wilmington *(G-9774)*
Dry Wall Associates Ltd......................D...... 302 737-3220
  Newark *(G-6475)*
Eastern Home Improvements Inc.........G...... 302 655-9920
  Wilmington *(G-10322)*
J & S General Contractors..................F...... 302 658-4499
  Wilmington *(G-11098)*
James Rice Jr Construction Co.............G...... 302 731-9323
  Newark *(G-6826)*
Joseph A Santillo Inc..........................G...... 302 661-7313
  Wilmington *(G-11186)*
JW Tull Contracting Svcs LLC..............F...... 302 494-8179
  Wilmington *(G-11212)*
Kristin Konstruction Company.............G...... 302 791-9670
  Claymont *(G-772)*
M W Fogarty Inc.................................G...... 302 658-5547
  Hockessin *(G-3083)*
Mebro Inc..E...... 302 992-0104
  Wilmington *(G-11613)*
National Restortn & Faclty Svc.............E...... 856 401-0100
  Wilmington *(G-11809)*
Renovate LLC....................................G...... 302 378-1768
  Middletown *(G-4218)*
Renzi Group Inc.................................G...... 302 588-2603
  Wilmington *(G-12381)*
Roberts Const Co...............................E...... 302 335-4141
  Frederica *(G-2411)*
Rosauri Builders & Remodelers...........G...... 302 234-8464
  Hockessin *(G-3140)*
Shure-Line Construction Inc................E...... 302 653-4610
  Kenton *(G-3185)*
Tolton Builders Inc..............................G...... 302 239-5357
  Hockessin *(G-3162)*
W D Pressley Inc.................................G...... 302 653-4381
  Smyrna *(G-8737)*
Zacs Inc..G...... 302 242-4653
  Magnolia *(G-3913)*

COMMERCIAL ART & GRAPHIC DESIGN SVCS

Aztec Copies LLC...............................F...... 302 575-1993
  Wilmington *(G-9204)*
De Nest Studio...................................G...... 302 836-1316
  Bear *(G-101)*
Graphics Unlimited Inc........................G...... 302 398-3898
  Harrington *(G-2842)*
Growth Inc..F...... 302 366-8586
  Newark *(G-6694)*
Promotion Zone LLC...........................G...... 302 832-8565
  Newark *(G-7269)*

COMMERCIAL ART & ILLUSTRATION SVCS

Visual Arts Studio Inc..........................G...... 302 652-0925
  Wilmington *(G-13094)*

COMMERCIAL EQPT WHOLESALERS, NEC

Burke Equipment Company.................E...... 302 248-7070
  Delmar *(G-975)*
Burke Equipment Company.................G...... 302 248-7070
  Delmar *(G-976)*
Jesco Inc...G...... 302 376-6946
  Middletown *(G-4114)*

COMMERCIAL EQPT, WHOLESALE: Restaurant, NEC

Brewster Products Inc.........................G...... 302 764-4463
  Wilmington *(G-9469)*
Elmer Schultz Services Inc...................G...... 302 655-8900
  Wilmington *(G-10382)*
Hy-Point Equipment Co.......................F...... 302 478-0388
  Wilmington *(G-10980)*
South Forks Inc..................................G...... 302 731-0444
  Newark *(G-7461)*

COMMERCIAL EQPT, WHOLESALE: Scales, Exc Laboratory

Widgeon Enterprises Inc......................G...... 302 846-9763
  Delmar *(G-1049)*

COMMERCIAL EQPT, WHOLESALE: Vending Machines, Coin-Operated

Vending Solutions LLC........................G...... 302 674-2222
  Dover *(G-2189)*

COMMERCIAL PHOTOGRAPHIC STUDIO

Colourworks Photographic Svcs...........G...... 302 428-0222
  Wilmington *(G-9778)*
Cut Out Image Inc..............................G...... 844 866-5577
  Newark *(G-6333)*
Herbert Studios..................................G...... 302 836-3122
  Newark *(G-6724)*

COMMERCIAL PRINTING & NEWSPAPER PUBLISHING COMBINED

Gatehuse Mdia Del Holdings Inc..........G...... 302 678-3616
  Dover *(G-1584)*
Hoy En Delaware LLC.........................G...... 302 854-0240
  Georgetown *(G-2562)*
Morning Report Research Inc..............G...... 302 730-3793
  Dover *(G-1872)*
News-Journal Company......................E...... 302 324-2500
  New Castle *(G-5569)*

COMMODITY CONTRACT TRADING COMPANIES

Bsr Trade LLC...................................G...... 646 250-4409
  Dover *(G-1240)*
Novin LLC...G...... 315 670-7979
  Wilmington *(G-11913)*
Social Enterprise LLC.........................G...... 718 417-4076
  New Castle *(G-5720)*
Sqs Global Solutions LLC....................F...... 302 691-9682
  Wilmington *(G-12718)*

COMMODITY CONTRACTS BROKERS, DEALERS

Monterey SW LLC...............................F...... 302 504-4901
  Newark *(G-7054)*
Monterey Swf LLC..............................F...... 302 504-4901
  Newark *(G-7055)*

COMMODITY INVESTORS

Rite Way Distributors..........................G...... 302 535-8507
  Felton *(G-2317)*

COMMON SAND MINING

Bardon U S Corporation......................G...... 302 552-3136
  Wilmington *(G-9253)*

COMMUNICATIONS CARRIER: Wired

Generation Consultants LLC................G...... 302 722-4884
  Newark *(G-6646)*

COMMUNICATIONS EQPT & SYSTEMS, NEC

Nt Ezlinq Holdings LLC.......................G...... 302 351-3051
  Wilmington *(G-11918)*
Phoenix Vitae Holdings LLC................G...... 302 351-3047
  Wilmington *(G-12127)*

COMMUNICATIONS EQPT REPAIR & MAINTENANCE

ET Communications LLC....................F...... 302 322-2222
  New Castle *(G-5296)*
Video Tech Center Inc........................E...... 302 691-7213
  Wilmington *(G-13080)*
Wireless Electronics Inc......................G...... 302 652-1301
  Wilmington *(G-13278)*

COMMUNICATIONS EQPT WHOLESALERS

Alliance International Elec...................G...... 302 838-3880
  Bear *(G-26)*
Microtune LP LLC...............................D...... 302 691-6037
  Wilmington *(G-11677)*

COMMUNICATIONS SVCS

Delmarva Communications Inc...........F...... 302 324-1230
  New Castle *(G-5244)*
Dynamic Packet Corp.........................F...... 302 448-2222
  Newark *(G-6484)*

COMMUNICATIONS SVCS: Data

Qbr Telecom Inc.................................F...... 302 510-1155
  Wilmington *(G-12274)*

COMMUNICATIONS SVCS, NEC

Bluestone Communication...................G...... 302 478-4200
  Wilmington *(G-9384)*
Cinemavericks Media LLC...................G...... 302 438-1144
  Wilmington *(G-9708)*
Clique Digital Media Mktg LLC.............G...... 305 704-2128
  Dover *(G-1294)*
Delaware First Media Corp..................G...... 302 857-7096
  Dover *(G-1370)*
Gai Communications Inc....................G...... 609 254-1470
  Newark *(G-6632)*
Influencers Lab Media LLC..................G...... 302 444-6990
  Wilmington *(G-11025)*
Jerry A Fletcher.................................G...... 302 875-9057
  Delmar *(G-1007)*
Legist Media Ltd.................................G...... 302 655-2730
  Wilmington *(G-11364)*
Phonecandiescom..............................G...... 215 385-1818
  Bear *(G-282)*
Rising Star Communication.................G...... 302 462-5474
  Seaford *(G-8379)*

COMMUNICATIONS SVCS: Cellular

Angle Wireless Wholesale LLC............G...... 302 883-7788
  Newark *(G-5969)*
Appa Inc...G...... 302 440-1448
  Dover *(G-1130)*
AT&T Corp..D...... 302 644-4529
  Rehoboth Beach *(G-7848)*
AT&T Mobility LLC.............................F...... 302 674-4888
  Dover *(G-1153)*
Cellco Partnership.............................G...... 302 530-4620
  Wilmington *(G-9611)*
Cellco Partnership.............................D...... 302 697-8340
  Camden *(G-547)*
Cellco Partnership.............................F...... 302 730-5200
  Dover *(G-1262)*
Cellco Partnership.............................G...... 302 653-8183
  Smyrna *(G-8592)*
Cellco Partnership.............................F...... 302 376-6049
  Middletown *(G-3983)*
Crossroads Wireless Holdg LLC..........E...... 405 946-1200
  Wilmington *(G-9905)*
Grahams Wireless Solutions Inc..........F...... 717 943-0717
  Millsboro *(G-4698)*
New Cingular Wireless Svcs Inc..........F...... 302 999-0055
  Wilmington *(G-11854)*
New Cingular Wireless Svcs Inc..........F...... 302 762-1366
  Wilmington *(G-11855)*
Redi Call Corp...................................E...... 302 856-9000
  Georgetown *(G-2633)*
Sprint...G...... 302 261-8500
  Newark *(G-7475)*
Sprint Spectrum LP............................E...... 302 993-3700
  Wilmington *(G-12717)*
T-Mobile...G...... 302 652-7738
  Wilmington *(G-12846)*
T-Mobile Usa Inc................................G...... 302 644-7222
  Rehoboth Beach *(G-8094)*
T-Mobile Usa Inc................................G...... 302 736-1980
  Dover *(G-2128)*
T-Mobile Usa Inc................................F...... 302 838-4500
  Bear *(G-345)*
Tdp Wireless Inc................................F...... 302 424-1900
  Dover *(G-2133)*
Verizon Communications Inc..............F...... 302 324-1385
  New Castle *(G-5815)*
Verizon Delaware LLC........................C...... 302 571-1571
  Wilmington *(G-13062)*
Verizon Wireless Inc..........................G...... 302 737-5028
  Newark *(G-7651)*
Voyyp Inc..G...... 833 342-5667
  Newark *(G-7665)*
WER Wireless Inc..............................F...... 302 478-7748
  Wilmington *(G-13158)*
WER Wireless of Concord Inc.............F...... 302 478-7748
  Wilmington *(G-13159)*

COMMUNICATIONS SVCS: Data

ARINC Ctrl & Info Systems LLC..........G...... 302 658-7581
  Wilmington *(G-9129)*
Axxess Marine LLC............................G...... 954 225-1744
  Lewes *(G-3361)*
Epthi Inc...G...... 917 821-1935
  Wilmington *(G-10429)*

COMMUNICATIONS SVCS: Data

Losemynumbercom LLC ....G....... 302 778-9741
  Wilmington *(G-11438)*
Providence Media LLC ....G....... 302 715-1757
  Laurel *(G-3274)*

COMMUNICATIONS SVCS: Internet Connectivity Svcs

3d Internet Group Inc ....G....... 302 376-7900
  Middletown *(G-3925)*
7p Networks LLC ....F....... 938 777-7662
  Lewes *(G-3317)*
Brainbase Inc ....G....... 412 515-9000
  Wilmington *(G-9414)*
C & B Internet Services LLC ....G....... 302 384-9804
  Wilmington *(G-9520)*
Ewebvalet Co Inc ....G....... 302 893-0903
  Wilmington *(G-10455)*
Ing Bank Fsb ....G....... 302 255-3750
  Wilmington *(G-11029)*
Mgj Enterprises Inc ....E....... 866 525-8529
  Wilmington *(G-11652)*

COMMUNICATIONS SVCS: Internet Host Svcs

Clouto Inc ....G....... 302 966-9282
  Newark *(G-6252)*
Coastal Images Inc ....G....... 302 539-6001
  Fenwick Island *(G-2333)*
Host Integrado Inc ....G....... 277 326-6719
  Lewes *(G-3547)*
Intohost Inc ....F....... 888 567-2607
  Wilmington *(G-11070)*
Keep In Touch Systems Inc ....G....... 510 868-8088
  Wilmington *(G-11233)*
Lnh Inc ....F....... 302 731-4948
  Newark *(G-6945)*
Siteage LLC ....F....... 302 380-3709
  Lewes *(G-3746)*

COMMUNICATIONS SVCS: Online Svc Providers

New Concept Technologies LLC ....E....... 518 533-5367
  Wilmington *(G-11860)*
Notify Technology Inc ....G....... 505 818-5888
  Newark *(G-7139)*
Skynethostingnet Inc ....F....... 302 384-1784
  Wilmington *(G-12644)*
Studentup Inc ....G....... 951 427-7563
  Newark *(G-7497)*

COMMUNICATIONS SVCS: Phone Cable, Svcs, Land Or Submarine

Verizon Delaware LLC ....F....... 302 629-4502
  Seaford *(G-8430)*

COMMUNICATIONS SVCS: Proprietary Online Svcs Networks

Instanode Inc ....G....... 352 327-8872
  Wilmington *(G-11042)*

COMMUNICATIONS SVCS: Telephone, Broker

Globaltec Networks Inc ....G....... 646 321-8627
  Wilmington *(G-10732)*

COMMUNICATIONS SVCS: Telephone, Data

Alphasure Technologies ....G....... 302 992-0900
  Wilmington *(G-9032)*

COMMUNICATIONS SVCS: Telephone, Local

Verizon Delaware LLC ....C....... 302 571-1571
  Wilmington *(G-13062)*

COMMUNICATIONS SVCS: Telephone, Local & Long Distance

MCI Communications Corporation ..F....... 302 791-4900
  Wilmington *(G-11598)*
Spring Communications Inc ....G....... 302 475-1052
  Wilmington *(G-12713)*
Sprint Communications Inc ....E....... 302 613-4004
  New Castle *(G-5731)*
Sprint Communications Inc ....E....... 302 604-6125
  Georgetown *(G-2664)*
Sprint Spectrum LP ....E....... 302 393-2060
  Milford *(G-4568)*
Sprint Spectrum LP ....E....... 302 322-1712
  New Castle *(G-5732)*
Telco Envirotrols Inc ....F....... 302 846-9103
  Delmar *(G-1036)*

COMMUNICATIONS SVCS: Telephone, Long Distance

C4-Nvis USA LLC ....G....... 213 465-5089
  Dover *(G-1246)*
Firing Distance ....G....... 302 337-9094
  Bridgeville *(G-471)*
Sigma Telecom LLC ....E....... 347 741-8397
  Wilmington *(G-12612)*

COMMUNICATIONS SVCS: Telephone, Voice

Alcatel-Lucent USA Inc ....E....... 302 529-3900
  Wilmington *(G-9003)*
Progressive Telecom LLC ....E....... 302 883-8883
  Wilmington *(G-12245)*

COMMUNITY ACTION AGENCY

Pathways of Delaware Inc ....D....... 302 573-5073
  Wilmington *(G-12032)*

COMMUNITY CENTER

Achieve Solutions ....G....... 302 598-1457
  Hockessin *(G-2950)*
Bellevue Community Center ....G....... 302 429-5859
  Wilmington *(G-9288)*
Bernard ND Ruth Siegel Jcc ....D....... 302 478-5660
  Wilmington *(G-9307)*
Bfpe International Inc ....F....... 302 346-4800
  Dover *(G-1200)*
Cancer Support Cmnty Del Inc ......G....... 302 995-2850
  Wilmington *(G-9549)*
Christiana Community Ctr Inc ....G....... 302 353-6796
  Christiana *(G-666)*
Claymont Community Center Inc ..E....... 302 792-2757
  Claymont *(G-721)*
Connections Community Support ..E....... 302 659-0512
  Townsend *(G-8773)*
Harrison Hse Cmnty Prgrams Inc ..G....... 302 427-8438
  New Castle *(G-5375)*
Jewish Community Center Inc ......E....... 302 478-5660
  Wilmington *(G-11152)*
Latin American Cmnty Ctr Corp ....D....... 302 655-7338
  Wilmington *(G-11336)*
Metropltan Wlmngton Urban Leag ..G....... 302 778-8300
  Wilmington *(G-11650)*
Neighborhood House Inc ....F....... 302 658-5404
  Wilmington *(G-11830)*
Precious Moments Edu ....F....... 302 697-9374
  Dover *(G-1979)*
South Coastal ....G....... 302 542-5668
  Frankford *(G-2389)*
William Hcks Andrson Cmnty Ctr ..E....... 302 571-4266
  Wilmington *(G-13213)*

COMMUNITY CENTERS: Adult

Absalom Jones Senior Center ....G....... 302 998-0363
  Wilmington *(G-8909)*
Brandy Wine Senior Center ....G....... 302 798-5562
  Claymont *(G-704)*
Brandywine Assisted Living ....B....... 302 436-0808
  Selbyville *(G-8460)*
Bridgeville Senior Center ....G....... 302 337-8771
  Bridgeville *(G-456)*
Cape Henlopen Senior Center ....G....... 302 227-2055
  Rehoboth Beach *(G-7883)*
Cheer Inc ....F....... 302 856-5641
  Georgetown *(G-2467)*
Cheer Inc ....G....... 302 645-9239
  Lewes *(G-3412)*
Claymore Senior Center Inc ....G....... 302 428-3170
  Wilmington *(G-9735)*
Delaware Senior Olympics Inc ....G....... 302 736-5698
  Dover *(G-1390)*
Division Svcs For Agng Adlts ....E....... 302 255-9390
  New Castle *(G-5255)*
Frederica Senior Center Inc ....G....... 302 335-4555
  Frederica *(G-2402)*
Harrington Senior Center Inc ....G....... 302 398-4224
  Harrington *(G-2847)*
Howard Weston Senior Center ......G....... 302 328-6425
  New Castle *(G-5406)*
Laurel Senior Center Inc ....G....... 302 875-2536
  Laurel *(G-3256)*
Lewes Senior Citizens Center ....G....... 302 645-9293
  Lewes *(G-3604)*
M O T Senior Citizen Center ....F....... 302 378-3041
  Middletown *(G-4138)*
Middltown Odssa Twnsend Snior ..G....... 302 378-4758
  Middletown *(G-4163)*
Milford Senior Center Inc ....F....... 302 422-3385
  Milford *(G-4504)*
Modern Maturity Center Inc ....C....... 302 734-1200
  Dover *(G-1869)*
New Castle Senior Center ....G....... 302 326-4209
  New Castle *(G-5565)*
Newark Senior Center Inc ....E....... 302 737-2336
  Newark *(G-7128)*
Oak Grove Senior Center Inc ....G....... 302 998-3319
  Wilmington *(G-11927)*
Retired Senior Volunteer ....G....... 610 565-5563
  Wilmington *(G-12395)*
Rose Hill Community Center ....F....... 302 656-8513
  New Castle *(G-5684)*
Salvation Army ....D....... 302 656-1696
  Wilmington *(G-12529)*
Sellers Senior Center Inc ....G....... 302 762-2050
  Wilmington *(G-12576)*
Senior Nanticoke Center Inc ....F....... 302 629-4939
  Seaford *(G-8396)*
St Patrick Center Inc ....G....... 302 652-6219
  Wilmington *(G-12728)*
Wilmington Senior Center Inc ....E....... 302 651-3400
  Wilmington *(G-13257)*

COMMUNITY CENTERS: Youth

Big Brthers Big Sisters of Del ....F....... 302 998-3577
  Wilmington *(G-9331)*
Girl Scouts of The Cheasapea ....E....... 302 456-7150
  Newark *(G-6656)*
Urbanpromise Wilmington Inc ....F....... 302 425-5502
  Wilmington *(G-13036)*

COMMUNITY DEVELOPMENT GROUPS

Central Delaware Habitat For ....G....... 302 526-2366
  Dover *(G-1267)*
Connections Community Support ..E....... 302 654-7120
  Wilmington *(G-9827)*
Cornerstone West Cmnty Dev Co ..G....... 302 658-4171
  Wilmington *(G-9863)*
Coverdale Community Council ......G....... 302 337-7179
  Bridgeville *(G-461)*
Delaware Center For Justice ....F....... 302 658-7174
  Wilmington *(G-10013)*
Eastside Bluprt Cmnty Dev Corp ..F....... 302 384-2350
  Wilmington *(G-10329)*
Family Outrch Multi-Purpse Com ..G....... 302 422-2158
  Lincoln *(G-3847)*
Food Bank of Delaware Inc ....E....... 302 424-3301
  Milford *(G-4416)*
Food Bank of Delaware Inc ....E....... 302 292-1305
  Newark *(G-6598)*
Health & Social Svcs Del Dept ......E....... 302 552-3530
  Wilmington *(G-10868)*
Loris Hands Inc ....G....... 302 440-5454
  Newark *(G-6950)*
Uzuakoli Dev & Cultural Assn ....G....... 302 465-3266
  Dover *(G-2185)*
West Rhoboth Cmnty Land Tr Inc ..G....... 302 260-9519
  Rehoboth Beach *(G-8112)*
Wilmington Renaissance Corp ....G....... 302 425-5500
  Wilmington *(G-13243)*

COMMUNITY SVCS EMPLOYMENT TRAINING PROGRAM

Delmarva Clergy United Inc ....F....... 302 422-2350
  Ellendale *(G-2259)*

COMMUNITY THEATER PRODUCTION SVCS

Friends of Capitol Theater Inc ....G....... 302 678-3583
  Dover *(G-1570)*

COMPACT LASER DISCS: Prerecorded

Saregama India Limited ....G....... 859 490-0156
  Newark *(G-7390)*

PRODUCT & SERVICES SECTION

COMPOST
Peninsula Compost Company LLC ...... G 215 595-4218
  New Castle *(G-5612)*

COMPRESSORS, AIR CONDITIONING: Wholesalers
Kompressed Air Delaware Inc ...... G 302 275-1985
  New Castle *(G-5469)*

COMPRESSORS: Air & Gas
De Sales and Service ...... G 302 456-1660
  Newark *(G-6354)*
Easy Lawn Inc ...... E 302 815-6500
  Greenwood *(G-2736)*
Linne Industries LLC ...... G 302 454-1439
  Newark *(G-6938)*

COMPRESSORS: Repairing
Keene Enterprises Inc ...... G 302 422-2856
  Ellendale *(G-2261)*
Kompressed Air Delaware Inc ...... G 302 275-1985
  New Castle *(G-5469)*

COMPRESSORS: Wholesalers
Jorc Industrial LLC ...... G 302 395-0310
  New Castle *(G-5443)*
Kaeser Compressors Inc ...... G 410 242-8793
  New Castle *(G-5449)*

COMPUTER & COMPUTER SOFTWARE STORES
Amdisvet LLC ...... G 302 514-9130
  Smyrna *(G-8568)*
Antenna House Inc ...... G 302 427-2456
  Newark *(G-5973)*
Bits & Bytes Inc ...... G 302 674-2999
  Dover *(G-1207)*
Biz TEC Inc ...... G 302 227-1967
  Rehoboth Beach *(G-7870)*
Cadapult Ltd ...... F 302 733-0477
  Newark *(G-6143)*
Cyberdaptive Inc ...... G 302 388-3506
  Newark *(G-6336)*
Gamestop Inc ...... F 302 266-7362
  Newark *(G-6637)*
Response Computer Group Inc ...... F 302 335-3400
  Milford *(G-4540)*
Secure Data Cmpt Solutions Inc ...... G 302 346-7327
  Dover *(G-2065)*

COMPUTER & COMPUTER SOFTWARE STORES: Peripheral Eqpt
Creative Micro Designs Inc ...... G 302 456-5800
  Newark *(G-6314)*
Diamond Computer Inc ...... G 302 674-4064
  Dover *(G-1420)*
PC Supplies Inc ...... G 302 368-4800
  Newark *(G-7189)*
Tower Business Machines Inc ...... G 302 395-1445
  New Castle *(G-5780)*

COMPUTER & COMPUTER SOFTWARE STORES: Personal Computers
Quinn Data Corporation ...... G 302 429-7450
  Wilmington *(G-12289)*

COMPUTER & COMPUTER SOFTWARE STORES: Software & Access
Aspenologies LLC ...... G 302 234-4346
  Wilmington *(G-9153)*
Computers Fixed Today ...... G 302 724-6411
  Wilmington *(G-9807)*
Laser Images of Delaware Inc ...... G 302 836-8610
  Bear *(G-229)*

COMPUTER & COMPUTER SOFTWARE STORES: Software, Bus/Non-Game
Altr Solutions LLC ...... F 888 757-2587
  Dover *(G-1114)*
Famoid Technology LLC ...... G 530 601-7284
  New Castle *(G-5303)*

Mtc Usa LLC ...... F 980 999-8888
  Newark *(G-7069)*
Singular Key Inc ...... F 408 753-5848
  Wilmington *(G-12631)*

COMPUTER & DATA PROCESSING EQPT REPAIR & MAINTENANCE
Confluent Corporation ...... G 301 440-4100
  Georgetown *(G-2481)*
Laser Images of Delaware Inc ...... G 302 836-8610
  Bear *(G-229)*
Motto Computer Inc ...... G 302 633-6783
  Wilmington *(G-11763)*
PC Supplies Inc ...... G 302 368-4800
  Newark *(G-7189)*
Response Computer Group Inc ...... F 302 335-3400
  Milford *(G-4540)*
Secure Data Cmpt Solutions Inc ...... G 302 346-7327
  Dover *(G-2065)*
Steven Abdill ...... G 443 243-6864
  Wilmington *(G-12758)*

COMPUTER & OFFICE MACHINE MAINTENANCE & REPAIR
Access Versalign Inc ...... G 302 225-7800
  Wilmington *(G-8914)*
Biz TEC Inc ...... G 302 227-1967
  Rehoboth Beach *(G-7870)*
Coastal It Consulting ...... G 302 226-9395
  Rehoboth Beach *(G-7893)*
Computer Jocks ...... G 302 544-6448
  Bear *(G-81)*
Curvature Inc ...... G 302 525-9525
  Newark *(G-6328)*
Diamond Computer Inc ...... G 302 674-4064
  Dover *(G-1420)*
Eagle Eye America Inc ...... G 302 392-3600
  Bear *(G-134)*
First Tech ...... E 302 421-3650
  Wilmington *(G-10557)*
Software Services of De Inc ...... G 302 654-3172
  Wilmington *(G-12672)*
Tech Impact ...... F 302 256-5015
  Wilmington *(G-12867)*
Teleplan Vdeocom Solutions Inc ...... F 302 323-8503
  New Castle *(G-5760)*
Tower Business Machines Inc ...... G 302 395-1445
  New Castle *(G-5780)*
Zerowait Corporation ...... F 302 996-9408
  Wilmington *(G-13349)*

COMPUTER & SFTWR STORE: Modem, Monitor, Terminal/Disk Drive
Shore Consultants Ltd ...... F 302 737-3375
  Newark *(G-7417)*
Software Services of De Inc ...... E 302 654-3172
  Wilmington *(G-12672)*

COMPUTER FACILITIES MANAGEMENT SVCS
Absolute Computer Support LLC ...... E 717 917-8900
  Newark *(G-5887)*
Datatech Enterprises Inc ...... F 540 370-0010
  Selbyville *(G-8478)*
Herbert R Martin Associates ...... G 302 239-1700
  Hockessin *(G-3046)*
Information Safeguard Inc ...... G 410 604-2660
  Wilmington *(G-11027)*
Insight Engineering Solutions ...... G 302 378-4842
  Townsend *(G-8797)*
Veteran It Pro LLC ...... F 302 824-3111
  Hockessin *(G-3167)*

COMPUTER GRAPHICS SVCS
Cadrender LLC ...... G 302 657-0700
  Wilmington *(G-9532)*
Cgs Infotech Inc ...... E 302 351-2434
  Wilmington *(G-9623)*
Fine Line It Consulting LLP ...... G 302 645-4549
  Lewes *(G-3496)*
Infinity Intellectuals Inc ...... C 302 565-4830
  Newark *(G-6778)*
Mobius New Media Inc ...... G 302 475-9880
  Wilmington *(G-11719)*
My Qme Inc ...... E 302 218-8730
  Wilmington *(G-11789)*

COMPUTER PROGRAMMING SVCS

Professionsale Inc ...... G 646 262-9101
  Bear *(G-293)*
SM Technomine Inc ...... F 312 492-4386
  Wilmington *(G-12647)*
Techno Goober ...... F 302 645-7177
  Lewes *(G-3780)*
Web N App LLC ...... G 810 309-8242
  Smyrna *(G-8741)*

COMPUTER HARDWARE REQUIREMENTS ANALYSIS
34m LLC ...... E 302 444-8290
  Newark *(G-5857)*
Genesec Inc ...... G 917 656-5742
  Claymont *(G-751)*

COMPUTER PERIPHERAL EQPT REPAIR & MAINTENANCE
Technicare Inc ...... G 302 322-7766
  Newark *(G-7545)*

COMPUTER PERIPHERAL EQPT, NEC
Creative Micro Designs Inc ...... G 302 456-5800
  Newark *(G-6314)*
East Coast Games Inc ...... F 302 838-0669
  Bear *(G-136)*
Hewlett-Packard World Trade ...... E 877 424-4536
  Wilmington *(G-10898)*
Xerox Corporation ...... G 585 422-0272
  Wilmington *(G-13318)*

COMPUTER PERIPHERAL EQPT, WHOLESALE
Bb Technologies Inc ...... G 302 652-2300
  Wilmington *(G-9268)*
Broadberry Data Systems LLC ...... E 302 295-1086
  Wilmington *(G-9481)*
Broadberry Data Systems LLC ...... G 800 496-9918
  Wilmington *(G-9482)*
Hoover Computer Services Inc ...... G 302 529-7050
  Wilmington *(G-10950)*
Hypertec Usa Inc ...... G 480 626-9000
  Dover *(G-1664)*
Iconic Tsunami LLC ...... G 302 223-3411
  Smyrna *(G-8657)*
Lan Rack Inc ...... G 949 587-5168
  Dover *(G-1764)*
PC Supplies Inc ...... G 302 368-4800
  Newark *(G-7189)*

COMPUTER PLOTTERS
Ametek Inc ...... D 302 456-4400
  Newark *(G-5962)*

COMPUTER PROCESSING SVCS
Hangster Inc ...... G 619 871-8005
  Wilmington *(G-10833)*
Hap LLC ...... G 302 645-7400
  Lewes *(G-3531)*

COMPUTER PROGRAMMING SVCS
Biomedic Data Systems Inc ...... A 302 628-4100
  Seaford *(G-8171)*
Boxhero Inc ...... G 827 867-4320
  Middletown *(G-3971)*
Channelpro Mobile LLC ...... F 757 620-4635
  Newark *(G-6188)*
Cim Concepts Incorporated ...... F 302 613-5400
  New Castle *(G-5161)*
Clymene LLC ...... G 888 679-3310
  Lewes *(G-3433)*
Commtrak Corporation ...... G 302 644-1600
  Lewes *(G-3443)*
Compassred Inc ...... G 302 383-2856
  Wilmington *(G-9803)*
Conci LLC ...... D 847 665-9285
  Wilmington *(G-9808)*
Congruence Consulting Group ...... G 320 290-6155
  Newark *(G-6286)*
Covant Solutions Inc ...... G 302 607-2678
  Newark *(G-6307)*
Cratis Solutions Inc ...... G 515 423-7259
  Dover *(G-1320)*
Datatech Enterprises Inc ...... F 540 370-0010
  Selbyville *(G-8478)*

COMPUTER PROGRAMMING SVCS

Discidium Technology Inc..................G...... 347 220-5979
  Newark *(G-6455)*
Eagle Eye America Inc........................G...... 302 392-3600
  Bear *(G-134)*
Ftl Technologies Corporation...............F...... 703 873-7801
  Lewes *(G-3505)*
Hoover Computer Services Inc............G...... 302 529-7050
  Wilmington *(G-10950)*
Itango Inc..G...... 302 648-2646
  Wilmington *(G-11091)*
Jsi Group LLC.....................................G...... 267 582-5850
  Hockessin *(G-3070)*
Maestrik Inc...E...... 312 925-3116
  Newark *(G-6971)*
Myschedule Inc....................................G...... 877 235-6825
  Wilmington *(G-11790)*
Naiva Solutions Inc..............................G...... 612 987-6350
  Newark *(G-7082)*
Nationwide Hlth Info Tech Inc..............G...... 302 295-5033
  Wilmington *(G-11815)*
Ninety One Holding Inc.......................E...... 212 203-7900
  Bethany Beach *(G-418)*
Noble Master..G...... 302 261-2018
  Lewes *(G-3660)*
PLM Consulting Inc..............................F...... 302 984-2698
  Wilmington *(G-12160)*
Progressive Software Cmpt Inc............C...... 302 479-9700
  Wilmington *(G-12244)*
Sumuri LLC..G...... 302 570-0015
  Camden *(G-601)*
Technosecure Corporation...................E...... 732 302-9005
  Bear *(G-350)*
Town of Middletown.............................G...... 302 378-2711
  Middletown *(G-4265)*
Town of Middletown.............................E...... 302 376-9950
  Middletown *(G-4264)*
US Telex Corporation...........................E...... 302 652-2707
  Wilmington *(G-13040)*
Vedaham Inc...F...... 302 250-4594
  Wilmington *(G-13055)*
Vensoft LLC..G...... 302 392-9000
  Wilmington *(G-13057)*
Veteran It Pro LLC................................F...... 302 824-3111
  Hockessin *(G-3167)*

COMPUTER PROGRAMMING SVCS: Custom

Applied Control Engrg Inc....................D...... 302 738-8800
  Newark *(G-5987)*
Cloud Software Development LLC.......G...... 703 957-9847
  Wilmington *(G-9747)*
Dream Weaver LLC..............................G...... 302 352-9473
  Wilmington *(G-10232)*
Kissflow Inc..C...... 650 396-7692
  Wilmington *(G-11276)*
Mssgme Inc..G...... 786 233-7592
  Dover *(G-1877)*
Server Management LLC.....................G...... 302 300-1745
  Wilmington *(G-12584)*
Software Services of De Inc.................E...... 302 654-3172
  Wilmington *(G-12672)*
Z Data Inc..G...... 302 566-5351
  Newark *(G-7734)*

COMPUTER RELATED MAINTENANCE SVCS

Antenna House Inc..............................G...... 302 427-2456
  Newark *(G-5973)*
Conectiv Communications Inc............E...... 302 224-1177
  Newark *(G-6282)*
Eagle Eye America Inc........................G...... 302 392-3600
  Bear *(G-134)*
Gmg Solutions LLC.............................E...... 302 781-3008
  Wilmington *(G-10734)*
Nspire Automation LLC.......................G...... 404 545-0821
  Wilmington *(G-11917)*
Ram Tech Systems Inc.......................G...... 302 832-6600
  Middletown *(G-4210)*
Securenetmd LLC................................E...... 302 645-7770
  Lewes *(G-3736)*
Symbiosys Consulting LLC..................F...... 302 507-7649
  Wilmington *(G-12830)*
Threatstop Inc......................................F...... 760 542-1550
  Dover *(G-2146)*
University of Delaware.........................C...... 302 831-6041
  Newark *(G-7621)*
Verito Technologies LLC......................F...... 855 583-7486
  Wilmington *(G-13061)*

COMPUTER RELATED SVCS, NEC

Digital Technology...............................F...... 416 829-8400
  Wilmington *(G-10153)*
Licensing Assurance LLC.....................F...... 305 851-3545
  Lewes *(G-3607)*
Naiva Solutions Inc..............................G...... 612 987-6350
  Newark *(G-7082)*
Network Security Services Inc.............F...... 703 319-0411
  Dover *(G-1895)*
Swit Inc..C...... 302 792-0175
  Wilmington *(G-12826)*

COMPUTER SERVICE BUREAU

Ipr International LLC...........................E...... 302 304-8774
  Wilmington *(G-11080)*
Wilkinson Technology Svcs LLC..........G...... 302 384-7770
  Wilmington *(G-13204)*

COMPUTER SOFTWARE DEVELOPMENT

Agora Net Inc.......................................F...... 302 224-2475
  Newark *(G-5920)*
Ampx2 Inc..G...... 650 521-5750
  Dover *(G-1121)*
Antitoxin Technologies Inc...................G...... 650 304-0608
  Dover *(G-1129)*
ARA Technologies Inc..........................G...... 215 605-5707
  Wilmington *(G-9109)*
Aum LLC...F...... 302 385-6767
  Wilmington *(G-9182)*
Autoweb Technologies Inc..................G...... 443 485-4200
  Wilmington *(G-9192)*
Bar Code Software Inc........................G...... 410 360-7455
  Frankford *(G-2346)*
Blair Computing Systems Inc..............F...... 302 453-8947
  Newark *(G-6091)*
Blaze Systems Corporation................G...... 302 733-7235
  Newark *(G-6092)*
Breckenridge Software Tech...............G...... 302 656-8460
  Wilmington *(G-9464)*
Brittons Wise Computers Inc..............G...... 302 659-0343
  Smyrna *(G-8587)*
Bryant Technologies Inc.....................G...... 302 289-2044
  Felton *(G-2276)*
Buzlin Inc...G...... 800 829-0115
  Camden *(G-542)*
Chemaxon LLC....................................G...... 281 528-0485
  Wilmington *(G-9645)*
Cloudbees Inc......................................F...... 323 842-7783
  Lewes *(G-3431)*
Codeship Inc..F...... 617 515-3664
  Lewes *(G-3440)*
Collections Marketing Center..............E...... 302 830-9262
  Wilmington *(G-9769)*
Conrep Inc...G...... 302 528-8383
  Middletown *(G-4007)*
Continuum Media LLC.........................G...... 310 295-9997
  Camden *(G-552)*
Corvant LLC...F...... 302 299-1570
  Newark *(G-6302)*
Dekadu Inc...G...... 763 390-3266
  Wilmington *(G-9996)*
DOE Technologies Inc.........................E...... 302 792-1285
  Wilmington *(G-10181)*
Endevor LLC..G...... 302 543-5055
  Wilmington *(G-10397)*
English Tech LLC.................................G...... 844 707-9904
  Dover *(G-1524)*
Epiq Systems Inc.................................E...... 302 574-2600
  Wilmington *(G-10426)*
Epotec Inc..C...... 302 654-3090
  Wilmington *(G-10427)*
Et International Inc...............................F...... 302 266-6426
  Newark *(G-6541)*
Giesela Inc...G...... 855 556-4338
  Newark *(G-6653)*
Got Health-E LLC................................G...... 203 583-5447
  Wilmington *(G-10755)*
Gw Solutions LLC................................G...... 240 578-5981
  Bethany Beach *(G-402)*
Healex Systems Ltd............................G...... 302 235-5750
  Wilmington *(G-10866)*
Horizon Systems Inc............................G...... 302 983-3203
  New Castle *(G-5404)*
Hubgets Inc..G...... 239 206-2995
  Wilmington *(G-10970)*
Hypergames Inc..................................G...... 424 343-6370
  Wilmington *(G-10982)*
Imagine Technologies..........................F...... 240 428-8406
  Newark *(G-6767)*

Implify Inc..E...... 302 533-2345
  Newark *(G-6769)*
Intelligent Systems Inc........................G...... 302 388-0566
  Newark *(G-6795)*
Inumsoft Inc...G...... 302 533-5403
  Bear *(G-191)*
Kortech Consulting Inc........................F...... 302 559-4612
  Bear *(G-220)*
Labware Inc...E...... 302 658-8444
  Wilmington *(G-11319)*
Live Typing Inc....................................E...... 415 670-9601
  Wilmington *(G-11412)*
Mentor Consultants Inc......................G...... 610 566-4004
  Wilmington *(G-11633)*
Microlog Corporation Maryland...........G...... 301 540-5501
  Rehoboth Beach *(G-8006)*
Microsoft Corporation.........................E...... 302 669-0200
  Newark *(G-7025)*
Moving Sciences LLC..........................G...... 617 871-9892
  Wilmington *(G-11764)*
Mymedchoices Inc...............................G...... 302 932-1920
  Hockessin *(G-3100)*
Omninet International Inc....................E...... 208 246-5022
  Wilmington *(G-11950)*
Pks & Company PA..............................G...... 302 645-5757
  Lewes *(G-3693)*
Polymorphic Software Inc....................G...... 786 612-0257
  Wilmington *(G-12185)*
Pxe Group LLC....................................G...... 561 295-1451
  Dover *(G-2000)*
Raas Infotek LLC.................................E...... 302 894-3184
  Newark *(G-7294)*
Rainmaker Software Group LLC..........G...... 800 616-6701
  Wilmington *(G-12307)*
Ritchie Sawyer Corporation................F...... 302 475-1971
  Wilmington *(G-12426)*
Rovier LLC...G...... 302 832-6726
  Newark *(G-7368)*
Safer Technologies LLC......................G...... 302 497-0333
  Wilmington *(G-12521)*
Scope One Inc.....................................G...... 415 429-9347
  Dover *(G-2061)*
Scorelogix LLC.....................................E...... 302 294-6532
  Newark *(G-7396)*
Supply Chain Consultants Inc.............E...... 302 738-9215
  Wilmington *(G-12812)*
Tech Central LLC.................................F...... 717 273-3301
  Wilmington *(G-12866)*
Toolook Inc..G...... 240 330-3307
  Wilmington *(G-12926)*
Touchstone Systems Inc.....................F...... 302 324-5322
  New Castle *(G-5779)*
Transactional Web Inc........................G...... 908 216-5054
  Wilmington *(G-12954)*
Trialogics LLC......................................F...... 302 313-9000
  Wilmington *(G-12969)*
True Intelligence Tech Inc...................G...... 979 209-0335
  Wilmington *(G-12987)*
Turnkey Lender Inc.............................G...... 888 299-4892
  Lewes *(G-3799)*
Volvant Inc...G...... 805 456-6464
  Wilmington *(G-13103)*
Vortex Labs LLC...................................G...... 302 231-1294
  Wilmington *(G-13104)*
We Cobble LLC....................................F...... 302 504-4294
  Wilmington *(G-13130)*
Web Applications Inc..........................G...... 302 834-0282
  Newark *(G-7680)*
Webstudy Inc.......................................G...... 888 326-4058
  Harbeson *(G-2802)*
Wgames Incorporated........................G...... 206 618-3699
  Wilmington *(G-13178)*
Xxl Cloud Inc.......................................G...... 302 298-0050
  Wilmington *(G-13324)*
Zenbanx Holding Ltd..........................G...... 310 749-3101
  Claymont *(G-829)*

COMPUTER SOFTWARE DEVELOPMENT & APPLICATIONS

1 Software Place..................................G...... 302 533-0344
  Newark *(G-5851)*
360tovisit Inc.......................................F...... 302 526-0575
  Newark *(G-5858)*
3rdgp LLC..G...... 905 330-3335
  Dover *(G-1069)*
A2ps Consulting and Sftwr LLC..........F...... 331 201-6101
  Wilmington *(G-8891)*
Accelertrain Company Limited...........G...... 413 599-0450
  Dover *(G-1079)*

PRODUCT & SERVICES SECTION — COMPUTER SOFTWARE DEVELOPMENT & APPLICATIONS

Company	Code	Phone
Adferns Media LLC — Dover (G-1086)	G	315 444-7720
Aila Pty Inc — Newark (G-5922)	E	626 693-0598
Angee Inc — Wilmington (G-9083)	E	650 320-1775
Animatra Inc — Lewes (G-3342)	G	303 350-9264
Annexus Health LLC — Wilmington (G-9087)	F	302 547-4154
Anotherai Inc — Lewes (G-3343)	G	408 987-1927
Apphive Inc — Newark (G-5984)	G	240 898-4661
Appic Stars LLC — Dover (G-1131)	G	903 224-6469
Apploye Inc — Newark (G-5989)	G	925 452-6102
Ask Connoisseur LLC — Claymont (G-695)	G	302 482-8026
Atoze Inc — Newark (G-6025)	G	415 992-7936
B&H Insurance LLC — Newark (G-6036)	E	302 995-2247
Babilonia Inc — Newark (G-6039)	G	415 237-3339
Bantam Technologies LLC — Wilmington (G-9245)	G	302 256-5823
Barclays PLC — Wilmington (G-9252)	E	302 622-8990
Bathwa Limited — New Castle (G-5068)	D	213 550-3812
Bbest LLC — Wilmington (G-9269)	F	302 581-9963
Birdie Ssot LLC — Dover (G-1205)	G	857 361-6883
Blix Inc — Newark (G-6094)	E	347 753-8035
Blu Dragon Studio Inc — Newark (G-6097)	G	302 722-6227
Bml App Development — Wilmington (G-9386)	G	302 528-7281
Bolt Innovation LLC — Dover (G-1220)	G	800 293-5249
Brown Eagle Inc — Wilmington (G-9489)	G	302 295-3816
Bsbv Inc — Lewes (G-3392)	G	631 201-2044
Bysness Inc — Wilmington (G-9518)	F	937 687-8701
Capture Technologies Inc — Wilmington (G-9559)	G	650 772-8006
Carzaty Inc — Dover (G-1258)	F	650 396-0144
Change Shop LLC — Newark (G-6187)	G	301 363-7188
Classroomapp Inc — Lewes (G-3426)	F	833 257-7761
Client Monster LLC — Newark (G-6250)	G	866 799-5433
Clinpharma Clinical RES LLC — Wilmington (G-9744)	G	646 961-3437
Construct App Inc — Wilmington (G-9834)	F	415 702-0634
Contact Info Inc — Dover (G-1312)	G	917 817-7939
Cubics Inc — Newark (G-6324)	G	302 261-5751
Cyber Seven Technologies LLC — Newark (G-6335)	G	302 635-7122
Data Age International LLC — Wilmington (G-9961)	E	302 760-9222
Data-Bi LLC — Wilmington (G-9962)	G	302 290-3138
Dax-Wave Consulting LLC — Wilmington (G-9974)	G	424 543-6662
DC Consulting Service LLC — Wilmington (G-9976)	F	617 594-9780
Delaware Beacon Network LLC — Wilmington (G-10006)	G	302 218-2755
Digital Penguin Inc — Newark (G-6448)	G	484 387-7803
Dining Software Group Inc — Camden (G-562)	G	720 236-9572
Drop Table LLC — Wilmington (G-10237)	G	650 669-8753
E2e LLC — Hockessin (G-3014)	G	703 906-5353
Ekalt LLC — Wilmington (G-10365)	G	302 300-4853
Epic Kings LLC — Claymont (G-739)	G	302 669-9018
Eventzilla Corporation — Wilmington (G-10444)	F	888 817-2837
Exa Solutions Inc — Newark (G-6548)	G	302 273-9320
Fabby Inc — Wilmington (G-10470)	F	408 891-7991
Famoid Technology LLC — New Castle (G-5303)	G	530 601-7284
Figgo Inc — Wilmington (G-6578)	F	734 560-1300
File Right LLC — Middletown (G-4070)	G	302 757-7107
Fitwise Inc — Middletown (G-4073)	G	812 929-2696
Fleek Inc — Wilmington (G-10572)	G	888 870-1291
Flowpay Corporation — Wilmington (G-10580)	G	720 425-3244
Franchise Command Inc — Newark (G-6611)	E	714 832-7767
Fx-Edge LLC — Lewes (G-3507)	E	718 404-9362
Gamers4gamers LLC — Newark (G-6636)	G	302 722-6289
Gatesair Inc — Wilmington (G-10676)	G	513 459-3400
Geo-Fence Inc — Lewes (G-1589)	G	763 516-8934
Getresponse Inc — Wilmington (G-10705)	G	302 573-3895
Ghg Enterprises LLC — Wilmington (G-10709)	G	817 705-0313
Gigkloud Inc — Lewes (G-3514)	F	301 375-5008
Global Exterior LLC — Middletown (G-4089)	G	302 722-1969
Golden Shell Corp — Dover (G-1599)	G	917 951-6118
Gossamer Games LLC — Lewes (G-3520)	G	302 645-7400
Gotit Inc — Dover (G-1602)	F	408 382-1300
Gyst Inc — Dover (G-1620)	G	631 680-4307
Har-Lex LLC — Wilmington (G-10835)	G	302 476-2322
Hashr8 Software LLC — Newark (G-6713)	G	702 473-0426
Hexact Inc — Newark (G-6726)	G	850 716-1616
Himalaya Trading Inc — Dover (G-1647)	G	702 833-0485
Homself Limited — Middletown (G-4108)	D	213 269-5469
Inbit Inc — Dover (G-1669)	G	302 603-7437
Infevo Technologies Co Ltd — Newark (G-6777)	G	626 703-8197
Informal Inc — Newark (G-6780)	G	415 504-2106
Innclude LLC — Wilmington (G-11037)	G	310 430-6552
Intouch Inc — Wilmington (G-11037)	G	302 313-2594
Intoyou Inc — Milford (G-4451)	G	818 309-5115
Iroi Management LLC — Lewes (G-3562)	F	516 373-5269
Itennisyou LLC — Newark (G-6810)	G	305 890-3234
Iveeapp Corp — Wilmington (G-11094)	G	610 999-6290
Ivychat Inc — Newark (G-6811)	F	201 567-5694
Joincube Inc — Dover (G-1706)	F	214 532-9997
Juni Holdings Inc — Wilmington (G-11209)	F	415 949-4860
Kaleido Health Solutions Inc — Wilmington (G-11221)	G	908 721-7020
Keyboarders LLC — Wilmington (G-11250)	G	302 438-8055
Keylent Inc — Wilmington (G-11251)	G	401 864-6498
Knowt Inc — Lewes (G-3585)	G	848 391-0575
Kwikbuck Inc — Wilmington (G-11305)	G	774 517-8959
Labware Global Services Inc — Wilmington (G-11321)	F	302 658-8444
Labware Holdings Inc — Wilmington (G-11322)	E	302 658-8444
LAp Studios Inc — Newark (G-6917)	F	213 357-0825
Lnbe LLC — Wilmington (G-11417)	G	302 393-2201
Loom Network Inc — Wilmington (G-11434)	G	404 939-1294
Lumulabs Inc — Newark (G-6957)	G	302 261-5284
Maan Softwares Inc — Lewes (G-3615)	E	531 203-9141
Made By Tilde Inc — Newark (G-6970)	G	302 766-7215
Madrona Labs Inc — Wilmington (G-11483)	G	216 375-1978
Makave International Trdg LLC — Dover (G-1812)	E	302 288-0670
Mara Labs Inc — Wilmington (G-11518)	E	650 564-4971
Mayjuun LLC — Lewes (G-3628)	G	865 300-7738
Medici Ventures Inc — Wilmington (G-11617)	G	801 319-7029
Metaquotes Software Corp — Wilmington (G-11648)	G	657 859-6918
Mican Technologies Inc — Bear (G-252)	G	302 703-0708
Microcom Tech LLC — Rehoboth Beach (G-8005)	G	858 775-5559
Middleware Inc — Wilmington (G-11683)	G	415 213-2625
Mightyinvoice LLC — Dover (G-1854)	G	302 415-3000
Minoti Inc — Lewes (G-3644)	F	720 725-0720
Miss Mafia LLC — Wilmington (G-11713)	G	800 246-2677
Mithril Cable Network Inc — Claymont (G-783)	F	213 373-4381
Mobile Alerts LLC — Dover (G-1867)	G	202 596-8709
Modern Masters Inc — Dover (G-1868)	G	240 800-6622
Morrow Limited — Montchanin (G-4987)	D	213 631-3534
Moscase Inc — Dover (G-1874)	G	786 520-8062
Must App Corp — Wilmington (G-11779)	F	905 537-5522
Neutec Corp — Dover (G-1896)	G	302 697-6752
New Concept Technologies LLC — Wilmington (G-11860)	E	518 533-5367
Next Music Inc — Wilmington (G-11881)	G	650 300-4881
Next Trucking Inc — Wilmington (G-11882)	E	213 568-0388
Novo Financial Corp — Dover (G-1906)	F	844 260-6800
Nvcomputers Inc — Wilmington (G-11924)	G	860 878-0525
Objects Worldwide Inc — Wilmington (G-11931)	G	703 623-7861
Omni Games Inc — Wilmington (G-11949)	F	302 652-4800
Orbeex Trading Inc — Wilmington (G-11970)	F	786 403-9124
Otw Technologies Inc — Dover (G-1926)	G	813 230-4212
Ovo Digital Services LLC — Wilmington (G-11986)	G	415 741-1615
Pathao Inc — Dover (G-1939)	G	845 242-3834
Pathscale Inc — Wilmington (G-12031)	E	408 520-0811
PDr Vc Ltd Liability Company — Wilmington (G-12056)	G	424 281-4669
Peeper Vehicle Technology Corp — Dover (G-1943)	G	800 971-4134
People Over Profit LLC — Dover (G-1947)	G	718 612-0328
Perkwiz Inc — Hockessin (G-3116)	G	702 866-9122
Petcube Inc — Wilmington (G-12093)	G	786 375-9065
Phly LLC — Wilmington (G-12122)	G	778 882-2391

Employee Codes: A=Over 500 employees, B=251-500 C=101-250, D=51-100, E=20-50, F=10-19, G=1-9

2020 Harris Directory of Delaware Businesses

Play US Media LLC ....G.... 302 924-5034
Dover *(G-1965)*
Playphone Inc ....G.... 415 307-0246
Dover *(G-1967)*
Playsight Interactive USA Inc ....F.... 800 246-2677
Wilmington *(G-12156)*
Pointlook Corporation ....G.... 415 448-6002
Wilmington *(G-12179)*
Precisioncure LLC ....G.... 302 622-9119
Wilmington *(G-12208)*
Project Assistants Inc ....E.... 302 477-9711
Wilmington *(G-12246)*
Protech Solutions Group LLC ....G.... 844 744-2418
Wilmington *(G-12254)*
Protocol Labs Inc ....F.... 302 703-7194
Wilmington *(G-12256)*
Purpose Ministries Inc ....G.... 302 753-0435
Newark *(G-7273)*
Qmobi Inc ....E.... 800 246-2677
Wilmington *(G-12275)*
Qsr Group LLC ....G.... 302 268-6909
Wilmington *(G-12276)*
Quavo Inc ....E.... 484 802-4693
Wilmington *(G-12284)*
Radiocut Inc ....G.... 302 613-1280
Wilmington *(G-12301)*
Rct Studio Inc ....G.... 669 255-1562
Wilmington *(G-12336)*
Reporting Solutions LLC ....G.... 857 284-3583
Newark *(G-7321)*
Royal Era LLC ....G.... 484 574-0260
Newark *(G-7369)*
Saferwatch LLC ....E.... 844 449-2824
Lewes *(G-3728)*
Sailnovo Limited ....D.... 213 550-3897
Dover *(G-2054)*
Scanta Inc ....E.... 302 645-7400
Lewes *(G-3732)*
Sensofusion Inc ....F.... 570 239-4912
Milton *(G-4967)*
Sherweb Inc ....G.... 888 567-6610
Newark *(G-7416)*
Shipshap LLC ....G.... 425 298-5215
Middletown *(G-4240)*
Shouldr LLC ....G.... 917 331-1384
Lewes *(G-3741)*
Singular Key Inc ....F.... 408 753-5848
Wilmington *(G-12631)*
Sitengle Technology LLC ....F.... 719 822-0710
Dover *(G-2086)*
Sketches and Pixels LLC ....G.... 312 834-4402
Newark *(G-7435)*
Skinary App Inc ....G.... 773 744-5407
Middletown *(G-4242)*
Smartstudents LLC ....G.... 302 597-6586
Wilmington *(G-12655)*
Softmogul Inc ....G.... 414 426-1650
Wilmington *(G-12671)*
Spearhead Inc ....G.... 347 670-2699
Bear *(G-331)*
Speedrid Ltd ....D.... 213 550-5462
Dover *(G-2097)*
Sqrin Technologies LLC ....G.... 540 330-1379
Lewes *(G-3761)*
Stylelabs Inc ....E.... 347 674-7993
Wilmington *(G-12782)*
Subcodevs Inc ....G.... 704 234-6780
Wilmington *(G-12784)*
Surge Networks Inc ....G.... 206 432-5047
Newark *(G-7515)*
Swit Inc ....C.... 302 792-0175
Wilmington *(G-12826)*
Sygul Inc ....E.... 315 384-1848
Newark *(G-7524)*
Tabella Inc ....G.... 415 799-2389
Newark *(G-7528)*
Thinkruptive Media Inc ....F.... 310 779-4748
Dover *(G-2142)*
Tiki Interactive Inc ....G.... 408 306-4393
Lewes *(G-3785)*
Toptracker LLC ....B.... 415 230-0131
Wilmington *(G-12934)*
Truck Lagbe Inc ....E.... 860 810-8677
Lewes *(G-3795)*
True Life Church Newark Inc ....G.... 302 283-9003
Bear *(G-361)*
Twyne Inc ....G.... 213 675-9518
Camden *(G-603)*
U Scope Solutions LLC ....F.... 844 872-6732
Wilmington *(G-13003)*
Uno Messenger LLC ....G.... 513 703-8091
Wilmington *(G-13033)*
Vam Apps Co ....G.... 786 220-4826
Wilmington *(G-13046)*
Veristuffcom Inc ....G.... 972 545-2434
Wilmington *(G-13060)*
Vertigo Group Inc ....F.... 302 298-0825
Wilmington *(G-13068)*
Vertrius Corp ....F.... 800 770-1913
Lewes *(G-3808)*
Vew Technologies Inc ....G.... 310 560-3814
Wilmington *(G-13073)*
Vpn Vpn Vpn Proxy ....G.... 415 758-8354
Lewes *(G-3810)*
W23 S12 Holdings LLC ....G.... 610 348-3825
Wilmington *(G-13110)*
Wabisabi Design Inc ....G.... 650 451-8501
Newark *(G-7673)*
Wallor Wearables LLC ....G.... 505 310-6099
Lewes *(G-3814)*
Webbrowser Media Inc ....G.... 302 830-3664
Wilmington *(G-13134)*
Whitaker LLC ....G.... 302 633-2740
Wilmington *(G-13187)*
Windy Weather World Inc ....G.... 650 204-7941
Claymont *(G-823)*
Workplace Rebels LLC ....G.... 917 771-8286
Dover *(G-2237)*
Workweek Inc ....G.... 423 708-4565
Dover *(G-2238)*
Wutap LLC ....G.... 610 457-3559
Newark *(G-7725)*
Wutopia Group US Ltd ....F.... 302 488-0248
Dover *(G-2241)*
Xerafy Inc ....G.... 817 938-4197
Wilmington *(G-13317)*
Yello Technologies Inc ....G.... 954 802-6089
Lewes *(G-3833)*
Youshop Inc ....E.... 302 526-0521
Dover *(G-2249)*
Youyu Home Technology LLC ....F.... 347 796-4305
Wilmington *(G-13336)*
Z Data Inc ....G.... 302 566-5351
Newark *(G-7735)*
Zilpa Ltd ....G.... 800 504-5368
Wilmington *(G-13351)*
Zir LLC ....G.... 203 524-1215
Lewes *(G-3835)*
Zumra Solutions LLC ....G.... 302 504-4423
Lewes *(G-3836)*

COMPUTER SOFTWARE SYSTEMS ANALYSIS & DESIGN: Custom

Afrikelist Corporation ....F.... 800 767-1744
Wilmington *(G-8974)*
Ardexo Inc ....G.... 855 617-7500
Dover *(G-1134)*
Aries Security LLC ....G.... 302 365-0026
Wilmington *(G-9128)*
Bits & Bytes Inc ....G.... 302 674-2999
Dover *(G-1207)*
Booking Bullet Inc ....G.... 416 988-2354
Newark *(G-6106)*
Computer Aid Inc ....C.... 302 831-5500
Newark *(G-6276)*
Decisivedge LLC ....G.... 302 299-1570
Newark *(G-6357)*
Done Again Software LLC ....G.... 301 466-7858
Lewes *(G-3469)*
Encross LLC ....F.... 302 351-2593
Wilmington *(G-10396)*
Extreme Scale Solutions LLC ....F.... 302 540-7149
Newark *(G-6558)*
Fabit Corp ....G.... 832 217-0864
Wilmington *(G-10471)*
Four Point Solutions Ltd ....E.... 613 907-6400
Wilmington *(G-10605)*
Gulch Group LLC ....G.... 202 697-1756
Rehoboth Beach *(G-7956)*
Inclind Inc ....G.... 302 856-2802
Lewes *(G-3556)*
Insight Engineering Solutions ....G.... 302 378-4842
Townsend *(G-8797)*
Lamed LLC ....G.... 302 597-9018
Newark *(G-6914)*
Pike Creek Computer Company ....F.... 302 239-5113
Wilmington *(G-12137)*
Polar Strategy Inc ....G.... 703 628-0001
Lewes *(G-3695)*
Professionals LLC ....G.... 302 295-2330
Wilmington *(G-12240)*
Ram Tech Systems Inc ....E.... 302 832-6600
Middletown *(G-4210)*
Rockey & Associates Inc ....G.... 610 640-4880
Lewes *(G-3723)*
Sain Cosmos LLC ....F.... 936 244-7017
Wilmington *(G-12523)*
Shore Consultants Ltd ....F.... 302 737-3375
Newark *(G-7417)*
Trifecta Health Solutions Inc ....G.... 614 582-4184
Middletown *(G-4268)*

COMPUTER SOFTWARE WRITERS

Foxfire Industries LLC ....G.... 817 602-4900
Newark *(G-6609)*
Severn Trent Inc ....E.... 302 427-5990
Wilmington *(G-12588)*
Tandem Hosted Resources Inc ....F.... 302 740-7099
Newark *(G-7537)*
Unite USA Inc ....E.... 609 915-9130
Wilmington *(G-13020)*

COMPUTER SOFTWARE WRITERS: Freelance

Cell Point LLC ....D.... 302 658-9200
Wilmington *(G-9610)*
Writingwizards Inc ....G.... 650 382-1357
Lewes *(G-3830)*

COMPUTER STORAGE DEVICES, NEC

Hewlett-Packard World Trade ....E.... 877 424-4536
Wilmington *(G-10898)*
Quantum Corporation ....G.... 302 737-7012
Newark *(G-7284)*
Zerowait Corporation ....F.... 302 996-9408
Wilmington *(G-13349)*

COMPUTER SYSTEMS ANALYSIS & DESIGN

Applied Control Engrg Inc ....D.... 302 738-8800
Newark *(G-5987)*
Cloudxperts LLC ....G.... 302 257-5686
Dover *(G-1295)*
Congruence Consulting Group ....G.... 320 290-6155
Newark *(G-6286)*
Indelible Blue Inc ....F.... 302 231-5200
Lewes *(G-3557)*
Vel Micro Works Incorporated ....G.... 302 239-4661
Hockessin *(G-3166)*
Xcs Corporation ....G.... 302 514-0600
Wilmington *(G-13316)*

COMPUTER TERMINALS

Hewlett-Packard World Trade ....E.... 877 424-4536
Wilmington *(G-10898)*
Isaac Fair Corporation ....E.... 302 324-8015
New Castle *(G-5426)*

COMPUTER-AIDED SYSTEM SVCS

Bluent LLC ....D.... 832 476-8459
Lewes *(G-3388)*

COMPUTERS, NEC

Anatrope Inc ....G.... 202 507-9441
Dover *(G-1123)*
Broadberry Data Systems LLC ....E.... 302 295-1086
Wilmington *(G-9481)*
Broadberry Data Systems LLC ....G.... 800 496-9918
Wilmington *(G-9482)*
Carter Firm LLC ....G.... 267 420-0717
Wilmington *(G-9582)*
Ecomo Inc ....G.... 412 567-3867
Dover *(G-1502)*
Hewlett-Packard World Trade ....E.... 877 424-4536
Wilmington *(G-10898)*
P M O Advisors L L C ....G.... 302 545-1159
Wilmington *(G-11995)*
Scientific Games Corporation ....F.... 302 737-4300
Newark *(G-7395)*
Sumuri LLC ....G.... 302 570-0015
Camden *(G-601)*
Weyl Enterprises Inc ....G.... 302 993-1248
Wilmington *(G-13176)*

PRODUCT & SERVICES SECTION

CONSTRUCTION MATERIALS, WHOLESALE: Building, Exterior

COMPUTERS, NEC, WHOLESALE

Info Systems LLC	C	302 633-9800
Wilmington (G-11026)		
Quinn Data Corporation	G	302 429-7450
Wilmington (G-12289)		

COMPUTERS, PERIPH & SOFTWARE, WHLSE: Personal & Home Entrtn

Tops International Corp	G	302 738-8889
Newark (G-7576)		

COMPUTERS, PERIPHERALS & SOFTWARE, WHOLESALE: Printers

Baytown Systems Inc	G	302 689-3421
Wilmington (G-9267)		
Cutler Industries Inc	G	302 689-3779
Wilmington (G-9928)		

COMPUTERS, PERIPHERALS & SOFTWARE, WHOLESALE: Software

34m LLC	E	302 444-8290
Newark (G-5857)		
AR Solutions Inc	F	609 751-9611
Claymont (G-693)		
Cadapult Ltd	F	302 733-0477
Newark (G-6143)		
Ergosix Corporation	G	844 603-1181
Dover (G-1530)		
Express Vpn LLC	G	310 601-8492
Newark (G-6554)		
Horizon Systems Inc	G	302 983-3203
New Castle (G-5404)		
Singular Key Inc	F	408 753-5848
Wilmington (G-12631)		
Superstore LLC	F	302 200-4933
Wilmington (G-12811)		
Trutrac LLC	G	833 878-8722
Wilmington (G-12989)		
We Cobble LLC	F	302 504-4294
Wilmington (G-13130)		

COMPUTERS: Personal

Blake Computers	G	540 843-0656
Milton (G-4869)		
Eluktronics Inc	F	302 380-3242
Newark (G-6520)		
It S Apples Oranges In	G	301 333-3696
Lewes (G-3564)		
Naughty Apple	G	954 300-7158
Wilmington (G-11820)		
Radiance Vr Inc	G	937 818-3988
Lewes (G-3706)		

CONCERT MANAGEMENT SVCS

Imcg Global Inc	G	800 559-6140
Lewes (G-3553)		

CONCRETE PLANTS

Buffalo Concrete Co Inc	G	302 378-4421
Wilmington (G-9501)		

CONCRETE PRDTS

American Precast Inc	G	302 629-6688
Seaford (G-8149)		
Ballistics Technology Intl Ltd	G	877 291-1111
Wilmington (G-9228)		
F Sartin Tyson Inc	F	302 834-4571
Saint Georges (G-8125)		
Glass Technologists Inc	G	240 682-0966
Middletown (G-4087)		

CONCRETE: Ready-Mixed

Atlantic Concrete Company Inc	D	302 422-8017
Milford (G-4312)		
Atlantic Concrete Company Inc	G	302 398-8920
Harrington (G-2815)		
Atlantic Concrete Company Inc	E	302 856-7847
Lewes (G-3354)		
Bardon U S Corporation	G	302 552-3136
Wilmington (G-9253)		
Cemex Materials LLC	E	302 378-8920
Middletown (G-3984)		
Chaney Enterprises	G	302 990-5039
Seaford (G-8189)		
Concrete Co Inc	G	302 652-1101
Wilmington (G-9814)		
Greggo & Ferrara Inc	E	302 834-3333
Bear (G-173)		
HMA Concrete LLC	F	302 777-1235
Wilmington (G-10921)		
Maddox Concrete Co Inc	G	302 656-2000
Wilmington (G-11482)		
Material Transit Inc	F	302 395-0556
New Castle (G-5512)		
Southgate Concrete Company	F	302 376-5280
Middletown (G-4247)		
Thoro-Goods Concrete Co Inc	E	302 934-8102
Dagsboro (G-938)		

CONDENSERS: Heat Transfer Eqpt, Evaporative

Baltimore Aircoil Company Inc	C	302 424-2583
Milford (G-4317)		

CONFECTIONERY PRDTS WHOLESALERS

A E Moore Incorporated	F	302 934-7055
Millsboro (G-4620)		
Harry Kenyon Incorporated	E	302 762-7776
New Castle (G-5376)		
King of Sweets Inc	F	302 730-8200
Dover (G-1750)		

CONFECTIONS & CANDY

Chocolate Swirl LLC	G	718 407-0034
Wilmington (G-9670)		
Leiny Snacks	F	302 494-2499
Wilmington (G-11367)		

CONFINEMENT SURVEILLANCE SYS MAINTENANCE & MONITORING SVCS

Ip Camera Warehouse LLC	G	302 358-2690
Wilmington (G-11079)		

CONNECTORS: Electrical

Whitaker LLC	G	302 633-2740
Wilmington (G-13187)		

CONSERVATION PROGRAMS ADMINISTRATION SVCS

Parks & Recreation Del Div	F	302 761-6963
Wilmington (G-12023)		
Parks & Recreation Del Div	F	302 571-7788
Wilmington (G-12024)		

CONSTRUCTION & MINING MACHINERY WHOLESALERS

Alban Tractor Co Inc	E	302 284-4100
Felton (G-2270)		
Atlantic Tractor LLC	F	302 834-0114
Newark (G-6022)		
Foulk Lawn & Equipment Co Inc	G	302 475-3233
Wilmington (G-10599)		
Giles & Ransome Inc	G	302 777-5800
New Castle (G-5353)		
Iron Source LLC	G	302 856-7545
Georgetown (G-2568)		
Jesco Inc	G	302 376-6946
Middletown (G-4114)		
Judd Brook 5 LLC	G	302 846-3355
Delmar (G-1011)		

CONSTRUCTION EQPT REPAIR SVCS

Heavy Equipment Rental Inc	F	302 654-5916
New Castle (G-5388)		
State Line Machine Inc	F	302 478-0285
Wilmington (G-12745)		

CONSTRUCTION EQPT: Buckets, Excavating, Clamshell, Etc

Bos Construction Company	G	302 875-9120
Laurel (G-3202)		

CONSTRUCTION EQPT: Bulldozers

Duane Edward Ruark	G	302 846-2332
Delmar (G-994)		

CONSTRUCTION EQPT: Line Markers, Self-Propelled

Marking Services Inc	G	302 478-0381
Wilmington (G-11538)		

CONSTRUCTION EQPT: Rakes, Land Clearing, Mechanical

Smw Sales LLC	F	302 875-7958
Laurel (G-3290)		

CONSTRUCTION EQPT: SCRAPERS, GRADERS, ROLLERS & SIMILAR EQPT

Meredith Salvage	G	302 349-4776
Greenwood (G-2752)		

CONSTRUCTION EQPT: Tractors

Cnh Cptal Oprting Lase Eqp Rcv	B	262 636-6011
Wilmington (G-9750)		

CONSTRUCTION EQPT: Wrecker Hoists, Automobile

Prela S Lynch	G	302 856-2130
Georgetown (G-2624)		

CONSTRUCTION MATERIALS, WHOLESALE: Air Ducts, Sheet Metal

Ducts Unlimited Inc	G	302 378-4125
Smyrna (G-8628)		

CONSTRUCTION MATERIALS, WHOLESALE: Brick, Exc Refractory

Delaware Brick Company	E	302 994-0948
Wilmington (G-10008)		

CONSTRUCTION MATERIALS, WHOLESALE: Building Stone

Christiana Materials Inc	F	302 633-5600
Wilmington (G-9688)		

CONSTRUCTION MATERIALS, WHOLESALE: Building Stone, Granite

Best Granite LLC	G	302 644-8302
Lewes (G-3378)		
Casale Marble Imports Inc	D	561 404-4213
Wilmington (G-9585)		
Pera Trading Inc	G	302 292-1750
Newark (G-7200)		

CONSTRUCTION MATERIALS, WHOLESALE: Building Stone, Marble

Landis Ltd	G	302 656-9024
Wilmington (G-11326)		
Marble Source Unlimited Inc	E	302 337-7665
Bridgeville (G-492)		

CONSTRUCTION MATERIALS, WHOLESALE: Building, Exterior

Delaware Building Supply Corp	E	302 424-3505
Milford (G-4377)		
Lowes Home Centers LLC	C	302 479-7799
Wilmington (G-11444)		
Lowes Home Centers LLC	C	302 934-3740
Millsboro (G-4727)		
Lowes Home Centers LLC	C	302 376-3006
Middletown (G-4137)		
Lowes Home Centers LLC	C	302 735-7500
Dover (G-1798)		
Lowes Home Centers LLC	C	302 645-0900
Lewes (G-3612)		
Lowes Home Centers LLC	C	302 834-8508
Bear (G-238)		
Lowes Home Centers LLC	C	302 697-0700
Camden (G-589)		
Lowes Home Centers LLC	C	302 781-1154
Newark (G-6953)		
Lowes Home Centers LLC	C	302 536-4000
Seaford (G-8296)		
Lowes Home Centers LLC	C	302 252-3228
New Castle (G-5488)		

Employee Codes: A=Over 500 employees, B=251-500 C=101-250, D=51-100, E=20-50, F=10-19, G=1-9

CONSTRUCTION MATERIALS, WHOLESALE: Building, Exterior

Marjam Supply Co Inc ....F 302 283-1020
  Newark *(G-6988)*
Metrie Inc ....G 302 337-0269
  Bridgeville *(G-499)*
State Line Building Supply ....F 302 436-8624
  Selbyville *(G-8549)*

CONSTRUCTION MATERIALS, WHOLESALE: Building, Interior

American Cedar & Millwork Inc ....D 302 645-9580
  Lewes *(G-3335)*
Delaware Flooring Supply Inc ....G 302 276-0031
  New Castle *(G-5230)*
P D Supply Inc ....G 302 655-3358
  Wilmington *(G-11994)*

CONSTRUCTION MATERIALS, WHOLESALE: Ceiling Systems & Prdts

Erco Ceilings Inc ....F 302 994-6200
  Wilmington *(G-10431)*
Erco Ceilings & Interiors Inc ....F 302 398-3200
  Harrington *(G-2838)*
Union Whl Acoustical Sup Co ....G 302 656-4462
  Wilmington *(G-13014)*

CONSTRUCTION MATERIALS, WHOLESALE: Cement

Jet Products LLC ....G 877 453-8868
  Wilmington *(G-11151)*

CONSTRUCTION MATERIALS, WHOLESALE: Ceramic, Exc Refractory

Marcus Materials Co ....G 302 731-7519
  Newark *(G-6984)*

CONSTRUCTION MATERIALS, WHOLESALE: Concrete Mixtures

Maddox Concrete Co Inc ....G 302 656-2000
  Wilmington *(G-11482)*

CONSTRUCTION MATERIALS, WHOLESALE: Door Frames

Crothers Doors and More I ....G 302 678-3667
  Camden Wyoming *(G-627)*

CONSTRUCTION MATERIALS, WHOLESALE: Doors, Garage

Hickman Overhead Door Company ....F 302 422-4249
  Milford *(G-4441)*

CONSTRUCTION MATERIALS, WHOLESALE: Gravel

Porter Sand & Gravel Inc ....G 302 335-5132
  Harrington *(G-2875)*

CONSTRUCTION MATERIALS, WHOLESALE: Lime, Exc Agricultural

Chemlime NJ Inc ....G 302 697-2115
  Magnolia *(G-3885)*

CONSTRUCTION MATERIALS, WHOLESALE: Limestone

Berkshire At Limestone ....G 302 635-7495
  Wilmington *(G-9304)*

CONSTRUCTION MATERIALS, WHOLESALE: Metal Buildings

Building Concepts America Inc ....E 302 292-0200
  Newark *(G-6131)*

CONSTRUCTION MATERIALS, WHOLESALE: Millwork

Wholesale Millwork Inc ....F 888 964-8746
  Seaford *(G-8437)*

CONSTRUCTION MATERIALS, WHOLESALE: Pallets, Wood

Dack Trading LLC ....G 917 576-4432
  Rehoboth Beach *(G-7907)*
Greenwood Pallet Co ....G 302 337-8181
  Bridgeville *(G-476)*
North American Hardwoods Ltd ....F 516 848-7729
  Wilmington *(G-11898)*
Rcd Timber Products Inc ....G 302 778-5700
  New Castle *(G-5668)*
Rehrig Penn Logistics Inc ....G 302 659-3337
  Smyrna *(G-8699)*

CONSTRUCTION MATERIALS, WHOLESALE: Paving Materials

Allan Myers Materials Inc ....G 302 734-8632
  Dover *(G-1108)*
Asphalt Paving Eqp & Sups ....G 302 683-0105
  Harbeson *(G-2773)*

CONSTRUCTION MATERIALS, WHOLESALE: Plywood

Fessenden Hall Incorporated ....F 302 674-4505
  Dover *(G-1549)*
Russell Plywood Inc ....F 302 689-0137
  New Castle *(G-5691)*

CONSTRUCTION MATERIALS, WHOLESALE: Prefabricated Structures

Aesops Gables Inc ....G 302 737-2683
  Newark *(G-5915)*
Door & Gate Co LLC ....G 888 505-6962
  Claymont *(G-734)*
F and M Equipment Ltd ....G 302 715-5382
  Laurel *(G-3229)*
George F Kempf Supply Co Inc ....G 302 658-3760
  Wilmington *(G-10698)*
Rew Material ....G 302 424-2125
  Milford *(G-4541)*

CONSTRUCTION MATERIALS, WHOLESALE: Roof, Asphalt/Sheet Metal

American Bldrs Contrs Sup Inc ....F 302 994-1166
  Wilmington *(G-9042)*
Goldis Enterprises Inc ....G 302 764-3100
  Wilmington *(G-10740)*
J & L Building Materials Inc ....F 302 504-0350
  New Castle *(G-5427)*
Quality Rofg Sup Lancaster Inc ....G 302 322-8322
  New Castle *(G-5658)*
S G Williams of Dover Inc ....F 302 678-1080
  Dover *(G-2050)*
Thomas Roofing Supply Company ....E 302 629-4521
  Seaford *(G-8421)*

CONSTRUCTION MATERIALS, WHOLESALE: Roofing & Siding Material

Goldis Holdings Inc ....D 302 764-3100
  Wilmington *(G-10741)*
Iko Manufacturing Inc ....D 302 764-3100
  Wilmington *(G-10999)*
Iko Sales Inc ....D 302 764-3100
  Wilmington *(G-11001)*
Mill Creek Metals Inc ....F 302 529-7020
  Claymont *(G-782)*
Quality Rofg Sup Lancaster Inc ....F 302 644-4115
  Lewes *(G-3703)*
SRS Distribution Inc ....F 240 965-8350
  Wilmington *(G-12719)*

CONSTRUCTION MATERIALS, WHOLESALE: Tile & Clay Prdts

Jack Parisi Tile Co Inc ....G 302 892-2455
  Wilmington *(G-11115)*

CONSTRUCTION MATERIALS, WHOLESALE: Wallboard

Builders Firstsource Inc ....E 302 731-0678
  Newark *(G-6129)*

CONSTRUCTION MATERIALS, WHOLESALE: Windows

American Bldrs Contrs Sup Inc ....F 302 994-1166
  Wilmington *(G-9042)*
Gunton Corporation ....G 302 999-0535
  Wilmington *(G-10803)*

CONSTRUCTION MATLS, WHOL: Lumber, Rough, Dressed/Finished

Grubb Lumber Company Inc ....E 302 652-2800
  Wilmington *(G-10791)*

CONSTRUCTION SITE PREPARATION SVCS

Melvin L Joseph Cnstr Co ....E 302 856-7396
  Georgetown *(G-2602)*
Pauls Paving Inc ....F 302 539-9123
  Frankford *(G-2379)*

CONSTRUCTION: Agricultural Building

W Enterprises LLC ....G 302 875-0430
  Laurel *(G-3303)*

CONSTRUCTION: Apartment Building

John Campanelli & Sons Inc ....G 302 239-8573
  Hockessin *(G-3067)*

CONSTRUCTION: Athletic & Recreation Facilities

Breakwater Construction Envmtl ....E 302 945-5800
  Millsboro *(G-4648)*

CONSTRUCTION: Athletic & Recreation Facilities

Custom Framers Inc ....E 302 684-5377
  Harbeson *(G-2781)*
Henderson Services Inc ....F 302 424-1999
  Milford *(G-4438)*
Lynx General Contracting ....G 302 368-9401
  Newark *(G-6961)*
Weavers Construction Inc ....G 302 270-8876
  Felton *(G-2326)*

CONSTRUCTION: Bridge

Ashland LLC ....E 302 594-5000
  Wilmington *(G-9151)*
Eastern Hwy Specialists Inc ....E 302 777-7673
  Wilmington *(G-10323)*
First State Crane Service ....F 302 398-8885
  Felton *(G-2292)*

CONSTRUCTION: Chemical Facility

Croda Uniqema Inc ....E 302 429-5599
  New Castle *(G-5210)*

CONSTRUCTION: Commercial & Institutional Building

Andrei S Remo ....G 302 569-4555
  Rehoboth Beach *(G-7843)*
Blackstone Building Group LLC ....G 302 824-4632
  Wilmington *(G-9364)*
Brandywine Contractors Inc ....G 302 325-2700
  New Castle *(G-5107)*
Broadpoint Construction LLC ....G 302 567-2100
  Rehoboth Beach *(G-7878)*
Brs Consulting Inc ....G 302 786-2326
  Harrington *(G-2819)*
Chilimidos LLC ....G 302 388-1880
  Hockessin *(G-2986)*
Consolidated LLC ....E 302 654-9001
  Wilmington *(G-9833)*
East Coast Minority Supplier ....E 302 656-3337
  Wilmington *(G-10320)*
Empire Investments Inc ....G 302 838-0631
  New Castle *(G-5289)*
First State Building LLC ....G 302 803-5082
  Wilmington *(G-10549)*
From Ground Up Construction ....G 302 747-0996
  Newark *(G-6625)*
Gettier Staffing Services Inc ....F 302 478-0911
  Wilmington *(G-10706)*
J A Moore & Sons Inc ....G 302 765-0110
  Wilmington *(G-11101)*

PRODUCT & SERVICES SECTION

CONSTRUCTION: Indl Building, Prefabricated

Jni CCC Jv1 .... G 302 654-6611
  Wilmington *(G-11162)*
Leon N Weiner & Associates Inc .... D 302 656-1354
  Wilmington *(G-11371)*
Mike Molitor Contractor LLC .... G 302 528-6300
  Hockessin *(G-3095)*
Pettitt Construction LLC .... G 302 690-0831
  Newark *(G-7208)*
Prestige Contractors Inc .... G 302 722-1032
  Wilmington *(G-12223)*
Roberts Wilbert .... G 215 867-5655
  Middletown *(G-4221)*
Smarter Home & Office LLC .... G 302 723-9313
  New Castle *(G-5718)*
Whiting-Turner Contracting Co .... E 302 292-0676
  Newark *(G-7693)*

CONSTRUCTION: Commercial & Office Building, New

Advance Construction Co Del .... F 302 697-9444
  Camden Wyoming *(G-611)*
Aecom Energy & Cnstr Inc .... F 302 234-1445
  Hockessin *(G-2952)*
Albert S Lambertson Inc .... G 302 734-9649
  Dover *(G-1101)*
Amakor Inc .... F 302 834-8664
  Delaware City *(G-947)*
Balfour Beatty LLC .... G 302 573-3873
  Wilmington *(G-9225)*
Bancroft Construction Company .... D 302 655-3434
  Wilmington *(G-9234)*
Bay Developers Inc .... F 302 736-0924
  Dover *(G-1179)*
Bellevue Holding Company .... E 302 655-1561
  Wilmington *(G-9291)*
Brandywine Contractors Inc .... G 302 325-2700
  New Castle *(G-5106)*
Bunting Construction Corp .... F 302 436-5124
  Selbyville *(G-8464)*
Cape Financial Services Inc .... F 302 645-6274
  Lewes *(G-3400)*
Carl Deputy & Son Builders LLC .... G 302 284-3041
  Felton *(G-2280)*
Choice Builders LLC .... G 302 856-7234
  Georgetown *(G-2470)*
Chrystal Holdings .... G 302 655-2398
  Wilmington *(G-9693)*
Commonwealth Contruction Co .... E 302 654-6611
  Wilmington *(G-9789)*
Conventional Builders Inc .... F 302 422-2429
  Houston *(G-3177)*
Crystal Holdings Inc .... D 302 421-5700
  Wilmington *(G-9909)*
Dal Construction .... G 302 538-5310
  Camden *(G-555)*
Del Homes Inc .... G 302 697-8204
  Magnolia *(G-3889)*
Deldeo Builders Inc .... F 302 791-0243
  Claymont *(G-733)*
Delmarva Builders Inc .... G 302 629-9123
  Bridgeville *(G-465)*
Deshong & Sons Contractors .... G 302 453-8500
  Newark *(G-6440)*
Diamond Hill Inc .... G 302 999-0302
  New Castle *(G-5251)*
Disabatino Construction Co .... C 302 652-3838
  Wilmington *(G-10164)*
Ebanks Construction LLC .... F 302 420-7584
  New Castle *(G-5279)*
Edge Construction Corp .... G 302 778-5200
  Wilmington *(G-10346)*
Edis Company .... E 302 421-5700
  Wilmington *(G-10350)*
Guardian Construction Co Inc .... D 302 834-1000
  New Castle *(G-5365)*
Hart Construction Co Inc .... F 302 737-7886
  Newark *(G-6712)*
Iacchetta Builders Inc .... G 302 436-4525
  Selbyville *(G-8505)*
John L Briggs & Co .... F 302 856-7033
  Georgetown *(G-2577)*
KB Coldiron Inc .... D 302 436-4224
  Selbyville *(G-8511)*
Kent Construction Co .... E 302 653-6469
  Smyrna *(G-8666)*
Locker Construction Inc .... G 302 239-2859
  Newark *(G-6946)*
Lockwood Design Construction .... G 302 684-4844
  Milton *(G-4925)*

M L Parker Construction Inc .... F 302 798-8530
  Claymont *(G-777)*
Mac Contractors Inc .... G 302 653-5765
  Smyrna *(G-8678)*
Mason Building Group Inc .... C 302 292-0600
  Newark *(G-6999)*
Miken Builders Inc .... E 302 537-4444
  Millville *(G-4851)*
Mitten Construction Co .... E 302 697-2124
  Dover *(G-1862)*
Moore Farms .... F 302 629-4999
  Georgetown *(G-2606)*
Mvl Structures Group LLC .... E 302 652-7580
  Wilmington *(G-11782)*
Mvl-Al Othman Al Zamel JV LLC .... E 832 302-2757
  Wilmington *(G-11783)*
Mvl-Saqa JV LLC .... E 832 302-2757
  Wilmington *(G-11784)*
Nason Construction Inc .... E 302 529-2510
  Wilmington *(G-11803)*
North East Contractors Inc .... E 302 286-6324
  Newark *(G-7138)*
Opus Design Build LLC .... D 952 656-4444
  Wilmington *(G-11965)*
Pettinaro Construction Co Inc .... G 302 999-0708
  Wilmington *(G-12102)*
Premier Builders Inc .... G 302 999-8500
  Wilmington *(G-12215)*
Regional Builders Inc .... G 302 628-8660
  Seaford *(G-8374)*
Reybold Construction Corp .... E 302 832-7100
  Bear *(G-304)*
Richard Y Johnson & Son Inc .... E 302 422-3732
  Lincoln *(G-3865)*
Robert C Peoples Inc .... D 302 834-5268
  Bear *(G-308)*
SC&a Construction Inc .... E 302 478-6030
  Wilmington *(G-12550)*
Shellys of Delaware Inc .... F 302 656-3337
  Wilmington *(G-12600)*
Silverside Contracting Inc .... G 302 798-1907
  Wilmington *(G-12619)*
Talley Brothers Inc .... F 302 224-5376
  Newark *(G-7536)*
Taylor Kline Inc .... F 302 328-8306
  New Castle *(G-5754)*
Vanguard Construction Inc .... G 302 697-9187
  Dover *(G-2187)*
Vari Development Corp .... G 302 479-5571
  Wilmington *(G-13050)*
Whayland Company Inc .... F 302 875-5445
  Laurel *(G-3309)*
Whayland Company LLC .... F 302 875-5445
  Laurel *(G-3310)*
Woods General Contracting .... G 302 856-4047
  Georgetown *(G-2708)*

CONSTRUCTION: Commercial & Office Buildings, Prefabricated

Ballard Builders LLC .... F 302 363-1677
  Clayton *(G-836)*

CONSTRUCTION: Condominium

Weather or Not Inc .... F 302 436-7533
  Selbyville *(G-8553)*

CONSTRUCTION: Dams, Waterways, Docks & Other Marine

CBI Services LLC .... F 302 325-8400
  New Castle *(G-5138)*
Interstate Construction Inc .... E 302 369-3590
  Newark *(G-6798)*

CONSTRUCTION: Dock

J & J Bulkheading .... G 302 436-2800
  Selbyville *(G-8507)*
W Sharp Paynter & Sons Inc .... G 302 684-8508
  Milton *(G-4979)*

CONSTRUCTION: Drainage System

Janette Redrow Ltd .... G 302 659-3934
  Townsend *(G-8800)*

CONSTRUCTION: Factory

Lynx General Contracting .... G 302 368-9401
  Newark *(G-6961)*

CONSTRUCTION: Farm Building

Dan H Beachy & Sons Inc .... G 302 492-1493
  Hartly *(G-2918)*
Humphries Construction Company .... G 302 349-9277
  Greenwood *(G-2744)*
Larry Hill Farms Inc .... F 302 875-0886
  Delmar *(G-1015)*
Warfel Construction Co Inc .... E 302 422-8927
  Milford *(G-4598)*
Westwood Farms Incorporated .... F 302 238-7141
  Millsboro *(G-4826)*

CONSTRUCTION: Food Prdts Manufacturing or Packing Plant

Essies Kitchen LLC .... G 302 465-2856
  Dover *(G-1531)*

CONSTRUCTION: Garage

Space Makers Inc .... G 302 322-4325
  Bear *(G-330)*

CONSTRUCTION: Greenhouse

Sunworks Corporation .... G 302 655-5772
  Wilmington *(G-12802)*
Wilmington .... G 302 357-4509
  Wilmington *(G-13221)*

CONSTRUCTION: Harbor

John T Rogers Jr .... G 302 945-3016
  Millsboro *(G-4715)*

CONSTRUCTION: Heavy

Lavond Mackey .... E 484 466-8055
  Wilmington *(G-11338)*

CONSTRUCTION: Heavy Highway & Street

Amears Contractors Inc .... G 302 791-7767
  Claymont *(G-690)*
Andrei S Remo .... G 302 569-4555
  Rehoboth Beach *(G-7843)*
Ashland LLC .... E 302 594-5000
  Wilmington *(G-9151)*
George & Lynch Inc .... C 302 736-3031
  Dover *(G-1590)*
Matts Management Family LLC .... F 302 732-3715
  Frankford *(G-2372)*
Mumford and Miller Con Inc .... C 302 378-7736
  Middletown *(G-4171)*
Rp Ventures and Holdings Inc .... E 410 398-3000
  New Castle *(G-5690)*
Sams Construction LLC .... E 302 654-6542
  Wilmington *(G-12534)*
Transportation Delaware Dept .... B 302 326-8950
  Bear *(G-357)*
Walo US Holdings Inc .... G 212 691-4537
  Dover *(G-2204)*

CONSTRUCTION: Indl Building & Warehouse

Bancroft Construction Company .... D 302 655-3434
  Wilmington *(G-9234)*
Disabatino Construction Co .... C 302 652-3838
  Wilmington *(G-10164)*
East Coast Minority Supplier .... E 302 656-3337
  Wilmington *(G-10320)*
Mario F Medori Inc .... G 302 239-4550
  Wilmington *(G-11528)*
Metro Steel Incorporated .... E 302 778-2288
  New Castle *(G-5519)*
Nason Construction Inc .... E 302 529-2510
  Wilmington *(G-11803)*
Penco Corporation .... G 302 629-7911
  Seaford *(G-8345)*
Rock Solid Contracting and Dev .... G 302 655-8250
  Wilmington *(G-12448)*
Skanska USA Building Inc .... E 215 495-8790
  Newark *(G-7434)*
Whiting-Turner Contracting Co .... E 302 292-0676
  Newark *(G-7693)*

CONSTRUCTION: Indl Building, Prefabricated

Advance Construction Co Del .... F 302 697-9444
  Camden Wyoming *(G-611)*

CONSTRUCTION: Indl Building, Prefabricated

Building Concepts America Inc............E......302 292-0200
Newark *(G-6131)*
Colonial Construction Company..........F......302 994-5705
Wilmington *(G-9774)*
Eastern Metals Inc..............................F......302 454-7886
Newark *(G-6499)*

CONSTRUCTION: Indl Buildings, New, NEC

Bristol Industrial Corporation..............F......302 322-1100
New Castle *(G-5115)*
Broadpoint Construction LLC.............G......302 567-2100
Rehoboth Beach *(G-7878)*
Conventional Builders Inc...................F......302 422-2429
Houston *(G-3177)*
Crystal Holdings Inc...........................D......302 421-5700
Wilmington *(G-9909)*
Deshong & Sons Contractors..............G......302 453-8500
Newark *(G-6440)*
Edis Company....................................E......302 421-5700
Wilmington *(G-10350)*
Gettier Staffing Services Inc................F......302 478-0911
Wilmington *(G-10706)*
Gfp Cement Contractors LLC..............F......302 998-7687
Wilmington *(G-10708)*
Guardian Envmtl Svcs Co Inc..............D......302 918-3070
Newark *(G-6695)*
Hart Construction Co Inc....................F......302 737-7886
Newark *(G-6712)*
John L Briggs & Co............................F......302 856-7033
Georgetown *(G-2577)*
Kent Construction Co..........................E......302 653-6469
Smyrna *(G-8666)*
Miken Builders Inc.............................E......302 537-4444
Millville *(G-4851)*
Mitten Construction Co......................E......302 697-2124
Dover *(G-1862)*
Pettinaro Construction Co Inc.............D......302 999-0708
Wilmington *(G-12102)*
Shellys of Delaware Inc......................F......302 656-3337
Wilmington *(G-12600)*
Talley Brothers Inc.............................E......302 224-5376
Newark *(G-7536)*
Whayland Company Inc......................F......302 875-5445
Laurel *(G-3309)*
Wohlsen Construction Company..........E......302 324-9900
Wilmington *(G-13284)*

CONSTRUCTION: Indl Plant

Koch Accounting Services LLC............E......877 446-8478
Wilmington *(G-11286)*

CONSTRUCTION: Land Preparation

George M Howard & Sons Inc.............G......302 645-9655
Rehoboth Beach *(G-7945)*
Mumford and Miller Con Inc...............C......302 378-7736
Middletown *(G-4171)*

CONSTRUCTION: Marine

George & Lynch Inc...........................C......302 736-3031
Dover *(G-1590)*
Merritt Marine Cnstr Inc....................G......302 436-2881
Selbyville *(G-8519)*
Precision Marine Construction............G......302 227-2711
Rehoboth Beach *(G-8035)*
Sun Marine Maintenance Inc..............F......302 539-6756
Frankford *(G-2391)*

CONSTRUCTION: Multi-family Dwellings, New

Breeze Construction LLC....................E......302 522-9201
Townsend *(G-8766)*
Joseph E Stevens & Father.................G......302 654-8556
Wilmington *(G-11189)*

CONSTRUCTION: Nonresidential Buildings, Custom

Regal Contractors LLC........................G......302 736-5000
Dover *(G-2019)*

CONSTRUCTION: Oil & Gas Pipeline Construction

US Bortek LLC...................................F......888 203-7686
Camden *(G-604)*
Voshell Bros Welding Inc....................E......302 674-1414
Dover *(G-2199)*

CONSTRUCTION: Parking Lot

Magowi Consulting Group LLC...........F......832 301-9230
Newark *(G-6972)*
Sanco Construction Co Inc.................G......302 633-4156
Wilmington *(G-12536)*
Terra Firma of Delmarva Inc..............F......302 846-3350
Delmar *(G-1037)*

CONSTRUCTION: Pipeline, NEC

Current Solutions...............................G......302 724-5243
Dover *(G-1330)*

CONSTRUCTION: Power & Communication Transmission Tower

Chris Kissell.....................................G......302 547-4800
Smyrna *(G-8593)*

CONSTRUCTION: Railroad & Subway

Asplundh Tree Expert Co...................B......302 678-4702
Dover *(G-1147)*

CONSTRUCTION: Refineries

Delaware City Refining Co LLC...........C......302 834-6000
Delaware City *(G-954)*

CONSTRUCTION: Residential, Nec

Atlantic Homes LLC............................G......302 947-0223
Lewes *(G-3356)*
B Doherty Inc....................................G......302 239-3500
Wilmington *(G-9211)*
Brandywine Exteriors Corp.................E......302 746-7134
Wilmington *(G-9431)*
Capano Management Company..........G......302 737-8056
Wilmington *(G-6149)*
Carl M Freeman Associates Inc..........D......302 436-3000
Ocean View *(G-7775)*
Cirillo Bros Inc..................................G......302 326-1540
New Castle *(G-5162)*
Custom Improvers Inc........................G......302 731-9246
Newark *(G-6332)*
Deldeo Builders Inc...........................F......302 791-0243
Claymont *(G-733)*
Diamond State Pole Bldings LLC.........G......302 387-1710
Felton *(G-2286)*
Disabatino Construction Co................C......302 652-3838
Wilmington *(G-10164)*
E A Zando Custom Designs Inc..........F......302 684-4601
Milton *(G-4900)*
East Coast Minority Supplier...............E......302 656-3337
Wilmington *(G-10320)*
Ebanks Construction LLC...................G......302 420-7584
New Castle *(G-5279)*
Empire Construction Company............G......302 235-2093
Newark *(G-6524)*
Equity Contracting LLC......................G......302 504-1468
Wilmington *(G-10430)*
Falcon Crest Inv Intl Inc....................G......240 701-1746
Wilmington *(G-10481)*
H & M Construction...........................G......302 645-6639
Lewes *(G-3527)*
H & T Builders Inc.............................G......302 422-0745
Milford *(G-4429)*
Henlopen Homes LLC........................G......302 684-0860
Milton *(G-4913)*
J Rocco Construction LLC..................G......302 856-4100
Georgetown *(G-2570)*
Martin Construction Svcs LLC............F......302 200-0885
Newark *(G-6994)*
Mazzola Systems Inc..........................G......302 738-6808
Newark *(G-7008)*
Nail It Down General Contrs..............G......302 698-3073
Dover *(G-1881)*
Newark Building Services LLC............G......302 377-7687
Newark *(G-7111)*
Nvr Inc...E......302 731-5770
Newark *(G-7140)*
Preferred Construction Inc.................G......302 322-9568
New Castle *(G-5637)*
Prestige Contractors Inc....................G......302 722-1032
Wilmington *(G-12223)*
Pro Clean Wilmington Inc..................G......302 836-8080
Delaware City *(G-964)*
Rapid Renovation and Repr LLC.........F......302 475-5400
Harrington *(G-2879)*
Roberts Wilbert................................215 867-5655
Middletown *(G-4221)*
Scuba World Inc................................F......302 698-1117
Dover *(G-2064)*
Separe Inc..E......302 736-5000
Dover *(G-2069)*
Shamrock Construction Inc................G......302 376-0320
Smyrna *(G-8713)*
Thomas Brothers LLC........................G......302 366-1316
Newark *(G-7562)*
Vvs Inc...G......302 827-2525
Lewes *(G-3812)*
Warren Reid.....................................E......302 877-0901
Laurel *(G-3304)*

CONSTRUCTION: School Building

Wohlsen Construction Company..........E......302 324-9900
Wilmington *(G-13284)*

CONSTRUCTION: Sewer Line

Epb Associates Inc............................F......302 475-7301
Wilmington *(G-10424)*
H I E Contractors Inc.........................F......302 224-3032
Newark *(G-6697)*
Hopkins Construction Inc...................E......302 337-3366
Bridgeville *(G-482)*
Teal Construction Inc........................D......302 276-6034
Dover *(G-2134)*
Tri-State Grouting LLC......................E......302 286-0701
Newark *(G-7587)*

CONSTRUCTION: Sidewalk

Brick Doctor Inc................................G......302 678-3380
Dover *(G-1231)*

CONSTRUCTION: Single-Family Housing

A Fields Unlimited LLC......................G......800 484-2331
Newark *(G-5866)*
Bartlett & Bartlett LLC......................G......302 653-7200
Clayton *(G-838)*
Battaglia Mechanical Inc...................E......302 325-6100
New Castle *(G-5071)*
Beazer Homes Corp..........................F......302 378-4161
Middletown *(G-3964)*
Bellevue Contractors LLC..................G......302 655-1522
Wilmington *(G-9289)*
Bellevue Remodel & Design LLC........G......302 482-7200
Wilmington *(G-9293)*
Black Dog Construction LLC..............G......302 530-4967
Newark *(G-6088)*
Capano Homes Inc...........................E......302 384-7980
Wilmington *(G-9553)*
Capstone Homes...............................G......302 684-4480
Milton *(G-4875)*
Cns Construction Corp......................E......302 224-0450
Newark *(G-6257)*
Commonwealth Construction.............G......302 654-6611
Wilmington *(G-9788)*
Comstock Custom Cabinets Inc.........G......302 422-2928
Milford *(G-4364)*
Conway Construction LLC.................G......302 453-9260
Newark *(G-6293)*
D P Investment L L C.......................G......302 998-7031
Wilmington *(G-9941)*
D&S Construction Company..............G......302 650-3209
Middletown *(G-4018)*
David Waters & Son..........................G......302 235-8653
Hockessin *(G-3001)*
Dead On Construction.......................G......302 462-5023
Selbyville *(G-8480)*
Del Homes Inc..................................E......302 730-1479
Dover *(G-1351)*
Delaware Homes Inc.........................F......302 223-6258
Smyrna *(G-8616)*
Delmarva Pole Building Sup Inc.........G......302 698-3636
Wyoming *(G-13361)*
Dimple Construction Inc...................G......302 559-7535
Bear *(G-119)*
Disabatino Construction Co...............C......302 652-3838
Wilmington *(G-10164)*
Double S Developers Inc...................F......302 838-8880
Bear *(G-126)*
G G + A LLC...................................F......302 376-6122
Middletown *(G-4082)*
George & Lynch Inc..........................E......302 238-7289
Millsboro *(G-4697)*
H&L Construction Corp.....................G......302 875-5634
Seaford *(G-8255)*
Habitat For Humanity.......................F......302 652-0365
Wilmington *(G-10815)*

Harvey Miller Construction ....G....... 302 674-4128
Dover ***(G-1637)***
Humphries Construction Company ....G....... 302 349-9277
Greenwood ***(G-2744)***
Impulse Construction ....G....... 302 644-0464
Lewes ***(G-3555)***
Integrity MGT Solution Inc ....G....... 302 270-8976
Clayton ***(G-857)***
Interfaith Cmnty Hsing of Del ....F....... 302 652-3991
Wilmington ***(G-11062)***
J & L Services Inc ....F....... 410 943-3355
Seaford ***(G-8274)***
J Culver Construction Inc ....G....... 302 337-8136
Bridgeville ***(G-485)***
J Kenneth Moore & Son Inc ....G....... 302 736-0563
Dover ***(G-1687)***
J Rocco Construction LLC ....G....... 302 856-4100
Georgetown ***(G-2570)***
Knotts Construction Inc ....G....... 302 475-7074
Wilmington ***(G-11283)***
Landmark Homes Inc ....G....... 302 242-1394
New Castle ***(G-5473)***
Mack Construction & Handy ....G....... 302 337-3448
Bridgeville ***(G-491)***
Mazzola Systems Inc ....F....... 302 738-6808
Newark ***(G-7008)***
Michael W Fogarty Gen Contr ....G....... 302 658-5547
Hockessin ***(G-3094)***
Minkers Construction Inc ....E....... 302 239-9239
Newark ***(G-7044)***
Moony and Zeager Inc ....G....... 302 593-8166
Wilmington ***(G-11742)***
Murphy Steel Inc ....E....... 302 366-8676
Newark ***(G-7073)***
Neighborhood House Inc ....F....... 302 658-5404
Wilmington ***(G-11830)***
Nvr Inc ....E....... 302 731-5770
Newark ***(G-7140)***
Onsite Construction Inc ....E....... 302 628-4244
Seaford ***(G-8337)***
Orjam Ltd ....F....... 302 482-5016
Wilmington ***(G-11974)***
Othg Inc ....G....... 302 421-9187
Wilmington ***(G-11982)***
Pano Development Inc ....G....... 302 428-1062
Wilmington ***(G-12014)***
Paoli Services Inc ....E....... 302 998-7031
Wilmington ***(G-12015)***
Patriot Government Svcs Inc ....G....... 302 655-3434
Wilmington ***(G-12035)***
Pettinaro Construction Co Inc ....D....... 302 999-0708
Wilmington ***(G-12102)***
Philadlphia Arms Town Hmes Inc ....F....... 302 503-7216
Ellendale ***(G-2262)***
Powell Construction L L C ....G....... 302 745-1146
Georgetown ***(G-2622)***
Pulte Home Corporation ....E....... 302 999-9525
New Castle ***(G-5654)***
Quality Construction Cleaning ....E....... 302 956-0752
Bridgeville ***(G-515)***
Reybold Homes Inc ....C....... 302 834-3000
Newark ***(G-7332)***
Richard D Whaley Cnstr LLC ....G....... 302 934-9525
Millsboro ***(G-4789)***
Rkj Construction Inc ....G....... 302 690-0959
Wilmington ***(G-12431)***
Rons Mobile Home Sales Inc ....G....... 302 398-9166
Harrington ***(G-2880)***
Sams Construction LLC ....E....... 302 654-6542
Wilmington ***(G-12533)***
Shockley Brothers Construction ....G....... 302 424-3255
Lincoln ***(G-3869)***
Stapen Construction Inc ....G....... 302 218-2190
Wilmington ***(G-12738)***
State Line Construction Inc ....F....... 302 349-4244
Greenwood ***(G-2764)***
Steven Schmith ....F....... 302 584-8394
Middletown ***(G-4248)***
Sussex Cnty Habitat For Humani ....G....... 302 855-1153
Georgetown ***(G-2674)***
Thomas F Cavanaugh ....G....... 302 995-2859
Wilmington ***(G-12900)***
Tricon Construction MGT Inc ....E....... 302 838-6500
New Castle ***(G-5793)***
Utilicon Solutions Ltd ....G....... 302 337-9980
Bridgeville ***(G-526)***
Wade Kimball Construction Inc ....F....... 302 284-4732
Camden Wyoming ***(G-661)***
Walan Specialty Cnstr Pdts LLC ....G....... 724 545-2300
Wilmington ***(G-13114)***
Weiner Development LLC ....E....... 302 764-9430
Wilmington ***(G-13139)***
Wilmington Housing Partnr Corp ....G....... 302 576-3000
Wilmington ***(G-13235)***

CONSTRUCTION: Single-family Housing, New

36 Builders Inc ....F....... 302 349-9480
Bridgeville ***(G-441)***
Accessible Home Builders Inc ....G....... 302 628-9571
Millsboro ***(G-4622)***
Albert S Lambertson Inc ....G....... 302 734-9649
Dover ***(G-1101)***
Aslin Inc ....G....... 302 674-1900
Dover ***(G-1145)***
Bancroft Homes Inc ....G....... 302 655-5461
Wilmington ***(G-9235)***
Bay Developers Inc ....F....... 302 736-0924
Dover ***(G-1179)***
Bay To Beach Builders Inc ....G....... 302 349-5099
Farmington ***(G-2266)***
Benjamin B Smith Builders Inc ....G....... 302 537-1916
Ocean View ***(G-7764)***
Beracah Homes Inc ....E....... 302 349-4561
Greenwood ***(G-2716)***
Bestfield Associates Inc ....F....... 302 633-6361
Wilmington ***(G-9315)***
Blenheim Management Company ....E....... 302 254-0100
Newark ***(G-6093)***
Boardwalk Builders Inc ....F....... 302 227-5754
Rehoboth Beach ***(G-7871)***
Bradley Arthur & Son Cnstr ....G....... 302 422-9391
Milford ***(G-4332)***
Brandywine Contractors Inc ....G....... 302 325-2700
New Castle ***(G-5107)***
Breeze Construction LLC ....G....... 302 522-9201
Townsend ***(G-8766)***
Brendon T Warfel Construction ....G....... 302 422-7814
Milford ***(G-4334)***
Bruce Mears Designer-Builder ....F....... 302 539-2355
Ocean View ***(G-7770)***
Bunting Construction Corp ....F....... 302 436-5124
Selbyville ***(G-8464)***
C & B Construct ....G....... 302 378-9862
Milford ***(G-4338)***
Cape Financial Services Inc ....F....... 302 645-6274
Lewes ***(G-3400)***
Carl Deputy & Son Builders LLC ....G....... 302 284-3041
Felton ***(G-2280)***
Charles A Zonko Builders Inc ....E....... 302 436-0222
Selbyville ***(G-8467)***
Charles R Reed ....G....... 302 284-3353
Felton ***(G-2282)***
Commonwealth Contruction Co ....E....... 302 654-6611
Wilmington ***(G-9789)***
Country Life Homes Milford De ....G....... 302 265-2257
Milford ***(G-4365)***
Cpr Construction Inc ....G....... 302 322-5770
New Castle ***(G-5207)***
Del Homes Inc ....G....... 302 697-8204
Magnolia ***(G-3889)***
Delaware Homes Inc ....G....... 302 378-9510
Townsend ***(G-8779)***
Delmarva Builders Inc ....G....... 302 629-9123
Bridgeville ***(G-465)***
Delpa Builders LLC ....F....... 302 731-7304
New Castle ***(G-5245)***
Deshong & Sons Contractors ....G....... 302 453-8500
Newark ***(G-6440)***
Dewson Construction Company ....E....... 302 427-2250
Wilmington ***(G-10131)***
Double Diamone Builders Inc ....F....... 302 945-2512
Millsboro ***(G-4682)***
Edge Construction Corp ....G....... 302 778-5200
Wilmington ***(G-10346)***
Empire Investments Inc ....G....... 302 838-0631
New Castle ***(G-5289)***
Garrison Custom Homes ....G....... 302 644-4008
Lewes ***(G-3508)***
George K Rickards Inc ....G....... 302 539-7550
Ocean View ***(G-7791)***
Gpe Construction LLC ....G....... 267 595-8942
Bear ***(G-169)***
Griffin Home Builders Inc ....F....... 302 629-5615
Seaford ***(G-8254)***
Gulfstream Development Corp ....G....... 302 539-6178
Ocean View ***(G-7792)***
H H Builders Inc ....G....... 302 735-9900
Dover ***(G-1622)***
Handler Builders Inc ....E....... 302 999-9200
Wilmington ***(G-10831)***
Handler Corporation ....E....... 302 999-9200
Wilmington ***(G-10832)***
Henlopen Homes Inc ....G....... 302 684-0860
Lewes ***(G-3541)***
Herring Creek Builders Inc ....G....... 302 684-3015
Milton ***(G-4914)***
Hickory Hill Builders Inc ....G....... 302 934-6109
Dagsboro ***(G-909)***
Hoenen & Mitchell Inc ....G....... 302 645-6193
Lewes ***(G-3543)***
Hugh H Hickman & Sons Inc ....F....... 302 539-9741
Bethany Beach ***(G-403)***
Iacchetta Builders Inc ....G....... 302 436-4525
Selbyville ***(G-8505)***
J B S Construction LLC ....G....... 302 349-5705
Greenwood ***(G-2746)***
J I Beiler Homes LLC ....G....... 302 697-1553
Camden ***(G-583)***
Jack Hickman Real Estate ....F....... 302 539-8000
Bethany Beach ***(G-406)***
John Campanelli & Sons Inc ....G....... 302 239-8573
Hockessin ***(G-3067)***
Joseph & Cummings Builder ....G....... 302 875-4279
Laurel ***(G-3244)***
Joseph E Stevens & Father ....G....... 302 654-8556
Wilmington ***(G-11189)***
Jsf Construction Co Inc ....G....... 302 999-9573
Wilmington ***(G-11204)***
Kaye Construction ....E....... 302 628-6962
Seaford ***(G-8285)***
Kersey Homes Inc ....G....... 302 934-8434
Millsboro ***(G-4717)***
Kokoszka & Sons Inc ....G....... 302 328-4807
New Castle ***(G-5468)***
Lane Builders LLC ....F....... 302 645-5555
Lewes ***(G-3591)***
Lenape Builders Inc ....F....... 302 376-3971
Middletown ***(G-4128)***
Leon N Weiner & Associates Inc ....D....... 302 656-1354
Wilmington ***(G-11371)***
Lighthouse Construction Inc ....F....... 302 677-1965
Magnolia ***(G-3898)***
LLC Schell Brothers ....E....... 302 376-0355
Middletown ***(G-4136)***
Lockwood Design Construction ....G....... 302 684-4844
Milton ***(G-4925)***
M L Parker Construction Inc ....F....... 302 798-8530
Claymont ***(G-777)***
Miken Builders Inc ....E....... 302 537-4444
Millville ***(G-4851)***
Morning Star Construction LLC ....F....... 302 539-0791
Dagsboro ***(G-923)***
Nvr Inc ....E....... 302 732-9900
Dagsboro ***(G-926)***
Oak Construction ....G....... 302 703-2013
Lewes ***(G-3663)***
R D Arnold Construction Inc ....F....... 610 255-4739
Middletown ***(G-4207)***
Rays Plumbing & Heating Svcs ....F....... 302 697-3936
Felton ***(G-2315)***
Restoration Guys LLC ....G....... 302 542-4045
Seaford ***(G-8378)***
Richard Y Johnson & Son Inc ....E....... 302 422-3732
Lincoln ***(G-3865)***
Robert C Peoples Inc ....D....... 302 834-5268
Bear ***(G-308)***
Rockland Builders Inc ....F....... 302 995-6800
Wilmington ***(G-12452)***
Rosauri Builders & Remodelers ....G....... 302 234-8464
Hockessin ***(G-3140)***
SC&a Construction Inc ....E....... 302 478-6030
Wilmington ***(G-12550)***
Schell Brothers LLC ....F....... 302 226-1994
Rehoboth Beach ***(G-8068)***
Shellys of Delaware Inc ....F....... 302 656-3337
Wilmington ***(G-12600)***
T J Lane Construction Inc ....G....... 302 734-1099
Dover ***(G-2126)***
Timothy B OHare Custom Bldr ....F....... 302 537-9559
Ocean View ***(G-7822)***
Tlbc LLC ....G....... 302 797-8700
Lewes ***(G-3787)***
Toll Brothers Inc ....E....... 302 832-1700
New Castle ***(G-5773)***
Tru General Contractor Inc ....G....... 302 354-0553
Wilmington ***(G-12985)***
Turnstone Builders LLC ....F....... 302 227-8876
Rehoboth Beach ***(G-8101)***

U and I Builders Inc.....G..... 302 697-1645
Dover *(G-2169)*
Vanguard Construction Inc.....G..... 302 697-9187
Dover *(G-2187)*
Vari Development Corp.....G..... 302 479-5571
Wilmington *(G-13050)*
Warfel Construction Co Inc.....E..... 302 422-8927
Milford *(G-4598)*
Wilson Construction Co Inc.....G..... 302 856-3115
Georgetown *(G-2704)*
Woods General Contracting.....G..... 302 856-4047
Georgetown *(G-2708)*
Yencer Builders Inc.....G..... 302 284-9989
Felton *(G-2327)*

CONSTRUCTION: Single-family Housing, Prefabricated

Liberto Development Ltd.....G..... 302 698-1104
Dover *(G-1782)*

CONSTRUCTION: Steel Buildings

Janette Redrow Ltd.....G..... 302 659-3534
Townsend *(G-8800)*

CONSTRUCTION: Street Surfacing & Paving

Baker & Sons Paving.....G..... 302 945-6333
Middletown *(G-3960)*
Bayside Sealcoating Supply.....G..... 302 697-6441
Camden Wyoming *(G-618)*
Brandywine Construction Co.....D..... 302 571-9773
New Castle *(G-5105)*
C&J Paving Inc.....F..... 302 684-0211
Milton *(G-4873)*
D E Leager Construction.....G..... 302 994-1060
Wilmington *(G-9939)*
Daisy Construction Company.....D..... 302 658-4417
Wilmington *(G-9947)*
David G Horsey & Sons Inc.....D..... 302 875-3033
Laurel *(G-3221)*
Ds Paving.....G..... 302 832-3748
Bear *(G-128)*
George P Stewart.....G..... 302 737-4927
Newark *(G-6648)*
James L Webb Paving Co Inc.....G..... 302 697-2000
Camden *(G-584)*
Jerrys Inc.....F..... 302 422-7676
Milford *(G-4457)*
Keoghs Contracting Company.....G..... 302 656-0058
New Castle *(G-5460)*
McKenzie Paving Inc.....F..... 302 376-8560
Middletown *(G-4150)*
McNeil Paving.....G..... 302 945-7131
Millsboro *(G-4738)*
Ralph Cahall & Son Paving.....D..... 302 653-4220
Smyrna *(G-8696)*
Road Site Construction Inc.....F..... 302 645-1922
Lewes *(G-3720)*
Rock Bottom Paving Inc.....G..... 800 728-3160
Felton *(G-2318)*
Straight Line Striping LLC.....G..... 302 228-3335
Georgetown *(G-2668)*
Whitemans Paving Inc.....G..... 302 378-1828
Townsend *(G-8832)*

CONSTRUCTION: Swimming Pools

Chas Pools Inc.....F..... 302 737-9224
Middletown *(G-3985)*
Clarks Glasgow Pools Inc.....F..... 302 834-0200
New Castle *(G-5175)*
Clarks Swimming Pools Inc.....G..... 302 629-8835
Seaford *(G-8198)*
Dover Pool & Patio Center Inc.....E..... 302 346-7665
Dover *(G-1465)*
Dover Pool & Patio Center Inc.....G..... 302 839-3300
Milford *(G-4392)*
Swift Pools Inc.....E..... 302 738-9800
Newark *(G-7522)*

CONSTRUCTION: Telephone & Communication Line

Yacht Anything Ltd.....G..... 302 226-3335
Rehoboth Beach *(G-8120)*

CONSTRUCTION: Utility Line

Asplundh Tree Expert Co.....B..... 302 678-4702
Dover *(G-1147)*
Brandywine Construction Co.....D..... 302 571-9773
New Castle *(G-5105)*
Bunting & Murray Cnstr Corp.....D..... 302 436-5144
Selbyville *(G-8463)*
CNJ Contracting LLC.....G..... 302 659-3750
Smyrna *(G-8600)*
Core & Main LP.....G..... 302 737-1500
Newark *(G-6297)*
David Bridge.....G..... 302 429-3317
Bear *(G-95)*
Dixie Construction Company Inc.....E..... 302 858-5007
Georgetown *(G-2511)*
Dycom Industries Inc.....G..... 302 613-0958
New Castle *(G-5269)*
Fast Pipe Lining East Inc.....F..... 302 368-7414
Newark *(G-6574)*
George & Lynch Inc.....C..... 302 736-3031
Dover *(G-1590)*
Phalco Inc.....G..... 302 654-2620
Wilmington *(G-12107)*
Standard Pipe Services LLC.....D..... 302 286-0701
Newark *(G-7480)*
Triton Construction Co Inc.....E..... 516 780-8100
New Castle *(G-5795)*
Utilisite Inc.....F..... 302 945-5022
Lewes *(G-3806)*
Wilmington Resources.....F..... 302 746-7162
Wilmington *(G-13244)*
Zober Contracting Services Inc.....G..... 302 270-3078
Dover *(G-2253)*

CONSTRUCTION: Warehouse

Dan H Beachy & Sons Inc.....G..... 302 492-1493
Hartly *(G-2918)*
Reybold Construction Corp.....E..... 302 832-7100
Bear *(G-304)*

CONSTRUCTION: Waste Water & Sewage Treatment Plant

Artesian Wastewater MD Inc.....E..... 302 453-6900
Newark *(G-6002)*
Artesian Wastewater MGT Inc.....E..... 302 453-6900
Newark *(G-6003)*
Crimson Group LLC.....G..... 301 252-3779
Newark *(G-6316)*
Jjid Inc.....E..... 302 836-0414
Bear *(G-201)*

CONSTRUCTION: Water Main

Merit Construction Engineers.....F..... 302 992-9810
Wilmington *(G-11644)*

CONSULTING SVC: Actuarial

American Diagnostic Svcs Inc.....G..... 302 628-4209
Seaford *(G-8146)*
Du Pont Delaware Inc.....G..... 302 774-1000
Wilmington *(G-10242)*
Prestege LLC.....G..... 302 312-8548
Newark *(G-7247)*

CONSULTING SVC: Business, NEC

Acuitive Inc.....G..... 214 738-1099
Wilmington *(G-8929)*
Acumen Strategies Inc.....G..... 302 218-3949
Hockessin *(G-2951)*
Aecom Usa Inc.....E..... 302 781-5963
Wilmington *(G-8963)*
African Wood Inc.....G..... 302 884-6738
Wilmington *(G-8973)*
American Gen Trdg Contg US Inc.....G..... 804 739-1480
Dover *(G-1119)*
Aquila of Delaware Inc.....F..... 302 999-1106
Wilmington *(G-9107)*
Assoction Brds Thlgcal Educatn.....G..... 302 654-7770
Wilmington *(G-9160)*
Atlantic Duncan Inc.....F..... 302 383-0740
Newark *(G-6020)*
B Rich Enterprises.....G..... 302 530-6865
Middletown *(G-3957)*
Bastianelli Group Inc.....G..... 302 658-1500
Newark *(G-6050)*
Bishop Enterprises Corporation.....E..... 302 379-2884
Wilmington *(G-9342)*
Burton Enterprises Inc.....G..... 302 838-0115
Bear *(G-57)*
C and L Bradford and Assoc.....G..... 302 529-8566
Wilmington *(G-9522)*
Cannon Cold Storage LLC.....E..... 302 337-5500
Bridgeville *(G-457)*
Capstone Homes LLC.....G..... 302 644-0300
Lewes *(G-3404)*
Cardiovascular Consultants of.....G..... 302 541-8138
Ocean View *(G-7774)*
Cda Group Inc.....G..... 302 793-0693
Claymont *(G-710)*
Cecon Group LLC.....G..... 302 994-8000
Wilmington *(G-9608)*
Cleaver.....G..... 302 659-1707
Smyrna *(G-8599)*
Cloudcoffer LLC.....E..... 412 620-3203
Wilmington *(G-9748)*
Cognitive Group LLC.....F..... 301 585-1444
Dover *(G-1302)*
Commonwealth Group.....G..... 302 995-6400
Wilmington *(G-9790)*
Congruence Consulting Group.....G..... 320 290-6155
Newark *(G-6286)*
Consulttive Rview Rhbilitation.....G..... 302 366-0356
Newark *(G-6290)*
Core Construction LLC.....G..... 302 449-4186
Smyrna *(G-8605)*
Corporations & Companies Inc.....G..... 302 652-4800
Wilmington *(G-9867)*
Countermeasures Assessment.....G..... 302 322-9600
New Castle *(G-5200)*
D & H Credit Services Inc.....F..... 302 832-6980
Newark *(G-6340)*
D E Enterprises LLC.....G..... 302 653-5493
Clayton *(G-841)*
De Novo Corporation.....E..... 302 234-7407
Wilmington *(G-9987)*
Delaware Innovation Space Inc.....G..... 302 695-2201
Wilmington *(G-10058)*
Design Tribe Republic LLC.....G..... 302 918-5279
Wilmington *(G-10124)*
Dolan Manufacturing Solutions.....G..... 302 378-4981
Middletown *(G-4040)*
Drh Enterprises LLC.....G..... 302 864-0060
Seaford *(G-8226)*
Ementum Inc.....E..... 866 984-1999
Milton *(G-4903)*
Encross LLC.....F..... 302 351-2593
Wilmington *(G-10396)*
Endocrinology Consultant.....G..... 302 734-2782
Dover *(G-1521)*
Endovascular Consultants LLC.....G..... 302 482-1333
Wilmington *(G-10398)*
Envision Consulting LLC.....G..... 302 658-9027
Wilmington *(G-10421)*
Envision Solution LLC.....F..... 302 442-7329
Wilmington *(G-10422)*
Etechpublish Inc.....G..... 302 294-1678
Newark *(G-6542)*
Fareed Services.....G..... 302 559-8594
Wilmington *(G-10499)*
First State Sealcoating.....G..... 302 632-1234
Camden Wyoming *(G-639)*
Georgetown Construction Co.....D..... 302 856-7601
Georgetown *(G-2544)*
Gift Solutions LLC.....G..... 585 317-4465
Newark *(G-6654)*
GL Gray Consulting Services LL.....G..... 302 698-3339
Magnolia *(G-3891)*
Global Dev Partners Inc.....G..... 480 330-7931
Wilmington *(G-10723)*
Good Home Solutions LLC.....G..... 302 540-3190
Wilmington *(G-10746)*
Graceland Group Inc.....G..... 302 226-1373
Dewey Beach *(G-1058)*
Grape Solutions.....G..... 201 784-9797
Wilmington *(G-10761)*
Greenwing Solutions Inc.....G..... 302 295-5690
Wilmington *(G-10782)*
H Clemons Consulting Inc.....E..... 302 295-5097
Wilmington *(G-10805)*
Har-Lex LLC.....G..... 302 476-2322
Wilmington *(G-10835)*
Hedgeforce LLC.....G..... 305 600-0085
Newark *(G-6720)*
Highdef Transportation LLC.....G..... 610 212-8596
Bear *(G-184)*
I AM Consulting Group Inc.....F..... 302 521-4999
Bear *(G-187)*
Incorporators USA LLC.....F..... 800 441-5940
Wilmington *(G-11015)*
Industry ARC.....F..... 614 588-8538
Wilmington *(G-11023)*

Inrg of Delaware Inc................................G....... 302 369-1412
Lewes *(G-3559)*
Intelligent Signage Inc............................G....... 302 762-4100
Wilmington *(G-11052)*
International Spine Pain..........................G....... 302 478-7001
Wilmington *(G-11067)*
Jackson Contracting Inc..........................F....... 302 678-2011
Dover *(G-1689)*
Jeris LLC...F....... 443 745-9023
Selbyville *(G-8508)*
JR Gettier & Associates Inc...................B....... 302 478-0911
Wilmington *(G-11202)*
Kfs Strategic MGT Svcs LLC..................F....... 302 545-7640
Bear *(G-217)*
Koala Enterprises Inc.............................G....... 302 436-9950
Frankford *(G-2370)*
Kramer Group LLC...................................G....... 717 368-2117
Wilmington *(G-11291)*
La Jolla Fincl Partners LLC....................G....... 858 864-0146
Wilmington *(G-11312)*
Leadership Caddie..................................F....... 302 743-6456
Bear *(G-232)*
Lens Tolic LLC...G....... 800 343-5697
Hockessin *(G-3081)*
Lindco..G....... 302 652-0708
Wilmington *(G-11393)*
Lityx LLC...G....... 888 548-9947
Wilmington *(G-11411)*
Maryann Metrinko LLC...........................G....... 410 643-1472
Lewes *(G-3623)*
Medevice Services LLC...........................G....... 877 202-1588
Dover *(G-1835)*
Mefta LLC..F....... 804 433-3566
Wilmington *(G-11622)*
Monterey Enterprises LLC......................G....... 302 504-4901
Newark *(G-7053)*
Mtk Enterprises LLC................................G....... 302 266-9611
Newark *(G-7070)*
My Benefit Advisor LLC...........................G....... 302 588-7242
Wilmington *(G-11786)*
Nabstar Hospitality..................................G....... 302 453-1700
Newark *(G-7080)*
Nations Equity Investments Inc..............G....... 302 257-9287
Wilmington *(G-11814)*
Netragy LLC...G....... 973 846-7018
Newark *(G-7094)*
New Castle Cnty Shoppers Guide..........E....... 302 325-6600
New Castle *(G-5554)*
New Covenant Elec Svcs Inc..................G....... 302 454-1165
Middletown *(G-4172)*
Newark Heritage Partners I LLC............F....... 302 283-0540
Newark *(G-7121)*
Nova Consultants Ltd..............................F....... 302 328-1686
New Castle *(G-5581)*
Nr Hudson Consulting Inc.......................G....... 302 875-5276
Laurel *(G-3267)*
Nucar Consulting Inc...............................E....... 302 696-6000
Odessa *(G-7831)*
Ocean First Enterprises LLC..................F....... 302 232-8547
Wilmington *(G-11933)*
Office Partners Xiv Bellevue..................G....... 302 691-2100
Wilmington *(G-11940)*
Orchard Park Group Inc..........................E....... 302 356-1139
New Castle *(G-5590)*
Paragon Group..F....... 302 798-5777
Claymont *(G-792)*
Performance Materials Na Inc................A....... 302 892-7009
Wilmington *(G-12085)*
Perrone Enterprises Inc..........................G....... 302 436-8031
Selbyville *(G-8530)*
Pmcaa Inc..G....... 302 439-6028
Wilmington *(G-12163)*
Princeton Coml Holdings LLC................G....... 302 449-4836
Newark *(G-7253)*
Project Widgets Inc..................................G....... 302 439-3414
Wilmington *(G-12249)*
Quinteccent Inc..G....... 443 838-5447
Selbyville *(G-8536)*
Rallypoint Solutions LLC.........................F....... 302 543-8087
Wilmington *(G-12308)*
Reading Assist Institute..........................F....... 302 425-4080
Wilmington *(G-12342)*
Renaissance Square LLC........................G....... 302 943-5118
Dover *(G-2024)*
RFS Enterprises Inc..................................G....... 302 888-0143
Wilmington *(G-12398)*
Ricore Inc...G....... 302 656-8158
New Castle *(G-5678)*
Rockledge Global Partners Ltd..............F....... 800 659-1102
Wilmington *(G-12456)*
Sandler Occptnal Mdicine Assoc...........E....... 302 369-0171
Newark *(G-7381)*
Sandy Knoll Enterprises LLC.................G....... 302 875-3916
Laurel *(G-3287)*
Santora CPA Group Pa.............................E....... 302 737-6200
Newark *(G-7385)*
Schatz Messick Enterprises LLC............G....... 302 398-8646
Harrington *(G-2883)*
Scio Risk Group Llc.................................F....... 302 897-1534
Wilmington *(G-12561)*
Sentinel-Sg LLC..G....... 580 458-9184
Wilmington *(G-12580)*
Sereduke Design Cons LLC....................G....... 302 478-3468
Wilmington *(G-12582)*
Siemanowski Consulting Inc...................G....... 302 368-1081
Newark *(G-7423)*
Sinnott Exc Consulting LLC....................G....... 302 656-2898
Wilmington *(G-12632)*
Spectrum Tax Consultants USA.............G....... 866 544-1408
Wilmington *(G-12700)*
Spine Group LLC.......................................G....... 302 595-3030
Wilmington *(G-12706)*
Sqs Global Solutions LLC.......................F....... 302 691-9682
Wilmington *(G-12718)*
Strategy House Inc...................................G....... 302 658-1500
Newark *(G-7494)*
Systems Tech & Science LLC..................G....... 703 757-2010
Dagsboro *(G-937)*
Tade Info Tech Solutions........................G....... 302 832-1449
Newark *(G-7529)*
Tarpon Strategies LLC............................G....... 215 806-2723
Newark *(G-7540)*
Tech Management Services Inc.............G....... 302 539-4837
Bethany Beach *(G-435)*
Trainor Consulting LLC...........................G....... 302 428-1677
Wilmington *(G-12950)*
Treehouse Wellness Center LLC...........F....... 302 893-1001
Wilmington *(G-12963)*
Trellist Inc..G....... 302 593-1432
Wilmington *(G-12965)*
Trinity Gold Consulting LLC...................G....... 302 476-9774
Wilmington *(G-12975)*
Virtual Business Entps LLC....................G....... 302 472-9100
Wilmington *(G-13089)*
Vtms LLC..G....... 302 264-9094
Dover *(G-2201)*
Wagamon Technology Group LLC..........G....... 302 424-1855
Milford *(G-4593)*
Wheeler Wolfenden & Dwares PA..........E....... 302 254-8240
Wilmington *(G-13184)*
Wiedmann Enterprises Inc.......................G....... 302 645-2028
Lewes *(G-3822)*
Yph Consultants LLC................................G....... 302 674-4766
Dover *(G-2250)*
Zahn Incorporated....................................G....... 302 425-3700
Wilmington *(G-13339)*
Zieta Technologies LLC............................F....... 302 252-5249
Wilmington *(G-13350)*

CONSULTING SVC: Computer

2ndquadrant Inc..G....... 650 378-1218
Wilmington *(G-8856)*
Ait Advanced Infotech Inc........................G....... 302 454-8620
Bear *(G-24)*
Aleric International Inc............................F....... 302 547-4846
Middletown *(G-3934)*
Applied Control Engrg Inc.......................D....... 302 738-8800
Newark *(G-5987)*
Apps Complex LLC....................................F....... 705 600-0729
Lewes *(G-3344)*
Biritek LLC..G....... 949 556-3943
Dover *(G-1206)*
Bluent LLC...D....... 832 476-8459
Lewes *(G-3388)*
Burgeon It Services LLC..........................F....... 302 613-0999
Wilmington *(G-9506)*
Capgemini America Inc............................G....... 302 656-7491
Wilmington *(G-9555)*
Computer Sciences Corporation............B....... 302 391-8347
Newark *(G-6277)*
Congruence Consulting Group..............G....... 320 290-6155
Newark *(G-6286)*
Conventra LLC...G....... 302 378-4461
Middletown *(G-4008)*
Counterpoint Software Inc.......................G....... 302 426-6500
Wilmington *(G-9875)*
Csols Inc..E....... 302 731-5290
Newark *(G-6322)*
Datatech Enterprises Inc.........................F....... 540 370-0010
Selbyville *(G-8478)*
Dax-Wave Consulting LLC.......................G....... 424 543-6662
Wilmington *(G-9974)*
Delasoft Inc..C....... 302 533-7912
New Castle *(G-5222)*
Dew Softech Inc..E....... 302 834-2555
Newark *(G-6441)*
Diamond Technologies Inc.......................E....... 302 421-8252
Wilmington *(G-10149)*
Diligent Bus Solutions LLC.......................G....... 302 897-5993
Newark *(G-6449)*
Discidium Technology Inc.........................G....... 347 220-5979
Newark *(G-6455)*
E-Dmz Security LLC..................................E....... 302 791-9370
Wilmington *(G-10312)*
E2e LLC...G....... 703 906-5353
Hockessin *(G-3014)*
Edward Land Consulting Inc....................G....... 302 838-7003
Bear *(G-140)*
Encross LLC...F....... 302 351-2593
Wilmington *(G-10396)*
Ets & Ycp LLC..G....... 302 525-4111
Newark *(G-6543)*
Even & Odd Minds LLC..............................F....... 619 663-7284
Wilmington *(G-10443)*
Feast Kitchen Inc..G....... 415 758-8779
Dover *(G-1545)*
Forward Discovery Inc...............................G....... 703 647-6364
Camden Wyoming *(G-641)*
Frontier Technologies Inc..........................G....... 302 225-2530
Wilmington *(G-10644)*
GBA Enterprises Inc...................................G....... 302 323-1080
New Castle *(G-5346)*
Genovesius Solutia LLC.............................G....... 302 252-7506
Hockessin *(G-3036)*
Headstream Inc...D....... 302 356-0156
Wilmington *(G-10865)*
Hoover Computer Services Inc.................G....... 302 529-7050
Wilmington *(G-10950)*
Horizon Systems Inc...................................G....... 302 983-3203
New Castle *(G-5404)*
Inetworkz LLC...F....... 407 401-9384
Lewes *(G-3558)*
Internet Working Technologies...............G....... 302 424-1855
Milford *(G-4450)*
Intrinsic Partners LLC................................D....... 610 388-0853
Wilmington *(G-11071)*
Inumsoft Inc..G....... 302 533-5403
Bear *(G-191)*
It Resources Inc..E....... 203 521-6945
Newark *(G-6809)*
Jhonston and Associates...........................G....... 302 368-9790
Newark *(G-6838)*
Keyboarders LLC..G....... 302 438-8055
Wilmington *(G-11250)*
Kogut Tech Consulting Inc.........................G....... 302 455-0388
Newark *(G-6901)*
Kortech Consulting Inc..............................F....... 302 559-4612
Bear *(G-220)*
Lambro Technologies LLC..........................G....... 302 351-2559
Wilmington *(G-11325)*
Liveware Inc..F....... 302 791-9446
Claymont *(G-775)*
Luxcore LLC..F....... 302 777-0538
Wilmington *(G-11457)*
Maan Softwares Inc....................................E....... 531 203-9141
Lewes *(G-3615)*
McSglobal Inc..G....... 302 427-6970
Wilmington *(G-11607)*
My Digital Shield...G....... 423 310-8977
Wilmington *(G-11787)*
Network Design Technologies...................G....... 610 991-2929
Wilmington *(G-11839)*
Partners Plus Inc..G....... 302 529-3700
New Castle *(G-5605)*
Pathscale Inc...E....... 408 520-0811
Wilmington *(G-12031)*
PLM Consulting Inc.....................................F....... 302 984-2698
Wilmington *(G-12160)*
Precisionists Inc..G....... 610 241-5354
Wilmington *(G-12209)*
Proactive Prfmce Solutions Inc.................F....... 302 375-0451
Newark *(G-7264)*
Raas Infotek LLC...E....... 302 894-3184
Newark *(G-7294)*
Ru Inc...C....... 917 346-0285
Wilmington *(G-12488)*
Sanjaban Corp..G....... 612 805-5971
Wilmington *(G-12540)*
SC Foster LLC...F....... 302 383-0201
Wilmington *(G-12548)*

CONSULTING SVC: Computer

Scicom Scntific Communications ....G....... 302 475-2694
 Wilmington *(G-12558)*
Sherweb Inc ....G....... 888 567-6610
 Newark *(G-7416)*
Sigma Data Systems Inc ....G....... 302 453-8812
 Newark *(G-7426)*
Solid Idea Solutions LLC ....G....... 646 982-2890
 Lewes *(G-3755)*
Syncretic Software Inc ....F....... 302 762-2600
 Wilmington *(G-12835)*
Tech International Corp ....G....... 302 478-2301
 Wilmington *(G-12868)*
Techno Soft Inc ....F....... 302 392-5200
 Wilmington *(G-12871)*
Tecs Plus ....G....... 302 437-6890
 Newark *(G-7550)*
Toptal LLC ....D....... 650 843-9206
 Wilmington *(G-12933)*
Total Risc Technology USA LLC ....D....... 972 422-9135
 Wilmington *(G-12940)*
Vensoft LLC ....E....... 302 392-9000
 Wilmington *(G-13057)*
Vitalus Technologies Inc ....G....... 302 383-9100
 Clayton *(G-873)*
Wahid Consultants LLC ....E....... 315 400-0955
 New Castle *(G-5821)*
Webbit ....G....... 302 725-6024
 Milford *(G-4600)*
Wenova Inc ....G....... 847 477-0489
 New Castle *(G-5829)*
Wyndham Group Inc ....G....... 704 905-9750
 Wilmington *(G-13312)*
Yes Hardsoft Solutions Inc ....G....... 609 632-0397
 Claymont *(G-828)*
Z Data Inc ....G....... 302 566-5351
 Newark *(G-7735)*
Ziras Technologies Inc ....F....... 302 286-7303
 Newark *(G-7741)*

CONSULTING SVC: Data Processing

3d Tech LLC ....G....... 610 268-2350
 Hockessin *(G-2947)*
Data-Bi LLC ....G....... 302 290-3138
 Wilmington *(G-9962)*
Ik Solutions Inc ....G....... 302 861-6775
 Newark *(G-6766)*
Implify Inc ....E....... 302 533-2345
 Newark *(G-6769)*
Inov8 Inc ....G....... 302 465-5124
 Camden Wyoming *(G-646)*
Orpheus Companies Ltd ....G....... 302 328-3451
 New Castle *(G-5592)*

CONSULTING SVC: Educational

Pyramid Educational Cons ....E....... 302 368-2515
 New Castle *(G-5655)*

CONSULTING SVC: Engineering

Aecom Global II LLC ....D....... 302 933-0200
 Millsboro *(G-4623)*
ARA Technologies Inc ....G....... 215 605-5707
 Wilmington *(G-9109)*
Arcadis US Inc ....E....... 302 658-1718
 Wilmington *(G-9120)*
Aries Security LLC ....G....... 302 365-0026
 Wilmington *(G-9128)*
Black & Veatch Corporation ....E....... 302 798-0200
 Wilmington *(G-9346)*
Cabe Associates Inc ....F....... 302 674-9280
 Dover *(G-1247)*
Cecon Group LLC ....G....... 302 994-8000
 Wilmington *(G-9608)*
Century Engineering Inc ....D....... 302 734-9188
 Dover *(G-1270)*
De Technologies Inc ....G....... 302 285-0353
 Middletown *(G-4021)*
Dedc LLC ....D....... 302 738-7172
 Newark *(G-6358)*
Duffield Associates Inc ....D....... 302 239-6634
 Wilmington *(G-10245)*
E-Merge Systems Inc ....G....... 302 894-3860
 Newark *(G-6493)*
Gahagan & Bryant Assoc Inc ....F....... 302 652-4948
 Wilmington *(G-10662)*
Gannett Fleming Inc ....E....... 302 378-2256
 Middletown *(G-4083)*
George Miles & Buhr LLC ....G....... 302 628-1421
 Seaford *(G-8253)*

Hillis-Carnes Engrg Assoc Inc ....E....... 302 744-9855
 Dover *(G-1646)*
Hough Associates Inc ....F....... 302 322-7800
 Newark *(G-6750)*
I 3 A LLC ....G....... 302 659-0909
 Smyrna *(G-8656)*
Karins Engineering Inc ....E....... 302 369-2900
 Newark *(G-6867)*
Kci Protection Tech LLC ....G....... 302 543-8340
 Newark *(G-6870)*
Kubota Research Associates ....G....... 302 683-0199
 Hockessin *(G-3072)*
Luriware Consulting Agricultur ....G....... 302 244-1947
 Dover *(G-1799)*
Lutz Engineering Inc ....G....... 302 479-9017
 Wilmington *(G-11456)*
Mahaffy & Associates Inc ....E....... 302 656-8381
 Middletown *(G-4141)*
On Board Engineering Corp ....G....... 302 613-5030
 New Castle *(G-5587)*
Paragon Engineering Corp ....E....... 302 762-6010
 Wilmington *(G-12016)*
Pennoni ....G....... 302 234-4600
 Newark *(G-7196)*
Pennoni Associates Inc ....E....... 302 684-8030
 Milton *(G-4947)*
Pennoni Associates Inc ....G....... 302 655-4451
 Newark *(G-7197)*
Power Delivery Solutions LLC ....E....... 302 260-3114
 Newark *(G-7236)*
Pro-Tech Engineering Inc ....E....... 302 998-1717
 Wilmington *(G-12236)*
RDS Engineering LLC ....G....... 417 763-3727
 Lewes *(G-3710)*
Robert A Chagnon ....G....... 302 489-1932
 Hockessin *(G-3138)*
Sargent & Lundy LLC ....G....... 302 622-7200
 Wilmington *(G-12542)*
Scott Engineering Inc ....G....... 302 736-3058
 Dover *(G-2062)*
Sinnott Exc Consulting LLC ....G....... 302 656-2898
 Wilmington *(G-12632)*
Taylor McCormick Inc ....E....... 302 738-0203
 Christiana *(G-682)*
Technology Transfers Inc ....G....... 302 234-4718
 Newark *(G-7547)*
Tetra Tech Inc ....F....... 302 738-7551
 Newark *(G-7559)*
TY Lin International Group ....G....... 302 883-3662
 Dover *(G-2168)*
Urban Engineers Inc ....G....... 302 689-0260
 New Castle *(G-5811)*
URS Group Inc ....D....... 302 731-7824
 Newark *(G-7634)*
Vandemark & Lynch Inc ....E....... 302 764-7635
 Wilmington *(G-13048)*
Whitman Requardt and Assoc LLP ....F....... 302 571-9001
 Dover *(G-13195)*

CONSULTING SVC: Executive Placement & Search

CBI Group LLc ....E....... 302 266-0860
 Newark *(G-6174)*
Christiana Consulting Inc ....G....... 302 454-7000
 Newark *(G-6221)*
Conducerent Incorporated ....G....... 302 543-8525
 Wilmington *(G-9816)*
Global Network Executive Inc ....F....... 302 251-8940
 Wilmington *(G-10728)*
Global Recruiters Network Inc ....G....... 302 455-9500
 Newark *(G-6667)*
Hornberger Management Company ...G....... 302 573-2541
 Wilmington *(G-10956)*
Howroyd-Wright Emplymnt Agcy ....G....... 302 738-4022
 Newark *(G-6752)*
Mwidm Inc ....E....... 302 298-0101
 Wilmington *(G-11785)*
Professional Recruiting Cons ....G....... 302 479-9550
 Wilmington *(G-12239)*
Ramona Clay ....G....... 866 448-0834
 Wilmington *(G-12314)*
Randstad Professionals Us LLC ....F....... 302 658-6181
 Wilmington *(G-12316)*

CONSULTING SVC: Financial Management

Abridge Partners LLC ....G....... 302 378-1882
 Middletown *(G-3928)*
America Group ....G....... 302 529-1320
 Wilmington *(G-9041)*

Bloom Consulting ....G....... 302 584-1592
 Wilmington *(G-9372)*
Boothe Investment Group ....G....... 302 734-7526
 Dover *(G-1221)*
Byron & Davis Cccc ....G....... 302 792-2334
 Wilmington *(G-9517)*
Cypress Capital Management LLC ....F....... 302 429-8436
 Wilmington *(G-9934)*
Daimlerchrysler N Amrca Financ ....G....... 302 292-6840
 Newark *(G-6344)*
Daniel M McDermott Chfc Cfp ....G....... 302 778-5677
 Wilmington *(G-9956)*
Delaware Incorporation Svcs ....F....... 302 658-1733
 Wilmington *(G-10057)*
Delaware Marketing Partners ....G....... 302 575-1610
 Wilmington *(G-10062)*
Diamond State Fincl Group Inc ....E....... 302 366-0366
 Newark *(G-6444)*
Dorey Financial Services Inc ....G....... 302 856-0970
 Georgetown *(G-2513)*
Douglas C Loew & Associates ....G....... 302 453-0550
 Newark *(G-6464)*
Fair Square Financial LLC ....G....... 571 205-0305
 Wilmington *(G-10475)*
Financial House Inc ....F....... 302 654-5451
 Wilmington *(G-10540)*
Inflection Point Ventures LP ....G....... 302 452-1120
 Newark *(G-6779)*
Insurance & Fincl Svcs Ltd Del ....G....... 302 234-1200
 Wilmington *(G-11044)*
Intercontinental Marketing ....G....... 302 429-7555
 Wilmington *(G-11056)*
Key Advisors Group LLC ....G....... 302 735-9909
 Dover *(G-1744)*
Lawter Planning Group Inc ....G....... 302 736-6065
 Dover *(G-1772)*
Mallard Advisors LLC ....F....... 302 239-1654
 Hockessin *(G-3086)*
Money Galaxy Inc ....F....... 302 319-2008
 Wilmington *(G-11731)*
Newrez LLC ....G....... 302 455-6600
 Middletown *(G-4174)*
Newton One Advisors ....F....... 302 731-1326
 Newark *(G-7130)*

CONSULTING SVC: Human Resource

ADP Pacific Inc ....G....... 302 657-4060
 Wilmington *(G-8942)*
Congruence Consulting Group ....G....... 320 290-6155
 Newark *(G-6286)*
Connecting Generations Inc ....F....... 302 656-2122
 Wilmington *(G-9825)*
Dfs Corporate Services LLC ....A....... 302 323-7191
 New Castle *(G-5250)*
Even & Odd Minds LLC ....F....... 619 663-7284
 Wilmington *(G-10443)*
Franklin Kennet LLC ....F....... 302 655-6536
 Wilmington *(G-10617)*
Functionalit Inc ....G....... 703 566-6624
 Selbyville *(G-8495)*
Fursan Consulting Services ....F....... 240 654-5784
 New Castle *(G-5336)*
Host Nation Perspectives LLC ....G....... 443 292-6702
 Selbyville *(G-8504)*
Modernthink LLC ....F....... 302 764-4477
 Wilmington *(G-11721)*
Weelwork Inc ....G....... 800 546-8607
 Claymont *(G-818)*
White & Associates ....G....... 302 765-3736
 Wilmington *(G-13188)*

CONSULTING SVC: Management

AA Smith & Associates LLC ....F....... 973 477-3052
 Middletown *(G-3926)*
Above and Beyond Coverage LLC ....E....... 201 417-5189
 Wilmington *(G-8907)*
Aesthtic Special Care Assoc PA ....F....... 302 482-4444
 Wilmington *(G-8967)*
All In One Brands LLC ....G....... 301 323-8144
 Dover *(G-1105)*
Anq LLC ....G....... 408 837-3678
 Wilmington *(G-9089)*
Arm Chair Scouts LLC ....F....... 315 360-8692
 Wilmington *(G-9130)*
Big Tomorrow LLC ....F....... 650 714-3912
 Wilmington *(G-9333)*
Blackgrid Consulting LLC ....G....... 302 319-2013
 Wilmington *(G-9348)*
Carr Paris ....F....... 302 401-1203
 Wilmington *(G-9578)*

PRODUCT & SERVICES SECTION

CONSULTING SVC: Online Technology

Company	Code	Phone
Cloud Services Solutions Inc — Wilmington (G-9746)	G	888 335-3132
Comprehensive Bus Cons Inc — Hockessin (G-2995)	G	302 635-7711
Conducerent Incorporated — Wilmington (G-9816)	G	302 543-8525
Core Value Global LLC — Wilmington (G-9860)	G	908 312-4070
Crimson Strategy Group LLP — Dover (G-1323)	G	302 503-5698
Csi Solutions LLC — Newark (G-6320)	F	202 506-7573
Da Vinci Ebusiness Ltd — Wilmington (G-9945)	G	610 399-3988
Decisivedge LLC — Newark (G-6357)	G	302 299-1570
Delaware State Education Assn — Dover (G-1396)	E	302 734-5834
Dreamville LLC — Lewes (G-3472)	G	662 524-0917
Drw Funding LLC — Dover (G-1481)	G	404 631-7127
Dumont Group LLC — New Castle (G-5265)	G	302 777-1003
Dynamic Devices LLC — Wilmington (G-10271)	F	302 994-2401
Enterprise Rsurce Planners Inc — Wilmington (G-10415)	G	800 716-3660
Esis Inc — Wilmington (G-10436)	G	215 640-1000
Femmepal Corporation — Lewes (G-3494)	E	888 406-0804
Financial Services — Wilmington (G-10541)	E	302 478-4707
Five Sixty Enterprise LLC — Wilmington (G-10566)	E	302 268-6530
Gale and Associates LLC — Dover (G-1578)	G	302 698-4253
Gateway International 360 LLC — New Castle (G-5345)	G	302 250-4990
Green Interest Enterprises LLC — Dover (G-1612)	G	228 355-0708
Grofos International LLC — Newark (G-6693)	G	302 635-4805
Gulf Development Partners LLC — Wilmington (G-10800)	G	646 334-1245
Ibr Group Inc — Newark (G-6760)	F	610 986-8545
Ignis Group LLC — Lewes (G-3552)	E	302 645-7400
Independent School MGT Inc — Wilmington (G-11018)	E	302 656-4944
Intrinsic Partners LLC — Wilmington (G-11071)	D	610 388-0853
Isis North America Inc — Lewes (G-3563)	G	508 653-7318
Johnston Associates — Newark (G-6848)	G	302 521-2984
Keen Consulting Inc — Georgetown (G-2580)	G	302 684-5270
Kelmar Associates LLC — Wilmington (G-11238)	D	781 213-6926
Kirk & Associates LLC — Christiana (G-672)	F	302 444-4733
Kortech Consulting Inc — Bear (G-220)	F	302 559-4612
Lifesource Consulting Svcs LLC — Dover (G-1784)	F	302 257-6247
Linda McCormick — Wilmington (G-11392)	G	443 987-2099
Longo and Associates LLP — Wilmington (G-11431)	G	302 477-7500
Maintenance Troubleshooting — Newark (G-6976)	G	302 692-0871
Management Options Inc — Newark (G-6980)	F	302 234-0836
Market Edge LLC — Wilmington (G-11534)	E	302 442-6800
Mid States Sales & Marketing — Wilmington (G-11680)	E	302 888-2475
Morning Report Research Inc — Dover (G-1872)	G	302 730-3793
Mwidm Inc — Wilmington (G-11785)	E	302 298-0101
My Market Quest Inc — Wilmington (G-11788)	F	213 265-9767
Nhb Advisors Inc — Wilmington (G-11886)	G	610 660-0060
Nova RE & Bus Consulting LLC — Lewes (G-3661)	F	302 258-2193
Oceanstar Technologies Inc — Bear (G-270)	G	302 542-1900
Omninet International Inc — Wilmington (G-11950)	E	208 246-5022
Omniway Corporation — Newark (G-7147)	F	302 738-5076
Openexo Inc — Dover (G-1919)	F	617 965-5057
Paul Associates — Wilmington (G-12039)	G	302 584-0064
Perry and Associates Inc — Hockessin (G-3117)	F	302 898-2327
Pierce Professional Services — Magnolia (G-3903)	G	302 331-1154
Pineal Consulting Group LLC — Newark (G-7218)	F	302 219-4822
Postal Associates Inc — Wilmington (G-12193)	G	302 584-1244
Precisionists Inc — Wilmington (G-12209)	G	610 241-5354
Quinteccent Inc — Selbyville (G-8536)	G	443 838-5447
Redleo Software Inc — Wilmington (G-12348)	F	302 691-9072
Sam Walts & Associates — Wilmington (G-12531)	G	302 777-2211
Second Chance Solutions LLC — Wilmington (G-12567)	G	302 204-0551
Sopo-360 LLC — Newark (G-7460)	G	703 585-3706
Timtec LLC — Newark (G-7567)	F	302 292-8500
Unique Creations By Chloe LLC — Wilmington (G-13016)	E	855 942-0477
Velocity Pointe LLC — Wilmington (G-13056)	G	302 351-8305
Veteran It Pro LLC — Hockessin (G-3167)	F	302 824-3111
Well Done Cleaning Services — Wilmington (G-13142)	G	443 407-3064
Wyndham Group Inc — Wilmington (G-13312)	G	704 905-9750
Xonex Relocation LLC — New Castle (G-5843)	D	302 323-9000
Zutz Risk Management — Wilmington (G-13355)	D	302 658-8000

CONSULTING SVC: Marketing Management

Company	Code	Phone
Adamlouis Ltd Liability Co — Wilmington (G-8932)	G	973 937-7524
Advanced Internet Solutions — Wilmington (G-8952)	G	302 584-4641
Avalanche Strategies LLC — Selbyville (G-8452)	C	302 436-7060
Breckenridge Software Tech — Wilmington (G-9464)	G	302 656-8460
Convergence Group Inc — Wilmington (G-9845)	F	302 234-7400
Cool Nerds Marketing Inc — Wilmington (G-9851)	F	302 304-3440
Cr24 LLC — Wilmington (G-9890)	F	888 427-9357
Design Tribe Republic LLC — Wilmington (G-10124)	G	302 918-5279
Dojupa LLC — Wilmington (G-10185)	G	302 300-2009
Encima Group Inc — Newark (G-6525)	D	302 352-1714
Epic Marketing Cons Corp — Middletown (G-4061)	E	302 285-9790
Gkua Inc — Wilmington (G-10718)	F	415 971-5341
Global Data Mining LLC — Lewes (G-3516)	G	551 208-1316
Grind or Starve LLC — Wilmington (G-10786)	G	302 322-1679
Honey Bee Seasonal Kit & Mkt — Wilmington (G-10947)	G	302 407-5579
Iconic Skus LLC — Wilmington (G-10989)	G	302 722-4547
Kc & Associates Inc — Wilmington (G-11231)	G	302 633-3300
KS Kitchen LLC — Newark (G-6904)	G	302 743-4349
Marketing Creators Inc — Wilmington (G-11536)	D	302 409-0344
Marketing Enterprise Capyuring — Wilmington (G-11537)	G	302 293-9250
Money Bax LLC — Lewes (G-3646)	G	302 360-8577
Montesino Associates — Wilmington (G-11736)	G	302 888-2355
Moore International LLC — Wilmington (G-11745)	G	302 603-7262
Mozeweb LLC — Newark (G-7065)	G	302 355-0692
Mtc Usa LLC — Newark (G-7069)	F	980 999-8888
My Qme Inc — Wilmington (G-11789)	E	302 218-8730
Ohana Companies Inc — Wilmington (G-11941)	F	302 225-5505
Project of Providence LLC — Wilmington (G-12247)	G	302 438-8970
Project Otr LLC — Wilmington (G-12248)	G	404 964-2244
Scottish Ventures LLC — New Castle (G-5695)	G	302 382-6057
Solace Lifesciences Inc — Wilmington (G-12674)	G	302 275-4195
Tecnologika Usa Inc — Wilmington (G-12874)	G	302 597-7611
Trellist Inc — Wilmington (G-12964)	E	302 778-1300
Vector Marketing Corp — Wilmington (G-13053)	G	716 373-6141
Vtms LLC — Dover (G-2201)	G	302 264-9094
Zir LLC — Lewes (G-3835)	G	203 524-1215
Zumra Solutions LLC — Lewes (G-3836)	G	302 504-4423

CONSULTING SVC: Online Technology

Company	Code	Phone
4sight Group LLC — Wilmington (G-8864)	G	800 490-2131
Aegisnet Inc — New Castle (G-5011)	E	302 325-2122
Almm Ventures LLC — Wilmington (G-9026)	G	302 778-1300
Applied Technologies Inc — Camden Wyoming (G-614)	G	302 670-4601
Axiom Resources LLC — Dover (G-1163)	F	410 756-0440
Bamboozle Web Services Inc — Newark (G-6041)	G	833 380-4600
Blackthorn Advisory Group LLC — Wilmington (G-9365)	G	302 442-6484
Compd Holdings Inc — Middletown (G-4005)	G	929 436-5252
Delmarvavoip LLC — Lewes (G-3460)	G	855 645-8647
Delt LLC — Newark (G-6431)	G	215 869-7409
Efotolabcom Inc — Wilmington (G-10361)	G	302 984-0807
Evocati Group Corporation — Dover (G-1533)	F	206 551-9087
Evonsys LLC — Wilmington (G-10451)	G	302 544-2156
G B Tech Inc — Middletown (G-4081)	E	302 378-5600
Goodworld Inc — Wilmington (G-10750)	G	845 325-2232
Icuelab LLC — Wilmington (G-6761)	G	302 983-8924
Iji Inc — Wilmington (G-10997)	E	732 485-9427
Instadapp Labs LLC — Lewes (G-3560)	G	469 605-1661
Intercontinental Tech LLC — Wilmington (G-11057)	G	302 984-2111
It Tigers LLC — Lewes (G-3565)	G	732 898-2793
Layercake LLC — Newark (G-6924)	G	571 449-7538
Lifesquared Inc — Dover (G-1785)	G	415 475-9090
Maven Security Consulting Inc — Bear (G-248)	G	302 365-6862
Net Monarch — Wilmington (G-11837)	G	302 994-9407
Paymenex Inc — Wilmington (G-12048)	D	302 504-6044
Play US Media LLC — Dover (G-1965)	G	302 924-5034
Private Family Network LLC — Dover (G-1988)	F	302 760-9684
Quickborn Consulting LLC — Wilmington (G-12288)	G	302 407-0922

Employee Codes: A=Over 500 employees, B=251-500, C=101-250, D=51-100, E=20-50, F=10-19, G=1-9

2020 Harris Directory of Delaware Businesses

CONSULTING SVC: Online Technology

Rave Business Systems LLC .... F 302 407-2270
　Lewes *(G-3708)*
Scinorx Technologies Inc .... G 302 268-5447
　Wilmington *(G-12560)*
Sendsafely LLC .... F 917 375-5891
　Newark *(G-7407)*
Skiplist Inc .... G 440 855-0319
　Newark *(G-7436)*
SM Technomine Inc .... F 312 492-4386
　Wilmington *(G-12647)*
Smart Armor Protected LLC .... E 480 823-8122
　Newark *(G-7444)*
Tapp Networks LLC .... G 302 222-3384
　Newark *(G-7539)*
Tekstrom Inc .... E 302 709-5900
　Wilmington *(G-12876)*
Ublerb .... G 773 569-9686
　Dover *(G-2171)*
Vls It Consulting Inc .... F 302 368-5656
　Newark *(G-7662)*
Vsg Business Solutions LLC .... E 302 261-3209
　Bear *(G-367)*
Wahed Inc .... E 646 961-7063
　Lewes *(G-3813)*
Warain Corp .... G 762 670-3452
　Wilmington *(G-13118)*
Xtium LLC .... E 302 351-6177
　Wilmington *(G-13323)*
Yesamerica Corporation .... F 800 872-1548
　Middletown *(G-4294)*

CONSULTING SVC: Personnel Management

BP Staffing Inc .... G 302 999-7213
　Wilmington *(G-9407)*

CONSULTING SVC: Sales Management

Bennett & Bennett Inc .... F 302 990-8939
　New Castle *(G-5081)*
Performance Based Results .... G 302 478-4443
　Talleyville *(G-8750)*

CONSULTING SVC: Telecommunications

ABC Systems Inc .... G 302 528-8875
　Newark *(G-5883)*
Alliance Bus Dev Concepts LLC .... F 803 814-4004
　Clayton *(G-832)*
C4-Nvis USA LLC .... G 213 465-5089
　Dover *(G-1246)*
Convergone Gvrnment Sltons LLC .... G 302 999-7020
　Wilmington *(G-9846)*
Flex Ip Solutions Inc .... G 610 359-5812
　Wilmington *(G-10573)*
McNichol Enterprises Inc .... F 302 633-9348
　Wilmington *(G-11606)*
Netinstincts Inc .... F 302 521-9478
　Wilmington *(G-11838)*
Qsr Group LLC .... G 302 268-6909
　Wilmington *(G-12276)*
Trinet Consultants Inc .... F 302 633-9348
　Wilmington *(G-12973)*
Verscom LLC .... E 866 238-9189
　Wilmington *(G-13065)*

CONSULTING SVCS, BUSINESS: Agricultural

Agricltral Assssmnts Intl Corp .... G 240 463-6677
　Laurel *(G-3191)*
East Coast Seed LLC .... G 302 856-7018
　Georgetown *(G-2518)*
Eden Green LLC .... F 817 999-1570
　Wilmington *(G-10344)*
Emerald Bioagriculture Corp .... F 517 882-7370
　Hockessin *(G-3019)*
J C Wells & Sons LP .... G 302 422-4732
　Milford *(G-4455)*
JD Rellek Company Inc .... G 302 284-7042
　Felton *(G-2298)*
Southern States Coop Inc .... G 302 875-3635
　Laurel *(G-3293)*

CONSULTING SVCS, BUSINESS: City Planning

ARC HUD VII Inc .... G 302 996-9400
　Wilmington *(G-9117)*

CONSULTING SVCS, BUSINESS: Communications

Elevationtv .... G 978 317-9285
　Wilmington *(G-10373)*

CONSULTING SVCS, BUSINESS: Energy Conservation

Ameresco Inc .... G 302 284-1480
　Felton *(G-2271)*
Ameresco Inc .... G 302 875-0696
　Georgetown *(G-2430)*
Cleantech Energy Solutions LLC .... G 301 704-2831
　Wilmington *(G-9738)*
Flexera Inc .... E 302 945-6870
　Harbeson *(G-2783)*
Suffex Conservation .... G 302 856-2105
　Georgetown *(G-2670)*
Umbrella Corporation .... E 302 603-7100
　Rehoboth Beach *(G-8104)*
Wise Power Systems Inc .... F 302 351-4613
　Wilmington *(G-13279)*

CONSULTING SVCS, BUSINESS: Environmental

Action Environmental Service .... G 302 798-3100
　Wilmington *(G-8926)*
Applied Research Assoc Inc .... D 302 677-4147
　Dover *(G-1133)*
Atlantic Resource Management .... F 302 539-2029
　Ocean View *(G-7756)*
Batta Inc .... E 302 737-3376
　Newark *(G-6051)*
Batta Environmental Assoc Inc .... E 302 737-3376
　Newark *(G-6052)*
Brightfields Inc .... E 302 656-9600
　Wilmington *(G-9477)*
Capitol Environmental Svcs Inc .... G 302 652-8999
　Newark *(G-6150)*
Cardno Inc .... F 302 395-1919
　Newark *(G-6154)*
Compliance Environmental Inc .... G 302 674-4427
　Dover *(G-1308)*
Cyclesolv LLC .... G 302 894-9400
　Newark *(G-6337)*
Eagle Us Inc .... A 484 913-0300
　Wilmington *(G-10315)*
Environmental Alliance Inc .... E 302 995-7544
　Wilmington *(G-10419)*
Environmental Consulting Svcs .... F 302 378-9881
　Middletown *(G-4059)*
Environmental Resources Inc .... G 302 436-9637
　Selbyville *(G-8489)*
Environmental Services Inc .... G 302 669-6812
　New Castle *(G-5292)*
Environmental Testing Inc .... G 302 378-5341
　Middletown *(G-4060)*
Envirotech Envmtl Consulting .... G 302 684-5201
　Lewes *(G-3483)*
Fshery Mid-Atlntic MGT Council .... F 302 674-2331
　Dover *(G-1571)*
Geo-Technology Associates Inc .... E 302 326-2100
　New Castle *(G-5351)*
Geo-Technology Associates Inc .... G 302 855-5775
　Georgetown *(G-2538)*
Gwantel Intl Corp Engrg & Tech .... G 302 377-6235
　Newark *(G-6696)*
Harvard Environmental Inc .... F 302 326-2333
　Bear *(G-178)*
Joseph T Hardy & Son Inc .... E 302 328-9457
　New Castle *(G-5446)*
Landmark Engineering Inc .... D 302 323-9377
　Newark *(G-6915)*
Mehar Investment Group LLC .... G 302 999-1888
　Wilmington *(G-11624)*
Six Angels Development Inc .... G 302 218-1548
　Wilmington *(G-12637)*
Sustainable-Generation LLC .... G 917 678-6947
　Wilmington *(G-12820)*
Ten Bears Environmental LLC .... G 302 731-8633
　Newark *(G-7556)*
Terra Systems Inc .... F 302 798-9553
　Claymont *(G-810)*
Wik Associates Inc .... F 302 322-2558
　Wilmington *(G-7694)*
Woods Hole Group Inc .... G 302 222-6720
　Dover *(G-2236)*

CONSULTING SVCS, BUSINESS: Publishing

Decoy Magazine .... G 302 644-9001
　Lewes *(G-3450)*
Gamut Color Inc .... G 302 652-7171
　Wilmington *(G-10668)*
Moghul Life Inc .... G 347 560-9124
　Wilmington *(G-11724)*

CONSULTING SVCS, BUSINESS: Safety Training Svcs

Atlantic Training LLC .... F 302 464-0341
　Middletown *(G-3951)*
Delaware Safety Council Inc .... G 302 276-0660
　New Castle *(G-5239)*
Ellis Fall Sfety Solutions LLC .... G 302 571-8470
　Wilmington *(G-10379)*
Fireside Partners Inc .... G 302 613-2165
　Dover *(G-1551)*
Yellow Pine Associates Inc .... G 302 994-9500
　Wilmington *(G-13326)*

CONSULTING SVCS, BUSINESS: Sys Engnrg, Exc Computer/Prof

Batescainelli LLC .... G 202 618-2040
　Rehoboth Beach *(G-7856)*
Bluestone AM LLC .... F 302 477-0370
　Wilmington *(G-9383)*
Carter Firm LLC .... G 267 420-0717
　Wilmington *(G-9582)*
Creative Micro Designs Inc .... G 302 456-5800
　Newark *(G-6314)*
Insight Engineering Solutions .... G 302 378-4842
　Townsend *(G-8797)*
Tek Electronics LLC .... G 302 449-6947
　Middletown *(G-4254)*
Tek Tree LLC .... F 302 368-2730
　Newark *(G-7551)*

CONSULTING SVCS, BUSINESS: Systems Analysis & Engineering

AC Group Inc .... G 201 840-5566
　Wilmington *(G-8910)*
E I Du Pont De Nemours & Co .... D 302 774-1000
　Newark *(G-6490)*
Professional Roof Services Inc .... G 302 731-5770
　Newark *(G-7266)*
Telgian Corporation .... E 480 753-5444
　Wilmington *(G-12880)*

CONSULTING SVCS, BUSINESS: Systems Analysis Or Design

Mentor Consultants Inc .... G 610 566-4004
　Wilmington *(G-11633)*

CONSULTING SVCS, BUSINESS: Testing, Educational Or Personnel

Aspira of Delaware Inc .... G 302 292-1463
　Newark *(G-6011)*
Multicultural A Delaware .... F 302 399-6118
　Dover *(G-1878)*

CONSULTING SVCS, BUSINESS: Urban Planning & Consulting

ARC HUD I Inc .... G 302 996-9400
　Wilmington *(G-9116)*
Delaware Family Voices Inc .... F 302 588-4908
　Wilmington *(G-10046)*
Diamond State CLT Inc .... F 800 282-0477
　Dover *(G-1424)*
Dvhd Inc .... G 302 584-3547
　Wilmington *(G-10270)*
Ncall Research Inc .... E 302 678-9400
　Dover *(G-1888)*
Wilmington Metropolitan Area P .... F 302 737-6205
　Newark *(G-7702)*

CONSULTING SVCS: Oil

ARC Offshore Investments Inc .... G 561 670-9938
　Wilmington *(G-9119)*
O&G Knwldge Shring Pltform LLC .... G 303 872-0533
　Wilmington *(G-11926)*

PRODUCT & SERVICES SECTION
CONTRACTORS: Carpentry, Cabinet Building & Installation

CONSULTING SVCS: Psychological

New Perspectives Inc .... G 302 489-0220
  Wilmington *(G-11869)*
Psychotherapeutic Svcs Assoc ...... E 302 672-7159
  Dover *(G-1997)*

CONSULTING SVCS: Scientific

Performance Cons Group Inc .... E 302 738-7532
  Newark *(G-7202)*
PSI-TEC Corporation .... G 425 943-9493
  Wilmington *(G-12259)*
Rama LLC .... G 202 596-9547
  Wilmington *(G-12312)*
Ribodynamics LLC .... G 518 339-6605
  Wilmington *(G-12405)*
Stride Services Inc .... F 302 540-4713
  Wilmington *(G-12776)*

CONSUMER PURCHASING SVCS

Domian International Svc LLC ...... G 804 837-3616
  Smyrna *(G-8624)*

CONTAINERS: Food & Beverage

Jmt Inter LLC .... G 302 312-5177
  Bear *(G-202)*

CONTAINERS: Glass

Glass Technologists Inc .... G 240 682-0966
  Middletown *(G-4087)*

CONTAINERS: Metal

Aquila Trading LLC .... G 302 290-5566
  Hockessin *(G-2959)*

CONTAINERS: Plastic

Axess Corporation .... G 302 292-8500
  New Castle *(G-5061)*
Graham Packaging Co Europe LLC .... E 302 453-9464
  Newark *(G-6680)*
Letica Corporation .... C 302 378-9853
  Middletown *(G-4130)*

CONTRACT FOOD SVCS

De Catering Inc .... E 302 607-7200
  Wilmington *(G-9985)*

CONTRACTOR: Framing

Custom Framers Inc .... E 302 684-5377
  Harbeson *(G-2781)*
H & M Construction .... G 302 645-6639
  Lewes *(G-3527)*
J R Brooks Custom Framing LLC .... G 302 538-3637
  Felton *(G-2296)*
Jbr Contractors Inc .... E 856 296-9594
  Millsboro *(G-4714)*
Mason Building Group Inc .... C 302 292-0600
  Newark *(G-6999)*
Menchaca Building Corp .... G 302 475-4581
  Wilmington *(G-11629)*

CONTRACTORS: Access Control System Eqpt

Certified Lock & Access LLC .... G 302 383-7507
  Wilmington *(G-9618)*

CONTRACTORS: Acoustical & Ceiling Work

Erco Ceilings & Interiors Inc .... F 302 994-6200
  Wilmington *(G-10432)*
J & G Acoustical Co .... E 302 285-3630
  Middletown *(G-4112)*
Master Interiors Inc .... E 302 368-9361
  Newark *(G-7000)*
Master Interiors Inc .... G 302 368-9361
  Milford *(G-4489)*
Peninsula Acoustical Co Inc .... G 302 653-3551
  Smyrna *(G-8687)*
Precision Drywall Inc .... E 415 550-8880
  Wilmington *(G-12205)*
Union Wholesale Co .... E 302 656-4462
  Wilmington *(G-13015)*

CONTRACTORS: Antenna Installation

Atechnologie LLC .... G 781 325-5230
  Wilmington *(G-9171)*
JW Tull Contracting Svcs LLC ...... F 302 494-8179
  Wilmington *(G-11212)*
Millennia Contracting Inc .... F 302 654-6200
  New Castle *(G-5529)*
Produce Marketing Assn Inc .... D 302 738-7100
  Newark *(G-7265)*
US Installation Group Inc .... F 302 994-1644
  Wilmington *(G-13039)*

CONTRACTORS: Asbestos Removal & Encapsulation

Astec Inc .... F 302 378-2717
  Middletown *(G-3946)*
County Environmental Inc .... E 302 322-8946
  New Castle *(G-5201)*

CONTRACTORS: Asphalt

Blacktop Sealcoating Inc .... G 302 234-2243
  Newark *(G-6090)*
Clarks Glasgow Pools Inc .... F 302 834-0200
  New Castle *(G-5175)*
Highland Construction LLC .... F 302 286-6990
  Bear *(G-185)*
New Castle Hot Mix Inc .... G 302 655-2119
  Wilmington *(G-11853)*
River Asphalt LLC .... G 302 934-0881
  Dagsboro *(G-932)*
Rp Ventures and Holdings Inc .... E 410 398-3000
  New Castle *(G-5690)*
Stripe-A-Lot Inc .... E 302 654-9175
  Wilmington *(G-12777)*
Triad Construction Company LLC .... E 302 652-3339
  New Castle *(G-5791)*
Victor Colbert Construction .... E 302 834-1174
  Newark *(G-7656)*

CONTRACTORS: Awning Installation

E W Brown Inc .... G 302 652-6612
  Wilmington *(G-10310)*
Gainor Awnings Inc .... G 302 998-8611
  Wilmington *(G-10663)*
Patio Systems Inc .... G 302 644-6540
  Lewes *(G-3680)*

CONTRACTORS: Banking Machine Installation & Svc

Riley Electric Inc .... G 302 276-3581
  Newark *(G-7341)*

CONTRACTORS: Bathtub Refinishing

Custom Porcelain Inc .... G 302 659-6590
  Townsend *(G-8777)*

CONTRACTORS: Boiler & Furnace

Burns & McBride Inc .... D 302 656-5110
  New Castle *(G-5121)*
Frederick Enterprises Inc .... E 302 994-5786
  Wilmington *(G-10627)*

CONTRACTORS: Bricklaying

Riddles Masonry .... G 302 238-7225
  Millsboro *(G-4791)*

CONTRACTORS: Bridge Painting

Marinis Bros Inc .... F 302 322-9663
  New Castle *(G-5506)*

CONTRACTORS: Building Board-up

LLC Schell Brothers .... F 302 226-1994
  Rehoboth Beach *(G-7988)*

CONTRACTORS: Building Eqpt & Machinery Installation

Greg Elect .... G 215 651-1477
  Hockessin *(G-3040)*

CONTRACTORS: Building Front Installation, Metal

Steel Suppliers Inc .... C 302 654-5243
  Wilmington *(G-12748)*
Tri-State Fbrction McHning LLC .... E 302 232-3133
  New Castle *(G-5788)*

CONTRACTORS: Building Sign Installation & Mntnce

Kent Sign Company Inc .... F 302 697-2181
  Dover *(G-1739)*
Kgc Enterprises Inc .... G 302 668-1835
  Wilmington *(G-11255)*

CONTRACTORS: Building Site Preparation

Eastern States Cnstr Svc Inc ...... D 302 995-2259
  Wilmington *(G-10326)*
Gateway Construction Inc .... G 302 653-4400
  Clayton *(G-852)*
Geotech LLC .... G 302 353-9769
  Newark *(G-6649)*
Harmony Construction Inc .... F 302 737-8700
  Newark *(G-6709)*
J & L Services Inc .... F 410 943-3355
  Seaford *(G-8274)*
Sunnyfield Contractors Inc .... F 302 674-8610
  Dover *(G-2114)*

CONTRACTORS: Cable TV Installation

Conectiv Energy Supply Inc .... D 302 454-0300
  Newark *(G-6283)*
Prince Telecom LLC .... D 302 324-1800
  New Castle *(G-5643)*
Tricomm Services Corporation ... G 302 454-2975
  Newark *(G-7590)*

CONTRACTORS: Carpentry Work

Beeline Services LLC .... G 302 376-7399
  Middletown *(G-3965)*
Comstock Custom Cabinets Inc .... G 302 422-2928
  Milford *(G-4364)*
Construction Unlimited Inc .... G 302 836-3140
  Bear *(G-83)*
De Nisio General Construction ... G 302 656-9460
  Wilmington *(G-9986)*
First State Carpentry LLC .... G 302 738-8849
  Newark *(G-6582)*
J & L Services Inc .... F 410 943-3355
  Seaford *(G-8274)*
Joseph E Stevens & Father .... G 302 654-8556
  Wilmington *(G-11189)*
Kevin Garber .... G 302 834-0639
  Bear *(G-216)*
Knight Construction .... G 610 496-6879
  Wilmington *(G-11280)*
Mark Ventresca Associates Inc ... G 302 239-3925
  Hockessin *(G-3089)*
Mastercrafters Inc .... E 302 678-1470
  Dover *(G-1825)*
Maxwell World .... G 937 463-3579
  Dagsboro *(G-918)*

CONTRACTORS: Carpentry, Cabinet & Finish Work

Ed Turulski Custom Woodworking .... G 302 658-2221
  Wilmington *(G-10342)*
Oceanic Ventures Inc .... G 302 645-5872
  Lewes *(G-3664)*
Rementer Brothers Inc .... G 302 249-4250
  Milton *(G-4956)*

CONTRACTORS: Carpentry, Cabinet Building & Installation

Coastal Cabinetry LLC .... G 302 542-4155
  Seaford *(G-8199)*
G2 Group Inc .... G 302 836-4202
  Bear *(G-163)*
Michael A OBrien & Sons .... G 302 994-2894
  Wilmington *(G-11656)*

Employee Codes: A=Over 500 employees, B=251-500
C=101-250, D=51-100, E=20-50, F=10-19, G=1-9

CONTRACTORS: Carpentry, Finish & Trim Work

CONTRACTORS: Carpentry, Finish & Trim Work
Urban Svcs Fcilities Maint LLC ....G....... 302 993-6363
  Wilmington *(G-13035)*
V & P Custom Finishers Inc ....G....... 302 376-6367
  Townsend *(G-8830)*

CONTRACTORS: Carpet Laying
Airbase Carpet Mart Abct Dist ....G....... 302 323-8800
  New Castle *(G-5019)*
Connolly Flooring Inc ....E....... 302 996-9470
  Wilmington *(G-9831)*
Edwards Paul Crpt Installation ....G....... 302 672-7847
  Dover *(G-1509)*
Facility Services Group Inc ....G....... 302 317-3029
  Wilmington *(G-10474)*
Modular Carpet Recycling Inc ....F....... 484 885-5890
  New Castle *(G-5534)*
New Castle County Flooring ....G....... 302 218-0507
  Newark *(G-7100)*

CONTRACTORS: Central Vacuum Cleaning System Installation
Preferred Security Inc ....G....... 302 834-7800
  Bear *(G-288)*

CONTRACTORS: Ceramic Floor Tile Installation
Mikes Ceramic Tile Inc ....G....... 302 376-5743
  Middletown *(G-4165)*

CONTRACTORS: Chimney Construction & Maintenance
Clean Sweep ....G....... 302 422-6085
  Milford *(G-4355)*
Roger Rullo Brick Pointing ....G....... 302 378-8100
  Middletown *(G-4223)*

CONTRACTORS: Closed Circuit Television Installation
Carzo & Associates Inc ....G....... 302 575-0336
  Wilmington *(G-9584)*

CONTRACTORS: Closet Organizers, Installation & Design
Atlantic Source Contg Inc ....G....... 302 645-5207
  Lewes *(G-3359)*

CONTRACTORS: Coating, Caulking & Weather, Water & Fire
Eastern Industrial Svcs Inc ....D....... 302 455-1400
  New Castle *(G-5278)*
K & R Seal Coating LLC ....G....... 302 530-3649
  Bear *(G-210)*

CONTRACTORS: Commercial & Office Building
Absolute Equity ....F....... 302 983-2591
  Delaware City *(G-945)*
Aviman Management LLC ....E....... 302 377-5788
  Wilmington *(G-9199)*
B Doherty Inc ....G....... 302 239-3500
  Wilmington *(G-9211)*
Breeze Construction LLC ....G....... 302 522-9201
  Townsend *(G-8766)*
Brendon T Warfel Construction ....G....... 302 422-7814
  Milford *(G-4334)*
Cirillo Bros Inc ....E....... 302 326-1540
  New Castle *(G-5162)*
Construction Unlimited Inc ....G....... 302 836-3140
  Bear *(G-83)*
Deiter Inc ....G....... 302 875-9167
  Georgetown *(G-2497)*
Delcon Builders Inc ....F....... 609 499-7747
  New Castle *(G-5243)*
Diamond State Pole Bldings LLC ....G....... 302 387-1710
  Felton *(G-2286)*
Insite Constructors Inc ....G....... 302 479-5555
  Wilmington *(G-10873)*
John Campanelli & Sons Inc ....G....... 302 239-8573
  Hockessin *(G-3067)*
Lighthouse Construction Inc ....F....... 302 677-1965
  Magnolia *(G-3898)*
Linda McCormick ....G....... 443 987-2099
  Wilmington *(G-11392)*
Martin Construction Svcs LLC ....F....... 302 200-0885
  Newark *(G-6994)*
Michael-Bruno LLC ....G....... 315 941-8514
  Wilmington *(G-11669)*
Milestone Construction Co Inc ....F....... 302 442-4252
  Newark *(G-7040)*
Moony and Zeager Inc ....G....... 302 593-8166
  Wilmington *(G-11742)*
Mundy Industrial Contrs Inc ....G....... 302 629-1100
  Seaford *(G-8314)*
Petrucon Construction Inc ....F....... 302 571-5781
  Wilmington *(G-12101)*
Preferred Construction Inc ....G....... 302 322-9568
  New Castle *(G-5637)*
Signature Furniture Svcs LLC ....E....... 302 691-1010
  New Castle *(G-5712)*
Simpson Gary Contracting LLC ....G....... 302 398-7733
  Harrington *(G-2889)*
Tycos General Contractors Inc ....G....... 302 478-9267
  Wilmington *(G-13002)*
White Eagle Integrations ....G....... 302 464-0550
  Middletown *(G-4285)*

CONTRACTORS: Communications Svcs
Airwave Technology ....G....... 302 734-7838
  Dover *(G-1098)*
Fiber One Inc ....F....... 302 834-0890
  Newark *(G-6577)*
Gatesair Inc ....G....... 513 459-3400
  Wilmington *(G-10676)*
Martel Inc ....F....... 302 744-9566
  Dover *(G-1821)*
Yacht Anything Ltd ....G....... 302 226-3335
  Rehoboth Beach *(G-8120)*

CONTRACTORS: Computer Installation
Assurance Media LLC ....E....... 302 892-3540
  Wilmington *(G-9162)*
Beacon Air Inc ....G....... 302 323-1688
  New Castle *(G-5077)*

CONTRACTORS: Concrete
A G Concrete Works LLC ....G....... 302 841-2227
  Dagsboro *(G-876)*
Boozer Excavation Co Inc ....G....... 302 542-0290
  Milton *(G-4870)*
Bradley & Sons Designer Con ....G....... 302 836-8031
  Bear *(G-55)*
Cipolloni Brothers LLC ....G....... 302 449-0960
  Smyrna *(G-8595)*
CNJ Contracting LLC ....G....... 302 659-3750
  Smyrna *(G-8600)*
Coastal Concrete Works LLC ....G....... 302 381-5261
  Harbeson *(G-2776)*
Concrete Services Inc ....F....... 302 883-2883
  Dover *(G-1310)*
Curbs Etc Inc ....G....... 302 653-3511
  Smyrna *(G-8608)*
Cutting of Precision Concrete ....G....... 302 543-5833
  Newport *(G-7746)*
D Gingerich Concrete & Masnry ....E....... 302 492-8662
  Hartly *(G-2917)*
Daisy Construction Company ....D....... 302 658-4417
  Wilmington *(G-9947)*
De Nisio General Construction ....G....... 302 656-9460
  Wilmington *(G-9986)*
Duncan S Concrete ....G....... 302 395-1552
  Bear *(G-129)*
East Coast Builders Inc ....F....... 302 629-3551
  Seaford *(G-8229)*
East Coast Poured Walls Inc ....G....... 302 430-0630
  Milford *(G-4399)*
F & N Vazquez Concrete LLC ....G....... 302 725-5305
  Lincoln *(G-3846)*
Francis Kelly Sons Inc ....G....... 302 999-7400
  Wilmington *(G-10610)*
Frank Deramo & Son Inc ....F....... 302 328-0102
  New Castle *(G-5328)*
Graydon Hurst & Son Inc ....G....... 302 762-2444
  Wilmington *(G-10765)*
Healy & Long Inc ....G....... 302 654-8039
  Wilmington *(G-10873)*
James L Webb Paving Co Inc ....G....... 302 697-2000
  Camden *(G-584)*
JT Hoover Concrete Inc ....E....... 302 832-7699
  Bear *(G-205)*
Kevins Masonry Concrete Co ....G....... 302 382-7259
  Felton *(G-2301)*
Lafazia Construction ....G....... 302 234-1300
  Wilmington *(G-11323)*
Leager Construction Inc ....G....... 302 653-8021
  Smyrna *(G-8671)*
M & M Construction Inc ....G....... 410 758-1071
  Odessa *(G-7829)*
Merit Construction Engineers ....F....... 302 992-9810
  Wilmington *(G-11644)*
Mumford and Miller Con Inc ....C....... 302 378-7736
  Middletown *(G-4171)*
Peninsula Masonry Inc ....E....... 302 684-3410
  Harbeson *(G-2795)*
Poured Foundations of De Inc ....G....... 302 234-2050
  Newark *(G-7235)*
Ralph Cahall & Son Paving ....D....... 302 653-4220
  Smyrna *(G-8696)*
Richard D Whaley Cnstr LLC ....G....... 302 934-9525
  Millsboro *(G-4789)*
RS Widdoes and Son Inc ....G....... 302 764-7455
  Wilmington *(G-12486)*
Shea Concrete Ltd ....E....... 302 422-7221
  Milford *(G-4558)*
Shore Masonry Inc ....G....... 302 945-5933
  Millsboro *(G-4800)*
Smith Concrete Inc ....G....... 302 270-9251
  Milford *(G-4562)*
Superior Foundations Inc ....E....... 302 293-7061
  Bear *(G-342)*
Superior Sealing Services D ....G....... 610 717-6237
  Bear *(G-343)*
Talley Brothers Inc ....E....... 302 224-5376
  Newark *(G-7536)*
Victor Colbert Construction ....E....... 302 368-7270
  Newark *(G-7657)*
Wsd Contracting Inc ....G....... 302 492-8606
  Hartly *(G-2944)*

CONTRACTORS: Concrete Block Masonry Laying
Esposito Mansory LLC ....F....... 302 996-4961
  Wilmington *(G-10437)*
M & L Contractors Inc ....F....... 302 436-9303
  Selbyville *(G-8513)*
Paragon Masonry Corporation ....E....... 302 798-7314
  Wilmington *(G-12017)*

CONTRACTORS: Concrete Pumping
Delmarva Concrete Pumping Inc ....G....... 302 537-4118
  Frankford *(G-2359)*
Trottys Concrete Pumping Inc ....F....... 302 732-3100
  Frankford *(G-2394)*

CONTRACTORS: Concrete Reinforcement Placing
M & M Construction Inc ....G....... 410 758-1071
  Odessa *(G-7829)*

CONTRACTORS: Construction Caulking
J & B Caulkers Co ....G....... 302 653-7325
  Townsend *(G-8799)*

CONTRACTORS: Construction Site Cleanup
Gemini Building Systems LLC ....D....... 302 654-5310
  Wilmington *(G-10688)*
Mebro Inc ....E....... 302 992-0104
  Wilmington *(G-11613)*

CONTRACTORS: Corrosion Control Installation
Line-X Delaware Inc ....F....... 302 672-7005
  Dover *(G-1791)*

CONTRACTORS: Countertop Installation
American Cabinetry LLC ....G....... 302 655-4064
  Wilmington *(G-9043)*
Everest Granite LLC ....G....... 302 229-4733
  Wilmington *(G-10445)*
Mastercrafters Inc ....E....... 302 678-1470
  Dover *(G-1825)*
That Granite Place LLC ....G....... 302 337-7490
  Bridgeville *(G-525)*

PRODUCT & SERVICES SECTION

CONTRACTORS: Fence Construction

Troy Granite Inc .... E 302 292-1750
Newark *(G-7596)*

CONTRACTORS: Curb & Sidewalk

J E Rispoli Contractor Inc .... E 302 999-1310
Wilmington *(G-11105)*

CONTRACTORS: Decontamination Svcs

Mold Medics Global LLC .... G 301 943-9428
Wilmington *(G-11726)*

CONTRACTORS: Demolition, Building & Other Structures

Burns & Fiorina Demolition .... G 732 888-1076
Newark *(G-6137)*
Design Contracting Inc .... G 302 429-6900
Wilmington *(G-10121)*
K & L Renovations LLC .... F 302 456-0373
Newark *(G-6862)*
Mid-Atlntic Dismantlement Corp .... F 302 678-9300
Dover *(G-1851)*
Thomas Building Group Inc .... E 302 283-0600
Newark *(G-7563)*

CONTRACTORS: Demountable Partition Installation

J & G Acoustical Co .... E 302 285-3630
Middletown *(G-4112)*

CONTRACTORS: Driveway

Pauls Paving Inc .... F 302 539-9123
Frankford *(G-2379)*
Yardscape Inc .... G 302 540-0311
Middletown *(G-4293)*

CONTRACTORS: Drywall

A L N Construction Inc .... D 302 292-1580
Newark *(G-5868)*
Camden Drywall Inc .... G 302 697-9653
Wyoming *(G-13359)*
Custom Drywall Inc .... G 302 369-3266
Newark *(G-6330)*
Dry Wall Inc .... E 302 838-6500
New Castle *(G-5262)*
Ed Hileman Drywall Inc .... G 302 436-6277
Selbyville *(G-8486)*
Heritage Interiors Inc .... E 302 369-3199
Newark *(G-6725)*
J Michaels Painting Inc .... F 302 738-8465
Newark *(G-6817)*
Kenco Drywall .... E 302 697-6489
Felton *(G-2300)*
M3 Contracting LLC .... E 302 781-3143
Newark *(G-6968)*
Rexmex Drywall LLC .... G 302 343-9140
Hartly *(G-2939)*
Spacecon LLC .... G 302 322-9285
New Castle *(G-5727)*
State Drywall Co Inc .... E 302 239-2843
Hockessin *(G-3148)*
Superior Drywall Inc .... F 302 732-9800
Dagsboro *(G-935)*
Three Bs Painting Contractors ..... G 302 227-1497
Rehoboth Beach *(G-8097)*
Tri-State Drywall LLC .... E 302 798-2709
Claymont *(G-812)*

CONTRACTORS: Earthmoving

Epb Associates Inc .... F 302 475-7301
Wilmington *(G-10424)*

CONTRACTORS: Electric Power Systems

Battaglia Associates Inc .... G 302 325-6100
New Castle *(G-5069)*
Cmy Solutions LLC .... G 321 732-1866
Newark *(G-6256)*
Electrical Power Systems Inc .... G 302 325-3502
New Castle *(G-5283)*
Roberts Electric Inc .... G 302 233-3017
Magnolia *(G-3907)*

CONTRACTORS: Electrical

A & B Electric .... G 302 349-4050
Greenwood *(G-2710)*

A C Electric Company .... G 302 764-7429
Wilmington *(G-8872)*
Advanced Power Generation .... G 302 375-6145
Claymont *(G-686)*
Aezi Electrical Services LLC .... G 302 547-5734
Middletown *(G-3932)*
AMP Electric LLC .... G 302 337-8050
Bridgeville *(G-446)*
Artisan Electrical Inc .... G 302 645-5844
Lewes *(G-3348)*
Arugie Enterprises Corp .... G 302 225-2000
Wilmington *(G-9145)*
Atr Electrical Services Inc .... G 302 373-7769
Middletown *(G-3954)*
Boxwood Electric Inc .... G 302 368-3257
New Castle *(G-5101)*
Cardenti Electric .... F 302 834-1278
Bear *(G-64)*
Chieffo Electric Inc .... E 302 292-6813
Middletown *(G-3986)*
Conectiv LLC .... C 202 872-2680
Wilmington *(G-9817)*
Defense Communication LLC ...... F 850 348-0708
Wilmington *(G-9993)*
Delcollo Security Technologies .... G 302 994-5400
Wilmington *(G-10100)*
Delmarva Communications Inc .... F 302 324-1230
New Castle *(G-5244)*
Electronic Systems Specialist ...... G 302 738-4165
Newark *(G-6510)*
Galloway Electric Co Inc .... F 302 453-8385
Newark *(G-6633)*
H & A Electric Co .... G 302 678-8252
Dover *(G-1621)*
Hockessin Electric Inc .... G 302 239-9332
Hockessin *(G-3052)*
Integrity Tech Solutions Inc .... G 302 369-9093
Newark *(G-6793)*
Kriss Contracting Inc .... G 302 492-3502
Hartly *(G-2932)*
Liberty Electric LLC .... G 410 275-9200
Bear *(G-234)*
P S C Contracting Inc .... G 302 838-2998
Delaware City *(G-962)*
Progressive Services Inc .... G 302 658-7260
Wilmington *(G-12243)*
Ram Electric Inc .... G 302 875-2356
Laurel *(G-3278)*
Riley Electric .... G 302 533-5918
Newark *(G-7340)*
S J Desmond Inc .... G 302 475-6520
Wilmington *(G-12507)*
Simplex Time Recorder LLC .... F 302 325-6300
New Castle *(G-5714)*
Stork Electric Inc .... G 302 654-9427
Wilmington *(G-12773)*
Transcore LP .... E 302 677-7262
Dover *(G-2159)*
White Eagle Electrical Contg ...... F 302 378-3366
Middletown *(G-4284)*

CONTRACTORS: Electronic Controls Installation

Service Unlimited Inc .... E 302 326-2665
New Castle *(G-5700)*

CONTRACTORS: Energy Management Control

Advanced Power Control Inc ...... D 302 368-0443
Newark *(G-5907)*
Federal Energy Inf .... F 858 521-3300
Wilmington *(G-10513)*

CONTRACTORS: Environmental Controls Installation

Erosion Control Services De .... E 302 218-8913
Bear *(G-145)*
George & Lynch Inc .... C 302 736-3031
Dover *(G-1590)*

CONTRACTORS: Erection & Dismantling, Poured Concrete Forms

Eclipes Erection Inc .... E 302 633-1421
Wilmington *(G-10337)*

CONTRACTORS: Excavating

Bobcat of New Castle LLC .... F 732 780-6880
New Castle *(G-5098)*
Bramble Construction Co Inc ..... F 302 856-6723
Georgetown *(G-2458)*
Bunting & Murray Cnstr Corp ..... D 302 436-5144
Selbyville *(G-8463)*
Castle Construction Del Inc .... E 302 326-3600
New Castle *(G-5136)*
Centerville Company Contrs ...... G 302 656-8666
Wilmington *(G-9613)*
Central Backhoe Service .... G 302 398-6420
Milton *(G-4877)*
Choptank Excavation .... G 302 378-8114
Middletown *(G-3987)*
CNJ Contracting LLC .... G 302 659-3750
Smyrna *(G-8600)*
Cygnet Construction Corp .... G 302 436-5212
Selbyville *(G-8475)*
D E Leager Construction .... G 302 994-1060
Wilmington *(G-9939)*
David G Horsey & Sons Inc .... D 302 875-3033
Laurel *(G-3221)*
Dirt Works Inc .... F 302 947-2429
Lewes *(G-3466)*
J & M Industries Inc .... G 302 575-0200
Wilmington *(G-11097)*
Jeff Bartsch Trckg Excvtg Inc ..... G 302 653-9329
Townsend *(G-8801)*
Jerrys Inc .... G 302 422-7676
Milford *(G-4457)*
Kaye Construction .... G 302 628-6962
Seaford *(G-8285)*
Leroy Betts Construction Inc ...... G 302 284-9193
Felton *(G-2303)*
M G Hamex Corporation .... F 302 832-9072
New Castle *(G-5493)*
Midway Services Inc .... G 302 422-8603
Lincoln *(G-3861)*
Pearce & Moretto Inc .... E 302 326-0707
New Castle *(G-5611)*
R & E Excavation LLC .... G 302 750-5226
New Castle *(G-5660)*
Ralph Cahall & Son Paving .... G 302 653-4220
Smyrna *(G-8696)*
Robert Keating Excavating .... G 302 239-4670
Hockessin *(G-3139)*
Swain Excavation Inc .... G 302 422-4349
Lincoln *(G-3872)*
Swift Construction Co Inc .... G 302 855-1011
Georgetown *(G-2685)*
W Sharp Paynter & Sons Inc ...... G 302 684-8508
Milton *(G-4979)*
Walter W Snyder .... G 302 378-1817
Middletown *(G-4280)*

CONTRACTORS: Exterior Concrete Stucco

Healy Long & Jevin Inc .... F 302 654-8039
Wilmington *(G-10874)*
O Morales Stucco Plaster Inc ..... G 302 834-8891
Bear *(G-269)*
Santo Stucco .... G 302 453-0901
Newark *(G-7384)*

CONTRACTORS: Exterior Painting

Nu-Look Painting Contractors ..... G 302 734-9203
Dover *(G-1910)*
Quality Finishers Inc .... G 302 325-1963
New Castle *(G-5657)*
Sundew Painting Inc .... E 302 994-7004
Wilmington *(G-12800)*
Superior Drywall Inc .... F 302 732-9800
Dagsboro *(G-935)*

CONTRACTORS: Fence Construction

A & R Fence Co Inc .... G 302 366-8550
Newark *(G-5864)*
Arcadia Fencing Inc .... G 302 398-7700
Harrington *(G-2812)*
B G Halko & Sons Inc .... G 302 322-2020
New Castle *(G-5063)*
Built-Rite Fence Co Inc .... G 302 366-8329
Newark *(G-6134)*
Delaware Valley Fence & Iron ..... G 302 322-8193
New Castle *(G-5242)*
Dickerson Fence Co Inc .... G 302 846-2227
Delmar *(G-993)*

CONTRACTORS: Fence Construction

Eastern Shore Porch Patio Inc .... E 302 436-9520
  Selbyville (G-8485)
Guardian Fence Co .... F 302 834-3044
  Middletown (G-4097)
Iron Hill Fence .... G 302 453-9060
  Newark (G-6807)
J & M Fencing Inc .... F 302 284-9674
  Felton (G-2295)
Nanticoke Fence LLC .... G 302 628-7808
  Seaford (G-8318)
Newark Fence Co .... G 302 368-5329
  Newark (G-7120)
Pierce Fence Company Inc .... F 302 674-1996
  Dover (G-1959)
Pioneer Fence Co Inc .... F 302 998-2892
  Wilmington (G-12143)
Sussex Fencing .... G 302 945-7008
  Millsboro (G-4807)

CONTRACTORS: Fiber Optic Cable Installation

Conectiv Communications Inc .... E 302 224-1177
  Newark (G-6282)
Emergncy Response Protocol LLC .... G 302 994-2600
  Wilmington (G-10391)
Rhino Cabling Group Inc .... F 302 312-1033
  Newark (G-7334)

CONTRACTORS: Fire Detection & Burglar Alarm Systems

Advanced Security Systems Inc .... G 302 998-7222
  Wilmington (G-8956)
Alarm Systems Co of Delaware .... G 302 239-7754
  Hockessin (G-2954)
B Safe Inc .... E 302 422-3916
  Dover (G-1167)
M D Electric LLC .... G 302 838-2852
  Bear (G-242)
Security Inc .... F 302 652-5276
  Claymont (G-802)
Security Instrument Corp Del .... D 302 998-2261
  Wilmington (G-12571)
Telgian Corporation .... E 480 753-5444
  Wilmington (G-12880)
Vector Security Inc .... E 302 422-7031
  Milford (G-4589)

CONTRACTORS: Fire Sprinkler System Installation Svcs

Armored Fire Protection LLC .... G 302 563-3516
  Townsend (G-8758)
Cmp Fire LLC .... G 410 620-2062
  Newark (G-6255)
Preferred Fire Protection .... F 302 256-0607
  Wilmington (G-12212)
Radius Services LLC .... D 302 993-0600
  Wilmington (G-12304)
Steven Brown & Associates Inc .... G 302 652-4722
  Wilmington (G-12759)
Telgian Corporation .... E 480 753-5444
  Wilmington (G-12880)

CONTRACTORS: Floor Laying & Other Floor Work

Anderson Floor Coverings Inc .... F 302 227-3244
  Rehoboth Beach (G-7842)
Creative Flooring Contrs Inc .... F 302 653-7521
  Smyrna (G-8607)
Creative Floors Inc .... F 302 455-9045
  Newark (G-6313)
Creative Kitchens and Floors .... G 302 629-3166
  Seaford (G-8214)
Delawres Fnest Hardwood Floors .... G 302 376-0742
  Middletown (G-4033)
Fasttrak .... E 302 761-5454
  Wilmington (G-10506)
Flooring Solutions Inc .... F 302 655-8001
  Wilmington (G-10576)
Margherita Vincent & Anthony .... G 302 834-9023
  Newark (G-6985)
Northeastern Coating Systems .... G 302 328-6545
  Wilmington (G-11905)
Spacecon LLC .... G 302 322-9285
  New Castle (G-5727)

CONTRACTORS: Flooring

Floor Coatings Etc Inc .... E 302 322-4177
  New Castle (G-5320)
J & T Concrete Inc .... F 302 368-4949
  Newark (G-6814)

CONTRACTORS: Food Svcs Eqpt Installation

Gregg & Sons Mechanical LLC .... G 302 223-8145
  Townsend (G-8790)

CONTRACTORS: Foundation & Footing

Seaford Concrete Products LLC .... G 302 628-6964
  Seaford (G-8387)

CONTRACTORS: Foundation Building

Corrado American LLC .... E 302 655-6501
  New Castle (G-5196)

CONTRACTORS: Garage Doors

Clark & Sons Inc .... E 302 998-7552
  Wilmington (G-9731)
Clark & Sons Inc .... G 302 856-3372
  Georgetown (G-2474)
Clark & Sons Overhead Doors .... E 302 998-7552
  Wilmington (G-9732)
Del-Mar Door Services Inc .... G 800 492-2392
  Middletown (G-4025)
Diamond State Door .... G 302 743-4667
  Wilmington (G-10142)
FB Door-Delaware LLC .... F 302 995-1000
  Newport (G-7749)
J & A Overhead Door Inc .... G 302 846-9915
  Delmar (G-1005)
Overhead Door Co Delmar Inc .... E 302 424-4400
  Milford (G-4520)
Pinnacle Garage Door Company .... G 302 505-4531
  Felton (G-2310)
Yoder Overhead Door Company .... G 302 875-0663
  Delmar (G-1050)

CONTRACTORS: Gasoline Pump Installation

Coastal Pump & Tank Inc .... F 302 398-3061
  Harrington (G-2826)
First State Petroleum Services .... G 302 398-9704
  Harrington (G-2841)

CONTRACTORS: General Electric

A & A Electrical Inc .... F 302 436-4800
  Frankford (G-2343)
A Plus Electric & Security .... G 302 455-1725
  Newark (G-5869)
Alliance Electric Inc .... F 302 366-0295
  Newark (G-5940)
Allied Elec Solutions Ltd .... F 302 893-0257
  Wilmington (G-9022)
Anaconda Prtctive Concepts Inc .... F 302 834-1125
  Newark (G-5965)
Anchor Electric Inc .... G 302 221-6111
  New Castle (G-5037)
Apple Electric Inc .... E 302 645-5105
  Rehoboth Beach (G-7845)
Associates Contracting Inc .... F 302 734-4311
  Dover (G-1150)
B & M Electric Inc .... G 302 745-3807
  Georgetown (G-2442)
Battaglia Electric Inc .... C 302 325-6100
  New Castle (G-5070)
Bauguess Electrical Svcs Inc .... G 302 737-5614
  Newark (G-6053)
Bausum & Duckett Elc Co Inc .... G 302 846-0536
  Delmar (G-973)
Boyces Electrical Service .... G 302 875-5877
  Laurel (G-3203)
BW Electric Inc .... E 302 566-6248
  Harrington (G-2821)
Byers Industrial Services LLC .... E 302 836-4790
  Bear (G-58)
Cahill Contracting .... F 302 378-9650
  Middletown (G-3979)
City Electric Contracting Co .... F 302 764-0775
  Wilmington (G-9721)
Construction MGT Svcs Inc .... A 302 478-4200
  Wilmington (G-9835)
Conti Electric of N J Inc .... G 302 996-3905
  Wilmington (G-9839)
Cox Electric Inc .... G 302 629-5448
  Seaford (G-8211)
Current Solutions Inc .... G 302 736-5210
  Camden Wyoming (G-629)
Daniel George Bebee Inc .... G 443 359-1542
  Laurel (G-3220)
Dave Smagala .... G 302 383-2761
  Claymont (G-729)
Devary Electric Inc .... G 302 674-4560
  Dover (G-1417)
Diamond Electric Inc .... E 302 697-3296
  Dover (G-1421)
Donald Eichholz .... G 302 792-1236
  Wilmington (G-10195)
Donaldson Electric .... G 302 660-7534
  Wilmington (G-10197)
East Coast Electric Inc .... F 302 998-1577
  Wilmington (G-10319)
Electrical Associates Inc .... G 302 678-1068
  Hartly (G-2921)
First State Electric Company .... E 302 322-0140
  New Castle (G-5315)
FM Electric Inc .... G 302 492-3900
  Marydel (G-3916)
Gerone C Hudson Elec Contr .... F 302 539-3332
  Frankford (G-2365)
Hatzel & Buehler Inc .... G 302 478-4200
  Wilmington (G-10853)
Hatzel & Buehler Inc .... C 302 798-5422
  Wilmington (G-10854)
Hazzard Electrical Contractors .... G 302 645-8457
  Lewes (G-3538)
I-Pulse Inc .... G 604 689-8765
  Wilmington (G-10984)
Integrated Wirg Solutions LLC .... E 302 999-8448
  Saint Georges (G-8126)
J R Pini Electrical Contrs .... F 302 368-2311
  Newark (G-6819)
James F Givens Inc .... G 302 875-5436
  Laurel (G-3242)
Jsf Construction Co Inc .... G 302 999-9573
  Wilmington (G-11204)
Kokoszka & Sons Inc .... G 302 328-4807
  New Castle (G-5468)
La Vere Electric Inc .... G 302 422-9185
  Milford (G-4469)
Lee Townsend Electrical Contr .... G 302 697-3432
  Dover (G-1778)
M Auger Enterprise Inc .... E 302 992-9922
  Wilmington (G-11470)
M Davis & Sons Inc .... C 302 998-3385
  Wilmington (G-11471)
Megee Plumbing & Heating Co .... D 302 856-6311
  Georgetown (G-2600)
Messina Charles Plbg & Elc Co .... D 302 674-5696
  Dover (G-1842)
Mid-Atlantic Elec Svcs Inc .... E 302 945-2555
  Millsboro (G-4745)
Mid-County Electric Inc .... F 302 934-8304
  Millsboro (G-4747)
Midshore Electrical Services .... G 302 945-2555
  Harbeson (G-2792)
Murphy Electric Inc .... F 302 644-0404
  Lewes (G-3652)
Nesmith & Company Inc .... E 215 755-4570
  Claymont (G-788)
Nickle Elec Companies Inc .... E 302 856-1006
  Georgetown (G-2609)
Nickle Elec Companies Inc .... C 302 453-4000
  Newark (G-7134)
P S C Electric Contractor Inc .... F 302 838-2998
  Delaware City (G-963)
Pace Electric .... G 302 328-2600
  Wilmington (G-12000)
Peter D Furness Elc Co Inc .... C 302 764-6030
  Wilmington (G-12094)
Power Plus Electrical Contg .... F 302 736-5070
  Dover (G-1978)
Preferred Electric Inc .... D 302 322-1217
  New Castle (G-5638)
Pro-Grade Electric LLC .... F 302 258-7745
  Georgetown (G-2628)
Q and R Electric LLC .... G 302 670-1817
  Newark (G-7276)
Rays Plumbing & Heating Svcs .... G 302 697-3936
  Felton (G-2315)
Remco Electric .... G 302 422-6833
  Milford (G-4536)
Satterfield & Ryan Inc .... F 302 422-4919
  Milford (G-4553)

PRODUCT & SERVICES SECTION

CONTRACTORS: Hydronics Heating

Shore Electric Inc..................................G......302 645-4503
  Lewes (G-3740)
Shure Line Electrical Inc........................G......302 856-3110
  Georgetown (G-2655)
Shure-Line Electrical Inc.......................D......302 389-1114
  Smyrna (G-8715)
Simmons Electrical Service LLC............G......410 543-1480
  Delmar (G-1030)
Solar Heating Inc..................................E......302 836-3943
  Bear (G-327)
Superior Electric Service Co..................E......302 658-5949
  Wilmington (G-12807)
Sure Line Electrical Inc.........................E......302 856-3110
  Georgetown (G-2672)
T A Rietdorf & Sons Inc.........................G......302 429-0341
  Wilmington (G-12844)
Tangent Cable Systems Inc...................E......302 994-4104
  Wilmington (G-12851)
Taylor Electric Service Inc....................G......302 422-3966
  Milford (G-4576)
Tc Electric Company Inc........................E......302 791-0378
  Wilmington (G-12856)
Thorn Electric Inc.................................F......302 653-4300
  Smyrna (G-8731)
Towles Electric Inc...............................G......302 674-4985
  Dover (G-2154)
Tri-State SEC & Contrls LLC..................F......302 299-2175
  Newark (G-7589)
Tri-State Technologies Inc....................E......302 658-5400
  Wilmington (G-12967)
Tudor Electric Inc.................................G......302 736-1444
  Dover (G-2165)
Tusi Brothers Inc..................................E......302 998-6383
  Wilmington (G-12994)
Vassallo Michael Elec Contr..................F......302 455-9405
  Newark (G-7646)
Wanex Electrical Service LLC................F......302 326-1700
  New Castle (G-5822)
Watts Electric Company.......................G......302 529-1183
  Wilmington (G-13123)
Wayne Bennett....................................G......302 436-2379
  Frankford (G-2397)
Wolanski & Sons Electric Inc.................G......302 999-0838
  Wilmington (G-13285)

CONTRACTORS: Glass Tinting, Architectural & Automotive

Gotshadeonline Inc..............................G......302 832-8468
  Bear (G-168)
Professional Window Tinting..................G......302 456-3456
  Newark (G-7267)
Shore Tint & More Inc..........................G......302 947-4624
  Harbeson (G-2800)

CONTRACTORS: Glass, Glazing & Tinting

1st Class Glass LLC..............................G......302 229-9203
  Wilmington (G-8849)
Atlas Glass & Metal LLC.......................G......302 456-5958
  Newark (G-6023)
Delaware Storefronts LLC.....................G......302 697-1850
  Dover (G-1400)
Eastern Home Improvements Inc...........G......302 655-9920
  Wilmington (G-10322)
Go-Glass Corporation...........................F......302 674-3390
  Dover (G-1596)
Gregory D Thacker................................G......302 239-0879
  Newark (G-6689)
Mikes Glass Service Inc........................F......302 658-7936
  Wilmington (G-11686)
MMR Associates Inc.............................G......302 883-2984
  Dover (G-1865)
New Castle Glass Inc............................G......302 322-6164
  New Castle (G-5558)
Newark Glass & Mirror Inc....................F......302 834-1158
  Bear (G-264)
Parags Glass Company.........................G......302 737-0101
  Newark (G-7176)
Premier Glass & Screen Inc..................F......302 732-3101
  Frankford (G-2380)
Service Glass Inc..................................F......302 629-9139
  Seaford (G-8397)
Superior Screen & Glass.......................F......302 541-5399
  Ocean View (G-7816)
West Ventures Inc................................G......307 737-9900
  New Castle (G-5830)
Zephyr Aluminum LLC...........................G......302 571-0585
  Wilmington (G-13348)

CONTRACTORS: Gutters & Downspouts

Coghan-Haes LLC..................................E......302 325-4210
  Wilmington (G-9759)
Hickman Overhead Door Company........F......302 422-4249
  Milford (G-4441)
M A K Roofing Inc.................................G......302 737-5380
  Newark (G-6963)
Milford Gutter Guys LLC.......................G......302 424-1931
  Lincoln (G-3862)
Sharp Raingutters.................................F......302 398-4873
  Harrington (G-2887)

CONTRACTORS: Heating & Air Conditioning

Blm Industries Inc................................G......302 238-7745
  Millsboro (G-4645)
Chesapeake Climate Control LLC...........E......302 732-6006
  Frankford (G-2353)
Clark Services Inc Delaware.................G......302 834-0556
  Bear (G-76)
Clark Services Inc of Del......................F......302 322-1118
  New Castle (G-5174)
Clarke Service Groupdotcom LLC..........F......302 875-0300
  Laurel (G-3216)
Climate Control Heating Inc..................G......302 349-5778
  Greenwood (G-2720)
Climate Solutions Services...................G......302 275-9919
  Wilmington (G-9742)
Ducts Unlimited Inc.............................G......302 378-4125
  Smyrna (G-8628)
Fletcher Plumbing Htg & AC Inc............F......302 653-6277
  Smyrna (G-8636)
Gold Star Services................................F......302 376-7677
  Newark (G-6671)
Harry L Adams Inc................................F......302 328-5268
  New Castle (G-5377)
K and B Hvac Svcs LLC........................G......302 846-3111
  Delmar (G-1012)
Manley Hvac Inc..................................G......302 998-4654
  Wilmington (G-11503)
McCrea Equipment Company Inc..........D......302 945-0821
  Harbeson (G-2791)
McMahon Heating & AC........................F......302 945-4300
  Lewes (G-3630)
National HVAC Service.........................E......570 825-2894
  Seaford (G-8327)
Pierce Total Comfort LLC......................F......302 378-7714
  Middletown (G-4191)
Preffered Mechanical Services.............G......302 993-1122
  Wilmington (G-12213)
Staplefords At Wilmington Inc..............G......302 762-0637
  Wilmington (G-12739)
Traps Plumbing Heating A/C................G......302 677-1775
  Dover (G-2161)
Tusi and Son Mechanical Inc................G......302 731-8228
  Newark (G-7602)

CONTRACTORS: Heating Systems Repair & Maintenance Svc

Bjk Plumbing & Heating LLC.................G......215 828-2556
  Magnolia (G-3882)
Summit Heating and AC LLC.................G......302 378-1203
  Townsend (G-8824)
Top Notch Htg & A C & Rfrgn................G......302 645-7171
  Lewes (G-3789)
Wilkins Fuel Co.....................................G......302 422-5597
  Milford (G-4605)
Willey and Co.......................................G......302 629-3327
  Laurel (G-3311)

CONTRACTORS: Highway & Street Construction, General

A P Croll & Son Inc...............................D......302 856-6177
  Georgetown (G-2419)
Allan Myers Md Inc...............................C......302 883-3501
  Dover (G-1109)
Austin & Bednash Construction.............E......302 376-5590
  Newark (G-6026)
Disabatino Enterprises LLC...................D......302 652-3838
  Wilmington (G-10165)
Dixie Construction Company Inc...........E......302 858-5007
  Georgetown (G-2511)
Eastern States Cnstr Svc Inc................D......302 995-2259
  Wilmington (G-10326)
Ffi General Contractor In.......................G......302 420-1242
  Wilmington (G-10527)
GF McLaughlin LLC................................G......302 279-6018
  Wilmington (G-10707)
Jjid Inc..E......302 836-0414
  Bear (G-201)
Martys Contracting...............................G......302 234-8690
  Hockessin (G-3091)
Material Supply Inc...............................E......302 658-6524
  Wilmington (G-11566)
Messick and Johnson LLc.....................G......302 628-3111
  Seaford (G-8308)
New Castle County Flooring.................G......302 218-0507
  Newark (G-7100)
Pacer International One LLC.................F......302 588-9500
  Wilmington (G-12003)
RS Widdoes and Son Inc......................G......302 764-7455
  Wilmington (G-12486)
Sweeten Companies Inc.......................G......302 737-6161
  Newark (G-7520)

CONTRACTORS: Highway & Street Paving

A-Del Construction Company Inc..........D......302 453-8286
  Newark (G-5871)
David M Sartin Sr.................................G......302 838-1074
  Bear (G-97)
Don Rogers Inc.....................................E......302 658-6524
  Wilmington (G-10193)
E Earle Downing Inc.............................E......302 656-9908
  Wilmington (G-10277)
Harmony Construction Inc....................G......302 737-8700
  Newark (G-6709)
Harrisons Asphalt Paving......................G......302 674-1255
  Dover (G-1633)
Melvin L Joseph Cnstr Co.....................E......302 856-7396
  Georgetown (G-2602)
Mitten Construction Co........................E......302 697-2124
  Dover (G-1862)
Naudain Enterprises LLC......................G......302 239-6840
  Hockessin (G-3102)
Palmer & Associates Inc.......................G......302 834-9329
  Bear (G-275)
Peninsula Pave & Seal LLC...................G......302 226-7283
  Georgetown (G-2615)
Peter Domanski & Sons........................G......302 475-3214
  Hockessin (G-3118)
Restoration Dynamics LLC....................G......302 378-3729
  Wilmington (G-12389)
Sanco Construction Co Inc...................G......302 633-4156
  Wilmington (G-12536)
South Jersey Paving.............................G......856 498-8647
  Bear (G-329)
Teal Construction Inc...........................D......302 276-6034
  Dover (G-2134)
Voshell Bros Welding Inc......................E......302 674-1414
  Dover (G-2199)
Wb Paving LLC.....................................G......302 838-1886
  Bear (G-373)

CONTRACTORS: Home & Office Intrs Finish, Furnish/Remodel

Linda McCormick...................................G......443 987-2099
  Wilmington (G-11392)
R & J Taylor Inc....................................G......302 368-7888
  Newark (G-7289)
Saienni Stairs LLC................................G......302 292-2699
  Newark (G-7377)

CONTRACTORS: Hotel & Motel Renovation

Petrucon Construction Inc....................F......302 571-5781
  Wilmington (G-12101)

CONTRACTORS: Hotel, Motel/Multi-Family Home Renovtn/Remodel

Bright Finish LLC...................................G......888 974-4747
  Smyrna (G-8586)
Kristin Konstruction Company..............G......302 791-9670
  Claymont (G-772)
Wit Services LLC..................................G......302 995-2983
  Wilmington (G-13280)

CONTRACTORS: Hydraulic Eqpt Installation & Svcs

White Drilling Corp...............................G......302 422-4057
  Lincoln (G-3873)

CONTRACTORS: Hydronics Heating

R S Bauer LLC......................................F......302 398-4668
  Harrington (G-2877)

CONTRACTORS: Indl Building Renovation, Remodeling & Repair

CONTRACTORS: Indl Building Renovation, Remodeling & Repair

- Breslin Contracting Inc .... E 302 322-0320
  New Castle *(G-5110)*
- Emment A Oat Contractor Inc .... G 302 999-1567
  Wilmington *(G-10393)*
- Jeffrey Hatch .... G 443 496-0449
  Marydel *(G-3919)*
- Kristin Konstruction Company .... G 302 791-9670
  Claymont *(G-772)*
- Mebro Inc .... E 302 992-0104
  Wilmington *(G-11613)*
- R W Home Services Inc .... F 302 539-4683
  Ocean View *(G-7810)*

CONTRACTORS: Insulation Installation, Building

- A S A P Insulation Inc .... F 302 836-9040
  Newark *(G-5870)*
- Blue Hen Insulation Inc .... G 302 424-4482
  Milford *(G-4327)*
- Dale Insulation Co of Delaware ..... G 302 324-9332
  New Castle *(G-5213)*
- Delmarva Spray Foam LLC .... F 302 752-1080
  Georgetown *(G-2509)*
- Eastern Industrial Svcs Inc .... D 302 455-1400
  New Castle *(G-5278)*
- H & C Insulation LLC .... G 302 448-0777
  Greenwood *(G-2743)*
- Newark Insulation Co Inc .... F 302 731-8970
  Newark *(G-7122)*
- Phillips Insulation Inc .... G 302 655-6523
  Wilmington *(G-12118)*
- Southland Insulators Del LLC .... D 302 854-0344
  Georgetown *(G-2662)*

CONTRACTORS: Kitchen & Bathroom Remodeling

- 1st State Accessibility LLC .... G 844 663-4396
  Wilmington *(G-8850)*
- 2 Days Bath LLC .... F 302 798-0103
  Wilmington *(G-8851)*
- Alan M Billingsley Jr .... G 302 998-7907
  Wilmington *(G-8998)*
- Allura Bath & Kitchen Inc .... G 302 731-2851
  Newark *(G-5944)*
- Atlantic Kitchen & Bath LLC .... G 302 947-9001
  Lewes *(G-3357)*
- Creative Kitchens and Floors .... G 302 629-3166
  Seaford *(G-8214)*
- Giorgi Kitchens Inc .... F 302 762-1121
  Wilmington *(G-10715)*
- Jeffrey Hatch .... G 443 496-0449
  Marydel *(G-3919)*

CONTRACTORS: Lighting Syst

- Light Action Inc .... F 302 328-7800
  New Castle *(G-5481)*
- Lightscapes Inc .... G 302 798-5451
  Wilmington *(G-11387)*

CONTRACTORS: Machinery Installation

- Bruce Industrial Co Inc .... D 302 655-9616
  New Castle *(G-5118)*
- Planned Poultry Renovation .... E 302 875-4196
  Laurel *(G-3273)*
- R & S Fabrication Inc .... F 302 629-0377
  Bridgeville *(G-516)*

CONTRACTORS: Masonry & Stonework

- Amer Masonry T A Marino .... G 302 834-1511
  New Castle *(G-5030)*
- Ashcraft Masonry Inc .... F 302 537-4298
  Ocean View *(G-7755)*
- Blair Carmean Masonry .... G 302 934-6103
  Georgetown *(G-2455)*
- Blue Hen Masonry Inc .... G 302 398-8737
  Greenwood *(G-2718)*
- CNJ Contracting LLC .... G 302 659-3750
  Smyrna *(G-8600)*
- Davis Young Associates Inc .... F 610 388-0932
  Yorklyn *(G-13365)*
- Enterprise Masonry Corporation ... E 302 764-6858
  Wilmington *(G-10413)*
- Falasco Masonry Inc .... G 302 697-8971
  Camden Wyoming *(G-636)*
- Fireplace Specialities LLC .... G 302 436-9250
  Selbyville *(G-8493)*
- J D Masonry Inc .... F 302 684-1009
  Harbeson *(G-2787)*
- J W Humphries Masonry .... G 302 284-0510
  Felton *(G-2297)*
- Jeandar Masonry Construction ..... G 302 994-2616
  Wilmington *(G-11137)*
- Joseph L Hinks .... G 302 875-2260
  Laurel *(G-3245)*
- L A Masonary Inc .... F 302 239-6833
  Newark *(G-6907)*
- Lawrence Legates Masnry Co Inc . G 302 422-8043
  Milford *(G-4472)*
- Lighthouse Masonry Inc .... G 302 945-1392
  Lewes *(G-3609)*
- Mainline Masonry Inc .... E 302 998-2499
  Middletown *(G-4142)*
- Mario Medori Inc .... F 302 656-8432
  Wilmington *(G-11529)*
- Mike Faella Inc .... G 302 475-2116
  Wilmington *(G-11685)*
- Nu-Tech Masonry Inc .... F 302 934-5660
  Millsboro *(G-4764)*
- Peninsula Masonry Inc .... E 302 684-3410
  Harbeson *(G-2795)*
- R F Gentner & Son .... G 302 947-2733
  Harbeson *(G-2796)*
- Restoration Dynamics LLC .... G 302 378-3729
  Wilmington *(G-12389)*
- Romano Masonry Inc .... E 302 368-4155
  Newark *(G-7362)*
- Shore Masonry Inc .... G 302 945-5933
  Millsboro *(G-4800)*
- South Delaware Masonry Inc .... G 302 378-1998
  Townsend *(G-8822)*
- Stonegate Granite .... G 302 500-8081
  Georgetown *(G-2667)*
- Thomas E OGrady Masonry .... G 302 378-8245
  Middletown *(G-4257)*
- Trenton Block Delaware Inc .... G 302 684-0112
  Milton *(G-4977)*
- Walter W Snyder .... G 302 378-1817
  Middletown *(G-4280)*
- Wilson Masonry Corp .... F 302 398-8240
  Harrington *(G-2908)*

CONTRACTORS: Mechanical

- A & A Mechanical Service Inc .... G 302 234-9949
  Hockessin *(G-2949)*
- Battaglia Electric Inc .... C 302 325-6100
  New Castle *(G-5070)*
- C & D Contractors Inc .... E 302 764-2020
  Wilmington *(G-9521)*
- Certified Mechanical Contrs .... G 302 559-3727
  Wilmington *(G-9619)*
- Christiana Mechanical Inc .... F 302 378-7308
  Middletown *(G-3989)*
- Custom Mechanical Inc .... E 302 537-1150
  Frankford *(G-2358)*
- D & C Mechanical LLC .... G 302 604-9025
  Greenwood *(G-2726)*
- Flo Mechanical LLC .... G 302 239-7299
  Hockessin *(G-3030)*
- Henderson Mechanical Inc .... G 302 629-3753
  Seaford *(G-8263)*
- ID Griffith Inc .... D 302 656-8253
  Wilmington *(G-10991)*
- J F Sobieski Mech Contrs Inc .... C 302 993-0103
  Wilmington *(G-11106)*
- Kmp Mechanical LLC .... G 410 392-6126
  Newark *(G-6898)*
- Liberty Mechanical LLC .... G 302 397-8863
  Wilmington *(G-11380)*
- M Davis & Sons Inc .... G 302 998-3385
  Wilmington *(G-11472)*
- Mdm McHncal Instlltion USA LLC . G 617 938-9634
  Wilmington *(G-11610)*
- Merit Mechanical Co Inc .... D 302 366-8601
  Newark *(G-7019)*
- Merit Services Inc .... G 302 366-8601
  Newark *(G-7020)*
- Modern Controls Inc .... E 302 325-6800
  New Castle *(G-5532)*
- Statewide Mechanical Inc .... G 302 376-6117
  Townsend *(G-8823)*
- Summit Mechanical Inc .... E 302 836-8814
  Bear *(G-340)*
- Tri-State Technologies Inc .... E 302 658-5400
  Wilmington *(G-12967)*
- William Delcampo Mechanical SE . G 302 992-9748
  Wilmington *(G-13207)*
- William G Day Company .... F 302 427-3700
  Wilmington *(G-13209)*
- William H McDaniel Inc .... F 302 764-2020
  Wilmington *(G-13212)*
- X/L Mechanical Inc .... G 203 233-3329
  Camden *(G-608)*
- Yerkie Corp .... G 302 653-1321
  Clayton *(G-875)*

CONTRACTORS: Millwrights

- Amazon Steel Construction Inc .... G 302 751-1146
  Milford *(G-4305)*
- Harrold & Son Inc .... G 302 629-9504
  Seaford *(G-8262)*

CONTRACTORS: Mobile Home Site Set-Up

- Messicks Mobile Homes Inc .... F 302 398-9166
  Harrington *(G-2867)*

CONTRACTORS: Multi-Family Home Remodeling

- Aruanno Enterprises Inc .... G 302 530-1217
  Middletown *(G-3943)*
- Dieste Mark Design Build LLC ...... F 301 921-9050
  Bethany Beach *(G-398)*
- H B P Inc .... E 302 378-9693
  Middletown *(G-4098)*

CONTRACTORS: Office Furniture Installation

- Advance Office Instlltions Inc .... E 302 777-5599
  New Castle *(G-5008)*
- Affordable Delivery Svcs LLC .... E 302 276-0246
  New Castle *(G-5016)*
- Gray Audograph Agency Inc .... E 302 658-1700
  New Castle *(G-5359)*
- Step By Step Furn Installation ...... G 302 834-8257
  Newark *(G-7488)*

CONTRACTORS: Oil & Gas Wells Pumping Svcs

- Delaware Storage & Pipeline Co ... G 302 736-1774
  Dover *(G-1399)*

CONTRACTORS: Oil/Gas Well Construction, Rpr/Dismantling Svcs

- Burton Hg & Company Inc .... F 302 245-3384
  Dagsboro *(G-887)*
- Cunningham Homes LLC .... G 267 473-0895
  Newark *(G-6326)*
- DH Tech Wilmington De .... G 215 680-9194
  Wilmington *(G-10136)*
- Dick Ennis Inc .... G 302 945-2627
  Lewes *(G-3464)*
- Greenamoyer Construction .... G 302 999-8235
  Wilmington *(G-10774)*
- Keyrock LLC .... G 818 605-7772
  Wilmington *(G-11252)*
- Property Doctors LLC .... G 302 249-7731
  Magnolia *(G-3905)*

CONTRACTORS: On-Site Mobile Home Repair Svcs

- First State Services .... G 302 985-1560
  Wilmington *(G-10554)*
- Pierson Culver LLC .... G 302 732-1145
  Dagsboro *(G-930)*

CONTRACTORS: On-Site Welding

- Amazon Steel Construction Inc .... G 302 751-1146
  Milford *(G-4305)*
- Collett & Son Welding Inc .... G 302 376-1830
  Townsend *(G-8770)*
- Collett and Sons Welding .... G 302 223-6525
  Smyrna *(G-8601)*
- R C Fabricators Inc .... D 302 573-8989
  Wilmington *(G-12293)*
- Sussex Machine Works Inc .... G 302 875-7958
  Laurel *(G-3297)*
- William Chambers and Son .... G 302 284-9655
  Viola *(G-8838)*

PRODUCT & SERVICES SECTION

CONTRACTORS: Plumbing

CONTRACTORS: Ornamental Metal Work

Tri-State Fbrction McHning LLC ....E....... 302 232-3133
  New Castle *(G-5788)*

CONTRACTORS: Paint & Wallpaper Stripping

Stracke Enterprises Inc ....G....... 302 743-6515
  Newark *(G-7492)*

CONTRACTORS: Painting & Wall Covering

Color Works Painting Inc ....F....... 302 324-8411
  New Castle *(G-5183)*
DPs Custom Painting LLC ....G....... 302 732-3232
  Frankford *(G-2360)*
Facepainting ....G....... 302 344-3145
  New Castle *(G-5302)*
J Michaels Painting Inc ....F....... 302 738-8465
  Newark *(G-6817)*
John Mobile Sndblst & Pain ....G....... 302 270-5627
  Hartly *(G-2928)*
Keystone Finishing Inc...............................F....... 925 825-2498
  Wilmington *(G-11254)*
McElroy & Son Inc ....F....... 302 995-2623
  Wilmington *(G-11595)*
O B Pntg & Powerwashing Inc..................G....... 302 238-7384
  Millsboro *(G-4765)*
Painters Local Union 277 ....G....... 302 994-7835
  Wilmington *(G-12006)*
Robert G Burke Painting Co ....F....... 302 998-2200
  Wilmington *(G-12438)*
Robert J Peoples Inc ....F....... 302 984-2017
  New Castle *(G-5680)*
Ronald W Peacock Inc................................F....... 302 571-9313
  Wilmington *(G-12470)*
Smith Superior Pntg Repr Svcs.................G....... 302 384-6575
  Wilmington *(G-12661)*
Taylor & Sons Inc ....G....... 302 856-6962
  Georgetown *(G-2686)*
Three Bs Painting Contractors ....G....... 302 227-1497
  Rehoboth Beach *(G-8097)*

CONTRACTORS: Painting, Commercial

Clean Hands LLC ....F....... 215 681-1435
  Smyrna *(G-8598)*
G T Painting Inc...F....... 302 734-7771
  Dover *(G-1577)*
Kent County Painting Inc ....F....... 302 994-9628
  Wilmington *(G-11244)*
Urban Svcs Fcilities Maint LLC ....G....... 302 993-6463
  Wilmington *(G-13035)*

CONTRACTORS: Painting, Commercial, Exterior

Burke Painting Co Inc ....F....... 302 998-8500
  Wilmington *(G-9507)*
Connor Charles & Sons Painting ....G....... 302 945-1746
  Georgetown *(G-2482)*
Robert J Peoples Inc ....F....... 302 322-0595
  Wilmington *(G-12440)*

CONTRACTORS: Painting, Indl

Cannon Sline LLC ....D....... 302 658-1420
  New Castle *(G-5131)*
Coatings Inc ....G....... 302 661-1962
  Wilmington *(G-9755)*
Maccari Companies Inc ....G....... 302 994-9628
  Wilmington *(G-11476)*

CONTRACTORS: Painting, Residential

Bell Painting & Wall Covering...................F....... 302 738-8854
  Newark *(G-6069)*
Cassidy Painting Inc ....E....... 302 683-0710
  Wilmington *(G-9588)*
D C Painting Corp ....G....... 302 218-1211
  Hockessin *(G-2999)*
J G M Associates ....G....... 302 645-2159
  Lewes *(G-3567)*
J Rocco Construction LLC ....G....... 302 856-4100
  Georgetown *(G-2570)*
James Hughes Company Inc ....G....... 302 239-4529
  Hockessin *(G-3065)*
Mayse Painting & Contg LLC ....G....... 443 553-6503
  Middletown *(G-4148)*
Regal Painting & Decorating ....F....... 302 994-8943
  Wilmington *(G-12354)*
Reis Enterprises LLC ....G....... 302 740-8382
  Bear *(G-301)*

Sundew Painting Inc ....E....... 302 684-5858
  Harbeson *(G-2801)*
Top Qality Indus Finishers Inc..................G....... 302 778-5005
  Wilmington *(G-12929)*
Wilkisons Marking Service Inc ....G....... 302 697-3669
  Dover *(G-2226)*

CONTRACTORS: Painting, Residential, Interior

Final Finishes Inc ....G....... 302 995-1850
  Wilmington *(G-10539)*
Jamestown Painting & Dctg Inc ....E....... 302 454-7344
  Newark *(G-6827)*
Jgarvey Enterprises Inc ....G....... 302 562-7282
  Wilmington *(G-11154)*

CONTRACTORS: Patio & Deck Construction & Repair

Coastal Sun Roms Prch Enclsres ....G....... 302 537-3679
  Frankford *(G-2355)*
J&J Contracting Co Inc ....G....... 302 227-0800
  Rehoboth Beach *(G-7969)*
J&J Systems ....G....... 302 239-2969
  Hockessin *(G-3063)*

CONTRACTORS: Pavement Marking

A1 Striping Inc...G....... 302 738-5016
  Newark *(G-5872)*
Asphalt Striping Svcs Del LLC ....G....... 302 456-9820
  Wilmington *(G-9154)*
Durrell Sandblasting & Pntg Co ....G....... 302 836-1113
  Newark *(G-6481)*

CONTRACTORS: Petroleum Storage Tanks, Pumping & Draining

Ecg Industries Inc ....G....... 302 453-0535
  Newark *(G-6502)*
Jbm Petroleum Service LLC ....G....... 302 752-6105
  Lincoln *(G-3857)*

CONTRACTORS: Pile Driving

First State Crane Service ....G....... 302 398-8885
  Felton *(G-2292)*

CONTRACTORS: Pipe & Boiler Insulating

County Insulation Co..................................D....... 302 322-8946
  New Castle *(G-5202)*

CONTRACTORS: Plaster & Drywall Work

Cook Plastering Inc ....F....... 302 737-0778
  Newark *(G-6295)*

CONTRACTORS: Plastering, Plain or Ornamental

O Morales Stucco Plaster Inc ....G....... 302 834-8891
  Bear *(G-269)*
Pauls Plastering Inc ....E....... 302 654-5583
  New Castle *(G-5609)*

CONTRACTORS: Plumbing

A and D Plumbing LLC ....G....... 302 387-9232
  Magnolia *(G-3877)*
A J Dauphin & Son Inc ....G....... 302 994-1454
  Wilmington *(G-8880)*
Angler Plumbing LLC ....G....... 302 293-5691
  Newark *(G-5970)*
Associates Contracting Inc.......................F....... 302 734-4311
  Dover *(G-1150)*
Back Bay Plumbing ....G....... 302 945-1210
  Millsboro *(G-4633)*
Battaglia Associates Inc ....G....... 302 325-6100
  New Castle *(G-5069)*
Bill Rust Plumbing ....G....... 302 422-6061
  Harrington *(G-2818)*
Breeding & Day Inc ....E....... 302 478-4585
  Wilmington *(G-9466)*
Budget Rooter Inc.......................................G....... 302 322-3011
  New Castle *(G-5120)*
Cahill Plumbing & Heating Inc.................G....... 302 894-1802
  Newark *(G-6144)*
Calfo & Haight Inc......................................E....... 302 998-3852
  Wilmington *(G-9536)*

Cesn Partners Inc ....F....... 302 537-1814
  Ocean View *(G-7776)*
Charles A Klein & Sons Inc 410 549-6960
  Selbyville *(G-8466)*
Charles Moon Plumbing & Htg ....G....... 302 798-6666
  Claymont *(G-713)*
Charles S Reskovitz Inc ....G....... 302 999-9455
  Wilmington *(G-9637)*
Chesapeake Plumbing & Htg Inc ....E....... 302 732-6006
  Frankford *(G-2354)*
Clendaniel Plbg Htg & Coolg ....G....... 302 684-3152
  Milton *(G-4880)*
Collins Mechanical Inc ....G....... 302 398-8877
  Harrington *(G-2828)*
Cooper Bros Inc ....F....... 302 323-0717
  New Castle *(G-5194)*
Daves Contracting Inc ....G....... 302 436-5129
  Selbyville *(G-8479)*
Del Campo Plumbing & Heating ....G....... 302 998-3648
  Wilmington *(G-9997)*
Domenic Di Donato Plbg Htg Inc............. 856 207-4919
  Wilmington *(G-10189)*
Elvin Schrock and Sons Inc......................G....... 302 349-4384
  Greenwood *(G-2737)*
Federal Mechanical Contractors ....F....... 302 656-2998
  New Castle *(G-5305)*
Flowrite Inc ....G....... 302 547-5657
  Bear *(G-156)*
Graydon Hurst & Son Inc ....G....... 302 762-2444
  Wilmington *(G-10765)*
Happy Hours ....G....... 302 422-9766
  Milford *(G-4435)*
Harry Caswell Inc ....E....... 302 945-5322
  Millsboro *(G-4704)*
Horizon Services Inc..................................G....... 302 762-1200
  Wilmington *(G-10955)*
J Stachon Plumbing LLC ....G....... 302 998-0938
  Wilmington *(G-11111)*
Joseph T Richardson Inc ....F....... 302 398-8101
  Harrington *(G-2859)*
K BS Plumbing Incorporated ....G....... 302 678-2757
  Dover *(G-1717)*
K C Weaver and Sons Inc ....G....... 302 994-8399
  Wilmington *(G-11214)*
M D Plumbing Drain Cleaning.................G....... 302 492-8880
  Marydel *(G-3920)*
M Davis & Sons Inc.....................................C....... 302 998-3385
  Wilmington *(G-11471)*
Malins Jim E Plumbing & Htg ....G....... 302 239-2755
  Hockessin *(G-3085)*
Miller John H Plumbing & Htg ....F....... 302 697-1012
  Camden *(G-591)*
Ocean View Plumbing Inc ....F....... 302 732-9117
  Dagsboro *(G-927)*
R A Chance Plumbing Inc ....G....... 302 292-1315
  Newark *(G-7291)*
R A Chance Plumbing Inc ....G....... 302 324-8200
  New Castle *(G-5661)*
Rabspan Inc..G....... 302 324-8104
  New Castle *(G-5664)*
Rays Plumbing & Heating Svcs................F....... 302 697-3936
  Felton *(G-2315)*
Red Dog Plumbing and Heating ....G....... 302 436-5024
  Selbyville *(G-8537)*
Robert Gears ....G....... 302 834-7487
  Frankford *(G-2383)*
Robert J Seward and Son ....G....... 302 378-9414
  Townsend *(G-8820)*
Rw Greer Inc ....G....... 302 764-0376
  Wilmington *(G-12499)*
Schlosser Assoc Mech Cntrs Inc ....E....... 302 738-7333
  Newark *(G-7393)*
Siegfried J Schulze Inc ....F....... 302 737-0403
  Newark *(G-7422)*
Stan Perkoskis Plumbing & Htg ....F....... 302 529-1220
  Wilmington *(G-12734)*
State Wide Plumbing Inc ....G....... 302 292-0924
  Newark *(G-7486)*
Stay True Plumbing ....G....... 302 464-1198
  Bear *(G-338)*
Tj S Plumbing Heating L ....G....... 302 228-7129
  Frankford *(G-2393)*
Wegman Bros Inc ....F....... 302 738-4328
  Newark *(G-7681)*
William D Shellady Inc ....D....... 302 652-3106
  Wilmington *(G-13206)*
William G Robelen Inc ....G....... 302 656-8726
  Wilmington *(G-13210)*

Employee Codes: A=Over 500 employees, B=251-500
C=101-250, D=51-100, E=20-50, F=10-19, G=1-9

CONTRACTORS: Pollution Control Eqpt Installation

Pradhan Energy Projects .... G 305 428-2123
  Hockessin (G-3124)

CONTRACTORS: Post Disaster Renovations

Marlings Inc .... F 302 325-1759
  New Castle (G-5509)
Phoenix Home Theater Inc .... F 302 295-1390
  Wilmington (G-12124)

CONTRACTORS: Prefabricated Window & Door Installation

R & J Taylor Inc .... G 302 368-7888
  Newark (G-7289)

CONTRACTORS: Refractory or Acid Brick Masonry

Rgp Holding Inc .... G 302 661-0117
  Wilmington (G-12399)

CONTRACTORS: Refrigeration

General Refrigeration Company .... E 302 846-3073
  Delmar (G-999)
Gregg & Sons Mechanical LLC .... G 302 223-8145
  Townsend (G-8790)
John Hiott Refrigeration & AC .... F 302 697-3050
  Camden Wyoming (G-648)

CONTRACTORS: Roof Repair

R R Roofing Inc 2 .... G 302 218-7474
  Wilmington (G-12297)

CONTRACTORS: Roofing

Apex Piping Systems Inc .... E 302 998-5272
  Wilmington (G-9096)
Bayside Exteriors LLC .... G 302 727-5288
  Lewes (G-3363)
Beckers Chimney and Roofg LLC ...... E 302 463-8294
  Wilmington (G-9280)
Best Roofing and Siding Co .... G 302 678-5700
  Dover (G-1197)
D Shinn Inc .... F 302 792-2033
  Wilmington (G-9943)
David Saunders General Contrs .... G 302 998-0056
  Wilmington (G-9973)
Delmarva Roofing & Coating Inc .... E 302 349-5174
  Greenwood (G-2728)
Eastern Metals Inc .... F 302 454-7886
  Newark (G-6499)
Farrell Roofing Inc .... E 302 378-7663
  Middletown (G-4069)
Francis Pollinger & Son Inc .... E 302 655-8097
  Wilmington (G-10612)
G Fedale General Contrs LLC .... F 302 225-7663
  Hockessin (G-3033)
G Fedale Roofing and Siding .... F 302 225-7663
  Wilmington (G-10658)
Gearhart Construction Inc .... G 302 674-5466
  Dover (G-1587)
H K Griffith Inc .... E 302 368-4635
  Newark (G-6698)
Hurlock Roofing Company .... E 302 654-2783
  Wilmington (G-10978)
Jsf Construction Co Inc .... G 302 999-9573
  Wilmington (G-11204)
Kirkin Roofing LLC .... G 302 483-7135
  New Castle (G-5466)
Lane Home Services Inc .... F 302 652-7663
  Wilmington (G-11329)
Let US Lift It Inc .... G 302 654-2221
  Wilmington (G-11376)
Martin J Burke Inc .... G 302 741-2638
  Dover (G-1823)
McConnell Bros Inc .... G 302 218-4240
  Wilmington (G-11588)
P & C Roofing Inc .... E 302 322-6767
  New Castle (G-5595)
Peter Domanski & Sons .... G 302 475-3214
  Hockessin (G-3118)
Robert Grant Inc .... F 302 422-6090
  Milford (G-4546)
Roofers Inc .... E 302 995-7027
  Wilmington (G-12473)

Tazelaar Roofing Service Inc .... G 302 697-2643
  Dover (G-2132)
Wertz & Co .... E 302 658-5186
  Wilmington (G-13161)
Wilkinson Roofing & Siding Inc .... E 302 998-0176
  Wilmington (G-13203)

CONTRACTORS: Roofing & Gutter Work

CTA Roofing & Waterproofing .... F 302 454-8551
  Newark (G-6323)
Quality Exteriors Inc .... F 302 398-9283
  Harrington (G-2876)

CONTRACTORS: Roustabout Svcs

Estate Servicing LLC .... G 302 731-1119
  Newark (G-6540)
Rock Solid Servicing LLC .... G 302 233-2569
  Magnolia (G-3908)

CONTRACTORS: Safety & Security Eqpt

Advanced Coatings Engrg LLC .... E 888 607-0000
  Newark (G-5904)
Preferred Security Inc .... G 302 834-7800
  Bear (G-288)
Technicare Inc .... G 302 322-7766
  Newark (G-7545)

CONTRACTORS: Sandblasting Svc, Building Exteriors

Cassidy Painting Inc .... E 302 683-0710
  Wilmington (G-9588)
Coatings Inc .... G 302 661-1962
  Wilmington (G-9755)
Durrell Sandblasting & Pntg Co .... G 302 836-1113
  Newark (G-6481)
Maccari Companies Inc .... G 302 994-9628
  Wilmington (G-11476)

CONTRACTORS: Screening, Window & Door

Newport Builders & Windowland .... F 302 994-3537
  Wilmington (G-11878)
Superior Screen & Glass .... F 302 541-5399
  Ocean View (G-7816)

CONTRACTORS: Septic System

C White & Sons LLC .... G 302 629-4848
  Seaford (G-8179)
Clean Delaware LLC .... E 302 684-4221
  Lewes (G-3427)
Cox Electric Inc .... G 302 629-5448
  Seaford (G-8211)
Cs Webb Daughters & Son Inc .... G 302 239-2801
  Hockessin (G-2998)
George M Howard & Sons Inc .... G 302 645-9655
  Rehoboth Beach (G-7945)
Leager Construction Inc .... G 302 653-8021
  Smyrna (G-8671)
Midway Services Inc .... G 302 422-8603
  Lincoln (G-3861)

CONTRACTORS: Sheet Metal Work, NEC

Ducts Unlimited Inc .... G 302 378-4125
  Smyrna (G-8628)
L & J Sheet Metal .... F 302 875-2822
  Laurel (G-3249)
Mastercraft Welding .... G 302 697-3932
  Dover (G-1824)
Mumford Sheet Metal Works Inc .... E 302 436-8251
  Selbyville (G-8527)
Pencader Mechanical Contrs .... G 302 368-9144
  Newark (G-7194)

CONTRACTORS: Sheet metal Work, Architectural

Tri-State Fbrction McHning LLC .... E 302 232-3133
  New Castle (G-5788)

CONTRACTORS: Sidewalk

Brick Doctor Inc .... G 302 678-3380
  Dover (G-1231)

CONTRACTORS: Siding

Delaware Siding Company Inc .... G 302 836-6971
  Bear (G-113)

Home Services Unlimited .... G 302 293-8726
  Newark (G-6740)
Interstate Steel Co Inc .... E 302 598-5159
  Newark (G-6800)
PJ Fitzpatrick Inc .... D 302 325-2360
  New Castle (G-5623)

CONTRACTORS: Single-Family Home Fire Damage Repair

First Choice Services Inc .... E 302 648-7877
  Dagsboro (G-901)
Gibellino Construction Co .... G 302 455-0500
  Newark (G-6652)
Mebro Inc .... E 302 992-0104
  Wilmington (G-11613)
National Restortn & Faclty Svc .... E 856 401-0100
  Wilmington (G-11809)

CONTRACTORS: Single-family Home General Remodeling

Advance Construction Co Del .... F 302 697-9444
  Camden Wyoming (G-611)
Atlantic Enterprises LLC .... G 302 542-5427
  Lewes (G-3355)
Beam Construction Inc .... G 302 537-2787
  Fenwick Island (G-2330)
C & K Builders LLC .... G 302 324-9811
  Bear (G-59)
C Wallace & Associates .... G 302 528-2182
  Hockessin (G-2973)
C&M Construction Company LLC .... E 302 663-0936
  Millsboro (G-4652)
Carrie Construction Inc .... G 302 239-5386
  Hockessin (G-2977)
Case Hndyman Svcs W Chster LLC .... G 302 234-6558
  Hockessin (G-2979)
Choice Rmdlg & Restoration Inc .... G 717 917-0601
  Hockessin (G-2987)
CK Construction Inc .... G 302 698-3207
  Camden (G-550)
Colonial Construction Company .... F 302 994-5705
  Wilmington (G-9774)
Custom Improvers Inc .... G 302 731-9246
  Newark (G-6332)
E D Custom Contracting Inc .... G 302 653-2646
  Clayton (G-844)
Eastern Shore Porch Patio Inc .... E 302 436-9520
  Selbyville (G-8485)
Francis Pollinger & Son Inc .... E 302 655-8097
  Wilmington (G-10612)
Hanco Inc .... G 302 734-9782
  Dover (G-1626)
Home Services LLC .... G 302 510-4580
  Wilmington (G-10940)
Homestar Remodeling LLC .... E 302 528-5898
  Wilmington (G-10943)
Jack Saxton Construction Co .... G 302 764-5683
  Wilmington (G-11116)
James A Peel & Sons Inc .... G 302 738-1468
  Newark (G-6825)
James Rice Jr Construction Co .... G 302 731-9323
  Newark (G-6826)
K E Smart & Sons Inc .... G 302 875-7002
  Laurel (G-3247)
Kairos Home Pros LLC .... G 302 233-7044
  Dover (G-1721)
Kings Contracting Inc .... G 302 677-0363
  Dover (G-1751)
Locker Construction Inc .... G 302 239-2859
  Newark (G-6946)
M W Fogarty Inc .... G 302 658-5547
  Hockessin (G-3083)
Mullico General Construction .... F 302 475-4400
  Wilmington (G-11773)
Paragon Contracting Inc .... G 302 697-6565
  Camden (G-595)
Parker Construction Inc .... G 302 798-8530
  Claymont (G-793)
Poolside Cnstr & Renovation .... G 302 436-9711
  Selbyville (G-8533)
Quality Builders Inc .... G 302 697-0664
  Camden (G-597)
Quality Finishers Inc .... G 302 325-1963
  New Castle (G-5657)
RC Hellings Inc .... F 302 798-6850
  Claymont (G-799)
Renzi Group Inc .... G 302 588-2603
  Wilmington (G-12381)

PRODUCT & SERVICES SECTION
CONTRACTORS: Warm Air Heating & Air Conditioning

Rubio Construction LLC .... G 302 377-0353
 Wilmington *(G-12489)*
S J Passwater General Cnstr .... G 302 422-1061
 Milford *(G-4550)*
Silverside Contracting Inc .... G 302 798-1907
 Wilmington *(G-12619)*
Twaddell Plumbing and Heating .... G 302 475-5577
 Wilmington *(G-12997)*
W D Pressley Inc .... G 302 653-4381
 Smyrna *(G-8737)*
Wertz & Co .... E 302 658-5186
 Wilmington *(G-13161)*

CONTRACTORS: Skylight Installation

Archer Exteriors Inc .... F 302 877-0650
 Georgetown *(G-2434)*

CONTRACTORS: Solar Energy Eqpt

Allied Elec Solutions Ltd .... F 302 893-0257
 Wilmington *(G-9022)*
Blue Skies Solar & Wind Power .... E 302 326-0856
 New Castle *(G-5097)*
Clean Energy Usa LLC .... G 302 227-1337
 Rehoboth Beach *(G-7891)*
CMI Electric Inc .... G 302 731-5556
 Newark *(G-6253)*
CMI Electric Inc .... E 302 731-5556
 Newark *(G-6254)*
Congo Capital Management LLC .... F 732 337-6643
 Wilmington *(G-9820)*
Kw Solar Solutions Inc .... G 302 838-8400
 Bear *(G-225)*
Kw Solar Solutions Inc .... G 302 838-8400
 Bear *(G-226)*
Rigid Builders LLC .... F 732 425-3443
 Georgetown *(G-2640)*

CONTRACTORS: Sound Eqpt Installation

Baby Tel Communications Inc .... G 302 368-3969
 Newark *(G-6040)*
Brandywine Electronics Corp .... F 302 324-9992
 Bear *(G-56)*
Hts 20 LLP .... G 800 690-2029
 Milton *(G-4916)*
Smartis .... G 302 653-8355
 Dover *(G-2089)*

CONTRACTORS: Special Trades, NEC

All Restored Inc .... G 302 222-3537
 Camden Wyoming *(G-613)*
Atlantic Business Contracting .... G 302 337-7490
 Bridgeville *(G-449)*
B & T Contracting .... F 302 492-8415
 Camden Wyoming *(G-616)*
Boyds Trailor Hitches .... G 302 697-9000
 Camden Wyoming *(G-619)*
Builders LLC General .... G 302 533-6528
 Newark *(G-6130)*
Hertiage Builders & Improvemen .... G 302 275-8675
 Bear *(G-182)*
Jbs Contracting .... G 302 543-7264
 Wilmington *(G-11135)*
Lacieah Inc .... G 302 365-5585
 Newark *(G-6912)*
N Mallari Gc Corp .... G 302 516-7738
 Newark *(G-7078)*
Summer Hill Custom Home Bldr .... G 302 462-5853
 Ocean View *(G-7815)*

CONTRACTORS: Specialized Public Building

Mind Body & Sole .... G 302 537-3668
 Bethany Beach *(G-415)*

CONTRACTORS: Spraying, Nonagricultural

Delmarva Spray Foam LLC .... F 302 752-1080
 Georgetown *(G-2509)*

CONTRACTORS: Sprinkler System

Bear Industries Inc .... D 302 368-1311
 Newark *(G-6065)*

CONTRACTORS: Stone Masonry

Colonial Masonry Ltd .... G 302 349-4945
 Greenwood *(G-2721)*
Joseph Rizzo & Sons Cnstr Co .... E 302 656-8116
 New Castle *(G-5445)*

Mario F Medori Inc .... G 302 239-4550
 Wilmington *(G-11528)*

CONTRACTORS: Store Fixture Installation

Superior Screen & Glass .... F 302 541-5399
 Ocean View *(G-7816)*

CONTRACTORS: Structural Iron Work, Structural

M Davis & Sons Inc .... C 302 998-3385
 Wilmington *(G-11471)*
Rapuano Iron Works Inc .... G 302 571-1809
 Wilmington *(G-12317)*

CONTRACTORS: Structural Steel Erection

Amazon Steel Construction Inc .... G 302 751-1146
 Milford *(G-4305)*
Atlas Wldg & Fabrication Inc .... E 302 326-1900
 New Castle *(G-5053)*
Deaven Development Corp .... G 302 994-5793
 Wilmington *(G-9991)*
Donald F Deaven Inc .... E 302 994-5793
 Wilmington *(G-10196)*
East Coast Erectors Inc .... G 302 323-1800
 New Castle *(G-5275)*
Emlyn Construction Co .... G 302 697-8247
 Dover *(G-1519)*
Falcon Steel Co .... D 302 571-0890
 Wilmington *(G-10482)*
H & T Builders Inc .... G 302 422-0745
 Milford *(G-4429)*
Mid-Atlantic Steel LLC .... E 302 323-1800
 New Castle *(G-5527)*
R C Fabricators Inc .... D 302 573-8989
 Wilmington *(G-12293)*
Summit Steel Inc .... D 302 325-3220
 New Castle *(G-5741)*
W F Construction Inc .... G 302 420-6747
 Newark *(G-7669)*

CONTRACTORS: Stucco, Interior

D M S Stucco Construction Co .... F 302 368-2618
 Newark *(G-6342)*
Stucco Smith Systems .... G 302 245-8179
 Selbyville *(G-8550)*

CONTRACTORS: Svc Station Eqpt

Aztech Contracting Inc .... F 302 526-2145
 Felton *(G-2273)*
Keene Enterprises Inc .... G 302 422-2856
 Ellendale *(G-2261)*

CONTRACTORS: Svc Station Eqpt Installation, Maint & Repair

Rnh Installation .... G 302 731-8900
 Newark *(G-7347)*

CONTRACTORS: Terrazzo Work

Consolidated Construction Svcs .... F 302 629-6070
 Seaford *(G-8205)*

CONTRACTORS: Tile Installation, Ceramic

Ceramic Tile Supply Co .... D 302 737-4968
 Newark *(G-6180)*
Jack Parisi Tile Co Inc .... G 302 892-2455
 Wilmington *(G-11115)*
Keystone Granite and Tile Inc .... G 302 323-0200
 New Castle *(G-5462)*
Pala Tile & Carpet Contrs Inc .... E 302 652-4500
 Wilmington *(G-12007)*
Peninsula Acoustical Co Inc .... G 302 653-3551
 Smyrna *(G-8687)*
Tile Market of Delaware Inc .... G 302 644-7100
 Lewes *(G-3786)*
Tile Market of Delaware Inc .... D 302 777-4663
 Wilmington *(G-12910)*
Tile Shop LLC .... G 302 250-4889
 Wilmington *(G-12911)*

CONTRACTORS: Tuck Pointing & Restoration

Premier Restoration Cnstr Inc .... F 302 832-1288
 Middletown *(G-4198)*

Vivid Colors Carpet LLC .... G 302 335-3933
 Frederica *(G-2415)*

CONTRACTORS: Underground Utilities

Bramble Construction Co Inc .... F 302 856-6723
 Georgetown *(G-2458)*
Eastern States Cnstr Svc Inc .... D 302 995-2259
 Wilmington *(G-10326)*
Joseph T Hardy & Son Inc .... E 302 328-9457
 New Castle *(G-5446)*
Melcar Underground Ltd .... E 484 653-8259
 Lewes *(G-3633)*
Tri-State Underground Inc .... F 302 836-8030
 Townsend *(G-8829)*
Tri-State Underground Inc .... G 302 293-9352
 Bear *(G-358)*
Underground Locating Services .... G 302 856-9626
 Georgetown *(G-2697)*
Utilicon Solutions Ltd .... G 302 337-9980
 Bridgeville *(G-526)*
Utility Lines Cnstr Svcs LLC .... F 302 337-9980
 Bridgeville *(G-527)*

CONTRACTORS: Unit Paver Installation

Brick Doctor Inc .... G 302 678-3380
 Dover *(G-1231)*

CONTRACTORS: Wall Covering

Kokoszka & Sons Inc .... G 302 328-4807
 New Castle *(G-5468)*

CONTRACTORS: Warm Air Heating & Air Conditioning

A & A Air Services Inc .... E 302 436-4800
 Frankford *(G-2342)*
A & H Plumbing & Heating Inc .... G 302 223-8027
 Clayton *(G-830)*
A-1 Air Conditioning Heating .... G 302 998-5634
 Newport *(G-7744)*
Affordable Heating & AC .... G 302 328-9220
 New Castle *(G-5017)*
After Hours Heating & Air .... G 302 945-3310
 Millsboro *(G-4624)*
Air Doctorx Inc .... G 302 492-1333
 Hartly *(G-2912)*
Amstel Mechanical Contractors .... G 302 836-6469
 New Castle *(G-5036)*
Arctec Air Heating & Cooling .... G 302 629-7129
 Bridgeville *(G-447)*
Around Clock Htg AC Inc .... G 302 856-9306
 Georgetown *(G-2435)*
Atlantic Refrigeration Inc .... E 302 645-9321
 Lewes *(G-3358)*
B Walls Son Htg & A Conditions .... F 302 856-4045
 Georgetown *(G-2443)*
Calvert Mechanical Systems Inc .... E 302 998-0460
 Wilmington *(G-9543)*
Coastal Mechanical .... D 302 994-9100
 Wilmington *(G-9754)*
Community Heating & AC .... G 302 422-6839
 Lincoln *(G-3843)*
Daniel D Rappa Inc .... F 302 994-1199
 Wilmington *(G-9955)*
Delaware Heating & AC .... F 302 738-4669
 Bear *(G-108)*
Delaware Heating & AC Svcs Inc .... E 302 738-4669
 Newark *(G-6383)*
Delmarva Refrigeration Inc .... G 302 846-2727
 Delmar *(G-992)*
Dewitt Heating and AC Inc .... G 267 228-7355
 Bear *(G-115)*
Donald Eichholz .... G 302 792-1236
 Wilmington *(G-10195)*
Eastern Shore Energy Inc .... E 302 697-9230
 Camden *(G-566)*
Esquire Plumbing & Heating Co .... G 302 378-7001
 Middletown *(G-4062)*
Ferrell Cooling & Heating Inc .... G 302 436-2922
 Selbyville *(G-8492)*
First Class Heating & AC Inc .... F 302 934-8900
 Millsboro *(G-4690)*
First Class Heating AC .... E 302 834-1036
 Newark *(G-6580)*
George H Burns Inc .... E 302 658-0752
 Wilmington *(G-10699)*
H & R Heating & AC .... E 302 323-9919
 New Castle *(G-5367)*

Employee Codes: A=Over 500 employees, B=251-500
C=101-250, D=51-100, E=20-50, F=10-19, G=1-9

2020 Harris Directory of Delaware Businesses

CONTRACTORS: Warm Air Heating & Air Conditioning

Hellens Heating & Air I .... G 302 945-1875
  Harbeson (G-2784)
Henry Eashum & Son Inc .... F 302 697-6164
  Camden (G-578)
Hentkowski Inc .... F 302 998-2257
  Wilmington (G-10887)
Hillside Oil Company Inc .... E 302 738-4144
  Newark (G-6729)
Hollingsworth Heating & AC .... G 302 422-7525
  Milford (G-4443)
Hyett Refrigeration Inc .... F 302 684-4600
  Harbeson (G-2786)
J E Pellegrino & Associates .... G 302 655-2565
  Wilmington (G-11104)
Jsf Construction Co Inc .... G 302 999-9573
  Wilmington (G-11204)
Maichle S Heating Air .... F 302 328-4822
  New Castle (G-5499)
Megee Plumbing & Heating Co .... D 302 856-6311
  Georgetown (G-2600)
Monroe Mechanical Contracting .... G 302 223-6020
  Clayton (G-865)
Morans Refrigeration Service .... F 703 642-1200
  Rehoboth Beach (G-8011)
National HVAC Service .... E 302 323-1776
  New Castle (G-5546)
North Star Heating & Air Inc .... E 302 732-3967
  Dagsboro (G-925)
Premier Heating & AC .... G 302 684-1888
  Milton (G-4953)
Quality Htg Ar-Cnditioning Inc .... D 302 654-5247
  Wilmington (G-12280)
Rays and Sons Mechanical LLC .... G 302 697-2100
  Seaford (G-8372)
Robert Mullin .... G 302 322-9002
  Wilmington (G-12441)
Russo Brothers Inc .... G 302 764-5562
  Wilmington (G-12497)
Rw Heating & Air Inc .... G 302 856-4330
  Harbeson (G-2798)
Scotts Refrigeration & AC .... G 302 732-3736
  Frankford (G-2386)
Service Unlimited Inc .... E 302 326-2665
  New Castle (G-5700)
Solar Heating Inc .... E 302 836-3943
  Bear (G-327)
Total Climate Control Inc .... G 302 836-6240
  Newark (G-7578)
Twaddell Plumbing and Heating .... G 302 475-5577
  Wilmington (G-12997)

CONTRACTORS: Water Intake Well Drilling Svc

Robert J Seward and Son .... G 302 378-9414
  Townsend (G-8820)

CONTRACTORS: Water Well Drilling

Delmarva Builders Inc .... G 302 629-9123
  Bridgeville (G-465)
Middletown Well Drilling Co .... G 302 378-9396
  Odessa (G-7830)
White Drilling Corp .... G 302 422-4057
  Lincoln (G-3873)

CONTRACTORS: Water Well Servicing

A C Schultes of Delaware Inc .... F 302 337-0700
  Bridgeville (G-442)
American Water Well System .... F 302 629-3796
  Seaford (G-8150)

CONTRACTORS: Waterproofing

Adam Basement .... G 302 983-8446
  Newark (G-5898)
CTA Roofing & Waterproofing .... F 302 454-8551
  Newark (G-6323)
Delmarva Roofing & Coating Inc .... E 302 349-5174
  Greenwood (G-2728)
East Coast Elastomerics Inc .... F 302 524-8004
  Selbyville (G-8484)
Farrell Roofing Inc .... E 302 378-7663
  Middletown (G-4069)
H2o Pro LLC .... G 302 321-7077
  Frankford (G-2367)
Mid-Atlantic Systems Dpn Inc .... G 301 206-9510
  Newark (G-7032)
Mid-Atlntic Wtrproofing MD Inc 855 692-4668
  Newark (G-7033)

CONTRACTORS: Well Bailing, Cleaning, Swabbing & Treating Svc

Adv Fuel Polishing Service .... G 302 477-1040
  Claymont (G-685)

CONTRACTORS: Well Cleaning Svcs

Willey and Co .... G 302 629-3327
  Laurel (G-3311)

CONTRACTORS: Window Treatment Installation

Dezins Unlimited Inc .... G 302 652-4545
  Wilmington (G-10135)
Interiors By Kim Inc .... G 302 537-2480
  Ocean View (G-7794)
Royal Treatments .... G 302 722-6733
  Smyrna (G-8705)

CONTRACTORS: Windows & Doors

Francis Pollinger & Son Inc .... E 302 655-8097
  Wilmington (G-10612)
Newport Builders & Windowland .... F 302 994-3537
  Wilmington (G-11878)

CONTRACTORS: Wood Floor Installation & Refinishing

Coffin Hardwood Flooring Inc .... G 302 934-6414
  Millsboro (G-4665)
Dominic A Di Febo & Sons .... F 302 425-5054
  Wilmington (G-10190)
Donald G Varnes & Sons Inc .... G 302 737-5953
  Newark (G-6461)
Edward Varnes Hardwood Floors .... F 302 292-0919
  Newark (G-6503)
Urban Svcs Fcilities Maint LLC .... G 302 993-6363
  Wilmington (G-13035)
Ziggys Inc .... F 302 453-1285
  Newark (G-7740)

CONTRACTORS: Wrecking & Demolition

D & D Contractors Inc .... F 302 378-9724
  Smyrna (G-8609)
Geotech LLC .... G 302 353-9769
  Newark (G-6649)
Green Earth Tech Group LLC .... E 302 257-5617
  Wilmington (G-10771)
Rpj Waste Services Inc .... G 302 653-9999
  Smyrna (G-8706)
Steven Augusiewicz Inc .... G 302 738-1919
  Bear (G-339)

CONTROL EQPT: Buses Or Trucks, Electric

Totaltrax Inc .... D 302 514-0600
  New Castle (G-5778)

CONTROL EQPT: Electric

Val-Tech Inc .... E 302 738-0500
  Newark (G-7638)

CONTROL PANELS: Electrical

Atlantic Control Systems Inc .... G 302 284-9700
  Felton (G-2272)
Panelmatic Inc .... G 302 324-9193
  New Castle (G-5600)
Panelmatic East Inc .... F 302 324-9193
  New Castle (G-5601)
Power Electronics Inc .... E 302 653-4822
  Clayton (G-868)

CONTROLS & ACCESS: Indl, Electric

Ultrafine Technologies Inc .... G 302 384-6513
  Wilmington (G-13009)

CONTROLS: Automatic Temperature

Sewickley Capital Inc .... G 302 793-4964
  Wilmington (G-12589)

CONTROLS: Environmental

Air Liquide America LP .... G 302 225-2132
  Wilmington (G-7032)
Energy Systems Tech Inc .... G 302 368-0443
  Newark (G-6528)

Val-Tech Inc .... E 302 738-0500
  Newark (G-7638)

CONTROLS: Marine & Navy, Auxiliary

Xrosswater USA LLC .... G 917 310-1344
  Newark (G-7726)

CONTROLS: Relay & Ind

Automation Inc .... F 302 999-0971
  Wilmington (G-9187)

CONVALESCENT HOME

Courtland Manor Inc .... D 302 674-0566
  Dover (G-1318)

CONVALESCENT HOMES

1080 Slver Lk Blvd Oprtons LLC .... C 610 444-6350
  Dover (G-1063)
500 South Dupont Boule .... E 302 422-8700
  Milford (G-4297)
Brandywine Nursing & Rehab .... C 302 683-0444
  Wilmington (G-9444)
Cadbury At Lewes Inc .... D 302 644-6382
  Lewes (G-3399)
Churchman Village Center LLC .... G 302 998-6900
  Newark (G-6234)
Exceptional Care For Children .... D 302 894-1001
  Newark (G-6551)
Five Star Senior Living Inc .... D 302 478-4296
  Wilmington (G-10570)
Genesis Eldercare Nat Ctrs Inc .... C 302 734-5990
  Dover (G-1588)
Green Valley Terrace Snf LLC .... C 302 934-7300
  Millsboro (G-4700)
Greenvlle Retirement Cmnty LLC .... C 302 658-6200
  Wilmington (G-10781)
Hcr Manorcare Med Svcs Fla LLC ...... C 302 239-8583
  Wilmington (G-10863)
Home of Merciful Rest Society .... C 302 652-3311
  Wilmington (G-10939)
Milton & Hattie Kutz Home Inc .... C 302 764-7000
  Wilmington (G-11700)
Peninsula Untd Mthdst Hmes Inc .... C 302 654-5101
  Wilmington (G-12064)
Regal Hgts Hlthcre Ctr LLC .... D 302 998-0181
  Hockessin (G-3133)
Regency Hlthcare Rehab Ctr LLC .... C 302 654-8400
  Wilmington (G-12355)
Weston Senior Living Center .... F 302 994-4434
  Wilmington (G-13170)

CONVENIENCE STORES

J William Gordy Fuel Co .... F 302 846-3425
  Delmar (G-1006)
Jeff Thomas .... G 302 762-9154
  Wilmington (G-11143)
Service Energy LLC .... D 302 734-7433
  Dover (G-2071)

CONVENTION & TRADE SHOW SVCS

Delaware 87ers LLC .... E 302 351-5385
  Wilmington (G-10000)
Greater Wilmington Convention .... G 302 652-4088
  Wilmington (G-10769)

CONVERTERS: Data

Audioscience Inc .... F 302 324-5333
  New Castle (G-5054)
Cisco Systems Inc .... G 302 492-1735
  Hartly (G-2916)

CONVERTERS: Rotary, Electrical

Junttan USA Inc .... G 302 500-1274
  Laurel (G-3246)

CONVEYORS & CONVEYING EQPT

Airsled Inc .... G 302 292-8911
  Newark (G-5928)
Amazon Steel Construction Inc .... G 302 751-1146
  Milford (G-4305)
CDI Inc Sofr System LLC .... G 302 536-7325
  Seaford (G-8184)
Holts Metal Works Inc .... G 302 628-1609
  Seaford (G-8266)

PRODUCT & SERVICES SECTION

COVERS: Slip Made Of Fabric, Plastic, Etc.

COOKING & FOOD WARMING EQPT: Commercial

Eagle Mhc Company ....B....... 302 653-3000
  Clayton *(G-847)*
Franke USA Holding Inc ....F....... 615 462-4000
  Wilmington *(G-10614)*
Jaa Industries LLC ....G....... 302 332-0388
  New Castle *(G-5433)*
Metal Msters Fdservice Eqp Inc ....C....... 302 653-3000
  Clayton *(G-863)*

COOKING & FOODWARMING EQPT: Coffee Brewing

Coffee Artisan LLC ....G....... 302 297-8800
  Millsboro *(G-4664)*

COOLING TOWERS: Metal

Creative Assemblies Inc ....F....... 302 956-6194
  Bridgeville *(G-462)*

COPPER ORES

CC Enterprises LLC ....G....... 302 265-3677
  Newark *(G-6175)*

COPY MACHINES WHOLESALERS

Blue Marble Logistics LLC ....F....... 302 661-4390
  Wilmington *(G-9378)*
Hilyards Inc ....E....... 302 995-2201
  Wilmington *(G-10913)*
Steven Abdill ....G....... 443 243-6864
  Wilmington *(G-12758)*

CORRECTIONAL INSTITUTIONS

Correction Delaware Department ....B....... 302 856-5280
  Georgetown *(G-2487)*

COSMETIC PREPARATIONS

Majalco LLC ....G....... 703 507-5298
  Wilmington *(G-11494)*
Sun Pharmaceuticals Corp ....F....... 302 678-6000
  Dover *(G-2113)*

COSMETICS & TOILETRIES

Brandywine Botanicals LLC ....G....... 302 354-4650
  Wilmington *(G-9419)*
Cdo USA Inc ....G....... 347 429-5110
  Wilmington *(G-9605)*
Goodales Naturals ....G....... 302 743-6455
  Newark *(G-6674)*
My Lip Stuff ....G....... 302 945-5922
  Lewes *(G-3653)*
Playtex Manufacturing Inc ....D....... 302 678-6000
  Dover *(G-1969)*
Prayon Inc ....G....... 302 449-0875
  Middletown *(G-4196)*
Succulents Soap Sand Scents ....G....... 302 757-0697
  Newark *(G-7499)*

COSMETICS WHOLESALERS

Pharmadel LLC ....F....... 302 322-1329
  New Castle *(G-5620)*
Sally Beauty Supply LLC ....G....... 302 629-5160
  Seaford *(G-8383)*

COSMETOLOGIST

J and J Hair Fashions ....G....... 302 422-5117
  Milford *(G-4454)*
James & Jesses Barbr & Buty Sp ....G....... 302 658-9617
  Wilmington *(G-11119)*
Resh LLC ....F....... 302 543-5469
  New Castle *(G-5674)*

COSMETOLOGY & BEAUTY SCHOOLS

Carme LLC ....F....... 302 832-8418
  Newark *(G-6157)*
Hair Academy Llc ....G....... 302 738-6251
  Newark *(G-6701)*

COSMETOLOGY & PERSONAL HYGIENE SALONS

Beautiful Lashes ....G....... 302 983-9521
  Wilmington *(G-9278)*

Cartessa Aesthetics ....G....... 302 332-1991
  Hockessin *(G-2978)*
Charlotte Wilson ....G....... 302 500-1440
  Seaford *(G-8191)*
Girls Auto Clinic LLC ....G....... 484 679-6394
  New Castle *(G-5354)*
Posh Salon ....F....... 302 655-7000
  Wilmington *(G-12189)*
Premiere Hair Design ....G....... 302 368-7711
  Newark *(G-7245)*
Trilogy Salon and Day Spa Inc ....E....... 302 292-3511
  Newark *(G-7591)*
Womens Wellness Ctr & Med Spa ....G....... 302 643-2500
  Newark *(G-7716)*

COSMETOLOGY SCHOOL

Delaware Learning Institue of ....F....... 302 732-6704
  Dagsboro *(G-895)*
Island of Misfits LLC ....G....... 302 732-6704
  Dagsboro *(G-912)*

COSTUME JEWELRY & NOVELTIES: Apparel, Exc Precious Metals

Goldmine Enterprises Inc ....G....... 302 834-4314
  Bear *(G-167)*

COSTUME JEWELRY & NOVELTIES: Bracelets, Exc Precious Metals

Mission Bracelets ....G....... 302 528-5065
  Smyrna *(G-8681)*

COSTUME JEWELRY & NOVELTIES: Exc Semi & Precious

Altschuler Micki Designs ....G....... 302 655-6867
  Wilmington *(G-9035)*
Go Ahead Make My Ring ....G....... 302 235-8172
  Newark *(G-6668)*

COUGH MEDICINES

Glaxosmithkline Holdings ....C....... 302 984-6932
  Wilmington *(G-10720)*

COUNCIL FOR SOCIAL AGENCY

Children Fmilies First Del Inc ....G....... 302 674-8384
  Dover *(G-1276)*
Childrens Advocacy Ctr of Del ....F....... 302 741-2123
  Dover *(G-1278)*
Delaware Hmanities Council Inc ....G....... 302 657-0650
  Wilmington *(G-10054)*
Powell Life Skills Inc ....C....... 302 378-2706
  Townsend *(G-8816)*

COUNTER & SINK TOPS

Counterparts LLC ....G....... 302 349-0400
  Greenwood *(G-2723)*
Solid Image Inc ....G....... 302 877-0901
  Laurel *(G-3291)*

COUNTRY CLUBS

Cavaliers of Delaware Inc ....D....... 302 731-5600
  Newark *(G-6173)*
Cripple Creek Golf & Cntry CLB ....E....... 302 539-1446
  Dagsboro *(G-894)*
Dale Maple Country Club Inc ....E....... 302 674-2505
  Dover *(G-1337)*
Greenville Country Club Inc ....E....... 302 652-3255
  Wilmington *(G-10779)*
Henlopen Acres Beach Club Inc ....G....... 302 227-9919
  Rehoboth Beach *(G-7960)*
Kings Creek Country Club Inc ....F....... 302 227-8951
  Rehoboth Beach *(G-7982)*
Newark Country Club ....E....... 302 368-7008
  Newark *(G-7114)*
Peninsula ....G....... 302 945-4768
  Millsboro *(G-4774)*
Rehoboth Beach Country Club ....D....... 302 227-3811
  Rehoboth Beach *(G-8049)*
Ronald L Barrows ....F....... 302 227-3616
  Rehoboth Beach *(G-8062)*
Saint Anthonys Club ....G....... 302 328-9440
  New Castle *(G-5693)*
Sussex Pines Country Club ....E....... 302 856-6283
  Georgetown *(G-2682)*

Wilmington Country Club ....C....... 302 655-6171
  Wilmington *(G-13228)*

COURIER OR MESSENGER SVCS

Brooks Courier Service Inc ....C....... 302 762-4661
  Wilmington *(G-9485)*
Mdnewsline Inc ....G....... 773 759-4363
  Dover *(G-1834)*
Tristate Courier & Carriage ....E....... 302 654-3345
  Wilmington *(G-12980)*
Yello Technologies Inc ....G....... 954 802-6089
  Lewes *(G-3833)*

COURIER SVCS, AIR: Letter Delivery, Private

Livingston Healthcare Svcs Inc ....B....... 302 631-5000
  Newark *(G-6944)*

COURIER SVCS, AIR: Package Delivery, Private

Federal Express Corporation ....D....... 302 577-2667
  Wilmington *(G-10515)*
Federal Express Corporation ....E....... 800 463-3339
  New Castle *(G-5304)*

COURIER SVCS: Air

Federal Express Corporation ....G....... 800 463-3339
  Wilmington *(G-10514)*
Fedex Ground Package Sys Inc ....G....... 800 463-3339
  New Castle *(G-5307)*
Jz Road & Air Cargo Lines Inc ....G....... 302 468-5988
  Newark *(G-6861)*
Midnite Air Corp ....E....... 614 296-1678
  Newark *(G-7036)*
Penobscot Properties LLC ....G....... 302 322-4477
  New Castle *(G-5616)*

COURIER SVCS: Ground

Brooks Courier Service Inc ....C....... 302 762-4661
  Wilmington *(G-9485)*
Carr Courier Service Inc ....G....... 302 846-9826
  Delmar *(G-979)*
Charles E Carlson ....G....... 302 284-3184
  Camden Wyoming *(G-623)*
Darlington Postal Company LLC ....G....... 410 917-4147
  Newark *(G-6346)*
Delaware Medical Courier ....G....... 302 670-1247
  Milton *(G-4888)*
Harrymirimax Logisitics ....F....... 302 784-5578
  New Castle *(G-5378)*

COURIER SVCS: Package By Vehicle

Livingston Healthcare Svcs Inc ....B....... 302 631-5000
  Newark *(G-6944)*
Parcels Inc ....G....... 302 888-1718
  Wilmington *(G-12018)*
Parcels Inc ....G....... 302 736-1777
  Dover *(G-1935)*

COURIER SVCS: Parcel By Vehicle

Agrima Postal Solutions LLC ....D....... 302 394-6939
  Lewes *(G-3328)*

COURT REPORTING SVCS

Chancery Court Reporters ....G....... 302 255-0515
  Wilmington *(G-9628)*
Dale Hawkins ....G....... 302 658-6697
  Wilmington *(G-9948)*
Federal Court Reporters ....G....... 302 573-6195
  Wilmington *(G-10512)*
Wilcox & Fetzer Ltd ....E....... 302 655-0477
  Wilmington *(G-13200)*

COURTS

Supreme Court United States ....E....... 302 252-2950
  Wilmington *(G-12814)*

COVERS: Canvas

Cape Canvas ....G....... 302 684-8201
  Milton *(G-4874)*

COVERS: Slip Made Of Fabric, Plastic, Etc.

Calloways Custom Interiors Co ....G....... 302 994-7931
  Wilmington *(G-9538)*

Employee Codes: A=Over 500 employees, B=251-500, C=101-250, D=51-100, E=20-50, F=10-19, G=1-9

2020 Harris Directory of Delaware Businesses

CRANE & AERIAL LIFT SVCS

Specialized Carier Systems Inc .... G 302 424-4548
Milford *(G-4567)*

CREATIVE SVCS: Advertisers, Exc Writers

Advangelists LLC .... G 734 546-4989
Wilmington *(G-8958)*
De Novo Corporation .... E 302 234-7407
Wilmington *(G-9987)*
Miller Mauro Group Inc .... G 302 426-6565
Wilmington *(G-11694)*
Plugdin Inc .... G 347 726-1831
Dover *(G-1972)*
Pond Publishing & Productions .... G 302 284-0200
Felton *(G-2313)*

CREDIT & OTHER FINANCIAL RESPONSIBILITY INSURANCE

Chubb Insurance Company .... G 302 477-1892
Wilmington *(G-9695)*

CREDIT AGENCIES: Federal & Federally Sponsored

Agfirst Farm Credit Bank .... G 302 734-7534
Dover *(G-1094)*
Agfirst Farm Credit Bank .... G 302 856-9081
Georgetown *(G-2425)*

CREDIT AGENCIES: Federal Land Banks

Mid Atlantic Farm Credit Aca .... D 302 734-7534
Dover *(G-1847)*

CREDIT AGENCIES: Student Loan Marketing Association

SLM Corporation .... D 302 451-0200
Newark *(G-7441)*
SLM Financial Corporation .... F 856 642-8300
Newark *(G-7442)*

CREDIT BUREAUS

Groupe Victoire LLC .... G 302 384-5355
Wilmington *(G-10790)*
Lexisnexis Risk Assets Inc .... A 800 458-9410
Wilmington *(G-11378)*
S Wallace Holdings LLC .... G 917 304-1164
Wilmington *(G-12509)*

CREDIT CARD SVCS

Applied Card Holdings Inc .... G 302 326-4200
Wilmington *(G-9101)*
Continental Finance Co LLC .... E 302 456-1930
Wilmington *(G-9840)*
Delaware Merchant Services .... G 302 838-9100
Wilmington *(G-10066)*
Dfs Corporate Services LLC .... B 302 735-3902
Dover *(G-1419)*
Fia Card Services Nat Assn .... D 800 362-6255
Wilmington *(G-10529)*
Fidelity National Fincl Inc .... D 302 658-2102
Wilmington *(G-10534)*
Mercantile Processing Inc .... G 302 524-8000
Millville *(G-4849)*
Perkwiz Inc .... G 702 866-9122
Hockessin *(G-3116)*

CREDIT INSTITUTIONS, SHORT-TERM BUS: Wrkg Capital Finance

Bizboost Inc .... G 732 865-8050
Wilmington *(G-9343)*
John Lovett Inc .... D 302 455-9460
Newark *(G-6843)*
Swift Financial LLC .... E 302 374-7019
Wilmington *(G-12825)*

CREDIT INSTITUTIONS, SHORT-TERM BUSINESS: Factoring Svcs

Oink Oink LLC .... G 302 924-5034
Dover *(G-1914)*

CREDIT INSTITUTIONS: Personal

Advance America Cash Advance .... F 302 999-0145
New Castle *(G-5007)*
Bank of New Castle .... G 800 347-3301
New Castle *(G-5066)*
Cash Advance Plus .... G 302 846-3900
Delmar *(G-980)*
Cash Advance Plus .... G 302 629-6266
Seaford *(G-8183)*
Citifinancial Inc .... G 302 834-6677
Bear *(G-73)*
Citifinancial Credit Company .... G 302 628-9253
Seaford *(G-8195)*
Citifinancial Credit Company .... G 302 834-6677
Bear *(G-74)*
Citifinancial Credit Company .... G 302 678-8226
Dover *(G-1283)*
E Z Cash of Delaware Inc .... G 302 424-4013
Milford *(G-4397)*
EZ Cash of New Hampshire Inc .... G 302 846-0464
Delmar *(G-998)*
EZ Loans Inc .... F 302 934-5563
Millsboro *(G-4688)*
Minute Loan Center .... G 302 994-6588
Wilmington *(G-11711)*
Moneykey - TX Inc .... G 866 255-1668
Wilmington *(G-11732)*
One Main Financial .... G 302 737-9456
Newark *(G-7151)*
SLM Corporation .... D 302 451-0200
Newark *(G-7441)*

CREDIT INSTITUTIONS: Short-Term Business

Armstrong Cork Finance LLC .... G 302 652-1520
Wilmington *(G-9133)*
Citifinancial Credit Company .... G 302 834-6677
Bear *(G-74)*
Citifinancial Credit Company .... G 302 678-8226
Dover *(G-1283)*
Dfs Corporate Services LLC .... B 302 735-3902
Dover *(G-1419)*
One Main Financial .... G 302 737-9456
Newark *(G-7151)*

CREDIT INVESTIGATION SVCS

D & H Credit Services Inc .... F 302 832-6980
Newark *(G-6340)*

CREDIT UNIONS: Federally Chartered

American Spirit Federal Cr Un .... F 302 738-4515
Newark *(G-5958)*
American Spirit Federal Cr Un .... F 302 738-4515
Newark *(G-5959)*
Chestnut Run Federal Cr Un .... F 302 999-2967
Wilmington *(G-9658)*
Community Pwered Federal Cr Un .... F 302 392-2930
Bear *(G-80)*
Community Pwered Federal Cr Un .... G 302 324-1441
New Castle *(G-5188)*
Community Twered Federal Cr Un .... G 302 994-3617
Wilmington *(G-9796)*
Community Twered Federal Cr Un .... F 302 368-2396
Newark *(G-6273)*
Del-One Federal Credit Union .... F 302 739-2390
Dover *(G-1353)*
Del-One Federal Credit Union .... G 302 739-4496
Dover *(G-1354)*
Del-One Federal Credit Union .... G 302 739-4496
Smyrna *(G-8614)*
Del-One Federal Credit Union .... G 302 424-2969
Milford *(G-4373)*
Del-One Federal Credit Union .... E 302 739-4496
Dover *(G-1355)*
Del-One Federal Credit Union .... G 302 577-2667
Wilmington *(G-9999)*
Del-One Federal Credit Union .... G 302 323-4578
New Castle *(G-5221)*
Del-One Federal Credit Union .... G 302 739-6389
Dover *(G-1356)*
Del-One Federal Credit Union .... G 302 856-5100
Georgetown *(G-2498)*
Delaware Aliance Federal Cr Un .... G 302 429-0404
New Castle *(G-5224)*
Delaware First Federal Cr Un .... F 302 998-0665
Wilmington *(G-10047)*
Delaware Rver Bay Auth Emplyee .... G 302 571-6320
New Castle *(G-5238)*
Delaware State Police Federal .... G 302 324-8141
New Castle *(G-5240)*
Delaware State Police Federal .... F 302 856-3501
Georgetown *(G-2503)*
Dexsta Federal Credit Union .... F 302 996-4893
Wilmington *(G-10132)*
Dexsta Federal Credit Union .... E 302 996-4893
Wilmington *(G-10133)*
Dexsta Federal Credit Union .... G 302 695-3888
Wilmington *(G-10134)*
Dfs Corporate Services LLC .... G 302 349-4512
Greenwood *(G-2730)*
Dover Federal Credit Union .... D 302 678-8000
Dover *(G-1449)*
Dover Federal Credit Union .... G 302 322-4230
New Castle *(G-5258)*
Edge Moor Dupont Employees .... G 302 761-2282
Wilmington *(G-10347)*
First State Federal Credit Un .... F 302 674-5281
Dover *(G-1556)*
First State Refinery .... G 302 838-8303
New Castle *(G-5317)*
Louviers Federal Credit Union .... E 302 571-9513
Wilmington *(G-11442)*
Louviers Federal Credit Union .... F 302 733-0426
Newark *(G-6952)*
New Castle County School Emplo .... F 302 613-5330
New Castle *(G-5555)*
New Cstle Cnty Del Em Fdral Cr .... G 302 395-5350
New Castle *(G-5568)*
Priority Plus Federal Cr Un .... G 302 633-6480
Wilmington *(G-12231)*
Provident Federal Credit Union .... F 302 734-1133
Dover *(G-1992)*
Sussex County Federal Cr Un .... E 302 629-0100
Seaford *(G-8414)*
Sussex County Federal Cr Un .... G 302 422-9110
Milford *(G-4573)*
Sussex County Federal Cr Un .... G 302 644-7111
Lewes *(G-3771)*
Sussex County Federal Cr Un .... G 302 322-7777
New Castle *(G-5745)*
Wilmington Police and Fire Fed .... G 302 654-0818
Wilmington *(G-13242)*

CREDIT UNIONS: State Chartered

Community Twered Federal Cr Un .... F 302 368-2396
Newark *(G-6273)*
Dexsta Federal Credit Union .... F 302 695-3888
Wilmington *(G-10134)*
Dover Federal Credit Union .... D 302 678-8000
Dover *(G-1449)*
Eagle One Federal Credit Union .... G 302 798-7749
Claymont *(G-738)*

CREMATORIES

Melsons Cape Hnlopen Crematory .... G 302 537-2441
Frankford *(G-2374)*

CRISIS CENTER

A Door of Hope Inc .... G 302 998-9000
Wilmington *(G-8876)*

CRISIS INTERVENTION CENTERS

Contactlifeline Inc .... F 302 761-9800
Wilmington *(G-9838)*
Ministry of Caring Inc .... G 302 652-5522
Wilmington *(G-11708)*
Ministry of Caring Inc .... G 302 652-0970
Wilmington *(G-11709)*

CRUCIBLES

Rhi Refractories Holding Co .... G 302 655-6497
Wilmington *(G-12400)*

CRUDE PETROLEUM & NATURAL GAS PRODUCTION

I-Pulse Inc .... G 604 689-8765
Wilmington *(G-10984)*

CRUDE PETROLEUM PRODUCTION

Nemours Energy .... G 302 655-4838
Wilmington *(G-11832)*
Sun Gabon Oil Company .... G 302 293-6000
Wilmington *(G-12793)*

CULTURE MEDIA

One EDM LLC .... E 908 399-0536
Wilmington (G-11954)

CUTLERY, NEC

Bio Medic Corporation .... F 302 628-4300
Seaford (G-8170)

CUTOUTS: Distribution

Deride Igo .... G 302 234-4121
Newark (G-6439)

CYCLIC CRUDES & INTERMEDIATES

BASF Corporation .... C 302 992-5600
Wilmington (G-9258)
Chemfirst Inc .... D 302 774-1000
Wilmington (G-9646)
Honeywell International Inc .... D 302 791-6700
Claymont (G-763)

CYLINDERS: Pressure

Anderson Group Inc .... G 302 478-6160
Wilmington (G-9078)

CYLINDERS: Pump

Site Work Safety Supplies Inc .... G 302 672-7011
Dover (G-2085)

DAIRY PRDTS WHOLESALERS: Fresh

Burris Logistics .... D 302 398-5050
Harrington (G-2820)
H C Davis Inc .... G 302 337-7001
Bridgeville (G-477)
Hillandale Farms of Pa Inc .... E 302 492-1537
Hartly (G-2927)
Natural Dairy Products Corp .... G 302 455-1261
Newark (G-7086)

DAIRY PRDTS: Butter

CD Cream .... G 302 832-5425
Delaware City (G-950)

DAIRY PRDTS: Dietary Supplements, Dairy & Non-Dairy Based

Botica Cbd Inc .... G 619 800-5857
Wilmington (G-9396)
Nuvim Inc .... G 302 827-4052
Lewes (G-3662)
Roxlor LLC .... G 302 778-4166
Wilmington (G-12481)
Tesla Nootropics Inc .... G 514 718-2270
Dover (G-2140)

DAIRY PRDTS: Evaporated Milk

Nestle Usa Inc .... C 302 325-0300
New Castle (G-5552)

DAIRY PRDTS: Frozen Desserts & Novelties

Dana E Herbert .... G 302 721-5798
Bear (G-93)
Sunshine Crepes .... G 302 537-1765
Bethany Beach (G-432)

DAIRY PRDTS: Ice Cream, Bulk

Big Chill Inc .... G 302 727-5568
Rehoboth Beach (G-7868)
Frazzberry .... G 302 543-7791
Wilmington (G-10622)

DAIRY PRDTS: Milk & Cream, Cultured & Flavored

Hy-Point Dairy Farms Inc .... C 302 478-1414
Wilmington (G-10979)

DAIRY PRDTS: Milk, Fluid

Kraft Heinz Company .... A 302 734-6100
Dover (G-1758)

DAIRY PRDTS: Milk, Processed, Pasteurized, Homogenized/Btld

Tuscan/Lehigh Dairies Inc .... F 302 398-8321
Harrington (G-2901)

DAIRY PRDTS: Processed Cheese

Heather Kraft .... G 302 927-0072
Dagsboro (G-908)

DAMAGED MERCHANDISE SALVAGING, SVCS ONLY

Fitzgerald Auto Salvage Inc .... D 302 422-7584
Lincoln (G-3849)

DANCE BAND

Smooth Sound Dance Band .... E 302 398-8467
Harrington (G-2891)

DANCE INSTRUCTOR & SCHOOL

A Dance Class .... G 302 422-2633
Milford (G-4301)
Barbaras Dance Academy .... G 302 883-4355
Dover (G-1172)
Dance Conservatory .... G 302 734-9717
Dover (G-1339)
Dancedelaware .... G 302 998-1222
Wilmington (G-9954)
Delaware Arts Conservatory .... F 302 595-4160
Bear (G-103)
Delaware Dance Center Inc .... G 302 454-1440
Wilmington (G-10035)
Delaware Dance Company Inc .... E 302 738-2023
Newark (G-6374)
Hockessin Dance Center Inc .... G 302 738-3838
Newark (G-6733)
Take Lead Dance Studio .... G 302 234-0909
Hockessin (G-3156)
Tri-State Cheernastics Inc .... G 302 322-4020
New Castle (G-5787)

DANCE INSTRUCTOR & SCHOOL SVCS

Brandywine Center For Dance & .... G 302 798-0124
Wilmington (G-9423)
Mid-Atlantic Ballet Inc .... G 302 266-6362
Newark (G-7028)

DATA PROCESSING & PREPARATION SVCS

Ample Business Solutions Inc .... E 302 752-4270
Wilmington (G-9071)
Analyttica Datalab Inc .... E 917 300-3325
Wilmington (G-9074)
Brandywine Cad Design Inc .... E 302 478-8334
Wilmington (G-9420)
Computer Aid Inc .... C 302 831-5500
Newark (G-6276)
Cyberdaptive Inc .... G 302 388-3506
Newark (G-6336)
Data-Bi LLC .... G 302 290-3138
Wilmington (G-9962)
Datatech Enterprises Inc .... F 540 370-0010
Selbyville (G-8478)
GOBLIN Technologies LLC .... G 844 733-5724
Newark (G-6669)
Herox Pbc .... F 604 681-3651
Wilmington (G-10894)
Invensis Inc .... C 302 351-3509
Wilmington (G-11072)
Native Communications LLC .... G 302 439-0640
Wilmington (G-11817)
Pointlook Corporation .... G 415 448-6002
Wilmington (G-12179)
Vpn Express Incorporated .... E 302 351-8029
Wilmington (G-13106)
Webstudy Inc .... G 888 326-4058
Harbeson (G-2802)

DATA PROCESSING SVCS

Computer Services of Delaware ..... G 302 697-8644
Dover (G-1309)
Conch Island .... G 302 226-9378
Rehoboth Beach (G-7899)
Data Drum Inc .... G 347 502-8485
Seaford (G-6347)
J P Morgan Services Inc .... A 302 634-1000
Newark (G-6818)

John Snow Labs Inc .... E 302 786-5227
Lewes (G-3574)
National Dcument MGT Solutions .. G 302 535-9263
Marydel (G-3921)
Planet Payment Solutions Inc .... E 516 670-3200
New Castle (G-5625)
Valiu Inc .... E 317 853-5081
Lewes (G-3807)

DATABASE INFORMATION RETRIEVAL SVCS

Xcs Corporation .... G 302 514-0600
Wilmington (G-13316)

DATING SVCS

Rendezvous Inc .... G 302 645-7400
Lewes (G-3715)

DEBT COUNSELING OR ADJUSTMENT SVCS: Individuals

Fresh Start Marketplace LLC .... F 302 240-3002
Dover (G-1569)
Shechinah Empower Center Inc .... G 302 858-4467
Georgetown (G-2653)

DECORATIVE WOOD & WOODWORK

Artisan Woodworks LLC .... G 302 841-5182
Harbeson (G-2772)
Cedar Neck Decor LLC .... G 918 497-7179
Dagsboro (G-891)
Dick Palmer Woodworking .... G 302 227-8419
Rehoboth Beach (G-7916)
Farlow-Taylor Construction .... G 302 436-9660
Selbyville (G-8490)

DEFENSE SYSTEMS & EQPT

Absolute Cyber Defense .... G 850 532-0233
Dover (G-1078)
First Line Defense LLC .... G 302 287-2764
Smyrna (G-8634)
Magen Tactical Defense .... G 484 589-0670
Claymont (G-779)
Raytheon Company .... C 302 656-1339
Wilmington (G-12332)

DEHUMIDIFIERS: Electric

Creative Assemblies Inc .... F 302 956-6194
Bridgeville (G-462)

DELIVERY SVCS, BY VEHICLE

Affordable Delivery Svcs LLC .... E 302 276-0246
New Castle (G-5016)
Atlas World Express LLC .... G 202 536-5238
Middletown (G-3953)
Drone Delivery Systems Corp .... G 757 903-5006
Lewes (G-3475)
Fedex Ground Package Sys Inc ..... G 800 463-3339
Seaford (G-8243)
Good To Go Delivery LLC .... F 302 893-2734
Wilmington (G-10747)
J & S Moving & Dlvry Svc LLC .... G 302 357-5675
Newark (G-6813)
Lns Delivery Inc .... G 302 448-6848
Millsboro (G-4722)
N and J Delivery Service LLC .... G 302 562-3220
Bear (G-259)
Qwintry LLC .... G 858 633-6353
Newark (G-7288)
SF Express Corporation .... F 302 407-6155
New Castle (G-5702)
Smf Deliveries LLC .... G 302 945-6693
Lewes (G-3749)
Triglias Transportation Co .... E 302 846-2141
Delmar (G-1042)

DENTAL EQPT

Delmarva Laboratories Inc .... G 302 645-2226
Milton (G-4891)
Tc Dental Equipment Services .... G 302 740-9049
Townsend (G-8826)

DENTAL EQPT & SPLYS

C&G Dental Studio LLC .... G 302 345-4995
Bear (G-60)
Delmarva 2000 Ltd .... G 302 645-2226
Milton (G-4889)

DENTAL EQPT & SPLYS

Dentsply Sirona Inc .... D 302 422-4511
  Milford (G-4388)
Dentsply Sirona Inc .... D 302 422-1043
  Milford (G-4389)
Dentsply Sirona Inc .... C 302 430-7474
  Milford (G-4390)
Phocal Therapy Inc .... G 917 803-7168
  Lewes (G-3688)

DENTAL EQPT & SPLYS WHOLESALERS

Dentsply Sirona Inc .... G 302 422-4511
  Milford (G-4387)

DENTAL EQPT & SPLYS: Enamels

Delaware Smile Center 302 285-7645
  Middletown (G-4032)
Healthy Smiles of Delaware PA ...... G 302 658-7200
  Wilmington (G-10872)

DENTAL EQPT & SPLYS: Glue

Kuraray America Inc .... F 302 992-4204
  Wilmington (G-11301)

DENTISTS' OFFICES & CLINICS

Aaron B Poleck D M D LLC .... G 302 623-4190
  Newark (G-5877)
Aaron B Poleck DDS .... G 302 533-7649
  Newark (G-5878)
Adam C Sydell DDS .... G 302 684-1100
  Milton (G-4860)
Alfred B Lauder DDS .... G 302 697-7188
  Camden Wyoming (G-612)
Areas USA Dd LLC .... G 302 674-1946
  Dover (G-1135)
Arthur L Young Dentist Jr .... G 302 737-9065
  Newark (G-6006)
Avalon Dental LLC Bldg G4 .... G 302 292-8899
  Newark (G-6030)
Barry Klassman DDS RES .... G 302 478-0475
  Wilmington (G-9256)
Bear-Glasgow Dental LLC .... G 302 836-9330
  Bear (G-49)
Beautiful Smiles of Delaware .... G 302 656-0558
  Wilmington (G-9279)
Bernard A Lewis DDS .... G 302 943-0456
  Dover (G-1194)
Bernardo Anthony J Jr Dr DDS ..... G 302 998-9244
  Wilmington (G-9308)
Blair A Jones DDS .... G 302 226-1115
  Lewes (G-3386)
Blog - Care First Dental Team .... G 302 741-2044
  Dover (G-1212)
Bright Dental .... E 302 376-7882
  Middletown (G-3973)
Cathy L Harris DDS .... G 302 453-1400
  Newark (G-6171)
Cha Moon DDS .... G 302 297-3750
  Newark (G-6182)
Charles J Veith DMD .... G 302 658-7354
  Wilmington (G-9632)
Christiana Family Dental Care ..... G 302 623-4190
  Newark (G-6224)
Christine Fox DDS .... G 302 703-2838
  Lewes (G-3419)
Christopher Baran DDS .... G 903 968-7467
  Wilmington (G-9692)
Christopher Fortin DDS .... G 302 422-9791
  Milford (G-4352)
Concord Dental .... G 302 836-3750
  Wilmington (G-9811)
David A King DDS .... G 302 998-0331
  Wilmington (G-9965)
Dd Snacks LLC .... G 302 652-3850
  Wilmington (G-9983)
Delaware Dental Care Centers ..... G 410 474-5520
  Dover (G-1363)
Delaware Mobile Dentistry .... G 302 698-9901
  Dover (G-1381)
Delaware Star Dental .... G 302 994-3093
  Wilmington (G-10085)
Dental Diagnostics & Services ..... G 302 655-2626
  Wilmington (G-10115)
Dental Sleep Solution .... G 302 235-8249
  Wilmington (G-10116)
Dougherty Dental Solutions LLC . G 302 475-3270
  Wilmington (G-10212)
Dover Fmly Csmtc Dentistry LLC . G 302 672-7766
  Dover (G-1450)

Dr Fay Mintz-Guttin DMD .... G 302 356-0392
  Wilmington (G-10222)
Dr Jeffrey E Felzer DMD PC .... G 302 995-6979
  Wilmington (G-10225)
Dr John Fontana III .... G 302 734-1950
  Dover (G-1477)
Dr Shefali Pandya .... G 302 421-9960
  Wilmington (G-10229)
Dr Weidong Yang Dental Office ... G 302 409-3050
  Bear (G-127)
Edward B Bayley DMD .... G 302 766-4633
  Wilmington (G-10355)
Edwin S Kuipers DDS .... G 302 455-0333
  Newark (G-6505)
Emory & Marier PA .... F 302 422-2020
  Milford (G-4405)
Enhanced Dental Care .... G 302 645-7200
  Rehoboth Beach (G-7927)
Equidental .... G 302 423-0851
  Dover (G-1526)
Erik S Bradley DDS .... G 302 239-5917
  Wilmington (G-10435)
Erin N Macko DDS LLC .... G 302 368-7463
  Newark (G-6538)
Family Denistry .... G 302 368-0054
  Newark (G-6567)
Family Dentistry Wilmington .... G 302 656-2434
  Wilmington (G-10489)
Franklin Pancko DDS .... G 302 674-1140
  Dover (G-1565)
Frederick N Hartman .... G 302 479-5068
  Wilmington (G-10628)
Freedom Dental Management Inc . G 302 836-3750
  Wilmington (G-6616)
G Leigh Cook DMD .... F 302 453-8700
  Newark (G-6631)
Gary R Collins DDS .... G 302 239-3531
  Wilmington (G-10674)
Gentle Touch Dentistry .... G 302 765-3373
  Wilmington (G-10696)
George E Frattali DDS .... G 302 651-4408
  Wilmington (G-10697)
Hammond M Knox DDS .... G 302 383-6696
  Newark (G-6704)
Harry He DDS .... G 302 836-3711
  Newark (G-6711)
Herbert T Casalena DDS .... F 302 984-1712
  Wilmington (G-10888)
J A Pyne Jr DDS PA .... G 302 994-7730
  Wilmington (G-11102)
Jeffrey L Cook D M D .... G 302 453-8700
  Newark (G-6831)
Jessica S Dicerbo DDS .... G 302 644-4460
  Rehoboth Beach (G-7972)
Jill Garrido DDS .... G 302 475-3110
  Wilmington (G-11158)
Jillann I Hounsell DDS .... G 302 239-5917
  Hockessin (G-3066)
Jillann I Hounsell DDS .... G 302 691-3000
  Wilmington (G-11159)
Jiten Patel DDS .... G 302 690-8629
  Milford (G-4458)
John A Capodanno DDS PA .... G 302 697-7859
  Dover (G-1701)
John H Hatfield DDS .... G 302 698-0567
  Dover (G-1705)
John J Thaler II DDS .... G 302 478-9000
  Wilmington (G-11173)
John Wasniewski III DMD .... G 302 832-1371
  Bear (G-203)
Joseph C Kelly DDS .... G 302 475-5555
  Wilmington (G-11188)
Judith E McCann DMD .... G 302 368-7463
  Wilmington (G-6857)
Julie Q Nies DDS .... G 302 242-9085
  Dover (G-1715)
Junior Anderson Dover .... G 302 376-7979
  Townsend (G-8803)
Karl J Zeren DDS .... G 302 644-2773
  Rehoboth Beach (G-7976)
Kelly Ann Hatton .... G 484 571-5369
  Wilmington (G-11237)
Laurie Jacobs .... G 302 239-6257
  Hockessin (G-3078)
Lisa A Fagioletti DMD LLC .... G 302 514-9064
  Smyrna (G-8673)
Lrk Dental .... G 302 629-7115
  Seaford (G-8297)
Mark B Brown DDS .... G 302 537-1200
  Bethany Beach (G-413)

Mary Sweeney-Lehr .... G 302 764-0589
  Wilmington (G-11558)
Maryann K Bailey DDS .... G 302 655-5822
  Wilmington (G-11560)
Michael Butterworth Dr .... G 302 732-9850
  Dagsboro (G-922)
Michael Matthias .... G 302 575-0100
  Wilmington (G-11662)
Mill Creek Select .... G 302 995-2090
  Wilmington (G-11688)
Milltown Dental LLC .... G 302 998-3332
  Wilmington (G-11697)
Neil G McAneny DDS .... G 302 368-0329
  Newark (G-7089)
Ofc Partners Xiv Bellevue .... G 302 439-3345
  Wilmington (G-11937)
Oral & Maxillofacial Surgery .... G 302 998-0331
  Wilmington (G-11967)
Park Place Dental .... G 302 652-3775
  Wilmington (G-12020)
Peter Patellis .... G 302 537-1200
  Bethany Beach (G-421)
Robert A Penna DMD .... G 302 623-4060
  Newark (G-7349)
Robert P Hart DDS .... G 302 328-1513
  New Castle (G-5681)
Russo Mary Claire Real Estate .... G 302 529-2653
  Wilmington (G-12498)
Rutledge Dental Assoc Inc .... G 302 378-8705
  Middletown (G-4228)
Sarah K Smith DDS .... G 302 442-3233
  Newark (G-7386)
Southern Delaware Dental Spec . G 302 855-9499
  Georgetown (G-2661)
Stanley Goleburn DDS .... G 302 297-3750
  Newark (G-7482)
Terry Bryan .... G 302 698-9901
  Dover (G-2139)
Two Dds LLC .... G 302 300-1259
  Middletown (G-4271)
Westside Family Healthcare Inc .. E 302 678-4622
  Dover (G-2217)
Westside Family Healthcare Inc .. F 302 575-1414
  Wilmington (G-13171)
Westside Family Healthcare Inc .. F 302 836-2864
  Bear (G-376)
Westside Family Healthcare Inc .. F 302 455-0900
  Newark (G-7689)
Westside Family Healthcare Inc .. F 302 656-8292
  Wilmington (G-13172)
Westside Family Healthcare Inc .. F 302 656-8292
  Wilmington (G-13173)
Woodmill Dental .... G 302 998-8588
  Wilmington (G-13298)
Woodmill Dental .... G 302 998-8588
  Wilmington (G-13299)
Wright Bruce B DDS Office RES .. G 302 227-8707
  Rehoboth Beach (G-8119)
Xgate Dental Inc .... G 302 613-2142
  Wilmington (G-13320)

DEPARTMENT STORES

Be Blessed Design Group LLC ..... G 302 561-3793
  Bear (G-45)
Cato Corporation .... G 302 854-9548
  Georgetown (G-2464)

DEPARTMENT STORES: Army-Navy Goods

AMC Museum Foundation .... G 302 677-5938
  Dover (G-1116)
Domian International Svc LLC ..... G 804 837-3616
  Smyrna (G-8624)

DEPARTMENT STORES: Country General

Country Store .... F 302 653-5111
  Kenton (G-3184)

DEPILATORIES, COSMETIC

Cosmetic Innovators LLC .... G 310 310-9784
  Wilmington (G-9870)

DEPOSIT INSURANCE

Gem Group LP .... G 302 762-2008
  Wilmington (G-10687)

DERMATOLOGICALS

Delaware Dermatologic ....G..... 302 593-8625
  Wilmington *(G-10038)*
Workroom Enterprises LLC ....G..... 417 621-5577
  Wilmington *(G-13304)*

DESIGN SVCS, NEC

313design Lab Inc ....G..... 929 399-6426
  Lewes *(G-3316)*
Angle Planning Concepts ....F..... 302 735-7526
  Dover *(G-1126)*
Chesapeake Design Center LLC ....G..... 302 875-8570
  Laurel *(G-3212)*
Custom Creations By Design ....G..... 302 482-2267
  Wilmington *(G-9925)*
Designer Consigner Inc ....G..... 302 239-4034
  Hockessin *(G-3008)*
Gt Designs Inc ....G..... 302 275-8100
  Middletown *(G-4096)*
Jl Mechanical Inc ....G..... 302 337-7855
  Bridgeville *(G-487)*
Johnny Janosik Inc ....G..... 302 875-5955
  Laurel *(G-3243)*
M R Designs Inc ....G..... 302 684-8082
  Milton *(G-4928)*
Nouvir Lightning Corporation ....G..... 302 628-9888
  Seaford *(G-8331)*
Pierce Design & Tool ....G..... 302 222-3339
  Dover *(G-1958)*
Vera Bradley Designs Inc ....G..... 302 733-0880
  Newark *(G-7650)*

DESIGN SVCS: Commercial & Indl

ABS Engineering LLC ....G..... 302 595-9081
  Newark *(G-5886)*
Cadtech Inc ....F..... 302 832-2255
  Bear *(G-61)*
Drafting By Design Inc ....G..... 302 292-8304
  Newark *(G-6472)*

DESIGN SVCS: Computer Integrated Systems

924 Inc ....E..... 302 656-6100
  Wilmington *(G-8870)*
Access Versalign Inc ....G..... 302 225-7800
  Wilmington *(G-8914)*
Aigc Games Inc ....G..... 214 499-8654
  Lewes *(G-3331)*
Blu Dragon Studio Inc ....G..... 302 722-6227
  Newark *(G-6097)*
Brittons Wise Computers Inc ....G..... 302 659-0343
  Smyrna *(G-8587)*
Datatech Enterprises Inc ....F..... 540 370-0010
  Selbyville *(G-8478)*
Dodd Health Innovation LLC ....G..... 410 598-7266
  Ocean View *(G-7784)*
E-Dmz Security LLC ....E..... 302 791-9370
  Wilmington *(G-10312)*
Enterprise Services LLC ....C..... 302 454-7622
  Newark *(G-6533)*
Genex Technologies Inc ....D..... 302 266-6161
  Newark *(G-6647)*
Gyst Inc ....G..... 631 680-4307
  Dover *(G-1620)*
Info Systems Inc ....C..... 302 633-9800
  Wilmington *(G-11026)*
Internet Business Pubg Corp ....F..... 302 875-7700
  Laurel *(G-3241)*
Itiyam LLC ....F..... 703 291-1600
  Wilmington *(G-11093)*
Linkedin Profile Services LLC ......F..... 703 679-7719
  Wilmington *(G-11397)*
M C Tek LLC ....G..... 302 644-9695
  Rehoboth Beach *(G-7992)*
Progressive Software Cmpt Inc ....C..... 302 479-9700
  Wilmington *(G-12244)*
Public Systems Inc ....E..... 302 326-4500
  New Castle *(G-5652)*
Scientific Games Corporation ......F..... 302 737-4300
  Newark *(G-7395)*
Sync It LLC ....G..... 904 697-1132
  Wilmington *(G-12832)*
Tandem Hosted Resources Inc ...F..... 302 740-7099
  Newark *(G-7537)*
United3 Services Inc ....G..... 302 233-5985
  Millsboro *(G-4817)*
Verizon Delaware LLC ....C..... 302 571-1571
  Wilmington *(G-13062)*

Webstudy Inc ....G..... 888 326-4058
  Harbeson *(G-2802)*

DETECTIVE & ARMORED CAR SERVICES

Black Dragon Corporation ....D..... 617 470-9230
  Newark *(G-6089)*

DETECTIVE AGENCY

Base Enterprise Inc ....G..... 302 337-0548
  Bridgeville *(G-452)*
Delaware Detective Group LLC ...G..... 302 373-3678
  Middletown *(G-4027)*
Lenar Detective Agency Inc ....C..... 302 994-3011
  Wilmington *(G-11369)*
Resort Investigation & Patrol ....E..... 302 539-5808
  Millville *(G-4855)*

DETOXIFICATION CENTERS, OUTPATIENT

Connections Community Support ..D..... 302 536-1952
  Seaford *(G-8204)*

DEVELOPING & LABORATORY SVCS: Motion Picture

Risingplatformproductions LLC ....G..... 660 283-0183
  Newark *(G-7344)*

DIAGNOSTIC SUBSTANCES

Carolyn A Drkowski Ht Ascp LLC ...G..... 443 831-4854
  Lewes *(G-3408)*
E I Du Pont De Nemours & Co ....D..... 302 695-5300
  Wilmington *(G-10306)*
Siemens Healthcare Diagnostics ..D..... 302 631-8006
  New Castle *(G-5710)*
Siemens Hlthcare Dgnostics Inc ..D..... 302 631-7357
  Newark *(G-7425)*

DIAGNOSTIC SUBSTANCES OR AGENTS: In Vitro

Easy Diagnostics ....G..... 302 674-4089
  Dover *(G-1501)*

DIATOMACEOUS EARTH MINING SVCS

Rgp Holding Inc ....G..... 302 661-0117
  Wilmington *(G-12399)*

DIET & WEIGHT REDUCING CENTERS

Jenny Craig Wght Loss Ctrs Inc ...G..... 302 477-9202
  Wilmington *(G-11149)*
Jenny Craig Wght Loss Ctrs Inc ...G..... 302 454-0991
  Newark *(G-6834)*

DIODES: Light Emitting

Dupont Displays Inc ....E..... 805 562-9293
  Wilmington *(G-10253)*
Jaykal Led Solutions Inc ....G..... 302 295-0015
  Harbeson *(G-2788)*

DIRECT SELLING ESTABLISHMENTS: Telemarketing

Redzun LLC ....G..... 512 657-4100
  Wilmington *(G-12349)*

DIRECT SELLING ESTABLSHS: Furnishings, Door-To-Door

Stuart Kingston Galleries Inc ....F..... 302 652-7978
  Wilmington *(G-12780)*

DISC JOCKEYS

Aqua Flow Sprinklers ....G..... 302 369-3629
  Newark *(G-5991)*
Mobile Muzic Inc ....G..... 302 998-5951
  Wilmington *(G-11718)*

DISCS & TAPE: Optical, Blank

National Tape Duplicators ....G..... 302 999-1110
  Wilmington *(G-11813)*

DISHES: Plastic, Exc Foam

Galleyware Company Inc ....G..... 302 996-9480
  Wilmington *(G-10666)*

DISINFECTING & DEODORIZING SVCS

R W Home Services Inc ....F..... 302 539-4683
  Ocean View *(G-7810)*

DISINFECTING SVCS

Air Quality Remediation LLC ....F..... 302 464-1050
  Townsend *(G-8755)*
Think Clean & Grounds Up LLC ...F..... 904 250-1614
  New Castle *(G-5767)*

DISKETTE DUPLICATING SVCS

Mozeweb LLC ....G..... 302 355-0692
  Newark *(G-7065)*
Petcube Inc ....E..... 786 375-9065
  Wilmington *(G-12093)*

DISPLAY LETTERING SVCS

Initial Trading Co ....G..... 302 428-1132
  Wilmington *(G-11034)*

DISTRIBUTORS: Motor Vehicle Engine

Main Office Inc ....G..... 302 732-3460
  Dagsboro *(G-916)*

DIVING EQPT STORES

Scuba World Inc ....F..... 302 698-1117
  Dover *(G-2064)*

DOCUMENT EMBOSSING SVCS

DLS Discovery LLC ....D..... 302 888-2060
  Wilmington *(G-10176)*

DOCUMENT STORAGE SVCS

Nrai Services LLC ....F..... 302 674-4089
  Dover *(G-1907)*

DOCUMENTATION CENTER

A Gentlemans Touch Inc ....F..... 302 655-7015
  Wilmington *(G-8878)*

DOOR & WINDOW REPAIR SVCS

Yoder Overhead Door Company ...G..... 302 875-0663
  Delmar *(G-1050)*

DOOR OPERATING SYSTEMS: Electric

Gentleman Door Company Inc ....G..... 302 239-4045
  Yorklyn *(G-13366)*

DOORS & WINDOWS WHOLESALERS: All Materials

Clearview Windows LLC ....G..... 302 491-6768
  Milford *(G-4356)*

DOORS: Garage, Overhead, Metal

Cheslantic Overhead Door ....G..... 443 880-0378
  Delmar *(G-983)*
Pinnacle Garage Door Company ...G..... 302 505-4531
  Felton *(G-2310)*

DOORS: Garage, Overhead, Wood

Pinnacle Garage Door Company ...G..... 302 505-4531
  Felton *(G-2310)*

DRAFTING SPLYS WHOLESALERS

Reprographics Center Inc ....G..... 302 328-5019
  New Castle *(G-5672)*

DRAFTING SVCS

Systems Approach Ltd ....G..... 302 743-6331
  Newark *(G-7526)*

DRAPERIES & CURTAINS

Emerson & Klair ....G..... 302 239-6362
  Hockessin *(G-3020)*
Mp Axle Inc ....G..... 302 478-6442
  Wilmington *(G-11765)*
Royal Treatments ....G..... 302 722-6733
  Smyrna *(G-8705)*

DRAPERIES & DRAPERY FABRICS, COTTON

Vertical Blind Factory Inc ....F...... 302 998-9616
  Wilmington (G-13067)

DRAPERIES: Plastic & Textile, From Purchased Materials

Barlows Upholstery Inc ....G...... 302 655-3955
  Wilmington (G-9255)
Butlers Sewing Center Inc ....G...... 302 629-9155
  Seaford (G-8178)
Calloways Custom Interiors Co ....G...... 302 994-7931
  Wilmington (G-9538)
Draperies Etc Inc ....F...... 302 422-7323
  Milford (G-4395)
G L K Inc ....G...... 302 697-3838
  Dover (G-1576)

DRAPERY & UPHOLSTERY STORES: Draperies

Dream Weaver Interiors Inc ....G...... 302 644-0800
  Rehoboth Beach (G-7921)

DRAWBACK SVCS: Customs

Damon Baca ....G...... 858 837-0800
  Dover (G-1338)

DRINKING PLACES: Alcoholic Beverages

Delcastle Golf Club Management ......E...... 302 998-9505
  Wilmington (G-10098)
Harrington Raceway Inc ....B...... 302 398-5346
  Harrington (G-2846)
Hollywood Grill Restaurant ....D...... 302 655-1348
  Wilmington (G-10930)
New Castle Sailing Club ....G...... 302 307-3060
  New Castle (G-5564)
Wilmington Country Club ....C...... 302 655-6171
  Wilmington (G-13228)

DRINKING PLACES: Beer Garden

Dewey Beer & Food Company LLC ..G...... 302 227-1182
  Dewey Beach (G-1056)

DRINKING WATER COOLERS WHOLESALERS: Mechanical

Reil Machines USA Inc ....F...... 905 488-9263
  Wilmington (G-12369)

DRONES: Target, Used By Ships, Metal

Firefly Drone Operations Llc ....G...... 305 206-6955
  Wilmington (G-10543)

DRUG CLINIC, OUTPATIENT

ARS New Castle LLC ....G...... 302 323-9400
  New Castle (G-5046)
Sleep Disorders Ctr-Christiana ....G...... 302 623-0650
  Newark (G-7440)

DRUG STORES

Prescription Center Inc ....G...... 302 764-8564
  Wilmington (G-12221)

DRUGS & DRUG PROPRIETARIES, WHOLESALE

Disrupt Pharma Tech Africa Inc ....G...... 312 945-8002
  Dover (G-1430)

DRUGS & DRUG PROPRIETARIES, WHOLESALE: Animal Medicines

Animal Health Sales Inc ....F...... 302 436-8286
  Selbyville (G-8448)

DRUGS & DRUG PROPRIETARIES, WHOLESALE: Patent Medicines

Sinuswars LLC ....F...... 212 901-0805
  Wilmington (G-12633)

DRUGS & DRUG PROPRIETARIES, WHOLESALE: Pharmaceuticals

A2a Intgrted Phrmceuticals LLC ....G...... 270 202-2461
  Lewes (G-3320)
A66 Inc ....G...... 800 444-0446
  Wilmington (G-8892)
Delaware Pharmacist Society ....G...... 302 659-3088
  Smyrna (G-8619)
Foresee Pharmaceuticals Inc ....G...... 302 396-5243
  Newark (G-6602)
Fulcrum Pharmacy MGT Inc ....G...... 302 658-8020
  Wilmington (G-10645)
Hannas Phrm Sup Co Inc ....F...... 302 571-8761
  Wilmington (G-10834)
Pharmerica Long-Term Care LLC ....D...... 302 454-8234
  Newark (G-7209)
Qps LLC ....C...... 302 369-3753
  Newark (G-7280)
Radius Rx Direct Inc ....G...... 302 658-9196
  Wilmington (G-12303)
SPI Pharma Inc ....E...... 302 262-3223
  Seaford (G-8407)
SPI Pharma Inc ....E...... 302 576-8500
  Wilmington (G-12704)
Wh Nutritionals LLC ....G...... 302 357-3611
  Wilmington (G-13179)
Xynomic Pharmaceuticals Inc ....F...... 650 430-7561
  Dover (G-2243)

DRUGS & DRUG PROPRIETARIES, WHOLESALE: Vitamins & Minerals

Makeshopncompany Inc ....F...... 302 999-9961
  New Castle (G-5503)

DRUGS ACTING ON THE CENTRAL NERVOUS SYSTEM & SENSE ORGANS

DRG Holdco Inc ....G...... 610 974-9760
  Wilmington (G-10234)

DRYCLEANING & LAUNDRY SVCS: Commercial & Family

AP Linens Inc ....E...... 302 430-0851
  Milford (G-4308)
Harry Louies Laundry & Dry Clg ....F...... 302 734-8195
  Dover (G-1634)
Main Gate Laundry ....G...... 302 998-9949
  Wilmington (G-11490)
Newark Chinese Ldry & Dry Clrs ......G...... 302 368-3305
  Newark (G-7112)
Selbyville Cleaners Inc ....E...... 302 249-3444
  Selbyville (G-8544)

DRYCLEANING PLANTS

Blue Swan Cleaners Inc ....F...... 302 652-7607
  Wilmington (G-9382)
City One Hour Cleaners ....G...... 302 658-0001
  Wilmington (G-9724)
Colton Cleaners ....F...... 302 234-9422
  Hockessin (G-2992)
Harry Louies Laundry & Dry Clg ....F...... 302 734-8195
  Dover (G-1634)
Joy Cleaners Inc ....G...... 302 656-3537
  Wilmington (G-11199)
Kims Cleaners ....G...... 302 656-2397
  Wilmington (G-11262)
Main Gate Laundry ....G...... 302 998-9949
  Wilmington (G-11490)
Newark Chinese Ldry & Dry Clrs ......G...... 302 368-3305
  Newark (G-7112)
Value Rate Cleaners ....G...... 302 477-9191
  Wilmington (G-13045)

DRYCLEANING SVC: Collecting & Distributing Agency

Parkway Dry Cleaners Inc ....G...... 302 737-2406
  Newark (G-7178)
Thompson Cleaners ....G...... 302 998-0935
  Wilmington (G-12903)
Towne & Country Cleaners Inc ....G...... 302 478-8911
  Wilmington (G-12944)

DRYCLEANING SVC: Drapery & Curtain

Brasures Carpet Care Inc ....G...... 302 436-5652
  Selbyville (G-8461)

Capitol Cleaners & Launderers ....G...... 302 674-0500
  Dover (G-1252)
Proclean Inc ....E...... 302 656-8080
  Delaware City (G-965)
Schroedl Company ....D...... 410 358-5500
  Wilmington (G-12556)

DUCTS: Sheet Metal

Ducts Unlimited Inc ....G...... 302 378-4125
  Smyrna (G-8628)

DURABLE GOODS WHOLESALERS, NEC

Active Supply LLC ....G...... 888 843-0243
  Bear (G-11)
Direct Importer LLC ....G...... 302 838-2183
  Newark (G-6451)
Kratom Foundation LLC ....G...... 302 645-7400
  Lewes (G-3586)
MidatIntic Auto Rstration Sups ....G...... 302 422-3812
  Milford (G-4495)
Paradise Grill ....G...... 302 945-4500
  Millsboro (G-4768)

DYES & PIGMENTS: Organic

E I Du Pont De Nemours & Co ....B...... 302 999-2826
  Wilmington (G-10283)
E I Du Pont De Nemours & Co ....A...... 302 485-3000
  Wilmington (G-10278)
E I Du Pont De Nemours & Co ....G...... 800 441-7515
  Wilmington (G-10290)
E I Du Pont De Nemours & Co ....B...... 302 892-5655
  Wilmington (G-10301)
Orient Corporation of America ....E...... 302 628-1300
  Seaford (G-8339)

DYES & TINTS: Household

Economic Laundry Solutions ....E...... 302 234-7627
  Hockessin (G-3017)

EARTH SCIENCE SVCS

Brightfields Inc ....E...... 302 656-9600
  Wilmington (G-9477)
Evergreen Resources Group LLC .....G...... 302 477-0189
  Wilmington (G-10449)
Moran Envmtl Recovery LLC ....F...... 302 322-6008
  Newark (G-7057)

EATING PLACES

Ask Connoisseur LLC ....G...... 302 482-8026
  Claymont (G-695)
Baywood Greens Golf Club ....E...... 302 947-9225
  Millsboro (G-4638)
Boardwalk Plaza Incorporated ....D...... 302 227-0441
  Rehoboth Beach (G-7872)
Camels Hump Inc ....F...... 302 227-5719
  Rehoboth Beach (G-7882)
Coastal Properties I LLC ....E...... 302 227-5800
  Rehoboth Beach (G-7895)
Delcastle Golf Club Management .....E...... 302 998-9505
  Wilmington (G-10098)
Diamond State Pty Rentl & Sls ....E...... 302 777-6677
  Wilmington (G-10146)
Djont/Jpm Wilmington Lsg LLC ....D...... 302 478-6000
  Wilmington (G-10172)
Doubltree Htels Suites Resorts ....E...... 302 478-6000
  Wilmington (G-10210)
Greenville Country Club Inc ....E...... 302 652-3255
  Wilmington (G-10779)
Harrington Raceway Inc ....B...... 302 398-5346
  Harrington (G-2846)
Jacks Bstro At Dvid Fnney Inn ....G...... 302 544-5172
  New Castle (G-5434)
King of Sweets Inc ....F...... 302 730-8200
  Dover (G-1750)
M & P Adventures Inc ....E...... 302 645-6271
  Lewes (G-3614)
Newark Country Club ....E...... 302 368-7008
  Newark (G-7114)
Routzhan Jessman ....F...... 302 398-4206
  Harrington (G-2881)
Seafood City Inc ....E...... 302 284-8486
  Felton (G-2319)
Swami Enterprises Inc ....G...... 302 999-8077
  Wilmington (G-12822)
Universty & Whist Club Wlmgton .....F...... 302 658-5125
  Wilmington (G-13031)

PRODUCT & SERVICES SECTION

Venus On Halfshell .... G 302 227-9292
　Dewey Beach *(G-1061)*
Wilmington Country Club .... C 302 655-6171
　Wilmington *(G-13228)*

EDITORIAL SVCS

Biblion .... G 302 644-2210
　Lewes *(G-3383)*
Dialog News Paper Inc .... G 302 573-3109
　Wilmington *(G-10138)*

EDUCATIONAL SVCS

Avkin Inc .... F 302 562-7468
　New Castle *(G-5059)*
Delaware Fncl Edcatn Alnce Inc .... G 302 674-0288
　Dover *(G-1371)*
Distillate Media LLC .... G 302 270-7945
　Dover *(G-1431)*
Enhanced Corporate Prfmce LLC .... E 302 545-8541
　Newark *(G-6529)*
Kind To Kids Foundation .... G 302 654-5440
　Wilmington *(G-11264)*
Rose Hill Community Center .... F 302 656-8513
　New Castle *(G-5684)*
Shechinah Empower Center Inc .... G 302 858-4467
　Georgetown *(G-2653)*

EDUCATIONAL SVCS, NONDEGREE GRANTING: Continuing Education

Austrlian Phystherapy Ctrs Ltd .... G 631 298-5367
　Wilmington *(G-9185)*
Pressley Ridge Foundation .... G 302 854-9782
　Georgetown *(G-2626)*

EGG WHOLESALERS

Hillandale Farms of Pa Inc .... E 302 492-1537
　Hartly *(G-2927)*

ELECTRIC & OTHER SERVICES COMBINED

Balanceco2 Inc .... F 302 494-9476
　Wilmington *(G-9224)*
Blue Energy International LLC .... G 480 941-5100
　Wilmington *(G-9376)*
Blue Energy Partners LLC .... F 480 941-5100
　Wilmington *(G-9377)*
Indian River Power LLC .... F 302 934-3527
　Dagsboro *(G-911)*
Tristar Solar Farm LLC .... G 626 457-1381
　Wilmington *(G-12979)*

ELECTRIC MOTOR REPAIR SVCS

Dills Electric .... G 302 674-3444
　Dover *(G-1426)*
Electric Motor Repair Svc .... G 302 322-1179
　New Castle *(G-5281)*
HP Motors Inc .... G 302 368-4543
　Newark *(G-6753)*
Warren Electric Co Inc .... G 302 629-9134
　Seaford *(G-8433)*

ELECTRIC POWER DISTRIBUTION TO CONSUMERS

Aspire Energy LLC .... G 330 682-7726
　Dover *(G-1146)*
Atlantic City Electric Company .... E 202 872-2000
　Newark *(G-6018)*
Blue Hen Utility Services Inc .... G 302 273-3167
　New Castle *(G-5094)*
Chesapeake Utilities Corp .... C 302 734-6799
　Dover *(G-1274)*
City of Dover .... E 302 736-7070
　Dover *(G-1290)*
Conectiv LLC .... E 302 429-3018
　Newark *(G-6281)*
Delmarva Power & Light Company .... C 302 454-0300
　Newark *(G-6426)*
Delmarva Power & Light Company .... E 302 429-3376
　Wilmington *(G-10103)*

ELECTRIC POWER GENERATION: Fossil Fuel

Domian International Svc LLC .... G 804 837-3616
　Smyrna *(G-8624)*

ELECTRIC POWER, COGENERATED

Clearwater Enrgy Resources LLC .... G 510 267-8921
　Wilmington *(G-9740)*

ELECTRIC SERVICES

Aci Energy Inc .... D 302 588-3024
　Wilmington *(G-8922)*
Calpine Corporation .... G 302 824-4779
　Wilmington *(G-9541)*
Carroll Brothers Electric LLC .... G 302 947-4754
　Millsboro *(G-4656)*
City of Milford .... E 302 422-1110
　Milford *(G-4354)*
Cogentrix Delaware Holdings .... B 847 908-2800
　Wilmington *(G-9758)*
Congo Capital Management LLC .... G 732 337-6643
　Wilmington *(G-9821)*
Delaware Municipal Elc Corp .... G 302 653-2733
　Smyrna *(G-8617)*
Elec Integrity .... F 302 388-3430
　Dover *(G-1512)*
Electrical Integrity LLC .... G 302 388-3430
　New Castle *(G-5282)*
Etechboys Inc .... G 800 549-4208
　Wilmington *(G-10440)*
Flemings Electrical Service .... G 302 258-9386
　Laurel *(G-3230)*
J Fredericks & Son Elec C .... G 302 733-0307
　Newark *(G-6816)*
KB Electrical Services .... G 302 276-5733
　Wilmington *(G-11230)*
Mid Atlantic Renewable Energy .... G 302 672-0741
　Dover *(G-1848)*
Municipal Services Commission .... F 302 323-2330
　New Castle *(G-5539)*
NRG Energy Inc .... C 302 934-3537
　Millsboro *(G-4763)*
Ridgewood Electric Power Tr V .... G 302 888-7444
　Wilmington *(G-12417)*
Ridgewood Electric Pwr Tr III .... F 302 888-7444
　Wilmington *(G-12418)*
St Delware Electrical .... G 302 857-5316
　Dover *(G-2100)*
Sustainable Energy Utility .... G 302 504-3071
　Wilmington *(G-12819)*

ELECTRIC SVCS, NEC: Power Generation

Calpine Corporation .... E 302 764-4478
　Wilmington *(G-9540)*
Calpine Operating Svcs Co Inc .... E 302 468-5400
　Wilmington *(G-9542)*
Captains Grant Solar 1 Inc .... G 410 375-2092
　Millsboro *(G-4655)*
Conectiv LLC .... C 202 872-2680
　Wilmington *(G-9817)*
Conectiv LLC .... F 800 375-7117
　Wilmington *(G-9818)*
Delmarva Power & Light Company .... C 302 454-4450
　Newark *(G-6428)*
Delmarva Power & Light Company .... C 302 454-0300
　Wilmington *(G-10104)*
Energy Center Dover LLC .... F 302 678-4666
　Dover *(G-1523)*
FPL Energy American Wind LLC .... G 302 655-0632
　Wilmington *(G-10609)*
Garrison Calpine .... G 302 562-5661
　Dover *(G-1579)*
Pepco Holdings LLC .... E 202 872-2000
　Newark *(G-7199)*
Pepco Holdings LLC .... E 202 872-2000
　Wilmington *(G-12080)*
Scituate Solar I LLC .... G 212 419-4843
　Wilmington *(G-12563)*
SFE Solar Energy Inc .... F 905 366-7037
　Wilmington *(G-12590)*

ELECTRICAL APPARATUS & EQPT WHOLESALERS

Anderson Group Inc .... G 302 478-6160
　Wilmington *(G-9078)*
Select Suppliers Ltd .... G 303 523-1813
　Dover *(G-2068)*
Siemens Corporation .... F 302 690-2046
　Newark *(G-7424)*
Tecot Electric Supply Co .... G 302 735-3300
　Dover *(G-2135)*
Todays Energy Solutions LLC .... G 302 438-0285
　Wilmington *(G-12921)*

ELECTRICAL EQPT: Automotive, NEC

Wesco Distribution Inc .... F 302 655-9611
　Wilmington *(G-13162)*

ELECTRICAL APPLIANCES, TELEVISIONS & RADIOS WHOLESALERS

Lowes Home Centers LLC .... C 302 479-7799
　Wilmington *(G-11444)*
Lowes Home Centers LLC .... C 302 934-3740
　Millsboro *(G-4727)*
Lowes Home Centers LLC .... C 302 376-3006
　Middletown *(G-4137)*
Lowes Home Centers LLC .... C 302 735-7500
　Dover *(G-1798)*
Lowes Home Centers LLC .... C 302 645-0900
　Lewes *(G-3612)*
Lowes Home Centers LLC .... C 302 834-8508
　Bear *(G-238)*
Lowes Home Centers LLC .... C 302 697-0700
　Camden *(G-589)*
Lowes Home Centers LLC .... C 302 781-1154
　Newark *(G-6953)*
Lowes Home Centers LLC .... C 302 536-4000
　Seaford *(G-8296)*
Lowes Home Centers LLC .... C 302 252-3228
　New Castle *(G-5488)*
Tanner Operations Inc .... F 302 464-2194
　Townsend *(G-8825)*

ELECTRICAL CONSTRUCTION MATERIALS WHOLESALERS

City Electric Supply Company .... G 302 777-5300
　Wilmington *(G-9722)*

ELECTRICAL CURRENT CARRYING WIRING DEVICES

DMC Power Inc .... F 302 276-0303
　New Castle *(G-5257)*
NGK Spark Plugs USA Holdg Inc .... G 302 288-0131
　Wilmington *(G-11885)*
Security Satellite .... G 302 376-0241
　Middletown *(G-4235)*

ELECTRICAL DEVICE PARTS: Porcelain, Molded

NGK Spark Plugs USA Holdg Inc .... G 302 288-0131
　Wilmington *(G-11885)*

ELECTRICAL EQPT & SPLYS

Dave Smagala .... G 302 383-2761
　Claymont *(G-729)*
Electric Beach Tanning Company .... G 302 730-8266
　Dover *(G-1513)*
Mohawk Electrical Systems Inc .... E 302 422-2500
　Milford *(G-4509)*
North American Brands Inc .... E 519 680-0385
　Wilmington *(G-11897)*
Precision Systems Inds LLC .... G 224 388-9837
　Wilmington *(G-12207)*
Thermal Transf Composites LLC .... G 302 635-7156
　Hockessin *(G-3159)*

ELECTRICAL EQPT REPAIR & MAINTENANCE

Blue Skies Solar & Wind Power .... E 302 326-0856
　New Castle *(G-5097)*
CMI Electric Inc .... E 302 731-5556
　Newark *(G-6253)*
Modern Controls Inc .... E 302 325-6800
　New Castle *(G-5532)*
Morton Electric Co .... G 302 645-9414
　Lewes *(G-3650)*
Qoe Inc .... G 302 455-1234
　Newark *(G-7279)*

ELECTRICAL EQPT REPAIR SVCS

Food Equipment Service Inc .... F 302 996-9363
　Wilmington *(G-10586)*
Naes Corporation .... F 856 299-0020
　New Castle *(G-5542)*

ELECTRICAL EQPT: Automotive, NEC

Htk Automotive USA Corp .... E 888 998-9366
　Wilmington *(G-10968)*

ELECTRICAL GOODS, WHOL: Antennas, Receiving/Satellite Dishes
Conectiv Energy Supply Inc ....D....... 302 454-0300
  Newark *(G-6283)*

ELECTRICAL GOODS, WHOL: Vid Camera-Aud Recorders/Camcorders
Brandywine Electronics Corp.................F....... 302 324-9992
  Bear *(G-56)*

ELECTRICAL GOODS, WHOLESALE: Air Conditioning Appliances
Gt World Machineries Usa Inc ....F....... 800 242-4935
  Christiana *(G-669)*

ELECTRICAL GOODS, WHOLESALE: Batteries, Storage, Indl
Ploeners Automotive Pdts Co ....G....... 302 655-4418
  Wilmington *(G-12161)*

ELECTRICAL GOODS, WHOLESALE: Capacitors
John R Seiberlich Inc ....D....... 302 356-2400
  New Castle *(G-5441)*
Semiconductorplus Inc ....G....... 302 330-7533
  Wilmington *(G-12577)*

ELECTRICAL GOODS, WHOLESALE: Closed Circuit Television Or TV
A V C Inc ....G....... 302 227-2549
  Rehoboth Beach *(G-7835)*

ELECTRICAL GOODS, WHOLESALE: Electrical Appliances, Major
ABC Sales & Service Inc ....E....... 302 652-3683
  Wilmington *(G-8899)*
Appliances Zone ....G....... 302 280-6073
  Delmar *(G-971)*
National Appliance Whse Inc ....G....... 302 543-7636
  Wilmington *(G-11805)*

ELECTRICAL GOODS, WHOLESALE: Electronic Parts
Alvatek Electronics LLC ....F....... 302 655-5870
  Wilmington *(G-9036)*
Atechnologie LLC ....G....... 781 325-5230
  Wilmington *(G-9171)*
Electronics Exchange Inc ....G....... 302 322-5401
  New Castle *(G-5285)*

ELECTRICAL GOODS, WHOLESALE: Fans, Household
Artisan Electrical Inc ....G....... 302 645-5844
  Lewes *(G-3348)*

ELECTRICAL GOODS, WHOLESALE: Fire Alarm Systems
Simplex Time Recorder LLC ....F....... 302 325-6300
  New Castle *(G-5714)*

ELECTRICAL GOODS, WHOLESALE: Fittings & Construction Mat
Bristol Industrial Corporation ....F....... 302 322-1100
  New Castle *(G-5115)*

ELECTRICAL GOODS, WHOLESALE: Generators
Allpower Generator Sales & Svc ....G....... 302 793-1690
  Claymont *(G-688)*
Powerback Service LLC ....G....... 302 934-1901
  Millsboro *(G-4785)*

ELECTRICAL GOODS, WHOLESALE: Household Appliances, NEC
Reil Machines USA Inc ....F....... 905 488-9263
  Wilmington *(G-12369)*

ELECTRICAL GOODS, WHOLESALE: Insulators
NGK North America Inc ....G....... 302 654-1344
  Wilmington *(G-11884)*

ELECTRICAL GOODS, WHOLESALE: Light Bulbs & Related Splys
Rigel Energy Group LLC ....F....... 888 624-9844
  Wilmington *(G-12421)*

ELECTRICAL GOODS, WHOLESALE: Lighting Fittings & Access
Ledtolight ....G....... 941 323-6664
  Wilmington *(G-11354)*

ELECTRICAL GOODS, WHOLESALE: Lighting Fixtures, Comm & Indl
American Neon Products Company ....F....... 302 856-3400
  Milford *(G-4306)*

ELECTRICAL GOODS, WHOLESALE: Mobile telephone Eqpt
Lumenty Technologies Inc ....F....... 971 331-3113
  Wilmington *(G-11449)*
Voxx Electronics Corp ....F....... 302 656-5303
  Wilmington *(G-13105)*

ELECTRICAL GOODS, WHOLESALE: Motor Ctrls, Starters & Relays
Electric Motor Wholesale Inc ....F....... 302 653-1844
  Camden Wyoming *(G-635)*

ELECTRICAL GOODS, WHOLESALE: Motors
Warren Electric Co Inc ....G....... 302 629-9134
  Seaford *(G-8433)*
WW Grainger Inc ....F....... 302 322-1840
  New Castle *(G-5842)*

ELECTRICAL GOODS, WHOLESALE: Radio & TV Or TV Eqpt & Parts
Delmarva Communications Inc ....F....... 302 324-1230
  New Castle *(G-5244)*

ELECTRICAL GOODS, WHOLESALE: Security Control Eqpt & Systems
A Plus Electric & Security ....G....... 302 455-1725
  Newark *(G-5869)*
S & B Pro Security LLC ....G....... 800 841-9907
  Dover *(G-2047)*
Securitech Inc ....F....... 302 996-9230
  Wilmington *(G-12570)*

ELECTRICAL GOODS, WHOLESALE: Signaling, Eqpt
Wilmington Resources ....F....... 302 746-7162
  Wilmington *(G-13244)*

ELECTRICAL GOODS, WHOLESALE: Sound Eqpt
Quality Distributors Inc ....G....... 917 335-6662
  Wilmington *(G-12279)*

ELECTRICAL GOODS, WHOLESALE: Switches, Exc Electronic, NEC
Semiconductorplus Inc ....G....... 302 330-7533
  Wilmington *(G-12577)*

ELECTRICAL GOODS, WHOLESALE: Telephone & Telegraphic Eqpt
WER Wireless Inc ....E....... 302 478-7748
  Wilmington *(G-13158)*

ELECTRICAL GOODS, WHOLESALE: Video Eqpt
Video Walltronics Inc ....G....... 302 328-4511
  New Castle *(G-5817)*

ELECTRICAL GOODS, WHOLESALE: Wire & Cable, Electronic
John R Seiberlich Inc ....D....... 302 356-2400
  New Castle *(G-5441)*

ELECTRICAL HOUSEHOLD APPLIANCE REPAIR
ABC Sales & Service Inc ....E....... 302 652-3683
  Wilmington *(G-8899)*
Del-Mar Appliance of Delaware ....G....... 302 674-2414
  Dover *(G-1352)*
Johns Washer Repair ....G....... 302 792-2333
  Claymont *(G-769)*
Kral Electronics Inc ....F....... 302 737-1300
  Newark *(G-6902)*
Micro Ovens of Delaware ....G....... 302 998-8444
  Wilmington *(G-11674)*
Quality Appliance Services ....G....... 302 766-4808
  Newark *(G-7282)*
Video Tech Center Inc ....E....... 302 691-7213
  Wilmington *(G-13080)*

ELECTRICAL INDL APPARATUS, NEC
Voltvault Inc ....G....... 302 981-5339
  Newark *(G-7664)*
Xerafy Inc ....G....... 817 938-4197
  Wilmington *(G-13317)*

ELECTRICAL SPLYS
Billows Electric Supply Co Inc ....G....... 302 996-9133
  Wilmington *(G-9338)*
Denney Electric Supply Del Inc ....G....... 302 934-8885
  Millsboro *(G-4677)*
Dover Electric Supply Co Inc ....E....... 302 674-0115
  Dover *(G-1447)*
Dover Electric Supply Co Inc ....G....... 302 645-0555
  Rehoboth Beach *(G-7920)*
Graybar Electric Company Inc ....G....... 302 322-2200
  New Castle *(G-5360)*
Griffith Industrial Supply ....G....... 302 731-0574
  Newark *(G-6691)*
Tecot Electric Supply Co ....G....... 302 368-9161
  Newark *(G-7549)*
Tri State Battery and Auto Elc ....F....... 302 292-2330
  Newark *(G-7584)*
United Electric Supply Co Inc ....C....... 800 322-3374
  New Castle *(G-5804)*
United Electric Supply Co Inc ....F....... 302 674-8351
  Dover *(G-2180)*
United Electric Supply Co Inc ....G....... 302 732-1291
  Dagsboro *(G-941)*

ELECTROMEDICAL EQPT
Direct Radiography Corp ....C....... 302 631-2700
  Newark *(G-6452)*
Slimstim Inc ....G....... 310 560-4950
  Wilmington *(G-12646)*

ELECTROMETALLURGICAL PRDTS
American Minerals Inc ....G....... 302 652-3301
  New Castle *(G-5033)*

ELECTRONIC COMPONENTS
Pbtv Global Inc ....F....... 302 292-1400
  Wilmington *(G-12050)*
Pierce Design & Tool ....G....... 302 222-3339
  Dover *(G-1958)*

ELECTRONIC PARTS & EQPT WHOLESALERS
Bellex International Corp ....G....... 302 791-5180
  Wilmington *(G-9294)*
Maxbright Inc ....E....... 281 616-7999
  Lewes *(G-3626)*
Servo2gocom Ltd ....E....... 877 378-0240
  Wilmington *(G-12586)*
Seth Ral & Associates Inc ....G....... 302 478-9020
  Wilmington *(G-12587)*
Vectorvance LLC ....G....... 347 779-9932
  Wilmington *(G-13054)*

ELECTRONIC SHOPPING
7c Infotech Inc ....G....... 717 288-8686
  Wilmington *(G-8866)*

PRODUCT & SERVICES SECTION

EMPLOYMENT SVCS: Labor Contractors

Carzaty Inc .... F 650 396-0144
  Dover *(G-1258)*
David Popovich LLC .... G 855 464-9653
  Wilmington *(G-9971)*
Dell Oem Inc .... G 302 294-0060
  Newark *(G-6425)*
Mymoroccanbazar Inc .... G 323 238-5747
  Newark *(G-7077)*
Sqs Global Solutions LLC .... F 302 691-9682
  Wilmington *(G-12718)*
Wna Infotech LLC .... E 302 668-5977
  Bear *(G-379)*

ELEMENTARY & SECONDARY SCHOOLS, PRIVATE NEC

Cacc Montessori School .... E 302 239-2917
  Hockessin *(G-2974)*

ELEMENTARY & SECONDARY SCHOOLS, PUBLIC

Smyrna School District .... E 302 653-3135
  Smyrna *(G-8721)*

ELEMENTARY & SECONDARY SCHOOLS, SPECIAL EDUCATION

Readhowyouwant LLC .... G 302 730-4560
  Dover *(G-2014)*

ELEMENTARY SCHOOLS, NEC

Catholic Docese Wilmington Inc ..... E 302 731-2210
  Newark *(G-6169)*

ELEMENTARY SCHOOLS, PRIVATE

Elementary Workshop Inc .... F 302 656-1498
  Wilmington *(G-10369)*
Newark Ctr For Creative Lrng .... F 302 368-7772
  Newark *(G-7115)*
Wilmington Montessori School .... D 302 475-0555
  Wilmington *(G-13238)*

ELEMENTARY SCHOOLS, PUBLIC

Caesar Rodney School District .... D 302 697-3207
  Dover *(G-1248)*
Capital School District .... G 302 678-8394
  Dover *(G-1250)*

ELEVATOR: Grain, Storage Only

Milford Grain Co Inc .... G 302 422-6752
  Milford *(G-4498)*

ELEVATORS & EQPT

MV Farinola Inc .... G 302 545-8492
  Wilmington *(G-11781)*

ELEVATORS WHOLESALERS

Atlantic Elevators .... G 302 537-8304
  Dagsboro *(G-878)*
Brandywine Elevator Co Inc .... G 866 636-0102
  Wilmington *(G-9430)*
Liberty Elevator Experts LLC .... G 302 650-4688
  Newark *(G-6934)*

ELEVATORS: Installation & Conversion

Brandywine Elevator Co Inc .... G 866 636-0102
  Wilmington *(G-9430)*

EMBLEMS: Embroidered

Initially Yours Inc .... G 302 999-0562
  Wilmington *(G-11035)*
Whisman John .... G 302 530-1676
  Wilmington *(G-13185)*

EMBROIDERING & ART NEEDLEWORK FOR THE TRADE

A Nod To Stella Embroidery .... G 302 697-6308
  Wyoming *(G-13358)*
Actors Attic .... G 302 734-8214
  Dover *(G-1084)*
Alice M Mehaffey .... G 302 697-1893
  Dover *(G-1104)*

Andrew Pipon .... G 949 337-2249
  Milford *(G-4307)*
Array of Monograms .... G 302 998-2381
  Seaford *(G-8154)*
Championship Apparel Corp .... G 302 731-5917
  Newark *(G-6186)*
Delvina I Willson .... G 302 659-3672
  Smyrna *(G-8623)*
Dream Weavers Embroidery .... G 302 998-4264
  Wilmington *(G-10233)*
Embroid Me LLC .... G 302 993-0204
  Wilmington *(G-10388)*
Flutterby Stitches & EMB .... G 302 531-7784
  Dover *(G-1560)*
In A Stitch .... G 302 678-2260
  Dover *(G-1668)*
Just One Embroiderer .... G 302 832-9655
  Bear *(G-206)*
Kitschy Stitch .... G 302 200-9889
  Lewes *(G-3582)*
Patricia Hoffmann .... G 203 247-2635
  Bethany Beach *(G-419)*
Pineapple Stitchery .... G 302 500-8050
  Georgetown *(G-2619)*
Shacraft .... G 302 995-6385
  Marshallton *(G-3914)*
Shields Brothers .... G 302 999-1094
  Wilmington *(G-12601)*

EMBROIDERING SVC

A Stitch In Time .... G 302 395-1306
  New Castle *(G-4994)*
Five Stars Embroidery .... G 443 466-9692
  Middletown *(G-4074)*
Hoopin It Up Embroidery .... G 302 945-5511
  Millsboro *(G-4706)*
Lids Corporation .... G 302 736-8465
  Dover *(G-1783)*
Marksman Embroidery .... G 302 223-6740
  Smyrna *(G-8679)*
Penny Cooper Sportswear & EMB .. G 302 325-3710
  New Castle *(G-5615)*
Rwm Embroidery & More LLC .... F 302 653-8384
  Smyrna *(G-8709)*
Sew There Embroidery .... G 302 545-0127
  Townsend *(G-8821)*
Stamford Screen Printing Inc .... G 302 654-2442
  Wilmington *(G-12733)*
T&T Custom Embroidery Inc .... G 302 420-9454
  Bear *(G-344)*

EMBROIDERY ADVERTISING SVCS

Atlantic Sun Screen Prtg Inc .... F 302 731-5100
  Newark *(G-6021)*
Midnight Blue Inc .... G 302 436-9665
  Selbyville *(G-8522)*
Red Sun Custom Apparel Inc .... E 302 988-8230
  Selbyville *(G-8538)*
Stephen Cropper .... G 302 732-3730
  Frankford *(G-2390)*
Unique Image LLC .... E 302 658-2266
  Wilmington *(G-13017)*

EMBROIDERY KITS

Monogram Specialties .... G 302 292-2424
  Newark *(G-7052)*

EMERGENCY & RELIEF SVCS

Forgotten Few Foundation Inc .... G 302 494-6212
  Wilmington *(G-10594)*
Sussex Community Crisis .... F 302 856-2246
  Georgetown *(G-2675)*

EMERGENCY ALARMS

G K Associates Inc .... G 302 381-2824
  Rehoboth Beach *(G-7940)*
Grillo Holdings Inc .... G 302 261-9668
  Wilmington *(G-10785)*

EMERGENCY SHELTERS

Brandywine Hundred Fire Co 1 ...... D 302 764-4901
  Wilmington *(G-9438)*
Door of Second Chances Inc .... E 302 898-3959
  Wilmington *(G-10201)*
Dover Interfaith Mission Fr Ho .... F 302 736-3600
  Dover *(G-1454)*

Dunamis-Homes of Divine .... G 302 393-5778
  Camden Wyoming *(G-631)*
Friendship House Incorporated ...... F 302 652-8033
  Wilmington *(G-10640)*
Sojourners Place Inc .... E 302 764-4592
  Wilmington *(G-12673)*

EMPLOYEE LEASING SVCS

Fladger & Associates Inc .... E 302 836-3100
  Bear *(G-155)*

EMPLOYMENT AGENCY SVCS

924 Inc .... E 302 656-6100
  Wilmington *(G-8870)*
Accu Personnel Inc .... F 302 384-8777
  Wilmington *(G-8917)*
Adecco Usa Inc .... G 302 669-4005
  New Castle *(G-5003)*
Altea Resources LLC .... D 713 242-1460
  Dover *(G-1113)*
Barrett Business Services Inc .... G 302 674-2206
  Dover *(G-1173)*
Careers Usa Inc .... G 302 737-3600
  New Castle *(G-5132)*
Caring N Action Nursing .... G 302 368-2273
  Newark *(G-6155)*
Centrix Hr .... G 302 777-7818
  Wilmington *(G-9616)*
Coastal Hospitality LLC .... G 302 304-3156
  Wilmington *(G-9752)*
Community Integrated Services ..... E 215 238-7411
  Milford *(G-4362)*
Computer Staffing Services LLC .... E 302 737-4920
  Newark *(G-6278)*
Contemprary Stffing Sltons Inc ...... G 302 328-1300
  New Castle *(G-5192)*
D-Staffing Consulting Svcs LLC ..... D 302 402-5678
  Dover *(G-1336)*
Delaware Valley Group LLC .... G 302 777-7007
  Wilmington *(G-10095)*
Dkmrbh Inc .... F 302 250-4428
  Wilmington *(G-10173)*
Hyper Jobs LLC .... E 786 667-0905
  Newark *(G-6757)*
Integrity Staffing Solutions .... A 302 661-8770
  Newark *(G-6792)*
Jobs For Delaware Graduates .... E 302 734-9341
  Dover *(G-1699)*
Joseph Moore .... G 302 478-5659
  Wilmington *(G-11194)*
Opus Financial Svcs USA Inc .... G 646 435-5616
  Wilmington *(G-11966)*
Premier Staffing Solutions Inc .... D 302 628-7700
  Seaford *(G-8362)*
Redleo Software Inc .... F 302 691-9072
  Wilmington *(G-12348)*
Relig Staffing Inc .... E 312 219-6786
  Dover *(G-2022)*
Service General Corp .... C 302 856-3500
  Georgetown *(G-2651)*
Trinity Cloud Company .... E 973 494-8190
  Wilmington *(G-12974)*
Whitecrow Research Inc .... F 908 752-4200
  Wilmington *(G-13193)*
Whitehook Solutions LLC .... G 302 222-5177
  Smyrna *(G-8744)*
Wilmington Senior Center Inc .... F 302 651-3440
  Wilmington *(G-13256)*

EMPLOYMENT SVCS: Labor Contractors

Congruence Consulting Group .... G 320 290-6155
  Newark *(G-6286)*
Elite Office Staff Inc .... D 302 387-4158
  Dover *(G-1514)*
Hastin-Karin Inc .... G 347 377-8415
  Wilmington *(G-10851)*
Kna Solutions LLC .... G 302 709-1215
  Dover *(G-1753)*
Marine Corps United States .... G 302 376-3590
  Middletown *(G-4145)*
Premier Staffing Solutions Inc .... G 302 344-5996
  Georgetown *(G-2625)*
Servicexpress Corporation .... A 302 854-9118
  Seaford *(G-8399)*
Servicexpress Corporation .... C 302 424-3500
  Milford *(G-4556)*
Servicexpress Corporation .... G 302 856-3500
  Georgetown *(G-2652)*

Employee Codes: A=Over 500 employees, B=251-500
C=101-250, D=51-100, E=20-50, F=10-19, G=1-9

2020 Harris Directory of Delaware Businesses

EMPLOYMENT SVCS: Labor Contractors

Silicon Valley Ht Partners LP .... G 213 272-0088
  Camden *(G-600)*
Staffmark Investment LLC .... G 302 422-0606
  Milford *(G-4569)*
Staffmark Investment LLC .... G 302 854-0650
  Georgetown *(G-2665)*

EMPLOYMENT SVCS: Model Registry

Barbizon of Delaware Inc .... E 302 658-6666
  Wilmington *(G-9249)*

EMPLOYMENT SVCS: Nurses' Registry

Christiana Care Home Health .... F 302 698-4300
  Camden *(G-549)*
Majestique Ventures & Hlth Cre .... E 302 633-4010
  Wilmington *(G-11495)*
Nurses Connection .... G 302 421-3687
  Wilmington *(G-11923)*

EMPLOYMENT SVCS: Registries

Delaware Registry Ltd .... G 302 477-9800
  Wilmington *(G-10078)*

ENGINEERING HELP SVCS

GSM Systems Inc .... F 302 284-8304
  Viola *(G-8836)*

ENGINEERING SVCS

Acorn Energy Inc .... G 302 656-1708
  Wilmington *(G-8923)*
Ai Construction Services LLC .... G 619 732-0250
  Middletown *(G-3933)*
Arenarts Inc .... F 302 408-0887
  Claymont *(G-694)*
Beacon Engineering LLC .... G 302 864-8825
  Georgetown *(G-2451)*
Beckley Associates LLC .... G 301 943-7343
  Ocean View *(G-7763)*
Brandywine Cad Design Inc .... E 302 478-8334
  Wilmington *(G-9420)*
Brightfields Inc .... E 302 656-9600
  Wilmington *(G-9477)*
Calvin R Clendaniel Associates .... G 302 422-5347
  Lincoln *(G-3840)*
Cmy Solutions LLC .... G 321 732-1866
  Newark *(G-6256)*
Cohawk .... G 302 422-5176
  Milford *(G-4361)*
Commerce Global Inc .... G 302 478-0853
  Wilmington *(G-9784)*
Corrosion Testing Laboratories .... F 302 454-8200
  Newark *(G-6301)*
Cotten Engineering LLC .... G 302 628-9164
  Seaford *(G-8209)*
Delaware Secretary of State .... E 302 472-7678
  Wilmington *(G-10083)*
Delmarva Power & Light Company .... G 302 454-4040
  Newark *(G-6427)*
Dupont Prfmce Coatings Inc .... A 302 892-1064
  Wilmington *(G-10258)*
E I Du Pont De Nemours & Co .... E 302 999-4356
  Wilmington *(G-10291)*
East West Engineering Inc .... G 302 528-0652
  Bear *(G-137)*
Evocati Group Corporation .... F 206 551-9087
  Dover *(G-1533)*
Gcora Corp .... G 302 310-1000
  Milford *(G-4421)*
Gif North America LLC .... B 703 969-9243
  Rehoboth Beach *(G-7948)*
Hardcore Cmpstes Oprations Llc .... D 302 442-5900
  New Castle *(G-5374)*
Jaed Corporation .... F 302 832-1652
  Bear *(G-196)*
Ji DCI Jv-Il .... F 302 652-4221
  Wilmington *(G-11156)*
Koch Accounting Services LLC .... E 877 446-8478
  Wilmington *(G-11286)*
Lindsay and Associates Limited .... G 703 631-5840
  Milton *(G-4924)*
Merge Industrial Solutions LLC .... E 302 400-2157
  Dover *(G-1838)*
Meridian Architects Engineers .... E 302 643-9928
  Milton *(G-4935)*
Michael-Bruno LLC .... G 315 941-8514
  Wilmington *(G-11669)*
Mig Consulting LLC .... G 302 999-1888
  Wilmington *(G-11684)*

Network Mapping Inc .... G 310 560-4142
  Wilmington *(G-11840)*
P C Bohler Engineering .... E 302 644-1155
  Rehoboth Beach *(G-8026)*
Phase Snsitive Innovations Inc .... F 302 456-9003
  Newark *(G-7210)*
Pilottown Engineering LLC .... G 302 703-1770
  Lewes *(G-3691)*
Precise Alignment Mch TI Co .... G 302 832-2922
  Newark *(G-7239)*
Quinteccent Inc .... G 443 838-5447
  Selbyville *(G-8536)*
Sauer Holdings Inc .... E 302 656-8989
  Wilmington *(G-12545)*
Spaceport Support Services .... G 302 524-4020
  Selbyville *(G-8547)*
Summer Consultants Inc .... F 484 493-4150
  Newark *(G-7502)*
Tech International Corp .... G 302 478-2301
  Wilmington *(G-12868)*
Techmer Engineered Solutions .... G 800 401-8181
  New Castle *(G-5758)*
Telgian Engrg & Consulting LLC .... F 480 282-5392
  Wilmington *(G-12881)*
Ten Bears Environmental LLC .... G 302 731-8633
  Newark *(G-7556)*
Tetra Tech Inc .... E 302 738-7551
  Newark *(G-7560)*
Trim Waste Management LLC .... G 802 738-2500
  Newark *(G-7592)*
Unitrack Industries Inc .... E 302 424-5050
  Milford *(G-4586)*
Xcs Corporation .... G 302 514-0600
  Wilmington *(G-13316)*

ENGINEERING SVCS: Aviation Or Aeronautical

Carzo & Associates Inc .... G 302 575-0336
  Wilmington *(G-9584)*
Delta Engineering Corporation .... F 302 325-9320
  New Castle *(G-5247)*
Dupont Aviation Corp .... E 302 996-8000
  New Castle *(G-5266)*

ENGINEERING SVCS: Building Construction

American Hardscapes LLC .... F 302 253-8237
  Georgetown *(G-2431)*
Magowi Consulting Group LLC .... F 832 301-9230
  Newark *(G-6972)*
Mvl Structures Group LLC .... E 302 652-7580
  Wilmington *(G-11782)*

ENGINEERING SVCS: Chemical

Delux Engineering LLC .... G 610 304-0606
  Newark *(G-6434)*

ENGINEERING SVCS: Civil

Apex Engineering Inc .... F 302 994-1900
  Wilmington *(G-9095)*
Batta Ramesh C Associates PA .... E 302 998-9463
  Wilmington *(G-9260)*
Becker Morgan Group Inc .... F 302 734-7950
  Dover *(G-1189)*
Blake and Vaughan Engrg Inc .... F 302 888-1780
  Wilmington *(G-9367)*
Cda Engineering Inc .... G 302 998-9202
  Wilmington *(G-9604)*
Cgc Consulting LLC .... G 302 489-2280
  Wilmington *(G-9622)*
Civil Engineering Assoc LLC .... G 302 376-8833
  Middletown *(G-3993)*
Foresite Assoc Inc .... G 302 351-3421
  New Castle *(G-5323)*
Ibi Group (us) Inc .... C 949 833-5588
  Wilmington *(G-10987)*
Integrated Solutions Planning .... G 302 297-9215
  Georgetown *(G-2567)*
Johnson Mirmiran Thompson Inc .... E 302 266-9600
  Newark *(G-6847)*
Kci Technologies Inc .... E 302 731-9176
  Newark *(G-6871)*
Kercher Group Inc .... F 302 894-1098
  Newark *(G-6875)*
Landmark Engineering Inc .... D 302 323-9377
  Newark *(G-6915)*
Landmark Engineering Inc .... G 302 734-9597
  Newark *(G-6916)*

Larson Engineering Inc .... G 302 731-7434
  Newark *(G-6918)*
Merit Construction Engineers .... F 302 992-9810
  Wilmington *(G-11643)*
Mountain Consulting Inc .... G 302 744-9875
  Dover *(G-1876)*
Pelsa Company Inc .... G 302 834-3771
  Newark *(G-7191)*
Rummel Klepper & Kahl LLP .... E 302 468-4880
  Wilmington *(G-12493)*
VD&I Holdings Inc .... D 302 764-7635
  Wilmington *(G-13052)*
Wallace Montgomery & Assoc LLP .... E 302 510-1080
  Newark *(G-7674)*
Woodin + Associates LLC .... F 302 378-7300
  Middletown *(G-4290)*

ENGINEERING SVCS: Construction & Civil

Aecom Usa Inc .... E 302 781-5963
  Wilmington *(G-8963)*
B E & K Inc .... B 302 452-9000
  Newark *(G-6033)*
B E & K Engineering Company .... G 302 452-9000
  Newark *(G-6034)*
Merestone Consultants Inc .... F 302 992-7900
  Wilmington *(G-11639)*
Merestone Consultants Inc .... G 302 226-5880
  Lewes *(G-3637)*
Premier Restoration Inc .... F 302 645-1611
  Lewes *(G-3696)*
Qbeck Inspection Group .... E 302 452-9257
  Newark *(G-7277)*
Retained Logic Group Inc .... G 302 530-3692
  Middletown *(G-4219)*
Techncal Stffing Resources LLC .... G 302 452-9933
  Newark *(G-7544)*

ENGINEERING SVCS: Electrical Or Electronic

AC Group Inc .... G 201 840-5566
  Wilmington *(G-8910)*
Ames Engineering Corp .... E 302 658-6945
  Wilmington *(G-9067)*
Em Photonics Inc .... F 302 456-9003
  Newark *(G-6522)*
Game Changing Industries LLC .... G 302 498-8321
  Wilmington *(G-10667)*
Suretronix Solutions LLC .... G 302 407-3146
  Wilmington *(G-12817)*

ENGINEERING SVCS: Energy conservation

Delmarva Energy Solutions LLC .... G 302 684-3418
  Milton *(G-4890)*

ENGINEERING SVCS: Fire Protection

South Bowers Volunteer Fire Co .... E 302 335-4666
  Milford *(G-4565)*
Telgian Corporation .... E 480 753-5444
  Wilmington *(G-12880)*
Yellow Pine Associates Inc .... G 302 994-9500
  Wilmington *(G-13326)*

ENGINEERING SVCS: Heating & Ventilation

Delaware Engineering & Design .... D 302 738-7172
  Newark *(G-6378)*

ENGINEERING SVCS: Industrial

Drafting By Design Inc .... G 302 292-8304
  Newark *(G-6472)*
Flowline Technologies Inc .... G 302 256-5825
  Wilmington *(G-10579)*

ENGINEERING SVCS: Marine

Biehl & Co LP .... G 302 594-9700
  Wilmington *(G-9327)*

ENGINEERING SVCS: Mechanical

Diamond Mechanical Inc .... E 302 697-7694
  Dover *(G-1422)*
Polar Mechanical Inc .... E 302 994-9566
  Wilmington *(G-12180)*

ENGINEERING SVCS: Professional

Philadelphia Control Systems .... G 302 368-4333
  Christiana *(G-675)*

PRODUCT & SERVICES SECTION

FABRICS: Canvas

ENGINEERING SVCS: Structural

Corporate Arcft Technical Svcs.............G....... 302 383-9400
  Wilmington *(G-9864)*
Criterium Jagiasi Engineers ....G....... 302 498-5600
  Wilmington *(G-9899)*
Edc LLC ....F....... 302 645-0777
  Lewes *(G-3478)*
Long & Tann & D Onofrio Inc ....G....... 302 477-1970
  Wilmington *(G-11430)*
Macintosh Engineering Inc ....F....... 302 252-9200
  Wilmington *(G-11480)*

ENGINES: Internal Combustion, NEC

Cummins Power Generation Inc............B....... 302 762-2027
  Wilmington *(G-9918)*

ENGRAVING SVC, NEC

Abba Monument Co Inc ....G....... 302 738-0272
  Newark *(G-5880)*

ENGRAVING SVCS: Tombstone

Abba Monument Co Inc ....G....... 302 738-0272
  Newark *(G-5880)*

ENGRAVINGS: Plastic

New Castle Engraving Co ....G....... 302 652-7551
  New Castle *(G-5557)*

ENTERTAINERS & ENTERTAINMENT GROUPS

Alex Vaughan Mobile Entrtnmnt...........G....... 302 674-2464
  Dover *(G-1102)*
Bihbrand Inc ....F....... 302 223-4330
  Lewes *(G-3384)*
Coastal Concerts Inc ....G....... 302 645-1539
  Lewes *(G-3437)*
Comfort Zone Jazz LLC ....G....... 302 745-2019
  Milton *(G-4882)*
E I Du Pont De Nemours & Co ....F....... 302 888-0200
  Wilmington *(G-10296)*
Everett Robinson ....F....... 302 530-6574
  Wilmington *(G-10446)*
Mid Atlantic Grand Prix LLC ....E....... 302 656-5278
  New Castle *(G-5522)*
Real Life Entertainment ....G....... 516 413-2782
  Newark *(G-7304)*
Studio J Entrmt & AP & Cof Bar ....G....... 410 422-3155
  Laurel *(G-3296)*

ENTERTAINMENT PROMOTION SVCS

Rhodeside Inc ....G....... 505 261-4568
  Wilmington *(G-12402)*
Worldwind Inc ....G....... 302 762-0556
  Wilmington *(G-13305)*

ENTERTAINMENT SVCS

Bobby Wilson Entertainment LLC.........G....... 302 233-6463
  Dover *(G-1217)*
Continuum Media LLC ....F....... 310 295-9997
  Camden *(G-552)*
Cube Media L L C ....G....... 716 239-2789
  Wilmington *(G-9915)*
Dj First Class ....F....... 302 345-0602
  New Castle *(G-5256)*
Dover Motorsports Inc ....G....... 302 328-6820
  New Castle *(G-5259)*
Gge Amusements ....G....... 302 227-0661
  Rehoboth Beach *(G-7947)*
Jammin Productions ....G....... 302 670-7302
  Dover *(G-1693)*
K&B Investors LLC ....G....... 302 357-9723
  Wilmington *(G-11216)*
Lune Rouge Entrmt USA Inc ....E....... 514 556-2101
  Wilmington *(G-11451)*
PDr Vc Ltd Liability Company..............G....... 424 281-4669
  Wilmington *(G-12056)*
Premier Entertainment III LLC ....E....... 302 674-4600
  Dover *(G-1982)*
Soucialize Inc ....G....... 916 803-1057
  Lewes *(G-3756)*
Zone Laser Tag Inc ....F....... 302 730-8888
  Dover *(G-2254)*

ENVELOPES

Owens Corningfibreboard..................G....... 302 654-4250
  Wilmington *(G-11987)*

ENVIRONMENTAL QUALITY PROGS ADMIN, GOVT: Recreational

City of Newark.................................E....... 302 366-7060
  Newark *(G-6243)*

EQUIPMENT: Rental & Leasing, NEC

Actors Attic ....G....... 302 734-8214
  Dover *(G-1084)*
Arrow Leasing Corp ....F....... 302 834-4546
  Bear *(G-36)*
Burke Equipment Company ....D....... 302 697-3200
  Felton *(G-2278)*
Carrier Rental Systems Inc ....E....... 302 836-3000
  Bear *(G-65)*
Chesapeake Supply & Eqp Co ....G....... 302 284-1000
  Felton *(G-2283)*
Coastal Rentals Hydraulics LLC...........G....... 302 251-3103
  Millville *(G-4840)*
Darby Leasing LLC ....G....... 302 477-0500
  Wilmington *(G-9960)*
Diamond Chemical & Supply Co ....E....... 302 656-7786
  Wilmington *(G-10139)*
Dover Rent-All Inc ....F....... 302 739-0860
  Dover *(G-1469)*
Grand Rental Station ....G....... 302 227-7368
  Rehoboth Beach *(G-7954)*
Groff Tractor & Equipment LLC............F....... 302 349-5760
  Greenwood *(G-2742)*
J&S Leasing Co Inc ....G....... 302 328-1066
  New Castle *(G-5432)*
Material Handling Supply Inc ....F....... 302 571-0176
  New Castle *(G-5511)*
Morton Electric Co ....G....... 302 645-9414
  Lewes *(G-3650)*
National Rig Rental LLC ....G....... 302 539-1963
  Frankford *(G-2378)*
Penske Truck Leasing Co LP ....E....... 302 325-9290
  New Castle *(G-5617)*
Professional Leasing Inc ....G....... 302 629-4350
  Seaford *(G-8365)*
Queen B Tbl Chair Rentals LLC ....G....... 215 960-6303
  Dover *(G-2002)*
Quillens Rent All Inc ....G....... 302 227-3151
  Rehoboth Beach *(G-8039)*
Right Way Flagging and Sign Co ....E....... 302 698-5229
  Camden Wyoming *(G-653)*
Ryder Truck Rental Inc ....E....... 302 798-1472
  Wilmington *(G-12501)*
Shell We Bounce ....G....... 302 727-5411
  Rehoboth Beach *(G-8073)*
Temp-Air Inc ....F....... 302 369-3880
  Newark *(G-7555)*
United Rentals North Amer Inc ....E....... 302 328-2900
  New Castle *(G-5807)*

ESTIMATING SVCS: Construction

Mainline Masonry Inc........................E....... 302 998-2499
  Middletown *(G-4142)*

ETHYLENE-PROPYLENE RUBBERS: EPDM Polymers

Cowie Technology Corp ....G....... 856 692-2828
  New Castle *(G-5206)*
Empower Materials Inc ....F....... 302 225-0100
  New Castle *(G-5290)*

EXCAVATING MACHINERY & EQPT WHOLESALERS

McClung-Logan Equipment Co Inc ......F....... 302 337-3400
  Bridgeville *(G-495)*

EXECUTIVE OFFICES: Federal, State & Local

Health & Social Svcs Del Dept............F....... 302 856-5586
  Georgetown *(G-2556)*
Historical & Cultural Afairs ....F....... 302 792-0285
  Claymont *(G-761)*
Historical & Cultural Afairs ....F....... 302 323-4453
  New Castle *(G-5396)*
Historical & Cultural Afairs ....F....... 302 739-3277
  Dover *(G-1650)*

EXERCISE EQPT STORES

Gym Source ....G....... 302 478-4069
  Wilmington *(G-10804)*

EXERCISE FACILITY

Cycology 202 LLC ....F....... 610 202-0518
  Lewes *(G-3447)*

EXERCISE SALON

Cnu Fit LLC ....G....... 302 744-9037
  Dover *(G-1298)*
Curves ....G....... 302 731-2617
  Newark *(G-6329)*
Curves For Women ....F....... 302 477-9400
  Wilmington *(G-9921)*

EXHAUST HOOD OR FAN CLEANING SVCS

Als Power Washing Service ....E....... 302 399-3406
  Dover *(G-1112)*
Hood Man LLC..................................G....... 302 422-4564
  Lincoln *(G-3855)*

EXHIBITORS, ITINERANT, MOTION PICTURE

Carmike Cinemas Inc ....E....... 302 734-5249
  Dover *(G-1256)*

EXPLOSIVES: Emulsions

Emulsion Products Company ....E....... 302 629-3505
  Seaford *(G-8236)*

EXTENDED CARE FACILITY

Green Acres Health Systems ....C....... 302 934-7300
  Millsboro *(G-4699)*

EXTERMINATING & FUMIGATING SVCS

Brasures Pest Control Inc ....E....... 302 436-8140
  Selbyville *(G-8462)*
Home Paramount Pest Control ....G....... 302 894-9201
  New Castle *(G-5401)*
Royal Pest Solutions Inc ....E....... 302 322-6665
  New Castle *(G-5688)*

EXTERMINATING PRDTS: Household Or Indl Use

Mark Wilson Diguardi ....G....... 302 897-6625
  Millsboro *(G-4735)*

EYEGLASSES

Luxottica of America Inc ....C....... 302 322-4131
  New Castle *(G-5491)*

FABRIC STORES

Loomcraft Textile & Supply Co ....F....... 302 454-3232
  Newark *(G-6948)*

FABRICATED METAL PRODUCTS, NEC

Hickory Hill Metal Fabrication..............G....... 302 382-6727
  Dover *(G-1643)*
Visionary Energy Systems Inc.............G....... 410 739-4342
  Dover *(G-2195)*

FABRICS: Alpacas, Cotton

C and C Alpaca Factory ....G....... 609 752-7894
  Lewes *(G-3397)*

FABRICS: Apparel & Outerwear, Broadwoven

Krisallis...G....... 610 522-7273
  Bear *(G-224)*

FABRICS: Broadwoven, Synthetic Manmade Fiber & Silk

Agree Arlington TX LLC ....G....... 302 683-3008
  Wilmington *(G-8980)*
Invista Capital Management LLC.........E....... 302 629-1100
  Seaford *(G-8272)*

FABRICS: Canvas

Aloft Canvas LLC ....G....... 302 893-0144
  New Castle *(G-5024)*

FABRICS: Canvas

Classic Canvas LLC .... G 443 359-0150
  Delmar (G-984)
Dannys Custom Upholstery .... G 302 436-8200
  Selbyville (G-8477)
Keiths Boat Canvas .... G 302 841-8081
  Georgetown (G-2581)
Magic Canvas .... G 302 312-4122
  Middletown (G-4140)
Uncorked Canvas Parties .... G 302 724-7625
  Dover (G-2175)
Uncorked Canvas Parties LLC .... G 302 659-1396
  Smyrna (G-8734)

FABRICS: Denims

Denim Duo-Vers .... G 302 632-6943
  Milford (G-4386)
Threads N Denims .... G 302 678-0642
  Dover (G-2145)

FABRICS: Jean

H D Lee Company Inc .... F 302 477-3930
  Wilmington (G-10807)

FABRICS: Nonwoven

Donner Corporation .... G 302 778-0844
  Wilmington (G-10199)
Dow Chemical Company .... B 302 368-4169
  Newark (G-6467)
Dupont Specialty Pdts USA LLC .... G 302 774-1000
  Wilmington (G-10263)

FABRICS: Nylon, Broadwoven

Baker Safety Equipment Inc .... G 302 376-9302
  Bear (G-44)

FABRICS: Shoe

Pointe Snaps .... G 260 602-0898
  Wilmington (G-12178)

FABRICS: Trimmings

Delaware Screen Printing Inc .... G 302 378-4231
  Middletown (G-4031)
Elwyn .... D 302 658-8860
  Wilmington (G-10385)
Health & Social Svcs Del Dept .... E 302 255-9800
  New Castle (G-5383)
Health & Social Svcs Del Dept .... E 302 255-9855
  New Castle (G-5385)

FACILITIES SUPPORT SVCS

Brandywine Zoo .... E 302 571-7747
  Wilmington (G-9462)
Brightfields Inc .... E 302 656-9600
  Wilmington (G-9477)
Cognitive Group LLC .... F 301 585-1444
  Dover (G-1302)
Day and Zimmermann Inc .... C 302 368-1609
  Newark (G-6350)
Ecg Industries Inc .... G 302 453-0535
  Newark (G-6502)
Focus Solutions Services Inc .... F 302 318-1345
  Newark (G-6597)
Professional Roof Services Inc .... G 302 731-5770
  Newark (G-7266)
Seaford Mission Inc .... F 302 629-2559
  Seaford (G-8393)

FACILITIES: Inspection & fixed

Drba Police Fund .... D 302 571-6326
  New Castle (G-5260)

FACILITY RENTAL & PARTY PLANNING SVCS

Delaware AG Museum & Vlg .... G 302 734-1618
  Dover (G-1357)
Eventc2 LLC .... G 301 467-5780
  Newark (G-6545)
Events A La Carte .... G 302 753-7462
  Middletown (G-4065)

FACSIMILE COMMUNICATION EQPT

B Williams Holding Corp .... F 302 656-8596
  Wilmington (G-9214)

FAMILY CLOTHING STORES

Garage .... G 302 453-1930
  Newark (G-6638)
Studio J Entrmt & AP & Cof Bar .... G 410 422-3155
  Laurel (G-3296)

FAMILY COUNSELING SVCS

Brownstein Meryl Med Lpcmh .... G 302 479-5060
  Wilmington (G-9491)
Children Youth & Their Fam .... F 302 628-2024
  Seaford (G-8193)
Delaware Guidance Services For .... F 302 455-9333
  Newark (G-6382)
Delaware Guidance Services For .... F 302 652-3948
  Wilmington (G-10048)
Newark Family Counceling Ctr .... G 302 368-6895
  Newark (G-7119)
Sussex Family Counseling LLC .... G 302 864-7970
  Georgetown (G-2680)

FAMILY OR MARRIAGE COUNSELING

Crossroads of Delaware .... G 302 744-9999
  Dover (G-1325)

FAMILY PLANNING CLINIC

Planned Parenthood of Delaware .... E 302 655-7293
  Wilmington (G-12150)
Planned Parenthood of Delaware .... E 302 678-5200
  Dover (G-1963)
Planned Parenthood of Delaware .... G 302 731-7801
  Newark (G-7222)
Sussex Pregnancy Care Center .... G 302 856-4344
  Georgetown (G-2683)

FARM & GARDEN MACHINERY WHOLESALERS

Atlantic Tractor LLC .... E 302 653-8536
  Clayton (G-835)
Burke Equipment Company .... E 302 248-7070
  Delmar (G-975)
Burke Equipment Company .... D 302 697-3200
  Felton (G-2278)
Farmers First Services Inc .... G 302 424-8340
  Milford (G-4410)
Newark Kubota Inc .... F 302 365-6000
  Newark (G-7123)

FARM PRDTS, RAW MATERIAL, WHOLESALE: Tobacco & Tobacco Prdts

Kirkwood Smoke Shop .... G 302 525-6718
  Newark (G-6893)

FARM PRDTS, RAW MATERIALS, WHOLESALE: Cotton Merchants

Tops International Corp .... G 302 738-8889
  Newark (G-7576)

FARM PRDTS, RAW MATERIALS, WHOLESALE: Farm Animals

Baxter Farms Inc .... G 302 856-1818
  Georgetown (G-2447)

FARM PRDTS, RAW MATERIALS, WHOLESALE: Oil Nuts, Kernel/Seed

African Wood Inc .... G 302 884-6738
  Wilmington (G-8973)

FARM SPLY STORES

Arkion Life Sciences LLC .... E 302 504-7400
  New Castle (G-5044)
Bryan & Brittingham Inc .... F 302 846-9500
  Delmar (G-974)
Clark Seed Company Inc .... G 302 653-9249
  Clayton (G-839)

FARM SPLYS WHOLESALERS

Hudson Farm Supply Co Inc .... G 302 398-3654
  Harrington (G-2853)
Joseph M L Sand & Gravel Co .... F 302 856-7396
  Georgetown (G-2578)

W Enterprises LLC .... G 302 875-0430
  Laurel (G-3303)
Whaleys Seed Store Inc .... G 302 875-7833
  Laurel (G-3308)

FARM SPLYS, WHOLESALE: Equestrian Eqpt

Chick Harness & Supply Inc .... E 302 398-4630
  Harrington (G-2824)

FARM SPLYS, WHOLESALE: Feed

Bryan & Brittingham Inc .... F 302 846-9500
  Delmar (G-974)
Standlee Hay Feed LLC .... G 302 737-5117
  Newark (G-7481)

FARM SPLYS, WHOLESALE: Garden Splys

Leons Garden World Ej Inc .... F 410 392-8630
  New Castle (G-5480)
Q Vandenberg & Sons Inc .... E 800 242-2852
  Wilmington (G-12273)

FARM SPLYS, WHOLESALE: Greenhouse Eqpt & Splys

Greenview Gardens Inc .... G 302 422-8109
  Lincoln (G-3852)
Pepper Greenhouses .... G 302 684-8092
  Milton (G-4948)

FARM SPLYS, WHOLESALE: Hay

Harvest Consumer Products LLC .... E 302 732-6624
  Dagsboro (G-907)

FASTENERS WHOLESALERS

Makk-O Industries Inc .... G 302 376-0160
  Townsend (G-8808)
Triangle Fastener Corporation .... F 302 322-0600
  New Castle (G-5792)

FASTENERS: Metal

Pennengineering Holdings LLC .... C 302 576-2746
  Wilmington (G-12069)

FASTENERS: Notions, Hooks & Eyes

Iron Lion Enterprises Inc .... G 302 628-8320
  Seaford (G-8273)

FAUCETS & SPIGOTS: Metal & Plastic

A and D Plumbing LLC .... G 302 387-9232
  Magnolia (G-3877)

FEDERAL SAVINGS & LOAN ASSOCIATIONS

Beneficial Oklahoma Inc .... F 302 529-8701
  Wilmington (G-9298)
Third Fdral Sav Ln Assn Clvlan .... G 302 661-2009
  Wilmington (G-12897)
Wilmington Savings Fund Soc .... G 302 571-7090
  Wilmington (G-13255)

FEDERAL SAVINGS BANKS

Barclays Bank Delaware .... B 302 255-8000
  Wilmington (G-9250)
Malvern Federal Savings Bank .... G 302 477-7305
  Montchanin (G-4986)
Wilmington Savings Fund Soc .... G 302 792-6043
  Claymont (G-821)
Wilmington Savings Fund Soc .... G 302 571-6516
  Wilmington (G-13250)

FELT: Polishing

Semiconductor Technologies .... G 302 420-1432
  Newark (G-7405)

FENCE POSTS: Iron & Steel

Delaware Valley Fence & Iron .... G 302 322-8193
  New Castle (G-5242)

FENCING DEALERS

Delaware Valley Fence & Iron .... G 302 322-8193
  New Castle (G-5242)

PRODUCT & SERVICES SECTION

FINANCIAL SVCS

FENCING MATERIALS: Plastic

Atlantic Aluminum Products Inc .... D 302 349-9091
  Greenwood (G-2713)
Delaware Valley Fence & Iron .... G 302 322-8193
  New Castle (G-5242)
Oxford Plastic Systems LLC .... G 800 567-9182
  Wilmington (G-11989)

FERRIES: Operating Across Rivers Or Within Harbors

Delaware River & Bay Authority .... E 800 643-3779
  Lewes (G-3457)

FERTILIZER, AGRICULTURAL: Wholesalers

Nutrien AG Solutions Inc .... F 302 422-3570
  Milford (G-4516)
Soil Service Inc .... G 302 629-7054
  Seaford (G-8404)

FERTILIZERS: NEC

Emerald Bioagriculture Corp .... F 517 882-7370
  Hockessin (G-3019)
Growmark Fs LLC .... D 302 422-3002
  Milford (G-4425)
Harvest Consumer Products LLC .... E 302 732-6624
  Dagsboro (G-907)
Nutrien AG Solutions Inc .... G 302 629-2780
  Seaford (G-8333)
Southern States Coop Inc .... F 302 732-6651
  Dagsboro (G-934)
Southern States Coop Inc .... G 302 875-3635
  Laurel (G-3293)
Southern States Coop Inc .... F 302 378-9841
  Middletown (G-4246)

FERTILIZERS: Nitrogenous

Growmark Fs LLC .... D 302 422-3002
  Milford (G-4425)
Southern States Coop Inc .... F 302 378-9841
  Middletown (G-4246)

FERTILIZERS: Phosphatic

Growmark Fs LLC .... G 302 422-3001
  Milford (G-4426)
Growmark Fs LLC .... D 302 422-3002
  Milford (G-4425)
Southern States Coop Inc .... F 302 378-9841
  Middletown (G-4246)

FIBER & FIBER PRDTS: Protein

Chesapeake Perl Inc .... F 302 533-3540
  Newark (G-6193)

FIBER & FIBER PRDTS: Synthetic Cellulosic

FMC Corporation .... D 302 451-0100
  Newark (G-6596)

FIBER OPTICS

Te Connectivity .... G 302 633-2740
  Wilmington (G-12864)

FILLERS & SEALERS: Wood

T B Painting Restoration .... G 610 283-4100
  Newark (G-7527)

FILM & SHEET: Unsuppported Plastic

Aearo Technologies LLC .... D 302 283-5497
  Newark (G-5913)
Axess Corporation .... G 302 292-8500
  New Castle (G-5061)
E I Du Pont De Nemours & Co .... F 302 774-1000
  Wilmington (G-10282)
Grayling Industries Inc .... E 770 751-9095
  Frederica (G-2403)

FILM DEVELOPING & PRINTING SVCS

Cameras Etc Inc .... G 302 453-9400
  Newark (G-6146)

FILM PROCESSING & FINISHING LABORATORY

Colourworks Photographic Svcs .... G 302 428-0222
  Wilmington (G-9778)
Delaware Color Lab .... G 302 529-1339
  Wilmington (G-10021)

FILTERS

Graver Separations Inc .... G 302 731-1700
  Newark (G-6683)
Precision Airconvey Corp .... F 302 999-8000
  Newark (G-7241)

FILTERS & STRAINERS: Pipeline

Atlantic Screen & Mfg Inc .... G 302 684-3197
  Milton (G-4865)

FILTERS: Air Intake, Internal Combustion Engine, Exc Auto

Airespa Worldwide Whl LLC .... G 908 227-4441
  Dover (G-1097)
Messick & Gray Cnstr Inc .... F 302 337-8445
  Bridgeville (G-498)

FILTERS: Motor Vehicle

Hayloft Enterprises Inc .... G 302 656-7600
  Wilmington (G-10857)

FILTRATION DEVICES: Electronic

Xergy Inc .... G 302 629-5768
  Harrington (G-2911)

FINANCIAL INVESTMENT ADVICE

20 20 Fincl Advisors of Del .... G 302 777-2020
  Wilmington (G-8852)
Ameriprise Financial Services .... G 302 476-8000
  Wilmington (G-9061)
Ameriprise Financial Svcs Inc .... F 302 543-5784
  Wilmington (G-9062)
Ameriprise Financial Svcs Inc .... G 302 475-5105
  Wilmington (G-9063)
Amerirpise .... G 302 656-7773
  Wilmington (G-9066)
Bank of New York Mellon Corp .... G 302 791-1700
  Wilmington (G-9244)
Barclays Financial Corporation .... G 302 652-6201
  Wilmington (G-9251)
Blackrock Financial Management .... G 302 797-2000
  Wilmington (G-9350)
Butler Financial Ltd .... G 302 778-2170
  Wilmington (G-9515)
Carey Ins & Fin Services Inc .... G 302 934-8383
  Dagsboro (G-888)
Cigna Holdings Inc .... F 215 761-1000
  Claymont (G-719)
Clipper Advisor LLC .... E 203 428-5251
  Wilmington (G-9745)
Coastal .... G 302 319-4061
  Wilmington (G-9751)
Crude Gold Research LLC .... F 646 681-7317
  Dover (G-1327)
Egs Financial Care Inc .... G 800 227-4000
  Wilmington (G-10363)
First Command Fincl Plg Inc .... F 302 535-8132
  Camden Wyoming (G-638)
First Un Fincl Investments Inc .... G 646 652-6580
  Wilmington (G-10558)
Hcac .... G 302 266-8100
  Newark (G-6714)
John Koziol Inc .... G 302 234-5430
  Hockessin (G-3068)
Michael Gioia .... G 302 479-7780
  Wilmington (G-11660)
Morgan Stnley Smith Barney LLC .... G 302 644-6600
  Rehoboth Beach (G-8013)
Ms Financing LLC .... F 212 276-1206
  Wilmington (G-11769)
New Visions Inv Group LLC .... G 302 299-6234
  Newark (G-7109)
Onemain Financial Group LLC .... G 302 834-6677
  Bear (G-273)
Onemain Financial Group LLC .... G 302 628-9253
  Seaford (G-8336)
Onemain Financial Group LLC .... G 302 674-3900
  Dover (G-1918)
Onemain Financial Group LLC .... G 302 422-9657
  Milford (G-4519)
Onemain Financial Group LLC .... G 302 478-8070
  Wilmington (G-11958)
Parkwood Trust Company .... G 302 426-1220
  Wilmington (G-12026)
Pfpc Worldwide Inc .... F 302 791-1700
  Wilmington (G-12105)
Playtex Investment Corporation .... G 302 678-6000
  Dover (G-1968)
Qienna Wealth Management Inc .... G 610 765-6008
  Newark (G-7278)
Rbc Capital Markets LLC .... G 302 252-9444
  Wilmington (G-12334)
Riverstone Financial II LLC .... G 302 295-5310
  Wilmington (G-12430)
Rk Advisors LLC .... G 302 561-5258
  Hockessin (G-3137)
Rouse Insurance and Fincl LL .... G 302 678-2223
  Dover (G-2044)
Saggio Management Group Inc .... G 302 659-6560
  Smyrna (G-8711)
Smithfeld Intl Investments Inc .... G 302 477-1358
  Wilmington (G-12662)
Swan Financial Group .... G 302 689-6095
  Frederica (G-2414)
Wells Fargo Clearing Svcs LLC .... E 302 731-2131
  Newark (G-7686)

FINANCIAL SVCS

Business At International LLC .... E 605 610-4885
  Lewes (G-3394)
Citifinancial Inc .... G 302 834-6677
  Bear (G-73)
Citigroup Inc .... G 302 631-3530
  Newark (G-6237)
City of Dover .... E 302 736-7035
  Dover (G-1289)
Comprehensive Bus Svcs LLC .... F 302 994-2000
  Newark (G-6274)
Coqonut Inc .... G 347 419-7709
  Wilmington (G-9857)
Cordjia LLC .... E 302 743-1297
  Newark (G-6296)
Fourth Floor .... G 302 472-8416
  Wilmington (G-10606)
Gensource Fincl Asrn Co LLC .... F 302 415-3030
  Wilmington (G-10695)
HARt Group LLC .... G 302 782-9742
  Dover (G-1636)
Hcac .... G 302 266-8100
  Newark (G-6714)
Local TV Finance LLC .... E 302 636-5401
  Wilmington (G-11420)
Lumber Industries Inc .... G 302 655-9651
  Wilmington (G-11448)
Mellon Private Wealth MGT .... G 302 421-2306
  Wilmington (G-11626)
Mitek Holdings Inc .... G 302 429-1816
  Wilmington (G-11715)
Morgan Stnley Smith Barney LLC .... G 302 636-5500
  Wilmington (G-11754)
National Opprtnities Unlimited .... F 913 905-2261
  New Castle (G-5547)
Newrez LLC .... G 302 455-6600
  Middletown (G-4174)
Novo Financial Corp .... F 844 260-6800
  Dover (G-1906)
Oink Oink LLC .... G 302 924-5034
  Dover (G-1914)
Power Financial Group Inc .... G 302 992-7971
  Wilmington (G-12196)
Premier Nat Ln & Lsg Group LLC .... G 302 295-2194
  Wilmington (G-12216)
Rockwood Financial Group Inc .... G 302 791-0237
  Wilmington (G-12457)
Sean E Chipman .... F 302 300-4307
  New Castle (G-5697)
Shopify Payments (usa) Inc .... G 613 241-2828
  Wilmington (G-12607)
Sovereign Capitl MGT Group Inc .... A 619 294-8989
  Wilmington (G-12689)
Springleaf Fincl Holdings LLC .... B 302 543-6767
  Wilmington (G-12715)
Sun Exchange Inc .... G 917 747-9527
  Lewes (G-3769)
Swift Financial LLC .... G 302 374-7019
  Wilmington (G-12825)
UBS Financial Services Inc .... F 302 657-5331
  Wilmington (G-13007)

FINANCIAL SVCS

Vitellus LLC .... G 718 782-3539
  Wilmington *(G-13096)*
Wilmington Trust Corporation .... E 302 651-8378
  Wilmington *(G-13263)*
Windy Inc .... F 224 707-0442
  Dover *(G-2234)*
Wmk Financing Inc .... E 302 576-2697
  Wilmington *(G-13283)*

FINISHING AGENTS: Textile

James Thompson & Company Inc .... E 302 349-4501
  Greenwood *(G-2748)*

FINISHING SCHOOLS, CHARM & MODELING

Barbizon of Delaware Inc .... E 302 658-6666
  Wilmington *(G-9249)*

FINISHING SVCS

Rbc Capital Markets LLC .... G 302 252-9444
  Wilmington *(G-12334)*

FIRE ARMS, SMALL: Shotguns Or Shotgun Parts, 30 mm & Below

Stockmarket .... G 302 697-8878
  Magnolia *(G-3909)*

FIRE CONTROL OR BOMBING EQPT: Electronic

Dp Fire & Safety Inc .... F 302 998-5430
  Wilmington *(G-10217)*

FIRE EXTINGUISHER SVC

Cmp Fire LLC .... G 410 620-2062
  Newark *(G-6255)*

FIRE EXTINGUISHERS, WHOLESALE

Delaware City Fire Co No 1 .... G 302 834-9336
  Delaware City *(G-952)*

FIRE INSURANCE UNDERWRITERS' LABORATORIES

21st Century N Amer Insur Co .... A 877 310-5687
  Wilmington *(G-8855)*

FIRE PROTECTION SVCS: Contracted

Allegiant Fire Protection LLC .... G 302 276-1300
  Newark *(G-5938)*
Bethany Beach Vlntr Fire Co .... E 302 539-7700
  Bethany Beach *(G-388)*
Brandywine Hundred Fire Co 1 .... D 302 764-4901
  Wilmington *(G-9438)*
Elsmere Fire Co 1 Inc .... G 302 999-0183
  Wilmington *(G-10383)*
Patriot Systems Inc .... G 302 472-9727
  Wilmington *(G-12036)*
Quality III Fire Protection .... G 302 762-8262
  Wilmington *(G-12281)*

FIRE PROTECTION, GOVERNMENT: Local

Christiana Fire Company .... G 302 834-2433
  Bear *(G-71)*

FIREARMS & AMMUNITION, EXC SPORTING, WHOLESALE

Airbase Carpet Mart Abct Dist .... G 302 323-8800
  New Castle *(G-5019)*
Freedom Materials .... G 302 281-0085
  Newark *(G-6617)*

FIREBRICK: Clay

Rgp Holding Inc .... G 302 661-0117
  Wilmington *(G-12399)*

FIREPLACE EQPT & ACCESS

Fireside Heart & Home .... G 302 337-3025
  Bridgeville *(G-470)*

FISH & SEAFOOD MARKETS

Seafood City Inc .... E 302 284-8486
  Felton *(G-2319)*

FISH & SEAFOOD WHOLESALERS

George and Son Seafood Market .... G 302 239-7204
  Hockessin *(G-3037)*
J A E Seafood .... E 302 765-2546
  Wilmington *(G-11100)*
Lewes Fishhouse & Produce Inc .... E 302 827-4074
  Lewes *(G-3600)*
Oceanside Seafood Mkt Deli LLC .... G 302 313-5158
  Lewes *(G-3666)*
Seafood City Inc .... E 302 284-8486
  Felton *(G-2319)*
Venus On Halfshell .... G 302 227-9292
  Dewey Beach *(G-1061)*
Wooley Bully Inc .... G 302 542-3613
  Millsboro *(G-4829)*

FITTINGS & ASSEMBLIES: Hose & Tube, Hydraulic Or Pneumatic

Mto Hose Solutions Inc .... G 302 266-6555
  Newark *(G-7071)*

FITTINGS: Pipe

American Insert Flange Co Inc .... F 302 777-7464
  Wilmington *(G-9050)*

FLEA MARKET

Catholic Docese Wilmington Inc .... G 302 764-2717
  Wilmington *(G-9595)*

FLIGHT TRAINING SCHOOLS

Horizon Helicopters Inc .... G 302 368-5135
  Newark *(G-6745)*

FLOOR COVERING STORES

A + Floor Store Inc .... F 302 698-2166
  Camden Wyoming *(G-609)*
Art Floor Inc .... E 302 636-9201
  Wilmington *(G-9135)*
Brasures Pest Control Inc .... E 302 436-8140
  Selbyville *(G-8462)*
Connolly Flooring Inc .... E 302 996-9470
  Wilmington *(G-9831)*
Interiors By Kim Inc .... G 302 537-2480
  Ocean View *(G-7794)*

FLOOR COVERING STORES: Carpets

Anderson Floor Coverings Inc .... F 302 227-3244
  Rehoboth Beach *(G-7842)*
Callaway Furniture Inc .... G 302 398-8858
  Harrington *(G-2823)*
Delaware Rug Co Inc .... G 302 998-8881
  Wilmington *(G-10082)*
Edwards Paul Crpt Installation .... G 302 672-7847
  Dover *(G-1509)*
L & L Carpet Discount Ctrs Inc .... G 302 292-3712
  Newark *(G-6906)*
Proclean Inc .... E 302 656-8080
  Delaware City *(G-965)*
Reiver Hyman & Co Inc .... G 302 764-2040
  Wilmington *(G-12371)*
Stuart Kingston Inc .... F 302 227-2524
  Rehoboth Beach *(G-8090)*

FLOOR COVERING STORES: Floor Tile

Pala Tile & Carpet Contrs Inc .... E 302 652-4500
  Wilmington *(G-12007)*

FLOOR COVERING STORES: Rugs

Brasures Carpet Care Inc .... G 302 436-5652
  Selbyville *(G-8461)*

FLOOR COVERING: Plastic

Cramaro Tarpaulin Systems Inc .... F 302 292-2170
  Newark *(G-6311)*

FLOOR COVERINGS WHOLESALERS

A + Floor Store Inc .... F 302 698-2166
  Camden Wyoming *(G-609)*
Art Floor Inc .... E 302 636-9201
  Wilmington *(G-9135)*
Coverdeck Systems Inc .... E 302 427-7578
  Wilmington *(G-9883)*
General Crpt-Mech Sply .... G 302 322-1847
  New Castle *(G-5348)*
L & L Carpet Discount Ctrs Inc .... G 302 292-3712
  Newark *(G-6906)*
Reiver Hyman & Co Inc .... G 302 764-2040
  Wilmington *(G-12371)*

FLOOR WAXING SVCS

L & M Services Inc .... F 302 658-3735
  Wilmington *(G-11306)*
Sussex Floor .... G 302 629-5620
  Seaford *(G-8415)*

FLOORING: Hard Surface

Maneto Inc .... G 302 656-4285
  Wilmington *(G-11501)*

FLOORING: Hardwood

Old Wood & Co LLC .... F 302 684-3600
  Harbeson *(G-2794)*

FLORIST: Flowers, Fresh

Kirks Flowers Inc .... E 302 737-3931
  Newark *(G-6890)*
Lakeside Greenhouses Inc .... G 302 875-2457
  Laurel *(G-3250)*

FLORISTS

Eggplant Inc .... G 302 737-1073
  Newark *(G-6509)*
Village Green Inc .... E 302 764-2234
  Wilmington *(G-13082)*

FLORISTS' ARTICLES: Pottery

Valuewrite .... G 302 593-0694
  Middletown *(G-4275)*

FLOTATION COMPANIES

Hudson Valley Investment Corp .... G 302 656-1825
  Wilmington *(G-10971)*

FLOTATION COMPANIES: Securities

PNC Bank National Association .... G 302 994-6337
  Wilmington *(G-12165)*
Ziv Investments Co .... F 302 573-5080
  Wilmington *(G-13352)*

FLOWERS & FLORISTS' SPLYS WHOLESALERS

Harvest Consumer Products LLC .... E 302 732-6624
  Dagsboro *(G-907)*
Sieck Wholesale Florist Inc .... F 302 356-2000
  New Castle *(G-5708)*

FLOWERS, FRESH, WHOLESALE

Lakeside Greenhouses Inc .... G 302 875-2457
  Laurel *(G-3250)*

FLUID POWER PUMPS & MOTORS

Smw Sales LLC .... F 302 875-7958
  Laurel *(G-3290)*

FOOD PRDTS, CANNED OR FRESH PACK: Vegetable Juices

Fresh Industries Ltd .... G 205 737-3747
  Rehoboth Beach *(G-7937)*

FOOD PRDTS, CANNED: Barbecue Sauce

Trisco Foods LLC .... D 719 352-3218
  Wilmington *(G-12978)*

FOOD PRDTS, CANNED: Chili Sauce, Tomato

Peppers Inc .... F 302 644-6900
  Lewes *(G-3684)*

FOOD PRDTS, CANNED: Fruits

Kraft Heinz Company .... A 302 734-6100
  Dover *(G-1758)*

PRODUCT & SERVICES SECTION

FOOD PRDTS: Chicken, Processed, Frozen

FOOD PRDTS, CANNED: Italian
Vincenza & Margherita Bistro ....G....... 302 479-7999
Wilmington *(G-13083)*

FOOD PRDTS, CANNED: Mexican, NEC
Freakin Fresh Salsa Inc.........................G....... 302 750-9789
Wilmington *(G-10623)*
Mariachi House ....G....... 302 635-7361
Hockessin *(G-3088)*

FOOD PRDTS, CANNED: Mushrooms
Mushroom Supply & Services Inc ....F....... 302 998-2008
Newark *(G-7074)*

FOOD PRDTS, CANNED: Vegetables
Hanover Foods Corporation ....C....... 302 653-9281
Clayton *(G-855)*

FOOD PRDTS, CONFECTIONERY, WHOLESALE: Snack Foods
Herr Foods Incorporated ....E....... 302 628-9161
Seaford *(G-8264)*

FOOD PRDTS, FISH & SEAFOOD, WHOLESALE: Seafood
Alaskawild Seafoods ....G....... 302 337-0710
Seaford *(G-8142)*
Febys Fishery Inc....................................E....... 302 998-9501
Wilmington *(G-10511)*
Harbor House Seafood Inc ....D....... 302 629-0444
Seaford *(G-8260)*
Meding & Son Seafood ....F....... 302 335-3944
Milford *(G-4491)*
Meltrone Inc..F....... 302 998-3457
Wilmington *(G-11628)*
Paul Sorvino Foods Inc ....G....... 302 547-1977
Wilmington *(G-12045)*
Southern Crab Company ....C....... 302 478-0181
Wilmington *(G-12687)*

FOOD PRDTS, FISH & SEAFOOD: Codfish, Salted
Lusotrading Corp.....................................G....... 302 288-0670
Wilmington *(G-11452)*

FOOD PRDTS, FISH & SEAFOOD: Seafood, Frozen, Prepared
Steven P Copp...G....... 302 645-9112
Lewes *(G-3765)*

FOOD PRDTS, FROZEN: Dinners, Packaged
Hanover Foods Corporation ....C....... 302 653-9281
Clayton *(G-855)*

FOOD PRDTS, FROZEN: Ethnic Foods, NEC
H&H Trading International LLC..............G....... 480 580-3911
Wilmington *(G-10811)*
Pictsweet Company ....D....... 302 337-8206
Bridgeville *(G-509)*

FOOD PRDTS, FROZEN: Fruits & Vegetables
Tropical Harvest Inc................................G....... 302 682-9463
Rehoboth Beach *(G-8099)*

FOOD PRDTS, FROZEN: Fruits, Juices & Vegetables
JG Townsend Jr & Co Inc.......................E....... 302 856-2525
Georgetown *(G-2574)*
Smoothies Soup and Sandwiches ....G....... 302 280-6183
Laurel *(G-3289)*

FOOD PRDTS, FROZEN: NEC
Nicola Pizza Inc......................................E....... 302 227-6511
Rehoboth Beach *(G-8017)*

FOOD PRDTS, FROZEN: Vegetables, Exc Potato Prdts
Hanover Foods Corporation ....C....... 302 653-9281
Clayton *(G-855)*

FOOD PRDTS, FRUITS & VEGETABLES, FRESH, WHOLESALE
Dole Fresh Fruit Company ....D....... 302 652-6484
Wilmington *(G-10187)*
Dole Fresh Fruit Company ....F....... 302 652-2215
Wilmington *(G-10188)*
Forever Fresh LLC ....G....... 302 510-8538
Wilmington *(G-10593)*
Pandol Bros Inc.......................................E....... 302 571-8923
Wilmington *(G-12013)*

FOOD PRDTS, FRUITS & VEGETABLES, FRESH, WHOLESALE: Fruits
Chiquita Brands LLC ....F....... 302 571-9781
Wilmington *(G-9668)*
David Oppenheimer and Co I LLC..........E....... 302 533-0779
Newark *(G-6349)*
Robert T Minner Jr ....G....... 302 422-9206
Greenwood *(G-2760)*
Willey Farms Inc.....................................D....... 302 378-8441
Townsend *(G-8833)*

FOOD PRDTS, FRUITS & VEGETABLES, FRESH, WHOLESALE: Vegetable
Thomas E Moore Inc ....F....... 302 674-1500
Kenton *(G-3187)*

FOOD PRDTS, MEAT & MEAT PRDTS, WHOLESALE: Fresh
H C Davis Inc ....G....... 302 337-7001
Bridgeville *(G-477)*
Ralph and Paul Adams Inc ....B....... 800 338-4727
Bridgeville *(G-517)*
South Forks Inc.......................................G....... 302 731-0344
Newark *(G-7461)*
West Dover Butcher Shop Inc ....E....... 302 734-5447
Dover *(G-2214)*

FOOD PRDTS, POULTRY, WHOLESALE: Poultry Prdts, NEC
Mountaire of Delmarva Inc.....................G....... 302 988-6207
Selbyville *(G-8526)*
Pet Poultry Products LLC ....E....... 302 337-8223
Bridgeville *(G-508)*

FOOD PRDTS, WHOL: Canned Goods, Fruit, Veg, Seafood/Meats
Ism ....G....... 302 656-2376
Wilmington *(G-11090)*

FOOD PRDTS, WHOLESALE: Beverages, Exc Coffee & Tea
Angry 8 LLC..F....... 203 304-9256
Newark *(G-5971)*

FOOD PRDTS, WHOLESALE: Chocolate
Chocolette Distribution LLC ....G....... 917 547-8905
Lewes *(G-3416)*

FOOD PRDTS, WHOLESALE: Coffee & Tea
African Wood Inc ....G....... 302 884-6738
Wilmington *(G-8973)*

FOOD PRDTS, WHOLESALE: Condiments
Freakin Fresh Salsa Inc ....G....... 302 750-9789
Wilmington *(G-10623)*

FOOD PRDTS, WHOLESALE: Cookies
Classic Cookies of Dowingtown..............G....... 302 494-9662
Wilmington *(G-9734)*

FOOD PRDTS, WHOLESALE: Corn
Baldwin Sayre Inc ....G....... 302 337-0309
Bridgeville *(G-451)*

FOOD PRDTS, WHOLESALE: Dog Food
Tail Bangers Inc ....E....... 302 947-4900
Millsboro *(G-4810)*

Tailbangers..D....... 302 934-1125
Millsboro *(G-4811)*

FOOD PRDTS, WHOLESALE: Dried or Canned Foods
South Forks Inc.......................................G....... 302 731-0344
Newark *(G-7461)*

FOOD PRDTS, WHOLESALE: Flavorings & Fragrances
Wen International Inc..............................G....... 845 354-1773
Wilmington *(G-13155)*

FOOD PRDTS, WHOLESALE: Grain Elevators
Mountaire Farms Delaware Inc...............G....... 302 398-3296
Harrington *(G-2869)*

FOOD PRDTS, WHOLESALE: Grains
Allen Harim Foods LLC ....E....... 302 629-9460
Seaford *(G-8144)*
Dack Trading LLC ....G....... 917 576-4432
Rehoboth Beach *(G-7907)*
Hopkins Granary Inc ....G....... 302 684-8525
Milton *(G-4915)*
Johnson Jr Henry & Son Farm ....G....... 302 436-8501
Selbyville *(G-8509)*
Laurel Grain Company ....G....... 302 875-4231
Laurel *(G-3253)*

FOOD PRDTS, WHOLESALE: Health
Tasteables..G....... 267 777-9143
Claymont *(G-809)*

FOOD PRDTS, WHOLESALE: Juices
Tuscan/Lehigh Dairies Inc......................F....... 302 398-8321
Harrington *(G-2901)*

FOOD PRDTS, WHOLESALE: Organic & Diet
Green Roots LLC ....G....... 516 643-2621
Lewes *(G-3522)*

FOOD PRDTS, WHOLESALE: Sandwiches
Scotts Co ....G....... 302 777-4779
Wilmington *(G-12564)*

FOOD PRDTS, WHOLESALE: Sauces
Peppers Inc..F....... 302 645-0812
Lewes *(G-3683)*

FOOD PRDTS, WHOLESALE: Specialty
Rondo Specialty Foods Ltd ....G....... 800 724-6636
New Castle *(G-5683)*

FOOD PRDTS, WHOLESALE: Spices & Seasonings
Spain Magic Rose LLC ....G....... 941 312-2051
Wilmington *(G-12691)*

FOOD PRDTS, WHOLESALE: Sugar, Refined
Lusotrading Corp.....................................G....... 302 288-0670
Wilmington *(G-11452)*

FOOD PRDTS, WHOLESALE: Tea
Firsd Tea North America LLC.................G....... 302 322-1255
New Castle *(G-5310)*

FOOD PRDTS, WHOLESALE: Water, Mineral Or Spring, Bottled
Evoqua Water Technologies LLC ....G....... 302 654-3712
Wilmington *(G-10452)*
Mr Natural Bottled Water Inc.................F....... 302 436-7700
Ocean View *(G-7803)*

FOOD PRDTS: Chicken, Processed, Frozen
New B & M Meats Inc.............................G....... 302 655-5331
Wilmington *(G-11849)*

Employee Codes: A=Over 500 employees, B=251-500
C=101-250, D=51-100, E=20-50, F=10-19, G=1-9

FOOD PRDTS: Cocoa & Cocoa Prdts

Interntnal Agrclture Prod Grou ....G....... 302 450-2008
 Smyrna *(G-8659)*

FOOD PRDTS: Coffee

Mbanza Coffee Inc ....G....... 813 403-8724
 Newark *(G-7010)*

FOOD PRDTS: Dessert Mixes & Fillings

Trisco Foods LLC ....D....... 719 352-3218
 Wilmington *(G-12978)*

FOOD PRDTS: Flour

McShares Inc ....G....... 302 656-3168
 Wilmington *(G-11608)*

FOOD PRDTS: Flour & Other Grain Mill Products

Kraft Heinz Company ....A....... 302 734-6100
 Dover *(G-1758)*

FOOD PRDTS: Fruit Juices

Juiceplus+ ....G....... 302 322-2616
 New Castle *(G-5447)*

FOOD PRDTS: Gelatin Dessert Preparations

Kraft Heinz Company ....A....... 302 734-6100
 Dover *(G-1758)*

FOOD PRDTS: Ice, Blocks

Blue Marlin Ice LLC ....G....... 302 697-7800
 Dover *(G-1214)*

FOOD PRDTS: Nuts & Seeds

Sunshine Nut Company LLC ....E....... 781 352-7766
 Lewes *(G-3770)*

FOOD PRDTS: Olive Oil

Lusotrading Corp ....G....... 302 288-0670
 Wilmington *(G-11452)*

FOOD PRDTS: Potato & Corn Chips & Similar Prdts

Fishers Popcorn Fenwick LLC ....E....... 302 539-8833
 Fenwick Island *(G-2336)*

FOOD PRDTS: Poultry Sausage, Lunch Meats/Other Poultry Prdts

Amerrican Express Shuttle Inc ....G....... 302 420-8377
 Newark *(G-5950)*

FOOD PRDTS: Poultry, Processed, NEC

Allen Biotech LLC ....A....... 302 629-9136
 Millsboro *(G-4626)*
Harim Usa Ltd ....G....... 302 629-9136
 Seaford *(G-8261)*
Perdue Farms Inc ....D....... 302 424-2600
 Milford *(G-4525)*

FOOD PRDTS: Preparations

All Peoples Food LLC ....G....... 302 690-4881
 Newark *(G-5935)*
Carlyle Cocoa Co LLC ....F....... 302 428-3800
 New Castle *(G-5134)*
Dr Dunner Usa Inc ....G....... 302 656-1950
 Wilmington *(G-10220)*
Phillip L Hrrs Fd/Cnsltnt ....G....... 302 270-2905
 Harrington *(G-2874)*
Super Suppers ....G....... 302 478-5935
 Wilmington *(G-12804)*

FOOD PRDTS: Seasonings & Spices

Andre Noel Thalia ....G....... 302 747-0813
 New Castle *(G-5038)*
Cook Awesome Food LLC ....G....... 302 990-2665
 Wilmington *(G-9850)*

FOOD PRDTS: Syrup, Maple

Grandma ZS Maple Haus ....G....... 412 297-3324
 Claymont *(G-757)*

FOOD PRDTS: Tea

Firsd Tea North America LLC ....G....... 302 322-1255
 New Castle *(G-5310)*
Martin Grey LLC ....G....... 302 990-0675
 Lewes *(G-3621)*

FOOD PRDTS: Vegetables, Freeze-Dried

Hanover Foods Corporation ....C....... 302 653-9281
 Clayton *(G-855)*

FOOD PRODUCTS MACHINERY

E I Du Pont De Nemours & Co ....D....... 302 695-5300
 Wilmington *(G-10306)*
Metal Msters Fdservice Eqp Inc ....C....... 302 653-3000
 Clayton *(G-863)*

FOOD STORES: Convenience, Chain

Om Shiv Groceries Inc ....G....... 302 856-7014
 Georgetown *(G-2611)*

FOOD STORES: Convenience, Independent

Newport Ventures Inc ....F....... 302 998-1693
 Wilmington *(G-11879)*
Peninsula Oil Co Inc ....E....... 302 422-6691
 Seaford *(G-8349)*

FOOD STORES: Cooperative

Hs Capital LLC ....G....... 302 598-2961
 Wilmington *(G-10964)*

FOOTWEAR, WHOLESALE: Shoe Access

Shoolex LLC ....G....... 866 697-3330
 Lewes *(G-3739)*

FOOTWEAR, WHOLESALE: Shoes

Jaiden Jewels Shoes and ACC ....G....... 302 659-2473
 Smyrna *(G-8661)*
Lehigh Vly Safety Sup Co Inc ....G....... 302 323-9166
 New Castle *(G-5477)*
Vivig Shoes ....F....... 302 427-2700
 Wilmington *(G-13098)*

FORGINGS

A T I Funding Corporation ....F....... 302 656-8937
 Wilmington *(G-8884)*
Square One Electric Service Co ....F....... 302 678-0400
 Dover *(G-2099)*
Tdy Holdings LLC ....G....... 302 254-4172
 Wilmington *(G-12863)*

FORGINGS: Bearing & Bearing Race, Nonferrous

Delaware Capital Formation Inc ....G....... 302 793-4921
 Wilmington *(G-10010)*

FORGINGS: Gear & Chain

Eager Gear ....G....... 302 727-5831
 Lewes *(G-3477)*
Timken Gears & Services Inc ....F....... 302 633-4600
 New Castle *(G-5770)*

FOUNDRIES: Nonferrous

Diamond State Props ....G....... 302 528-7146
 Bear *(G-117)*

FOUNDRIES: Steel Investment

Consoldted Fabrication Constrs ....E....... 302 654-9001
 Wilmington *(G-9832)*
S P S International Inv Co ....G....... 302 478-9055
 Wilmington *(G-12508)*
Tajan Holdings & Investments ....G....... 302 300-1183
 Middletown *(G-4253)*

FRANCHISES, SELLING OR LICENSING

1000 Degrees Pizzeria ....G....... 609 382-3022
 Wilmington *(G-8841)*

Kohr Brothers Inc ....F....... 302 227-9354
 Rehoboth Beach *(G-7983)*

FREIGHT CAR LOADING & UNLOADING SVCS

Burris Logistics ....D....... 302 839-4531
 Milford *(G-4337)*
Elite Trnspt & Logistics Inc ....F....... 302 348-8480
 Wilmington *(G-10378)*
Lantransit Enterprises LLC ....F....... 302 722-4800
 Lewes *(G-3592)*
PCI of Virginia LLC ....F....... 302 655-7300
 New Castle *(G-5610)*
Port Contractors Inc ....D....... 302 655-7300
 New Castle *(G-5632)*

FREIGHT FORWARDING ARRANGEMENTS

Amh Enterprises LLC ....E....... 302 337-0300
 Bridgeville *(G-445)*
Blockfreight Inc ....F....... 614 350-2252
 Lewes *(G-3387)*
Cargoex Inc ....G....... 800 850-9493
 Wilmington *(G-9569)*
Evanix Enterprises LLC ....G....... 302 384-1806
 Middletown *(G-4064)*
Pteris Global (usa) Inc ....F....... 516 593-5633
 Dover *(G-1998)*
Tc Trans Inc ....G....... 302 339-7952
 Georgetown *(G-2687)*
Triglia Express Inc ....E....... 302 846-2248
 Delmar *(G-1040)*

FREIGHT FORWARDING ARRANGEMENTS: Domestic

Faustin Enterprises LLC ....G....... 302 543-2687
 Wilmington *(G-10508)*
Transcore LP ....E....... 302 838-7429
 Middletown *(G-4266)*

FREIGHT FORWARDING ARRANGEMENTS: Foreign

Port To Port Intl Corp ....E....... 302 654-2444
 New Castle *(G-5633)*

FREIGHT TRANSPORTATION ARRANGEMENTS

Achieve Logistic Systems ....G....... 302 654-4701
 Wilmington *(G-8921)*
Bettan Trucking LLC ....E....... 302 841-3834
 Lewes *(G-3380)*
Briscoe Trucking Inc ....F....... 302 836-1327
 Newark *(G-6123)*
City Mist LLC ....G....... 302 342-1377
 New Castle *(G-5171)*
Gjv Inc ....G....... 302 455-1600
 Newark *(G-6659)*
MA Transportation LLC ....G....... 302 588-5435
 Millsboro *(G-4730)*
MD Freight & Logistics LLC ....G....... 804 347-1196
 Dover *(G-1833)*
New Creation Logistics Inc ....F....... 302 438-3154
 Newark *(G-7103)*
New Hope Vehicle Exports LLC ....G....... 302 275-6482
 Wilmington *(G-11863)*
Ohmyzip ....E....... 302 322-8792
 New Castle *(G-5586)*
Pacific Cargo LLC ....G....... 302 521-6317
 Wilmington *(G-12004)*
Penn Del Carriers LLC ....G....... 484 424-3768
 New Castle *(G-5614)*
SF Logistics Limited ....E....... 302 317-3954
 New Castle *(G-5703)*
Trinity Logistics Inc ....G....... 302 595-2116
 New Castle *(G-5794)*
UPS Supply Chain Solutions Inc ....F....... 302 631-5259
 Newark *(G-7631)*
Wentzel Transportation ....G....... 302 355-9465
 Smyrna *(G-8743)*

FRICTION MATERIAL, MADE FROM POWDERED METAL

Joseph T Ryerson & Son Inc ....E....... 302 366-0555
 Newark *(G-6851)*

PRODUCT & SERVICES SECTION
FURNITURE WHOLESALERS

FRUIT & VEGETABLE MARKETS

Vinces Produce Inc .... G 302 322-0386
  New Castle *(G-5818)*
Willey Farms Inc .... D 302 378-8441
  Townsend *(G-8833)*

FRUITS & VEGETABLES WHOLESALERS: Fresh

7day Farmers Market LLC .... G 302 476-8924
  Wilmington *(G-8867)*
Ernie Deangelis .... F 302 226-9533
  Rehoboth Beach *(G-7928)*
Estia Hospitality Group Inc .... F 302 798-5319
  Claymont *(G-741)*
Vinces Produce Inc .... G 302 322-0386
  New Castle *(G-5818)*

FUEL ADDITIVES

Fairville Products Inc .... G 302 425-4400
  Wilmington *(G-10477)*
Innospec Inc .... G 302 454-8100
  Newark *(G-6783)*

FUEL DEALERS, NEC

Stump B Gone Inc .... G 302 737-7779
  Newark *(G-7498)*

FUEL OIL DEALERS

Burns & McBride Inc .... D 302 656-5110
  New Castle *(G-5121)*
C L Burchenal Oil Co Inc .... G 302 697-1517
  Camden *(G-543)*
Clark Services Inc Delaware .... G 302 834-0556
  Bear *(G-76)*
Durrell Sandblasting & Pntg Co .... G 302 836-1113
  Newark *(G-6481)*
Foraker Oil Inc .... G 302 834-7595
  Delaware City *(G-957)*
H R Phillips Inc .... E 302 422-4518
  Milford *(G-4430)*
Hillside Oil Company Inc .... E 302 738-4144
  Newark *(G-6729)*
J H Wilkerson & Son Inc .... G 302 422-4306
  Milford *(G-4456)*
Schlosser Assoc Mech Cntrs Inc .... E 302 738-7333
  Newark *(G-7393)*
Service Energy LLC .... D 302 734-7433
  Dover *(G-2071)*
Service Energy LLC .... F 302 645-9050
  Lewes *(G-3737)*
Shellhorn & Hill Inc .... D 302 654-4200
  Wilmington *(G-12599)*
Smokeys Gulf Service Inc .... G 302 378-2451
  Middletown *(G-4245)*
Wilkins Fuel Co .... G 302 422-5597
  Milford *(G-4605)*
Will C & Will Fuels .... G 302 366-1915
  Newark *(G-7695)*

FUELS: Ethanol

Advanced Bio-Energy Tech Inc .... G 347 363-9927
  Dover *(G-1088)*
Judy Tim Fuel Inc .... G 302 349-5895
  Greenwood *(G-2749)*
Lynch Heights Fuel Corp .... G 302 422-9195
  Milford *(G-4481)*
Memorial Super Fuel .... G 215 512-1012
  New Castle *(G-5515)*
Plaza Fuel .... G 302 275-6242
  Wilmington *(G-12157)*
Simar Fuel Inc .... G 302 304-1969
  Smyrna *(G-8716)*
Vital Renewable Energy Company .... G 202 595-2944
  Wilmington *(G-13095)*

FUELS: Jet

Transtate Jet Service Inc .... G 302 346-3102
  Dover *(G-2160)*

FUELS: Oil

Prime Products Usa Inc .... G 302 528-3866
  Wilmington *(G-12226)*

FUND RAISING ORGANIZATION, NON-FEE BASIS

Beth Sholom Congregation .... D 302 734-5578
  Dover *(G-1199)*
Georgetown Playground & Pk Inc .... G 302 856-7111
  Georgetown *(G-2547)*
Homes For Life Foundation .... F 302 571-1217
  Wilmington *(G-10942)*
Knights York Cross of Honour .... G 302 731-4817
  Newark *(G-6900)*
March of Dimes Inc .... G 302 225-1020
  Wilmington *(G-11521)*

FUNDRAISING SVCS

6 Star Fundraising LLC .... G 302 250-5085
  Newark *(G-5861)*
African Markets Fund LLC .... G 703 944-1514
  Dover *(G-1092)*
Aids Delaware Inc .... G 302 652-6776
  Wilmington *(G-8986)*
Beebe Medical Foundation .... G 302 644-2900
  Lewes *(G-3373)*

FUNERAL DIRECTOR

Bennie Smith Funeral Home Inc .... G 302 934-9019
  Millsboro *(G-4643)*
Berry Short Funeral Home Inc .... G 302 422-8091
  Milford *(G-4324)*
Direct Cremation Services Del .... F 302 656-6873
  Wilmington *(G-10160)*
Dohery Funeral Homes Inc .... G 302 999-8277
  Wilmington *(G-10184)*
Gore Funeral Services .... G 610 364-9900
  New Castle *(G-5357)*
Melson Funeral Services Ltd .... G 302 732-9000
  Frankford *(G-2373)*

FUNERAL HOME

A Douglas Melson .... G 302 732-6606
  Frankford *(G-2344)*
Austin Cox Home Services .... G 410 334-6406
  Georgetown *(G-2441)*
Beeson Funeral Home .... G 302 764-2900
  Wilmington *(G-9281)*
Bennie Smith Funeral Home Inc .... G 302 678-8747
  Dover *(G-1193)*
Charles P Arcaro Funeral Home .... G 302 658-9095
  Wilmington *(G-9635)*
Congo Funeral Home .... F 302 652-6640
  Wilmington *(G-9822)*
Delaware Prof Fnrl Svcs Inc .... E 302 731-5459
  Newark *(G-6404)*
Ews Funeral Home .... G 302 494-1847
  Bear *(G-146)*
Faries Funeral Directors Inc .... G 302 653-8816
  Smyrna *(G-8633)*
Gebhart Funeral Home Inc .... E 302 798-7726
  Claymont *(G-750)*
Hannigan Short Disharoonk .... G 302 875-3637
  Laurel *(G-3237)*
House of Wright Mortuary .... F 302 762-8448
  Wilmington *(G-10960)*
James T Chandler & Son Inc .... F 302 478-7100
  Wilmington *(G-11124)*
John F Yasik Funeral Services .... G 302 428-9986
  Wilmington *(G-11169)*
John F Yasik Inc .... G 302 652-5114
  Wilmington *(G-11170)*
Krienen-Griffith Inc .... G 302 994-9614
  Wilmington *(G-11295)*
Lofland Funeral Home Inc .... G 302 422-5416
  Milford *(G-4476)*
McCrery Funeral Homes Inc .... G 302 478-2204
  Wilmington *(G-11592)*
Melson Funeral Services .... G 302 945-9000
  Millsboro *(G-4741)*
Michael A Mealey & Sons Inc .... F 302 652-5913
  Wilmington *(G-11654)*
Michael A Mealey & Sons Inc .... F 302 654-3005
  Wilmington *(G-11655)*
Parsell Funeral Entps Inc .... G 302 645-9520
  Lewes *(G-3679)*
Robert T Jones & Foard Inc .... G 302 731-4627
  Newark *(G-7352)*
Ryland Funeral Home Inc .... G 302 764-7711
  Wilmington *(G-12503)*
Short Funeral Home Inc .... G 302 846-9814
  Delmar *(G-1028)*

Short Funeral Home Inc .... G 302 875-3637
  Laurel *(G-3288)*
Spicer Mullikin Funeral Homes .... E 302 368-9500
  New Castle *(G-5729)*
Spicer Mullikin Funeral Homes .... F 302 368-9500
  Newark *(G-7471)*
Thomas E Melvin Son Inc .... G 302 398-3884
  Harrington *(G-2899)*
Torbert Funeral Chapel Inc .... F 302 734-3341
  Dover *(G-2153)*
Trader Funeral Home Inc .... G 302 734-4620
  Dover *(G-2158)*
Warwick Funeral Home .... G 302 368-9500
  Newark *(G-7677)*
Watson Funeral Home Inc .... F 302 934-7842
  Millsboro *(G-4824)*
Watson-Yates Funeral Home Inc .... G 302 629-8561
  Seaford *(G-8435)*
Zwaanendael LLC .... G 302 645-6466
  Lewes *(G-3837)*

FUNERAL HOMES & SVCS

Edward R Bell .... G 302 658-1555
  Wilmington *(G-10358)*

FUNGICIDES OR HERBICIDES

Corteva Inc .... E 302 485-3000
  Wilmington *(G-9869)*

FURNACES & OVENS: Indl

Nabertherm Inc .... G 302 322-3665
  New Castle *(G-5541)*

FURNITURE & CABINET STORES: Custom

G2 Group Inc .... G 302 836-4202
  Bear *(G-163)*
Group Three Inc .... G 302 658-4158
  Wilmington *(G-10789)*

FURNITURE REFINISHING SVCS

Melroys Furniture Refinishing .... G 302 645-1856
  Lewes *(G-3636)*

FURNITURE STORES

Carolina Street Garden & Home .... G 302 539-2405
  Fenwick Island *(G-2332)*
Couture Denim LLC .... G 302 220-8339
  New Castle *(G-5204)*
Furniture Whl Connection Inc .... F 302 836-6000
  Bear *(G-162)*
Kenton Chair Shop .... F 302 653-2411
  Clayton *(G-859)*
Kirk Cabinetry LLC .... G 302 220-3377
  Wilmington *(G-11271)*
Maryann Metrinko LLC .... G 410 643-1472
  Lewes *(G-3623)*
Rite Way Distributors .... G 302 535-8507
  Felton *(G-2317)*

FURNITURE STORES: Office

Callaway Furniture Inc .... G 302 398-8858
  Harrington *(G-2823)*
W B Mason Co Inc .... C 888 926-2766
  Newark *(G-7667)*

FURNITURE STORES: Outdoor & Garden

Eastern Shore Porch Patio Inc .... E 302 436-9520
  Selbyville *(G-8485)*

FURNITURE UPHOLSTERY REPAIR SVCS

Colliers Trim Shop Inc .... G 302 227-8398
  Rehoboth Beach *(G-7897)*

FURNITURE WHOLESALERS

Docs Medical LLC .... G 301 401-1489
  Bear *(G-122)*
Furniture Whl Connection Inc .... F 302 836-6000
  Bear *(G-162)*
L F Systems Corp .... G 302 322-0460
  New Castle *(G-5471)*
Laytons Umbrellas .... G 302 249-1958
  Laurel *(G-3257)*

Employee Codes: A=Over 500 employees, B=251-500
C=101-250, D=51-100, E=20-50, F=10-19, G=1-9

2020 Harris Directory of
Delaware Businesses

FURNITURE, HOUSEHOLD: Wholesalers

Browne USA Inc .... E 302 326-4802
  New Castle (G-5116)

FURNITURE, OFFICE: Wholesalers

Corporate Interiors Inc .... D 302 322-1008
  New Castle (G-5195)
Richert Inc .... E 302 684-0696
  Milton (G-4961)

FURNITURE, WHOLESALE: Racks

Lan Rack Inc .... G 949 587-5168
  Dover (G-1764)

FURNITURE: Cabinets & Vanities, Medicine, Metal

Zwd Products Corporation .... B 302 326-8200
  New Castle (G-5848)

FURNITURE: Chairs, Household Wood

Kenton Chair Shop .... F 302 653-2411
  Clayton (G-859)

FURNITURE: Foundations & Platforms

Design Specific US Inc .... G 650 318-6473
  Wilmington (G-10123)

FURNITURE: Hospital

Tarpon Strategies LLC .... G 215 806-2723
  Newark (G-7540)

FURNITURE: Household, Metal

Tri-State Fbrction McHning LLC .... E 302 232-3133
  New Castle (G-5788)

FURNITURE: Household, NEC

Michael Pdmnczky Cnsrvator LLC ..... G 302 388-0656
  Wilmington (G-11664)

FURNITURE: Household, Wood

Astral Plane Woodworks Inc .... G 302 654-8666
  Wilmington (G-9166)
Butler Woodcrafters .... G 302 764-0744
  Wilmington (G-9516)
Group Three Inc .... G 302 658-4158
  Wilmington (G-10789)
Initial Trading Co .... G 302 428-1132
  Wilmington (G-11034)
Kirk Cabinetry LLC .... G 302 220-3377
  Wilmington (G-11271)
Mtb Artisans LLC .... G 303 475-9024
  Wilmington (G-11772)
Quilted Heirlooms .... G 302 354-6061
  Middletown (G-4206)
Slice of Wood LLC .... G 315 335-0917
  Delaware City (G-967)

FURNITURE: Institutional, Exc Wood

Butler Woodcrafters .... G 302 764-0744
  Wilmington (G-9516)
Turning Point Collection LLC .... G 302 416-0092
  Wilmington (G-12993)

FURNITURE: Juvenile, Wood

Brandywine Valley Woodworking .... G 302 743-5640
  Wilmington (G-9459)

FURNITURE: Laboratory

L F Systems Corp .... F 302 322-0460
  New Castle (G-5471)

FURNITURE: Mattresses, Box & Bedsprings

Plushbeds Inc .... G 888 758-7423
  Wilmington (G-12162)

FURNITURE: Office, Exc Wood

Business Slip LLC .... G 302 563-3660
  Wilmington (G-9512)

FURNITURE: Office, Wood

Butler Woodcrafters .... G 302 764-0744
  Wilmington (G-9516)
Corporate Interiors Inc .... D 302 322-1008
  New Castle (G-5195)
Heirloom Creations .... G 302 659-1817
  Smyrna (G-8651)
Registry Furniture Inc .... G 626 297-9508
  Wilmington (G-12365)

FURNITURE: Picnic Tables Or Benches, Park

Acorn Site Furnishings .... G 302 249-4979
  Bridgeville (G-443)

FURNITURE: Sleep

Panda Sleep Inc .... G 302 760-9754
  Dover (G-1931)

FURNITURE: Upholstered

Barlows Upholstery Inc .... G 302 655-3955
  Wilmington (G-9255)
Charles Andrews .... G 302 378-7116
  Townsend (G-8769)

GAMBLING MACHINE, OPERATIONS

Dover Downs Inc .... A 302 674-4600
  Dover (G-1445)

GAMBLING: Lotteries

Scientific Games Corporation .... F 302 737-4300
  Newark (G-7395)

GAME MACHINES, COIN-OPERATED, WHOLESALE

International Game Technology .... F 302 674-3177
  Dover (G-1682)

GAMES & TOYS: Banks

Affiliate Venture Group .... G 302 379-6961
  Wilmington (G-8969)

GAMES & TOYS: Board Games, Children's & Adults'

Tetris Company LLC .... G 302 656-1950
  Wilmington (G-12886)

GAMES & TOYS: Electronic

Philymack Games LLC .... G 302 658-7581
  Wilmington (G-12121)
Top Dog Best Games LLC .... G 949 859-8869
  Wilmington (G-12927)
Yotta Games LLC .... G 425 247-0756
  Wilmington (G-13329)

GAMES & TOYS: Game Machines, Exc Coin-Operated

Zone Systems Inc .... F 302 730-8888
  Dover (G-2255)

GAMES & TOYS: Models, Boat & Ship, Toy & Hobby

Aero-Marine Laminates Inc .... F 302 628-3944
  Seaford (G-8141)

GAMING: Slot Machines

Delaware Racing Association .... B 302 355-1000
  Newark (G-6405)
Delaware Racing Association .... A 302 994-2521
  Newark (G-10076)

GARAGE DOOR REPAIR SVCS

Hickman Overhead Door Company .... F 302 422-4249
  Milford (G-4441)
Pinnacle Garage Door Company .... G 302 505-4531
  Felton (G-2310)
Precision Door Service .... G 302 343-6394
  Wilmington (G-12204)

GARMENT: Pressing & cleaners' agents

Sepia Cleaners .... G 302 656-0700
  Wilmington (G-12581)

GAS & OIL FIELD EXPLORATION SVCS

Butamax Advanced Biofuels LLC ...... G 302 695-3617
  Wilmington (G-9513)
E I Du Pont De Nemours & Co .... F 302 774-1000
  Wilmington (G-10294)
I-Pulse Inc .... G 604 689-8765
  Wilmington (G-10984)
Penn Virginia Holding Corp .... C 302 288-0158
  Wilmington (G-12067)
Rangeland Nm LLC .... G 800 316-6660
  Dover (G-2009)
Sun Orient Exploration Company .... G 302 293-6000
  Wilmington (G-12797)

GAS & OIL FIELD SVCS, NEC

Aim Metals & Alloys USA Inc .... G 212 450-4519
  Wilmington (G-8989)
Atlantic Oil & Gas LLC .... G 302 898-2862
  Townsend (G-8760)
Lone Star Global Services Inc .... G 302 744-9800
  Dover (G-1795)
TCI Inspections USA LLC .... G 302 261-5208
  Wilmington (G-12858)

GAS & OTHER COMBINED SVCS

Peninsula Energy Svcs Co Inc .... F 302 734-6799
  Dover (G-1945)

GAS APPLIANCE REPAIR SVCS

Hayes Sewing Machine Company ..... F 302 764-9033
  Wilmington (G-10856)

GAS FIELD MACHINERY & EQPT

Tdw Delaware Inc .... G 302 594-9880
  New Castle (G-5755)

GAS PRODUCTION & DISTRIBUTION

Conectiv Energy Supply Inc .... D 302 454-0300
  Newark (G-6283)
Osaka Gas USA Corporation .... G 302 658-7581
  Wilmington (G-11979)

GAS STATIONS

E I Du Pont De Nemours & Co .... G 302 772-0016
  New Castle (G-5271)
J William Gordy Fuel Co .... F 302 846-3425
  Delmar (G-1006)
Logue Brothers Inc .... F 302 762-1896
  Wilmington (G-11427)
Shellhorn & Hill Inc .... D 302 654-4200
  Wilmington (G-12599)
Walls Service Center Inc .... G 302 422-8110
  Milford (G-4596)

GASES: Helium

Helium3 Tech and Services LLC .... G 302 766-2856
  Newark (G-6721)

GASES: Hydrogen

Occidental Chemical Corp .... G 302 834-3800
  New Castle (G-5585)

GASES: Indl

Air Liquide America LP .... G 302 225-2132
  Wilmington (G-8992)
Air Lqide Advanced Separations .... G 302 225-1100
  Newport (G-7745)
Air Lqide Advanced Tech US LLC ..... G 302 225-1100
  Newark (G-5925)
Air Lqide Advanced Tech US LLC ..... E 302 225-1100
  Wilmington (G-8993)
Airgas Usa LLC .... E 302 834-7404
  Delaware City (G-946)
E I Du Pont De Nemours & Co .... G 302 366-5763
  Newark (G-6491)
Keen Compressed Gas Co .... E 302 594-4545
  New Castle (G-5456)
Pure Air Holdings Corp .... G 302 655-7130
  Wilmington (G-12270)

PRODUCT & SERVICES SECTION

GLASS: Stained

GASES: Nitrogen
Messer LLC .... E 302 798-9342
  Claymont *(G-781)*

GASES: Oxygen
AAL Drtc .... G 302 229-5891
  Newark *(G-5875)*

GASKETS
Miller Metal Fabrication Inc .... D 302 337-2291
  Bridgeville *(G-501)*

GASKETS & SEALING DEVICES
Delaware Thrmplastic Specialty .... G 302 424-4722
  Milford *(G-4381)*
Greene Tweed of Delaware Inc .... G 302 888-2560
  Wilmington *(G-10778)*
Watson-Marlow Flow Smart Inc .... E 302 536-6388
  Seaford *(G-8434)*

GASOLINE FILLING STATIONS
Careys Inc .... E 302 875-5674
  Laurel *(G-3207)*
Horton and Bros Inc .... G 302 738-7221
  Newark *(G-6747)*
Jeff Thomas .... G 302 762-9154
  Wilmington *(G-11143)*
Manor Exxon Inc .... G 302 834-6691
  Bear *(G-243)*
Meadowood Mobil Station .... G 302 731-5602
  Newark *(G-7013)*
Millcreek Texaco Station .... G 302 571-8489
  Wilmington *(G-11691)*
Newport Ventures Inc .... F 302 998-1693
  Wilmington *(G-11879)*
Om Shiv Groceries Inc .... G 302 856-7014
  Georgetown *(G-2611)*
Sals Auto Services Inc .... G 302 654-1168
  Wilmington *(G-12526)*
Smokeys Gulf Service Inc .... G 302 378-2451
  Middletown *(G-4245)*

GASOLINE WHOLESALERS
H R Phillips Inc .... E 302 422-4518
  Milford *(G-4430)*
J William Gordy Fuel Co .... F 302 846-3425
  Delmar *(G-1006)*

GEARS: Power Transmission, Exc Auto
David Brown Gear Systems USA .... G 540 416-2062
  Wilmington *(G-9966)*
David Brown Gear Systems USA .... G 540 943-8375
  Wilmington *(G-9967)*

GEMSTONE & INDL DIAMOND MINING SVCS
Asbury Carbons Inc .... G 302 652-0266
  Wilmington *(G-9146)*

GENERAL & INDUSTRIAL LOAN INSTITUTIONS
Delaware Title Loans Inc .... F 302 368-2131
  Newark *(G-6419)*
Delaware Title Loans Inc .... F 302 629-8843
  Seaford *(G-8221)*
Delaware Title Loans Inc .... G 302 328-7482
  New Castle *(G-5241)*
Delaware Title Loans Inc .... G 302 653-8315
  Smyrna *(G-8621)*

GENERAL COUNSELING SVCS
A Seed Hope Counseling Ctr LLC .... G 302 605-6702
  Wilmington *(G-8883)*
Adirondack Bhvral Hlthcare LLC .... G 302 832-1282
  Christiana *(G-665)*
Balanced Mind Cnseling Ctr LLC .... G 302 377-6911
  Middletown *(G-3962)*
Bellwether Behavioral Health .... F 856 769-2042
  Bear *(G-50)*
Brandywine Counseling .... E 302 762-7120
  Wilmington *(G-9426)*
Bridge Counseling Center LLC .... G 302 856-9190
  Georgetown *(G-2459)*
Catholic Charities Inc .... G 302 674-1600
  Dover *(G-1261)*
Center For A Pstive Hmnity LLC .... G 302 703-1036
  Felton *(G-2281)*
Counseling Services Inc .... G 302 894-1477
  Wilmington *(G-9874)*
Delaware Councl On Gmblng Prbl ...... G 302 226-5041
  Rehoboth Beach *(G-7911)*
Fellowship Hlth Resources Inc .... F 302 854-0626
  Georgetown *(G-2528)*
Jewish Family Service of Del .... G 302 798-0600
  Claymont *(G-768)*
Khanyi Media Corporation .... G 302 482-8142
  Wilmington *(G-11257)*
Middletown Counseling .... G 302 376-0621
  Middletown *(G-4155)*
Millenium Counseling .... G 302 995-9188
  Wilmington *(G-11692)*
Mind and Body Consortium LLC .... E 302 674-2380
  Dover *(G-1860)*
Pike Creek Psychological Ctr PA .... F 302 738-6859
  Newark *(G-7217)*
Shechinah Empower Center Inc .... G 302 858-4467
  Georgetown *(G-2653)*
Suburban Psychiatric Svcs LLC .... F 302 999-9834
  Wilmington *(G-12787)*
Survivors Abuse In Rcovery Inc .... G 302 651-0181
  Wilmington *(G-12818)*

GENERAL MERCHANDISE, NONDURABLE, WHOLESALE
Domian International Svc LLC .... G 804 837-3616
  Smyrna *(G-8624)*
Eecoo LLC .... E 315 503-1477
  Newark *(G-6507)*
Grupo Acosta Ecuador Limited .... C 302 231-2981
  Wilmington *(G-10792)*
Site Source Contractor Supply .... G 302 322-0444
  Bear *(G-323)*
Tansley Associates (usa) Inc .... F 403 569-8566
  Wilmington *(G-12852)*
Tarpon Strategies LLC .... G 215 806-2723
  Newark *(G-7540)*

GENERATOR REPAIR SVCS
Roys Electrical Service Inc .... G 302 674-3199
  Cheswold *(G-663)*

GENERATORS: Automotive & Aircraft
Solavitek Engineering Inc .... G 514 949-6981
  Newark *(G-7455)*

GENERATORS: Electric
Cummins Power Generation Inc .... B 302 762-2027
  Wilmington *(G-9918)*

GENERATORS: Gas
Bif III Holtwood LLC .... E 819 561-2722
  Wilmington *(G-9328)*

GERIATRIC RESIDENTIAL CARE FACILITY
Catholic Mnstry To Elderly Inc .... F 302 368-2784
  Newark *(G-6170)*
Churchman Village Center LLC .... G 302 998-6900
  Newark *(G-6234)*
Connections Community Support .... D 302 389-1118
  Smyrna *(G-8603)*
Green Valley Pavilion .... E 302 653-5085
  Smyrna *(G-8646)*
Ingleside Homes Inc .... D 302 575-0250
  Wilmington *(G-11031)*

GERIATRIC SOCIAL SVCS
Chase Center On River .... G 302 655-2187
  Wilmington *(G-9641)*
Cornerstone Senior Center .... G 302 836-6463
  Bear *(G-85)*
Health & Social Svcs Del Dept .... D 302 391-3505
  New Castle *(G-5387)*
Ingleside Homes Inc .... D 302 575-0250
  Wilmington *(G-11031)*
Tri-State Cheernastics Inc .... G 302 322-4020
  New Castle *(G-5787)*

GIFT SHOP
Beth Sholom Congregation .... D 302 734-5578
  Dover *(G-1199)*
Coiffure Ltd .... G 302 652-3443
  Wilmington *(G-9763)*
Good Samaritan Aid .... G 302 875-2425
  Laurel *(G-3233)*
Junior Bd of Christiana Care .... G 302 733-1100
  Newark *(G-6858)*
Old Country Garden Center Inc .... E 302 652-3317
  Wilmington *(G-11943)*
Stuart Kingston Galleries Inc .... F 302 652-7978
  Wilmington *(G-12780)*

GIFT, NOVELTY & SOUVENIR STORES: Party Favors
Forever Inc .... G 302 368-1440
  Newark *(G-6604)*
Fulton Paper Company .... F 302 594-0400
  Wilmington *(G-10648)*
Henninger Printing Co Inc .... G 302 934-8119
  Millsboro *(G-4705)*

GIFTS & NOVELTIES: Wholesalers
Alias Inc .... G 302 481-5556
  Wilmington *(G-9010)*
Custom Decor Inc .... E 302 735-7600
  Dover *(G-1332)*
Guinevere Associates Inc .... G 302 635-7798
  Wilmington *(G-10799)*

GLASS FABRICATORS
Glass Technologists Inc .... G 240 682-0966
  Middletown *(G-4087)*

GLASS PRDTS, FROM PURCHASED GLASS: Insulating
Hensco LLC .... G 302 423-1638
  Harrington *(G-2849)*

GLASS PRDTS, FROM PURCHASED GLASS: Windshields
Cannon Enterprises .... G 302 629-6746
  Seaford *(G-8181)*

GLASS PRDTS, PRESSED OR BLOWN: Scientific Glassware
R and H Filter Co Inc .... G 302 856-2129
  Georgetown *(G-2632)*

GLASS STORES
Go-Glass Corporation .... F 302 674-3390
  Dover *(G-1596)*
Newark Glass & Mirror Inc .... F 302 834-1158
  Bear *(G-264)*

GLASS, AUTOMOTIVE: Wholesalers
Pgw Auto Glass LLC .... G 302 793-1486
  Claymont *(G-794)*
Safelite Glass Corp .... G 877 800-2727
  Dover *(G-2053)*
Safelite Glass Corp .... F 302 656-4640
  Wilmington *(G-12519)*

GLASS: Fiber
Psp Corp .... G 302 764-7730
  Wilmington *(G-12260)*

GLASS: Leaded
Gregory D Thacker .... G 302 239-0879
  Newark *(G-6689)*

GLASS: Pressed & Blown, NEC
Global Scientific Glass Inc .... G 302 429-9330
  Wilmington *(G-10730)*
Gregory D Thacker .... G 302 239-0879
  Newark *(G-6689)*
Studio On 24 Inc .... G 302 644-4424
  Lewes *(G-3767)*

GLASS: Stained
Charles Ogden .... G 305 606-4512
  Wilmington *(G-9634)*

Employee Codes: A=Over 500 employees, B=251-500
C=101-250, D=51-100, E=20-50, F=10-19, G=1-9

2020 Harris Directory of Delaware Businesses

GLASS: Stained

Victorian Glassworks .... G 302 798-4847
  Wilmington *(G-13078)*

GLASSWARE WHOLESALERS

Duralex Usa Inc .... D 302 326-4804
  New Castle *(G-5267)*

GLASSWARE: Laboratory

Miles Scientific Corporation .... F 302 737-6960
  Newark *(G-7039)*

GLASSWARE: Laboratory & Medical

Shamrock Glass Co Inc .... F 302 629-5500
  Seaford *(G-8400)*

GLOBAL POSITIONING SYSTEMS & EQPT

Geo-Fence Inc .... G 763 516-8934
  Dover *(G-1589)*

GLOVES: Fabric

Kaul Glove and Mfg Co .... D 302 292-2660
  New Castle *(G-5454)*
Masley Enterprises Inc .... E 302 427-9885
  Wilmington *(G-11561)*

GLOVES: Leather, Work

Kaul Glove and Mfg Co .... D 302 292-2660
  New Castle *(G-5454)*

GLOVES: Welders'

Masley Enterprises Inc .... E 302 427-9885
  Wilmington *(G-11561)*

GOLF COURSES: Public

American Classic Golf Club LLC ... G 302 703-6662
  Lewes *(G-3336)*
Arpago Corp .... G 302 645-7955
  Lewes *(G-3347)*
Back Creek Golf Shop .... E 302 378-6499
  Middletown *(G-3958)*
Bayside Golf LLC DBA Bear Trap .. F 302 537-5600
  Ocean View *(G-7760)*
Bayside Resort Golf Club .... E 302 436-3400
  Selbyville *(G-8453)*
Baywood Greens Golf Club .... E 302 947-9225
  Millsboro *(G-4638)*
Baywood Greens Golf Club .... E 302 947-9800
  Millsboro *(G-4639)*
Bear Trap Partners .... F 302 537-5600
  Ocean View *(G-7761)*
City of Seaford Inc .... F 302 629-2890
  Seaford *(G-8197)*
Delaware Park Racing LLC .... G 302 994-6700
  Wilmington *(G-10073)*
Delcastle Golf Club .... G 302 995-1990
  Wilmington *(G-10097)*
Delcastle Golf Club Management . E 302 998-9505
  Wilmington *(G-10098)*
Dover Golf Center .... G 302 674-8275
  Dover *(G-1451)*
Frog Hollow Golf Course .... E 302 376-6500
  Middletown *(G-4079)*
Garrisons Lake Golf Club .... G 302 659-1206
  Smyrna *(G-8639)*
Golf Course At Garrisons Lake ..... G 302 659-1206
  Smyrna *(G-8644)*
Greens At Broadview LLC .... G 302 684-3000
  Milton *(G-4910)*
Jonathans Landing .... E 302 697-8204
  Magnolia *(G-3896)*
Lynx Golf Ltd .... G 778 755-4107
  Dover *(G-1809)*
Meadowbrook Golf Group Inc ..... G 302 571-9041
  Wilmington *(G-11611)*
Odessa National Golf Crse LLC ... F 302 464-1007
  Townsend *(G-8814)*
Par 3 Inc .... G 302 674-8275
  Dover *(G-1934)*
Peninsula At Long Neck LLC .... G 302 947-4717
  Millsboro *(G-4775)*
Rock Manor Golf Course .... G 302 295-1400
  Wilmington *(G-12447)*
Rookery Golf Courses South .... G 302 422-7010
  Milford *(G-4548)*
Vinces Sports Center Inc .... G 302 738-4859
  Newark *(G-7659)*

Worcester Golf Club Inc .... F 610 222-0200
  Milton *(G-4981)*

GOLF EQPT

Abbey Lein Inc .... G 302 239-2712
  Newark *(G-5881)*
Rope-It Golf LLC .... G 305 767-3481
  Wilmington *(G-12474)*

GOLF GOODS & EQPT

Baywood Greens Golf Club .... E 302 947-9225
  Millsboro *(G-4638)*
Delcastle Golf Club Management . E 302 998-9505
  Wilmington *(G-10098)*

GOVERNMENT, EXECUTIVE OFFICES: Mayors'

City of Newark .... F 302 366-0457
  Newark *(G-6242)*

GOVERNMENT, GENERAL: Administration

Delaware Secretary of State .... F 302 736-7400
  Dover *(G-1389)*
Delaware Secretary of State .... G 302 834-8046
  Bear *(G-112)*

GOVERNMENT, GENERAL: Administration, Local

City of Dover .... E 302 736-7035
  Dover *(G-1289)*

GOVERNMENT, GENERAL: Administration, State

Children Youth & Their Fam .... F 302 628-2024
  Seaford *(G-8193)*

GRADING SVCS

Bramble Construction Co Inc ...... F 302 856-6723
  Georgetown *(G-2458)*

GRANITE: Cut & Shaped

Keystone Granite and Tile Inc .... G 302 323-0200
  New Castle *(G-5462)*

GRANITE: Dimension

Everest Granite LLC .... G 302 229-4733
  Wilmington *(G-10445)*

GRANTMAKING FOUNDATIONS

East Side Cmmty Lrng Cntr Fndt .. G 302 762-5834
  Wilmington *(G-10321)*
Resurrection Center .... G 302 762-8311
  Wilmington *(G-12391)*
Udaan Inc .... F 267 408-3001
  Bear *(G-363)*

GRAPHIC ARTS & RELATED DESIGN SVCS

9193 4323 Quebec Inc .... G 855 824-0795
  Newark *(G-5862)*
Brand Design Co Inc .... G 302 234-2356
  Yorklyn *(G-13364)*
Dean Dsign/Marketing Group Inc . G 717 898-9800
  Lincoln *(G-3844)*
Envision It Publications LLC ...... G 800 329-9411
  Bear *(G-144)*
Eye35design LLC .... G 470 236-3933
  Dover *(G-1535)*
Green Crescent LLC .... G 800 735-9620
  Dover *(G-1611)*
Gulch Group LLC .... G 202 697-1756
  Rehoboth Beach *(G-7956)*
Hamilton Associates .... G 302 629-4949
  Seaford *(G-8257)*
Integrated Solutions Planning .... G 302 297-9215
  Georgetown *(G-2567)*
Mitchell Associates Inc .... G 302 594-9400
  Wilmington *(G-11714)*
Pixxy Solutions LLC .... E 631 609-6686
  Claymont *(G-795)*
Precision Color Graphics LLC ...... G 302 661-2595
  Wilmington *(G-12202)*

Sunshine Graphics and Printing .. G 302 724-5127
  Dover *(G-2115)*
Xcs Corporation .... G 302 514-0600
  Wilmington *(G-13316)*

GRASSES: Artificial & Preserved

Close Cuts Lawn Svc & Ldscpg ... G 302 422-2248
  Milford *(G-4358)*

GRAVEL MINING

Sussex Sand & Gravel Inc .... G 302 628-6962
  Seaford *(G-8418)*

GROCERIES WHOLESALERS, NEC

326 Associates LP .... G 302 328-4101
  New Castle *(G-4990)*
Legacy Foods LLC .... G 302 656-5540
  Wilmington *(G-11360)*
P-Ks Wholesale Grocer Inc .... F 302 656-5540
  Wilmington *(G-11998)*

GROCERIES, GENERAL LINE WHOLESALERS

Camels Hump Inc .... F 302 227-5719
  Rehoboth Beach *(G-7882)*
Jcholley LLC .... G 302 653-6659
  Bear *(G-199)*
Moran Foods LLC .... F 302 798-5042
  Claymont *(G-785)*

GROUP DAY CARE CENTER

A Leap of Faith Inc .... F 302 543-6256
  Wilmington *(G-8881)*
All My Children Inc .... F 302 995-9191
  Wilmington *(G-9015)*
Angels In Heaven .... G 302 398-7820
  Harrington *(G-2811)*
Angels Lindas .... E 302 328-3700
  New Castle *(G-5039)*
Army & Air Force Exchange Svc .. D 302 677-3716
  Dover *(G-1138)*
Atlantic Dawn Ltd .... F 302 737-8854
  Newark *(G-6019)*
Beach Babies Child Care .... F 302 378-4778
  Townsend *(G-8763)*
Beverlys Help In Hand .... G 302 651-9304
  Wilmington *(G-9321)*
Bright Horizons Chld Ctrs LLC .... D 302 456-8913
  Newark *(G-6119)*
Bright Horizons Chld Ctrs LLC .... G 302 282-6378
  Wilmington *(G-9474)*
Bright Horizons Chld Ctrs LLC .... E 302 477-1023
  Wilmington *(G-9475)*
Bright Horizons Chld Ctrs LLC .... E 302 453-2050
  Newark *(G-6120)*
Bright Stars Home Daycare .... G 302 378-8142
  Middletown *(G-3975)*
Brilliant Little Minds .... G 302 376-9889
  Middletown *(G-3976)*
Brown Lisha .... G 302 832-9529
  Newark *(G-6126)*
Catholic Charities Inc .... G 302 674-1600
  Dover *(G-1261)*
Celebree Holding Inc .... G 302 834-0436
  Bear *(G-69)*
Children First Lrng Ctr Inc .... G 302 674-5227
  Dover *(G-1275)*
Children S Secret Garden .... F 302 730-1717
  Dover *(G-1277)*
Connections Development Corp .. G 302 436-3292
  Frankford *(G-2356)*
Cozy Critters Child Care Corp .... E 302 541-8210
  Frankford *(G-2357)*
Creative Minds Daycare .... G 302 378-0741
  Townsend *(G-8775)*
Deanne Naples Family Daycare .. G 302 376-1408
  Middletown *(G-4022)*
Dis Daycare .... F 302 888-0350
  Wilmington *(G-10162)*
Dover Educational & Cmnty Ctr .. F 302 883-3092
  Dover *(G-1446)*
Dovers Childrens Villag .... F 302 672-6476
  Dover *(G-1473)*
Educational Enrichment Center .. E 302 478-8697
  Wilmington *(G-10354)*
Eisele Celine .... G 302 684-3201
  Milton *(G-4902)*

PRODUCT & SERVICES SECTION — HALFWAY GROUP HOME, PERSONS WITH SOCIAL OR PERSONAL PROBLEMS

Emma Jefferies Day Care .... G 302 762-3235
  Wilmington *(G-10392)*
Favored Childcare Academy Inc .... G 302 698-1266
  Dover *(G-1543)*
Gift Love Early Learning Ctr .... G 302 659-1984
  Smyrna *(G-8641)*
Graceland Daycare .... G 302 698-0414
  Magnolia *(G-3892)*
Greenbank Child Dev Ctr .... G 302 994-8574
  Wilmington *(G-10775)*
Hilltop Lutheran Neighborhd .... E 302 656-3224
  Wilmington *(G-10910)*
Karries Daycare .... G 302 328-7369
  New Castle *(G-5451)*
Kids Inc .... G 302 422-9099
  Milford *(G-4467)*
Kidscom Daycare .... G 302 544-5655
  New Castle *(G-5464)*
Kidz Akademy Corp .... G 302 732-6077
  Dagsboro *(G-913)*
Kindercare Learning Ctrs LLC .... E 302 234-8680
  Hockessin *(G-3071)*
Kindercare Learning Ctrs LLC .... F 302 834-6931
  Newark *(G-6888)*
Kindercare Learning Ctrs LLC .... F 302 322-3102
  New Castle *(G-5465)*
Kindercare Learning Ctrs LLC .... E 302 475-2212
  Wilmington *(G-11265)*
Kindercare Learning Ctrs LLC .... F 302 731-7138
  Wilmington *(G-11266)*
Kingdom Kids Day Care .... F 302 492-0207
  Hartly *(G-2931)*
Lil Red Hen Nursery Schl Inc .... E 302 846-2777
  Delmar *(G-1017)*
Little Blessings Daycare .... F 302 655-8962
  Wilmington *(G-11401)*
Little Folks Too Day Care .... G 302 652-3420
  Wilmington *(G-11402)*
Little Folks Too Day Care .... E 302 652-1238
  Wilmington *(G-11403)*
Little Star Inc .... F 302 995-2920
  Wilmington *(G-11408)*
Little Steps Daycare .... G 302 654-4867
  Wilmington *(G-11409)*
Lynns Home Daycare .... G 302 337-0186
  Bridgeville *(G-490)*
Marlette R Lofland .... G 302 628-1521
  Bridgeville *(G-494)*
Mary E Herring Daycare Center .... G 302 652-5978
  Wilmington *(G-11557)*
Maxines Daycare .... G 302 652-7242
  Wilmington *(G-11580)*
MI-Dee Inc .... E 302 453-7326
  Newark *(G-7022)*
Moms House Inc .... G 302 678-8688
  Dover *(G-1870)*
Mother Hubbard Child Care Ctr .... F 302 368-7584
  Newark *(G-7063)*
Neenee Wees Daycare .... G 302 730-3630
  Dover *(G-1891)*
Over Rainbow Daycare .... G 302 328-6574
  New Castle *(G-5594)*
Patricia Degirolano Day Care .... G 302 947-2874
  Millsboro *(G-4770)*
Patricia Disario Day Care .... G 302 737-8889
  Newark *(G-7182)*
Pirulos Child Care Center LLC .... G 302 836-3520
  Newark *(G-7220)*
Precious Little Angels Daycare .... G 302 378-2912
  Townsend *(G-8817)*
Precious Moments Day Care .... G 302 856-2346
  Georgetown *(G-2623)*
Regina Coleman .... G 215 476-4682
  Wilmington *(G-12357)*
Renzi Rust Inc .... F 302 424-4470
  Milford *(G-4538)*
Rising Stars Child Care Inc .... F 302 998-7682
  Wilmington *(G-12424)*
Rosa M Custis .... G 302 934-0541
  Millsboro *(G-4795)*
Sandy Rose Inc .... F 302 454-1649
  Newark *(G-7383)*
Scalias Day Care Center Inc .... F 302 366-1430
  Newark *(G-7392)*
Shelias Childcare Center .... G 302 472-9648
  Wilmington *(G-12597)*
Shells Child Care Center III .... F 302 398-9778
  Harrington *(G-2888)*
Slaughter Neck Educational and .... G 302 684-1834
  Lincoln *(G-3870)*
Small Wonder Day Care Inc .... E 302 654-2269
  Wilmington *(G-12651)*
Step Up Daycare .... G 302 762-3183
  Wilmington *(G-12752)*
Sunshine Home Daycare .... G 302 674-2009
  Dover *(G-2116)*
Susan T Fischer .... G 302 832-2570
  Newark *(G-7517)*
Tender Loving Kare .... E 302 464-1014
  Middletown *(G-4256)*
Tinas Tiny Tots Daycare .... G 302 536-7077
  Seaford *(G-8424)*
Toddlers Tech Inc .... F 302 655-4487
  Wilmington *(G-12923)*
Universal Design Company .... G 302 328-8391
  New Castle *(G-5809)*
V Quinton Inc .... F 302 449-1711
  Middletown *(G-4274)*
Wagstaff Day Care Center Inc .... F 302 998-7818
  Wilmington *(G-13112)*

GROUP FOSTER HOME

Elizabeth W Murphey School Inc .... D 302 734-7478
  Dover *(G-1515)*
Pressley Ridge Foundation .... G 302 366-0490
  Christiana *(G-678)*

GROUP HOSPITALIZATION PLANS

American Life Insurance Co .... D 302 594-2000
  Wilmington *(G-9053)*

GUARD PROTECTIVE SVCS

Bennett Det Prtective Agcy Inc .... G 302 734-2480
  Dover *(G-1192)*
Global Protection MGT LLC .... D 302 425-4190
  Wilmington *(G-10729)*
Int Investigation Security Inc .... G 609 727-8317
  Lewes *(G-3561)*

GUARD SVCS

ADT LLC .... F 302 918-1016
  Newark *(G-5902)*
Advantage Security Inc .... F 302 652-3060
  Wilmington *(G-8960)*
Command Security Corporation .... C 302 478-7003
  Wilmington *(G-9782)*
Delaware Academy Pub Safety SEC .. F 302 377-1465
  New Castle *(G-5223)*
Dupont Esl Security .... E 302 695-1657
  Wilmington *(G-10254)*
Ironhouse Security Group Inc .... G 443 312-9932
  Dover *(G-1684)*
Multi-Cble Adv SEC Sltns Inc .... G 703 909-6239
  Wilmington *(G-11774)*
Social Security Administration .... G 302 736-3688
  Dover *(G-2092)*

GUIDED MISSILES & SPACE VEHICLES

Lockheed Martin Overseas LLC .... G 301 897-6923
  Wilmington *(G-11422)*

GUTTERS: Sheet Metal

S G Williams & Bros Co .... F 302 656-8167
  Wilmington *(G-12506)*

GYMNASTICS INSTRUCTION

Little Gym of Ncc .... G 302 543-5524
  Wilmington *(G-11404)*
Olympiad Schools Inc .... F 302 636-0606
  Wilmington *(G-11946)*
Tri-State Cheernastics Inc .... G 302 322-4020
  New Castle *(G-5787)*

HAIR DRESSING, FOR THE TRADE

Bombshell Beauty Inc .... G 302 559-3011
  Wilmington *(G-9392)*

HAIR STYLIST: Men

Haircut & Company Inc .... F 302 239-3236
  Newark *(G-6702)*
House of Hair .... G 302 697-6088
  Dover *(G-1657)*
Toms Barber Shop .... G 302 992-9635
  Wilmington *(G-12925)*

HAIRDRESSERS

Altered Images Hair Studio .... G 302 234-2151
  Newark *(G-5947)*
Artistic Designs Salon .... G 302 644-2009
  Lewes *(G-3349)*
Bad Hair Day Inc .... E 302 226-4247
  Rehoboth Beach *(G-7853)*
C KS Hairport Ltd Salon & Spa .... G 302 645-2246
  Lewes *(G-3398)*
Cheveux Inc .... E 302 731-9202
  Newark *(G-6195)*
Christophers Hair Design .... G 302 378-1988
  Middletown *(G-3990)*
Coiffure Ltd .... G 302 652-3443
  Wilmington *(G-9763)*
Fabrizio Salon .... F 302 254-3432
  Wilmington *(G-10473)*
Family Comb & Scissors .... G 302 398-8570
  Harrington *(G-2840)*
Ferrari Hair Studio Ltd .... G 302 731-7505
  Wilmington *(G-10525)*
George Marcus Salon Inc .... F 302 475-7530
  Wilmington *(G-10702)*
Glossgirl Inc .... G 302 888-4520
  Wilmington *(G-10733)*
Hair 2 Please .... G 302 378-3349
  Middletown *(G-4101)*
Hair Artistry .... G 302 645-7167
  Lewes *(G-3529)*
Hair Designs By Regina .... G 302 652-8089
  Wilmington *(G-10819)*
Hair Levels .... G 302 212-0842
  Wilmington *(G-10821)*
Head Quarters Barbershop .... G 646 423-6767
  Wilmington *(G-4106)*
Headquarters 2 Inc .... F 302 731-9600
  Newark *(G-6715)*
JM Virgin Hair Company .... G 856 383-8588
  New Castle *(G-5440)*
Mark IV Beauty Salon Inc .... G 302 737-4994
  Newark *(G-6990)*
Maxim Hair & Nails LLC .... G 410 920-8656
  Selbyville *(G-8517)*
Mdm Hair Studio .... G 302 312-6052
  Middletown *(G-4151)*
Michaelangelos Hair Designs .... G 302 734-8343
  Dover *(G-1846)*
Mr Chris Hair Design .... G 302 658-2121
  Wilmington *(G-11766)*
New Trend Hair Salon .... G 302 998-3331
  Wilmington *(G-11871)*
Petite Hair Designs .... G 302 945-2595
  Millsboro *(G-4781)*
Pizazz Beauty Studio .... G 302 761-9820
  Wilmington *(G-12146)*
Ralphs Scissors Sensations .... G 302 764-2744
  Wilmington *(G-12311)*
Rape of The Locke Inc .... G 302 368-5370
  Newark *(G-7297)*
Regis Corporation .... G 302 856-2575
  Georgetown *(G-2634)*
Regis Corporation .... F 302 454-2800
  Newark *(G-7311)*
Rene Delyn Designs Inc .... F 302 736-6070
  Dover *(G-2028)*
Robins Hair & Tanning .... G 302 529-9000
  Wilmington *(G-12443)*
Salon Rispoli Inc .... G 302 731-9202
  Newark *(G-7380)*
Scissor Wizards Inc .... G 302 475-9575
  Wilmington *(G-12562)*
Shear Magic Hair Design .... F 302 836-4001
  Bear *(G-318)*
Styles By US .... G 302 629-3244
  Seaford *(G-8410)*
Todds .... F 302 658-0387
  Wilmington *(G-12924)*
Visions Hair Design .... G 302 477-0820
  Wilmington *(G-13093)*
Vivians Style .... G 302 645-9444
  Lewes *(G-3809)*
Yankee Clippers Hair Designer .... G 302 422-2748
  Milford *(G-4615)*

HALFWAY GROUP HOME, PERSONS WITH SOCIAL OR PERSONAL PROBLEMS

Fellowship Hlth Resources Inc .... F 302 854-0626
  Georgetown *(G-2528)*

Employee Codes: A=Over 500 employees, B=251-500
C=101-250, D=51-100, E=20-50, F=10-19, G=1-9

HANDBAGS

Fellowship Hlth Resources Inc .... F 302 856-7642
  Georgetown (G-2529)
Keystone Autism Services .... F 302 731-3115
  Newark (G-6880)

HANDBAGS

Frontgate LLC .... G 302 245-6654
  Bethany Beach (G-400)
Lamar Bags .... G 302 492-8566
  Hartly (G-2933)
Tradeway Corporation .... G 302 834-1957
  New Castle (G-5782)

HARDWARE

Bronco Manufacturing Inc .... G 302 475-1210
  Wilmington (G-9484)
D C Mitchell LLC .... G 302 998-1181
  Wilmington (G-9938)
Gibbons Innovations Inc .... G 302 265-4220
  Lincoln (G-3851)

HARDWARE & EQPT: Stage, Exc Lighting

Staging Dimensions Inc .... F 302 328-4100
  New Castle (G-5735)
Staging Dimesions Inc .... F 302 328-4100
  New Castle (G-5736)

HARDWARE STORES

Bryan & Brittingham Inc .... F 302 846-9500
  Delmar (G-974)
D F Quillen & Sons Inc .... E 302 227-2531
  Rehoboth Beach (G-7906)
Mechanics Paradise Inc .... F 302 652-8863
  New Castle (G-5513)

HARDWARE STORES: Chainsaws

Suburban Lawn & Equipment Inc ...... G 302 475-4300
  Wilmington (G-12785)
T & T Small Engines Inc .... G 302 492-8677
  Hartly (G-2943)

HARDWARE STORES: Door Locks & Lock Sets

Allied Lock & Safe Company .... G 302 658-3172
  Wilmington (G-9023)

HARDWARE STORES: Tools

Case Construction Inc .... E 302 737-3800
  Newark (G-6164)

HARDWARE WHOLESALERS

Clark & Sons Overhead Doors .... E 302 998-7552
  Wilmington (G-9732)
Integrity Corporation Inc .... F 410 392-8665
  Newark (G-6790)
Mumford Sheet Metal Works Inc ...... E 302 436-8251
  Selbyville (G-8527)
Ron Ell Hardware Inc .... F 302 328-8997
  New Castle (G-5682)
Standard Industrial Supply Co .... G 302 656-1631
  Wilmington (G-12735)

HARDWARE, WHOLESALE: Bolts

Building Fasteners Inc .... G 302 738-0671
  Newark (G-6132)

HARDWARE, WHOLESALE: Builders', NEC

Foss-Brown Inc .... F 610 940-6040
  Wilmington (G-10598)
Sumuri LLC .... G 302 570-0015
  Camden (G-601)
T & C Enterprise Incorporated .... G 302 934-8080
  Millsboro (G-4809)

HARDWARE, WHOLESALE: Nozzles

Petroserv Inc .... G 302 398-3260
  Harrington (G-2873)

HARDWARE, WHOLESALE: Nuts

Acurio LLC .... G 201 932-8160
  Wilmington (G-8931)

HARDWARE, WHOLESALE: Power Tools & Access

WW Grainger Inc .... F 302 322-1840
  New Castle (G-5842)

HARDWARE, WHOLESALE: Security Devices, Locks

Allied Lock & Safe Company .... G 302 658-3172
  Wilmington (G-9023)

HARDWARE: Rubber

Acurio LLC .... G 201 932-8160
  Wilmington (G-8931)

HARNESS HORSE RACING

Dover Downs Inc .... A 302 674-4600
  Dover (G-1445)
Harrington Raceway Inc .... F 302 398-4920
  Harrington (G-2845)

HARNESSES, HALTERS, SADDLERY & STRAPS

Fairway Manufacturing Company ...... G 302 398-4630
  Harrington (G-2839)

HEAD START CENTER, EXC IN CONJUNCTION WITH SCHOOL

Early Childhood Lab .... G 302 857-6731
  Dover (G-1496)
Estelles Child Dev Ctr Inc .... F 302 792-9065
  New Castle (G-5294)
Head Start Harrington .... G 302 398-9196
  Harrington (G-2848)
Heart Start Er Training Inc .... G 302 420-1917
  Wilmington (G-10876)
New Castle County Head Start .... F 302 452-1500
  Newark (G-7101)
New Castle County Head Start .... E 302 999-8480
  Wilmington (G-11852)
New Castle County Head Start .... F 302 832-2212
  Bear (G-262)
New Direction Early Headstart .... G 302 831-0584
  Newark (G-7104)
Rose Hill Community Center .... F 302 656-8513
  New Castle (G-5684)
Telamon Corp Head Start Prgram ..... D 302 653-3766
  Smyrna (G-8729)
Telamon Corporation .... E 302 736-5933
  Dover (G-2136)
Thomas Jffrson Lrng Foundation ..... F 302 856-3300
  Georgetown (G-2691)
Timber Heart Learning Center .... F 302 674-2565
  Dover (G-2148)
White Oak Head Start .... G 302 736-5933
  Dover (G-2224)
Wilmington Head Start .... G 302 762-8038
  Wilmington (G-13231)
Wilmington Headstart Inc .... G 302 421-3620
  Wilmington (G-13232)
Wilmington Headstart Inc .... E 302 762-8038
  Wilmington (G-13233)

HEALTH & ALLIED SERVICES, NEC

166th Medical Squadron .... D 302 323-3385
  New Castle (G-4989)
Access Quality Healthcare .... G 302 947-4437
  Millsboro (G-4621)
Acuhealth & Wellness .... G 302 438-4493
  Middletown (G-3930)
Animatra Inc .... G 303 350-9264
  Lewes (G-3342)
Bancroft Behavioral Health Inc .... G 302 502-3255
  Newark (G-6043)
Beachview Family Health .... G 302 537-8318
  Millville (G-4835)
Brandx Heirloom Tomatoes .... G 302 287-1782
  Townsend (G-8765)
Claymont Methadone Clinic .... G 855 244-7803
  Claymont (G-722)
Compassonate Certification Ctr .... G 888 316-9085
  Middletown (G-4004)
Das Financial Health LLC .... G 570 947-7931
  Dover (G-1341)
Delaware Eye Clinics .... G 302 645-2338
  Milton (G-4887)
Delaware Health and Fitnes LLC ...... G 302 584-7531
  Hockessin (G-3004)
Delaware Med Care Assoc LLC .... G 302 633-9033
  Newark (G-6393)
Douglas Morrow .... G 302 750-9161
  Wilmington (G-10213)
Dover Behavorl Hlth 249 .... G 302 741-0140
  Dover (G-1442)
Dr Debra Wolf Encore Health .... G 302 737-1918
  Newark (G-6470)
Eternal Health LLC .... G 302 635-7421
  Wilmington (G-10441)
Fidelity Mntal Hlth Sltons LLC .... G 302 304-2974
  Dover (G-1550)
First State Health & Wellness .... G 302 684-1995
  Milton (G-4906)
Fusion Health Works .... G 302 543-4714
  Wilmington (G-10651)
Green Clinics Laboratory LLC .... G 302 734-5050
  Dover (G-1610)
Health Support Services .... G 302 287-4952
  Wilmington (G-10870)
Javed Gilani MD .... G 302 478-7160
  Wilmington (G-11130)
Life At St Frncis Hlthcare Inc .... G 302 660-3297
  Wilmington (G-11383)
Lily Intrnl Medicine Asscs LLC .... G 302 424-1000
  Milford (G-4474)
Medical Reimbursement Sol .... G 516 809-6812
  Millsboro (G-4740)
Medicine Woman .... G 302 684-8048
  Milton (G-4933)
Middelaware Family Medicine .... G 302 724-5125
  Dover (G-1853)
Mind Mechanix .... G 302 503-5142
  Milford (G-4505)
One Stop Medical Inc .... G 302 450-4479
  Milford (G-4518)
Paradigm Health LLC .... G 301 233-7221
  Bear (G-277)
Patient First Medical LLC .... G 302 536-7740
  Seaford (G-8341)
Pearl Clinic LLC .... G 302 648-2099
  Millsboro (G-4772)
Peninsula Health LLC .... G 302 945-0440
  Millsboro (G-4777)
Pivotal Medical .... G 302 299-5795
  Bethany Beach (G-422)
Precision Care & Wellness LLC .... G 302 407-5222
  Wilmington (G-12201)
Regional Medical Group LLC .... G 302 993-7890
  Wilmington (G-12359)
Rekindle Family Medicine .... G 302 565-4799
  Wilmington (G-12372)
Repotmecom Inc .... G 301 315-2344
  Georgetown (G-2637)
Rose Health Center Inc .... G 302 441-5987
  Lewes (G-3725)
Select Health Services LLC .... G 504 737-4300
  Newark (G-7403)
Spirits Path To Wellness LLC .... G 302 998-0074
  Wilmington (G-12707)
Sussex Eye Care & Medical Asso ..... G 302 644-8007
  Lewes (G-3772)
Telemed Health Group .... G 561 922-3953
  Dover (G-2137)
Transforming Wellness LLC .... G 302 249-2526
  Millville (G-4856)
United Medical Clinics of De .... F 302 451-5607
  Bear (G-365)
Wellness and Rejuvenation .... G 732 977-6958
  Millsboro (G-4825)
Wellness From Within .... G 717 884-3908
  Lewes (G-3818)

HEALTH & WELFARE COUNCIL

Easter Seal Delaware .... E 302 856-7364
  Georgetown (G-2519)
Ministry of Caring Inc .... C 302 652-8947
  Wilmington (G-11704)

HEALTH AIDS: Exercise Eqpt

Movetec Fitness Equipment LLC ..... G 302 563-4487
  Newark (G-7064)

HEALTH CLUBS

B Fit Enterprises ....F 302 292-1785
  Newark (G-6035)
Body and Soul Fitness LLC ....G 302 536-1278
  Seaford (G-8172)
Crossfit Bear ....G 302 540-4394
  Bear (G-89)
Crossfit Diamond State LLC ....G 201 803-1159
  Wilmington (G-9904)
Crossfit Dover LLC ....G 302 242-5400
  Magnolia (G-3888)
Energy Gym ....F 302 436-9001
  Selbyville (G-8488)
Forever Fit Foundation ....G 302 698-5201
  Dover (G-1561)
Frontline Crossfit ....G 302 229-6467
  New Castle (G-5332)
Higher Power Yoga and Fitness ....G 302 526-2077
  Dover (G-1644)
Missy Muller ....G 302 376-0760
  Middletown (G-4167)
Ricks Fitness & Health Inc ....G 302 684-0316
  Milton (G-4962)
Womens Fitness ....G 302 239-5088
  Wilmington (G-13291)

HEALTH INSURANCE CARRIERS

Chesapeake Rehab Equipment Inc ....G 302 266-6234
  Newark (G-6194)
Cigna Holdings Inc ....F 215 761-1000
  Claymont (G-719)
Highmarks Inc ....B 302 421-3000
  Wilmington (G-10905)

HEALTH MAINTENANCE ORGANIZATION: Insurance Only

Aetna Hose Hook & Ladder Co 9 ....E 302 454-3305
  Newark (G-5916)
Aetna Inc ....G 860 808-3458
  Newark (G-5918)
Coventry Health Care Inc ....G 302 995-6100
  Newark (G-6308)
Coventry Health Care Del Inc ....D 302 995-6100
  Wilmington (G-9881)

HEALTH PRACTITIONERS' OFFICES, NEC

Akhtar Javed ....G 606 515-3698
  Magnolia (G-3879)
Amy Donovan ....G 302 245-8957
  Lewes (G-3337)
Annette Rickolt ....G 302 285-4200
  Middletown (G-3940)
Brandywine Pain Center ....F 302 998-2585
  Wilmington (G-9447)
Catherine Kotalis ....G 302 526-1470
  Dover (G-1259)
Christina Newton ....G 302 454-2400
  Bear (G-72)
Christine W Maynard MD ....G 302 995-7073
  Wilmington (G-9691)
Christopher A Bowens MD ....G 302 834-3700
  Newark (G-6231)
Delaware Vein Center ....G 302 258-8853
  Georgetown (G-2505)
Dorilyn English PHD ....G 302 655-6506
  Wilmington (G-10202)
Dorinda F Dove ....G 302 658-2229
  Wilmington (G-10203)
Eric Barsky ....G 856 495-6988
  Newark (G-6536)
Family Care Associates ....G 302 454-8880
  Newark (G-6566)
Healing Adults & Adolescents ....G 302 836-4000
  Bear (G-180)
Javed Gilani MD ....G 302 478-7160
  Wilmington (G-11130)
Jill Dusak ....G 302 652-4705
  Wilmington (G-11157)
John Johnson Dr ....G 302 999-7104
  Wilmington (G-11174)
Laurie Ann Fishinger ....G 570 460-4370
  Millsboro (G-4718)
Lucila Carmichael Rn ....G 302 324-8901
  New Castle (G-5489)
Lynn Holiday Shynea ....G 302 674-4700
  Dover (G-1808)
Mary Dodson ....G 302 479-0100
  Wilmington (G-11556)

Maryruth L Nich ....G 302 623-1929
  Newark (G-6998)
Melissa A Wolf ....G 716 465-7093
  Lewes (G-3635)
Naomi Ruth Howard ....G 828 284-8721
  Smyrna (G-8684)
Primary Care Delaware L L C ....G 302 744-9645
  Dover (G-1986)
Reddish Walton ....G 302 629-4787
  Seaford (G-8373)
Roberto A Uribe PHD ....G 302 524-0814
  Newark (G-7353)
Tammy S Bennett ....G 302 875-6550
  Laurel (G-3298)
Timothy W McHugh ....G 302 633-1280
  Bear (G-353)

HEALTH SCREENING SVCS

Bayhealth Medical Center Inc ....D 302 744-7033
  Dover (G-1181)
Johnny Walker Enterprises LLC ....G 408 500-6439
  Lewes (G-3575)
Sleep Disorders Center ....G 302 645-3186
  Lewes (G-3747)

HEALTH SYSTEMS AGENCY

AARP ....F 202 434-2277
  Wilmington (G-8895)
Leukemia & Lymphoma Soc Inc ....G 302 661-7300
  Wilmington (G-11377)
Long Term Care Residents Div ....F 302 424-8600
  Milford (G-4477)
Quinn-Miller Group Inc ....G 302 738-9742
  Wilmington (G-12290)

HEARING AID REPAIR SVCS

Delaware Hearing Aids ....G 302 652-3558
  Wilmington (G-10051)

HEARING TESTING SVCS

Vision & Hearing Inc ....G 302 475-8897
  Wilmington (G-13091)

HEAT EXCHANGERS: After Or Inter Coolers Or Condensers, Etc

Baltimore Aircoil Company Inc ....C 302 424-2583
  Milford (G-4317)

HEAT TREATING: Metal

Industrial Metal Treating Corp ....F 302 656-1677
  Wilmington (G-11021)

HEATERS: Room & Wall, Including Radiators

World Class Products LLC ....G 302 737-1441
  Newark (G-7720)

HEATING & AIR CONDITIONING EQPT & SPLYS WHOLESALERS

A & A Mechanical Service Inc ....G 302 234-9949
  Hockessin (G-2949)
Building Systems and Svcs Inc ....E 302 996-0900
  Wilmington (G-9503)
Lycon Investment Company ....G 302 732-0940
  Dagsboro (G-915)
United Refrigeration Inc ....G 302 322-1836
  New Castle (G-5806)
WJC of Delaware LLC ....F 302 323-9600
  New Castle (G-5839)

HEAVY DISTILLATES

Ashland LLC ....E 302 594-5000
  Wilmington (G-9151)

HEELS, BOOT OR SHOE: Rubber, Composition Or Fiber

Vulcan International Corp ....F 302 428-3181
  Wilmington (G-13107)

HELICOPTERS

Central Pacific Helicopters ....G 760 786-4163
  Lewes (G-3411)

HELP SUPPLY SERVICES

Bestemps ....G 302 674-4357
  Dover (G-1198)
BP Staffing Inc ....G 302 999-7213
  Wilmington (G-9407)
County of Kent ....D 302 735-2180
  Dover (G-1317)
Integrity Staffing Solutions ....A 520 276-7775
  Newark (G-6791)
Timber Ridge Inc ....E 302 239-9239
  Hockessin (G-3161)
Transworld Diversfd Svcs Inc ....F 302 777-5902
  Wilmington (G-12959)

HIGHWAY & STREET MAINTENANCE SVCS

Transportation Delaware Dept ....E 302 653-4128
  Middletown (G-4267)

HISTORICAL SOCIETY

Friends of Bellaca Airfield ....G 302 322-3816
  New Castle (G-5331)
Historical Society of Del Inc ....E 302 322-8411
  New Castle (G-5397)
Historical Society of Delaware ....E 302 655-7161
  Wilmington (G-10919)
Maxwell World 937 463-3579
  Dagsboro (G-918)
Milton Historical Society ....F 302 684-1010
  Milton (G-4941)
New Castle Historical Society ....G 302 322-2794
  New Castle (G-5560)
Odessa Historic Foundation ....E 302 378-4119
  Odessa (G-7832)
Rehoboth Beach Historical Soc ....G 302 227-7310
  Rehoboth Beach (G-8052)

HOBBY & COLLECTORS SVCS

Linda & Richard Partnership ....G 302 697-9758
  Dover (G-1790)

HOBBY, TOY & GAME STORES: Chess, Backgammon/Other Drbl Games

Days of Knights ....G 302 366-0963
  Newark (G-6351)

HOLDING COMPANIES, NEC

Educational Assets Corp ....G 302 288-0149
  Wilmington (G-10353)
Faith Fmly Friends Holdg LLC ....F 202 256-4524
  Lewes (G-3490)
Global Innovation Holding LLC ....G 877 276-7701
  Wilmington (G-10727)
Ibi Group (delaware) Inc ....C 614 818-4900
  Wilmington (G-10986)
Instant Global Services Corp ....G 302 514-1047
  Dover (G-1679)
Integrated Green Partners LLC ....G 402 871-8347
  Wilmington (G-11049)
Maruko Holdings Usa LLC ....G 917 515-2776
  Lewes (G-3622)
Nazhat Enterprises Holdings 415 670-9262
  Dover (G-1887)
Willow Tree Equity Holding LLC ....F 213 479-4077
  Lewes (G-3826)
Yhp Holdings LLC 302 636-5401
  Wilmington (G-13327)

HOLDING COMPANIES: Banks

Advantage Delaware ....G 302 365-5398
  Bear (G-14)
Bank of New York Mellon ....G 302 421-2207
  Wilmington (G-9241)
Bank of New York Mellon Corp ....G 302 416-6283
  Wilmington (G-9242)
Cbc Holding Inc ....C 302 254-2000
  Wilmington (G-9600)

HOLDING COMPANIES: Investment, Exc Banks

ALC Funding Corporation ....G 302 656-8923
  Wilmington (G-9002)
Ampco Ues Sub Inc ....G 302 691-6420
  Wilmington (G-9070)
Belchim Crop Prtection US Corp ....F 302 407-3590
  Wilmington (G-9284)

HOLDING COMPANIES: Investment, Exc Banks

Blockweather Holdings LLC .... G 844 644-6837
  Dover *(G-1211)*
Chestnut Investors II Inc .... E 302 478-5142
  Wilmington *(G-9657)*
Clyde Bergemann Pwr Group LLC .... D 770 557-3600
  Lewes *(G-3432)*
Complex Systems Inc .... G 302 651-8300
  Wilmington *(G-9805)*
Crystal Penn Avenue LP .... D 302 846-0613
  Delmar *(G-987)*
Eri Investments Inc .... F 302 656-8089
  Wilmington *(G-10434)*
Gcg Capital LLC .... B 302 703-7610
  Lewes *(G-3509)*
Griffen Corporate Services .... F 302 576-2890
  Wilmington *(G-10783)*
Hall International Ind Corp .... F 302 777-2290
  Wilmington *(G-10825)*
Just Be Holdings LLC .... G 833 454-5273
  Newark *(G-6859)*
Lela Capital LLC .... F 917 428-0304
  Ocean View *(G-7799)*
Limewood Investments Del Inc .... G 302 656-8915
  Wilmington *(G-11391)*
Mangrove Holdings LLC .... F 305 587-2950
  Wilmington *(G-11502)*
Mera Usa LLC .... G 305 577-3443
  Wilmington *(G-11635)*
Midway LLC .... G 302 378-9156
  Middletown *(G-4164)*
Morgan Stnley Intl Hldings Inc .... D 302 657-2000
  Wilmington *(G-11753)*
North Face Apparel Corp .... E 336 424-7755
  Wilmington *(G-11899)*
Oni Acquisition Corp .... G 212 271-3800
  Wilmington *(G-11959)*
Persona Group LLC .... G 302 335-5221
  Magnolia *(G-3902)*
Pitney Bowes Intl Holdings .... F 302 656-8595
  Wilmington *(G-12144)*
Progressive Investment Co Inc .... F 302 656-8597
  Wilmington *(G-12242)*
Rfpc & Wabtec .... G 302 573-3977
  Wilmington *(G-12397)*
Stewart Law Firm .... E 302 652-5200
  Wilmington *(G-12763)*
Suthar Holding Corporation .... E 302 291-2490
  Lewes *(G-3774)*
Sybounheuang Group Inc .... G 302 999-9339
  Wilmington *(G-12827)*

HOLDING COMPANIES: Personal, Exc Banks

Adh Holdings LLC .... G 302 482-4138
  Wilmington *(G-8937)*
Anglin Associates LLC .... F 302 653-3500
  Clayton *(G-833)*
Hchc Uk Holdings Inc .... F 302 225-5007
  Wilmington *(G-10861)*
Hsi Service Corp .... F 302 369-3709
  Newark *(G-6755)*
Hunte Corporate Enterprise LLC .... G 212 710-1341
  Wilmington *(G-10975)*
Labware Global Services Inc .... F 302 658-8444
  Wilmington *(G-11321)*
Labware Holdings Inc .... E 302 658-8444
  Wilmington *(G-11322)*
Playtex Marketing Corp .... G 302 678-6000
  Dover *(G-1970)*
Qps Holdings LLC .... F 302 369-5601
  Newark *(G-7281)*

HOLDING COMPANIES: Public Utility

Exco Inc .... D 905 477-3065
  Wilmington *(G-10458)*
P&L Transportation Inc .... G 800 444-2580
  Wilmington *(G-11997)*
Thales Holding Corporation .... A 302 326-0830
  New Castle *(G-5766)*

HOME CENTER STORES

Home Depot USA Inc .... C 302 838-6818
  Newark *(G-6739)*
Home Depot USA Inc .... C 302 395-1260
  New Castle *(G-5400)*
Home Depot USA Inc .... C 302 735-8864
  Dover *(G-1652)*
Lowes Home Centers LLC .... C 302 376-3006
  Middletown *(G-4137)*
Lowes Home Centers LLC .... C 302 645-0900
  Lewes *(G-3612)*
Lowes Home Centers LLC .... C 302 834-8508
  Bear *(G-238)*
Lowes Home Centers LLC .... C 302 536-4000
  Seaford *(G-8296)*
Lowes Home Centers LLC .... C 302 252-3228
  New Castle *(G-5488)*

HOME ENTERTAINMENT EQPT: Electronic, NEC

Maxbright Inc .... E 281 616-7999
  Lewes *(G-3626)*

HOME FOR THE DESTITUTE

Sunday Breakfast Mission .... F 302 656-8542
  Wilmington *(G-12799)*

HOME FOR THE MENTALLY HANDICAPPED

Advo Opco LLC .... A 302 365-8051
  Bear *(G-16)*
Advoserv Inc .... E 302 365-8050
  Bear *(G-17)*
Advoserv Nj Inc .... F 302 365-8050
  Bear *(G-18)*
Connections Community Support .... D 302 984-2302
  Wilmington *(G-9826)*
Keystone Service Systems Inc .... C 302 286-7234
  Newark *(G-6881)*
Keystone Service Systems Inc .... G 302 273-3952
  Newark *(G-6882)*
National Mentor Holdings Inc .... F 302 934-0512
  Millsboro *(G-4761)*

HOME FOR THE MENTALLY RETARDED, EXC SKILLED OR INTERMEDIATE

Lauren Farms Group Home .... G 302 836-1379
  Bear *(G-230)*

HOME FURNISHINGS WHOLESALERS

Rite Way Distributors .... G 302 535-8507
  Felton *(G-2317)*
Seth Ral & Associates Inc .... G 302 478-9020
  Wilmington *(G-12587)*

HOME HEALTH CARE SVCS

Acts Rtrmnt-Life Cmmnities Inc .... A 302 654-5101
  Wilmington *(G-8928)*
Addus Healthcare Inc .... G 302 995-9010
  Wilmington *(G-8936)*
Addus Healthcare Inc .... E 302 424-4842
  Milford *(G-4302)*
Aegle Health .... G 302 468-0235
  New Castle *(G-5012)*
Affinity Homecare Services .... G 302 264-9363
  Dover *(G-1091)*
Almost Home Day Care .... G 302 220-6731
  Newark *(G-5946)*
Always Best Care .... G 302 409-3710
  Milton *(G-4862)*
Amedisys Inc .... E 302 678-4764
  Dover *(G-1117)*
Anderson Lawn & Home Care .... G 302 376-7115
  Middletown *(G-3938)*
Angels Visiting .... G 302 691-8700
  Wilmington *(G-9085)*
At Home Care Agency .... G 302 883-2059
  Dover *(G-1151)*
At Home Infucare LLC .... G 302 883-2059
  Dover *(G-1152)*
Atkins Home Health Aid Agency .... G 302 832-0315
  Bear *(G-42)*
Bayada Home Health Care Inc .... G 302 322-2300
  New Castle *(G-5074)*
Bayada Home Health Care Inc .... G 302 655-1333
  Wilmington *(G-9264)*
Bc Home Health Care Services .... G 302 746-7844
  Claymont *(G-700)*
Bills Home Care Service LLC .... G 302 526-2071
  Dover *(G-1203)*
Biotek Remedys Inc .... E 877 246-9104
  New Castle *(G-5092)*
Blue Ridge Home Care Inc .... G 302 397-8211
  Dover *(G-1215)*
By The Shore .... G 302 462-0496
  Milton *(G-4871)*
Cain Home Health Services .... F 302 268-6919
  Wilmington *(G-9535)*
Careportmd LLC .... F 302 202-3020
  Wilmington *(G-9567)*
Caring For Life Inc .... E 302 892-2214
  New Castle *(G-5133)*
Caring Hearts Home Care LLC .... G 302 734-9000
  Hartly *(G-2914)*
Caring Matters Home Care .... G 302 993-1121
  Camden *(G-545)*
Caroline M Wiesner .... G 877 220-9755
  Wilmington *(G-9575)*
Carpe Vita Home Care .... G 302 482-4305
  Wilmington *(G-9576)*
Chesapeakecaregivers LLC .... G 302 841-9686
  Seaford *(G-8192)*
Christiana Care Infusion .... G 302 623-0345
  Newark *(G-6219)*
Cindys Home Away From Hme Fam ... G 302 378-0487
  Middletown *(G-3991)*
Comfort Care At Home Inc .... E 302 737-8078
  Newark *(G-6266)*
Dedicated To Home Care LLC .... G 484 470-5013
  New Castle *(G-5220)*
Delaware Home Health Care .... F 302 856-3600
  Georgetown *(G-2500)*
Delaware Hospice Inc .... E 302 678-4444
  Dover *(G-1378)*
Delaware Hospice Inc .... E 302 856-7717
  Milford *(G-4379)*
Dover Health Care Center LLC .... G 302 270-5238
  Dover *(G-1452)*
Envolve Inc .... B 314 349-3571
  Wilmington *(G-10423)*
Epic Health Services Inc .... G 302 504-4092
  Christiana *(G-668)*
Excellent Home Care .... G 302 327-0147
  New Castle *(G-5299)*
Expert Home Care .... G 856 870-6691
  Middletown *(G-4066)*
Fogarty Inc .... G 610 731-4804
  Seaford *(G-8246)*
General Hlthcare Resources LLC .... C 302 998-0469
  Wilmington *(G-10691)*
Generations Home Care Inc .... E 302 322-3100
  Wilmington *(G-10692)*
Grace Visitation Services .... D 302 329-9475
  Milton *(G-4909)*
Griswold Home Care .... G 302 750-4564
  Wilmington *(G-10787)*
Hallies Helping Hands Home .... G 844 277-8911
  Townsend *(G-8792)*
Healthy At Home Care LLC .... G 571 228-5935
  Rehoboth Beach *(G-7958)*
Heartland Hospice Services LLC .... D 302 737-7080
  Newark *(G-6718)*
Heartland Hospice Services LLC .... D 419 252-5743
  Newark *(G-6719)*
Home Care Assistance De .... G 856 625-9934
  Bear *(G-186)*
Home Health Corp America Inc .... F 302 678-4764
  Dover *(G-1653)*
Home Health Heartfel .... G 302 660-2686
  Wilmington *(G-10936)*
Home Health Services By TLC .... E 302 322-5510
  Wilmington *(G-10937)*
Home Instead Senior Care .... G 302 697-6435
  Dover *(G-1654)*
Homewatch Caregivers .... G 302 644-1888
  Lewes *(G-3545)*
Homewatch Caregivers LLC .... F 302 691-5358
  Wilmington *(G-10944)*
Ind Swift Laboratories Inc .... G 302 233-1564
  Dover *(G-1670)*
Ingleside Homes Inc .... D 302 575-0250
  Wilmington *(G-11031)*
Kindheart Homecare .... G 484 479-6582
  Middletown *(G-4124)*
La Red Health Care .... G 757 709-5072
  Georgetown *(G-2586)*
Lieske E2e Home Hlth Care Inc .... E 302 898-1563
  Middletown *(G-4131)*
Lifetime Skills Services LLC .... E 302 378-2911
  Middletown *(G-4132)*
Lynne Betts .... G 302 265-5602
  Seaford *(G-8298)*
Macklyn Home Care .... G 302 690-9397
  Wilmington *(G-11481)*
Macklyn Home Care .... G 302 253-8208
  Georgetown *(G-2594)*

PRODUCT & SERVICES SECTION

Maxim Healthcare Services Inc .... F 302 478-3434
  Wilmington *(G-11579)*
Mayjuun LLC .... G 865 300-7738
  Lewes *(G-3628)*
National Mentor Holdings Inc .... E 732 627-9890
  Millsboro *(G-4760)*
National Mentor Holdings Inc .... F 302 934-0512
  Millsboro *(G-4761)*
Near and Dear Home Care .... G 302 530-6498
  Newark *(G-7088)*
Neighborly Home Care .... G 610 420-1868
  Wilmington *(G-11831)*
No Place Like Home LLC .... G 302 528-8682
  Bear *(G-266)*
Nurse Next Door Home Care Svcs .... G 302 264-1021
  Camden *(G-594)*
Nurses N Kids Inc .... E 302 424-1770
  Milford *(G-4515)*
Option Care Enterprises Inc .... E 302 355-6100
  Newark *(G-7158)*
Pennsula Home Care LLC .... G 302 629-4914
  Seaford *(G-8351)*
Perry & Assoc .... G 302 472-8701
  Wilmington *(G-12088)*
Philadelph Ft Ankl Asscts .... G 215 465-5342
  Wilmington *(G-12112)*
Phyllis M Green .... G 302 354-6986
  Bear *(G-283)*
Premier Immediate Med Care LLC .... G 610 226-6200
  Hockessin *(G-3125)*
Private Duty Home Care .... G 302 482-3502
  Wilmington *(G-12232)*
Pro 2 Respiratory Services .... G 302 514-9843
  Smyrna *(G-8693)*
R&R Homecare .... G 302 478-3448
  Wilmington *(G-12299)*
Ridgaway Philips of Delaware .... G 302 323-1436
  New Castle *(G-5679)*
Right At Home .... G 302 652-1550
  Wilmington *(G-12422)*
Robert Bird .... F 302 654-4003
  Wilmington *(G-12435)*
Saint Home Health Care .... G 302 514-9597
  Milford *(G-4551)*
Senior Home Help LLC .... G 302 335-4243
  Felton *(G-2320)*
Seniortech Inc .... G 302 234-1274
  Hockessin *(G-3143)*
Shorecare of Delaware .... G 302 724-5235
  Dover *(G-2080)*
Shorecare of Delaware .... G 302 724-5235
  Dover *(G-2081)*
Special Care Inc .... F 302 644-6990
  Lewes *(G-3760)*
Special Care Inc .... G 302 456-9904
  Wilmington *(G-12695)*
T & L Consulting Services LLC .... G 302 573-1585
  Wilmington *(G-12843)*
TLC Home Care .... G 302 983-5720
  Wilmington *(G-12917)*
Trinity Home Health Care Corp .... E 302 838-2710
  Newark *(G-7594)*
Trinity Home Health Care LLC .... G 410 620-9366
  Newark *(G-7595)*
Vitas Healthcare Corporation .... D 302 451-4000
  Newark *(G-7661)*
Vna of Delaware .... G 302 454-5422
  Newark *(G-7663)*
Wow Tech USA Ltd .... G 613 828-6678
  Wilmington *(G-13306)*

HOME IMPROVEMENT & RENOVATION CONTRACTOR AGENCY

A Fields Unlimited LLC .... G 800 484-2331
  Newark *(G-5866)*
Bennett & Bennett Inc .... F 302 990-8939
  New Castle *(G-5081)*
Community Services Corporation ..... F 302 368-4400
  Newark *(G-6272)*
Dream Clean Team LP .... F 302 981-5154
  Newark *(G-6473)*
Gb Home Improvement .... G 302 654-5411
  Wilmington *(G-10681)*
White Eagle Integrations .... G 302 464-0550
  Middletown *(G-4285)*

HOMEBUILDERS & OTHER OPERATIVE BUILDERS

Broadpoint Construction LLC .... G 302 567-2100
  Rehoboth Beach *(G-7878)*
J D Construction .... G 302 292-8789
  Newark *(G-6815)*
No Joke I LLC .... G 302 395-0882
  New Castle *(G-5573)*
Nvr Inc .... E 302 731-5770
  Newark *(G-7140)*

HOMEFURNISHING STORES: Cutlery

Willey Knives Inc .... G 302 349-4070
  Greenwood *(G-2768)*

HOMEFURNISHING STORES: Fireplaces & Wood Burning Stoves

Walls Farm and Garden Ctr Inc .... G 302 422-4565
  Milford *(G-4594)*

HOMEFURNISHING STORES: Lighting Fixtures

Colonial Electric Supply Co .... F 302 998-9993
  New Castle *(G-5181)*
Denney Electric Supply Del Inc .... G 302 934-8885
  Millsboro *(G-4677)*
Grossman Electric Supply Inc .... G 302 655-5561
  New Castle *(G-5364)*
Light Action Inc .... F 302 328-7800
  New Castle *(G-5481)*

HOMEFURNISHING STORES: Window Furnishings

Rementer Brothers Inc .... G 302 249-4250
  Milton *(G-4956)*

HOMEFURNISHINGS & SPLYS, WHOLESALE: Decorative

Selling Dreams LLC .... G 302 746-7999
  Claymont *(G-803)*
Williams-Sonoma Stores Inc .... E 302 368-7707
  Newark *(G-7700)*

HOMEFURNISHINGS, WHOLESALE: Blankets

Advacare LLC .... G 302 448-5045
  Wilmington *(G-8944)*

HOMEFURNISHINGS, WHOLESALE: Draperies

F Schumacher & Co .... C 302 454-3200
  Newark *(G-6561)*

HOMEFURNISHINGS, WHOLESALE: Fireplace Eqpt & Access

Fireside Heart & Home .... G 302 337-3025
  Bridgeville *(G-470)*

HOMEFURNISHINGS, WHOLESALE: Kitchenware

Franke USA Holding Inc .... F 615 462-4000
  Wilmington *(G-10614)*
Middletown Kitchen and Bath .... G 302 376-5766
  Middletown *(G-4158)*

HOMEFURNISHINGS, WHOLESALE: Sheets, Textile

Avs Industries LLC .... G 302 221-1705
  New Castle *(G-5060)*
Microdry Inc .... G 302 416-3021
  Wilmington *(G-11675)*
Ready Set Textiles Inc .... G 302 518-6583
  Rehoboth Beach *(G-8045)*

HOMEMAKERS' SVCS

Reliable Home Services LLC .... G 302 246-6000
  Wilmington *(G-12375)*

HOMES FOR THE ELDERLY

Home For Aged Wmn-Mnquadale HM ... C 302 654-1810
  Wilmington *(G-10935)*
Peninsula Untd Mthdst Hmes Inc ..... G 302 235-6800
  Hockessin *(G-3114)*
Peninsula Untd Mthdst Hmes Inc ..... C 302 654-5101
  Wilmington *(G-12064)*
Sacred Heart Village I Inc .... E 302 428-0801
  Wilmington *(G-12513)*
Sacred Heart Village II Inc .... G 302 428-3702
  Wilmington *(G-12514)*
Westminster Village Dover .... G 302 744-3527
  Dover *(G-2216)*

HOMES, MODULAR: Wooden

Cool Branch Associates LLC .... G 302 629-5363
  Seaford *(G-8206)*
Henlopen Homes Inc .... G 302 684-0860
  Lewes *(G-3541)*

HONES

Spectrum Hone & Lace Llc .... G 313 268-5455
  Newark *(G-7469)*

HOOKS: Gate

Fencemaxcom Inc .... G 302 343-9063
  Hartly *(G-2922)*

HORSES WHOLESALERS

Andy Mast .... G 302 653-5014
  Dover *(G-1125)*

HORSES, RACING

Sharp Farm .... G 302 652-7729
  Wilmington *(G-12594)*
Sharp Farm .... F 302 378-9606
  Middletown *(G-4239)*

HORSESHOEING SVCS

Michael Matthew Sponaugle .... G 302 566-1010
  Harrington *(G-2868)*

HOSES & BELTING: Rubber & Plastic

Industrial Valves & Fittings .... F 302 326-2494
  New Castle *(G-5417)*

HOSPITALS: AMA Approved Residency

Christiana Care Hlth Svcs Inc .... C 302 623-7201
  Newark *(G-6217)*

HOSPITALS: Children's

Lawall Prosthetics - Orthotics .... G 302 677-0693
  Dover *(G-1769)*

HOSPITALS: Chronic Disease

Health & Social Svcs Del Dept .... A 302 223-1000
  Smyrna *(G-8650)*

HOSPITALS: Maternity

Home of Divine Providence Inc .... G 302 654-1184
  Wilmington *(G-10938)*

HOSPITALS: Medical & Surgical

Ai Dupont Hosp For Children .... A 302 651-4620
  Wilmington *(G-8984)*
Atlantic General Hospital Corp .... F 302 524-5007
  Selbyville *(G-8451)*
Bayhealth Med Ctr Inc-OCC Hlth ...... E 302 678-1303
  Dover *(G-1180)*
Bayhealth Medical Center Inc .... A 302 422-3311
  Milford *(G-4320)*
Bayhealth Medical Center Inc .... E 302 422-3311
  Dover *(G-1182)*
Bayview Endoscopy Center .... F 302 644-0455
  Lewes *(G-3365)*
Beebe Healthcare .... G 302 934-5052
  Millsboro *(G-4641)*
Beebe Hospital Hs .... G 302 645-3565
  Lewes *(G-3369)*
Beebe Medical Center Inc .... C 302 645-3100
  Rehoboth Beach *(G-7862)*

Employee Codes: A=Over 500 employees, B=251-500
C=101-250, D=51-100, E=20-50, F=10-19, G=1-9

HOSPITALS: Medical & Surgical

Beebe Medical Center Inc .... A 302 645-3300
  Lewes (G-3370)
Beebe Medical Center Inc .... C 302 645-3300
  Lewes (G-3371)
Beebe Medical Center Inc .... E 302 645-3629
  Lewes (G-3372)
Beebe Medical Center Inc .... E 302 947-9767
  Millsboro (G-4642)
Beebe Medical Center Inc .... G 302 856-9729
  Georgetown (G-2453)
Brandywine Veterinary Hospital .... G 302 476-8779
  Wilmington (G-9460)
Brian Costleigh LLC .... G 302 645-3775
  Rehoboth Beach (G-7876)
Cancer Care Ctrs At Bay Hlth .... F 302 674-4401
  Dover (G-1249)
Catholic Health East .... G 302 325-4900
  New Castle (G-5137)
Cedar Tree Surgical Center .... F 302 945-9766
  Millsboro (G-4658)
Central Del Endoscopy Unit .... G 302 677-1617
  Dover (G-1264)
Central Delaware Surgery Ctr .... F 302 744-6801
  Dover (G-1268)
Christana Care Vsclar Spcalist .... F 302 733-5700
  Newark (G-6203)
Christiana Care .... G 302 654-4925
  Wilmington (G-9675)
Christiana Care .... F 302 633-3750
  Wilmington (G-9676)
Christiana Care Health Sys Inc .... F 302 623-7500
  Wilmington (G-9677)
Christiana Care Health Sys Inc .... G 302 733-1000
  Newark (G-6212)
Christiana Care Health Sys Inc .... G 302 449-3000
  Middletown (G-3988)
Christiana Care Health Sys Inc .... F 302 733-5700
  Newark (G-6213)
Christiana Care Health Sys Inc .... C 302 733-1000
  Wilmington (G-9679)
Christiana Care Hlth Svcs Inc .... F 302 327-5820
  New Castle (G-5154)
Christiana Care Hlth Svcs Inc .... B 302 733-1900
  Newark (G-6215)
Christiana Care Hlth Svcs Inc .... C 302 327-3959
  New Castle (G-5155)
Christiana Care Hlth Svcs Inc .... E 302 733-5437
  Newark (G-6216)
Christiana Care Hlth Svcs Inc .... G 302 733-1805
  Wilmington (G-9684)
Cuhiana Care Health System .... G 302 733-1780
  Newark (G-6325)
Cynthia Crosser DC Fiama .... G 302 239-5014
  Wilmington (G-9933)
David E Driban .... G 302 322-0860
  New Castle (G-5216)
Delaware Bay Surgical Svc PA .... F 302 645-5650
  Lewes (G-3454)
Delaware Center For Oral Srgry .... F 302 369-1000
  Newark (G-6367)
Delaware Outpatient Center .... D 302 738-0300
  Newark (G-6401)
Endoscopy Center of Delaware .... F 302 892-2710
  Newark (G-6527)
Envision Healthcare Corp .... F 302 644-3852
  Lewes (G-3485)
Frenius Medical Care .... G 302 421-9177
  Wilmington (G-10633)
Healthpartners Delmarva LLC .... G 302 744-6008
  Dover (G-1641)
Hospitalists of Delaware .... G 302 984-2577
  Wilmington (G-10958)
Iqarus Americas Inc .... E 407 222-5726
  Wilmington (G-11081)
Jr Board of Kent Gen Hospital .... G 302 744-7128
  Dover (G-1710)
Kent General Hospital .... G 302 744-7688
  Dover (G-1734)
Kent General Hospital .... G 302 378-1199
  Middletown (G-4120)
Kent General Hospital .... E 302 430-5731
  Milford (G-4463)
Kent General Hospital .... G 302 653-2010
  Smyrna (G-8667)
Nemours Foundation .... A 302 651-4000
  Wilmington (G-11833)
North Wilmington Womens Center .... G 302 529-7900
  Wilmington (G-11902)
Peninsula Regional Medical Ctr .... G 302 436-8004
  Selbyville (G-8529)
Peninsula Regional Medical Ctr .... F 302 732-8400
  Dagsboro (G-929)
Rockford Center .... D 302 996-5480
  Newark (G-7354)
Route 24 Animal Hospital .... G 302 945-2330
  Millsboro (G-4796)
Select Medical Corporation .... D 302 421-4545
  Wilmington (G-12574)
Southern Delaware Surgery Ctr .... F 302 644-6992
  Rehoboth Beach (G-8084)
St Francis Family Care .... G 302 554-5127
  New Castle (G-5734)
St Francis Hospital .... G 302 369-9370
  Newark (G-7477)
St Francis Hospital Inc .... A 616 685-3538
  Wilmington (G-12722)
Trinity Health Corporation .... F 302 421-4100
  Wilmington (G-12976)
Womens Health Ctr Christn Care .... F 302 428-5810
  Wilmington (G-13292)
World Hospital Inc .... G 609 254-3391
  Bear (G-380)

HOSPITALS: Mental Retardation

Cadia Rhabilitation Pike Creek .... E 302 455-0808
  Wilmington (G-9529)
Oak Hrc New Castle LLC .... D 302 328-2580
  New Castle (G-5584)

HOSPITALS: Mental, Exc For The Mentally Retarded

Psychotherapeutic Services .... E 302 672-7159
  Dover (G-1994)

HOSPITALS: Psychiatric

Alternative Solutions .... G 302 542-9081
  Georgetown (G-2429)
Children Youth & Their Fam .... D 302 577-4270
  New Castle (G-5147)
Health & Social Svcs Del Dept .... F 302 255-2700
  New Castle (G-5384)
Health & Social Svcs Del Dept .... A 302 255-2700
  New Castle (G-5386)
Phc Inc .... F 313 831-3500
  New Castle (G-5621)
Rockford Center .... D 302 996-5480
  Newark (G-7354)
Social Health Innovations Inc .... G 917 476-9355
  Dover (G-2091)

HOSPITALS: Rehabilitation, Alcoholism

1212 Corporation .... G 302 764-4048
  Wilmington (G-8844)
Brandywine Counseling .... F 302 454-3020
  Newark (G-6116)
Central Delaware Committee .... G 302 854-0172
  Georgetown (G-2466)
Children Fmilies First Del Inc .... E 302 856-2388
  Georgetown (G-2468)
Horizon House Inc .... G 302 798-1960
  Claymont (G-764)

HOSPITALS: Rehabilitation, Drug Addiction

Advanced Treatment Systems .... F 302 792-0700
  Claymont (G-687)
Aquila of Delaware Inc .... G 302 856-9746
  Georgetown (G-2432)
Crest Central .... F 302 736-0576
  Dover (G-1322)
Thresholds Inc .... G 302 827-4478
  Lewes (G-3783)
Westside N Begnings Yth Imprvm .... G 302 227-5442
  Rehoboth Beach (G-8113)

HOSPITALS: Specialty, NEC

B M A Central Delaware .... G 302 678-5718
  Dover (G-1165)
Compassionate Care Hospice .... G 302 856-1486
  Georgetown (G-2480)
Encompass Health Corporation .... C 302 464-3400
  Middletown (G-4058)
Presbyterian Senior Living .... C 302 744-3600
  Dover (G-1984)
Select Specialty Hospital .... D 302 421-4590
  Wilmington (G-12575)

HOTEL & MOTEL RESERVATION SVCS

Lookinn Inc .... G 302 839-2088
  Dover (G-1796)
Smart Hospitality & MGT LLC .... E 212 444-1989
  Wilmington (G-12654)

HOTEL: Franchised

764 Dover Leipsic LLC .... F 302 736-1204
  Dover (G-1071)
Atlantic Budget Inn Millsboro .... E 302 934-6711
  Millsboro (G-4632)
Blue Hen Hotel LLC .... G 302 266-0354
  Newark (G-6099)
Comfort Suites .... F 302 628-5400
  Seaford (G-8202)
Comfort Suites Motel .... G 302 266-6600
  Hockessin (G-2993)
Rama Corporation .... E 302 266-6600
  Hockessin (G-3128)
Towne Place Suites By Marriott .... F 302 369-6212
  Newark (G-7580)
Wilmington Christiana Cou .... F 302 456-3800
  Newark (G-7701)

HOTEL: YMCA/YMHA

Young Mens Christian Associat .... C 302 571-6900
  Wilmington (G-13332)
Young MNS Chrstn Assn Wlmngton ...... E 302 221-9622
  Wilmington (G-13334)

HOTELS & MOTELS

44 New England Management Co .... E 302 479-7900
  Wilmington (G-8862)
900 F Street Owner LLC .... D 212 355-1500
  Wilmington (G-8869)
Boardwalk Plaza Incorporated .... D 302 227-0441
  Rehoboth Beach (G-7872)
Brighton Hotels LLC .... E 302 227-5780
  Rehoboth Beach (G-7877)
Canal New Orleans Hotel LLC .... E 504 962-0500
  Wilmington (G-9548)
Everest Hotel Group LLC .... F 213 272-0088
  Camden (G-569)
Everest Sonoma Management LLC ...... D 213 272-0088
  Camden (G-570)
Green Room Restaurant .... E 302 594-3100
  Wilmington (G-10773)
Homewood Suites .... E 302 565-2100
  Wilmington (G-10945)
Kenny Simpler .... G 302 226-2900
  Rehoboth Beach (G-7978)
Luxiasuites LLC .... E 302 778-2900
  Wilmington (G-11459)
Luxiasuites LLC .... G 302 426-1200
  Wilmington (G-11461)
Milford Lodging LLC .... E 302 839-5000
  Milford (G-4500)
New Orleans Hotel Equity LLC .... G 302 757-7300
  Wilmington (G-11868)
Packem Associates Partnership .... G 302 227-5780
  Rehoboth Beach (G-8027)
Pagoda Hotel Inc .... A 808 922-1233
  New Castle (G-5597)
Premier Entertainment III LLC .... E 302 674-4600
  Dover (G-1982)
Residence Inn Dover .... F 302 677-0777
  Dover (G-2033)
Resort Custom Homes .... G 302 645-8222
  Lewes (G-3717)
Sabre Amb LLC .... E 302 299-1400
  New Castle (G-5692)
Zwaanendael LLC .... G 302 645-6466
  Lewes (G-3837)

HOUSE & BABYSITTING SVCS

Selwor Enterprises Inc .... F 302 454-9454
  Newark (G-7404)

HOUSEHOLD APPLIANCE REPAIR SVCS

Kelly Appliance Service .... G 302 628-5396
  Seaford (G-8286)

HOUSEHOLD APPLIANCE STORES

Johns Washer Repair .... G 302 792-2333
  Claymont (G-769)

PRODUCT & SERVICES SECTION

Kelly Appliance Service .... G 302 628-5396
  Seaford *(G-8286)*
Lowes Home Centers LLC .... C 302 479-7799
  Wilmington *(G-11444)*
Lowes Home Centers LLC .... C 302 934-3740
  Millsboro *(G-4727)*
Lowes Home Centers LLC .... C 302 376-3006
  Middletown *(G-4137)*
Lowes Home Centers LLC .... C 302 735-7500
  Dover *(G-1798)*
Lowes Home Centers LLC .... C 302 645-0900
  Lewes *(G-3612)*
Lowes Home Centers LLC .... C 302 834-8508
  Bear *(G-238)*
Lowes Home Centers LLC .... C 302 697-0700
  Camden *(G-589)*
Lowes Home Centers LLC .... C 302 781-1154
  Newark *(G-6953)*
Lowes Home Centers LLC .... C 302 536-4000
  Seaford *(G-8296)*
Lowes Home Centers LLC .... C 302 252-3228
  New Castle *(G-5488)*

HOUSEHOLD APPLIANCE STORES: Electric

Del-Mar Appliance of Delaware .... G 302 674-2414
  Dover *(G-1352)*
Delmarva Refrigeration Inc .... G 302 846-2727
  Delmar *(G-992)*

HOUSEHOLD APPLIANCE STORES: Electric Household, Major

ABC Sales & Service Inc .... E 302 652-3683
  Wilmington *(G-8899)*
C B Joe TV & Appliances Inc .... F 302 322-7600
  New Castle *(G-5125)*
Interiors By Kim Inc .... G 302 537-2480
  Ocean View *(G-7794)*

HOUSEHOLD APPLIANCE STORES: Garbage Disposals

Clean Earth New Castle Inc .... E 302 427-6633
  New Castle *(G-5177)*

HOUSEHOLD APPLIANCE STORES: Gas Appliances

Hatfield Gas Connections Inc .... G 302 945-2354
  Lewes *(G-3536)*
Schagrin Gas Co .... E 302 378-2000
  Middletown *(G-4232)*

HOUSEHOLD ARTICLES, EXC FURNITURE: Cut Stone

Anta Import/Export LLC .... G 302 653-4542
  Clayton *(G-834)*

HOUSEHOLD FURNISHINGS, NEC

Bethany Resort Furn Whse .... G 302 251-4101
  Selbyville *(G-8456)*
Bethrant Industries LLC .... G 484 343-5435
  New Castle *(G-5088)*
Katherine Klyc Intl LLC .... G 917 312-0789
  New Castle *(G-5452)*

HOUSEKEEPING & MAID SVCS

D A Jones Inc .... G 302 836-9238
  Selbyville *(G-8476)*
J & W Mc Cormick Ltd .... E 302 798-0336
  Wilmington *(G-11099)*
Maids For You Inc .... F 302 328-9050
  New Castle *(G-5500)*
Markatos Services Inc .... E 302 792-0606
  Wilmington *(G-11532)*
Merry Maids Inc .... F 302 698-9038
  Dover *(G-1841)*
TMI Company Store Holding Corp .... E 302 992-0220
  Wilmington *(G-12920)*

HOUSES: Rooming & Boarding

Ministry of Caring Inc .... G 302 652-0904
  Wilmington *(G-11706)*

HOUSEWARES, ELECTRIC: Heating Units, Electric Appliances

Econat Inc .... G 201 925-5239
  Middletown *(G-4048)*

HOUSEWARES, ELECTRIC: Roasters

McGinnis Farms LLC .... G 302 841-8175
  Dagsboro *(G-920)*

HOUSEWARES: Dishes, Plastic

Pacifico Industrial Ltd .... E 213 435-1181
  Newark *(G-7170)*

HOUSING AUTHORITY OPERATOR

Cabell Corp .... G 302 398-8125
  Harrington *(G-2822)*
Elf Homes Inc .... G 650 918-7829
  Wilmington *(G-10374)*
Lutheran Senior Svcs of Dover .... F 302 674-1408
  Dover *(G-1807)*

HUMAN RESOURCE, SOCIAL WORK & WELFARE ADMINISTRATION SVCS

Health & Social Svcs Del Dept .... F 302 337-8261
  Bridgeville *(G-480)*
Health & Social Svcs Del Dept .... D 302 391-3505
  New Castle *(G-5387)*

HUMANE SOCIETIES

Delaware Humane Association .... E 302 571-0111
  Wilmington *(G-10055)*
Delaware S P C A .... E 302 998-2281
  Newark *(G-6409)*
Delaware S P C A .... G 302 856-6361
  Georgetown *(G-2502)*
Delaware Spca .... G 302 698-3006
  Camden *(G-559)*
Faithful Friends Inc .... D 302 427-8514
  Wilmington *(G-10479)*
Kent County Scty For The Prvnt .... E 302 698-3006
  Camden *(G-587)*
Spca .... G 302 698-3006
  Newark *(G-7465)*

HYDRAULIC EQPT REPAIR SVC

Anderson Group Inc .... G 302 478-6160
  Wilmington *(G-9078)*
Sussex Hydraulics Sales & Svcs .... G 302 846-9702
  Delmar *(G-1033)*

ICE

Hanover Foods Corporation .... C 302 653-9281
  Clayton *(G-855)*
Kimos Hawaiian Shave Ice .... G 302 998-1763
  Wilmington *(G-11261)*
Rockford Ice .... G 302 478-7280
  Wilmington *(G-12449)*
Seaford Ice .... G 302 629-2562
  Seaford *(G-8390)*
Seaford Ice Inc .... G 302 629-2562
  Seaford *(G-8391)*

ICE CREAM & ICES WHOLESALERS

Hy-Point Dairy Farms Inc .... C 302 478-1414
  Wilmington *(G-10979)*

INCINERATORS

Chemfirst Inc .... D 302 774-1000
  Wilmington *(G-9646)*

INDL & PERSONAL SVC PAPER WHOLESALERS

Forever Inc .... G 302 368-1440
  Newark *(G-6604)*
Freedom Paper Company LLC .... G 443 542-5845
  Wilmington *(G-10629)*

INDL & PERSONAL SVC PAPER, WHOL: Bags, Paper/Disp Plastic

Forever Inc .... E 302 594-0400
  Wilmington *(G-10592)*

Fulton Paper Company .... F 302 594-0400
  Wilmington *(G-10648)*
Wayden Inc .... G 302 798-1642
  Claymont *(G-817)*

INDL & PERSONAL SVC PAPER, WHOL: Paper, Wrap/Coarse/Prdts

A E Moore Incorporated .... F 302 934-7055
  Millsboro *(G-4620)*
Diamond Chemical & Supply Co .... E 302 656-7786
  Wilmington *(G-10139)*
Forever Inc .... G 302 449-2100
  Middletown *(G-4076)*

INDL & PERSONAL SVC PAPER, WHOLESALE: Boxes & Containers

Pet Poultry Products LLC .... E 302 337-8223
  Bridgeville *(G-508)*

INDL & PERSONAL SVC PAPER, WHOLESALE: Towels, Paper

Orlando J Camp & Associates .... G 302 478-3720
  Wilmington *(G-11975)*

INDL EQPT CLEANING SVCS

Richards Investment Group Corp .... G 302 399-0450
  Smyrna *(G-8701)*

INDL EQPT SVCS

Industrial Resource Netwrk Inc .... F 302 888-2905
  Wilmington *(G-11022)*
Progressive Systems Inc .... G 302 732-3321
  Frankford *(G-2381)*

INDL MACHINERY & EQPT WHOLESALERS

Accudyne Systems Inc .... E 302 369-5390
  Newark *(G-5889)*
Advance Marine LLC .... G 302 656-2111
  Wilmington *(G-8947)*
Autotype Holdings (usa) Inc .... C 302 378-3100
  Middletown *(G-3956)*
Billy Warren Son .... G 302 349-5767
  Greenwood *(G-2717)*
Experienced Auto Parts Inc .... G 302 322-3344
  New Castle *(G-5301)*
First State Automation LLC .... G 302 743-4798
  New Castle *(G-5314)*
Firstchoice Group America LLC .... G 425 242-8626
  Lewes *(G-3499)*
Groff Tractor & Equipment LLC .... F 302 349-5760
  Greenwood *(G-2742)*
Lundberg Tech Inc - America .... G 302 738-2500
  Newark *(G-6958)*
Lweco Group LLC .... G 302 296-8035
  Millsboro *(G-4728)*
McCabes Mechanical Service Inc .... F 302 854-9001
  Georgetown *(G-2599)*
Mechanics Paradise Inc .... F 302 652-8863
  New Castle *(G-5513)*
Messick & Gray Cnstr Inc .... E 302 337-8777
  Bridgeville *(G-497)*
Pascale Industries Inc .... F 302 421-9400
  New Castle *(G-5606)*
Skab International Corporation .... G 412 475-2221
  Dover *(G-2087)*
Supercritical Fluid Tech .... G 302 738-3420
  Newark *(G-7511)*
Uet International Inc .... G 302 834-0234
  Bear *(G-364)*
Vallen Distribution Inc .... G 302 992-5604
  Wilmington *(G-13044)*
Vallen Distribution Inc .... G 856 542-1453
  Delaware City *(G-968)*
World Wide Trading Brokers .... G 302 368-7041
  Newark *(G-7722)*

INDL MACHINERY REPAIR & MAINTENANCE

Brooks Machine Inc .... G 302 674-5900
  Dover *(G-1235)*
Bruce Industrial Co Inc .... D 302 655-9616
  New Castle *(G-5118)*
C H P T Manufacturing Inc .... G 302 856-7660
  Georgetown *(G-2461)*
Cooper Bearings Inc .... F 302 858-5056
  Georgetown *(G-2484)*

INDL MACHINERY REPAIR & MAINTENANCE

F and M Equipment Ltd ....G....... 302 715-5382
  Laurel *(G-3229)*
Fiduks Industrial Services Inc ....F 302 994-2534
  Wilmington *(G-10536)*
Groff Tractor & Equipment LLC ....F 302 349-5760
  Greenwood *(G-2742)*
International Electrical Svcs ....G....... 302 438-6096
  Wilmington *(G-11065)*
Messick & Gray Cnstr Inc ....E 302 337-8777
  Bridgeville *(G-497)*
Messick & Gray Cnstr Inc ....F 302 337-8445
  Bridgeville *(G-498)*
Shark Service Center LLC ....G....... 302 337-8233
  Bridgeville *(G-520)*
Square One Electric Service Co ....F 302 678-0400
  Dover *(G-2099)*
Xerox Corporation ....E 302 792-5100
  Wilmington *(G-13319)*

INDL PROCESS INSTRUMENTS: Analyzers

Romer Labs Technology Inc ....E 855 337-6637
  Newark *(G-7363)*

INDL PROCESS INSTRUMENTS: Control

Acorn Energy Inc ....G....... 302 656-1708
  Wilmington *(G-8923)*
K-Tron Investment Co ....E 856 589-0500
  Wilmington *(G-11217)*
Testek Aerospace Holdings LLC ....G....... 302 658-7581
  Wilmington *(G-12885)*

INDL PROCESS INSTRUMENTS: Digital Display, Process Variables

DLS Discovery ....G....... 302 654-3345
  Wilmington *(G-10175)*
Quboai Corporation ....G....... 484 889-5789
  Wilmington *(G-12285)*

INDL PROCESS INSTRUMENTS: Indl Flow & Measuring

Eeco Inc ....G....... 302 456-1448
  Newark *(G-6506)*

INDL PROCESS INSTRUMENTS: On-Stream Gas Or Liquid Analysis

American Meter Holdings Corp ....G....... 302 477-0208
  Wilmington *(G-9054)*

INDL PROCESS INSTRUMENTS: Water Quality Monitoring/Cntrl Sys

Ecomo Inc ....G....... 412 567-3867
  Dover *(G-1502)*
Engineered Systems & Designs ....G....... 302 456-0446
  Wilmington *(G-10402)*

INDL SPLYS WHOLESALERS

E-Industrial Suppliers LLC ....G....... 302 251-6210
  Wilmington *(G-10313)*
Eastern Shore Equipment Co ....G....... 302 697-3300
  Camden Wyoming *(G-633)*
Greenberg Supply Co Inc ....E 302 656-4496
  Wilmington *(G-10777)*
Griffith Industrial Supply ....G....... 302 731-0574
  Newark *(G-6691)*
Industrial Products of Del ....F 302 328-6648
  New Castle *(G-5415)*
Motion Industries Inc ....F 302 462-3130
  Delmar *(G-1023)*
MSC Industrial Direct Co Inc ....F 302 998-1214
  Wilmington *(G-11771)*
Rhino Lnngs Del Auto Style Inc ....F 302 368-4660
  Newark *(G-7335)*
Sid Tool Co Inc ....F 302 322-5441
  New Castle *(G-5707)*
Standard Industrial Supply Co ....G....... 302 656-1631
  Wilmington *(G-12735)*
State Line Machine Inc ....F 302 478-0285
  Wilmington *(G-12745)*
Summit Aviation Inc ....D....... 302 834-5400
  Middletown *(G-4250)*
Urie & Blanton Inc ....G....... 302 658-8604
  Wilmington *(G-13037)*
W T Schrider & Sons Inc ....F 302 934-1900
  Millsboro *(G-4822)*

Wesco Distribution Inc ....F 302 655-9611
  Wilmington *(G-13162)*

INDL SPLYS, WHOL: Fasteners, Incl Nuts, Bolts, Screws, Etc

Building Fasteners Inc ....G....... 302 738-0671
  Newark *(G-6132)*
Fastenal Company ....G....... 302 424-4149
  Milford *(G-4411)*
Froggys Industrial Supply Inc ....G....... 302 508-2340
  Smyrna *(G-8637)*
Integra Services Tech Inc ....F 302 792-0346
  Claymont *(G-765)*
Skyline Supply Inc ....G....... 302 894-9190
  Newark *(G-7438)*

INDL SPLYS, WHOLESALE: Abrasives

Arlon Partners Inc ....G....... 302 595-1234
  Bear *(G-35)*

INDL SPLYS, WHOLESALE: Bearings

Applied Constructal Inc ....G....... 203 606-1656
  Bethel *(G-440)*
Philadlphia Ball Rller Bearing ....G....... 215 727-0982
  Wilmington *(G-12113)*
Power Trans Inc ....G....... 302 322-7110
  New Castle *(G-5634)*
Ruby Industrial Tech LLC ....G....... 302 674-2943
  Dover *(G-2045)*

INDL SPLYS, WHOLESALE: Drums, New Or Reconditioned

First State Steel Drum Co ....G....... 302 655-2422
  New Castle *(G-5318)*
Industrial Resource Netwrk Inc ....F 302 888-2905
  Wilmington *(G-11022)*
Petroserv Inc ....G....... 302 398-3260
  Harrington *(G-2873)*

INDL SPLYS, WHOLESALE: Electric Tools

WW Grainger Inc ....F 302 322-1840
  New Castle *(G-5842)*

INDL SPLYS, WHOLESALE: Filters, Indl

Dfc Industries Inc ....G....... 215 292-1572
  New Castle *(G-5249)*
Phoenix Filtration Inc ....G....... 302 998-8805
  Wilmington *(G-12123)*

INDL SPLYS, WHOLESALE: Fittings

Mitusha International Corp ....G....... 302 674-2977
  Dover *(G-1863)*
Vertex Industries Inc ....G....... 302 472-0601
  Wilmington *(G-13066)*

INDL SPLYS, WHOLESALE: Hydraulic & Pneumatic Pistons/Valves

Bristol Industrial Corporation ....F 302 322-1100
  New Castle *(G-5115)*

INDL SPLYS, WHOLESALE: Power Transmission, Eqpt & Apparatus

Electric Motor Wholesale Inc ....F 302 653-1844
  Camden Wyoming *(G-635)*

INDL SPLYS, WHOLESALE: Rubber Goods, Mechanical

Delmarva Rubber & Gasket Co ....G....... 302 424-8300
  Bridgeville *(G-466)*
Polymart Inc ....G....... 302 656-1470
  Hockessin *(G-3122)*
Trelltex Inc ....F 302 738-4313
  Newark *(G-7583)*

INDL SPLYS, WHOLESALE: Tools

Carney Machinery Co ....G....... 302 571-8382
  Wilmington *(G-9574)*

INDL SPLYS, WHOLESALE: Tools, NEC

Case Construction Inc ....E 302 737-3800
  Newark *(G-6164)*

Independent Metal Strap Co Inc ....E 516 621-0030
  Dover *(G-1671)*

INDL SPLYS, WHOLESALE: Valves & Fittings

GTS Technical Sales LLC ....G....... 302 778-1362
  Wilmington *(G-10795)*
John R Seiberlich Inc ....D....... 302 356-2400
  New Castle *(G-5441)*
Precision Flow LLC ....F 302 544-4417
  New Castle *(G-5636)*
Royal Instruments Inc ....G....... 302 328-5900
  New Castle *(G-5686)*

INDL TOOL GRINDING SVCS

J & A Grinding Inc ....F 302 368-8760
  Newark *(G-6812)*

INDUSTRIAL & COMMERCIAL EQPT INSPECTION SVCS

First State Inspection Agency ....G....... 302 422-3859
  Milford *(G-4413)*
Food Equipment Service Inc ....F 302 996-9363
  Wilmington *(G-10586)*
Phalco Inc ....G....... 302 654-2620
  Wilmington *(G-12107)*

INFORMATION BUREAU SVCS

Government Information Center ....G....... 302 857-3020
  Dover *(G-1604)*
Info Solutions North Amer LLC ....F 302 793-9200
  New Castle *(G-5418)*

INFORMATION RETRIEVAL SERVICES

American Domain Names LLC ....F 253 785-0332
  Wilmington *(G-9044)*
Braincore Inc ....F 302 999-9221
  New Castle *(G-5103)*
Digital Whale LLC ....G....... 302 526-0115
  Camden *(G-561)*
Eagle Eye America Inc ....G....... 302 392-3600
  Bear *(G-134)*
Homeland SEC Verification LLC ....G....... 888 791-4614
  Wilmington *(G-10941)*
Instanode Inc ....G....... 352 327-8872
  Wilmington *(G-11042)*
Lexisnexis Risk Assets Inc ....A 800 458-9410
  Wilmington *(G-11378)*
Plai Apps Inc ....G....... 661 678-3740
  Dover *(G-1962)*
Veteran It Pro LLC ....F 302 824-3111
  Hockessin *(G-3167)*
Webstudy Inc ....G....... 888 326-4058
  Harbeson *(G-2802)*

INFORMATION SVCS: Consumer

Grofos International LLC ....G....... 302 635-4805
  Newark *(G-6693)*
Storyworth Inc ....G....... 415 967-1531
  Claymont *(G-808)*

INGOTS: Steel

Chemfirst Inc ....D....... 302 774-1000
  Wilmington *(G-9646)*

INK: Printing

C & A Ink ....G....... 302 565-9866
  Newark *(G-6140)*
Digital Ink Sciences LLC ....G....... 951 757-0027
  Wilmington *(G-10152)*
Do It Wiser LLC ....G....... 800 816-0944
  Wilmington *(G-10179)*

INNS

Baymont Inn & Suites Newark ....G....... 302 453-1700
  Newark *(G-6056)*
Dogfish Inn ....G....... 302 644-8292
  Lewes *(G-3468)*
Inn At Wilmington ....E 302 479-7900
  Wilmington *(G-11036)*
Inn LLC A-1 Dash ....G....... 302 368-7964
  Newark *(G-6781)*
Inns of Rehoboth Beach LLC ....G....... 302 645-8003
  Rehoboth Beach *(G-7968)*
Jacks Bstro At Dvid Fnney Inn ....G....... 302 544-5172
  New Castle *(G-5434)*

PRODUCT & SERVICES SECTION

INSULATION & ROOFING MATERIALS: Wood, Reconstituted

Relax Inn .... G 302 875-1554
  Laurel (G-3279)
Seaside Inn .... F 302 251-5000
  Fenwick Island (G-2340)

INSECTICIDES

Sharda USA LLC .... G 610 350-6930
  Hockessin (G-3145)

INSPECTION & TESTING SVCS

Mumford-Bjorkman Associates .... F 302 655-8234
  Wilmington (G-11775)

INSPECTION SVCS, TRANSPORTATION

Integrated Dynmc Solutions LLC .... G 818 406-8500
  Camden (G-582)

INSTRUMENTS & METERS: Measuring, Electric

Spectr-Physics Hldings USA Inc .... G 302 478-4600
  Wilmington (G-12698)

INSTRUMENTS, LAB: Spectroscopic/Optical Properties Measuring

Denovix Inc .... E 302 442-6911
  Wilmington (G-10110)

INSTRUMENTS, LABORATORY: Differential Thermal Analysis

Ttna Energy Systems LLC .... G 302 384-9147
  Wilmington (G-12990)

INSTRUMENTS, LABORATORY: Gas Analyzing

Apollo Scitech LLC .... G 302 861-6557
  Newark (G-5983)

INSTRUMENTS, LABORATORY: Infrared Analytical

Wilmington Infrared Tech .... G 302 234-6761
  Wilmington (G-13236)

INSTRUMENTS, LABORATORY: Mass Spectrometers

Mstm LLC .... G 302 239-4447
  Newark (G-7068)

INSTRUMENTS, MEASURING & CNTRL: Gauges, Auto, Computer

Peeper Vehicle Technology Corp .... G 800 971-4134
  Dover (G-1943)

INSTRUMENTS, MEASURING & CNTRL: Testing, Abrasion, Etc

Industrial Physics Inc .... G 302 613-5600
  New Castle (G-5414)

INSTRUMENTS, MEASURING & CNTRLG: Thermometers/Temp Sensors

Spekciton Biosciences LLC .... G 302 353-2694
  Wilmington (G-12702)

INSTRUMENTS, MEASURING & CONTROLLING: Breathalyzers

Toxtrap Inc .... G 302 698-1400
  Dover (G-2156)

INSTRUMENTS, MEASURING/CNTRL: Gauging, Ultrasonic Thickness

Solvetech Inc .... G 302 798-5400
  Wilmington (G-12680)

INSTRUMENTS, MEASURING/CNTRLG: Meters, Nuclear Rad Cnt Rate

Quarta-Rad Inc .... G 201 877-2002
  Wilmington (G-12283)

INSTRUMENTS, SURGICAL & MEDICAL: Blood & Bone Work

Caveman Design Inc .... G 302 234-9969
  Hockessin (G-2980)
W L Gore & Associates Inc .... C 302 368-3700
  Newark (G-7672)

INSTRUMENTS, SURGICAL & MEDICAL: Optometers

Optometry Associates PC .... G 302 654-6490
  Wilmington (G-11964)

INSTRUMENTS, SURGICAL/MED: Microsurgical, Exc Electromedical

Delaware Instrument Lab LLC .... G 302 737-6250
  Newark (G-6389)

INSTRUMENTS: Analytical

Axess Corporation .... G 302 292-8500
  New Castle (G-5061)
B & W Tek Inc .... D 302 368-7788
  Newark (G-6032)
B&W Tek LLC .... D 302 368-7824
  Newark (G-6038)
Bia Separations Inc .... G 510 740-4045
  Wilmington (G-9326)
Bonna-Agela Technologies Inc .... D 302 438-8798
  Hockessin (G-2966)
M&M Mass Spec Consulting LLC .... G 302 250-4488
  Newark (G-6967)
Markes International Inc .... G 302 656-5500
  Wilmington (G-11533)
Ribodynamics LLC .... G 518 339-6605
  Wilmington (G-12405)
Separation Methods Tech Inc .... F 302 368-0610
  Newark (G-7408)
Sisuaq Scientific .... G 302 739-3073
  Wilmington (G-12635)
Supercritical Fluid Tech .... G 302 738-3420
  Newark (G-7511)
Supercritical Fluid Tech .... G 302 738-3420
  Newark (G-7512)

INSTRUMENTS: Elec Lab Stds, Resist, Inductance/Capacitance

Aim Research Co .... G 302 235-5940
  Hockessin (G-2953)

INSTRUMENTS: Flow, Indl Process

Delaware Capital Formation Inc .... G 302 793-4921
  Wilmington (G-10010)

INSTRUMENTS: Indl Process Control

Ametek Inc .... D 302 456-4400
  Newark (G-5962)
Hexagon Metrology Inc .... G 302 351-3580
  Wilmington (G-10899)
McCabes Mechanical Service Inc .... F 302 854-9001
  Georgetown (G-2599)

INSTRUMENTS: Laser, Scientific & Engineering

Spectr-Physics Hldings USA Inc .... G 302 478-4600
  Wilmington (G-12698)

INSTRUMENTS: Measurement, Indl Process

Applied Analytics Inc .... E 781 791-5005
  Newark (G-5985)

INSTRUMENTS: Measuring & Controlling

1 A Lifesafer Inc .... G 800 634-3077
  Harrington (G-2803)
1 A Lifesafer Inc .... G 800 634-3077
  Seaford (G-8132)
1 A Lifesafer Inc .... G 800 634-3077
  Georgetown (G-2416)
1 A Lifesafer Inc .... G 800 634-3077
  Harbeson (G-2771)
1 A Lifesafer Inc .... G 800 634-3077
  Millsboro (G-4617)
1 A Lifesafer Inc .... G 800 634-3077
  Newark (G-5850)

1 A Lifesafer Inc .... G 800 634-3077
  Dover (G-1062)
1 A Lifesafer Inc .... G 800 634-3077
  Milford (G-4296)
1 A Lifesafer Inc .... G 800 634-3077
  Lewes (G-3315)
1 A Lifesafer Inc .... G 800 634-3077
  Claymont (G-683)
A S I Controls .... G 302 629-7730
  Seaford (G-8135)
Arrim LLC .... G 617 697-7914
  Wilmington (G-9134)
Avatar Instruments Inc .... G 302 703-6865
  Lewes (G-3360)
Hanbang Group .... G 626 506-7585
  Newark (G-6705)
Horney Industrial Electronics .... G 302 337-3600
  Bridgeville (G-483)
Maintenance Troubleshooting .... G 302 692-0871
  Newark (G-6976)
Millennium Prcess Contrls Svcs .... F 302 455-1717
  Bear (G-256)
Sepax Technologies Inc .... F 302 366-1101
  Newark (G-7409)
Testex Inc .... G 302 731-5693
  Newark (G-7558)

INSTRUMENTS: Measuring Electricity

Advance Nanotech Inc .... G 212 583-0080
  Wilmington (G-8948)
Agilent Technologies Inc .... A 408 345-8886
  Wilmington (G-8978)
Agilent Technologies Inc .... A 877 424-4536
  Wilmington (G-8979)
Engineered Systems & Designs .... G 302 456-0446
  Wilmington (G-10402)

INSTRUMENTS: Medical & Surgical

Clarius Mobile Health Corp .... G 778 800-9975
  Lewes (G-3425)
Delamed Supplies Inc .... G 917 517-4492
  Claymont (G-731)
Denco Inc .... G 302 798-4200
  Wilmington (G-10108)
Docs Medical LLC .... G 301 401-1489
  Bear (G-122)
E I Du Pont De Nemours & Co .... E 302 996-4000
  Wilmington (G-10293)
Fbk Medical Tubing Inc .... E 302 855-0585
  Georgetown (G-2527)
Hologic Inc .... E 302 631-2700
  Newark (G-6738)
Moor Instruments Inc .... G 302 798-7470
  Wilmington (G-11743)
Smith & Nephew Holdings Inc .... G 302 884-6720
  Wilmington (G-12659)

INSTRUMENTS: Optical, Analytical

Creative Devices Inc .... G 302 378-5433
  Middletown (G-4014)

INSTRUMENTS: Test, Digital, Electronic & Electrical Circuits

AC Group Inc .... G 201 840-5566
  Wilmington (G-8910)
Suretronix Solutions LLC .... G 302 407-3146
  Wilmington (G-12817)

INSTRUMENTS: Test, Electrical, Engine

Pcu Systems LLC .... G 888 780-9728
  Wilmington (G-12053)

INSTRUMENTS: Thermal Property Measurement

Ta Instruments - Waters LLC .... C 302 427-4000
  New Castle (G-5751)

INSULATION & ROOFING MATERIALS: Wood, Reconstituted

Jcr Systems LLC .... G 302 420-6072
  New Castle (G-5439)

Employee Codes: A=Over 500 employees, B=251-500
C=101-250, D=51-100, E=20-50, F=10-19, G=1-9

2020 Harris Directory of Delaware Businesses

INSULATION MATERIALS WHOLESALERS

Thomco Inc.............G....... 302 454-0361
Newark *(G-7564)*

INSULATION: Fiberglass

Ipm Inc.............G....... 302 328-4030
New Castle *(G-5424)*

INSULATORS, PORCELAIN: Electrical

NGK North America Inc.............G....... 302 654-1344
Wilmington *(G-11884)*

INSURANCE AGENCIES & BROKERS

American Life Insurance Co.............D....... 302 594-2000
Wilmington *(G-9053)*
Assurance Partners Intl.............F....... 302 478-0173
Wilmington *(G-9163)*
Bob Simmons Agency.............G....... 302 698-1970
Dover *(G-1216)*
Denise Beam.............G....... 302 539-1900
Ocean View *(G-7783)*
Emory Agency Inc.............G....... 302 855-2100
Georgetown *(G-2522)*
Eric Cline.............G....... 302 629-3984
Seaford *(G-8238)*
George H Bunting Jr.............G....... 302 227-3891
Rehoboth Beach *(G-7944)*
Hartle Brian State Farm Agency.............G....... 302 322-1741
New Castle *(G-5379)*
Jack Lewis.............G....... 302 475-2010
Wilmington *(G-11114)*
John Borden.............G....... 302 674-2992
Dover *(G-1703)*
John C Leverage.............G....... 302 629-3525
Seaford *(G-8281)*
Kathy Safford.............G....... 302 734-8268
Dover *(G-1724)*
Katie Bennett.............G....... 302 697-2650
Camden *(G-586)*
Lawrence Agencies Inc.............G....... 302 995-6936
Wilmington *(G-11344)*
Mark Penuel.............G....... 302 856-7724
Georgetown *(G-2597)*
Metropolitan Life Insur Co.............E....... 302 738-0888
Newark *(G-7021)*
Metropolitan Life Insur Co.............F....... 302 734-5803
Dover *(G-1844)*
Moore Insurance & Financial.............G....... 302 999-9101
Wilmington *(G-11744)*
New York Life Insurance Co.............E....... 302 369-8500
Newark *(G-7110)*
Patrick J McCabe.............G....... 302 368-3711
Newark *(G-7183)*
Phil Hill.............G....... 302 678-0499
Dover *(G-1954)*
Progressive Casualty Insur Co.............G....... 302 734-7360
Dover *(G-1990)*
Robert F Mullen Insurance Agcy.............G....... 302 322-5331
Bear *(G-309)*
Sanderson Albidress Agency.............G....... 302 368-3010
Wilmington *(G-12539)*
Schanne Mark State Farm Insur.............G....... 302 422-7231
Milford *(G-4554)*
Stacy K Gates.............G....... 302 368-1968
Newark *(G-7478)*
Starr Wright Insur Agcy Inc.............E....... 302 483-0190
Wilmington *(G-12743)*
State Farm Insurance.............G....... 302 832-0344
Newark *(G-7485)*
State Farm Mutl Auto Insur Co.............D....... 302 434-3333
Wilmington *(G-12744)*
Terry White.............G....... 302 652-4969
Newark *(G-7557)*
Zavier J Decaire.............F....... 302 658-0218
Wilmington *(G-13341)*

INSURANCE AGENTS, NEC

AIG AIG.............G....... 302 252-4683
Wilmington *(G-8987)*
Allen Insurance Group.............F....... 302 654-8823
Wilmington *(G-9019)*
B&H Insurance LLC.............E....... 302 995-2247
Newark *(G-6036)*
Bishop Associates.............G....... 302 838-1270
Newark *(G-6084)*
C Edgar Wood Inc.............E....... 302 674-3500
Dover *(G-1245)*
Carey Jr James E Inc.............G....... 302 934-8383
Dagsboro *(G-889)*
Chambers Insurance Agency Inc.............G....... 302 655-5300
Wilmington *(G-9625)*
Charles M Wallace.............G....... 302 998-1412
Wilmington *(G-9633)*
Clark Bffone Mtthews Insur AGC.............E....... 302 322-2261
New Castle *(G-5173)*
Cnc Insurance Associates Inc.............F....... 302 678-3860
Dover *(G-1296)*
Collender Griffith Chang Inc.............G....... 302 992-0600
Wilmington *(G-9772)*
Commercial Insurance Assoc.............G....... 610 436-4608
Newark *(G-6268)*
Concord Agency Inc.............G....... 302 478-4000
Wilmington *(G-9809)*
Davis Insurance Group Inc.............G....... 302 652-4700
Montchanin *(G-4985)*
Douglas Bennetti Insur Agcy.............G....... 302 724-4490
Dover *(G-1440)*
Douglas C Loew & Associates.............G....... 302 453-0550
Newark *(G-6464)*
Downs Insurance Associates.............G....... 302 422-8863
Milford *(G-4394)*
Drass Insurance Agency Inc.............G....... 302 998-1331
Wilmington *(G-10231)*
Farm Financial Services Inc.............G....... 302 854-9760
Georgetown *(G-2526)*
Fidelity National Info Svcs.............F....... 302 658-2102
Wilmington *(G-10535)*
Fox Point Programs Inc.............F....... 800 499-7242
Claymont *(G-747)*
Fusura LLC.............D....... 302 397-2200
Wilmington *(G-10652)*
George J Weiner Associates.............F....... 302 658-0218
Wilmington *(G-10701)*
Hoeschel Inv & Insur Group.............F....... 302 738-3535
Newark *(G-6734)*
Insurance & Financial Svcs Inc.............E....... 302 239-5895
Wilmington *(G-11043)*
Insurance & Fincl Svcs Ltd Del.............G....... 302 234-1200
Wilmington *(G-11044)*
Insurance Associates Inc.............F....... 302 368-0888
Newark *(G-6786)*
Insurance Market Inc.............E....... 302 875-7591
Laurel *(G-3239)*
Insurance Market Inc.............G....... 302 934-9006
Millsboro *(G-4709)*
Insurance Office America Inc.............G....... 302 764-1000
Wilmington *(G-11046)*
KT&d Inc.............F....... 302 429-8500
Wilmington *(G-11298)*
L & D Insurance Services LLC.............G....... 302 235-2288
Hockessin *(G-3073)*
L & W Insurance Inc.............G....... 302 674-3500
Dover *(G-1760)*
Lisa Broadbent Insurance Inc.............F....... 302 731-0044
Newark *(G-6939)*
Lyons Insurance Agency Inc.............E....... 302 227-7100
Wilmington *(G-11466)*
Mary Bryan Inc.............F....... 302 875-5099
Laurel *(G-3262)*
McComrick Insurance Services.............G....... 302 732-6655
Dagsboro *(G-919)*
Muncie Insurance Services.............G....... 302 678-2800
Dover *(G-1879)*
Nickle Insurance.............G....... 302 654-0347
Wilmington *(G-11888)*
Occidental L Transamerica.............F....... 302 477-9700
Wilmington *(G-11932)*
Pfister Insurance Inc.............G....... 302 674-3100
Dover *(G-1953)*
Poland & Sullivan Insurance.............F....... 302 738-3535
Newark *(G-7229)*
Prominent Insurance Svcs Inc.............G....... 302 351-3368
Wilmington *(G-12251)*
Rawlins Ferguson Jones & Lewis.............G....... 302 337-8231
Bridgeville *(G-518)*
Records Gebhart Agency Inc.............G....... 302 653-9211
Smyrna *(G-8698)*
Rhue & Associates Inc.............G....... 302 422-3058
Milford *(G-4542)*
Richard A Parsons Agency Inc.............G....... 302 674-2810
Dover *(G-2035)*
S T Good Insurance Inc.............E....... 215 969-8385
Newark *(G-7374)*
Select Financial Group.............G....... 302 424-7777
Milford *(G-4555)*
W C Ungerer Insurance Agency.............G....... 302 368-8505
Newark *(G-7668)*
Williams Insurance Agency Inc.............E....... 302 227-2501
Rehoboth Beach *(G-8116)*
Williams Insurance Agency Inc.............G....... 302 239-5500
Wilmington *(G-13217)*
Work First Casualty Company.............F....... 302 477-1710
Wilmington *(G-13302)*

INSURANCE BROKERS, NEC

Business Insurance Services.............G....... 302 655-5300
Wilmington *(G-9511)*
Donald C Savoy Inc.............G....... 888 992-6755
Newark *(G-6460)*
Donald C Savoy Inc.............G....... 302 697-4100
Dover *(G-1437)*
Fred S Smalls Insurance.............F....... 302 633-1980
Wilmington *(G-10626)*
Kelly & Assoc Insur Group Inc.............G....... 302 661-6324
Wilmington *(G-11236)*
Marsh USA Inc.............E....... 302 888-4300
Wilmington *(G-11543)*
New Castle Insurance Ltd.............F....... 302 328-6111
New Castle *(G-5561)*
Nickle Insurance Agency Inc.............G....... 302 834-9700
Delaware City *(G-961)*
Surplus & Excess Line Ltd.............G....... 302 653-5016
Smyrna *(G-8727)*
Wilgus Associates Inc.............E....... 302 539-7511
Bethany Beach *(G-438)*
Wilgus Associates Inc.............F....... 302 644-2960
Lewes *(G-3823)*

INSURANCE CARRIERS: Automobile

Chrissinger and Baumberger.............F....... 302 777-0100
Wilmington *(G-9672)*
Liberty Mutual Fire Insur Co.............E....... 302 993-0500
Wilmington *(G-11381)*
Reese Agency Inc.............G....... 302 678-5656
Dover *(G-2018)*
Steadfast Insurance Company.............G....... 847 605-6000
Dover *(G-2106)*

INSURANCE CARRIERS: Bank Deposit

Raymond James Fincl Svcs Inc.............G....... 302 227-0330
Rehoboth Beach *(G-8041)*

INSURANCE CARRIERS: Dental

Highmarks Inc.............G....... 302 421-3000
Wilmington *(G-10906)*

INSURANCE CARRIERS: Direct Accident & Health

Ace American Insurance Company.............F....... 302 476-6000
Wilmington *(G-8919)*
American Life Insurance Co.............D....... 302 594-2000
Wilmington *(G-9053)*
American-Amicable Holding Inc.............G....... 302 427-0355
Wilmington *(G-9059)*
Harrington Insurance.............G....... 302 883-5000
Dover *(G-1629)*
Highmarks Inc.............G....... 302 674-8492
Dover *(G-1645)*

INSURANCE CARRIERS: Disability

Citicorp Del-Lease Inc.............D....... 302 323-3801
New Castle *(G-5166)*
Delphi Financial Group Inc.............E....... 302 478-5142
Wilmington *(G-10105)*

INSURANCE CARRIERS: Hospital & Medical

Coventry Health Care Inc.............G....... 800 833-7423
Newark *(G-6309)*

INSURANCE CARRIERS: Life

American Income Life Insurance.............E....... 610 277-9499
Wilmington *(G-9048)*
American-Amicable Holding Inc.............G....... 302 427-0355
Wilmington *(G-9059)*
Cigna Corporate Services LLC.............D....... 302 792-4906
Wilmington *(G-9703)*
Cigna Global Holdings Inc.............F....... 302 797-3469
Claymont *(G-718)*
Cigna Holdings Inc.............F....... 215 761-1000
Claymont *(G-719)*
Citicorp Del-Lease Inc.............D....... 302 323-3801
New Castle *(G-5166)*

PRODUCT & SERVICES SECTION
INVESTMENT ADVISORY SVCS

Donald C Savoy Inc ....G....... 888 992-6755
 Newark *(G-6460)*
Entourage Financial Group LLC............G....... 302 352-9473
 Wilmington *(G-10417)*
Hackney Business Solutions LLC..........G....... 843 496-7236
 Newark *(G-6700)*
Highmarks Inc ....G....... 302 421-3000
 Wilmington *(G-10906)*
Penn Mutual Life Insurance Co ....F....... 302 655-7151
 Wilmington *(G-12066)*
Principal Financial Group Inc ....D....... 302 993-8045
 Wilmington *(G-12228)*

INSURANCE CARRIERS: Property & Casualty

AAA Club Alliance Inc ....F....... 302 674-8020
 Dover *(G-1075)*
American Gen Lf Insur Co Del ....F....... 302 575-5200
 Wilmington *(G-9046)*
Cigna Holdings Inc ....F....... 215 761-1000
 Claymont *(G-719)*
Highmarks Inc ....G....... 302 421-3000
 Wilmington *(G-10906)*
Liberty Mutual Insurance Co................E....... 302 993-0500
 Wilmington *(G-11382)*
Progressive Casualty Insur Co ....G....... 302 734-7360
 Dover *(G-1990)*

INSURANCE CARRIERS: Title

Intercoastal Title Agency Inc ....G....... 302 478-7752
 Wilmington *(G-11053)*
Stewart Title Guaranty Company ....F....... 302 651-9201
 Wilmington *(G-12766)*

INSURANCE CLAIM ADJUSTERS, NOT EMPLOYED BY INSURANCE COMPANY

Delaware Insur Guarantee Assn ....G....... 302 456-3656
 Newark *(G-6390)*
Penn Del Adjustment Service ....G....... 302 999-0196
 Bear *(G-281)*
Perry and Associates Services ....G....... 302 581-3092
 Wilmington *(G-12089)*

INSURANCE CLAIM PROCESSING, EXC MEDICAL

Integra ADM Group Inc ....F....... 800 959-3518
 Seaford *(G-8271)*

INSURANCE EDUCATION SVCS

Entourage Financial Group LLC............G....... 302 352-9473
 Wilmington *(G-10417)*

INSURANCE INFORMATION & CONSULTING SVCS

Muncie Insurance Services...................G....... 302 629-9414
 Seaford *(G-8313)*
Regulatory Insurance Services ....G....... 302 678-2444
 Dover *(G-2021)*
Usi Inc ....D....... 302 658-8000
 Wilmington *(G-13041)*

INSURANCE INFORMATION BUREAUS

Lexisnexis Risk Assets Inc ....A....... 800 458-9410
 Wilmington *(G-11378)*

INSURANCE: Agents, Brokers & Service

21st Century Insurance Company ....G....... 302 252-2000
 Wilmington *(G-8854)*
AAA Club Alliance Inc ....F....... 302 283-4300
 Newark *(G-5874)*
Affordable Insur Netwrk Del.................G....... 302 392-4500
 Bear *(G-21)*
Affordable Insurance ....G....... 302 834-9641
 Bear *(G-22)*
AIG Federal Savings Bank ....E....... 302 661-8992
 Wilmington *(G-8988)*
Axa Equitable Life Insur Co ....F....... 302 655-7231
 Wilmington *(G-9201)*
Bosco Insurance Agency ....G....... 302 678-0647
 Dover *(G-1222)*
Calvin Sheets ....G....... 302 832-0600
 Bear *(G-63)*
Chesapeake Insurance Advisors ....F....... 302 544-6900
 New Castle *(G-5145)*

Dewberry Insurance Agency Inc ....G....... 302 995-9550
 Wilmington *(G-10130)*
Dick Broadbent Insurance ....G....... 302 998-0137
 Wilmington *(G-10150)*
Endurnce Reinsurance Corp Amer ....F....... 973 898-9575
 Wilmington *(G-10399)*
First Access Inc ....F....... 949 455-4027
 Wilmington *(G-10544)*
Franklin T Varone Inc..........................G....... 302 475-6200
 Wilmington *(G-10619)*
Geico Corporation ....G....... 302 998-9192
 Wilmington *(G-10686)*
Harrington Realty Inc ....E....... 302 736-0800
 Dover *(G-1630)*
Independent School MGT Inc ....E....... 302 656-4944
 Wilmington *(G-11018)*
Insley Insurance & Fincl Svc ....G....... 302 286-0777
 Newark *(G-6784)*
John Koziol Inc ....G....... 302 234-5430
 Hockessin *(G-3068)*
Kevin Lammers Ins ....G....... 302 283-1210
 Newark *(G-6878)*
Marvel Agency Inc ....E....... 302 422-7844
 Milford *(G-4488)*
McCall Brooks Insurance Agency ....G....... 302 475-8200
 Wilmington *(G-11585)*
Morgan Stanley ....E....... 302 644-6600
 Rehoboth Beach *(G-8012)*
Nationwide Corporation ....G....... 302 761-9611
 New Castle *(G-5548)*
Nationwide Insurance Co ....G....... 302 678-2223
 Dover *(G-1884)*
Nationwide Mutual Insurance Co ....G....... 302 479-5560
 Wilmington *(G-11816)*
Nationwide Mutual Insurance Co ....F....... 302 234-5430
 Hockessin *(G-3101)*
Peninsula Health Alliance Inc ....G....... 302 856-9778
 Georgetown *(G-2614)*
Planet Payment Solutions Inc ....E....... 516 670-3200
 New Castle *(G-5625)*
Prudential Insur Co of Amer ....E....... 302 734-7877
 Dover *(G-1993)*
Prudential Insur Co of Amer ....G....... 302 378-8811
 Middletown *(G-4201)*
Richard E Small Inc ....G....... 302 875-7199
 Laurel *(G-3280)*
Sheets Insurance Inc ....G....... 302 832-0441
 Bear *(G-320)*
Short Insurance Associates ....G....... 302 629-0999
 Seaford *(G-8401)*
Standard Insurance Company ....G....... 302 322-9922
 New Castle *(G-5738)*
Steinebach Robert and Assoc ....G....... 302 328-1212
 Christiana *(G-680)*
Thomas R Wyshock ....G....... 302 645-5070
 Lewes *(G-3782)*
Tom Wiseley Insurance Agency ....G....... 302 832-7700
 Newark *(G-7574)*
Travel Co Inc ....G....... 302 652-6263
 Wilmington *(G-12960)*
Truitt Insurance Agency Inc ....G....... 302 645-9344
 Lewes *(G-3796)*
Virgil P Ellwanger...............................G....... 302 934-8083
 Millsboro *(G-4820)*
Weymouth Swyze Crroon Insur In ....F....... 302 655-3705
 Wilmington *(G-13177)*

INTEGRATED CIRCUITS, SEMICONDUCTOR NETWORKS, ETC

Suretronix Solutions LLC.....................G....... 302 407-3146
 Wilmington *(G-12817)*
Wiregateit LLC ....G....... 302 538-1304
 Newark *(G-7712)*

INTERIOR DECORATING SVCS

Bernardon PC ....F....... 302 622-9550
 Wilmington *(G-9309)*
Carolina Street Garden & Home ....G....... 302 539-2405
 Fenwick Island *(G-2332)*
Delaware Valley Field Svcs LLC ....G....... 302 384-8617
 Wilmington *(G-10094)*
Dream Weaver Interiors Inc ....G....... 302 644-0800
 Rehoboth Beach *(G-7921)*
Kirks Flowers Inc ....E....... 302 737-3931
 Newark *(G-6890)*
Maryann Metrinko LLC ....G....... 410 643-1472
 Lewes *(G-3623)*
Regal Painting & Decorating ....G....... 302 994-8943
 Wilmington *(G-12354)*

INTERIOR DESIGN SVCS, NEC

Abha Architects Inc ....E....... 302 658-6426
 Wilmington *(G-8902)*
Arqitecture LLC ....G....... 302 777-5666
 Winterthur *(G-13356)*
Bar & Associates Ltd ....G....... 302 999-9233
 Wilmington *(G-9246)*
Buck Simpers Archt + Assoc Inc ....F....... 302 658-9300
 Wilmington *(G-9498)*
Contract Environments Inc ....G....... 302 658-0668
 Wilmington *(G-9843)*
Dcc Design Group LLC.......................G....... 302 777-2100
 Wilmington *(G-9978)*
Holland Corp ....G....... 302 245-5645
 Selbyville *(G-8503)*
Lynn and Rachel Walsh ....G....... 302 422-2893
 Milford *(G-4482)*
Mark Showell Interiors Ltd ....F....... 302 227-2272
 Rehoboth Beach *(G-7999)*
Plain & Fancy Inc ....G....... 302 656-9901
 Wilmington *(G-12148)*
Stuart Kingston Galleries Inc ....F....... 302 652-7978
 Wilmington *(G-12780)*
Zahn Incorporated ....G....... 302 425-3700
 Wilmington *(G-13339)*

INTERIOR DESIGNING SVCS

Design Services Ltd............................G....... 302 475-5663
 Wilmington *(G-10122)*
Echelon Interiors LLC..........................G....... 302 519-9151
 Rehoboth Beach *(G-7924)*
Mitchell Associates Inc ....E....... 302 594-9400
 Wilmington *(G-11714)*
Nancy Conklin Interiors.......................G....... 302 655-0877
 Wilmington *(G-11796)*

INTERIOR REPAIR SVCS

Colliers Trim Shop Inc ....G....... 302 227-8398
 Rehoboth Beach *(G-7897)*

INTERMEDIATE CARE FACILITY

Brookdale Senior Living Inc ....E....... 302 239-3200
 Hockessin *(G-2970)*
Chancellor Care Ctr of Delmar ....C....... 302 846-3077
 Delmar *(G-982)*
Home of Merciful Rest Society ....C....... 302 652-3311
 Wilmington *(G-10939)*
Ingleside Homes Inc ....E....... 302 984-0950
 Wilmington *(G-11032)*
Little Sisters of The Poor ....D....... 302 368-5886
 Newark *(G-6941)*
Lutheran Senior Services Inc ....E....... 302 654-4490
 Wilmington *(G-11454)*
Martin Luther Homes East Inc ....G....... 302 475-4920
 Wilmington *(G-11550)*
Mary Campbell Center Inc ....C....... 302 762-6025
 Wilmington *(G-11555)*
Mosaic ....G....... 302 456-5995
 Newark *(G-7062)*
Premier Healthcare Inc ....E....... 302 731-5576
 Newark *(G-7244)*
Seaside Pointe ....G....... 302 226-8750
 Rehoboth Beach *(G-8072)*
Summit At Hockessin ....G....... 302 235-8388
 Hockessin *(G-3153)*

INVENTOR

Elevationtv...G....... 978 317-9285
 Wilmington *(G-10373)*

INVENTORY COMPUTING SVCS

Retail Services Wis Corp......................D....... 302 477-0667
 Wilmington *(G-12392)*

INVERTERS: Nonrotating Electrical

Orange Power Electric Inc ....G....... 205 886-5815
 Wilmington *(G-11969)*

INVESTMENT ADVISORY SVCS

Ameriprise Financial Svcs Inc ....E....... 302 468-8200
 Wilmington *(G-9064)*
Ameriprise Financial Svcs Inc ....F....... 302 475-2357
 Wilmington *(G-9065)*
Ashford Capital Management ....F....... 302 655-1750
 Wilmington *(G-9149)*

Employee Codes: A=Over 500 employees, B=251-500
C=101-250, D=51-100, E=20-50, F=10-19, G=1-9

INVESTMENT ADVISORY SVCS

Biddle Capital Management Inc............G...... 302 369-6789
Newark *(G-6079)*
Blackrock Instnl Mgt Corp..................D...... 302 797-2000
Wilmington *(G-9354)*
Brown Advisory Incorporated............G...... 302 351-7600
Wilmington *(G-9487)*
Brown Brothers Harriman & Co..........F...... 302 552-4040
Wilmington *(G-9488)*
Diversified Financial Cons.................G...... 302 765-3500
Wilmington *(G-10170)*
Fidelity Income Advisors Co...............E...... 302 223-9444
Wilmington *(G-10533)*
Friess Associates LLC.......................G...... 302 656-3017
Wilmington *(G-10642)*
Glenmede Trust Co Nat Assn.............G...... 302 661-2900
Wilmington *(G-10721)*
Global Financial Advisors Netw..........G...... 302 697-3565
Rehoboth Beach *(G-7949)*
Independence Wealth Advisors..........G...... 302 763-1180
Hockessin *(G-3058)*
Integrated Wealth MGT LLC...............G...... 302 442-4233
Wilmington *(G-11051)*
Investment Property Services L..........G...... 302 994-3907
Wilmington *(G-11073)*
Kalmar Investments Inc......................E...... 302 658-7575
Wilmington *(G-11222)*
Mallard Advisors LLC.........................E...... 302 737-4546
Newark *(G-6979)*
Mallard Advisors LLC.........................F...... 302 239-1654
Hockessin *(G-3086)*
Swarthmore Financial Services..........G...... 302 325-0700
New Castle *(G-5746)*
Topkis Financial Advisors LLC............G...... 302 654-4444
Wilmington *(G-12932)*
United Brokerage Packaging..............G...... 302 294-6782
Newark *(G-7612)*
Wbi Capital Advisors LLC...................G...... 856 361-6362
Wilmington *(G-13127)*
Wilmington Trust Corporation.............E...... 302 651-8378
Wilmington *(G-13263)*

INVESTMENT BANKERS

Citibank Overseas Inv Corp.................F...... 302 323-3600
New Castle *(G-5164)*
Kensington Cross Ltd.........................F...... 888 999-9360
Rehoboth Beach *(G-7979)*
Rsl Investors Inc................................E...... 302 478-5142
Wilmington *(G-12487)*
Skajaquoda Capital LLC.....................F...... 302 504-4448
Wilmington *(G-12641)*

INVESTMENT COUNSELORS

Cleantech Energy Solutions LLC........G...... 301 704-2831
Wilmington *(G-9738)*
Marvin & Palmer Associates...............E...... 302 573-3570
Wilmington *(G-11554)*

INVESTMENT FIRM: General Brokerage

Assurance Partners Intl......................F...... 302 478-0173
Wilmington *(G-9163)*
Cawsl Enterprises Inc........................G...... 302 478-6160
Wilmington *(G-9597)*
Cfd Group Inc....................................E...... 242 698-1039
Wilmington *(G-9620)*
Defense Shield Trust.........................E...... 540 815-8248
Wilmington *(G-9994)*
Delaware Valley Brokerage Inc..........G...... 302 477-9700
Wilmington *(G-10092)*
Detroit Desl Rmnfacturing Corp.........G...... 302 427-3564
Wilmington *(G-10125)*
Morgan Garanty Intl Fincl Corp..........E...... 302 634-1000
Newark *(G-7058)*
Peters Alan E Peters & Assoc...........G...... 302 656-1007
Wilmington *(G-12099)*
United Telecommunications...............E...... 302 654-6108
Wilmington *(G-13027)*

INVESTMENT FUNDS, NEC

Bombay Hook Ltd..............................G...... 302 571-8644
Wilmington *(G-9391)*
Breakthrugh Cpitl Partners LLC..........G...... 212 381-4420
Lewes *(G-3391)*
Merrill Lynch Pierce Fenner...............D...... 302 571-5100
Wilmington *(G-11646)*
National Holding Investment Co.........F...... 302 573-3887
Wilmington *(G-11806)*
Revod Corporation............................G...... 302 477-1795
Wilmington *(G-12396)*
Stella ABG Acquisition Inc..................G...... 302 654-6682
Wilmington *(G-12751)*
Thales Inc..G...... 302 326-0830
New Castle *(G-5765)*

INVESTMENT FUNDS: Open-Ended

ADP Capital Management Inc............G...... 302 657-4060
Wilmington *(G-8941)*
Blackrock Mncpl Income Inv Qlt..........G...... 800 441-7762
Wilmington *(G-9358)*
Daniels + Tansey LLP........................G...... 302 594-1070
Wilmington *(G-9957)*
Elliott Holdings Corporation................F...... 650 241-8646
Middletown *(G-4056)*
Global Currents Inv MGT LLC............F...... 302 476-3800
Wilmington *(G-10722)*
Vital Renewable Energy Company.....G...... 202 595-2944
Wilmington *(G-13095)*

INVESTMENT OFFICES: Management, Closed-End

African Markets Fund LLC..................G...... 703 944-1514
Dover *(G-1092)*
Atlas Management Inc.......................G...... 302 576-2749
Wilmington *(G-9180)*
Blackrock Income Trust Inc................G...... 800 441-7762
Wilmington *(G-9353)*
Blackrock Mncpl 2030 Trget Ter........G...... 800 882-0052
Wilmington *(G-9357)*
Blackrock Mnhldngs Cal Qlty Fu........G...... 800 441-7762
Wilmington *(G-9359)*
Blackrock Mnhldngs NJ Qlty Fun........G...... 800 441-7762
Wilmington *(G-9360)*
Blackrock NY Mncpl Income Qlty........G...... 800 441-7762
Wilmington *(G-9361)*

INVESTMENT OFFICES: Money Market Mutual

Black Rock Inc...................................F...... 302 797-2009
Wilmington *(G-9347)*
Blackrock Funds II..............................F...... 302 797-2000
Wilmington *(G-9351)*
Blackrock Global Long.......................G...... 302 797-2000
Wilmington *(G-9352)*
Blackrock Intermediate.......................F...... 302 797-2000
Wilmington *(G-9355)*
Blackrock LNG-Hrzon Eqity Fund.......G...... 800 441-7762
Wilmington *(G-9356)*
Brandywine Fund Inc.........................F...... 302 656-3017
Wilmington *(G-9434)*
Dupont Capital Management Corp.....G...... 302 477-6000
Wilmington *(G-10250)*
Government Portfolio LLC..................F...... 301 718-9742
Rehoboth Beach *(G-7952)*

INVESTMENT OFFICES: Mutual Fund Sales, On Own Account

H S B C Overseas Corp De................F...... 302 657-8400
Wilmington *(G-10810)*

INVESTORS, NEC

Acopia LLC..D...... 302 286-5172
Newark *(G-5893)*
Bell Rock Capital LLC........................F...... 302 227-7607
Rehoboth Beach *(G-7865)*
Carpenter Investments Inc.................G...... 302 656-5664
Wilmington *(G-9577)*
Cigna Corporation..............................G...... 302 792-4906
Wilmington *(G-9705)*
Cigna Real Estate Inc........................G...... 302 476-3337
Wilmington *(G-9706)*
Dd & E Investment Group Inc.............G...... 302 319-2780
Wilmington *(G-9982)*
Dt Investment Partners LLC...............G...... 302 442-6203
Wilmington *(G-10238)*
Fas Mart / Shore Stop 286 LLC..........G...... 302 366-9694
Newark *(G-6573)*
GPM Investments LLC.......................F...... 302 436-6330
Selbyville *(G-8496)*
Green DOT Capital LLC.....................G...... 302 395-0500
Bear *(G-171)*
Hs Capital LLC...................................G...... 302 317-3614
Wilmington *(G-10965)*
J A Banks & Associates LLC.............F...... 914 260-2003
Smyrna *(G-8660)*
Kpv Enterprises Llc............................G...... 302 500-9669
Bear *(G-221)*
Landmark Homes...............................G...... 302 388-8557
Dover *(G-1765)*
Lcd Wealth Management LLC...........G...... 302 294-0013
Hockessin *(G-3080)*
Llb Acquisition LLC............................G...... 212 750-8300
Wilmington *(G-11414)*
Obsidian Investors LLC......................G...... 954 560-1499
Middletown *(G-4177)*
Partnrre Cpitl Invstments Corp...........F...... 608 347-5824
Wilmington *(G-12028)*
Pcms Holdings Inc.............................G...... 302 281-3600
Wilmington *(G-12052)*
Pga Acquisitions V LLC.....................G...... 302 355-3500
Wilmington *(G-12106)*
PNC Bank National Association.........G...... 302 326-4710
New Castle *(G-5626)*
Questar Capital Corporation..............G...... 302 856-9778
Georgetown *(G-2631)*
Weepor Company Inc.........................G...... 302 575-9945
Wilmington *(G-13137)*
Ws One Investment Usa LLC.............F...... 302 317-2610
New Castle *(G-5841)*
Wsfs Investment Group Inc................G...... 302 573-3258
Wilmington *(G-13308)*

INVESTORS: Real Estate, Exc Property Operators

Aimco/Bethesda GP LLC....................E...... 303 757-8101
Wilmington *(G-8990)*
D M Peoples Investment Corp............G...... 302 836-1500
Bear *(G-92)*
Lc Associates LLC.............................F...... 302 235-2500
Hockessin *(G-3079)*
McCray Investments..........................G...... 302 836-8569
Newark *(G-7012)*
Pacer International One LLC..............F...... 302 588-9500
Wilmington *(G-12003)*
Scottish Ventures LLC........................G...... 302 382-6057
New Castle *(G-5695)*
Svea Real Estate Group LLC.............F...... 855 262-9665
Dover *(G-2122)*

IRON ORES

American Minerals Partnership..........C...... 302 652-3301
New Castle *(G-5034)*
Banfield & Temperley Inc....................G...... 347 878-6057
Dover *(G-1169)*

IRRIGATION EQPT WHOLESALERS

O A Newton & Son Company.............E...... 302 337-3782
Bridgeville *(G-504)*
Tucker Mechanical Service Inc..........G...... 302 536-7730
Seaford *(G-8426)*
Walls Irrigation Inc.............................F...... 302 422-2262
Milford *(G-4595)*

IRRIGATION SYSTEMS, NEC Water Distribution Or Sply Systems

Atlantic Water Products......................E...... 302 326-1166
New Castle *(G-5052)*
County of Sussex...............................F...... 302 947-0864
Millsboro *(G-4670)*

JANITORIAL & CUSTODIAL SVCS

ABM Industries Incorporated..............E...... 302 999-1898
Wilmington *(G-8905)*
ABM Janitorial Services Inc................A...... 302 571-9900
Wilmington *(G-8906)*
Advanced Bizz Innovations LLC........G...... 302 397-1162
Townsend *(G-8753)*
All Clean Services..............................G...... 302 378-7376
Townsend *(G-8756)*
All Pro Maids Inc................................E...... 302 645-9247
Lewes *(G-3334)*
Alvins Professional Services..............F...... 302 544-6634
New Castle *(G-5028)*
Arrowsmith Cleaning Solutions..........G...... 302 377-5614
Townsend *(G-8759)*
Bravo Building Services Inc................A...... 302 322-5959
New Castle *(G-5108)*
Briggs Services LLC..........................G...... 302 569-5230
Ellendale *(G-2258)*
Catch-A-Web Cleaning Inc................E...... 302 836-1970
Bear *(G-67)*

PRODUCT & SERVICES SECTION

Chaffin Cleaning Service Inc .... E 302 369-2704
  Newark *(G-6183)*
Clean Force Building Services .... F 302 494-9330
  Newark *(G-6247)*
David Jenkins .... G 302 304-5568
  Bear *(G-96)*
Delmarva Cleaning & Maint Inc .... C 302 734-1856
  Dover *(G-1409)*
Delores Welch .... G 302 856-7989
  Georgetown *(G-2510)*
Don-Lee Margin Corporation .... E 302 629-7567
  Seaford *(G-8225)*
Dream Clean Team LP .... F 302 981-5154
  Newark *(G-6473)*
Dss - Integrity LLC .... E 302 677-0111
  Dover *(G-1482)*
Dss Services Inc .... F 302 677-0111
  Dover *(G-1483)*
Dss Urban Joint Venture LLC .... E 302 677-0111
  Dover *(G-1484)*
Dust Away Cleaning Svcs Inc .... E 302 658-8803
  Wilmington *(G-10269)*
Eckels Family LLC .... E 302 465-5224
  Felton *(G-2290)*
Efficient Services Inc .... G 302 629-2124
  Seaford *(G-8234)*
Elite Commercial Cleaning Inc .... D 302 366-8900
  Newark *(G-6514)*
Harmon Investments LLC .... G 302 383-2176
  Wilmington *(G-10837)*
JBA Enterprises .... F 302 834-6685
  Bear *(G-198)*
Master Klean Company .... G 302 539-4290
  Ocean View *(G-7802)*
Mid-Atlantic Services A-Team .... D 302 984-9559
  Wilmington *(G-11681)*
Mid-Atlantic Services A-Team .... E 302 628-3403
  Seaford *(G-8310)*
Otis Kamara .... G 443 207-2643
  Dover *(G-1925)*
Pride Klean Inc .... E 302 994-8500
  Wilmington *(G-12225)*
Proclean .... G 302 654-1074
  New Castle *(G-5649)*
Ras Addis & Associates Inc .... F 302 571-1683
  Wilmington *(G-12318)*
Simply Clean Jantr Svcs Inc .... E 302 744-9100
  Dover *(G-2084)*
Slater Fireplaces Inc .... G 302 999-1200
  Wilmington *(G-12645)*
Stl & Associates LLC .... G 302 359-2801
  Smyrna *(G-8725)*
Superior Commercial Cleaning .... G 302 897-2544
  Newark *(G-7513)*
Todds Janitorial Service Inc .... G 302 378-8212
  Middletown *(G-4262)*
Top of The Line Jantr Svcs .... F 302 645-2668
  Lewes *(G-3790)*

JANITORIAL EQPT & SPLYS WHOLESALERS

Diamond Chemical & Supply Co .... E 302 656-7786
  Wilmington *(G-10139)*
Goorland and Mann Inc .... G 302 655-1514
  Wilmington *(G-10752)*
Source Supply Inc .... F 302 328-5110
  New Castle *(G-5723)*
South Forks Inc .... G 302 731-0344
  Newark *(G-7461)*
State Janitorial Supply Co .... G 302 734-4814
  Dover *(G-2104)*
Wholesale Janitor Supply Co .... G 302 655-5722
  Wilmington *(G-13197)*

JEWELRY FINDINGS & LAPIDARY WORK

Gem Merchant LLC .... G 734 274-1280
  Lewes *(G-3510)*

JEWELRY REPAIR SVCS

Bellingers Jewelers .... G 302 227-6410
  Rehoboth Beach *(G-7866)*
Continental Jewelers Inc .... F 302 475-2000
  Wilmington *(G-9841)*
Del Haven of Wilmington Inc .... G 302 999-9040
  Newark *(G-6361)*
Michael Gallagher Jewelers .... G 302 836-2925
  Bear *(G-254)*
Turquoise Shop Inc .... F 302 366-7448
  Newark *(G-7601)*
Whittens Fine Jewelry .... G 302 995-7464
  Wilmington *(G-13196)*

JEWELRY STORES

Charles Allen Ltd .... G 302 475-5048
  Wilmington *(G-9630)*
T K O Designs Inc .... G 302 539-6992
  Bethany Beach *(G-434)*
Whittens Fine Jewelry .... G 302 995-7464
  Wilmington *(G-13196)*

JEWELRY STORES: Precious Stones & Precious Metals

Alex and Ani LLC .... G 302 731-1420
  Newark *(G-5930)*
Alex and Ani LLC .... G 302 227-7360
  Rehoboth Beach *(G-7839)*
Bellingers Jewelers .... G 302 227-6410
  Rehoboth Beach *(G-7866)*
Continental Jewelers Inc .... F 302 475-2000
  Wilmington *(G-9841)*
Del Haven of Wilmington Inc .... G 302 999-9040
  Newark *(G-6361)*
First State Coin Co .... G 302 734-7776
  Dover *(G-1554)*
Michael Gallagher Jewelers .... G 302 836-2925
  Bear *(G-254)*
Precision Jewelry Inc .... G 302 422-7138
  Milford *(G-4528)*
Silver Works Inc .... F 302 227-1707
  Rehoboth Beach *(G-8076)*
Stuart Kingston Galleries Inc .... G 302 652-7978
  Wilmington *(G-12780)*
Turquoise Shop Inc .... F 302 366-7448
  Newark *(G-7601)*
Wholesale Jewelry Outlet Inc .... G 302 994-5114
  Wilmington *(G-13198)*

JEWELRY STORES: Watches

Bridgewater Jewelers .... G 302 328-2101
  New Castle *(G-5113)*

JEWELRY, WHOLESALE

Wholesale Jewelry Outlet Inc .... G 302 994-5114
  Wilmington *(G-13198)*

JEWELRY: Decorative, Fashion & Costume

Anya International LLC .... E 847 850-0920
  Newark *(G-5976)*
Swarovski US Holding Limited .... G 302 737-4811
  Newark *(G-7518)*
T K O Designs Inc .... G 302 539-6992
  Bethany Beach *(G-434)*

JEWELRY: Precious Metal

Alex and Ani LLC .... G 302 731-1420
  Newark *(G-5930)*
Alex and Ani LLC .... G 302 227-7360
  Rehoboth Beach *(G-7839)*
Charles Allen Ltd .... G 302 475-5048
  Wilmington *(G-9630)*
Juwelo Usa Inc .... G 888 471-7614
  Wilmington *(G-11211)*
Lolahsoul Jewelry Inc .... G 888 771-7087
  Wilmington *(G-11429)*
Olga N Ganoudis Jewelry .... G 302 421-9820
  Wilmington *(G-11945)*
Rck Soliatire LLC .... F 551 358-8400
  Rehoboth Beach *(G-8043)*
Silver Works Inc .... F 302 227-1707
  Rehoboth Beach *(G-8076)*

JIGS & FIXTURES

Pcu Systems LLC .... G 888 780-9728
  Wilmington *(G-12053)*

JOB COUNSELING

Elwyn .... D 302 658-8860
  Wilmington *(G-10385)*
Opportunity Center Inc .... D 302 762-0300
  New Castle *(G-5589)*

JOB PRINTING & NEWSPAPER PUBLISHING COMBINED

Communicate U Media LLC .... G 610 453-6501
  Middletown *(G-4001)*

JOB TRAINING & VOCATIONAL REHABILITATION SVCS

Academy Massage & Bdy Work Ltd .... G 302 392-6768
  Bear *(G-10)*
Easter Seal Delaware .... E 302 856-7364
  Georgetown *(G-2519)*
Easter Seal Delaware .... E 302 678-3353
  Dover *(G-1499)*
Health & Social Svcs Del Dept .... E 302 255-9800
  New Castle *(G-5383)*
Health & Social Svcs Del Dept .... E 302 255-9855
  New Castle *(G-5385)*
Leadership Caddie .... F 302 743-6456
  Bear *(G-232)*
Leadership Institute Inc .... F 302 368-7292
  Newark *(G-6925)*
Service Quest .... G 302 235-0173
  Hockessin *(G-3144)*

JOB TRAINING SVCS

Corelink Ministries .... G 610 505-6043
  Wilmington *(G-9861)*
Fursan Consulting Services .... F 240 654-5784
  New Castle *(G-5336)*
Jobs For Delaware Graduates .... G 302 995-7175
  Wilmington *(G-11163)*
Telamon Corp/Early Chldhd Pgrm ...... G 302 934-1642
  Georgetown *(G-2690)*
Telamon Corporation .... F 302 398-9196
  Harrington *(G-2898)*
Telamon Corporation .... G 302 684-3234
  Milton *(G-4975)*
Telamon Corporation .... G 302 629-5557
  Seaford *(G-8420)*
Telamon Corporation .... G 302 424-2335
  Milford *(G-4577)*

JOISTS: Long-Span Series, Open Web Steel

Engineering Incorporated .... G 302 995-6862
  Wilmington *(G-10403)*

JUICE, FROZEN: Wholesalers

Copra Inc .... G 917 224-1727
  Wilmington *(G-9855)*

JUNIOR COLLEGE, NEC

Delaware Tchncal Cmnty College ...... C 302 259-6160
  Georgetown *(G-2504)*

KIDNEY DIALYSIS CENTERS

Bio-Mdcal Applications Del Inc .... G 302 366-0129
  Newark *(G-6081)*
Bio-Mdical Applications of Del .... E 302 998-7568
  Newark *(G-6082)*
DSI Laurel LLC .... D 302 715-3060
  Laurel *(G-3224)*
Fresenius Med Care S Delaware .... F 302 934-6342
  Millsboro *(G-4694)*
Fresenius Med Cre N Delaware .... E 302 239-4704
  Hockessin *(G-3032)*
Fresenius Medical Care .... E 302 736-1340
  Dover *(G-1567)*
Fresenius Medical Care .... E 302 337-8789
  Bridgeville *(G-473)*
Fresenius Medical Care N Amer .... F 302 328-9044
  New Castle *(G-5330)*
Fresenius Medical Care N Amer .... G 302 633-6228
  Wilmington *(G-10635)*
Fresenius Medical Care Nephr .... G 302 836-6093
  Bear *(G-161)*
Fresenius Medical Care Vero Be .... E 302 453-8834
  Newark *(G-6621)*
Fresenius Usa Inc .... F 302 422-9739
  Milford *(G-4417)*
Fresenius Usa Inc .... E 302 455-0454
  Newark *(G-6622)*
Fresenius Usa Inc .... E 302 658-7469
  Wilmington *(G-10636)*
Liberty Dalysis Wilmington LLC .... F 302 429-0142
  Wilmington *(G-11379)*

KIDNEY DIALYSIS CENTERS

National Medical Care Inc ....F...... 302 658-7469
  Wilmington *(G-11808)*
Renal Care Center Dover.................E...... 302 678-5718
  Dover *(G-2025)*
Renal Care Group Inc ....E...... 302 678-8744
  Dover *(G-2026)*

KINDERGARTEN

Kindercare Learning Ctrs LLC.................F...... 302 834-6931
  Newark *(G-6888)*
Limestone Country Day School.................F...... 302 239-9041
  Wilmington *(G-11388)*

KITCHEN ARTICLES: Semivitreous Earthenware

Pony Run Kitchens LLC ....G...... 302 492-3006
  Hartly *(G-2937)*

KITCHEN CABINET STORES, EXC CUSTOM

American Cabinetry LLC.................G...... 302 655-4064
  Wilmington *(G-9043)*

KITCHEN CABINETS WHOLESALERS

Allura Bath & Kitchen Inc.................G...... 302 731-2851
  Newark *(G-5944)*
Cabinetry Unlimited LLC.................E...... 302 436-5030
  Selbyville *(G-8465)*
Robinson Export & Import Corp.................G...... 410 219-7200
  Millsboro *(G-4794)*

KITCHEN TOOLS & UTENSILS WHOLESALERS

Lekue USA Inc ....D...... 302 326-4805
  New Castle *(G-5478)*
Rosle U S A Corp ....E...... 302 326-4801
  New Castle *(G-5685)*

KITCHEN UTENSILS: Food Handling & Processing Prdts, Wood

Hillandale Farms Delaware Inc.................E...... 302 492-3644
  Hartly *(G-2926)*

KITCHEN UTENSILS: Wooden

Coastal Woodcraft ....G...... 302 856-7947
  Georgetown *(G-2475)*

KITCHENWARE: Plastic

Pony Run Kitchens LLC ....G...... 302 492-3006
  Hartly *(G-2937)*

LABOR RESOURCE SVCS

Employers Bench Inc ....F...... 973 757-1912
  Christiana *(G-667)*

LABOR UNION

American Postal Workers Union ....E...... 302 322-8994
  New Castle *(G-5035)*
Diamond State Teleml Un ....F...... 302 999-1100
  Wilmington *(G-10148)*
General Teamsters Local Un 326.................G...... 302 328-2387
  New Castle *(G-5349)*
Iron Workers Local 451 ....G...... 302 994-0946
  Wilmington *(G-11082)*
Laborers Intl Un N Amer ....G...... 302 654-2880
  Newark *(G-6911)*
Laborers Intl Un N Amer ....F...... 302 934-7376
  Georgetown *(G-2588)*
Millwrights Local Union 1548.................F...... 410 355-0011
  Wilmington *(G-11698)*
National Assn Ltr Carriers ....G...... 302 652-2933
  Newport *(G-7751)*
Plumbers Pipefitters Local 74.................G...... 302 636-7400
  Newark *(G-7223)*
Transport Wkrs Un Amer Intl Un ....G...... 302 652-1503
  Wilmington *(G-12957)*
United Steelworkers ....E...... 302 999-0412
  Wilmington *(G-13026)*
United Tele Wkrs Local 13101.................G...... 302 737-0400
  Newark *(G-7616)*

LABORATORIES, TESTING: Food

E I Du Pont De Nemours & Co ....D...... 302 695-5300
  Wilmington *(G-10306)*
Wm Systems Inc ....G...... 302 450-4482
  Wilmington *(G-13282)*

LABORATORIES, TESTING: Forensic

Alias Technology LLC ....G...... 302 856-9488
  Georgetown *(G-2428)*

LABORATORIES, TESTING: Metallurgical

MMR Group Inc ....E...... 302 328-0500
  New Castle *(G-5531)*

LABORATORIES, TESTING: Prdt Certification, Sfty/Performance

Red Lion Medical Safety Inc ....G...... 302 731-8600
  Newark *(G-7306)*

LABORATORIES, TESTING: Product Testing

Evans ....G...... 302 629-0545
  Seaford *(G-8240)*

LABORATORIES, TESTING: Soil Analysis

Ecg Industries Inc ....G...... 302 453-0535
  Newark *(G-6502)*
Geo-Technology Associates Inc ....E...... 302 326-2100
  New Castle *(G-5351)*

LABORATORIES, TESTING: Water

Element Mtls Tech Wlmngton Inc.................F...... 302 636-0202
  Wilmington *(G-10368)*
Envirocorp Inc.................F...... 302 398-3869
  Harrington *(G-2837)*
Eurofins Qc Inc ....F...... 302 276-0432
  New Castle *(G-5297)*
R L Laboratories Inc ....F...... 302 328-1686
  New Castle *(G-5663)*

LABORATORIES: Biological

Exalenz Bioscience Inc ....G...... 888 392-5369
  Wilmington *(G-10456)*

LABORATORIES: Biological Research

Arkion Life Sciences LLC.................E...... 302 504-7400
  New Castle *(G-5044)*
Charles River Labs Intl Inc.................G...... 302 292-8888
  Newark *(G-6190)*
Delaware Innovation Space Inc ....G...... 302 695-2201
  Wilmington *(G-10058)*
E I Du Pont De Nemours & Co ....D...... 302 774-1000
  Wilmington *(G-10308)*
Frontier Scientific Inc ....G...... 302 266-6891
  Newark *(G-6626)*
Penn Labs Inc.................F...... 215 751-4000
  Wilmington *(G-12065)*

LABORATORIES: Biotechnology

Advanced Materials Technology ....G...... 302 477-2510
  Wilmington *(G-8953)*
Algorithm Sciences LLC ....G...... 734 904-9491
  Wilmington *(G-9009)*
Biomatik Usa LLC.................F...... 416 273-4858
  Wilmington *(G-9340)*
E I Du Pont De Nemours & Co ....G...... 302 774-1000
  Wilmington *(G-10288)*
Ezy Biotech LLC.................G...... 212 247-4261
  Wilmington *(G-10467)*
Fraunhofer Usa Inc ....D...... 302 369-1708
  Newark *(G-6613)*
Jenrin Discovery LLC.................G...... 302 379-1679
  Wilmington *(G-11150)*
Napigen Inc.................G...... 302 419-8117
  Wilmington *(G-11801)*
Neurorx Inc ....F...... 202 340-1352
  Wilmington *(G-11846)*
Sdix LLC ....D...... 302 456-6789
  Newark *(G-7398)*
Separation Methods Tech Inc ....F...... 302 368-0610
  Newark *(G-7408)*
Timtec LLC ....F...... 302 292-8500
  Newark *(G-7567)*
White Dog Labs Inc.................F...... 302 220-4760
  New Castle *(G-5832)*

PRODUCT & SERVICES SECTION

Wilmington Pharmatech Co LLC.................E...... 302 737-9916
  Newark *(G-7703)*

LABORATORIES: Blood Analysis

Laboratory Corporation America ....E...... 302 234-0493
  Hockessin *(G-3076)*

LABORATORIES: Commercial Nonphysical Research

431 Corporation ....G...... 352 385-1427
  Bear *(G-1)*
China Monitor Inc.................F...... 302 351-2324
  Wilmington *(G-9667)*
Digital Wish Inc ....G...... 802 375-6721
  Milton *(G-4895)*
Incenco International ....F...... 302 478-8400
  Wilmington *(G-11012)*
Wboc Inc ....F...... 302 734-9262
  Dover *(G-2207)*

LABORATORIES: Dental

All Denture Center ....F...... 302 656-8202
  Wilmington *(G-9013)*
Chromium Dental LLC ....F...... 302 731-5582
  Newark *(G-6233)*
Sonshine Dental Labs Inc ....F...... 302 731-5582
  Newark *(G-7459)*
Welsh Family Dentistry ....G...... 302 836-3711
  Hockessin *(G-3172)*
Wilmington & Newark Dental ....G...... 302 571-0526
  Wilmington *(G-13222)*

LABORATORIES: Dental & Medical X-Ray

Breast Imaging Center.................E...... 302 623-9729
  Newark *(G-6117)*
Clinical Breast Imaging ....G...... 302 658-4800
  Wilmington *(G-9743)*
Delaware Imaging Network ....G...... 302 449-5400
  Middletown *(G-4028)*
Delaware Imaging Network ....F...... 302 644-2590
  Newark *(G-6388)*
F P T & W Medical Associates ....F...... 800 421-2368
  Wilmington *(G-10469)*
Molecular Imaging Services Inc ....G...... 302 450-4505
  Bear *(G-257)*
Omega Imaging Associates LLC ....G...... 302 654-5245
  Wilmington *(G-11947)*

LABORATORIES: Dental, Crown & Bridge Production

Mittelman Dental Lab.................F...... 302 798-7440
  Claymont *(G-784)*
National Dentex LLC ....D...... 302 661-6000
  New Castle *(G-5544)*
Precision Dental Laboratory ....G...... 302 478-5608
  Wilmington *(G-12203)*

LABORATORIES: Electronic Research

Ultrafine Technologies Inc ....G...... 302 384-6513
  Wilmington *(G-13009)*

LABORATORIES: Environmental Research

Environmental Consulting Svcs.................F...... 302 378-9881
  Middletown *(G-4059)*
Environmental Protection Agcy ....A...... 302 739-9917
  Dover *(G-1525)*

LABORATORIES: Medical

Allied Diagnstc Pathology Cons.................G...... 302 575-8103
  Wilmington *(G-9021)*
Arcpoint Labs ....G...... 302 268-6560
  Wilmington *(G-9125)*
Beebe Medical Foundation ....G...... 302 684-8579
  Milton *(G-4868)*
Brandywine Imaging LLC ....E...... 302 654-5300
  Wilmington *(G-9440)*
CD Diagnostics Inc ....F...... 302 367-7770
  Claymont *(G-709)*
Clinpharma Clinical RES LLC ....G...... 646 961-3437
  Wilmington *(G-9744)*
Delaware Diagnostic Labs LLC ....G...... 302 996-9585
  Newark *(G-6376)*
Delaware Public Health Lab ....G...... 302 223-1520
  Smyrna *(G-8620)*

Delaware Womens Imaging LLC......E...... 302 738-9100
  Newark (G-6422)
Glaxosmithkline Holdings......C...... 302 984-6932
  Wilmington (G-10720)
Laboratory Corporation America......G...... 302 653-5119
  Smyrna (G-8669)
Laboratory Corporation America......G...... 302 735-4694
  Dover (G-1763)
Laboratory Corporation America......G...... 302 655-5673
  New Castle (G-5472)
Laboratory Corporation America......E...... 302 998-7340
  Wilmington (G-11317)
Maria Lazar MD......G...... 302 838-2210
  Newark (G-6986)
Omega Imaging Associates LLC......F...... 302 995-2037
  Wilmington (G-11948)
Paul Renzi......G...... 302 478-3166
  Wilmington (G-12043)
Professional Imaging......G...... 302 653-3522
  Smyrna (G-8694)
Quest Diagnostics Incorporated......F...... 302 322-4651
  New Castle (G-5659)
Quest Diagnostics Incorporated......G...... 302 478-1100
  Wilmington (G-12286)
Quest Diagnostics Incorporated......G...... 302 735-4555
  Dover (G-2003)
Quest Diagnostics Incorporated......G...... 302 455-0720
  Newark (G-7287)

LABORATORIES: Medical Pathology

Armed Forces Med Examiner Sys......D...... 302 346-8653
  Dover (G-1137)
Christiana Care Health Sys Inc......B...... 302 733-1601
  Newark (G-6207)
Delaware Clinical & Labortry......G...... 302 999-8095
  Wilmington (G-10019)
Laboratory Corporation America......G...... 302 731-0244
  Newark (G-6910)

LABORATORIES: Noncommercial Research

A66 Inc......G...... 800 444-0446
  Wilmington (G-8892)
Delaware Community Foundation......F...... 302 571-8004
  Wilmington (G-10023)
Delaware Nature Society......D...... 302 239-1283
  Hockessin (G-3006)
Disaster Research Center......E...... 302 831-6618
  Newark (G-6454)
Global Institute......G...... 732 776-7360
  Newark (G-6666)
Indonesian Cultural Institute......G...... 302 981-7780
  Newark (G-6773)
Mid Atlantic Pain Institute......G...... 302 369-1700
  Milford (G-4494)
Smid Aerospace Corporation......G...... 443 205-0881
  Bear (G-326)
Society For Acupuncture RES Inc......F...... 302 222-1832
  Lewes (G-3752)
Tdm Pharmaceutical RES LLC......G...... 302 832-1008
  Newark (G-7543)
Towle Institute......G...... 302 993-1408
  Wilmington (G-12943)
University of Delaware......E...... 302 831-4811
  Newark (G-7620)

LABORATORIES: Physical Research, Commercial

Alpha Omega Scientific LLC......G...... 302 415-4499
  New Castle (G-5026)
Batescainelli LLC......G...... 202 618-2040
  Rehoboth Beach (G-7856)
Beatdapp Inc......G...... 310 903-0244
  Dover (G-1185)
C M-Tec Inc......G...... 302 369-6166
  Newark (G-6141)
Cowie Technology Corp......G...... 302 998-7037
  Wilmington (G-9885)
Dupont Specialty Pdts USA LLC......E...... 302 695-3295
  Wilmington (G-10262)
E I Du Pont De Nemours & Co......E...... 805 562-5307
  Wilmington (G-10304)
M-Cap Technologies Intl......G...... 302 695-5329
  Wilmington (G-11474)
MMR Group Inc......E...... 302 328-0500
  New Castle (G-5531)
Modern Water Inc......E...... 302 669-6900
  New Castle (G-5533)
Partnership For De Estuary......G...... 302 655-4990
  Wilmington (G-12027)

Stride Services Inc......F...... 302 540-4713
  Wilmington (G-12776)
Synchrgnix Info Strategies LLC......E...... 302 892-4800
  Wilmington (G-12833)
W7energy LLC......G...... 302 897-1653
  Wilmington (G-13111)
Warehouse Technology Inc......G...... 302 516-7791
  New Castle (G-5823)

LABORATORIES: Testing

Agro Lab......G...... 302 265-2734
  Harrington (G-2805)
Cogtest Inc......F...... 302 454-1265
  Newark (G-6259)
Laboratory Corporation America......E...... 302 651-9502
  Wilmington (G-11315)
Laboratory Corporation America......G...... 302 376-6146
  Middletown (G-4126)
Laboratory Corporation America......G...... 302 449-0246
  Middletown (G-4127)
Laboratory Corporation America......G...... 302 629-3182
  Seaford (G-8289)
Laboratory Corporation America......G...... 302 834-6845
  Bear (G-227)
Laboratory Corporation America......G...... 302 834-1359
  Newark (G-6908)
Laboratory Corporation America......E...... 302 737-3525
  Newark (G-6909)
Laboratory Corporation America......E...... 302 798-2520
  Wilmington (G-11316)
Laboratory Corporation America......E...... 302 994-8575
  Wilmington (G-11318)
Medlab Environmental Testing......G...... 302 655-5227
  New Castle (G-5514)
Quest Diagnostics Incorporated......F...... 302 537-3862
  Millville (G-4853)
Quest Diagnostics Incorporated......E...... 302 424-4504
  Milford (G-4532)
Quest Diagnostics Incorporated......G...... 302 628-3078
  Seaford (G-8366)
Quest Diagnostics Incorporated......F...... 302 239-5273
  Wilmington (G-12287)
Quest Diagnostics Incorporated......G...... 302 376-8675
  Middletown (G-4205)

LABORATORIES: Testing

3sigma Labs Inc......G...... 925 236-2618
  Wilmington (G-8859)
Accugenix Inc......E...... 302 292-8888
  Newark (G-5890)
Agera Laboratories......G...... 302 888-1500
  Wilmington (G-8975)
Christiana Care Health Sys Inc......G...... 302 477-6500
  Wilmington (G-9680)
Compact Membrane Systems Inc......E...... 302 999-7996
  Wilmington (G-9797)
Corrosion Testing Laboratories......F...... 302 454-8200
  Newark (G-6301)
Integrity Testlabs LLC......D...... 302 325-2365
  New Castle (G-5421)
K & S Technical Services Inc......G...... 302 737-9133
  Newark (G-6864)
Lehigh Testing Laboratories......E...... 302 328-0500
  New Castle (G-5476)
Lewis Research Inc......G...... 302 644-0881
  Lewes (G-3606)
Micron Incorporated......G...... 302 998-1184
  Wilmington (G-11676)
Mid-Atlantic Envmtl Labs Inc......F...... 302 654-1340
  New Castle (G-5525)
Midi Labs Inc......E...... 302 737-4297
  Newark (G-7035)
Quinteccent Inc......G...... 443 838-5447
  Selbyville (G-8536)
Stereochemical Inc......G...... 302 266-0700
  Newark (G-7490)
Tell Lab......G...... 302 831-7121
  Newark (G-7554)

LABORATORY APPARATUS & FURNITURE

Bio Medic Corporation......F...... 302 628-4300
  Seaford (G-8170)
Life Sciences Intl LLC......G...... 603 436-9444
  Wilmington (G-11385)
Nanodrop Technologies LLC......E...... 302 479-7707
  Wilmington (G-11798)

LABORATORY CHEMICALS: Organic

Cfg Lab Inc......G...... 302 261-3403
  Wilmington (G-9621)
Invista Capital Management LLC......E...... 302 629-1100
  Seaford (G-8272)
Urbn Steamlab LLC......G...... 267 738-3096
  Lewes (G-3803)

LABORATORY EQPT, EXC MEDICAL: Wholesalers

Bio Medic Corporation......F...... 302 628-4300
  Seaford (G-8170)
Buchi Corporation......D...... 302 652-3000
  New Castle (G-5119)
Miles Scientific Corporation......F...... 302 737-6960
  Newark (G-7039)

LABORATORY EQPT: Clinical Instruments Exc Medical

Safeguard Dx Laboratory......G...... 888 919-8275
  Wilmington (G-12517)

LABORATORY EQPT: Incubators

Delaware Technology Park Inc......G...... 302 452-1100
  Newark (G-6417)

LABORATORY INSTRUMENT REPAIR SVCS

General Separation Tech Inc......G...... 302 533-5646
  Newark (G-6645)

LAMINATED PLASTICS: Plate, Sheet, Rod & Tubes

Fbk Medical Tubing Inc......E...... 302 855-0585
  Georgetown (G-2527)
Franklin Fibre-Lamitex Corp......E...... 302 652-3621
  Wilmington (G-10616)
Ipd Technologies LLC......G...... 302 533-8850
  Newark (G-6805)
New Process Fibre Company Inc......D...... 302 349-4535
  Greenwood (G-2757)

LAMP & LIGHT BULBS & TUBES

Acuity Brands Lighting Inc......E...... 302 476-2055
  New Castle (G-5002)
Blue Arrow Contract Manufactur......G...... 302 738-2583
  Newark (G-6098)
Glass Technologists Inc......G...... 240 682-0966
  Middletown (G-4087)

LAND SUBDIVIDERS & DEVELOPERS: Commercial

Commonwealth Group LLC......E...... 302 472-7200
  Wilmington (G-9791)
D & D Contractors Inc......F...... 302 378-9724
  Smyrna (G-8609)
Donne Delle & Associates Inc......E...... 302 325-1111
  Newark (G-6462)
Eastern States Develpment Inc......G...... 302 998-0683
  Wilmington (G-10327)
McConnell Development Inc......G...... 302 428-0712
  Wilmington (G-11589)
Riverfront Dev Corp Del......F...... 302 425-4890
  Wilmington (G-12427)
Sybounheuang Group Inc......G...... 302 999-9339
  Wilmington (G-12827)

LAND SUBDIVIDERS & DEVELOPERS: Residential

Barclay Farms......G...... 302 697-6939
  Camden (G-539)
Gulfstream Development Corp......G...... 302 539-6178
  Ocean View (G-7792)
Interfaith Cmnty Hsing of Del......F...... 302 652-3991
  Wilmington (G-11062)
Jack Hickman Real Estate......F...... 302 539-8000
  Bethany Beach (G-406)
Ocean Atlantic Management LLC......F...... 302 227-3573
  Rehoboth Beach (G-8020)
Reybold Construction Corp......E...... 302 832-7100
  Bear (G-304)
Salt Pond Associates......F...... 302 539-2750
  Bethany Beach (G-430)

LAND SUBDIVIDERS & DEVELOPERS: Residential

Tony Ashburn Inc .... G 302 677-1940
  Dover *(G-2151)*

LAND SUBDIVISION & DEVELOPMENT

Del Homes Inc .... G 302 697-8204
  Magnolia *(G-3889)*
Edward B De Seta & Associates .... G 302 428-1313
  Wilmington *(G-10356)*
Ferm Development LLC .... G 302 792-1102
  Wilmington *(G-10521)*
First Power LLC 610 247-5750
  Wilmington *(G-10547)*
Glasgow Medical Associates PA .... G 302 836-8350
  Newark *(G-6662)*
Leon N Weiner & Associates Inc .... D 302 656-1354
  Wilmington *(G-11371)*
Parkway Gravel Inc .... D 302 658-5241
  New Castle *(G-5603)*
Patterson Price RE LLC .... G 302 366-0200
  Newark *(G-7184)*
Patterson Price RE LLC .... F 302 378-9550
  Middletown *(G-4181)*
Riverfront Development Corp .... F 302 425-4890
  Wilmington *(G-12428)*
Roizman & Associates Inc .... G 302 426-9688
  Wilmington *(G-12465)*
Woodlawn Trustees Inc .... E 302 655-6215
  Wilmington *(G-13297)*

LASER SYSTEMS & EQPT

Alphasense Inc .... G 302 998-1116
  Wilmington *(G-9031)*

LAUNDRIES, EXC POWER & COIN-OPERATED

Harry Louies Laundry & Dry Clg .... F 302 734-8195
  Dover *(G-1634)*
North Hills Cleaners Inc .... F 302 764-1234
  Wilmington *(G-11900)*

LAUNDRY & DRYCLEANER AGENTS

Capitol Cleaners & Launderers .... D 302 674-1511
  Dover *(G-1251)*
Capitol Cleaners & Launderers 302 674-0500
  Dover *(G-1252)*

LAUNDRY & DRYCLEANING SVCS, EXC COIN-OPERATED: Garment Press

Blue Swan Cleaners Inc .... F 302 652-7607
  Wilmington *(G-9382)*
Marvi Cleaners Limited Inc .... G 302 764-3077
  Wilmington *(G-11553)*

LAUNDRY & DRYCLEANING SVCS, EXC COIN-OPERATED: Pickup

McKelvey Hires Dry Cleaning .... F 302 998-9191
  Wilmington *(G-11601)*

LAUNDRY & DRYCLEANING SVCS, EXC COIN-OPERATED: Retail Agent

Capitol Cleaners & Launderers .... G 302 378-4744
  Middletown *(G-3981)*

LAUNDRY & GARMENT SVCS, NEC

Honey Alteration .... G 302 519-2031
  Lewes *(G-3546)*

LAUNDRY & GARMENT SVCS, NEC: Fur Cleaning, Repairing/Storage

Joy Cleaners Inc .... G 302 656-3537
  Wilmington *(G-11199)*

LAUNDRY & GARMENT SVCS, NEC: Garment Alteration & Repair

Marvi Cleaners Limited Inc .... G 302 764-3077
  Wilmington *(G-11553)*

LAUNDRY & GARMENT SVCS, NEC: Garment Making, Alter & Repair

Curzon Corp .... E 302 655-5551
  Wilmington *(G-9922)*

LAUNDRY & GARMENT SVCS: Tailor Shop, Exc Custom/Merchant

Candlelight Bridal Formal Tlrg .... G 302 934-8009
  Millsboro *(G-4654)*

LAUNDRY SVC: Indl Eqpt

Domain Hr Solutions .... F 302 357-9401
  Middletown *(G-4041)*
Nixon Uniform Service Inc .... C 302 325-2875
  New Castle *(G-5571)*

LAUNDRY SVCS: Indl

Jwr 1 LLC .... G 302 379-9951
  Bear *(G-209)*

LAWN & GARDEN EQPT

East Coast Perennials Inc .... G 302 945-5853
  Millsboro *(G-4683)*
Easy Lawn Inc .... E 302 815-6500
  Greenwood *(G-2736)*
Erosion Control Products Corp .... F 302 815-6500
  Greenwood *(G-2739)*
Hydroseeding Company LLC .... E 302 815-6500
  Greenwood *(G-2745)*

LAWN & GARDEN EQPT STORES

Atlantic Tractor LLC .... F 302 834-0114
  Newark *(G-6022)*
Delaware Hardscape Supply LLC .... G 302 996-6464
  Wilmington *(G-10049)*
Pughs Service Inc .... F 302 678-2408
  Dover *(G-1999)*
Tull Brothers Inc .... E 302 629-3071
  Seaford *(G-8427)*
Woodward Enterprises Inc .... F 302 378-2849
  Middletown *(G-4291)*

LAWN MOWER REPAIR SHOP

Foulk Lawn & Equipment Co Inc .... G 302 475-3233
  Wilmington *(G-10599)*
Pughs Service Inc .... F 302 678-2408
  Dover *(G-1999)*
Suburban Lawn & Equipment Inc .... G 302 475-4300
  Wilmington *(G-12785)*
Talleys Garage Inc .... G 302 652-0463
  Wilmington *(G-12850)*

LEASING & RENTAL SVCS: Computer Hardware, Exc Finance

34m LLC .... E 302 444-8290
  Newark *(G-5857)*

LEASING & RENTAL SVCS: Cranes & Aerial Lift Eqpt

Active Crane Rentals Inc .... E 302 998-1000
  Wilmington *(G-8927)*
Don D Corp .... E 302 994-5793
  Wilmington *(G-10192)*
First State Crane Service .... F 302 398-8885
  Felton *(G-2292)*
Raven Crane & Equipment Co LLC ...... G 302 998-1000
  New Castle *(G-5667)*

LEASING & RENTAL: Automobile With Driver

In The Drivers Seat .... G 302 475-3361
  Wilmington *(G-11009)*

LEASING & RENTAL: Construction & Mining Eqpt

Blade Platforms LLC .... G 646 431-1666
  Wilmington *(G-9366)*
Chesapeake Supply & Eqp Co .... G 302 284-1000
  Felton *(G-2283)*
Dozr Ltd .... E 844 218-3697
  Wilmington *(G-10216)*
Eagle Power and Equipment Corp .... F 302 652-3028
  New Castle *(G-5274)*
Heavy Equipment Rental Inc .... F 302 654-5716
  New Castle *(G-6260)*
Interstate Aerials LLC .... G 302 838-1117
  Bear *(G-190)*

Iron Source LLC .... G 302 856-7545
  Georgetown *(G-2568)*
Judd Brook 5 LLC .... G 302 846-3355
  Delmar *(G-1011)*
Knight Hauling Inc .... G 610 494-6800
  Wilmington *(G-11281)*
Sunbelt Rentals Inc .... F 302 907-1921
  Delmar *(G-1032)*
Sunbelt Rentals Inc .... G 302 669-0595
  New Castle *(G-5743)*

LEASING & RENTAL: Medical Machinery & Eqpt

American Homepatient Inc .... D 302 454-4941
  Newark *(G-5953)*
Apria Healthcare LLC .... E 302 737-7979
  Newark *(G-5990)*
Broad Creek Medical Service .... F 302 629-0202
  Seaford *(G-8174)*
Lincare Inc .... G 302 424-8302
  Felton *(G-2305)*
Quinn-Miller Group Inc .... G 302 738-9742
  Wilmington *(G-12290)*
Univita of Florida Inc .... E 239 936-4449
  Wilmington *(G-13032)*

LEASING & RENTAL: Mobile Home Sites

Bayshore Inc .... G 302 539-7200
  Ocean View *(G-7758)*
Canterbury Homes Inc .... G 302 284-0351
  Felton *(G-2279)*
Carlisle Group .... G 302 475-3010
  Wilmington *(G-9572)*
Colonial East LP .... F 302 644-4758
  Lewes *(G-3442)*
Dis Inc .... F 302 834-1633
  Newark *(G-6453)*
Equity Lifestyle Prpts Inc .... G 302 645-5770
  Lewes *(G-3486)*
Equity Lifestyle Prpts Inc .... G 302 945-1544
  Millsboro *(G-4686)*
Holly Hill Estates .... G 302 653-7503
  Smyrna *(G-8653)*
Hometown America LLC .... G 302 945-5186
  Lewes *(G-3544)*
Love Creek Marina MBL Hm Site .... F 302 448-6492
  Lewes *(G-3611)*
Millcreek Mobile Hm Pk Land Co .... F 302 998-3045
  Wilmington *(G-11690)*
Nanticoke Shores Assoc LLC .... F 302 945-1500
  Millsboro *(G-4759)*
Pine Acres Inc .... F 302 945-2000
  Lewes *(G-3692)*
Pinewood Acres MBL Hm Pk L L C ...... G 302 678-1004
  Dover *(G-1960)*
Reybold Group of Companies Inc .... G 302 834-2544
  Bear *(G-306)*
Shady Park Inc .... G 302 436-8441
  Selbyville *(G-8545)*
Sun Communities Inc .... G 302 335-5444
  Frederica *(G-2413)*
Sun Communities Inc .... G 302 227-8118
  Rehoboth Beach *(G-8091)*
Theta Vest Inc .... F 302 227-3745
  Rehoboth Beach *(G-8096)*
Tunnell Companies LP .... E 302 945-9300
  Millsboro *(G-4816)*
Waterford Mhc Inc .... G 302 834-9514
  Bear *(G-371)*
White House Beach Inc .... F 302 945-3032
  Millsboro *(G-4827)*

LEASING & RENTAL: Modular Office Trailers

Sussex Suites LLC .... G 302 856-3351
  Georgetown *(G-2684)*

LEASING & RENTAL: Other Real Estate Property

Carl M Freeman Associates Inc .... C 302 539-6961
  Bethany Beach *(G-391)*
Cigna Real Estate Inc .... G 302 476-3337
  Wilmington *(G-9706)*
Coldwell Bnkr Cml Amato Assoc .... G 302 224-7700
  Newark *(G-6260)*
Double R Holdings Inc .... G 302 645-5555
  Lewes *(G-3470)*

PRODUCT & SERVICES SECTION

LEGAL SVCS: General Practice Attorney or Lawyer

First Class Properties Del LLC .... G 302 677-0770
  Dover (G-1552)
Hensco LLC .... G 302 423-1638
  Harrington (G-2849)
Long & Foster Real Estate Inc .... G 302 227-3821
  Rehoboth Beach (G-7991)
Parkway Gravel Inc .... D 302 658-5241
  New Castle (G-5603)
Pettinaro Construction Co Inc .... D 302 999-0708
  Wilmington (G-12102)
Resortquest Delaware RE LLC .... F 302 541-8999
  Bethany Beach (G-428)
Shipyard Center LLC .... G 302 999-0708
  Wilmington (G-12605)
Tunnell Companies LP .... E 302 945-9300
  Millsboro (G-4816)
Wilgus Associates Inc .... F 302 644-2960
  Lewes (G-3823)

LEASING & RENTAL: Trucks, Without Drivers

Bayshore Ford Truck Sales Inc .... D 302 656-3160
  New Castle (G-5075)
D E Leager Construction .... G 302 994-1060
  Wilmington (G-9939)
Livingston Healthcare Svcs Inc .... B 302 631-5000
  Newark (G-6944)
Martin Newark Dealership Inc .... C 302 454-9300
  Newark (G-6996)
Morton Electric Co .... G 302 645-9414
  Lewes (G-3650)
Penske Truck Leasing Co LP .... F 302 994-7899
  Wilmington (G-12076)
Penske Truck Leasing Co LP .... E 302 325-9290
  New Castle (G-5617)
Penske Truck Leasing Corp .... F 302 629-5373
  Seaford (G-8352)
Penske Truck Leasing Corp .... F 302 658-3255
  Wilmington (G-12077)
Penske Truck Leasing Corp .... G 302 260-7039
  Rehoboth Beach (G-8030)
Penske Truck Leasing Corp .... G 302 449-9294
  Middletown (G-4188)
Spallco Enterprises Inc .... G 302 762-3825
  Wilmington (G-12692)
Tat Trucking Inc .... F 302 261-5444
  Bear (G-347)
U Haul Co Independent Dealers .... G 302 424-3189
  Milford (G-4582)
U Haul Company Independent Dlr .... G 302 369-8230
  Newark (G-7605)
U Haul Neighborhood Dealer .... G 302 613-0207
  Bear (G-362)
U-Haul International Inc .... G 302 762-6445
  Wilmington (G-13004)
U-Haul Neighborhood Dealer .... G 302 644-4316
  Lewes (G-3800)
U-Haul Neighborhood Dealer .... G 302 703-0376
  Lewes (G-3801)
U-Haul Neighborhood Dealer .... G 302 326-1875
  New Castle (G-5800)
U-Haul Neighborhood Dealer .... G 302 449-7379
  Middletown (G-4272)
Watkins System Inc .... E 302 658-8561
  New Castle (G-5827)

LEASING & RENTAL: Utility Trailers & RV's

Morton Electric Co .... G 302 645-9414
  Lewes (G-3650)
Penske Truck Leasing Co LP .... E 302 325-9290
  New Castle (G-5617)

LEASING: Passenger Car

Delaware Motor Sales Inc .... C 302 656-3100
  Wilmington (G-10067)
Esl Inc .... G 302 629-4553
  Seaford (G-8239)
Future Ford Sales Inc .... D 302 999-0261
  Wilmington (G-10654)
Martin Newark Dealership Inc .... C 302 454-9300
  Newark (G-6996)
New Car Connection .... F 302 328-7000
  New Castle (G-5553)
Professional Leasing Inc .... G 302 629-4350
  Seaford (G-8365)
Star States Leasing Corp .... E 302 283-4500
  (G-7484)
Winner Ford of Newark Inc .... G 302 731-2415
  Newark (G-7710)

Winner Group Inc .... E 302 292-8200
  Newark (G-7711)

LEASING: Residential Buildings

Baynum Enterprises Inc .... D 302 629-6104
  Seaford (G-8163)
Baynum Enterprises Inc .... E 302 875-4477
  Laurel (G-3196)
Baynum Enterprises Inc .... E 302 934-8699
  Millsboro (G-4635)
Chandler Heights II LP .... F 302 629-8048
  Seaford (G-8188)
Chelten Preservation Assoc LLC .... F 302 322-6323
  New Castle (G-5142)
Interfaith Cmnty Hsing of Del .... F 302 652-3991
  Wilmington (G-11062)
J & S General Contractors .... F 302 658-4499
  Wilmington (G-11098)
Prudential Gallo Realty .... F 302 645-6661
  Lewes (G-3700)

LEATHER & CUT STOCK WHOLESALERS

Monseco Leather LLC .... F 302 235-1777
  Hockessin (G-3098)

LEATHER GOODS, EXC FOOTWEAR, GLOVES, LUGGAGE/BELTING, WHOL

Masley Enterprises Inc .... E 302 427-9885
  Wilmington (G-11561)

LEATHER GOODS: Feed Bags, Horse

Andy Mast .... G 302 653-5014
  Dover (G-1125)

LEATHER GOODS: Garments

Tough Luck LLC .... G 302 644-8001
  Lewes (G-3792)

LEATHER GOODS: Harnesses Or Harness Parts

Jarel Industries LLC .... G 336 782-0697
  Camden (G-585)

LEATHER GOODS: Wallets

Trihold Inc .... G 302 475-4517
  Wilmington (G-12972)

LEATHER, LEATHER GOODS & FURS, WHOLESALE

Francis Enterprises LLC .... F 302 276-1316
  New Castle (G-5327)

LEATHER: Indl Prdts

Exco Inc .... D 905 477-3065
  Wilmington (G-10458)

LEATHER: Saddlery

Fairway Manufacturing Company .... G 302 398-4630
  Harrington (G-2839)

LECTURE BUREAU

Bki Enterprises LLC .... G 302 541-5317
  Ocean View (G-7768)

LEGAL AID SVCS

Community Legal Aid Society .... D 302 757-7001
  Wilmington (G-9795)
Legal Services Corp Delaware .... G 302 575-0408
  Wilmington (G-11361)
UAW-GM Legal Services Plan .... F 302 562-8212
  Newark (G-7606)

LEGAL OFFICES & SVCS

American Incorporators Ltd .... F 302 421-5752
  Wilmington (G-9049)
Barnett Tom D Law Firm .... G 302 855-9252
  Georgetown (G-2446)
Brown Shels Bauregard LLC .... G 302 226-2270
  Dover (G-1237)
Capitol Credit Services Inc .... F 302 678-1735
  Dover (G-1253)

Cogency Global Inc .... G 800 483-1140
  Dover (G-1301)
Corp1 Inc .... F 720 644-6144
  Dover (G-1313)
Countermeasures Assessment .... G 302 322-9600
  New Castle (G-5200)
CSC Corporate Domains Inc .... F 902 746-5201
  Wilmington (G-9910)
Delaware Claims Agency LLC .... G 212 957-2180
  Wilmington (G-10017)
Delaware Department Finance .... E 302 739-5291
  Dover (G-1364)
Delaware Tchncal Cmnty College .... G 302 259-6160
  Georgetown (G-2504)
Law Office Laura A Yiengst LLC .... G 302 264-9780
  Dover (G-1767)
Legalnature LLC .... G 888 881-1139
  Dover (G-1779)
Poolside Cnstr & Renovation .... G 302 436-9711
  Selbyville (G-8533)
Prentice-Hall Corp System Inc .... F 302 636-5440
  Wilmington (G-12220)
Thomson Reuters (grc) Inc .... A 212 227-7357
  Wilmington (G-12904)
Vps Services LLC .... G 302 376-6710
  Middletown (G-4278)
Whitaker Corporation .... F 302 633-2740
  Wilmington (G-13186)
Whittington & Aulgur .... F 302 378-1661
  Odessa (G-7833)

LEGAL PROCESS SERVERS

Brandywine Process Servers .... G 302 475-2600
  Wilmington (G-9451)
Golt Adj Service Inc .... E 302 798-5500
  Wilmington (G-10744)

LEGAL SVCS: Administrative & Government Law

Brown Stone Nimeroff LLC .... E 302 428-8142
  Wilmington (G-9490)

LEGAL SVCS: Bankruptcy Law

Doroshow Pasquale Karwitz Sieg .... F 302 934-9400
  Millsboro (G-4681)
Doroshow Pasquale Karwitz Sieg .... F 302 424-7744
  Milford (G-4391)
Doroshow Pasquale Karwitz Sieg .... F 302 832-3200
  Bear (G-124)
Doroshow Pasquale Karwitz Sieg .... F 302 998-0100
  Wilmington (G-10205)
Richard S Cobb Esquire .... F 302 467-4430
  Wilmington (G-12411)

LEGAL SVCS: Criminal Law

Malik John S Atty At Law .... G 302 427-2247
  Wilmington (G-11496)
Ronald D Jr Attorney At Law .... G 302 856-9860
  Georgetown (G-2642)

LEGAL SVCS: Debt Collection Law

Patrick Scanlon PA .... G 302 424-1996
  Milford (G-4523)

LEGAL SVCS: Divorce & Family Law

Gonser and Gonser P A .... G 302 478-4445
  Wilmington (G-10745)

LEGAL SVCS: General Practice Attorney or Lawyer

Allmond & Eastburn .... G 302 764-2193
  Wilmington (G-9025)
Archer & Greiner PC .... G 302 858-5151
  Georgetown (G-2433)
Ashby & Geddes .... E 302 654-1888
  Wilmington (G-9148)
Baird Mandalas Brockstedt LLC .... F 302 677-0061
  Dover (G-1168)
Balick & Balick Pllc .... G 302 658-4265
  Wilmington (G-9226)
Ballard Spahr LLP .... G 302 252-4465
  Wilmington (G-9227)
Barros Mc Namara Malkwcz & Tay .... E 302 734-8400
  Dover (G-1174)

Employee Codes: A=Over 500 employees, B=251-500
C=101-250, D=51-100, E=20-50, F=10-19, G=1-9

LEGAL SVCS: General Practice Attorney or Lawyer

Name	Code	Phone
Benesch Friedlander Coplan &	F	216 363-4500
Wilmington (G-9301)		
Beverly L Bove PA	G	302 777-3500
Wilmington (G-9320)		
Blank Rome LLP	E	302 425-6400
Wilmington (G-9368)		
Bonnie M Benson PA	G	302 697-4900
Camden (G-541)		
Brown Shiels & OBrien	F	302 734-4766
Dover (G-1236)		
Bruce A Rogers PA	G	302 856-7161
Georgetown (G-2460)		
Carmine Potter & Associates	G	302 832-6000
Newark (G-6158)		
Carmine Potter & Associates	F	302 658-8940
Wilmington (G-9573)		
Casarino Christman Shalk	E	302 594-4500
Wilmington (G-9586)		
Charles S Knothe Inc	G	302 478-8800
Wilmington (G-9636)		
Charles Slanina	G	302 234-1605
Hockessin (G-2983)		
Ciconte Roseman & Wasserman	F	302 658-7101
Wilmington (G-9701)		
Cindy L Szabo	G	302 855-9505
Georgetown (G-2472)		
Cohen Seglias Pallas	E	302 425-5089
Wilmington (G-9761)		
Cole Schotz PC	E	302 984-9541
Wilmington (G-9767)		
Community Legal Aid Society	F	302 856-0038
Georgetown (G-2479)		
Cooch & Taylor Attys	F	302 652-3641
Wilmington (G-9847)		
Cooch and Taylor A Prof Assn	E	302 984-3800
Wilmington (G-9848)		
Cooper Levenson PA	G	302 838-2600
Bear (G-84)		
Cozen OConnor	F	302 295-2000
Wilmington (G-9886)		
Crossland and Associates	G	302 658-2100
Hockessin (G-2996)		
Curley & Benton LLC	G	302 674-3333
Dover (G-1329)		
Cynthia L Carroll	G	302 733-0411
Newark (G-6338)		
Dalton & Associates PA	G	302 652-2050
Wilmington (G-9950)		
David A Dorey Esq	F	302 425-6400
Wilmington (G-9964)		
De Workers Cmpnstion Legal Ctr	G	302 888-1111
Hockessin (G-3002)		
Deirde A McCartney	G	302 644-8330
Lewes (G-3451)		
Delaware Counsel Group LLP	G	302 543-4870
Rockland (G-8123)		
Delaware Law Office of Larry	G	302 286-6336
Newark (G-6392)		
Doroshow Pasquale Karwitz Sieg	E	302 998-2397
Wilmington (G-10204)		
Doroshow Pasquale Karwitz Sieg	F	302 674-7100
Dover (G-1438)		
Dorsey and Whitney Del LLP	G	302 425-7171
Wilmington (G-10206)		
Eckert Smans Chrin Mellott LLC	D	302 574-7400
Wilmington (G-10336)		
Elzufon Austin Reardon Tarlov	G	302 644-0144
Lewes (G-3481)		
Elzufon Austin Reardon Tarlov	E	302 428-3181
Wilmington (G-10386)		
Eric M Doroshow	G	302 934-9400
Millsboro (G-4687)		
Ferrara Haley & Bevis	F	302 656-7247
Wilmington (G-10524)		
Ferry Joseph & Pearce PA	G	302 856-3706
Georgetown (G-2530)		
Ferry Joseph & Pearce PA	F	302 575-1555
Wilmington (G-10526)		
Fox Rothschild LLP	F	302 654-7444
Wilmington (G-10608)		
Franta Rchard E Attrney At Law	G	302 428-1800
Wilmington (G-10620)		
Frederick K Funk	G	302 368-6233
Newark (G-6614)		
Freibott Law Firm	F	302 633-9000
Wilmington (G-10631)		
Giordano Delcollo & Werb LLC	G	302 234-6855
Wilmington (G-10714)		
Goldfein & Hosmer PC	G	302 656-3301
Wilmington (G-10739)		
Grady & Hampton LLC	G	302 678-1265
Dover (G-1606)		
Grant & Eisenhofer PA	D	302 622-7000
Wilmington (G-10760)		
GSB&b LLC	G	302 425-5800
Wilmington (G-10793)		
Haller & Hudson	G	302 856-4525
Georgetown (G-2554)		
Hartnett & Hartnett	G	302 239-4220
Hockessin (G-3043)		
Harvey Macelree Ltd	F	302 654-4454
Wilmington (G-10848)		
Heckler & Frabizzio PA	F	302 573-4800
Wilmington (G-10879)		
Heiman Gouge & Kaufman LLP	G	302 658-1800
Wilmington (G-10880)		
Herdeg Dupont Dalle Pazze LLP	G	302 655-6500
Wilmington (G-10891)		
Hogan & Veith PA	G	302 656-7540
Wilmington (G-10924)		
Hudson Jnes Jaywork Fisher LLC	E	302 734-7401
Dover (G-1661)		
Jackson Thmas C Attrney At Law	G	302 736-1723
Dover (G-1690)		
James L Holzman	E	302 888-6500
Wilmington (G-11122)		
Jeffrey K Martin PC	G	302 777-4681
Wilmington (G-11144)		
John E Sullivan	G	302 234-6855
Wilmington (G-11168)		
John Williams PA	G	302 571-4780
Wilmington (G-11176)		
Joseph A Hurley PA	G	302 658-8980
Wilmington (G-11184)		
Joseph Longobardi Atty	G	302 575-1502
Wilmington (G-11193)		
Joseph W Benson PA	G	302 656-8811
Wilmington (G-11195)		
Katharine L Mayer Atty	F	302 984-6312
Wilmington (G-11227)		
Katherine Laffey	G	302 651-7999
Wilmington (G-11228)		
Kenneth R Schuster	G	302 984-1000
Wilmington (G-11241)		
Kimberly A Leaman PA	G	301 261-4115
Selbyville (G-8512)		
Knepper & Stratton	G	302 658-1717
Dover (G-1754)		
Laffey Kathryn J The Law Off	G	302 651-7999
Wilmington (G-11324)		
Law Office of R l Masten Jr	G	302 358-2044
Newark (G-6921)		
Lawrence Levinson Attorney	G	302 656-6393
Wilmington (G-11346)		
Leech Tshman Fscaldo Lampl LLC	G	302 421-9379
Wilmington (G-11357)		
Legal Services of Delaware	F	302 575-0408
Wilmington (G-11362)		
Leonard L Williams	G	302 652-3141
Wilmington (G-11373)		
Liguori Morris & Reddin	G	302 678-9900
Dover (G-1788)		
Linarducci & Butler PA	G	302 325-2400
New Castle (G-5483)		
Loizides & Associates PC	G	302 654-0248
Wilmington (G-11428)		
Lyons David J Law Office	G	302 777-5698
Wilmington (G-11464)		
Macelree & Harvey Ltd	G	302 654-4454
Wilmington (G-11473)		
Marks ONeill OBrien Doher	E	302 658-6538
Wilmington (G-11540)		
Maron Mrvel Brdley Anderson PA	D	302 425-5177
Wilmington (G-11524)		
Mattleman Weinroth & Miller PC	G	302 731-8349
Newark (G-7003)		
McCarter & English LLP	D	302 984-6300
Wilmington (G-11586)		
McGivney Kluger & Cook PC	F	302 656-1200
Wilmington (G-11596)		
McLaughlin Gordon L Law Office	G	302 651-7979
Wilmington (G-11602)		
McLaughlin Morton Holdg Co LLC	F	302 426-1313
Wilmington (G-11603)		
Michael B Joseph	F	302 656-0123
Wilmington (G-11658)		
Michael P Morton PA	G	302 426-1313
Wilmington (G-11663)		
Montgomery McCracken	E	302 504-7800
Wilmington (G-11739)		
Mooney & Andrew PA	G	302 856-3070
Georgetown (G-2605)		
Morgan Lewis International LLC	G	302 574-3000
Wilmington (G-11751)		
Morris and Morris	G	302 426-0400
Wilmington (G-11755)		
Morris James LLP	F	302 655-2599
Wilmington (G-11756)		
Morris James LLP	F	302 888-6800
Wilmington (G-11757)		
Morris James LLP	E	302 260-7290
Rehoboth Beach (G-8014)		
Morris James LLP	G	302 678-8815
Dover (G-1873)		
Morris James LLP	D	302 888-6863
Wilmington (G-11758)		
Morris Jmes Htchens Wllams LLP	G	302 368-4200
Newark (G-7059)		
Morris Nchols Arsht Tnnell LLP	C	302 658-9200
Wilmington (G-11759)		
Nolan Williams & Plumhoff	E	410 823-7800
Newark (G-7135)		
Nolte & Brodoway PA	G	302 777-1700
Wilmington (G-11893)		
O Kelly Ernst Belli Wallen LLC	G	302 778-4001
Wilmington (G-11925)		
Patricia P McGonigle	F	302 888-7605
Wilmington (G-12034)		
Phillips Gldmn McLghln & Hll	E	302 655-4200
Wilmington (G-12116)		
Potter Anderson & Corroon LLP	C	302 984-6000
Wilmington (G-12195)		
Rahaim & Saints Attys At Law	F	302 892-9200
Wilmington (G-12306)		
Raskaukas Joseph C Aty Law	G	302 537-2000
Bethany Beach (G-425)		
Raymond E Tomassetti Esq	G	302 539-3041
Fenwick Island (G-2339)		
Raymond E Tomassetti Esq	G	302 995-2840
Wilmington (G-12326)		
Reger Rizzo & Darnall LLP	G	302 652-3611
Wilmington (G-12356)		
Richards Layton & Finger P A	E	302 651-7700
Wilmington (G-12412)		
Richards Layton & Finger P A	B	302 651-7700
Wilmington (G-12413)		
Ridrodsky & Long PA	F	302 691-8822
Wilmington (G-12419)		
Robinson Grayson and Ward PA	G	302 655-6262
Wilmington (G-12444)		
Roger D Anderson	E	302 652-8400
Wilmington (G-12464)		
Rosen Moss Snyder Bleefeld	G	302 475-8060
Wilmington (G-12475)		
Rosner Law Group LLC	G	302 295-4877
Wilmington (G-12478)		
Ross Aronstam & Moritz LLP	F	302 576-1600
Wilmington (G-12479)		
Saul Ewing Arnstein & Lehr LLP	E	302 654-1413
Wilmington (G-12546)		
Schmittinger & Rodriguez PA	D	302 674-0140
Dover (G-2059)		
Schnader Hrrson Sgal Lewis LLP	D	302 888-4554
Wilmington (G-12554)		
Schoenbeck & Schoenbeck PA	G	302 239-9316
Wilmington (G-12555)		
Schwartz & Schwartz Atty At La	G	302 678-8700
Dover (G-2060)		
Seitz Vanogtrop & Green	F	302 888-0600
Wilmington (G-12573)		
Skadden Arps Slate Meagher	C	302 651-3000
Wilmington (G-12639)		
Skadden Arps Slate Meagher & F	B	302 651-3000
Wilmington (G-12640)		
Smith Fnberg McCrtney Berl LLP	E	302 644-8330
Lewes (G-3750)		
Smith Katzenstein & Furlow LLP	E	302 652-8400
Wilmington (G-12660)		
Steen Waehler Schrider Fox LLC	G	302 539-7900
Ocean View (G-7814)		
Steven J Stirparo	G	302 479-9555
Wilmington (G-12761)		
Stevens & Lee PC	E	302 654-5180
Wilmington (G-12762)		
Tarabicos Grosso	G	302 757-7800
New Castle (G-5753)		
Thomas J Allingham II	E	302 651-3000
Wilmington (G-12901)		
Tighe and Cottrell PA	F	302 658-6400
Wilmington (G-12909)		

PRODUCT & SERVICES SECTION

LIGHTING FIXTURES, NEC

Tunnell & Raysor PA .... E 302 856-7313
  Georgetown *(G-2696)*
Tunnell & Raysor PA .... G 302 226-4420
  Rehoboth Beach *(G-8100)*
Tunnell & Raysor PA .... G 302 644-4442
  Lewes *(G-3798)*
Tybout Redfearn & Pell PA .... D 302 658-6901
  Wilmington *(G-13001)*
Vance A Funk III .... G 302 368-2561
  Newark *(G-7643)*
Vivian A Houghton Esquire .... G 302 658-0518
  Wilmington *(G-13097)*
Weber Gallagher Simpson .... G 302 346-6377
  Dover *(G-2209)*
Weik Nitsche & Dougherty .... E 302 655-4040
  Wilmington *(G-13138)*
Wharton Levin Ehrmantraut .... G 302 252-0090
  Wilmington *(G-13181)*
White and Williams LLP .... F 302 654-0424
  Wilmington *(G-13189)*
Whittington & Aulgur .... G 302 235-5800
  Yorklyn *(G-13368)*
Wilbraham Lawler & Buba PC .... G 302 421-9922
  Wilmington *(G-13199)*
William E Ward PA .... F 302 225-3350
  Wilmington *(G-13208)*
William W Erhart PA .... G 302 651-0113
  Wilmington *(G-13216)*
Williams Law Firm PA .... G 302 575-0873
  Wilmington *(G-13218)*
Woloshin and Lynch Associates .... F 302 449-2606
  Middletown *(G-4289)*
Womble Bond Dickinson (us) LLP .... D 302 252-4320
  Wilmington *(G-13289)*
Young and Malmberg PA .... F 302 672-5600
  Dover *(G-2247)*

LEGAL SVCS: General Practice Law Office

Archer & Greiner PC .... G 302 777-4350
  Wilmington *(G-9122)*
Atlantic Law Group LLC .... E 302 854-0380
  Georgetown *(G-2439)*
Betts & Abram PA LLC .... G 302 856-7755
  Georgetown *(G-2454)*
Biggs & Battaglia .... F 302 655-9677
  Wilmington *(G-9335)*
Boudart & Mensinger LLP .... G 302 428-0100
  Wilmington *(G-9397)*
Community Legal Aid Society .... G 302 674-8500
  Dover *(G-1306)*
Curran James P Law Offices .... G 302 894-1111
  Newark *(G-6327)*
Delaware Counsel Group LLP .... G 302 576-9600
  Wilmington *(G-10028)*
Draper & Goldberg Pllc .... G 302 448-4040
  Georgetown *(G-2514)*
Drinker Biddle & Reath LLP .... F 302 467-4200
  Wilmington *(G-10236)*
Fish & Richardson PC .... E 302 652-5070
  Wilmington *(G-10560)*
Flowers Counsel Group LLC .... G 302 656-7370
  Wilmington *(G-10578)*
Fuqua & Yori P A .... F 302 856-7777
  Georgetown *(G-2536)*
Gary A Bryde PA .... G 302 239-3700
  Hockessin *(G-3035)*
Gill Edward Law Offices of .... F 302 854-5400
  Georgetown *(G-2548)*
Gordon Fournaris Mammarella PA .... E 302 652-2900
  Wilmington *(G-10754)*
Hamilton Pepper LLP .... E 302 777-6500
  Wilmington *(G-10828)*
Harris Berger LLC .... G 302 665-1140
  Wilmington *(G-10842)*
Heiman Aber Goldlust & Baker .... E 302 658-1800
  Wilmington *(G-10881)*
Hudson Jnes Jaywork Fisher LLC .... F 302 227-9441
  Rehoboth Beach *(G-7966)*
Jacobs & Crumplar PA .... E 302 656-5445
  Wilmington *(G-11117)*
Karen Y Vcks Law Offces of LLC .... G 302 674-1100
  Dover *(G-1722)*
Kimmel Carter Roman & Peltz .... F 302 565-6100
  Christiana *(G-671)*
Knepper & Stratton .... G 302 658-1717
  Wilmington *(G-11279)*
Labaton Sucharow LLP .... F 302 573-6938
  Wilmington *(G-11313)*
Landis Rath & Cobb LLP .... F 302 467-4400
  Wilmington *(G-11327)*

Law Office of James Curra .... G 302 894-1111
  Newark *(G-6920)*
Law Offices Gary R Dodge PA .... G 302 674-5400
  Dover *(G-1768)*
Lyons Doughty & Veldhuis .... D 302 428-1670
  Wilmington *(G-11465)*
Manning Gross + Massenburg LLP .... F 302 657-2100
  Wilmington *(G-11504)*
Margolis Edelstein .... E 302 888-1112
  Wilmington *(G-11524)*
Marshall Dennehey .... E 302 552-4300
  Wilmington *(G-11545)*
Martin Daniel D & Assoc LLC .... G 302 658-2884
  Wilmington *(G-11549)*
Monzack Mersky McLaughlin 302 656-8162
  Wilmington *(G-11741)*
Murphy & Landon PC .... F 302 472-8100
  Wilmington *(G-11776)*
Novak Druce Cnnlly Bv+qigg LLP .... C 302 252-9922
  Wilmington *(G-11911)*
Office John M Law .... G 302 427-2369
  Wilmington *(G-11939)*
P A Bayard .... D 302 429-4212
  Wilmington *(G-11991)*
Parkowski Guerke & Swayze PA .... E 302 678-3262
  Dover *(G-1936)*
Parkway Law LLC .... G 302 449-0400
  Townsend *(G-8815)*
Philip M Finestrauss PA .... G 302 984-1600
  Wilmington *(G-12114)*
R Stokes Nolte Esquire & .... G 302 777-1700
  Wilmington *(G-12298)*
Ramunno & Ramunno & Scerba PA .... F 302 656-9400
  Wilmington *(G-12315)*
Reilly Janiczek & McDevitt PC .... F 302 777-1700
  Wilmington *(G-12370)*
Roeberg Moore & Associates PA .... F 302 658-4757
  Wilmington *(G-12463)*
Rosenthal Monhait Goddess PA .... F 302 656-4433
  Wilmington *(G-12477)*
Schab & Barnett PA .... G 302 856-9024
  Georgetown *(G-2648)*
Smith Firm LLC .... G 302 875-5595
  Seaford *(G-8403)*
Smith Fnberg McCrtney Berl LLP .... E 302 856-7082
  Georgetown *(G-2657)*
Snyder Associates PA .... G 302 657-8300
  Wilmington *(G-12667)*
Street & Ellis P A .... G 302 735-8408
  Dover *(G-2110)*
Stumpf Vickers and Sandy .... F 302 856-3561
  Georgetown *(G-2669)*
Weiss & Saville PA .... G 302 656-0400
  Wilmington *(G-13140)*
Werb & Sullivan .... F 302 652-1100
  Wilmington *(G-13160)*
Whittington & Aulgur .... F 302 378-1661
  Middletown *(G-4286)*
Wilson Halbrook & Bayard PA .... F 302 856-0015
  Georgetown *(G-2705)*
Young & McNelis .... G 302 674-8822
  Dover *(G-2246)*
Young Cnway Strgatt Taylor LLP .... C 302 571-6600
  Wilmington *(G-13330)*

LEGAL SVCS: Immigration & Naturalization Law

La Esperanza Inc .... F 302 854-9262
  Georgetown *(G-2585)*

LEGAL SVCS: Malpractice & Negligence Law

Marin Bayard .... G 302 658-4200
  Wilmington *(G-11525)*

LEGAL SVCS: Real Estate Law

Sergovic & Carmean P A .... G 302 855-1260
  Georgetown *(G-2649)*
Sergovic Carmean Weidman .... F 302 855-0551
  Georgetown *(G-2650)*
Ward & Taylor LLC .... G 302 227-1403
  Rehoboth Beach *(G-8108)*
Ward & Taylor LLC .... E 302 225-3350
  Wilmington *(G-13119)*

LEGAL SVCS: Securities Law

Supreme Court of The State Del .... G 302 255-0544
  Wilmington *(G-12815)*

LEGAL SVCS: Specialized Law Offices, Attorney

Bifferato Gentilotti LLC .... G 302 429-1900
  Wilmington *(G-9329)*
Bifferato Gentilotti LLC .... G 302 429-1900
  Wilmington *(G-9330)*
Bodell Bove LLC .... F 302 655-6749
  Wilmington *(G-9390)*
Business Centric Svcs Group .... G 302 984-3800
  Wilmington *(G-9509)*
Cross & Simon LLC 302 777-4200
  Wilmington *(G-9903)*
David I Walsh Esquire PA .... G 302 498-0760
  Lewes *(G-3448)*
Greenberg Praurig LLC .... E 302 661-7000
  Wilmington *(G-10776)*
Law Firm .... F 302 472-4900
  Wilmington *(G-11340)*
Losco and Marconi PA .... G 302 656-7776
  Wilmington *(G-11437)*
Pratcher Krayer LLC .... G 302 803-5291
  Wilmington *(G-12197)*
Rhoades & Morrow LLC .... F 302 427-9500
  Wilmington *(G-12401)*
Stewart Law Firm .... G 302 652-5200
  Wilmington *(G-12763)*
Wilks Lukoff & Bracegirdle LLC .... G 302 225-0850
  Wilmington *(G-13205)*

LEGITIMATE LIVE THEATER PRODUCERS

Clear Space Theatre Company .... G 302 227-2270
  Rehoboth Beach *(G-7892)*
Dickens Parlour Theatre .... G 302 829-1071
  Millville *(G-4842)*

LESSORS: Farm Land

JG Townsend Jr & Co Inc .... E 302 856-2525
  Georgetown *(G-2574)*
Vance Phillips Inc .... G 302 542-1501
  Laurel *(G-3301)*

LIABILITY INSURANCE

AAA Club Alliance Inc .... B 302 299-4700
  Wilmington *(G-8893)*
Highmarks Inc .... G 302 421-3000
  Wilmington *(G-10906)*

LIFE INSURANCE CARRIERS

Cigna Corporation .... C 302 792-4906
  Wilmington *(G-9704)*
First Lincoln Holdings Inc .... E 302 429-4900
  Wilmington *(G-10546)*

LIFESAVING & SURVIVAL EQPT, EXC MEDICAL, WHOLESALE

Anderson Group Inc .... G 302 478-6160
  Wilmington *(G-9078)*
Honeywell Safety Pdts USA Inc .... F 302 636-5401
  Wilmington *(G-10948)*

LIGHTERS, CIGARETTE & CIGAR, WHOLESALE

Books & Tobaccos Inc .... F 302 994-3156
  Wilmington *(G-9393)*

LIGHTING EQPT: Outdoor

Sun-In-One Inc .... G 302 762-3100
  Wilmington *(G-12798)*

LIGHTING FIXTURES WHOLESALERS

Colonial Electric Supply Co .... F 302 998-9993
  New Castle *(G-5181)*
Diversified Lighting Assoc Inc .... G 302 286-6370
  Wilmington *(G-10171)*
Grossman Electric Supply Inc .... G 302 655-5561
  New Castle *(G-5364)*

LIGHTING FIXTURES, NEC

Detweilers Lighting .... G 302 678-5804
  Hartly *(G-2919)*
Evergreen Led .... G 302 218-7819
  Townsend *(G-8785)*

LIGHTING FIXTURES, NEC

Ledtolight...G...... 941 323-6664
Wilmington *(G-11354)*
Newport..G...... 302 995-2840
Wilmington *(G-11877)*
Smb Lighting...G...... 302 733-0664
Newark *(G-7448)*

LIGHTING FIXTURES: Indl & Commercial

Acuity Brands Lighting Inc...................E...... 302 476-2055
New Castle *(G-5002)*
Illumination Technology Inc..................G...... 410 430-5349
Delmar *(G-1004)*
Pemco Lighting Products Inc...............G...... 302 892-9000
Wilmington *(G-12061)*
Pemco Lighting Products LLC.............G...... 302 892-9000
Wilmington *(G-12062)*
Rigel Energy Group LLC.......................F...... 888 624-9844
Wilmington *(G-12421)*
Way To Go Led Lighting Company......F...... 844 312-4574
Newark *(G-7679)*

LIGHTING FIXTURES: Motor Vehicle

Arrow Safety Device Co........................F...... 302 856-2516
Selbyville *(G-8450)*
G K Associates Inc...............................G...... 302 381-2824
Rehoboth Beach *(G-7940)*

LIGHTING FIXTURES: Residential

Acuity Brands Lighting Inc...................E...... 302 476-2055
New Castle *(G-5002)*
Fme Lighting LLC..................................G...... 877 234-8460
Rehoboth Beach *(G-7936)*
Pemco Lighting Products Inc...............G...... 302 892-9000
Wilmington *(G-12061)*

LIGHTING FIXTURES: Residential, Electric

Jaykal Led Solutions Inc......................G...... 302 295-0015
Harbeson *(G-2788)*

LIMOUSINE SVCS

Bayside Limousine................................F...... 302 644-6999
Millsboro *(G-4636)*
Buker Limousine & Trnsp Svc..............F...... 302 234-7600
Newark *(G-6135)*
Citywide Transportation Inc..................F...... 302 792-0159
Wilmington *(G-9727)*
Class Limousine Service......................G...... 302 653-1166
Smyrna *(G-8597)*
Dnd Limousine Service.........................E...... 302 998-5856
Wilmington *(G-10178)*
Eagle Limousine Inc..............................C...... 302 325-4200
New Castle *(G-5273)*
First Class Limousine...........................G...... 302 836-9500
New Castle *(G-5313)*
Genes Limousine Service Inc..............E...... 410 479-8470
Bridgeville *(G-474)*
Harding Limo Bus Cnnection LLC.......G...... 302 376-1818
Middletown *(G-4104)*
Limo Exchange......................................F...... 302 322-1200
New Castle *(G-5482)*
Limousine Unlimited LLC.....................F...... 302 284-1100
Felton *(G-2304)*
New Castle Shuttle and Taxi SE..........G...... 302 326-1855
New Castle *(G-5566)*
Primetime Limousine............................F...... 302 425-5599
Wilmington *(G-12227)*
Roadrunner Express Inc......................E...... 302 426-9551
Wilmington *(G-12433)*
Stars Transportation LLC.....................G...... 770 530-1843
Harrington *(G-2893)*

LINEN SPLY SVC

All Star Linen and Uniform Co.............G...... 302 897-9003
Wilmington *(G-9016)*
Capitol Cleaners & Launderers............D...... 302 674-1511
Dover *(G-1251)*
Selbyville Cleaners Inc.........................E...... 302 249-3444
Selbyville *(G-8544)*

LINEN SPLY SVC: Towel

Socal Auto Supply Inc..........................D...... 818 717-9982
Lewes *(G-3751)*

LINEN SPLY SVC: Uniform

Alsco Inc..E...... 302 322-2136
New Castle *(G-5027)*

Palace Laundry Inc...............................E...... 302 322-2136
New Castle *(G-5598)*

LINEN STORES

Initial Trading Co...................................G...... 302 428-1132
Wilmington *(G-11034)*

LININGS: Fabric, Apparel & Other, Exc Millinery

Be Blessed Design Group LLC............G...... 302 561-3793
Bear *(G-45)*

LIP BALMS

Lip Balm Land LLC................................G...... 302 319-9919
Wilmington *(G-11399)*

LIQUEFIED PETROLEUM GAS DEALERS

Petroleum Equipment Inc.....................E...... 302 734-7433
Dover *(G-1951)*

LIQUEFIED PETROLEUM GAS WHOLESALERS

Sherman Heating Oils Inc....................G...... 302 684-4008
Milton *(G-4968)*
Sherman Heating Oils Inc....................F...... 302 684-4008
Milton *(G-4969)*

LOAN CORRESPONDENTS

True Access Capital Corp....................F...... 302 652-6774
Wilmington *(G-12986)*

LOBBYING SVCS

Willis Groupllc.......................................G...... 302 632-9898
Dover *(G-2229)*

LOCKS

Black & Decker Inc................................G...... 860 827-3861
Newark *(G-6087)*

LOCKSMITHS

Allied Lock & Safe Company................G...... 302 658-3172
Wilmington *(G-9023)*
Certified Lock & Access LLC...............G...... 302 383-7507
Wilmington *(G-9618)*

LOGGING

Summers Logging LLC.........................G...... 302 234-8725
Hockessin *(G-3152)*
Whitetail Country Log & Hlg.................G...... 302 846-3982
Delmar *(G-1048)*

LOGGING CAMPS & CONTRACTORS

American Timber Brokerage.................G...... 302 655-8471
Wilmington *(G-9058)*
Aslin Inc...G...... 302 674-1900
Dover *(G-1145)*
D&C Logging..G...... 302 846-3982
Delmar *(G-990)*
High Vue Logging Inc...........................G...... 302 697-3606
Camden *(G-579)*

LOOSELEAF BINDERS

Cann-Erikson Bindery Inc....................F...... 302 995-6636
Wilmington *(G-9550)*
L E Stansell Inc.....................................G...... 302 475-1534
Wilmington *(G-11308)*

LOTIONS OR CREAMS: Face

Glaxosmithkline Holdings....................C...... 302 984-6932
Wilmington *(G-10720)*
Laboratoires Esthederm USA Inc........G...... 514 270-3763
Wilmington *(G-11314)*

LOTIONS: SHAVING

Remarle..G...... 215 245-6644
Middletown *(G-4216)*

LUBRICANTS: Corrosion Preventive

Nalco Company LLC.............................E...... 856 423-6417
New Castle *(G-5543)*

LUBRICATING OIL & GREASE WHOLESALERS

Chemours Company Fc LLC................F...... 302 773-1267
Wilmington *(G-9650)*
Sandy Brae Laboratories Inc..............G...... 302 456-0446
Newark *(G-7382)*
Vp Racing Fuels Inc.............................G...... 302 368-1500
Newark *(G-7666)*

LUGGAGE & BRIEFCASES

Travelway Group USA Inc....................G...... 514 331-3130
Wilmington *(G-12961)*

LUGGAGE WHOLESALERS

Blu H20 Ltd...G...... 302 875-4810
Laurel *(G-3201)*

LUMBER & BLDG MATLS DEALER, RET: Garage Doors, Sell/Install

Hickman Overhead Door Company.....F...... 302 422-4249
Milford *(G-4441)*
Precision Door Service.........................G...... 302 343-6394
Wilmington *(G-12204)*

LUMBER & BLDG MATRLS DEALERS, RET: Bath Fixtures, Eqpt/Sply

Zenith Home Corp.................................B...... 302 326-8200
New Castle *(G-5845)*

LUMBER & BLDG MTRLS DEALERS, RET: Greenhouse Kits, Prefab

Pepper Greenhouses.............................G...... 302 684-8092
Milton *(G-4948)*

LUMBER & BLDG MTRLS DEALERS, RET: Windows, Storm, Wood/Metal

Newport Builders & Windowland..........F...... 302 994-3537
Wilmington *(G-11878)*

LUMBER & BUILDING MATERIALS DEALER, RET: Door & Window Prdts

Mark Ventresca Associates Inc...........G...... 302 239-3925
Hockessin *(G-3089)*

LUMBER & BUILDING MATERIALS DEALER, RET: Masonry Matls/Splys

Allan Myers Materials Inc....................G...... 302 734-8632
Dover *(G-1108)*
Casale Marble Imports Inc..................D...... 561 404-4213
Wilmington *(G-9585)*

LUMBER & BUILDING MATERIALS DEALERS, RET: Solar Heating Eqpt

African Wood Inc...................................G...... 302 884-6738
Wilmington *(G-8973)*

LUMBER & BUILDING MATERIALS DEALERS, RETAIL: Brick

Delaware Brick Company.....................E...... 302 994-0948
Wilmington *(G-10008)*

LUMBER & BUILDING MATERIALS DEALERS, RETAIL: Countertops

Cabinetry Unlimited LLC......................E...... 302 436-5030
Selbyville *(G-8465)*

LUMBER & BUILDING MATERIALS DEALERS, RETAIL: Modular Homes

Dick Ennis Inc.......................................G...... 302 945-2627
Lewes *(G-3464)*
Vaughan Bckley Modular Sls Inc........G...... 215 259-7509
Wilmington *(G-13051)*

PRODUCT & SERVICES SECTION
MACHINERY & EQPT, INDL, WHOLESALE: Recycling

LUMBER & BUILDING MATERIALS DEALERS, RETAIL: Tile, Ceramic
Jack Parisi Tile Co Inc .... G 302 892-2455
  Wilmington *(G-11115)*

LUMBER: Hardwood Dimension
Delmarva Hardwood Products .... F 302 349-4101
  Laurel *(G-3222)*

LUMBER: Hardwood Dimension & Flooring Mills
Gordys Lumber Inc .... F 302 875-3502
  Laurel *(G-3234)*
Grubb Lumber Company Inc .... E 302 652-2800
  Wilmington *(G-10791)*
Warren Truss Co .... F 302 368-8566
  Newark *(G-7676)*

LUMBER: Rails, Fence, Round Or Split
Delaware Valley Fence & Iron .... G 302 322-8193
  New Castle *(G-5242)*

LUMBER: Treated
Glory Contracting .... G 302 275-5430
  Townsend *(G-8789)*

LUMBER: Veneer, Hardwood
Maneto Inc .... G 302 656-4285
  Wilmington *(G-11501)*

MACHINE PARTS: Stamped Or Pressed Metal
Bear Forge and Machine Co Inc .... G 302 322-5199
  Bear *(G-47)*

MACHINE SHOPS
Deangelis & Son Inc .... G 302 337-8699
  Bridgeville *(G-464)*
Nanticoke Consulting Inc .... G 302 424-0750
  Greenwood *(G-2755)*

MACHINE TOOL ACCESS: Diamond Cutting, For Turning, Etc
Applied Diamond Inc .... G 302 999-1132
  Wilmington *(G-9102)*
Ddk .... F 302 999-1132
  Wilmington *(G-9984)*

MACHINE TOOL ACCESS: Pushers
Alexis Wirt .... G 302 654-4236
  Wilmington *(G-9005)*
Petal Pushers LLC .... G 302 945-0350
  Lewes *(G-3685)*

MACHINE TOOL ACCESS: Tools & Access
Mechanical Systems Intl Corp .... F 302 453-8315
  Newark *(G-7014)*

MACHINE TOOLS, METAL CUTTING: Tool Replacement & Rpr Parts
Mazzpac LLC .... G 973 641-9159
  Newark *(G-7009)*
Seaford Machine Works Inc .... F 302 629-6034
  Seaford *(G-8392)*

MACHINE TOOLS, METAL FORMING: Mechanical, Pneumatic Or Hyd
Miller Metal Fabrication Inc .... D 302 337-2291
  Bridgeville *(G-501)*

MACHINE TOOLS: Metal Cutting
Diy Tool Supply LLC .... G 302 253-8461
  Georgetown *(G-2512)*
Paul A Lange .... G 302 378-1706
  Middletown *(G-4183)*

MACHINE TOOLS: Metal Forming
Delaware Capital Formation Inc .... G 302 793-4921
  Wilmington *(G-10010)*

MACHINERY & EQPT FINANCE LEASING
B Williams Holding Corp .... F 302 656-8596
  Wilmington *(G-9214)*
Pinnacle Funding Inc .... G 302 657-0160
  Wilmington *(G-12142)*

MACHINERY & EQPT, AGRICULTURAL, WHOL: Farm Eqpt Parts/Splys
Binkley Hurst LP .... G 302 628-3135
  Seaford *(G-8169)*
Tull Brothers Inc .... E 302 629-3071
  Seaford *(G-8427)*

MACHINERY & EQPT, AGRICULTURAL, WHOLESALE: Agricultural, NEC
Messick & Gray Cnstr Inc .... E 302 337-8777
  Bridgeville *(G-497)*
Messick & Gray Cnstr Inc .... F 302 337-8445
  Bridgeville *(G-498)*

MACHINERY & EQPT, AGRICULTURAL, WHOLESALE: Farm Implements
Hoober Inc .... D 717 768-8231
  Middletown *(G-4109)*

MACHINERY & EQPT, AGRICULTURAL, WHOLESALE: Garden, NEC
Whaleys Seed Store Inc .... G 302 875-7833
  Laurel *(G-3308)*

MACHINERY & EQPT, AGRICULTURAL, WHOLESALE: Landscaping Eqpt
All Rock & Mulch LLC .... G 302 838-7625
  Bear *(G-25)*
Delaware Hardscape Supply LLC .... G 302 996-6464
  Wilmington *(G-10049)*

MACHINERY & EQPT, AGRICULTURAL, WHOLESALE: Lawn & Garden
W Enterprises LLC .... G 302 875-0430
  Laurel *(G-3303)*
Woodward Enterprises Inc .... F 302 378-2849
  Middletown *(G-4291)*

MACHINERY & EQPT, AGRICULTURAL, WHOLESALE: Poultry Eqpt
Bunting & Bertrand Inc .... F 302 732-6836
  Frankford *(G-2351)*
Peninsula Poultry Eqp Co Inc .... F 302 875-0889
  Laurel *(G-3270)*

MACHINERY & EQPT, AGRICULTURAL, WHOLESALE: Tractors
Judd Brook 5 LLC .... G 302 846-3355
  Delmar *(G-1011)*

MACHINERY & EQPT, INDL, WHOL: Brewery Prdts Mfrg, Commercial
Wilmington .... G 302 357-4509
  Wilmington *(G-13221)*

MACHINERY & EQPT, INDL, WHOL: Controlling Instruments/Access
Instruments & Thermal Products .... G 302 378-6290
  Townsend *(G-8798)*

MACHINERY & EQPT, INDL, WHOLESALE: Chemical Process
Kahl Company Inc .... G 302 478-8450
  Wilmington *(G-11220)*
Schlegel Associates Inc .... G 302 477-1810
  Wilmington *(G-12553)*

MACHINERY & EQPT, INDL, WHOLESALE: Cranes
Jaa Industries LLC .... G 302 332-0388
  New Castle *(G-5433)*

MACHINERY & EQPT, INDL, WHOLESALE: Drilling, Exc Bits
Automation Air Inc .... G 973 875-6676
  Bridgeville *(G-450)*

MACHINERY & EQPT, INDL, WHOLESALE: Engines & Parts, Diesel
Careys Diesel Inc .... F 302 678-3797
  Leipsic *(G-3313)*

MACHINERY & EQPT, INDL, WHOLESALE: Fans
WW Grainger Inc .... F 302 322-1840
  New Castle *(G-5842)*

MACHINERY & EQPT, INDL, WHOLESALE: Food Manufacturing
Franke USA Holding Inc .... F 615 462-4000
  Wilmington *(G-10614)*
JLJ Enterprises Inc .... F 302 398-0229
  Harrington *(G-2857)*

MACHINERY & EQPT, INDL, WHOLESALE: Food Product Manufacturng
Delaware Capital Formation Inc .... G 302 793-4921
  Wilmington *(G-10010)*
Delaware Capital Holdings Inc .... G 302 793-4921
  Wilmington *(G-10011)*

MACHINERY & EQPT, INDL, WHOLESALE: Hydraulic Systems
Benz Hydraulics Inc .... F 302 328-6648
  New Castle *(G-5082)*
Fiduks Industrial Services Inc .... F 302 994-2534
  Wilmington *(G-10537)*
Sussex Hydraulics Sales & Svcs .... G 302 846-9702
  Delmar *(G-1033)*

MACHINERY & EQPT, INDL, WHOLESALE: Indl Machine Parts
Mitusha International Corp .... G 302 674-2977
  Dover *(G-1863)*
Phalco Inc .... G 302 654-2620
  Wilmington *(G-12107)*
Power Trans Inc .... F 302 337-3016
  Bridgeville *(G-512)*

MACHINERY & EQPT, INDL, WHOLESALE: Lift Trucks & Parts
Cod Lift Truck Inc .... G 302 656-7731
  Wilmington *(G-9757)*

MACHINERY & EQPT, INDL, WHOLESALE: Machine Tools & Access
Arnold International Inc .... G 302 266-4441
  Newark *(G-5998)*
Fiduks Industrial Services Inc .... F 302 994-2534
  Wilmington *(G-10536)*

MACHINERY & EQPT, INDL, WHOLESALE: Measure/Test, Electric
Testing Machines Inc .... E 302 613-5600
  New Castle *(G-5764)*

MACHINERY & EQPT, INDL, WHOLESALE: Metal Refining
Philadlphia Ball Rller Bearing .... G 215 727-0982
  Wilmington *(G-12113)*

MACHINERY & EQPT, INDL, WHOLESALE: Recycling
Technicare Inc .... G 302 322-7766
  Newark *(G-7545)*

MACHINERY & EQPT, INDL, WHOLESALE: Robots

Automation Partnership .... G 302 478-9060
  Wilmington *(G-9188)*

MACHINERY & EQPT, INDL, WHOLESALE: Safety Eqpt

Cintas Corporation No 2 .... G 302 765-6460
  Wilmington *(G-9709)*
Ellis Ladder Improvements .... G 302 571-8470
  Wilmington *(G-10380)*
First State Distributors Inc .... G 302 655-8266
  Wilmington *(G-10551)*
Sussex Protection Service LLC .... F 302 337-0209
  Bridgeville *(G-522)*
Totaltrax Inc .... D 302 514-0600
  New Castle *(G-5778)*

MACHINERY & EQPT, INDL, WHOLESALE: Sawmill

Advanced Machinery Sales Inc .... F 302 322-2226
  New Castle *(G-5009)*
Eastern Shore Metals LLC .... F 302 629-6629
  Seaford *(G-8231)*

MACHINERY & EQPT, INDL, WHOLESALE: Tractors, Indl

Traction Wholesale Center Inc .... G 302 743-8473
  Wilmington *(G-12946)*

MACHINERY & EQPT, INDL, WHOLESALE: Water Pumps

Square One Electric Service Co .... F 302 678-0400
  Dover *(G-2099)*

MACHINERY & EQPT, INDL, WHOLESALE: Woodworking

Asw Machinery Inc .... F 899 792-5288
  New Castle *(G-5049)*

MACHINERY & EQPT, WHOLESALE: Bailey Bridges

Bristol Industrial Corporation .... F 302 322-1100
  New Castle *(G-5115)*

MACHINERY & EQPT, WHOLESALE: Construction, General

Chesapeake Supply & Eqp Co .... G 302 284-1000
  Felton *(G-2283)*
E-Industrial Suppliers LLC .... G 302 251-6210
  Wilmington *(G-10313)*
Eagle Power and Equipment Corp .... F 302 652-3028
  New Castle *(G-5274)*
Fmj Electrical Contracting .... G 215 669-2085
  Claymont *(G-746)*
Industrial Products of Del .... F 302 328-6648
  New Castle *(G-5415)*
S G Williams & Bros Co .... F 302 656-8167
  Wilmington *(G-12506)*
Th White General Contract .... G 302 945-1829
  Millsboro *(G-4812)*

MACHINERY & EQPT, WHOLESALE: Contractors Materials

Foley Incorporated .... E 302 328-4131
  Bear *(G-157)*
Price Is Right Contracting LLC .... F 215 760-1416
  Wilmington *(G-12224)*

MACHINERY & EQPT, WHOLESALE: Masonry

Delaware Brick Company .... G 302 883-2507
  Dover *(G-1361)*

MACHINERY & EQPT, WHOLESALE: Oil Field Eqpt

Wm Systems Inc .... G 302 450-4482
  Wilmington *(G-13282)*

MACHINERY & EQPT: Farm

Easy Lawn Inc .... E 302 815-6500
  Greenwood *(G-2736)*
Farmers Harvest Inc .... G 302 734-7708
  Dover *(G-1541)*
James Atkinson .... G 302 236-7499
  Harrington *(G-2854)*
Lumi Cases LLC .... G 302 525-6971
  Newark *(G-6956)*

MACHINERY & EQPT: Gas Producers, Generators/Other Rltd Eqpt

Kissangen Inc .... E 414 446-4182
  Newark *(G-6895)*

MACHINERY & EQPT: Liquid Automation

Steven Abdill .... G 443 243-6864
  Wilmington *(G-12758)*

MACHINERY BASES

A B Fab & Machining LLC .... G 302 293-4945
  New Castle *(G-4991)*

MACHINERY, COMMERCIAL LAUNDRY: Washing, Incl Coin-Operated

Service General Corp .... C 302 856-3500
  Georgetown *(G-2651)*

MACHINERY, FOOD PRDTS: Food Processing, Smokers

Fishing Inc .... G 302 999-9961
  Wilmington *(G-10563)*

MACHINERY, MAILING: Mailing

B Williams Holding Corp .... F 302 656-8596
  Wilmington *(G-9214)*

MACHINERY, METALWORKING: Rotary Slitters, Metalworking

Junttan USA Inc .... G 302 500-1274
  Laurel *(G-3246)*

MACHINERY, OFFICE: Stapling, Hand Or Power

Black & Decker Inc .... G 860 827-3861
  Newark *(G-6087)*

MACHINERY, PRINTING TRADES: Printing Trade Parts & Attchts

Roller Service Corporation .... E 302 737-5000
  Newark *(G-7361)*

MACHINERY/EQPT, AGRICULTURAL, WHOL: Wind Mach, Frost Protctn

Bluewater Wind LLC .... G 302 731-7020
  Lewes *(G-3389)*

MACHINERY/EQPT, INDL, WHOL: Cleaning, High Press, Sand/Steam

Barrys Cleaning Service .... G 302 653-0110
  Clayton *(G-837)*
John J Buckley Associates Inc .... G 302 475-5443
  Wilmington *(G-11172)*
John R Seiberlich Inc .... D 302 356-2400
  New Castle *(G-5441)*
Progressive Systems Inc .... G 302 732-3321
  Frankford *(G-2381)*

MACHINERY: Construction

Advance Marine LLC .... G 302 656-2111
  Wilmington *(G-8947)*
Teksolv Usd Inc .... G 302 738-1050
  Newark *(G-7552)*
Xcmg Machinery Us LLC .... G 786 796-1094
  Wilmington *(G-13315)*

MACHINERY: Cryogenic, Industrial

Cae(us) Inc .... G 813 885-7481
  Wilmington *(G-9533)*

MACHINERY: Custom

Trim Waste Management LLC .... G 302 738-2500
  Newark *(G-7592)*

MACHINERY: Engraving

Laser Marking Works LLC .... G 786 307-6203
  Wilmington *(G-11333)*

MACHINERY: Industrial, NEC

Croesus Inc .... G 302 472-9260
  Wilmington *(G-9902)*
State Line Machine Inc .... G 302 875-2248
  Laurel *(G-3295)*

MACHINERY: Metalworking

Pennengineering Holdings LLC .... C 302 576-2746
  Wilmington *(G-12069)*

MACHINERY: Packaging

Ames Engineering Corp .... E 302 658-6945
  Wilmington *(G-9067)*
Telesonic PC Inc .... G 302 658-6945
  Wilmington *(G-12878)*
Telesonic PC Inc .... G 302 658-6945
  Wilmington *(G-12879)*

MACHINERY: Plastic Working

Negri Bossi Usa Inc .... F 302 328-8020
  New Castle *(G-5550)*
Sewickley Capital Inc .... G 302 793-4964
  Wilmington *(G-12589)*

MACHINERY: Printing Presses

Ferrante & Associates Inc .... G 781 891-4328
  Wilmington *(G-10522)*

MACHINISTS' TOOLS: Precision

Advanced Metal Concepts Inc .... F 302 421-9905
  Middletown *(G-3931)*

MAGAZINES, WHOLESALE

Suburban Marketing Associates .... D 302 656-8440
  Wilmington *(G-12786)*

MAGNESITE MINING

Rhi Refractories Holding Co .... G 302 655-6497
  Wilmington *(G-12400)*

MAIL-ORDER BOOK CLUBS

Cedar Lane Inc .... F 302 328-7232
  New Castle *(G-5139)*

MAIL-ORDER HOUSE, NEC

F D Hammond Enterprises Inc .... F 302 424-8455
  Milford *(G-4407)*

MAIL-ORDER HOUSES: Computer Eqpt & Electronics

Bolt Innovation LLC .... G 800 293-5249
  Dover *(G-1220)*
Loadbalancerorginc .... G 888 867-9504
  Wilmington *(G-11418)*

MAIL-ORDER HOUSES: Computer Software

Kintyre Solutions LLC .... G 888 636-0010
  Wilmington *(G-11269)*

MAIL-ORDER HOUSES: General Merchandise

DOT Matrix Inc .... G 917 657-4918
  Dover *(G-1439)*
Himalaya Trading Inc .... G 702 833-0485
  Dover *(G-1647)*
Magneco LLC .... G 302 613-0080
  Wilmington *(G-11487)*

PRODUCT & SERVICES SECTION

MANAGEMENT CONSULTING SVCS: Management Engineering

MAILBOX RENTAL & RELATED SVCS

Dabvasan Inc .... G 302 529-1100
  Wilmington (G-9946)
Gjv Inc .... G 302 455-1600
  Newark (G-6659)
Global Shipping Center LLC .... G 302 798-4321
  Claymont (G-754)
Mail Stop .... G 302 947-4704
  Millsboro (G-4731)

MAILING & MESSENGER SVCS

Itconnectus Inc .... G 302 531-1139
  Dover (G-1685)
Mail Rooms Ltd .... G 302 629-4838
  Seaford (G-8300)

MAILING LIST: Compilers

Bcd Systems .... G 302 328-2070
  New Castle (G-5076)

MAILING SVCS, NEC

Copy Craft Inc .... E 302 633-1313
  Wilmington (G-9856)
D & B Printing and Mailing Inc .... G 302 838-7111
  Newark (G-6339)
Mail Center .... G 302 422-2200
  Milford (G-4483)

MANAGEMENT CONSULTING SVCS: Administrative

Central Firm LLC .... G 610 470-9836
  Wilmington (G-9615)
County of Sussex .... E 302 855-7878
  Georgetown (G-2490)
MV Farinola Inc .... G 302 545-8492
  Wilmington (G-11781)
TLC Personal Assistants .... G 302 290-9902
  Wilmington (G-12918)

MANAGEMENT CONSULTING SVCS: Automation & Robotics

ABS Engineering LLC .... G 302 595-9081
  Newark (G-5886)
Pro Automated Inc .... D 302 294-6121
  Newark (G-7262)

MANAGEMENT CONSULTING SVCS: Banking & Finance

DCH Auto Group (usa) Inc .... G 302 478-4600
  Wilmington (G-9980)
P A Aba Intl Inc .... F 800 979-5106
  Lewes (G-3675)

MANAGEMENT CONSULTING SVCS: Business

924 Inc .... E 302 656-6100
  Wilmington (G-8870)
Blue Ridge Air Inc .... G 302 323-4800
  New Castle (G-5096)
Circus Associates Intelligence .... E 757 663-7864
  Lewes (G-3422)
Cognition Group Inc .... G 302 454-1265
  Wilmington (G-9760)
Dominring Blgcal RES Group LLC .. F 951 327-8062
  Rehoboth Beach (G-7919)
F D Hammond Enterprises Inc ...... F 302 424-8455
  Milford (G-4407)
Fiscal Associates .... F 302 894-0500
  Newark (G-6588)
Gavinsolmonese .... F 302 655-8997
  Wilmington (G-10680)
Government Mrktplace Ltd Lblty ... E 302 297-9694
  Newark (G-6679)
Hat Blue Group LLC .... F 225 288-2962
  Lewes (G-3535)
Iceteccom Inc .... G 302 477-1792
  Wilmington (G-10988)
Incenco International .... F 302 478-8400
  Wilmington (G-11012)
Kch Ventures LLC .... G 302 737-6260
  Newark (G-6869)
Kfs Strategic MGT Svcs LLC .... F 302 545-7640
  Bear (G-217)

Positioneering LLC .... G 302 415-3200
  Wilmington (G-12191)
Printify LLC .... G 415 968-6351
  Wilmington (G-12230)
Pyramid Group MGT Svcs Corp .... G 302 737-1770
  Newark (G-7275)
Sfin 3 Inc .... G 302 472-9276
  Wilmington (G-12591)
Strategic Solutions Intl Inc .... G 302 525-6313
  Newark (G-7493)
Supply Chain Consultants Inc .... E 302 738-9215
  Wilmington (G-12812)
V2s Corporation .... D 302 384-9947
  Wilmington (G-13042)
Winner Group Management Inc .... E 302 571-5200
  Wilmington (G-13273)

MANAGEMENT CONSULTING SVCS: Business Planning & Organizing

Countermeasures Assessment ...... G 302 322-9600
  New Castle (G-5200)
Delaware Registered Agents .... G 302 733-0600
  Newark (G-6406)
Dss International LLC .... G 302 836-0270
  Newark (G-6476)
Hardin & Associates Inc .... G 302 654-9923
  Wilmington (G-10836)
Resources For Human Dev Inc ..... E 302 691-7574
  Wilmington (G-12387)
Resources For Human Dev Inc ..... E 302 731-5283
  Newark (G-7326)
Vironex Envmtl Field Svcs Inc .... E 302 661-1400
  Wilmington (G-13088)
Wang Consultants Inc .... G 626 483-0265
  Wilmington (G-13117)

MANAGEMENT CONSULTING SVCS: Compensation & Benefits Planning

Batescainelli LLC .... G 202 618-2040
  Rehoboth Beach (G-7856)

MANAGEMENT CONSULTING SVCS: Construction Project

Alliance Bus Dev Concepts LLC .... F 803 814-4004
  Clayton (G-832)
Austin Alliance Electric Inc .... E 843 297-8078
  Wilmington (G-9184)
Brs Consulting Inc .... G 302 786-2326
  Harrington (G-2819)
Emory Hill & Company .... D 302 322-4400
  New Castle (G-5287)
Mountain Consulting Inc .... G 302 744-9875
  Dover (G-1876)
Ubivis Management LLC .... E 833 824-8476
  Rehoboth Beach (G-8103)
Vcg LLC .... G 302 336-8151
  Dover (G-2188)

MANAGEMENT CONSULTING SVCS: Corporate Objectives & Policies

K and L Gates .... G 302 416-7000
  Wilmington (G-11213)
McNichol Enterprises Inc .... F 302 633-9348
  Wilmington (G-11606)

MANAGEMENT CONSULTING SVCS: Corporation Organizing

Company Corporation .... D 302 636-5440
  Wilmington (G-9798)
Corporate Holding Services .... G 302 428-0515
  Wilmington (G-9865)
Delaware Intercorp Inc .... G 302 266-9367
  Wilmington (G-10059)
Phs Corporate Services Inc .... G 302 571-1128
  Wilmington (G-12128)

MANAGEMENT CONSULTING SVCS: Distribution Channels

Moghul Life Inc .... G 347 560-9124
  Wilmington (G-11724)

MANAGEMENT CONSULTING SVCS: Food & Beverage

Haccp Navigator LLC .... G 302 531-7922
  Lincoln (G-3853)
Red Clay Consolidated Schl Dst ... G 302 992-5580
  Wilmington (G-12347)

MANAGEMENT CONSULTING SVCS: Franchising

United Worldwide Express LLC ..... G 347 651-5111
  Wilmington (G-13029)

MANAGEMENT CONSULTING SVCS: General

Exo Works Inc .... G 302 531-1139
  Dover (G-1534)
Ezprohub LLC .... G 302 327-4222
  Newark (G-6560)
On Point Partners LLC .... G 302 655-5606
  Wilmington (G-11952)
Siriusiq Mobile LLC .... F 888 414-2047
  Newark (G-7433)
Xcutivescom Inc .... G 888 245-9996
  Dover (G-2242)

MANAGEMENT CONSULTING SVCS: Hospital & Health

Delaware Healthcare Assn .... G 302 674-2853
  Dover (G-1376)
Ecsquared Inc .... G 302 750-8554
  Wilmington (G-10341)
Mediguide America LLC .... E 302 425-5900
  Wilmington (G-11619)
Metropolitan Revenue Assoc LLC . G 302 449-7490
  New Castle (G-5520)
Nemours Hlth & Prevention Svcs .. G 302 366-1929
  Newark (G-7092)
Perinatal Assocation Delaware ..... E 302 654-1088
  Wilmington (G-12086)
Sweat Social LLC .... G 504 510-1973
  Dover (G-2123)
Tipton Communications Group ..... G 302 454-7901
  Newark (G-7568)

MANAGEMENT CONSULTING SVCS: Incentive Or Award Program

American Institute For Pub Svc ..... G 302 622-9101
  Wilmington (G-9051)

MANAGEMENT CONSULTING SVCS: Industrial & Labor

Red Clay Inc .... G 302 239-2018
  Hockessin (G-3132)

MANAGEMENT CONSULTING SVCS: Industry Specialist

Adjuvant Research Services Inc ... F 302 737-5513
  Newark (G-5900)
Express Legal Documents LLC .... E 212 710-1374
  Wilmington (G-10463)

MANAGEMENT CONSULTING SVCS: Information Systems

Intercontinental Tech LLC .... G 302 984-2111
  Wilmington (G-11057)
It Tigers LLC .... G 732 898-2793
  Lewes (G-3565)
Kintyre Solutions LLC .... G 888 636-0010
  Wilmington (G-11269)
Lockheed Martin Overseas LLC ... G 301 897-6923
  Wilmington (G-11422)
Mentor Consultants Inc .... G 610 566-4004
  Wilmington (G-11633)

MANAGEMENT CONSULTING SVCS: Management Engineering

Core Functions LLC .... G 443 956-9626
  Selbyville (G-8471)

MANAGEMENT CONSULTING SVCS: Manufacturing

Delaware Mfg EXT Partnr Inc..............G........ 302 283-3131
  Newark *(G-6395)*

MANAGEMENT CONSULTING SVCS: Merchandising

Kmh Contracting.............................G........ 302 331-4894
  Magnolia *(G-3897)*

MANAGEMENT CONSULTING SVCS: New Products & Svcs

Ascension Industries LLC................G........ 302 659-1778
  Smyrna *(G-8576)*
Delaware Enterprises Inc ....E........ 302 324-5660
  New Castle *(G-5228)*
Global Vision Xtreme Corp ....F........ 302 287-4822
  Claymont *(G-755)*

MANAGEMENT CONSULTING SVCS: Programmed Instruction

Jack Donovan....................................G........ 410 715-0504
  Millsboro *(G-4711)*

MANAGEMENT CONSULTING SVCS: Public Utilities

Cmy Solutions LLC ....G........ 321 732-1866
  Newark *(G-6256)*

MANAGEMENT CONSULTING SVCS: Quality Assurance

Advanced Systems Inc....................G........ 302 368-1211
  Newark *(G-5908)*
Genovesius Solutia LLC ....G........ 302 252-7506
  Hockessin *(G-3036)*

MANAGEMENT CONSULTING SVCS: Real Estate

Eco SBC 2015-1 REO 167061 LLC...E........ 302 652-8013
  Wilmington *(G-10340)*
Harvey Hanna & Associates Inc .....G........ 302 323-9300
  Newport *(G-7750)*
Merion Realty Services LLC ....G........ 302 656-8543
  Wilmington *(G-11642)*
Pabian Ventures LLC ....G........ 302 762-1992
  Wilmington *(G-11999)*
Sweeny and Associates ....G........ 302 453-1645
  Newark *(G-7519)*
Wartrude Services Inc ....F........ 302 213-3944
  Wilmington *(G-13120)*

MANAGEMENT CONSULTING SVCS: Restaurant & Food

De Catering Inc................................E........ 302 607-7200
  Wilmington *(G-9985)*

MANAGEMENT CONSULTING SVCS: Retail Trade Consultant

Golden Thorns Inc............................G........ 861 598-6748
  Lewes *(G-3519)*

MANAGEMENT CONSULTING SVCS: Training & Development

Alder Associates LLC......................G........ 360 833-0988
  Wilmington *(G-9004)*
David G Major Associates Inc ....E........ 703 642-7450
  Millsboro *(G-4673)*
Enhanced Corporate Prfmce LLC ...E........ 302 545-8541
  Newark *(G-6529)*
Momentum Management Group Inc...G........ 302 477-9730
  Wilmington *(G-11728)*
Parent Information Ctr Del Inc........G........ 302 999-7394
  Wilmington *(G-12019)*

MANAGEMENT CONSULTING SVCS: Transportation

Integrated AVI Solutions LLC..........G........ 302 351-3427
  Wilmington *(G-11047)*

Simpler Logistics LLC......................G........ 800 619-8321
  Wilmington *(G-12626)*

MANAGEMENT SERVICES

1995 Property Management Inc.....G........ 302 745-1187
  Seaford *(G-8133)*
Agile 1 ....F........ 302 791-6900
  Wilmington *(G-8977)*
AMC - Commercial Inc...................G........ 302 229-0051
  Claymont *(G-689)*
Ameken Network Group Inc ....F........ 302 545-3472
  Claymont *(G-691)*
Apartment Communities Corp.......D........ 302 656-7781
  Wilmington *(G-9094)*
Atlantic Management.....................G........ 302 222-3919
  Rehoboth Beach *(G-7850)*
Avantys Health LLC........................G........ 302 521-2848
  Wilmington *(G-9196)*
Balfour Beatty LLC ....G........ 302 573-3873
  Wilmington *(G-9225)*
Bayshore Records MGT LLC ....G........ 302 731-4477
  Newark *(G-6058)*
Beachview Mgmt Inc......................G........ 302 227-3280
  Georgetown *(G-2450)*
C and L Bradford and Assoc..........G........ 302 529-8566
  Wilmington *(G-9522)*
Cafe Management Associates ......G........ 302 655-4959
  Wilmington *(G-9534)*
Cap Managment Services LLC .....G........ 302 846-0120
  Delmar *(G-978)*
Capano Management Company ...D........ 302 429-8700
  Wilmington *(G-9554)*
Chubb INA Ovrseas Holdings Inc..F........ 302 476-6000
  Wilmington *(G-9694)*
Columbus Inn Management I........G........ 302 429-8700
  Wilmington *(G-9779)*
Coventry Health Care Inc..............G........ 800 833-7423
  Newark *(G-6309)*
Davin Management Group LLC....F........ 302 367-6563
  Bear *(G-99)*
Dax-Wave Consulting LLC ....G........ 424 543-6662
  Wilmington *(G-9974)*
Delaware Innovation Space Inc ....G........ 302 695-2201
  Wilmington *(G-10058)*
Dnrec Air Waste Management ......G........ 302 739-9406
  Dover *(G-1435)*
Easy Corp Ltd ....F........ 302 824-0109
  Wilmington *(G-10331)*
Eprintit Usa Inc................................F........ 613 299-7105
  Wilmington *(G-10428)*
Erickson Management.....................G........ 302 235-0855
  Newark *(G-6537)*
Faith Family Management Co........G........ 302 832-5936
  Newark *(G-6564)*
First State Management LLC........G........ 302 268-8176
  Lincoln *(G-3848)*
Harvey Development Co.................C........ 302 323-9300
  New Castle *(G-5381)*
Hlh Construction MGT Svcs Inc....F........ 302 654-7508
  Wilmington *(G-10920)*
Integrated Solutions Planning........G........ 302 297-9215
  Georgetown *(G-2567)*
J P Morgan Services Inc................A........ 302 634-1000
  Newark *(G-6818)*
J&D Management..............................G........ 302 239-2489
  Hockessin *(G-3062)*
K W Lands LLC................................E........ 302 674-2200
  Dover *(G-1718)*
Magetti Gorup LLC.........................D........ 302 355-5540
  Wilmington *(G-11485)*
Majalco LLC ....G........ 703 507-5298
  Wilmington *(G-11494)*
Marta Group....................................G........ 302 737-2008
  Newark *(G-6993)*
McNeil and Fmly MGT Group LLC..F........ 302 830-3267
  Wilmington *(G-11605)*
Merman Management Inc...............G........ 302 456-9904
  Wilmington *(G-11645)*
Mid Atlantic Grand Prix LLC ....E........ 302 656-5278
  New Castle *(G-5522)*
Mosaic..C........ 302 456-5995
  Newark *(G-7062)*
New Balance Retail Management...G........ 302 230-3062
  Wilmington *(G-11850)*
Prosperity Unlimited Ente..............G........ 302 379-2494
  Middletown *(G-4200)*
Richman Wealth Management ......G........ 443 536-6936
  Rehoboth Beach *(G-8058)*
Roberts Property MGT LLC ....G........ 302 537-5371
  Bethany Beach *(G-429)*

Safe Harbor Property MGT LLC....G........ 302 436-9882
  Selbyville *(G-8542)*
Saggio Management Group Inc ...G........ 302 659-6560
  Smyrna *(G-8710)*
Service General Corp.....................C........ 302 856-3500
  Georgetown *(G-2651)*
Severn Trent Inc..............................E........ 302 427-5990
  Wilmington *(G-12588)*
Six Plus Inc......................................G........ 302 652-3296
  Wilmington *(G-12638)*
Smart Printing MGT LLC ....G........ 855 549-4900
  Newark *(G-7447)*
St Anthonys Housing Mgt Corp....G........ 302 421-3756
  Wilmington *(G-12721)*
Syngenta Corporation ....E........ 302 425-2000
  Wilmington *(G-12836)*
Telamon Corp Head Start Prgram..D........ 302 653-3766
  Smyrna *(G-8729)*
Tgx Holdings Inc.............................C........ 212 260-6300
  Wilmington *(G-12890)*
Thomson Reuters (grc) Inc...........A........ 212 227-7357
  Wilmington *(G-12904)*
Tpw Management LLC...................G........ 302 227-7878
  Lewes *(G-3793)*
Twin Hearts Management LLC.....G........ 302 777-5700
  Dover *(G-2167)*
Vest Management Inc....................G........ 302 856-3100
  Georgetown *(G-2700)*
Waste Management Inc ....F........ 302 854-5304
  Laurel *(G-3305)*
Whispering Meadows LLC............G........ 302 698-1073
  Dover *(G-2223)*
Wilmington Trust Corporation ......E........ 302 651-8378
  Wilmington *(G-13263)*
Winifred Ellen Erbe........................G........ 302 541-0889
  Frankford *(G-2399)*

MANAGEMENT SVCS, FACILITIES SUPPORT: Environ Remediation

Dibiasos Clg Rstration Svc Inc......G........ 302 376-7111
  Townsend *(G-8784)*
Environmental Versacorp................G........ 302 798-1839
  Wilmington *(G-10420)*
H2o Pro LLC ....G........ 302 321-7077
  Frankford *(G-2367)*

MANAGEMENT SVCS: Administrative

Advance Central Services Inc.......E........ 302 830-9732
  Wilmington *(G-8945)*
Cetaris Inc.......................................G........ 416 679-9555
  Dover *(G-1271)*
Clearwater Ergny Resources LLC..G........ 510 267-8921
  Wilmington *(G-9740)*
Crystal Holdings Inc.......................D........ 302 421-5700
  Wilmington *(G-9909)*
Hyas US Inc....................................G........ 250 327-9743
  Wilmington *(G-10981)*

MANAGEMENT SVCS: Business

Antebellum Hospitality Inc............G........ 302 436-4375
  Selbyville *(G-8449)*
Aquatic Management.....................G........ 302 235-1818
  Wilmington *(G-9106)*
Ardexo Inc ....G........ 855 617-7500
  Dover *(G-1134)*
Brownstone LLC ....G........ 302 300-4370
  New Castle *(G-5117)*
Business Integration Solution ......G........ 302 355-3512
  Newark *(G-6139)*
Case Management Services.........G........ 302 354-3711
  Wilmington *(G-9587)*
Ceo-Hqcom LLC.............................G........ 302 883-8555
  Hockessin *(G-2982)*
Cht Holdings LLC............................F........ 954 864-2008
  Lewes *(G-3421)*
Cloud Services Solutions Inc........G........ 888 335-3132
  Wilmington *(G-9746)*
CSC Entity Services LLC..............G........ 302 654-7584
  Wilmington *(G-9911)*
Dis Management.............................G........ 302 543-4481
  Wilmington *(G-10163)*
Everett Robinson............................F........ 302 530-6574
  Wilmington *(G-10446)*
Highmarks Inc................................G........ 302 421-3000
  Wilmington *(G-10906)*
Keystate Corporate MGT LLC......G........ 302 425-5158
  Wilmington *(G-11253)*
Lawrence Kennedy.........................F........ 302 533-5880
  Newark *(G-6923)*

M C Tek LLC ....G.... 302 644-9695
Rehoboth Beach *(G-7992)*
Minatee Business Group ....G.... 302 543-5092
Wilmington *(G-11703)*
Moorway Painting Management ....G.... 302 764-5002
Wilmington *(G-11747)*
Natural House Inc ....G.... 302 218-0338
Newark *(G-7087)*
Orion Group LLC ....G.... 302 357-9137
Wilmington *(G-11973)*
Peek Performance Group LLC ....E.... 480 242-6087
Wilmington *(G-12059)*
Pro Pest Management of De Inc ....F.... 302 994-2847
Wilmington *(G-12233)*
Prorank Business Solutions LLC ....G.... 302 256-0642
Wilmington *(G-12253)*
Registred Agnts Legal Svcs LLC ....G.... 302 427-6970
Wilmington *(G-12364)*
Right Property MGT Co LLC ....F.... 302 227-1155
Rehoboth Beach *(G-8059)*
Secure Management ....G.... 302 999-8342
Middletown *(G-4234)*
Signature Property Management ....G.... 302 212-2381
Lewes *(G-3745)*
Strands Prprty Prservation LLC ....G.... 302 381-9792
Millsboro *(G-4805)*
Tdc Partners Ltd ....G.... 302 827-2137
Lewes *(G-3779)*
Teksolv Usd Inc ....D.... 302 738-1050
Newark *(G-7553)*
Tm Management LLC ....G.... 302 654-4940
Wilmington *(G-12919)*
Totaltranslogistics LLC ....G.... 302 325-4245
New Castle *(G-5777)*
Wellington Management Group ....G.... 215 569-8900
Wilmington *(G-13143)*
Xenith Solutions LLC ....G.... 703 963-3523
Selbyville *(G-8556)*

MANAGEMENT SVCS: Construction

Bellevue Holding Company ....E.... 302 655-1561
Wilmington *(G-9291)*
Bpgs Construction LLC ....D.... 302 691-2111
Wilmington *(G-9412)*
Brandywine Contractors Inc ....G.... 302 325-2700
New Castle *(G-5107)*
Buck Simpers Archt + Assoc Inc ....F.... 302 658-9300
Wilmington *(G-9498)*
Bz Construction Services Inc ....G.... 302 999-7505
Wilmington *(G-9519)*
C & S Consultants Inc ....G.... 302 236-5211
Milford *(G-4339)*
Construction MGT Svcs Inc ....A.... 302 478-4200
Wilmington *(G-9835)*
Craftsman Cbntry Woodworks Inc ....G.... 302 841-5274
Selbyville *(G-8472)*
J T Mican & Associates Inc ....G.... 302 323-8152
New Castle *(G-5431)*
Keep Selling Property LLC ....G.... 302 235-3066
New Castle *(G-5458)*
Lighthouse Construction Inc ....F.... 302 677-1965
Magnolia *(G-3898)*
Locker Construction Inc ....G.... 302 239-2859
Newark *(G-6946)*
Montchanin Design Group Inc ....F.... 302 652-3008
Wilmington *(G-11735)*
Omniway Corporation ....F.... 302 738-5076
Newark *(G-7147)*
Palmetto MGT & Engrg LLC ....C.... 302 993-2766
Wilmington *(G-12009)*
Providence At Heritage Sh ....G.... 302 337-1040
Bridgeville *(G-513)*
Unity Construction Inc ....E.... 302 998-0531
Wilmington *(G-13030)*
Wohlsen Construction Company ....E.... 302 324-9900
Wilmington *(G-13284)*

MANAGEMENT SVCS: Financial, Business

Affinity Wealth Management ....F.... 302 652-6767
Wilmington *(G-8971)*
Corrado Management Svcs LLC ....E.... 302 225-0700
New Castle *(G-5198)*
Ekww Inc ....G.... 302 234-2877
Hockessin *(G-3018)*
Glen Playa Inc ....G.... 302 703-7512
Lewes *(G-3515)*
Hfm Investment Advisors Inc ....G.... 302 234-9777
Newark *(G-6727)*
Kubera Global Solutions LLC ....F.... 480 241-5124
Wilmington *(G-11299)*

Lau & Assoc Ltd ....F.... 302 792-5955
Wilmington *(G-11337)*
Lutheran Community Services ....G.... 302 654-8886
Wilmington *(G-11453)*
Walnut Green Asset MGT LL ....G.... 302 689-3798
Wilmington *(G-13116)*

MANAGEMENT SVCS: Hospital

Christiana Care Health Sys Inc ....B.... 302 733-1601
Newark *(G-6207)*
Christiana Care Health Sys Inc ....F.... 302 623-0390
Newark *(G-6208)*
Christiana Care Health Sys Inc ....G.... 302 366-1929
Newark *(G-6211)*
Christiana Care Health Sys Inc ....C.... 302 733-1000
Wilmington *(G-9679)*

MANAGEMENT SVCS: Hotel Or Motel

Atlantic Management Ltd ....F.... 302 645-9511
Rehoboth Beach *(G-7851)*
Axia Management ....B.... 302 674-2200
Dover *(G-1162)*
Crestline Hotels & Resorts LLC ....C.... 302 655-0400
Wilmington *(G-9898)*
Eagle Hospitality Group LLC ....F.... 302 678-8388
Dover *(G-1493)*
Everest Hotel Group LLC ....F.... 213 272-0088
Camden *(G-569)*
Procaccianti Group LLC ....E.... 401 946-4600
Wilmington *(G-12237)*

MANAGEMENT SVCS: Personnel

Inov8 Inc ....G.... 302 465-5124
Camden Wyoming *(G-646)*

MANAGEMENT SVCS: Restaurant

Aark Network Inc ....D.... 302 399-3945
Newark *(G-5876)*
Ashby Management Corporation ....G.... 302 894-1200
Newark *(G-6009)*
Cactus Annies Restaurant & Bar ....F.... 302 655-9004
Wilmington *(G-9528)*
McDonalds ....G.... 302 674-2095
Dover *(G-1832)*
Mera Rd 2 LLC ....G.... 305 577-3443
Wilmington *(G-11634)*
Sodel Concepts II LLC ....G.... 302 228-3786
Rehoboth Beach *(G-8080)*

MANGANESE ORES MINING

American Minerals Partnership ....C.... 302 652-3301
New Castle *(G-5034)*

MANHOLES & COVERS: Metal

Ej Usa Inc ....F.... 302 378-1100
Middletown *(G-4051)*

MANPOWER POOLS

Manpowergroup Inc ....G.... 302 674-8600
Dover *(G-1813)*

MANUFACTURED & MOBILE HOME DEALERS

Bayshore Inc ....G.... 302 539-7200
Ocean View *(G-7758)*
Love Creek Marina MBL Hm Site ....F.... 302 448-6492
Lewes *(G-3611)*
Rons Mobile Home Sales Inc ....G.... 302 398-9166
Harrington *(G-2880)*
Theta Vest Inc ....F.... 302 227-3745
Rehoboth Beach *(G-8096)*

MANUFACTURING INDUSTRIES, NEC

Albatross Industries LLC ....G.... 850 447-2150
Lewes *(G-3333)*
American Industries LLC ....G.... 302 585-0129
Milton *(G-4863)*
Bambu Candles LLC ....G.... 917 903-2563
Newark *(G-6042)*
Bell Manufacturing Company Inc ....G.... 302 703-2684
Lewes *(G-3376)*
Bold Industries LLC ....G.... 302 858-7237
Frankford *(G-2348)*
Botts Industries ....G.... 302 934-1628
Millsboro *(G-4647)*

Chimpark LLC ....G.... 226 219-7771
New Castle *(G-5150)*
Coastal Wood Industries ....G.... 302 398-9601
Harrington *(G-2827)*
Curry Industries LLC ....G.... 732 858-1794
Dover *(G-1331)*
Eastern Shore Lite Industries ....G.... 302 653-8687
Clayton *(G-848)*
Footcare Technologies Inc ....G.... 704 301-6966
Milton *(G-4907)*
Gardner Industries Inc ....G.... 302 448-9195
Seaford *(G-8249)*
Gibson Industries ....G.... 302 653-7874
Clayton *(G-854)*
Good Manufacturing Practices ....G.... 302 222-6808
Dover *(G-1601)*
Goodwill Industries Delaware ....G.... 302 337-8561
Bridgeville *(G-475)*
Grayling Industries Inc ....G.... 302 629-6860
Frederica *(G-2404)*
Hackett Industries LLC ....G.... 302 357-2539
Wilmington *(G-10816)*
Haunted Industries ....G.... 302 836-5823
Bear *(G-179)*
Invisible Hand Labs LLC ....G.... 434 989-9642
Wilmington *(G-11074)*
Island Genius LLC ....G.... 888 529-5506
Wilmington *(G-11089)*
J M Industries ....G.... 302 893-0363
Hockessin *(G-3061)*
Jjs Industries LP ....G.... 302 690-2957
Wilmington *(G-11161)*
Kershaw Industries ....G.... 302 464-1051
Middletown *(G-4121)*
Laytons Umbrellas ....G.... 302 249-1958
Laurel *(G-3257)*
M and J Industries ....G.... 302 559-5005
Wilmington *(G-11468)*
Macknyfe Specialties ....G.... 302 239-4904
Hockessin *(G-3084)*
Maf Industries ....G.... 302 249-1254
Seaford *(G-8299)*
Martial Industries LLC ....G.... 302 983-5742
Middletown *(G-4147)*
Maws Tails Mfg ....G.... 302 740-7664
Milton *(G-4932)*
Mazindustries ....G.... 302 292-3636
Newark *(G-7007)*
Michael J Munroe ....G.... 804 240-7188
Magnolia *(G-3899)*
MMR Industries Inc ....G.... 302 999-9561
Wilmington *(G-11717)*
Mnr Industries LLC ....G.... 443 485-6213
Dover *(G-1866)*
Myrle Manufacturing LLC ....G.... 302 249-9408
Greenwood *(G-2754)*
National Industries For The Bl ....G.... 302 477-0860
Wilmington *(G-11807)*
Northernsigs Mfg LLC ....G.... 302 383-9270
Wilmington *(G-11908)*
Pandaciti LLC ....G.... 226 219-7771
New Castle *(G-5599)*
Polytechnic Resources Inc ....G.... 302 629-4221
Seaford *(G-8359)*
R M Bell Industries Inc ....G.... 302 542-3747
Lewes *(G-3705)*
Roman Industries Inc ....G.... 302 420-9420
Wilmington *(G-12467)*
Rowe Industries Inc ....G.... 443 458-5569
Georgetown *(G-2644)*
S&D Industries LLC ....G.... 703 801-3643
Wilmington *(G-12510)*
Sandwich Inc ....G.... 647 360-8300
Lewes *(G-3729)*
Sdg Defense Industry LLC ....G.... 302 526-4800
New Castle *(G-5696)*
Still Industries Inc ....G.... 302 368-8832
Newark *(G-7491)*
Syf Industries ....G.... 302 384-6214
Wilmington *(G-12828)*
US Green Battery Inc ....G.... 347 723-5963
New Castle *(G-5812)*
Uzin Utz Manufacturing N Amer ....G.... 336 456-4624
Dover *(G-2184)*
Vetcon Industries LLC ....G.... 850 207-6723
Newark *(G-7655)*
Westlake Chemical Products ....G.... 302 691-6028
Wilmington *(G-13169)*
Westmor Industries ....G.... 302 398-3253
Harrington *(G-2906)*

Employee Codes: A=Over 500 employees, B=251-500
C=101-250, D=51-100, E=20-50, F=10-19, G=1-9
2020 Harris Directory of
Delaware Businesses
865
PRDT & SVC

MANUFACTURING INDUSTRIES, NEC

Westmor Industries .... G 302 956-0243
  Bridgeville (G-533)
What If Y Not Everything Inc .... G 732 898-0241
  Dover (G-2218)
Whet Industries Inc .... G 302 236-2182
  Newark (G-7690)

MARBLE, BUILDING: Cut & Shaped

Stone Express .... G 302 376-8876
  Middletown (G-4249)

MARINAS

Barsgr LLC .... G 302 645-6665
  Lewes (G-3362)
Bayshore Inc .... G 302 539-7200
  Ocean View (G-7758)
Delaware Bay Launch Service .... F 302 422-7604
  Milford (G-4376)
Fenwick Island Marine LLC .... G 302 436-4702
  Selbyville (G-8491)
Indian River Captains Assoc .... G 302 227-3071
  Rehoboth Beach (G-7967)
Jack Hickman Real Estate .... F 302 539-8000
  Bethany Beach (G-406)
Love Creek Marina MBL Hm Site .... F 302 448-6492
  Lewes (G-3611)
South Shore Provisions LLC .... G 443 614-2442
  Selbyville (G-8546)
Summit North Marina .... F 302 836-1800
  Bear (G-341)
Walkers Marine Corporation .... G 302 629-8666
  Seaford (G-8432)

MARINE BASIN OPERATIONS

Marshall Hotels & Resorts Inc .... E 302 227-1700
  Rehoboth Beach (G-8000)

MARINE CARGO HANDLING SVCS

Advance Marine LLC .... G 302 656-2111
  Wilmington (G-8947)

MARINE CARGO HANDLING SVCS: Waterfront Terminal Operations

Diamond State Port Corporation .... D 302 472-7678
  Wilmington (G-10144)

MARINE ENGINE REPAIR SVCS

Almars Outboard Service & Sls .... G 302 328-8541
  New Castle (G-5023)
Clifton Leasing Co Inc .... E 302 674-2300
  Dover (G-1293)
Rudy Marine Inc .... F 302 999-8735
  Wilmington (G-12491)

MARINE HARDWARE

Marinhrdwremfg/Forcebeyond Inc .... G 302 691-4787
  Newark (G-6987)

MARINE SPLY DEALERS

Eastern Group Inc .... E 302 737-6603
  Newark (G-6497)
Hilton Marine Supply Company .... G 302 994-3365
  Wilmington (G-10912)

MARINE SPLYS WHOLESALERS

Bethany Auto Parts Inc .... G 302 539-0555
  Ocean View (G-7765)
Eastern Group Inc .... E 302 737-6603
  Newark (G-6497)

MARKETS: Meat & fish

Lewes Fishhouse & Produce Inc .... E 302 827-4074
  Lewes (G-3600)

MARKING DEVICES

Franklin Rubber Stamp Co Inc .... F 302 654-8841
  Wilmington (G-10618)
Golden Rubber Stamp Co .... G 302 658-7343
  Wilmington (G-10738)
Stamps By Impression .... G 302 645-7191
  Lewes (G-3762)

MARTIAL ARTS INSTRUCTION

Aikikai Foundation of Delaware .... G 302 369-2454
  Newark (G-5921)
American Karate Studios .... E 302 737-9500
  Newark (G-5954)
American Martial Arts Inst .... F 302 834-4060
  Bear (G-27)
Elevated Studios Hq .... G 302 407-3229
  Wilmington (G-10372)
Rigbys Karate Academy .... G 302 735-9637
  Dover (G-2036)

MASSAGE PARLOR & STEAM BATH SVCS

Essencia Salon and Day Spa .... G 302 234-9144
  Hockessin (G-3023)
Sanctuary Spa and Saloon .... F 302 475-1469
  Wilmington (G-12537)

MASSAGE PARLORS

Alternative Therapy LLC .... G 302 368-0800
  Newark (G-5949)
Cnu Fit LLC .... G 302 744-9037
  Dover (G-1298)
Deep Muscle Therapy Center Del .... F 302 397-8073
  Wilmington (G-9992)
Hand & Spa .... G 302 478-1700
  Wilmington (G-10830)
Stephanie Galbraith .... G 302 290-2235
  Wilmington (G-12753)
Therapy At Beach .... G 302 313-5555
  Lewes (G-3781)

MASSAGE THERAPIST

Hockessin Chrpractic Centre PA .... G 302 239-8550
  Hockessin (G-3048)
Jackson Massage and Cft .... G 302 525-6808
  Newark (G-6822)
Massage By Alicia .... G 352 401-4328
  Wilmington (G-11563)
Medical Massage Delaware LLC .... G 888 757-1951
  Newark (G-7016)

MATERIALS HANDLING EQPT WHOLESALERS

Airsled Inc .... G 302 292-8911
  Newark (G-5928)
Bruce Industrial Co Inc .... D 302 655-9616
  New Castle (G-5118)
Catalyst Handling Resources .... E 302 798-2200
  Claymont (G-708)
Eastern Lift Truck Co Inc .... G 302 286-6660
  Newark (G-6498)
Eastern Lift Truck Co Inc .... F 302 875-4031
  Laurel (G-3226)
Material Handling Supply Inc .... F 302 571-0176
  New Castle (G-5511)
McCall Handling Co .... F 302 846-2334
  Delmar (G-1019)
O A Newton & Son Company .... G 302 337-3782
  Bridgeville (G-504)

MATTRESS STORES

Able Whelling and Machiene .... G 302 436-1929
  Selbyville (G-8446)
Plushbeds Inc .... G 888 758-7423
  Wilmington (G-12162)

MEAL DELIVERY PROGRAMS

Meals On Wheels Delaware Inc .... G 302 656-6451
  Wilmington (G-11612)
Meals On Whels of Lwes Rhoboth .... G 302 645-7449
  Lewes (G-3631)
Ministry of Caring Inc .... G 302 658-6123
  Wilmington (G-11707)

MEAT & FISH MARKETS: Freezer Provisioners, Meat

Murrys of Maryland Inc .... G 302 328-3361
  New Castle (G-5540)

MEAT & FISH MARKETS: Seafood

Febys Fishery Inc .... E 302 998-9501
  Wilmington (G-10511)

Meding & Son Seafood .... F 302 335-3944
  Milford (G-4491)
Meltrone Inc .... F 302 998-3457
  Wilmington (G-11628)

MEAT & MEAT PRDTS WHOLESALERS

B & M Meats Inc .... F 302 655-5521
  Wilmington (G-9210)
Estia Hospitality Group Inc .... F 302 798-5319
  Claymont (G-741)
Lewes Fishhouse & Produce Inc .... E 302 827-4074
  Lewes (G-3600)
Sure Good Foods USA LLC .... E 905 288-1136
  Newark (G-7514)

MEAT MARKETS

Jabez Corp .... F 302 475-7600
  Wilmington (G-11113)
West Dover Butcher Shop Inc .... G 302 734-5447
  Dover (G-2214)

MEAT PRDTS: Boxed Beef, From Slaughtered Meat

Cbbc Opco LLC .... G 863 967-0636
  Wilmington (G-9599)

MEAT PRDTS: Prepared Beef Prdts From Purchased Beef

New B & M Meats Inc .... G 302 655-5331
  Wilmington (G-11849)

MEAT PRDTS: Sausages, From Purchased Meat

Kirby & Holloway Provisions Co .... E 302 398-3705
  Harrington (G-2863)

MEAT PRDTS: Scrapple, From Purchased Meat

Ralph and Paul Adams Inc .... B 800 338-4727
  Bridgeville (G-517)

MEAT PROCESSED FROM PURCHASED CARCASSES

AES Foods .... G 302 420-8377
  Newark (G-5914)

MEATS, PACKAGED FROZEN: Wholesalers

Murrys of Maryland Inc .... G 302 328-3361
  New Castle (G-5540)

MEDICAL & HOSPITAL EQPT WHOLESALERS

Aracent Healthcare LLC .... G 302 478-8865
  Wilmington (G-9110)
Cardiomo Care Inc .... F 929 360-5107
  Wilmington (G-9566)
Dienay Distribution Corp .... G 732 766-0814
  Middletown (G-4039)
Osskin USA Inc .... G 302 266-8200
  Newark (G-7162)
Siemens Hlthcare Dgnostics Inc .... D 302 631-7357
  Newark (G-7425)
Synergy Medical USA Inc .... F 302 444-0163
  Newark (G-7525)
World Wide Trading Brokers .... G 302 368-7041
  Newark (G-7722)

MEDICAL & SURGICAL SPLYS: Abdominal Support, Braces/Trusses

Independence Prosthtcs-Ortho .... G 302 369-9476
  Newark (G-6770)

MEDICAL & SURGICAL SPLYS: Crutches & Walkers

Roll-A-Bout Corporation .... G 302 736-6151
  Frederica (G-2412)

PRODUCT & SERVICES SECTION
MEMBERSHIP ORGANIZATIONS, BUSINESS: Merchants' Association

MEDICAL & SURGICAL SPLYS: Dressings, Surgical
Johnson & Johnson .... E 302 652-3840
Wilmington *(G-11179)*

MEDICAL & SURGICAL SPLYS: Limbs, Artificial
Harry J Lawall & Son Inc .... F 302 429-7630
Wilmington *(G-10844)*

MEDICAL & SURGICAL SPLYS: Orthopedic Appliances
Delmarv Orthtcs & Prosthtcs .... G 302 678-8311
Dover *(G-1407)*
Zimmer US Inc .... G 617 272-0062
Camden Wyoming *(G-662)*

MEDICAL & SURGICAL SPLYS: Personal Safety Eqpt
Dads Workwear Inc .... G 302 663-0068
Laurel *(G-3219)*
Ilc Dover LP .... B 302 335-3911
Frederica *(G-2407)*
Jarel Industries LLC .... G 336 782-0697
Camden *(G-585)*
New Ilc Dover Inc .... F 302 335-3911
Frederica *(G-2410)*

MEDICAL & SURGICAL SPLYS: Prosthetic Appliances
Choy Wilson Cdgn .... G 302 424-4141
Milford *(G-4351)*

MEDICAL & SURGICAL SPLYS: Supports, Abdominal, Ankle, Etc
Christana Ctr For Wns Wellness .... G 302 454-9800
Newark *(G-6204)*

MEDICAL & SURGICAL SPLYS: Welders' Hoods
Thomas E Moore Inc .... G 302 653-2000
Kenton *(G-3186)*

MEDICAL CENTERS
Abby Medical Center .... G 302 999-0003
Newark *(G-5882)*
Allergy Associates PA .... G 302 834-3401
Newark *(G-5939)*
Beebe Medical Center Inc .... D 302 393-2056
Milford *(G-4321)*
Beebe Medical Center Inc .... D 302 541-4175
Millville *(G-4836)*
Beebe Medical Center Inc .... D 302 645-3289
Rehoboth Beach *(G-7863)*
Beebe Medical Center Inc .... C 302 645-3010
Rehoboth Beach *(G-7864)*
Beebe Physician Network Inc .... E 302 645-1805
Lewes *(G-3374)*
Coastal Pain Care Physcians PA .... F 302 644-8330
Lewes *(G-3438)*
Concentra Inc .... F 302 738-0103
Newark *(G-6279)*
Concord Med Spine & Pain Ctr .... G 302 652-1107
Wilmington *(G-9813)*
Critical Care Systems Intl Inc .... G 302 765-4132
Wilmington *(G-9900)*
Family Medical Centre PA .... F 302 678-0510
Dover *(G-1539)*
Family Medicine Ctr Naticchia .... G 302 477-3300
Wilmington *(G-10493)*
Frensenius Medical Ctr .... G 302 762-2903
Wilmington *(G-10634)*
Limestone Medical Center Inc .... D 302 992-0500
Wilmington *(G-11389)*
Ocean Medical Imaging Del LLC .... G 302 684-5151
Milton *(G-4943)*
Rescue Surgical Solutions LLC .... G 302 722-5877
Newark *(G-7324)*
Trinity Medical Center PA .... G 302 846-0618
Delmar *(G-1043)*
VA Medical Center .... F 302 994-2511
Wilmington *(G-13043)*

Veterans Health Administration .... G 302 994-1660
Wilmington *(G-13071)*

MEDICAL EQPT: Laser Systems
Litecure LLC .... E 302 709-0408
New Castle *(G-5485)*

MEDICAL EQPT: MRI/Magnetic Resonance Imaging Devs, Nuclear
Silverside Open Mri Imaging .... G 302 246-2000
Wilmington *(G-12621)*

MEDICAL FIELD ASSOCIATION
Asssction Pathology Chairs Inc .... G 301 634-7880
Wilmington *(G-9161)*
Medical Society of Delaware .... E 302 366-1400
Newark *(G-7018)*

MEDICAL HELP SVCS
County of Sussex .... D 302 854-5050
Georgetown *(G-2489)*
Eden Hill Express Care LLC .... E 302 674-1999
Dover *(G-1504)*

MEDICAL SUNDRIES: Rubber
LRC North America Inc .... E 302 427-2845
Wilmington *(G-11446)*

MEDICAL SVCS ORGANIZATION
Cpr Solutions Inc .... G 302 477-1114
Wilmington *(G-9889)*
Delaware Health Net Inc .... G 410 788-9715
Wilmington *(G-10050)*
Delaware Occupational Health S .... E 302 368-5100
Newark *(G-6400)*
Diocese of Wilmington .... E 302 368-0146
Wilmington *(G-10158)*
La Red Health Center Inc .... D 302 855-1233
Georgetown *(G-2587)*
Laurel Highschool Wellness Ctr .... G 302 875-6164
Laurel *(G-3254)*
Nanticoke Health Services Inc .... G 302 629-6611
Seaford *(G-8323)*
Panzeea .... F 770 573-3672
Seaford *(G-8340)*

MEDICAL, DENTAL & HOSPITAL EQPT, WHOL: Dentists' Prof Splys
Rhondium Corporation .... F 800 771-4364
Wilmington *(G-12403)*

MEDICAL, DENTAL & HOSPITAL EQPT, WHOL: Hosptl Eqpt/Furniture
Junior Bd of Christiana Care .... G 302 733-1100
Newark *(G-6858)*

MEDICAL, DENTAL & HOSPITAL EQPT, WHOLESALE: Med Eqpt & Splys
First Choice Home Med Equipt .... E 302 323-8700
New Castle *(G-5312)*
Hannas Phrm Sup Co Inc .... F 302 571-8761
Wilmington *(G-10834)*
Jaco LLC .... G 302 645-8068
Milton *(G-4920)*
Linda McCormick .... G 443 987-2099
Wilmington *(G-11392)*
Marosa Surgical Industries .... F 302 674-0907
New Castle *(G-5510)*
Medical Technologies Intl .... E 760 837-4778
Dover *(G-1836)*
Medrep Inc .... G 302 571-0263
Wilmington *(G-11621)*
Medtix LLC .... E 302 645-8070
Milford *(G-4492)*
Medtix LLC .... F 302 265-4550
Lewes *(G-3632)*
Peninsula Home Health Care .... F 302 629-5672
Seaford *(G-8348)*
Personal Health PDT Dev LLC .... E 888 901-6150
Wilmington *(G-12091)*
Prescription Center Inc .... G 302 764-8564
Wilmington *(G-12221)*

Purushas Picks Inc .... G 302 918-7663
Bear *(G-295)*
Quinn-Miller Group Inc .... G 302 738-9742
Wilmington *(G-12290)*
Smith & Nephew Holdings Inc .... G 302 884-6720
Wilmington *(G-12659)*

MEDICAL, DENTAL & HOSPITAL EQPT, WHOLESALE: Medical Lab
Broad Creek Medical Service .... F 302 629-0202
Seaford *(G-8174)*
Gaudlitz Inc .... G 202 468-3876
Dover *(G-1585)*

MEDICAL, DENTAL & HOSPITAL EQPT, WHOLESALE: Safety
Anderson Group Inc .... G 302 478-6160
Wilmington *(G-9078)*
Baker Safety Equipment Inc .... G 302 376-9302
Bear *(G-44)*

MEDICAL, DENTAL & HOSPITAL EQPT, WHOLESALE: Therapy
Hysiotherapy Associates Inc .... E 610 444-1270
Wilmington *(G-10983)*

MEDITATION THERAPY
Dental Sleep Solution .... G 302 235-8249
Wilmington *(G-10116)*

MELAMINE RESINS: Melamine-Formaldehyde
Oci Melamine Americas Inc .... G 800 615-8284
Wilmington *(G-11934)*

MEMBER ORGS, CIVIC, SOCIAL & FRATERNAL: Bars & Restaurants
Delaware City Recreation Club .... G 302 834-9900
Delaware City *(G-953)*
Polish Library Association .... G 302 652-9555
Wilmington *(G-12183)*
Wilmington Club Inc .... E 302 658-4287
Wilmington *(G-13226)*

MEMBERSHIP HOTELS
Airbnb Inc .... G 415 800-5959
Wilmington *(G-8994)*
Innpros Inc .... F 302 326-2500
Bear *(G-188)*

MEMBERSHIP ORGANIZATIONS, BUSINESS: Better Business Bureau
Better Business Bureau of De .... G 302 221-5255
New Castle *(G-5089)*

MEMBERSHIP ORGANIZATIONS, BUSINESS: Community Affairs & Svcs
Establishing Black Men LLC .... G 215 432-7469
Claymont *(G-740)*
Nemours Hlth & Prevention Svcs .... G 302 366-1929
Newark *(G-7092)*
Pride of Delaware Lodge .... G 215 453-9236
Newark *(G-7251)*

MEMBERSHIP ORGANIZATIONS, BUSINESS: Contractors' Association
Assocted Bldrs Cntrs Del Chpte .... G 302 328-1111
New Castle *(G-5048)*
Dtg General Contractor .... G 321 439-0893
Wilmington *(G-10239)*

MEMBERSHIP ORGANIZATIONS, BUSINESS: Merchants' Association
Clark Associates Inc .... E 302 421-9950
New Castle *(G-5172)*
Delaware Racing Association .... D 302 994-6700
Wilmington *(G-10075)*
Stapler Athletic Association .... G 302 652-9769
Wilmington *(G-12740)*

MEMBERSHIP ORGANIZATIONS, CIVIC, SOCIAL & FRAT: Tenant Assoc

Sussex Cnty Manufactrd Housing.........G....... 302 945-2122
  Millsboro (G-4806)

MEMBERSHIP ORGANIZATIONS, CIVIC, SOCIAL/FRAT: Boy Scout Org

Del-Mr-Va Cncil Inc Boy Scuts.............E....... 302 622-3300
  Wilmington (G-9998)

MEMBERSHIP ORGANIZATIONS, CIVIC, SOCIAL/FRAT: Rec Assoc

Police Athc Leag Wlmington Inc ....G....... 302 764-6170
  Wilmington (G-12181)
Wilmington Trap Association ....E....... 302 834-9320
  Newark (G-7708)

MEMBERSHIP ORGANIZATIONS, CIVIC, SOCIAL/FRAT: Social Assoc

Eastern Bison Association ....F....... 434 660-6036
  Greenwood (G-2735)
Natio Assoc For The Advan of ....F....... 302 655-0998
  Wilmington (G-11804)

MEMBERSHIP ORGANIZATIONS, CIVIC, SOCIAL/FRAT: Youth Orgs

Bear-Glasgow YMCA ....G....... 302 836-9622
  Newark (G-6066)
Boys & Girls Club of De ....G....... 302 677-6376
  Dover (G-1224)
Boys & Girls Club of Milford ....G....... 302 422-4453
  Milford (G-4330)
Boys & Girls Clubs Del Inc ....F....... 302 422-3757
  Milford (G-4331)
Boys & Girls Clubs Del Inc ....B....... 302 658-1870
  Wilmington (G-9404)
Boys & Girls Clubs Del Inc ....E....... 302 836-6464
  Newark (G-6112)
Boys & Girls Clubs Del Inc ....F....... 302 655-8569
  New Castle (G-5102)
Boys & Girls Clubs Del Inc ....G....... 302 678-5182
  Dover (G-1225)
Boys & Girls Clubs Del Inc ....G....... 302 678-5182
  Dover (G-1226)
Boys & Girls Clubs Del Inc ....F....... 302 656-1386
  Wilmington (G-9405)
Boys & Girls Clubs Del Inc ....E....... 302 655-4591
  Wilmington (G-9406)
Boys & Girls Clubs Del Inc ....G....... 302 856-4903
  Georgetown (G-2457)
Boys & Girls Clubs Del Inc ....E....... 302 628-3789
  Seaford (G-8173)
Boys & Girls Clubs of America ....F....... 302 659-5610
  Smyrna (G-8584)
Boys & Girls Clubs of America ....G....... 302 875-1200
  Laurel (G-3204)
Boys Girls Clubs ....G....... 302 260-9864
  Rehoboth Beach (G-7873)
Georgetown Boys and Girls Club........F....... 302 856-4903
  Georgetown (G-2542)
Girls Incorporate of Delaware ....E....... 302 575-1041
  Wilmington (G-10716)
Kristol Ctr For Jewish Lf Inc ....G....... 302 453-0479
  Newark (G-6903)
Police Athletic League Del ....G....... 302 656-9501
  New Castle (G-5631)
Public Allies Deleware Inc ....G....... 302 573-4438
  Wilmington (G-12265)
Seaford Police Dept ....E....... 302 629-6644
  Seaford (G-8394)
Wilmington Youth Organization............G....... 302 761-9030
  Wilmington (G-13267)
Young Mens Christian Associat ....D....... 302 296-9622
  Rehoboth Beach (G-8121)
YWCA Delaware ....F....... 302 224-4060
  Newark (G-7733)

MEMBERSHIP ORGANIZATIONS, NEC: Amateur Sports Promotion

Skim USA..F....... 302 227-4011
  Rehoboth Beach (G-8078)

MEMBERSHIP ORGANIZATIONS, NEC: Art Council

Christina Cultural Arts Center ....E....... 302 652-0101
  Wilmington (G-9690)

MEMBERSHIP ORGANIZATIONS, NEC: Automobile Owner Association

AAA Club Alliance Inc ....B....... 302 368-8175
  Newark (G-5873)
AAA Club Alliance Inc ....F....... 302 674-8020
  Dover (G-1075)

MEMBERSHIP ORGANIZATIONS, NEC: Charitable

A Fresh Start Clg Svcs Corp ....G....... 302 257-1099
  Newark (G-5867)
Afgceaa Corporation ....G....... 617 314-0814
  Wilmington (G-8972)
American Soc Cytopathology Inc.........G....... 302 543-6583
  Wilmington (G-9056)
Association Educational Publr ....F....... 302 295-8350
  Wilmington (G-9158)
Astrazeneca Foundation ....G....... 302 886-3000
  Wilmington (G-9167)
Athari Inc ....F....... 312 358-4933
  Dover (G-1154)
Because Love Allows Compassion......E....... 302 674-2496
  Dover (G-1188)
Benevlent Prtective Order Elks ....E....... 302 736-1903
  Dover (G-1191)
Bethany Beach Vlntr Fire Co ....E....... 302 539-7700
  Bethany Beach (G-388)
Blessed Giving ....G....... 302 856-4551
  Georgetown (G-2456)
Blindsight Delaware LLC ....E....... 302 998-5913
  Wilmington (G-9370)
Brain Injury Association Del ....F....... 302 346-2083
  Dover (G-1228)
Cape Henlopen Senior Center ....G....... 302 227-2055
  Rehoboth Beach (G-7883)
Catholic Docese Wilmington Inc ....G....... 302 764-2717
  Wilmington (G-9595)
Challenge Program ....G....... 302 655-0945
  Wilmington (G-9624)
Child Inc ....E....... 302 762-8989
  Wilmington (G-9661)
Collegiate Network Inc ....G....... 302 652-4600
  Wilmington (G-9771)
Curiosity Service Foundation ....G....... 302 628-4140
  Seaford (G-8215)
Dcrac ....G....... 302 298-3289
  Wilmington (G-9981)
Delaware Chpr Amer Acdmy Pedtc ....G....... 302 218-1075
  Newark (G-6369)
Delaware Comm Reinvstmnt Actn ......G....... 302 298-3250
  Wilmington (G-10022)
Delaware Lacrosse Foundation............F....... 302 831-8661
  Wilmington (G-10061)
Dewey Artist Collaboration Inc.............G....... 302 212-9798
  Rehoboth Beach (G-7915)
East Sussex Moose Lodge ....G....... 302 436-2088
  Frankford (G-2361)
Fairwinds Baptist Church Inc ....G....... 302 322-1029
  Bear (G-149)
Family & Friends Caring Perola...........F....... 302 683-0611
  Wilmington (G-10484)
Foundation Source Philanthropi ....E....... 800 839-1754
  Wilmington (G-10603)
Frets4vetsorg ....G....... 302 382-1426
  Georgetown (G-2534)
Gene and Taffin A Ray Family ....F....... 800 839-1754
  Wilmington (G-10690)
Gods Way To Recovery Inc ....G....... 302 856-7375
  Georgetown (G-2549)
Harrison House Cmnty Program ....E....... 302 595-3370
  Newark (G-6710)
Iaad ....F....... 302 234-0214
  Newark (G-6758)
Independent Resources Inc ....F....... 302 765-0191
  Wilmington (G-11017)
Keith D Stoltz Foundation ....F....... 302 654-3600
  Wilmington (G-11234)
Khan Family Foundation Inc ....G....... 800 839-1754
  Wilmington (G-11256)
Kind To Kids Foundation ....G....... 302 654-5440
  Wilmington (G-11264)
Knights York Cross of Honour ....G....... 302 731-4817
  Newark (G-6900)
Leukemia & Lymphoma Soc Inc ....G....... 302 661-7300
  Wilmington (G-11377)
Lewes Senior Citizens Center ....G....... 302 645-9293
  Lewes (G-3604)
Lituation Creative Designs Inc ....F....... 302 494-4399
  Wilmington (G-11410)
Lodge Lane Assisted Living ....E....... 302 757-8100
  Wilmington (G-11424)
Mass For The Homeless Inc ....G....... 302 368-1030
  Wilmington (G-11562)
Millsboro Art League Inc ....G....... 302 934-6440
  Millsboro (G-4748)
Ministry of Caring Inc ....G....... 302 428-3702
  Wilmington (G-11705)
Morning After Inc ....G....... 302 562-5190
  Hartly (G-2936)
Nehemiah Gtwy Cmnty Dev Corp ......G....... 302 655-0803
  Wilmington (G-11829)
Norbertine Fathers ....G....... 302 449-1840
  Middletown (G-4175)
Pressley Ridge Foundation ....G....... 302 854-9782
  Georgetown (G-2626)
Read-Alouddelaware Inc ....G....... 302 656-5256
  Wilmington (G-12341)
Rotary International ....F....... 302 738-0827
  Newark (G-7366)
Society of St Vincent De Paul ....G....... 302 328-5166
  Wilmington (G-12668)
Summer Lrng Collaborative Inc...........G....... 860 751-9887
  Wilmington (G-12791)
Unidel Foundation Inc ....G....... 302 658-9200
  Wilmington (G-13010)
Water Is Life Kenya Inc ....G....... 302 894-7335
  Newark (G-7678)
Welfare Foundation Inc ....G....... 302 683-8200
  Wilmington (G-13141)
What Is Your Voice Inc ....F....... 443 653-2067
  Lewes (G-3820)

MEMBERSHIP ORGANIZATIONS, NEC: Christian Science Reading Rm

Christian Science Reading Room ....F....... 302 227-7650
  Rehoboth Beach (G-7888)

MEMBERSHIP ORGANIZATIONS, NEC: Food Co-Operative

Harvest Ministries Inc ....E....... 302 846-3001
  Delmar (G-1002)

MEMBERSHIP ORGANIZATIONS, NEC: Literary, Film Or Cultural

Rising Sunset Publishing LLC..............G....... 877 231-5425
  Newark (G-7343)

MEMBERSHIP ORGANIZATIONS, NEC: Personal Interest

Delaware Ctr For Hrtclture Inc ....F....... 302 658-6262
  Wilmington (G-10032)
Delaware Friends of Folk ....G....... 302 678-1423
  Dover (G-1372)
Moms Club..G....... 302 738-8822
  Wilmington (G-11729)
Retrosheet Inc ....G....... 302 731-1570
  Newark (G-7329)

MEMBERSHIP ORGANIZATIONS, NEC: Reading Room, Religious Mat

Christian Science Reading Room ....G....... 302 456-1428
  Newark (G-6206)

MEMBERSHIP ORGANIZATIONS, POLITICAL: Political Fundraising

Republican State Committee Del..........G....... 302 668-1954
  Wilmington (G-12384)

MEMBERSHIP ORGANIZATIONS, PROF: Education/Teacher Assoc

American Philosophical Assn ....F....... 302 831-1112
  Newark (G-5956)
International Literacy Assn ....D....... 302 731-1600
  Newark (G-6797)

PRODUCT & SERVICES SECTION — MEMBERSHIP SPORTS & RECREATION CLUBS

Jones Francina .... G 302 245-4139
  Delmar *(G-1010)*
Navy League of United States .... G 302 456-4410
  Wilmington *(G-11824)*

MEMBERSHIP ORGANIZATIONS, PROFESSIONAL: Health Association

American Lung Association .... G 302 674-9701
  Dover *(G-1120)*
Central and Southern Delaware .... G 302 545-8067
  Milford *(G-4345)*
Delaware Health Care Comm .... F 302 739-2730
  Dover *(G-1374)*
Delaware Health Info Netwrk .... F 302 678-0220
  Dover *(G-1375)*
National Society Inc 302 656-9572
  Wilmington *(G-11811)*

MEMBERSHIP ORGANIZATIONS, REL: Churches, Temples & Shrines

Church of God In Christ .... F 302 678-1949
  Dover *(G-1282)*

MEMBERSHIP ORGANIZATIONS, RELIGIOUS: Baptist Church

Fairwinds Baptist Church Inc .... G 302 322-1029
  Bear *(G-149)*
Ogletown Baptist Church .... E 302 737-2511
  Newark *(G-7144)*

MEMBERSHIP ORGANIZATIONS, RELIGIOUS: Catholic Church

Diocese of Wilmington .... E 302 368-0146
  Wilmington *(G-10158)*

MEMBERSHIP ORGANIZATIONS, RELIGIOUS: Episcopal Church

Diocesan Council Inc .... E 302 475-4688
  Wilmington *(G-10157)*

MEMBERSHIP ORGANIZATIONS, RELIGIOUS: Lutheran Church

Hilltop Lutheran Neighborhd .... E 302 656-3224
  Wilmington *(G-10910)*
St Stephens Evang Lutheran Ch .... G 302 652-7623
  Wilmington *(G-12729)*

MEMBERSHIP ORGANIZATIONS, RELIGIOUS: Methodist Church

Bethel United Methodist Church .... E 302 645-9426
  Lewes *(G-3379)*
Chester Bethel United Methodis .... F 302 475-3549
  Wilmington *(G-9656)*
Ebenezer United Methdst Chruch ...... F 302 731-9495
  Newark *(G-6500)*
Newark United Methodist .... E 302 368-8774
  Newark *(G-7129)*
Seaford Mission Inc .... F 302 629-2559
  Seaford *(G-8393)*
St Marks United Methodist Ch .... E 302 994-0400
  Wilmington *(G-12726)*

MEMBERSHIP ORGANIZATIONS, RELIGIOUS: Nonchurch

Ministry of Caring Inc .... G 302 428-3702
  Wilmington *(G-11705)*

MEMBERSHIP ORGANIZATIONS, RELIGIOUS: Presbyterian Church

Elsmere Presbyterian Church .... F 302 998-6365
  Wilmington *(G-10384)*
Faith Presbyterian Church .... F 302 764-8615
  Wilmington *(G-10478)*

MEMBERSHIP ORGANIZATIONS, RELIGIOUS: Religious Instruction

Northern Del Youth For Chrst .... G 302 995-6937
  Wilmington *(G-11906)*

MEMBERSHIP ORGS, CIVIC, SOCIAL & FRAT: Dwelling-Related

Longview Farms Civic Assn .... G 302 475-6684
  Wilmington *(G-11432)*

MEMBERSHIP ORGS, CIVIC, SOCIAL & FRAT: Girl Scout

Girl Scouts of The Cheasapea .... E 302 456-7150
  Newark *(G-6656)*

MEMBERSHIP ORGS, CIVIC, SOCIAL & FRATERNAL: Civic Assoc

Benevolent Protectve Ordr Elks .... F 302 629-2458
  Seaford *(G-8165)*
East Sussex Moose Lodge .... G 302 436-2088
  Frankford *(G-2361)*
Greater Dover Foundation .... G 302 734-2513
  Dover *(G-1609)*
Hall Burke VFW Post 5447 Inc .... F 302 798-2052
  Wilmington *(G-10824)*
League of Wmen Vters New Cstle ..... F 302 571-8948
  Wilmington *(G-11349)*
Loyal Order Mose Lwes Rehoboth .... G 302 684-4004
  Lewes *(G-3613)*
Moose International Inc .... G 302 684-4004
  Lewes *(G-3649)*
Pride of Delaw .... G 302 861-6857
  Newark *(G-7250)*
Rotary International .... F 302 378-2488
  Middletown *(G-4224)*
Rotary International .... F 302 227-5862
  Rehoboth Beach *(G-8063)*
Willow Run Civic Association .... G 302 994-2250
  Wilmington *(G-13219)*

MEMBERSHIP ORGS, CIVIC, SOCIAL & FRATERNAL: Condo Assoc

1122 Condominium .... G 302 234-4860
  New Castle *(G-4988)*
1401 Condominium Association .... E 302 656-8171
  Wilmington *(G-8847)*
Baynard House Condominiums .... G 302 319-3740
  Wilmington *(G-9266)*
Brandywine Park Condos .... G 302 655-2262
  Wilmington *(G-9448)*
Coffee Run Condo Council Inc .... G 302 239-4134
  Hockessin *(G-2991)*
Council of Devon .... F 302 658-5366
  Wilmington *(G-9873)*
Hamilton House Condominium .... G 302 658-7787
  Wilmington *(G-10827)*
Helopen Condominium Council .... G 302 227-6409
  Rehoboth Beach *(G-7959)*
Mallerd Lakes .... F 443 783-2993
  Selbyville *(G-8514)*
Mariners Court Condo Assn .... E 443 742-7812
  Rehoboth Beach *(G-7998)*
One Commerce Ctr Condo Council ... G 302 573-2513
  Wilmington *(G-11953)*
One Virginia .... G 302 227-9533
  Rehoboth Beach *(G-8023)*
Park Plaza Condo Association .... G 302 658-3526
  Wilmington *(G-12021)*
Rockford Park Condominium Home .. G 302 658-7842
  Wilmington *(G-12451)*
Solutions Property Management .... G 302 581-9060
  Rehoboth Beach *(G-8081)*
Star of The Sea Assoc of Ownrs .... G 302 227-6006
  Rehoboth Beach *(G-8086)*
Tiffany Pines I Condo Assn .... G 302 227-0913
  Rehoboth Beach *(G-8098)*

MEMBERSHIP ORGS, CIVIC, SOCIAL & FRATERNAL: Protection

Center For Inland Bays Inc .... G 302 226-8105
  Rehoboth Beach *(G-7885)*
Delaware Wild Lands Inc .... G 302 378-2736
  Odessa *(G-7825)*
Millcreek Foundation .... G 302 239-3811
  Hockessin *(G-3096)*
The Nature Conservancy .... F 302 654-4707
  Wilmington *(G-12891)*

MEMBERSHIP ORGS, CIVIC, SOCIAL & FRATERNAL: University Club

Alpha PHI Delta Fraternity .... E 302 531-7854
  Camden *(G-536)*

MEMBERSHIP ORGS, CIVIC, SOCIAL/FRAT: Educator's Assoc

Indo-American Association Del .... F 302 234-0214
  Newark *(G-6772)*
Intercollegiate Studies Inst .... D 302 656-3292
  Wilmington *(G-11054)*

MEMBERSHIP ORGS, LABOR UNIONS/SIMILAR: Employees' Assoc

Christina Education Assn .... F 302 454-7700
  Newark *(G-6228)*
Contemprary Stffing Sltons Inc .... G 302 328-1300
  New Castle *(G-5192)*

MEMBERSHIP ORGS, LABOR UNIONS: Collective Bargaining

American Federation .... G 302 283-1330
  Newark *(G-5951)*
United Auto Workers Local 435 .... F 302 995-6001
  Newark *(G-7611)*

MEMBERSHIP SPORTS & RECREATION CLUBS

20dollar Club Association .... G 978 908-6047
  Wilmington *(G-8853)*
American Sports Licensing .... D 302 288-0122
  Wilmington *(G-9057)*
Bayside At Bthany Lkes Clbhuse .... F 302 539-4378
  Ocean View *(G-7759)*
Bayside Sports Club LLC .... F 302 436-3550
  Selbyville *(G-8454)*
Big Stone Hunting Club .... G 302 424-7592
  Milford *(G-4326)*
Bob Lafazia .... G 302 633-1456
  Wilmington *(G-9389)*
Brandywine Lacrosse Club .... G 302 249-1840
  Wilmington *(G-9441)*
Brandywine Volleyball Club .... G 302 898-6452
  Wilmington *(G-9461)*
Bridgeville Lions Club Inc .... E 302 629-9543
  Bridgeville *(G-455)*
Cambridge Club Assoc Partn .... G 302 674-3500
  Hockessin *(G-2975)*
Camden-Wyoming Rotary Club .... G 302 697-2724
  Camden Wyoming *(G-622)*
Can Collecting Club .... G 302 420-5768
  Wilmington *(G-9547)*
Champions Club 215 380-1273
  Magnolia *(G-3884)*
Clementes Clubhouse .... G 302 455-0936
  Newark *(G-6249)*
Club Mantis Boxing LLC .... G 302 943-2580
  Lincoln *(G-3842)*
Coastal Club Schell Brothers .... G 302 966-0063
  Lewes *(G-3435)*
Credit Share Club LLC .... G 302 401-6450
  Dover *(G-1321)*
Del Bay Retriever Club .... G 302 678-8583
  Dover *(G-1350)*
Delaware Lacrosse Foundation .... F 302 831-8661
  Wilmington *(G-10061)*
Delaware Riders Basbal CLB Inc .... G 302 475-1915
  Wilmington *(G-10080)*
Delaware Trail Spinners .... G 302 738-0177
  Newark *(G-6420)*
Diamond State Curling Club .... G 856 577-3747
  Hockessin *(G-3009)*
Down Under Boxing Club .... G 302 745-4392
  Bridgeville *(G-467)*
Emblem At Christiana Clubhouse ...... G 302 525-6692
  Newark *(G-6523)*
Factory Sports .... G 302 313-4186
  Lewes *(G-3489)*
Hagerty Drivers Club LLC .... G 302 504-6086
  Wilmington *(G-10817)*
Hartly Ruritan Club .... G 302 492-8337
  Hartly *(G-2924)*
Hellenic Univ CLB Wilmington .... G 302 479-8811
  Wilmington *(G-10883)*

MEMBERSHIP SPORTS & RECREATION CLUBS

Hockessin Soccer Club .... F 302 234-1444
  Hockessin *(G-3054)*
Hunt Wandendale Club .... G 302 945-3369
  Millsboro *(G-4707)*
Itennisyou LLC .... G 305 890-3234
  Newark *(G-6810)*
Little Gym .... G 302 856-2310
  Georgetown *(G-2592)*
Little League Baseball Inc .... G 302 276-0375
  New Castle *(G-5486)*
Mako Swim Club LLC .... G 631 682-2131
  Harbeson *(G-2790)*
Michael Lo Sapio .... G 201 919-2643
  Townsend *(G-8810)*
Middletown Sports Complex LLC .... G 302 299-8630
  Middletown *(G-4160)*
Millsboro Little League .... F 302 934-1806
  Millsboro *(G-4751)*
Milton Garden Club .... G 302 684-8315
  Milton *(G-4940)*
New Castle Sailing Club .... G 302 307-3060
  New Castle *(G-5564)*
Northeast Rally Club .... G 302 934-1246
  Millsboro *(G-4762)*
Pike Creek Court Club Inc .... D 302 239-6688
  Wilmington *(G-12138)*
Polish American Civic Assn .... G 302 652-9324
  Wilmington *(G-12182)*
Rehoboth Bay Sailing Assn .... G 302 227-9008
  Rehoboth Beach *(G-8048)*
Resort Poker League .... G 302 604-8706
  Selbyville *(G-8539)*
Rockland Sports LLC .... D 302 654-4435
  Wilmington *(G-12454)*
Sache Social Club .... G 302 287-4813
  Wilmington *(G-12512)*
Salem County Amateur Radio CLB .... G 302 689-8127
  Wilmington *(G-12524)*
Skim USA .... F 302 227-4011
  Rehoboth Beach *(G-8078)*
Spring Lake Bath & Tennis Club .... G 302 227-6136
  Rehoboth Beach *(G-8085)*
Studio 11 .... F 302 622-9959
  Wilmington *(G-12781)*
Terrace Athletic Club Inc .... G 302 652-9059
  New Castle *(G-5762)*
Vacation Club .... G 302 628-1144
  Seaford *(G-8429)*
Velo Amis .... G 302 757-2783
  Newark *(G-7649)*
Wilmington Aquatic Club Inc .... G 302 322-2487
  New Castle *(G-5835)*
Wilmington Turners Club .... F 302 658-9011
  Wilmington *(G-13266)*
Womens Civic Club Bethany Bch .... G 302 539-7515
  Bethany Beach *(G-439)*
Womens Tennis C N C C .... G 302 762-2078
  Wilmington *(G-13293)*
Woodland Ferry Beagle Club .... G 302 856-2186
  Georgetown *(G-2707)*
YMCA Central Branch LLC .... F 302 571-6950
  Wilmington *(G-13328)*
Young Mens Christian Associat .... D 302 571-6935
  Wilmington *(G-13331)*
Young Mens Christian Associat .... D 302 296-9622
  Rehoboth Beach *(G-8121)*
Young Mens Christian Associat .... C 302 571-6900
  Wilmington *(G-13332)*
Young MNS Chrstn Assn Wlmngton .... E 302 221-9622
  Wilmington *(G-13334)*

MEN'S & BOYS' CLOTHING STORES

Dads Workwear Inc .... G 302 663-0068
  Laurel *(G-3219)*

MEN'S & BOYS' CLOTHING WHOLESALERS, NEC

Grand National USA Inc .... G 416 746-3511
  Wilmington *(G-10758)*
H D Lee Company Inc .... F 302 477-3930
  Wilmington *(G-10807)*

MEN'S & BOYS' SPORTSWEAR WHOLESALERS

Gbg USA Inc .... G 888 342-7243
  Wilmington *(G-10683)*

MEN'S & BOYS' UNDERWEAR WHOLESALERS

Majdell Group USA Inc .... G 302 722-8223
  Newark *(G-6977)*

MEN'S & BOYS' WORK CLOTHING WHOLESALERS

Kaul Glove and Mfg Co .... D 302 292-2660
  New Castle *(G-5454)*

MEN'S CLOTHING STORES: Everyday, Exc Suits & Sportswear

Designer Braids and Trade .... G 718 783-9078
  Middletown *(G-4037)*

MENTAL HEALTH CLINIC, OUTPATIENT

Advanced Behavioral Care Inc .... G 410 599-7400
  Lewes *(G-3326)*
Aod Smyma 43 .... G 302 659-5060
  Smyrna *(G-8573)*
Applied Biofeedback Solutions .... G 302 674-3225
  Dover *(G-1132)*
Connections .... G 302 221-6605
  New Castle *(G-5190)*
Connections Community Support .... D 302 653-1505
  Smyrna *(G-8604)*
Dima II Inc .... G 302 427-0787
  Wilmington *(G-10155)*
Doris V Obenshain .... G 302 448-1450
  Middletown *(G-4043)*
Fellowship Hlth Resources Inc .... G 302 422-6699
  Milford *(G-4412)*
Focus Behavioral Health .... F 302 762-2285
  Wilmington *(G-10584)*
Focus Health Care Delaware LLC .... D 302 395-1111
  New Castle *(G-5322)*
Health & Social Svcs Del Dept .... F 302 368-6700
  Newark *(G-6716)*
Health & Social Svcs Del Dept .... G 302 283-7500
  Newark *(G-6717)*
Joselow Beth Lpcmh .... G 302 644-0130
  Lewes *(G-3578)*
Kent Sussex Community Services .... F 302 384-6926
  Dover *(G-1740)*
Marc Wsburg Lpcmh Mntal Hlth C .... G 302 798-4400
  Wilmington *(G-11520)*
McCormick Assoc Middletown LLC .... G 302 449-0710
  Middletown *(G-4149)*
Mental Health Assn In Del .... G 302 654-6833
  Wilmington *(G-11632)*
Northeast Treatment Ctrs Inc .... E 302 691-0140
  Wilmington *(G-11904)*
On National Alliance .... E 302 427-0787
  Wilmington *(G-11951)*
Point Hope Brain Injury Spport .... G 302 731-7676
  New Castle *(G-5629)*
Psychotherapeutic Svc Assn Inc .... G 302 284-8370
  Dover *(G-1996)*
R H D Brandywine Hills .... E 302 764-3660
  Wilmington *(G-12296)*
Richard L Todd PHD .... G 302 853-0559
  Milton *(G-4958)*
Safe Space Delaware Inc .... F 302 691-7946
  Wilmington *(G-12516)*
Shauna Sullivan Lcsw .... G 302 383-6826
  Wilmington *(G-12595)*
Talk With Twila Ministries .... G 302 525-6472
  Newark *(G-7535)*

MENTAL HEALTH PRACTITIONERS' OFFICES

Pike Creek Psychological Ctr PA .... F 302 738-6859
  Newark *(G-7217)*
Psychological Services .... G 302 489-0213
  Wilmington *(G-12262)*

MERCHANDISING MACHINE OPERATORS: Vending

Efficient Services Inc .... G 302 629-2124
  Seaford *(G-8234)*

METAL CUTTING SVCS

BLJ&d Flagging Llc .... F 302 272-0574
  Dover *(G-1210)*

Metal Shop .... F 302 846-2988
  Delmar *(G-1020)*

METAL DETECTORS

Eastern Shore Metal Detectors .... G 302 628-1985
  Seaford *(G-8230)*

METAL FABRICATORS: Architechtural

Custom Mechanical Inc .... G 302 537-5611
  Bethany Beach *(G-393)*
Murphy Steel Inc .... E 302 366-8676
  Newark *(G-7073)*

METAL FABRICATORS: Plate

Air Liquide America LP .... G 302 225-2132
  Wilmington *(G-8992)*
Elanco Inc .... G 302 731-8500
  Bear *(G-142)*

METAL FABRICATORS: Sheet

AG & G Sheet Metal Inc .... G 302 653-4111
  Smyrna *(G-8562)*
Allied Precision Inc .... G 302 376-6844
  Middletown *(G-3936)*
Atlas Wldg & Fabrication Inc .... E 302 326-1900
  New Castle *(G-5053)*
Custom Mechanical Inc .... G 302 537-5611
  Bethany Beach *(G-393)*
Custom Mechanical Inc .... E 302 537-1150
  Frankford *(G-2358)*
Custom Sheet Metal of Delaware .... G 302 998-6865
  Wilmington *(G-9926)*
East Coast Machine Works .... G 302 349-5180
  Greenwood *(G-2734)*
L & J Sheet Metal .... F 302 875-2822
  Laurel *(G-3249)*
M Cubed Technologies Inc .... D 302 454-8600
  Newark *(G-6964)*
Mastercraft Welding .... G 302 697-3932
  Dover *(G-1824)*
McCabes Mechanical Service Inc .... F 302 854-9001
  Georgetown *(G-2599)*
Metal-Tech Inc .... E 302 322-7770
  New Castle *(G-5518)*
Murphy Steel Inc .... E 302 366-8676
  Newark *(G-7073)*
Power Electronics Inc .... E 302 653-4822
  Clayton *(G-868)*
Quality Htg Ar-Cnditioning Inc .... D 302 654-5247
  Wilmington *(G-12280)*
Ronald P Wilson .... G 302 539-4139
  Frankford *(G-2384)*
V E Guerrazzi Inc .... F 302 369-5557
  Newark *(G-7636)*

METAL FABRICATORS: Structural, Ship

Hardcore Cmpstes Oprations Llc .... D 302 442-5900
  New Castle *(G-5374)*
SIP Inc of Delaware .... G 302 654-4533
  Wilmington *(G-12634)*

METAL MINING SVCS

Joseph T Ryerson & Son Inc .... E 302 366-0555
  Newark *(G-6851)*
Nanoshel LLC .... G 302 268-6163
  Wilmington *(G-11799)*

METAL SERVICE CENTERS & OFFICES

Metal Partners Rebar LLC .... F 215 791-3491
  New Castle *(G-5517)*
Vulcraft Sales Corp .... F 302 427-5832
  Wilmington *(G-13108)*

METAL SLITTING & SHEARING

Eastern Shore Metals LLC .... F 302 629-6629
  Seaford *(G-8231)*

METAL STAMPINGS: Ornamental

George Products Company Inc .... F 302 449-0199
  Middletown *(G-4086)*

PRODUCT & SERVICES SECTION

MOLDS: Indl

METALS SVC CENTERS & WHOLESALERS: Casting, Rough, Iron/Steel
- Calmet Corporation .... E 714 505-6765
  Wilmington *(G-9539)*

METALS SVC CENTERS & WHOLESALERS: Piling, Iron & Steel
- Bristol Industrial Corporation .... F 302 322-1100
  New Castle *(G-5115)*

METALS SVC CENTERS & WHOLESALERS: Pipe & Tubing, Steel
- Petroserv Inc .... G 302 398-3260
  Harrington *(G-2873)*
- Vertex Industries Inc .... G 302 472-0601
  Wilmington *(G-13066)*

METALS SVC CENTERS & WHOLESALERS: Sheets, Metal
- Miller Metal Fabrication Inc .... D 302 337-2291
  Bridgeville *(G-501)*

METALS SVC CENTERS & WHOLESALERS: Steel
- B & B Industries Inc .... F 302 655-6156
  Wilmington *(G-9207)*
- Boyds Trailor Hitches .... G 302 697-9000
  Camden Wyoming *(G-619)*
- Bushwick Metals LLC .... G 302 328-0590
  New Castle *(G-5123)*
- Delta Sales Corp .... D 302 436-6063
  Selbyville *(G-8481)*
- East Coast Stainless Inc .... G 302 366-0675
  Newark *(G-6495)*
- East Coast Stainless & Alloys .... F 302 366-0675
  Newark *(G-6496)*
- Industrial Stl Structures Inc .... E 302 275-8892
  New Castle *(G-5416)*
- Steel and Metal Service .... G 302 322-9960
  New Castle *(G-5739)*
- Steel Suppliers Inc .... C 302 654-5243
  Wilmington *(G-12748)*

METALS SVC CTRS & WHOLESALERS: Aluminum Bars, Rods, Etc
- S G Williams & Bros Co .... F 302 656-8167
  Wilmington *(G-12506)*

METALWORK: Miscellaneous
- Cox Industries Inc .... G 302 332-8470
  Newark *(G-6310)*
- International Electrical Svcs .... G 302 438-6096
  Wilmington *(G-11065)*
- Regen Solutions LLC .... G 323 362-4336
  Dover *(G-2020)*

METALWORK: Ornamental
- Asa V Peugh Inc .... F 302 629-7969
  Seaford *(G-8156)*
- Deaven Development Corp .... G 302 994-5793
  Wilmington *(G-9991)*
- Donald F Deaven Inc .... E 302 994-5793
  Wilmington *(G-10196)*

METALWORKING MACHINERY WHOLESALERS
- Brooks Machine Inc .... G 302 674-5900
  Dover *(G-1235)*

METERING DEVICES: Gas Meters, Domestic & Large Cap, Indl
- American Meter Holdings Corp ..... G 302 477-0208
  Wilmington *(G-9054)*

METERING DEVICES: Water Quality Monitoring & Control Systems
- Meterpro Services Inc .... G 302 227-8596
  Rehoboth Beach *(G-8004)*

MICROFILM SVCS
- Data MGT Internationale Inc .... E 302 656-1151
  New Castle *(G-5215)*

MICROWAVE COMPONENTS
- AC Group Inc .... G 201 840-5566
  Wilmington *(G-8910)*
- Intelexmicro Inc .... G 302 907-9545
  Laurel *(G-3240)*

MICROWAVE OVENS: Household
- Five In One Oven Inc .... G 888 401-3911
  Newark *(G-6591)*

MILK, FLUID: Wholesalers
- Tuscan/Lehigh Dairies Inc .... F 302 398-8321
  Harrington *(G-2901)*

MILLWORK
- Aderyn Woodworks .... G 219 229-5070
  New Castle *(G-5004)*
- Aldas Refinishing Company .... G 302 528-5028
  Hockessin *(G-2955)*
- Bancroft Carpentry Company .... G 302 655-3434
  Wilmington *(G-9233)*
- Brandywine Mill Work .... G 302 652-3008
  Wilmington *(G-9442)*
- Craigs Woodworks LLC .... G 302 998-4201
  Wilmington *(G-9892)*
- Daniel A Yoder .... G 302 730-4076
  Dover *(G-1340)*
- Delaware Millwork .... G 302 376-8324
  Middletown *(G-4029)*
- Doug Green Woodworking .... G 302 652-6522
  Wilmington *(G-10211)*
- Espositos Woodworking & Cnstr ... G 302 245-5474
  Milton *(G-4904)*
- Frankford Custom Woodworks Inc . F 302 732-9570
  Frankford *(G-2363)*
- Georges Custom Woodworking ...... G 302 541-4599
  Dagsboro *(G-903)*
- Group Three Inc .... G 302 658-4158
  Wilmington *(G-10789)*
- Grubb Lumber Company Inc .... E 302 652-2800
  Wilmington *(G-10791)*
- Johns Woodworking LLC .... G 302 492-3527
  Hartly *(G-2929)*
- Kauffman Woodworks .... G 302 836-1976
  Bear *(G-213)*
- Koty Inc .... E 302 654-2665
  Wilmington *(G-11290)*
- Lanning Woodworks .... G 302 353-4726
  Wilmington *(G-11330)*
- Leroy A Coblentz .... G 302 343-7434
  Hartly *(G-2934)*
- Lulla Woodworking .... G 302 841-8800
  Ocean View *(G-7801)*
- Mary Costas Woodworking .... G 302 227-6255
  Rehoboth Beach *(G-8002)*
- Mastermark Woodworking Inc ...... G 302 945-9131
  Millsboro *(G-4737)*
- Mennos Woodworks .... G 302 381-5525
  Greenwood *(G-2751)*
- Monge Woodworking .... G 302 455-0175
  Newark *(G-7050)*
- New Look Home Inc .... G 302 994-4397
  Wilmington *(G-11866)*
- OBryan Woodworks .... G 302 398-8202
  Harrington *(G-2870)*
- ONeill Woodworking LLC .... G 443 669-3458
  Lewes *(G-3669)*
- Peirce James Townsend III .... G 302 449-2279
  Middletown *(G-4187)*
- Taylor Woodworks .... G 302 697-0155
  Magnolia *(G-3910)*
- Tj Custom Woodworks Inc .... G 302 563-8535
  Newark *(G-7569)*
- Wolf Wood Works LLC .... G 302 275-7227
  Wilmington *(G-13286)*
- Woodworks .... G 302 995-0800
  Wilmington *(G-13301)*
- Wyoming Millwork Co .... G 302 684-3150
  Milton *(G-4983)*
- Wyoming Millwork Co .... E 302 697-8650
  Camden *(G-607)*

MINE EXPLORATION SVCS: Nonmetallic Minerals
- Reliance Egleford Upstream LLC ... G 302 472-7437
  Wilmington *(G-12376)*

MINERAL WOOL
- Schmidt & Assoc .... G 610 255-3540
  Ocean View *(G-7811)*

MINIATURE GOLF COURSES
- Vinces Sports Center Inc .... G 302 738-4859
  Newark *(G-7659)*

MISC FIN INVEST ACT: Shares, RE, Entertain & Eqpt, Sales
- Hollie Enterprises LLC .... G 903 721-1904
  Wilmington *(G-10927)*
- Pacer International One LLC .... F 302 588-9500
  Wilmington *(G-12003)*
- Sks Enterprise .... D 302 310-2511
  Newark *(G-7437)*

MIXERS: Hot Metal
- Contractor Materials LLC .... E 302 658-5241
  New Castle *(G-5193)*

MIXTURES & BLOCKS: Asphalt Paving
- Christiana Materials Inc .... F 302 633-5600
  Wilmington *(G-9688)*
- Driveway Mint Pvng/Slcting LLC ... G 302 228-2644
  Bridgeville *(G-468)*
- Gardner-Gibson Inc .... G 302 628-4290
  Seaford *(G-8250)*
- Material Supply Inc .... E 302 658-6524
  Wilmington *(G-11566)*

MOBILE COMMUNICATIONS EQPT
- Interdgital Communications Inc .... D 610 878-7800
  Wilmington *(G-11058)*
- Interdigital Inc .... G 302 281-3600
  Wilmington *(G-11059)*
- Interdigital Wireless Inc .... D 302 281-3600
  Wilmington *(G-11061)*

MOBILE HOME DEALERS: Mobile Home Eqpt
- T & C Enterprise Incorporated ...... G 302 934-8080
  Millsboro *(G-4809)*

MOBILE HOMES
- Atlantic Realty Management .... G 302 629-0770
  Seaford *(G-8158)*
- Hippo Trailer .... G 302 854-6661
  Georgetown *(G-2558)*

MOBILE HOMES WHOLESALERS
- T & C Enterprise Incorporated ...... G 302 934-8080
  Millsboro *(G-4809)*

MOBILE HOMES, EXC RECREATIONAL
- CMH Capital Inc .... G 302 651-7947
  Wilmington *(G-9749)*

MODELS: General, Exc Toy
- Rosas Greek Btq .... G 302 678-2147
  Dover *(G-2043)*

MOLDED RUBBER PRDTS
- Fabreeka Intl Holdings Inc .... F 302 452-2500
  Newark *(G-6562)*

MOLDINGS: Picture Frame
- Carol Boyd Heron .... G 302 645-0551
  Lewes *(G-3407)*

MOLDS: Indl
- Mold Busters LLC .... G 302 339-2204
  Harbeson *(G-2793)*

MONEY ORDER ISSUANCE SVCS

Juni Holdings Inc ....F 415 949-4860
  Wilmington (G-11209)
Oink Oink LLC ....G 302 924-5034
  Dover (G-1914)

MONTESSORI CHILD DEVELOPMENT CENTER

A Childs Potential ....G 302 249-6929
  Lewes (G-3319)
Capital School District ....G 302 678-8394
  Dover (G-1250)
Claremont School LLC ....G 302 478-4531
  Wilmington (G-9729)
Hockessin Montessori School ....E 302 234-1240
  Hockessin (G-3053)
Lewes Montessori School ....G 302 644-7482
  Lewes (G-3602)
New Day Montessori ....G 302 235-2554
  Wilmington (G-11862)
Newark Montessori Preschool ....G 302 366-1481
  Newark (G-7124)

MONUMENTS & GRAVE MARKERS, EXC TERRAZZO

S & F Monuments ....G 302 722-8045
  Newark (G-7372)

MONUMENTS: Concrete

Wm V Sipple & Son Inc ....G 302 422-4214
  Milford (G-4611)

MONUMENTS: Cut Stone, Exc Finishing Or Lettering Only

Abba Monument Co Inc ....G 302 738-0272
  Newark (G-5880)

MORTGAGE BANKERS

Anniemac Home Mortgage LLC ....E 302 234-2956
  Wilmington (G-9088)
Castle Mortage Services Inc ....F 302 366-0912
  Newark (G-6167)
Freedom Mortgage Corporation ....F 302 368-7100
  Newark (G-6618)
Gilpin Mortgage ....F 302 656-5400
  Wilmington (G-10712)
Mortgage America Inc ....G 302 239-0600
  Wilmington (G-11760)
Mortgage Network Solutions LLC ....E 302 252-0100
  Wilmington (G-11761)
P B Investment Corp ....G 302 266-7920
  Newark (G-7167)
Premier Capital Holding ....G 302 730-1010
  Dover (G-1981)
Wells Fargo Home Mortgage Inc ....G 302 227-5700
  Rehoboth Beach (G-8111)
Wells Fargo Home Mortgage Inc ....G 302 239-6300
  Hockessin (G-3171)

MOTEL

Adams Oceanfront Resort ....F 302 227-3030
  Dewey Beach (G-1051)
Admiral Hotel ....G 302 227-2103
  Rehoboth Beach (G-7837)
Admiral West Inc ....E 609 729-0031
  Wilmington (G-8939)
Anchorage Motel Inc ....G 302 645-8320
  Rehoboth Beach (G-7841)
Atlantic View Motel ....F 302 227-3878
  Dewey Beach (G-1052)
Beacon Motel ....E 302 645-4888
  Lewes (G-3368)
Bell Buoy Motel ....G 302 227-6000
  Dewey Beach (G-1054)
Coastal Properties I LLC ....E 302 227-5800
  Rehoboth Beach (G-7895)
Cooper Simpler Associates Inc ....G 302 227-2999
  Rehoboth Beach (G-7901)
Country Villa Motel ....G 814 938-8330
  Milford (G-4366)
Courtyard Newark At Ud ....F 302 737-0900
  Newark (G-6306)
Delaware Motel and Rv Park ....G 302 328-3114
  New Castle (G-5232)

Dewey Beach House ....E 302 227-4000
  Dewey Beach (G-1055)
George Metz ....G 302 227-4343
  Rehoboth Beach (G-7946)
High Seas Motel ....G 302 227-2022
  Rehoboth Beach (G-7964)
Moore Partnership ....F 302 227-5253
  Dewey Beach (G-1059)
Moores Enterprises Inc ....F 302 227-8200
  Rehoboth Beach (G-8010)
New Castle Lodging Corporation ....F 302 654-5544
  New Castle (G-5562)
Pelican Bay Group Inc ....G 302 945-5900
  Millsboro (G-4773)
Red Mill Inn ....G 302 645-9736
  Lewes (G-3711)
Rehoboth Inn LLC ....G 302 226-2410
  Rehoboth Beach (G-8054)
Sandcastle Motel ....G 302 227-0400
  Rehoboth Beach (G-8066)
Shriji Hospitality (not Llc) ....F 302 654-5544
  New Castle (G-5706)
Superlodge ....G 302 654-5544
  Wilmington (G-12809)
Sussex Sands Inc ....G 302 539-8200
  Fenwick Island (G-2341)
Umiya Inc ....G 302 674-4011
  Dover (G-2173)

MOTEL: Franchised

Bethany Beach Bed & Breakfast ....G 301 651-2278
  Bethany Beach (G-385)
Lomas Properties LLC ....G 302 260-9245
  Rehoboth Beach (G-7990)
Nab Motel Inc ....F 302 656-9431
  Wilmington (G-11793)
Shree Kishna Inc ....F 302 839-5000
  Milford (G-4560)

MOTION PICTURE & VIDEO DISTRIBUTION

Bernieface Productions LLC ....G 302 561-0273
  Bear (G-51)
Bew Productions ....G 302 547-8661
  Wilmington (G-9322)
Brewster Products Inc ....G 302 798-1988
  New Castle (G-5111)
CB Productions ....G 302 715-1015
  Laurel (G-3209)
Digital Heart Productions ....G 302 737-6158
  Newark (G-6446)
Far Flung Bungy LLC ....F 302 421-8226
  Wilmington (G-10497)
Fish & Monkey Productions LLC ....F 302 897-4318
  Wilmington (G-10559)
J Alexander Productions LLC ....F 302 559-6667
  Wilmington (G-11103)
J Chance Productions ....G 302 322-2251
  New Castle (G-5428)
Jam Productions ....G 302 369-3629
  Newark (G-6824)
Kamproductions ....G 302 228-1852
  Lincoln (G-3858)
Michael Woody Productions ....F 302 584-2082
  Bear (G-255)
New Cndlelight Productions Inc ....E 302 475-2313
  Wilmington (G-11856)
Nkognito Productions LLC ....G 302 943-0399
  Magnolia (G-3901)
Peristalsis Productions Inc ....G 302 366-1106
  Newark (G-7204)
Short Wars Productions LLC ....F 302 932-0707
  Wilmington (G-12609)
Trauma Film Production PR LLC ....G 623 582-2287
  Dover (G-2162)

MOTION PICTURE & VIDEO PRODUCTION SVCS

Avian Productions Inc ....G 302 526-0542
  Dover (G-1161)
Continuum Media LLC ....F 310 295-9997
  Camden (G-552)
Electro Sound Systems Inc ....F 302 543-2292
  Newport (G-7748)
Imcg Global Inc ....G 800 559-6140
  Lewes (G-3553)
Maxwell World ....G 937 463-3579
  Dagsboro (G-918)
Productions For Purpose Inc ....G 302 388-9883
  Middletown (G-4199)

Waco Lid Films Inc ....G 302 378-7053
  Townsend (G-8831)

MOTION PICTURE DISTRIBUTION

Echelon Studios Inc ....F 800 208-9052
  Wilmington (G-10335)

MOTION PICTURE DISTRIBUTION, EXCLUSIVE OF PRODUCTION

Moghul Life Inc ....G 347 560-9124
  Wilmington (G-11724)

MOTOR REPAIR SVCS

F and D Equipment & Repair LLC ....G 302 378-1999
  Middletown (G-4068)
Roys Electrical Service Inc ....G 302 674-3199
  Cheswold (G-663)

MOTOR VEHICLE ASSEMBLY, COMPLETE: Autos, Incl Specialty

Penske Performance Inc ....D 302 656-2082
  Wilmington (G-12075)

MOTOR VEHICLE ASSEMBLY, COMPLETE: Fire Department Vehicles

Aetna Hose Hook and Ladder Co ....G 302 454-3300
  Newark (G-5917)

MOTOR VEHICLE DEALERS: Automobiles, New & Used

Bayshore Ford Truck Sales Inc ....D 302 656-3160
  New Castle (G-5075)
Brandywine Chrysler Jeep Dodge ....D 302 998-0458
  Wilmington (G-9424)
Delaware Motor Sales Inc ....C 302 656-3100
  Wilmington (G-10067)
Diamond Motor Sports Inc ....D 302 697-3222
  Dover (G-1423)
Dover Volkswagen Inc ....E 302 734-4761
  Dover (G-1472)
Future Ford Sales Inc ....D 302 999-0261
  Wilmington (G-10654)
IG Burton & Company Inc ....D 302 422-3041
  Milford (G-4447)
IG Burton & Company Inc ....E 302 629-2800
  Seaford (G-8269)
IG Burton & Company Inc ....E 302 424-3041
  Milford (G-4448)
Martin Newark Dealership Inc ....C 302 454-9300
  Newark (G-6996)
NAPA M3 Inc ....G 719 660-6263
  Wilmington (G-11800)
New Car Connection ....F 302 328-7000
  New Castle (G-5553)
Porter Nissan Buick Newark ....D 302 368-6300
  Newark (G-7233)
Rittenhouse Motor Co Inc ....E 302 731-5059
  Newark (G-7345)
Townsend Bros Inc ....D 302 674-0100
  Dover (G-2155)
Willis Ford Inc ....E 302 653-5900
  Smyrna (G-8746)
Winner Ford of Newark Inc ....C 302 731-2415
  Newark (G-7710)
Winner Group Inc ....B 302 764-5900
  Wilmington (G-13272)
Winner Group Inc ....E 302 292-8200
  Newark (G-7711)
Winner Infiniti Inc ....E 302 764-5900
  Wilmington (G-13274)
Winners Circle Inc ....E 302 661-2100
  Wilmington (G-13276)

MOTOR VEHICLE DEALERS: Cars, Used Only

4n Car Inc ....G 302 856-7434
  Georgetown (G-2417)
Armigers Auto Center Inc ....G 302 875-7642
  Laurel (G-3193)
Automotive Services Inc ....F 302 762-0100
  Wilmington (G-9190)
Brasures Body Shop Inc ....G 302 732-6157
  Frankford (G-2349)

PRODUCT & SERVICES SECTION

MUSEUMS

Deals On Wheels Inc .... E 302 999-9955
  Wilmington *(G-9988)*
European Coach Werkes Inc .... G 302 436-2277
  Frankford *(G-2362)*
Lifetime Skills Services LLC .... E 302 378-2911
  Middletown *(G-4132)*
Sports Car Service Inc .... F 302 764-7439
  Wilmington *(G-12709)*
United Auto Sales Inc .... G 302 325-3000
  New Castle *(G-5803)*

MOTOR VEHICLE DEALERS: Pickups, New & Used

Harvey Mack Sales & Svc Inc .... E 302 324-8340
  New Castle *(G-5382)*
Lee Mc Neill Associates .... G 302 593-6172
  Wilmington *(G-11356)*

MOTOR VEHICLE DEALERS: Trucks, Tractors/Trailers, New & Used

Clifton Leasing Co Inc .... E 302 674-2300
  Dover *(G-1293)*
Wellers Tire Service Inc .... F 302 337-8228
  Bridgeville *(G-531)*

MOTOR VEHICLE PARTS & ACCESS: Acceleration Eqpt

Autoport Inc .... E 302 658-5100
  New Castle *(G-5057)*

MOTOR VEHICLE PARTS & ACCESS: Instrument Board Assemblies

Smartwheel Inc .... G 617 542-7400
  Wilmington *(G-12656)*

MOTOR VEHICLE PARTS & ACCESS: Trailer Hitches

Horizon Intl Holdings LLC .... A 302 636-5401
  Wilmington *(G-10954)*

MOTOR VEHICLE PARTS & ACCESS: Transmissions

Sword Parts LLC .... G 302 246-1346
  Rehoboth Beach *(G-8093)*

MOTOR VEHICLE RACING & DRIVER SVCS

Advanced Motorsports .... G 302 629-3301
  Seaford *(G-8139)*
Penske Performance Inc .... D 302 656-2082
  Wilmington *(G-12075)*

MOTOR VEHICLE SPLYS & PARTS WHOLESALERS: New

Dover Automotive Inc .... G 302 653-9234
  Smyrna *(G-8625)*
Gaudlitz Inc .... G 202 468-3876
  Dover *(G-1585)*
IG Burton & Company Inc .... E 302 629-2800
  Seaford *(G-8269)*
Mto Hose Solutions Inc .... G 302 266-6555
  Newark *(G-7071)*

MOTOR VEHICLE SPLYS & PARTS WHOLESALERS: Used

Bridgeville Auto Center Inc .... F 302 337-3100
  Bridgeville *(G-454)*
Fred Drake Automotive Inc .... G 302 378-4877
  Townsend *(G-8788)*
Lkq Northeast Inc .... G 800 223-0171
  Dover *(G-1793)*

MOTOR VEHICLES & CAR BODIES

International Std Elc Corp .... F 302 427-3769
  Wilmington *(G-11068)*
North ATL Intl Ocean Carier .... G 786 275-5352
  New Castle *(G-5576)*
Revnation Ltd Liability Co .... G 202 672-4120
  Magnolia *(G-3906)*
Star Campus II .... G 302 514-7586
  Newark *(G-7483)*

MOTOR VEHICLES, WHOLESALE: Fire Trucks

Delmarva Pump Center Inc .... E 302 492-1245
  Marydel *(G-3915)*

MOTOR VEHICLES, WHOLESALE: Recreational, All-Terrain

Walls Farm and Garden Ctr Inc .... G 302 422-4565
  Milford *(G-4594)*

MOTOR VEHICLES, WHOLESALE: Trailers, Truck, New & Used

Harvey Mack Sales & Svc Inc .... E 302 324-8340
  New Castle *(G-5382)*
Utility/Eastern .... E 302 337-7400
  Bridgeville *(G-528)*

MOTOR VEHICLES, WHOLESALE: Truck bodies

Autoport Inc .... E 302 658-5100
  New Castle *(G-5057)*

MOTOR VEHICLES, WHOLESALE: Trucks, commercial

Lee Mc Neill Associates .... G 302 593-6172
  Wilmington *(G-11356)*
Tri-State Truck & Eqp Sls LLC .... G 302 276-1253
  New Castle *(G-5789)*

MOTORCYCLE DEALERS

NAPA M3 Inc .... G 719 660-6263
  Wilmington *(G-11800)*

MOTORCYCLE DEALERS: Bicycles, Motorized

Victor Kornbluth .... G 302 791-9777
  Claymont *(G-815)*

MOTORCYCLE PARTS & ACCESS DEALERS

Charles Offroad .... G 443 365-0630
  Laurel *(G-3211)*
Rommel Cycles LLC .... D 302 658-8800
  Smyrna *(G-8703)*

MOTORCYCLE REPAIR SHOPS

Charles Offroad .... G 443 365-0630
  Laurel *(G-3211)*
Freedom Cycle LLC .... G 302 286-6900
  Newark *(G-6615)*
Rommel Cycles LLC .... D 302 658-8800
  Smyrna *(G-8703)*

MOTORCYCLES & RELATED PARTS

Infinity Choppers .... G 302 249-7282
  Georgetown *(G-2565)*

MOTORS: Generators

All American Electric Svcs LLC .... G 410 479-0277
  Greenwood *(G-2712)*
Ametek Inc .... D 302 456-4400
  Newark *(G-5962)*
Arex Holding Inc .... G 646 216-2091
  Wilmington *(G-9126)*
Eeco Inc .... G 302 456-1448
  Newark *(G-6506)*
Renewable Energy Resources Inc .... G 302 544-0054
  Georgetown *(G-2635)*

MOVIE THEATERS, EXC DRIVE-IN

Assoc Community Talents Inc .... G 302 378-7038
  Middletown *(G-3944)*
Associated Cmnty Talents Inc .... G 302 378-1200
  Middletown *(G-3945)*
Cinemark Usa Inc .... G 302 994-7280
  Wilmington *(G-9707)*
Foot Light Production Inc .... F 302 645-7220
  Lewes *(G-3502)*
Regal Cinemas Inc .... E 302 479-0753
  Wilmington *(G-12353)*
Regal Cinemas Inc .... D 302 834-8515
  Christiana *(G-679)*
Rich Hebert & Associates .... G 202 255-3474
  Selbyville *(G-8541)*
Westown Movies LLC .... G 330 244-1633
  Middletown *(G-4283)*
Wilkins Enterprises .... G 302 732-3744
  Dagsboro *(G-944)*

MOVING SVC & STORAGE: Local

Bayshore Trnsp Sys Inc .... F 302 366-0220
  Newark *(G-6060)*
Delaware Moving & Storage Inc .... D 302 322-0311
  Bear *(G-110)*
On-Demand Services LLC .... G 302 388-1215
  New Castle *(G-5588)*

MOVING SVC: Local

Berry International Inc .... G 302 674-1300
  Dover *(G-1196)*
Move Crew .... G 302 290-4684
  New Castle *(G-5537)*
Muvers Inc .... G 888 508-4849
  Wilmington *(G-11780)*

MOVING SVC: Long-Distance

American Van Storage Corp .... E 302 369-0900
  Newark *(G-5961)*
Bayshore Trnsp Sys Inc .... D 302 366-0220
  Newark *(G-6059)*
Holman Moving Systems LLC .... D 302 323-9000
  New Castle *(G-5399)*

MULTI-SVCS CENTER

University of Delaware .... E 302 831-2501
  Newark *(G-7622)*
West End Neighborhood Hse Inc .... G 302 654-2131
  Wilmington *(G-13165)*
West End Neighborhood Hse Inc .... D 302 658-4171
  Wilmington *(G-13166)*

MUSEUMS

AMC Museum Foundation .... G 302 677-5938
  Dover *(G-1116)*
Biggs Swell C Mseum Amercn Art .... G 302 674-2111
  Dover *(G-1201)*
Commission On Archvs In Hstory .... G 302 335-5544
  Frederica *(G-2400)*
Delaware AG Museum & Vlg .... G 302 734-1618
  Dover *(G-1357)*
Delaware Art Museum Inc .... E 302 571-9590
  Wilmington *(G-10001)*
Delaware Children S Museum .... G 302 654-2340
  Wilmington *(G-10015)*
Delaware Childrens Museum Inc .... G 302 654-2340
  Wilmington *(G-10016)*
Delaware Museum of Natural .... E 302 658-9111
  Wilmington *(G-10068)*
Eleuthrian Mlls-Hgley Fndtion .... C 302 658-2400
  Wilmington *(G-10370)*
Filipino Heritg & Arts Museum .... G 302 731-5899
  Newark *(G-6579)*
For Delaware Center .... F 302 656-6466
  Wilmington *(G-10589)*
Hale Byrnes House .... F 302 998-3792
  Newark *(G-6703)*
Historical & Cultural Affairs .... F 302 792-0285
  Claymont *(G-761)*
Historical & Cultural Affairs .... F 302 323-4453
  New Castle *(G-5396)*
Historical & Cultural Affairs .... F 302 739-3277
  Dover *(G-1650)*
Historical Society of Del Inc .... E 302 295-2400
  Wilmington *(G-10918)*
Lewes Historical Society .... G 302 645-7670
  Lewes *(G-3601)*
Nanticoke Indian Museum .... G 302 945-7022
  Millsboro *(G-4758)*
Overfalls Maritime Museum .... D 302 644-8050
  Lewes *(G-3674)*
Rehoboth Art League Inc .... G 302 227-8408
  Rehoboth Beach *(G-8047)*
Rockwood Museum .... G 302 761-4340
  Wilmington *(G-12458)*
Sewell C Biggs Trust .... F 302 674-2111
  Dover *(G-2073)*
Winterthur Museum .... G 302 740-9771
  Wilmington *(G-13277)*

MUSEUMS

PRODUCT & SERVICES SECTION

Winterthur Museum Garden & Lib........E....... 302 888-4600
  Winterthur *(G-13357)*

MUSEUMS & ART GALLERIES

Kalmar Nyckel Foundation...................G....... 302 429-7447
  Wilmington *(G-11223)*
Somerville Manning Gallery................G....... 302 652-0271
  Wilmington *(G-12681)*

MUSIC ARRANGING & COMPOSING SVCS

Dj First Class......................................F....... 302 345-0602
  New Castle *(G-5256)*
Ibg Enterprise Inc...............................G....... 302 494-5017
  New Castle *(G-5408)*

MUSIC BROADCASTING SVCS

Digital Broadcast Corporation............F....... 215 285-0912
  Wilmington *(G-10151)*
Donald Walker...................................G....... 240 507-9805
  Harrington *(G-2834)*

MUSIC DISTRIBUTION SYSTEM SVCS

Dmg Clearances Inc..........................G....... 302 239-6337
  Hockessin *(G-3010)*

MUSIC RECORDING PRODUCER

Bitta Monk Entertainment Inc............G....... 916 969-4430
  Newark *(G-6085)*
Blue Pie Productions USA LLC..........F....... 917 817-7174
  Wilmington *(G-9380)*

MUSIC VIDEO PRODUCTION SVCS

Brandywine Electronics Corp.............F....... 302 324-9992
  Bear *(G-56)*

MUSICAL ENTERTAINERS

Levi Calling..G....... 302 449-0017
  Townsend *(G-8806)*
Milford Community Band Inc.............D....... 302 422-6304
  Milford *(G-4497)*
Raymond Entrmt Group LLC.............G....... 302 731-2000
  Newark *(G-7300)*

MUSICAL INSTRUMENT REPAIR

Flute Pro Shop Inc.............................G....... 302 479-5000
  Wilmington *(G-10583)*

MUSICAL INSTRUMENTS & ACCESS: NEC

Bb Custom Instruments.....................G....... 302 339-3826
  Georgetown *(G-2449)*
Victor Kornbluth.................................G....... 302 791-9777
  Claymont *(G-815)*

MUSICAL INSTRUMENTS & PARTS: Percussion

Imperial Dynasty Arts Program..........F....... 302 521-8551
  Wilmington *(G-11008)*

MUSICAL INSTRUMENTS & SPLYS STORES: Organs

Earle Teate Music..............................G....... 302 736-1937
  Dover *(G-1495)*

MUSICAL INSTRUMENTS & SPLYS STORES: Pianos

Flute Pro Shop Inc.............................G....... 302 479-5000
  Wilmington *(G-10583)*

MUSICAL INSTRUMENTS: Guitars & Parts, Electric & Acoustic

Cara Guitars Manufacturing...............E....... 302 521-0119
  Wilmington *(G-9562)*

NAIL SALONS

4 Seasons Nails & Spa......................G....... 302 663-9474
  Millsboro *(G-4619)*
A R Nails..G....... 302 858-4592
  Georgetown *(G-2420)*
Allure Salon.......................................G....... 302 653-6125
  Smyrna *(G-8566)*
Angel Nails..F....... 302 449-5067
  Middletown *(G-3939)*
Currie Hair Skin Nailss......................G....... 302 777-7755
  Wilmington *(G-9920)*
Cuts & Styles Barley Mill Inc.............G....... 302 999-8059
  Wilmington *(G-9929)*
Gemini Hair Designs..........................G....... 302 654-9371
  Wilmington *(G-10689)*
Joanne Reuther..................................G....... 302 945-8707
  Lewes *(G-3571)*
Lee Nails..G....... 302 674-5001
  Dover *(G-1777)*
Les Nails..G....... 302 449-5290
  Middletown *(G-4129)*
Lon Spa Inc.......................................G....... 302 368-4595
  Newark *(G-6947)*
Lux Spa & Nails.................................G....... 302 834-4899
  Bear *(G-241)*
N&D Nail Salon..................................G....... 302 834-4899
  Bear *(G-261)*
Nail Pros..G....... 302 674-2988
  Dover *(G-1882)*
Perfect Nails......................................G....... 302 731-1964
  Newark *(G-7201)*
Precious Nails....................................G....... 302 292-1690
  Wilmington *(G-12200)*
Pretty Nails..G....... 302 628-3937
  Seaford *(G-8363)*
Sky Nails..G....... 302 322-5949
  New Castle *(G-5715)*
Something Unique Inc.......................G....... 302 678-0555
  Dover *(G-2094)*
Star Nail Salon...................................G....... 302 498-0702
  Wilmington *(G-12741)*
Star Nails & Spa................................G....... 302 798-6245
  Wilmington *(G-12742)*
Sunlight Salon LLC............................G....... 302 456-1799
  Newark *(G-7507)*
Today Nails..G....... 302 286-7937
  Newark *(G-7572)*
Top Nails..G....... 302 644-2261
  Lewes *(G-3788)*

NAILS WHOLESALERS

Chez Nichole Hair & Nail Salon.........E....... 302 654-8888
  Wilmington *(G-9659)*

NATIONAL SECURITY, GOVERNMENT: Air Force

Army & Air Force Exchange Svc.......D....... 302 677-3716
  Dover *(G-1138)*
Army & Air Force Exchange Svc.......G....... 302 677-6365
  Dover *(G-1139)*
Army & Air Force Exchange Svc.......G....... 302 734-8262
  Dover *(G-1140)*
US Dept of the Air Force....................B....... 302 677-2525
  Dover *(G-2183)*

NATIONAL SECURITY, GOVERNMENT: Army

Armed Forces Med Examiner Sys.....D....... 302 346-8653
  Dover *(G-1137)*

NATURAL GAS COMPRESSING SVC, On-Site

TEC-Con Inc......................................G....... 610 583-8770
  New Castle *(G-5757)*

NATURAL GAS DISTRIBUTION TO CONSUMERS

Chesapeake Utilities Corp.................C....... 302 734-6799
  Dover *(G-1274)*
Conectiv LLC.....................................C....... 202 872-2680
  Wilmington *(G-9817)*
Conectiv Energy Supply Inc..............D....... 302 454-0300
  Newark *(G-6283)*
Delmarva Power & Light Company...C....... 302 454-0300
  Wilmington *(G-10104)*
Pepco Holdings LLC..........................E....... 202 872-2000
  Wilmington *(G-12080)*

NATURAL GAS TRANSMISSION & DISTRIBUTION

Conectiv Energy Supply Inc..............D....... 302 454-0300
  Newark *(G-6283)*
Sandpiper Energy Inc........................E....... 302 736-7656
  Dover *(G-2057)*

NATURAL PROPANE PRODUCTION

Party Gas...G....... 302 730-3880
  Dover *(G-1938)*

NATURAL RESOURCE PRESERVATION SVCS

Delaware Secretary of State..............F....... 302 736-7400
  Dover *(G-1389)*
Fort Delaware Society.......................G....... 302 834-1630
  Delaware City *(G-959)*
Landmark Engineering Inc.................D....... 302 323-9377
  Newark *(G-6915)*
New Castle Conservation Dst...........E....... 302 832-3100
  Newark *(G-7099)*
Sussex Conservation District............E....... 302 856-2105
  Georgetown *(G-2676)*

NAUTICAL REPAIR SVCS

Midlantic Marine Center Inc..............F....... 302 436-2628
  Selbyville *(G-8521)*
Reliable Trailer Inc............................F....... 856 962-7900
  Felton *(G-2316)*

NAVIGATIONAL SYSTEMS & INSTRUMENTS

Spectr-Physics Hldings USA Inc.......G....... 302 478-4600
  Wilmington *(G-12698)*

NEIGHBORHOOD DEVELOPMENT GROUP

Fort Miles Historical Assn Inc............G....... 302 645-0753
  Lewes *(G-3503)*
Ggc Inc..G....... 267 893-8052
  Lincoln *(G-3850)*
Northern Del Youth For Chrst...........G....... 302 995-6937
  Wilmington *(G-11906)*

NEW & USED CAR DEALERS

Bullfeathers Auto Sound Inc.............G....... 302 846-0434
  Laurel *(G-3205)*
Delmarva Pump Center Inc..............E....... 302 492-1245
  Marydel *(G-3915)*
Indian River Golf Cars Dr Wldg.........G....... 302 947-2044
  Millsboro *(G-4708)*
Martin Dealership..............................G....... 302 738-5200
  Newark *(G-6995)*
Richard Addington Co.......................G....... 302 422-2668
  Milford *(G-4543)*

NEWS SYNDICATES

Associated Press................................G....... 302 737-1628
  Newark *(G-6012)*

NEWSPAPERS & PERIODICALS NEWS REPORTING SVCS

Nk Consulting Inc..............................F....... 330 269-5775
  Wilmington *(G-11891)*

NEWSPAPERS, WHOLESALE

Distribution Marketing of Del.............G....... 302 658-6397
  Wilmington *(G-10168)*

NONDURABLE GOODS WHOLESALERS, NEC

Dillon Distributors LLC......................G....... 302 226-9700
  Rehoboth Beach *(G-7917)*

NOTARIES PUBLIC

Zicherheit LLC...................................F....... 302 510-3718
  Selbyville *(G-8557)*

NOVELTIES, DURABLE, WHOLESALE

Prepaid Legal Service Inc..................F....... 302 836-1985
  Bear *(G-291)*

NOZZLES & SPRINKLERS Lawn Hose

Aqua Flow Sprinklers.........................G....... 302 369-3629
  Newark *(G-5991)*

NUCLEAR DETECTORS: Solid State

Quarta-Rad Inc...................................G....... 201 877-2002
  Wilmington *(G-12283)*

NUCLEAR ELECTRIC POWER GENERATION

Nuclear Service Organization ....G....... 302 888-3000
Wilmington *(G-11922)*

NURSERIES & LAWN & GARDEN SPLY STORES, RETAIL: Fertilizer

Soil Service Inc ....G....... 302 629-7054
Seaford *(G-8404)*

NURSERIES & LAWN/GARDEN SPLY STORE, RET: Lawnmowers/Tractors

Burke Equipment Company ....D....... 302 697-3200
Felton *(G-2278)*
Foulk Lawn & Equipment Co Inc ....G....... 302 475-3233
Wilmington *(G-10599)*
Hockessin Tractor Inc........................G....... 302 239-4201
Hockessin *(G-3055)*
Suburban Lawn & Equipment Inc.......G....... 302 475-4300
Wilmington *(G-12785)*
T & T Small Engines Inc ....G....... 302 492-8677
Hartly *(G-2943)*
Walls Farm and Garden Ctr Inc ....G....... 302 422-4565
Milford *(G-4594)*

NURSERIES & LAWN/GARDEN SPLY STORES, RET: Garden Splys/Tools

Lords Landscaping Inc.......................E....... 302 539-6119
Millville *(G-4847)*
Talleys Garage Inc ....G....... 302 652-0463
Wilmington *(G-12850)*

NURSERIES/LAWN/GRDN SPLY STORE, RET: Nursery Stck, Seed/Bulb

Clark Seed Company Inc....................G....... 302 653-9249
Clayton *(G-839)*
Delaware Lawn & Tree Service ....F....... 302 834-7406
Bear *(G-109)*
Hudson Farm Supply Co Inc..............G....... 302 398-3654
Harrington *(G-2853)*
Itea Inc ....G....... 302 328-3716
Bear *(G-193)*
Richard Belotti ....F....... 302 934-7585
Georgetown *(G-2639)*
Willey Farms Inc................................D....... 302 378-8441
Townsend *(G-8833)*

NURSERY & GARDEN CENTERS

Bartons Landscaping/Lawn Inc...........E....... 302 629-2213
Seaford *(G-8162)*
Countryside Lawn & Landscape ....E....... 302 832-1320
Newark *(G-6304)*
Leons Garden World Ej Inc ....F....... 410 392-8630
New Castle *(G-5480)*
Old Country Garden Center Inc..........E....... 302 652-3317
Wilmington *(G-11943)*

NURSERY SCHOOLS

Bethel United Methodist Church ....E....... 302 645-9426
Lewes *(G-3379)*
Loving Care Nursery School...............G....... 302 653-6990
Smyrna *(G-8676)*
Odessa Early Education Center ....G....... 302 376-5254
Townsend *(G-8813)*
Playhouse Nursery School ....G....... 302 747-7007
Dover *(G-1966)*

NURSERY STOCK, WHOLESALE

Sterling Nursery Inc...........................G....... 302 653-7060
Smyrna *(G-8724)*
Willey Farms Inc................................D....... 302 378-8441
Townsend *(G-8833)*

NURSING & PERSONAL CARE FACILITIES, NEC

A and H Nursing Administra ....G....... 302 544-4474
Bear *(G-3)*
Infusion Care Delaware Home ....G....... 302 423-2511
Wilmington *(G-11028)*
Lodge Lane Assisted Living ....E....... 302 757-8100
Wilmington *(G-11424)*
Miss Kittys Kiddies ....G....... 302 571-1547
Wilmington *(G-11712)*
Nicole L Scott Np-C Adult ....G....... 302 690-1692
Hockessin *(G-3104)*
North Eastern Waffles LLC ....G....... 302 697-2226
Dover *(G-1901)*
Oncology Care Home ....G....... 610 274-2437
Newark *(G-7149)*
Quality Care Homes LLC ....G....... 302 858-3999
Lewes *(G-3702)*
Quality Lawn Care Home RE ....G....... 302 331-5892
Camden Wyoming *(G-652)*
United Adult Care Ltd ....G....... 302 725-0708
Harrington *(G-2902)*

NURSING CARE FACILITIES: Skilled

100 St Clire Drv Oprations LLC ....C....... 610 444-6350
Hockessin *(G-2945)*
100 St Clire Drv Oprations LLC ....G....... 302 234-5420
Hockessin *(G-2946)*
1203 Walker Rd Operations LLC ....C....... 302 735-8800
Dover *(G-1064)*
1203 Walker Rd Operations LLC ....A....... 610 444-6350
Dover *(G-1065)*
700 Marvel Road Operations LLC ......A....... 302 422-3303
Milford *(G-4298)*
715 East King St Oprations LLC ....G....... 302 628-3000
Seaford *(G-8134)*
810 Suth Broom St Oprtions LLC ....C....... 302 655-1375
Wilmington *(G-8868)*
Beebe School of Nursing ....F....... 302 645-3251
Lewes *(G-3375)*
Birth Center Holistic Women ....F....... 302 658-2229
Newark *(G-6083)*
Brandywine Snior Lving MGT LLC .....D....... 302 226-8750
Rehoboth Beach *(G-7874)*
Cadia Rhabilitation Silverside ....E....... 302 478-8889
Wilmington *(G-9530)*
Cadia Rverside Healthcare Svcs ....G....... 302 455-0808
Wilmington *(G-9531)*
Capitol Nursg & Rhb Cntr LLC ....C....... 302 734-1199
Dover *(G-1254)*
Chancellor Care Ctr of Delmar............C....... 302 846-3077
Delmar *(G-982)*
Christiana Care Hlth Svcs Inc.............F....... 302 733-6510
Newark *(G-6218)*
Commonspirit Health..........................D....... 302 234-5420
Hockessin *(G-2994)*
Compassionate Care Hospice of........D....... 302 994-1704
Wilmington *(G-9801)*
Country Meadow Propco LLC.............G....... 330 633-0555
Dover *(G-1315)*
Courtland Manor Inc ....D....... 302 674-0566
Dover *(G-1318)*
Emeritus Corporation ....E....... 302 674-4407
Dover *(G-1517)*
Five Star Quality Care Inc ....G....... 302 266-9255
Newark *(G-6592)*
Five Star Quality Care Inc ....G....... 302 366-0160
Newark *(G-6593)*
Five Star Quality Care Inc ....D....... 302 655-6249
Wilmington *(G-10568)*
Five Star Quality Care Inc ....G....... 302 792-5115
Wilmington *(G-10569)*
Five Star Senior Living Inc ....D....... 302 283-0540
Newark *(G-6594)*
Genesis Halthcare - Main Voice.........G....... 302 536-6390
Seaford *(G-8251)*
Genesis Healthcare Corporation ....G....... 302 422-3754
Milford *(G-4422)*
Genesis Healthcare Seafood Ctr ....C....... 302 629-3575
Seaford *(G-8252)*
Green Valley Pavilion.........................E....... 302 653-5085
Smyrna *(G-8646)*
Harrison Snior Lving Gorgetown ....G....... 302 856-4574
Georgetown *(G-2555)*
Health & Social Svcs Del Dept...........A....... 302 223-1000
Smyrna *(G-8650)*
Hillside Center ....F....... 302 652-1181
Wilmington *(G-10909)*
Home For Aged Wmn-Mnquadale HM ...C....... 302 654-1810
Wilmington *(G-10935)*
Ingleside Homes Inc..........................E....... 302 984-0950
Wilmington *(G-11032)*
Ivy Gables LLC ....F....... 302 475-9400
Wilmington *(G-11095)*
Just Like Home ....G....... 302 653-0605
Smyrna *(G-8665)*
Manor House ....F....... 302 629-4368
Seaford *(G-8301)*
New Castle HEAlth&rehab Cntr ....C....... 302 328-2580
New Castle *(G-5559)*
Nursing Board....................................G....... 302 744-4500
Dover *(G-1911)*
Odyssey Healthcare Inc ....E....... 302 478-1297
Wilmington *(G-11936)*
Onix Silverside LLC ....D....... 484 731-2500
Wilmington *(G-11960)*
Parkview Covalescent Center.............G....... 302 655-0955
Wilmington *(G-12025)*
Peninsula Untd Mthdst Hmes Inc ....B....... 302 235-6810
Hockessin *(G-3113)*
Presbyterian Senior Living ....C....... 302 744-3600
Dover *(G-1984)*
Public Health Nursing........................F....... 302 856-5136
Georgetown *(G-2630)*
Riverside Healthcare Center ....G....... 302 764-2615
Wilmington *(G-12429)*
Rockland Place ....E....... 302 777-3099
Wilmington *(G-12453)*
Steven E Diamond M D ....G....... 302 655-8868
Wilmington *(G-12760)*
Summit Retirement Community ....F....... 888 933-2300
Hockessin *(G-3154)*
Sunrise Senior Living LLC ....D....... 302 475-9163
Wilmington *(G-12801)*

NURSING HOME, EXC SKILLED & INTERMEDIATE CARE FACILITY

Broadmeadow Investment LLC ....C....... 302 449-3400
Middletown *(G-3977)*
Brookdale Senior Living Inc ....E....... 302 239-3200
Hockessin *(G-2970)*
Capitol Nursg & Rhb Cntr LLC ....C....... 302 734-1199
Dover *(G-1254)*
Green Valley Pavilion.........................E....... 302 653-5085
Smyrna *(G-8646)*
Hillside Center ....F....... 302 652-1181
Wilmington *(G-10909)*
Presbyterian Senior Living ....C....... 302 744-3600
Dover *(G-1984)*

NUTRITION SVCS

Dupont De Nemours Inc ....B....... 302 774-1000
Wilmington *(G-10251)*
New U Nutrition Inc............................G....... 302 543-4555
Wilmington *(G-11872)*
Produce For Btter Hlth Fndtion ....E....... 302 235-2329
Hockessin *(G-3126)*

NYLON FIBERS

Durafiber Tech DFT Entps Inc............D....... 704 912-3770
Wilmington *(G-10268)*
E I Du Pont De Nemours & Co ....A....... 302 485-3000
Wilmington *(G-10278)*
E I Du Pont De Nemours & Co ....G....... 800 441-7515
Wilmington *(G-10290)*
E I Du Pont De Nemours & Co ....B....... 302 892-5655
Wilmington *(G-10301)*
Specialty Products N&H Inc...............G....... 302 774-1000
Wilmington *(G-12697)*

OFC/CLINIC OF MED DRS: Special, Phys Or Surgeon, Eye Or ENT

David B Ettinger DMD MD ....G....... 302 369-1000
Newark *(G-6348)*
Delaware Eye Institute PA ....E....... 302 645-2300
Rehoboth Beach *(G-7912)*
Delaware Eye Surgery Center ....G....... 302 645-2300
Rehoboth Beach *(G-7913)*
E N T Associates ....F....... 302 674-3752
Dover *(G-1491)*
Gabriel Jr Timoteo R MD ....G....... 302 998-0300
Wilmington *(G-10661)*
Wilm Otolarngology ....F....... 302 658-0404
Wilmington *(G-13220)*

OFC/CLINIC OF MED DRS: Specl, Phys Or Surgeon, Occup & Indl

Children Youth & Their Fam ....E....... 302 633-2600
Wilmington *(G-9663)*

OFC/CLINIC, MED DRS: Specl, Phys Or Surgeon, Infect Disease

John F Reinhardt MD PA ....G....... 302 731-0800
Newark *(G-6842)*

OFC/CLINIC, MED DRS: Specl, Phys Or Surgeon, Infect Disease

PRODUCT & SERVICES SECTION

Marshall T Williams MD PHD ....F....... 302 994-9692
  Newark *(G-6992)*
Zarraga & Zarraga Internl Medc ....G....... 302 422-9140
  Milford *(G-4616)*

OFCS & CLINICS, MEDICAL DRS: Specl, Physician Or Surgn, ENT

Delaware Ear Nose & Throat Hea ....G....... 302 738-6014
  Newark *(G-6377)*
Ent Allergy Center ....G....... 302 629-3400
  Seaford *(G-8237)*
Ent and Allergy Delaware LLC ....F....... 302 998-0300
  Wilmington *(G-10406)*
Family Ear Nose & Throad ....E....... 302 998-0300
  Wilmington *(G-10490)*
Family Ent Physicians Inc ....E....... 302 998-0300
  Wilmington *(G-10491)*
Hearsay Services of Delaware ....G....... 302 422-3312
  Milford *(G-4437)*
Jiao Junfang MD ....G....... 302 453-1342
  Smyrna *(G-8664)*
Michael T Teixido MD ....G....... 302 998-0300
  Wilmington *(G-11668)*
Nanticoke Ear Nose and Throat ....G....... 302 629-9067
  Seaford *(G-8317)*
Otolaryngology Consultants ....F....... 302 328-1331
  Hockessin *(G-3108)*
Paul Imber Do ....G....... 302 478-5647
  Wilmington *(G-12042)*

OFFICE EQPT & ACCESSORY CUSTOMIZING SVCS

Laser Tone Bus Systems LLC ....G....... 302 335-2510
  Milford *(G-4471)*

OFFICE EQPT WHOLESALERS

Autotote Canada Inc ....C....... 302 737-4300
  Newark *(G-6029)*
Digital Office Solutions Inc ....F....... 302 286-6706
  Newark *(G-6447)*
Laser Tone Bus Systems LLC ....G....... 302 335-2510
  Milford *(G-4471)*
Michelet Finance Inc ....G....... 302 427-8751
  Wilmington *(G-11671)*
No Nonsense Office Mchs LLC ....G....... 302 856-7381
  Georgetown *(G-2610)*
Ricoh Usa Inc ....F....... 302 573-3562
  Wilmington *(G-12415)*

OFFICE EQPT, WHOLESALE: Duplicating Machines

Xerox Corporation ....E....... 302 792-5100
  Wilmington *(G-13319)*

OFFICE EQPT, WHOLESALE: Photocopy Machines

Canon Solutions America Inc ....E....... 302 792-8700
  Wilmington *(G-9551)*
Ricoh Usa Inc ....D....... 302 737-8000
  Newark *(G-7339)*

OFFICE FURNITURE REPAIR & MAINTENANCE SVCS

Advance Office Instltions Inc ....E....... 302 777-5599
  New Castle *(G-5008)*

OFFICE MANAGEMENT SVCS

Signature Group Management Co ....G....... 302 691-1010
  New Castle *(G-5713)*

OFFICE SPLY & STATIONERY STORES

Forever Inc ....G....... 302 368-1440
  Newark *(G-6604)*
Fulton Paper Company ....F....... 302 594-0400
  Wilmington *(G-10648)*
Henninger Printing Co Inc ....G....... 302 934-8119
  Millsboro *(G-4705)*

OFFICE SPLY & STATIONERY STORES: Office Forms & Splys

Creative Promotions ....G....... 302 697-7896
  Camden *(G-553)*

Mail Rooms Ltd ....G....... 302 629-4838
  Seaford *(G-8300)*

OFFICE SPLYS, NEC, WHOLESALE

Total Services Inc ....G....... 302 575-1132
  New Castle *(G-5776)*

OFFICES & CLINICS DOCTORS OF MED: Intrnl Med Practitioners

Andrew Nowakowski MD PA ....G....... 410 838-8900
  Bear *(G-29)*
D C Medical Services LLC ....G....... 302 855-0915
  Georgetown *(G-2492)*
Jarrell Benson Giles & Sweeney ....F....... 302 678-4488
  Dover *(G-1694)*
Total Care Physicians ....G....... 302 836-4200
  Newark *(G-7577)*
Zarek Donohue LLC ....E....... 302 543-5454
  Wilmington *(G-13340)*

OFFICES & CLINICS DRS OF MED: Psychiatrists/Psychoanalysts

Christiana Counseling ....G....... 302 995-1680
  Wilmington *(G-9686)*

OFFICES & CLINICS HLTH PRACTITNRS: Psychiatric Social Wrkr

Connections Community Support ....D....... 302 984-2302
  Wilmington *(G-9826)*

OFFICES & CLINICS OF DENTISTS: Dental Clinic

Allan C Goldfeder DMD ....G....... 302 994-1782
  Wilmington *(G-9017)*
Apex Dental Center LLC ....G....... 302 633-7550
  Newark *(G-5980)*
Bear Glasgow Dental ....F....... 302 836-3750
  Newark *(G-6064)*
Blue Hen Dental LLC ....G....... 302 538-0448
  Smyrna *(G-8582)*
Charles D Calhoon DDS P ....G....... 302 731-0202
  Wilmington *(G-9631)*
Dental Group ....G....... 302 645-8993
  Lewes *(G-3461)*
Graylyn Dental ....G....... 302 475-5555
  Wilmington *(G-10767)*
Hounsell Dental LLC ....G....... 302 691-8132
  Wilmington *(G-10959)*
Modern Dental ....G....... 302 478-1748
  Wilmington *(G-11720)*
New Concept Dental ....G....... 302 778-3822
  Wilmington *(G-11859)*
Pace Enterprises LLC ....G....... 302 529-2500
  Wilmington *(G-12001)*
Peninsula Dental LLC ....G....... 302 297-3750
  Millsboro *(G-4776)*
Sedation Center PA ....G....... 302 678-3384
  Dover *(G-2066)*
Sparkle Mobile Dental Services ....G....... 302 762-4322
  Wilmington *(G-12694)*
Swiatowicz Dental Associates ....G....... 302 476-8185
  Wilmington *(G-12824)*

OFFICES & CLINICS OF DENTISTS: Dental Clinics & Offices

Milunsky Family Dentistry ....G....... 610 566-5322
  Wilmington *(G-11701)*
Milunsky Family Dentistry PC ....G....... 610 872-8042
  Wilmington *(G-11702)*
Premier Dentistry Christiana ....G....... 302 366-7636
  Newark *(G-7243)*
Robert C Director DDS ....G....... 302 658-7358
  Wilmington *(G-12436)*
Tigani Family Dentistry PA ....G....... 302 571-8740
  Wilmington *(G-12908)*
Your Dentistry Today Inc ....G....... 302 575-0100
  Wilmington *(G-13335)*

OFFICES & CLINICS OF DENTISTS: Dental Surgeon

Alvis D Burris ....G....... 302 697-3125
  Camden *(G-537)*
Bruce G Fay DMD PA ....G....... 302 778-3822
  Wilmington *(G-9494)*

Carter Karen DMD ....G....... 302 832-2200
  Bear *(G-66)*
Christianna Dental Center ....G....... 302 369-3200
  Newark *(G-6227)*
Christina Ctr For Oral Surgery ....G....... 302 328-3053
  New Castle *(G-5160)*
Dann J Gladnick Dmd PA ....G....... 302 654-7243
  Wilmington *(G-9959)*
Devon Sadlowski DMD ....F....... 302 735-8940
  Dover *(G-1418)*
Douglas Ditty DMD MD ....G....... 302 644-2977
  Lewes *(G-3471)*
Eugene M DAmico III DDS PA ....G....... 302 292-1600
  Newark *(G-6544)*
First State Oral & M ....G....... 302 674-4450
  Dover *(G-1558)*
Hockessin Dental ....G....... 302 239-7277
  Hockessin *(G-3051)*
Joseph F Spera DMD PA ....G....... 302 475-1122
  Wilmington *(G-11190)*
Louis K Rafetto DMD ....G....... 302 477-1800
  Wilmington *(G-11440)*
Marta Blackhurst DMD ....G....... 302 478-1504
  Wilmington *(G-11548)*
Michael L Cahoon Dr ....G....... 302 644-4171
  Lewes *(G-3640)*
Mullen Thomas R DMD PA ....G....... 302 629-3588
  Seaford *(G-8312)*
Raymond W Petrunich ....G....... 302 836-3565
  Newark *(G-7303)*
Thomas Dougherty DDS ....G....... 302 239-2500
  Wilmington *(G-12899)*
Thomas Jenkins DMD ....F....... 302 426-0526
  Wilmington *(G-12902)*
Thomas W Mercer DMD ....G....... 302 678-2942
  Dover *(G-2144)*
Zachary Chipman DMD PA ....G....... 302 994-8696
  Wilmington *(G-13338)*

OFFICES & CLINICS OF DENTISTS: Dentists' Office

Access Dental LLC ....G....... 302 674-3303
  Dover *(G-1080)*
Alan R Levine DDS ....F....... 302 475-3743
  Wilmington *(G-8999)*
Alexis A Senholzi DMD ....G....... 302 234-2728
  Hockessin *(G-2956)*
Alfred Lauder DDS ....G....... 302 678-9742
  Dover *(G-1103)*
All Smiles Family & Cosme ....G....... 302 734-5303
  Dover *(G-1107)*
Anna Marie Mazoch DDS PA ....G....... 302 998-9594
  Wilmington *(G-9086)*
Arthur W Henry DDS Inc ....G....... 302 734-8101
  Dover *(G-1141)*
Avalon Dental ....G....... 302 999-8822
  Wilmington *(G-9195)*
Baker James Ccjr DDS ....G....... 302 658-9511
  Wilmington *(G-9222)*
Blue Diamond Dental PA ....G....... 302 655-8387
  Wilmington *(G-9375)*
Brafman Family Dentistry PC ....F....... 302 732-3852
  Dagsboro *(G-885)*
Brandywine Dental Care ....G....... 302 421-9960
  Wilmington *(G-9429)*
Brian A Wisk ....G....... 302 653-5011
  Smyrna *(G-8585)*
Brian McAllister DDS ....G....... 302 376-0617
  Middletown *(G-3972)*
Brice Darla M DDS Ms ....G....... 302 478-4700
  Wilmington *(G-9470)*
Bruce E Matthews DDS PA ....G....... 302 234-2440
  Hockessin *(G-2971)*
Bruce E Matthews DDS PA ....F....... 302 475-9220
  Wilmington *(G-9493)*
Caimar Corporation ....G....... 302 653-5011
  Smyrna *(G-8589)*
Christine E Fox DDS ....G....... 302 732-9850
  Dagsboro *(G-892)*
Clay White Dental Associates ....F....... 302 731-4225
  Newark *(G-6245)*
Collins Associates ....F....... 302 834-4000
  Newark *(G-6261)*
Conley & Wright DDS ....G....... 302 645-6671
  Rehoboth Beach *(G-7900)*
Connie F Cicorelli DDS PA ....G....... 302 798-5797
  Wilmington *(G-9849)*
Cook & Cook Ltd Partnership ....E....... 302 428-0109
  Wilmington *(G-9849)*

PRODUCT & SERVICES SECTION **OFFICES & CLINICS OF DENTISTS: Dentists' Office**

Listing	Code	Phone
Cook G Legih DDS& Cook Jefry	G	302 378-4416
Middletown (G-4009)		
Crescent Dental Associates	G	302 230-0000
Wilmington (G-9897)		
Crescent Dental Associates	G	302 836-6968
Bear (G-88)		
Curtis J Leciejewski DDS PA	G	302 226-7960
Rehoboth Beach (G-7905)		
Cynthia A Mumma DDS	G	302 652-2451
Wilmington (G-9932)		
D B Nibouar DDS	F	302 239-0502
Wilmington (G-9937)		
D R Deakyne DDS	G	302 653-6661
Smyrna (G-8610)		
D S Williams DMD PA	G	302 239-5272
Wilmington (G-9942)		
David E Mastrota DMD PA	G	302 654-0100
Wilmington (G-9969)		
David L Isaacs DDS	G	302 654-2904
Wilmington (G-9970)		
Deakyne Dental Associates PA	G	302 653-6661
Smyrna (G-8612)		
Deborah J Halligan DDS	G	302 738-5766
Newark (G-6356)		
Delaware Dentistry	G	302 475-6900
Wilmington (G-10036)		
Delaware Gentle Dental Group	G	302 514-6200
Smyrna (G-8615)		
Delaware Modern Dental LLC	G	302 366-8668
Newark (G-6396)		
Dental Associates PA	G	302 571-0878
Wilmington (G-10111)		
Dental Associates Delaware PA	E	302 477-4900
Wilmington (G-10112)		
Dental Associates Delaware PA	E	302 378-8600
Middletown (G-4035)		
Dental Associates Delaware PA	G	302 477-4900
Wilmington (G-10113)		
Dental Associates Hockessin	G	302 239-5917
Wilmington (G-10114)		
Dentistry For Children	F	302 475-7640
Wilmington (G-10117)		
Dominic Gioffre DDS PA	F	302 239-0410
Wilmington (G-10191)		
Dover Dental Associates	F	302 734-7634
Dover (G-1444)		
Dover Junior A DDS	G	302 836-3750
Newark (G-6466)		
Dr Amit Dua	G	302 239-5917
Hockessin (G-3011)		
Dr Bruce Matthews DDS	G	302 234-2440
Hockessin (G-3012)		
Dr Christopher Burns	G	302 674-8331
Dover (G-1475)		
Dr Clyde A Maxwell Jr	G	302 765-3373
Wilmington (G-10219)		
Dr Dawn Grandison DDS	G	302 678-3384
Dover (G-1476)		
Dr Howard Giles - Wilmington	G	302 477-4900
Wilmington (G-10223)		
Dr James Kramer	G	302 436-5133
Selbyville (G-8483)		
Dr Robert M Collins	G	302 239-3655
Wilmington (G-10228)		
Dr Robert Webster	G	302 674-1080
Dover (G-1479)		
Edward S Yalisove DDS PA	G	302 658-4124
Wilmington (G-10359)		
Edwin S Kuipers DDS	G	302 652-3775
Wilmington (G-10360)		
Elkington I Kent DDS	G	302 629-3008
Seaford (G-8235)		
Eric S Balliet	F	302 856-7423
Georgetown (G-2524)		
Eugene M DAmico III DDS PA	G	302 376-3700
Middletown (G-4063)		
Family Dental Associates Inc	F	302 674-8810
Dover (G-1537)		
Family Dental Care	G	302 999-7600
Wilmington (G-10487)		
Family Dental Center	F	302 656-8266
Wilmington (G-10488)		
Family Dentistry Milford PA	G	302 422-6924
Milford (G-4409)		
Foulk Road Dental & Associates	F	302 652-3775
Wilmington (G-10602)		
Fred L Wright DDS	G	302 239-1641
Wilmington (G-10624)		
Gary L Waite DMD	G	302 239-8586
Wilmington (G-10673)		
Glenwood Dental Associates LLP	G	302 653-5011
Smyrna (G-8642)		
Gonce William E Dr DDS PA	G	302 235-2400
Hockessin (G-3039)		
H Dean McSpadden DDS	G	302 239-5917
Hockessin (G-3042)		
H Dean McSpadden DDS	G	302 571-0680
Wilmington (G-10808)		
Ignacio S Gispert DDS	G	302 322-2303
New Castle (G-5410)		
Isaacs Isacs Fmly Dentistry PA	F	302 654-1328
Wilmington (G-11088)		
J Michael Fay DDS PA	F	302 998-2244
Wilmington (G-11108)		
J R Forshey DMD PA	G	302 322-0245
New Castle (G-5430)		
J R Williamson DDS	G	302 734-8887
Dover (G-1688)		
J S McKelvey DDS	F	302 239-0303
Wilmington (G-11110)		
James S Pillsbury DDS	G	302 734-0330
Dover (G-1692)		
James Tigani III DDS	G	302 571-8740
Wilmington (G-11125)		
Jay J Harris PC	G	302 453-1400
Newark (G-6829)		
Jeanette Y Son Dentist	G	302 998-8283
Wilmington (G-11138)		
Jeena M Jolly DDS	G	302 655-2626
Wilmington (G-11141)		
Jeffrey A Bright DMD	E	302 832-1371
Middletown (G-4113)		
Jennifer L Joseph DDS	G	302 239-6677
Wilmington (G-11147)		
Jerome C Kayatta DDS	G	302 737-6761
Newark (G-6835)		
John C Lynch DDS PA	G	302 629-7115
Seaford (G-8282)		
John N Russo DDS	F	302 652-3775
Wilmington (G-11175)		
John Nista DDS	G	302 292-1552
Newark (G-6845)		
John Wasniewski DMD	G	302 266-0200
Newark (G-6850)		
Joseph Cornatzer DDS	G	302 239-5917
Hockessin (G-3069)		
Kelly Walker DDS	G	302 832-2200
Bear (G-214)		
King & Minsk PA Inc	F	302 475-3270
Wilmington (G-11268)		
Kirkwood Dental Associates PA	F	302 994-2582
Wilmington (G-11274)		
Kirkwood Dental Associates PA	G	302 834-7700
Newark (G-6892)		
L F Conlin DDS	G	302 764-0930
Wilmington (G-11310)		
Laima V Anthaney DMD	G	302 645-4726
Lewes (G-3588)		
Laurel Dental	G	302 875-4271
Laurel (G-3252)		
Leo J Kituskie DDS	G	302 479-3937
Wilmington (G-11370)		
Lois James DDS	G	302 537-4500
Ocean View (G-7800)		
Louis P Martin DDS	G	302 994-4900
Wilmington (G-11441)		
Mark A Fortunato	E	302 477-4900
Wilmington (G-11530)		
Mark C Gladnick DDS	G	302 994-2660
Wilmington (G-11531)		
Mark Wieczorek Dmd PC	F	302 838-3384
Bear (G-246)		
Marta Biskup DDS	G	302 478-0000
Wilmington (G-11547)		
Mary Ziomek DDS	G	301 984-9646
Milton (G-4931)		
Mercer Dental Associates	G	302 664-1385
Milton (G-4934)		
Michael A Poleck DDS	G	302 644-4100
Lewes (G-3639)		
Michael A Poleck DDS PA	G	302 994-7730
Wilmington (G-11657)		
Michael J Ryan DDS	G	302 378-8600
Middletown (G-4153)		
Michael T Rosen DDS PA	G	866 561-5067
Wilmington (G-11667)		
Middletown Family Dentist	G	302 376-1959
Middletown (G-4156)		
Monica Mehring DDS	F	302 368-0054
Newark (G-7051)		
Ms Governors Square Shopping C	G	302 838-3384
Bear (G-258)		
Nathaniel Jon Bent DDS PA	G	302 731-4907
Newark (G-7084)		
Neena Mukkamala DDS	G	302 734-5305
Dover (G-1890)		
Neil G McAneny DDS PC	F	302 731-4907
Newark (G-7090)		
New Castle Dental Assoc PA	F	302 328-1513
New Castle (G-5556)		
Newark Dental Assoc Inc	E	302 737-5170
Newark (G-7117)		
Nicholas J Puntrieri	G	302 834-7700
Newark (G-7131)		
Norman M Lippman DDS	G	302 674-1140
Dover (G-1900)		
Norman S Steward DDS PA	G	302 422-9791
Milford (G-4514)		
Paul G Collins DDS	G	302 934-8005
Millsboro (G-4771)		
Paul R Christian DMD	G	302 376-9600
Middletown (G-4184)		
Premier Comprehensive Dental	G	302 378-3131
Middletown (G-4197)		
Progresive Dental Arts	F	302 455-9569
Newark (G-7268)		
Progressive Dental Arts	G	302 234-2222
Wilmington (G-12241)		
R M Quinn DDS	F	302 674-8000
Dover (G-2007)		
Ralph Tomases DDS PA	G	302 652-8656
Wilmington (G-12310)		
Raymond L Para DDS	G	302 234-2728
Hockessin (G-3130)		
Rebekah Fedele DMD PA	G	302 994-9555
Wilmington (G-12345)		
Rehoboth Beach Dent	G	302 226-7960
Rehoboth Beach (G-8050)		
Richard E Chodroff DMD	G	302 995-6979
Wilmington (G-12406)		
Richard J Tananis DDS LLC	G	302 875-4271
Laurel (G-3281)		
Richard S Jacobs DDS	G	302 792-2648
Claymont (G-800)		
Rodriguez Marieve O Dmd PA	G	302 655-5862
Wilmington (G-12462)		
Russell J Tibbetts DDS PA	G	302 479-5959
Wilmington (G-12496)		
Sattar A Syed DMD PA	G	302 994-3093
Wilmington (G-12544)		
Silly Smiles LLC	G	302 838-1865
Newark (G-7429)		
Silverside Dental Associates	G	302 478-4700
Wilmington (G-12620)		
Small Wonder Dental	G	302 525-6463
Newark (G-7443)		
Smile Brite Dental Care LLC	G	302 384-8448
Wilmington (G-12657)		
Smile Brite Dental Care LLC	F	302 838-8306
Newark (G-7449)		
Smile Place	G	302 514-6200
Smyrna (G-8717)		
Smile Solutions By Emmi Dental	G	302 999-8113
Wilmington (G-12658)		
Smiles Jolly PA	G	302 378-3384
Middletown (G-4244)		
Smyrna Dental Center PA	G	302 223-6194
Smyrna (G-8718)		
Southern Dental LLC	G	302 536-7589
Seaford (G-8406)		
Stanley H Goloskov DDS PA	G	302 475-0600
Wilmington (G-12737)		
Stephen A Niemoeller DMD PA	G	302 737-3320
Newark (G-7489)		
Steven Alban DDS PA	G	302 422-9637
Milford (G-4570)		
Thomas Baldwin DDS	G	302 829-1243
Ocean View (G-7820)		
Thomas Postlethwait DDS	G	302 674-8283
Dover (G-2143)		
Timothy and Rosemary Clay DMD	F	302 998-0500
Wilmington (G-12912)		
Todd Rowen DMD	G	302 994-5887
Wilmington (G-12922)		
Townsend Fmly Cosmtc Dentistry	G	302 376-7979
Townsend (G-8827)		
Victor J Venturena DDS	G	302 656-0558
Wilmington (G-13076)		
Victor L Gregory Jr DMD	G	302 239-1827
Wilmington (G-13077)		

Employee Codes: A=Over 500 employees, B=251-500
C=101-250, D=51-100, E=20-50, F=10-19, G=1-9

2020 Harris Directory of Delaware Businesses

OFFICES & CLINICS OF DENTISTS: Dentists' Office

W H Thomas DDS .... G 302 697-1152
  Dover *(G-2202)*
Wahl Family Dentistry .... E 302 655-1228
  Wilmington *(G-13113)*
Weatherhill Dental .... G 302 239-6677
  Wilmington *(G-13132)*
William Gonce .... G 302 235-2400
  Newark *(G-7698)*
William P Smith DDS .... G 302 737-7274
  Newark *(G-7699)*
Wilmington Dental Assoc PA .... F 302 654-6915
  Wilmington *(G-13229)*

OFFICES & CLINICS OF DENTISTS: Endodontist

Aloe & Carr PA .... G 302 736-6631
  Dover *(G-1111)*
John B Fontana Jr DDS .... G 302 656-2434
  Wilmington *(G-11167)*
Prudent Endodontics .... G 302 475-3803
  Wilmington *(G-12258)*
Suk-Young Carr DDS .... G 302 736-6631
  Dover *(G-2112)*

OFFICES & CLINICS OF DENTISTS: Oral Pathologist

B James Rogge DDS .... G 302 736-1423
  Dover *(G-1164)*
Maxillofacial Southern De Oral .... G 302 644-2977
  Lewes *(G-3627)*

OFFICES & CLINICS OF DENTISTS: Pedodontist

Coastal Kids Pediatric Dntstry .... G 302 644-4460
  Rehoboth Beach *(G-7894)*
Lawrence A Louie DMD .... G 302 674-5437
  Dover *(G-1770)*

OFFICES & CLINICS OF DENTISTS: Periodontist

Barry Kayne DDS .... G 302 456-0400
  Newark *(G-6048)*
Delaware Periodontics .... G 302 658-7871
  Wilmington *(G-10074)*
Emil W Tetzner D M D .... G 302 744-9900
  Dover *(G-1518)*
G W Keller DDS .... F 302 652-3586
  Wilmington *(G-10659)*
Margaret M Munley DDS .... G 302 475-2626
  Wilmington *(G-11523)*

OFFICES & CLINICS OF DENTISTS: Prosthodontist

Delmarva Prosthodontics .... G 302 674-8331
  Dover *(G-1411)*
Michele Broder .... G 302 652-1533
  Wilmington *(G-11670)*
Park Place Dental .... G 302 455-0333
  Newark *(G-7177)*
Ramon Galvan .... G 201 797-7172
  Wilmington *(G-12313)*

OFFICES & CLINICS OF DENTISTS: Specialist, Maxillofacial

G B Lyons DDS .... F 302 654-1765
  Wilmington *(G-10657)*
Marsico & Weinstien DDS .... G 302 998-8474
  Wilmington *(G-11546)*
Oral Mxllfcial Srgery Assoc PA .... F 302 655-6183
  Wilmington *(G-11968)*
Peter F Subach .... G 302 995-1870
  Wilmington *(G-12095)*
Southern Del Assoc Dntl Spc .... G 302 226-1606
  Rehoboth Beach *(G-8082)*

OFFICES & CLINICS OF DENTISTS: Specialist, Practitioners

Jr Walter J Kaminski DDS .... F 302 738-3666
  Christiana *(G-670)*
Qlean Implants Inc .... G 302 613-0804
  Rehoboth Beach *(G-8038)*
S D Nemcic DDS .... G 302 734-1950
  Dover *(G-2049)*

OFFICES & CLINICS OF DOCTORS OF MEDICINE: Allergist

Abby L Allen Fnp .... G 302 856-1773
  Georgetown *(G-2421)*
Allergy Associates PA Inc .... F 302 798-8070
  Wilmington *(G-9020)*
Asthma and Allergy Care Del .... G 302 995-2952
  Wilmington *(G-9164)*
Ent and Allergy Delaware LLC .... E 302 478-8467
  Wilmington *(G-10405)*
Ent and Allergy Delaware LLC .... G 302 832-8700
  Newark *(G-6530)*
Joel R Temple MD .... G 302 678-1343
  Dover *(G-1700)*
Peninsula Allergy and Asthma .... G 302 734-4434
  Dover *(G-1944)*

OFFICES & CLINICS OF DOCTORS OF MEDICINE: Anesthesiologist

Advanced Anesthesiology & Pain .... G 302 283-3300
  Wilmington *(G-8949)*
Allied Anesthesia Assoc LLC .... G 302 547-3620
  Dover *(G-1110)*
Eugene E Godfrey Do .... G 302 674-1356
  Dover *(G-1532)*
First State Anesthesia Svcs .... G 302 225-2990
  Newark *(G-6581)*
Milford Anesthesia Assoc LLC .... A 203 783-1831
  Newark *(G-7041)*
Outpatient Ansthsia Spclists PA .... F 302 995-1860
  Wilmington *(G-11984)*
P A Anesthesia Services .... G 302 709-4709
  New Castle *(G-5596)*

OFFICES & CLINICS OF DOCTORS OF MEDICINE: Dermatologist

Attitude LLC None .... G 302 422-3356
  Milford *(G-4313)*
Burke Dermatology .... F 302 703-6585
  Rehoboth Beach *(G-7881)*
Burke Dermatology .... G 302 734-3376
  Dover *(G-1242)*
Burke Dermatology .... G 302 230-3376
  Newark *(G-6136)*
Delaware Dermatolgy PA .... G 302 736-1800
  Dover *(G-1366)*
Dr Fanny Berg P C .... G 302 475-8000
  Wilmington *(G-10221)*
Michael K Rosenthal .... G 302 652-3469
  Wilmington *(G-11661)*
Mitchell C Stickler MD Inc .... F 302 644-6400
  Lewes *(G-3645)*
New Image Laser and Skin Care .... G 302 537-4336
  Ocean View *(G-7804)*
Panzer Dermatology Assoc PA .... G 302 633-7550
  Newark *(G-7174)*
Paul Sica MD .... G 302 652-3469
  Wilmington *(G-12044)*

OFFICES & CLINICS OF DOCTORS OF MEDICINE: Dispensary

Columbia Care New York LLC .... G 302 297-8614
  Smyrna *(G-8602)*
Corizon Health Inc .... D 302 266-8230
  Newark *(G-6298)*

OFFICES & CLINICS OF DOCTORS OF MEDICINE: Endocrinologist

Advanced Endoscopy Center LLC .... G 302 678-0725
  Dover *(G-1089)*
Center For Human Reproduction .... F 302 738-4600
  Newark *(G-6178)*
James H Hays MD .... G 302 633-1212
  Wilmington *(G-11121)*
Manveen Duggal MD .... G 302 734-5438
  Dover *(G-1817)*
Rodney Baltazar .... G 302 283-3300
  Middletown *(G-4222)*
Seaford Endoscopy Center .... G 302 629-7177
  Seaford *(G-8388)*

OFFICES & CLINICS OF DOCTORS OF MEDICINE: Gastronomist

Caruso Richard F MD PA .... G 302 645-6698
  Lewes *(G-3410)*
Central Del Endoscopy Unit .... F 302 422-3393
  Milford *(G-4324)*
Donald A Girard MD .... G 302 633-5755
  Wilmington *(G-10194)*
First State Gastroenterology A .... G 302 677-1617
  Dover *(G-1557)*
Gastroenterology Associates PA .... E 302 738-5300
  Newark *(G-6641)*
GI Associates of Delaware .... G 302 678-5008
  Dover *(G-1592)*
GI Specialists of De .... G 302 832-1545
  Newark *(G-6651)*
Nanticoke Gastroenterology .... G 302 629-2229
  Seaford *(G-8319)*
Parviz Sorouri Md PA .... G 302 453-9171
  Newark *(G-7179)*
William M Kaplan MD .... G 302 422-3393
  Milford *(G-4606)*

OFFICES & CLINICS OF DOCTORS OF MEDICINE: Gynecologist

Affinity Womens Health LLC .... G 302 468-4320
  Bear *(G-20)*
Bay Area Womens Care .... G 302 424-2200
  Milford *(G-4318)*
Birth Center Holistic Women .... F 302 658-2229
  Newark *(G-6083)*
Brandywine Ob Gyn .... G 302 477-1375
  Wilmington *(G-9445)*
Christana Ctr For Wns Wellness .... G 302 454-9800
  Newark *(G-6204)*
Dcmfm At Christiana Care .... G 302 543-7543
  Newark *(G-6352)*
Dedicated To Women Ob Gyn .... E 302 674-0223
  Dover *(G-1348)*
Dedicated To Women Obgyn .... F 302 285-5545
  Middletown *(G-4024)*
Delaware Obgyn & Womens Health .... G 302 730-0633
  Dover *(G-1383)*
Delawre Ctr For Mtrnal & Fetal .... E 302 319-5680
  Newark *(G-6424)*
Duque Nieva MD PA .... G 302 838-9712
  Bear *(G-130)*
Just For Women Ob/Gyn PA .... F 302 224-9400
  Newark *(G-6860)*
Khan Ob Gyn Associates .... F 302 735-8720
  Dover *(G-1745)*
M Imran MD .... G 302 453-7399
  Newark *(G-6966)*
Maternity Associates PA .... G 302 478-7973
  Wilmington *(G-11567)*
Nanticoke Obgyn Associates P A .... F 302 629-2434
  Seaford *(G-8326)*
Pike Creek Assoc In Wns Care .... F 302 995-7062
  Wilmington *(G-12134)*
Reproductive Associates Del PA .... G 302 478-8000
  Wilmington *(G-12382)*
Uma Chatterjee MD .... G 302 995-7500
  Newark *(G-7608)*
Women First LLC .... G 302 368-3257
  Newark *(G-7714)*
Womens Medical Center Inc .... G 302 629-5409
  Seaford *(G-8442)*
Womens Wellness Ctr & Med Spa .... G 302 643-2500
  Newark *(G-7716)*

OFFICES & CLINICS OF DOCTORS OF MEDICINE: Hematologist

Delaware Clncal Lab Physcans P .... E 302 737-7700
  Newark *(G-6370)*
Michael W Lankiewicz MD .... G 302 737-7700
  Newark *(G-7023)*

OFFICES & CLINICS OF DOCTORS OF MEDICINE: Nephrologist

Nephrology Associates PA .... E 302 225-0451
  Newark *(G-7093)*

OFFICES & CLINICS OF DOCTORS OF MEDICINE: Neurologist

Boulos Magdy I MD PA .... G 302 571-9750
  Wilmington *(G-9399)*
Center For Neurology .... D 302 422-0800
  Milford *(G-4344)*
Chesapeake Neurology Service .... G 302 563-7253
  Wilmington *(G-9655)*
Comprhensive Neurology Ctr LLC .... F 302 996-9010
  Newark *(G-6275)*
Neuro Ophthalmologic Asso .... G 302 792-1616
  Claymont *(G-789)*
Neurology Associates PA .... E 302 731-3017
  Newark *(G-7095)*
Neurosurgical Associates PA .... G 302 738-9543
  Newark *(G-7097)*
P A Cnmri .... D 302 678-8100
  Dover *(G-1928)*
Robert J Varipapa MD .... G 302 678-8100
  Dover *(G-2037)*
Stephen F Penny MD .... G 302 678-8100
  Dover *(G-2108)*

OFFICES & CLINICS OF DOCTORS OF MEDICINE: Neurosurgeon

Delaware Nurosurgical Group PA .... F 302 731-3017
  Newark *(G-6399)*
Neurosurgery Consultants PA .... G 302 738-9145
  Newark *(G-7096)*

OFFICES & CLINICS OF DOCTORS OF MEDICINE: Obstetrician

Bayside Health Assn Chartered .... E 302 645-4700
  Lewes *(G-3364)*
Duque Nieva MD PA .... G 302 655-2048
  Wilmington *(G-10266)*
Elias Mamberg MD .... G 302 428-0337
  Wilmington *(G-10375)*
Joaquin Cabrera MD .... G 302 629-8977
  Seaford *(G-8280)*
Jose Picazo M D P A .... G 302 738-6535
  Newark *(G-6850)*
Maternity Gynecology Assoc PA .... E 302 368-9000
  Newark *(G-7002)*
Ob-Gyn Associates of Dover P A .... E 302 674-0223
  Dover *(G-1912)*
Pregnacy Health Center .... G 302 698-9311
  Dover *(G-1980)*
Reproductive Associates Del PA .... E 302 623-4242
  Newark *(G-7322)*
Women To Women Ob/Gyn Assoc PA ... G 302 778-2229
  Wilmington *(G-13290)*

OFFICES & CLINICS OF DOCTORS OF MEDICINE: Oncologist

Medical Oncology Hematology .... E 302 999-8095
  Newark *(G-7017)*
Nanticoke Health Services Inc .... E 302 628-6344
  Seaford *(G-8321)*
Onpoint Oncology Inc .... G 610 274-0188
  Newark *(G-7154)*
Regional Hmatology Oncology PA .... E 302 731-7782
  Wilmington *(G-12358)*

OFFICES & CLINICS OF DOCTORS OF MEDICINE: Ophthalmologist

Boyd Jeffrey MD .... G 302 454-8800
  Newark *(G-6111)*
Cataract and Laser Center LLC .... F 302 454-8802
  Newark *(G-6168)*
Charles Wang MD PA .... G 302 655-1500
  Wilmington *(G-9639)*
David C Larned MD .... G 302 655-7600
  Wilmington *(G-9968)*
Delaware Eye Surgeons .... G 302 956-0285
  Wilmington *(G-10045)*
Delaware Ophthalmology Cons PA .... E 302 479-3937
  Wilmington *(G-10070)*
Douglas J Lavenburg MD PA .... F 302 993-0722
  Newark *(G-6465)*
Epstein Kplan Opthlmlogist LLP .... G 302 322-4444
  New Castle *(G-5293)*
Eye Care of Delaware .... E 302 454-8800
  Newark *(G-6559)*
Eye Consultants LLC .... G 302 998-2333
  Wilmington *(G-10464)*
Eye Physicians and Surgeons PA .... E 302 225-1018
  Wilmington *(G-10465)*
Family Medicine At Greenville .... F 302 429-5870
  Wilmington *(G-10492)*
Gary I Markowitz MD .... G 302 422-5155
  Milford *(G-4420)*
Halpern Opthalmology Assoc .... G 302 678-2210
  Dover *(G-1624)*
John R Stump MD .... G 302 422-3937
  Milford *(G-4459)*
Kalin Eye Assoc .... G 302 292-2020
  Newark *(G-6866)*
Millsboro Eye Care LLC .... G 302 684-2020
  Milton *(G-4938)*
Retinovitreous Associates Ltd .... F 302 351-1087
  Wilmington *(G-12393)*
Retinovitreous Associates Ltd .... G 302 351-1085
  Wilmington *(G-12394)*
Robinson & Cook Eyes Surgical .... E 302 645-2300
  Rehoboth Beach *(G-8060)*
Vision Center of Delaware Inc .... F 302 656-8867
  Wilmington *(G-13092)*

OFFICES & CLINICS OF DOCTORS OF MEDICINE: Pathologist

Assoction Pathology Chairs Inc .... G 301 634-7880
  Wilmington *(G-9161)*
Doctors Pathology Services PA .... E 302 677-0000
  Dover *(G-1436)*
Orthopaedic Specialists PA .... E 302 655-9494
  Wilmington *(G-11978)*

OFFICES & CLINICS OF DOCTORS OF MEDICINE: Pediatrician

Abigail E Martin M D .... G 302 651-4000
  Wilmington *(G-8903)*
Alfred Idpont Hosp For Chldren .... A 302 651-4000
  Wilmington *(G-9008)*
Atlantic Adult & Pediatric .... F 302 644-1300
  Lewes *(G-3352)*
Bayada Home Health Care Inc .... D 302 424-8200
  Milford *(G-4319)*
Beacon Pediatrics LLC .... F 302 645-8212
  Rehoboth Beach *(G-7860)*
Brandi Wine Pediatric Inc .... G 302 478-7805
  Wilmington *(G-9416)*
Brdly M Winston Pdrtcs Prctc .... G 302 424-1650
  Milford *(G-4333)*
Caridad Rosal MA MD .... E 302 653-6174
  Smyrna *(G-8591)*
Choudhary Arabinda K MD .... G 302 651-4000
  Wilmington *(G-9671)*
Cntrl De Gstroenterolgyassoc I .... G 302 678-9002
  Dover *(G-1297)*
Coastal Kid Watch .... F 302 537-0793
  Millville *(G-4839)*
Delaware Modern Pediatrics .... F 302 392-2077
  Newark *(G-6397)*
Edwin C Katzman MD .... G 302 368-2501
  Newark *(G-6504)*
Edwina C Granada MD .... G 302 629-7555
  Seaford *(G-8232)*
Fataneh M Ziari MD .... G 302 836-8533
  Newark *(G-6575)*
First State Pediatrics LLC .... F 302 292-1559
  Newark *(G-6584)*
Francis Mase Pediatrics .... F 302 762-5656
  Wilmington *(G-10611)*
Future Bright Pediatrics .... G 302 883-3266
  Dover *(G-1574)*
Future Bright Pediatrics LLC .... F 302 538-6258
  Camden *(G-573)*
Janice Tildon-Burton MD .... G 302 832-1124
  Newark *(G-6828)*
Kathleen M Cronan MD .... E 302 651-5860
  Wilmington *(G-11229)*
Kaza Medical Group Inc .... F 302 674-2616
  Dover *(G-1725)*
Kent Pediatrics LLC .... G 302 264-9691
  Dover *(G-1737)*
Kerry S Kirifides MD PA .... G 302 918-6400
  Newark *(G-6876)*
Khan Pediatrics Inc .... G 302 449-5791
  Wilmington *(G-6884)*
Kiddocs .... G 302 892-3300
  Wilmington *(G-11258)*
Kids Teens Pediatrics of Dover .... G 302 538-5624
  Dover *(G-1749)*
Lowell Scott MD PA .... G 302 684-1119
  Milton *(G-4926)*
Luis L David MD PA .... G 302 422-9768
  Milford *(G-4480)*
Macfarlane A Radford MD PA .... F 302 633-6338
  Wilmington *(G-11478)*
Matthew Gotthold Dr .... G 302 762-6222
  Wilmington *(G-11569)*
Matthew Gotthold Dr .... G 302 762-6222
  Wilmington *(G-11570)*
Michael A Mc Culloch MD .... G 302 651-6600
  Wilmington *(G-11653)*
Nemours Foundation .... G 302 422-4559
  Milford *(G-4512)*
Nemours Foundation .... E 302 651-6811
  Wilmington *(G-11834)*
Nemours Foundation .... G 302 651-4400
  Wilmington *(G-11835)*
Nemours Fundation Pension Plan .... E 302 629-5030
  Seaford *(G-8329)*
Nemours Fundation Pension Plan .... C 302 836-7820
  Newark *(G-7091)*
New Ark Pediatrics Inc .... F 302 738-4800
  Newark *(G-7098)*
Newark Pediatrician Inc .... F 302 738-4800
  Newark *(G-7126)*
P A Brandywine Pediatrics .... F 302 479-9610
  Wilmington *(G-11992)*
Paul C Anisman M D .... G 302 651-6600
  Wilmington *(G-12040)*
Pediatric & Adolescent Center .... G 302 684-0561
  Milton *(G-4946)*
Pediatric Associates PA .... E 302 368-8612
  Newark *(G-7190)*
Persephone Jones MD .... G 302 651-4000
  Wilmington *(G-12090)*
Pike Creek Pediatric Assoc .... F 302 239-7755
  Wilmington *(G-12140)*
Quinn Pediatric Dentistry .... G 302 674-8000
  Dover *(G-2004)*
Robert A Heinle M D .... G 302 651-6400
  Wilmington *(G-12434)*

OFFICES & CLINICS OF DOCTORS OF MEDICINE: Psychiatrist

Carol A Tavani MD .... G 302 454-9900
  Newark *(G-6160)*
F H Everett & Associates Inc .... G 302 674-2380
  Dover *(G-1536)*
Harmonious Mind LLC .... G 302 668-1059
  Wilmington *(G-10838)*
Perspective Counseling Center .... G 302 677-1758
  Felton *(G-2309)*
Serene Minds .... G 302 478-6199
  Wilmington *(G-12583)*

OFFICES & CLINICS OF DOCTORS OF MEDICINE: Radiologist

Delaware Diagnostic Group LLC .... G 302 472-5555
  Wilmington *(G-10040)*
Delaware Imaging Network .... G 302 836-4200
  Newark *(G-6386)*
Delaware Imaging Network .... E 302 652-3016
  Newark *(G-6387)*
Delaware Imaging Network .... G 302 449-5400
  Middletown *(G-4028)*
Delaware Imaging Network .... F 302 644-2590
  Newark *(G-6388)*
Delaware Imaging Network .... G 302 478-1100
  Wilmington *(G-10056)*
Delaware Open M R I .... G 302 479-5400
  Wilmington *(G-10069)*
Delaware Open M R I & C T .... G 302 734-5800
  Dover *(G-1384)*
Delaware Open M R I LLC .... G 302 449-2300
  Middletown *(G-4030)*
Imaging Group Delaware PA .... G 302 421-4300
  Wilmington *(G-11005)*
Jeanes Radiology Associates PC .... G 302 738-1700
  Newark *(G-6830)*
Limestone Open Mri LLC .... F 302 246-2001
  Wilmington *(G-11390)*
Limestone Open Mri LLC .... G 302 834-4500
  Bear *(G-235)*
Mid Delaware Imaging Inc .... F 302 734-9888
  Dover *(G-1849)*

Mri Consultants LLC ..... G 302 295-3367
Newark *(G-7067)*
Omega Imaging Associates LLC ..... E 302 738-9300
Newark *(G-7146)*
Omega Imaging Associates LLC ..... G 302 654-5245
Wilmington *(G-11947)*
Open Mri At Trolley Square LLC ..... F 302 472-5555
Wilmington *(G-11961)*
Pike Creek Imaging Center ..... F 302 995-2037
Wilmington *(G-12139)*
Radiation Oncology ..... E 302 733-1830
Newark *(G-7295)*
Radiology Associates Inc ..... E 302 832-5590
Wilmington *(G-12302)*
Silverside Open Mri Imaging ..... G 302 246-2000
Wilmington *(G-12621)*
Southern Delaware Imaging LLP ..... F 302 645-7919
Lewes *(G-3758)*
Trolley Sq Opn Mri & Imgng Ctr ..... F 302 472-5555
Wilmington *(G-12983)*

OFFICES & CLINICS OF DOCTORS OF MEDICINE: Surgeon

Advanced Surgical Specialists ..... G 302 475-4900
Wilmington *(G-8957)*
Aesthtic Plstic Surgery Del PA ..... F 302 656-0214
Wilmington *(G-8966)*
Arminio Joseph A MD & Assoc PA ..... F 302 654-6245
Wilmington *(G-9132)*
Cape Surgical Associates PA ..... G 302 645-7050
Lewes *(G-3403)*
Colon Rectal Surgery Assoc Del ..... F 302 737-5444
Newark *(G-6262)*
Del Marva Hand Specialists LLC ..... G 302 644-0940
Lewes *(G-3452)*
Delaware Plstic/Recons Srgy PA ..... G 302 994-8492
Newark *(G-6403)*
Delaware Soc Orthpd Surgeons ..... G 302 366-1400
Newark *(G-6413)*
Delaware Surgery Center LLC ..... E 302 730-0217
Dover *(G-1401)*
Delaware Surgical Group PA ..... G 302 892-2100
Wilmington *(G-10088)*
Delmarva Bariatric Fitnes Ctr ..... G 410 341-6180
Lewes *(G-3459)*
Delmarva Surgery Center ..... G 302 369-1700
Newark *(G-6429)*
Dover Oral and Maxillofacial S ..... G 302 674-1140
Dover *(G-1463)*
First State Surgery Center LLC ..... F 302 683-0700
Newark *(G-6586)*
Glasgow Medical Associates PA ..... G 302 836-3539
Newark *(G-6661)*
Institute of Christiana ..... F 302 892-9900
Newark *(G-6785)*
John T Malcynski MD ..... G 302 424-7522
Milford *(G-4460)*
Lewes Surgery Center ..... G 302 644-3466
Lewes *(G-3605)*
Matthew W Lawrence Do ..... F 302 652-6050
Wilmington *(G-11573)*
Medical Associates Bear Inc ..... G 302 832-6768
Bear *(G-250)*
Mid Atlantic Surgical Practice ..... F 302 652-6050
Wilmington *(G-11679)*
Minimally Invasive Surgcl & Ne ..... E 302 738-0300
Newark *(G-7043)*
P A Ortho-Surg ..... G 302 658-4800
Wilmington *(G-11993)*
Premiere Oral and Facial Surg ..... G 302 273-8300
Wilmington *(G-12219)*
Raafat Z Abdel-Misih MD ..... G 302 658-7533
Wilmington *(G-12300)*
Ramachandra U Hosmane MD ..... G 302 645-2274
Lewes *(G-3707)*
Rockland Surgery Center LP ..... E 302 999-0200
Wilmington *(G-12455)*
St Francis Bariatric Center ..... G 302 421-4121
Newark *(G-7476)*
Sunwise Drmatology Surgery LLC ..... G 302 378-7981
Middletown *(G-4251)*
Surgical Associates PA ..... F 302 346-4502
Dover *(G-2119)*
Wolf Creek Surgeons PA ..... F 302 678-3627
Dover *(G-2235)*
Zabel PLStc&recnstrctve Surgry ..... G 302 996-6400
Newark *(G-7736)*

OFFICES & CLINICS OF DOCTORS OF MEDICINE: Surgeon, Plastic

Abel Center For Oculofacial ..... G 302 998-3220
Wilmington *(G-8901)*
Advanced Plastic Surgery Cente ..... F 302 623-4004
Newark *(G-5906)*
Asher B Carey III ..... G 302 678-3443
Dover *(G-1144)*
Brandywine Cosmetic Surgery ..... G 302 652-3331
Wilmington *(G-9425)*
Brandywine Cosmetic Surgery ..... G 302 652-3331
Newark *(G-6115)*
Christiana Csmtc Srgry Cnsltnt ..... F 302 368-9611
Newark *(G-6222)*
Delaware Plastic & Recon ..... F 302 994-8492
Newark *(G-6402)*
Dr Mehdi Balakhani ..... G 302 368-8900
Wilmington *(G-10227)*
Joseph J Danyo MD ..... G 302 888-0508
Wilmington *(G-11192)*
Laser & Plastic Surgery Center ..... G 302 674-4865
Dover *(G-1766)*
Malek Abdollah Dr ..... G 302 994-8492
Newark *(G-6978)*
Peninsula Plastic Surgery PC ..... G 302 663-0119
Millsboro *(G-4778)*
Peter R Coggins MD ..... G 302 655-1115
Wilmington *(G-12097)*

OFFICES & CLINICS OF DOCTORS OF MEDICINE: Urologist

Andrew J Glick MD ..... E 302 652-8990
Wilmington *(G-9079)*
Brandywine Urology Cons PA ..... E 302 652-8990
Wilmington *(G-9457)*
Urology Assoc Southern Del PA ..... G 302 422-5569
Milford *(G-4588)*
Urology Associates Dover PA ..... E 302 674-1728
Dover *(G-2182)*

OFFICES & CLINICS OF DOCTORS, MEDICINE: Gen & Fam Practice

Abad & Salameda PA ..... G 302 652-4705
Wilmington *(G-8897)*
Abigail Family Medicine LLC ..... G 302 738-3770
Newark *(G-5884)*
All About Women LLC ..... E 302 224-8400
Newark *(G-5932)*
Andreas Rauer MD PA ..... G 302 734-1760
Dover *(G-1124)*
Andrew Weinstein MD Inc ..... G 302 428-1675
Wilmington *(G-9082)*
Arthritis and Osteoporosis LLC ..... G 302 628-8300
Seaford *(G-8155)*
Atlantic Family Physician LLC ..... G 302 856-4092
Georgetown *(G-2437)*
Atlantic Family Physicians ..... G 302 856-4092
Milton *(G-4864)*
Aviado Domingo G MD ..... G 302 430-7600
Milford *(G-4316)*
Bhaskar Palekar MD PA ..... G 302 645-1805
Lewes *(G-3381)*
Brandywine Care L L C ..... F 302 658-5822
Wilmington *(G-9421)*
Brandywine Family Medicine ..... G 302 475-5000
Wilmington *(G-9432)*
Bruce C Turner MD ..... G 302 366-0938
Newark *(G-6128)*
Ccmc Inc ..... G 302 477-9660
Wilmington *(G-9602)*
Central Delaware Fmly Medicine ..... F 302 735-1616
Dover *(G-1266)*
Christiana Neonatal Practice ..... F 302 733-2410
Newark *(G-6226)*
Christopher H Wendel Md PA ..... G 302 540-2979
Hockessin *(G-2988)*
Connections Development Corp ..... F 302 984-3380
Wilmington *(G-9829)*
Curtis A Smith ..... G 302 875-6800
Laurel *(G-3218)*
David G Reyes MD ..... G 302 735-7780
Dover *(G-1344)*
Dover Family Physicians PA ..... E 302 734-2500
Dover *(G-1448)*
Duque Nieva MD PA ..... G 302 655-5661
Wilmington *(G-10267)*
Elva G Pearson MD ..... G 302 623-4144
Newark *(G-6521)*
Family Health Delaware Inc ..... G 302 734-2444
Dover *(G-1538)*
Family Practice Center ..... F 302 645-2833
Lewes *(G-3491)*
Family Practice Cntr of New CA ..... G 302 999-0933
Newark *(G-6569)*
Family Practice Hockessin PA ..... G 302 239-4500
Hockessin *(G-3027)*
First State Vein and Laser Ctr ..... G 302 294-0700
Wilmington *(G-10556)*
Georgetown Family Medicine ..... F 302 856-4092
Georgetown *(G-2545)*
Horizons Family Practice PA ..... F 302 918-6300
Newark *(G-6746)*
Ian Myers MD LLC ..... G 302 832-7600
Newark *(G-6759)*
III John F Glenn MD ..... G 302 735-8850
Dover *(G-1667)*
Internal Medicine Delaware LLC ..... G 302 261-2269
Middletown *(G-4111)*
James Fierro Do PA ..... G 302 529-2255
Wilmington *(G-11120)*
John Hocutt Jr MD ..... G 302 475-7800
Wilmington *(G-11171)*
Jose D Manalo MD PA Inc ..... G 302 655-0355
Wilmington *(G-11183)*
K V Associates Inc ..... G 302 322-1353
New Castle *(G-5448)*
Kathryn L Ford Fmly Practice ..... G 302 674-8088
Dover *(G-1723)*
Kirk Family Practice ..... G 302 423-2049
Wilmington *(G-11272)*
Kristen Smith ..... F 302 623-6320
Wilmington *(G-11296)*
Lawrence M Lewandoski MD ..... G 302 698-1100
Dover *(G-1771)*
Lee M Dennis MD ..... G 302 735-1888
Dover *(G-1776)*
Longneck Family Practice ..... G 302 947-9767
Millsboro *(G-4726)*
Lowell Scott MD PA ..... G 302 684-1119
Milford *(G-4478)*
M Diana Metzger MD ..... F 302 731-0942
Newark *(G-6965)*
Marita F Fallorina MD ..... G 302 322-0660
New Castle *(G-5507)*
Mark Glassner MD ..... F 302 369-9002
Newark *(G-6989)*
Mark W Wingel ..... G 302 239-6200
Hockessin *(G-3090)*
Mary Kobak MD ..... G 302 623-0260
Newark *(G-6997)*
Medical Center of Harrington ..... G 302 398-8704
Harrington *(G-2866)*
Mid-Atlantic Fmly Practice LLC ..... E 302 934-0944
Millsboro *(G-4746)*
Mid-Atlantic Fmly Practice LLC ..... F 302 644-6860
Lewes *(G-3641)*
Middltown Familycare Assoc LLC ..... F 302 378-4779
Middletown *(G-4162)*
Milford Medical Associates PA ..... F 302 424-0600
Milford *(G-4501)*
Millsboro Family Practice PA ..... G 302 934-5626
Millsboro *(G-4749)*
Milton Enterprises Inc ..... G 302 684-2000
Milton *(G-4939)*
Milton Family Practice ..... F 302 684-2000
Lewes *(G-3642)*
Nanticoke Health Services Inc ..... E 302 629-4240
Seaford *(G-8320)*
Nanticoke Health Services Inc ..... E 302 856-7099
Georgetown *(G-2608)*
Nanticoke Health Services Inc ..... D 302 629-3923
Seaford *(G-8322)*
Narinder Singh MD ..... G 302 737-2600
Newark *(G-7083)*
Ovation Health Intl LLC ..... G 302 765-7595
Wilmington *(G-11985)*
Patricia H Purcell MD ..... G 302 428-1142
Wilmington *(G-12033)*
Paul H Aguillon MD ..... G 302 629-6664
Seaford *(G-8342)*
Peninsula Regional Medical Ctr ..... F 302 732-8400
Dagsboro *(G-929)*
Physician Dspnsng Solutions ..... E 302 734-7246
Wilmington *(G-12129)*
Premiere Physicians PA ..... G 302 762-6675
Newark *(G-7246)*

Quality Family Physicians PA................G....... 302 235-2351
Hockessin *(G-3127)*
Rebecca Jaffee MD................F....... 302 992-0200
Wilmington *(G-12344)*
Richard L Sherry MD................F....... 302 475-1880
Wilmington *(G-12410)*
Richard L Sherry MD................F....... 302 836-3937
Newark *(G-7338)*
Robert Donlick MD................G....... 302 653-8916
Smyrna *(G-8702)*
Schwartz Eric Wm MD................E....... 302 234-5770
Hockessin *(G-3142)*
Southside Family Practice................G....... 302 735-1880
Dover *(G-2096)*
Stoney Batter Family Medicine................E....... 302 234-9109
Wilmington *(G-12770)*
Teresa H Keller MD................G....... 302 422-2022
Milford *(G-4578)*
Theresa Little MD................G....... 302 735-1616
Dover *(G-2141)*
Tooze & Easter MD PA................E....... 302 735-8700
Dover *(G-2152)*
Total Care Physicians................E....... 302 998-2977
Wilmington *(G-12937)*
Total Care Physicians................E....... 302 798-0666
Wilmington *(G-12938)*
Tri-State Health................G....... 302 368-2563
Newark *(G-7588)*
Van Buren Medical Associates................E....... 302 998-1151
Wilmington *(G-13047)*
Visionquest Eye Care Center................E....... 302 678-3545
Dover *(G-2196)*
Wayne I Tucker................G....... 302 838-1100
Bear *(G-372)*
Westside Family Healthcare Inc................F....... 302 836-2864
Bear *(G-376)*
William A Ellert MD................G....... 302 369-9370
Newark *(G-7696)*
Wilson Family Practice................G....... 302 422-6677
Milford *(G-4609)*

OFFICES & CLINICS OF DRS OF MED: Cardiologist & Vascular

Ashish B Parikh................F....... 302 338-9444
Newark *(G-6010)*
Bellevue Heart Group LLC................G....... 302 468-4500
Wilmington *(G-9290)*
Cardiology Consultants................F....... 302 645-1233
Lewes *(G-3405)*
Cardiology Consultants................G....... 302 541-8138
Millville *(G-4838)*
Cardiology Physicans PA Inc................E....... 302 366-8600
Newark *(G-6153)*
Cardiology Specialists................G....... 302 453-0624
Wilmington *(G-9565)*
Christiana Care Health Sys Inc................G....... 302 477-6500
Wilmington *(G-9680)*
Christopher A Bowens MD................G....... 302 834-3700
Newark *(G-6231)*
Clinic By Sea................G....... 302 644-0999
Lewes *(G-3429)*
Clinical Crdlgy Spcialists LLC................G....... 302 834-3700
Newark *(G-6251)*
Delaware Crdovascular Assoc PA................F....... 302 644-7676
Lewes *(G-3456)*
Delaware Crdovascular Assoc PA................G....... 302 993-7676
Newark *(G-6371)*
Delaware Crdovascular Assoc PA................F....... 302 734-7676
Dover *(G-1362)*
Delaware Crdovascular Assoc PA................F....... 302 543-4800
Wilmington *(G-10030)*
Delaware Heart & Vascular PA................G....... 302 734-1414
Dover *(G-1377)*
Eranga Cardiology................G....... 302 747-7486
Dover *(G-1529)*
Henlopen Cardiology PA................G....... 302 645-7671
Rehoboth Beach *(G-7961)*
Ierardi Vascular Clinic LLC................G....... 302 655-8272
Newark *(G-6763)*
Nanticoke Cardiology................E....... 302 629-9099
Seaford *(G-8316)*
P A Alfieri Cardiology................E....... 302 731-0001
Wilmington *(G-11990)*
Palermo Francis A MD Facc PA................G....... 302 994-1100
Newark *(G-7171)*
Philips B Eric DMD PA................F....... 302 738-7303
Newark *(G-7213)*
Surgical Nanticoke Assoc PA................G....... 302 629-8662
Seaford *(G-8411)*

Vascular Specialists Del PA................G....... 302 733-5700
Newark *(G-7645)*
Westover Cardiology................G....... 302 482-2035
Middletown *(G-4282)*

OFFICES & CLINICS OF DRS OF MED: Clinic, Op by Physicians

Delaware Sleep Dsrder Ctrs LLC................E....... 302 669-6141
Wilmington *(G-10084)*
Eden Hill Medical Center LLC................G....... 302 883-0097
Dover *(G-1505)*
First State Medical Assoc LLC................G....... 302 999-8169
Wilmington *(G-10552)*
Glasgow Medical Center LLC................C....... 302 836-8350
Newark *(G-6664)*
Hcsg Regal Hghts Regal41................G....... 302 998-0181
Hockessin *(G-3044)*
Heritage Medical Associates PA................G....... 302 998-3334
Wilmington *(G-10893)*
Kent General Hospital Inc................G....... 302 430-5705
Milford *(G-4464)*
Kentmere Healthcare Cnsltng................G....... 302 478-7600
Wilmington *(G-11245)*
Morgan Kalman Clinic................F....... 610 869-5757
Wilmington *(G-11750)*
Shore Community Medical................G....... 302 827-4365
Rehoboth Beach *(G-8074)*
Sleep Disorder Center Del Inc................G....... 302 224-6000
Newark *(G-7439)*
Veterans Health Administration................B....... 302 994-2511
Wilmington *(G-13070)*
Westside Family Healthcare Inc................F....... 302 575-1414
Wilmington *(G-13171)*
Westside Family Healthcare Inc................F....... 302 455-0900
Newark *(G-7689)*
Westside Family Healthcare Inc................F....... 302 656-8292
Wilmington *(G-13172)*
Westside Family Healthcare Inc................F....... 302 656-8292
Wilmington *(G-13173)*

OFFICES & CLINICS OF DRS OF MED: Em Med Ctr, Freestanding

Newark Emergency Center Inc................E....... 302 738-4300
Newark *(G-7118)*

OFFICES & CLINICS OF DRS OF MED: Health Maint Org Or HMO

Textronics Inc................F....... 302 351-2109
Wilmington *(G-12889)*

OFFICES & CLINICS OF DRS OF MED: Physician/Surgeon, Int Med

Associates In Medicine PA................G....... 302 645-6644
Lewes *(G-3350)*
Bethany Primary Care................G....... 302 537-1100
Bethany Beach *(G-390)*
Blanca O Lim MD................E....... 302 653-1669
Smyrna *(G-8581)*
Christiana Care Health Sys Inc................G....... 302 529-1975
Wilmington *(G-9678)*
Christiana Care Hlth Svcs Inc................F....... 302 623-0100
Newark *(G-6214)*
Delaware Institue Pain MGT................G....... 302 698-3994
Camden *(G-558)*
Delaware Primary Care LLC................G....... 302 730-0554
Dover *(G-1388)*
Delaware Surgical Arts................G....... 302 225-0177
Newark *(G-6416)*
Dr Monika Gupta PA................G....... 302 737-5074
Newark *(G-6471)*
Edward S Jaoude................E....... 302 684-2020
Milton *(G-4901)*
Gary Quiroga................G....... 302 697-3352
Dover *(G-1580)*
Georgetown Medical Assoc LLC................F....... 302 856-3737
Georgetown *(G-2546)*
Harsha Tankala MD................G....... 302 674-1818
Dover *(G-1635)*
Health Care Assoc PA................G....... 302 684-2033
Milton *(G-4912)*
Infectious Disease Association................G....... 302 368-2883
Newark *(G-6775)*
Infusion Solutions of De................F....... 302 674-4627
Dover *(G-1677)*
Internal Medicine Associates................F....... 302 633-1700
Wilmington *(G-11064)*

Internal Medicine Bridgeville................G....... 302 337-3300
Bridgeville *(G-484)*
Internal Medicine Dover PA................G....... 302 678-4488
Dover *(G-1681)*
Irene C Szeto MD................G....... 302 832-1560
Bear *(G-192)*
Irwin L Lifrak MD PC................G....... 302 654-7317
Wilmington *(G-11085)*
Joseph Bryer MD................G....... 302 426-9440
Wilmington *(G-11187)*
Laurel Medical Group................G....... 302 875-7753
Laurel *(G-3255)*
Lewes Surgical and Med Assoc................F....... 302 945-9730
Millsboro *(G-4719)*
Loughran Medical Group PA................G....... 302 479-8464
Wilmington *(G-11439)*
Pasquale Fucci MD................G....... 302 652-4705
Wilmington *(G-12030)*
Prospect Crozer LLC................G....... 302 798-8785
Claymont *(G-797)*
R G Altschuler MD................G....... 302 652-3771
Wilmington *(G-12295)*
Seth Ivins Dr MD................G....... 302 824-7280
Newark *(G-7411)*
Smyrna Medical Associates PA................E....... 302 653-6174
Smyrna *(G-8719)*
Ty Jennifer MD................G....... 302 651-4459
Wilmington *(G-13000)*

OFFICES & CLINICS OF DRS OF MED: Physician/Surgeon, Phy Med

Anthony Lee Cucuzzella MD................F....... 302 623-4370
Newark *(G-5974)*
Frank Falco MD................F....... 302 392-6501
Bear *(G-160)*
Klaus Dr Robert MD................G....... 302 422-3500
Wilmington *(G-11277)*
Rehabilitation Associates PA................G....... 302 832-8894
Newark *(G-7314)*
Total Health & Rehabilitation................G....... 302 999-9202
Wilmington *(G-12939)*

OFFICES & CLINICS OF DRS OF MEDICINE: Med Clinic, Pri Care

Alpha Care Medical LLC................G....... 302 398-0888
Harrington *(G-2807)*
Alpha Care Medical LLC................G....... 800 818-8680
Millsboro *(G-4628)*
Christiana Care Health Sys Inc................G....... 302 428-4110
Claymont *(G-717)*
Christiana Care Hlth Svcs Inc................G....... 302 477-3960
Wilmington *(G-9683)*
Delaware Medical Care Inc................E....... 302 225-6868
Wilmington *(G-10065)*
Foundtion For A Btter Tomorrow................G....... 302 674-1397
Dover *(G-1563)*
IPC Healthcare Inc................E....... 302 368-2630
Newark *(G-6804)*
Nemours Foundation................C....... 302 629-5030
Seaford *(G-8328)*
Southbrdge Med Advsory Council................E....... 302 655-6187
Wilmington *(G-12686)*

OFFICES & CLINICS OF DRS OF MEDICINE: Physician, Orthopedic

Bruce E Katz M D................G....... 302 478-5500
Wilmington *(G-9492)*
Cape Medical Associates PA................F....... 302 645-2805
Lewes *(G-3402)*
Casscells Orthopaedics Sp................G....... 302 832-6220
Newark *(G-6166)*
Center For Intrvntnal Pain SPI................G....... 302 792-1370
Wilmington *(G-9612)*
Christopher Casscells MD................G....... 302 832-6220
Newark *(G-6232)*
Debay Surgical Service................F....... 302 644-4954
Lewes *(G-3449)*
Delaware Orthopaedic Specialis................E....... 302 633-3555
Wilmington *(G-10071)*
Delaware Orthopedic................G....... 302 730-0840
Dover *(G-1385)*
Delaware Pain & Spine Center................G....... 302 737-0800
Wilmington *(G-10072)*
Dushuttle Richard P MD PA................F....... 302 678-8447
Dover *(G-1488)*
Lewes Orthopedic Ctr................G....... 302 645-4939
Lewes *(G-3603)*

PRDT & SVC

Employee Codes: A=Over 500 employees, B=251-500
C=101-250, D=51-100, E=20-50, F=10-19, G=1-9
2020 Harris Directory of Delaware Businesses
881

OFFICES & CLINICS OF DRS OF MEDICINE: Physician, Orthopedic

Michael L Mattern MD PA .... F 302 734-3416
  Dover *(G-1845)*
Mid Atlantic Spine .... F 302 369-1700
  Newark *(G-7027)*
Morgan Kalman Clinic PA .... F 302 529-5500
  Wilmington *(G-11749)*
Orthopdic Assoc Suthern Del PA ..... E 302 644-3311
  Lewes *(G-3673)*
Orthopedic Properties LLC .... G 302 998-2310
  Newark *(G-7159)*
Orthopedic Specialists .... E 302 351-4848
  Newark *(G-7160)*
Orthopedic Spine Center P A .... G 302 734-9700
  Dover *(G-1923)*
Peter F Townsend MD .... E 302 633-3555
  Wilmington *(G-12096)*
Premier Othpdic Bone Jint Care ...... G 302 422-6506
  Milford *(G-4529)*
Regional Orthopaedic Assoc .... E 302 633-3555
  Wilmington *(G-12360)*
Summit Orthopaedic HM Care LLC ... G 302 703-0800
  Lewes *(G-3768)*

OFFICES & CLINICS OF DRS OF MEDICINE: Pulmonary

Amick Mart J MD .... F 302 633-1700
  Wilmington *(G-9069)*
Kent Pulmonary Associates LLC ...... G 302 674-7155
  Dover *(G-1738)*
Milford Pulmonary Assoc LLC .... G 302 424-3100
  Milford *(G-4502)*
Pulmonary & Sleep Cons LLC .... G 302 994-4060
  Wilmington *(G-12267)*
Pulmonary Associates PA .... G 302 656-2213
  Wilmington *(G-12268)*
Wilmington Medical Associates .... F 302 478-0400
  Wilmington *(G-13237)*

OFFICES & CLINICS OF DRS OF MEDICINE: Rheumatology

Jose A Pando MD .... F 302 644-2302
  Lewes *(G-3576)*

OFFICES & CLINICS OF DRS, MED: Specialized Practitioners

Alfieri Anthony D Do Facc .... G 302 397-8199
  Wilmington *(G-9007)*
Dover Pulmonary PA .... G 302 734-0400
  Dover *(G-1468)*
Health & Social Svcs Del Dept .... G 302 577-3420
  Wilmington *(G-10867)*
International Spine Pain .... G 302 478-7001
  Wilmington *(G-11067)*
Lawall Prosthetics - Orthotics .... G 302 677-0693
  Dover *(G-1769)*
Lawall Prosthetics - Orthotics .... F 302 427-3668
  Wilmington *(G-11341)*
Lawall Prosthetics - Orthotics .... E 302 429-7625
  Wilmington *(G-11342)*
Pain MGT & Rehabilitation Ctr .... F 302 734-7246
  Dover *(G-1929)*
Rehabilitation Associates .... G 302 529-8783
  Newark *(G-7313)*

OFFICES & CLINICS OF HEALTH PRACTITIONERS: Nurse & Med Asst

Aston Home Health .... F 302 421-3686
  Wilmington *(G-9165)*
Bayada Home Health Care Inc .... G 302 655-1333
  Wilmington *(G-9264)*
Bayada Home Health Care Inc .... D 302 424-8200
  Milford *(G-4319)*

OFFICES & CLINICS OF HEALTH PRACTITIONERS: Nutrition

Brdly M Winston Pdrtcs Prctc .... G 302 424-1650
  Milford *(G-4333)*
Hcr Manor Care Svc Fla III Inc .... G 302 764-0181
  Wilmington *(G-10862)*
Kalin Eye Assoc .... G 302 292-2020
  Newark *(G-6866)*

OFFICES & CLINICS OF HEALTH PRACTITIONERS: Nutritionist

Select Physical Therapy .... G 302 760-9966
  Dover *(G-2067)*

OFFICES & CLINICS OF HEALTH PRACTITIONERS: Occu Therapist

Nanticoke Memorial Hosp Inc .... G 302 629-6875
  Seaford *(G-8325)*

OFFICES & CLINICS OF HEALTH PRACTITIONERS: Physical Therapy

All Therapy LLC .... G 302 376-5578
  Middletown *(G-3935)*
ATI Holdings LLC .... E 302 422-6670
  Milford *(G-4310)*
ATI Holdings LLC .... E 302 993-1450
  Wilmington *(G-9173)*
ATI Holdings LLC .... E 302 836-5670
  Bear *(G-40)*
ATI Holdings LLC .... E 302 226-2230
  Rehoboth Beach *(G-7849)*
ATI Holdings LLC .... E 302 894-1600
  Newark *(G-6016)*
ATI Holdings LLC .... E 302 285-0700
  Middletown *(G-3947)*
ATI Holdings LLC .... E 302 659-3102
  Smyrna *(G-8577)*
ATI Holdings LLC .... E 302 994-1200
  Wilmington *(G-9174)*
ATI Holdings LLC .... E 302 786-3008
  Harrington *(G-2814)*
ATI Holdings LLC .... E 302 536-5562
  Seaford *(G-8157)*
ATI Holdings LLC .... E 302 838-2165
  Newark *(G-6017)*
ATI Holdings LLC .... E 302 677-0100
  Dover *(G-1155)*
ATI Holdings LLC .... E 302 392-3400
  Bear *(G-41)*
ATI Holdings LLC .... E 302 475-7500
  Wilmington *(G-9175)*
ATI Holdings LLC .... E 302 351-0302
  Wilmington *(G-9176)*
ATI Holdings LLC .... E 302 741-0200
  Dover *(G-1156)*
ATI Holdings LLC .... E 302 654-1700
  New Castle *(G-5050)*
ATI Holdings LLC .... E 302 656-2521
  Wilmington *(G-9177)*
ATI Holdings LLC .... E 302 297-0700
  Millsboro *(G-4631)*
ATI Holdings LLC .... F 302 658-7800
  Wilmington *(G-9178)*
Back Clinic Inc .... F 302 995-2100
  Wilmington *(G-9220)*
Basco Physical Therapy .... G 302 730-1294
  Dover *(G-1176)*
Christiana Care Hlth Svcs Inc .... F 302 428-6662
  Wilmington *(G-9681)*
Christiana Care Hlth Svcs Inc .... E 302 477-3300
  Wilmington *(G-9682)*
Christiana Care Hlth Svcs Inc .... E 302 327-5555
  New Castle *(G-5156)*
Chuck B Barker Pt Dpt Ocs Atc .... G 302 730-4800
  Dover *(G-1281)*
Coastal Care Physical Therapy .... G 480 236-3863
  Selbyville *(G-8469)*
Cristy Anna Care Physcl Thrapy ...... G 302 378-6111
  Middletown *(G-4015)*
Delaware Curative .... G 302 836-5670
  Bear *(G-107)*
Delaware Curative Workshop .... D 302 656-2521
  Wilmington *(G-10033)*
Delaware Orthopedic and Sports ..... E 302 653-8389
  Smyrna *(G-8618)*
Dynamic Therapy Services LLC .... F 302 691-5603
  Newark *(G-6485)*
Dynamic Therapy Services LLC .... F 302 526-2148
  Dover *(G-1489)*
Dynamic Therapy Services LLC .... F 302 376-4315
  Middletown *(G-4046)*
Dynamic Therapy Services LLC .... F 302 778-0810
  Wilmington *(G-10273)*
Dynamic Therapy Services LLC .... F 302 544-4388
  New Castle *(G-5270)*
Dynamic Therapy Services LLC .... F 302 703-2355
  Lewes *(G-3476)*
Dynamic Therapy Services LLC .... G 302 292-3454
  Newark *(G-6486)*
Dynamic Therapy Services LLC .... F 302 998-9880
  Wilmington *(G-10274)*
Dynamic Therapy Services LLC .... E 302 834-1550
  Bear *(G-131)*
Hillside Center .... F 302 652-1181
  Wilmington *(G-10909)*
Lakeside Physical Therapy LLC .... F 302 280-6920
  Laurel *(G-3251)*
Mike Walsh Physical Therapy .... G 302 724-5593
  Dover *(G-1855)*
Orthopaedic & Sports Phys .... G 302 683-0782
  Wilmington *(G-11977)*
Peak Cryotherapy .... G 302 502-3160
  Wilmington *(G-12057)*
Performance Physcl Therapy Inc ..... F 302 234-2288
  Hockessin *(G-3115)*
Phoenix Rehabilitation and Hea .... G 302 725-5720
  Milford *(G-4526)*
Phoenix Rhbilitation Hlth Svcs .... G 302 764-2008
  Wilmington *(G-12125)*
Physical Therapist .... G 302 983-4151
  Middletown *(G-4190)*
Physiotherapy Associates Inc .... G 302 655-8989
  Wilmington *(G-12130)*
Physiotherapy Associates Inc .... F 302 674-1269
  Dover *(G-1957)*
Physiotherapy Associates Inc .... G 610 444-1270
  Wilmington *(G-12131)*
Physiotherapy Corporation .... G 302 628-8568
  Seaford *(G-8357)*
Prelude Therapeutics Inc .... E 302 644-5427
  Wilmington *(G-12214)*
Premier Physical Therapy & .... G 302 389-7855
  Smyrna *(G-8691)*
Pro Physical Therapy PA .... F 302 654-1700
  New Castle *(G-5647)*
Pro Physl Therapy Ftns Acct .... F 302 658-7800
  Wilmington *(G-12234)*
Southern Del Physcl Therapy .... G 302 947-4460
  Millsboro *(G-4802)*
Southern Del Physcl Therapy .... G 302 854-9600
  Georgetown *(G-2660)*
Southern Del Physcl Therapy .... G 302 659-0173
  Smyrna *(G-8723)*
Southern Del Physcl Therapy .... G 302 227-2008
  Rehoboth Beach *(G-8083)*
Southern Del Physcl Therapy .... F 302 644-2530
  Lewes *(G-3757)*
Specialty Rehabilitation Inc .... F 302 709-0440
  Newark *(G-7468)*
Spine & Orthopedic Specialist .... G 302 633-1280
  Newark *(G-7472)*
Thrive Physical Therapy .... G 302 834-8400
  Middletown *(G-4258)*
Tidewater Physcl Thrpy and REB .... G 302 684-2829
  Milton *(G-4976)*
Tidewater Physcl Thrpy and REB .... G 302 856-2446
  Georgetown *(G-2693)*
Tidewater Physcl Thrpy and REB .... G 302 398-7982
  Harrington *(G-2900)*
Tidewater Physcl Thrpy and REB .... G 302 537-7260
  Ocean View *(G-7821)*
Tidewater Physcl Thrpy and REB .... G 302 629-4024
  Seaford *(G-8422)*
Tidewater Physcl Thrpy and REB .... G 302 945-5111
  Lewes *(G-3784)*
Total Health & Rehabilitation .... G 302 999-9202
  Wilmington *(G-12939)*
Wellness Health Inc .... G 302 424-4100
  Milford *(G-4601)*
Wilderman Physical Therapy LLC .... G 717 873-6836
  Wilmington *(G-13201)*
Woodlyn Physical Therapy Inc .... G 610 583-1133
  Newark *(G-7718)*

OFFICES & CLINICS OF HEALTH PRACTITIONERS: Physiotherapist

Austrlian Phystherapy Ctrs Ltd .... G 631 298-5367
  Wilmington *(G-9185)*
Blue Hen Physical Therapy Inc .... E 302 453-1588
  Newark *(G-6100)*
Physical Therapy Services Inc .... E 302 678-3100
  Dover *(G-1955)*
Rehabilitation Consultants Inc .... E 302 478-5240
  Wilmington *(G-12367)*

PRODUCT & SERVICES SECTION — OPERATOR: Apartment Buildings

Zuber & Associates Inc .... G 302 478-1618
Wilmington *(G-13353)*

OFFICES & CLINICS OF HEALTH PRACTITIONERS: Speech Pathology

Speech Clinic .... E 302 999-0702
Wilmington *(G-12701)*

OFFICES & CLINICS OF HEALTH PRACTITIONERS: Speech Specialist

Speech Therapeutics Inc .... G 302 234-9226
Hockessin *(G-3147)*

OFFICES & CLINICS OF HEALTH PRACTITIONERS: Speech Therapist

Ellingsen & Associates .... F 302 650-6437
Newark *(G-6517)*

OFFICES & CLINICS OF HEALTH PRACTRS: Clinical Psychologist

Associates In Hlth Psychology .... F 302 428-0205
Wilmington *(G-9156)*
Kathryn M Gehret .... G 610 420-7233
Lewes *(G-3581)*
Marsha S Eddorlov .... G 302 994-4014
Wilmington *(G-11544)*
New Perspectives Inc .... G 302 489-0220
Wilmington *(G-11869)*
Norman S Broudy M D .... G 302 655-7110
Wilmington *(G-11896)*
Pike Creek Psychlogical Ctr PA .... G 302 449-2223
Middletown *(G-4192)*
Samuel Blumberg PHD .... G 302 652-7733
Wilmington *(G-12535)*
Wilmington Psychiatric Svcs .... G 302 999-8602
Newark *(G-7704)*
Yanez & De Yanez MD PC .... G 302 655-2991
Wilmington *(G-13325)*

OFFICES & CLINICS OF HLTH PRACTITIONERS: Reg/Practical Nurse

Michelle S Jones .... G 302 651-4801
Wilmington *(G-11673)*
Nurse Next Door Home Care Svcs .... G 302 264-1021
Camden *(G-594)*

OFFICES & CLINICS OF OPTOMETRISTS: Specialist, Contact Lens

Halpern Eye Associates Inc .... G 302 734-5861
Middletown *(G-4102)*

OFFICES & CLINICS OF OPTOMETRISTS: Specialist, Optometrists

Allan S Tocker Od .... G 302 995-9060
Wilmington *(G-9018)*
Bryan K Sterling LLC .... G 302 734-3511
Dover *(G-1239)*
Halpern Eye Associates Inc .... G 302 537-0234
Millville *(G-4846)*
Halpern Eye Associates Inc .... E 302 734-5861
Dover *(G-1623)*
Halpern Eye Associates Inc .... G 302 422-2020
Milford *(G-4432)*
Halpern Eye Associates Inc .... G 302 653-3400
Smyrna *(G-8649)*
Howard B Stromwasser .... G 302 368-4424
Newark *(G-6751)*
In Vision Eye Care Inc .... G 302 235-7031
Hockessin *(G-3057)*
Kneisley Eye Care PA .... G 302 224-3000
Newark *(G-6899)*
Simon Eye Associates PA .... G 302 655-8180
Wilmington *(G-12623)*
Simon Eye Associates PA .... F 302 239-1389
Wilmington *(G-12624)*
Steve O Quillin Od .... G 302 398-8404
Harrington *(G-2894)*
Susan J Betts Od .... G 302 629-6691
Seaford *(G-8412)*
Sussex Eye Center PA .... G 302 856-2020
Georgetown *(G-2679)*
Sussex Eye Center PA .... G 302 436-2020
Selbyville *(G-8551)*

OIL & GAS FIELD MACHINERY

Us Engineering Corporation .... F 302 645-7400
Lewes *(G-3804)*

OIL BURNER REPAIR SVCS

Burns & McBride Inc .... D 302 656-5110
New Castle *(G-5121)*

OIL FIELD MACHINERY & EQPT

Delaware Capital Holdings Inc .... G 302 793-4921
Wilmington *(G-10011)*

OIL FIELD SVCS, NEC

Accurate-Energy LLC .... G 302 947-9560
Lewes *(G-3323)*
Mabel R Cole .... G 302 378-2792
Middletown *(G-4139)*
Tdw Services Inc .... F 302 594-9880
New Castle *(G-5756)*

OILS & ESSENTIAL OILS

Carbocycle Co .... G 212 214-4068
Wilmington *(G-9564)*

OILS & GREASES: Lubricating

Castrol Industrial N Amer Inc .... D 302 934-9100
Millsboro *(G-4657)*
Chem Tech Inc .... G 302 798-9675
Wilmington *(G-9644)*
Restore Incorporated .... F 302 655-6257
Wilmington *(G-12390)*

OILS: Lubricating

Robert Elgart Automotive .... G 800 220-7777
Newark *(G-7350)*
Ultrachem Inc .... F 302 325-9880
New Castle *(G-5801)*

OLD AGE ASSISTANCE

Sussex County Senior Ctr Svcs .... G 302 539-2671
Ocean View *(G-7817)*

OLEFINS

Hercules International Ltd LLC .... G 302 594-5000
Wilmington *(G-10889)*
Hercules LLC .... C 302 594-5000
Wilmington *(G-10890)*

ON-LINE DATABASE INFORMATION RETRIEVAL SVCS

Aidbits Inc .... G 647 692-3494
Lewes *(G-3330)*
Hughes Network Systems LLC .... G 302 335-4138
Frederica *(G-2406)*
Merix LLC .... G 425 659-1425
Lewes *(G-3638)*
Quantumfly LLC .... F 312 618-5739
Dover *(G-2001)*

OPERA COMPANIES

Operadelaware Inc .... G 302 658-8063
Wilmington *(G-11962)*

OPERATIVE BUILDERS: Condominiums

Carl M Freeman Associates Inc .... C 302 539-6961
Bethany Beach *(G-391)*
Construction Layout Services .... G 302 998-1800
Newark *(G-6289)*
Del Homes Inc .... G 302 697-8204
Magnolia *(G-3889)*
Hudson Management & Entps LLC .... G 302 645-9464
Milton *(G-4917)*

OPERATIVE BUILDERS: Cooperative Apartment

Berman Development Corp .... G 302 323-9522
New Castle *(G-5084)*

OPERATOR TRAINING, COMPUTER

Magowi Consulting Group LLC .... F 832 301-9230
Newark *(G-6972)*

Majalco LLC .... G 703 507-5298
Wilmington *(G-11494)*
Process Academy LLC .... G 302 415-3104
Wilmington *(G-12238)*
Sumuri LLC .... G 302 570-0015
Camden *(G-601)*

OPERATOR: Apartment Buildings

Admirals Club Apts2c .... E 302 737-8496
Newark *(G-5901)*
Ai Enterprises .... G 302 764-2342
Wilmington *(G-8985)*
Aion Prides Court LLC .... G 302 737-2085
Newark *(G-5923)*
Aion University Village LLC .... G 302 366-8000
Newark *(G-5924)*
Alban Associates .... G 302 656-1827
Wilmington *(G-9001)*
Apartment Communities Inc .... F 302 798-9100
Claymont *(G-692)*
Appoquinimink Development Inc .... G 302 378-0878
Middletown *(G-3942)*
Belmont Villa Condominiums .... G 302 368-1633
Newark *(G-6071)*
Berman Development Corp .... G 302 323-1197
New Castle *(G-5083)*
Bethel Villa Associates LP .... G 302 426-9688
Wilmington *(G-9316)*
Bethel Villas 2009 Assoc LP .... G 610 278-1733
Wilmington *(G-9317)*
Better Homes of Laurel Inc .... G 302 875-4281
Laurel *(G-3199)*
Boston Land Co Mgt Svcs Inc .... G 302 571-0100
Wilmington *(G-9395)*
Brandywine Hills Apartments .... E 302 764-3242
Wilmington *(G-9436)*
Brandywine I & 2 Apts .... F 302 475-8600
Wilmington *(G-9439)*
Buford Manlove Grdns Assoc LP .... E 302 652-3991
Hockessin *(G-2972)*
Burlington Manor Associates .... F 609 387-3184
Wilmington *(G-9508)*
Cabell Corp .... G 302 398-8125
Harrington *(G-2822)*
Capano Management Company .... G 302 737-8056
Newark *(G-6149)*
Carl M Freeman Associates Inc .... C 302 539-6961
Bethany Beach *(G-391)*
Carleton Court Associates LP .... F 302 454-1800
Wilmington *(G-9571)*
Carvel Gardens Associates LP .... G 302 875-4281
Laurel *(G-3208)*
Cavalier Group .... G 302 429-8700
Wilmington *(G-9596)*
Cavalier Group .... E 302 368-7437
Newark *(G-6172)*
Chasemont Apartments .... G 302 731-0784
Newark *(G-6191)*
Christiana Village Apts .... G 302 427-0403
Wilmington *(G-9689)*
Christiana Wood LLC .... G 302 322-1172
New Castle *(G-5158)*
City Systems Inc .... G 302 655-9914
Wilmington *(G-9725)*
Clyde Spinelli .... G 302 328-7679
New Castle *(G-5178)*
Colonial Inv Managment Co .... G 302 736-0674
Dover *(G-1303)*
Colonial Rlty Assoc Ltd Partnr .... F 302 737-1254
Newark *(G-6264)*
Colony North Apartments .... F 302 762-0405
Wilmington *(G-9777)*
Community Housing Inc .... G 302 652-3991
Wilmington *(G-9793)*
Compton Pk Prsrvtion Assoc LLC .... F 302 654-4369
Wilmington *(G-9806)*
Country Village Apartments .... G 302 674-0991
Dover *(G-1316)*
D C J L Partnership .... G 302 328-8040
New Castle *(G-5211)*
Dack Realty Corp .... G 302 792-2737
Claymont *(G-726)*
Delaware Equity Fund IV .... G 302 655-1420
Wilmington *(G-10044)*
Doyjul Apartments .... F 302 998-0088
Wilmington *(G-10215)*
Dunbarton Oaks Associates .... G 302 856-7719
Georgetown *(G-2516)*
East Coast Property MGT Inc .... F 302 629-8612
Milford *(G-4400)*

OPERATOR: Apartment Buildings

Eastern Property Group Inc .... G 302 764-7112
  Wilmington *(G-10324)*
Eastern Prosperity Group .... G 302 764-7112
  Wilmington *(G-10325)*
Eastlake Apartments LLC .... F 302 764-0215
  Wilmington *(G-10328)*
Egg Harbor City Apartments LLC .... G 302 543-6514
  Wilmington *(G-10362)*
Evergreen Realty .... E 302 999-8805
  Wilmington *(G-10447)*
Evergreen Realty Inc .... G 302 998-0354
  Wilmington *(G-10448)*
Farrand Village Apartments .... G 302 998-5796
  Wilmington *(G-10501)*
First Montgomery Properties .... E 302 834-8272
  Bear *(G-152)*
Forest Park Apartments .... G 302 737-6151
  Wilmington *(G-10591)*
Frankel Enterprises Inc .... G 302 652-6364
  Wilmington *(G-10615)*
Galman Group Inc .... G 302 737-5550
  Newark *(G-6635)*
Georgetown Manor Apartments .... G 302 328-6231
  New Castle *(G-5352)*
Governors Place Townhomes .... G 302 653-6655
  Smyrna *(G-8645)*
Harbor Club Apartments .... E 302 738-3561
  Newark *(G-6708)*
Harbour Towne Associates LP .... G 302 645-1003
  Lewes *(G-3533)*
Iacono - Summer Chase .... F 302 994-2505
  Wilmington *(G-10985)*
J & S General Contractors .... F 302 658-4499
  Wilmington *(G-11098)*
Kbf Associates LP .... G 302 328-5400
  New Castle *(G-5455)*
Kimberton Apartments Assoc LP .... F 302 368-0116
  Newark *(G-6887)*
Leo Ritter & Co .... G 302 674-1375
  Dover *(G-1781)*
Leon N Weiner & Associates Inc .... G 302 737-9574
  Newark *(G-6932)*
Leon N Weiner & Associates Inc .... G 860 447-2282
  Wilmington *(G-11372)*
Leon N Weiner & Associates Inc .... G 302 856-2251
  Georgetown *(G-2590)*
Leon N Weiner & Associates Inc .... F 302 322-6323
  New Castle *(G-5479)*
Leon N Weiner & Associates Inc .... G 302 422-3343
  Milford *(G-4473)*
Leon N Weiner & Associates Inc .... G 302 798-3446
  Claymont *(G-773)*
Lexington Green Apartments .... G 302 322-8959
  Newark *(G-6933)*
Louis Capano and Associates .... G 302 738-8000
  Newark *(G-6951)*
Lsref4 Lighthouse Corp Acqstn .... G 302 737-8500
  Newark *(G-6954)*
Luther Towers IV Dover Inc .... F 302 674-1408
  Dover *(G-1802)*
Luther Village I Dover Inc .... F 302 674-1408
  Dover *(G-1804)*
Luxiasuites LLC .... G 302 654-8527
  Wilmington *(G-11458)*
Main Twers Prsrvtion Assoc LLC .... F 302 737-9574
  Newark *(G-6975)*
Management Associates Inc .... F 302 652-3991
  Wilmington *(G-11498)*
Market Street Preservation Inc .... G 302 422-8255
  Milford *(G-4486)*
Market Street Preservation LP .... G 302 422-8255
  Milford *(G-4487)*
Martys Contracting .... G 302 234-8690
  Hockessin *(G-3091)*
Mid-Atlantic Realty Co Inc .... G 302 322-9500
  New Castle *(G-5526)*
Mid-Atlantic Realty Co Inc .... G 302 738-5325
  Newark *(G-7030)*
Mid-Atlantic Realty Co Inc .... G 302 737-3110
  Newark *(G-7031)*
Milford Housing Development .... E 302 678-0300
  Dover *(G-1856)*
Millsboro Village I LLC .... G 302 678-9400
  Millsboro *(G-4752)*
Mispillion III .... G 302 422-4429
  Milford *(G-4507)*
ML Newark LLC .... F 302 737-2868
  Wilmington *(G-7048)*
New Alden-Berkley Assoc LLC .... F 207 774-5341
  Wilmington *(G-11848)*

New Colony North Enterprises .... G 302 762-0405
  Wilmington *(G-11857)*
New Compton Towne Assoc LP .... G 302 571-0217
  Wilmington *(G-11858)*
New R V Associates L P .... G 302 798-6878
  Claymont *(G-790)*
New Wndsor Apartments Assoc LP .... G 302 656-1354
  Wilmington *(G-11874)*
Old Landing II LP .... G 302 934-1871
  Millsboro *(G-4767)*
Owners Management Company .... G 302 422-0740
  Milford *(G-4521)*
Panco Management Corporation .... F 302 366-1875
  Newark *(G-7173)*
Panco Management Corporation .... G 302 995-6152
  Wilmington *(G-12011)*
Panco Management Corporation .... G 302 475-9337
  Wilmington *(G-12012)*
Park View .... G 302 429-7288
  Wilmington *(G-12022)*
Parson Thorne Realty Assoc LP .... E 302 422-9367
  Milford *(G-4522)*
Pennrose Management Company .... G 302 571-8295
  Wilmington *(G-12070)*
Pettinaro Enterprises LLC .... E 302 999-0708
  Wilmington *(G-12103)*
Phase Flats II L P .... G 717 291-1911
  Wilmington *(G-12109)*
Phase I Flats L P .... G 717 291-1911
  Wilmington *(G-12110)*
Prides Court Apartments .... G 302 737-2085
  Newark *(G-7252)*
Providence Hall Associates LP .... E 518 828-4700
  Wilmington *(G-12257)*
Prudential Gallo Realty .... F 302 645-6661
  Lewes *(G-3700)*
Robino Management Group Inc .... G 302 734-2944
  Dover *(G-2038)*
Rockwood Apartments .... F 302 832-8823
  Newark *(G-7355)*
Roizman & Associates Inc .... G 302 426-9688
  Wilmington *(G-12465)*
School Bell Apartments LP .... G 302 328-9500
  Bear *(G-314)*
Seaford Preservation Assoc LLC .... F 302 629-6416
  Seaford *(G-8395)*
Service General Corp .... C 302 856-3500
  Georgetown *(G-2651)*
Sheldon Limited Partnership .... G 302 738-3048
  Newark *(G-7414)*
Shelter Development LLC .... G 302 737-4999
  Newark *(G-7415)*
Silver Springs Apartments .... G 302 992-0800
  Wilmington *(G-12617)*
South Gate Realty Assoc LLP .... G 302 368-4535
  Claymont *(G-806)*
St James Place Associates .... F 302 764-6450
  Wilmington *(G-12723)*
Stoltz Realty Co .... G 302 656-8543
  Wilmington *(G-12769)*
Stoltz Realty Co .... F 302 798-8500
  Claymont *(G-807)*
Stoneybrook Presvtn Assoc LLC .... F 302 764-9430
  Wilmington *(G-12772)*
Summit Properties Inc .... G 302 737-3747
  Newark *(G-7505)*
Top of Hllbrndywine Apartments .... G 302 798-9971
  Wilmington *(G-12928)*
Town and Country Trust .... F 302 328-8700
  Bear *(G-356)*
Udel Holdings LLC .... E 877 833-8737
  Newark *(G-7607)*
Udr Inc .... G 302 674-8887
  Dover *(G-2172)*
University Village Apartment .... G 302 731-5972
  Newark *(G-7630)*
Vance Phillips Inc .... G 302 542-1501
  Laurel *(G-3301)*
Victoria Mews LP Delnware Vall .... G 302 489-2000
  Hockessin *(G-3168)*
Victorian Apartments LLC .... G 302 678-0968
  Dover *(G-2192)*
Village At Fox Point .... G 302 762-7480
  Wilmington *(G-13081)*
Village Windhover Apartments .... F 302 834-1168
  Newark *(G-7658)*
Vintage Properties LLC .... G 302 994-4442
  Wilmington *(G-13084)*
Walden LLC .... G 302 998-8112
  Wilmington *(G-13115)*

West Minister Management .... G 302 678-4515
  Dover *(G-2215)*
Westwood Properties Ltd .... G 302 655-0274
  Wilmington *(G-13174)*
Whatcoat Village Assoc LLC .... F 856 596-0500
  Dover *(G-2221)*
Windsor Forest Town Homes .... G 302 328-1260
  New Castle *(G-5838)*
Woodacres Associates LP .... F 302 792-0243
  Claymont *(G-826)*
Woodland Hill Preservation .... F 302 764-6450
  Wilmington *(G-13296)*
Woods Edge Apartments .... G 302 762-8300
  Wilmington *(G-13300)*
Woolard Properties .... G 302 731-1944
  Newark *(G-7719)*
Xsc Ip LLC .... E 305 384-6700
  Wilmington *(G-13322)*
Zwaanendael LLC .... G 302 645-6466
  Lewes *(G-3837)*

OPERATOR: Nonresidential Buildings

302 Properties LLC .... G 302 753-8383
  Newark *(G-5856)*
A-Stover Management Group LLC .... F 866 299-0709
  Bear *(G-6)*
Cigna Global Holdings Inc .... F 302 797-3469
  Claymont *(G-718)*
Cigna Real Estate Inc .... G 302 476-3337
  Wilmington *(G-9706)*
Covenant Properties I .... G 302 234-5655
  Wilmington *(G-9880)*
Delaware Occupational Health S .... E 302 368-5100
  Newark *(G-6400)*
Delport Holding Company .... G 302 655-7300
  New Castle *(G-5246)*
Fusco Management Inc .... E 302 328-6251
  New Castle *(G-5338)*
Habitat America LLC .... E 302 875-3525
  Laurel *(G-3236)*
Kenco Group Inc .... E 302 629-4295
  Seaford *(G-8287)*
Market Street Center Inc .... G 302 856-9024
  Georgetown *(G-2598)*
McLeen Properties .... G 302 482-1486
  Wilmington *(G-11604)*
Parkway Gravel Inc .... D 302 658-5241
  New Castle *(G-5603)*
Pbe Companies LLC .... E 617 346-7459
  Wilmington *(G-12049)*
Property Improvements LLC .... G 610 692-5343
  Bethany Beach *(G-424)*
Silver Lining Solutions LLC .... G 302 691-7100
  Wilmington *(G-12616)*
Unity Construction Inc .... E 302 998-0531
  Wilmington *(G-13030)*
Vintage Properties LLC .... G 302 994-2505
  Wilmington *(G-13085)*
Wwd Inc .... G 302 994-4553
  Wilmington *(G-13310)*

OPHTHALMIC GOODS

Essilor America Holding Co Inc .... F 214 496-4000
  Wilmington *(G-10439)*

OPHTHALMIC GOODS WHOLESALERS

Essilor America Holding Co Inc .... F 214 496-4000
  Wilmington *(G-10439)*

OPHTHALMIC GOODS, NEC, WHOLESALE: Frames

Jim Kounnas Optometrists .... G 302 722-6197
  Wilmington *(G-11160)*

OPHTHALMIC GOODS: Frames, Lenses & Parts, Eyeglasses

Jim Kounnas Optometrists .... G 302 722-6197
  Wilmington *(G-11160)*

OPTICAL GOODS STORES

Allan S Tocker Od .... G 302 995-9060
  Wilmington *(G-9018)*

PRODUCT & SERVICES SECTION

OPTICAL GOODS STORES: Contact Lenses, Prescription

W Lee Mackewiz Od PA .... G 302 834-2020
   Bear *(G-368)*

OPTICAL GOODS STORES: Eyeglasses, Prescription

Jim Kounnas Optometrists .... G 302 722-6197
   Wilmington *(G-11160)*

OPTICAL INSTRUMENTS & LENSES

Atlantic Industrial Optics .... G 302 856-7905
   Georgetown *(G-2438)*
Docs Medical LLC .... G 301 401-1489
   Bear *(G-122)*
Spectr-Physics Hldings USA Inc .... G 302 478-4600
   Wilmington *(G-12698)*

OPTICAL SCANNING SVCS

Court Record & Data MGT Svcs .... G 732 955-6567
   Wilmington *(G-9877)*
Creaform USA Inc .... G 407 732-4103
   Newark *(G-6312)*

OPTOMETRISTS' OFFICES

Amy M Farrall OD LLC .... G 302 737-5777
   Newark *(G-5964)*
Chambers Optometrist .... G 302 543-6492
   Wilmington *(G-9626)*
Delaware Eye Care Center .... E 302 674-1121
   Dover *(G-1368)*
Dr Andrew Berman .... G 302 678-1000
   Dover *(G-1474)*
Halpern Eye Associates Inc .... F 302 629-6816
   Seaford *(G-8256)*
Halpern Eye Associates Inc .... G 302 838-0800
   Bear *(G-176)*
In Vision Eye Care .... F 302 655-1952
   Wilmington *(G-11010)*
John M Otto Od .... G 302 623-0170
   Newark *(G-6844)*
Joseph G Goldberg Od .... G 302 999-1286
   Wilmington *(G-11191)*
Larry Wallis .... G 856 456-3925
   Wilmington *(G-11331)*
Ronald S Pogach Od RES .... G 302 994-3300
   Newark *(G-7364)*
Simon Eye Associates PA .... E 302 834-4305
   Bear *(G-322)*
Timothy Westgate .... G 302 629-9197
   Seaford *(G-8423)*

ORCHESTRAS & BANDS

First State Strings Inc .... G 302 331-7362
   Camden Wyoming *(G-640)*
Wilmington String Ensemble .... E 302 764-1201
   Wilmington *(G-13258)*

ORGANIZATIONS & UNIONS: Labor

American Federation of State .... F 302 323-2121
   New Castle *(G-5031)*
Delaware Nature Society .... D 302 239-1283
   Hockessin *(G-3006)*
Delaware State Education Assn .... E 302 734-5834
   Dover *(G-1396)*
Delaware State Education Assn .... G 302 366-8440
   Newark *(G-6415)*
Pace Local 2 898 .... G 302 737-8898
   Newark *(G-7169)*
Smart .... F 302 655-6084
   New Castle *(G-5717)*

ORGANIZATIONS, NEC

American Frnds of The Ryal Soc .... G 302 295-4959
   Wilmington *(G-9045)*
Attention Dficit Disorder Assn .... G 302 478-0255
   Talleyville *(G-8749)*
Blackwater Village Association .... G 302 541-4700
   Dagsboro *(G-883)*
Friends of University Sussex .... F 302 295-4959
   Wilmington *(G-10639)*
Hispanic American Assn of Del .... G 302 562-2705
   Newark *(G-6730)*
National Guard Association Del .... F 302 326-7125
   New Castle *(G-5545)*
Plantation Lakes Homeowners .... G 302 934-5200
   Millsboro *(G-4782)*

ORGANIZATIONS: Civic & Social

Arise Africa Foundation Inc .... G 877 829-5500
   New Castle *(G-5043)*
Best Buddies International Inc .... G 302 691-3187
   Wilmington *(G-9313)*
Community Business Dev Corp .... G 302 544-1709
   Newark *(G-6271)*
Del Ray Foundatins LLC .... G 302 272-6153
   Milford *(G-4372)*
Delaware Ffa Foundation Inc .... G 302 857-6493
   Dover *(G-1369)*
Delaware Nature Society .... D 302 239-1283
   Hockessin *(G-3006)*
Delaware Retired Schl Prsnl .... E 302 674-8252
   Wilmington *(G-10079)*
Early Foundations Therapeutic .... G 302 384-6905
   Wilmington *(G-10316)*
Farpath Foundation .... G 302 645-8328
   Lewes *(G-3492)*
Freelee Foundation .... G 302 607-8053
   Newark *(G-6619)*
Lincoln Community Hall Inc .... G 302 242-1747
   Lincoln *(G-3859)*
Maplewood Home Owners Clubhous .... G 302 645-9925
   Rehoboth Beach *(G-7997)*
Noor Foundation International .... G 302 234-8860
   Hockessin *(G-3105)*
Objective Zero Foundation .... F 202 573-9660
   Wilmington *(G-11930)*
Omega PSI PHI Fraternity .... G 908 463-2197
   Dover *(G-1917)*
PHI Service Co .... F 302 451-5224
   Newark *(G-7212)*
Raskob Foundation For Catholic .... F 302 655-4440
   Wilmington *(G-12319)*
Richardson Park Community .... E 302 428-1247
   Wilmington *(G-12414)*
Salvation Army .... E 302 654-8808
   Wilmington *(G-12530)*
Solar Foundations Usa Inc .... F 855 738-7200
   New Castle *(G-5721)*
South Bowers Ladies Auxiliary .... E 302 335-4135
   Milford *(G-4564)*
St Stephens Evang Lutheran Ch .... G 302 652-7623
   Wilmington *(G-12729)*
United Tele Wkrs Local 13101 .... G 302 737-0400
   Wilmington *(G-7616)*
Wdbid Management Company .... D 302 425-5374
   Wilmington *(G-13129)*
YWCA Delaware .... D 302 655-0039
   Wilmington *(G-13337)*

ORGANIZATIONS: Educational Research Agency

Delaware Acdemy of Mdicine Inc .... F 302 733-3900
   Newark *(G-6363)*

ORGANIZATIONS: Medical Research

Analytical Biological Svcs Inc .... E 302 654-4492
   Wilmington *(G-9073)*
Atria Medical Inc .... G 407 334-5190
   Dover *(G-1158)*

ORGANIZATIONS: Noncommercial Biological Research

Delaware Native Plants Society .... G 302 735-8918
   Dover *(G-1382)*

ORGANIZATIONS: Professional

American Heart Association Inc .... F 302 454-0613
   Newark *(G-5952)*
American Lung Assn of Del .... G 302 737-6414
   Newark *(G-5955)*
Association For The Rights .... F 302 996-9400
   Wilmington *(G-9159)*
Bethany Dental Association .... G 302 537-1200
   Bethany Beach *(G-389)*
Cramer & Dimichele PA .... G 302 293-1230
   Wilmington *(G-9893)*
Dcor .... G 302 227-9341
   Rehoboth Beach *(G-7908)*
Delaware Association .... G 302 622-9177
   Wilmington *(G-10002)*

ORGANIZATIONS: Veterans' Membership

Delaware Association For Blind .... F 302 998-5913
   Wilmington *(G-10003)*
Delaware Helpline Inc .... F 302 255-1810
   Wilmington *(G-10052)*
Delaware Rural Water Assn .... G 302 424-3792
   Milford *(G-4380)*
Family Practice Association PA .... E 302 656-5416
   Wilmington *(G-10494)*
LLC Levy Wilson .... F 302 888-1088
   Wilmington *(G-11415)*
Nonprofit Bus Solutions LLC .... F 302 353-4606
   Wilmington *(G-11894)*
Seamens Center Wilmington Inc .... F 302 575-1300
   Wilmington *(G-12565)*
State Education Agency Di .... F 302 739-4111
   Dover *(G-2103)*
Volume Mob Inc .... G 302 433-6629
   Wilmington *(G-13101)*

ORGANIZATIONS: Religious

Christ Ch Episcpal Preschool .... E 302 472-0021
   Wilmington *(G-9673)*
Covenant Asset Mgmt & Financl .... G 302 324-5655
   New Castle *(G-5205)*
Fellowship Hlth Resources Inc .... F 302 856-7642
   Georgetown *(G-2529)*
Jewish Federation of Delaware .... F 302 478-5660
   Wilmington *(G-11153)*
Purpose Ministries Inc .... G 302 753-0435
   Newark *(G-7273)*
Salvation Army .... C 302 934-3730
   Millsboro *(G-4797)*
Samson Communications Inc .... F 302 424-1013
   Lincoln *(G-3867)*

ORGANIZATIONS: Research Institute

Delaware Vly Outcomes RES LLC .... G 302 444-9363
   Newark *(G-6421)*
Epic Research LLC .... G 703 297-8121
   Wilmington *(G-10425)*
Galvin Industries LLC .... G 703 505-7860
   Georgetown *(G-2537)*
Invistas Applied RES Centre .... F 302 731-6800
   Newark *(G-6802)*
Minder Foundation .... G 917 477-7661
   Lewes *(G-3643)*
Signal Garden Research Corp .... G 708 715-3646
   Lewes *(G-3743)*
Thomson Reuters (grc) Inc .... A 212 227-7357
   Wilmington *(G-12904)*
Ubinet Inc .... G 302 722-6015
   Wilmington *(G-13006)*
University of Delaware .... F 302 831-2833
   Newark *(G-7624)*
Zinger Enterprizes Inc .... G 302 381-6761
   Laurel *(G-3312)*

ORGANIZATIONS: Scientific Research Agency

Avantix Labratories Inc .... F 302 832-1008
   Newark *(G-6031)*

ORGANIZATIONS: Veterans' Membership

American Legion .... G 302 398-3566
   Harrington *(G-2809)*
American Legion .... G 302 628-5221
   Seaford *(G-8147)*
American Legion Log Cabin .... G 302 629-9915
   Seaford *(G-8148)*
American Lgion Amblance Stn 64 .... G 302 653-6465
   Smyrna *(G-8569)*
Battle Proven Foundation .... G 703 216-1986
   Dover *(G-1178)*
Brenden Bailey & Chandler VFW .... G 302 239-0797
   Hockessin *(G-2969)*
Delaware Veterans Home Inc .... D 302 424-6000
   Milford *(G-4382)*
Diamond State Home Auxiliary .... G 302 652-9331
   Newport *(G-7747)*
Disabled American Veterans .... E 302 697-9061
   Camden *(G-563)*
Oak Orchard-Riverdale American .... F 302 945-1673
   Millsboro *(G-4766)*
V F W Post Home .... G 302 366-8438
   Newark *(G-7637)*
V F W Sussex Mem Post 7422 .... G 302 934-9967
   Millsboro *(G-4819)*

Employee Codes: A=Over 500 employees, B=251-500
C=101-250, D=51-100, E=20-50, F=10-19, G=1-9

ORGANIZATIONS: Veterans' Membership

V F W Virgil Wilson Post .... G 302 629-3092
Seaford *(G-8428)*
Veterans of Foreign Wars Newmn .... G 302 653-8801
Smyrna *(G-8736)*
VFW Post 6483 .... G 302 422-4412
Milford *(G-4591)*
Walter L Fox Post 2 Inc .... E 302 674-1741
Dover *(G-2205)*

ORTHODONTIST

A D Alpine DMD .... F 302 239-4600
Wilmington *(G-8875)*
Ahl Orthodontics .... G 302 678-3000
Dover *(G-1096)*
Ali S Husain Orthodontist .... F 302 838-1400
Newark *(G-5931)*
Alpine Rafetto Orthodontics .... G 302 239-2304
Wilmington *(G-9033)*
Anzilotti Orthodontics .... G 302 750-0117
Wilmington *(G-9093)*
Clifford L Anzilotti DDS PC .... F 302 475-2050
Wilmington *(G-9741)*
Clifford L Anzilotti DDS PC .... F 302 378-2778
Middletown *(G-3997)*
Delaware Valley Orthodontics .... G 302 239-3531
Wilmington *(G-10096)*
Fred S Fink Orthodontist .... G 302 478-6930
Wilmington *(G-10625)*
Gordon C Honig DMD PA .... G 302 737-6333
Newark *(G-6678)*
Gordon C Honig DMD PA .... G 302 696-4020
Middletown *(G-4091)*
Greeley & Nista Orthodontics .... F 302 475-4102
Wilmington *(G-10770)*
Johnson Orthodontics .... G 302 645-5554
Rehoboth Beach *(G-7973)*
Kidd Robert W III DDS .... F 302 678-1440
Dover *(G-1747)*
Mattern & Piccioni Md PA .... F 302 730-8060
Dover *(G-1827)*
Michael S Wirosloff DMD .... G 302 998-8588
Wilmington *(G-11665)*
OConnor Orthodontics .... G 302 678-1441
Dover *(G-1913)*
Orthodontics On Silver Lake .... G 302 672-7776
Dover *(G-1921)*
Orthodontics On Silver Lake PA .... G 302 672-7776
Dover *(G-1922)*
Penna Orthodontics .... G 302 998-8783
Wilmington *(G-12068)*
Rawlins Orthodontics .... G 302 239-3533
Wilmington *(G-12324)*
Sussex Orthodontics .... G 302 644-4100
Dover *(G-2121)*

OUTBOARD MOTOR DEALERS

Almars Outboard Service & Sls .... G 302 328-8541
New Castle *(G-5023)*

OUTLETS: Electric, Convenience

Leggs Hanes Bali Playtex Otlt .... G 302 227-8943
Rehoboth Beach *(G-7985)*

OUTREACH PROGRAM

Beautiful Gate Outreach Center .... F 302 472-3002
Wilmington *(G-9277)*
Child Inc .... E 302 762-8989
Wilmington *(G-9661)*
Ministry of Caring Inc .... G 302 652-0969
Wilmington *(G-11710)*
N U Friendship Outreach Inc .... G 302 836-0404
Bear *(G-260)*
One Village Alliance Inc .... G 302 275-1715
Wilmington *(G-11957)*
Outreach Team LLC .... G 302 744-9550
Dover *(G-1927)*
Samaritan Outreach .... G 302 594-9476
Wilmington *(G-12532)*

PACKAGED FROZEN FOODS WHOLESALERS, NEC

Burris Logistics .... D 302 398-5050
Harrington *(G-2820)*
DOT Foods Inc .... D 302 300-4239
Bear *(G-125)*
H C Davis Inc .... G 302 337-7001
Bridgeville *(G-477)*

JG Townsend Jr & Co Inc .... E 302 856-2525
Georgetown *(G-2574)*
JG Townsend Jr Frz Foods Inc .... E 302 856-2525
Georgetown *(G-2575)*

PACKAGING & LABELING SVCS

Cpmg Inc .... G 302 429-8688
Wilmington *(G-9888)*
Customs Benefits .... G 302 798-2884
Wilmington *(G-9927)*
E I Du Pont De Nemours & Co .... A 302 999-5072
Wilmington *(G-10303)*
Montesino Technologies Inc .... G 302 888-2355
Wilmington *(G-11737)*

PACKAGING MATERIALS, WHOLESALE

A Womans Touch Moving & Pkg .... G 302 265-4729
Rehoboth Beach *(G-7836)*
K K American Corporation .... G 302 738-8982
Bear *(G-211)*
Mid-Atlantic Packaging Company .... E 800 284-1332
Dover *(G-1850)*
Taghleef Industries LLC .... G 302 326-5500
Newark *(G-7530)*

PACKAGING MATERIALS: Paper

Mercantile Press Inc .... F 302 764-6884
Wilmington *(G-11636)*
Printpack Inc .... C 302 323-4000
New Castle *(G-5645)*

PACKAGING MATERIALS: Plastic Film, Coated Or Laminated

Zacros America Inc .... C 302 368-7354
Newark *(G-7737)*

PACKAGING MATERIALS: Polystyrene Foam

Baytown Packhouse Inc .... G 936 340-2122
Newark *(G-6061)*
Prezoom LLC .... G 302 414-8204
New Castle *(G-5640)*

PACKAGING: Blister Or Bubble Formed, Plastic

Richard Earl Fisher .... G 302 598-1957
Wilmington *(G-12407)*

PACKING & CRATING SVC

Atlas Van Lines Agents .... E 302 369-0900
Newark *(G-6024)*
On-Demand Services LLC .... G 302 388-1215
New Castle *(G-5588)*

PACKING SVCS: Shipping

Cpmg Inc .... G 302 429-8688
Wilmington *(G-9888)*
Marlex Pharmaceuticals Inc .... E 302 328-3355
New Castle *(G-5508)*

PAGERS: One-way

Integrated Data Corp .... G 302 295-5057
Wilmington *(G-11048)*

PAINT & PAINTING SPLYS STORE

Moorway Painting Management .... G 302 764-5002
Wilmington *(G-11747)*

PAINT STORE

Mammeles Inc .... G 302 998-0541
Wilmington *(G-11497)*

PAINTING SVC: Metal Prdts

Metal-Tech Inc .... E 302 322-7770
New Castle *(G-5518)*
Prestige Powder Finishing Inc .... F 302 737-7500
Newark *(G-7249)*

PAINTS & ALLIED PRODUCTS

Modified Thermoset Resins Inc .... G 302 235-3710
Wilmington *(G-11722)*
Steves Painting Plus .... G 302 684-8938
Lincoln *(G-3871)*

PRODUCT & SERVICES SECTION

PAINTS, VARNISHES & SPLYS WHOLESALERS

F Schumacher & Co .... C 302 454-3200
Newark *(G-6561)*
T B Painting Restoration .... G 610 283-4100
Newark *(G-7527)*

PAINTS, VARNISHES & SPLYS, WHOLESALE: Paints

B F Shin of Salisbury Inc .... G 302 652-3521
Wilmington *(G-9212)*
First State Distributors Inc .... G 302 655-8266
Wilmington *(G-10551)*
Mammeles Inc .... G 302 998-0541
Wilmington *(G-11497)*

PALLETS

Dans Pallets & Services .... G 302 836-4848
Bear *(G-94)*
Greenwood Pallet Co .... G 302 337-8181
Bridgeville *(G-476)*

PALLETS: Plastic

Plasti Pallets Corp .... G 302 737-1977
Christiana *(G-676)*

PALLETS: Wooden

Rcd Timber Products Inc .... G 302 778-5700
New Castle *(G-5668)*

PAPER & BOARD: Die-cut

Cann-Erikson Bindery Inc .... F 302 995-6636
Wilmington *(G-9550)*

PAPER MANUFACTURERS: Exc Newsprint

Action Unlimited Resources Inc .... E 302 323-1455
New Castle *(G-5001)*
Advanced Thermal Packaging .... G 302 326-2222
New Castle *(G-5010)*
Deadcow Computers .... G 302 239-5974
Newark *(G-6355)*
Norkol Converting Corporation .... E 302 283-1080
Newark *(G-7136)*

PAPER PRDTS: Panty Liners, Made From Purchased Materials

Edgewell Personal Care Company .... A 302 678-6191
Dover *(G-1507)*

PAPER PRDTS: Sanitary

Docs Medical LLC .... G 301 401-1489
Bear *(G-122)*
Playtex Manufacturing Inc .... D 302 678-6000
Dover *(G-1969)*
Playtex Products LLC .... F 302 678-6000
Dover *(G-1971)*

PAPER PRDTS: Tampons, Sanitary, Made From Purchased Material

Edgewell Personal Care LLC .... B 302 678-6000
Dover *(G-1506)*

PAPER PRDTS: Towels, Napkins/Tissue Paper, From Purchd Mtrls

BETz&betz Enterprises LLC .... G 302 602-0613
Wilmington *(G-9318)*
Socal Auto Supply Inc .... D 818 717-9982
Lewes *(G-3751)*

PAPER: Coated & Laminated, NEC

Mercantile Press Inc .... F 302 764-6884
Wilmington *(G-11636)*

PAPER: Gift Wrap

K&B Investors LLC .... G 302 357-9723
Wilmington *(G-11216)*

PRODUCT & SERVICES SECTION

PARKING GARAGE
Colonial Parking Inc .... G 302 651-3618
  Wilmington *(G-9776)*
Landmark Parking Inc .... F 302 651-3610
  Wilmington *(G-11328)*
Wilmington Parking Authority .... E 302 655-4442
  Wilmington *(G-13241)*

PARKING LOTS
City of Newark .... F 302 366-0457
  Newark *(G-6242)*
Colonial Parking Inc .... E 302 651-3600
  Wilmington *(G-9775)*
Sp Plus Corporation .... G 302 652-1410
  Wilmington *(G-12690)*

PARKING LOTS & GARAGES
Go Go Go Inc .... G 302 645-7400
  Lewes *(G-3517)*

PARTITIONS & FIXTURES: Except Wood
J and J Display .... G 302 628-4190
  Seaford *(G-8275)*

PARTS: Metal
Anthony J Nappa .... G 716 888-0553
  Magnolia *(G-3880)*

PARTY & SPECIAL EVENT PLANNING SVCS
Celebrations Design Group Ltd .... G 302 793-3893
  Claymont *(G-711)*
Km Klacko & Associate .... G 302 652-1482
  Wilmington *(G-11278)*
Knowland Group LLC .... F 302 645-9777
  Lewes *(G-3584)*

PASSENGER AIRLINE SVCS
Travel Agency .... G 302 381-0205
  Lewes *(G-3794)*
United Air Lines Inc .... F 872 825-1911
  Wilmington *(G-13021)*

PASSENGER TRAIN SVCS
Alfreda Hicks LLC .... G 302 312-8721
  New Castle *(G-5022)*

PATCHING PLASTER: Household
Franklin Jester PA .... G 302 368-3080
  Newark *(G-6612)*

PATENT OWNERS & LESSORS
Idpa Holdings Inc .... G 302 281-3600
  Wilmington *(G-10993)*
Idtp Holdings Inc .... G 302 281-3600
  Wilmington *(G-10994)*
Interdigital Belgium LLC .... G 302 281-3600
  Wilmington *(G-11060)*

PATENT SOLICITOR
Fish & Richardson PC .... E 302 652-5070
  Wilmington *(G-10561)*

PATTERNS: Indl
Patterns .... G 302 654-9075
  Rockland *(G-8124)*

PAVERS
Stockley Materials LLC .... G 302 856-7601
  Georgetown *(G-2666)*

PAVING MIXTURES
Ashland LLC .... E 302 594-5000
  Wilmington *(G-9151)*
Diamond Materials LLC .... D 302 658-6524
  Wilmington *(G-10140)*

PAYROLL SVCS
City of Dover .... G 302 736-7018
  Dover *(G-1288)*
Global Merchant Partners LLC .... G 302 425-3567
  Rehoboth Beach *(G-7950)*

Payroll Management Assistants .... G 302 456-6816
  Newark *(G-7188)*
Sean E Chipman .... F 302 300-4307
  New Castle *(G-5697)*

PENSION & RETIREMENT PLAN CONSULTANTS
Benefit Administrators Del .... G 302 234-1978
  Wilmington *(G-9299)*
Risk Consultan .... G 302 655-3350
  Wilmington *(G-12425)*

PENSION FUNDS
Benefit Services Unlimited .... E 302 479-5696
  Wilmington *(G-9300)*

PENSIONS
American General .... G 302 575-5200
  Wilmington *(G-9047)*

PERFORMING ARTS CENTER PRODUCTION SVCS
Everett Robinson .... F 302 530-6574
  Wilmington *(G-10446)*
Grand Opera House Inc .... E 302 652-5577
  Wilmington *(G-10759)*
Heidis Academy of Prfrmg Arts .... F 302 293-7868
  Bear *(G-181)*
Joshua M Freeman Foundation .... F 302 436-3003
  Selbyville *(G-8510)*

PERSONAL & HOUSEHOLD GOODS REPAIR, NEC
A & R Fence Co Inc .... G 302 366-8550
  Newark *(G-5864)*
Homeimprovement E B&S .... G 302 465-1828
  Dover *(G-1655)*
Woodward Enterprises Inc .... F 302 378-2849
  Middletown *(G-4291)*

PERSONAL APPEARANCE SVCS
Fresh Start Transformations .... G 302 219-0221
  Newark *(G-6623)*
Snap Fitness .... G 302 741-2444
  Dover *(G-2090)*

PERSONAL CARE FACILITY
Compassionate Care .... G 302 654-5401
  Wilmington *(G-9799)*
Compassionate Care Hospi of Ce .... G 302 993-9090
  Wilmington *(G-9800)*
Delaware Hospice .... G 302 934-9018
  Millsboro *(G-4675)*
Delaware Hospice Inc .... D 302 478-5707
  Newark *(G-6384)*
Elderly Comfort Corporation .... F 302 530-6680
  Wilmington *(G-10367)*
Milton & Hattie Kutz Home Inc .... C 302 764-7000
  Wilmington *(G-11700)*
Seasons Hspice Plltive Care De .... E 847 692-1000
  Newark *(G-7399)*

PERSONAL CREDIT INSTITUTION: Indl Loan Bank, Non Deposit
Citifinancial Services Inc .... G 302 875-2813
  Laurel *(G-3214)*

PERSONAL CREDIT INSTITUTIONS: Auto Loans, Incl Insurance
Auto Equity Loans .... G 302 834-2500
  Bear *(G-43)*
Auto Equity Loans .... G 302 731-0073
  Newark *(G-6028)*
Auto Equity Loans .... G 302 998-3009
  Wilmington *(G-9186)*
Northeastern Title Loans .... G 302 672-7895
  Dover *(G-1902)*

PERSONAL CREDIT INSTITUTIONS: Consumer Finance Companies
Beneficial Consumer Disc Co .... G 302 425-2500
  Wilmington *(G-9297)*

John Lovett Inc .... D 302 455-9460
  Newark *(G-6843)*
Mariner Finance LLC .... G 302 628-3970
  Seaford *(G-8304)*
Mariner Finance LLC .... G 302 384-6047
  Wilmington *(G-11527)*
Marlette Funding LLC .... G 302 358-2730
  Wilmington *(G-11541)*
Noble Finance Corp .... G 302 995-2760
  Dover *(G-1899)*

PERSONAL CREDIT INSTITUTIONS: Finance Licensed Loan Co's, Sm
Northeastern Title Loans .... G 302 326-2210
  New Castle *(G-5579)*

PERSONAL CREDIT INSTITUTIONS: Financing, Autos, Furniture
Coastal Credit LLC .... G 302 734-1312
  Dover *(G-1300)*
Falcidian LLC .... G 302 656-5500
  Wilmington *(G-10480)*

PERSONAL CREDIT INSTITUTIONS: Install Sales Finance
Delaware Depository Svc Co LLC .... G 302 762-2635
  Wilmington *(G-10037)*

PERSONAL CREDIT INSTITUTIONS: Licensed Loan Companies, Small
College Avenue Student Ln LLC .... D 302 684-6070
  Wilmington *(G-9770)*

PERSONAL DOCUMENT & INFORMATION SVCS
Adpese LLC .... G 302 223-5411
  Wilmington *(G-8943)*

PERSONAL FINANCIAL SVCS
Covenant Asset Mgmt & Financl .... G 302 324-5655
  New Castle *(G-5205)*
Oink Oink LLC .... G 302 924-5034
  Dover *(G-1914)*
Paxful Inc .... F 865 272-9385
  Wilmington *(G-12047)*

PERSONAL INVESTIGATION SVCS
T & B Invstgtions SEC Agcy LLC .... G 302 476-4087
  Middletown *(G-4252)*

PERSONAL SVCS
B P Services .... G 302 399-4132
  Dover *(G-1166)*
Whole Child App Inc .... F 302 570-2002
  Lewes *(G-3821)*

PEST CONTROL IN STRUCTURES SVCS
Accurate Pest Control Company .... E 302 875-2725
  Laurel *(G-3189)*
Bug Rite Extreminator Comp .... G 302 738-4373
  Wilmington *(G-9502)*
Corteva Inc .... E 302 485-3000
  Wilmington *(G-9869)*
Delmar Termite & Pest Control .... G 302 658-5010
  Wilmington *(G-10101)*
Diamond Pest Control .... G 302 654-2300
  Wilmington *(G-10141)*
Maguire & Sons Inc .... G 302 798-1200
  Wilmington *(G-11488)*
Rentokil North America Inc .... F 302 337-8100
  Bridgeville *(G-519)*
Royal Pest Management .... G 302 322-3600
  New Castle *(G-5687)*
Royal Termite & Pest Ctrl Inc .... E 302 322-3600
  New Castle *(G-5689)*
Total Pest Solutions .... G 302 275-7159
  Camden Wyoming *(G-660)*
Tri State Termite & Pest Ctrl .... G 302 239-0512
  Newark *(G-7585)*
True Pest Control Services .... G 302 834-0867
  Middletown *(G-4270)*

PEST CONTROL SVCS

Activ Pest & Lawn Inc	F	302 645-1502
Lewes *(G-3324)*

Delaware Mosquito Control LLC ....G........ 302 504-6757
  Newark *(G-6398)*
Elkton Exterminating Co Inc ....F........ 302 368-9116
  Newark *(G-6516)*
Guy Bug ....G........ 302 242-5254
  Dover *(G-1619)*
Ladybug Pest Management Inc ....G........ 302 846-2295
  Delmar *(G-1014)*
Orkin LLC ....F........ 302 322-9569
  New Castle *(G-5591)*
Rentokil North America Inc ....F........ 302 325-2687
  Newark *(G-7319)*
Terminix Intl Co Ltd Partnr ....E........ 302 653-4866
  New Castle *(G-5761)*

PESTICIDES WHOLESALERS

Growmark Fs LLC ....G........ 302 422-3001
  Milford *(G-4426)*
Growmark Fs LLC ....D........ 302 422-3002
  Milford *(G-4425)*
Nutrien AG Solutions Inc ....G........ 302 629-2780
  Seaford *(G-8333)*

PET FOOD WHOLESALERS

Beaverdam Pet Food ....G........ 302 349-5299
  Greenwood *(G-2714)*
Food For Pets USA Inc ....G........ 514 831-4876
  Newark *(G-6599)*

PET SPLYS

Anything Under Sun LLC ....G........ 302 292-1023
  Newark *(G-5977)*
Dog Anya ....G........ 302 456-0108
  Newark *(G-6458)*
Icy Pup ....G........ 302 777-1776
  Fenwick Island *(G-2337)*
K9 Natural Foods USA LLC ....E........ 855 596-2887
  Wilmington *(G-11219)*

PET SPLYS WHOLESALERS

Animal Health Sales Inc ....F........ 302 436-8286
  Selbyville *(G-8448)*

PET-SITTING SVC: In-Home

Weather or Not Dog Walkers ....G........ 302 304-8399
  Wilmington *(G-13131)*

PETROLEUM & PETROLEUM PRDTS, WHOL Svc Station Splys, Petro

Pep-Up Inc ....G........ 302 645-2600
  Rehoboth Beach *(G-8031)*
Pep-Up Inc ....F........ 302 856-2555
  Georgetown *(G-2617)*

PETROLEUM & PETROLEUM PRDTS, WHOLESALE Crude Oil

Conectiv LLC ....C........ 202 872-2680
  Wilmington *(G-9817)*

PETROLEUM & PETROLEUM PRDTS, WHOLESALE Fuel Oil

Adams Oil Co Inc ....G........ 302 629-4531
  Seaford *(G-8138)*
C L Burchenal Oil Co Inc ....G........ 302 697-1517
  Camden *(G-543)*
Smokeys Gulf Service Inc ....G........ 302 378-2451
  Middletown *(G-4245)*

PETROLEUM & PETROLEUM PRDTS, WHOLESALE: Bulk Stations

Peninsula Oil Co Inc ....E........ 302 422-6691
  Seaford *(G-8349)*

PETROLEUM BULK STATIONS & TERMINALS

Du Pont Elastomers LP ....D........ 302 774-1000
  Wilmington *(G-10243)*

E I Du Pont De Nemours & Co ....G........ 302 772-0016
  New Castle *(G-5271)*
Service Oil Company ....E........ 302 734-7433
  Dover *(G-2072)*

PETROLEUM PRDTS WHOLESALERS

Petroleum Equipment Inc ....E........ 302 734-7433
  Dover *(G-1951)*
Petroleum Equipment Inc ....G........ 302 422-4281
  Dover *(G-1952)*
Service Energy LLC ....G........ 302 734-7433
  New Castle *(G-5699)*
Service Energy LLC ....D........ 302 734-7433
  Dover *(G-2071)*
Service Energy LLC ....F........ 302 645-9050
  Lewes *(G-3737)*
Shellhorn & Hill Inc ....D........ 302 654-4200
  Wilmington *(G-12599)*

PETROLEUM REFINERY INSPECTION SVCS

Jbm Petroleum Service LLC ....G........ 302 752-6105
  Lincoln *(G-3857)*

PHARMACEUTICAL PREPARATIONS: Druggists' Preparations

A2a Intgrted Phrmceuticals LLC ....G........ 270 202-2461
  Lewes *(G-3320)*
Ayala Pharmaceuticals Inc ....F........ 857 444-0553
  Wilmington *(G-9202)*
Therapy Architects ....G........ 610 246-5705
  Wilmington *(G-12894)*
Zeneca Holdings Inc ....E........ 302 886-3000
  Wilmington *(G-13344)*

PHARMACEUTICAL PREPARATIONS: Medicines, Capsule Or Ampule

Adesis Inc ....E........ 302 323-4880
  New Castle *(G-5005)*
Ilgen Inc ....G........ 518 369-0069
  Wilmington *(G-11004)*

PHARMACEUTICAL PREPARATIONS: Pills

Drnaturalhealing Inc ....G........ 302 265-2213
  Milford *(G-4396)*

PHARMACEUTICAL PREPARATIONS: Powders

Veramorph LLC ....G........ 401 473-1318
  Wilmington *(G-13058)*

PHARMACEUTICAL PREPARATIONS: Proprietary Drug PRDTS

LRC North America Inc ....E........ 302 427-2845
  Wilmington *(G-11446)*

PHARMACEUTICAL PREPARATIONS: Tinctures

Champions + Legends Corp ....G........ 702 605-2522
  Wilmington *(G-9627)*

PHARMACEUTICALS

A66 Inc ....G........ 800 444-0446
  Wilmington *(G-8892)*
Aeolus Pharmaceuticals Inc ....G........ 949 481-9825
  Wilmington *(G-8964)*
Alyvant Therapeutics Inc ....G........ 646 767-5878
  Wilmington *(G-9037)*
Angita Pharmard LLC ....G........ 302 234-6794
  Hockessin *(G-2958)*
Astrazeneca LP ....A........ 302 886-3000
  Wilmington *(G-9168)*
Astrazeneca Pharmaceuticals LP ....A........ 302 286-3500
  Newark *(G-6013)*
Auragin LLC ....G........ 800 383-5109
  Wilmington *(G-9183)*
Bristol-Myers Squibb Company ....E........ 800 321-1335
  Wilmington *(G-9479)*
Colgate-Palmolive Company ....B........ 302 428-1554
  Wilmington *(G-9768)*
Dupont Nutrition and Health ....G........ 302 451-0112
  Wilmington *(G-6478)*
E I Du Pont De Nemours & Co ....B........ 302 892-5655
  Wilmington *(G-10301)*

E I Du Pont De Nemours & Co ....A........ 302 485-3000
  Wilmington *(G-10278)*
E I Du Pont De Nemours & Co ....G........ 800 441-7515
  Wilmington *(G-10290)*
FMC Corporation ....D........ 302 451-0100
  Newark *(G-6596)*
Fulcrum Pharmacy MGT Inc ....G........ 302 658-8020
  Wilmington *(G-10645)*
Genesis Laboratories Inc ....G........ 832 217-8585
  Wilmington *(G-10693)*
Glaxosmithkline Capital Inc ....G........ 302 656-5280
  Wilmington *(G-10719)*
Glycomira LLC ....G........ 704 651-9789
  Dover *(G-1595)*
Grant Pharmaceuticals Inc ....G........ 855 364-7268
  Newark *(G-6681)*
Incyte Corporation ....C........ 302 498-6700
  Wilmington *(G-11016)*
Marlex Pharmaceuticals Inc ....E........ 302 328-3355
  New Castle *(G-5508)*
Medimmune LLC ....G........ 301 398-1200
  Wilmington *(G-11620)*
Merck & Co Inc ....E........ 410 860-2227
  Millsboro *(G-4742)*
Merck and Company Inc ....E........ 302 934-8051
  Millsboro *(G-4743)*
Merck Holdings LLC ....G........ 302 234-1401
  Wilmington *(G-11637)*
Modulation Therapeutics Inc ....G........ 813 784-0033
  Wilmington *(G-11723)*
Neuracon Biotech Inc ....G........ 813 966-3129
  Wilmington *(G-11843)*
Neurolixis Inc ....G........ 215 910-2261
  Wilmington *(G-11845)*
New Life Medicals LLC ....G........ 302 478-7973
  Wilmington *(G-11865)*
New Nordic US Inc ....G........ 514 390-2316
  Wilmington *(G-11867)*
Noramco Inc ....E........ 302 761-2923
  Wilmington *(G-11895)*
Novartis Corporation ....B........ 302 992-5610
  Wilmington *(G-11912)*
Novo Nordisk Pharma Inc ....G........ 302 691-6181
  Wilmington *(G-11914)*
Novo Nrdisk US Coml Hldngs Inc ....G........ 302 691-6181
  Wilmington *(G-11915)*
Pharma E Market LLC ....F........ 302 737-3711
  Hockessin *(G-3119)*
Pharmunion LLC ....G........ 415 307-5128
  Wilmington *(G-12108)*
Platinum US Distribution Inc ....G........ 905 364-8713
  Wilmington *(G-12153)*
Shire North American Group Inc ....G........ 484 595-8800
  Wilmington *(G-12606)*
Snow Pharmaceuticals LLC ....G........ 302 436-8855
  Frankford *(G-2388)*
Urigen Pharmaceuticals Inc ....G........ 732 640-0160
  Wilmington *(G-13038)*
Zeneca Inc ....G........ 302 886-3000
  Wilmington *(G-13345)*

PHARMACEUTICALS: Medicinal & Botanical Prdts

Jmsp USA LLC ....G........ 337 254-1451
  Camden Wyoming *(G-647)*
Personal Health PDT Dev LLC ....E........ 888 901-6150
  Wilmington *(G-12091)*

PHOTOCOPY MACHINES

B Williams Holding Corp ....F........ 302 656-8596
  Wilmington *(G-9214)*

PHOTOCOPYING & DUPLICATING SVCS

Amer Inc ....G........ 302 654-2498
  Wilmington *(G-9039)*
ARC Document Solutions Inc ....E........ 302 654-2365
  Wilmington *(G-9114)*
Braun Engineering & Surveying ....F........ 302 698-0701
  Camden Wyoming *(G-621)*
Copy Craft Inc ....G........ 302 633-1313
  Wilmington *(G-9856)*
Fedex Office & Print Svcs Inc ....E........ 302 475-9501
  Wilmington *(G-10517)*
Fedex Office & Print Svcs Inc ....G........ 302 652-2151
  Wilmington *(G-10518)*
Fedex Office & Print Svcs Inc ....F........ 302 368-5080
  Newark *(G-6576)*
Fedex Office & Print Svcs Inc ....G........ 302 996-0264
  Wilmington *(G-10519)*

PRODUCT & SERVICES SECTION

Garile Inc .... E 302 366-0848
  Newark *(G-6639)*
Medical Copy Services .... G 302 654-4741
  Wilmington *(G-11616)*
Mr Copy Inc .... G 302 227-4666
  Rehoboth Beach *(G-8015)*

PHOTOELECTRIC CELLS: Electronic Eye, Solid State

Laser Management Group LLC .... G 302 992-9030
  Wilmington *(G-11332)*

PHOTOFINISHING LABORATORIES

Fujifilm Imaging Colorants Inc .... D 302 472-1245
  New Castle *(G-5335)*

PHOTOGRAMMATIC MAPPING SVCS

Haymy Resources LLC .... G 402 218-6787
  Lewes *(G-3537)*

PHOTOGRAPHIC CONTROL SYSTEMS: Electronic

Metatron Inc .... G 619 550-4668
  Dover *(G-1843)*

PHOTOGRAPHIC EQPT & SPLYS

Motopods LLC .... G 818 641-4299
  Dover *(G-1875)*

PHOTOGRAPHIC EQPT & SPLYS WHOLESALERS

Fujifilm Imaging Colorants Inc .... E 302 477-8022
  New Castle *(G-5334)*
Waco Lid Films Inc .... G 302 378-7053
  Townsend *(G-8831)*

PHOTOGRAPHIC EQPT & SPLYS, WHOLESALE: Printing Apparatus

Autotype Holdings (usa) Inc .... C 302 378-3100
  Middletown *(G-3956)*

PHOTOGRAPHIC EQPT & SPLYS: Reels, Film

AM Custom Tackle Inc .... G 302 945-7921
  Millsboro *(G-4629)*

PHOTOGRAPHIC EQPT & SPLYS: Tripods, Camera & Projector

Integrated Technology Systems .... G 302 429-0560
  Wilmington *(G-11050)*

PHOTOGRAPHIC EQPT/SPLYS, WHOL: Cameras/Projectors/Eqpt/Splys

Cameras Etc Inc .... F 302 764-9400
  Wilmington *(G-9545)*

PHOTOGRAPHIC SVCS

Avalanche Strategies LLC .... C 302 436-7060
  Selbyville *(G-8452)*

PHOTOGRAPHY SVCS: Commercial

Dean Digital Imaging Inc .... G 302 655-6992
  Wilmington *(G-9989)*
Floyd Dean Inc .... G 302 655-7193
  Wilmington *(G-10581)*

PHOTOGRAPHY SVCS: Portrait Studios

Lifetouch Portrait Studios Inc .... G 302 453-8080
  Newark *(G-6935)*
Lifetouch Portrait Studios Inc .... F 302 734-9870
  Dover *(G-1786)*
Little Nests Portraits .... F 610 459-8622
  Wilmington *(G-11405)*

PHOTOGRAPHY SVCS: Still Or Video

Aperture Photography .... G 302 377-6590
  Middletown *(G-3941)*
Belles and Beaus Photography .... G 302 368-2468
  Newark *(G-6070)*

Blue Hen Photography .... G 302 690-3259
  Bear *(G-53)*
Everett Robinson .... F 302 530-6574
  Wilmington *(G-10446)*
Foschi Studio .... G 302 439-4457
  Wilmington *(G-10597)*
Gramonoli Enterprises Inc .... G 302 227-1288
  Rehoboth Beach *(G-7953)*
Gs Racing Photos .... G 302 855-1165
  Georgetown *(G-2551)*
Gunn Shot Photography .... G 302 399-3094
  Smyrna *(G-8647)*
Joseph A Dudeck .... G 302 559-5552
  Middletown *(G-4116)*
Kari Heverin Photography .... G 302 943-0176
  Townsend *(G-8804)*
Photography By Dennis McD .... G 610 678-0318
  Milton *(G-4951)*
Portrait Innovations Inc .... G 302 477-1696
  Wilmington *(G-12188)*
Tpp Acquisition Inc .... F 302 674-4805
  Dover *(G-2157)*
West Photography .... G 302 858-6003
  Georgetown *(G-2703)*
Youngs Studio of Photography .... G 302 736-2661
  Dover *(G-2248)*

PHOTOGRAPHY: Aerial

Firefly Drone Operations Llc .... G 305 206-6955
  Wilmington *(G-10543)*
Horizon Helicopters Inc .... G 302 368-5135
  Newark *(G-6745)*

PHYSICAL EXAMINATION & TESTING SVCS

Delaware Medical Associates PA .... F 302 475-2535
  Wilmington *(G-10064)*
Diagnostic Medical Services .... G 302 292-2700
  Newark *(G-6442)*
Exam Master Corporation .... E 302 378-3842
  Newark *(G-6549)*
Halo Medical Technologies LLC .... G 302 475-2300
  Wilmington *(G-10826)*
Heckessin Health Partners .... G 302 234-2597
  Hockessin *(G-3045)*
Womens Imaging Center Delaware .... E 302 738-9494
  Newark *(G-7715)*

PHYSICAL FITNESS CENTERS

Bear-Glasgow YMCA .... G 302 836-9622
  Newark *(G-6066)*
Curves International Inc .... G 302 698-1481
  Camden *(G-554)*
David L Townsend Co Inc .... G 302 378-7967
  Smyrna *(G-8611)*
Fitness Mtivation Inst of Amer .... G 302 628-3488
  Seaford *(G-8245)*
Golds Gym .... G 302 226-4653
  Rehoboth Beach *(G-7951)*
Harts Two .... G 302 741-2119
  Camden Wyoming *(G-644)*
HB Fitness Delaware Inc .... F 302 384-7245
  Wilmington *(G-10859)*
Legion Transformation Ctr LLC .... G 302 543-4922
  Wilmington *(G-11363)*
Lillys Personal Training .... G 302 538-6723
  Dover *(G-1789)*
More Than Fitness Inc .... G 302 690-5655
  Wilmington *(G-11748)*
National Fitness LLC .... G 301 841-8066
  Bethany Beach *(G-417)*
Neuro Fitness Therapy .... G 302 753-2700
  Wilmington *(G-11844)*
Pike Creek Court Club Inc .... D 302 239-6688
  Wilmington *(G-12138)*
Plexus Fitness .... F 302 654-9642
  Wilmington *(G-12159)*
Retro Fitness .... E 302 276-0828
  Bear *(G-303)*
Semp Wellness LLC .... G 302 525-9612
  Newark *(G-7406)*
Silverback Gyms LLC .... G 302 539-8282
  Ocean View *(G-7813)*
Smakkfitness LLC .... G 213 280-7569
  Wilmington *(G-12649)*
Snap Fitness .... G 302 741-2444
  Dover *(G-2090)*
Taekwondo Fitness Ctr of Del .... G 302 836-8264
  Bear *(G-346)*

PHYSICIANS' OFFICES & CLINICS: Medical doctors

W23 S12 Holdings LLC .... G 610 348-3825
  Wilmington *(G-13110)*
Young Mens Christian Associat .... D 302 571-6935
  Wilmington *(G-13331)*
Young Mens Christian Associat .... D 302 296-9622
  Rehoboth Beach *(G-8121)*
Young Mens Christian Associat .... F 302 472-9622
  Wilmington *(G-13333)*
Young Mens Christian Associat .... C 302 571-6900
  Wilmington *(G-13332)*
YWCA Delaware .... D 302 655-0039
  Wilmington *(G-13337)*
YWCA Delaware .... F 302 224-4060
  Newark *(G-7733)*

PHYSICAL FITNESS CLUBS WITH TRAINING EQPT

American Martial Arts Inst .... F 302 834-4060
  Bear *(G-27)*
Anytime Fitness .... G 302 475-2404
  Wilmington *(G-9092)*
Anytime Fitness .... G 302 738-3040
  Newark *(G-5978)*
Anytime Fitness .... G 302 653-4496
  Smyrna *(G-8572)*
Kirkwood Ftnes Racquetball CLB .... F 302 529-1865
  Wilmington *(G-11275)*
Tri-State Cheernastics Inc .... G 302 322-4020
  New Castle *(G-5787)*

PHYSICIANS' OFFICES & CLINICS: Medical

Camp Chiropractic Inc .... G 302 378-2899
  Middletown *(G-3980)*
Christiana Medical Group PA .... G 302 366-1800
  Newark *(G-6225)*
Cynthia P Mangubat MD .... G 302 674-1356
  Dover *(G-1334)*
Deborah Kirk .... G 302 653-6022
  Smyrna *(G-8613)*
Delaware County Pain MGT .... G 302 575-1145
  Wilmington *(G-10029)*
Delaware Interventional Spine .... G 302 674-8444
  Dover *(G-1379)*
Dr Azarcon & Assoc .... G 302 478-2969
  Wilmington *(G-10218)*
Du Pont Lynne M MD .... G 302 777-7966
  Wilmington *(G-10240)*
Glasgow Medical Associates PA .... F 302 836-8350
  Newark *(G-6663)*
John Johnson Dr .... G 302 999-7104
  Wilmington *(G-11174)*
Michael Butterworth Dr .... G 302 732-9850
  Dagsboro *(G-922)*
North Bay Medical Associates .... F 302 731-4620
  Newark *(G-7137)*
Robert S Callahan MD PA .... G 302 731-0942
  Newark *(G-7351)*
Roger Alexander MD .... G 302 422-5223
  Milford *(G-4547)*
Spine Care of Delaware .... G 302 894-1900
  Newark *(G-7473)*
Stewart Septimus MD .... G 302 992-9940
  Wilmington *(G-12764)*
Sussex Pain Relief Center LLC .... E 302 519-0100
  Georgetown *(G-2681)*
William B Funk MD .... F 302 731-0900
  Newark *(G-7697)*
Wilmington Otolrynglgy Assc .... G 302 658-0404
  Wilmington *(G-13239)*

PHYSICIANS' OFFICES & CLINICS: Medical doctors

A Center For Mntal Wllness Inc .... F 302 674-1397
  Dover *(G-1074)*
A I Dupont Hospital For Child .... G 302 651-4186
  Wilmington *(G-8879)*
Aaron S Chidekel M D .... G 302 651-6400
  Wilmington *(G-8894)*
Adriane Hohmann .... G 302 253-2020
  Georgetown *(G-2424)*
Alyvant Therapeutics Inc .... G 646 767-5878
  Wilmington *(G-9037)*
Amy Wachter MD .... G 302 661-3070
  Wilmington *(G-9072)*
Andre M D Hoffman .... G 302 892-2710
  Wilmington *(G-5967)*
Andrey Georgieff MD .... G 302 998-1866
  Newark *(G-5968)*

Angela Saldarriaga ....G.... 302 633-1182
Wilmington *(G-9084)*
Antonio C Narvaez MD ....G.... 302 453-1002
Newark *(G-5975)*
Armand De MD Sanctic ....F.... 302 475-2535
Wilmington *(G-9131)*
Athena T Jolly M D ....G.... 302 454-3020
Newark *(G-6014)*
Bayhealth Medical Group Ent ....G.... 302 339-8040
Georgetown *(G-2448)*
Beacon Medical Group PA ....G.... 302 947-9767
Rehoboth Beach *(G-7859)*
Beebe Medical Center Inc ....G.... 302 856-9729
Georgetown *(G-2453)*
Beth A Renzulli M D ....G.... 302 449-0420
Middletown *(G-3966)*
Bhaskar S Palekar MD PA ....G.... 302 645-1806
Lewes *(G-3382)*
Bijan K Sorouri MD PA ....G.... 302 453-9171
Newark *(G-6080)*
BMA of Smyrna ....G.... 302 659-5220
Smyrna *(G-8583)*
Bradford Family Physicians LLC ....G.... 302 730-3750
Dover *(G-1227)*
Cardio-Kinetics Inc ....E.... 302 738-6635
Newark *(G-6152)*
Central Del Gstrntrology Assoc ....G.... 302 422-3393
Milford *(G-4347)*
Chistine E Woods ....G.... 302 709-4497
Newark *(G-6201)*
Christiana Care ....F.... 302 633-3750
Wilmington *(G-9676)*
Christiana Care Health Sys Inc ....F.... 302 733-2410
Newark *(G-6210)*
Christiana Care Health Sys Inc ....F.... 302 659-4401
Smyrna *(G-8594)*
Christine W Maynard M D ....G.... 302 225-6110
Newark *(G-6230)*
Claravall Odilon ....G.... 302 875-7753
Laurel *(G-3215)*
Cnmri ....G.... 302 422-0800
Milford *(G-4360)*
Coastal Kids Pediatric Dntstry ....G.... 302 644-4460
Rehoboth Beach *(G-7894)*
Deborah A Wingel Do ....G.... 302 239-6200
Hockessin *(G-3003)*
Douglas R Johnston M D ....G.... 302 651-4000
Wilmington *(G-10214)*
Duncan Elisabeth D MD ....G.... 302 677-2730
Dover *(G-1486)*
Dynamic Therapy Services LLC ....F.... 302 526-2148
Dover *(G-1489)*
Elizabeth Jackovic MD ....G.... 302 623-0240
Newark *(G-6515)*
Erik M D Stancofski ....G.... 302 645-7050
Lewes *(G-3487)*
Eugene M DAmico III DDS PA ....G.... 302 292-1600
Newark *(G-6544)*
Fenwick Medical Center ....G.... 302 539-2399
Fenwick Island *(G-2335)*
Fresenius Medical Care Souther ....E.... 302 678-2181
Dover *(G-1568)*
George Mtstsos MD Crdiolgy LLC ....G.... 302 482-2035
Wilmington *(G-10703)*
Gilani Malik Javed MD ....G.... 302 737-8116
Wilmington *(G-10710)*
Habib Bolourchi MD Facc ....G.... 302 645-7672
Rehoboth Beach *(G-7957)*
Harry A Lehman III Md PA ....F.... 302 629-5050
Bridgeville *(G-479)*
Healthy Outcomes LLC ....G.... 302 856-4022
Georgetown *(G-2557)*
Helena Schroyer MD ....G.... 302 429-5870
Wilmington *(G-10882)*
Indian River Golf Cars Dr Wldg ....G.... 302 947-2044
Millsboro *(G-4708)*
IPC Healthcare ....G.... 302 984-2577
Newark *(G-6803)*
Jay D Lufty MD ....F.... 302 658-0404
Wilmington *(G-11131)*
Jeff Ezell Dr ....G.... 302 654-5955
Wilmington *(G-11142)*
Jennifer M D Hung ....G.... 302 644-0690
Rehoboth Beach *(G-7971)*
John D Mannion M D ....G.... 302 744-7980
Dover *(G-1704)*
Jonathan L Kates M D ....G.... 302 730-4366
Dover *(G-1707)*
Jose H Austria MD ....G.... 302 645-8954
Lewes *(G-3577)*
Joseph A Kuhn MD LLC ....G.... 302 656-3801
Wilmington *(G-11185)*
Joseph G Goldberg Od ....G.... 302 999-1286
Wilmington *(G-11191)*
Joseph Schwartz Psyd ....G.... 302 213-3287
Rehoboth Beach *(G-7974)*
Joseph Schwartz Psyd ....G.... 302 213-3287
Lewes *(G-3579)*
Joshua Kalin MD ....G.... 302 737-6900
Newark *(G-6852)*
K F W Medical Inst De LLC ....G.... 302 533-6406
Newark *(G-6865)*
Khaja Yezdani MD ....F.... 302 322-1794
New Castle *(G-5463)*
Lakeside Physical Therapy LLC ....F.... 302 280-6920
Laurel *(G-3251)*
Long Neck Med Entreprises LLC ....G.... 302 945-9730
Millsboro *(G-4723)*
Lynnanne Kasarda MD ....G.... 302 655-5822
Wilmington *(G-11463)*
Mark Menendez ....G.... 302 644-8500
Lewes *(G-3619)*
Melissa A Mackel Do ....G.... 302 674-4070
Dover *(G-1837)*
Michael Matthias ....G.... 302 575-0100
Wilmington *(G-11662)*
Michelle E Papa Do ....G.... 302 656-5424
Wilmington *(G-11672)*
Mike Walsh Physical Therapy ....G.... 302 724-5593
Dover *(G-1855)*
Milford Medical Associates PA ....G.... 302 329-9517
Milton *(G-4937)*
Mymedchoices Inc ....G.... 302 932-1920
Hockessin *(G-3100)*
Nancy A Union MD ....G.... 302 645-6644
Lewes *(G-3654)*
New Castle Family Care PA ....G.... 302 275-3428
Newark *(G-7102)*
Novacare Rehabilitation ....G.... 302 674-4192
Dover *(G-1904)*
Pamela M D Leclaire ....G.... 302 677-2600
Dover *(G-1930)*
Patrick Swier Mdpa Kar ....G.... 302 645-7737
Lewes *(G-3681)*
Peninsula Regional Medical Ctr ....G.... 302 436-8004
Selbyville *(G-8529)*
Persante Sleep Center ....G.... 302 508-2130
Smyrna *(G-8688)*
R M Villasenor MD ....G.... 302 629-4078
Seaford *(G-8368)*
Rafi Soofi MD ....G.... 302 999-1644
Wilmington *(G-12305)*
Ricks Fitness & Health Inc ....G.... 302 684-0316
Milton *(G-4962)*
Rochelle E Haas M D ....G.... 302 651-5600
Wilmington *(G-12446)*
Rosalina Dejesus-Jiloca MD ....F.... 302 629-4238
Seaford *(G-8382)*
Ryan C Gough MD ....G.... 302 677-6527
Dover *(G-2046)*
Samaha Michel R MD ....G.... 302 422-3100
Milford *(G-4552)*
Shashikala Patel MD ....G.... 302 737-5074
Newark *(G-7413)*
Southern Delaware Med Group ....G.... 302 424-3900
Dover *(G-2095)*
Southern Delaware Med Group PA ....E.... 302 424-3900
Milford *(G-4566)*
Spine Group LLC ....G.... 302 595-3030
Wilmington *(G-12706)*
Stephen F Wetherill MD ....G.... 302 478-3700
Wilmington *(G-12755)*
Stone Harbor Square LLC ....G.... 302 227-5227
Rehoboth Beach *(G-8088)*
Surgical Critical Assoc ....G.... 302 623-4370
Newark *(G-7516)*
Terry L Horton ....G.... 302 320-4900
Wilmington *(G-12884)*
Timothy Liveright MD ....G.... 302 655-7293
Wilmington *(G-12914)*
Trinity Medical Assoc ....G.... 302 762-6675
Wilmington *(G-12977)*
Tru Beauti LLC ....E.... 302 353-9249
Middletown *(G-4269)*
W Lee Mackewiz Od PA ....G.... 302 834-2020
Bear *(G-368)*
Westside Family Healthcare Inc ....C.... 302 652-2455
New Castle *(G-5831)*
Zeina Jeha Md MPH ....G.... 302 503-4200
Lewes *(G-3834)*

PHYSICIANS' OFFICES & CLINICS: Osteopathic

Abby Medical Center ....G.... 302 999-0003
Newark *(G-5882)*
Alan Warrington Do ....G.... 302 239-9599
Wilmington *(G-9000)*
Alfieri Anthony D Do Facc ....G.... 302 397-8199
Wilmington *(G-9007)*
Andrew W Donohue D O ....G.... 302 999-7386
Wilmington *(G-9081)*
Anthony A Vasile Do ....G.... 302 764-2072
Wilmington *(G-9090)*
Battaglia Joseph A & Diamond ....G.... 302 655-8868
Wilmington *(G-9261)*
Brandywine Family Medicine ....G.... 302 475-5000
Wilmington *(G-9432)*
Christiana Care ....G.... 302 654-4925
Wilmington *(G-9675)*
Christiana Care Health Sys Inc ....F.... 302 659-4401
Smyrna *(G-8594)*
Cynthia P Mangubat MD ....G.... 302 674-1356
Dover *(G-1334)*
Dr Jason Parker Do ....G.... 302 651-5874
Wilmington *(G-10224)*
Dr Jillian G Stevens Do ....G.... 302 762-7332
Wilmington *(G-10226)*
Dr Marisa E Conti Do ....G.... 302 678-4488
Dover *(G-1478)*
Dr Ronald R Blanck Do ....G.... 302 541-4137
Fenwick Island *(G-2334)*
Family Doctors ....G.... 302 368-3600
Newark *(G-6568)*
Family Medicine Smyrna Clayton ....G.... 302 653-1050
Smyrna *(G-8631)*
Family Practice Hockessin PA ....G.... 302 239-4500
Hockessin *(G-3027)*
International Spine Pain ....G.... 302 478-7001
Wilmington *(G-11067)*
John B Coll Do ....G.... 302 678-8100
Dover *(G-1702)*
Joseph Parise Do ....G.... 302 735-8855
Dover *(G-1709)*
Milford Medical Associates PA ....G.... 302 329-9517
Milton *(G-4937)*
N O Biasotto Do ....G.... 302 998-1211
Newark *(G-7079)*
Nicholas O Biasotto Co ....G.... 302 998-1235
Newark *(G-7132)*
P A Womencare ....G.... 302 731-2900
Newark *(G-7166)*
Paul Imber Do ....G.... 302 478-5647
Wilmington *(G-12042)*
Pulmonary & Sleep Cons LLC ....G.... 302 994-4060
Wilmington *(G-12267)*
Ralph Burdick Do ....G.... 302 834-3600
Delaware City *(G-966)*
Robert S Callahan MD PA ....G.... 302 731-0942
Newark *(G-7351)*
Southern Delaware Med Group ....G.... 302 424-3900
Dover *(G-2095)*
Sullivan Anna Marie Do ....G.... 302 454-1680
Newark *(G-7501)*
To Do Yard Guys ....G.... 302 947-9475
Millsboro *(G-4813)*
Total Care Physicians ....G.... 302 836-4200
Newark *(G-7577)*
Trinity Medical Center PA ....G.... 302 846-0618
Delmar *(G-1043)*
Urology Assoc Southern Del PA ....G.... 302 422-5569
Milford *(G-4588)*
Vincent Lobo Dr PA ....G.... 302 398-8163
Harrington *(G-2905)*

PICTURE FRAMES: Wood

Carspecken-Scott Inc ....G.... 302 762-7955
Wilmington *(G-9581)*

PICTURE FRAMING SVCS, CUSTOM

Acanthus & Reed Ltd ....G.... 212 628-9290
New Castle *(G-4999)*
Carspecken-Scott Inc ....G.... 302 655-7173
Wilmington *(G-9580)*
George Hardcastle & Sons Inc ....G.... 302 655-5230
Wilmington *(G-10700)*
Youve Been Framed ....G.... 302 366-8029
Newark *(G-7732)*

PRODUCT & SERVICES SECTION

PIECE GOODS, NOTIONS & DRY GOODS, WHOL: Textiles, Woven
Yoko Trading .... G 302 353-4506
  Newark *(G-7730)*

PIECE GOODS, NOTIONS & DRY GOODS, WHOL: Yard Goods, Woven
F Schumacher & Co .... C 302 454-3200
  Newark *(G-6561)*

PIECE GOODS, NOTIONS & OTHER DRY GOODS, WHOLESALE: Bridal
Henninger Printing Co Inc .... G 302 934-8119
  Millsboro *(G-4705)*

PIECE GOODS, NOTIONS & OTHER DRY GOODS, WHOLESALE: Fabrics
Loomcraft Textile & Supply Co .... F 302 454-3232
  Newark *(G-6948)*
Wayne Industries Inc .... G 302 478-6160
  Wilmington *(G-13126)*

PIECE GOODS, NOTIONS/DRY GOODS, WHOL: Fabrics, Synthetic
W L Gore & Associates Inc .... C 302 368-3700
  Newark *(G-7672)*

PIECE GOODS, NOTIONS/DRY GOODS, WHOL: Sewing Splys/Notions
Delaware D G Co LLC .... F 302 731-0500
  Newark *(G-6373)*

PILOT SVCS: Aviation
Aero Ways Inc .... F 302 324-9970
  New Castle *(G-5014)*
Haymy Resources LLC .... G 402 218-6787
  Lewes *(G-3537)*
Partsquarry-Aviation Div .... G 302 703-7195
  Wilmington *(G-12029)*
Webro Holdings LLC .... G 302 314-3334
  Rehoboth Beach *(G-8109)*

PIPE & FITTING: Fabrication
Baltimore Aircoil Company Inc .... C 302 424-2583
  Milford *(G-4317)*
Thermal Pipe Systems Inc .... G 302 999-1588
  Wilmington *(G-12895)*

PIPE SECTIONS, FABRICATED FROM PURCHASED PIPE
Atlantic Screen & Mfg Inc .... G 302 684-3197
  Milton *(G-4865)*

PIPE, IRRIGATION: Concrete
Smw Sales LLC .... F 302 875-7958
  Laurel *(G-3290)*

PIPE: Irrigation, Sheet Metal
Atlantic Screen & Mfg Inc .... G 302 684-3197
  Milton *(G-4865)*

PIPELINE & POWER LINE INSPECTION SVCS
Federal Technical Associates .... G 302 697-7951
  Dover *(G-1547)*

PIPELINE TERMINAL FACILITIES: Independent
J M Aja Transportation LLC .... G 302 562-6028
  Wilmington *(G-11107)*
Reddix Transportation Inc .... F 302 249-9331
  Lewes *(G-3712)*

PIPELINES: Natural Gas
Eastern Shore Natural Gas Co .... F 302 734-6716
  Dover *(G-1500)*

PIPES & TUBES
Apex Piping Systems Inc .... D 302 995-6136
  Wilmington *(G-9097)*

PIPES & TUBES: Steel
Emeca/Spe Usa LLC .... G 302 875-0760
  Laurel *(G-3228)*
Handy & Harman .... G 302 697-9521
  Camden *(G-574)*
Handytube Corporation .... D 302 697-9521
  Camden *(G-576)*
Handytube Corporation .... D 302 697-9521
  Camden *(G-577)*
Iko Sales Ltd .... D 302 764-3100
  Wilmington *(G-11002)*
Psp Corp .... G 302 764-7730
  Wilmington *(G-12260)*

PIPES & TUBES: Welded
Apex Piping Systems Inc .... D 302 995-6136
  Wilmington *(G-9097)*

PLANING MILLS: Millwork
Boxwood Planing Mill Inc .... G 302 999-0249
  Wilmington *(G-9402)*

PLANT CARE SVCS
Village Green Inc .... E 302 764-2234
  Wilmington *(G-13082)*

PLANTS, POTTED, WHOLESALE
Village Green Inc .... E 302 764-2234
  Wilmington *(G-13082)*

PLANTS: Artificial & Preserved
Desangosse US Inc .... G 302 691-6137
  Wilmington *(G-10119)*

PLASTIC COLORING & FINISHING
Dongjin Usa Inc .... F 302 691-8510
  Wilmington *(G-10198)*

PLASTICS FILM & SHEET
Ajedium Film Group LLC .... G 302 452-6609
  Newark *(G-5929)*
Dupont De Nemours Inc .... B 302 774-1000
  Wilmington *(G-10251)*
Printpack Inc .... C 302 323-4000
  New Castle *(G-5645)*

PLASTICS FILM & SHEET: Photographic & X-Ray
Fuji Film .... F 302 477-8000
  New Castle *(G-5333)*

PLASTICS FILM & SHEET: Polyethylene
Wilmington Fibre Specialty Co .... E 302 328-7525
  New Castle *(G-5836)*

PLASTICS FILM & SHEET: Polypropylene
Delstar Technologies Inc .... C 302 378-8888
  Middletown *(G-4034)*
Taghleef Industries Inc .... B 302 326-5500
  Newark *(G-7531)*
Taghleef Industries Inc .... D 302 326-5500
  Newark *(G-7532)*

PLASTICS FILM & SHEET: Polyvinyl
Kuraray America Inc .... F 302 992-4204
  Wilmington *(G-11301)*

PLASTICS MATERIAL & RESINS
Aearo Technologies LLC .... D 302 283-5497
  Newark *(G-5913)*
Ashland LLC .... E 302 594-5000
  Wilmington *(G-9151)*
Delmarva Plastics Co .... G 302 398-1000
  Harrington *(G-2832)*
Division-Developmental Dsblts .... G 302 836-2110
  Bear *(G-121)*

PLATING & POLISHING SVC

Dow Chemical Company .... C 302 366-0500
  Newark *(G-6468)*
Dupont Prfmce Elastomers LLC .... B 302 774-1000
  Wilmington *(G-10259)*
Dupont Specialty Pdts USA LLC .... E 302 774-1000
  Newark *(G-6479)*
Himont Inc .... G 302 996-6000
  Wilmington *(G-10914)*
Ineos Chlor Americas Inc .... G 302 529-9601
  Wilmington *(G-11024)*
Invista Capital Management LLC .... G 302 683-3000
  Wilmington *(G-11075)*
Invista Capital Management LLC .... E 877 446-8478
  Wilmington *(G-11076)*
Invista Capital Management LLC .... A 302 731-6882
  Newark *(G-6801)*
Invista SARL .... G 302 683-3001
  Wilmington *(G-11077)*
Precision Polyolefins LLC .... G 301 588-3709
  Wilmington *(G-12206)*
T P Composites Inc .... G 610 358-9001
  New Castle *(G-5749)*
Techmer Engnered Solutions LLC .... D 610 548-5032
  New Castle *(G-5759)*

PLASTICS PROCESSING
Ensinger Penn Fibre Inc .... E 302 349-4505
  Greenwood *(G-2738)*
New Process Fibre Company Inc .... D 302 349-4535
  Greenwood *(G-2757)*
Philly Plastics Corp .... G 718 435-4808
  Wilmington *(G-12119)*

PLASTICS: Finished Injection Molded
Gaudlitz Inc .... G 202 468-3876
  Dover *(G-1585)*
Imcg Global Inc .... G 800 559-6140
  Lewes *(G-3553)*
Negri Bossi North America Inc .... G 302 328-8020
  New Castle *(G-5549)*

PLASTICS: Injection Molded
Atlantis Industries Corp .... E 302 684-8542
  Georgetown *(G-2440)*
Craig Technologies Inc .... E 302 628-9900
  Seaford *(G-8213)*
Custom America .... G 856 516-1103
  Wilmington *(G-9924)*
Forcebeyond Inc .... E 302 995-6588
  Wilmington *(G-10590)*
Mohawk Plastic Products Inc .... G 302 424-4324
  Milford *(G-4510)*
Precise Technology Inc .... G 302 737-4638
  Newark *(G-7240)*

PLASTICS: Molded
Crown Molding Man .... G 302 455-1204
  Newark *(G-6317)*
Molded Components Inc .... G 302 588-2240
  Wilmington *(G-11727)*

PLASTICS: Polystyrene Foam
Aearo Technologies LLC .... D 302 283-5497
  Newark *(G-5913)*
Dupont De Nemours Inc .... B 302 774-1000
  Wilmington *(G-10251)*
Fluorogistx LLC .... F 302 479-7614
  Wilmington *(G-10582)*

PLASTICS: Thermoformed
Wilmington Fibre Specialty Co .... E 302 328-7525
  New Castle *(G-5836)*

PLATEMAKING SVC: Letterpress
Union Press Printing Inc .... G 302 652-0496
  Wilmington *(G-13013)*

PLATES: Steel
Evraz Clymont Stl Holdings Inc .... B 302 792-5400
  Claymont *(G-743)*

PLATING & POLISHING SVC
Aurista Technologies Inc .... F 302 792-4900
  Claymont *(G-696)*

PLATING SVC: NEC

Industraplate Corp .... F 302 654-5210
  Wilmington *(G-11020)*
Old School Plating .... G 302 345-0350
  Bear *(G-271)*

PLAYGROUND EQPT

Liberty Parks and Playgrounds .... G 302 659-5083
  Clayton *(G-862)*

PLUMBING & HEATING EQPT & SPLY, WHOL: Htg Eqpt/Panels, Solar

Sun-In-One Inc .... G 302 762-3100
  Wilmington *(G-12798)*
Sweeten Companies Inc .... G 302 737-6161
  Newark *(G-7520)*

PLUMBING & HEATING EQPT & SPLY, WHOLESALE: Hydronic Htg Eqpt

Delmarva Refrigeration Inc .... G 302 846-2727
  Delmar *(G-992)*
Sid Harvey Industries Inc .... G 302 746-7760
  Claymont *(G-805)*

PLUMBING & HEATING EQPT & SPLYS WHOLESALERS

Delaware Plumbing Supply Co .... F 302 656-5437
  New Castle *(G-5233)*
Greenberg Supply Co Inc .... E 302 656-4496
  Wilmington *(G-10777)*
Hajoca Corporation .... F 302 764-6000
  Wilmington *(G-10823)*
Penco Corporation .... G 302 698-3108
  Camden *(G-596)*

PLUMBING & HEATING EQPT & SPLYS, WHOL: Pipe/Fitting, Plastic

Briggs Company .... E 302 328-9471
  New Castle *(G-5114)*

PLUMBING & HEATING EQPT & SPLYS, WHOL: Plumbing Fitting/Sply

Core & Main LP .... G 302 684-3452
  Milton *(G-4883)*
Dover Plumbing Supply Co .... F 302 674-0333
  Dover *(G-1464)*
Ferguson Enterprises LLC .... E 302 656-4421
  Wilmington *(G-10520)*
Ferguson Enterprises LLC .... G 302 747-2032
  Dover *(G-1548)*
Ferguson Enterprises LLC .... G 302 934-6040
  Millsboro *(G-4689)*
Ferguson Enterprises LLC .... G 302 322-2836
  New Castle *(G-5309)*
Mumford Sheet Metal Works Inc .... E 302 436-8251
  Selbyville *(G-8527)*
Northeastern Supply Inc .... G 302 698-1414
  Camden *(G-593)*
Northeastern Supply Inc .... G 302 378-7880
  Middletown *(G-4176)*
Penco Corporation .... G 302 227-9188
  Rehoboth Beach *(G-8029)*
Penco Corporation .... G 302 738-3212
  Newark *(G-7195)*
Penco Corporation .... D 302 629-7911
  Seaford *(G-8343)*
Vertex Industries Inc .... G 302 472-0601
  Wilmington *(G-13066)*

PLUMBING & HEATING EQPT & SPLYS, WHOL: Plumbng/Heatng Valves

Bristol Industrial Corporation .... F 302 322-1100
  New Castle *(G-5115)*

PLUMBING & HEATING EQPT & SPLYS, WHOL: Water Purif Eqpt

Graver Technologies LLC .... C 302 731-1700
  Newark *(G-6684)*
Schagrin Gas Co .... E 302 378-2000
  Middletown *(G-4232)*
Waterlogic Usa Inc .... C 302 323-2100
  New Castle *(G-5826)*

PLUMBING FIXTURES

Ferguson Enterprises LLC .... G 302 747-2032
  Dover *(G-1548)*

PODIATRISTS' OFFICES

Advanced Foot & Ankle Center ...... G 302 355-0056
  Newark *(G-5905)*
Brandywine Podiatry PA .... G 302 658-1129
  Wilmington *(G-9450)*
Delaware Foot & Ankle Assoc .... G 302 834-3575
  Newark *(G-6380)*
Delaware Podiatrist Medicine .... G 302 674-9255
  Dover *(G-1387)*
Delaware Valley Ent Inc .... G 302 427-2444
  Wilmington *(G-10093)*
Edwin M Mow DPM Facfas .... G 302 424-1760
  Milford *(G-4403)*
Foot & Ankle Associates .... F 302 652-5767
  Wilmington *(G-10587)*
Foot & Ankle Ctr of Delaware .... G 302 945-1221
  Millsboro *(G-4692)*
Foot Care Group Inc .... E 302 998-0178
  Wilmington *(G-10588)*
Foot Care Group Inc .... F 302 285-0292
  Middletown *(G-4075)*
Garcia Podiatry Group .... G 302 994-5956
  Wilmington *(G-10669)*
James F Palmer .... G 302 629-6162
  Seaford *(G-8277)*
James F Palmer .... G 302 644-3980
  Lewes *(G-3570)*
John Hocutt Jr MD .... G 302 475-7800
  Wilmington *(G-11171)*
Lisa Ryan Hobbs DPM .... G 302 629-3000
  Seaford *(G-8295)*
Raymond V Feehery Jr DPM .... G 302 999-8511
  Newark *(G-7302)*
Southern Delaware Foot .... G 302 404-5915
  Seaford *(G-8405)*
Sussex Podiatry Group .... G 302 645-8555
  Lewes *(G-3773)*
Tri State Foot & Ankle Ctr LLC ...... G 302 475-1299
  Wilmington *(G-12966)*

POINT OF SALE DEVICES

Global Merchant Partners LLC ...... G 302 425-3567
  Rehoboth Beach *(G-7950)*
Huawei Technologies Svc LLC .... C 888 548-2934
  Dover *(G-1659)*

POLICE PROTECTION: Local Government

Town of Middletown .... E 302 376-9950
  Middletown *(G-4264)*

POLISHING SVC: Metals Or Formed Prdts

Rohm and Haas Electronic .... F 302 366-0500
  Newark *(G-7357)*

POLYETHYLENE RESINS

Celanese International Corp .... G 972 443-4000
  Wilmington *(G-9609)*

POLYHYDRIC ALCOHOL ESTERS, AMINOS, ETC

Dupont Tate Lyle Bio Pdts LLC ...... G 865 408-1962
  Wilmington *(G-10264)*

POLYTETRAFLUOROETHYLENE RESINS

Intech Services Inc .... G 302 366-8530
  Newark *(G-6788)*
W L Gore & Associates Inc .... C 302 368-3700
  Newark *(G-7672)*

POLYURETHANE RESINS

Polymer Technologies Inc .... D 302 738-9001
  Newark *(G-7231)*

POLYVINYL CHLORIDE RESINS

Formosa Plastics Corp Delaware .... C 302 836-2200
  Delaware City *(G-958)*

PORCELAIN: Chemical

Intelligent Building Mtls LLC .... G 302 261-9922
  Newark *(G-6794)*

PORTRAITS, WHOLESALE

Little Nests Portraits .... F 610 459-8622
  Wilmington *(G-11405)*

POSTAL STATION SVC, CONTRACTED

Bayville Postal Svc .... G 302 436-2715
  Selbyville *(G-8455)*

POTPOURRI

Millies Scented Rocks LLC .... G 302 331-9232
  Magnolia *(G-3900)*

POTTERY

B & F Ceramics .... G 302 475-4721
  Wilmington *(G-9209)*
Joel Gonzalez .... G 302 562-6878
  Middletown *(G-4115)*
Katlyn Co Ceramics .... G 302 528-1322
  Bear *(G-212)*
Robert McMann .... G 302 329-9413
  Milton *(G-4964)*

POULTRY & POULTRY PRDTS WHOLESALERS

Eastern Shore Poultry Company .... B 302 855-1350
  Georgetown *(G-2520)*
Jabez Corp .... F 302 475-7600
  Wilmington *(G-11113)*

POULTRY & SMALL GAME SLAUGHTERING & PROCESSING

Mountaire Farms Delaware Inc ..... F 302 934-1100
  Millsboro *(G-4756)*
Mountaire Farms Inc .... F 302 988-6200
  Selbyville *(G-8523)*
Perdue Farms Inc .... G 302 629-3216
  Seaford *(G-8353)*
Perdue Farms Inc .... E 302 337-2210
  Bridgeville *(G-507)*
Perdue Farms Inc .... G 410 543-3424
  Seaford *(G-8354)*
Perdue Farms Incorporated .... G 302 855-5635
  Georgetown *(G-2618)*

POWDER: Metal

Ametek Inc .... D 302 456-4400
  Newark *(G-5962)*

POWER TRANSMISSION EQPT: Mechanical

Pierce Design & Tool .... G 302 222-3339
  Dover *(G-1958)*

PRECIOUS METALS WHOLESALERS

First State Coin Co .... G 302 734-7776
  Dover *(G-1554)*

PRECIOUS STONES & METALS, WHOLESALE

Alamad Investments LLC .... G 833 311-8899
  Lewes *(G-3332)*

PRECIOUS STONES WHOLESALERS

Gem Merchant LLC .... G 734 274-1280
  Lewes *(G-3510)*
Stuart Kingston Inc .... F 302 227-2524
  Rehoboth Beach *(G-8090)*

PRERECORDED TAPE, CD/RECORD STORES: Video Tapes, Prerecorded

Video Den .... G 302 628-9835
  Seaford *(G-8431)*

PRODUCT & SERVICES SECTION

PRERECORDED TAPE, COMPACT DISC & RECORD STORES

Studio J Entrmt & AP & Cof Bar ....G....... 410 422-3155
  Laurel *(G-3296)*

PRESCHOOL CENTERS

A Childs World LLC ....F....... 302 322-9386
  Bear *(G-4)*
Academy of Early Learning......................G....... 302 659-0750
  Smyrna *(G-8560)*
Acclaim Academy LLC ....E....... 215 848-7827
  Wilmington *(G-8916)*
Ave Preschool ....F....... 302 422-8775
  Milford *(G-4315)*
Babes On Square ....G....... 302 477-9190
  Wilmington *(G-9219)*
Beach Babies Child Care ....E....... 302 644-1585
  Lewes *(G-3366)*
Bear Early Education Center ....G....... 302 836-5000
  Newark *(G-6063)*
Beginnings and Beyond Inc ....F....... 302 734-2464
  Dover *(G-1190)*
Boost Learning LLC..................................G....... 302 691-5821
  Wilmington *(G-9394)*
Building Blocks Academy Ltd ....F....... 302 284-8797
  Felton *(G-2277)*
Carmen R Benitez ....G....... 302 793-2061
  Claymont *(G-707)*
Catholic Docese Wilmington Inc.............E....... 302 731-2210
  Newark *(G-6169)*
Cdb Ventures Inc ....E....... 302 235-0414
  Hockessin *(G-2981)*
Children First Preschool ....G....... 302 239-3544
  Hockessin *(G-2985)*
Childrens Beach House Inc ....F....... 302 645-9184
  Lewes *(G-3413)*
Christ Ch Episcpal Preschool..................E....... 302 472-0021
  Wilmington *(G-9673)*
Corporate Kids Lrng Ctr Inc....................E....... 302 678-0688
  Dover *(G-1314)*
Covenant Preschool ....F....... 302 764-8503
  Wilmington *(G-9879)*
Developing Minds Preschool..................G....... 302 995-9611
  Wilmington *(G-10129)*
Discovery Island Preschool ....F....... 302 732-7529
  Dagsboro *(G-898)*
Early Learning Center ....E....... 302 239-3033
  Hockessin *(G-3015)*
Ebenezer United Methdst Chruch ....F....... 302 731-9495
  Newark *(G-6500)*
Education Svcs Unlimited LLC...............F....... 302 650-4210
  Wilmington *(G-10352)*
Elaine Leonard ....F....... 302 376-5553
  Middletown *(G-4052)*
Expanding Our Kids World ....E....... 302 659-0293
  Smyrna *(G-8630)*
Fairchild Day School ....G....... 302 478-4646
  Wilmington *(G-10476)*
First Steps Preschool-Milford ....G....... 302 424-4470
  Milford *(G-4415)*
Foulk Pre-Schl & Day Cre Cntr ....G....... 302 529-1580
  Wilmington *(G-10600)*
Foulk Pre-Schl & Day Cre Cntr ....G....... 302 478-3047
  Wilmington *(G-10601)*
Funstep Inc ....F....... 302 731-9618
  Newark *(G-6629)*
Gb Jacobs LLC...E....... 302 378-9100
  Middletown *(G-4084)*
Good Beginnings Preschool....................G....... 302 875-5507
  Laurel *(G-3232)*
Green Acres Pre School ....F....... 302 378-9250
  Odessa *(G-7827)*
Guardian Angel Child Care ....G....... 302 428-3620
  Wilmington *(G-10796)*
Happy Kids Academy Inc ....E....... 302 369-6929
  Newark *(G-6706)*
Hartly Family Learning Ctr LLC ....F....... 302 492-1152
  Hartly *(G-2923)*
Karen Schreiber ....G....... 302 628-3007
  Seaford *(G-8284)*
Karen Schreiber ....G....... 302 875-7733
  Laurel *(G-3248)*
Kids Cottage LLC ....E....... 302 644-7690
  Rehoboth Beach *(G-7981)*
Kids Nest Day Care ....G....... 302 731-7017
  Newark *(G-6886)*
Kidz Ink ....E....... 302 838-1500
  Bear *(G-218)*

Kidz Ink ....G....... 302 376-1700
  Middletown *(G-4123)*
La Petite Academy Inc............................E....... 302 234-2574
  Hockessin *(G-3075)*
Learning Care Group Inc ....G....... 302 235-5702
  Wilmington *(G-11350)*
Learning Express Academy ....E....... 302 737-8260
  Newark *(G-6926)*
Learning Express Preschool ....F....... 302 737-8990
  Newark *(G-6927)*
Learning Years Preschool ....G....... 302 241-4781
  Dover *(G-1774)*
Limestone Country Day School ....G....... 302 239-9041
  Wilmington *(G-11388)*
Little Einsteins Preschool ....G....... 302 933-0600
  Millsboro *(G-4721)*
Little Learner Inc ....F....... 302 798-5570
  Claymont *(G-774)*
Little Pople Child Dev Ctr Inc.................F....... 302 836-5900
  Bear *(G-237)*
Little Scholars Learning Ctr....................F....... 302 656-8785
  Wilmington *(G-11407)*
Little School Inc ....F....... 302 734-3040
  Dover *(G-1792)*
Little Stars Inc ....F....... 302 737-9759
  Newark *(G-6942)*
Mahavir LLC ....E....... 302 651-7995
  Wilmington *(G-11489)*
Milford Early Learning Center ....G....... 302 331-6612
  Camden Wyoming *(G-649)*
Mother Goose Childrens Center.............G....... 302 934-8454
  Millsboro *(G-4754)*
Newark Christian Childcare ....E....... 302 369-3000
  Newark *(G-7113)*
Newark Day-Nursery Association ....E....... 302 731-4925
  Newark *(G-7116)*
Newark United Methodist ....E....... 302 368-8774
  Newark *(G-7129)*
Panda Early Education Ctr Inc................E....... 302 832-1891
  Christiana *(G-674)*
Panda Early Education Ctr Inc................F....... 302 832-1891
  Bear *(G-276)*
Passion Care Services Inc ....F....... 302 832-2622
  Bear *(G-278)*
Patricia McKay ....G....... 302 563-5334
  Bear *(G-280)*
Primeros Pasos Inc ....G....... 302 856-7406
  Georgetown *(G-2627)*
Rainbow Day Care & Pre-Sch ....G....... 302 628-1020
  Seaford *(G-8370)*
Selwor Enterprises Inc ....F....... 302 454-9454
  Newark *(G-7404)*
Smalls Stepping Stone ....E....... 302 652-3011
  Wilmington *(G-12653)*
St Marks United Methodist Ch ....E....... 302 994-0400
  Wilmington *(G-12726)*
St Michaels School Inc...........................E....... 302 656-3389
  Wilmington *(G-12727)*
Sussex Prschool Erly Care Ctrs ....G....... 302 732-7529
  Seaford *(G-8417)*
Tadpole Academy LLC ....G....... 302 658-2141
  Wilmington *(G-12848)*
Telamon Corporation Headstart ....F....... 302 875-7718
  Laurel *(G-3299)*
Tutor Time Learning Ctrs LLC ....E....... 302 235-5701
  Wilmington *(G-12995)*
Tutor Time Lrng Systems Inc ....E....... 302 478-7366
  Wilmington *(G-12996)*
United Cerebral Palsy of De ....F....... 302 856-3490
  Georgetown *(G-2698)*
Village Sq Acdemy Lrng Ctr LLC............G....... 302 539-5000
  Ocean View *(G-7823)*
West Wilmington Svnth Day Adv...........G....... 302 998-3961
  Wilmington *(G-13168)*
Whatcoat Christian Preschool................G....... 302 698-2108
  Dover *(G-2219)*
Wilmington Montessori School ....D....... 302 475-0555
  Wilmington *(G-13238)*

PRESS SVCS

Dover Post Co Inc ....D....... 302 678-3616
  Dover *(G-1467)*

PRESSES

Eastern Shore Metals LLC ....F....... 302 629-6629
  Seaford *(G-8231)*

PRESTRESSED CONCRETE PRDTS

Concrete Bldg Systems Del Inc..............E....... 302 846-3645
  Delmar *(G-986)*

PRINT CARTRIDGES: Laser & Other Computer Printers

Kent-Sussex Industries Inc....................B....... 302 422-4014
  Milford *(G-4466)*

PRINTED CIRCUIT BOARDS

Rogers Corporation ....E....... 302 834-2100
  Bear *(G-312)*
Suretronix Solutions LLC ....G....... 302 407-3146
  Wilmington *(G-12817)*

PRINTERS & PLOTTERS

On Demand Services LLC ....G....... 302 388-1215
  Newark *(G-7148)*

PRINTING & BINDING: Books

Moghul Life Inc ....G....... 347 560-9124
  Wilmington *(G-11724)*

PRINTING & ENGRAVING: Invitation & Stationery

Brodie Invitations....................................G....... 302 999-7889
  Wilmington *(G-9483)*

PRINTING MACHINERY

E I Du Pont De Nemours & Co ....E....... 805 562-5307
  Wilmington *(G-10304)*
My Qme Inc ....E....... 302 218-8730
  Wilmington *(G-11789)*
Spratley Publishing ....G....... 267 779-7353
  Wilmington *(G-12712)*

PRINTING MACHINERY, EQPT & SPLYS: Wholesalers

Deangelis & Son Inc ....G....... 302 337-8699
  Bridgeville *(G-464)*

PRINTING TRADES MACHINERY & EQPT REPAIR SVCS

Deangelis & Son Inc ....G....... 302 337-8699
  Bridgeville *(G-464)*

PRINTING, COMMERCIAL: Bags, Plastic, NEC

Jeb Plastics Inc ....G....... 302 479-9223
  Wilmington *(G-11139)*

PRINTING, COMMERCIAL: Business Forms, NEC

Advanced Office Systems & Sups ....G....... 302 629-7505
  Seaford *(G-8140)*
Best Office Pros ....G....... 302 629-4561
  Seaford *(G-8167)*

PRINTING, COMMERCIAL: Decals, NEC

Promotion Zone LLC ....G....... 302 832-8565
  Newark *(G-7269)*

PRINTING, COMMERCIAL: Promotional

Unique Image LLC ....E....... 302 658-2266
  Wilmington *(G-13017)*

PRINTING, COMMERCIAL: Screen

Benjamin Tanei ....G....... 302 521-2033
  Townsend *(G-8764)*
Cosmic Custom Screen Printing ....G....... 302 933-0920
  Millsboro *(G-4668)*
Diamond State Graphics Inc ....F....... 302 325-1100
  New Castle *(G-5252)*
Dragons Lair Printing LLC ....G....... 302 798-4465
  Claymont *(G-735)*
Factors Etc Inc ....D....... 302 834-1625
  Bear *(G-148)*
Go Tees LLC ....G....... 708 703-1788
  Middletown *(G-4090)*

Lasting Impression Inc A......G...... 302 762-9200
Wilmington *(G-11335)*
Logo Motive Inc......G...... 302 645-2959
Rehoboth Beach *(G-7989)*
Meade Inc......G...... 302 262-3394
Seaford *(G-8306)*
Middletown Ink LLC......G...... 302 725-0705
Middletown *(G-4157)*
Midnight Blue Inc......F...... 302 436-9665
Selbyville *(G-8522)*
New Image Inc......G...... 302 738-6824
Newark *(G-7106)*
Remline Corp......E...... 302 737-7228
Newark *(G-7316)*
Ronan Gill LLC......F...... 877 549-7712
Wilmington *(G-12471)*
Sportz Tees......G...... 302 280-6076
Laurel *(G-3294)*
Stamford Screen Printing Inc......G...... 302 654-2442
Wilmington *(G-12733)*
Superior Graphic & Printing......G...... 302 290-3475
Wilmington *(G-12808)*
Ten Talents Enterprises Inc......G...... 302 409-0718
Middletown *(G-4255)*

PRINTING, LITHOGRAPHIC: Color

Delta Forms Inc......F...... 302 652-3266
Wilmington *(G-10106)*

PRINTING, LITHOGRAPHIC: Decals

Skinify LLC......F...... 302 212-5689
Rehoboth Beach *(G-8079)*

PRINTING, LITHOGRAPHIC: Maps

Rockford Map Gallery LLC......G...... 302 740-1851
Wilmington *(G-12450)*

PRINTING, LITHOGRAPHIC: Promotional

Stephen Cropper......G...... 302 732-3730
Frankford *(G-2390)*

PRINTING, LITHOGRAPHIC: Schedules, Transportation

Horizon Aeronautics Inc......G...... 409 504-2645
Wilmington *(G-10952)*

PRINTING, LITHOGRAPHIC: Transfers, Decalcomania Or Dry

Factors Etc Inc......D...... 302 834-1625
Bear *(G-148)*

PRINTING: Books

Aafton Research & Media Inc......G...... 617 407-6619
Dover *(G-1076)*
Pmb Associates LLC......G...... 302 436-0111
Selbyville *(G-8531)*
Print Shack Inc......G...... 302 629-4430
Seaford *(G-8364)*

PRINTING: Commercial, NEC

AIA......G...... 302 407-2252
New Castle *(G-5018)*
Amer Inc......G...... 302 654-2498
Wilmington *(G-9039)*
B-Line Printing......G...... 302 628-1311
Seaford *(G-8160)*
Compass Graphics......G...... 302 378-1977
Middletown *(G-4003)*
Corlo Services Inc......G...... 302 737-3207
Newark *(G-6299)*
Creative Promotions......G...... 302 697-7896
Camden *(G-553)*
D & D Screen Printing......G...... 302 349-4231
Greenwood *(G-2727)*
Delaware Screen Printing Inc......G...... 302 378-4231
Middletown *(G-4031)*
Design Craft......G...... 302 834-3720
Delaware City *(G-956)*
Encore Designs Inc......G...... 302 798-5678
Wilmington *(G-10395)*
Fbk Graphico Inc......G...... 302 743-4784
Wilmington *(G-10509)*
Fedex Office & Print Svcs Inc......G...... 302 996-0264
Wilmington *(G-10519)*
First Class Cards LLC......G...... 302 653-0111
Clayton *(G-850)*
Max One Printing......G...... 302 897-9050
Bear *(G-249)*
Patio Printing Co Inc......G...... 302 328-6881
New Castle *(G-5608)*
Richard J Wadsley......G...... 302 545-7162
Middletown *(G-4220)*
Sunshine Graphics and Printing......G...... 302 724-5127
Dover *(G-2115)*
Sussex Printing Corp......D...... 302 629-9303
Seaford *(G-8416)*
To A Tee Printing......G...... 302 525-6336
Newark *(G-7571)*
Unique Tracking LLC......G...... 912 220-3522
Wilmington *(G-13019)*
Village Graphics LLC......G...... 302 697-9288
Dover *(G-2193)*
Zzhouse Inc......G...... 302 354-3474
New Castle *(G-5849)*

PRINTING: Gravure, Business Form & Card

Blue Heron Ent Inc......G...... 302 834-1521
Bear *(G-54)*
Stephen Cropper......G...... 302 732-3730
Frankford *(G-2390)*

PRINTING: Gravure, Labels

Ancar Enterprises LLC......G...... 302 477-1884
Wilmington *(G-9075)*

PRINTING: Gravure, Rotogravure

Promotion Zone LLC......G...... 302 832-8565
Newark *(G-7269)*
Scientific Games Corporation......F...... 302 737-4300
Newark *(G-7395)*

PRINTING: Letterpress

Stanley Golden......G...... 302 652-5626
Wilmington *(G-12736)*

PRINTING: Lithographic

A+ Printing......G...... 302 273-3147
Wilmington *(G-8888)*
AlphaGraphics Franchising Inc......G...... 302 559-8369
Wilmington *(G-9030)*
Ancar Enterprises LLC......G...... 302 477-1884
Wilmington *(G-9075)*
Ancar Enterprises LLC......F...... 302 453-2600
Newark *(G-5966)*
Associates International Inc......D...... 302 656-4500
Wilmington *(G-9157)*
Axial Medical Printing Inc......G...... 518 620-4479
Claymont *(G-697)*
Bgdedge Inc......G...... 302 477-1734
Wilmington *(G-9325)*
Bgi Print Solutions......G...... 302 234-2825
Newark *(G-6077)*
Bgi Print Solutions......G...... 302 234-2825
Newark *(G-6078)*
Bills Printers Service......G...... 302 798-0482
Claymont *(G-702)*
Chapis Drafting & Blue Print......G...... 302 629-6373
Seaford *(G-8190)*
Chick Harness & Supply Inc......E...... 302 398-4630
Harrington *(G-2824)*
Coko Prints......G...... 302 507-1683
Wilmington *(G-9765)*
Conventioneer Pubg Co Inc......G...... 301 487-3907
Georgetown *(G-2483)*
D & B Printing and Mailing Inc......G...... 302 838-7111
Newark *(G-6339)*
DC Printing Inc......G...... 302 545-6666
Wilmington *(G-9977)*
Delaware Screen Printing Inc......G...... 302 378-4231
Middletown *(G-4031)*
Delaware State Printing......G...... 302 228-9431
Dover *(G-1397)*
Depro-Serical USA Inc......G...... 302 368-8040
Townsend *(G-8783)*
Dover Post Co Inc......D...... 302 678-3616
Dover *(G-1467)*
Edythe L Pridgen......G...... 302 652-8887
Bear *(G-141)*
Fannon Color Printing LLC......G...... 302 227-2164
Rehoboth Beach *(G-7931)*
Fedex Office & Print Svcs Inc......G...... 302 996-0264
Wilmington *(G-10519)*
Fishtail Print Company......G...... 302 408-4800
Rehoboth Beach *(G-7934)*
Fishtail Print Company......G...... 302 682-3053
Rehoboth Beach *(G-7935)*
Gannett Co Inc......D...... 302 325-6600
New Castle *(G-5343)*
Garile Inc......E...... 302 366-0848
Newark *(G-6639)*
Health & Social Svcs Del Dept......E...... 302 255-9800
New Castle *(G-5383)*
Health & Social Svcs Del Dept......E...... 302 255-9855
New Castle *(G-5385)*
Jerry O Thompson Prntng......G...... 302 832-1309
Bear *(G-200)*
Job Printing......G...... 302 907-0416
Delmar *(G-1008)*
Kardmaster Graphics......E...... 610 434-5262
Wilmington *(G-11225)*
Lights Out Screen Printing Co......G...... 302 409-0560
Wilmington *(G-11386)*
Lord Printing LLC......G...... 302 439-3253
Wilmington *(G-11435)*
Mail Rooms Ltd......G...... 302 629-4838
Seaford *(G-8300)*
Markizon Printing......G...... 610 715-7989
Wilmington *(G-11539)*
Marthann Print Center LLC......G...... 267 884-8130
Dover *(G-1822)*
Mgl Screen Printing......G...... 302 450-6250
Clayton *(G-864)*
Morales Screen Printing......G...... 302 465-8179
Dover *(G-1871)*
New Image Inc......G...... 302 738-6824
Newark *(G-7106)*
Newphoenix Screen Printing......G...... 302 747-8991
Dover *(G-1897)*
Nexsigns LLC......G...... 302 508-2615
Clayton *(G-866)*
One Hour Printing......G...... 302 220-1684
Newark *(G-7150)*
Prince Manufacturing Co......F...... 646 747-4208
New Castle *(G-5641)*
Print Coast 2 Coast......G...... 302 381-4610
Lewes *(G-3697)*
Print On This......G...... 302 235-9475
Newark *(G-7254)*
Printcurement......G...... 302 249-6100
New Castle *(G-5644)*
Printed Solid Inc......F...... 302 439-0098
Newark *(G-7255)*
Printit Solutions......G...... 302 380-3838
Dover *(G-1987)*
Prints and Princesses......G...... 703 881-1057
Newark *(G-7256)*
Pulsar Print LLC......G...... 302 394-9202
New Castle *(G-5653)*
Rcd Printing......G...... 302 424-8467
Milford *(G-4533)*
Rescue Printig......G...... 302 286-7266
Newark *(G-7323)*
Smart International Inc......G...... 302 451-9517
Newark *(G-7445)*
Southern Printing......G...... 302 832-3475
New Castle *(G-5725)*
Star Art Inc......G...... 302 261-6732
Bear *(G-337)*
Stratis Visuals LLC......G...... 860 482-1208
Newark *(G-7495)*
Sussex Printing Corp......D...... 302 629-9303
Seaford *(G-8416)*
Thoroughthreads......G...... 302 356-0502
Wilmington *(G-12905)*
UNI Printing Solutionsllc......G...... 631 438-6045
New Castle *(G-5802)*
W B Mason Co Inc......C...... 888 926-2766
Newark *(G-7667)*
Zeal Print Co LLC......G...... 302 407-5745
Wilmington *(G-13342)*

PRINTING: Offset

Academy Business Mch & Prtg Co......G...... 302 654-3200
Wilmington *(G-8912)*
Amer Inc......G...... 302 654-2498
Wilmington *(G-9039)*
Armor Graphics Inc......G...... 302 737-8790
Newark *(G-5996)*
Ben-Dom Printing Company......F...... 302 737-9144
Newark *(G-6072)*
Brandywine Graphics Inc......G...... 302 655-7571
Wilmington *(G-9435)*

PRODUCT & SERVICES SECTION

Coastal Printing Company .... G 302 537-1700
  Ocean View *(G-7780)*
Communications Printing Inc .... G 302 229-9369
  Newark *(G-6270)*
Copy Craft Inc .... E 302 633-1313
  Wilmington *(G-9856)*
DMD Business Forms & Prtg Co .... G 302 998-8200
  Wilmington *(G-10177)*
Dover Litho Printing Co .... F 302 698-5292
  Dover *(G-1457)*
Dover Post Co Inc .... D 302 653-2083
  Dover *(G-1466)*
Duck Creek Printing LLC .... G 302 653-5121
  Smyrna *(G-8627)*
Grm Pro Imaging LLC .... G 302 999-8162
  Wilmington *(G-10788)*
I N I Holdings Inc .... G 302 674-3600
  Dover *(G-1665)*
Independent Newsmedia USA Inc ...... D 302 674-3600
  Dover *(G-1672)*
Luke Destefano Inc .... G 302 455-0710
  Newark *(G-6955)*
McClafferty Printing Company .... E 302 652-8112
  Wilmington *(G-11587)*
Mercantile Press Inc .... F 302 764-6884
  Wilmington *(G-11636)*
News Print Shop .... G 302 337-8283
  Bridgeville *(G-502)*
OConnell Speedy Printing Inc .... G 302 656-1475
  Wilmington *(G-11935)*
Penney Enterprises Inc .... G 302 629-4430
  Seaford *(G-8350)*
Print-N-Press Inc .... G 302 994-6665
  Wilmington *(G-12229)*
Rogers Graphics Inc .... F 302 856-0028
  Georgetown *(G-2641)*
Rogers Graphics Inc .... G 302 422-6694
  Harbeson *(G-2797)*
Sprint Quality Printing Inc .... G 302 478-0720
  Wilmington *(G-12716)*
Stanley Golden .... G 302 652-5626
  Wilmington *(G-12736)*
Union Press Printing Inc .... G 302 652-0496
  Wilmington *(G-13013)*
William N Cann Inc .... E 302 995-0820
  Wilmington *(G-13215)*

PRINTING: Screen, Broadwoven Fabrics, Cotton

Carter Printing and Design .... G 302 655-2343
  New Castle *(G-5135)*
D By D Printing LLC .... G 302 659-3373
  Dover *(G-1335)*

PRINTING: Screen, Fabric

Atlantic Sun Screen Prtg Inc .... F 302 731-5100
  Newark *(G-6021)*
Dream Graphics .... G 302 328-6264
  New Castle *(G-5261)*
Jairus Enterprises Inc .... G 302 834-1625
  Bear *(G-197)*
Kathy Stabley .... G 302 322-7884
  New Castle *(G-5453)*
Lasting Impression Inc A .... G 302 762-9200
  Wilmington *(G-11335)*
Red Sun Custom Apparel Inc .... E 302 988-8230
  Selbyville *(G-8538)*
Stephen Cropper .... G 302 732-3730
  Frankford *(G-2390)*
Unique Image LLC .... E 302 658-2266
  Wilmington *(G-13017)*
Whisman John .... G 302 530-1676
  Wilmington *(G-13185)*

PRIVATE INVESTIGATOR SVCS

Alpha Omega Invstgtons Wrkmans ..... G 302 323-8111
  New Castle *(G-5025)*
JR Gettier & Associates Inc .... B 302 478-0911
  Wilmington *(G-11202)*
S & H Enterprises Inc .... F 302 999-9911
  Wilmington *(G-12505)*

PROBATION OFFICE

Supreme Court United States .... E 302 252-2950
  Wilmington *(G-12814)*

PRODUCT ENDORSEMENT SVCS

Industrial Training Cons Inc .... F 302 266-6100
  Newark *(G-6774)*

PRODUCTION CREDIT ASSOCIATION, AGRICULTURAL

Mid Atlantic Farm Credit Aca .... D 302 734-7534
  Dover *(G-1847)*

PROFESSIONAL EQPT & SPLYS, WHOLESALE: Analytical Instruments

Joint Anlytcl Systms (amrcs) .... G 302 607-0088
  Newark *(G-6849)*

PROFESSIONAL EQPT & SPLYS, WHOLESALE: Law Enforcement

Toxtrap Inc .... G 302 698-1400
  Dover *(G-2156)*

PROFESSIONAL EQPT & SPLYS, WHOLESALE: Optical Goods

Elsicon Inc .... F 302 266-7030
  Newark *(G-6519)*

PROFESSIONAL EQPT & SPLYS, WHOLESALE: Theatrical

Main Light Industries Inc .... C 302 998-8017
  Wilmington *(G-11491)*

PROGRAM ADMIN, GOVT: Energy Devpt & Conservation Agency

City of Dover .... E 302 736-7070
  Dover *(G-1290)*

PROGRAM ADMINISTRATION, GOVERNMENT: Social & Human Resources

Inov8 Inc .... G 302 465-5124
  Camden Wyoming *(G-646)*

PROGRAM ADMINISTRATION, GOVERNMENT: Social & Manpower, State

Children Youth & Their Fam .... G 302 577-6011
  Wilmington *(G-9662)*
Health & Social Svcs Del Dept .... F 302 255-9500
  Dover *(G-1640)*

PROMOTION SVCS

Middletown Main Street Inc .... G 302 378-2977
  Middletown *(G-4159)*
Remline Corp .... E 302 737-7228
  Newark *(G-7316)*
Spark Productions LLC .... G 302 436-0183
  Selbyville *(G-8548)*

PROPELLERS: Boat & Ship, Machined

Proper Pitch LLC .... G 302 436-5442
  Selbyville *(G-8534)*

PROPERTY & CASUALTY INSURANCE AGENTS

Chubb US Holding Inc .... A 215 640-1000
  Wilmington *(G-9696)*
Cigna Global Holdings Inc .... F 302 797-3469
  Claymont *(G-718)*
Reese Agency Inc .... G 302 678-5656
  Dover *(G-2018)*

PROPERTY DAMAGE INSURANCE

AAA Club Alliance Inc .... B 302 299-4700
  Wilmington *(G-8893)*
Nuclear Electric Insurance Ltd .... D 302 888-3000
  Wilmington *(G-11921)*
Wentworth Group .... G 302 998-2115
  Wilmington *(G-13156)*

PUBLIC FINANCE, TAX & MONETARY POLICY, GOVT: Lottery Cntrl

Delaware Department Finance .... E 302 739-5291
  Dover *(G-1364)*

PUBLIC HEALTH PROGRAM ADMINISTRATION, GOVERNMENT: State

Health & Social Svcs Del Dept .... E 302 255-9855
  New Castle *(G-5385)*
Health & Social Svcs Del Dept .... D 302 857-5000
  Dover *(G-1639)*
Health & Social Svcs Del Dept .... E 302 255-9800
  New Castle *(G-5383)*

PUBLIC HEALTH PROGRAMS ADMINISTRATION SVCS

Children Youth & Their Fam .... D 302 577-4270
  New Castle *(G-5147)*
Children Youth & Their Fam .... E 302 633-2600
  Wilmington *(G-9663)*
Health & Social Svcs Del Dept .... F 302 368-6700
  Newark *(G-6716)*
Health & Social Svcs Del Dept .... A 302 223-1000
  Smyrna *(G-8650)*
Health & Social Svcs Del Dept .... E 302 577-3420
  Wilmington *(G-10867)*
Health & Social Svcs Del Dept .... E 302 552-3530
  Wilmington *(G-10868)*
Health & Social Svcs Del Dept .... A 302 255-2700
  New Castle *(G-5386)*
Health & Social Svcs Del Dept .... G 302 283-7500
  Newark *(G-6717)*
Health & Social Svcs Del Dept .... D 302 391-3505
  New Castle *(G-5387)*

PUBLIC LIBRARY

Historical Society of Delaware .... E 302 655-7161
  Wilmington *(G-10919)*

PUBLIC RELATIONS & PUBLICITY SVCS

Bgp Publicity Inc .... G 302 234-9500
  Hockessin *(G-2964)*

PUBLIC RELATIONS SVCS

Aloysius Butlr Clark Assoc Inc .... D 302 655-1552
  Wilmington *(G-9029)*
Kimos Hawaiian Shave Ice .... G 302 998-1763
  Wilmington *(G-11261)*
One System Incorporated .... F 888 311-1110
  Wilmington *(G-11956)*
The Ascendant Group Inc .... F 302 450-4494
  Newark *(G-7561)*
Tipton Communications Group .... G 302 454-7901
  Newark *(G-7568)*

PUBLISHERS: Art Copy & Poster

Qoro LLC .... G 302 322-5900
  New Castle *(G-5656)*

PUBLISHERS: Book

A Chance To Write It LLC .... G 202 256-4524
  Lewes *(G-3318)*
Cedar Lane Inc .... F 302 328-7232
  New Castle *(G-5139)*
Cosmic Strands LLC .... G 302 660-3268
  Wilmington *(G-9871)*
Kevin Fleming .... G 302 227-4994
  Rehoboth Beach *(G-7980)*
Medical Society of Delaware .... E 302 366-1400
  Newark *(G-7018)*
Meta Galaxic Publishing Inc .... G 302 245-7939
  Wilmington *(G-11647)*
Miller Publishing Inc .... G 302 576-6579
  Wilmington *(G-11695)*
Pond Publishing & Productions .... G 302 284-0200
  Felton *(G-2313)*
Readhowyouwant LLC .... G 302 730-4560
  Dover *(G-2014)*
Talents Publishing LLC .... G 302 353-4574
  Newark *(G-7534)*
When Poets Dream Inc .... G 818 738-6954
  Dover *(G-2222)*

PUBLISHERS: Books, No Printing

Birdsong Books .... G 302 378-7274
Middletown *(G-3968)*
Liveware Inc .... F 302 791-9446
Claymont *(G-775)*
Royal Era LLC .... G 484 574-0260
Newark *(G-7369)*
Thi (us) Inc .... G 302 792-1444
Claymont *(G-811)*
Wiley-Liss Inc .... G 302 429-8627
Wilmington *(G-13202)*

PUBLISHERS: Directories, Telephone

Coastal Images Inc .... G 302 539-6001
Fenwick Island *(G-2333)*
Verizon Delaware LLC .... C 302 571-1571
Wilmington *(G-13062)*

PUBLISHERS: Magazines, No Printing

Action Enterprise Inc .... E 302 537-7223
Fenwick Island *(G-2328)*
Delaware Italian-American .... G 302 545-6406
Wilmington *(G-10060)*
Living Well Magazine .... G 302 355-0929
Newark *(G-6943)*
Martinelli Holdings LLC .... E 302 656-1809
Wilmington *(G-11551)*
Simply Stylng-Schl of Csmtlgy .... G 302 778-1885
Wilmington *(G-12628)*
Suburban Publishing Inc .... E 302 656-1809
Wilmington *(G-12788)*
T S N Publishing Co Inc .... G 302 655-6483
Wilmington *(G-12845)*
U Transit Inc .... G 302 227-1197
Rehoboth Beach *(G-8102)*

PUBLISHERS: Miscellaneous

1300 Publishing Company LLC .... G 302 268-2684
Wilmington *(G-8845)*
321 Down Street Press Inc .... G 302 376-3965
Middletown *(G-3924)*
Associates International Inc .... D 302 656-4500
Wilmington *(G-9157)*
Beech Hill Press .... G 302 588-0315
Newark *(G-6067)*
Bottle of Smoke Press .... G 302 399-1856
Dover *(G-1223)*
Buchspot LLC .... G 302 715-1253
Lewes *(G-3393)*
Byzantium Sky Press .... G 302 258-6116
Milton *(G-4872)*
Cameck Publishing .... G 302 598-4799
Wilmington *(G-9544)*
Capital Gaines LLC .... G 302 433-6777
Wilmington *(G-9557)*
Cherryrich Publishing .... G 302 533-6354
Newark *(G-6192)*
Chesapeake Seaglass Jewelry .... G 410 778-4999
Selbyville *(G-8468)*
Chip Vickio .... G 302 448-0211
Millsboro *(G-4660)*
Cnwynn Publications .... G 484 753-1568
Dover *(G-1299)*
Cruz Publishing Group .... G 302 287-2938
Dover *(G-1328)*
Crystal Diamond Publishing .... G 302 737-2130
Newark *(G-6319)*
Delaware Guitar School .... G 302 697-2341
Wyoming *(G-13360)*
Devils Party Press .... G 310 904-3660
Milton *(G-4893)*
Emw Publications .... G 302 438-9879
Hockessin *(G-3022)*
Fruitbearer Publishing LLC .... G 302 856-6649
Georgetown *(G-2535)*
Grow USA Press .... G 302 725-5195
Milford *(G-4424)*
Harman Hay Publications Inc .... G 302 669-9144
Bear *(G-177)*
Harmoniously Pbc .... G 302 291-1106
Wilmington *(G-10839)*
Hill Publishing Inc .... G 917 826-3722
Newark *(G-6728)*
Hindin Media LLC .... G 302 463-4612
Wilmington *(G-10915)*
Hither Creek Press .... G 603 387-3444
Milford *(G-4442)*

Hobo News Press Inc .... G 302 235-1066
Newark *(G-6732)*
Impress .... G 302 645-8411
Lewes *(G-3554)*
Independent School MGT Inc .... E 302 656-4944
Wilmington *(G-11018)*
Joseph M Press Mr .... G 302 378-2053
Middletown *(G-4117)*
Kardmaster Graphics .... E 610 434-5262
Wilmington *(G-11225)*
Kitty Jazzy Publishing .... G 302 897-8842
Newark *(G-6896)*
L & B Publishing .... G 302 743-4061
Newark *(G-6905)*
Litcharts LLC .... G 646 481-4807
Wilmington *(G-11400)*
MJM Publishing .... G 302 943-3590
Felton *(G-2307)*
New Castle Cnty Shoppers Guide .... E 302 325-6600
New Castle *(G-5554)*
Pagetech .... G 845 624-4911
Lewes *(G-3676)*
Pat Press .... G 302 836-2955
Bear *(G-279)*
Pixorize Inc .... G 737 529-4404
Wilmington *(G-12145)*
PMC Publications LLC .... G 302 268-4480
Newark *(G-7224)*
Postimpressions Incorporated .... G 302 656-2271
Wilmington *(G-12194)*
Powers Publishing Group .... G 302 519-8575
Millsboro *(G-4786)*
Prestwick House Inc .... E 302 659-2070
Smyrna *(G-8692)*
Psychoanalytic Electronic .... G 949 495-3332
Wilmington *(G-12261)*
Publication Print .... G 302 992-2040
Wilmington *(G-12266)*
Reed Elsevier Capital Inc .... F 302 427-9299
Wilmington *(G-12350)*
Responsible Publishing .... G 609 412-9621
Wilmington *(G-12388)*
Review .... E 302 831-2771
Newark *(G-7330)*
Rhino Smart Publications .... G 302 737-3422
Newark *(G-7336)*
Rlk Press Inc .... G 267 565-5138
Wilmington *(G-12432)*
Russell D Earnest & Assoc .... G 302 659-0730
Clayton *(G-870)*
Russell D Earnest Assoc .... G 302 659-0730
Hartly *(G-2941)*
Sociomatry Press .... G 302 313-5341
Lewes *(G-3753)*
Socraticlaw Co Inc .... G 302 654-9191
Wilmington *(G-12669)*
Speedy Publishing LLC .... G 888 248-4521
Newark *(G-7470)*
Spotlight Publications LLC .... G 302 504-1329
Wilmington *(G-12711)*
Sujo Music Publishing .... G 302 731-8575
Newark *(G-7500)*
Syncretic Press .... G 443 723-8355
Wilmington *(G-12834)*
Wallflowers Press .... G 302 454-1411
Newark *(G-7675)*
Willow Winters Publishing LLC .... G 570 885-2513
Middletown *(G-4287)*
Wilson Publications LLC .... G 215 237-2344
Bear *(G-378)*
Yellow Light Publishing LLC .... G 302 242-0990
Greenwood *(G-2770)*

PUBLISHERS: Music Book & Sheet Music

Melody Entertainment USA Inc .... G 305 505-7659
Wilmington *(G-11627)*
Percebe Music Inc .... G 850 341-9594
Dover *(G-1949)*

PUBLISHERS: Newsletter

T S N Publishing Co Inc .... G 302 655-6483
Wilmington *(G-12845)*

PUBLISHERS: Newspaper

Fifty Plus Monthly .... G 302 645-2938
Milton *(G-4905)*
Gatehouse Media Inc .... D 302 678-3616
Dover *(G-1583)*

Get Real On Line Classifieds .... G 302 234-6522
Hockessin *(G-3038)*
High Tide News .... G 302 727-0390
Selbyville *(G-8501)*
Hola Delaware LLC .... G 302 832-3620
Newark *(G-6735)*
Info Titan LLC .... G 510 495-4117
Dover *(G-1676)*
Sussex Countian .... G 302 856-0026
Dover *(G-2120)*
Sussex Post .... G 302 629-5505
Milford *(G-4574)*
Wilmington Trust Sp Services .... A 302 427-7650
Wilmington *(G-13264)*

PUBLISHERS: Newspapers, No Printing

Community Publications Inc .... F 302 239-4644
Middletown *(G-4002)*
Dover Post Co Inc .... G 302 378-9531
Middletown *(G-4044)*
First State Press LLC .... G 302 731-9058
Newark *(G-6585)*
Gannett Co Inc .... D 302 325-6600
New Castle *(G-5343)*
I N I Holdings Inc .... G 302 674-3600
Dover *(G-1665)*
Independent Newsmedia USA Inc .... D 302 674-3600
Dover *(G-1672)*
Morning Star Publications Inc .... F 302 629-9788
Seaford *(G-8311)*
New Castle Weekly Inc .... G 302 328-6005
New Castle *(G-5567)*

PUBLISHERS: Pamphlets, No Printing

Kardmaster Graphics .... E 610 434-5262
Wilmington *(G-11225)*

PUBLISHERS: Periodical, With Printing

Envision It Publications LLC .... G 800 329-9411
Bear *(G-144)*

PUBLISHERS: Periodicals, Magazines

Burris & Baxter Communications .... G 302 454-8511
Newark *(G-6138)*
Business History Conference .... G 302 658-2400
Wilmington *(G-9510)*
Henlopen Design LLC .... G 302 265-4330
Lewes *(G-3540)*
Hudson Valley Investment Corp .... G 302 656-1825
Wilmington *(G-10971)*
Todays Latino Magazine .... G 302 981-5131
Middletown *(G-4260)*

PUBLISHING & BROADCASTING: Internet Only

Aag La LLC .... G 305 801-7900
Dover *(G-1077)*
Additive Mfg Tech Inc .... G 540 577-9260
Wilmington *(G-8935)*
Birthdayboxio Inc .... G 302 990-2616
Wilmington *(G-9341)*
Distillate Media LLC .... G 302 270-7945
Dover *(G-1431)*
Finding A Voice Inc .... G 315 333-7567
Lewes *(G-3495)*
Glimpse Global Inc .... G 305 216-7667
Dover *(G-1593)*
Govbizconnect Inc .... G 860 341-1925
Dover *(G-1603)*
Green Pages Technologies Inc .... G 626 497-6363
Newark *(G-6686)*
Hotelrunner Inc .... E 302 956-9616
Newark *(G-6749)*
Intouch Inc .... G 302 313-2594
Dover *(G-1683)*
Lsf Networks LLC .... G 213 537-2402
Wilmington *(G-11447)*
Lumhaa LLC .... G 916 517-9972
Wilmington *(G-11450)*
Market Keys LLC .... G 205 800-0285
Wilmington *(G-11535)*
Pixstorm LLC .... G 617 365-4949
Dover *(G-1961)*
Red Ghost Interactive LLC .... G 385 485-9100
Middletown *(G-4213)*
Robotick New Media Network LLC .... G 213 219-3083
Dover *(G-2039)*

Ryan Media Lab Inc ....G....... 302 360-8847
  Lewes *(G-3727)*
Si360 Inc ....F....... 800 849-6058
  Newark *(G-7420)*
Sourcing Time LLC ....G....... 302 409-0890
  Wilmington *(G-12685)*
Web Advantage Inc ....F....... 302 479-7634
  Wilmington *(G-13133)*
Webcasting Media LLC ....G....... 302 261-5178
  Lewes *(G-3817)*
Wherebyus Enterprises Inc ....G....... 305 988-0808
  Claymont *(G-819)*
Wna Infotech LLC ....E....... 302 668-5977
  Bear *(G-379)*
Workaway Ventures Inc ....G....... 843 608-9108
  Wilmington *(G-13303)*
X Leader LLC ....G....... 800 345-2677
  Lewes *(G-3831)*
Yesllama LLC ....G....... 714 270-8731
  Dover *(G-2244)*

PUBLISHING & PRINTING: Books

Dragon Cloud Inc ....A....... 702 508-2676
  Wilmington *(G-10230)*
Heartfelt Books Publishing ....G....... 866 557-6522
  Wilmington *(G-10877)*
Moghul Life Inc ....G....... 347 560-9124
  Wilmington *(G-11724)*

PUBLISHING & PRINTING: Comic Books

Wutopia Group US Ltd ....F....... 302 488-0248
  Dover *(G-2241)*

PUBLISHING & PRINTING: Guides

Sussex Printing Corp ....D....... 302 629-9303
  Seaford *(G-8416)*

PUBLISHING & PRINTING: Magazines: publishing & printing

AB Creative Publishing LLC ....G....... 202 802-6909
  Wilmington *(G-8896)*
Advance Magazine Publs Inc ....D....... 302 830-4630
  Wilmington *(G-8946)*
CIO Story LLC ....G....... 408 915-5559
  Wilmington *(G-9710)*
Conde Nast International Inc ....E....... 515 243-3273
  Wilmington *(G-9815)*
Crafts Report Publishing Co ....F....... 302 656-2209
  Wilmington *(G-9891)*
Decoy Magazine ....G....... 302 644-9001
  Lewes *(G-3450)*
Hypebeast Inc ....E....... 714 791-0755
  Dover *(G-1663)*
Student Media Group ....F....... 302 607-2580
  Newark *(G-7496)*

PUBLISHING & PRINTING: Newsletters, Business Svc

Edit Inc ....G....... 302 478-7069
  Wilmington *(G-10351)*

PUBLISHING & PRINTING: Newspapers

Cape Gazette Ltd ....E....... 302 645-7700
  Lewes *(G-3401)*
Coastal Point ....F....... 302 539-1788
  Ocean View *(G-7779)*
County Women S Journal ....G....... 302 236-1435
  Lewes *(G-3446)*
Delaware Grapevine LLC ....G....... 302 731-8400
  Newark *(G-6381)*
Delawareblack Com LLC ....G....... 302 388-1444
  Newark *(G-6423)*
Dover Post Co Inc ....D....... 302 653-2083
  Dover *(G-1466)*
Dover Post Inc ....G....... 304 222-6025
  Milford *(G-4393)*
Hearst Media Services Conn LLC ....E....... 203 330-6231
  Wilmington *(G-10875)*
Independent Newsmedia Inc USA ....G....... 302 422-1200
  Milford *(G-4449)*
Independent Newsmedia USA Inc ....C....... 302 674-3600
  Dover *(G-1673)*
K2 Advanced Media LLC ....G....... 408 305-7007
  Wilmington *(G-11218)*
L E York Law LLC ....G....... 302 234-8338
  Wilmington *(G-11309)*

Peter Shin ....G....... 302 498-0977
  Wilmington *(G-12098)*
Review ....E....... 302 831-2771
  Newark *(G-7330)*
Smyrna News & Tobacco ....G....... 302 653-9620
  Smyrna *(G-8720)*
Spark ....G....... 302 324-2203
  New Castle *(G-5728)*
Wave Newspaper ....F....... 302 537-1881
  Bethany Beach *(G-437)*

PUBLISHING & PRINTING: Textbooks

Linguatext Ltd ....G....... 302 453-8695
  Newark *(G-6936)*

PULP MILLS

Penco Corporation ....G....... 302 629-7911
  Seaford *(G-8345)*

PUMPS

C H P T Manufacturing Inc ....G....... 302 856-7660
  Georgetown *(G-2461)*
Easy Lawn Inc ....E....... 302 815-6500
  Greenwood *(G-2736)*

PUMPS & PUMPING EQPT REPAIR SVCS

Modern Controls Inc ....E....... 302 325-6800
  New Castle *(G-5532)*

PUMPS & PUMPING EQPT WHOLESALERS

Aquaflow Pump & Supply Company .....F....... 302 834-1311
  Bear *(G-33)*
Pump and Corrosion Tech Inc ....G....... 302 655-3490
  Wilmington *(G-12269)*
Steven Brown & Associates Inc ....G....... 302 652-4722
  Wilmington *(G-12759)*
United Rentals North Amer Inc ....G....... 302 907-0292
  Delmar *(G-1046)*

PUPPETS & MARIONETTES

Pam Pipes & Puppets ....G....... 302 999-0078
  Wilmington *(G-12010)*

PURCHASING SVCS

E I Du Pont De Nemours & Co ....B....... 302 892-8832
  Wilmington *(G-10284)*
Global Merchant Partners LLC ....G....... 302 425-3567
  Rehoboth Beach *(G-7950)*
Msb Enterprise Partners LLC ....G....... 302 947-0736
  Millsboro *(G-4757)*

PURIFICATION & DUST COLLECTION EQPT

Air Natures Way Inc ....G....... 302 738-3063
  Newark *(G-5926)*

QUARTZ CRYSTALS: Electronic

Atlantic Industrial Optics ....G....... 302 856-7905
  Georgetown *(G-2438)*

QUILTING SVC & SPLYS, FOR THE TRADE

Grassy Creek Quilting ....G....... 302 528-1653
  Claymont *(G-758)*

RACETRACKS

Premier Entertainment III LLC ....E....... 302 674-4600
  Dover *(G-1982)*

RACETRACKS: Auto

Dover Intl Speedway Inc ....G....... 302 857-2114
  Dover *(G-1455)*
Dover Motorsports Inc ....G....... 302 328-6820
  New Castle *(G-5259)*
Dover Motorsports Inc ....D....... 302 883-6500
  Dover *(G-1460)*
U S 13 Dragway Inc ....D....... 302 875-1911
  Delmar *(G-1044)*

RACETRACKS: Horse

Delaware Racing Association ....B....... 302 355-1000
  Newark *(G-6405)*
Delaware Racing Association ....A....... 302 994-2521
  Wilmington *(G-10076)*

RADIO & TELEVISION COMMUNICATIONS EQUIPMENT

3d Microwave LLC ....G....... 302 497-0223
  Laurel *(G-3188)*
Gatesair Inc ....G....... 513 459-3400
  Wilmington *(G-10676)*
Quinteccent Inc ....G....... 443 838-5447
  Selbyville *(G-8536)*

RADIO BROADCASTING & COMMUNICATIONS EQPT

C4-Nvis USA LLC ....G....... 213 465-5089
  Dover *(G-1246)*

RADIO BROADCASTING STATIONS

887 The Bridge ....F....... 302 422-6909
  Milford *(G-4299)*
Beasley Broadcast Group Inc ....E....... 302 765-1160
  Wilmington *(G-9275)*
Beasley FM Acquisition Corp ....G....... 302 765-1160
  Wilmington *(G-9276)*
Delmarva Broadcasting Co Inc ....E....... 302 422-7575
  Milford *(G-4383)*
Heritage Sports Rdo Netwrk LLC ....G....... 302 492-1132
  Hartly *(G-2925)*
Iheartmedia Inc ....D....... 302 395-9800
  New Castle *(G-5411)*
Lnp Media Group Inc ....G....... 302 422-7575
  Milford *(G-4475)*
Porter Broadcasting ....G....... 302 535-8809
  Dover *(G-1977)*
Priority Radio Inc ....G....... 302 540-5690
  Newark *(G-7257)*
Samson Communications Inc ....F....... 302 424-1013
  Lincoln *(G-3867)*
Voice Radio LLC ....G....... 302 858-5118
  Georgetown *(G-2701)*
Wafl Wyus Broadcasting Inc ....E....... 302 422-7575
  Milford *(G-4592)*
Wjwk ....G....... 302 856-2567
  Georgetown *(G-2706)*
Wrdx ....G....... 302 395-9739
  New Castle *(G-5840)*

RADIO REPAIR SHOP, NEC

C B Joe TV & Appliances Inc ....F....... 302 322-7600
  New Castle *(G-5125)*

RADIO, TELEVISION & CONSUMER ELECTRONICS STORES: Eqpt, NEC

Solace Lifesciences Inc ....G....... 302 275-4195
  Wilmington *(G-12674)*

RADIO, TELEVISION & CONSUMER ELECTRONICS STORES: TV Sets

G & S TV & Antenna ....G....... 302 422-5733
  Milford *(G-4419)*

RADIO, TV & CONSUMER ELEC STORES: Tape Recorders/Players

Video Den ....G....... 302 628-9835
  Seaford *(G-8431)*

RADIO, TV & CONSUMER ELECTRONICS: VCR & Access

Brandywine Electronics Corp ....F....... 302 324-9992
  Bear *(G-56)*
Cameras Etc Inc ....F....... 302 764-9400
  Wilmington *(G-9545)*

RADIO, TV/CONSUMER ELEC STORES: Antennas, Satellite Dish

Airwave Technology ....G....... 302 734-7838
  Dover *(G-1098)*

RAILROAD CAR RENTING & LEASING SVCS

Road & Rail Services Inc ....B....... 302 731-2552
  Newark *(G-7348)*

RAILROAD CAR REPAIR SVCS

Dana Railcare Inc .... E 302 652-8550
Wilmington *(G-9952)*
Delaware Car Company .... E 302 655-6665
Wilmington *(G-10012)*

RAILROAD CARGO LOADING & UNLOADING SVCS

All Around Moverz .... G 302 494-9925
Wilmington *(G-9012)*
All In One Transportation LLC .... D 302 482-3222
Wilmington *(G-9014)*
Aloha Movers .... F 302 559-4310
Wilmington *(G-9028)*
Altra Cargo Inc .... G 302 256-0748
Wilmington *(G-9034)*
Atlantic Bulk Ltd .... F 302 378-6300
Middletown *(G-3950)*
Bay Shippers LLC .... G 302 652-5005
New Castle *(G-5072)*
Dolphin Ship Services Ltd .... G 302 832-0410
Bear *(G-123)*
Harrymirimax Logisitics .... F 302 784-5578
New Castle *(G-5378)*
Menno Freight Logistics LLC .... G 302 229-8137
Wilmington *(G-11631)*
National Auto Movers LLC .... G 302 229-9256
Smyrna *(G-8685)*
North Atlantic Ocean Ship .... G 302 652-3782
New Castle *(G-5577)*
Walter Doring .... G 302 727-6773
Rehoboth Beach *(G-8107)*

RAILROAD EQPT

Delaware Car Company .... E 302 655-6665
Wilmington *(G-10012)*

RAILROAD EQPT & SPLYS WHOLESALERS

Brakes Engine & Tracks LLC .... G 302 476-9450
Wilmington *(G-9415)*

RAILROAD EQPT: Street Cars & Eqpt

Revnation Ltd Liability Co .... G 202 672-4120
Magnolia *(G-3906)*

RAILROAD MAINTENANCE & REPAIR SVCS

Road & Rail Services Inc .... B 302 731-2552
Newark *(G-7348)*

RAILROAD TIES: Concrete

Rocla Concrete Tie Inc .... E 302 836-5304
Bear *(G-311)*

RAILROADS: Long Haul

CSX Transportation Inc .... E 302 998-8613
Wilmington *(G-9913)*
Delaware Coast Line RR Co .... G 302 422-9200
Milford *(G-4378)*
Transflo Terminal Services Inc .... F 302 994-3853
Wilmington *(G-12956)*

RAZORS, RAZOR BLADES

Cobra Razors .... G 302 540-0464
Wilmington *(G-9756)*

REAL ESTATE AGENCIES & BROKERS

Bellevue Realty Co .... F 302 655-1818
Wilmington *(G-9292)*
Bpg Real Estate Services LLC .... G 302 478-1190
Wilmington *(G-9410)*
Burton Realty Inc .... G 302 945-5100
Millsboro *(G-4650)*
Callaway Farnell and Moore .... G 302 629-4514
Seaford *(G-8180)*
Carthage Group Inc .... G 610 931-8493
Newark *(G-6163)*
Cooperealty Associates Inc .... E 302 629-6693
Seaford *(G-8207)*
D M F Associates Inc .... G 302 539-0606
Bethany Beach *(G-395)*
Dee & Doreens Team .... F 302 677-0030
Dover *(G-1349)*
Dover Consulting Services Inc .... G 302 736-1365
Dover *(G-1443)*
ERA Harrington Realty .... E 302 674-4663
Dover *(G-1527)*
Fox & Roach LLC .... E 302 239-2343
Hockessin *(G-3031)*
Golden Coastal Realty .... F 302 360-0226
Lewes *(G-3518)*
Green Oak Real Estate LP .... D 212 359-7800
Wilmington *(G-10772)*
Imaging Neuroscience Real Est .... G 302 731-9656
Newark *(G-6768)*
Jack Lingo Inc Realtor .... F 302 947-9030
Lewes *(G-3568)*
Jack Lingo Realtor .... E 302 645-2207
Lewes *(G-3569)*
Joe Maggio Realty .... G 302 539-9300
Bethany Beach *(G-407)*
Jones Enterprises Incorporated .... G 888 639-1194
Wilmington *(G-11181)*
Lc Homes Inc .... G 302 429-8700
Wilmington *(G-11347)*
Legum & Norman Mid-West LLC .... G 302 227-8448
Lewes *(G-3594)*
Long & Foster Companies Inc .... E 302 539-9040
Bethany Beach *(G-410)*
Long & Foster Companies Inc .... G 302 539-9767
Bethany Beach *(G-411)*
Marvel Agency Inc .... E 302 422-7844
Milford *(G-4488)*
New Castle Cnty Bd of Realtors .... G 302 762-6100
Wilmington *(G-11851)*
Nickle Insurance Agency Inc .... G 302 834-9700
Delaware City *(G-961)*
Ocean Atlantic Associates LLC .... F 302 227-3573
Rehoboth Beach *(G-8019)*
Patterson-Schwartz & Assoc Inc .... B 302 234-5250
Hockessin *(G-3112)*
Patterson-Schwartz & Assoc Inc .... F 302 285-5100
Middletown *(G-4182)*
Patterson-Schwartz & Assoc Inc .... E 302 672-9400
Dover *(G-1942)*
Pettinaro Construction Co Inc .... E 302 832-8823
Newark *(G-7207)*
Prudential Fox and Roach Realt .... G 302 378-9500
Bear *(G-294)*
Smalls Real Estate Company .... F 302 633-1985
Wilmington *(G-12652)*
Stoltz Realty Co .... E 302 656-8543
Wilmington *(G-12769)*
Stoltz Realty Co .... F 302 798-8500
Claymont *(G-807)*
Trans Un Sttlment Slutions Inc .... D 800 916-8800
Wilmington *(G-12953)*
Valley Stream Village Apts .... G 302 733-0844
Newark *(G-7642)*
Warner Tansey Inc .... G 302 539-3001
Bethany Beach *(G-436)*
Wilgus Associates Inc .... G 302 539-7511
Bethany Beach *(G-438)*
Yvonne Hall Inc .... G 302 677-1300
Dover *(G-2251)*

REAL ESTATE AGENCIES: Buying

CD Clean Energy and Infrastruc .... G 480 653-8450
Wilmington *(G-9603)*
First Class Properties Del LLC .... G 302 677-0770
Dover *(G-1552)*
Grapetree Inc .... G 302 655-1950
Wilmington *(G-10762)*

REAL ESTATE AGENCIES: Commercial

4 Corners LLC .... G 302 723-2264
Wilmington *(G-8860)*
Brandywine Realty Trust .... G 302 655-5900
Wilmington *(G-9453)*
Brandywood Plaza Assoc LLC .... G 302 633-9134
Wilmington *(G-9463)*
Broker Post .... G 302 628-8467
Seaford *(G-8175)*
Capital Commercial Realty LLC .... G 302 734-4400
Wilmington *(G-9556)*
CB Richard Ellis RE Svcs LLC .... G 302 661-6700
Wilmington *(G-9598)*
Cbre Inc .... G 302 661-6700
Wilmington *(G-9601)*
Cushman & Wakefield Del Inc .... G 302 655-9621
Wilmington *(G-9923)*
Delaware RE Advisors LLC .... G 302 998-4030
Wilmington *(G-10077)*
Kw Commercial .... G 302 299-1123
Wilmington *(G-11304)*
McConnell Johnson RE Co LLC .... F 302 421-2000
Wilmington *(G-11590)*
Moore & Lind Inc .... G 302 934-8818
Millsboro *(G-4753)*
Musi Commercial Properties Inc .... G 302 594-1000
Wilmington *(G-11778)*
Nnn 824 North Market St LLC .... F 302 652-8013
Wilmington *(G-11892)*
Svn Commercial Real Estate .... F 410 543-2440
Delmar *(G-1034)*
Team Wilson .... G 302 888-1088
Wilmington *(G-12865)*

REAL ESTATE AGENCIES: Leasing & Rentals

Beimac LLC .... G 302 677-1965
Magnolia *(G-3881)*
Bpg Real Estate Services LLC .... E 302 777-2000
Wilmington *(G-9411)*
Chichester Business Park LLC .... G 302 379-3140
Wilmington *(G-9660)*
Dreamville LLC .... G 662 524-0917
Lewes *(G-3472)*
First Montgomery Properties .... E 302 834-8272
Bear *(G-152)*
Galloway Leasing Inc .... F 302 453-8385
Newark *(G-6634)*
J A Banks & Associates LLC .... F 914 260-2003
Smyrna *(G-8660)*
Obsidian Investors LLC .... G 954 560-1499
Middletown *(G-4177)*
Penflex III LLC .... G 302 998-0683
Wilmington *(G-12063)*
R J Farms Inc .... G 302 629-2520
Seaford *(G-8367)*
Resortquest Delaware RE LLC .... G 302 436-1100
Selbyville *(G-8540)*
Resortquest Delaware RE LLC .... F 302 541-8999
Bethany Beach *(G-428)*
Seagreen Bicycle LLP .... G 302 226-2323
Rehoboth Beach *(G-8070)*
Springside LLC .... G 302 838-7223
Newark *(G-7474)*
Summit Bridge Inv Prpts LLC .... G 410 499-1456
Newark *(G-7503)*
United Group Real Estate LLC .... E 929 999-1277
New Castle *(G-5805)*

REAL ESTATE AGENCIES: Multiple Listing Svc

Greenlea LLC .... G 302 227-7868
Rehoboth Beach *(G-7955)*
L3d LLC .... G 302 677-0031
Dover *(G-1761)*

REAL ESTATE AGENCIES: Rental

Fairville Management Co LLC .... F 302 489-2000
Hockessin *(G-3026)*
Luther Martin Foundation Dover .... G 302 674-1408
Dover *(G-1800)*
St Andrews Apartments .... F 302 834-8600
Bear *(G-334)*

REAL ESTATE AGENCIES: Residential

A C Emsley & Associates .... G 302 429-9191
Wilmington *(G-8873)*
Berkshire Hataway Home Svcs .... F 302 235-6431
Hockessin *(G-2963)*
Burns & Ellis Realty Co .... E 302 674-4220
Dover *(G-1243)*
C M L Management .... G 302 537-5599
Ocean View *(G-7771)*
C21 Gold Key Realty .... G 302 250-6801
Newark *(G-6142)*
Calatlantic Group Inc .... G 302 834-5472
Bear *(G-62)*
Century 21 Fantini Realty .... F 302 798-6688
Claymont *(G-712)*
Century 21 Mann & Sons .... D 302 227-9477
Rehoboth Beach *(G-7886)*
Century 21 Tom Livizos Inc .... G 302 737-9000
Newark *(G-6179)*
Coldwell Banker .... F 302 539-4086
Bethany Beach *(G-392)*
Coldwell Banker Rehoboth Resrt .... E 302 227-5000
Rehoboth Beach *(G-7896)*
Coldwell Bnkr Coml Amato Assoc .... G 302 224-7700
Newark *(G-6260)*

Cole Realty Inc..........F....... 302 764-4700
Wilmington *(G-9766)*
Debbie Reed..........F....... 302 227-3818
Rehoboth Beach *(G-7909)*
Delaware Realty Group Inc..........G....... 302 227-4800
Rehoboth Beach *(G-7914)*
ERA Harrington Realty..........E....... 302 363-1796
Dover *(G-1528)*
Fox & Roach LP..........E....... 302 836-2888
Bear *(G-158)*
Fox & Roach LP..........E....... 302 477-5500
Wilmington *(G-10607)*
Gallo Realty Inc..........G....... 888 624-6794
Bethany Beach *(G-401)*
Gallo Realty Inc..........G....... 302 945-7368
Rehoboth Beach *(G-7942)*
Goldenopp RE Solutions..........G....... 908 565-0510
Bear *(G-166)*
Harrington Realty Inc..........E....... 302 422-2424
Dover *(G-1631)*
Home Finders Real Estate Co..........G....... 302 655-8091
Wilmington *(G-10934)*
Home Team Realty..........F....... 302 629-7711
Seaford *(G-8267)*
Jack Lingo Inc Realtor..........E....... 302 227-3883
Rehoboth Beach *(G-7970)*
Keller Williams Realty Ce..........G....... 302 653-3624
Dover *(G-1730)*
Leslie Kopp Inc..........F....... 302 541-5207
Bethany Beach *(G-409)*
Long & Foster Real Estate Inc..........G....... 302 227-3821
Rehoboth Beach *(G-7991)*
Maggio/Shields Teams..........F....... 302 226-3770
Rehoboth Beach *(G-7994)*
Max RE Associates Inc..........E....... 302 453-3200
Newark *(G-7005)*
Max RE Associates Inc..........D....... 302 477-3900
Wilmington *(G-11578)*
Max RE Central..........F....... 302 234-3800
Hockessin *(G-3092)*
Nt Philadelphia LLC..........G....... 302 384-8967
Wilmington *(G-11919)*
Ocean Atlantic Agency Inc..........F....... 302 227-6767
Rehoboth Beach *(G-8018)*
Patterson Price RE LLC..........G....... 302 366-0200
Newark *(G-7184)*
Patterson Price RE LLC..........F....... 302 378-9550
Middletown *(G-4181)*
Patterson-Schwartz & Assoc Inc..........D....... 302 733-7000
Newark *(G-7185)*
Patterson-Schwartz & Assoc Inc..........E....... 302 429-4500
Wilmington *(G-12038)*
Prudential Gallo Realty..........F....... 302 645-6661
Lewes *(G-3700)*
RE Max of Wilmington..........E....... 302 234-2500
Wilmington *(G-12337)*
RE Max of Wilmington..........E....... 302 657-8000
Wilmington *(G-12338)*
RE/Max Horizons Inc..........E....... 302 678-4300
Dover *(G-2013)*
Real Estate Partners LLC..........G....... 302 656-0251
Wilmington *(G-12343)*
Rehoboth Realty Inc..........E....... 302 227-5000
Rehoboth Beach *(G-8055)*
Remax 1st Choice LLC..........G....... 302 378-8700
Middletown *(G-4217)*
Remax By Sea..........E....... 302 541-5000
Bethany Beach *(G-427)*
Remax Coast & Country..........G....... 302 645-0800
Lewes *(G-3714)*
Remax Sunvest Realty Corp..........E....... 302 995-1589
Wilmington *(G-12378)*
Richard Bryan..........F....... 302 645-6100
Lewes *(G-3718)*
Riggin Group..........G....... 302 235-2903
Hockessin *(G-3136)*
Rita Lynn Inc..........G....... 302 422-3904
Milford *(G-4544)*
Robinson Realestate..........G....... 302 629-4574
Seaford *(G-8381)*
Tom Wright Real Estate..........D....... 302 234-6026
Hockessin *(G-3163)*
Vickie York At Beach Realty..........G....... 302 539-2145
Millville *(G-4857)*
Wanamakers Associates LLC..........G....... 302 834-3491
Bear *(G-370)*
Watsons Auction & Realty Svc..........G....... 302 422-2392
Milford *(G-4599)*

REAL ESTATE AGENCIES: Selling

Crowley and Assoc Rlty Inc..........F....... 302 227-6131
Rehoboth Beach *(G-7904)*
JG Townsend Jr & Co Inc..........E....... 302 856-2525
Georgetown *(G-2574)*

REAL ESTATE AGENTS & MANAGERS

A-Stover Management Group LLC..........F....... 866 299-0709
Bear *(G-6)*
Babilonia Inc..........G....... 415 237-3339
Newark *(G-6039)*
Better Homes Laurel II Inc..........G....... 302 875-4282
Laurel *(G-3198)*
Bpg Office Invstors III/IV LLC..........F....... 302 691-2100
Wilmington *(G-9408)*
Brandywine Fine Properties..........F....... 302 691-3052
Wilmington *(G-9433)*
Carl M Freeman Associates Inc..........C....... 302 539-6961
Bethany Beach *(G-391)*
Cigna Real Estate Inc..........G....... 302 476-3337
Wilmington *(G-9706)*
Commonwealth Trust Co..........F....... 302 658-7214
Wilmington *(G-9792)*
E B D Management Inc..........G....... 302 428-1313
Wilmington *(G-10275)*
Ear Enterprise LLC..........G....... 302 836-8334
Bear *(G-135)*
H T G Consulting LLC..........E....... 302 322-4100
New Castle *(G-5368)*
Harrington Realty Inc..........E....... 302 736-0800
Dover *(G-1630)*
Harvey Development Co..........C....... 302 323-9300
New Castle *(G-5381)*
Hollywood Grill Restaurant..........D....... 302 655-1348
Wilmington *(G-10930)*
Lielles Investments LLC..........E....... 215 874-0770
Lewes *(G-3608)*
Local Investments LLC..........G....... 302 422-0731
Wilmington *(G-11419)*
Magron Inc..........G....... 302 324-8094
New Castle *(G-5498)*
Margaret Harris-Nemtuda..........G....... 302 477-5500
Wilmington *(G-11522)*
Nanticoke Shores Assoc LLC..........F....... 302 945-1500
Millsboro *(G-4759)*
Ocean View Farms Inc..........G....... 302 537-4042
Ocean View *(G-7808)*
Pacer International One LLC..........F....... 302 588-9500
Wilmington *(G-12003)*
Pettinaro Construction Co Inc..........D....... 302 999-0708
Wilmington *(G-12102)*
Planned Residential Communites..........F....... 302 475-4621
Wilmington *(G-12151)*
Princeton Coml Holdings LLC..........G....... 302 449-4836
Newark *(G-7253)*
Rocky Lac LLC..........F....... 302 440-5561
Bear *(G-310)*
Rush Realty LLC..........G....... 302 219-6707
Smyrna *(G-8707)*
Sovereign Capitl MGT Group Inc..........A....... 619 294-8989
Wilmington *(G-12689)*
Stormblade Inc..........G....... 302 206-1631
Dover *(G-2109)*
Topaz & Associates LLC..........F....... 302 448-8914
Newark *(G-7575)*
Tunnell Companies LP..........E....... 302 945-9300
Millsboro *(G-4816)*
Vitellus LLC..........G....... 718 782-3539
Wilmington *(G-13096)*
Wilgus Associates Inc..........F....... 302 644-2960
Lewes *(G-3823)*
Wilsons Auction Sales Inc..........G....... 302 422-3454
Lincoln *(G-3874)*

REAL ESTATE APPRAISERS

Agvisory LLC..........G....... 302 270-5165
Lewes *(G-3329)*
Appraisal Associates Inc..........G....... 302 652-0710
Wilmington *(G-9104)*
H D C Inc..........G....... 302 323-9300
Wilmington *(G-10806)*
Landmark Associates of Del..........G....... 302 645-7070
Lewes *(G-3590)*
Newmarkkfsm..........G....... 302 655-0600
Wilmington *(G-11876)*
Pencader Associates..........G....... 302 838-7838
Newark *(G-7193)*
Steven Sachs Appraisal Access..........G....... 302 477-9676
Talleyville *(G-8752)*

Wells Agency Inc..........G....... 302 422-2121
Milford *(G-4602)*

REAL ESTATE AUCTION

Sks Enterprise..........D....... 302 310-2511
Newark *(G-7437)*

REAL ESTATE BOARDS

Sussex County Assn Realtors..........G....... 302 855-2300
Georgetown *(G-2677)*

REAL ESTATE BROKERS: Manufactured Homes, On-Site

Howard M Joseph Inc..........G....... 302 335-1300
Milford *(G-4446)*
Manufctured Hsing Concepts LLC..........D....... 302 934-8848
Millsboro *(G-4734)*

REAL ESTATE ESCROW AGENCIES

Delaware Corporate Agents Inc..........G....... 302 762-8637
Wilmington *(G-10026)*

REAL ESTATE FIDUCIARIES' OFFICES

Arhc McNwdny01 LLC..........E....... 518 213-1000
Wilmington *(G-9127)*
Frontline LLC..........G....... 302 526-0877
Lewes *(G-3504)*

REAL ESTATE INVESTMENT TRUSTS

Acadia Realty Trust..........G....... 302 479-5510
Wilmington *(G-8913)*
All United Prpts Solutions LLC..........F....... 310 853-2223
Camden *(G-535)*
Bpg Office Partners Viii LLC..........E....... 302 250-3065
Wilmington *(G-9409)*
K&B Investors LLC..........G....... 302 357-9723
Wilmington *(G-11216)*
New Windsor Associates LLC..........G....... 207 774-5341
Wilmington *(G-11873)*
Southwest American Corp..........G....... 302 652-7003
Wilmington *(G-12688)*
St Lawrence Grant Ave Trust..........G....... 302 652-7978
Wilmington *(G-12724)*

REAL ESTATE LISTING SVCS

Cap Title of Delaware LLC..........G....... 302 537-3788
Ocean View *(G-7773)*

REAL ESTATE MANAGERS: Condominium

Brandywine Valley Properties..........G....... 302 475-7660
Wilmington *(G-9458)*
Mid-Atlantic Realty Co Inc..........E....... 302 658-7642
Newark *(G-7029)*

REAL ESTATE MANAGERS: Cooperative Apartment

Palladian Management LLC..........F....... 302 737-1971
Newark *(G-7172)*

REAL ESTATE OPERATORS, EXC DEVELOPERS: Apartment Hotel

Apartment Communities Corp..........D....... 302 656-7781
Wilmington *(G-9094)*
Appleby Apartments Assoc LP..........G....... 302 219-5014
New Castle *(G-5041)*
Barrettes Run Apartments..........G....... 302 368-3400
Newark *(G-6047)*
Brandywine Apartment Assoc LP..........F....... 302 475-8600
Wilmington *(G-9417)*
Brookside Plaza Apartments LLC..........G....... 302 737-2008
Newark *(G-6125)*
Chelten Apartments Assoc LP..........F....... 302 322-6323
Wilmington *(G-9643)*
Cranston Hall Apartments..........G....... 302 999-7001
Wilmington *(G-9894)*
Foxwood Apts Rehab..........G....... 302 366-8790
Newark *(G-6610)*
Galloway Court Apts..........G....... 302 328-0488
New Castle *(G-5341)*
Georgtown Prsrvation Assoc LLC..........G....... 302 856-1557
Wilmington *(G-10704)*
Iron Hill Apartments Assoc..........G....... 302 366-8228
Newark *(G-6806)*

PRDT & SVC

REAL ESTATE OPERATORS, EXC DEVELOPERS: Apartment Hotel

Rp Management Inc ....G...... 302 798-6878
  Claymont *(G-801)*
Schoolhouse Trust Inc ....F...... 302 322-6161
  Bear *(G-315)*
University Garden Associates ....G...... 302 368-3823
  Newark *(G-7617)*
Westover Management Company LP....G...... 302 738-5775
  Newark *(G-7687)*
Westover Management Company LP....F...... 302 731-1638
  Newark *(G-7688)*
Woodland Apartments LP ....G...... 302 994-9003
  Wilmington *(G-13295)*

REAL ESTATE OPERATORS, EXC DEVELOPERS: Commercial/Indl Bldg

AAA Club Alliance Inc ....B...... 302 299-4700
  Wilmington *(G-8893)*
Aftermath Services LLC ....E...... 302 357-3780
  Dover *(G-1093)*
Ai Enterprises ....G...... 302 764-2342
  Wilmington *(G-8985)*
Belco Inc ....G...... 302 655-1561
  Wilmington *(G-9286)*
Chabbott Ptrosky Coml Realtors ....G...... 302 678-3276
  Dover *(G-1272)*
Church Street Associates ....G...... 302 227-1599
  Rehoboth Beach *(G-7889)*
Cigna Holdings Inc ....F...... 215 761-1000
  Claymont *(G-719)*
Commerce Associates LP ....G...... 302 573-2500
  Wilmington *(G-9783)*
Dover Rent-All Inc ....F...... 302 739-0860
  Dover *(G-1469)*
Emory Hill RE Svcs Inc ....D...... 302 322-9500
  New Castle *(G-5288)*
Executive Offices Inc ....G...... 302 323-8100
  New Castle *(G-5300)*
Glasgow Shopping Center Corp ....G...... 302 836-1503
  Bear *(G-165)*
Gordy Management Inc ....G...... 302 322-3723
  New Castle *(G-5356)*
H R Phillips Inc ....E...... 302 422-4518
  Milford *(G-4430)*
Melchiorre and Melchiorre ....F...... 302 645-6311
  Lewes *(G-3634)*
Prudential Gallo Realty ....F...... 302 645-6661
  Lewes *(G-3700)*
Rodney Square Associates ....G...... 302 652-1536
  Wilmington *(G-12461)*
Tudor Enterprises L L C ....G...... 302 736-8255
  Dover *(G-2166)*
United Outdoor Advertising ....G...... 302 652-3177
  Wilmington *(G-13025)*

REAL ESTATE OPERATORS, EXC DEVELOPERS: Residential Hotel

Hub Associates ....G...... 302 674-2200
  Dover *(G-1660)*

REAL ESTATE OPERATORS, EXC DEVELOPERS: Retirement Hotel

BNai Brith Snior Ctzens Hsing ....G...... 302 798-6846
  Claymont *(G-703)*
Ingleside Homes Inc ....E...... 302 984-0950
  Wilmington *(G-11032)*
Ingleside Rtrment Aprtmnts LLC ....D...... 302 575-0250
  Wilmington *(G-11033)*
Lorelton ....E...... 302 573-3580
  Wilmington *(G-11436)*
Luther Towers III Dover Inc ....E...... 302 674-1408
  Dover *(G-1801)*
Luther Towers of Dover Inc ....E...... 302 674-1408
  Dover *(G-1803)*
Luther Village II Dover Inc ....F...... 302 674-1408
  Dover *(G-1805)*
Luther Village of Dover ....G...... 302 674-3780
  Dover *(G-1806)*
Lutheran Senior Services Inc ....G...... 302 654-4490
  Wilmington *(G-11455)*
Lutheran Snr Srvcs Ssx Cnty ....G...... 302 684-1668
  Milton *(G-4927)*
Main Towers Assoicates LP ....G...... 302 761-7327
  Wilmington *(G-11492)*
Stoneybrook Associates LP ....F...... 302 764-6450
  Wilmington *(G-12771)*

REAL ESTATE OPERATORS, EXC DEVELOPERS: Shopping Ctr

Concord Mall LLC ....E...... 302 478-9271
  Wilmington *(G-9812)*

REAL ESTATE OPS, EXC DEVELOPER: Residential Bldg, 4 Or Less

Ai Enterprises ....G...... 302 764-2342
  Wilmington *(G-8985)*
Cigna Holdings Inc ....F...... 215 761-1000
  Claymont *(G-719)*
Melchiorre and Melchiorre ....F...... 302 645-6311
  Lewes *(G-3634)*
Veterans Re-Entry Resources ....F...... 302 384-2350
  Wilmington *(G-13072)*
Wild Meadows Homes ....D...... 302 730-4700
  Dover *(G-2225)*
Zwaanendael LLC ....G...... 302 645-6466
  Lewes *(G-3837)*

RECREATIONAL & SPORTING CAMPS

Camp Arrowhead Busine ....G...... 302 448-6919
  Wilmington *(G-9546)*
Dave Arletta ....E...... 302 475-8013
  Wilmington *(G-9963)*
Matts Fish Camp Lewes De LLC ....G...... 302 539-4415
  Lewes *(G-3624)*

RECREATIONAL DEALERS: Camper & Travel Trailers

Delmarva Rv Center Inc ....E...... 302 424-4505
  Milford *(G-4385)*

RECREATIONAL VEHICLE REPAIR SVCS

True Mobility Inc ....G...... 302 836-4110
  New Castle *(G-5797)*

RECREATIONAL VEHICLE REPAIRS

Delmarva Rv Center Inc ....E...... 302 424-4505
  Milford *(G-4385)*

RECYCLABLE SCRAP & WASTE MATERIALS WHOLESALERS

Ewaste Express ....G...... 302 691-8052
  Wilmington *(G-10454)*
Newark Recycling Center Inc ....G...... 302 737-7300
  Newark *(G-7127)*

RECYCLING: Paper

Eco Plastic Products Del Inc ....G...... 302 575-9227
  Wilmington *(G-10339)*
Revolution Recovery Del LLC ....F...... 302 356-3000
  New Castle *(G-5676)*

REELS: Cable, Metal

Delmaco Manufacturing Inc ....F...... 302 856-6345
  Georgetown *(G-2506)*

REFINERS & SMELTERS: Gold, Secondary

M and R ....G...... 302 421-9838
  Wilmington *(G-11469)*

REFINERS & SMELTERS: Nonferrous Metal

Diamond State Recycling Corp ....E...... 302 655-1501
  Wilmington *(G-10147)*

REFINING: Petroleum

Discount Oil LLC ....G...... 302 737-6560
  Bear *(G-120)*
E I Du Pont De Nemours & Co ....E...... 302 452-9000
  Newark *(G-6492)*
E I Du Pont De Nemours & Co ....G...... 302 772-0016
  New Castle *(G-5271)*
Honeywell International Inc ....D...... 302 791-6700
  Claymont *(G-763)*
Innospec Inc ....F...... 302 454-8100
  Newark *(G-6782)*
Reliance Egleford Upstream LLC ....G...... 302 472-7437
  Wilmington *(G-12362)*
Sun Malaysia Petroleum Company ....G...... 302 293-6000
  Wilmington *(G-12794)*
Sun Noordzee Oil Company ....G...... 302 293-6000
  Wilmington *(G-12796)*

REFRACTORIES: Clay

Rhi Refractories Holding Co ....G...... 302 655-6497
  Wilmington *(G-12400)*

REFRIGERATION & HEATING EQUIPMENT

Beach Mobile Home Supply ....G...... 302 945-5611
  Millsboro *(G-4640)*
Eeco Inc ....G...... 302 456-1448
  Newark *(G-6506)*
Munters Corporation ....F...... 302 798-2455
  Claymont *(G-787)*
Trane US Inc ....E...... 302 395-0200
  New Castle *(G-5783)*

REFRIGERATION EQPT & SPLYS WHOLESALERS

Berry Refrigeration Co ....E...... 302 733-0933
  Newark *(G-6073)*
Greenberg Supply Co Inc ....E...... 302 656-4496
  Wilmington *(G-10777)*
R E Michel Company LLC ....G...... 302 678-0250
  Dover *(G-2006)*
R E Michel Company LLC ....G...... 302 645-0585
  Lewes *(G-3704)*
Thermo King Corporation ....E...... 302 907-0345
  Delmar *(G-1038)*
Thermo King Corporation ....E...... 302 907-0345
  Delmar *(G-1039)*
United Refrigeration Inc ....G...... 302 322-1836
  New Castle *(G-5806)*
WW Grainger Inc ....F...... 302 322-1840
  New Castle *(G-5842)*

REFRIGERATION EQPT & SPLYS, WHOLESALE: Commercial Eqpt

Delmarva Refrigeration Inc ....G...... 302 846-2727
  Delmar *(G-992)*
John R Seiberlich Inc ....D...... 302 356-2400
  New Castle *(G-5441)*

REFRIGERATION EQPT: Complete

Bluchill Inc ....G...... 302 658-2638
  New Castle *(G-5093)*

REFRIGERATION REPAIR SVCS

Delmarva Refrigeration Inc ....G...... 302 846-2727
  Delmar *(G-992)*
Morans Refrigeration Service ....F...... 703 642-1200
  Rehoboth Beach *(G-8011)*
Roto-Rooter Services Company ....E...... 302 659-7637
  Newark *(G-7367)*

REFRIGERATION SVC & REPAIR

United Technologies Corp ....F...... 800 227-7437
  New Castle *(G-5808)*

REFUSE SYSTEMS

BFI Waste Services LLC ....D...... 302 284-4440
  Felton *(G-2274)*
BFI Waste Services LLC ....E...... 302 658-4097
  Wilmington *(G-9324)*
Blue Hen Bzzrds Dspose-All LLC ....F...... 302 856-0913
  Millsboro *(G-4646)*
Mid Atlantic Waste System ....F...... 610 497-2405
  New Castle *(G-5523)*
Mid-Shore Envmtl Svcs Inc ....F...... 302 736-5504
  Bridgeville *(G-500)*
Tri-State Waste Solutions Inc ....E...... 302 622-8600
  New Castle *(G-5790)*
Waste Management Delaware Inc ....C...... 302 994-0944
  Wilmington *(G-13121)*
Waste Management Delaware Inc ....G...... 302 854-5301
  Laurel *(G-3306)*
Waste Management Michigan Inc ....G...... 302 655-1360
  New Castle *(G-5824)*

REGULATION & ADMIN, GOVT: Port Authority/Dist, Nonoperating

Delaware Secretary of State ....E...... 302 472-7678
  Wilmington *(G-10083)*

PRODUCT & SERVICES SECTION

REGULATION/ADMIN, GOVT: Water Vessel & Port Regultng Agency

Delaware River & Bay Authority .... E 800 643-3779
  Lewes *(G-3457)*

REHABILITATION CENTER, OUTPATIENT TREATMENT

Acupoint Therapeutics .... G 302 734-7716
  Dover *(G-1085)*
Advancexing Pain & Rehabltatn .... F 302 384-7439
  Newark *(G-5910)*
Ah Therapy Services LLC .... G 302 379-0528
  Wilmington *(G-8982)*
All The Difference Inc .... F 302 738-6353
  Newark *(G-5936)*
Angelic Therapy .... G 717 870-4618
  Lewes *(G-3339)*
Barker Benchark Therpy & Rehab .... G 302 659-7552
  Smyrna *(G-8580)*
Body Ease Therapy .... G 610 314-0780
  Newark *(G-6103)*
Body/Mind & Spirit Massage Thr .... G 302 453-8151
  Newark *(G-6104)*
Brandywine Occpational Therapy .... G 302 740-4798
  Wilmington *(G-9446)*
Brownstarr Therapy .... G 302 838-2645
  Newark *(G-6127)*
Capitol Nursg & Rhb Cntr LLC .... C 302 734-1199
  Dover *(G-1254)*
Cardio-Kinetics Inc .... E 302 738-6635
  Newark *(G-6152)*
Chelsea McHugh Music Therapy .... G 302 827-2335
  Milton *(G-4878)*
Chuck B Barker Pt Dpt Ocs Atc .... G 302 730-4800
  Dover *(G-1281)*
Defy Therapy Services LLC .... G 302 290-9562
  Wilmington *(G-9995)*
Delaware Back PAln&sprts Rehab .... D 302 529-8783
  Newark *(G-6364)*
Delaware Curative Workshop .... D 302 656-2521
  Wilmington *(G-10033)*
Delaware Rehabilitation Inst .... G 302 831-0315
  Newark *(G-6407)*
Delaware Spine Rehabilitation .... G 302 883-2292
  Dover *(G-1394)*
Dynamic Therapy Services LLC .... G 302 280-6953
  Laurel *(G-3225)*
Dynamic Therapy Services LLC .... G 302 566-6624
  Harrington *(G-2836)*
Easter Seal Delaware .... E 302 678-3353
  Dover *(G-1499)*
Elwyn .... D 302 658-8860
  Wilmington *(G-10385)*
Emory Massage Therapy .... G 302 290-0003
  Dover *(G-1520)*
Empowered Therapy Services .... G 302 234-4820
  Hockessin *(G-3021)*
First State Rehab Home LLC .... G 443 252-7367
  Wilmington *(G-10553)*
Henlopen Music Therapy SE .... G 302 593-7784
  Lewes *(G-3542)*
Hope Rising Therapy .... G 302 273-3194
  Newark *(G-6744)*
Hysiotherapy Associates Inc .... E 610 444-1270
  Wilmington *(G-10983)*
Informed Touch Massage Therapy .... G 302 229-8239
  Townsend *(G-8796)*
Intouch Body Therapy LLC .... G 302 537-0510
  Bethany Beach *(G-404)*
Jan Stern Eqine Asssted Thrapy .... G 302 234-9835
  Wilmington *(G-11127)*
Lake Therapy Creations .... G 410 920-7130
  Newark *(G-6913)*
Lewes Expressive Therapy .... G 302 727-3275
  Lewes *(G-3599)*
Matrix Rehabilitation Delaware .... G 302 424-1714
  Milford *(G-4490)*
Mend ME Massage Therapy Inc .... G 302 229-1250
  Wilmington *(G-11630)*
Moore Physcial Therapy .... G 302 654-8142
  Wilmington *(G-11746)*
Necessary Luxury .... G 302 764-4032
  Wilmington *(G-11827)*
Novacare Rehabilitation .... G 302 537-7762
  Ocean View *(G-7805)*
Novacare Rehabilitation .... G 302 597-9256
  Bear *(G-268)*
Novacare Rehabilitation Dover .... G 302 760-9966
  Dover *(G-1905)*
Novacare Rehabilitation Seafor .... G 302 990-2951
  Seaford *(G-8332)*
Occupational Therapy Sour .... G 302 234-2273
  Hockessin *(G-3107)*
On The Spot Massage .... G 302 545-5200
  Bear *(G-272)*
Oneness Massage Therapy .... G 302 893-0348
  Newark *(G-7153)*
Pace Inc .... E 302 999-9812
  Wilmington *(G-12002)*
Pain & Sleep Therapy Center .... G 302 314-1409
  Wilmington *(G-12005)*
Premier Spine & Rehab .... G 302 730-4878
  Dover *(G-1983)*
Premier Spine and Rehab .... G 302 404-5293
  Seaford *(G-8361)*
Presicson Pain Rhbltation Svcs .... G 302 827-2321
  Rehoboth Beach *(G-8036)*
Pro Rehab Chiropractic .... G 302 200-9102
  Lewes *(G-3698)*
Rehabitation Consultants .... E 302 478-2131
  Wilmington *(G-12368)*
Relaxing Tours LLC .... G 610 905-3852
  Greenwood *(G-2759)*
S T Progressive Strides .... G 410 775-8103
  Bear *(G-313)*
Swedish Massage Therapy .... G 302 841-3166
  Ocean View *(G-7819)*
Therapy Concierge .... G 302 319-3040
  Bear *(G-351)*
Therapy Services of Delaw .... G 302 239-2285
  Hockessin *(G-3158)*
Tidewater Physcl Thrpy and REB .... G 302 629-4024
  Seaford *(G-8422)*
Tidewater Physcl Thrpy and REB .... G 302 945-5111
  Lewes *(G-3784)*
Total Health & Rehabilitation .... G 302 999-9202
  Wilmington *(G-12939)*
Unique Massage Therapy .... G 302 359-5982
  Dover *(G-2178)*
Wilmington Pain/Rehab Cntr PA .... G 302 575-1776
  Wilmington *(G-13240)*
Worlds Best Massage Therapy .... G 302 366-8777
  Newark *(G-7723)*
Zen Therapy & Body Work .... G 302 252-1733
  Wilmington *(G-13343)*

REHABILITATION SVCS

Carpe Dia Organization .... G 302 333-7546
  Newark *(G-6161)*
Connections Community Support .... D 302 984-2302
  Wilmington *(G-9826)*
Connections Community Support .... F 302 654-9289
  Wilmington *(G-9828)*
Delaware Dagnstc Rehabilitatio .... G 302 777-3955
  Wilmington *(G-10034)*
Delaware Diagnostic & Rehab .... G 302 777-3955
  Wilmington *(G-10039)*
Hillside Center .... F 302 652-1181
  Wilmington *(G-10909)*
Jungle Gym LLC .... F 302 734-1515
  Dover *(G-1716)*
Open Door Inc .... F 302 731-1504
  Newark *(G-7155)*
Phc Inc .... F 313 831-3500
  New Castle *(G-5621)*
Puzzles of Life .... G 302 339-0327
  Wilmington *(G-12272)*
Tidewater Physcl Thrpy and REB .... G 302 684-2829
  Milton *(G-4976)*

REINSURANCE CARRIERS: Accident & Health

Architect Engineer Ins Co Risk .... G 302 658-2342
  Wilmington *(G-9123)*

RELIGIOUS SCHOOL

Harvest Community Dev Corp .... E 302 654-2613
  Wilmington *(G-10847)*

RELOCATION SVCS

Business Move Solutions Inc .... E 302 324-0080
  New Castle *(G-5124)*

REMOVERS & CLEANERS

Coatings With A Purpose Inc .... G 302 462-1465
  Georgetown *(G-2476)*

RENT-A-CAR SVCS

Avis Rent A Car System Inc .... F 302 322-2092
  New Castle *(G-5058)*
Budget Rent A Car System Inc .... G 302 652-0629
  Wilmington *(G-9500)*
Dela Belle Inv Group Corp .... G 901 279-2742
  Middletown *(G-4026)*
Enterprise Lsg Phladelphia LLC .... G 302 425-4404
  Wilmington *(G-10409)*
Enterprise Lsg Phladelphia LLC .... G 302 479-7829
  Wilmington *(G-10410)*
Enterprise Lsg Phladelphia LLC .... G 302 732-3534
  Dagsboro *(G-900)*
Hertz Corporation .... E 302 654-8312
  Wilmington *(G-10895)*
Hertz Corporation .... E 302 428-0637
  New Castle *(G-5390)*
Hertz Corporation .... E 302 428-0637
  New Castle *(G-5391)*
Hertz Corporation .... E 302 428-0637
  Wilmington *(G-10896)*
Hertz Corporation .... E 302 428-0637
  New Castle *(G-5392)*
Hertz Local Edition Corp .... G 302 678-0700
  Dover *(G-1642)*
Kent Leasing Company Inc .... E 302 697-3000
  Dover *(G-1736)*
Spallco Enterprises Inc .... G 302 368-5950
  Newark *(G-7463)*
Spallco Enterprises Inc .... G 302 762-3825
  Wilmington *(G-12692)*
Winner Group Inc .... B 302 764-5900
  Wilmington *(G-13272)*
Wreck Masters Demo Derby .... F 302 368-5544
  Bear *(G-381)*

RENTAL CENTERS: Furniture

Aarons Sales & Leasing .... G 302 628-8870
  Seaford *(G-8136)*
American Furniture Rentals Inc .... E 302 323-1682
  New Castle *(G-5032)*

RENTAL CENTERS: General

Milford Rent All Inc .... G 302 422-0100
  Milford *(G-4503)*
United Rentals North Amer Inc .... F 302 846-0955
  Delmar *(G-1045)*

RENTAL CENTERS: Party & Banquet Eqpt & Splys

Aardvark Party Rentals LLC .... G 302 331-1929
  Bear *(G-8)*
Action Rental Inc .... G 302 366-0749
  Newark *(G-5894)*
Diamond State Pty Rentl & Sls .... E 302 777-6677
  Wilmington *(G-10146)*
Milford Rental Center Inc .... G 302 422-0315
  Dover *(G-1857)*
Rent Co Inc .... F 302 674-1177
  Dover *(G-2029)*

RENTAL CENTERS: Tools

Home Depot USA Inc .... C 302 838-6818
  Newark *(G-6739)*
Home Depot USA Inc .... C 302 395-1260
  New Castle *(G-5400)*
Home Depot USA Inc .... C 302 735-8864
  Dover *(G-1652)*

RENTAL SVCS: Appliance

Brewster Products Inc .... G 302 798-1988
  Wilmington *(G-9468)*
Rent-A-Center Inc .... G 302 653-3701
  Smyrna *(G-8700)*
Rent-A-Center Inc .... E 302 322-4335
  New Castle *(G-5671)*
Rent-A-Center Inc .... G 302 731-7900
  Newark *(G-7317)*
Rent-A-Center Inc .... G 302 654-7700
  Wilmington *(G-12380)*
Rent-A-Center Inc .... G 302 678-4676
  Dover *(G-2030)*
Rent-A-Center Inc .... G 302 838-7333
  Bear *(G-302)*
Rent-A-Center Inc .... G 302 674-5060
  Dover *(G-2031)*

RENTAL SVCS: Appliance

Rent-A-Center Inc ....G....... 302 934-6700
Millsboro (G-4788)
Rent-A-Center Inc ....G....... 302 629-8925
Seaford (G-8377)
Rent-A-Center Inc ....G....... 302 734-3505
Dover (G-2032)
Rent-A-Center Inc ....G....... 302 856-9200
Georgetown (G-2636)
Rent-A-Center Inc ....G....... 302 422-1230
Milford (G-4537)

RENTAL SVCS: Audio-Visual Eqpt & Sply

A V Resources Inc ....G....... 302 994-1488
Wilmington (G-8886)
Brandywine Electronics Corp ....F....... 302 324-9992
Bear (G-56)
Mid South Audio LLC ....G....... 302 856-6993
Georgetown (G-2603)

RENTAL SVCS: Business Machine & Electronic Eqpt

B Williams Holding Corp ....F....... 302 656-8596
Wilmington (G-9214)

RENTAL SVCS: Clothing

Candlelight Bridal Formal Tlrg ....G....... 302 934-8009
Millsboro (G-4654)
Nixon Unf Rntl Svc of Lncaster ....G....... 302 656-2774
New Castle (G-5570)

RENTAL SVCS: Electronic Eqpt, Exc Computers

Junttan USA Inc ....G....... 302 500-1274
Laurel (G-3246)

RENTAL SVCS: Eqpt, Theatrical

Gobos Togo Inc ....G....... 302 426-1898
New Castle (G-5355)
Main Light Industries Inc ....C....... 302 998-8017
Wilmington (G-11491)

RENTAL SVCS: Home Cleaning & Maintenance Eqpt

Ten Talents Enterprises Inc ....G....... 302 409-0718
Middletown (G-4255)

RENTAL SVCS: Home Entertainment Eqpt

Excape Entertainment US Ltd ....G....... 949 943-9219
Wilmington (G-10457)

RENTAL SVCS: Office Facilities & Secretarial Svcs

1313 Innovation ....G....... 302 407-0420
Wilmington (G-8846)
Hq Global Workplaces Inc ....G....... 302 295-4800
Wilmington (G-10963)
Regus Corporation ....G....... 302 318-1300
Newark (G-7312)
Regus Corporation ....G....... 302 295-4800
Wilmington (G-12366)

RENTAL SVCS: Propane Eqpt

Total Construction Rentals Inc ....F....... 302 575-1132
New Castle (G-5775)

RENTAL SVCS: Stores & Yards Eqpt

Action Unlimited Resources Inc ....E....... 302 323-1455
New Castle (G-5001)

RENTAL SVCS: Tuxedo

Boutique The Bridal Ltd ....G....... 302 335-5948
Milford (G-4329)
Bridal & Tuxedo Outlet Inc ....:....... 302 731-8802
Newark (G-6118)
Formal Affairs Inc ....F....... 302 737-1519
Newark (G-6606)
Matthew Smith ....G....... 302 654-4853
Wilmington (G-11572)

RENTAL SVCS: Vending Machine

Gge Amusements ....G....... 302 227-0661
Rehoboth Beach (G-7947)
Gian-Co ....E....... 302 798-7100
Claymont (G-753)

RENTAL SVCS: Video Cassette Recorder & Access

Video Den ....G....... 302 628-9835
Seaford (G-8431)

RENTAL SVCS: Video Disk/Tape, To The General Public

Pat Cirelli ....G....... 302 322-6751
New Castle (G-5607)
Video Den ....G....... 302 628-9835
Seaford (G-8431)

RENTAL SVCS: Work Zone Traffic Eqpt, Flags, Cones, Etc

Enterprise Flasher Co Inc ....F....... 302 999-0856
Wilmington (G-10407)
Sussex Protection Service LLC ....F....... 302 337-0209
Bridgeville (G-522)

RENTAL: Passenger Car

Ace Rent-A-Car Inc ....E....... 302 368-5950
Newark (G-5892)
Burke Equipment Company ....F....... 302 629-7500
Delmar (G-977)
Ean Holdings LLC ....G....... 302 422-1167
Milford (G-4398)
Ean Holdings LLC ....G....... 302 674-5553
Dover (G-1494)
Ean Holdings LLC ....G....... 302 376-5606
Middletown (G-4047)
Enterprise Lsg Phladelphia LLC ....G....... 302 266-7777
Newark (G-6531)
Enterprise Lsg Phladelphia LLC ....G....... 302 656-5464
Wilmington (G-10411)
Enterprise Lsg Phladelphia LLC ....G....... 302 761-4545
Wilmington (G-10412)
Enterprise Lsg Phladelphia LLC ....G....... 302 292-0524
Newark (G-6532)
Enterprise Rent-A-Car ....G....... 302 323-0850
New Castle (G-5291)
Enterprise Rent-A-Car ....G....... 302 934-1216
Millsboro (G-4685)
Enterprise Rent-A-Car ....G....... 302 575-1021
Wilmington (G-10414)
Enterprise Rent-A-Car ....G....... 302 653-4330
Smyrna (G-8629)
Go4spin ....G....... 310 400-2588
Wilmington (G-10735)

RENTAL: Portable Toilet

A-1 Sanitation Service Inc ....F....... 302 322-1074
New Castle (G-4995)
AAA Portable Restroom Co Inc ....G....... 909 981-0090
Camden Wyoming (G-610)

RENTAL: Trucks, With Drivers

Michael A Sinclair Inc ....G....... 302 834-8144
Bear (G-253)

RENTAL: Video Tape & Disc

California Video 2 ....G....... 302 477-6944
Wilmington (G-9537)
Extreme Audio & Video ....G....... 302 533-7404
Newark (G-6555)

REPAIR SERVICES, NEC

Bg Truck & Trailor Repair ....G....... 302 455-9171
Middletown (G-3967)
Community Auto Repair ....G....... 302 856-3333
Georgetown (G-2478)
Croosroads Auto Repair Inc ....G....... 302 436-9100
Selbyville (G-8473)
Earls Place LLC ....G....... 302 538-8909
Felton (G-2289)
Econerd ....G....... 302 669-9279
Middletown (G-4049)
Lion Totalcare Inc ....E....... 610 444-1700
Wilmington (G-11398)

REPAIR TRAINING, COMPUTER

Carter Firm LLC ....G....... 267 420-0717
Wilmington (G-9582)
Global Computers Networks LLC ....G....... 484 686-8374
Middletown (G-4088)

REPOSSESSION SVCS

A1 Nationwide LLC ....G....... 302 327-9302
Wilmington (G-8889)

RESEARCH & DEVELOPMENT SVCS, COMMERCIAL: Engineering Lab

Applied Research Assoc Inc ....D....... 302 677-4147
Dover (G-1133)

RESEARCH, DEV & TESTING SVCS, COMM: Chem Lab, Exc Testing

Stereochemical Inc ....G....... 302 266-0700
Newark (G-7490)

RESEARCH, DEVEL & TEST SVCS, COMM: Sociological & Education

Readhowyouwant LLC ....G....... 302 730-4560
Dover (G-2014)

RESEARCH, DEVELOPMENT & TEST SVCS, COMM: Business Analysis

Ka Analytics & Tech LLC ....G....... 800 520-8178
Dover (G-1720)
Sparkia Inc ....G....... 302 636-5440
Wilmington (G-12693)

RESEARCH, DEVELOPMENT & TEST SVCS, COMM: Cmptr Hardware Dev

Aries Security LLC ....G....... 302 365-0026
Wilmington (G-9128)
Moscase Inc ....G....... 786 520-8062
Dover (G-1874)
Omnimaven Inc ....G....... 302 378-8918
Middletown (G-4178)
Research & Innovation Co ....G....... 302 281-3600
Wilmington (G-12385)
Romie LLC ....G....... 866 698-0052
Wilmington (G-12468)

RESEARCH, DEVELOPMENT & TEST SVCS, COMM: Research, Exc Lab

Ayala Pharmaceuticals Inc ....F....... 857 444-0553
Wilmington (G-9202)
Circus Associates Intelligence ....E....... 757 663-7864
Lewes (G-3422)

RESEARCH, DEVELOPMENT & TESTING SVCS, COMM: Agricultural

Nichino America Inc ....E....... 302 636-9001
Wilmington (G-11887)

RESEARCH, DEVELOPMENT & TESTING SVCS, COMM: Bus Economic Sve

Taq Incorporated ....G....... 302 734-8300
Dover (G-2130)

RESEARCH, DEVELOPMENT & TESTING SVCS, COMM: Natural Resource

Environmental Testing Inc ....G....... 302 378-5341
Middletown (G-4060)
University of Delaware ....B....... 302 831-8149
Newark (G-7627)
University of Delaware ....D....... 302 831-6300
Newark (G-7628)

RESEARCH, DEVELOPMENT & TESTING SVCS, COMM: Research Lab

Diversified Chemical Pdts Inc ....G....... 302 656-5293
Wilmington (G-10169)
Dupont Displays Inc ....E....... 805 562-9293
Wilmington (G-10253)
Frontier Scientific Svcs Inc ....G....... 302 266-6891
Newark (G-6627)

PRODUCT & SERVICES SECTION

RESEARCH, DEVELOPMENT & TESTING SVCS, COMMERCIAL: Business

Fast Intrcnnect Tchologies Inc .... G 302 465-5344
  Dover *(G-1542)*

RESEARCH, DEVELOPMENT & TESTING SVCS, COMMERCIAL: Education

University of Delaware .... E 302 831-2136
  Newark *(G-7626)*

RESEARCH, DEVELOPMENT & TESTING SVCS, COMMERCIAL: Energy

Delaware Sstnble Enrgy Utility .... G 302 883-3038
  Dover *(G-1395)*
Ener-G Group Inc .... F 917 281-0020
  Wilmington *(G-10400)*
IEC .... E 302 831-6231
  Newark *(G-6762)*
Sun Coal & Coke LLC .... A 630 824-1000
  Wilmington *(G-12792)*

RESEARCH, DEVELOPMENT & TESTING SVCS, COMMERCIAL: Medical

Fbk Medical Tubing Inc .... E 302 855-0585
  Georgetown *(G-2527)*
Merck Holdings LLC .... G 302 234-1401
  Wilmington *(G-11637)*

RESEARCH, DEVELOPMENT & TESTING SVCS, COMMERCIAL: Physical

Red Clay Inc .... G 302 239-2018
  Hockessin *(G-3132)*

RESEARCH, DEVELOPMENT SVCS, COMMERCIAL: Indl Lab

Chuck George Inc .... E 302 994-7444
  Wilmington *(G-9697)*

RESEARCH, DVLPT & TEST SVCS, COMM: Mkt Analysis or Research

Environics Analytics Inc .... E 302 600-0304
  Wilmington *(G-10418)*
Ibope Media LLC .... G 305 529-0062
  Lewes *(G-3549)*
Ivychat Inc .... F 201 567-5694
  Newark *(G-6811)*
Kc & Associates Inc .... G 302 633-3300
  Wilmington *(G-11231)*
Remline Corp .... E 302 737-7228
  Newark *(G-7316)*
Sanosil International LLC .... F 302 454-8102
  New Castle *(G-5694)*
SM Technomine Inc .... F 312 492-4386
  Wilmington *(G-12647)*

RESEARCH, DVLPT & TESTING SVCS, COMM: Mkt, Bus & Economic

Gbc International Corp .... G 404 860-2533
  Wilmington *(G-10682)*
Willowflare LLC .... G 312 428-0159
  Lewes *(G-3827)*

RESEARCH, DVLPT & TESTING SVCS, COMM: Survey, Mktg

Envision It Publications LLC .... G 800 329-9411
  Bear *(G-144)*
Pelsa Company Inc .... G 302 834-3771
  Newark *(G-7191)*
Wherebyus Enterprises Inc .... G 305 988-0808
  Claymont *(G-819)*

RESERVATION SVCS

Bookaway .... E 888 250-3414
  Newark *(G-6105)*

RESIDENTIAL CARE FOR CHILDREN

Children Fmilies First Del Inc .... E 302 629-6996
  Seaford *(G-8194)*
New Vision Services Inc .... F 484 350-6495
  Newark *(G-7108)*

RESIDENTIAL CARE FOR THE HANDICAPPED

Chimes Inc .... G 302 678-3270
  Dover *(G-1279)*
Chimes Inc .... D 302 452-3400
  Newark *(G-6199)*
Choice For Cmnty Lvng-Byview 1 .... G 302 328-4176
  New Castle *(G-5151)*
Choices For Community Living .... G 302 398-0446
  Harrington *(G-2825)*

RESIDENTIAL MENTAL HEALTH & SUBSTANCE ABUSE FACILITIES

Active Day Inc .... F 302 831-6774
  Newark *(G-5896)*
Advoserv Nj Inc .... D 302 365-8050
  Bear *(G-19)*
Assisted Living Concepts LLC .... G 302 735-8800
  Dover *(G-1148)*
Changing Faces Inc .... F 302 397-4164
  Lincoln *(G-3841)*
Correction Delaware Department .... B 302 856-5280
  Georgetown *(G-2487)*
Dunamis-Homes of Divine .... G 302 393-5778
  Camden Wyoming *(G-631)*
Elderwood Village Dover LLC .... D 516 496-1505
  Dover *(G-1511)*
Gateway House Inc .... F 302 571-8885
  Wilmington *(G-10677)*
Heritage At Milford .... F 302 422-8700
  Milford *(G-4439)*
Kencrest Services .... G 302 834-3365
  Saint Georges *(G-8127)*
Little Sisters of The Poor .... D 302 368-5886
  Newark *(G-6941)*
Living Harvest Interntl Minst .... G 302 757-4273
  Wilmington *(G-11413)*
Majalco LLC .... G 703 507-5298
  Wilmington *(G-11494)*
National Mentor Holdings Inc .... E 732 627-9890
  Millsboro *(G-4760)*
People In Transition Inc .... G 302 784-5214
  New Castle *(G-5618)*
Sunrise Senior Living LLC .... D 302 475-9163
  Wilmington *(G-12801)*
Visionquest Nonprofit Corp .... E 302 735-1666
  Dover *(G-2197)*
Windsor Place .... G 302 239-3200
  Hockessin *(G-3174)*
Young Mens Christian Associat .... C 302 571-6900
  Wilmington *(G-13332)*

RESIDENTIAL MENTALLY HANDICAPPED FACILITIES

Community Alternatives Ind Inc .... F 302 323-1436
  New Castle *(G-5187)*
Community Systems and Svcs Inc .... C 302 325-1500
  New Castle *(G-5189)*
Mosaic .... C 302 456-5995
  Newark *(G-7060)*
Mossaic .... G 302 428-1680
  Wilmington *(G-11762)*
RES-Care Inc .... E 302 323-1436
  New Castle *(G-5673)*

RESIDENTIAL REMODELERS

Advance Wndw/Sprior Siding Inc .... F 302 324-8890
  Newark *(G-5903)*
Aruanno Enterprises Inc .... G 302 530-1217
  Middletown *(G-3943)*
Astute General Contracting LLC .... G 302 383-4942
  Wilmington *(G-9169)*
Connell Construction Co .... G 302 738-9428
  Newark *(G-6287)*
D F Quillen & Sons Inc .... E 302 227-2531
  Rehoboth Beach *(G-7906)*
Dugan Dt Roofing Inc .... G 302 636-9300
  Wilmington *(G-10246)*
Eastern Home Improvements Inc .... G 302 655-9920
  Wilmington *(G-10322)*
J & S General Contractors .... F 302 658-4499
  Wilmington *(G-11098)*
Jeffrey Hatch .... G 443 496-0449
  Marydel *(G-3919)*
Joseph Devane Enterprises Inc .... F 302 703-0493
  New Castle *(G-5444)*
Kelly Maintenance Ltd Inc .... G 302 539-3956
  Ocean View *(G-7797)*
Kristin Konstruction Company .... G 302 791-9670
  Claymont *(G-772)*
Mark Ventresca Associates Inc .... G 302 239-3925
  Hockessin *(G-3089)*
PJ Fitzpatrick Inc .... D 302 325-2360
  New Castle *(G-5623)*
Preferred Contractors Inc .... G 302 798-5457
  Wilmington *(G-12211)*
Rcw Renovations Inc .... G 302 239-3714
  Hockessin *(G-3131)*
Signature Cnstr Svcs LLC .... F 302 691-1010
  New Castle *(G-5711)*
Space Makers Inc .... G 302 322-4325
  Bear *(G-330)*
Williamson Building Corp .... G 302 644-0605
  Lewes *(G-3825)*

RESORT HOTEL: Franchised

422 Hotel LLC .... D 401 946-4600
  Wilmington *(G-8861)*

RESORT HOTELS

Beach House Services .... G 302 645-2554
  Milton *(G-4867)*
Bethany Beach Ocean .... E 302 539-3201
  Bethany Beach *(G-387)*
Breakers Associates .... E 302 227-6688
  Rehoboth Beach *(G-7875)*
Gulab Management Inc .... F 302 422-8089
  Milford *(G-4427)*
Henlopen Hotel Inc .... F 302 227-2551
  Rehoboth Beach *(G-7962)*
Riverdale Park LLC .... G 302 945-2475
  Millsboro *(G-4792)*
Sands Inc .... D 302 227-2511
  Rehoboth Beach *(G-8067)*
Simpler and Sons LLC .... G 302 296-4400
  Rehoboth Beach *(G-8077)*
Surf Club .... G 302 227-7059
  Dewey Beach *(G-1060)*

RESPIRATORY THERAPY CLINIC

Christiana Care Health Sys Inc .... F 302 623-0390
  Newark *(G-6208)*
Christina Care Vna .... E 302 327-5212
  New Castle *(G-5159)*
Jennifer Lopez Moya Rpt .... G 302 836-1495
  Newark *(G-6832)*

RESTAURANTS: Delicatessen

Oceanside Seafood Mkt Deli LLC .... G 302 313-5158
  Lewes *(G-3666)*

RESTAURANTS: Full Svc, American

Delaware Beer Works Inc .... E 302 836-2739
  Bear *(G-104)*
Vincenza & Margherita Bistro .... G 302 479-7999
  Wilmington *(G-13083)*

RESTAURANTS: Full Svc, Family, Independent

Country Villa Motel .... F 814 938-8330
  Milford *(G-4366)*
Hollywood Grill Restaurant .... D 302 655-1348
  Wilmington *(G-10930)*
Pagoda Hotel Inc .... A 808 922-1233
  New Castle *(G-5597)*

RESTAURANTS: Full Svc, Seafood

Dogfish Head Inc .... F 302 226-2739
  Rehoboth Beach *(G-7918)*
Febys Fishery Inc .... E 302 998-9501
  Wilmington *(G-10511)*
Meding & Son Seafood .... F 302 335-3944
  Milford *(G-4491)*

RESTAURANTS: Limited Svc, Coffee Shop

Point Coffee Shop and Bakery .... G 302 260-9734
  Rehoboth Beach *(G-8033)*

RESTAURANTS: Limited Svc, Fast-Food, Chain

McDonalds .... G 302 674-2095
Dover *(G-1832)*

RESTAURANTS: Limited Svc, Frozen Yogurt Stand

Kohr Brothers Inc .... F 302 227-9354
Rehoboth Beach *(G-7983)*

RESTAURANTS: Limited Svc, Pizza

1000 Degrees Pizzeria .... G 609 382-3022
Wilmington *(G-8841)*
Baynum Enterprises Inc .... D 302 629-6104
Seaford *(G-8163)*
Baynum Enterprises Inc .... E 302 875-4477
Laurel *(G-3196)*
Baynum Enterprises Inc .... E 302 934-8699
Millsboro *(G-4635)*
Nicola Pizza Inc .... E 302 227-6211
Rehoboth Beach *(G-8017)*

RESTAURANTS: Limited Svc, Sandwiches & Submarines Shop

Estia Hospitality Group Inc .... F 302 798-5319
Claymont *(G-741)*

RESTROOM CLEANING SVCS

Crystal Graham .... F 302 669-9318
Middletown *(G-4016)*
Diamond State Commercial Clg .... G 215 888-2575
Bear *(G-116)*

RESUME WRITING SVCS

Linkedin Profile Services LLC .... F 703 679-7719
Wilmington *(G-11397)*

RETAIL BAKERY: Bread

Bimbo Bakeries Usa Inc .... E 302 328-0837
New Castle *(G-5091)*

RETAIL BAKERY: Doughnuts

Swami Enterprises Inc .... G 302 999-8077
Wilmington *(G-12822)*

RETAIL FIREPLACE STORES

Fireside Heart & Home .... G 302 337-3025
Bridgeville *(G-470)*
Slater Fireplaces Inc .... G 302 999-1200
Wilmington *(G-12645)*

RETAIL STORES, NEC

Dbd Wholesale LLC .... G 215 301-6277
Wilmington *(G-9975)*
Rockford Ice .... G 302 478-7280
Wilmington *(G-12449)*

RETAIL STORES: Alarm Signal Systems

Hardwood Direct LLC .... G 302 378-3692
Middletown *(G-4105)*

RETAIL STORES: Alcoholic Beverage Making Eqpt & Splys

Carol Boyd Heron .... G 302 645-0551
Lewes *(G-3407)*
Roys Electrical Service Inc .... G 302 674-3199
Cheswold *(G-663)*

RETAIL STORES: Audio-Visual Eqpt & Splys

A V Resources Inc .... G 302 994-1488
Wilmington *(G-8886)*

RETAIL STORES: Awnings

Coastal Sun Roms Prch Enclsres .... G 302 537-3679
Frankford *(G-2355)*
Prestige Powder Inc .... G 302 737-7086
Newark *(G-7248)*

RETAIL STORES: Batteries, Non-Automotive

Htk Automotive USA Corporation .... E 310 504-2283
Wilmington *(G-10969)*

RETAIL STORES: Business Machines & Eqpt

Excel Business Systems Inc .... E 302 453-1500
Newark *(G-6550)*
Gray Audograph Agency Inc .... E 302 658-1700
New Castle *(G-5359)*
Mark D Garrett .... G 302 674-2825
Dover *(G-1818)*
Qoe Inc .... G 302 455-1234
Newark *(G-7279)*
Tower Business Machines Inc .... G 302 395-1445
New Castle *(G-5780)*

RETAIL STORES: Cake Decorating Splys

Cannons Cake and Candy Sups .... G 302 738-3321
Newark *(G-6148)*

RETAIL STORES: Cleaning Eqpt & Splys

Goorland Enterprises LLC .... G 302 229-4573
Wilmington *(G-10753)*

RETAIL STORES: Coins

First State Coin Co .... G 302 734-7776
Dover *(G-1554)*

RETAIL STORES: Communication Eqpt

Visual Communications Inc .... G 302 792-9500
Claymont *(G-816)*

RETAIL STORES: Cosmetics

Sally Beauty Supply LLC .... G 302 629-5160
Seaford *(G-8383)*

RETAIL STORES: Electronic Parts & Eqpt

Denney Electric Supply Del Inc .... G 302 934-8885
Millsboro *(G-4677)*
Power Trans Inc .... F 302 337-3016
Bridgeville *(G-512)*
Xenopia LLC .... G 302 703-7050
Lewes *(G-3832)*

RETAIL STORES: Farm Eqpt & Splys

Erosion Control Products Corp .... F 302 815-6500
Greenwood *(G-2739)*
Farmers Harvest Inc .... G 302 734-7708
Dover *(G-1541)*
Hydroseeding Company LLC .... E 302 815-6500
Greenwood *(G-2745)*
W Enterprises LLC .... G 302 875-0430
Laurel *(G-3303)*

RETAIL STORES: Farm Tractors

Newark Kubota Inc .... F 302 365-6000
Newark *(G-7123)*

RETAIL STORES: Fire Extinguishers

Dp Fire & Safety Inc .... F 302 998-5430
Wilmington *(G-10217)*

RETAIL STORES: Flags

Henninger Printing Co Inc .... G 302 934-8119
Millsboro *(G-4705)*

RETAIL STORES: Hair Care Prdts

Designer Braids and Trade .... G 718 783-9078
Middletown *(G-4037)*
Total Beauty Supply Inc .... G 302 798-4647
Wilmington *(G-12936)*

RETAIL STORES: Hearing Aids

Delaware Hearing Aids .... G 302 652-3558
Wilmington *(G-10051)*
Hearsay Services of Delaware .... G 302 422-3312
Milford *(G-4437)*

RETAIL STORES: Ice

Kimos Hawaiian Shave Ice .... G 302 998-1763
Wilmington *(G-11261)*

RETAIL STORES: Medical Apparatus & Splys

American Homepatient Inc .... D 302 454-4941
Newark *(G-5953)*
Chesapeake Rehab Equipment Inc .... G 302 266-6234
Newark *(G-6194)*
Dentsply Sirona Inc .... G 302 422-4511
Milford *(G-4387)*
Marosa Surgical Industries .... F 302 674-0907
New Castle *(G-5510)*
Mid Atlntic Scientific Svc Inc .... G 302 328-4440
New Castle *(G-5524)*
Purushas Picks Inc .... G 302 918-7663
Bear *(G-295)*
Quinn-Miller Group Inc .... G 302 738-9742
Wilmington *(G-12290)*
True Mobility Inc .... G 302 836-4110
New Castle *(G-5797)*

RETAIL STORES: Mobile Telephones & Eqpt

Crossroads Wireless Holdg LLC .... E 405 946-1200
Wilmington *(G-9905)*
Interdgital Communications Inc .... D 610 878-7800
Wilmington *(G-11058)*
Interdigital Inc .... G 302 281-3600
Wilmington *(G-11059)*
Interdigital Wireless Inc .... D 302 281-3600
Wilmington *(G-11061)*
WER Wireless of Concord Inc .... F 302 478-7748
Wilmington *(G-13159)*

RETAIL STORES: Monuments, Finished To Custom Order

Abba Monument Co Inc .... G 302 738-0272
Newark *(G-5880)*

RETAIL STORES: Motors, Electric

HP Motors Inc .... G 302 368-4543
Newark *(G-6753)*

RETAIL STORES: Orthopedic & Prosthesis Applications

Independence Prosthtcs-Ortho .... G 302 369-9476
Newark *(G-6770)*
Lawall Prosthetics - Orthotics .... F 302 427-3668
Wilmington *(G-11341)*

RETAIL STORES: Plumbing & Heating Splys

Collins Mechanical Inc .... E 302 398-8877
Harrington *(G-2828)*
Delaware Plumbing Supply Co .... F 302 656-5437
New Castle *(G-5233)*

RETAIL STORES: Safety Splys & Eqpt

Enterprise Flasher Co Inc .... F 302 999-0856
Wilmington *(G-10407)*

RETAIL STORES: Swimming Pools, Above Ground

Clarks Swimming Pools Inc .... G 302 629-8835
Seaford *(G-8198)*

RETAIL STORES: Telephone & Communication Eqpt

A V C Inc .... G 302 227-2549
Rehoboth Beach *(G-7835)*
Goldstar- Cash LLC .... G 302 427-2535
Wilmington *(G-10742)*
Verizon Wireless Inc .... G 302 737-5028
Newark *(G-7651)*
Yerkie Corp .... G 302 653-1321
Clayton *(G-875)*

RETAIL STORES: Telephone Eqpt & Systems

Cellco Partnership .... F 302 376-6049
Middletown *(G-3983)*
Key-Tel Communications Inc .... G 302 475-3066
Wilmington *(G-11249)*

RETAIL STORES: Tents

Tee Pees From Rattlesnks .... G 302 654-0709
Wilmington *(G-12875)*

PRODUCT & SERVICES SECTION

RETAIL STORES: Theatrical Eqpt & Splys
Actors Attic .... G 302 734-8214
Dover *(G-1084)*

RETAIL STORES: Tombstones
Cecil Vault & Memorial Co Inc .... G 302 994-3806
Wilmington *(G-9606)*

RETAIL STORES: Vaults & Safes
Short Funeral Home Inc .... G 302 846-9814
Delmar *(G-1028)*
Short Funeral Home Inc .... G 302 875-3637
Laurel *(G-3288)*

RETAIL STORES: Water Purification Eqpt
Graver Technologies LLC .... C 302 731-1700
Newark *(G-6684)*
Watercraft LLC .... G 302 757-0786
Wilmington *(G-13122)*

RETIREMENT COMMUNITIES WITH NURSING
Little Sisters of The Poor .... D 302 368-5886
Newark *(G-6941)*

REUPHOLSTERY SVCS
Barlows Upholstery Inc .... G 302 655-3955
Wilmington *(G-9255)*
Calloways Custom Interiors Co .... G 302 994-7931
Wilmington *(G-9538)*
Charles Andrews .... G 302 378-7116
Townsend *(G-8769)*

RIDING STABLES
Wellspring Farm Inc .... G 302 798-2407
Wilmington *(G-13154)*

ROAD CONSTRUCTION EQUIPMENT WHOLESALERS
Sun Piledriving Equipment LLC .... G 302 539-6756
Frankford *(G-2392)*

ROCK SALT MINING
Oceanport LLC .... F 302 792-2212
Claymont *(G-791)*

ROLLS & ROLL COVERINGS: Rubber
Pascale Industries Inc .... F 302 421-9400
New Castle *(G-5606)*

ROOFING GRANULES
Iko Southeast Inc .... E 815 936-9600
Wilmington *(G-11003)*

ROOFING MATERIALS: Asphalt
Goldis Enterprises Inc .... G 302 764-3100
Wilmington *(G-10740)*
Goldis Holdings Inc .... D 302 764-3100
Wilmington *(G-10741)*
Iko Industries Inc .... G 302 764-3100
Wilmington *(G-10998)*
Iko Production Inc .... D 302 764-3100
Wilmington *(G-11000)*
Monroe Iko Inc .... D 302 764-3100
Wilmington *(G-11734)*

ROOMING & BOARDING HOUSES: Dormitory, Commercially Operated
Beacon Hospitality .... G 302 249-0502
Georgetown *(G-2452)*

ROOMING & BOARDING HOUSES: Lodging House, Exc Organization
DSU Student Housing LLC .... G 302 857-9566
Dover *(G-1485)*

RUBBER
Dupont Specialty Pdts USA LLC .... C 302 451-0717
Newark *(G-6480)*

Rogers Corporation .... C 302 834-2100
Bear *(G-312)*

RUBBER PRDTS
Brandywine Rubber Mills LLC .... G 267 499-3993
Wilmington *(G-9454)*

RUBBER PRDTS: Automotive, Mechanical
Hat Blue Group LLC .... F 225 288-2962
Lewes *(G-3535)*

RUBBER PRDTS: Silicone
Arlon LLC .... C 302 834-2100
Bear *(G-34)*

RUBBER STAMP, WHOLESALE
Golden Rubber Stamp Co .... G 302 658-7343
Wilmington *(G-10738)*

RUGS : Tufted
Maneto Inc .... G 302 656-4285
Wilmington *(G-11501)*

SADDLERY STORES
Chick Harness & Supply Inc .... E 302 398-4630
Harrington *(G-2824)*

SAFETY EQPT & SPLYS WHOLESALERS
McDonald Safety Equipment Inc ...... F 302 999-0151
Wilmington *(G-11594)*

SALES PROMOTION SVCS
Alexander Rv Service Center .... G 302 653-3250
Smyrna *(G-8563)*
SC Marketing US Inc .... G 714 352-4992
Wilmington *(G-12549)*

SAND & GRAVEL
Bear Materials LLC .... G 302 658-5241
New Castle *(G-5078)*
Cook Hauling LLC .... G 302 378-6451
Middletown *(G-4010)*
Goldsboro Sand and Gravel .... G 410 310-0402
Camden Wyoming *(G-643)*
Legacy Vulcan LLC .... G 302 875-5733
Seaford *(G-8292)*
Legacy Vulcan LLC .... G 302 875-0748
Georgetown *(G-2589)*
Lewis Sand and Gravel LLC .... G 302 238-0169
Millsboro *(G-4720)*
Material Transit Inc .... F 302 395-0556
New Castle *(G-5512)*
Parkway Gravel Inc .... G 302 326-0554
New Castle *(G-5604)*
Pkwy Gravel .... G 302 328-5182
New Castle *(G-5624)*

SAND MINING
Joseph M L Sand & Gravel Co .... F 302 856-7396
Georgetown *(G-2578)*

SAND: Hygrade
Stockley Materials LLC .... G 302 856-7601
Georgetown *(G-2666)*

SAND: Silica
American Minerals Inc .... G 302 652-3301
New Castle *(G-5033)*

SANDBLASTING SVC: Building Exterior
Bright Finish LLC .... G 888 974-4747
Smyrna *(G-8586)*
RPR Environmental Solutions .... G 302 362-0687
Lincoln *(G-3866)*

SANITARY SVCS: Disease Control
Infectious Diseases Cons PA .... F 302 994-9692
Newark *(G-6776)*

SANITARY SVCS: Environmental Cleanup
C&H Environmental Services .... G 302 376-0178
Middletown *(G-3978)*
County Environmental Inc .... E 302 322-8946
New Castle *(G-5201)*
Dupont North America Inc .... B 302 774-1000
Wilmington *(G-10256)*
Guardian Envmtl Svcs Co Inc .... D 302 918-3070
Newark *(G-6695)*
Hazardous Waste .... G 302 739-9403
Dover *(G-1638)*
Preferred Enviromental .... G 610 364-1106
Clayton *(G-869)*
R W Home Services Inc .... F 302 539-4683
Ocean View *(G-7810)*
Terra Systems Inc .... F 302 798-9553
Claymont *(G-810)*

SANITARY SVCS: Hazardous Waste, Collection & Disposal
Bestrans Inc .... D 302 824-0909
New Castle *(G-5087)*
Brightfields Inc .... E 302 656-9600
Wilmington *(G-9477)*
Clean Earth New Castle Inc .... E 302 427-6633
New Castle *(G-5177)*

SANITARY SVCS: Liquid Waste Collection & Disposal
Clean Delaware Inc .... F 302 684-4221
Milton *(G-4879)*

SANITARY SVCS: Nonhazardous Waste Disposal Sites
International Petro Corp Del .... D 302 421-9306
Wilmington *(G-11066)*

SANITARY SVCS: Oil Spill Cleanup
Delaware Bay & River .... F 302 645-7861
Lewes *(G-3453)*

SANITARY SVCS: Refuse Collection & Disposal Svcs
Delaware Solid Waste Authority ...... E 302 378-1407
Townsend *(G-8781)*
First State Disposal .... F 302 644-3885
Lewes *(G-3498)*
Goodeals Inc .... G 302 999-1737
Wilmington *(G-10748)*
Independent Transfer Operators ..... G 302 420-4289
Hockessin *(G-3059)*
KRC Waste Management Inc .... G 302 999-9276
Wilmington *(G-11294)*
Republic Services Inc .... E 302 658-4097
Wilmington *(G-12383)*
Toss That Junk LLC .... G 302 326-3867
Bear *(G-355)*
Waste Masters Solutions LLC .... G 302 824-0909
New Castle *(G-5825)*

SANITARY SVCS: Rubbish Collection & Disposal
Buzzards Inc .... G 302 945-3500
Millsboro *(G-4651)*
Draw Incorporated .... G 410 208-9513
Greenwood *(G-2732)*
Randolphs Refuse Service Inc .... G 302 658-5674
New Castle *(G-5665)*
Wasteflo LLC .... G 410 202-0802
Laurel *(G-3307)*

SANITARY SVCS: Sanitary Landfill, Operation Of
Cherry Island LLC .... F 302 658-5241
New Castle *(G-5144)*
Delaware Solid Waste Authority ...... E 302 764-2732
Dover *(G-1393)*
Ecg Industries Inc .... G 302 453-0535
Newark *(G-6502)*

SANITARY SVCS: Sewage Treatment Facility

James Powell .... G 302 539-2351
  Frankford *(G-2369)*

SANITARY SVCS: Waste Materials, Recycling

Able Recycling Inc .... F 302 324-1760
  Wilmington *(G-8904)*
Choice Medwaste LLC .... G 302 366-1187
  Newark *(G-6202)*
Ciancon Global LLC .... E 302 365-0956
  Wilmington *(G-9699)*
Commodities Plus Inc .... G 302 376-5219
  Newark *(G-6269)*
D & J Recycling Inc .... G 302 422-0163
  Milford *(G-4368)*
Data Guard Recycling Inc .... G 302 337-8870
  Bridgeville *(G-463)*
Delaware Recyclable Products .... F 302 655-1360
  New Castle *(G-5235)*
Delaware Solid Waste Authority .... E 302 739-5361
  Dover *(G-1392)*
Diamond State Recycling Corp .... E 302 655-1501
  Wilmington *(G-10147)*
Holland Mulch Inc .... F 302 765-3100
  Wilmington *(G-10926)*
Independent Disposal Services .... D 302 378-5400
  Townsend *(G-8795)*
Kaye Construction .... E 302 628-6962
  Seaford *(G-8285)*
Kroegers Salvage Inc .... F 302 381-7082
  Bridgeville *(G-489)*
Magnus Environmental Corp .... E 302 655-4443
  New Castle *(G-5497)*
Modular Carpet Recycling Inc .... F 484 885-5890
  New Castle *(G-5534)*
Perdue-Agrirecycle LLC .... E 302 628-2360
  Seaford *(G-8355)*
Rapid Recycling Inc .... G 302 324-5360
  New Castle *(G-5666)*
RE Community Holdings II Inc .... G 302 778-9793
  New Castle *(G-5669)*
Solutions of Advant-Edge .... G 302 533-6858
  Newark *(G-7456)*

SANITATION CHEMICALS & CLEANING AGENTS

Beauty Max Inc .... G 302 735-1705
  Dover *(G-1186)*
Dow Chemical Company .... B 302 368-4169
  Newark *(G-6467)*
Playtex Manufacturing Inc .... D 302 678-6000
  Dover *(G-1969)*

SATELLITE COMMUNICATIONS EQPT

Oros Communications LLC .... G 954 228-7399
  Wilmington *(G-11976)*
Ted Johnson Enterprises .... G 302 349-5925
  Greenwood *(G-2765)*

SATELLITES: Communications

Dorsia Alliance Ltd .... G 302 492-5052
  Wilmington *(G-10207)*
Newcosmos LLC .... G 302 838-1935
  Bear *(G-265)*

SAVINGS INSTITUTIONS: Federally Chartered

Artisans Bank Inc .... G 302 674-3214
  Dover *(G-1142)*
Capital One National Assn .... G 302 645-1360
  Rehoboth Beach *(G-7884)*
Ing Bank Fsb .... E 302 658-2200
  Wilmington *(G-11030)*
Wilmington Savings Fund Soc .... G 302 571-6500
  Wilmington *(G-13252)*
Wilmington Savings Fund Soc .... E 302 226-5648
  Rehoboth Beach *(G-8117)*

SAWING & PLANING MILLS

Byler Sawmill .... G 302 730-4208
  Dover *(G-1244)*
Gordys Lumber Inc .... F 302 875-3502
  Laurel *(G-3234)*
Grubb Lumber Company Inc .... E 302 652-2800
  Wilmington *(G-10791)*
Reserves At Sawmill .... G 302 424-1910
  Milford *(G-4539)*
Rocla Concrete Tie Inc .... E 302 836-5304
  Bear *(G-311)*
Swartzentruber Sawmill Co .... G 302 492-1665
  Hartly *(G-2942)*
Woodchuck Enterprises Inc .... G 302 239-8336
  Hockessin *(G-3175)*

SAWING & PLANING MILLS: Custom

Frank Bartsch Saw Mill .... G 302 653-9721
  Townsend *(G-8787)*

SCALE REPAIR SVCS

Widgeon Enterprises Inc .... G 302 846-9763
  Delmar *(G-1049)*

SCANNING DEVICES: Optical

Ncs Pearson Inc .... D 302 736-8006
  Dover *(G-1889)*

SCHOOL BUS SVC

Achieve Logistic Systems .... G 302 654-4701
  Wilmington *(G-8921)*
B&P Transit .... F 302 653-8466
  Smyrna *(G-8579)*
Boulden Buses Inc .... E 302 998-5463
  Wilmington *(G-9398)*
Christina School District .... B 302 454-2281
  Newark *(G-6229)*
Colonial School District .... C 302 323-2700
  New Castle *(G-5182)*
D&N Bus Service Inc .... F 302 422-3869
  Milford *(G-4369)*
Dawson Bus Service Inc .... D 302 697-9501
  Camden *(G-556)*
Dawson Bus Service Inc .... F 302 678-2594
  Dover *(G-1345)*
Dianes Bus Service .... F 302 629-4336
  Seaford *(G-8223)*
E A Slack Bus Service Inc .... G 302 697-2012
  Camden Wyoming *(G-632)*
First Student Inc .... C 302 995-9607
  Newark *(G-6587)*
Knotts Incorporated .... D 302 322-0554
  New Castle *(G-5467)*
Lambden Bus Service .... G 302 629-4358
  Seaford *(G-8290)*
Larkins Bus Service LLC .... F 302 653-5855
  Clayton *(G-861)*
Lehanes Bus Service Inc .... E 302 328-7100
  New Castle *(G-5475)*
Sutton Bus & Truck Co Inc .... D 302 995-7444
  Wilmington *(G-12821)*

SCHOOL FOR PHYSICALLY HANDICAPPED, NEC

Pressley Ridge Foundation .... G 302 366-0490
  Christiana *(G-678)*

SCIENTIFIC EQPT REPAIR SVCS

Igal Biochemical LLC .... G 302 525-2090
  Newark *(G-6765)*
Mid Atlntic Scientific Svc Inc .... G 302 328-4440
  New Castle *(G-5524)*

SCIENTIFIC INSTRUMENTS WHOLESALERS

Igal Biochemical LLC .... G 302 525-2090
  Newark *(G-6765)*
K & S Technical Services Inc .... G 302 737-9133
  Newark *(G-6864)*

SCRAP & WASTE MATERIALS, WHOLESALE: Auto Wrecking For Scrap

Delaware Auto Salvage Inc .... G 302 322-2328
  New Castle *(G-5225)*
Lkq Northeast Inc .... G 800 223-0171
  Dover *(G-1793)*

SCRAP & WASTE MATERIALS, WHOLESALE: Ferrous Metal

Billy Warren Son .... G 302 349-5767
  Greenwood *(G-2717)*

SCRAP & WASTE MATERIALS, WHOLESALE: Junk & Scrap

Murrays Motors .... G 302 628-0500
  Seaford *(G-8315)*

SCRAP & WASTE MATERIALS, WHOLESALE: Metal

Diamond State Recycling Corp .... E 302 655-1501
  Wilmington *(G-10147)*
Joseph Smith & Sons Inc .... G 302 492-8091
  Hartly *(G-2930)*
Network Scrap Metal Corp .... G 910 202-0655
  Wilmington *(G-11841)*
Steel and Metal Service .... G 302 322-9960
  New Castle *(G-5739)*

SCRUBBERS: CATV System

302 Aquatics LLC .... G 302 222-4807
  Dover *(G-1068)*

SEALANTS

Delchem Inc .... F 302 426-1800
  Wilmington *(G-10099)*

SEALING COMPOUNDS: Sealing, synthetic rubber or plastic

Max Seal Inc .... F 619 946-2650
  Lewes *(G-3625)*

SEALS: Hermetic

Century Seals Inc .... E 302 629-0324
  Seaford *(G-8185)*

SEARCH & NAVIGATION SYSTEMS

Pilots Assn For Bay River Del .... E 302 645-2229
  Lewes *(G-3690)*

SEARCH & RESCUE SVCS

Destiny Rescue Intl Inc .... G 574 529-2238
  Lewes *(G-3463)*
Mid Sussex Rescue Squad Inc .... E 302 945-2680
  Millsboro *(G-4744)*

SECRETARIAL & COURT REPORTING

Garile Inc .... E 302 366-0848
  Newark *(G-6639)*

SECRETARIAL SVCS

Maples Fiduciary Svcs Del Inc .... G 302 338-9130
  Wilmington *(G-11517)*

SECURE STORAGE SVC: Document

Ardexo Inc .... G 855 617-7500
  Dover *(G-1134)*
Iron Mountain Incorporated .... G 610 636-1424
  New Castle *(G-5425)*
Lifestyle Document MGT Inc .... G 302 856-6387
  Georgetown *(G-2591)*

SECURE STORAGE SVC: Household & Furniture

Secure Self Storage .... G 302 832-0400
  New Castle *(G-5698)*

SECURITIES DEALING

Brown Brothers Harriman & Co .... F 302 552-4040
  Wilmington *(G-9488)*

SECURITY & COMMODITY EXCHANGES

Delaware Bd Trade Holdings Inc .... F 302 298-0600
  Wilmington *(G-10005)*

SECURITY CONTROL EQPT & SYSTEMS

Golage Inc .... G 302 526-1181
  Dover *(G-1597)*
Net Monarch .... G 302 994-9407
  Wilmington *(G-11837)*
Securitech Inc .... F 302 996-9230
  Wilmington *(G-12570)*

PRODUCT & SERVICES SECTION

Solenis LLC .... B 866 337-1533
  Wilmington *(G-12677)*

SKATING RINKS: Roller

Delaware Skating Center Ltd .... E 302 697-3218
  Dover *(G-1391)*
Delaware Skating Center Ltd .... E 302 366-0473
  Newark *(G-6412)*
Skateworld Inc .... E 302 875-2121
  Seaford *(G-8402)*

SKILL TRAINING CENTER

Advanced Training Acadmey .... F 302 369-8800
  Newark *(G-5909)*
Industrial Training Cons Inc .... F 302 266-6100
  Newark *(G-6774)*

SKIN CARE PRDTS: Suntan Lotions & Oils

Richard Earl Fisher .... G 302 598-1957
  Wilmington *(G-12407)*

SLAG PRDTS

Prince Minerals LLC .... F 646 747-4200
  New Castle *(G-5642)*

SMALL BUSINESS INVESTMENT COMPANIES

Frascella Enterprises Inc .... E 267 467-4496
  Claymont *(G-748)*
Knight Capital Funding LLC .... E 888 523-4363
  Dover *(G-1755)*

SOAPS & DETERGENTS

Capriottis of Milford .... G 302 424-3309
  Milford *(G-4340)*
Suds Bar Soap & Essentials LLC .... G 302 674-1303
  Dover *(G-2111)*

SOCIAL CLUBS

Delaware Saengerbund Lib Assn .... G 302 366-9454
  Newark *(G-6410)*
Supreme Grand Lodge of U S A .... G 302 998-3549
  Wilmington *(G-12816)*
Universty & Whist Club Wlmgton .... F 302 658-5125
  Wilmington *(G-13031)*
Wilmington Elks Home Inc .... G 302 652-0313
  Wilmington *(G-13230)*

SOCIAL SERVICES INFORMATION EXCHANGE

Simplymiddle .... F 302 200-0102
  Newark *(G-7432)*
Simplymiddle LLC .... F 302 217-3460
  Wilmington *(G-12629)*
Veterans Re-Entry Resources .... F 302 384-2350
  Wilmington *(G-13072)*

SOCIAL SERVICES, NEC

ARC Finance Ltd .... G 914 478-3851
  Wilmington *(G-9115)*
Article 19 Inc .... G 302 295-4959
  Wilmington *(G-9138)*
Fathers Day Gala Inc .... G 302 981-4117
  Wilmington *(G-10507)*
Hidden Acres Rest Home Inc .... F 302 492-1962
  Marydel *(G-3918)*
Homeward Bound Inc .... F 302 737-2241
  Newark *(G-6741)*
Meghan House Inc .... G 302 253-8261
  Georgetown *(G-2601)*
Royal Mission & Ministries .... G 302 249-8863
  Laurel *(G-3286)*
Saint Georges Cultr & Arts Rev .... G 302 836-8202
  Saint Georges *(G-8129)*
Volunteers For Adolescent .... G 302 658-3331
  Wilmington *(G-13102)*

SOCIAL SVCS CENTER

Brandywine Center For Autism .... G 302 762-2636
  Wilmington *(G-9422)*
Catholic Charities Inc .... G 302 856-9578
  Georgetown *(G-2463)*
Catholic Charities Inc .... E 302 573-3122
  Wilmington *(G-9592)*

Catholic Charities Inc .... F 302 654-1184
  Wilmington *(G-9593)*
Catholic Charities Inc .... G 302 674-1600
  Dover *(G-1260)*
Catholic Charities Inc .... E 302 655-9624
  Wilmington *(G-9594)*
Catholic Charities Inc .... G 302 684-8694
  Milton *(G-4876)*
Child Inc .... C 302 832-5451
  Newark *(G-6197)*
Children Fmilies First Del Inc .... G 302 674-8384
  Dover *(G-1276)*
Delaware Breast Cancer Coalit .... G 302 644-6844
  Lewes *(G-3455)*
Delaware Breast Cancer Coalit .... F 302 778-1102
  Wilmington *(G-10007)*
Delaware Hiv Services Inc .... F 302 654-5471
  Wilmington *(G-10053)*
Epilepsy Foundation of Del .... G 302 999-9313
  Newark *(G-6535)*
Friendship House Incorporated .... F 302 652-8133
  Wilmington *(G-10641)*
Independent Resources Inc .... F 302 735-4599
  Dover *(G-1674)*
La Esperanza Inc .... F 302 854-9262
  Georgetown *(G-2585)*
Lutheran Community Services .... G 302 654-8886
  Wilmington *(G-11453)*
Peoples Place II Inc .... G 302 422-8033
  Milford *(G-4524)*
Point of Hope Inc .... G 302 731-7676
  Christiana *(G-677)*
Rauma Survivors Foundation .... G 302 275-9705
  Wilmington *(G-12323)*
Reeds Refuge Center Inc .... D 302 428-1830
  Wilmington *(G-12351)*
Salvation Army .... F 302 628-2020
  Seaford *(G-8384)*
St Anthonys Community Center .... E 302 421-3721
  Wilmington *(G-12720)*
Turning Point At Peoples Place .... G 302 424-2420
  Milford *(G-4580)*
United Cerebral Palsy of De .... F 302 764-6216
  Wilmington *(G-13022)*
Way Home Inc .... G 302 856-9870
  Georgetown *(G-2702)*
Whatcoat Social Service Agency .... F 302 734-0319
  Dover *(G-2220)*

SOCIAL SVCS, HANDICAPPED

ARC of Delaware .... E 302 996-9400
  Wilmington *(G-9118)*
Autism Delaware Inc .... F 302 224-6020
  Newark *(G-6027)*
Blossom Philadelphia .... F 215 242-4200
  Wilmington *(G-9373)*
Easter Seal Delaware .... C 302 324-4444
  New Castle *(G-5276)*
Horizon House of Delaware Inc .... E 302 658-2392
  Wilmington *(G-10953)*
Pioneer House .... E 302 286-0892
  Newark *(G-7219)*
Special Olympics Inc .... F 302 831-4653
  Newark *(G-7466)*

SOCIAL SVCS: Individual & Family

A Bail Bond By Resto & Co Inc .... G 302 312-7714
  New Castle *(G-4992)*
Allow ME Errand Service LLC .... F 302 480-0954
  Newark *(G-5942)*
Alzheimers Assn Del Chapter .... C 302 633-4420
  Wilmington *(G-9038)*
ARC A Resource Ctr For Youth .... G 302 658-6134
  Wilmington *(G-9113)*
Bear-Glasgow YMCA .... G 302 836-9622
  Newark *(G-6066)*
Children Fmilies First Del Inc .... E 302 856-2388
  Georgetown *(G-2468)*
Childrens Choice Inc .... G 302 731-9512
  Newark *(G-6198)*
Connections Community Support .... D 302 536-1952
  Seaford *(G-8204)*
Cosey Gabre .... G 302 233-0658
  Felton *(G-2284)*
Delaware Adlescent Program Inc .... E 302 531-0257
  Camden *(G-557)*
Delaware Breast Cancer Coalit .... G 302 672-6435
  Dover *(G-1360)*
Delaware Clitn Agnst Dmstc Vln .... G 302 658-2958
  Wilmington *(G-10020)*

SOCIAL SVCS: Individual & Family

Delaware Ctr For Hmless Vtrans .... F 302 898-2647
  Wilmington *(G-10031)*
Delaware Guidance Ser .... E 302 678-3020
  Dover *(G-1373)*
Delaware Juniors Volleyball .... G 302 463-4218
  Newark *(G-6391)*
Delaware Teen Challenge Inc .... F 302 629-8824
  Seaford *(G-8220)*
Delaware Wic Program .... G 302 741-2900
  Dover *(G-1405)*
Delaware Wic Program .... G 302 857-5000
  Dover *(G-1406)*
Dimarquez Intl Ministries Inc .... F 302 256-4847
  New Castle *(G-5253)*
Dover Educational & Cmnty Ctr .... F 302 883-3092
  Dover *(G-1446)*
Elohim Community Dev Corp .... G 302 856-4551
  Georgetown *(G-2521)*
F H Everett & Associates Inc .... G 302 674-2380
  Dover *(G-1536)*
Family Cnsling Ctr St Puls Inc .... F 302 576-4136
  Wilmington *(G-10486)*
Family Promise of Northern New .... G 302 998-2222
  Wilmington *(G-10495)*
First State Cmnty Action Agcy .... D 302 856-7761
  Georgetown *(G-2532)*
Freedom Ctr For Ind Living Inc .... G 302 376-4399
  Middletown *(G-4077)*
Friends & Family Practice .... G 302 537-3740
  Millville *(G-4845)*
Gem-Gradually Expanding Minds .... G 302 322-3701
  Newark *(G-6643)*
Good Samaritan Aid .... G 302 875-2425
  Laurel *(G-3233)*
Habitat For Humanity .... F 302 652-0365
  Wilmington *(G-10815)*
Habitat For Humanity Intl Inc .... G 302 855-1156
  Georgetown *(G-2553)*
Health & Social Svcs Del Dept .... F 302 337-8261
  Bridgeville *(G-480)*
Health & Social Svcs Del Dept .... D 302 857-5000
  Dover *(G-1639)*
Health & Social Svcs Del Dept .... E 302 552-3530
  Wilmington *(G-10868)*
Home For Aged Wmn-Mnquadale HM ... C 302 654-1810
  Wilmington *(G-10935)*
Hrnx LLC .... F 844 700-0090
  Dover *(G-1658)*
Idrch3 Ministries .... G 302 344-6957
  Camden *(G-581)*
Keystone Service Systems Inc .... G 302 273-3952
  Newark *(G-6882)*
Kristina Brandis .... G 516 457-2717
  Middletown *(G-4125)*
Lisa R Savage .... G 302 353-7052
  Newark *(G-6940)*
Luz D Reynoso .... G 302 358-6237
  Newark *(G-6959)*
Martin Luther Homes East Inc .... G 302 475-4920
  Wilmington *(G-11550)*
MB Veterans Center LLC .... G 302 384-2350
  Wilmington *(G-11582)*
Merakey USA .... D 302 325-3540
  New Castle *(G-5516)*
My Sisters Place Inc .... G 302 737-5303
  Newark *(G-7076)*
Nehemiah Gtwy Cmnty Dev Corp .... G 302 655-0803
  Wilmington *(G-11829)*
Open Door Inc .... G 302 629-7900
  Seaford *(G-8338)*
Patricia Ayers .... G 609 335-8923
  Newark *(G-7181)*
Pauls House Inc .... F 302 384-2350
  Wilmington *(G-12046)*
Peoples Settlement Assc of WI .... E 302 658-4133
  Wilmington *(G-12079)*
Prison Ministries Delaware Inc .... F 302 737-2792
  Newark *(G-7260)*
Rain of Light Inc .... G 302 312-7642
  Newark *(G-7296)*
Reach Riverside Dev Corp .... G 302 540-1698
  Wilmington *(G-12340)*
Resources For Human Dev Inc .... D 215 951-0300
  Newark *(G-7327)*
Ronald McDonald House Delaware .... F 302 428-5299
  Wilmington *(G-12469)*
Ryerson Geralyn .... G 302 547-3060
  Wilmington *(G-12502)*
Salvation Army .... C 302 934-3730
  Millsboro *(G-4797)*

SOCIAL SVCS: Individual & Family

Company		Phone
Salvation Army ... Wilmington *(G-12528)*	E	302 996-9400
Shelatia J Dennis ... Dover *(G-2075)*	G	302 465-0630
Shepherd Place Inc ... Dover *(G-2076)*	F	302 678-1909
Sussex Pregnancy Care Center ... Georgetown *(G-2683)*	G	302 856-4344
Tatsapod-Aame ... Wilmington *(G-12854)*	F	302 897-8963
Transitional Youth ... Greenwood *(G-2767)*	F	302 423-7543
Troy Farmer ... Bear *(G-360)*	G	888 711-0094
United Way of Delaware Inc ... Wilmington *(G-13028)*	E	302 573-3700
Unity Perspectives Inc ... Milford *(G-4587)*	G	302 265-2854
Veterans Re-Entry Resources ... Wilmington *(G-13072)*	F	302 384-2350
Wellspring Counseling Services ... Smyrna *(G-8742)*	G	302 373-8904
Young Mens Christian Associat ... Wilmington *(G-13332)*	C	302 571-6900
Young Mens Christian Associat ... Rehoboth Beach *(G-8121)*	D	302 296-9622
YWCA Delaware ... Newark *(G-7733)*	F	302 224-4060

SOCIAL WORKER

Company		Phone
American Institute For Pub Svc ... Wilmington *(G-9051)*	G	302 622-9101
Karen Kim Zogheib Lcsw ... Wilmington *(G-11226)*	G	786 897-3022
Tranquility Counseling Inc ... Newark *(G-7581)*	G	302 636-0700

SOFT DRINKS WHOLESALERS

Company		Phone
Elizabeth Beverage Company LLC ... New Castle *(G-5286)*	G	302 322-9895
Pepsi-Cola Btlg of Wilmington ... Wilmington *(G-12081)*	C	302 761-4848
Pepsi-Cola Metro Btlg Co Inc ... Wilmington *(G-12082)*	C	302 764-6770
Valentina Liquors ... Newark *(G-7641)*	G	302 368-3264

SOFTWARE PUBLISHERS: Application

Company		Phone
7c Infotech Inc ... Wilmington *(G-8866)*	G	717 288-8686
Abcware LLC ... Wilmington *(G-8900)*	G	888 755-1485
Advice Wallet Inc ... Wilmington *(G-8961)*	F	510 280-2475
AEG International LLC ... Laurel *(G-3190)*	G	302 750-6411
All Lives Matter LLC ... Dover *(G-1106)*	G	252 767-9291
Allosentry LLC ... Newark *(G-5941)*	G	617 838-7608
Almond Toc Inc ... Wilmington *(G-9027)*	G	347 756-2318
Anchor App Inc ... Wilmington *(G-9076)*	G	302 421-6890
Anvil Enterprises LLC ... Wilmington *(G-9091)*	G	323 230-9376
Audtra Benefit Corp ... Dover *(G-1159)*	G	800 991-5156
Baabao Inc ... Wilmington *(G-9216)*	G	415 990-6767
Basemark Inc ... Dover *(G-1177)*	G	832 483-7093
Bbhotel Corp ... Wilmington *(G-9270)*	G	939 272-3953
Bijoti Inc ... Wilmington *(G-9336)*	F	908 916-7764
Biritek LLC ... Dover *(G-1206)*	G	949 556-3943
Calmeet Inc ... Newark *(G-6145)*	G	469 223-0863
Cansurround Pbc ... Wilmington *(G-9552)*	G	302 540-2270
Chameleon City Inc ... Newark *(G-6184)*	G	415 964-0054
Chatngo Corporation ... Wilmington *(G-9642)*	G	302 504-4291
Coditas Inc ... Lewes *(G-3441)*	G	888 220-6200
Colorimetrix Inc ... New Castle *(G-5184)*	G	347 560-0037
Communicate U Media LLC ... Middletown *(G-4001)*	G	610 453-6501
Conventra LLC ... Middletown *(G-4008)*	G	302 378-4461
Coqonut Inc ... Wilmington *(G-9857)*	G	347 419-7709
Cryptomarket Inc ... Wilmington *(G-9908)*	G	860 222-0318
Digital Penguin Inc ... Newark *(G-6448)*	G	484 387-7803
Discidium Technology Inc ... Newark *(G-6455)*	G	347 220-5979
Done Again Software LLC ... Lewes *(G-3469)*	G	301 466-7858
Dresslikeme LLC ... Dover *(G-1480)*	G	302 450-1046
Eitv USA Inc ... Wilmington *(G-10364)*	G	305 517-7715
Eksab Corporation ... Camden *(G-567)*	G	319 371-1669
Enclave Digital Development Co ... Lewes *(G-3482)*	G	203 807-0400
Famoid Technology LLC ... New Castle *(G-5303)*	G	530 601-7284
Farnam Hall Ventures LLC ... Wilmington *(G-10500)*	G	347 687-2152
Feastfox Inc ... Dover *(G-1546)*	G	650 250-6887
Fever Labs Inc ... Camden *(G-571)*	G	646 781-7359
Fitovate LLC ... Wilmington *(G-10565)*	G	302 463-9790
Foxfire Industries LLC ... Newark *(G-6609)*	G	817 602-4900
Free Psychic Reading LLC ... Dover *(G-1566)*	G	305 439-1455
Full Game Ahead USA LLC ... Wilmington *(G-10646)*	G	302 281-0102
Giesela Inc ... Newark *(G-6653)*	G	855 556-4338
Givfolio LLC ... Newark *(G-6657)*	G	213 949-1964
Global Computers Networks LLC ... Middletown *(G-4088)*	G	484 686-8374
Go Go Go Inc ... Lewes *(G-3517)*	G	302 645-7400
Gulch Group LLC ... Rehoboth Beach *(G-7956)*	G	202 697-1756
Halligan LLC ... Lewes *(G-3530)*	G	314 488-9400
Harbin LLC ... Lewes *(G-3532)*	G	302 219-3320
Hoard Inc ... Wilmington *(G-10922)*	F	980 333-1703
Hullo Inc ... Dover *(G-1662)*	G	415 939-6534
Hungrosity LLC ... Wilmington *(G-10972)*	G	401 527-1133
Hyper Jobs LLC ... Newark *(G-6757)*	E	786 667-0905
Idf Connect Inc ... Wilmington *(G-10992)*	G	888 765-1611
Innclude LLC ... Wilmington *(G-11037)*	G	310 430-6552
Island Boy Enterprise LLC ... Bethany Beach *(G-405)*	G	904 347-4563
Itango Inc ... Wilmington *(G-11091)*	G	302 648-2646
Johnny Walker Enterprises LLC ... Lewes *(G-3575)*	G	408 500-6439
Joto Inc ... Wilmington *(G-11197)*	G	260 337-3362
Kankana LLC ... Wilmington *(G-11224)*	G	302 597-6998
Kera Cable Products LLC ... Dover *(G-1743)*	G	917 383-4013
Keystack Inc ... Newark *(G-6879)*	G	510 629-5099
Knowt Inc ... Lewes *(G-3585)*	F	848 391-0575
Life Before Us LLC ... Wilmington *(G-11384)*	G	917 690-3380
Lifesquared Inc ... Dover *(G-1785)*	G	415 475-9090
Localspin LLC ... Wilmington *(G-11421)*	G	917 232-7203
Locksign LLC ... Lewes *(G-3610)*	G	917 573-6582
Lookinn Inc ... Dover *(G-1796)*	G	302 839-2088
Magneco LLC ... Wilmington *(G-11487)*	G	302 613-0080
Merix LLC ... Lewes *(G-3638)*	G	425 659-1425
Mm Mobile LLC ... Dover *(G-1864)*	G	917 297-9534
Moving Sciences LLC ... Wilmington *(G-11764)*	G	617 871-9892
Mresource LLC ... Wilmington *(G-11768)*	G	312 608-4789
My Easy Team LLC ... Newark *(G-7075)*	G	302 722-6821
Next Generation Plant Svcs Inc ... Wilmington *(G-11880)*	G	302 654-7584
Noble Master ... Lewes *(G-3660)*	G	302 261-2018
Office Bpo LLC ... Wilmington *(G-11938)*	G	248 716-5136
Open Barn Inc ... Lewes *(G-3670)*	G	669 254-7747
Oppa Inc ... Lewes *(G-3671)*	G	732 540-0308
Oppameet LLC ... Lewes *(G-3672)*	G	732 540-0308
Ordering Inc ... Wilmington *(G-11972)*	F	888 443-6203
Oto Global Inc ... Newark *(G-7163)*	G	966 597-9694
Paypergigs Inc ... Newark *(G-7187)*	A	917 336-2162
Pbtv Global Inc ... Wilmington *(G-12050)*	F	302 292-1400
Peas and Love Corporation ... Wilmington *(G-12058)*	G	301 537-3593
Peeper Vehicle Technology Corp ... Wilmington *(G-1943)*	G	800 971-4134
Pfpc Worldwide Inc ... Wilmington *(G-12105)*	F	302 791-1700
Play US Media LLC ... Dover *(G-1965)*	G	302 924-5034
Pointless Technology LLC ... Dover *(G-1975)*	G	917 403-2264
Red Rhino Labs LLC ... Newark *(G-7307)*	G	650 275-2464
Refrating LLC ... New Castle *(G-5670)*	G	617 358-2789
Remote Inc ... Wilmington *(G-12379)*	G	302 636-5440
SEI Robotics Corporation ... Newark *(G-7402)*	C	858 752-8675
Sinc Business Corporation ... Wilmington *(G-12630)*	G	480 210-1798
Statwhiz Ventures LLC ... Wilmington *(G-12746)*	G	310 819-5427
Stay Prime Inc ... Wilmington *(G-12747)*	G	612 770-6753
Stealthorg LLC ... Dover *(G-2107)*	G	302 724-6461
Sweat Social LLC ... Dover *(G-2123)*	G	504 510-1973
Sysod Inc ... Wilmington *(G-12838)*	G	973 333-4848
Tableart LLC ... Wilmington *(G-12847)*	G	650 587-8769
Topiary Tech LLC ... Wilmington *(G-12931)*	G	302 636-5440
Tricky Minute Games Inc ... Wilmington *(G-12971)*	G	302 319-5137
Trumove Inc ... Lewes *(G-3797)*	G	917 379-7427
Ufo Development Group Inc ... Lewes *(G-3802)*	G	408 995-3217
Unadori LLC ... Dover *(G-2174)*	G	917 539-2128
Unfold Creative LLC ... Dover *(G-2176)*	G	509 850-1337
Version 40 Software LLC ... Magnolia *(G-3911)*	G	302 270-0245
Vitellus LLC ... Wilmington *(G-13096)*	G	718 782-3539
Wavertech LLC ... Wilmington *(G-13124)*	G	877 735-0897
Wbi Capital Advisors LLC ... Wilmington *(G-13127)*	G	856 361-6362
Wepro LLC ... Wilmington *(G-13157)*	G	310 650-8622
Winker Labs LLC ... Wilmington *(G-13271)*	G	630 449-8130

Wutap LLC .... G 610 457-3559
Newark (G-7725)
Zumidian .... G 302 219-3500
Wilmington (G-13354)

SOFTWARE PUBLISHERS: Business & Professional

Altr Solutions LLC .... F 888 757-2587
Dover (G-1114)
Apploye Inc .... G 925 452-6102
Newark (G-5989)
Babel Inc .... G 866 327-3465
Wilmington (G-9218)
Batescainelli LLC .... G 202 618-2040
Rehoboth Beach (G-7856)
Business Services Corp .... G 302 645-0400
Lewes (G-3395)
Clairvyant Technosolutions Inc .... E 302 999-7172
Wilmington (G-9728)
CT Corporation System .... E 302 658-4968
Wilmington (G-9914)
Directrestore LLC .... F 650 276-0384
Dover (G-1428)
Donr LLC .... G 857 400-8679
Wilmington (G-10200)
Dream Weaver LLC .... G 302 352-9473
Wilmington (G-10232)
Eclipse Software Inc .... G 212 727-1136
Wilmington (G-10338)
Floristware Inc .... G 888 531-3012
Wilmington (G-10577)
Flowpay Corporation .... G 720 425-3244
Wilmington (G-10580)
Four Point Solutions Ltd .... E 613 907-6400
Wilmington (G-10605)
Freshbooks Usa Inc .... G 416 525-5384
Wilmington (G-10637)
Get Takeout LLC .... G 800 785-6218
Lewes (G-3513)
Inspectware .... G 302 999-9601
Wilmington (G-11041)
Labware Global Services Inc .... F 302 658-8444
Wilmington (G-11321)
Labware Holdings Inc .... E 302 658-8444
Wilmington (G-11322)
Laurel Bridge Software Inc .... G 302 453-0222
Newark (G-6919)
Lityx LLC .... G 888 548-9947
Wilmington (G-11411)
Lognex Inc .... G 786 650-7755
Wilmington (G-11426)
Machine Learning Systems LLC .... G 302 299-2621
Wilmington (G-11479)
Medibid .... G 888 855-6334
Wilmington (G-11615)
Mindcentral Inc .... G 302 273-1011
Newark (G-7042)
Perceri LLC .... G 217 721-8731
Dover (G-1950)
Point of Sale Technologies .... G 302 659-5119
Clayton (G-867)
Process Academy LLC .... G 302 415-3104
Wilmington (G-12238)
Promenta LLC .... G 302 552-2922
Wilmington (G-12250)
Prosift LLC .... G 302 678-2386
Dover (G-1991)
Quantus Innovations LLC .... G 302 356-1661
Wilmington (G-12282)
Raad360 LLC .... F 855 722-3360
Newark (G-7293)
Retrocode Inc .... G 302 570-0002
Newark (G-7328)
Rfx Analyst Inc .... G 302 244-5650
Dover (G-2034)
Ru Inc .... C 917 346-0285
Wilmington (G-12488)
Singular Key Inc .... F 408 753-5848
Wilmington (G-12631)
Siriusiq Mobile LLC .... F 888 414-2047
Newark (G-7433)
Switchedon Inc .... E 415 271-1172
Lewes (G-3775)
Voice 4 Impact Inc .... G 484 410-0111
Wilmington (G-13099)
Zimple Inc .... G 877 494-6753
Dover (G-2252)

SOFTWARE PUBLISHERS: Computer Utilities

Advangelists LLC .... G 734 546-4989
Wilmington (G-8958)
Bayesian Health Inc .... G 408 205-8035
Wilmington (G-9265)
Ifi Inc .... G 718 791-7669
Newark (G-6764)

SOFTWARE PUBLISHERS: Education

Acumen Health Technologies LLC .... F 800 941-0356
Wilmington (G-8930)
Crossknowledge .... D 646 699-5983
Dover (G-1324)
Edaura Inc .... G 707 330-9836
Wilmington (G-10343)
Fluent Forever Inc .... F 262 725-1707
Lewes (G-3501)
Iexperienceilearn LLC .... G 718 704-4870
New Castle (G-5409)
Lyra Software Inc .... G 347 506-5287
Newark (G-6962)
Odyssey Technologies LLC .... D 302 525-8184
Newark (G-7143)
Paperbasket LLC .... G 516 360-3500
Dover (G-1933)
Percebe Music Inc .... G 850 341-9594
Dover (G-1949)
Rogue Elephants LLC .... G 979 264-2845
Lewes (G-3724)
Scholarjet PBc .... G 617 407-9851
Lewes (G-3733)

SOFTWARE PUBLISHERS: Home Entertainment

Alfa-Order LLC .... G 302 319-2663
Wilmington (G-9006)
Fabmanianet .... G 302 994-5801
Wilmington (G-10472)
Fun Bakery LLC .... G 858 220-0946
Dover (G-1572)
Neon Dojo LLC .... G 650 275-2395
Dover (G-1892)
Neon Fun LLC .... G 858 220-0946
Dover (G-1893)
Relytv LLC .... G 213 373-5988
Dover (G-2023)
Tap 99 LLC .... G 301 541-7395
Wilmington (G-12853)
Taply LLC .... G 650 275-2395
Dover (G-2129)

SOFTWARE PUBLISHERS: NEC

Accessquint LLC .... F 302 351-4064
Wilmington (G-8915)
Acorn Energy Inc .... G 302 656-1708
Wilmington (G-8923)
Aeres Corporation .... G 858 926-8626
New Castle (G-5013)
Aivo America Corp .... G 415 849-2288
Dover (G-1099)
Amdisvet LLC .... G 302 514-9130
Smyrna (G-8568)
Anamo Inc .... G 702 852-2992
Dover (G-1122)
App Pros LLC .... G 646 441-0788
Wilmington (G-9098)
Ardexo Inc .... G 855 617-7500
Dover (G-1134)
Atapy Software LLC .... G 657 221-9370
Lewes (G-3351)
Beatdapp Inc .... G 310 903-0244
Dover (G-1185)
Biomechsys Incorporated .... G 818 305-4436
Dover (G-1204)
Blaze Systems Corporation .... G 302 733-7235
Newark (G-6092)
Bluevault LLC .... F 302 425-4367
Wilmington (G-9385)
Chart Exchange .... G 850 376-6435
Claymont (G-714)
Charter Dynamics LLC .... G 888 260-4579
Wilmington (G-9640)
Conformit .... G 302 451-9167
Newark (G-6285)
Cosmodog Software Inc .... G 302 762-2437
Wilmington (G-9872)
Cybele Software Inc .... G 302 892-9625
Wilmington (G-9931)
Cyber 20/20 Inc .... F 203 802-8742
Newark (G-6334)
Cyberwolf Software Inc .... G 302 324-8442
Bear (G-91)
Damon Baca .... G 858 837-0800
Dover (G-1338)
Datatech Enterprises Inc .... F 540 370-0010
Selbyville (G-8478)
Derby Software LLC .... G 502 435-1371
Dover (G-1415)
Dimensional Insight Inc .... G 302 791-0687
Wilmington (G-10156)
Dodd Health Innovation LLC .... G 410 598-7266
Ocean View (G-7784)
Dxc Technology Company .... G 302 391-2762
Newark (G-6482)
Eagle Eye America Inc .... G 302 392-3600
Bear (G-134)
Easy Analytic Software Inc .... G 302 762-4271
Wilmington (G-10330)
Enth Inc .... G 630 986-8700
Wilmington (G-10416)
Famealy Inc .... G 650 492-5009
Newark (G-6565)
Heavy Key Studios LLC .... G 302 356-6832
New Castle (G-5389)
Hells Kitchen Software Ltd .... G 302 983-5644
Newark (G-6722)
Henderson Software .... G 302 239-7573
Wilmington (G-10884)
Ithaca Holdco 2 LLC .... G 650 385-5000
Wilmington (G-11092)
KOA Technologies LLC .... G 760 471-5726
Wilmington (G-11285)
Labware Inc .... G 302 658-8444
Wilmington (G-11320)
Loadbalancerorginc .... G 888 867-9504
Wilmington (G-11418)
Marble City Software Inc .... G 302 658-2583
Wilmington (G-11519)
Matter Music Inc .... F 650 793-7749
Wilmington (G-11568)
Mimix Company .... G 305 916-8602
Dover (G-1859)
Money Galaxy Inc .... F 302 319-2008
Wilmington (G-11731)
Mwidm Inc .... E 302 298-0101
Wilmington (G-11785)
Nerd Boy LLC .... G 302 857-0243
Dover (G-1894)
Nevron Software LLC .... F 302 792-0175
Wilmington (G-11847)
Nortonlifelock Inc .... G 650 527-8000
Wilmington (G-11909)
Outcome Associates LLC .... G 302 368-3637
Newark (G-7164)
Pangeamart Inc .... G 914 374-0913
Lewes (G-3677)
Pharmacy Technologies Inc .... G 877 655-3846
Lewes (G-3686)
Platenger LLC .... G 302 298-0896
Wilmington (G-12152)
Qrepublik Inc .... G 559 475-8262
Claymont (G-798)
Ram Tech Systems Inc .... E 302 832-6600
Middletown (G-4210)
Re-Up App Inc .... G 267 972-1183
Wilmington (G-12339)
Readyb Inc .... G 323 813-8710
Dover (G-2015)
Renderapps LLC .... G 919 274-0582
Dover (G-2027)
Rendezvous Inc .... G 302 645-7400
Lewes (G-3715)
Shore Consultants Ltd .... F 302 737-3375
Newark (G-7417)
Sitwa Group LLC .... G 786 802-4155
Wilmington (G-12636)
Software Bananas LLC .... G 302 348-8488
Newark (G-7453)
Solufy Corp .... E 877 476-5839
Wilmington (G-12679)
Stream App LLC .... G 610 420-5864
Wilmington (G-12775)
Symmetry Dimensions Inc .... F 302 918-5536
Wilmington (G-12831)
Thoroughbred Software Intl .... G 302 339-8383
Georgetown (G-2692)

SOFTWARE PUBLISHERS: NEC

Tom Miller Remodeling..................G....... 302 674-1637
  Dover *(G-2150)*
Verde Advantage Group LLC ....G....... 302 333-5701
  Wilmington *(G-13059)*
Vshield Software Corp ....G....... 302 531-0855
  Dover *(G-2200)*
Walltag Inc.....................................G....... 917 725-1715
  Lewes *(G-3815)*
Webstudy Inc................................G....... 888 326-4058
  Harbeson *(G-2802)*
Xapix Inc......................................G....... 408 508-4324
  Wilmington *(G-13313)*
Yorokobi Inc ....G....... 323 591-3466
  Newark *(G-7731)*

SOFTWARE PUBLISHERS: Operating Systems

Cyber Seven Technologies LLC ....G....... 302 635-7122
  Newark *(G-6335)*
Isaac Fair Corporation.....................E....... 302 324-8015
  New Castle *(G-5426)*
Romie LLC ....G....... 866 698-0052
  Wilmington *(G-12468)*
Sumuri LLC...................................G....... 302 570-0015
  Camden *(G-601)*
Talk Aware LLC ....G....... 302 645-7400
  Lewes *(G-3776)*

SOFTWARE PUBLISHERS: Publisher's

Appmotion Inc................................G....... 347 513-6533
  Wilmington *(G-9103)*
Bk 2 Si LLC ....G....... 800 246-2677
  Wilmington *(G-9344)*
Core Purchase LLC........................G....... 616 328-5715
  Wilmington *(G-9859)*
Genex Technologies Inc..................D....... 302 266-6161
  Newark *(G-6647)*
Global Gaming Business ....G....... 302 994-3898
  Wilmington *(G-10725)*
Queryloop Inc................................G....... 412 253-6265
  Newark *(G-7286)*

SOFTWARE TRAINING, COMPUTER

Bits & Bytes Inc.............................G....... 302 674-2999
  Dover *(G-1207)*
Conventra LLC ....G....... 302 378-4461
  Middletown *(G-4008)*
Discidium Technology Inc................G....... 347 220-5979
  Newark *(G-6455)*
Inov8 Inc ....G....... 302 465-5124
  Camden Wyoming *(G-646)*
Kortech Consulting Inc ....F....... 302 559-4612
  Bear *(G-220)*

SOLAR CELLS

Dupont De Nemours Inc ....B....... 302 774-1000
  Wilmington *(G-10251)*
Solar Unlimited North Amer LLC ....G....... 302 542-4580
  Lewes *(G-3754)*

SOLAR HEATING EQPT

Solar Foundations Usa Inc...............G....... 518 935-3360
  Newark *(G-7454)*

SOLID CONTAINING UNITS: Concrete

Rhi Refractories Holding Co ....G....... 302 655-6497
  Wilmington *(G-12400)*

SOUND EQPT: Electric

Max Virtual LLC ....G....... 302 525-8112
  Newark *(G-7006)*

SOUND RECORDING STUDIOS

DOE Technologies Inc ....E....... 302 792-1285
  Wilmington *(G-10181)*
Great I AM Prod Studios Inc ....G....... 302 463-2483
  New Castle *(G-5361)*
Mid South Audio LLC ....G....... 302 856-6993
  Georgetown *(G-2603)*

SPACE FLIGHT OPERATIONS, EXC GOVERNMENT

Nexus Services America LLC ....G....... 800 946-4626
  Wilmington *(G-11883)*

SPAS

1110 On Parkway Nedi Spa ....F....... 302 576-1110
  Wilmington *(G-8843)*
Afterglo Beauty Spa........................G....... 302 537-7546
  Millville *(G-4832)*
Alternative Therapy LLC ....G....... 302 368-0800
  Newark *(G-5949)*
Avenue Day Spa ....F....... 302 227-5649
  Rehoboth Beach *(G-7852)*
Christophers Hair Design ....G....... 302 378-1988
  Middletown *(G-3990)*
Haus of Lacquer LLC ....E....... 302 690-0309
  Wilmington *(G-10855)*
Hockessin Day Spa ....G....... 302 234-7573
  Hockessin *(G-3050)*
Jennifers Spa ....G....... 302 740-6363
  Newark *(G-6833)*
La Bella Vita Salon & Day Spa ....G....... 302 883-2597
  Dover *(G-1762)*
Last Tangle Salon and Spa ....G....... 302 653-6638
  Smyrna *(G-8670)*
Sanctuary Spa and Saloon ....F....... 302 475-1469
  Wilmington *(G-12537)*
Spa At Corolla Inc ....F....... 302 292-2858
  Wilmington *(G-7462)*
Via Mdical Day Spa Pasca Salon .....G....... 302 757-2830
  Wilmington *(G-13074)*

SPEAKER SYSTEMS

Soundboks Inc...............................G....... 213 436-5888
  Wilmington *(G-12684)*

SPECIAL EDUCATION SCHOOLS, PUBLIC

Lake Forest School District ....F....... 302 398-8945
  Harrington *(G-2864)*

SPECIALIZED LEGAL SVCS

Central Firm LLC............................G....... 610 470-9836
  Wilmington *(G-9615)*
Delaware Bus Incorporators Inc.......G....... 302 996-5819
  Wilmington *(G-10009)*
Express Legal Documents LLC ....E....... 212 710-1374
  Wilmington *(G-10463)*
Harvard Business Services Inc ....E....... 302 645-7400
  Lewes *(G-3534)*

SPECIALTY FOOD STORES: Health & Dietetic Food

Hockessin Chrpractic Centre PA.......G....... 302 239-8550
  Hockessin *(G-3048)*

SPECIALTY OUTPATIENT CLINICS, NEC

Behavioral Health Assoc..................G....... 302 429-6200
  Wilmington *(G-9282)*
Delmarva Surgery Ctr ....G....... 443 245-3470
  Newark *(G-6430)*
Family Planning ....G....... 302 856-5225
  Georgetown *(G-2525)*
Health & Social Svcs Del Dept ....D....... 302 857-5000
  Dover *(G-1639)*
Iveeapp Corp ....G....... 610 999-6290
  Wilmington *(G-11094)*
Kenneth Butler ....G....... 302 561-8114
  Newark *(G-6874)*
Management Pain LLC ....G....... 302 543-5180
  Wilmington *(G-11499)*
Midatlantic Pain Institute..................D....... 302 369-1700
  Newark *(G-7034)*
National Stress Clinic LLC ....G....... 646 571-8627
  Wilmington *(G-11812)*
Nemours Foundation ....A....... 302 651-4000
  Wilmington *(G-11836)*
US Dept of the Air Force ....B....... 302 677-2525
  Dover *(G-2183)*

SPECULATIVE BUILDERS: Single-Family Housing

Benchmark Builders Inc ....E....... 302 995-6945
  Wilmington *(G-9295)*
Cape Financial Services Inc............F....... 302 645-6274
  Lewes *(G-3400)*
Creative Builders Inc ....G....... 302 228-8153
  Harbeson *(G-2780)*
Gearhart Construction Inc ....G....... 302 674-5466
  Dover *(G-1587)*

PRODUCT & SERVICES SECTION

Pulte Home Corporation..................E....... 302 378-9091
  Middletown *(G-4203)*

SPEED READING INSTRUCTION

Reading Assist Institute ....F....... 302 425-4080
  Wilmington *(G-12342)*

SPICE & HERB STORES

Andre Noel Thalia..........................G....... 302 747-0813
  New Castle *(G-5038)*

SPORTING & ATHLETIC GOODS: Balls, Baseball, Football, Etc

Beachballs Com LLC ....G....... 302 628-8888
  Seaford *(G-8164)*

SPORTING & ATHLETIC GOODS: Bowling Pins

Vulcan International Corp ....F....... 302 428-3181
  Wilmington *(G-13107)*

SPORTING & ATHLETIC GOODS: Cricket Eqpt, NEC

National Cricket Associates.............G....... 302 454-7294
  Newark *(G-7085)*

SPORTING & ATHLETIC GOODS: Driving Ranges, Golf, Electronic

Golfclub LLC ....G....... 908 770-7892
  Wilmington *(G-10743)*

SPORTING & ATHLETIC GOODS: Fishing Eqpt

Bullens Bucktails Inc ....G....... 302 998-6288
  Wilmington *(G-9504)*

SPORTING & ATHLETIC GOODS: Game Calls

Bubba Game Calls ....G....... 302 332-2004
  Townsend *(G-8767)*
Competition Game Calls ....G....... 302 345-7463
  Wilmington *(G-9804)*
Devastator Game Calls LLC ....G....... 302 875-5328
  Laurel *(G-3223)*

SPORTING & ATHLETIC GOODS: Gymnasium Eqpt

Robert Fickling..............................G....... 980 422-4754
  Wilmington *(G-12437)*

SPORTING & ATHLETIC GOODS: Lacrosse Eqpt & Splys, NEC

Foldfast Goals LLC.........................G....... 302 478-7881
  Wilmington *(G-10585)*

SPORTING & ATHLETIC GOODS: Mitts & Gloves, Baseball

Masley Enterprises Inc ....E....... 302 427-9885
  Wilmington *(G-11561)*

SPORTING & ATHLETIC GOODS: Rods & Rod Parts, Fishing

JC Zimny Rod Co...........................G....... 302 998-9187
  Wilmington *(G-11136)*

SPORTING & ATHLETIC GOODS: Scoops, Crab & Fish

Prouse Enterprises LLC ....G....... 302 846-9000
  Milford *(G-4531)*

SPORTING & ATHLETIC GOODS: Shafts, Golf Club

Black & Decker Inc.........................G....... 860 827-3861
  Newark *(G-6087)*

SPORTING & ATHLETIC GOODS: Shooting Eqpt & Splys, General

J & V Shooters Supply ....G....... 302 422-5417
Milford *(G-4453)*

SPORTING & ATHLETIC GOODS: Skateboards

Kinetic Skateboarding ....G....... 856 375-2236
Wilmington *(G-11267)*
Planet X Skateboards ....G....... 484 886-9287
Wilmington *(G-12149)*

SPORTING & ATHLETIC GOODS: Snowshoes

Gym Source ....G....... 302 478-4069
Wilmington *(G-10804)*

SPORTING & ATHLETIC GOODS: Strings, Tennis Racket

Racqueteer ....G....... 302 378-1596
Middletown *(G-4209)*

SPORTING & REC GOODS, WHOLESALE: Camping Eqpt & Splys

Light My Fire Inc ....G....... 239 777-0878
Dover *(G-1787)*

SPORTING & RECREATIONAL GOODS & SPLYS WHOLESALERS

Shorty USA Inc ....G....... 302 234-7750
Hockessin *(G-3146)*
Sporting Goods Properties ....G....... 302 774-1000
Wilmington *(G-12708)*
Switch Inc ....G....... 302 738-7499
Newark *(G-7523)*
Versatile Impex Inc ....G....... 302 369-9480
Newark *(G-7652)*

SPORTING & RECREATIONAL GOODS, WHOLESALE: Diving

Posidon Adventure Inc ....F....... 302 543-5024
Wilmington *(G-12190)*

SPORTING & RECREATIONAL GOODS, WHOLESALE: Exercise

Signature Fitness Eqp LLC ....G....... 888 657-5357
Lewes *(G-3744)*

SPORTING & RECREATIONAL GOODS, WHOLESALE: Fishing

Old Inlet Bait and Tackle Inc ....F....... 302 227-7974
Rehoboth Beach *(G-8022)*

SPORTING & RECREATIONAL GOODS, WHOLESALE: Fitness

James Sutton ....F....... 302 328-5438
New Castle *(G-5435)*

SPORTING & RECREATIONAL GOODS, WHOLESALE: Gymnasium

Spring Floor Tech LLC ....G....... 302 528-3474
New Castle *(G-5730)*

SPORTING & RECREATIONAL GOODS, WHOLESALE: Outboard Motors

Eastern Group Inc ....E....... 302 737-6603
Newark *(G-6497)*

SPORTING CAMPS

Ed Hunt Inc ....G....... 302 339-8443
Dover *(G-1503)*

SPORTING FIREARMS WHOLESALERS

First State Firearms & ACC LLC ....G....... 302 322-1126
New Castle *(G-5316)*
Millers Gun Center Inc ....G....... 302 328-9747
New Castle *(G-5530)*

SPORTING GOODS

Asferik LLC ....G....... 302 981-6519
Wilmington *(G-9147)*
Disrupt Industries Delaware ....G....... 424 229-9300
Dover *(G-1429)*
Par 4 Golf Inc ....G....... 302 227-5663
Rehoboth Beach *(G-8028)*
Rukket LLC ....G....... 855 478-5538
Wilmington *(G-12492)*
Sjm Sales Inc ....G....... 302 697-6748
Camden Wyoming *(G-657)*
Sling With ME ....G....... 302 424-0111
Milford *(G-4561)*

SPORTING GOODS STORES, NEC

Midway Fitness Center ....G....... 302 645-0407
Rehoboth Beach *(G-8007)*
Rukket LLC ....G....... 855 478-5538
Wilmington *(G-12492)*
Shorty USA Inc ....G....... 302 234-7750
Hockessin *(G-3146)*
Summit North Marina ....F....... 302 836-1800
Bear *(G-341)*
Wilmington Country Club ....C....... 302 655-6171
Wilmington *(G-13228)*

SPORTING GOODS STORES: Bait & Tackle

Old Inlet Bait and Tackle Inc ....F....... 302 227-7974
Rehoboth Beach *(G-8022)*

SPORTING GOODS STORES: Firearms

Millers Gun Center Inc ....G....... 302 328-9747
New Castle *(G-5530)*
Noble Eagle Sales LLC ....F....... 302 736-5166
Dover *(G-1898)*
Police & Fire Rod & Gun Club ....G....... 302 655-0304
New Castle *(G-5630)*
Shooters Choice Inc ....G....... 302 736-5166
Dover *(G-2079)*

SPORTING GOODS STORES: Fishing Eqpt

South Shore Provisions LLC ....G....... 443 614-2442
Selbyville *(G-8546)*

SPORTING GOODS STORES: Martial Arts Eqpt & Splys

Rigbys Karate Academy ....G....... 302 735-9637
Dover *(G-2036)*

SPORTING GOODS STORES: Team sports Eqpt

Racqueteer ....G....... 302 378-1596
Middletown *(G-4209)*

SPORTING GOODS: Surfboards

Fells Point Surf Co LLC ....G....... 302 212-2005
Dewey Beach *(G-1057)*
Hague Surfboards ....G....... 302 745-9336
Lewes *(G-3528)*

SPORTS APPAREL STORES

Cato Corporation ....G....... 302 854-9548
Georgetown *(G-2464)*
Huzala Inc ....G....... 313 404-6941
Newark *(G-6756)*
Ronan Gill LLC ....F....... 877 549-7712
Wilmington *(G-12471)*

SPORTS CLUBS, MANAGERS & PROMOTERS

Five Star Franchising LLC ....G....... 646 838-3992
Wilmington *(G-10567)*

SPORTS TEAMS & CLUBS: Baseball

Wilmington Blue Rocks Baseball ....F....... 302 888-2015
Wilmington *(G-13224)*

SPRINGS: Wire

Delmaco Manufacturing Inc ....F....... 302 856-6345
Georgetown *(G-2506)*

STAFFING, EMPLOYMENT PLACEMENT

A&F Group LLC ....G....... 302 504-9937
Wilmington *(G-8887)*
Access Labor Service Inc ....F....... 302 326-2575
New Castle *(G-5000)*
Alpha Technologies Consulting ....F....... 302 898-2862
Townsend *(G-8757)*
Bernard and Bernard Inc ....G....... 302 999-7213
Wilmington *(G-9306)*
Exclusively Legal Inc ....F....... 302 239-5990
Hockessin *(G-3025)*
Insignia Global Corporation ....G....... 302 310-4107
Wilmington *(G-11039)*
Opportunity Center Inc ....D....... 302 762-0300
New Castle *(G-5589)*
Robert Half International Inc ....E....... 302 252-3162
Wilmington *(G-12439)*

STAGE LIGHTING SYSTEMS

Main Light Industries Inc ....C....... 302 998-8017
Wilmington *(G-11491)*

STAINLESS STEEL

ATI Flat Rlled Pdts Hldngs LLC ....G....... 302 368-7350
Newark *(G-6015)*

STAIRCASES & STAIRS, WOOD

Richard Hrrmann Strbilders Inc ....G....... 302 654-4329
Wilmington *(G-12408)*

STAMPINGS: Automotive

Shiloh Industries Inc ....G....... 302 656-1950
Wilmington *(G-12602)*

STATE CREDIT UNIONS, NOT FEDERALLY CHARTERED

Seaford Federal Credit Union ....G....... 302 629-7852
Seaford *(G-8389)*

STATE SAVINGS BANKS, NOT FEDERALLY CHARTERED

Artisans Bank Inc ....G....... 302 656-8188
Wilmington *(G-9139)*
Artisans Bank Inc ....D....... 302 658-6881
Wilmington *(G-9140)*
Artisans Bank Inc ....G....... 302 838-6700
Newark *(G-6007)*
Artisans Bank Inc ....G....... 302 479-2553
Wilmington *(G-9141)*
Artisans Bank Inc ....G....... 302 479-2550
Wilmington *(G-9142)*
Artisans Bank Inc ....G....... 302 674-3214
Dover *(G-1142)*
Artisans Bank Inc ....G....... 302 993-8220
Wilmington *(G-9143)*
Artisans Bank Inc ....G....... 302 738-3744
Wilmington *(G-9144)*
Artisans Bank Inc ....G....... 302 834-8800
Bear *(G-38)*
Artisans Bank Inc ....G....... 302 430-7681
Milford *(G-4309)*
Artisans Bank Inc ....G....... 302 296-0155
Rehoboth Beach *(G-7847)*

STATIC ELIMINATORS: Ind

Dane Waters ....G....... 302 377-9999
Claymont *(G-727)*

STATIONARY & OFFICE SPLYS, WHOLESALE: Looseleaf Binders

L E Stansell Inc ....G....... 302 475-1534
Wilmington *(G-11308)*

STATIONERY & OFFICE SPLYS WHOLESALERS

Nitro Impact Inc ....F....... 347 694-7000
Wilmington *(G-11890)*

STATUARY GOODS, EXC RELIGIOUS: Wholesalers

All Classics Ltd .... G 302 738-2190
Newark *(G-5933)*

STEEL & ALLOYS: Tool & Die

Link Metals LLC .... G 302 295-5066
Wilmington *(G-11396)*

STEEL FABRICATORS

Amazon Steel Construction Inc .... G 302 751-1146
Milford *(G-4305)*
Anchor Enterprises .... G 302 629-7969
Seaford *(G-8151)*
Asa V Peugh Inc .... F 302 629-7969
Seaford *(G-8156)*
Crystal Steel Fabricators Inc .... G 302 846-0277
Delmar *(G-988)*
Custom Mechanical Inc .... G 302 537-5611
Bethany Beach *(G-393)*
Deaven Development Corp .... G 302 994-5793
Wilmington *(G-9991)*
Donald F Deaven Inc .... E 302 994-5793
Wilmington *(G-10196)*
Eagle Erectors Inc .... E 302 832-9586
Bear *(G-133)*
East Coast Erectors Inc .... E 302 323-1800
New Castle *(G-5275)*
First State Fabrication LLC .... G 302 875-2417
Seaford *(G-8244)*
Industrial Products of Del .... F 302 328-6648
New Castle *(G-5415)*
Iron Works Inc .... F 302 684-1887
Milton *(G-4918)*
K & S Ironworks .... F 302 658-0040
Middletown *(G-4119)*
Messick & Gray Cnstr Inc .... E 302 337-8777
Bridgeville *(G-497)*
Messick & Gray Cnstr Inc .... F 302 337-8445
Bridgeville *(G-498)*
Miller Metal Fabrication Inc .... D 302 337-2291
Bridgeville *(G-501)*
MJM Fabrications Inc .... G 302 764-0163
Wilmington *(G-11716)*
Phillips Fabrication .... G 302 875-4424
Laurel *(G-3272)*
Potts Wldg Boiler Repr Co Inc .... C 302 453-2550
Newark *(G-7234)*
R C Fabricators Inc .... D 302 573-8989
Wilmington *(G-12293)*
Rivas Ulises .... G 302 454-8595
Newark *(G-7346)*
Ronald P Wilson .... G 302 539-4139
Frankford *(G-2384)*
Spg International LLC .... G 404 823-3934
Marydel *(G-3922)*
Tri-State Fbrction McHning LLC .... E 302 232-3133
New Castle *(G-5788)*

STEEL MILLS

Eagle Erectors Inc .... E 302 832-9586
Bear *(G-133)*
Greenbrook Tms Neurohealth Ctr ...... G 302 994-4010
Bear *(G-172)*
Stainless Steel Invest Inc .... G 800 499-7833
Wilmington *(G-12732)*

STEEL, HOT-ROLLED: Sheet Or Strip

Ah (uk) Inc .... G 302 288-0115
Wilmington *(G-8981)*

STEEL: Cold-Rolled

Stainless Alloys Inc .... G 800 499-7833
Wilmington *(G-12731)*
Stainless Steel Invest Inc .... G 800 499-7833
Wilmington *(G-12732)*

STENCILS

Hot Shot Concepts .... G 302 947-1808
Harbeson *(G-2785)*

STEVEDORING SVCS

Delaware River Stevedores Inc .... G 302 657-0472
Wilmington *(G-10081)*

Murphy Marine Services Inc .... B 302 571-4700
Wilmington *(G-11777)*

STOCK SHAPES: Plastic

Quantum Polymers Corporation .... F 302 737-7012
Newark *(G-7285)*

STONE: Crushed & Broken, NEC

Contractors Materials LLC .... G 302 656-6066
Wilmington *(G-9844)*
Pioneer Materials .... G 302 284-3580
Felton *(G-2311)*

STONE: Quarrying & Processing, Own Stone Prdts

H&K Group Inc .... G 302 934-7635
Dagsboro *(G-906)*

STORES: Auto & Home Supply

Martin Newark Dealership Inc .... C 302 454-9300
Newark *(G-6996)*
New Creation Logistics Inc .... F 302 438-3154
Newark *(G-7103)*
Winner Ford of Newark Inc .... C 302 731-2415
Newark *(G-7710)*
Winner Group Inc .... E 302 292-8200
Newark *(G-7711)*
Wreck Masters Demo Derby .... F 302 368-5544
Bear *(G-381)*

STRAPS: Bindings, Textile

Wayne Industries Inc .... G 302 478-6160
Wilmington *(G-13126)*

STUCCO

Best Stucco LLC .... G 302 650-3620
New Castle *(G-5086)*
Santo Stucco .... G 302 453-0901
Newark *(G-7384)*

STUDIOS: Artist's

Delaware Arts Conservatory .... F 302 595-4160
Bear *(G-103)*

STUDIOS: Artists & Artists' Studios

Agriculture United States Dept .... G 302 741-2600
Dover *(G-1095)*

SUB-LESSORS: Real Estate

West Orange Office Exec Pk LLC .... F 973 320-3227
Wilmington *(G-13167)*

SUBSCRIPTION FULFILLMENT SVCS: Magazine, Newspaper, Etc

Nk Consulting Inc .... F 330 269-5775
Wilmington *(G-11891)*
Thinkruptive Media Inc .... F 310 779-4748
Dover *(G-2142)*

SUBSTANCE ABUSE CLINICS, OUTPATIENT

Central Delaware Committee .... E 302 735-7790
Dover *(G-1265)*
Connections CSP Inc Dover .... G 302 672-9276
Dover *(G-1311)*
Corinthian House .... G 302 858-1493
Georgetown *(G-2485)*
Corizon LLC .... F 302 998-3958
Wilmington *(G-9862)*
Delaware Councl On Gmblng Prbl ...... G 302 655-3261
Wilmington *(G-10027)*
Foundtion For A Btter Tomorrow .... G 302 674-1397
Dover *(G-1563)*
Hogar Crea Int of Delaware .... G 302 762-2875
Wilmington *(G-10925)*
Hudson House Services .... G 302 856-4363
Georgetown *(G-2563)*

SUGAR SUBSTITUTES: Organic

SPI Holding Company .... B 800 789-9755
Wilmington *(G-12703)*

SUMMER CAMPS, EXC DAY & SPORTS INSTRUCTIONAL

Hoops For Hope Delaware .... F 302 229-7600
Wilmington *(G-10949)*
Hope House Daycare .... F 302 407-3404
Wilmington *(G-10951)*
Win From Wthin Xc Camp/Tatnall .... E 302 494-5312
Wilmington *(G-13269)*

SUMMER THEATER

Rehoboth Summer Chld Theatre .... F 302 227-6766
Rehoboth Beach *(G-8056)*

SUNDRIES & RELATED PRDTS: Medical & Laboratory, Rubber

W L Gore & Associates Inc .... C 302 368-3700
Newark *(G-7672)*

SUNROOMS: Prefabricated Metal

Betterlving Ptio Snroms Dlmrva .... G 302 251-0000
Dagsboro *(G-882)*
Coastal Sun Roms Prch Enclsres .... G 302 537-3679
Frankford *(G-2355)*
Sweeten Companies Inc .... G 302 737-6161
Newark *(G-7520)*

SUPERMARKETS & OTHER GROCERY STORES

GBA Enterprises Inc .... G 302 323-1080
New Castle *(G-5346)*

SURFACE ACTIVE AGENTS: Oils & Greases

Richard Earl Fisher .... G 302 598-1957
Wilmington *(G-12407)*

SURGICAL & MEDICAL INSTRUMENTS WHOLESALERS

Tarpon Strategies LLC .... G 215 806-2723
Newark *(G-7540)*

SURGICAL APPLIANCES & SPLYS

Delmarva Laboratories Inc .... G 302 645-2226
Milton *(G-4891)*
E&N Surgical LLC .... G 860 471-0786
Wilmington *(G-10311)*
Family Respiratory & Med Supl .... G 302 653-3602
Smyrna *(G-8632)*
Mih International LLC .... G 301 908-4233
Newark *(G-7038)*

SURGICAL EQPT: See Also Instruments

Datwyler Pharma Packg USA Inc .... G 302 603-8020
Middletown *(G-4019)*

SURGICAL IMPLANTS

Frizbee Medical Inc .... G 424 901-1534
Wilmington *(G-10643)*

SURVEYING & MAPPING: Land Parcels

Batta Ramesh C Associates PA .... E 302 998-9463
Wilmington *(G-9260)*
Braun Engineering & Surveying .... F 302 698-0701
Camden Wyoming *(G-621)*
Charles D Murphy Associates .... F 302 422-7327
Milford *(G-4348)*
Christian Raymond F & Assoc .... G 302 738-3016
Newark *(G-6205)*
Clifton L Bakhsh Jr Inc .... F 302 378-8009
Middletown *(G-3998)*
Coast Survey .... G 302 645-7184
Lewes *(G-3434)*
Compass Point Associates LLC .... G 302 684-2980
Harbeson *(G-2777)*
Davis Bowen & Friedel Inc .... E 302 424-1441
Milford *(G-4371)*
Firefly Drone Operations Llc .... G 305 206-6955
Wilmington *(G-10543)*
Landmark Engineering Inc .... D 302 323-9377
Newark *(G-6915)*
Landmark Engineering Inc .... G 302 734-9597
Newark *(G-6916)*

PRODUCT & SERVICES SECTION

TANKS: Fuel, Including Oil & Gas, Metal Plate

Landtech LLC .... G 302 539-2366
  Ocean View *(G-7798)*
Lewis Miller Inc .... G 302 629-9895
  Seaford *(G-8293)*
McBride and Ziegler Inc .... E 302 737-9138
  Newark *(G-7011)*
Merestone Consultants Inc .... F 302 992-7900
  Wilmington *(G-11639)*
Merestone Consultants Inc .... F 302 226-5880
  Lewes *(G-3637)*
Morris & Ritchie Assoc Inc .... E 302 855-5734
  Georgetown *(G-2607)*
Morris & Ritchie Assoc Inc .... F 302 326-2200
  New Castle *(G-5536)*
Professional Roof Services Inc ..... G 302 731-5770
  Newark *(G-7266)*
Retained Logic Group Inc .... G 302 530-3692
  Middletown *(G-4219)*
Robert Larimore .... G 302 730-8682
  Camden Wyoming *(G-654)*
Scott Engineering Inc .... G 302 736-3058
  Dover *(G-2062)*
Simpler Surveying & Associates ... G 302 539-7873
  Frankford *(G-2387)*
Woodin + Associates LLC .... F 302 378-7300
  Middletown *(G-4290)*

SURVEYING INSTRUMENTS WHOLESALERS

Survey Supply Inc .... G 302 422-3338
  Milford *(G-4572)*
Trimble Navigation Limited .... G 302 368-2434
  Newark *(G-7593)*

SURVEYING SVCS: Aerial Digital Imaging

Amplified Gchmical Imaging LLC .. G 302 266-2428
  Newark *(G-5963)*

SURVEYING SVCS: Photogrammetric Engineering

Adams Kemp Associates Inc .... G 302 856-6699
  Georgetown *(G-2423)*
Design Consultants Group LLC .... E 302 684-8030
  Milton *(G-4892)*
Rod-AES Surveryors Co .... G 302 993-1059
  Wilmington *(G-12459)*

SVC ESTABLISH EQPT, WHOLESALE: Carpet/Rug Clean Eqpt & Sply

Grime Busters USA Inc .... G 302 834-7006
  Newark *(G-6692)*

SVC ESTABLISHMENT EQPT & SPLYS WHOLESALERS

Richard J Leach Upholstery .... G 302 764-2067
  Wilmington *(G-12409)*

SVC ESTABLISHMENT EQPT, WHOL: Cleaning & Maint Eqpt & Splys

East Coast Cleaning Co LLC .... F 302 762-6820
  Wilmington *(G-10318)*
Eastern Shore Equipment Co .... G 302 697-3300
  Camden Wyoming *(G-633)*
Goorland Enterprises LLC .... G 302 229-4573
  Wilmington *(G-10753)*

SVC ESTABLISHMENT EQPT, WHOL: Concrete Burial Vaults & Boxes

Hollie Enterprises LLC .... G 903 721-1904
  Wilmington *(G-10927)*

SVC ESTABLISHMENT EQPT, WHOL: Stress Reducing Eqpt, Electric

Solace Lifesciences Inc .... G 302 275-4195
  Wilmington *(G-12674)*

SVC ESTABLISHMENT EQPT, WHOLESALE: Beauty Parlor Eqpt & Sply

Cad Import Inc .... E 302 628-4178
  New Castle *(G-5128)*
Central America Distrs LLC .... F 302 628-4178
  Georgetown *(G-2465)*

Sally Beauty Supply LLC .... G 302 731-0285
  Newark *(G-7378)*
Sally Beauty Supply LLC .... G 302 995-6197
  Wilmington *(G-12525)*
Sally Beauty Supply LLC .... G 302 674-2201
  Dover *(G-2056)*
Sally Beauty Supply LLC .... G 302 737-8837
  Newark *(G-7379)*
Total Beauty Supply Inc .... G 302 798-4647
  Wilmington *(G-12936)*

SVC ESTABLISHMENT EQPT, WHOLESALE: Firefighting Eqpt

Hoopes Fire Prevention Inc .... F 302 323-0220
  Newark *(G-6743)*

SVC ESTABLISHMENT EQPT, WHOLESALE: Laundry Eqpt & Splys

Blue Sky Clean .... G 302 584-5800
  Wilmington *(G-9381)*

SVC ESTABLISHMENT EQPT, WHOLESALE: Sprinkler Systems

Lightscapes Inc .... G 302 798-5451
  Wilmington *(G-11387)*
Steven Brown & Associates Inc .... G 302 652-4722
  Wilmington *(G-12759)*

SVC ESTABLISHMENT EQPT, WHOLESALE: Vending Machines & Splys

Vending Solutions LLC .... G 302 674-2222
  Dover *(G-2189)*

SWIMMING POOL & HOT TUB CLEANING & MAINTENANCE SVCS

Carter Pool Management LLC .... F 302 236-6952
  Lewes *(G-3409)*
Henderson Services Inc .... F 302 424-1999
  Milford *(G-4438)*

SWIMMING POOL SPLY STORES

Dover Pool & Patio Center Inc ...... E 302 346-7665
  Dover *(G-1465)*

SWITCHES: Electronic

Hollingsead International LLC .... B 302 855-5888
  Georgetown *(G-2559)*
Val-Tech Inc .... E 302 738-0500
  Newark *(G-7638)*

SWITCHES: Electronic Applications

Tricklestar Inc .... G 888 700-1098
  Wilmington *(G-12970)*

SYMPHONY ORCHESTRA

Delaware Symphony Association .. D 302 656-7442
  Wilmington *(G-10089)*
Dover Symphony Orchestra Inc .... G 302 734-1701
  Dover *(G-1471)*

SYSTEMS ENGINEERING: Computer Related

Averest Inc .... G 302 281-2062
  Wilmington *(G-9198)*
Cyber Seven Technologies LLC ... G 302 635-7122
  Newark *(G-6335)*
Dennek LLC .... G 302 703-0790
  Wilmington *(G-10109)*
Sharlay Computer Systems .... G 302 588-3170
  Smyrna *(G-8714)*

SYSTEMS INTEGRATION SVCS

Cim Concepts Incorporated .... F 302 613-5400
  New Castle *(G-5161)*
Data-Bi LLC .... G 302 290-3138
  Wilmington *(G-9962)*
Ebc Systems LLC .... G 302 472-1896
  Wilmington *(G-10334)*
Sevone Inc .... E 302 319-5400
  Newark *(G-7412)*
Smartis .... G 302 653-8355
  Dover *(G-2089)*

SYSTEMS INTEGRATION SVCS: Local Area Network

Insight Engineering Solutions .... G 302 378-4842
  Townsend *(G-8797)*

SYSTEMS INTEGRATION SVCS: Office Computer Automation

Ardexo Inc .... G 855 617-7500
  Dover *(G-1134)*
Batescainelli LLC .... G 202 618-2040
  Rehoboth Beach *(G-7856)*
Majalco LLC .... G 703 507-5298
  Wilmington *(G-11494)*
Medictek Inc .... F 302 351-4924
  Wilmington *(G-11618)*
PHD Technology Solutions LLC ... E 410 961-7895
  Newark *(G-7211)*

SYSTEMS SOFTWARE DEVELOPMENT SVCS

Bothub Ai Limited .... F 669 278-7485
  Newark *(G-6108)*
Cloudcoffer LLC .... E 412 620-3203
  Wilmington *(G-9748)*
Encross LLC .... F 302 351-2593
  Wilmington *(G-10396)*
Horizon Systems Inc .... G 302 983-3203
  New Castle *(G-5404)*
Inclind Inc .... G 302 856-2802
  Lewes *(G-3556)*
Knowpro LLC .... G 772 538-6477
  Wilmington *(G-11284)*
Kortech Consulting Inc .... F 302 559-4612
  Bear *(G-220)*
Omnimaven Inc .... G 302 378-8918
  Middletown *(G-4178)*
Panzeea .... F 770 573-3672
  Seaford *(G-8340)*
Pentius Inc .... E 855 825-3778
  Wilmington *(G-12078)*
Play US Media LLC .... G 302 924-5034
  Dover *(G-1965)*
Rave Business Systems LLC .... F 302 407-2270
  Lewes *(G-3708)*
Recoveryip Innovations LLC .... G 617 901-3414
  Newark *(G-7305)*
Riders App Inc .... G 347 484-4344
  Wilmington *(G-12416)*
Sahave Inc .... F 630 401-5211
  Wilmington *(G-12522)*
Sensofusion Inc .... F 570 239-4912
  Milton *(G-4967)*
Systmade Technologies LLC .... F 888 944-3546
  Dover *(G-2124)*
Versatus Corp .... G 203 293-3597
  Wilmington *(G-13064)*

TABLE OR COUNTERTOPS, PLASTIC LAMINATED

Cabinetry Unlimited LLC .... E 302 436-5030
  Selbyville *(G-8465)*
Michael A OBrien & Sons .... G 302 994-2894
  Wilmington *(G-11656)*

TABLEWARE: Vitreous China

Saenger Porcelain .... G 302 738-5349
  Newark *(G-7375)*

TAILORS: Custom

Classic Image Inc .... G 302 658-7281
  New Castle *(G-5176)*
Matthew Smith .... G 302 654-4853
  Wilmington *(G-11572)*

TANKS & OTHER TRACKED VEHICLE CMPNTS

Intech Services .... G 302 366-1442
  Newark *(G-6787)*

TANKS: Fuel, Including Oil & Gas, Metal Plate

Atom Alloys LLC .... G 786 975-3771
  Wilmington *(G-9181)*

TANKS: Plastic & Fiberglass

Justin Tanks LLC ....E...... 302 856-3521
  Georgetown *(G-2579)*

TANNING SALON EQPT & SPLYS, WHOLESALE

M & M Marketing Group LLC ....G...... 321 274-5352
  Wilmington *(G-11467)*

TANNING SALONS

Beach Tans and Hair Design ....G...... 302 645-8267
  Rehoboth Beach *(G-7858)*
Electric Beach Tanning Company ....G...... 302 730-8266
  Dover *(G-1513)*
Endless Summer Tanning Salon ....G...... 302 369-0455
  Newark *(G-6526)*
Hollywood Tan ....G...... 302 995-2692
  Wilmington *(G-10932)*
Hollywood Tans ....G...... 302 478-8267
  Wilmington *(G-10933)*
Robins Hair & Tanning ....G...... 302 529-9000
  Wilmington *(G-12443)*
Tantini LLC ....G...... 302 444-4024
  Newark *(G-7538)*
U Tan Inc ....G...... 302 674-8040
  Dover *(G-2170)*

TANTALITE MINING

African Markets Fund LLC ....G...... 703 944-1514
  Dover *(G-1092)*

TARGET DRONES

Firefly Drone Operations Llc ....G...... 305 206-6955
  Wilmington *(G-10543)*

TARPAULINS, WHOLESALE

Cramaro Tarpaulin Systems Inc ....F...... 302 292-2170
  Newark *(G-6311)*

TATTOO PARLORS

Everybody Needs Ink ....G...... 302 633-0866
  Wilmington *(G-10450)*
Independent Studio Inc ....G...... 302 436-5581
  Selbyville *(G-8506)*
Poppycock Tattoo ....G...... 302 543-7973
  Wilmington *(G-12187)*

TAX RETURN PREPARATION SVCS

Adkins & Assoc CPA ....G...... 302 737-2390
  Wilmington *(G-8938)*
Advantage Delaware LLC ....G...... 302 479-7764
  Wilmington *(G-8959)*
Affordable Tax Services LLC ....G...... 302 399-3867
  Bear *(G-23)*
Basic Block Corp ....F...... 302 645-2000
  Rehoboth Beach *(G-7855)*
David Wentworth ....G...... 302 856-3272
  Georgetown *(G-2493)*
Dbw Tax Services ....G...... 302 276-0428
  Bear *(G-100)*
Ekww Inc ....G...... 302 234-2877
  Hockessin *(G-3018)*
Elite Tax Services LLC ....G...... 302 256-0401
  Wilmington *(G-10377)*
H&R Block Inc ....G...... 302 934-6178
  Millsboro *(G-4702)*
H&R Block Inc ....F...... 302 378-8931
  Middletown *(G-4100)*
H&R Block Inc ....F...... 302 999-7488
  Wilmington *(G-10812)*
H&R Block Inc ....F...... 302 328-7320
  New Castle *(G-5370)*
H&R Block Inc ....F...... 302 652-3286
  New Castle *(G-5371)*
H&R Block Inc ....F...... 302 836-2700
  Bear *(G-174)*
H&R Block Inc ....F...... 302 478-9140
  Wilmington *(G-10813)*
H&R Block Inc ....F...... 302 479-5717
  Newark *(G-6699)*
H&R Block Inc ....F...... 302 478-6300
  Wilmington *(G-10814)*
Horty & Horty PA ....E...... 302 730-4560
  Dover *(G-1656)*
Jackson Hewitt Inc ....G...... 302 934-7430
  Millsboro *(G-4712)*
Jackson Hewitt Tax Service ....G...... 302 629-4548
  Seaford *(G-8276)*
Kelly Robert & Assoc LLC ....F...... 302 737-7785
  Newark *(G-6873)*
Michael Eller Income Tax Svc ....G...... 302 652-5916
  Wilmington *(G-11659)*
Miller & Associates PA ....G...... 302 234-0678
  Wilmington *(G-11693)*
Oates Consultants LLC ....G...... 302 477-0109
  Wilmington *(G-11929)*
Papaleo Rosen Chelf & Pinder ....F...... 302 644-8600
  Lewes *(G-3678)*
Prefered Tax Service Inc ....G...... 302 654-4388
  Wilmington *(G-12210)*
R E Wlllams Prof Acctg Frm Tax ....G...... 302 598-7171
  Wilmington *(G-12294)*
Ronald Midaugh ....F...... 410 860-1040
  Dover *(G-2041)*
Sandra S Gulledge CPA ....G...... 302 674-1585
  Dover *(G-2058)*
Slacum & Doyle Tax Service LLC ....E...... 302 734-1850
  Dover *(G-2088)*
Tax Management Service Inc ....G...... 703 845-5900
  Milford *(G-4575)*
Tax Masters of Delaware ....G...... 302 832-1313
  Bear *(G-348)*
Thomson Reuters (grc) Inc ....A...... 212 227-7357
  Wilmington *(G-12904)*
Wahid Consultants LLC ....E...... 315 400-0955
  New Castle *(G-5821)*
Walls & Davenport Inc ....G...... 302 653-4779
  Smyrna *(G-8739)*
Wentworth Inc ....F...... 302 629-6284
  Seaford *(G-8436)*

TAXI CABS

Aryvve Technologies LLC ....G...... 678 977-1252
  Dover *(G-1143)*
City Cab of Delware Inc ....G...... 302 734-5968
  Dover *(G-1286)*
City Cab of Delware Inc ....F...... 302 227-8294
  Rehoboth Beach *(G-7890)*
City Cab of Delware Inc ....G...... 302 734-5968
  Dover *(G-1287)*
Delmarva Transportation Inc ....G...... 302 349-0840
  Greenwood *(G-2729)*
U S Express Taxi Company LLC ....G...... 302 357-1908
  New Castle *(G-5799)*
Zizo Taxi Cab LLC ....G...... 302 528-5663
  Newark *(G-7742)*

TECHNICAL WRITING SVCS

Technical Writers Inc ....E...... 302 477-1972
  Wilmington *(G-12869)*

TELECOMMUNICATION EQPT REPAIR SVCS, EXC TELEPHONES

Smith Brothers Communication ....G...... 302 293-5224
  Newark *(G-7450)*

TELECOMMUNICATION SYSTEMS & EQPT

Targus U S A ....G...... 302 644-2311
  Lewes *(G-3778)*

TELECOMMUNICATIONS CARRIERS & SVCS: Wired

Azur Gcs Inc ....G...... 302 884-6713
  Wilmington *(G-9205)*
Cellco Partnership ....E...... 302 653-8183
  Smyrna *(G-8592)*
Cellco Partnership ....F...... 302 376-6049
  Middletown *(G-3983)*
Conectiv Communications Inc ....E...... 302 224-1177
  Newark *(G-6282)*
Consult Dynamics Inc ....G...... 302 654-1019
  Wilmington *(G-9837)*
Home Media One LLC ....G...... 302 644-0307
  Georgetown *(G-2560)*
Jsi Group LLC ....G...... 267 582-5850
  Hockessin *(G-3070)*
Key-Tel Communications Inc ....G...... 302 475-3066
  Wilmington *(G-11249)*
MCI LLC ....F...... 302 407-5034
  Wilmington *(G-11599)*
MCI LLC ....G...... 302 293-0028
  Wilmington *(G-11600)*
Qsr Group LLC ....G...... 302 268-6909
  Wilmington *(G-12276)*
Scientific Games Corporation ....F...... 302 737-4300
  Newark *(G-7395)*
Traitel Telecom Corp ....E...... 619 331-1913
  Wilmington *(G-12951)*
Under/Comm Inc ....F...... 302 424-1554
  Milford *(G-4583)*
Utility Audit Group Inc ....G...... 302 398-8505
  Harrington *(G-2903)*
Verizon Delaware LLC ....E...... 302 761-6079
  Wilmington *(G-13063)*
Verizon Delaware LLC ....E...... 302 422-1430
  Milford *(G-4590)*
Verizon Wireless Inc ....G...... 302 737-5028
  Newark *(G-7651)*
Vps International LLC ....F...... 800 493-9356
  Lewes *(G-3811)*

TELECOMMUNICATIONS CARRIERS & SVCS: Wireless

Spring Communications Inc ....G...... 302 297-2000
  Millsboro *(G-4803)*

TELECONFERENCING SVCS

Conference Group LLC ....E...... 302 224-8255
  Newark *(G-6284)*

TELEMARKETING BUREAUS

Interactive Marketing Services ....E...... 302 456-9810
  Newark *(G-6796)*
MBNA Marketing Systems Inc ....A...... 302 456-8588
  Wilmington *(G-11583)*
Nettel Partners LLC ....F...... 215 290-7383
  Rehoboth Beach *(G-8016)*
SM Technomine Inc ....F...... 312 492-4386
  Wilmington *(G-12648)*
SM Technomine Inc ....F...... 312 492-4386
  Wilmington *(G-12647)*
Strategic Fund Raising Inc ....E...... 651 649-0404
  Wilmington *(G-12774)*

TELEPHONE ANSWERING SVCS

Applied Virtual Solutions LLC ....G...... 302 312-8548
  Newark *(G-5988)*
Bayshore Communications Inc ....F...... 302 737-2164
  Newark *(G-6057)*
Shore Answer LLC ....F...... 302 253-8381
  Georgetown *(G-2654)*
Stericycle Comm Solutions Inc ....F...... 302 656-0630
  Wilmington *(G-12757)*

TELEPHONE CENTRAL OFFICE EQPT: Dial Or Manual

Central Firm LLC ....G...... 610 470-9836
  Wilmington *(G-9615)*

TELEPHONE EQPT INSTALLATION

Advanced Networking Inc ....F...... 302 442-6199
  Wilmington *(G-8954)*
Communications & Wiring Co ....G...... 302 539-0809
  Dagsboro *(G-893)*
Gray Audograph Agency Inc ....E...... 302 658-1700
  New Castle *(G-5359)*

TELEPHONE EQPT: NEC

Bio Medic Corporation ....F...... 302 628-4300
  Seaford *(G-8170)*
Siemens ....G...... 302 220-1544
  Wilmington *(G-12611)*
Siemens AG ....G...... 302 836-2933
  Bear *(G-321)*
Siemens Corporation ....G...... 302 220-1544
  New Castle *(G-5709)*

TELEPHONE SET REPAIR SVCS

Martel Inc ....F...... 302 744-9566
  Dover *(G-1821)*

TELEPHONE SVCS

World Wide Com Corporation ....F...... 646 810-8624
  Newark *(G-7721)*

PRODUCT & SERVICES SECTION

TIRE RECAPPING & RETREADING

TELEPHONE: Automatic Dialers

Shiv Baba LLC .... F 703 314-1203
 Dover *(G-2077)*

TELEPHONE: Fiber Optic Systems

2nu Photonics LLC .... G 302 388-2261
 Newark *(G-5854)*
Photon Programming .... G 302 328-2925
 New Castle *(G-5622)*
Versitron Inc .... D 302 894-0699
 Newark *(G-7653)*

TELEVISION BROADCASTING STATIONS

Abc Inc .... G 302 429-0189
 Wilmington *(G-8898)*
Draper Communications Inc .... F 302 684-8962
 Milton *(G-4898)*
Gtv Live Shopping LLC .... G 844 694-8688
 Hockessin *(G-3041)*
Thales Holding Corporation .... A 302 326-0830
 New Castle *(G-5766)*
Wboc Inc .... F 302 734-9262
 Dover *(G-2207)*

TELEVISION FILM PRODUCTION SVCS

Everett Robinson .... F 302 530-6574
 Wilmington *(G-10446)*
Melody Entertainment USA Inc .... G 305 505-7659
 Wilmington *(G-11627)*
Teleduction Associates Inc .... G 302 429-0303
 Wilmington *(G-12877)*

TELEVISION REPAIR SHOP

Als TV Service .... G 302 653-3711
 Smyrna *(G-8567)*
Computers Fixed Today .... G 302 724-6411
 Wilmington *(G-9807)*
Far Rezolutions Inc .... G 302 547-6850
 Newark *(G-6570)*
G & S TV & Antenna .... G 302 422-5733
 Milford *(G-4419)*
Overture LLC .... G 302 226-1940
 Rehoboth Beach *(G-8025)*

TEMPORARY HELP SVCS

Access Labor Service Inc .... E 302 741-2575
 Dover *(G-1081)*
Adecco Usa Inc .... G 302 457-4059
 Newark *(G-5899)*
Aerotek Inc .... E 302 561-6300
 New Castle *(G-5015)*
Barrett Business Services Inc .... G 302 674-2206
 Dover *(G-1173)*
Benitime Solutions Inc .... G 302 476-8097
 Wilmington *(G-9302)*
Career Associates Inc .... G 302 674-4357
 Dover *(G-1255)*
Interim Health Care .... G 302 322-2743
 New Castle *(G-5422)*
Interim Healthcare Del LLC .... C 302 322-2743
 Smyrna *(G-8658)*
J&J Staffing Resources Inc .... G 302 738-7800
 Newark *(G-6821)*
Kelly Services Inc .... F 302 323-4748
 New Castle *(G-5459)*
Kelly Services Inc .... G 302 674-8087
 Dover *(G-1731)*
Placers Inc of Delaware .... F 302 709-0973
 Newark *(G-7221)*
Staffmark Investment LLC .... E 302 834-2303
 Bear *(G-336)*

TEMPORARY RELIEF SVCS

Methodist Mission and Church E ..... G 302 225-5862
 Wilmington *(G-11649)*
Ministry of Caring Inc .... G 302 652-0904
 Wilmington *(G-11706)*
People Builders Inc .... G 302 250-0716
 Newark *(G-7198)*
Techno Relief Limited .... G 416 453-9393
 Wilmington *(G-12870)*

TEN PIN CENTERS

AMF Bowling Centers Inc .... E 302 998-5316
 Wilmington *(G-9068)*

Bowlerama Inc .... E 302 654-0704
 New Castle *(G-5100)*
Delaware Womens Bowling Assn ..... F 302 834-7002
 Bear *(G-114)*
Inspection Lanes .... G 302 853-1003
 Georgetown *(G-2566)*
Inspection Lanes .... G 302 744-2514
 Dover *(G-1678)*
Milford Bowling Lanes Inc .... G 302 422-9456
 Milford *(G-4496)*
Millsboro Lanes Inc .... F 302 934-0400
 Millsboro *(G-4750)*
Pleasant Hill Lanes Inc .... E 302 998-8811
 Wilmington *(G-12158)*

TENTS: All Materials

Tee Pees From Rattlesnks .... G 302 654-0709
 Wilmington *(G-12875)*

TESTERS: Physical Property

Testing Machines Inc .... E 302 613-5600
 New Castle *(G-5764)*

TEXTILE PRDTS: Hand Woven & Crocheted

Ajs Crochets .... G 302 257-0381
 Dover *(G-1100)*
Crochet Creations By Debbie .... G 302 287-2462
 Wilmington *(G-9901)*

TEXTILE: Finishing, Cotton Broadwoven

James Thompson & Company Inc ... E 302 349-4501
 Greenwood *(G-2748)*

TEXTILE: Finishing, Raw Stock NEC

James Thompson & Company Inc ... E 302 349-4501
 Greenwood *(G-2748)*

TEXTILE: Goods, NEC

Hodges International Inc .... G 310 874-8516
 Dover *(G-1651)*

TEXTILES: Jute & Flax Prdts

Garage .... G 302 453-1930
 Newark *(G-6638)*

THEATER COMPANIES

Delaware Theatre Company .... E 302 594-1100
 Wilmington *(G-10090)*

THEATRICAL LIGHTING SVCS

Light Action Inc .... F 302 328-7800
 New Castle *(G-5481)*

THEATRICAL PRODUCERS & SVCS

Earle Teate Music .... G 302 736-1937
 Dover *(G-1495)*
Pieces of A Dream Inc .... G 302 593-6172
 Wilmington *(G-12132)*
Wilmington String Ensemble .... E 302 764-1201
 Wilmington *(G-13258)*

THERMOELECTRIC DEVICES: Solid State

Thermoelectrics Unlimited Inc .... G 302 764-6618
 Wilmington *(G-12896)*

THERMOPLASTIC MATERIALS

Dupont De Nemours Inc .... B 302 774-1000
 Wilmington *(G-10251)*
E I Du Pont De Nemours & Co .... B 302 654-8198
 Wilmington *(G-10297)*
E I Du Pont De Nemours & Co .... B 302 999-2826
 Wilmington *(G-10283)*
E I Du Pont De Nemours & Co .... A 302 485-3000
 Wilmington *(G-10278)*
E I Du Pont De Nemours & Co .... G 800 441-7515
 Wilmington *(G-10290)*
E I Du Pont De Nemours & Co .... B 302 892-5655
 Wilmington *(G-10301)*

THREAD & YARN, RUBBER: Fabric Covered

Conlin Corporation .... E 302 633-9174
 Wilmington *(G-9823)*

TICKET OFFICES & AGENCIES: Theatrical

B & B Tickettown Inc .... G 302 656-9797
 Wilmington *(G-9208)*
Michael Schwartz .... F 302 791-9999
 Wilmington *(G-11666)*

TILE: Wall & Floor, Ceramic

Micahs General Contracting .... G 302 437-4068
 Bear *(G-251)*

TILE: Wall, Ceramic

Maneto Inc .... G 302 656-4285
 Wilmington *(G-11501)*

TIMBER PRDTS WHOLESALERS

JG Townsend Jr & Co Inc .... E 302 856-2525
 Georgetown *(G-2574)*

TIN ORE MINING

African Markets Fund LLC .... G 703 944-1514
 Dover *(G-1092)*

TIRE & TUBE REPAIR MATERIALS, WHOLESALE

EZ Manufacturing Company LLC ... G 302 653-6567
 Clayton *(G-849)*
Tire Sales LLC .... E 302 994-2900
 New Castle *(G-5772)*

TIRE DEALERS

Admiral Tire .... G 302 734-5911
 Dover *(G-1087)*
Ajacks Tire Service Inc .... G 302 834-5200
 New Castle *(G-5020)*
Bargain Tire & Service Inc .... F 302 764-8900
 Wilmington *(G-9254)*
Bridgestone Ret Operations LLC ... G 302 422-4508
 Milford *(G-4335)*
Bridgestone Ret Operations LLC ... F 302 995-2487
 Wilmington *(G-9472)*
Bridgestone Ret Operations LLC ... F 302 734-4522
 Dover *(G-1232)*
Bridgestone Ret Operations LLC ... G 302 656-2529
 New Castle *(G-5112)*
Carl King Tire Co Inc .... F 302 644-4070
 Lewes *(G-3406)*
Carl King Tire Co Inc .... E 302 697-9506
 Camden *(G-546)*
Clarksville Auto Service Ctr 302 539-1700
 Ocean View *(G-7777)*
Cochran-Trivits Inc .... G 302 328-2945
 New Castle *(G-5179)*
Delaware Tire Center Inc .... F 302 674-0234
 Dover *(G-1402)*
Delaware Tire Center Inc .... G 302 368-2531
 Newark *(G-6418)*
Diamond State Tire Inc .... F 302 836-1919
 Bear *(G-118)*
Els Tire Service Inc .... F 302 834-1997
 Newark *(G-6518)*
Furrs Tire Service Inc .... G 302 678-0800
 Dover *(G-1573)*
Goodyear Tire & Rubber Company . G 302 737-2461
 Newark *(G-6677)*
Goodyear Tire & Rubber Company . F 302 998-0428
 Wilmington *(G-10751)*
Kirkwood Tires Inc .... G 302 737-2460
 Newark *(G-6894)*
Monro Inc .... G 302 846-2732
 Delmar *(G-1022)*
Sports Car Tire Inc .... E 302 571-8473
 Wilmington *(G-12710)*
Tbc Retail Group Inc .... E 302 478-8013
 Wilmington *(G-12855)*
Tire Sales & Service Inc .... E 302 658-8955
 Wilmington *(G-12916)*
Wellers Tire Service Inc .... F 302 337-8228
 Bridgeville *(G-531)*

TIRE RECAPPING & RETREADING

Clarksville Auto Service Ctr .... E 302 539-1700
 Ocean View *(G-7777)*
Diamond State Tire Inc .... F 302 836-1919
 Bear *(G-118)*

Employee Codes: A=Over 500 employees, B=251-500
C=101-250, D=51-100, E=20-50, F=10-19, G=1-9

TIRES & INNER TUBES

BF Disc Inc ....G....... 302 691-6351
  Wilmington (G-9323)
Michelin Corporation ....G....... 864 458-4698
  Newark (G-7024)

TIRES & TUBES WHOLESALERS

Bargain Tire & Service Inc ....F....... 302 764-8900
  Wilmington (G-9254)
Cochran-Trivits Inc ....G....... 302 328-2945
  New Castle (G-5179)
Tire Rack Inc ....D....... 302 325-8260
  New Castle (G-5771)

TIRES & TUBES, WHOLESALE: Automotive

Admiral Tire ....G....... 302 734-5911
  Dover (G-1087)
Bridgestone Ret Operations LLC ....G....... 302 422-4508
  Milford (G-4335)
Carl King Tire Co Inc ....E....... 302 697-9506
  Camden (G-546)
Carl King Tire Co Inc ....F....... 302 644-4070
  Lewes (G-3406)
Delaware Tire Center Inc ....F....... 302 674-0234
  Dover (G-1402)
Delaware Tire Center Inc ....F....... 302 368-2531
  Newark (G-6418)
Goodyear Tire & Rubber Company ....F....... 302 998-0428
  Wilmington (G-10751)
Tbc Retail Group Inc ....E....... 302 478-8013
  Wilmington (G-12855)
Traction Wholesale Center Inc ....G....... 302 743-8473
  Wilmington (G-12946)
Wellers Tire Service Inc ....F....... 302 337-8228
  Bridgeville (G-531)

TIRES & TUBES, WHOLESALE: Truck

Els Tire Service Inc ....F....... 302 834-1997
  Newark (G-6518)
Tire Sales & Service Inc ....E....... 302 658-8955
  Wilmington (G-12916)

TITANIUM MILL PRDTS

Titanium Black Exec Sltons LLC ....G....... 813 785-7842
  Dover (G-2149)

TITLE & TRUST COMPANIES

Brennan Title Company ....G....... 302 541-0400
  Frankford (G-2350)

TITLE ABSTRACT & SETTLEMENT OFFICES

Delaware Settlement Services ....G....... 302 731-2500
  Newark (G-6411)
Old Republic Nat Title Insur ....F....... 302 661-1997
  Wilmington (G-11944)
Trans Un Sttlment Slutions Inc ....D....... 800 916-8800
  Wilmington (G-12953)

TITLE INSURANCE: Real Estate

First American Title Insur Co ....F....... 302 855-2120
  Georgetown (G-2531)
First American Title Insur Co ....G....... 302 421-9440
  Wilmington (G-10545)
Harrington Insurance ....G....... 302 883-5000
  Dover (G-1629)
Old Republic Nat Title Insur ....G....... 302 734-3570
  Dover (G-1915)

TOBACCO & PRDTS, WHOLESALE: Cigars

Cigarette City Inc ....E....... 302 836-4889
  Newark (G-6235)
Guy & Lady Barrel LLC ....G....... 302 399-3069
  Dover (G-1618)
Harry Kenyon Incorporated ....E....... 302 762-7776
  New Castle (G-5376)

TOBACCO & PRDTS, WHOLESALE: Smokeless

51 and Prospect ....G....... 443 944-1934
  Newark (G-5860)
Delmar Vapor Lounge ....G....... 302 907-0125
  Delmar (G-991)
Flavors & More Inc ....G....... 917 887-9241
  Wilmington (G-10571)

Vape Escape ....G....... 302 737-8273
  Newark (G-7644)

TOBACCO & TOBACCO PRDTS WHOLESALERS

J&J Contracting Co Inc ....G....... 302 227-0800
  Rehoboth Beach (G-7969)

TOBACCO STORES & STANDS

Cigarette City Inc ....E....... 302 836-4889
  Newark (G-6235)

TOBACCO: Cigarettes

Emerald Industries LLC ....G....... 302 450-1416
  Wilmington (G-10390)

TOILETRIES, COSMETICS & PERFUME STORES

Cosmetic Innovators LLC ....G....... 310 310-9784
  Wilmington (G-9870)
Haloali Teeth Whitening LLC ....G....... 302 300-4042
  Claymont (G-760)
Victorias Scret Pink Main Line ....G....... 302 644-1035
  Rehoboth Beach (G-8106)

TOILETRIES, WHOLESALE: Toiletries

Hotel Environments Inc ....G....... 302 234-9294
  Hockessin (G-3056)
Mid States Sales & Marketing ....E....... 302 888-2475
  Wilmington (G-11680)

TOILETS, PORTABLE, WHOLESALE

A1 Sanitation Service Inc ....F....... 302 653-9591
  Smyrna (G-8559)

TOLL BRIDGE OPERATIONS

Delaware River & Bay Authority ....E....... 302 571-6474
  New Castle (G-5236)
Delaware River & Bay Authority ....C....... 302 571-6303
  New Castle (G-5237)

TOLL OPERATIONS

Paybysky Inc ....G....... 519 641-1771
  Lewes (G-3682)

TOOLS & EQPT: Used With Sporting Arms

Pkg LLC ....G....... 269 651-8640
  Wilmington (G-12147)

TOOLS: Hand

Connor Marketing Inc ....G....... 302 376-6037
  Middletown (G-4006)
Danaher Corporation ....G....... 302 798-5741
  Wilmington (G-9953)
Easy Lawn Inc ....E....... 302 815-6500
  Greenwood (G-2736)

TOOLS: Hand, Power

Black & Decker Corporation ....G....... 302 738-0250
  Newark (G-6086)
Eeco Inc ....G....... 302 456-1448
  Newark (G-6506)
Rhi Refractories Holding Co ....G....... 302 655-6497
  Wilmington (G-12400)

TOURIST INFORMATION BUREAU

Kent County Tourism Corp ....G....... 302 734-1736
  Dover (G-1733)

TOWELS: Paper

Procter & Gamble Paper Pdts Co ....B....... 302 678-2600
  Dover (G-1989)

TOWING & TUGBOAT SVC

Buntings Garage Inc ....F....... 302 732-9021
  Dagsboro (G-886)

TOWING SVCS: Marine

Dick Ennis Inc ....G....... 302 945-2627
  Lewes (G-3464)

Wilmington Tug Inc ....E....... 302 652-1666
  Wilmington (G-13265)

TOYS

Sandebbarnanricway Corp ....G....... 302 475-2705
  Wilmington (G-12538)

TOYS & HOBBY GOODS & SPLYS, WHOLESALE: Video Games

Gamestop Inc ....F....... 302 266-7362
  Newark (G-6637)
Guidance Gaming ....F....... 724 708-2321
  Dover (G-1614)
Workplace Rebels LLC ....G....... 917 771-8286
  Dover (G-2237)

TOYS: Dolls, Stuffed Animals & Parts

Gelfand Group Inc ....G....... 310 666-2362
  Camden Wyoming (G-642)
Linda & Richard Partnership ....G....... 302 697-9758
  Dover (G-1790)

TOYS: Kites

East Coast Kite Sports ....G....... 302 359-0749
  Magnolia (G-3890)
Kite ....G....... 302 324-9569
  Bear (G-219)

TOYS: Rubber

Forte Sports Incorporated ....G....... 302 731-0776
  Newark (G-6607)

TRACTOR REPAIR SVCS

Hockessin Tractor Inc ....G....... 302 239-4201
  Hockessin (G-3055)

TRADERS: Commodity, Contracts

Mefta LLC ....F....... 804 433-3566
  Wilmington (G-11622)

TRADERS: Security

Futuretech Inv Group Inc ....F....... 302 476-9529
  Newark (G-6630)

TRAFFIC CONTROL FLAGGING SVCS

Highway Traffic Controllers ....E....... 302 697-7117
  Camden Wyoming (G-645)
Right Way Flagging and Sign Co ....E....... 302 698-5229
  Camden Wyoming (G-653)

TRAILER PARKS

Delaware Motel and Rv Park ....G....... 302 328-3114
  New Castle (G-5232)
Tuckahoe Acres Camping Resort ....G....... 302 539-1841
  Dagsboro (G-940)

TRAILERS & PARTS: Truck & Semi's

24 Hr Truck Services LLC ....G....... 609 516-7307
  Newark (G-5853)
Utility/Eastern ....E....... 302 337-7400
  Bridgeville (G-528)

TRAILERS & TRAILER EQPT

Pessagno Equipment Inc ....G....... 302 738-7001
  Newark (G-7205)

TRAILERS: Bodies

Kruger Trailers Inc ....G....... 302 856-2577
  Georgetown (G-2584)

TRANSLATION & INTERPRETATION SVCS

Deafinitions & Interpreting ....F....... 302 563-7714
  Bear (G-102)
Green Crescent LLC ....G....... 800 735-9620
  Dover (G-1611)
One Hour Translation Inc ....G....... 800 720-3722
  Lewes (G-3668)
Sayhi LLC ....G....... 860 631-7725
  Wilmington (G-12547)

PRODUCT & SERVICES SECTION

TRANSPORTATION AGENTS & BROKERS

Burris Freight Management LLC .... D 800 805-8135
  Milford *(G-4336)*
Delaware Trnsp Svcs Inc .... G 302 981-6562
  Dover *(G-1404)*
Hollywell Logistics LLC .... D 267 901-4272
  Wilmington *(G-10929)*
Makeshopncompany Inc .... F 302 999-9961
  New Castle *(G-5503)*

TRANSPORTATION ARRANGEMENT SVCS, PASS: Sightseeing Tour Co's

U Transit Inc .... G 302 227-1197
  Rehoboth Beach *(G-8102)*

TRANSPORTATION ARRANGEMENT SVCS, PASSENGER: Airline Ticket

Advantage Travel Inc .... G 302 674-8747
  Bear *(G-15)*

TRANSPORTATION ARRANGEMENT SVCS, PASSENGER: Carpool/Vanpool

Fleek Inc .... G 888 870-1291
  Wilmington *(G-10572)*

TRANSPORTATION ARRANGEMENT SVCS, PASSENGER: Tours, Conducted

Fare4air LLC .... F 844 663-4040
  Wilmington *(G-10498)*
Posidon Adventure Inc .... F 302 543-5024
  Wilmington *(G-12190)*

TRANSPORTATION ARRANGEMNT SVCS, PASS: Travel Tour Pkgs, Whol

Promotora Systems Inc .... G 302 304-3147
  Wilmington *(G-12252)*

TRANSPORTATION BROKERS: Truck

Aku Transport Inc .... G 302 500-8127
  Georgetown *(G-2427)*
Hollie Enterprises LLC .... G 903 721-1904
  Wilmington *(G-10927)*
North American Trnspt Co Inc .... G 856 696-5483
  New Castle *(G-5575)*
Pyramid Transport Inc .... E 302 337-9340
  Bridgeville *(G-514)*
Trinity Logistics Inc .... C 302 253-3900
  Seaford *(G-8425)*

TRANSPORTATION EPQT & SPLYS, WHOL: Aircraft Engs/Eng Parts

Arteaga Properties LLC .... G 808 339-6906
  Wilmington *(G-9136)*

TRANSPORTATION EPQT & SPLYS, WHOLESALE: Marine Crafts/Splys

Hilton Corp .... G 302 994-3465
  Wilmington *(G-10911)*

TRANSPORTATION EPQT/SPLYS, WHOL: Marine Propulsn Mach/Eqpt

Hilton Marine Supply Company .... G 302 994-3465
  Wilmington *(G-10912)*

TRANSPORTATION EQPT & SPLYS WHOLESALERS, NEC

Janette Redrow Ltd .... G 302 659-3534
  Townsend *(G-8800)*
Summit Aviation Inc .... D 302 834-5400
  Middletown *(G-4250)*

TRANSPORTATION PROGRAMS REGULATION & ADMINISTRATION SVCS

Delaware Dept Transportation .... C 302 577-3278
  Dover *(G-1365)*
Transportation Delaware Dept .... B 302 326-8950
  Bear *(G-357)*
Transportation Delaware Dept .... E 302 653-4128
  Middletown *(G-4267)*

Transportation Delaware Dept .... G 302 658-8960
  Wilmington *(G-12958)*

TRANSPORTATION SVCS, AIR, NONSCHEDULED: Air Cargo Carriers

Jz Road & Air Cargo Lines Inc .... G 302 468-5988
  Newark *(G-6861)*

TRANSPORTATION SVCS, AIR, NONSCHEDULED: Helicopter Carriers

Horizon Helicopters Inc .... G 302 368-5135
  Newark *(G-6745)*

TRANSPORTATION SVCS, DEEP SEA: Intercoastal, Freight

OSG America LP .... G 212 578-1922
  Newark *(G-7161)*
Vader LLC .... F 302 565-9684
  Bear *(G-366)*

TRANSPORTATION SVCS, NEC

Adkess Transport Services LLC .... G 978 235-3924
  Bear *(G-13)*
AEG International LLC .... G 302 750-6411
  Laurel *(G-3190)*
AV Logistics LLC .... G 302 725-5407
  Milford *(G-4314)*
Base Line Transports L .... G 302 438-3092
  Middletown *(G-3963)*
Bluedot Technologies Inc .... G 415 800-1890
  Newark *(G-6102)*
Compassionate Care Trnspt LLC .... G 215 847-9836
  Wilmington *(G-9802)*
Crown Shipping .... G 617 909-3357
  Dover *(G-1326)*
Dixon Brothers LLC .... F 302 377-8289
  Newark *(G-6456)*
E-Lyte Transportation .... G 808 269-0283
  Dover *(G-1492)*
Ed Hunt Inc .... G 302 339-8443
  Dover *(G-1503)*
H Juarez Transport Inc .... G 302 407-5102
  Wilmington *(G-10809)*
J & J Bus Service .... F 302 744-9002
  Dover *(G-1686)*
John A Donovan .... G 302 540-7512
  Newark *(G-6841)*
Kinoland Logistics LLC .... G 302 565-4505
  Newark *(G-6889)*
L&J Transportation LLC .... G 302 234-3366
  Hockessin *(G-3074)*
MED Transport LLC .... E 513 257-7626
  Wilmington *(G-11614)*
Meridian Limo LLC .... G 800 462-1550
  Dover *(G-1839)*
P&P Horse Transportation .... G 302 388-7687
  Newark *(G-7168)*
Rivera Transportation Inc .... G 302 258-9023
  Laurel *(G-3282)*
Robert Bryan .... G 302 875-5099
  Laurel *(G-3284)*
Ruan T119 .... G 302 376-9300
  Middletown *(G-4225)*
Savannah Logistics LLC .... G 302 893-7251
  Middletown *(G-4230)*
Schiff Transport LLC .... G 302 398-8014
  Harrington *(G-2885)*
Spirit-Trans Inc .... G 302 290-9830
  Bear *(G-333)*
St Logistics .... G 302 407-5931
  Wilmington *(G-12725)*
Trans Logistics LLC .... F 267 244-6550
  Wilmington *(G-12952)*
Trial Transport Logistics .... G 302 383-5907
  Wilmington *(G-12968)*
Wayman Transportation Svc .... G 302 363-5139
  Magnolia *(G-3912)*
Yellow Trans .... F 302 628-2805
  Seaford *(G-8445)*

TRANSPORTATION SVCS, WATER: River, Exc St Lawrence Seaway

Delaware Bay Launch Service .... F 302 422-7604
  Milford *(G-4376)*

TRANSPORTATION SVCS, WATER: Water Taxis

Delaware Bay Launch Service .... F 302 422-7604
  Milford *(G-4376)*

TRANSPORTATION SVCS: Airport

Arrow Shuttle Service .... G 302 836-5658
  Bear *(G-37)*
City Wide Transportation Inc .... F 302 792-1225
  Claymont *(G-720)*
Delaware Trnsp Svcs Inc .... G 302 981-6562
  Dover *(G-1404)*
Gold Label Transportation LLC .... G 302 668-2383
  Newark *(G-6670)*

TRANSPORTATION SVCS: Airport Limousine, Scheduled Svcs

Preferred Trnsp Systems LLC .... G 302 323-0828
  Bear *(G-290)*

TRANSPORTATION SVCS: Bus Line Operations

Dover Leasing Co Inc .... F 302 674-2300
  Dover *(G-1456)*

TRANSPORTATION SVCS: Bus Line, Intercity

Chambers Bus Service Inc .... E 302 284-9655
  Viola *(G-8834)*

TRANSPORTATION SVCS: Highway, Intercity, Special Svcs

RE Calloway Trnsp Inc .... E 302 422-2471
  Houston *(G-3182)*

TRANSPORTATION SVCS: Railroad Terminals

Tcar Holdings LLC .... G 720 328-0944
  Wilmington *(G-12857)*

TRANSPORTATION SVCS: Vanpool Operation

Preferred Trnsp Systems LLC .... G 302 323-0828
  Bear *(G-290)*

TRANSPORTATION: Air, Nonscheduled Passenger

Transcontinental Airways Corp .... F 202 817-2020
  Wilmington *(G-12955)*

TRANSPORTATION: Air, Nonscheduled, NEC

Integrated Dynmc Solutions LLC ...... G 818 406-8500
  Camden *(G-582)*
Interjet West Inc .... F 209 848-0290
  Wilmington *(G-11063)*
Penobscot Properties LLC .... G 302 322-4477
  New Castle *(G-5616)*

TRANSPORTATION: Air, Scheduled Freight

United Parcel Service Inc .... G 302 453-7462
  Newark *(G-7614)*

TRANSPORTATION: Air, Scheduled Passenger

Penobscot Properties LLC .... G 302 322-4477
  New Castle *(G-5616)*

TRANSPORTATION: Bus Transit Systems

Academy Express .... G 302 537-4805
  Ocean View *(G-7753)*
Hilton Bus Service .... E 302 697-7676
  Camden *(G-580)*
Matthew Smith Bus Service .... E 302 734-9311
  Dover *(G-1828)*

TRANSPORTATION: Bus Transit Systems

Spikes Coach Lines .... G 302 438-3644
  Wilmington *(G-12705)*

Employee Codes: A=Over 500 employees, B=251-500
C=101-250, D=51-100, E=20-50, F=10-19, G=1-9

Xinnix Ticketing Inc ....G....... 302 778-1818
Wilmington *(G-13321)*

TRANSPORTATION: Deep Sea Foreign Freight

New Hope Vehicle Exports LLC............G....... 302 275-6482
Wilmington *(G-11863)*

TRANSPORTATION: Deep Sea Passenger

Cruise One................G....... 302 698-6468
Camden Wyoming *(G-628)*

TRANSPORTATION: Local Passenger, NEC

Executive Transportation Inc..........G....... 302 337-3455
Greenwood *(G-2740)*
Lisa M Horsey................G....... 302 725-5767
Lincoln *(G-3860)*
Macklyn Home Care................G....... 302 690-9397
Wilmington *(G-11481)*

TRANSPORTATION: Transit Systems, NEC

Dans Taxi & Shuttle................G....... 302 383-8826
Claymont *(G-728)*
Dcat Transit LLC................G....... 302 855-1231
Georgetown *(G-2495)*
Delaware Transportation Auth..........F....... 302 760-2000
Dover *(G-1403)*
Direct Mobile Transit Inc................F....... 302 218-5106
Wilmington *(G-10161)*
Gg Shuttle Service................G....... 302 684-8818
Milton *(G-4908)*
Shamrock Services LLC................G....... 302 519-7609
Lewes *(G-3738)*
United Transit Company L L C..........G....... 302 838-3575
Saint Georges *(G-8131)*

TRANSPORTATION: Trolley Systems

U Transit Inc................G....... 302 227-1197
Rehoboth Beach *(G-8102)*

TRAVEL AGENCIES

AAA Club Alliance Inc................B....... 302 299-4700
Wilmington *(G-8893)*
AAA Club Alliance Inc................F....... 302 674-8020
Dover *(G-1075)*
Aba Travl & Ent Inc................G....... 305 374-0838
Lewes *(G-3321)*
Advantage Travel Inc................G....... 302 674-8747
Bear *(G-15)*
Al Jusant Travel................G....... 302 427-2594
Wilmington *(G-8997)*
Ans Corporation................G....... 410 296-8330
Rehoboth Beach *(G-7844)*
Bethany Travel Inc................G....... 302 933-0955
Millsboro *(G-4644)*
Cruise Holidays Brandywine Vly..........F....... 302 239-6400
Hockessin *(G-2997)*
Cruise One................G....... 302 698-6468
Camden Wyoming *(G-628)*
Cruise Shoppe Inc................G....... 302 737-7220
Bear *(G-90)*
Cruiseone................G....... 302 945-4620
Millsboro *(G-4672)*
Fare4air LLC................F....... 844 663-4040
Wilmington *(G-10498)*
International Travel Network..........G....... 415 840-0207
Wilmington *(G-11069)*
Journeys LLC................G....... 302 384-7843
Wilmington *(G-11198)*
Kcs Sensational Vacations..........G....... 267 886-0991
Dover *(G-1726)*
Mymoroccanbazar Inc................G....... 323 238-5747
Newark *(G-7077)*
Ocean Travel................G....... 302 227-1607
Rehoboth Beach *(G-8021)*
Preferred Travel................G....... 302 838-8966
Bear *(G-289)*
Red Carpet Travel Agency Inc..........E....... 302 475-1220
Wilmington *(G-12346)*
Travel Travel Newark Inc................G....... 302 737-5555
Newark *(G-7582)*
Visamtion LLC................G....... 302 268-2177
New Castle *(G-5819)*
Windham Enterprises Inc................G....... 302 678-5777
Dover *(G-2231)*

TRAVEL ARRANGEMENT SVCS: Passenger

Twyne Inc................G....... 213 675-9518
Camden *(G-603)*

TRAVELER ACCOMMODATIONS, NEC

1102 West Street Ltd Partnr..........E....... 302 429-7600
Wilmington *(G-8842)*
190 Stadium LLC................F....... 302 659-3635
Smyrna *(G-8558)*
44 Aasha Hospitality Assoc LLC..........E....... 302 674-3784
Dover *(G-1070)*
44 New England Management Co..........E....... 302 477-9500
Wilmington *(G-8863)*
700 Nrth King St Wlmington LLC..........C....... 302 655-0400
Wilmington *(G-8865)*
A & G Kramedas Associates LLC..........F....... 302 674-3300
Dover *(G-1072)*
A & G Realty LLC................E....... 302 674-3300
Dover *(G-1073)*
Amaa Management Corporation..........F....... 302 677-0505
Dover *(G-1115)*
Americinn International LLC..........F....... 302 398-3900
Harrington *(G-2810)*
Beacon Hospitality................G....... 302 249-0502
Georgetown *(G-2452)*
Bear Hospitality Inc................G....... 302 326-2500
Bear *(G-48)*
Best Western Goldleaf Ht LLC..........F....... 302 226-1100
Rehoboth Beach *(G-7867)*
Best Western Newark................G....... 302 738-3400
Newark *(G-6074)*
Bpg Hotel Partners X LLC..........D....... 302 453-9700
Newark *(G-6113)*
Buccini/Pollin Group Inc..........C....... 302 691-2100
Wilmington *(G-9497)*
Chapman Hospitality Inc..........E....... 302 738-3400
Newark *(G-6189)*
Chudasama Enterprises LLC..........G....... 302 856-7532
Georgetown *(G-2471)*
Colonial Oaks Hotel LLC..........E....... 302 645-7766
Rehoboth Beach *(G-7898)*
Comfort Inn & Suites................F....... 302 737-3900
Newark *(G-6267)*
Concord Towers Inc................D....... 302 737-2700
Newark *(G-6280)*
Country Inns Suites................G....... 302 266-6400
Newark *(G-6303)*
Courtyard Management Corp..........C....... 302 429-7600
Wilmington *(G-9878)*
Courtyard Management Corp..........E....... 302 456-3800
Newark *(G-6305)*
Creative Courtyards................G....... 302 226-1994
Rehoboth Beach *(G-7903)*
Days Inn and Suites Seaford..........F....... 302 629-4300
Seaford *(G-8218)*
Days Inn Dover Downtown..........E....... 302 674-8002
Dover *(G-1346)*
Delaware Hotel Associates LP..........D....... 302 792-2700
Claymont *(G-732)*
Dhm Wilmington LLC................D....... 302 656-8952
Wilmington *(G-10137)*
Dipna Inc................E....... 302 478-0300
Wilmington *(G-10159)*
Djont/Jpm Wilmington Lsg LLC..........D....... 302 478-6000
Wilmington *(G-10172)*
Doubltree Htels Suites Resorts..........E....... 302 478-6000
Wilmington *(G-10210)*
Dover Hospitality Group LLC..........E....... 302 677-0900
Dover *(G-1453)*
Dpnl LLC................F....... 302 366-8097
Newark *(G-6469)*
Driftwood Hospitality MGT LLC..........D....... 302 655-0400
Wilmington *(G-10235)*
Dutch Village Motel Inc..........F....... 302 328-6246
New Castle *(G-5268)*
Eastern Hospitality Management..........F....... 302 322-9480
New Castle *(G-5277)*
Econo Lodge Inn Suites Resort..........F....... 302 227-0500
Rehoboth Beach *(G-7925)*
ESA P Portfolio LLC................F....... 302 283-0800
Newark *(G-6539)*
Express Hotel Inc................G....... 302 227-4030
Rehoboth Beach *(G-7929)*
Four Points By Sheraton..........G....... 302 266-6600
Newark *(G-6608)*
Gracelawn Memorial Park Inc..........E....... 302 654-6158
New Castle *(G-5358)*
Gulab Management Inc................G....... 302 398-4206
Harrington *(G-2844)*
Gulab Management Inc................D....... 302 934-6126
Milford *(G-4428)*
Gulab Management Inc................E....... 302 734-4433
Dover *(G-1615)*
Gurukrupa Inc................G....... 302 328-6691
New Castle *(G-5366)*
Hampton Inn................F....... 302 629-4500
Seaford *(G-8258)*
Hampton Inn................F....... 302 422-4320
Milford *(G-4434)*
Hampton Inn Middletown..........F....... 302 378-5656
Middletown *(G-4103)*
Hampton Inn Seaford................G....... 302 629-4500
Seaford *(G-8259)*
Hampton Inn-Dover................G....... 302 736-3500
Dover *(G-1625)*
Holiday Inn Express................F....... 302 227-4030
Rehoboth Beach *(G-7965)*
Holiday Inn Express................E....... 302 398-8800
Harrington *(G-2850)*
Holiday Inn Select................D....... 302 792-2700
Claymont *(G-762)*
Hollywood Grill Restaurant..........D....... 302 655-1348
Wilmington *(G-10930)*
Hollywood Grill Restaurant..........F....... 302 629-4500
Seaford *(G-8265)*
Hollywood Grill Restaurant..........D....... 302 479-2000
Wilmington *(G-10931)*
Hollywood Grill Restaurant..........E....... 302 737-3900
Newark *(G-6736)*
Homewood Suites Newark..........G....... 302 453-9700
Newark *(G-6742)*
Interstate Hotels Resorts Inc..........E....... 302 792-2700
Claymont *(G-766)*
J & P Management Inc................F....... 302 854-9400
Georgetown *(G-2569)*
Jay Ambe Inc................F....... 302 654-5400
New Castle *(G-5436)*
Jay Devi Inc................F....... 302 777-4700
New Castle *(G-5437)*
Jay Ganesh LLC................G....... 302 322-1800
New Castle *(G-5438)*
Jaysons LLC................E....... 302 656-9436
Wilmington *(G-11133)*
K W Lands LLC................E....... 302 674-2200
Dover *(G-1718)*
K W Lands North LLC................E....... 302 678-0600
Dover *(G-1719)*
Keval Corp................F....... 302 453-9100
Newark *(G-6877)*
Khanna Entps Ltd A Ltd Partnr..........E....... 302 266-6400
Newark *(G-6885)*
Kw Garden................E....... 302 735-7770
Dover *(G-1759)*
Lila Keshav Hospitality LLC..........F....... 302 696-2272
Middletown *(G-4133)*
MainStay Suites................F....... 302 678-8383
Dover *(G-1811)*
Mark One LLC................F....... 302 735-4700
Dover *(G-1819)*
Marriott International Inc..........G....... 800 441-7048
Newark *(G-6991)*
Midway Ventures LLC................E....... 302 645-8003
Rehoboth Beach *(G-8009)*
Mj Wilmington Hotel Assoc LP..........E....... 302 454-1500
Newark *(G-7046)*
Mj Wilmington Hotel Assoc LP..........C....... 302 454-1500
Newark *(G-7047)*
Nacstar................E....... 302 453-1700
Newark *(G-7081)*
Nazar Dover LLC................E....... 302 747-5050
Dover *(G-1886)*
Paul Amos................F....... 302 541-9200
Bethany Beach *(G-420)*
Pde I LLC................D....... 302 654-8300
Wilmington *(G-12054)*
Priya Realty Corp................G....... 302 737-5050
Newark *(G-7261)*
Quality Inn................F....... 302 292-1500
Newark *(G-7283)*
Quintasian LLC................E....... 302 674-3784
Dover *(G-2005)*
Red Roof................G....... 302 368-8521
Newark *(G-7308)*
Red Roof Inns Inc................F....... 302 292-2870
Newark *(G-7309)*
Residence Inn By Marriott LLC..........E....... 302 453-9200
Newark *(G-7325)*
Resort Hotel LLC................E....... 302 226-1515
Rehoboth Beach *(G-8057)*

PRODUCT & SERVICES SECTION
TRUCKING: Except Local

RI Heritage Inn Topeka Inc ....E 785 271-8903
  Wilmington *(G-12404)*
Rodeway Inn ....E 302 227-0401
  Rehoboth Beach *(G-8061)*
Routzhan Jessman ....F 302 398-4206
  Harrington *(G-2881)*
Sage Hospitality Resources LLC ....E 302 292-1500
  Newark *(G-7376)*
Seper 8 Motel ....E 302 734-5701
  Dover *(G-2070)*
Shiv Sagar Inc ....F 302 674-3800
  Dover *(G-2078)*
Shree Lalji LLC ....G 302 730-8009
  Dover *(G-2082)*
Shri SAI Dover LLC ....E 302 747-5050
  Dover *(G-2083)*
Shri Swami Narayan LLC ....E 302 738-3198
  Newark *(G-7418)*
Skyways Motor Lodge Corp ....E 302 328-6666
  New Castle *(G-5716)*
Sleep Inn & Suites ....E 302 645-6464
  Lewes *(G-3748)*
Sonesta ....E 302 453-9200
  Newark *(G-7458)*
Sun Hotel Inc ....G 302 322-0711
  New Castle *(G-5742)*
Sunny Hospitality LLC ....F 302 226-0700
  Rehoboth Beach *(G-8092)*
Sunny Hospitality LLC ....F 302 398-3900
  Harrington *(G-2895)*
Super Eight Dover ....G 302 734-5701
  Dover *(G-2117)*
Tru By Hilton Georgetown LLC ....E 302 515-2100
  Georgetown *(G-2695)*
Tucson Hotels LP ....D 678 830-2438
  Wilmington *(G-12991)*
Veer Hotels Inc ....G 302 398-3900
  Harrington *(G-2904)*
Wilmington Hotel Venture ....C 302 655-0400
  Wilmington *(G-13234)*

TRAVELERS' AID

PDr Vc Ltd Liability Company ....G 424 281-4669
  Wilmington *(G-12056)*

TRUCK & BUS BODIES: Farm Truck

Kruger Trailers Inc ....G 302 856-2577
  Georgetown *(G-2584)*

TRUCK & FREIGHT TERMINALS & SUPPORT ACTIVITIES

Kimbles AVI Lgistical Svcs Inc ....G 334 663-4954
  Georgetown *(G-2582)*

TRUCK BODIES: Body Parts

T & J Murray Worldwide Svcs ....F 302 736-1790
  Dover *(G-2125)*

TRUCK BODY SHOP

Stokes Garage Inc ....G 302 994-0613
  Wilmington *(G-12768)*

TRUCK DRIVER SVCS

Triglia Trans Co ....E 302 846-3795
  Delmar *(G-1041)*
Walker & Sons Inc ....F 302 653-5635
  Smyrna *(G-8738)*

TRUCK GENERAL REPAIR SVC

All American Truck Brokers ....G 302 654-6101
  Wilmington *(G-9011)*
B & F Towing & Salvage Co Inc ....E 302 328-4146
  New Castle *(G-5062)*
Blue Hen Spring Works Inc ....F 302 422-6500
  Milford *(G-4328)*
Coastal Towing Inc ....G 302 645-6300
  Lewes *(G-3439)*
Delaware Fleet Service Inc ....G 302 778-5000
  New Castle *(G-5229)*
Delmarva Pump Center Inc ....E 302 492-1245
  Marydel *(G-3915)*
Durkee Automotive Inc ....G 302 798-5656
  Claymont *(G-737)*
H & H Truck and Trailer Repair ....G 302 653-1446
  Smyrna *(G-8648)*
Isaacs Automotive Inc ....G 302 995-2519
  Wilmington *(G-11087)*
Shark Service Center LLC ....G 302 337-8233
  Bridgeville *(G-520)*
Truck Tech Inc ....F 302 832-8000
  New Castle *(G-5796)*
Universalfleet ....G 302 428-0661
  New Castle *(G-5810)*

TRUCK PAINTING & LETTERING SVCS

Penuel Sign Co ....G 302 856-7265
  Georgetown *(G-2616)*

TRUCK PARTS & ACCESSORIES: Wholesalers

All American Truck Brokers ....G 302 654-6101
  Wilmington *(G-9011)*
Harvey Mack Sales & Svc Inc ....E 302 324-8340
  New Castle *(G-5382)*
Keller Truck Parts Inc ....G 302 658-5107
  Wilmington *(G-11235)*
Ploeners Automotive Pdts Co ....G 302 655-4418
  Wilmington *(G-12161)*
T & J Murray Worldwide Svcs ....F 302 736-1790
  Dover *(G-2125)*
Transaxle LLC ....G 302 322-8300
  New Castle *(G-5785)*

TRUCKING & HAULING SVCS: Contract Basis

Contractual Carriers Inc ....E 302 453-1420
  Newark *(G-6292)*
Hab Nab Trucking Inc ....E 302 245-6900
  Bridgeville *(G-478)*
Old Dominion Freight Line Inc ....E 302 337-8793
  Bridgeville *(G-505)*
Penny Express Inc ....G 302 571-0544
  Wilmington *(G-12072)*
Schwerman Trucking Co ....E 302 832-3103
  Bear *(G-316)*
Triglias Transportation Co ....E 302 846-2141
  Delmar *(G-1042)*
Warren W Seaver ....G 302 674-8969
  Dover *(G-2206)*

TRUCKING & HAULING SVCS: Furniture Moving & Storage, Local

Advance Office Instltions Inc ....E 302 777-5599
  New Castle *(G-5008)*
Dunkley Enterprises LLC ....G 302 275-0100
  Odessa *(G-7826)*

TRUCKING & HAULING SVCS: Garbage, Collect/Transport Only

Buzzards Inc ....G 302 945-3500
  Millsboro *(G-4651)*
Wasteflo LLC ....G 410 202-0802
  Laurel *(G-3307)*

TRUCKING & HAULING SVCS: Haulage & Cartage, Light, Local

Harmony Trucking Inc ....G 302 633-5600
  Wilmington *(G-10840)*
High Tide Trucking Inc ....G 302 846-3537
  Delmar *(G-1003)*

TRUCKING & HAULING SVCS: Heavy, NEC

Banks Farm LLC ....G 302 542-4100
  Dagsboro *(G-881)*
Bear Concrete Construction ....E 302 834-3333
  Newark *(G-6062)*
Material Transit Inc ....F 302 395-0556
  New Castle *(G-5512)*

TRUCKING & HAULING SVCS: Liquid Petroleum, Exc Local

Marine Lubricants Inc ....G 302 429-7570
  Wilmington *(G-11526)*

TRUCKING & HAULING SVCS: Mail Carriers, Contract

Eastern Mail Transport Inc ....F 302 838-0500
  Bear *(G-139)*

TRUCKING & HAULING SVCS: Mobile Homes

Messicks Mobile Homes Inc ....F 302 398-9166
  Harrington *(G-2867)*
Pierson Culver LLC ....G 302 732-1145
  Dagsboro *(G-930)*

TRUCKING, ANIMAL

Andrew Simoff Horse Trnsp ....G 302 994-1433
  Wilmington *(G-9080)*

TRUCKING, AUTOMOBILE CARRIER

Co Fs Holding Company LLC ....G 302 894-1244
  Newark *(G-6258)*
T A H First Inc ....G 302 653-6114
  Smyrna *(G-8728)*
Yrc Inc ....G 302 322-5111
  New Castle *(G-5844)*

TRUCKING, DUMP

All American Truck Brokers ....G 302 654-6101
  Wilmington *(G-9011)*
Geotech LLC ....G 302 353-9769
  Newark *(G-6649)*
Morris E Justice Inc ....G 302 539-7731
  Dagsboro *(G-924)*
Reddix Trucking Inc ....G 302 745-1277
  Lewes *(G-3713)*
Sutton Bus & Truck Co Inc ....D 302 995-7444
  Wilmington *(G-12821)*
Wagner N J & Sons Trucking ....F 302 242-7731
  Felton *(G-2325)*
Walleys Trucking Inc ....G 302 893-8652
  Bear *(G-369)*

TRUCKING, REFRIGERATED: Long-Distance

Burris Logistics ....E 302 221-4100
  New Castle *(G-5122)*
William R Knotts & Son Inc ....F 302 674-3496
  Dover *(G-2227)*

TRUCKING: Except Local

A Duie Pyle Inc ....D 302 326-9440
  New Castle *(G-4993)*
Adam Hobbs & Son Inc ....F 302 697-2090
  Felton *(G-2269)*
Armed Forces Driving School ....G 302 981-6903
  Newark *(G-5995)*
Armstrong Relocation Co LLC ....G 302 323-9000
  New Castle *(G-5045)*
Asi Transport LLC ....G 302 349-9460
  Bridgeville *(G-448)*
Atlantic Bulk Carriers ....F 302 378-6300
  Middletown *(G-3949)*
Baq Logistics LLC ....G 302 401-6466
  Dover *(G-1171)*
Benson Enterprise Inc ....G 302 344-9183
  Seaford *(G-8166)*
Christiana Motor Freight Inc ....F 302 655-6271
  New Castle *(G-5157)*
City Mist LLC ....G 302 342-1377
  New Castle *(G-5171)*
Delaware Moving & Storage Inc .....D 302 322-0311
  Bear *(G-110)*
Diamond State Corporation ....D 302 674-1300
  Dover *(G-1425)*
E & J Trucking Inc ....G 302 349-4284
  Greenwood *(G-2733)*
Eastern Mail Transport Inc ....F 302 838-0500
  Bear *(G-139)*
Eric Hobbs Trucking Inc ....E 302 697-2090
  Viola *(G-8835)*
Foodliner Inc ....D 302 368-4204
  Newark *(G-6600)*
Freehold Cartage Inc ....G 302 658-2005
  New Castle *(G-5329)*
George W Oppel ....G 302 398-4433
  Houston *(G-3178)*
Hobbs Enterprises Inc ....G 302 697-2090
  Viola *(G-8837)*
Holman Moving Systems LLC ....B 302 323-9000
  New Castle *(G-5398)*

Employee Codes: A=Over 500 employees, B=251-500
C=101-250, D=51-100, E=20-50, F=10-19, G=1-9

2020 Harris Directory of
Delaware Businesses

TRUCKING: Except Local

Jeff Bartsch Trckg Excvtg Inc	G	302 653-9329
Townsend (G-8801)		
Mark IV Transportation Co Inc	E	302 337-9898
Bridgeville (G-493)		
Mawuli Logistics LLC	G	302 544-5129
Newark (G-7004)		
Montgomery Kenneth John	G	302 992-0484
Wilmington (G-11740)		
On-Demand Services LLC	G	302 388-1215
New Castle (G-5588)		
Parker Express Inc	E	302 221-5777
New Castle (G-5602)		
Phoenix Trnsp & Logistics Inc	G	302 348-8814
Wilmington (G-12126)		
R W Morgan Farms Inc	G	302 542-7740
Lincoln (G-3864)		
Reed Trucking Company	D	302 684-8585
Milton (G-4955)		
Ruan Transport Corporation	G	302 696-3270
Middletown (G-4226)		
Tc Logistics Incorporated	F	302 470-8557
Bear (G-349)		
Trinity 3 Enterprises Inc	G	267 973-2666
Bear (G-359)		
Ultimate Express Inc	F	443 523-0800
Selbyville (G-8552)		
Xpo Logistics Freight Inc	E	302 629-5228
Seaford (G-8444)		

TRUCKING: Local, With Storage

Bayshore Trnsp Sys Inc	D	302 366-0220
Newark (G-6059)		
Bennett & Bennett Inc	F	302 990-8939
New Castle (G-5081)		
Buntings Garage Inc	F	302 732-9021
Dagsboro (G-886)		
Christiana Motor Freight Inc	F	302 655-6271
New Castle (G-5157)		
Contractual Carriers Inc	E	302 453-1420
Newark (G-6292)		
Davis Trucking & Family LLC	F	302 381-6358
Millsboro (G-4674)		
Diamond State Corporation	D	302 674-1300
Dover (G-1425)		
Hollie Enterprises LLC	G	903 721-1904
Wilmington (G-10927)		
Holman Moving Systems LLC	B	302 323-9000
New Castle (G-5398)		
Holman Moving Systems LLC	D	302 323-9000
New Castle (G-5399)		
New Creation Logistics Inc	F	302 438-3154
Newark (G-7103)		
Penske Truck Leasing Corp	G	302 449-9294
Middletown (G-4188)		
United Distribution Inc	F	302 429-0400
Wilmington (G-13024)		
Whipper Snapper Transport LLC	G	302 265-2437
Milford (G-4604)		

TRUCKING: Local, Without Storage

A Collins Trucking Inc	G	302 438-8334
Bear (G-5)		
Aoz Food and Gas LLC	G	302 981-2966
Newark (G-5979)		
Asi Transport LLC	G	302 349-9460
Bridgeville (G-448)		
Beth Trucking Inc	G	918 814-2970
Newark (G-6075)		
BFI Waste Services LLC	E	302 658-4097
Wilmington (G-9324)		
Bk Lord Trucking	G	302 284-7890
Felton (G-2275)		
Bloomfield Trucking Inc	G	302 834-6922
Middletown (G-3970)		
C&J Paving Inc	F	302 684-0211
Milton (G-4873)		
Connolly Options LLC	E	302 998-2016
New Castle (G-5191)		
Courtesy Trnsp Svcs Inc	D	302 322-9722
New Castle (G-5203)		
Cr Newlin Trucking Inc	G	302 678-9124
Dover (G-1319)		
Dawn Arrow Inc	E	302 328-9695
New Castle (G-5217)		
Delp Trucking	G	302 275-6541
Smyrna (G-8622)		
Deo Trucking	G	302 744-9832
Dover (G-1414)		
Dependable Trucking Inc	F	302 655-6271
New Castle (G-5248)		

Diamond State Express LLC	G	302 563-3514
Wilmington (G-10143)		
Elizabeth Malbert	G	302 422-9015
Lincoln (G-3845)		
Far Trucking LLC	G	302 266-8034
Newark (G-6571)		
First Chice Auto Trck Mddltown	G	302 376-6333
Middletown (G-4071)		
Foraker Oil Inc	G	302 834-7595
Delaware City (G-957)		
Gens Trucking Inc	G	302 421-3522
New Castle (G-5350)		
H G Investments LLC	E	302 734-5017
Magnolia (G-3894)		
Hab Nab Trucking Inc	G	302 245-6900
Bridgeville (G-478)		
Highland Construction LLC	F	302 286-6990
Bear (G-185)		
James Poole	G	215 407-4046
Smyrna (G-8662)		
Jkb Corp	E	302 734-5017
Dover (G-1698)		
John T Brown Inc	G	302 398-8518
Harrington (G-2858)		
Johnny Walker Enterprises LLC	G	408 500-6439
Lewes (G-3575)		
L A S Trucking LLC	G	302 439-4433
Wilmington (G-11307)		
M & W Trucking Inc	G	302 655-6994
New Castle (G-5492)		
Morris CT Trucking Inc	G	302 653-2396
Smyrna (G-8682)		
Murry Trucking Llc	G	302 653-4811
Smyrna (G-8683)		
On-Demand Services LLC	G	302 388-1215
New Castle (G-5588)		
PB Trucking Inc	F	302 841-3209
Greenwood (G-2758)		
Penny Express Inc	G	302 571-0544
Wilmington (G-12072)		
R & W Transportation Corp	G	703 670-5483
Wilmington (G-12292)		
R&R Logistics Inc	G	302 629-4255
Seaford (G-8369)		
Richard Woinski Trucking	G	302 644-1579
Lewes (G-3719)		
Sardo & Sons Warehousing Inc	G	302 369-2100
Newark (G-7387)		
Scottys Trucking Inc	G	302 629-5156
Seaford (G-8385)		
Sentinel Transportation LLC	F	302 477-1640
Wilmington (G-12579)		
Sharon Construction Inc	F	302 999-1345
Wilmington (G-12593)		
Shirkey Trucking Corp	G	302 349-2791
Greenwood (G-2763)		
Smart Plus Transport LLC	G	347 963-0980
Newark (G-7446)		
Specialized Carier Systems Inc	G	302 424-4548
Milford (G-4567)		
Tmk Trucking LLC	G	302 449-5131
Middletown (G-4259)		
Unique Pro-Co LLC	G	302 723-2365
Wilmington (G-13018)		
V & A Trucking LLC	G	302 276-5548
Newark (G-7635)		
W Gifford Inc	G	302 420-6112
Newark (G-7670)		
Whites Family Trucking LLC	G	302 393-1401
Ellendale (G-2264)		
Whitetail Country Log & Hlg	G	302 846-3982
Delmar (G-1048)		
Wwc III	F	302 238-7778
Millsboro (G-4830)		

TRUCKING: Long-Distance, Less Than Truckload

Fedex Freight Corporation	E	800 218-6570
New Castle (G-5306)		
Jz Road & Air Cargo Lines Inc	G	302 468-5988
Newark (G-6861)		

TRUCKS & TRACTORS: Industrial

3M Company	C	302 286-2480
Newark (G-5859)		
Airsled Inc	G	302 292-8911
Newark (G-5928)		
Wwc III Trucking LLC	G	302 238-7778
Millsboro (G-4831)		

TRUCKS, INDL: Wholesalers

Four States LLC	F	302 655-3400
New Castle (G-5325)		

TRUCKS: Forklift

Shipley Associates Inc	G	302 652-1766
Wilmington (G-12604)		

TRUNKS

Snickers Ditch Trunk Company	G	302 325-1762
New Castle (G-5719)		

TRUSSES & FRAMING: Prefabricated Metal

All-Span Inc	E	302 349-9460
Bridgeville (G-444)		

TRUSSES: Wood, Roof

Sam Yoder and Son LLC	C	302 398-4711
Greenwood (G-2762)		
Warren Truss Co	F	302 368-8566
Newark (G-7676)		
Warren Truss Co	G	302 337-9470
Bridgeville (G-530)		

TRUST COMPANIES: National With Deposits, Commercial

Capital One National Assn	F	302 658-3302
Wilmington (G-9558)		
PNC Bancorp Inc	E	302 427-5896
Wilmington (G-12164)		
PNC Bank National Association	G	302 337-3500
Bridgeville (G-511)		
PNC Bank National Association	E	302 934-3106
Millsboro (G-4783)		
PNC Bank National Association	F	302 733-7150
Newark (G-7225)		
PNC Bank National Association	G	302 733-7170
Newark (G-7226)		
PNC Bank National Association	F	302 537-2600
Bethany Beach (G-423)		
PNC Bank National Association	G	302 378-4441
Middletown (G-4194)		
PNC Bank National Association	F	302 429-1761
Wilmington (G-12167)		
PNC Bank National Association	F	302 832-8750
Bear (G-284)		
PNC Bank National Association	F	302 478-7822
Wilmington (G-12171)		
PNC Bank National Association	G	302 235-4010
Wilmington (G-12172)		
PNC Bank National Association	F	302 838-6782
Bear (G-285)		
PNC Bank National Association	G	302 993-3000
Wilmington (G-12173)		
PNC Bank National Association	F	302 735-2160
Dover (G-1974)		
PNC Bank National Association	F	302 645-4500
Lewes (G-3694)		
PNC Bank National Association	F	302 855-0400
Georgetown (G-2621)		

TRUST COMPANIES: State Accepting Deposits, Commercial

Bank of Delmarva	G	302 226-8900
Rehoboth Beach (G-7854)		
Calvin B Taylor Bnkg Berlin MD	G	302 541-0500
Ocean View (G-7772)		
Citizens Bank National Assn	G	302 734-0231
Dover (G-1285)		
Citizens Bank National Assn	G	302 653-9245
Smyrna (G-8596)		
Citizens Bank National Assn		302 477-1205
Wilmington (G-9715)		
Community Bank Delaware	E	302 348-8600
Lewes (G-3444)		
Discover Bank	E	302 349-4512
Greenwood (G-2731)		
Manufacturers & Traders Tr Co	G	302 285-3277
Middletown (G-4143)		
Manufacturers & Traders Tr Co	G	302 472-3233
Wilmington (G-11506)		
Manufacturers & Traders Tr Co	F	302 735-2010
Dover (G-1814)		
Manufacturers & Traders Tr Co	F	302 855-2160
Milford (G-4485)		

PRODUCT & SERVICES SECTION

Manufacturers & Traders Tr Co .... F 302 651-1757
  Wilmington (G-11508)
Manufacturers & Traders Tr Co .... F 302 651-1803
  Wilmington (G-11509)
Manufacturers & Traders Tr Co .... F 302 651-1544
  Wilmington (G-11510)
Manufacturers & Traders Tr Co .... F 302 656-1260
  Wilmington (G-11511)
Manufacturers & Traders Tr Co .... G 302 856-4405
  Georgetown (G-2596)
PNC Bank National Association .... F 302 733-7160
  Newark (G-7227)
PNC Bank National Association .... F 302 629-5000
  Seaford (G-8358)
PNC Bank National Association .... F 302 733-7192
  New Castle (G-5628)

TRUST MANAGEMENT SVC, EXC EDUCATIONAL, RELIGIOUS & CHARITY

Brandywine Trust Co .... E 302 234-5750
  Hockessin (G-2968)
Wells Fargo Delaware Trust Co .... G 302 575-2002
  Wilmington (G-13153)

TRUST MANAGEMENT SVCS: Charitable

Delaware Community Foundation .... F 302 571-8004
  Wilmington (G-10023)
Milton & Hattie Kutz Foundaton .... F 302 427-2100
  Wilmington (G-11699)
Play For Good Inc .... G 312 520-9788
  Wilmington (G-12154)

TRUST MANAGEMENT SVCS: Educational

Simply Styling-Schl of Csmtlgy .... G 302 778-1885
  Wilmington (G-12628)

TRUST MANAGEMENT SVCS: Personal Investment

Bank of New York Mellon Corp .... G 302 421-2335
  Wilmington (G-9243)

TRUST MGMT SVCS: Priv Estate, Personal Invest/Vacation Fund

Boothe Investment Group .... G 302 734-7526
  Dover (G-1221)

TUBING, COLD-DRAWN: Mech Or Hypodermic Sizes, Stainless

Handytube Corporation .... D 302 697-9521
  Camden (G-575)

TUBING: Electrical Use, Quartz

Atlantic Industrial Optics .... G 302 856-7905
  Georgetown (G-2438)

TUBING: Plastic

Fbk Medical Tubing Inc .... E 302 855-0585
  Georgetown (G-2527)
Tpi Partners Inc .... D 302 855-0139
  Georgetown (G-2694)

TURBINE GENERATOR SET UNITS: Hydraulic, Complete

Junttan USA Inc .... G 302 500-1274
  Laurel (G-3246)

TURBINES & TURBINE GENERATOR SETS

Everlift Wind Technology .... G 240 683-9787
  Lewes (G-3488)
Garrett Motion Inc .... G 973 867-7017
  Wilmington (G-10671)
Kissangen Inc .... E 414 446-4182
  Newark (G-6895)
Webro Holdings LLC .... G 302 314-3334
  Rehoboth Beach (G-8109)
Wing2wind Technology Inc .... G 240 683-9787
  Lewes (G-3828)

TURKEY PROCESSING & SLAUGHTERING

Jcr Enterprises Inc .... E 302 629-9163
  Seaford (G-8279)

TYPESETTING SVC

Amer Inc .... G 302 654-2498
  Wilmington (G-9039)
Associates International Inc .... D 302 656-4500
  Wilmington (G-9157)
Ben-Dom Printing Company .... F 302 737-9144
  Newark (G-6072)
Dover Post Co Inc .... D 302 678-3616
  Dover (G-1467)
Garile Inc .... E 302 366-0848
  Newark (G-6639)
Stanley Golden .... G 302 652-5626
  Wilmington (G-12736)
Sussex Printing Corp .... D 302 629-9303
  Seaford (G-8416)
William N Cann Inc .... E 302 995-0820
  Wilmington (G-13215)

UNISEX HAIR SALONS

1401 Hair Designs Ltd .... G 302 655-1401
  Wilmington (G-8848)
Above Beyond Unisex Hair Salon .... G 302 276-0187
  New Castle (G-4998)
All About U Evada Concept .... G 302 539-1925
  Millville (G-4833)
Babe Styling Studio Inc .... G 302 543-7738
  Wilmington (G-9217)
Brandon Tatum .... G 302 564-7428
  Selbyville (G-8459)
Carol Inc .... E 302 386-4362
  Newark (G-6159)
Chez Nichole Hair & Nail Salon .... E 302 654-8888
  Wilmington (G-9659)
Gc New Castle Inc .... G 302 544-6128
  New Castle (G-5347)
Great Clips .... G 302 478-2022
  Wilmington (G-10768)
Hair Sensations Inc .... G 302 731-0920
  New Castle (G-5372)
Hairworks Inc .... F 302 656-0566
  Wilmington (G-10822)
Head Quarters .... G 302 798-1639
  Wilmington (G-10864)
Jersey Clippers LLC .... E 302 956-0138
  Bridgeville (G-486)
Jk Tangles Hair Salon .... F 302 698-1006
  Dover (G-1697)
Mastercuts .... G 302 674-0300
  Dover (G-1826)
Maxines Hair Happenings Inc .... G 302 875-4055
  Laurel (G-3263)
Nu Attitude Styling Salon Ltd .... G 302 734-8638
  Dover (G-1908)
Penache Beauty Salon .... G 302 731-5912
  Newark (G-7192)
Premier Solutions Intl .... G 302 477-1334
  Wilmington (G-12218)
Ratner Companies LC .... F 302 226-9822
  Rehoboth Beach (G-8040)
Ratner Companies LC .... F 302 678-8081
  Dover (G-2010)
Ratner Companies LC .... G 302 999-7724
  Wilmington (G-12321)
Ratner Companies LC .... F 302 836-3749
  Bear (G-297)
Ratner Companies LC .... E 302 366-9032
  Newark (G-7299)
Ratner Companies LC .... F 302 376-3568
  Middletown (G-4212)
Ratner Companies LC .... F 302 537-4624
  Millville (G-4854)
Ratner Companies LC .... F 302 478-9978
  Wilmington (G-12322)
Regis Corporation .... G 302 376-6165
  Middletown (G-4214)
Regis Corporation .... G 302 654-4477
  Wilmington (G-12361)
Regis Corporation .... G 302 430-0881
  Milford (G-4535)
Regis Corporation .... G 302 697-6220
  Camden (G-598)
Regis Corporation .... G 302 834-1272
  Bear (G-299)
Regis Corporation .... G 302 227-9730
  Rehoboth Beach (G-8046)
Regis Corporation .... F 302 834-9916
  Bear (G-300)
Regis Corporation .... G 302 629-2916
  Seaford (G-8375)

USED MERCHANDISE STORES: Furniture

Regis Corporation .... G 302 628-0484
  Seaford (G-8376)
Regis Corporation .... G 302 478-5065
  Wilmington (G-12362)
Royal Hair Design LLC .... G 302 312-4569
  Smyrna (G-8704)
Salon By Dominic .... F 302 239-8282
  Hockessin (G-3141)
Sophisticuts Inc .... G 302 834-7427
  Bear (G-328)
Supercuts Inc .... G 302 475-5001
  Wilmington (G-12805)
Sylvia Saienna .... G 302 683-9082
  Wilmington (G-12829)
Town and Country Salon Inc .... E 302 737-1855
  Newark (G-7579)
Ultimate Images Inc .... G 302 479-0292
  Wilmington (G-13008)
Uppercut Inc .... G 302 736-1661
  Dover (G-2181)
Xanadu Concepts LLC .... G 302 449-2677
  Middletown (G-4292)

UNIVERSITY

University of Delaware .... F 302 831-2802
  Newark (G-7629)
University of Delaware .... F 302 831-2792
  Newark (G-7619)
University of Delaware .... E 302 831-4811
  Newark (G-7620)
University of Delaware .... C 302 831-6041
  Newark (G-7621)
University of Delaware .... E 302 831-2501
  Newark (G-7622)
University of Delaware .... E 302 831-2961
  Newark (G-7623)
University of Delaware .... F 302 831-2833
  Newark (G-7624)
University of Delaware .... C 302 831-1141
  Newark (G-7625)
University of Delaware .... E 302 831-2136
  Newark (G-7626)
University of Delaware .... B 302 831-8149
  Newark (G-7627)
University of Delaware .... D 302 831-6300
  Newark (G-7628)

UPHOLSTERY WORK SVCS

Color Dye Systems and Co .... G 302 454-1754
  Newark (G-6265)
Timothy Blawn .... G 302 697-3843
  Camden Wyoming (G-659)

URBAN PLANNING & COMMUNITY & RURAL DEVELOPMENT SVCS

One Village Alliance Inc .... G 302 275-1715
  Wilmington (G-11957)

USED CAR DEALERS

Delaware Public Auto Auction .... E 302 656-0500
  New Castle (G-5234)
Future Ford Sales Inc .... D 302 999-0261
  Wilmington (G-10654)
New Car Connection .... F 302 328-7000
  New Castle (G-5553)
Preferred Auto and Cycle LLC .... G 302 855-0169
  Dagsboro (G-931)
Winner Ford of Newark Inc .... C 302 731-2415
  Newark (G-7710)
Wolfs Elite Autos .... G 302 999-9199
  Wilmington (G-13287)

USED MERCHANDISE STORES

Fred Drake Automotive Inc .... G 302 378-4877
  Townsend (G-8788)
Goodwill Inds Del Del Cnty Inc .... E 302 761-4640
  Wilmington (G-10749)

USED MERCHANDISE STORES: Furniture

Goodeals Inc .... G 302 999-1737
  Wilmington (G-10748)

Employee Codes: A=Over 500 employees, B=251-500
C=101-250, D=51-100, E=20-50, F=10-19, G=1-9

2020 Harris Directory of Delaware Businesses

UTENSILS: Household, Cooking & Kitchen, Metal
Idylc Homes LLC ....G...... 302 295-3719
Wilmington *(G-10995)*

UTILITY TRAILER DEALERS
Utility/Eastern..E...... 302 337-7400
Bridgeville *(G-528)*

VACATION LODGES
Re/Max Realty Group-Rentals..................F...... 302 227-4800
Rehoboth Beach *(G-8044)*

VACUUM CLEANER REPAIR SVCS
Master Klean Company ....G...... 302 539-4290
Ocean View *(G-7802)*

VACUUM CLEANER STORES
Master Klean Company ....G...... 302 539-4290
Ocean View *(G-7802)*

VACUUM CLEANERS: Household
Healthy Homes De Inc ....G...... 302 998-1001
Wilmington *(G-10871)*

VALUE-ADDED RESELLERS: Computer Systems
Blue Ocean Systems LLC ....G...... 866 355-5989
Wilmington *(G-9379)*
Central Firm LLC ....G...... 610 470-9836
Wilmington *(G-9615)*
Consult Dynamics Inc ....E...... 302 654-1019
Wilmington *(G-9837)*
Delaware Business Systems Inc ....E...... 302 395-0900
New Castle *(G-5226)*
Discidium Technology Inc ....G...... 347 220-5979
Newark *(G-6455)*
Polar Strategy Inc ....G...... 703 628-0001
Lewes *(G-3695)*
Ram Tech Systems Inc ....E...... 302 832-6600
Middletown *(G-4210)*

VALVES
Mid Atlantic Industrial Sales ....G...... 302 698-6356
Camden *(G-590)*

VALVES & PIPE FITTINGS
Solar Unlimited North Amer LLC ....G...... 302 542-4580
Lewes *(G-3754)*

VALVES: Indl
Eeco Inc ....G...... 302 456-1448
Newark *(G-6506)*
Potts Wldg Boiler Repr Co Inc ....C...... 302 453-2550
Newark *(G-7234)*

VALVES: Regulating & Control, Automatic
Automation & Controls Tech LLC ....G...... 913 908-4344
Milton *(G-4866)*

VARIETY STORE MERCHANDISE, WHOLESALE
Atg Trading LLC ....G...... 909 348-0620
Wilmington *(G-9172)*

VARIETY STORES
Historical Society of Delware.................E...... 302 655-7161
Wilmington *(G-10919)*
Stuart Kingston Inc.................................F...... 302 227-2524
Rehoboth Beach *(G-8090)*

VEHICLES: All Terrain
Affordable Recreation LLC ....G...... 603 635-2101
Lewes *(G-3327)*

VENDING MACHINE OPERATORS: Candy & Snack Food
Vending Solutions LLC ....G...... 302 674-2222
Dover *(G-2189)*

VENDING MACHINE OPERATORS: Sandwich & Hot Food
Columbia Vending Service Inc ....F...... 302 856-7000
Delmar *(G-985)*

VENDING MACHINE REPAIR SVCS
Columbia Vending Service Inc ....F...... 302 856-7000
Delmar *(G-985)*

VENDING MACHINES & PARTS
Vending Solutions LLC ....G...... 302 674-2222
Dover *(G-2189)*

VENTILATING EQPT: Metal
Faust Sheet Metal Works Inc ....G...... 302 645-9509
Lewes *(G-3493)*

VENTURE CAPITAL COMPANIES
Aurum Capital Ventures Inc ....G...... 877 467-7780
Dover *(G-1160)*
Joyce Co ....E...... 302 353-4011
Wilmington *(G-11200)*
Jsc Ventures LLC ....D...... 302 336-8151
Dover *(G-1712)*
Medici Ventures Inc ....E...... 801 319-7029
Wilmington *(G-11617)*
Nikko Capital Investments Ltd ....E...... 832 324-5335
Lewes *(G-3659)*

VESSELS: Process, Indl, Metal Plate
Apex Piping Systems Inc ....D...... 302 995-6136
Wilmington *(G-9097)*
Newarc Welding & Fabricating ....G...... 302 658-5214
Wilmington *(G-11875)*

VETERANS AFFAIRS ADMINISTRATION SVCS
Delaware Secretary of State...................G...... 302 834-8046
Bear *(G-112)*

VETERANS' AFFAIRS ADMINISTRATION, GOVERNMENT: Federal
Veterans Health Administration..............B...... 302 994-2511
Wilmington *(G-13070)*
Veterans Health Administration..............G...... 302 994-1660
Wilmington *(G-13071)*

VIDEO PRODUCTION SVCS
Cornerstone Media Production ....G...... 302 855-9380
Georgetown *(G-2486)*
Ken-Del Productions Inc ....F...... 302 999-1111
Wilmington *(G-11239)*
Point Eght Third Prdctions LLC ....G...... 302 317-9419
Wilmington *(G-12177)*

VIDEO TAPE PRODUCTION SVCS
OK Video ....F...... 302 762-2333
Wilmington *(G-11942)*
Pond Publishing & Productions..............G...... 302 284-0200
Felton *(G-2313)*

VINYL RESINS, NEC
Bilcare Research Inc..............................D...... 302 838-3200
Delaware City *(G-949)*
Kuraray America Inc ....F...... 302 992-4204
Wilmington *(G-11301)*

VISA PROCUREMENT SVCS
University of Delaware ....F...... 302 831-2792
Newark *(G-7619)*

VISITING NURSE
Bayada Home Health Care Inc ....D...... 302 424-8200
Milford *(G-4319)*
Bayada Home Health Care Inc ....D...... 302 655-1333
Wilmington *(G-9263)*
Bayada Home Health Care Inc ....F...... 856 231-1000
New Castle *(G-5073)*
Bayada Home Health Care Inc ....G...... 302 836-1000
Newark *(G-6055)*
Christana Care HM Hlth Cmnty S ....B...... 302 327-5583
New Castle *(G-5152)*
Christiana Care Home Health ....F...... 302 995-8448
Wilmington *(G-9685)*
Christiana Care Home Health ....F...... 302 698-4300
Camden *(G-549)*
Comfort Keepers ....G...... 302 378-0994
Townsend *(G-8771)*
Health Care Consultants Inc ....C...... 302 892-9210
Wilmington *(G-10869)*
Interim Healthcare Del LLC ....C...... 302 322-2743
Smyrna *(G-8658)*

VISUAL COMMUNICATIONS SYSTEMS
Versitron Inc..D...... 302 894-0699
Newark *(G-7653)*

VITAMINS: Natural Or Synthetic, Uncompounded, Bulk
Phoenix Intl Resources LLC ....G...... 954 309-0120
Lewes *(G-3689)*

VOCATIONAL TRAINING AGENCY
Chimes Inc..G...... 302 382-4500
New Castle *(G-5148)*
Easter Seal Delaware ....C...... 302 324-4444
New Castle *(G-5276)*
Goodwill Inds Del Del Cnty Inc ....E...... 302 761-4640
Wilmington *(G-10749)*

WALL COVERING STORE
Interiors By Kim Inc ....G...... 302 537-2480
Ocean View *(G-7794)*

WALLPAPER STORE
East Coast Minority Supplier ....E...... 302 656-3337
Wilmington *(G-10320)*

WAREHOUSING & STORAGE FACILITIES, NEC
Ariio Inc ....G...... 562 481-8717
Dover *(G-1136)*
Delaware Direct Inc................................E...... 302 658-8223
Wilmington *(G-10042)*
Meherrin AG & Chem Co ....G...... 302 337-0330
Bridgeville *(G-496)*

WAREHOUSING & STORAGE, REFRIGERATED: Cold Storage Or Refrig
Blue Marlin Ice LLC ....G...... 302 697-7800
Dover *(G-1214)*
Citrosuco North America Inc ....F...... 302 652-8763
Wilmington *(G-9720)*
United States Cold Storage Inc ....E...... 302 422-7536
Milford *(G-4584)*
United States Cold Storage Inc ....E...... 302 422-7536
Milford *(G-4585)*

WAREHOUSING & STORAGE, REFRIGERATED: Frozen Or Refrig Goods
Burris Logistics......................................E...... 302 221-4100
New Castle *(G-5122)*

WAREHOUSING & STORAGE: General
American Van Storage Corp ....E...... 302 369-0900
Newark *(G-5961)*
D & S Warehousing Inc ....E...... 302 731-7440
Newark *(G-6341)*
First State Warehousing.........................D...... 302 426-0802
New Castle *(G-5319)*
Intercontinental Chem Svcs Inc ....E...... 302 654-6800
Wilmington *(G-11055)*
Kenco Group Inc ....E...... 302 629-4295
Seaford *(G-8287)*
Penco Corporation ....D...... 302 629-7911
Seaford *(G-8343)*
Sardo & Sons Warehousing Inc ....G...... 302 369-2100
Newark *(G-7387)*
Sardo & Sons Warehousing Inc ....E...... 302 737-3000
Newark *(G-7388)*
Sardo & Sons Warehousing Inc ....F...... 302 369-0852
Newark *(G-7389)*

PRODUCT & SERVICES SECTION

WELDING REPAIR SVC

Standard Distributing Co Inc .... E 302 674-4591
 Dover (G-2102)

WAREHOUSING & STORAGE: General

Advance Office Instltions Inc .... E 302 777-5599
 New Castle (G-5008)
Allstate Van & Storage Corp .... E 302 369-0230
 Newark (G-5943)
American Prtable Mini Stor Inc .... G 302 934-9898
 Millsboro (G-4630)
Burris Logistics .... E 302 221-4100
 New Castle (G-5122)
Burris Logistics .... D 302 398-5050
 Harrington (G-2820)
Cannon Cold Storage LLC .... E 302 337-5500
 Bridgeville (G-457)
Ceco Inc .... E 302 732-3919
 Dagsboro (G-890)
Delaware Moving & Storage Inc .... D 302 322-0311
 Bear (G-110)
DOT Foods Inc .... D 302 300-4239
 Bear (G-125)
Iovate Health Sciences USA Inc .... E 888 334-4448
 Wilmington (G-11078)
Mtc Delaware LLC .... G 302 654-3400
 New Castle (G-5538)
New Creation Logistics Inc .... F 302 438-3154
 Newark (G-7103)
On-Demand Services LLC .... G 302 388-1215
 New Castle (G-5588)
Penco Corporation .... G 302 629-3061
 Seaford (G-8344)
Tops International Corp .... G 302 738-8889
 Newark (G-7576)

WAREHOUSING & STORAGE: Miniwarehouse

Love Creek Marina MBL Hm Site .... F 302 448-6492
 Lewes (G-3611)
Mc Ginnis Commercial RE .... G 302 736-2700
 Dover (G-1831)
Record Storage Center Inc .... G 302 674-8571
 Dover (G-2016)

WAREHOUSING & STORAGE: Oil & Gasoline, Caverns For Hire

Magellan Midstream Partners LP .... F 302 654-3717
 Wilmington (G-11484)

WAREHOUSING & STORAGE: Self Storage

Brandywine Chemical Company .... G 302 656-5428
 New Castle (G-5104)
Central Storage .... G 302 678-1919
 Dover (G-1269)
Hardy Development .... G 302 436-4496
 Selbyville (G-8499)
Secure Self Storage .... G 302 832-0400
 New Castle (G-5698)
Sentinel Self Storage .... G 302 999-0704
 Wilmington (G-12578)

WARM AIR HEATING & AC EQPT & SPLYS, WHOLESALE Air Filters

John R Seiberlich Inc .... D 302 356-2400
 New Castle (G-5441)

WARM AIR HEATING/AC EQPT/SPLYS, WHOL Warm Air Htg Eqpt/Splys

Berry Refrigeration Co .... E 302 733-0933
 Newark (G-6073)
R E Michel Company LLC .... G 302 678-0250
 Dover (G-2006)
R E Michel Company LLC .... G 302 645-0585
 Lewes (G-3704)
R E Michel Company LLC .... G 302 368-9410
 Newark (G-7292)
WW Grainger Inc .... F 302 322-1840
 New Castle (G-5842)

WASHERS

Lemay Enterprises Inc .... G 302 659-3278
 Townsend (G-8805)
Mr Window Washer .... G 302 588-3624
 Claymont (G-786)

WASTE CLEANING SVCS

Board of Public Works Inc .... G 302 645-6450
 Lewes (G-3390)
Delaware Rural Water Assn .... G 302 398-9633
 Harrington (G-2830)
HCC Corporation LLC .... G 302 421-9306
 Wilmington (G-10860)

WATCH REPAIR SVCS

Bridgewater Jewelers .... G 302 328-2101
 New Castle (G-5113)

WATCHES

Aurista Technologies Inc .... F 302 792-4900
 Claymont (G-696)

WATER SOFTENER SVCS

A and D Plumbing LLC .... G 302 387-9232
 Magnolia (G-3877)
Atlantic Water Products .... E 302 326-1166
 New Castle (G-5052)
Delmarva Water Solutions .... G 302 674-0509
 Dover (G-1412)
Dibiasos Clg Rstration Svc Inc .... G 302 376-7111
 Townsend (G-8784)
Watercraft LLC .... G 302 757-0786
 Wilmington (G-13122)

WATER SOFTENING WHOLESALERS

Condor Technologies Inc .... G 302 698-4444
 Camden (G-551)

WATER SPLY: Irrigation

Atlantic Irrigation Spc Inc .... G 302 846-3527
 Delmar (G-972)
First State Landscaping .... F 302 420-8604
 Bear (G-153)
Impact Irrgation Solutions Inc .... G 484 723-3600
 Wilmington (G-11007)
Jobes Landscape Inc .... G 302 945-0195
 Lewes (G-3572)
Vincent Farms Inc .... C 302 875-5707
 Laurel (G-3302)

WATER SUPPLY

Artesian Resources Corporation .... G 302 453-6900
 Newark (G-6000)
Artesian Utility Dev Inc .... E 800 332-5114
 Newark (G-6001)
Artesian Water Company Inc .... E 302 453-6900
 Newark (G-6004)
Artesian Water Maryland Inc .... E 302 453-6900
 Newark (G-6005)
Camdenwyoming Sewer & Wtr Auth .... F 302 697-6372
 Camden (G-544)
City of Wilmington .... E 302 576-2584
 Wilmington (G-9723)
Core & Main LP .... G 302 684-3452
 Milton (G-4883)
Core & Main LP .... G 302 737-1500
 Newark (G-6297)
J H Wilkerson & Son Inc .... G 302 422-4306
 Milford (G-4456)
Long Neck Water Co .... G 302 947-9600
 Millsboro (G-4724)
Municipal Services Commission .... F 302 323-2330
 New Castle (G-5539)
Naamans Creek Watershed .... G 302 475-3037
 Wilmington (G-11792)
National Waterworks Inc .... G 302 653-9096
 Milton (G-4942)
Suez North America Inc .... F 302 633-5670
 Wilmington (G-12789)
Suez Water Delaware Inc .... D 302 633-5905
 Wilmington (G-12790)
Sussex Shores Water Co Corp .... G 302 539-7611
 Bethany Beach (G-433)
Tidewater Utilities Inc .... D 302 674-8056
 Dover (G-2147)

WATER TREATMENT EQPT: Indl

Aquion Inc .... G 847 725-3000
 Wilmington (G-9108)
Graver Technologies LLC .... C 302 731-1700
 Newark (G-6684)

Sanosil International LLC .... F 302 454-8102
 New Castle (G-5694)
Suez North America Inc .... F 302 633-5670
 Wilmington (G-12789)
Verisoft Inc .... G 602 908-7151
 Dover (G-2190)
Watercraft LLC .... G 302 757-0786
 Wilmington (G-13122)

WATER: Pasteurized & Mineral, Bottled & Canned

Domian International Svc LLC .... G 804 837-3616
 Smyrna (G-8624)
Mr Natural Bottled Water .... G 302 436-7700
 Frankford (G-2376)

WATERPROOFING COMPOUNDS

Aquacast Liner LLC .... D 302 535-3728
 Newark (G-5993)
Jcr Systems LLC .... G 302 420-6072
 New Castle (G-5439)

WEATHER RELATED SVCS

Congo Capital Management LLC .... F 732 337-6643
 Wilmington (G-9820)

WEB SEARCH PORTALS: Internet

Rippl Labs Inc .... F 551 427-1997
 Wilmington (G-12423)
Search LLC .... E 858 348-4584
 Lewes (G-3734)

WEIGHING MACHINERY & APPARATUS

Spectr-Physics Hldings USA Inc .... G 302 478-4600
 Wilmington (G-12698)

WELDING EQPT & SPLYS WHOLESALERS

Airgas Inc .... G 302 575-1822
 Wilmington (G-8996)
Airgas Usa LLC .... F 302 286-5400
 Newark (G-5927)
E E Rosser Inc .... G 302 762-9643
 Wilmington (G-10276)
G & E Welding Supply Co .... F 302 322-9353
 New Castle (G-5339)
Praxair Distribution Inc .... G 302 654-8755
 Wilmington (G-12198)
Urie & Blanton Inc .... G 302 658-8604
 Wilmington (G-13037)

WELDING EQPT REPAIR SVCS

Metal Shop .... F 302 846-2988
 Delmar (G-1020)

WELDING EQPT: Electric

Ef Technologies Inc .... G 302 451-1088
 Newark (G-6508)

WELDING REPAIR SVC

3rd State Welding Supply LLC .... G 302 777-1088
 Wilmington (G-8858)
Allied Precision Inc .... G 302 376-6844
 Middletown (G-3936)
Basher & Son Enterprises Inc .... G 302 239-6584
 Hockessin (G-2962)
Bear Forge and Machine Co Inc .... G 302 322-5199
 Bear (G-47)
Bg Welding LLC .... G 302 228-7260
 Bridgeville (G-453)
Boyds Trailor Hitches .... G 302 697-9000
 Camden Wyoming (G-619)
Boyds Welding Inc .... G 302 697-9000
 Camden Wyoming (G-620)
Bruces Welding Inc .... G 302 629-3891
 Seaford (G-8176)
C&C Welding .... G 402 414-2485
 New Castle (G-5126)
Cat Welding LLC .... G 302 846-3509
 Delmar (G-981)
Chets Welding Service .... G 302 492-1003
 Hartly (G-2915)
Chuck George Inc .... E 302 994-7444
 Wilmington (G-9697)
Dana S Wright .... G 610 563-6070
 Newark (G-6345)

WELDING REPAIR SVC

Davis Welding Service Llc .... G 302 465-3004
  Seaford (G-8217)
Dempseys Specialized Services .... G 302 530-7856
  Newark (G-6436)
Diamond State Welding LLC .... G 302 644-8489
  Milton (G-4894)
East Coast Machine Works .... G 302 349-5180
  Greenwood (G-2734)
George Swire Sr .... G 302 690-6995
  Clayton (G-853)
George W Plummer & Son Inc .... G 302 645-9531
  Lewes (G-3511)
Gj Chalfant Welding .... G 302 545-6404
  Newark (G-6658)
GJ Chalfant Welding LLC .... G 302 983-0822
  Port Penn (G-7834)
Graydie Welding LLC .... G 302 753-0695
  Wilmington (G-10764)
Haines Fabrication & Mch LLC .... F 302 436-1929
  Selbyville (G-8497)
Hot Rod Welding .... G 302 725-5485
  Harrington (G-2851)
Indian River Golf Cars Dr Wldg .... G 302 947-2044
  Millsboro (G-4708)
Joe Falco Portable Welding .... G 302 998-1115
  Wilmington (G-11164)
Js Knotts Inc .... G 302 284-4888
  Felton (G-2299)
Jumpers Welding Inc .... G 302 519-7941
  Middletown (G-4118)
K L Vincent Welding Svc Inc .... F 302 398-9357
  Harrington (G-2860)
L & J Sheet Metal .... F 302 875-2822
  Laurel (G-3249)
Leland Oakley Welding .... G 302 469-5746
  Felton (G-2302)
Leroy H Smith .... G 302 875-5976
  Laurel (G-3258)
Lloyds Wldg & Fabrication LLC .... G 302 384-7662
  Wilmington (G-11416)
Marvel Portable Welding Inc .... G 302 732-9480
  Dagsboro (G-917)
Mastercraft Welding .... G 302 697-3932
  Dover (G-1824)
Metal-Tech Inc .... E 302 322-7770
  New Castle (G-5518)
Miller JW Wldg Boiler Repr Co .... G 302 449-1575
  Middletown (G-4166)
Mitchell S Welding LLC .... G 302 632-1089
  Camden Wyoming (G-650)
Moore Qlty Wldg Fbrication LLC .... G 302 731-4818
  Newark (G-7056)
Moore Quality Welding Fab .... G 302 250-7136
  Middletown (G-4169)
Newarc Welding Inc .... G 302 376-1801
  Middletown (G-4173)
Nicks Welding Repair LLC .... G 302 545-1494
  Wilmington (G-11889)
Peninsula Technical Services I .... G 302 907-0554
  Delmar (G-1025)
Pts Professional Welding .... G 302 632-2079
  Houston (G-3180)
R & J Welding & Fabrication .... G 302 236-5618
  Laurel (G-3276)
R C Fabricators Inc .... D 302 573-8989
  Wilmington (G-12293)
Richard M White Welding .... G 302 684-4461
  Milton (G-4959)
Ronald P Wilson .... G 302 539-4139
  Frankford (G-2384)
Sapps Welding Service .... G 302 491-6319
  Lincoln (G-3868)
Seaford Machine Works Inc .... F 302 629-6034
  Seaford (G-8392)
Terrys Welding LLC .... G 302 349-5260
  Greenwood (G-2766)
Truck Tech Inc .... F 302 832-8000
  New Castle (G-5796)
Welding By Jackson .... G 302 846-3090
  Delmar (G-1047)
William Stele Wldg Fabrication .... G 302 422-7444
  Milford (G-4607)

WELDING SPLYS, EXC GASES: Wholesalers

G & E Welding Supply Co .... F 302 322-9353
  New Castle (G-5339)
Keen Compressed Gas Co .... F 302 594-4545
  Wilmington (G-11232)
Keen Compressed Gas Co .... G 302 736-6814
  Dover (G-1728)
Keen Compressed Gas Co .... E 302 594-4545
  New Castle (G-5456)
Keen Compressed Gas Co Inc .... G 610 583-8770
  New Castle (G-5457)
Roberts Oxygen Company Inc .... G 302 337-9666
  Seaford (G-8380)

WESTERN APPAREL STORES

Chick Harness & Supply Inc .... E 302 398-4630
  Harrington (G-2824)

WHEELCHAIR LIFTS

Design Specific US Inc .... G 650 318-6473
  Wilmington (G-10123)

WHEELCHAIRS

Wheelchair Mechanix .... G 302 478-0858
  Wilmington (G-13182)

WHISTLES

Clean As A Whistle .... G 302 757-5024
  Newark (G-6246)
Clean As A Whistle Inc .... G 302 376-1388
  Middletown (G-3996)
Under Whistle .... G 302 250-8400
  Newark (G-7610)

WIG & HAIRPIECE STORES

Key To Beauty .... G 302 398-9460
  Harrington (G-2861)

WINDOW BLIND REPAIR SVCS

Vertical Blind Factory Inc .... F 302 998-9616
  Wilmington (G-13067)

WINDOW CLEANING SVCS

City Window Cleaning of Del .... E 302 633-0633
  Wilmington (G-9726)
Clearview Windows LLC .... G 302 491-6768
  Milford (G-4356)
TNT Window Cleaning .... G 302 326-2411
  Newark (G-7570)

WINDOW FURNISHINGS WHOLESALERS

Gb Shades LLC .... G 302 798-3028
  Claymont (G-749)

WINE & DISTILLED ALCOHOLIC BEVERAGES WHOLESALERS

Sleigh Financial Inc .... G 302 684-2929
  Milton (G-4970)

WIRE

Priscilla Lancaster .... G 302 792-8305
  Claymont (G-796)
Wire Works .... G 302 792-8305
  Claymont (G-824)

WIRE & CABLE: Aluminum

Gelfand Group Inc .... G 310 666-2362
  Camden Wyoming (G-642)

WIRE & WIRE PRDTS

Wire Works .... G 302 792-8305
  Claymont (G-824)

WIRE FENCING & ACCESS WHOLESALERS

J & M Fencing Inc .... F 302 284-9674
  Felton (G-2295)
Master-Halco Inc .... F 302 475-6714
  Wilmington (G-11564)

WIRE ROPE CENTERS

Barry USA Inc .... G 800 305-2673
  Newark (G-6049)
Barry USA Inc .... G 800 305-2673
  Dover (G-1175)

WIRE: Communication

First State Controls Inc .... F 302 559-7822
  Wilmington (G-10550)

W L Gore & Associates Inc .... C 302 368-3700
  Newark (G-7672)

WOMEN'S & CHILDREN'S CLOTHING WHOLESALERS, NEC

Cato Corporation .... G 302 854-9548
  Georgetown (G-2464)
Crazy Ladyz LLC .... F 302 541-4040
  Ocean View (G-7781)
Great Graphic Originals Ltd .... G 302 734-7600
  Dover (G-1608)
H D Lee Company Inc .... F 302 477-3930
  Wilmington (G-10807)
Lacoste Usa Inc .... G 302 227-9575
  Rehoboth Beach (G-7984)

WOMEN'S & GIRLS' SPORTSWEAR WHOLESALERS

Gbg USA Inc .... G 888 342-7243
  Wilmington (G-10683)

WOMEN'S CLOTHING STORES

Designer Braids and Trade .... G 718 783-9078
  Middletown (G-4037)
Garage .... G 302 453-1930
  Newark (G-6638)

WOMEN'S CLOTHING STORES: Ready-To-Wear

Cato Corporation .... G 302 854-9548
  Georgetown (G-2464)

WOOD & WOOD BY-PRDTS, WHOLESALE

Flw Wood Products Inc .... G 410 259-4674
  Dagsboro (G-902)

WOOD CHIPS, WHOLESALE

Global Entp Worldwide LLC .... D 713 260-9687
  Wilmington (G-10724)

WOOD PRDTS

Butler Woodcrafters .... G 302 764-0744
  Wilmington (G-9516)

WOOD PRDTS: Applicators

Nanticoke Industries LLC .... G 302 245-8825
  Seaford (G-8324)

WOOD PRDTS: Lasts, Boot & Shoe

Vulcan International Corp .... F 302 428-3181
  Wilmington (G-13107)

WOOD PRDTS: Mulch Or Sawdust

Delaware Animal Products LLC .... G 302 423-7754
  Milford (G-4374)
Stockley Materials LLC .... G 302 856-7601
  Georgetown (G-2666)

WOOD PRDTS: Mulch, Wood & Bark

Harvest Consumer Products LLC .... E 302 732-6624
  Dagsboro (G-907)

WOOD PRDTS: Novelties, Fiber

Charles Ogden .... G 305 606-4512
  Wilmington (G-9634)

WOOD PRDTS: Trophy Bases

Kenco Trophy Sales .... G 302 846-3339
  Delmar (G-1013)

WOOD TREATING: Wood Prdts, Creosoted

Wood Expressions Incorporated .... G 302 738-6189
  Newark (G-7717)

WREATHS: Artificial

Denices Ragged Wreath .... G 302 220-7377
  Newark (G-6437)
Lily Wreaths .... G 202 251-6004
  Harrington (G-2865)

PRODUCT & SERVICES SECTION

X-RAY EQPT & TUBES

Direct Radiography Corp ....C....... 302 631-2700
  Newark *(G-6452)*
E I Du Pont De Nemours & Co ....E....... 302 996-4000
  Wilmington *(G-10293)*
Hologic Inc..C....... 302 631-2846
  Newark *(G-6737)*

YARN MILLS: Rewinding

Clover Yarns Inc................................G....... 302 422-4518
  Milford *(G-4359)*

YOGURT WHOLESALERS

Yogo Factory ....G....... 302 266-4506
  Newark *(G-7728)*
Yogurt City ....G....... 302 292-8881
  Newark *(G-7729)*

YOUTH CAMPS

Bear-Glasgow YMCA ....G....... 302 836-9622
  Newark *(G-6066)*
Young Mens Christian Associat ....D....... 302 296-9622
  Rehoboth Beach *(G-8121)*
YWCA Delaware ....F....... 302 224-4060
  Newark *(G-7733)*